Peterson's Graduate Programs in the Humanities, Arts & Social Sciences

2011

Peterson's Publishing

PETERSON'S Publishing

About Peterson's Publishing
To succeed on your lifelong educational journey, you will need accurate, dependable, and practical tools and resources. That is why Peterson's is everywhere education happens. Because whenever and however you need education content delivered, you can rely on Peterson's to provide the information, know-how, and guidance to help you reach your goals. Tools to match the right students with the right school. It's here. Personalized resources and expert guidance. It's here. Comprehensive and dependable education content—delivered whenever and however you need it. It's all here.

For more information, contact Peterson's Publishing, 2000 Lenox Drive, Lawrenceville, NJ 08648; 800-338-3282 Ext. 54229; or find us online at www.petersonspublishing.com.

Stephen Clemente, Managing Director, Publishing and Institutional Research; Bernadette Webster, Director of Publishing; Jill C. Schwartz, Editor; Ken Britschge, Research Project Manager; Courtney Foust, Amy L. Weber, Research Associates; Phyllis Johnson, Programmer; Ray Golaszewski, Manufacturing Manager; Linda M. Williams, Composition Manager; Karen Mount, Danielle Vreeland, Shannon White, Client Relations Representatives

ISSN 1097-1076
ISBN-13: 978-0-7689-2853-2
ISBN-10: 0-7689-2853-2

Printed in the United States of America

10 9 8 7 6 5 4 3 2 1 13 12 11

Forty-fifth Edition

By producing this book on recycled paper (40% post-consumer waste) 145 trees were saved.

CONTENTS

A Note from the Peterson's Editors vii

THE GRADUATE ADVISER 1

The Admissions Process 3

Financial Support 5

Accreditation and Accrediting Agencies 9

How to Use These Guides 13

DIRECTORY OF INSTITUTIONS WITH PROGRAMS IN HUMANITIES, ARTS & SOCIAL SCIENCES

Directory of Institutions and Their Offerings 19

ACADEMIC AND PROFESSIONAL PROGRAMS IN ARTS AND ARCHITECTURE

Section 1: Applied Arts and Design 85
Program Directories
- Applied Arts and Design—General 86
- Computer Art and Design 90
- Graphic Design 95
- Illustration 99
- Industrial Design 100
- Interior Design 101
- Medical Illustration 105
- Photography 105
- Textile Design 110

Close-Ups 113

Section 2: Architecture 121
Program Directories
- Architectural History 122
- Architecture 122
- Building Science 131
- Environmental Design 132
- Historic Preservation 133
- Landscape Architecture 135
- Lighting Design 139
- Urban Design 140

Close-Ups 143

Section 3: Art and Art History 149
Program Directories
- Art/Fine Arts 150
- Art History 170
- Arts Administration 180
- Art Therapy 183
- Decorative Arts 185
- Museum Studies 186

Close-Ups 191

Section 4: Comparative and Interdisciplinary Arts 201
Program Directory
- Comparative and Interdisciplinary Arts 202

Section 5: Film, Television, and Video 203
Program Directories
- Film, Television, and Video Production 204
- Film, Television, and Video Theory and Criticism 210

Section 6: Performing Arts 213
Program Directories
- Dance 214
- Music 217
- Theater 245
- Therapies—Dance, Drama, and Music 258

Close-Up 261

ACADEMIC AND PROFESSIONAL PROGRAMS IN THE HUMANITIES

Section 7: History 265
Program Directories
- History 266
- History of Medicine 294
- History of Science and Technology 294
- Medieval and Renaissance Studies 296
- Public History 299

Close-Up 303

Section 8: Humanities 305
Program Directories
- Humanities 306
- Liberal Studies 310

Section 9: Language and Literature 319
Program Directories
- Asian Languages 320
- Celtic Languages 322
- Chinese 322
- Classics 323

Comparative Literature 330
English 336
French 369
German 380
Italian 387
Japanese 390
Near and Middle Eastern Languages 392
Portuguese 394
Romance Languages 396
Russian 398
Scandinavian Languages 400
Slavic Languages 401
Spanish 403
Close-Ups 417

Section 10: Linguistic Studies 423
Program Directories
Linguistics 424
Translation and Interpretation 435
Close-Up 437

Section 11: Philosophy and Ethics 439
Program Directories
Ethics 440
Philosophy 442

Section 12: Religious Studies 457
Program Directories
Missions and Missiology 458
Pastoral Ministry and Counseling 461
Religion 475
Theology 487
Close-Ups 511

Section 13: Writing 517
Program Directories
Technical Writing 518
Writing 519

ACADEMIC AND PROFESSIONAL PROGRAMS IN INTERDISCIPLINARY STUDIES

Section 14: Interdisciplinary Studies 539
Program Directory
Interdisciplinary Studies 540
Close-Up 551

ACADEMIC AND PROFESSIONAL PROGRAMS IN THE SOCIAL SCIENCES

Section 15: Area and Cultural Studies 555
Program Directories
African-American Studies 556
African Studies 558
American Indian/Native American Studies 560
American Studies 561
Asian-American Studies 567
Asian Studies 567
Canadian Studies 573
Cultural Studies 574
East European and Russian Studies 578
Ethnic Studies 579
Folklore 580
Gender Studies 581
Hispanic Studies 583
Holocaust and Genocide Studies 585
Jewish Studies 586
Latin American Studies 589
Near and Middle Eastern Studies 592
Northern Studies 596
Pacific Area/Pacific Rim Studies 596
Western European Studies 597
Women's Studies 599
Close-Up 607

Section 16: Communication and Media 609
Program Directories
Communication—General 610
Arts Journalism 632
Broadcast Journalism 632
Corporate and Organizational Communication 633
Health Communication 638
Internet and Interactive Multimedia 639
Journalism 642
Mass Communication 648
Media Studies 654
Publishing 661
Rhetoric 662
Speech and Interpersonal Communication 666
Technical Communication 671
Close-Ups 673

Section 17: Conflict Resolution and Mediation/Peace Studies 687
Program Directory
Conflict Resolution and Mediation/Peace Studies 688

Section 18: Criminology and Forensics 695
Program Directories
Criminal Justice and Criminology 696
Forensic Sciences 717
Close-Up 721

Section 19: Economics 723
Program Directories
Agricultural Economics and Agribusiness 724
Applied Economics 729
Economic Development 732
Economics 735
International Economics 756
Mineral Economics 757
Close-Up 759

Section 20: Family and Consumer Sciences 761
Program Directories
Family and Consumer Sciences-General 762
Child and Family Studies 766
Child Development 774
Clothing and Textiles 776
Consumer Economics 778
Gerontology 781

Section 21: Geography 789
Program Directories
Geographic Information Systems 790
Geography 794

Section 22: Military and Defense Studies 805
Program Directories
Military and Defense Studies 806
National Security 807
Close-Up 809

Section 23: Political Science and International Affairs 811
Program Directories
International Affairs 812
International Development 824
International Trade Policy 826
Political Science 827
Close-Ups 849

Section 24: Psychology and Counseling 859
Program Directories
Psychology—General 860
Addictions/Substance Abuse Counseling 900
Clinical Psychology 904
Cognitive Sciences 925
Counseling Psychology 931
Developmental Psychology 956
Experimental Psychology 961
Forensic Psychology 968
Genetic Counseling 970
Health Psychology 971
Human Development 975
Industrial and Organizational Psychology 983
Marriage and Family Therapy 992
Psychoanalysis and Psychotherapy 1005
Rehabilitation Counseling 1005
School Psychology 1012
Social Psychology 1031
Sport Psychology 1043
Thanatology 1045
Transpersonal and Humanistic Psychology 1045
Close-Ups 1047

Section 25: Public, Regional, and Industrial Affairs 1109
Program Directories
Disability Studies 1110
Emergency Management 1110
Homeland Security 1113
Industrial and Labor Relations 1115
Philanthropic Studies 1118
Public Administration 1119
Public Affairs 1146
Public Policy 1151
Rural Planning and Studies 1163
Sustainable Development 1164
Urban and Regional Planning 1167
Urban Studies 1177
Close-Ups 1181

Section 26: Social Sciences 1197
Program Directory
Social Sciences 1198

Section 27: Sociology, Anthropology, and Archaeology 1203
Program Directories
Anthropology 1204
Applied Social Research 1217
Archaeology 1217
Biological Anthropology 1222
Demography and Population Studies 1222
Rural Sociology 1224
Sociology 1224
Survey Methodology 1243
Close-Up 1245

APPENDIXES

Institutional Changes Since the 2010 Edition 1249

Abbreviations Used in the Guides 1250

INDEXES

Close-Ups and Displays 1271

Directories and Subject Areas 1273

Directories and Subject Areas in This Book 1281

A Note from the Peterson's Editors

The six volumes of Peterson's *Graduate and Professional Programs*, the only annually updated reference work of its kind, provide wide-ranging information on the graduate and professional programs offered by accredited colleges and universities in the United States, U.S. territories, and Canada and by those institutions outside the United States that are accredited by U.S. accrediting bodies. More than 44,000 individual academic and professional programs at more than 2,200 institutions are listed. Peterson's *Graduate and Professional Programs* have been used for more than forty years by prospective graduate and professional students, placement counselors, faculty advisers, and all others interested in postbaccalaureate education.

Graduate & Professional Programs: An Overview contains information on institutions as a whole, while the other books in the series are devoted to specific academic and professional fields:

Graduate Programs in the Humanities, Arts & Social Sciences

Graduate Programs in the Biological Sciences

Graduate Programs in the Physical Sciences, Mathematics, Agricultural Sciences, the Environment & Natural Resources

Graduate Programs in Engineering & Applied Sciences

Graduate Programs in Business, Education, Health, Information Studies, Law & Social Work

The books may be used individually or as a set. For example, if you have chosen a field of study but do not know what institution you want to attend or if you have a college or university in mind but have not chosen an academic field of study, it is best to begin with the Overview guide.

Graduate & Professional Programs: An Overview presents several directories to help you identify programs of study that might interest you; you can then research those programs further in the other books in the series by using the Directory of Graduate and Professional Programs by Field, which lists 500 fields and gives the names of those institutions that offer graduate degree programs in each.

For geographical or financial reasons, you may be interested in attending a particular institution and will want to know what it has to offer. You should turn to the Directory of Institutions and Their Offerings, which lists the degree programs available at each institution. As in the Directory of Graduate and Professional Programs by Field, the level of degrees offered is also indicated.

All books in the series include advice on graduate education, including topics such as admissions tests, financial aid, and accreditation. **The Graduate Adviser** includes two essays and information about accreditation. The first essay, "The Admissions Process," discusses general admission requirements, admission tests, factors to consider when selecting a graduate school or program, when and how to apply, and how admission decisions are made. Special information for international students and tips for minority students are also included. The second essay, "Financial Support," is an overview of the broad range of support available at the graduate level. Fellowships, scholarships, and grants; assistantships and internships; federal and private loan programs, as well as Federal Work-Study; and the GI bill are detailed. This essay concludes with advice on applying for need-based financial aid. "Accreditation and Accrediting Agencies" gives information on accreditation and its purpose and lists institutional accrediting agencies first and then specialized accrediting agencies relevant to each volume's specific fields of study.

With information on more than 44,000 graduate programs in 500 disciplines, Peterson's *Graduate and Professional Programs* give you all the information you need about the programs that are of interest to you in three formats: **Profiles** (capsule summaries of basic information), **Displays** (information that an institution or program wants to emphasize), and **Close-Ups** (written by administrators, with more expansive information than the **Profiles**, emphasizing different aspects of the programs). By using these various formats of program information, coupled with **Appendixes** and **Indexes** covering directories and subject areas for all six books, you will find that these guides provide the most comprehensive, accurate, and up-to-date graduate study information available.

Find Us on Facebook® and Follow Us on Twitter™

Join the grad school conversation on Facebook® and Twitter™ at www.facebook.com/usgradschools and www.twitter.com/usgradschools. Peterson's expert resources are available to help you as you search for the right graduate program for you.

Peterson's publishes a full line of resources with information you need to guide you through the graduate admissions process. Peterson's publications can be found at college libraries and career centers and your local bookstore or library—or visit us on the Web at www.petersonspublishing.com. Peterson's books are now also available as eBooks.

Colleges and universities will be pleased to know that Peterson's helped you in your selection. Admissions staff members are more than happy to answer questions, address specific problems, and help in any way they can. The editors at Peterson's wish you great success in your graduate program search!

THE GRADUATE ADVISER

The Admissions Process

Generalizations about graduate admissions practices are not always helpful because each institution has its own set of guidelines and procedures. Nevertheless, some broad statements can be made about the admissions process that may help you plan your strategy.

Factors Involved in Selecting a Graduate School or Program

Selecting a graduate school and a specific program of study is a complex matter. Quality of the faculty; program and course offerings; the nature, size, and location of the institution; admission requirements; cost; and the availability of financial assistance are among the many factors that affect one's choice of institution. Other considerations are job placement and achievements of the program's graduates and the institution's resources, such as libraries, laboratories, and computer facilities. If you are to make the best possible choice, you need to learn as much as you can about the schools and programs you are considering before you apply.

The following steps may help you narrow your choices.

- Talk to alumni of the programs or institutions you are considering to get their impressions of how well they were prepared for work in their fields of study.
- Remember that graduate school requirements change, so be sure to get the most up-to-date information possible.
- Talk to department faculty members and the graduate adviser at your undergraduate institution. They often have information about programs of study at other institutions.
- Visit the Web sites of the graduate schools in which you are interested to request a graduate catalog. Contact the department chair in your chosen field of study for additional information about the department and the field.
- Visit as many campuses as possible. Call ahead for an appointment with the graduate adviser in your field of interest and be sure to check out the facilities and talk to students.

General Requirements

Graduate schools and departments have requirements that applicants for admission must meet. Typically, these requirements include undergraduate transcripts (which provide information about undergraduate grade point average and course work applied toward a major), admission test scores, and letters of recommendation. Most graduate programs also ask for an essay or personal statement that describes your personal reasons for seeking graduate study. In some fields, such as art and music, portfolios or auditions may be required in addition to other evidence of talent. Some institutions require that the applicant have an undergraduate degree in the same subject as the intended graduate major.

Most institutions evaluate each applicant on the basis of the applicant's total record, and the weight accorded any given factor varies widely from institution to institution and from program to program.

The Application Process

You should begin the application process at least one year before you expect to begin your graduate study. Find out the application deadline for each institution (many are provided in the **Profile** section of this guide). Go to the institution's Web site and find out if you can apply online. If not, request a paper application form. Fill out this form thoroughly and neatly. Assume that the school needs all the information it is requesting and that the admissions officer will be sensitive to the neatness and overall quality of what you submit. Do not supply more information than the school requires.

The institution may ask at least one question that will require a three- or four-paragraph answer. Compose your response on the assumption that the admissions officer is interested in both what you think and how you express yourself. Keep your statement brief and to the point, but, at the same time, include all pertinent information about your past experiences and your educational goals. Individual statements vary greatly in style and content, which helps admissions officers differentiate among applicants. Many graduate departments give considerable weight to the statement in making their admissions decisions, so be sure to take the time to prepare a thoughtful and concise statement.

If recommendations are a part of the admissions requirements, carefully choose the individuals you ask to write them. It is generally best to ask current or former professors to write the recommendations, provided they are able to attest to your intellectual ability and motivation for doing the work required of a graduate student. It is advisable to provide stamped, preaddressed envelopes to people being asked to submit recommendations on your behalf.

Completed applications, including references, transcripts, and admission test scores, should be received at the institution by the specified date.

Be advised that institutions do not usually make admissions decisions until all materials have been received. Enclose a self-addressed postcard with your application, requesting confirmation of receipt. Allow at least ten days for the return of the postcard before making further inquiries.

If you plan to apply for financial support, it is imperative that you file your application early.

ADMISSION TESTS

The major testing program used in graduate admissions is the Graduate Record Examinations (GRE) testing program, sponsored by the GRE Board and administered by Educational Testing Service, Princeton, New Jersey.

The Graduate Record Examinations testing program consists of a General Test and eight Subject Tests. The General Test measures critical thinking, verbal reasoning, quantitative reasoning, and analytical writing skills. It is offered as an Internet-based test (iBT) in the United States, Canada, and many other countries.

The typical computer-based General Test consists of one 30-minute verbal reasoning section, one 45-minute quantitative reasoning sections, one 45-minute issue analysis (writing) section, and one 30-minute argument analysis (writing) section. In addition, an unidentified verbal or quantitative section that doesn't count toward a score may be included and an identified research section that is not scored may also be included.

The Subject Tests measure achievement and assume undergraduate majors or extensive background in the following eight disciplines:

- Biochemistry, Cell and Molecular Biology
- Biology
- Chemistry
- Computer Science
- Literature in English
- Mathematics
- Physics
- Psychology

The Subject Tests are available three times per year as paper-based administrations around the world. Testing time is approximately 2 hours and 50 minutes. You can obtain more information about the GRE by visiting the ETS Web site at www.ets.org or consulting the *GRE Information and Registration Bulletin*. The *Bulletin* can be obtained at many undergraduate colleges. You can also download it from the ETS Web site or obtain it by contacting Graduate Record Examinations, Educational Testing Service, P.O. Box 6000, Princeton, NJ 08541-6000; phone: 609-771-7670.

If you expect to apply for admission to a program that requires any of the GRE tests, you should select a test date well in advance of the application deadline. Scores on the computer-based General Test are reported within ten to fifteen days; scores on the paper-based Subject Tests are reported within six weeks.

Another testing program, the Miller Analogies Test (MAT), is administered at more than 500 Controlled Testing Centers, licensed by Harcourt Assessment, Inc., in the United States, Canada, and other countries. The MAT computer-based test is now available. Testing time is 60 minutes. The test consists of 120 partial analogies. You can obtain the *Candidate Information Booklet,* which contains a list of test centers and instructions for taking the test, from http://www.milleranalogies.com or by calling 800-622-3231 (toll-free).

Check the specific requirements of the programs to which you are applying.

How Admission Decisions Are Made

The program you apply to is directly involved in the admissions process. Although the final decision is usually made by the graduate dean (or an associate) or the faculty admissions committee, recommendations from faculty members in your intended field are important. At some institutions, an interview is incorporated into the decision process.

A Special Note for International Students

In addition to the steps already described, there are some special considerations for international students who intend to apply for graduate study in the United States. All graduate schools require an indication of competence in English. The purpose of the Test of English as a Foreign Language (TOEFL) is to evaluate the English proficiency of people who are nonnative speakers of English and want to study at colleges and universities where English is the language of instruction. The TOEFL is administered by Educational Testing Service (ETS) under the general direction of a policy board established by the College Board and the Graduate Record Examinations Board.

The TOEFL iBT assesses the four basic language skills: listening, reading, writing, and speaking. It was administered for the first time in September 2005, and ETS continues to introduce the TOEFL iBT in selected cities. The Internet-based test is administered at secure, official test centers. The testing time is approximately 4 hours. Because the TOEFL iBT includes a speaking section, the Test of Spoken English (TSE) is no longer needed.

The TOEFL is also offered in the paper-based format in areas of the world where Internet-based testing is not available. The paper-based TOEFL consists of three sections—listening comprehension, structure and written expression, and reading comprehension. The testing time is approximately 3 hours. The Test of Written English (TWE) is also given. The TWE is a 30-minute essay that measures the examinee's ability to compose in English. Examinees receive a TWE score separate from their TOEFL score. The *Information Bulletin* contains information on local fees and registration procedures.

Additional information and registration materials are available from TOEFL Services, Educational Testing Service, P.O. Box 6151, Princeton, New Jersey 08541-6151. Phone: 609-771-7100. Web site: www.toefl.org.

International students should apply especially early because of the number of steps required to complete the admissions process. Furthermore, many United States graduate schools have a limited number of spaces for international students, and many more students apply than the schools can accommodate.

International students may find financial assistance from institutions very limited. The U.S. government requires international applicants to submit a certification of support, which is a statement attesting to the applicant's financial resources. In addition, international students *must* have health insurance coverage.

Tips for Minority Students

Indicators of a university's values in terms of diversity are found both in its recruitment programs and its resources directed to student success. Important questions: Does the institution vigorously recruit minorities for its graduate programs? Is there funding available to help with the costs associated with visiting the school? Are minorities represented in the institution's brochures or Web site or on their faculty rolls? What campus-based resources or services (including assistance in locating housing or career counseling and placement) are available? Is funding available to members of underrepresented groups?

At the program level, it is particularly important for minority students to investigate the "climate" of a program under consideration. How many minority students are enrolled and how many have graduated? What opportunities are there to work with diverse faculty and mentors whose research interests match yours? How are conflicts resolved or concerns addressed? How interested are faculty in building strong and supportive relations with students? "Climate" concerns should be addressed by posing questions to various individuals, including faculty members, current students, and alumni.

Information is also available through various organizations, such as the Hispanic Association of Colleges & Universities (HACU), and publications such as *Diverse Issues in Higher Education* and *Hispanic Outlook* magazine. There are also books devoted to this topic, such as *The Multicultural Student's Guide to Colleges* by Robert Mitchell.

Financial Support

The range of financial support at the graduate level is very broad. The following descriptions will give you a general idea of what you might expect and what will be expected of you as a financial support recipient.

Fellowships, Scholarships, and Grants

These are usually outright awards of a few hundred to many thousands of dollars with no service to the institution required in return. Fellowships and scholarships are usually awarded on the basis of merit and are highly competitive. Grants are made on the basis of financial need or special talent in a field of study. Many fellowships, scholarships, and grants not only cover tuition, fees, and supplies but also include stipends for living expenses with allowances for dependents. However, the terms of each should be examined because some do not permit recipients to supplement their income with outside work. Fellowships, scholarships, and grants may vary in the number of years for which they are awarded.

In addition to the availability of these funds at the university or program level, many excellent fellowship programs are available at the national level and may be applied for before and during enrollment in a graduate program. A listing of many of these programs can be found at the Council of Graduate Schools' Web site: http://www.cgsnet.org. There is a wealth of information in the "Programs" and "Awards" sections.

Assistantships and Internships

Many graduate students receive financial support through assistantships, particularly involving teaching or research duties. It is important to recognize that such appointments should not be viewed simply as employment relationships but rather should constitute an integral and important part of a student's graduate education. As such, the appointments should be accompanied by strong faculty mentoring and increasingly responsible apprenticeship experiences. The specific nature of these appointments in a given program should be considered in selecting that graduate program.

TEACHING ASSISTANTSHIPS

These usually provide a salary and full or partial tuition remission and may also provide health benefits. Unlike fellowships, scholarships, and grants, which require no service to the institution, teaching assistantships require recipients to provide the institution with a specific amount of undergraduate teaching, ideally related to the student's field of study. Some teaching assistants are limited to grading papers, compiling bibliographies, taking notes, or monitoring laboratories. At some graduate schools, teaching assistants must carry lighter course loads than regular full-time students.

RESEARCH ASSISTANTSHIPS

These are very similar to teaching assistantships in the manner in which financial assistance is provided. The difference is that recipients are given basic research assignments in their disciplines rather than teaching responsibilities. The work required is normally related to the student's field of study; in most instances, the assistantship supports the student's thesis or dissertation research.

ADMINISTRATIVE INTERNSHIPS

These are similar to assistantships in application of financial assistance funds, but the student is given an assignment on a part-time basis, usually as a special assistant with one of the university's administrative offices. The assignment may not necessarily be directly related to the recipient's discipline.

RESIDENCE HALL AND COUNSELING ASSISTANTSHIPS

These assistantships are frequently assigned to graduate students in psychology, counseling, and social work, but they may be offered to students in other disciplines, especially if the student has worked in this capacity during his or her undergraduate years. Duties can vary from being available in a dean's office for a specific number of hours for consultation with undergraduates to living in campus residences and being responsible for both counseling and administrative tasks or advising student activity groups. Residence hall assistantships often include a room and board allowance and, in some cases, tuition assistance and stipends. Contact the Housing and Student Life Office for more information.

Health Insurance

The availability and affordability of health insurance is an important issue and one that should be considered in an applicant's choice of institution and program. While often included with assistantships and fellowships, this is not always the case and, even if provided, the benefits may be limited. It is important to note that the U.S. government requires international students to have health insurance.

The GI Bill

This provides financial assistance for students who are veterans of the United States armed forces. If you are a veteran, contact your local Veterans Administration office to determine your eligibility and to get full details about benefits. There are a number of programs that offer educational benefits to current military enlistees. Some states have tuition assistance programs for members of the National Guard. Contact the VA office at the college for more information.

Federal Work-Study Program (FWS)

Employment is another way some students finance their graduate studies. The federally funded Federal Work-Study Program provides eligible students with employment opportunities, usually in public and private nonprofit organizations. Federal funds pay up to 75 percent of the wages, with the remainder paid by the employing agency. FWS is available to graduate students who demonstrate financial need. Not all schools have these funds, and some only award them to undergraduates. Each school sets its application deadline and work-study earnings limits. Wages vary and are related to the type of work done. You must file the Free Application for Federal Student Aid (FAFSA) to be eligible for this program.

Loans

Many graduate students borrow to finance their graduate programs when other sources of assistance (which do not have to be repaid) prove insufficient. You should always read and understand the terms of any loan program before submitting your application.

FEDERAL DIRECT LOANS

Federal Direct Stafford Loans. The Federal Direct Stafford Loan Program offers low-interest loans to students with the Department of Education acting as the lender.

There are two components of the Federal Stafford Loan program. Under the *subsidized* component of the program, the federal government pays the interest on the loan while you are enrolled in graduate school on at least a half-time basis, during the six-month grace period after you drop below half-time enrollment, as well as during any period of deferment. Under the *unsubsidized* component of the program, you pay the interest on the loan from the day proceeds are issued. Eligibility for the federal subsidy is based on demonstrated financial need as determined by the financial aid office from the information you provide on the FAFSA. A cosigner is not required, since the loan is not based on creditworthiness.

Although *unsubsidized* Federal Direct Stafford Loans may not be as desirable as *subsidized* Federal Direct Stafford Loans from the student's perspective, they are a useful source of support for those who may not qualify for the subsidized loans or who need additional financial assistance.

Graduate students may borrow up to $20,500 per year through the Direct Stafford Loan Program, up to a cumulative maximum of $138,500, including undergraduate borrowing. This may include up to $8500 in *subsidized* Direct Stafford Loans annually, depending on eligibility, up to a cumulative maximum of $65,500, including undergraduate borrowing. The amount of the loan borrowed through the *unsubsidized* Direct Stafford Loan Program equals the total amount of the loan (as much as $20,500) minus your eligibility for a *subsidized* Direct Loan (as much as $8500). You may borrow up to the cost of attendance at the school in which you are enrolled or will attend, minus estimated financial assistance from other federal, state, and private sources, up to a maximum of $20,500.

Direct Stafford Loans made on or after July 1, 2006, carry a fixed interest rate of 6.8% both for in-school and in-repayment borrowers.

A fee is deducted from the loan proceeds upon disbursement. Loans with a first disbursement on or after July 1, 2010 have a borrower origination fee of 1 percent. The Department of Education offers a 0.5 percent origination fee rebate incentive. Borrowers must make their first twelve payments on time in order to retain the rebate.

Under the *subsidized* Federal Direct Stafford Loan Program, repayment begins six months after your last date of enrollment on at least a half-time basis. Under the *unsubsidized* program, repayment of interest begins within thirty days from disbursement of the loan proceeds, and repayment of the principal begins six months after your last enrollment on at least a half-time basis. Some borrowers may choose to defer interest payments while they are in school. The accrued interest is added to the loan balance when the borrower begins repayment. There are several repayment options.

Federal Perkins Loans. The Federal Perkins Loan is available to students demonstrating financial need and is administered directly by the school. Not all schools have these funds, and some may award them to undergraduates only. Eligibility is determined from the information you provide on the FAFSA. The school will notify you of your eligibility.

Eligible graduate students may borrow up to $6000 per year, up to a maximum of $40,000, including undergraduate borrowing (even if your previous Perkins Loans have been repaid). The interest rate for Federal Perkins Loans is 5 percent, and no interest accrues while you remain in school at least half-time. There are no guarantee, loan, or disbursement fees. Repayment begins nine months after your last date of enrollment on at least a half-time basis and may extend over a maximum of ten years with no prepayment penalty.

Federal Direct Graduate PLUS Loans. Effective July 1, 2006, graduate and professional students are eligible for Graduate PLUS loans. This program allows students to borrow up to the cost of attendance, less any other aid received. These loans have a fixed interest rate of 7.9 percent, and interest begins to accrue at the time of disbursement. The PLUS loans do involve a credit check; a PLUS borrower may obtain a loan with a cosigner if his or her credit is not good enough. Grad PLUS loans may be deferred while a student in school and for the six months following a drop below half-time enrollment. For more information, contact your college financial aid office.

Deferring Your Federal Loan Repayments. If you borrowed under the Federal Direct Stafford Loan Program, Federal Direct Loan Program, or the Federal Perkins Loan Program for previous undergraduate or graduate study, your repayments may be deferred when you return to graduate school, depending on when you borrowed and under which program.

There are other deferment options available if you are temporarily unable to repay your loan. Information about these deferments is provided at your entrance and exit interviews. If you believe you are eligible for a deferment of your loan repayments, you must contact your lender or loan servicer to request a deferment form. The deferment must be filed prior to the time your repayment is due, and it must be refiled when it expires if you remain eligible for deferment at that time.

SUPPLEMENTAL (PRIVATE) LOANS

Many lending institutions offer supplemental loan programs and other financing plans, such as the ones described here, to students seeking additional assistance in meeting their education expenses. Some loan programs target all types of graduate students; others are designed specifically for business, law, or medical students. In addition, you can use private loans not specifically designed for education to help finance your graduate degree.

If you are considering borrowing through a supplemental or private loan program, you should carefully consider the terms and be sure to "read the fine print." Check with the program sponsor for the most current terms that will be applicable to the amounts you intend to borrow for graduate study. Most supplemental loan programs for graduate study offer unsubsidized, credit-based loans. In general, a credit-ready borrower is one who has a satisfactory credit history or no credit history at all. A creditworthy borrower generally must pass a credit test to be eligible to borrow or act as a cosigner for the loan funds.

Many supplemental loan programs have minimum and maximum annual loan limits. Some offer amounts equal to the cost of attendance minus any other aid you will receive for graduate study. If you are planning to borrow for several years of graduate study, consider whether there is a cumulative or aggregate limit on the amount you may borrow. Often this cumulative or aggregate limit will include any amounts you borrowed and have not repaid for undergraduate or previous graduate study.

The combination of the annual interest rate, loan fees, and the repayment terms you choose will determine how much you will repay over time. Compare these features in combination before you decide which loan program to use. Some loans offer interest rates that are adjusted monthly, some quarterly, some annually. Some offer interest rates that are lower during the in-school, grace, and deferment periods and then increase when you begin repayment. Some programs include a loan "origination" fee, which is usually deducted from the principal amount you receive when the loan is disbursed and must be repaid along with the interest and other principal when you graduate, withdraw from school, or drop below half-time study. Sometimes the loan fees are reduced if you borrow with a qualified cosigner. Some programs allow you to defer interest and/or principal payments while you are enrolled in graduate school. Many programs allow you to capitalize your interest payments; the interest due on your loan is added to the outstanding balance of your loan, so you don't have to repay immediately, but this increases the amount you owe. Other programs allow you to pay the interest as you go, which reduces the amount you later have to repay. The private loan market is very competitive, and your financial aid office can help you evaluate these programs.

Applying for Need-Based Financial Aid

Schools that award federal and institutional financial assistance based on need will require you to complete the FAFSA and, in some cases, an institutional financial aid application.

If you are applying for federal student assistance, you **must** complete the FAFSA. A service of the U.S. Department of Education, the FAFSA is free to all applicants. Most applicants apply online at www.fafsa.ed.gov. Paper applications are available at the financial aid office of your local college.

After your FAFSA information has been processed, you will receive a Student Aid Report (SAR). If you provided an e-mail address on the FAFSA, this will be sent to you electronically; otherwise, it will be mailed to your home address.

Follow the instructions on the SAR if you need to correct information reported on your original application. If your situation changes after you file your FAFSA, contact your financial aid officer to discuss amending your information. You can also appeal your financial aid award if you have extenuating circumstances.

If you would like more information on federal student financial aid, visit the FAFSA Web site or download the most recent version of *Funding Education Beyond High School: The Guide to Federal Student Aid* at http://studentaid.ed.gov/students/publications/student_guide/index.html. This guide is also available in Spanish.

The U.S. Department of Education also has a toll-free number for questions concerning federal student aid programs. The number is 1-800-4-FED AID (1-800-433-3243). If you are hearing impaired, call toll-free, 1-800-730-8913.

Summary

Remember that these are generalized statements about financial assistance at the graduate level. Because each institution allots its aid differently, you should communicate directly with the school and the specific department of interest to you. It is not unusual, for example, to find that an endowment vested within a specific department supports one or more fellowships. You may fit its requirements and specifications precisely.

Accreditation and Accrediting Agencies

Colleges and universities in the United States, and their individual academic and professional programs, are accredited by nongovernmental agencies concerned with monitoring the quality of education in this country. Agencies with both regional and national jurisdictions grant accreditation to institutions as a whole, while specialized bodies acting on a nationwide basis—often national professional associations—grant accreditation to departments and programs in specific fields.

Institutional and specialized accrediting agencies share the same basic concerns: the purpose an academic unit—whether university or program—has set for itself and how well it fulfills that purpose, the adequacy of its financial and other resources, the quality of its academic offerings, and the level of services it provides. Agencies that grant institutional accreditation take a broader view, of course, and examine university-wide or college-wide services with which a specialized agency may not concern itself.

Both types of agencies follow the same general procedures when considering an application for accreditation. The academic unit prepares a self-evaluation, focusing on the concerns mentioned above and usually including an assessment of both its strengths and weaknesses; a team of representatives of the accrediting body reviews this evaluation, visits the campus, and makes its own report; and finally, the accrediting body makes a decision on the application. Often, even when accreditation is granted, the agency makes a recommendation regarding how the institution or program can improve. All institutions and programs are also reviewed every few years to determine whether they continue to meet established standards; if they do not, they may lose their accreditation.

Accrediting agencies themselves are reviewed and evaluated periodically by the U.S. Department of Education and the Council for Higher Education Accreditation (CHEA). Recognized agencies adhere to certain standards and practices, and their authority in matters of accreditation is widely accepted in the educational community.

This does not mean, however, that accreditation is a simple matter, either for schools wishing to become accredited or for students deciding where to apply. Indeed, in certain fields the very meaning and methods of accreditation are the subject of a good deal of debate. For their part, those applying to graduate school should be aware of the safeguards provided by regional accreditation, especially in terms of degree acceptance and institutional longevity. Beyond this, applicants should understand the role that specialized accreditation plays in their field, as this varies considerably from one discipline to another. In certain professional fields, it is necessary to have graduated from a program that is accredited in order to be eligible for a license to practice, and in some fields the federal government also makes this a hiring requirement. In other disciplines, however, accreditation is not as essential, and there can be excellent programs that are not accredited. In fact, some programs choose not to seek accreditation, although most do.

Institutions and programs that present themselves for accreditation are sometimes granted the status of candidate for accreditation, or what is known as "preaccreditation." This may happen, for example, when an academic unit is too new to have met all the requirements for accreditation. Such status signifies initial recognition and indicates that the school or program in question is working to fulfill all requirements; it does not, however, guarantee that accreditation will be granted.

Institutional Accrediting Agencies—Regional

MIDDLE STATES ASSOCIATION OF COLLEGES AND SCHOOLS
Accredits institutions in Delaware, District of Columbia, Maryland, New Jersey, New York, Pennsylvania, Puerto Rico, and the Virgin Islands.
Dr. Elizabeth Sibolski, Acting President
Middle States Commission on Higher Education
3624 Market Street, Second Floor West
Philadelphia, Pennsylvania 19104
Phone: 267-284-5000
Fax: 215-662-5501
E-mail: info@msche.org
Web: www.msche.org

NEW ENGLAND ASSOCIATION OF SCHOOLS AND COLLEGES
Accredits institutions in Connecticut, Maine, Massachusetts, New Hampshire, Rhode Island, and Vermont.
Barbara E. Brittingham, Director
Commission on Institutions of Higher Education
209 Burlington Road, Suite 201
Bedford, Massachusetts 01730-1433
Phone: 781-271-0022
Fax: 781-271-0950
E-mail: CIHE@neasc.org
Web: www.neasc.org

NORTH CENTRAL ASSOCIATION OF COLLEGES AND SCHOOLS
Accredits institutions in Arizona, Arkansas, Colorado, Illinois, Indiana, Iowa, Kansas, Michigan, Minnesota, Missouri, Nebraska, New Mexico, North Dakota, Ohio, Oklahoma, South Dakota, West Virginia, Wisconsin, and Wyoming.
Dr. Sylvia Manning, President
The Higher Learning Commission
230 South LaSalle Street, Suite 7-500
Chicago, Illinois 60604-1413
Phone: 312-263-0456
Fax: 312-263-7462
E-mail: smanning@hlcommission.org
Web: www.ncahigherlearningcommission.org

NORTHWEST COMMISSION ON COLLEGES AND UNIVERSITIES
Accredits institutions in Alaska, Idaho, Montana, Nevada, Oregon, Utah, and Washington.
Dr. Sandra E. Elman, President
8060 165th Avenue, NE, Suite 100
Redmond, Washington 98052
Phone: 425-558-4224
Fax: 425-376-0596
E-mail: selman@nwccu.org
Web: www.nwccu.org

SOUTHERN ASSOCIATION OF COLLEGES AND SCHOOLS
Accredits institutions in Alabama, Florida, Georgia, Kentucky, Louisiana, Mississippi, North Carolina, South Carolina, Tennessee, Texas, and Virginia.
Belle S. Wheelan, President
Commission on Colleges
1866 Southern Lane
Decatur, Georgia 30033-4097
Phone: 404-679-4500
Fax: 404-679-4558
E-mail: questions@sacscoc.org
Web: www.sacsoc.org

WESTERN ASSOCIATION OF SCHOOLS AND COLLEGES
Accredits institutions in California, Guam, and Hawaii.
Ralph A. Wolff, President and Executive Director
Accrediting Commission for Senior Colleges and Universities
985 Atlantic Avenue, Suite 100
Alameda, California 94501
Phone: 510-748-9001
Fax: 510-748-9797
E-mail: www.wascsenior.org
Web: www.wascweb.org/contact

Institutional Accrediting Agencies—Other

ACCREDITING COUNCIL FOR INDEPENDENT COLLEGES AND SCHOOLS
Albert C. Gray, Ph.D., Executive Director and CEO
750 First Street, NE, Suite 980
Washington, DC 20002-4241
Phone: 202-336-6780
Fax: 202-842-2593
E-mail: info@acics.org
Web: www.acics.org

DISTANCE EDUCATION AND TRAINING COUNCIL (DETC)
Accrediting Commission
Michael P. Lambert, Executive Director
1601 18th Street, NW, Suite 2
Washington, DC 20009
Phone: 202-234-5100
Fax: 202-332-1386
E-mail: detc@detc.org
Web: www.detc.org

Specialized Accrediting Agencies

[Only *Graduate & Professional Programs: An Overview* of *Peterson's Graduate and Professional Programs* Series includes the complete list of specialized accrediting groups recognized by the U.S. Department of Education and the Council on Higher Education Accreditation (CHEA). The list in this book is abridged.]

ART AND DESIGN
Samuel Hope, Executive Director
Karen P. Moynahan, Associate Director
National Association of Schools of Art and Design (NASAD)
Commission on Accreditation
11250 Roger Bacon Drive, Suite 21
Reston, Virginia 20190-5243
Phone: 703-437-0700
Fax: 703-437-6312
E-mail: info@arts-accredit.org
Web: www.arts-accredit.org

CLINICAL PASTORAL EDUCATION
Teresa E. Snorton, Executive Director
Accreditation Commission
Association for Clinical Pastoral Education, Inc.
1549 Claremont Road, Suite 103
Decatur, Georgia 30033-4611
Phone: 404-320-1472
Fax: 404-320-0849
E-mail: acpe@acpe.edu
Web: www.acpe.edu

DANCE
Samuel Hope, Executive Director
Karen P. Moynahan, Associate Director
National Association of Schools of Dance (NASD)
Commission on Accreditation
11250 Roger Bacon Drive, Suite 21
Reston, Virginia 20190-5248
Phone: 703-437-0700
Fax: 703-437-6312
E-mail: info@arts-accredit.org
Web: www.arts-accredit.org

DIETETICS
Ulric K. Chung, Ph.D., Executive Director
American Dietetic Association
Commission on Accreditation for Dietetics Education (CADE-ADA)
120 South Riverside Plaza, Suite 2000
Chicago, Illinois 60606-6995
Phone: 800-877-1600
Fax: 312-899-4817
E-mail: cade@eatright.org
Web: www.eatright.org/cade

INTERIOR DESIGN
Holly Mattson, Executive Director
Council for Interior Design Accreditation
206 Grandview Avenue, Suite 350
Grand Rapids, Michigan 49503-4014
Phone: 616-458-0400
Fax: 616-458-0460
E-mail: info@accredit-id.org
Web: www.accredit-id.org

JOURNALISM AND MASS COMMUNICATIONS
Susanne Shaw, Executive Director
Accrediting Council on Education in Journalism and Mass Communications (ACEJMC)
School of Journalism
Stauffer-Flint Hall
University of Kansas
1435 Jayhawk Boulevard
Lawrence, Kansas 66045-7575
Phone: 785-864-3973
Fax: 785-864-5225
E-mail: sshaw@ku.edu
Web: www2.ku.edu/~acejmc

LANDSCAPE ARCHITECTURE
Ronald C. Leighton, Executive Director
Landscape Architectural Accreditation Board
American Society of Landscape Architects
636 Eye Street, NW
Washington, DC 20001-3736
Phone: 202-898-2444
Fax: 202-898-1185
E-mail: info@asla.org
Web: www.asla.org

MARRIAGE AND FAMILY THERAPY
Jeff S. Harmon, Director of Accreditation Services
Commission on Accreditation for Marriage and Family Therapy Education
American Association for Marriage and Family Therapy
112 South Alfred Street
Alexandria, Virginia 22314-3061
Phone: 703-838-9808
Fax: 703-838-9805
E-mail: coamfle@aamft.org
Web: www.aamft.org

MEDICAL ILLUSTRATION
Commission on Accreditation of Allied Health Education Programs (CAAHEP)
Kathleen Megivern, Executive Director
1361 Park Street
Clearwater, Florida 33756
Phone: 727-210-2350
Fax: 727-210-2354
E-mail: mail@caahep.org
Web: www.caahep.org

MUSIC
Samuel Hope, Executive Director
Karen P. Moynahan, Associate Director
National Association of Schools of Music (NASM)
Commission on Accreditation
11250 Roger Bacon Drive, Suite 21
Reston, Virginia 20190-5248
Phone: 703-437-0700
Fax: 703-437-6312
E-mail: info@arts-accredit.org
Web: www.arts-accredit.org

PLANNING
Shonagh Merits, Executive Director
American Institute of Certified Planners/Association of Collegiate Schools of Planning/American Planning Association
Planning Accreditation Board (PAB)
53 West Jackson Boulevard, Suite 1315
Chicago, Illinois 60604
Phone: 312-334-1271
Fax: 312-334-1273
E-mail: pab@planning.org
Web: www.planningaccreditationboard.org

PSYCHOLOGY AND COUNSELING
Susan Zlotlow, Executive Director
Office of Program Consultation and Accreditation
American Psychological Association
750 First Street, NE
Washington, DC 20002-4242
Phone: 202-336-5979
Fax: 202-336-5978
E-mail: apaaccred@apa.org
Web: www.apa.org/ed/accreditation

Carol L. Bobby, Executive Director
Council for Accreditation of Counseling and Related Educational Programs (CACREP)
1001 North Fairfax Street, Suite 510
Alexandria, Virginia 22314
Phone: 703-535-5990
Fax: 703-739-6209
E-mail: cacrep@cacrep.org
Web: www.cacrep.org

PUBLIC AFFAIRS AND ADMINISTRATION
Crystal Calarusse, Executive Director
Commission on Peer Review and Accreditation
National Association of Schools of Public Affairs and Administration
1120 G Street, NW, Suite 730
Washington, DC 20005
Phone: 202-628-8965
Fax: 202-626-4978
E-mail: calarusse@naspaa.org
Web: www.naspaa.org

SPEECH-LANGUAGE PATHOLOGY AND AUDIOLOGY
Patrima L. Tice, Director of Credentialing
American Speech-Language-Hearing Association
Council on Academic Accreditation in Audiology and Speech-Language Pathology
2200 Research Boulevard
Rockville, Maryland 20850-3289
Phone: 301-296-5796
Fax: 301-296-8750
E-mail: ptice@asha.org
Web: www.asha.org/academic/accreditation/default.htm

TECHNOLOGY
Michale S. McComis, Ed.D., Executive Director
Accrediting Commission of Career Schools and Colleges
2101 Wilson Boulevard, Suite 302
Arlington, Virginia 22201
Phone: 703-247-4212
Fax: 703-247-4533
E-mail: mccomis@accsct.org
Web: www.accs.org

THEATER
Samuel Hope, Executive Director
Karen P. Moynahan, Associate Director
National Association of Schools of Theatre
Commission on Accreditation
11250 Roger Bacon Drive, Suite 21
Reston, Virginia 20190
Phone: 703-437-0700
Fax: 703-437-6312
E-mail: info@arts-accredit.org
Web: www.arts-accredit.org

THEOLOGY
Bernard Fryshman, Executive Vice President
Association of Advanced Rabbinical and Talmudic Schools (AARTS)
Accreditation Commission
11 Broadway, Suite 405
New York, New York 10004
Phone: 212-363-1991
Fax: 212-533-5335
E-mail: BFryshman@nyit.edu

Daniel O. Aleshire, Executive Director
Association of Theological Schools in the United States and Canada (ATS)
Commission on Accrediting
10 Summit Park Drive
Pittsburgh, Pennsylvania 15275-1110
Phone: 412-788-6505
Fax: 412-788-6510
E-mail: ats@ats.edu
Web: www.ats.edu

Dr. Russell G. Fitzgerald, Executive Director
Transnational Association of Christian Colleges and Schools (TRACS)
Accreditation Commission
P.O. Box 328
Forest, Virginia 24551
Phone: 434-525-9539
Fax: 434-525-9538
E-mail: info@tracs.org
Web: www.tracs.org

How to Use These Guides

As you identify the particular programs and institutions that interest you, you can use both the ***Graduate & Professional Programs: An Overview*** volume and the specialized volumes in the series to obtain detailed information.

- ***Graduate Programs in the Physical Sciences, Mathematics, Agricultural Sciences, the Environment & Natural Resources***
- ***Graduate Programs in Engineering & Applied Sciences***
- ***Graduate Programs the Humanities, Arts & Social Sciences***
- ***Graduate Programs in the Biological Sciences***
- ***Graduate Programs in Business, Education, Health, Information Studies, Law & Social Work***

Each of the specialized volumes in the series is divided into sections that contain one or more directories devoted to programs in a particular field. If you do not find a directory devoted to your field of interest in a specific volume, consult "Directories and Subject Areas" (located at the end of each volume). After you have identified the correct volume, consult the "Directories and Subject Areas in This Book" index, which shows (as does the more general directory) what directories cover subjects not specifically named in a directory or section title.

Each of the specialized volumes in the series has a number of general directories. These directories have entries for the largest unit at an institution granting graduate degrees in that field. For example, the general Engineering and Applied Sciences directory in the ***Graduate Programs in Engineering & Applied Sciences*** volume consists of **Profiles** for colleges, schools, and departments of engineering and applied sciences.

General directories are followed by other directories, or sections, that give more detailed information about programs in particular areas of the general field that has been covered. The general Engineering and Applied Sciences directory, in the previous example, is followed by nineteen sections with directories in specific areas of engineering, such as Chemical Engineering, Industrial/Management Engineering, and Mechanical Engineering.

Because of the broad nature of many fields, any system of organization is bound to involve a certain amount of overlap. Environmental studies, for example, is a field whose various aspects are studied in several types of departments and schools. Readers interested in such studies will find information on relevant programs in the ***Graduate Programs in the Biological Sciences*** volume under Ecology and Environmental Biology; in the ***Graduate Programs in the Physical Sciences, Mathematics, Agricultural Sciences, the Environment & Natural Resources*** volume under Environmental Management and Policy and Natural Resources; in the ***Graduate Programs in Engineering & Applied Sciences*** volume under Energy Management and Policy and Environmental Engineering; and in the ***Graduate Programs in Business, Education, Health, Information Studies, Law & Social Work*** volume under Environmental and Occupational Health. To help you find all of the programs of interest to you, the introduction to each section within the specialized volumes includes, if applicable, a paragraph suggesting other sections and directories with information on related areas of study.

Directory of Institutions with Programs in the Humanities, Arts & Social Sciences

This directory lists institutions in alphabetical order and includes beneath each name the academic fields in which each institution offers graduate programs. The degree level in each field is also indicated, provided that the institution has supplied that information in response to Peterson's Annual Survey of Graduate and Professional Institutions. An M indicates that a master's degree program is offered; a D indicates that a doctoral degree program is offered; a P indicates that the first professional degree is offered; an O signifies that other advanced degrees (e.g., certificates or specialist degrees) are offered; and an * (asterisk) indicates that a **Close-Up** and/or **Display** is located in this volume. See the index, "Close-Ups and Displays," for the specific page number.

Profiles of Academic and Professional Programs in the Specialized Volumes

Each section of **Profiles** has a table of contents that lists the Program Directories, **Displays**, and **Close-Ups.** Program Directories consist of the **Profiles** of programs in the relevant fields, with **Displays** following if programs have chosen to include them. **Close-Ups,** which are more individualized statements, again if programs have chosen to submit them, are also listed.

The **Profiles** found in the 500 directories in the specialized volumes provide basic data about the graduate units in capsule form for quick reference. To make these directories as useful as possible, **Profiles** are generally listed for an institution's smallest academic unit within a subject area. In other words, if an institution has a College of Liberal Arts that administers many related programs, the **Profile** for the individual program (e.g., Program in History), not the entire College, appears in the directory.

There are some programs that do not fit into any current directory and are not given individual **Profiles**. The directory structure is reviewed annually in order to keep this number to a minimum and to accommodate major trends in graduate education.

The following outline describes the **Profile** information found in the guides and explains how best to use that information. Any item that does not apply to or was not provided by a graduate unit is omitted from its listing. The format of the **Profiles** is constant, making it easy to compare one institution with another and one program with another.

Identifying Information. The institution's name, in boldface type, is followed by a complete listing of the administrative structure for that field of study. (For example, University of Akron, Buchtel College of Arts and Sciences, Department of Theoretical and Applied Mathematics, Program in Mathematics.) The last unit listed is the one to which all information in the **Profile** pertains. The institution's city, state, and zip code follow.

Offerings. Each field of study offered by the unit is listed with all postbaccalaureate degrees awarded. Degrees that are not preceded by a specific concentration are awarded in the general field listed in the unit name. Frequently, fields of study are broken down into subspecializations, and those appear following the degrees awarded; for example, "Offerings in secondary education (M.Ed.), including English education, mathematics education, science education." Students enrolled in the M.Ed. program would be able to specialize in any of the three fields mentioned.

Professional Accreditation. Some **Profiles** indicate whether a program is professionally accredited. Because it is possible for a program to receive or lose professional accreditation at any time, students entering fields in which accreditation is important to a career should verify the status of programs by contacting either the chairperson or the appropriate accrediting association.

Jointly Offered Degrees. Explanatory statements concerning programs that are offered in cooperation with other institutions are included in the list of degrees offered. This occurs most commonly on a regional basis (for example, two state universities offering a cooperative Ph.D. in special education) or where the specialized nature of the institutions encourages joint efforts (a J.D./M.B.A. offered by a law school at an institution with no formal business programs and an institution with a business school but lacking a law school). Only programs that are truly cooperative are listed; those involving only limited course work at another institution are not. Interested students should contact the heads of such units for further information.

Part-Time and Evening/Weekend Programs. When information regarding the availability of part-time or evening/weekend study appears in the **Profile**, it means that students are able to earn a degree exclusively through such study.

Postbaccalaureate Distance Learning Degrees. A postbaccalaureate distance learning degree program signifies that course requirements can be fulfilled with minimal or no on-campus study.

Faculty. Figures on the number of faculty members actively involved with graduate students through teaching or research are separated into full-and part-time as well as men and women whenever the information has been supplied.

Students. Figures for the number of students enrolled in graduate and professional programs pertain to the semester of highest enrollment from the 2009–10 academic year. These figures are broken down into full-and part-time and men and women whenever the data have been supplied. Information on the number of matriculated students enrolled in the unit who are members of a minority group or are international students appears here. The average age of the matriculated students is followed by the number of applicants, the percentage accepted, and the number enrolled for fall 2009.

Degrees Awarded. The number of degrees awarded in the calendar year is listed. Many doctoral programs offer a terminal master's degree if students leave the program after completing only part of the requirements for a doctoral degree; that is indicated here. All degrees are classified into one of four types: master's, doctoral, first professional, and other advanced degrees. A unit may award one or several degrees at a given level; however, the data are only collected by type and may therefore represent several different degree programs.

Degree Requirements. The information in this section is also broken down by type of degree, and all information for a degree level pertains to all degrees of that type unless otherwise specified. Degree requirements are collected in a simplified form to provide some very basic information on the nature of the program and on foreign language, thesis or dissertation, comprehensive exam, and registration requirements. Many units also provide a short list of additional requirements, such as fieldwork or an internship. For complete information on graduation requirements, contact the graduate school or program directly.

Entrance Requirements. Entrance requirements are broken down into the four degree levels of master's, doctoral, first professional, and other advanced degrees. Within each level, information may be provided in two basic categories: entrance exams and other requirements. The entrance exams are identified by the standard acronyms used by the testing agencies, unless they are not well known. Other entrance requirements are quite varied, but they often contain an undergraduate or graduate grade point average (GPA). Unless otherwise stated, the GPA is calculated on a 4.0 scale and is listed as a minimum required for admission. Additional exam requirements/recommendations for international students may be listed here. Application deadlines for domestic and international students, the application fee, and whether electronic applications are accepted may be listed here. Note that the deadline should be used for reference only; these dates are subject to change, and students interested in applying should always contact the graduate unit directly about application procedures and deadlines.

Expenses. The typical cost of study for the 2009–10 academic year is given in two basic categories: tuition and fees. Cost of study may be quite complex at a graduate institution. There are often sliding scales for part-time study, a different cost for first-year students, and other variables that make it impossible to completely cover the cost of study for each graduate program. To provide the most usable information, figures are given for full-time study for a full year where available and for part-time study in terms of a per-unit rate (per credit, per semester hour, etc.). Occasionally, variances may be noted in tuition and fees for reasons such as the type of program, whether courses are taken during the day or evening, whether courses are at the master's or doctoral level, or other institution-specific reasons. Expenses are usually subject to change; for exact costs at any given time, contact your chosen schools and programs directly. Keep in mind that the tuition of Canadian institutions is usually given in Canadian dollars.

Financial Support. This section contains data on the number of awards administered by the institution and given to graduate students during the 2009–10 academic year. The first figure given represents the total number of students receiving financial support enrolled in that unit. If the unit has provided information on graduate appointments, these are broken down into three major categories: fellowships give money to graduate students to cover the cost of study and living expenses and are not based on a work obligation or research commitment, research assistantships provide stipends to graduate students for assistance in a formal research project with a faculty member, and teaching assistantships provide stipends to graduate students for teaching or for assisting faculty members in teaching undergraduate classes. Within each category, figures are given for the total number of awards, the average yearly amount per award, and whether full or partial tuition reimbursements are awarded. In addition to graduate appointments, the availability of several other financial aid sources is covered in this section. Tuition waivers are routinely part of a graduate appointment, but units sometimes waive part or all of a student's tuition even if a graduate appointment is not available. Federal Work-Study is made available to students who demonstrate need and meet the federal guidelines; this form of aid normally includes 10 or more hours of work per week in an office of the institution. Institutionally sponsored loans are low-interest loans available to graduate students to cover both educational and living expenses. Career-related internships or fieldwork offer money to students who are participating in a formal off-campus research project or practicum. Grants, scholarships, traineeships, unspecified assistantships, and other awards may also be noted. The availability of financial support to part-time students is also indicated here.

Some programs list the financial aid application deadline and the forms that need to be completed for students to be eligible for financial awards. There are two forms: FAFSA, the Free Application for Federal Student Aid, which is required for federal aid, and the CSS PROFILE®.

Faculty Research. Each unit has the opportunity to list several keyword phrases describing the current research involving faculty members and graduate students. Space limitations prevent the unit from listing complete information on all research programs. The total expenditure for funded research from the previous academic year may also be included.

Unit Head and Application Contact. The head of the graduate program for each unit is listed with academic title and telephone and fax numbers and e-mail address if available. In addition to the unit head, many graduate programs list a separate contact for application and admission information, which follows the listing for the unit head. If no unit head or application contact is given, you should contact the overall institution for information on graduate admissions.

Displays and Close-Ups

The **Displays** and **Close-Ups** are supplementary insertions submitted by deans, chairs, and other administrators who wish to offer an additional, more individualized statement to readers. A number of graduate school and program administrators have attached a **Display** ad near the **Profile** listing. Here you will find information that an institution or program wants to emphasize. The **Close-Ups** are by their very nature more expansive and flexible than the **Profiles**, and the administrators who have written them may emphasize different aspects of their programs. All of the **Close-Ups** are organized in the same way (with the exception of a few that describe research and training opportunities instead of degree programs), and in each one you will find information on the same basic topics, such as programs of study, research facilities, tuition and fees, financial aid, and application procedures. If an institution or program has submitted a **Close-Up**, a boldface cross-reference appears below its **Profile**. As with the **Displays**, all of the **Close-Ups** in the guides have been submitted by choice; the absence of a **Display** or **Close-Up** does not reflect any type of editorial judgment on the part of Peterson's, and their presence in the guides should not be taken as an indication of status, quality, or approval. Statements regarding a university's objectives and accomplishments are a reflection of its own beliefs and are not the opinions of the Peterson's editors.

Appendixes

This section contains two appendixes. The first, "Institutional Changes Since the 2010 Edition," lists institutions that have closed, merged, or changed their name or status since the last edition of the guides. The second, "Abbreviations Used in the Guides," gives abbreviations of degree names, along with what those abbreviations stand for. These appendixes are identical in all six volumes of ***Peterson's Graduate and Professional Programs***.

Indexes

There are three indexes presented here. The first index, "Close-Ups and Displays," gives page references for all programs that have chosen to place **Close-Ups** and **Displays** in this volume. It is arranged alphabetically by institution; within institutions, the arrangement is alphabetical by subject area. It is not an index to all programs in the book's directories of **Profiles**; readers must refer to the directories themselves for **Profile** information on programs that have not submitted the additional, more individualized statements. The second index, "Directories and Subject Areas in Other Books in This Series", gives book references for the directories in the specialized volumes and also includes cross-references for subject area names not used in the directory structure, for example, "Computing Technology (see Computer Science)." The third index, "Directories and Subject Areas in This Book," gives page references for the directories in this volume and cross-references for subject area names not used in this volume's directory structure.

Data Collection Procedures

The information published in the directories and **Profiles** of all the books is collected through Peterson's Annual Survey of Graduate and Professional Institutions. The survey is sent each spring to more than 2,200 institutions offering postbaccalaureate degree programs, including accredited institutions in the United States, U.S. territories, and Canada and those institutions outside the United States that are accredited by U.S. accrediting bodies. Deans and other administrators complete these surveys, providing information on programs in the 500 academic and professional fields covered in the guides as well as overall institutional information. While every effort has been made to ensure the accuracy and completeness of the data, information is sometimes unavailable or changes occur after publication deadlines. All usable information received in time for publication has been included. The omission of any particular item from a directory or **Profile** signifies either that the item is not applicable to the institution or program or that information was not available. **Profiles** of programs scheduled to begin during the 2010–11 academic year cannot, obviously, include statistics on enrollment or, in many cases, the number of faculty members. If no usable data were submitted by an institution, its name, address, and program name appear in order to indicate the availability of graduate work.

Criteria for Inclusion in This Guide

To be included in this guide, an institution must have full accreditation or be a candidate for accreditation (preaccreditation) status by an institutional or specialized accrediting body recognized by the U.S. Department of Education or the Council for Higher Education Accreditation (CHEA). Institutional accrediting bodies, which review each institution as a whole, include the six regional associations of schools and colleges (Middle States, New England, North Central, Northwest, Southern, and Western), each of which is responsible for a specified portion of the United States and its territories. Other institutional accrediting bodies are national in scope and accredit specific kinds of institutions (e.g., Bible colleges, independent colleges, and rabbinical and Talmudic schools). Program registration by the New York State Board of Regents is considered to be the equivalent of institutional accreditation, since the board requires that all programs offered by an institution meet its standards before recognition is granted. A Canadian institution must be chartered and authorized to grant degrees by the provincial government, affiliated with a chartered institution, or accredited by a recognized U.S. accrediting body. This guide also includes institutions outside the United States that are accredited by these U.S. accrediting bodies. There are recognized specialized or professional accrediting bodies in more than fifty different fields, each of which is authorized to accredit institutions or specific programs in its particular field. For specialized institutions that offer programs in one field only, we designate this to be the equivalent of institutional accreditation. A full explanation of the accrediting process and complete information on recognized institutional (regional and national) and specialized accrediting bodies can be found online at www.chea.org or at www.ed.gov/admins/finaid/accred/index.html.

DIRECTORY OF INSTITUTIONS WITH PROGRAMS IN HUMANITIES, ARTS & SOCIAL SCIENCES

ABILENE CHRISTIAN UNIVERSITY
Clinical Psychology M
Communication—General M
Conflict Resolution and Mediation/Peace Studies M,O
Counseling Psychology M
English M
Gerontology M,O
Liberal Studies M
Marriage and Family Therapy M
Missions and Missiology M
Pastoral Ministry and Counseling M,D
Psychology—General M
Rhetoric M
School Psychology O
Theology P,M
Writing M

ACADEMY OF ART UNIVERSITY
Applied Arts and Design—General M
Architecture M
Art/Fine Arts M
Clothing and Textiles M
Computer Art and Design M
Film, Television, and Video Production M
Graphic Design M
Illustration M
Industrial Design M
Interior Design M
Internet and Interactive Multimedia M
Photography M
Textile Design M

ACADIA UNIVERSITY
Clinical Psychology M
English M
Geographic Information Systems M
Political Science M
Psychology—General M
Sociology M
Theology P,M,D

ADAMS STATE COLLEGE
Art/Fine Arts M
History M

ADELPHI UNIVERSITY
Art/Fine Arts M
Clinical Psychology D
Counseling Psychology M
Emergency Management O
Gerontology M,O
Psychology—General M,D
Public Administration O
School Psychology M
Writing M

ADLER GRADUATE SCHOOL
Counseling Psychology M,O
Industrial and Organizational Psychology M,O
Marriage and Family Therapy M,O
Psychoanalysis and Psychotherapy M,O

ADLER SCHOOL OF PROFESSIONAL PSYCHOLOGY
Addictions/Substance Abuse Counseling M,D,O
Art Therapy M,D,O
Clinical Psychology M,D,O
Counseling Psychology M,D,O
Criminal Justice and Criminology M,D,O
Forensic Psychology M,D,O
Gerontology M,D,O
Health Psychology M,D,O
Industrial and Organizational Psychology M,D,O
Marriage and Family Therapy M,D,O
Psychology—General M,D,O*
Rehabilitation Counseling M,D,O
Sport Psychology M,D,O

ALABAMA AGRICULTURAL AND MECHANICAL UNIVERSITY
Agricultural Economics and Agribusiness M
Clinical Psychology M,O
Counseling Psychology M,O
Family and Consumer Sciences-General M,D
Music M
Psychology—General M,O
School Psychology M,O
Urban and Regional Planning M

ALABAMA STATE UNIVERSITY
Music M

ALASKA PACIFIC UNIVERSITY
Counseling Psychology M
Interdisciplinary Studies M
Liberal Studies M

ALBANY STATE UNIVERSITY
Criminal Justice and Criminology M
Economic Development M
Economics M
Forensic Sciences M
Music M
Public Administration M
Public Policy M

ALBERTUS MAGNUS COLLEGE
Art Therapy M
Liberal Studies M

ALCORN STATE UNIVERSITY
Agricultural Economics and Agribusiness M

ALFRED UNIVERSITY
Applied Arts and Design—General M
Art/Fine Arts M,D
Computer Art and Design M
Internet and Interactive Multimedia M
School Psychology M,D,O

ALLIANCE THEOLOGICAL SEMINARY
Missions and Missiology P,M
Pastoral Ministry and Counseling P,M
Theology P,M

ALLIANT INTERNATIONAL UNIVERSITY–FRESNO
Clinical Psychology D
Forensic Psychology D
Industrial and Organizational Psychology M,D
Psychology—General D

ALLIANT INTERNATIONAL UNIVERSITY–IRVINE
Forensic Psychology D
Forensic Sciences D
Marriage and Family Therapy M,D
School Psychology M,D,O

ALLIANT INTERNATIONAL UNIVERSITY–LOS ANGELES
Addictions/Substance Abuse Counseling M
Clinical Psychology D
Forensic Psychology D
Gerontology M
Industrial and Organizational Psychology M,D
Marriage and Family Therapy M
Psychology—General M,D
School Psychology M,D,O

ALLIANT INTERNATIONAL UNIVERSITY–MÉXICO CITY
Counseling Psychology M
International Affairs M

ALLIANT INTERNATIONAL UNIVERSITY–SACRAMENTO
Clinical Psychology D
Industrial and Organizational Psychology D
Marriage and Family Therapy M
Psychology—General M,D

ALLIANT INTERNATIONAL UNIVERSITY–SAN DIEGO
Clinical Psychology M,D
Industrial and Organizational Psychology M,D
International Affairs M
Marriage and Family Therapy M,D
Psychology—General M,D
School Psychology M,D,O

ALLIANT INTERNATIONAL UNIVERSITY–SAN FRANCISCO
Clinical Psychology D,O
Industrial and Organizational Psychology M,D
Psychology—General M,D,O
School Psychology M,D,O

ALVERNIA UNIVERSITY
Liberal Studies M
Social Psychology M

AMBERTON UNIVERSITY
Counseling Psychology M
Interdisciplinary Studies M

AMBROSE UNIVERSITY COLLEGE
Cultural Studies P,M,O
Missions and Missiology P,M,O
Religion P,M,O
Theology P,M,O

AMERICAN BAPTIST SEMINARY OF THE WEST
Pastoral Ministry and Counseling P,M
Theology P,M

AMERICAN CONSERVATORY THEATER
Theater M,O

AMERICAN FILM INSTITUTE CONSERVATORY
Film, Television, and Video Production M

AMERICAN GRADUATE SCHOOL IN PARIS
International Affairs M,D

AMERICAN INTERCONTINENTAL UNIVERSITY ONLINE
Industrial and Organizational Psychology M

AMERICAN INTERNATIONAL COLLEGE
Clinical Psychology M
Corporate and Organizational Communication M
Forensic Psychology M
Psychology—General M,D
Public Administration M

AMERICAN JEWISH UNIVERSITY
Jewish Studies M
Theology M

AMERICAN PUBLIC UNIVERSITY SYSTEM
Conflict Resolution and Mediation/Peace Studies M
Criminal Justice and Criminology M
Emergency Management M
History M
Homeland Security M
Humanities M
International Affairs M
Military and Defense Studies M
National Security M
Political Science M
Public Administration M

AMERICAN UNIVERSITY
American Studies M,D,O
Anthropology M,D,O
Applied Economics M,D,O
Applied Social Research M,O
Art History M
Art/Fine Arts M
Arts Administration M,O
Broadcast Journalism M
Clinical Psychology D
Communication—General M*
Comparative Literature M
Conflict Resolution and Mediation/Peace Studies M,D,O
Criminal Justice and Criminology M,D
Cultural Studies M,D,O
Economics M,D,O
Ethics M,D,O
Experimental Psychology M
Film, Television, and Video Production M
French O
History M,D
Interdisciplinary Studies M
International Affairs M,D,O*

- International Development M,D,O
- Journalism M
- Latin American Studies M,O
- Mass Communication M,D,O
- Media Studies M
- Philosophy M
- Political Science M,D,O
- Psychology—General D
- Public Administration M,D,O
- Public Affairs M
- Public Policy M
- Russian O
- Social Psychology M
- Sociology M,O
- Spanish M,O
- Sustainable Development M,D,O
- Translation and Interpretation M,O
- Western European Studies M,D,O
- Writing M

THE AMERICAN UNIVERSITY IN CAIRO

- Anthropology M
- Broadcast Journalism M
- Communication—General M
- Comparative Literature M
- Demography and Population Studies M,O
- Economics M
- English M
- Gender Studies M,O
- Journalism M
- Mass Communication M
- Near and Middle Eastern Languages M,O
- Near and Middle Eastern Studies M,O
- Political Science M
- Public Administration M,O
- Public Policy M,O
- Sociology M
- Women's Studies M,O

THE AMERICAN UNIVERSITY OF ATHENS

- Corporate and Organizational Communication M
- Political Science M

AMERICAN UNIVERSITY OF BEIRUT

- Agricultural Economics and Agribusiness M
- Anthropology M
- Archaeology M
- Economics M
- English M
- Health Psychology M
- History M
- Near and Middle Eastern Languages M
- Near and Middle Eastern Studies M
- Philosophy M
- Political Science M
- Psychology—General M
- Public Administration M
- Sociology M
- Urban and Regional Planning M,D
- Urban Design M,D

THE AMERICAN UNIVERSITY OF PARIS

- Communication—General M
- Conflict Resolution and Mediation/Peace Studies M
- Cultural Studies M
- International Affairs M
- Near and Middle Eastern Studies M
- Public Policy M

AMERICAN UNIVERSITY OF PUERTO RICO

- Art History M
- Criminal Justice and Criminology M

AMERICAN UNIVERSITY OF SHARJAH

- Public Administration M
- Translation and Interpretation M
- Urban and Regional Planning M

AMRIDGE UNIVERSITY

- Counseling Psychology P,M,D
- Marriage and Family Therapy P,M,D
- Pastoral Ministry and Counseling P,M,D
- Religion P,M,D
- Theology P,M,D

ANDERSON UNIVERSITY (IN)

- Missions and Missiology P,M,D
- Theology P,M,D

ANDERSON UNIVERSITY (SC)

- Criminal Justice and Criminology M
- Pastoral Ministry and Counseling M

ANDOVER NEWTON THEOLOGICAL SCHOOL

- Theology P,M,D

ANDREW JACKSON UNIVERSITY

- Criminal Justice and Criminology M
- Public Administration M

ANDREWS UNIVERSITY

- Architecture M
- Communication—General M
- Counseling Psychology D
- Developmental Psychology M,D
- Economics M
- English M
- History M
- International Development M
- Music M
- Pastoral Ministry and Counseling P,M,D,O
- Psychology—General M,D,O
- School Psychology M,O
- Social Psychology M
- Theology P,M,D,O

ANGELO STATE UNIVERSITY

- Communication—General M
- Counseling Psychology M
- English M
- History M
- Industrial and Organizational Psychology M
- Interdisciplinary Studies M
- Journalism M
- Psychology—General M
- Public Administration M

ANNA MARIA COLLEGE

- Art/Fine Arts M,O
- Counseling Psychology M
- Criminal Justice and Criminology M
- Emergency Management M,O
- Pastoral Ministry and Counseling M
- Public Administration M

ANTIOCH UNIVERSITY LOS ANGELES

- Clinical Psychology M
- Psychology—General M
- Writing M,O

ANTIOCH UNIVERSITY MIDWEST

- Art/Fine Arts M
- Comparative Literature M
- Conflict Resolution and Mediation/Peace Studies M
- Counseling Psychology M
- Film, Television, and Video Production M
- Liberal Studies M
- Psychology—General M
- Theater M
- Writing M

ANTIOCH UNIVERSITY NEW ENGLAND

- Clinical Psychology M,D
- Counseling Psychology M
- Interdisciplinary Studies M
- Marriage and Family Therapy M,D
- Psychology—General M,D,O
- Therapies—Dance, Drama, and Music M

ANTIOCH UNIVERSITY SANTA BARBARA

- Clinical Psychology D
- Psychology—General M

ANTIOCH UNIVERSITY SEATTLE

- Corporate and Organizational Communication M
- Industrial and Organizational Psychology M
- Psychology—General M,D

APEX SCHOOL OF THEOLOGY

- Theology P,M,D

APPALACHIAN BIBLE COLLEGE

- Pastoral Ministry and Counseling M

APPALACHIAN STATE UNIVERSITY

- American Studies M
- Child Development M
- Clinical Psychology M,O
- Criminal Justice and Criminology M
- Cultural Studies M
- English M
- Experimental Psychology M,O
- Family and Consumer Sciences-General M
- Geographic Information Systems M
- Geography M
- Gerontology M
- Health Psychology M,O
- History M
- Industrial and Organizational Psychology M,O
- International Affairs M
- Marriage and Family Therapy M
- Music M
- Political Science M
- Psychology—General M,O
- Public Administration M
- Public History M
- Romance Languages M
- School Psychology M
- Social Psychology M
- Sustainable Development M
- Therapies—Dance, Drama, and Music M

AQUINAS INSTITUTE OF THEOLOGY

- Pastoral Ministry and Counseling P,M,D,O
- Theology P,M,D,O

ARCADIA UNIVERSITY

- Child Development M,D,O
- Conflict Resolution and Mediation/Peace Studies M
- English M
- Forensic Sciences M
- Genetic Counseling M
- Humanities M
- International Affairs M
- Psychology—General M,D,O
- School Psychology M
- Social Psychology M
- Theater M,D,O

ARGOSY UNIVERSITY, ATLANTA

- Clinical Psychology M,D,O
- Forensic Psychology M,D,O
- Health Psychology M,D,O
- Industrial and Organizational Psychology M,D,O
- Marriage and Family Therapy M,D,O
- Psychology—General M,D,O*
- Social Psychology M,D,O
- Sport Psychology M,D,O

ARGOSY UNIVERSITY, CHICAGO

- Clinical Psychology M,D*
- Counseling Psychology D
- Forensic Psychology D
- Health Psychology D
- Human Development D
- Industrial and Organizational Psychology M,D
- Marriage and Family Therapy D
- Psychoanalysis and Psychotherapy D
- Psychology—General M,D
- Public Administration M,D
- Social Psychology M,D

ARGOSY UNIVERSITY, DALLAS

- Clinical Psychology M,D*
- Forensic Psychology M
- Industrial and Organizational Psychology M
- Psychology—General M,D
- Public Administration M,D,O
- School Psychology M,D
- Social Psychology M

ARGOSY UNIVERSITY, DENVER
Clinical Psychology M,D
Counseling Psychology M,D
Forensic Psychology M,D
Industrial and Organizational Psychology M,D
Marriage and Family Therapy M,D
Psychology—General M,D*
Public Administration M,D

ARGOSY UNIVERSITY, HAWAI'I
Addictions/Substance Abuse Counseling O
Clinical Psychology M,D,O
Counseling Psychology D
Forensic Psychology M
Marriage and Family Therapy M
Psychology—General M,D,O*
School Psychology M

ARGOSY UNIVERSITY, INLAND EMPIRE
Clinical Psychology M,D
Counseling Psychology M,D
Forensic Psychology M,D
Industrial and Organizational Psychology M,D
Marriage and Family Therapy M,D
Psychology—General M,D*
Public Administration M,D
Sport Psychology M,D

ARGOSY UNIVERSITY, LOS ANGELES
Clinical Psychology M,D*
Counseling Psychology M,D
Forensic Psychology M,D
Marriage and Family Therapy M,D
Psychology—General M,D
Public Administration M,D

ARGOSY UNIVERSITY, NASHVILLE
Counseling Psychology M,D*
Psychology—General M,D

ARGOSY UNIVERSITY, ORANGE COUNTY
Clinical Psychology M,D
Counseling Psychology M,D
Forensic Psychology M
Marriage and Family Therapy M,D
Psychology—General M,D*
Public Administration M,D,O
Sport Psychology M

ARGOSY UNIVERSITY, PHOENIX
Clinical Psychology M,D
Counseling Psychology M
Forensic Psychology M
Industrial and Organizational Psychology M
Psychology—General M,D*
Public Administration M,D
School Psychology M,D
Sport Psychology M,D

ARGOSY UNIVERSITY, SALT LAKE CITY
Counseling Psychology M,D
Forensic Psychology M,D
Marriage and Family Therapy M,D
Psychology—General M,D*
Public Administration M,D

ARGOSY UNIVERSITY, SAN DIEGO
Clinical Psychology M,D
Counseling Psychology M,D*
Forensic Psychology M,D
Marriage and Family Therapy M,D
Psychology—General M,D
Public Administration M,D

ARGOSY UNIVERSITY, SAN FRANCISCO BAY AREA
Clinical Psychology M,D
Counseling Psychology M,D
Forensic Psychology M
Psychology—General M,D*
Public Administration M,D
Sport Psychology M,D

ARGOSY UNIVERSITY, SARASOTA
Counseling Psychology M,D
Forensic Psychology M,D
Marriage and Family Therapy M,D
Pastoral Ministry and Counseling M,D
Psychology—General M,D*
Public Administration M,D,O
School Psychology M,D,O
Social Psychology M,D

ARGOSY UNIVERSITY, SCHAUMBURG
Clinical Psychology M,D,O*
Corporate and Organizational Communication M,D,O
Counseling Psychology M,D,O
Forensic Psychology M,D,O
Health Psychology M,D,O
Industrial and Organizational Psychology M,D,O
Marriage and Family Therapy M,D,O
Psychology—General M,D,O
Public Administration M,D,O
Social Psychology M,D,O

ARGOSY UNIVERSITY, SEATTLE
Clinical Psychology M,D,O*
Counseling Psychology M,D
Psychology—General M,D,O
Public Administration M,D

ARGOSY UNIVERSITY, TAMPA
Clinical Psychology M,D
Counseling Psychology M,D
Industrial and Organizational Psychology M,D
Marriage and Family Therapy M,D
Psychology—General M,D*
Public Administration M,D

ARGOSY UNIVERSITY, TWIN CITIES
Clinical Psychology M,D,O
Forensic Psychology M,D,O
Health Psychology M,D,O
Industrial and Organizational Psychology M,D,O
Marriage and Family Therapy M,D,O
Psychology—General M,D,O*
Public Administration M,D

ARGOSY UNIVERSITY, WASHINGTON DC
Clinical Psychology M,D*
Counseling Psychology M,D
Forensic Psychology M,D
Health Psychology M,D
Marriage and Family Therapy M,D
Psychology—General M,D
Public Administration M,D,O
Social Psychology M,D

ARIZONA STATE UNIVERSITY
Agricultural Economics and Agribusiness M,D
Anthropology M,D
Applied Arts and Design—General M
Architectural History D
Architecture M
Art/Fine Arts M,D
Building Science M
Child and Family Studies M,D
Chinese M
Clinical Psychology D
Cognitive Sciences D
Communication—General M,D
Comparative Literature M,D
Computer Art and Design M
Counseling Psychology D
Criminal Justice and Criminology M,D
Cultural Studies M
Dance M
Developmental Psychology D
Economics D
English M,D
Environmental Design D
Film, Television, and Video Production M
French M
Gender Studies D
Geographic Information Systems M,D
Geography M,D
German M
Gerontology M,O
History M,D
Human Development M,D
Industrial Design M
Interdisciplinary Studies M
Interior Design M
Japanese M
Journalism M
Landscape Architecture M
Latin American Studies M,D
Linguistics M,D
Marriage and Family Therapy M,D
Mass Communication M
Media Studies M
Museum Studies M,D
Music M,D
Philosophy M,D
Political Science M,D
Psychology—General M,D
Public Affairs M,D
Public History M,D
Public Policy P,M
Religion M,D
Social Psychology D
Social Sciences M,D
Sociology M,D
Spanish M,D
Speech and Interpersonal Communication M,D
Sustainable Development M,D
Theater M,D
Therapies—Dance, Drama, and Music M,D
Urban and Regional Planning M,D
Urban Design M
Writing M

ARKANSAS STATE UNIVERSITY—JONESBORO
Art/Fine Arts M
Communication—General M,O
Criminal Justice and Criminology M,O
English M,O
Gerontology M,D,O
Historic Preservation M,D
History M,O
Journalism M
Media Studies M
Music M,O
Political Science M,O
Public Administration M,O
Rehabilitation Counseling M,O
School Psychology M,O
Sociology M,O
Speech and Interpersonal Communication M,O
Theater M,O

ARKANSAS TECH UNIVERSITY
Art/Fine Arts M
Communication—General M
Emergency Management M
English M
History M
Journalism M
Psychology—General M
Social Sciences M
Spanish M

ARMSTRONG ATLANTIC STATE UNIVERSITY
Criminal Justice and Criminology M
History M
Liberal Studies M

ART CENTER COLLEGE OF DESIGN
Applied Arts and Design—General M*
Art/Fine Arts M
Computer Art and Design M
Environmental Design M
Film, Television, and Video Production M
Industrial Design M

THE ART INSTITUTE OF BOSTON AT LESLEY UNIVERSITY
Art/Fine Arts M

THE ART INSTITUTE OF CALIFORNIA–SAN FRANCISCO
Art/Fine Arts M
Film, Television, and Video Production M

ASBURY THEOLOGICAL SEMINARY
Missions and Missiology M,D,O

*M—master's degree; P—first professional degree; D—doctorate; O—other advanced degree; *—Close-Up and/or Display*

Pastoral Ministry and Counseling M,D,O
Theology M,D,O

ASBURY UNIVERSITY
Child and Family Studies M
Classics M
English M
French M
Spanish M
Writing M

ASHLAND THEOLOGICAL SEMINARY
History P,M,D,O
Pastoral Ministry and Counseling P,M,D,O
Theology P,M,D,O

ASHLAND UNIVERSITY
History M
Political Science M
Writing M

ASSEMBLIES OF GOD THEOLOGICAL SEMINARY
Cultural Studies P,M,D
Missions and Missiology P,M,D
Pastoral Ministry and Counseling P,M,D
Theology P,M,D
Women's Studies P,M,D

ASSOCIATED MENNONITE BIBLICAL SEMINARY
Conflict Resolution and Mediation/Peace Studies P,M,O
Missions and Missiology P,M,O
Theology P,M,O

ASSUMPTION COLLEGE
Child and Family Studies M,O
Counseling Psychology M,O
Economics M,O
Psychology—General M,O
Rehabilitation Counseling M,O
School Psychology M,O

ATHABASCA UNIVERSITY
Art Therapy M,O
Counseling Psychology M,O
Cultural Studies M
Interdisciplinary Studies M
International Development M
Psychology—General M,O

THE ATHENAEUM OF OHIO
Pastoral Ministry and Counseling P,M,O
Theology P,M,O

ATLANTIC COLLEGE
Graphic Design M

ATLANTIC SCHOOL OF THEOLOGY
Pastoral Ministry and Counseling P,M,O
Theology P,M,O

ATLANTIC UNIVERSITY
Transpersonal and Humanistic Psychology M

A.T. STILL UNIVERSITY OF HEALTH SCIENCES
Gerontology M,D

AUBURN UNIVERSITY
Agricultural Economics and Agribusiness M,D
Applied Economics M,D
Architecture M
Building Science M
Child and Family Studies M,D
Clothing and Textiles M
Communication—General M
Economics M
English M,D*
Experimental Psychology M,D
Geography M
History M,D
Human Development M,D
Industrial and Organizational Psychology M,D
Industrial Design M
Landscape Architecture M
Mass Communication M
Political Science M,D
Psychology—General M,D
Public Administration M,D
Rehabilitation Counseling M,D
Rural Sociology M
Sociology M
Spanish M
Urban and Regional Planning M

AUBURN UNIVERSITY MONTGOMERY
Criminal Justice and Criminology M
Liberal Studies M
Political Science M,D
Psychology—General M
Public Administration M,D

AUGUSTA STATE UNIVERSITY
Political Science M
Psychology—General M

AUSTIN COLLEGE
Theater M

AUSTIN GRADUATE SCHOOL OF THEOLOGY
Theology M

AUSTIN PEAY STATE UNIVERSITY
Communication—General M
English M
Military and Defense Studies M
Music M
Psychology—General M,O

AUSTIN PRESBYTERIAN THEOLOGICAL SEMINARY
Pastoral Ministry and Counseling P,M,D
Theology P,M,D

AVE MARIA UNIVERSITY
Pastoral Ministry and Counseling M,D
Theology M,D

AVILA UNIVERSITY
Counseling Psychology M
Psychology—General M

AZUSA PACIFIC UNIVERSITY
Art/Fine Arts M
Clinical Psychology M,D
Ethics M
Marriage and Family Therapy M,D
Music M
Pastoral Ministry and Counseling P,M
Psychology—General M,D
Religion M
School Psychology M
Theology M,D

BABEL UNIVERSITY SCHOOL OF TRANSLATION
Translation and Interpretation M

BAKER UNIVERSITY
Conflict Resolution and Mediation/Peace Studies M
Liberal Studies M

BAKKE GRADUATE UNIVERSITY
Pastoral Ministry and Counseling M,D

BALL STATE UNIVERSITY
Anthropology M
Architecture M
Art/Fine Arts M
Clinical Psychology M
Cognitive Sciences M
Communication—General M
Counseling Psychology M,D
English M,D
Family and Consumer Sciences-General M
Gerontology M
Historic Preservation M
History M
Journalism M
Landscape Architecture M
Linguistics D
Political Science M
Psychology—General M
Public Administration M
Rhetoric M
School Psychology M,D,O
Social Psychology M
Social Sciences M
Sociology M
Speech and Interpersonal Communication M
Urban and Regional Planning M
Urban Design M
Writing M,D

BANGOR THEOLOGICAL SEMINARY
Theology P,M,D

BANK STREET COLLEGE OF EDUCATION
Child and Family Studies M

BAPTIST BIBLE COLLEGE
Cultural Studies P,M
Pastoral Ministry and Counseling P,M
Theology P,M

BAPTIST BIBLE COLLEGE OF PENNSYLVANIA
Missions and Missiology P,M,D
Pastoral Ministry and Counseling P,M,D
Religion P,M,D
Theology P,M,D

BAPTIST MISSIONARY ASSOCIATION THEOLOGICAL SEMINARY
Theology P,M

BAPTIST THEOLOGICAL SEMINARY AT RICHMOND
Pastoral Ministry and Counseling P,D
Religion P,D
Theology P,D

BARD COLLEGE
Art History M,D
Art/Fine Arts M
Decorative Arts M,D
Museum Studies M
Music M
Photography M

BARD GRADUATE CENTER FOR STUDIES IN THE DECORATIVE ARTS, DESIGN, AND CULTURE
Art History M,D*
Decorative Arts M,D

BARRY UNIVERSITY
Art/Fine Arts M
Clinical Psychology M,O
Communication—General M,O
Corporate and Organizational Communication M,O
Liberal Studies M
Marriage and Family Therapy M,O
Pastoral Ministry and Counseling M,D
Photography M
Psychology—General M,O
Public Administration M
Rehabilitation Counseling M,O
School Psychology M,O
Sport Psychology M
Theology M,D

BASTYR UNIVERSITY
Health Psychology M

BAYAMÓN CENTRAL UNIVERSITY
Criminal Justice and Criminology M
Industrial and Organizational Psychology M
Psychology—General M
Rehabilitation Counseling M

BAYLOR UNIVERSITY
American Studies M
Clinical Psychology M,D
Communication—General M
Economics M
English M,D
History M
Interdisciplinary Studies M,D
International Affairs M,D
Journalism M
Museum Studies M
Music M
Philosophy M,D
Political Science M,D
Psychology—General M,D
Public Administration M,D
Public Policy M,D
Religion M,D
Sociology M,D
Spanish M

Theater M
Theology P,M,D

BELHAVEN UNIVERSITY (MS)
Public Administration M

BELLARMINE UNIVERSITY
Communication—General M
Religion M

BELLEVUE UNIVERSITY
Criminal Justice and Criminology M,D
Public Administration M,D

BELMONT UNIVERSITY
English M
Music M
Writing M

BEMIDJI STATE UNIVERSITY
Counseling Psychology M
English M

BENEDICTINE UNIVERSITY
Clinical Psychology M
Emergency Management M

BENNINGTON COLLEGE
Dance M
English M
French M
Music M
Spanish M
Theater M
Writing M

BERNARD M. BARUCH COLLEGE OF THE CITY UNIVERSITY OF NEW YORK
Corporate and Organizational Communication M
Economics M
Industrial and Labor Relations M
Industrial and Organizational Psychology M,D,O
Public Administration M

BETHANY THEOLOGICAL SEMINARY
Conflict Resolution and Mediation/Peace Studies P,M,O
Pastoral Ministry and Counseling P,M,O
Religion P,M,O
Theology P,M,O

BETHANY UNIVERSITY
Clinical Psychology M

BETHEL COLLEGE
Pastoral Ministry and Counseling M
Theology M

BETHEL SEMINARY
Marriage and Family Therapy P,M,D,O
Missions and Missiology P,M,D,O
Pastoral Ministry and Counseling P,M,D,O
Theology P,M,D,O

BETHEL UNIVERSITY (MN)
Communication—General M,O
Counseling Psychology M
Developmental Psychology M
Gerontology M
Social Psychology M

BETHESDA CHRISTIAN UNIVERSITY
Music P,M
Religion P,M
Theology P,M

BETH HAMEDRASH SHAAREI YOSHER INSTITUTE
Theology

BETH HATALMUD RABBINICAL COLLEGE
Theology

BETH MEDRASH GOVOHA
Theology

BETHUNE-COOKMAN UNIVERSITY
Theology M

BEULAH HEIGHTS UNIVERSITY
Religion M

BEXLEY HALL EPISCOPAL SEMINARY
Theology P,M

BIBLICAL THEOLOGICAL SEMINARY
Missions and Missiology P,M,D,O
Pastoral Ministry and Counseling P,M,D,O
Theology P,M,D,O

BIOLA UNIVERSITY
Cultural Studies M,D,O
Ethics P,M,D
Linguistics M,D,O
Missions and Missiology M,D,O
Psychology—General M,D
Religion P,M,D
Theology P,M,D

BIRMINGHAM-SOUTHERN COLLEGE
Music M
Public Administration M

BLESSED JOHN XXIII NATIONAL SEMINARY
Theology P

BOB JONES UNIVERSITY
Art/Fine Arts P,M,D,O
English P,M,D,O
Film, Television, and Video Production P,M,D,O
Graphic Design P,M,D,O
History P,M,D,O
Illustration P,M,D,O
Journalism P,M,D,O
Media Studies P,M,D,O
Music P,M,D,O
Pastoral Ministry and Counseling P,M,D,O
Religion P,M,D,O
Rhetoric P,M,D,O
Speech and Interpersonal Communication P,M,D,O

Theater P,M,D,O
Theology P,M,D,O

BOISE STATE UNIVERSITY
Art/Fine Arts M
Communication—General M
Criminal Justice and Criminology M
English M
History M
Interdisciplinary Studies M
Music M
Public Administration M
Public Policy M
Technical Communication M
Writing M

BORICUA COLLEGE
Latin American Studies M

BOSTON ARCHITECTURAL COLLEGE
Architecture M
Interior Design M

BOSTON COLLEGE
Classics M
Counseling Psychology M,D
Developmental Psychology M,D
East European and Russian Studies M
Economics D
English M,D
French M,D
History M,D
Italian M,D
Linguistics M
Pastoral Ministry and Counseling P,M,D,O
Philosophy M,D
Political Science M,D
Psychology—General M,D
Russian M
Slavic Languages M
Sociology M,D
Spanish M,D
Theology P,M,D,O
Western European Studies M,D

THE BOSTON CONSERVATORY
Music M,O
Theater M

BOSTON GRADUATE SCHOOL OF PSYCHOANALYSIS
Counseling Psychology M
Psychoanalysis and Psychotherapy M,D,O
Psychology—General M

BOSTON UNIVERSITY
African Studies M,O
African-American Studies M
American Studies D
Anthropology M,D
Archaeology M,D
Art History M,D,O
Art/Fine Arts M
Arts Administration M,O
Broadcast Journalism M
Classics M,D
Cognitive Sciences M,D
Communication—General M*
Counseling Psychology D
Criminal Justice and Criminology M

Economic Development M
Economics M,D
English M,D
Film, Television, and Video Production M
Film, Television, and Video Theory and Criticism M
French M,D
Geographic Information Systems M,D
Geography M,D
Graphic Design M
Historic Preservation M
History M,D
Human Development M,D,O
Interdisciplinary Studies M
International Affairs M,D,O
Journalism M
Liberal Studies M
Linguistics M,D
Mass Communication M
Media Studies M
Museum Studies M,D,O
Music M,D,O
Philosophy M,D
Political Science M,D
Psychology—General M,D
Public Administration M
Religion M,D
Romance Languages M,D
Sociology M,D
Spanish M,D
Theater M,O
Theology P,M,D
Urban and Regional Planning M
Urban Studies M
Writing M,D

BOWIE STATE UNIVERSITY
Corporate and Organizational Communication M,O
Counseling Psychology M
English M
Public Administration M

BOWLING GREEN STATE UNIVERSITY
American Studies M,D
Applied Arts and Design—General M
Art History M
Art/Fine Arts M
Child and Family Studies M
Clinical Psychology M,D
Communication—General M,D
Computer Art and Design M
Counseling Psychology M
Criminal Justice and Criminology M
Demography and Population Studies M,D
Developmental Psychology M,D
Economics M
English M,D
Experimental Psychology M,D
Family and Consumer Sciences-General M
Film, Television, and Video Production M,D
French M
German M
Graphic Design M
History M,D
Human Development M

*M—master's degree; P—first professional degree; D—doctorate; O—other advanced degree; *—Close-Up and/or Display*

Industrial and Organizational Psychology	M,D
Interdisciplinary Studies	M,D
Music	M,D
Philosophy	M,D
Political Science	
Psychology—General	M,D
Public Administration	M
Rehabilitation Counseling	M
Rhetoric	M,D
School Psychology	M,O
Social Psychology	M,D
Sociology	M,D
Spanish	M
Speech and Interpersonal Communication	M,D
Technical Communication	M,D
Theater	M,D
Writing	M,D

BRADLEY UNIVERSITY

Applied Arts and Design—General	M
Art/Fine Arts	M
Comparative and Interdisciplinary Arts	M
English	M
Human Development	M
Illustration	M
Liberal Studies	M
Photography	M

BRANDEIS UNIVERSITY

Anthropology	M,D
Art/Fine Arts	O
Child and Family Studies	M,D
Classics	M,O
Cognitive Sciences	M,D
Communication—General	M,O
Conflict Resolution and Mediation/Peace Studies	M
Cultural Studies	M
Developmental Psychology	M,D
Disability Studies	D
Economics	M,D
English	M,D
Gender Studies	M,D
Genetic Counseling	M
History	M,D
International Affairs	M,D
International Development	M
Jewish Studies	M,D
Linguistics	M
Music	M,D
Near and Middle Eastern Languages	M,D
Near and Middle Eastern Studies	M,D
Philosophy	M
Political Science	M,D
Psychology—General	M,D
Public Policy	M
Social Psychology	M,D
Sociology	M,D
Sustainable Development	M
Theater	M
Women's Studies	M,D

BRANDON UNIVERSITY

Music	M
Rural Planning and Studies	M,O

BRENAU UNIVERSITY

Interior Design	M
Psychology—General	M

BRIDGEWATER STATE UNIVERSITY

Criminal Justice and Criminology	M
English	M
Psychology—General	M
Public Administration	M

BRIERCREST SEMINARY

Marriage and Family Therapy	M
Missions and Missiology	M
Pastoral Ministry and Counseling	P,M
Religion	P,M
Theology	P,M

BRIGHAM YOUNG UNIVERSITY

Anthropology	M
Art History	M
Art/Fine Arts	M
Child and Family Studies	M,D
Clinical Psychology	M,D
Communication—General	M
Comparative and Interdisciplinary Arts	M
Comparative Literature	M
Counseling Psychology	M,D,O
English	M
Film, Television, and Video Production	M
French	M
Geography	M
German	M
Human Development	M,D
Humanities	M
Industrial Design	M
Linguistics	M,O
Marriage and Family Therapy	M,D
Mass Communication	M
Music	M
Political Science	M
Portuguese	M
Psychology—General	M,D
Public Administration	M
Public Policy	M
Rhetoric	M
School Psychology	M,D,O
Social Psychology	M,D
Sociology	M
Spanish	M
Theater	M
Writing	M

BROCK UNIVERSITY

Child and Family Studies	M
Classics	M
Comparative Literature	M
Cultural Studies	M
Disability Studies	M,O
Economics	M
English	M
Geography	M
History	M
Human Development	M,D
International Affairs	M
Philosophy	M
Political Science	M
Psychology—General	M,D
Public Policy	M
Social Psychology	M,D
Sociology	M

BROOKLYN COLLEGE OF THE CITY UNIVERSITY OF NEW YORK

Art History	M,D
Art/Fine Arts	M,D
Counseling Psychology	M,D,O
Economics	M
English	M,D
Experimental Psychology	M,D
Film, Television, and Video Production	M
French	M,D
History	M,D
Industrial and Organizational Psychology	M
International Affairs	M,D
Internet and Interactive Multimedia	M,O
Jewish Studies	M
Liberal Studies	M
Media Studies	M
Music	M,D,O
Photography	M,D
Political Science	M,D
Psychology—General	M,D
Public Policy	M,D
School Psychology	M,O
Social Psychology	M
Sociology	M,D
Spanish	M,D
Speech and Interpersonal Communication	M,D
Thanatology	M
Theater	M,D
Urban Studies	M,D
Writing	M

BROOKS INSTITUTE

Photography	M

BROWN UNIVERSITY

American Studies	M,D
Anthropology	M,D
Archaeology	M,D
Art History	M,D
Classics	M,D
Cognitive Sciences	M,D
Comparative Literature	D
Developmental Psychology	D
East European and Russian Studies	M,D
Economics	D
English	D
French	D
German	D
Hispanic Studies	M,D
History	M,D
Italian	D
Jewish Studies	D
Latin American Studies	M,D
Linguistics	M,D
Museum Studies	M,D
Music	D
Philosophy	M,D
Political Science	D
Psychology—General	D
Public Policy	M
Religion	D
Russian	M,D
Slavic Languages	M,D
Social Psychology	D
Sociology	M,D
Theater	M,D
Western European Studies	M,D
Writing	M

BRYN ATHYN COLLEGE OF THE NEW CHURCH

Religion	P,M
Theology	P,M

BRYN MAWR COLLEGE

Archaeology	M,D
Art History	M,D
Classics	M,D
Clinical Psychology	D
Developmental Psychology	D
French	M,D
Psychology—General	D

BUCKNELL UNIVERSITY

English	M
Psychology—General	M
School Psychology	M

BUFFALO STATE COLLEGE, STATE UNIVERSITY OF NEW YORK

Applied Economics	M
Criminal Justice and Criminology	M
Economics	M
English	M
Historic Preservation	M,O
History	M
Interdisciplinary Studies	M

BUTLER UNIVERSITY

English	M
History	M
Music	M

CALDWELL COLLEGE

Art Therapy	M
Counseling Psychology	M
Pastoral Ministry and Counseling	M
Psychology—General	M,D

CALIFORNIA BAPTIST UNIVERSITY

Counseling Psychology	M
English	M
Forensic Psychology	M
Music	M
Pastoral Ministry and Counseling	M
Public Administration	M
School Psychology	M

CALIFORNIA COAST UNIVERSITY

Psychology—General	M

CALIFORNIA COLLEGE OF THE ARTS

Applied Arts and Design—General	M
Architecture	M
Art/Fine Arts	M
Film, Television, and Video Production	M
Film, Television, and Video Theory and Criticism	M
Museum Studies	M
Photography	M
Textile Design	M
Writing	M

CALIFORNIA INSTITUTE OF INTEGRAL STUDIES

Anthropology	M,D
Art Therapy	M,D
Asian Studies	M,D
Clinical Psychology	M,D
Counseling Psychology	M,D
Health Psychology	M,D

Humanities M,D
Philosophy M,D
Psychology—General M,D
Religion M,D
Social Psychology M,D
Theology M,D
Therapies—Dance, Drama, and Music M,D
Women's Studies M,D
Writing M,D

CALIFORNIA INSTITUTE OF TECHNOLOGY

Social Sciences M,D

CALIFORNIA INSTITUTE OF THE ARTS

Applied Arts and Design—General M,O
Art/Fine Arts M,O
Dance M,O
Film, Television, and Video Production M,O
Graphic Design M,O
Music M,O
Photography M,O
Theater M,O
Writing M,O

CALIFORNIA LUTHERAN UNIVERSITY

Clinical Psychology M,D
Marriage and Family Therapy M,D
Psychology—General M,D
Public Administration M
Public Policy M

CALIFORNIA POLYTECHNIC STATE UNIVERSITY, SAN LUIS OBISPO

Agricultural Economics and Agribusiness M
Architecture M
English M
History M
Political Science M
Psychology—General M
Urban and Regional Planning M

CALIFORNIA STATE POLYTECHNIC UNIVERSITY, POMONA

Architecture M
Economics M
English M
History M
Landscape Architecture M
Psychology—General M
Public Administration M
Urban and Regional Planning M

CALIFORNIA STATE UNIVERSITY, BAKERSFIELD

Anthropology M
Counseling Psychology M
English M
History M
Interdisciplinary Studies M
Psychology—General M
Public Administration M
Sociology M
Spanish M

CALIFORNIA STATE UNIVERSITY, CHICO

Anthropology M
Art History M
Art/Fine Arts M
Communication—General M
English M
Geography M
History M
Interdisciplinary Studies M
Marriage and Family Therapy M
Museum Studies M
Music M
Political Science M
Psychology—General M
Public Administration M
Rural Planning and Studies M
Social Sciences M
Urban and Regional Planning M

CALIFORNIA STATE UNIVERSITY, DOMINGUEZ HILLS

Applied Social Research M,O
Clinical Psychology M
Conflict Resolution and Mediation/Peace Studies M
English M,O
Humanities M
Marriage and Family Therapy M
Psychology—General M
Public Administration M
Rhetoric M,O
Sociology M,O

CALIFORNIA STATE UNIVERSITY, EAST BAY

Anthropology M
Communication—General M
Economics M
English M
Geography M
History M
Humanities M
Interdisciplinary Studies M,O
Internet and Interactive Multimedia M
Music M
Public Administration M

CALIFORNIA STATE UNIVERSITY, FRESNO

Applied Arts and Design—General M
Art/Fine Arts M
Communication—General M
Criminal Justice and Criminology M
English M
Family and Consumer Sciences-General M
History M
International Affairs M
Journalism M
Linguistics M
Marriage and Family Therapy M
Mass Communication M
Music M
Psychology—General M
Public Administration M
Rehabilitation Counseling M
Spanish M
Sport Psychology M
Writing M

CALIFORNIA STATE UNIVERSITY, FULLERTON

American Studies M
Anthropology M
Applied Arts and Design—General M
Art History M
Art/Fine Arts M
Clinical Psychology M
Communication—General M
Comparative Literature M
Dance M
Economics M
English M
Film, Television, and Video Production M
French M
Geography M
German M
Gerontology M
History M
Journalism M
Linguistics M
Media Studies M
Music M
Photography M
Political Science M
Psychology—General M
Public Administration M
Social Psychology M
Sociology M
Spanish M
Speech and Interpersonal Communication M
Theater M

CALIFORNIA STATE UNIVERSITY, LONG BEACH

African Studies M
American Studies M
Anthropology M
Art History M
Art/Fine Arts M
Asian Studies M
Asian-American Studies M
Communication—General M
Consumer Economics M
Criminal Justice and Criminology M
Dance M
Economics M
Emergency Management M
English M
Family and Consumer Sciences-General M
French M
Geography M
German M
Gerontology M
History M
Industrial and Organizational Psychology M
Interdisciplinary Studies M
Latin American Studies M
Linguistics M
Marriage and Family Therapy M
Medieval and Renaissance Studies M
Music M
Near and Middle Eastern Studies M
Philosophy M
Political Science M
Psychology—General M
Public Administration M
Public Policy M
Religion M
Spanish M
Sport Psychology M
Theater M
Western European Studies M
Writing M

CALIFORNIA STATE UNIVERSITY, LOS ANGELES

Anthropology M
Applied Arts and Design—General M
Art History M
Art Therapy M
Art/Fine Arts M
Child and Family Studies M
Child Development M
Communication—General M
Criminal Justice and Criminology M
Economics M
English M
Film, Television, and Video Production M
French M
Geography M
Graphic Design M
Hispanic Studies M
History M
Latin American Studies M
Music M
Philosophy M
Photography M
Political Science M
Psychology—General M
Public Administration M
Rehabilitation Counseling M,D
School Psychology M,D
Sociology M
Spanish M
Speech and Interpersonal Communication M
Textile Design M
Theater M

CALIFORNIA STATE UNIVERSITY, MONTEREY BAY

Interdisciplinary Studies M
Public Policy M

CALIFORNIA STATE UNIVERSITY, NORTHRIDGE

Anthropology M
Archaeology M
Art History M
Art/Fine Arts M
Clinical Psychology M
Communication—General M
Comparative Literature M
English M
Experimental Psychology M
Family and Consumer Sciences-General M
Film, Television, and Video Production M
Geography M
Hispanic Studies M
History M
Interdisciplinary Studies M
Journalism M
Linguistics M
Marriage and Family Therapy M
Mass Communication M
Music M
Political Science M
Psychology—General M
Public Administration M

*M—master's degree; P—first professional degree; D—doctorate; O—other advanced degree; *—Close-Up and/or Display*

Rhetoric	M
School Psychology	M
Sociology	M
Spanish	M
Speech and Interpersonal Communication	M
Theater	M
Writing	M

CALIFORNIA STATE UNIVERSITY, SACRAMENTO

Anthropology	M
Art/Fine Arts	M
Communication—General	M
Counseling Psychology	M
Criminal Justice and Criminology	M
Dance	M
English	M
French	M
German	M
International Affairs	M
Liberal Studies	M
Music	M
Political Science	M
Psychology—General	M
Public Administration	M
Public History	M
Public Policy	M
School Psychology	M
Sociology	M
Spanish	M
Theater	M
Writing	M

CALIFORNIA STATE UNIVERSITY, SAN BERNARDINO

Art/Fine Arts	M
Child Development	M
Clinical Psychology	M
Communication—General	M
Corporate and Organizational Communication	M
Counseling Psychology	M
Criminal Justice and Criminology	M
English	M
Experimental Psychology	M
Human Development	M
Industrial and Organizational Psychology	M
Interdisciplinary Studies	M
National Security	M
Psychology—General	M
Public Administration	M
Rehabilitation Counseling	M
Social Sciences	M
Spanish	M
Theater	M
Writing	M

CALIFORNIA STATE UNIVERSITY, SAN MARCOS

English	M
Psychology—General	M
Sociology	M
Spanish	M
Writing	M

CALIFORNIA STATE UNIVERSITY, STANISLAUS

Art/Fine Arts	O
Child Development	M,O
Criminal Justice and Criminology	M
English	M,O
Genetic Counseling	M
Gerontology	O
History	M
Interdisciplinary Studies	M
International Affairs	M
Psychology—General	M,O
Public Administration	M
Rhetoric	M,O
Sustainable Development	M
Writing	M,O

CALIFORNIA UNIVERSITY OF PENNSYLVANIA

Criminal Justice and Criminology	M
School Psychology	M
Social Sciences	M
Sport Psychology	M

CALUMET COLLEGE OF SAINT JOSEPH

Criminal Justice and Criminology	M

CALVARY BIBLE COLLEGE AND THEOLOGICAL SEMINARY

Pastoral Ministry and Counseling	P,M
Theology	P,M

CALVIN THEOLOGICAL SEMINARY

Missions and Missiology	P,M,D
Pastoral Ministry and Counseling	P,M,D
Religion	P,M,D
Theology	P,M,D

CAMBRIDGE COLLEGE

Addictions/Substance Abuse Counseling	M,O
Conflict Resolution and Mediation/Peace Studies	M
Counseling Psychology	M,O
Forensic Psychology	M,O
Interdisciplinary Studies	M,D,O
Marriage and Family Therapy	M,O
Psychology—General	M,O
School Psychology	M,D,O

CAMERON UNIVERSITY

Psychology—General	M

CAMPBELLSVILLE UNIVERSITY

Music	M
Social Sciences	M
Theology	M

CAMPBELL UNIVERSITY

Interdisciplinary Studies	M
Theology	P,M,D

CANADIAN SOUTHERN BAPTIST SEMINARY

Theology	P,M

CANISIUS COLLEGE

Corporate and Organizational Communication	M
School Psychology	M
Social Psychology	M

CAPE BRETON UNIVERSITY

Economic Development	M

CAPELLA UNIVERSITY

Addictions/Substance Abuse Counseling	M,D,O
Child and Family Studies	M,D,O
Clinical Psychology	M,D,O
Counseling Psychology	M,D,O
Criminal Justice and Criminology	M,D,O
Developmental Psychology	M,D,O
Emergency Management	M,D
Gerontology	M,D
Industrial and Organizational Psychology	M,D,O
Marriage and Family Therapy	M,D,O
Psychology—General	M,D,O
Public Administration	M,D
School Psychology	M,D,O
Sport Psychology	M,D,O

CAPITAL BIBLE SEMINARY

Pastoral Ministry and Counseling	P,M,O
Theology	P,M,O

CAPITAL UNIVERSITY

Music	M

CARDINAL STRITCH UNIVERSITY

Applied Arts and Design—General	M
Clinical Psychology	M
Graphic Design	M
History	M
Liberal Studies	M
Music	M
Pastoral Ministry and Counseling	M
Psychology—General	M
Religion	M

CAREY THEOLOGICAL COLLEGE

Theology	P,M,D

CARIBBEAN UNIVERSITY

Art History	M,D
Criminal Justice and Criminology	M,D
Museum Studies	M,D

CARLETON UNIVERSITY

Anthropology	M
Architecture	M
Art History	M
Canadian Studies	M,D
Cognitive Sciences	D
Communication—General	M,D
Comparative Literature	D
Conflict Resolution and Mediation/Peace Studies	M,O
East European and Russian Studies	M,O
Economics	M,D
English	M,D
Film, Television, and Video Production	M
French	M
Geography	M,D
History	M,D
Industrial Design	M
International Affairs	M,D
Journalism	M,D
Linguistics	M
Music	M
Philosophy	M
Political Science	M,D
Psychology—General	M,D
Public Administration	M,D
Public Policy	M,D
Sociology	M,D
Western European Studies	M,O

CARLOS ALBIZU UNIVERSITY

Clinical Psychology	M,D
Industrial and Organizational Psychology	M,D
Psychology—General	M,D

CARLOS ALBIZU UNIVERSITY, MIAMI CAMPUS

Clinical Psychology	M,D
Counseling Psychology	M,D
Industrial and Organizational Psychology	M,D
Marriage and Family Therapy	M,D
Psychology—General	M,D
School Psychology	M,D

CARLOW UNIVERSITY

Counseling Psychology	M
Humanities	M
Writing	M

CARNEGIE MELLON UNIVERSITY

African Studies	M,D
African-American Studies	M,D
Applied Arts and Design—General	D
Architecture	M,D
Art/Fine Arts	M
Arts Administration	M
Building Science	M,D
Cognitive Sciences	D
Communication—General	M,D
Comparative Literature	M,D
Computer Art and Design	M,D
Corporate and Organizational Communication	M
Criminal Justice and Criminology	M
Cultural Studies	M,D
Developmental Psychology	D
Economics	D
English	M,D
Film, Television, and Video Production	M
Gender Studies	M,D
History of Science and Technology	M,D
History	M,D
Industrial and Labor Relations	M,D
Linguistics	D
Media Studies	M
Music	M
Philosophy	M,D
Psychology—General	D
Public Administration	M
Public Policy	M,D
Publishing	M
Rhetoric	M,D
Social Psychology	D
Social Sciences	D
Technical Writing	M
Theater	M
Urban Design	M,D
Writing	M

CAROLINA EVANGELICAL DIVINITY SCHOOL
- Pastoral Ministry and Counseling D
- Theology P,M

CASE WESTERN RESERVE UNIVERSITY
- Anthropology M,D
- Art History M,D
- Clinical Psychology D
- Cognitive Sciences M
- Comparative Literature M
- Dance M
- Economics M
- English M,D
- Experimental Psychology D
- French M
- Genetic Counseling M
- History M,D
- Industrial and Labor Relations M
- Linguistics M
- Museum Studies M,D
- Music M,D
- Political Science M,D
- Psychology—General D
- Sociology M,D
- Theater M

CASTLETON STATE COLLEGE
- Forensic Psychology M
- Psychology—General M

THE CATHOLIC DISTANCE UNIVERSITY
- Theology M

CATHOLIC THEOLOGICAL UNION AT CHICAGO
- Missions and Missiology P,M,D,O
- Pastoral Ministry and Counseling P,M,D,O
- Theology P,M,D,O

THE CATHOLIC UNIVERSITY OF AMERICA
- American Studies M,D
- Anthropology M
- Architecture M
- Classics M,D
- Clinical Psychology M,D
- Computer Art and Design M
- Cultural Studies M
- Economics M
- English M,D
- Experimental Psychology M,D
- History M,D
- International Affairs M,D
- Medieval and Renaissance Studies M,D,O
- Music M,D,O
- Near and Middle Eastern Languages M,D
- Near and Middle Eastern Studies M,D
- Pastoral Ministry and Counseling P,M,D,O
- Philosophy M,D,O
- Political Science M,D
- Psychology—General M,D
- Religion P,M,D,O
- Rhetoric M,D
- Sociology M
- Spanish M,D
- Theater M
- Theology P,M,D,O
- Urban and Regional Planning M
- Urban Design M
- Western European Studies M,D

CEDAR CREST COLLEGE
- Forensic Sciences M

CENTENARY COLLEGE
- Counseling Psychology M

CENTRAL BAPTIST THEOLOGICAL SEMINARY
- Missions and Missiology P,M,O
- Theology P,M,O

CENTRAL BAPTIST THEOLOGICAL SEMINARY OF VIRGINIA BEACH
- Theology P,M

CENTRAL CONNECTICUT STATE UNIVERSITY
- Communication—General M,O
- Corporate and Organizational Communication M,O
- Criminal Justice and Criminology M
- English M,O
- French M,O
- Geography M
- German M,O
- Health Psychology M
- History M,O
- International Affairs M
- Italian M,O
- Marriage and Family Therapy M,O
- Psychology—General M
- Rehabilitation Counseling M,O
- School Psychology M,O
- Social Psychology M
- Spanish M,O

CENTRAL EUROPEAN UNIVERSITY
- Anthropology M,D
- Economics M,D
- Gender Studies M,D
- History M,D
- Humanities M,D
- International Affairs M,D
- Medieval and Renaissance Studies M,D
- Philosophy M,D
- Political Science M,D
- Public Policy M,D
- Social Sciences M,D
- Sociology M,D

CENTRAL MICHIGAN UNIVERSITY
- American Indian/Native American Studies M
- American Studies M,D,O
- Child and Family Studies M,O
- Clinical Psychology M,D
- Clothing and Textiles M,O
- Communication—General M
- Corporate and Organizational Communication M,O
- Counseling Psychology M,D,O
- Cultural Studies M
- Economics M
- English M
- Experimental Psychology M,D
- Family and Consumer Sciences-General M,O
- Film, Television, and Video Production M
- Film, Television, and Video Theory and Criticism M
- Gender Studies M
- History M,D,O
- Human Development M,O
- Humanities M
- Industrial and Organizational Psychology M,D
- International Affairs M,O
- Mass Communication M
- Media Studies M
- Music M
- Political Science M,O
- Psychology—General M,D,O
- Public Administration M,O
- School Psychology D,O
- Spanish M
- Speech and Interpersonal Communication M
- Western European Studies M,D,O
- Writing M

CENTRAL WASHINGTON UNIVERSITY
- Art/Fine Arts M
- Child and Family Studies M
- Counseling Psychology M
- English M
- Experimental Psychology M
- Family and Consumer Sciences-General M
- History M
- Interdisciplinary Studies M
- Music M
- Psychology—General M
- School Psychology M
- Theater M

CENTRAL YESHIVA TOMCHEI TMIMIM-LUBAVITCH
- Theology

CENTRO DE ESTUDIOS AVANZADOS DE PUERTO RICO Y EL CARIBE
- History M,D
- Latin American Studies M,D

CHAMINADE UNIVERSITY OF HONOLULU
- Conflict Resolution and Mediation/Peace Studies M
- Counseling Psychology M
- Criminal Justice and Criminology M,O
- Forensic Sciences M
- Homeland Security M,O
- Pastoral Ministry and Counseling M
- Theology M

CHAPMAN UNIVERSITY
- Cultural Studies D
- Disability Studies D
- Economics P,M
- English M
- Film, Television, and Video Production M
- Health Communication M
- International Affairs M
- Marriage and Family Therapy M
- School Psychology M,D,O
- Writing M

CHARLESTON SOUTHERN UNIVERSITY
- Criminal Justice and Criminology M

CHATHAM UNIVERSITY
- Computer Art and Design M
- Counseling Psychology M,D
- Developmental Psychology M,D
- Film, Television, and Video Production M
- Health Psychology M,D
- Industrial and Organizational Psychology M,D
- Interior Design M
- Landscape Architecture M
- Marriage and Family Therapy M,D
- Sport Psychology M,D
- Writing M

CHESTNUT HILL COLLEGE
- Clinical Psychology M,D,O
- Counseling Psychology M,O
- Gerontology M,O
- Psychology—General M,D,O
- Religion M,O

CHEYNEY UNIVERSITY OF PENNSYLVANIA
- Public Administration M

THE CHICAGO SCHOOL OF PROFESSIONAL PSYCHOLOGY
- Clinical Psychology M,D
- Forensic Psychology M,D
- Industrial and Organizational Psychology M,D
- Psychology—General M,D
- School Psychology O

THE CHICAGO SCHOOL OF PROFESSIONAL PSYCHOLOGY AT DOWNTOWN LOS ANGELES
- Clinical Psychology M,D
- Forensic Psychology D
- Industrial and Organizational Psychology M
- Marriage and Family Therapy M,D
- Psychology—General M,D

THE CHICAGO SCHOOL OF PROFESSIONAL PSYCHOLOGY AT GRAYSLAKE
- Clinical Psychology M
- Counseling Psychology M
- School Psychology O

THE CHICAGO SCHOOL OF PROFESSIONAL PSYCHOLOGY AT IRVINE
- Clinical Psychology D
- Forensic Psychology D
- Marriage and Family Therapy M,D
- Psychology—General D

*M—master's degree; P—first professional degree; D—doctorate; O—other advanced degree; *—Close-Up and/or Display*

THE CHICAGO SCHOOL OF PROFESSIONAL PSYCHOLOGY AT WESTWOOD
Clinical Psychology M
Marriage and Family Therapy M,D
Psychology—General D

THE CHICAGO SCHOOL OF PROFESSIONAL PSYCHOLOGY: ONLINE
Forensic Psychology M,O
Industrial and Organizational Psychology M,D,O
Psychology—General M,D

CHICAGO STATE UNIVERSITY
Criminal Justice and Criminology M
Economic Development M
English M
Geography M
History M
Writing M

CHICAGO THEOLOGICAL SEMINARY
Ethics P,M,D
Pastoral Ministry and Counseling P,M,D
Religion P,M,D
Theology P,M,D

CHRISTENDOM COLLEGE
Theology M

CHRISTIAN BROTHERS UNIVERSITY
Religion M

CHRISTIAN THEOLOGICAL SEMINARY
Marriage and Family Therapy P,M,D
Pastoral Ministry and Counseling P,M,D
Religion P,M,D
Theology P,M,D

CHRISTIE'S EDUCATION
Art History M
Museum Studies M

CHRIST THE KING SEMINARY
Pastoral Ministry and Counseling P,M,O
Theology P,M,O

CHURCH DIVINITY SCHOOL OF THE PACIFIC
Theology P,M,D,O

CHURCH OF GOD THEOLOGICAL SEMINARY
Pastoral Ministry and Counseling P,M,D
Theology P,M,D

CINCINNATI CHRISTIAN UNIVERSITY
Pastoral Ministry and Counseling M
Religion P,M
Theology P,M

THE CITADEL, THE MILITARY COLLEGE OF SOUTH CAROLINA
English M
History M
Psychology—General M,O
School Psychology O
Social Sciences M

CITY COLLEGE OF THE CITY UNIVERSITY OF NEW YORK
Architecture M
Art History M
Art/Fine Arts M
Clinical Psychology M,D
Counseling Psychology M
Economics M
English M
Experimental Psychology M,D
Graphic Design M
History M
International Affairs M
Landscape Architecture M
Media Studies M
Museum Studies M
Music M
Psychology—General M,D
Public Administration M,D
Sociology M
Spanish M
Sustainable Development M
Urban Design M
Writing M

CITY UNIVERSITY OF SEATTLE
Counseling Psychology M
School Psychology M,O

CLAREMONT GRADUATE UNIVERSITY
African Studies M,D,O
American Studies M,D,O
Art/Fine Arts M
Arts Administration M
Cognitive Sciences M,D,O
Comparative Literature M,D
Computer Art and Design M
Cultural Studies M,D,O
Developmental Psychology M,D,O
Economic Development M,D,O
Economics M,D,O
English M,D
Ethics M,D
Film, Television, and Video Theory and Criticism M,D
Health Psychology M,D,O
History M,D,O
Human Development M,D,O
Humanities M,D,O
Industrial and Organizational Psychology M,D,O
International Affairs M,D
International Economics M,D,O
Media Studies M,D,O
Museum Studies M,D,O
Music M,D
Philosophy M,D
Photography M
Political Science M,D
Psychology—General M,D,O
Public Policy M,D,O
Religion M,D
Social Psychology M,D,O
Theology M,D
Western European Studies M,D,O
Women's Studies M,D
Writing M,D

CLAREMONT SCHOOL OF THEOLOGY
Ethics M,D
Pastoral Ministry and Counseling M,D
Religion M,D
Theology P,M,D

CLARION UNIVERSITY OF PENNSYLVANIA
Communication—General M
English M

CLARK ATLANTA UNIVERSITY
African-American Studies M,D
Criminal Justice and Criminology M
Economics M
English M,D
History M,D
Political Science M,D
Public Administration M
Romance Languages M,D
Sociology M
Women's Studies M,D

CLARK UNIVERSITY
American Studies M,D
Clinical Psychology D
Communication—General M
Developmental Psychology D
Economics D
English M
Geographic Information Systems M
Geography M,D
History M,D,O
Holocaust and Genocide Studies D
International Development M
Liberal Studies M
Psychology—General D
Public Administration M,O
Social Psychology D
Sustainable Development M
Urban and Regional Planning M

CLAYTON STATE UNIVERSITY
Liberal Studies M

CLEMSON UNIVERSITY
Architecture M
Art/Fine Arts M
Communication—General M,D
Computer Art and Design M
Counseling Psychology M
English M
Environmental Design D
Historic Preservation M
History M
Human Development M
Humanities D
Industrial and Organizational Psychology D
Landscape Architecture M
Psychology—General M,D
Public Affairs D
Rhetoric D
Social Sciences D
Sociology M
Urban and Regional Planning M
Writing M

CLEVELAND INSTITUTE OF MUSIC
Music M,D,O

CLEVELAND STATE UNIVERSITY
Addictions/Substance Abuse Counseling M,O
Art History M
Art/Fine Arts M
Clinical Psychology M,D,O
Communication—General M,O
Counseling Psychology M,D,O
Economic Development M,D,O
Economics M,D,O
English M
Experimental Psychology M,D,O
French M
Geographic Information Systems M,D,O
Gerontology M,D,O
Health Communication M,O
History M
Industrial and Labor Relations P,M
Industrial and Organizational Psychology M,D,O
Latin American Studies M
Linguistics M
Museum Studies M,D
Music M
Philosophy M,O
Psychology—General M,D,O
Public Administration M,O
School Psychology M,D,O
Sociology M
Spanish M
Sport Psychology M
Urban and Regional Planning M,O
Urban Design M,O
Urban Studies M,D,O
Writing M

COLGATE ROCHESTER CROZER DIVINITY SCHOOL
Theology P,M,D,O

THE COLLEGE AT BROCKPORT, STATE UNIVERSITY OF NEW YORK
American Studies M
Art/Fine Arts M
Arts Administration M,O
Communication—General M
Counseling Psychology M,O
Dance M
English M
History M
Liberal Studies M
Psychology—General M
Public Administration M,O
Writing M

COLLÈGE DOMINICAIN DE PHILOSOPHIE ET DE THÉOLOGIE
Philosophy M,D
Theology M,D,O

COLLEGE OF CHARLESTON
Arts Administration M,O
Communication—General M
Corporate and Organizational Communication O
English M
Historic Preservation M
History M
Public Administration M
Translation and Interpretation O

COLLEGE OF EMMANUEL AND ST. CHAD
- Theology P,M

COLLEGE OF MOUNT ST. JOSEPH
- Pastoral Ministry and Counseling M,O
- Theology M,O

THE COLLEGE OF NEW JERSEY
- Addictions/Substance Abuse Counseling M,O
- English M
- Marriage and Family Therapy O

THE COLLEGE OF NEW ROCHELLE
- Art Therapy M
- Art/Fine Arts M
- Communication—General M,O
- Counseling Psychology M,O
- Gerontology M,O
- Graphic Design M
- School Psychology M
- Social Psychology M

COLLEGE OF NOTRE DAME OF MARYLAND
- Communication—General M
- Liberal Studies M

COLLEGE OF SAINT ELIZABETH
- Counseling Psychology M,O
- Criminal Justice and Criminology M
- Forensic Psychology M,O
- Psychology—General M,O
- Public Administration M
- Theology M

COLLEGE OF ST. JOSEPH
- Addictions/Substance Abuse Counseling M
- Clinical Psychology M
- Counseling Psychology M
- Psychology—General M
- School Psychology M
- Social Psychology M

THE COLLEGE OF SAINT ROSE
- English M
- History M
- Mass Communication M
- Music M
- Political Science M
- School Psychology M,O

COLLEGE OF STATEN ISLAND OF THE CITY UNIVERSITY OF NEW YORK
- Counseling Psychology M
- English M
- Film, Television, and Video Theory and Criticism M
- History M
- Liberal Studies M
- Media Studies M

COLLEGE OF THE HUMANITIES AND SCIENCES, HARRISON MIDDLETON UNIVERSITY
- Comparative Literature M,D
- Humanities M,D
- Interdisciplinary Studies M,D
- Philosophy M,D
- Religion M,D
- Social Sciences M,D

THE COLLEGE OF WILLIAM AND MARY
- Addictions/Substance Abuse Counseling M,D
- American Studies M,D
- Anthropology M,D
- Experimental Psychology M
- History M,D
- Marriage and Family Therapy M,D
- Public Policy M
- School Psychology M,O

COLLÈGE UNIVERSITAIRE DE SAINT-BONIFACE
- Canadian Studies M

COLORADO CHRISTIAN UNIVERSITY
- Counseling Psychology M

THE COLORADO COLLEGE
- American Studies M
- Humanities M
- Liberal Studies M

COLORADO SCHOOL OF MINES
- International Affairs M,O
- Mineral Economics M,D

COLORADO STATE UNIVERSITY
- Agricultural Economics and Agribusiness M,D
- Anthropology M
- Art/Fine Arts M
- Child and Family Studies M,D
- Consumer Economics M
- Economics M,D
- English M
- History M
- Human Development M,D
- Mass Communication M,D
- Music M
- Philosophy M
- Political Science M,D
- Psychology—General M,D
- Sociology M,D
- Speech and Interpersonal Communication M
- Technical Communication M,D
- Technical Writing M,D
- Writing M

COLORADO TECHNICAL UNIVERSITY COLORADO SPRINGS
- Conflict Resolution and Mediation/Peace Studies M,D
- Criminal Justice and Criminology M

COLORADO TECHNICAL UNIVERSITY DENVER
- Conflict Resolution and Mediation/Peace Studies M
- Criminal Justice and Criminology M

COLORADO TECHNICAL UNIVERSITY SIOUX FALLS
- Criminal Justice and Criminology M

COLUMBIA COLLEGE (MO)
- Criminal Justice and Criminology M

COLUMBIA COLLEGE (SC)
- Conflict Resolution and Mediation/Peace Studies M,O

COLUMBIA COLLEGE CHICAGO
- Arts Administration M
- Comparative and Interdisciplinary Arts M
- Film, Television, and Video Production M
- Journalism M
- Media Studies M
- Music M
- Photography M
- Therapies—Dance, Drama, and Music M,O
- Writing M

COLUMBIA INTERNATIONAL UNIVERSITY
- Cultural Studies P,M,D,O
- Missions and Missiology P,M,D,O
- Pastoral Ministry and Counseling P,M,D,O
- Theology P,M,D,O

COLUMBIA SOUTHERN UNIVERSITY
- Criminal Justice and Criminology M

COLUMBIA THEOLOGICAL SEMINARY
- Theology P,M,D

COLUMBIA UNIVERSITY
- African Studies O
- African-American Studies M
- American Studies M
- Anthropology M,D
- Archaeology M,D
- Architecture M,D
- Art History M,D
- Art/Fine Arts M
- Asian Languages M,D
- Asian Studies M,D,O
- Classics M,D
- Communication—General M,D
- Comparative Literature M,D
- Conflict Resolution and Mediation/Peace Studies M
- Corporate and Organizational Communication M
- East European and Russian Studies M,O
- Economics M,D
- English M,D
- Environmental Design M
- Ethics M
- Experimental Psychology M,D
- Film, Television, and Video Production M
- French M,D
- German M,D
- Historic Preservation M,O
- History M,D
- Interdisciplinary Studies M
- International Affairs M
- Italian M,D
- Jewish Studies M,D
- Journalism M,D
- Landscape Architecture M
- Latin American Studies M,O
- Liberal Studies M
- Medieval and Renaissance Studies M
- Music M,D
- Near and Middle Eastern Languages M,D
- Near and Middle Eastern Studies M,D,O
- Philosophy M,D
- Photography M
- Political Science M,D
- Psychology—General M,D
- Public Administration M
- Public Policy M
- Religion M,D
- Romance Languages M,D
- Russian M,D
- Slavic Languages M,D
- Social Psychology M,D
- Social Sciences M
- Sociology M,D
- Spanish M,D
- Sustainable Development M,D
- Theater M,D*
- Urban and Regional Planning M,D
- Western European Studies M,O
- Writing M

COLUMBUS STATE UNIVERSITY
- Counseling Psychology M,D,O
- Criminal Justice and Criminology M
- Public Administration M

CONCORDIA LUTHERAN SEMINARY
- Theology P,O

CONCORDIA SEMINARY
- Theology P,M,D,O

CONCORDIA THEOLOGICAL SEMINARY
- Theology P,M,D

CONCORDIA UNIVERSITY (CA)
- Applied Social Research M
- Cultural Studies M
- International Affairs M
- Religion M
- Theology M

CONCORDIA UNIVERSITY (CANADA)
- Anthropology M
- Applied Arts and Design—General O
- Art History M,D
- Art Therapy M
- Art/Fine Arts M
- Child and Family Studies M
- Clinical Psychology M,D,O
- Communication—General M,D,O
- Computer Art and Design O
- Economic Development O
- Economics M,D,O
- English M
- Film, Television, and Video Production M
- Film, Television, and Video Theory and Criticism M
- French M,O
- Geography M,D,O

*M—master's degree; P—first professional degree; D—doctorate; O—other advanced degree; *—Close-Up and/or Display*

History M,D
Humanities D
Interdisciplinary Studies M,D
Internet and Interactive Multimedia M,O
Jewish Studies M
Journalism O
Linguistics M,O
Media Studies M,D,O
Music O
Philosophy M
Political Science M,D
Psychology—General M,D
Public Administration M,D
Public Affairs O
Public Policy M,D
Religion M,D
Rural Planning and Studies M,D,O
Sociology M
Theology M
Translation and Interpretation M,O
Urban and Regional Planning O
Urban Studies M,O
Writing M

CONCORDIA UNIVERSITY CHICAGO

Counseling Psychology M
Gerontology M
Liberal Studies M
Music M
Psychology—General M
Religion M

CONCORDIA UNIVERSITY, NEBRASKA

Pastoral Ministry and Counseling M

CONCORDIA UNIVERSITY, ST. PAUL

Child and Family Studies M,O
Criminal Justice and Criminology M
Pastoral Ministry and Counseling M,O
Theology M,O

CONCORDIA UNIVERSITY WISCONSIN

Child and Family Studies M
Corporate and Organizational Communication M
Counseling Psychology M
Music M
Psychology—General M
Public Administration M

CONCORD UNIVERSITY

Geography M
Psychology—General M

CONNECTICUT COLLEGE

Psychology—General M

CONSERVATORIO DE MUSICA

Music O

CONVERSE COLLEGE

English M
History M
Liberal Studies M
Marriage and Family Therapy O
Music M
Political Science M

CONWAY SCHOOL OF LANDSCAPE DESIGN

Landscape Architecture M

COOPER UNION FOR THE ADVANCEMENT OF SCIENCE AND ART

Architecture M

COPPIN STATE UNIVERSITY

Addictions/Substance Abuse Counseling M
Criminal Justice and Criminology M
Rehabilitation Counseling M

CORBAN UNIVERSITY

Pastoral Ministry and Counseling M

CORCORAN COLLEGE OF ART AND DESIGN

Decorative Arts M
Interior Design M

CORNELL UNIVERSITY

African Studies M,D
African-American Studies M,D
Agricultural Economics and Agribusiness M
American Studies M,D
Anthropology D
Applied Economics M,D
Archaeology M,D
Architectural History M,D
Architecture M,D
Art History D
Art/Fine Arts M
Asian Languages M,D
Asian Studies M,D
Building Science M,D
Child and Family Studies D
Chinese M,D
Classics D
Clothing and Textiles M,D
Cognitive Sciences D
Communication—General M,D
Comparative Literature D
Computer Art and Design M,D
Conflict Resolution and Mediation/Peace Studies M,D
Consumer Economics M,D
Cultural Studies M,D
Demography and Population Studies M,D
Developmental Psychology D
East European and Russian Studies M,D
Economic Development M,D
Economics M,D
English M,D
Environmental Design M
Ethnic Studies M,D
Experimental Psychology D
Family and Consumer Sciences-General M,D
French D
Gender Studies M,D
German M,D
Historic Preservation M,D
History of Science and Technology M,D
History M,D
Human Development D
Industrial and Labor Relations M,D*
Interior Design M
International Affairs D
International Development M
Italian D
Japanese M,D
Jewish Studies M,D
Landscape Architecture M
Latin American Studies M,D
Linguistics M,D
Medieval and Renaissance Studies M,D
Music M,D
Near and Middle Eastern Studies M,D
Philosophy D
Photography M
Political Science D
Psychology—General D
Public Affairs M*
Public Policy M,D
Religion D
Romance Languages M,D
Rural Planning and Studies M
Rural Sociology M,D
Scandinavian Languages M,D
Slavic Languages M,D
Social Psychology M,D
Sociology M,D
Spanish D
Textile Design M,D
Theater D
Urban and Regional Planning M,D
Urban Design M,D
Western European Studies M,D
Women's Studies M,D
Writing M,D

COVENANT THEOLOGICAL SEMINARY

Theology P,M,D,O

CRANBROOK ACADEMY OF ART

Applied Arts and Design—General M
Architecture M
Art/Fine Arts M
Graphic Design M
Photography M
Textile Design M

CREIGHTON UNIVERSITY

Conflict Resolution and Mediation/Peace Studies M,O
English M
International Affairs M
Liberal Studies M
Social Psychology M
Theology M
Writing M

THE CRISWELL COLLEGE

Jewish Studies P,M
Pastoral Ministry and Counseling P,M
Theology P,M

CROWN COLLEGE

Theology M

CUMBERLAND UNIVERSITY

Public Administration M

CUNY GRADUATE SCHOOL OF JOURNALISM

Journalism M*

CURRY COLLEGE

Criminal Justice and Criminology M

CURTIS INSTITUTE OF MUSIC

Music M

DALHOUSIE UNIVERSITY

Anthropology M,D
Architecture M
Classics M,D
Clinical Psychology M,D
Economics M,D
English M,D
French M,D
German M
History M,D
Interdisciplinary Studies D
International Development M
Music M
Philosophy M,D
Political Science M,D
Psychology—General M,D
Public Administration M,O
Rural Planning and Studies M
Sociology M,D
Urban and Regional Planning M

DALLAS BAPTIST UNIVERSITY

Conflict Resolution and Mediation/Peace Studies M
Corporate and Organizational Communication M
Counseling Psychology M
Criminal Justice and Criminology M
Experimental Psychology M
Interdisciplinary Studies M
Liberal Studies M
Missions and Missiology M
Pastoral Ministry and Counseling M

DALLAS THEOLOGICAL SEMINARY

Media Studies M,D,O
Missions and Missiology M,D,O
Pastoral Ministry and Counseling M,D,O
Theology M,D,O

DARKEI NOAM RABBINICAL COLLEGE

Theology

DARTMOUTH COLLEGE

Cognitive Sciences D
Comparative Literature M
Liberal Studies M
Music M
Psychology—General D

DEFIANCE COLLEGE

Criminal Justice and Criminology M

DELAWARE STATE UNIVERSITY

Historic Preservation M

DELAWARE VALLEY COLLEGE

Agricultural Economics and Agribusiness M

DELL'ARTE INTERNATIONAL SCHOOL OF PHYSICAL THEATRE

Theater M

DELTA STATE UNIVERSITY

Criminal Justice and Criminology M
Urban and Regional Planning M

DENVER SEMINARY

Marriage and Family Therapy P,M,D,O
Pastoral Ministry and Counseling P,M,D,O
Religion P,M,D,O
Theology P,M,D,O

DEPAUL UNIVERSITY

Clinical Psychology M,D
Communication—General M
Computer Art and Design M,D
Corporate and Organizational Communication M
Economics M
English M
Experimental Psychology M,D
History M
Human Development M,D
Industrial and Organizational Psychology M,D
Interdisciplinary Studies M
Internet and Interactive Multimedia M,D
Journalism M
Media Studies M
Music M,O
Philosophy M,D
Psychology—General M,D
Public Administration M,O
Public Affairs M,O
Public Policy M,O
Publishing M
Rhetoric M
Social Psychology M,D
Sociology M
Technical Writing M
Theater M
Urban and Regional Planning M,O
Writing M

DESALES UNIVERSITY

Criminal Justice and Criminology M

DEVRY UNIVERSITY

Communication—General M
Public Administration M

DIGITAL MEDIA ARTS COLLEGE

Computer Art and Design M
Graphic Design M
Media Studies M

DOMINICAN HOUSE OF STUDIES, PONTIFICAL FACULTY OF THE IMMACULATE CONCEPTION

Theology P,M,O

DOMINICAN SCHOOL OF PHILOSOPHY AND THEOLOGY

Philosophy M
Theology P,O

DOMINICAN UNIVERSITY

Pastoral Ministry and Counseling M

DOMINICAN UNIVERSITY OF CALIFORNIA

Counseling Psychology M
Gerontology M
Humanities M
Marriage and Family Therapy M
Sustainable Development M

DOWLING COLLEGE

Liberal Studies M

DRAKE UNIVERSITY

Communication—General M
Public Administration M

DREW UNIVERSITY

English M
French M
History M,D
Holocaust and Genocide Studies M,D,O
Humanities M,D,O
Interdisciplinary Studies M,D,O
Italian M
Spanish M
Theater M
Theology P,M,D,O
Translation and Interpretation M
Writing M

DREXEL UNIVERSITY

Applied Arts and Design—General M
Art Therapy M,O
Arts Administration M
Clinical Psychology D
Communication—General M
Computer Art and Design M
Corporate and Organizational Communication M
Economics M,D,O
Emergency Management M
Film, Television, and Video Production M
Forensic Psychology D
Health Psychology D
History of Science and Technology M
Homeland Security M
Interior Design M
Journalism M
Marriage and Family Therapy M,D
Mass Communication M
Psychology—General M,D
Publishing M
Technical Communication M
Technical Writing M
Textile Design M
Therapies—Dance, Drama, and Music M,O

DRURY UNIVERSITY

Architecture M
Art/Fine Arts M
Communication—General M
Criminal Justice and Criminology M

DUKE UNIVERSITY

Anthropology D
Art History D
Art/Fine Arts D
Asian Studies M,O
Biological Anthropology D
Classics D
Clinical Psychology D
Cognitive Sciences D
Comparative Literature D
Developmental Psychology D
Economics M,D
English D
Experimental Psychology D
French D
German D
Health Psychology D
History M,D
Human Development D
Humanities M
International Development M,O
Latin American Studies M,D
Liberal Studies M
Music M,D
Philosophy M,D
Political Science M,D
Psychology—General D
Public Policy M,D,O
Religion M,D
Slavic Languages M
Sociology M,D
Spanish D
Theology P,M,D

DUQUESNE UNIVERSITY

Clinical Psychology D
Communication—General M,D
Conflict Resolution and Mediation/Peace Studies M,O
English M,D
Ethics M
Forensic Sciences M
History M
Internet and Interactive Multimedia M,O
Liberal Studies M
Museum Studies M
Music M,O
Philosophy M,D
Psychology—General D
Public Administration M,O
Public Policy M,O
Rhetoric M,D
School Psychology M,D,O
Theology M,D

EARLHAM SCHOOL OF RELIGION

Religion P,M
Theology P,M

EAST CAROLINA UNIVERSITY

Addictions/Substance Abuse Counseling M
American Studies M
Anthropology M
Art/Fine Arts M
Child and Family Studies M
Child Development M
Clinical Psychology M
Criminal Justice and Criminology M
Economics M
English M
Geography M
Health Communication M
Health Psychology D
History M
International Affairs M
Marriage and Family Therapy M
Music M
Political Science M
Psychology—General M
Public Administration M
Rehabilitation Counseling M
School Psychology
Sociology M
Therapies—Dance, Drama, and Music M
Western European Studies M

EAST CENTRAL UNIVERSITY

Criminal Justice and Criminology M
Psychology—General M
Rehabilitation Counseling M

EASTERN ILLINOIS UNIVERSITY

Art/Fine Arts M
Clinical Psychology M,O
Consumer Economics M
Economics M
English M
Family and Consumer Sciences-General M
Gerontology M
History M
Music M
Political Science M
Psychology—General M,O
Public History M
School Psychology M,O
Speech and Interpersonal Communication M

EASTERN KENTUCKY UNIVERSITY

Clinical Psychology M,O
Criminal Justice and Criminology M
English M
History M
Industrial and Organizational Psychology M,O
Music M
Political Science M
Psychology—General M,O
Public Administration M
School Psychology M,O
Urban and Regional Planning M
Writing M

EASTERN MENNONITE UNIVERSITY

Conflict Resolution and Mediation/Peace Studies M,O
Pastoral Ministry and Counseling P,M,O
Religion P,M,O
Theology P,M,O

*M—master's degree; P—first professional degree; D—doctorate; O—other advanced degree; *—Close-Up and/or Display*

EASTERN MICHIGAN UNIVERSITY
Addictions/Substance Abuse Counseling M
African-American Studies O
American Studies M,O
Applied Economics M
Art/Fine Arts M
Arts Administration M
Child and Family Studies M
Clinical Psychology M,D
Clothing and Textiles M
Communication—General M
Criminal Justice and Criminology M
Cultural Studies M
Economic Development M
Economics M
English M,O
French M,O
Gender Studies M,O
Geographic Information Systems M,O
Geography M,O
German M,O
Gerontology M,O
Hispanic Studies M,O
Historic Preservation M,O
History M,O
Interior Design M
International Economics M
Japanese M,O
Linguistics M
Music M
Psychology—General M,D
Public Administration M,O
Public Policy M,O
Social Psychology M,O
Social Sciences M,O
Sociology M
Spanish M,O
Technical Communication M,O
Theater M
Urban and Regional Planning M,O
Women's Studies M,O
Writing M,O

EASTERN NAZARENE COLLEGE
Counseling Psychology M
Marriage and Family Therapy M

EASTERN NEW MEXICO UNIVERSITY
Anthropology M
Communication—General M
English M

EASTERN UNIVERSITY
Counseling Psychology M,O
Economic Development M
International Development M
Marriage and Family Therapy D
Missions and Missiology D
Pastoral Ministry and Counseling D
School Psychology M,O
Social Psychology M,O
Theology P,M,D
Urban and Regional Planning M
Urban Studies M

EASTERN VIRGINIA MEDICAL SCHOOL
Art Therapy M
Clinical Psychology D

EASTERN WASHINGTON UNIVERSITY
Clinical Psychology M
Communication—General M
Counseling Psychology M
English M
Experimental Psychology M
History M
Interdisciplinary Studies M
Music M
Psychology—General M
Public Administration M
Rhetoric M
School Psychology M
Sport Psychology M
Technical Communication M
Urban and Regional Planning M
Writing M

EAST STROUDSBURG UNIVERSITY OF PENNSYLVANIA
History M
Political Science M

EAST TENNESSEE STATE UNIVERSITY
Art History M
Art/Fine Arts M
Clinical Psychology M
Communication—General M
Computer Art and Design M
Criminal Justice and Criminology M
Economic Development M
Economics M
English M
Gerontology M,O
History M
Human Development M
Liberal Studies M
Marriage and Family Therapy M
Psychology—General M
Sociology M
Urban and Regional Planning M
Urban Studies M

ECUMENICAL THEOLOGICAL SEMINARY
Pastoral Ministry and Counseling D
Theology P

EDEN THEOLOGICAL SEMINARY
Theology P,M,D

EDGEWOOD COLLEGE
Marriage and Family Therapy M
Religion M

EDINBORO UNIVERSITY OF PENNSYLVANIA
Art/Fine Arts M
Clinical Psychology M
Communication—General M,O
Media Studies M,O
Psychology—General M
Rehabilitation Counseling M,O
Social Sciences M

ELMHURST COLLEGE
English M
Industrial and Organizational Psychology M

ELMS COLLEGE
Religion M

ELON UNIVERSITY
Internet and Interactive Multimedia M

EMERSON COLLEGE
Broadcast Journalism M
Communication—General M
Corporate and Organizational Communication M
Health Communication M
Journalism M
Media Studies M
Publishing M
Theater M
Writing M

EMILY CARR INSTITUTE OF ART + DESIGN
Applied Arts and Design—General M
Art/Fine Arts M
Computer Art and Design M

EMMANUEL SCHOOL OF RELIGION
Missions and Missiology P,M,D
Pastoral Ministry and Counseling P,M,D
Religion P,M,D
Theology P,M,D

EMORY & HENRY COLLEGE
American Studies M
History M

EMORY UNIVERSITY
Anthropology D
Art History D
Clinical Psychology D
Cognitive Sciences D
Comparative Literature D,O
Demography and Population Studies M
Developmental Psychology D
Economics D
English D,O
Ethics P,M,D
Film, Television, and Video Theory and Criticism M,D,O
French D,O
Gerontology M
History D
Interdisciplinary Studies D
Jewish Studies M
Music M
Near and Middle Eastern Studies D,O
Philosophy D,O
Political Science D
Portuguese D,O
Psychology—General D
Religion D,O
Sociology M,D
Spanish D,O
Theology P,M,D
Women's Studies D,O

EMPORIA STATE UNIVERSITY
Art Therapy M
Clinical Psychology M
Counseling Psychology M
English M
History M
Industrial and Organizational Psychology M
Music M
Psychology—General M
Rehabilitation Counseling M
School Psychology M,O

EPISCOPAL DIVINITY SCHOOL
Theology P,M,D,O

ERIKSON INSTITUTE
Child Development M
Developmental Psychology M,O
Human Development M,O

ERSKINE THEOLOGICAL SEMINARY
Theology P,M,D

EVANGELICAL SEMINARY OF PUERTO RICO
Theology P,M,D

EVANGELICAL THEOLOGICAL SEMINARY
Marriage and Family Therapy P,M
Missions and Missiology P,M
Pastoral Ministry and Counseling P,M
Theology P,M

EVANGEL UNIVERSITY
Clinical Psychology M
Counseling Psychology M
Psychology—General M
School Psychology M

EVEREST UNIVERSITY
Criminal Justice and Criminology M

EVEREST UNIVERSITY
Criminal Justice and Criminology M

EVEREST UNIVERSITY
Criminal Justice and Criminology M

EVEREST UNIVERSITY
Criminal Justice and Criminology M

THE EVERGREEN STATE COLLEGE
Public Administration M

EXCELSIOR COLLEGE
Liberal Studies M

FAIRFIELD UNIVERSITY
American Studies M
Communication—General M
Industrial and Organizational Psychology M,O
Marriage and Family Therapy M
Psychology—General M,O
School Psychology M,O
Writing M

FAIRLEIGH DICKINSON UNIVERSITY, COLLEGE AT FLORHAM

Corporate and Organizational Communication	M
Counseling Psychology	M
Industrial and Organizational Psychology	M
Psychology—General	M,O
Public Administration	M
Writing	M

FAIRLEIGH DICKINSON UNIVERSITY, METROPOLITAN CAMPUS

Art/Fine Arts	M
Clinical Psychology	M,D
Communication—General	M
Comparative Literature	M
English	M
Experimental Psychology	M,O
Forensic Psychology	M
History	M
Homeland Security	M
International Affairs	M
Media Studies	M
Political Science	M
Psychology—General	M,D,O
Public Administration	M,O
School Psychology	M,D

FAIRMONT STATE UNIVERSITY

Criminal Justice and Criminology	M

FAITH BAPTIST BIBLE COLLEGE AND THEOLOGICAL SEMINARY

Pastoral Ministry and Counseling	P,M
Religion	P,M
Theology	P,M

FAITH EVANGELICAL LUTHERAN SEMINARY

Theology	P,M,D

FASHION INSTITUTE OF TECHNOLOGY

Applied Arts and Design—General	M*
Art History	M
Arts Administration	M
Clothing and Textiles	M
Illustration	M
Museum Studies	M

FAYETTEVILLE STATE UNIVERSITY

Criminal Justice and Criminology	M
English	M
History	M
Political Science	M
Psychology—General	M
Sociology	M

FELICIAN COLLEGE

Counseling Psychology	M*

FERRIS STATE UNIVERSITY

Applied Arts and Design—General	M
Art/Fine Arts	M
Criminal Justice and Criminology	M

FIELDING GRADUATE UNIVERSITY

Clinical Psychology	M,D,O
Human Development	M,D,O
Psychology—General	M,D,O

FISK UNIVERSITY

Clinical Psychology	M
Psychology—General	M

FITCHBURG STATE UNIVERSITY

Communication—General	M,O
Counseling Psychology	M
English	M,O
History	M,O
Interdisciplinary Studies	O
Technical Writing	M,O

FIVE TOWNS COLLEGE

Music	M,D

FLORIDA AGRICULTURAL AND MECHANICAL UNIVERSITY

African-American Studies	M
Agricultural Economics and Agribusiness	M
Architecture	M
Criminal Justice and Criminology	M
Economics	M
History	M
International Affairs	M
Journalism	M
Landscape Architecture	M
Political Science	M
Psychology—General	M
Public Administration	M
School Psychology	M
Social Psychology	M
Social Sciences	M
Sociology	M

FLORIDA ATLANTIC UNIVERSITY

Anthropology	M
Applied Arts and Design—General	M
Art/Fine Arts	M
Communication—General	M,O
Comparative and Interdisciplinary Arts	D
Comparative Literature	M
Computer Art and Design	M
Counseling Psychology	M,D,O
Criminal Justice and Criminology	M
Economic Development	M,O
Economics	M
English	M
Environmental Design	M,O
Film, Television, and Video Production	M,O
Film, Television, and Video Theory and Criticism	M,O
French	M
Geography	M
Graphic Design	M
History	M,O
Journalism	M,O
Liberal Studies	M
Linguistics	M
Marriage and Family Therapy	M,D,O
Music	M
Political Science	M
Psychology—General	M,D
Public Administration	M,D
Rehabilitation Counseling	M,D,O
Sociology	M
Spanish	M
Sustainable Development	M,O
Theater	M
Urban and Regional Planning	M,O
Women's Studies	M,O
Writing	M

FLORIDA GULF COAST UNIVERSITY

Criminal Justice and Criminology	M
English	M
Forensic Sciences	M
History	M
Interdisciplinary Studies	M
Public Administration	M

FLORIDA INSTITUTE OF TECHNOLOGY

Clinical Psychology	M,D
Communication—General	M
Corporate and Organizational Communication	M
Emergency Management	M
Industrial and Organizational Psychology	M,D
Psychology—General	M,D*
Public Administration	M
Technical Communication	M

FLORIDA INTERNATIONAL UNIVERSITY

African Studies	M
Architecture	M
Art/Fine Arts	M
Asian Studies	M
Conflict Resolution and Mediation/Peace Studies	O
Counseling Psychology	M
Criminal Justice and Criminology	M
Economics	M,D
English	M
Forensic Sciences	M
History	M,D
Interior Design	M
International Affairs	M,D
Landscape Architecture	M
Latin American Studies	M
Liberal Studies	M
Linguistics	M
Mass Communication	M
Music	M
Political Science	M,D
Psychology—General	M,D
Public Administration	M,D
Rehabilitation Counseling	M
Religion	M
School Psychology	M,O
Sociology	M,D
Spanish	M,D
Writing	M

FLORIDA STATE UNIVERSITY

Archaeology	M,D
Art History	M,D,O
Art/Fine Arts	M
Arts Administration	M,D
Asian Studies	M
Child and Family Studies	M,D
Classics	M,D
Clinical Psychology	D
Cognitive Sciences	D
Communication—General	M,D
Corporate and Organizational Communication	M,D
Counseling Psychology	M,D,O
Criminal Justice and Criminology	M,D
Dance	M
Demography and Population Studies	M
Developmental Psychology	D
East European and Russian Studies	M
Economics	M,D
English	M,D
Family and Consumer Sciences-General	M,D
Film, Television, and Video Production	M
French	M,D
Geographic Information Systems	M,D
Geography	M,D
German	M
History	M,D
Interior Design	M
International Affairs	M
Italian	M
Marriage and Family Therapy	M,D
Mass Communication	M,D
Media Studies	M,D
Museum Studies	M,D,O
Music	M,D
Philosophy	M,D
Political Science	M,D
Psychology—General	M,D
Public Administration	M,D,O
Public History	M,D
Public Policy	M,D,O
Rehabilitation Counseling	M,D,O
Religion	M,D
Rhetoric	M,D
School Psychology	M,O
Slavic Languages	M
Social Psychology	D
Sociology	M,D
Spanish	M,D
Speech and Interpersonal Communication	M,D
Sport Psychology	M,D,O
Theater	M,D
Therapies—Dance, Drama, and Music	M,D
Urban and Regional Planning	M,D
Writing	M,D

FONTBONNE UNIVERSITY

Art/Fine Arts	M
Family and Consumer Sciences-General	M
Theater	M

FORDHAM UNIVERSITY

Classics	M,D
Clinical Psychology	D
Communication—General	M
Corporate and Organizational Communication	M
Counseling Psychology	M,D,O

*M—master's degree; P—first professional degree; D—doctorate; O—other advanced degree; *—Close-Up and/or Display*

Developmental Psychology D
Economic Development M,O
Economics M,D,O
English M,D
Ethics M,O
History M,D
International Affairs M,O
International Development M,O
International Economics M,O
Latin American Studies M,O
Liberal Studies M
Mass Communication M
Media Studies M
Medieval and Renaissance Studies M,O
Pastoral Ministry and Counseling M,D,O
Philosophy M,D
Political Science M
Psychology—General D
Religion M,D,O
School Psychology M,D,O
Sociology M
Theology M,D
Urban Studies M

FORT HAYS STATE UNIVERSITY
Art/Fine Arts M
Communication—General M
English M
Geography M
History M
Liberal Studies M
Psychology—General M,O
School Psychology O

FORT VALLEY STATE UNIVERSITY
Counseling Psychology M
Rehabilitation Counseling M

FRAMINGHAM STATE COLLEGE
Art/Fine Arts M
Psychology—General M
Public Administration M
Spanish M

FRANCISCAN SCHOOL OF THEOLOGY
Theology P,M

FRANCISCAN UNIVERSITY OF STEUBENVILLE
Counseling Psychology M
Philosophy M
Theology M

FRANCIS MARION UNIVERSITY
Clinical Psychology M
Counseling Psychology M
Psychology—General M
School Psychology M

FRANKLIN PIERCE UNIVERSITY
Interdisciplinary Studies M,D,O

FRANKLIN UNIVERSITY
Corporate and Organizational Communication M

FRANK LLOYD WRIGHT SCHOOL OF ARCHITECTURE
Architecture M

FREDERICK S. PARDEE RAND GRADUATE SCHOOL
Public Policy D

FREED-HARDEMAN UNIVERSITY
Ethics M
Pastoral Ministry and Counseling M
Theology P,M

FRESNO PACIFIC UNIVERSITY
Conflict Resolution and Mediation/Peace Studies M
Interdisciplinary Studies M
School Psychology M

FRIENDS UNIVERSITY
Marriage and Family Therapy M
Theology M

FROSTBURG STATE UNIVERSITY
Counseling Psychology M
Interdisciplinary Studies M
Psychology—General M

FULLER THEOLOGICAL SEMINARY
Clinical Psychology D
Marriage and Family Therapy M,O
Missions and Missiology P,M,D
Music P,M,D
Pastoral Ministry and Counseling P,M,D
Psychology—General M,D,O
Theology P,M,D

FULL SAIL UNIVERSITY
Art/Fine Arts M
Computer Art and Design M
Graphic Design M
Internet and Interactive Multimedia M
Media Studies M

GALLAUDET UNIVERSITY
Clinical Psychology D
Counseling Psychology M
Developmental Psychology M,O
Linguistics M,D
Psychology—General M,D,O
School Psychology M,O

GANNON UNIVERSITY
Counseling Psychology D
English M
Gerontology O
Pastoral Ministry and Counseling M,O
Public Administration M,O

GARDNER-WEBB UNIVERSITY
Counseling Psychology M
English M
Missions and Missiology P,D
Pastoral Ministry and Counseling P,D
Psychology—General M
School Psychology M
Theology P,D

GARRETT-EVANGELICAL THEOLOGICAL SEMINARY
Music P,M,D
Pastoral Ministry and Counseling P,M,D
Theology P,M,D

GENERAL THEOLOGICAL SEMINARY
Pastoral Ministry and Counseling P,M,D,O
Religion P,M,D,O
Theology P,M,D,O

GENEVA COLLEGE
Counseling Psychology M
Marriage and Family Therapy M
Psychology—General M

GEORGE FOX UNIVERSITY
Clinical Psychology M,D
Counseling Psychology M,O
Marriage and Family Therapy M,O
Missions and Missiology P,M,D,O
Pastoral Ministry and Counseling P,M,D,O
Psychology—General M,D
School Psychology M,O
Theology P,M,D,O

GEORGE MASON UNIVERSITY
Anthropology M,D
Art History M*
Arts Administration M,O
Cognitive Sciences M,D,O
Communication—General M,D
Conflict Resolution and Mediation/Peace Studies M,D,O
Criminal Justice and Criminology M,D
Cultural Studies D
Dance M
Economics M,D,O
English M,D,O
Folklore M,D,O
Forensic Sciences M,D,O
Geographic Information Systems M,D,O
Geography M
Gerontology M,O
Graphic Design M
History M,D
Homeland Security M,D,O
Interdisciplinary Studies M
International Affairs M
Internet and Interactive Multimedia M,D,O
Linguistics M,D,O
Music M,D,O
Philosophy M,O
Political Science M,D,O
Psychology—General M,D,O
Public Administration M,D,O
Public Affairs M,D,O
Public Policy M,D*
School Psychology O
Social Sciences M,D,O
Sociology M,D
Sustainable Development M,D,O
Writing M

GEORGETOWN UNIVERSITY
American Studies M,D
Communication—General M
Comparative Literature M,D
Conflict Resolution and Mediation/Peace Studies M
East European and Russian Studies M
Economic Development D
Economics D
English M
Ethics M,D
German M,D
History M,D
Humanities M,D
Industrial and Labor Relations D
Interdisciplinary Studies M,D
International Affairs P,M,D
Internet and Interactive Multimedia M
Journalism M,D
Latin American Studies M
Liberal Studies M,D
Linguistics M,D,O
Media Studies M,D
Medieval and Renaissance Studies M,D
Near and Middle Eastern Languages M,D
Near and Middle Eastern Studies M,D,O
Philosophy M,D
Political Science M,D
Psychology—General D
Public Policy M,D
Religion M,D
Spanish M,D
Theology D
Western European Studies M

THE GEORGE WASHINGTON UNIVERSITY
American Studies M,D
Anthropology M,D
Art History M
Art Therapy M
Art/Fine Arts M
Asian Studies M
Clinical Psychology D
Cognitive Sciences D
Communication—General M
Criminal Justice and Criminology M
East European and Russian Studies M
Economics M,D
Emergency Management M,D,O
English M,D
Folklore M,D
Forensic Sciences M
Geography M
Historic Preservation M,D
History M,D
Human Development M
Industrial and Organizational Psychology M,D
Interior Design M
International Affairs M
International Development M
International Trade Policy M
Latin American Studies M
Mass Communication M
Military and Defense Studies M
Museum Studies M,O
Near and Middle Eastern Studies M
Philosophy M,D
Photography M
Political Science M,D
Psychology—General D
Public Administration M,D
Public Affairs M
Public Policy M,D
Publishing M
Rehabilitation Counseling M
Religion M
Social Psychology M,D
Sociology M
Theater M
Western European Studies M
Women's Studies M,D,O

GEORGIA COLLEGE & STATE UNIVERSITY

Criminal Justice and Criminology	M
English	M
History	M
Public Administration	M
Public History	M
Therapies—Dance, Drama, and Music	M
Writing	M

GEORGIA INSTITUTE OF TECHNOLOGY

Architecture	M,D
Building Science	M,D
Computer Art and Design	M,D
Economic Development	M,D
Economics	M
Experimental Psychology	M,D
Geographic Information Systems	M,D
History of Science and Technology	M,D
Industrial and Organizational Psychology	M,D
International Affairs	M,D
Internet and Interactive Multimedia	M,D
Psychology—General	M,D
Public Policy	M,D
Urban and Regional Planning	M,D
Urban Design	M,D

GEORGIAN COURT UNIVERSITY

Counseling Psychology	M,O
Pastoral Ministry and Counseling	M,O
Theology	M,O

GEORGIA SOUTHERN UNIVERSITY

Applied Economics	M
Art/Fine Arts	M
English	M
History	M
Music	M
Psychology—General	M,D
Public Administration	M
School Psychology	M,O
Sociology	M
Spanish	M

GEORGIA STATE UNIVERSITY

Anthropology	M
Art History	M
Art/Fine Arts	M
Communication—General	M,D
Counseling Psychology	M,D,O
Criminal Justice and Criminology	M,D,O
Economic Development	M,D,O
Economics	M,D
Emergency Management	M,D,O
English	M,D
Film, Television, and Video Production	M,D
French	M,O
Geographic Information Systems	O
Geography	M
German	M,O
Gerontology	M
Historic Preservation	M,O
History	M,D
Latin American Studies	M,D,O
Linguistics	M,D
Mass Communication	M,D
Music	M
Philosophy	M
Photography	M,D
Political Science	M,D
Psychology—General	M,D
Public Administration	M,D,O
Public Policy	M,D,O
Rehabilitation Counseling	M
Religion	M
Rhetoric	M,D
School Psychology	M,D,O
Sociology	M,D
Spanish	M,O
Speech and Interpersonal Communication	M,D
Translation and Interpretation	O
Urban and Regional Planning	M,D,O
Women's Studies	M,O
Writing	M,D

GLOBAL UNIVERSITY

Missions and Missiology	P,M
Theology	P,M

GODDARD COLLEGE

Comparative and Interdisciplinary Arts	M
Counseling Psychology	M
Industrial and Organizational Psychology	M
Interdisciplinary Studies	M
Writing	M

GOLDEN GATE BAPTIST THEOLOGICAL SEMINARY

Pastoral Ministry and Counseling	P,M,D,O
Theology	P,M,D,O

GOLDEN GATE UNIVERSITY

Psychology—General	M,D,O

GONZAGA UNIVERSITY

Communication—General	M
Counseling Psychology	M
Pastoral Ministry and Counseling	M
Philosophy	M
Religion	M

GORDON-CONWELL THEOLOGICAL SEMINARY

Archaeology	P,M,D
Missions and Missiology	P,M,D
Pastoral Ministry and Counseling	P,M,D
Religion	P,M,D
Theology	P,M,D

GOUCHER COLLEGE

Arts Administration	M
Cultural Studies	M
Historic Preservation	M
Writing	M

GOVERNORS STATE UNIVERSITY

Addictions/Substance Abuse Counseling	M
Art/Fine Arts	M
Communication—General	M
Counseling Psychology	M
English	M
Media Studies	M
Political Science	M
Psychology—General	M
Public Administration	M

GRACE COLLEGE

Counseling Psychology	M

GRACELAND UNIVERSITY (IA)

Pastoral Ministry and Counseling	M
Religion	M

GRACE THEOLOGICAL SEMINARY

Cultural Studies	P,M,D,O
Missions and Missiology	P,M,D,O
Pastoral Ministry and Counseling	P,M,D,O
Theology	P,M,D,O

GRACE UNIVERSITY

Counseling Psychology	M
Pastoral Ministry and Counseling	M
Theology	M

GRADUATE INSTITUTE OF APPLIED LINGUISTICS

Linguistics	M,O

GRADUATE SCHOOL AND UNIVERSITY CENTER OF THE CITY UNIVERSITY OF NEW YORK

Anthropology	D
Archaeology	D
Architectural History	D
Art History	D
Classics	M,D
Clinical Psychology	D
Cognitive Sciences	D
Comparative Literature	M,D
Criminal Justice and Criminology	D
Developmental Psychology	D
Economics	D
English	D
Experimental Psychology	D
French	D
German	M,D
History	D
Industrial and Organizational Psychology	D
Interdisciplinary Studies	M,D
Italian	M,D
Liberal Studies	M
Linguistics	M,D
Medieval and Renaissance Studies	M,D
Music	D
Philosophy	M,D
Political Science	M,D
Psychology—General	D
Public Policy	M,D
Social Psychology	D
Sociology	D
Spanish	D
Theater	D
Urban Studies	M,D
Women's Studies	M,D

GRADUATE THEOLOGICAL UNION

Art History	M,D,O
Cultural Studies	M,D,O
Ethics	M,D,O
Jewish Studies	M,D,O
Religion	M,D,O
Social Sciences	M,D,O
Theology	M,D,O

GRAMBLING STATE UNIVERSITY

Criminal Justice and Criminology	M
English	M,D
Mass Communication	M
Political Science	M
Public Administration	M

GRAND CANYON UNIVERSITY

Addictions/Substance Abuse Counseling	M

GRAND RAPIDS THEOLOGICAL SEMINARY OF CORNERSTONE UNIVERSITY

Missions and Missiology	P,M
Pastoral Ministry and Counseling	P,M
Religion	P,M
Theology	P,M

GRAND VALLEY STATE UNIVERSITY

Communication—General	M
Criminal Justice and Criminology	M
English	M
Public Administration	M
School Psychology	M

GRATZ COLLEGE

Holocaust and Genocide Studies	M,O
Jewish Studies	M,O
Music	M,O

GREENVILLE COLLEGE

Pastoral Ministry and Counseling	M

HAMLINE UNIVERSITY

Liberal Studies	M,O
Public Administration	M,D,O

HAMPTON UNIVERSITY

Pastoral Ministry and Counseling	M

HARDING UNIVERSITY

Counseling Psychology	M
Marriage and Family Therapy	M
Pastoral Ministry and Counseling	M

HARDING UNIVERSITY GRADUATE SCHOOL OF RELIGION

Pastoral Ministry and Counseling	P,M,D
Religion	P,M,D
Theology	P,M,D

HARDIN-SIMMONS UNIVERSITY

English	M
History	M
Marriage and Family Therapy	M
Music	M
Pastoral Ministry and Counseling	M,D
Psychology—General	M
Religion	M
Theology	P,M,D

*M—master's degree; P—first professional degree; D—doctorate; O—other advanced degree; *—Close-Up and / or Display*

HARRISBURG UNIVERSITY OF SCIENCE AND TECHNOLOGY

Public Administration	M

HARTFORD SEMINARY

Pastoral Ministry and Counseling	M,D,O
Religion	M,D,O
Theology	M,D,O

HARVARD UNIVERSITY

African Studies	D
African-American Studies	D
American Studies	D
Anthropology	M,D
Archaeology	M,D
Architectural History	D
Architecture	M,D
Art History	D
Asian Languages	M,D
Asian Studies	M,D
Celtic Languages	D
Chinese	D
Classics	D
Cognitive Sciences	M,D
Communication—General	M,O
Comparative Literature	D
Demography and Population Studies	M,D
Developmental Psychology	D
East European and Russian Studies	M
Economics	D
English	M,D,O
Experimental Psychology	D
French	M,D
German	D
History of Science and Technology	M,D
History	D
Human Development	M,D
International Affairs	P,D
International Development	M
Italian	M,D
Japanese	D
Jewish Studies	M,D
Journalism	M,O
Landscape Architecture	M,D
Liberal Studies	M,O
Linguistics	D
Medieval and Renaissance Studies	D
Museum Studies	M,O
Music	M,D
Near and Middle Eastern Languages	M,D
Near and Middle Eastern Studies	M,D
Philosophy	M,D
Political Science	M,D,O
Portuguese	M,D
Psychology—General	D
Public Administration	M
Public Policy	M,D
Religion	D
Russian	D
Scandinavian Languages	D
Slavic Languages	D
Social Psychology	D
Sociology	D
Spanish	M,D
Technical Communication	M
Theology	P,M,D
Urban and Regional Planning	M,D
Urban Design	M

HAWAI'I PACIFIC UNIVERSITY

Communication—General	M*
Economics	M
Military and Defense Studies	M*
Sustainable Development	M*

HAZELDEN GRADUATE SCHOOL OF ADDICTION STUDIES

Addictions/Substance Abuse Counseling	M,O

HEBREW COLLEGE

Jewish Studies	M,O
Music	M,O
Theology	M

HEBREW UNION COLLEGE–JEWISH INSTITUTE OF RELIGION (CA)

Jewish Studies	M,D
Theology	P

HEBREW UNION COLLEGE–JEWISH INSTITUTE OF RELIGION (NY)

Jewish Studies	M
Music	M
Near and Middle Eastern Languages	D
Theology	P,D

HEBREW UNION COLLEGE–JEWISH INSTITUTE OF RELIGION (OH)

Jewish Studies	P,M,D
Near and Middle Eastern Studies	M,D
Religion	M,D
Theology	P

HEC MONTREAL

Applied Economics	M
Arts Administration	O
Corporate and Organizational Communication	O
Sustainable Development	O

HEIDELBERG UNIVERSITY

Counseling Psychology	M

HENDERSON STATE UNIVERSITY

Counseling Psychology	M
Liberal Studies	M

HERITAGE BAPTIST COLLEGE AND HERITAGE THEOLOGICAL SEMINARY

Pastoral Ministry and Counseling	P,M,D,O
Theology	P,M,D,O

HERITAGE CHRISTIAN UNIVERSITY

Classics	M
Pastoral Ministry and Counseling	M
Religion	M

HERITAGE UNIVERSITY

English	M

HIGH POINT UNIVERSITY

History	M

HILLSDALE FREE WILL BAPTIST COLLEGE

Pastoral Ministry and Counseling	M

HIRAM COLLEGE

Interdisciplinary Studies	M

HODGES UNIVERSITY

Criminal Justice and Criminology	M
Interdisciplinary Studies	M
Psychology—General	M
Public Administration	M

HOFSTRA UNIVERSITY

Applied Social Research	M
Art Therapy	M
Art/Fine Arts	M
Clinical Psychology	D
Communication—General	M
Comparative Literature	M
Counseling Psychology	M,O
English	M
Film, Television, and Video Production	M
French	M
German	M
Gerontology	M,O
Human Development	D
Humanities	M,D
Industrial and Organizational Psychology	M,D
Journalism	M
Linguistics	M,D
Marriage and Family Therapy	M
Music	M
Psychology—General	M,D
Rehabilitation Counseling	M,O
Rhetoric	M
Russian	M
School Psychology	D
Social Psychology	D
Sociology	M
Spanish	M
Speech and Interpersonal Communication	M
Writing	M

HOLLINS UNIVERSITY

Art/Fine Arts	M,O
Dance	M
English	M
Film, Television, and Video Production	M
Film, Television, and Video Theory and Criticism	M
Humanities	M,O
Interdisciplinary Studies	M,O
Liberal Studies	M,O
Music	M,O
Social Sciences	M,O
Theater	M
Writing	M

HOLMES INSTITUTE

Pastoral Ministry and Counseling	M

HOLY APOSTLES COLLEGE AND SEMINARY

Theology	P,M,O

HOLY CROSS GREEK ORTHODOX SCHOOL OF THEOLOGY

Theology	P,M

HOLY FAMILY UNIVERSITY

Counseling Psychology	M
Criminal Justice and Criminology	M

HOLY NAMES UNIVERSITY

Counseling Psychology	M,O
Forensic Psychology	M,O
Music	M,O
Pastoral Ministry and Counseling	M,O
Religion	M,O

HOOD COLLEGE

Art/Fine Arts	M,O
Human Development	M,O
Humanities	M
Psychology—General	M,O
Public Administration	M
Thanatology	M,O

HOOD THEOLOGICAL SEMINARY

Theology	P,M,D

HOPE INTERNATIONAL UNIVERSITY

International Development	M
Marriage and Family Therapy	M
Missions and Missiology	M
Music	M
Religion	M

HOUGHTON COLLEGE

Music	M

HOUSTON BAPTIST UNIVERSITY

Counseling Psychology	M
Liberal Studies	M
Pastoral Ministry and Counseling	M
Psychology—General	M
Theology	M

HOUSTON GRADUATE SCHOOL OF THEOLOGY

Pastoral Ministry and Counseling	P,M,D
Theology	P,M,D

HOWARD PAYNE UNIVERSITY

Pastoral Ministry and Counseling	M

HOWARD UNIVERSITY

African Studies	M,D
Applied Arts and Design—General	M
Art History	M
Art/Fine Arts	M
Clinical Psychology	M,D
Communication—General	M,D
Corporate and Organizational Communication	M,D
Counseling Psychology	M,D,O
Developmental Psychology	M,D
Economics	M,D
English	M,D
Experimental Psychology	M,D
Film, Television, and Video Production	M
French	M
History	M,D
Human Development	M
Mass Communication	M,D
Media Studies	M,D
Music	M

Philosophy	M
Photography	M
Political Science	M,D
Psychology—General	M,D
Public Administration	M
School Psychology	M,D,O
Social Psychology	M,D
Sociology	M,D
Spanish	M
Theology	P,M,D

HULT INTERNATIONAL BUSINESS SCHOOL (UNITED STATES)

Conflict Resolution and Mediation/Peace Studies	M
International Affairs	M
National Security	M
Political Science	M

HUMBOLDT STATE UNIVERSITY

Counseling Psychology	M
English	M
Film, Television, and Video Production	M
Psychology—General	M
School Psychology	M
Social Sciences	M
Sociology	M
Theater	M

HUNTER COLLEGE OF THE CITY UNIVERSITY OF NEW YORK

Anthropology	M
Applied Social Research	M
Art History	M
Art/Fine Arts	M
Classics	M
Cognitive Sciences	M
Economics	M
English	M
French	M
Geographic Information Systems	M,O
Geography	M,O
History	M
Italian	M
Media Studies	M
Music	M
Psychology—General	M
Rehabilitation Counseling	M
Romance Languages	M
Social Psychology	M
Sociology	M
Spanish	M
Theater	M
Urban and Regional Planning	M
Urban Studies	M
Writing	M

HUNTINGTON UNIVERSITY

Pastoral Ministry and Counseling	M

HUSSON UNIVERSITY

Counseling Psychology	M
Criminal Justice and Criminology	M

IDAHO STATE UNIVERSITY

Anthropology	M
Art/Fine Arts	M
Clinical Psychology	D
Counseling Psychology	M,D,O
English	M,D,O
Geographic Information Systems	M,O
History	M
Interdisciplinary Studies	M
Marriage and Family Therapy	M,D,O
Political Science	M,D
Psychology—General	M,D
Public Administration	M
Rhetoric	M
School Psychology	M,D,O
Sociology	M
Speech and Interpersonal Communication	M
Theater	M

ILIFF SCHOOL OF THEOLOGY

Pastoral Ministry and Counseling	P,M,D
Religion	P,M,D
Theology	P,M,D

ILLINOIS INSTITUTE OF TECHNOLOGY

Applied Arts and Design—General	M,D,O
Architecture	M,D*
Clinical Psychology	M,D
Communication—General	M,D
Corporate and Organizational Communication	M
Industrial and Organizational Psychology	M,D
Landscape Architecture	M,D
Psychology—General	M,D
Public Administration	M
Rehabilitation Counseling	M,D
Technical Writing	M,D

ILLINOIS STATE UNIVERSITY

Agricultural Economics and Agribusiness	M
Archaeology	M
Art History	M
Art/Fine Arts	M
Clinical Psychology	M,D,O
Communication—General	M
Counseling Psychology	M,D,O
Criminal Justice and Criminology	M
Developmental Psychology	M,D,O
Economics	M
English	M,D
Experimental Psychology	M,D,O
Family and Consumer Sciences-General	M
French	M
German	M
Graphic Design	M
History	M
Industrial and Organizational Psychology	M,D,O
Music	M
Photography	M
Political Science	M
Psychology—General	M,D,O
School Psychology	D,O
Sociology	M
Spanish	M
Textile Design	M
Theater	M
Writing	M

IMMACULATA UNIVERSITY

Clinical Psychology	M,D,O
Communication—General	M
Counseling Psychology	M,D,O
Psychology—General	M,D,O
School Psychology	M,D,O
Therapies—Dance, Drama, and Music	M

INDIANA STATE UNIVERSITY

Art/Fine Arts	M
Clinical Psychology	M,D
Communication—General	M
Comparative Literature	M
Consumer Economics	M
Counseling Psychology	M,D,O
Criminal Justice and Criminology	M
English	M
Family and Consumer Sciences-General	M
Geography	M,D
Graphic Design	M
History	M
Linguistics	M,O
Media Studies	M
Music	M
Photography	M
Political Science	M
Psychology—General	M,D
Public Administration	M
School Psychology	M,D,O
Writing	M

INDIANA TECH

Criminal Justice and Criminology	M

INDIANA UNIVERSITY BLOOMINGTON

African Studies	M
African-American Studies	M
Anthropology	M,D
Art History	M,D
Art/Fine Arts	M,D
Asian Languages	M,D
Asian Studies	M,D
Child and Family Studies	M,D
Chinese	M,D
Classics	M,D
Cognitive Sciences	M,D
Communication—General	M,D
Comparative Literature	M,D
Computer Art and Design	M,D
Counseling Psychology	M,D,O
Criminal Justice and Criminology	M,D
Developmental Psychology	M,D
East European and Russian Studies	M,O
Economic Development	M,D,O
Economics	M,D
English	M,D
Film, Television, and Video Theory and Criticism	M,D
Folklore	M,D
French	M,D
Gender Studies	D
Geography	M,D
German	M,D
History of Science and Technology	M,D
History	M,D
Human Development	M,D
International Affairs	M,D,O
Italian	M,D
Japanese	M,D
Journalism	M,D
Latin American Studies	M
Linguistics	M,D
Mass Communication	M,D
Media Studies	M,D
Medieval and Renaissance Studies	M,D
Music	M,D,O
Near and Middle Eastern Languages	M,D
Philosophy	M,D
Political Science	M,D
Portuguese	M,D
Psychology—General	M,D
Public Administration	M,D,O
Public Affairs	M,D,O*
Public Policy	M,D,O
Religion	M,D
Rhetoric	M,D
School Psychology	M,D,O
Slavic Languages	M,D
Social Psychology	M,D
Social Sciences	P,M,D,O
Sociology	M,D
Spanish	M,D
Speech and Interpersonal Communication	M,D
Theater	M,D
Western European Studies	M
Writing	M,D

INDIANA UNIVERSITY KOKOMO

Liberal Studies	M
Public Administration	M,O

INDIANA UNIVERSITY NORTHWEST

Criminal Justice and Criminology	M,O
Public Administration	M,O
Public Affairs	M,O

INDIANA UNIVERSITY OF PENNSYLVANIA

Archaeology	M
Art/Fine Arts	M
Clinical Psychology	D
Communication—General	M,D
Criminal Justice and Criminology	M,D
Emergency Management	M
English	M,D
Geography	M
History	M
Industrial and Labor Relations	M
Linguistics	M,D
Media Studies	M,D
Music	M
Political Science	M
Psychology—General	M,D
Public Affairs	M
Rhetoric	M,D
School Psychology	D,O
Sociology	M
Writing	M,D

INDIANA UNIVERSITY–PURDUE UNIVERSITY FORT WAYNE

Communication—General	M
English	M,O
Liberal Studies	M
Marriage and Family Therapy	M,O
Public Affairs	M,O
Sociology	M

*M—master's degree; P—first professional degree; D—doctorate; O—other advanced degree; *—Close-Up and/or Display*

INDIANA UNIVERSITY–PURDUE UNIVERSITY INDIANAPOLIS

Addictions/Substance Abuse Counseling M,D
Applied Arts and Design—General M
Art/Fine Arts M
Child and Family Studies M
Clinical Psychology M,D
Criminal Justice and Criminology M
Economics M
English M
Gender Studies M
Geographic Information Systems M,O
History M
Industrial and Organizational Psychology M
Internet and Interactive Multimedia M,D
Liberal Studies M,D,O
Museum Studies M,O
Music M
Philanthropic Studies M,D
Philosophy M,O
Political Science M,O
Psychology—General M,D
Public Administration M
Public Affairs M
Public History M
Public Policy M
Rehabilitation Counseling M,D
Sociology M

INDIANA UNIVERSITY SOUTH BEND

English M
Liberal Studies M
Music M
Psychology—General M
Public Administration M,O
Public Affairs M,O

INDIANA UNIVERSITY SOUTHEAST

Liberal Studies M

INDIANA WESLEYAN UNIVERSITY

Addictions/Substance Abuse Counseling M
Counseling Psychology M
Marriage and Family Therapy M
Pastoral Ministry and Counseling M
Social Psychology M
Theology P,M

INSTITUTE FOR CHRISTIAN STUDIES

Philosophy M,D
Political Science M,D
Theology M,D

INSTITUTE OF PUBLIC ADMINISTRATION

Public Administration M,O

INSTITUTE OF TRANSPERSONAL PSYCHOLOGY

Clinical Psychology M,D
Counseling Psychology M,D
Pastoral Ministry and Counseling M
Psychology—General M,D,O
Transpersonal and Humanistic Psychology M,D,O

Women's Studies M

THE INSTITUTE OF WORLD POLITICS

Military and Defense Studies M,O
National Security M,O
Political Science M,O
Public Affairs M,O
Public Policy M,O

INSTITUTO CENTROAMERICANO DE ADMINISTRACIÓN DE EMPRESAS

Agricultural Economics and Agribusiness M
Economics M
Sustainable Development M

INSTITUTO TECNOLOGICO DE SANTO DOMINGO

Human Development M
Linguistics M
Marriage and Family Therapy M
Psychology—General M

INSTITUTO TECNOLÓGICO Y DE ESTUDIOS SUPERIORES DE MONTERREY, CAMPUS CENTRAL DE VERACRUZ

Humanities M

INSTITUTO TECNOLÓGICO Y DE ESTUDIOS SUPERIORES DE MONTERREY, CAMPUS CIUDAD DE MÉXICO

Economics M,D
Humanities M,D

INSTITUTO TECNOLÓGICO Y DE ESTUDIOS SUPERIORES DE MONTERREY, CAMPUS CIUDAD JUÁREZ

Humanities M
Public Administration M

INSTITUTO TECNOLÓGICO Y DE ESTUDIOS SUPERIORES DE MONTERREY, CAMPUS CIUDAD OBREGÓN

Communication—General M
International Affairs M

INSTITUTO TECNOLÓGICO Y DE ESTUDIOS SUPERIORES DE MONTERREY, CAMPUS ESTADO DE MÉXICO

Architecture M,D
Humanities M,D

INSTITUTO TECNOLÓGICO Y DE ESTUDIOS SUPERIORES DE MONTERREY, CAMPUS IRAPUATO

Architecture M,D
Humanities M,D

INSTITUTO TECNOLÓGICO Y DE ESTUDIOS SUPERIORES DE MONTERREY, CAMPUS MONTERREY

Communication—General M,D

INTER AMERICAN UNIVERSITY OF PUERTO RICO, AGUADILLA CAMPUS

Counseling Psychology M

Criminal Justice and Criminology M

INTER AMERICAN UNIVERSITY OF PUERTO RICO, METROPOLITAN CAMPUS

American Studies M,D
Counseling Psychology M,D
Criminal Justice and Criminology M
English M
History M,D
Industrial and Labor Relations M,D
Industrial and Organizational Psychology M,D
Pastoral Ministry and Counseling D
Psychology—General M,D
School Psychology M,D
Spanish M
Theology D
Women's Studies M

INTER AMERICAN UNIVERSITY OF PUERTO RICO, PONCE CAMPUS

Criminal Justice and Criminology M
Spanish M

INTER AMERICAN UNIVERSITY OF PUERTO RICO, SAN GERMÁN CAMPUS

Art/Fine Arts M
Counseling Psychology M,D
Photography M
Psychology—General M,D
School Psychology M,D

INTERDENOMINATIONAL THEOLOGICAL CENTER

Theology P,M,D

INTERNATIONAL BAPTIST COLLEGE

Pastoral Ministry and Counseling M,D
Theology M

INTERNATIONAL TECHNOLOGICAL UNIVERSITY

Computer Art and Design M

INTERNATIONAL UNIVERSITY IN GENEVA

Communication—General M
Media Studies M

IONA COLLEGE

Counseling Psychology M
Criminal Justice and Criminology M
English M
Experimental Psychology M
History M
Industrial and Organizational Psychology M
Italian M
Journalism M
Marriage and Family Therapy M,O
Mass Communication M
Pastoral Ministry and Counseling M,O
Psychology—General M
School Psychology M
Spanish M

IOWA STATE UNIVERSITY OF SCIENCE AND TECHNOLOGY

Agricultural Economics and Agribusiness M,D
Anthropology M
Applied Arts and Design—General M
Architecture M
Child and Family Studies M,D
Clothing and Textiles M,D
Cognitive Sciences D
Consumer Economics M,D
Corporate and Organizational Communication M,D
Counseling Psychology D
Economics M,D
English M,D
Family and Consumer Sciences-General M
Graphic Design M
History of Science and Technology M,D
History M,D
Human Development M,D
Interdisciplinary Studies M
Interior Design M
Journalism M
Landscape Architecture M
Mass Communication M
Political Science M
Psychology—General D
Public Administration M
Rhetoric M,D
Rural Planning and Studies M,D
Rural Sociology M,D
Social Psychology D
Sociology M,D
Sustainable Development M,D
Urban and Regional Planning M
Writing M,D

ITHACA COLLEGE

Communication—General M
Music M

JACKSON STATE UNIVERSITY

Clinical Psychology D
Criminal Justice and Criminology M
English M
History M
Mass Communication M
Political Science M
Psychology—General D
Public Administration M,D
Public Affairs M
Public Policy M,D
Rehabilitation Counseling M,O
Sociology M
Urban and Regional Planning M

JACKSONVILLE STATE UNIVERSITY

Criminal Justice and Criminology M
Emergency Management M
English M
History M
Liberal Studies M
Music M
Political Science M
Psychology—General M

JAMES MADISON UNIVERSITY
Art History M
Art/Fine Arts M
Clinical Psychology M,D,O
Counseling Psychology M,O
English M
History M
Music D
Photography M
Political Science M
Psychology—General M,D,O
Public Administration M
School Psychology M,D,O
Technical Writing M
Textile Design M

JESUIT SCHOOL OF THEOLOGY AT BERKELEY
Theology P,M,D,O

THE JEWISH THEOLOGICAL SEMINARY
Jewish Studies M,D
Music M
Religion M,D*
Theology M,D,O*

JEWISH UNIVERSITY OF AMERICA
Jewish Studies P,D
Pastoral Ministry and Counseling M,D

JOHN BROWN UNIVERSITY
Marriage and Family Therapy M
Pastoral Ministry and Counseling M

JOHN CARROLL UNIVERSITY
Corporate and Organizational Communication M
Counseling Psychology M,O
English M
History M
Humanities M
Religion M

JOHN F. KENNEDY UNIVERSITY
Art/Fine Arts M
Comparative and Interdisciplinary Arts M
Counseling Psychology M
Health Psychology M
Industrial and Organizational Psychology M,O
Interdisciplinary Studies M
Museum Studies M,O
Psychology—General M,D,O
Sport Psychology M
Transpersonal and Humanistic Psychology M

JOHN JAY COLLEGE OF CRIMINAL JUSTICE OF THE CITY UNIVERSITY OF NEW YORK
Criminal Justice and Criminology M,D
Forensic Psychology M,D
Forensic Sciences M,D
Public Administration M
Public Policy M,D

THE JOHNS HOPKINS UNIVERSITY
Addictions/Substance Abuse Counseling M,D
Anthropology D
Applied Economics M
Art History M,D
Asian Studies M,D,O
Classics D
Clinical Psychology M,D
Cognitive Sciences D
Communication—General M
Comparative Literature D
Criminal Justice and Criminology M
Demography and Population Studies M,D
Economics D
Emergency Management M,O
English D
French D
Genetic Counseling M,D
Geography M,D
German D
Health Communication M,D
History of Science and Technology M,D
History D
Homeland Security M,O
International Affairs M,D,O
International Development M,D,O
International Economics M,D,O
Italian D
Liberal Studies M,O
Medical Illustration M
Military and Defense Studies M
Museum Studies M
Music M,D,O
Near and Middle Eastern Studies D
Philosophy M,D
Political Science M,D,O
Psychology—General D
Public Policy M*
Romance Languages D
School Psychology M,O
Social Sciences M,D
Sociology D
Spanish D
Technical Writing M
Writing M

JOHNSON BIBLE COLLEGE
Marriage and Family Therapy M
Theology M

JOHNSON STATE COLLEGE
Art/Fine Arts M

JONES INTERNATIONAL UNIVERSITY
Conflict Resolution and Mediation/Peace Studies M
Corporate and Organizational Communication M

THE JUDGE ADVOCATE GENERAL'S SCHOOL, U.S. ARMY
Military and Defense Studies M

JUDSON UNIVERSITY
Architecture M

THE JUILLIARD SCHOOL
Music M,D,O

KANSAS STATE UNIVERSITY
Agricultural Economics and Agribusiness M,D
Applied Arts and Design—General M
Architecture M
Art/Fine Arts M
Child and Family Studies M,D
Clothing and Textiles M,D
Communication—General M
Consumer Economics D
Economics M,D
English M
Family and Consumer Sciences-General M,D
French M
Geography M,D
German M
History M,D
Human Development M,D
International Affairs M
Landscape Architecture M
Marriage and Family Therapy M,D
Mass Communication M
Music M
National Security M,D
Political Science M
Psychology—General M,D
Public Administration M
Rhetoric M
Sociology M,D
Spanish M
Speech and Interpersonal Communication M
Theater M
Urban and Regional Planning M

KAPLAN UNIVERSITY, DAVENPORT CAMPUS
Criminal Justice and Criminology M
Political Science M,O

KEAN UNIVERSITY
Addictions/Substance Abuse Counseling M
Art/Fine Arts M
Clinical Psychology D
Communication—General M
Counseling Psychology M
Criminal Justice and Criminology M
Graphic Design M
Holocaust and Genocide Studies M
Industrial and Organizational Psychology M
Liberal Studies M
Marriage and Family Therapy O
Political Science M
Psychology—General M
Public Administration M
School Psychology D,O
Sociology M
Spanish M
Writing M

KEENE STATE COLLEGE
School Psychology M,O

KEHILATH YAKOV RABBINICAL SEMINARY
Theology

KEISER UNIVERSITY
Criminal Justice and Criminology M

KENNESAW STATE UNIVERSITY
American Studies M
Conflict Resolution and Mediation/Peace Studies M
Public Administration M
Writing M

KENRICK-GLENNON SEMINARY
Theology P,M

KENT STATE UNIVERSITY
Anthropology M
Architecture M,O
Art History M
Art/Fine Arts M
Biological Anthropology D
Child and Family Studies M
Classics M,D
Clinical Psychology M,D
Communication—General M,D
Comparative Literature M,D
Criminal Justice and Criminology M
Economics M
English M,D
Experimental Psychology M,D
French M,D
Geography M,D
German M,D
Gerontology M
Graphic Design M
Historic Preservation M,O
History M,D
Human Development M,D
Illustration M
Japanese M,D
Journalism M
Liberal Studies M
Mass Communication M
Music M,D
Philosophy M
Political Science M,D
Psychology—General M,D
Public Administration M
Public Policy M,D
Rehabilitation Counseling M,O
Rhetoric M,D
Russian M,D
School Psychology M,D,O
Social Psychology M
Sociology M,D
Spanish M,D
Textile Design M
Theater M
Translation and Interpretation M,D
Urban Design M,O
Writing M,D

KENTUCKY CHRISTIAN UNIVERSITY
Religion M
Theology M

KENTUCKY STATE UNIVERSITY
International Affairs M
Public Administration M

KEUKA COLLEGE
Criminal Justice and Criminology M

*M—master's degree; P—first professional degree; D—doctorate; O—other advanced degree; *—Close-Up and/or Display*

KNOX COLLEGE
- Theology P,M,D

KNOX THEOLOGICAL SEMINARY
- Missions and Missiology M
- Pastoral Ministry and Counseling D
- Religion M
- Theology P,M,O

KOL YAAKOV TORAH CENTER
- Theology O

KUTZTOWN UNIVERSITY OF PENNSYLVANIA
- Counseling Psychology M
- English M
- Marriage and Family Therapy M
- Media Studies M
- Public Administration M

LAGUNA COLLEGE OF ART & DESIGN
- Art/Fine Arts M

LAKE FOREST COLLEGE
- Liberal Studies M

LAKEHEAD UNIVERSITY
- Clinical Psychology M,D
- Economics M
- English M
- Experimental Psychology M,D
- Gerontology M,D
- History M
- Psychology—General M,D
- Sociology M
- Women's Studies M,D

LAKELAND COLLEGE
- Theology M

LAMAR UNIVERSITY
- Applied Arts and Design—General M
- Art History M
- Art/Fine Arts M
- Clinical Psychology M
- Criminal Justice and Criminology M
- English M
- Family and Consumer Sciences-General M,O
- History M
- Industrial and Organizational Psychology M
- Music M
- Photography M
- Political Science M
- Psychology—General M
- Public Administration M
- Social Psychology M
- Theater M

LANCASTER BIBLE COLLEGE & GRADUATE SCHOOL
- Pastoral Ministry and Counseling M
- Theology M

LANCASTER THEOLOGICAL SEMINARY
- Art History P,M,D,O
- Ethics P,M,D,O
- Religion P,M,D,O
- Theology P,M,D,O

LANGSTON UNIVERSITY
- Rehabilitation Counseling M

LA SALLE UNIVERSITY
- Clinical Psychology M,D
- Corporate and Organizational Communication M
- Counseling Psychology M
- East European and Russian Studies M
- Hispanic Studies M
- History M
- Latin American Studies M
- Marriage and Family Therapy D
- Pastoral Ministry and Counseling M
- Psychology—General D
- Rehabilitation Counseling D
- Religion M
- Theology M

LASELL COLLEGE
- Communication—General M,O
- Corporate and Organizational Communication M,O

LA SIERRA UNIVERSITY
- Communication—General M
- English M
- Pastoral Ministry and Counseling P,M
- Religion P,M
- School Psychology M,O
- Writing M

LAURA AND ALVIN SIEGAL COLLEGE OF JUDAIC STUDIES
- Holocaust and Genocide Studies M
- Humanities M
- Jewish Studies M

LAURENTIAN UNIVERSITY
- Applied Social Research M
- Experimental Psychology M
- History M
- Human Development M
- Humanities M
- Psychology—General M
- Sociology M
- Technical Writing O

LAWRENCE TECHNOLOGICAL UNIVERSITY
- Architecture M
- Interior Design M
- Technical Communication M

LEBANESE AMERICAN UNIVERSITY
- International Affairs M

LEE UNIVERSITY
- Counseling Psychology M
- Music M
- Religion M
- Theology M

LEHIGH UNIVERSITY
- American Studies M,D
- Counseling Psychology M,D,O
- Economics M,D
- English M,D
- History M,D
- Human Development M,D
- Interdisciplinary Studies M,D
- International Development M,O
- Political Science M
- Psychology—General M,D
- School Psychology D,O
- Sociology M

LEHMAN COLLEGE OF THE CITY UNIVERSITY OF NEW YORK
- Art/Fine Arts M
- English M
- History M
- Spanish M

LENOIR-RHYNE UNIVERSITY
- School Psychology M
- Social Psychology M

LESLEY UNIVERSITY
- Art Therapy M,D,O
- Art/Fine Arts M
- Clinical Psychology M,D,O
- Counseling Psychology M
- Health Psychology M
- Interdisciplinary Studies M
- International Affairs M,O
- Psychology—General M,D,O
- School Psychology M
- Social Psychology M,D,O
- Sustainable Development M
- Therapies—Dance, Drama, and Music M,D,O
- Urban and Regional Planning M
- Women's Studies M
- Writing M

LEWIS & CLARK COLLEGE
- Addictions/Substance Abuse Counseling M
- Counseling Psychology M,O
- Cultural Studies M,O
- Marriage and Family Therapy M
- Psychology—General M,O
- School Psychology M,O
- Social Psychology M

LEWIS UNIVERSITY
- Counseling Psychology M
- Criminal Justice and Criminology M
- Public Administration M

LEXINGTON THEOLOGICAL SEMINARY
- Theology P,M,D

LIBERTY UNIVERSITY
- Communication—General M
- Counseling Psychology M,D
- Pastoral Ministry and Counseling M,D
- Religion P,M,D
- Theology P,M,D

LIM COLLEGE
- Textile Design M

LINCOLN CHRISTIAN SEMINARY
- Pastoral Ministry and Counseling P,M,D
- Theology P,M,D

LINCOLN UNIVERSITY (MO)
- Criminal Justice and Criminology M,O
- History M,O
- Political Science M,O
- Public Administration M,O
- Public Policy M,O
- Social Sciences M,O
- Sociology M,O

LINDENWOOD UNIVERSITY
- American Studies M
- Art/Fine Arts M
- Communication—General M,O
- Counseling Psychology M,D,O
- Criminal Justice and Criminology M,O
- Gerontology M,O
- International Affairs M
- Public Administration M
- School Psychology M,D,O
- Theater M
- Writing M,O

LINDSEY WILSON COLLEGE
- Counseling Psychology M
- Human Development M

LIPSCOMB UNIVERSITY
- Conflict Resolution and Mediation/Peace Studies M,O
- Counseling Psychology M,O
- Psychology—General M,O
- Religion P,M
- Theology P,M

LOCK HAVEN UNIVERSITY OF PENNSYLVANIA
- Liberal Studies M

LOGOS EVANGELICAL SEMINARY
- Theology P,M,D

LOMA LINDA UNIVERSITY
- Child and Family Studies M,D,O
- Pastoral Ministry and Counseling M,O
- Psychology—General D
- Religion M

LONG ISLAND UNIVERSITY AT RIVERHEAD
- Homeland Security M,O

LONG ISLAND UNIVERSITY, BRENTWOOD CAMPUS
- Counseling Psychology M
- Criminal Justice and Criminology M

LONG ISLAND UNIVERSITY, BROOKLYN CAMPUS
- Clinical Psychology D
- Comparative Literature M
- Computer Art and Design M
- Economics M
- English M
- History M,O
- International Affairs M,O
- Political Science M
- Psychology—General M,D
- Public Administration M
- School Psychology M
- Social Sciences M,O
- Urban Studies M
- Writing M

LONG ISLAND UNIVERSITY, C.W. POST CAMPUS
- Art Therapy M
- Art/Fine Arts M
- Clinical Psychology D

- Computer Art and Design M
- Criminal Justice and Criminology M
- English M
- Gerontology M,O
- History M
- Interdisciplinary Studies M
- International Affairs M
- Internet and Interactive Multimedia M
- Music M
- Political Science M
- Psychology—General M,D
- Public Administration M,O
- Social Sciences M
- Spanish M
- Theater M

LONG ISLAND UNIVERSITY, ROCKLAND GRADUATE CAMPUS

- Counseling Psychology M
- Gerontology M,O
- Public Administration M,O

LONG ISLAND UNIVERSITY, WESTCHESTER GRADUATE CAMPUS

- Counseling Psychology M
- School Psychology M

LONGWOOD UNIVERSITY

- Criminal Justice and Criminology M
- English M
- Writing M

LONGY SCHOOL OF MUSIC

- Music M,O

LORAS COLLEGE

- Pastoral Ministry and Counseling M
- Psychology—General M
- Theology M

LOUISIANA STATE UNIVERSITY AND AGRICULTURAL AND MECHANICAL COLLEGE

- Agricultural Economics and Agribusiness M,D
- Anthropology M,D
- Applied Arts and Design—General M
- Architecture M
- Art History M
- Art/Fine Arts M
- Clinical Psychology M,D
- Cognitive Sciences M,D
- Communication—General M,D
- Comparative Literature M,D
- Developmental Psychology M,D
- Economics M,D
- English M,D
- Family and Consumer Sciences-General M,D
- French M,D
- Geography M,D
- Graphic Design M
- Hispanic Studies M
- History M,D
- Industrial and Organizational Psychology M,D
- Landscape Architecture M
- Liberal Studies M
- Linguistics M,D
- Mass Communication M,D
- Media Studies M,D
- Music M,D
- Philosophy M
- Photography M
- Political Science M,D
- Psychology—General M,D
- Public Administration M,D
- School Psychology M,D
- Sociology M,D
- Theater M,D
- Writing M,D

LOUISIANA STATE UNIVERSITY HEALTH SCIENCES CENTER

- Rehabilitation Counseling M

LOUISIANA STATE UNIVERSITY IN SHREVEPORT

- Counseling Psychology M
- Liberal Studies M
- School Psychology O

LOUISIANA TECH UNIVERSITY

- Applied Arts and Design—General M
- Art/Fine Arts M
- Counseling Psychology M,D
- Economics M,D
- English M
- Family and Consumer Sciences-General M
- Graphic Design M
- History M
- Industrial and Organizational Psychology M,D
- Interior Design M
- Photography M
- Psychology—General M,D
- Speech and Interpersonal Communication M

LOUISVILLE PRESBYTERIAN THEOLOGICAL SEMINARY

- Religion P,M,D
- Theology P,M,D

LOYOLA MARYMOUNT UNIVERSITY

- English M
- Film, Television, and Video Production M
- Marriage and Family Therapy M
- Pastoral Ministry and Counseling M
- Philosophy M
- School Psychology M
- Theology M
- Writing M

LOYOLA UNIVERSITY CHICAGO

- Clinical Psychology M,D
- Cognitive Sciences M
- Corporate and Organizational Communication M
- Counseling Psychology D
- Criminal Justice and Criminology M
- Developmental Psychology M,D
- English M,D
- History M,D
- Industrial and Labor Relations M
- Pastoral Ministry and Counseling M,O
- Philosophy M,D
- Political Science M,D
- Psychology—General M,D
- Public History M,D
- School Psychology D,O
- Social Psychology M,D
- Sociology M,D
- Spanish M
- Theology P,M,D,O
- Urban and Regional Planning M,O
- Urban Studies M,D

LOYOLA UNIVERSITY MARYLAND

- Clinical Psychology M,D,O
- Counseling Psychology M,O
- Liberal Studies M
- Pastoral Ministry and Counseling M,D,O
- Psychology—General M,D,O

LOYOLA UNIVERSITY NEW ORLEANS

- Criminal Justice and Criminology M
- Music M
- Theology M,O
- Therapies—Dance, Drama, and Music M

LUBBOCK CHRISTIAN UNIVERSITY

- Theology M

LUTHERAN SCHOOL OF THEOLOGY AT CHICAGO

- Pastoral Ministry and Counseling P,M,D
- Theology P,M,D

LUTHERAN THEOLOGICAL SEMINARY

- Ethics P,M,D
- Pastoral Ministry and Counseling P,M,D
- Religion P,M,D
- Theology P,M,D

LUTHERAN THEOLOGICAL SEMINARY AT GETTYSBURG

- Pastoral Ministry and Counseling P,M,D
- Religion P,M,D
- Theology P,M,D

THE LUTHERAN THEOLOGICAL SEMINARY AT PHILADELPHIA

- Pastoral Ministry and Counseling P,M,D,O
- Religion P,M,D,O
- Theology P,M,D,O

LUTHERAN THEOLOGICAL SOUTHERN SEMINARY

- Theology P,M,D

LUTHER RICE UNIVERSITY

- Missions and Missiology P,M,D
- Pastoral Ministry and Counseling P,M,D
- Theology P,M,D

LUTHER SEMINARY

- Theology P,M,D

LYNCHBURG COLLEGE

- English M
- History M
- Music M
- Social Psychology M

LYNN UNIVERSITY

- Criminal Justice and Criminology M,O
- Emergency Management M,O
- Mass Communication M
- Media Studies M
- Music M,O
- Psychology—General M,O

MACHZIKEI HADATH RABBINICAL COLLEGE

- Theology O

MADONNA UNIVERSITY

- Clinical Psychology M
- Criminal Justice and Criminology M
- Liberal Studies M
- Pastoral Ministry and Counseling M
- Psychology—General M
- Theology M

MAHARISHI UNIVERSITY OF MANAGEMENT

- Asian Studies M,D

MAINE COLLEGE OF ART

- Art/Fine Arts M

MALONE UNIVERSITY

- Theology M

MANHATTAN SCHOOL OF MUSIC

- Music M,D,O

MANHATTANVILLE COLLEGE

- Liberal Studies M
- Writing M

MANSFIELD UNIVERSITY OF PENNSYLVANIA

- Music M
- Psychology—General M

MAPLE SPRINGS BAPTIST BIBLE COLLEGE AND SEMINARY

- Pastoral Ministry and Counseling P,M,D,O
- Theology P,M,D,O

MARANATHA BAPTIST BIBLE COLLEGE

- Cultural Studies M
- Pastoral Ministry and Counseling M
- Theology M

MARIETTA COLLEGE

- Corporate and Organizational Communication M
- Psychology—General M

MARIST COLLEGE

- Corporate and Organizational Communication M
- Counseling Psychology M,O
- Psychology—General M,O
- Public Administration M
- School Psychology M,O

MARLBORO COLLEGE

- Internet and Interactive Multimedia M

*M—master's degree; P—first professional degree; D—doctorate; O—other advanced degree; *—Close-Up and/or Display*

MARQUETTE UNIVERSITY

Clinical Psychology	M,D
Communication—General	M
Economics	M
English	M,D
Ethics	M,D
Health Communication	M
History	M,D
Interdisciplinary Studies	M,D
International Affairs	M
Journalism	M
Mass Communication	M
Media Studies	M
Medieval and Renaissance Studies	M,D
Philosophy	M,D
Political Science	M
Psychology—General	M,D
Public Administration	M
Spanish	M
Speech and Interpersonal Communication	M
Theology	M,D

MARSHALL UNIVERSITY

Art/Fine Arts	M
Classics	M
Clinical Psychology	M,D
Communication—General	M
Criminal Justice and Criminology	M
English	M
Family and Consumer Sciences-General	M
Geography	M
History	M
Humanities	M
Industrial and Organizational Psychology	M,D
Journalism	M
Mass Communication	M
Music	M
Political Science	M
Psychology—General	M,D
School Psychology	O
Sociology	M
Spanish	M

MARS HILL GRADUATE SCHOOL

Counseling Psychology	M
Religion	M
Theology	M

MARTIN UNIVERSITY

Pastoral Ministry and Counseling	M
Psychology—General	M
Social Psychology	M

MARY BALDWIN COLLEGE

English	M
Theater	M

MARYGROVE COLLEGE

English	M
Translation and Interpretation	O

MARYLAND INSTITUTE COLLEGE OF ART

Art/Fine Arts	M,O
Graphic Design	M
Photography	M

MARYLHURST UNIVERSITY

Art Therapy	M,O
Counseling Psychology	M,O
Interdisciplinary Studies	M
Public Administration	M
Public Policy	M
Sustainable Development	M
Theology	P,M

MARYMOUNT UNIVERSITY

Counseling Psychology	M,O
English	M
Forensic Psychology	M
Humanities	M
Interior Design	M
Pastoral Ministry and Counseling	M,O

MARYVILLE UNIVERSITY OF SAINT LOUIS

Addictions/Substance Abuse Counseling	M,O
Marriage and Family Therapy	M,O
Rehabilitation Counseling	M,O
Therapies—Dance, Drama, and Music	M

MARYWOOD UNIVERSITY

Architecture	M
Art Therapy	M,O
Art/Fine Arts	M
Clinical Psychology	M,D
Communication—General	M
Corporate and Organizational Communication	M,O
Counseling Psychology	M
Criminal Justice and Criminology	M
Film, Television, and Video Production	M
Gerontology	M
Graphic Design	M
Health Communication	M,O
Human Development	D
Illustration	M
Interdisciplinary Studies	M
Interior Design	M
Media Studies	M
Photography	M
Psychology—General	M
Public Administration	M
School Psychology	O
Textile Design	M
Therapies—Dance, Drama, and Music	M,O

MASSACHUSETTS COLLEGE OF ART AND DESIGN

Applied Arts and Design—General	M
Architecture	M
Art/Fine Arts	M
Film, Television, and Video Production	M
Photography	M
Textile Design	M
Theater	M

MASSACHUSETTS INSTITUTE OF TECHNOLOGY

Archaeology	M,D,O
Architectural History	M,D
Architecture	M,D
Art History	M,D
Cognitive Sciences	D
Economics	M,D
History of Science and Technology	D
Humanities	M
Linguistics	D
Media Studies	M,D
Philosophy	D
Political Science	M,D
Social Sciences	D
Technical Writing	M
Urban and Regional Planning	M,D
Urban Studies	M,D
Writing	M

MASSACHUSETTS MARITIME ACADEMY

Emergency Management	M

MASSACHUSETTS SCHOOL OF PROFESSIONAL PSYCHOLOGY

Clinical Psychology	M,D,O
Counseling Psychology	M,D,O
Forensic Psychology	M,D,O
Industrial and Organizational Psychology	M,D,O
Psychology—General	M,D,O
School Psychology	M,D,O

THE MASTER'S COLLEGE AND SEMINARY

Pastoral Ministry and Counseling	P,M,D
Theology	P,M,D

MCCORMICK THEOLOGICAL SEMINARY

Pastoral Ministry and Counseling	P,M,D,O
Theology	P,M,D,O

MCDANIEL COLLEGE

Liberal Studies	M

MCGILL UNIVERSITY

Agricultural Economics and Agribusiness	M
Anthropology	M,D
Architecture	M,D,O
Art History	M,D
Asian Studies	M,D
Clinical Psychology	M,D
Communication—General	M,D
Counseling Psychology	M,D,O
Developmental Psychology	M,D,O
Economics	M,D
English	M,D
Experimental Psychology	M,D
Forensic Sciences	M,D,O
French	M,D
Genetic Counseling	M,D
Geography	M,D
German	M,D
Hispanic Studies	M,D
History of Medicine	M,D
History	M,D
International Development	M,D,O
Italian	M,D
Jewish Studies	M
Linguistics	M,D
Music	M,D
Near and Middle Eastern Studies	M,D,O
Philosophy	M,D
Political Science	M,D
Psychology—General	M,D
Religion	M,D
Russian	M,D
School Psychology	M,D,O
Sociology	M,D,O
Theology	M,D
Urban and Regional Planning	M,D

MCKENDREE UNIVERSITY

Counseling Psychology	M

MCMASTER UNIVERSITY

Anthropology	M,D
Classics	M,D
Cultural Studies	M,D
Economics	M,D
English	M,D
French	M
Geography	M,D
History	M,D
Industrial and Labor Relations	M
International Affairs	M,D
Pastoral Ministry and Counseling	P,M,D,O
Philosophy	M,D
Political Science	M,D
Psychology—General	M,D
Public Administration	M,D
Public Affairs	M,D
Public Policy	M,D
Religion	M,D
Sociology	M,D
Theology	P,M,D,O

MCNEESE STATE UNIVERSITY

Addictions/Substance Abuse Counseling	M
Counseling Psychology	M
English	M
Experimental Psychology	M
Psychology—General	M
School Psychology	M
Writing	M

MEADVILLE LOMBARD THEOLOGICAL SCHOOL

Pastoral Ministry and Counseling	P,M,D
Theology	P,M,D

MEDAILLE COLLEGE

Counseling Psychology	M
Psychology—General	M

MEDICAL COLLEGE OF GEORGIA

Medical Illustration	M

MEMORIAL UNIVERSITY OF NEWFOUNDLAND

Anthropology	M,D
Archaeology	M,D
Classics	M
Economics	M
English	M,D
Experimental Psychology	M,D
Folklore	M,D
French	M
Gender Studies	M,D
Geography	M,D
German	M
History	M,D
Humanities	M
Industrial and Labor Relations	M
Linguistics	M,D
Music	M,D
Philosophy	M
Political Science	M
Psychology—General	M,D
Religion	M
Social Psychology	M,D
Sociology	M,D
Sport Psychology	M
Women's Studies	M

MEMPHIS COLLEGE OF ART
Applied Arts and Design—General M
Art/Fine Arts M*
Computer Art and Design M

MEMPHIS THEOLOGICAL SEMINARY
Theology P,M,D

MENNONITE BRETHREN BIBLICAL SEMINARY
Marriage and Family Therapy M,O
Missions and Missiology M
Pastoral Ministry and Counseling M
Theology P,M

MERCER UNIVERSITY
Music P,M
Theology P,M,D

MERCY COLLEGE
Addictions/Substance Abuse Counseling M,O
Counseling Psychology M,O
English M
Marriage and Family Therapy M,O
Psychology—General M
School Psychology M

MERCYHURST COLLEGE
Biological Anthropology M
Criminal Justice and Criminology M,O
Forensic Sciences M

MEREDITH COLLEGE
Music M

MESIVTA OF EASTERN PARKWAY–YESHIVA ZICHRON MEILECH
Theology

MESIVTA TIFERETH JERUSALEM OF AMERICA
Theology

MESIVTA TORAH VODAATH RABBINICAL SEMINARY
Theology

MESSIAH COLLEGE
Counseling Psychology M,O
Marriage and Family Therapy M,O
Music M

METHODIST THEOLOGICAL SCHOOL IN OHIO
Theology P,M,D

METHODIST UNIVERSITY
Criminal Justice and Criminology M

METROPOLITAN COLLEGE OF NEW YORK
Corporate and Organizational Communication M
Media Studies M
Public Administration M

METROPOLITAN STATE UNIVERSITY
Liberal Studies M
Psychology—General M
Public Administration M,O
Technical Writing M

MIAMI INTERNATIONAL UNIVERSITY OF ART & DESIGN
Art/Fine Arts M
Computer Art and Design M
Film, Television, and Video Production M
Graphic Design M*
Interior Design M

MIAMI UNIVERSITY
Architecture M
Art/Fine Arts M
Child and Family Studies M
Economics M
English M,D
French M
Geography M
Gerontology M,D
History M
Music M
Philosophy M
Political Science M
Psychology—General D
Religion M
School Psychology M,O
Theater M

MICHIGAN SCHOOL OF PROFESSIONAL PSYCHOLOGY
Clinical Psychology M,D
Psychology—General M,D
Transpersonal and Humanistic Psychology M,D

MICHIGAN STATE UNIVERSITY
African Studies M,D
African-American Studies M,D
Agricultural Economics and Agribusiness M,D
American Studies M,D
Anthropology M,D
Art/Fine Arts M
Child and Family Studies M,D
Child Development M,D
Communication—General M,D
Computer Art and Design M
Criminal Justice and Criminology M,D
Economics M,D
English M,D
Environmental Design M,D
Forensic Sciences M,D
French M,D
Geography M,D
German M,D
Health Communication M
Hispanic Studies M,D
History M,D
Industrial and Labor Relations M,D
Interior Design M,D
Journalism M
Latin American Studies D
Linguistics M,D
Marriage and Family Therapy M,D
Media Studies M,D
Music M,D
Philosophy M,D
Political Science M,D
Portuguese M,D
Psychology—General M,D
Rehabilitation Counseling M,D,O
Rhetoric M,D
Romance Languages M,D
School Psychology M,D,O
Sociology M,D
Spanish M,D
Theater M
Therapies—Dance, Drama, and Music M,D
Urban and Regional Planning M,D
Writing M,D

MICHIGAN TECHNOLOGICAL UNIVERSITY
Archaeology M,D
Historic Preservation D
Mineral Economics M
Rhetoric M,D
Sustainable Development O
Technical Communication M,D

MICHIGAN THEOLOGICAL SEMINARY
Counseling Psychology P,M,O
Religion P,M,O
Theology P,M,O

MID-AMERICA BAPTIST THEOLOGICAL SEMINARY
Theology P,M,D

MID-AMERICA BAPTIST THEOLOGICAL SEMINARY NORTHEAST BRANCH
Theology P

MID-AMERICA CHRISTIAN UNIVERSITY
Counseling Psychology M
Marriage and Family Therapy M
Pastoral Ministry and Counseling M
Public Administration M

MIDAMERICA NAZARENE UNIVERSITY
Counseling Psychology M,O

MID-AMERICA REFORMED SEMINARY
Theology P,M

MIDDLEBURY COLLEGE
Chinese M
English M
French M,D
German M,D
Italian M,D
Russian M,D
Spanish M,D

MIDDLE TENNESSEE STATE UNIVERSITY
Child and Family Studies M
Child Development M
Clinical Psychology M,O
Counseling Psychology M,O
Criminal Justice and Criminology M
Economics M,D
English M,D
Experimental Psychology M,O
Gerontology O
History M
Industrial and Organizational Psychology M,O
Mass Communication M
Music M
Psychology—General M
Public History M,D
School Psychology M,O
Social Sciences M
Sociology M

MIDWESTERN BAPTIST THEOLOGICAL SEMINARY
Archaeology P,M,D,O
Linguistics P,M,D,O
Missions and Missiology P,M,D,O
Music P,M,D,O
Pastoral Ministry and Counseling P,M,D,O
Religion P,M,D,O
Theology P,M,D,O

MIDWESTERN STATE UNIVERSITY
Criminal Justice and Criminology M
English M
History M
Political Science M
Psychology—General M
Public Administration M

MIDWESTERN UNIVERSITY, DOWNERS GROVE CAMPUS
Clinical Psychology M,D

MIDWESTERN UNIVERSITY, GLENDALE CAMPUS
Clinical Psychology D

MIDWEST UNIVERSITY
Theology P,M,D

MILLERSVILLE UNIVERSITY OF PENNSYLVANIA
Clinical Psychology M
Emergency Management M
English M
French M
German M
History M
Psychology—General M
School Psychology M
Spanish M

MILLS COLLEGE
Art/Fine Arts M
Dance M
English M
Illustration M
Interdisciplinary Studies M,O
Music M
Photography M
Public Policy M
Writing M

MINNEAPOLIS COLLEGE OF ART AND DESIGN
Applied Arts and Design—General M
Art/Fine Arts M,O
Computer Art and Design O
Film, Television, and Video Production M
Graphic Design M,O
Illustration M
Photography M
Sustainable Development O

*M—master's degree; P—first professional degree; D—doctorate; O—other advanced degree; *—Close-Up and/or Display*

MINNESOTA STATE UNIVERSITY MANKATO

- Anthropology M
- Art/Fine Arts M
- Clinical Psychology M,D
- Communication—General M,O
- English M,O
- Ethnic Studies M,O
- French M
- Gender Studies M,O
- Geographic Information Systems M,O
- Geography M,O
- Gerontology M,O
- History M
- Industrial and Organizational Psychology M,D
- Interdisciplinary Studies M
- Marriage and Family Therapy M,D,O
- Music M
- Psychology—General M,D
- Public Administration M
- Rehabilitation Counseling M
- School Psychology M,D
- Social Psychology M,D,O
- Sociology M
- Spanish M
- Technical Communication M,O
- Theater M
- Urban and Regional Planning M,O
- Urban Studies M,O
- Women's Studies M,O
- Writing M,O

MINNESOTA STATE UNIVERSITY MOORHEAD

- Liberal Studies M
- Public Administration M
- School Psychology M,O
- Writing M

MINOT STATE UNIVERSITY

- Criminal Justice and Criminology M
- School Psychology O

MIRRER YESHIVA

- Theology

MISSISSIPPI COLLEGE

- Art/Fine Arts M
- Communication—General M
- Corporate and Organizational Communication M
- Counseling Psychology M,O
- Criminal Justice and Criminology M,O
- English M
- History M,O
- Liberal Studies M
- Marriage and Family Therapy M,O
- Music M
- Political Science M,O
- Social Sciences M,O

MISSISSIPPI STATE UNIVERSITY

- Agricultural Economics and Agribusiness M
- American Studies M,D
- Anthropology M
- Applied Economics M,D
- Architecture M
- Clinical Psychology M,D
- Cognitive Sciences M,D
- Computer Art and Design M
- Economics M,D
- English M
- Experimental Psychology M,D
- French M
- German M
- History M,D
- Interdisciplinary Studies M,D
- Landscape Architecture M
- Political Science M,D
- Psychology—General M,D
- Public Administration M,D
- Public Policy M,D
- School Psychology M,D,O
- Sociology M,D
- Spanish M
- Western European Studies M,D

MISSISSIPPI VALLEY STATE UNIVERSITY

- Criminal Justice and Criminology M

MISSOURI BAPTIST UNIVERSITY

- Pastoral Ministry and Counseling M,O

MISSOURI SOUTHERN STATE UNIVERSITY

- Criminal Justice and Criminology M

MISSOURI STATE UNIVERSITY

- Anthropology M
- Art/Fine Arts M
- Child and Family Studies M
- Clinical Psychology M
- Communication—General M
- Criminal Justice and Criminology M
- English M
- Experimental Psychology M
- Family and Consumer Sciences-General M
- Geography M
- History M
- Industrial and Organizational Psychology M
- Interior Design M
- International Affairs M*
- Military and Defense Studies M
- Music M
- Political Science M
- Psychology—General M
- Public Administration M
- Religion M
- Social Psychology M
- Spanish M
- Textile Design M
- Theater M
- Urban and Regional Planning M

MOLLOY COLLEGE

- Criminal Justice and Criminology M
- Therapies—Dance, Drama, and Music M

MONMOUTH UNIVERSITY

- American Studies M
- Communication—General M,O
- Corporate and Organizational Communication M,O
- Counseling Psychology M,O
- Criminal Justice and Criminology M,O
- English M
- History M
- Homeland Security M,O
- Liberal Studies M
- Psychology—General M,O
- Public Policy M
- Rhetoric M
- Western European Studies M
- Writing M

MONTANA STATE UNIVERSITY

- American Indian/Native American Studies M
- Architecture M
- Art/Fine Arts M
- Consumer Economics M
- English M
- Film, Television, and Video Production M
- History M,D
- Human Development M
- Psychology—General M
- Public Administration M
- School Psychology M,D,O

MONTANA STATE UNIVERSITY BILLINGS

- Communication—General M
- Interdisciplinary Studies M
- Psychology—General M
- Public Administration M
- Rehabilitation Counseling M

MONTANA TECH OF THE UNIVERSITY OF MONTANA

- Interdisciplinary Studies M
- Technical Communication M

MONTCLAIR STATE UNIVERSITY

- Addictions/Substance Abuse Counseling M,D,O
- Anthropology O
- Art History M,O
- Art/Fine Arts M,O
- Arts Administration M
- Clinical Psychology M,O
- Communication—General M
- Conflict Resolution and Mediation/Peace Studies M,O
- Corporate and Organizational Communication M
- Counseling Psychology M,D,O
- Economics M
- English M,O
- French M,O
- Geographic Information Systems M,D,O
- History M,O
- Industrial and Organizational Psychology M,O
- Italian M,O
- Linguistics M,O
- Marriage and Family Therapy M,O
- Music M,O
- Philosophy M,D
- Political Science M
- Psychology—General M,O
- School Psychology M,O
- Social Psychology M,D,O
- Social Sciences M,O
- Sociology M
- Spanish M,O
- Speech and Interpersonal Communication M
- Theater M
- Therapies—Dance, Drama, and Music M,O
- Translation and Interpretation M,O
- Urban and Regional Planning O

MONTEREY INSTITUTE OF INTERNATIONAL STUDIES

- International Affairs M*
- International Trade Policy M
- Public Administration M
- Translation and Interpretation M*

MOODY BIBLE INSTITUTE

- Pastoral Ministry and Counseling P,M,O
- Theology P,M,O
- Urban Studies P,M,O

MOORE COLLEGE OF ART & DESIGN

- Art/Fine Arts M
- Interior Design M

MORAVIAN THEOLOGICAL SEMINARY

- Theology P,M

MOREHEAD STATE UNIVERSITY

- Art/Fine Arts M
- Clinical Psychology M
- Communication—General M
- Counseling Psychology M
- Criminal Justice and Criminology M
- English M
- Experimental Psychology M
- Gerontology M
- Graphic Design M
- Music M
- Psychology—General M
- Public Administration M
- Public Policy M
- Sociology M

MORGAN STATE UNIVERSITY

- African-American Studies M,D
- Architecture M
- Economics M
- English M,D
- History M,D
- International Affairs M
- Landscape Architecture M
- Music M
- Psychology—General M,D
- Sociology M
- Urban and Regional Planning M

MOUNTAIN STATE UNIVERSITY

- Criminal Justice and Criminology M
- Interdisciplinary Studies M
- Psychology—General M

MOUNT ALOYSIUS COLLEGE

- Criminal Justice and Criminology M
- Psychology—General M

Social Psychology	M

MOUNT ANGEL SEMINARY

Theology	P,M

MOUNT HOLYOKE COLLEGE

Psychology—General	M

MOUNT IDA COLLEGE

Interior Design	M

MOUNT MARTY COLLEGE

Pastoral Ministry and Counseling	M

MOUNT MARY COLLEGE

Art Therapy	M
English	M
Pastoral Ministry and Counseling	M
Social Psychology	M

MOUNT ST. MARY'S COLLEGE

Counseling Psychology	M
Humanities	M
Marriage and Family Therapy	M
Psychology—General	M
Religion	M

MOUNT ST. MARY'S UNIVERSITY

Theology	P,M

MOUNT SAINT VINCENT UNIVERSITY

Child and Family Studies	M
Gerontology	M
School Psychology	M
Women's Studies	M

MOUNT SINAI SCHOOL OF MEDICINE OF NEW YORK UNIVERSITY

Genetic Counseling	M,D

MOUNT VERNON NAZARENE UNIVERSITY

Theology	M

MURRAY STATE UNIVERSITY

Clinical Psychology	M
Corporate and Organizational Communication	M
Economics	M
English	M
History	M
Mass Communication	M
Music	M
Psychology—General	M
Public Affairs	M
Writing	M

NAROPA UNIVERSITY

Art Therapy	M
Asian Languages	M
Clinical Psychology	M
Counseling Psychology	M
Psychoanalysis and Psychotherapy	M
Religion	M
Social Psychology	M
Theater	M
Theology	P
Therapies—Dance, Drama, and Music	M
Transpersonal and Humanistic Psychology	M
Writing	M

NASHOTAH HOUSE

Theology	P,M,O

NATIONAL DEFENSE INTELLIGENCE COLLEGE

Military and Defense Studies	M

NATIONAL DEFENSE UNIVERSITY

Conflict Resolution and Mediation/Peace Studies	M
Homeland Security	M
Military and Defense Studies	M
National Security	M

NATIONAL-LOUIS UNIVERSITY

Corporate and Organizational Communication	M,O
Health Psychology	M,D,O
Human Development	M,D,O
Industrial and Organizational Psychology	M,D,O
Psychology—General	M,D,O
Public Policy	M
School Psychology	M,D,O
Social Psychology	M,D,O
Writing	M,O

NATIONAL THEATRE CONSERVATORY

Theater	M,O

NATIONAL UNIVERSITY

Art/Fine Arts	M
Communication—General	M
Computer Art and Design	M
Conflict Resolution and Mediation/Peace Studies	M
Corporate and Organizational Communication	M
Counseling Psychology	M
Criminal Justice and Criminology	M
Economics	M
English	M
Forensic Sciences	M
History	M
Homeland Security	M
Humanities	M
Internet and Interactive Multimedia	M
Media Studies	M
Psychology—General	M
Public Administration	M
School Psychology	M
Writing	M

NATIONAL UNIVERSITY OF SINGAPORE

Public Administration	M,D
Public Affairs	M,D
Public Policy	M,D

NAVAL POSTGRADUATE SCHOOL

International Affairs	M
Military and Defense Studies	M,D
National Security	M
Political Science	M

NAVAL WAR COLLEGE

National Security	M

NAZARENE THEOLOGICAL SEMINARY

Missions and Missiology	P,M,D
Theology	P,M,D

NAZARETH COLLEGE OF ROCHESTER

Art Therapy	M
Liberal Studies	M
Therapies—Dance, Drama, and Music	M

NEBRASKA WESLEYAN UNIVERSITY

Forensic Sciences	M
History	M

NER ISRAEL RABBINICAL COLLEGE

Theology	M,D,O

NER ISRAEL YESHIVA COLLEGE OF TORONTO

Theology	

NEUMANN UNIVERSITY

Pastoral Ministry and Counseling	M,O

NEW BRUNSWICK THEOLOGICAL SEMINARY

Pastoral Ministry and Counseling	D
Theology	P,M,D

NEW ENGLAND COLLEGE

Counseling Psychology	M
International Affairs	M
Public Policy	M
Writing	M

NEW ENGLAND CONSERVATORY OF MUSIC

Music	M,D,O

NEW JERSEY CITY UNIVERSITY

Art/Fine Arts	M
Counseling Psychology	M
Criminal Justice and Criminology	M
Music	M
School Psychology	M,O
Urban Studies	M

NEW JERSEY INSTITUTE OF TECHNOLOGY

Architecture	M
Emergency Management	M,D
History	M
Technical Communication	M
Urban Studies	D

NEW LIFE THEOLOGICAL SEMINARY

Religion	M

NEWMAN THEOLOGICAL COLLEGE

Theology	P,M

NEWMAN UNIVERSITY

Theology	M

NEW MEXICO HIGHLANDS UNIVERSITY

American Studies	M
Anthropology	M
Clinical Psychology	M
English	M
Internet and Interactive Multimedia	M
Media Studies	M
Psychology—General	M
Public Affairs	M
Rhetoric	M
School Psychology	M
Sociology	M
Writing	M

NEW MEXICO STATE UNIVERSITY

Agricultural Economics and Agribusiness	M,D
Anthropology	M
Applied Arts and Design—General	M
Art History	M
Art/Fine Arts	M
Communication—General	M
Corporate and Organizational Communication	M,D
Counseling Psychology	M,D,O
Criminal Justice and Criminology	M
Economic Development	M,D
Economics	M,D
English	M,D
Family and Consumer Sciences-General	M
Geography	M
History	M
Interdisciplinary Studies	M,D
Music	M
Photography	M
Political Science	M
Psychology—General	M,D
Rhetoric	M,D
School Psychology	M,D,O
Sociology	M
Spanish	M
Writing	M,D

NEW ORLEANS BAPTIST THEOLOGICAL SEMINARY

Music	M,D
Pastoral Ministry and Counseling	P,M,D
Theology	P,M,D

NEW SAINT ANDREWS COLLEGE

Religion	M,O
Theology	M,O

THE NEW SCHOOL: A UNIVERSITY

Anthropology	M,D
Applied Arts and Design—General	M
Applied Social Research	M,D
Architecture	M
Art/Fine Arts	M
Clinical Psychology	M,D
Cognitive Sciences	M,D
Computer Art and Design	M
Decorative Arts	M
Developmental Psychology	M,D
Economics	M,D
History	M,D
Interior Design	M

*M—master's degree; P—first professional degree; D—doctorate; O—other advanced degree; *—Close-Up and/or Display*

International Affairs	M
International Economics	M,D
Liberal Studies	M
Lighting Design	M
Media Studies	M,O
Music	M
Philosophy	M,D
Photography	M
Political Science	M,D
Psychology—General	M,D
Public Policy	D
Social Sciences	M,D
Sociology	M,D
Textile Design	M
Theater	M
Urban Studies	M
Writing	M

NEWSCHOOL OF ARCHITECTURE & DESIGN

Architecture	M

NEW YORK ACADEMY OF ART

Art/Fine Arts	M

NEW YORK FILM ACADEMY

Film, Television, and Video Production	M

NEW YORK INSTITUTE OF TECHNOLOGY

Architecture	M
Art/Fine Arts	M
Communication—General	M
Computer Art and Design	M
Counseling Psychology	M
Graphic Design	M
Industrial and Labor Relations	M,O
Urban Design	M

NEW YORK MEDICAL COLLEGE

Emergency Management	O

NEW YORK SCHOOL OF INTERIOR DESIGN

Interior Design	M
Sustainable Development	M

NEW YORK STUDIO SCHOOL OF DRAWING, PAINTING AND SCULPTURE

Art/Fine Arts	M,O

NEW YORK THEOLOGICAL SEMINARY

Theology	P,M,D

NEW YORK UNIVERSITY

African Studies	M,D,O
American Studies	M,D
Anthropology	M,D
Applied Arts and Design—General	M
Applied Economics	M,D,O
Archaeology	M,D
Art History	M,D
Art Therapy	M
Art/Fine Arts	M,D,O
Arts Administration	M
Asian Studies	M,D
Classics	M,D,O
Cognitive Sciences	M,D,O
Communication—General	M,D
Comparative Literature	M,D
Computer Art and Design	M
Conflict Resolution and Mediation/Peace Studies	M
Corporate and Organizational Communication	M
Counseling Psychology	M,D,O
Cultural Studies	M,D,O
Dance	M,D
Developmental Psychology	M,D
Economics	M,D,O
English	M,D,O
Film, Television, and Video Production	M
Film, Television, and Video Theory and Criticism	M,D
French	M,D,O
German	M,D
Graphic Design	M
Hispanic Studies	M,D
Historic Preservation	
History	M,D,O
Human Development	M,D,O
Humanities	M,O
Industrial and Organizational Psychology	M,D,O
Interdisciplinary Studies	M*
International Affairs	M,D,O
Internet and Interactive Multimedia	M
Italian	M,D
Jewish Studies	M,D,O
Journalism	M,D,O
Latin American Studies	M,D,O
Linguistics	M,D,O
Media Studies	M,D
Museum Studies	M,D,O
Music	M,D,O
National Security	M
Near and Middle Eastern Studies	M,D,O
Philosophy	M,D
Political Science	M,D
Portuguese	M,D
Psychoanalysis and Psychotherapy	M,D,O
Psychology—General	M,D,O
Public Administration	M,D,O
Public History	M,D,O
Publishing	M
Religion	M,O
Romance Languages	M,D
Russian	M
Slavic Languages	M
Social Psychology	M,D,O
Social Sciences	M,O
Sociology	M,D
Spanish	M,D
Speech and Interpersonal Communication	M,D
Theater	M,D,O
Therapies—Dance, Drama, and Music	M
Translation and Interpretation	M,D
Urban and Regional Planning	M,O
Western European Studies	M
Writing	M,D

NIAGARA UNIVERSITY

Criminal Justice and Criminology	M
Interdisciplinary Studies	M
School Psychology	M,O

NICHOLLS STATE UNIVERSITY

Counseling Psychology	M,O
School Psychology	M,O

NICHOLS COLLEGE

Criminal Justice and Criminology	M

THE NIGERIAN BAPTIST THEOLOGICAL SEMINARY

Music	P,M,D,O
Pastoral Ministry and Counseling	P,M,D,O
Theology	P,M,D,O

NORFOLK STATE UNIVERSITY

Art/Fine Arts	M
Clinical Psychology	M
Communication—General	M
Criminal Justice and Criminology	M
Media Studies	M
Music	M
Psychology—General	M,D
Social Psychology	M
Sociology	M
Urban Studies	M

NORTH CAROLINA AGRICULTURAL AND TECHNICAL STATE UNIVERSITY

African-American Studies	M
Agricultural Economics and Agribusiness	M
Applied Economics	M
English	M
Rehabilitation Counseling	M,D

NORTH CAROLINA CENTRAL UNIVERSITY

Criminal Justice and Criminology	M
English	M
Family and Consumer Sciences-General	M
History	M
Music	M
Psychology—General	M
Public Administration	M
Social Psychology	M
Sociology	M

NORTH CAROLINA STATE UNIVERSITY

Agricultural Economics and Agribusiness	M
Anthropology	M
Applied Arts and Design—General	M,D
Architecture	M
Clothing and Textiles	D
Communication—General	M
Computer Art and Design	D
Developmental Psychology	D
Economics	M,D
English	M
Experimental Psychology	D
French	M
Geographic Information Systems	M,D
Graphic Design	M
History	M
Industrial and Organizational Psychology	D
Industrial Design	M
International Affairs	M
Landscape Architecture	M
Liberal Studies	M
Psychology—General	D
Public Administration	M,D
Public History	M
Rhetoric	D
School Psychology	D
Social Psychology	M
Sociology	M,D
Spanish	M
Technical Communication	M
Writing	M

NORTH CENTRAL COLLEGE

Liberal Studies	M

NORTHCENTRAL UNIVERSITY

Marriage and Family Therapy	M,D,O
Psychology—General	M,D,O

NORTH DAKOTA STATE UNIVERSITY

Agricultural Economics and Agribusiness	M
Child and Family Studies	M,D
Child Development	M,D
Clinical Psychology	M,D
Cognitive Sciences	M,D
Communication—General	M,D
Consumer Economics	M,D
Criminal Justice and Criminology	M,D
Emergency Management	M,D
English	M
Family and Consumer Sciences-General	M
Gerontology	M,D
Health Psychology	M,D
History	M,D
Human Development	D
Marriage and Family Therapy	M,D
Mass Communication	M,D
Music	M,D
Psychology—General	M,D
Social Psychology	M,D
Social Sciences	M,D
Sociology	M,D
Speech and Interpersonal Communication	M,D

NORTHEASTERN ILLINOIS UNIVERSITY

English	M
Geography	M
Gerontology	M
History	M
Linguistics	M
Music	M
Political Science	M
Speech and Interpersonal Communication	M
Writing	M

NORTHEASTERN SEMINARY AT ROBERTS WESLEYAN COLLEGE

Theology	P,M,D

NORTHEASTERN STATE UNIVERSITY

American Studies	M
Communication—General	M
Counseling Psychology	M
Criminal Justice and Criminology	M
English	M
Psychology—General	M

NORTHEASTERN UNIVERSITY

Applied Economics	M,D
Architecture	M
Art/Fine Arts	M
Communication—General	M
Counseling Psychology	M,D,O
Criminal Justice and Criminology	M,D
Cultural Studies	M
Economics	M,D
English	M,D,O
Experimental Psychology	M,D
History	M,D
Interdisciplinary Studies	D
International Affairs	M,D,O
Journalism	M
Media Studies	M
Political Science	M,D,O
Psychology—General	M,D,O
Public Administration	M,D,O
Public Affairs	M,D,O
Public History	M,D
Public Policy	M,D
Rehabilitation Counseling	M
School Psychology	D,O
Sociology	M,D
Speech and Interpersonal Communication	D
Urban and Regional Planning	M
Urban Studies	M,D,O

NORTHERN ARIZONA UNIVERSITY

Anthropology	M
Archaeology	M
Clinical Psychology	M
Communication—General	M
Counseling Psychology	D
Criminal Justice and Criminology	M,O
English	M
Ethnic Studies	O
Gender Studies	O
Geographic Information Systems	M,O
Geography	M,O
Health Psychology	M
History	M,D
Human Development	O
Liberal Studies	M
Linguistics	M,D,O
Music	M
Political Science	M,D,O
Psychology—General	M
Public Administration	M,D,O
School Psychology	M,D
Social Psychology	M
Sociology	M
Spanish	M
Sustainable Development	M
Technical Writing	M
Women's Studies	O
Writing	M

NORTHERN BAPTIST THEOLOGICAL SEMINARY

Pastoral Ministry and Counseling	P,M,D
Theology	P,M,D

NORTHERN ILLINOIS UNIVERSITY

Anthropology	M
Art/Fine Arts	M
Child and Family Studies	M
Communication—General	M
Dance	M
Economics	M,D
English	M,D
French	M
Geography	M
History	M,D
Music	M,O
Philosophy	M
Political Science	M,D
Psychology—General	M,D
Public Administration	M
Romance Languages	M
Sociology	M
Spanish	M
Theater	M

NORTHERN KENTUCKY UNIVERSITY

Communication—General	M,O
English	M,O
Health Psychology	M,O
Industrial and Organizational Psychology	M,O
Liberal Studies	M,O
Marriage and Family Therapy	M,O
Media Studies	M,O
Music	M,O
Public Administration	M,O
Public History	M,O
Rhetoric	M,O
Social Psychology	M,O
Writing	M,O

NORTHERN MICHIGAN UNIVERSITY

Criminal Justice and Criminology	M
English	M
Psychology—General	M
Public Administration	M
Writing	M

NORTH GEORGIA COLLEGE & STATE UNIVERSITY

Public Administration	M
Social Psychology	M

NORTH GREENVILLE UNIVERSITY

Pastoral Ministry and Counseling	M

NORTH PARK THEOLOGICAL SEMINARY

Pastoral Ministry and Counseling	M,O
Theology	P,M,D

NORTHWEST BAPTIST SEMINARY

Theology	P,M,D,O

NORTHWESTERN OKLAHOMA STATE UNIVERSITY

Counseling Psychology	M

NORTHWESTERN STATE UNIVERSITY OF LOUISIANA

Archaeology	M
Art/Fine Arts	M
Clinical Psychology	M
English	M
Historic Preservation	M
Music	M
Psychology—General	M

NORTHWESTERN UNIVERSITY

African Studies	O
African-American Studies	D
American Studies	M
Anthropology	D
Art History	D
Art/Fine Arts	M
Broadcast Journalism	M
Clinical Psychology	D
Cognitive Sciences	D
Communication—General	M,D
Comparative Literature	M,D,O
Corporate and Organizational Communication	M
Counseling Psychology	M
Economics	M,D
English	M,D*
Ethics	M
Film, Television, and Video Production	M,D
French	D,O
Gender Studies	
Genetic Counseling	M
German	D
History	M,D
Human Development	D
International Affairs	P,M,O
Internet and Interactive Multimedia	M
Italian	D,O
Journalism	M
Liberal Studies	M
Linguistics	M,D
Marriage and Family Therapy	M
Media Studies	M,D
Music	M,D,O
Philosophy	D
Political Science	M,D
Psychology—General	D
Public Administration	M
Public Policy	M,D
Publishing	M
Religion	M
Slavic Languages	D
Social Psychology	D
Social Sciences	M,O
Sociology	D
Speech and Interpersonal Communication	M,D
Theater	M,D
Writing	M

NORTHWEST MISSOURI STATE UNIVERSITY

Agricultural Economics and Agribusiness	M
English	M
Geographic Information Systems	M,O
Geography	M,O
History	M
Psychology—General	M

NORTHWEST NAZARENE UNIVERSITY

Marriage and Family Therapy	M
Missions and Missiology	P,M
Pastoral Ministry and Counseling	P,M
Religion	P,M
School Psychology	M
Social Psychology	M

NORTHWEST UNIVERSITY

Counseling Psychology	M,D
Cultural Studies	M
Missions and Missiology	M
Pastoral Ministry and Counseling	M
Psychology—General	M,D
Theology	M

NORWICH UNIVERSITY

American Studies	M
Conflict Resolution and Mediation/Peace Studies	M
Ethnic Studies	M
Gender Studies	M
International Affairs	M
Military and Defense Studies	M
Public Administration	M

NOTRE DAME COLLEGE (OH)

Pastoral Ministry and Counseling	M,O

NOTRE DAME DE NAMUR UNIVERSITY

Art Therapy	M
Clinical Psychology	M
English	M,O
Marriage and Family Therapy	M
Music	M,O
Psychology—General	M
Public Administration	M
Public Affairs	M

NOTRE DAME SEMINARY

Theology	P,M

NOVA SOUTHEASTERN UNIVERSITY

Child and Family Studies	M,D
Clinical Psychology	D,O
Conflict Resolution and Mediation/Peace Studies	M,D
Counseling Psychology	M
Criminal Justice and Criminology	M*
Humanities	M
Interdisciplinary Studies	M
Marriage and Family Therapy	M,D,O
Psychology—General	M,D,O
Public Administration	M
School Psychology	O
Social Sciences	M
Spanish	M,O

NSCAD UNIVERSITY

Applied Arts and Design—General	M
Art/Fine Arts	M

NYACK COLLEGE

Social Sciences	M

OAKLAND CITY UNIVERSITY

Theology	P,D

OAKLAND UNIVERSITY

Counseling Psychology	M,D,O
Economics	O
English	M
History	M
Liberal Studies	M
Linguistics	M,O
Music	M,D
Public Administration	M

*M—master's degree; P—first professional degree; D—doctorate; O—other advanced degree; *—Close-Up and/or Display*

OAKWOOD UNIVERSITY

Pastoral Ministry and Counseling	M

OBERLIN COLLEGE

Music	M,O

OBLATE SCHOOL OF THEOLOGY

Pastoral Ministry and Counseling	P,M,D,O
Religion	P,M,D,O
Theology	P,M,D,O

OCCIDENTAL COLLEGE

Liberal Studies	M

OHIO DOMINICAN UNIVERSITY

Liberal Studies	M
Theology	M

THE OHIO STATE UNIVERSITY

African Studies	M
African-American Studies	M
Agricultural Economics and Agribusiness	M,D
Anthropology	M,D
Architecture	M
Art History	M,D
Art/Fine Arts	M
Arts Administration	M
Asian Languages	M,D
Child and Family Studies	M,D
Chinese	M,D
Classics	M,D
Clinical Psychology	M,D
Clothing and Textiles	M,D
Cognitive Sciences	M,D
Communication—General	M,D
Consumer Economics	M,D
Dance	D
Developmental Psychology	M,D
East European and Russian Studies	M
Economics	M,D
English	M,D
French	M,D
Geography	M,D
German	M,D
History	M,D
Human Development	M,D
Industrial and Labor Relations	M,D
Industrial Design	M
Interdisciplinary Studies	M,D
Interior Design	M
Italian	M,D
Japanese	M,D
Journalism	M
Landscape Architecture	M
Linguistics	M,D
Music	M,D
Near and Middle Eastern Languages	M,D
Philosophy	M,D
Political Science	M,D
Portuguese	M,D
Psychology—General	M,D
Public Affairs	M,D
Rural Sociology	M,D
Slavic Languages	M,D
Social Psychology	M,D
Sociology	M,D
Spanish	M,D
Theater	M,D
Urban and Regional Planning	M,D
Women's Studies	M,D

OHIO UNIVERSITY

African Studies	M
Applied Economics	M
Art History	M
Art/Fine Arts	M
Asian Studies	M
Child and Family Studies	M
Child Development	M
Clinical Psychology	D
Clothing and Textiles	M
Communication—General	M,D
Comparative and Interdisciplinary Arts	D
Corporate and Organizational Communication	M,D
Economics	M
English	M,D
Experimental Psychology	D
Family and Consumer Sciences-General	M
Film, Television, and Video Production	M
Film, Television, and Video Theory and Criticism	M
French	M
Geography	M
Graphic Design	M
Health Communication	M,D
History	M,D
Industrial and Organizational Psychology	D
International Affairs	M
International Development	M
Journalism	M,D
Latin American Studies	M
Linguistics	M
Media Studies	M,D
Music	M,O
Philosophy	M
Photography	M
Political Science	M
Psychology—General	D
Public Administration	M
Rehabilitation Counseling	M,D
Rhetoric	M,D
Social Sciences	M
Sociology	M
Spanish	M
Speech and Interpersonal Communication	M,D
Theater	M
Therapies—Dance, Drama, and Music	M,O

OHR HAMEIR THEOLOGICAL SEMINARY

Theology	

OKLAHOMA CHRISTIAN UNIVERSITY

Pastoral Ministry and Counseling	P,M
Theology	P,M

OKLAHOMA CITY UNIVERSITY

Art/Fine Arts	M
Comparative Literature	M
Corporate and Organizational Communication	M
Criminal Justice and Criminology	M
Dance	M
Liberal Studies	M
Mass Communication	M
Music	M
Philosophy	M
Religion	M
Sociology	M
Theater	M
Writing	M

OKLAHOMA STATE UNIVERSITY

Agricultural Economics and Agribusiness	M,D
Applied Arts and Design—General	M,D
Child and Family Studies	M,D
Clinical Psychology	M,D
Clothing and Textiles	M,D
Consumer Economics	M,D
Economics	M,D
Emergency Management	M,D
English	M,D
Family and Consumer Sciences-General	M,D
Geography	M,D
History	M,D
Human Development	M,D
International Affairs	M,D,O
Landscape Architecture	M,D
Mass Communication	M
Music	M
Philosophy	M
Political Science	M,D
Psychology—General	M,D
Sociology	M,D
Theater	M
Writing	M,D

OKLAHOMA STATE UNIVERSITY CENTER FOR HEALTH SCIENCES

Forensic Psychology	M,O
Forensic Sciences	M,O

OLD DOMINION UNIVERSITY

Applied Economics	M
Clinical Psychology	D
Conflict Resolution and Mediation/Peace Studies	M,D
Criminal Justice and Criminology	D
Economics	M
English	M,D
Experimental Psychology	D
History	M
Humanities	M
Industrial and Organizational Psychology	D
International Affairs	M,D
Linguistics	M
Psychology—General	M,D
Public Administration	M,D
Sociology	M
Urban Studies	D
Women's Studies	M,D
Writing	M

OLIVET NAZARENE UNIVERSITY

Religion	M
Theology	M

ORAL ROBERTS UNIVERSITY

Marriage and Family Therapy	P,M,D
Missions and Missiology	P,M,D
Near and Middle Eastern Languages	P,M,D
Pastoral Ministry and Counseling	P,M,D
Theology	P,M,D

OREGON HEALTH & SCIENCE UNIVERSITY

Gerontology	M,O

OREGON STATE UNIVERSITY

Agricultural Economics and Agribusiness	M,D
Anthropology	M
Child and Family Studies	M,D
Clothing and Textiles	M,D
Economics	M,D
English	M
Family and Consumer Sciences-General	M
Geography	M,D
Gerontology	M
History of Science and Technology	M,D
History	M,D
Human Development	M,D
Interdisciplinary Studies	M

OREGON STATE UNIVERSITY–CASCADES

School Psychology	M
Social Psychology	M

OTIS COLLEGE OF ART AND DESIGN

Art/Fine Arts	M
Graphic Design	M
Photography	M
Writing	M

OTTAWA UNIVERSITY

Art Therapy	M
Counseling Psychology	M
Marriage and Family Therapy	M
Pastoral Ministry and Counseling	M
School Psychology	M

OUR LADY OF HOLY CROSS COLLEGE

Marriage and Family Therapy	M

OUR LADY OF THE LAKE UNIVERSITY OF SAN ANTONIO

Communication—General	M
Counseling Psychology	M,D
English	M
Human Development	M
Marriage and Family Therapy	M,D
Psychology—General	M,D
School Psychology	M,D
Writing	M

OXFORD GRADUATE SCHOOL

Child and Family Studies	M,D
Religion	M,D

PACE UNIVERSITY

Addictions/Substance Abuse Counseling	M
Clinical Psychology	M,D
Counseling Psychology	M
Economics	M
Forensic Sciences	M
Homeland Security	M
Internet and Interactive Multimedia	M,D,O
Psychology—General	M
Public Administration	M
Publishing	M,O
School Psychology	M,D
Theater	M

PACIFICA GRADUATE INSTITUTE
Clinical Psychology M,D
Counseling Psychology M,D
Psychology—General M,D

PACIFIC LUTHERAN THEOLOGICAL SEMINARY
Theology P,M,D,O

PACIFIC LUTHERAN UNIVERSITY
Marriage and Family Therapy M
Writing M

PACIFIC NORTHWEST COLLEGE OF ART
Applied Arts and Design—General M
Art/Fine Arts M

PACIFIC OAKS COLLEGE
Human Development M
Marriage and Family Therapy M

PACIFIC SCHOOL OF RELIGION
Religion P,M,D,O
Theology P,M,D,O

PACIFIC UNIVERSITY
Psychology—General M,D
Writing M

PALM BEACH ATLANTIC UNIVERSITY
Addictions/Substance Abuse Counseling M
Counseling Psychology M
Marriage and Family Therapy M

PALO ALTO UNIVERSITY
Clinical Psychology D
Psychology—General M,D

PARK UNIVERSITY
Emergency Management M
Public Administration M
Public Affairs M

PAYNE THEOLOGICAL SEMINARY
Theology P

PENN STATE HARRISBURG
American Studies M,D
Humanities M,D
Psychology—General M,D
Public Affairs M,D

PENN STATE UNIVERSITY PARK
Agricultural Economics and Agribusiness M,D
Anthropology M,D
Architecture M
Art History M,D
Art/Fine Arts M,D
Child and Family Studies M,D
Communication—General M,D
Counseling Psychology M,D
Demography and Population Studies M,D
Economics M,D
English M,D
French M,D
Geography M,D
German M,D
History M,D
Human Development M,D
Industrial and Labor Relations M,O
Landscape Architecture M
Linguistics M,D
Music M,D
Philosophy M,D
Political Science M,D
Psychology—General M,D
Rural Sociology M,D
School Psychology M,D
Sociology M,D
Spanish M,D
Theater M
Writing M,D

PENNSYLVANIA ACADEMY OF THE FINE ARTS
Art/Fine Arts M,O

PEPPERDINE UNIVERSITY
American Studies M
Clinical Psychology M,D
Communication—General M
Conflict Resolution and Mediation/Peace Studies M
Economics M
History M
Humanities M
International Affairs M
Marriage and Family Therapy M,D
Political Science M
Psychology—General M,D
Public Administration M
Public Policy M
Religion P,M

PERU STATE COLLEGE
Economics M

PHILADELPHIA BIBLICAL UNIVERSITY
Pastoral Ministry and Counseling M
Theology P,M

PHILADELPHIA COLLEGE OF OSTEOPATHIC MEDICINE
Clinical Psychology M,D,O
Counseling Psychology M,D,O
Forensic Sciences M
Health Psychology M,D,O
Industrial and Organizational Psychology M,D,O
Psychology—General M,D,O*
School Psychology M,D,O

PHILADELPHIA UNIVERSITY
Architecture M
Clothing and Textiles M
Computer Art and Design M
Emergency Management M
Sustainable Development M
Textile Design M

PHILLIPS GRADUATE INSTITUTE
Clinical Psychology D
Marriage and Family Therapy M,D

PHILLIPS THEOLOGICAL SEMINARY
Ethics P,M,D
Missions and Missiology P,M,D
Music P,M,D
Pastoral Ministry and Counseling D
Theology P,M,D

PHOENIX SEMINARY
Counseling Psychology P,M,D,O
Cultural Studies P,M,D,O
Pastoral Ministry and Counseling P,M,D,O
Theology P,M,D,O
Women's Studies P,M,D,O

PIEDMONT BAPTIST COLLEGE AND GRADUATE SCHOOL
Theology M,D

PITTSBURGH THEOLOGICAL SEMINARY
Theology P,M,D

PITTSBURG STATE UNIVERSITY
Art/Fine Arts M
Communication—General M
English M
Graphic Design M,O
History M
Music M
Psychology—General M
School Psychology O
Social Psychology M
Theater M

POINT LOMA NAZARENE UNIVERSITY
Religion M

POINT PARK UNIVERSITY
Communication—General M*
Criminal Justice and Criminology M
Journalism M
Mass Communication M
Music M
Theater M

POLYTECHNIC INSTITUTE OF NYU
Communication—General O
Criminal Justice and Criminology M,D,O
Film, Television, and Video Production O
History of Science and Technology M
Humanities M,O
Interdisciplinary Studies M
Internet and Interactive Multimedia M,O
Journalism M
Psychology—General M,O
Technical Communication O
Technical Writing M

POLYTECHNIC INSTITUTE OF NYU, LONG ISLAND GRADUATE CENTER
Interdisciplinary Studies M

POLYTECHNIC INSTITUTE OF NYU, WESTCHESTER GRADUATE CENTER
Criminal Justice and Criminology M
Interdisciplinary Studies M

POLYTECHNIC UNIVERSITY OF PUERTO RICO
Landscape Architecture M

PONCE SCHOOL OF MEDICINE
Clinical Psychology D

PONTIFICAL CATHOLIC UNIVERSITY OF PUERTO RICO
Clinical Psychology M,D
Criminal Justice and Criminology M
Hispanic Studies M,O
History M
Industrial and Organizational Psychology M,D
Psychology—General M,D
Public Administration M
Rehabilitation Counseling M
Spanish M,O
Theology P

PONTIFICAL COLLEGE JOSEPHINUM
Theology P,M

PONTIFICIA UNIVERSIDAD CATOLICA MADRE Y MAESTRA
Architecture M
Criminal Justice and Criminology M
History M
Industrial and Labor Relations M
Interior Design M

PORTLAND STATE UNIVERSITY
Anthropology M,D,O
Applied Economics M,D
Applied Social Research M,D
Art/Fine Arts M
Conflict Resolution and Mediation/Peace Studies M
Criminal Justice and Criminology M,D
Economics M,D,O
English M
French M
Geography M,D
German M
Gerontology O
History M
Japanese M
Music M
Political Science M,D
Psychology—General M,D,O
Public Administration M,D
Sociology M,D,O
Spanish M
Speech and Interpersonal Communication M,O
Theater M
Urban and Regional Planning M
Urban Studies M,D

PRAIRIE VIEW A&M UNIVERSITY
Agricultural Economics and Agribusiness M
Architecture M
Clinical Psychology M,D
English M
Family and Consumer Sciences-General M
Forensic Psychology M,D
Sociology M
Urban Design M

*M—master's degree; P—first professional degree; D—doctorate; O—other advanced degree; *—Close-Up and/or Display*

PRATT INSTITUTE

Applied Arts and Design—General M,O*
Architecture M*
Art History M
Art Therapy M
Art/Fine Arts M
Arts Administration M
Graphic Design M
Historic Preservation M
Industrial Design M
Interior Design M
Internet and Interactive Multimedia M
Photography M
Therapies—Dance, Drama, and Music M
Urban and Regional Planning M
Urban Design M

PRESCOTT COLLEGE

Art Therapy M
Counseling Psychology M
Health Psychology M
Humanities M
Psychoanalysis and Psychotherapy M

PRINCETON THEOLOGICAL SEMINARY

Religion P,M,D
Theology P,M,D

PRINCETON UNIVERSITY

Anthropology D
Archaeology D
Architecture M,D
Asian Studies D
Classics D
Comparative Literature D
Demography and Population Studies D,O
Economics D,O
English D
French D
German D
History of Science and Technology D
History D
International Affairs M,D
Music D
Near and Middle Eastern Studies M,D
Philosophy D
Political Science D
Portuguese D
Psychology—General D
Public Affairs M,D,O
Public Policy M,D
Religion D
Russian D
Slavic Languages D
Sociology D,O
Spanish D

PROVIDENCE COLLEGE

American Studies M
Economics M
History M
Religion M
Theology M

PROVIDENCE COLLEGE AND THEOLOGICAL SEMINARY

Counseling Psychology P,M,D,O
Missions and Missiology P,M,D,O
Pastoral Ministry and Counseling P,M,D,O
Theology P,M,D,O

PURCHASE COLLEGE, STATE UNIVERSITY OF NEW YORK

Art History M
Art/Fine Arts M
Dance M
Music M
Theater M

PURDUE UNIVERSITY

Agricultural Economics and Agribusiness M,D
American Studies M,D
Anthropology M,D
Applied Arts and Design—General M
Art/Fine Arts M
Child and Family Studies M,D
Child Development M,D
Clothing and Textiles M,D
Communication—General M,D
Comparative Literature M,D
Consumer Economics M,D
Economics D
English M,D
Family and Consumer Sciences-General M,D
French M,D
German M,D
History M,D
Human Development M,D
Linguistics M,D
Marriage and Family Therapy M,D
Philosophy M,D
Political Science M,D
Psychology—General D
Sociology M,D
Spanish M,D
Sport Psychology M,D
Theater M
Writing M,D

PURDUE UNIVERSITY CALUMET

Communication—General M
Counseling Psychology M
English M
History M
Marriage and Family Therapy M
School Psychology M

QUEENS COLLEGE OF THE CITY UNIVERSITY OF NEW YORK

Art History M
Art/Fine Arts M
Clinical Psychology M
English M
Family and Consumer Sciences-General M
French M
History M
Italian M
Liberal Studies M
Linguistics M
Music M
Psychology—General M
Romance Languages M
School Psychology M,O
Social Sciences M
Sociology M
Spanish M
Urban Studies M
Writing M

QUEEN'S UNIVERSITY AT KINGSTON

Canadian Studies M,D
Classics M
Clinical Psychology M,D
Cognitive Sciences M,D
Communication—General M,D
Developmental Psychology M,D
English M,D
French M,D
Gender Studies M,D
Geography M,D
German M,D
Hispanic Studies M
Industrial and Labor Relations M
International Affairs M,D
Philosophy M,D
Political Science M,D
Psychology—General M,D
Public Policy M
Religion M
Social Psychology M,D
Sociology M,D
Spanish M
Sport Psychology M,D
Theology P,M,O
Urban and Regional Planning M
Women's Studies M,D

QUEENS UNIVERSITY OF CHARLOTTE

Corporate and Organizational Communication M
Writing M

QUINCY UNIVERSITY

Counseling Psychology M
School Psychology M
Theology M

QUINNIPIAC UNIVERSITY

Communication—General M
Internet and Interactive Multimedia M
Journalism M

RABBI ISAAC ELCHANAN THEOLOGICAL SEMINARY

Theology O

RABBINICAL ACADEMY MESIVTA RABBI CHAIM BERLIN

Theology O

RABBINICAL COLLEGE BETH SHRAGA

Theology

RABBINICAL COLLEGE BOBOVER YESHIVA B'NEI ZION

Theology

RABBINICAL COLLEGE CH'SAN SOFER

Theology

RABBINICAL COLLEGE OF LONG ISLAND

Theology

RABBINICAL SEMINARY M'KOR CHAIM

Theology

RABBINICAL SEMINARY OF AMERICA

Theology

RADFORD UNIVERSITY

Art/Fine Arts M
Clinical Psychology M
Corporate and Organizational Communication M
Counseling Psychology M,D
Criminal Justice and Criminology M
English M
Experimental Psychology M
Industrial and Organizational Psychology M
Music M
Psychology—General M
School Psychology M,O
Therapies—Dance, Drama, and Music M

RAMAPO COLLEGE OF NEW JERSEY

Liberal Studies M

RECONSTRUCTIONIST RABBINICAL COLLEGE

Theology P,M,D,O

REED COLLEGE

Liberal Studies M

REFORMED PRESBYTERIAN THEOLOGICAL SEMINARY

Theology P,M,D

REFORMED THEOLOGICAL SEMINARY–CHARLOTTE CAMPUS

Pastoral Ministry and Counseling P,M,D
Religion P,M,D
Theology P,M,D

REFORMED THEOLOGICAL SEMINARY–JACKSON CAMPUS

Marriage and Family Therapy P,M,D,O
Missions and Missiology P,M,D,O
Pastoral Ministry and Counseling P,M,D,O
Theology P,M,D,O

REFORMED THEOLOGICAL SEMINARY–ORLANDO CAMPUS

Pastoral Ministry and Counseling P,M,D
Theology P,M,D

REFORMED THEOLOGICAL SEMINARY–WASHINGTON D.C.

Religion P,M
Theology P,M

REGENT COLLEGE

Theology P,M,O

REGENT'S AMERICAN COLLEGE LONDON

International Affairs M

REGENT UNIVERSITY

American Studies M
Clinical Psychology M,D,O
Communication—General M,D
Computer Art and Design M,D
Counseling Psychology M,D,O
Economics M
Film, Television, and Video Production M,D
Homeland Security M
International Affairs M
International Economics M
Journalism M,D

Missions and Missiology P,M,D
Near and Middle Eastern Studies M
Pastoral Ministry and Counseling P,M,D
Political Science M
Public Administration M
Public Policy M
Social Psychology M,D,O
Theater M,D
Theology P,M,D

REGIS COLLEGE (CANADA)

Pastoral Ministry and Counseling P,M,D,O
Philosophy P,M,D,O
Theology P,M,D,O

REGIS COLLEGE (MA)

Corporate and Organizational Communication M

REGIS UNIVERSITY

Art/Fine Arts M,O
Arts Administration M,O
Communication—General M,O
Conflict Resolution and Mediation/Peace Studies M,O
Counseling Psychology M,O
Criminal Justice and Criminology M,O
Interdisciplinary Studies M,O
Marriage and Family Therapy M,O
Music M,O
Psychology—General M,O
Social Psychology M,O
Social Sciences M,O
Technical Writing M,O

REINHARDT UNIVERSITY

Music M

RENSSELAER POLYTECHNIC INSTITUTE

Applied Arts and Design—General M,D
Architecture M
Art/Fine Arts M,D
Cognitive Sciences D
Communication—General M,D
Computer Art and Design M,D
Economics M
History of Science and Technology M,D
Interdisciplinary Studies M,D
Lighting Design M
Rhetoric M,D
Speech and Interpersonal Communication M,D
Sustainable Development M,D
Technical Communication M

RHODE ISLAND COLLEGE

Art/Fine Arts M
Arts Administration M
English M
History M
Psychology—General M
Public Administration M
Theater M
Writing M

RHODE ISLAND SCHOOL OF DESIGN

Applied Arts and Design—General M
Architecture M
Art/Fine Arts M
Computer Art and Design M
Graphic Design M
Industrial Design M
Interior Design M
Landscape Architecture M
Photography M
Textile Design M

RICE UNIVERSITY

African Studies D
American Studies D
Anthropology M,D
Archaeology M,D
Architecture M,D
Art History D
Cognitive Sciences M,D
Economics M,D
English M,D
History M,D
Industrial and Organizational Psychology M,D
Jewish Studies D
Liberal Studies M
Linguistics M,D
Music M,D
Near and Middle Eastern Studies D
Philosophy M,D
Political Science D
Psychology—General M,D
Religion D
Sociology D
Urban Design M,D

THE RICHARD STOCKTON COLLEGE OF NEW JERSEY

Criminal Justice and Criminology M
Holocaust and Genocide Studies M

RICHMOND, THE AMERICAN INTERNATIONAL UNIVERSITY IN LONDON

Art History M
International Affairs M

RICHMONT GRADUATE UNIVERSITY

Counseling Psychology M
Marriage and Family Therapy M
Psychology—General M

RIDER UNIVERSITY

French O
German O
School Psychology O
Spanish O

RIVIER COLLEGE

Counseling Psychology M,D,O
English M
Writing M

ROBERT MORRIS UNIVERSITY

Internet and Interactive Multimedia M,D

ROBERTS WESLEYAN COLLEGE

Child and Family Studies M
Pastoral Ministry and Counseling M
School Psychology M

ROCHESTER COLLEGE

Missions and Missiology M

ROCHESTER INSTITUTE OF TECHNOLOGY

Art/Fine Arts M
Communication—General M
Computer Art and Design M
Criminal Justice and Criminology M
Film, Television, and Video Production M
Gerontology M,O
Graphic Design M
Industrial Design M
Interdisciplinary Studies M
Internet and Interactive Multimedia M,O
Media Studies M
Medical Illustration M
Photography M
Psychology—General M
Public Policy M
Sustainable Development D
Technical Communication O

ROGER WILLIAMS UNIVERSITY

Architecture M
Criminal Justice and Criminology M
Forensic Psychology M
Public Administration M

ROLLINS COLLEGE

Liberal Studies M

ROOSEVELT UNIVERSITY

Anthropology M
Applied Economics M
Clinical Psychology M,D
Communication—General M
Corporate and Organizational Communication M
Economics M
English M
Gender Studies M,O
History M
Industrial and Organizational Psychology M
Journalism M
Music M,O
Political Science M
Psychology—General D
Public Administration M
Sociology M
Spanish M
Theater M
Women's Studies M,O
Writing M

ROSALIND FRANKLIN UNIVERSITY OF MEDICINE AND SCIENCE

Interdisciplinary Studies D
Psychology—General M,D

ROSEMONT COLLEGE

Counseling Psychology M
English M
Publishing M
Writing M

ROWAN UNIVERSITY

Clinical Psychology M
Counseling Psychology M
Criminal Justice and Criminology M
Music M
Psychology—General M
School Psychology M,O
Theater M
Writing M

ROYAL MILITARY COLLEGE OF CANADA

Military and Defense Studies M,D

ROYAL ROADS UNIVERSITY

Conflict Resolution and Mediation/Peace Studies M,O
Emergency Management M,O

RUTGERS, THE STATE UNIVERSITY OF NEW JERSEY, CAMDEN

Child Development M,D
Criminal Justice and Criminology M
English M
History M
International Affairs M
International Development M
Liberal Studies M
Psychology—General M
Public Administration M
Public History M
Public Policy M
Writing M

RUTGERS, THE STATE UNIVERSITY OF NEW JERSEY, NEWARK

American Studies M,D
Cognitive Sciences D*
Criminal Justice and Criminology D
Economics M
English M
History M
International Affairs M,D
Liberal Studies M
Music M
Political Science M
Psychology—General D
Public Administration M,D
Public Policy M,D
Social Psychology D
Urban Studies M,D
Writing M

RUTGERS, THE STATE UNIVERSITY OF NEW JERSEY, NEW BRUNSWICK

African Studies D
African-American Studies D
Agricultural Economics and Agribusiness M
Anthropology M,D
Applied Arts and Design—General M
Art History M,D,O
Art/Fine Arts M
Asian Studies D
Classics M,D
Clinical Psychology M,D
Cognitive Sciences D
Communication—General D

*M—master's degree; P—first professional degree; D—doctorate; O—other advanced degree; *—Close-Up and/or Display*

Comparative Literature M,D
Counseling Psychology M
Economics M,D
English D
French M,D
Gender Studies M,D
Geography M,D
German M,D
Health Psychology D
Historic Preservation M,D,O
History of Medicine D
History of Science and Technology D
History D
Industrial and Labor Relations M,D*
Industrial and Organizational Psychology M,D
Interdisciplinary Studies D
International Affairs D
Italian M,D
Linguistics D
Medieval and Renaissance Studies D
Music M,D,O
Philosophy D
Political Science D
Psychology—General M,D
Public Policy M,D
School Psychology M,D
Social Psychology D
Sociology M,D
Spanish M,D
Theater M
Translation and Interpretation M,D
Urban and Regional Planning M,D
Women's Studies M,D
Writing M

RYERSON UNIVERSITY
Arts Administration M

SACRED HEART MAJOR SEMINARY
Pastoral Ministry and Counseling P,M
Theology P,M

SACRED HEART SCHOOL OF THEOLOGY
Theology P,M

SACRED HEART UNIVERSITY
Criminal Justice and Criminology M
Gerontology M
Internet and Interactive Multimedia M,O
Religion M

SAGE GRADUATE SCHOOL
Child and Family Studies M
Counseling Psychology M
Forensic Psychology M,O
Gerontology M,O
Psychology—General M
Public Administration M,O
Social Psychology M

SAGINAW VALLEY STATE UNIVERSITY
Communication—General M
Media Studies M
Public Administration M

ST. AMBROSE UNIVERSITY
Criminal Justice and Criminology M
Pastoral Ministry and Counseling M

ST. ANDREW'S COLLEGE IN WINNIPEG
Theology P

ST. AUGUSTINE'S SEMINARY OF TORONTO
Pastoral Ministry and Counseling P,M,O
Theology P,M,O

SAINT BERNARD'S SCHOOL OF THEOLOGY AND MINISTRY
Pastoral Ministry and Counseling P,M,O
Theology P,M,O

ST. BONAVENTURE UNIVERSITY
Corporate and Organizational Communication M
Counseling Psychology M,O
English M
Social Psychology M,O

ST. CATHERINE UNIVERSITY
Theology M

ST. CHARLES BORROMEO SEMINARY, OVERBROOK
Religion M
Theology P,M

ST. CLOUD STATE UNIVERSITY
Applied Economics M
Archaeology M
Child and Family Studies M
Criminal Justice and Criminology M
Economics M
English M
Geography M
Gerontology M
Historic Preservation M
History M
Industrial and Organizational Psychology M
Marriage and Family Therapy M
Mass Communication M
Music M
Psychology—General M,D
Rehabilitation Counseling M
Social Psychology M

ST. EDWARD'S UNIVERSITY
Computer Art and Design M
Conflict Resolution and Mediation/Peace Studies M,O
Counseling Psychology M,O
Ethics M
Humanities M,O
Liberal Studies M,O
Public Administration M,O
Social Sciences M,O

SAINT FRANCIS SEMINARY
Pastoral Ministry and Counseling P,M
Theology P,M

ST. FRANCIS XAVIER UNIVERSITY
Cultural Studies M

ST. JOHN FISHER COLLEGE
Counseling Psychology M
International Affairs M

ST. JOHN'S COLLEGE (MD)
Liberal Studies M

ST. JOHN'S COLLEGE (NM)
Asian Languages M
Asian Studies M
Liberal Studies M

ST. JOHN'S SEMINARY (CA)
Pastoral Ministry and Counseling P,M
Theology P,M

SAINT JOHN'S SEMINARY (MA)
Religion P,M
Theology P,M

SAINT JOHN'S UNIVERSITY (MN)
Music P,M
Pastoral Ministry and Counseling P,M
Theology P,M

ST. JOHN'S UNIVERSITY (NY)
African Studies M,O
Asian Studies M,O
Clinical Psychology D
Criminal Justice and Criminology M
English M,D
Experimental Psychology M
History M,D
International Affairs M
Liberal Studies M
Pastoral Ministry and Counseling P,M,O
Philosophy M
Political Science M,O
Psychology—General M,D
Rehabilitation Counseling M,D,O
School Psychology M,D
Sociology M
Spanish M,O
Theology P,M,O

SAINT JOSEPH COLLEGE
Counseling Psychology M
Gerontology M,O
Human Development M,O
Marriage and Family Therapy M
Social Psychology M

SAINT JOSEPH'S COLLEGE
Music M,O

ST. JOSEPH'S SEMINARY
Theology P,M

SAINT JOSEPH'S UNIVERSITY
Criminal Justice and Criminology M,O
Gerontology M,O
Homeland Security M,O
Industrial and Organizational Psychology M,O
Psychology—General M,O
Writing M

ST. LAWRENCE UNIVERSITY
Human Development M,O

SAINT LEO UNIVERSITY
Criminal Justice and Criminology M
Pastoral Ministry and Counseling M
Theology M

SAINT LOUIS UNIVERSITY
American Studies M,D
Clinical Psychology M,D
Communication—General M
English M,D
Experimental Psychology M,D
French M
Geographic Information Systems M,D,O
History M,D
Human Development M,D,O
Industrial and Organizational Psychology M,D
Marriage and Family Therapy M,D,O
Philosophy M,D
Political Science M
Psychology—General M,D
Public Administration M,D,O
Public Policy M,D,O
Spanish M
Theology M,D
Urban Studies M,D,O

SAINT LOUIS UNIVERSITY–MADRID CAMPUS
English M
Spanish M*

SAINT MARTIN'S UNIVERSITY
Counseling Psychology M
Social Psychology M

SAINT MARY-OF-THE-WOODS COLLEGE
Art Therapy M,O
Pastoral Ministry and Counseling M,O
Theology M,O
Therapies—Dance, Drama, and Music M

SAINT MARY'S COLLEGE OF CALIFORNIA
Marriage and Family Therapy M
Writing M

SAINT MARY SEMINARY AND GRADUATE SCHOOL OF THEOLOGY
Theology P,M,D

ST. MARY'S SEMINARY AND UNIVERSITY
Theology P,M,D,O*

SAINT MARY'S UNIVERSITY (CANADA)
Canadian Studies M,O
Criminal Justice and Criminology M
Gender Studies M
History M
Industrial and Organizational Psychology M,D
International Development M,O
Philosophy M
Psychology—General M,D
Religion M
Theology M
Women's Studies M

ST. MARY'S UNIVERSITY (UNITED STATES)

Addictions/Substance Abuse Counseling	M,D,O
Clinical Psychology	M
Communication—General	M
Counseling Psychology	M
English	M
Industrial and Organizational Psychology	M
International Affairs	M
Marriage and Family Therapy	M,D
Pastoral Ministry and Counseling	M
Political Science	M
Psychology—General	M
Public Administration	M
Social Psychology	M
Theology	M

SAINT MARY'S UNIVERSITY OF MINNESOTA

Arts Administration	M
Counseling Psychology	M
Geographic Information Systems	M,O
Human Development	M
Marriage and Family Therapy	M,O
Pastoral Ministry and Counseling	M,O
Philanthropic Studies	M

SAINT MEINRAD SCHOOL OF THEOLOGY

Theology	P,M

SAINT MICHAEL'S COLLEGE

Clinical Psychology	M
Theology	M,O

ST. NORBERT COLLEGE

Liberal Studies	M
Theology	M

ST. PATRICK'S SEMINARY & UNIVERSITY

Theology	P,M

SAINT PAUL SCHOOL OF THEOLOGY

Theology	P,M,D

SAINT PAUL UNIVERSITY

Conflict Resolution and Mediation/Peace Studies	M
Counseling Psychology	M
Marriage and Family Therapy	M
Missions and Missiology	M
Pastoral Ministry and Counseling	M,D,O
Theology	M,D,O

ST. PETERSBURG THEOLOGICAL SEMINARY

Jewish Studies	P,M,D
Pastoral Ministry and Counseling	P,M,D
Theology	P,M,D

SAINT PETER'S COLLEGE

Criminal Justice and Criminology	M

ST. PETER'S SEMINARY

Theology	P,M

SAINTS CYRIL AND METHODIUS SEMINARY

Pastoral Ministry and Counseling	P,M
Theology	P,M

ST. STEPHEN'S COLLEGE

Pastoral Ministry and Counseling	M,D
Theology	M,D

ST. THOMAS UNIVERSITY

Arts Administration	M
Communication—General	M,D,O
Counseling Psychology	M
Criminal Justice and Criminology	M,O
Film, Television, and Video Production	M
Hispanic Studies	M,O
Marriage and Family Therapy	M,O
Pastoral Ministry and Counseling	M,D,O
Public Administration	M,O
Theology	M,D,O

ST. TIKHON'S ORTHODOX THEOLOGICAL SEMINARY

Theology	P

SAINT VINCENT DE PAUL REGIONAL SEMINARY

Theology	P,M

SAINT VINCENT SEMINARY

Theology	P,M

ST. VLADIMIR'S ORTHODOX THEOLOGICAL SEMINARY

Music	P,M,D
Theology	P,M,D

SAINT XAVIER UNIVERSITY

Counseling Psychology	M,O
English	M,O
Psychology—General	M,O
Writing	M,O

SALEM STATE COLLEGE

Counseling Psychology	M,O
Criminal Justice and Criminology	M
English	M
Geography	M
History	M
Psychology—General	M
Spanish	M

SALISBURY UNIVERSITY

Conflict Resolution and Mediation/Peace Studies	M
English	M
Geographic Information Systems	M
History	M
Writing	M

SALVE REGINA UNIVERSITY

Art Therapy	M,O
Counseling Psychology	M,O
Criminal Justice and Criminology	M
Homeland Security	M,O
Humanities	M,D,O
International Affairs	M,O
Rehabilitation Counseling	M,O

SAMFORD UNIVERSITY

Music	M
Theology	P,M,D

SAM HOUSTON STATE UNIVERSITY

Clinical Psychology	M,D
Criminal Justice and Criminology	M,D
Dance	M
English	M
Family and Consumer Sciences-General	M
Forensic Sciences	M,D
History	M
Humanities	M,D
Music	M
Political Science	M
Psychology—General	M,D
Public Administration	M
Sociology	M
Speech and Interpersonal Communication	M,D

SAN DIEGO STATE UNIVERSITY

Anthropology	M
Applied Arts and Design—General	M
Art History	M
Art/Fine Arts	M
Asian Studies	M
Child and Family Studies	M
Child Development	M
Clinical Psychology	M,D
Communication—General	M
Criminal Justice and Criminology	M
Economics	M
Emergency Management	M,D
English	M
Environmental Design	M
Film, Television, and Video Production	M
Geography	M,D
Gerontology	M
Graphic Design	M
Health Psychology	M,D
History	M
Industrial and Organizational Psychology	M,D
Interdisciplinary Studies	M
Interior Design	M
Internet and Interactive Multimedia	M
Latin American Studies	M
Liberal Studies	M
Linguistics	M,O
Media Studies	M
Music	M
Philosophy	M
Political Science	M
Psychology—General	M,D
Public Administration	M
Rehabilitation Counseling	M
Rhetoric	M
Romance Languages	M
School Psychology	M
Sociology	M
Spanish	M
Theater	M
Urban and Regional Planning	M
Western European Studies	M
Women's Studies	M
Writing	M

SAN FRANCISCO ART INSTITUTE

Applied Arts and Design—General	M,O
Art History	M
Art/Fine Arts	M,O
Film, Television, and Video Production	M,O
Museum Studies	M
Photography	M,O
Urban Studies	M

SAN FRANCISCO CONSERVATORY OF MUSIC

Music	M

SAN FRANCISCO STATE UNIVERSITY

Anthropology	M
Art History	M
Art/Fine Arts	M
Asian-American Studies	M
Chinese	M
Classics	M
Comparative Literature	M
Counseling Psychology	M
Cultural Studies	M
Economics	M
English	M,O
Ethnic Studies	M
Family and Consumer Sciences-General	M
Film, Television, and Video Production	M
Film, Television, and Video Theory and Criticism	M
French	M
Geography	M
German	M
Gerontology	M
History	M
Humanities	M
Industrial Design	M
International Affairs	M
Italian	M
Japanese	M
Linguistics	M
Marriage and Family Therapy	M
Media Studies	M
Museum Studies	M
Music	M
Philosophy	M,O
Political Science	M
Psychology—General	M
Public Administration	M
Public Policy	M
Rehabilitation Counseling	M
Spanish	M
Speech and Interpersonal Communication	M
Theater	M
Women's Studies	M
Writing	M

SAN FRANCISCO THEOLOGICAL SEMINARY

Theology	P,M,D

SAN JOSE STATE UNIVERSITY

Anthropology	M
Applied Arts and Design—General	M
Applied Economics	M
Art History	M
Art/Fine Arts	M
Child and Family Studies	M
Clinical Psychology	M

*M—master's degree; P—first professional degree; D—doctorate; O—other advanced degree; *—Close-Up and/or Display*

Communication—General M
Comparative Literature M
Computer Art and Design M
Criminal Justice and Criminology M
Economics M
English M
Experimental Psychology M
Film, Television, and Video Production M
French M
Geographic Information Systems M,O
Geography M,O
Gerontology M,O
Hispanic Studies M
History M
Illustration M
Industrial and Organizational Psychology M
Interdisciplinary Studies M
Linguistics M,O
Mass Communication M
Music M
Philosophy M
Photography M
Psychology—General M
Public Administration M
Sociology M
Spanish M
Speech and Interpersonal Communication M
Theater M
Urban and Regional Planning M,O

SANTA CLARA UNIVERSITY

Agricultural Economics and Agribusiness M
Counseling Psychology M
Health Psychology M
Music M
Pastoral Ministry and Counseling M
Religion M

SARAH LAWRENCE COLLEGE

Child Development M
Dance M
Genetic Counseling M
History M
Interdisciplinary Studies M
Theater M
Women's Studies M
Writing M

SAVANNAH COLLEGE OF ART AND DESIGN

Applied Arts and Design—General M
Architectural History M
Architecture M
Art History M
Art/Fine Arts M
Arts Administration M
Computer Art and Design M
Film, Television, and Video Production M
Film, Television, and Video Theory and Criticism M
Graphic Design M
Historic Preservation M
Illustration M
Industrial Design M
Interior Design M
Internet and Interactive Multimedia M
Media Studies M
Music M
Photography M
Textile Design M
Theater M
Urban Design M
Writing M

SAVANNAH STATE UNIVERSITY

Public Administration M
Urban Studies M

SAYBROOK UNIVERSITY

Clinical Psychology M,D
Counseling Psychology M
Health Psychology M,D
Marriage and Family Therapy M,D
Psychology—General M,D
Sustainable Development M,D
Transpersonal and Humanistic Psychology M,D

SCHILLER INTERNATIONAL UNIVERSITY

International Affairs M

SCHILLER INTERNATIONAL UNIVERSITY (UNITED KINGDOM)

Corporate and Organizational Communication M
International Affairs M

SCHOOL OF ADVANCED AIR AND SPACE STUDIES

Military and Defense Studies M

THE SCHOOL OF PROFESSIONAL PSYCHOLOGY AT FOREST INSTITUTE

Clinical Psychology M,D,O
Counseling Psychology M,D,O
Marriage and Family Therapy M,D,O
Psychology—General M,D,O

SCHOOL OF THE ART INSTITUTE OF CHICAGO

Applied Arts and Design—General M
Architecture M
Art History M,O
Art Therapy M
Art/Fine Arts M
Arts Administration M
Arts Journalism M
Film, Television, and Video Production M
Graphic Design M
Historic Preservation M
Interior Design M
Journalism M
Music M
Photography M
Textile Design M,O
Writing M,O

SCHOOL OF THE MUSEUM OF FINE ARTS, BOSTON

Art/Fine Arts M

SCHOOL OF VISUAL ARTS (NY)

Applied Arts and Design—General M
Art Therapy M
Art/Fine Arts M
Computer Art and Design M
Film, Television, and Video Production M
Illustration M
Internet and Interactive Multimedia M
Photography M

SEABURY-WESTERN THEOLOGICAL SEMINARY

Music P,M,D,O
Theology P,M,D,O

SEATTLE PACIFIC UNIVERSITY

Clinical Psychology D
Industrial and Organizational Psychology M,D
Marriage and Family Therapy M,O
Theology P,M
Writing M

SEATTLE UNIVERSITY

Criminal Justice and Criminology M
Pastoral Ministry and Counseling M
Psychology—General M
Public Administration M
School Psychology M,O
Theology P,M,O
Transpersonal and Humanistic Psychology M

SEMINARY OF THE IMMACULATE CONCEPTION

Pastoral Ministry and Counseling P,M,D,O
Theology P,M,D,O

SEMINARY OF THE SOUTHWEST

Pastoral Ministry and Counseling P,M,O
Religion P,M,O
Theology P,M,O

SETON HALL UNIVERSITY

Art/Fine Arts M
Asian Languages M
Asian Studies M
Chinese M
Communication—General M
Corporate and Organizational Communication M
Counseling Psychology M,D
English M
Experimental Psychology M
History M
Holocaust and Genocide Studies M
International Affairs M*
Jewish Studies M
Marriage and Family Therapy M,D,O
Museum Studies M
Pastoral Ministry and Counseling P,M,O
Psychology—General M,D,O
Public Administration M,O
Public Policy M,O
Religion P,M,O
School Psychology O
Speech and Interpersonal Communication M
Theology P,M,O
Writing M

SETON HILL UNIVERSITY

Art Therapy M,O
Holocaust and Genocide Studies O
Marriage and Family Therapy M
Writing M

SEWANEE: THE UNIVERSITY OF THE SOUTH

English M
Theology P,M,D
Writing M

SHASTA BIBLE COLLEGE

Pastoral Ministry and Counseling M

SHAW UNIVERSITY

Theology P,M

SHENANDOAH UNIVERSITY

Arts Administration M,D,O
Dance M,D,O
Music M,D,O
Public Administration M,D,O
Therapies—Dance, Drama, and Music M,D,O

SHIPPENSBURG UNIVERSITY OF PENNSYLVANIA

Addictions/Substance Abuse Counseling M,O
Communication—General M
Counseling Psychology M,O
Criminal Justice and Criminology M
Geography M
Gerontology M,O
History M,O
Marriage and Family Therapy M,O
Psychology—General M
Public Administration M
Public History M,O
Social Psychology M,O
Sociology M

SH'OR YOSHUV RABBINICAL COLLEGE

Theology

SIMMONS COLLEGE

Corporate and Organizational Communication M
Cultural Studies M
English M
Gender Studies M
History M
Psychology—General M,D
Public History O
Spanish M

SIMON FRASER UNIVERSITY

Anthropology M,D
Archaeology M,D
Communication—General M,D
Comparative and Interdisciplinary Arts M
Criminal Justice and Criminology M,D
Economics M,D
English M,D
French M
Geography M,D
Gerontology M,D
History M,D
Internet and Interactive Multimedia M,D
Latin American Studies M
Liberal Studies M
Linguistics M,D

Philosophy M,D
Political Science M,D
Psychology—General M,D
Public Policy M
Publishing M
Sociology M,D
Urban Studies M,O
Women's Studies M,D

SIMPSON COLLEGE

Criminal Justice and Criminology M

SIMPSON UNIVERSITY

Counseling Psychology M
Missions and Missiology P,M
Pastoral Ministry and Counseling P,M

SIOUX FALLS SEMINARY

Marriage and Family Therapy M
Pastoral Ministry and Counseling P,M
Religion M
Theology M,D,O

SIT GRADUATE INSTITUTE

Conflict Resolution and Mediation/Peace Studies M
International Affairs M
Near and Middle Eastern Studies M
Sustainable Development M

SKIDMORE COLLEGE

Liberal Studies M

SLIPPERY ROCK UNIVERSITY OF PENNSYLVANIA

English M
History M
Sustainable Development M
Writing M

SMITH COLLEGE

Dance M
French M
History M
Theater M

SOJOURNER-DOUGLASS COLLEGE

Public Administration M

SOKA UNIVERSITY OF AMERICA

Japanese O

SONOMA STATE UNIVERSITY

Anthropology M
Counseling Psychology M
English M
History M
Interdisciplinary Studies M
Marriage and Family Therapy M
Political Science M
Public Administration M
Public History M
Writing M

SOUTH CAROLINA STATE UNIVERSITY

Agricultural Economics and Agribusiness M
Child and Family Studies M
Family and Consumer Sciences-General M
Rehabilitation Counseling M

SOUTH DAKOTA STATE UNIVERSITY

Clothing and Textiles M
Communication—General M
Economics M
English M
Family and Consumer Sciences-General M
Geography M
Human Development M
Interior Design M
Journalism M
Rural Sociology M,D

SOUTHEASTERN BAPTIST THEOLOGICAL SEMINARY

Ethics P,M,D
Missions and Missiology P,M,D
Music P,M,D
Philosophy P,M,D
Psychology—General P,M,D
Theology P,M,D
Women's Studies P,M,D

SOUTHEASTERN LOUISIANA UNIVERSITY

Addictions/Substance Abuse Counseling M
Communication—General M
English M
History M
Marriage and Family Therapy M
Music M
Psychology—General M
Social Psychology M
Sociology M
Writing M

SOUTHEASTERN OKLAHOMA STATE UNIVERSITY

Social Psychology M

SOUTHEASTERN UNIVERSITY (FL)

Counseling Psychology M
Pastoral Ministry and Counseling M

SOUTHEAST MISSOURI STATE UNIVERSITY

Counseling Psychology M,O
Criminal Justice and Criminology M
English M
Forensic Sciences M
History M
Public Administration M
School Psychology M,O

SOUTHERN ADVENTIST UNIVERSITY

Counseling Psychology M
Missions and Missiology M
Psychology—General M
Religion M
Theology M

SOUTHERN ARKANSAS UNIVERSITY–MAGNOLIA

Counseling Psychology M
Public Administration M

SOUTHERN BAPTIST THEOLOGICAL SEMINARY

Missions and Missiology P,M,D
Music P,M,D
Pastoral Ministry and Counseling P,M,D
Philosophy P,M,D
Religion P,M,D
Theology P,M,D

SOUTHERN CALIFORNIA INSTITUTE OF ARCHITECTURE

Architecture M

SOUTHERN CALIFORNIA SEMINARY

Counseling Psychology P,M,D
Psychology—General P,M,D
Religion P,M,D
Theology P,M,D

SOUTHERN CONNECTICUT STATE UNIVERSITY

English M
History M
Political Science M
Psychology—General M
School Psychology M,O
Sociology M
Sport Psychology M
Urban Studies M
Women's Studies M

SOUTHERN EVANGELICAL SEMINARY

Jewish Studies M,D,O
Missions and Missiology P,M,O
Near and Middle Eastern Studies M,D,O
Pastoral Ministry and Counseling P,M,O
Philosophy M,D,O
Religion P,M,D,O
Theology P,M,D,O

SOUTHERN ILLINOIS UNIVERSITY CARBONDALE

Agricultural Economics and Agribusiness M
Anthropology M,D
Applied Arts and Design—General M
Architecture M
Art/Fine Arts M
Clinical Psychology M,D
Communication—General M,D
Counseling Psychology M,D
Criminal Justice and Criminology M
Cultural Studies M
Economics M,D
English M,D
Experimental Psychology M,D
Geography M,D
History M,D
Human Development M,D
Journalism D
Linguistics M
Mass Communication M
Media Studies M
Music M
Philosophy M,D
Political Science M,D
Psychology—General M,D
Public Administration M
Rehabilitation Counseling M,D
Rhetoric M,D
Sociology M,D
Speech and Interpersonal Communication M,D
Theater M,D
Writing M

SOUTHERN ILLINOIS UNIVERSITY EDWARDSVILLE

Art Therapy M
Art/Fine Arts M
Clinical Psychology M
Corporate and Organizational Communication O
Economics M
English M,O
Geography M
History M
Industrial and Organizational Psychology M
Mass Communication M
Media Studies O
Museum Studies O
Music M
Psychology—General M,O
Public Administration M
School Psychology O
Sociology M
Speech and Interpersonal Communication M
Writing M

SOUTHERN METHODIST UNIVERSITY

Anthropology M,D
Applied Economics M,D
Art History M
Art/Fine Arts M
Arts Administration
Clinical Psychology D
Communication—General M
Conflict Resolution and Mediation/Peace Studies M,O
Dance M
Economics M,D
English M,D
Film, Television, and Video Production M
History M,D
Liberal Studies M
Medieval and Renaissance Studies M
Music M,O
Photography M
Psychology—General D
Religion M,D
Theater M
Theology P,M,D

SOUTHERN NAZARENE UNIVERSITY

Counseling Psychology M
Marriage and Family Therapy M
Psychology—General M
Religion M
Theology M

SOUTHERN NEW HAMPSHIRE UNIVERSITY

Addictions/Substance Abuse Counseling M,O
Child Development M,O
Clinical Psychology M,O
Economic Development M,D
Psychology—General M,O
Public Policy M,D
Writing M,O

*M—master's degree; P—first professional degree; D—doctorate; O—other advanced degree; *—Close-Up and/or Display*

SOUTHERN OREGON UNIVERSITY

Counseling Psychology	M
Interdisciplinary Studies	M
Psychology—General	M

SOUTHERN POLYTECHNIC STATE UNIVERSITY

Communication—General	M,O
Corporate and Organizational Communication	M,O
Graphic Design	M,O
Internet and Interactive Multimedia	M,O
Technical Communication	M,O

SOUTHERN UNIVERSITY AND AGRICULTURAL AND MECHANICAL COLLEGE

Criminal Justice and Criminology	M
History	M
Mass Communication	M
Political Science	M
Psychology—General	M
Public Administration	M
Public Policy	D
Rehabilitation Counseling	M
Social Sciences	M

SOUTHERN UTAH UNIVERSITY

Arts Administration	M
Communication—General	M
Forensic Sciences	M
Public Administration	M

SOUTHERN WESLEYAN UNIVERSITY

Pastoral Ministry and Counseling	M

SOUTH UNIVERSITY (AL)

Counseling Psychology	M

SOUTH UNIVERSITY (FL)

Counseling Psychology	M*

SOUTH UNIVERSITY (GA)

Counseling Psychology	M*
Criminal Justice and Criminology	M

SOUTH UNIVERSITY (SC)

Counseling Psychology	M*

SOUTH UNIVERSITY (VA)

Counseling Psychology	M*

SOUTH UNIVERSITY (VA)

Counseling Psychology	M*

SOUTHWESTERN ASSEMBLIES OF GOD UNIVERSITY

Counseling Psychology	M
History	M
Missions and Missiology	P,M
Pastoral Ministry and Counseling	P,M
Religion	P,M
Theology	P,M

SOUTHWESTERN BAPTIST THEOLOGICAL SEMINARY

Music	M,D,O
Theology	P,M,D,O

SOUTHWESTERN CHRISTIAN UNIVERSITY

Missions and Missiology	M
Pastoral Ministry and Counseling	M

SOUTHWESTERN COLLEGE (KS)

Criminal Justice and Criminology	M

SOUTHWESTERN COLLEGE (NM)

Art Therapy	M
Counseling Psychology	M,O
Health Psychology	O
Psychology—General	O
Social Psychology	O
Thanatology	M,O

SOUTHWESTERN OKLAHOMA STATE UNIVERSITY

Music	M
School Psychology	M

SPALDING UNIVERSITY

Clinical Psychology	M,D
Communication—General	M
Corporate and Organizational Communication	M
Psychology—General	M,D
Writing	M

SPERTUS INSTITUTE OF JEWISH STUDIES

Jewish Studies	M,D

SPRING ARBOR UNIVERSITY

Child and Family Studies	M
Communication—General	M
Counseling Psychology	M
Pastoral Ministry and Counseling	M
Theology	M

SPRINGFIELD COLLEGE

Addictions/Substance Abuse Counseling	M
Art Therapy	M,O
Counseling Psychology	M,O
Industrial and Organizational Psychology	M,O
Marriage and Family Therapy	M,O
Rehabilitation Counseling	M
Social Psychology	M
Sport Psychology	M,D,O

SPRING HILL COLLEGE

Art/Fine Arts	M
English	M
Ethics	M
History	M
Liberal Studies	M
Pastoral Ministry and Counseling	M
Theology	M

STANFORD UNIVERSITY

Anthropology	M,D
Art/Fine Arts	M,D
Asian Studies	M
Child and Family Studies	D
Chinese	M,D
Classics	M,D
Communication—General	M,D
Comparative Literature	D
Counseling Psychology	D
Developmental Psychology	D
East European and Russian Studies	M
Economics	D
English	M,D
French	M,D
German	M,D
History	M,D
Humanities	M
Interdisciplinary Studies	M,D
International Affairs	M
Italian	M,D
Japanese	M,D
Journalism	M,D
Linguistics	M,D
Music	M,D
Philosophy	M,D
Political Science	M,D
Psychology—General	D
Religion	M,D
Russian	M,D
Slavic Languages	M,D
Sociology	D
Spanish	M,D
Theater	D

STARR KING SCHOOL FOR THE MINISTRY

Theology	P

STATE UNIVERSITY OF NEW YORK AT BINGHAMTON

Anthropology	M,D
Art History	M,D
Clinical Psychology	M,D
Cognitive Sciences	M,D
Comparative Literature	M,D
Cultural Studies	M,D
Economics	M,D
English	M,D
French	M
Geography	M
History	M,D
Italian	M
Music	M
Philosophy	M,D
Political Science	M,D
Psychology—General	M,D
Public Administration	M
Public Policy	M,D
Sociology	M,D
Spanish	M,O
Theater	M
Translation and Interpretation	M,O

STATE UNIVERSITY OF NEW YORK AT FREDONIA

English	M
Interdisciplinary Studies	M
Music	M

STATE UNIVERSITY OF NEW YORK AT NEW PALTZ

Art/Fine Arts	M
Counseling Psychology	M
English	M
Music	M
Psychology—General	M
Therapies—Dance, Drama, and Music	M

STATE UNIVERSITY OF NEW YORK AT OSWEGO

Art/Fine Arts	M
Child and Family Studies	M
Consumer Economics	M
Counseling Psychology	M,O
English	M
History	M
School Psychology	M,O

STATE UNIVERSITY OF NEW YORK AT PLATTSBURGH

Liberal Studies	M
Psychology—General	M,O
School Psychology	M,O

STATE UNIVERSITY OF NEW YORK COLLEGE AT CORTLAND

American Studies	O
English	M
History	M

STATE UNIVERSITY OF NEW YORK COLLEGE AT ONEONTA

Family and Consumer Sciences-General	M
Museum Studies	M

STATE UNIVERSITY OF NEW YORK COLLEGE AT POTSDAM

Communication—General	M
English	M
Music	M

STATE UNIVERSITY OF NEW YORK COLLEGE OF ENVIRONMENTAL SCIENCE AND FORESTRY

Communication—General	M,D
Landscape Architecture	M
Urban and Regional Planning	M,D
Urban Design	M

STATE UNIVERSITY OF NEW YORK EMPIRE STATE COLLEGE

Industrial and Labor Relations	M
Liberal Studies	M
Public Policy	M

STATE UNIVERSITY OF NEW YORK INSTITUTE OF TECHNOLOGY

Sociology	M

STEPHEN F. AUSTIN STATE UNIVERSITY

Applied Arts and Design—General	M
Art/Fine Arts	M
Communication—General	M
English	M
Family and Consumer Sciences-General	M
History	M
Interdisciplinary Studies	M
Mass Communication	M
Music	M
Psychology—General	M
Public Administration	M
School Psychology	M

STEPHENS COLLEGE

Counseling Psychology	M
Marriage and Family Therapy	M

STETSON UNIVERSITY

English	M
Marriage and Family Therapy	M

STEVENS INSTITUTE OF TECHNOLOGY

Communication—General	M,D,O
Computer Art and Design	M,D,O
Corporate and Organizational Communication	O
Internet and Interactive Multimedia	M,D,O

STEVENSON UNIVERSITY

Forensic Sciences	M

STONY BROOK UNIVERSITY, STATE UNIVERSITY OF NEW YORK

Addictions/Substance Abuse Counseling	M
African Studies	M
Anthropology	M,D
Art History	M,D
Art/Fine Arts	M
Clinical Psychology	D
Comparative Literature	M,D
Cultural Studies	M,D
Economics	M,D
English	M,D,O
Experimental Psychology	D
French	M
Health Psychology	D
Hispanic Studies	M,D
History	M,D
Italian	M
Liberal Studies	M,O
Linguistics	M,D
Music	M,D
Philosophy	M,D
Political Science	M,D
Psychology—General	D
Public Policy	M
Romance Languages	M
Social Psychology	D
Social Sciences	M,O
Sociology	M,D
Theater	M
Women's Studies	O
Writing	M,O

STRAYER UNIVERSITY

Public Administration	M

SUFFOLK UNIVERSITY

Applied Arts and Design—General	M
Clinical Psychology	D
Communication—General	M
Corporate and Organizational Communication	M
Counseling Psychology	M,O
Criminal Justice and Criminology	M
Economics	M,D
Ethics	M
Graphic Design	M
Interior Design	M
Political Science	M,O
Psychology—General	D
Public Administration	M,O
Public Policy	M
Women's Studies	M

SULLIVAN UNIVERSITY

Conflict Resolution and Mediation/Peace Studies	P,M

SUL ROSS STATE UNIVERSITY

Applied Arts and Design—General	M
Art History	M
Art/Fine Arts	M
Criminal Justice and Criminology	M
English	M
History	M
Political Science	M
Psychology—General	M
Public Administration	M
Textile Design	M

SYRACUSE UNIVERSITY

Addictions/Substance Abuse Counseling	O
African Studies	M
African-American Studies	M
Anthropology	M,D
Applied Arts and Design—General	M
Architecture	M
Art History	M
Art/Fine Arts	M
Arts Journalism	M
Broadcast Journalism	M
Child and Family Studies	M,D
Clinical Psychology	M,D
Communication—General	M,D*
Computer Art and Design	M
Conflict Resolution and Mediation/Peace Studies	O
Disability Studies	O
Economics	M,D,O
English	M,D
Experimental Psychology	D
Film, Television, and Video Production	M
Film, Television, and Video Theory and Criticism	M
Forensic Sciences	M
French	M
Gender Studies	O
Geography	M,D
Historic Preservation	O
History	M,D
Illustration	M
International Affairs	
Journalism	M
Latin American Studies	O
Linguistics	M
Marriage and Family Therapy	M
Mass Communication	M,D
Media Studies	M
Museum Studies	M
Music	M
Near and Middle Eastern Studies	O
Philosophy	M,D
Photography	M
Political Science	M,D,O
Public Administration	M,D,O
Public Policy	O
Religion	M,D
Rhetoric	M,D
School Psychology	M,D,O
Social Psychology	D
Social Sciences	M,D
Sociology	M,D
Spanish	M
Textile Design	M
Western European Studies	O
Women's Studies	O
Writing	M,D

TALMUDIC COLLEGE OF FLORIDA

Theology	M,D

TARLETON STATE UNIVERSITY

Counseling Psychology	M,O
Criminal Justice and Criminology	M
Economics	M
English	M
History	M
Liberal Studies	M
Political Science	M
School Psychology	M,O

TAYLOR COLLEGE AND SEMINARY

Cultural Studies	P,M,O
Missions and Missiology	P,M,O
Theology	P,M,O

TAYLOR UNIVERSITY

Religion	M

TEACHERS COLLEGE, COLUMBIA UNIVERSITY

Anthropology	M,D
Arts Administration	M
Clinical Psychology	D
Communication—General	M,D
Counseling Psychology	M,D
Developmental Psychology	M,D
Economics	M,D
History	M,D
Industrial and Organizational Psychology	M,D
Interdisciplinary Studies	M,D
Linguistics	M,D
Political Science	M,D
Rehabilitation Counseling	M
School Psychology	M,D
Social Psychology	M,D
Sociology	M,D

TELSHE YESHIVA–CHICAGO

Jewish Studies	O

TEMPLE BAPTIST SEMINARY

Archaeology	P,M,D
Religion	P,M,D
Theology	P,M,D

TEMPLE UNIVERSITY

African-American Studies	M,D
Anthropology	D
Art History	M,D
Art/Fine Arts	M
Arts Administration	M,D
Clinical Psychology	D
Cognitive Sciences	D
Communication—General	M,D
Corporate and Organizational Communication	M,D
Counseling Psychology	M,D
Criminal Justice and Criminology	M,D
Dance	M,D
Developmental Psychology	D
English	M,D
Film, Television, and Video Production	M
Geography	M
Graphic Design	M
History	M,D
Industrial and Organizational Psychology	M
Journalism	M
Liberal Studies	M
Linguistics	M
Mass Communication	D
Media Studies	M,D
Music	M,D
Philosophy	M,D
Photography	M
Political Science	M,D
Psychology—General	D
Religion	M,D
School Psychology	M,D
Social Psychology	D
Sociology	M,D
Spanish	M,D
Textile Design	M
Theater	M
Therapies—Dance, Drama, and Music	M,D
Urban and Regional Planning	M
Urban Studies	M
Writing	M

TENNESSEE STATE UNIVERSITY

Counseling Psychology	M,D
Criminal Justice and Criminology	M
English	M
Family and Consumer Sciences-General	M
Psychology—General	M,D
Public Administration	M,D
School Psychology	M,D

TENNESSEE TECHNOLOGICAL UNIVERSITY

English	M

TEXAS A&M INTERNATIONAL UNIVERSITY

Counseling Psychology	M
Criminal Justice and Criminology	M
English	M,D
Hispanic Studies	M,D
History	M
Political Science	M
Psychology—General	M
Public Administration	M
Social Sciences	M
Sociology	M
Spanish	M,D

TEXAS A&M UNIVERSITY

Agricultural Economics and Agribusiness	M,D
Anthropology	M,D
Architecture	M,D
Art/Fine Arts	M,D
Clinical Psychology	M,D
Cognitive Sciences	M,D
Communication—General	M,D
Counseling Psychology	M,D
Developmental Psychology	M,D
Economics	M,D
English	M,D
Geography	M,D
History	M,D
Homeland Security	M,O
Human Development	M,D
Industrial and Organizational Psychology	M,D

*M—master's degree; P—first professional degree; D—doctorate; O—other advanced degree; *—Close-Up and/or Display*

International Affairs	M,O
International Development	M,O
Landscape Architecture	M,D
National Security	M,O
Philosophy	M,D
Political Science	M,D
Psychology—General	M,D
Public Administration	M,O
Public Affairs	M,O
Public Policy	M,O
School Psychology	M,D
Social Psychology	M,D
Sociology	M,D*
Spanish	M,D
Urban and Regional Planning	M,D

TEXAS A&M UNIVERSITY–COMMERCE

Art History	M
Art/Fine Arts	M
Cognitive Sciences	M,D
Counseling Psychology	M,D
Economics	M
English	M,D
History	M
Music	M
Psychology—General	M,D
Social Sciences	M
Sociology	M
Spanish	M,D
Speech and Interpersonal Communication	M
Theater	M

TEXAS A&M UNIVERSITY–CORPUS CHRISTI

Art/Fine Arts	M
English	M
History	M
Psychology—General	M
Public Administration	M

TEXAS A&M UNIVERSITY–KINGSVILLE

Agricultural Economics and Agribusiness	M
Art/Fine Arts	M
English	M
Family and Consumer Sciences-General	M
Gerontology	M
History	M
Political Science	M
Psychology—General	M
Sociology	M
Spanish	M

TEXAS A&M UNIVERSITY–TEXARKANA

Counseling Psychology	M
English	M
Interdisciplinary Studies	M
Psychology—General	M

TEXAS CHRISTIAN UNIVERSITY

Art History	M
Art/Fine Arts	M
Cognitive Sciences	M,D
English	M,D
Experimental Psychology	M,D
History	M,D
Journalism	M
Liberal Studies	M
Music	M,D,O
Psychology—General	M,D
Rhetoric	M,D
Social Psychology	M,D
Speech and Interpersonal Communication	M

TEXAS SOUTHERN UNIVERSITY

Art/Fine Arts	M
Communication—General	M
Criminal Justice and Criminology	M,D
English	M
Family and Consumer Sciences-General	M
History	M
Music	M
Psychology—General	M
Public Administration	M
Sociology	M
Urban and Regional Planning	M,D

TEXAS STATE UNIVERSITY–SAN MARCOS

Anthropology	M
Child and Family Studies	M
Communication—General	M
Computer Art and Design	M
Criminal Justice and Criminology	M,D
English	M
Geographic Information Systems	M,D
Geography	M,D
Graphic Design	M
Health Psychology	M
History	M
Interdisciplinary Studies	M
International Affairs	M
Mass Communication	M
Music	M
Political Science	M
Psychology—General	M
Public Administration	M
Rhetoric	M
School Psychology	M
Sociology	M
Spanish	M
Technical Communication	M
Theater	M
Writing	M

TEXAS TECH UNIVERSITY

Agricultural Economics and Agribusiness	M,D
Anthropology	M
Applied Economics	M,D
Architecture	M
Art/Fine Arts	M,D
Child and Family Studies	M,D
Classics	M
Clinical Psychology	M,D
Communication—General	M
Consumer Economics	M,D
Counseling Psychology	M,D
Dance	M,D
Economics	M,D
English	M,D
Environmental Design	M,D
Experimental Psychology	M,D
Family and Consumer Sciences-General	M,D
French	M
German	M
Gerontology	M,D
Historic Preservation	M
History	M,D
Human Development	M,D
Humanities	M,D
Interdisciplinary Studies	M
Interior Design	M,D
Landscape Architecture	M
Linguistics	M
Marriage and Family Therapy	M,D
Mass Communication	M,D
Museum Studies	M
Music	M,D
Philosophy	M
Political Science	M,D
Psychology—General	M,D
Public Administration	M,D
Rhetoric	M,D
Romance Languages	M,D
Sociology	M
Spanish	M,D
Technical Writing	M,D
Theater	M,D

TEXAS TECH UNIVERSITY HEALTH SCIENCES CENTER

Rehabilitation Counseling	M

TEXAS WESLEYAN UNIVERSITY

Counseling Psychology	M,D
Marriage and Family Therapy	M,D

TEXAS WOMAN'S UNIVERSITY

Art/Fine Arts	M
Child and Family Studies	M,D
Child Development	M,D
Counseling Psychology	M,D,O
Dance	M,D
English	M,D
History	M
Marriage and Family Therapy	M,D
Music	M
Political Science	M
Psychology—General	M,D,O
Rhetoric	M,D
School Psychology	M,D,O
Sociology	M,D
Theater	M
Women's Studies	M,D

THOMAS EDISON STATE COLLEGE

Homeland Security	O
Liberal Studies	M
Public Administration	O

THOMAS JEFFERSON UNIVERSITY

Marriage and Family Therapy	M

THOMAS UNIVERSITY

Rehabilitation Counseling	M
Social Psychology	M

TIFFIN UNIVERSITY

Criminal Justice and Criminology	M
Forensic Psychology	M
Homeland Security	M
Humanities	M

TORONTO SCHOOL OF THEOLOGY

Theology	P,M,D

TOURO COLLEGE

Jewish Studies	M

TOWSON UNIVERSITY

Art/Fine Arts	M
Child and Family Studies	O
Clinical Psychology	M
Communication—General	M,O
Corporate and Organizational Communication	M
Counseling Psychology	O
Forensic Sciences	M
Geography	M
Gerontology	M,O
Homeland Security	M,O
Humanities	M
Internet and Interactive Multimedia	D,O
Jewish Studies	M
Liberal Studies	M
Music	M
School Psychology	O
Social Sciences	M
Theater	M
Women's Studies	M,O
Writing	M

TRENT UNIVERSITY

American Indian/Native American Studies	M,D
Anthropology	M
Canadian Studies	M,D
Cultural Studies	D
Geography	M,D

TREVECCA NAZARENE UNIVERSITY

Counseling Psychology	M
Marriage and Family Therapy	M
Psychology—General	M,D
Religion	M
Theology	M

TRINE UNIVERSITY

Criminal Justice and Criminology	M

TRINITY BAPTIST COLLEGE

Pastoral Ministry and Counseling	M

TRINITY COLLEGE

American Studies	M
Economics	M
English	M
Public Policy	M

TRINITY INTERNATIONAL UNIVERSITY

Archaeology	P,M,D,O
Communication—General	M
Counseling Psychology	P,M,D,O
Missions and Missiology	P,M,D,O
Pastoral Ministry and Counseling	P,M,D,O
Theology	P,M,D,O

TRINITY INTERNATIONAL UNIVERSITY, SOUTH FLORIDA CAMPUS

Counseling Psychology	M
Religion	M,O

TRINITY LUTHERAN SEMINARY

Music	P,M
Pastoral Ministry and Counseling	P,M
Theology	P,M

TRINITY SCHOOL FOR MINISTRY

Missions and Missiology	P,M,D,O
Pastoral Ministry and Counseling	P,M,D,O

Religion P,M,D,O
Theology P,M,D,O

TRINITY UNIVERSITY
School Psychology M

TRINITY (WASHINGTON) UNIVERSITY
Communication—General M
National Security M

TRINITY WESTERN UNIVERSITY
Counseling Psychology M
English M
History M
Humanities M
Interdisciplinary Studies M
Linguistics M
Pastoral Ministry and Counseling P,M,D
Philosophy M
Theology P,M,D

TROPICAL AGRICULTURE RESEARCH AND HIGHER EDUCATION CENTER
Agricultural Economics and Agribusiness M,D

TROY UNIVERSITY
Addictions/Substance Abuse Counseling M,O
Clinical Psychology M,O
Criminal Justice and Criminology M,O
Economic Development M
History M
International Affairs M
Music M
National Security M
Political Science M
Public Administration M
Rehabilitation Counseling M,O
School Psychology M,O
Social Psychology M,O

TRUMAN STATE UNIVERSITY
English M
Music M

TUFTS UNIVERSITY
Archaeology M
Art History M
Art/Fine Arts M
Child and Family Studies M,D,O
Child Development M,D,O
Classics M
Conflict Resolution and Mediation/Peace Studies M,D
Economics M
English M,D
Family and Consumer Sciences-General M,D,O
French M
German M
Health Communication M
History M,D
International Affairs M,D
International Development M,D
Museum Studies O
Music M
Philosophy M
Psychology—General M,D
Public Administration O
Public Policy M
School Psychology M,O
Theater M,D

Urban and Regional Planning M
Urban Studies M

TUI UNIVERSITY
Conflict Resolution and Mediation/Peace Studies M,D
Criminal Justice and Criminology M,D
Emergency Management M,D,O
Public Administration M,D

TULANE UNIVERSITY
Anthropology M,D
Architecture M
Art History M
Art/Fine Arts M
Classics M
Dance M
Economics M,D
English M,D
French M,D
Health Communication M
History M,D
Interdisciplinary Studies D
International Development M,D
Latin American Studies M,D
Liberal Studies M
Music M
Philosophy M,D
Political Science M,D
Portuguese M,D
Psychology—General M,D
Sociology M,D
Spanish M,D
Theater M

TUSKEGEE UNIVERSITY
Agricultural Economics and Agribusiness M

TYNDALE UNIVERSITY COLLEGE & SEMINARY
Missions and Missiology P,M,O
Pastoral Ministry and Counseling P,M,O
Theology P,M,O

UNIFICATION THEOLOGICAL SEMINARY
Theology P,M,D

UNIFORMED SERVICES UNIVERSITY OF THE HEALTH SCIENCES
Clinical Psychology D
Psychology—General D

UNION COLLEGE (KY)
Clinical Psychology M
Counseling Psychology M
Psychology—General M
School Psychology M

UNION GRADUATE COLLEGE
Chinese M,O
Classics M,O

UNION INSTITUTE & UNIVERSITY
Clinical Psychology M,D
Counseling Psychology M
Cultural Studies M
Developmental Psychology M
History M

Industrial and Organizational Psychology M
Interdisciplinary Studies M,D
Marriage and Family Therapy D
Psychology—General M
Public Policy M,D
Writing M

UNION THEOLOGICAL SEMINARY AND PRESBYTERIAN SCHOOL OF CHRISTIAN EDUCATION
Theology P,M,D

UNION THEOLOGICAL SEMINARY IN THE CITY OF NEW YORK
Theology P,M,D

UNION UNIVERSITY
Cultural Studies M
Pastoral Ministry and Counseling M,D
Religion M,D

UNITED STATES ARMY COMMAND AND GENERAL STAFF COLLEGE
Military and Defense Studies M

UNITED STATES INTERNATIONAL UNIVERSITY
Counseling Psychology M
International Affairs M

UNITED TALMUDICAL SEMINARY
Theology

UNITED THEOLOGICAL SEMINARY
Theology P,M,D

UNITED THEOLOGICAL SEMINARY OF THE TWIN CITIES
Art/Fine Arts P,M,D,O
Asian Studies P,M,D,O
Conflict Resolution and Mediation/Peace Studies P,M,D,O
Ethnic Studies P,M,D,O
Humanities P,M,D,O
Pastoral Ministry and Counseling P,M,D,O
Religion P,M,D,O
Theology P,M,D,O
Women's Studies P,M,D,O

UNIVERSIDAD ADVENTISTA DE LAS ANTILLAS
History M
Spanish M

UNIVERSIDAD AUTONOMA DE GUADALAJARA
Architecture M,D
Computer Art and Design M,D
Corporate and Organizational Communication M,D
Film, Television, and Video Production M,D
Internet and Interactive Multimedia M,D
Philosophy M,D
Public Policy M,D
Spanish M,D

Translation and Interpretation M,D

UNIVERSIDAD CENTRAL DEL CARIBE
Addictions/Substance Abuse Counseling M

UNIVERSIDAD CENTRAL DEL ESTE
Public Policy P,M,D

UNIVERSIDAD DE IBEROAMERICA
Clinical Psychology P,M,D
Forensic Psychology P,M,D

UNIVERSIDAD DE LAS AMERICAS, A.C.
International Affairs M
Marriage and Family Therapy M
Psychology—General M

UNIVERSIDAD DE LAS AMÉRICAS–PUEBLA
American Studies M
Anthropology M
Archaeology M
Computer Art and Design M
Economics M
English M
Linguistics M
Psychology—General M

UNIVERSIDAD DEL ESTE
Agricultural Economics and Agribusiness M
Criminal Justice and Criminology M
Public Policy M

UNIVERSIDAD DEL TURABO
Art/Fine Arts M
Arts Administration M
Conflict Resolution and Mediation/Peace Studies M
Counseling Psychology M,D,O
Criminal Justice and Criminology M
Forensic Sciences M

UNIVERSIDAD FLET
Theology M

UNIVERSIDAD METROPOLITANA
Communication—General M
Hispanic Studies M

UNIVERSITÉ DE MONCTON
Economics M
French M,D
History M
Public Administration M

UNIVERSITÉ DE MONTRÉAL
Anthropology M,D
Art History M,D
Classics
Communication—General M,D,O
Comparative Literature M,D
Criminal Justice and Criminology M,D
Demography and Population Studies M,D
Developmental Psychology M,D,O

*M—master's degree; P—first professional degree; D—doctorate; O—other advanced degree; *—Close-Up and/or Display*

Economics M,D
Emergency Management O
English M,D
Environmental Design M,D,O
Film, Television, and Video Theory and Criticism M,D
French M,D
Genetic Counseling
Geography M,D,O
German M
Gerontology O
Hispanic Studies M,D
History M,D
Industrial and Labor Relations M,D,O
International Affairs
Linguistics M,D,O
Museum Studies M
Music M,D,O
Philosophy M,D
Political Science M,D
Psychology—General M,D
Public Policy
Rehabilitation Counseling O
Sociology M,D
Spanish M
Theology M,D,O
Translation and Interpretation M,D,O

UNIVERSITÉ DE SHERBROOKE

Canadian Studies M,D
Comparative Literature M,D
Conflict Resolution and Mediation/Peace Studies P,M,D,O
Economics M
Ethics M,D,O
French M,D
Geography M,D
Gerontology M
History M
Linguistics M,D
Philosophy M,D,O
Psychology—General M
Religion M,D,O
Theater M,D
Theology M,D,O

UNIVERSITÉ DU QUÉBEC À CHICOUTIMI

Art/Fine Arts M
Canadian Studies M
Comparative Literature M
Ethics O
French O
Linguistics M
Theology M,D

UNIVERSITÉ DU QUÉBEC À MONTRÉAL

Art History M,D
Art/Fine Arts M
Communication—General M,D
Comparative Literature M,D
Dance M
Economics M,D
Geographic Information Systems O
Geography M
History M,D
Linguistics M,D
Museum Studies M
Philosophy M,D
Political Science M,D
Psychology—General D
Public Administration M
Religion M,D
Sociology M,D
Urban Studies M,D

UNIVERSITÉ DU QUÉBEC À RIMOUSKI

Comparative Literature M,D
Ethics M,O
Social Psychology M
Urban and Regional Planning M,D,O

UNIVERSITÉ DU QUÉBEC À TROIS-RIVIÈRES

Communication—General M,O
Comparative Literature M
Industrial and Labor Relations O
Philosophy M,D
Psychology—General D,O

UNIVERSITÉ DU QUÉBEC, ÉCOLE NATIONALE D'ADMINISTRATION PUBLIQUE

Public Administration D,O
Urban Studies M

UNIVERSITÉ DU QUÉBEC EN OUTAOUAIS

Industrial and Labor Relations M,D,O
Urban and Regional Planning M

UNIVERSITÉ DU QUÉBEC, INSTITUT NATIONAL DE LA RECHERCHE SCIENTIFIQUE

Demography and Population Studies M,D
Urban Studies M,D

UNIVERSITÉ LAVAL

Agricultural Economics and Agribusiness M
Anthropology M,D
Archaeology M,D
Architecture M
Art History M,D
Art/Fine Arts M
Clinical Psychology D
Comparative Literature M,D
Consumer Economics O
Economics M,D
English M,D
Ethics O
Ethnic Studies M,D
Film, Television, and Video Theory and Criticism M,D
Geographic Information Systems M,O
Geography M,D
Gerontology O
Graphic Design M
History M,D
Industrial and Labor Relations M,D
International Affairs M,D
Journalism O
Linguistics M,D
Mass Communication M,D
Museum Studies O
Music M,D
Philosophy M,D
Political Science M,D
Psychology—General D
Religion M,D
Rural Planning and Studies O
Social Psychology D
Sociology M,D
Spanish M,D
Theater M,D
Theology M,D
Translation and Interpretation M,O
Urban and Regional Planning M,D
Women's Studies O

UNIVERSITY AT ALBANY, STATE UNIVERSITY OF NEW YORK

African Studies M
African-American Studies M
Anthropology M,D
Art/Fine Arts M
Clinical Psychology M,D,O
Communication—General M,D
Counseling Psychology M,D,O
Criminal Justice and Criminology M,D
Demography and Population Studies M,D,O
Economics M,D,O
English M,D
Experimental Psychology M,D,O
Forensic Sciences M,D
French M,D
Geographic Information Systems M,O
Geography M,O
History M,D,O
Industrial and Organizational Psychology M,D,O
Italian M
Latin American Studies M,O
Liberal Studies M
Philosophy M,D
Political Science M,D
Psychology—General M,D,O
Public Administration M,D,O
Public History M,D,O
Public Policy M,D,O
Rehabilitation Counseling M
Russian M,O
School Psychology M,D,O
Social Psychology M,D,O
Sociology M,D,O
Spanish M,D
Theater M
Translation and Interpretation M,O
Urban and Regional Planning M
Urban Studies M,D,O
Women's Studies M,D

UNIVERSITY AT BUFFALO, THE STATE UNIVERSITY OF NEW YORK

American Studies M,D
Anthropology M,D
Architecture M
Art History M,O
Art/Fine Arts M,O
Classics M,D,O
Clinical Psychology M,D
Cognitive Sciences M,D
Communication—General M,D
Comparative Literature M,D
Counseling Psychology M,D,O
Economics M,D,O
English M,D
French M,D,O
Geographic Information Systems M,D,O
Geography M,D,O
German M,D,O
History M,D
Linguistics M,D
Media Studies M,O
Museum Studies M,O
Music M,D
Philosophy M,D
Political Science M,D
Psychology—General M,D
Rehabilitation Counseling M,D,O
Romance Languages M,D
Social Psychology M,D
Sociology M,D
Spanish M,D,O
Urban and Regional Planning M
Urban Design M

UNIVERSITY OF ADVANCING TECHNOLOGY

Internet and Interactive Multimedia M

THE UNIVERSITY OF AKRON

Arts Administration M
Child and Family Studies M
Child Development M
Clothing and Textiles M
Communication—General M
Counseling Psychology M,D
Economics M
English M
Geographic Information Systems M
Geography M
History M,D
Industrial and Organizational Psychology M,D
Marriage and Family Therapy M
Music M
Political Science M
Psychology—General M,D
Public Administration M
School Psychology M
Social Psychology M
Sociology M,D
Spanish M
Theater M
Urban and Regional Planning M
Urban Studies M,D
Writing M

THE UNIVERSITY OF ALABAMA

American Studies M
Anthropology M,D
Art History M
Art/Fine Arts M
Child and Family Studies M
Clinical Psychology D
Clothing and Textiles M
Communication—General M,D
Consumer Economics M
Criminal Justice and Criminology M
Economics M,D
English M,D
Experimental Psychology D
Family and Consumer Sciences-General M,D
Film, Television, and Video Production M
French M,D
Geography M
German M,D
History M,D
Human Development M
Interior Design M
Journalism M
Mass Communication D
Media Studies M
Music M,D
Photography M

Political Science M,D
Psychology—General D
Public Administration M,D
Rhetoric M,D
Romance Languages M,D
Spanish M,D
Speech and Interpersonal Communication M
Theater M
Women's Studies M
Writing M,D

THE UNIVERSITY OF ALABAMA AT BIRMINGHAM

Anthropology M
Art History M
Communication—General M
Criminal Justice and Criminology M
English M
History M
Psychology—General M,D
Public Administration M
Sociology M

THE UNIVERSITY OF ALABAMA IN HUNTSVILLE

Criminal Justice and Criminology O
English M,O
History M
Interdisciplinary Studies M,D,O
Psychology—General M
Public Affairs M
Technical Writing M,O

UNIVERSITY OF ALASKA ANCHORAGE

Anthropology M
Clinical Psychology M,D
English M
Interdisciplinary Studies M
Psychology—General M,D
Public Administration M
Social Psychology M,D
Writing M

UNIVERSITY OF ALASKA FAIRBANKS

Anthropology M,D
Art/Fine Arts M
Clinical Psychology D
Communication—General M
Computer Art and Design M
Corporate and Organizational Communication M
Criminal Justice and Criminology M
Cultural Studies M
Economics M
English M
Geography M,D
History M
Interdisciplinary Studies M,D
Linguistics M
Music M
Northern Studies M
Photography M
Psychology—General D
Rural Planning and Studies M
Social Psychology M,D
Sustainable Development M,D
Writing M

UNIVERSITY OF ALASKA SOUTHEAST

Public Administration M

UNIVERSITY OF ALBERTA

Agricultural Economics and Agribusiness M,D
Anthropology M,D
Applied Arts and Design—General M
Archaeology M,D
Art History M
Art/Fine Arts M
Asian Studies M
Chinese M
Classics M,D
Clothing and Textiles M,D
Communication—General M
Counseling Psychology M,D
Criminal Justice and Criminology M,D
Demography and Population Studies M,D
East European and Russian Studies M,D
Economics M,D
English M,D
Family and Consumer Sciences-General M,D
Folklore M,D
French M,D
German M,D
Hispanic Studies M,D
History M,D
Industrial and Labor Relations D
Italian M,D
Japanese M
Linguistics M,D
Music M,D
Philosophy M,D
Political Science M,D
Psychology—General M,D
Rural Sociology M,D
School Psychology M,D
Slavic Languages M,D
Sociology M,D
Theater M

THE UNIVERSITY OF ARIZONA

Agricultural Economics and Agribusiness M
American Indian/Native American Studies M,D
Anthropology M,D
Architecture M
Art History M,D
Art/Fine Arts M
Asian Studies M,D
Child and Family Studies M
Classics M
Communication—General M,D
Dance M
Economics M,D
English M,D
Family and Consumer Sciences-General M,D
French M
Geography M,D
German M
History M,D
Human Development M
Interdisciplinary Studies M,D
Landscape Architecture M
Latin American Studies M
Linguistics M,D
Media Studies M
Music M,D
Near and Middle Eastern Studies M,D
Philosophy M,D
Political Science M,D
Psychology—General M,D
Public Administration M,D
Public Policy M,D
Rehabilitation Counseling M,D
Rhetoric D
Russian M
Sociology D
Spanish M,D
Theater M
Urban and Regional Planning M
Women's Studies M,D
Writing M

UNIVERSITY OF ARKANSAS

Agricultural Economics and Agribusiness M
Anthropology M,D
Art/Fine Arts M
Communication—General M
Comparative Literature M,D
Economics M,D
English M,D
Family and Consumer Sciences-General M
French M
Geography M
German M
History M,D
Interdisciplinary Studies M,D
Journalism M
Music M
Philosophy M,D
Political Science M
Psychology—General M,D
Public Administration M
Public Policy D
Rehabilitation Counseling M,D
Sociology M
Spanish M
Theater M
Translation and Interpretation M
Writing M

UNIVERSITY OF ARKANSAS AT LITTLE ROCK

Art History M
Art/Fine Arts M
Conflict Resolution and Mediation/Peace Studies O
Criminal Justice and Criminology M,D
Gerontology O
Journalism M
Liberal Studies M
Marriage and Family Therapy O
Mass Communication M
Psychology—General M
Public Administration M
Public Affairs M,O
Public History M
Rehabilitation Counseling M,O
Rhetoric M
Speech and Interpersonal Communication M
Technical Writing M
Writing M

UNIVERSITY OF ARKANSAS AT PINE BLUFF

Addictions/Substance Abuse Counseling M

UNIVERSITY OF ARKANSAS FOR MEDICAL SCIENCES

Genetic Counseling M

UNIVERSITY OF ATLANTA

Social Sciences P,M,D,O

UNIVERSITY OF BALTIMORE

Applied Arts and Design—General M
Computer Art and Design M,D
Conflict Resolution and Mediation/Peace Studies M
Counseling Psychology M
Criminal Justice and Criminology M
Ethics M
Graphic Design M,D
Industrial and Organizational Psychology M
Psychology—General M
Public Administration M,D
Publishing M
Writing M

UNIVERSITY OF BRIDGEPORT

Conflict Resolution and Mediation/Peace Studies M
International Affairs M

THE UNIVERSITY OF BRITISH COLUMBIA

Agricultural Economics and Agribusiness M
Anthropology M,D
Archaeology M,D
Architecture M
Art History M,D,O
Art/Fine Arts M,D,O
Asian Studies M,D
Classics M,D
Clinical Psychology M,D
Cognitive Sciences M,D
Counseling Psychology M,D,O
Developmental Psychology M,D
East European and Russian Studies M,D
Economics M,D
English M,D
Film, Television, and Video Production M,O
Film, Television, and Video Theory and Criticism M,O
French M,D
Genetic Counseling M
Geography M,D
German M,D
Health Psychology M,D
Hispanic Studies M,D
History M,D
Human Development M,D,O
International Affairs M
Journalism M
Landscape Architecture M
Linguistics M,D
Museum Studies M,D,O
Music M,D
Philosophy M,D
Political Science M,D
Psychology—General M,D
Public History M,D

*M—master's degree; P—first professional degree; D—doctorate; O—other advanced degree; *—Close-Up and/or Display*

Religion M,D
School Psychology M,D,O
Social Psychology M,D
Sociology M,D
Theater M,D
Urban and Regional Planning M,D
Western European Studies M
Writing M,O

UNIVERSITY OF CALGARY

Anthropology M,D
Archaeology M,D
Architecture M,D
Art/Fine Arts M
Classics M,D
Clinical Psychology M,D
Communication—General M,D
Counseling Psychology M,D
Economics M,D
English M,D
Environmental Design M,D
Geography M,D
German M
History M,D
Human Development M,D
Linguistics M,D
Military and Defense Studies M,D
Music M,D
Philosophy M,D
Political Science M,D
Psychology—General M,D
Religion M,D
School Psychology M,D
Sociology M,D
Theater M

UNIVERSITY OF CALIFORNIA, BERKELEY

Addictions/Substance Abuse Counseling O
African-American Studies D
Agricultural Economics and Agribusiness D
Anthropology D
Applied Arts and Design—General M,O
Archaeology M,D
Architectural History M,D
Architecture M,D
Art History D
Art/Fine Arts M,O
Asian Languages M,D
Asian Studies M,D
Building Science M,D
Chinese D
Classics M,D
Comparative Literature D
Counseling Psychology O
Demography and Population Studies M,D
Economics D
English D
Environmental Design M,D
Ethnic Studies D
Folklore M
French D
Geography D
German D
Hispanic Studies D
History of Science and Technology D
History M,D
Human Development M,D
Industrial and Labor Relations D
Interior Design O
International Affairs M,D
Italian D
Japanese D
Jewish Studies D
Journalism M
Landscape Architecture M,D,O
Latin American Studies M
Linguistics D
Music D
Near and Middle Eastern Studies M,D
Philosophy D
Political Science D
Psychology—General D
Public Policy M,D
Religion D
Rhetoric D
Romance Languages D
Russian D
Scandinavian Languages D
Slavic Languages D
Sociology D
Spanish D
Sustainable Development O
Theater D
Urban and Regional Planning M,D
Urban Design M,D
Writing O

UNIVERSITY OF CALIFORNIA, DAVIS

Agricultural Economics and Agribusiness M,D
American Indian/Native American Studies M,D
Anthropology M,D
Art History M
Art/Fine Arts M
Child Development M
Clothing and Textiles M
Communication—General M
Comparative Literature D
Cultural Studies M,D
Economics M,D
English M,D
Forensic Sciences M
French D
Geography M,D
German M,D
History M,D
Human Development D
Linguistics M,D
Music M,D
Philosophy M,D
Political Science M,D
Psychology—General D
Sociology M,D
Spanish M,D
Textile Design M
Theater M,D
Urban and Regional Planning M
Writing M,D

UNIVERSITY OF CALIFORNIA, IRVINE

Anthropology M,D
Art History M,D
Art/Fine Arts M
Asian Languages M,D
Chinese M,D
Classics M,D
Comparative Literature M,D
Criminal Justice and Criminology M,D
Dance M
Demography and Population Studies M
Economics M,D
English M,D
French M,D
Genetic Counseling M
German M,D
History M,D
Japanese M,D
Music M
Philosophy M,D
Political Science D
Psychology—General D
Social Sciences M,D
Sociology M,D
Spanish M,D
Theater M,D
Urban and Regional Planning M,D
Urban Studies M,D
Writing M

UNIVERSITY OF CALIFORNIA, LOS ANGELES

African Studies M
African-American Studies M
American Indian/Native American Studies M
Anthropology M,D
Applied Arts and Design—General M
Applied Social Research M,D
Archaeology M,D
Architecture M,D
Art History M,D
Art/Fine Arts M
Asian Languages M,D
Asian Studies M,D
Asian-American Studies M
Classics M,D
Comparative Literature M,D
Dance M,D
Economics M,D
English M,D
Film, Television, and Video Production M,D,O
French M,D
Geography M,D
German M,D
Hispanic Studies D
History M,D
Italian M,D
Latin American Studies M
Linguistics M,D
Music M,D
Near and Middle Eastern Languages M,D
Near and Middle Eastern Studies M,D
Philosophy M,D
Political Science M,D
Portuguese M
Psychology—General M,D
Public Policy M
Scandinavian Languages M
Slavic Languages M,D
Sociology M,D
Spanish M
Theater M,D
Urban and Regional Planning M,D
Urban Design M,D
Women's Studies M,D

UNIVERSITY OF CALIFORNIA, MERCED

Cognitive Sciences M,D
Social Sciences M,D

UNIVERSITY OF CALIFORNIA, RIVERSIDE

Anthropology M,D
Art History M
Art/Fine Arts M
Asian Studies M
Classics D
Comparative Literature M,D
Dance M,D
Economics M,D*
English M,D
Ethnic Studies D
Hispanic Studies M,D
Historic Preservation M,D
History M,D
Museum Studies M,D
Music M,D
Philosophy M,D
Political Science M,D
Psychology—General M,D
School Psychology M,D
Sociology M,D
Spanish M,D
Writing M

UNIVERSITY OF CALIFORNIA, SAN DIEGO

Anthropology D
Art/Fine Arts M,D
Clinical Psychology D
Cognitive Sciences D
Communication—General M,D
Comparative Literature M,D
Economics M,D
English M
Ethnic Studies M,D
French M
German M
History of Science and Technology M,D
History M,D
International Affairs M,D
Jewish Studies M,D
Latin American Studies M
Linguistics D
Music M,D
Pacific Area/Pacific Rim Studies M,D
Philosophy D
Political Science M,D
Psychology—General D
Sociology D
Spanish M
Theater M,D

UNIVERSITY OF CALIFORNIA, SAN FRANCISCO

Anthropology D
History of Science and Technology M,D
Sociology D

UNIVERSITY OF CALIFORNIA, SANTA BARBARA

Agricultural Economics and Agribusiness M,D
Anthropology M,D
Archaeology M,D
Art History D
Art/Fine Arts M,D
Asian Languages M,D
Asian Studies M,D
Child and Family Studies M,D
Classics M,D
Clinical Psychology M,D
Cognitive Sciences M,D
Communication—General D
Comparative Literature D
Counseling Psychology M,D
Developmental Psychology M,D
Economics M,D
English D
Film, Television, and Video Production D
French M,D
Geography M,D
German M,D
Hispanic Studies M,D

History	D
Human Development	D
International Affairs	M,D
Latin American Studies	M,D
Linguistics	M,D
Media Studies	M,D
Medieval and Renaissance Studies	M,D
Music	M,D
Philosophy	D
Political Science	M,D
Portuguese	M,D
Psychology—General	M,D
Religion	M,D
School Psychology	M,D
Sociology	D
Spanish	M,D
Speech and Interpersonal Communication	D
Theater	M,D
Women's Studies	M,D

UNIVERSITY OF CALIFORNIA, SANTA CRUZ

Anthropology	D
Applied Economics	M
Archaeology	D
Art/Fine Arts	M
Communication—General	O
Comparative Literature	M,D
Computer Art and Design	M
Economics	D
English	M,D
History	M,D
Humanities	D
Illustration	O
International Affairs	D
Linguistics	M,D
Music	M,D
Philosophy	M,D
Political Science	D
Psychology—General	D
Social Sciences	D
Sociology	D
Technical Writing	O
Theater	O
Writing	M

UNIVERSITY OF CENTRAL ARKANSAS

Computer Art and Design	M
Counseling Psychology	M
Economic Development	M
Economics	M
English	M
Family and Consumer Sciences-General	M
Film, Television, and Video Production	M
Geographic Information Systems	M,O
Geography	M,O
History	M
Music	M
Psychology—General	M,D
School Psychology	M,D
Social Psychology	M

UNIVERSITY OF CENTRAL FLORIDA

Anthropology	M
Art/Fine Arts	M
Child and Family Studies	M,O
Clinical Psychology	M,D
Communication—General	M
Computer Art and Design	M
Criminal Justice and Criminology	M,O
Economics	M,D
Emergency Management	M,O
English	M
Experimental Psychology	M,D
Film, Television, and Video Production	M
Forensic Sciences	M,D,O
Gerontology	M,O
History	M
Homeland Security	M,O
Industrial and Organizational Psychology	M,D
Interdisciplinary Studies	M
Internet and Interactive Multimedia	M
Latin American Studies	M,D,O
Marriage and Family Therapy	M,O
Music	M
Political Science	M
Psychology—General	M,D
Public Administration	M,O
Public Affairs	D
School Psychology	O
Sociology	M,D,O
Spanish	M
Theater	M
Urban and Regional Planning	M,O
Writing	M

UNIVERSITY OF CENTRAL MISSOURI

Counseling Psychology	M,D,O
Criminal Justice and Criminology	M
English	M
Gerontology	M
History	M
Mass Communication	M
Music	M
Psychology—General	M
Sociology	M
Speech and Interpersonal Communication	M
Theater	M

UNIVERSITY OF CENTRAL OKLAHOMA

Addictions/Substance Abuse Counseling	M
American Studies	M
Applied Arts and Design—General	M
Counseling Psychology	M
Criminal Justice and Criminology	M
English	M
Family and Consumer Sciences-General	M
Gerontology	M
History	M
Human Development	M
Interior Design	M
International Affairs	M
Museum Studies	M
Music	M
Political Science	M
Psychology—General	M
Urban Studies	M
Writing	M

UNIVERSITY OF CHICAGO

Anthropology	M,D
Archaeology	M,D
Art History	M,D
Art/Fine Arts	M
Asian Languages	M,D
Asian Studies	M,D
Classics	M,D
Comparative Literature	M,D
Economics	D
English	M,D
Film, Television, and Video Theory and Criticism	M,D
French	M,D
German	M,D
History	D
Human Development	D
Humanities	M
Interdisciplinary Studies	D
International Affairs	M
Italian	M,D
Latin American Studies	M
Linguistics	M,D
Media Studies	M,D
Music	M,D
Near and Middle Eastern Languages	M,D
Near and Middle Eastern Studies	M,D
Philosophy	M,D
Political Science	D
Psychology—General	D
Public Policy	M,D
Religion	P,M,D
Romance Languages	M,D
Slavic Languages	M,D
Social Sciences	M,D
Sociology	D
Spanish	M,D
Theology	P,M,D

UNIVERSITY OF CINCINNATI

Anthropology	M
Applied Arts and Design—General	M
Architecture	M
Art History	M
Art/Fine Arts	M
Arts Administration	M,D
Classics	M,D
Clinical Psychology	D
Communication—General	M
Criminal Justice and Criminology	M,D
Economics	M
English	M,D
Experimental Psychology	D
French	M,D
Genetic Counseling	M
Geography	M,D
German	M,D
Graphic Design	M
History	M,D
Industrial and Labor Relations	M
Industrial Design	M
Interdisciplinary Studies	D
Interior Design	M
Music	M,D,O
Philosophy	M,D
Political Science	M,D
Psychology—General	D
Romance Languages	M,D
School Psychology	D,O
Sociology	M,D
Spanish	M,D
Textile Design	M
Theater	M,D
Urban and Regional Planning	M
Women's Studies	M,O

UNIVERSITY OF COLORADO AT BOULDER

Anthropology	M,D
Art History	M
Art/Fine Arts	M
Asian Studies	M,D
Chinese	M,D
Classics	M,D
Communication—General	M,D
Comparative Literature	M,D
Dance	M,D
Economics	M,D
English	M,D
French	M,D
Geography	M,D
German	M
History	M,D
International Affairs	M,D
Japanese	M,D
Journalism	M,D
Linguistics	M,D
Mass Communication	M,D
Media Studies	D
Museum Studies	M
Music	M,D
Philosophy	M,D
Photography	M
Political Science	M,D
Psychology—General	M,D
Public Policy	M,D
Religion	M
Sociology	D
Spanish	M,D
Theater	M,D
Writing	M,D

UNIVERSITY OF COLORADO AT COLORADO SPRINGS

Communication—General	M
Criminal Justice and Criminology	M
Geography	M
History	M
Psychology—General	M,D
Public Administration	M
Public Affairs	M
Sociology	M

UNIVERSITY OF COLORADO DENVER

Anthropology	M
Architecture	M
Clinical Psychology	D
Communication—General	M
Counseling Psychology	M,O
Criminal Justice and Criminology	M
Economics	M
English	M,O
Genetic Counseling	M,D
Geographic Information Systems	M,D
Health Psychology	D
History	M
Humanities	M
Landscape Architecture	M
Linguistics	M,O
Music	M
Political Science	M
Psychology—General	M
Public Administration	M
Public Affairs	D
Social Sciences	M
Sociology	M
Spanish	M
Technical Communication	M
Urban and Regional Planning	M,D

*M—master's degree; P—first professional degree; D—doctorate; O—other advanced degree; *—Close-Up and/or Display*

Urban Design	M

UNIVERSITY OF CONNECTICUT

African Studies	M
Agricultural Economics and Agribusiness	M,D
Anthropology	M,D
Art History	M
Art/Fine Arts	M
Child and Family Studies	M,D,O
Clinical Psychology	M,D,O
Cognitive Sciences	M,D,O
Communication—General	M
Comparative Literature	M,D
Corporate and Organizational Communication	D
Counseling Psychology	M,D,O
Developmental Psychology	M,D,O
Economics	M,D
English	M,D
Experimental Psychology	M,D,O
French	M,D
Geographic Information Systems	M,D,O
Geography	M,D,O
German	M,D
Health Psychology	M,D,O
History	M,D
Homeland Security	M
Human Development	M,D,O
Industrial and Organizational Psychology	M,D,O
International Affairs	M
Italian	M,D
Jewish Studies	M
Latin American Studies	M
Linguistics	M,D
Medieval and Renaissance Studies	M,D
Music	M,D,O
Philosophy	M,D
Political Science	M,D
Psychology—General	M,D,O
Public Administration	M,O
School Psychology	M,D,O
Social Psychology	M,D,O
Sociology	M,D
Spanish	M,D
Sustainable Development	M
Theater	M
Western European Studies	M

UNIVERSITY OF DALLAS

American Studies	M
Art/Fine Arts	M
Comparative Literature	D
English	M
Humanities	M
Pastoral Ministry and Counseling	M
Philosophy	M,D
Political Science	M,D
Psychology—General	M
Theology	M

UNIVERSITY OF DAYTON

Clinical Psychology	M
Communication—General	M
English	M
Human Development	M,O
Pastoral Ministry and Counseling	M,D
Psychology—General	M
Public Administration	M
School Psychology	M,O
Social Psychology	M,O
Theology	M,D

UNIVERSITY OF DELAWARE

Agricultural Economics and Agribusiness	M
American Studies	M
Applied Arts and Design—General	M
Art History	M,D
Art/Fine Arts	M
Child and Family Studies	M,D
Clinical Psychology	D
Clothing and Textiles	M
Cognitive Sciences	D
Communication—General	M
Criminal Justice and Criminology	M,D
Economics	M,D
English	M,D
French	M
Geography	M,D
German	M
Historic Preservation	M,D
History of Science and Technology	M,D
History	M,D
Human Development	M,D
International Affairs	M,D
Liberal Studies	M
Linguistics	M,D
Music	M
Political Science	M,D
Psychology—General	D
Public Administration	M*
Public Policy	M,D
School Psychology	M,D,O
Social Psychology	D
Sociology	M,D
Spanish	M
Theater	M
Urban Studies	M,D

UNIVERSITY OF DENVER

Anthropology	M
Art History	M
Art/Fine Arts	M
Child and Family Studies	M,D,O
Clinical Psychology	M,D
Communication—General	M,O
Computer Art and Design	M
Counseling Psychology	M,D,O
Criminal Justice and Criminology	M,O
Economics	M
English	M,D
Film, Television, and Video Production	M
Geographic Information Systems	M,O
Geography	M,D
International Affairs	M,D
Liberal Studies	M,O
Mass Communication	M
Media Studies	M
Museum Studies	M
Music	M,O
Psychology—General	M,D
Public Policy	M
Religion	M,D
School Psychology	M,D,O
Speech and Interpersonal Communication	M,D
Theology	D
Translation and Interpretation	M,O

UNIVERSITY OF DETROIT MERCY

Addictions/Substance Abuse Counseling	M,O
Clinical Psychology	M,D
Criminal Justice and Criminology	M
Industrial and Organizational Psychology	M
Liberal Studies	M
Military and Defense Studies	M
Psychology—General	M,D,O
Religion	M
School Psychology	O

UNIVERSITY OF DUBUQUE

Communication—General	M
Theology	P,M,D

UNIVERSITY OF EVANSVILLE

Public Administration	M

THE UNIVERSITY OF FINDLAY

Liberal Studies	M
Public Administration	M

UNIVERSITY OF FLORIDA

African Studies	O
Agricultural Economics and Agribusiness	M,D
Anthropology	M,D
Architecture	M,D
Art History	M,D
Art/Fine Arts	M,D
Arts Administration	M
Building Science	M,D
Classics	M,D
Clinical Psychology	D
Cognitive Sciences	M,D
Communication—General	M,D
Computer Art and Design	M,D
Counseling Psychology	M,D
Criminal Justice and Criminology	M,D
Developmental Psychology	M,D
Economics	M,D
English	M,D
Family and Consumer Sciences-General	M
Forensic Sciences	M,O
French	M,D
Gender Studies	M,O
Geography	M,D
German	M,D
Graphic Design	M,D
Health Communication	M,D,O
Health Psychology	D
History	M,D
Interior Design	M,D
International Affairs	M
International Development	M,D,O
Internet and Interactive Multimedia	M,D
Journalism	M
Landscape Architecture	M,D
Latin American Studies	M,O
Linguistics	M,D,O
Marriage and Family Therapy	M,D,O
Mass Communication	M,D
Media Studies	M
Museum Studies	M,D
Music	M,D
Philosophy	M,D
Photography	M,D
Political Science	M,D,O
Psychology—General	M,D
Public Affairs	M,D,O
Rehabilitation Counseling	M
Religion	M,D
School Psychology	M,D,O
Social Psychology	M,D
Social Sciences	M
Sociology	M,D
Spanish	M,D
Sport Psychology	M,D
Theater	M
Urban and Regional Planning	M,D
Women's Studies	M,O
Writing	M,D

UNIVERSITY OF GEORGIA

Agricultural Economics and Agribusiness	M,D
Anthropology	M,D
Applied Economics	M,D
Archaeology	M,D
Art History	M
Art/Fine Arts	M
Child and Family Studies	M,D,O
Classics	M
Clothing and Textiles	M,D
Communication—General	M,D
Comparative Literature	M,D
Consumer Economics	M,D
Economics	M,D
English	M,D
Environmental Design	M
Family and Consumer Sciences-General	M,D
French	M
Geography	M,D
German	M
Gerontology	O
Historic Preservation	M
History	M,D
Interior Design	M,D
Internet and Interactive Multimedia	M
Journalism	M,D
Landscape Architecture	M
Linguistics	M,D
Mass Communication	M,D
Music	M,D
Philosophy	M,D
Political Science	M,D
Psychology—General	M,D
Public Administration	M,D
Public Policy	M,D
Religion	M
Romance Languages	M,D
Sociology	M,D
Spanish	M
Speech and Interpersonal Communication	M,D
Sustainable Development	M,D
Theater	M,D
Women's Studies	O
Writing	M,D

UNIVERSITY OF GREAT FALLS

Counseling Psychology	M
Criminal Justice and Criminology	M

UNIVERSITY OF GUAM

Art/Fine Arts	M
English	M
Graphic Design	M
Pacific Area/Pacific Rim Studies	M
Public Administration	M

UNIVERSITY OF GUELPH

Agricultural Economics and Agribusiness	M,D
Anthropology	M,D
Art/Fine Arts	M
Child and Family Studies	M,D
Clinical Psychology	M,D
Cognitive Sciences	M,D
Comparative Literature	D
Consumer Economics	M
Criminal Justice and Criminology	M,D
Demography and Population Studies	M,D
Economics	M,D
English	M
French	M
Geography	M,D
History	M,D
Human Development	M,D
Industrial and Organizational Psychology	M,D
International Development	M,D
Landscape Architecture	M
Marriage and Family Therapy	M,D
Medieval and Renaissance Studies	D
Philosophy	M,D
Political Science	M
Psychology—General	M,D
Public Administration	M
Public Policy	M
Rural Planning and Studies	M,D
Social Psychology	M,D
Sociology	M,D
Theater	M
Western European Studies	M

UNIVERSITY OF HARTFORD

Architecture	M
Art/Fine Arts	M
Clinical Psychology	M,D
Communication—General	M
Experimental Psychology	M
Music	M,D,O
Psychology—General	M,D
School Psychology	M

UNIVERSITY OF HAWAII AT HILO

Asian Studies	M
Counseling Psychology	M
Cultural Studies	M,D

UNIVERSITY OF HAWAII AT MANOA

American Studies	M,D,O
Anthropology	M,D
Architecture	D
Art History	M
Art/Fine Arts	M
Asian Languages	M,D
Asian Studies	O
Chinese	M,D,O
Clinical Psychology	M,D,O
Communication—General	M,O
Conflict Resolution and Mediation/Peace Studies	O
Dance	M,D
Demography and Population Studies	O
Disability Studies	O
Economics	M,D
Emergency Management	O
English	M,D
French	M
Geography	M,D,O
Historic Preservation	O
History	M,D
Japanese	M,D,O
Linguistics	M,D
Museum Studies	O
Music	M,D
Pacific Area/Pacific Rim Studies	M,O
Philosophy	M,D
Political Science	M,D
Psychology—General	M,D,O
Public Administration	M,O
Public Policy	O
Religion	M
Social Psychology	M,D,O
Sociology	M,D
Spanish	M
Speech and Interpersonal Communication	M
Theater	M,D
Urban and Regional Planning	M,D,O
Women's Studies	O

UNIVERSITY OF HOUSTON

Anthropology	M
Architecture	M
Art/Fine Arts	M
Communication—General	M
Computer Art and Design	M
Counseling Psychology	M,D
Economics	M,D
Family and Consumer Sciences-General	M
Graphic Design	M
Health Communication	M
Hispanic Studies	M,D
History	M,D
Human Development	M
Linguistics	M,D
Mass Communication	M
Music	M,D
Philosophy	M
Photography	M
Political Science	M,D
Psychology—General	M,D
Public History	M,D
Sociology	M
Spanish	M
Speech and Interpersonal Communication	M
Theater	M
Writing	M,D

UNIVERSITY OF HOUSTON–CLEAR LAKE

Clinical Psychology	M
Criminal Justice and Criminology	M
Cultural Studies	M
English	M
History	M
Humanities	M
Marriage and Family Therapy	M
Psychology—General	M
School Psychology	M
Sociology	M

UNIVERSITY OF HOUSTON–DOWNTOWN

Criminal Justice and Criminology	M
English	M
Technical Communication	M
Writing	M

UNIVERSITY OF HOUSTON–VICTORIA

Counseling Psychology	M
Economic Development	M
Interdisciplinary Studies	M
Psychology—General	M
Publishing	M
School Psychology	M

UNIVERSITY OF IDAHO

Agricultural Economics and Agribusiness	M
Anthropology	M
Applied Arts and Design—General	M
Applied Economics	M
Architecture	M
Art/Fine Arts	M
Consumer Economics	M
English	M
Geography	M,D
History	M,D
Interdisciplinary Studies	M
Landscape Architecture	M
Music	M
Political Science	M,D
Psychology—General	M
Public Administration	M
Public Affairs	M,D
School Psychology	O
Social Sciences	M
Theater	M
Urban and Regional Planning	M
Writing	M

UNIVERSITY OF ILLINOIS AT CHICAGO

Anthropology	M,D
Architecture	M
Art History	M,D
Art/Fine Arts	M
Communication—General	M,D
Criminal Justice and Criminology	M,D
Disability Studies	M,D
Economics	M,D
English	M,D
Forensic Sciences	M
French	M
Geography	M
German	M,D
Graphic Design	M
Hispanic Studies	M,D
History	M,D
Human Development	M,D
Industrial Design	M
Linguistics	M
Medical Illustration	M
Philosophy	M,D
Photography	M
Political Science	M,D
Psychology—General	D
Public Administration	M,D
Sociology	M,D
Spanish	M,D
Urban and Regional Planning	M,D
Writing	M,D

UNIVERSITY OF ILLINOIS AT SPRINGFIELD

Addictions/Substance Abuse Counseling	M
Child and Family Studies	M
Communication—General	M
English	M
Gerontology	M
History	M
Human Development	M
Interdisciplinary Studies	M
Journalism	M
Political Science	M
Public Administration	M,D
Public History	M
Social Sciences	M

UNIVERSITY OF ILLINOIS AT URBANA–CHAMPAIGN

African Studies	M
Agricultural Economics and Agribusiness	M,D
Anthropology	M,D
Applied Arts and Design—General	M,D
Architecture	M,D
Art History	M,D
Art/Fine Arts	M
Asian Languages	M,D
Asian Studies	M,D
Classics	M,D
Communication—General	M,D
Comparative Literature	M,D
Consumer Economics	M,D
Dance	M
East European and Russian Studies	M
Economics	M,D
English	M,D
French	M,D
Geography	M,D
German	M,D
Graphic Design	M
History	M,D
Human Development	M,D
Industrial and Labor Relations	M,D
Industrial Design	M
Italian	M,D
Journalism	M
Landscape Architecture	M,D
Latin American Studies	M
Linguistics	M,D
Media Studies	M,D
Music	M,D,O
Philosophy	M,D
Photography	M
Political Science	M,D
Portuguese	M,D
Psychology—General	M,D
Slavic Languages	M,D
Sociology	M,D
Spanish	M,D
Theater	M,D
Urban and Regional Planning	M,D
Western European Studies	M
Writing	M,D

UNIVERSITY OF INDIANAPOLIS

Art/Fine Arts	M
Clinical Psychology	M,D
Counseling Psychology	M,D
English	M
Gerontology	M,O
History	M
International Affairs	M
Psychology—General	M,D

*M—master's degree; P—first professional degree; D—doctorate; O—other advanced degree; *—Close-Up and/or Display*

- Sociology M

THE UNIVERSITY OF IOWA

- African-American Studies M
- American Studies M,D
- Anthropology M,D
- Art History M,D
- Art/Fine Arts M
- Asian Studies M
- Classics M,D
- Communication—General M,D
- Comparative Literature M,D
- Counseling Psychology M,D,O
- Dance M
- Economics D
- English M,D
- Film, Television, and Video Production M
- Film, Television, and Video Theory and Criticism M,D
- French M,D
- Geography M,D
- German M,D
- History M,D
- Journalism M
- Linguistics M,D
- Mass Communication M,D
- Media Studies M,D
- Music M,D
- Philosophy M,D
- Political Science M,D
- Psychology—General M,D,O
- Rehabilitation Counseling M,D
- Religion M,D
- Rhetoric M,D
- School Psychology M,D,O
- Social Psychology M,D
- Sociology M,D
- Spanish M,D
- Sport Psychology M,D
- Theater M
- Translation and Interpretation M
- Urban and Regional Planning M
- Women's Studies D
- Writing M,D

THE UNIVERSITY OF KANSAS

- African Studies M,O
- African-American Studies M,O
- American Indian/Native American Studies M
- American Studies M,D
- Anthropology M,D
- Applied Arts and Design—General M
- Architecture M,D,O
- Art History M,D
- Art/Fine Arts M
- Asian Languages M
- Asian Studies M
- Classics M
- Clinical Psychology M,D
- Cognitive Sciences M,D
- Communication—General M,D
- Computer Art and Design M
- Counseling Psychology M,D
- Developmental Psychology M,D
- East European and Russian Studies M
- Economics M,D
- English M,D
- Film, Television, and Video Theory and Criticism M,D
- French M,D
- Geography M,D
- German M,D
- Gerontology M,D,O
- History M,D
- Interdisciplinary Studies M,D
- International Affairs M
- Journalism M
- Latin American Studies M,O
- Linguistics M,D
- Media Studies M,D
- Museum Studies M,O
- Music M,D
- Near and Middle Eastern Studies M
- Philosophy M,D
- Political Science M,D
- Psychology—General M,D
- Public Administration M,D
- Rehabilitation Counseling M,D
- Religion M
- School Psychology D,O
- Slavic Languages M,D
- Social Psychology M,D
- Social Sciences M,D
- Sociology M,D
- Spanish M,D
- Theater M,D
- Therapies—Dance, Drama, and Music M
- Urban and Regional Planning M
- Writing M,D

UNIVERSITY OF KENTUCKY

- Agricultural Economics and Agribusiness M,D
- Anthropology M,D
- Applied Arts and Design—General M
- Architecture M
- Art History M
- Art/Fine Arts M
- Child and Family Studies M,D
- Classics M
- Clinical Psychology M,D
- Clothing and Textiles M
- Communication—General M,D
- Counseling Psychology M,D,O
- Economics M,D
- English M,D
- Experimental Psychology M,D
- French M
- Geography M,D
- German M
- Gerontology D
- Hispanic Studies M,D
- Historic Preservation M
- History M,D
- Interior Design M
- International Affairs M
- Music M,D
- Philosophy M,D
- Political Science M,D
- Psychology—General M,D
- Public Administration M,D
- Rehabilitation Counseling M,D
- School Psychology M,D,O
- Sociology M,D
- Theater M

UNIVERSITY OF LA VERNE

- Child and Family Studies M
- Child Development M
- Clinical Psychology D
- Counseling Psychology M
- Gerontology M,O
- Marriage and Family Therapy M
- Psychology—General M,D
- Public Administration M,D
- Social Psychology D

UNIVERSITY OF LETHBRIDGE

- Addictions/Substance Abuse Counseling M,D
- American Indian/Native American Studies M,D
- Anthropology M,D
- Archaeology M,D
- Art/Fine Arts M,D
- Canadian Studies M,D
- Counseling Psychology M,D
- Economics M,D
- English M,D
- French M,D
- Geographic Information Systems M,D
- Geography M,D
- German M,D
- History M,D
- Media Studies M,D
- Music M,D
- Philosophy M,D
- Political Science M,D
- Psychology—General M,D
- Religion M,D
- Social Sciences M,D
- Sociology M,D
- Spanish M,D
- Theater M,D
- Urban Studies M,D
- Women's Studies M,D

UNIVERSITY OF LOUISIANA AT LAFAYETTE

- American Studies D
- Cognitive Sciences D
- Communication—General M
- English M,D
- Folklore M,D
- French M,D
- History M
- Mass Communication M
- Music M
- Psychology—General M
- Rehabilitation Counseling M
- Rhetoric M,D
- Writing M,D

UNIVERSITY OF LOUISIANA AT MONROE

- Addictions/Substance Abuse Counseling M
- Communication—General M
- Criminal Justice and Criminology M
- English M
- Experimental Psychology M
- Gerontology M,O
- History M
- Marriage and Family Therapy M,D
- Music M
- Psychology—General M,O
- School Psychology M,O

UNIVERSITY OF LOUISVILLE

- Addictions/Substance Abuse Counseling M,D,O
- African Studies M
- African-American Studies M
- Anthropology M
- Art History M,D
- Art/Fine Arts M,D
- Clinical Psychology D
- Communication—General M
- Criminal Justice and Criminology M
- English M,D
- Experimental Psychology D
- French M
- Geography M
- Gerontology M,D,O
- History M,O
- Humanities M,D
- Interdisciplinary Studies M,D
- Marriage and Family Therapy M,D,O
- Museum Studies M,D
- Music M
- Philosophy M
- Political Science M
- Psychology—General D
- Public Administration M,D
- Public Affairs M,D
- Public History M,O
- Public Policy M,D
- Rhetoric M,D
- Sociology M
- Spanish M
- Theater M
- Urban and Regional Planning M,D
- Urban Studies M,D
- Women's Studies M,O
- Writing M,D

UNIVERSITY OF MAINE

- Agricultural Economics and Agribusiness M
- Clinical Psychology M,D
- Communication—General M
- Developmental Psychology M,D
- Economics M
- English M
- Experimental Psychology M,D
- French M
- History M,D
- Human Development M
- Interdisciplinary Studies D
- Liberal Studies M
- Music M
- Psychology—General M,D
- Public Administration M,D*
- Social Psychology M,D

UNIVERSITY OF MANAGEMENT AND TECHNOLOGY

- Criminal Justice and Criminology M
- Public Administration M,O

UNIVERSITY OF MANITOBA

- Agricultural Economics and Agribusiness M,D
- American Indian/Native American Studies M
- Anthropology M,D
- Architecture M
- Canadian Studies M
- Child and Family Studies M
- Classics M
- Clinical Psychology M,D
- Clothing and Textiles M
- Disability Studies M
- Economics M,D
- English M,D
- Family and Consumer Sciences-General M
- French M,D
- Geography M,D
- German M

History M,D
Interdisciplinary Studies M,D
Interior Design M
Landscape Architecture M
Linguistics M,D
Museum Studies M,D
Music M
Northern Studies M
Philosophy M
Political Science M
Psychology—General M,D
Public Administration M
Religion M,D
School Psychology M,D
Slavic Languages M
Sociology M,D
Urban and Regional Planning M

UNIVERSITY OF MARY

Addictions/Substance Abuse Counseling M
School Psychology M
Social Psychology M

UNIVERSITY OF MARY HARDIN-BAYLOR

Counseling Psychology M
Marriage and Family Therapy M
Psychology—General M
School Psychology M
Social Psychology M

UNIVERSITY OF MARYLAND, BALTIMORE

Gerontology M,D

UNIVERSITY OF MARYLAND, BALTIMORE COUNTY

Art/Fine Arts M
Cognitive Sciences D
Communication—General M
Dance M
Developmental Psychology D
Economics M,D
Geographic Information Systems M,O
Geography M,D
Gerontology M,D
History M
Industrial and Organizational Psychology M
Linguistics M
Music O
Psychology—General M,D
Public Policy M,D
Social Sciences D
Sociology M,O
Theater M
Urban Studies M,D
Women's Studies O

UNIVERSITY OF MARYLAND, COLLEGE PARK

Agricultural Economics and Agribusiness M,D
American Studies M,D
Anthropology M
Architecture M
Art History M,D
Art Therapy M,D,O
Art/Fine Arts M
Broadcast Journalism M,D
Child and Family Studies M,D
Classics M
Clinical Psychology M,D
Cognitive Sciences D
Communication—General M,D
Comparative Literature M,D
Counseling Psychology M,D,O
Criminal Justice and Criminology M,D
Dance M
Developmental Psychology M,D
Economics M,D
English M,D
Experimental Psychology M,D
Family and Consumer Sciences-General M,D
French M,D
Geography M,D
German M,D
Historic Preservation M,O
History M,D
Human Development M,D
Industrial and Organizational Psychology M,D
Japanese M,D
Jewish Studies M
Journalism M,D
Linguistics M,D
Marriage and Family Therapy M,D
Media Studies M,D
Music M,D
Near and Middle Eastern Languages M,O
Philosophy M,D
Political Science D
Portuguese M,D
Psychology—General M,D
Public Administration M
Public Policy M,D
Rehabilitation Counseling M,D,O
School Psychology M,D,O
Social Psychology M,D
Sociology M,D
Spanish M,D
Speech and Interpersonal Communication M,D
Survey Methodology M,D
Sustainable Development M
Theater M,D
Urban and Regional Planning M,D
Women's Studies M,D
Writing M,D

UNIVERSITY OF MARYLAND EASTERN SHORE

Criminal Justice and Criminology M
Rehabilitation Counseling M

UNIVERSITY OF MASSACHUSETTS AMHERST

African-American Studies M,D
Agricultural Economics and Agribusiness M,D
Anthropology M,D
Architecture M
Art History M
Art/Fine Arts M
Child and Family Studies M,D,O
Chinese M
Classics M
Clinical Psychology M,D
Cognitive Sciences M,D
Communication—General M,D
Comparative Literature M,D
Conflict Resolution and Mediation/Peace Studies M,D
Developmental Psychology M,D
Economics M,D
English M,D
French M
Geography M
German M,D
Historic Preservation M
History of Science and Technology M,D
History M,D
Industrial and Labor Relations M
Interior Design M
Italian M
Japanese M
Landscape Architecture M
Linguistics M,D
Music M,D
Philosophy M,D
Political Science M,D
Portuguese M,D
Psychology—General M,D
Public Administration M
Public History M,D
Public Policy M
Scandinavian Languages M,D
School Psychology M,D,O
Social Psychology M,D
Sociology M,D
Spanish M,D
Theater M
Urban and Regional Planning M,D
Writing M,D

UNIVERSITY OF MASSACHUSETTS BOSTON

American Studies M
Archaeology M
Clinical Psychology D
Conflict Resolution and Mediation/Peace Studies M,O
Counseling Psychology M,O
English M
Forensic Psychology M,O
Gerontology M,D,O
History M
Linguistics M
Marriage and Family Therapy M,O
Political Science M,D,O
Public Affairs M
Public History M
Public Policy D
Rehabilitation Counseling M,O
School Psychology M,O
Sociology M
Women's Studies M,D,O

UNIVERSITY OF MASSACHUSETTS DARTMOUTH

Applied Arts and Design—General M
Art/Fine Arts M,O
Clinical Psychology M,O
Computer Art and Design M
Graphic Design M
Illustration M
Latin American Studies M,D
Photography M
Portuguese M,D
Psychology—General M,O
Public Policy M,O
Textile Design M,O
Writing M,O

UNIVERSITY OF MASSACHUSETTS LOWELL

Criminal Justice and Criminology M
Economic Development M,O
Economics M,O
Music M
Psychology—General M
Social Psychology M
Sociology M,O
Sustainable Development M,D,O

UNIVERSITY OF MEDICINE AND DENTISTRY OF NEW JERSEY

Counseling Psychology M,D,O
Interdisciplinary Studies M,D
Rehabilitation Counseling M,D

UNIVERSITY OF MEMPHIS

African-American Studies M,D,O
Anthropology M
Archaeology M,O
Architecture M
Art History M,O
Art/Fine Arts M,O
Clinical Psychology M,D,O
Communication—General M,D
Comparative Literature M,D,O
Counseling Psychology M,D
Criminal Justice and Criminology M
Economics M,D
English M,D,O
Experimental Psychology M,D,O
Family and Consumer Sciences-General M
Film, Television, and Video Production M,D
French M
Graphic Design M,O
History M,D
Interior Design M,O
Journalism M
Liberal Studies M
Linguistics M,D,O
Music M,D,O
Philosophy M,D
Photography M,O
Political Science M
Psychology—General M,D,O
Public Administration M
Public Policy M
Rehabilitation Counseling M,D
School Psychology M,D,O
Social Sciences M
Sociology M
Spanish M
Theater M
Urban and Regional Planning M
Writing M,D,O

UNIVERSITY OF MIAMI

Architecture M
Art History M
Art/Fine Arts M
Broadcast Journalism M,D
Clinical Psychology M,D
Communication—General M,D
Counseling Psychology D

*M—master's degree; P—first professional degree; D—doctorate; O—other advanced degree; *—Close-Up and/or Display*

Developmental Psychology	M,D
Economic Development	M,D
Economics	M,D
English	M,D
Film, Television, and Video Production	M,D
Film, Television, and Video Theory and Criticism	M,D
French	D
Geography	M
Graphic Design	M
History	M,D
International Affairs	M,D
International Economics	M,D
Internet and Interactive Multimedia	M
Journalism	M,D
Latin American Studies	M
Liberal Studies	M
Marriage and Family Therapy	M,O
Music	M,D,O
Philosophy	M,D
Photography	M
Political Science	M
Psychology—General	M,D
Romance Languages	D
Sociology	M,D
Spanish	M,D
Therapies—Dance, Drama, and Music	M,D,O
Urban Design	M
Writing	M,D

UNIVERSITY OF MICHIGAN

American Studies	M,D
Anthropology	D
Applied Arts and Design—General	M
Applied Economics	M
Archaeology	D
Architecture	M,D
Art History	D
Art/Fine Arts	M
Asian Languages	M,D
Asian Studies	M,D,O
Classics	M,D,O
Clinical Psychology	D
Communication—General	D
Comparative Literature	D
Dance	M
Developmental Psychology	D
East European and Russian Studies	M,O
Economics	M,D
English	M,D,O
Experimental Psychology	D
Film, Television, and Video Theory and Criticism	D,O
French	D
Genetic Counseling	M,D
German	M,D
History	D,O
Jewish Studies	M,D,O
Landscape Architecture	M,D
Linguistics	D
Mass Communication	D
Media Studies	M
Medieval and Renaissance Studies	O
Music	M,D,O
Near and Middle Eastern Languages	M,D
Near and Middle Eastern Studies	M,D
Philosophy	M,D
Political Science	M,D
Psychology—General	D,O
Public Policy	M,D
Religion	M,D
Romance Languages	D
Russian	M,D
Slavic Languages	M,D
Social Psychology	D
Social Sciences	D
Sociology	D,O
Spanish	D
Survey Methodology	M,D,O
Sustainable Development	M,D
Theater	M,D
Urban and Regional Planning	M,D,O
Urban Design	M
Women's Studies	D,O
Writing	M

UNIVERSITY OF MICHIGAN–DEARBORN

Clinical Psychology	M
Health Psychology	M
Liberal Studies	M
Public Administration	M,O
Public Policy	M

UNIVERSITY OF MICHIGAN–FLINT

American Studies	M
English	M
Public Administration	M
Social Sciences	M

UNIVERSITY OF MINNESOTA, DULUTH

Anthropology	M
Art/Fine Arts	M
Criminal Justice and Criminology	M
English	M
Graphic Design	M
Liberal Studies	M
Music	M
Sociology	M

UNIVERSITY OF MINNESOTA, TWIN CITIES CAMPUS

American Studies	D
Anthropology	M,D
Applied Arts and Design—General	M,D,O
Applied Economics	M,D
Archaeology	M,D
Architecture	M
Art History	M,D
Art/Fine Arts	M
Asian Languages	D
Asian Studies	D
Child and Family Studies	M,D
Child Development	M,D
Classics	M,D
Clinical Psychology	D
Clothing and Textiles	M,D,O
Cognitive Sciences	D
Communication—General	M,D,O
Comparative Literature	D
Counseling Psychology	D
Cultural Studies	D
Dance	M,D
Economic Development	M
Economics	D
English	M,D
French	M,D
Genetic Counseling	M,D
Geographic Information Systems	M
German	M,D
History of Medicine	M,D
History of Science and Technology	M,D
History	M,D
Industrial and Labor Relations	M,D
Industrial and Organizational Psychology	D
Interdisciplinary Studies	D
Interior Design	M,D,O
International Development	M
Landscape Architecture	M
Linguistics	M,D
Marriage and Family Therapy	M,D
Mass Communication	M,D
Medieval and Renaissance Studies	M,D
Music	M,D
Philosophy	M,D
Political Science	D
Portuguese	M,D
Psychology—General	D
Public Affairs	M
Public Policy	M
Religion	M,D
Scandinavian Languages	M,D
School Psychology	M,D,O
Social Psychology	D
Sociology	M,D
Spanish	M,D
Textile Design	M,D,O
Theater	M,D
Urban and Regional Planning	M
Women's Studies	D

UNIVERSITY OF MISSISSIPPI

American Studies	M
Anthropology	M
Art History	M
Art/Fine Arts	M
Classics	M
Clinical Psychology	M,D
Economics	M,D
English	M,D
Experimental Psychology	M,D
Family and Consumer Sciences-General	M
French	M
German	M
History	M,D
Journalism	M
Music	M,D
Philosophy	M
Political Science	M,D
Psychology—General	M,D
Sociology	M
Spanish	M

UNIVERSITY OF MISSOURI

Agricultural Economics and Agribusiness	M,D
Anthropology	M,D
Archaeology	M,D
Architecture	M
Art History	M,D
Art/Fine Arts	M
Child and Family Studies	M,D
Classics	M,D
Clothing and Textiles	M
Communication—General	M,D
Comparative Literature	M,D
Computer Art and Design	M
Conflict Resolution and Mediation/Peace Studies	M
Consumer Economics	M
Counseling Psychology	M,D,O
Economics	M,D
English	M,D
Environmental Design	M
Family and Consumer Sciences-General	M,D
French	M,D
Geography	M
German	M
History	M,D
Human Development	M,D
Journalism	M,D
Music	M
Philosophy	M,D
Political Science	M,D
Psychology—General	M,D
Public Affairs	M
Religion	M
Romance Languages	M,D
Rural Sociology	M,D
School Psychology	M,D,O
Sociology	M,D
Spanish	M,D
Theater	M,D

UNIVERSITY OF MISSOURI–KANSAS CITY

Art History	M,D
Art/Fine Arts	M,D
Clinical Psychology	M,D
Counseling Psychology	M,D,O
Criminal Justice and Criminology	M
Economics	M,D
English	M,D
Health Psychology	M,D
History	M,D
Interdisciplinary Studies	D
Media Studies	M,D
Music	M,D
Political Science	M,D
Psychology—General	M,D
Public Administration	M,D
Public Affairs	M,D
Romance Languages	M
Social Psychology	M,D
Sociology	M,D
Theater	M
Writing	M,D

UNIVERSITY OF MISSOURI–ST. LOUIS

Clinical Psychology	M,D,O
Communication—General	M
Criminal Justice and Criminology	M,D
Economics	M,O
English	M,O
Gerontology	M,O
Industrial and Organizational Psychology	M,D,O
Linguistics	M,O
Museum Studies	M,O
Philosophy	M
Political Science	M,D
Psychology—General	M,D,O
Public Administration	M,D,O
Public Policy	M,D,O
School Psychology	D,O
Social Psychology	M,D,O
Writing	M,O

UNIVERSITY OF MOBILE

Marriage and Family Therapy	M
Religion	M
Theology	M

THE UNIVERSITY OF MONTANA

Anthropology	M,D
Art/Fine Arts	M
Clinical Psychology	M,D,O

Communication—General	M
Counseling Psychology	M,D,O
Criminal Justice and Criminology	M
Developmental Psychology	M,D,O
Economics	M
English	M
Experimental Psychology	M,D,O
French	M
Geographic Information Systems	M
Geography	M
German	M
History	M,D
Interdisciplinary Studies	M,D
Jewish Studies	M
Journalism	M
Linguistics	M,D
Music	M
Philosophy	M
Political Science	M
Psychology—General	M,D,O
Public Administration	M
Rural Planning and Studies	M
Rural Sociology	M
School Psychology	M,D,O
Sociology	M
Spanish	M
Theater	M
Writing	M

UNIVERSITY OF MONTEVALLO

English	M
Marriage and Family Therapy	M
Social Psychology	M

UNIVERSITY OF NEBRASKA AT KEARNEY

English	M
History	M
School Psychology	M,O
Writing	M

UNIVERSITY OF NEBRASKA AT OMAHA

Communication—General	M
Criminal Justice and Criminology	M,D
Developmental Psychology	M,D,O
Economics	M
English	M,O
Geography	M,O
Gerontology	M,O
History	M
Industrial and Organizational Psychology	M,D,O
Music	M
Political Science	M
Psychology—General	M,D,O
Public Administration	M,D,O
School Psychology	M,D,O
Technical Communication	M,O
Theater	M
Writing	M,O

UNIVERSITY OF NEBRASKA–LINCOLN

Agricultural Economics and Agribusiness	M,D
Anthropology	M
Archaeology	M,D
Architecture	M,D
Art History	M
Art/Fine Arts	M
Child and Family Studies	M,D
Child Development	M,D
Classics	M
Clinical Psychology	M,D
Clothing and Textiles	M,D
Cognitive Sciences	M,D,O
Communication—General	M,D
Comparative Literature	M,D
Consumer Economics	M,D
Corporate and Organizational Communication	M,D
Counseling Psychology	M,D,O
Developmental Psychology	M,D,O
Economics	M,D
English	M,D
Family and Consumer Sciences-General	M,D
French	M,D
Geography	M,D
German	M,D
Gerontology	M,D
History	M,D
Human Development	M,D,O
Interior Design	M,D
Journalism	M
Marriage and Family Therapy	M,D
Mass Communication	M
Music	M,D
Philosophy	M,D
Political Science	M,D,O
Psychology—General	M,D
Public Policy	M,D,O
Rhetoric	M,D
School Psychology	M,D,O
Social Psychology	M,D
Sociology	M,D
Spanish	M,D
Speech and Interpersonal Communication	M,D
Survey Methodology	M,D
Theater	M
Urban and Regional Planning	M,D
Writing	M,D

UNIVERSITY OF NEVADA, LAS VEGAS

Addictions/Substance Abuse Counseling	M,O
Anthropology	M,D
Architecture	M
Art/Fine Arts	M
Communication—General	M
Criminal Justice and Criminology	M
Economics	M
Emergency Management	M,D,O
English	M,D
Ethics	M
Film, Television, and Video Production	M
Forensic Sciences	M,O
Hispanic Studies	M,O
History	M,D
Journalism	M
Marriage and Family Therapy	M,O
Media Studies	M
Music	M,D
Political Science	M,D
Psychology—General	D
Public Administration	M,D,O
Public Affairs	M,D,O
Public Policy	M
Rehabilitation Counseling	M,O
Sociology	M,D
Spanish	M,O
Theater	M
Translation and Interpretation	M,O
Women's Studies	O
Writing	M,D

UNIVERSITY OF NEVADA, RENO

Agricultural Economics and Agribusiness	M,D
Anthropology	M,D
Applied Economics	M,D
Art/Fine Arts	M
Child and Family Studies	M
Clinical Psychology	D
Cognitive Sciences	M,D
Criminal Justice and Criminology	M
Economics	M
English	M,D
French	M
Geography	M,D
German	M
History	M,D
Human Development	M
Journalism	M
Music	M
Philosophy	M
Political Science	M,D
Psychology—General	M,D
Public Administration	M
Social Psychology	D
Sociology	M
Spanish	M
Speech and Interpersonal Communication	M
Western European Studies	D

UNIVERSITY OF NEW BRUNSWICK FREDERICTON

Anthropology	M
Applied Economics	M
Classics	M
Clinical Psychology	M,D
Conflict Resolution and Mediation/Peace Studies	M
Economics	M
English	M,D
Experimental Psychology	M,D
History	M,D
Interdisciplinary Studies	M,D
Philosophy	M
Political Science	M
Psychology—General	M,D
Public Administration	M
Public Policy	M
Sociology	M,D
Sustainable Development	M

UNIVERSITY OF NEW BRUNSWICK SAINT JOHN

Clinical Psychology	M,D
Experimental Psychology	M,D
Psychology—General	M,D

UNIVERSITY OF NEW ENGLAND

Addictions/Substance Abuse Counseling	M,O
Gerontology	M,O

UNIVERSITY OF NEW HAMPSHIRE

Art/Fine Arts	M
Child and Family Studies	M
Comparative Literature	M,D
Economics	M,D
English	M,D
History	M,D
Liberal Studies	M
Linguistics	M,D
Marriage and Family Therapy	M
Museum Studies	M,D
Music	M
Political Science	M
Psychology—General	D
Public Administration	M,O
Sociology	M,D
Spanish	M
Writing	M,D

UNIVERSITY OF NEW HAVEN

Conflict Resolution and Mediation/Peace Studies	M,O
Criminal Justice and Criminology	M,O
Emergency Management	M,O
Forensic Psychology	M,O
Forensic Sciences	M,O
Geographic Information Systems	M,O
Homeland Security	M,O
Industrial and Labor Relations	M,O
Industrial and Organizational Psychology	M,O
National Security	M,O
Public Administration	M,O
Social Psychology	M,O
Urban and Regional Planning	M,O

UNIVERSITY OF NEW MEXICO

American Studies	M,D
Anthropology	M,D
Architecture	M
Art History	M,D
Art/Fine Arts	M
Child and Family Studies	M,D
Clinical Psychology	M,D
Communication—General	M,D
Comparative Literature	M,D
Dance	M
Economics	M,D
English	M,D
French	M,D
Geography	M
German	M,D
Historic Preservation	O
History	M,D
Landscape Architecture	M
Latin American Studies	M,D
Linguistics	M,D
Music	M
Philosophy	M,D
Political Science	M,D
Portuguese	M,D
Psychology—General	M,D
Public Administration	M
Sociology	M,D
Spanish	M,D
Theater	M
Urban and Regional Planning	M
Urban Design	O
Women's Studies	O

*M—master's degree; P—first professional degree; D—doctorate; O—other advanced degree; *—Close-Up and/or Display*

Writing M,D

UNIVERSITY OF NEW ORLEANS

Art/Fine Arts M
Arts Administration M
Economics D
English M
Film, Television, and Video Production M
Geography M
History M
Music M
Political Science M,D
Psychology—General M,D
Public Administration M
Romance Languages M
Sociology M
Theater M
Urban and Regional Planning M
Urban Studies M,D

UNIVERSITY OF NORTH ALABAMA

Criminal Justice and Criminology M
English M
History M

THE UNIVERSITY OF NORTH CAROLINA AT ASHEVILLE

Liberal Studies M

THE UNIVERSITY OF NORTH CAROLINA AT CHAPEL HILL

Anthropology M,D
Archaeology M,D
Art History M,D
Art/Fine Arts M
Classics M,D
Clinical Psychology D
Cognitive Sciences D
Communication—General M,D
Comparative Literature M,D
Developmental Psychology D
East European and Russian Studies M
Economics M,D
English M,D
Experimental Psychology D
Folklore M
French M,D
Geography M,D
German M,D
History M,D
Italian M,D
Latin American Studies M,D,O
Linguistics M,D
Mass Communication M,D
Music M,D
Philosophy M,D
Political Science M,D
Portuguese M,D
Psychology—General D
Public Administration M
Public Policy D
Rehabilitation Counseling M,D
Religion M,D
Romance Languages M,D
Russian M,D
School Psychology M,D
Slavic Languages M,D
Social Psychology D
Sociology M,D
Spanish M,D
Theater M
Urban and Regional Planning M,D

THE UNIVERSITY OF NORTH CAROLINA AT CHARLOTTE

Architecture M
Child Development M,D
Clinical Psychology M
Communication—General M
Criminal Justice and Criminology M
Dance M
Economics M
English M
Geography M,D
Gerontology M
Health Psychology D
History M
Industrial and Organizational Psychology M,D
Latin American Studies M
Liberal Studies M
Psychology—General M,D
Public Administration M,D
Public Policy M,D
Religion M
Social Psychology M
Sociology M
Spanish M
Theater M

THE UNIVERSITY OF NORTH CAROLINA AT GREENSBORO

Applied Economics M
Architecture M,O
Art/Fine Arts M
Child and Family Studies M,D
Classics M
Clinical Psychology M,D
Cognitive Sciences M,D
Communication—General M
Conflict Resolution and Mediation/Peace Studies M,O
Counseling Psychology M,D,O
Criminal Justice and Criminology M
Dance M
Developmental Psychology M,D
Economic Development M,D,O
Economics D
English M,D
Family and Consumer Sciences-General M,D,O
Film, Television, and Video Production M
French M
Gender Studies M,O
Genetic Counseling M
Geographic Information Systems M,D,O
Geography M,D,O
Gerontology M,O
Hispanic Studies M,O
Historic Preservation M,O
History M,D,O
Human Development M,D
Interior Design M,O
Liberal Studies M
Marriage and Family Therapy M,D,O
Media Studies M
Museum Studies M,D,O
Music M,D
Political Science M,O
Psychology—General M,D
Public Affairs M,O
Rhetoric M,D
School Psychology M,D,O
Social Psychology M,D
Sociology M

Spanish M,O
Technical Writing M,D,O
Textile Design M,D
Theater M
Women's Studies M,D,O
Writing M

THE UNIVERSITY OF NORTH CAROLINA AT PEMBROKE

Public Administration M

UNIVERSITY OF NORTH CAROLINA SCHOOL OF THE ARTS

Arts Administration M
Film, Television, and Video Production M
Music M
Theater M

THE UNIVERSITY OF NORTH CAROLINA WILMINGTON

Criminal Justice and Criminology M
English M
Gerontology M
Hispanic Studies M,O
History M
Liberal Studies M
Psychology—General M
Public Administration M
Sociology M
Writing M

UNIVERSITY OF NORTH DAKOTA

Applied Economics M
Art/Fine Arts M
Clinical Psychology M,D
Communication—General M,D
Counseling Psychology M
Criminal Justice and Criminology D
English M,D
Experimental Psychology M,D
Forensic Psychology M,D
Geography M
History M,D
Linguistics M
Music M,D
Psychology—General M,D
Public Administration M
Sociology M
Theater M

UNIVERSITY OF NORTHERN BRITISH COLUMBIA

Disability Studies M,D,O
Gender Studies M,D,O
History M,D,O
Interdisciplinary Studies M,D,O
International Affairs M,D,O
Political Science M,D,O
Psychology—General M,D,O

UNIVERSITY OF NORTHERN COLORADO

Art/Fine Arts M
Communication—General M
Counseling Psychology D
English M
Gerontology M
History M
Music M,D
Psychology—General M,D
Rehabilitation Counseling M,D
School Psychology D,O
Sociology M
Spanish M

UNIVERSITY OF NORTHERN IOWA

Art/Fine Arts M
Communication—General M
Criminal Justice and Criminology M
English M
French M
Gender Studies M
Geography M
German M
History M
Music M
Political Science M
Psychology—General M
Public Policy M
School Psychology M,O
Social Sciences M
Sociology M
Spanish M
Women's Studies M

UNIVERSITY OF NORTH FLORIDA

Counseling Psychology M
Criminal Justice and Criminology M
English M
Ethics M,O
Gerontology M,O
History M
Philosophy M,O
Psychology—General M
Public Administration M
Rehabilitation Counseling M,O
Translation and Interpretation M
Writing M

UNIVERSITY OF NORTH TEXAS

Anthropology M
Applied Arts and Design—General M
Applied Economics M
Art History M,D,O
Art/Fine Arts M
Child and Family Studies M,O
Clinical Psychology M,D
Clothing and Textiles M
Communication—General M
Counseling Psychology M,D
Criminal Justice and Criminology M
Economics M
English M,D
Experimental Psychology M,D
Film, Television, and Video Production M
French M
Geography M
Gerontology M,D,O
Health Psychology M,D
History M,D
Human Development M,O
Industrial and Labor Relations M
Interdisciplinary Studies M
Journalism M,O
Museum Studies M,D,O
Music M,D
Philosophy M,D
Political Science M,D
Psychology—General M,D
Public Administration M,D
Rehabilitation Counseling M
Religion M,D
School Psychology M

Sociology M,D
Spanish M
Writing M,D

UNIVERSITY OF NORTH TEXAS HEALTH SCIENCE CENTER AT FORT WORTH

Forensic Sciences M,D

UNIVERSITY OF NOTRE DAME

Applied Arts and Design—General M
Architecture M
Art History M
Art/Fine Arts M
Cognitive Sciences D
Comparative Literature D
Conflict Resolution and Mediation/Peace Studies M,D
Counseling Psychology D
Developmental Psychology D
Economics M,D
English M,D
French M
Graphic Design M
History of Science and Technology M,D
History M,D
Industrial Design M
Italian M
Latin American Studies M
Medieval and Renaissance Studies M,D
Philosophy D
Photography M
Political Science D
Psychology—General D
Religion M
Romance Languages M
Sociology D
Spanish M
Theology P,M,D
Writing M

UNIVERSITY OF OKLAHOMA

American Indian/Native American Studies M
Anthropology M,D
Applied Arts and Design—General M
Architecture M
Art History M
Art/Fine Arts M
Communication—General M,D
Counseling Psychology D
Dance M
Economics M,D
English M,D
Film, Television, and Video Production M
French M,D
Geography M,D
German M
History of Science and Technology M,D
History M,D
Interdisciplinary Studies M,D
International Affairs M
Journalism M
Landscape Architecture M
Liberal Studies M
Mass Communication M
Museum Studies M
Music M,D
Philosophy M,D
Photography M
Political Science M,D
Psychology—General M,D
Public Administration M
School Psychology M,D
Social Psychology M
Sociology M,D
Spanish M,D
Theater M
Urban and Regional Planning M
Writing M

UNIVERSITY OF OKLAHOMA HEALTH SCIENCES CENTER

Genetic Counseling M

UNIVERSITY OF OKLAHOMA—TULSA

Architecture M
Emergency Management M
Homeland Security M
Music O
Urban Design M
Urban Studies M

UNIVERSITY OF OREGON

Anthropology M,D
Architecture M
Art History M,D
Art/Fine Arts M
Arts Administration M
Asian Languages M,D
Asian Studies M
Chinese M,D
Classics M
Clinical Psychology D
Cognitive Sciences M,D
Communication—General M,D
Comparative Literature M,D
Dance M
Developmental Psychology M,D
Economics M,D
English M,D
Folklore M
French M
Geography M,D
German M,D
Historic Preservation M
History M,D
Interdisciplinary Studies M
Interior Design M
International Affairs M
Italian M
Japanese M,D
Journalism M,D
Landscape Architecture M
Linguistics M,D
Media Studies M
Music M,D
Philosophy M,D
Political Science M,D
Psychology—General M,D
Public Policy M
Romance Languages M,D
Russian M
Social Psychology M,D
Sociology M,D
Spanish M
Theater M,D
Urban and Regional Planning M
Writing M

UNIVERSITY OF OTTAWA

Anthropology M
Canadian Studies D
Classics M,D
Communication—General M
Criminal Justice and Criminology M,D
Economics M,D
English M,D
French M,D
Geography M,D
History M,D
Interdisciplinary Studies D,O
International Development M
Linguistics M,D
Music M,O
Philosophy M,D
Political Science M,D
Psychology—General D
Public Administration D,O
Religion M,D
Sociology M
Spanish M,D
Theater M
Translation and Interpretation M,D
Women's Studies M

UNIVERSITY OF PENNSYLVANIA

African Studies M,D
Anthropology M,D
Applied Economics D
Archaeology M,D
Architecture M,D,O*
Art History M,D
Art/Fine Arts M
Asian Studies M,D
Classics M,D
Communication—General D
Comparative Literature M,D
Computer Art and Design M
Counseling Psychology M,D
Criminal Justice and Criminology M,D
Demography and Population Studies M,D
Economics M,D
English M,D
Ethics M,D
French M,D
German M,D
Historic Preservation M,O
History of Science and Technology M,D
History M,D
Human Development M,D
International Affairs M
Italian M,D
Landscape Architecture M,O
Liberal Studies M
Linguistics M,D
Music M,D
Near and Middle Eastern Studies M,D
Philosophy M,D
Political Science M,D
Psychology—General D
Public Administration M*
Public Policy M,D
Religion D
Romance Languages M,D
Sociology M,D
Spanish M,D
Urban and Regional Planning M,D,O
Urban Design D
Writing M,D

UNIVERSITY OF PHOENIX

Criminal Justice and Criminology M
Gerontology M
Marriage and Family Therapy M
Psychology—General M
Public Administration M
Social Psychology M

UNIVERSITY OF PHOENIX–ATLANTA CAMPUS

Criminal Justice and Criminology M
Public Administration M

UNIVERSITY OF PHOENIX–AUGUSTA CAMPUS

Criminal Justice and Criminology M
Public Administration M

UNIVERSITY OF PHOENIX–AUSTIN CAMPUS

Criminal Justice and Criminology M
Psychology—General M
Public Administration M

UNIVERSITY OF PHOENIX–BAY AREA CAMPUS

Criminal Justice and Criminology M
Marriage and Family Therapy M
Public Administration M

UNIVERSITY OF PHOENIX–BIRMINGHAM CAMPUS

Criminal Justice and Criminology M
Gerontology M
Psychology—General M
Public Administration M

UNIVERSITY OF PHOENIX–CENTRAL FLORIDA CAMPUS

Public Administration M

UNIVERSITY OF PHOENIX–CENTRAL VALLEY CAMPUS

Gerontology M
Marriage and Family Therapy M
Public Administration M

UNIVERSITY OF PHOENIX–CHATTANOOGA CAMPUS

Criminal Justice and Criminology M
Gerontology M
Psychology—General M
Public Administration M

UNIVERSITY OF PHOENIX–CHEYENNE CAMPUS

Criminal Justice and Criminology M
Psychology—General M
Public Administration M

UNIVERSITY OF PHOENIX–CINCINNATI CAMPUS

Criminal Justice and Criminology M
Psychology—General M
Public Administration M

UNIVERSITY OF PHOENIX–CLEVELAND CAMPUS

Criminal Justice and Criminology M
Psychology—General M
Public Administration M

UNIVERSITY OF PHOENIX–COLUMBUS GEORGIA CAMPUS

Criminal Justice and Criminology M
Public Administration M

*M—master's degree; P—first professional degree; D—doctorate; O—other advanced degree; *—Close-Up and/or Display*

UNIVERSITY OF PHOENIX–COLUMBUS OHIO CAMPUS
Criminal Justice and Criminology M
Psychology—General M
Public Administration M

UNIVERSITY OF PHOENIX–DALLAS CAMPUS
Criminal Justice and Criminology M
Psychology—General M
Public Administration M

UNIVERSITY OF PHOENIX–DENVER CAMPUS
Criminal Justice and Criminology M
Marriage and Family Therapy M
Psychology—General M
Public Administration M
School Psychology M
Social Psychology M

UNIVERSITY OF PHOENIX–DES MOINES CAMPUS
Criminal Justice and Criminology M
Public Administration M

UNIVERSITY OF PHOENIX–EASTERN WASHINGTON CAMPUS
Public Administration M

UNIVERSITY OF PHOENIX–HARRISBURG CAMPUS
Criminal Justice and Criminology M
Psychology—General M
Public Administration M

UNIVERSITY OF PHOENIX–HAWAII CAMPUS
Criminal Justice and Criminology M
Gerontology M
Marriage and Family Therapy M
Psychology—General M
Public Administration M
Social Psychology M

UNIVERSITY OF PHOENIX–HOUSTON CAMPUS
Criminal Justice and Criminology M
Psychology—General M
Public Administration M

UNIVERSITY OF PHOENIX–IDAHO CAMPUS
Criminal Justice and Criminology M
Psychology—General M
Public Administration M

UNIVERSITY OF PHOENIX–INDIANAPOLIS CAMPUS
Criminal Justice and Criminology M
Psychology—General M
Public Administration M

UNIVERSITY OF PHOENIX–JERSEY CITY CAMPUS
Criminal Justice and Criminology M
Psychology—General M
Public Administration M

UNIVERSITY OF PHOENIX–KANSAS CITY CAMPUS
Criminal Justice and Criminology M
Public Administration M
Social Psychology M

UNIVERSITY OF PHOENIX–LAS VEGAS CAMPUS
Counseling Psychology M
Criminal Justice and Criminology M
Marriage and Family Therapy M
Psychology—General M
Public Administration M
School Psychology M

UNIVERSITY OF PHOENIX–LOUISIANA CAMPUS
Criminal Justice and Criminology M
Psychology—General M
Public Administration M

UNIVERSITY OF PHOENIX–MADISON CAMPUS
Public Administration M

UNIVERSITY OF PHOENIX–MADISON CAMPUS
Internet and Interactive Multimedia M
Public Administration M

UNIVERSITY OF PHOENIX–MARYLAND CAMPUS
Criminal Justice and Criminology M
Psychology—General M
Public Administration M

UNIVERSITY OF PHOENIX–MEMPHIS CAMPUS
Criminal Justice and Criminology M
Public Administration M

UNIVERSITY OF PHOENIX–METRO DETROIT CAMPUS
Criminal Justice and Criminology M

UNIVERSITY OF PHOENIX–MINNEAPOLIS/ST. LOUIS PARK CAMPUS
Public Administration M
Social Psychology M

UNIVERSITY OF PHOENIX–NEW MEXICO CAMPUS
Criminal Justice and Criminology M
Marriage and Family Therapy M
Psychology—General M

UNIVERSITY OF PHOENIX–NORTHERN NEVADA CAMPUS
Criminal Justice and Criminology M
Marriage and Family Therapy M
Psychology—General M
Public Administration M
School Psychology M

UNIVERSITY OF PHOENIX–NORTHERN VIRGINIA CAMPUS
Criminal Justice and Criminology M
Public Administration M

UNIVERSITY OF PHOENIX–NORTH FLORIDA CAMPUS
Public Administration M

UNIVERSITY OF PHOENIX–NORTHWEST ARKANSAS CAMPUS
Criminal Justice and Criminology M
Public Administration M

UNIVERSITY OF PHOENIX–OKLAHOMA CITY CAMPUS
Criminal Justice and Criminology M
Psychology—General M

UNIVERSITY OF PHOENIX–OMAHA CAMPUS
Criminal Justice and Criminology M
Public Administration M

UNIVERSITY OF PHOENIX–OREGON CAMPUS
Criminal Justice and Criminology M
Psychology—General M
Public Administration M

UNIVERSITY OF PHOENIX–PHILADELPHIA CAMPUS
Criminal Justice and Criminology M
Psychology—General M
Public Administration M

UNIVERSITY OF PHOENIX–PHOENIX CAMPUS
Gerontology M,O
Marriage and Family Therapy M,O
Psychology—General M,O
Social Psychology M,O

UNIVERSITY OF PHOENIX–PITTSBURGH CAMPUS
Criminal Justice and Criminology M
Psychology—General M
Public Administration M

UNIVERSITY OF PHOENIX–PUERTO RICO CAMPUS
Counseling Psychology M
Marriage and Family Therapy M
School Psychology M

UNIVERSITY OF PHOENIX–RICHMOND CAMPUS
Criminal Justice and Criminology M
Psychology—General M
Public Administration M

UNIVERSITY OF PHOENIX–SACRAMENTO VALLEY CAMPUS
Counseling Psychology M
Criminal Justice and Criminology M
Marriage and Family Therapy M
Psychology—General M
Public Administration M

UNIVERSITY OF PHOENIX–ST. LOUIS CAMPUS
Criminal Justice and Criminology M
Public Administration M

UNIVERSITY OF PHOENIX–SAN ANTONIO CAMPUS
Criminal Justice and Criminology M
Psychology—General M
Public Administration M

UNIVERSITY OF PHOENIX–SAN DIEGO CAMPUS
Criminal Justice and Criminology M
Marriage and Family Therapy M
Public Administration M

UNIVERSITY OF PHOENIX–SAVANNAH CAMPUS
Criminal Justice and Criminology M
Public Administration M

UNIVERSITY OF PHOENIX–SOUTHERN ARIZONA CAMPUS
Criminal Justice and Criminology M,O
Marriage and Family Therapy M,O
Psychology—General M,O

UNIVERSITY OF PHOENIX–SOUTHERN CALIFORNIA CAMPUS
Criminal Justice and Criminology M,O
Marriage and Family Therapy M,O
Psychology—General M,O
Public Administration M

UNIVERSITY OF PHOENIX–SOUTHERN COLORADO CAMPUS
Criminal Justice and Criminology M
Gerontology M
Marriage and Family Therapy M
Psychology—General M
Public Administration M
School Psychology M,O
Social Psychology M

UNIVERSITY OF PHOENIX–SOUTH FLORIDA CAMPUS
Public Administration M

UNIVERSITY OF PHOENIX–SPRINGFIELD CAMPUS
Criminal Justice and Criminology M
Public Administration M

UNIVERSITY OF PHOENIX–TULSA CAMPUS
Criminal Justice and Criminology M
Psychology—General M

UNIVERSITY OF PHOENIX–UTAH CAMPUS
Counseling Psychology M
School Psychology M

UNIVERSITY OF PHOENIX–WESTERN WASHINGTON CAMPUS
Criminal Justice and Criminology M
Public Administration M

UNIVERSITY OF PHOENIX–WEST FLORIDA CAMPUS

Public Administration	M

UNIVERSITY OF PITTSBURGH

African Studies	O
Anthropology	M,D
Architectural History	M,D
Art History	M,D
Asian Studies	M,O
Classics	M,D
Cognitive Sciences	D
Communication—General	M,D
Criminal Justice and Criminology	M,D
Cultural Studies	M,D
Developmental Psychology	M,D
Disability Studies	O
East European and Russian Studies	O
Economics	M,D
Emergency Management	M,D,O
English	M,D
French	M,D
Genetic Counseling	M
Geographic Information Systems	M,D
German	M,D
Gerontology	M,D,O
Hispanic Studies	M,D
History of Science and Technology	M,D
History	M,D
Interdisciplinary Studies	D
International Affairs	M,D,O
International Development	M,O
Italian	M
Latin American Studies	O
Linguistics	M,D
Military and Defense Studies	M
Music	M,D
National Security	M
Philosophy	M,D
Political Science	M,D
Psychology—General	M,D
Public Administration	M,D,O
Public Policy	M,D,O
Rehabilitation Counseling	M
Religion	M,D
Slavic Languages	M,D
Sociology	M,D
Spanish	M,D
Theater	M,D
Urban and Regional Planning	M,O
Western European Studies	O
Women's Studies	O
Writing	M,D

UNIVERSITY OF PORTLAND

Communication—General	M
Corporate and Organizational Communication	M
Music	M
Pastoral Ministry and Counseling	M
Theater	M

UNIVERSITY OF PRINCE EDWARD ISLAND

Geography	M

UNIVERSITY OF PUERTO RICO, MAYAGÜEZ CAMPUS

Agricultural Economics and Agribusiness	M
English	M
Hispanic Studies	M

UNIVERSITY OF PUERTO RICO, MEDICAL SCIENCES CAMPUS

Demography and Population Studies	M
Gerontology	M,O

UNIVERSITY OF PUERTO RICO, RÍO PIEDRAS

Architecture	M
Clinical Psychology	M,D
Communication—General	M
Comparative Literature	M
Economics	M
English	M,D
Family and Consumer Sciences-General	M
Hispanic Studies	M,D
History	M,D
Industrial and Organizational Psychology	M,D
Journalism	M
Linguistics	M,D
Mass Communication	M
Philosophy	M
Psychology—General	M,D
Public Administration	M
Rehabilitation Counseling	M
Social Psychology	M,D
Sociology	M
Translation and Interpretation	M,O
Urban and Regional Planning	M

UNIVERSITY OF PUGET SOUND

Counseling Psychology	M
Pastoral Ministry and Counseling	M

UNIVERSITY OF REDLANDS

Geographic Information Systems	M
Music	M

UNIVERSITY OF REGINA

American Indian/Native American Studies	M
Anthropology	M
Art/Fine Arts	M
Canadian Studies	M,D
Clinical Psychology	M,D
Criminal Justice and Criminology	M
Economics	M,D,O
English	M,D
Experimental Psychology	M,D
French	M
Geography	M,D
Gerontology	M
History	M,D
Linguistics	M
Music	M,D
Philosophy	M
Political Science	M
Psychology—General	M,D
Public Administration	M,D,O
Public Policy	M,D,O
Religion	M,D
Social Sciences	M,D
Sociology	M,D
Women's Studies	M

UNIVERSITY OF RHODE ISLAND

Child and Family Studies	M
Clinical Psychology	M,D
Clothing and Textiles	M
Communication—General	M
Counseling Psychology	M
Economics	M,D
English	M,D
Forensic Sciences	M,D,O
Gerontology	M,D
History	M
Industrial and Labor Relations	M
International Affairs	M
Music	M
Political Science	M
Psychology—General	M,D
Public Administration	M
Public Policy	M
School Psychology	M,D
Spanish	M
Sport Psychology	M

UNIVERSITY OF ROCHESTER

Art History	M,D
Art/Fine Arts	M,D*
Clinical Psychology	M,D
Cognitive Sciences	M,D
Developmental Psychology	M,D
Economics	M,D
Emergency Management	M,D,O
English	M,D
History	M,D
Marriage and Family Therapy	M
Music	M,D
Philosophy	M,D
Political Science	M,D
Psychology—General	M,D
Social Psychology	M,D

UNIVERSITY OF SAINT FRANCIS (IN)

Art/Fine Arts	M
Counseling Psychology	M
Pastoral Ministry and Counseling	M
Psychology—General	M

UNIVERSITY OF SAINT MARY

Psychology—General	M

UNIVERSITY OF SAINT MARY OF THE LAKE–MUNDELEIN SEMINARY

Theology	P,M,D

UNIVERSITY OF ST. MICHAEL'S COLLEGE

Jewish Studies	P,M,D,O
Pastoral Ministry and Counseling	P,M,D,O
Theology	P,M,D,O

UNIVERSITY OF ST. THOMAS (MN)

Art History	M
Corporate and Organizational Communication	M
Counseling Psychology	M,D,O
English	M
Human Development	M,D,O
Marriage and Family Therapy	M,D,O
Pastoral Ministry and Counseling	M
Psychology—General	M,D,O
Religion	M
Theology	P,M

UNIVERSITY OF ST. THOMAS (TX)

Liberal Studies	M
Philosophy	M,D
Theology	P,M

UNIVERSITY OF SAN DIEGO

Conflict Resolution and Mediation/Peace Studies	M
Counseling Psychology	M
History	M
International Affairs	M
Marriage and Family Therapy	M
Theater	M

UNIVERSITY OF SAN FRANCISCO

Asian Studies	M
Counseling Psychology	M,D
Economics	M
International Affairs	M
International Development	M
Internet and Interactive Multimedia	M
Marriage and Family Therapy	M,D
Pacific Area/Pacific Rim Studies	M
Public Administration	M
Public Affairs	M
Writing	M

UNIVERSITY OF SASKATCHEWAN

Agricultural Economics and Agribusiness	M,D,O
Anthropology	M
Archaeology	M,D
Art/Fine Arts	M
Canadian Studies	M,D
East European and Russian Studies	M
Economics	M,O
English	M,D
French	M
Gender Studies	M,D
Geography	M,D
German	M
History	M,D
Industrial and Labor Relations	M
Music	M
Philosophy	M
Political Science	M
Psychology—General	M,D
Public Affairs	M,D
Public Policy	M,D
Religion	M
Sociology	M,D
Theater	M
Women's Studies	M,D

THE UNIVERSITY OF SCRANTON

Counseling Psychology	M,O
History	M
Rehabilitation Counseling	M
Social Psychology	M
Theology	M

UNIVERSITY OF SOUTH AFRICA

Anthropology	M,D
Archaeology	M,D
Art History	M,D

*M—master's degree; P—first professional degree; D—doctorate; O—other advanced degree; *—Close-Up and/or Display*

Classics	M,D
Clinical Psychology	M,D
Communication—General	M,D
Counseling Psychology	M,D
Criminal Justice and Criminology	M,D
Economics	M,D
English	M,D
Ethics	M,D
Family and Consumer Sciences-General	M,D
French	M,D
Geography	M,D
German	M,D
History	M,D
Human Development	M,D
Industrial and Organizational Psychology	M,D
Italian	M,D
Linguistics	M,D
Missions and Missiology	M,D
Music	M,D
Near and Middle Eastern Languages	M,D
Near and Middle Eastern Studies	M,D
Pastoral Ministry and Counseling	M,D
Philosophy	M,D
Political Science	M,D
Portuguese	M,D
Psychology—General	M,D
Public Administration	M,D
Religion	M,D
Romance Languages	M,D
Russian	M,D
Sociology	M,D
Spanish	M,D
Theology	M,D

UNIVERSITY OF SOUTH ALABAMA

Communication—General	M
English	M
Gerontology	O
History	M
Psychology—General	M
Public Administration	M
Rehabilitation Counseling	M,D
School Psychology	M,D
Sociology	M

UNIVERSITY OF SOUTH CAROLINA

Anthropology	M,D
Art History	M
Art/Fine Arts	M
Clinical Psychology	M,D
Comparative Literature	M,D
Consumer Economics	M
Criminal Justice and Criminology	M,D
Economics	M,D
English	M,D
Experimental Psychology	M,D
French	M,D
Genetic Counseling	M
Geography	M,D
German	M,D
Gerontology	O
Historic Preservation	M,O
History	M,D,O
International Affairs	M,D
Journalism	M,D
Linguistics	M,D,O
Media Studies	M
Museum Studies	M,O
Music	M,D,O
Philosophy	M,D
Political Science	M,D
Psychology—General	M,D
Public Administration	M
Public History	M,O
Rehabilitation Counseling	M,O
Religion	M
School Psychology	D
Social Psychology	M,D
Sociology	M,D
Spanish	M,D
Speech and Interpersonal Communication	M,D
Theater	M,D
Women's Studies	O
Writing	M,D

UNIVERSITY OF SOUTH CAROLINA AIKEN

Clinical Psychology	M

THE UNIVERSITY OF SOUTH DAKOTA

Art/Fine Arts	M
Clinical Psychology	M,D
Communication—General	M
English	M,D
History	M
Interdisciplinary Studies	M
Music	M
Political Science	M,D
Psychology—General	M,D
Public Administration	M,D
Theater	M

UNIVERSITY OF SOUTHERN CALIFORNIA

American Studies	D
Architecture	M,D
Art History	M,D,O
Art/Fine Arts	M,D,O
Arts Administration	M
Asian Languages	M,D
Asian Studies	M,D
Broadcast Journalism	M
Child and Family Studies	M,D
Classics	M,D
Clinical Psychology	M,D
Cognitive Sciences	M,D
Communication—General	M,D*
Comparative Literature	M,D
Computer Art and Design	M
Corporate and Organizational Communication	M,D
Developmental Psychology	M,D
Economic Development	M,D
Economics	M,D
English	M,D
Film, Television, and Video Production	M,O
Film, Television, and Video Theory and Criticism	M,D
Geographic Information Systems	M,D,O
Geography	M,D,O
Gerontology	M,D,O
Health Communication	M
History	M,D
International Affairs	M,D
Internet and Interactive Multimedia	M,D
Journalism	M
Linguistics	M,D
Marriage and Family Therapy	M
Mass Communication	M,D
Media Studies	M,D
Music	M,D,O
Philosophy	M,D
Photography	M
Political Science	M,D
Psychology—General	M,D
Public Administration	M,D
Public Policy	M,O
Slavic Languages	M,D
Social Psychology	M,D
Sociology	D
Speech and Interpersonal Communication	M,D
Sustainable Development	M,D,O
Theater	M
Urban and Regional Planning	M,D,O
Writing	M,D

UNIVERSITY OF SOUTHERN INDIANA

Liberal Studies	M
Public Administration	M

UNIVERSITY OF SOUTHERN MAINE

American Studies	M
Counseling Psychology	M,O
Music	M
Public Policy	M,D,O
Rehabilitation Counseling	M,O
School Psychology	M,D
Urban and Regional Planning	M,O
Writing	M

UNIVERSITY OF SOUTHERN MISSISSIPPI

Anthropology	M
Child and Family Studies	M
Clinical Psychology	M,D
Counseling Psychology	M,D
Criminal Justice and Criminology	M,D
Economic Development	M,D
Economics	M,D
English	M,D
Experimental Psychology	M,D
Geography	M,D
History	M,D
International Affairs	M,D
International Development	M,D
Marriage and Family Therapy	M
Mass Communication	M,D
Music	M,D
Philosophy	M
Political Science	M,D
Psychology—General	M,D
School Psychology	M,D
Speech and Interpersonal Communication	M,D
Theater	M

UNIVERSITY OF SOUTH FLORIDA

African Studies	M
American Studies	M
Anthropology	M,D
Architecture	M
Art History	M
Art/Fine Arts	M
Classics	M
Clinical Psychology	D
Cognitive Sciences	D
Communication—General	M,D
Criminal Justice and Criminology	M,D
Economics	M,D
English	M,D
Film, Television, and Video Theory and Criticism	M
French	M
Geography	M,D
Gerontology	M,D
History	M,D
Humanities	M
Industrial and Organizational Psychology	D
Interdisciplinary Studies	M,D
International Affairs	M,D
Latin American Studies	M,D
Linguistics	M
Mass Communication	M
Music	M,D
Philosophy	M,D
Political Science	M,D
Psychology—General	D
Public Administration	M,D
Rehabilitation Counseling	M
Religion	M
School Psychology	M,D,O
Sociology	M,D
Spanish	M
Women's Studies	M

THE UNIVERSITY OF TAMPA

Economics	M

THE UNIVERSITY OF TENNESSEE

Anthropology	M,D
Archaeology	M,D
Architecture	M
Art/Fine Arts	M
Child and Family Studies	M,D
Clinical Psychology	M,D
Clothing and Textiles	M,D
Communication—General	M,D
Consumer Economics	M,D
Counseling Psychology	M,D
Criminal Justice and Criminology	M,D
Economics	M,D
English	M,D
Experimental Psychology	M,D
Family and Consumer Sciences-General	D
French	M,D
Geography	M,D
German	M,D
Gerontology	M
Graphic Design	M
History	M,D
Industrial and Organizational Psychology	D
Italian	D
Journalism	M,D
Landscape Architecture	M
Linguistics	D
Media Studies	M,D
Music	M
Philosophy	M,D
Photography	M
Political Science	M,D
Portuguese	D
Psychology—General	M,D
Public Administration	M
Rehabilitation Counseling	M,D
Religion	M,D

Russian D
School Psychology M,D,O
Sociology M,D
Spanish M,D
Speech and Interpersonal Communication M,D
Theater M

THE UNIVERSITY OF TENNESSEE AT CHATTANOOGA

Criminal Justice and Criminology M
English M,O
Experimental Psychology M
Industrial and Organizational Psychology M
Music M
Psychology—General M
Public Administration M,O
Rhetoric M,O
School Psychology O
Social Psychology M
Writing M,O

THE UNIVERSITY OF TENNESSEE AT MARTIN

Child and Family Studies M
Child Development M
Family and Consumer Sciences-General M
Social Psychology M

THE UNIVERSITY OF TEXAS AT ARLINGTON

Anthropology M
Architecture M
Art/Fine Arts M
Communication—General M
Criminal Justice and Criminology M
Economics M
English M,D
Experimental Psychology M,D
French M
Health Psychology M,D
History M,D
Humanities M
Industrial and Organizational Psychology M,D
Interdisciplinary Studies M
Landscape Architecture M
Linguistics M,D
Music M
Political Science M
Psychology—General M,D
Public Administration M
Public Affairs D
Sociology M
Spanish M
Urban and Regional Planning M

THE UNIVERSITY OF TEXAS AT AUSTIN

African Studies M,D
American Studies M,D
Anthropology M,D
Applied Arts and Design—General M
Archaeology M,D
Architectural History M,D
Architecture M,D
Art History M,D
Art/Fine Arts M
Asian Languages M,D
Asian Studies M,D
Child and Family Studies M,D
Child Development M,D
Classics M,D
Cognitive Sciences M,D
Communication—General M,D
Comparative Literature M,D
Counseling Psychology M,D
Dance M,D
East European and Russian Studies M
Economics M,D
English M,D
Family and Consumer Sciences-General M,D
Film, Television, and Video Production M,D
Folklore M,D
French M,D
Geography M,D
German M,D
Hispanic Studies M
Historic Preservation M,D
History M,D
Human Development M,D
Italian M,D
Journalism M,D
Landscape Architecture M,D
Latin American Studies M,D
Linguistics M,D
Media Studies M,D
Mineral Economics M
Music M,D
Near and Middle Eastern Languages M,D
Near and Middle Eastern Studies M,D
Philosophy D
Political Science D
Portuguese M,D
Psychology—General D
Public Affairs M,D
Public History M,D
Public Policy M,D
Romance Languages M,D
School Psychology M,D
Slavic Languages M,D
Sociology M,D
Spanish M,D
Sport Psychology M,D
Theater M,D
Urban and Regional Planning M,D
Urban Design M,D
Writing M,D

THE UNIVERSITY OF TEXAS AT BROWNSVILLE

English M
History M
Interdisciplinary Studies M
Political Science M
Psychology—General M
Public Administration M
Public Policy M
Spanish M

THE UNIVERSITY OF TEXAS AT DALLAS

Child and Family Studies M,D
Cognitive Sciences M,D
Communication—General M,D
Comparative Literature M,D
Criminal Justice and Criminology M,D
Economics M,D*
Geographic Information Systems M,D
Humanities M,D
Interdisciplinary Studies M
Latin American Studies M,D
Political Science M,D
Psychology—General M,D
Public Administration D
Public Affairs M,D
Public Policy M,D
Sociology M

THE UNIVERSITY OF TEXAS AT EL PASO

Art/Fine Arts M
Clinical Psychology M,D
Communication—General M
Economics M
English M,D,O
Experimental Psychology M,D
Gender Studies O
History M,D
Homeland Security M,O
Interdisciplinary Studies M
Latin American Studies M,O
Liberal Studies M
Linguistics M,O
Military and Defense Studies M,O
Music M
National Security M,O
Philosophy M
Political Science M
Psychology—General M,D
Public Administration M,O
Public Policy M,O
Rehabilitation Counseling M
Rhetoric M,D,O
Sociology M,O
Spanish M,O
Women's Studies O
Writing M,D,O

THE UNIVERSITY OF TEXAS AT SAN ANTONIO

Anthropology M,D
Architecture M
Art History M
Art/Fine Arts M
Communication—General M
Criminal Justice and Criminology M
Cultural Studies M,D
Demography and Population Studies D
Economics M
English M,D
History M
Interdisciplinary Studies M
Music M,O
Political Science M
Psychology—General M
Public Administration M
Sociology M
Spanish M

THE UNIVERSITY OF TEXAS AT TYLER

Art History M
Art/Fine Arts M
Clinical Psychology M
Communication—General M
Counseling Psychology M
Criminal Justice and Criminology M
English M
History M
Interdisciplinary Studies M
Marriage and Family Therapy M
Political Science M
Psychology—General M
Public Administration M
School Psychology M
Social Sciences M
Sociology M

THE UNIVERSITY OF TEXAS HEALTH SCIENCE CENTER AT HOUSTON

Genetic Counseling M

THE UNIVERSITY OF TEXAS MEDICAL BRANCH

Humanities M,D

THE UNIVERSITY OF TEXAS OF THE PERMIAN BASIN

Clinical Psychology M
Criminal Justice and Criminology M
English M
Experimental Psychology M
History M
Political Science M
Psychology—General M
Spanish M

THE UNIVERSITY OF TEXAS–PAN AMERICAN

Art/Fine Arts M
Clinical Psychology M
Communication—General M
Criminal Justice and Criminology M
Economics D
English M
Experimental Psychology M
History M
Interdisciplinary Studies M
Music M
Psychology—General M
Public Administration M
Rehabilitation Counseling M
School Psychology M
Sociology M
Spanish M
Theater M

THE UNIVERSITY OF TEXAS SOUTHWESTERN MEDICAL CENTER AT DALLAS

Clinical Psychology D
Medical Illustration M
Rehabilitation Counseling M

THE UNIVERSITY OF THE ARTS

Art/Fine Arts M*
Industrial Design M
Museum Studies M
Music M

UNIVERSITY OF THE DISTRICT OF COLUMBIA

Clinical Psychology M
Counseling Psychology M
English M
Public Administration M

UNIVERSITY OF THE FRASER VALLEY

Criminal Justice and Criminology M

*M—master's degree; P—first professional degree; D—doctorate; O—other advanced degree; *—Close-Up and/or Display*

UNIVERSITY OF THE INCARNATE WORD
- Communication—General M,O
- Interdisciplinary Studies M
- Religion M

UNIVERSITY OF THE PACIFIC
- Communication—General M
- Criminal Justice and Criminology P,M,D
- International Affairs P,M,D
- Music M
- Psychology—General M
- Public Policy P,M,D
- School Psychology M,D,O
- Therapies—Dance, Drama, and Music M

UNIVERSITY OF THE ROCKIES
- Psychology—General M,D

UNIVERSITY OF THE SACRED HEART
- Broadcast Journalism M,O
- Communication—General M,O
- Conflict Resolution and Mediation/Peace Studies M
- Cultural Studies M
- Film, Television, and Video Production M,O
- Internet and Interactive Multimedia M,O
- Writing M,O

UNIVERSITY OF THE SCIENCES IN PHILADELPHIA
- Health Psychology M
- Technical Writing M,O

UNIVERSITY OF THE SOUTHWEST
- Counseling Psychology M

UNIVERSITY OF THE VIRGIN ISLANDS
- Public Administration M

UNIVERSITY OF THE WEST
- Religion M,D

THE UNIVERSITY OF TOLEDO
- Clinical Psychology M,D
- Cognitive Sciences M,D
- Communication—General O
- Criminal Justice and Criminology M,O
- Economics M
- English M,O
- Experimental Psychology M,D
- French M
- Geographic Information Systems M,O
- Geography M,O
- German M
- Gerontology O
- History M,D
- Homeland Security M,O
- Liberal Studies M
- Music M
- Philosophy M
- Political Science M
- Psychology—General M,D
- Public Administration M,O
- School Psychology M,D,O
- Social Psychology M,D,O
- Sociology M
- Spanish M
- Urban and Regional Planning M,O
- Writing M,O

UNIVERSITY OF TORONTO
- Anthropology M,D
- Architecture M
- Art History M,D
- Art/Fine Arts M,D
- Asian Studies M,D
- Classics M,D
- Comparative Literature M,D
- Criminal Justice and Criminology M,D
- East European and Russian Studies M
- Economics M,D
- English M,D
- French M,D
- Genetic Counseling M,D
- Geography M,D
- German M,D
- History of Science and Technology M,D
- History M,D
- Industrial and Labor Relations M,D
- Italian M,D
- Linguistics M,D
- Medieval and Renaissance Studies M,D
- Museum Studies M,D
- Music M,D
- Near and Middle Eastern Studies M,D
- Philosophy M,D
- Political Science M,D
- Portuguese M,D
- Psychology—General M,D
- Religion M,D
- Slavic Languages M,D
- Sociology M,D
- Spanish M,D
- Theater M,D
- Urban and Regional Planning M,D
- Urban Design M,D

UNIVERSITY OF TRINITY COLLEGE
- Music P,M,D,O
- Pastoral Ministry and Counseling P,M,D,O
- Theology P,M,D,O

UNIVERSITY OF TULSA
- Anthropology M
- Art/Fine Arts M
- Clinical Psychology M,D
- English M,D
- History M
- Industrial and Organizational Psychology M,D
- Psychology—General M,D
- Public Policy P,M,O

UNIVERSITY OF UTAH
- American Studies M,D
- Anthropology M,D
- Architecture M
- Art History M
- Art/Fine Arts M
- Asian Studies M
- Child and Family Studies M
- Clinical Psychology D
- Communication—General M,D
- Comparative Literature M,D
- Consumer Economics M
- Counseling Psychology M,D
- Dance M
- Economics M,D
- English M,D
- Film, Television, and Video Production M
- French M,D
- Geography M,D
- German M,D
- Gerontology M,O
- Graphic Design M
- History M,D
- Human Development M
- Humanities M
- International Affairs M
- Linguistics M,D
- Music M,D
- Near and Middle Eastern Languages M,D
- Near and Middle Eastern Studies M,D
- Philosophy M,D
- Photography M
- Political Science M,D
- Psychology—General D
- Public Administration M
- Rhetoric M,D
- School Psychology M,D
- Sociology M,D
- Spanish M,D
- Urban and Regional Planning M,D
- Writing M,D

UNIVERSITY OF VERMONT
- Agricultural Economics and Agribusiness M
- Applied Economics M
- Classics M
- Clinical Psychology D
- Communication—General M
- Counseling Psychology M
- English M
- French M
- German M
- Historic Preservation M
- History M
- Interdisciplinary Studies M
- Psychology—General D
- Public Administration M

UNIVERSITY OF VICTORIA
- Anthropology M
- Art History M,D
- Art/Fine Arts M
- Asian Studies M
- Child and Family Studies M,D
- Classics M,D
- Clinical Psychology M,D
- Computer Art and Design M
- Conflict Resolution and Mediation/Peace Studies M,D
- Counseling Psychology M,D
- Developmental Psychology M,D
- Economics M,D
- English M,D
- Experimental Psychology M,D
- Film, Television, and Video Production M
- French M
- Geography M,D
- German M
- Hispanic Studies M
- History M,D
- Human Development M,D
- Italian M
- Linguistics M,D
- Music M,D
- Pacific Area/Pacific Rim Studies M
- Philosophy M
- Photography M
- Political Science M,D
- Psychology—General M,D
- Public Administration M,D
- Social Psychology M,D
- Sociology M,D
- Theater M
- Writing M

UNIVERSITY OF VIRGINIA
- Anthropology M,D
- Archaeology M,D
- Architectural History M,D
- Architecture M
- Art History M,D
- Asian Studies M
- Classics M,D
- Clinical Psychology D
- Economics M,D
- English M,D,O
- French M,D
- German M,D
- History M,D
- Interdisciplinary Studies M,D
- International Affairs M,D
- Italian M
- Landscape Architecture M
- Linguistics M
- Music M,D
- Philosophy M,D
- Political Science M,D
- Psychology—General M,D
- Public Policy M
- Religion M,D
- Romance Languages M,D
- School Psychology M,D
- Slavic Languages M,D
- Sociology M,D
- Spanish M,D
- Theater M
- Urban and Regional Planning M,O
- Writing M

UNIVERSITY OF WASHINGTON
- Anthropology M,D
- Applied Arts and Design—General M
- Architecture M,D,O
- Art History M,D
- Art/Fine Arts M
- Asian Languages M,D
- Asian Studies M,D
- Chinese M,D
- Classics M,D
- Clinical Psychology D
- Cognitive Sciences D
- Communication—General M,D
- Comparative Literature M,D
- Dance M
- Demography and Population Studies M,D
- Developmental Psychology D
- East European and Russian Studies M
- Economics M,D
- English M,D
- French M,D
- Geography M,D
- German M,D
- Hispanic Studies M
- Historic Preservation O
- History M,D
- Human Development M,D
- Industrial Design M
- International Affairs M
- Italian M,D
- Japanese M,D
- Landscape Architecture M
- Lighting Design M,D,O
- Linguistics M,D
- Museum Studies M

Music	M,D
Near and Middle Eastern Studies	M,D
Philosophy	M,D
Photography	M
Political Science	M,D
Portuguese	M
Psychology—General	D
Public Administration	M,D
Public Affairs	M,D
Public Policy	M,D
Religion	M,D
Romance Languages	M,D
Russian	M,D
Scandinavian Languages	M,D
School Psychology	M,D
Slavic Languages	M,D
Social Psychology	D
Social Sciences	M,D
Sociology	M,D
Spanish	M
Sustainable Development	P,M,D
Technical Communication	M,D
Theater	M,D
Urban and Regional Planning	M,D
Urban Design	M,D,O
Women's Studies	D
Writing	M

UNIVERSITY OF WASHINGTON, BOTHELL

Cultural Studies	M
Public Policy	M

UNIVERSITY OF WASHINGTON, TACOMA

Interdisciplinary Studies	M

UNIVERSITY OF WATERLOO

Anthropology	M
Architecture	M
Art/Fine Arts	M
Economic Development	M
Economics	M,D
English	M,D
French	M,D
Geography	M,D
German	M,D
History	M,D
International Affairs	M,D
Near and Middle Eastern Studies	M
Philosophy	M,D
Political Science	M,D
Psychology—General	M,D
Public Affairs	M
Religion	D
Russian	M,D
Sociology	M,D
Technical Writing	M,D
Urban and Regional Planning	M,D

THE UNIVERSITY OF WESTERN ONTARIO

Anthropology	M,D
Classics	M
Comparative Literature	M,D
Counseling Psychology	M
Economics	M,D
English	M,D
French	M,D
Geography	M,D
History	M,D
Interdisciplinary Studies	M,D
Journalism	M
Media Studies	M,D
Music	M,D
Philosophy	M,D
Political Science	M,D
Psychology—General	M,D
Sociology	M,D
Spanish	M,D
Sustainable Development	M,D

UNIVERSITY OF WEST FLORIDA

Anthropology	M
Archaeology	M
Communication—General	M
Counseling Psychology	M
Criminal Justice and Criminology	M
English	M
Gerontology	M
Historic Preservation	M
History	M
Humanities	M
Industrial and Organizational Psychology	M
Military and Defense Studies	M
Political Science	M
Psychology—General	M
Public Administration	M
Public History	M
Sociology	M
Writing	M

UNIVERSITY OF WEST GEORGIA

Counseling Psychology	M,D,O
Criminal Justice and Criminology	M
English	M
History	M,O
Museum Studies	M,O
Music	M
Psychology—General	M,D
Public Administration	M,O
Public History	M,O
Rural Planning and Studies	M,O
Sociology	M

UNIVERSITY OF WINDSOR

Art/Fine Arts	M
Clinical Psychology	M,D
Communication—General	M
Criminal Justice and Criminology	M,D
Economics	M
English	M
History	M
Philosophy	M
Political Science	M
Psychology—General	M,D
Social Psychology	M,D
Sociology	M,D
Writing	M

THE UNIVERSITY OF WINNIPEG

History	M
Marriage and Family Therapy	P,M,O
Public Administration	M
Religion	M
Theology	P,M,O

UNIVERSITY OF WISCONSIN–EAU CLAIRE

English	M
History	M
Psychology—General	M,O
School Psychology	M,O

UNIVERSITY OF WISCONSIN–LA CROSSE

Psychology—General	M,O
School Psychology	M,O

UNIVERSITY OF WISCONSIN–MADISON

African Studies	M,D
African-American Studies	M
Agricultural Economics and Agribusiness	M,D
American Studies	M,D
Anthropology	D
Applied Arts and Design—General	M,D
Applied Economics	M,D
Archaeology	D
Art History	M,D
Art/Fine Arts	M
Arts Administration	M
Asian Languages	M,D
Asian Studies	M,D
Child and Family Studies	M,D
Chinese	M,D
Classics	M,D
Clinical Psychology	D
Cognitive Sciences	D
Communication—General	M,D
Comparative Literature	M,D
Consumer Economics	M,D
Counseling Psychology	D
Developmental Psychology	D
Economics	D
English	M,D
Family and Consumer Sciences-General	M,D
Film, Television, and Video Theory and Criticism	M,D
Folklore	M,D
French	M,D,O
Genetic Counseling	M
Geographic Information Systems	M,D,O
Geography	M,D,O
German	M,D
History of Science and Technology	M,D
History	M,D
Human Development	M,D
Italian	M,D
Japanese	M,D
Jewish Studies	M,D
Journalism	M,D
Landscape Architecture	M
Latin American Studies	M,D
Linguistics	M,D
Mass Communication	M,D
Media Studies	M,D
Music	M,D
Near and Middle Eastern Languages	M,D
Near and Middle Eastern Studies	M,D
Philosophy	M,D
Political Science	D
Portuguese	M,D
Psychology—General	D
Public Affairs	M
Rehabilitation Counseling	M,D
Rhetoric	M,D
Rural Sociology	M,D
Scandinavian Languages	M,D
Slavic Languages	M,D
Social Psychology	D
Social Sciences	D
Sociology	M,D
Spanish	M,D
Speech and Interpersonal Communication	M,D
Sustainable Development	M
Theater	M,D
Urban and Regional Planning	M,D
Women's Studies	M,D
Writing	M,D

UNIVERSITY OF WISCONSIN–MILWAUKEE

African Studies	D
Anthropology	M,D,O
Architecture	M,D,O
Art History	M,O
Art/Fine Arts	M
Classics	M,O
Clinical Psychology	M,D
Communication—General	M,D,O
Comparative Literature	M,D,O
Conflict Resolution and Mediation/Peace Studies	M,D,O
Counseling Psychology	M,D
Criminal Justice and Criminology	M
Dance	M
Developmental Psychology	M,D
Economics	M,D
English	M,D,O
Film, Television, and Video Production	M
French	M,O
Geographic Information Systems	M,O
Geography	M,D
German	M,O
Gerontology	M,D,O
Historic Preservation	M,D,O
History	M,D
Industrial and Labor Relations	M,O
Interdisciplinary Studies	D
Italian	M,O
Jewish Studies	M,O
Liberal Studies	M
Linguistics	M,D,O
Marriage and Family Therapy	M,D,O
Media Studies	M,O
Museum Studies	M,D,O
Music	M,O
Philosophy	M
Political Science	M,D
Psychology—General	M,D
Public Administration	M
Rhetoric	M,D,O
School Psychology	D,O
Slavic Languages	M,O
Social Psychology	M,D
Sociology	M
Spanish	M,O
Technical Communication	M,D,O
Theater	M
Translation and Interpretation	M,O
Urban and Regional Planning	M,O
Urban Studies	M,D
Writing	M,D,O

UNIVERSITY OF WISCONSIN–OSHKOSH

English	M

*M—master's degree; P—first professional degree; D—doctorate; O—other advanced degree; *—Close-Up and/or Display*

Experimental Psychology	M
Industrial and Organizational Psychology	M
Psychology—General	M
Public Administration	M

UNIVERSITY OF WISCONSIN–PLATTEVILLE

Criminal Justice and Criminology	M

UNIVERSITY OF WISCONSIN–RIVER FALLS

Art/Fine Arts	M
School Psychology	M,O

UNIVERSITY OF WISCONSIN–STEVENS POINT

Communication—General	M
Corporate and Organizational Communication	M
English	M
Family and Consumer Sciences-General	M
History	M
Human Development	M
Mass Communication	M
Speech and Interpersonal Communication	M

UNIVERSITY OF WISCONSIN–STOUT

Child and Family Studies	M
Counseling Psychology	M
Human Development	M
Marriage and Family Therapy	M
Psychology—General	M
Rehabilitation Counseling	M
School Psychology	M,O

UNIVERSITY OF WISCONSIN–SUPERIOR

Art History	M
Art Therapy	M
Art/Fine Arts	M
Communication—General	M
Mass Communication	M
School Psychology	M
Social Psychology	M
Speech and Interpersonal Communication	M
Theater	M

UNIVERSITY OF WISCONSIN–WHITEWATER

Communication—General	M
Corporate and Organizational Communication	M
Mass Communication	M
Psychology—General	M,O
School Psychology	M,O
Social Psychology	M

UNIVERSITY OF WYOMING

Agricultural Economics and Agribusiness	M
American Studies	M
Anthropology	M,D
Applied Economics	M
Child Development	M
Communication—General	M
Consumer Economics	M
Economics	M,D
English	M
French	M
Geography	M
German	M
History	M
International Affairs	M
Music	M
Philosophy	M
Political Science	M
Psychology—General	M,D
Public Administration	M
Rural Planning and Studies	M
Sociology	M
Spanish	M
Writing	M

UPPER IOWA UNIVERSITY

Criminal Justice and Criminology	M
Homeland Security	M
Public Administration	M

URBANA UNIVERSITY

Criminal Justice and Criminology	M

URSULINE COLLEGE

Art Therapy	M
Historic Preservation	M
Liberal Studies	M
Theology	M

UTAH STATE UNIVERSITY

American Studies	M
Applied Economics	M
Art/Fine Arts	M
Child and Family Studies	M,D
Clinical Psychology	M,D
Communication—General	M
Consumer Economics	M
Counseling Psychology	M,D
Disability Studies	M,D,O
Economics	M,D
English	M
Family and Consumer Sciences-General	M,D
Folklore	M
Geography	M,D
History	M
Human Development	M,D
Interior Design	M
Landscape Architecture	M
Marriage and Family Therapy	M,D
Political Science	M
Psychology—General	M,D
Rehabilitation Counseling	M
School Psychology	M,D
Sociology	M,D
Theater	M
Urban and Regional Planning	M,D
Writing	M

UTICA COLLEGE

Criminal Justice and Criminology	M
Liberal Studies	M

VALDOSTA STATE UNIVERSITY

Clinical Psychology	M,O
Counseling Psychology	M,O
Criminal Justice and Criminology	M
English	M
History	M
Industrial and Organizational Psychology	M,O
Marriage and Family Therapy	M
Psychology—General	M,O
School Psychology	M,O
Sociology	M

VALPARAISO UNIVERSITY

Asian Studies	M
Clinical Psychology	M,O
Communication—General	M
Counseling Psychology	M,O
English	M,O
Ethics	M,O
Gerontology	M,O
History	M,O
International Economics	M
Liberal Studies	M,O
Media Studies	M
Psychology—General	M,O
School Psychology	
Theology	M,O

VANCOUVER SCHOOL OF THEOLOGY

Theology	P,M,O

VANDERBILT UNIVERSITY

Anthropology	M,D
Child and Family Studies	M
Classics	M
Economic Development	M,D
Economics	P,M,D
English	M,D
French	M,D
German	M,D
History	M,D
Human Development	M
Latin American Studies	M
Liberal Studies	M
Philosophy	M,D
Political Science	M,D
Portuguese	M,D
Psychology—General	M,D
Public Policy	M,D
Religion	M,D
Sociology	M,D
Spanish	M,D
Theology	P,M
Urban and Regional Planning	M
Writing	M

VANGUARD UNIVERSITY OF SOUTHERN CALIFORNIA

Clinical Psychology	M
Religion	M
Theology	M

VICTORIA UNIVERSITY

Theology	P,M,D,O

VILLANOVA UNIVERSITY

Communication—General	M
English	M*
Hispanic Studies	M*
History	M*
Humanities	M
Liberal Studies	M
Philosophy	D
Political Science	M*
Psychology—General	M*
Public Administration	M
Theater	M
Theology	M*

VIRGINIA COLLEGE AT BIRMINGHAM

Criminal Justice and Criminology	M

VIRGINIA COMMONWEALTH UNIVERSITY

Applied Arts and Design—General	M
Applied Social Research	M,O
Architectural History	M,D
Art History	M,D
Art/Fine Arts	M,D
Clinical Psychology	D
Communication—General	D
Counseling Psychology	M,D,O
Criminal Justice and Criminology	M,O
Economics	M
Emergency Management	M,O
English	M
Forensic Sciences	M
Gender Studies	O
Geographic Information Systems	O
Gerontology	M,D,O
Historic Preservation	O
History	M,D
Homeland Security	M,O
Humanities	M,D,O
Interdisciplinary Studies	M
Interior Design	M
Internet and Interactive Multimedia	M
Journalism	M
Mass Communication	M
Media Studies	D
Museum Studies	M,D
Music	M
Photography	M
Political Science	M,D,O
Psychology—General	D
Public Administration	M,O
Public Affairs	M,D,O
Public Policy	D
Rehabilitation Counseling	M,O
Rhetoric	M
Sociology	M
Theater	M
Urban and Regional Planning	M,O
Writing	M

VIRGINIA POLYTECHNIC INSTITUTE AND STATE UNIVERSITY

Agricultural Economics and Agribusiness	M,D
Applied Arts and Design—General	M,D
Applied Economics	M,D
Architecture	M,D
Child and Family Studies	M,D
Child Development	M,D
Clinical Psychology	M,D
Clothing and Textiles	M,D
Communication—General	M
Consumer Economics	M,D
Developmental Psychology	M,D
Economic Development	M,D
Economics	M,D
English	M,D
Environmental Design	D
Geographic Information Systems	D
Geography	M,D
Gerontology	M,D

History of Science and Technology	M,D
History	M
Human Development	M,D
Industrial and Organizational Psychology	M,D
Interdisciplinary Studies	M,D
Interior Design	M,D
International Affairs	M,D
International Development	M,D
International Economics	M,D
Landscape Architecture	M,D
Liberal Studies	M,O
Marriage and Family Therapy	M,D
National Security	M,O
Philosophy	M
Political Science	M,O
Psychology—General	M,D
Public Administration	M,D
Public Affairs	M,D
Public Policy	M,D
Rural Planning and Studies	M,D
Sociology	M,D
Theater	M
Urban and Regional Planning	M,D

VIRGINIA STATE UNIVERSITY

Clinical Psychology	M,D
Economics	M
English	M
Health Psychology	M,D
History	M
Interdisciplinary Studies	M
Psychology—General	M,D

VIRGINIA THEOLOGICAL SEMINARY

Theology	P,M,D

VIRGINIA UNION UNIVERSITY

Theology	P,D

VIRGINIA UNIVERSITY OF LYNCHBURG

Religion	P

WAKE FOREST UNIVERSITY

Communication—General	M
English	M
Liberal Studies	M
Psychology—General	M
Religion	M
Speech and Interpersonal Communication	M

WALDEN UNIVERSITY

Child and Family Studies	M,D
Clinical Psychology	M,D,O
Conflict Resolution and Mediation/Peace Studies	M,D,O
Counseling Psychology	M,D,O
Criminal Justice and Criminology	M,D,O
Developmental Psychology	M,D,O
Forensic Psychology	M,D,O
Health Psychology	M,D,O
Homeland Security	M,D,O
Industrial and Organizational Psychology	M,D,O
International Affairs	M,D,O
Marriage and Family Therapy	M,D
Psychology—General	M,D,O
Public Administration	M,D,O
Public Policy	M,D,O
Social Psychology	M,D,O
Sustainable Development	M,D,O

WALLA WALLA UNIVERSITY

Counseling Psychology	M

WALSH UNIVERSITY

Counseling Psychology	M
Theology	M

WARNER PACIFIC COLLEGE

Ethics	M
Pastoral Ministry and Counseling	M
Religion	M
Theology	M

WARREN WILSON COLLEGE

Writing	M

WARTBURG THEOLOGICAL SEMINARY

Theology	P,M

WASHBURN UNIVERSITY

Clinical Psychology	M
Criminal Justice and Criminology	M
Liberal Studies	M
Psychology—General	M

WASHINGTON ADVENTIST UNIVERSITY

Counseling Psychology	M
Public Administration	M
Religion	M

WASHINGTON COLLEGE

English	M
History	M
Psychology—General	M

WASHINGTON STATE UNIVERSITY

Agricultural Economics and Agribusiness	M,D,O
American Studies	M,D
Anthropology	M,D
Applied Economics	M,D,O
Archaeology	M,D
Architecture	M
Art/Fine Arts	M
Asian Studies	M,D
Clinical Psychology	M,D
Clothing and Textiles	M,D
Communication—General	M,D
Computer Art and Design	M
Corporate and Organizational Communication	M,D
Counseling Psychology	M,D,O
Criminal Justice and Criminology	M,D
Cultural Studies	M,D
Demography and Population Studies	M,D
Economics	M,D,O
English	M,D
Ethnic Studies	M,D
Experimental Psychology	M,D
Health Communication	M,D
History	M,D
Human Development	M
Interdisciplinary Studies	D
Interior Design	M,D
International Affairs	M,D
Landscape Architecture	M,D
Media Studies	M,D
Music	M
Philosophy	M
Photography	M
Political Science	M,D
Psychology—General	M,D
Public History	M,D
Public Policy	M,D
School Psychology	M,D,O
Social Psychology	M,D
Sociology	M,D
Spanish	M
Western European Studies	M,D
Women's Studies	M,D

WASHINGTON STATE UNIVERSITY SPOKANE

Architecture	M,D
Criminal Justice and Criminology	M,D
Interior Design	M,D
Landscape Architecture	M,D

WASHINGTON STATE UNIVERSITY VANCOUVER

History	M
Public Affairs	M

WASHINGTON THEOLOGICAL UNION

Theology	P,M,D

WASHINGTON UNIVERSITY IN ST. LOUIS

Anthropology	D
Archaeology	M,D
Architecture	M
Art History	M,D
Art/Fine Arts	M
Asian Languages	M,D
Asian Studies	M
Chinese	M,D
Classics	M
Clinical Psychology	D
Comparative Literature	M,D
Economics	D
English	M,D
Experimental Psychology	D
French	M,D
German	M,D
History	M,D
Japanese	M,D
Music	M,D
Philosophy	M,D
Political Science	M,D
Psychology—General	D
Public Policy	M
Romance Languages	M,D
Social Psychology	D
Spanish	M,D
Speech and Interpersonal Communication	M,D
Urban Design	M
Writing	M

WAYLAND BAPTIST UNIVERSITY

Counseling Psychology	M
Criminal Justice and Criminology	M
Homeland Security	M
Interdisciplinary Studies	M
Pastoral Ministry and Counseling	M
Public Administration	M
Religion	M

WAYNESBURG UNIVERSITY

Addictions/Substance Abuse Counseling	M,D
Clinical Psychology	M,D
Counseling Psychology	M,D

WAYNE STATE COLLEGE

Communication—General	M

WAYNE STATE UNIVERSITY

Addictions/Substance Abuse Counseling	O
Anthropology	M,D
Applied Arts and Design—General	M
Art History	M
Art/Fine Arts	M
Child and Family Studies	O
Classics	M
Clinical Psychology	M,D,O
Cognitive Sciences	M,D
Communication—General	M,D
Comparative Literature	M
Conflict Resolution and Mediation/Peace Studies	M,O
Corporate and Organizational Communication	M,D
Criminal Justice and Criminology	M
Developmental Psychology	M,D
Economic Development	O
Economics	M,D,O
English	M,D
French	M
Geography	M
German	M,D
Gerontology	O
History	M,D
Human Development	M
Industrial and Labor Relations	M
Industrial and Organizational Psychology	M,D
Italian	M
Linguistics	M
Media Studies	M,D
Music	M,O
Near and Middle Eastern Studies	M
Philosophy	M,D
Political Science	M,D
Psychology—General	M,D
Public Administration	M
Rehabilitation Counseling	M,D,O
Russian	M,D
School Psychology	M,D,O
Sociology	M,D
Spanish	M
Speech and Interpersonal Communication	M,D
Sustainable Development	O
Theater	M,D
Urban and Regional Planning	M
Writing	M,D

WEBBER INTERNATIONAL UNIVERSITY

Criminal Justice and Criminology	M

*M—master's degree; P—first professional degree; D—doctorate; O—other advanced degree; *—Close-Up and/or Display*

WEBER STATE UNIVERSITY

English M

WEBSTER UNIVERSITY

Art/Fine Arts M
Arts Administration M
Communication—General M
Corporate and Organizational Communication M
Counseling Psychology M
Criminal Justice and Criminology M,D,O
Gerontology M
International Affairs M
Media Studies M
Music M
Public Administration M,D,O

WENTWORTH INSTITUTE OF TECHNOLOGY

Architecture M

WESLEYAN UNIVERSITY

Liberal Studies M,O
Music M,D

WESLEY BIBLICAL SEMINARY

Marriage and Family Therapy P,M
Missions and Missiology P,M
Pastoral Ministry and Counseling P,M
Religion P,M
Theology P,M

WESLEY THEOLOGICAL SEMINARY

Theology P,M,D

WEST CHESTER UNIVERSITY OF PENNSYLVANIA

Anthropology M,O
Classics M,O
Clinical Psychology M,O
Communication—General M
Criminal Justice and Criminology M
Economics M
Emergency Management M,O
English M,O
Ethics M,O
French M,O
Geographic Information Systems M,O
Geography M,O
German M,O
Gerontology M,O
Health Psychology M,O
History M,O
Holocaust and Genocide Studies M,O
Industrial and Organizational Psychology M,O
Music M,O
Philosophy M,O
Political Science M,O
Psychology—General M,O
Public Administration M,O
Public Affairs M,O
Sociology M,O
Spanish M,O
Sustainable Development M,O
Urban and Regional Planning M,O
Women's Studies M,O

WESTERN CAROLINA UNIVERSITY

Applied Arts and Design—General M
Art/Fine Arts M
English M
History M
Music M
Psychology—General M
Public Affairs M
School Psychology M
Social Psychology M

WESTERN CONNECTICUT STATE UNIVERSITY

Art/Fine Arts M
Criminal Justice and Criminology M
English M
History M
Illustration M
Social Psychology M
Writing M

WESTERN ILLINOIS UNIVERSITY

Clinical Psychology M,O
Communication—General M
Criminal Justice and Criminology M,O
Economics M,O
English M,O
Geographic Information Systems M,O
Geography M,O
Graphic Design M,O
History M
Internet and Interactive Multimedia M,O
Liberal Studies M
Museum Studies M
Music M
Political Science M,O
Psychology—General M,O
Public Administration M,O
School Psychology M,O
Social Psychology M,O
Sociology M
Sustainable Development M,O
Theater M

WESTERN INTERNATIONAL UNIVERSITY

Public Administration M

WESTERN KENTUCKY UNIVERSITY

Anthropology M
Communication—General M
Comparative Literature M
English M
Geography M
History M
Interdisciplinary Studies M
Political Science M
Psychology—General M,O
School Psychology M,O
Sociology M
Writing M

WESTERN MICHIGAN UNIVERSITY

Anthropology M
Applied Arts and Design—General M
Applied Economics M,D
Clinical Psychology M,D
Communication—General M
Corporate and Organizational Communication M
Counseling Psychology M,D
Economics M,D
English M,D
Experimental Psychology M,D
Family and Consumer Sciences-General M
Geography M,O
Graphic Design M
History M,D
Industrial and Organizational Psychology M,D
Marriage and Family Therapy M,D
Medieval and Renaissance Studies M
Music M
Philosophy M
Political Science M,D
Psychology—General M,D
Public Administration M,D,O
Public Affairs M,D,O
Rehabilitation Counseling M
Religion M
Sociology M,D
Spanish M,D
Therapies—Dance, Drama, and Music M
Writing M,D

WESTERN NEW ENGLAND COLLEGE

Psychology—General D,O

WESTERN NEW MEXICO UNIVERSITY

Interdisciplinary Studies M
School Psychology M

WESTERN OREGON UNIVERSITY

Criminal Justice and Criminology M
Music M
Rehabilitation Counseling M

WESTERN SEMINARY

Pastoral Ministry and Counseling P,M,D,O
Religion M,O
Theology M,D,O
Women's Studies M

WESTERN SEMINARY–SACRAMENTO CAMPUS

Marriage and Family Therapy P,M
Pastoral Ministry and Counseling P,M
Theology P,M

WESTERN SEMINARY–SAN JOSE CAMPUS

Marriage and Family Therapy P,M
Pastoral Ministry and Counseling P,M
Theology P,M

WESTERN THEOLOGICAL SEMINARY

Theology P,M,D

WESTERN WASHINGTON UNIVERSITY

Anthropology M
Counseling Psychology M
English M
Experimental Psychology M
Geography M
History M
Music M
Political Science M
Psychology—General M
Rehabilitation Counseling M

WESTFIELD STATE COLLEGE

Counseling Psychology M
Criminal Justice and Criminology M
English M
History M
Psychology—General M

WESTMINSTER CHOIR COLLEGE OF RIDER UNIVERSITY

Music M

WESTMINSTER COLLEGE (UT)

Communication—General M
Counseling Psychology M
Writing M

WESTMINSTER SEMINARY CALIFORNIA

Religion P,M
Theology P,M

WESTMINSTER THEOLOGICAL SEMINARY

Missions and Missiology P,M,D,O
Pastoral Ministry and Counseling P,M,D,O
Religion P,M,D,O
Theology P,M,D,O

WEST TEXAS A&M UNIVERSITY

Agricultural Economics and Agribusiness M
Art/Fine Arts M
Communication—General M
Criminal Justice and Criminology M
Economics M
English M
History M
Interdisciplinary Studies M
Music M
Political Science M
Psychology—General M

WEST VIRGINIA STATE UNIVERSITY

Media Studies M

WEST VIRGINIA UNIVERSITY

African Studies M,D
African-American Studies M,D
Agricultural Economics and Agribusiness M
American Studies M,D
Applied Social Research M
Art History M
Art/Fine Arts M
Asian Studies M,D
Child and Family Studies M
Clinical Psychology M,D
Communication—General M,D
Corporate and Organizational Communication M,D,O
Counseling Psychology D

Developmental Psychology	M,D
Economic Development	M,D
Economics	M,D
English	M,D
Forensic Sciences	M,D
French	M
Geographic Information Systems	M,D
Geography	M,D
Graphic Design	M
History of Science and Technology	M,D
History	M,D
Human Development	M,D
Industrial and Labor Relations	M
International Affairs	M,D
International Economics	M,D
Journalism	M,O
Latin American Studies	M,D
Liberal Studies	M
Linguistics	M
Music	M,D
Political Science	M,D
Psychology—General	M,D
Public Administration	M
Public Policy	M,D
Rehabilitation Counseling	M
Sociology	M
Spanish	M
Sport Psychology	M,D
Sustainable Development	D
Theater	M
Urban and Regional Planning	M,D
Writing	M

WHEATON COLLEGE

American Studies	M
Archaeology	M
Clinical Psychology	M,D
Cultural Studies	M,O
Missions and Missiology	M,O
Pastoral Ministry and Counseling	M,D
Psychology—General	M,D
Religion	M
Theology	M,D

WHEELOCK COLLEGE

Child and Family Studies	M
Human Development	M

WHITTIER COLLEGE

Child Development	M

WHITWORTH UNIVERSITY

Theology	M

WICHITA STATE UNIVERSITY

Anthropology	M
Art/Fine Arts	M
Clinical Psychology	D
Communication—General	M
Criminal Justice and Criminology	M
Economics	M
English	M
Gerontology	M
History	M
Liberal Studies	M
Music	M
Psychology—General	D
Public Administration	M
School Psychology	M,O
Social Psychology	D
Sociology	M
Spanish	M
Writing	M

WIDENER UNIVERSITY

Clinical Psychology	D
Criminal Justice and Criminology	M
Liberal Studies	M
Psychology—General	
Public Administration	M

WILBERFORCE UNIVERSITY

Rehabilitation Counseling	M

WILFRID LAURIER UNIVERSITY

Archaeology	M
Classics	M
Cognitive Sciences	M,D
Communication—General	M
Cultural Studies	M
Developmental Psychology	M,D
Economics	M
English	M,D
Ethics	P,M,D,O
Film, Television, and Video Theory and Criticism	M,D
Geography	M,D
History	M,D
International Affairs	M,D
Pastoral Ministry and Counseling	P,M,D,O
Philosophy	M
Political Science	M
Psychology—General	M,D
Public Policy	M
Religion	M,D
Social Psychology	M,D
Sociology	M
Theology	P,M,D,O
Therapies—Dance, Drama, and Music	M

WILKES UNIVERSITY

Writing	M

WILLIAM CAREY UNIVERSITY

Counseling Psychology	M
Psychology—General	M

WILLIAM PATERSON UNIVERSITY OF NEW JERSEY

Art/Fine Arts	M
Clinical Psychology	M
Communication—General	M
Counseling Psychology	M
English	M
History	M
Music	M
Public Policy	M
Sociology	M

WILLIAMS COLLEGE

Art History	M

WILLIAM WOODS UNIVERSITY

Agricultural Economics and Agribusiness	M,O

WILMINGTON UNIVERSITY

Criminal Justice and Criminology	M
Gerontology	M
Homeland Security	M
Internet and Interactive Multimedia	M
Public Administration	M
Social Psychology	M

WINEBRENNER THEOLOGICAL SEMINARY

Theology	P,M,D

WINONA STATE UNIVERSITY

English	M

WINSTON-SALEM STATE UNIVERSITY

Rehabilitation Counseling	M

WINTHROP UNIVERSITY

Art/Fine Arts	M
Arts Administration	M
English	M
History	M
Liberal Studies	M
Music	M
Psychology—General	M,O
Spanish	M

WISCONSIN SCHOOL OF PROFESSIONAL PSYCHOLOGY

Clinical Psychology	M,D
Psychology—General	M,D

WOODBURY UNIVERSITY

Architecture	M

WORCESTER POLYTECHNIC INSTITUTE

Interdisciplinary Studies	M,D,O
Social Sciences	M,D,O

WORCESTER STATE COLLEGE

History	M
School Psychology	M,O
Spanish	M

WRIGHT INSTITUTE

Clinical Psychology	M,D
Counseling Psychology	M,D
Psychology—General	M,D

WRIGHT STATE UNIVERSITY

Applied Economics	M
Clinical Psychology	D
Criminal Justice and Criminology	M
Economics	M
English	M
History	M
Humanities	M
Industrial and Organizational Psychology	M,D
Interdisciplinary Studies	M
Music	M
Psychology—General	M,D
Public Administration	M
Rehabilitation Counseling	M
Rhetoric	M
Urban Studies	M
Writing	M

WYCLIFFE COLLEGE

Religion	P,M,D,O
Theology	P,M,D,O

XAVIER UNIVERSITY

Clinical Psychology	M,D
Criminal Justice and Criminology	M
English	M
Experimental Psychology	M,D
Industrial and Organizational Psychology	M,D
Pastoral Ministry and Counseling	M
Psychology—General	M,D
Theology	M

XAVIER UNIVERSITY OF LOUISIANA

Pastoral Ministry and Counseling	M
Theology	M

YALE UNIVERSITY

African Studies	M
African-American Studies	D
American Studies	D
Anthropology	M,D
Applied Arts and Design—General	M
Archaeology	M,D
Architecture	M,D
Art History	D
Art/Fine Arts	M
Asian Languages	D
Asian Studies	M
Classics	M,D
Clinical Psychology	D
Cognitive Sciences	D
Comparative Literature	D
Developmental Psychology	D
East European and Russian Studies	M,D
Economic Development	M
Economics	M,D
English	M,D
Environmental Design	M,D
Film, Television, and Video Theory and Criticism	D
French	M,D
German	D
Graphic Design	M
History of Medicine	M,D
History of Science and Technology	M,D
History	M,D
International Affairs	M
International Economics	M
Italian	D
Latin American Studies	D
Linguistics	D
Medieval and Renaissance Studies	M,D
Music	M,D,O
Near and Middle Eastern Languages	M,D
Near and Middle Eastern Studies	M,D
Philosophy	D
Photography	M
Political Science	D
Portuguese	D
Psychology—General	D
Religion	D
Russian	D
Slavic Languages	D
Social Psychology	D
Social Sciences	M,D
Sociology	D
Spanish	D
Theater	M,D,O
Theology	P,M

YESHIVA BETH MOSHE

Theology	O

YESHIVA DERECH CHAIM

Religion	D

*M—master's degree; P—first professional degree; D—doctorate; O—other advanced degree; *—Close-Up and/or Display*

YESHIVA KARLIN STOLIN RABBINICAL INSTITUTE

Theology	O

YESHIVA OF NITRA RABBINICAL COLLEGE

Theology	

YESHIVA SHAAR HATORAH TALMUDIC RESEARCH INSTITUTE

Theology	

YESHIVATH ZICHRON MOSHE

Theology	O

YESHIVA TORAS CHAIM TALMUDICAL SEMINARY

Theology	

YESHIVA UNIVERSITY

Clinical Psychology	D
Counseling Psychology	M
Health Psychology	D
Jewish Studies	M,D
Psychology—General	M,D
School Psychology	D

YORK UNIVERSITY

Anthropology	M,D
Applied Arts and Design—General	M
Art History	M,D
Art/Fine Arts	M,D
Communication—General	M,D
Dance	M
Disability Studies	M,D
Economics	M,D
Emergency Management	M
English	M,D
Film, Television, and Video Production	M,D
French	M
Geography	M,D
History	M,D
Humanities	M,D
Interdisciplinary Studies	M
International Affairs	M
Linguistics	M,D
Music	M,D
Philosophy	M,D
Political Science	M,D
Psychology—General	M,D
Public Administration	M,D
Public Affairs	M
Public Policy	M
Social Sciences	M
Sociology	M,D
Theater	M,D
Translation and Interpretation	M
Women's Studies	M,D

YOUNGSTOWN STATE UNIVERSITY

Counseling Psychology	M
Criminal Justice and Criminology	M
Economics	M
English	M
History	M
Music	M
Psychology—General	M
School Psychology	M

ACADEMIC AND PROFESSIONAL PROGRAMS IN ARTS AND ARCHITECTURE

Section 1
Applied Arts and Design

This section contains a directory of institutions offering graduate work in applied arts and design, followed by in-depth entries submitted by institutions that chose to prepare detailed program descriptions. Additional information about programs listed in the directory but not augmented by an in-depth entry may be obtained by writing directly to the dean of a graduate school or chair of a department at the address given in the directory.

For programs offering related work, see also in this book *Architecture* and *Art and Art History*. In another guide in this series:

Graduate Programs in Business, Education, Health, Information Studies, Law & Social Work

See *Advertising and Public Relations*

CONTENTS

Program Directories

Applied Arts and Design—General 86
Computer Art and Design 90
Graphic Design 95
Illustration 99
Industrial Design 100
Interior Design 101
Medical Illustration 105
Photography 105
Textile Design 110

Close-Ups

Art Center College of Design 113
Fashion Institute of Technology 115
Miami International University of Art & Design 117
Pratt Institute 119

See also:

Columbia University—Film, Theater Arts, Visual Arts, and Writing 261
Memphis College of Art—Studio Practice and Art Education 195
Syracuse University—Communications 683
The University of the Arts—Graduate Studies 199

Applied Arts and Design—General

Academy of Art University, Graduate Program, School of Advertising, San Francisco, CA 94105-3410. Offers MFA. Part-time programs available. Postbaccalaureate distance learning degree programs offered (no on-campus study). *Degree requirements:* For master's, thesis, final review. *Entrance requirements:* For master's, minimum GPA of 3.0, portfolio. Electronic applications accepted.

Alfred University, Graduate School, New York State College of Ceramics, School of Art and Design, Alfred, NY 14802-1205. Offers ceramic art (MFA); electronic integrated arts (MFA); glass art (MFA); sculpture (MFA). *Accreditation:* NASAD. *Degree requirements:* For master's, exhibit. *Entrance requirements:* For master's, portfolio. Additional exam requirements/recommendations for international students: Required—TOEFL (minimum score 550 paper-based; 213 computer-based; 80 iBT), IELTS (minimum score 6). Electronic applications accepted. *Expenses:* Tuition: Full-time $33,296; part-time $708 per credit hour. Required fees: $880; $144 per year. Full-time tuition and fees vary according to program. *Faculty research:* Ceramic sculpture, functional ceramics, wood, mixed media, hot and cold glass.

Arizona State University, Graduate College, College of Design, Program in Design, Tempe, AZ 85287. Offers arts/media/engineering (MSD); healthcare and healing environments (MSD); industrial design (MSD); interaction design (MSD); interior design (MSD); new product innovation (MSD); visual communication design (MSD). *Accreditation:* NASAD. *Degree requirements:* For master's, thesis optional. *Entrance requirements:* For master's, GRE General Test, design portfolio.

Art Center College of Design, Graduate Division, Pasadena, CA 91103. Offers MFA, MS. *Accreditation:* NASAD. *Faculty:* 15 full-time (4 women), 26 part-time/adjunct (17 women). *Students:* 135 full-time (53 women), 38 part-time (16 women); includes 38 minority (3 African Americans, 2 American Indian/Alaska Native, 29 Asian Americans or Pacific Islanders, 4 Hispanic Americans), 42 international. Average age 28. 251 applicants, 39% accepted, 45 enrolled. In 2009, 36 master's awarded. *Degree requirements:* For master's, thesis, studio project. *Entrance requirements:* For master's, portfolio. Additional exam requirements/recommendations for international students: Required—TOEFL (minimum score 100 iBT). *Application deadline:* For fall admission, 2/1 priority date for domestic and international students; for spring admission, 10/1 priority date for domestic and international students. Applications are processed on a rolling basis. *Expenses:* Tuition: Full-time $16,737. *Financial support:* In 2009–10, 149 students received support; teaching assistantships, career-related internships or fieldwork, Federal Work-Study, and scholarships/grants available. Financial award application deadline: 3/1. *Faculty research:* Computer graphics, automobile aerodynamics. *Unit head:* Kit Barron, VP of Admission and Enrollment Services. *Application contact:* Kit Barron, VP of Admission and Enrollment Services.

See Close-Up on page 113.

Bowling Green State University, Graduate College, College of Arts and Sciences, School of Art, Bowling Green, OH 43403. Offers 2-D studio art (MA, MFA); 3-D studio art (MA, MFA); art education (MA); art history (MA); computer art (MA); design (MFA); digital arts (MFA); graphics (MFA). *Accreditation:* NASAD. Part-time programs available. *Degree requirements:* For master's, thesis or alternative, final exhibit (MFA). *Entrance requirements:* For master's, GRE General Test (MA), slide portfolio (15-20 slides). Additional exam requirements/recommendations for international students: Required—TOEFL. Electronic applications accepted. *Faculty research:* Computer animation and virtual reality, Spanish still-life painting from 1600 to 1800, art and psychotherapy, Japanese wood-firing techniques in ceramics, non-toxic printmaking technologies.

Bradley University, Graduate School, Slane College of Communications and Fine Arts, Department of Art, Peoria, IL 61625-0002. Offers ceramics (MA, MFA); drawing/illustration (MA, MFA); interdisciplinary art (MA, MFA); painting (MA, MFA); photography (MA, MFA); printmaking (MA, MFA); sculpture (MA, MFA); visual communication and design (MA, MFA). *Accreditation:* NASAD. Part-time programs available. *Degree requirements:* For master's, comprehensive exam, thesis, final exhibit. *Entrance requirements:* For master's, portfolio, 2 letters of recommendation. Additional exam requirements/recommendations for international students: Required—TOEFL (minimum score 550 paper-based; 213 computer-based; 79 iBT).

California College of the Arts, Graduate Programs, Program in Design, San Francisco, CA 94107. Offers MFA. *Degree requirements:* For master's, thesis, exhibit. *Entrance requirements:* For master's, appropriate bachelor's degree, portfolio, resume, letters of recommendation. Additional exam requirements/recommendations for international students: Required—TOEFL (minimum score 600 paper-based; 250 computer-based). Electronic applications accepted.

California College of the Arts, Graduate Programs, Program in Design Strategy, San Francisco, CA 94107. Offers MBA.

California Institute of the Arts, School of Art, Valencia, CA 91355-2340. Offers art (MFA, Adv C); graphic design (MFA, Adv C); photography (MFA, Adv C). *Accreditation:* NASAD (one or more programs are accredited). *Degree requirements:* For master's, final project. *Entrance requirements:* For master's, portfolio. Additional exam requirements/recommendations for international students: Required—TOEFL. Electronic applications accepted.

California State University, Fresno, Division of Graduate Studies, College of Arts and Humanities, Department of Art and Design, Fresno, CA 93740-8027. Offers art (MA). Part-time and evening/weekend programs available. *Degree requirements:* For master's, thesis or alternative. *Entrance requirements:* For master's, GRE General Test, minimum GPA of 3.0, portfolio. Additional exam requirements/recommendations for international students: Required—TOEFL. Electronic applications accepted. *Faculty research:* Art history, graphic design, studio art.

California State University, Fullerton, Graduate Studies, College of the Arts, Department of Art, Fullerton, CA 92834-9480. Offers art (MA, MFA), including ceramics (MFA), crafts, creative photography (MFA), design (MFA), drawing and painting, printmaking (MFA), sculpture; art history (MA); design (MA). *Accreditation:* NASAD (one or more programs are accredited). Part-time programs available. *Students:* 47 full-time (29 women), 38 part-time (23 women); includes 24 minority (2 African Americans, 12 Asian Americans or Pacific Islanders, 10 Hispanic Americans), 10 international. Average age 34. 76 applicants, 28% accepted, 19 enrolled. In 2009, 20 master's awarded. *Degree requirements:* For master's, project or thesis. *Entrance requirements:* For master's, minimum GPA of 2.5 in last 60 units of course work, portfolio. Application fee: $55. *Expenses:* Tuition, nonresident: full-time $11,160; part-time $373 per credit. Required fees: $1440 per term. Tuition and fees vary according to course load, degree level and program. *Financial support:* Career-related internships or fieldwork, Federal Work-Study, institutionally sponsored loans, and scholarships/grants available. Support available to part-time students. Financial award application deadline: 3/1; financial award applicants required to submit FAFSA. *Unit head:* Larry Johnson, Chair, 657-278-3471. *Application contact:* Admissions/Applications, 657-278-2371.

California State University, Los Angeles, Graduate Studies, College of Arts and Letters, Department of Art, Los Angeles, CA 90032-8530. Offers art (MA), including art education, art history, art therapy, ceramics, metals, and textiles, design (MA, MFA), painting, sculpture, and graphic arts, photography; fine arts (MFA), including crafts, design (MA, MFA), studio arts. *Accreditation:* NASAD (one or more programs are accredited). Part-time and evening/weekend programs available. *Faculty:* 12 full-time (6 women), 1 part-time/adjunct (0 women). *Students:* 28 full-time (21 women), 40 part-time (28 women); includes 22 minority (1 African American, 6 Asian Americans or Pacific Islanders, 15 Hispanic Americans), 9 international. Average age 37. 30 applicants, 100% accepted, 12 enrolled. In 2009, 17 master's awarded. *Degree requirements:* For master's, comprehensive exam, project or thesis. *Entrance requirements:* For master's, portfolio. Additional exam requirements/recommendations for international students: Required—TOEFL (minimum score 500 paper-based; 173 computer-based). *Application deadline:* For fall admission, 5/1 for domestic and international students. Applications are processed on a rolling basis. Application fee: $55. Electronic applications accepted. *Financial support:* Federal Work-Study available. Support available to part-time students. Financial award application deadline: 3/1. *Faculty research:* The artist and the book, conceptual art, ceramic processes, computer graphics, architectural graphics. *Unit head:* Dr. Abbas Daneshvari, Chair, 323-343-4010, Fax: 323-343-4045, E-mail: adanesh@calstatela.edu. *Application contact:* Dr. Cheryl L. Ney, Associate Vice President for Academic Affairs and Dean of Graduate Studies, 323-343-3820, Fax: 323-343-5653, E-mail: cney@cslanet.calstatela.edu.

Cardinal Stritch University, College of Arts and Sciences, Department of Art, Milwaukee, WI 53217-3985. Offers visual studies (MA). Part-time and evening/weekend programs available. *Degree requirements:* For master's, thesis, portfolio, exhibit. *Entrance requirements:* For master's, minimum GPA of 2.75; 3 letters of recommendation.

Carnegie Mellon University, College of Fine Arts, School of Design, Program in Design, Pittsburgh, PA 15213-3891. Offers PhD. *Accreditation:* NASAD. *Degree requirements:* For doctorate, one foreign language, comprehensive exam, thesis/dissertation. *Entrance requirements:* For doctorate, GRE, portfolio of relevant work. Additional exam requirements/recommendations for international students: Required—TOEFL (minimum score 600 paper-based; 250 computer-based). *Faculty research:* Design theory, typography and information design, new product development, organizational behavior, interaction design.

Concordia University, School of Graduate Studies, Faculty of Fine Arts, Department of Design and Computation Arts, Montréal, QC H3G 1M8, Canada. Offers digital technologies in design art practice (Certificate).

Cranbrook Academy of Art, Graduate School, Program in Fine Arts, Bloomfield Hills, MI 48303-0801. Offers ceramics (MFA); design (MFA), including graphic design; fiber arts (MFA); metalsmithing (MFA); painting (MFA); photography (MFA); printmaking (MFA); sculpture (MFA). *Accreditation:* NASAD. *Degree requirements:* For master's, thesis, exhibit. *Entrance requirements:* Additional exam requirements/recommendations for international students: Required—TOEFL (minimum score 550 paper-based; 213 computer-based).

Drexel University, Antoinette Westphal College of Media Arts and Design, Philadelphia, PA 19104-2875. Offers arts administration (MS); digital media (MS); fashion design (MS); interior architecture and design (MS); television management (MS); MS/MBA. *Accreditation:* NASAD. Part-time and evening/weekend programs available. *Entrance requirements:* For master's, interview. Additional exam requirements/recommendations for international students: Required—TOEFL. Electronic applications accepted. *Expenses:* Contact institution.

Emily Carr Institute of Art + Design, Program in Applied Arts, Vancouver, BC V6H 3R9, Canada. Offers design (MAA); media arts (MAA); visual arts (MAA). *Degree requirements:* For master's, internship, thesis project. *Entrance requirements:* For master's, minimum overall GPA of 3.0, visual portfolio, 3 letters of recommendation. Additional exam requirements/recommendations for international students: Required—TOEFL (minimum score 570 paper-based; 230 computer-based; 84 iBT), IELTS (minimum score 6.5), Michigan English Language Assessment Battery (minimum score 81). *Application deadline:* For fall admission, 1/15 for domestic students. Application fee: $75 Canadian dollars. Electronic applications accepted. Tuition and fees charges are reported in Canadian dollars. *Expenses:* Tuition, state resident: full-time $11,355 Canadian dollars. Tuition, nonresident: full-time $11,355 Canadian dollars. Required fees: $134.70 Canadian dollars. *Unit head:* Renee Van Halm, Interim Dean, Graduate Studies and Research, E-mail: masters@ecuad.ca. *Application contact:* Graduate Studies Contact, 604-844-3850.

Fashion Institute of Technology, School of Graduate Studies, New York, NY 10001-5992. Offers MA, MPS. *Accreditation:* NASAD. Part-time and evening/weekend programs available. *Faculty:* 8 full-time (6 women), 60 part-time/adjunct (34 women). *Students:* 127 full-time (110 women), 79 part-time (71 women); includes 21 minority (5 African Americans, 1 American Indian/Alaska Native, 6 Asian Americans or Pacific Islanders, 9 Hispanic Americans), 39 international. Average age 30. 368 applicants, 36% accepted, 105 enrolled. In 2009, 76 master's awarded. *Degree requirements:* For master's, one foreign language, thesis, internship. *Entrance requirements:* For master's, GRE or GMAT, portfolio, letters of recommendation, resume. Additional exam requirements/recommendations for international students: Required—TOEFL (minimum score 550 paper-based; 213 computer-based). *Application deadline:* For fall admission, 1/15 priority date for domestic and international students. Applications are processed on a rolling basis. Application fee: $50. Electronic applications accepted. *Expenses:* Tuition, state resident: full-time $8198; part-time $342 per credit. Tuition, nonresident: full-time $12,972; part-time $541 per credit. Required fees: $450. *Financial support:* In 2009–10, 68 students received support. Federal Work-Study and scholarships/grants available. Financial award applicants required to submit FAFSA. *Faculty research:* Fashion history, material conservation, international marketing and global sourcing, sustainable economic development, luxury braiding in China. *Unit head:* Dr. Reginetta Haboucha, Acting Dean, 212-217-4300, Fax: 212-217-5156. *Application contact:* Carole deSantis, Administrative Secretary, Graduate Admissions, 212-217-4314, Fax: 212-217-5156, E-mail: carole_desantis@fitnyc.edu.

See Close-Up on page 115.

Ferris State University, Kendall College of Art and Design, Big Rapids, MI 49307. Offers MFA. *Accreditation:* NASAD. Part-time programs available. *Faculty:* 13 full-time (9 women). *Students:* 27 full-time (16 women), 26 part-time (18 women); includes 4 minority (3 African Americans, 1 Asian American or Pacific Islander). Average age 33. 29 applicants, 45% accepted, 13 enrolled. In 2009, 12 master's awarded. *Degree requirements:* For master's, thesis, seminars. *Entrance requirements:* For master's, portfolio, 3 letters of recommendation, curriculum vitae. Additional exam requirements/recommendations for international students: Required—TOEFL (minimum score 500 paper-based; 173 computer-based; 61 iBT). *Application deadline:* For fall admission, 2/15 priority date for domestic and international students; for spring admission, 11/1 priority date for domestic and international students. Applications are processed on a rolling basis. Application fee: $30. *Financial support:* In 2009–10, 26 students received support, including 4 fellowships (averaging $8,530 per year); unspecified assistantships and half-tuition scholarships ($6317 average), graduate assistantships ($5309 average) also available. Financial award application deadline: 2/15; financial award applicants required to submit FAFSA. *Unit head:* Dr. Oliver H. Evans, President and Vice Chancellor, 616-451-2787. *Application contact:* Sandra Britton, Director of Enrollment Management, 616-451-2787, Fax: 616-836-9689, E-mail: brittons@ferris.edu.

Florida Atlantic University, Dorothy F. Schmidt College of Arts and Letters, Department of Visual Arts and Art History, Boca Raton, FL 33431-0991. Offers art education (MAT); ceramics (MFA); computer art (MFA); graphic design (MFA); painting (MFA). *Faculty:* 23 full-time (12 women), 17 part-time/adjunct (11 women). *Students:* 15 full-time (11 women), 11 part-time (6 women); includes 7 minority (1 African American, 6 Hispanic Americans), 3 international. Average age 31. 19 applicants, 21% accepted, 0 enrolled. In 2009, 5 master's awarded. *Degree requirements:* For master's, one foreign language, project. *Entrance requirements:* For master's, GRE General Test, minimum GPA of 3.0 during last 60 hours of course work, slide portfolio. *Application deadline:* For fall admission, 2/21 for domestic and international students; for spring admission, 10/1 for domestic and international students. Application fee: $30. Electronic applications accepted. *Expenses:* Tuition, state resident: full-time $7055; part-time $293.94 per credit hour. Tuition, nonresident: full-time $22,096; part-time $920.66 per credit hour. *Financial support:* Research assistantships with full tuition reimbursements, teaching assistantships with full tuition reimbursements, career-related internships or fieldwork, Federal Work-Study, and institutionally sponsored loans available. Financial award applicants required to submit FAFSA. *Faculty research:* Painting, ceramics (traditional and non-traditional), installation, video and interactive sculpture. *Unit head:* Dr. Linda Johnson, Chair, 561-297-3870, Fax: 561-297-3078, E-mail: ljohnson@fau.edu. *Application contact:* James A. Novak, Associate Professor/Graduate Coordinator/Advisor, 561-297-2430, Fax: 561-297-3078, E-mail: jnovak@fau.edu.

Howard University, Graduate School, Division of Fine Arts, Department of Art, Program in Fine Arts, Washington, DC 20059-0002. Offers 3D reality (sculpture and ceramics) (MFA); design (MFA); electronic studio (MFA); painting (MFA); photography (MFA). *Accreditation:* NASAD. *Degree requirements:* For master's, comprehensive exam, thesis, exhibit. *Entrance requirements:* For master's, minimum GPA of 3.0, portfolio.

Illinois Institute of Technology, Graduate College, Institute of Design, Chicago, IL 60616-3793. Offers M Des, MDM, PhD, M Des/MBA. Part-time programs available. *Faculty:* 10 full-time (1 woman), 11 part-time/adjunct (1 woman). *Students:* 118 full-time (57 women), 24 part-time (14 women); includes 24 minority (3 African Americans, 3 American Indian/Alaska Native, 17 Asian Americans or Pacific Islanders, 1 Hispanic American), 44 international. Average age 30. 180 applicants, 66% accepted, 51 enrolled. In 2009, 56 master's, 1 doctorate awarded. Terminal master's awarded for partial completion of doctoral program. *Degree requirements:* For master's, comprehensive exam; for doctorate, 2 foreign languages, comprehensive exam, thesis/dissertation. *Entrance requirements:* For master's, GRE General Test or GMAT (for MDes/MBA), Bachelor's Degree, min GPA of 3.0, official transcripts, portfolio, prior work experience, 3 letters of recommendation from professional contacts, statement of education and career goals, interview; for doctorate, GRE General Test, Master's Degree, official transcripts, portfolio, 2-5 years of work experience, 3 letters of recommendation, statement of research interests, interview. Additional exam requirements/recommendations for international students: Required—TOEFL (minimum score 600 paper-based; 100 iBT). *Application deadline:* For fall admission, 2/15 priority date for domestic students, 2/15 for international students; for spring admission, 10/15 priority date for domestic students, 9/15 for international students. Application fee: $75. *Expenses:* Contact institution. *Financial support:* In 2009–10, fellowships (averaging $5,400 per year), research assistantships (averaging $10,000 per year), teaching assistantships (averaging $10,000 per year) were awarded; career-related internships or fieldwork, Federal Work-Study, institutionally sponsored loans, scholarships/grants, health care benefits, and unspecified assistantships also available. Support available to part-time students. Financial award applicants required to submit FAFSA. *Faculty research:* Design planning, human-centered design, new product definition, interactive systems, context-sensitive design. *Unit head:* Patrick Whitney, Dean, 312-595-4900, Fax: 312-595-4901, E-mail: patrick.whitney@iit.edu. *Application contact:* Rachel Dean, Director of Admissions and Retention, 312-595-4906, Fax: 312-596-4901, E-mail: rdean@id.iit.edu.

Indiana University–Purdue University Indianapolis, Herron School of Art and Design, Indianapolis, IN 46202-2896. Offers art education (MAE); furniture design (MFA); printmaking (MFA); sculpture (MFA); visual communication (MFA). Part-time and evening/weekend programs available. *Faculty:* 2 full-time (both women). *Students:* 36 full-time (21 women), 11 part-time (all women); includes 6 minority (2 Asian Americans or Pacific Islanders, 4 Hispanic Americans), 6 international. Average age 31. 60 applicants, 60% accepted, 20 enrolled. In 2009, 1 master's awarded. *Entrance requirements:* For master's, portfolio, 44 hours of course work in art history and studio art. *Application deadline:* For fall admission, 6/1 priority date for domestic students, 3/15 priority date for international students; for spring admission, 11/1 priority date for domestic students, 10/15 priority date for international students. Applications are processed on a rolling basis. Application fee: $55 ($65 for international students). Electronic applications accepted. *Financial support:* Career-related internships or fieldwork, Federal Work-Study, institutionally sponsored loans, scholarships/grants, and tuition waivers (partial) available. Support available to part-time students. Total annual research expenditures: $6,097. *Unit head:* Valerie Eickmeier, Dean, 317-278-9470, Fax: 317-278-9471, E-mail: herron@iupui.edu. *Application contact:* Herron Student Services Office, 317-378-9400, E-mail: herrart@iupui.edu.

Iowa State University of Science and Technology, Graduate College, College of Design, Department of Art and Design, Ames, IA 50011. Offers art and design (MA); graphic design (MFA); integrated visual arts (MFA); interior design (MFA). Part-time programs available. *Faculty:* 34 full-time (20 women), 1 (woman) part-time/adjunct. *Students:* 44 full-time (35 women), 9 part-time (6 women); includes 2 minority (1 African American, 1 Asian American or Pacific Islander), 14 international. 27 applicants, 63% accepted, 10 enrolled. In 2009, 11 master's awarded. *Degree requirements:* For master's, thesis (for some programs). *Entrance requirements:* For master's, GRE General Test, resume, supplemental departmental form. Additional exam requirements/recommendations for international students: Required—TOEFL (minimum score 550 paper-based; 79 iBT) or IELTS (minimum score 6.5). *Application deadline:* For fall admission, 5/1 priority date for domestic and international students. Applications are processed on a rolling basis. Application fee: $40 ($90 for international students). Electronic applications accepted. *Expenses:* Tuition, state resident: full-time $6716. Tuition, nonresident: full-time $8908. Tuition and fees vary according to course level, course load, program and student level. *Financial support:* In 2009–10, 19 research assistantships with full and partial tuition reimbursements (averaging $7,850 per year) were awarded; teaching assistantships with full and partial tuition reimbursements, career-related internships or fieldwork, Federal Work-Study, institutionally sponsored loans, and tuition waivers (partial) also available. Support available to part-time students. Financial award application deadline: 2/15; financial award applicants required to submit FAFSA. *Faculty research:* Computer applications, fire safety, human factors in design, art and design education, fine arts, craft design. *Unit head:* Roger Baer, Chair, 515-294-6724, Fax: 515-294-2725, E-mail: artdn@iastate.edu. *Application contact:* Roger Baer, Chair, 515-294-6724, Fax: 515-294-2725, E-mail: artdn@iastate.edu.

Kansas State University, Graduate School, College of Human Ecology, Department of Apparel, Textiles, and Interior Design, Manhattan, KS 66506. Offers design (MS); general apparel and textile (MS); marketing (MS); merchandising (MS); product development (MS). *Faculty:* 10 full-time (8 women), 1 (woman) part-time/adjunct. *Students:* 7 full-time (5 women), 15 part-time (12 women); includes 3 minority (1 African American, 1 Asian American or Pacific Islander, 1 Hispanic American). Average age 29. 13 applicants, 85% accepted, 7 enrolled. In 2009, 3 master's awarded. *Degree requirements:* For master's, thesis optional, residency. *Entrance requirements:* For master's, GRE General Test, minimum undergraduate GPA of 3.0. Additional exam requirements/recommendations for international students: Required—TOEFL (minimum score 600 paper-based; 250 computer-based). *Application deadline:* For fall admission, 2/1 priority date for domestic and international students; for spring admission, 8/1 priority date for domestic and international students. Applications are processed on a rolling basis. Application fee: $40 ($55 for international students). Electronic applications accepted. *Financial support:* In 2009–10, 3 research assistantships (averaging $14,460 per year), 5 teaching assistantships with full tuition reimbursements (averaging $10,590 per year) were awarded; career-related internships or fieldwork, Federal Work-Study, institutionally sponsored loans, and scholarships/grants also available. Support available to part-time students. Financial award application deadline: 3/1; financial award applicants required to submit FAFSA. *Faculty research:* Apparel marketing and consumer behavior, protective and functional clothing and textiles, social and environmental responsibility, apparel design, new product development. Total annual research expenditures: $40,303. *Unit head:* Jana Hawley, Head, 785-532-6993, Fax: 785-532-3796, E-mail: hawleyj@ksu.edu. *Application contact:* Gina Jackson, Application Contact, 785-532-6693, Fax: 785-532-3796, E-mail: gjackson@ksu.edu.

Lamar University, College of Graduate Studies, College of Fine Arts and Communication, Department of Art, Beaumont, TX 77710. Offers art history (MA); photography (MA); studio art (MA); visual design (MA). Part-time and evening/weekend programs available. *Faculty:* 6 full-time (3 women). *Students:* 3 full-time (1 woman), 1 (woman) part-time. Average age 45. 5 applicants, 60% accepted, 3 enrolled. *Degree requirements:* For master's, thesis. *Entrance requirements:* For master's, GRE General Test, minimum GPA of 2.5 in last 60 hours of undergraduate course work. Additional exam requirements/recommendations for international students: Required—TOEFL. *Application deadline:* For fall admission, 8/1 priority date for domestic students; for spring admission, 12/1 for domestic students. Applications are processed on a rolling basis. Application fee: $25 ($50 for international students). *Financial support:* Fellowships, career-related internships or fieldwork, Federal Work-Study, and scholarships/grants available. Financial award application deadline: 4/1. *Faculty research:* Nineteenth century academic paintings, metal casting, pigment color stability, computer-modified photography, manipulated photography. *Unit head:* Donna M. Meeks, Chair, 409-880-8141, Fax: 409-880-1799, E-mail: meeksdm@lub002.lamar.edu. *Application contact:* Debbie Piper, Coordinator of Graduate Admissions, 409-880-8356, Fax: 409-880-8414, E-mail: gradmissions@hal.lamar.edu.

Louisiana State University and Agricultural and Mechanical College, Graduate School, College of Art and Design, Baton Rouge, LA 70803. Offers M Arch, MA, MFA, MLA. *Accreditation:* ASLA (one or more programs are accredited); NASAD (one or more programs are accredited). Part-time programs available. *Students:* 114 full-time (63 women), 10 part-time (5 women); includes 12 minority (4 African Americans, 6 Asian Americans or Pacific Islanders, 2 Hispanic Americans), 12 international. Average age 28. 183 applicants, 36% accepted, 38 enrolled. In 2009, 40 master's awarded. *Degree requirements:* For master's, thesis. *Entrance requirements:* For master's, GRE General Test, minimum GPA of 3.0. Additional exam requirements/recommendations for international students: Required—TOEFL (minimum score 550 paper-based; 213 computer-based; 79 iBT) or IELTS (minimum score 6.5). *Application deadline:* For fall admission, 1/25 priority date for domestic students, 5/15 for international students; for spring admission, 10/15 for international students. Applications are processed on a rolling basis. Application fee: $50 ($70 for international students). Electronic applications accepted. *Financial support:* In 2009–10, 100 students received support, including 27 research assistantships with partial tuition reimbursements available (averaging $7,470 per year), 45 teaching assistantships with partial tuition reimbursements available (averaging $6,767 per year); fellowships, career-related internships or fieldwork, Federal Work-Study, institutionally sponsored loans, scholarships/grants, health care benefits, tuition waivers (full and partial), and unspecified assistantships also available. Support available to part-time students. Financial award applicants required to submit FAFSA. *Faculty research:* Creative studio work, site design, computer applications, historic preservation, energy conservation. Total annual research expenditures: $114,998. *Unit head:* David Cronrath, Dean, 225-578-5400, Fax: 225-578-5040, E-mail: dc1@lsu.edu. *Application contact:* Theresa Mooney, Academic Counselor, 225-578-5400, Fax: 225-578-1445, E-mail: deacon1@lsu.edu.

Louisiana Tech University, Graduate School, College of Liberal Arts, School of Art, Ruston, LA 71272. Offers art and graphic design (MFA); photography (MFA); studio art (MFA). *Accreditation:* NASAD. Part-time programs available. *Degree requirements:* For master's, exhibit. *Entrance requirements:* For master's, GRE General Test, portfolio.

Massachusetts College of Art and Design, Graduate Programs, Program in Fine Arts, Boston, MA 02115-5882. Offers ceramics (MFA); design (MFA); fibers (MFA); film/video (MFA); glass (MFA); media and performing arts (MFA); metals/jewelry (MFA); painting (MFA); photography (MFA); printmaking (MFA); sculpture (MFA). *Accreditation:* NASAD. *Faculty:* 10 full-time (5 women), 8 part-time/adjunct (6 women). *Students:* 89 full-time (56 women), 12 part-time (8 women); includes 8 minority (5 Asian Americans or Pacific Islanders, 3 Hispanic Americans), 10 international. Average age 34. 295 applicants, 24% accepted, 40 enrolled. In 2009, 44 master's awarded. *Degree requirements:* For master's, thesis, exhibit. *Entrance requirements:* For master's, 12 units of course work in art history, portfolio, resume, letters of reference, interview. Additional exam requirements/recommendations for international students: Required—TOEFL (minimum score 563 paper-based; 223 computer-based; 85 iBT); Recommended—IELTS (minimum score 6.5). *Application deadline:* For fall admission, 1/15 for domestic and international students. Application fee: $75. Electronic applications accepted. *Expenses:* Tuition, state resident: full-time $18,450; part-time $615 per credit. Tuition, nonresident: full-time $18,450; part-time $615 per credit. Tuition and fees vary according to program. *Financial support:* In 2009–10, 50 research assistantships (averaging $2,000 per year), 40 teaching assistantships (averaging $2,000 per year) were awarded; career-related internships or fieldwork, Federal Work-Study, and clerical/technical assistantships ($2000) also available. Support available to part-time students. Financial award application deadline: 5/1; financial award applicants required to submit FAFSA. *Unit head:* George Creamer, Dean of Graduate Programs, 617-879-7163, Fax: 617-879-7171, E-mail: creamer@massart.edu. *Application contact:* George Creamer, Dean of Graduate Programs, 617-879-7163, Fax: 617-879-7171, E-mail: creamer@massart.edu.

Memphis College of Art, Graduate Programs, Memphis, TN 38104-2764. Offers art education (MA, MAT); computer arts (MFA); studio art (MFA). *Accreditation:* NASAD. *Faculty:* 25 full-time (13 women), 8 part-time/adjunct (6 women). *Students:* 19 full-time (12 women), 71 part-time (48 women); includes 20 minority (16 African Americans, 3 Asian Americans or Pacific Islanders, 1 Hispanic American), 1 international. Average age 31. 83 applicants, 59% accepted, 34 enrolled. In 2009, 19 master's awarded. *Degree requirements:* For master's, thesis. *Entrance requirements:* For master's, portfolio, interview, resume. Additional exam requirements/recommendations for international students: Required—TOEFL (minimum score 525 paper-based; 195 computer-based). *Application deadline:* For fall admission, 3/1 for domestic and international students; for spring admission, 11/1 for domestic and international students. Applications are processed on a rolling basis. Application fee: $50. Electronic applications accepted. *Expenses:* Tuition: Full-time $23,000; part-time $958 per credit hour. Required fees: $600; $200 per course. Tuition and fees vary according to program. *Financial support:* In 2009–10, 90 students received support. Career-related internships or fieldwork, Federal Work-Study, scholarships/grants, and unspecified assistantships available. Support available to part-time students. Financial award application deadline: 8/1; financial award applicants required to submit FAFSA. *Unit head:* Robert E. Miller, Dean of Academic Affairs, 901-272-5100, Fax: 901-272-5158, E-mail: rmiller@mca.edu. *Application contact:* Annette Moore, Dean of Admissions, 901-272-5151, Fax: 901-272-5158, E-mail: amoore@mca.edu.

See Close-Up on page 195.

Minneapolis College of Art and Design, Program in Visual Studies, Minneapolis, MN 55404-4347. Offers animation (MFA); comic art (MFA); drawing (MFA); filmmaking (MFA); fine arts (MFA); furniture design (MFA); graphic design (MFA); illustration (MFA); interactive media (MFA); painting (MFA); photography (MFA); printmaking (MFA); sculpture (MFA). *Accreditation:* NASAD. Part-time programs available. *Faculty:* 42 full-time (13 women). *Students:* 12 full-time (2 women), 18 part-time (8 women). Average age 27. 166 applicants, 28% accepted, 12 enrolled. In 2009, 10 master's awarded. *Degree requirements:* For master's, thesis, thesis exhibit. *Entrance requirements:* For master's, portfolio of visual artwork, resume, 3 letters of recommendation. Additional exam requirements/recommendations for international students: Required—TOEFL (minimum score 550 paper-based; 213 computer-based; 79 iBT). *Application deadline:* For fall admission, 1/15 for domestic and international students. Application fee: $50. Electronic applications accepted. *Expenses:* Tuition: Full-time $29,500; part-time $985 per credit. Required fees: $100. *Financial support:* In 2009–10, 23 students received support, including 15 teaching assistantships (averaging $6,000 per year); career-related internships or fieldwork, Federal Work-Study, scholarships/grants, and unspecified assistantships also available. Support available to part-time students. Financial award application deadline: 3/15; financial award applicants required to submit FAFSA. *Faculty research:* Visual arts: animation, comic art, drawing, filmmaking, furniture design, graphic design, illustration, interactive media, painting, photography, printmaking, sculpture. *Unit head:* Carole Fisher, Graduate Director, 612-874-3629, E-mail: carole_fisher@mcad.edu. *Application contact:* William Mullen, Vice President of Enrollment Management, 612-874-3760, Fax: 612-874-3701, E-mail: william_mullen@mcad.edu.

New Mexico State University, Graduate School, College of Arts and Sciences, Department of Art, Las Cruces, NM 88003-8001. Offers art history (MA); ceramics (MA, MFA); design (MA, MFA); drawing (MFA); metals (MA, MFA); painting (MFA); photography (MFA); printmaking (MA, MFA); sculpture (MA, MFA). *Faculty:* 11 full-time (6 women), 2 part-time/adjunct (1 woman). *Students:* 32 full-time (15 women); includes 8 minority (2 American Indian/Alaska

Applied Arts and Design—General

New Mexico State University (continued)

Native, 6 Hispanic Americans). Average age 31. 33 applicants, 55% accepted, 7 enrolled. In 2009, 8 master's awarded. *Degree requirements:* For master's, comprehensive exam (for some programs), thesis, thesis exhibit. *Entrance requirements:* For master's, portfolio, 10-page paper (art history). *Application deadline:* For fall admission, 2/15 for domestic students; for winter admission, 10/15 for domestic students; for spring admission, 7/15 for domestic students. Application fee: $30 ($50 for international students). Electronic applications accepted. *Expenses:* Tuition, state resident: full-time $4080; part-time $223 per credit. Tuition, nonresident: full-time $14,256; part-time $647 per credit. Required fees: $1278; $639 per semester. *Financial support:* In 2009–10, 1 research assistantship (averaging $7,900 per year), 29 teaching assistantships (averaging $9,092 per year) were awarded; Federal Work-Study and health care benefits also available. Support available to part-time students. Financial award application deadline: 3/1; financial award applicants required to submit FAFSA. *Faculty research:* Painting, graphic design, sculpture, printmaking, drawing, ceramics, photography, jewelry. *Unit head:* Spencer D. Fidler, Head, 575-646-1705, Fax: 575-646-8036, E-mail: sfidler@nmsu.edu. *Application contact:* Spencer D. Fidler, Head, 575-646-1705, Fax: 575-646-8036, E-mail: sfidler@nmsu.edu.

The New School: A University, Parsons The New School for Design, Program in Transdisciplinary Design (TransDesign), New York, NY 10011. Offers MFA. *Degree requirements:* For master's, thesis. *Financial support:* Teaching assistantships available. *Unit head:* Jamer Hunt, Chair, 212-229-8950 Ext. 3152, E-mail: huntj@newschool.edu. *Application contact:* David Norris, Director of Admissions, 212-229-8989 Ext. 4023, Fax: 212-229-8975, E-mail: norrisd@newschool.edu.

New York University, Tisch School of the Arts Asia, Singapore, NY 248923, Singapore. Offers animation and digital arts (MFA); dramatic writing (MFA); film production (MFA). *Entrance requirements:* Additional exam requirements/recommendations for international students: Required—TOEFL (minimum score 610 paper-based; 250 computer-based; 105 iBT). Electronic applications accepted. *Expenses:* Tuition: Full-time $30,528; part-time $1272 per credit. Required fees: $2177.

New York University, Tisch School of the Arts, Department of Design for Stage and Film, New York, NY 10012-1019. Offers MFA. *Faculty:* 10 full-time, 11 part-time/adjunct. *Students:* 58 full-time (35 women); includes 7 minority (2 African Americans, 1 American Indian/Alaska Native, 3 Asian Americans or Pacific Islanders, 1 Hispanic American). Average age 28. 139 applicants, 22% accepted, 20 enrolled. In 2009, 20 master's awarded. *Degree requirements:* For master's, thesis. *Entrance requirements:* For master's, interview, portfolio. Additional exam requirements/recommendations for international students: Required—TOEFL (minimum score 620 paper-based; 260 computer-based; 105 iBT), IELTS. *Application deadline:* For fall admission, 1/1 priority date for domestic and international students. Application fee: $60. Electronic applications accepted. *Expenses:* Tuition: Full-time $30,528; part-time $1272 per credit. Required fees: $2177. *Financial support:* In 2009–10, 28 students received support, including 12 fellowships with full and partial tuition reimbursements available; Federal Work-Study, institutionally sponsored loans, tuition waivers (partial), and unspecified assistantships also available. Financial award application deadline: 2/15; financial award applicants required to submit FAFSA. *Unit head:* Susan Hilferty, Chair, 212-998-1950, Fax: 212-998-1953, E-mail: tisch.design@nyu.edu. *Application contact:* Dan Sandford, Director of Graduate Admissions, 212-998-1918, Fax: 212-995-4060, E-mail: tisch.gradadmissions@nyu.edu.

North Carolina State University, Graduate School, College of Design, Program in Art and Design, Raleigh, NC 27695. Offers MAD. *Degree requirements:* For master's, thesis optional. Electronic applications accepted.

North Carolina State University, Graduate School, College of Design, Program in Design, Raleigh, NC 27695. Offers PhD. *Degree requirements:* For doctorate, thesis/dissertation. *Entrance requirements:* For doctorate, GRE. Electronic applications accepted. *Faculty research:* Design and cognition, children's environments, community design, ecological design, sustainable communities and urban spatial development.

NSCAD University, Program in Fine Arts, Halifax, NS B3J 3J6, Canada. Offers craft (MFA); design (M Des); fine and media arts (MFA). *Degree requirements:* For master's, thesis, exhibit. *Entrance requirements:* For master's, portfolio, at least 5 art history classes. Additional exam requirements/recommendations for international students: Required—Michigan English Language Assessment Battery (minimum score: 80), CanTEST (minimum score: 4.5), CAEL (minimum score: 70); Recommended—TOEFL (minimum score 575 paper-based; 233 computer-based; 90 iBT), IELTS (minimum score 6.5).

Oklahoma State University, College of Human Environmental Sciences, Department of Design, Housing and Merchandising, Stillwater, OK 74078. Offers MS, PhD. *Faculty:* 16 full-time (12 women), 4 part-time/adjunct (3 women). *Students:* 11 full-time (8 women), 20 part-time (18 women); includes 3 minority (1 African American, 1 Asian American or Pacific Islander, 1 Hispanic American), 10 international. Average age 32. 23 applicants, 43% accepted, 7 enrolled. In 2009, 6 master's, 1 doctorate awarded. *Degree requirements:* For master's, thesis (for some programs); for doctorate, comprehensive exam, thesis/dissertation. *Entrance requirements:* For master's and doctorate, GRE or GMAT. Additional exam requirements/recommendations for international students: Required—TOEFL (minimum score 550 paper-based; 79 iBT). *Application deadline:* For fall admission, 3/1 priority date for international students; for spring admission, 8/1 priority date for international students. Applications are processed on a rolling basis. Application fee: $40 ($75 for international students). Electronic applications accepted. *Expenses:* Tuition, state resident: full-time $3716; part-time $154.85 per credit hour. Tuition, nonresident: full-time $14,448; part-time $602 per credit hour. Required fees: $1772; $73.85 per credit hour. One-time fee: $50. Tuition and fees vary according to course load and campus/location. *Financial support:* In 2009–10, 13 research assistantships (averaging $11,781 per year), 7 teaching assistantships (averaging $14,158 per year) were awarded; career-related internships or fieldwork, Federal Work-Study, scholarships/grants, health care benefits, tuition waivers (partial), and unspecified assistantships also available. Support available to part-time students. Financial award application deadline: 3/1; financial award applicants required to submit FAFSA. *Faculty research:* Environmental sciences design, housing and merchandising; creativity and physical environment; product development, production and evaluation; experimental learning and critical thinking; technology strategies and assessment; customer expectation and satisfaction. *Unit head:* Dr. Randall Russ, Interim Head, 405-744-5049, Fax: 405-744-6910. *Application contact:* Dr. Gordon Emslie, Dean, 405-744-6368, Fax: 405-744-0355, E-mail: grad-i@okstate.edu.

Pacific Northwest College of Art, Program in Applied Craft and Design, Portland, OR 97209. Offers MFA. Program offered in collaboration with Oregon College of Art & Craft. *Entrance requirements:* For master's, resume, 2 letters of recommendation, portfolio.

Pratt Institute, School of Art and Design, Brooklyn, NY 11205-3899. Offers MFA, MID, MPS, MS, Adv C, MS/MFA, MS/MS. *Accreditation:* NASAD (one or more programs are accredited). Part-time programs available. *Faculty:* 41 full-time (17 women), 200 part-time/adjunct (99 women). *Students:* 921 full-time (707 women), 67 part-time (51 women); includes 161 minority (36 African Americans, 72 Asian Americans or Pacific Islanders, 53 Hispanic Americans), 300 international. Average age 28. 1,724 applicants, 54% accepted, 360 enrolled. In 2009, 371 master's awarded. *Degree requirements:* For master's, thesis. *Entrance requirements:* Additional exam requirements/recommendations for international students: Required—TOEFL. *Application deadline:* For fall admission, 1/5 for domestic and international students; for spring admission, 10/1 for domestic and international students. Application fee: $50 ($90 for international students). Electronic applications accepted. *Expenses:* Tuition: Full-time $22,734. Required fees: $1280. *Financial support:* Career-related internships or fieldwork, Federal Work-Study, institutionally sponsored loans, scholarships/grants, health care benefits, and unspecified assistantships available. Support available to part-time students. Financial award application deadline: 2/1; financial award applicants required to submit FAFSA. *Faculty research:* Painting, sculpture, and printmaking; package, interior, and communications design; art therapy; graphic and industrial design; four-dimensional design. *Unit head:* Concetta Stewart, Dean, 718-636-3619. *Application contact:* Young Hah, Director of Graduate Admissions, 718-636-3683, Fax: 718-399-4242, E-mail: yhah@pratt.edu.

See Close-Up on page 119.

Purdue University, Graduate School, College of Liberal Arts, Department of Visual and Performing Arts, West Lafayette, IN 47907. Offers art and design (MA); theatre (MA, MFA). *Accreditation:* NASAD; NAST. Part-time programs available. *Degree requirements:* For master's, terminal exhibit, project, or thesis. *Entrance requirements:* Additional exam requirements/recommendations for international students: Required—TOEFL. Electronic applications accepted. *Faculty research:* Design, fine arts, photography, acting, directing, theatre technology.

Rensselaer Polytechnic Institute, Graduate School, School of Humanities and Social Sciences, Department of Science and Technology Studies, Troy, NY 12180-3590. Offers design studies (MS, PhD); policy studies (MS, PhD); science studies (MS, PhD); sustainability studies (MS, PhD); technology studies (MS, PhD). Part-time programs available. *Faculty:* 16 full-time (6 women). *Students:* 21 full-time (8 women), 3 part-time (1 woman); includes 6 Asian Americans or Pacific Islanders. Average age 27. 19 applicants, 42% accepted, 5 enrolled. In 2009, 1 master's, 9 doctorates awarded. Terminal master's awarded for partial completion of doctoral program. *Degree requirements:* For master's, thesis (for some programs); for doctorate, comprehensive exam, thesis/dissertation. *Entrance requirements:* For master's and doctorate, GRE General Test. Additional exam requirements/recommendations for international students: Required—TOEFL (minimum score 600 paper-based; 250 computer-based). *Application deadline:* For fall admission, 1/15 priority date for domestic students, 1/15 for international students. Applications are processed on a rolling basis. Application fee: $75. Electronic applications accepted. *Expenses:* Tuition: Full-time $38,100. *Financial support:* In 2009–10, 22 students received support, including 5 fellowships (averaging $22,000 per year), 1 research assistantship with full tuition reimbursement available (averaging $16,500 per year), 10 teaching assistantships with full tuition reimbursements available (averaging $16,500 per year); career-related internships or fieldwork, institutionally sponsored loans, and tuition waivers (partial) also available. Financial award application deadline: 1/15. *Faculty research:* Communities and technology, social dimensions of IT and biotechnology, ethics and policy, design. Total annual research expenditures: $75,000. *Unit head:* Dr. Sharon Anderson-Gold, Chair, 518-276-8837, Fax: 518-276-2659, E-mail: anders@rpi.edu. *Application contact:* Dr. Edward J. Woodhouse, Director of Graduate Studies, 518-276-8506, Fax: 518-276-2659, E-mail: woodhouse@rpi.edu.

Rhode Island School of Design, Graduate Studies, Providence, RI 02903-2784. Offers M Arch, MA, MAT, MFA, MIA, MID, MLA. *Accreditation:* NASAD (one or more programs are accredited). *Degree requirements:* For master's, thesis, exhibit. *Entrance requirements:* For master's, portfolio, 3 letters of recommendation. Additional exam requirements/recommendations for international students: Required—TOEFL (minimum score 580 paper-based; 237 computer-based), IELTS (minimum score 6.5). Electronic applications accepted. *Faculty research:* Ceramics, glass, graphic design, sculpture, jewelry/metalsmithing, photography, painting, industrial design, architecture.

Rutgers, The State University of New Jersey, New Brunswick, Mason Gross School of the Arts, Department of Theater Arts, Piscataway, NJ 08854-8097. Offers acting (MFA); design (MFA); directing (MFA); playwriting (MFA); stage management (MFA). *Degree requirements:* For master's, thesis (for some programs), performance project. *Entrance requirements:* For master's, audition, interview, portfolio. Electronic applications accepted. *Faculty research:* Faculty of working professional.

San Diego State University, Graduate and Research Affairs, College of Professional Studies and Fine Arts, School of Art, Design and Art History, San Diego, CA 92182. Offers art history (MA); studio arts (MA, MFA), including applied design, environmental design, graphic design, interior design, painting and printmaking, sculpture. *Accreditation:* NASAD (one or more programs are accredited). *Degree requirements:* For master's, variable foreign language requirement, thesis. *Entrance requirements:* For master's, GRE General Test, bachelor's degree in related field, slide portfolio, typed slide information sheet, 2 letters of recommendation. Additional exam requirements/recommendations for international students: Required—TOEFL. Electronic applications accepted.

San Francisco Art Institute, Graduate Program, Department of Design and Technology, San Francisco, CA 94133. Offers MFA, Certificate. Part-time programs available. *Degree requirements:* For master's and Certificate, oral reviews. *Entrance requirements:* For master's and Certificate, portfolio. Additional exam requirements/recommendations for international students: Required—TOEFL (minimum score 580 paper-based; 237 computer-based). Electronic applications accepted.

San Jose State University, Graduate Studies and Research, College of Humanities and the Arts, School of Art and Design, San Jose, CA 95192-0001. Offers animation/illustration (MA); art history (MA); digital media arts (MFA); photography (MFA); pictorial arts (MFA); spatial arts (MFA). *Accreditation:* NASAD (one or more programs are accredited). *Students:* 48 full-time (27 women), 24 part-time (16 women); includes 13 minority (3 African Americans, 6 Asian Americans or Pacific Islanders, 4 Hispanic Americans), 2 international. Average age 36. 69 applicants, 23% accepted, 16 enrolled. In 2009, 17 master's awarded. *Entrance requirements:* For master's, GRE. *Application deadline:* For fall admission, 6/29 for domestic students; for spring admission, 11/30 for domestic students. Applications are processed on a rolling basis. Application fee: $59. Electronic applications accepted. *Financial support:* Applicants required to submit FAFSA. *Unit head:* John Loomis, Director, 408-924-4320, Fax: 408-924-4326. *Application contact:* John Loomis, Director, 408-924-4320, Fax: 408-924-4326.

Savannah College of Art and Design, Graduate School, Savannah, GA 31402-3146. Offers advertising design (MA, MFA); animation (MA, MFA); architectural history (MA, MFA); architecture (M Arch); art history (MA, MFA); arts administration (MA); broadcast design (MA, MFA); cinema studies (MA); commercial photography (MA); digital photography (MA); documentary photography (MA); fashion (MA, MFA); fibers (MA, MFA); film and television (MA, MFA); furniture design (MA, MFA); graphic design (MA, MFA); historic preservation (MA, MFA); illustration (MA, MFA); illustration design (MA); industrial design (MA, MFA); interactive design and game development (MA, MFA); interior design (MA, MFA); metals and jewelry (MA, MFA); painting (MA, MFA); performing arts (MA, MFA); photography (MA, MFA); printmaking (MA, MFA); production design (MA, MFA); professional education (MA); professional writing (MFA); sculpture (MA, MFA); sequential art (MA, MFA); sound design (MA, MFA); urban design and development (MA); visual effects (MA, MFA). Part-time programs available. Postbaccalaureate distance learning degree programs offered (no on-campus study). *Degree requirements:* For master's, thesis, internship. *Entrance requirements:* For master's, interview, 3 letters of recommendation. Additional exam requirements/recommendations for international students: Required—TOEFL (minimum score 500 paper-based; 133 computer-based). Electronic applications accepted. *Expenses:* Tuition: Full-time $28,515; part-time $627 per credit hour. One-time fee: $500. Tuition and fees vary according to course load. *Faculty research:* Urban planning for diverse communities, photovoltaics-powered environmental control, computer-aided design and virtual reality, multimedia design.

School of the Art Institute of Chicago, Graduate Division, Department of Architecture, Interior Architecture, and Designed Objects, Program in Designed Objects, Chicago, IL 60603-3103. Offers M Des. *Entrance requirements:* Additional exam requirements/recommendations for international students: Required—TOEFL, IELTS.

School of the Art Institute of Chicago, Graduate Division, Department of Architecture, Interior Architecture, and Designed Objects, Program in Design for Emerging Technologies,

Chicago, IL 60603-3103. Offers MFA. *Entrance requirements:* Additional exam requirements/recommendations for international students: Required—TOEFL, IELTS.

School of the Art Institute of Chicago, Graduate Division, Department of Architecture, Interior Architecture, and Designed Objects, Program in Interior Architecture, Chicago, IL 60603-3103. Offers M Arc. *Entrance requirements:* Additional exam requirements/recommendations for international students: Required—TOEFL, IELTS.

School of Visual Arts, Graduate Programs, Branding Department, New York, NY 10010-3994. Offers MPS.

School of Visual Arts, Graduate Programs, Design Department, New York, NY 10010-3994. Offers MFA. *Accreditation:* NASAD. *Degree requirements:* For master's, final review, project or thesis. *Entrance requirements:* For master's, portfolio. Additional exam requirements/recommendations for international students: Required—TOEFL (minimum score 550 paper-based; 213 computer-based; 79 iBT). Electronic applications accepted. *Expenses:* Contact institution.

School of Visual Arts, Graduate Programs, Program in Design Criticism, New York, NY 10010-3994. Offers MFA.

Southern Illinois University Carbondale, Graduate School, College of Liberal Arts, School of Art and Design, Carbondale, IL 62901-4701. Offers ceramics (MFA); drawing (MFA); fiber/weaving (MFA); glass (MFA); jewelry (MFA); metalsmithing/blacksmithing (MFA); painting (MFA); printmaking (MFA); sculpture (MFA). *Accreditation:* NASAD. *Degree requirements:* For master's, thesis or alternative. *Entrance requirements:* For master's, minimum GPA of 2.7, portfolio, slides. Additional exam requirements/recommendations for international students: Required—TOEFL. *Faculty research:* Prints/woodcuts, foundry, watercolor.

Stephen F. Austin State University, Graduate School, College of Fine Arts, School of Art, Nacogdoches, TX 75962. Offers art (MA); design (MFA); drawing (MFA); painting (MFA); sculpture (MFA). *Accreditation:* NASAD. Part-time programs available. *Degree requirements:* For master's, comprehensive exam, thesis, exhibit. *Entrance requirements:* For master's, GRE General Test, portfolio. Additional exam requirements/recommendations for international students: Required—TOEFL. *Faculty research:* Printmaking, jewelry, photography, ceramics, art history.

Suffolk University, New England School of Art and Design, Boston, MA 02108-2770. Offers graphic design (MA); interior design (MA). *Accreditation:* CIDA; NASAD. Part-time and evening/weekend programs available. *Faculty:* 22 full-time (12 women), 7 part-time/adjunct (2 women). *Students:* 51 full-time (47 women), 85 part-time (75 women); includes 13 minority (1 African American, 1 American Indian/Alaska Native, 7 Asian Americans or Pacific Islanders, 4 Hispanic Americans), 12 international. Average age 30. 99 applicants, 68% accepted, 37 enrolled. In 2009, 40 master's awarded. *Entrance requirements:* For master's, art portfolio, interview, 2 letters of recommendation, resume. Additional exam requirements/recommendations for international students: Required—TOEFL (minimum score 550 paper-based; 213 computer-based; 80 iBT). *Application deadline:* For fall admission, 6/15 priority date for domestic students, 6/15 for international students; for spring admission, 11/1 priority date for domestic students, 11/1 for international students. Applications are processed on a rolling basis. Application fee: $50. Electronic applications accepted. *Expenses:* Contact institution. *Financial support:* In 2009–10, 76 students received support, including 9 fellowships with partial tuition reimbursements available (averaging $7,444 per year). Financial award application deadline: 4/1. *Faculty research:* Adaptive re-use of historical structures, universal design, American architecture history, interior design to reduce inefficiency, meditation SPA. *Unit head:* William Davis, Director, 617-994-4264, Fax: 617-994-4250, E-mail: wdavis@suffolk.edu. *Application contact:* Judith Reynolds, Director of Graduate Admissions, 617-573-8302, Fax: 617-305-1733, E-mail: grad.admission@suffolk.edu.

Sul Ross State University, School of Arts and Sciences, Department of Fine Arts and Communication, Alpine, TX 79832. Offers art education (M Ed); art history (M Ed); studio art (M Ed), including ceramics, design, drawing, jewelry, painting, printmaking, sculpture, weaving. Part-time programs available. *Degree requirements:* For master's, oral or written exam. *Entrance requirements:* For master's, GRE General Test, minimum GPA of 2.5 in last 60 hours of undergraduate work. *Faculty research:* Ceramic sculpture, watercolor, wood sculpture, rock art.

Syracuse University, College of Visual and Performing Arts, Program in Art Video, Syracuse, NY 13244. Offers MFA. *Accreditation:* NASAD. Part-time programs available. Postbaccalaureate distance learning degree programs offered (no on-campus study). *Students:* 9 full-time (7 women); includes 2 minority (1 African American, 1 Hispanic American), 4 international. Average age 28. 11 applicants, 27% accepted, 1 enrolled. In 2009, 1 master's awarded. *Degree requirements:* For master's, thesis or alternative. *Entrance requirements:* For master's, portfolio. Additional exam requirements/recommendations for international students: Required—TOEFL (minimum score 100 iBT). *Application deadline:* For fall admission, 2/1 priority date for domestic and international students. Application fee: $75. Electronic applications accepted. *Expenses:* Tuition: Full-time $26,808; part-time $1117 per credit. Required fees: $1024. *Financial support:* Fellowships with full tuition reimbursements, teaching assistantships with full and partial tuition reimbursements, Federal Work-Study and tuition waivers (partial) available. Financial award application deadline: 1/1; financial award applicants required to submit FAFSA. *Unit head:* Heath Hanlin, Department Chair, 315-443-21033, E-mail: hahanlin@syr.edu. *Application contact:* Harriett Conti, Assistant Dean for Recruitment and Admissions, 315-443-5755, E-mail: hmconti@syr.edu.

University of Alberta, Faculty of Graduate Studies and Research, Department of Art and Design, Edmonton, AB T6G 2E1, Canada. Offers drawing (MFA); history of art, design, and visual culture (MA); industrial design (M Des); painting (MFA); printmaking (MFA); sculpture (MFA); visual communication design (M Des). *Faculty:* 19 full-time (7 women). *Students:* 28 full-time (16 women), 12 part-time (8 women). Average age 25. 66 applicants, 26% accepted, 12 enrolled. In 2009, 10 master's awarded. *Degree requirements:* For master's, thesis. *Entrance requirements:* For master's, portfolio (MFA and MDES). Additional exam requirements/recommendations for international students: Required—TOEFL (minimum score 550 paper-based; 213 computer-based). *Application deadline:* For fall admission, 2/1 for domestic and international students. Application fee: $0. Tuition and fees charges are reported in Canadian dollars. *Expenses:* Tuition, area resident: Full-time $4626 Canadian dollars; part-time $99.72 Canadian dollars per unit. International tuition: $8216 Canadian dollars full-time. Required fees: $3590 Canadian dollars; $99.72 Canadian dollars per unit. $215 Canadian dollars per term. *Financial support:* In 2009–10, 29 students received support, including 5 research assistantships (averaging $3,300 per year), 13 teaching assistantships (averaging $8,100 per year); scholarships/grants and unspecified assistantships also available. Financial award application deadline: 2/1. *Unit head:* Dr. Liz Ingram, Acting Chair, 780-492-3261, Fax: 780-492-7870. *Application contact:* Sharon Orescan, Administrative Assistant, 780-492-5712, Fax: 780-492-7870, E-mail: artdes@ualberta.ca.

University of Baltimore, Graduate School, The Yale Gordon College of Liberal Arts, Program in Integrated Design, Baltimore, MD 21201-5779. Offers MFA. Part-time and evening/weekend programs available. *Entrance requirements:* Additional exam requirements/recommendations for international students: Required—TOEFL (minimum score 550 paper-based; 213 computer-based). Electronic applications accepted. *Expenses:* Contact institution. *Faculty research:* Information and graphics design, economics, hypermedia communications.

University of California, Berkeley, Graduate Division, College of Environmental Design, Master of Arts in Design Program, Berkeley, CA 94720-1500. Offers MA. *Students:* 8 full-time (4 women). Average age 33. 13 applicants, 3 enrolled. In 2009, 1 master's awarded. *Degree requirements:* For master's, thesis. *Entrance requirements:* For master's, GRE General Test, minimum GPA of 3.0, portfolio, 3 letters of recommendation. Additional exam requirements/recommendations for international students: Required—TOEFL. *Application deadline:* For fall admission, 2/1 for domestic students. Application fee: $70 ($90 for international students). *Financial support:* Unspecified assistantships available. *Unit head:* Prof. Anthony Dubovsky, Chair, 510-642-4942. *Application contact:* Lois H. Ito Koch, Student Affairs Officer, 510-642-5577, Fax: 510-643-5607, E-mail: likoch@berkeley.edu.

University of California, Berkeley, UC Berkeley Extension, Certificate Programs in Art and Design, Berkeley, CA 94720-1500. Offers interior design and interior architecture (Certificate); landscape architecture (Certificate); visual arts (Postbaccalaureate Certificate). *Unit head:* Diana Wu, Dean, 510-642-4181. *Application contact:* Art and Design, 415-284-1041, E-mail: visualarts@unex.berkeley.edu.

University of California, Los Angeles, Graduate Division, School of the Arts and Architecture, Department of Design/Media Arts, Los Angeles, CA 90095. Offers MFA. *Degree requirements:* For master's, comprehensive exam. *Entrance requirements:* For master's, portfolio, 20 slides and/or videotape, minimum GPA of 3.0. Additional exam requirements/recommendations for international students: Required—TOEFL. Electronic applications accepted.

University of Central Oklahoma, College of Graduate Studies and Research, College of Arts, Media, and Design, Department of Design and Interior Design, Edmond, OK 73034-5209. Offers MFA. Part-time programs available. Postbaccalaureate distance learning degree programs offered (minimal on-campus study). *Entrance requirements:* Additional exam requirements/recommendations for international students: Required—TOEFL (minimum score 550 paper-based; 213 computer-based). Electronic applications accepted. *Expenses:* Tuition, state resident: full-time $4128; part-time $172 per credit hour. Tuition, nonresident: full-time $10,373; part-time $432.20 per credit hour. Required fees: $433.20; $18.05 per credit hour.

University of Cincinnati, Graduate School, College of Design, Architecture, Art, and Planning, School of Design, Cincinnati, OH 45221. Offers fashion design (M Des); graphic design (M Des); industrial design (M Des); interaction design (M Des); product development (M Des). *Accreditation:* NASAD. *Degree requirements:* For master's, thesis. *Entrance requirements:* For master's, undergraduate degree in design or related field, 2 years of work experience in design or related field. Additional exam requirements/recommendations for international students: Required—TOEFL. Electronic applications accepted. *Faculty research:* Design theory, interdisciplinary design topics.

University of Delaware, College of Arts and Sciences, Department of Art, Newark, DE 19716. Offers MA, MFA. *Degree requirements:* For master's, exposition paper final exhibition. *Entrance requirements:* For master's, portfolio of creative work. Electronic applications accepted. *Faculty research:* Painting, printmaking, ceramics, photography, sculpture.

University of Idaho, College of Graduate Studies, College of Art and Architecture, Department of Art and Design, Moscow, ID 83844-2282. Offers art (MAT, MFA). *Accreditation:* NASAD. *Faculty:* 4 full-time. *Students:* 16 full-time, 11 part-time. In 2009, 4 master's awarded. *Degree requirements:* For master's, thesis (for some programs). *Entrance requirements:* For master's, minimum GPA of 2.8. *Application deadline:* For fall admission, 8/1 for domestic students; for spring admission, 12/15 for domestic students. Application fee: $55 ($60 for international students). *Expenses:* Tuition, state resident: full-time $6120. Tuition, nonresident: full-time $17,712. *Financial support:* Research assistantships, teaching assistantships available. Financial award application deadline: 2/15. *Faculty research:* Information design. *Unit head:* William Woolston, Chair, 208-885-7837. *Application contact:* William Woolston, Chair, 208-885-7837.

University of Illinois at Urbana–Champaign, Graduate College, College of Fine and Applied Arts, School of Art and Design, Champaign, IL 61820. Offers Ed M, MA, MFA, PhD. *Accreditation:* NASAD. *Faculty:* 48 full-time (21 women), 3 part-time/adjunct (1 woman). *Students:* 90 full-time (65 women), 9 part-time (4 women); includes 12 minority (2 American Indian/Alaska Native, 7 Asian Americans or Pacific Islanders, 3 Hispanic Americans), 25 international. 264 applicants, 10% accepted, 26 enrolled. In 2009, 31 master's, 9 doctorates awarded. *Entrance requirements:* For master's, minimum GPA of 3.0. *Application deadline:* Applications are processed on a rolling basis. Application fee: $60 ($75 for international students). Electronic applications accepted. *Financial support:* In 2009–10, 17 fellowships, 11 research assistantships, 55 teaching assistantships were awarded; tuition waivers (full and partial) also available. *Unit head:* Nan Goggin, Director, 217-333-0855, Fax: 217-244-7688, E-mail: goggin@illinois.edu. *Application contact:* Marsha K. Biddle, Coordinator of Graduate Academic Affairs, 217-333-0642, Fax: 217-244-7688, E-mail: mbiddle@illinois.edu.

The University of Kansas, Graduate Studies, School of Architecture, Design, and Planning, Department of Design, Lawrence, KS 66045. Offers design (MA, MFA); design management (MA); interaction design (MA). *Accreditation:* NASAD (one or more programs are accredited). *Students:* 7 full-time (4 women), 19 part-time (12 women), 1 international. Average age 34. 16 applicants, 88% accepted, 12 enrolled. In 2009, 2 master's awarded. *Degree requirements:* For master's, thesis. *Entrance requirements:* For master's, portfolio, 3 letters of recommendation, minimum GPA of 3.0. Additional exam requirements/recommendations for international students: Required—TOEFL, IELTS. *Application deadline:* For fall admission, 2/1 for domestic and international students; for spring admission, 10/15 for domestic students. Application fee: $45 ($55 for international students). Electronic applications accepted. *Expenses:* Tuition, state resident: full-time $6492; part-time $270.50 per credit hour. Tuition, nonresident: full-time $15,510; part-time $646.25 per credit hour. Required fees: $847; $70.56 per credit hour. Tuition and fees vary according to course load and program. *Financial support:* Fellowships, teaching assistantships with full and partial tuition reimbursements, Federal Work-Study, scholarships/grants, and unspecified assistantships available. Financial award application deadline: 2/1; financial award applicants required to submit FAFSA. *Faculty research:* Interaction design, design management, photography, graphic design, industrial design. *Unit head:* Prof. Gregory Thomas, Chairperson, 785-864-4401. *Application contact:* Prof. Gregory Thomas, Chairperson, 785-864-4401.

University of Kentucky, Graduate School, College of Design, Lexington, KY 40506-0032. Offers M Arch, MAIDM, MHP, MSIDM. *Accreditation:* NASAD. *Entrance requirements:* For master's, GRE, minimum GPA of 2.75. Additional exam requirements/recommendations for international students: Required—TOEFL (minimum score 550 paper-based; 213 computer-based). Electronic applications accepted.

University of Massachusetts Dartmouth, Graduate School, College of Visual and Performing Arts, Program in Visual Design, North Dartmouth, MA 02747-2300. Offers digital media (MFA); graphic design (MFA); illustration (MFA); photography (MFA); typography (MFA). *Accreditation:* NASAD. *Faculty:* 17 full-time (7 women), 3 part-time/adjunct (2 women). *Students:* 6 full-time (4 women), 1 (woman) part-time. Average age 35. 25 applicants, 44% accepted, 2 enrolled. In 2009, 2 master's awarded. *Degree requirements:* For master's, visual thesis. *Entrance requirements:* For master's, portfolio, interview, minimum GPA of 3.0, 3 letters of recommendation. Additional exam requirements/recommendations for international students: Required—TOEFL (minimum score 500 paper-based). *Application deadline:* For fall admission, 2/1 priority date for domestic students, 12/1 priority date for international students. Applications are processed on a rolling basis. Application fee: $40 ($60 for international students). Electronic applications accepted. *Expenses:* Tuition, state resident: full-time $2071; part-time $86.29 per credit. Tuition, nonresident: full-time $8099; part-time $337.46 per credit. Required fees: $9446. Tuition and fees vary according to class time, course load and reciprocity agreements. *Financial support:* In 2009–10, 5 teaching assistantships with full tuition reimbursements (averaging $3,088 per year) were awarded; Federal Work-Study and unspecified assistantships also available. Support available to part-time students. Financial award application deadline: 3/1; financial award applicants required to submit FAFSA. Total annual research expenditures: $1,000. *Unit head:* Memory Holloway, Director, 508-999-8554, E-mail: mholloway@umassd.edu. *Application contact:* Elan Turcotte-Shamski, Graduate Admissions Officer, 508-999-8604, Fax: 508-999-8183, E-mail: graduate@umassd.edu.

Applied Arts and Design—General

University of Michigan, Horace H. Rackham School of Graduate Studies, School of Art and Design, Ann Arbor, MI 48109. Offers art and design (MFA). *Accreditation:* NASAD. *Degree requirements:* For master's, thesis, exhibit (MFA), slide lecture. *Entrance requirements:* For master's, portfolio. Additional exam requirements/recommendations for international students: Required—TOEFL, IELTS. Electronic applications accepted. *Expenses:* Tuition, state resident: full-time $17,286; part-time $1099 per credit hour. Tuition, nonresident: full-time $34,944; part-time $2080 per credit hour. Required fees: $95 per semester. Tuition and fees vary according to course load, degree level and program. *Faculty research:* Creative expression, commercial design, preparation for teaching.

University of Minnesota, Twin Cities Campus, Graduate School, College of Design, Department of Design, Housing, and Apparel, Minneapolis, MN 55455-0213. Offers apparel (MA, MS, PhD); design communication (MA, MS, PhD); housing studies (MA, MS, PhD, Postbaccalaureate Certificate); interactive design (MFA); interior design (MA, MS, PhD). Part-time programs available. *Degree requirements:* For master's and Postbaccalaureate Certificate, comprehensive exam, thesis (for some programs); for doctorate, comprehensive exam, thesis/dissertation. *Entrance requirements:* For master's, GRE General Test, minimum GPA of 3.0 (preferred), portfolio, 3 letters of recommendation; for doctorate, GRE General Test, minimum GPA of 3.0 (preferred), portfolio, 3 letters of recommendation, writing sample; for Post-baccalaureate Certificate, GRE General Test, minimum GPA of 3.0 (preferred). Additional exam requirements/recommendations for international students: Required—TOEFL (minimum score 550 paper-based; 213 computer-based; 79 iBT). Electronic applications accepted. *Faculty research:* Housing policy and community development; consumer behavior; interactive design; design history; social, cultural, and behavioral issues related to designed environments.

University of North Texas, Robert B. Toulouse School of Graduate Studies, College of Visual Arts and Design, Department of Design, Denton, TX 76203. Offers MFA. *Accreditation:* NASAD. *Degree requirements:* For master's, problem or thesis. *Entrance requirements:* Additional exam requirements/recommendations for international students: Required—proof of English language proficiency; Recommended—TOEFL (minimum score 550 paper-based; 213 computer-based; 79 iBT). *Application deadline:* Applications are processed on a rolling basis. Application fee: $50 ($75 for international students). Electronic applications accepted. *Expenses:* Tuition, state resident: full-time $4298; part-time $239 per contact hour. Tuition, nonresident: full-time $9878; part-time $549 per contact hour. Required fees: $265 per contact hour. *Financial support:* Fellowships, teaching assistantships available. Financial award applicants required to submit FAFSA. *Faculty research:* Color, lighting, sustainable design, hand sewing techniques, ethics.

University of Notre Dame, Graduate School, College of Arts and Letters, Division of Humanities, Department of Art, Art History, and Design, Notre Dame, IN 46556. Offers art history (MA); design (MFA), including graphic design, industrial design; studio art (MFA), including ceramics, painting, photography, printmaking, sculpture. *Accreditation:* NASAD. *Degree requirements:* For master's, comprehensive exam (for some programs), thesis. *Entrance requirements:* For master's, GRE General Test, minimum GPA of 3.0. Additional exam requirements/recommendations for international students: Required—TOEFL (minimum score 600 paper-based; 250 computer-based; 80 iBT). Electronic applications accepted. *Faculty research:* Studio art practice in ceramics, printing, photography, printmaking and sculpture, graphic design and industrial design, digital imaging in design and photography, Renaissance and American art history, contemporary art theory and criticism.

University of Oklahoma, Graduate College, College of Fine Arts, School of Drama, Norman, OK 73019. Offers acting (MFA); design (MFA); directing (MFA); drama (MA). *Accreditation:* NAST. *Students:* 10 full-time (4 women), 1 (woman) part-time; includes 1 minority (American Indian/Alaska Native), 1 international. 12 applicants, 33% accepted, 3 enrolled. In 2009, 4 master's awarded. *Degree requirements:* For master's, comprehensive exam, thesis (MA), departmental qualifying exam. *Entrance requirements:* For master's, BA with 36 hours in drama, auditions. Additional exam requirements/recommendations for international students: Required—TOEFL (minimum score 550 paper-based; 213 computer-based). *Application deadline:* For fall admission, 6/1 for domestic students, 4/1 for international students; for spring admission, 11/1 for domestic students, 9/1 for international students. Applications are processed on a rolling basis. Application fee: $40 ($90 for international students). Electronic applications accepted. *Expenses:* Tuition, state resident: full-time $3744; part-time $156 per credit hour. Tuition, nonresident: full-time $13,577; part-time $565.70 per credit hour. Required fees: $2415; $90.10 per credit hour. *Financial support:* In 2009–10, 2 research assistantships with partial tuition reimbursements (averaging $9,586 per year), 9 teaching assistantships with partial tuition reimbursements (averaging $9,586 per year) were awarded; unspecified assistantships also available. Financial award application deadline: 4/7; financial award applicants required to submit FAFSA. *Faculty research:* Directing, costume design, lighting design, dramaturgy. *Unit head:* Dr. Tom Orr, Director, 405-325-4021, Fax: 405-325-0400, E-mail: thorr@ou.edu. *Application contact:* Dr. Judith Pender, Graduate Liaison, 405-325-5319, Fax: 405-325-0400, E-mail: jmpender@ou.edu.

The University of Texas at Austin, Graduate School, College of Fine Arts, Department of Art and Art History, Program in Design, Austin, TX 78712-1111. Offers MFA. *Accreditation:* NASAD. *Degree requirements:* For master's, thesis, oral exam, exhibition. *Entrance requirements:* For master's, minimum GPA of 3.0, portfolio. Electronic applications accepted.

University of Washington, Graduate School, College of Arts and Sciences, School of Art, Division of Design, Seattle, WA 98195. Offers industrial design (MFA); visual communication design (MFA).

University of Wisconsin–Madison, Graduate School, School of Human Ecology, Program in Design Studies, Madison, WI 53706-1380. Offers MFA, MS, PhD. *Degree requirements:* For master's, thesis (for some programs); for doctorate, comprehensive exam, thesis/dissertation. *Entrance requirements:* For master's, portfolio, scholarly paper, 3 letters of recommendation from faculty; for doctorate, letters of recommendation, scholarly paper. Additional exam requirements/recommendations for international students: Required—TOEFL (minimum score 580 paper-based; 237 computer-based). *Expenses:* Tuition, state resident: part-time $594 per credit. Tuition, nonresident: part-time $1504 per credit. Required fees: $65 per credit. Tuition and fees vary according to course load, program and reciprocity agreements. *Faculty research:* Feng shui, material culture, behavior and environment, use of pattern to enhance environment, design visualization.

Virginia Commonwealth University, Graduate School, School of the Arts, Department of Graphic Design, Richmond, VA 23284-9005. Offers design/visual communications (MFA); interior environment (MFA); photography and film (MFA). *Accreditation:* NASAD. *Degree requirements:* For master's, thesis, exhibition. *Entrance requirements:* For master's, portfolio. *Faculty research:* Film, photography, interior environments, visual communication.

Virginia Polytechnic Institute and State University, Graduate School, College of Architecture and Urban Studies, School of Architecture and Design, Blacksburg, VA 24061. Offers architecture (M Arch, MS); architecture design research (PhD). *Accreditation:* NAAB. *Faculty:* 57 full-time (19 women). *Students:* 166 full-time (75 women), 21 part-time (8 women); includes 64 minority (1 African American, 41 American Indian/Alaska Native, 7 Asian Americans or Pacific Islanders, 15 Hispanic Americans), 15 international. Average age 28. 378 applicants, 36% accepted, 65 enrolled. In 2009, 58 master's awarded. *Entrance requirements:* For master's and doctorate, GRE, GMAT. Additional exam requirements/recommendations for international students: Required—TOEFL (minimum score 550 paper-based; 213 computer-based). *Application deadline:* For fall admission, 5/15 for international students; for spring admission, 10/15 for international students. Applications are processed on a rolling basis. Application fee: $65. Electronic applications accepted. *Expenses:* Tuition, area resident: Full-time $10,228; part-time $459 per credit hour. Tuition, nonresident: full-time $17,892; part-time $865 per credit hour. Required fees: $1966; $451 per semester. *Financial support:* In 2009–10, 5 fellowships with full tuition reimbursements (averaging $600 per year), 4 research assistantships with full tuition reimbursements (averaging $4,917 per year), 50 teaching assistantships with full tuition reimbursements (averaging $9,268 per year) were awarded; career-related internships or fieldwork, Federal Work-Study, scholarships/grants, and unspecified assistantships also available. Financial award application deadline: 1/15. *Faculty research:* Computer applications in design, building technology, architectural design theory, solar/passive energy design, building assembly. Total annual research expenditures: $253,759. *Unit head:* Dr. Steve R. Thompson, Dean, 540-231-9931, Fax: 540-231-9938, E-mail: stthomp2@vt.edu. *Application contact:* Dr. Steve R. Thompson, Dean, 540-231-9931, Fax: 540-231-9938, E-mail: stthomp2@vt.edu.

Wayne State University, College of Fine, Performing and Communication Arts, Department of Art and Art History, Program in Design and Merchandising, Detroit, MI 48202. Offers MA. *Degree requirements:* For master's, one foreign language. *Entrance requirements:* Additional exam requirements/recommendations for international students: Required—TOEFL (minimum score 550 paper-based; 213 computer-based); Recommended—TWE (minimum score 6). Electronic applications accepted.

Western Carolina University, Graduate School, College of Fine and Performing Arts, School of Art and Design, Cullowhee, NC 28723. Offers MFA. Part-time programs available. *Students:* 13 full-time (8 women), 3 part-time (1 woman). Average age 34. 23 applicants, 26% accepted, 6 enrolled. In 2009, 9 master's awarded. *Degree requirements:* For master's, thesis. *Entrance requirements:* For master's, GRE, appropriate undergraduate degree, portfolio, letters of recommendation. Additional exam requirements/recommendations for international students: Required—TOEFL (minimum score 550 paper-based; 270 computer-based; 79 iBT). *Application deadline:* For fall admission, 3/1 for domestic students. Application fee: $45. *Financial support:* In 2009–10, 10 students received support, including 10 teaching assistantships with full and partial tuition reimbursements available (averaging $7,500 per year); fellowships, research assistantships with full and partial tuition reimbursements available, career-related internships or fieldwork, institutionally sponsored loans, scholarships/grants, and unspecified assistantships also available. Financial award application deadline: 3/31; financial award applicants required to submit FAFSA. *Faculty research:* Art and society, visual literacy, vernacular cultural studies and oral history, environments for aging, health and leisure. *Unit head:* Richard Tichich, Chair, 828-227-7210, Fax: 828-227-7505, E-mail: rtichich@email.wcu.edu. *Application contact:* Admissions Specialist for Fine and Performing Arts, 828-227-7398, Fax: 828-227-7480, E-mail: gradsch@email.wcu.edu.

Western Michigan University, Graduate College, College of Fine Arts, Gwen Frostic School of Art, Kalamazoo, MI 49008. Offers art education (MA); studio art (MFA). *Accreditation:* NASAD (one or more programs are accredited). *Degree requirements:* For master's, thesis or alternative.

Yale University, School of Art, New Haven, CT 06520. Offers graphic design (MFA); painting/printmaking (MFA); photography (MFA); sculpture (MFA). *Faculty:* 7 full-time (3 women), 36 part-time/adjunct (12 women). *Students:* 119 full-time (62 women); includes 17 minority (4 African Americans, 6 Asian Americans or Pacific Islanders, 7 Hispanic Americans), 25 international. Average age 28. 1,266 applicants, 5% accepted, 58 enrolled. In 2009, 57 master's awarded. *Degree requirements:* For master's, thesis (for some programs). *Entrance requirements:* Additional exam requirements/recommendations for international students: Required—TOEFL (minimum score 550 paper-based; 250 computer-based; 100 iBT). *Application deadline:* For fall admission, 1/5 for domestic and international students. Application fee: $100. Electronic applications accepted. *Expenses:* Contact institution. *Financial support:* In 2009–10, 90 students received support, including 54 teaching assistantships (averaging $1,900 per year); Federal Work-Study, scholarships/grants, and unspecified assistantships also available. Financial award application deadline: 3/1; financial award applicants required to submit FAFSA. *Unit head:* Robert Storr, Dean, 203-432-2606. *Application contact:* Patricia Ann DeChiara, Director of Academic Affairs, 203-432-2600, E-mail: artschool.info@yale.edu.

York University, Faculty of Graduate Studies, Faculty of Fine Arts, Program in Design, Toronto, ON M3J 1P3, Canada. Offers M Des. Electronic applications accepted.

Computer Art and Design

Academy of Art University, Graduate Program, School of Web Design and New Media, San Francisco, CA 94105-3410. Offers MFA. Part-time and evening/weekend programs available. *Degree requirements:* For master's, thesis, final review. *Entrance requirements:* For master's, portfolio. Electronic applications accepted.

Alfred University, Graduate School, New York State College of Ceramics, School of Art and Design, Alfred, NY 14802-1205. Offers ceramic art (MFA); electronic integrated arts (MFA); glass art (MFA); sculpture (MFA). *Accreditation:* NASAD. *Degree requirements:* For master's, exhibit. *Entrance requirements:* For master's, portfolio. Additional exam requirements/recommendations for international students: Required—TOEFL (minimum score 550 paper-based; 213 computer-based; 80 iBT), IELTS (minimum score 6). Electronic applications accepted. *Expenses:* Tuition: Full-time $33,296; part-time $708 per credit hour. Required fees: $880; $144 per year. Full-time tuition and fees vary according to program. *Faculty research:* Ceramic sculpture, functional ceramics, wood, mixed media, hot and cold glass.

Arizona State University, Graduate College, College of Design, Program in Design, Tempe, AZ 85287. Offers arts/media/engineering (MSD); healthcare and healing environments (MSD); industrial design (MSD); interaction design (MSD); interior design (MSD); new product innovation (MSD); visual communication design (MSD). *Accreditation:* NASAD. *Degree requirements:* For master's, thesis optional. *Entrance requirements:* For master's, GRE General Test, design portfolio.

Art Center College of Design, Graduate Division, Department of Media Design, Pasadena, CA 91103. Offers MFA. *Accreditation:* NASAD. *Faculty:* 8 full-time (3 women). *Students:* 15 full-time (7 women), 5 part-time (2 women), 10 international. Average age 29. 93 applicants, 35% accepted, 15 enrolled. In 2009, 13 master's awarded. *Degree requirements:* For master's, thesis, studio project. *Entrance requirements:* For master's, portfolio. Additional exam requirements/recommendations for international students: Required—TOEFL (minimum score 600 paper-based; 250 computer-based; 100 iBT). *Application deadline:* For fall admission, 2/1 for domestic students, 2/1 priority date for international students. Application fee: $50 ($70 for international students). *Expenses:* Tuition: Full-time $16,737. *Financial support:* Teaching assistantships, career-related internships or fieldwork, Federal Work-Study, and scholarships/grants available. Support available to part-time students. Financial award application deadline: 2/1; financial award applicants required to submit FAFSA. *Unit head:* Anne Burdick, Chair,

626-396-2359, E-mail: anne.burdick@artcenter.edu. *Application contact:* Kevin Wingate, 626-396-2469.

See Close-Up on page 113.

Bowling Green State University, Graduate College, College of Arts and Sciences, School of Art, Bowling Green, OH 43403. Offers 2-D studio art (MA, MFA); 3-D studio art (MA, MFA); art education (MA); art history (MA); computer art (MA); design (MFA); digital arts (MFA); graphics (MFA). *Accreditation:* NASAD. Part-time programs available. *Degree requirements:* For master's, thesis or alternative, final exhibit (MFA). *Entrance requirements:* For master's, GRE General Test (MA), slide portfolio (15-20 slides). Additional exam requirements/recommendations for international students: Required—TOEFL. Electronic applications accepted. *Faculty research:* Computer animation and virtual reality, Spanish still-life painting from 1600 to 1800, art and psychotherapy, Japanese wood-firing techniques in ceramics, non-toxic printmaking technologies.

Carnegie Mellon University, College of Fine Arts, School of Design, Program in Interaction Design, Pittsburgh, PA 15213-3891. Offers M Des, PhD. Part-time programs available. *Degree requirements:* For master's, thesis. *Entrance requirements:* For master's, GRE, portfolio of relevant work. Additional exam requirements/recommendations for international students: Required—TOEFL (minimum score 600 paper-based; 250 computer-based). *Faculty research:* Interaction and emotion, visual interface design, robotics, visualization and diagramming, design theory.

The Catholic University of America, School of Architecture and Planning, Washington, DC 20064. Offers cultural studies/sacred space (M Arch); design technologies (M Arch); digital media (M Arch); urban design (M Arch). Part-time programs available. *Faculty:* 20 full-time (7 women), 34 part-time/adjunct (4 women). *Students:* 110 full-time (46 women), 37 part-time (16 women); includes 40 minority (12 African Americans, 11 Asian Americans or Pacific Islanders, 17 Hispanic Americans), 9 international. Average age 27. 154 applicants, 80% accepted, 55 enrolled. In 2009, 39 master's awarded. *Degree requirements:* For master's, thesis. *Entrance requirements:* For master's, GRE (minimum score: 1000), minimum GPA of 2.8, portfolio, statement of purpose, official copies of academic transcripts, three letters of recommendation. Additional exam requirements/recommendations for international students: Required—TOEFL (minimum score 580 paper-based; 237 computer-based). *Application deadline:* For fall admission, 1/15 priority date for domestic students, 1/15 for international students; for spring admission, 10/15 priority date for domestic students, 10/15 for international students. Applications are processed on a rolling basis. Application fee: $55. Electronic applications accepted. *Expenses:* Contact institution. *Financial support:* Fellowships, research assistantships, teaching assistantships, Federal Work-Study, scholarships/grants, tuition waivers (full and partial), and unspecified assistantships available. Financial award application deadline: 2/1; financial award applicants required to submit FAFSA. *Faculty research:* Architectural history, cultural studies/scared space, design technologies, digital media, real estate development, urban design. *Unit head:* Randall Ott, Dean, 202-319-5784, Fax: 202-319-2023, E-mail: ott@cua.edu. *Application contact:* Julie Schwing, Director of Graduate Admissions, 202-319-5057, Fax: 202-319-6533, E-mail: cua-admissions@cua.edu.

Chatham University, Program in Film and Digital Technology, Pittsburgh, PA 15232-2826. Offers emerging media (MFA). Part-time and evening/weekend programs available. *Students:* 11 full-time (7 women), 6 part-time (3 women). Average age 29. 19 applicants, 79% accepted, 13 enrolled. *Degree requirements:* For master's, thesis, capstone project. *Entrance requirements:* Additional exam requirements/recommendations for international students: Required—TOEFL (minimum score 600 paper-based; 250 computer-based; 100 iBT), IELTS (minimum score 6.5), TWE. *Application deadline:* For fall admission, 7/1 priority date for domestic students, 6/1 priority date for international students; for spring admission, 12/1 priority date for domestic students, 11/1 priority date for international students. Applications are processed on a rolling basis. Application fee: $45. Electronic applications accepted. *Financial support:* Applicants required to submit FAFSA. *Unit head:* Dr. Prajna Parasher, Director, 412-365-1182, E-mail: parasher@chatham.edu. *Application contact:* Dory Perry, Associate Director of Graduate Admissions, 412-365-2758, Fax: 412-365-1609, E-mail: gradadmissions@chatham.edu.

Claremont Graduate University, Graduate Programs, School of Arts and Humanities, Department of Art, Claremont, CA 91711. Offers digital media (MA, MFA); drawing (MA, MFA); installation (MA, MFA); new genre (MA, MFA); painting (MA, MFA); performance (MA, MFA); photography (MA, MFA); sculpture (MA, MFA). Part-time programs available. *Faculty:* 4 full-time (1 woman). *Students:* 61 full-time (32 women), 1 part-time (0 women); includes 14 minority (1 African American, 6 Asian Americans or Pacific Islanders, 7 Hispanic Americans), 4 international. Average age 33. In 2009, 33 master's awarded. *Degree requirements:* For master's, final project show. *Entrance requirements:* For master's, BA in art or BFA, slide review. Additional exam requirements/recommendations for international students: Required—TOEFL (minimum score 550 paper-based; 213 computer-based; 80 iBT). *Application deadline:* For fall admission, 2/1 priority date for domestic students. Applications are processed on a rolling basis. Application fee: $60. Electronic applications accepted. *Expenses:* Contact institution. *Financial support:* Fellowships, research assistantships, teaching assistantships, Federal Work-Study, institutionally sponsored loans, and scholarships/grants available. Support available to part-time students. Financial award application deadline: 2/15; financial award applicants required to submit FAFSA. *Faculty research:* Acoustic sculpture, feminization of abstraction, installation sculpture. *Unit head:* David Pagel, Chair, 909-607-2479, Fax: 909-607-1276, E-mail: david.pagel@cgu.edu. *Application contact:* Pat Evans, Program Administrator, 909-607-9292, Fax: 909-607-1276, E-mail: patricia.evans@cgu.edu.

Clemson University, Graduate School, College of Engineering and Science, School of Computing, Program in Digital Production Arts, Clemson, SC 29634. Offers MFA. *Students:* 18 full-time (3 women), 3 part-time (1 woman); includes 3 minority (1 African American, 2 Asian Americans or Pacific Islanders), 4 international. Average age 26. 22 applicants, 55% accepted, 5 enrolled. In 2009, 2 master's awarded. *Degree requirements:* For master's, thesis. *Entrance requirements:* For master's, GRE General Test, portfolio. Additional exam requirements/recommendations for international students: Required—TOEFL. *Application deadline:* For fall admission, 4/15 for domestic and international students; for spring admission, 9/15 for international students. Applications are processed on a rolling basis. Application fee: $70 ($80 for international students). Electronic applications accepted. *Expenses:* Tuition, state resident: full-time $8684; part-time $528 per credit hour. Tuition, nonresident: full-time $15,330; part-time $1078 per credit hour. Required fees: $736; $37 per semester. Part-time tuition and fees vary according to course load and program. *Financial support:* In 2009–10, 11 students received support, including 3 research assistantships with partial tuition reimbursements available (averaging $19,530 per year), 1 teaching assistantship with partial tuition reimbursement available (averaging $10,440 per year); fellowships with full and partial tuition reimbursements available, career-related internships or fieldwork, institutionally sponsored loans, scholarships/grants, health care benefits, and unspecified assistantships also available. Support available to part-time students. *Unit head:* Dr. Larry F. Hodges, Chair, 864-656-7552, Fax: 864-656-0145, E-mail: lfh@clemson.edu. *Application contact:* Timothy A. Davis, Coordinator, 864-656-3891, Fax: 864-656-0204, E-mail: tadavis@cs.clemson.edu.

Concordia University, School of Graduate Studies, Faculty of Fine Arts, Department of Design and Computation Arts, Montréal, QC H3G 1M8, Canada. Offers digital technologies in design art practice (Certificate).

Cornell University, Graduate School, Graduate Fields of Architecture, Art and Planning, Field of Architecture, Ithaca, NY 14853-0001. Offers architectural design (M Arch); architectural science (MS); building technology and environmental science (MS); computer graphics (MS); history of architecture (MA, PhD); history of urban development (MA, PhD); theory and criticism of architecture (M Arch); urban design (M Arch). *Faculty:* 38 full-time (12 women). *Students:* 100 full-time (45 women); includes 14 minority (2 African Americans, 6 Asian Americans or Pacific Islanders, 6 Hispanic Americans), 38 international. Average age 28. 558 applicants, 18% accepted, 44 enrolled. In 2009, 42 master's, 3 doctorates awarded. *Degree requirements:* For master's, one foreign language, thesis (MA, MS); for doctorate, 2 foreign languages, comprehensive exam, thesis/dissertation. *Entrance requirements:* For master's, GRE General Test, 5 year bachelor's degree in architecture, portfolio (M Arch), 3 letters of recommendation; for doctorate, GRE General Test, 3 letters of recommendation. Additional exam requirements/recommendations for international students: Required—TOEFL (minimum score 600 paper-based; 250 computer-based; 77 iBT). *Application deadline:* For fall admission, 1/15 priority date for domestic students. Application fee: $70. Electronic applications accepted. *Expenses:* Tuition: Full-time $29,500. Required fees: $70. Full-time tuition and fees vary according to degree level, program and student level. *Financial support:* In 2009–10, 16 students received support, including 2 fellowships with full tuition reimbursements available, 1 research assistantship with full tuition reimbursement available, 10 teaching assistantships with full tuition reimbursements available; institutionally sponsored loans, scholarships/grants, health care benefits, tuition waivers (full and partial), and unspecified assistantships also available. Financial award applicants required to submit FAFSA. *Faculty research:* Architectural design and urban design, theory and criticism of architecture, computer graphics, building technology and environmental science, history of architecture and history of urban-development. *Unit head:* Director of Graduate Studies, 607-255-6701, Fax: 607-255-0291. *Application contact:* Graduate Field Assistant, 607-255-6701, Fax: 607-255-0291, E-mail: cuarch@cornell.edu.

DePaul University, College of Computing and Digital Media, Chicago, IL 60604. Offers business information technology (MS); computational finance (MS); computer and information sciences (PhD); computer game development (MS); computer graphics and motion technology (MS); computer science (MS); computer, information and network security (MS), including applied technology; digital cinema (MFA, MS), including information technology project management (MS); e-commerce technology (MS); human-computer interaction (MS); information systems (MS); information technology (MA); information technology project management (MS); software engineering (MS); telecommunications systems (MS); JD/MS. Part-time and evening/weekend programs available. Postbaccalaureate distance learning degree programs offered (no on-campus study). *Faculty:* 78 full-time (16 women), 191 part-time/adjunct (51 women). *Students:* 922 full-time (239 women), 887 part-time (209 women); includes 466 minority (193 African Americans, 3 American Indian/Alaska Native, 162 Asian Americans or Pacific Islanders, 108 Hispanic Americans), 276 international. Average age 31. 853 applicants, 67% accepted, 294 enrolled. In 2009, 444 master's, 4 doctorates awarded. *Degree requirements:* For master's, thesis (for some programs); for doctorate, comprehensive exam, thesis/dissertation. *Entrance requirements:* For master's, GRE or GMAT (MS in computational finance only), bachelor's degree; for doctorate, GRE, master's degree in computer science. Additional exam requirements/recommendations for international students: Required—TOEFL (minimum score 550 paper-based; 213 computer-based), IELTS (minimum score 6.5), Pearson Test of English (minimum score 53). *Application deadline:* For fall admission, 8/15 priority date for domestic students, 6/1 priority date for international students; for winter admission, 12/15 priority date for domestic students, 9/15 priority date for international students; for spring admission, 3/1 priority date for domestic students, 12/15 priority date for international students. Applications are processed on a rolling basis. Application fee: $25. Electronic applications accepted. *Expenses:* Contact institution. *Financial support:* In 2009–10, 69 students received support, including 6 fellowships with full tuition reimbursements available (averaging $25,858 per year), 75 teaching assistantships with full and partial tuition reimbursements available (averaging $5,780 per year); research assistantships, Federal Work-Study, scholarships/grants, tuition waivers (full and partial), and unspecified assistantships also available. Support available to part-time students. Financial award application deadline: 4/30; financial award applicants required to submit FAFSA. *Faculty research:* Bioinformatics, visual computing, graphics and animation, high performance and scientific computing, databases. Total annual research expenditures: $790,000. *Unit head:* Dr. David Miller, Dean, 312-362-8381, Fax: 312-362-5185. *Application contact:* Dr. Liz Friedman, Assistant Dean of Student Services, 312-362-5384, Fax: 312-362-5327, E-mail: efriedm2@cdm.depaul.edu.

Digital Media Arts College, Graduate Programs, Boca Raton, FL 33431. Offers graphic design (MFA); special FX animation (MFA).

Drexel University, Antoinette Westphal College of Media Arts and Design, Program in Digital Media, Philadelphia, PA 19104-2875. Offers MS. *Degree requirements:* For master's, thesis (including oral presentation, written statement, and copy of completed media work). *Entrance requirements:* For master's, interview. Additional exam requirements/recommendations for international students: Required—TOEFL. Electronic applications accepted.

East Tennessee State University, School of Graduate Studies, College of Business and Technology, Department of Technology and Geomatics, Johnson City, TN 37614. Offers digital media (MS); engineering technology (MS); industrial arts/technology education (MS). Part-time programs available. *Degree requirements:* For master's, thesis or alternative, final oral exam. *Entrance requirements:* For master's, bachelor's degree in technical or related area, minimum GPA of 3.0. Additional exam requirements/recommendations for international students: Required—TOEFL (minimum score 550 paper-based; 213 computer-based). *Faculty research:* Computer-integrated manufacturing, technology education, CAD/CAM, organizational change.

Emily Carr Institute of Art + Design, Program in Digital Media, Vancouver, BC V5T 1E1, Canada. Offers MDM. *Faculty:* 8 full-time (2 women), 7 part-time/adjunct (5 women). *Degree requirements:* For master's, internship. *Entrance requirements:* For master's, portfolio, minimum undergraduate B+ average, 3 reference letters. Additional exam requirements/recommendations for international students: Required—TOEFL (minimum score 86 iBT). Electronic applications accepted. Tuition and fees charges are reported in Canadian dollars. *Expenses:* Tuition, province resident: full-time $11,355 Canadian dollars. Tuition, Canadian resident: full-time $11,355 Canadian dollars. Required fees: $134.70 Canadian dollars. *Unit head:* Dr. Gerri Sinclair, Executive Director, 778-370-1001. *Application contact:* Dr. Gerri Sinclair, Executive Director, 778-370-1001.

Florida Atlantic University, Dorothy F. Schmidt College of Arts and Letters, Department of Visual Arts and Art History, Boca Raton, FL 33431-0991. Offers art education (MAT); ceramics (MFA); computer art (MFA); graphic design (MFA); painting (MFA). *Faculty:* 23 full-time (12 women), 17 part-time/adjunct (11 women). *Students:* 15 full-time (11 women), 11 part-time (6 women); includes 7 minority (1 African American, 6 Hispanic Americans), 3 international. Average age 31. 19 applicants, 21% accepted, 0 enrolled. In 2009, 5 master's awarded. *Degree requirements:* For master's, one foreign language, project. *Entrance requirements:* For master's, GRE General Test, minimum GPA of 3.0 during last 60 hours of course work, slide portfolio. *Application deadline:* For fall admission, 2/21 for domestic and international students; for spring admission, 10/1 for domestic and international students. Application fee: $30. Electronic applications accepted. *Expenses:* Tuition, state resident: full-time $7055; part-time $293.94 per credit hour. Tuition, nonresident: full-time $22,096; part-time $920.66 per credit hour. *Financial support:* Research assistantships with full tuition reimbursements, teaching assistantships with full tuition reimbursements, career-related internships or fieldwork, Federal Work-Study, and institutionally sponsored loans available. Financial award applicants required to submit FAFSA. *Faculty research:* Painting, ceramics (traditional and non-traditional), installation, video and interactive sculpture. *Unit head:* Dr. Linda Johnson, Chair, 561-297-3870, Fax: 561-297-3078, E-mail: ljohnson@fau.edu. *Application contact:* James A. Novak, Associate Professor/Graduate Coordinator/Advisor, 561-297-2430, Fax: 561-297-3078, E-mail: jnovak@fau.edu.

Full Sail University, Game Design Master of Science Program—Campus, Winter Park, FL 32792-7437. Offers MS.

Georgia Institute of Technology, Graduate Studies and Research, Ivan Allen College of Policy and International Affairs, School of Literature, Communication and Culture, Atlanta, GA 30332-0001. Offers digital media (MS, PhD); human computer interaction (MSHCI). *Degree requirements:* For master's, thesis or alternative. *Entrance requirements:* Additional exam requirements/recommendations for international students: Required—TOEFL. Electronic applications accepted. *Faculty research:* New media studies.

Computer Art and Design

Indiana University Bloomington, School of Informatics, Bloomington, IN 47408. Offers bioinformatics (MS); chemical informatics (MS); computer science (MS, PhD); health informatics (MS); human computer interaction (MS); informatics (PhD); laboratory informatics (MS); media arts and science (MS); music informatics (MS); security informatics (MS); MS/PhD. PhD offered through University Graduate School. Part-time programs available. Postbaccalaureate distance learning degree programs offered (no on-campus study). *Faculty:* 63 full-time (12 women). *Students:* 367 full-time (93 women), 32 part-time (11 women); includes 18 minority (4 African Americans, 1 American Indian/Alaska Native, 11 Asian Americans or Pacific Islanders, 2 Hispanic Americans), 254 international. Average age 27. 676 applicants, 52% accepted, 146 enrolled. In 2009, 82 master's, 18 doctorates awarded. Terminal master's awarded for partial completion of doctoral program. *Degree requirements:* For master's, thesis optional; for doctorate, comprehensive exam, thesis/dissertation, oral and written exams. *Entrance requirements:* For master's and doctorate, GRE, letters of reference. Additional exam requirements/recommendations for international students: Required—TOEFL. *Application deadline:* For fall admission, 1/15 for domestic students, 12/1 for international students. Application fee: $55 ($65 for international students). Electronic applications accepted. *Financial support:* In 2009–10, 2 fellowships with full and partial tuition reimbursements (averaging $20,000 per year), 41 research assistantships (averaging $14,000 per year), 84 teaching assistantships (averaging $13,000 per year) were awarded; Federal Work-Study, institutionally sponsored loans, scholarships/grants, health care benefits, tuition waivers (full and partial), and unspecified assistantships also available. Support available to part-time students. Total annual research expenditures: $2 million. *Unit head:* Dr. David Leake, Associate Dean for Graduate Studies, 812-855-9756, E-mail: leake@cs.indiana.edu. *Application contact:* Rachel Lawmaster, Manager of Graduate Admissions and Studies, 812-856-3622, Fax: 812-856-3825, E-mail: raclee@indiana.edu.

International Technological University, Program in Digital Arts, Santa Clara, CA 95050. Offers MA.

Long Island University, Brooklyn Campus, Richard L. Conolly College of Liberal Arts and Sciences, Department of Media Arts, Brooklyn, NY 11201-8423. Offers MA. Part-time and evening/weekend programs available. *Degree requirements:* For master's, integrated thesis project. *Entrance requirements:* For master's, 2 letters of recommendation. Additional exam requirements/recommendations for international students: Required—TOEFL (minimum score 500 paper-based; 173 computer-based). *Faculty research:* Film noir, art and photography, new media/new aesthetic.

Long Island University, C.W. Post Campus, School of Visual and Performing Arts, Department of Theatre, Film, Dance and Arts Management, Brookville, NY 11548-1300. Offers interactive multimedia (MA); theatre (MA). Part-time and evening/weekend programs available. *Degree requirements:* For master's, thesis. *Entrance requirements:* For master's, placement exam. Electronic applications accepted. *Faculty research:* Playwriting, intercultural dance and theatre, translation, Suzuki, set and costume design.

Memphis College of Art, Graduate Programs, Memphis, TN 38104-2764. Offers art education (MA, MAT); computer arts (MFA); studio art (MFA). *Accreditation:* NASAD. *Faculty:* 25 full-time (13 women), 8 part-time/adjunct (6 women). *Students:* 19 full-time (12 women), 71 part-time (48 women); includes 20 minority (16 African Americans, 3 Asian Americans or Pacific Islanders, 1 Hispanic American), 1 international. Average age 31. 83 applicants, 59% accepted, 34 enrolled. In 2009, 19 master's awarded. *Degree requirements:* For master's, thesis. *Entrance requirements:* For master's, portfolio, interview, resume. Additional exam requirements/recommendations for international students: Required—TOEFL (minimum score 525 paper-based; 195 computer-based). *Application deadline:* For fall admission, 3/1 for domestic and international students; for spring admission, 11/1 for domestic and international students. Applications are processed on a rolling basis. Application fee: $50. Electronic applications accepted. *Expenses:* Tuition: Full-time $23,000; part-time $958 per credit hour. Required fees: $600; $200 per course. Tuition and fees vary according to program. *Financial support:* In 2009–10, 90 students received support. Career-related internships or fieldwork, Federal Work-Study, scholarships/grants, and unspecified assistantships available. Support available to part-time students. Financial award application deadline: 8/1; financial award applicants required to submit FAFSA. *Unit head:* Robert E. Miller, Dean of Academic Affairs, 901-272-5100, Fax: 901-272-5158, E-mail: rmiller@mca.edu. *Application contact:* Annette Moore, Dean of Admissions, 901-272-5151, Fax: 901-272-5158, E-mail: amoore@mca.edu.

See Close-Up on page 195.

Miami International University of Art & Design, Program in Computer Animation, Miami, FL 33132-1418. Offers MFA. Postbaccalaureate distance learning degree programs offered. *Application contact:* Office of Graduate Admissions, 305-428-5700.

See Close-Up on page 117.

Michigan State University, The Graduate School, College of Communication Arts and Sciences, Department of Telecommunication, Information Studies, and Media, East Lansing, MI 48824. Offers digital media arts and technology (MA); information and telecommunication management (MA); information, policy and society (MA); serious game design (MA). *Faculty:* 15 full-time (3 women). *Students:* 35 full-time (10 women), 28 part-time (6 women); includes 8 minority (4 African Americans, 3 Asian Americans or Pacific Islanders, 1 Hispanic American), 18 international. Average age 29. 57 applicants, 56% accepted. In 2009, 13 degrees awarded. *Entrance requirements:* Additional exam requirements/recommendations for international students: Required—TOEFL. Electronic applications accepted. *Financial support:* In 2009–10, 1 research assistantship with tuition reimbursement (averaging $13,239 per year), 5 teaching assistantships with tuition reimbursements (averaging $11,902 per year) were awarded. Total annual research expenditures: $741,489. *Unit head:* Dr. Charles Steinfield, Chairperson, 517-355-8372, Fax: 517-355-1292, E-mail: steinfie@msu.edu. *Application contact:* Rachel Iseler, Academic Programs Coordinator, 517-432-3676, Fax: 517-355-1292, E-mail: tism@msu.edu.

Minneapolis College of Art and Design, Certificate Programs, Minneapolis, MN 55404-4347. Offers design (Certificate); fine arts (Certificate); graphic design (Certificate); media (Certificate); sustainable design (Certificate). Part-time programs available. Postbaccalaureate distance learning degree programs offered. *Faculty:* 42 full-time (29 women). *Students:* 4 full-time (2 women), 22 part-time (19 women). Average age 24. In 2009, 15 Certificates awarded. *Degree requirements:* For Certificate, final project. *Entrance requirements:* For degree, resume, portfolio, letter of recommendation. Additional exam requirements/recommendations for international students: Required—TOEFL (minimum score 550 paper-based; 213 computer-based; 79 iBT). *Application deadline:* For fall admission, 1/15 for domestic and international students; for spring admission, 10/15 for domestic and international students. Application fee: $50. Electronic applications accepted. *Expenses:* Tuition: Full-time $29,500; part-time $985 per credit. Required fees: $100. *Financial support:* Career-related internships or fieldwork and scholarships/grants available. Financial award application deadline: 3/15; financial award applicants required to submit FAFSA. *Faculty research:* Visual arts. *Unit head:* Howard Oransky, Director of Continuing Studies, 612-874-3778, E-mail: howard_oransky@mcad.edu. *Application contact:* Howard Oransky, Director of Continuing Studies, 612-874-3778, Fax: 612-874-3701, E-mail: howard_oransky@mcad.edu.

Mississippi State University, College of Architecture, Art and Design, Mississippi State, MS 39762. Offers MS. *Accreditation:* NASAD. *Faculty:* 20 full-time (6 women). *Students:* 8 full-time (7 women), 2 part-time (1 woman); includes 2 minority (both African Americans), 2 international. Average age 27. 14 applicants, 79% accepted, 7 enrolled. In 2009, 9 master's awarded. *Degree requirements:* For master's, comprehensive exam, thesis, final written and oral exam. *Entrance requirements:* For master's, GRE General Test, essay stating intent and aspirations for study, portfolio, minimum GPA of 3.0. Additional exam requirements/recommendations for international students: Required—TOEFL (minimum score 600 paper-based; 250 computer-based; 100 iBT); Recommended—IELTS (minimum score 7.5). *Application deadline:* For fall admission, 7/1 for domestic students, 5/1 for international students; for spring admission, 11/1 for domestic students, 9/1 for international students. Applications are processed on a rolling basis. Application fee: $40. Electronic applications accepted. *Expenses:* Tuition, state resident: full-time $2575.50; part-time $286.25 per credit hour. Tuition, nonresident: full-time $6510; part-time $723.50 per credit hour. Tuition and fees vary according to course load. *Financial support:* In 2009–10, 2 research assistantships with full tuition reimbursements (averaging $9,000 per year), 1 teaching assistantship (averaging $9,000 per year) were awarded; career-related internships or fieldwork, Federal Work-Study, institutionally sponsored loans, and unspecified assistantships also available. Financial award application deadline: 4/1; financial award applicants required to submit FAFSA. *Faculty research:* Digital art in architecture, process change and management, multi-media databases, 3-D modeling and animation, virtual archaeology. *Unit head:* James L. West, Dean/Professor, 662-325-2202, Fax: 662-325-8872, E-mail: jwest@caad.msstate.edu. *Application contact:* James L. West, Dean/Professor, 662-325-2202, Fax: 662-325-8872, E-mail: jwest@caad.msstate.edu.

National University, Academic Affairs, School of Media and Communication, Department of Media, La Jolla, CA 92037-1011. Offers digital cinema (MFA); educational and instructional technology (MS); video game production and design (MFA). Part-time and evening/weekend programs available. Postbaccalaureate distance learning degree programs offered (no on-campus study). *Faculty:* 9 full-time (4 women), 13 part-time/adjunct (4 women). *Students:* 68 full-time (26 women), 118 part-time (45 women); includes 64 minority (29 African Americans, 10 Asian Americans or Pacific Islanders, 25 Hispanic Americans), 1 international. Average age 39. 118 applicants, 100% accepted, 70 enrolled. In 2009, 58 master's awarded. *Degree requirements:* For master's, thesis. *Entrance requirements:* For master's, interview, minimum GPA of 2.5. Additional exam requirements/recommendations for international students: Required—TOEFL (minimum score 550 paper-based; 213 computer-based; 79 iBT), IELTS (minimum score 6). *Application deadline:* Applications are processed on a rolling basis. Application fee: $60 ($65 for international students). Electronic applications accepted. *Expenses:* Tuition: Part-time $338 per quarter hour. *Financial support:* Career-related internships or fieldwork, institutionally sponsored loans, scholarships/grants, and tuition waivers (partial) available. Support available to part-time students. Financial award application deadline: 6/30; financial award applicants required to submit FAFSA. *Unit head:* Dr. Timothy Langdell, Department Chair, 310-662-2149, Fax: 858-309-3450, E-mail: tlangdell@nu.edu. *Application contact:* Dominick Giovanniello, Associate Regional Dean—San Diego, 800-NAT-UNIV, Fax: 858-541-7792, E-mail: dgiovann@nu.edu.

The New School: A University, Parsons The New School for Design, Program in Design and Technology, New York, NY 10011. Offers MFA. *Accreditation:* NASAD. *Faculty:* 11 full-time (8 women). *Students:* 167 full-time (90 women), 8 part-time (5 women); includes 40 minority (10 African Americans, 23 Asian Americans or Pacific Islanders, 7 Hispanic Americans), 63 international. Average age 27. 289 applicants, 79% accepted, 101 enrolled. In 2009, 64 master's awarded. *Degree requirements:* For master's, thesis, exam, written essay. *Entrance requirements:* For master's, portfolio. Additional exam requirements/recommendations for international students: Required—TOEFL (minimum score 580 paper-based; 237 computer-based; 92 iBT). *Application deadline:* For fall admission, 2/1 for domestic and international students. Application fee: $50. Electronic applications accepted. *Financial support:* Federal Work-Study, scholarships/grants, and tuition waivers (full and partial) available. Support available to part-time students. Financial award application deadline: 3/1; financial award applicants required to submit FAFSA. *Unit head:* Anezka Sebek, Chair, 212-229-8908 Ext. 4343, E-mail: sebeka@newschool.edu. *Application contact:* David Norris, Director of Admissions, 212-229-8989 Ext. 4023, Fax: 212-229-8975, E-mail: norrisd@newschool.edu.

New York Institute of Technology, Graduate Division, School of Arts and Sciences, Program in Fine Arts, Old Westbury, NY 11568-8000. Offers computer graphics and animation (MFA); fine arts and technology (MFA); graphic design (MFA). Part-time and evening/weekend programs available. *Students:* 17 full-time (8 women), 15 part-time (8 women); includes 5 African Americans, 1 Asian American or Pacific Islander, 4 Hispanic Americans, 7 international. Average age 32. In 2009, 2 master's awarded. *Degree requirements:* For master's, thesis or alternative. *Entrance requirements:* Additional exam requirements/recommendations for international students: Required—TOEFL (minimum score 550 paper-based; 213 computer-based). *Application deadline:* For fall admission, 7/1 priority date for domestic students; for spring admission, 12/1 priority date for domestic students. Applications are processed on a rolling basis. Application fee: $50. Electronic applications accepted. *Expenses:* Tuition: Part-time $825 per credit. *Financial support:* Research assistantships, career-related internships or fieldwork, Federal Work-Study, institutionally sponsored loans, tuition waivers (partial), and unspecified assistantships available. Support available to part-time students. Financial award applicants required to submit FAFSA. *Unit head:* Dr. Roger Yu, Dean, 516-686-7700, Fax: 516-686-1192, E-mail: ryu@nyit.edu. *Application contact:* Dr. Jacquelyn Nealon, Vice President for Enrollment Services, 516-686-7925, Fax: 516-686-7597, E-mail: jnealon@nyit.edu.

New York University, School of Continuing and Professional Studies, Division for Media Industry Studies and Design, Center for Advanced Digital Applications, New York, NY 10012-1019. Offers digital imaging and design (MS), including 2D or 3D production. Part-time programs available. *Faculty:* 2 full-time (1 woman), 21 part-time/adjunct (2 women). *Students:* 40 full-time (20 women), 38 part-time (12 women); includes 15 minority (3 African Americans, 8 Asian Americans or Pacific Islanders, 4 Hispanic Americans). Average age 31. 56 applicants, 77% accepted, 28 enrolled. In 2009, 44 master's awarded. *Degree requirements:* For master's, thesis, research and documentation, project. *Entrance requirements:* For master's, GRE or GMAT (recommended), portfolio, 2 letters of recommendation, resume. Additional exam requirements/recommendations for international students: Required—TOEFL (minimum score 600 paper-based; 250 computer-based; 100 iBT), TWE. *Application deadline:* For fall admission, 2/1 priority date for domestic and international students; for spring admission, 10/15 priority date for domestic students, 8/15 priority date for international students. Applications are processed on a rolling basis. Application fee: $75. Electronic applications accepted. *Expenses:* Tuition: Full-time $30,528; part-time $1272 per credit. Required fees: $2177. *Financial support:* In 2009–10, 35 students received support, including 35 fellowships with tuition reimbursements available (averaging $3,136 per year); career-related internships or fieldwork and scholarships/grants also available. Support available to part-time students. Financial award application deadline: 3/1; financial award applicants required to submit FAFSA. *Unit head:* Patricia Heard-Greene, Director, 212-992-3269, Fax: 212-992-3386, E-mail: patricia.heard-greene@nyu.edu. *Application contact:* Wang Kathy, Assistant Director, 212-992-3370, Fax: 212-992-3377, E-mail: cada@nyu.edu.

New York University, School of Continuing and Professional Studies, Division for Media Industry Studies and Design, Program in Graphic Communications Management and Technology, New York, NY 10012-1019. Offers MA. Part-time and evening/weekend programs available. *Faculty:* 1 (woman) full-time, 12 part-time/adjunct (3 women). *Students:* 24 full-time (15 women), 87 part-time (56 women); includes 22 minority (6 African Americans, 1 American Indian/Alaska Native, 11 Asian Americans or Pacific Islanders, 4 Hispanic Americans). Average age 32. 44 applicants, 82% accepted, 25 enrolled. In 2009, 42 master's awarded. *Degree requirements:* For master's, thesis, capstone, research course. *Entrance requirements:* For master's, GRE General Test or GMAT (for recent graduates), resume, 2 letters of recommendation. Additional exam requirements/recommendations for international students: Required—TOEFL (minimum score 600 paper-based; 250 computer-based; 100 iBT), TWE. *Application deadline:* For fall admission, 2/1 priority date for domestic and international students; for spring admission, 10/15 priority date for domestic students, 8/15 priority date for international students. Applications are processed on a rolling basis. Application fee: $75. Electronic applications accepted. *Expenses:* Tuition: Full-time $30,528; part-time $1272 per credit. Required fees: $2177. *Financial support:* In 2009–10, 53 students received support, including 56 fellowships (averaging $2,451 per year); scholarships/grants and tuition waivers (partial) also available. Support available to part-time students. Financial award application deadline: 3/1; financial award applicants required to submit FAFSA. *Unit head:* Bonnie Blake, Director, 212-992-3222,

Fax: 212-992-3386, E-mail: bonnie.blake@nyu.edu. *Application contact:* Ansley Dunn, Program Administrator, 212-992-3283, Fax: 212-992-3233, E-mail: ansley.dunn@nyu.edu.

New York University, Tisch School of the Arts Asia, Singapore, NY 248923, Singapore. Offers animation and digital arts (MFA); dramatic writing (MFA); film production (MFA). *Entrance requirements:* Additional exam requirements/recommendations for international students: Required—TOEFL (minimum score 610 paper-based; 250 computer-based; 105 iBT). Electronic applications accepted. *Expenses:* Tuition: Full-time $30,528; part-time $1272 per credit. Required fees: $2177.

North Carolina State University, Graduate School, College of Humanities and Social Sciences, Program in Communication, Rhetoric, and Digital Media, Raleigh, NC 27695. Offers PhD.

Philadelphia University, School of Design and Media, Program in Digital Design, Philadelphia, PA 19144. Offers MS. *Accreditation:* NASAD. *Entrance requirements:* For master's, portfolio. Additional exam requirements/recommendations for international students: Required—TOEFL (minimum score 550 paper-based; 213 computer-based; 79 iBT). Electronic applications accepted.

Regent University, Graduate School, School of Communication and the Arts, Virginia Beach, VA 23464-9800. Offers acting (MFA); acting and directing (MFA); cinema arts/television arts (MA); communication (MA, PhD); digital media (MA); directing for cinema/TV (MA); journalism (MA); producing for cinema/TV (MA); script and screenwriting (MFA); theatre (MA). Part-time programs available. Postbaccalaureate distance learning degree programs offered (minimal on-campus study). *Faculty:* 27 full-time (3 women), 24 part-time/adjunct (8 women). *Students:* 120 full-time (65 women), 160 part-time (82 women); includes 70 minority (53 African Americans, 2 American Indian/Alaska Native, 4 Asian Americans or Pacific Islanders, 11 Hispanic Americans), 10 international. Average age 31. 221 applicants, 58% accepted, 62 enrolled. In 2009, 61 master's, 13 doctorates awarded. *Degree requirements:* For master's, thesis or alternative; for doctorate, thesis/dissertation. *Entrance requirements:* For master's, GRE General Test or MAT, minimum undergraduate GPA of 3.0, writing sample, computer literacy survey, recommendation, resume, interview, audition (MFA programs); for doctorate, GRE General Test, minimum graduate GPA of 3.0, writing sample, computer literacy survey, recommendation, interview, transcripts. Additional exam requirements/recommendations for international students: Required—TOEFL (minimum score 577 paper-based; 233 computer-based). *Application deadline:* For fall admission, 3/1 priority date for domestic students; for spring admission, 10/1 priority date for domestic students. Applications are processed on a rolling basis. Application fee: $50. Electronic applications accepted. *Expenses:* Contact institution. *Financial support:* In 2009–10, 229 students received support; fellowships with full and partial tuition reimbursements available, career-related internships or fieldwork, scholarships/grants, tuition waivers (full and partial), and unspecified assistantships available. Support available to part-time students. Financial award application deadline: 9/1; financial award applicants required to submit FAFSA. *Faculty research:* Southern gospel music, education and entertainment, celebrities and the media, journalism and ethics, C. S. Lewis. *Unit head:* Michael Patrick, Dean, 757-352-4970, Fax: 757-352-4279, E-mail: michpat@regent.edu. *Application contact:* Matthew Chadwick, Director of Admissions, 800-373-5504, Fax: 757-352-4381, E-mail: admissions@regent.edu.

Rensselaer Polytechnic Institute, Graduate School, School of Humanities and Social Sciences, Department of the Arts, Program in Electronic Arts, Troy, NY 12180-3590. Offers MFA, PhD. *Faculty:* 14 full-time (8 women). *Students:* 17 full-time (6 women), 2 part-time (both women); includes 3 minority (2 Asian Americans or Pacific Islanders, 1 Hispanic American), 1 international. Average age 28. 74 applicants, 34% accepted, 9 enrolled. In 2009, 5 master's awarded. *Degree requirements:* For master's, thesis in the form of a large-scale creative project; for doctorate, comprehensive exam, dissertation or creative project and dissertation text. *Entrance requirements:* For master's, portfolio; for doctorate, MA, MM, MS or MFA; portfolio; scholarly writing sample (previous thesis or publication); evidence of research-based creative orientation. Additional exam requirements/recommendations for international students: Required—TOEFL (minimum score 570 paper-based; 230 computer-based; 89 iBT), IELTS (minimum score 6.5). *Application deadline:* For fall admission, 1/15 for domestic and international students. Applications are processed on a rolling basis. Application fee: $75. Electronic applications accepted. *Expenses:* Tuition: Full-time $38,100. *Financial support:* In 2009–10, 15 students received support, including 7 fellowships with full tuition reimbursements available (averaging $16,000 per year), 8 teaching assistantships with full tuition reimbursements available (averaging $16,000 per year); unspecified assistantships also available. Financial award application deadline: 1/15. *Faculty research:* Computer music, video art, Net art, interactivity, bio art. *Unit head:* Mary Anne Staniszewski, Acting Head, 518-276-4784, Fax: 518-276-4370, E-mail: stanim@rpi.edu. *Application contact:* Jennifer Mumby, Graduate Program Administrator, 518-276-4784, Fax: 518-276-4370, E-mail: mumbyj@rpi.edu.

Rhode Island School of Design, Graduate Studies, Program in Digital Media, Providence, RI 02903-2784. Offers MFA. *Entrance requirements:* Additional exam requirements/recommendations for international students: Required—TOEFL (minimum score 580 paper-based; 237 computer-based), IELTS (minimum score 6.5).

Rochester Institute of Technology, Graduate Enrollment Services, College of Imaging Arts and Sciences, School of Design, Program in Computer Graphics Design, Rochester, NY 14623-5603. Offers MFA. *Accreditation:* NASAD. Part-time programs available. *Students:* 59 full-time (25 women), 12 part-time (7 women); includes 6 minority (2 African Americans, 1 American Indian/Alaska Native, 2 Asian Americans or Pacific Islanders, 1 Hispanic American), 43 international. Average age 29. 45 applicants, 60% accepted, 19 enrolled. In 2009, 9 master's awarded. *Degree requirements:* For master's, thesis. *Entrance requirements:* For master's, portfolio, minimum GPA of 3.0. Additional exam requirements/recommendations for international students: Required—TOEFL (minimum score 550 paper-based; 213 computer-based; 79 iBT), or IELTS (minimum score 6.5). *Application deadline:* For fall admission, 2/15 priority date for domestic and international students. Applications are processed on a rolling basis. Application fee: $50. Electronic applications accepted. *Expenses:* Tuition: Full-time $31,533; part-time $876 per credit hour. Required fees: $210. *Financial support:* In 2009–10, 50 students received support; research assistantships with partial tuition reimbursements available, teaching assistantships with partial tuition reimbursements available, career-related internships or fieldwork, institutionally sponsored loans, scholarships/grants, and unspecified assistantships available. Support available to part-time students. Financial award application deadline: 8/30; financial award applicants required to submit FAFSA. *Unit head:* Chris Jackson, Graduate Coordinator, 585-475-2688, Fax: 585-475-7533, E-mail: cbjpgd@rit.edu. *Application contact:* Diane Ellison, Assistant Vice President, Graduate Enrollment Services, 585-475-2229, Fax: 585-475-7164, E-mail: gradinfo@rit.edu.

St. Edward's University, School of Management and Business, Area of Digital Media Management, Austin, TX 78704. Offers MBA. *Students:* 34 full-time (14 women); includes 11 minority (2 African Americans, 2 Asian Americans or Pacific Islanders, 7 Hispanic Americans). Average age 26. 39 applicants, 64% accepted, 22 enrolled. In 2009, 11 master's awarded. *Entrance requirements:* For master's, GRE or GMAT, interview, 2 letters of recommendation, minimum GPA of 3.0 in last 60 hours of course work. Additional exam requirements/recommendations for international students: Required—TOEFL (minimum score 550 paper-based; 213 computer-based; 79 iBT) or IELTS (minimum score 6). *Application deadline:* For fall admission, 2/15 priority date for domestic and international students. Applications are processed on a rolling basis. Application fee: $45 ($50 for international students). Electronic applications accepted. *Expenses:* Contact institution. *Financial support:* Scholarships/grants available. *Unit head:* Russell Rains, Director, 512-428-1220, Fax: 512-448-8492, E-mail: russellr@stedwards.edu. *Application contact:* Kay L. Arnold, Assistant Director of Admissions, 512-233-1661, Fax: 512-428-1032, E-mail: kayla@stedwards.edu.

San Jose State University, Graduate Studies and Research, College of Humanities and the Arts, School of Art and Design, San Jose, CA 95192-0001. Offers animation/illustration (MA); art history (MA); digital media arts (MFA); photography (MFA); pictorial arts (MFA); spatial arts (MFA). *Accreditation:* NASAD (one or more programs are accredited). *Students:* 48 full-time (27 women), 24 part-time (16 women); includes 13 minority (3 African Americans, 6 Asian Americans or Pacific Islanders, 4 Hispanic Americans), 2 international. Average age 36. 69 applicants, 23% accepted, 16 enrolled. In 2009, 17 master's awarded. *Entrance requirements:* For master's, GRE. *Application deadline:* For fall admission, 6/29 for domestic students; for spring admission, 11/30 for domestic students. Applications are processed on a rolling basis. Application fee: $59. Electronic applications accepted. *Financial support:* Applicants required to submit FAFSA. *Unit head:* John Loomis, Director, 408-924-4320, Fax: 408-924-4326. *Application contact:* John Loomis, Director, 408-924-4320, Fax: 408-924-4326.

Savannah College of Art and Design, Graduate School, Program in Animation, Savannah, GA 31402-3146. Offers MA, MFA. Part-time programs available. *Degree requirements:* For master's, thesis, internships. *Entrance requirements:* For master's, interview, portfolio. Additional exam requirements/recommendations for international students: Required—TOEFL (minimum score 450 paper-based; 133 computer-based). Electronic applications accepted. *Expenses:* Tuition: Full-time $28,515; part-time $627 per credit hour. One-time fee: $500. Tuition and fees vary according to course load.

Savannah College of Art and Design, Graduate School, Program in Broadcast Design, Savannah, GA 31402-3146. Offers MA, MFA. Part-time programs available. *Degree requirements:* For master's, thesis, internships. *Entrance requirements:* For master's, interview, portfolio. Additional exam requirements/recommendations for international students: Required—TOEFL (minimum score 450 paper-based; 133 computer-based). Electronic applications accepted. *Expenses:* Tuition: Full-time $28,515; part-time $627 per credit hour. One-time fee: $500. Tuition and fees vary according to course load.

Savannah College of Art and Design, Graduate School, Program in Digital Photography, Savannah, GA 31402-3146. Offers MA. Part-time programs available. *Degree requirements:* For master's, thesis. *Entrance requirements:* For master's, interview, portfolio. Additional exam requirements/recommendations for international students: Required—TOEFL (minimum score 450 paper-based; 133 computer-based). Electronic applications accepted. *Expenses:* Tuition: Full-time $28,515; part-time $627 per credit hour. One-time fee: $500. Tuition and fees vary according to course load.

Savannah College of Art and Design, Graduate School, Program in Interactive Design and Game Development, Savannah, GA 31402-3146. Offers MA, MFA. Part-time programs available. *Degree requirements:* For master's, thesis, internships. *Entrance requirements:* For master's, interview, portfolio. Additional exam requirements/recommendations for international students: Required—TOEFL (minimum score 450 paper-based; 133 computer-based). Electronic applications accepted. *Expenses:* Tuition: Full-time $28,515; part-time $627 per credit hour. One-time fee: $500. Tuition and fees vary according to course load.

School of Visual Arts, Graduate Programs, Computer Art Department, New York, NY 10010-3994. Offers MFA. *Accreditation:* NASAD. *Degree requirements:* For master's, final review, project or thesis. *Entrance requirements:* For master's, portfolio. Additional exam requirements/recommendations for international students: Required—TOEFL (minimum score 550 paper-based; 213 computer-based; 79 iBT). Electronic applications accepted.

Stevens Institute of Technology, Graduate School, Charles V. Schaefer Jr. School of Engineering, Department of Computer Science, Hoboken, NJ 07030. Offers computer graphics (Certificate); computer science (MS, PhD); computer systems (Certificate); database management systems (Certificate); distributed systems (Certificate); elements of computer science (Certificate); enterprise computing (Certificate); enterprise security and information assurance (Certificate); health informatics (Certificate); multimedia experience and management (Certificate); networks and systems administration (Certificate); security and privacy (Certificate); service oriented computing (Certificate); software design (Certificate); theoretical computer science (Certificate). Part-time and evening/weekend programs available. Terminal master's awarded for partial completion of doctoral program. *Degree requirements:* For master's, thesis optional; for doctorate, variable foreign language requirement, comprehensive exam, thesis/dissertation. *Entrance requirements:* For master's and doctorate, GRE, minimum GPA of 3.0. Additional exam requirements/recommendations for international students: Required—TOEFL. Electronic applications accepted. *Expenses:* Tuition: Full-time $9900; part-time $1100 per credit. Required fees: $286 per semester. *Faculty research:* Semantics, reliability theory, programming language, cyber security.

Syracuse University, College of Visual and Performing Arts, Program in Computer Art, Syracuse, NY 13244. Offers MFA. *Students:* 4 full-time (0 women). Average age 25. 16 applicants, 19% accepted, 0 enrolled. In 2009, 1 master's awarded. *Degree requirements:* For master's, thesis or alternative. *Entrance requirements:* For master's, portfolio. Additional exam requirements/recommendations for international students: Required—TOEFL (minimum score 100 iBT). *Application deadline:* For fall admission, 2/1 priority date for domestic and international students. Application fee: $75. Electronic applications accepted. *Expenses:* Tuition: Full-time $26,808; part-time $1117 per credit. Required fees: $1024. *Financial support:* Fellowships with tuition reimbursements, teaching assistantships with tuition reimbursements available. Financial award application deadline: 1/1; financial award applicants required to submit FAFSA. *Unit head:* Heath Hanlin, Chair, 315-443-1033, E-mail: hahanlin@syr.edu. *Application contact:* Harriett Conti, Assistant Dean for Recruitment and Admissions, 315-443-5755, E-mail: hmconti@syr.edu.

Texas State University–San Marcos, Graduate School, College of Fine Arts and Communication, Department of Art and Design, Program in Communication Design, San Marcos, TX 78666. Offers MFA. *Faculty:* 3 full-time (1 woman). *Students:* 10 full-time (4 women), 22 part-time (9 women); includes 6 minority (3 Asian Americans or Pacific Islanders, 3 Hispanic Americans), 3 international. Average age 34. 23 applicants, 35% accepted, 8 enrolled. *Degree requirements:* For master's, comprehensive exam, thesis (for some programs). *Entrance requirements:* For master's, minimum GPA of 2.75 on last 60 hours of undergraduate work, 20-work portfolio. Additional exam requirements/recommendations for international students: Required—TOEFL (minimum score 550 paper-based; 213 computer-based). *Application deadline:* For fall admission, 3/15 for domestic and international students. Applications are processed on a rolling basis. Application fee: $40 ($90 for international students). Electronic applications accepted. *Expenses:* Tuition, state resident: full-time $5784; part-time $241 per credit hour. Tuition, nonresident: part-time $551 per credit hour. Required fees: $1728; $48 per credit hour. $306. Tuition and fees vary according to course load. *Financial support:* In 2009–10, 24 students received support, including 5 teaching assistantships (averaging $5,481 per year); Federal Work-Study and institutionally sponsored loans also available. Support available to part-time students. Financial award application deadline: 4/1; financial award applicants required to submit FAFSA. *Unit head:* William Meek, Program Advisor, 512-245-0311, E-mail: w.meek@txstate.edu. *Application contact:* Dr. J. Michael Willoughby, Dean of Graduate School, 512-245-2581, Fax: 512-245-8365, E-mail: gradcollege@txstate.edu.

Universidad Autonoma de Guadalajara, Graduate Programs, Guadalajara, Mexico. Offers administrative law and justice (LL M); advertising and corporate communications (MA); architecture (M Arch); business (MBA); computational science (MCC); education (Ed M, Ed D); English-Spanish translation (MA); fiscal law (MA); integrated management of digital animation (MA); international business (MIB); international corporate law (LL M); internet technologies (MS); labor health (MS); manufacturing systems (MMS); philosophy (MA, PhD); power electronics (MS); quality systems (MQS); renewable energy (MS); social evaluation of projects (MBA); strategic market research (MBA); teaching mathematics (MA).

Universidad de las Américas–Puebla, Division of Graduate Studies, School of Humanities, Program in Information Design, Puebla, Mexico. Offers MA. Part-time and evening/weekend

Computer Art and Design

Universidad de las Américas–Puebla (continued)

programs available. *Degree requirements:* For master's, one foreign language, thesis. *Entrance requirements:* Additional exam requirements/recommendations for international students: Required—TOEFL. *Faculty research:* Typography, project development, organizational image.

University of Alaska Fairbanks, College of Liberal Arts, Department of Art, Fairbanks, AK 99775-5640. Offers art (MFA); ceramics (MFA); computer art (MFA); drawing (MFA); Native arts (MFA); painting (MFA); photography (MFA); printmaking (MFA); sculpture (MFA). Part-time programs available. *Faculty:* 7 full-time (2 women), 4 part-time/adjunct (3 women). *Students:* 7 full-time (3 women), 2 part-time (0 women); includes 1 minority (American Indian/Alaska Native). Average age 33. 10 applicants, 30% accepted, 2 enrolled. In 2009, 2 master's awarded. *Degree requirements:* For master's, comprehensive exam, thesis, oral exam, oral defense. *Entrance requirements:* For master's, portfolio. Additional exam requirements/recommendations for international students: Required—TOEFL (minimum score 550 paper-based; 213 computer-based; 80 iBT). *Application deadline:* For fall admission, 6/1 for domestic students, 3/1 for international students; for spring admission, 10/15 for domestic students, 9/1 for international students. Applications are processed on a rolling basis. Application fee: $60. Electronic applications accepted. *Expenses:* Tuition, state resident: full-time $7584; part-time $316 per credit. Tuition, nonresident: full-time $15,504; part-time $646 per credit. Required fees: $23 per credit. $135 per semester. Tuition and fees vary according to course level, course load and reciprocity agreements. *Financial support:* In 2009–10, 1 fellowship (averaging $13,500 per year), 4 teaching assistantships (averaging $12,058 per year) were awarded; research assistantships, Federal Work-Study, scholarships/grants, health care benefits, and unspecified assistantships also available. Support available to part-time students. Financial award application deadline: 7/1; financial award applicants required to submit FAFSA. *Faculty research:* Computer art, survey of arts in Alaska, found object art, visualization and animation, painting from the wilderness. *Unit head:* Todd Sherman, Chair, 907-474-7530, Fax: 907-474-5853, E-mail: fyart@uaf.edu. *Application contact:* Todd Sherman, Chair, 907-474-7530, Fax: 907-474-5853, E-mail: fyart@uaf.edu.

University of Baltimore, Graduate School, The Yale Gordon College of Liberal Arts, School of Information Arts and Technologies, Baltimore, MD 21201-5779. Offers communications design (DCD); human-computer interaction (MS); interaction design and information technology (MS). Part-time and evening/weekend programs available. *Entrance requirements:* For master's, GRE or MAT, minimum undergraduate GPA of 3.0. Additional exam requirements/recommendations for international students: Required—TOEFL (minimum score 550 paper-based; 213 computer-based).

University of California, Santa Cruz, Division of Graduate Studies, Division of the Arts, Program in Digital Arts and New Media, Santa Cruz, CA 95064. Offers MFA. *Entrance requirements:* Additional exam requirements/recommendations for international students: Required—TOEFL; Recommended—IELTS. Electronic applications accepted.

University of Central Arkansas, Graduate School, College of Fine Arts and Communication, Program in Digital Filmmaking, Conway, AR 72035-0001. Offers MFA. *Accreditation:* NASAD. *Faculty:* 5 full-time (0 women). *Students:* 24 full-time (6 women), 3 part-time (0 women); includes 2 minority (1 African American, 1 Asian American or Pacific Islander), 1 international. Average age 28. 9 applicants, 89% accepted, 6 enrolled. In 2009, 1 master's awarded. *Degree requirements:* For master's, thesis. *Entrance requirements:* For master's, GRE General Test, minimum GPA of 2.7. Additional exam requirements/recommendations for international students: Required—TOEFL (minimum score 550 paper-based; 213 computer-based). *Application deadline:* For fall admission, 3/1 priority date for domestic and international students; for spring admission, 10/1 priority date for domestic and international students. Applications are processed on a rolling basis. Application fee: $25 ($50 for international students). *Expenses:* Tuition, state resident: full-time $5136; part-time $214 per credit hour. Required fees: $379.50; $127 per term. Tuition and fees vary according to course level, course load and campus/location. *Financial support:* Unspecified assistantships available. *Unit head:* Dr. Joseph Anderson, Chair, 501-450-3162, E-mail: josepha@uca.edu. *Application contact:* Brenda Herring, Admissions Assistant, 501-450-5065, Fax: 501-450-5678, E-mail: bherring@uca.edu.

University of Central Florida, College of Arts and Humanities, Department of Art, Orlando, FL 32816. Offers studio art and the computer (MFA). *Faculty:* 24 full-time (5 women), 6 part-time/adjunct (2 women). *Students:* 20 full-time (14 women); includes 2 minority (both Asian Americans or Pacific Islanders). Average age 30. 20 applicants, 60% accepted, 10 enrolled. In 2009, 10 master's awarded. Application fee: $30. Electronic applications accepted. *Expenses:* Tuition, state resident: part-time $306.31 per credit hour. Tuition, nonresident: part-time $1099.01 per credit hour. Part-time tuition and fees vary according to degree level and program. *Financial support:* In 2009–10, 2 fellowships (averaging $5,300 per year), 3 research assistantships (averaging $3,200 per year), 2 teaching assistantships (averaging $6,400 per year) were awarded; scholarships/grants and unspecified assistantships also available. *Unit head:* Jack Lew, Interim Chair, 407-823-3145, Fax: 407-823-6470. *Application contact:* Jack Lew, Interim Chair, 407-823-3145, Fax: 407-823-6470.

University of Central Florida, College of Arts and Humanities, Division of Film and Digital Media, Orlando, FL 32816. Offers interactive entertainment (MS). *Students:* 50 full-time (5 women), 49 part-time (5 women); includes 31 minority (5 African Americans, 5 Asian Americans or Pacific Islanders, 21 Hispanic Americans), 6 international. Average age 25. 92 applicants, 64% accepted, 49 enrolled. In 2009, 31 master's awarded. Application fee: $30. *Expenses:* Tuition, state resident: part-time $306.31 per credit hour. Tuition, nonresident: part-time $1099.01 per credit hour. Part-time tuition and fees vary according to degree level and program. *Financial support:* In 2009–10, 1 student received support, including 1 fellowship with partial tuition reimbursement available (averaging $10,000 per year), 3 research assistantships (averaging $3,200 per year), 2 teaching assistantships (averaging $6,400 per year). *Unit head:* Dr. Jose Maunez-Cuadra, Interim Chair, 407-823-2121, Fax: 407-317-7094, E-mail: info@fiea.ucf.edu. *Application contact:* Dr. Jose Maunez-Cuadra, Interim Chair, 407-823-2121, Fax: 407-317-7094, E-mail: info@fiea.ucf.edu.

University of Denver, Division of Arts, Humanities and Social Sciences, Department of Digital Media Studies, Denver, CO 80208. Offers MA. Part-time programs available. *Faculty:* 1 (woman) full-time. *Students:* 1 full-time (0 women), 12 part-time (6 women); includes 2 minority (1 African American, 1 Hispanic American). Average age 30. 22 applicants, 86% accepted, 6 enrolled. In 2009, 3 master's awarded. *Application deadline:* Applications are processed on a rolling basis. Application fee: $50. Electronic applications accepted. *Expenses:* Tuition: Full-time $34,596; part-time $961 per quarter hour. Required fees: $4 per quarter hour. Tuition and fees vary according to course load, campus/location and program. *Unit head:* Dr. Anne McCall, Dean, 303-871-4449. *Application contact:* Chris Coleman, Information Contact, 303-871-7716, E-mail: ccolem22@du.edu.

University of Denver, Division of Arts, Humanities and Social Sciences, School of Art and Art History, Denver, CO 80208. Offers art history (MA); art history/museum studies (MA); electronic media arts and design (MFA). *Accreditation:* NASAD. Part-time programs available. *Faculty:* 16 full-time (11 women), 9 part-time/adjunct (5 women). *Students:* 15 full-time (14 women), 7 part-time (6 women); includes 1 minority (Hispanic American). Average age 29. 55 applicants, 51% accepted, 14 enrolled. In 2009, 10 master's awarded. *Degree requirements:* For master's, one foreign language, research paper. *Entrance requirements:* For master's, GRE. Additional exam requirements/recommendations for international students: Required—TOEFL. *Application deadline:* Applications are processed on a rolling basis. Application fee: $50. Electronic applications accepted. *Expenses:* Tuition: Full-time $34,596; part-time $961 per quarter hour. Required fees: $4 per quarter hour. Tuition and fees vary according to course load, campus/location and program. *Financial support:* Career-related internships or fieldwork, Federal Work-Study, institutionally sponsored loans, and scholarships/grants available. Support available to part-time students. Financial award application deadline: 3/1; financial award applicants required to submit FAFSA. *Faculty research:* Images of women in alchemical manuscripts and books, Giovanni Benedetto, Salvatore Castiglione. *Unit head:* Dr. Annette Stott, Director, 303-871-2846. *Application contact:* Dr. Annabeth Headrick, Graduate Advisor, 303-871-3574, E-mail: saah-interest@du.edu.

University of Florida, Graduate School, College of Engineering and College of Liberal Arts and Sciences, Department of Computer and Information Science and Engineering, Gainesville, FL 32611. Offers computer engineering (ME, MS, PhD); computer science (MS); digital arts and sciences (MS). Part-time programs available. *Degree requirements:* For master's, thesis (for some programs); for doctorate, thesis/dissertation. *Entrance requirements:* For master's and doctorate, GRE General Test, minimum GPA of 3.0. Additional exam requirements/recommendations for international students: Required—TOEFL (minimum score 550 paper-based; 213 computer-based). Electronic applications accepted. *Faculty research:* Artificial intelligence, networks security, distributed computing, parallel processing system, vision and visualization, database systems.

University of Florida, Graduate School, College of Fine Arts, School of Art and Art History, Gainesville, FL 32611. Offers art (MFA), including ceramics, creative photography, drawing, electronic intermedia, graphic design, painting, printmaking, sculpture; art education (MA); art history (MA, PhD); digital arts and sciences (MA); museology (museum studies) (MA). *Accreditation:* NASAD. *Degree requirements:* For master's, variable foreign language requirement, project or thesis (MFA). *Entrance requirements:* For master's, portfolio (MFA), writing sample (MA), GRE General Test or minimum GPA of 3.0. Additional exam requirements/recommendations for international students: Required—TOEFL (minimum score 550 paper-based; 213 computer-based). Electronic applications accepted. *Faculty research:* Studio production, art historical studies of style context.

University of Houston, College of Liberal Arts and Social Sciences, Department of Art, Houston, TX 77204. Offers art (MA); graphic communication (MFA); interdisciplinary practice and emerging forms (MFA); painting (MFA); photography/digital media (MFA); sculpture (MFA). *Faculty:* 10 full-time (6 women), 7 part-time/adjunct (3 women). *Students:* 35 full-time (20 women); includes 5 minority (2 African Americans, 1 Asian American or Pacific Islander, 2 Hispanic Americans), 4 international. Average age 32. 61 applicants, 31% accepted, 13 enrolled. In 2009, 12 master's awarded. *Entrance requirements:* For master's, GRE General Test, includes baccalaureate degree and portfolio. Additional exam requirements/recommendations for international students: Required—TOEFL. *Application deadline:* For fall admission, 2/1 for domestic and international students. Application fee: $25 ($75 for international students). Electronic applications accepted. *Expenses:* Tuition, state resident: full-time $7676; part-time $320 per credit hour. Tuition, nonresident: full-time $14,324; part-time $597 per credit hour. Required fees: $3034. *Financial support:* In 2009–10, 22 teaching assistantships with full tuition reimbursements (averaging $10,400 per year) were awarded; career-related internships or fieldwork, Federal Work-Study, institutionally sponsored loans, scholarships/grants, health care benefits, and unspecified assistantships also available. Support available to part-time students. Financial award application deadline: 3/10. *Faculty research:* Painting, sculpture, photography/installation/video, graphic design and typography, art history (Pre-Columbian to Surrealism). *Unit head:* Dr. John Reed, Chairperson, 713-743-3001, Fax: 713-743-2823, E-mail: jreed@uh.edu. *Application contact:* Cathy Hunt, Graduate Advisor and Instructional Assistant Professor, 713-743-2830, Fax: 713-743-2823, E-mail: chunt@uh.edu.

The University of Kansas, Graduate Studies, School of Architecture, Design, and Planning, Department of Design, Lawrence, KS 66045. Offers design (MA, MFA); design management (MA); interaction design (MA). *Accreditation:* NASAD (one or more programs are accredited). *Students:* 7 full-time (4 women), 19 part-time (12 women), 1 international. Average age 34. 16 applicants, 88% accepted, 12 enrolled. In 2009, 2 master's awarded. *Degree requirements:* For master's, thesis. *Entrance requirements:* For master's, portfolio, 3 letters of recommendation, minimum GPA of 3.0. Additional exam requirements/recommendations for international students: Required—TOEFL, IELTS. *Application deadline:* For fall admission, 2/1 for domestic and international students; for spring admission, 10/15 for domestic students. Application fee: $45 ($55 for international students). Electronic applications accepted. *Expenses:* Tuition, state resident: full-time $6492; part-time $270.50 per credit hour. Tuition, nonresident: full-time $15,510; part-time $646.25 per credit hour. Required fees: $847; $70.56 per credit hour. Tuition and fees vary according to course load and program. *Financial support:* Fellowships, teaching assistantships with full and partial tuition reimbursements, Federal Work-Study, scholarships/grants, and unspecified assistantships available. Financial award application deadline: 2/1; financial award applicants required to submit FAFSA. *Faculty research:* Interaction design, design management, photography, graphic design, industrial design. *Unit head:* Prof. Gregory Thomas, Chairperson, 785-864-4401. *Application contact:* Prof. Gregory Thomas, Chairperson, 785-864-4401.

University of Massachusetts Dartmouth, Graduate School, College of Visual and Performing Arts, Program in Visual Design, North Dartmouth, MA 02747-2300. Offers digital media (MFA); graphic design (MFA); illustration (MFA); photography (MFA); typography (MFA). *Accreditation:* NASAD. *Faculty:* 17 full-time (7 women), 3 part-time/adjunct (2 women). *Students:* 6 full-time (4 women), 1 (woman) part-time. Average age 35. 25 applicants, 44% accepted, 2 enrolled. In 2009, 2 master's awarded. *Degree requirements:* For master's, visual thesis. *Entrance requirements:* For master's, portfolio, interview, minimum GPA of 3.0, 3 letters of recommendation. Additional exam requirements/recommendations for international students: Required—TOEFL (minimum score 500 paper-based). *Application deadline:* For fall admission, 2/1 priority date for domestic students, 12/1 priority date for international students. Applications are processed on a rolling basis. Application fee: $40 ($60 for international students). Electronic applications accepted. *Expenses:* Tuition, state resident: full-time $2071; part-time $86.29 per credit. Tuition, nonresident: full-time $8099; part-time $337.46 per credit. Required fees: $9446. Tuition and fees vary according to class time, course load and reciprocity agreements. *Financial support:* In 2009–10, 5 teaching assistantships with full tuition reimbursements (averaging $3,088 per year) were awarded; Federal Work-Study and unspecified assistantships also available. Support available to part-time students. Financial award application deadline: 3/1; financial award applicants required to submit FAFSA. Total annual research expenditures: $1,000. *Unit head:* Memory Holloway, Director, 508-999-8554, E-mail: mholloway@umassd.edu. *Application contact:* Elan Turcotte-Shamski, Graduate Admissions Officer, 508-999-8604, Fax: 508-999-8183, E-mail: graduate@umassd.edu.

University of Missouri, Graduate School, College of Human Environmental Science, Department of Architectural Studies, Columbia, MO 65211. Offers design with digital media (MA, MS); environmental design (MS). *Entrance requirements:* For master's, GRE General Test, minimum GPA of 3.0. Additional exam requirements/recommendations for international students: Required—TOEFL (minimum score 500 paper-based; 173 computer-based; 61 iBT).

University of Pennsylvania, School of Engineering and Applied Science, Computer Graphics and Game Technology Program, Philadelphia, PA 19104. Offers MSE. *Students:* 14 full-time (2 women), 4 part-time (1 woman); includes 4 minority (all Asian Americans or Pacific Islanders), 9 international. 60 applicants, 48% accepted, 11 enrolled. In 2009, 14 master's awarded. Application fee: $70. *Expenses:* Tuition: Full-time $25,660; part-time $4758 per course. Required fees: $2152; $270 per course. Tuition and fees vary according to course load, degree level and program.

University of Southern California, Graduate School, School of Cinematic Arts, Division of Animation and Digital Arts, Los Angeles, CA 90089. Offers MFA. *Faculty:* 8 full-time (5 women), 14 part-time/adjunct (5 women). *Students:* 43 full-time (20 women); includes 9 minority (2 African Americans, 1 American Indian/Alaska Native, 2 Asian Americans or Pacific Islanders, 4 Hispanic Americans), 12 international. In 2009, 13 master's awarded. *Degree requirements:* For master's, thesis, digital media and research. *Application deadline:* For fall admission, 12/1 for domestic and international students. Electronic applications accepted. *Expenses:* Contact institution. *Financial support:* In 2009–10, 21 students received support, including 6 fellowships with partial tuition reimbursements available; career-related internships or fieldwork, scholarships/grants, and tuition waivers (partial) also available. Financial award application deadline: 3/9; financial award applicants required to submit FAFSA. *Faculty research:* Science visualization, visual effects, experimental animation, documentary visualization, motion graphics. *Unit head:* Sheila M. Sofian, Department Chair and Associate Professor, 213-740-7595, Fax: 213-740-5869, E-mail: ssofian@cinema.usc.edu. *Application contact:* Daphne M. Sigismondi, Assistant Director, 213-740-3986, Fax: 213-740-5869, E-mail: dsigismondi@cinema.usc.edu.

University of Victoria, Faculty of Graduate Studies, Faculty of Fine Arts, Department of Visual Arts, Victoria, BC V8W 2Y2, Canada. Offers digital multimedia (MFA); drawing (MFA); painting (MFA); photography (MFA); sculpture (MFA); video (MFA). *Degree requirements:* For master's, exhibit, oral exam. *Entrance requirements:* For master's, portfolio, BFA. Additional exam requirements/recommendations for international students: Required—TOEFL (minimum score 575 paper-based; 233 computer-based), IELTS (minimum score 7). Electronic applications accepted.

Washington State University, Graduate School, College of Liberal Arts, Department of Fine Arts, Pullman, WA 99164. Offers ceramics (MFA); digital media (MFA); drawing (MFA); painting (MFA); photography (MFA); print making (MFA); sculpture (MFA). *Faculty:* 10. *Students:* 15 full-time (8 women); includes 2 minority (1 African American, 1 Hispanic American). Average age 29. 30 applicants, 20% accepted, 5 enrolled. In 2009, 5 master's awarded. *Degree requirements:* For master's, comprehensive exam (for some programs), thesis, exhibit, oral exam. *Entrance requirements:* For master's, GRE, Graduate School application, statement of intent indicating your area(s) of focus, the subject of your work, the concepts and issues you are exploring, and how you foresee your work evolving within the program, portfolio of no more than 15 images on CD/DVD,inventory list with the title, medium, size and approximate date of completion for each work. Additional exam requirements/recommendations for international students: Required—TOEFL (minimum score 550 paper-based; 213 computer-based), IELTS. *Application deadline:* For fall admission, 1/10 for domestic and international students. Application fee: $50. Electronic applications accepted. *Financial support:* In 2009–10, fellowships with full and partial tuition reimbursements (averaging $3,114 per year), research assistantships with full and partial tuition reimbursements (averaging $13,917 per year), teaching assistantships with full and partial tuition reimbursements (averaging $13,056 per year) were awarded; career-related internships or fieldwork, Federal Work-Study, institutionally sponsored loans, tuition waivers (partial), and unspecified assistantships also available. Financial award application deadline: 2/15; financial award applicants required to submit FAFSA. *Faculty research:* Polynesian art, museum representation, number theory. *Unit head:* Dr. Chris Watts, Interim Chair, 509-335-7107, Fax: 509-335-7742, E-mail: cjwatts@wsu.edu. *Application contact:* Graduate School Admissions, 800-GRADWSU, Fax: 509-335-1949, E-mail: gradsch@wsu.edu.

Graphic Design

Academy of Art University, Graduate Program, School of Graphic Design, San Francisco, CA 94105-3410. Offers MFA. *Accreditation:* NASAD. Part-time programs available. Postbaccalaureate distance learning degree programs offered (no on-campus study). *Degree requirements:* For master's, final review. *Entrance requirements:* For master's, minimum GPA of 3.0, portfolio. Electronic applications accepted.

Atlantic College, Program in Graphic Arts, Guaynabo, PR 00970. Offers digital graphic design (MGD). Part-time programs available. *Degree requirements:* For master's, thesis. *Entrance requirements:* For master's, minimum GPA of 3.0, 2 letters of recommendation, portfolio, interview. *Faculty research:* Digital design, technology.

Bob Jones University, Graduate Programs, Greenville, SC 29614. Offers accountancy (MS); Bible (MA); Bible translation (MA); Biblical studies (Certificate); broadcast management (MS); business administration (MBA); church history (MA, PhD); church ministries (MA); church music (MM); cinema and video production (MA); counseling (MS); curriculum and instruction (Ed D); divinity (M Div); dramatic production (MA); educational leadership (MS, Ed D, Ed S); elementary education (M Ed, MAT); English (M Ed, MA, MAT); fine arts (MA); graphic design (MA); history (M Ed, MA); illustration (MA); interpretative speech (MA); mathematics (M Ed, MAT); medical missions (Certificate); ministry (MM, D Min); multi-categorical special education (M Ed, MAT); music (M Ed); New Testament interpretation (PhD); Old Testament interpretation (PhD); orchestral instrument performance (MM); organ performance (MM); pastoral studies (MA); personnel services (MS, Ed S); piano pedagogy (MM); piano performance (MM); platform arts (MA); radio and television broadcasting (MS); rhetoric and public address (MA); secondary education (M Ed); studio art (MA); teaching Bible (MA); theology (MA, PhD); voice performance (MM); youth ministries (MA); M Div/MM.

Boston University, College of Fine Arts, School of Visual Arts, Program in Graphic Design, Boston, MA 02215. Offers MFA. *Students:* 26 full-time (23 women), 3 part-time (all women), 13 international. Average age 29. 81 applicants, 41% accepted, 15 enrolled. In 2009, 14 master's awarded. *Entrance requirements:* For master's, portfolio. Additional exam requirements/recommendations for international students: Required—TOEFL. *Application deadline:* For fall admission, 2/15 for domestic students, 2/15 priority date for international students. Applications are processed on a rolling basis. Application fee: $70. *Expenses:* Tuition: Full-time $37,910; part-time $1184 per credit hour. Required fees: $386; $40 per semester. Part-time tuition and fees vary according to class time, course level, degree level and program. *Financial support:* Fellowships, teaching assistantships available. Financial award application deadline: 2/15. *Unit head:* Alston Purvis, Chairman, 617-353-3371, E-mail: apurvis@bu.edu. *Application contact:* Mark Krone, Manager, Graduate Admissions, 617-353-3350, E-mail: arts@bu.edu.

Bowling Green State University, Graduate College, College of Arts and Sciences, School of Art, Bowling Green, OH 43403. Offers 2-D studio art (MA, MFA); 3-D studio art (MA, MFA); art education (MA); art history (MA); computer art (MA); design (MFA); digital arts (MFA); graphics (MFA). *Accreditation:* NASAD. Part-time programs available. *Degree requirements:* For master's, thesis or alternative, final exhibit (MFA). *Entrance requirements:* For master's, GRE General Test (MA), slide portfolio (15-20 slides). Additional exam requirements/recommendations for international students: Required—TOEFL. Electronic applications accepted. *Faculty research:* Computer animation and virtual reality, Spanish still-life painting from 1600 to 1800, art and psychotherapy, Japanese wood-firing techniques in ceramics, non-toxic printmaking technologies.

California Institute of the Arts, School of Art, Valencia, CA 91355-2340. Offers art (MFA, Adv C); graphic design (MFA, Adv C); photography (MFA, Adv C). *Accreditation:* NASAD (one or more programs are accredited). *Degree requirements:* For master's, final project. *Entrance requirements:* For master's, portfolio. Additional exam requirements/recommendations for international students: Required—TOEFL. Electronic applications accepted.

California State University, Los Angeles, Graduate Studies, College of Arts and Letters, Department of Art, Los Angeles, CA 90032-8530. Offers art (MA), including art education, art history, art therapy, ceramics, metals, and textiles, design (MA, MFA), painting, sculpture, and graphic arts, photography; fine arts (MFA), including crafts, design (MA, MFA), studio arts. *Accreditation:* NASAD (one or more programs are accredited). Part-time and evening/weekend programs available. *Faculty:* 12 full-time (6 women), 1 part-time/adjunct (0 women). *Students:* 28 full-time (21 women), 40 part-time (28 women); includes 22 minority (1 African American, 6 Asian Americans or Pacific Islanders, 15 Hispanic Americans), 9 international. Average age 37. 30 applicants, 100% accepted, 12 enrolled. In 2009, 17 master's awarded. *Degree requirements:* For master's, comprehensive exam, project or thesis. *Entrance requirements:* For master's, portfolio. Additional exam requirements/recommendations for international students: Required—TOEFL (minimum score 500 paper-based; 173 computer-based). *Application deadline:* For fall admission, 5/1 for domestic and international students. Applications are processed on a rolling basis. Application fee: $55. Electronic applications accepted. *Financial support:* Federal Work-Study available. Support available to part-time students. Financial award application deadline: 3/1. *Faculty research:* The artist and the book, conceptual art, ceramic processes, computer graphics, architectural graphics. *Unit head:* Dr. Abbas Daneshvari, Chair, 323-343-4010, Fax: 323-343-4045, E-mail: adanesh@calstatela.edu. *Application contact:* Dr. Cheryl L. Ney, Associate Vice President for Academic Affairs and Dean of Graduate Studies, 323-343-3820, Fax: 323-343-5653, E-mail: cney@cslanet.calstatela.edu.

Cardinal Stritch University, College of Arts and Sciences, Department of Art, Milwaukee, WI 53217-3985. Offers visual studies (MA). Part-time and evening/weekend programs available. *Degree requirements:* For master's, thesis, portfolio, exhibit. *Entrance requirements:* For master's, minimum GPA of 2.75; 3 letters of recommendation.

City College of the City University of New York, Graduate School, College of Liberal Arts and Science, Division of the Humanities and Arts, Department of Art, Program in Fine Arts, New York, NY 10031-9198. Offers advertising design (MFA); ceramic design (MFA); painting (MFA); printmaking (MFA); sculpture (MFA); wood and metal design (MFA). *Degree requirements:* For master's, thesis exhibit. *Entrance requirements:* For master's, 20 slide portfolio. Additional exam requirements/recommendations for international students: Required—TOEFL (minimum score 577 paper-based; 90 iBT). Electronic applications accepted.

The College of New Rochelle, Graduate School, Division of Art and Communication Studies, Program in Studio Art, New Rochelle, NY 10805-2308. Offers MS. Part-time and evening/weekend programs available. *Degree requirements:* For master's, apprenticeship. *Entrance requirements:* For master's, portfolio, 36 credits of course work in studio art. *Faculty research:* Experimental computer graphics.

Cranbrook Academy of Art, Graduate School, Program in Fine Arts, Bloomfield Hills, MI 48303-0801. Offers ceramics (MFA); design (MFA), including graphic design; fiber arts (MFA); metalsmithing (MFA); painting (MFA); photography (MFA); printmaking (MFA); sculpture (MFA). *Accreditation:* NASAD. *Degree requirements:* For master's, thesis, exhibit. *Entrance requirements:* Additional exam requirements/recommendations for international students: Required—TOEFL (minimum score 550 paper-based; 213 computer-based).

Digital Media Arts College, Graduate Programs, Boca Raton, FL 33431. Offers graphic design (MFA); special FX animation (MFA).

Florida Atlantic University, Dorothy F. Schmidt College of Arts and Letters, Department of Visual Arts and Art History, Boca Raton, FL 33431-0991. Offers art education (MAT); ceramics (MFA); computer art (MFA); graphic design (MFA); painting (MFA). *Faculty:* 23 full-time (12 women), 17 part-time/adjunct (11 women). *Students:* 15 full-time (11 women), 11 part-time (6 women); includes 7 minority (1 African American, 6 Hispanic Americans), 3 international. Average age 31. 19 applicants, 21% accepted, 0 enrolled. In 2009, 5 master's awarded. *Degree requirements:* For master's, one foreign language, project. *Entrance requirements:* For master's, GRE General Test, minimum GPA of 3.0 during last 60 hours of course work, slide portfolio. *Application deadline:* For fall admission, 2/21 for domestic and international students; for spring admission, 10/1 for domestic and international students. Application fee: $30. Electronic applications accepted. *Expenses:* Tuition, state resident: full-time $7055; part-time $293.94 per credit hour. Tuition, nonresident: full-time $22,096; part-time $920.66 per credit hour. *Financial support:* Research assistantships with full tuition reimbursements, teaching assistantships with full tuition reimbursements, career-related internships or fieldwork, Federal Work-Study, and institutionally sponsored loans available. Financial award applicants required to submit FAFSA. *Faculty research:* Painting, ceramics (traditional and non-traditional), installation, video and interactive sculpture. *Unit head:* Dr. Linda Johnson, Chair, 561-297-3870, Fax: 561-297-3078, E-mail: ljohnson@fau.edu. *Application contact:* James A. Novak, Associate Professor/Graduate Coordinator/Advisor, 561-297-2430, Fax: 561-297-3078, E-mail: jnovak@fau.edu.

Full Sail University, Game Design Master of Science Program—Campus, Winter Park, FL 32792-7437. Offers MS.

George Mason University, College of Visual and Performing Arts, Program in Visual Technologies, Fairfax, VA 22030. Offers art and visual technology (MA, MFA); art education (MAT); graphic design (MA). *Faculty:* 21 full-time (11 women), 31 part-time/adjunct (18 women). *Students:* 20 full-time (14 women), 18 part-time (14 women); includes 6 minority (1 African American, 2 Asian Americans or Pacific Islanders, 3 Hispanic Americans), 1 international. Average age 32. 46 applicants, 48% accepted, 17 enrolled. In 2009, 10 master's awarded. *Degree requirements:* For master's, thesis, apprenticeship in business; dissertation or project. *Entrance requirements:* For master's, BA or BFA, portfolio, resume, 3 letters of reference. Additional exam requirements/recommendations for international students: Required—TOEFL. *Application deadline:* For fall admission, 1/15 for domestic students. Application fee: $75. Electronic applications accepted. *Expenses:* Tuition, state resident: full-time $7568; part-time $315.33 per credit hour. Tuition, nonresident: full-time $21,704; part-time $904.33 per credit hour. Required fees: $2184; $91 per credit hour. *Financial support:* Teaching assistantships, career-related internships or fieldwork, Federal Work-Study, unspecified assistantships, and health care benefits (full-time research or teaching assistantship recipients) available. Support available to part-time students. Financial award application deadline: 3/1; financial award applicants required to submit FAFSA. *Faculty research:* Digital arts, painting, photography, print-making, sculpture; combined art forms in in-disciplinary projects including installation, performance, publishing, time or writing based; combined creative and critical approaches. *Unit head:* Dr. Scott M. Martin, Director, 703-993-4574, Fax: 703-993-8995, E-mail: smartin4@gmu.edu. *Application contact:* Dr. Scott M. Martin, Director, 703-993-4574, Fax: 703-993-8995, E-mail: smartin4@gmu.edu.

Illinois State University, Graduate School, College of Fine Arts, School of Art, Normal, IL 61790-2200. Offers art history (MA, MS); ceramics (MFA, MS); drawing (MFA, MS); fibers (MFA, MS); glass (MFA, MS); graphic design (MFA, MS); metals (MFA, MS); painting (MFA, MS); photography (MFA, MS); printmaking (MFA, MS); sculpture (MFA, MS). *Accreditation:* NASAD (one or more programs are accredited). *Degree requirements:* For master's, thesis or alternative, internship. *Entrance requirements:* For master's, portfolio, sample of scholarly writing. *Faculty research:* General operations support: Normal Editions Workshop for FY2007.

Indiana State University, School of Graduate Studies, College of Arts and Sciences, Department of Art, Terre Haute, IN 47809. Offers ceramics (MA, MFA); drawing (MA, MFA); graphic design (MA, MFA); painting (MA, MFA); photography (MA, MFA); printmaking (MA, MFA); sculpture (MA, MFA). *Accreditation:* NASAD (one or more programs are accredited). Part-time programs available. *Degree requirements:* For master's, thesis or alternative,

Graphic Design

Indiana State University (continued)
departmental qualifying exam. *Entrance requirements:* For master's, portfolio. Additional exam requirements/recommendations for international students: Required—TOEFL (minimum score 550 paper-based).

Iowa State University of Science and Technology, Graduate College, College of Design, Department of Art and Design, Ames, IA 50011. Offers art and design (MA); graphic design (MFA); integrated visual arts (MFA); interior design (MFA). Part-time programs available. *Faculty:* 34 full-time (20 women), 1 (woman) part-time/adjunct. *Students:* 44 full-time (35 women), 9 part-time (6 women); includes 2 minority (1 African American, 1 Asian American or Pacific Islander), 14 international. 27 applicants, 63% accepted, 10 enrolled. In 2009, 11 master's awarded. *Degree requirements:* For master's, thesis (for some programs). *Entrance requirements:* For master's, GRE General Test, resume, supplemental departmental form. Additional exam requirements/recommendations for international students: Required—TOEFL (minimum score 550 paper-based; 79 iBT) or IELTS (minimum score 6.5). *Application deadline:* For fall admission, 5/1 priority date for domestic and international students. Applications are processed on a rolling basis. Application fee: $40 ($90 for international students). Electronic applications accepted. *Expenses:* Tuition, state resident: full-time $6716. Tuition, nonresident: full-time $8908. Tuition and fees vary according to course level, course load, program and student level. *Financial support:* In 2009–10, 19 research assistantships with full and partial tuition reimbursements (averaging $7,850 per year) were awarded; teaching assistantships with full and partial tuition reimbursements, career-related internships or fieldwork, Federal Work-Study, institutionally sponsored loans, and tuition waivers (partial) also available. Support available to part-time students. Financial award application deadline: 2/15; financial award applicants required to submit FAFSA. *Faculty research:* Computer applications, fire safety, human factors in design, art and design education, fine arts, craft design. *Unit head:* Roger Baer, Chair, 515-294-6724, Fax: 515-294-2725, E-mail: artdn@iastate.edu. *Application contact:* Roger Baer, Chair, 515-294-6724, Fax: 515-294-2725, E-mail: artdn@iastate.edu.

Kean University, College of Visual and Performing Arts, Program in Graphic Communication Technology Management, Union, NJ 07083. Offers MS. Part-time and evening/weekend programs available. *Faculty:* 12 full-time (3 women). *Students:* 6 full-time (4 women), 10 part-time (6 women); includes 5 minority (1 African American, 1 Asian American or Pacific Islander, 3 Hispanic Americans), 3 international. Average age 32. 7 applicants, 86% accepted, 3 enrolled. In 2009, 10 master's awarded. *Degree requirements:* For master's, research component. *Entrance requirements:* For master's, minimum GPA of 3.0, 2 letters of recommendation, departmental interview. *Application deadline:* For fall admission, 5/1 for domestic students; for spring admission, 11/1 for domestic students. Application fee: $60 ($150 for international students). Electronic applications accepted. *Expenses:* Tuition, state resident: full-time $10,440; part-time $435 per credit. Tuition, nonresident: full-time $14,160; part-time $590 per credit. Required fees: $2642; $110 per credit. Part-time tuition and fees vary according to course load and degree level. *Financial support:* In 2009–10, 2 research assistantships with full tuition reimbursements (averaging $3,263 per year) were awarded; unspecified assistantships also available. *Unit head:* Dr. Cyril Nwako, Program Coordinator, 908-737-3530, E-mail: cnwako@kean.edu. *Application contact:* Dorothy Rowe, Pre-Admissions Coordinator, 908-737-5928, Fax: 908-737-5965, E-mail: drowe@kean.edu.

Kent State University, College of Communication and Information, School of Visual Communication Design, Kent, OH 44242-0001. Offers MA, MFA. *Accreditation:* NASAD. Part-time programs available. *Degree requirements:* For master's, thesis, portfolios. *Entrance requirements:* For master's, portfolio (studio majors), minimum GPA of 2.75, GPA of 3.0 in major. *Faculty research:* Graphic design.

Louisiana State University and Agricultural and Mechanical College, Graduate School, College of Art and Design, School of Art, Program in Studio Art, Baton Rouge, LA 70803. Offers ceramics (MFA); graphic design (MFA); painting and drawing (MFA); photography (MFA); printmaking (MFA); sculpture (MFA). *Accreditation:* NASAD. *Students:* 46 full-time (31 women), 2 part-time (0 women); includes 1 African American, 4 Asian Americans or Pacific Islanders, 6 international. Average age 29. 74 applicants, 20% accepted. In 2009, 11 master's awarded. *Degree requirements:* For master's, thesis. *Entrance requirements:* For master's, minimum GPA of 3.0. Additional exam requirements/recommendations for international students: Required—TOEFL (minimum score 550 paper-based; 213 computer-based; 79 iBT), IELTS (minimum score 6.5). *Application deadline:* For fall admission, 1/25 priority date for domestic students, 5/15 for international students; for spring admission, 10/15 for international students. Applications are processed on a rolling basis. Electronic applications accepted. *Financial support:* In 2009–10, 25 students received support; research assistantships with partial tuition reimbursements available, teaching assistantships, career-related internships or fieldwork, Federal Work-Study, institutionally sponsored loans, scholarships/grants, and unspecified assistantships available. Support available to part-time students. Financial award application deadline: 3/15. *Unit head:* Tom Neff, Graduate Coordinator, 225-578-5411, Fax: 225-578-1445, E-mail: tneff@lsu.edu. *Application contact:* Tom Neff, Graduate Coordinator, 225-578-5411, Fax: 225-578-1445, E-mail: tneff@lsu.edu.

Louisiana Tech University, Graduate School, College of Liberal Arts, School of Art, Ruston, LA 71272. Offers art and graphic design (MFA); photography (MFA); studio art (MFA). *Accreditation:* NASAD. Part-time programs available. *Degree requirements:* For master's, exhibit. *Entrance requirements:* For master's, GRE General Test, portfolio.

Maryland Institute College of Art, Graduate Studies, Program in Graphic Design, Baltimore, MD 21217. Offers MFA. *Faculty:* 2 full-time (both women), 5 part-time/adjunct (3 women). *Students:* 18 full-time (11 women); includes 2 minority (1 Asian American or Pacific Islander, 1 Hispanic American), 2 international. Average age 27. In 2009, 9 master's awarded. *Degree requirements:* For master's, thesis, exhibit. *Entrance requirements:* For master's, 40 credits in studio art, 6 credits in art history, portfolio. Additional exam requirements/recommendations for international students: Required—TOEFL (minimum score 550 paper-based; 213 computer-based). *Application deadline:* For fall admission, 1/15 for domestic and international students. Application fee: $50. *Expenses:* Tuition: Full-time $33,000; part-time $1375 per credit hour. Required fees: $1090; $545 per semester. *Financial support:* In 2009–10, 16 students received support, including 3 fellowships (averaging $17,274 per year), 13 teaching assistantships (averaging $1,800 per year); career-related internships or fieldwork and scholarships/grants also available. Financial award application deadline: 3/1; financial award applicants required to submit FAFSA. *Unit head:* Ellen Lupton, Director, 410-225-2382, Fax: 410-669-1141. *Application contact:* Scott G. Kelly, Associate Dean of Graduate Admission, 410-225-2256, Fax: 410-225-2408, E-mail: graduate@mica.edu.

Marywood University, Academic Affairs, Insalaco College of Creative and Performing Arts, Art Department, Program in Studio Art, Scranton, PA 18509-1598. Offers advertising design (MA); ceramics (MA); clay (MA); graphic design (MA); illustration (MA); painting (MA); photography (MA); printmaking (MA); sculpture (MA); weaving (MA). *Accreditation:* NASAD. *Students:* 6 full-time (5 women), 7 part-time (all women); includes 1 minority (Asian American or Pacific Islander). Average age 38. 5 applicants, 80% accepted. In 2009, 6 master's awarded. *Entrance requirements:* Additional exam requirements/recommendations for international students: Required—TOEFL (minimum score 550 paper-based; 213 computer-based; 79 iBT). *Application deadline:* For fall admission, 4/1 priority date for domestic students, 3/31 priority date for international students; for spring admission, 11/1 priority date for domestic students, 8/31 priority date for international students. Applications are processed on a rolling basis. Application fee: $35. Electronic applications accepted. *Expenses:* Tuition: Part-time $715 per credit. Required fees: $270 per semester. Tuition and fees vary according to degree level, campus/location and program. *Financial support:* Career-related internships or fieldwork, scholarships/grants, and unspecified assistantships available. Support available to part-time students. Financial award application deadline: 6/30; financial award applicants required to submit FAFSA. *Faculty research:* Texture and line in clay, cast bronze sculpture, color theories, book art and illustration, sculptural form. *Application contact:* Tammy Manka, Assistant Director of Graduate Admissions, 866-279-9663, E-mail: tmanka@marywood.edu.

Marywood University, Academic Affairs, Insalaco College of Creative and Performing Arts, Art Department, Program in Visual Arts, Scranton, PA 18509-1598. Offers advertising design (MFA); clay (MFA); graphic design (MFA); illustration (MFA); metals (MFA); painting (MFA); photography (MFA); printmaking (MFA). *Accreditation:* NASAD. *Students:* 16 full-time (13 women), 29 part-time (16 women); includes 2 minority (both Asian Americans or Pacific Islanders), 2 international. Average age 37. In 2009, 11 master's awarded. *Entrance requirements:* Additional exam requirements/recommendations for international students: Required—TOEFL (minimum score 550 paper-based; 213 computer-based; 79 iBT). *Application deadline:* For fall admission, 4/1 priority date for domestic students, 3/31 priority date for international students; for spring admission, 11/1 priority date for domestic students, 8/31 priority date for international students. Applications are processed on a rolling basis. Application fee: $35. Electronic applications accepted. *Expenses:* Contact institution. *Financial support:* Career-related internships or fieldwork, scholarships/grants, and unspecified assistantships available. Support available to part-time students. Financial award application deadline: 6/30; financial award applicants required to submit FAFSA. *Faculty research:* Mariology, exploration of visual imagery, explorations involving drawing on the loom, clay as sculptural medium, oil paintings. *Application contact:* Tammy Manka, Assistant Director of Graduate Admissions, 866-279-9663, E-mail: tmanka@marywood.edu.

Miami International University of Art & Design, Program in Graphic Design, Miami, FL 33132-1418. Offers MA, MFA. Postbaccalaureate distance learning degree programs offered. *Application contact:* Office of Graduate Admissions, 305-428-5700.

See Close-Up on page 117.

Minneapolis College of Art and Design, Certificate Programs, Minneapolis, MN 55404-4347. Offers design (Certificate); fine arts (Certificate); graphic design (Certificate); media (Certificate); sustainable design (Certificate). Part-time programs available. Postbaccalaureate distance learning degree programs offered. *Faculty:* 42 full-time (29 women). *Students:* 4 full-time (2 women), 22 part-time (19 women). Average age 24. In 2009, 15 Certificates awarded. *Degree requirements:* For Certificate, final project. *Entrance requirements:* For degree, resume, portfolio, letter of recommendation. Additional exam requirements/recommendations for international students: Required—TOEFL (minimum score 550 paper-based; 213 computer-based; 79 iBT). *Application deadline:* For fall admission, 1/15 for domestic and international students; for spring admission, 10/15 for domestic and international students. Application fee: $50. Electronic applications accepted. *Expenses:* Tuition: Full-time $29,500; part-time $985 per credit. Required fees: $100. *Financial support:* Career-related internships or fieldwork and scholarships/grants available. Financial award application deadline: 3/15; financial award applicants required to submit FAFSA. *Faculty research:* Visual arts. *Unit head:* Howard Oransky, Director of Continuing Studies, 612-874-3778, E-mail: howard_oransky@mcad.edu. *Application contact:* Howard Oransky, Director of Continuing Studies, 612-874-3778, Fax: 612-874-3701, E-mail: howard_oransky@mcad.edu.

Minneapolis College of Art and Design, Program in Visual Studies, Minneapolis, MN 55404-4347. Offers animation (MFA); comic art (MFA); drawing (MFA); filmmaking (MFA); fine arts (MFA); furniture design (MFA); graphic design (MFA); illustration (MFA); interactive media (MFA); painting (MFA); photography (MFA); printmaking (MFA); sculpture (MFA). *Accreditation:* NASAD. Part-time programs available. *Faculty:* 42 full-time (13 women). *Students:* 12 full-time (2 women), 18 part-time (8 women). Average age 27. 166 applicants, 28% accepted, 12 enrolled. In 2009, 10 master's awarded. *Degree requirements:* For master's, thesis exhibit. *Entrance requirements:* For master's, portfolio of visual artwork, resume, 3 letters of recommendation. Additional exam requirements/recommendations for international students: Required—TOEFL (minimum score 550 paper-based; 213 computer-based; 79 iBT). *Application deadline:* For fall admission, 1/15 for domestic and international students. Application fee: $50. Electronic applications accepted. *Expenses:* Tuition: Full-time $29,500; part-time $985 per credit. Required fees: $100. *Financial support:* In 2009–10, 23 students received support, including 15 teaching assistantships (averaging $6,000 per year); career-related internships or fieldwork, Federal Work-Study, scholarships/grants, and unspecified assistantships also available. Support available to part-time students. Financial award application deadline: 3/15; financial award applicants required to submit FAFSA. *Faculty research:* Visual arts: animation, comic art, drawing, filmmaking, furniture design, graphic design, illustration, interactive media, painting, photography, printmaking, sculpture. *Unit head:* Carole Fisher, Graduate Director, 612-874-3629, E-mail: carole_fisher@mcad.edu. *Application contact:* William Mullen, Vice President of Enrollment Management, 612-874-3760, Fax: 612-874-3701, E-mail: william_mullen@mcad.edu.

Morehead State University, Graduate Programs, Caudill College of Arts, Humanities and Social Sciences, Department of Art and Design, Morehead, KY 40351. Offers art education (MA); graphic design (MA); studio art (MA). Part-time and evening/weekend programs available. *Faculty:* 9 full-time (3 women), 2 part-time/adjunct (1 woman). *Students:* 9 full-time (4 women), 3 part-time (2 women). Average age 31. 5 applicants, 60% accepted, 3 enrolled. In 2009, 7 master's awarded. *Degree requirements:* For master's, comprehensive exam, thesis (for some programs), oral exam during exhibition. *Entrance requirements:* For master's, GRE General Test, minimum undergraduate GPA of 3.0 in major, 2.5 overall; portfolio; bachelor's degree in art. Additional exam requirements/recommendations for international students: Required—TOEFL (minimum score 500 paper-based; 173 computer-based). *Application deadline:* For fall admission, 8/1 priority date for domestic and international students; for spring admission, 12/1 priority date for domestic and international students. Applications are processed on a rolling basis. Application fee: $30. Electronic applications accepted. *Expenses:* Tuition, state resident: full-time $6318; part-time $351 per credit hour. Tuition, nonresident: full-time $15,804; part-time $878 per credit hour. *Financial support:* In 2009–10, 3 research assistantships (averaging $10,000 per year), 2 teaching assistantships (averaging $10,000 per year) were awarded; career-related internships or fieldwork, Federal Work-Study, and unspecified assistantships also available. Financial award application deadline: 3/15; financial award applicants required to submit FAFSA. *Faculty research:* Computer art, painting, drawing, ceramics, photography. *Unit head:* Robert Franzini, Chair, 606-783-2193, Fax: 606-783-5048, E-mail: r.franzi@moreheadstate.edu. *Application contact:* Michelle Barber, Graduate Recruitment and Retention Assistant Director, 606-783-5127, Fax: 606-783-5061, E-mail: m.barber@moreheadstate.edu.

New York Institute of Technology, Graduate Division, School of Arts and Sciences, Program in Fine Arts, Old Westbury, NY 11568-8000. Offers computer graphics and animation (MFA); fine arts and technology (MFA); graphic design (MFA). Part-time and evening/weekend programs available. *Students:* 17 full-time (8 women), 15 part-time (8 women); includes 5 African Americans, 1 Asian American or Pacific Islander, 4 Hispanic Americans, 7 international. Average age 32. In 2009, 2 master's awarded. *Degree requirements:* For master's, thesis or alternative. *Entrance requirements:* Additional exam requirements/recommendations for international students: Required—TOEFL (minimum score 550 paper-based; 213 computer-based). *Application deadline:* For fall admission, 7/1 priority date for domestic students; for spring admission, 12/1 priority date for domestic students. Applications are processed on a rolling basis. Application fee: $50. Electronic applications accepted. *Expenses:* Tuition: Part-time $825 per credit. *Financial support:* Research assistantships, career-related internships or fieldwork, Federal Work-Study, institutionally sponsored loans, tuition waivers (partial), and unspecified assistantships available. Support available to part-time students. Financial award applicants required to submit FAFSA. *Unit head:* Dr. Roger Yu, Dean, 516-686-7700, Fax: 516-686-1192, E-mail: ryu@nyit.edu. *Application contact:* Dr. Jacquelyn Nealon, Vice President for Enrollment Services, 516-686-7925, Fax: 516-686-7597, E-mail: jnealon@nyit.edu.

New York University, School of Continuing and Professional Studies, Division for Media Industry Studies and Design, Program in Graphic Communications Management and Technology, New York, NY 10012-1019. Offers MA. Part-time and evening/weekend programs available. *Faculty:* 1 (woman) full-time, 12 part-time/adjunct (3 women). *Students:* 24 full-time (15 women), 87 part-time (56 women); includes 22 minority (6 African Americans, 1 American

Indian/Alaska Native, 11 Asian Americans or Pacific Islanders, 4 Hispanic Americans). Average age 32. 44 applicants, 82% accepted, 25 enrolled. In 2009, 42 master's awarded. *Degree requirements:* For master's, thesis, capstone, research course. *Entrance requirements:* For master's, GRE General Test or GMAT (for recent graduates), resume, 2 letters of recommendation. Additional exam requirements/recommendations for international students: Required—TOEFL (minimum score 600 paper-based; 250 computer-based; 100 iBT), TWE. *Application deadline:* For fall admission, 2/1 priority date for domestic and international students; for spring admission, 10/15 priority date for domestic students, 8/15 priority date for international students. Applications are processed on a rolling basis. Application fee: $75. Electronic applications accepted. *Expenses:* Tuition: Full-time $30,528; part-time $1272 per credit. Required fees: $2177. *Financial support:* In 2009–10, 53 students received support, including 56 fellowships (averaging $2,451 per year); scholarships/grants and tuition waivers (partial) also available. Support available to part-time students. Financial award application deadline: 3/1; financial award applicants required to submit FAFSA. *Unit head:* Bonnie Blake, Director, 212-992-3222, Fax: 212-992-3386, E-mail: bonnie.blake@nyu.edu. *Application contact:* Ansley Dunn, Program Administrator, 212-992-3283, Fax: 212-992-3233, E-mail: ansley.dunn@nyu.edu.

North Carolina State University, Graduate School, College of Design, Department of Graphic Design, Raleigh, NC 27695. Offers MGD. *Accreditation:* NASAD. *Degree requirements:* For master's, thesis optional, oral exam. *Entrance requirements:* For master's, GRE General Test, portfolio. Electronic applications accepted. *Faculty research:* Typography, graphic design, interaction design, design and cognition, design and culture.

Ohio University, Graduate College, College of Fine Arts, School of Art, Athens, OH 45701-2979. Offers art history (MA); ceramics (MFA); graphic design (MFA); painting (MFA); photography (MFA); printmaking (MFA); sculpture (MFA). Part-time programs available. *Faculty:* 30 full-time (16 women), 7 part-time/adjunct (3 women). *Students:* 53 full-time (30 women), 4 part-time (all women); includes 3 minority (2 Asian Americans or Pacific Islanders, 1 Hispanic American), 4 international. 150 applicants, 33% accepted, 28 enrolled. In 2009, 22 master's awarded. *Degree requirements:* For master's, thesis. *Entrance requirements:* For master's, portfolio. Additional exam requirements/recommendations for international students: Required—TOEFL (minimum score 550 paper-based; 80 iBT) or IELTS Academic (minimum score 6.5). *Application deadline:* For fall admission, 2/1 for domestic and international students. Application fee: $50 ($55 for international students). Electronic applications accepted. *Expenses:* Tuition, state resident: full-time $7839; part-time $323 per quarter hour. Tuition, nonresident: full-time $15,831; part-time $654 per quarter hour. Required fees: $2931. *Financial support:* Teaching assistantships with full and partial tuition reimbursements, career-related internships or fieldwork, Federal Work-Study, institutionally sponsored loans, scholarships/grants, tuition waivers (partial), and unspecified assistantships available. Financial award application deadline: 2/1. *Faculty research:* Vapor fired ceramics, video installation, art theory, digital photography, mixed and interdisciplinary media work. *Unit head:* David LaPalombara, Director, 740-593-4290, Fax: 740-593-0457, E-mail: lapalomb@ohio.edu. *Application contact:* Rosemarie Basile, Chair, Graduate Programs, 740-593-4281, Fax: 740-593-0457, E-mail: basile@ohio.edu.

Otis College of Art and Design, Program in Graphic Design, Los Angeles, CA 90045-9785. Offers MFA. *Faculty:* 1 (woman) full-time. *Students:* 14 full-time (9 women); includes 4 minority (2 African Americans, 1 Asian American or Pacific Islander, 1 Hispanic American), 5 international. 93 applicants, 18% accepted, 5 enrolled. *Entrance requirements:* Additional exam requirements/recommendations for international students: Required—TOEFL (minimum score 600 paper-based; 250 computer-based). Electronic applications accepted. *Expenses:* Tuition: Full-time $33,200. Required fees: $700. *Unit head:* Kali Nikitas, Chair, Graduate Studies, 310-665-6820, Fax: 310-665-6843, E-mail: jhayes@otis.edu. *Application contact:* Information Contact, 310-665-6820, Fax: 310-665-6821, E-mail: admissions@otis.edu.

Pittsburg State University, Graduate School, College of Technology, Departments of Graphics and Imaging Technologies and Technology Management, Pittsburg, KS 66762. Offers human resource development (MS); industrial education (Ed S); technology (MS), including printing management. *Degree requirements:* For master's, thesis or alternative. *Expenses:* Tuition, state resident: full-time $4212; part-time $176 per credit. Tuition, nonresident: full-time $11,530; part-time $480 per credit. Required fees: $940; $43 per credit. Tuition and fees vary according to course level, course load, degree level, campus/location, reciprocity agreements and student level.

Pratt Institute, School of Art and Design, Program in Communications Design, New York, NY 10011. Offers MS. *Accreditation:* NASAD. Part-time programs available. *Faculty:* 5 full-time (2 women), 33 part-time/adjunct (9 women). *Students:* 192 full-time (147 women), 33 part-time (23 women); includes 38 minority (7 African Americans, 21 Asian Americans or Pacific Islanders, 10 Hispanic Americans), 106 international. Average age 27. 252 applicants, 69% accepted, 73 enrolled. In 2009, 78 master's awarded. *Degree requirements:* For master's, thesis. *Entrance requirements:* For master's, portfolio, letters of recommendation. Additional exam requirements/recommendations for international students: Required—TOEFL (minimum score 575 paper-based; 233 computer-based; 90 iBT). *Application deadline:* For fall admission, 1/5 for domestic and international students; for spring admission, 10/1 for domestic and international students. Application fee: $50 ($90 for international students). Electronic applications accepted. *Expenses:* Tuition: Full-time $22,734. Required fees: $1280. *Financial support:* Career-related internships or fieldwork, Federal Work-Study, institutionally sponsored loans, scholarships/grants, and unspecified assistantships available. Support available to part-time students. Financial award application deadline: 2/1; financial award applicants required to submit FAFSA. *Faculty research:* Graphics, film, photography, media presentations, computer graphics for community service organizations. *Unit head:* Jeffrey Bellantoni, Chairperson, 212-647-7573, E-mail: jbell189@pratt.edu. *Application contact:* Young Hah, Director of Graduate Admissions, 718-636-3683, Fax: 718-399-4242, E-mail: yhah@pratt.edu.

See Close-Up on page 119.

Pratt Institute, School of Art and Design, Program in Digital Arts, Brooklyn, NY 11205-3899. Offers MFA, MS/MFA. *Accreditation:* NASAD. *Faculty:* 6 full-time (1 woman), 17 part-time/adjunct (8 women). *Students:* 55 full-time (30 women), 1 (woman) part-time; includes 6 minority (2 African Americans, 2 Asian Americans or Pacific Islanders, 2 Hispanic Americans), 30 international. Average age 29. 140 applicants, 29% accepted, 10 enrolled. In 2009, 19 master's awarded. *Degree requirements:* For master's, thesis, exhibit. *Entrance requirements:* For master's, portfolio or video tape, letters of recommendation. Additional exam requirements/recommendations for international students: Required—TOEFL (minimum score 550 paper-based; 213 computer-based; 79 iBT). *Application deadline:* For fall admission, 1/5 for domestic and international students; for spring admission, 10/1 for domestic and international students. Applications are processed on a rolling basis. Application fee: $50 ($90 for international students). Electronic applications accepted. *Expenses:* Tuition: Full-time $22,734. Required fees: $1280. *Financial support:* Career-related internships or fieldwork, Federal Work-Study, institutionally sponsored loans, scholarships/grants, health care benefits, and unspecified assistantships available. Support available to part-time students. Financial award application deadline: 2/1; financial award applicants required to submit FAFSA. *Unit head:* Peter Patchen, Chair, 718-636-3693, E-mail: ppatchen@pratt.edu. *Application contact:* Young Hah, Director of Graduate Admissions, 718-636-3683, Fax: 718-399-4242, E-mail: yhah@pratt.edu.

See Close-Up on page 119.

Rhode Island School of Design, Graduate Studies, Division of Architecture and Design, Department of Graphic Design, Providence, RI 02903-2784. Offers MFA. *Accreditation:* NASAD. *Degree requirements:* For master's, thesis, exhibit. *Entrance requirements:* For master's, portfolio, 3 letters of recommendation. Additional exam requirements/recommendations for international students: Required—TOEFL (minimum score 580 paper-based; 237 computer-based), IELTS (minimum score 6.5).

Rochester Institute of Technology, Graduate Enrollment Services, College of Imaging Arts and Sciences, School of Design, Program in Computer Graphics Design, Rochester, NY 14623-5603. Offers MFA. *Accreditation:* NASAD. Part-time programs available. *Students:* 59 full-time (25 women), 12 part-time (7 women); includes 6 minority (2 African Americans, 1 American Indian/Alaska Native, 2 Asian Americans or Pacific Islanders, 1 Hispanic American), 43 international. Average age 29. 45 applicants, 60% accepted, 19 enrolled. In 2009, 9 master's awarded. *Degree requirements:* For master's, thesis. *Entrance requirements:* For master's, portfolio, minimum GPA of 3.0. Additional exam requirements/recommendations for international students: Required—TOEFL (minimum score 550 paper-based; 213 computer-based; 79 iBT) or IELTS (minimum score 6.5). *Application deadline:* For fall admission, 2/15 priority date for domestic and international students. Applications are processed on a rolling basis. Application fee: $50. Electronic applications accepted. *Expenses:* Tuition: Full-time $31,533; part-time $876 per credit hour. Required fees: $210. *Financial support:* In 2009–10, 50 students received support; research assistantships with partial tuition reimbursements available, teaching assistantships with partial tuition reimbursements available, career-related internships or fieldwork, institutionally sponsored loans, scholarships/grants, and unspecified assistantships available. Support available to part-time students. Financial award application deadline: 8/30; financial award applicants required to submit FAFSA. *Unit head:* Chris Jackson, Graduate Coordinator, 585-475-2688, Fax: 585-475-7533, E-mail: cbjpgd@rit.edu. *Application contact:* Diane Ellison, Assistant Vice President, Graduate Enrollment Services, 585-475-2229, Fax: 585-475-7164, E-mail: gradinfo@rit.edu.

Rochester Institute of Technology, Graduate Enrollment Services, College of Imaging Arts and Sciences, School of Design, Program in Graphic Design, Rochester, NY 14623-5603. Offers MFA. *Accreditation:* NASAD. Part-time programs available. *Students:* 20 full-time (16 women); includes 1 Hispanic American, 9 international. Average age 27. 64 applicants, 50% accepted, 16 enrolled. In 2009, 4 master's awarded. *Degree requirements:* For master's, thesis (for some programs). *Entrance requirements:* For master's, portfolio, minimum GPA of 3.0. Additional exam requirements/recommendations for international students: Required—TOEFL (minimum score 550 paper-based; 213 computer-based; 79 iBT), or IELTS (minimum score 6.5). *Application deadline:* For fall admission, 2/15 priority date for domestic and international students. Applications are processed on a rolling basis. Application fee: $50. *Expenses:* Tuition: Full-time $31,533; part-time $876 per credit hour. Required fees: $210. *Financial support:* In 2009–10, 15 students received support; teaching assistantships with partial tuition reimbursements available, career-related internships or fieldwork, institutionally sponsored loans, scholarships/grants, and unspecified assistantships available. Support available to part-time students. Financial award application deadline: 2/15; financial award applicants required to submit FAFSA. *Unit head:* Deborah Beardslee, Graduate Coordinator, 585-475-2668, Fax: 585-475-7533, E-mail: dabfaa@rit.edu. *Application contact:* Diane Ellison, Assistant Vice President, Graduate Enrollment Services, 585-475-2229, Fax: 585-475-7164, E-mail: gradinfo@rit.edu.

Rochester Institute of Technology, Graduate Enrollment Services, College of Imaging Arts and Sciences, School of Print Media, Program in Print Media, Rochester, NY 14623-5603. Offers MS. Part-time programs available. Postbaccalaureate distance learning degree programs offered (minimal on-campus study). *Students:* 26 full-time (11 women), 4 part-time (0 women); includes 2 Asian Americans or Pacific Islanders, 1 Hispanic American, 22 international. Average age 27. 13 applicants, 69% accepted, 9 enrolled. In 2009, 18 master's awarded. *Entrance requirements:* For master's, minimum GPA of 3.0. Additional exam requirements/recommendations for international students: Required—TOEFL (minimum score 550 paper-based; 213 computer-based; 79 iBT), or IELTS (minimum score 6.5). *Application deadline:* For fall admission, 2/15 priority date for domestic and international students. Applications are processed on a rolling basis. Application fee: $50. Electronic applications accepted. *Expenses:* Tuition: Full-time $31,533; part-time $876 per credit hour. Required fees: $210. *Financial support:* In 2009–10, 12 students received support; research assistantships with partial tuition reimbursements available, teaching assistantships with partial tuition reimbursements available, career-related internships or fieldwork, institutionally sponsored loans, scholarships/grants, and unspecified assistantships available. Support available to part-time students. Financial award applicants required to submit FAFSA. *Unit head:* Dr. Patricia Sorce, Administrative Chair, 585-475-2728, Fax: 585-475-5336, E-mail: spminfo@rit.edu. *Application contact:* Diane Ellison, Assistant Vice President, Graduate Enrollment Services, 585-475-2229, Fax: 585-475-7164, E-mail: gradinfo@rit.edu.

San Diego State University, Graduate and Research Affairs, College of Professional Studies and Fine Arts, School of Art, Design and Art History, San Diego, CA 92182. Offers art history (MA); studio arts (MA, MFA), including applied design, environmental design, graphic design, interior design, painting and printmaking, sculpture. *Accreditation:* NASAD (one or more programs are accredited). *Degree requirements:* For master's, variable foreign language requirement, thesis. *Entrance requirements:* For master's, GRE General Test, bachelor's degree in related field, slide portfolio, typed slide information sheet, 2 letters of recommendation. Additional exam requirements/recommendations for international students: Required—TOEFL. Electronic applications accepted.

Savannah College of Art and Design, Graduate School, Program in Advertising Design, Savannah, GA 31402-3146. Offers MA, MFA. Part-time programs available. *Degree requirements:* For master's, thesis, internships. *Entrance requirements:* For master's, interview, portfolio. Additional exam requirements/recommendations for international students: Required—TOEFL (minimum score 450 paper-based; 133 computer-based). Electronic applications accepted. *Expenses:* Tuition: Full-time $28,515; part-time $627 per credit hour. One-time fee: $500. Tuition and fees vary according to course load.

Savannah College of Art and Design, Graduate School, Program in Graphic Design, Savannah, GA 31402-3146. Offers MA, MFA. Part-time programs available. *Degree requirements:* For master's, thesis, exhibit, internships. *Entrance requirements:* For master's, interview, portfolio. Additional exam requirements/recommendations for international students: Required—TOEFL (minimum score 450 paper-based; 133 computer-based). Electronic applications accepted. *Expenses:* Tuition: Full-time $28,515; part-time $627 per credit hour. One-time fee: $500. Tuition and fees vary according to course load.

School of the Art Institute of Chicago, Graduate Division, Department of Visual Communication, Chicago, IL 60603-3103. Offers MFA. *Entrance requirements:* Additional exam requirements/recommendations for international students: Required—TOEFL, IELTS.

Southern Polytechnic State University, School of Arts and Sciences, Department of English, Technical Communication, and Media Arts, Marietta, GA 30060-2896. Offers communications management (Graduate Certificate); content development (Graduate Certificate); information and instructional design (MSIID); information design and communication (MS); instructional design (Graduate Certificate); technical and professional communication (Graduate Certificate); visual communication and graphics (Graduate Certificate). Part-time and evening/weekend programs available. Postbaccalaureate distance learning degree programs offered (no on-campus study). *Faculty:* 4 full-time (3 women), 1 part-time/adjunct (0 women). *Students:* 5 full-time (all women), 50 part-time (32 women); includes 18 African Americans, 2 international. Average age 38. 32 applicants, 94% accepted, 26 enrolled. In 2009, 8 master's awarded. *Degree requirements:* For master's, thesis or internship; for Graduate Certificate, thesis optional, 18 hours completed through thesis option (6 hours), internship option (6 hours) or advanced coursework option (6 hours). *Entrance requirements:* For master's, GRE, statement of purpose, writing sample, professional recommendations, timed essay; for Graduate Certificate, writing sample, professional recommendations. Additional exam requirements/recommendations for international students: Required—TOEFL (minimum score 550 paper-based; 213 computer-based; 79 iBT), IELTS (minimum score 6.5). *Application deadline:* For fall admission, 5/1 priority date for domestic students, 7/1 priority date for international students; for spring admission, 9/1 priority date for domestic students, 11/1 priority date for international students. Applications are processed on a rolling basis. Application fee: $20. Electronic applications accepted. *Expenses:* Tuition, state resident: full-time $2896; part-time $181 per credit hour. Tuition, nonresident: full-time $11,552; part-time $722 per credit hour. Required fees: $1096;

Graphic Design

Southern Polytechnic State University (continued)
$1096 per year. *Financial support:* In 2009–10, 1 research assistantship with full tuition reimbursement (averaging $4,000 per year), 1 teaching assistantship with partial tuition reimbursement (averaging $4,000 per year) were awarded; career-related internships or fieldwork, Federal Work-Study, scholarships/grants, and unspecified assistantships also available. Support available to part-time students. Financial award application deadline: 5/1; financial award applicants required to submit FAFSA. *Faculty research:* Usability, user-centered design, instructional design, information architecture, information design. *Unit head:* Dr. Mark Nunes, Chair, 678-915-7202, Fax: 678-915-7425, E-mail: mnunes@spsu.edu. *Application contact:* Nikki Palamiotis, Director of Graduate Studies, 678-915-4276, Fax: 678-915-7292, E-mail: npalamio@spsu.edu.

Suffolk University, New England School of Art and Design, Program in Graphic Design, Boston, MA 02108-2770. Offers MA. *Entrance requirements:* For master's, portfolio, interview, statement of professional goals, official transcripts, 2 letters of recommendation, resume. Application fee: $50. *Expenses:* Tuition: Full-time $33,000; part-time $1100 per credit. Required fees: $20. Tuition and fees vary according to program. *Unit head:* Rita Daly, Director, 617-573-1530, Fax: 617-994-4250. *Application contact:* Judith Reynolds, Director of Graduate Admissions, 617-573-8302, Fax: 617-305-1733, E-mail: grad.admission@suffolk.edu.

Temple University, Graduate School, Tyler School of Art, Department of Graphic Arts and Design, Philadelphia, PA 19122-6096. Offers graphic and interactive design (MFA); photography (MFA); printmaking (MFA). *Degree requirements:* For master's, essay, exhibit. *Entrance requirements:* For master's, minimum GPA of 3.0; slide portfolio, 40 credits in studio art; 12 credits in art history. Additional exam requirements/recommendations for international students: Required—TOEFL (minimum score 550 paper-based; 213 computer-based; 79 iBT). Electronic applications accepted.

Texas State University–San Marcos, Graduate School, College of Fine Arts and Communication, Department of Art and Design, Program in Communication Design, San Marcos, TX 78666. Offers MFA. *Faculty:* 3 full-time (1 woman). *Students:* 10 full-time (4 women), 22 part-time (9 women); includes 6 minority (3 Asian Americans or Pacific Islanders, 3 Hispanic Americans), 3 international. Average age 34. 23 applicants, 35% accepted, 8 enrolled. *Degree requirements:* For master's, comprehensive exam, thesis (for some programs). *Entrance requirements:* For master's, minimum GPA of 2.75 on last 60 hours of undergraduate work, 20-work portfolio. Additional exam requirements/recommendations for international students: Required—TOEFL (minimum score 550 paper-based; 213 computer-based). *Application deadline:* For fall admission, 3/15 for domestic and international students. Applications are processed on a rolling basis. Application fee: $40 ($90 for international students). Electronic applications accepted. *Expenses:* Tuition, state resident: full-time $5784; part-time $241 per credit hour. Tuition, nonresident: part-time $551 per credit hour. Required fees: $1728; $48 per credit hour. $306. Tuition and fees vary according to course load. *Financial support:* In 2009–10, 24 students received support, including 5 teaching assistantships (averaging $5,481 per year); Federal Work-Study and institutionally sponsored loans also available. Support available to part-time students. Financial award application deadline: 4/1; financial award applicants required to submit FAFSA. *Unit head:* William Meek, Program Advisor, 512-245-0311, E-mail: w.meek@txstate.edu. *Application contact:* Dr. J. Michael Willoughby, Dean of Graduate School, 512-245-2581, Fax: 512-245-8365, E-mail: gradcollege@txstate.edu.

Université Laval, Faculty of Architecture, Planning and Visual Arts, School of Visual Arts, Programs in Visual Arts, Québec, QC G1K 7P4, Canada. Offers graphic design and multimedia (MA); visual arts (MA). *Degree requirements:* For master's, thesis (for some programs). *Entrance requirements:* For master's, technical exam, interview, mastery of pertinent software, knowledge of French. Electronic applications accepted.

University of Baltimore, Graduate School, The Yale Gordon College of Liberal Arts, Program in Publications Design, Baltimore, MD 21201-5779. Offers MA. Part-time and evening/weekend programs available. *Degree requirements:* For master's, seminar project. *Entrance requirements:* For master's, minimum GPA of 3.0, portfolio, interview. Additional exam requirements/recommendations for international students: Required—TOEFL (minimum score 550 paper-based; 213 computer-based). Electronic applications accepted. *Faculty research:* Communication theory, graphic design, media technology.

University of Baltimore, Graduate School, The Yale Gordon College of Liberal Arts, School of Information Arts and Technologies, Doctoral Program in Communications Design, Baltimore, MD 21201-5779. Offers DCD. Part-time and evening/weekend programs available. *Entrance requirements:* For doctorate, minimum GPA of 3.2, previous graduate study in related discipline, portfolio, resume. Electronic applications accepted.

University of Cincinnati, Graduate School, College of Design, Architecture, Art, and Planning, School of Design, Cincinnati, OH 45221. Offers fashion design (M Des); graphic design (M Des); industrial design (M Des); interaction design (M Des); product development (M Des). *Accreditation:* NASAD. *Degree requirements:* For master's, thesis. *Entrance requirements:* For master's, undergraduate degree in design or related field, 2 years of work experience in design or related field. Additional exam requirements/recommendations for international students: Required—TOEFL. Electronic applications accepted. *Faculty research:* Design theory, interdisciplinary design topics.

University of Florida, Graduate School, College of Fine Arts, School of Art and Art History, Gainesville, FL 32611. Offers art (MFA), including ceramics, creative photography, drawing, electronic intermedia, graphic design, painting, printmaking, sculpture; art education (MA); art history (MA, PhD); digital arts and sciences (MA); museology (museum studies) (MA). *Accreditation:* NASAD. *Degree requirements:* For master's, variable foreign language requirement, project or thesis (MFA). *Entrance requirements:* For master's, portfolio (MFA), writing sample (MA), GRE General Test or minimum GPA of 3.0. Additional exam requirements/recommendations for international students: Required—TOEFL (minimum score 550 paper-based; 213 computer-based). Electronic applications accepted. *Faculty research:* Studio production, art historical studies of style context.

University of Guam, Office of Graduate Studies, College of Liberal Arts and Social Sciences, Division of Fine Arts, Mangilao, GU 96923. Offers ceramics (MA); graphics (MA); painting (MA). *Degree requirements:* For master's, thesis or alternative, exhibit, final oral exam. *Entrance requirements:* For master's, GRE General Test, portfolio. Additional exam requirements/recommendations for international students: Required—TOEFL.

University of Houston, College of Liberal Arts and Social Sciences, Department of Art, Houston, TX 77204. Offers art (MA); graphic communication (MFA); interdisciplinary practice and emerging forms (MFA); painting (MFA); photography/digital media (MFA); sculpture (MFA). *Faculty:* 10 full-time (6 women), 7 part-time/adjunct (3 women). *Students:* 35 full-time (20 women); includes 5 minority (2 African Americans, 1 Asian American or Pacific Islander, 2 Hispanic Americans), 4 international. Average age 32. 61 applicants, 31% accepted, 13 enrolled. In 2009, 12 master's awarded. *Entrance requirements:* For master's, GRE General Test, includes baccalaureate degree and portfolio. Additional exam requirements/recommendations for international students: Required—TOEFL. *Application deadline:* For fall admission, 2/1 for domestic and international students. Application fee: $25 ($75 for international students). Electronic applications accepted. *Expenses:* Tuition, state resident: full-time $7676; part-time $320 per credit hour. Tuition, nonresident: full-time $14,324; part-time $597 per credit hour. Required fees: $3034. *Financial support:* In 2009–10, 22 teaching assistantships with full tuition reimbursements (averaging $10,400 per year) were awarded; career-related internships or fieldwork, Federal Work-Study, institutionally sponsored loans, scholarships/grants, health care benefits, and unspecified assistantships also available. Support available to part-time students. Financial award application deadline: 3/10. *Faculty research:* Painting, sculpture, photography/installation/video, graphic design and typography, art history (Pre-Columbian to Surrealism). *Unit head:* Dr. John Reed, Chairperson, 713-743-3001, Fax: 713-743-2823, E-mail: jreed@uh.edu. *Application contact:* Cathy Hunt, Graduate Advisor and Instructional Assistant Professor, 713-743-2830, Fax: 713-743-2823, E-mail: chunt@uh.edu.

University of Illinois at Chicago, Graduate College, College of Architecture and Art, School of Art and Design, Chicago, IL 60607-7128. Offers electronic visualization (MFA); film animation (MFA); graphic design (MFA); industrial design (MFA); photography (MFA); studio arts (MFA). *Accreditation:* NASAD. *Degree requirements:* For master's, thesis, exhibit. *Entrance requirements:* For master's, MAT, portfolio. Additional exam requirements/recommendations for international students: Required—TOEFL. Electronic applications accepted.

University of Illinois at Urbana–Champaign, Graduate College, College of Fine and Applied Arts, School of Art and Design, Program in Design and Media, Champaign, IL 61820. Offers art and design (MFA), including new media; graphic design (MFA); industrial design (MFA). *Accreditation:* NASAD. *Students:* 18 full-time (9 women), 2 part-time (1 woman); includes 2 minority (both Asian Americans or Pacific Islanders), 10 international. 109 applicants, 7% accepted, 8 enrolled. In 2009, 4 master's awarded. *Entrance requirements:* For master's, minimum GPA of 3.0. Additional exam requirements/recommendations for international students: Required—TOEFL (minimum score 550 paper-based; 213 computer-based; 79 iBT). *Application deadline:* Applications are processed on a rolling basis. Application fee: $60 ($75 for international students). Electronic applications accepted. *Financial support:* Fellowships, research assistantships, teaching assistantships, tuition waivers (full and partial) available. *Unit head:* Ernest Scott, Chair, 217-333-1579, E-mail: ernscott@illinois.edu. *Application contact:* Marsha Biddle, Coordinator of Graduate Academic Affairs, 217-333-0642, Fax: 217-244-7688, E-mail: mbiddle@illinois.edu.

University of Massachusetts Dartmouth, Graduate School, College of Visual and Performing Arts, Program in Visual Design, North Dartmouth, MA 02747-2300. Offers digital media (MFA); graphic design (MFA); illustration (MFA); photography (MFA); typography (MFA). *Accreditation:* NASAD. *Faculty:* 17 full-time (7 women), 3 part-time/adjunct (2 women). *Students:* 6 full-time (4 women), 1 (woman) part-time. Average age 35. 25 applicants, 44% accepted, 2 enrolled. In 2009, 2 master's awarded. *Degree requirements:* For master's, visual thesis. *Entrance requirements:* For master's, portfolio, interview, minimum GPA of 3.0, 3 letters of recommendation. Additional exam requirements/recommendations for international students: Required—TOEFL (minimum score 500 paper-based). *Application deadline:* For fall admission, 2/1 priority date for domestic students, 12/1 priority date for international students. Applications are processed on a rolling basis. Application fee: $40 ($60 for international students). Electronic applications accepted. *Expenses:* Tuition, state resident: full-time $2071; part-time $86.29 per credit. Tuition, nonresident: full-time $8099; part-time $337.46 per credit. Required fees: $9446. Tuition and fees vary according to class time, course load and reciprocity agreements. *Financial support:* In 2009–10, 5 teaching assistantships with full tuition reimbursements (averaging $3,088 per year) were awarded; Federal Work-Study and unspecified assistantships also available. Support available to part-time students. Financial award application deadline: 3/1; financial award applicants required to submit FAFSA. Total annual research expenditures: $1,000. *Unit head:* Memory Holloway, Director, 508-999-8554, E-mail: mholloway@umassd.edu. *Application contact:* Elan Turcotte-Shamski, Graduate Admissions Officer, 508-999-8604, Fax: 508-999-8183, E-mail: graduate@umassd.edu.

University of Memphis, Graduate School, College of Communication and Fine Arts, Department of Art, Memphis, TN 38152. Offers art (Graduate Certificate); art history (MA), including Egyptian art and archaeology, general art history; ceramics (MFA); graphic design (MFA); interior design (MFA); painting (MFA); printmaking/photography (MFA); sculpture (MFA). *Accreditation:* NASAD (one or more programs are accredited). *Faculty:* 20 full-time (7 women), 4 part-time/adjunct (2 women). *Students:* 39 full-time (26 women), 10 part-time (8 women); includes 4 African Americans, 1 Asian American or Pacific Islander, 1 international. Average age 29. 44 applicants, 77% accepted, 22 enrolled. In 2009, 16 master's, 5 other advanced degrees awarded. *Degree requirements:* For master's, 2 foreign languages, comprehensive exam, thesis. *Entrance requirements:* For master's, GRE General Test or MAT, portfolio (MFA). *Application deadline:* For fall admission, 8/1 for domestic students; for spring admission, 12/1 for domestic students. Applications are processed on a rolling basis. Application fee: $35 ($60 for international students). *Expenses:* Tuition, state resident: full-time $6246; part-time $347 per credit hour. Tuition, nonresident: full-time $15,894; part-time $883 per credit hour. Required fees: $1160. Full-time tuition and fees vary according to course load, degree level and program. *Financial support:* In 2009–10, 38 students received support; research assistantships with full tuition reimbursements available, teaching assistantships with full tuition reimbursements available, Federal Work-Study, scholarships/grants, and unspecified assistantships available. Financial award application deadline: 2/15; financial award applicants required to submit FAFSA. *Faculty research:* Online collaborative learning, advanced art history studies, electronic publishing/design, studio arts, architectural studies. *Unit head:* Prof. Richard Lou, Chair, 901-678-2216, Fax: 901-678-2735, E-mail: gmyatt@memphis.edu. *Application contact:* Greely Myat, Graduate Studies Coordinator, 901-678-2650.

University of Miami, Graduate School, College of Arts and Sciences, Department of Art and Art History, Coral Gables, FL 33124. Offers art history (MA); ceramics/glass (MFA); graphic design/multimedia (MFA); painting (MFA); photography/digital imaging (MFA); printmaking (MFA); sculpture (MFA). Part-time programs available. *Degree requirements:* For master's, variable foreign language requirement, thesis, exhibit (MFA), comprehensive exam (MA). *Entrance requirements:* For master's, GRE General Test (MA), research paper (MA), slide portfolio (MFA). Additional exam requirements/recommendations for international students: Required—TOEFL. Electronic applications accepted. *Faculty research:* Installation art, public art.

University of Minnesota, Duluth, Graduate School, School of Fine Arts, Department of Art and Design, Duluth, MN 55812-2496. Offers graphic design (MFA). Part-time programs available. *Faculty:* 15 full-time (10 women), 6 part-time/adjunct (5 women). *Students:* 7 full-time (4 women), 1 part-time (0 women), 2 international. Average age 26. 11 applicants, 18% accepted, 2 enrolled. In 2009, 2 master's awarded. *Degree requirements:* For master's, final exhibit, project, supporting paper. *Entrance requirements:* For master's, minimum GPA of 3.0, writing sample, slide portfolio. Additional exam requirements/recommendations for international students: Required—TOEFL (minimum score 550 paper-based; 213 computer-based). *Application deadline:* For fall admission, 4/15 for domestic and international students; for spring admission, 11/1 for domestic and international students. Application fee: $55 ($75 for international students). *Financial support:* In 2009–10, 8 students received support, including research assistantships with full tuition reimbursements available (averaging $13,000 per year), teaching assistantships with full tuition reimbursements available (averaging $13,000 per year); career-related internships or fieldwork, institutionally sponsored loans, scholarships/grants, health care benefits, and unspecified assistantships also available. Financial award application deadline: 3/15. *Faculty research:* Motion graphics, graphic design history, interactive design, typography, education. Total annual research expenditures: $50,000. *Unit head:* Prof. Janice Kmetz, Director of Graduate Studies, 218-726-8150, E-mail: jkmetz@d.umn.edu. *Application contact:* M. J. Leone, Executive Administrative Specialist, 218-726-7523, Fax: 218-726-6970, E-mail: grad@d.umn.edu.

University of Notre Dame, Graduate School, College of Arts and Letters, Division of Humanities, Department of Art, Art History, and Design, Notre Dame, IN 46556. Offers art history (MA); design (MFA), including graphic design, industrial design; studio art (MFA), including ceramics, painting, photography, printmaking, sculpture. *Accreditation:* NASAD. *Degree requirements:* For master's, comprehensive exam (for some programs), thesis. *Entrance requirements:* For master's, GRE General Test, minimum GPA of 3.0. Additional exam requirements/recommendations for international students: Required—TOEFL (minimum score 600 paper-based; 250 computer-based; 80 iBT). Electronic applications accepted. *Faculty research:* Studio art practice in ceramics, printing, photography, printmaking and sculpture, graphic design and industrial design, digital imaging in design and photography, Renaissance and American art history, contemporary art theory and criticism.

The University of Tennessee, Graduate School, College of Arts and Sciences, School of Art, Knoxville, TN 37996. Offers ceramics (MFA); drawing (MFA); graphic design (MFA); inter-area studies (MFA); media arts (MFA); painting (MFA); printmaking (MFA); sculpture (MFA); watercolor (MFA). *Accreditation:* NASAD. *Degree requirements:* For master's, thesis or alternative, exhibit. *Entrance requirements:* For master's, portfolio, minimum GPA of 2.7. Additional exam requirements/recommendations for international students: Required—TOEFL. Electronic applications accepted. *Expenses:* Tuition, state resident: full-time $6826; part-time $380 per semester hour. Tuition, nonresident: full-time $21,844; part-time $1147 per semester hour. Tuition and fees vary according to program.

University of Utah, The Graduate School, College of Fine Arts, Department of Art and Art History, Salt Lake City, UT 84112-0380. Offers art history (MA); ceramics (MFA); community-based art education (MFA); drawing (MFA); graphic design (MFA); painting (MFA); photography/digital imaging (MFA); printmaking (MFA); sculpture/intermedia (MFA). *Faculty:* 24 full-time (11 women). *Students:* 20 full-time (15 women), 2 part-time (both women), 1 international. Average age 31. 59 applicants, 24% accepted, 9 enrolled. In 2009, 11 master's awarded. *Degree requirements:* For master's, variable foreign language requirement, comprehensive exam (for some programs), thesis or alternative, exhibit and final project paper (for MFA). *Entrance requirements:* For master's, CD portfolio (MFA), writing sample (MA), curriculum vitae, letters of recommendation. Additional exam requirements/recommendations for international students: Required—TOEFL (minimum score 575 paper-based; 183 computer-based; 75 iBT). *Application deadline:* For fall admission, 1/2 priority date for domestic and international students. Application fee: $55 ($65 for international students). Electronic applications accepted. *Expenses:* Tuition, state resident: full-time $4004; part-time $1674 per semester. Tuition, nonresident: full-time $14,134; part-time $5915 per semester. Required fees: $324 per semester. Tuition and fees vary according to course load, degree level and program. *Financial support:* In 2009–10, 2 fellowships, 6 research assistantships with partial tuition reimbursements, 34 teaching assistantships with partial tuition reimbursements were awarded; Federal Work-Study, institutionally sponsored loans, scholarships/grants, tuition waivers (partial), unspecified assistantships, and stipends also available. Financial award application deadline: 1/2; financial award applicants required to submit FAFSA. *Faculty research:* Studio art, European art history, Asian art history, Latin American art history, twentieth century/contemporary art history. Total annual research expenditures: $8,748. *Unit head:* Dr. Elizabeth A. Peterson, Chair, 801-581-7012, Fax: 801-585-6171, E-mail: elizabeth.peterson@art.utah.edu. *Application contact:* Prof. John O'Connell, Director of Graduate Studies, 801-581-8677, Fax: 801-585-6171, E-mail: j.oconnell@utah.edu.

Western Illinois University, School of Graduate Studies, College of Education and Human Services, Department of Instructional Design and Technology, Macomb, IL 61455-1390. Offers distance learning (Certificate); graphic applications (Certificate); instructional design and technology (MS); multimedia (Certificate); technology integration in education (Certificate); training development (Certificate). Part-time programs available. Postbaccalaureate distance learning degree programs offered (no on-campus study). *Students:* 23 full-time (13 women), 56 part-time (37 women); includes 18 minority (12 African Americans, 2 American Indian/Alaska Native, 3 Asian Americans or Pacific Islanders, 1 Hispanic American), 8 international. Average age 36. 18 applicants, 72% accepted. In 2009, 25 master's, 2 other advanced degrees awarded. *Degree requirements:* For master's, thesis or alternative. *Entrance requirements:* Additional exam requirements/recommendations for international students: Required—TOEFL (minimum score 550 paper-based; 213 computer-based; 80 iBT). *Application deadline:* Applications are processed on a rolling basis. Application fee: $30. Electronic applications accepted. *Expenses:* Tuition, state resident: full-time $4486; part-time $249.21 per credit hour. Tuition, nonresident: full-time $8972; part-time $498.42 per credit hour. Required fees: $72.62 per credit hour. *Financial support:* In 2009–10, 16 students received support, including 11 research assistantships with full tuition reimbursements available (averaging $7,280 per year), 5 teaching assistantships with full tuition reimbursements available (averaging $8,400 per year). Financial award applicants required to submit FAFSA. *Unit head:* Dr. Hoyet Hemphill, Chairperson, 309-298-1952. *Application contact:* Evelyn Hoing, Assistant Director of Graduate Studies, 309-298-1806, Fax: 309-298-2345, E-mail: grad-office@wiu.edu.

Western Michigan University, Graduate College, College of Fine Arts, Gwen Frostic School of Art, Kalamazoo, MI 49008. Offers art education (MA); studio art (MFA). *Accreditation:* NASAD (one or more programs are accredited). *Degree requirements:* For master's, thesis or alternative.

West Virginia University, College of Creative Arts, Division of Art and Design, Morgantown, WV 26506. Offers art education (MA); art history (MA); ceramics (MFA); graphic design (MFA); painting (MFA); printmaking (MFA); sculpture (MFA); studio art (MA). *Accreditation:* NASAD. *Degree requirements:* For master's, thesis, exhibit. *Entrance requirements:* For master's, minimum GPA of 2.75, portfolio. Additional exam requirements/recommendations for international students: Required—TOEFL. *Expenses:* Contact institution. *Faculty research:* Medieval art history.

Yale University, School of Art, New Haven, CT 06520. Offers graphic design (MFA); painting/printmaking (MFA); photography (MFA); sculpture (MFA). *Faculty:* 7 full-time (3 women), 36 part-time/adjunct (12 women). *Students:* 119 full-time (62 women); includes 17 minority (4 African Americans, 6 Asian Americans or Pacific Islanders, 7 Hispanic Americans), 25 international. Average age 28. 1,266 applicants, 5% accepted, 58 enrolled. In 2009, 57 master's awarded. *Degree requirements:* For master's, thesis (for some programs). *Entrance requirements:* Additional exam requirements/recommendations for international students: Required—TOEFL (minimum score 550 paper-based; 250 computer-based; 100 iBT). *Application deadline:* For fall admission, 1/5 for domestic and international students. Application fee: $100. Electronic applications accepted. *Expenses:* Contact institution. *Financial support:* In 2009–10, 90 students received support, including 54 teaching assistantships (averaging $1,900 per year); Federal Work-Study, scholarships/grants, and unspecified assistantships also available. Financial award application deadline: 3/1; financial award applicants required to submit FAFSA. *Unit head:* Robert Storr, Dean, 203-432-2606. *Application contact:* Patricia Ann DeChiara, Director of Academic Affairs, 203-432-2600, E-mail: artschool.info@yale.edu.

Illustration

Academy of Art University, Graduate Program, School of Illustration, San Francisco, CA 94105-3410. Offers MFA. *Accreditation:* NASAD. Part-time programs available. Postbaccalaureate distance learning degree programs offered (no on-campus study). *Degree requirements:* For master's, final review. *Entrance requirements:* For master's, minimum GPA of 3.0, portfolio. Electronic applications accepted.

Bob Jones University, Graduate Programs, Greenville, SC 29614. Offers accountancy (MS); Bible (MA); Bible translation (MA); Biblical studies (Certificate); broadcast management (MS); business administration (MBA); church history (MA, PhD); church ministries (MA); church music (MM); cinema and video production (MA); counseling (MS); curriculum and instruction (Ed D); divinity (M Div); dramatic production (MA); educational leadership (MS, Ed D, Ed S); elementary education (M Ed, MAT); English (M Ed, MA, MAT); fine arts (MA); graphic design (MA); history (M Ed, MA); illustration (MA); interpretative speech (MA); mathematics (M Ed, MAT); medical missions (Certificate); ministry (MM, D Min); multi-categorical special education (M Ed, MAT); music (M Ed); New Testament interpretation (PhD); Old Testament interpretation (PhD); orchestral instrument performance (MM); organ performance (MM); pastoral studies (MA); personnel services (MS, Ed S); piano pedagogy (MM); piano performance (MM); platform arts (MA); radio and television broadcasting (MS); rhetoric and public address (MA); secondary education (M Ed); studio art (MA); teaching Bible (MA); theology (MA, PhD); voice performance (MM); youth ministries (MA); M Div/MM.

Bradley University, Graduate School, Slane College of Communications and Fine Arts, Department of Art, Peoria, IL 61625-0002. Offers ceramics (MA, MFA); drawing/illustration (MA, MFA); interdisciplinary art (MA, MFA); painting (MA, MFA); photography (MA, MFA); printmaking (MA, MFA); sculpture (MA, MFA); visual communication and design (MA, MFA). *Accreditation:* NASAD. Part-time programs available. *Degree requirements:* For master's, comprehensive exam, thesis, final exhibit. *Entrance requirements:* For master's, portfolio, 2 letters of recommendation. Additional exam requirements/recommendations for international students: Required—TOEFL (minimum score 550 paper-based; 213 computer-based; 79 iBT).

Fashion Institute of Technology, School of Graduate Studies, Program in Illustration, New York, NY 10001-5992. Offers MA. *Entrance requirements:* Additional exam requirements/recommendations for international students: Required—TOEFL (minimum score 550 paper-based; 213 computer-based). Electronic applications accepted. *Expenses:* Tuition, state resident: full-time $8198; part-time $342 per credit. Tuition, nonresident: full-time $12,972; part-time $541 per credit. Required fees: $450.

Kent State University, College of Communication and Information, School of Visual Communication Design, Kent, OH 44242-0001. Offers MA, MFA. *Accreditation:* NASAD. Part-time programs available. *Degree requirements:* For master's, thesis, portfolios. *Entrance requirements:* For master's, portfolio (studio majors), minimum GPA of 2.75, GPA of 3.0 in major. *Faculty research:* Graphic design.

Marywood University, Academic Affairs, Insalaco College of Creative and Performing Arts, Art Department, Program in Studio Art, Scranton, PA 18509-1598. Offers advertising design (MA); ceramics (MA); clay (MA); graphic design (MA); illustration (MA); painting (MA); photography (MA); printmaking (MA); sculpture (MA); weaving (MA). *Accreditation:* NASAD. *Students:* 6 full-time (5 women), 7 part-time (all women); includes 1 minority (Asian American or Pacific Islander). Average age 38. 5 applicants, 80% accepted. In 2009, 6 master's awarded. *Entrance requirements:* Additional exam requirements/recommendations for international students: Required—TOEFL (minimum score 550 paper-based; 213 computer-based; 79 iBT). *Application deadline:* For fall admission, 4/1 priority date for domestic students, 3/31 priority date for international students; for spring admission, 11/1 priority date for domestic students, 8/31 priority date for international students. Applications are processed on a rolling basis. Application fee: $35. Electronic applications accepted. *Expenses:* Tuition: Part-time $715 per credit. Required fees: $270 per semester. Tuition and fees vary according to degree level, campus/location and program. *Financial support:* Career-related internships or fieldwork, scholarships/grants, and unspecified assistantships available. Support available to part-time students. Financial award application deadline: 6/30; financial award applicants required to submit FAFSA. *Faculty research:* Texture and line in clay, cast bronze sculpture, color theories, book art and illustration, sculptural form. *Application contact:* Tammy Manka, Assistant Director of Graduate Admissions, 866-279-9663, E-mail: tmanka@marywood.edu.

Marywood University, Academic Affairs, Insalaco College of Creative and Performing Arts, Art Department, Program in Visual Arts, Scranton, PA 18509-1598. Offers advertising design (MFA); clay (MFA); graphic design (MFA); illustration (MFA); metals (MFA); painting (MFA); photography (MFA); printmaking (MFA). *Accreditation:* NASAD. *Students:* 16 full-time (13 women), 29 part-time (16 women); includes 2 minority (both Asian Americans or Pacific Islanders), 2 international. Average age 37. In 2009, 11 master's awarded. *Entrance requirements:* Additional exam requirements/recommendations for international students: Required—TOEFL (minimum score 550 paper-based; 213 computer-based; 79 iBT). *Application deadline:* For fall admission, 4/1 priority date for domestic students, 3/31 priority date for international students; for spring admission, 11/1 priority date for domestic students, 8/31 priority date for international students. Applications are processed on a rolling basis. Application fee: $35. Electronic applications accepted. *Expenses:* Contact institution. *Financial support:* Career-related internships or fieldwork, scholarships/grants, and unspecified assistantships available. Support available to part-time students. Financial award application deadline: 6/30; financial award applicants required to submit FAFSA. *Faculty research:* Mariology, exploration of visual imagery, explorations involving drawing on the loom, clay as sculptural medium, oil paintings. *Application contact:* Tammy Manka, Assistant Director of Graduate Admissions, 866-279-9663, E-mail: tmanka@marywood.edu.

Mills College, Graduate Studies, Department of English, Oakland, CA 94613-1000. Offers book art and creative writing (MFA); creative writing, poetry (MFA); creative writing, prose (MFA); English and American literature (MA). Part-time programs available. *Faculty:* 10 full-time (8 women), 16 part-time/adjunct (13 women). *Students:* 92 full-time (71 women), 5 part-time (4 women); includes 26 minority (11 African Americans, 1 American Indian/Alaska Native, 8 Asian Americans or Pacific Islanders, 6 Hispanic Americans). Average age 31. 176 applicants, 85% accepted, 42 enrolled. In 2009, 63 master's awarded. *Degree requirements:* For master's, comprehensive exam, thesis. *Entrance requirements:* For master's, manuscript, writing sample. Additional exam requirements/recommendations for international students: Required—TOEFL. *Application deadline:* For fall admission, 2/1 priority date for domestic students; for spring admission, 11/1 for domestic students. Applications are processed on a rolling basis. Application fee: $50. Electronic applications accepted. *Expenses:* Tuition: Full-time $26,326; part-time $6584 per course. Required fees: $896. One-time fee: $896 part-time. Tuition and fees vary according to program. *Financial support:* In 2009–10, 85 students received support, including 85 fellowships (averaging $7,587 per year), 35 teaching assistantships with partial tuition reimbursements available (averaging $2,667 per year); scholarships/grants also available. Support available to part-time students. Financial award application deadline: 2/1; financial award applicants required to submit FAFSA. *Faculty research:* Creative writing, African-American literature, Victorian women writers, theories of sexuality, Shakespeare. *Unit head:* Dr. Cynthia Scheinberg, Chair, 510-430-2213, E-mail: cyns@mills.edu. *Application contact:* Jessica King, Graduate Admission Specialist, 510-430-3305, Fax: 510-430-2159, E-mail: grad-studies@mills.edu.

Minneapolis College of Art and Design, Program in Visual Studies, Minneapolis, MN 55404-4347. Offers animation (MFA); comic art (MFA); drawing (MFA); filmmaking (MFA); fine arts (MFA); furniture design (MFA); graphic design (MFA); illustration (MFA); interactive media (MFA); painting (MFA); photography (MFA); printmaking (MFA); sculpture (MFA). *Accreditation:* NASAD. Part-time programs available. *Faculty:* 42 full-time (13 women). *Students:* 12 full-time (2 women), 18 part-time (8 women). Average age 27. 166 applicants, 28% accepted, 12 enrolled. In 2009, 10 master's awarded. *Degree requirements:* For master's, thesis, thesis exhibit. *Entrance requirements:* For master's, portfolio of visual artwork, resume, 3 letters of recommendation. Additional exam requirements/recommendations for international students: Required—TOEFL (minimum score 550 paper-based; 213 computer-based; 79 iBT). *Application deadline:* For fall admission, 1/15 for domestic and international students. Application fee: $50. Electronic applications accepted. *Expenses:* Tuition: Full-time $29,500; part-time $985 per credit. Required fees: $100. *Financial support:* In 2009–10, 23 students received support,

Illustration

Minneapolis College of Art and Design (continued)
including 15 teaching assistantships (averaging $6,000 per year); career-related internships or fieldwork, Federal Work-Study, scholarships/grants, and unspecified assistantships also available. Support available to part-time students. Financial award application deadline: 3/15; financial award applicants required to submit FAFSA. *Faculty research:* Visual arts: animation, comic art, drawing, filmmaking, furniture design, graphic design, illustration, interactive media, painting, photography, printmaking, sculpture. *Unit head:* Carole Fisher, Graduate Director, 612-874-3629, E-mail: carole_fisher@mcad.edu. *Application contact:* William Mullen, Vice President of Enrollment Management, 612-874-3760, Fax: 612-874-3701, E-mail: william_mullen@mcad.edu.

San Jose State University, Graduate Studies and Research, College of Humanities and the Arts, School of Art and Design, San Jose, CA 95192-0001. Offers animation/illustration (MA); art history (MA); digital media arts (MFA); photography (MFA); pictorial arts (MFA); spatial arts (MFA). *Accreditation:* NASAD (one or more programs are accredited). *Students:* 48 full-time (27 women), 24 part-time (16 women); includes 13 minority (3 African Americans, 6 Asian Americans or Pacific Islanders, 4 Hispanic Americans), 2 international. Average age 36. 69 applicants, 23% accepted, 16 enrolled. In 2009, 17 master's awarded. *Entrance requirements:* For master's, GRE. *Application deadline:* For fall admission, 6/29 for domestic students; for spring admission, 11/30 for domestic students. Applications are processed on a rolling basis. Application fee: $59. Electronic applications accepted. *Financial support:* Applicants required to submit FAFSA. *Unit head:* John Loomis, Director, 408-924-4320, Fax: 408-924-4326. *Application contact:* John Loomis, Director, 408-924-4320, Fax: 408-924-4326.

Savannah College of Art and Design, Graduate School, Program in Illustration, Savannah, GA 31402-3146. Offers MA, MFA. Part-time programs available. *Degree requirements:* For master's, thesis, exhibit, internships. *Entrance requirements:* For master's, interview, portfolio. Additional exam requirements/recommendations for international students: Required—TOEFL (minimum score 450 paper-based; 133 computer-based). Electronic applications accepted. *Expenses:* Tuition: Full-time $28,515; part-time $627 per credit hour. One-time fee: $500. Tuition and fees vary according to course load.

Savannah College of Art and Design, Graduate School, Program in Illustration Design, Savannah, GA 31402-3146. Offers MA. Part-time programs available. *Degree requirements:* For master's, thesis. *Entrance requirements:* For master's, interview, portfolio. Additional exam requirements/recommendations for international students: Required—TOEFL (minimum score 450 paper-based; 133 computer-based). Electronic applications accepted. *Expenses:* Tuition: Full-time $28,515; part-time $627 per credit hour. One-time fee: $500. Tuition and fees vary according to course load.

Savannah College of Art and Design, Graduate School, Program in Sequential Art, Savannah, GA 31402-3146. Offers MA, MFA. Part-time programs available. *Degree requirements:* For master's, thesis, exhibit, internships. *Entrance requirements:* For master's, interview, portfolio. Additional exam requirements/recommendations for international students: Required—TOEFL (minimum score 450 paper-based; 133 computer-based). Electronic applications accepted. *Expenses:* Tuition: Full-time $28,515; part-time $627 per credit hour. One-time fee: $500. Tuition and fees vary according to course load.

School of Visual Arts, Graduate Programs, Illustration Department, New York, NY 10010-3994. Offers MFA. *Accreditation:* NASAD. *Degree requirements:* For master's, final review, project or thesis. *Entrance requirements:* For master's, portfolio. Additional exam requirements/recommendations for international students: Required—TOEFL (minimum score 550 paper-based; 213 computer-based; 79 iBT). Electronic applications accepted.

Syracuse University, College of Visual and Performing Arts, Program in Illustration, Syracuse, NY 13244. Offers MFA. *Students:* 2 full-time (1 woman), 1 part-time (0 women); includes 1 minority (Asian American or Pacific Islander). Average age 25. 18 applicants, 33% accepted, 1 enrolled. In 2009, 3 master's awarded. *Entrance requirements:* For master's, portfolio. Additional exam requirements/recommendations for international students: Required—TOEFL (minimum score 100 iBT). *Application deadline:* For fall admission, 2/1 priority date for domestic and international students. Application fee: $75. Electronic applications accepted. *Expenses:* Tuition: Full-time $26,808; part-time $1117 per credit. Required fees: $1024. *Financial support:* Fellowships with tuition reimbursements, teaching assistantships with tuition reimbursements available. Financial award application deadline: 1/1. *Unit head:* Errol Willett, Chair, 315-443-3830, E-mail: eswillett@syr.edu. *Application contact:* Harriett Conti, Assistant Dean for Recruitment and Admissions, 315-443-5755, E-mail: hmconti@syr.edu.

University of California, Santa Cruz, Division of Graduate Studies, Division of Physical and Biological Sciences, Program in Science Communication, Santa Cruz, CA 95064. Offers science illustration (Certificate); science writing (Certificate). *Entrance requirements:* For degree, GRE General Test, GRE Subject Test, bachelor's degree in science. Electronic applications accepted.

University of Massachusetts Dartmouth, Graduate School, College of Visual and Performing Arts, Program in Visual Design, North Dartmouth, MA 02747-2300. Offers digital media (MFA); graphic design (MFA); illustration (MFA); photography (MFA); typography (MFA). *Accreditation:* NASAD. *Faculty:* 17 full-time (7 women), 3 part-time/adjunct (2 women). *Students:* 6 full-time (4 women), 1 (woman) part-time. Average age 35. 25 applicants, 44% accepted, 2 enrolled. In 2009, 2 master's awarded. *Degree requirements:* For master's, visual thesis. *Entrance requirements:* For master's, portfolio, interview, minimum GPA of 3.0, 3 letters of recommendation. Additional exam requirements/recommendations for international students: Required—TOEFL (minimum score 500 paper-based). *Application deadline:* For fall admission, 2/1 priority date for domestic students, 12/1 priority date for international students. Applications are processed on a rolling basis. Application fee: $40 ($60 for international students). Electronic applications accepted. *Expenses:* Tuition, state resident: full-time $2071; part-time $86.29 per credit. Tuition, nonresident: full-time $8099; part-time $337.46 per credit. Required fees: $9446. Tuition and fees vary according to class time, course load and reciprocity agreements. *Financial support:* In 2009–10, 5 teaching assistantships with full tuition reimbursements (averaging $3,088 per year) were awarded; Federal Work-Study and unspecified assistantships also available. Support available to part-time students. Financial award application deadline: 3/1; financial award applicants required to submit FAFSA. Total annual research expenditures: $1,000. *Unit head:* Memory Holloway, Director, 508-999-8554, E-mail: mholloway@umassd.edu. *Application contact:* Elan Turcotte-Shamski, Graduate Admissions Officer, 508-999-8604, Fax: 508-999-8183, E-mail: graduate@umassd.edu.

Western Connecticut State University, Division of Graduate Studies, School of Visual and Performing Arts, Department of Art, Danbury, CT 06810-6885. Offers illustration (MFA); painting (MFA). Part-time programs available. *Faculty:* 3 full-time (2 women), 3 part-time/adjunct (0 women). *Students:* 23 full-time (14 women); includes 1 minority (African American), 2 international. Average age 31. In 2009, 10 master's awarded. *Degree requirements:* For master's, individual exhibition of artwork, review of student's progress prior to admission to final semester, completion of program in 6 years. *Entrance requirements:* For master's, portfolio review, minimum GPA of 2.5. Additional exam requirements/recommendations for international students: Recommended—TOEFL (minimum score 550 paper-based; 213 computer-based; 79 iBT), IELTS (minimum score 6). *Application deadline:* For fall admission, 8/5 priority date for domestic students; for spring admission, 1/5 priority date for domestic students. Application fee: $50. *Expenses:* Tuition, state resident: full-time $5012; part-time $278 per credit hour. Tuition, nonresident: full-time $13,962; part-time $284 per credit hour. Required fees: $3886; $139 per credit hour. Full-time tuition and fees vary according to course load and program. Part-time tuition and fees vary according to course level, degree level and program. *Financial support:* In 2009–10, 8 students received support. Scholarships/grants available. Financial award application deadline: 5/1; financial award applicants required to submit FAFSA. *Unit head:* Margaret Grimes, Graduate Co-Coordinator, 203-837-8402, Fax: 203-837-8945, E-mail: grimesm@wcsu.edu. *Application contact:* Chris Shankle, Associate Director of Graduate Studies, 203-837-9005, Fax: 203-837-8326, E-mail: shanklec@wcsu.edu.

Industrial Design

Academy of Art University, Graduate Program, School of Industrial Design, San Francisco, CA 94105-3410. Offers MFA. Part-time programs available. Postbaccalaureate distance learning degree programs offered (no on-campus study). *Degree requirements:* For master's, final review. *Entrance requirements:* For master's, portfolio. Electronic applications accepted.

Arizona State University, Graduate College, College of Design, Program in Design, Tempe, AZ 85287. Offers arts/media/engineering (MSD); healthcare and healing environments (MSD); industrial design (MSD); interaction design (MSD); interior design (MSD); new product innovation (MSD); visual communication design (MSD). *Accreditation:* NASAD. *Degree requirements:* For master's, thesis optional. *Entrance requirements:* For master's, GRE General Test, design portfolio.

Art Center College of Design, Graduate Division, Industrial Design Department, Pasadena, CA 91103. Offers environmental design (MS); product design (MS). *Accreditation:* NASAD. *Faculty:* 8 part-time/adjunct (1 woman). *Students:* 9 full-time (4 women), 5 part-time (4 women). Average age 29. 87 applicants, 25% accepted, 9 enrolled. In 2009, 9 master's awarded. *Degree requirements:* For master's, thesis, studio project. *Entrance requirements:* For master's, portfolio. Additional exam requirements/recommendations for international students: Required—TOEFL (minimum score 600 paper-based; 250 computer-based; 100 iBT). *Application deadline:* For fall admission, 2/1 for domestic and international students. Application fee: $50 ($70 for international students). *Expenses:* Tuition: Full-time $16,737. *Financial support:* Teaching assistantships, career-related internships or fieldwork, Federal Work-Study, and scholarships/grants available. Financial award application deadline: 2/1. *Unit head:* Andrew Ogden, Chair, 626-396-2464. *Application contact:* Maritza Hererra, 626-396-2464.

See Close-Up on page 113.

Auburn University, Graduate School, College of Architecture, Design, and Construction, Department of Industrial Design, Auburn University, AL 36849. Offers MID. *Accreditation:* NASAD. Part-time programs available. *Faculty:* 17 full-time (3 women). *Students:* 11 full-time (7 women), 7 part-time (3 women); includes 2 minority (1 African American, 1 Asian American or Pacific Islander), 5 international. Average age 26. 31 applicants, 35% accepted, 7 enrolled. In 2009, 6 master's awarded. *Entrance requirements:* For master's, GRE General Test. *Application deadline:* For fall admission, 9/1 for domestic students; for spring admission, 3/1 for domestic students. Applications are processed on a rolling basis. Application fee: $50 ($60 for international students). Electronic applications accepted. *Expenses:* Tuition, state resident: full-time $6240. Tuition, nonresident: full-time $18,720. International tuition: $18,938 full-time. Required fees: $492. Tuition and fees vary according to course load, program and reciprocity agreements. *Financial support:* Federal Work-Study available. Support available to part-time students. Financial award application deadline: 3/15; financial award applicants required to submit FAFSA. *Faculty research:* Design of space living facilities, color use in business communications. *Unit head:* Clark E. Lundell, Head, 334-844-2364. *Application contact:* Dr. George Flowers, Dean of the Graduate School, 334-844-2125.

Brigham Young University, Graduate Studies, Ira A. Fulton College of Engineering and Technology, School of Technology, Provo, UT 84602-1001. Offers construction management (MS); information technology (MS); manufacturing systems (MS); technology and engineering education (MS). *Faculty:* 25 full-time (0 women). *Students:* 23 full-time (3 women); includes 3 minority (2 Asian Americans or Pacific Islanders, 1 Hispanic American). Average age 25. 14 applicants, 71% accepted, 6 enrolled. In 2009, 13 master's awarded. *Degree requirements:* For master's, thesis. *Entrance requirements:* For master's, GRE General Test, GMAT (construction management), minimum GPA of 3.0 in last 60 hours of course work. Additional exam requirements/recommendations for international students: Required—TOEFL (minimum score 580 paper-based; 237 computer-based; 85 iBT). *Application deadline:* For fall admission, 2/15 for domestic and international students; for winter admission, 9/15 for domestic and international students; for spring admission, 2/15 for domestic and international students. Application fee: $50. Electronic applications accepted. *Expenses:* Tuition: Full-time $5580; part-time $301 per credit hour. Tuition and fees vary according to student's religious affiliation. *Financial support:* In 2009–10, 9 research assistantships (averaging $4,774 per year), 7 teaching assistantships (averaging $4,481 per year) were awarded; fellowships, career-related internships or fieldwork also available. Financial award application deadline: 2/1. *Faculty research:* Real time process control in IT, electronic physical design, processing and non-linear systems, networking, computerized systems in CM. Total annual research expenditures: $52,000. *Unit head:* Val D. Hawks, Director, 801-422-6300, Fax: 801-422-0490, E-mail: hawksv@byu.edu. *Application contact:* Ronald E. Terry, Graduate Coordinator, 801-422-4297, Fax: 801-422-0490, E-mail: ralowe@byu.edu.

Carleton University, Faculty of Graduate Studies, Faculty of Engineering and Design, School of Industrial Design, Ottawa, ON K1S 5B6, Canada. Offers M Des. *Degree requirements:* For master's, thesis optional. *Entrance requirements:* For master's, honors degree. Additional exam requirements/recommendations for international students: Required—TOEFL.

North Carolina State University, Graduate School, College of Design, Department of Industrial Design, Raleigh, NC 27695. Offers MID. *Accreditation:* NASAD. Part-time programs available. *Degree requirements:* For master's, thesis optional, oral exam, project. *Entrance requirements:* For master's, GRE General Test (recommended), portfolio. Electronic applications accepted. *Faculty research:* Computer graphics, ergonomics, product design.

The Ohio State University, Graduate School, College of the Arts, Department of Industrial, Interior, and Visual Communication Design, Columbus, OH 43210. Offers MA, MFA. *Accreditation:* NASAD. Part-time programs available. *Faculty:* 14. *Students:* 29 full-time (15 women), 9 part-time (4 women); includes 2 minority (both African Americans), 8 international. Average age 28. In 2009, 14 master's awarded. *Degree requirements:* For master's, project or thesis. *Entrance requirements:* For master's, bachelor's degree in interior space, graphics, product design, or related field. Additional exam requirements/recommendations for international students: Recommended—TOEFL (minimum score 600 paper-based; 250 computer-based). *Application deadline:* For fall admission, 8/15 priority date for domestic students, 7/1 priority date for international students; for winter admission, 12/1 priority date for domestic students, 11/1 priority date for international students; for spring admission, 3/1 priority date for domestic students, 2/1 priority date for international students. Applications are processed on a rolling basis. Application fee: $40 ($50 for international students). Electronic applications accepted. *Expenses:* Tuition, state resident: full-time $10,683. Tuition, nonresident: full-time $25,923. Tuition and fees vary according to course load and program. *Financial support:* Fellowships, research assistantships, teaching assistantships, career-related internships or fieldwork, Federal Work-Study, institutionally sponsored loans, and unspecified assistantships available. Support available to part-time students. Financial award application deadline: 5/1. *Unit head:* R. Brian Stone, Graduate Studies Committee Chair, 614-688-6746, Fax: 614-292-0217, E-mail: stone.158@osu.edu. *Application contact:* 614-292-9444, Fax: 614-292-3895, E-mail: domestic.grad@osu.edu.

Pratt Institute, School of Art and Design, Program in Industrial Design, Brooklyn, NY 11205-3899. Offers MID. *Accreditation:* NASAD. Part-time programs available. *Faculty:* 6 full-time (1 woman), 26 part-time/adjunct (8 women). *Students:* 78 full-time (50 women), 2 part-time (both women); includes 16 minority (2 African Americans, 11 Asian Americans or Pacific Islanders, 3 Hispanic Americans), 12 international. Average age 29. 247 applicants, 27% accepted, 26 enrolled. In 2009, 19 master's awarded. *Degree requirements:* For master's, thesis. *Entrance requirements:* For master's, portfolio, letters of recommendation. Additional exam requirements/recommendations for international students: Required—TOEFL (minimum score 575 paper-based; 233 computer-based; 100 iBT). *Application deadline:* For fall admission, 1/5 for domestic and international students; for spring admission, 10/1 for domestic and international students. Application fee: $50 ($90 for international students). Electronic applications accepted. *Expenses:* Tuition: Full-time $22,734. Required fees: $1280. *Financial support:* Career-related internships or fieldwork, Federal Work-Study, institutionally sponsored loans, scholarships/grants, health care benefits, and unspecified assistantships available. Support available to part-time students. Financial award application deadline: 2/1; financial award applicants required to submit FAFSA. *Faculty research:* Universal design, design ethics, sustainability in design. *Unit head:* Matthew Burger, Chairperson, 718-636-3520, Fax: 718-636-3553, E-mail: mburger@pratt.edu. *Application contact:* Young Hah, Director of Graduate Admissions, 718-636-3683, Fax: 718-399-4242, E-mail: yhah@pratt.edu.

See Close-Up on page 119.

Pratt Institute, School of Art and Design, Program in Package Design, New York, NY 10011. Offers MS. *Accreditation:* NASAD. Part-time programs available. *Faculty:* 5 full-time (2 women), 33 part-time/adjunct (9 women). *Students:* 21 full-time (20 women), 4 part-time (all women); includes 6 minority (2 African Americans, 4 Asian Americans or Pacific Islanders), 12 international. Average age 27. 24 applicants, 83% accepted, 6 enrolled. In 2009, 10 master's awarded. *Degree requirements:* For master's, thesis. *Entrance requirements:* For master's, portfolio, letters of recommendation. Additional exam requirements/recommendations for international students: Required—TOEFL (minimum score 575 paper-based; 233 computer-based; 90 iBT). *Application deadline:* For fall admission, 1/5 for domestic and international students; for spring admission, 10/1 for domestic and international students. Application fee: $50 ($90 for international students). Electronic applications accepted. *Expenses:* Tuition: Full-time $22,734. Required fees: $1280. *Financial support:* Career-related internships or fieldwork, Federal Work-Study, institutionally sponsored loans, scholarships/grants, health care benefits, and unspecified assistantships available. Support available to part-time students. Financial award application deadline: 2/1; financial award applicants required to submit FAFSA. *Unit head:* Jeffrey Bellantoni, Chairperson, 212-647-7573, E-mail: jbell189@pratt.edu. *Application contact:* Young Hah, Director of Graduate Admissions, 718-636-3683, Fax: 718-399-4242, E-mail: yhah@pratt.edu.

See Close-Up on page 119.

Rhode Island School of Design, Graduate Studies, Division of Architecture and Design, Department of Industrial Design, Providence, RI 02903-2784. Offers MID. *Accreditation:* NASAD. *Degree requirements:* For master's, thesis, exhibit. *Entrance requirements:* For master's, portfolio, 3 letters of recommendation. Additional exam requirements/recommendations for international students: Required—TOEFL (minimum score 580 paper-based; 237 computer-based), IELTS (minimum score 6.5).

Rochester Institute of Technology, Graduate Enrollment Services, College of Imaging Arts and Sciences, School of Design, Program in Industrial Design, Rochester, NY 14623-5603. Offers MFA. *Accreditation:* NASAD. Part-time programs available. *Students:* 25 full-time (9 women), 2 part-time (1 woman); includes 1 Asian American or Pacific Islander, 16 international. Average age 30. 112 applicants, 21% accepted, 6 enrolled. In 2009, 15 master's awarded. *Degree requirements:* For master's, thesis (for some programs). *Entrance requirements:* For master's, portfolio, minimum GPA of 3.0. Additional exam requirements/recommendations for international students: Required—TOEFL (minimum score 550 paper-based; 213 computer-based; 79 iBT), or IELTS (minimum score 6.5). *Application deadline:* For fall admission, 2/15 priority date for domestic and international students. Applications are processed on a rolling basis. Application fee: $50. Electronic applications accepted. *Expenses:* Tuition: Full-time $31,533; part-time $876 per credit hour. Required fees: $210. *Financial support:* In 2009–10, 15 students received support; teaching assistantships with partial tuition reimbursements available, career-related internships or fieldwork, institutionally sponsored loans, scholarships/grants, and unspecified assistantships available. Support available to part-time students. Financial award application deadline: 8/30; financial award applicants required to submit FAFSA. *Unit head:* David Morgan, Graduate Coordinator, 585-475-2668, Fax: 585-475-7533, E-mail: dcmfaa@rit.edu. *Application contact:* Diane Ellison, Assistant Vice President, Graduate Enrollment Services, 585-475-2229, Fax: 585-475-7164, E-mail: gradinfo@rit.edu.

San Francisco State University, Division of Graduate Studies, College of Creative Arts, Department of Design and Industry, San Francisco, CA 94132-1722. Offers industrial arts (MA).

Savannah College of Art and Design, Graduate School, Program in Industrial Design, Savannah, GA 31402-3146. Offers MA, MFA. Part-time programs available. *Degree requirements:* For master's, thesis, exhibit, internships. *Entrance requirements:* For master's, interview, portfolio. Additional exam requirements/recommendations for international students: Required—TOEFL (minimum score 450 paper-based; 133 computer-based). Electronic applications accepted. *Expenses:* Tuition: Full-time $28,515; part-time $627 per credit hour. One-time fee: $500. Tuition and fees vary according to course load.

University of Cincinnati, Graduate School, College of Design, Architecture, Art, and Planning, School of Design, Cincinnati, OH 45221. Offers fashion design (M Des); graphic design (M Des); industrial design (M Des); interaction design (M Des); product development (M Des). *Accreditation:* NASAD. *Degree requirements:* For master's, thesis. *Entrance requirements:* For master's, undergraduate degree in design or related field, 2 years of work experience in design or related field. Additional exam requirements/recommendations for international students: Required—TOEFL. Electronic applications accepted. *Faculty research:* Design theory, interdisciplinary design topics.

University of Illinois at Chicago, Graduate College, College of Architecture and Art, School of Art and Design, Chicago, IL 60607-7128. Offers electronic visualization (MFA); film animation (MFA); graphic design (MFA); industrial design (MFA); photography (MFA); studio arts (MFA). *Accreditation:* NASAD. *Degree requirements:* For master's, thesis, exhibit. *Entrance requirements:* For master's, MAT, portfolio. Additional exam requirements/recommendations for international students: Required—TOEFL. Electronic applications accepted.

University of Illinois at Urbana–Champaign, Graduate College, College of Fine and Applied Arts, School of Art and Design, Program in Design and Media, Champaign, IL 61820. Offers art and design (MFA), including new media; graphic design (MFA); industrial design (MFA). *Accreditation:* NASAD. *Students:* 18 full-time (9 women), 2 part-time (1 woman); includes 2 minority (both Asian Americans or Pacific Islanders), 10 international. 109 applicants, 7% accepted, 8 enrolled. In 2009, 4 master's awarded. *Entrance requirements:* For master's, minimum GPA of 3.0. Additional exam requirements/recommendations for international students: Required—TOEFL (minimum score 550 paper-based; 213 computer-based; 79 iBT). *Application deadline:* Applications are processed on a rolling basis. Application fee: $60 ($75 for international students). Electronic applications accepted. *Financial support:* Fellowships, research assistantships, teaching assistantships, tuition waivers (full and partial) available. *Unit head:* Ernest Scott, Chair, 217-333-1579, E-mail: ernscott@illinois.edu. *Application contact:* Marsha Biddle, Coordinator of Graduate Academic Affairs, 217-333-0642, Fax: 217-244-7688, E-mail: mbiddle@illinois.edu.

University of Notre Dame, Graduate School, College of Arts and Letters, Division of Humanities, Department of Art, Art History, and Design, Notre Dame, IN 46556. Offers art history (MA); design (MFA), including graphic design, industrial design; studio art (MFA), including ceramics, painting, photography, printmaking, sculpture. *Accreditation:* NASAD. *Degree requirements:* For master's, comprehensive exam (for some programs), thesis. *Entrance requirements:* For master's, GRE General Test, minimum GPA of 3.0. Additional exam requirements/recommendations for international students: Required—TOEFL (minimum score 600 paper-based; 250 computer-based; 80 iBT). Electronic applications accepted. *Faculty research:* Studio art practice in ceramics, printing, photography, printmaking and sculpture, graphic design and industrial design, digital imaging in design and photography, Renaissance and American art history, contemporary art theory and criticism.

The University of the Arts, College of Art and Design, Department of Industrial Design, Philadelphia, PA 19102-4944. Offers MID. *Accreditation:* NASAD. *Degree requirements:* For master's, thesis. *Entrance requirements:* For master's, portfolio. Additional exam requirements/recommendations for international students: Required—TOEFL (minimum score 550 paper-based; 213 computer-based).

See Close-Up on page 199.

University of Washington, Graduate School, College of Arts and Sciences, School of Art, Division of Design, Seattle, WA 98195. Offers industrial design (MFA); visual communication design (MFA).

Interior Design

Academy of Art University, Graduate Program, School of Interior Architecture and Design, San Francisco, CA 94105-3410. Offers MFA. Part-time programs available. Postbaccalaureate distance learning degree programs offered (no on-campus study). *Degree requirements:* For master's, final review. *Entrance requirements:* For master's, portfolio. Electronic applications accepted.

Arizona State University, Graduate College, College of Design, Program in Design, Tempe, AZ 85287. Offers arts/media/engineering (MSD); healthcare and healing environments (MSD); industrial design (MSD); interaction design (MSD); interior design (MSD); new product innovation (MSD); visual communication design (MSD). *Accreditation:* NASAD. *Degree requirements:* For master's, thesis optional. *Entrance requirements:* For master's, GRE General Test, design portfolio.

Boston Architectural College, Graduate Programs, Boston, MA 02115-2795. Offers architecture (M Arch); interior design (MID). *Accreditation:* CIDA. *Degree requirements:* For master's, thesis. *Entrance requirements:* For master's, portfolio (recommended). Electronic applications accepted.

Brenau University, Graduate Programs, School of Fine Arts and Humanities, Gainesville, GA 30501. Offers interior design (MID). Part-time programs available. *Faculty:* 2 full-time (both women). *Students:* 1 (woman) full-time, 4 part-time (all women). Average age 28. 1 applicant, 100% accepted, 0 enrolled. In 2009, 6 master's awarded. *Degree requirements:* For master's, thesis, internship. *Entrance requirements:* For master's, portfolio review, minimum GPA of 3.0. Additional exam requirements/recommendations for international students: Required—TOEFL (minimum score 500 paper-based). *Application deadline:* Applications are processed on a rolling basis. Application fee: $35. Electronic applications accepted. *Unit head:* Dr. Andrea Birch, Dean, E-mail: abirch@brenau.edu. *Application contact:* Christina White, Dean of Admissions, 770-718-5320, Fax: 770-718-5338.

Chatham University, Program in Interior Architecture, Pittsburgh, PA 15232-2826. Offers MIA. Part-time and evening/weekend programs available. Postbaccalaureate distance learning degree programs offered (no on-campus study). *Students:* 17 full-time (14 women), 6 part-time (5 women). Average age 37. 30 applicants, 63% accepted, 8 enrolled. In 2009, 6 master's awarded. *Entrance requirements:* Additional exam requirements/recommendations for international students: Required—TOEFL (minimum score 600 paper-based; 250 computer-based; 100 iBT), IELTS (minimum score 6.5), TWE. *Application deadline:* For fall admission, 7/1 priority date for domestic students, 6/1 priority date for international students; for spring admission, 12/1 priority date for domestic students, 11/1 priority date for international students. Applications are processed on a rolling basis. Application fee: $45. Electronic applications accepted. *Financial support:* Applicants required to submit FAFSA. *Faculty research:* Sustainability. *Unit head:* Prof. Lori Anthony, Director, 412-365-2977, E-mail: lanthony@chatham.edu. *Application contact:* Michael May, Director of Graduate Admissions, 412-365-1141, Fax: 412-365-1609, E-mail: gradadmissions@chatham.edu.

Corcoran College of Art and Design, Graduate Programs, Washington, DC 20006-4804. Offers art education (MAT); history of decorative arts (MA); interior design (MA). *Accreditation:* NASAD. Part-time programs available. *Entrance requirements:* Additional exam requirements/recommendations for international students: Required—TOEFL.

Cornell University, Graduate School, Graduate Fields of Human Ecology, Field of Design and Environmental Analysis, Ithaca, NY 14853-0001. Offers applied research in human-environment relations (MS); facilities planning and management (MS); housing and design (MS); human factors and ergonomics (MS); human-environment relations (MS); interior design (MA, MPS). *Faculty:* 14 full-time (6 women). *Students:* 20 full-time (16 women); includes 3 minority (2 Asian Americans or Pacific Islanders, 1 Hispanic American), 2 international. Average age 27. 43 applicants, 30% accepted, 12 enrolled. In 2009, 3 master's awarded. *Degree requirements:* For master's, thesis. *Entrance requirements:* For master's, GRE General Test, portfolio or slides of recent work; bachelor's degree in interior design, architecture or related design discipline; 2 letters of recommendation. Additional exam requirements/recommendations for international students: Required—TOEFL (minimum score 600 paper-based; 250 computer-based; 105 iBT). *Application deadline:* For fall admission, 2/1 priority date for domestic students. Application fee: $70. Electronic applications accepted. *Expenses:* Tuition: Full-time

Interior Design

Cornell University (continued)
$29,500. Required fees: $70. Full-time tuition and fees vary according to degree level, program and student level. *Financial support:* In 2009–10, 13 students received support, including 1 fellowship with full tuition reimbursement available, 5 teaching assistantships with full tuition reimbursements available; research assistantships with full tuition reimbursements available, institutionally sponsored loans, scholarships/grants, health care benefits, tuition waivers (full and partial), and unspecified assistantships also available. Financial award applicants required to submit FAFSA. *Faculty research:* Facility planning and management, environmental psychology, housing, interior design, ergonomics and human factors. *Unit head:* Director of Graduate Studies, 607-255-2168, Fax: 607-255-0305. *Application contact:* Graduate Field Assistant, 607-255-2168, Fax: 607-255-0305, E-mail: deagrad@cornell.edu.

Drexel University, Antoinette Westphal College of Media Arts and Design, Program in Interior Architecture and Design, Philadelphia, PA 19104-2875. Offers MS. *Accreditation:* NASAD. *Degree requirements:* For master's, comprehensive exam, thesis, graduate review. *Entrance requirements:* For master's, interview. Additional exam requirements/recommendations for international students: Required—TOEFL. Electronic applications accepted. *Faculty research:* History of commercial interiors, hospice spaces, environmental sculpture, painting.

Eastern Michigan University, Graduate School, College of Technology, School of Engineering Technology, Program in Interior Design, Ypsilanti, MI 48197. Offers MS. Part-time and evening/weekend programs available. Postbaccalaureate distance learning degree programs offered (minimal on-campus study). *Students:* 8 full-time (7 women), 18 part-time (16 women); includes 2 minority (1 African American, 1 Asian American or Pacific Islander), 3 international. Average age 37. In 2009, 1 master's awarded. *Entrance requirements:* Additional exam requirements/recommendations for international students: Required—TOEFL. *Application deadline:* Applications are processed on a rolling basis. Application fee: $35. Tuition and fees vary according to course level. *Financial support:* Fellowships, research assistantships with full tuition reimbursements, teaching assistantships with full tuition reimbursements, career-related internships or fieldwork, Federal Work-Study, institutionally sponsored loans, scholarships/grants, tuition waivers (partial), and unspecified assistantships available. Support available to part-time students. Financial award applicants required to submit FAFSA. *Unit head:* Dr. Shinming Shyu, Program Coordinator, 734-487-6419, Fax: 734-487-8755, E-mail: sshyu@emich.edu. *Application contact:* Dr. Shinming Shyu, Program Coordinator, 734-487-6419, Fax: 734-487-8755, E-mail: sshyu@emich.edu.

Florida International University, College of Architecture and the Arts, School of Architecture, Interior Design Program, Miami, FL 33199. Offers MA, MID. *Faculty:* 1 (woman) full-time. *Students:* 28 full-time (24 women), 2 part-time (both women); includes 17 minority (2 African Americans, 1 Asian American or Pacific Islander, 14 Hispanic Americans), 4 international. Average age 30. 29 applicants, 24% accepted, 6 enrolled. In 2009, 4 degrees awarded. *Entrance requirements:* For master's, GRE or minimum GPA of 3.0 in upper-level undergraduate work, portfolio. Additional exam requirements/recommendations for international students: Required—TOEFL (minimum score 550 paper-based; 80 iBT). *Application deadline:* For fall admission, 2/1 for domestic and international students. Application fee: $30. Electronic applications accepted. *Expenses:* Tuition, state resident: full-time $8008; part-time $4004 per year. Tuition, nonresident: full-time $20,104; part-time $10,052 per year. Required fees: $298; $149 per term. *Financial support:* Institutionally sponsored loans and scholarships/grants available. Financial award application deadline: 3/1; financial award applicants required to submit FAFSA. *Unit head:* Dr. Brian Schriner, Interim Dean, 305-348-6742, Fax: 305-348-2650, E-mail: schriner@fiu.edu. *Application contact:* Prof. Janine King, Graduate Program Director, 305-348-6630, Fax: 305-348-2650, E-mail: janine.king@fiu.edu.

Florida State University, The Graduate School, College of Visual Arts, Theatre and Dance, Department of Interior Design, Tallahassee, FL 32306. Offers MA, MFA, MS. *Accreditation:* NASAD (one or more programs are accredited). *Faculty:* 8 full-time (3 women), 4 part-time/adjunct (3 women). *Students:* 35 full-time (33 women), 8 part-time (all women); includes 6 minority (4 African Americans, 1 Asian American or Pacific Islander, 1 Hispanic American), 1 international. Average age 30. 13 applicants, 92% accepted, 12 enrolled. In 2009, 14 master's awarded. *Degree requirements:* For master's, thesis or alternative. *Entrance requirements:* For master's, GRE General Test, minimum GPA of 3.0 during previous 2 years. Additional exam requirements/recommendations for international students: Required—TOEFL (minimum score 550 paper-based). Application fee: $30. Electronic applications accepted. *Expenses:* Tuition, state resident: full-time $7413. Tuition, nonresident: full-time $22,567. *Financial support:* In 2009–10, 1 fellowship (averaging $18,000 per year), 2 research assistantships with tuition reimbursements (averaging $3,200 per year), 10 teaching assistantships with tuition reimbursements (averaging $3,200 per year) were awarded; career-related internships or fieldwork and unspecified assistantships also available. Financial award applicants required to submit FAFSA. *Faculty research:* Graphics techniques, history of interiors, technical proficiencies, computer-aided design and drafting, historic restoration. *Unit head:* Eric Wiedegreen, Chairman, 850-645-2504, Fax: 850-644-3112, E-mail: ewiedegr@fsu.edu. *Application contact:* Dr. Lisa Waxman, Director of Graduate Studies, 850-644-8326, Fax: 850-644-3112, E-mail: lwaxman@mailer.fsu.edu.

The George Washington University, Columbian College of Arts and Sciences, Department of Fine Arts and Art History, Program in Interior Design, Washington, DC 20052. Offers MFA. *Students:* 19 full-time (16 women), 28 part-time (all women); includes 12 minority (6 African Americans, 4 Asian Americans or Pacific Islanders, 2 Hispanic Americans), 4 international. Average age 30. 34 applicants, 76% accepted, 8 enrolled. In 2009, 12 master's awarded. *Entrance requirements:* Additional exam requirements/recommendations for international students: Required—TOEFL (minimum score 550 paper-based; 213 computer-based; 80 iBT). *Application deadline:* For fall admission, 3/1 for domestic students, 1/15 for international students; for spring admission, 10/1 for domestic students, 9/1 for international students. *Financial support:* Application deadline: 1/15. *Unit head:* Thomas K. Brown, Chair, 202-994-9067, E-mail: thbrown@gwu.edu. *Application contact:* Information Contact, 202-994-6085, Fax: 202-994-8657, E-mail: art@gwu.edu.

Iowa State University of Science and Technology, Graduate College, College of Design, Department of Art and Design, Ames, IA 50011. Offers art and design (MA); graphic design (MFA); integrated visual arts (MFA); interior design (MFA). Part-time programs available. *Faculty:* 34 full-time (20 women), 1 (woman) part-time/adjunct. *Students:* 44 full-time (35 women), 9 part-time (6 women); includes 2 minority (1 African American, 1 Asian American or Pacific Islander), 14 international. 27 applicants, 63% accepted, 10 enrolled. In 2009, 11 master's awarded. *Degree requirements:* For master's, thesis (for some programs). *Entrance requirements:* For master's, GRE General Test, resume, supplemental departmental form. Additional exam requirements/recommendations for international students: Required—TOEFL (minimum score 550 paper-based; 79 iBT) or IELTS (minimum score 6.5). *Application deadline:* For fall admission, 5/1 priority date for domestic and international students. Applications are processed on a rolling basis. Application fee: $40 ($90 for international students). Electronic applications accepted. *Expenses:* Tuition, state resident: full-time $6716. Tuition, nonresident: full-time $8908. Tuition and fees vary according to course level, course load, program and student level. *Financial support:* In 2009–10, 19 research assistantships with full and partial tuition reimbursements (averaging $7,850 per year) were awarded; teaching assistantships with full and partial tuition reimbursements, career-related internships or fieldwork, Federal Work-Study, institutionally sponsored loans, and tuition waivers (partial) also available. Support available to part-time students. Financial award application deadline: 2/15; financial award applicants required to submit FAFSA. *Faculty research:* Computer applications, fire safety, human factors in design, art and design education, fine arts, craft design. *Unit head:* Roger Baer, Chair, 515-294-6724, Fax: 515-294-2725, E-mail: artdn@iastate.edu. *Application contact:* Roger Baer, Chair, 515-294-6724, Fax: 515-294-2725, E-mail: artdn@iastate.edu.

Lawrence Technological University, College of Architecture and Design, Southfield, MI 48075-1058. Offers architecture (M Arch); interior design (MID). *Accreditation:* NASAD. Part-time and evening/weekend programs available. *Faculty:* 9 full-time (2 women), 12 part-time/adjunct (3 women). *Students:* 5 full-time (3 women), 157 part-time (57 women); includes 28 minority (13 African Americans, 1 American Indian/Alaska Native, 10 Asian Americans or Pacific Islanders, 4 Hispanic Americans), 13 international. Average age 32. 150 applicants, 63% accepted, 68 enrolled. In 2009, 107 master's awarded. *Degree requirements:* For master's, thesis. *Entrance requirements:* For master's, portfolio. Additional exam requirements/recommendations for international students: Required—TOEFL (minimum score 550 paper-based; 213 computer-based; 79 iBT). *Application deadline:* For fall admission, 2/1 priority date for domestic students, 2/1 for international students; for winter admission, 11/1 priority date for domestic students, 11/1 for international students; for spring admission, 2/1 priority date for domestic students, 2/1 for international students. Applications are processed on a rolling basis. Application fee: $50. Electronic applications accepted. *Expenses:* Tuition: Full-time $11,320; part-time $798 per credit hour. *Financial support:* In 2009–10, 105 students received support. Federal Work-Study available. Financial award application deadline: 4/1; financial award applicants required to submit FAFSA. *Unit head:* Glen LeRoy, Dean, 248-204-2800, Fax: 248-204-2900, E-mail: archdean@ltu.edu. *Application contact:* Jane Rohrback, Director of Admissions, 248-204-3160, Fax: 248-204-3188, E-mail: admissions@ltu.edu.

Louisiana Tech University, Graduate School, College of Liberal Arts, School of Architecture, Ruston, LA 71272. Offers interior design (MFA). *Entrance requirements:* For master's, GRE General Test.

Marymount University, School of Arts and Sciences, Program in Interior Design, Arlington, VA 22207-4299. Offers MA. *Accreditation:* CIDA. Part-time and evening/weekend programs available. *Faculty:* 5 full-time (4 women), 3 part-time/adjunct (2 women). *Students:* 25 full-time (all women), 31 part-time (27 women); includes 18 minority (8 African Americans, 7 Asian Americans or Pacific Islanders, 3 Hispanic Americans), 2 international. Average age 33. 18 applicants, 100% accepted, 8 enrolled. In 2009, 18 master's awarded. *Degree requirements:* For master's, thesis or alternative. *Entrance requirements:* For master's, GRE, National Council for Interior Design Qualification (NCIDQ) exam, or National Council of Architectural Registration Boards (NCARB) Architectural Registration Exam, 2 letters of recommendation, interview, resume, personal statement, portfolio. Additional exam requirements/recommendations for international students: Required—TOEFL (minimum score 600 paper-based; 250 computer-based; 96 iBT), IELTS (minimum score 6.5). *Application deadline:* For fall admission, 6/24 for domestic students, 7/1 for international students; for spring admission, 11/11 for domestic students, 10/15 for international students. Applications are processed on a rolling basis. Application fee: $40. Electronic applications accepted. *Expenses:* Tuition: Full-time $13,050; part-time $725 per credit hour. Required fees: $135; $7.50 per credit hour. *Financial support:* In 2009–10, 4 students received support; research assistantships with full and partial tuition reimbursements available, career-related internships or fieldwork, Federal Work-Study, scholarships/grants, and unspecified assistantships available. Support available to part-time students. Financial award applicants required to submit FAFSA. *Unit head:* Dr. Robert Meden, Chair, 703-284-1574, Fax: 703-284-3859, E-mail: robin.wagner@marymount.edu. *Application contact:* Francesca Reed, Director, Graduate Admissions, 703-284-5901, Fax: 703-527-3815, E-mail: grad.admissions@marymount.edu.

Marywood University, Academic Affairs, School of Architecture, Scranton, PA 18509-1598. Offers architecture (M Arch); studio art (MA), including interior design. *Students:* 2 part-time (both women). Average age 25. In 2009, 6 master's awarded. *Entrance requirements:* Additional exam requirements/recommendations for international students: Required—TOEFL (minimum score 550 paper-based; 213 computer-based; 79 iBT). *Expenses:* Tuition: Part-time $715 per credit. Required fees: $270 per semester. Tuition and fees vary according to degree level, campus/location and program. *Financial support:* Career-related internships or fieldwork, scholarships/grants, and unspecified assistantships available. Support available to part-time students. Financial award application deadline: 6/30; financial award applicants required to submit FAFSA. *Unit head:* Gregory K. Hunt, Founding Dean, 570-348-6211 Ext. 4536, E-mail: gkhunt@marywood.edu. *Application contact:* Tammy Manka, Assistant Director of Graduate Admissions, 866-279-9663, E-mail: tmanka@marywood.edu.

Miami International University of Art & Design, Program in Interior Design, Miami, FL 33132-1418. Offers MFA. *Application contact:* Office of Graduate Admissions, 305-428-5700.

See Close-Up on page 117.

Michigan State University, The Graduate School, College of Agriculture and Natural Resources and College of Social Science, School of Planning, Design and Construction, East Lansing, MI 48824. Offers construction management (MS, PhD); environmental design (MA); interior design and facilities management (MA); international planning studies (MIPS); urban and regional planning (MURP). *Faculty:* 25 full-time (12 women). *Students:* 56 full-time (21 women), 25 part-time (12 women); includes 4 minority (1 African American, 2 Asian Americans or Pacific Islanders, 1 Hispanic American), 53 international. Average age 30. 122 applicants, 57% accepted. In 2009, 34 degrees awarded. *Degree requirements:* For master's, thesis or alternative. *Entrance requirements:* Additional exam requirements/recommendations for international students: Required—TOEFL. *Application deadline:* Applications are processed on a rolling basis. Electronic applications accepted. *Financial support:* In 2009–10, 16 research assistantships with tuition reimbursements (averaging $13,001 per year), 2 teaching assistantships with tuition reimbursements (averaging $13,599 per year) were awarded. Total annual research expenditures: $281,011. *Unit head:* Dr. Scott G. Witter, Director, 517-432-6379, Fax: 517-432-8108, E-mail: witter@msu.edu. *Application contact:* Dawn Brown, Graduate Secretary, 517-432-3393, Fax: 517-432-3772, E-mail: browndaw@msu.edu.

Missouri State University, Graduate College, College of Natural and Applied Sciences, Department of Fashion and Interior Design, Springfield, MO 65897. Offers secondary education (MS Ed), including consumer sciences. Part-time programs available. *Faculty:* 2 full-time (both women), 1 (woman) part-time/adjunct. *Students:* 3 part-time (all women). Average age 47. 2 applicants, 50% accepted, 0 enrolled. *Degree requirements:* For master's, comprehensive exam, thesis or alternative. *Entrance requirements:* For master's, 9-12 teaching certification (MS Ed), minimum GPA of 3.0 (MNAS). Additional exam requirements/recommendations for international students: Required—TOEFL (minimum score 550 paper-based; 213 computer-based; 79 iBT). *Application deadline:* For fall admission, 7/20 priority date for domestic students, 5/1 for international students; for spring admission, 12/20 priority date for domestic students, 9/1 for international students. Applications are processed on a rolling basis. Application fee: $35 ($50 for international students). Electronic applications accepted. *Expenses:* Tuition, state resident: full-time $3852; part-time $214 per credit hour. Tuition, nonresident: full-time $7524; part-time $418 per credit hour. Required fees: $696; $172 per semester. Tuition and fees vary according to course level, course load, degree level and program. *Financial support:* Career-related internships or fieldwork, Federal Work-Study, institutionally sponsored loans, scholarships/grants, and unspecified assistantships available. Financial award application deadline: 3/31; financial award applicants required to submit FAFSA. *Unit head:* Dr. Paula Kemp, Head, 417-836-5497, Fax: 417-836-4341, E-mail: paulakemp@missouristate.edu. *Application contact:* Eric Eckert, Coordinator of Graduate Admissions and Recruitment, 417-836-5331, Fax: 417-836-6200, E-mail: ericeckert@missouristate.edu.

Moore College of Art & Design, Program in Interior Design, Philadelphia, PA 19103. Offers MFA. Evening/weekend programs available. *Degree requirements:* For master's, thesis, internship, thesis exhibition. *Entrance requirements:* For master's, minimum GPA of 3.0, on-site interview, portfolio, 3 letters of recommendation, resume.

Mount Ida College, Program in Interior Design, Newton, MA 02459-3310. Offers MSM. *Accreditation:* NASAD. Part-time and evening/weekend programs available. Postbaccalaureate distance learning degree programs offered (minimal on-campus study). *Faculty:* 3 full-time (2 women). *Students:* 4 part-time (all women). Average age 30. 4 applicants, 100% accepted, 4 enrolled. *Entrance requirements:* For master's, portfolio. Additional exam requirements/recommendations for international students: Required—TOEFL (minimum score 550 paper-based; 220 computer-based; 79 iBT); Recommended—IELTS (minimum score 5.5). *Application deadline:* For fall admission, 8/15 for domestic and international students; for spring admission, 1/3 for domestic and international students. Applications are processed on a rolling basis. Application fee: $50. Electronic applications accepted. *Expenses:* Tuition: Part-time $650 per credit. *Financial support:* Teaching assistantships, Federal Work-Study available. Financial award applicants required to submit FAFSA. *Unit head:* Rose Botti-Salitsky, Director, 617-928-4644, E-mail: rbottisalitsky@mountida.edu. *Application contact:* Jay Titus, Dean of Admissions, 617-928-4553, Fax: 617-928-4507, E-mail: jtitus@mountida.edu.

The New School: A University, Parsons The New School for Design, Program in Interior Design, New York, NY 10011. Offers MFA. *Faculty:* 5 full-time (3 women). *Students:* 12 full-time (7 women); includes 2 minority (1 African American, 1 Hispanic American), 4 international. Average age 29. 107 applicants, 25% accepted, 12 enrolled. *Degree requirements:* For master's, thesis. *Entrance requirements:* For master's, portfolio. Additional exam requirements/recommendations for international students: Required—TOEFL (minimum score 580 paper-based; 237 computer-based; 92 iBT). *Application deadline:* For fall admission, 2/1 for domestic and international students. Application fee: $50. Electronic applications accepted. *Financial support:* Federal Work-Study and scholarships/grants available. Support available to part-time students. *Unit head:* Jonsara Ruth, Dean, 212-229-8955 Ext. 2923, E-mail: ruthj@newschool.edu. *Application contact:* David Norris, Director of Admissions, 212-229-8989 Ext. 4023, Fax: 212-229-8975, E-mail: norrisd@newschool.edu.

The New School: A University, Parsons The New School for Design, Program in Lighting Design, New York, NY 10011. Offers MFA. *Accreditation:* NASAD. *Faculty:* 3 full-time (0 women). *Students:* 44 full-time (27 women), 1 (woman) part-time; includes 9 minority (1 African American, 5 Asian Americans or Pacific Islanders, 3 Hispanic Americans), 18 international. Average age 28. 74 applicants, 54% accepted, 22 enrolled. In 2009, 17 master's awarded. *Degree requirements:* For master's, thesis. *Entrance requirements:* For master's, portfolio. Additional exam requirements/recommendations for international students: Required—TOEFL (minimum score 580 paper-based; 237 computer-based; 92 iBT). *Application deadline:* For fall admission, 2/1 for domestic and international students. Application fee: $50. Electronic applications accepted. *Financial support:* Federal Work-Study, scholarships/grants, and tuition waivers (partial) available. Support available to part-time students. Financial award application deadline: 3/1; financial award applicants required to submit FAFSA. *Unit head:* Derek Porter, Chair, 212-229-8955 Ext. 2924, E-mail: porterd@newschool.edu. *Application contact:* David Norris, Director of Admissions, 212-229-8989 Ext. 4023, Fax: 212-229-8975, E-mail: norrisd@newschool.edu.

New York School of Interior Design, Program in Interior Design, New York, NY 10021-5110. Offers MFA. *Accreditation:* NASAD. *Faculty:* 12 part-time/adjunct (7 women). *Students:* 33 full-time (27 women); includes 8 minority (2 African Americans, 5 Asian Americans or Pacific Islanders, 1 Hispanic American). Average age 30. 89 applicants, 69% accepted, 33 enrolled. *Degree requirements:* For master's, thesis. *Entrance requirements:* For master's, portfolio, undergraduate degree in interior design or closely related field. Additional exam requirements/recommendations for international students: Required—TOEFL (minimum score 550 paper-based; 213 computer-based; 79 iBT). *Application deadline:* For fall admission, 3/1 priority date for domestic and international students. Applications are processed on a rolling basis. Application fee: $50 ($75 for international students). Electronic applications accepted. *Expenses:* Tuition: Full-time $24,250. *Financial support:* In 2009–10, 2 research assistantships (averaging $10,000 per year) were awarded; career-related internships or fieldwork, Federal Work-Study, institutionally sponsored loans, and scholarships/grants also available. Financial award application deadline: 8/1; financial award applicants required to submit FAFSA. *Faculty research:* History, theory, aesthetics, sociology, and green design; landscape, lighting, furniture, product, and set design. *Unit head:* Scott Ageloff, Dean, 212-472-1500 Ext. 301, Fax: 212-288-6577, E-mail: sageloff@nysid.edu. *Application contact:* David T. Sprouls, Director of Admissions, 212-472-1500 Ext. 202, Fax: 212-472-1867, E-mail: dsprouls@nysid.edu.

New York School of Interior Design, Program in Interior Design (Post-Professional Level), New York, NY 10021-5110. Offers MFA. *Faculty:* 12 part-time/adjunct (7 women). *Students:* 19 full-time (14 women); includes 12 minority (2 African Americans, 7 Asian Americans or Pacific Islanders, 3 Hispanic Americans), 1 international. Average age 27. 89 applicants, 33% accepted, 12 enrolled. In 2009, 1 master's awarded. *Degree requirements:* For master's, thesis. *Entrance requirements:* For master's, portfolio. Additional exam requirements/recommendations for international students: Required—TOEFL (minimum score 550 paper-based; 213 computer-based; 79 iBT). *Application deadline:* For fall admission, 3/1 priority date for domestic and international students; for spring admission, 10/1 priority date for domestic and international students. Applications are processed on a rolling basis. Application fee: $50 ($75 for international students). Electronic applications accepted. *Expenses:* Tuition: Full-time $24,250. *Financial support:* In 2009–10, 3 research assistantships (averaging $10,000 per year) were awarded; career-related internships or fieldwork, Federal Work-Study, institutionally sponsored loans, and scholarships/grants also available. Financial award application deadline: 8/1; financial award applicants required to submit FAFSA. *Application contact:* Scott Ageloff, Dean, 212-472-1500 Ext. 301, Fax: 212-288-6577, E-mail: sageloff@nysid.edu.

The Ohio State University, Graduate School, College of the Arts, Department of Industrial, Interior, and Visual Communication Design, Columbus, OH 43210. Offers MA, MFA. *Accreditation:* NASAD. Part-time programs available. *Faculty:* 14. *Students:* 29 full-time (15 women), 9 part-time (4 women); includes 2 minority (both African Americans), 8 international. Average age 28. In 2009, 14 master's awarded. *Degree requirements:* For master's, project or thesis. *Entrance requirements:* For master's, bachelor's degree in interior space, graphics, product design, or related field. Additional exam requirements/recommendations for international students: Recommended—TOEFL (minimum score 600 paper-based; 250 computer-based). *Application deadline:* For fall admission, 8/15 priority date for domestic students, 7/1 priority date for international students; for winter admission, 12/1 priority date for domestic students, 11/1 priority date for international students; for spring admission, 3/1 priority date for domestic students, 2/1 priority date for international students. Applications are processed on a rolling basis. Application fee: $40 ($50 for international students). Electronic applications accepted. *Expenses:* Tuition, state resident: full-time $10,683. Tuition, nonresident: full-time $25,923. Tuition and fees vary according to course load and program. *Financial support:* Fellowships, research assistantships, teaching assistantships, career-related internships or fieldwork, Federal Work-Study, institutionally sponsored loans, and unspecified assistantships available. Support available to part-time students. Financial award application deadline: 5/1. *Unit head:* R. Brian Stone, Graduate Studies Committee Chair, 614-688-6746, Fax: 614-292-0217, E-mail: stone.158@osu.edu. *Application contact:* 614-292-9444, Fax: 614-292-3895, E-mail: domestic.grad@osu.edu.

Pontificia Universidad Catolica Madre y Maestra, Graduate School, Santiago, Dominican Republic. Offers administration (M Adm); architecture of interiors (M Arch); architecture of tourist lodgings (M Arch); banking and financial management (M Mgmt); civil law (LL M); construction administration (ME); corporate business law (LL M); criminal procedure law (LL M); environmental engineering (ME, MEE); finance (M Mgmt); history applied to education (M Ed); human resources (EMBA); insurance (M Mgmt); international business (M Mgmt); labor law and Social Security (LL M); logistics management (ME); marketing (M Mgmt); renewable energy (ME); strategic cost management (M Mgmt). *Entrance requirements:* For master's, curriculum vitae, interview.

Pratt Institute, School of Art and Design, Program in Interior Design, Brooklyn, NY 11205-3899. Offers MS. *Accreditation:* NASAD. Part-time programs available. *Faculty:* 4 full-time (1 woman), 27 part-time/adjunct (10 women). *Students:* 169 full-time (141 women), 7 part-time (5 women); includes 32 minority (3 African Americans, 17 Asian Americans or Pacific Islanders, 12 Hispanic Americans), 61 international. Average age 28. 245 applicants, 64% accepted, 63 enrolled. In 2009, 53 master's awarded. *Degree requirements:* For master's, thesis. *Entrance requirements:* For master's, portfolio, letters of recommendation. Additional exam requirements/recommendations for international students: Required—TOEFL (minimum score 575 paper-based; 233 computer-based; 90 iBT). *Application deadline:* For fall admission, 1/5 for domestic and international students; for spring admission, 10/1 for domestic and international students. Application fee: $50 ($90 for international students). Electronic applications accepted. *Expenses:* Tuition: Full-time $22,734. Required fees: $1280. *Financial support:* Career-related internships or fieldwork, Federal Work-Study, institutionally sponsored loans, scholarships/grants, health care benefits, and unspecified assistantships available. Support available to part-time students. Financial award application deadline: 2/1; financial award applicants required to submit FAFSA. *Unit head:* Anita Cooney, Chairperson, 718-636-3630, Fax: 718-636-3553, E-mail: acooney@pratt.edu. *Application contact:* Young Hah, Director of Graduate Admissions, 718-636-3683, Fax: 718-399-4242, E-mail: yhah@pratt.edu.

See Close-Up on page 119.

Rhode Island School of Design, Graduate Studies, Division of Architecture and Design, Department of Interior Architecture, Providence, RI 02903-2784. Offers MIA. *Degree requirements:* For master's, thesis, exhibit. *Entrance requirements:* For master's, portfolio, 3 letters of recommendation. Additional exam requirements/recommendations for international students: Required—TOEFL (minimum score 580 paper-based; 237 computer-based), IELTS (minimum score 6.5).

San Diego State University, Graduate and Research Affairs, College of Professional Studies and Fine Arts, School of Art, Design and Art History, San Diego, CA 92182. Offers art history (MA); studio arts (MA, MFA), including applied design, environmental design, graphic design, interior design, painting and printmaking, sculpture. *Accreditation:* NASAD (one or more programs are accredited). *Degree requirements:* For master's, variable foreign language requirement, thesis. *Entrance requirements:* For master's, GRE General Test, bachelor's degree in related field, slide portfolio, typed slide information sheet, 2 letters of recommendation. Additional exam requirements/recommendations for international students: Required—TOEFL. Electronic applications accepted.

Savannah College of Art and Design, Graduate School, Program in Interior Design, Savannah, GA 31402-3146. Offers MA, MFA. Part-time programs available. *Degree requirements:* For master's, thesis, internship. *Entrance requirements:* For master's, interview, portfolio. Additional exam requirements/recommendations for international students: Required—TOEFL (minimum score 450 paper-based; 133 computer-based). Electronic applications accepted. *Expenses:* Tuition: Full-time $28,515; part-time $627 per credit hour. One-time fee: $500. Tuition and fees vary according to course load.

School of the Art Institute of Chicago, Graduate Division, Department of Architecture, Interior Architecture, and Designed Objects, Chicago, IL 60603-3103. Offers architecture (M Arc); design for emerging technologies (MFA); designed objects (M Des); interior architecture (M Arc). *Entrance requirements:* Additional exam requirements/recommendations for international students: Required—TOEFL, IELTS.

South Dakota State University, Graduate School, College of Education and Human Sciences, Department of Apparel Merchandising and Interior Design, Brookings, SD 57007. Offers MFCS. Part-time and evening/weekend programs available. Postbaccalaureate distance learning degree programs offered. *Entrance requirements:* Additional exam requirements/recommendations for international students: Required—TOEFL (minimum score 550 paper-based; 213 computer-based; 79 iBT). *Faculty research:* Rural internet shopping, professional development in apparel merchandising, gender, aesthetics.

Suffolk University, New England School of Art and Design, Program in Interior Design, Boston, MA 02108-2770. Offers MA. *Entrance requirements:* For master's, statement of professional goals, official transcripts, 2 letters of recommendation, resume. Application fee: $50. *Expenses:* Tuition: Full-time $33,000; part-time $1100 per credit. Required fees: $20. Tuition and fees vary according to program. *Unit head:* Karen Clarke, Program Director, 617-573-8785, Fax: 617-536-0461, E-mail: kclarke@suffolk.edu. *Application contact:* Judith Reynolds, Director of Graduate Admissions, 617-573-8302, Fax: 617-305-1733, E-mail: grad.admission@suffolk.edu.

Texas Tech University, Graduate School, College of Human Sciences, Department of Design, Lubbock, TX 79409. Offers environmental design (MS); interior and environmental design (PhD). *Faculty:* 4 full-time (2 women). *Students:* 8 full-time (7 women), 12 part-time (9 women); includes 2 minority (1 Asian American or Pacific Islander, 1 Hispanic American), 6 international. Average age 29. 19 applicants, 63% accepted, 5 enrolled. In 2009, 1 master's awarded. *Degree requirements:* For master's, thesis or alternative; for doctorate, thesis/dissertation. *Entrance requirements:* For master's and doctorate, GRE. Application fee: $50 ($75 for international students). *Expenses:* Tuition, state resident: full-time $5100; part-time $213 per credit hour. Tuition, nonresident: full-time $11,748; part-time $490 per credit hour. Required fees: $2298; $50 per credit hour. $555 per semester. *Financial support:* Research assistantships, teaching assistantships available. Financial award application deadline: 4/15. *Faculty research:* Meanings in the built environment, influence of technology on pedagogic environments, interior design components, computer usage in interior design, design and evaluation of physical environments for the elderly and physically and mentally challenged. Total annual research expenditures: $64,146. *Unit head:* Dr. Cherif M. Amor, Interim Chair, 806-742-3050, Fax: 806-742-1639, E-mail: cherif.amor@ttu.edu. *Application contact:* Dr. JoAnn Shroyer, Graduate Programs Director, 806-742-3050 Ext. 228, Fax: 806-742-1639, E-mail: joann.shroyer@ttu.edu.

The University of Alabama, Graduate School, College of Human Environmental Sciences, Department of Clothing, Textiles, and Interior Design, Tuscaloosa, AL 35487. Offers MSHES. *Faculty:* 5 full-time (all women). *Students:* 1 (woman) full-time. Average age 55. *Degree requirements:* For master's, comprehensive exam, thesis optional. *Entrance requirements:* For master's, GRE General Test or MAT, minimum GPA of 3.0. *Application deadline:* For fall admission, 7/6 for domestic students. Applications are processed on a rolling basis. Application fee: $50 ($60 for international students). *Expenses:* Tuition, state resident: full-time $7000. Tuition, nonresident: full-time $19,200. *Financial support:* In 2009–10, 1 research assistantship with full tuition reimbursement (averaging $8,100 per year), 2 teaching assistantships with full tuition reimbursements (averaging $8,100 per year) were awarded; fellowships, career-related internships or fieldwork, Federal Work-Study, and scholarships/grants also available. Financial award application deadline: 3/15. *Faculty research:* Archeological textiles, textile science, material culture, social psychology, international trade. *Unit head:* Dr. Carolyn Callis, Chair and Associate Professor, 205-348-6176, Fax: 205-348-0022, E-mail: ccallis@ches.ua.edu. *Application contact:* Dr. Carolyn Callis, Chair and Associate Professor, 205-348-6176, Fax: 205-348-0022, E-mail: ccallis@ches.ua.edu.

University of California, Berkeley, UC Berkeley Extension, Certificate Programs in Art and Design, Berkeley, CA 94720-1500. Offers interior design and interior architecture (Certificate); landscape architecture (Certificate); visual arts (Postbaccalaureate Certificate). *Unit head:* Diana Wu, Dean, 510-642-4181. *Application contact:* Art and Design, 415-284-1041, E-mail: visualarts@unex.berkeley.edu.

University of Central Oklahoma, College of Graduate Studies and Research, College of Arts, Media, and Design, Department of Design and Interior Design, Edmond, OK 73034-5209. Offers MFA. Part-time programs available. Postbaccalaureate distance learning degree programs offered (minimal on-campus study). *Entrance requirements:* Additional exam requirements/recommendations for international students: Required—TOEFL (minimum score 550 paper-based; 213 computer-based). Electronic applications accepted. *Expenses:* Tuition, state resident: full-time $4128; part-time $172 per credit hour. Tuition, nonresident: full-time $10,373; part-time $432.20 per credit hour. Required fees: $433.20; $18.05 per credit hour.

University of Central Oklahoma, College of Graduate Studies and Research, College of Education, Department of Human Environmental Sciences, Edmond, OK 73034-5209. Offers

Interior Design

University of Central Oklahoma (continued)
family and child studies (MS); family and consumer science education (MS); interior design (MS); nutrition-food management (MS). Part-time programs available. *Entrance requirements:* Additional exam requirements/recommendations for international students: Required—TOEFL (minimum score 550 paper-based; 213 computer-based). Electronic applications accepted. *Expenses:* Tuition, state resident: full-time $4128; part-time $172 per credit hour. Tuition, nonresident: full-time $10,373; part-time $432.20 per credit hour. Required fees: $433.20; $18.05 per credit hour. *Faculty research:* Dietetics and food science.

University of Cincinnati, Graduate School, College of Design, Architecture, Art, and Planning, School of Architecture and Interior Design, Cincinnati, OH 45221. Offers architecture (M Arch). *Accreditation:* NASAD. *Degree requirements:* For master's, one foreign language, thesis. *Entrance requirements:* Additional exam requirements/recommendations for international students: Required—TOEFL. *Faculty research:* Theory and history of architecture.

University of Florida, Graduate School, College of Design, Construction and Planning, Department of Interior Design, Gainesville, FL 32611. Offers MID, PhD. *Entrance requirements:* For master's, GRE General Test, minimum GPA of 3.0. Additional exam requirements/recommendations for international students: Required—TOEFL.

University of Georgia, Graduate School, College of Family and Consumer Sciences, Department of Textiles, Merchandising, and Interiors, Athens, GA 30602. Offers historic costume and textiles (MS); merchandising/international trade (MS); textile analysis (PhD); textile chemical processes (PhD); textile products and standards (PhD); textile science (MS). *Faculty:* 13 full-time (9 women). *Students:* 18 full-time (15 women), 6 part-time (all women); includes 3 minority (2 African Americans, 1 Hispanic American), 6 international. 20 applicants, 50% accepted, 9 enrolled. In 2009, 5 master's awarded. *Degree requirements:* For master's, thesis; for doctorate, thesis/dissertation. *Entrance requirements:* For master's and doctorate, GRE General Test. *Application deadline:* For fall admission, 7/1 priority date for domestic students; for spring admission, 11/15 for domestic students. Application fee: $50. Electronic applications accepted. *Expenses:* Tuition, state resident: full-time $6000; part-time $250 per credit hour. Tuition, nonresident: full-time $20,904; part-time $871 per credit hour. Required fees: $730 per semester. *Financial support:* Fellowships, research assistantships, teaching assistantships, unspecified assistantships available. *Unit head:* Dr. Patricia K. Hunt-Hurst, Department Head, 706-542-4888, Fax: 706-542-0410, E-mail: phunt@fcs.uga.edu. *Application contact:* Dr. Patricia K. Hunt-Hurst, Department Head, 706-542-4888, Fax: 706-542-0410, E-mail: phunt@fcs.uga.edu.

University of Kentucky, Graduate School, College of Design, Program in Interior Design, Merchandising, and Textiles, Lexington, KY 40506-0032. Offers MAIDM, MSIDM. *Degree requirements:* For master's, comprehensive exam, thesis optional. *Entrance requirements:* For master's, GRE General Test, minimum undergraduate GPA of 2.75. Additional exam requirements/recommendations for international students: Required—TOEFL (minimum score 550 paper-based; 213 computer-based). Electronic applications accepted. *Faculty research:* Interior design, apparel merchandising, textile evaluation, creativity in design, social-psychological aspects of dress and interiors.

University of Manitoba, Faculty of Graduate Studies, Faculty of Architecture, Department of Interior Design, Winnipeg, MB R3T 2N2, Canada. Offers MID. *Accreditation:* CIDA.

University of Massachusetts Amherst, Graduate School, College of Humanities and Fine Arts, Department of Art, Programs in Architecture and Design, Amherst, MA 01003. Offers architecture and design (M Arch); historic preservation (MS); interior design (MS). Part-time programs available. *Students:* 43 full-time (15 women); includes 5 minority (1 African American, 2 Asian Americans or Pacific Islanders, 2 Hispanic Americans), 7 international. Average age 30. 100 applicants, 64% accepted, 21 enrolled. In 2009, 12 master's awarded. *Degree requirements:* For master's, thesis or alternative. *Entrance requirements:* For master's, GRE General Test (M Arch), portfolio. Additional exam requirements/recommendations for international students: Required—TOEFL (minimum score 550 paper-based; 213 computer-based; 80 iBT), IELTS (minimum score 6.5). *Application deadline:* For fall admission, 2/1 for domestic and international students. Applications are processed on a rolling basis. Application fee: $50 ($65 for international students). Electronic applications accepted. *Expenses:* Tuition, state resident: full-time $2640; part-time $110 per credit. Tuition, nonresident: full-time $9936; part-time $414 per credit. Tuition and fees vary according to course load. *Financial support:* Fellowships, research assistantships, teaching assistantships, career-related internships or fieldwork, Federal Work-Study, scholarships/grants, traineeships, health care benefits, tuition waivers (full), and unspecified assistantships available. Support available to part-time students. Financial award application deadline: 2/1. *Unit head:* Dr. Ray K. Mann, Graduate Program Director, 413-545-0943, Fax: 413-545-3929. *Application contact:* Jean M. Ames, Supervisor of Admissions, 413-545-0722, Fax: 413-577-0100, E-mail: gradadm@grad.umass.edu.

University of Memphis, Graduate School, College of Communication and Fine Arts, Department of Art, Memphis, TN 38152. Offers art (Graduate Certificate); art history (MA), including Egyptian art and archaeology, general art history; ceramics (MFA); graphic design (MFA); interior design (MFA); painting (MFA); printmaking/photography (MFA); sculpture (MFA). *Accreditation:* NASAD (one or more programs are accredited). *Faculty:* 20 full-time (7 women), 4 part-time/adjunct (2 women). *Students:* 39 full-time (26 women), 10 part-time (8 women); includes 4 African Americans, 1 Asian American or Pacific Islander, 1 international. Average age 29. 44 applicants, 77% accepted, 22 enrolled. In 2009, 16 master's, 5 other advanced degrees awarded. *Degree requirements:* For master's, 2 foreign languages, comprehensive exam, thesis. *Entrance requirements:* For master's, GRE General Test or MAT, portfolio (MFA). *Application deadline:* For fall admission, 8/1 for domestic students; for spring admission, 12/1 for domestic students. Applications are processed on a rolling basis. Application fee: $35 ($60 for international students). *Expenses:* Tuition, state resident: full-time $6246; part-time $347 per credit hour. Tuition, nonresident: full-time $15,894; part-time $883 per credit hour. Required fees: $1160. Full-time tuition and fees vary according to course load, degree level and program. *Financial support:* In 2009–10, 38 students received support; research assistantships with full tuition reimbursements available, teaching assistantships with full tuition reimbursements available, Federal Work-Study, scholarships/grants, and unspecified assistantships available. Financial award application deadline: 2/15; financial award applicants required to submit FAFSA. *Faculty research:* Online collaborative learning, advanced art history studies, electronic publishing/design, studio arts, architectural studies. *Unit head:* Prof. Richard Lou, Chair, 901-678-2216, Fax: 901-678-2735, E-mail: gmyatt@memphis.edu. *Application contact:* Greely Myat, Graduate Studies Coordinator, 901-678-2650.

University of Minnesota, Twin Cities Campus, Graduate School, College of Design, Department of Design, Housing, and Apparel, Minneapolis, MN 55455-0213. Offers apparel (MA, MS, PhD); design communication (MA, MS, PhD); housing studies (MA, MS, PhD, Postbaccalaureate Certificate); interactive design (MFA); interior design (MA, MS, PhD). Part-time programs available. *Degree requirements:* For master's and Postbaccalaureate Certificate, comprehensive exam, thesis (for some programs); for doctorate, comprehensive exam, thesis/dissertation. *Entrance requirements:* For master's, GRE General Test, minimum GPA of 3.0 (preferred), portfolio, 3 letters of recommendation; for doctorate, GRE General Test, minimum GPA of 3.0 (preferred), portfolio, 3 letters of recommendation, writing sample; for Postbaccalaureate Certificate, GRE General Test, minimum GPA of 3.0 (preferred). Additional exam requirements/recommendations for international students: Required—TOEFL (minimum score 550 paper-based; 213 computer-based; 79 iBT). Electronic applications accepted. *Faculty research:* Housing policy and community development; consumer behavior; interactive design; design history; social, cultural, and behavioral issues related to designed environments.

University of Nebraska–Lincoln, Graduate College, College of Architecture, Department of Architecture, Lincoln, NE 68588. Offers architecture (M Arch, MS, PhD); interior design (MS); M Arch/MBA; M Arch/MCRP. *Entrance requirements:* Additional exam requirements/recommendations for international students: Required—TOEFL. Electronic applications accepted.

The University of North Carolina at Greensboro, Graduate School, School of Human Environmental Sciences, Department of Interior Architecture, Greensboro, NC 27412-5001. Offers historic preservation (Certificate); interior architecture (MS); museum studies (Certificate). *Degree requirements:* For master's, thesis. *Entrance requirements:* For master's, GRE General Test or MAT, bachelor's degree in interior design, interview, portfolio. Additional exam requirements/recommendations for international students: Required—TOEFL. Electronic applications accepted.

University of Oregon, Graduate School, School of Architecture and Allied Arts, Department of Architecture, Eugene, OR 97403. Offers architecture (M Arch); interior architecture (MI Arch). *Accreditation:* CIDA. *Degree requirements:* For master's, thesis (for some programs). *Entrance requirements:* For master's, GRE General Test. Additional exam requirements/recommendations for international students: Required—TOEFL. *Faculty research:* Innovation in housing design and design production, climate responsive design, passive heating and cooling, computer software development for design applications, vernacular architecture.

Utah State University, School of Graduate Studies, College of Humanities, Arts and Social Sciences, Program in Interior Design, Logan, UT 84322. Offers MS. Part-time programs available. Postbaccalaureate distance learning degree programs offered. *Entrance requirements:* For master's, GRE General Test, MAT, minimum GPA of 3.0. Additional exam requirements/recommendations for international students: Required—TOEFL.

Virginia Commonwealth University, Graduate School, School of the Arts, Department of Graphic Design, Richmond, VA 23284-9005. Offers design/visual communications (MFA); interior environment (MFA); photography and film (MFA). *Accreditation:* NASAD. *Degree requirements:* For master's, thesis, exhibition. *Entrance requirements:* For master's, portfolio. *Faculty research:* Film, photography, interior environments, visual communication.

Virginia Polytechnic Institute and State University, Graduate School, College of Liberal Arts and Human Sciences, Department of Apparel, Housing, and Resource Management, Blacksburg, VA 24061. Offers apparel business and economics (MS, PhD); apparel product design and analysis (MS, PhD); apparel quality analysis (MS, PhD); consumer studies (MS, PhD); family financial management (MS, PhD); household equipment (MS, PhD); housing (MS, PhD); interior design (MS, PhD); resource management (MS, PhD). *Faculty:* 14 full-time (all women). *Students:* 10 full-time (9 women), 5 part-time (all women); includes 9 minority (1 African American, 6 American Indian/Alaska Native, 1 Asian American or Pacific Islander, 1 Hispanic American). Average age 34. 6 applicants. In 2009, 3 master's, 5 doctorates awarded. *Entrance requirements:* For master's and doctorate, GRE, GMAT. Additional exam requirements/recommendations for international students: Required—TOEFL (minimum score 550 paper-based; 213 computer-based). *Application deadline:* For fall admission, 5/15 for international students; for spring admission, 10/15 for international students. Applications are processed on a rolling basis. Application fee: $65. Electronic applications accepted. *Expenses:* Tuition, area resident: Full-time $10,228; part-time $459 per credit hour. Tuition, nonresident: full-time $17,892; part-time $865 per credit hour. Required fees: $1966; $451 per semester. *Financial support:* In 2009–10, 6 teaching assistantships with full tuition reimbursements (averaging $13,546 per year) were awarded; career-related internships or fieldwork, Federal Work-Study, scholarships/grants, and unspecified assistantships also available. Financial award application deadline: 1/15. *Faculty research:* Housing for elderly, affordable housing, household time use, phosphate laundry study, economic well-living. Total annual research expenditures: $27,151. *Unit head:* Dr. LuAnn R. Gaskill, Dean, 540-231-4781, Fax: 540-231-3250, E-mail: lagaskil@vt.edu. *Application contact:* Julia Beemish, Information Contact, 540-231-8881, Fax: 540-231-3250, E-mail: jbeamish@vt.edu.

Washington State University, Graduate School, College of Agricultural, Human, and Natural Resource Sciences, Department of Apparel, Merchandising, Design, and Textiles, Pullman, WA 99164. Offers apparel, merchandising, design and textiles (MA); interdisciplinary (PhD); interior design (MA). Part-time programs available. *Faculty:* 8. *Students:* 6 full-time (all women), 4 part-time (all women); includes 1 minority (Asian American or Pacific Islander), 2 international. Average age 33. 10 applicants, 20% accepted, 1 enrolled. In 2009, 3 master's awarded. *Degree requirements:* For master's, comprehensive exam (for some programs), thesis, oral exam; for doctorate, comprehensive exam, thesis/dissertation. *Entrance requirements:* For master's, GRE, minimum GPA of 3.0, 3 writing samples, 3 letters of recommendation, portfolio. Additional exam requirements/recommendations for international students: Required—TOEFL, IELTS. *Application deadline:* For fall admission, 1/11 priority date for domestic students, 1/10 for international students; for spring admission, 7/1 for domestic and international students. Applications are processed on a rolling basis. Application fee: $50. Electronic applications accepted. *Financial support:* In 2009–10, research assistantships with full and partial tuition reimbursements (averaging $14,634 per year), 5 teaching assistantships with full and partial tuition reimbursements (averaging $13,383 per year) were awarded; career-related internships or fieldwork, Federal Work-Study, institutionally sponsored loans, and scholarships/grants also available. Financial award application deadline: 2/15; financial award applicants required to submit FAFSA. *Faculty research:* Product development, design theory, cultural diversity, computer design accessibility. *Unit head:* Dr. Karen K. Leonas, Department Chair, 509-335-1233, Fax: 509-355-7299, E-mail: kleonas@wsu.edu. *Application contact:* Graduate School Admissions, 800-GRADWSU, Fax: 509-335-1949, E-mail: gradsch@wsu.edu.

Washington State University Spokane, Graduate Programs, Interdisciplinary Design Institute, Spokane, WA 99210. Offers architecture (M Arch, MS); design (Dr DES); interior design (MA); landscape architecture (MS). Part-time programs available. *Faculty:* 7. *Students:* 9 full-time (6 women), 2 part-time (both women); includes 1 minority (Asian American or Pacific Islander), 5 international. Average age 35. In 2009, 18 master's awarded. *Degree requirements:* For master's, comprehensive exam (for some programs), thesis (for some programs); for doctorate, comprehensive exam, thesis/dissertation. *Entrance requirements:* For master's, minimum GPA of 3.0, portfolio of design work, 3 letters of recommendation (M Arch); for doctorate, minimum graduate GPA of 3.5. Additional exam requirements/recommendations for international students: Required—TOEFL (minimum score 550 paper-based; 213 computer-based). *Application deadline:* For fall admission, 1/10 priority date for domestic students, 1/10 for international students; for spring admission, 7/1 priority date for domestic students, 7/1 for international students. Application fee: $50. *Expenses:* Tuition, state resident: part-time $423 per credit. Tuition, nonresident: part-time $1032 per credit. *Financial support:* In 2009–10, research assistantships with full and partial tuition reimbursements (averaging $14,634 per year), teaching assistantships with full and partial tuition reimbursements (averaging $13,383 per year) were awarded. Financial award application deadline: 2/15. *Faculty research:* Environment-behavior relationships, land use and environmental planning, urban space as interior design, art and architectural aesthetics. Total annual research expenditures: $84,000. *Unit head:* Dr. Nancy H. Blossom, Director, 509-358-7513, E-mail: blossom@wsu.edu. *Application contact:* Graduate School Admissions, 800-GRADWSU, Fax: 509-335-1949, E-mail: gradsch@wsu.edu.

Medical Illustration

The Johns Hopkins University, School of Medicine, Graduate Programs in Medicine, Department of Art as Applied to Medicine, Baltimore, MD 21205. Offers medical and biological illustration (MA). *Accreditation:* ARCMI. *Faculty:* 8 full-time (2 women), 15 part-time/adjunct (7 women). *Students:* 12 full-time (9 women), 1 (woman) part-time, 3 international. Average age 24. 37 applicants, 19% accepted, 6 enrolled. In 2009, 3 master's awarded. *Degree requirements:* For master's, thesis. *Application deadline:* For fall admission, 1/15 for domestic and international students. Applications are processed on a rolling basis. Application fee: $85. Electronic applications accepted. *Financial support:* In 2009–10, 13 students received support, including 12 fellowships with partial tuition reimbursements available (averaging $17,000 per year), 4 teaching assistantships (averaging $500 per year); institutionally sponsored loans, scholarships/grants, tuition waivers (partial), and unspecified assistantships also available. Financial award application deadline: 5/31; financial award applicants required to submit FAFSA. *Faculty research:* Visualization; digital media; animation and 3D modeling; instructional design; facial prosthetics and anaplastology. *Unit head:* Gary Lees, Chairman and Director, 410-955-3213, Fax: 410-955-1085, E-mail: medart-info@jhmi.edu. *Application contact:* Dacia M. Balch, Administrative Coordinator, 410-955-3213, Fax: 410-955-1085, E-mail: medart-info@jhmi.edu.

Medical College of Georgia, School of Graduate Studies, Program in Medical Illustration, Augusta, GA 30912. Offers MS. *Accreditation:* ARCMI. *Degree requirements:* For master's, thesis or alternative, project. *Entrance requirements:* For master's, GRE General Test, portfolio. Additional exam requirements/recommendations for international students: Required—TOEFL (minimum score 550 paper-based; 213 computer-based; 79 iBT). Electronic applications accepted. Full-time tuition and fees vary according to campus/location, program and student level. *Faculty research:* Digital visual communication modalities, information science education, Southwestern Native American art pedagogy, medical illustration pedagogy, public health/visual education.

Rochester Institute of Technology, Graduate Enrollment Services, College of Imaging Arts and Sciences, School of Art, Program in Medical Illustration, Rochester, NY 14623-5603. Offers MFA. Part-time programs available. *Students:* 3 full-time (2 women), 3 part-time (2 women); includes 2 Asian Americans or Pacific Islanders. Average age 31. 9 applicants, 78% accepted, 4 enrolled. In 2009, 1 master's awarded. *Degree requirements:* For master's, thesis. *Entrance requirements:* For master's, portfolio, minimum GPA of 3.0. Additional exam requirements/recommendations for international students: Required—TOEFL (minimum score 550 paper-based; 213 computer-based; 79 iBT), or IELTS (minimum score 6.5). *Application deadline:* For fall admission, 2/15 priority date for domestic and international students. Applications are processed on a rolling basis. Application fee: $50. Electronic applications accepted. *Expenses:* Tuition: Full-time $31,533; part-time $876 per credit hour. Required fees: $210. *Financial support:* In 2009–10, 3 students received support; teaching assistantships with partial tuition reimbursements available, career-related internships or fieldwork, institutionally sponsored loans, scholarships/grants, and unspecified assistantships available. Support available to part-time students. Financial award applicants required to submit FAFSA. *Unit head:* Don Arday, Administrative Chair, 585-475-7562, Fax: 585-475-6447, E-mail: facpgd@rit.edu. *Application contact:* Diane Ellison, Assistant Vice President, Graduate Enrollment Services, 585-475-2229, Fax: 585-475-7164, E-mail: gradinfo@rit.edu.

University of Illinois at Chicago, Graduate College, College of Applied Health Sciences, Program in Biomedical Visualization, Chicago, IL 60607-7128. Offers MS. *Accreditation:* ARCMI. *Degree requirements:* For master's, thesis. *Entrance requirements:* For master's, GRE General Test, minimum GPA of 2.75. Additional exam requirements/recommendations for international students: Required—TOEFL. Electronic applications accepted. *Expenses:* Contact institution. *Faculty research:* Medical illustration, graphics, reconstruction, anatomical modeling.

The University of Texas Southwestern Medical Center at Dallas, Southwestern Graduate School of Biomedical Sciences, Division of Applied Science, Biomedical Communications Program, Dallas, TX 75390. Offers MA. *Accreditation:* ARCMI. *Students:* 16 full-time (11 women); includes 5 minority (3 Asian Americans or Pacific Islanders, 2 Hispanic Americans), 1 international. Average age 27. 19 applicants, 32% accepted, 5 enrolled. In 2009, 6 master's awarded. *Degree requirements:* For master's, thesis. *Entrance requirements:* For master's, GRE General Test, minimum GPA of 3.0. *Application deadline:* For spring admission, 9/1 priority date for domestic students. Applications are processed on a rolling basis. Application fee: $0. Electronic applications accepted. *Financial support:* In 2009–10, 4 teaching assistantships were awarded; career-related internships or fieldwork and institutionally sponsored loans also available. Financial award application deadline: 3/1; financial award applicants required to submit FAFSA. *Faculty research:* Breast self-examination to indigent populations. *Unit head:* Lewis E. Calver, Chair, 214-648-4699, Fax: 214-648-5353, E-mail: lcalve@mednet.swmed.edu. *Application contact:* Sonja Shryer, Education Coordinator, 214-648-4634, Fax: 214-648-5353, E-mail: marcelle.hanson@utsouthwestern.edu.

Photography

Academy of Art University, Graduate Program, School of Photography, San Francisco, CA 94105-3410. Offers MFA. *Accreditation:* NASAD. Part-time programs available. Post-baccalaureate distance learning degree programs offered (no on-campus study). *Degree requirements:* For master's, final review. *Entrance requirements:* For master's, portfolio. Electronic applications accepted.

Bard College, International Center of Photography, Annandale-on-Hudson, NY 12504. Offers advanced photographic studies (MFA).

Barry University, School of Arts and Sciences, Department of Fine Arts, Miami Shores, FL 33161-6695. Offers photography (MA, MFA). *Degree requirements:* For master's, thesis (for some programs). *Entrance requirements:* For master's, GRE General Test, minimum GPA of 3.0. Electronic applications accepted. *Faculty research:* Inclusion education, exceptional education, art-based assessments.

Bradley University, Graduate School, Slane College of Communications and Fine Arts, Department of Art, Peoria, IL 61625-0002. Offers ceramics (MA, MFA); drawing/illustration (MA, MFA); interdisciplinary art (MA, MFA); painting (MA, MFA); photography (MA, MFA); printmaking (MA, MFA); sculpture (MA, MFA); visual communication and design (MA, MFA). *Accreditation:* NASAD. Part-time programs available. *Degree requirements:* For master's, comprehensive exam, thesis, final exhibit. *Entrance requirements:* For master's, portfolio, 2 letters of recommendation. Additional exam requirements/recommendations for international students: Required—TOEFL (minimum score 550 paper-based; 213 computer-based; 79 iBT).

Brooklyn College of the City University of New York, Division of Graduate Studies, Department of Art, Brooklyn, NY 11210-2889. Offers art history (MA, PhD); digital art (MFA); drawing and painting (MFA); photography (MFA); printmaking (MFA); sculpture (MFA). Part-time programs available. *Students:* 27 full-time (14 women), 20 part-time (15 women); includes 11 minority (2 African Americans, 3 Asian Americans or Pacific Islanders, 6 Hispanic Americans), 2 international. Average age 30. 123 applicants, 49% accepted, 26 enrolled. In 2009, 14 master's awarded. *Degree requirements:* For master's, thesis. *Entrance requirements:* For master's, bachelor's degree in art, portfolio, 2 letters of recommendation. Additional exam requirements/recommendations for international students: Required—TOEFL (minimum score 500 paper-based; 173 computer-based; 61 iBT). *Application deadline:* For fall admission, 2/1 priority date for domestic students, 2/1 for international students. Applications are processed on a rolling basis. Application fee: $125. Electronic applications accepted. *Expenses:* Tuition, area resident: Full-time $7360; part-time $310 per credit hour. Tuition, state resident: full-time $7360; part-time $310 per credit hour. Tuition, nonresident: full-time $13,800; part-time $575 per credit hour. International tuition: $13,800 full-time. Required fees: $140.10 per semester. *Financial support:* Career-related internships or fieldwork, Federal Work-Study, institutionally sponsored loans, scholarships/grants, and painting awards available. Support available to part-time students. Financial award application deadline: 5/1; financial award applicants required to submit FAFSA. *Unit head:* Dr. Michael Mallory, Chairperson, 718-951-5181, E-mail: mmallory@brooklyn.cuny.edu. *Application contact:* Hernan Sierra, Graduate Admissions Coordinator, 718-951-4536, Fax: 718-951-4506, E-mail: grads@brooklyn.cuny.edu.

Brooks Institute, Graduate Program in Professional Photography, Santa Barbara, CA 93101. Offers MFA. Evening/weekend programs available. *Degree requirements:* For master's, thesis. *Entrance requirements:* For master's, portfolio review testing procedure (written exam), minimum GPA of 3.0, 3 letters of recommendation. Additional exam requirements/recommendations for international students: Required—TOEFL (minimum score 580 paper-based; 237 computer-based). Electronic applications accepted.

California College of the Arts, Graduate Programs, Programs in Fine Art, San Francisco, CA 94107. Offers ceramics (MFA); film/video/performance (MFA); glass (MFA); jewelry/metal arts (MFA); painting/drawing (MFA); photography (MFA); printmaking (MFA); sculpture (MFA); textiles (MFA); wood/furniture (MFA). *Accreditation:* NASAD. *Degree requirements:* For master's, thesis, exhibit. *Entrance requirements:* For master's, appropriate bachelor's degree, portfolio. Additional exam requirements/recommendations for international students: Required—TOEFL (minimum score 600 paper-based; 250 computer-based). Electronic applications accepted.

California Institute of the Arts, School of Art, Valencia, CA 91355-2340. Offers art (MFA, Adv C); graphic design (MFA, Adv C); photography (MFA, Adv C). *Accreditation:* NASAD (one or more programs are accredited). *Degree requirements:* For master's, final project. *Entrance requirements:* For master's, portfolio. Additional exam requirements/recommendations for international students: Required—TOEFL. Electronic applications accepted.

California State University, Fullerton, Graduate Studies, College of the Arts, Department of Art, Fullerton, CA 92834-9480. Offers art (MA, MFA), including ceramics (MFA), crafts, creative photography (MFA), design (MFA), drawing and painting, printmaking (MFA), sculpture; art history (MA); design (MA). *Accreditation:* NASAD (one or more programs are accredited). Part-time programs available. *Students:* 47 full-time (29 women), 38 part-time (23 women); includes 24 minority (2 African Americans, 12 Asian Americans or Pacific Islanders, 10 Hispanic Americans), 10 international. Average age 34. 76 applicants, 28% accepted, 19 enrolled. In 2009, 20 master's awarded. *Degree requirements:* For master's, project or thesis. *Entrance requirements:* For master's, minimum GPA of 2.5 in last 60 units of course work, portfolio. Application fee: $55. *Expenses:* Tuition, nonresident: full-time $11,160; part-time $373 per credit. Required fees: $1440 per term. Tuition and fees vary according to course load, degree level and program. *Financial support:* Career-related internships or fieldwork, Federal Work-Study, institutionally sponsored loans, and scholarships/grants available. Support available to part-time students. Financial award application deadline: 3/1; financial award applicants required to submit FAFSA. *Unit head:* Larry Johnson, Chair, 657-278-3471. *Application contact:* Admissions/Applications, 657-278-2371.

California State University, Los Angeles, Graduate Studies, College of Arts and Letters, Department of Art, Los Angeles, CA 90032-8530. Offers art (MA), including art education, art history, art therapy, ceramics, metals, and textiles, design (MA, MFA), painting, sculpture, and graphic arts, photography; fine arts (MFA), including crafts, design (MA, MFA), studio arts. *Accreditation:* NASAD (one or more programs are accredited). Part-time and evening/weekend programs available. *Faculty:* 12 full-time (6 women), 1 part-time/adjunct (0 women). *Students:* 28 full-time (21 women), 40 part-time (28 women); includes 22 minority (1 African American, 6 Asian Americans or Pacific Islanders, 15 Hispanic Americans), 9 international. Average age 37. 30 applicants, 100% accepted, 12 enrolled. In 2009, 17 master's awarded. *Degree requirements:* For master's, comprehensive exam, project or thesis. *Entrance requirements:* For master's, portfolio. Additional exam requirements/recommendations for international students: Required—TOEFL (minimum score 500 paper-based; 173 computer-based). *Application deadline:* For fall admission, 5/1 for domestic and international students. Applications are processed on a rolling basis. Application fee: $55. Electronic applications accepted. *Financial support:* Federal Work-Study available. Support available to part-time students. Financial award application deadline: 3/1. *Faculty research:* The artist and the book, conceptual art, ceramic processes, computer graphics, architectural graphics. *Unit head:* Dr. Abbas Daneshvari, Chair, 323-343-4010, Fax: 323-343-4045, E-mail: adanesh@calstatela.edu. *Application contact:* Dr. Cheryl L. Ney, Associate Vice President for Academic Affairs and Dean of Graduate Studies, 323-343-3820, Fax: 323-343-5653, E-mail: cney@cslanet.calstatela.edu.

Claremont Graduate University, Graduate Programs, School of Arts and Humanities, Department of Art, Claremont, CA 91711. Offers digital media (MA, MFA); drawing (MA, MFA); installation (MA, MFA); new genre (MA, MFA); painting (MA, MFA); performance (MA, MFA); photography (MA, MFA); sculpture (MA, MFA). Part-time programs available. *Faculty:* 4 full-time (1 woman). *Students:* 61 full-time (32 women), 1 part-time (0 women); includes 14 minority (1 African American, 6 Asian Americans or Pacific Islanders, 7 Hispanic Americans), 4 international. Average age 33. In 2009, 33 master's awarded. *Degree requirements:* For master's, final project show. *Entrance requirements:* For master's, BA in art or BFA, slide review. Additional exam requirements/recommendations for international students: Required—TOEFL (minimum score 550 paper-based; 213 computer-based; 80 iBT). *Application deadline:* For fall admission, 2/1 priority date for domestic students. Applications are processed on a rolling basis. Application fee: $60. Electronic applications accepted. *Expenses:* Contact institution. *Financial support:* Fellowships, research assistantships, teaching assistantships, Federal Work-Study, institutionally sponsored loans, and scholarships/grants available. Support available to part-time students. Financial award application deadline: 2/15; financial award applicants required to submit FAFSA. *Faculty research:* Acoustic sculpture, feminization of abstraction, installation sculpture. *Unit head:* David Pagel, Chair, 909-607-2479, Fax: 909-607-1276, E-mail: david.pagel@cgu.edu. *Application contact:* Pat Evans, Program Administrator, 909-607-9292, Fax: 909-607-1276, E-mail: patricia.evans@cgu.edu.

Columbia College Chicago, Graduate School, Department of Photography, Chicago, IL 60605-1996. Offers MA, MFA. *Degree requirements:* For master's, thesis, project. *Entrance requirements:* For master's, minimum GPA of 3.0, portfolio. Additional exam requirements/recommendations for international students: Required—TOEFL (minimum score 550 paper-based; 213 computer-based). Electronic applications accepted. *Expenses:* Tuition: Part-time $651 per credit hour. Required fees: $651 per credit hour. $205 per semester. One-time fee: $285 part-time. Tuition and fees vary according to program.

Photography

Columbia University, School of the Arts, Visual Arts Division, New York, NY 10027. Offers new genres (MFA); painting (MFA); photography (MFA); printmaking (MFA); sculpture (MFA). *Degree requirements:* For master's, thesis. *Entrance requirements:* For master's, 3 letters of recommendation, portfolio, resume. Additional exam requirements/recommendations for international students: Required—TOEFL (minimum score 600 paper-based; 250 computer-based; 100 iBT). Electronic applications accepted.

See Close-Up on page 261.

Cornell University, Graduate School, Graduate Fields of Architecture, Art and Planning, Field of Art, Ithaca, NY 14853-0001. Offers creative visual arts (MFA), including painting, photography, printmaking, sculpture. *Faculty:* 22 full-time (8 women). *Students:* 10 full-time (6 women); includes 1 minority (Hispanic American), 2 international. Average age 31. 142 applicants, 6% accepted, 6 enrolled. In 2009, 6 master's awarded. *Degree requirements:* For master's, thesis, exhibit. *Entrance requirements:* For master's, slide portfolio of 10-20 slides, 3 letters of recommendation, resume. Additional exam requirements/recommendations for international students: Required—TOEFL (minimum score 550 paper-based; 213 computer-based; 77 iBT). *Application deadline:* For fall admission, 2/15 for domestic students. Application fee: $70. Electronic applications accepted. *Expenses:* Tuition: Full-time $29,500. Required fees: $70. Full-time tuition and fees vary according to degree level, program and student level. *Financial support:* In 2009–10, 10 students received support, including 6 teaching assistantships with full tuition reimbursements available; fellowships with full tuition reimbursements available, research assistantships with full tuition reimbursements available, institutionally sponsored loans, scholarships/grants, health care benefits, tuition waivers (full and partial), and unspecified assistantships also available. Financial award applicants required to submit FAFSA. *Faculty research:* Painting, sculpture, photography, printmaking. *Unit head:* Director of Graduate Studies, 607-255-6730, Fax: 607-255-3462. *Application contact:* Graduate Field Assistant, 607-255-6730, Fax: 607-255-3462, E-mail: artinfo@cornell.edu.

Cranbrook Academy of Art, Graduate School, Program in Fine Arts, Bloomfield Hills, MI 48303-0801. Offers ceramics (MFA); design (MFA), including graphic design; fiber arts (MFA); metalsmithing (MFA); painting (MFA); photography (MFA); printmaking (MFA); sculpture (MFA). *Accreditation:* NASAD. *Degree requirements:* For master's, thesis, exhibit. *Entrance requirements:* Additional exam requirements/recommendations for international students: Required—TOEFL (minimum score 550 paper-based; 213 computer-based).

The George Washington University, Columbian College of Arts and Sciences, Department of Fine Arts and Art History, Washington, DC 20052. Offers art history (MA), including art history, museum training; ceramics (MFA); drawing/painting (MFA); interior design (MFA); new media (MFA); photography (MFA); sculpture (MFA). *Accreditation:* CIDA. Part-time and evening/weekend programs available. *Faculty:* 18 full-time (9 women), 41 part-time/adjunct (27 women). *Students:* 47 full-time (41 women), 33 part-time (all women); includes 15 minority (6 African Americans, 5 Asian Americans or Pacific Islanders, 4 Hispanic Americans), 4 international. Average age 28. 131 applicants, 60% accepted, 26 enrolled. In 2009, 36 master's awarded. *Entrance requirements:* For master's, GRE General Test, bachelor's degree in field, minimum GPA of 3.0. Additional exam requirements/recommendations for international students: Required—TOEFL (minimum score 550 paper-based; 213 computer-based; 80 iBT). *Application deadline:* For fall admission, 3/1 priority date for domestic students, 1/15 priority date for international students; for spring admission, 10/1 priority date for domestic students, 9/1 priority date for international students. Applications are processed on a rolling basis. Application fee: $60. Electronic applications accepted. *Financial support:* In 2009–10, 12 students received support; fellowships, teaching assistantships, career-related internships or fieldwork, Federal Work-Study, and tuition waivers available. Financial award application deadline: 1/15. *Unit head:* Thomas K. Brown, Chair, 202-994-9067, E-mail: thbrown@gwu.edu. *Application contact:* Information Contact, 202-994-6085, Fax: 202-994-8657, E-mail: art@gwu.edu.

Georgia State University, College of Arts and Sciences, Department of Communication, Atlanta, GA 30302-3083. Offers film/video/digital imaging (MA); human communication and social influence (MA); mass communication (MA); moving image studies (PhD); public communication (PhD). Part-time programs available. *Degree requirements:* For master's, one foreign language, thesis or alternative; for doctorate, comprehensive exam, thesis/dissertation. *Entrance requirements:* For master's and doctorate, GRE General Test. Additional exam requirements/recommendations for international students: Required—TOEFL (minimum score 80 computer-based). Electronic applications accepted. *Faculty research:* Critical/cultural studies, rhetoric studies, film/media studies, mass communications/journalism, audience studies.

Howard University, Graduate School, Division of Fine Arts, Department of Art, Program in Fine Arts, Washington, DC 20059-0002. Offers 3D reality (sculpture and ceramics) (MFA); design (MFA); electronic studio (MFA); painting (MFA); photography (MFA). *Accreditation:* NASAD. *Degree requirements:* For master's, comprehensive exam, thesis, exhibit. *Entrance requirements:* For master's, minimum GPA of 3.0, portfolio.

Illinois State University, Graduate School, College of Fine Arts, School of Art, Normal, IL 61790-2200. Offers art history (MA, MS); ceramics (MFA, MS); drawing (MFA, MS); fibers (MFA, MS); glass (MFA, MS); graphic design (MFA, MS); metals (MFA, MS); painting (MFA, MS); photography (MFA, MS); printmaking (MFA, MS); sculpture (MFA, MS). *Accreditation:* NASAD (one or more programs are accredited). *Degree requirements:* For master's, thesis or alternative, internship. *Entrance requirements:* For master's, portfolio, sample of scholarly writing. *Faculty research:* General operations support: Normal Editions Workshop for FY2007.

Indiana State University, School of Graduate Studies, College of Arts and Sciences, Department of Art, Terre Haute, IN 47809. Offers ceramics (MA, MFA); drawing (MA, MFA); graphic design (MA, MFA); painting (MA, MFA); photography (MA, MFA); printmaking (MA, MFA); sculpture (MA, MFA). *Accreditation:* NASAD (one or more programs are accredited). Part-time programs available. *Degree requirements:* For master's, thesis or alternative, departmental qualifying exam. *Entrance requirements:* For master's, portfolio. Additional exam requirements/recommendations for international students: Required—TOEFL (minimum score 550 paper-based).

Inter American University of Puerto Rico, San Germán Campus, Graduate Studies Center, Program in Fine Arts, San Germán, PR 00683-5008. Offers ceramics (MFA); drawing (MFA); engraving (MFA); painting (MFA); photography (MFA); sculpture (MFA). *Degree requirements:* For master's, comprehensive exam, thesis. *Entrance requirements:* For master's, GRE General Test or EXADEP, minimum GPA of 3.0.

James Madison University, The Graduate School, College of Visual and Performing Arts, School of Art and Art History, Harrisonburg, VA 22807. Offers art education (MA); art history (MA); ceramics (MFA); drawing/painting (MFA); metal/jewelry (MFA); photography (MFA); printmaking (MFA); sculpture (MFA); studio art (MA); weaving/fibers (MFA). *Accreditation:* NASAD. Part-time programs available. *Faculty:* 11 full-time (6 women), 1 (woman) part-time/adjunct. *Students:* 10 full-time (8 women); includes 1 minority (African American). Average age 27. In 2009, 4 master's awarded. *Degree requirements:* For master's, thesis (for some programs). *Entrance requirements:* For master's, GRE General Test, language exam in French or German, portfolio, 3 letters of recommendation, research paper. Additional exam requirements/recommendations for international students: Required—TOEFL. *Application deadline:* For fall admission, 2/15 priority date for domestic students, 2/15 for international students; for spring admission, 10/15 priority date for domestic students, 10/15 for international students. Applications are processed on a rolling basis. Application fee: $55. Electronic applications accepted. *Expenses:* Tuition, area resident: Part-time $305 per credit hour. Tuition, state resident: part-time $305 per credit hour. Tuition, nonresident: part-time $890 per credit hour. *Financial support:* In 2009–10, 8 students received support, including 3 teaching assistantships with full tuition reimbursements available (averaging $8,664 per year); Federal Work-Study also available. Financial award application deadline: 3/1; financial award applicants required to submit FAFSA. *Unit head:* Leslie M. Bellavance, Academic Unit Head, 540-568-6216. *Application contact:* Lynette M. Bible, Director of Graduate Admissions, 540-568-6395, Fax: 540-568-7860, E-mail: biblelm@jmu.edu.

Lamar University, College of Graduate Studies, College of Fine Arts and Communication, Department of Art, Beaumont, TX 77710. Offers art history (MA); photography (MA); studio art (MA); visual design (MA). Part-time and evening/weekend programs available. *Faculty:* 6 full-time (3 women). *Students:* 3 full-time (1 woman), 1 (woman) part-time. Average age 45. 5 applicants, 60% accepted, 3 enrolled. *Degree requirements:* For master's, thesis. *Entrance requirements:* For master's, GRE General Test, minimum GPA of 2.5 in last 60 hours of undergraduate course work. Additional exam requirements/recommendations for international students: Required—TOEFL. *Application deadline:* For fall admission, 8/1 priority date for domestic students; for spring admission, 12/1 for domestic students. Applications are processed on a rolling basis. Application fee: $25 ($50 for international students). *Financial support:* Fellowships, career-related internships or fieldwork, Federal Work-Study, and scholarships/grants available. Financial award application deadline: 4/1. *Faculty research:* Nineteenth century academic paintings, metal casting, pigment color stability, computer-modified photography, manipulated photography. *Unit head:* Donna M. Meeks, Chair, 409-880-8141, Fax: 409-880-1799, E-mail: meeksdm@lub002.lamar.edu. *Application contact:* Debbie Piper, Coordinator of Graduate Admissions, 409-880-8356, Fax: 409-880-8414, E-mail: gradmissions@hal.lamar.edu.

Louisiana State University and Agricultural and Mechanical College, Graduate School, College of Art and Design, School of Art, Program in Studio Art, Baton Rouge, LA 70803. Offers ceramics (MFA); graphic design (MFA); painting and drawing (MFA); photography (MFA); printmaking (MFA); sculpture (MFA). *Accreditation:* NASAD. *Students:* 46 full-time (31 women), 2 part-time (0 women); includes 1 African American, 4 Asian Americans or Pacific Islanders, 6 international. Average age 29. 74 applicants, 20% accepted. In 2009, 11 master's awarded. *Degree requirements:* For master's, thesis. *Entrance requirements:* For master's, minimum GPA of 3.0. Additional exam requirements/recommendations for international students: Required—TOEFL (minimum score 550 paper-based; 213 computer-based; 79 iBT), IELTS (minimum score 6.5). *Application deadline:* For fall admission, 1/25 priority date for domestic students, 5/15 for international students; for spring admission, 10/15 for international students. Applications are processed on a rolling basis. Electronic applications accepted. *Financial support:* In 2009–10, 25 students received support; research assistantships with partial tuition reimbursements available, teaching assistantships, career-related internships or fieldwork, Federal Work-Study, institutionally sponsored loans, scholarships/grants, and unspecified assistantships available. Support available to part-time students. Financial award application deadline: 3/15. *Unit head:* Tom Neff, Graduate Coordinator, 225-578-5411, Fax: 225-578-1445, E-mail: tneff@lsu.edu. *Application contact:* Tom Neff, Graduate Coordinator, 225-578-5411, Fax: 225-578-1445, E-mail: tneff@lsu.edu.

Louisiana Tech University, Graduate School, College of Liberal Arts, School of Art, Ruston, LA 71272. Offers art and graphic design (MFA); photography (MFA); studio art (MFA). *Accreditation:* NASAD. Part-time programs available. *Degree requirements:* For master's, exhibit. *Entrance requirements:* For master's, GRE General Test, portfolio.

Maryland Institute College of Art, Graduate Studies, Program in Photographic and Electronic Media, Baltimore, MD 21217. Offers MFA. *Accreditation:* NASAD. *Faculty:* 1 full-time (0 women), 2 part-time/adjunct (1 woman). *Students:* 21 full-time (7 women); includes 3 minority (2 African Americans, 1 Hispanic American), 3 international. Average age 31. In 2009, 12 master's awarded. *Degree requirements:* For master's, thesis, exhibit. *Entrance requirements:* For master's, portfolio, 40 studio credits, 6 credits in art history. Additional exam requirements/recommendations for international students: Required—TOEFL (minimum score 550 paper-based; 213 computer-based). *Application deadline:* For fall admission, 1/15 for domestic and international students. Application fee: $60. *Expenses:* Tuition: Full-time $33,000; part-time $1375 per credit hour. Required fees: $1090; $545 per semester. *Financial support:* In 2009–10, 21 students received support, including 2 fellowships (averaging $17,274 per year), 22 teaching assistantships (averaging $1,800 per year); career-related internships or fieldwork and scholarships/grants also available. Financial award application deadline: 3/1; financial award applicants required to submit FAFSA. *Unit head:* Timothy Druckrey, Director, 410-225-2405, Fax: 410-669-1141. *Application contact:* Scott G. Kelly, Associate Dean of Graduate Admission, 410-225-2256, Fax: 410-225-2408, E-mail: graduate@mica.edu.

Marywood University, Academic Affairs, Insalaco College of Creative and Performing Arts, Art Department, Program in Studio Art, Scranton, PA 18509-1598. Offers advertising design (MA); ceramics (MA); clay (MA); graphic design (MA); illustration (MA); painting (MA); photography (MA); printmaking (MA); sculpture (MA); weaving (MA). *Accreditation:* NASAD. *Students:* 6 full-time (5 women), 7 part-time (all women); includes 1 minority (Asian American or Pacific Islander). Average age 38. 5 applicants, 80% accepted. In 2009, 6 master's awarded. *Entrance requirements:* Additional exam requirements/recommendations for international students: Required—TOEFL (minimum score 550 paper-based; 213 computer-based; 79 iBT). *Application deadline:* For fall admission, 4/1 priority date for domestic students, 3/31 priority date for international students; for spring admission, 11/1 priority date for domestic students, 8/31 priority date for international students. Applications are processed on a rolling basis. Application fee: $35. Electronic applications accepted. *Expenses:* Tuition: Part-time $715 per credit. Required fees: $270 per semester. Tuition and fees vary according to degree level, campus/location and program. *Financial support:* Career-related internships or fieldwork, scholarships/grants, and unspecified assistantships available. Support available to part-time students. Financial award application deadline: 6/30; financial award applicants required to submit FAFSA. *Faculty research:* Texture and line in clay, cast bronze sculpture, color theories, book art and illustration, sculptural form. *Application contact:* Tammy Manka, Assistant Director of Graduate Admissions, 866-279-9663, E-mail: tmanka@marywood.edu.

Marywood University, Academic Affairs, Insalaco College of Creative and Performing Arts, Art Department, Program in Visual Arts, Scranton, PA 18509-1598. Offers advertising design (MFA); clay (MFA); graphic design (MFA); illustration (MFA); metals (MFA); painting (MFA); photography (MFA); printmaking (MFA). *Accreditation:* NASAD. *Students:* 16 full-time (13 women), 29 part-time (16 women); includes 2 minority (both Asian Americans or Pacific Islanders), 2 international. Average age 37. In 2009, 11 master's awarded. *Entrance requirements:* Additional exam requirements/recommendations for international students: Required—TOEFL (minimum score 550 paper-based; 213 computer-based; 79 iBT). *Application deadline:* For fall admission, 4/1 priority date for domestic students, 3/31 priority date for international students; for spring admission, 11/1 priority date for domestic students, 8/31 priority date for international students. Applications are processed on a rolling basis. Application fee: $35. Electronic applications accepted. *Expenses:* Contact institution. *Financial support:* Career-related internships or fieldwork, scholarships/grants, and unspecified assistantships available. Support available to part-time students. Financial award application deadline: 6/30; financial award applicants required to submit FAFSA. *Faculty research:* Mariology, exploration of visual imagery, explorations involving drawing on the loom, clay as sculptural medium, oil paintings. *Application contact:* Tammy Manka, Assistant Director of Graduate Admissions, 866-279-9663, E-mail: tmanka@marywood.edu.

Massachusetts College of Art and Design, Graduate Programs, Program in Fine Arts, Boston, MA 02115-5882. Offers ceramics (MFA); design (MFA); fibers (MFA); film/video (MFA); glass (MFA); media and performing arts (MFA); metals/jewelry (MFA); painting (MFA); photography (MFA); printmaking (MFA); sculpture (MFA). *Accreditation:* NASAD. *Faculty:* 10 full-time (5 women), 8 part-time/adjunct (6 women). *Students:* 89 full-time (56 women), 12 part-time (8 women); includes 8 minority (5 Asian Americans or Pacific Islanders, 3 Hispanic Americans), 10 international. Average age 34. 295 applicants, 24% accepted, 40 enrolled. In 2009, 44 master's awarded. *Degree requirements:* For master's, thesis, exhibit. *Entrance requirements:* For master's, 12 units of course work in art history, portfolio, resume, letters of reference, interview. Additional exam requirements/recommendations for international students:

Required—TOEFL (minimum score 563 paper-based; 223 computer-based; 85 iBT); Recommended—IELTS (minimum score 6.5). *Application deadline:* For fall admission, 1/15 for domestic and international students. Application fee: $75. Electronic applications accepted. *Expenses:* Tuition, state resident: full-time $18,450; part-time $615 per credit. Tuition, nonresident: full-time $18,450; part-time $615 per credit. Tuition and fees vary according to program. *Financial support:* In 2009–10, 50 research assistantships (averaging $2,000 per year), 40 teaching assistantships (averaging $2,000 per year) were awarded; career-related internships or fieldwork, Federal Work-Study, and clerical/technical assistantships ($2000) also available. Support available to part-time students. Financial award application deadline: 5/1; financial award applicants required to submit FAFSA. *Unit head:* George Creamer, Dean of Graduate Programs, 617-879-7163, Fax: 617-879-7171, E-mail: creamer@massart.edu. *Application contact:* George Creamer, Dean of Graduate Programs, 617-879-7163, Fax: 617-879-7171, E-mail: creamer@massart.edu.

Mills College, Graduate Studies, Department of Art, Oakland, CA 94613-1000. Offers ceramics (MFA); intermedia (MFA); painting (MFA); photography (MFA); sculpture (MFA). *Faculty:* 7 full-time (5 women), 8 part-time/adjunct (5 women). *Students:* 22 full-time (13 women); includes 3 minority (2 Asian Americans or Pacific Islanders, 1 Hispanic American). Average age 31. 107 applicants, 21% accepted, 12 enrolled. In 2009, 10 master's awarded. *Degree requirements:* For master's, thesis or alternative, exhibit. *Entrance requirements:* For master's, portfolio. Additional exam requirements/recommendations for international students: Required—TOEFL. *Application deadline:* For fall admission, 2/1 for domestic students; for spring admission, 11/1 for domestic students. Application fee: $50. *Expenses:* Contact institution. *Financial support:* In 2009–10, 22 students received support, including 22 fellowships (averaging $8,938 per year), 13 teaching assistantships with partial tuition reimbursements available (averaging $13,055 per year); scholarships/grants and unspecified assistantships also available. Financial award application deadline: 2/1; financial award applicants required to submit FAFSA. *Faculty research:* Contemporary Chinese/American art, Asian art, performance art, feminist theory, installation. *Unit head:* Mary-Ann Milford, Chairperson, 510-430-3142, Fax: 510-430-3314. *Application contact:* Jessica King, Graduate Admission Specialist, 510-430-3305, Fax: 510-430-2159, E-mail: grad-studies@mills.edu.

Minneapolis College of Art and Design, Program in Visual Studies, Minneapolis, MN 55404-4347. Offers animation (MFA); comic art (MFA); drawing (MFA); filmmaking (MFA); fine arts (MFA); furniture design (MFA); graphic design (MFA); illustration (MFA); interactive media (MFA); painting (MFA); photography (MFA); printmaking (MFA); sculpture (MFA). *Accreditation:* NASAD. Part-time programs available. *Faculty:* 42 full-time (13 women). *Students:* 12 full-time (2 women), 18 part-time (8 women). Average age 27. 166 applicants, 28% accepted, 12 enrolled. In 2009, 10 master's awarded. *Degree requirements:* For master's, thesis, thesis exhibit. *Entrance requirements:* For master's, portfolio of visual artwork, resume, 3 letters of recommendation. Additional exam requirements/recommendations for international students: Required—TOEFL (minimum score 550 paper-based; 213 computer-based; 79 iBT). *Application deadline:* For fall admission, 1/15 for domestic and international students. Application fee: $50. Electronic applications accepted. *Expenses:* Tuition: Full-time $29,500; part-time $985 per credit. Required fees: $100. *Financial support:* In 2009–10, 23 students received support, including 15 teaching assistantships (averaging $6,000 per year); career-related internships or fieldwork, Federal Work-Study, scholarships/grants, and unspecified assistantships also available. Support available to part-time students. Financial award application deadline: 3/15; financial award applicants required to submit FAFSA. *Faculty research:* Visual arts: animation, comic art, drawing, filmmaking, furniture design, graphic design, illustration, interactive media, painting, photography, printmaking, sculpture. *Unit head:* Carole Fisher, Graduate Director, 612-874-3629, E-mail: carole_fisher@mcad.edu. *Application contact:* William Mullen, Vice President of Enrollment Management, 612-874-3760, Fax: 612-874-3701, E-mail: william_mullen@mcad.edu.

New Mexico State University, Graduate School, College of Arts and Sciences, Department of Art, Las Cruces, NM 88003-8001. Offers art history (MA); ceramics (MA, MFA); design (MA, MFA); drawing (MFA); metals (MA, MFA); painting (MFA); photography (MFA); printmaking (MA, MFA); sculpture (MA, MFA). *Faculty:* 11 full-time (6 women), 2 part-time/adjunct (1 woman). *Students:* 32 full-time (15 women); includes 8 minority (2 American Indian/Alaska Native, 6 Hispanic Americans). Average age 31. 33 applicants, 55% accepted, 7 enrolled. In 2009, 8 master's awarded. *Degree requirements:* For master's, comprehensive exam (for some programs), thesis, thesis exhibit. *Entrance requirements:* For master's, portfolio, 10-page paper (art history). *Application deadline:* For fall admission, 2/15 for domestic students; for winter admission, 10/15 for domestic students; for spring admission, 7/15 for domestic students. Application fee: $30 ($50 for international students). Electronic applications accepted. *Expenses:* Tuition, state resident: full-time $4080; part-time $223 per credit. Tuition, nonresident: full-time $14,256; part-time $647 per credit. Required fees: $1278; $639 per semester. *Financial support:* In 2009–10, 1 research assistantship (averaging $7,900 per year), 29 teaching assistantships (averaging $9,092 per year) were awarded; Federal Work-Study and health care benefits also available. Support available to part-time students. Financial award application deadline: 3/1; financial award applicants required to submit FAFSA. *Faculty research:* Painting, graphic design, sculpture, printmaking, drawing, ceramics, photography, jewelry. *Unit head:* Spencer D. Fidler, Head, 575-646-1705, Fax: 575-646-8036, E-mail: sfidler@nmsu.edu. *Application contact:* Spencer D. Fidler, Head, 575-646-1705, Fax: 575-646-8036, E-mail: sfidler@nmsu.edu.

The New School: A University, Parsons The New School for Design, Program in Photography, New York, NY 10011. Offers MFA. *Faculty:* 10 full-time (3 women). *Students:* 11 full-time (6 women), 24 part-time (16 women); includes 2 minority (1 American Indian/Alaska Native, 1 Asian American or Pacific Islander), 12 international. Average age 27. 110 applicants, 33% accepted, 15 enrolled. In 2009, 8 master's awarded. *Degree requirements:* For master's, thesis. *Entrance requirements:* For master's, portfolio. Additional exam requirements/recommendations for international students: Required—TOEFL (minimum score 580 paper-based; 237 computer-based; 93 iBT). *Application deadline:* For fall admission, 2/1 for domestic and international students. Application fee: $50. Electronic applications accepted. *Financial support:* Federal Work-Study, scholarships/grants, and tuition waivers (full and partial) available. Support available to part-time students. Financial award application deadline: 3/1; financial award applicants required to submit FAFSA. *Unit head:* James Ramer, Chair, 212-229-8923 Ext. 4243, E-mail: ramerj@newschool.edu. *Application contact:* David Norris, Director of Admissions, 212-229-8989 Ext. 4023, Fax: 212-229-8975, E-mail: norrisd@newschool.edu.

Ohio University, Graduate College, College of Fine Arts, School of Art, Athens, OH 45701-2979. Offers art history (MA); ceramics (MFA); graphic design (MFA); painting (MFA); photography (MFA); printmaking (MFA); sculpture (MFA). Part-time programs available. *Faculty:* 30 full-time (16 women), 7 part-time/adjunct (3 women). *Students:* 53 full-time (30 women), 4 part-time (all women); includes 3 minority (2 Asian Americans or Pacific Islanders, 1 Hispanic American), 4 international. 150 applicants, 33% accepted, 28 enrolled. In 2009, 22 master's awarded. *Degree requirements:* For master's, thesis. *Entrance requirements:* For master's, portfolio. Additional exam requirements/recommendations for international students: Required—TOEFL (minimum score 550 paper-based; 80 iBT) or IELTS Academic (minimum score 6.5). *Application deadline:* For fall admission, 2/1 for domestic and international students. Application fee: $50 ($55 for international students). Electronic applications accepted. *Expenses:* Tuition, state resident: full-time $7839; part-time $323 per quarter hour. Tuition, nonresident: full-time $15,831; part-time $654 per quarter hour. Required fees: $2931. *Financial support:* Teaching assistantships with full and partial tuition reimbursements, career-related internships or fieldwork, Federal Work-Study, institutionally sponsored loans, scholarships/grants, tuition waivers (partial), and unspecified assistantships available. Financial award application deadline: 2/1. *Faculty research:* Vapor fired ceramics, video installation, art theory, digital photography, mixed and interdisciplinary media work. *Unit head:* David LaPalombara, Director, 740-593-4290, Fax: 740-593-0457, E-mail: lapalomb@ohio.edu. *Application contact:* Rosemarie Basile, Chair, Graduate Programs, 740-593-4281, Fax: 740-593-0457, E-mail: basile@ohio.edu.

Ohio University, Graduate College, Scripps College of Communication, School of Visual Communication, Athens, OH 45701-2979. Offers MA. *Accreditation:* NASAD. *Faculty:* 11 full-time (2 women). *Students:* 29 full-time (14 women), 5 part-time (3 women); includes 5 minority (2 African Americans, 1 American Indian/Alaska Native, 2 Hispanic Americans), 5 international. 46 applicants, 50% accepted, 16 enrolled. In 2009, 18 master's awarded. *Entrance requirements:* For master's, minimum GPA of 2.5, portfolio. Additional exam requirements/recommendations for international students: Required—TOEFL (minimum score 600 paper-based; 100 iBT) or IELTS (minimum score 7). *Application deadline:* For fall admission, 2/1 for domestic students, 12/14 for international students. Application fee: $50 ($55 for international students). Electronic applications accepted. *Expenses:* Tuition, state resident: full-time $7839; part-time $323 per quarter hour. Tuition, nonresident: full-time $15,831; part-time $654 per quarter hour. Required fees: $2931. *Financial support:* Federal Work-Study, institutionally sponsored loans, and tuition waivers (partial) available. Financial award applicants required to submit FAFSA. *Faculty research:* Photojournalism (including documentary photography), commercial photography (including illustrative photography), picture editing, informational graphics/publication design, interactive multimedia, and visual media management. *Unit head:* Terry Eiler, Director, 740-595-4895, E-mail: eiler@ohio.edu. *Application contact:* Stan Alost, Assistant Director, 740-597-1778, Fax: 740-593-0190, E-mail: alost@ohio.edu.

Otis College of Art and Design, Program in Fine Arts, Los Angeles, CA 90045-9785. Offers new genres (MFA); painting (MFA); photography (MFA); sculpture (MFA). *Accreditation:* NASAD. *Faculty:* 7 part-time/adjunct (3 women). *Students:* 19 full-time (10 women), 2 part-time (both women); includes 4 minority (1 American Indian/Alaska Native, 1 Asian American or Pacific Islander, 2 Hispanic Americans), 3 international. Average age 32. 199 applicants, 21% accepted, 10 enrolled. In 2009, 10 master's awarded. *Degree requirements:* For master's, thesis. *Entrance requirements:* For master's, portfolio. Additional exam requirements/recommendations for international students: Required—TOEFL (minimum score 600 paper-based; 250 computer-based). *Application deadline:* For fall admission, 2/1 for domestic and international students; for spring admission, 11/1 for domestic and international students. Application fee: $50. Electronic applications accepted. *Expenses:* Tuition: Full-time $33,200. Required fees: $700. *Financial support:* Career-related internships or fieldwork, Federal Work-Study, scholarships/grants, and tuition waivers (partial) available. Financial award applicants required to submit FAFSA. *Unit head:* Roy Dowell, Chair, 310-665-6893, Fax: 310-665-6998, E-mail: grads@otis.edu. *Application contact:* Information Contact, 310-665-6820, Fax: 310-665-6821, E-mail: admissions@otis.edu.

Pratt Institute, School of Art and Design, Program in Fine Arts, Brooklyn, NY 11205-3899. Offers new forms (MFA); painting and drawing (MFA); photography (MFA); printmaking (MFA); sculpture (MFA). *Accreditation:* NASAD. Part-time programs available. *Faculty:* 8 full-time (2 women), 30 part-time/adjunct (15 women). *Students:* 130 full-time (79 women), 2 part-time (both women); includes 13 minority (2 African Americans, 4 Asian Americans or Pacific Islanders, 7 Hispanic Americans), 37 international. Average age 28. 299 applicants, 60% accepted, 66 enrolled. In 2009, 82 master's awarded. *Degree requirements:* For master's, thesis, exhibit. *Entrance requirements:* For master's, portfolio, letters of recommendation. Additional exam requirements/recommendations for international students: Required—TOEFL (minimum score 550 paper-based; 213 computer-based; 79 iBT). *Application deadline:* For fall admission, 1/5 for domestic and international students; for spring admission, 10/1 for domestic and international students. Application fee: $50 ($90 for international students). Electronic applications accepted. *Expenses:* Tuition: Full-time $22,734. Required fees: $1280. *Financial support:* Career-related internships or fieldwork, Federal Work-Study, institutionally sponsored loans, scholarships/grants, health care benefits, and unspecified assistantships available. Support available to part-time students. Financial award application deadline: 2/1; financial award applicants required to submit FAFSA. *Unit head:* Donna Moran, Chairperson, 718-636-3602, E-mail: dmoran@pratt.edu. *Application contact:* Young Hah, Director of Graduate Admissions, 718-636-3683, Fax: 718-399-4242, E-mail: yhah@pratt.edu.

See Close-Up on page 119.

Rhode Island School of Design, Graduate Studies, Division of Fine Arts, Department of Photography, Providence, RI 02903-2784. Offers MFA. *Accreditation:* NASAD. *Degree requirements:* For master's, thesis, exhibit. *Entrance requirements:* For master's, portfolio, 3 letters of recommendation. Additional exam requirements/recommendations for international students: Required—TOEFL (minimum score 580 paper-based; 237 computer-based), IELTS (minimum score 6.5).

Rochester Institute of Technology, Graduate Enrollment Services, College of Imaging Arts and Sciences, School of Photographic Arts and Sciences, Program in Imaging Arts, Rochester, NY 14623-5603. Offers MFA. *Accreditation:* NASAD. Part-time programs available. *Students:* 66 full-time (35 women), 17 part-time (10 women); includes 1 African American, 2 Asian Americans or Pacific Islanders, 3 Hispanic Americans, 31 international. Average age 29. 165 applicants, 36% accepted, 22 enrolled. In 2009, 23 master's awarded. *Degree requirements:* For master's, thesis, exhibit. *Entrance requirements:* For master's, portfolio, minimum GPA of 3.0. Additional exam requirements/recommendations for international students: Required—TOEFL (minimum score 550 paper-based; 213 computer-based; 79 iBT), or IELTS (minimum score 6.5). *Application deadline:* For fall admission, 2/15 priority date for domestic and international students. Applications are processed on a rolling basis. Application fee: $50. Electronic applications accepted. *Expenses:* Tuition: Full-time $31,533; part-time $876 per credit hour. Required fees: $210. *Financial support:* In 2009–10, 45 students received support; fellowships with partial tuition reimbursements available, research assistantships with partial tuition reimbursements available, teaching assistantships with partial tuition reimbursements available, career-related internships or fieldwork, institutionally sponsored loans, scholarships/grants, tuition waivers (partial), and unspecified assistantships available. Support available to part-time students. Financial award application deadline: 8/30; financial award applicants required to submit FAFSA. *Unit head:* Angela Kelly, MFA Coordinator, 585-475-2717, Fax: 585-475-5804, E-mail: spasinfo@rit.edu. *Application contact:* Diane Ellison, Assistant Vice President, Graduate Enrollment Services, 585-475-2229, Fax: 585-475-7164, E-mail: gradinfo@rit.edu.

San Francisco Art Institute, Graduate Program, Department of Photography, San Francisco, CA 94133. Offers MFA, Certificate. *Accreditation:* NASAD. Part-time programs available. *Degree requirements:* For master's and Certificate, oral reviews. *Entrance requirements:* For master's and Certificate, portfolio. Additional exam requirements/recommendations for international students: Required—TOEFL (minimum score 580 paper-based; 237 computer-based). Electronic applications accepted.

San Jose State University, Graduate Studies and Research, College of Humanities and the Arts, School of Art and Design, San Jose, CA 95192-0001. Offers animation/illustration (MA); art history (MA); digital media arts (MFA); photography (MFA); pictorial arts (MFA); spatial arts (MFA). *Accreditation:* NASAD (one or more programs are accredited). *Students:* 48 full-time (27 women), 24 part-time (16 women); includes 13 minority (3 African Americans, 6 Asian Americans or Pacific Islanders, 4 Hispanic Americans), 2 international. Average age 36. 69 applicants, 23% accepted, 16 enrolled. In 2009, 17 master's awarded. *Entrance requirements:* For master's, GRE. *Application deadline:* For fall admission, 6/29 for domestic students; for spring admission, 11/30 for domestic students. Applications are processed on a rolling basis. Application fee: $59. Electronic applications accepted. *Financial support:* Applicants required to submit FAFSA. *Unit head:* John Loomis, Director, 408-924-4320, Fax: 408-924-4326. *Application contact:* John Loomis, Director, 408-924-4320, Fax: 408-924-4326.

Savannah College of Art and Design, Graduate School, Program in Commercial Photography, Savannah, GA 31402-3146. Offers MA. Part-time programs available. *Degree requirements:* For master's, thesis. *Entrance requirements:* For master's, interview, portfolio. Additional exam requirements/recommendations for international students: Required—TOEFL (minimum score 450 paper-based; 133 computer-based). Electronic applications accepted. *Expenses:* Tuition: Full-time $28,515; part-time $627 per credit hour. One-time fee: $500. Tuition and fees vary according to course load.

Photography

Savannah College of Art and Design, Graduate School, Program in Digital Photography, Savannah, GA 31402-3146. Offers MA. Part-time programs available. *Degree requirements:* For master's, thesis. *Entrance requirements:* For master's, interview, portfolio. Additional exam requirements/recommendations for international students: Required—TOEFL (minimum score 450 paper-based; 133 computer-based). Electronic applications accepted. *Expenses:* Tuition: Full-time $28,515; part-time $627 per credit hour. One-time fee: $500. Tuition and fees vary according to course load.

Savannah College of Art and Design, Graduate School, Program in Documentary Photography, Savannah, GA 31402-3146. Offers MA. Part-time programs available. *Degree requirements:* For master's, thesis. *Entrance requirements:* For master's, interview, portfolio. Additional exam requirements/recommendations for international students: Required—TOEFL (minimum score 450 paper-based; 133 computer-based). Electronic applications accepted. *Expenses:* Tuition: Full-time $28,515; part-time $627 per credit hour. One-time fee: $500. Tuition and fees vary according to course load.

Savannah College of Art and Design, Graduate School, Program in Photography, Savannah, GA 31402-3146. Offers MA, MFA. Part-time programs available. *Degree requirements:* For master's, thesis, exhibit, internships. *Entrance requirements:* For master's, interview, portfolio. Additional exam requirements/recommendations for international students: Required—TOEFL (minimum score 450 paper-based; 133 computer-based). Electronic applications accepted. *Expenses:* Tuition: Full-time $28,515; part-time $627 per credit hour. One-time fee: $500. Tuition and fees vary according to course load.

School of the Art Institute of Chicago, Graduate Division, Department of Photography, Chicago, IL 60603-3103. Offers MFA. *Accreditation:* NASAD. *Entrance requirements:* Additional exam requirements/recommendations for international students: Required—TOEFL.

School of Visual Arts, Graduate Programs, Digital Photography Department, New York, NY 10010-3994. Offers MPS. *Degree requirements:* For master's, thesis or project. *Entrance requirements:* For master's, portfolio. Additional exam requirements/recommendations for international students: Required—TOEFL (minimum score 550 paper-based; 213 computer-based; 79 iBT). Electronic applications accepted.

School of Visual Arts, Graduate Programs, Program in Photography, Video and Related Media, New York, NY 10010-3994. Offers MFA. *Accreditation:* NASAD. *Degree requirements:* For master's, final review, project or thesis. *Entrance requirements:* For master's, portfolio. Additional exam requirements/recommendations for international students: Required—TOEFL (minimum score 550 paper-based; 213 computer-based; 79 iBT). Electronic applications accepted.

Southern Methodist University, Meadows School of the Arts, Division of Art, Dallas, TX 75275. Offers studio art (MFA), including ceramics, drawing, painting, photography, printmaking, sculpture. *Accreditation:* NASAD. *Faculty:* 12 full-time (3 women), 3 part-time/adjunct (1 woman). *Students:* 9 full-time (4 women); includes 1 minority (Hispanic American), 1 international. Average age 29. 35 applicants, 20% accepted, 6 enrolled. In 2009, 4 master's awarded. *Degree requirements:* For master's, thesis or alternative, exhibit. *Entrance requirements:* For master's, BFA or equivalent, letters of recommendation, portfolio. Additional exam requirements/recommendations for international students: Required—TOEFL (minimum score 550 paper-based; 213 computer-based; 80 iBT). *Application deadline:* For fall admission, 2/15 for domestic and international students. Application fee: $75. *Financial support:* In 2009–10, 5 fellowships (averaging $32,914 per year), 5 teaching assistantships (averaging $3,000 per year) were awarded; scholarships/grants and unspecified assistantships also available. Financial award application deadline: 3/1; financial award applicants required to submit FAFSA. *Faculty research:* American stoneware, Southwestern furniture traditions, photographic apparatus and techniques, American ceramists, architecture. Total annual research expenditures: $20,000. *Unit head:* James W. Sullivan, Chair, 214-768-2489, E-mail: jsulliva@smu.edu. *Application contact:* Jean Cherry, Director of Graduate Admissions and Records, 214-768-3765, Fax: 214-768-3272, E-mail: jcherry@smu.edu.

Syracuse University, College of Visual and Performing Arts, Program in Art Photography, Syracuse, NY 13244. Offers MFA. *Accreditation:* NASAD. *Students:* 12 full-time (8 women), 1 part-time (0 women); includes 1 minority (Asian American or Pacific Islander), 2 international. Average age 30. 28 applicants, 25% accepted, 5 enrolled. In 2009, 6 master's awarded. *Degree requirements:* For master's, thesis or alternative. *Entrance requirements:* For master's, portfolio. Additional exam requirements/recommendations for international students: Required—TOEFL (minimum score 100 iBT). *Application deadline:* For fall admission, 2/1 priority date for domestic and international students. Application fee: $75. Electronic applications accepted. *Expenses:* Tuition: Full-time $26,808; part-time $1117 per credit. Required fees: $1024. *Financial support:* Fellowships with full tuition reimbursements, research assistantships with full and partial tuition reimbursements, teaching assistantships with full and partial tuition reimbursements, tuition waivers (partial) available. Financial award application deadline: 1/1; financial award applicants required to submit FAFSA. *Unit head:* Heath Hanlin, Department Chair, 315-443-1033, E-mail: hahanlin@syr.edu. *Application contact:* Harriett Conti, Assistant Dean for Recruitment and Admissions, 315-443-5755, E-mail: hmconti@syr.edu.

Syracuse University, S. I. Newhouse School of Public Communications, Program in Photography, Syracuse, NY 13244. Offers MS. *Students:* 14 full-time (6 women), 5 part-time (4 women); includes 1 minority (Asian American or Pacific Islander), 1 international. Average age 28. 12 applicants, 75% accepted, 2 enrolled. In 2009, 5 master's awarded. *Degree requirements:* For master's, thesis optional, special project. *Entrance requirements:* For master's, GRE General Test, portfolio. Additional exam requirements/recommendations for international students: Required—TOEFL (minimum score 600 paper-based; 250 computer-based; 100 iBT). *Application deadline:* For fall admission, 2/1 priority date for domestic and international students. Application fee: $45. Electronic applications accepted. *Expenses:* Tuition: Full-time $26,808; part-time $1117 per credit. Required fees: $1024. *Financial support:* Fellowships with tuition reimbursements, research assistantships with tuition reimbursements, teaching assistantships with tuition reimbursements, Federal Work-Study and tuition waivers (partial) available. Financial award application deadline: 2/1. *Unit head:* Anthony R. Golden, Director, 315-443-2304, Fax: 315-443-3946. *Application contact:* Martha Coria, Graduate Admissions, 315-443-5749, Fax: 315-443-1834, E-mail: pcgrad@syr.edu.

See Close-Up on page 683.

Temple University, Graduate School, Tyler School of Art, Department of Graphic Arts and Design, Philadelphia, PA 19122-6096. Offers graphic and interactive design (MFA); photography (MFA); printmaking (MFA). *Degree requirements:* For master's, essay, exhibit. *Entrance requirements:* For master's, minimum GPA of 3.0; slide portfolio, 40 credits in studio art; 12 credits in art history. Additional exam requirements/recommendations for international students: Required—TOEFL (minimum score 550 paper-based; 213 computer-based; 79 iBT). Electronic applications accepted.

The University of Alabama, Graduate School, College of Arts and Sciences, Department of Art, Tuscaloosa, AL 35487. Offers art history (MA); studio art (MA, MFA), including ceramics, painting, photography, printmaking, sculpture. *Accreditation:* NASAD. Part-time programs available. *Faculty:* 16 full-time (8 women), 1 part-time/adjunct (0 women). *Students:* 17 full-time (10 women), 4 part-time (all women); includes 1 minority (Asian American or Pacific Islander), 1 international. Average age 31. 31 applicants, 39% accepted, 7 enrolled. In 2009, 1 degree awarded. *Degree requirements:* For master's, one foreign language, comprehensive exam (for some programs), oral exam, thesis statement, exhibit (studio art), thesis (art history). *Entrance requirements:* For master's, GRE General Test or MAT (art history), minimum GPA of 3.0, BFA or equivalent (studio art). Additional exam requirements/recommendations for international students: Required—TOEFL (minimum score 550 paper-based; 213 computer-based). *Application deadline:* For fall admission, 3/15 for domestic and international students; for spring admission, 10/15 for domestic and international students. Applications are processed on a rolling basis. Application fee: $50 ($60 for international students). Electronic applications accepted. *Expenses:* Tuition, state resident: full-time $7000. Tuition, nonresident: full-time $19,200. *Financial support:* In 2009–10, 2 fellowships with full tuition reimbursements (averaging $14,000 per year), 13 teaching assistantships with full and partial tuition reimbursements (averaging $9,206 per year) were awarded; career-related internships or fieldwork, institutionally sponsored loans, scholarships/grants, and unspecified assistantships also available. Financial award application deadline: 7/14. *Faculty research:* Nineteenth century American art history, Chinese art history, Baroque art history, twentieth century art history, Asian art history. *Unit head:* William T. Dooley, Chairperson, 205-348-1890, Fax: 205-348-0287, E-mail: wtdooley@bama.ua.edu. *Application contact:* Craig R. Wedderspoon, Graduate Coordinator, 205-348-1898, Fax: 205-348-0287, E-mail: cwedders@bama.edu.

University of Alaska Fairbanks, College of Liberal Arts, Department of Art, Fairbanks, AK 99775-5640. Offers art (MFA); ceramics (MFA); computer art (MFA); drawing (MFA); Native arts (MFA); painting (MFA); photography (MFA); printmaking (MFA); sculpture (MFA). Part-time programs available. *Faculty:* 7 full-time (2 women), 4 part-time/adjunct (3 women). *Students:* 7 full-time (3 women), 2 part-time (0 women); includes 1 minority (American Indian/Alaska Native). Average age 33. 10 applicants, 30% accepted, 2 enrolled. In 2009, 2 master's awarded. *Degree requirements:* For master's, comprehensive exam, thesis, oral exam, oral defense. *Entrance requirements:* For master's, portfolio. Additional exam requirements/recommendations for international students: Required—TOEFL (minimum score 550 paper-based; 213 computer-based; 80 iBT). *Application deadline:* For fall admission, 6/1 for domestic students, 3/1 for international students; for spring admission, 10/15 for domestic students, 9/1 for international students. Applications are processed on a rolling basis. Application fee: $60. Electronic applications accepted. *Expenses:* Tuition, state resident: full-time $7584; part-time $316 per credit. Tuition, nonresident: full-time $15,504; part-time $646 per credit. Required fees: $23 per credit. $135 per semester. Tuition and fees vary according to course level, course load and reciprocity agreements. *Financial support:* In 2009–10, 1 fellowship (averaging $13,500 per year), 4 teaching assistantships (averaging $12,058 per year) were awarded; research assistantships, Federal Work-Study, scholarships/grants, health care benefits, and unspecified assistantships also available. Support available to part-time students. Financial award application deadline: 7/1; financial award applicants required to submit FAFSA. *Faculty research:* Computer art, survey of arts in Alaska, found object art, visualization and animation, painting from the wilderness. *Unit head:* Todd Sherman, Chair, 907-474-7530, Fax: 907-474-5853, E-mail: fyart@uaf.edu. *Application contact:* Todd Sherman, Chair, 907-474-7530, Fax: 907-474-5853, E-mail: fyart@uaf.edu.

University of Colorado at Boulder, Graduate School, College of Arts and Sciences, Department of Art and Art History, Boulder, CO 80309. Offers art history (MA), including 19th century art, contemporary art criticism, early 20th century art, Russian and Soviet art; ceramics (MFA); drawing (MFA); painting (MFA); photography and media arts (MFA); printmaking (MFA); sculpture (MFA). *Faculty:* 28 full-time (13 women). *Students:* 42 full-time (25 women), 1 (woman) part-time; includes 9 minority (1 American Indian/Alaska Native, 3 Asian Americans or Pacific Islanders, 5 Hispanic Americans), 1 international. Average age 31. 224 applicants, 6% accepted, 14 enrolled. In 2009, 17 master's awarded. *Degree requirements:* For master's, variable foreign language requirement, comprehensive exam, thesis (for some programs). *Entrance requirements:* For master's, GRE General Test, minimum undergraduate GPA of 3.0, portfolio. *Application deadline:* For fall admission, 1/15 priority date for domestic students, 12/1 for international students. Application fee: $50 ($60 for international students). *Financial support:* In 2009–10, 6 fellowships (averaging $1,713 per year), 13 research assistantships (averaging $5,087 per year) were awarded; Federal Work-Study, scholarships/grants, and tuition waivers (full) also available. Financial award application deadline: 1/15. *Faculty research:* Drawing, painting, ceramics, sculpture, photography and media arts, printmaking, Russian and Soviet art, early twentieth century art, contemporary art criticism, nineteenth century art. Total annual research expenditures: $10,586.

University of Florida, Graduate School, College of Fine Arts, School of Art and Art History, Gainesville, FL 32611. Offers art (MFA), including ceramics, creative photography, drawing, electronic intermedia, graphic design, painting, printmaking, sculpture; art education (MA); art history (MA, PhD); digital arts and sciences (MA); museology (museum studies) (MA). *Accreditation:* NASAD. *Degree requirements:* For master's, variable foreign language requirement, project or thesis (MFA). *Entrance requirements:* For master's, portfolio (MFA), writing sample (MA), GRE General Test or minimum GPA of 3.0. Additional exam requirements/recommendations for international students: Required—TOEFL (minimum score 550 paper-based; 213 computer-based). Electronic applications accepted. *Faculty research:* Studio production, art historical studies of style context.

University of Houston, College of Liberal Arts and Social Sciences, Department of Art, Houston, TX 77204. Offers art (MA); graphic communication (MFA); interdisciplinary practice and emerging forms (MFA); painting (MFA); photography/digital media (MFA); sculpture (MFA). *Faculty:* 10 full-time (6 women), 7 part-time/adjunct (3 women). *Students:* 35 full-time (20 women); includes 5 minority (2 African Americans, 1 Asian American or Pacific Islander, 2 Hispanic Americans), 4 international. Average age 32. 61 applicants, 31% accepted, 13 enrolled. In 2009, 12 master's awarded. *Entrance requirements:* For master's, GRE General Test, includes baccalaureate degree and portfolio. Additional exam requirements/recommendations for international students: Required—TOEFL. *Application deadline:* For fall admission, 2/1 for domestic and international students. Application fee: $25 ($75 for international students). Electronic applications accepted. *Expenses:* Tuition, state resident: full-time $7676; part-time $320 per credit hour. Tuition, nonresident: full-time $14,324; part-time $597 per credit hour. Required fees: $3034. *Financial support:* In 2009–10, 22 teaching assistantships with full tuition reimbursements (averaging $10,400 per year) were awarded; career-related internships or fieldwork, Federal Work-Study, institutionally sponsored loans, scholarships/grants, health care benefits, and unspecified assistantships also available. Support available to part-time students. Financial award application deadline: 3/10. *Faculty research:* Painting, sculpture, photography/installation/video, graphic design and typography, art history (Pre-Columbian to Surrealism). *Unit head:* Dr. John Reed, Chairperson, 713-743-3001, Fax: 713-743-2823, E-mail: jreed@uh.edu. *Application contact:* Cathy Hunt, Graduate Advisor and Instructional Assistant Professor, 713-743-2830, Fax: 713-743-2823, E-mail: chunt@uh.edu.

University of Illinois at Chicago, Graduate College, College of Architecture and Art, School of Art and Design, Chicago, IL 60607-7128. Offers electronic visualization (MFA); film animation (MFA); graphic design (MFA); industrial design (MFA); photography (MFA); studio arts (MFA). *Accreditation:* NASAD. *Degree requirements:* For master's, thesis, exhibit. *Entrance requirements:* For master's, MAT, portfolio. Additional exam requirements/recommendations for international students: Required—TOEFL. Electronic applications accepted.

University of Illinois at Urbana–Champaign, Graduate College, College of Fine and Applied Arts, School of Art and Design, Program in Studio Arts, Champaign, IL 61820. Offers art and design (MFA); crafts (MFA); metals (MFA); painting (MFA); photography (MFA); sculpture (MFA). *Accreditation:* NASAD. *Students:* 22 full-time (15 women), 2 part-time (1 woman); includes 5 minority (2 American Indian/Alaska Native, 2 Asian Americans or Pacific Islanders, 1 Hispanic American), 5 international. 86 applicants, 12% accepted, 10 enrolled. In 2009, 12 master's awarded. *Entrance requirements:* For master's, minimum GPA of 3.0. Additional exam requirements/recommendations for international students: Required—TOEFL (minimum score 550 paper-based; 213 computer-based; 79 iBT). *Application deadline:* Applications are processed on a rolling basis. Application fee: $60 ($75 for international students). Electronic applications accepted. *Financial support:* Fellowships, research assistantships, teaching assistantships, tuition waivers (full and partial) available. *Unit head:* Timothy Van Laar, Chair, 217-333-6611, E-mail: tvanlaar@illinois.edu. *Application contact:* Marsha Biddle, Assistant to the Associate Director, 217-333-0642, Fax: 217-244-7688, E-mail: mbiddle@illinois.edu.

University of Massachusetts Dartmouth, Graduate School, College of Visual and Performing Arts, Program in Visual Design, North Dartmouth, MA 02747-2300. Offers digital media (MFA);

graphic design (MFA); illustration (MFA); photography (MFA); typography (MFA). *Accreditation:* NASAD. *Faculty:* 17 full-time (7 women), 3 part-time/adjunct (2 women). *Students:* 6 full-time (4 women), 1 (woman) part-time. Average age 35. 25 applicants, 44% accepted, 2 enrolled. In 2009, 2 master's awarded. *Degree requirements:* For master's, visual thesis. *Entrance requirements:* For master's, portfolio, interview, minimum GPA of 3.0, 3 letters of recommendation. Additional exam requirements/recommendations for international students: Required—TOEFL (minimum score 500 paper-based). *Application deadline:* For fall admission, 2/1 priority date for domestic students, 12/1 priority date for international students. Applications are processed on a rolling basis. Application fee: $40 ($60 for international students). Electronic applications accepted. *Expenses:* Tuition, state resident: full-time $2071; part-time $86.29 per credit. Tuition, nonresident: full-time $8099; part-time $337.46 per credit. Required fees: $9446. Tuition and fees vary according to class time, course load and reciprocity agreements. *Financial support:* In 2009–10, 5 teaching assistantships with full tuition reimbursements (averaging $3,088 per year) were awarded; Federal Work-Study and unspecified assistantships also available. Support available to part-time students. Financial award application deadline: 3/1; financial award applicants required to submit FAFSA. Total annual research expenditures: $1,000. *Unit head:* Memory Holloway, Director, 508-999-8554, E-mail: mholloway@umassd.edu. *Application contact:* Elan Turcotte-Shamski, Graduate Admissions Officer, 508-999-8604, Fax: 508-999-8183, E-mail: graduate@umassd.edu.

University of Memphis, Graduate School, College of Communication and Fine Arts, Department of Art, Memphis, TN 38152. Offers art (Graduate Certificate); art history (MA), including Egyptian art and archaeology, general art history; ceramics (MFA); graphic design (MFA); interior design (MFA); painting (MFA); printmaking/photography (MFA); sculpture (MFA). *Accreditation:* NASAD (one or more programs are accredited). *Faculty:* 20 full-time (7 women), 4 part-time/adjunct (2 women). *Students:* 39 full-time (26 women), 10 part-time (8 women); includes 4 African Americans, 1 Asian American or Pacific Islander, 1 international. Average age 29. 44 applicants, 77% accepted, 22 enrolled. In 2009, 16 master's, 5 other advanced degrees awarded. *Degree requirements:* For master's, 2 foreign languages, comprehensive exam, thesis. *Entrance requirements:* For master's, GRE General Test or MAT, portfolio (MFA). *Application deadline:* For fall admission, 8/1 for domestic students; for spring admission, 12/1 for domestic students. Applications are processed on a rolling basis. Application fee: $35 ($60 for international students). *Expenses:* Tuition, state resident: full-time $6246; part-time $347 per credit hour. Tuition, nonresident: full-time $15,894; part-time $883 per credit hour. Required fees: $1160. Full-time tuition and fees vary according to course load, degree level and program. *Financial support:* In 2009–10, 38 students received support; research assistantships with full tuition reimbursements available, teaching assistantships with full tuition reimbursements available, Federal Work-Study, scholarships/grants, and unspecified assistantships available. Financial award application deadline: 2/15; financial award applicants required to submit FAFSA. *Faculty research:* Online collaborative learning, advanced art history studies, electronic publishing/design, studio arts, architectural studies. *Unit head:* Prof. Richard Lou, Chair, 901-678-2216, Fax: 901-678-2735, E-mail: gmyatt@memphis.edu. *Application contact:* Greely Myat, Graduate Studies Coordinator, 901-678-2650.

University of Miami, Graduate School, College of Arts and Sciences, Department of Art and Art History, Coral Gables, FL 33124. Offers art history (MA); ceramics/glass (MFA); graphic design/multimedia (MFA); painting (MFA); photography/digital imaging (MFA); printmaking (MFA); sculpture (MFA). Part-time programs available. *Degree requirements:* For master's, variable foreign language requirement, thesis, exhibit (MFA), comprehensive exam (MA). *Entrance requirements:* For master's, GRE General Test (MA), research paper (MA), slide portfolio (MFA). Additional exam requirements/recommendations for international students: Required—TOEFL. Electronic applications accepted. *Faculty research:* Installation art, public art.

University of Notre Dame, Graduate School, College of Arts and Letters, Division of Humanities, Department of Art, Art History, and Design, Notre Dame, IN 46556. Offers art history (MA); design (MFA), including graphic design, industrial design; studio art (MFA), including ceramics, painting, photography, printmaking, sculpture. *Accreditation:* NASAD. *Degree requirements:* For master's, comprehensive exam (for some programs), thesis. *Entrance requirements:* For master's, GRE General Test, minimum GPA of 3.0. Additional exam requirements/recommendations for international students: Required—TOEFL (minimum score 600 paper-based; 250 computer-based; 80 iBT). Electronic applications accepted. *Faculty research:* Studio art practice in ceramics, printing, photography, printmaking and sculpture, graphic design and industrial design, digital imaging in design and photography, Renaissance and American art history, contemporary art theory and criticism.

University of Oklahoma, Graduate College, College of Fine Arts, School of Art and Art History, Norman, OK 73019. Offers art (MA, MFA); art history (MA, MFA); ceramics (MFA); film and video (MFA); painting (MFA); photography (MFA); printmaking (MFA); visual communications (MFA). *Faculty:* 27 full-time (11 women). *Students:* 25 full-time (13 women), 13 part-time (12 women); includes 8 minority (2 African Americans, 5 American Indian/Alaska Native, 1 Asian American or Pacific Islander), 6 international. 36 applicants, 53% accepted, 11 enrolled. In 2009, 4 master's awarded. *Degree requirements:* For master's, thesis (MA), exhibit (MFA), departmental qualifying exam. *Entrance requirements:* For master's, GRE General Test (MA), bachelor's degree in art (MFA) or art history (MA), minimum GPA of 3.0 in last 60 undergraduate hours, 3 letters of recommendation, written research paper. Additional exam requirements/recommendations for international students: Required—TOEFL (minimum score 550 paper-based; 213 computer-based). *Application deadline:* For fall admission, 2/1 priority date for domestic students, 2/1 for international students; for spring admission, 10/1 for domestic and international students. Applications are processed on a rolling basis. Application fee: $40 ($90 for international students). Electronic applications accepted. *Expenses:* Tuition, state resident: full-time $3744; part-time $156 per credit hour. Tuition, nonresident: full-time $13,577; part-time $565.70 per credit hour. Required fees: $2415; $90.10 per credit hour. *Financial support:* In 2009–10, 26 students received support, including 17 research assistantships with partial tuition reimbursements available (averaging $9,940 per year), 1 teaching assistantship with partial tuition reimbursement available (averaging $9,586 per year); career-related internships or fieldwork, Federal Work-Study, institutionally sponsored loans, scholarships/grants, health care benefits, tuition waivers (full and partial), and unspecified assistantships also available. Financial award application deadline: 4/7; financial award applicants required to submit FAFSA. *Faculty research:* Native American art history and art of the American West, contemporary and figurative sculpture, painting and print making, graphic design, media. Total annual research expenditures: $34,861. *Unit head:* Mary Jo Watson, Director, 405-325-2691, Fax: 405-325-1668, E-mail: mjwatson@ou.edu. *Application contact:* Jonathan Hils, Graduate Liaison, 405-325-2691, Fax: 405-325-1668, E-mail: hils@ou.edu.

University of Southern California, Graduate School, Roski School of Fine Arts, Graduate Programs in Fine Arts, Los Angeles, CA 90089. Offers painting/drawing (MFA); photography (MFA); sculpture/new genres (MFA). *Faculty:* 5 full-time (3 women), 1 part-time/adjunct (0 women). *Students:* 16 full-time (5 women); includes 2 minority (1 Asian American or Pacific Islander, 1 Hispanic American), 3 international. Average age 27. 312 applicants, 3% accepted, 8 enrolled. In 2009, 8 master's awarded. *Degree requirements:* For master's, thesis. *Entrance requirements:* For master's, portfolio and artist statement, 3 ltrs of recommendation. Additional exam requirements/recommendations for international students: Required—TOEFL (minimum score 600 paper-based; 250 computer-based; 100 iBT). *Application deadline:* For fall admission, 2/1 for domestic and international students. Application fee: $85. Electronic applications accepted. *Expenses:* Tuition: Full-time $25,980; part-time $1315 per unit. Required fees: $554. One-time fee: $35 full-time. Full-time tuition and fees vary according to degree level and program. *Financial support:* In 2009–10, 16 students received support, including 3 research assistantships (averaging $3,500 per year), 13 teaching assistantships with full tuition reimbursements available (averaging $9,500 per year); health care benefits and unspecified assistantships also available. Financial award application deadline: 2/1. *Faculty research:* Film and community growth, adolescence and transgenderism. *Unit head:* Charlie White, MFA Director, 213-743-1804, Fax: 213-743-1817. *Application contact:* Dwayne Moser, MFA Coordinator, 213-743-1804, Fax: 213-743-1817, E-mail: dmoser@usc.edu.

The University of Tennessee, Graduate School, College of Arts and Sciences, School of Art, Knoxville, TN 37996. Offers ceramics (MFA); drawing (MFA); graphic design (MFA); inter-area studies (MFA); media arts (MFA); painting (MFA); printmaking (MFA); sculpture (MFA); watercolor (MFA). *Accreditation:* NASAD. *Degree requirements:* For master's, thesis or alternative, exhibit. *Entrance requirements:* For master's, portfolio, minimum GPA of 2.7. Additional exam requirements/recommendations for international students: Required—TOEFL. Electronic applications accepted. *Expenses:* Tuition, state resident: full-time $6826; part-time $380 per semester hour. Tuition, nonresident: full-time $21,844; part-time $1147 per semester hour. Tuition and fees vary according to program.

University of Utah, The Graduate School, College of Fine Arts, Department of Art and Art History, Salt Lake City, UT 84112-0380. Offers art history (MA); ceramics (MFA); community-based art education (MFA); drawing (MFA); graphic design (MFA); painting (MFA); photography/digital imaging (MFA); printmaking (MFA); sculpture/intermedia (MFA). *Faculty:* 24 full-time (11 women). *Students:* 20 full-time (15 women), 2 part-time (both women), 1 international. Average age 31. 59 applicants, 24% accepted, 9 enrolled. In 2009, 11 master's awarded. *Degree requirements:* For master's, variable foreign language requirement, comprehensive exam (for some programs), thesis or alternative, exhibit and final project paper (for MFA). *Entrance requirements:* For master's, CD portfolio (MFA), writing sample (MA), curriculum vitae, letters of recommendation. Additional exam requirements/recommendations for international students: Required—TOEFL (minimum score 575 paper-based; 183 computer-based; 75 iBT). *Application deadline:* For fall admission, 1/2 priority date for domestic and international students. Application fee: $55 ($65 for international students). Electronic applications accepted. *Expenses:* Tuition, state resident: full-time $4004; part-time $1674 per semester. Tuition, nonresident: full-time $14,134; part-time $5915 per semester. Required fees: $324 per semester. Tuition and fees vary according to course load, degree level and program. *Financial support:* In 2009–10, 2 fellowships, 6 research assistantships with partial tuition reimbursements, 34 teaching assistantships with partial tuition reimbursements were awarded; Federal Work-Study, institutionally sponsored loans, scholarships/grants, tuition waivers (partial), unspecified assistantships, and stipends also available. Financial award application deadline: 1/2; financial award applicants required to submit FAFSA. *Faculty research:* Studio art, European art history, Asian art history, Latin American art history, twentieth century/contemporary art history. Total annual research expenditures: $8,748. *Unit head:* Dr. Elizabeth A. Peterson, Chair, 801-581-7012, Fax: 801-585-6171, E-mail: elizabeth.peterson@art.utah.edu. *Application contact:* Prof. John O'Connell, Director of Graduate Studies, 801-581-8677, Fax: 801-585-6171, E-mail: j.oconnell@utah.edu.

University of Victoria, Faculty of Graduate Studies, Faculty of Fine Arts, Department of Visual Arts, Victoria, BC V8W 2Y2, Canada. Offers digital multimedia (MFA); drawing (MFA); painting (MFA); photography (MFA); sculpture (MFA); video (MFA). *Degree requirements:* For master's, exhibit, oral exam. *Entrance requirements:* For master's, portfolio, BFA. Additional exam requirements/recommendations for international students: Required—TOEFL (minimum score 575 paper-based; 233 computer-based), IELTS (minimum score 7). Electronic applications accepted.

University of Washington, Graduate School, College of Arts and Sciences, School of Art, Division of Art, Seattle, WA 98195. Offers painting and drawing (MFA); photography (MFA). *Degree requirements:* For master's, thesis, exhibit. *Entrance requirements:* For master's, BFA or equivalent academic work in art, 20 slide portfolio. Additional exam requirements/recommendations for international students: Required—TOEFL. Electronic applications accepted.

Virginia Commonwealth University, Graduate School, School of the Arts, Department of Graphic Design, Richmond, VA 23284-9005. Offers design/visual communications (MFA); interior environment (MFA); photography and film (MFA). *Accreditation:* NASAD. *Degree requirements:* For master's, thesis, exhibition. *Entrance requirements:* For master's, portfolio. *Faculty research:* Film, photography, interior environments, visual communication.

Washington State University, Graduate School, College of Liberal Arts, Department of Fine Arts, Pullman, WA 99164. Offers ceramics (MFA); digital media (MFA); drawing (MFA); painting (MFA); photography (MFA); print making (MFA); sculpture (MFA). *Faculty:* 10. *Students:* 15 full-time (8 women); includes 2 minority (1 African American, 1 Hispanic American). Average age 29. 30 applicants, 20% accepted, 5 enrolled. In 2009, 5 master's awarded. *Degree requirements:* For master's, comprehensive exam (for some programs), thesis, exhibit, oral exam. *Entrance requirements:* For master's, GRE, Graduate School application, statement of intent indicating your area(s) of focus, the subject of your work, the concepts and issues you are exploring, and how you foresee your work evolving within the program, portfolio of no more than 15 images on CD/DVD,inventory list with the title, medium, size and approximate date of completion for each work. Additional exam requirements/recommendations for international students: Required—TOEFL (minimum score 550 paper-based; 213 computer-based), IELTS. *Application deadline:* For fall admission, 1/10 for domestic and international students. Application fee: $50. Electronic applications accepted. *Financial support:* In 2009–10, fellowships with full and partial tuition reimbursements (averaging $3,114 per year), research assistantships with full and partial tuition reimbursements (averaging $13,917 per year), teaching assistantships with full and partial tuition reimbursements (averaging $13,056 per year) were awarded; career-related internships or fieldwork, Federal Work-Study, institutionally sponsored loans, tuition waivers (partial), and unspecified assistantships also available. Financial award application deadline: 2/15; financial award applicants required to submit FAFSA. *Faculty research:* Polynesian art, museum representation, number theory. *Unit head:* Dr. Chris Watts, Interim Chair, 509-335-7107, Fax: 509-335-7742, E-mail: cjwatts@wsu.edu. *Application contact:* Graduate School Admissions, 800-GRADWSU, Fax: 509-335-1949, E-mail: gradsch@wsu.edu.

Yale University, School of Art, New Haven, CT 06520. Offers graphic design (MFA); painting/printmaking (MFA); photography (MFA); sculpture (MFA). *Faculty:* 7 full-time (3 women), 36 part-time/adjunct (12 women). *Students:* 119 full-time (62 women); includes 17 minority (4 African Americans, 6 Asian Americans or Pacific Islanders, 7 Hispanic Americans), 25 international. Average age 28. 1,266 applicants, 5% accepted, 58 enrolled. In 2009, 57 master's awarded. *Degree requirements:* For master's, thesis (for some programs). *Entrance requirements:* Additional exam requirements/recommendations for international students: Required—TOEFL (minimum score 550 paper-based; 250 computer-based; 100 iBT). *Application deadline:* For fall admission, 1/5 for domestic and international students. Application fee: $100. Electronic applications accepted. *Expenses:* Contact institution. *Financial support:* In 2009–10, 90 students received support, including 54 teaching assistantships (averaging $1,900 per year); Federal Work-Study, scholarships/grants, and unspecified assistantships also available. Financial award application deadline: 3/1; financial award applicants required to submit FAFSA. *Unit head:* Robert Storr, Dean, 203-432-2606. *Application contact:* Patricia Ann DeChiara, Director of Academic Affairs, 203-432-2600, E-mail: artschool.info@yale.edu.

Textile Design

Academy of Art University, Graduate Program, School of Fashion, San Francisco, CA 94105-3410. Offers fashion design (MFA); fashion merchandising (MFA); fashion textiles (MFA); knitwear (MFA). Part-time programs available. Postbaccalaureate distance learning degree programs offered (no on-campus study). *Degree requirements:* For master's, thesis, final review. *Entrance requirements:* For master's, minimum GPA of 3.0, portfolio. Electronic applications accepted.

California College of the Arts, Graduate Programs, Programs in Fine Art, San Francisco, CA 94107. Offers ceramics (MFA); film/video/performance (MFA); glass (MFA); jewelry/metal arts (MFA); painting/drawing (MFA); photography (MFA); printmaking (MFA); sculpture (MFA); textiles (MFA); wood/furniture (MFA). *Accreditation:* NASAD. *Degree requirements:* For master's, thesis, exhibit. *Entrance requirements:* For master's, appropriate bachelor's degree, portfolio. Additional exam requirements/recommendations for international students: Required—TOEFL (minimum score 600 paper-based; 250 computer-based). Electronic applications accepted.

California State University, Los Angeles, Graduate Studies, College of Arts and Letters, Department of Art, Los Angeles, CA 90032-8530. Offers art (MA), including art education, art history, art therapy, ceramics, metals, and textiles, design (MA, MFA), painting, sculpture, and graphic arts, photography; fine arts (MFA), including crafts, design (MA, MFA), studio arts. *Accreditation:* NASAD (one or more programs are accredited). Part-time and evening/weekend programs available. *Faculty:* 12 full-time (6 women), 1 part-time/adjunct (0 women). *Students:* 28 full-time (21 women), 40 part-time (28 women); includes 22 minority (1 African American, 6 Asian Americans or Pacific Islanders, 15 Hispanic Americans), 9 international. Average age 37. 30 applicants, 100% accepted, 12 enrolled. In 2009, 17 master's awarded. *Degree requirements:* For master's, comprehensive exam, project or thesis. *Entrance requirements:* For master's, portfolio. Additional exam requirements/recommendations for international students: Required—TOEFL (minimum score 500 paper-based; 173 computer-based). *Application deadline:* For fall admission, 5/1 for domestic and international students. Applications are processed on a rolling basis. Application fee: $55. Electronic applications accepted. *Financial support:* Federal Work-Study available. Support available to part-time students. Financial award application deadline: 3/1. *Faculty research:* The artist and the book, conceptual art, ceramic processes, computer graphics, architectural graphics. *Unit head:* Dr. Abbas Daneshvari, Chair, 323-343-4010, Fax: 323-343-4045, E-mail: adanesh@calstatela.edu. *Application contact:* Dr. Cheryl L. Ney, Associate Vice President for Academic Affairs and Dean of Graduate Studies, 323-343-3820, Fax: 323-343-5653, E-mail: cney@cslanet.calstatela.edu.

Cornell University, Graduate School, Graduate Fields of Human Ecology, Field of Textiles, Ithaca, NY 14853-0001. Offers apparel design (MA, MPS); fiber science (MS, PhD); polymer science (MS, PhD); textile science (MS, PhD). *Faculty:* 17 full-time (7 women). *Students:* 21 full-time (16 women); includes 1 minority (Hispanic American), 12 international. Average age 30. 26 applicants, 19% accepted, 3 enrolled. In 2009, 1 master's, 4 doctorates awarded. *Degree requirements:* For master's, thesis (MA, MS), project paper (MPS); for doctorate, comprehensive exam, thesis/dissertation. *Entrance requirements:* For master's, GRE General Test, 2 letters of recommendation, portfolio (functional apparel design); for doctorate, GRE General Test, 2 letters of recommendation. Additional exam requirements/recommendations for international students: Required—TOEFL (minimum score 600 paper-based; 250 computer-based; 77 iBT). *Application deadline:* For fall admission, 3/1 for domestic students; for spring admission, 10/1 for domestic students. Application fee: $70. Electronic applications accepted. *Expenses:* Tuition: Full-time $29,500. Required fees: $70. Full-time tuition and fees vary according to degree level, program and student level. *Financial support:* In 2009–10, 19 students received support, including 2 teaching assistantships with full tuition reimbursements available; fellowships with full tuition reimbursements available, research assistantships with full tuition reimbursements available, institutionally sponsored loans, scholarships/grants, health care benefits, tuition waivers (full and partial), and unspecified assistantships also available. Financial award applicants required to submit FAFSA. *Faculty research:* Apparel design, consumption, mass customization, 3-D body scanning. *Unit head:* Director of Graduate Studies, 607-255-3151, Fax: 607-255-1093. *Application contact:* Graduate Field Assistant, 607-255-3151, Fax: 607-255-1093, E-mail: textiles_grad@cornell.edu.

Cranbrook Academy of Art, Graduate School, Program in Fine Arts, Bloomfield Hills, MI 48303-0801. Offers ceramics (MFA); design (MFA), including graphic design; fiber arts (MFA); metalsmithing (MFA); painting (MFA); photography (MFA); printmaking (MFA); sculpture (MFA). *Accreditation:* NASAD. *Degree requirements:* For master's, thesis, exhibit. *Entrance requirements:* Additional exam requirements/recommendations for international students: Required—TOEFL (minimum score 550 paper-based; 213 computer-based).

Drexel University, Antoinette Westphal College of Media Arts and Design, Program in Fashion Design, Philadelphia, PA 19104-2875. Offers MS. *Accreditation:* NASAD. *Degree requirements:* For master's, thesis, portfolio review. *Entrance requirements:* For master's, interview. Additional exam requirements/recommendations for international students: Required—TOEFL. Electronic applications accepted.

Illinois State University, Graduate School, College of Fine Arts, School of Art, Normal, IL 61790-2200. Offers art history (MA, MS); ceramics (MFA, MS); drawing (MFA, MS); fibers (MFA, MS); glass (MFA, MS); graphic design (MFA, MS); metals (MFA, MS); painting (MFA, MS); photography (MFA, MS); printmaking (MFA, MS); sculpture (MFA, MS). *Accreditation:* NASAD (one or more programs are accredited). *Degree requirements:* For master's, thesis or alternative, internship. *Entrance requirements:* For master's, portfolio, sample of scholarly writing. *Faculty research:* General operations support: Normal Editions Workshop for FY2007.

James Madison University, The Graduate School, College of Visual and Performing Arts, School of Art and Art History, Harrisonburg, VA 22807. Offers art education (MA); art history (MA); ceramics (MFA); drawing/painting (MFA); metal/jewelry (MFA); photography (MFA); printmaking (MFA); sculpture (MFA); studio art (MA); weaving/fibers (MFA). *Accreditation:* NASAD. Part-time programs available. *Faculty:* 11 full-time (6 women), 1 (woman) part-time/adjunct. *Students:* 10 full-time (8 women); includes 1 minority (African American). Average age 27. In 2009, 4 master's awarded. *Degree requirements:* For master's, thesis (for some programs). *Entrance requirements:* For master's, GRE General Test, language exam in French or German, portfolio, 3 letters of recommendation, research paper. Additional exam requirements/recommendations for international students: Required—TOEFL. *Application deadline:* For fall admission, 2/15 priority date for domestic students, 2/15 for international students; for spring admission, 10/15 priority date for domestic students, 10/15 for international students. Applications are processed on a rolling basis. Application fee: $55. Electronic applications accepted. *Expenses:* Tuition, area resident: Part-time $305 per credit hour. Tuition, state resident: part-time $305 per credit hour. Tuition, nonresident: part-time $890 per credit hour. *Financial support:* In 2009–10, 8 students received support, including 3 teaching assistantships with full tuition reimbursements available (averaging $8,664 per year); Federal Work-Study also available. Financial award application deadline: 3/1; financial award applicants required to submit FAFSA. *Unit head:* Leslie M. Bellavance, Academic Unit Head, 540-568-6216. *Application contact:* Lynette M. Bible, Director of Graduate Admissions, 540-568-6395, Fax: 540-568-7860, E-mail: biblelm@jmu.edu.

Kent State University, College of the Arts, School of Art, Kent, OH 44242-0001. Offers art education (MA); art history (MA); crafts (MA, MFA), including ceramics (MA), glass, jewelry/metals, textiles/art; fine art (MA, MFA), including drawing/painting, printmaking, sculpture. *Accreditation:* NASAD (one or more programs are accredited). *Degree requirements:* For master's, one foreign language, thesis. *Entrance requirements:* For master's, undergraduate degree in proposed area of study (for fine arts and crafts programs); minimum overall GPA of 2.75 (3.0 for art major); 3 letters of recommendation; portfolio (15-20 slides for MA, 20-25 for MFA). Additional exam requirements/recommendations for international students: Required—TOEFL. Electronic applications accepted.

LIM College, MBA Program, New York, NY 10022-5268. Offers entrepreneurship (MBA); fashion management (MBA).

Marywood University, Academic Affairs, Insalaco College of Creative and Performing Arts, Art Department, Program in Studio Art, Scranton, PA 18509-1598. Offers advertising design (MA); ceramics (MA); clay (MA); graphic design (MA); illustration (MA); painting (MA); photography (MA); printmaking (MA); sculpture (MA); weaving (MA). *Accreditation:* NASAD. *Students:* 6 full-time (5 women), 7 part-time (all women); includes 1 minority (Asian American or Pacific Islander). Average age 38. 5 applicants, 80% accepted. In 2009, 6 master's awarded. *Entrance requirements:* Additional exam requirements/recommendations for international students: Required—TOEFL (minimum score 550 paper-based; 213 computer-based; 79 iBT). *Application deadline:* For fall admission, 4/1 priority date for domestic students, 3/31 priority date for international students; for spring admission, 11/1 priority date for domestic students, 8/31 priority date for international students. Applications are processed on a rolling basis. Application fee: $35. Electronic applications accepted. *Expenses:* Tuition: Part-time $715 per credit. Required fees: $270 per semester. Tuition and fees vary according to degree level, campus/location and program. *Financial support:* Career-related internships or fieldwork, scholarships/grants, and unspecified assistantships available. Support available to part-time students. Financial award application deadline: 6/30; financial award applicants required to submit FAFSA. *Faculty research:* Texture and line in clay, cast bronze sculpture, color theories, book art and illustration, sculptural form. *Application contact:* Tammy Manka, Assistant Director of Graduate Admissions, 866-279-9663, E-mail: tmanka@marywood.edu.

Massachusetts College of Art and Design, Graduate Programs, Program in Fine Arts, Boston, MA 02115-5882. Offers ceramics (MFA); design (MFA); fibers (MFA); film/video (MFA); glass (MFA); media and performing arts (MFA); metals/jewelry (MFA); painting (MFA); photography (MFA); printmaking (MFA); sculpture (MFA). *Accreditation:* NASAD. *Faculty:* 10 full-time (5 women), 8 part-time/adjunct (6 women). *Students:* 89 full-time (56 women), 12 part-time (8 women); includes 8 minority (5 Asian Americans or Pacific Islanders, 3 Hispanic Americans), 10 international. Average age 34. 295 applicants, 24% accepted, 40 enrolled. In 2009, 44 master's awarded. *Degree requirements:* For master's, thesis, exhibit. *Entrance requirements:* For master's, 12 units of course work in art history, portfolio, resume, letters of reference, interview. Additional exam requirements/recommendations for international students: Required—TOEFL (minimum score 563 paper-based; 223 computer-based; 85 iBT); Recommended—IELTS (minimum score 6.5). *Application deadline:* For fall admission, 1/15 for domestic and international students. Application fee: $75. Electronic applications accepted. *Expenses:* Tuition, state resident: full-time $18,450; part-time $615 per credit. Tuition, nonresident: full-time $18,450; part-time $615 per credit. Tuition and fees vary according to program. *Financial support:* In 2009–10, 50 research assistantships (averaging $2,000 per year), 40 teaching assistantships (averaging $2,000 per year) were awarded; career-related internships or fieldwork, Federal Work-Study, and clerical/technical assistantships ($2000) also available. Support available to part-time students. Financial award application deadline: 5/1; financial award applicants required to submit FAFSA. *Unit head:* George Creamer, Dean of Graduate Programs, 617-879-7163, Fax: 617-879-7171, E-mail: creamer@massart.edu. *Application contact:* George Creamer, Dean of Graduate Programs, 617-879-7163, Fax: 617-879-7171, E-mail: creamer@massart.edu.

Missouri State University, Graduate College, College of Natural and Applied Sciences, Department of Fashion and Interior Design, Springfield, MO 65897. Offers secondary education (MS Ed), including consumer sciences. Part-time programs available. *Faculty:* 2 full-time (both women), 1 (woman) part-time/adjunct. *Students:* 3 part-time (all women). Average age 47. 2 applicants, 50% accepted, 0 enrolled. *Degree requirements:* For master's, comprehensive exam, thesis or alternative. *Entrance requirements:* For master's, 9-12 teaching certification (MS Ed), minimum GPA of 3.0 (MNAS). Additional exam requirements/recommendations for international students: Required—TOEFL (minimum score 550 paper-based; 213 computer-based; 79 iBT). *Application deadline:* For fall admission, 7/20 priority date for domestic students, 5/1 for international students; for spring admission, 12/20 priority date for domestic students, 9/1 for international students. Applications are processed on a rolling basis. Application fee: $35 ($50 for international students). Electronic applications accepted. *Expenses:* Tuition, state resident: full-time $3852; part-time $214 per credit hour. Tuition, nonresident: full-time $7524; part-time $418 per credit hour. Required fees: $696; $172 per semester. Tuition and fees vary according to course level, course load, degree level and program. *Financial support:* Career-related internships or fieldwork, Federal Work-Study, institutionally sponsored loans, scholarships/grants, and unspecified assistantships available. Financial award application deadline: 3/31; financial award applicants required to submit FAFSA. *Unit head:* Dr. Paula Kemp, Head, 417-836-5497, Fax: 417-836-4341, E-mail: paulakemp@missouristate.edu. *Application contact:* Eric Eckert, Coordinator of Graduate Admissions and Recruitment, 417-836-5331, Fax: 417-836-6200, E-mail: ericeckert@missouristate.edu.

The New School: A University, Parsons The New School for Design, Program in Fashion Design and Society, New York, NY 10011. Offers MFA. *Unit head:* Shelley Fox, Director, 212-229-8966 Ext. 2746, E-mail: foxs@newschool.edu. *Application contact:* David Norris, Director of Admissions, 212-229-8989 Ext. 4023, Fax: 212-229-8975, E-mail: norrisd@newschool.edu.

The New School: A University, Parsons The New School for Design, Program in Fashion Studies, New York, NY 10011. Offers MA. *Faculty:* 2. *Degree requirements:* For master's, thesis. *Unit head:* Director, 212-229-8989. *Application contact:* David Norris, Director of Admissions, 212-229-8989 Ext. 4023, Fax: 212-229-8975, E-mail: norrisd@newschool.edu.

Philadelphia University, School of Engineering and Textiles, Program in Textile Design, Philadelphia, PA 19144. Offers MS. *Accreditation:* NASAD. Part-time programs available. *Entrance requirements:* For master's, GRE or MAT, minimum GPA of 2.8. Additional exam requirements/recommendations for international students: Required—TOEFL (minimum score 550 paper-based; 213 computer-based; 79 iBT). Electronic applications accepted.

Rhode Island School of Design, Graduate Studies, Division of Fine Arts, Department of Textiles, Providence, RI 02903-2784. Offers MFA. *Accreditation:* NASAD. *Degree requirements:* For master's, thesis, exhibit. *Entrance requirements:* For master's, portfolio, 3 letters of recommendation. Additional exam requirements/recommendations for international students: Required—TOEFL (minimum score 580 paper-based; 237 computer-based), IELTS (minimum score 6.5).

Savannah College of Art and Design, Graduate School, Program in Fashion, Savannah, GA 31402-3146. Offers MA, MFA. Part-time programs available. *Degree requirements:* For master's, thesis, internship. *Entrance requirements:* For master's, interview, portfolio. Additional exam requirements/recommendations for international students: Required—TOEFL (minimum score 450 paper-based; 133 computer-based). Electronic applications accepted. *Expenses:* Tuition: Full-time $28,515; part-time $627 per credit hour. One-time fee: $500. Tuition and fees vary according to course load.

Savannah College of Art and Design, Graduate School, Program in Fibers, Savannah, GA 31402-3146. Offers MA, MFA. Part-time programs available. *Degree requirements:* For master's, thesis, internship. *Entrance requirements:* For master's, interview, portfolio. Additional exam requirements/recommendations for international students: Required—TOEFL (minimum score 450 paper-based; 133 computer-based). Electronic applications accepted. *Expenses:* Tuition: Full-time $28,515; part-time $627 per credit hour. One-time fee: $500. Tuition and fees vary according to course load.

School of the Art Institute of Chicago, Graduate Division, Program in Fashion, Body, and Garment, Chicago, IL 60603-3103. Offers M Des, Certificate.

Sul Ross State University, School of Arts and Sciences, Department of Fine Arts and Communication, Alpine, TX 79832. Offers art education (M Ed); art history (M Ed); studio art (M Ed), including ceramics, design, drawing, jewelry, painting, printmaking, sculpture, weaving. Part-time programs available. *Degree requirements:* For master's, oral or written exam. *Entrance requirements:* For master's, GRE General Test, minimum GPA of 2.5 in last 60 hours of undergraduate work. *Faculty research:* Ceramic sculpture, watercolor, wood sculpture, rock art.

Syracuse University, College of Visual and Performing Arts, Program in Fiber Arts/Material Studies, Syracuse, NY 13244. Offers MFA. *Students:* 3 full-time (all women), 1 international. Average age 25. 6 applicants, 50% accepted, 2 enrolled. *Degree requirements:* For master's, thesis or alternative. *Entrance requirements:* For master's, portfolio. Additional exam requirements/recommendations for international students: Required—TOEFL (minimum score 100 iBT). *Application deadline:* For fall admission, 2/1 priority date for domestic and international students. Application fee: $75. Electronic applications accepted. *Expenses:* Tuition: Full-time $26,808; part-time $1117 per credit. Required fees: $1024. *Financial support:* Fellowships with full and partial tuition reimbursements, teaching assistantships with full and partial tuition reimbursements available. Financial award application deadline: 1/1; financial award applicants required to submit FAFSA. *Unit head:* Errol Willett, Chair, 315-443-3830, E-mail: eswillett@syr.edu. *Application contact:* Harriett Conti, Assistant Dean for Recruitment and Admissions, 315-443-5755, E-mail: hmconti@syr.edu.

Temple University, Graduate School, Tyler School of Art, Department of Crafts, Philadelphia, PA 19122-6096. Offers ceramics/glass (MFA); fibers and fabric design (MFA); metals/jewelry/CAD-CAM (MFA). *Degree requirements:* For master's, essay, exhibit. *Entrance requirements:* For master's, minimum GPA of 3.0, slide portfolio, 40 credits in studio art, 12 credits in art history. Additional exam requirements/recommendations for international students: Required—TOEFL (minimum score 550 paper-based; 213 computer-based; 79 iBT). Electronic applications accepted.

University of California, Davis, Graduate Studies, Program in Textile Arts and Costume Design, Davis, CA 95616. Offers MFA. *Degree requirements:* For master's, presentation of an individual project/body of work. *Entrance requirements:* For master's, minimum GPA of 3.0, portfolio. Additional exam requirements/recommendations for international students: Required—TOEFL (minimum score 550 paper-based; 213 computer-based). Electronic applications accepted. *Faculty research:* Historic ethnographic and contemporary costume and textile design, computer-aided design.

University of Cincinnati, Graduate School, College of Design, Architecture, Art, and Planning, School of Design, Cincinnati, OH 45221. Offers fashion design (M Des); graphic design (M Des); industrial design (M Des); interaction design (M Des); product development (M Des). *Accreditation:* NASAD. *Degree requirements:* For master's, thesis. *Entrance requirements:* For master's, undergraduate degree in design or related field, 2 years of work experience in design or related field. Additional exam requirements/recommendations for international students: Required—TOEFL. Electronic applications accepted. *Faculty research:* Design theory, interdisciplinary design topics.

University of Massachusetts Dartmouth, Graduate School, College of Visual and Performing Arts, Program in Artisanry, North Dartmouth, MA 02747-2300. Offers ceramics (MFA, Postbaccalaureate Certificate); fibers (MFA); fibers/textiles (Postbaccalaureate Certificate); jewelry/metals (MFA, Postbaccalaureate Certificate); wood/furniture design (MFA, Postbaccalaureate Certificate). *Accreditation:* NASAD. *Faculty:* 7 full-time (4 women), 5 part-time/adjunct (3 women). *Students:* 14 full-time (12 women), 13 part-time (7 women); includes 3 minority (2 Asian Americans or Pacific Islanders, 1 Hispanic American), 3 international. Average age 29. 37 applicants, 57% accepted, 12 enrolled. In 2009, 9 master's awarded. *Degree requirements:* For master's, thesis, visual thesis. *Entrance requirements:* For master's, portfolio, interview, minimum GPA of 3.0, 3 letters of recommendation. Additional exam requirements/recommendations for international students: Required—TOEFL (minimum score 500 paper-based). *Application deadline:* For fall admission, 2/1 for domestic students, 12/1 for international students. Applications are processed on a rolling basis. Application fee: $40 ($60 for international students). Electronic applications accepted. *Expenses:* Tuition, state resident: full-time $2071; part-time $86.29 per credit. Tuition, nonresident: full-time $8099; part-time $337.46 per credit. Required fees: $9446. Tuition and fees vary according to class time, course load and reciprocity agreements. *Financial support:* In 2009–10, 2 fellowships with full tuition reimbursements (averaging $5,333 per year), 1 research assistantship with full tuition reimbursement (averaging $7,400 per year), 14 teaching assistantships with full tuition reimbursements (averaging $3,088 per year) were awarded; Federal Work-Study and unspecified assistantships also available. Support available to part-time students. Financial award application deadline: 3/1; financial award applicants required to submit FAFSA. *Faculty research:* Historic European tapestry, computerized weaving. Total annual research expenditures: $4,000. *Unit head:* Memory Holloway, Director, 508-999-8010, E-mail: mholloway@umassd.edu. *Application contact:* Elan Turcotte-Shamski, Graduate Admissions Officer, 508-999-8604, Fax: 508-999-8183, E-mail: graduate@umassd.edu.

University of Minnesota, Twin Cities Campus, Graduate School, College of Design, Department of Design, Housing, and Apparel, Minneapolis, MN 55455-0213. Offers apparel (MA, MS, PhD); design communication (MA, MS, PhD); housing studies (MA, MS, PhD, Postbaccalaureate Certificate); interactive design (MFA); interior design (MA, MS, PhD). Part-time programs available. *Degree requirements:* For master's and Postbaccalaureate Certificate, comprehensive exam, thesis (for some programs); for doctorate, comprehensive exam, thesis/dissertation. *Entrance requirements:* For master's, GRE General Test, minimum GPA of 3.0 (preferred), portfolio, 3 letters of recommendation; for doctorate, GRE General Test, minimum GPA of 3.0 (preferred), portfolio, 3 letters of recommendation, writing sample; for Postbaccalaureate Certificate, GRE General Test, minimum GPA of 3.0 (preferred). Additional exam requirements/recommendations for international students: Required—TOEFL (minimum score 550 paper-based; 213 computer-based; 79 iBT). Electronic applications accepted. *Faculty research:* Housing policy and community development; consumer behavior; interactive design; design history; social, cultural, and behavioral issues related to designed environments.

The University of North Carolina at Greensboro, Graduate School, School of Human Environmental Sciences, Department of Consumer, Apparel, and Retail Studies, Greensboro, NC 27412-5001. Offers MS, PhD. *Degree requirements:* For master's, one foreign language; for doctorate, one foreign language, thesis/dissertation. *Entrance requirements:* For master's and doctorate, GRE General Test. Additional exam requirements/recommendations for international students: Required—TOEFL. Electronic applications accepted. *Faculty research:* Impact of phosphate removal, protective clothing for pesticide workers, fabric hand: subjective and objective measurements.

ArtCenter

ART CENTER COLLEGE OF DESIGN

Programs of Study

Art Center's graduate programs provide a framework in which students can pursue advanced studies in media design, broadcast cinema (film), art, and industrial design. The graduate programs enable students to broaden their practical, conceptual, and analytical skills by providing a balance between professional and theoretical approaches to art and design practice.

Every program has its own graduate seminar, which brings artists, designers, and critics to the campus regularly. Each program's curriculum allows students to follow their own interests and direction, yet is designed to ensure that every student covers comprehensive course material and receives critical feedback. In addition to regular meetings with graduate faculty members, students benefit from interaction with visiting artists and designers.

Broadcast cinema, Art Center's M.F.A. program for filmmakers, is focused on the creation of works for existing, emerging, and future forms of broadcast and theatrical distribution. The traditional term "broadcast" represents the College's exploration of the vast potential of satellite distribution and "cinema" represents innovation in visual aesthetics and content. Early development of each student's individual creative identity is a priority. Students may choose to specialize in any creative leadership roles in filmmaking. The program encourages students to explore new content, forms, and methods of storytelling.

The M.F.A. program in media design is for students who are interested in exploring the future of communication in an information-saturated, media-driven world. This interdisciplinary program encourages innovation and experimentation, theoretical research, the development of technological sophistication, and individual creativity. Students work in state-of-the-art facilities under the direction of a diverse faculty of accomplished designers, technology specialists, theorists, and thought leaders, and meet regularly with visiting artists, scholars, and entrepreneurs.

An M.S. degree is offered in industrial design. This graduate program encourages students with a background in product or environmental design to expand their knowledge and expertise while emphasizing experimentation, innovation, and multidisciplinary research. Particular emphasis is placed on broadening students' intellectual grasp of design issues, using digital and written media for communication, and realizing the full potential of the creative process. The first year of the program is spent in a joint multidisciplinary project. Students work closely with a distinguished core faculty and with many visiting specialists.

The M.F.A. program in art brings together students and a varied faculty composed of internationally known artists. The size of the program—about 35 students and 7 graduate advisers—allows for intensive one-on-one dialogue while offering sufficient diversity to generate critical exchange and controversy. The program emphasizes both making and theorizing the art object and provides studios for independent work as well as classes in theory and technique.

Research Facilities

The James Lemont Fogg Memorial Library contains 92,000 volumes of books and periodicals, and 9,000 videotapes and DVDs of rare features, animation, documentaries, advertising, computer graphics, and instructional programs. A photo reference collection contains more than 90,000 pictures. The Rare Book Room houses limited and signed editions, portfolios, and other materials. Subscriptions are maintained for more than 400 magazines, and online subscriptions provide access to thousands of magazine articles and images. A CD-ROM workstation can be used to view a collection of more than 350 interactive CD-ROMs. Occidental College's library of more than 1 million volumes serves as another resource for Art Center students.

Art Center maintains state-of-the-art studios and shops, including a rapid-modeling machine that creates three-dimensional prototype models. Archetype Press, a 3,000-square-foot facility, houses fourteen presses and 2,400 drawers of rare type from American and European foundries. Students have access to a wide range of interactive multimedia and digital resources for exploring and refining their ideas, including sixty Silicon Graphics workstations, 140 Apple Macintosh computers, twelve Compaq Professional NT workstations, and the latest design software available.

In addition, the Wind Tunnel facility at Art Center's South Campus includes the New Ecology of Things (N.E.T.) research lab, dedicated to exploring a future world of interactive networked technologies. The lab includes a collection of experimental media and technologies, including custom hardware and software created by the media design faculty.

Financial Aid

Graduate students may apply for scholarships by meeting priority deadlines. Scholarships are awarded by a graduate scholarship committee. Candidates must demonstrate financial need and present an exceptional portfolio of work for scholarship consideration. Grants and loans, including the California Graduate Fellowship and FFELP Loan Program, are available. Teaching assistantships are also available.

Cost of Study

The cost of tuition for 2010 is $16,737 per fifteen-week semester.

Living and Housing Costs

The College does not currently maintain dormitories. A wide variety of housing is available in Pasadena and neighboring communities. The average cost of rent and food per semester is approximately $5000.

Student Group

Approximately 130 graduate students, of whom 60 percent are men and 40 percent are women, are enrolled in the College.

Student Outcomes

Most students pursue careers as practicing artists and designers within their professions.

Location

Art Center is located in Pasadena, California, a residential community near Los Angeles. With two campuses, one in a striking glass and steel facility on the hillsides of Pasadena and the other near old town Pasadena, the College is a short distance from greater Los Angeles. Students benefit from their proximity to art galleries, advertising and design agencies, and the entertainment industry.

The College

A private, nonprofit institution, Art Center College of Design was founded in 1930 with the purpose of educating students for distinguished careers in the visual arts professions. The total enrollment, including undergraduates, is 1,600. Eighteen percent of students are international and represent forty-seven different countries. The College is accredited by WASC and NASAD.

Applying

Applicants for the art program may apply for entry in any of the three scheduled terms each year: fall, spring, or summer. Applications are accepted on a rolling admissions basis, with consideration given as long as space is available in a class. Spaces in most graduate programs are extremely limited and may require application a number of semesters in advance. Media design and industrial design applicants may apply only for the fall semester, and the application deadline for these programs is February 1. Broadcast cinema students start in the fall only and applications are reviewed on a rolling basis. The art program is six semesters in length and the broadcast cinema is four semesters in length. The media design program offers a two- and three-year option. Applicants may consult the Admissions Office about the status of any entering class.

Correspondence and Information

Admissions Office
Art Center College of Design
1700 Lida Street
Pasadena, California 91103

Phone: 626-396-2373
Fax: 626-795-0578
E-mail: admissions@artcenter.edu
Web site: http://www.artcenter.edu

Art Center College of Design

THE FACULTY

The faculty members are core faculty advisers for graduate programs. Graduate students have access to a wide variety of classes and additional faculty members at Art Center.

Media Design Program

Anne Burdick, Chair; M.F.A., California Institute of the Arts. Designer, writer, editor. Work is included in the Museum of Modern Art in New York and the San Francisco Museum of Modern Art. Publications include *Eye, I.D., Idea, Adobe Think Tank,* and *Emigre* magazines. Awards include the Leipzig Award (Most Beautiful Book in the World), AIGA 50 Books/50 Covers, I.D. Interactive Design Annual, Webby Award, ACD 100, and others. Projects include electronic corpora and text-dictionaries with the Austrian Academy of Sciences, experimental fiction at the Walker Art Center's Gallery 9, and books of literary/media criticism by authors such as Marshall McLuhan and N. Katherine Hayles. Burdick has been the design editor of *Electronic Book Review* since 1995.

Sean Donahue, M.F.A., Art Center College of Design. Principal of ResearchCenteredDesign, a Los Angeles–based design practice. His practice consists of professional commissions, self-initiated research, design advocacy, education, and publishing. Donahue has lectured and published internationally at RISD, RCA, and North Carolina State University, where he was also the 2004 Designer-in-Residence. Published research: the University of Cambridge, Princeton Architectural Press, MIT Press, and *I.D.* magazine.

Tim Durfee, M.Arch., Yale. He is a partner of the Los Angeles firm of Durfee | Regn which has created—in collaboration with other designers—award-winning exhibitions for LACMA, the Hammer, Huntington Library, Pacific Design Center, UCLA, the Indianapolis Museum of Art, the International Center for Photography in New York, and a permanent exhibition for Target Corporation's headquarters in Minneapolis. He also collaborates with artists, including Ultraworld at the Centre Pompidou's L'ARC in Paris with Doug Aitken in 2005. He has developed interface prototypes and production designs for SF MOMA and LAUNCH and an award-winning Web site for LACMA.

Ben Hooker, M.A., B.Sc., Royal College of Art (London). Collaborates with architects, industrial designers, and computer scientists working in the field of human-computer interaction, resulting in computer-generated data landscapes merging with real, physical spaces. He is also a member of the Visiting Faculty at Intel's Research Lab in Berkeley. Clients include Shona Kitchen; San Jose International Airport, and projects for Vitra Design Museum and Art Center College of Design.

Philip Van Allen, B.A., California, Santa Cruz. Interaction designer/producer/technologist for experimental information and entertainment systems with a research focus on interactive objects and spaces, productive interaction (productiveinteraction.com) and interactive audio. Background in music recording and software development. Principal: Commotion New Media. Clients: Infiniti, George P. Johnson, Interval Research, Philips, Yahoo/Launch Media, Virgin Interactive Entertainment, Art Center College of Design, Nestlé, U2, The Germs. Teacher: ACCD, Santa Monica College, McGill University. Interactive art collaborations: Yoko Ono, Kim Abeles. Exhibitions: Nucleus Gallery, SIGGRAPH Virtual Lounge. Publications: Founded mid-nineties magazine ArtCommotion.com, DIS 2004 ACM conference proceedings, USC Annenberg Online Journalism Review.

Industrial Design Program

Andrew Ogden, Chair; B.S., Art Center College of Design. Vice president and executive designer, Walt Disney Imagineering; designer, Honda R&D North America.

Mark Andersen, B.S., Art Center College of Design. Designer; founder/owner, ZoomOutDesign. Clients: Zaca Inc. and BioControl Inc. Exhibitions: *Brewery Art Walk 2005–06,* Los Angeles. Awards: IDSA silver for Zaca SpaceCab, IDSA bronze for Hycore Biomedical accuPINCH, and honorable mention, "Why Design?", Art Center faculty grant for 3-D digital modeling research.

Katherine Bennett, B.S.I.D., Philadelphia College of Art. Design research, product development, information architecture, strategic planning. Clients: Johnson Controls International, Avery Dennison. Formerly with Donald Chadwick Associates, Hauser, Saul Bass, Henry Dreyfuss Associates. Projects: contract and residential furniture, consumer products, equipment and instrumentation, communications. Publications (periodicals): *Los Angeles Times, Innovation, Modern Photography.*

Richard Keyes, B.F.A., Art Center College of Design. Owner, Keyes Design; former designer, Steven Jacobs, Fulton & Green, the Graphics Studio. Clients: Warner Brothers Records, Atlantic Richfield, Guess? Jeans, Convergent Technologies, His Holiness the Dalai Lama, Empire Berol (color consulting), Homebody, Los Angeles Housing Department, Parson's Engineering (design consultant). Former instructor: California State University, Los Angeles; Los Angeles Valley College; UCLA Extension.

Steven Montgomery, B.A., Michigan State. Industrial designer; principal, BioDesign, specializing in medical and consumer product design; former project manager for S. G. Hauser Associates, Inc.; designer, Huck & Studer Design, KMH Associates. Clients: Johnson & Johnson, Baxter Healthcare Corporation, Becton Dickinson, Omron Healthcare, Cepheid, Panasonic, Technicolor, Boeing/Teague, Bissell, Thomson Electronics, Reebok, Acer, Whirlpool, Hyundai, Honda R&D, Goldstar, Caterpillar, DaimlerChrysler, Nokia, Microsoft, Disney. Awards: IDSA.

Geoff Wardle, M.Des., Royal College of Art (London). Corporate design experience: British Leyland, Chrysler Europe, Saab, Ford Asia Pacific. Design consultant: Tatra, Czech Republic; TVS-Suzuki, India. Former chair of Transportation Design, Art Center Europe.

Broadcast Cinema Program

Robert W. Peterson, Chair; B.F.A., Art Center College of Design. Director/Director of Photography. Production design, visual effects design, commercials, music videos, documentary films, television, theater. Clients: 20th Century Fox, Paramount, Columbia, Universal, United Artists. Awards: Clio, Belding, Council for Advancement of Secondary Education, New York Film Festival.

Jean-Pierre Geuens, Ph.D., USC. Professor of Cinema, Los Angeles City College. Author: *Film Production Theory.* Publications: *Film Quarterly, Film Criticism, Spectator, LA/CA Journal.*

John Hartzog, Ph.D., USC. Director, Learning Resource Center, California State University, Northridge. Publications: *Film Quarterly, Magill Cinema Annual, Academe.*

Victoria Hochberg, B.A., Antioch College. Fulbright Fellowship. Writer/director: feature films, television, documentaries, music videos. Television: *Sex and the City, Ghost Whisperer, Kitchen Confidential, Reaper.* Feature writer: *The Love of Good Women,* performed with the San Francisco Mime Troupe, Pantomime Theatre of New York. Awards: two Emmy awards for writing and directing, four nominations and two Directors Guild of America awards, Writers Guild of America Award nomination. Member: National Board of the Directors Guild of America, including the Special Projects and Creative Rights Committees.

Eric Sherman, B.A., Yale. Director, cinematographer, producer: *Pep Squad, Mystic Nights & Pirate Fights, After Freedom.* President, Film Transform. Author: *The Director's Event, Directing The Film, Frame by Frame, Selling Your Film, Home Entertainment–The Ultimate Movie Marketplace.* Publications: *Moviemaker.* Awards: Montreal Film Festival, Audience Award, Methodfest *(After Freedom),* New York, Bilbao, Columbus Film Festivals, Peabody Broadcasting Award. Member: Board of Trustees, American Cinematheque; Board of Directors, Film Forum.

Fine Art Program

Jeremy Gilbert-Rolfe, Chair; M.F.A., Florida State. Paintings exhibited nationally and internationally since 1971. Major publications include *Immanence and Contradiction: Recent Essays on the Artistic Device* and *Beyond Piety: Critical Essays on the Visual Arts, 1986–1993.* Recipient, John Simon Guggenheim Memorial Fellowship and the Frank Jewett Mather Award for distinction in art or architectural criticism.

Lita Albuquerque, B.A., UCLA. In the 1970s and 1980s, Albuquerque was a seminal part of the California Light and Space movement and a pioneer in Process Art, Environmental Art, and Earth Art. In recent years, she completed an installation on the pyramids in Egypt called Sol Star. She is currently preparing for a global project at the North and South Poles.

Walead Beshty, M.F.A., Yale. Exhibitions: Hirschhorn Museum, Washington D.C.; Museum of Modern Art, New York; The Tate Britain, U.K.; Armand Hammer Museum of Art, Los Angeles; Whitney Museum of American Art, New York; Wallspace, New York. Faculty: Art Institute of Chicago, Bard College, Roski Graduate School of Fine Arts–UCLA, CalArts.

Stan Douglas, M.F.A., Emily Carr Institute. Exhibitions: Vancouver Art Gallery; Waterloo Art Gallery, Ontario; Joslyn Art Museum, Omaha; The Art Institute of Chicago; Institute of Contemporary Arts, London; Galerie Nationale du Jeu de Paume, Paris. Faculty: Professor of Photography and Digital Media, Universität der Künste, Berlin, 2004–06.

Diana Maria Thater, M.F.A., Art Center College of Design. Exhibitions: Dia Center for the Arts, the Museum of Modern Art, the Saint Louis Art Museum, the Renaissance Society at the University of Chicago, Walker Center for the Arts, Portland Art Museum, Vienna Secession, the Basel Kunsthalle, and the Salzburger Kunstverein, among many others. Grants: NEA and the Etants-Donnes Foundation, Guggenheim Fellowship, 2005–06.

Annette Weisser, M.A., Academy of Media Arts (Cologne). Solo exhibitions include *Annette Weisser/Ingo Vetter: Works 1996–2006,* Westphalian State Museum of Art and Culture, Munster (2006); *NameGame,* Hall for Art, Luneburg (2003); *NameGame,* platform ev, Berlin and Forum Citypark, , Graz (2002); *What counts is to absorb all the antitheses at once, rather than resolving them,* Bethany Arthouse, Berlin (1998); *Tableau,* Current Art Society, Munster (1998).

Located on 175 wooded acres in Pasadena, Hillside Campus has been home to Art Center since 1976. The main building is a dramatic postmodern steel-and-glass bridge structure spanning an arroyo in the San Raphael Hills, just above the Rose Bowl.

FASHION INSTITUTE OF TECHNOLOGY

State University of New York

School of Graduate Studies

Programs of Study

The Fashion Institute of Technology (FIT), a State University of New York (SUNY) college of art and design, business, and technology, is home to a mix of innovative achievers, creative thinkers, and industry pioneers. FIT fosters interdisciplinary initiatives, advances research, and provides access to an international network of professionals. With selective admissions and a reputation for excellence, FIT offers its diverse student body access to world-class faculty, dynamic and relevant curricula, and a superior education at an affordable cost. It offers seven programs of graduate study leading to the Master of Arts (M.A.), Master of Fine Arts (M.F.A.), and Master of Professional Studies (M.P.S.) degrees. The programs in Art Market: Principles and Practices; Exhibition Design; Fashion and Textile Studies: History, Theory, Museum Practice; and Sustainable Interior Environments lead to the M.A. degree. The Illustration program leads to the M.F.A. degree. The M.P.S. degree programs are Cosmetics and Fragrance Marketing and Management, and Global Fashion Management.

Art Market: Principles and Practices is a 48-credit, full- or part-time M.A. program preparing students for careers in the business, collection, and exhibition of art. The curriculum includes art history, writing for the art market, gallery design and operation, business practices, computer technology for the art world, marketing, valuation and appraisal, exhibition theory, and art law and professional ethics. Students are required to complete a relevant internship and to research and write a master's qualifying paper. Graduating students must also complete a practicum in which they assemble a group show from concept to execution at a New York City gallery.

Cosmetics and Fragrance Marketing and Management is a 36-credit, part-time M.P.S. program providing industry professionals with high-level management skills and an interdisciplinary, global perspective. The curriculum is designed to encompass three skill sets that leaders in the cosmetics and fragrance industries have identified as crucial to managerial success: core business skills such as management, corporate finance, international business, and management communication; marketing skills such as advanced marketing theory, marketing communications, and market research and strategy; and technical and creative competencies such as cosmetics and fragrance product knowledge, retail and creative management, and an intellectual foundation in beauty and fashion culture. A global component sends students abroad for an intensive week of meetings with industry leaders. The program culminates in a capstone seminar.

The 36-credit, full-time Exhibition Design M.A. program prepares students for careers in the exhibition design and visual display production industry. The studio-driven, one-year course of study focuses on the designer's role within the exhibition team, with emphasis on the development of both design and fabrication skills. Studio projects—such as museum and gallery design, traveling exhibits, and corporate collections—are linked to graphic, lighting, and presentation courses. All graduating students complete an independent, theme-driven design project. Students are also required to complete a related internship.

The 48-credit, full- or part-time Fashion and Textile Studies: History, Theory, Museum Practice M.A. program prepares students for professional curatorial, conservation, education, and other scholarly careers that focus on historic clothing, accessories, textiles, and related materials. The curriculum incorporates conservation skills, current collections management methods, exhibition techniques, art historical methodologies, material culture studies, and gender studies and utilizes the resources of The Museum at FIT, one of the world's largest collections of clothing, textiles, and accessories. Students may elect either a conservation or curatorial emphasis; they may also select up to two independent study courses with an appropriate focus on their chosen specialization. All students are required to complete an internship in the field, write a master's qualifying paper based on original research, and take an active role in a yearlong course culminating in a professional exhibition.

Global Fashion Management is a 36-credit, full-time M.P.S. program offered in collaboration with Hong Kong Polytechnic University in Hong Kong and the Institut Français de la Mode in Paris, preparing current fashion executives for senior managerial positions. The course of study is completed in a three-semester period and includes one intensive seminar course taught in each of the three participating institutions. The curriculum includes courses in production management and the supply chain, global marketing and fashion brand management, current technologies in the fashion industry, international team management, international culture and business, challenges to profitability, and politics and world trade.

The 60-credit evening and weekend Illustration M.F.A. program is designed for working professionals seeking advanced study to further develop their skills as master illustrators. The program focuses on high-level techniques, new media applications, and illustration business practices. The curriculum encompasses digital and traditional studio methods, entrepreneurial research and writing, and opportunities in new and emerging markets. The program features assignments that mirror marketplace demands and specifications, regular guest lecturers, a visit to West Coast film and entertainment studios, and regular off-campus involvement in New York City's art and design world. Students complete a visual thesis project and an independently researched and written master's thesis.

Sustainable Interior Environments is a 36-credit, two-year, part-time evening and weekend M.A. program for established professionals, including practicing interior designers, architects, facilities planners, and managers. The program's intensive, hands-on curriculum focuses on the principles and theories of sustainable design as they apply to the built environment. Through experiential learning, specialized science courses, case studies, and research, students acquire a deep understanding of human psychological, physiological, and ergonomic needs, as well as information about toxic substances, pollution prevention, environmental systems, energy efficiency, and resource conservation. A graduate seminar guides students toward their research-oriented capstone project.

Research Facilities

The School of Graduate Studies is primarily located in the campus's Shirley Goodman Resource Center, which also houses the Gladys Marcus Library and The Museum at FIT. School of Graduate Studies facilities include conference rooms; a fully equipped conservation laboratory; a multipurpose laboratory for conservation projects and the dressing of mannequins; storage facilities for costume and textile materials; a graduate student lounge with computer and printer access; a graduate student library reading room with computers, reference materials, and copies of past classes' qualifying and thesis papers; specialized wireless classrooms; and classrooms equipped with model stands, easels, and drafting tables.

The Gladys Marcus Library houses more than 300,000 volumes of print, nonprint, and digital resources. Specialized holdings include industry reference materials, manufacturers' catalogues, original fashion sketches and scrapbooks, portfolios of plates, photographs, and sample books. The FIT Digital Library provides access to over 90 searchable online databases.

The Museum at FIT houses one of the world's most important collections of clothing and textiles and is the only museum in New York City dedicated to the art of fashion. The permanent collection encompasses more than 50,000 garments and accessories dating from the eighteenth century, with particular strength in twentieth-century fashion, as well as 30,000 textiles and 300,000 textile swatches. Each year, nearly 100,000 visitors are drawn to the museum's award-winning exhibitions and public programs.

Financial Aid

FIT directly administers its institutional grants and scholarships. Federal funding administered by the college may include Federal Supplemental Educational Opportunity Grants, Federal Perkins Loans, federally subsidized and unsubsidized loans for students and parents, and the Federal Work-Study Program. New York State residents who meet state guidelines for eligibility may also receive Educational Opportunity Program funds. Priority for institutionally administered funds is given to students enrolled and designated as full-time.

Cost of Study

Tuition for New York State residents is $4099 per semester, or $342 per credit. Out-of-state residents' tuition is $6972 per semester, or $582 per credit. Tuition and fees are subject to change at the discretion of FIT's Board of Trustees. Additional expenses—for class materials, textbooks, and travel—may apply and vary per program.

Living and Housing Costs

Residence facilities are available to graduate students. Traditional residence hall accommodations (including meal plan) cost from $5685 to $5850 per semester. Apartment-style housing options (not including meal plan) cost from $4825 to $8760 per semester.

Student Group

Enrollment in the School of Graduate Studies is approximately 200 students per academic year, allowing considerable individualized advisement. Students come to FIT from throughout the country and around the world.

Student Outcomes

Art Market: Principles and Practices graduates find employment as art gallery directors, public art program directors, art consultants for private and corporate collections, art foundation administrators, museum marketing and development directors, independent curators, auction house department heads, and artists' representatives. Students in the Cosmetics and Fragrance Marketing and Management and Global Fashion Management programs maintain full-time employment in the industry while working toward their degree, which provides the basis for advancement to positions of upper-level managerial responsibility. Graduates of the Exhibition Design program find employment with architectural and exhibition design firms, museums, historic trusts, and special-events companies. Graduates of the Fashion and Textile Studies: History, Theory, Museum Practice program find positions as museum curators, research specialists, collections managers and registrars, historic house directors, museum educators, independent exhibition curators, corporate curators, fashion and textile historians, costume and textile conservators, auction house department specialists and researchers, vintage clothing and textile dealers, and consultants. Students in the Illustration program graduate with a personal vision, an entrepreneurial spirit, and the skills needed to succeed as freelance illustrators. Students in the Sustainable Interior Environments program gain highly marketable expertise that enables them to advance in their current employment, as well as assume leadership positions in the design industry, educational institutions, and research centers.

Location

FIT is connected to New York City, to students, and to careers. Located in Manhattan's Chelsea neighborhood, it places students at the heart of the advertising, visual arts, fashion, business, and communications industries. Students gain unparalleled exposure to their field through guest lectures, field trips, internships, and sponsored competitions. The location provides access to major museums, galleries, and auction houses as well as dining, entertainment, and shopping options. The campus is near subway, bus, and commuter rail lines.

Applying

Applicants to all School of Graduate Studies programs must hold a baccalaureate degree in an appropriate major from an accredited college or university, with a cumulative GPA of 3.0 or higher. International students from non-English-speaking countries are required to submit minimum TOEFL scores of 550 on the written test, 213 on the computer test, or 80 on the Internet test. Students applying to the Art Market: Principles and Practices; Fashion and Textile Studies: History, Theory, Museum Practice; and Global Fashion Management programs must submit GRE scores. Each major has additional, specialized prerequisites for admission; for detailed information, students should visit the School of Graduate Studies on FIT's Web site.

Domestic and international students use the same application when seeking admission. The deadline for completed applications with transcripts and supplemental materials is February 15 for Art Market: Principles and Practices; Exhibition Design; Fashion and Textile Studies: History, Theory, Museum Practice; Illustration; Global Fashion Management; and Sustainable Interior Environments. The deadline for Cosmetics and Fragrance Marketing and Management is March 15. After the deadline dates, applicants are considered on a rolling admissions basis. Candidates may apply online at http://www.fitnyc.edu/gradstudies.

Correspondence and Information

School of Graduate Studies
Room E315
Fashion Institute of Technology
Seventh Avenue at 27th Street
New York, New York 10001-5992

Phone: 212-217-4300
Fax: 212-217-4301
E-mail: gradinfo@fitnyc.edu
Web site: http://www.fitnyc.edu/gradstudies

Fashion Institute of Technology

THE FACULTY

Art Market: Principles and Practices
Katherine Jánszky Michaelsen, Associate Chairperson; Ph.D., Columbia.
Catherine Hannah Behrend, M.B.A., NYU; Certificate in Executive Education, INSEAD (France).
Ágnes Berecz, Ph.D., Sorbonne (Paris).
Elizabeth Grady, Ph.D., Northwestern.
Christine Helm, M.Ed., Columbia Teachers College.
John Lee, B.A., Vassar.
Sheri L. Pasquarella, B.A., Stony Brook, SUNY.
Clayton Press, Ph.D. candidate, Southern Illinois.
Lucille A. Roussin, Ph.D., Columbia; J.D., Yeshiva.
Martha Schwendener, M.A., Texas at Austin.
Beth Miller Servetar, M.F.A., Bennington.
Gayle M. Skluzacek, B.A., Barat.

Cosmetics and Fragrance Marketing and Management
Stephen Kanlian, Associate Chairperson; M.P.A., Pennsylvania.
Bruce Abramson, M.P.S., Fashion Institute of Technology; M.B.A., Fordham.
Jean Broom, M.S.W., Minnesota; M.M., Northwestern.
Dorothy C. Foster, J.D., Fordham.
Judy Galloway, A.B., Mary Baldwin.
Bradley Horowitz, M.B.A., Fordham.
Guillermo Jimenez, J.D., Berkeley.
Janice Levine, M.P.S., Fashion Institute of Technology.
Mary C. Manning, Institute of Marketing (England) and Kingston Upon Thames (England).
Mark Polson, M.P.S., Fashion Institute of Technology.
Cynthia Strite, Ph.D. candidate, Columbia Teachers College.
Mary Tumolo, former Vice President, Promotional Marketing, Lancôme, L'Oreal USA.
Pamela Vaile, M.B.A., Pace.
Karen Young, B.A., Denver.

Exhibition Design
Brenda Cowan, Associate Chairperson; M.S.Ed., Bank Street College of Education.
Norman Bleckner, B.I.D., Pratt.
Robin Drake, B.S., Pratt.
John Katimaris, M.F.A., Parsons; RA, AIA, IES, IIDA.
Lucian J. Leone, B.I.D., Pratt.
Ran Lerner, M.I.D., Domus Academy (Italy).
Scott Lundberg, M.I.D., Pratt.
Karl Matsuda, Certificate in Art, Cooper Union.
John Newman, M.A., Parsons; IES.
Michael Stiller, B.A., Bard.
Michele Y. T. Washington, M.S., Pratt.

Fashion and Textile Studies: History, Theory, Museum Practice
Denyse Montegut, Associate Chairperson; Ph.D. candidate, Delaware.
June Burns Bové, M.A., NYU.
Nancy Deihl, M.A., NYU.
Judith Eisenberg, M.A., Wichita State.
Rebecca Fifield, M.A., George Washington.
Lourdes M. Font, Ph.D., NYU.
Désirée Koslin, M.F.A., CUNY, City College; Ph.D., NYU.
Diane Maglio, M.A., Fashion Institute of Technology.
Elizabeth McMahon, Ph.D. candidate, Bard Graduate Center.
Sarah Scaturro, M.A., Fashion Institute of Technology.
Rebecca Shea, M.A., Fashion Institute of Technology.
Valerie Soll, B.A., Oregon.
Denise Stone, M.A., Fashion Institute of Technology.

Global Fashion Management
Pamela Ellsworth, Associate Chairperson; M.P.S., Fashion Institute of Technology.
Praveen K. Chaudhry, Ph.D., Pennsylvania.
Virginia Cutchin, M.B.A., CUNY, Baruch.
Tom Nastos, B.A., Fashion Institute of Technology.
Jeanette Nostra, B.S., Goddard.

Illustration
Melanie Reim, Associate Chairperson; M.F.A., Syracuse.
Daniel Abraham, A.B., Chicago, J.D., Miami (Florida).
Steve Brodner, B.F.A., Cooper Union.
Elliot Cowan, Master's Diploma, Melbourne (Australia).
Salvatore Catalano, B.A., SUNY Empire State College.
Peter Cusack, M.A., Syracuse.
Vincent DiFate, M.A., Syracuse.
Michael De Feo, Temple.
Dennis Dittrich, M.F.A., Syracuse.
Daniel Filippone, M.F.A., New York Academy of Art.
Michael Hyde, M.F.A., Columbia; Ph.D., NYU.
Amy Lemmon, Ph.D., Cincinnati.
Albert Lorenz, M.S., Columbia.
William Low, M.A., Syracuse.
Daniel Pelavin, M.F.A., Cranbrook Academy of Art.
Cheryl Phelps, B.F.A., Memphis College of Art.
Zina Saunders, Cooper Union.
Stanley Solomon, Ph.D., NYU.
Chris Spollen, B.F.A., Parsons.
Nancy Stahl, Arizona.
Murray Tinkelman, Cooper Union.
Carmile S. Zaino, B.F.A., Parsons.

Sustainable Interior Environments
Grazyna Pilatowicz, Acting Chairperson, M.A., Lublin (Poland).
Fiona Cousin, M.St., Cambridge (England).
Ronald Eligator, M.S., Yale.
John Katimaris, M.F.A., Parsons, RA, AIA, IES, IIDA.
Susan Kaplan, B.A., CUNY, Queens, B.Arch., CUNY, City College.
Arthur H. Kopelman, M.Phil., Ph.D., CUNY Graduate Center.
Karen R. Pearson, Ph.D., Washington State.
Matthew A. Postal, M.Phil., Ph.D., CUNY Graduate Center.
Nora J. Rubinstein, M.Phil., Ph.D., CUNY Graduate Center.

The faculty members listed above constitute a partial listing. Guest lecturers are not included.

Miami International University of Art & Design™

MIAMI INTERNATIONAL UNIVERSITY OF ART & DESIGN

Master's Programs

Programs of Study

Miami International University of Art & Design offers Master of Fine Arts degrees in computer animation, film, graphic design, interior design, and visual arts. A Master of Arts program is available in graphic design.

Many of the programs require students to take a course in teaching methodologies, enabling them to learn the language of the industry. In addition, students discover techniques that help them to communicate within an area of expertise. Aesthetics, planning, research, and writing are also important elements in rounding out the educational experience.

Most degrees require six quarters of study, for a total of 90 credits. Course work varies by program, and the detailed curriculum may be viewed online at http://www.artinstitutes.edu/miami.

Research Facilities

Miami International University of Art & Design is located within a 60,000-square-foot academic and administration building. The facility includes industry-related equipment, a painting and sculpture studio, a production facility, and an editing facility. There are also interior design and fashion resource rooms.

Financial Aid

Financial aid is available to those who qualify. Students who require financial assistance to attend Miami International University of Art & Design must first submit a Free Application for Federal Student Aid (FAFSA) and then meet with a financial aid officer to determine the amount of aid needed and the types of aid available.

Cost of Study

Tuition and other fees vary by graduate program and are due in full prior to matriculation for each quarter of study.

Living and Housing Costs

Students should contact the University for information on housing options and living expenses.

Student Group

Individuals enrolled in graduate programs at Miami International University of Art & Design come from a variety of backgrounds. Students (graduate and undergraduate) at the school are from out of state and across America; many also come from other countries.

Student Outcomes

The University works to foster the students' desire to maintain high levels of professionalism in their chosen careers. Special emphasis is placed on helping students to reach their personal, academic, and career goals. As part of this objective, the Office of Career Services works with students throughout their education and after graduation, offering career assessment and planning, job search assistance, and networking opportunities.

Location

Miami is a culturally rich region that celebrates events year-round, including the African-American Heritage Festival, Haitian Heritage Week, the Viva Mexico Celebration, the Israel Independence Celebration, and Asian Cultural Week. The city is home to professional sports teams, and residents enjoy the sandy beaches, international cuisine, local clubs, the historic Art Deco District, Coral Gables, and Key Biscayne. The Florida Keys, Disney World, and the Bahamas are all just a short trip away.

The University

Students are creative, competitive, and open to new ideas. The University's faculty consists of full-time and part-time professors, many of whom have advanced degrees and professional experience in their respective fields.

Student clubs and organizations include AIGA, American Society of Interior Designers (ASID), International Student Club, and Student Council.

Miami International University of Art & Design and its branch campuses, The Art Institute of Jacksonville and The Art Institute of Tampa, are accredited by the Commission on Colleges of the Southern Association of Colleges and Schools to award the master's, bachelor's, and associate degrees. Contact the Commission on Colleges at 1866 Southern Lane, Decatur, Georgia 30033-4097 or call 404-679-4500 for questions about the accreditation of Miami International University of Art & Design.

Miami International University of Art & Design is licensed by the Commission for Independent Education, Florida Department of Education. Additional information regarding this institution may be obtained by contacting the Commission at 325 West Gaines Street, Suite 1414, Tallahassee, Florida 32399-0400; phone: 888-224-6684.

Applying

Applicants are interviewed, either in person or by telephone, to explore their background and interest in program offerings. Each applicant's transcript and essay are evaluated by the Admissions Acceptance Committee, which reserves the right to request additional records of accomplishment in core academic courses. There is a $50 application fee.

International students' transcripts must be prepared in English or include a complete and official English translation. Proof of English language proficiency or enrollment in the school's English as a second language (ESL) course is required for all prospective international students.

To obtain an application, make arrangements for an interview, or tour the school, prospective students should contact the University at the address listed in this description.

Correspondence and Information

Miami International University of Art & Design
1501 Biscayne Boulevard, Suite 100
Miami, Florida 33132-1418
Phone: 305-428-5700
800-225-9023 (toll-free)
Fax: 305-374-5933
Web site: http://www.artinstitutes.edu/miami

Miami International University of Art & Design

THE FACULTY AND THEIR RESEARCH

At Miami International University of Art & Design, students find an experienced faculty focused on providing students with the skills needed for the marketplace. Many faculty members are researchers and practitioners in their fields, who bring their experience into the classroom. These members are qualified to prepare students to face the challenges of the real world. The faculty members of the school are committed to the personal and professional development of their students.

The Art Institute of Atlanta; The Art Institute of Atlanta–Decatur[1]; The Art Institute of Austin[2]; The Art Institute of California–Hollywood; The Art Institute of California–Inland Empire; The Art Institute of California–Los Angeles; The Art Institute of California–Orange County; The Art Institute of California–Sacramento; The Art Institute of California–San Diego; The Art Institute of California–San Francisco; The Art Institute of California–Sunnyvale; The Art Institute of Charleston[1]; The Art Institute of Charlotte; The Art Institute of Colorado; The Art Institute of Dallas; The Art Institute of Fort Lauderdale; The Art Institute of Fort Worth[3]; The Art Institute of Houston; The Art Institute of Houston–North[2]; The Art Institute of Indianapolis[4]; The Art Institute of Jacksonville[5]; The Art Institute of Las Vegas; The Art Institute of Michigan; The Art Institute of New York City; The Art Institute of Ohio–Cincinnati[6]; The Art Institute of Philadelphia; The Art Institute of Phoenix; The Art Institute of Pittsburgh; The Art Institute of Portland; The Art Institute of Raleigh–Durham; The Art Institute of Salt Lake City; The Art Institute of Seattle; The Art Institute of Tampa[5]; The Art Institute of Tennessee–Nashville[1,7]; The Art Institute of Tucson; The Art Institute of Vancouver; The Art Institute of Virginia Beach[1,8]; The Art Institute of Washington[1,8]; The Art Institute of Washington–Northern Virginia[1,8]; The Art Institute of York–Pennsylvania; The Art Institutes International–Kansas City; The Art Institutes International Minnesota; The Illinois Institute of Art–Chicago; The Illinois Institute of Art–Schaumburg; Miami International University of Art & Design; The New England Institute of Art.

[1]A branch of The Art Institute of Atlanta

[2]A branch of The Art Institute of Houston

[3]A branch of The Art Institute of Dallas

[4]The Art Institute of Indianapolis is regulated by the Indiana Commission on Proprietary Education, 302 West Washington Street, Room E201, Indianapolis, Indiana 46204, AC-0080

[5]A branch of Miami International University of Art & Design

[6]The Art Institute of Ohio–Cincinnati, 8845 Governors Hill Drive, Suite 100, Cincinnati, Ohio 45249-3317, OH Reg. #04-01-1698B

[7]The Art Institute of Tennessee–Nashville is authorized for operation as a postsecondary educational institution by the Tennessee Higher Education Commission.

[8]Certified by the State Council of Higher Education to operate in Virginia.

PRATT INSTITUTE

School of Art and Design

Programs of Study

Pratt has been educating professionals for productive careers in the fields of art and design since its founding in 1887. Pratt's School of Art and Design, one of the largest of its kind, offers an outstanding professional art and design education taught by a faculty of working professionals who bring high standards and current practices to the classroom. Faculty members have received more than eighteen Tiffany, Fulbright, and Guggenheim awards as well as other prestigious professional awards. Pratt's graduate interior design program was ranked first nationally by *DesignIntelligence* in 2010; graduate industrial design was ranked fifth. *U.S. News and World Report* ranked Pratt's interior design program first in the country; graduate fine art was ranked fifteenth, and industrial design was ranked fourth.

Pratt offers master's degrees in a variety of programs, including Master of Fine Arts in digital arts, history of art and design, or studio arts (new forms–nontraditional investigations, painting and drawing, photography, printmaking, sculpture); Master of Science in art and design education (teacher certification), communications and package design, dance/movement therapy, history of art and design, or interior design; Master of Industrial Design; and Master of Professional Studies in art therapy, art therapy–special education, arts and cultural management, or design management. A postbaccalaureate New York State certification program for the teaching of art in grades pre-K–12 is available for fine arts graduate students. Art therapy majors electing a special education concentration are eligible for provisional New York State teaching certification. Pratt also offers a dual degree in fine arts and library and information science, a dual degree in art history and library science, and a dual degree in digital arts and library science as well as various certificates for holders of the M.S. in library science including museum studies, archives, and library and information studies.

Graduates of Pratt's design programs have the competitive edge needed to obtain top administrative and creative positions in design studios, businesses, various industries, and arts organizations; graduates of the digital arts program may also work in interactive media or computer animation. Art and design education graduates are prepared to pursue teaching careers in pre-K–12 schools, museums and cultural institutions, or colleges. Graduates of the creative arts therapy program work in psychiatric, medical rehabilitation, geriatric and family therapy, school, substance abuse, and child-life settings. They also learn to work with a variety of patient populations, including patients with eating disorders and the homeless.

All graduate art and design curricula include supportive course work in the humanities. Students can choose from a wide array of course offerings, including art and design history, comparative literature, philosophy, foreign languages, and social sciences. The graduate programs require the completion of 34 to 68 credits (75 credits for the M.S./M.F.A. dual-degree program) and last from 2 to 3 years, depending on the curriculum and the number of prerequisites that have not been met at the time of admission. For the granting of degrees, all of the graduate programs require the submission of a thesis or a comparable effort. For the M.F.A., an exhibition and supporting corollary statement are required. Candidates for the M.S. and the M.I.D. degrees must present a thesis project that demonstrates a meaningful contribution to design and documents the supportive research that informs all phases of design and construction. For the M.P.S. in art therapy and the M.S. in dance/movement therapy, the thesis project may involve research, an extended case study, the development of a project implementing innovative techniques in therapy, or the opportunity to publish an article. For the M.P.S. in design management, the thesis project is the preparation of a business case study.

Research Facilities

The Pratt Library contains 186,589 bound volumes, serial backfiles, and other material (including government documents); 251,603 audiovisual materials; and 3,996 microforms and subscribes to 925 periodicals.

Pratt maintains numerous studios, shops, and technical facilities for work in all media as well as state-of-the-art computer facilities. Computer graphics labs include state-of-the-art Macintosh, PC/NT, and UNIX operating systems as well as digital video and audio systems. Pratt also has extensive gallery space for exhibitions.

Financial Aid

Financial aid awards are offered through a variety of institutional, state, and federally funded programs. These include Graduate Scholarships awarded by departments to incoming students on the basis of merit, endowed and restricted scholarships for continuing students, Federal Perkins Loan and Federal Work-Study Programs, the Tuition Assistance Program of New York State, and Pratt loans and student help. Assistantships are awarded on a competitive basis to continuing students in all departments. Special alumni-sponsored fellowships are also available.

Cost of Study

Graduate tuition for 2010–11 is $22,734 per year (18 credits, $1263 per credit) and student fees are $1280 per year. The cost of books and supplies varies widely, depending on the program in which the student is enrolled. Updated cost information is available at http://www.pratt.edu/costs_and_budgeting.

Living and Housing Costs

Campus housing continues to be expanded to meet students' needs and is available for single students on a first-come, first-served basis. Housing costs average $16,808 per academic year. Pratt offers limited graduate student housing two blocks away from the campus. There is a plentiful supply of moderately priced rentals in the immediate area and in adjacent neighborhoods for married students seeking housing and for those students choosing to reside off campus.

Student Group

In educating more than four generations of students to be creative, technically skilled, and adaptable professionals, Pratt has gained an international reputation that attracts more than 4,700 undergraduate and graduate students annually from forty-nine states and over seventy countries.

Location

Pratt Institute's 25-acre, parklike main campus is situated among the turn-of-the-century mansions, Victorian brownstones, and wide, tree-lined boulevards of Clinton Hill, one of Brooklyn's landmark-designated historic neighborhoods. Midtown Manhattan, the heart of New York City, is only 25 minutes away by subway and offers students a vast array of professional, cultural, and recreational opportunities. Pratt also maintains a satellite facility in Manhattan's Chelsea district. Pratt Manhattan houses the Institute's graduate arts and cultural management, communications/packaging design, design management, facilities management, historic preservation, library and information science, and urban design; it also offers Associate of Occupational Studies (A.O.S.) and Associate of Applied Science (A.A.S.) degree programs.

The Institute

A private, nonsectarian institute of higher education, Pratt Institute was founded by the industrialist and philanthropist Charles Pratt. Changing with the needs and requirements of the professional world for which it prepares its graduates, Pratt today educates 2,998 undergraduate and 1,709 graduate students for careers in art and design, architecture, and library and information science.

Applying

The deadline for applications and all supporting materials, including portfolio, is January 5. Applicants should include everything in one package, including recommendations in sealed envelopes with the reference's signature across the flap. Early submission of applications with all necessary credentials is highly desirable. For applicants who intend to file for financial aid, applications and all supporting documents should be received no later than January 5 for the fall semester and October 1 for the spring semester. Applications received after these dates are considered if openings exist in a particular program.

Correspondence and Information

Graduate Admissions Office
Pratt Institute
200 Willoughby Avenue
Brooklyn, New York 11205

Phone: 718-636-3514
800-331-0834 (toll-free)
Fax: 718-399-4242
E-mail: admissions@pratt.edu
Web site: http://www.pratt.edu
http://www.pratt.edu/admiss/request (to request information)

Pratt Institute

THE FACULTY

Concetta Stewart, Dean; Ph.D., Rutgers.

Art and Design Education
Amy Brook Snider, Chair; Ph.D., NYU. Lisa Baumwell, Associate Professor; Ph.D., NYU. Lisa Capone; Adjunct Instructor; M.F.A., Pratt. Nancy Doyle, Visiting Instructor; M.S., CUNY, Hunter. Ascha Kells Drake, Visiting Instructor; M.F.A., Cranbrook Academy of Art. Sandra Edmonds, Adjunct Assistant Professor; Ph.D., Columbia. Mary Elmer-Dewitt, Adjunct Instructor; M.S., Pratt. Shari Fischberg (Lederman), Visiting Professor; Ph.D., Columbia. Graham Guerra, Visiting Instructor; M.F.A., Yale. Miki Iwamura, Visiting Instructor; B.F.A., Rhode Island School of Design. McKendree Key, Visiting Instructor; B.F.A., Colorado College. Heather Lewis, Assistant Professor; Ph.D., NYU. Josh Millis, Visiting Instructor; M.F.A., Art Institute of Chicago. Kristina Lamour Sansone, Visiting Professor; M.F.A., Yale. Theodora Skipitares, Assistant Professor; M.F.A., NYU. Melinda Wax, Visiting Assistant Professor; M.S., Pratt. Aileen Wilson, Associate Professor; Ed.M., Columbia.

Arts and Cultural Management
Mary McBride, Chair; Ph.D., NYU. Monica Shay, Assistant Professor; M.P.S., Regis University (Colorado). Sally Block, Visiting Assistant Professor. Laurie Cumbo, Visiting Assistant Professor; M.A., NYU. Michele Ferenz, Visiting Assistant Professor; M.A., Harvard. Young Hah, Visiting Assistant Professor. Radiah Harper, Visiting Assistant Professor; M.S., Bank Street College of Education. Jeffrey Klein, Visiting Assistant Professor. Bonita Kolb, Visiting Assistant Professor; Ph.D., Golden Gate. Sheila McDaniel, Visiting Assistant Professor. Elissa Moorhead, Visiting Assistant Professor. Mario Moorhead, Visiting Assistant Professor. Susan Schear, Visiting Assistant Professor. Vida Schreibman, Visiting Associate Professor; M.A., NYU. Jennifer Scott, Visiting Assistant Professor; M.A., Michigan–Dearborn. Christopher Shrum, Visiting Assistant Professor; M.A.; NYU. Denise Tahara, Visiting Assistant Professor; Ph.D., NYU. Jacqueline Tarry, Visiting Assistant Professor. Yolanda Trincere, Visiting Assistant Professor; Ph.D., NYU.

Communications/Package Design
Jeff Bellantoni, Chair; M.F.A., Virginia Commonwealth. Michelle Hinebrook, Assistant Chair and Adjunct Instructor; M.F.A., Cranbrook Academy of Art. Chava Ben-Amos, Professor; B.A., Bezalel Art Academy (Jerusalem, Israel). Warren Bernard, Adjunct Assistant Instructor; M.S., Pratt. Andrew Brenits, Visiting Assistant Professor; M.P.S., Pratt. Jean Brennan, Adjunct Assistant Professor; M.S., Pratt. Steve Burnett, Visiting Associate Professor; M.F.A., Pratt. Tom Delaney, Visiting Instructor. Antonio Dispigna, Professor; M.S., Pratt. Tom Dolle, Adjunct Professor; B.F.A., Rhode Island School of Design. Kevin Gatta, Professor; M.S., Pratt. Bob Gill, Adjunct Associate Professor. J. Roger Guilfoyle, Adjunct Professor; B.A., Creighton. J. Graham Hanson, Adjunct Associate Professor; B.F.A., Iowa State. William Hilson, Adjunct Professor. Milton Kass, Visiting Assistant Professor; B.I.D., Pratt. Alvin Katz, Visiting Associate Professor. Saima Kazmi, Visiting Instructor; M.S., Pratt. Kimberly Kiser, Visiting Instructor; M.S., Pratt. Tom Klinkowstein, Adjunct Professor; M.S., Syracuse. Gusty Lange, Adjunct Associate Professor; M.P.S., Pratt. Eunsun Lee, Adjunct Assistant Professor; M.S., Pratt. Alex Liebergesell, Adjunct Assistant Professor; M.F.A., Yale. Marilyn Lyons, Adjunct Associate Professor. Sandie Maxa, Visiting Assistant Professor; M.F.A., Virginia Commonwealth. Scott Menchin, Visiting Associate Professor. Ann Morris, Visiting Assistant Professor; M.A., CUNY, Hunter. Eric O'Toole, Adjunct Assistant Professor; B.I.D., Pratt. Peter Jay Pultorak, Visiting Instructor; B.A., Notre Dame. Marc Rosen, Visiting Associate Professor; M. S., Pratt. William Schiffmiller, Visiting Assistant Professor; M.P.S., Pratt. Marc Schneider, Adjunct Assistant Professor; M.S., NYU. Christie Shin, Visiting Instructor; M.S., Pratt. Cheryl Stockton, Visiting Assistant Professor; B.A., Point Park College. Jim Warner, Visiting Assistant Professor; B.F.A., Massachusetts College of Art. Alisa Zamir, Professor; M.S., Pratt.

Creative Arts Therapy
Jean Davis, Chair, Adjunct Associate Professor; M.P.S. Pratt. Linda Siegel, Director of Graduate Art Therapy Program, Assistant Professor. Joan Wittig, Director of Graduate Dance/Movement Therapy Program, Assistant Professor; M.S., CUNY, Hunter. Josephine Abbenante, Adjunct Assistant Professor; M.A., Louisville. Claudia Bader, Visiting Instructor. Donna Bassin, Visiting Associate Professor. Beate Becker, Adjunct Associate Professor; M.S., CUNY, Hunter. Joachim Boenig, Adjunct Assistant Professor. Kimberly Bush, Visiting Instructor; M.F.A., Parsons. Angela Cooper, Visiting Instructor. Barbara Cooper, Adjunct Associate Professor. Carol Cox, Visiting Assistant Professor. Christina Devereaux, Visiting Assistant Professor; M.A., UCLA. Alison Gigl-George, Adjunct Assistant Professor. Blair Glaser, Visiting Instructor. Stephanie Gorski, Visiting Instructor; M.P.S., Pratt. Corinna Hiller, Visiting Instructor; M.S., CUNY, Hunter. Valerie Hubbs, Visiting Instructor; M.S., CUNY, Hunter. Melissa Klay, Visiting Instructor; Ph.D., Pacifica Graduate. Judith Luongo, Adjunct Associate Professor. Julie Miller, Visiting Instructor. Virginia Reed, Visiting Assistant Professor. Madeline Rugh, Visiting Associate Professor; Ph.D., Oklahoma. Dina Schapiro, Adjunct Instructor. Jean Seibel, Visiting Instructor. Ann Smith, Visiting Instructor; Ph.D., Fielding Graduate University. Laurel Thompson, Professor. Susan Tortora, Visiting Assistant Professor. Elissa White, Visiting Assistant Professor. Robert Wolf, Visiting Assistant Professor. Eva Young, Visiting Instructor. Christine Zimbelmann, Visiting Instructor.

Design Management
Mary McBride, Chair; Ph.D., NYU. Christopher Collette, Adjunct Assistant Professor; M.A., Denison University. Laurence DeGaetano, Adjunct Assistant Professor; M.B.A., NYU. Roger Dunbar, Visiting Professor; Ph.D., Cornell. Scott Fiaschetti, Visiting Associate Professor. Steven Fuhrmann, Visiting Assistant Professor. Larry Gibbs, Visiting Assistant Professor. Richard Green, Professor. Francine Martini, Visiting Assistant Professor. Jacqueline McCormack, Adjunct Associate Professor; M.P.S., Pratt. James Murray, Visiting Assistant Professor; M.P.S., Pratt. Jo Ann Stonier, Visiting Assistant Professor; J.D., St. John's (New York). Marvin Waldman, Visiting Assistant Professor; M.B.A., CUNY, Baruch.

Digital Arts
Peter Patchen, Chair; M.F.A., Oregon. Melissa Lundquist, Assistant Chair and Adjunct Assistant Professor; M.F.A., Yale. Rick Barry, Professor; M.F.A. Pratt. Thomas Bonè, Visiting Assistant Professor. Liubomir Borissov, Associate Professor; Ph.D., Columbia. Svjetlana Bukvich-Nichols, Visiting Associate Professor; M.F.A., Rensselaer. Edward Darino, Adjunct Associate Professor; M.F.A., NYU. Marianna Ellenberg, Visiting Instructor; M.A. Slade School of Art. Carla Gannis, Visiting Instructor; M.F.A., Boston University. Kay Hines, Visiting Instructor; B.A., Barnard. Everett Kane, Visiting Associate Professor; M.F.A., Art Center College of Design. Lara Kohl, Adjunct Assistant Professor; M.F.A., Art Institute of Chicago. Linda Lauro-Lazin, Adjunct Associate Professor. Peter Mackey, Professor; M.F.A., USC. Robert O'Neill, Adjunct Assistant Professor; M.F.A., Parsons. Michael O'Rourke, Professor; Ed.M., Harvard. Samantha Olschan, Visiting Instructor; M.F.A., Art Institute of Chicago. Gap-Yuel Seo, Visiting Instructor; B.F.A., Pratt. Claudia Tait, Associate Professor; M.F.A., Maryland. Lee Wolland, Visiting Instructor.

Fine Arts
Donna Moran, Chair; M.F.A., Pratt. Sheila Pepe, Assistant Chair; M.F.A., School of the Museum of Fine Arts. David Alban, Visiting Assistant Professor; M.F.A., Cranbrook Academy of Art. Adam Apostolos, Visiting Instructor. Michael Brennan, Adjunct Instructor; M.F.A., Pratt. Mona Brody, Visiting Assistant Professor; M.F.A., Norwich. Richard Budelis, Associate Professor. James Costanzo, Adjunct Associate Professor; M.F.A., Iowa. Kelly Driscoll, Assistant Professor; M.F.A., CUNY, City College. Brad Ewing, Visiting Instructor; M.F.A., Rhode Island School of Design. Allen Frame, Adjunct Associate Professor. Linda Francis, Adjunct Professor; M.A., CUNY, Hunter. Joseph Fyfe, Visiting Assistant Professor; B.F.A., University of the Arts. Jonathan Goodman, Adjunct Associate Professor. Eric Heist, Visiting Assistant Professor; M.F.A., CUNY, Hunter. Licio Isolani, Professor. Shirley Kaneda, Associate Professor; B.F.A., Parsons. Julian Kreimer, Visiting Associate Professor. Catherine Lecleire, Adjunct Assistant Professor; M.F.A., USC. Jenny Lee, Adjunct Professor. Marc Lepson, Visiting Associate Professor; M.F.A., Art Institute of Chicago. Naohisa Matsumoto, Visiting Instructor. J. Martin Mazorra, Visiting Assistant Professor; M.F.A., American. Dennis McNett, Adjunct Assistant Professor; M.F.A., Pratt. Jennifer Melby, Visiting Assistant Professor. Anne Messner, Adjunct Professor; B.F.A., Pratt. Robert Morgan, Adjunct Professor; Ph.D., NYU. James Moroney, Associate Professor; M.F.A., Pratt. Cyrilla Mozenter, Adjunct Professor; M.F.A., Pratt. Dominique Nahas, Visiting Assistant Professor. Ross Neher, Adjunct Professor. Thirwell Nolen, Adjunct Assistant Professor. Coleman O'Connell, Visiting Assistant Professor. Catherine Redmond, Adjunct Associate Professor; B.A., Harpur College. Howard Rosenthal, Visiting Associate Professor; M.F.A., Pratt. Miriam Schaer, Visiting Assistant Professor; B.F.A., School of Visual Arts. Linda Schrank, Adjunct Professor; M.A., NYU. Carla Shapiro, Visiting Assistant Professor. Elise Siegel, Visiting Assistant Professor. Lori Sikorski, Adjunct Assistant Professor; M.F.A., Pratt. Robbin Silverberg, Adjunct Assistant Professor; B.A., Princeton. Joseph Smith, Professor; B.F.A., Pratt. Tim Spelios, Visiting Associate Professor; B.F.A., Illinois. Craig Taylor, Visiting Assistant Professor. Marjorie Welish, Adjunct Professor. Elizabeth Whalley, Visiting Assistant Professor; M.F.A., CUNY, Brooklyn. Christopher White, Adjunct Assistant Professor; B.A., Harvard. Robert Zakarian, Professor.

History of Art and Design
Steven Zucker, Chair; Ph.D., CUNY Graduate Center. Gayle Rodda Kurtz, Assistant Chair; Ph.D., CUNY Graduate Center. Sam Bryan, Adjunct Associate Professor; D.A., Carnegie Mellon. Sandra Cheng, Visiting Assistant Professor; Ph.D., Delaware. Edward DeCarbo, Adjunct Associate Professor; Ph.D., Indiana. Eva Diaz, Assistant Professor; M.A., Princeton. Mary Edwards, Adjunct Professor; Ph.D., Columbia. Diana Gisolfi, Professor; Ph.D., Yale. Dimitri Hazzikostas, Assistant Professor; Ph.D., Columbia. Frima Fox Hofrichter; Ph.D., Rutgers. Vivien Knussi, Adjunct Instructor; M.A., Tufts. Marilyn Kushner, Visiting Professor; Ph.D., Northwestern. Marsha Morton, Professor; Ph.D., NYU. Antoinette Owen, Visiting Associate Professor; M.A., SUNY, Cooperstown Graduate Program. Joyce Polistena, Adjunct Associate Professor; Ph.D. Katarina V. Posch, Associate Professor; Ph.D., Tokyo University of the Arts. Vanessa Rocco, Adjunct Assistant Professor; Ph.D., CUNY Graduate Center. Ann Schoenfeld, Adjunct Assistant Professor; Ph.D., CUNY Graduate Center. Dorothy Shepard, Adjunct Professor; Ph.D., Bryn Mawr. Borhua Wang, Adjunct Associate Professor; Ph.D., Columbia.

Industrial Design
Steve Diskin, Chair. M.Arch., Harvard. Leonard Bacich, Professor. Harvey Bernstein, Adjunct Professor; M.S., Pratt. Fred Blumlein, Adjunct Professor. Matthew Burger; B.I.D, Pratt. Gine Caspi, Visiting Professor. Linda Celentano, Adjunct Associate Professor; B.I.D., Pratt. Gihyun Cho, Adjunct Professor. Allan Chochinov, Adjunct Associate Professor. Kevin Crowley, Visiting Assistant Professor. Lucia DeRespinis, Adjunct Professor; B.I.D., Pratt. Patrick Fenton, Visiting Instructor. Kathryn Filla, Adjunct Professor. Colin Gentle, Visiting Instructor; B.Eng., Connecticut. Mark Goetz, Adjunct Professor. William Gordon, Visiting Instructor. Bruce Hannah, Professor; B.I.D., Pratt. Kate Hixon, Adjunct Associate Professor. Benjamin Hopson, Visiting Instructor. Jeffrey Kapec, Visiting Associate Professor; B.I.D., Pratt. Noah King, Visiting Instructor; B.I.D., Pratt. Robert Langhorn, Visiting Assistant Professor. Jay Levy, Visiting Assistant Professor. Jong Lim, Adjunct Professor; M.F.A., Pratt. Steven Mercurio, Visiting Associate Professor. Frank Millero III, Visiting Assistant Professor; M.I.D., Pratt. Katrin Mueller-Russo, Adjunct Associate Professor. Samantha Murphy, Visiting Instructor. Shigeru Natsume, Visiting Associate Professor. Daniel November, Professor. Judith Nylen, Visiting Assistant Professor; M.L.S, M.F.A., Pratt. Jeanne Pfordresher, Adjunct Instructor. Timothy Richartz, Adjunct Assistant Professor. Andrew Roberto, Visiting Instructor; M.F.A., SUNY at New Paltz. Molly Roberts, Visiting Associate Professor; M.I.D., Pratt. Willy Schwenzfeier, Visiting Instructor. Arthur Sempliner, Adjunct Assistant Professor. Martin Skalski, Professor. Kimberly Snyder, Adjunct Associate Professor. Jordan Steckel, Adjunct Associate Professor; B.F.A., Yale. Karen Stone, Adjunct Associate Professor; M.I.D., Pratt. Irvin Tepper, Adjunct Professor; M.F.A., Washington (Seattle). Jonathan Thayer, Assistant Professor. William Tolbert, Visiting Associate Professor. Brett Tom, Visiting Instructor. Scott Vandervoort, Adjunct Instructor. Kim Walter, Visiting Assistant Professor. Seth Weiner, Visiting Instructor. Joel Wennerstrom, Adjunct Assistant Professor; M.I.D., Pratt. Julia Wheeler, Visiting Instructor. Hyukjae Yoo, Adjunct Associate Professor; M.I.D., Pratt.

Interior Design
Anita Cooney, Chair; B.A., Brown, B.Arch., Pratt. Jennifer Logun, Assistant Chair; M.Arch., Florida. Eric Ansel, Visiting Assistant Professor; M.F.A., Art Institute of Chicago, M.Arch., Pratt. Tarek Ashkar, Visiting Assistant Professor; M.Arch., Harvard. Mary Burke, Visiting Assistant Professor. Amy Campos, Visiting Assistant Professor; M.Arch., Columbia. Lisa Casertano, Visiting Assistant Professor; M.S. Columbia. Ike Cheung, Visiting Assistant Professor; B.Arch., Pratt. Melissa Ciccetti, Visiting Assistant Professor; M.Arch., Pennsylvania. Glen Coben, Visiting Assistant Professor; B.Arch., Cornell. James Conti, Adjunct Associate Professor; M.F.A., Ohio State. Mateo Antonio deCardena, Visiting Assistant Professor; B.Arch., Cooper Union. Robin Drake, Visiting Assistant Professor; B.S., Pratt. Joann Eckstut, Visiting Assistant Professor; B.A., Columbia. Jayme Elterman, Visiting Assistant Professor; Bachelor of Environmental Design, Texas A&M. Ron Eng, Visiting Assistant Professor; M.Arch., MIT. Philip Farrell, Adjunct Professor; M.S., Pratt. William Feuerman, Visiting Assistant Professor; M.S., Columbia. Antonio Furgiuele, Visiting Assistant Professor. Pavlina Gantcheva, Visiting Assistant Professor; M.S. Columbia. Jennifer Gieseking, Visiting Assistant Professor; M.A., Columbia. Jennifer Hanlin, Visiting Assistant Professor; M.Arch., Harvard. Claudia Hernandez, Visiting Assistant Professor; M.S., Columbia. Juliet Hernandez, Visiting Assistant Professor; M.Arch., Harvard. Jim Johnson, Visiting Assistant Professor; M.Arch., Texas at Austin. Mi-Young Kang, Visiting Assistant Professor; M.S., Pratt. Sheryl Kasak, Visiting Assistant Professor; M.A., Columbia. Vanessa Keith, Visiting Assistant Professor; M.Arch., Pennsylvania. Margaret Kirk, Visiting Instructor; M.Arch., Pratt. Annie Kwon, Visiting Assistant Professor; M.S., Columbia. Scott Larrabee, Visiting Assistant Professor. John Lee, Visiting Assistant Professor; M.Arch., Harvard. Meg Lipke, Visiting Assistant Professor; M.F.A. Cornell. Jason Livingston, Visiting Assistant Professor; M.F.A., NYU. Cam Lorendo, Visiting Assistant Professor; B.A., Parsons. Carmen Malvar, Adjunct Assistant Professor. William Mangold, Adjunct Assistant Professor; Ph.D., CUNY Graduate Center. Gregory Marinic, Visiting Assistant Professor; M.Arch., Maryland, College Park. Juan Matiz, Visiting Assistant Professor; B.Arch., Pratt. Molly McKnight, Visiting Assistant Professor; B.Arch., Arizona. Anthony Mekel, Adjunct Assistant Professor; B.Arch., Pratt. Christopher Metz, Visiting Assistant Professor; B.Arch., Kansas State. Francine Monaco, Adjunct Associate Professor; B.Arch., Cincinnati. Julie Torres Moskovitz, Visiting Assistant Professor; M.Arch., Pennsylvania. Stephen Mullins, Visiting Assistant Professor; M.F.A., Architectural Association (London). Tetsu Ohara, Visiting Assistant Professor; M.Arch., Harvard. Jon Otis, Professor; M.S., Massachusetts. Dae Park, Visiting Assistant Professor. Andrew Pettit, Adjunct Associate Professor; B.Arch., Pratt. Salvatore Raffone, Visiting Assistant Professor; M.Arch., Harvard. Woody Rainey, Visiting Assistant Professor; B.Arch., Utah. Christian Rietzke, Visiting Assistant Professor. Gustav Rohrs, Professor; B.Arch., MIT. Edward Russell, Adjunct Assistant Professor; M.F.A., Parsons. Hazel Siegel, Visiting Assistant Professor; M.F.A., CUNY, Hunter. Andrew Simons, Visiting Assistant Professor; B.F.A., Carnegie Mellon. Steve Smith, Adjunct Associate Professor; B.S., Pratt. Joanna Sohn, Visiting Assistant Professor; M.S., Pratt. Keena Suh, Adjunct Assistant Professor; M.Arch., Columbia. Myonggi Sul, Professor; M.S., Pratt. Yutaka Takiura, Visiting Associate Professor; M.Arch., Pennsylvania. Madeleine Taylor, Visiting Assistant Professor; M.S., Columbia. Karin Tehve, Visiting Assistant Professor; M.Arch., Harvard. Omar Toro-Vaca, Visiting Assistant Professor; B.Arch., Pratt. Jack Travis, Adjunct Assistant Professor; M.Arch., Illinois at Urbana-Champaign. Dominic Walbridge, Visiting Assistant Professor; M.Arch., Syracuse. Corey Yurkovich, Visiting Assistant Professor; M.Arch., Kent State. Michael Zuckerman, Adjunct Associate Professor; B.Arch., CUNY, City College.

Section 2
Architecture

This section contains a directory of institutions offering graduate work in architecture, followed by in-depth entries submitted by institutions that chose to prepare detailed program descriptions. Additional information about programs listed in the directory but not augmented by an in-depth entry may be obtained by writing directly to the dean of a graduate school or chair of a department at the address given in the directory.

For programs offering related work, see also in this book *Applied Arts and Design, Art and Art History,* and *Public, Regional, and Industrial Affairs. In another guide in this series:*

Graduate Programs in Engineering & Applied Sciences
See *Civil and Environmental Engineering*

CONTENTS

Program Directories

Architectural History 122
Architecture 122
Building Science 131
Environmental Design 132
Historic Preservation 133
Landscape Architecture 135
Lighting Design 139
Urban Design 140

Close-Ups and Display

Illinois Institute of Technology 143
Architecture (Display) 125
Pratt Institute 145
University of Pennsylvania 147

See also:

Art Center College of Design—Art and Design 113
University of Delaware—Urban Affairs and Public Policy 1195

Architectural History

Arizona State University, Graduate College, College of Design, Program in Environmental Design and Planning, Tempe, AZ 85287. Offers design (PhD); history, theory, and criticism (PhD); planning (PhD). *Degree requirements:* For doctorate, thesis/dissertation.

Cornell University, Graduate School, Graduate Fields of Architecture, Art and Planning, Field of Architecture, Ithaca, NY 14853-0001. Offers architectural design (M Arch); architectural science (MS); building technology and environmental science (MS); computer graphics (MS); history of architecture (MA, PhD); history of urban development (MA, PhD); theory and criticism of architecture (M Arch); urban design (M Arch). *Faculty:* 38 full-time (12 women). *Students:* 100 full-time (45 women); includes 14 minority (2 African Americans, 6 Asian Americans or Pacific Islanders, 6 Hispanic Americans), 38 international. Average age 28. 558 applicants, 18% accepted, 44 enrolled. In 2009, 42 master's, 3 doctorates awarded. *Degree requirements:* For master's, one foreign language, thesis (MA, MS); for doctorate, 2 foreign languages, comprehensive exam, thesis/dissertation. *Entrance requirements:* For master's, GRE General Test, 5 year bachelor's degree in architecture, portfolio (M Arch), 3 letters of recommendation; for doctorate, GRE General Test, 3 letters of recommendation. Additional exam requirements/recommendations for international students: Required—TOEFL (minimum score 600 paper-based; 250 computer-based; 77 iBT). *Application deadline:* For fall admission, 1/15 priority date for domestic students. Application fee: $70. Electronic applications accepted. *Expenses:* Tuition: Full-time $29,500. Required fees: $70. Full-time tuition and fees vary according to degree level, program and student level. *Financial support:* In 2009–10, 16 students received support, including 2 fellowships with full tuition reimbursements available, 1 research assistantship with full tuition reimbursement available, 10 teaching assistantships with full tuition reimbursements available; institutionally sponsored loans, scholarships/grants, health care benefits, tuition waivers (full and partial), and unspecified assistantships also available. Financial award applicants required to submit FAFSA. *Faculty research:* Architectural design and urban design, theory and criticism of architecture, computer graphics, building technology and environmental science, history of architecture and history of urban-development. *Unit head:* Director of Graduate Studies, 607-255-6701, Fax: 607-255-0291. *Application contact:* Graduate Field Assistant, 607-255-6701, Fax: 607-255-0291, E-mail: cuarch@cornell.edu.

Graduate School and University Center of the City University of New York, Graduate Studies, Program in Art History, New York, NY 10016-4039. Offers architecture (PhD); graphic arts (PhD); painting (PhD); photography (PhD); sculpture (PhD). *Faculty:* 16 full-time (11 women). *Students:* 177 full-time (143 women), 10 part-time (all women); includes 14 minority (3 African Americans, 2 Asian Americans or Pacific Islanders, 9 Hispanic Americans), 18 international. Average age 34. 82 applicants, 54% accepted, 23 enrolled. In 2009, 9 doctorates awarded. *Degree requirements:* For doctorate, 2 foreign languages, thesis/dissertation. *Entrance requirements:* For doctorate, GRE General Test. Additional exam requirements/recommendations for international students: Required—TOEFL. *Application deadline:* For fall admission, 4/15 for domestic students; for spring admission, 11/15 for domestic students. Application fee: $125. Electronic applications accepted. *Financial support:* In 2009–10, 91 students received support, including 70 fellowships, 4 research assistantships, 12 teaching assistantships; career-related internships or fieldwork, Federal Work-Study, institutionally sponsored loans, and tuition waivers (full and partial) also available. Financial award application deadline: 2/1; financial award applicants required to submit FAFSA. *Unit head:* Dr. Kevin Murphy, Executive Officer, 212-817-8035, Fax: 212-817-1502, E-mail: kmurphy@gc.cuny.edu. *Application contact:* Les Gribben, Director of Admissions, 212-817-7470, Fax: 212-817-1624, E-mail: lgribben@gc.cuny.edu.

Harvard University, Graduate School of Arts and Sciences, Department of History of Art and Architecture, Cambridge, MA 02138. Offers ancient art (PhD); ancient Near Eastern art (PhD); baroque art (PhD); Byzantine art (PhD); classical art (PhD); Indian art (PhD); Islamic art (PhD); Japanese and Chinese art (PhD); medieval art (PhD); modern art (PhD); Renaissance and modern architecture (PhD); Renaissance art (PhD). *Degree requirements:* For doctorate, variable foreign language requirement, thesis/dissertation, general exams; reading exams in French, German, and Italian. *Entrance requirements:* For doctorate, GRE General Test. Additional exam requirements/recommendations for international students: Required—TOEFL. *Expenses:* Tuition: Full-time $33,696. Required fees: $1126. Full-time tuition and fees vary according to program.

Massachusetts Institute of Technology, School of Architecture and Planning, Department of Architecture, Cambridge, MA 02139-4307. Offers architecture (M Arch, PhD), including building technology (PhD), design and computation (PhD), history and theory of architecture (PhD), history and theory of art (PhD); architecture studies (SM Arch S); building technology (SMBT); visual studies (SM Vis S). *Faculty:* 35 full-time (9 women). *Students:* 221 full-time (113 women); includes 34 minority (4 African Americans, 2 American Indian/Alaska Native, 21 Asian Americans or Pacific Islanders, 7 Hispanic Americans), 81 international. Average age 28. 1,011 applicants, 14% accepted, 75 enrolled. In 2009, 71 master's, 12 doctorates awarded. *Degree requirements:* For master's, thesis; for doctorate, comprehensive exam, thesis/dissertation. *Entrance requirements:* For master's, GRE General Test (for some programs), portfolio (for some programs); for doctorate, GRE General Test (for some programs). Additional exam requirements/recommendations for international students: Required—TOEFL or IELTS. *Application deadline:* For fall admission, 12/15 for domestic and international students. Application fee: $75. Electronic applications accepted. *Expenses:* Tuition: Full-time $37,510; part-time $585 per unit. Required fees: $272. *Financial support:* In 2009–10, 211 students received support, including 153 fellowships with tuition reimbursements available (averaging $17,293 per year), 26 research assistantships with tuition reimbursements available (averaging $24,640 per year), 24 teaching assistantships with tuition reimbursements available (averaging $27,324 per year); career-related internships or fieldwork, Federal Work-Study, institutionally sponsored loans, scholarships/grants, health care benefits, and unspecified assistantships also available. *Faculty research:* Architecture and urbanism, building technology and sustainability, computation and design, history, contemporary visual art practice, theory, and criticism. Total annual research expenditures: $1.9 million. *Unit head:* Prof. Yung Ho Chang, Department Head, 617-253-7791, E-mail: arch@mit.edu. *Application contact:* Admissions Coordinator, 617-253-7387, Fax: 617-253-8993, E-mail: arch@mit.edu.

Savannah College of Art and Design, Graduate School, Program in Architectural History, Savannah, GA 31402-3146. Offers MA, MFA. Part-time programs available. *Degree requirements:* For master's, one foreign language, thesis, internship. *Entrance requirements:* For master's, interview, research paper. Additional exam requirements/recommendations for international students: Required—TOEFL (minimum score 450 paper-based; 133 computer-based). Electronic applications accepted. *Expenses:* Tuition: Full-time $28,515; part-time $627 per credit hour. One-time fee: $500. Tuition and fees vary according to course load.

University of California, Berkeley, Graduate Division, College of Environmental Design, Department of Architecture, Berkeley, CA 94720-1500. Offers architecture (M Arch); building science (MS, PhD); building structures, construction and materials (MS, PhD); design theories, methods, and practices (MS, PhD); environmental design in developing countries (MS, PhD); history of architecture and urbanism (MS, PhD); social and cultural processes in architecture and urbanism (MS, PhD); M Arch/MCP; M Arch/MS; MLA/M Arch. *Students:* 156 full-time (91 women). Average age 30. 935 applicants, 60 enrolled. In 2009, 42 master's, 12 doctorates awarded. *Degree requirements:* For master's, thesis; for doctorate, thesis/dissertation, qualifying exam. *Entrance requirements:* For master's and doctorate, GRE General Test, minimum GPA of 3.0, 3 letters of recommendation. Additional exam requirements/recommendations for international students: Required—TOEFL. Application fee: $70 ($90 for international students). Electronic applications accepted. *Financial support:* Unspecified assistantships available. *Unit head:* Prof. Gail Brager, Chair, 510-642-4942. *Application contact:* Lois H. Ito Koch, Student Affairs Officer, 510-642-5577, Fax: 510-643-5607, E-mail: archgrad@berkeley.edu.

University of Pittsburgh, School of Arts and Sciences, Department of History of Art and Architecture, Pittsburgh, PA 15260. Offers MA, PhD. *Faculty:* 13 full-time (7 women). *Students:* 34 full-time (28 women), 1 (woman) part-time; includes 7 minority (all Asian Americans or Pacific Islanders). Average age 33. 51 applicants, 18% accepted, 4 enrolled. In 2009, 5 master's, 5 doctorates awarded. Terminal master's awarded for partial completion of doctoral program. *Degree requirements:* For master's, one foreign language, thesis; for doctorate, 2 foreign languages, comprehensive exam, thesis/dissertation. *Entrance requirements:* For doctorate, GRE General Test, 3 letters of recommendation, writing sample, foreign language questionnaire. Additional exam requirements/recommendations for international students: Required—TOEFL (minimum score 550 paper-based; 213 computer-based; 80 iBT). *Application deadline:* For fall admission, 1/15 for domestic and international students. Application fee: $50. Electronic applications accepted. *Expenses:* Tuition, state resident: full-time $16,402; part-time $665 per credit. Tuition, nonresident: full-time $28,694; part-time $1175 per credit. Required fees: $690; $175 per term. Tuition and fees vary according to program. *Financial support:* In 2009–10, 28 students received support, including 16 fellowships with full tuition reimbursements available (averaging $17,822 per year), 12 teaching assistantships with full tuition reimbursements available (averaging $15,675 per year); research assistantships with full tuition reimbursements available, career-related internships or fieldwork, Federal Work-Study, scholarships/grants, health care benefits, and tuition waivers (partial) also available. Financial award application deadline: 1/15. *Faculty research:* Asian, medieval, Renaissance/Baroque, modern art and architecture, contemporary. Total annual research expenditures: $10,000. *Unit head:* Dr. Kirk Savage, Chair, 412-648-2405, Fax: 412-648-2792, E-mail: ksa@pitt.edu. *Application contact:* Dr. Josh Ellenbogen, Director, Graduate Studies, 412-648-2400, Fax: 412-648-2792, E-mail: jme23@pitt.edu.

The University of Texas at Austin, Graduate School, School of Architecture, Austin, TX 78712-1111. Offers architecture (M Arch); community and regional planning (MSCRP, PhD); historic preservation (MS); history of architecture (MA, PhD); landscape architecture (MLA); urban design (MSUD); JD/MSCRP; MSCRP/MA; MSCRP/PhD. *Degree requirements:* For doctorate, thesis/dissertation. *Entrance requirements:* For master's and doctorate, GRE General Test. Additional exam requirements/recommendations for international students: Required—TOEFL (minimum score 550 paper-based; 213 computer-based). Electronic applications accepted.

University of Virginia, College and Graduate School of Arts and Sciences, McIntire Department of Art, Charlottesville, VA 22904-4130. Offers classical art and archaeology (MA, PhD); history of art and architecture (MA, PhD). *Degree requirements:* For master's, one foreign language, thesis, defense; for doctorate, 2 foreign languages, comprehensive exam, thesis/dissertation, defense. *Entrance requirements:* For master's and doctorate, GRE General Test, writing sample. Additional exam requirements/recommendations for international students: Recommended—TOEFL (minimum score 600 paper-based; 250 computer-based; 90 iBT), IELTS (minimum score 7). Electronic applications accepted. *Faculty research:* Classical art, renaissance art and architecture, American material culture.

University of Virginia, School of Architecture, Department of Architectural History, Charlottesville, VA 22903. Offers M Arch H, PhD. *Faculty:* 7 full-time (3 women). *Students:* 27 full-time (23 women), 2 part-time (0 women); includes 1 minority (Hispanic American), 3 international. Average age 30. 23 applicants, 74% accepted, 7 enrolled. In 2009, 6 master's awarded. *Degree requirements:* For master's, one foreign language, thesis. *Entrance requirements:* For master's, GRE General Test, 3 letters of recommendation. Additional exam requirements/recommendations for international students: Required—TOEFL (minimum score 600 paper-based; 250 computer-based; 90 iBT). *Application deadline:* For fall admission, 1/5 for domestic and international students. Applications are processed on a rolling basis. Application fee: $60. Electronic applications accepted. *Financial support:* Career-related internships or fieldwork, Federal Work-Study, and institutionally sponsored loans available. Financial award applicants required to submit FAFSA. *Faculty research:* Urban form, nineteenth and twentieth century American architecture. *Unit head:* Louis Nelson, Chair, 434-924-1428, Fax: 434-982-2678, E-mail: lnelson@virginia.edu. *Application contact:* Graduate Admissions Officer, 434-924-6442, E-mail: arch-admissions@virginia.edu.

Virginia Commonwealth University, Graduate School, School of the Arts, Department of Art History, Richmond, VA 23284-9005. Offers architectural history (MA); art history (MA, PhD); historical studies (MA); museum studies (MA). *Accreditation:* NASAD. *Degree requirements:* For master's, thesis; for doctorate, comprehensive exam, thesis/dissertation. *Entrance requirements:* For master's and doctorate, GRE General Test. *Faculty research:* Modern, nineteenth century, Renaissance, American, and Medieval art.

Architecture

Academy of Art University, Graduate Program, School of Architecture, San Francisco, CA 94105-3410. Offers M Arch. Part-time programs available. *Degree requirements:* For master's, final review. *Entrance requirements:* For master's, portfolio, bachelor's degree in architecture or related field. Electronic applications accepted.

Andrews University, School of Graduate Studies, Division of Architecture, Berrien Springs, MI 49104. Offers M Arch. *Faculty:* 8 full-time (2 women), 1 part-time/adjunct (0 women). *Students:* 15 full-time (6 women); includes 5 minority (3 African Americans, 2 Hispanic Americans). Average age 25. 30 applicants, 63% accepted, 11 enrolled. In 2009, 25 master's awarded. *Entrance requirements:* For master's, GRE. Additional exam requirements/recommendations for international students: Required—TOEFL (minimum score 550 paper-based). Application fee: $40. *Unit head:* Carey Carscallen, Director, 269-471-6003. *Application contact:* Carolyn Hurst, Supervisor of Graduate Admission, 800-253-2874, Fax: 269-471-6321, E-mail: graduate@andrews.edu.

Arizona State University, Graduate College, College of Design, School of Architecture and Landscape Architecture, Tempe, AZ 85287. Offers architecture (M Arch); building design (MS); landscape architecture (MLA); urban design (MUD); MA/MBA. *Degree requirements:* For master's, thesis optional. *Entrance requirements:* For master's, GRE General Test, design portfolio.

Auburn University, Graduate School, College of Architecture, Design, and Construction, Auburn University, AL 36849. Offers MBS, MCP, MDB, MID, MLA, MPA/MCP. Part-time programs available. *Faculty:* 61 full-time (12 women), 6 part-time/adjunct (2 women). *Students:* 111

full-time (41 women), 43 part-time (12 women); includes 12 minority (8 African Americans, 1 Asian American or Pacific Islander, 3 Hispanic Americans), 22 international. Average age 26. 250 applicants, 58% accepted, 97 enrolled. In 2009, 37 master's awarded. *Entrance requirements:* For master's, GRE General Test. *Application deadline:* For fall admission, 7/7 for domestic students; for spring admission, 11/24 for domestic students. Applications are processed on a rolling basis. Application fee: $50 ($60 for international students). Electronic applications accepted. *Expenses:* Contact institution. *Financial support:* Fellowships, Federal Work-Study available. Support available to part-time students. Financial award application deadline: 3/15; financial award applicants required to submit FAFSA. *Unit head:* Prof. Dan D. Bennett, Dean, 334-844-4524. *Application contact:* Dr. George Flowers, Dean of the Graduate School, 334-844-2125.

Ball State University, Graduate School, College of Architecture and Planning, Department of Architecture, Program in Architecture, Muncie, IN 47306-1099. Offers M Arch. *Degree requirements:* For master's, thesis. *Entrance requirements:* For master's, minimum undergraduate B average, portfolio, writing sample.

Boston Architectural College, Graduate Programs, Boston, MA 02115-2795. Offers architecture (M Arch); interior design (MID). *Accreditation:* CIDA. *Degree requirements:* For master's, thesis. *Entrance requirements:* For master's, portfolio (recommended). Electronic applications accepted.

California College of the Arts, Graduate Programs, Program in Architecture, San Francisco, CA 94107. Offers M Arch. *Degree requirements:* For master's, thesis. *Entrance requirements:* For master's, appropriate bachelor's degree, portfolio, resume, minimum 2 letters of recommendation. Additional exam requirements/recommendations for international students: Required—TOEFL (minimum score 600 paper-based; 250 computer-based).

California Polytechnic State University, San Luis Obispo, College of Architecture and Environmental Design, Department of Architecture, San Luis Obispo, CA 93407. Offers MS. Part-time programs available. *Faculty:* 4 full-time (0 women), 2 part-time/adjunct (1 woman). *Students:* 16 full-time (7 women), 4 part-time (2 women); includes 4 minority (1 Asian American or Pacific Islander, 3 Hispanic Americans). Average age 29. 29 applicants, 76% accepted, 13 enrolled. In 2009, 8 master's awarded. *Degree requirements:* For master's, thesis. *Entrance requirements:* For master's, GRE, minimum GPA of 3.0, 2 letters of recommendation. Additional exam requirements/recommendations for international students: Required—TOEFL (minimum score 550 paper-based; 213 computer-based), or IELTS (minimum score 6). *Application deadline:* For fall admission, 7/1 for domestic students, 11/30 for international students; for winter admission, 11/1 for domestic students, 6/30 for international students. Applications are processed on a rolling basis. Application fee: $55. Electronic applications accepted. *Expenses:* Tuition, nonresident: full-time $11,160; part-time $248 per unit. Required fees: $7134; $1553 per quarter. *Financial support:* Research assistantships, teaching assistantships, Federal Work-Study and institutionally sponsored loans available. Support available to part-time students. Financial award application deadline: 3/2; financial award applicants required to submit FAFSA. *Faculty research:* Computer-assisted design, decision support systems, building science, facilities management. Total annual research expenditures: $2.4 million. *Unit head:* Dr. Jens Pohl, Graduate Coordinator, 805-756-2841, Fax: 805-756-1500, E-mail: jpohl@calpoly.edu. *Application contact:* Dr. James Maraviglia, Assistant Vice President for Admissions, Recruitment and Financial Aid, 805-756-2311, Fax: 805-756-5400, E-mail: admissions@calpoly.edu.

California State Polytechnic University, Pomona, Academic Affairs, College of Environmental Design, Program in Architecture, Pomona, CA 91768-2557. Offers M Arch. Part-time programs available. *Students:* 57 full-time (31 women), 10 part-time (7 women); includes 18 minority (1 African American, 11 Asian Americans or Pacific Islanders, 6 Hispanic Americans), 3 international. Average age 29. 150 applicants, 21% accepted, 20 enrolled. In 2009, 21 master's awarded. *Degree requirements:* For master's, thesis or alternative. *Application deadline:* For fall admission, 5/1 for domestic students; for winter admission, 10/15 priority date for domestic students; for spring admission, 1/20 priority date for domestic students. Applications are processed on a rolling basis. Application fee: $55. Electronic applications accepted. *Expenses:* Tuition, nonresident: full-time $6696; part-time $248 per credit. Required fees: $5487; $3237 per term. Tuition and fees vary according to course load, degree level and program. *Financial support:* Career-related internships or fieldwork, Federal Work-Study, and institutionally sponsored loans available. Support available to part-time students. Financial award application deadline: 3/2; financial award applicants required to submit FAFSA. *Unit head:* Kip Dickson, Graduate Coordinator, 909-869-2682, Fax: 909-869-4331, E-mail: kadickson@csupomona.edu. *Application contact:* Scott J. Duncan, Director, Admissions, 909-869-3258, Fax: 909-869-4529, E-mail: sjduncan@csupomona.edu.

Carleton University, Faculty of Graduate Studies, Faculty of Engineering and Design, School of Architecture, Ottawa, ON K1S 5B6, Canada. Offers design studies (M Arch). *Degree requirements:* For master's, thesis. *Entrance requirements:* For master's, honors degree. Additional exam requirements/recommendations for international students: Required—TOEFL. *Faculty research:* Theoretical issues in architecture and culture, cultural diversity, architecture and technoscientific culture.

Carnegie Mellon University, College of Fine Arts, School of Architecture, Pittsburgh, PA 15213-3891. Offers architectural engineering construction management (M Sc); architecture (MSA); architecture, engineering, and construction management (PhD); building performance and diagnostics (M Sc, PhD); computational design (M Sc, PhD); sustainable design (M Sc); urban design (M Sc). Terminal master's awarded for partial completion of doctoral program. *Degree requirements:* For doctorate, thesis/dissertation. *Entrance requirements:* For master's and doctorate, GRE General Test. Additional exam requirements/recommendations for international students: Required—TOEFL.

The Catholic University of America, School of Architecture and Planning, Washington, DC 20064. Offers cultural studies/sacred space (M Arch); design technologies (M Arch); digital media (M Arch); urban design (M Arch). Part-time programs available. *Faculty:* 20 full-time (7 women), 34 part-time/adjunct (4 women). *Students:* 110 full-time (46 women), 37 part-time (16 women); includes 40 minority (12 African Americans, 11 Asian Americans or Pacific Islanders, 17 Hispanic Americans), 9 international. Average age 27. 154 applicants, 80% accepted, 55 enrolled. In 2009, 39 master's awarded. *Degree requirements:* For master's, thesis. *Entrance requirements:* For master's, GRE (minimum score: 1000), minimum GPA of 2.8, portfolio, statement of purpose, official copies of academic transcripts, three letters of recommendation. Additional exam requirements/recommendations for international students: Required—TOEFL (minimum score 580 paper-based; 237 computer-based). *Application deadline:* For fall admission, 1/15 priority date for domestic students, 1/15 for international students; for spring admission, 10/15 priority date for domestic students, 10/15 for international students. Applications are processed on a rolling basis. Application fee: $55. Electronic applications accepted. *Expenses:* Contact institution. *Financial support:* Fellowships, research assistantships, teaching assistantships, Federal Work-Study, scholarships/grants, tuition waivers (full and partial), and unspecified assistantships available. Financial award application deadline: 2/1; financial award applicants required to submit FAFSA. *Faculty research:* Architectural history, cultural studies/scared space, design technologies, digital media, real estate development, urban design. *Unit head:* Randall Ott, Dean, 202-319-5784, Fax: 202-319-2023, E-mail: ott@cua.edu. *Application contact:* Julie Schwing, Director of Graduate Admissions, 202-319-5057, Fax: 202-319-6533, E-mail: cua-admissions@cua.edu.

City College of the City University of New York, Graduate School, School of Architecture and Environmental Studies, Program in Architecture, New York, NY 10031-9198. Offers M Arch. *Students:* 40 full-time (20 women), 1 (woman) part-time; includes 29 minority (6 African Americans, 10 Asian Americans or Pacific Islanders, 13 Hispanic Americans), 8 international. 209 applicants, 53% accepted. In 2009, 27 master's awarded. *Entrance requirements:* For master's, GRE. Additional exam requirements/recommendations for international students: Required—TOEFL (minimum score 550 paper-based; 213 computer-based). *Application deadline:* For fall admission, 1/15 for domestic students. Application fee: $125. *Unit head:* Brad Horn, Head, 212-650-8319. *Application contact:* Sarah Morales, Information Contact, 212-650-8748, E-mail: archgrad@ccny.cuny.edu.

Clemson University, Graduate School, College of Architecture, Arts, and Humanities, Department of Architecture, Clemson, SC 29634. Offers M Arch, MS. *Faculty:* 23 full-time (4 women), 8 part-time/adjunct (2 women). *Students:* 74 full-time (35 women), 2 part-time (both women); includes 7 minority (3 African Americans, 3 Asian Americans or Pacific Islanders, 1 Hispanic American), 4 international. Average age 26. 205 applicants, 52% accepted, 42 enrolled. In 2009, 17 master's awarded. *Degree requirements:* For master's, thesis. *Entrance requirements:* For master's, GRE General Test, portfolio. Additional exam requirements/recommendations for international students: Required—TOEFL, IELTS. *Application deadline:* For fall admission, 2/1 for domestic students, 4/15 for international students; for spring admission, 9/15 for international students. Applications are processed on a rolling basis. Application fee: $70 ($80 for international students). Electronic applications accepted. *Expenses:* Tuition, state resident: full-time $8684; part-time $528 per credit hour. Tuition, nonresident: full-time $15,330; part-time $1078 per credit hour. Required fees: $736; $37 per semester. Part-time tuition and fees vary according to course load and program. *Financial support:* In 2009–10, 34 students received support, including 9 fellowships with full and partial tuition reimbursements available (averaging $3,323 per year); research assistantships with partial tuition reimbursements available, teaching assistantships with partial tuition reimbursements available, career-related internships or fieldwork, institutionally sponsored loans, scholarships/grants, health care benefits, and unspecified assistantships also available. Support available to part-time students. Financial award application deadline: 2/15; financial award applicants required to submit FAFSA. *Faculty research:* Color and computers, light energy, theory and philosophy, architecture for education, architecture for health. Total annual research expenditures: $408,626. *Unit head:* Dr. Jose Caban, Chair, 864-656-3898, Fax: 864-656-0204, E-mail: jcaban@clemson.edu. *Application contact:* Michelle McLane, Student Services, 864-656-3938, Fax: 864-656-1810, E-mail: wking@clemson.edu.

Columbia University, Graduate School of Architecture, Planning, and Preservation, Program in Advanced Architectural Design, New York, NY 10027. Offers MS. *Entrance requirements:* For master's, GRE General Test.

Columbia University, Graduate School of Architecture, Planning, and Preservation, Program in Architecture, New York, NY 10027. Offers M Arch, PhD, M Arch/MS. PhD offered through the Graduate School of Arts and Science. *Degree requirements:* For master's, thesis optional. *Entrance requirements:* For master's, GRE General Test.

Cooper Union for the Advancement of Science and Art, Irwin S. Chanin School of Architecture, New York, NY 10003-7120. Offers M Arch II. *Faculty:* 14 full-time (3 women), 19 part-time/adjunct (6 women). *Students:* 7 full-time (2 women), 5 international. 100 applicants, 11% accepted, 7 enrolled. *Degree requirements:* For master's, thesis. *Entrance requirements:* For master's, GRE, 1 year of work experience, 3 letters of recommendation, resume or curriculum vitae, essay, portfolio, interview. Additional exam requirements/recommendations for international students: Required—TOEFL. *Application deadline:* For fall admission, 2/1 for domestic students. Application fee: $65. *Expenses:* Tuition: Full-time $35,000. Required fees: $1650. *Financial support:* In 2009–10, 7 students received support. Tuition waivers and all admitted students receive a full-tuition scholarship for the length of their study available. Financial award application deadline: 5/1; financial award applicants required to submit CSS PROFILE or FAFSA. *Unit head:* Dr. Anthony Vidler, Dean. *Application contact:* Susan Cohen, Student Contact, 212-353-4120, E-mail: admissions@cooper.edu.

Cornell University, Graduate School, Graduate Fields of Architecture, Art and Planning, Field of Architecture, Ithaca, NY 14853-0001. Offers architectural design (M Arch); architectural science (MS); building technology and environmental science (MS); computer graphics (MS); history of architecture (MA, PhD); history of urban development (MA, PhD); theory and criticism of architecture (M Arch); urban design (M Arch). *Faculty:* 38 full-time (12 women). *Students:* 100 full-time (45 women); includes 14 minority (2 African Americans, 6 Asian Americans or Pacific Islanders, 6 Hispanic Americans), 38 international. Average age 28. 558 applicants, 18% accepted, 44 enrolled. In 2009, 42 master's, 3 doctorates awarded. *Degree requirements:* For master's, one foreign language, thesis (MA, MS); for doctorate, 2 foreign languages, comprehensive exam, thesis/dissertation. *Entrance requirements:* For master's, GRE General Test, 5 year bachelor's degree in architecture, portfolio (M Arch), 3 letters of recommendation; for doctorate, GRE General Test, 3 letters of recommendation. Additional exam requirements/recommendations for international students: Required—TOEFL (minimum score 600 paper-based; 250 computer-based; 77 iBT). *Application deadline:* For fall admission, 1/15 priority date for domestic students. Application fee: $70. Electronic applications accepted. *Expenses:* Tuition: Full-time $29,500. Required fees: $70. Full-time tuition and fees vary according to degree level, program and student level. *Financial support:* In 2009–10, 16 students received support, including 2 fellowships with full tuition reimbursements available, 1 research assistantship with full tuition reimbursement available, 10 teaching assistantships with full tuition reimbursements available; institutionally sponsored loans, scholarships/grants, health care benefits, tuition waivers (full and partial), and unspecified assistantships also available. Financial award applicants required to submit FAFSA. *Faculty research:* Architectural design and urban design, theory and criticism of architecture, computer graphics, building technology and environmental science, history of architecture and history of urban-development. *Unit head:* Director of Graduate Studies, 607-255-6701, Fax: 607-255-0291. *Application contact:* Graduate Field Assistant, 607-255-6701, Fax: 607-255-0291, E-mail: cuarch@cornell.edu.

Cranbrook Academy of Art, Graduate School, Program in Architecture, Bloomfield Hills, MI 48303-0801. Offers M Arch. *Degree requirements:* For master's, thesis, exhibit. *Entrance requirements:* Additional exam requirements/recommendations for international students: Required—TOEFL (minimum score 550 paper-based; 213 computer-based).

Dalhousie University, Faculty of Architecture and Planning, Halifax, NS B3J 2X4, Canada. Offers M Arch, M Eng, M Plan, MEDS, MPS. *Degree requirements:* For master's, thesis. *Entrance requirements:* Additional exam requirements/recommendations for international students: Required—TOEFL, IELTS, 1 of 5 approved tests: TOEFL, IELTS, CANTEST, CAEL, Michigan English Language Assessment Battery. Electronic applications accepted.

Drury University, Hammons School of Architecture, Springfield, MO 65802. Offers M Arch. *Degree requirements:* For master's, thesis project.

Florida Agricultural and Mechanical University, Division of Graduate Studies, Research, and Continuing Education, School of Architecture, Tallahassee, FL 32307-3200. Offers architectural studies (MS Arch); architecture (professional) (M Arch); landscape architecture (MLA). Part-time programs available. *Faculty:* 20 full-time (6 women). *Students:* 52 full-time (20 women), 11 part-time (3 women); includes 44 minority (41 African Americans, 1 Asian American or Pacific Islander, 2 Hispanic Americans), 3 international. In 2009, 11 master's awarded. *Degree requirements:* For master's, thesis. *Entrance requirements:* For master's, GRE General Test, minimum GPA of 3.0, portfolio. Additional exam requirements/recommendations for international students: Required—TOEFL (minimum score 550 paper-based). *Application deadline:* For fall admission, 5/1 for domestic students, 1/15 for international students; for spring admission, 11/1 for domestic students. Application fee: $30. *Financial support:* Fellowships, research assistantships, teaching assistantships, Federal Work-Study, institutionally sponsored loans, scholarships/grants, and tuition waivers (partial) available. Financial award application deadline: 5/1. *Faculty research:* Environmental technology, post-occupancy evaluation, building economics, design methods, computer-aided design. *Unit head:* Rodner Wright, Dean, 850-599-3244. *Application contact:* Dr. Chanta M. Haywood, Dean of Graduate Studies, Research, and Continuing Education, 850-599-3315, Fax: 850-599-3727.

Architecture

Florida International University, College of Architecture and the Arts, Miami, FL 33199. Offers M Arch, MA, MFA, MID, MLA, MM, MS. *Accreditation:* ASLA. Part-time and evening/weekend programs available. *Faculty:* 58 full-time (19 women). *Students:* 230 full-time (123 women), 33 part-time (15 women); includes 166 minority (10 African Americans, 6 Asian Americans or Pacific Islanders, 150 Hispanic Americans), 17 international. Average age 28. 289 applicants, 28% accepted, 76 enrolled. In 2009, 68 master's awarded. *Degree requirements:* For master's, thesis (for some programs). *Entrance requirements:* For master's, GRE (depending on program), minimum GPA of 3.0 (upper-level coursework). Additional exam requirements/recommendations for international students: Required—TOEFL (minimum score 550 paper-based; 80 iBT). *Application deadline:* For fall admission, 6/1 for domestic students, 4/1 for international students; for spring admission, 10/1 for domestic students, 9/1 for international students. Applications are processed on a rolling basis. Application fee: $30. Electronic applications accepted. *Expenses:* Tuition, state resident: full-time $8008; part-time $4004 per year. Tuition, nonresident: full-time $20,104; part-time $10,052 per year. Required fees: $298; $149 per term. *Financial support:* Institutionally sponsored loans and scholarships/grants available. Financial award application deadline: 3/1; financial award applicants required to submit FAFSA. *Unit head:* Dr. Brian Schriner, Acting Dean, 305-348-3181, Fax: 305-348-6716, E-mail: brian.schriner@fiu.edu. *Application contact:* Nanett Rojas, Assistant Director of Graduate Admissions, 305-348-7442, Fax: 305-348-7441, E-mail: gradadm@fiu.edu.

Florida International University, College of Architecture and the Arts, School of Architecture, Architecture Program, Miami, FL 33199. Offers M Arch, MA. Part-time and evening/weekend programs available. *Faculty:* 12 full-time (3 women). *Students:* 142 full-time (70 women), 7 part-time (3 women); includes 106 minority (4 African Americans, 3 Asian Americans or Pacific Islanders, 99 Hispanic Americans), 6 international. Average age 26. 172 applicants, 28% accepted, 45 enrolled. In 2009, 37 master's awarded. *Entrance requirements:* For master's, GRE or minimum GPA of 3.0 in upper-level undergraduate work, portfolio. Additional exam requirements/recommendations for international students: Required—TOEFL (minimum score 550 paper-based; 80 iBT). *Application deadline:* For fall admission, 2/1 for domestic and international students. Application fee: $30. Electronic applications accepted. *Expenses:* Tuition, state resident: full-time $8008; part-time $4004 per year. Tuition, nonresident: full-time $20,104; part-time $10,052 per year. Required fees: $298; $149 per term. *Financial support:* Institutionally sponsored loans and scholarships/grants available. Financial award application deadline: 3/1; financial award applicants required to submit FAFSA. *Unit head:* Prof. Brian Schriner, Interim Dean, 305-348-6442, Fax: 305-348-2650, E-mail: schriner@fiu.edu. *Application contact:* Prof. Adam Drisin, Graduate Program Director, 305-348-7077, Fax: 305-348-2650, E-mail: drisina@fiu.edu.

Frank Lloyd Wright School of Architecture, Graduate Program, Scottsdale, AZ 85261-4430. Offers M Arch. Summer session held in Spring Green, WI. *Degree requirements:* For master's, thesis or alternative. *Entrance requirements:* For master's, interviews, portfolio. Additional exam requirements/recommendations for international students: Required—TOEFL.

Georgia Institute of Technology, Graduate Studies and Research, College of Architecture, City and Regional Planning Program, Atlanta, GA 30332-0001. Offers city and regional planning (PhD); economic development (MCRP); environmental planning and management (MCRP); geographic information systems (MCRP); land and community development (MCRP); land use planning (MCRP); transportation (MCRP); urban design (MCRP); MCP/MSCE. *Accreditation:* ACSP. *Degree requirements:* For master's, thesis, internship. *Entrance requirements:* For master's, GRE General Test, minimum GPA of 2.7. Additional exam requirements/recommendations for international students: Required—TOEFL. Electronic applications accepted.

Georgia Institute of Technology, Graduate Studies and Research, College of Architecture, Doctoral Program in Architecture, Atlanta, GA 30332-0001. Offers PhD. Part-time programs available. Postbaccalaureate distance learning degree programs offered. *Degree requirements:* For doctorate, comprehensive exam, thesis/dissertation. *Entrance requirements:* For doctorate, GRE General Test. Additional exam requirements/recommendations for international students: Required—TOEFL (minimum score 600 paper-based; 250 computer-based). Electronic applications accepted.

Georgia Institute of Technology, Graduate Studies and Research, College of Architecture, Master's Program in Architecture, Atlanta, GA 30332-0001. Offers M Arch, MS, M Arch/MCRP. Part-time programs available. *Degree requirements:* For master's, thesis or alternative. *Entrance requirements:* For master's, GRE General Test. Additional exam requirements/recommendations for international students: Required—TOEFL (minimum score 600 paper-based; 250 computer-based). Electronic applications accepted.

Georgia Institute of Technology, Graduate Studies and Research, College of Architecture, Program in Building Construction, Atlanta, GA 30332-0001. Offers building construction (PhD); integrated facility management (MS); integrated project delivery systems (MS); residential construction development (MS). Part-time and evening/weekend programs available. *Entrance requirements:* For master's and doctorate, GRE or GMAT. Additional exam requirements/recommendations for international students: Required—TOEFL (minimum score 550 paper-based; 213 computer-based). Electronic applications accepted. *Faculty research:* Design-build, mold, indoor air quality, real estate.

Harvard University, Graduate School of Arts and Sciences, Committee on Architecture, Landscape Architecture, and Urban Planning, Cambridge, MA 02138. Offers architecture (PhD); landscape architecture (PhD); urban planning (PhD). *Degree requirements:* For doctorate, one foreign language, thesis/dissertation, oral exam. *Entrance requirements:* For doctorate, GRE General Test. Additional exam requirements/recommendations for international students: Required—TOEFL. *Expenses:* Tuition: Full-time $33,696. Required fees: $1126. Full-time tuition and fees vary according to program.

Harvard University, Graduate School of Design, Department of Architecture, Cambridge, MA 02138. Offers M Arch. *Faculty:* 14 full-time (5 women), 60 part-time/adjunct (17 women). *Students:* 334 full-time (153 women); includes 84 minority (6 African Americans, 4 American Indian/Alaska Native, 58 Asian Americans or Pacific Islanders, 16 Hispanic Americans), 81 international. Average age 27. In 2009, 104 master's awarded. *Degree requirements:* For master's, thesis (for some programs). *Entrance requirements:* For master's, GRE General Test. Additional exam requirements/recommendations for international students: Required—TOEFL (minimum score 600 paper-based; 250 computer-based; 104 iBT). *Application deadline:* For fall admission, 12/15 for domestic and international students. Application fee: $85. Electronic applications accepted. *Expenses:* Tuition: Full-time $33,696. Required fees: $1126. Full-time tuition and fees vary according to program. *Financial support:* Federal Work-Study and scholarships/grants available. Financial award application deadline: 2/4; financial award applicants required to submit FAFSA. *Unit head:* P. Scott Cohen, Chair, 617-495-2591. *Application contact:* Gail Gustafson, Director of Admissions, 617-495-5453, Fax: 617-495-8949, E-mail: ggustafson@gsd.harvard.edu.

Harvard University, Graduate School of Design, Program in Design, Cambridge, MA 02138. Offers Dr DES. *Students:* 32 full-time (15 women); includes 2 minority (1 Asian American or Pacific Islander, 1 Hispanic American), 21 international. Average age 35. In 2009, 9 doctorates awarded. *Entrance requirements:* For doctorate, GRE General Test. Additional exam requirements/recommendations for international students: Required—TOEFL (minimum score 600 paper-based; 250 computer-based; 104 iBT). *Application deadline:* For fall admission, 1/14 for domestic and international students. Application fee: $85. Electronic applications accepted. *Expenses:* Tuition: Full-time $33,696. Required fees: $1126. Full-time tuition and fees vary according to program. *Financial support:* Teaching assistantships, Federal Work-Study and scholarships/grants available. Financial award application deadline: 2/4; financial award applicants required to submit FAFSA. *Unit head:* Antoine Picon, Director, 617-495-2337. *Application contact:* Gail Gustafson, Director of Admissions, 617-495-5453, Fax: 617-495-8949, E-mail: ggustafson@gsd.harvard.edu.

Harvard University, Graduate School of Design, Program in Design Studies, Cambridge, MA 02138. Offers M Des S. *Students:* 66 full-time (24 women); includes 14 minority (12 Asian Americans or Pacific Islanders, 2 Hispanic Americans), 26 international. Average age 31. In 2009, 25 master's awarded. *Entrance requirements:* For master's, GRE General Test. Additional exam requirements/recommendations for international students: Required—TOEFL (minimum score 600 paper-based; 250 computer-based; 104 iBT). *Application deadline:* For fall admission, 1/14 for domestic and international students. Application fee: $85. Electronic applications accepted. *Expenses:* Tuition: Full-time $33,696. Required fees: $1126. Full-time tuition and fees vary according to program. *Financial support:* Federal Work-Study and scholarships/grants available. Financial award application deadline: 2/4; financial award applicants required to submit FAFSA. *Unit head:* Martin Bechthold, Director, 617-495-2337. *Application contact:* Gail Gustafson, Director of Admissions, 617-495-5453, Fax: 617-495-8949, E-mail: ggustafson@gsd.harvard.edu.

Illinois Institute of Technology, Graduate College, College of Architecture, Chicago, IL 60616-3793. Offers architecture (M Arch, MS Arch, PhD); integrated building delivery (M IBD); landscape architecture (MLA). Part-time programs available. *Faculty:* 40 full-time (5 women), 55 part-time/adjunct (15 women). *Students:* 205 full-time (93 women), 30 part-time (11 women); includes 14 minority (3 African Americans, 4 Asian Americans or Pacific Islanders, 7 Hispanic Americans), 97 international. Average age 29. 479 applicants, 67% accepted, 76 enrolled. In 2009, 54 master's, 2 doctorates awarded. *Degree requirements:* For master's, thesis (for some programs); for doctorate, comprehensive exam, thesis/dissertation. *Entrance requirements:* For master's, GRE General Test, Applicants must have a college grade point average of 3.0 on a 4.0 point scale. ; for doctorate, GRE General Test, minimum GPA of 3.5, official transcripts, portfolio, 3 letters of recommendation, professional statement. Additional exam requirements/recommendations for international students: Required—TOEFL (minimum score 550 paper-based; 80 iBT). *Application deadline:* For fall admission, 1/15 for domestic students, 1/1 for international students. Applications are processed on a rolling basis. Application fee: $50. Electronic applications accepted. *Expenses:* Tuition: Full-time $17,550; part-time $888 per credit hour. Required fees: $850; $7.50 per credit hour. One-time fee: $50 full-time. Full-time tuition and fees vary according to program. *Financial support:* In 2009–10, 125 teaching assistantships (averaging $4,000 per year) were awarded; fellowships, career-related internships or fieldwork, Federal Work-Study, institutionally sponsored loans, scholarships/grants, and health care benefits also available. Support available to part-time students. Financial award applicants required to submit FAFSA. *Faculty research:* Sustainability and environmental design, comprehensive tall building design, innovative materials technology, advanced structural systems, digital design methods. *Unit head:* Donna V. Robertson, John and Jeanne Rowe Chair, 312-567-3230, Fax: 312-567-5820, E-mail: robertson@iit.edu. *Application contact:* Donna V. Robertson, John and Jeanne Rowe Chair, 312-567-3230, Fax: 312-567-5820, E-mail: robertson@iit.edu.

See Display on page 125 and Close-Up on page 143.

Instituto Tecnológico y de Estudios Superiores de Monterrey, Campus Estado de México, Professional and Graduate Division, Estado de Mexico, Mexico. Offers administration of information technologies (MITA); architecture (M Arch); business administration (GMBA, MBA); computer sciences (MCS, PhD); education (M Ed); educational institution administration (MAD); educational technology and innovation (PhD); electronic commerce (MEC); environmental systems (MS); finance (MAF); humanistic studies (MHS); information sciences and knowledge management (MISKM); information systems (MS); manufacturing systems (MS); marketing (MEM); quality systems and productivity (MS); science and materials engineering (PhD); telecommunications management (MTM). Part-time programs available. Postbaccalaureate distance learning degree programs offered (minimal on-campus study). *Degree requirements:* For master's, one foreign language, thesis (for some programs); for doctorate, one foreign language, thesis/dissertation. *Entrance requirements:* For master's, E-PAEP 500, interview; for doctorate, E-PAEP 500, research proposal. Additional exam requirements/recommendations for international students: Required—TOEFL (minimum score 550 paper-based). *Faculty research:* Surface treatments by plasmas, mechanical properties, robotics, graphical computing, mechatronics security protocols.

Instituto Tecnológico y de Estudios Superiores de Monterrey, Campus Irapuato, Graduate Programs, Irapuato, Mexico. Offers administration (MBA); administration of information technology (MAIT); administration of telecommunications (MAT); architecture (M Arch); computer science (MCS); education (M Ed); educational administration (MEA); educational innovation and technology (DEIT); educational technology (MET); electronic commerce (MBA); environmental administration and planning (MEAP); environmental systems (MES); finances (MBA); humanistic studies (MHS); international management for Latin American executives (MIMLAE); library and information science (MLIS); manufacturing quality management (MMQM); marketing research (MBA).

Iowa State University of Science and Technology, Graduate College, College of Design, Department of Architecture, Ames, IA 50011. Offers architectural studies (MSAS); architecture (M Arch); M Arch/MBA; M Arch/MCRP; M Arch/MS. *Faculty:* 27 full-time (9 women), 2 part-time/adjunct (1 woman). *Students:* 49 full-time (22 women), 3 part-time (1 woman); includes 3 minority (all Hispanic Americans), 14 international. 79 applicants, 66% accepted, 24 enrolled. In 2009, 13 master's awarded. *Degree requirements:* For master's, thesis (for some programs). *Entrance requirements:* For master's, GRE General Test, portfolio, letters of reference. Additional exam requirements/recommendations for international students: Required—TOEFL (minimum score 600 paper-based; 79 iBT) or IELTS (minimum score 7). *Application deadline:* For fall admission, 1/4 priority date for domestic and international students. Applications are processed on a rolling basis. Application fee: $40 ($90 for international students). Electronic applications accepted. *Expenses:* Tuition, state resident: full-time $6716. Tuition, nonresident: full-time $8908. Tuition and fees vary according to course level, course load, program and student level. *Financial support:* In 2009–10, 30 students received support, including 2 research assistantships with full and partial tuition reimbursements available (averaging $7,210 per year), 27 teaching assistantships with tuition reimbursements available (averaging $7,850 per year); career-related internships or fieldwork, Federal Work-Study, institutionally sponsored loans, tuition waivers (partial), and unspecified assistantships also available. Support available to part-time students. Financial award application deadline: 2/1; financial award applicants required to submit FAFSA. *Faculty research:* Computer-aided architectural design, social dimensions of urban architecture, designing for the elderly, energy utilization in buildings, architectural theory. *Unit head:* Dr. Calvin F. Lewis, Chair, 515-294-2665, Fax: 515-294-1440, E-mail: calewis@iastate.edu. *Application contact:* Dr. Marwan Ghandour, Director of Graduate Education, 515-294-3543, E-mail: jejonas@iastate.edu.

Judson University, Graduate Programs, Elgin, IL 60123-1498. Offers architecture (M Arch); literacy (M Ed); organizational leadership (MA); teaching (M Ed). Part-time and evening/weekend programs available. Postbaccalaureate distance learning degree programs offered (no on-campus study). *Degree requirements:* For master's, comprehensive exam (for some programs), thesis. *Entrance requirements:* For master's, interviews.

Kansas State University, Graduate School, College of Architecture, Planning and Design, Department of Architecture, Manhattan, KS 66506. Offers M Arch. Part-time programs available. *Faculty:* 21 full-time (3 women). *Students:* 115 full-time (40 women), 11 part-time (2 women); includes 4 minority (1 African American, 3 Hispanic Americans), 12 international. Average age 23. 98 applicants, 85% accepted, 80 enrolled. In 2009, 58 master's awarded. *Degree requirements:* For master's, thesis optional, residency. *Entrance requirements:* For master's, portfolio, minimum GPA of 3.0. Additional exam requirements/recommendations for international students: Required—TOEFL (minimum score 600 paper-based). *Application deadline:* For fall admission, 2/1 priority date for domestic and international students; for spring admission, 8/1 priority date for domestic and international students. Applications are processed on a rolling basis. Application fee: $80. Electronic applications accepted. *Financial support:* In 2009–10, 5 teaching assistantships with full tuition reimbursements (averaging $10,863 per year) were awarded; research assistantships, institutionally sponsored loans and scholarships/grants also available. Support available to part-time students. Financial award application deadline: 3/1; financial award applicants required to submit FAFSA. *Faculty research:* Design theory, environment behavior and place studies, ecological and sustainable design. Total annual research expenditures: $77,632. *Unit head:* Peter Magyar, Head, 785-532-5953, Fax: 785-532-6722, E-mail: pmagyar@ksu.edu. *Application contact:* Todd Gabbard, Director, 785-532-1129, Fax: 785-532-6722, E-mail: rtodd@ksu.edu.

Kent State University, College of Architecture and Environmental Design, Kent, OH 44242-0001. Offers architecture (M Arch); preservation architecture (Certificate); urban design (M Arch, MUD, Certificate). Part-time programs available. *Degree requirements:* For master's, thesis optional. *Entrance requirements:* For master's, GRE, portfolio, minimum GPA of 2.75, 3 letters of reference, resume, undergraduate architecture degree. Additional exam requirements/recommendations for international students: Required—TOEFL (minimum score 550 paper-based). Electronic applications accepted. *Faculty research:* History and theory, building technology, landscape architecture and urbanism, urbanism, sustainable development.

Lawrence Technological University, College of Architecture and Design, Southfield, MI 48075-1058. Offers architecture (M Arch); interior design (MID). *Accreditation:* NASAD. Part-time and evening/weekend programs available. *Faculty:* 9 full-time (2 women), 12 part-time/adjunct (3 women). *Students:* 5 full-time (3 women), 157 part-time (57 women); includes 28 minority (13 African Americans, 1 American Indian/Alaska Native, 10 Asian Americans or Pacific Islanders, 4 Hispanic Americans), 13 international. Average age 32. 150 applicants, 63% accepted, 68 enrolled. In 2009, 107 master's awarded. *Degree requirements:* For master's, thesis. *Entrance requirements:* For master's, portfolio. Additional exam requirements/recommendations for international students: Required—TOEFL (minimum score 550 paper-based; 213 computer-based; 79 iBT). *Application deadline:* For fall admission, 2/1 priority date for domestic students, 2/1 for international students; for winter admission, 11/1 priority date for domestic students, 11/1 for international students; for spring admission, 2/1 priority date for domestic students, 2/1 for international students. Applications are processed on a rolling basis. Application fee: $50. Electronic applications accepted. *Expenses:* Tuition: Full-time $11,320; part-time $798 per credit hour. *Financial support:* In 2009–10, 105 students received support. Federal Work-Study available. Financial award application deadline: 4/1; financial award applicants required to submit FAFSA. *Unit head:* Glen LeRoy, Dean, 248-204-2800, Fax: 248-204-2900, E-mail: archdean@ltu.edu. *Application contact:* Jane Rohrback, Director of Admissions, 248-204-3160, Fax: 248-204-3188, E-mail: admissions@ltu.edu.

Louisiana State University and Agricultural and Mechanical College, Graduate School, College of Art and Design, School of Architecture, Baton Rouge, LA 70803. Offers M Arch. Part-time programs available. *Faculty:* 12 full-time (2 women). *Students:* 25 full-time (8 women), 3 part-time (1 woman); includes 3 minority (1 African American, 1 Asian American or Pacific Islander, 1 Hispanic American), 1 international. Average age 27. 36 applicants, 44% accepted, 12 enrolled. In 2009, 10 master's awarded. *Degree requirements:* For master's, thesis. *Entrance requirements:* For master's, GRE General Test, minimum GPA of 3.0. Additional exam requirements/recommendations for international students: Required—TOEFL (minimum score 550 paper-based; 213 computer-based; 79 iBT) or IELTS (minimum score 6.5). *Application deadline:* For fall admission, 1/25 priority date for domestic students, 5/15 for international students; for spring admission, 10/15 for international students. Applications are processed on a rolling basis. Application fee: $50 ($70 for international students). Electronic applications accepted. *Financial support:* In 2009–10, 24 students received support, including 9 research assistantships with full and partial tuition reimbursements available (averaging $7,489 per year), 1 teaching assistantship with full and partial tuition reimbursement available (averaging $9,300 per year); fellowships, career-related internships or fieldwork, Federal Work-Study, institutionally sponsored loans, scholarships/grants, health care benefits, tuition waivers (full and partial), and unspecified assistantships also available. Support available to part-time students. Financial award application deadline: 3/1; financial award applicants required to submit FAFSA. *Faculty research:* Architectural design, history of architecture, sustainable design, digital fabrication, community design. Total annual research expenditures: $43,755. *Unit head:* Jori Erdman, Director, 225-578-6885, Fax: 225-578-2168, E-mail: jerdman@lsu.edu. *Application contact:* David Bertolini, Graduate Coordinator, 225-578-6885, Fax: 225-578-2168, E-mail: dbertoli@lsu.edu.

Marywood University, Academic Affairs, School of Architecture, Scranton, PA 18509-1598. Offers architecture (M Arch); studio art (MA), including interior design. *Students:* 2 part-time (both women). Average age 25. In 2009, 6 master's awarded. *Entrance requirements:* Additional exam requirements/recommendations for international students: Required—TOEFL (minimum score 550 paper-based; 213 computer-based; 79 iBT). *Expenses:* Tuition: Part-time $715 per credit. Required fees: $270 per semester. Tuition and fees vary according to degree level, campus/location and program. *Financial support:* Career-related internships or fieldwork, scholarships/grants, and unspecified assistantships available. Support available to part-time students. Financial award application deadline: 6/30; financial award applicants required to submit FAFSA. *Unit head:* Gregory K. Hunt, Founding Dean, 570-348-6211 Ext. 4536, E-mail: gkhunt@marywood.edu. *Application contact:* Tammy Manka, Assistant Director of Graduate Admissions, 866-279-9663, E-mail: tmanka@marywood.edu.

Massachusetts College of Art and Design, Graduate Programs, Program in Architecture, Boston, MA 02115-5882. Offers M Arch. Part-time programs available. *Faculty:* 3 full-time (2 women), 13 part-time/adjunct (3 women). *Students:* 21 full-time (9 women), 1 part-time (0 women); includes 4 minority (2 African Americans, 2 Asian Americans or Pacific Islanders), 2 international. *Degree requirements:* For master's, thesis. *Entrance requirements:* For master's, portfolio, resume, college transcripts, statement of purpose, letters of reference, interview. Additional exam requirements/recommendations for international students: Required—TOEFL (minimum score 563 paper-based; 223 computer-based; 85 iBT); Recommended—IELTS (minimum score 6.5). *Application deadline:* For fall admission, 1/15 for domestic and international students. Application fee: $75. Electronic applications accepted. *Expenses:* Contact institution. *Financial support:* Teaching assistantships ($2000) available. Financial award application deadline: 3/1; financial award applicants required to submit FAFSA. *Unit head:* George Creamer, Dean of Graduate Programs, 617-879-7163, Fax: 617-879-7171, E-mail: creamer@massart.edu. *Application contact:* George Creamer, Dean of Graduate Programs, 617-879-7163, Fax: 617-879-7171, E-mail: creamer@massart.edu.

Massachusetts Institute of Technology, School of Architecture and Planning, Department of Architecture, Cambridge, MA 02139-4307. Offers architecture (M Arch, PhD), including building technology (PhD), design and computation (PhD), history and theory of architecture (PhD), history and theory of art (PhD); architecture studies (SM Arch S); building technology (SMBT); visual studies (SM Vis S). *Faculty:* 35 full-time (9 women). *Students:* 221 full-time (113 women); includes 34 minority (4 African Americans, 2 American Indian/Alaska Native, 21 Asian Americans or Pacific Islanders, 7 Hispanic Americans), 81 international. Average age 28. 1,011 applicants, 14% accepted, 75 enrolled. In 2009, 71 master's, 12 doctorates awarded. *Degree requirements:* For master's, thesis; for doctorate, comprehensive exam, thesis/dissertation. *Entrance requirements:* For master's, GRE General Test (for some programs), portfolio (for some programs); for doctorate, GRE General Test (for some programs). Additional exam requirements/recommendations for international students: Required—TOEFL or IELTS. *Application deadline:* For fall admission, 12/15 for domestic and international students. Application fee: $75. Electronic applications accepted. *Expenses:* Tuition: Full-time $37,510; part-time $585 per unit. Required fees: $272. *Financial support:* In 2009–10, 211 students received support, including 153

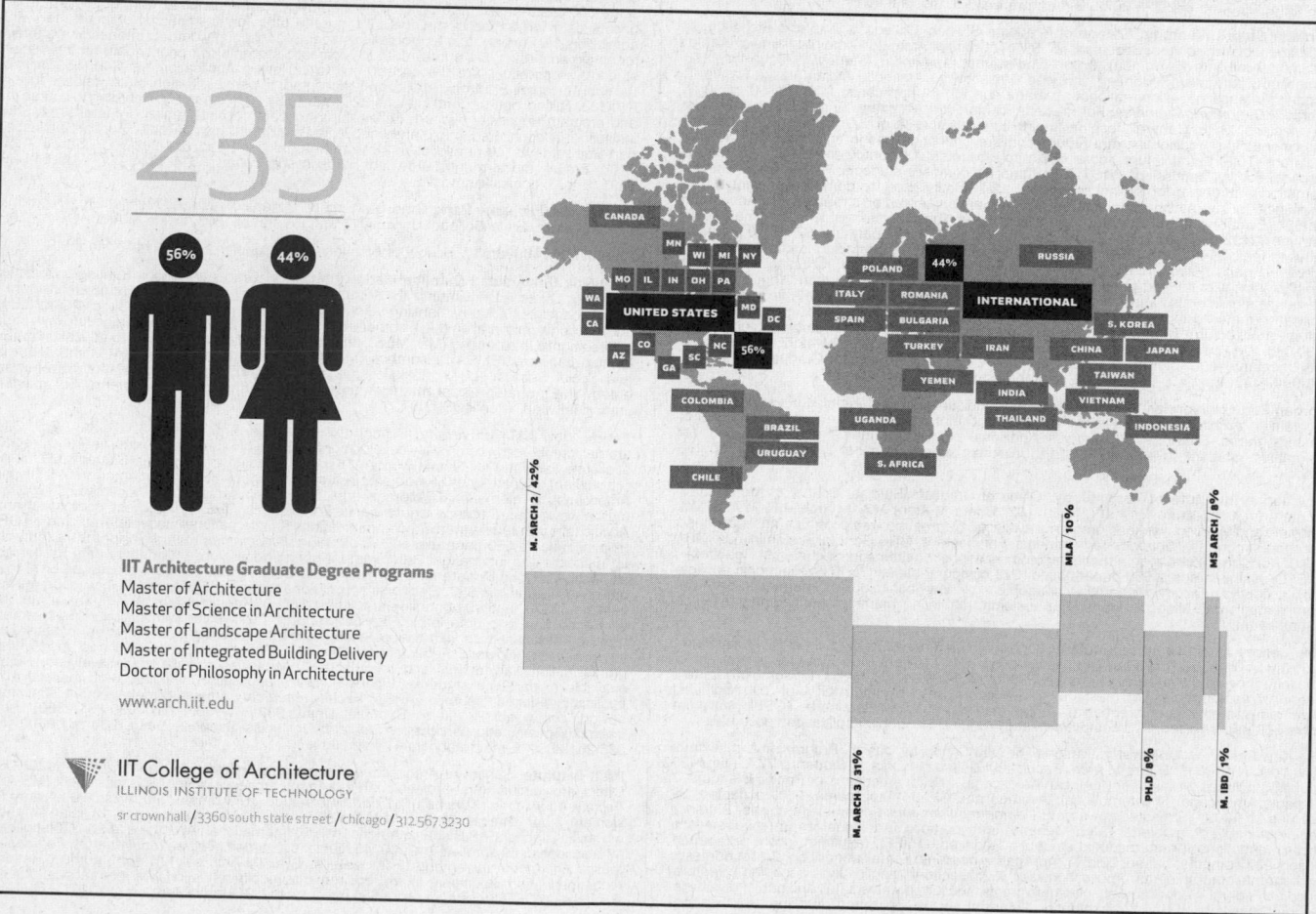

Architecture

Massachusetts Institute of Technology (continued)
fellowships with tuition reimbursements available (averaging $17,293 per year), 26 research assistantships with tuition reimbursements available (averaging $24,640 per year), 24 teaching assistantships with tuition reimbursements available (averaging $27,324 per year); career-related internships or fieldwork, Federal Work-Study, institutionally sponsored loans, scholarships/grants, health care benefits, and unspecified assistantships also available. *Faculty research:* Architecture and urbanism, building technology and sustainability, computation and design, history, contemporary visual art practice, theory, and criticism. Total annual research expenditures: $1.9 million. *Unit head:* Prof. Yung Ho Chang, Department Head, 617-253-7791, E-mail: arch@mit.edu. *Application contact:* Admissions Coordinator, 617-253-7387, Fax: 617-253-8993, E-mail: arch@mit.edu.

McGill University, Faculty of Graduate and Postdoctoral Studies, Faculty of Engineering, School of Architecture, Montréal, QC H3A 2T5, Canada. Offers affordable homes (M Arch II, Diploma); architectural history and theory (M Arch II); architecture (PhD); domestic environment (M Arch II); domestic environments (Diploma); minimum cost housing in developing countries (M Arch II, Diploma); professional architecture (M Arch I).

Miami University, Graduate School, School of Fine Arts, Department of Architecture, Oxford, OH 45056. Offers M Arch. *Students:* 28 full-time (10 women), 1 (woman) part-time; includes 2 minority (1 Asian American or Pacific Islander, 1 Hispanic American), 6 international. *Entrance requirements:* For master's, portfolio, minimum undergraduate GPA of 3.0 during previous 2 years or 3.0 overall. Additional exam requirements/recommendations for international students: Required—TOEFL. Application fee: $50. *Expenses:* Tuition, state resident: full-time $11,280. Tuition, nonresident: full-time $24,912. Required fees: $516. *Financial support:* Fellowships with full tuition reimbursements, research assistantships, teaching assistantships, Federal Work-Study, health care benefits, tuition waivers (full), and unspecified assistantships available. Financial award application deadline: 3/1. *Unit head:* Dr. John Weigand, Chair, 513-529-4903. *Application contact:* Craig Hinrichs, Associate Professor, Director of Graduate Studies, 513-529-7210, E-mail: arcid@muohio.edu.

Mississippi State University, College of Architecture, Art and Design, Mississippi State, MS 39762. Offers MS. *Accreditation:* NASAD. *Faculty:* 20 full-time (6 women). *Students:* 8 full-time (7 women), 2 part-time (1 woman); includes 2 minority (both African Americans), 2 international. Average age 27. 14 applicants, 79% accepted, 7 enrolled. In 2009, 9 master's awarded. *Degree requirements:* For master's, comprehensive exam, thesis, final written and oral exam. *Entrance requirements:* For master's, GRE General Test, essay stating intent and aspirations for study, portfolio, minimum GPA of 3.0. Additional exam requirements/recommendations for international students: Required—TOEFL (minimum score 600 paper-based; 250 computer-based; 100 iBT); Recommended—IELTS (minimum score 7.5). *Application deadline:* For fall admission, 7/1 for domestic students, 5/1 for international students; for spring admission, 11/1 for domestic students, 9/1 for international students. Applications are processed on a rolling basis. Application fee: $40. Electronic applications accepted. *Expenses:* Tuition, state resident: full-time $2575.50; part-time $286.25 per credit hour. Tuition, nonresident: full-time $6510; part-time $723.50 per credit hour. Tuition and fees vary according to course load. *Financial support:* In 2009–10, 2 research assistantships with full tuition reimbursements (averaging $9,000 per year), 1 teaching assistantship (averaging $9,000 per year) were awarded; career-related internships or fieldwork, Federal Work-Study, institutionally sponsored loans, and unspecified assistantships also available. Financial award application deadline: 4/1; financial award applicants required to submit FAFSA. *Faculty research:* Digital art in architecture, process change and management, multi-media databases, 3-D modeling and animation, virtual archaeology. *Unit head:* James L. West, Dean/Professor, 662-325-2202, Fax: 662-325-8872, E-mail: jwest@caad.msstate.edu. *Application contact:* James L. West, Dean/Professor, 662-325-2202, Fax: 662-325-8872, E-mail: jwest@caad.msstate.edu.

Montana State University, College of Graduate Studies, College of Arts and Architecture, Department of Architecture, Bozeman, MT 59717. Offers M Arch. Part-time programs available. *Faculty:* 19 full-time (5 women), 9 part-time/adjunct (4 women). *Students:* 70 full-time (16 women), 18 part-time (7 women); includes 3 minority (1 American Indian/Alaska Native, 2 Hispanic Americans), 4 international. Average age 25. 89 applicants. In 2009, 50 master's awarded. *Degree requirements:* For master's, comprehensive exam. *Entrance requirements:* For master's, GRE General Test, minimum cumulative GPA of 3.0, portfolio, 3 letters of recommendation. Additional exam requirements/recommendations for international students: Required—TOEFL (minimum score 550 paper-based; 213 computer-based). *Application deadline:* For fall admission, 7/15 priority date for domestic students, 5/15 priority date for international students; for spring admission, 12/1 priority date for domestic students, 10/1 priority date for international students. Applications are processed on a rolling basis. Application fee: $30. Electronic applications accepted. *Expenses:* Tuition, state resident: full-time $5635; part-time $3492 per year. Tuition, nonresident: full-time $17,212; part-time $7865.10 per year. Required fees: $1441; $153.15 per credit. Tuition and fees vary according to course load and program. *Financial support:* In 2009–10, 40 students received support, including 36 teaching assistantships with full and partial tuition reimbursements available; Federal Work-Study and scholarships/grants also available. Financial award application deadline: 3/1; financial award applicants required to submit FAFSA. *Faculty research:* Sustainable design, architectural history, architectural graphics, community planning. Total annual research expenditures: $130,080. *Unit head:* Fatih Rifki, Director, 406-994-4290, Fax: 406-994-4257, E-mail: fatih.rifki@montana.edu. *Application contact:* Dr. Carl A. Fox, Vice Provost for Graduate Education, 406-994-4145, Fax: 406-994-7433, E-mail: gradstudy@montana.edu.

Morgan State University, School of Graduate Studies, Institute of Architecture and Planning, Program in Architecture, Baltimore, MD 21251. Offers M Arch. *Degree requirements:* For master's, thesis. *Entrance requirements:* Additional exam requirements/recommendations for international students: Required—TOEFL (minimum score 550 paper-based; 213 computer-based).

New Jersey Institute of Technology, Office of Graduate Studies, School of Architecture, Program in Architecture, Newark, NJ 07102. Offers M Arch, MS, M Arch/MIP, M Arch/MS. Part-time and evening/weekend programs available. *Degree requirements:* For master's, thesis (for some programs). *Entrance requirements:* For master's, GRE General Test, minimum GPA of 3.0. Additional exam requirements/recommendations for international students: Required—TOEFL (minimum score 550 paper-based; 213 computer-based; 79 iBT). Electronic applications accepted. *Faculty research:* Management of new technologies, information systems management, operations management systems, marketing management, human resource management.

New Jersey Institute of Technology, Office of Graduate Studies, School of Architecture, Program in Infrastructure Planning, Newark, NJ 07102. Offers MIP. Part-time and evening/weekend programs available. *Degree requirements:* For master's, thesis (for some programs). *Entrance requirements:* For master's, GRE General Test, minimum GPA of 3.0. Additional exam requirements/recommendations for international students: Required—TOEFL (minimum score 550 paper-based; 213 computer-based; 79 iBT). Electronic applications accepted.

The New School: A University, Parsons The New School for Design, Program in Architecture, New York, NY 10011. Offers M Arch. *Faculty:* 5 full-time (1 woman). *Students:* 77 full-time (38 women); includes 14 minority (3 African Americans, 4 Asian Americans or Pacific Islanders, 7 Hispanic Americans), 7 international. Average age 26. 351 applicants, 35% accepted, 39 enrolled. In 2009, 19 master's awarded. *Degree requirements:* For master's, thesis. *Entrance requirements:* For master's, GRE General Test, portfolio. Additional exam requirements/recommendations for international students: Required—TOEFL (minimum score 580 paper-based; 237 computer-based; 92 iBT). *Application deadline:* For fall admission, 2/1 for domestic and international students. Application fee: $50. Electronic applications accepted. *Financial support:* Federal Work-Study, scholarships/grants, and tuition waivers (full and partial) available. Support available to part-time students. Financial award application deadline: 3/1; financial award applicants required to submit FAFSA. *Unit head:* David Lewis, Director, 212-229-8955 Ext. 2915, E-mail: lewisd@newschool.edu. *Application contact:* David Norris, Director of Admissions, 212-229-8989 Ext. 4023, Fax: 212-229-8975, E-mail: norrisd@newschool.edu.

Newschool of Architecture & Design, Program in Architecture, San Diego, CA 92101-6634. Offers M Arch, MS. Part-time and evening/weekend programs available. *Degree requirements:* For master's, thesis. *Entrance requirements:* For master's, portfolio, interview. *Faculty research:* Urban studies, regional studies, environmental design, structures, cross-cultural studies.

New York Institute of Technology, Graduate Division, School of Architecture and Design, Old Westbury, NY 11568-8000. Offers urban and regional design (M Arch). Part-time programs available. *Students:* 20 full-time (13 women), 2 part-time (both women); includes 2 minority (1 Asian American or Pacific Islander, 1 Hispanic American), 14 international. Average age 27. In 2009, 7 master's awarded. *Degree requirements:* For master's, thesis. *Entrance requirements:* For master's, minimum QPA of 2.85, portfolio. Additional exam requirements/recommendations for international students: Required—TOEFL (minimum score 550 paper-based; 213 computer-based). *Application deadline:* For fall admission, 7/1 priority date for domestic students; for spring admission, 12/1 priority date for domestic students. Applications are processed on a rolling basis. Application fee: $50. Electronic applications accepted. *Expenses:* Tuition: Part-time $825 per credit. *Financial support:* Research assistantships with partial tuition reimbursements, institutionally sponsored loans and tuition waivers (full and partial) available. Support available to part-time students. Financial award applicants required to submit FAFSA. *Faculty research:* Affordable housing, urban modeling and simulation, transport systems and infrastructure, relationships of policy and form. *Unit head:* Judith DiMaio, Dean, 516-686-7594, Fax: 516-686-7921, E-mail: jdimaio@nyit.edu. *Application contact:* Dr. Jacquelyn Nealon, Vice President for Enrollment Services, 516-686-7925, Fax: 516-686-7597, E-mail: jnealon@nyit.edu.

North Carolina State University, Graduate School, College of Design, School of Architecture, Raleigh, NC 27695. Offers M Arch. *Degree requirements:* For master's, thesis optional, oral exam, project. *Entrance requirements:* For master's, GRE General Test, portfolio. Electronic applications accepted. *Faculty research:* Architectural design, architectural history and theory, construction materials, sustainable design.

Northeastern University, College of Arts, Media and Design, School of Architecture, Boston, MA 02115-5096. Offers M Arch. *Faculty:* 12 full-time (4 women), 26 part-time/adjunct (10 women). *Students:* 21 full-time (10 women), 5 part-time (2 women); includes 1 Hispanic American. 102 applicants, 52% accepted, 24 enrolled. In 2009, 50 master's awarded. *Entrance requirements:* Additional exam requirements/recommendations for international students: Required—TOEFL or IELTS. *Application deadline:* For fall admission, 2/1 priority date for domestic and international students. Applications are processed on a rolling basis. Application fee: $50. Electronic applications accepted. *Financial support:* Federal Work-Study and scholarships/grants available. Support available to part-time students. Financial award application deadline: 3/1; financial award applicants required to submit FAFSA. *Unit head:* Peter Wiederspahn, Chair, 617-373-4637, Fax: 617-373-7080, E-mail: p.wiederspahn@neu.edu. *Application contact:* Jo-Anne Dickinson, Administrative Assistant, 617-373-5990, Fax: 617-373-7281, E-mail: gsas@neu.edu.

The Ohio State University, Graduate School, College of Engineering, Austin E. Knowlton School of Architecture, Program in Architecture, Columbus, OH 43210. Offers M Arch, MAS. *Faculty:* 16. *Students:* 79 full-time (30 women), 4 part-time (1 woman); includes 8 minority (1 American Indian/Alaska Native, 2 Asian Americans or Pacific Islanders, 5 Hispanic Americans), 9 international. Average age 26. In 2009, 24 master's awarded. *Degree requirements:* For master's, thesis optional. *Entrance requirements:* For master's, GRE General Test. Additional exam requirements/recommendations for international students: Required—TOEFL (minimum score 600 paper-based; 250 computer-based). *Application deadline:* For fall admission, 8/15 priority date for domestic students, 7/1 priority date for international students; for winter admission, 12/1 priority date for domestic students, 11/1 priority date for international students; for spring admission, 3/1 priority date for domestic students, 2/1 priority date for international students. Applications are processed on a rolling basis. Application fee: $40 ($50 for international students). Electronic applications accepted. *Expenses:* Tuition, state resident: full-time $10,683. Tuition, nonresident: full-time $25,923. Tuition and fees vary according to course load and program. *Financial support:* Fellowships, research assistantships, Federal Work-Study, institutionally sponsored loans, and unspecified assistantships available. Support available to part-time students. *Unit head:* John McMorrough, Section Head, 614-292-8461, Fax: 614-282-7106, E-mail: mcmorrough.1@osu.edu. *Application contact:* 614-292-9444, Fax: 614-292-3895, E-mail: domestic.grad@osu.edu.

Penn State University Park, Graduate School, College of Arts and Architecture, Department of Architecture, State College, University Park, PA 16802-1503. Offers M Arch.

Philadelphia University, School of Architecture, Philadelphia, PA 19144. Offers MS.

Pontificia Universidad Catolica Madre y Maestra, Graduate School, Santiago, Dominican Republic. Offers administration (M Adm); architecture of interiors (M Arch); architecture of tourist lodgings (M Arch); banking and financial management (M Mgmt); civil law (LL M); construction administration (ME); corporate business law (LL M); criminal procedure law (LL M); environmental engineering (ME, MEE); finance (M Mgmt); history applied to education (M Ed); human resources (EMBA); insurance (M Mgmt); international business (M Mgmt); labor law and Social Security (LL M); logistics management (ME); marketing (M Mgmt); renewable energy (ME); strategic cost management (M Mgmt). *Entrance requirements:* For master's, curriculum vitae, interview.

Prairie View A&M University, School of Architecture, Prairie View, TX 77446-0519. Offers architecture (M Arch); community development (MCD). Part-time and evening/weekend programs available. *Faculty:* 4 full-time (1 woman), 6 part-time/adjunct (2 women). *Students:* 29 full-time (10 women), 35 part-time (14 women); includes 59 minority (54 African Americans, 5 Hispanic Americans), 3 international. Average age 28. 63 applicants, 100% accepted. In 2009, 39 master's awarded. *Entrance requirements:* For master's, GRE General Test, portfolio (M Arch). Additional exam requirements/recommendations for international students: Required—TOEFL (minimum score 550 paper-based). *Application deadline:* For fall admission, 6/1 priority date for domestic and international students; for spring admission, 11/1 priority date for domestic students, 10/1 priority date for international students. Applications are processed on a rolling basis. Application fee: $50. Electronic applications accepted. *Expenses:* Tuition, state resident: full-time $2200. Tuition, nonresident: full-time $5600. Required fees: $1720. Tuition and fees vary according to course load. *Financial support:* Fellowships with tuition reimbursements, research assistantships with tuition reimbursements, teaching assistantships, career-related internships or fieldwork, Federal Work-Study, institutionally sponsored loans, scholarships/grants, tuition waivers (full and partial), and unspecified assistantships available. Support available to part-time students. Financial award application deadline: 3/1; financial award applicants required to submit FAFSA. *Faculty research:* Community management, sustainable design. *Unit head:* Dr. Ikhlas Sabouni, Dean, 936-261-9800, Fax: 936-261-2350, E-mail: isabouni@pvamu.edu. *Application contact:* Dr. Ikhlas Sabouni, Dean, 936-261-9800, Fax: 936-261-2350, E-mail: isabouni@pvamu.edu.

Pratt Institute, School of Architecture, Program in Architecture, Brooklyn, NY 11205-3899. Offers architecture (first-professional) (M Arch); architecture (post-professional) (MS Arch). *Faculty:* 10 full-time (3 women), 47 part-time/adjunct (18 women). *Students:* 199 full-time (108 women), 4 part-time (all women); includes 35 minority (4 African Americans, 13 Asian Americans or Pacific Islanders, 18 Hispanic Americans), 56 international. Average age 26. 770 applicants, 47% accepted, 80 enrolled. In 2009, 45 master's awarded. *Degree requirements:* For master's, thesis. *Entrance requirements:* For master's, GRE (M Arch only), B Arch, portfolio, letters of recommendation. Additional exam requirements/recommendations for international students: Required—TOEFL (minimum score 550 paper-based; 213 computer-based; 79 iBT). *Application* *deadline:* For fall admission, 1/5 for domestic and international students; for spring admission, 10/1 for domestic and international students. Application fee: $50 ($90 for international students). Electronic applications accepted. *Expenses:* Tuition: Full-time $22,734. Required fees: $1280. *Financial support:* Career-related internships or fieldwork, Federal Work-Study, institutionally sponsored loans, scholarships/grants, health care benefits, and unspecified assistantships available. Support available to part-time students. Financial award application deadline: 2/1; financial award applicants required to submit FAFSA. *Faculty research:* Design theory, advanced structural systems, urban investigations. *Unit head:* William J. Mac Donald, Chairperson, 718-636-4308, E-mail: wmacdona@pratt.edu. *Application contact:* Young Hah, Director of Graduate Admissions, 718-636-3683, Fax: 718-399-4242, E-mail: yhah@pratt.edu.

See Close-Up on page 145.

Princeton University, Graduate School, School of Architecture, Princeton, NJ 08544-1019. Offers M Arch, PhD. Terminal master's awarded for partial completion of doctoral program. *Degree requirements:* For master's, thesis; for doctorate, 2 foreign languages, comprehensive exam, thesis/dissertation. *Entrance requirements:* For master's, GRE General Test, design portfolio, math, 2 semesters of physics, and art/architecture survey; for doctorate, GRE General Test, samples of written work. Additional exam requirements/recommendations for international students: Required—TOEFL (minimum score 600 paper-based; 260 computer-based). Electronic applications accepted. *Faculty research:* Design, urban studies, landscape architecture, media and information technologies in architecture.

Rensselaer Polytechnic Institute, Graduate School, School of Architecture, MS Program in Architectural Sciences, Troy, NY 12180-3590. Offers acoustics (MS); built ecologies (MS); lighting (MS). *Faculty:* 15 full-time (4 women), 8 part-time/adjunct (1 woman). *Students:* 20 full-time (2 women), 1 part-time (0 women); includes 1 Asian American or Pacific Islander, 1 Hispanic American, 4 international. Average age 21. 46 applicants, 54% accepted, 11 enrolled. In 2009, 22 master's awarded. *Degree requirements:* For master's, thesis. *Entrance requirements:* For master's, GRE General Test. Additional exam requirements/recommendations for international students: Required—TOEFL (minimum score 570 paper-based; 230 computer-based; 89 iBT), IELTS (minimum score 6.5). *Application deadline:* For fall admission, 1/1 priority date for domestic and international students. Applications are processed on a rolling basis. Application fee: $75. Electronic applications accepted. *Expenses:* Tuition: Full-time $38,100. *Financial support:* In 2009–10, 5 students received support, including 4 research assistantships with tuition reimbursements available (averaging $16,500 per year), 1 teaching assistantship with tuition reimbursement available (averaging $16,500 per year); institutionally sponsored loans and unspecified assistantships also available. Financial award application deadline: 1/1. *Faculty research:* Acoustics: modeling, auralization, signal processing; built ecologies: emerging materials and technologies, sustainable built environments; lighting: energy-efficient lighting, product development, daylighting, transportation, lighting, light and health, solid state lighting. *Unit head:* Prof. Ted Krueger, Head, Graduate Programs, 518-276-6466, E-mail: krueger@rpi.edu. *Application contact:* Erin Bermingham, Senior Program Administrator, 518-276-3986, Fax: 518-276-3034, E-mail: bermie@rpi.edu.

Rhode Island School of Design, Graduate Studies, Division of Architecture and Design, Department of Architecture, Providence, RI 02903-2784. Offers M Arch. *Degree requirements:* For master's, thesis, exhibit. *Entrance requirements:* For master's, portfolio, 3 letters of recommendation. Additional exam requirements/recommendations for international students: Required—TOEFL (minimum score 580 paper-based; 237 computer-based), IELTS (minimum score 6.5).

Rice University, Graduate Programs, School of Architecture, Houston, TX 77251-1892. Offers architecture (M Arch, D Arch); urban design (M Arch). *Faculty:* 16 full-time (5 women), 21 part-time/adjunct (4 women). *Students:* 81 full-time (36 women); includes 10 minority (1 African American, 5 Asian Americans or Pacific Islanders, 4 Hispanic Americans), 10 international. 324 applicants, 18% accepted, 26 enrolled. In 2009, 28 master's awarded. *Degree requirements:* For master's, thesis optional; for doctorate, thesis/dissertation. *Entrance requirements:* For master's and doctorate, GRE. Additional exam requirements/recommendations for international students: Required—TOEFL (minimum score 600 paper-based; 250 computer-based; 100 iBT). *Application deadline:* For fall admission, 12/31 priority date for domestic and international students. Application fee: $70. Electronic applications accepted. *Financial support:* In 2009–10, 79 fellowships (averaging $12,950 per year) were awarded. *Unit head:* Sarah Whiting, Dean, School of Architecture, 713-348-4044, Fax: 713-348-5277, E-mail: sarah.whiting@rice.edu. *Application contact:* Kathleen H. Roberts, Graduate Coordinator, 713-348-5202, Fax: 713-348-5277, E-mail: kroberts@rice.edu.

Roger Williams University, School of Architecture, Art and Historic Preservation, Bristol, RI 02809. Offers architecture (M Arch). Students often begin 5-6 year dual degree sequence as undergraduates. *Degree requirements:* For master's, thesis. *Entrance requirements:* For master's, portfolio, 2 letters of recommendation. Additional exam requirements/recommendations for international students: Recommended—IELTS. Electronic applications accepted. *Expenses:* Contact institution.

Savannah College of Art and Design, Graduate School, Program in Architecture, Savannah, GA 31402-3146. Offers M Arch. Part-time programs available. *Degree requirements:* For master's, thesis, internship. *Entrance requirements:* For master's, interview, portfolio. Additional exam requirements/recommendations for international students: Required—TOEFL (minimum score 450 paper-based; 133 computer-based). Electronic applications accepted. *Expenses:* Tuition: Full-time $28,515; part-time $627 per credit hour. One-time fee: $500. Tuition and fees vary according to course load. *Faculty research:* Computer-aided design, photovoltaics-powered environmental control.

School of the Art Institute of Chicago, Graduate Division, Department of Architecture, Interior Architecture, and Designed Objects, Chicago, IL 60603-3103. Offers architecture (M Arc); design for emerging technologies (MFA); designed objects (M Des); interior architecture (M Arc). *Entrance requirements:* Additional exam requirements/recommendations for international students: Required—TOEFL, IELTS.

Southern California Institute of Architecture, Graduate Program in Architecture, Los Angeles, CA 90013. Offers M Arch. *Degree requirements:* For master's, thesis, final project. *Entrance requirements:* For master's, GRE General Test, portfolio of architectural and creative work, letters of recommendation. *Faculty research:* Architectural theory.

Southern Illinois University Carbondale, Graduate School, College of Applied Science, School of Architecture, Carbondale, IL 62901-4701. Offers M Arch.

Syracuse University, School of Architecture, Syracuse, NY 13244. Offers M Arch I, M Arch II. *Faculty:* 36 full-time (11 women), 13 part-time/adjunct (3 women). *Students:* 98 full-time (43 women), 2 part-time (0 women); includes 17 minority (6 African Americans, 3 Asian Americans or Pacific Islanders, 8 Hispanic Americans), 16 international. Average age 26. 229 applicants, 52% accepted, 39 enrolled. In 2009, 33 master's awarded. *Degree requirements:* For master's, thesis. *Entrance requirements:* For master's, GRE General Test, interview, portfolio. Additional exam requirements/recommendations for international students: Required—TOEFL (minimum score 100 iBT). *Application deadline:* For fall admission, 2/1 priority date for domestic and international students. Applications are processed on a rolling basis. Application fee: $75. Electronic applications accepted. *Expenses:* Tuition: Full-time $26,808; part-time $1117 per credit. Required fees: $1024. *Financial support:* Fellowships with full and partial tuition reimbursements, research assistantships with full and partial tuition reimbursements, teaching assistantships with full and partial tuition reimbursements, Federal Work-Study, institutionally sponsored loans, scholarships/grants, health care benefits, tuition waivers (full and partial), and unspecified assistantships available. Financial award application deadline: 1/1. *Faculty research:* Urban design, urban mapping, building systems, landscape, theory. *Unit head:* Mark Robbins, Dean, 315-443-1041, Fax: 315-443-5082. *Application contact:* Mark Linder, Graduate Director, 315-443-1041, Fax: 315-443-5082.

Texas A&M University, College of Architecture, Department of Architecture, College Station, TX 77843. Offers architecture (M Arch, MS Arch, PhD); visualization science (MS). *Faculty:* 36. *Students:* 147 full-time (64 women), 18 part-time (5 women); includes 22 minority (3 African Americans, 1 American Indian/Alaska Native, 7 Asian Americans or Pacific Islanders, 11 Hispanic Americans), 73 international. Average age 24. In 2009, 41 master's, 11 doctorates awarded. *Degree requirements:* For master's, comprehensive exam, thesis; for doctorate, comprehensive exam, thesis/dissertation. *Entrance requirements:* For master's, GRE General Test, portfolio, letters of recommendation; for doctorate, GRE General Test. Additional exam requirements/recommendations for international students: Required—TOEFL. *Application deadline:* For fall admission, 1/15 priority date for domestic and international students. Applications are processed on a rolling basis. Application fee: $50 ($75 for international students). Electronic applications accepted. *Expenses:* Tuition, state resident: full-time $3991; part-time $221.74 per credit hour. Tuition, nonresident: full-time $9049; part-time $502.74 per credit hour. *Financial support:* Fellowships, research assistantships, teaching assistantships, career-related internships or fieldwork, Federal Work-Study, institutionally sponsored loans, and scholarships/grants available. Financial award application deadline: 1/15; financial award applicants required to submit FAFSA. *Faculty research:* Energy optimization, architecture pedagogy, environment and behavior. *Unit head:* Glen Mills, Head, 979-845-1015, Fax: 979-862-1571, E-mail: gmills@archmail.tamu.edu. *Application contact:* 979-845-6582, Fax: 979-862-7119, E-mail: gradoff@archone.tamu.edu.

Texas Tech University, Graduate School, College of Architecture, Post-Professional Program in Architecture, Lubbock, TX 79409. Offers MS. Part-time programs available. *Students:* 4 full-time (1 woman), 5 part-time (2 women); includes 1 minority (Hispanic American), 3 international. Average age 28. 11 applicants, 27% accepted, 0 enrolled. In 2009, 4 master's awarded. *Degree requirements:* For master's, thesis. *Entrance requirements:* For master's, GRE General Test, portfolio. Additional exam requirements/recommendations for international students: Required—TOEFL (minimum score 550 paper-based; 213 computer-based). *Application deadline:* For fall admission, 3/1 priority date for domestic students; for spring admission, 11/1 priority date for domestic students. Applications are processed on a rolling basis. Application fee: $50 ($75 for international students). Electronic applications accepted. *Expenses:* Tuition, state resident: full-time $5100; part-time $213 per credit hour. Tuition, nonresident: full-time $11,748; part-time $490 per credit hour. Required fees: $2298; $50 per credit hour. $555 per semester. *Financial support:* Research assistantships with partial tuition reimbursements, teaching assistantships with partial tuition reimbursements, career-related internships or fieldwork, Federal Work-Study, and institutionally sponsored loans available. Support available to part-time students. Financial award application deadline: 4/15; financial award applicants required to submit FAFSA. *Faculty research:* Historic preservation, visualization, community development and design, sustainable architecture, international architecture. *Unit head:* Haq Saif, Associate Dean of Research and Post-Professional Graduate Studies, 806-742-3136, Fax: 806-742-2855, E-mail: saif.haq@ttu.edu. *Application contact:* Lori Rodriguez, Academic Program Assistant, 806-742-3136 Ext. 272, Fax: 806-742-2855, E-mail: lori.rodriguez@ttu.edu.

Texas Tech University, Graduate School, College of Architecture, Professional Program in Architecture, Lubbock, TX 79409. Offers M Arch, M Arch/MBA. Part-time programs available. *Students:* 89 full-time (20 women), 12 part-time (0 women); includes 24 minority (2 Asian Americans or Pacific Islanders, 22 Hispanic Americans), 3 international. Average age 25. 74 applicants, 65% accepted, 30 enrolled. In 2009, 48 master's awarded. *Degree requirements:* For master's, thesis. *Entrance requirements:* For master's, GRE General Test, portfolio. Additional exam requirements/recommendations for international students: Required—TOEFL (minimum score 550 paper-based; 213 computer-based). *Application deadline:* For fall admission, 3/1 priority date for international students; for spring admission, 11/1 priority date for international students. Applications are processed on a rolling basis. Application fee: $50 ($75 for international students). Electronic applications accepted. *Expenses:* Tuition, state resident: full-time $5100; part-time $213 per credit hour. Tuition, nonresident: full-time $11,748; part-time $490 per credit hour. Required fees: $2298; $50 per credit hour. $555 per semester. *Financial support:* Research assistantships with partial tuition reimbursements, teaching assistantships with partial tuition reimbursements, career-related internships or fieldwork, Federal Work-Study, and institutionally sponsored loans available. Support available to part-time students. Financial award application deadline: 4/15; financial award applicants required to submit FAFSA. *Faculty research:* Historical preservation; visualization; community design; digital design and construction; healthcare facilities. *Unit head:* Clifton Ellis, Associate Dean for Academics, 806-742-3136, Fax: 806-742-2855, E-mail: architecture.programs@ttu.edu. *Application contact:* Lori Rodriguez, Academic Program Assistant, 806-742-3136 Ext. 247, Fax: 806-742-2855, E-mail: lori.rodriguez@ttu.edu.

Tulane University, School of Architecture, New Orleans, LA 70118-5669. Offers M Arch, MPS. Part-time programs available. *Degree requirements:* For master's, thesis. *Entrance requirements:* For master's, GRE, portfolio. Additional exam requirements/recommendations for international students: Required—TOEFL. *Expenses:* Contact institution. *Faculty research:* Design topics, preservation and environmental conservation, architecture and human health, computing.

Universidad Autonoma de Guadalajara, Graduate Programs, Guadalajara, Mexico. Offers administrative law and justice (LL M); advertising and corporate communications (MA); architecture (M Arch); business (MBA); computational science (MCC); education (Ed M, Ed D); English-Spanish translation (MA); fiscal law (MA); integrated management of digital animation (MA); international business (MIB); international corporate law (LL M); internet technologies (MS); labor health (MS); manufacturing systems (MMS); philosophy (MA, PhD); power electronics (MS); quality systems (MQS); renewable energy (MS); social evaluation of projects (MBA); strategic market research (MBA); teaching mathematics (MA).

Université Laval, Faculty of Architecture, Planning and Visual Arts, School of Architecture, Program in Architecture, Québec, QC G1K 7P4, Canada. Offers M Arch, M Sc. Part-time programs available. *Degree requirements:* For master's, thesis (for some programs). *Entrance requirements:* For master's, mastery of software (CAO), knowledge of French and English. Electronic applications accepted.

University at Buffalo, the State University of New York, Graduate School, School of Architecture and Planning, Department of Architecture, Buffalo, NY 14260. Offers M Arch, M Arch/MBA, M Arch/MFA, M Arch/MUP. *Faculty:* 21 full-time (8 women), 18 part-time/adjunct (5 women). *Students:* 125 full-time (46 women), 11 part-time (6 women); includes 7 minority (1 African American, 3 Asian Americans or Pacific Islanders, 3 Hispanic Americans), 22 international. Average age 25. 284 applicants, 46% accepted, 49 enrolled. In 2009, 40 master's awarded. *Degree requirements:* For master's, thesis or alternative, project. *Entrance requirements:* For master's, GRE, portfolio, 3 letters of recommendation, minimum GPA of 3.0. Additional exam requirements/recommendations for international students: Required—TOEFL (minimum score 550 paper-based; 213 computer-based; 79 iBT), or IELTS (minimum score 6.5). *Application deadline:* For fall admission, 1/15 for domestic and international students. Application fee: $75. Electronic applications accepted. *Financial support:* In 2009–10, 4 fellowships with full tuition reimbursements (averaging $9,600 per year), 4 research assistantships with full and partial tuition reimbursements (averaging $6,573 per year), 28 teaching assistantships with partial tuition reimbursements (averaging $4,800 per year) were awarded; career-related internships or fieldwork, Federal Work-Study, institutionally sponsored loans, scholarships/grants, health care benefits, tuition waivers (partial), and unspecified assistantships also available. Support available to part-time students. Financial award application deadline: 3/1; financial award applicants required to submit FAFSA. *Faculty research:* Inclusive design, material culture, situated technologies, sustainable urban and natural environments. Total annual research expenditures: $1.3 million. *Unit head:* Mehrdad Hadighi, Chair, 716-829-3483 Ext. 105, Fax: 716-829-3256, E-mail: hadighi@buffalo.edu. *Application contact:* Deborah R. Smith, Assistant to the Chair, 716-829-3485 Ext. 105, Fax: 716-829-3256, E-mail: drs5@buffalo.edu.

Architecture

The University of Arizona, College of Architecture and Landscape Architecture, School of Architecture, Tucson, AZ 85721. Offers M Arch. *Faculty:* 8. *Students:* 20 full-time (8 women), 6 part-time (2 women); includes 2 minority (both American Indian/Alaska Native), 9 international. Average age 31. 42 applicants, 43% accepted, 10 enrolled. In 2009, 14 master's awarded. *Entrance requirements:* For master's, GRE, 3 letters of recommendation, statement of purpose, portfolio, resume. Additional exam requirements/recommendations for international students: Required—TOEFL (minimum score 550 paper-based; 213 computer-based; 79 iBT). *Application deadline:* For fall admission, 2/1 for domestic students, 12/1 for international students; for spring admission, 2/1 for domestic and international students. Application fee: $75. Electronic applications accepted. *Expenses:* Tuition, state resident: full-time $9028. Tuition, nonresident: full-time $24,890. *Financial support:* In 2009–10, 23 teaching assistantships with full tuition reimbursements (averaging $10,184 per year) were awarded; research assistantships with full tuition reimbursements, health care benefits and unspecified assistantships also available. Total annual research expenditures: $41,435. *Unit head:* Mary Hardin, Interim Director, 520-621-6752, E-mail: mchardin@u.arizona.edu. *Application contact:* Linda Erasmus, 520-621-9819, Fax: 520-621-8700, E-mail: erasmus@email.arizona.edu.

The University of British Columbia, Faculty of Applied Science, School of Architecture and Landscape Architecture, Vancouver, BC V6T 1Z2, Canada. Offers architecture (M Arch, MASA); landscape architecture (MASLA, MLA). *Degree requirements:* For master's, thesis. *Entrance requirements:* For master's, portfolio, resume, 3 reference letters. Additional exam requirements/recommendations for international students: Required—TOEFL (minimum score 600 paper-based; 250 computer-based; 100 iBT). Electronic applications accepted. *Expenses:* Contact institution. *Faculty research:* Energy and resource use of buildings, advanced design research, urban design and community activism, advanced research in computer applications, cultural studies.

University of Calgary, Faculty of Graduate Studies, Faculty of Environmental Design, Calgary, AB T2N 1N4, Canada. Offers architecture (M Arch); environmental design (M Env Des, PhD). *Degree requirements:* For master's, thesis; for doctorate, thesis/dissertation. *Entrance requirements:* For master's, minimum GPA of 3.0; for doctorate, minimum GPA of 3.5. Additional exam requirements/recommendations for international students: Required—TOEFL (minimum score 550 paper-based; 213 computer-based). *Faculty research:* Sustainable development in architecture, planning and product design, energy and environment, impact assessment, ecotourism.

University of California, Berkeley, Graduate Division, College of Environmental Design, Department of Architecture, Berkeley, CA 94720-1500. Offers architecture (M Arch); building science (MS, PhD); building structures, construction and materials (MS, PhD); design theories, methods, and practices (MS, PhD); environmental design in developing countries (MS, PhD); history of architecture and urbanism (MS, PhD); social and cultural processes in architecture and urbanism (MS, PhD); M Arch/MCP; M Arch/MS; MLA/M Arch. *Students:* 156 full-time (91 women). Average age 30. 935 applicants, 60 enrolled. In 2009, 42 master's, 12 doctorates awarded. *Degree requirements:* For master's, thesis; for doctorate, thesis/dissertation, qualifying exam. *Entrance requirements:* For master's and doctorate, GRE General Test, minimum GPA of 3.0, 3 letters of recommendation. Additional exam requirements/recommendations for international students: Required—TOEFL. Application fee: $70 ($90 for international students). Electronic applications accepted. *Financial support:* Unspecified assistantships available. *Unit head:* Prof. Gail Brager, Chair, 510-642-4942. *Application contact:* Lois H. Ito Koch, Student Affairs Officer, 510-642-5577, Fax: 510-643-5607, E-mail: archgrad@berkeley.edu.

University of California, Los Angeles, Graduate Division, School of the Arts and Architecture, Department of Architecture and Urban Design, Los Angeles, CA 90095. Offers M Arch, MA, PhD. *Degree requirements:* For master's, thesis or alternative, comprehensive exam or design project; for doctorate, 2 foreign languages, thesis/dissertation, oral and written qualifying exams. *Entrance requirements:* For master's and doctorate, GRE General Test, portfolio. Additional exam requirements/recommendations for international students: Required—TOEFL. Electronic applications accepted. *Faculty research:* Urban poverty and low wage labor markets; environmental planning and politics; international political economy; physical planning, urban design, planning history; housing and land development; transportation and land use; critical urban and regional studies.

University of Cincinnati, Graduate School, College of Design, Architecture, Art, and Planning, School of Architecture and Interior Design, Cincinnati, OH 45221. Offers architecture (M Arch). *Accreditation:* NASAD. *Degree requirements:* For master's, one foreign language, thesis. *Entrance requirements:* Additional exam requirements/recommendations for international students: Required—TOEFL. *Faculty research:* Theory and history of architecture.

University of Colorado Denver, College of Architecture and Planning, Program in Architecture, Denver, CO 80217-3364. Offers M Arch. Part-time programs available. *Students:* 285 full-time (126 women), 17 part-time (9 women); includes 30 minority (5 African Americans, 10 Asian Americans or Pacific Islanders, 15 Hispanic Americans), 11 international. 326 applicants, 65% accepted, 91 enrolled. In 2009, 89 master's awarded. *Degree requirements:* For master's, thesis optional. *Entrance requirements:* For master's, GRE or minimum GPA of 3.0, portfolio, course work in trigonometry and physics. Additional exam requirements/recommendations for international students: Required—TOEFL (minimum score 550 paper-based; 213 computer-based). *Application deadline:* For fall admission, 3/15 for domestic students; for spring admission, 10/1 for domestic students. Application fee: $50 ($75 for international students). *Financial support:* Teaching assistantships, career-related internships or fieldwork, Federal Work-Study, institutionally sponsored loans, and scholarships/grants available. Financial award application deadline: 4/1; financial award applicants required to submit FAFSA. *Faculty research:* Architectural design; history, theory, and criticism of architecture; regional and environmental issues; sustainability; intervention and transformation in the urban and rural landscape. *Unit head:* Hans Morgenthaler, Chair, 303-556-4227, Fax: 303-556-3687, E-mail: hans.morgenthaler@ucdenver.edu. *Application contact:* Heather Zertuche, Administrative Assistant II, 303-556-3382, Fax: 303-556-3687, E-mail: anpdeansoffice@storm.cudenver.edu.

University of Florida, Graduate School, College of Design, Construction and Planning, Doctoral Program in Design, Construction and Planning, Gainesville, FL 32611. Offers PhD. *Degree requirements:* For doctorate, thesis/dissertation. *Entrance requirements:* For doctorate, GRE General Test, minimum GPA of 3.2. Additional exam requirements/recommendations for international students: Required—TOEFL. Electronic applications accepted. *Faculty research:* Architecture, building construction, urban and regional planning.

University of Florida, Graduate School, College of Design, Construction and Planning, School of Architecture, Gainesville, FL 32611. Offers M Arch, MSAS, PhD.

University of Hartford, College of Engineering, Technology and Architecture, Program in Architecture, West Hartford, CT 06117-1599. Offers M Arch. *Entrance requirements:* For master's, 3 letters of recommendation, portfolio. Additional exam requirements/recommendations for international students: Required—TOEFL (minimum score 550 paper-based; 213 computer-based).

University of Hawaii at Manoa, School of Architecture, Honolulu, HI 96822. Offers D Arch. *Expenses:* Tuition, state resident: full-time $8900; part-time $372 per credit. Tuition, nonresident: full-time $21,400; part-time $898 per credit. Required fees: $207 per semester. *Faculty research:* Housing, future cities, environmental studies, preservation, professional practice.

University of Houston, College of Architecture, Houston, TX 77204. Offers MA, MS. *Faculty:* 15 full-time (2 women), 16 part-time/adjunct (2 women). *Students:* 67 full-time (33 women), 7 part-time (3 women); includes 13 minority (2 African Americans, 7 Asian Americans or Pacific Islanders, 4 Hispanic Americans), 15 international. Average age 28. 111 applicants, 50% accepted, 32 enrolled. In 2009, 27 master's awarded. *Entrance requirements:* For master's, GRE General Test. Additional exam requirements/recommendations for international students: Required—TOEFL (minimum score 550 paper-based; 79 iBT), IELTS (minimum score 6.5). *Application deadline:* For fall admission, 2/1 priority date for domestic and international students; for spring admission, 10/1 priority date for domestic and international students. Applications are processed on a rolling basis. Application fee: $50. Electronic applications accepted. *Expenses:* Tuition, state resident: full-time $7676; part-time $320 per credit hour. Tuition, nonresident: full-time $14,324; part-time $597 per credit hour. Required fees: $3034. *Financial support:* In 2009–10, 1 fellowship with full tuition reimbursement (averaging $9,700 per year), 2 teaching assistantships with full tuition reimbursements (averaging $9,200 per year) were awarded; research assistantships with full tuition reimbursements, career-related internships or fieldwork, Federal Work-Study, institutionally sponsored loans, scholarships/grants, health care benefits, and unspecified assistantships also available. Support available to part-time students. Financial award application deadline: 2/1. *Faculty research:* Community based design; twentieth century architecture, urbanism, and design; extreme environments; design build; green building components and digital technology. *Unit head:* Dr. Patricia Oliver, Dean, 713-743-2400, Fax: 713-743-2358, E-mail: poliver@central.uh.edu. *Application contact:* Thomas M. Colbert, Director of Graduate Studies, 713-743-2380, Fax: 713-743-2358, E-mail: tcolbert@uh.edu.

University of Idaho, College of Graduate Studies, College of Art and Architecture, Department of Architecture and Interior Design, Moscow, ID 83844-2282. Offers M Arch, MS. *Faculty:* 12 full-time, 1 part-time/adjunct. *Students:* 51 full-time, 6 part-time. In 2009, 46 master's awarded. *Entrance requirements:* For master's, minimum GPA of 2.8. *Application deadline:* For fall admission, 8/1 for domestic students; for spring admission, 12/15 for domestic students. Application fee: $55 ($60 for international students). *Expenses:* Tuition, state resident: full-time $6120. Tuition, nonresident: full-time $17,712. *Financial support:* Research assistantships, teaching assistantships available. Financial award application deadline: 2/15. *Faculty research:* Sustainable interior environments, multi-hazard design, environmental technologies for sustainable architectural design. *Unit head:* Diane Armpriest, Chair, 208-885-6781. *Application contact:* Diane Armpriest, Chair, 208-885-6781.

University of Illinois at Chicago, Graduate College, College of Architecture and Art, School of Architecture, Chicago, IL 60607-7128. Offers architecture (M Arch, MS Arch); architecture in health design (MS Arch). *Entrance requirements:* For master's, GRE General Test, portfolio, minimum GPA of 3.0. Additional exam requirements/recommendations for international students: Required—TOEFL. Electronic applications accepted. *Faculty research:* Housing values, elderly housing, design theory, deconstructivism.

University of Illinois at Urbana–Champaign, Graduate College, College of Fine and Applied Arts, School of Architecture, Champaign, IL 61820. Offers architectural studies (MS); architecture (M Arch, PhD); M Arch/MBA; M Arch/MS; M Arch/MUP; MCS/M Arch; MRP/JD. *Faculty:* 34 full-time (7 women), 5 part-time/adjunct (1 woman). *Students:* 188 full-time (76 women), 5 part-time (2 women); includes 37 minority (4 African Americans, 1 American Indian/Alaska Native, 19 Asian Americans or Pacific Islanders, 13 Hispanic Americans), 33 international. 422 applicants, 20% accepted, 71 enrolled. In 2009, 83 master's, 3 doctorates awarded. *Entrance requirements:* For master's, minimum GPA of 3.0; portfolio; for doctorate, GRE, minimum GPA of 3.0; portfolio. Additional exam requirements/recommendations for international students: Required—TOEFL (minimum score 590 paper-based; 243 computer-based; 96 iBT), or IELTS (minimum score 6.5). *Application deadline:* Applications are processed on a rolling basis. Application fee: $60 ($75 for international students). Electronic applications accepted. *Financial support:* In 2009–10, 32 fellowships, 16 research assistantships, 35 teaching assistantships were awarded; tuition waivers (full and partial) also available. *Unit head:* David Chasco, Director, 217-333-1331, Fax: 217-244-8866, E-mail: dchasco@illinois.edu. *Application contact:* Christopher R. Wilcock, Admissions and Records Officer, 217-244-4723, Fax: 217-244-8866, E-mail: cwilcock@illinois.edu.

The University of Kansas, Graduate Studies, School of Architecture, Design, and Planning, Program in Architecture, Lawrence, KS 66045. Offers architecture (PhD); facility management (AC); management option (M Arch); professional track (M Arch); M Arch/MBA; M Arch/MUP. *Faculty:* 20 full-time (5 women). *Students:* 122 full-time (48 women), 19 part-time (11 women); includes 14 minority (6 African Americans, 2 American Indian/Alaska Native, 2 Asian Americans or Pacific Islanders, 4 Hispanic Americans), 11 international. Average age 25. 113 applicants, 65% accepted, 37 enrolled. In 2009, 76 master's awarded. Terminal master's awarded for partial completion of doctoral program. *Degree requirements:* For master's, thesis or alternative, 1 summer abroad; for doctorate, comprehensive exam, thesis/dissertation. *Entrance requirements:* For master's, portfolio, minimum GPA of 3.0; for doctorate, GRE, portfolio. Additional exam requirements/recommendations for international students: Required—TOEFL. *Application deadline:* For fall admission, 3/1 priority date for domestic and international students; for spring admission, 11/1 priority date for domestic and international students. Applications are processed on a rolling basis. Application fee: $45 ($55 for international students). Electronic applications accepted. *Expenses:* Tuition, state resident: full-time $6492; part-time $270.50 per credit hour. Tuition, nonresident: full-time $15,510; part-time $646.25 per credit hour. Required fees: $847; $70.56 per credit hour. Tuition and fees vary according to course load and program. *Financial support:* Fellowships, research assistantships with partial tuition reimbursements, teaching assistantships with full and partial tuition reimbursements, scholarships/grants, health care benefits, and unspecified assistantships available. Financial award application deadline: 2/1; financial award applicants required to submit FAFSA. *Faculty research:* Design build, sustainability, emergent technology, healthy places, urban design. *Unit head:* Prof. Keith Diaz Moore, Chair, 785-864-5088, Fax: 785-864-5185, E-mail: archku@ku.edu. *Application contact:* Gera Elliott, Admissions Coordinator, 785-864-3167, Fax: 785-864-5185, E-mail: archku@ku.edu.

University of Kentucky, Graduate School, College of Design, School of Architecture, Lexington, KY 40506-0032. Offers M Arch. *Degree requirements:* For master's, comprehensive exam. *Entrance requirements:* For master's, GRE General Test, minimum undergraduate GPA of 2.75. Additional exam requirements/recommendations for international students: Required—TOEFL (minimum score 550 paper-based; 213 computer-based). Electronic applications accepted.

University of Manitoba, Faculty of Graduate Studies, Faculty of Architecture, Department of Architecture, Winnipeg, MB R3T 2N2, Canada. Offers M Arch. *Degree requirements:* For master's, thesis or alternative.

University of Maryland, College Park, Academic Affairs, School of Architecture, Planning and Preservation, Program in Architecture, College Park, MD 20742. Offers M Arch, M Arch/MCP. Part-time and evening/weekend programs available. *Faculty:* 22 full-time (7 women), 2 part-time/adjunct (0 women). *Students:* 85 full-time (51 women), 1 part-time (0 women); includes 18 minority (2 African Americans, 1 American Indian/Alaska Native, 8 Asian Americans or Pacific Islanders, 7 Hispanic Americans), 6 international. 311 applicants, 37% accepted, 61 enrolled. In 2009, 50 master's awarded. *Entrance requirements:* For master's, GRE General Test, portfolio, minimum GPA of 3.0, letters of recommendation. Additional exam requirements/recommendations for international students: Required—TOEFL. *Application deadline:* For fall admission, 12/15 for domestic and international students; for spring admission, 6/1 for international students. Applications are processed on a rolling basis. Application fee: $60. Electronic applications accepted. *Expenses:* Tuition, area resident: Part-time $471 per credit hour. Tuition, state resident: part-time $471 per credit hour. Tuition, nonresident: part-time $1016 per credit hour. Required fees: $337.04 per term. *Financial support:* In 2009–10, 51 teaching assistantships with tuition reimbursements (averaging $15,137 per year) were awarded; fellowships, research assistantships, career-related internships or fieldwork, Federal Work-Study, and scholarships/grants also available. Support available to part-time students. Financial award applicants required to submit FAFSA. *Faculty research:* Design, history, theory. Total annual research expenditures: $49,718. *Unit head:* Madlen Simon, Director, 301-405-8677, Fax: 301-314-9583, E-mail: mgsimon@umd.edu. *Application contact:* Dean of Graduate School, 301-405-0358.

University of Massachusetts Amherst, Graduate School, College of Humanities and Fine Arts, Department of Art, Programs in Architecture and Design, Amherst, MA 01003. Offers architecture and design (M Arch); historic preservation (MS); interior design (MS). Part-time programs available. *Students:* 43 full-time (15 women); includes 5 minority (1 African American, 2 Asian Americans or Pacific Islanders, 2 Hispanic Americans), 7 international. Average age 30. 100 applicants, 64% accepted, 21 enrolled. In 2009, 12 master's awarded. *Degree requirements:* For master's, thesis or alternative. *Entrance requirements:* For master's, GRE General Test (M Arch), portfolio. Additional exam requirements/recommendations for international students: Required—TOEFL (minimum score 550 paper-based; 213 computer-based; 80 iBT), IELTS (minimum score 6.5). *Application deadline:* For fall admission, 2/1 for domestic and international students. Applications are processed on a rolling basis. Application fee: $50 ($65 for international students). Electronic applications accepted. *Expenses:* Tuition, state resident: full-time $2640; part-time $110 per credit. Tuition, nonresident: full-time $9936; part-time $414 per credit. Tuition and fees vary according to course load. *Financial support:* Fellowships, research assistantships, teaching assistantships, career-related internships or fieldwork, Federal Work-Study, scholarships/grants, traineeships, health care benefits, tuition waivers (full), and unspecified assistantships available. Support available to part-time students. Financial award application deadline: 2/1. *Unit head:* Dr. Ray K. Mann, Graduate Program Director, 413-545-0943, Fax: 413-545-3929. *Application contact:* Jean M. Ames, Supervisor of Admissions, 413-545-0722, Fax: 413-577-0100, E-mail: gradadm@grad.umass.edu.

University of Memphis, Graduate School, College of Communication and Fine Arts, Department of Architecture, Memphis, TN 38152. Offers M Arch. *Faculty:* 4 full-time (1 woman), 1 part-time/adjunct (0 women). *Students:* 11 full-time (8 women), 1 part-time (0 women); includes 4 minority (3 African Americans, 1 American Indian/Alaska Native), 2 international. Average age 29. 5 applicants, 80% accepted, 4 enrolled. *Expenses:* Tuition, state resident: full-time $6246; part-time $347 per credit hour. Tuition, nonresident: full-time $15,894; part-time $883 per credit hour. Required fees: $1160. Full-time tuition and fees vary according to course load, degree level and program. *Financial support:* In 2009–10, 7 students received support; research assistantships with full tuition reimbursements available, teaching assistantships with full tuition reimbursements available, Federal Work-Study, scholarships/grants, and unspecified assistantships available. Financial award application deadline: 2/15; financial award applicants required to submit FAFSA. *Unit head:* Dr. Michael D. Hagge, Chair, 901-678-2724, Fax: 901-678-1755, E-mail: mdhagge@memphis.edu. *Application contact:* Sherry Brian, Coordinator of Graduate Studies, 901-678-3302, Fax: 901-678-1755.

University of Miami, Graduate School, School of Architecture, Coral Gables, FL 33124. Offers architecture (M Arch); suburb and town design (M Arch). *Entrance requirements:* For master's, GRE General Test, minimum GPA of 3.0, portfolio. Additional exam requirements/recommendations for international students: Required—TOEFL. Electronic applications accepted. *Faculty research:* Housing, town planning, retrofit.

University of Michigan, Taubman College of Architecture and Urban Planning, Doctoral Studies in Architecture, Ann Arbor, MI 48109. Offers PhD. Offered through the Horace H. Rackham School of Graduate Studies. Terminal master's awarded for partial completion of doctoral program. *Degree requirements:* For doctorate, comprehensive exam, thesis/dissertation, oral defense of dissertation, preliminary exam, practicum. *Entrance requirements:* For doctorate, GRE General Test. Additional exam requirements/recommendations for international students: Required—TOEFL (minimum score 560 paper-based; 220 computer-based; 100 iBT). Electronic applications accepted. *Expenses:* Contact institution. *Faculty research:* Environment and behavior, environmental technology, history-theory, design process and methods.

University of Michigan, Taubman College of Architecture and Urban Planning, Master of Architecture Program, Ann Arbor, MI 48109-2069. Offers M Arch, M Sc, M Arch/M Eng, M Arch/MSE, M Arch/MUP, MBA/M Arch. *Entrance requirements:* For master's, GRE, 3 recommendations, resume, portfolio. Additional exam requirements/recommendations for international students: Required—TOEFL (minimum score 600 paper-based; 250 computer-based; 100 iBT). Electronic applications accepted. *Expenses:* Contact institution.

University of Minnesota, Twin Cities Campus, Graduate School, College of Design, School of Architecture, Minneapolis, MN 55455-0213. Offers architecture (M Arch); sustainable design (MS). First professional and post-professional tracks available in M Arch program. *Degree requirements:* For master's, thesis (for some programs). *Entrance requirements:* For master's, GRE General Test, suggested GPA of 3.0, portfolio. Additional exam requirements/recommendations for international students: Required—TOEFL (minimum score 550 paper-based; 213 computer-based; 79 iBT). *Expenses:* Contact institution. *Faculty research:* History, daylighting, computer-aided design, sustainable design, structures.

University of Missouri, Graduate School, College of Human Environmental Science, Department of Architectural Studies, Columbia, MO 65211. Offers design with digital media (MA, MS); environmental design (MS). *Entrance requirements:* For master's, GRE General Test, minimum GPA of 3.0. Additional exam requirements/recommendations for international students: Required—TOEFL (minimum score 500 paper-based; 173 computer-based; 61 iBT).

University of Nebraska–Lincoln, Graduate College, College of Architecture, Department of Architecture, Graduate Program in Architecture, Lincoln, NE 68588. Offers MS, PhD. *Degree requirements:* For master's, comprehensive exam, thesis. *Entrance requirements:* For master's, GRE General Test. Additional exam requirements/recommendations for international students: Required—TOEFL (minimum score 550 paper-based; 213 computer-based). Electronic applications accepted. *Faculty research:* Housing, environmental design, architectural history, sustainable design, rural architecture.

University of Nebraska–Lincoln, Graduate College, College of Architecture, Department of Architecture, Professional Program in Architecture, Lincoln, NE 68588. Offers M Arch, M Arch/MBA, M Arch/MCRP. *Entrance requirements:* For master's, GRE General Test. Additional exam requirements/recommendations for international students: Required—TOEFL. *Faculty research:* Housing, environmental design, architectural history, sustainable design, rural architecture.

University of Nevada, Las Vegas, Graduate College, College of Fine Arts, School of Architecture, Las Vegas, NV 89154. Offers M Arch. Part-time programs available. *Faculty:* 10 full-time (1 woman), 3 part-time/adjunct (0 women). *Students:* 28 full-time (11 women), 11 part-time (4 women); includes 8 minority (1 African American, 2 Asian Americans or Pacific Islanders, 5 Hispanic Americans), 3 international. Average age 31. 61 applicants, 54% accepted, 18 enrolled. In 2009, 11 master's awarded. *Degree requirements:* For master's, thesis (for some programs), professional project. *Entrance requirements:* For master's, GRE General Test (minimum score 410 verbal, 430 quantitative). Additional exam requirements/recommendations for international students: Required—TOEFL (minimum score 550 paper-based; 213 computer-based; 80 iBT), IELTS (minimum score 7). *Application deadline:* For fall admission, 2/1 priority date for domestic and international students. Applications are processed on a rolling basis. Application fee: $60 ($95 for international students). Electronic applications accepted. *Financial support:* In 2009–10, 10 students received support, including 6 research assistantships with partial tuition reimbursements available (averaging $12,500 per year), 4 teaching assistantships with partial tuition reimbursements available (averaging $12,500 per year); institutionally sponsored loans, scholarships/grants, health care benefits, and unspecified assistantships also available. Financial award application deadline: 3/1. *Faculty research:* Passive solar architecture and solar water distillation, urban design frameworks involving applications of IT tools to address issues of sustainable urban life, creative processes considered as leadership in project development, architecture of George Barber, design guidelines for educational facilities. *Unit head:* Dr. Attila Lawrence, Chair/ Professor, 702-895-3031, Fax: 702-895-1119, E-mail: attila.lawrence@unlv.edu. *Application contact:* Graduate College Admissions Evaluator, 702-895-3320, Fax: 702-895-4180, E-mail: gradcollege@unlv.edu.

University of New Mexico, Graduate School, School of Architecture and Planning, Program in Architecture, Albuquerque, NM 87131-2039. Offers M Arch. *Faculty:* 28 full-time (10 women), 22 part-time/adjunct (7 women). *Students:* 80 full-time (24 women), 25 part-time (5 women); includes 38 minority (1 African American, 8 American Indian/Alaska Native, 4 Asian Americans or Pacific Islanders, 25 Hispanic Americans), 8 international. Average age 32. 103 applicants, 59% accepted, 33 enrolled. In 2009, 28 master's awarded. *Degree requirements:* For master's, thesis (for some programs), review. *Entrance requirements:* For master's, experience in field. Additional exam requirements/recommendations for international students: Required—TOEFL (minimum score 550 paper-based; 213 computer-based; 79 iBT). *Application deadline:* For fall admission, 2/1 priority date for domestic students. Application fee: $50. Electronic applications accepted. *Expenses:* Tuition, state resident: full-time $2099; part-time $233.20 per credit hour. Tuition, nonresident: full-time $6650. Required fees: $25 per semester. Tuition and fees vary according to course load, program and reciprocity agreements. *Financial support:* In 2009–10, 56 students received support, including 7 fellowships, 26 research assistantships with partial tuition reimbursements available (averaging $6,000 per year); scholarships/grants, health care benefits, and unspecified assistantships also available. Financial award application deadline: 3/1; financial award applicants required to submit FAFSA. *Faculty research:* Professional practice, design theory, sustainable environments, architecture and children, environment and behavior. *Unit head:* Geraldine Forbes Isais, Director, 505-277-3303, Fax: 505-277-0076, E-mail: gforbes@unm.edu. *Application contact:* Elizabeth Rowe, Senior Academic Advisor, 505-277-1303, Fax: 505-277-0076, E-mail: mitziv@unm.edu.

The University of North Carolina at Charlotte, Graduate School, College of Arts and Architecture, Charlotte, NC 28223-0001. Offers architecture (M Arch). *Faculty:* 45 full-time (15 women), 3 part-time/adjunct (1 woman). *Students:* 75 full-time (41 women), 7 part-time (5 women); includes 8 African Americans, 4 Asian Americans or Pacific Islanders, 1 Hispanic American. Average age 27. 73 applicants, 66% accepted, 37 enrolled. In 2009, 25 master's awarded. *Degree requirements:* For master's, project or thesis. *Entrance requirements:* For master's, GRE General Test or GMAT, portfolio, resume. Additional exam requirements/recommendations for international students: Required—TOEFL (minimum score 557 paper-based; 220 computer-based; 83 iBT). *Application deadline:* For fall admission, 2/15 for domestic students, 1/31 for international students. Application fee: $55. Electronic applications accepted. *Financial support:* In 2009–10, 16 students received support, including 16 teaching assistantships (averaging $8,338 per year); career-related internships or fieldwork, institutionally sponsored loans, scholarships/grants, and unspecified assistantships also available. Support available to part-time students. Financial award application deadline: 4/1; financial award applicants required to submit FAFSA. *Faculty research:* Daylighting and energy control, urban design, history and theory, construction techniques. Total annual research expenditures: $131,156. *Unit head:* Kenneth A. Lambla, Dean, 704-687-4024, Fax: 704-687-3353, E-mail: kalambla@uncc.edu. *Application contact:* Kathy B. Giddings, Director of Graduate Admissions, 704-687-5503, Fax: 704-687-3279, E-mail: gradadm@uncc.edu.

The University of North Carolina at Greensboro, Graduate School, School of Human Environmental Sciences, Department of Interior Architecture, Greensboro, NC 27412-5001. Offers historic preservation (Certificate); interior architecture (MS); museum studies (Certificate). *Degree requirements:* For master's, thesis. *Entrance requirements:* For master's, GRE General Test or MAT, bachelor's degree in interior design, interview, portfolio. Additional exam requirements/recommendations for international students: Required—TOEFL. Electronic applications accepted.

University of Notre Dame, Graduate School, School of Architecture, Notre Dame, IN 46556. Offers architectural design and urbanism (M ADU); architecture (M Arch). *Degree requirements:* For master's, thesis or alternative. *Entrance requirements:* For master's, GRE General Test, portfolio. Additional exam requirements/recommendations for international students: Required—TOEFL (minimum score 600 paper-based; 250 computer-based; 80 iBT). Electronic applications accepted. *Faculty research:* Architectural theory, urban design, classical and traditional architecture and urbanism.

University of Oklahoma, Graduate College, College of Architecture, Division of Architecture, Norman, OK 73019-0390. Offers M Arch. Part-time programs available. *Faculty:* 31 full-time (8 women). *Students:* 23 full-time (9 women), 8 part-time (3 women); includes 7 minority (2 American Indian/Alaska Native, 2 Asian Americans or Pacific Islanders, 3 Hispanic Americans), 9 international. 29 applicants, 90% accepted, 14 enrolled. In 2009, 12 master's awarded. *Degree requirements:* For master's, thesis or alternative, portfolio, project. *Entrance requirements:* For master's, GRE General Test, portfolio. Additional exam requirements/recommendations for international students: Required—TOEFL (minimum score 550 paper-based; 213 computer-based). *Application deadline:* For fall admission, 4/1 for domestic and international students; for spring admission, 11/1 for domestic students, 9/1 for international students. Applications are processed on a rolling basis. Application fee: $40 ($90 for international students). Electronic applications accepted. *Expenses:* Tuition, state resident: full-time $3744; part-time $156 per credit hour. Tuition, nonresident: full-time $13,577; part-time $565.70 per credit hour. Required fees: $2415; $90.10 per credit hour. *Financial support:* In 2009–10, 13 students received support, including 4 teaching assistantships with partial tuition reimbursements available (averaging $9,586 per year); career-related internships or fieldwork, Federal Work-Study, scholarships/grants, tuition waivers (partial), and unspecified assistantships also available. Support available to part-time students. Financial award applicants required to submit FAFSA. *Faculty research:* Sustainability, regionalism, facilities management. Total annual research expenditures: $465,876. *Unit head:* Nickolas L. Harm, Interim Director, 405-325-2444, Fax: 405-325-7558, E-mail: nharm@ou.edu. *Application contact:* Terry Patterson, Professor/Graduate Liaison, 405-325-3869, Fax: 405-325-7558, E-mail: tpatterson@ou.edu.

University of Oklahoma, Graduate College, College of Architecture, Division of Construction Science, Norman, OK 73019-0390. Offers MS. Part-time and evening/weekend programs available. *Students:* 9 full-time (3 women), 25 part-time (7 women); includes 2 minority (both African Americans), 7 international. 17 applicants, 88% accepted, 9 enrolled. In 2009, 5 master's awarded. *Degree requirements:* For master's, thesis or alternative, portfolio, project. *Entrance requirements:* For master's, GRE General Test, portfolio. Additional exam requirements/recommendations for international students: Required—TOEFL (minimum score 600 paper-based; 250 computer-based). *Application deadline:* For fall admission, 4/1 for domestic and international students; for spring admission, 11/1 for domestic students, 9/1 for international students. Applications are processed on a rolling basis. Application fee: $40 ($90 for international students). Electronic applications accepted. *Expenses:* Tuition, state resident: full-time $3744; part-time $156 per credit hour. Tuition, nonresident: full-time $13,577; part-time $565.70 per credit hour. Required fees: $2415; $90.10 per credit hour. *Financial support:* In 2009–10, 21 students received support, including 2 research assistantships with partial tuition reimbursements available (averaging $11,543 per year), 3 teaching assistantships with partial tuition reimbursements available (averaging $9,586 per year); career-related internships or fieldwork, scholarships/grants, tuition waivers (partial), and unspecified assistantships also available. Support available to part-time students. Financial award applicants required to submit FAFSA. *Faculty research:* Online education, highway construction, lean construction, Hispanic construction worker design/safety, online instructional design. *Unit head:* Kenneth Robson, Director, 405-325-2444, Fax: 405-325-7558, E-mail: krobson@ou.edu. *Application contact:* Richard C. Ryan, Professor, 405-325-3976, Fax: 405-325-7558, E-mail: rryan@ou.edu.

University of Oklahoma—Tulsa, Urban Design Studio, Tulsa, OK 74135-2512. Offers architectural urban studies (MS); urban design (M Arch).

University of Oregon, Graduate School, School of Architecture and Allied Arts, Department of Architecture, Eugene, OR 97403. Offers architecture (M Arch); interior architecture (MI Arch). *Accreditation:* CIDA. *Degree requirements:* For master's, thesis (for some programs). *Entrance requirements:* For master's, GRE General Test. Additional exam requirements/recommendations for international students: Required—TOEFL. *Faculty research:* Innovation in housing design

Architecture

University of Oregon (continued)
and design production, climate responsive design, passive heating and cooling, computer software development for design applications, vernacular architecture.

University of Pennsylvania, School of Design, Graduate Group in Architecture, Philadelphia, PA 19104. Offers architecture (PhD); real estate design and development (PhD); urban design (PhD). Part-time programs available. *Faculty:* 16 full-time (5 women), 13 part-time/adjunct (3 women). *Students:* 266 full-time (126 women), 7 part-time (2 women); includes 49 minority (6 African Americans, 2 American Indian/Alaska Native, 28 Asian Americans or Pacific Islanders, 13 Hispanic Americans), 81 international. 894 applicants, 38% accepted, 127 enrolled. In 2009, 6 doctorates awarded. *Degree requirements:* For doctorate, 2 foreign languages, comprehensive exam, thesis/dissertation, qualifying exam, final exam. *Entrance requirements:* For doctorate, GRE General Test, B Arch, M Arch, portfolio, writing sample. Additional exam requirements/recommendations for international students: Required—TOEFL. *Application deadline:* For fall admission, 1/2 priority date for domestic students. Application fee: $70. *Expenses:* Tuition: Full-time $25,660; part-time $4758 per course. Required fees: $2152; $270 per course. Tuition and fees vary according to course load, degree level and program. *Financial support:* Fellowships, research assistantships, teaching assistantships, institutionally sponsored loans, scholarships/grants, traineeships, health care benefits, and unspecified assistantships available. *Faculty research:* Theory, history, technology, representation, visualization, landscape, urban design, historic preservation.

See Close-Up on page 147.

University of Pennsylvania, School of Design, Master of Architecture Program, Philadelphia, PA 19104. Offers architecture (M Arch); real estate design and development (Certificate); urban design (Certificate). *Degree requirements:* For master's, thesis (for some programs). *Entrance requirements:* For master's and Certificate, GRE, portfolio. Additional exam requirements/recommendations for international students: Required—TOEFL. *Expenses:* Tuition: Full-time $25,660; part-time $4758 per course. Required fees: $2152; $270 per course. Tuition and fees vary according to course load, degree level and program. *Faculty research:* Computer modeling, metropolitan and regional urbanism, contemporary architectural theory structure and technology.

See Close-Up on page 147.

University of Puerto Rico, Río Piedras, School of Architecture, San Juan, PR 00931-3300. Offers M Arch. Part-time programs available. *Degree requirements:* For master's, comprehensive exam, thesis, design project. *Entrance requirements:* For master's, PAEG or GRE, bachelor's degree in architecture, interview, minimum GPA of 3.0, portfolio, 2 letters of recommendation.

University of Southern California, Graduate School, School of Architecture, Los Angeles, CA 90089. Offers M Arch, MBS, MHP, ML Arch, MLA, PhD, M Arch/M Pl, MLA/M Pl. Part-time programs available. *Students:* 187 full-time (91 women), 3 part-time (2 women); includes 33 minority (2 African Americans, 1 American Indian/Alaska Native, 15 Asian Americans or Pacific Islanders, 15 Hispanic Americans), 93 international. 415 applicants, 42% accepted, 92 enrolled. In 2009, 40 master's awarded. *Degree requirements:* For master's, thesis; for doctorate, 2 foreign languages, thesis/dissertation. *Entrance requirements:* For master's and doctorate, GRE. Additional exam requirements/recommendations for international students: Required—TOEFL (minimum score 100 iBT). *Application deadline:* For fall admission, 12/1 priority date for domestic students, 11/1 priority date for international students. Applications are processed on a rolling basis. Application fee: $85. Electronic applications accepted. *Expenses:* Tuition: Full-time $25,980; part-time $1315 per unit. Required fees: $554. One-time fee: $35 full-time. Full-time tuition and fees vary according to degree level and program. *Faculty research:* Digital technology in design, environmental intelligent design, creative responses to natural forces, urban place-making via landscape architecture, preservation and economic revitalization of communities and cultural landscape. *Unit head:* Dean Qingyun Ma, Dean, 213-740-2723, E-mail: archdean@usc.edu. *Application contact:* Julette Sanders, Director of Graduate Admissions, 213-821-2168, E-mail: archgrad@usc.edu.

University of South Florida, Graduate School, College of The Arts, School of Architecture and Community Design, Tampa, FL 33620-9951. Offers M Arch. *Faculty:* 10 full-time (2 women), 11 part-time/adjunct (5 women). *Students:* 72 full-time (30 women), 57 part-time (25 women); includes 43 minority (6 African Americans, 2 American Indian/Alaska Native, 7 Asian Americans or Pacific Islanders, 28 Hispanic Americans), 4 international. Average age 32. 83 applicants, 43% accepted, 22 enrolled. In 2009, 28 master's awarded. *Degree requirements:* For master's, comprehensive exam, thesis. *Entrance requirements:* For master's, GRE General Test, minimum GPA of 3.0 in last 60 hours of coursework. Additional exam requirements/recommendations for international students: Required—TOEFL (minimum score 550 paper-based; 213 computer-based). *Application deadline:* For fall admission, 2/1 priority date for domestic students, 1/2 for international students. Applications are processed on a rolling basis. Application fee: $30. Electronic applications accepted. *Financial support:* In 2009–10, 20 students received support, including 1 fellowship (averaging $7,500 per year), teaching assistantships (averaging $9,001 per year); Federal Work-Study, scholarships/grants, and unspecified assistantships also available. *Faculty research:* Community design, sustainability, portable classrooms. Total annual research expenditures: $27,090. *Unit head:* Prof. Robert MacLeod, School Director, 813-974-6015, Fax: 813-974-2557, E-mail: rmacleod@arch.usf.edu. *Application contact:* Mildred Abreu, Academic Advisor, 813-974-1216, Fax: 813-974-2557, E-mail: abreu@arch.usf.edu.

The University of Tennessee, Graduate School, College of Architecture and Design, Program in Architecture, Knoxville, TN 37996. Offers architecture (professional) (M Arch); architecture (research) (M Arch). *Degree requirements:* For master's, thesis. *Entrance requirements:* For master's, GRE General Test, minimum GPA of 3.0, 3 letters of recommendation, samples of portfolio work (highly recommended for professional track). Additional exam requirements/recommendations for international students: Required—TOEFL (minimum score 550 paper-based). *Expenses:* Tuition, state resident: full-time $6826; part-time $380 per semester hour. Tuition, nonresident: full-time $21,844; part-time $1147 per semester hour. Tuition and fees vary according to program.

The University of Texas at Arlington, Graduate School, School of Architecture, Program in Architecture, Arlington, TX 76019. Offers M Arch, M Arch/MCRP. *Faculty:* 24 full-time (4 women), 1 part-time/adjunct (0 women). *Students:* 149 full-time (54 women), 30 part-time (14 women); includes 50 minority (3 African Americans, 19 Asian Americans or Pacific Islanders, 28 Hispanic Americans), 25 international. 126 applicants, 98% accepted, 50 enrolled. In 2009, 38 master's awarded. *Entrance requirements:* For master's, GRE General Test (minimum score 1000 verbal and quantitative), minimum GPA of 3.0, portfolio, 3 letters of recommendation. Additional exam requirements/recommendations for international students: Required—TOEFL (minimum score 550 paper-based; 213 computer-based). *Application deadline:* For fall admission, 6/6 for domestic students, 4/4 for international students; for spring admission, 10/17 for domestic students, 9/5 for international students. Applications are processed on a rolling basis. Application fee: $35 ($60 for international students). Electronic applications accepted. *Financial support:* In 2009–10, 12 research assistantships with full and partial tuition reimbursements (averaging $4,824 per year), 16 teaching assistantships with full and partial tuition reimbursements (averaging $4,824 per year) were awarded; career-related internships or fieldwork, scholarships/grants, and unspecified assistantships also available. Financial award application deadline: 6/1; financial award applicants required to submit FAFSA. *Unit head:* Donald Gatzke, Director, 817-272-2801, Fax: 817-272-5098, E-mail: gatzke@uta.edu. *Application contact:* David Jones, Associate Dean, 817-272-2801, Fax: 817-272-5098, E-mail: djonesarch@uta.edu.

The University of Texas at Austin, Graduate School, School of Architecture, Austin, TX 78712-1111. Offers architecture (M Arch); community and regional planning (MSCRP, PhD); historic preservation (MS); history of architecture (MA, PhD); landscape architecture (MLA); urban design (MSUD); JD/MSCRP; MSCRP/MA; MSCRP/PhD. *Degree requirements:* For doctorate, thesis/dissertation. *Entrance requirements:* For master's and doctorate, GRE General Test. Additional exam requirements/recommendations for international students: Required—TOEFL (minimum score 550 paper-based; 213 computer-based). Electronic applications accepted.

The University of Texas at San Antonio, College of Architecture, San Antonio, TX 78249-0617. Offers M Arch, MS Arch. *Faculty:* 19 full-time (6 women). *Students:* 77 full-time (27 women), 22 part-time (8 women); includes 42 minority (4 African Americans, 1 Asian American or Pacific Islander, 37 Hispanic Americans), 8 international. Average age 29. 67 applicants, 66% accepted, 30 enrolled. In 2009, 32 master's awarded. *Degree requirements:* For master's, comprehensive exam (for some programs), thesis (for some programs). *Entrance requirements:* For master's, GRE General Test, minimum GPA of 3.0 in last 60 hours and in all architecture courses. Additional exam requirements/recommendations for international students: Required—TOEFL (minimum score 500 paper-based; 173 computer-based; 61 iBT), IELTS (minimum score 5). *Application deadline:* For fall admission, 7/1 for domestic students, 4/1 for international students; for spring admission, 11/1 for domestic students, 9/1 for international students. Applications are processed on a rolling basis. Application fee: $45 ($80 for international students). Electronic applications accepted. *Expenses:* Tuition, state resident: full-time $3975; part-time $221 per contact hour. Tuition, nonresident: full-time $13,947; part-time $775 per contact hour. Required fees: $1853. *Financial support:* In 2009–10, 22 students received support, including 36 research assistantships (averaging $6,691 per year); career-related internships or fieldwork, scholarships/grants, and unspecified assistantships also available. Total annual research expenditures: $60,720. *Unit head:* Julius M. Gribou, Dean, 210-458-3090, Fax: 210-458-3016, E-mail: julius.gribou@utsa.edu. *Application contact:* Robert Baron, Graduate Advisor, 210-458-3010, E-mail: rbaron@utsa.edu.

University of Toronto, School of Graduate Studies, Social Sciences Division, Faculty of Architecture, Landscape and Design, Toronto, ON M5S 1A1, Canada. Offers M Arch, MLA, MUD. *Accreditation:* ASLA. *Entrance requirements:* For master's, minimum B average; 3 letters of reference; resume; 3 writing samples; 5 samples of design work, drawing, or work in a related field. Additional exam requirements/recommendations for international students: Required—TOEFL (minimum score 580 paper-based; 237 computer-based), TWE (minimum score 5), Michigan English Language Assessment Battery (minimum score: 85), IELTS (minimum score: 7) or COPE (minimum score: 4). *Expenses:* Contact institution.

University of Utah, The Graduate School, College of Architecture and Planning, School of Architecture, Salt Lake City, UT 84112. Offers architectural studies (MS); architecture (M Arch); M Arch/MBA. Part-time programs available. *Faculty:* 6 full-time (2 women), 4 part-time/adjunct (1 woman). *Students:* 98 full-time (33 women), 5 part-time (3 women); includes 6 minority (2 Asian Americans or Pacific Islanders, 4 Hispanic Americans), 9 international. Average age 28. 89 applicants, 62% accepted, 36 enrolled. In 2009, 36 master's awarded. *Degree requirements:* For master's, thesis (for some programs), comprehensive project. *Entrance requirements:* For master's, minimum undergraduate GPA of 3.0. Additional exam requirements/recommendations for international students: Required—TOEFL (minimum score 550 paper-based; 173 computer-based). *Application deadline:* For fall admission, 1/1 for domestic and international students. Application fee: $55 ($65 for international students). Electronic applications accepted. *Expenses:* Contact institution. *Financial support:* In 2009–10, 41 students received support, including 19 fellowships with partial tuition reimbursements available, 2 research assistantships with partial tuition reimbursements available, 22 teaching assistantships with partial tuition reimbursements available; career-related internships or fieldwork, Federal Work-Study, and scholarships/grants also available. Financial award application deadline: 3/1; financial award applicants required to submit FAFSA. *Faculty research:* History, design, acoutics, photography, structures, architecture of American West, architectural communication and representation, impact of technology, design build. Total annual research expenditures: $12,045. *Unit head:* Prescott Muir, Director, 801-585-5354. *Application contact:* Mayra Focht, Admissions Advisor, 801-585-5354, Fax: 801-581-8217, E-mail: focht@arch.utah.edu.

University of Virginia, School of Architecture, Department of Architecture and Landscape Architecture, Charlottesville, VA 22903. Offers architecture (M Arch); landscape architecture (M Land Arch). *Faculty:* 25 full-time (10 women), 3 part-time/adjunct (2 women). *Students:* 110 full-time (73 women); includes 14 minority (5 African Americans, 7 Asian Americans or Pacific Islanders, 2 Hispanic Americans), 8 international. Average age 27. 556 applicants, 16% accepted, 22 enrolled. In 2009, 52 master's awarded. *Entrance requirements:* For master's, GRE General Test, 3 letters of recommendation, portfolio. Additional exam requirements/recommendations for international students: Required—TOEFL (minimum score 600 paper-based; 250 computer-based; 90 iBT). *Application deadline:* For fall admission, 1/5 for domestic and international students. Applications are processed on a rolling basis. Application fee: $60. Electronic applications accepted. *Financial support:* Career-related internships or fieldwork, Federal Work-Study, and institutionally sponsored loans available. Financial award applicants required to submit FAFSA. *Unit head:* Craig Barton, Chair, 434-924-1493, Fax: 434-982-2678, E-mail: ceb8x@virginia.edu. *Application contact:* Graduate Admissions Officer, 434-924-6442, E-mail: arch-admissions@virginia.edu.

University of Washington, Graduate School, College of Built Environments, Department of Architecture, Seattle, WA 98195. Offers architecture (M Arch, MS); built environment (PhD); design computing (Certificate); design firm leadership and management (Certificate); historic preservation (Certificate); lighting (Certificate); urban design (Certificate). *Degree requirements:* For master's, thesis. *Entrance requirements:* For master's, GRE General Test, minimum GPA of 3.0, portfolio, 3 letters of recommendation. Additional exam requirements/recommendations for international students: Required—TOEFL. *Faculty research:* Lighting, materials, computing theory, media, culture, environment.

University of Waterloo, Graduate Studies, Faculty of Engineering, School of Architecture, Waterloo, ON N2L 3G1, Canada. Offers M Arch. Part-time programs available. *Degree requirements:* For master's, thesis. *Entrance requirements:* For master's, bachelor's degree in pre-professional architecture. Electronic applications accepted.

University of Wisconsin–Milwaukee, Graduate School, School of Architecture and Urban Planning, Department of Architecture, Milwaukee, WI 53201-0413. Offers architecture (PhD); preservation studies (Certificate); M Arch/MUP. *Faculty:* 26 full-time (4 women). *Students:* 150 full-time (48 women), 11 part-time (7 women); includes 16 minority (4 African Americans, 1 American Indian/Alaska Native, 5 Asian Americans or Pacific Islanders, 6 Hispanic Americans), 13 international. Average age 30. 147 applicants, 51% accepted, 33 enrolled. In 2009, 26 master's, 2 doctorates awarded. *Degree requirements:* For master's, comprehensive exam, thesis; for doctorate, comprehensive exam, thesis/dissertation. *Entrance requirements:* For master's, GRE General Test, portfolio. Additional exam requirements/recommendations for international students: Required—TOEFL (minimum score 600 paper-based; 250 computer-based; 100 iBT), IELTS (minimum score 7). *Application deadline:* For fall admission, 1/1 priority date for domestic students; for spring admission, 9/1 for domestic students. Applications are processed on a rolling basis. Application fee: $45 ($75 for international students). *Expenses:* Tuition, state resident: full-time $8800. Tuition, nonresident: full-time $20,760. Tuition and fees vary according to program and reciprocity agreements. *Financial support:* In 2009–10, 21 teaching assistantships were awarded; career-related internships or fieldwork and unspecified assistantships also available. Support available to part-time students. Financial award application deadline: 4/15. Total annual research expenditures: $239,719. *Unit head:* Joan Simuncak, Representative, 414-229-4015, Fax: 414-229-6976, E-mail: joanarch@uwm.edu. *Application contact:* Josef Stagg, General Information Contact, 414-229-4032, Fax: 414-229-6967, E-mail: jstagg@uwm.edu.

Virginia Polytechnic Institute and State University, Graduate School, College of Architecture and Urban Studies, School of Architecture and Design, Blacksburg, VA 24061. Offers architecture (M Arch, MS); architecture design research (PhD). *Accreditation:* NASAD. *Faculty:* 57 full-time (19 women). *Students:* 166 full-time (75 women), 21 part-time (8 women); includes 64 minority (1 African American, 41 American Indian/Alaska Native, 7 Asian Americans or Pacific Islanders, 15 Hispanic Americans), 15 international. Average age 28. 378 applicants, 36% accepted, 65 enrolled. In 2009, 58 master's awarded. *Entrance requirements:* For master's and doctorate, GRE, GMAT. Additional exam requirements/recommendations for international students: Required—TOEFL (minimum score 550 paper-based; 213 computer-based). *Application deadline:* For fall admission, 5/15 for international students; for spring admission, 10/15 for international students. Applications are processed on a rolling basis. Application fee: $65. Electronic applications accepted. *Expenses:* Tuition, area resident: Full-time $10,228; part-time $459 per credit hour. Tuition, nonresident: full-time $17,892; part-time $865 per credit hour. Required fees: $1966; $451 per semester. *Financial support:* In 2009–10, 5 fellowships with full tuition reimbursements (averaging $600 per year), 4 research assistantships with full tuition reimbursements (averaging $4,917 per year), 50 teaching assistantships with full tuition reimbursements (averaging $9,268 per year) were awarded; career-related internships or fieldwork, Federal Work-Study, scholarships/grants, and unspecified assistantships also available. Financial award application deadline: 1/15. *Faculty research:* Computer applications in design, building technology, architectural design theory, solar/passive energy design, building assembly. Total annual research expenditures: $253,759. *Unit head:* Dr. Steve R. Thompson, Dean, 540-231-9931, Fax: 540-231-9938, E-mail: stthomp2@vt.edu. *Application contact:* Dr. Steve R. Thompson, Dean, 540-231-9931, Fax: 540-231-9938, E-mail: stthomp2@vt.edu.

Washington State University, Graduate School, College of Engineering and Architecture, School of Architecture and Construction Management, Pullman, WA 99164. Offers architecture (M Arch); architecture design theory (MS). *Faculty:* 16. *Students:* 51 full-time (24 women), 6 part-time (2 women); includes 8 minority (5 Asian Americans or Pacific Islanders, 3 Hispanic Americans), 2 international. Average age 27. 131 applicants, 38% accepted, 28 enrolled. In 2009, 22 master's awarded. *Degree requirements:* For master's, comprehensive exam (for some programs), thesis, oral exam. *Entrance requirements:* For master's, GRE General Test, minimum GPA of 3.0, 3 letters of recommendation. Additional exam requirements/recommendations for international students: Required—TOEFL, IELTS. *Application deadline:* For fall admission, 1/10 priority date for domestic and international students. Applications are processed on a rolling basis. Application fee: $50. *Financial support:* In 2009–10, 25 students received support, including 2 fellowships (averaging $2,000 per year), research assistantships with full and partial tuition reimbursements available (averaging $13,917 per year), 12 teaching assistantships with full and partial tuition reimbursements available (averaging $13,056 per year); career-related internships or fieldwork, Federal Work-Study, institutionally sponsored loans, and tuition waivers (partial) also available. Financial award application deadline: 3/1; financial award applicants required to submit FAFSA. *Faculty research:* Cultural, technological, and environmental design. *Unit head:* Dr. Greg Kessler, Director, 509-335-5539, Fax: 509-335-6132, E-mail: gkessler@acm.wsu.edu. *Application contact:* Graduate School Admissions, 800-GRADWSU, Fax: 509-335-1949, E-mail: gradsch@wsu.edu.

Washington State University Spokane, Graduate Programs, Interdisciplinary Design Institute, Spokane, WA 99210. Offers architecture (M Arch, MS); design (Dr DES); interior design (MA); landscape architecture (MS). Part-time programs available. *Faculty:* 7. *Students:* 9 full-time (6 women), 2 part-time (both women); includes 1 minority (Asian American or Pacific Islander), 5 international. Average age 35. In 2009, 18 master's awarded. *Degree requirements:* For master's, comprehensive exam (for some programs), thesis (for some programs); for doctorate, comprehensive exam, thesis/dissertation. *Entrance requirements:* For master's, minimum GPA of 3.0, portfolio of design work, 3 letters of recommendation (M Arch); for doctorate, minimum graduate GPA of 3.5. Additional exam requirements/recommendations for international students: Required—TOEFL (minimum score 550 paper-based; 213 computer-based). *Application deadline:* For fall admission, 1/10 priority date for domestic students, 1/10 for international students; for spring admission, 7/1 priority date for domestic students, 7/1 for international students. Application fee: $50. *Expenses:* Tuition, state resident: part-time $423 per credit. Tuition, nonresident: part-time $1032 per credit. *Financial support:* In 2009–10, research assistantships with full and partial tuition reimbursements (averaging $14,634 per year), teaching assistantships with full and partial tuition reimbursements (averaging $13,383 per year) were awarded. Financial award application deadline: 2/15. *Faculty research:* Environment-behavior relationships, land use and environmental planning, urban space as interior design, art and architectural aesthetics. Total annual research expenditures: $84,000. *Unit head:* Dr. Nancy H. Blossom, Director, 509-358-7513, E-mail: blossom@wsu.edu. *Application contact:* Graduate School Admissions, 800-GRADWSU, Fax: 509-335-1949, E-mail: gradsch@wsu.edu.

Washington University in St. Louis, Sam Fox School of Design and Visual Arts, Program in Architecture, St. Louis, MO 63130-4899. Offers M Arch, MLA, M Arch/MBA, M Arch/MCM, M Arch/MSW, M Arch/MUD, MLA/M Arch. *Degree requirements:* For master's, final project. *Entrance requirements:* For master's, GRE General Test, portfolio. Additional exam requirements/recommendations for international students: Required—TOEFL (minimum score 550 paper-based; 213 computer-based; 80 iBT), TWE. Electronic applications accepted. *Faculty research:* Urban design development issues.

Wentworth Institute of Technology, Department of Architecture, Boston, MA 02115-5998. Offers built environment (M Arch); form and culture (M Arch); tectonic studies (M Arch). *Faculty:* 11 full-time (2 women), 13 part-time/adjunct (1 woman). *Students:* 84 full-time (28 women); includes 3 minority (1 Asian American or Pacific Islander, 2 Hispanic Americans). Average age 23. 116 applicants, 82% accepted, 84 enrolled. *Degree requirements:* For master's, thesis project. *Entrance requirements:* For master's, GRE (external candidates), portfolio, references, minimum GPA of 3.0. Additional exam requirements/recommendations for international students: Required—TOEFL (minimum score 525 paper-based; 197 computer-based). *Application deadline:* For fall admission, 1/15 priority date for domestic and international students. Applications are processed on a rolling basis. Application fee: $50. Electronic applications accepted. *Expenses:* Tuition: Full-time $29,300. Required fees: $925. *Financial support:* In 2009–10, 42 students received support. Federal Work-Study and scholarships/grants available. Financial award applicants required to submit FAFSA. *Unit head:* Dr. Glenn Wiggins, Department Head, 617-989-4470, E-mail: wigginsg@wit.edu. *Application contact:* Maureen Dischino, Executive Director of Admissions, 617-989-4009, Fax: 617-989-4010, E-mail: dischinom@wit.edu.

Woodbury University, School of Architecture, Burbank, CA 91504-1099. Offers architecture (M Arch); real estate development (M Arch). *Faculty:* 2 full-time (1 woman), 4 part-time/adjunct (1 woman). *Students:* 22 full-time (5 women); includes 7 minority (2 African Americans, 4 Asian Americans or Pacific Islanders, 1 Hispanic American), 4 international. Average age 31. In 2009, 8 master's awarded. *Degree requirements:* For master's, thesis. *Entrance requirements:* For master's, 3 letters of recommendation, portfolio. Additional exam requirements/recommendations for international students: Required—TOEFL (minimum score 550 paper-based; 213 computer-based), IELTS (minimum score 7). *Application deadline:* For fall admission, 3/1 priority date for domestic and international students. Application fee: $60. *Expenses:* Contact institution. *Unit head:* Norman Millar, Chair, 318-767-0888 Ext. 130, Fax: 318-504-9320, E-mail: norman.millar@woodbury.edu. *Application contact:* Debra Abel, Administrative Director, 619-235-2900, Fax: 619-235-2901, E-mail: debra.abel@woodbury.edu.

Yale University, School of Architecture, New Haven, CT 06520. Offers M Arch, M Env Des, MEM, PhD, M Arch/M Env Des, M Arch/MBA. *Faculty:* 18 full-time (6 women), 74 part-time/adjunct (18 women). *Students:* 195 full-time (82 women); includes 33 minority (1 African American, 23 Asian Americans or Pacific Islanders, 9 Hispanic Americans), 35 international. 802 applicants, 16% accepted, 65 enrolled. In 2009, 66 master's awarded. *Entrance requirements:* For master's, GRE General Test, design portfolio. Additional exam requirements/recommendations for international students: Required—TOEFL. *Application deadline:* For fall admission, 1/3 for domestic students. *Expenses:* Contact institution. *Financial support:* In 2009–10, 164 students received support; fellowships, teaching assistantships, Federal Work-Study and institutionally sponsored loans available. Financial award application deadline: 2/1. *Unit head:* Robert A. M. Stern, Dean, 203-432-2279, Fax: 203-432-7175. *Application contact:* 203-432-2291, Fax: 203-432-6576.

Building Science

Arizona State University, Graduate College, College of Design, School of Architecture and Landscape Architecture, Tempe, AZ 85287. Offers architecture (M Arch); building design (MS); landscape architecture (MLA); urban design (MUD); MA/MBA. *Degree requirements:* For master's, thesis optional. *Entrance requirements:* For master's, GRE General Test, design portfolio.

Auburn University, Graduate School, College of Architecture, Design, and Construction, Department of Building Science, Auburn University, AL 36849. Offers building science (MBS); construction management (MBS). *Faculty:* 18 full-time (1 woman), 3 part-time/adjunct (1 woman). *Students:* 23 full-time (6 women), 25 part-time (3 women); includes 3 minority (1 African American, 2 Hispanic Americans), 4 international. Average age 27. 83 applicants, 60% accepted, 42 enrolled. In 2009, 7 master's awarded. *Entrance requirements:* For master's, GRE General Test. *Application deadline:* For fall admission, 7/17 for domestic students; for spring admission, 11/24 for domestic students. Applications are processed on a rolling basis. Application fee: $50 ($60 for international students). Electronic applications accepted. *Expenses:* Tuition, state resident: full-time $6240. Tuition, nonresident: full-time $18,720. International tuition: $18,938 full-time. Required fees: $492. Tuition and fees vary according to course load, program and reciprocity agreements. *Financial support:* Application deadline: 3/15. *Unit head:* John D. Murphy, Head, 334-844-4518. *Application contact:* Dr. George Flowers, Dean of the Graduate School, 334-844-2125.

Auburn University, Graduate School, College of Architecture, Design, and Construction, Program in Design-Build, Auburn University, AL 36849. Offers MDB. *Faculty:* 10 full-time (1 woman). *Students:* 20 full-time (4 women), 1 part-time (0 women), 1 international. Average age 25. 41 applicants, 54% accepted, 21 enrolled. In 2009, 10 master's awarded. Application fee: $50 ($60 for international students). *Expenses:* Tuition, state resident: full-time $6240. Tuition, nonresident: full-time $18,720. International tuition: $18,938 full-time. Required fees: $492. Tuition and fees vary according to course load, program and reciprocity agreements. *Financial support:* Applicants required to submit FAFSA. *Unit head:* Dan D. Bennett, Dean, 334-844-4524. *Application contact:* Dr. George Flowers, Dean of the Graduate School, 334-844-2125.

Carnegie Mellon University, College of Fine Arts, School of Architecture, Pittsburgh, PA 15213-3891. Offers architectural engineering construction management (M Sc); architecture (MSA); architecture, engineering, and construction management (PhD); building performance and diagnostics (M Sc, PhD); computational design (M Sc, PhD); sustainable design (M Sc); urban design (M Sc). Terminal master's awarded for partial completion of doctoral program. *Degree requirements:* For doctorate, thesis/dissertation. *Entrance requirements:* For master's and doctorate, GRE General Test. Additional exam requirements/recommendations for international students: Required—TOEFL.

Cornell University, Graduate School, Graduate Fields of Architecture, Art and Planning, Field of Architecture, Ithaca, NY 14853-0001. Offers architectural design (M Arch); architectural science (MS); building technology and environmental science (MS); computer graphics (MS); history of architecture (MA, PhD); history of urban development (MA, PhD); theory and criticism of architecture (M Arch); urban design (M Arch). *Faculty:* 38 full-time (12 women). *Students:* 100 full-time (45 women); includes 14 minority (2 African Americans, 6 Asian Americans or Pacific Islanders, 6 Hispanic Americans), 38 international. Average age 28. 558 applicants, 18% accepted, 44 enrolled. In 2009, 42 master's, 3 doctorates awarded. *Degree requirements:* For master's, one foreign language, thesis (MA, MS); for doctorate, 2 foreign languages, comprehensive exam, thesis/dissertation. *Entrance requirements:* For master's, GRE General Test, 5 year bachelor's degree in architecture, portfolio (M Arch), 3 letters of recommendation; for doctorate, GRE General Test, 3 letters of recommendation. Additional exam requirements/recommendations for international students: Required—TOEFL (minimum score 600 paper-based; 250 computer-based; 77 iBT). *Application deadline:* For fall admission, 1/15 priority date for domestic students. Application fee: $70. Electronic applications accepted. *Expenses:* Tuition: Full-time $29,500. Required fees: $70. Full-time tuition and fees vary according to degree level, program and student level. *Financial support:* In 2009–10, 16 students received support, including 2 fellowships with full tuition reimbursements available, 1 research assistantship with full tuition reimbursement available, 10 teaching assistantships with full tuition reimbursements available; institutionally sponsored loans, scholarships/grants, health care benefits, tuition waivers (full and partial), and unspecified assistantships also available. Financial award applicants required to submit FAFSA. *Faculty research:* Architectural design and urban design, theory and criticism of architecture, computer graphics, building technology and environmental science, history of architecture and history of urban-development. *Unit head:* Director of Graduate Studies, 607-255-6701, Fax: 607-255-0291. *Application contact:* Graduate Field Assistant, 607-255-6701, Fax: 607-255-0291, E-mail: cuarch@cornell.edu.

Georgia Institute of Technology, Graduate Studies and Research, College of Architecture, Program in Building Construction, Atlanta, GA 30332-0001. Offers building construction (PhD); integrated facility management (MS); integrated project delivery systems (MS); residential construction development (MS). Part-time and evening/weekend programs available. *Entrance requirements:* For master's and doctorate, GRE or GMAT. Additional exam requirements/recommendations for international students: Required—TOEFL (minimum score 550 paper-based; 213 computer-based). Electronic applications accepted. *Faculty research:* Design-build, mold, indoor air quality, real estate.

University of California, Berkeley, Graduate Division, College of Environmental Design, Department of Architecture, Berkeley, CA 94720-1500. Offers architecture (M Arch); building science (MS, PhD); building structures, construction and materials (MS, PhD); design theories, methods, and practices (MS, PhD); environmental design in developing countries (MS, PhD); history of architecture and urbanism (MS, PhD); social and cultural processes in architecture and urbanism (MS, PhD); M Arch/MCP; M Arch/MS; MLA/M Arch. *Students:* 156 full-time (91 women). Average age 30. 935 applicants, 60 enrolled. In 2009, 42 master's, 12 doctorates awarded. *Degree requirements:* For master's, thesis; for doctorate, thesis/dissertation, qualifying exam. *Entrance requirements:* For master's and doctorate, GRE General Test, minimum GPA of 3.0, 3 letters of recommendation. Additional exam requirements/recommendations for international students: Required—TOEFL. Application fee: $70 ($90 for international students). Electronic applications accepted. *Financial support:* Unspecified assistantships available. *Unit head:* Prof. Gail Brager, Chair, 510-642-4942. *Application contact:* Lois H. Ito Koch, Student Affairs Officer, 510-642-5577, Fax: 510-643-5607, E-mail: archgrad@berkeley.edu.

University of Florida, Graduate School, College of Design, Construction and Planning, M. E. Rinker, Sr. School of Building Construction, Gainesville, FL 32611. Offers MBC, MICM, MSBC,

Building Science

University of Florida (continued)
PhD. Part-time programs available. *Degree requirements:* For master's, thesis. *Entrance requirements:* For master's, GRE General Test, minimum GPA of 3.0. Additional exam requirements/recommendations for international students: Required—TOEFL. Electronic applications accepted. *Faculty research:* Safety, affordable housing, construction management, environmental issues, sustainable construction.

Environmental Design

Arizona State University, Graduate College, College of Design, Program in Environmental Design and Planning, Tempe, AZ 85287. Offers design (PhD); history, theory, and criticism (PhD); planning (PhD). *Degree requirements:* For doctorate, thesis/dissertation.

Art Center College of Design, Graduate Division, Industrial Design Department, Pasadena, CA 91103. Offers environmental design (MS); product design (MS). *Accreditation:* NASAD. *Faculty:* 8 part-time/adjunct (1 woman). *Students:* 9 full-time (4 women), 5 part-time (4 women). Average age 29. 87 applicants, 25% accepted, 9 enrolled. In 2009, 9 master's awarded. *Degree requirements:* For master's, thesis, studio project. *Entrance requirements:* For master's, portfolio. Additional exam requirements/recommendations for international students: Required—TOEFL (minimum score 600 paper-based; 250 computer-based; 100 iBT). *Application deadline:* For fall admission, 2/1 for domestic and international students. Application fee: $50 ($70 for international students). *Expenses:* Tuition: Full-time $16,737. *Financial support:* Teaching assistantships, career-related internships or fieldwork, Federal Work-Study, and scholarships/grants available. Financial award application deadline: 2/1. *Unit head:* Andrew Ogden, Chair, 626-396-2464. *Application contact:* Maritza Hererra, 626-396-2464.

See Close-Up on page 113.

Clemson University, Graduate School, College of Architecture, Arts, and Humanities, Program in Planning, Design and the Built Environment, Clemson, SC 29634. Offers PhD. *Faculty:* 21 full-time (6 women). *Students:* 18 full-time (3 women), 3 part-time (0 women), 5 international. Average age 37. 25 applicants, 44% accepted, 7 enrolled. In 2009, 5 doctorates awarded. *Entrance requirements:* For doctorate, GRE General Test. Additional exam requirements/recommendations for international students: Required—TOEFL. *Application deadline:* For fall admission, 1/1 for domestic and international students. Applications are processed on a rolling basis. Application fee: $70 ($80 for international students). Electronic applications accepted. *Expenses:* Tuition, state resident: full-time $8684; part-time $528 per credit hour. Tuition, nonresident: full-time $15,330; part-time $1078 per credit hour. Required fees: $736; $37 per semester. Part-time tuition and fees vary according to course load and program. *Financial support:* In 2009–10, 14 students received support, including 2 fellowships with full and partial tuition reimbursements available (averaging $7,000 per year), 7 teaching assistantships with partial tuition reimbursements available (averaging $21,829 per year); career-related internships or fieldwork, institutionally sponsored loans, scholarships/grants, health care benefits, and unspecified assistantships also available. Support available to part-time students. *Unit head:* Roger Liska, Interim Director, 864-656-3878, E-mail: riggor@clemson.edu. *Application contact:* Mickey Lauria, Concentration Coordinator, 864-656-0520, E-mail: mlauria@clemson.edu.

Columbia University, School of Continuing Education, Program in Landscape Design, New York, NY 10027. Offers MS. Part-time programs available. *Faculty:* 11 part-time/adjunct (3 women). *Students:* 27 part-time (20 women); includes 3 minority (2 African Americans, 1 Asian American or Pacific Islander), 2 international. 25 applicants, 88% accepted, 14 enrolled. In 2009, 17 master's awarded. *Entrance requirements:* For master's, minimum undergraduate GPA of 3.0. Additional exam requirements/recommendations for international students: Required—American Language Program placement test. *Application deadline:* For fall admission, 4/15 for domestic students. Application fee: $50. *Financial support:* Institutionally sponsored loans available. Financial award applicants required to submit FAFSA. *Unit head:* Joseph Disponzio, Program Director, 212-854-9699, E-mail: jd52@columbia.edu. *Application contact:* Bryce Weinert, Admissions Adviser, 212-854-9666, E-mail: sce-apply@columbia.edu.

Cornell University, Graduate School, Graduate Fields of Human Ecology, Field of Design and Environmental Analysis, Ithaca, NY 14853-0001. Offers applied research in human-environment relations (MS); facilities planning and management (MS); housing and design (MS); human factors and ergonomics (MS); human-environment relations (MS); interior design (MA, MPS). *Faculty:* 14 full-time (6 women). *Students:* 20 full-time (16 women); includes 3 minority (2 Asian Americans or Pacific Islanders, 1 Hispanic American), 2 international. Average age 27. 43 applicants, 30% accepted, 12 enrolled. In 2009, 3 master's awarded. *Degree requirements:* For master's, thesis. *Entrance requirements:* For master's, GRE General Test, portfolio or slides of recent work; bachelor's degree in interior design, architecture or related design discipline; 2 letters of recommendation. Additional exam requirements/recommendations for international students: Required—TOEFL (minimum score 600 paper-based; 250 computer-based; 105 iBT). *Application deadline:* For fall admission, 2/1 priority date for domestic students. Application fee: $70. Electronic applications accepted. *Expenses:* Tuition: Full-time $29,500. Required fees: $70. Full-time tuition and fees vary according to degree level, program and student level. *Financial support:* In 2009–10, 13 students received support, including 1 fellowship with full tuition reimbursement available, 5 teaching assistantships with full tuition reimbursements available; research assistantships with full tuition reimbursements available, institutionally sponsored loans, scholarships/grants, health care benefits, tuition waivers (full and partial), and unspecified assistantships also available. Financial award applicants required to submit FAFSA. *Faculty research:* Facility planning and management, environmental psychology, housing, interior design, ergonomics and human factors. *Unit head:* Director of Graduate Studies, 607-255-2168, Fax: 607-255-0305. *Application contact:* Graduate Field Assistant, 607-255-2168, Fax: 607-255-0305, E-mail: deagrad@cornell.edu.

Florida Atlantic University, College of Architecture, Urban and Public Affairs, School of Urban and Regional Planning, Boca Raton, FL 33431-0991. Offers economic development and tourism (Certificate); environmental planning (Certificate); sustainable community planning (Certificate); urban and regional planning (MURP); visual planning technology (Certificate). *Accreditation:* ACSP. Part-time and evening/weekend programs available. *Faculty:* 8 full-time (6 women), 1 (woman) part-time/adjunct. *Students:* 28 full-time (17 women), 12 part-time (4 women); includes 11 minority (2 African Americans, 1 Asian American or Pacific Islander, 8 Hispanic Americans), 3 international. Average age 31. 70 applicants, 47% accepted, 7 enrolled. In 2009, 14 master's awarded. *Entrance requirements:* For master's, GRE General Test, minimum GPA of 3.0. Additional exam requirements/recommendations for international students: Required—TOEFL. *Application deadline:* For fall admission, 7/1 priority date for domestic students, 2/15 for international students; for spring admission, 11/1 priority date for domestic students, 7/15 for international students. Applications are processed on a rolling basis. Application fee: $30. *Expenses:* Tuition, state resident: full-time $7055; part-time $293.94 per credit hour. Tuition, nonresident: full-time $22,096; part-time $920.66 per credit hour. *Financial support:* Fellowships with full tuition reimbursements, research assistantships, career-related internships or fieldwork, Federal Work-Study, institutionally sponsored loans, and tuition waivers (partial) available. Financial award application deadline: 4/1. *Faculty research:* Growth management, urban design, computer applications/geographical information systems, environmental planning. *Unit head:* Dr. Jaap Vos, Chair, 954-762-5653, Fax: 954-762-5673, E-mail: jvos@fau.edu. *Application contact:* Dr. Jaap Vos, Chair, 954-762-5653, Fax: 954-762-5673, E-mail: jvos@fau.edu.

Michigan State University, The Graduate School, College of Agriculture and Natural Resources and College of Social Science, School of Planning, Design and Construction, East Lansing, MI 48824. Offers construction management (MS, PhD); environmental design (MA); interior design and facilities management (MA); international planning studies (MIPS); urban and regional planning (MURP). *Faculty:* 25 full-time (12 women). *Students:* 56 full-time (21 women), 25 part-time (12 women); includes 4 minority (1 African American, 2 Asian Americans or Pacific Islanders, 1 Hispanic American), 53 international. Average age 30. 122 applicants, 57% accepted. In 2009, 34 degrees awarded. *Degree requirements:* For master's, thesis or alternative. *Entrance requirements:* Additional exam requirements/recommendations for international students: Required—TOEFL. *Application deadline:* Applications are processed on a rolling basis. Electronic applications accepted. *Financial support:* In 2009–10, 16 research assistantships with tuition reimbursements (averaging $13,001 per year), 2 teaching assistantships with tuition reimbursements (averaging $13,599 per year) were awarded. Total annual research expenditures: $281,011. *Unit head:* Dr. Scott G. Witter, Director, 517-432-6379, Fax: 517-432-8108, E-mail: witter@msu.edu. *Application contact:* Dawn Brown, Graduate Secretary, 517-432-3393, Fax: 517-432-3772, E-mail: browndaw@msu.edu.

San Diego State University, Graduate and Research Affairs, College of Professional Studies and Fine Arts, School of Art, Design and Art History, San Diego, CA 92182. Offers art history (MA); studio arts (MA, MFA), including applied design, environmental design, graphic design, interior design, painting and printmaking, sculpture. *Accreditation:* NASAD (one or more programs are accredited). *Degree requirements:* For master's, variable foreign language requirement, thesis. *Entrance requirements:* For master's, GRE General Test, bachelor's degree in related field, slide portfolio, typed slide information sheet, 2 letters of recommendation. Additional exam requirements/recommendations for international students: Required—TOEFL. Electronic applications accepted.

Texas Tech University, Graduate School, College of Human Sciences, Department of Design, Lubbock, TX 79409. Offers environmental design (MS); interior and environmental design (PhD). *Faculty:* 4 full-time (2 women). *Students:* 8 full-time (7 women), 12 part-time (9 women); includes 2 minority (1 Asian American or Pacific Islander, 1 Hispanic American), 6 international. Average age 29. 19 applicants, 63% accepted, 5 enrolled. In 2009, 1 master's awarded. *Degree requirements:* For master's, thesis or alternative; for doctorate, thesis/dissertation. *Entrance requirements:* For master's and doctorate, GRE. Application fee: $50 ($75 for international students). *Expenses:* Tuition, state resident: full-time $5100; part-time $213 per credit hour. Tuition, nonresident: full-time $11,748; part-time $490 per credit hour. Required fees: $2298; $50 per credit hour. $555 per semester. *Financial support:* Research assistantships, teaching assistantships available. Financial award application deadline: 4/15. *Faculty research:* Meanings in the built environment, influence of technology on pedagogic environments, interior design components, computer usage in interior design, design and evaluation of physical environments for the elderly and physically and mentally challenged. Total annual research expenditures: $64,146. *Unit head:* Dr. Cherif M. Amor, Interim Chair, 806-742-3050, Fax: 806-742-1639, E-mail: cherif.amor@ttu.edu. *Application contact:* Dr. JoAnn Shroyer, Graduate Programs Director, 806-742-3050 Ext. 228, Fax: 806-742-1639, E-mail: joann.shroyer@ttu.edu.

Université de Montréal, Faculty of Environmental Design and Planning, Montréal, QC H3C 3J7, Canada. Offers M Sc A, M Urb, PhD, DESS. *Accreditation:* ACSP. *Degree requirements:* For doctorate, thesis/dissertation, general exam. Electronic applications accepted. *Expenses:* Contact institution. *Faculty research:* Wayfinding, environmental evaluation, housing studies, urban design, urban and regional planning.

University of Calgary, Faculty of Graduate Studies, Faculty of Environmental Design, Calgary, AB T2N 1N4, Canada. Offers architecture (M Arch); environmental design (M Env Des, PhD). *Degree requirements:* For master's, thesis; for doctorate, thesis/dissertation. *Entrance requirements:* For master's, minimum GPA of 3.0; for doctorate, minimum GPA of 3.5. Additional exam requirements/recommendations for international students: Required—TOEFL (minimum score 550 paper-based; 213 computer-based). *Faculty research:* Sustainable development in architecture, planning and product design, energy and environment, impact assessment, ecotourism.

University of California, Berkeley, Graduate Division, College of Environmental Design, Department of Landscape Architecture and Environmental Planning, Berkeley, CA 94720-1500. Offers landscape architecture (MLA), including environmental planning, landscape design and site planning, urban and community design; landscape architecture and environmental planning (PhD); MLA/M Arch; MLA/MCP. *Accreditation:* ASLA (one or more programs are accredited). *Faculty:* 13 full-time, 6 part-time/adjunct. *Students:* 69 full-time (49 women). Average age 30. 252 applicants, 24 enrolled. In 2009, 31 master's, 1 doctorate awarded. *Degree requirements:* For master's, professional project or thesis; for doctorate, one foreign language, thesis/dissertation, qualifying exam. *Entrance requirements:* For master's, GRE General Test, minimum GPA of 3.0, portfolio; for doctorate, GRE General Test, master's degree (strongly recommended), minimum GPA of 3.0, sample of written work, 3 letters of recommendation. *Application deadline:* For fall admission, 12/15 for domestic students. Application fee: $70 ($90 for international students). *Financial support:* Fellowships, research assistantships, teaching assistantships, career-related internships or fieldwork, Federal Work-Study, institutionally sponsored loans, and unspecified assistantships available. *Unit head:* Prof. Linda Jewell, Chair, 510-642-4022, Fax: 510-643-6166. *Application contact:* Yong No, Student Affairs Officer, 510-642-2965, Fax: 510-643-6166, E-mail: laepgrad@berkeley.edu.

University of California, Berkeley, Graduate Division, College of Environmental Design, Master of Arts in Design Program, Berkeley, CA 94720-1500. Offers MA. *Students:* 8 full-time (4 women). Average age 33. 13 applicants, 3 enrolled. In 2009, 1 master's awarded. *Degree requirements:* For master's, thesis. *Entrance requirements:* For master's, GRE General Test, minimum GPA of 3.0, portfolio, 3 letters of recommendation. Additional exam requirements/recommendations for international students: Required—TOEFL. *Application deadline:* For fall admission, 2/1 for domestic students. Application fee: $70 ($90 for international students). *Financial support:* Unspecified assistantships available. *Unit head:* Prof. Anthony Dubovsky, Chair, 510-642-4942. *Application contact:* Lois H. Ito Koch, Student Affairs Officer, 510-642-5577, Fax: 510-643-5607, E-mail: likoch@berkeley.edu.

University of Georgia, Graduate School, College of Environment and Design, Athens, GA 30602. Offers environmental planning and design (MEPD); historic preservation (MHP); landscape architecture (MLA). *Faculty:* 25 full-time (8 women). *Students:* 86 full-time (59 women), 24 part-time (10 women); includes 2 Asian Americans or Pacific Islanders, 9 international. 240 applicants, 33% accepted, 33 enrolled. In 2009, 32 master's awarded. *Application deadline:* For fall admission, 7/1 priority date for domestic students; for spring admission, 11/15 for domestic students. Application fee: $50. *Expenses:* Tuition, state resident: full-time $6000; part-time $250 per credit hour. Tuition, nonresident: full-time $20,904; part-time $871 per credit hour. Required fees: $730 per semester. *Unit head:* Dean Daniels J. Nadenicek, Acting Dean, 706-542-1100, Fax: 706-542-4485, E-mail: dnadeni@uga.edu. *Application contact:*

Prof. Brian J. LaHaie, Director of Enrolled Student Services, 706-542-4704, Fax: 706-542-4236, E-mail: blahaie@uga.edu.

University of Missouri, Graduate School, College of Human Environmental Science, Department of Architectural Studies, Columbia, MO 65211. Offers design with digital media (MA, MS); environmental design (MS). *Entrance requirements:* For master's, GRE General Test, minimum GPA of 3.0. Additional exam requirements/recommendations for international students: Required—TOEFL (minimum score 500 paper-based; 173 computer-based; 61 iBT).

Virginia Polytechnic Institute and State University, Graduate School, College of Architecture and Urban Studies, Program in Environmental Design and Planning, Blacksburg, VA 24061. Offers PhD. *Students:* 23 full-time (12 women), 8 part-time (2 women); includes 15 minority (11 American Indian/Alaska Native, 2 Asian Americans or Pacific Islanders, 2 Hispanic Americans). Average age 35. 5 applicants, 60% accepted, 2 enrolled. In 2009, 10 doctorates awarded. *Entrance requirements:* For doctorate, GRE, GMAT. Additional exam requirements/recommendations for international students: Required—TOEFL (minimum score 550 paper-based; 213 computer-based). *Application deadline:* For fall admission, 5/15 for international students; for spring admission, 10/15 for international students. Applications are processed on a rolling basis. Application fee: $65. Electronic applications accepted. *Expenses:* Tuition, area resident: Full-time $10,228; part-time $459 per credit hour. Tuition, nonresident: full-time $17,892; part-time $865 per credit hour. Required fees: $1966; $451 per semester. *Financial support:* Teaching assistantships, career-related internships or fieldwork, Federal Work-Study, scholarships/grants, and unspecified assistantships available. Financial award application deadline: 1/15. *Faculty research:* Urban studies, architecture, landscape planning. *Unit head:* Dr. Patrick Miller, Head, 540-231-5582, Fax: 540-231-9938, E-mail: pmiller@vt.edu. *Application contact:* Chris Coon, Information Contact, 540-231-5582, Fax: 540-231-9938, E-mail: garch@vt.edu.

Yale University, School of Architecture, New Haven, CT 06520. Offers M Arch, M Env Des, MEM, PhD, M Arch/M Env Des, M Arch/MBA. *Faculty:* 18 full-time (6 women), 74 part-time/adjunct (18 women). *Students:* 195 full-time (82 women); includes 33 minority (1 African American, 23 Asian Americans or Pacific Islanders, 9 Hispanic Americans), 35 international. 802 applicants, 16% accepted, 65 enrolled. In 2009, 66 master's awarded. *Entrance requirements:* For master's, GRE General Test, design portfolio. Additional exam requirements/recommendations for international students: Required—TOEFL. *Application deadline:* For fall admission, 1/3 for domestic students. *Expenses:* Contact institution. *Financial support:* In 2009–10, 164 students received support; fellowships, teaching assistantships, Federal Work-Study and institutionally sponsored loans available. Financial award application deadline: 2/1. *Unit head:* Robert A. M. Stern, Dean, 203-432-2279, Fax: 203-432-7175. *Application contact:* 203-432-2291, Fax: 203-432-6576.

Historic Preservation

Arkansas State University—Jonesboro, Graduate School, College of Humanities and Social Sciences, Heritage Studies Program, Jonesboro, State University, AR 72467. Offers MA, PhD. Part-time programs available. *Faculty:* 2 full-time (1 woman), 2 part-time/adjunct (1 woman). *Students:* 14 full-time (11 women), 27 part-time (14 women); includes 6 minority (all African Americans), 2 international. Average age 41. 17 applicants, 41% accepted, 6 enrolled. In 2009, 6 master's, 2 doctorates awarded. *Degree requirements:* For master's, comprehensive exam, thesis or alternative, portfolio; for doctorate, comprehensive exam, thesis/dissertation, portfolio. *Entrance requirements:* For master's, GRE, MAT or GMAT, appropriate bachelor's degree, letters of reference, official transcript, interview, letter of interest, writing sample, immunization records; for doctorate, GRE, MAT, or GMAT, appropriate bachelor's or master's degree, interview, letters of reference, official transcript, letter of interest, writing sample, immunization records. Additional exam requirements/recommendations for international students: Required—TOEFL (minimum score 550 paper-based; 213 computer-based; 79 iBT), IELTS (minimum score 6). *Application deadline:* For fall admission, 7/1 for domestic and international students. Applications are processed on a rolling basis. Application fee: $50. Electronic applications accepted. *Expenses:* Tuition, state resident: full-time $3744; part-time $208 per credit hour. Tuition, nonresident: full-time $9540; part-time $530 per credit hour. Required fees: $896; $47 per credit hour. $25 per term. One-time fee: $50. Tuition and fees vary according to course load and program. *Financial support:* In 2009–10, 8 students received support; fellowships, teaching assistantships, career-related internships or fieldwork, scholarships/grants, tuition waivers (partial), and unspecified assistantships available. Financial award application deadline: 7/1; financial award applicants required to submit FAFSA. *Unit head:* Dr. Clyde Milner, Director, 870-972-3509, Fax: 870-972-3207, E-mail: cmilner@astate.edu. *Application contact:* Dr. Andrew Sustich, Dean of the Graduate School, 870-972-3029, Fax: 870-972-3857, E-mail: sustich@astate.edu.

Ball State University, Graduate School, College of Architecture and Planning, Department of Architecture, Program in Historic Preservation, Muncie, IN 47306-1099. Offers M Arch, MS. *Degree requirements:* For master's, thesis. *Entrance requirements:* For master's, minimum undergraduate B average, portfolio, writing sample.

Boston University, Graduate School of Arts and Sciences, Program in Preservation Studies, Boston, MA 02215. Offers MA, JD/MA. *Students:* 2 full-time (both women), 9 part-time (7 women). Average age 35. 26 applicants, 62% accepted, 3 enrolled. In 2009, 2 master's awarded. *Degree requirements:* For master's, one foreign language, thesis or alternative, internship. *Entrance requirements:* For master's, GRE General Test, scholarly writing sample, 3 letters of recommendation. Additional exam requirements/recommendations for international students: Required—TOEFL (minimum score 550 paper-based; 213 computer-based). *Application deadline:* For fall admission, 4/1 for domestic and international students; for spring admission, 11/15 for domestic and international students. Application fee: $70. Electronic applications accepted. *Expenses:* Tuition: Full-time $37,910; part-time $1184 per credit hour. Required fees: $386; $40 per semester. Part-time tuition and fees vary according to class time, course level, degree level and program. *Financial support:* In 2009–10, 2 research assistantships with partial tuition reimbursements were awarded; career-related internships or fieldwork, Federal Work-Study, and unspecified assistantships also available. Support available to part-time students. Financial award application deadline: 1/15; financial award applicants required to submit FAFSA. *Unit head:* Claire Dempsey, Director, 617-353-9910, Fax: 617-353-2556, E-mail: dempseyc@bu.edu. *Application contact:* Jessica Hill, Senior Program Coordinator, 617-353-2948, Fax: 617-353-2556, E-mail: jesshill@bu.edu.

Buffalo State College, State University of New York, The Graduate School, Faculty of Arts and Humanities, Department of Art Conservation, Buffalo, NY 14222-1095. Offers art conservation (CAS); conservation of historic works and art works (MA). *Degree requirements:* For master's, final oral exam; for CAS, internship. *Entrance requirements:* For master's, GRE General Test, minimum GPA of 2.8. Additional exam requirements/recommendations for international students: Required—TOEFL (minimum score 550 paper-based; 213 computer-based). *Faculty research:* Mechanics of deterioration of art, conservation of materials.

Clemson University, Graduate School, College of Architecture, Arts, and Humanities, Department of Planning and Landscape Architecture, Program in Historic Preservation, Clemson, SC 29634. Offers MS. *Students:* 22 full-time (18 women), 1 international. Average age 26. 47 applicants, 57% accepted, 11 enrolled. In 2009, 12 master's awarded. *Entrance requirements:* For master's, GRE General Test. Additional exam requirements/recommendations for international students: Required—TOEFL. *Application deadline:* For fall admission, 2/15 for domestic and international students. Applications are processed on a rolling basis. Application fee: $70 ($80 for international students). Electronic applications accepted. *Expenses:* Tuition, state resident: full-time $8684; part-time $528 per credit hour. Tuition, nonresident: full-time $15,330; part-time $1078 per credit hour. Required fees: $736; $37 per semester. Part-time tuition and fees vary according to course load and program. *Financial support:* In 2009–10, 22 students received support, including 22 fellowships with full and partial tuition reimbursements available (averaging $9,909 per year); research assistantships with partial tuition reimbursements available, teaching assistantships with partial tuition reimbursements available, career-related internships or fieldwork, institutionally sponsored loans, scholarships/grants, health care benefits, and unspecified assistantships also available. Support available to part-time students. *Unit head:* Dr. Elaine M. Worzala, Chair, 864-656-3657, Fax: 864-656-0204, E-mail: eworzal@clemson.edu. *Application contact:* Ashley Robbins, Coordinator, 864-937-9596, Fax: 864-656-0204, E-mail: arobbin@clemson.edu.

College of Charleston, Graduate School, School of the Arts, Program in Historic Preservation, Charleston, SC 29424-0001. Offers MS. *Faculty:* 7 full-time (1 woman). *Entrance requirements:* For master's, GRE. Additional exam requirements/recommendations for international students: Required—TOEFL. Electronic applications accepted. *Financial support:* Scholarships/grants available. Financial award applicants required to submit FAFSA. *Unit head:* Dr. Robert Russell, Director, 843-953-6352, E-mail: russellr@cofc.edu. *Application contact:* Susan Hallatt, Director of Graduate Admissions, 843-953-5614, Fax: 843-953-1434, E-mail: hallatts@cofc.edu.

Columbia University, Graduate School of Architecture, Planning, and Preservation, Program in Historic Preservation, New York, NY 10027. Offers MS, Certificate, M Arch/MS, MS/MS. *Degree requirements:* For master's, thesis. *Entrance requirements:* For master's, GRE General Test.

Cornell University, Graduate School, Graduate Fields of Architecture, Art and Planning, Field of City and Regional Planning, Ithaca, NY 14853-0001. Offers city and regional planning (MRP, PhD); environmental planning and design (MRP, PhD); historic preservation planning (MA); international development planning (MRP, PhD); planning theory and systems analysis (MRP, PhD); regional economics and development planning (MRP, PhD); regional science (MRP, PhD); social and health systems planning (MRP, PhD); urban and regional theory (MRP, PhD); urban planning history (MRP, PhD). *Accreditation:* ACSP (one or more programs are accredited). *Faculty:* 32 full-time (11 women). *Students:* 127 full-time (70 women); includes 19 minority (5 African Americans, 8 Asian Americans or Pacific Islanders, 6 Hispanic Americans), 22 international. Average age 30. 331 applicants, 46% accepted, 68 enrolled. In 2009, 50 master's, 4 doctorates awarded. *Degree requirements:* For master's, thesis (MA); for doctorate, comprehensive exam, thesis/dissertation. *Entrance requirements:* For master's and doctorate, GRE General Test, 2 letters of recommendation. Additional exam requirements/recommendations for international students: Required—TOEFL (minimum score 600 paper-based; 250 computer-based; 77 iBT). *Application deadline:* For fall admission, 1/10 for domestic students. Application fee: $70. Electronic applications accepted. *Expenses:* Tuition: Full-time $29,500. Required fees: $70. Full-time tuition and fees vary according to degree level, program and student level. *Financial support:* In 2009–10, 24 students received support, including 3 teaching assistantships with full tuition reimbursements available; fellowships with full tuition reimbursements available, research assistantships with full tuition reimbursements available, institutionally sponsored loans, scholarships/grants, health care benefits, tuition waivers (full and partial), and unspecified assistantships also available. Financial award applicants required to submit FAFSA. *Faculty research:* Land use planning, economic development, international development, historic preservation, community development. *Unit head:* Director of Graduate Studies, 607-255-6848, Fax: 607-255-1971. *Application contact:* Graduate Field Assistant, 607-255-6848, Fax: 607-255-1971, E-mail: crp_admissions@cornell.edu.

Delaware State University, Graduate Programs, Department of History, Philosophy and Political Sciences, Dover, DE 19901-2277. Offers historic preservation (MA). *Entrance requirements:* Additional exam requirements/recommendations for international students: Required—TOEFL (minimum score 550 paper-based). Electronic applications accepted.

Eastern Michigan University, Graduate School, College of Arts and Sciences, Department of Geography and Geology, Program in Historic Preservation, Ypsilanti, MI 48197. Offers heritage interpretation and tourism (MS); historic preservation (MS, Graduate Certificate). Part-time and evening/weekend programs available. Postbaccalaureate distance learning degree programs offered (minimal on-campus study). *Students:* 23 full-time (15 women), 61 part-time (43 women); includes 2 minority (both African Americans), 1 international. Average age 36. In 2009, 26 master's, 5 other advanced degrees awarded. *Entrance requirements:* Additional exam requirements/recommendations for international students: Required—TOEFL. *Application deadline:* Applications are processed on a rolling basis. Application fee: $35. Tuition and fees vary according to course level. *Financial support:* Fellowships, research assistantships with full tuition reimbursements, teaching assistantships with full tuition reimbursements, career-related internships or fieldwork, Federal Work-Study, institutionally sponsored loans, scholarships/grants, tuition waivers (partial), and unspecified assistantships available. Support available to part-time students. Financial award applicants required to submit FAFSA. *Application contact:* Dr. Ted Ligibel, Program Advisor, 734-487-0232, Fax: 734-487-6979, E-mail: tligibel@emich.edu.

The George Washington University, Columbian College of Arts and Sciences, Department of American Studies, Washington, DC 20052. Offers American studies (PhD); folklife (MA); historic preservation (MA); material culture (MA). Part-time and evening/weekend programs available. *Faculty:* 10 full-time (4 women), 5 part-time/adjunct (4 women). *Students:* 24 full-time (16 women), 26 part-time (14 women); includes 7 minority (5 African Americans, 1 Asian American or Pacific Islander, 1 Hispanic American), 3 international. Average age 31. 116 applicants, 43% accepted, 17 enrolled. In 2009, 10 master's, 4 doctorates awarded. Terminal master's awarded for partial completion of doctoral program. *Degree requirements:* For master's, comprehensive exam; for doctorate, one foreign language, thesis/dissertation, general exam. *Entrance requirements:* For master's and doctorate, GRE General Test, minimum GPA of 3.0. Additional exam requirements/recommendations for international students: Required—TOEFL (minimum score 550 paper-based; 213 computer-based; 80 iBT). *Application deadline:* For fall admission, 1/15 priority date for domestic and international students; for spring admission, 10/1 for domestic students. Application fee: $60. *Financial support:* In 2009–10, 22 students received support; fellowships, research assistantships, teaching assistantships, career-related internships or fieldwork, Federal Work-Study, institutionally sponsored loans, and tuition waivers available. Financial award application deadline: 1/15. *Unit head:* James A. Miller, Chair, 202-994-6743, E-mail: jam@gwu.edu. *Application contact:* Information Contact, 202-994-6070, Fax: 202-994-8651, E-mail: amst@gwu.edu.

Georgia State University, College of Arts and Sciences, Department of History, Program in Heritage Preservation, Atlanta, GA 30302-3083. Offers MHP, Certificate. Part-time and evening/weekend programs available. *Degree requirements:* For master's, exam, internship or thesis. *Entrance requirements:* For master's, GRE General Test, minimum GPA of 3.0. Additional

Historic Preservation

Georgia State University (continued)
exam requirements/recommendations for international students: Required—TOEFL. Electronic applications accepted. *Faculty research:* Historic preservation, local history, public history, museum studies.

Goucher College, Historic Preservation Program, Baltimore, MD 21204-2794. Offers MA. Part-time and evening/weekend programs available. Postbaccalaureate distance learning degree programs offered (minimal on-campus study). *Degree requirements:* For master's, thesis. *Entrance requirements:* For master's, 2 years of post-baccalaureate work or volunteer experience. *Expenses:* Contact institution.

Kent State University, College of Architecture and Environmental Design, Kent, OH 44242-0001. Offers architecture (M Arch); preservation architecture (Certificate); urban design (M Arch, MUD, Certificate). Part-time programs available. *Degree requirements:* For master's, thesis optional. *Entrance requirements:* For master's, GRE, portfolio, minimum GPA of 2.75, 3 letters of reference, resume, undergraduate architecture degree. Additional exam requirements/recommendations for international students: Required—TOEFL (minimum score 550 paper-based). Electronic applications accepted. *Faculty research:* History and theory, building technology, landscape architecture and urbanism, urbanism, sustainable development.

Michigan Technological University, Graduate School, College of Sciences and Arts, Department of Social Sciences, Program in Industrial Heritage and Archeology, Houghton, MI 49931. Offers PhD. Part-time programs available. *Degree requirements:* For doctorate, comprehensive exam, thesis/dissertation. *Entrance requirements:* Additional exam requirements/recommendations for international students: Required—TOEFL (minimum score 550 paper-based; 213 computer-based). Electronic applications accepted.

New York University, Graduate School of Arts and Science, Institute of Fine Arts, Program in Conservation Training, New York, NY 10012-1019. Offers MA/Diploma. *Application deadline:* For fall admission, 1/4 for domestic students. Application fee: $90. *Expenses:* Tuition: Full-time $30,528; part-time $1272 per credit. Required fees: $2177. *Financial support:* Career-related internships or fieldwork, Federal Work-Study, and institutionally sponsored loans available. Financial award application deadline: 1/4; financial award applicants required to submit FAFSA. *Unit head:* Hannelore Roemich, Chair, Conservation Center, 212-992-5800, Fax: 212-992-5807, E-mail: ifa.program@nyu.edu. *Application contact:* Michele Marincola, Director, 212-992-5800, Fax: 212-992-5807, E-mail: ifa.program@nyu.edu.

Northwestern State University of Louisiana, Graduate Studies and Research, Program in Heritage Resources, Natchitoches, LA 71497. Offers MA. *Degree requirements:* For master's, comprehensive exam, thesis or alternative. *Entrance requirements:* For master's, GRE General Test, minimum undergraduate GPA of 2.5.

Pratt Institute, School of Architecture, Program in Historic Preservation, New York, NY 10011. Offers MS. Part-time programs available. *Faculty:* 4 part-time/adjunct (1 woman). *Students:* 35 full-time (26 women), 2 part-time (both women); includes 5 minority (3 African Americans, 1 Asian American or Pacific Islander, 1 Hispanic American), 3 international. Average age 27. 56 applicants, 95% accepted, 19 enrolled. In 2009, 6 master's awarded. *Entrance requirements:* For master's, writing sample, bachelor's degree, transcripts, letters of recommendation, portfolio. Additional exam requirements/recommendations for international students: Required—TOEFL (minimum score 550 paper-based; 213 computer-based; 79 iBT). *Application deadline:* For fall admission, 1/5 for domestic and international students; for spring admission, 10/1 for domestic and international students. Application fee: $50 ($90 for international students). Electronic applications accepted. *Expenses:* Tuition: Full-time $22,734. Required fees: $1280. *Financial support:* Career-related internships or fieldwork, Federal Work-Study, institutionally sponsored loans, scholarships/grants, health care benefits, and unspecified assistantships available. Support available to part-time students. Financial award application deadline: 2/1; financial award applicants required to submit FAFSA. *Unit head:* Eric Allison, Coordinator, 212-647-7532, E-mail: eallison@pratt.edu. *Application contact:* Young Hah, Director of Graduate Admissions, 718-636-3683, Fax: 718-399-4242, E-mail: yhah@pratt.edu.

See Close-Up on page 145.

Rutgers, The State University of New Jersey, New Brunswick, Graduate School-New Brunswick, Program in Art History, Piscataway, NJ 08854-8097. Offers art history (MA, PhD); curatorial studies (Certificate); historic preservation (Certificate). Part-time programs available. Terminal master's awarded for partial completion of doctoral program. *Degree requirements:* For master's, one foreign language, comprehensive exam; for doctorate, 2 foreign languages, comprehensive exam, thesis/dissertation. *Entrance requirements:* For master's and doctorate, GRE General Test, writing sample. Additional exam requirements/recommendations for international students: Required—TOEFL (minimum score 550 paper-based; 213 computer-based). Electronic applications accepted. *Faculty research:* Ancient and medieval art and architecture; Renaissance and Baroque art and architecture; modern and contemporary art and architecture; Italian studies; the arts of Asia, Africa, and the Americas.

St. Cloud State University, School of Graduate Studies, College of Social Sciences, Program in Cultural Resource Management Archeology, St. Cloud, MN 56301-4498. Offers MS. *Students:* 13 full-time (3 women), 7 part-time (3 women); includes 1 minority (American Indian/Alaska Native). 10 applicants, 100% accepted, 0 enrolled. *Entrance requirements:* For master's, GRE General Test, minimum GPA of 2.75. Additional exam requirements/recommendations for international students: Required—Michigan English Language Assessment Battery; Recommended—TOEFL (minimum score 550 paper-based; 213 computer-based). *Application deadline:* For fall admission, 6/1 for domestic students, 4/1 for international students. Application fee: $35. *Unit head:* Dr. Mark Muniz, Coordinator, 320-308-4162, E-mail: mpmuniz@stcloudstate.edu. *Application contact:* Linda Lou Krueger, School of Graduate Studies, 320-308-2113, Fax: 320-308-5371, E-mail: lekrueger@stcloudstate.edu.

Savannah College of Art and Design, Graduate School, Program in Historic Preservation, Savannah, GA 31402-3146. Offers MA, MFA. Part-time programs available. *Degree requirements:* For master's, thesis, internship. *Entrance requirements:* For master's, interview, research paper. Additional exam requirements/recommendations for international students: Required—TOEFL (minimum score 450 paper-based; 133 computer-based). Electronic applications accepted. *Expenses:* Tuition: Full-time $28,515; part-time $627 per credit hour. One-time fee: $500. Tuition and fees vary according to course load.

School of the Art Institute of Chicago, Graduate Division, Program in Historic Preservation, Chicago, IL 60603-3103. Offers MSHP. *Entrance requirements:* Additional exam requirements/recommendations for international students: Required—TOEFL, IELTS.

Syracuse University, School of Information Studies, Program in Cultural Heritage Preservation, Syracuse, NY 13244. Offers CAS. Part-time programs available. *Degree requirements:* For CAS, internships. *Entrance requirements:* Additional exam requirements/recommendations for international students: Required—TOEFL (minimum score 100 iBT). *Application deadline:* For fall admission, 2/1 priority date for domestic and international students; for spring admission, 10/15 for domestic students, 10/15 priority date for international students. Applications are processed on a rolling basis. Application fee: $75. Electronic applications accepted. *Expenses:* Tuition: Full-time $26,808; part-time $1117 per credit. Required fees: $1024. *Unit head:* Kenneth Lavender, Dean, 315-443-6890, E-mail: klavende@syr.edu. *Application contact:* Susan Corieri, Director of Enrollment Management, 315-443-2575, E-mail: ist@syr.edu.

Texas Tech University, Graduate School, Program in Museum Science and Heritage Management, Lubbock, TX 79409. Offers heritage management (MS); museum science (MA). Part-time programs available. *Faculty:* 6 full-time (4 women), 1 part-time/adjunct (0 women). *Students:* 31 full-time (26 women), 7 part-time (6 women); includes 4 minority (1 African American, 3 Hispanic Americans). Average age 27. 34 applicants, 68% accepted, 14 enrolled. In 2009, 9 master's awarded. *Degree requirements:* For master's, thesis. *Entrance requirements:* For master's, GRE General Test. Additional exam requirements/recommendations for international students: Required—TOEFL (minimum score 550 paper-based; 213 computer-based). *Application deadline:* For fall admission, 3/1 priority date for international students; for spring admission, 11/1 priority date for international students. Applications are processed on a rolling basis. Application fee: $50 ($75 for international students). Electronic applications accepted. *Expenses:* Tuition, state resident: full-time $5100; part-time $213 per credit hour. Tuition, nonresident: full-time $11,748; part-time $490 per credit hour. Required fees: $2298; $50 per credit hour. $555 per semester. *Financial support:* In 2009–10, 2 research assistantships with partial tuition reimbursements (averaging $6,720 per year), 2 teaching assistantships with partial tuition reimbursements (averaging $8,018 per year) were awarded; career-related internships or fieldwork, Federal Work-Study, and institutionally sponsored loans also available. Support available to part-time students. Financial award application deadline: 4/15; financial award applicants required to submit FAFSA. *Faculty research:* Lubbock Lake Landmark; regional American fine art; museum education; Southern Plains cultural and natural heritage; natural science research. Total annual research expenditures: $48,569. *Unit head:* Dr. Eileen G. Johnson, Chair, 806-742-2442, Fax: 806-742-1136, E-mail: eileen.johnson@ttu.edu. *Application contact:* Claudia Cory, Assistant to the Director, 806-742-2442 Ext. 222, Fax: 806-742-1136, E-mail: claudia.cory@ttu.edu.

University of California, Riverside, Graduate Division, Department of History, Riverside, CA 92521-0102. Offers archival management (MA); historic preservation (MA); history (MA, PhD); museum curatorship (MA). Part-time programs available. Terminal master's awarded for partial completion of doctoral program. *Degree requirements:* For master's, one foreign language, comprehensive exam, internship report and oral exams, or thesis; for doctorate, 2 foreign languages, thesis/dissertation, qualifying exams, teaching experience. *Entrance requirements:* For master's, GRE General Test, minimum GPA of 3.2; for doctorate, GRE General Test, MA in history, minimum GPA of 3.2. Additional exam requirements/recommendations for international students: Required—TOEFL (minimum score 550 paper-based; 213 computer-based; 80 iBT). Electronic applications accepted. *Faculty research:* Native American history, United States, public history, Russia, Europe.

University of Delaware, College of Arts and Sciences, Program in Art Conservation, Newark, DE 19716. Offers practicing art conservation (MS). *Degree requirements:* For master's, internship, portfolio, oral exam, oral presentation. *Entrance requirements:* For master's, GRE General Test, course work in chemistry, art history/anthropology and studio art; minimum of 400 hours of conservation experience. Electronic applications accepted. *Faculty research:* Emergency response cleaning techniques, degradation process, art history, artists, materials, techniques of preservation and treatment.

University of Delaware, College of Human Services, Education and Public Policy, Center for Energy and Environmental Policy, Program in Urban Affairs and Public Policy, Newark, DE 19716. Offers community development and nonprofit leadership (MA); energy and environmental policy (MA); governance, planning and management (PhD); historic preservation (MA); social and urban policy (PhD); technology, environment and society (PhD). Part-time programs available. Terminal master's awarded for partial completion of doctoral program. *Degree requirements:* For master's, analytical paper or thesis; for doctorate, thesis/dissertation. *Entrance requirements:* For master's, GRE General Test, minimum GPA of 3.0; for doctorate, GRE General Test, minimum GPA of 3.5. Additional exam requirements/recommendations for international students: Required—TOEFL. Electronic applications accepted. *Faculty research:* Political economy; social policy analysis; technology and society; historic preservation; urban policy.

See Close-Up on page 1195.

University of Georgia, Graduate School, College of Environment and Design, Program in Historic Preservation, Athens, GA 30602. Offers MHP. *Students:* 28 full-time (19 women), 15 part-time (8 women); includes 1 minority (Asian American or Pacific Islander). 42 applicants, 71% accepted, 16 enrolled. In 2009, 21 master's awarded. *Degree requirements:* For master's, thesis. *Entrance requirements:* For master's, GRE General Test. *Application deadline:* For fall admission, 7/1 priority date for domestic students; for spring admission, 11/15 for domestic students. Application fee: $50. Electronic applications accepted. *Expenses:* Tuition, state resident: full-time $6000; part-time $250 per credit hour. Tuition, nonresident: full-time $20,904; part-time $871 per credit hour. Required fees: $730 per semester. *Financial support:* Fellowships, research assistantships, teaching assistantships, unspecified assistantships available. *Unit head:* Prof. John C. Waters, Graduate Coordinator, 706-542-4706, Fax: 706-542-4236, E-mail: jcwaters@uga.edu. *Application contact:* Graduate Coordinator.

University of Hawaii at Manoa, Graduate Division, College of Arts and Humanities, Department of American Studies, Program in Historic Preservation, Honolulu, HI 96822. Offers Graduate Certificate. Part-time programs available. *Students:* 7 full-time (5 women), 10 part-time (7 women); includes 9 minority (1 African American, 1 American Indian/Alaska Native, 6 Asian Americans or Pacific Islanders, 1 Hispanic American). Average age 35. 11 applicants, 82% accepted, 8 enrolled. In 2009, 6 Graduate Certificates awarded. *Entrance requirements:* Additional exam requirements/recommendations for international students: Required—TOEFL (minimum score 600 paper-based; 250 computer-based; 100 iBT), IELTS (minimum score 7). *Application deadline:* For fall admission, 3/1 for domestic and international students; for spring admission, 9/1 for domestic and international students. Application fee: $60. *Expenses:* Tuition, state resident: full-time $8900; part-time $372 per credit. Tuition, nonresident: full-time $21,400; part-time $898 per credit. Required fees: $207 per semester. *Financial support:* In 2009–10, 1 student received support, including 4 fellowships (averaging $1,675 per year), 1 teaching assistantship (averaging $14,382 per year). *Application contact:* Robert Perkinson, Graduate Chair, 808-956-8570, Fax: 808-956-4733, E-mail: perk@hawaii.edu.

University of Kentucky, Graduate School, College of Design, Department of Historic Preservation, Lexington, KY 40506-0032. Offers MHP. *Degree requirements:* For master's, comprehensive exam. *Entrance requirements:* For master's, GRE General Test, minimum undergraduate GPA of 2.75. Additional exam requirements/recommendations for international students: Required—TOEFL (minimum score 550 paper-based; 213 computer-based). Electronic applications accepted.

University of Maryland, College Park, Academic Affairs, School of Architecture, Planning and Preservation, Program in Historic Preservation, College Park, MD 20742. Offers MHP, Certificate. *Faculty:* 6 full-time (3 women), 2 part-time/adjunct (1 woman). *Students:* 15 full-time (12 women), 6 part-time (2 women); includes 1 minority (African American), 1 international. 41 applicants, 46% accepted, 7 enrolled. In 2009, 14 master's awarded. *Degree requirements:* For Certificate, thesis. *Entrance requirements:* For master's, GRE, minimum GPA of 3.0, 3 letters of recommendation, writing sample. Additional exam requirements/recommendations for international students: Required—TOEFL. *Application deadline:* For fall admission, 12/15 for domestic and international students; for spring admission, 6/1 for international students. Applications are processed on a rolling basis. Application fee: $60. Electronic applications accepted. *Expenses:* Tuition, area resident: Part-time $471 per credit hour. Tuition, state resident: part-time $471 per credit hour. Tuition, nonresident: part-time $1016 per credit hour. Required fees: $337.04 per term. *Financial support:* In 2009–10, 10 teaching assistantships (averaging $14,440 per year) were awarded; fellowships, career-related internships or fieldwork and tuition waivers also available. *Unit head:* Donald Linebaugh, Director, 301-405-6309, Fax: 301-314-9583, E-mail: dwline@umd.edu. *Application contact:* Dean of Graduate School, 301-405-0358.

University of Massachusetts Amherst, Graduate School, College of Humanities and Fine Arts, Department of Art, Programs in Architecture and Design, Amherst, MA 01003. Offers architecture and design (M Arch); historic preservation (MS); interior design (MS). Part-time programs available. *Students:* 43 full-time (15 women); includes 5 minority (1 African American, 2 Asian Americans or Pacific Islanders, 2 Hispanic Americans), 7 international. Average age 30. 100 applicants, 64% accepted, 21 enrolled. In 2009, 12 master's awarded. *Degree requirements:* For master's, thesis or alternative. *Entrance requirements:* For master's, GRE

General Test (M Arch), portfolio. Additional exam requirements/recommendations for international students: Required—TOEFL (minimum score 550 paper-based; 213 computer-based; 80 iBT), IELTS (minimum score 6.5). *Application deadline:* For fall admission, 2/1 for domestic and international students. Applications are processed on a rolling basis. Application fee: $50 ($65 for international students). Electronic applications accepted. *Expenses:* Tuition, state resident: full-time $2640; part-time $110 per credit. Tuition, nonresident: full-time $9936; part-time $414 per credit. Tuition and fees vary according to course load. *Financial support:* Fellowships, research assistantships, teaching assistantships, career-related internships or fieldwork, Federal Work-Study, scholarships/grants, traineeships, health care benefits, tuition waivers (full), and unspecified assistantships available. Support available to part-time students. Financial award application deadline: 2/1. *Unit head:* Dr. Ray K. Mann, Graduate Program Director, 413-545-0943, Fax: 413-545-3929. *Application contact:* Jean M. Ames, Supervisor of Admissions, 413-545-0722, Fax: 413-577-0100, E-mail: gradadm@grad.umass.edu.

University of New Mexico, Graduate School, School of Architecture and Planning, Program in Historic Preservation and Regionalism, Albuquerque, NM 87131-2039. Offers Graduate Certificate. Part-time and evening/weekend programs available. *Students:* 1 full-time (0 women), 10 part-time (4 women); includes 1 minority (Hispanic American), 1 international. Average age 45. 10 applicants, 90% accepted, 5 enrolled. *Application deadline:* For fall admission, 11/1 priority date for domestic students; for spring admission, 3/1 priority date for domestic students. Application fee: $50. Electronic applications accepted. *Expenses:* Tuition, state resident: full-time $2099; part-time $233.20 per credit hour. Tuition, nonresident: full-time $6650. Required fees: $25 per semester. Tuition and fees vary according to course load, program and reciprocity agreements. *Financial support:* Career-related internships or fieldwork and scholarships/grants available. Support available to part-time students. *Unit head:* Chris Wilson, Director, 505-277-3303, Fax: 505-277-0897, E-mail: chwilson@unm.edu. *Application contact:* Chris Wilson, Director, 505-277-3303, Fax: 505-277-0897, E-mail: chwilson@unm.edu.

The University of North Carolina at Greensboro, Graduate School, School of Human Environmental Sciences, Department of Interior Architecture, Greensboro, NC 27412-5001. Offers historic preservation (Certificate); interior architecture (MS); museum studies (Certificate). *Degree requirements:* For master's, thesis. *Entrance requirements:* For master's, GRE General Test or MAT, bachelor's degree in interior design, interview, portfolio. Additional exam requirements/recommendations for international students: Required—TOEFL. Electronic applications accepted.

University of Oregon, Graduate School, School of Architecture and Allied Arts, Program in Historic Preservation, Eugene, OR 97403. Offers MS. *Degree requirements:* For master's, thesis, internship. *Entrance requirements:* For master's, participation in Pacific Northwest Field School. Additional exam requirements/recommendations for international students: Required—TOEFL. *Faculty research:* Vernacular architecture, Native American architecture, masonry structure and details, wood construction systems, cultural landscapes.

University of Pennsylvania, School of Design, Graduate Group in Historic Preservation, Philadelphia, PA 19104. Offers conservation and heritage management (Certificate); historic conservation (Certificate); historic preservation (MS). Part-time programs available. *Faculty:* 2 full-time (0 women), 2 part-time/adjunct (0 women). *Students:* 46 full-time (40 women), 2 part-time (1 woman); includes 6 minority (2 African Americans, 2 Asian Americans or Pacific Islanders, 2 Hispanic Americans), 2 international. 83 applicants, 89% accepted, 25 enrolled. In 2009, 20 master's, 6 other advanced degrees awarded. *Degree requirements:* For master's, thesis. *Entrance requirements:* For master's, GRE. Additional exam requirements/recommendations for international students: Required—TOEFL. *Application deadline:* For fall admission, 1/2 priority date for domestic students. Application fee: $70. *Expenses:* Tuition: Full-time $25,660; part-time $4758 per course. Required fees: $2152; $270 per course. Tuition and fees vary according to course load, degree level and program. *Financial support:* Fellowships, research assistantships, teaching assistantships, career-related internships or fieldwork, Federal Work-Study, institutionally sponsored loans, scholarships/grants, and tuition waivers (partial) available. Support available to part-time students. Financial award applicants required to submit FAFSA. *Faculty research:* Historic building technology, architectural conservation, architectural theory, preservation in the Third World.

See Close-Up on page 147.

University of South Carolina, The Graduate School, College of Arts and Sciences, Department of History, Program in Public History, Columbia, SC 29208. Offers archives (MA); historic preservation (MA); museum (MA); museum management (Certificate); MLIS/MA. *Degree requirements:* For master's, one foreign language, thesis, internship. *Entrance requirements:* For master's, GRE General Test, writing sample. Additional exam requirements/recommendations for international students: Required—TOEFL. Electronic applications accepted. *Faculty research:* Museum studies, historic preservation, archives administration.

The University of Texas at Austin, Graduate School, School of Architecture, Austin, TX 78712-1111. Offers architecture (M Arch); community and regional planning (MSCRP, PhD); historic preservation (MS); history of architecture (MA, PhD); landscape architecture (MLA); urban design (MSUD); JD/MSCRP; MSCRP/MA; MSCRP/PhD. *Degree requirements:* For doctorate, thesis/dissertation. *Entrance requirements:* For master's and doctorate, GRE General Test. Additional exam requirements/recommendations for international students: Required—TOEFL (minimum score 550 paper-based; 213 computer-based). Electronic applications accepted.

University of Vermont, Graduate College, College of Arts and Sciences, Program in Historic Preservation, Burlington, VT 05405. Offers MS. *Students:* 24 (13 women). 26 applicants, 92% accepted, 13 enrolled. In 2009, 11 master's awarded. *Entrance requirements:* For master's, GRE General Test, sample project or equivalent. Additional exam requirements/recommendations for international students: Required—TOEFL (minimum score 550 paper-based; 213 computer-based; 80 iBT). *Application deadline:* For fall admission, 3/1 for domestic students. Application fee: $40. Electronic applications accepted. *Expenses:* Tuition, state resident: part-time $508 per credit hour. Tuition, nonresident: part-time $1281 per credit hour. *Financial support:* Fellowships, teaching assistantships available. Financial award application deadline: 3/1. *Faculty research:* Architectural environment. *Unit head:* T. Visser, Director, 802-656-3180. *Application contact:* T. Visser, Director, 802-656-3180.

University of Washington, Graduate School, College of Built Environments, Interdisciplinary Program in Historic Preservation, Seattle, WA 98195. Offers Certificate. Offered in cooperation with the Departments of Architecture, Landscape Architecture, and Urban Design and Planning. Part-time programs available. Electronic applications accepted. *Faculty research:* History of the built environment, historic preservation planning, vernacular architecture, ethnic and gender issues in preservation, restoration.

University of West Florida, College of Arts and Sciences: Arts, Department of History, Pensacola, FL 32514-5750. Offers historic preservation (MA); history (MA); military history (MA); public history (MA). Part-time and evening/weekend programs available. *Faculty:* 5 full-time (1 woman), 1 part-time/adjunct (0 women). *Students:* 14 full-time (6 women), 23 part-time (12 women); includes 5 minority (2 African Americans, 1 American Indian/Alaska Native, 1 Asian American or Pacific Islander, 1 Hispanic American). Average age 31. 26 applicants, 73% accepted, 9 enrolled. In 2009, 10 master's awarded. *Degree requirements:* For master's, thesis or alternative. *Entrance requirements:* For master's, GRE General Test, minimum GPA of 3.0, minimum 15 hours of upper-level history courses. Additional exam requirements/recommendations for international students: Required—TOEFL (minimum score 550 paper-based; 213 computer-based). *Application deadline:* For fall admission, 6/1 for domestic students, 5/15 for international students; for spring admission, 11/1 for domestic students, 10/1 for international students. Applications are processed on a rolling basis. Application fee: $30. *Expenses:* Tuition, state resident: full-time $4982; part-time $260 per credit hour. Tuition, nonresident: full-time $20,059; part-time $919 per credit hour. Required fees: $1247; $52 per credit hour. *Financial support:* In 2009–10, 2 teaching assistantships with partial tuition reimbursements (averaging $5,000 per year) were awarded; unspecified assistantships also available. Financial award application deadline: 4/15; financial award applicants required to submit FAFSA. *Unit head:* Dr. John J. Clune, Chairperson, 850-474-2680. *Application contact:* Terry McCray, Assistant Director of Graduate Admissions, 850-473-7718, Fax: 850-473-7714, E-mail: gradadmissions@uwf.edu.

University of Wisconsin–Milwaukee, Graduate School, School of Architecture and Urban Planning, Department of Architecture, Milwaukee, WI 53201-0413. Offers architecture (PhD); preservation studies (Certificate); M Arch/MUP. *Faculty:* 26 full-time (4 women). *Students:* 150 full-time (48 women), 11 part-time (7 women); includes 16 minority (4 African Americans, 1 American Indian/Alaska Native, 5 Asian Americans or Pacific Islanders, 6 Hispanic Americans), 13 international. Average age 30. 147 applicants, 51% accepted, 33 enrolled. In 2009, 26 master's, 2 doctorates awarded. *Degree requirements:* For master's, comprehensive exam, thesis; for doctorate, comprehensive exam, thesis/dissertation. *Entrance requirements:* For master's, GRE General Test, portfolio. Additional exam requirements/recommendations for international students: Required—TOEFL (minimum score 600 paper-based; 250 computer-based; 100 iBT), IELTS (minimum score 7). *Application deadline:* For fall admission, 1/1 priority date for domestic students; for spring admission, 9/1 for domestic students. Applications are processed on a rolling basis. Application fee: $45 ($75 for international students). *Expenses:* Tuition, state resident: full-time $8800. Tuition, nonresident: full-time $20,760. Tuition and fees vary according to program and reciprocity agreements. *Financial support:* In 2009–10, 21 teaching assistantships were awarded; career-related internships or fieldwork and unspecified assistantships also available. Support available to part-time students. Financial award application deadline: 4/15. Total annual research expenditures: $239,719. *Unit head:* Joan Simuncak, Representative, 414-229-4015, Fax: 414-229-6976, E-mail: joanarch@uwm.edu. *Application contact:* Josef Stagg, General Information Contact, 414-229-4032, Fax: 414-229-6967, E-mail: jstagg@uwm.edu.

Ursuline College, School of Graduate Studies, Program in Historic Preservation, Pepper Pike, OH 44124-4398. Offers MA. Part-time programs available. *Faculty:* 1 (woman) full-time, 2 part-time/adjunct (0 women). *Students:* 4 full-time (all women), 5 part-time (all women); includes 1 minority (African American). Average age 32. 6 applicants, 67% accepted, 4 enrolled. *Degree requirements:* For master's, thesis. *Entrance requirements:* For master's, minimum undergraduate GPA of 3.0. Additional exam requirements/recommendations for international students: Required—TOEFL (minimum score 500 paper-based; 173 computer-based). *Application deadline:* For fall admission, 8/1 priority date for domestic students. Applications are processed on a rolling basis. Application fee: $25. *Expenses:* Tuition: Full-time $14,544; part-time $808 per credit hour. Required fees: $230; $75 per semester. *Financial support:* In 2009–10, 4 students received support. Federal Work-Study available. Financial award application deadline: 3/1. *Unit head:* Bari Stith, 440-646-8135. *Application contact:* Melanie Steele, Secretary, 440-646-8199, Fax: 440-684-6138, E-mail: gradsch@ursuline.edu.

Virginia Commonwealth University, Graduate School, College of Humanities and Sciences, Wilder School of Government and Public Affairs, Department of Urban Studies and Planning, Program in Historic Preservation Planning, Richmond, VA 23284-9005. Offers Certificate.

Landscape Architecture

Arizona State University, Graduate College, College of Design, School of Architecture and Landscape Architecture, Tempe, AZ 85287. Offers architecture (M Arch); building design (MS); landscape architecture (MLA); urban design (MUD); MA/MBA. *Degree requirements:* For master's, thesis optional. *Entrance requirements:* For master's, GRE General Test, design portfolio.

Auburn University, Graduate School, College of Architecture, Design, and Construction, Program in Landscape Architecture, Auburn University, AL 36849. Offers MLA. *Accreditation:* ASLA. *Faculty:* 26 full-time (6 women), 3 part-time/adjunct (1 woman). *Students:* 33 full-time (11 women), 4 part-time (3 women); includes 2 minority (1 African American, 1 Hispanic American), 10 international. Average age 26. 56 applicants, 70% accepted, 17 enrolled. In 2009, 7 master's awarded. *Entrance requirements:* For master's, 3 letters of recommendation. Application fee: $50 ($60 for international students). *Expenses:* Tuition, state resident: full-time $6240. Tuition, nonresident: full-time $18,720. International tuition: $18,938 full-time. Required fees: $492. Tuition and fees vary according to course load, program and reciprocity agreements. *Financial support:* Applicants required to submit FAFSA. *Unit head:* Charlene Lebleu, Chair, 334-844-4516. *Application contact:* Dr. George Flowers, Dean of the Graduate School, 334-844-2125.

Ball State University, Graduate School, College of Architecture and Planning, Department of Landscape Architecture, Muncie, IN 47306-1099. Offers MLA. *Accreditation:* ASLA. *Degree requirements:* For master's, thesis. *Entrance requirements:* For master's, writing sample.

California State Polytechnic University, Pomona, Academic Affairs, College of Environmental Design, Program in Landscape Architecture, Pomona, CA 91768-2557. Offers M Land Arch. *Accreditation:* ASLA. Part-time programs available. *Students:* 51 full-time (24 women), 5 part-time (1 woman); includes 10 minority (1 African American, 1 American Indian/Alaska Native, 7 Asian Americans or Pacific Islanders, 1 Hispanic American), 2 international. Average age 32. 82 applicants, 27% accepted, 16 enrolled. In 2009, 13 master's awarded. *Degree requirements:* For master's, thesis or alternative. *Application deadline:* For fall admission, 5/1 priority date for domestic students; for winter admission, 10/15 priority date for domestic students; for spring admission, 1/20 priority date for domestic students. Applications are processed on a rolling basis. Application fee: $55. Electronic applications accepted. *Expenses:* Tuition, nonresident: full-time $6696; part-time $248 per credit. Required fees: $5487; $3237 per term. Tuition and fees vary according to course load, degree level and program. *Financial support:* Career-related internships or fieldwork, Federal Work-Study, and institutionally sponsored loans available. Support available to part-time students. Financial award application deadline: 3/2; financial award applicants required to submit FAFSA. *Unit head:* Dr. Gerald O. Taylor, Interim Chair/Associate Professor, 909-869-6891, Fax: 909-869-4460, E-mail: lagradprog@csupomona.edu. *Application contact:* Scott J. Duncan, Director, Admissions, 909-869-3258, Fax: 909-869-4529, E-mail: sjduncan@csupomona.edu.

Chatham University, Program in Landscape Architecture, Pittsburgh, PA 15232-2826. Offers landscape architecture (ML Arch); landscape studies (MA). Part-time and evening/weekend programs available. *Students:* 25 full-time (15 women), 16 part-time (10 women). Average age 31. 27 applicants, 56% accepted, 15 enrolled. In 2009, 6 master's awarded. *Degree*

Landscape Architecture

Chatham University (continued)
requirements: For master's, thesis, capstone project. *Entrance requirements:* Additional exam requirements/recommendations for international students: Required—TOEFL (minimum score 600 paper-based; 250 computer-based; 100 iBT), IELTS (minimum score 6.5), TWE. *Application deadline:* For fall admission, 7/1 priority date for domestic students, 6/1 priority date for international students; for spring admission, 12/1 priority date for domestic students, 11/1 priority date for international students. Applications are processed on a rolling basis. Application fee: $45. Electronic applications accepted. *Financial support:* Career-related internships or fieldwork available. Financial award applicants required to submit FAFSA. *Faculty research:* Sustainability. *Unit head:* Dr. Safei Hamed, Director, 412-365-1899, E-mail: shamed@chatham.edu. *Application contact:* Michael May, Director of Graduate Admissions, 412-365-1825, Fax: 412-365-1609, E-mail: gradadmissions@chatham.edu.

City College of the City University of New York, Graduate School, School of Architecture and Environmental Studies, New York, NY 10031-9198. Offers architecture (M Arch); landscape architecture (MLA); urban design (MUP). Part-time programs available. *Degree requirements:* For master's, thesis. *Entrance requirements:* For master's, portfolio, professional degree in architecture or equivalent. Additional exam requirements/recommendations for international students: Required—TOEFL (minimum score 550 paper-based; 213 computer-based).

Clemson University, Graduate School, College of Architecture, Arts, and Humanities, Department of Planning and Landscape Architecture, Program in Landscape Architecture, Clemson, SC 29634. Offers MLA. *Accreditation:* ASLA. *Students:* 28 full-time (10 women), 4 part-time (all women); includes 4 minority (all Hispanic Americans), 5 international. Average age 31. 36 applicants, 81% accepted, 6 enrolled. In 2009, 12 master's awarded. *Entrance requirements:* For master's, GRE General Test. Additional exam requirements/recommendations for international students: Required—TOEFL. *Application deadline:* For fall admission, 2/15 for domestic students, 4/15 for international students. Applications are processed on a rolling basis. Application fee: $70 ($80 for international students). Electronic applications accepted. *Expenses:* Tuition, state resident: full-time $8684; part-time $528 per credit hour. Tuition, nonresident: full-time $15,330; part-time $1078 per credit hour. Required fees: $736; $37 per semester. Part-time tuition and fees vary according to course load and program. *Financial support:* In 2009–10, 21 students received support, including 2 teaching assistantships with partial tuition reimbursements available (averaging $6,960 per year); fellowships with partial tuition reimbursements available, research assistantships with partial tuition reimbursements available, career-related internships or fieldwork, institutionally sponsored loans, scholarships/grants, health care benefits, and unspecified assistantships also available. Support available to part-time students. *Unit head:* Dr. Elaine M. Worzala, Chair, 864-656-3657, Fax: 864-656-7519, E-mail: eworzal@clemson.edu. *Application contact:* Dr. Umit Yilmaz, Coordinator, 864-656-7349, Fax: 864-656-7519, E-mail: uyilmaz@clemson.edu.

Columbia University, School of Continuing Education, Program in Landscape Design, New York, NY 10027. Offers MS. Part-time programs available. *Faculty:* 11 part-time/adjunct (3 women). *Students:* 27 part-time (20 women); includes 3 minority (2 African Americans, 1 Asian American or Pacific Islander), 2 international. 25 applicants, 88% accepted, 14 enrolled. In 2009, 17 master's awarded. *Entrance requirements:* For master's, minimum undergraduate GPA of 3.0. Additional exam requirements/recommendations for international students: Required—American Language Program placement test. *Application deadline:* For fall admission, 4/15 for domestic students. Application fee: $50. *Financial support:* Institutionally sponsored loans available. Financial award applicants required to submit FAFSA. *Unit head:* Joseph Disponzio, Program Director, 212-854-9699, E-mail: jd52@columbia.edu. *Application contact:* Bryce Weinert, Admissions Adviser, 212-854-9666, E-mail: sce-apply@columbia.edu.

Conway School of Landscape Design, Graduate Program in Landscape Design, Conway, MA 01341-0179. Offers MS. *Degree requirements:* For master's, projects. *Faculty research:* Restoration of native plant communities; integration of humanities, environment, and design.

Cornell University, Graduate School, Graduate Fields of Agriculture and Life Sciences and Graduate Fields of Architecture, Art and Planning, Field of Landscape Architecture, Ithaca, NY 14853-0001. Offers MLA. *Accreditation:* ASLA. *Faculty:* 24 full-time (8 women). *Students:* 53 full-time (21 women); includes 4 minority (2 Asian Americans or Pacific Islanders, 2 Hispanic Americans), 7 international. Average age 31. 133 applicants, 35% accepted, 20 enrolled. In 2009, 11 master's awarded. *Degree requirements:* For master's, project or thesis. *Entrance requirements:* For master's, GRE General Test (recommended), portfolio, 2 letters of recommendation. Additional exam requirements/recommendations for international students: Required—TOEFL (minimum score 550 paper-based; 213 computer-based; 77 iBT). *Application deadline:* For fall admission, 2/15 priority date for domestic students. Applications are processed on a rolling basis. Application fee: $70. Electronic applications accepted. *Expenses:* Tuition: Full-time $29,500. Required fees: $70. Full-time tuition and fees vary according to degree level, program and student level. *Financial support:* In 2009–10, 11 students received support; fellowships with full tuition reimbursements available, research assistantships with full tuition reimbursements available, teaching assistantships with full tuition reimbursements available, institutionally sponsored loans, scholarships/grants, health care benefits, tuition waivers (full and partial), and unspecified assistantships available. Financial award applicants required to submit FAFSA. *Faculty research:* Urban horticulture and landscape design, urban design research, cultural landscape history, women in landscape architecture, landscape design language, Japanese landscape architecture. *Unit head:* Director of Graduate Studies, 607-254-9552. *Application contact:* Graduate School Application Requests, Caldwell Hall, 607-254-9552, E-mail: lafield@cornell.edu.

Florida Agricultural and Mechanical University, Division of Graduate Studies, Research, and Continuing Education, School of Architecture, Tallahassee, FL 32307-3200. Offers architectural studies (MS Arch); architecture (professional) (M Arch); landscape architecture (MLA). Part-time programs available. *Faculty:* 20 full-time (6 women). *Students:* 52 full-time (20 women), 11 part-time (3 women); includes 44 minority (41 African Americans, 1 Asian American or Pacific Islander, 2 Hispanic Americans), 3 international. In 2009, 11 master's awarded. *Degree requirements:* For master's, thesis. *Entrance requirements:* For master's, GRE General Test, minimum GPA of 3.0, portfolio. Additional exam requirements/recommendations for international students: Required—TOEFL (minimum score 550 paper-based). *Application deadline:* For fall admission, 5/1 for domestic students, 1/15 for international students; for spring admission, 11/1 for domestic students. Application fee: $30. *Financial support:* Fellowships, research assistantships, teaching assistantships, Federal Work-Study, institutionally sponsored loans, scholarships/grants, and tuition waivers (partial) available. Financial award application deadline: 5/1. *Faculty research:* Environmental technology, post-occupancy evaluation, building economics, design methods, computer-aided design. *Unit head:* Rodner Wright, Dean, 850-599-3244. *Application contact:* Dr. Chanta M. Haywood, Dean of Graduate Studies, Research, and Continuing Education, 850-599-3315, Fax: 850-599-3727.

Florida International University, College of Architecture and the Arts, School of Architecture, Landscape Architecture Program, Miami, FL 33199. Offers MA, MLA. Part-time programs available. *Faculty:* 2 full-time (1 woman). *Students:* 27 full-time (12 women), 2 part-time (1 woman); includes 15 minority (1 African American, 14 Hispanic Americans), 1 international. Average age 28. 32 applicants, 19% accepted, 6 enrolled. In 2009, 13 master's awarded. *Entrance requirements:* For master's, GRE or minimum GPA of 3.0 in upper-level undergraduate work, portfolio. Additional exam requirements/recommendations for international students: Required—TOEFL (minimum score 550 paper-based; 80 iBT). *Application deadline:* For fall admission, 2/1 for domestic and international students. Application fee: $30. Electronic applications accepted. *Expenses:* Tuition, state resident: full-time $8008; part-time $4004 per year. Tuition, nonresident: full-time $20,104; part-time $10,052 per year. Required fees: $298; $149 per term. *Financial support:* Institutionally sponsored loans and scholarships/grants available. Financial award application deadline: 3/1; financial award applicants required to submit FAFSA. *Unit head:* Dr. Brian Schriner, Interim Dean, 305-348-6442, Fax: 305-348-6716, E-mail: schriner@fiu.edu. *Application contact:* Prof. Marta Canaves, Graduate Program Director, 305-348-1886, Fax: 305-348-6716, E-mail: marta.canaves@fiu.edu.

Harvard University, Graduate School of Arts and Sciences, Committee on Architecture, Landscape Architecture, and Urban Planning, Cambridge, MA 02138. Offers architecture (PhD); landscape architecture (PhD); urban planning (PhD). *Degree requirements:* For doctorate, one foreign language, thesis/dissertation, oral exam. *Entrance requirements:* For doctorate, GRE General Test. Additional exam requirements/recommendations for international students: Required—TOEFL. *Expenses:* Tuition: Full-time $33,696. Required fees: $1126. Full-time tuition and fees vary according to program.

Harvard University, Graduate School of Design, Department of Landscape Architecture, Cambridge, MA 02138. Offers MLA. *Accreditation:* ASLA. *Faculty:* 7 full-time (2 women), 37 part-time/adjunct (17 women). *Students:* 104 full-time (70 women); includes 12 minority (8 Asian Americans or Pacific Islanders, 4 Hispanic Americans), 31 international. Average age 28. In 2009, 37 master's awarded. *Entrance requirements:* For master's, GRE General Test. Additional exam requirements/recommendations for international students: Required—TOEFL (minimum score 600 paper-based; 250 computer-based; 104 iBT). *Application deadline:* For fall admission, 1/14 for domestic and international students. Application fee: $85. Electronic applications accepted. *Expenses:* Tuition: Full-time $33,696. Required fees: $1126. Full-time tuition and fees vary according to program. *Financial support:* Federal Work-Study and scholarships/grants available. Financial award application deadline: 2/4; financial award applicants required to submit FAFSA. *Unit head:* Charles Waldheim, Chair, 617-495-2573. *Application contact:* Gail Gustafson, Director of Admissions, 617-495-5453, Fax: 617-495-8949, E-mail: ggustafson@gsd.harvard.edu.

Illinois Institute of Technology, Graduate College, College of Architecture, Chicago, IL 60616-3793. Offers architecture (M Arch, MS Arch, PhD); integrated building delivery (M IBD); landscape architecture (MLA). Part-time programs available. *Faculty:* 40 full-time (5 women), 55 part-time/adjunct (15 women). *Students:* 205 full-time (93 women), 30 part-time (11 women); includes 14 minority (3 African Americans, 4 Asian Americans or Pacific Islanders, 7 Hispanic Americans), 97 international. Average age 29. 479 applicants, 67% accepted, 76 enrolled. In 2009, 54 master's, 2 doctorates awarded. *Degree requirements:* For master's, thesis (for some programs); for doctorate, comprehensive exam, thesis/dissertation. *Entrance requirements:* For master's, GRE General Test, Applicants must have a college grade point average of 3.0 on a 4.0 point scale. ; for doctorate, GRE General Test, minimum GPA of 3.5, official transcripts, portfolio, 3 letters of recommendation, professional statement. Additional exam requirements/recommendations for international students: Required—TOEFL (minimum score 550 paper-based; 80 iBT). *Application deadline:* For fall admission, 1/15 for domestic students, 1/1 for international students. Applications are processed on a rolling basis. Application fee: $50. Electronic applications accepted. *Expenses:* Tuition: Full-time $17,550; part-time $888 per credit hour. Required fees: $850; $7.50 per credit hour. One-time fee: $50 full-time. Full-time tuition and fees vary according to program. *Financial support:* In 2009–10, 125 teaching assistantships (averaging $4,000 per year) were awarded; fellowships, career-related internships or fieldwork, Federal Work-Study, institutionally sponsored loans, scholarships/grants, and health care benefits also available. Support available to part-time students. Financial award applicants required to submit FAFSA. *Faculty research:* Sustainability and environmental design, comprehensive tall building design, innovative materials technology, advanced structural systems, digital design methods. *Unit head:* Donna V. Robertson, John and Jeanne Rowe Chair, 312-567-3230, Fax: 312-567-5820, E-mail: robertson@iit.edu. *Application contact:* Donna V. Robertson, John and Jeanne Rowe Chair, 312-567-3230, Fax: 312-567-5820, E-mail: robertson@iit.edu.

See Close-Up on page 143.

Iowa State University of Science and Technology, Graduate College, College of Design, Department of Landscape Architecture, Ames, IA 50011. Offers MLA, MCRP/MLA. *Accreditation:* ASLA. Part-time programs available. *Faculty:* 12 full-time (4 women), 1 part-time/adjunct (0 women). *Students:* 6 full-time (4 women), 1 (woman) part-time; includes 1 minority (Hispanic American), 1 international. 17 applicants, 0% accepted, 0 enrolled. In 2009, 4 master's awarded. *Degree requirements:* For master's, thesis. *Entrance requirements:* For master's, GRE (highly recommended), portfolio. Additional exam requirements/recommendations for international students: Required—TOEFL (minimum score 600 paper-based; 100 iBT) or IELTS (minimum score 7). *Application deadline:* For fall admission, 2/1 priority date for domestic and international students. Applications are processed on a rolling basis. Application fee: $40 ($90 for international students). Electronic applications accepted. *Expenses:* Tuition, state resident: full-time $6716. Tuition, nonresident: full-time $8908. Tuition and fees vary according to course level, course load, program and student level. *Financial support:* In 2009–10, 3 research assistantships with full and partial tuition reimbursements (averaging $7,850 per year), 2 teaching assistantships with full and partial tuition reimbursements (averaging $7,850 per year) were awarded; career-related internships or fieldwork, Federal Work-Study, institutionally sponsored loans, tuition waivers (partial), and unspecified assistantships also available. Support available to part-time students. Financial award application deadline: 2/15; financial award applicants required to submit FAFSA. *Faculty research:* Landscape ecology, geographic information systems, landscape perception, historic preservation, resource management, design. Total annual research expenditures: $1.2 million. *Unit head:* Dr. Douglas Johnston, Chair, 515-294-6942, Fax: 515-294-2348, E-mail: landarch@iastate.edu. *Application contact:* Dr. Paul F. Anderson, Director of Graduate Education, 515-294-8958, E-mail: landarch@iastate.edu.

Kansas State University, Graduate School, College of Architecture, Planning and Design, Department of Landscape Architecture and Regional and Community Planning, Manhattan, KS 66506. Offers MLA. *Accreditation:* ASLA. Part-time programs available. *Faculty:* 16 full-time (4 women), 3 part-time/adjunct (1 woman). *Students:* 47 full-time (19 women); includes 4 minority (1 African American, 2 Asian Americans or Pacific Islanders, 1 Hispanic American), 8 international. Average age 27. 52 applicants, 65% accepted, 19 enrolled. In 2009, 36 master's awarded. *Degree requirements:* For master's, thesis, residency, oral exam. *Entrance requirements:* For master's, portfolio. Additional exam requirements/recommendations for international students: Required—TOEFL (minimum score 600 paper-based). *Application deadline:* For fall admission, 2/1 priority date for domestic and international students; for spring admission, 8/1 priority date for domestic and international students. Applications are processed on a rolling basis. Application fee: $80. Electronic applications accepted. *Financial support:* In 2009–10, 1 research assistantship (averaging $8,500 per year), 13 teaching assistantships with full tuition reimbursements (averaging $8,205 per year) were awarded; fellowships, career-related internships or fieldwork, Federal Work-Study, institutionally sponsored loans, and scholarships/grants also available. Support available to part-time students. Financial award application deadline: 3/15; financial award applicants required to submit FAFSA. *Faculty research:* Community planning and design, design and planning theory, geospatial technology infrastructure, watershed restoration, landscape ecology. Total annual research expenditures: $17,414. *Unit head:* Dr. Dan Donelin, Head, 785-532-5961, Fax: 785-532-6722, E-mail: dandon@ksu.edu. *Application contact:* Jody Fronce, Application Contact, 785-532-5961, Fax: 785-532-6722, E-mail: la-rcp@ksu.edu.

Louisiana State University and Agricultural and Mechanical College, Graduate School, College of Art and Design, School of Landscape Architecture, Baton Rouge, LA 70803. Offers MLA. *Accreditation:* ASLA. *Faculty:* 13 full-time (3 women). *Students:* 34 full-time (16 women), 1 (woman) part-time; includes 3 minority (1 African American, 1 Asian American or Pacific Islander, 1 Hispanic American), 6 international. Average age 29. 63 applicants, 41% accepted, 9 enrolled. In 2009, 12 master's awarded. *Degree requirements:* For master's, thesis. *Entrance requirements:* For master's, GRE General Test, minimum GPA of 3.0. Additional exam requirements/recommendations for international students: Required—TOEFL (minimum score 550 paper-based; 213 computer-based; 79 iBT) or IELTS (minimum score 6.5). *Application deadline:* For fall admission, 1/25 priority date for domestic students, 5/15 for international students; for spring admission, 10/15 for international students. Applications are processed on a rolling basis. Application fee: $50 ($70 for international students). Electronic applications accepted. *Financial support:* In 2009–10, 32 students received support, including 15 research assistantships with full and partial tuition reimbursements available (averaging $6,500 per year), 1 teaching assistantship with partial tuition reimbursement available (averaging $5,400 per year); fellowships, career-related internships or fieldwork, Federal Work-Study, institutionally sponsored loans, health care benefits, and unspecified assistantships also available. Financial award application deadline: 7/1; financial award applicants required to submit FAFSA. *Faculty research:* Digital representation, cultural landscapes, urban infrastructure, community design. Total annual research expenditures: $7,675. *Unit head:* Elizabeth Mossop, Director, 225-578-1434, Fax: 225-578-1445, E-mail: emossop@lsu.edu. *Application contact:* Elizabeth Mossop, Director, 225-578-1434, Fax: 225-578-1445, E-mail: emossop@lsu.edu.

Mississippi State University, College of Agriculture and Life Sciences, Department of Landscape Architecture, Mississippi State, MS 39762. Offers MLA. Part-time programs available. *Faculty:* 11 full-time (0 women). *Students:* 22 full-time (4 women), 7 part-time (1 woman); includes 2 minority (1 Asian American or Pacific Islander, 1 Hispanic American), 1 international. Average age 30. 22 applicants, 86% accepted, 11 enrolled. In 2009, 4 master's awarded. *Degree requirements:* For master's, thesis. *Entrance requirements:* For master's, GRE or minimum GPA of 3.0 in upper-division major emphasis courses from an accredited university, minimum GPA of 2.8 on bachelor's degree. Additional exam requirements/recommendations for international students: Required—TOEFL (minimum score 600 paper-based; 250 computer-based; 100 iBT); Recommended—IELTS (minimum score 7.5). *Application deadline:* For fall admission, 7/1 for domestic students, 5/1 for international students; for spring admission, 10/1 for domestic students, 9/1 for international students. Applications are processed on a rolling basis. Application fee: $40. Electronic applications accepted. *Expenses:* Tuition, state resident: full-time $2575.50; part-time $286.25 per credit hour. Tuition, nonresident: full-time $6510; part-time $723.50 per credit hour. Tuition and fees vary according to course load. *Financial support:* In 2009–10, 4 research assistantships (averaging $12,166 per year), 3 teaching assistantships with full and partial tuition reimbursements (averaging $7,120 per year) were awarded; Federal Work-Study, institutionally sponsored loans, tuition waivers (partial), and unspecified assistantships also available. Financial award application deadline: 4/1; financial award applicants required to submit FAFSA. *Faculty research:* Design pedagogy, low impact development, conservation planning, wildlife/urban interfacing planning, sustainable communities, watershed planning, historical landscapes, decision support system development, Center for Sustainable Design. *Unit head:* Sadik C. Artunc, Professor and Head, 662-325-4554, Fax: 662-325-7893, E-mail: sartunc@lalc.msstate.edu. *Application contact:* Christopher Campany, Professor and Graduate Coordinator, 662-325-3012, Fax: 662-325-7893, E-mail: ccampany@lalc.msstate.edu.

Morgan State University, School of Graduate Studies, Institute of Architecture and Planning, Program in Landscape Architecture, Baltimore, MD 21251. Offers MLA, MSLA. *Accreditation:* ASLA. *Degree requirements:* For master's, thesis. *Entrance requirements:* Additional exam requirements/recommendations for international students: Required—TOEFL (minimum score 550 paper-based; 213 computer-based). *Faculty research:* Philosophy and design, urban design, design history and theory, computer-aided design and community design.

North Carolina State University, Graduate School, College of Design, Department of Landscape Architecture, Raleigh, NC 27695. Offers MLA. *Accreditation:* ASLA. *Degree requirements:* For master's, thesis optional, oral exam, project. *Entrance requirements:* For master's, GRE General Test (recommended), portfolio. Electronic applications accepted. *Faculty research:* Community development and co-operative engagement, landscape planning and design.

The Ohio State University, Graduate School, College of Engineering, Austin E. Knowlton School of Architecture, Program in Landscape Architecture, Columbus, OH 43210. Offers M Land Arch. *Accreditation:* ASLA. *Faculty:* 8. *Students:* 25 full-time (9 women), 4 part-time (all women), 3 international. Average age 28. In 2009, 5 master's awarded. *Degree requirements:* For master's, thesis or alternative. *Entrance requirements:* For master's, GRE General Test. Additional exam requirements/recommendations for international students: Required—TOEFL (minimum score 600 paper-based; 250 computer-based). *Application deadline:* For fall admission, 8/15 priority date for domestic students, 7/1 priority date for international students; for winter admission, 12/1 priority date for domestic students, 11/1 priority date for international students; for spring admission, 3/1 priority date for domestic students, 2/1 priority date for international students. Applications are processed on a rolling basis. Application fee: $40 ($50 for international students). Electronic applications accepted. *Expenses:* Tuition, state resident: full-time $10,683. Tuition, nonresident: full-time $25,923. Tuition and fees vary according to course load and program. *Financial support:* Fellowships, Federal Work-Study, institutionally sponsored loans, and unspecified assistantships available. Support available to part-time students. *Unit head:* Jane Amidon, Section Head, 614-292-0081, Fax: 614-292-7106, E-mail: amidon.2@osu.edu. *Application contact:* 614-292-9444, Fax: 614-292-3895, E-mail: domestic.grad@osu.edu.

Oklahoma State University, College of Agricultural Science and Natural Resources, Department of Horticulture and Landscape Architecture, Stillwater, OK 74078. Offers agriculture (M Ag); crop science (PhD); environmental science (PhD); horticulture (MS); plant science (PhD). *Accreditation:* ASLA. *Faculty:* 21 full-time (2 women), 2 part-time/adjunct (1 woman). *Students:* 14 part-time (6 women); includes 2 minority (1 African American, 1 American Indian/Alaska Native), 6 international. Average age 28. 23 applicants, 48% accepted, 7 enrolled. In 2009, 3 master's awarded. *Degree requirements:* For master's, thesis (for some programs); for doctorate, comprehensive exam, thesis/dissertation. *Entrance requirements:* For master's and doctorate, GRE or GMAT. Additional exam requirements/recommendations for international students: Required—TOEFL (minimum score 550 paper-based; 79 iBT). *Application deadline:* For fall admission, 3/1 priority date for international students; for spring admission, 8/1 priority date for international students. Applications are processed on a rolling basis. Application fee: $40 ($75 for international students). Electronic applications accepted. *Expenses:* Tuition, state resident: full-time $3716; part-time $154.85 per credit hour. Tuition, nonresident: full-time $14,448; part-time $602 per credit hour. Required fees: $1772; $73.85 per credit hour. One-time fee: $50. Tuition and fees vary according to course load and campus/location. *Financial support:* In 2009–10, 12 research assistantships (averaging $15,748 per year) were awarded; career-related internships or fieldwork, Federal Work-Study, scholarships/grants, health care benefits, tuition waivers (partial), and unspecified assistantships also available. Support available to part-time students. Financial award application deadline: 3/1; financial award applicants required to submit FAFSA. *Faculty research:* Stress and postharvest physiology; water utilization and runoff; IPM systems and nursery, turf, floriculture, vegetable, net and fruit produces and natural resources, food extraction, and processing; public garden management. *Unit head:* Dr. Dale Maronek, Head, 405-744-5414, Fax: 405-744-9709. *Application contact:* Dr. Gordon Emslie, Dean, 405-744-6368, Fax: 405-744-0355, E-mail: grad-i@okstate.edu.

Penn State University Park, Graduate School, College of Arts and Architecture, Department of Landscape Architecture, State College, University Park, PA 16802-1503. Offers MLA, MS. *Accreditation:* ASLA.

Polytechnic University of Puerto Rico, Graduate School, Hato Rey, PR 00919. Offers business administration (MBA), including general studies, management of information systems, management of international enterprises; civil engineering (ME, MS); computer engineering (ME, MS); computer science (MS); electrical engineering (ME, MS); engineering management (MEM); environmental management (MEPM); landscape architecture (M Land Arch); manufacturing competitiveness (MMC, MS); manufacturing engineering (ME, MS). Part-time and evening/weekend programs available. *Entrance requirements:* For master's, 3 letters of recommendation.

Rhode Island School of Design, Graduate Studies, Division of Architecture and Design, Department of Landscape Architecture, Providence, RI 02903-2784. Offers MLA. *Accreditation:* ASLA. *Degree requirements:* For master's, thesis, exhibit. *Entrance requirements:* For master's, portfolio, 3 letters of recommendation. Additional exam requirements/recommendations for international students: Required—TOEFL (minimum score 580 paper-based; 237 computer-based), IELTS (minimum score 6.5).

State University of New York College of Environmental Science and Forestry, Department of Landscape Architecture, Syracuse, NY 13210-2779. Offers community design and planning (MLA, MS); cultural landscape studies and conservation (MLA, MS); landscape and urban ecology (MLA, MS). *Accreditation:* ASLA (one or more programs are accredited). *Degree requirements:* For master's, comprehensive exam (for some programs), thesis (for some programs). *Entrance requirements:* For master's, GRE General Test, minimum GPA of 3.0. Additional exam requirements/recommendations for international students: Required—TOEFL (paper-based 550, computer-based 213, iBT 80) or IELTS (6) or STEP Aiken (Grade 1). *Faculty research:* Site analysis and design, city and regional planning, community environments.

Texas A&M University, College of Architecture, Department of Landscape Architecture and Urban Planning, College Station, TX 77843. Offers land development (MSLD); landscape architecture (MLA); urban and regional science (PhD); urban planning (MUP). *Accreditation:* ACSP (one or more programs are accredited); ASLA (one or more programs are accredited). *Faculty:* 28. *Students:* 159 full-time (60 women), 17 part-time (10 women); includes 15 minority (5 African Americans, 1 American Indian/Alaska Native, 1 Asian American or Pacific Islander, 8 Hispanic Americans), 97 international. Average age 31. In 2009, 50 master's, 9 doctorates awarded. Terminal master's awarded for partial completion of doctoral program. *Degree requirements:* For master's, thesis optional, professional internship; for doctorate, comprehensive exam, thesis/dissertation, methods statistics seminar. *Entrance requirements:* For master's, GMAT or GRE General Test, portfolio (MLA), minimum GPA of 3.0; for doctorate, GMAT or GRE General Test. Additional exam requirements/recommendations for international students: Required—TOEFL. *Application deadline:* For fall admission, 2/1 priority date for domestic students; for spring admission, 8/1 for domestic students. Applications are processed on a rolling basis. Application fee: $50 ($75 for international students). Electronic applications accepted. *Expenses:* Tuition, state resident: full-time $3991; part-time $221.74 per credit hour. Tuition, nonresident: full-time $9049; part-time $502.74 per credit hour. *Financial support:* In 2009–10, fellowships with tuition reimbursements (averaging $1,000 per year), research assistantships with partial tuition reimbursements (averaging $8,100 per year), teaching assistantships with partial tuition reimbursements (averaging $11,250 per year) were awarded; career-related internships or fieldwork, institutionally sponsored loans, and scholarships/grants also available. Financial award application deadline: 4/1; financial award applicants required to submit FAFSA. *Faculty research:* Erosion control/water quality, geographic information systems/spatial information technology, transport hazards, international sustainable development. *Unit head:* Head, 979-845-1019, Fax: 979-862-1784. *Application contact:* Graduate Office, 979-845-6582, Fax: 979-845-4491, E-mail: t-morris@tamu.edu.

Texas Tech University, Graduate School, College of Agricultural Sciences and Natural Resources, Department of Landscape Architecture, Lubbock, TX 79409. Offers MLA. *Accreditation:* ASLA. Part-time programs available. *Faculty:* 4 full-time (0 women). *Students:* 7 full-time (2 women), 5 part-time (2 women), 2 international. Average age 29. 16 applicants, 88% accepted, 1 enrolled. In 2009, 2 master's awarded. *Entrance requirements:* For master's, GRE General Test. Additional exam requirements/recommendations for international students: Required—TOEFL (minimum score 550 paper-based; 213 computer-based). *Application deadline:* For fall admission, 3/1 priority date for international students; for spring admission, 11/1 priority date for international students. Applications are processed on a rolling basis. Application fee: $50 ($75 for international students). Electronic applications accepted. *Expenses:* Tuition, state resident: full-time $5100; part-time $213 per credit hour. Tuition, nonresident: full-time $11,748; part-time $490 per credit hour. Required fees: $2298; $50 per credit hour. $555 per semester. *Financial support:* In 2009–10, 1 teaching assistantship with partial tuition reimbursement (averaging $7,785 per year) was awarded; research assistantships with partial tuition reimbursements, Federal Work-Study and institutionally sponsored loans also available. Support available to part-time students. Financial award application deadline: 4/15; financial award applicants required to submit FAFSA. *Faculty research:* Computer-aided design, environmental planning and design, therapeutic landscapes, geographic information systems in planning, creative problem solving, site planning. *Unit head:* Alon Kvashny, Chair, 806-742-2894, Fax: 806-742-0770, E-mail: alon.kvashny@ttu.edu. *Application contact:* John C. Billing, Graduate Coordinator, 806-742-2858, Fax: 806-742-0770, E-mail: john.billing@ttu.edu.

The University of Arizona, College of Architecture and Landscape Architecture, School of Landscape Architecture, Tucson, AZ 85721. Offers ML Arch. *Accreditation:* ASLA. *Faculty:* 4. *Students:* 37 full-time (21 women), 11 part-time (6 women); includes 3 minority (2 Asian Americans or Pacific Islanders, 1 Hispanic American), 2 international. Average age 34. 59 applicants, 53% accepted, 17 enrolled. In 2009, 13 master's awarded. *Degree requirements:* For master's, thesis. *Entrance requirements:* For master's, minimum GPA of 3.2, 3 letters of reference, statement of intent, portfolio, transcripts. Additional exam requirements/recommendations for international students: Required—TOEFL (minimum score 600 paper-based). *Application deadline:* For fall admission, 1/15 for domestic and international students. Application fee: $75. Electronic applications accepted. *Expenses:* Tuition, state resident: full-time $9028. Tuition, nonresident: full-time $24,890. *Financial support:* In 2009–10, 9 research assistantships with full tuition reimbursements (averaging $10,184 per year) were awarded; teaching assistantships with full tuition reimbursements, career-related internships or fieldwork, scholarships/grants, health care benefits, tuition waivers (full), and unspecified assistantships also available. Financial award application deadline: 1/31. *Faculty research:* Children's environments, cultural landscapes, arid lands plant communities, geographic information systems and science (GS), computer-aided drafting and design (CAD). Total annual research expenditures: $80,123. *Unit head:* Prof. Ronald R. Stoltz, Director, 520-626-7730, Fax: 520-626-6448, E-mail: rstoltz@u.arizona.edu. *Application contact:* Debi A. Romero, Administrative Assistant, 520-621-1004, Fax: 520-626-6448, E-mail: landarch@u.arizona.edu.

The University of British Columbia, Faculty of Applied Science, School of Architecture and Landscape Architecture, Program in Landscape Architecture, Vancouver, BC V6T 1Z1, Canada. Offers MASLA, MLA. *Accreditation:* ASLA (one or more programs are accredited). *Degree requirements:* For master's, comprehensive exam or thesis. *Entrance requirements:* For master's, portfolio. Additional exam requirements/recommendations for international students: Required—TOEFL (minimum score 560 paper-based; 220 computer-based). Electronic applications accepted. *Faculty research:* Landscape design, urban-rural interface, urban ecology, sustainable development, collaborative planning and community forestry.

University of California, Berkeley, Graduate Division, College of Environmental Design, Department of Landscape Architecture and Environmental Planning, Berkeley, CA 94720-1500. Offers landscape architecture (MLA), including environmental planning, landscape design and site planning, urban and community design; landscape architecture and environmental planning (PhD); MLA/M Arch; MLA/MCP. *Accreditation:* ASLA (one or more programs are accredited). *Faculty:* 13 full-time, 6 part-time/adjunct. *Students:* 69 full-time (49 women). Average age 30. 252 applicants, 24 enrolled. In 2009, 31 master's, 1 doctorate awarded. *Degree requirements:* For master's, professional project or thesis; for doctorate, one foreign language, thesis/dissertation, qualifying exam. *Entrance requirements:* For master's, GRE General Test, minimum GPA of 3.0, portfolio; for doctorate, GRE General Test, master's degree (strongly recommended), minimum GPA of 3.0, sample of written work, 3 letters of recommendation. *Application deadline:* For fall admission, 12/15 for domestic students. Application fee: $70 ($90 for international students). *Financial support:* Fellowships, research assistantships, teaching assistantships, career-related internships or fieldwork, Federal Work-Study, institutionally sponsored loans, and unspecified assistantships available. *Unit head:* Prof. Linda Jewell, Chair, 510-642-4022, Fax: 510-643-6166. *Application contact:* Yong No, Student Affairs Officer, 510-642-2965, Fax: 510-643-6166, E-mail: laepgrad@berkeley.edu.

University of California, Berkeley, UC Berkeley Extension, Certificate Programs in Art and Design, Berkeley, CA 94720-1500. Offers interior design and interior architecture (Certificate);

Landscape Architecture

University of California, Berkeley (continued)
landscape architecture (Certificate); visual arts (Postbaccalaureate Certificate). *Unit head:* Diana Wu, Dean, 510-642-4181. *Application contact:* Art and Design, 415-284-1041, E-mail: visualarts@unex.berkeley.edu.

University of Colorado Denver, College of Architecture and Planning, Program in Landscape Architecture, Denver, CO 80217-3364. Offers MLA. *Accreditation:* ASLA. Part-time programs available. *Students:* 88 full-time (52 women), 4 part-time (3 women); includes 3 minority (2 African Americans, 1 Asian American or Pacific Islander), 6 international. 90 applicants, 84% accepted, 26 enrolled. In 2009, 31 master's awarded. *Degree requirements:* For master's, thesis optional. *Entrance requirements:* For master's, GRE or minimum GPA of 3.0, portfolio. Additional exam requirements/recommendations for international students: Required—TOEFL (minimum score 550 paper-based; 213 computer-based). *Application deadline:* For fall admission, 3/15 for domestic students; for spring admission, 10/1 for domestic students. Application fee: $50 ($75 for international students). *Financial support:* Teaching assistantships, career-related internships or fieldwork, Federal Work-Study, institutionally sponsored loans, and scholarships/grants available. Financial award application deadline: 3/1; financial award applicants required to submit FAFSA. *Faculty research:* Landscape architectural design theory and process, urban design, advanced landscape technologies, landscape planning. *Unit head:* Austin Allen, Chair, 303-556-8564, Fax: 303-556-3687, E-mail: austin.allen@ucdenver.edu. *Application contact:* Jenny Richardson, Administrative Assistant II, 303-492-8010, Fax: 303-556-3687, E-mail: jenny.richardson@colorado.edu.

University of Florida, Graduate School, College of Design, Construction and Planning, Department of Landscape Architecture, Gainesville, FL 32611. Offers MLA, PhD. *Accreditation:* ASLA. Part-time programs available. *Degree requirements:* For master's, thesis, internship. *Entrance requirements:* For master's, GRE General Test, minimum GPA of 3.0. Electronic applications accepted. *Faculty research:* Landscape reclamation, community development, landscape ethics, land-use planning, international conservation.

University of Georgia, Graduate School, College of Environment and Design, Program in Landscape Architecture, Athens, GA 30602. Offers MLA. *Accreditation:* ASLA. *Students:* 50 full-time (35 women), 8 part-time (2 women); includes 1 minority (Asian American or Pacific Islander), 9 international. 61 applicants, 38% accepted, 17 enrolled. In 2009, 11 master's awarded. *Degree requirements:* For master's, thesis. *Entrance requirements:* For master's, GRE General Test. Additional exam requirements/recommendations for international students: Required—TOEFL. *Application deadline:* For fall admission, 7/1 for domestic students; for spring admission, 11/15 priority date for domestic students. Application fee: $50. Electronic applications accepted. *Expenses:* Contact institution. *Financial support:* In 2009–10, 20 students received support; fellowships, research assistantships, teaching assistantships, tuition waivers (partial) and unspecified assistantships available. *Unit head:* Dr. Brian LaHaie, Graduate Coordinator, 706-542-4704, Fax: 706-542-4236, E-mail: blahaie@uga.edu. *Application contact:* Dr. Brian LaHaie, Graduate Coordinator, 706-542-4704, E-mail: blahaie@uga.edu.

University of Guelph, Graduate Program Services, Ontario Agricultural College, School of Environmental Design and Rural Development, Landscape Architecture Program, Guelph, ON N1G 2W1, Canada. Offers MLA. *Accreditation:* ASLA. *Degree requirements:* For master's, thesis. *Entrance requirements:* For master's, minimum B- average during previous 2 years of honors degree, portfolio and questionnaire. Additional exam requirements/recommendations for international students: Required—TOEFL (minimum score 600 paper-based; 250 computer-based; 89 iBT), IELTS (minimum score 7), Canadian Academic Language Assessment, Michigan English Language Assessment Battery. Electronic applications accepted. *Faculty research:* Land planning, human factors in design, landscape assessment (biophysical and cultural), landscape ecology and restoration, community design.

University of Idaho, College of Graduate Studies, College of Art and Architecture, Department of Landscape Architecture, Moscow, ID 83844-2282. Offers MS. *Accreditation:* ASLA. *Faculty:* 3 full-time, 1 part-time/adjunct. *Students:* 8 full-time, 2 part-time. In 2009, 1 master's awarded. Application fee: $55 ($60 for international students). *Expenses:* Tuition, state resident: full-time $6120. Tuition, nonresident: full-time $17,712. *Unit head:* Stephen R. Drown, Chair, 208-885-7902, E-mail: larch@uidaho.edu. *Application contact:* Stephen R. Drown, Chair, 208-885-7902, E-mail: larch@uidaho.edu.

University of Illinois at Urbana–Champaign, Graduate College, College of Fine and Applied Arts, Department of Landscape Architecture, Champaign, IL 61820. Offers MLA, PhD, MLA/MUP. *Accreditation:* ASLA. *Faculty:* 12 full-time (6 women). *Students:* 44 full-time (25 women), 1 part-time (0 women); includes 3 minority (1 African American, 2 Hispanic Americans), 20 international. 95 applicants, 37% accepted, 17 enrolled. In 2009, 12 master's, 1 doctorate awarded. *Entrance requirements:* For master's, GRE, minimum GPA of 3.0; portfolio; for doctorate, GRE, minimum GPA of 3.0. Additional exam requirements/recommendations for international students: Required—TOEFL (minimum score 570 paper-based; 230 computer-based; 89 iBT). *Application deadline:* Applications are processed on a rolling basis. Application fee: $60 ($75 for international students). Electronic applications accepted. *Financial support:* In 2009–10, 8 fellowships, 9 research assistantships, 15 teaching assistantships were awarded; tuition waivers (full and partial) also available. *Unit head:* Margaret Elen Deming, Head, 217-333-0176, Fax: 217-244-4568, E-mail: medeming@illinois.edu. *Application contact:* Carol Emmerling-DiNovo, Assistant Head, 214-244-0994, Fax: 214-244-4568, E-mail: cemmer@illinois.edu.

University of Manitoba, Faculty of Graduate Studies, Faculty of Architecture, Department of Landscape Architecture, Winnipeg, MB R3T 2N2, Canada. Offers M Land Arch. *Accreditation:* ASLA. *Degree requirements:* For master's, thesis or alternative.

University of Massachusetts Amherst, Graduate School, College of Social and Behavioral Sciences, Department of Landscape Architecture and Regional Planning, Program in Landscape Architecture, Amherst, MA 01003. Offers MLA, MLA/MRP. *Accreditation:* ASLA. Part-time programs available. *Students:* 29 full-time (16 women), 8 part-time (5 women); includes 1 minority (Hispanic American), 7 international. Average age 32. 73 applicants, 64% accepted, 13 enrolled. In 2009, 8 master's awarded. *Degree requirements:* For master's, thesis or alternative. *Entrance requirements:* For master's, GRE General Test, portfolio. Additional exam requirements/recommendations for international students: Required—TOEFL (minimum score 550 paper-based; 213 computer-based; 80 iBT), IELTS (minimum score 6.5). *Application deadline:* For fall admission, 2/1 for domestic and international students. Applications are processed on a rolling basis. Application fee: $50 ($65 for international students). Electronic applications accepted. *Expenses:* Tuition, state resident: full-time $2640; part-time $110 per credit. Tuition, nonresident: full-time $9936; part-time $414 per credit. Tuition and fees vary according to course load. *Financial support:* Fellowships, research assistantships, teaching assistantships, career-related internships or fieldwork, Federal Work-Study, scholarships/grants, traineeships, health care benefits, tuition waivers (full), and unspecified assistantships available. Support available to part-time students. Financial award application deadline: 2/1. *Unit head:* Dr. Mark S. Lindhult, Graduate Program Director, 413-545-2266, Fax: 413-545-1772. *Application contact:* Jean M. Ames, Supervisor of Admissions, 413-545-0722, Fax: 413-577-0010, E-mail: gradadm@grad.umass.edu.

University of Massachusetts Amherst, Graduate School, College of Social and Behavioral Sciences, Department of Landscape Architecture and Regional Planning, Program in Landscape Architecture and Regional Planning, Amherst, MA 01003. Offers MLA/MRP. *Accreditation:* ACSP; ASLA. Part-time programs available. *Students:* 8 full-time (6 women), 2 international. Average age 30. 10 applicants, 80% accepted, 3 enrolled. *Entrance requirements:* Additional exam requirements/recommendations for international students: Required—TOEFL (minimum score 550 paper-based; 213 computer-based; 80 iBT), IELTS (minimum score 6.5). *Application deadline:* For fall admission, 2/1 for domestic and international students. Applications are processed on a rolling basis. Application fee: $50 ($65 for international students). Electronic applications accepted. *Expenses:* Tuition, state resident: full-time $2640; part-time $110 per credit. Tuition, nonresident: full-time $9936; part-time $414 per credit. Tuition and fees vary according to course load. *Financial support:* Fellowships, research assistantships, teaching assistantships, career-related internships or fieldwork, Federal Work-Study, scholarships/grants, traineeships, health care benefits, tuition waivers (full), and unspecified assistantships available. Support available to part-time students. Financial award application deadline: 2/1. *Unit head:* Dr. Robert L. Ryan, Graduate Program Director, 413-545-2266, Fax: 413-545-1772. *Application contact:* Jean M. Ames, Supervisor of Admissions, 413-545-0721, Fax: 413-577-0010, E-mail: gradadm@grad.umass.edu.

University of Michigan, School of Natural Resources and Environment, Program in Landscape Architecture, Ann Arbor, MI 48109. Offers MLA, PhD, MLA/M Arch, MLA/MBA, MLA/MUP. Offered through the Horace H. Rackham School of Graduate Studies. *Accreditation:* ASLA (one or more programs are accredited). *Faculty:* 5 full-time (3 women), 1 part-time/adjunct (0 women). *Students:* 40 full-time (29 women); includes 8 minority (all Asian Americans or Pacific Islanders), 5 international. Average age 27. 65 applicants. In 2009, 5 master's, 2 doctorates awarded. *Degree requirements:* For master's, thesis, practicum or group project; for doctorate, comprehensive exam, thesis/dissertation, oral defense of dissertation, preliminary exam. *Entrance requirements:* For master's, GRE General Test; for doctorate, GRE General Test, master's degree, portfolio. Additional exam requirements/recommendations for international students: Required—TOEFL (minimum score 560 paper-based; 220 computer-based; 84 iBT) or IELTS (minimum score 6.5). *Application deadline:* For fall admission, 1/5 priority date for domestic and international students. Applications are processed on a rolling basis. Application fee: $60 ($75 for international students). *Expenses:* Tuition, state resident: full-time $17,286; part-time $1099 per credit hour. Tuition, nonresident: full-time $34,944; part-time $2080 per credit hour. Required fees: $95 per semester. Tuition and fees vary according to course load, degree level and program. *Financial support:* Fellowships with tuition reimbursements, research assistantships with tuition reimbursements, teaching assistantships with tuition reimbursements, career-related internships or fieldwork, Federal Work-Study, institutionally sponsored loans, scholarships/grants, health care benefits, and unspecified assistantships available. Support available to part-time students. Financial award application deadline: 1/5; financial award applicants required to submit FAFSA. *Faculty research:* Historic landscape documentation, landscape architecture, landscape perception, sustainable design, ecological design. Total annual research expenditures: $139,000. *Unit head:* Chris Ellis, Professor, 734-764-6453, Fax: 734-734-2195, E-mail: cdellis@umich.edu. *Application contact:* Adam Ancira, Recruiting and Admissions Coordinator, 734-764-6453, Fax: 734-936-2195, E-mail: snre.admissions@umich.edu.

University of Minnesota, Twin Cities Campus, Graduate School, College of Design, Department of Landscape Architecture, Minneapolis, MN 55455-0213. Offers MLA, MS. *Accreditation:* ASLA (one or more programs are accredited). *Degree requirements:* For master's, thesis (MS). *Entrance requirements:* For master's, GRE General Test (MS), suggested GPA of 3.0. Additional exam requirements/recommendations for international students: Required—TOEFL (minimum score 550 paper-based; 213 computer-based; 79 iBT). Electronic applications accepted. *Expenses:* Contact institution. *Faculty research:* Landscape history, landscape ecology, urban design, sustainable design, public art/space.

University of New Mexico, Graduate School, School of Architecture and Planning, Program in Landscape Architecture, Albuquerque, NM 87131-2039. Offers MLA. *Accreditation:* ASLA. Part-time programs available. *Faculty:* 3 full-time (2 women), 6 part-time/adjunct (3 women). *Students:* 50 full-time (26 women), 8 part-time (6 women); includes 4 minority (all Hispanic Americans), 8 international. Average age 33. 48 applicants, 60% accepted, 18 enrolled. In 2009, 20 master's awarded. *Degree requirements:* For master's, comprehensive exam, thesis optional, portfolio review, thesis studio. *Entrance requirements:* For master's, minimum GPA of 3.0. Additional exam requirements/recommendations for international students: Required—TOEFL. *Application deadline:* For fall admission, 2/15 priority date for domestic students; for spring admission, 11/1 for domestic students. Applications are processed on a rolling basis. Application fee: $50. Electronic applications accepted. *Expenses:* Contact institution. *Financial support:* In 2009–10, 25 students received support, including 10 fellowships (averaging $1,000 per year), 10 research assistantships with partial tuition reimbursements available (averaging $3,000 per year); scholarships/grants, health care benefits, tuition waivers (partial), and unspecified assistantships also available. Financial award application deadline: 3/1; financial award applicants required to submit FAFSA. *Faculty research:* Cultural landscape studies, urban design and sustainability, landscape and infrastructure. *Unit head:* Dr. Alfred Simon, Director, 505-277-4120, Fax: 505-277-0897, E-mail: asimon@unm.edu. *Application contact:* Beth Rowe, Senior Academic Advisor, 505-277-1303, Fax: 505-277-0076, E-mail: erowe@unm.edu.

University of Oklahoma, Graduate College, College of Architecture, Division of Landscape Architecture, Norman, OK 73019-0390. Offers MLA, MRCP/MLA. *Accreditation:* ASLA. Part-time programs available. *Faculty:* 1 full-time (0 women). *Students:* 11 full-time (4 women), 3 part-time (1 woman); includes 2 minority (1 Asian American or Pacific Islander, 1 Hispanic American), 2 international. 20 applicants, 100% accepted, 6 enrolled. In 2009, 5 master's awarded. *Degree requirements:* For master's, comprehensive exam, portfolio, project. *Entrance requirements:* For master's, GRE General Test, portfolio. Additional exam requirements/recommendations for international students: Required—TOEFL (minimum score 550 paper-based; 213 computer-based). *Application deadline:* For fall admission, 4/1 for domestic and international students; for spring admission, 11/1 for domestic students, 9/1 for international students. Applications are processed on a rolling basis. Application fee: $40 ($90 for international students). Electronic applications accepted. *Expenses:* Tuition, state resident: full-time $3744; part-time $156 per credit hour. Tuition, nonresident: full-time $13,577; part-time $565.70 per credit hour. Required fees: $2415; $90.10 per credit hour. *Financial support:* In 2009–10, 5 students received support, including 5 research assistantships with partial tuition reimbursements available (averaging $9,586 per year); career-related internships or fieldwork, Federal Work-Study, institutionally sponsored loans, scholarships/grants, and unspecified assistantships also available. Financial award applicants required to submit FAFSA. *Faculty research:* Sustainable urban design, greenways, community-based design and planning, site design and site planning, meaning in built environments. *Unit head:* Marjorie Callahan, Associate Dean, 405-325-3865, Fax: 405-325-7558, E-mail: mcallahan@ou.edu. *Application contact:* Marjorie Callahan, Associate Dean, 405-325-3865, Fax: 405-325-7558, E-mail: mcallahan@ou.edu.

University of Oregon, Graduate School, School of Architecture and Allied Arts, Department of Landscape Architecture, Eugene, OR 97403. Offers MLA. *Accreditation:* ASLA. *Degree requirements:* For master's, thesis or alternative, project. *Entrance requirements:* For master's, portfolio. Additional exam requirements/recommendations for international students: Required—TOEFL. *Faculty research:* Design, landscape planning analysis, history and theory, computer applications.

University of Pennsylvania, School of Design, Program in Landscape Architecture and Regional Planning, Philadelphia, PA 19104. Offers landscape architecture and regional planning (MLA); landscape studies (Certificate). *Accreditation:* ASLA (one or more programs are accredited). Part-time programs available. *Faculty:* 4 full-time (2 women), 6 part-time/adjunct (2 women). *Students:* 106 full-time (70 women), 2 part-time (both women); includes 9 minority (2 African Americans, 1 American Indian/Alaska Native, 5 Asian Americans or Pacific Islanders, 1 Hispanic American), 33 international. 244 applicants, 50% accepted, 50 enrolled. In 2009, 33 master's, 3 Certificates awarded. *Degree requirements:* For master's, thesis optional. *Entrance requirements:* For master's, GRE, portfolio. Additional exam requirements/recommendations for international students: Required—TOEFL. *Application deadline:* For fall admission, 1/2 priority date for domestic students. Application fee: $70. *Expenses:* Tuition: Full-time $25,660; part-time $4758 per course. Required fees: $2152; $270 per course. Tuition and fees vary according to course load, degree level and program. *Financial support:* Fellowships, research assistantships, teaching assistantships, career-related internships or fieldwork, Federal Work-Study, and institutionally sponsored loans available. Financial award applicants required to submit FAFSA. *Faculty research:* Early landscape architecture, natural distribution through landslides, urban gardens, landscape registration, watershed studies.

See Close-Up on page 147.

The University of Tennessee, Graduate School, College of Architecture and Design, Program in Landscape Architecture, Knoxville, TN 37996. Offers landscape architecture (MLA); landscape architecture (research) (MA, MS). *Degree requirements:* For master's, oral exam, project and thesis optional (MLA), oral exam and thesis (MA, MS). *Entrance requirements:* For master's, GRE General Test, minimum GPA of 3.0, 3 letters of recommendation, samples of portfolio work. Additional exam requirements/recommendations for international students: Required—TOEFL (minimum score 550 paper-based). *Expenses:* Tuition, state resident: full-time $6826; part-time $380 per semester hour. Tuition, nonresident: full-time $21,844; part-time $1147 per semester hour. Tuition and fees vary according to program.

The University of Texas at Arlington, Graduate School, School of Architecture, Program in Landscape Architecture, Arlington, TX 76019. Offers MLA. *Accreditation:* ASLA. Part-time and evening/weekend programs available. *Students:* 26 full-time (18 women), 12 part-time (9 women); includes 5 minority (2 African Americans, 3 Hispanic Americans), 11 international. 20 applicants, 95% accepted, 10 enrolled. In 2009, 7 master's awarded. *Degree requirements:* For master's, thesis. *Entrance requirements:* For master's, GRE General Test, minimum GPA of 3.0, portfolio. Additional exam requirements/recommendations for international students: Required—TOEFL (minimum score 550 paper-based; 213 computer-based). *Application deadline:* For fall admission, 6/16 for domestic students. Applications are processed on a rolling basis. Application fee: $35 ($50 for international students). *Financial support:* In 2009–10, 1 research assistantship with partial tuition reimbursement (averaging $4,824 per year), 2 teaching assistantships with partial tuition reimbursements (averaging $4,824 per year) were awarded; fellowships, career-related internships or fieldwork and tuition waivers (partial) also available. Financial award application deadline: 6/1; financial award applicants required to submit FAFSA. *Unit head:* Dr. Pat D. Taylor, Program Director, 817-272-2801, Fax: 817-272-5098, E-mail: pdt@uta.edu. *Application contact:* David Jones, Associate Dean, 817-272-2801, Fax: 817-272-5098, E-mail: djonesarch@uta.edu.

The University of Texas at Austin, Graduate School, School of Architecture, Austin, TX 78712-1111. Offers architecture (M Arch); community and regional planning (MSCRP, PhD); historic preservation (MS); history of architecture (MA, PhD); landscape architecture (MLA); urban design (MSUD); JD/MSCRP; MSCRP/MA; MSCRP/PhD. *Degree requirements:* For doctorate, thesis/dissertation. *Entrance requirements:* For master's and doctorate, GRE General Test. Additional exam requirements/recommendations for international students: Required—TOEFL (minimum score 550 paper-based; 213 computer-based). Electronic applications accepted.

University of Virginia, School of Architecture, Department of Architecture and Landscape Architecture, Program in Landscape Architecture, Charlottesville, VA 22903. Offers M Land Arch. *Accreditation:* ASLA. *Faculty:* 8 full-time (5 women). *Students:* 44 full-time (34 women); includes 2 minority (1 African American, 1 Asian American or Pacific Islander), 5 international. Average age 28. 145 applicants, 17% accepted, 4 enrolled. In 2009, 16 master's awarded. *Entrance requirements:* For master's, GRE General Test, 3 letters of recommendation; portfolio. Additional exam requirements/recommendations for international students: Required—TOEFL (minimum score 600 paper-based; 250 computer-based; 90 iBT). *Application deadline:* For fall admission, 1/16 for domestic and international students. Applications are processed on a rolling basis. Application fee: $60. Electronic applications accepted. *Financial support:* Applicants required to submit FAFSA. *Faculty research:* History of landscape architecture. *Unit head:* Kristina Hill, Director, 434-924-1044, Fax: 434-982-2678, E-mail: kzhill@virginia.edu. *Application contact:* Graduate Admissions Officer, 434-924-6442, Fax: 434-982-2678, E-mail: arch-admissions@virginia.edu.

University of Washington, Graduate School, College of Built Environments, Department of Landscape Architecture, Seattle, WA 98195. Offers MLA. *Accreditation:* ASLA. *Degree requirements:* For master's, thesis. *Entrance requirements:* For master's, GRE, minimum GPA of 3.0. Additional exam requirements/recommendations for international students: Required—TOEFL. *Faculty research:* Cultural landscape, history of gardens, urban stream restoration, campus master planning, urban ecology.

University of Wisconsin–Madison, Graduate School, College of Agricultural and Life Sciences, Department of Landscape Architecture, Madison, WI 53076. Offers MA, MS. *Accreditation:* ASLA. Part-time programs available. *Degree requirements:* For master's, thesis. *Entrance requirements:* For master's, GRE (recommended), samples of creative work. Additional exam requirements/recommendations for international students: Required—TOEFL (minimum score 580 paper-based; 237 computer-based). Electronic applications accepted. *Expenses:* Tuition, state resident: part-time $594 per credit. Tuition, nonresident: part-time $1504 per credit. Required fees: $65 per credit. Tuition and fees vary according to course load, program and reciprocity agreements. *Faculty research:* Urban/landscape ecology, land restoration, cultural resource preservation, community design, conservation design.

Utah State University, School of Graduate Studies, College of Humanities, Arts and Social Sciences, Department of Landscape Architecture and Environmental Planning, Logan, UT 84322: Offers bioregional planning (MS); landscape architecture (MLA). *Accreditation:* ASLA (one or more programs are accredited). *Degree requirements:* For master's, thesis. *Entrance requirements:* For master's, GRE General Test, minimum GPA of 3.0. Additional exam requirements/recommendations for international students: Required—TOEFL. *Faculty research:* Visual resource management, planning for wildlife, agricultural land preservation, watershed planning, community planning and design.

Virginia Polytechnic Institute and State University, Graduate School, College of Architecture and Urban Studies, Department of Landscape Architecture, Blacksburg, VA 24061. Offers MLA, PhD. *Accreditation:* ASLA. *Students:* 38 full-time (23 women), 7 part-time (4 women); includes 12 minority (7 American Indian/Alaska Native, 2 Asian Americans or Pacific Islanders, 3 Hispanic Americans), 4 international. Average age 29. 33 applicants, 45% accepted, 12 enrolled. In 2009, 10 master's awarded. *Entrance requirements:* For master's and doctorate, GRE, GMAT. Additional exam requirements/recommendations for international students: Required—TOEFL (minimum score 550 paper-based; 213 computer-based). *Application deadline:* For fall admission, 5/15 for international students; for spring admission, 10/15 for international students. Applications are processed on a rolling basis. Application fee: $65. Electronic applications accepted. *Expenses:* Tuition, area resident: Full-time $10,228; part-time $459 per credit hour. Tuition, nonresident: full-time $17,892; part-time $865 per credit hour. Required fees: $1966; $451 per semester. *Financial support:* Career-related internships or fieldwork, Federal Work-Study, scholarships/grants, and unspecified assistantships available. Financial award application deadline: 1/15. *Faculty research:* Land planning issues in rural areas, landscape perception and visual management theory, universal design, accessibility, ecological and cultural processes. *Unit head:* Dr. Brian F. Katen, Dean, 540-231-7505, Fax: 540-231-3367, E-mail: bkaten@vt.edu. *Application contact:* Mintai Kim, Information Contact, 540-231-9872, Fax: 540-231-3367, E-mail: mintkim@vt.edu.

Virginia Polytechnic Institute and State University, Graduate School, College of Architecture and Urban Studies, School of Public and International Affairs, Blacksburg, VA 24061. Offers environmental planning and policy (MURP); government and international affairs (MPIA); housing, community and economic development (MURP); international development planning (MURP); land use and physical planning (MURP); planning, governance and globalization (PhD), including environmental planning and landscape analysis, physical planning and urban design, public and international affairs, urban and environmental design and planning; urban and regional planning (MURP). *Accreditation:* ACSP. *Faculty:* 27 full-time (11 women), 2 part-time/adjunct (1 woman). *Students:* 73 full-time (51 women), 65 part-time (39 women); includes 15 minority (4 African Americans, 1 American Indian/Alaska Native, 6 Asian Americans or Pacific Islanders, 4 Hispanic Americans), 10 international. Average age 29. 86 applicants, 67% accepted, 40 enrolled. In 2009, 26 master's, 1 doctorate awarded. *Entrance requirements:* Additional exam requirements/recommendations for international students: Required—TOEFL (minimum score 550 paper-based; 213 computer-based). *Application deadline:* For fall admission, 5/15 for international students; for spring admission, 10/15 for international students. Applications are processed on a rolling basis. Application fee: $45. Electronic applications accepted. *Financial support:* In 2009–10, 1 teaching assistantship with full tuition reimbursement (averaging $5,560 per year) was awarded; career-related internships or fieldwork, Federal Work-Study, scholarships/grants, and unspecified assistantships also available. Financial award application deadline: 4/1. *Faculty research:* Design theory, environmental planning, town planning, transportation planning. *Unit head:* Dr. John Randolph, Dean, 540-231-6971, Fax: 540-231-9938, E-mail: energy@vt.edu. *Application contact:* Krystal D. Wright, Information Contact, 540-231-*5683, Fax: 540-231-9938, E-mail: garch@vt.edu.

Washington State University, Graduate School, College of Agricultural, Human, and Natural Resource Sciences, Department of Horticulture and Landscape Architecture, Pullman, WA 99164. Offers horticulture (MS, PhD); landscape architecture (MSLA). *Accreditation:* ASLA. Part-time programs available. *Degree requirements:* For master's, comprehensive exam (for some programs), thesis (for some programs), oral exam; for doctorate, comprehensive exam, thesis/dissertation, oral exam, written exam. *Entrance requirements:* For master's and doctorate, GRE General Test, GRE Subject Test, minimum GPA of 3.0, 3 letters of recommendation. Additional exam requirements/recommendations for international students: Required—TOEFL (minimum score 550 paper-based). Electronic applications accepted. *Faculty research:* Post-harvest physiology, genetics/plant breeding, molecular biology.

Washington State University Spokane, Graduate Programs, Interdisciplinary Design Institute, Spokane, WA 99210. Offers architecture (M Arch, MS); design (Dr DES); interior design (MA); landscape architecture (MS). Part-time programs available. *Faculty:* 7. *Students:* 9 full-time (6 women), 2 part-time (both women); includes 1 minority (Asian American or Pacific Islander), 5 international. Average age 35. In 2009, 18 master's awarded. *Degree requirements:* For master's, comprehensive exam (for some programs), thesis (for some programs); for doctorate, comprehensive exam, thesis/dissertation. *Entrance requirements:* For master's, minimum GPA of 3.0, portfolio of design work, 3 letters of recommendation (M Arch); for doctorate, minimum graduate GPA of 3.5. Additional exam requirements/recommendations for international students: Required—TOEFL (minimum score 550 paper-based; 213 computer-based). *Application deadline:* For fall admission, 1/10 priority date for domestic students, 1/10 for international students; for spring admission, 7/1 priority date for domestic students, 7/1 for international students. Application fee: $50. *Expenses:* Tuition, state resident: part-time $423 per credit. Tuition, nonresident: part-time $1032 per credit. *Financial support:* In 2009–10, research assistantships with full and partial tuition reimbursements (averaging $14,634 per year), teaching assistantships with full and partial tuition reimbursements (averaging $13,383 per year) were awarded. Financial award application deadline: 2/15. *Faculty research:* Environment-behavior relationships, land use and environmental planning, urban space as interior design, art and architectural aesthetics. Total annual research expenditures: $84,000. *Unit head:* Dr. Nancy H. Blossom, Director, 509-358-7513, E-mail: blossom@wsu.edu. *Application contact:* Graduate School Admissions, 800-GRADWSU, Fax: 509-335-1949, E-mail: gradsch@wsu.edu.

Lighting Design

The New School: A University, Parsons The New School for Design, Program in Lighting Design, New York, NY 10011. Offers MFA. *Accreditation:* NASAD. *Faculty:* 3 full-time (0 women). *Students:* 44 full-time (27 women), 1 (woman) part-time; includes 9 minority (1 African American, 5 Asian Americans or Pacific Islanders, 3 Hispanic Americans), 18 international. Average age 28. 74 applicants, 54% accepted, 22 enrolled. In 2009, 17 master's awarded. *Degree requirements:* For master's, thesis. *Entrance requirements:* For master's, portfolio. Additional exam requirements/recommendations for international students: Required—TOEFL (minimum score 580 paper-based; 237 computer-based; 92 iBT). *Application deadline:* For fall admission, 2/1 for domestic and international students. Application fee: $50. Electronic applications accepted. *Financial support:* Federal Work-Study, scholarships/grants, and tuition waivers (partial) available. Support available to part-time students. Financial award application deadline: 3/1; financial award applicants required to submit FAFSA. *Unit head:* Derek Porter, Chair, 212-229-8955 Ext. 2924, E-mail: porterd@newschool.edu. *Application contact:* David Norris, Director of Admissions, 212-229-8989 Ext. 4023, Fax: 212-229-8975, E-mail: norrisd@newschool.edu.

Rensselaer Polytechnic Institute, Graduate School, School of Architecture, MS Program in Architectural Sciences, Troy, NY 12180-3590. Offers acoustics (MS); built ecologies (MS); lighting (MS). *Faculty:* 15 full-time (4 women), 8 part-time/adjunct (1 woman). *Students:* 20 full-time (2 women), 1 part-time (0 women); includes 1 Asian American or Pacific Islander, 1 Hispanic American, 4 international. Average age 21. 46 applicants, 54% accepted, 11 enrolled. In 2009, 22 master's awarded. *Degree requirements:* For master's, thesis. *Entrance requirements:* For master's, GRE General Test. Additional exam requirements/recommendations for international students: Required—TOEFL (minimum score 570 paper-based; 230 computer-based; 89 iBT), IELTS (minimum score 6.5). *Application deadline:* For fall admission, 1/1 priority date for domestic and international students. Applications are processed on a rolling basis. Application fee: $75. Electronic applications accepted. *Expenses:* Tuition: Full-time $38,100. *Financial support:* In 2009–10, 5 students received support, including 4 research assistantships with tuition reimbursements available (averaging $16,500 per year), 1 teaching assistantship with tuition reimbursement available (averaging $16,500 per year); institutionally sponsored loans and unspecified assistantships also available. Financial award application deadline: 1/1. *Faculty research:* Acoustics: modeling, auralization, signal processing; built ecologies: emerging materials and technologies, sustainable built environments; lighting: energy-efficient lighting, product development, daylighting, transportation, lighting, light and health, solid state lighting. *Unit head:* Prof. Ted Krueger, Head, Graduate Programs, 518-276-6466, E-mail: krueger@rpi.edu. *Application contact:* Erin Bermingham, Senior Program Administrator, 518-276-3986, Fax: 518-276-3034, E-mail: bermie@rpi.edu.

Rensselaer Polytechnic Institute, Graduate School, School of Architecture, MS Program in Lighting, Troy, NY 12180-3590. Offers MS. Part-time programs available. *Faculty:* 5 full-time (2 women), 5 part-time/adjunct (3 women). *Students:* 8 full-time (6 women), 1 part-time (0 women). Average age 26. 16 applicants, 63% accepted, 4 enrolled. In 2009, 6 master's awarded. Terminal master's awarded for partial completion of doctoral program. *Degree requirements:* For master's, comprehensive exam (for some programs), thesis. *Entrance*

Lighting Design

Rensselaer Polytechnic Institute (continued)

requirements: For master's, GRE General Test, letters of recommendation, resume, portfolio or sample of research writing. Additional exam requirements/recommendations for international students: Required—TOEFL (minimum score 570 paper-based; 230 computer-based; 89 iBT), IELTS (minimum score 6.5). *Application deadline:* For fall admission, 1/1 priority date for domestic and international students. Applications are processed on a rolling basis. Application fee: $75. Electronic applications accepted. *Expenses:* Tuition: Full-time $38,100. *Financial support:* In 2009–10, 5 students received support, including 5 research assistantships with full tuition reimbursements available (averaging $16,500 per year); fellowships, teaching assistantships, career-related internships or fieldwork, institutionally sponsored loans, scholarships/grants, and unspecified assistantships also available. Financial award application deadline: 1/1. *Faculty research:* Energy-efficient lighting, lighting product development, lighting design demonstration, daylighting, transportation lighting. Total annual research expenditures: $3.7 million. *Unit head:* Prof. Ted Krueger, Head, Graduate Programs, 518-276-6466. *Application contact:* Erin Bermingham, Senior Program Administrator, Graduate Programs, 518-276-3986, Fax: 518-276-3034, E-mail: bermie@rpi.edu.

University of Washington, Graduate School, College of Built Environments, Department of Architecture, Seattle, WA 98195. Offers architecture (M Arch, MS); built environment (PhD); design computing (Certificate); design firm leadership and management (Certificate); historic preservation (Certificate); lighting (Certificate); urban design (Certificate). *Degree requirements:* For master's, thesis. *Entrance requirements:* For master's, GRE General Test, minimum GPA of 3.0, portfolio, 3 letters of recommendation. Additional exam requirements/recommendations for international students: Required—TOEFL. *Faculty research:* Lighting, materials, computing theory, media, culture, environment.

Urban Design

American University of Beirut, Graduate Programs, Faculty of Engineering and Architecture, Beirut, Lebanon. Offers civil engineering (ME, PhD); electrical and computer engineering (ME, PhD); engineering management (MEM); environmental and water resources (ME); environmental and water resources engineering (PhD); environmental technology (MSES); mechanical engineering (ME, PhD); urban design (MUD); urban planning and policy (MUP). Part-time programs available. *Degree requirements:* For master's, one foreign language, comprehensive exam, thesis (for some programs); for doctorate, one foreign language, comprehensive exam, thesis/dissertation, publications. *Entrance requirements:* For master's, letters of recommendation; for doctorate, letters of recommendation, master's degree, transcripts, curriculum vitae, interview. Additional exam requirements/recommendations for international students: Required—TOEFL (minimum score 600 paper-based; 250 computer-based; 100 iBT), IELTS (minimum score 7.5). Electronic applications accepted.

Arizona State University, Graduate College, College of Design, School of Architecture and Landscape Architecture, Tempe, AZ 85287. Offers architecture (M Arch); building design (MS); landscape architecture (MLA); urban design (MUD); MA/MBA. *Degree requirements:* For master's, thesis optional. *Entrance requirements:* For master's, GRE General Test, design portfolio.

Ball State University, Graduate School, College of Architecture and Planning, Department of Architecture, Program in Urban Design, Muncie, IN 47306-1099. Offers MUD.

Carnegie Mellon University, College of Fine Arts, School of Architecture, Pittsburgh, PA 15213-3891. Offers architectural engineering construction management (M Sc); architecture (MSA); architecture, engineering, and construction management (PhD); building performance and diagnostics (M Sc, PhD); computational design (M Sc, PhD); sustainable design (M Sc); urban design (M Sc). Terminal master's awarded for partial completion of doctoral program. *Degree requirements:* For doctorate, thesis/dissertation. *Entrance requirements:* For master's and doctorate, GRE General Test. Additional exam requirements/recommendations for international students: Required—TOEFL.

The Catholic University of America, School of Architecture and Planning, Washington, DC 20064. Offers cultural studies/sacred space (M Arch); design technologies (M Arch); digital media (M Arch); urban design (M Arch). Part-time programs available. *Faculty:* 20 full-time (7 women), 34 part-time/adjunct (4 women). *Students:* 110 full-time (46 women), 37 part-time (16 women); includes 40 minority (12 African Americans, 11 Asian Americans or Pacific Islanders, 17 Hispanic Americans), 9 international. Average age 27. 154 applicants, 80% accepted, 55 enrolled. In 2009, 39 master's awarded. *Degree requirements:* For master's, thesis. *Entrance requirements:* For master's, GRE (minimum score: 1000), minimum GPA of 2.8, portfolio, statement of purpose, official copies of academic transcripts, three letters of recommendation. Additional exam requirements/recommendations for international students: Required—TOEFL (minimum score 580 paper-based; 237 computer-based). *Application deadline:* For fall admission, 1/15 priority date for domestic students, 1/15 for international students; for spring admission, 10/15 priority date for domestic students, 10/15 for international students. Applications are processed on a rolling basis. Application fee: $55. Electronic applications accepted. *Expenses:* Contact institution. *Financial support:* Fellowships, research assistantships, teaching assistantships, Federal Work-Study, scholarships/grants, tuition waivers (full and partial), and unspecified assistantships available. Financial award application deadline: 2/1; financial award applicants required to submit FAFSA. *Faculty research:* Architectural history, cultural studies/scared space, design technologies, digital media, real estate development, urban design. *Unit head:* Randall Ott, Dean, 202-319-5784, Fax: 202-319-2023, E-mail: ott@cua.edu. *Application contact:* Julie Schwing, Director of Graduate Admissions, 202-319-5057, Fax: 202-319-6533, E-mail: cua-admissions@cua.edu.

City College of the City University of New York, Graduate School, School of Architecture and Environmental Studies, Program in Urban Design, New York, NY 10031-9198. Offers MUP. Part-time programs available. *Degree requirements:* For master's, thesis. *Entrance requirements:* For master's, portfolio, professional degree in architecture or equivalent. Additional exam requirements/recommendations for international students: Required—TOEFL (minimum score 550 paper-based; 213 computer-based). *Faculty research:* Real estate, planning, law.

Cleveland State University, College of Graduate Studies, Maxine Goodman Levin College of Urban Affairs, Program in Urban Planning, Design, and Development, Cleveland, OH 44115. Offers geographic information systems (Certificate); local and urban management (Certificate); urban economic development (Certificate); urban planning, design, and development (MUPDD); urban real estate development and finance (Certificate); JD/MUPDD. *Accreditation:* ACSP. Part-time and evening/weekend programs available. *Degree requirements:* For master's, project or thesis. *Entrance requirements:* For master's, GRE General Test (minimum 50th percentile verbal and quantitative, 4.0 analytical writing), minimum GPA of 3.0. Additional exam requirements/recommendations for international students: Required—TOEFL (minimum score 525 paper-based; 197 computer-based; 65 iBT). Electronic applications accepted. *Faculty research:* Housing and neighborhood development, urban housing policy, environmental sustainability, economic development.

Cornell University, Graduate School, Graduate Fields of Architecture, Art and Planning, Field of Architecture, Ithaca, NY 14853-0001. Offers architectural design (M Arch); architectural science (MS); building technology and environmental science (MS); computer graphics (MS); history of architecture (MA, PhD); history of urban development (MA, PhD); theory and criticism of architecture (M Arch); urban design (M Arch). *Faculty:* 38 full-time (12 women). *Students:* 100 full-time (45 women); includes 14 minority (2 African Americans, 6 Asian Americans or Pacific Islanders, 6 Hispanic Americans), 38 international. Average age 28. 558 applicants, 18% accepted, 44 enrolled. In 2009, 42 master's, 3 doctorates awarded. *Degree requirements:* For master's, one foreign language, thesis (MA, MS); for doctorate, 2 foreign languages, comprehensive exam, thesis/dissertation. *Entrance requirements:* For master's, GRE General Test, 5 year bachelor's degree in architecture, portfolio (M Arch), 3 letters of recommendation; for doctorate, GRE General Test, 3 letters of recommendation. Additional exam requirements/recommendations for international students: Required—TOEFL (minimum score 600 paper-based; 250 computer-based; 77 iBT). *Application deadline:* For fall admission, 1/15 priority date for domestic students. Application fee: $70. Electronic applications accepted. *Expenses:* Tuition: Full-time $29,500. Required fees: $70. Full-time tuition and fees vary according to degree level, program and student level. *Financial support:* In 2009–10, 16 students received support, including 2 fellowships with full tuition reimbursements available, 1 research assistantship with full tuition reimbursement available, 10 teaching assistantships with full tuition reimbursements available; institutionally sponsored loans, scholarships/grants, health care benefits, tuition waivers (full and partial), and unspecified assistantships also available. Financial award applicants required to submit FAFSA. *Faculty research:* Architectural design and urban design, theory and criticism of architecture, computer graphics, building technology and environmental science, history of architecture and history of urban-development. *Unit head:* Director of Graduate Studies, 607-255-6701, Fax: 607-255-0291. *Application contact:* Graduate Field Assistant, 607-255-6701, Fax: 607-255-0291, E-mail: cuarch@cornell.edu.

Georgia Institute of Technology, Graduate Studies and Research, College of Architecture, City and Regional Planning Program, Atlanta, GA 30332-0001. Offers city and regional planning (PhD); economic development (MCRP); environmental planning and management (MCRP); geographic information systems (MCRP); land and community development (MCRP); land use planning (MCRP); transportation (MCRP); urban design (MCRP); MCP/MSCE. *Accreditation:* ACSP. *Degree requirements:* For master's, thesis, internship. *Entrance requirements:* For master's, GRE General Test, minimum GPA of 2.7. Additional exam requirements/recommendations for international students: Required—TOEFL. Electronic applications accepted.

Harvard University, Graduate School of Design, Department of Urban Planning and Design, Cambridge, MA 02138. Offers urban planning (MUP); urban planning and design (MAUD, MLAUD). *Accreditation:* ACSP (one or more programs are accredited). *Faculty:* 5 full-time (2 women), 31 part-time/adjunct (6 women). *Students:* 110 full-time (45 women); includes 19 minority (3 African Americans, 1 American Indian/Alaska Native, 11 Asian Americans or Pacific Islanders, 4 Hispanic Americans), 42 international. Average age 29. In 2009, 59 master's awarded. *Entrance requirements:* For master's, GRE General Test. Additional exam requirements/recommendations for international students: Required—TOEFL (minimum score 600 paper-based; 250 computer-based; 104 iBT). *Application deadline:* For fall admission, 1/14 for domestic and international students. Application fee: $85. Electronic applications accepted. *Expenses:* Tuition: Full-time $33,696. Required fees: $1126. Full-time tuition and fees vary according to program. *Financial support:* Federal Work-Study and scholarships/grants available. Financial award application deadline: 2/4; financial award applicants required to submit FAFSA. *Unit head:* Rahul Mehrotra, Chair, 617-495-2521. *Application contact:* Gail Gustafson, Director of Admissions, 617-495-5453, Fax: 617-495-8949, E-mail: ggustafson@gsd.harvard.edu.

Kent State University, College of Architecture and Environmental Design, Kent, OH 44242-0001. Offers architecture (M Arch); preservation architecture (Certificate); urban design (M Arch, MUD, Certificate). Part-time programs available. *Degree requirements:* For master's, thesis optional. *Entrance requirements:* For master's, GRE, portfolio, minimum GPA of 2.75, 3 letters of reference, resume, undergraduate architecture degree. Additional exam requirements/recommendations for international students: Required—TOEFL (minimum score 550 paper-based). Electronic applications accepted. *Faculty research:* History and theory, building technology, landscape architecture and urbanism, urbanism, sustainable development.

New York Institute of Technology, Graduate Division, School of Architecture and Design, Old Westbury, NY 11568-8000. Offers urban and regional design (M Arch). Part-time programs available. *Students:* 20 full-time (13 women), 2 part-time (both women); includes 2 minority (1 Asian American or Pacific Islander, 1 Hispanic American), 14 international. Average age 27. In 2009, 7 master's awarded. *Degree requirements:* For master's, thesis. *Entrance requirements:* For master's, minimum QPA of 2.85, portfolio. Additional exam requirements/recommendations for international students: Required—TOEFL (minimum score 550 paper-based; 213 computer-based). *Application deadline:* For fall admission, 7/1 priority date for domestic students; for spring admission, 12/1 priority date for domestic students. Applications are processed on a rolling basis. Application fee: $50. Electronic applications accepted. *Expenses:* Tuition: Part-time $825 per credit. *Financial support:* Research assistantships with partial tuition reimbursements, institutionally sponsored loans and tuition waivers (full and partial) available. Support available to part-time students. Financial award applicants required to submit FAFSA. *Faculty research:* Affordable housing, urban modeling and simulation, transport systems and infrastructure, relationships of policy and form. *Unit head:* Judith DiMaio, Dean, 516-686-7594, Fax: 516-686-7921, E-mail: jdimaio@nyit.edu. *Application contact:* Dr. Jacquelyn Nealon, Vice President for Enrollment Services, 516-686-7925, Fax: 516-686-7597, E-mail: jnealon@nyit.edu.

Prairie View A&M University, School of Architecture, Prairie View, TX 77446-0519. Offers architecture (M Arch); community development (MCD). Part-time and evening/weekend programs available. *Faculty:* 4 full-time (1 woman), 6 part-time/adjunct (2 women). *Students:* 29 full-time (10 women), 35 part-time (14 women); includes 59 minority (54 African Americans, 5 Hispanic Americans), 3 international. Average age 28. 63 applicants, 100% accepted. In 2009, 39 master's awarded. *Entrance requirements:* For master's, GRE General Test, portfolio (M Arch). Additional exam requirements/recommendations for international students: Required—TOEFL (minimum score 550 paper-based). *Application deadline:* For fall admission, 6/1 priority date for domestic and international students; for spring admission, 11/1 priority date for domestic students, 10/1 priority date for international students. Applications are processed on a rolling basis. Application fee: $50. Electronic applications accepted. *Expenses:* Tuition, state resident: full-time $2200. Tuition, nonresident: full-time $5600. Required fees: $1720. Tuition and fees vary according to course load. *Financial support:* Fellowships with tuition reimbursements, research assistantships with tuition reimbursements, teaching assistantships, career-related internships or fieldwork, Federal Work-Study, institutionally sponsored loans, scholarships/grants, tuition waivers (full and partial), and unspecified assistantships available. Support available to part-time students. Financial award application deadline: 3/1; financial award applicants required to submit FAFSA. *Faculty research:* Community management, sustainable design. *Unit head:* Dr. Ikhlas Sabouni, Dean, 936-261-9800, Fax: 936-261-2350, E-mail: isabouni@pvamu.edu. *Application contact:* Dr. Ikhlas Sabouni, Dean, 936-261-9800, Fax: 936-261-2350, E-mail: isabouni@pvamu.edu.

Pratt Institute, School of Architecture, Program in Architecture and Urban Design, Brooklyn, NY 11205-3899. Offers architecture and urban design (post-profession) (MS). *Faculty:* 4

part-time/adjunct (2 women). *Students:* 16 full-time (8 women); includes 2 minority (1 African American, 1 Asian American or Pacific Islander), 13 international. Average age 25. 61 applicants, 26% accepted, 8 enrolled. In 2009, 6 master's awarded. *Degree requirements:* For master's, thesis. *Entrance requirements:* For master's, portfolio, letters of recommendation. Additional exam requirements/recommendations for international students: Required—TOEFL (minimum score 550 paper-based; 213 computer-based; 79 iBT). *Application deadline:* For fall admission, 1/5 for domestic and international students; for spring admission, 10/1 for domestic and international students. Applications are processed on a rolling basis. Application fee: $50 ($90 for international students). Electronic applications accepted. *Expenses:* Tuition: Full-time $22,734. Required fees: $1280. *Financial support:* Career-related internships or fieldwork, Federal Work-Study, institutionally sponsored loans, scholarships/grants, health care benefits, and unspecified assistantships available. Support available to part-time students. Financial award application deadline: 2/1; financial award applicants required to submit FAFSA. *Faculty research:* Urban development process; historical, social, and economic implications of planning. *Unit head:* William J. Mac Donald, Chairperson, 718-399-4357, E-mail: wmacdona@pratt.edu. *Application contact:* Young Hah, Director of Graduate Admissions, 718-636-3683, Fax: 718-399-4242, E-mail: yhah@pratt.edu.

See Close-Up on page 145.

Rice University, Graduate Programs, School of Architecture, Houston, TX 77251-1892. Offers architecture (M Arch, D Arch); urban design (M Arch). *Faculty:* 16 full-time (5 women), 21 part-time/adjunct (4 women). *Students:* 81 full-time (36 women); includes 10 minority (1 African American, 5 Asian Americans or Pacific Islanders, 4 Hispanic Americans), 10 international. 324 applicants, 18% accepted, 26 enrolled. In 2009, 28 master's awarded. *Degree requirements:* For master's, thesis optional; for doctorate, thesis/dissertation. *Entrance requirements:* For master's and doctorate, GRE. Additional exam requirements/recommendations for international students: Required—TOEFL (minimum score 600 paper-based; 250 computer-based; 100 iBT). *Application deadline:* For fall admission, 12/31 priority date for domestic and international students. Application fee: $70. Electronic applications accepted. *Financial support:* In 2009–10, 79 fellowships (averaging $12,950 per year) were awarded. *Unit head:* Sarah Whiting, Dean, School of Architecture, 713-348-4044, Fax: 713-348-5277, E-mail: sarah.whiting@rice.edu. *Application contact:* Kathleen H. Roberts, Graduate Coordinator, 713-348-5202, Fax: 713-348-5277, E-mail: kroberts@rice.edu.

Savannah College of Art and Design, Graduate School, Program in Urban Design and Development, Savannah, GA 31402-3146. Offers MA. Part-time programs available. *Degree requirements:* For master's, thesis. *Entrance requirements:* For master's, interview, portfolio. Additional exam requirements/recommendations for international students: Required—TOEFL (minimum score 450 paper-based; 133 computer-based). *Expenses:* Tuition: Full-time $28,515; part-time $627 per credit hour. One-time fee: $500. Tuition and fees vary according to course load.

State University of New York College of Environmental Science and Forestry, Department of Landscape Architecture, Syracuse, NY 13210-2779. Offers community design and planning (MLA, MS); cultural landscape studies and conservation (MLA, MS); landscape and urban ecology (MLA, MS). *Accreditation:* ASLA (one or more programs are accredited). *Degree requirements:* For master's, comprehensive exam (for some programs), thesis (for some programs). *Entrance requirements:* For master's, GRE General Test, minimum GPA of 3.0. Additional exam requirements/recommendations for international students: Required—TOEFL (paper-based 550, computer-based 213, iBT 80) or IELTS (6) or STEP Aiken (Grade 1). *Faculty research:* Site analysis and design, city and regional planning, community environments.

University at Buffalo, the State University of New York, Graduate School, School of Architecture and Planning, Department of Urban and Regional Planning, Buffalo, NY 14260. Offers MUP, JD/MUP, M Arch/MUP. *Accreditation:* ACSP. Part-time programs available. *Faculty:* 13 full-time (3 women), 8 part-time/adjunct (2 women). *Students:* 77 full-time (36 women), 19 part-time (11 women); includes 15 minority (13 African Americans, 2 Hispanic Americans), 16 international. Average age 28. 147 applicants, 62% accepted, 39 enrolled. In 2009, 39 master's awarded. *Degree requirements:* For master's, thesis or alternative, project. *Entrance requirements:* For master's, minimum GPA of 3.0, resume, 3 letters of recommendation. Additional exam requirements/recommendations for international students: Required—TOEFL (minimum score 550 paper-based; 213 computer-based; 79 iBT), or IELTS (minimum score 6.5). *Application deadline:* For fall admission, 3/1 priority date for domestic and international students; for spring admission, 10/31 priority date for domestic students, 10/1 priority date for international students. Applications are processed on a rolling basis. Application fee: $75. Electronic applications accepted. *Financial support:* In 2009–10, 3 fellowships with full tuition reimbursements (averaging $9,600 per year), 15 research assistantships with full and partial tuition reimbursements (averaging $5,044 per year), 9 teaching assistantships with partial tuition reimbursements (averaging $6,400 per year) were awarded; career-related internships or fieldwork, Federal Work-Study, institutionally sponsored loans, scholarships/grants, health care benefits, tuition waivers (partial), and unspecified assistantships also available. Support available to part-time students. Financial award application deadline: 3/1; financial award applicants required to submit FAFSA. *Faculty research:* Community development and urban management, economic and international development, environmental and land use planning, GIS and spatial modeling, urban design and physical planning. Total annual research expenditures: $341,108. *Unit head:* Dr. Niraj Verma, Professor and Chair, 716-829-2133 Ext. 109, Fax: 716-829-3256, E-mail: nverma@buffalo.edu. *Application contact:* Donna M. Rogalski, Assistant to the Chair, 716-829-2133 Ext. 109, Fax: 716-829-3256, E-mail: dmr1@buffalo.edu.

University of California, Berkeley, Graduate Division, College of Environmental Design, Department of Architecture, Berkeley, CA 94720-1500. Offers architecture (M Arch); building science (MS, PhD); building structures, construction and materials (MS, PhD); design theories, methods, and practices (MS, PhD); environmental design in developing countries (MS, PhD); history of architecture and urbanism (MS, PhD); social and cultural processes in architecture and urbanism (MS, PhD); M Arch/MCP; M Arch/MS; MLA/M Arch. *Students:* 156 full-time (91 women). Average age 30. 935 applicants, 60 enrolled. In 2009, 42 master's, 12 doctorates awarded. *Degree requirements:* For master's, thesis; for doctorate, thesis/dissertation, qualifying exam. *Entrance requirements:* For master's and doctorate, GRE General Test, minimum GPA of 3.0, 3 letters of recommendation. Additional exam requirements/recommendations for international students: Required—TOEFL. Application fee: $70 ($90 for international students). Electronic applications accepted. *Financial support:* Unspecified assistantships available. *Unit head:* Prof. Gail Brager, Chair, 510-642-4942. *Application contact:* Lois H. Ito Koch, Student Affairs Officer, 510-642-5577, Fax: 510-643-5607, E-mail: archgrad@berkeley.edu.

University of California, Berkeley, Graduate Division, College of Environmental Design, Department of Landscape Architecture and Environmental Planning, Berkeley, CA 94720-1500. Offers landscape architecture (MLA), including environmental planning, landscape design and site planning, urban and community design; landscape architecture and environmental planning (PhD); MLA/M Arch; MLA/MCP. *Accreditation:* ASLA (one or more programs are accredited). *Faculty:* 13 full-time, 6 part-time/adjunct. *Students:* 69 full-time (49 women). Average age 30. 252 applicants, 24 enrolled. In 2009, 31 master's, 1 doctorate awarded. *Degree requirements:* For master's, professional project or thesis; for doctorate, one foreign language, thesis/dissertation, qualifying exam. *Entrance requirements:* For master's, GRE General Test, minimum GPA of 3.0, portfolio; for doctorate, GRE General Test, master's degree (strongly recommended), minimum GPA of 3.0, sample of written work, 3 letters of recommendation. *Application deadline:* For fall admission, 12/15 for domestic students. Application fee: $70 ($90 for international students). *Financial support:* Fellowships, research assistantships, teaching assistantships, career-related internships or fieldwork, Federal Work-Study, institutionally sponsored loans, and unspecified assistantships available. *Unit head:* Prof. Linda Jewell, Chair, 510-642-4022, Fax: 510-643-6166. *Application contact:* Yong No, Student Affairs Officer, 510-642-2965, Fax: 510-643-6166, E-mail: laepgrad@berkeley.edu.

University of California, Berkeley, Graduate Division, College of Environmental Design, Group in Urban Design, Berkeley, CA 94720-1500. Offers MUD. *Faculty:* 13 full-time, 6 part-time/adjunct. *Students:* 9 full-time (4 women). Average age 29. 46 applicants, 9 enrolled. *Degree requirements:* For master's, professional project or thesis. *Entrance requirements:* For master's, GRE General Test, minimum GPA of 3.0, portfolio, 3 letters of recommendation. *Application deadline:* For fall admission, 1/5 for domestic students. Application fee: $70 ($90 for international students). *Financial support:* Unspecified assistantships available. *Unit head:* Prof. Peter Bosselmann, Chair, 510-642-4022. *Application contact:* Jaime Lee, Student Affairs Officer, 510-642-2965, Fax: 510-643-6166, E-mail: laepgrad@berkeley.edu.

University of California, Los Angeles, Graduate Division, School of the Arts and Architecture, Department of Architecture and Urban Design, Los Angeles, CA 90095. Offers M Arch, MA, PhD. *Degree requirements:* For master's, thesis or alternative, comprehensive exam or design project; for doctorate, 2 foreign languages, thesis/dissertation, oral and written qualifying exams. *Entrance requirements:* For master's and doctorate, GRE General Test, portfolio. Additional exam requirements/recommendations for international students: Required—TOEFL. Electronic applications accepted. *Faculty research:* Urban poverty and low wage labor markets; environmental planning and politics; international political economy; physical planning, urban design, planning history; housing and land development; transportation and land use; critical urban and regional studies.

University of Colorado Denver, College of Architecture and Planning, Program in Urban Design, Denver, CO 80217-3364. Offers MUD. Part-time programs available. *Students:* 11 full-time (7 women), 2 part-time (both women); includes 2 minority (1 Asian American or Pacific Islander, 1 Hispanic American), 3 international. 27 applicants, 44% accepted, 8 enrolled. In 2009, 22 master's awarded. *Degree requirements:* For master's, thesis optional. *Entrance requirements:* For master's, BA in architecture, minimum GPA of 3.0, portfolio. Additional exam requirements/recommendations for international students: Required—TOEFL (minimum score 550 paper-based; 213 computer-based). *Application deadline:* For fall admission, 3/15 for domestic students; for spring admission, 10/1 for domestic students. Application fee: $50 ($75 for international students). *Financial support:* Career-related internships or fieldwork, Federal Work-Study, institutionally sponsored loans, and scholarships/grants available. Financial award application deadline: 3/1; financial award applicants required to submit FAFSA. *Faculty research:* Architecture of the city, architectural experimentation and exploration, composition and decomposition, intervention and transformation in the urban and rural landscape. *Unit head:* Tom Clark, Chair, 303-556-3296, Fax: 303-492-6163, E-mail: tom.clark@ucdenver.edu. *Application contact:* Heather Zertuche, Administrative Assistant II, 303-556-3382, Fax: 303-556-3687, E-mail: anpdeansoffice@storm.cudenver.edu.

University of Miami, Graduate School, School of Architecture, Program in Suburb and Town Design, Coral Gables, FL 33124. Offers M Arch. *Entrance requirements:* For master's, GRE General Test, minimum GPA of 3.0, portfolio. Additional exam requirements/recommendations for international students: Required—TOEFL. Electronic applications accepted.

University of Michigan, Taubman College of Architecture and Urban Planning, Master of Urban Design Program, Ann Arbor, MI 48109-2069. Offers MUD. *Entrance requirements:* For master's, GRE General Test, 5 year bachelor of architecture, M Arch, bachelor of landscape architecture, master of landscape architecture, or MUP; portfolio. Additional exam requirements/recommendations for international students: Required—TOEFL (minimum score 560 paper-based; 220 computer-based; 84 iBT). *Expenses:* Contact institution.

University of New Mexico, Graduate School, School of Architecture and Planning, Program in Town Design, Albuquerque, NM 87131-2039. Offers Graduate Certificate. Part-time programs available. *Application deadline:* For fall admission, 3/1 for domestic students; for spring admission, 11/1 for domestic students. Application fee: $50. Electronic applications accepted. *Expenses:* Tuition, state resident: full-time $2099; part-time $233.20 per credit hour. Tuition, nonresident: full-time $6650. Required fees: $25 per semester. Tuition and fees vary according to course load, program and reciprocity agreements. *Unit head:* Mark C. Childs, Director, 505-277-5059, Fax: 505-277-0076, E-mail: mchilds@unm.edu. *Application contact:* Mark C. Childs, Director, 505-277-5059, Fax: 505-277-0076, E-mail: mchilds@unm.edu.

University of Oklahoma—Tulsa, Urban Design Studio, Tulsa, OK 74135-2512. Offers architectural urban studies (MS); urban design (M Arch).

University of Pennsylvania, School of Design, Graduate Group in Architecture, Philadelphia, PA 19104. Offers architecture (PhD); real estate design and development (PhD); urban design (PhD). Part-time programs available. *Faculty:* 16 full-time (5 women), 13 part-time/adjunct (3 women). *Students:* 266 full-time (126 women), 7 part-time (2 women); includes 49 minority (6 African Americans, 2 American Indian/Alaska Native, 28 Asian Americans or Pacific Islanders, 13 Hispanic Americans), 81 international. 894 applicants, 38% accepted, 127 enrolled. In 2009, 6 doctorates awarded. *Degree requirements:* For doctorate, 2 foreign languages, comprehensive exam, thesis/dissertation, qualifying exam, final exam. *Entrance requirements:* For doctorate, GRE General Test, B Arch, M Arch, portfolio, writing sample. Additional exam requirements/recommendations for international students: Required—TOEFL. *Application deadline:* For fall admission, 1/2 priority date for domestic students. Application fee: $70. *Expenses:* Tuition: Full-time $25,660; part-time $4758 per course. Required fees: $2152; $270 per course. Tuition and fees vary according to course load, degree level and program. *Financial support:* Fellowships, research assistantships, teaching assistantships, institutionally sponsored loans, scholarships/grants, traineeships, health care benefits, and unspecified assistantships available. *Faculty research:* Theory, history, technology, representation, visualization, landscape, urban design, historic preservation.

See Close-Up on page 147.

The University of Texas at Austin, Graduate School, School of Architecture, Austin, TX 78712-1111. Offers architecture (M Arch); community and regional planning (MSCRP, PhD); historic preservation (MS); history of architecture (MA, PhD); landscape architecture (MLA); urban design (MSUD); JD/MSCRP; MSCRP/MA; MSCRP/PhD. *Degree requirements:* For doctorate, thesis/dissertation. *Entrance requirements:* For master's and doctorate, GRE General Test. Additional exam requirements/recommendations for international students: Required—TOEFL (minimum score 550 paper-based; 213 computer-based). Electronic applications accepted.

University of Toronto, School of Graduate Studies, Social Sciences Division, Department of Geography, Toronto, ON M5S 1A1, Canada. Offers geography (M Sc, MA, PhD); planning (M Sc Pl); urban design studies (MUD). Part-time programs available. *Degree requirements:* For master's, thesis optional; for doctorate, thesis/dissertation. *Entrance requirements:* For master's, bachelor's degree or equivalent in geography or a closely related field, minimum B+ average in each of 2 final years of degree, 3 letters of reference; for doctorate, master of geography degree, minimum A–average.

University of Washington, Graduate School, College of Built Environments, Department of Urban Design and Planning, Seattle, WA 98195. Offers strategic planning for critical infrastructures (MSCPI); urban design and planning (PhD); urban planning (MUP). *Accreditation:* ACSP (one or more programs are accredited). *Degree requirements:* For master's, thesis or alternative; for doctorate, thesis/dissertation. *Entrance requirements:* For master's and doctorate, GRE General Test, minimum GPA of 3.0. Additional exam requirements/recommendations for international students: Required—TOEFL. *Faculty research:* Land-use and growth management, urban form and travel behavior, geographic information systems/remote sensing, historic preservation, urban ecology and environmental planning.

University of Washington, Graduate School, College of Built Environments, Interdisciplinary Program in Urban Design, Seattle, WA 98195. Offers Certificate. Electronic applications accepted. *Faculty research:* Urban design process; urban form; place theory; place analysis; race, class, and gender in community design.

Urban Design

Washington University in St. Louis, Sam Fox School of Design and Visual Arts, Program in Urban Design, St. Louis, MO 63130-4899. Offers MUD, M Arch/MUD, MUD/MSW. *Entrance requirements:* For master's, GRE General Test, portfolio. Additional exam requirements/recommendations for international students: Required—TOEFL (minimum score 600 paper-based; 250 computer-based; 100 iBT), TWE. *Faculty research:* Urban design development issues: city revitalization, sustainability and suburbanization; urban history and visualization of urban form.

IIT College of Architecture
ILLINOIS INSTITUTE OF TECHNOLOGY

ILLINOIS INSTITUTE OF TECHNOLOGY

College of Architecture

Programs of Study

The Illinois Institute of Technology (IIT) College of Architecture's graduate degree programs emphasize the integration of architectural design, theory, and technology. Through rigorous work and critical thought, the College promotes innovation and underscores refinement with the objective of developing outstanding proficiency in the practice of architecture and landscape architecture. The College offers five master's programs and a Ph.D. program.

The Master of Architecture first professional degree is accredited by the National Architectural Accreditation Board (NAAB). The program is developed around a sequence of five semester-long studios that culminate with the master's project during the final semester. Candidates who hold a pre-professional architecture degree may qualify for up to one year of advanced standing in the program.

The Master of Science in Architecture offers advanced architectural study that builds upon knowledge acquired from a first professional degree. The program combines courses and in-depth research concerning a specific area of concentration, culminating in the completion of a thesis. A Master of Science in Architecture with a specialization in sustainable new cities is also available.

The Master of Integrated Building Delivery program educates architects to more actively participate in, guide, and/or undertake the full range of entrepreneurial and innovative activities comprising design, develop, and build initiatives.

The Master of Landscape Architecture program is the only professional program of its kind in Chicago. The program was awarded accreditation by the Landscape Architectural Accreditation Board (LAAB) in fall 2010.

A Ph.D. program, Doctor of Philosophy in Architecture, is available for those advanced graduate students who plan to pursue careers in the academic and research fields and/or in the area of advanced professional practice within the domain of architecture.

Research Facilities

The College facilities include the Graham Resource Center, which provides books, serials, videos, online databases, and other resources to support faculty and student research and reference needs. The Architecture Materials Lab has a complete wood, metal, and plastics shop, which includes a CNC milling machine, three Universal laser cutters, and flatbed router. The College offers robust computing resources and houses two computer labs for student use and instruction spaces that are equipped with necessary software, printers, and plotters.

Financial Aid

The College of Architecture offers merit-based scholarships and fellowships, which are given exclusively to incoming students of the highest academic standing for use in their first year of graduate study. The graduate college Dean's Fellowships vary in amount each year and range from $8775 to $14,625 for the 2010–11 academic year. The College of Architecture Dean's Scholarships in the amount of $6000 are awarded for the first academic year.

Teaching assistantships are available to qualified graduate students after they have completed their first year of study.

Cost of Study

For the 2011–12 academic year, the estimated tuition and fees are $31,183 for the master's programs (based on 30 credit hours) and $19,483 for the Ph.D. program (based on 18 credit hours). These rates are based on the 2010–11 tuition rates and are subject to annual increases.

Living and Housing Costs

For the 2011–12 academic year, the College estimates $12,530 for living expenses and supplies. However, these expenses can vary greatly depending upon the type of housing and supply needs. While the majority of the graduate students live off campus, there are graduate apartments available on campus. For more information regarding the on-campus apartments, please visit IIT's housing office online at http://www.iit.edu/housing.

Student Group

The College of Architecture has a population of 235 degree-seeking graduate students and more than 900 students in the College in total, including those in the undergraduate program. At the graduate level, the population is 56 percent men and 44 percent women, with an international student population composing 44 percent of the graduate programs.

The College has degree options for students with or without a background in architecture. The majority of the graduate students are pursuing studies on a full-time basis.

Student Outcomes

Recent graduates of the program have been hired at several Chicago firms including Murphy/Jahn, Studio Gang, Dirk Denison Architects, and Wolff Landscape Architecture. Graduates can be found in both national and international firms, from New York to Hong Kong.

While many of the graduates go on to work in architecture firms, the degree programs provide a comprehensive design education, which can be applied to a variety of fields.

Location

The College is located in Chicago, one of the most vibrant, culturally diverse, and beautiful cities in the United States. The setting enriches architectural education by exposing the complexities of the urban environment, including issues of urban planning, affordable housing, transportation planning, historic preservation, adaptive reuse, and other trends that are transforming the city and field today.

The Institute

IIT's prominence is intertwined with the architectural and cultural legacy of Chicago, recognized internationally for its heritage of leadership in the architectural profession. The College forged its modernist reputation at the hands of Ludwig Mies van der Rohe. Unifying art and technology, his vision found expression in the campus he designed for IIT—a campus selected in 1976 by the AIA national membership as one of the top 200 architectural achievements in the United States.

Applying

Admission to the IIT College of Architecture's graduate programs is handled directly by the College of Architecture. The fall 2011 application deadline for the Master of Architecture and Master of Science in Architecture programs is January 15, with admission decisions released in March. The Master of Landscape Architecture and Master of Integrated Building Delivery have rolling admissions. The Ph.D. application deadline is April 15.

For information on the application requirements, please see the College's graduate admissions Web site at http://www.iit.edu/arch/admission/graduate.

Correspondence and Information

Graduate Admissions
IIT College of Architecture
S.R. Crown Hall
3360 South State Street
Chicago, Illinois 60616-3793
Phone: 312-567-3230
Fax: 312-567-5820
E-mail: arch@iit.edu
Web site: http://www.arch.iit.edu

Illinois Institute of Technology

THE FACULTY AND THEIR RESEARCH

Peter Beltemacchi, Associate Professor and Associate Dean; M.S., IIT. Urban design, city and regional planning.
Thomas Brock, Assistant Professor; M.Arch., Pennsylvania. Architectural design, construction technologies, digital media.
Marshall Brown, Assistant Professor; M.Arch., MAUD, Harvard. Architectural design and theory, urbanism.
Timothy Brown, Studio Associate Professor, Director of Admissions, and Director of International Affairs; M. Arch., Illinois at Chicago. Architectural design and theory.
Susan Conger-Austin, Assistant Professor; M.Arch., Princeton. Architectural design and theory.
Dirk Denison, Associate Professor and Director of Thesis; M.Arch., Harvard. Architectural design, community design, community planning.
John Durbrow, Assistant Professor; B.Arch., Rice. Architectural design, materials and technologies, planning, furniture design.
Mahjoub Elnimeiri, Professor and Director of Ph.D. in Architecture Program; Ph.D., Northwestern. Structural engineering, sustainability.
Martin Felsen, Studio Associate Professor; M.S., Columbia. Architectural design, urban design, digital technologies.
Frank Flury, Associate Professor; M.Arch., Karlsruhe (Germany). Architectural design, design/build.
David Goodman, Studio Associate Professor; M.Arch., Harvard. Architectural design and theory.
Gerald Horn, Studio Professor. Architectural design, mixed-use development, design analysis.
David Hovey, Associate Professor; M.S.Arch., IIT. Architectural design, medium- and high-density housing, design analysis, real estate development.
Chris Karidis, Studio Professor; B.Arch., IIT. Architectural design, building technology.
Thomas Kearns, Studio Associate Professor; B.Arch., Iowa State. Architectural design and theory, digital technologies.
Sean Keller, Assistant Professor; Ph.D. Harvard. Architectural history and theory.
Robert Krawczyk, Associate Professor and Director, Undergraduate Programs; B.Arch., Illinois at Chicago. Computer-aided design, advanced digital applications.
Ron Krueck, Studio Professor; B.Arch., IIT. Architectural design and theory.
Eva Kultermann, Assistant Professor; M.S., Oxford Brookes (England). Design and theory, design build, sustainability.
Peter Land, Professor; M.Arch., Carnegie Tech. Innovative structures; building technologies and materials; low-energy design; high-density, low-rise housing; urbanism and planning.
Harry Francis Mallgrave, Professor and Director, International Center for Sustainable New Cities; Ph.D., Pennsylvania. History and theory of architecture.
Thomas J. McLeish, Studio Associate Professor; M.S., MIT. Digital technology in practice, digital design and fabrication.
Jonathan Miller, Studio Associate Professor; M.F.A., NYU. Architectural design and theory; film studies.
Kathleen Nagle, Studio Associate Professor; M.Arch., Harvard. Architectural design, introduction to architecture.
Richard Nelson, Studio Associate Professor and Director for Buildings and Operations; M.Arch., Washington (St. Louis). Architectural design and building technology.
Peter L. Osler, Assistant Professor and Director, Landscape Architecture Program; M.L.A., M. Arch., Harvard.
Alphonso Peluso, Studio Assistant Professor; B.Arch., IIT. Digital design.
Paul Pettigrew, Studio Associate Professor; M.Arch., MIT. Architectural design, furniture design and build.
Benjamin R. Riley, Assistant Professor; M. Arch., Columbia. Architectural design, building technology, visual training.
Donna V. Robertson, Professor, Dean, and John and Jeanne Rowe Chair; M.Arch., Virginia. Architectural design and practice, preservation, case study methodology.
Christopher Rockey, Assistant Professor; B.S., M.Arch., Illinois at Urbana-Champaign. Structural engineering, constructability, efficiency.
Peter Roesch, Studio Associate Professor; M.S.Arch., IIT. Architectural design, medium- and high-density housing, urban design.
John Ronan, Associate Professor and Director, Advanced Studios; M.Arch., Harvard. Architectural design, material investigation.
Andrew Schachman, Studio Assistant Professor; M.Arch. Illinois at Chicago. Architectural design and theory.
George Schipporeit, Associate Professor. Building technology and systems, high-rise design, medium- and high-density housing, sustainable new cities.
Christian Stutzki, Studio Professor; Ph.D., RWTH Aachen (Germany). Structural engineering, facade and glass technology.
Arthur Takeuchi, Associate Professor; M.S.Arch., IIT. Space problem, visual training, building systems.
Catherine Wetzel, Associate Professor; M.Arch., Pennsylvania. Architectural design and practice.
Antony Wood, Studio Associate Professor and Executive Director, Council on Tall Buildings and Urban Habitat (CTBUH); Ph.D., Nottingham (UK). Tall buildings and sustainable design.

S.R. Crown Hall on the campus of Illinois Institute of Technology.

PRATT INSTITUTE

School of Architecture

Programs of Study

The School of Architecture is dedicated to maintaining the connection between design theory and practice and to extending the range of knowledge necessary to an understanding of the built environment. The diversity of programs within the School and the accessibility of other programs within the Institute enable students to pursue a wide range of interests. Students can take electives in fine arts, film, digital arts, industrial design, furniture design, interior design, and photography as well as electives in advanced architectural theory, design, technology, and management. The School has many internationally recognized faculty members who bring to the graduate programs a strong theoretical base and the high standards of their professional work. The programs are distinguished by strong studio cultures and creative approaches to architectural design. Many special courses are offered in contemporary theoretical and critical issues, advanced computing and media, building technology, architectural history, and experimental structures. The electronic laboratory is a fifty-station PC-based facility that offers instruction in a wide variety of two-dimensional and three-dimensional design programs. Students are exposed to the professional world through optional internship programs that place them in outstanding New York architectural offices, public agencies, and nonprofit design institutions, giving them firsthand work experience and credit towards their degree.

The School of Architecture offers at total of seven graduate programs. There are two graduate architecture programs: the first professional accredited Master of Architecture (M.Arch.) and the postprofessional Master of Architecture (M.S.Arch.). There are also five Master of Science programs: architecture and urban design, city and regional planning, environmental systems management, facilities management, and historic preservation.

The three-year M.Arch. first professional program is designed for students holding a four-year undergraduate program in any field, including architecture. Graduate courses and seminars are designed to familiarize students with all aspects of the discipline and practice of architecture. Design studios at Pratt find many of their coordinates within the rich territory of New York City. However, the program also reaches into areas worldwide and into other frames, such as global marketplaces, digital worlds, and historical, theoretical, and political networks. This program is fully accredited by NAAB. Students with a B.S. in architecture or other nonprofessional degree should apply for this M.Arch. program. The postprofessional M.S.Arch., a summer/fall/spring program, is for those who hold an accredited architecture degree or the equivalent. The program takes three semesters to complete. Students with significant professional experience can also apply for work credit, which reduces total credit-hour requirements. The postprofessional M.S.Arch. allows intensive theoretical and technical engagement of architecture and the city and stresses research and experimentation concentrating on the relations between architecture and other urban forms, scales, and forces. Research is conducted primarily within the analytic and synthetic content of the design studio and culminates in a required thesis.

The Master of Science in architecture and urban design program is intended for students who are interested in careers that enhance the growth and development of the built urban environments, the context for an urban laboratory. The 33-credit program requires 17 hours of design studio and research, with the balance of the credits in required courses in urban history, theory, infrastructure, and implementation and electives in law, transportation, housing, and preservation. The program is open to those with professional undergraduate degrees in architecture and is a summer/fall/spring program.

The four programs offered by Pratt's Programs for Sustainable Planning and Development (PSPD)—the M.S. in city and regional planning (CRP), the M.S. in environmental systems management (ESM), the M.S. in historic preservation, and the M.S. in facilities management—emphasize planning and preservation practice rooted in the principles of sustainability, equity, and public participation.

The curricula are designed to build the professional skills and knowledge of students who desire to affect the built, natural, and social environments of the nation's cities and communities in positive ways. CRP and ESM courses are offered in the evenings, enabling students to work full-time. The city and regional planning program offers specializations in community development, environmental planning, physical planning, and preservation planning. The CRP program requires the completion of 60 credits, including the thesis or the Demonstration of Professional Competence course. The ESM program requires 40 credits of course work.

Students with undergraduate degrees in architecture and engineering may have up to 9 credits waived in either the CRP or ESM program.

PSPD's historic preservation program is a two-year graduate program leading to the M.S. in historic preservation. The program, designed primarily for full-time students and based at the Manhattan campus, is a 44-credit sequence of courses that provides studies in community planning, history, interpretation, design, policy, and regulatory practice.

Recognizing that today's field of preservation requires more than curatorial management, the program fosters the knowledge preservationists must have in order to participate in policy-making to revitalize urban areas, suburban communities, and rural landscapes. With its urban focus, the program emphasizes hands-on work and makes extensive use of New York City's rich resources.

All four graduate programs in the PSPD maintain strong ties with Pratt's architecture and design programs and with the Pratt Center for Community Development, an innovative center for the practice of planning, design, and policy work that focuses on increasing quality of life and affecting social change in New York City's diverse communities.

The M.S. in facilities management program prepares individuals to assume leadership roles in corporations, institutions, and government. The degree requires the completion of 45 credits of course work and the 5-credit Demonstration of Professional Competence course, for a total of 50 credits. Students entering the program with prior professional experience or graduate work in related fields may be eligible for advanced standing; up to 12 credits may be waived. The facilities management program, accredited by IFMA, is offered at the Pratt Manhattan Center on an evening schedule, allowing maximum flexibility to combine full-time work with study and research. Students may take courses in any of the programs in PSPD.

Research Facilities

The Pratt Library has grown with the Institute to house one of the finest collections of reference material on art, design, and architecture. Recently remodeled and expanded to accommodate its growing collection, the library contains 186,589 bound volumes, serial backfiles, and other material, including government documents; 251,603 audiovisual materials; and 3,996 microforms and subscribes to 925 periodicals.

Pratt maintains numerous studios, shops, and technical facilities for work in all media, as well as state-of-the-art computer facilities. Pratt also has extensive gallery space for the exhibition of works by the student body, alumni, faculty members, and well-known architects and designers.

Financial Aid

Financial aid is offered through a variety of programs funded by the institution and the federal and state governments. These include Federal Perkins Loan and Federal Work-Study programs, the Tuition Assistance Program of New York State, and Pratt loans and student help. Graduate scholarships are awarded to entering students on a competitive basis. Fellowships and assistantships are awarded on a competitive basis to continuing students in all departments. Special alumni-sponsored fellowships are also available.

Cost of Study

Graduate tuition for 2010–11 is $30,312 per year (24 credits, $1263 per credit). Student fees are $1280 per semester. The cost of books and supplies varies widely, depending on the program in which the student is enrolled.

Living and Housing Costs

Campus housing continues to be expanded to meet student needs and is available for single students on a first-come, first-served basis. Housing costs average $16,808 per academic year. There is a plentiful supply of moderately priced rentals in the immediate area and in adjacent neighborhoods for married students seeking housing as well as for those students choosing to reside off campus.

Student Group

There are more than 375 students enrolled in Pratt's School of Architecture graduate programs; 52 percent are women. They come from all parts of the United States and the world. The graduate programs are noted for an exceptional placement ratio, with more than 85 percent of the graduating students finding employment before graduation.

Location

Pratt Institute is located in the Clinton Hill section of Brooklyn, on a 25-acre park-like campus. Pratt's Manhattan campus houses the Institute's graduate arts and cultural management, communications design, design management, facilities management, historic preservation, and library and information science programs as well as offering courses in architecture, city and regional planning, creative arts therapy, and urban design.

The Institute

A private, nonsectarian institute of higher education, Pratt Institute was founded in 1887 by the industrialist and philanthropist Charles Pratt. Today, Pratt educates 2,998 undergraduates and 1,709 graduate students for careers in art and design, architecture, and library and information science.

Applying

The application deadline is January 5. Early submission of applications, together with all necessary credentials, is highly desirable. For the applicant who intends to file for merit-based scholarships, applications and all supporting documents need to be received no later than January 5 for the fall semester and October 1 for the spring semester. All application materials must be received by January 5, or soon thereafter. Materials should be submitted in one package that includes the three letters of recommendation in sealed envelopes with the reference's signature across the flap.

Correspondence and Information

Graduate Admissions Office
Pratt Institute
200 Willoughby Avenue
Brooklyn, New York 11205
Phone: 718-636-3514
800-331-0834 (toll-free outside New York State)
Fax: 718-399-4242
E-mail: admissions@pratt.edu
Web site: http://www.pratt.edu

Pratt Institute

THE FACULTY

Thomas Hanrahan, Dean; M.Arch., Harvard; AIA, NCARB.

Architecture

William MacDonald, Professor and Chair; M.S., Columbia.
Philip Parker, Assistant Chair; M.Arch., Yale.
Gilland Akos, Visiting Assistant Professor.
Phillip Anzalone, Visiting Assistant Professor; M.Arch., Columbia.
Ezra Ardolino, Adjunct Assistant Professor.
Alexandra Barker, Adjunct Assistant Professor; M.Arch., Harvard.
Stephanie Bayard, Adjunct Assistant Professor; M.A., Columbia.
Karen Brandt, Visiting Professor; M.Arch., Harvard.
Dan Bucsescu, Adjunct Professor.
Theodore Calvin, Visiting Professor; M.S., Columbia.
Amber Chapin, Visiting Assistant Professor.
Manuel DeLanda, Adjunct Professor; B.F.A., School of Visual Arts.
Livio Dimitriu, Adjunct Professor.
Jeremy Edmiston, Adjunct Assistant Professor; M.S., Columbia.
Giuiano Fiorenzoli, Professor; M.A.S., MIT; M.Arch., Florence (Italy).
Erik Ghenoiu, Visiting Assistant Professor.
Jose Gonzalez, Visiting Assistant Professor.
Lara Guerra, Visiting Instructor.
Matthew Herman, Visiting Assistant Professor.
Michael Hollander, Visiting Associate Professor; M.Arch.
Alicia Imperiale, Visiting Assistant Professor; Ph.D. candidate, Princeton.
Catherine Ingraham, Professor, Ph.D.
Hina Jamelle, Visiting Assistant Professor.
Robert Kearns, Visiting Assistant Professor.
Michael Kennedy, Visiting Instructor.
Nico Kienzl, Visiting Instructor; D.Des., Harvard.
Karel Klein, Adjunct Associate Professor; M.Arch., Columbia.
Kevin Kleyla, Visiting Assistant Professor.
Carisima Koenig, Visiting Instructor.
M. Ferda Kolatan, Visiting Assistant Professor.
Craig Konyk, Adjunct Associate Professor.
Sameer Kumar, Adjunct Assistant Professor; M.Arch.
David Lallemant, Adjunct Assistant Professor; B.S.
Thomas Leeser, Adjunct Associate Professor.
Peter Macapia, Adjunct Assistant Professor; Ph.D., Columbia.
Radhi Majmuder, Visiting Assistant Professor.
Alexandru Marin, Adjunct Assistant Professor.
Natalia Martinez, Adjunct Instructor.
Katherine Mearns, Visiting Assistant Professor.
Tali Mejicovsky, Visiting Instructor; B.S., B.A., Pennsylvania.
Robert Mezquiti, Visiting Instructor; M.Arch.
Nilay Oza, Visiting Assistant Professor; M.S.Arch., MIT.
David Ruy, Adjunct Associate Professor; M.Arch., Columbia.
Maria Sieira, Adjunct Instructor; M.Arch., Pennsylvania.
Henry Smith-Miller, Adjunct Professor; M.Arch., Pennsylvania.
Jeremy Snyder, Visiting Assistant Professor.
Nathaniel Stanton, Adjunct Associate Professor.
Michael Szivos, Visiting Assistant Professor.
Jeffrey Taras, Visiting Instructor; M.Arch., Columbia.
Meredith Tenhoor, Visiting Instructor; Ph.D. candidate, Princeton.
Kenneth Tracy, Visiting Assistant Professor.
Maria Ludovica Tramontin, Adjunct Assistant Professor; Ph.D., Cagliari (Italy).
Jason Vigneri-Beane, Adjunct Assistant Professor; M.Arch., Iowa State.
Aaron White, Visiting Instructor; M.Arch., Pratt.
J. Christopher Whitelaw, Visiting Instructor; M.Arch., Columbia.
Lebbeus Woods, Adjunct Professor.

Urban Design

William MacDonald, Professor and Chair; M.S., Columbia.
Vito Hannibal Acconci, Adjunct Associate Professor; M.F.A., Iowa.
Nicholas Agneta, Visiting Assistant Professor, IDP Coordinator; B.Arch, Cooper Union; AIA.
Karen Brandt, Visiting Professor; M.A., Harvard.
Meta Brunzema, Adjunct Assistant Professor; M.Arch., Columbia.
Steven Chang, Adjunct Assistant Professor; B.Arch. Berkeley; AIA.
Robert Kearns, Adjunct Assistant Professor; M.A.E., Penn State; PE.
Carisima Koenig, Visiting Instructor.
Sameer Kumar, Adjunct Assistant Professor; M.Arch., Pennsylvania.
Charles Kwan, Visiting Instructor, M.Arch., Pratt.
Franklin Lee, Visiting Instructor; M.S., Columbia.
Carla Leitao, Adjunct Assistant Professor.
Teresa Llorente, Adjunct Assistant Professor, M.S., Columbia.
Elliot Maltby, Adjunct Associate Professor; M.L.A., Berkeley.
Victoria Marshall, Adjunct Associate Professor; M.L.A., Pennsylvania.
Signe Nielsen, Adjunct Professor, B.S., Pratt.
Gregory Okshteyn, Adjunct Assistant Professor; M.S.A.A.D., Columbia; AIA.
David Ruy, Adjunct Associate Professor.
Anne Save de Beaurecueil, Visiting Instructor; B.Arch., Caltech.
Richard Scherr, Adjunct Professor, M.S.Arch., Columbia.
Maria Sieira, Adjunct Instructor, M.Arch., Pennsylvania.
Roland Snooks, Adjunct Assistant Professor; M.S., Columbia.
Michael Szivos, Visiting Assistant Professor, M.S.A.A.D., Columbia.
Maria Ludoviica Tramontin, Adjunct Assistant Professor, Ph.D., Cagliari (Italy).
Jason Vigneri-Beane, Adjunct Assistant Professor, M.Arch., Iowa State.

Planning and the Environment (City and Regional Planning and Environmental Systems Management)

John Shapiro, Chair, Associate Professor; M.S.C.R.P., Pratt; AICP.
Eric Allison, Adjunct Associate Professor and Coordinator; Ph.D., Columbia.
Moshe Adler, Visiting Associate Professor; Ph.D., UCLA.
Robert Alpern, Visiting Associate Professor; I.L.B., Yale.
Erica Avrami, Visiting Instructor; Ph.D. candidate, Rutgers.
Jenifer Becker, Visiting Assistant Professor; M.S.CRP, Pratt.
Chris Benedict, Visiting Instructor; B.Arch., Cooper Union.
Michael Bobker, Visiting Assistant Professor, M.S., NYIT.
Viren Brahmbhatt, Visiting Assistant Professor; M.S.
Carlton Brown, Visiting Instructor; B.A., Princeton.
Joan Byron, Visiting Assistant Professor, B.Arch, Pratt.
Darryl Cabbagestalk, Visiting Assistant Professor; J.D., Pace.
Damon Chaky, Assistant Professor, Ph.D., Rensselaer.
Carter Craft, Visiting Assistant Professor, M.U.P., NYU.
Ramon Cruz, Visiting Assistant Professor.
Rayna Erlich, Visiting Instructor.
Stefanie Feldman, Visiting Assistant Professor; M.S., NJIT.
Roland Gebhardt, Visiting Assistant Professor; M.A., Hamburg (Germany).
Henry Gifford, Visiting Instructor.
Eva Hanhardt, Adjunct Assistant Professor; M.U.P., NYU.
Catherine Herman, Visiting Assistant Professor, M.S.C.R.P, Pratt.
George Jacquemart, Visiting Assistant Professor, M.S.U.P., Stanford; PE.
Larissa Justine Heilner, Visiting Assistant Professor; M.L.A., Pennsylvania.
Tanushri Kumar, Visiting Assistant Professor.
Brad Lander, Visiting Assistant Professor; M.S.CRP, Pratt.
Frank Lang, Visiting Assistant Professor.
Paul Mankiewicz, Visiting Associate Professor; Ph.D., CUNY.
Jonathan Martin, Visiting Assistant Professor; Ph.D., Cornell.
William Menking, Professor; M.S., London; M.S.CRP, Pratt.
Gita Nandan, Visiting Assistant Professor; M.Arch., Berkeley.
Steven Romalewski, Visiting Assistant Professor; M.S., Columbia.
Ariella Rosenberg, Visiting Assistant Professor; M.S., MIT.
Ron Shiffman, Professor; M.S.CRP, Pratt.
Anika Singh, Visiting Assistant Professor; J.D., NYU.
Mathy Stanislaus, Visiting Assistant Professor; J.D., IIT.
Ira Stern, Visiting Assistant Professor; M.S.CRP, Pratt.
Gelvin Stevenson, Visiting Associate Professor; Ph.D., Washington (St. Louis).
Samara Swanston, Visiting Assistant Professor; J.D., St. John's (New York).
Val Washington, Visiting Assistant Professor; J.D., Albany Law.
Vicki Weiner, Adjunct Associate Professor; M.S., Columbia.
Edward Perry Winston, Visiting Assistant Professor; M.Arch., Rice.
Ayse Yonder, Associate Professor; Ph.D., Berkeley.
Catherine Zidar, Visiting Assistant Professor; M.S.CRP, Pratt.

Historic Preservation

William MacDonald, Chair; M.S., Columbia.
Eric Allison, Adjunct Associate Professor and Coordinator; Ph.D., Columbia.
Erica Avrami, Visiting Assistant Professor; Ph.D. candidate, Rutgers.
Ned Kaufman, Adjunct Associate Professor; Ph.D., Yale.
Jane McNamara, Visiting Assistant Professor; M.A., NYU.
Marcia Reaven, Visiting Assistant Professor; Ph.D. candidate, NYU.
Theodore Prudon, Visiting Associate Professor; Ph.D., Columbia.
Vicki Weiner, Visiting Assistant Professor; M.S., Columbia.
Kevin Wolfe, Visiting Assistant Professor; M.Arch., Columbia.

Facilities Management and Construction Management

Harriet Markis, Assistant Professor and Chair; M. Engr., Cornell.
Matthias Ebinger, Visiting Assistant Professor, Dipl.-Ing. (FH), Germany.
William Henry, Visiting Assistant Professor; B.A., NYU.
Keith Keppler, Visiting Assistant Professor; M.B.A., USC.
Stephen Lograsso, Visiting Assistant Professor; B.S., NYIT.
Mary J. Matthews, Professor; M.S., Boston College.
Martin J. McManus, Visiting Assistant Professor; B.B.A., Pace.
Russell Olson, Visiting Assistant Professor; M.S., Pratt.
John E. Osborn, Visiting Associate Professor; J.D., South Carolina.
Edward D. Re Jr., Adjunct Associate Professor; M.S., Pratt.
Carol Reznikoff, Adjunct Associate Professor, M.S., Pratt.

UNIVERSITY OF PENNSYLVANIA

School of Design

Programs of Study

For men and women who wish to study design and planning within a rich, cross-disciplinary context, the University of Pennsylvania's School of Design offers exceptional opportunities. Founded more than 100 years ago, the School is known throughout the world for its exceptional mix of programs, and for fostering seminal thought about the way we shape and are shaped by the natural and man-made environment.

The School offers professional master's degrees in fine arts, architecture, environmental building design, landscape architecture, city planning, urban spatial analytics, and historic preservation. The School places great emphasis on interdisciplinary study. A series of both dual-degree options and certificates is offered to enable students to take their creative and intellectual study and research in depth across conventional departmental or program boundaries. Collaborative studios and cooperative programming with Penn's Wharton School, School of Engineering, and School of Arts and Sciences provide students with opportunities to interact with the multiple disciplines they are likely to encounter later in professional practice. To Ph.D. candidates, the graduate groups in architecture and city and regional planning offer advanced study for teaching and research.

Research Facilities

The Architectural Archives of the University of Pennsylvania preserves the works of more than 400 designers from the eighteenth century to the present and includes the Louis I. Kahn Collection. The Architectural Conservation Laboratory of the graduate program in historic preservation is devoted to advanced training and research in the conservation of the built environment. The PennDesign Computing Center supports a variety of computing activities, including CAD, GIS, and urban simulation modeling, as well as database, spreadsheet, and word processing applications. The Fabrication Center includes both conventional and computer-driven equipment. The University of Pennsylvania library is a composite of fourteen campus libraries, of which the Jerome and Anne Fisher Fine Arts Library is one, as well as the Perkins Rare Architectural Book Collection and the Slide Collection.

Financial Aid

The School of Design provides students with assistance in planning for and securing adequate financing for graduate school. New students need to apply for fellowships and scholarships at the time of application to their chosen department. Diversity scholarships are available.

Cost of Study

The tuition and general fee for full-time graduate students in the School of Design is $40,056 for the 2010–11 academic year. This includes a general fee of $2152. The 2010–11 nine-month budget is estimated at $63,620, which includes tuition and fees, room, board, and all other expenses.

Living and Housing Costs

There are several residential options offering both apartment and suite living arrangements for single and married students as well as students with families. Many graduate students live off campus, where housing is available at varying costs that begin at approximately $450 per month.

Student Group

The student body is drawn from all over the United States, from many other countries, and from a variety of undergraduate disciplines. There is an enrollment of approximately 625 full-time students. An active PennDesign Student Council and a University Graduate and Professional Student Association provide the opportunity for interaction among the departments and the twelve schools of the University.

Location

Philadelphia was founded more than 300 years ago and is famous for its historic significance. It is today, the nation's sixth-largest city, the home to major cultural institutions, and a vibrant mosaic of many cultures. Philadelphia and the surrounding region act as a laboratory for PennDesign students and faculty members.

The University and The School

Founded in 1740 by Benjamin Franklin, the University of Pennsylvania is composed of twelve graduate and professional schools and four undergraduate schools. The guiding philosophy of "one university" connotes the spirit of cooperation unifying the diverse intellectual and social activities of the University. PennDesign students are encouraged to take advantage of courses offered by the other graduate and professional schools through electives and audits.

Applying

Applicants to each degree program in the School of Design must submit an online application form, application fee, three letters of recommendation, official transcripts, and GRE scores. In addition, there are specific requirements for portfolios, or written statements by individual departments. The application fee is $70. The application deadline is December 15 for the Master of Architecture, Ph.D., and M.S. programs, and January 12 for all other programs.

Correspondence and Information

Office of Admissions
School of Design
110 Meyerson Hall
University of Pennsylvania
Philadelphia, Pennsylvania 19104-6311
Phone: 215-898-6520
Fax: 215-573-3927
E-mail: admissions@design.upenn.edu
Web site: http://www.design.upenn.edu

University of Pennsylvania

THE FACULTY AND THEIR RESEARCH

Architecture
Tony Atkin, M.Arch., Adjunct Associate Professor. Cultural and architectural design.
Cecil Balmond, M.Sc., Paul Philippe Cret Practice Professor of Architecture. Structural engineering, design.
William Braham, Ph.D., Associate Professor and Interim Chair. Design and building systems, lighting, color.
Winka Dubbeldam, M.Arch., Practice Professor. Design practice.
Homa Farjadi, M.Arch., Practice Professor. Design practice.
Richard Farley, M.Arch., Adjunct Associate Professor. Structures, architecture practice.
Annette Fierro, M.Arch., Associate Professor. Construction technology, design.
Helene Furján, Ph.D., Assistant Professor. History and theory.
Gary A. Hack, Ph.D., Professor. Urban design and physical planning.
Mark Alan Hughes, Ph.D., Distinguished Senior Fellow. Urban policy and practice.
Stephen Kieran, M.Arch., Adjunct Professor. Building systems, design.
Simon Kim, M.Arch., Assistant Professor. Architecture, computation, interaction.
David Leatherbarrow, Ph.D., Professor and Chair, Graduate Group. History and theory of architecture.
Ali Malkawi, Ph.D., Professor. Energy systems and design.
Peter McCleary, D.I.C., Emeritus Professor. Philosophy and history of architectural technology.
Detlef Mertins, Ph.D., Professor. History and theory.
Enrique Norten, M.Arch., Practice Professor. Design.
Ali Rahim, M.Arch., Associate Professor. Design theory and digital media.
Witold Rybczynski, M.Arch., Meyerson Professor of Urbanism. Design history and theory.
Marilyn Jordan Taylor, M.Arch., Dean and Paley Professor. Urban design and planning.
James Timberlake, M.Arch., Adjunct Professor. Building systems, design.
Franca Trubiano, Ph.D., Assistant Professor. Construction technology, architectural ecologies.
Cathrine Veikos, M.Arch., Assistant Professor. Digital methods and design.
Marion Weiss, M.Arch., Professor. Design, drawing, urbanism.
Richard Wesley, M.Arch., Adjunct Associate Professor and Undergraduate Chair. Design, theory.
Yun Kyu Yi, Ph.D., Assistant Professor. Environmental design and building performance.

City and Regional Planning
Jonathan Barnett, M.Arch., Practice Professor of City and Regional Planning. Physical planning and urban design.
Eugenie L. Birch, Ph.D., Nussdorf Professor of Urban Research and Education and Chair, Graduate Group. History of planning, inner-city revitalization, international planning.
Thomas L. Daniels, Ph.D., Professor of Urban Research. Growth management, watershed protection, farmland preservation.
Gary A. Hack, Ph.D., Professor. Urban design and physical planning.
Amy Hillier, Ph.D., Assistant Professor. Geographic information systems.
Y. David Hsu, Ph.D., Assistant Professor. Urban infrastructure systems.
John Keene, M.C.P., Emeritus Professor. Environmental planning and law.
John Landis, Ph.D., Crossways Professor and Chair. Growth management, transportation and land use, planning history.
Michael Larice, Ph.D., Associate Professor. Community and regional planning.
Harris Steinberg, M.Arch., Adjunct Assistant Professor. Professional practice.
Marilyn Jordan Taylor, M.Arch., Dean and Paley Professor. Urban design and planning.
Domenic Vitiello, Ph.D., Assistant Professor. Urban studies.
Rachel Weinberger, Ph.D., Assistant Professor. Transportation and land use.
Laura Wolf-Powers, Ph.D., Assistant Professor. Community and economic development.
Robert Yaro, M.C.P., Practice Professor. Regional planning and growth strategies.

Fine Arts
Terry Adkins, M.F.A., M.S., Professor. Sculpture.
Sharka Brod Hyland, M.F.A., Adjunct Assistant Professor. Graphic design, digital imaging.
Joshua Mosley, M.F.A., Associate Professor and Interim Chair. Digital animation.
Matthew Ritchie, B.F.A., Distinguished Senior Fellow. Painting and installation.
Julie Schneider, M.F.A., Adjunct Associate Professor. Drawing and painting.
Jackie Tileston, M.F.A., Associate Professor. Painting.

Historic Preservation
David De Long, Ph.D., Emeritus Professor. Historic preservation, history and theory of architecture.
Michael Henry, M.S., Adjunct Professor. Building pathology and diagnostics.
Randall Mason, Ph.D., Associate Professor and Chair. Preservation planning, cultural policy, site management.
Frank Matero, M.S., Professor and Director, Architecture Conservation Laboratory. Building and conservation technology.
John Milner, B.Arch., Adjunct Professor. Restoration and adaptive reuse of historic buildings, design of new buildings.

Landscape Architecture and Regional Planning
James Corner, M.L.A., Professor and Chair. Landscape urbanism.
Raffaella Fabiani Giannetto, Ph.D., Assistant Professor. Landscape history and theory.
John Dixon Hunt, Ph.D., Professor Emeritus. Landscape history and theory.
Anuradha Mathur, M.L.A., Associate Professor. Landscape design and theory.
Karen M'Closkey, M.L.A., Assistant Professor. Landscape design and theory.
Cora Olgyay, M.L.A., Adjunct Assistant Professor. Landscape materials.
Laurie Olin, B.Arch., Practice Professor. Design practice.
Lucinda Sanders, M.L.A., Adjunct Associate Professor. Design practice.
C. Dana Tomlin, Ph.D., Professor. Geographic information systems.

Section 3
Art and Art History

This section contains a directory of institutions offering graduate work in art and art history, followed by in-depth entries submitted by institutions that chose to prepare detailed program descriptions. Additional information about programs listed in the directory but not augmented by an in-depth entry may be obtained by writing directly to the dean of a graduate school or chair of a department at the address given in the directory.

For programs offering related work, see also in this book *Applied Arts and Design; Architecture; Area and Cultural Studies; Film, Television, and Video; Performing Arts;* and *Sociology, Anthropology, and Archaeology.* In another guide in this series:

Graduate Programs in Business, Education, Health, Information Studies, Law & Social Work

See *Subject Areas (Art Education)*

CONTENTS

Program Directories

Art/Fine Arts 150
Art History 170
Arts Administration 180
Art Therapy 183
Decorative Arts 185
Museum Studies 186

Close-Ups

Bard Graduate Center: Decorative Arts, Design History, and Material Culture 191
George Mason University 193
Memphis College of Art 195
University of Rochester 197
The University of the Arts 199

See also:

Adler School of Professional Psychology—Psychology 1047
Art Center College of Design—Art and Design 113
Columbia University—Film, Theater Arts, Visual Arts, and Writing 261
Fashion Institute of Technology—Fashion and Textile Studies 115
Miami International University of Art & Design—Art and Design 117
Pratt Institute—Art and Design 119
University of Pennsylvania—Design 147

Art/Fine Arts

Academy of Art University, Graduate Program, School of Fine Art, San Francisco, CA 94105-3410. Offers figurative painting (MFA); non-figurative painting (MFA); printmaking (MFA); sculpture (MFA). *Accreditation:* NASAD. Part-time programs available. Postbaccalaureate distance learning degree programs offered (no on-campus study). *Degree requirements:* For master's, final review. *Entrance requirements:* For master's, minimum GPA of 3.0, portfolio. Electronic applications accepted.

Adams State College, The Graduate School, Department of Art, Alamosa, CO 81102. Offers MA. Part-time programs available. *Degree requirements:* For master's, thesis, departmental qualifying exam. *Entrance requirements:* For master's, GRE General Test or MAT, minimum undergraduate GPA of 2.75.

Adelphi University, Graduate School of Arts and Sciences, Department of Art and Art History, Garden City, NY 11530-0701. Offers MA. Part-time programs available. *Students:* 15 part-time (12 women), 3 international. Average age 38. In 2009, 8 master's awarded. *Degree requirements:* For master's, art exhibit. *Entrance requirements:* For master's, portfolio, 2 letters of recommendation. Additional exam requirements/recommendations for international students: Required—TOEFL (minimum score 550 paper-based; 213 computer-based; 80 iBT). *Application deadline:* For fall admission, 5/1 for international students; for spring admission, 12/1 for international students. Applications are processed on a rolling basis. Application fee: $50. Electronic applications accepted. *Expenses:* Tuition: Full-time $28,340; part-time $830 per credit. Required fees: $600; $250 per credit. Full-time tuition and fees vary according to course load and program. *Financial support:* Research assistantships with full and partial tuition reimbursements, career-related internships or fieldwork, Federal Work-Study, institutionally sponsored loans, and unspecified assistantships available. Financial award application deadline: 2/15; financial award applicants required to submit FAFSA. *Unit head:* David Hornung, Chairperson, 516-877-4458, E-mail: hornung@adelphi.edu. *Application contact:* Christine Murphy, Director of Admissions, 516-877-3050, Fax: 516-877-3039, E-mail: graduateadmissions@adelphi.edu.

Alfred University, Graduate School, New York State College of Ceramics, School of Art and Design, Alfred, NY 14802-1205. Offers ceramic art (MFA); electronic integrated arts (MFA); glass art (MFA); sculpture (MFA). *Accreditation:* NASAD. *Degree requirements:* For master's, exhibit. *Entrance requirements:* For master's, portfolio. Additional exam requirements/recommendations for international students: Required—TOEFL (minimum score 550 paper-based; 213 computer-based; 80 iBT), IELTS (minimum score 6). Electronic applications accepted. *Expenses:* Tuition: Full-time $33,296; part-time $708 per credit hour. Required fees: $880; $144 per year. Full-time tuition and fees vary according to program. *Faculty research:* Ceramic sculpture, functional ceramics, wood, mixed media, hot and cold glass.

Alfred University, Graduate School, New York State College of Ceramics, School of Engineering, Alfred, NY 14802-1205. Offers biomedical materials engineering science (MS); ceramic engineering (MS); ceramics (PhD); electrical engineering (MS); glass science (MS, PhD); materials science and engineering (MS, PhD); mechanical engineering (MS). *Degree requirements:* For master's, thesis; for doctorate, thesis/dissertation. *Entrance requirements:* Additional exam requirements/recommendations for international students: Required—TOEFL (minimum score 590 paper-based; 243 computer-based). Electronic applications accepted. *Expenses:* Contact institution. *Faculty research:* Fine-particle technology, x-ray diffraction, superconductivity, electronic materials.

American University, College of Arts and Sciences, Department of Art, Programs in Painting, Sculpture and Printmaking, Washington, DC 20016-8004. Offers MFA. *Students:* 20 full-time (15 women), 1 (woman) part-time; includes 2 minority (1 Asian American or Pacific Islander, 1 Hispanic American), 1 international. Average age 29. 53 applicants, 42% accepted, 10 enrolled. In 2009, 9 master's awarded. *Degree requirements:* For master's, comprehensive exam, thesis. *Entrance requirements:* For master's, GRE, portfolio. *Application deadline:* For fall admission, 1/15 priority date for domestic students. Application fee: $80. *Expenses:* Tuition: Full-time $22,266; part-time $1237 per credit hour. Required fees: $430. Tuition and fees vary according to program. *Financial support:* Teaching assistantships with tuition reimbursements, career-related internships or fieldwork, Federal Work-Study, and institutionally sponsored loans available. Support available to part-time students. Financial award application deadline: 1/15. *Faculty research:* Drawing. *Unit head:* Luis Silva, Chair, 202-885-1682, Fax: 202-885-1132. *Application contact:* Glenna K. Haynie, Administrative Coordinator, 202-885-1671.

Anna Maria College, Graduate Division, Program in Education, Paxton, MA 01612. Offers early childhood education (M Ed); education (CAGS); elementary education (M Ed); English language arts (M Ed); visual arts (M Ed). Part-time and evening/weekend programs available. *Entrance requirements:* For master's, bachelor's degree in liberal arts or sciences, minimum GPA of 3.0. Additional exam requirements/recommendations for international students: Required—TOEFL (minimum score 500 paper-based). Electronic applications accepted.

Anna Maria College, Graduate Division, Program in Visual Arts, Paxton, MA 01612. Offers art and visual art (MA); teacher of visual art (M Ed). Part-time and evening/weekend programs available. *Degree requirements:* For master's, thesis. *Entrance requirements:* For master's, minimum GPA of 2.7, undergraduate major in art, portfolio. Additional exam requirements/recommendations for international students: Required—TOEFL (minimum score 500 paper-based). Electronic applications accepted.

Antioch University Midwest, Graduate Programs, Individualized Liberal and Professional Studies Program, Yellow Springs, OH 45387-1609. Offers liberal and professional studies (MA), including counseling, creative writing, education, film studies, liberal studies, management, modern literature, psychology, theatre, visual arts. Part-time and evening/weekend programs available. Postbaccalaureate distance learning degree programs offered (minimal on-campus study). *Faculty:* 1 full-time (0 women), 2 part-time/adjunct (1 woman). *Students:* 23 full-time (13 women), 41 part-time (30 women); includes 13 minority (11 African Americans, 2 Hispanic Americans). Average age 40. 21 applicants, 76% accepted, 15 enrolled. In 2009, 24 master's awarded. *Degree requirements:* For master's, thesis or alternative. *Entrance requirements:* For master's, resume, 2 letters of reference. *Application deadline:* For fall admission, 8/1 for domestic students; for winter admission, 12/1 for domestic students; for spring admission, 3/10 for domestic students. Applications are processed on a rolling basis. Application fee: $50. Electronic applications accepted. *Expenses:* Contact institution. *Financial support:* Federal Work-Study available. Financial award applicants required to submit FAFSA. *Unit head:* Dr. Jon Saari, Chair, 937-769-1879, Fax: 937-769-1807, E-mail: jsaari@antioch.edu. *Application contact:* Seth Gordon, Assistant Director of Admissions, 937-769-1800 Ext. 1825, Fax: 937-769-1804, E-mail: sgordon@antioch.edu.

Arizona State University, Graduate College, Herberger College of the Arts, School of Art, Tempe, AZ 85287. Offers MA, MFA, PhD.

Arkansas State University—Jonesboro, Graduate School, College of Fine Arts, Department of Art, Jonesboro, State University, AR 72467. Offers MA. *Accreditation:* NASAD. Part-time programs available. *Faculty:* 9 full-time (4 women). *Students:* 2 full-time (1 woman), 3 part-time (2 women). Average age 39. 2 applicants, 50% accepted, 1 enrolled. In 2009, 3 master's awarded. *Degree requirements:* For master's, comprehensive exam, thesis. *Entrance requirements:* For master's, GRE General Test or MAT, portfolio, appropriate bachelor's degree, letters of reference, writing sample. Additional exam requirements/recommendations for international students: Required—TOEFL (minimum score 550 paper-based; 213 computer-based; 79 iBT), IELTS (minimum score 6). *Application deadline:* Applications are processed on a rolling basis. Application fee: $30 ($40 for international students). Electronic applications accepted. *Expenses:* Tuition, state resident: full-time $3744; part-time $208 per credit hour. Tuition, nonresident: full-time $9540; part-time $530 per credit hour. Required fees: $896; $47 per credit hour. $25 per term. One-time fee: $50. Tuition and fees vary according to course load and program. *Financial support:* In 2009–10, 3 students received support; teaching assistantships, career-related internships or fieldwork, scholarships/grants, and unspecified assistantships available. Financial award application deadline: 7/1; financial award applicants required to submit FAFSA. *Unit head:* Curtis Steele, Chair, 870-972-3050, Fax: 870-972-3932, E-mail: csteele@astate.edu. *Application contact:* Dr. Andrew Sustich, Dean of the Graduate School, 870-972-3029, Fax: 870-972-3857, E-mail: sustich@astate.edu.

Arkansas Tech University, Graduate College, College of Arts and Humanities, Russellville, AR 72801. Offers communication (MLA); English (M Ed, MA); fine arts (MLA); history (MA); multi-media journalism (MA); psychology (MS); social science (MLA); Spanish (MA, MLA); teaching English as a second language (MA, MLA). Part-time programs available. *Students:* 39 full-time (30 women), 80 part-time (63 women); includes 11 minority (3 African Americans, 1 American Indian/Alaska Native, 1 Asian American or Pacific Islander, 6 Hispanic Americans), 23 international. Average age 33. In 2009, 70 master's awarded. *Degree requirements:* For master's, comprehensive exam (for some programs), thesis (for some programs), project. *Entrance requirements:* For master's, GRE General Test or MAT. Additional exam requirements/recommendations for international students: Required—TOEFL (minimum score 550 paper-based; 213 computer-based; 79 iBT), IELTS (minimum score 6). *Application deadline:* For fall admission, 3/1 priority date for domestic students, 5/1 priority date for international students; for spring admission, 10/1 priority date for domestic and international students. Applications are processed on a rolling basis. Application fee: $0 ($50 for international students). Electronic applications accepted. *Expenses:* Tuition, state resident: full-time $3438; part-time $191 per hour. Tuition, nonresident: full-time $6876; part-time $382 per hour. Required fees: $482; $9 per credit hour. $140 per semester. Tuition and fees vary according to course load. *Financial support:* In 2009–10, teaching assistantships with full tuition reimbursements (averaging $4,000 per year); research assistantships, career-related internships or fieldwork, Federal Work-Study, scholarships/grants, health care benefits, and unspecified assistantships also available. Support available to part-time students. Financial award application deadline: 4/15; financial award applicants required to submit FAFSA. *Unit head:* Dr. Micheal Tarver, Dean, 479-968-0274, Fax: 479-964-0812, E-mail: mtarver@atu.edu. *Application contact:* Dr. Mary B. Gunter, Dean of Graduate College, 479-968-0398, Fax: 479-964-0542, E-mail: graduate.school@atu.edu.

Art Center College of Design, Graduate Division, Fine Arts Department, Pasadena, CA 91103. Offers MFA. *Accreditation:* NASAD. *Faculty:* 7 full-time (4 women), 19 part-time/adjunct (9 women). *Students:* 33 full-time (17 women), 2 part-time (1 woman); includes 6 minority (3 American Indian/Alaska Native, 3 Asian Americans or Pacific Islanders), 5 international. Average age 27. 42 applicants, 45% accepted, 7 enrolled. In 2009, 5 master's awarded. *Degree requirements:* For master's, thesis, studio project. *Entrance requirements:* For master's, portfolio. Additional exam requirements/recommendations for international students: Required—TOEFL (minimum score 600 paper-based; 250 computer-based; 100 iBT). *Application deadline:* For fall admission, 3/1 priority date for domestic students; for winter admission, 9/15 priority date for domestic students. Applications are processed on a rolling basis. Application fee: $50 ($70 for international students). *Expenses:* Tuition: Full-time $16,737. *Financial support:* Teaching assistantships, career-related internships or fieldwork, Federal Work-Study, and scholarships/grants available. Financial award application deadline: 3/1. *Unit head:* Dr. Jeremy Gilbert-Rolfe, Chair, 626-584-8424. *Application contact:* Seb Bailey, 626-396-4222.

See Close-Up on page 113.

The Art Institute of Boston at Lesley University, Program in Visual Arts, Boston, MA 02215-2598. Offers MFA. *Accreditation:* NASAD.

The Art Institute of California–San Francisco, Master of Fine Arts Program, San Francisco, CA 94102. Offers computer animation (MFA).

Azusa Pacific University, College of Liberal Arts and Sciences, Program in Fine Arts in Visual Art, Azusa, CA 91702-7000. Offers MFA. *Accreditation:* NASAD.

Ball State University, Graduate School, College of Fine Arts, Department of Art, Muncie, IN 47306-1099. Offers art (MA); art education (MA, MAE). *Accreditation:* NASAD.

Bard College, Milton Avery Graduate School of the Arts, Annandale-on-Hudson, NY 12504. Offers MFA. *Degree requirements:* For master's, thesis, project, 8-week summer residency, independent study. *Entrance requirements:* For master's, interview, portfolio, 2 letters of recommendation, history of work in the arts. Additional exam requirements/recommendations for international students: Required—TOEFL (minimum score 550 paper-based; 213 computer-based). Electronic applications accepted. *Faculty research:* Original work in painting, writing, sculpture, photography, video/film, sound/music.

Barry University, School of Arts and Sciences, Department of Fine Arts, Miami Shores, FL 33161-6695. Offers photography (MA, MFA). *Degree requirements:* For master's, thesis (for some programs). *Entrance requirements:* For master's, GRE General Test, minimum GPA of 3.0. Electronic applications accepted. *Faculty research:* Inclusion education, exceptional education, art-based assessments.

Bob Jones University, Graduate Programs, Greenville, SC 29614. Offers accountancy (MS); Bible (MA); Bible translation (MA); Biblical studies (Certificate); broadcast management (MS); business administration (MBA); church history (MA, PhD); church ministries (MA); church music (MM); cinema and video production (MA); counseling (MS); curriculum and instruction (Ed D); divinity (M Div); dramatic production (MA); educational leadership (MS, Ed D, Ed S); elementary education (M Ed, MAT); English (M Ed, MA, MAT); fine arts (MA); graphic design (MA); history (M Ed, MA); illustration (MA); interpretative speech (MA); mathematics (M Ed, MAT); medical missions (Certificate); ministry (MM, D Min); multi-categorical special education (M Ed, MAT); music (M Ed); New Testament interpretation (PhD); Old Testament interpretation (PhD); orchestral instrument performance (MM); organ performance (MM); pastoral studies (MA); personnel services (MS, Ed S); piano pedagogy (MM); piano performance (MM); platform arts (MA); radio and television broadcasting (MS); rhetoric and public address (MA); secondary education (M Ed); studio art (MA); teaching Bible (MA); theology (MA, PhD); voice performance (MM); youth ministries (MA); M Div/MM.

Boise State University, Graduate College, College of Arts and Sciences, Department of Art, Program in Visual Arts, Boise, ID 83725-0399. Offers MFA. *Accreditation:* NASAD. Part-time programs available. *Degree requirements:* For master's, thesis. *Entrance requirements:* For master's, minimum GPA of 3.0, portfolio. Additional exam requirements/recommendations for international students: Required—TOEFL (minimum score 587 paper-based; 240 computer-based). Electronic applications accepted. *Expenses:* Tuition, state resident: full-time $3106; part-time $209 per credit. Tuition, nonresident: part-time $284 per credit.

Boston University, College of Fine Arts, School of Visual Arts, Boston, MA 02215. Offers art education (MA); graphic design (MFA); painting (MFA); sculpture (MFA); studio teaching (MA). *Faculty:* 17 full-time, 4 part-time/adjunct. *Students:* 28 full-time (20 women), 1 (woman) part-time; includes 8 minority (2 Asian Americans or Pacific Islanders, 6 Hispanic Americans), 1 international. Average age 28. 281 applicants, 28% accepted. In 2009, 38 master's awarded. *Entrance requirements:* For master's, portfolio. Additional exam requirements/recommendations for international students: Required—TOEFL. *Application deadline:* For fall admission, 2/15 for domestic and international students. Applications are processed on a rolling basis. Application fee: $70. *Expenses:* Tuition: Full-time $37,910; part-time $1184 per credit hour. Required fees: $386; $40 per semester. Part-time tuition and fees vary according to class time, course level, degree level and program. *Financial support:* Fellowships, teaching assistantships available.

Financial award application deadline: 2/15. *Unit head:* Lynne Allen, Director, 617-353-3371. *Application contact:* Mark Krone, Manager, Graduate Admissions, 617-353-3350, E-mail: arts@bu.edu.

Bowling Green State University, Graduate College, College of Arts and Sciences, School of Art, Bowling Green, OH 43403. Offers 2-D studio art (MA, MFA); 3-D studio art (MA, MFA); art education (MA); art history (MA); computer art (MA); design (MFA); digital arts (MFA); graphics (MFA). *Accreditation:* NASAD. Part-time programs available. *Degree requirements:* For master's, thesis or alternative, final exhibit (MFA). *Entrance requirements:* For master's, GRE General Test (MA), slide portfolio (15-20 slides). Additional exam requirements/recommendations for international students: Required—TOEFL. Electronic applications accepted. *Faculty research:* Computer animation and virtual reality, Spanish still-life painting from 1600 to 1800, art and psychotherapy, Japanese wood-firing techniques in ceramics, non-toxic printmaking technologies.

Bradley University, Graduate School, Slane College of Communications and Fine Arts, Department of Art, Peoria, IL 61625-0002. Offers ceramics (MA, MFA); drawing/illustration (MA, MFA); interdisciplinary art (MA, MFA); painting (MA, MFA); photography (MA, MFA); printmaking (MA, MFA); sculpture (MA, MFA); visual communication and design (MA, MFA). *Accreditation:* NASAD. Part-time programs available. *Degree requirements:* For master's, comprehensive exam, thesis, final exhibit. *Entrance requirements:* For master's, portfolio, 2 letters of recommendation. Additional exam requirements/recommendations for international students: Required—TOEFL (minimum score 550 paper-based; 213 computer-based; 79 iBT).

Brandeis University, Graduate School of Arts and Sciences, Program in Studio Art, Waltham, MA 02454-9110. Offers Certificate. *Faculty:* 13 full-time (5 women), 2 part-time/adjunct (both women). *Students:* 14 full-time (7 women); includes 1 minority (Hispanic American). 22 applicants, 100% accepted, 10 enrolled. In 2009, 4 Certificates awarded. *Degree requirements:* For Certificate, thesis, exhibit of work. *Entrance requirements:* For degree, resume, sample of work, studio work, letters of recommendation. Additional exam requirements/recommendations for international students: Required—TOEFL (minimum score 600 paper-based; 250 computer-based; 100 iBT); Recommended—IELTS (minimum score 7). *Application deadline:* Applications are processed on a rolling basis. Application fee: $75. Electronic applications accepted. *Expenses:* Contact institution. *Financial support:* In 2009–10, 14 teaching assistantships with partial tuition reimbursements were awarded; scholarships/grants and tuition waivers (partial) also available. Financial award application deadline: 4/15; financial award applicants required to submit FAFSA. *Faculty research:* Painting, sculpture, three-dimensional design, printmaking, drawing. *Unit head:* Sean Downey, Faculty Coordinator, 781-736-2660, Fax: 781-736-2672, E-mail: sdowney@brandeis.edu. *Application contact:* Joy Vlachos, Department Administrator, 781-736-2655, Fax: 781-736-2672, E-mail: vlachos@brandeis.edu.

Brigham Young University, Graduate Studies, College of Fine Arts and Communications, Department of Visual Arts, Provo, UT 84602-6414. Offers art education (MA); art history (MA); studio art (MFA). Art education applications accepted biennially. *Accreditation:* NASAD. *Faculty:* 24 full-time (7 women), 2 part-time/adjunct (1 woman). *Students:* 33 full-time (22 women); includes 4 minority (all Asian Americans or Pacific Islanders). Average age 26. 32 applicants, 38% accepted, 11 enrolled. In 2009, 9 master's awarded. *Degree requirements:* For master's, one foreign language, thesis (art history), selected project (MFA), curriculum project (art education). *Entrance requirements:* For master's, GRE (art history), minimum GPA of 3.0 (MFA, MA in art education), 3.3 (MA in art history), portfolio in slide form (MFA), writing samples (MA in art education, art history). Additional exam requirements/recommendations for international students: Required—TOEFL (minimum score 500 paper-based). *Application deadline:* For fall admission, 2/1 for domestic and international students. Application fee: $50. Electronic applications accepted. *Expenses:* Tuition: Full-time $5580; part-time $301 per credit hour. Tuition and fees vary according to student's religious affiliation. *Financial support:* In 2009–10, 27 students received support; research assistantships, teaching assistantships with partial tuition reimbursements available, scholarships/grants and tuition waivers (partial) available. Financial award application deadline: 2/1. *Faculty research:* Methodology-standards-assessment, medieval architecture, classical/Islamic eighteenth and nineteenth century art, Netherlandish art, contemporary art. Total annual research expenditures: $83,932. *Unit head:* Prof. Linda A. Reynolds, Chair, 801-422-4429, Fax: 801-422-0695, E-mail: sullivan@byu.edu. *Application contact:* Sharon Lyn Heelis, Secretary, 801-422-4429, Fax: 801-422-0695, E-mail: sharon_heelis@byu.edu.

Brooklyn College of the City University of New York, Division of Graduate Studies, Department of Art, Brooklyn, NY 11210-2889. Offers art history (MA, PhD); digital art (MFA); drawing and painting (MFA); photography (MFA); printmaking (MFA); sculpture (MFA). Part-time programs available. *Students:* 27 full-time (14 women), 20 part-time (15 women); includes 11 minority (2 African Americans, 3 Asian Americans or Pacific Islanders, 6 Hispanic Americans), 2 international. Average age 30. 123 applicants, 49% accepted, 26 enrolled. In 2009, 14 master's awarded. *Degree requirements:* For master's, thesis. *Entrance requirements:* For master's, bachelor's degree in art, portfolio, 2 letters of recommendation. Additional exam requirements/recommendations for international students: Required—TOEFL (minimum score 500 paper-based; 173 computer-based; 61 iBT). *Application deadline:* For fall admission, 2/1 priority date for domestic students, 2/1 for international students. Applications are processed on a rolling basis. Application fee: $125. Electronic applications accepted. *Expenses:* Tuition, area resident: Full-time $7360; part-time $310 per credit hour. Tuition, state resident: full-time $7360; part-time $310 per credit hour. Tuition, nonresident: full-time $13,800; part-time $575 per credit hour. International tuition: $13,800 full-time. Required fees: $140.10 per semester. *Financial support:* Career-related internships or fieldwork, Federal Work-Study, institutionally sponsored loans, scholarships/grants, and painting awards available. Support available to part-time students. Financial award application deadline: 5/1; financial award applicants required to submit FAFSA. *Unit head:* Dr. Michael Mallory, Chairperson, 718-951-5181, E-mail: mmallory@brooklyn.cuny.edu. *Application contact:* Hernan Sierra, Graduate Admissions Coordinator, 718-951-4536, Fax: 718-951-4506, E-mail: grads@brooklyn.cuny.edu.

California College of the Arts, Graduate Programs, Program in Visual and Critical Studies, San Francisco, CA 94107. Offers MA. *Degree requirements:* For master's, thesis, exhibit. *Entrance requirements:* For master's, appropriate bachelor's degree, portfolio. Additional exam requirements/recommendations for international students: Required—TOEFL (minimum score 600 paper-based; 250 computer-based). Electronic applications accepted.

California College of the Arts, Graduate Programs, Programs in Fine Art, San Francisco, CA 94107. Offers ceramics (MFA); film/video/performance (MFA); glass (MFA); jewelry/metal arts (MFA); painting/drawing (MFA); photography (MFA); printmaking (MFA); sculpture (MFA); textiles (MFA); wood/furniture (MFA). *Accreditation:* NASAD. *Degree requirements:* For master's, thesis, exhibit. *Entrance requirements:* For master's, appropriate bachelor's degree, portfolio. Additional exam requirements/recommendations for international students: Required—TOEFL (minimum score 600 paper-based; 250 computer-based). Electronic applications accepted.

California Institute of the Arts, School of Art, Valencia, CA 91355-2340. Offers art (MFA, Adv C); graphic design (MFA, Adv C); photography (MFA, Adv C). *Accreditation:* NASAD (one or more programs are accredited). *Degree requirements:* For master's, final project. *Entrance requirements:* For master's, portfolio. Additional exam requirements/recommendations for international students: Required—TOEFL. Electronic applications accepted.

California State University, Chico, Graduate School, College of Humanities and Fine Arts, Department of Art and Art History, Program in Fine Arts, Chico, CA 95929-0722. Offers MFA. *Accreditation:* NASAD. *Students:* 15 full-time (9 women), 1 (woman) part-time; includes 3 minority (all Hispanic Americans). Average age 34. 24 applicants, 33% accepted, 4 enrolled. In 2009, 2 master's awarded. *Degree requirements:* For master's, thesis or alternative. *Entrance requirements:* For master's, 2 letters of recommendation. Additional exam requirements/recommendations for international students: Required—TOEFL (minimum score 550 paper-based; 213 computer-based; 80 iBT), IELTS (minimum score 6.5). *Application deadline:* For fall admission, 3/1 priority date for domestic students, 3/1 for international students; for spring admission, 9/15 priority date for domestic students, 9/15 for international students. Applications are processed on a rolling basis. Application fee: $55. Electronic applications accepted. *Unit head:* Dr. Cameron Crawford, Graduate Coordinator, 530-898-6860. *Application contact:* Dr. Cameron Crawford, Graduate Coordinator, 530-898-6860.

California State University, Fresno, Division of Graduate Studies, College of Arts and Humanities, Department of Art and Design, Fresno, CA 93740-8027. Offers art (MA). Part-time and evening/weekend programs available. *Degree requirements:* For master's, thesis or alternative. *Entrance requirements:* For master's, GRE General Test, minimum GPA of 3.0, portfolio. Additional exam requirements/recommendations for international students: Required—TOEFL. Electronic applications accepted. *Faculty research:* Art history, graphic design, studio art.

California State University, Fullerton, Graduate Studies, College of the Arts, Department of Art, Fullerton, CA 92834-9480. Offers art (MA, MFA), including ceramics (MFA), crafts, creative photography (MFA), design (MFA), drawing and painting, printmaking (MFA), sculpture; art history (MA); design (MA). *Accreditation:* NASAD (one or more programs are accredited). Part-time programs available. *Students:* 47 full-time (29 women), 38 part-time (23 women); includes 24 minority (2 African Americans, 12 Asian Americans or Pacific Islanders, 10 Hispanic Americans), 10 international. Average age 34. 76 applicants, 28% accepted, 19 enrolled. In 2009, 20 master's awarded. *Degree requirements:* For master's, project or thesis. *Entrance requirements:* For master's, minimum GPA of 2.5 in last 60 units of course work, portfolio. Application fee: $55. *Expenses:* Tuition, nonresident: full-time $11,160; part-time $373 per credit. Required fees: $1440 per term. Tuition and fees vary according to course load, degree level and program. *Financial support:* Career-related internships or fieldwork, Federal Work-Study, institutionally sponsored loans, and scholarships/grants available. Support available to part-time students. Financial award application deadline: 3/1; financial award applicants required to submit FAFSA. *Unit head:* Larry Johnson, Chair, 657-278-3471. *Application contact:* Admissions/Applications, 657-278-2371.

California State University, Long Beach, Graduate Studies, College of the Arts, Department of Art, Long Beach, CA 90840. Offers art education (MA); art history (MA); studio art (MA, MFA). *Accreditation:* NASAD. Part-time programs available. *Faculty:* 81 full-time (49 women), 1 (woman) part-time/adjunct. *Students:* 84 full-time (54 women), 44 part-time (31 women); includes 35 minority (2 American Indian/Alaska Native, 16 Asian Americans or Pacific Islanders, 17 Hispanic Americans), 5 international. Average age 34. 183 applicants, 37% accepted, 43 enrolled. *Degree requirements:* For master's, thesis (for some programs). *Entrance requirements:* For master's, minimum GPA of 3.0 in last 60 hours. *Application deadline:* For fall admission, 7/1 for domestic students; for spring admission, 12/1 for domestic students. Applications are processed on a rolling basis. Application fee: $55. Electronic applications accepted. *Expenses:* Required fees: $1802 per semester. Part-time tuition and fees vary according to course load. *Financial support:* Federal Work-Study, institutionally sponsored loans, and scholarships/grants available. Financial award application deadline: 3/2. *Unit head:* Prof. David Hadlock, Chair, 562-985-7908, Fax: 562-985-1650, E-mail: dhadlock@csulb.edu. *Application contact:* Margaret Black, Graduate Advisor, 562-985-7910, Fax: 562-985-1650.

California State University, Los Angeles, Graduate Studies, College of Arts and Letters, Department of Art, Los Angeles, CA 90032-8530. Offers art (MA), including art education, art history, art therapy, ceramics, metals, and textiles, design (MA, MFA), painting, sculpture, and graphic arts, photography; fine arts (MFA), including crafts, design (MA, MFA), studio arts. *Accreditation:* NASAD (one or more programs are accredited). Part-time and evening/weekend programs available. *Faculty:* 12 full-time (6 women), 1 part-time/adjunct (0 women). *Students:* 28 full-time (21 women), 40 part-time (28 women); includes 22 minority (1 African American, 6 Asian Americans or Pacific Islanders, 15 Hispanic Americans), 9 international. Average age 37. 30 applicants, 100% accepted, 12 enrolled. In 2009, 17 master's awarded. *Degree requirements:* For master's, comprehensive exam, project or thesis. *Entrance requirements:* For master's, portfolio. Additional exam requirements/recommendations for international students: Required—TOEFL (minimum score 500 paper-based; 173 computer-based). *Application deadline:* For fall admission, 5/1 for domestic and international students. Applications are processed on a rolling basis. Application fee: $55. Electronic applications accepted. *Financial support:* Federal Work-Study available. Support available to part-time students. Financial award application deadline: 3/1. *Faculty research:* The artist and the book, conceptual art, ceramic processes, computer graphics, architectural graphics. *Unit head:* Dr. Abbas Daneshvari, Chair, 323-343-4010, Fax: 323-343-4045, E-mail: adanesh@calstatela.edu. *Application contact:* Dr. Cheryl L. Ney, Associate Vice President for Academic Affairs and Dean of Graduate Studies, 323-343-3820, Fax: 323-343-5653, E-mail: cney@cslanet.calstatela.edu.

California State University, Northridge, Graduate Studies, College of Arts, Media, and Communication, Department of Art, Northridge, CA 91330. Offers art education (MA); art history (MA); studio art (MA, MFA); visual communications (MA, MFA). *Accreditation:* NASAD. *Faculty:* 22 full-time (12 women), 42 part-time/adjunct (16 women). *Students:* 27 full-time (21 women), 29 part-time (23 women); includes 14 minority (2 African Americans, 1 American Indian/Alaska Native, 6 Asian Americans or Pacific Islanders, 5 Hispanic Americans), 3 international. Average age 35. 84 applicants, 29% accepted, 14 enrolled. In 2009, 29 master's awarded. *Application deadline:* For fall admission, 11/30 for domestic students. Application fee: $55. *Financial support:* Application deadline: 3/1. *Unit head:* Prof. Edward Alfano, Chair, 818-677-2242, E-mail: art.dept@csun.edu. *Application contact:* Prof. Edward Alfano, Chair, 818-677-2242, E-mail: art.dept@csun.edu.

California State University, Sacramento, Graduate Studies, College of Arts and Letters, Department of Art, Sacramento, CA 95819. Offers studio art (MA). *Accreditation:* NASAD. Part-time programs available. *Degree requirements:* For master's, thesis or alternative, departmental qualifying exam, writing proficiency exam. *Entrance requirements:* For master's, minimum GPA of 3.0 during previous 2 years. Additional exam requirements/recommendations for international students: Required—TOEFL. Electronic applications accepted.

California State University, San Bernardino, Graduate Studies, College of Arts and Letters, Department of Art, San Bernardino, CA 92407-2397. Offers art (MA); art/graphics (MA). *Accreditation:* NASAD. *Faculty:* 4 full-time (1 woman). *Students:* 10 full-time (3 women), 10 part-time (7 women); includes 10 minority (2 African Americans, 8 Hispanic Americans), 1 international. Average age 39. 23 applicants, 65% accepted, 4 enrolled. *Entrance requirements:* Additional exam requirements/recommendations for international students: Required—TOEFL. *Application deadline:* For fall admission, 8/31 priority date for domestic students. Application fee: $55. *Unit head:* Dr. Sant Khalsa, Chair/Professor, 909-537-5808, Fax: 909-537-7068, E-mail: santk@csusb.edu. *Application contact:* Olivia Rosas, Director of Admissions, 909-537-7577, Fax: 909-537-7034, E-mail: orosas@csusb.edu.

California State University, Stanislaus, College of the Arts, Department of Art, Turlock, CA 95382. Offers printmaking (Certificate). *Accreditation:* NASAD. Part-time programs available. *Degree requirements:* For Certificate, portfolio submission, exhibition participation. *Entrance requirements:* For degree, BA in arts, minimum GPA of 2.50, portfolio evaluation, 3 letters of reference. Electronic applications accepted.

Carnegie Mellon University, College of Fine Arts, School of Art, Pittsburgh, PA 15213-3891. Offers MFA. *Accreditation:* NASAD. *Degree requirements:* For master's, thesis, exhibit. *Entrance requirements:* For master's, portfolio. Additional exam requirements/recommendations for international students: Required—TOEFL.

Central Washington University, Graduate Studies and Research, College of Arts and Humanities, Department of Art, Ellensburg, WA 98926. Offers MA, MFA. *Faculty:* 8 full-time (4 women). *Students:* 3 full-time (2 women). 4 applicants, 75% accepted, 3 enrolled. In 2009, 3 master's awarded. *Degree requirements:* For master's, thesis or alternative. *Entrance requirements:* For master's, minimum GPA of 3.0, portfolio. Additional exam requirements/recommendations for international students: Required—TOEFL (minimum score 550 paper-

Art/Fine Arts

Central Washington University (continued)

based; 213 computer-based; 79 iBT). *Application deadline:* For fall admission, 2/1 for domestic students; for winter admission, 10/1 for domestic students; for spring admission, 1/1 for domestic students. Applications are processed on a rolling basis. Application fee: $50. Electronic applications accepted. *Expenses:* Tuition, state resident: full-time $7353; part-time $245 per credit. Tuition, nonresident: full-time $16,383; part-time $546 per credit. Required fees: $882. Tuition and fees vary according to degree level. *Financial support:* In 2009–10, 1 research assistantship with full and partial tuition reimbursement (averaging $9,145 per year), 2 teaching assistantships with full and partial tuition reimbursements (averaging $9,145 per year) were awarded; Federal Work-Study, health care benefits, and unspecified assistantships also available. Financial award application deadline: 3/1; financial award applicants required to submit FAFSA. *Unit head:* Dr. Liahna Armstrong, Interim Chair, 509-963-2665, Fax: 209-963-1918. *Application contact:* Justine Eason, Admissions Program Coordinator, 509-963-3103, Fax: 509-963-1799, E-mail: masters@cwu.edu.

City College of the City University of New York, Graduate School, College of Liberal Arts and Science, Division of the Humanities and Arts, Department of Art, Program in Fine Arts, New York, NY 10031-9198. Offers advertising design (MFA); ceramic design (MFA); painting (MFA); printmaking (MFA); sculpture (MFA); wood and metal design (MFA). *Degree requirements:* For master's, thesis exhibit. *Entrance requirements:* For master's, 20 slide portfolio. Additional exam requirements/recommendations for international students: Required—TOEFL (minimum score 577 paper-based; 90 iBT). Electronic applications accepted.

Claremont Graduate University, Graduate Programs, School of Arts and Humanities, Department of Art, Claremont, CA 91711. Offers digital media (MA, MFA); drawing (MA, MFA); installation (MA, MFA); new genre (MA, MFA); painting (MA, MFA); performance (MA, MFA); photography (MA, MFA); sculpture (MA, MFA). Part-time programs available. *Faculty:* 4 full-time (1 woman). *Students:* 61 full-time (32 women), 1 part-time (0 women); includes 14 minority (1 African American, 6 Asian Americans or Pacific Islanders, 7 Hispanic Americans), 4 international. Average age 33. In 2009, 33 master's awarded. *Degree requirements:* For master's, final project show. *Entrance requirements:* For master's, BA in art or BFA, slide review. Additional exam requirements/recommendations for international students: Required—TOEFL (minimum score 550 paper-based; 213 computer-based; 80 iBT). *Application deadline:* For fall admission, 2/1 priority date for domestic students. Applications are processed on a rolling basis. Application fee: $60. Electronic applications accepted. *Expenses:* Contact institution. *Financial support:* Fellowships, research assistantships, teaching assistantships, Federal Work-Study, institutionally sponsored loans, and scholarships/grants available. Support available to part-time students. Financial award application deadline: 2/15; financial award applicants required to submit FAFSA. *Faculty research:* Acoustic sculpture, feminization of abstraction, installation sculpture. *Unit head:* David Pagel, Chair, 909-607-2479, Fax: 909-607-1276, E-mail: david.pagel@cgu.edu. *Application contact:* Pat Evans, Program Administrator, 909-607-9292, Fax: 909-607-1276, E-mail: patricia.evans@cgu.edu.

Clemson University, Graduate School, College of Architecture, Arts, and Humanities, Department of Art, Program in Visual Arts, Clemson, SC 29634. Offers MFA. *Accreditation:* NASAD. *Students:* 20 full-time (7 women); includes 1 minority (Hispanic American). Average age 30. 43 applicants, 19% accepted, 6 enrolled. In 2009, 5 master's awarded. *Entrance requirements:* For master's, GRE General Test, portfolio. Additional exam requirements/recommendations for international students: Required—TOEFL. *Application deadline:* For fall admission, 3/15 for domestic students, 4/15 for international students; for spring admission, 9/15 for international students. Application fee: $70 ($80 for international students). Electronic applications accepted. *Expenses:* Tuition, state resident: full-time $8684; part-time $528 per credit hour. Tuition, nonresident: full-time $15,330; part-time $1078 per credit hour. Required fees: $736; $37 per semester. Part-time tuition and fees vary according to course load and program. *Financial support:* In 2009–10, 20 students received support, including 10 fellowships with full and partial tuition reimbursements available (averaging $2,280 per year); research assistantships, teaching assistantships, career-related internships or fieldwork, institutionally sponsored loans, scholarships/grants, health care benefits, and unspecified assistantships also available. Support available to part-time students. Financial award applicants required to submit FAFSA. *Unit head:* Michael V. Vatalaro, Chair, 864-656-3881, Fax: 864-656-0204, E-mail: vatalam@clemson.edu. *Application contact:* Dave Detrich, Coordinator, 864-656-3890, Fax: 864-656-0204.

Cleveland State University, College of Graduate Studies, College of Liberal Arts and Social Sciences, Department of Art, Cleveland, OH 44115. Offers art education (M Ed); art history (MA).

The College at Brockport, State University of New York, School of Arts, Humanities and Social Sciences, Visual Studies Workshop, Brockport, NY 14420-2997. Offers visual studies (MFA). *Students:* 9 full-time (6 women), 6 part-time (2 women); includes 1 minority (African American). 16 applicants, 69% accepted, 9 enrolled. In 2009, 8 master's awarded. *Degree requirements:* For master's, thesis or alternative, internship, final project. *Entrance requirements:* For master's, slides, portfolio, video or CD/DVD, including work description; letters of recommendation; minimum GPA of 3.0; statement of objectives. Additional exam requirements/recommendations for international students: Required—TOEFL (minimum score 550 paper-based; 213 computer-based; 79 iBT). *Application deadline:* For fall admission, 2/15 priority date for domestic and international students. Application fee: $50. Electronic applications accepted. *Expenses:* Tuition, state resident: full-time $8370; part-time $349 per credit. Tuition, nonresident: full-time $13,250; part-time $522 per credit. *Financial support:* Federal Work-Study and scholarships/grants available. Support available to part-time students. Financial award application deadline: 3/15; financial award applicants required to submit FAFSA. *Faculty research:* Photography, film, video, digital media, artists' books. *Unit head:* Tate Shaw, Executive Director, 585-442-8676, Fax: 585-442-1992, E-mail: tshaw@brockport.edu. *Application contact:* Kristen Merola, MFA Coordinator, 585-442-8676, Fax: 585-442-1992, E-mail: kmerola@brockport.edu.

The College of New Rochelle, Graduate School, Division of Art and Communication Studies, Program in Studio Art, New Rochelle, NY 10805-2308. Offers MS. Part-time and evening/weekend programs available. *Degree requirements:* For master's, apprenticeship. *Entrance requirements:* For master's, portfolio, 36 credits of course work in studio art. *Faculty research:* Experimental computer graphics.

Colorado State University, Graduate School, College of Liberal Arts, Department of Art, Fort Collins, CO 80523-1779. Offers MFA. *Faculty:* 21 full-time (9 women), 1 part-time/adjunct (0 women). *Students:* 18 full-time (12 women), 5 part-time (3 women); includes 1 minority (Asian American or Pacific Islander), 1 international. Average age 32. 44 applicants, 20% accepted, 6 enrolled. In 2009, 7 master's awarded. *Degree requirements:* For master's, comprehensive exam (for some programs), thesis (for some programs), exhibition. *Entrance requirements:* For master's, portfolio, letters of recommendation. Additional exam requirements/recommendations for international students: Required—TOEFL. *Application deadline:* For fall admission, 2/1 priority date for domestic students; for spring admission, 10/15 priority date for domestic students. Applications are processed on a rolling basis. Application fee: $50. Electronic applications accepted. *Expenses:* Contact institution. *Financial support:* In 2009–10, 9 students received support, including 9 teaching assistantships with tuition reimbursements available (averaging $8,220 per year); fellowships, research assistantships, Federal Work-Study, institutionally sponsored loans, scholarships/grants, health care benefits, and unspecified assistantships also available. Support available to part-time students. Financial award application deadline: 3/1; financial award applicants required to submit FAFSA. *Faculty research:* African art history, bronze castings, etching/lithography, pre-Columbian art history, contemporary crafts. Total annual research expenditures: $22,600. *Unit head:* Gary W. Voss, Chair, 970-491-5192, E-mail: gary.voss@colostate.edu. *Application contact:* Tom Lundberg, Graduate Coordinator, 970-491-5734, E-mail: thomas.lundberg@colostate.edu.

Columbia University, School of the Arts, Visual Arts Division, New York, NY 10027. Offers new genres (MFA); painting (MFA); photography (MFA); printmaking (MFA); sculpture (MFA). *Degree requirements:* For master's, thesis. *Entrance requirements:* For master's, 3 letters of recommendation, portfolio, resume. Additional exam requirements/recommendations for international students: Required—TOEFL (minimum score 600 paper-based; 250 computer-based; 100 iBT). Electronic applications accepted.

See Close-Up on page 261.

Concordia University, School of Graduate Studies, Faculty of Fine Arts, Department of Studio Arts, Montréal, QC H3G 1M8, Canada. Offers studio arts (MFA), including film production, open media, painting, photography, print media, sculpture, ceramics and fibers. *Degree requirements:* For master's, thesis or alternative. *Entrance requirements:* For master's, portfolio.

Cornell University, Graduate School, Graduate Fields of Architecture, Art and Planning, Field of Art, Ithaca, NY 14853-0001. Offers creative visual arts (MFA), including painting, photography, printmaking, sculpture. *Faculty:* 22 full-time (8 women). *Students:* 10 full-time (6 women); includes 1 minority (Hispanic American), 2 international. Average age 31. 142 applicants, 6% accepted, 6 enrolled. In 2009, 6 master's awarded. *Degree requirements:* For master's, thesis, exhibit. *Entrance requirements:* For master's, slide portfolio of 10-20 slides, 3 letters of recommendation, resume. Additional exam requirements/recommendations for international students: Required—TOEFL (minimum score 550 paper-based; 213 computer-based; 77 iBT). *Application deadline:* For fall admission, 2/15 for domestic students. Application fee: $70. Electronic applications accepted. *Expenses:* Tuition: Full-time $29,500. Required fees: $70. Full-time tuition and fees vary according to degree level, program and student level. *Financial support:* In 2009–10, 10 students received support, including 6 teaching assistantships with full tuition reimbursements available; fellowships with full tuition reimbursements available, research assistantships with full tuition reimbursements available, institutionally sponsored loans, scholarships/grants, health care benefits, tuition waivers (full and partial), and unspecified assistantships also available. Financial award applicants required to submit FAFSA. *Faculty research:* Painting, sculpture, photography, printmaking. *Unit head:* Director of Graduate Studies, 607-255-6730, Fax: 607-255-3462. *Application contact:* Graduate Field Assistant, 607-255-6730, Fax: 607-255-3462, E-mail: artinfo@cornell.edu.

Cranbrook Academy of Art, Graduate School, Program in Fine Arts, Bloomfield Hills, MI 48303-0801. Offers ceramics (MFA); design (MFA), including graphic design; fiber arts (MFA); metalsmithing (MFA); painting (MFA); photography (MFA); printmaking (MFA); sculpture (MFA). *Accreditation:* NASAD. *Degree requirements:* For master's, thesis, exhibit. *Entrance requirements:* Additional exam requirements/recommendations for international students: Required—TOEFL (minimum score 550 paper-based; 213 computer-based).

Drury University, Program in Studio Art and Theory, Springfield, MO 65802. Offers MA. *Entrance requirements:* For master's, GRE or MAT. Additional exam requirements/recommendations for international students: Required—TOEFL. Electronic applications accepted.

Duke University, Graduate School, Department of Art, Art History and Visual Studies, Durham, NC 27708-0764. Offers PhD. *Faculty:* 16 full-time. *Students:* 38 full-time (33 women); includes 6 minority (2 African Americans, 1 Asian American or Pacific Islander, 3 Hispanic Americans), 10 international. 79 applicants, 19% accepted, 8 enrolled. In 2009, 3 doctorates awarded. *Degree requirements:* For doctorate, thesis/dissertation. *Entrance requirements:* For doctorate, GRE General Test. Additional exam requirements/recommendations for international students: Required—TOEFL (minimum score 550 paper-based; 213 computer-based; 83 iBT), IELTS (minimum score 7). *Application deadline:* For fall admission, 12/8 priority date for domestic and international students. Application fee: $75. Electronic applications accepted. *Financial support:* Fellowships, teaching assistantships available. Financial award application deadline: 12/8. *Unit head:* Gennifer Weisenfeld, Director of Graduate Studies, 919-684-2224, Fax: 919-684-4398, E-mail: gennifer.weisenfeld@duke.edu. *Application contact:* Thomas Steffen, Director of Admissions, 919-684-3913, E-mail: grad-admissions@duke.edu.

East Carolina University, Graduate School, College of Fine Arts and Communication, School of Art and Design, Greenville, NC 27858-4353. Offers MA, MA Ed, MFA. *Accreditation:* NASAD (one or more programs are accredited). Part-time and evening/weekend programs available. *Degree requirements:* For master's, comprehensive exam, thesis (for some programs). *Entrance requirements:* For master's, GRE General Test or MAT, portfolio. Additional exam requirements/recommendations for international students: Required—TOEFL.

Eastern Illinois University, Graduate School, College of Arts and Humanities, Department of Art, Charleston, IL 61920-3099. Offers art (MA); art education (MA). *Accreditation:* NASAD. *Faculty:* 18 full-time (7 women). *Students:* 11 applicants, 64% accepted. In 2009, 7 master's awarded. *Degree requirements:* For master's, thesis or alternative, portfolio. *Application deadline:* For fall admission, 3/31 priority date for domestic students. Applications are processed on a rolling basis. Application fee: $30. *Expenses:* Tuition, state resident: full-time $9434; part-time $239 per credit hour. Tuition, nonresident: full-time $23,774; part-time $717 per credit hour. Required fees: $802.63. *Financial support:* In 2009–10, research assistantships with tuition reimbursements (averaging $7,200 per year), 6 teaching assistantships with tuition reimbursements (averaging $7,200 per year) were awarded. *Unit head:* Glenn Hild, Chairperson, 217-581-3410. *Application contact:* Chris Kahler, Coordinator, 217-581-6259, E-mail: cbkahler@eiu.edu.

Eastern Michigan University, Graduate School, College of Arts and Sciences, Department of Art, Program in Studio Art, Ypsilanti, MI 48197. Offers MA, MFA. Part-time and evening/weekend programs available. Postbaccalaureate distance learning degree programs offered (minimal on-campus study). *Students:* 10 full-time (5 women), 19 part-time (15 women); includes 4 minority (3 African Americans, 1 Asian American or Pacific Islander). Average age 44. 29 applicants, 45% accepted, 9 enrolled. In 2009, 11 master's awarded. *Application deadline:* Applications are processed on a rolling basis. Application fee: $35. Tuition and fees vary according to course level. *Financial support:* Fellowships, research assistantships with full tuition reimbursements, teaching assistantships with full tuition reimbursements, career-related internships or fieldwork, Federal Work-Study, institutionally sponsored loans, scholarships/grants, and unspecified assistantships available. Support available to part-time students. *Unit head:* Prof. Christopher Bocklage, Graduate Coordinator, 734-487-1268, Fax: 734-487-2324, E-mail: christopher.bocklage@emich.edu. *Application contact:* Prof. Christopher Bocklage, Graduate Coordinator, 734-487-1268, Fax: 734-487-2324, E-mail: christopher.bocklage@emich.edu.

East Tennessee State University, School of Graduate Studies, College of Arts and Sciences, Department of Art and Design, Johnson City, TN 37614. Offers art education (MA); art history (MA); studio art (MA, MFA). *Accreditation:* NASAD. *Degree requirements:* For master's, thesis, exhibit, oral exam (MFA). *Entrance requirements:* For master's, GRE General Test, portfolio (MFA), bachelor's degree in art, minimum GPA of 3.0. Additional exam requirements/recommendations for international students: Required—TOEFL (minimum score 550 paper-based; 213 computer-based). *Faculty research:* History of sculpture, art and senior citizens, encaustic paintings, digital media in art history.

Edinboro University of Pennsylvania, School of Graduate Studies and Research, School of Liberal Arts, Department of Art, Edinboro, PA 16444. Offers art (MA); fine arts (MFA), including ceramics, jewelry/metalsmithing, painting, printmaking, sculpture. *Accreditation:* NASAD. Evening/weekend programs available. *Faculty:* 15 full-time (10 women), 1 (woman) part-time/adjunct. *Students:* 28 full-time (9 women), 19 part-time (16 women); includes 2 minority (1 Asian American or Pacific Islander, 1 Hispanic American). Average age 30. In 2009, 7 master's awarded. *Degree requirements:* For master's, comprehensive exam, thesis or alternative, competency exam, exhibit, portfolio. *Entrance requirements:* For master's, GRE or MAT, interview, minimum QPA of 2.5, portfolio. *Application deadline:* Applications are processed on a rolling basis. Application fee: $30. Electronic applications accepted. *Expenses:* Tuition, state resident: full-time $6666; part-time $370 per credit. Tuition, nonresident: full-time $10,666;

part-time $593 per credit. Required fees: $2206.28. One-time fee: $204 part-time. *Financial support:* In 2009–10, 23 research assistantships with full and partial tuition reimbursements (averaging $4,050 per year) were awarded; Federal Work-Study, scholarships/grants, and unspecified assistantships also available. Financial award application deadline: 2/15; financial award applicants required to submit FAFSA. *Unit head:* Prof. John Lysak, Program Head, 814-732-2271, E-mail: jlysak@edinboro.edu. *Application contact:* Prof. John Lysak, Program Head, 814-732-2271, E-mail: jlysak@edinboro.edu.

Emily Carr Institute of Art + Design, Program in Applied Arts, Vancouver, BC V6H 3R9, Canada. Offers design (MAA); media arts (MAA); visual arts (MAA). *Degree requirements:* For master's, internship, thesis project. *Entrance requirements:* For master's, minimum overall GPA of 3.0, visual portfolio, 3 letters of recommendation. Additional exam requirements/recommendations for international students: Required—TOEFL (minimum score 570 paper-based; 230 computer-based; 84 iBT), IELTS (minimum score 6.5), Michigan English Language Assessment Battery (minimum score 81). *Application deadline:* For fall admission, 1/15 for domestic students. Application fee: $75 Canadian dollars. Electronic applications accepted. Tuition and fees charges are reported in Canadian dollars. *Expenses:* Tuition, state resident: full-time $11,355 Canadian dollars. Tuition, nonresident: full-time $11,355 Canadian dollars. Required fees: $134.70 Canadian dollars. *Unit head:* Renee Van Halm, Interim Dean, Graduate Studies and Research, E-mail: masters@ecuad.ca. *Application contact:* Graduate Studies Contact, 604-844-3850.

Fairleigh Dickinson University, Metropolitan Campus, University College: Arts, Sciences, and Professional Studies, School of Art and Media Studies, Teaneck, NJ 07666-1914. Offers MA. *Students:* 15 full-time (12 women), 11 part-time (7 women), 5 international. Average age 28. 16 applicants, 81% accepted, 8 enrolled. In 2009, 7 master's awarded. *Application deadline:* Applications are processed on a rolling basis. Application fee: $40. *Application contact:* Susan Brooman, University Director of Graduate Admissions, 201-692-2554, Fax: 201-692-2560, E-mail: globaleducation@fdu.edu.

Ferris State University, Kendall College of Art and Design, Big Rapids, MI 49307. Offers MFA. *Accreditation:* NASAD. Part-time programs available. *Faculty:* 13 full-time (9 women). *Students:* 27 full-time (16 women), 26 part-time (18 women); includes 4 minority (3 African Americans, 1 Asian American or Pacific Islander). Average age 33. 29 applicants, 45% accepted, 13 enrolled. In 2009, 12 master's awarded. *Degree requirements:* For master's, thesis, seminars. *Entrance requirements:* For master's, portfolio, 3 letters of recommendation, curriculum vitae. Additional exam requirements/recommendations for international students: Required—TOEFL (minimum score 500 paper-based; 173 computer-based; 61 iBT). *Application deadline:* For fall admission, 2/15 priority date for domestic and international students; for spring admission, 11/1 priority date for domestic and international students. Applications are processed on a rolling basis. Application fee: $30. *Financial support:* In 2009–10, 26 students received support, including 4 fellowships (averaging $8,530 per year); unspecified assistantships and half-tuition scholarships ($6317 average), graduate assistantships ($5309 average) also available. Financial award application deadline: 2/15; financial award applicants required to submit FAFSA. *Unit head:* Dr. Oliver H. Evans, President and Vice Chancellor, 616-451-2787. *Application contact:* Sandra Britton, Director of Enrollment Management, 616-451-2787, Fax: 616-836-9689, E-mail: brittons@ferris.edu.

Florida Atlantic University, Dorothy F. Schmidt College of Arts and Letters, Department of Visual Arts and Art History, Boca Raton, FL 33431-0991. Offers art education (MAT); ceramics (MFA); computer art (MFA); graphic design (MFA); painting (MFA). *Faculty:* 23 full-time (12 women), 17 part-time/adjunct (11 women). *Students:* 15 full-time (11 women), 11 part-time (6 women); includes 7 minority (1 African American, 6 Hispanic Americans), 3 international. Average age 31. 19 applicants, 21% accepted, 0 enrolled. In 2009, 5 master's awarded. *Degree requirements:* For master's, one foreign language, project. *Entrance requirements:* For master's, GRE General Test, minimum GPA of 3.0 during last 60 hours of course work, slide portfolio. *Application deadline:* For fall admission, 2/21 for domestic and international students; for spring admission, 10/1 for domestic and international students. Application fee: $30. Electronic applications accepted. *Expenses:* Tuition, state resident: full-time $7055; part-time $293.94 per credit hour. Tuition, nonresident: full-time $22,096; part-time $920.66 per credit hour. *Financial support:* Research assistantships with full tuition reimbursements, teaching assistantships with full tuition reimbursements, career-related internships or fieldwork, Federal Work-Study, and institutionally sponsored loans available. Financial award applicants required to submit FAFSA. *Faculty research:* Painting, ceramics (traditional and non-traditional), installation, video and interactive sculpture. *Unit head:* Dr. Linda Johnson, Chair, 561-297-3870, Fax: 561-297-3078, E-mail: ljohnson@fau.edu. *Application contact:* James A. Novak, Associate Professor/Graduate Coordinator/Advisor, 561-297-2430, Fax: 561-297-3078, E-mail: jnovak@fau.edu.

Florida International University, College of Architecture and the Arts, School of Art and Art History, Miami, FL 33199. Offers visual arts (MFA). *Accreditation:* NASAD. Part-time and evening/weekend programs available. *Faculty:* 14 full-time (6 women). *Students:* 10 full-time (6 women), 1 (woman) part-time; includes 4 minority (all Hispanic Americans), 1 international. Average age 28. 25 applicants, 16% accepted, 4 enrolled. In 2009, 2 master's awarded. *Entrance requirements:* For master's, minimum GPA of 3.0 (upper level coursework), 3 letters of recommendation, 20 slides of creative work. Additional exam requirements/recommendations for international students: Required—TOEFL (minimum score 550 paper-based; 80 iBT). *Application deadline:* For fall admission, 2/1 for domestic and international students. Application fee: $30. Electronic applications accepted. *Expenses:* Tuition, state resident: full-time $8008; part-time $4004 per year. Tuition, nonresident: full-time $20,104; part-time $10,052 per year. Required fees: $298; $149 per term. *Financial support:* Institutionally sponsored loans and scholarships/grants available. Financial award application deadline: 3/1; financial award applicants required to submit FAFSA. *Unit head:* Dr. Juan Martinez, Chair, 305-348-3539, Fax: 305-348-0513, E-mail: juan.martinez@fiu.edu. *Application contact:* Susie Novoa, Graduate Secretary, 305-348-2897, Fax: 305-348-0513, E-mail: susan.novoa@fiu.edu.

Florida State University, The Graduate School, College of Visual Arts, Theatre and Dance, Department of Art, Tallahassee, FL 32306. Offers studio art (MFA). *Accreditation:* NASAD. *Faculty:* 19 full-time (10 women). *Students:* 32 full-time (22 women); includes 4 minority (2 African Americans, 1 Asian American or Pacific Islander, 1 Hispanic American). Average age 26. 77 applicants, 18% accepted, 14 enrolled. In 2009, 8 master's awarded. *Degree requirements:* For master's, thesis, exhibit. *Entrance requirements:* For master's, portfolio, minimum GPA of 3.0. Additional exam requirements/recommendations for international students: Required—TOEFL (minimum score 550 paper-based). *Application deadline:* For fall admission, 2/23 priority date for domestic students, 2/23 for international students. Application fee: $30. Electronic applications accepted. *Expenses:* Tuition, state resident: full-time $7413. Tuition, nonresident: full-time $22,567. *Financial support:* In 2009–10, 32 students received support, including 22 research assistantships with partial tuition reimbursements available (averaging $5,000 per year), 10 teaching assistantships with partial tuition reimbursements available (averaging $5,400 per year); Federal Work-Study, institutionally sponsored loans, and unspecified assistantships also available. Financial award application deadline: 2/23; financial award applicants required to submit FAFSA. *Faculty research:* Photography, painting, sculpture, printmaking, ceramics. *Unit head:* Terry L. Hogan, Interim Chairperson, 850-644-6474, Fax: 850-644-8977, E-mail: lhogan@admin.fsu.edu. *Application contact:* Holly Hannessian, Graduate Director, 850-644-6474, Fax: 850-644-8977, E-mail: hhanessian@fsu.edu.

Fontbonne University, Graduate Programs, Department of Fine Arts, St. Louis, MO 63105-3098. Offers art (MA); fine arts (MFA); theater education (MA). Part-time and evening/weekend programs available. *Faculty:* 6 full-time (2 women), 5 part-time/adjunct (4 women). *Students:* 7 full-time (4 women), 6 part-time (5 women); includes 1 minority (African American). Average age 37. In 2009, 8 master's awarded. *Degree requirements:* For master's, thesis exhibit (MFA). *Entrance requirements:* For master's, minimum GPA of 3.0, portfolio. *Application deadline:* For fall admission, 8/1 priority date for domestic students. Applications are processed on a rolling basis. Application fee: $25. *Expenses:* Tuition: Part-time $562 per credit hour. *Financial support:* In 2009–10, teaching assistantships (averaging $2,500 per year). Support available to part-time students. Financial award application deadline: 4/1; financial award applicants required to submit FAFSA. *Unit head:* Catherine Connor-Talasek, Chairperson, 314-889-1431, Fax: 314-889-4545, E-mail: cconnor@fontbonne.edu. *Application contact:* Catherine Connor-Talasek, Chairperson, 314-889-1431, Fax: 314-889-4545, E-mail: cconnor@fontbonne.edu.

Fort Hays State University, Graduate School, College of Arts and Sciences, Department of Art, Hays, KS 67601-4099. Offers studio art (MFA). Part-time programs available. *Degree requirements:* For master's, comprehensive exam, thesis. *Entrance requirements:* For master's, slides. Additional exam requirements/recommendations for international students: Required—TOEFL (minimum score 550 paper-based; 213 computer-based; 79 iBT). Electronic applications accepted. *Faculty research:* Migration art of Germanic tribes, iconographic and stylistic development, graphic design, photography, lithography.

Framingham State College, Division of Graduate and Continuing Education, Program in Art, Framingham, MA 01701-9101. Offers M Ed.

Full Sail University, Education Media Design and Technology Master of Science Program—Online, Winter Park, FL 32792-7437. Offers MS. Postbaccalaureate distance learning degree programs offered (no on-campus study). *Entrance requirements:* Additional exam requirements/recommendations for international students: Required—TOEFL (minimum score 550 paper-based; 213 computer-based; 79 iBT).

Full Sail University, Media Design Master of Fine Arts Program—Online, Winter Park, FL 32792-7437. Offers MFA. Postbaccalaureate distance learning degree programs offered.

The George Washington University, Columbian College of Arts and Sciences, Department of Fine Arts and Art History, Washington, DC 20052. Offers art history (MA), including art history, museum training; ceramics (MFA); drawing/painting (MFA); interior design (MFA); new media (MFA); photography (MFA); sculpture (MFA). *Accreditation:* CIDA. Part-time and evening/weekend programs available. *Faculty:* 18 full-time (9 women), 41 part-time/adjunct (27 women). *Students:* 47 full-time (41 women), 33 part-time (all women); includes 15 minority (6 African Americans, 5 Asian Americans or Pacific Islanders, 4 Hispanic Americans), 4 international. Average age 28. 131 applicants, 60% accepted, 26 enrolled. In 2009, 36 master's awarded. *Entrance requirements:* For master's, GRE General Test, bachelor's degree in field, minimum GPA of 3.0. Additional exam requirements/recommendations for international students: Required—TOEFL (minimum score 550 paper-based; 213 computer-based; 80 iBT). *Application deadline:* For fall admission, 3/1 priority date for domestic students, 1/15 priority date for international students; for spring admission, 10/1 priority date for domestic students, 9/1 priority date for international students. Applications are processed on a rolling basis. Application fee: $60. Electronic applications accepted. *Financial support:* In 2009–10, 12 students received support; fellowships, teaching assistantships, career-related internships or fieldwork, Federal Work-Study, and tuition waivers available. Financial award application deadline: 1/15. *Unit head:* Thomas K. Brown, Chair, 202-994-9067, E-mail: thbrown@gwu.edu. *Application contact:* Information Contact, 202-994-6085, Fax: 202-994-8657, E-mail: art@gwu.edu.

Georgia Southern University, Jack N. Averitt College of Graduate Studies, College of Liberal Arts and Social Sciences, Department of Art, Statesboro, GA 30460. Offers fine arts (MFA). *Accreditation:* NASAD. Part-time programs available. *Students:* 21 full-time (12 women), 5 part-time (3 women); includes 3 minority (2 African Americans, 1 Hispanic American), 1 international. Average age 32. 15 applicants, 67% accepted, 8 enrolled. In 2009, 2 master's awarded. *Degree requirements:* For master's, thesis, exhibition. *Entrance requirements:* For master's, minimum GPA of 3.0; 18 semester hours of course work in studio art, 9 in art history; portfolio; letters of reference. Additional exam requirements/recommendations for international students: Required—TOEFL (minimum score 550 paper-based; 213 computer-based). *Application deadline:* For fall admission, 3/1 priority date for domestic and international students; for spring admission, 10/1 priority date for domestic students, 10/1 for international students. Applications are processed on a rolling basis. Application fee: $50. Electronic applications accepted. *Expenses:* Tuition, state resident: full-time $5040; part-time $210 per credit hour. Tuition, nonresident: full-time $20,136; part-time $839 per credit hour. Required fees: $1644. *Financial support:* In 2009–10, 22 students received support, including research assistantships with partial tuition reimbursements available (averaging $7,200 per year), teaching assistantships with partial tuition reimbursements available (averaging $7,200 per year); career-related internships or fieldwork, Federal Work-Study, scholarships/grants, tuition waivers (partial), and unspecified assistantships also available. Support available to part-time students. Financial award application deadline: 4/15; financial award applicants required to submit FAFSA. *Faculty research:* International design trends; graphic design social awareness campaigns; functional design; public sculpture; fine art painting, drawing, printmaking, paper and book arts; folk art; Georgia artists archive. *Unit head:* Dr. Patricia Carter, Chair, 912-478-5358, Fax: 912-478-5104, E-mail: pwcarter@georgiasouthern.edu. *Application contact:* Dr. Charles Ziglar, Coordinator for Graduate Student Recruitment, 912-478-5635, Fax: 912-478-0740, E-mail: gradadmissions@georgiasouthern.edu.

Georgia State University, College of Arts and Sciences, Ernest G. Welch School of Art and Design, Program in Studio Art, Atlanta, GA 30302-3083. Offers MFA. *Accreditation:* NASAD. *Degree requirements:* For master's, thesis, exhibit, presentations, screening. *Entrance requirements:* For master's, portfolio. Additional exam requirements/recommendations for international students: Required—TOEFL (minimum score 550 paper-based; 213 computer-based). Electronic applications accepted. *Faculty research:* Photography, drawing/painting, printmaking, sculpture, ceramics.

Governors State University, College of Arts and Sciences, Program in Art, University Park, IL 60466-0975. Offers MA. Part-time and evening/weekend programs available. *Degree requirements:* For master's, thesis or alternative. *Entrance requirements:* For master's, portfolio, bachelor's degree in humanities. *Faculty research:* Historical study of art of selected ethnic groups of southwestern Zaire.

Hofstra University, School of Education, Health, and Human Services, Department of Curriculum and Teaching, Program in Fine Arts Education, Hempstead, NY 11549. Offers MA, MS Ed. Part-time and evening/weekend programs available. *Students:* 27 full-time (25 women), 9 part-time (7 women); includes 1 minority (Hispanic American). Average age 29. 28 applicants, 89% accepted, 16 enrolled. In 2009, 10 master's awarded. *Degree requirements:* For master's, one foreign language, thesis or alternative, teaching portfolio. *Entrance requirements:* For master's, 2 letters of recommendation, portfolio, teacher certification (MA). Additional exam requirements/recommendations for international students: Required—TOEFL (minimum score 550 paper-based; 213 computer-based; 80 iBT). *Application deadline:* Applications are processed on a rolling basis. Application fee: $60. Electronic applications accepted. *Expenses:* Tuition: Full-time $16,200; part-time $900 per credit hour. Required fees: $970; $145 per term. Tuition and fees vary according to program. *Financial support:* In 2009–10, 24 students received support, including 3 fellowships with full and partial tuition reimbursements available (averaging $2,868 per year); research assistantships with full and partial tuition reimbursements available, Federal Work-Study, institutionally sponsored loans, scholarships/grants, tuition waivers (full and partial), and unspecified assistantships also available. Support available to part-time students. Financial award applicants required to submit FAFSA. *Faculty research:* Art education and interdisciplinary curricula, teacher/artist role in identity issues, early childhood art education, marginalization of the arts in education, gender issues. *Unit head:* Dr. Susan G. Zwirn, Program Director, 516-463-4976, Fax: 516-463-6196, E-mail: catsgz@hofstra.edu. *Application contact:* Carol Drummer, Dean of Graduate Admissions, 516-463-4876, Fax: 516-463-4664, E-mail: gradstudent@hofstra.edu.

Hollins University, Graduate Programs, Program in Liberal Studies, Roanoke, VA 24020-1603. Offers humanities (MALS); interdisciplinary studies (MALS); justice and legal studies

Art/Fine Arts

Hollins University (continued)
(MALS); liberal studies (CAS); social science (MALS); visual and performing arts (MALS). Part-time and evening/weekend programs available. *Faculty:* 7 full-time (1 woman), 4 part-time/adjunct (2 women). *Students:* 23 full-time (22 women), 73 part-time (57 women); includes 15 minority (13 African Americans, 2 Asian Americans or Pacific Islanders), 4 international. Average age 39. 31 applicants, 94% accepted, 25 enrolled. In 2009, 30 master's awarded. *Degree requirements:* For master's, thesis. *Entrance requirements:* For master's, letters of recommendation, interview. Additional exam requirements/recommendations for international students: Required—TOEFL (minimum score 550 paper-based; 213 computer-based; 79 iBT). *Application deadline:* For fall admission, 7/1 priority date for domestic and international students; for spring admission, 12/10 priority date for domestic and international students. Applications are processed on a rolling basis. Application fee: $40. Electronic applications accepted. *Expenses:* Tuition: Full-time $27,780; part-time $295 per contact hour. Required fees: $280; $70 per unit. Part-time tuition and fees vary according to course load and program. *Financial support:* In 2009–10, 31 students received support, including 2 fellowships (averaging $902 per year); Federal Work-Study and scholarships/grants also available. Support available to part-time students. Financial award application deadline: 7/15; financial award applicants required to submit FAFSA. *Faculty research:* Elderly blacks, film, feminist economics, US voting patterns, Wagner, diversity. *Unit head:* Dr. Edward A. Lynch, Director, 540-362-6475, Fax: 540-362-6288, E-mail: elynch@hollins.edu. *Application contact:* Cathy S. Koon, Manager of Graduate Services, 540-362-6326, Fax: 540-362-6288, E-mail: ckoon@hollins.edu.

Hood College, Graduate School, Program in Ceramic Arts, Frederick, MD 21701-8575. Offers ceramic arts (Certificate); ceramics (MFA). Part-time and evening/weekend programs available. *Faculty:* 1 (woman) full-time, 8 part-time/adjunct (5 women). *Students:* 4 full-time (3 women), 32 part-time (25 women). Average age 38. 10 applicants, 90% accepted, 8 enrolled. In 2009, 8 other advanced degrees awarded. *Degree requirements:* For master's, comprehensive exam. *Entrance requirements:* For master's, minimum GPA of 2.75; for Certificate, portfolio. Additional exam requirements/recommendations for international students: Required—TOEFL (minimum score 575 paper-based; 231 computer-based; 89 iBT). *Application deadline:* For fall admission, 7/15 for domestic and international students; for spring admission, 12/15 for domestic and international students. Applications are processed on a rolling basis. Application fee: $35. Electronic applications accepted. *Expenses:* Tuition: Full-time $6480; part-time $360 per credit. Required fees: $100; $50 per term. *Financial support:* Applicants required to submit FAFSA. *Unit head:* Joyce Michaud, Director, 301-696-3526, E-mail: jmichaud@hood.edu. *Application contact:* Dr. Allen P. Flora, Dean of Graduate School, 301-696-3811, Fax: 301-696-3597, E-mail: gofurther@hood.edu.

Howard University, Graduate School, Division of Fine Arts, Department of Art, Program in Fine Arts, Washington, DC 20059-0002. Offers 3D reality (sculpture and ceramics) (MFA); design (MFA); electronic studio (MFA); painting (MFA); photography (MFA). *Accreditation:* NASAD. *Degree requirements:* For master's, comprehensive exam, thesis, exhibit. *Entrance requirements:* For master's, minimum GPA of 3.0, portfolio.

Hunter College of the City University of New York, Graduate School, School of Arts and Sciences, Department of Art, Program in Studio Art, New York, NY 10021-5085. Offers fine arts (MFA). Part-time and evening/weekend programs available. *Faculty:* 11 full-time (6 women). *Students:* 10 full-time (7 women), 113 part-time (61 women); includes 9 minority (1 African American, 1 American Indian/Alaska Native, 3 Asian Americans or Pacific Islanders, 4 Hispanic Americans). Average age 30. 727 applicants, 8% accepted, 34 enrolled. In 2009, 46 master's awarded. *Degree requirements:* For master's, exhibit, project. *Entrance requirements:* For master's, minimum of 24 credits of course work in studio art and 9 credits of course work in art history, portfolio. Additional exam requirements/recommendations for international students: Required—TOEFL. *Application deadline:* For fall admission, 2/1 for domestic students; for spring admission, 10/1 for domestic students. Application fee: $125. *Expenses:* Tuition, state resident: full-time $7360; part-time $310 per credit. Required fees: $250 per semester. *Financial support:* Career-related internships or fieldwork, Federal Work-Study, scholarships/grants, and tuition waivers (partial) available. Support available to part-time students. Financial award application deadline: 4/15. *Faculty research:* Color theory, public printmaking and environmental commissions in painting and sculpture, graphics, ceramics, contemporary film and video. *Unit head:* Joel Carreiro, Graduate Adviser, 212-650-3398, E-mail: grad.arthistoryadvisor@hunter.cuny.edu. *Application contact:* William Zlata, Director for Graduate Admissions, 212-772-4482, Fax: 212-650-3336, E-mail: admissions@hunter.cuny.edu.

Idaho State University, Office of Graduate Studies, College of Arts and Sciences, Department of Art and Pre-Architecture, Pocatello, ID 83209-8004. Offers art (MFA). Part-time programs available. *Faculty:* 4 full-time (0 women). *Students:* 9 full-time (3 women), 5 part-time (1 woman); includes 1 minority (Hispanic American). Average age 40. *Degree requirements:* For master's, comprehensive exam, thesis, exhibit, 2 year minimum participation in program, oral exam. *Entrance requirements:* For master's, GRE General Test, GMAT or MAT, minimum GPA of 3.0 in all upper-division classes, portfolio of work, 3 letters of recommendation. Additional exam requirements/recommendations for international students: Required—TOEFL (minimum score 550 paper-based; 213 computer-based; 80 iBT). *Application deadline:* For fall admission, 3/15 for domestic and international students; for spring admission, 10/15 for domestic and international students. Applications are processed on a rolling basis. Application fee: $55. Electronic applications accepted. *Expenses:* Tuition, state resident: full-time $3318; part-time $297 per credit hour. Tuition, nonresident: full-time $13,120; part-time $437 per credit hour. Required fees: $2530. Tuition and fees vary according to program. *Financial support:* In 2009–10, 3 teaching assistantships with full and partial tuition reimbursements (averaging $12,282 per year) were awarded; Federal Work-Study, institutionally sponsored loans, scholarships/grants, traineeships, health care benefits, tuition waivers (full and partial), and unspecified assistantships also available. Support available to part-time students. Financial award application deadline: 1/1; financial award applicants required to submit FAFSA. *Faculty research:* Computerized weaving, anodizing refractory metals, viscosity printing, neon, ceramic shell casting. *Unit head:* Rudy Kovacs, Chair, 208-282-2488, Fax: 208-282-4741, E-mail: kovarudo@isu.edu. *Application contact:* Tami Carson, Graduate School Technical Records Specialist, 208-282-2150, Fax: 208-282-4847, E-mail: carstami@isu.edu.

Illinois State University, Graduate School, College of Fine Arts, Program in Arts Technology, Normal, IL 61790-2200. Offers MS. *Accreditation:* NASAD. *Degree requirements:* For master's, thesis or alternative.

Illinois State University, Graduate School, College of Fine Arts, School of Art, Normal, IL 61790-2200. Offers art history (MA, MS); ceramics (MFA, MS); drawing (MFA, MS); fibers (MFA, MS); glass (MFA, MS); graphic design (MFA, MS); metals (MFA, MS); painting (MFA, MS); photography (MFA, MS); printmaking (MFA, MS); sculpture (MFA, MS). *Accreditation:* NASAD (one or more programs are accredited). *Degree requirements:* For master's, thesis or alternative, internship. *Entrance requirements:* For master's, portfolio, sample of scholarly writing. *Faculty research:* General operations support: Normal Editions Workshop for FY2007.

Indiana State University, School of Graduate Studies, College of Arts and Sciences, Department of Art, Terre Haute, IN 47809. Offers ceramics (MA, MFA); drawing (MA, MFA); graphic design (MA, MFA); painting (MA, MFA); photography (MA, MFA); printmaking (MA, MFA); sculpture (MA, MFA). *Accreditation:* NASAD (one or more programs are accredited). Part-time programs available. *Degree requirements:* For master's, thesis or alternative, departmental qualifying exam. *Entrance requirements:* For master's, portfolio. Additional exam requirements/recommendations for international students: Required—TOEFL (minimum score 550 paper-based).

Indiana University Bloomington, University Graduate School, College of Arts and Sciences, Henry Radford Hope School of Fine Arts, Bloomington, IN 47405-7000. Offers MA, MFA, PhD. *Accreditation:* NASAD (one or more programs are accredited). *Faculty:* 17 full-time (10 women). *Students:* 134 full-time (95 women), 12 part-time (7 women); includes 6 minority (1 African American, 1 American Indian/Alaska Native, 3 Asian Americans or Pacific Islanders, 1 Hispanic American), 14 international. Average age 30. 262 applicants, 31% accepted, 54 enrolled. In 2009, 32 master's, 4 doctorates awarded. *Degree requirements:* For doctorate, 2 foreign languages, thesis/dissertation. *Entrance requirements:* For master's, portfolio (MFA); for doctorate, minimum GPA of 3.0. Additional exam requirements/recommendations for international students: Required—TOEFL. *Application deadline:* For fall admission, 1/15 priority date for domestic students, 12/15 for international students; for spring admission, 9/1 for domestic and international students. Applications are processed on a rolling basis. Application fee: $55 ($65 for international students). *Financial support:* Fellowships with tuition reimbursements, research assistantships with tuition reimbursements, teaching assistantships with tuition reimbursements, career-related internships or fieldwork, Federal Work-Study, scholarships/grants, tuition waivers (full and partial), and stipends available. Financial award application deadline: 2/15. *Faculty research:* Infrared reflectography, Italian Renaissance painters, hand papermaking, British Romantic landscape painting, late nineteenth century American art. *Unit head:* Paul Brown, Director, 812-855-7498. *Application contact:* Brad Wicklund, Graduate Services Coordinator, 812-855-7766, E-mail: bwicklun@indiana.edu.

Indiana University of Pennsylvania, School of Graduate Studies and Research, College of Fine Arts, Department of Art, Program in Art, Indiana, PA 15705-1087. Offers MA, MFA. *Accreditation:* NASAD. Part-time programs available. *Faculty:* 9 full-time (3 women). *Students:* 13 full-time (3 women), 12 part-time (7 women); includes 2 minority (1 African American, 1 Asian American or Pacific Islander), 4 international. Average age 29. 29 applicants, 48% accepted, 9 enrolled. In 2009, 2 master's awarded. *Degree requirements:* For master's, thesis optional. *Entrance requirements:* For master's, 3 letters of recommendation, portfolio. Additional exam requirements/recommendations for international students: Required—TOEFL. *Application deadline:* For fall admission, 7/1 priority date for domestic students; for spring admission, 11/1 for domestic students. Applications are processed on a rolling basis. Application fee: $40. *Expenses:* Tuition, state resident: full-time $6666; part-time $370 per credit hour. Tuition, nonresident: full-time $10,666; part-time $593 per credit hour. Required fees: $813 per semester. *Financial support:* In 2009–10, 1 fellowship (averaging $500 per year), 12 research assistantships with full and partial tuition reimbursements (averaging $3,987 per year) were awarded; career-related internships or fieldwork and Federal Work-Study also available. Support available to part-time students. Financial award application deadline: 3/15; financial award applicants required to submit FAFSA. *Unit head:* Dr. James Nestor, 724-357-2593, E-mail: nestor@iup.edu. *Application contact:* Dr. James Nestor, Graduate Coordinator, 724-357-2593, E-mail: nestor@iup.edu.

Indiana University–Purdue University Indianapolis, Herron School of Art and Design, Indianapolis, IN 46202-2896. Offers art education (MAE); furniture design (MFA); printmaking (MFA); sculpture (MFA); visual communication (MFA). Part-time and evening/weekend programs available. *Faculty:* 2 full-time (both women). *Students:* 36 full-time (21 women), 11 part-time (all women); includes 6 minority (2 Asian Americans or Pacific Islanders, 4 Hispanic Americans), 6 international. Average age 31. 60 applicants, 60% accepted, 20 enrolled. In 2009, 1 master's awarded. *Entrance requirements:* For master's, portfolio, 44 hours of course work in art history and studio art. *Application deadline:* For fall admission, 6/1 priority date for domestic students, 3/15 priority date for international students; for spring admission, 11/1 priority date for domestic students, 10/15 priority date for international students. Applications are processed on a rolling basis. Application fee: $55 ($65 for international students). Electronic applications accepted. *Financial support:* Career-related internships or fieldwork, Federal Work-Study, institutionally sponsored loans, scholarships/grants, and tuition waivers (partial) available. Support available to part-time students. Total annual research expenditures: $6,097. *Unit head:* Valerie Eickmeier, Dean, 317-278-9470, Fax: 317-278-9471, E-mail: herron@iupui.edu. *Application contact:* Herron Student Services Office, 317-378-9400, E-mail: herrart@iupui.edu.

Inter American University of Puerto Rico, San Germán Campus, Graduate Studies Center, Program in Fine Arts, San Germán, PR 00683-5008. Offers ceramics (MFA); drawing (MFA); engraving (MFA); painting (MFA); photography (MFA); sculpture (MFA). *Degree requirements:* For master's, comprehensive exam, thesis. *Entrance requirements:* For master's, GRE General Test or EXADEP, minimum GPA of 3.0.

James Madison University, The Graduate School, College of Visual and Performing Arts, School of Art and Art History, Harrisonburg, VA 22807. Offers art education (MA); art history (MA); ceramics (MFA); drawing/painting (MFA); metal/jewelry (MFA); photography (MFA); printmaking (MFA); sculpture (MFA); studio art (MA); weaving/fibers (MFA). *Accreditation:* NASAD. Part-time programs available. *Faculty:* 11 full-time (6 women), 1 (woman) part-time/adjunct. *Students:* 10 full-time (8 women); includes 1 minority (African American). Average age 27. In 2009, 4 master's awarded. *Degree requirements:* For master's, thesis (for some programs). *Entrance requirements:* For master's, GRE General Test, language exam in French or German, portfolio, 3 letters of recommendation, research paper. Additional exam requirements/recommendations for international students: Required—TOEFL. *Application deadline:* For fall admission, 2/15 priority date for domestic students, 2/15 for international students; for spring admission, 10/15 priority date for domestic students, 10/15 for international students. Applications are processed on a rolling basis. Application fee: $55. Electronic applications accepted. *Expenses:* Tuition, area resident: Part-time $305 per credit hour. Tuition, state resident: part-time $305 per credit hour. Tuition, nonresident: part-time $890 per credit hour. *Financial support:* In 2009–10, 8 students received support, including 3 teaching assistantships with full tuition reimbursements available (averaging $8,664 per year); Federal Work-Study also available. Financial award application deadline: 3/1; financial award applicants required to submit FAFSA. *Unit head:* Leslie M. Bellavance, Academic Unit Head, 540-568-6216. *Application contact:* Lynette M. Bible, Director of Graduate Admissions, 540-568-6395, Fax: 540-568-7860, E-mail: biblelm@jmu.edu.

John F. Kennedy University, Graduate School of Holistic Studies, Department of Arts and Consciousness, Program in Studio Arts, Pleasant Hill, CA 94523-4817. Offers MFA. Part-time and evening/weekend programs available. *Degree requirements:* For master's, thesis or alternative. *Entrance requirements:* For master's, interview, portfolio. Additional exam requirements/recommendations for international students: Required—TOEFL. *Expenses:* Contact institution.

Johnson State College, Program in Studio Arts, Johnson, VT 05656. Offers drawing (MFA); mixed media (MFA); painting (MFA); sculpture (MFA). Part-time programs available. Post-baccalaureate distance learning degree programs offered (minimal on-campus study). *Entrance requirements:* For master's, portfolio. Additional exam requirements/recommendations for international students: Required—TOEFL. *Expenses:* Contact institution.

Kansas State University, Graduate School, College of Arts and Sciences, Department of Art, Manhattan, KS 66506. Offers MFA. *Accreditation:* NASAD. Part-time programs available. *Faculty:* 17 full-time (5 women), 1 part-time/adjunct (0 women). *Students:* 14 full-time (6 women). Average age 31. 13 applicants, 46% accepted, 6 enrolled. In 2009, 7 master's awarded. *Degree requirements:* For master's, thesis, gallery exhibit. *Entrance requirements:* For master's, slides of artistic work, portfolio. Additional exam requirements/recommendations for international students: Required—TOEFL (minimum score 550 paper-based; 213 computer-based). *Application deadline:* For fall admission, 2/1 priority date for domestic and international students; for spring admission, 8/1 priority date for domestic and international students. Applications are processed on a rolling basis. Application fee: $40 ($55 for international students). Electronic applications accepted. *Financial support:* In 2009–10, 14 teaching assistantships with full tuition reimbursements (averaging $8,923 per year) were awarded; research assistantships, career-related internships or fieldwork, Federal Work-Study, institutionally sponsored loans, and scholarships/grants also available. Support available to part-time students. Financial award application deadline: 3/1; financial award applicants required to submit FAFSA. *Faculty research:* Drawing, painting, sculpture, metalsmithing, visual communication. *Unit head:* Gerry Craig, Head, 785-532-6605, Fax: 785-532-0334, E-mail: gkcraig@ksu.edu. *Application contact:* Elliot Pujol, Director, 785-532-6605, Fax: 785-532-0334, E-mail: hepujol@ksu.edu.

Kean University, College of Visual and Performing Arts, Union, NJ 07083. Offers MA, MS. Part-time and evening/weekend programs available. *Faculty:* 26 full-time (8 women). *Students:* 23 full-time (17 women), 57 part-time (41 women); includes 18 minority (9 African Americans, 3 Asian Americans or Pacific Islanders, 6 Hispanic Americans), 5 international. Average age 38. 33 applicants, 91% accepted, 19 enrolled. In 2009, 35 master's awarded. *Degree requirements:* For master's, comprehensive exam (for some programs), thesis (for some programs). *Entrance requirements:* For master's, minimum GPA of 3.0, 3 letters of recommendation, portfolio. *Application deadline:* For fall admission, 5/1 for domestic students; for spring admission, 11/1 for domestic students. Application fee: $60 ($150 for international students). Electronic applications accepted. *Expenses:* Tuition, state resident: full-time $10,440; part-time $435 per credit. Tuition, nonresident: full-time $14,160; part-time $590 per credit. Required fees: $2642; $110 per credit. Part-time tuition and fees vary according to course load and degree level. *Financial support:* In 2009–10, 5 research assistantships with full tuition reimbursements (averaging $3,263 per year) were awarded; unspecified assistantships also available. *Unit head:* Dr. Holly Logue, Dean, 908-737-4376, Fax: 908-737-4377, E-mail: hlogue@kean.edu. *Application contact:* Ann-Marie Kay, Assistant Director of Graduate Admissions, 908-737-4723, Fax: 908-737-5965, E-mail: grad-adm@kean.edu.

Kent State University, College of the Arts, School of Art, Kent, OH 44242-0001. Offers art education (MA); art history (MA); crafts (MA, MFA), including ceramics (MA), glass, jewelry/metals, textiles/art; fine art (MA, MFA), including drawing/painting, printmaking, sculpture. *Accreditation:* NASAD (one or more programs are accredited). *Degree requirements:* For master's, one foreign language, thesis. *Entrance requirements:* For master's, undergraduate degree in proposed area of study (for fine arts and crafts programs); minimum overall GPA of 2.75 (3.0 for art major); 3 letters of recommendation; portfolio (15-20 slides for MA, 20-25 for MFA). Additional exam requirements/recommendations for international students: Required—TOEFL. Electronic applications accepted.

Laguna College of Art & Design, Graduate Program, Laguna Beach, CA 92651-1136. Offers painting (MFA). *Accreditation:* NASAD. *Entrance requirements:* For master's, BA with a studio concentration or BFA, minimum GPA of 3.0 in studio subjects, portfolio, resume. Additional exam requirements/recommendations for international students: Required—TOEFL (minimum score 550 paper-based). Electronic applications accepted.

Lamar University, College of Graduate Studies, College of Fine Arts and Communication, Department of Art, Beaumont, TX 77710. Offers art history (MA); photography (MA); studio art (MA); visual design (MA). Part-time and evening/weekend programs available. *Faculty:* 6 full-time (3 women). *Students:* 3 full-time (1 woman), 1 (woman) part-time. Average age 45. 5 applicants, 60% accepted, 3 enrolled. *Degree requirements:* For master's, thesis. *Entrance requirements:* For master's, GRE General Test, minimum GPA of 2.5 in last 60 hours of undergraduate course work. Additional exam requirements/recommendations for international students: Required—TOEFL. *Application deadline:* For fall admission, 8/1 priority date for domestic students; for spring admission, 12/1 for domestic students. Applications are processed on a rolling basis. Application fee: $25 ($50 for international students). *Financial support:* Fellowships, career-related internships or fieldwork, Federal Work-Study, and scholarships/grants available. Financial award application deadline: 4/1. *Faculty research:* Nineteenth century academic paintings, metal casting, pigment color stability, computer-modified photography, manipulated photography. *Unit head:* Donna M. Meeks, Chair, 409-880-8141, Fax: 409-880-1799, E-mail: meeksdm@lub002.lamar.edu. *Application contact:* Debbie Piper, Coordinator of Graduate Admissions, 409-880-8356, Fax: 409-880-8414, E-mail: gradmissions@hal.lamar.edu.

Lehman College of the City University of New York, Division of Arts and Humanities, Department of Art, Bronx, NY 10468-1589. Offers MA, MFA. Part-time and evening/weekend programs available. *Entrance requirements:* For master's, 33 undergraduate credits in art, interview, portfolio. *Faculty research:* Graphic art, modern and contemporary art, sculpture, primitive and pre-Columbian art, medieval art.

Lesley University, Graduate School of Arts and Social Sciences, Program in Visual Arts, Cambridge, MA 02138-2790. Offers MFA. Postbaccalaureate distance learning degree programs offered. *Entrance requirements:* For master's, portfolio. Additional exam requirements/recommendations for international students: Required—TOEFL (minimum score 550 paper-based; 213 computer-based; 80 iBT). *Expenses:* Contact institution.

Lindenwood University, Graduate Programs, School of Fine and Performing Arts, St. Charles, MO 63301-1695. Offers arts management (MA); communication arts (MA); studio art (MA, MFA); theatre (MA, MFA). Part-time programs available. *Faculty:* 15 full-time (6 women), 5 part-time/adjunct (2 women). *Students:* 31 full-time (17 women), 13 part-time (9 women); includes 3 minority (all African Americans), 5 international. Average age 32. 6 applicants, 2 enrolled. In 2009, 9 master's awarded. *Degree requirements:* For master's, thesis (for some programs). *Entrance requirements:* For master's, audition or interview, minimum GPA of 3.0, submission of portfolio, letter of recommendation. Additional exam requirements/recommendations for international students: Required—TOEFL (minimum score 550 paper-based; 213 computer-based; 80 iBT). *Application deadline:* For fall admission, 8/27 priority date for domestic and international students; for spring admission, 1/28 priority date for domestic and international students. Applications are processed on a rolling basis. Application fee: $30 ($100 for international students). Electronic applications accepted. *Expenses:* Tuition: Full-time $12,960; part-time $370 per credit hour. Required fees: $340. One-time fee: $30 full-time. Tuition and fees vary according to course level and course load. *Financial support:* In 2009–10, 37 students received support. Career-related internships or fieldwork, institutionally sponsored loans, tuition waivers (partial), and unspecified assistantships available. Financial award application deadline: 6/30; financial award applicants required to submit FAFSA. *Unit head:* Donnell Walsh, Dean of Fine Arts, 636-949-4853, Fax: 636-949-4910, E-mail: dwalsh@lindenwood.edu. *Application contact:* Brett Barger, Dean of Evening Admissions and Extension Campuses, 636-949-4934, Fax: 636-949-4109, E-mail: adultadmissions@lindenwood.edu.

Long Island University, C.W. Post Campus, School of Visual and Performing Arts, Department of Art, Brookville, NY 11548-1300. Offers art (MA); art education (MS); clinical art therapy (MA); fine art and design (MFA). Part-time and evening/weekend programs available. *Degree requirements:* For master's, thesis. Electronic applications accepted. *Faculty research:* Painting, sculpture, installation, computers, video.

Louisiana State University and Agricultural and Mechanical College, Graduate School, College of Art and Design, School of Art, Program in Studio Art, Baton Rouge, LA 70803. Offers ceramics (MFA); graphic design (MFA); painting and drawing (MFA); photography (MFA); printmaking (MFA); sculpture (MFA). *Accreditation:* NASAD. *Students:* 46 full-time (31 women), 2 part-time (0 women); includes 1 African American, 4 Asian Americans or Pacific Islanders, 6 international. Average age 29. 74 applicants, 20% accepted. In 2009, 11 master's awarded. *Degree requirements:* For master's, thesis. *Entrance requirements:* For master's, minimum GPA of 3.0. Additional exam requirements/recommendations for international students: Required—TOEFL (minimum score 550 paper-based; 213 computer-based; 79 iBT), IELTS (minimum score 6.5). *Application deadline:* For fall admission, 1/25 priority date for domestic students, 5/15 for international students; for spring admission, 10/15 for international students. Applications are processed on a rolling basis. Electronic applications accepted. *Financial support:* In 2009–10, 25 students received support; research assistantships with partial tuition reimbursements available, teaching assistantships, career-related internships or fieldwork, Federal Work-Study, institutionally sponsored loans, scholarships/grants, and unspecified assistantships available. Support available to part-time students. Financial award application deadline: 3/15. *Unit head:* Tom Neff, Graduate Coordinator, 225-578-5411, Fax: 225-578-1445, E-mail: tneff@lsu.edu. *Application contact:* Tom Neff, Graduate Coordinator, 225-578-5411, Fax: 225-578-1445, E-mail: tneff@lsu.edu.

Louisiana Tech University, Graduate School, College of Liberal Arts, School of Art, Ruston, LA 71272. Offers art and graphic design (MFA); photography (MFA); studio art (MFA). *Accreditation:* NASAD. Part-time programs available. *Degree requirements:* For master's, exhibit. *Entrance requirements:* For master's, GRE General Test, portfolio.

Maine College of Art, Program in Studio Arts, Portland, ME 04101. Offers MFA. *Accreditation:* NASAD. *Degree requirements:* For master's, thesis. *Entrance requirements:* Additional exam requirements/recommendations for international students: Required—TOEFL (minimum score 550 paper-based; 213 computer-based). Electronic applications accepted.

Marshall University, Academic Affairs Division, College of Fine Arts, Department of Art, Huntington, WV 25755. Offers MA. Evening/weekend programs available. *Faculty:* 11 full-time (5 women), 11 part-time/adjunct (10 women). *Students:* 6 full-time (3 women), 4 part-time (3 women); includes 1 minority (American Indian/Alaska Native), 1 international. Average age 29. In 2009, 4 master's awarded. *Degree requirements:* For master's, thesis optional. *Entrance requirements:* For master's, GRE General Test, portfolio. Application fee: $40. *Unit head:* Prof. Byron Clercx, Chair, 304-696-5451, Fax: 304-696-6505, E-mail: clercx@marshall.edu. *Application contact:* Information Contact, 304-746-1900, Fax: 304-746-1902, E-mail: services@marshall.edu.

Maryland Institute College of Art, Graduate Studies, Fine Arts Post Baccalaureate Certificate Program, Baltimore, MD 21217. Offers Certificate. *Faculty:* 1 full-time (0 women), 2 part-time/adjunct (both women). *Students:* 19 full-time (14 women); includes 1 minority (African American), 2 international. Average age 28. In 2009, 17 Certificates awarded. *Degree requirements:* For Certificate, thesis. *Entrance requirements:* For degree, portfolio, 40 studio credits, 6 credits in art history. Additional exam requirements/recommendations for international students: Required—TOEFL (minimum score 550 paper-based; 213 computer-based; 80 iBT). *Application deadline:* For fall admission, 1/15 for domestic and international students; for spring admission, 10/1 for domestic and international students. Application fee: $60. *Expenses:* Tuition: Full-time $33,000; part-time $1375 per credit hour. Required fees: $1090; $545 per semester. *Financial support:* In 2009–10, 19 students received support, including 24 fellowships (averaging $6,500 per year); scholarships/grants also available. Financial award application deadline: 3/1; financial award applicants required to submit FAFSA. *Unit head:* William Schmidt, Director, 410-230-0568, Fax: 410-225-2408. *Application contact:* Scott G. Kelly, Associate Dean of Graduate Admission, 410-225-2256, Fax: 410-225-2408, E-mail: graduate@mica.edu.

Maryland Institute College of Art, Graduate Studies, Hoffberger School of Painting, Baltimore, MD 21217. Offers MFA. *Accreditation:* NASAD. *Faculty:* 4 full-time (3 women), 2 part-time/adjunct (1 woman). *Students:* 14 full-time (8 women); includes 2 minority (1 African American, 1 Hispanic American), 3 international. Average age 29. In 2009, 8 master's awarded. *Degree requirements:* For master's, thesis, exhibit. *Entrance requirements:* For master's, portfolio, 40 studio credits, 6 credits in art history. Additional exam requirements/recommendations for international students: Required—TOEFL (minimum score 550 paper-based; 213 computer-based; 80 iBT). *Application deadline:* For fall admission, 1/15 for domestic and international students. Application fee: $60. *Expenses:* Tuition: Full-time $33,000; part-time $1375 per credit hour. Required fees: $1090; $545 per semester. *Financial support:* In 2009–10, 14 students received support, including 1 fellowship (averaging $17,274 per year), 12 teaching assistantships (averaging $1,800 per year); career-related internships or fieldwork and scholarships/grants also available. Financial award application deadline: 3/1; financial award applicants required to submit FAFSA. *Unit head:* Timothy App, Director, 410-225-5273, Fax: 410-225-5275, E-mail: graduate@mica.edu. *Application contact:* Scott G. Kelly, Associate Dean of Graduate Admission, 410-225-2256, Fax: 410-225-2408, E-mail: graduate@mica.edu.

Maryland Institute College of Art, Graduate Studies, Mount Royal School of Art, Baltimore, MD 21217. Offers painting (MFA). *Faculty:* 1 (woman) full-time, 4 part-time/adjunct (1 woman). *Students:* 27 full-time (14 women); includes 2 minority (1 African American, 1 Asian American or Pacific Islander), 4 international. Average age 27. In 2009, 10 master's awarded. *Degree requirements:* For master's, thesis, exhibit. *Entrance requirements:* For master's, 40 credits in studio art, 6 credits in art history, portfolio. Additional exam requirements/recommendations for international students: Required—TOEFL (minimum score 550 paper-based; 213 computer-based; 80 iBT). *Application deadline:* For fall admission, 1/15 for domestic and international students. Application fee: $60. *Expenses:* Tuition: Full-time $33,000; part-time $1375 per credit hour. Required fees: $1090; $545 per semester. *Financial support:* In 2009–10, 25 students received support, including 4 fellowships (averaging $17,274 per year), 21 teaching assistantships (averaging $1,800 per year); career-related internships or fieldwork and scholarships/grants also available. Financial award application deadline: 3/1; financial award applicants required to submit FAFSA. *Unit head:* Frances Barth, Director, 410-225-2347, Fax: 410-225-5275, E-mail: graduate@mica.edu. *Application contact:* Scott G. Kelly, Associate Dean of Graduate Admission, 410-225-2256, Fax: 410-225-2408, E-mail: graduate@mica.edu.

Maryland Institute College of Art, Graduate Studies, Program in Community Arts, Baltimore, MD 21217. Offers MA. Part-time programs available. *Faculty:* 2 full-time (1 woman), 7 part-time/adjunct (all women). *Students:* 2 full-time (both women), 23 part-time (19 women); includes 4 minority (3 African Americans, 1 Asian American or Pacific Islander), 3 international. Average age 30. In 2009, 9 master's awarded. *Degree requirements:* For master's, thesis. *Entrance requirements:* For master's, portfolio, 40 studio credits, 6 credits in art history. Additional exam requirements/recommendations for international students: Required—TOEFL (minimum score 550 paper-based; 213 computer-based). *Application deadline:* For fall admission, 1/15 for domestic and international students. Application fee: $60. *Expenses:* Tuition: Full-time $33,000; part-time $1375 per credit hour. Required fees: $1090; $545 per semester. *Financial support:* In 2009–10, 21 students received support, including 1 fellowship (averaging $17,274 per year); teaching assistantships, career-related internships or fieldwork and scholarships/grants also available. Financial award application deadline: 3/1; financial award applicants required to submit FAFSA. *Unit head:* Ken Krafchek, Director, 410-225-2587, Fax: 410-225-2574. *Application contact:* Scott G. Kelly, Associate Dean of Graduate Admission, 410-225-2256, Fax: 410-225-2408, E-mail: graduate@mica.edu.

Maryland Institute College of Art, Graduate Studies, Program in Studio Art, Baltimore, MD 21217. Offers MFA. Offered during summer only. Part-time programs available. *Faculty:* 2 full-time (1 woman), 2 part-time/adjunct (1 woman). *Students:* 11 full-time (9 women), 27 part-time (17 women); includes 2 minority (1 American Indian/Alaska Native, 1 Hispanic American), 2 international. Average age 37. In 2009, 9 master's awarded. *Degree requirements:* For master's, thesis. *Entrance requirements:* For master's, portfolio, 40 studio credits, 6 credits in art history. Additional exam requirements/recommendations for international students: Required—TOEFL (minimum score 550 paper-based; 213 computer-based). *Application deadline:* For fall admission, 1/15 for domestic and international students. Application fee: $60. *Expenses:* Tuition: Full-time $33,000; part-time $1375 per credit hour. Required fees: $1090; $545 per semester. *Financial support:* In 2009–10, 27 students received support, including 5 fellowships (averaging $7,400 per year); teaching assistantships, career-related internships or fieldwork and scholarships/grants also available. Financial award application deadline: 3/1; financial award applicants required to submit FAFSA. *Unit head:* Zlata Baum, Director, 410-225-2297, Fax: 410-225-2257. *Application contact:* Scott G. Kelly, Associate Dean of Graduate Admission, 410-225-2256, Fax: 410-225-2408, E-mail: graduate@mica.edu.

Maryland Institute College of Art, Graduate Studies, Rinehart School of Sculpture, Baltimore, MD 21217. Offers MFA. *Accreditation:* NASAD. *Faculty:* 1 (woman) full-time. *Students:* 11 full-time (6 women); includes 1 minority (Asian American or Pacific Islander), 1 international. Average age 25. In 2009, 4 master's awarded. *Degree requirements:* For master's, thesis, exhibit. *Entrance requirements:* For master's, portfolio, 40 studio credits, 6 credits in art history. Additional exam requirements/recommendations for international students: Required—TOEFL (minimum score 550 paper-based; 213 computer-based). *Application deadline:* For fall admission, 1/15 for domestic and international students. Application fee: $60. *Expenses:* Tuition: Full-time $33,000; part-time $1375 per credit hour. Required fees: $1090; $545 per semester. *Financial support:* In 2009–10, 11 students received support, including 2 fellowships (averaging $17,274 per year), 9 teaching assistantships (averaging $1,800 per year); career-related internships or fieldwork and scholarships/grants also available. Financial award application deadline: 3/1; financial award applicants required to submit FAFSA. *Unit head:*

Art/Fine Arts

Maryland Institute College of Art (continued)
Maren Hassinger, Director, 410-225-2271, Fax: 410-225-2408. *Application contact:* Scott G. Kelly, Associate Dean of Graduate Admission, 410-225-2256, Fax: 410-225-2408, E-mail: graduate@mica.edu.

Marywood University, Academic Affairs, Insalaco College of Creative and Performing Arts, Art Department, Program in Studio Art, Scranton, PA 18509-1598. Offers advertising design (MA); ceramics (MA); clay (MA); graphic design (MA); illustration (MA); painting (MA); photography (MA); printmaking (MA); sculpture (MA); weaving (MA). *Accreditation:* NASAD. *Students:* 6 full-time (5 women), 7 part-time (all women); includes 1 minority (Asian American or Pacific Islander). Average age 38. 5 applicants, 80% accepted. In 2009, 6 master's awarded. *Entrance requirements:* Additional exam requirements/recommendations for international students: Required—TOEFL (minimum score 550 paper-based; 213 computer-based; 79 iBT). *Application deadline:* For fall admission, 4/1 priority date for domestic students, 3/31 priority date for international students; for spring admission, 11/1 priority date for domestic students, 8/31 priority date for international students. Applications are processed on a rolling basis. Application fee: $35. Electronic applications accepted. *Expenses:* Tuition: Part-time $715 per credit. Required fees: $270 per semester. Tuition and fees vary according to degree level, campus/location and program. *Financial support:* Career-related internships or fieldwork, scholarships/grants, and unspecified assistantships available. Support available to part-time students. Financial award application deadline: 6/30; financial award applicants required to submit FAFSA. *Faculty research:* Texture and line in clay, cast bronze sculpture, color theories, book art and illustration, sculptural form. *Application contact:* Tammy Manka, Assistant Director of Graduate Admissions, 866-279-9663, E-mail: tmanka@marywood.edu.

Marywood University, Academic Affairs, Insalaco College of Creative and Performing Arts, Art Department, Program in Visual Arts, Scranton, PA 18509-1598. Offers advertising design (MFA); clay (MFA); graphic design (MFA); illustration (MFA); metals (MFA); painting (MFA); photography (MFA); printmaking (MFA). *Accreditation:* NASAD. *Students:* 16 full-time (13 women), 29 part-time (16 women); includes 2 minority (both Asian Americans or Pacific Islanders), 2 international. Average age 37. In 2009, 11 master's awarded. *Entrance requirements:* Additional exam requirements/recommendations for international students: Required—TOEFL (minimum score 550 paper-based; 213 computer-based; 79 iBT). *Application deadline:* For fall admission, 4/1 priority date for domestic students, 3/31 priority date for international students; for spring admission, 11/1 priority date for domestic students, 8/31 priority date for international students. Applications are processed on a rolling basis. Application fee: $35. Electronic applications accepted. *Expenses:* Contact institution. *Financial support:* Career-related internships or fieldwork, scholarships/grants, and unspecified assistantships available. Support available to part-time students. Financial award application deadline: 6/30; financial award applicants required to submit FAFSA. *Faculty research:* Mariology, exploration of visual imagery, explorations involving drawing on the loom, clay as sculptural medium, oil paintings. *Application contact:* Tammy Manka, Assistant Director of Graduate Admissions, 866-279-9663, E-mail: tmanka@marywood.edu.

Marywood University, Academic Affairs, School of Architecture, Scranton, PA 18509-1598. Offers architecture (M Arch); studio art (MA), including interior design. *Students:* 2 part-time (both women). Average age 25. In 2009, 6 master's awarded. *Entrance requirements:* Additional exam requirements/recommendations for international students: Required—TOEFL (minimum score 550 paper-based; 213 computer-based; 79 iBT). *Expenses:* Tuition: Part-time $715 per credit. Required fees: $270 per semester. Tuition and fees vary according to degree level, campus/location and program. *Financial support:* Career-related internships or fieldwork, scholarships/grants, and unspecified assistantships available. Support available to part-time students. Financial award application deadline: 6/30; financial award applicants required to submit FAFSA. *Unit head:* Gregory K. Hunt, Founding Dean, 570-348-6211 Ext. 4536, E-mail: gkhunt@marywood.edu. *Application contact:* Tammy Manka, Assistant Director of Graduate Admissions, 866-279-9663, E-mail: tmanka@marywood.edu.

Massachusetts College of Art and Design, Graduate Programs, Program in Fine Arts, Boston, MA 02115-5882. Offers ceramics (MFA); design (MFA); fibers (MFA); film/video (MFA); glass (MFA); media and performing arts (MFA); metals/jewelry (MFA); painting (MFA); photography (MFA); printmaking (MFA); sculpture (MFA). *Accreditation:* NASAD. *Faculty:* 10 full-time (5 women), 8 part-time/adjunct (6 women). *Students:* 89 full-time (56 women), 12 part-time (8 women); includes 8 minority (5 Asian Americans or Pacific Islanders, 3 Hispanic Americans), 10 international. Average age 34. 295 applicants, 24% accepted, 40 enrolled. In 2009, 44 master's awarded. *Degree requirements:* For master's, thesis, exhibit. *Entrance requirements:* For master's, 12 units of course work in art history, portfolio, resume, letters of reference, interview. Additional exam requirements/recommendations for international students: Required—TOEFL (minimum score 563 paper-based; 223 computer-based; 85 iBT); Recommended—IELTS (minimum score 6.5). *Application deadline:* For fall admission, 1/15 for domestic and international students. Application fee: $75. Electronic applications accepted. *Expenses:* Tuition, state resident: full-time $18,450; part-time $615 per credit. Tuition, nonresident: full-time $18,450; part-time $615 per credit. Tuition and fees vary according to program. *Financial support:* In 2009–10, 50 research assistantships (averaging $2,000 per year), 40 teaching assistantships (averaging $2,000 per year) were awarded; career-related internships or fieldwork, Federal Work-Study, and clerical/technical assistantships ($2000) also available. Support available to part-time students. Financial award application deadline: 5/1; financial award applicants required to submit FAFSA. *Unit head:* George Creamer, Dean of Graduate Programs, 617-879-7163, Fax: 617-879-7171, E-mail: creamer@massart.edu. *Application contact:* George Creamer, Dean of Graduate Programs, 617-879-7163, Fax: 617-879-7171, E-mail: creamer@massart.edu.

Memphis College of Art, Graduate Programs, Program in Studio Art, Memphis, TN 38104-2764. Offers MFA. *Accreditation:* NASAD. Part-time programs available. *Faculty:* 25 full-time (13 women), 8 part-time/adjunct (6 women). *Students:* 18 full-time (11 women), 1 (woman) part-time; includes 2 minority (both African Americans). Average age 28. 59 applicants, 42% accepted, 10 enrolled. In 2009, 10 degrees awarded. *Degree requirements:* For master's, thesis. *Entrance requirements:* For master's, portfolio, interview, resume. Additional exam requirements/recommendations for international students: Required—TOEFL (minimum score 525 paper-based; 195 computer-based). *Application deadline:* For fall admission, 3/1 for domestic and international students; for spring admission, 11/1 for domestic and international students. Application fee: $50. Electronic applications accepted. *Expenses:* Tuition: Full-time $23,000; part-time $958 per credit hour. Required fees: $600; $200 per course. Tuition and fees vary according to program. *Financial support:* In 2009–10, 19 students received support, including 5 teaching assistantships (averaging $2,500 per year); career-related internships or fieldwork, Federal Work-Study, scholarships/grants, and unspecified assistantships also available. Financial award application deadline: 8/1; financial award applicants required to submit FAFSA. *Unit head:* Howard Paine, Director of MFA Graduate Program, 901-272-5100, Fax: 901-272-5158, E-mail: hpaine@mca.edu. *Application contact:* Annette Moore, Dean of Admissions, 901-272-5151, Fax: 901-272-5158, E-mail: amoore@mca.edu.

See Close-Up on page 195.

Miami International University of Art & Design, Program in Visual Arts, Miami, FL 33132-1418. Offers MFA. Postbaccalaureate distance learning degree programs offered. *Application contact:* Office of Graduate Admissions, 305-428-5700.

See Close-Up on page 117.

Miami University, Graduate School, School of Fine Arts, Department of Art, Program in Studio Art, Oxford, OH 45056. Offers MFA. *Accreditation:* NASAD. *Degree requirements:* For master's, thesis, final project. *Entrance requirements:* For master's, portfolio, minimum undergraduate GPA of 3.0 during previous 2 years or 2.75 overall. *Application deadline:* For fall admission, 2/1 priority date for domestic students. Applications are processed on a rolling basis. Application fee: $35. *Expenses:* Tuition, state resident: full-time $11,280. Tuition, nonresident: full-time $24,912. Required fees: $516. *Financial support:* Application deadline: 3/1. *Unit head:* Prof. Ellen Price, Graduate Director, 513-529-7128, E-mail: priceej@muohio.edu. *Application contact:* Prof. Ellen Price, Graduate Director, 513-529-7128, E-mail: priceej@muohio.edu.

Michigan State University, The Graduate School, College of Arts and Letters, Department of Art and Art History, East Lansing, MI 48824. Offers studio art (MFA). *Faculty:* 25 full-time (12 women). *Students:* 16 full-time (9 women), 2 part-time (1 woman); includes 2 minority (1 American Indian/Alaska Native, 1 Hispanic American), 2 international. Average age 29. 31 applicants, 16% accepted. In 2009, 6 master's awarded. *Entrance requirements:* For master's, minimum GPA of 3.0, portfolio, resume. Additional exam requirements/recommendations for international students: Required—TOEFL, Michigan State University ELT (minimum score 85), Michigan Michigan English Language Assessment Battery (minimum score 83). *Application deadline:* Applications are processed on a rolling basis. Electronic applications accepted. *Expenses:* Tuition, state resident: part-time $478.25 per credit hour. Tuition, nonresident: part-time $966.50 per credit hour. Part-time tuition and fees vary according to program. *Financial support:* In 2009–10, 1 research assistantship with tuition reimbursement (averaging $6,061 per year), 11 teaching assistantships with tuition reimbursements (averaging $5,653 per year) were awarded. Total annual research expenditures: $841. *Unit head:* Prof. Thomas G. Berding, Chairperson, 517-355-7612, Fax: 517-432-3938, E-mail: berding@msu.edu. *Application contact:* Andrea Worful, Graduate Secretary, 517-355-7612, Fax: 517-432-3938, E-mail: artgrad@msu.edu.

Mills College, Graduate Studies, Department of Art, Oakland, CA 94613-1000. Offers ceramics (MFA); intermedia (MFA); painting (MFA); photography (MFA); sculpture (MFA). *Faculty:* 7 full-time (5 women), 8 part-time/adjunct (5 women). *Students:* 22 full-time (13 women); includes 3 minority (2 Asian Americans or Pacific Islanders, 1 Hispanic American). Average age 31. 107 applicants, 21% accepted, 12 enrolled. In 2009, 10 master's awarded. *Degree requirements:* For master's, thesis or alternative, exhibit. *Entrance requirements:* For master's, portfolio. Additional exam requirements/recommendations for international students: Required—TOEFL. *Application deadline:* For fall admission, 2/1 for domestic students; for spring admission, 11/1 for domestic students. Application fee: $50. *Expenses:* Contact institution. *Financial support:* In 2009–10, 22 students received support, including 22 fellowships (averaging $8,938 per year), 13 teaching assistantships with partial tuition reimbursements available (averaging $13,055 per year); scholarships/grants and unspecified assistantships also available. Financial award application deadline: 2/1; financial award applicants required to submit FAFSA. *Faculty research:* Contemporary Chinese/American art, Asian art, performance art, feminist theory, installation. *Unit head:* Mary-Ann Milford, Chairperson, 510-430-3142, Fax: 510-430-3314. *Application contact:* Jessica King, Graduate Admission Specialist, 510-430-3305, Fax: 510-430-2159, E-mail: grad-studies@mills.edu.

Minneapolis College of Art and Design, Certificate Programs, Minneapolis, MN 55404-4347. Offers design (Certificate); fine arts (Certificate); graphic design (Certificate); media (Certificate); sustainable design (Certificate). Part-time programs available. Postbaccalaureate distance learning degree programs offered. *Faculty:* 42 full-time (29 women). *Students:* 4 full-time (2 women), 22 part-time (19 women). Average age 24. In 2009, 15 Certificates awarded. *Degree requirements:* For Certificate, final project. *Entrance requirements:* For degree, resume, portfolio, letter of recommendation. Additional exam requirements/recommendations for international students: Required—TOEFL (minimum score 550 paper-based; 213 computer-based; 79 iBT). *Application deadline:* For fall admission, 1/15 for domestic and international students; for spring admission, 10/15 for domestic and international students. Application fee: $50. Electronic applications accepted. *Expenses:* Tuition: Full-time $29,500; part-time $985 per credit. Required fees: $100. *Financial support:* Career-related internships or fieldwork and scholarships/grants available. Financial award application deadline: 3/15; financial award applicants required to submit FAFSA. *Faculty research:* Visual arts. *Unit head:* Howard Oransky, Director of Continuing Studies, 612-874-3778, E-mail: howard_oransky@mcad.edu. *Application contact:* Howard Oransky, Director of Continuing Studies, 612-874-3778, Fax: 612-874-3701, E-mail: howard_oransky@mcad.edu.

Minneapolis College of Art and Design, Program in Visual Studies, Minneapolis, MN 55404-4347. Offers animation (MFA); comic art (MFA); drawing (MFA); filmmaking (MFA); fine arts (MFA); furniture design (MFA); graphic design (MFA); illustration (MFA); interactive media (MFA); painting (MFA); photography (MFA); printmaking (MFA); sculpture (MFA). *Accreditation:* NASAD. Part-time programs available. *Faculty:* 42 full-time (13 women). *Students:* 12 full-time (2 women), 18 part-time (8 women). Average age 27. 166 applicants, 28% accepted, 12 enrolled. In 2009, 10 master's awarded. *Degree requirements:* For master's, thesis, thesis exhibit. *Entrance requirements:* For master's, portfolio of visual artwork, resume, 3 letters of recommendation. Additional exam requirements/recommendations for international students: Required—TOEFL (minimum score 550 paper-based; 213 computer-based; 79 iBT). *Application deadline:* For fall admission, 1/15 for domestic and international students. Application fee: $50. Electronic applications accepted. *Expenses:* Tuition: Full-time $29,500; part-time $985 per credit. Required fees: $100. *Financial support:* In 2009–10, 23 students received support, including 15 teaching assistantships (averaging $6,000 per year); career-related internships or fieldwork, Federal Work-Study, scholarships/grants, and unspecified assistantships also available. Support available to part-time students. Financial award application deadline: 3/15; financial award applicants required to submit FAFSA. *Faculty research:* Visual arts: animation, comic art, drawing, filmmaking, furniture design, graphic design, illustration, interactive media, painting, photography, printmaking, sculpture. *Unit head:* Carole Fisher, Graduate Director, 612-874-3629, E-mail: carole_fisher@mcad.edu. *Application contact:* William Mullen, Vice President of Enrollment Management, 612-874-3760, Fax: 612-874-3701, E-mail: william_mullen@mcad.edu.

Minnesota State University Mankato, College of Graduate Studies, College of Arts and Humanities, Department of Art, Mankato, MN 56001. Offers art education (MS); studio art (MA); teaching art (MAT). *Accreditation:* NASAD (one or more programs are accredited). Part-time programs available. *Students:* 5 full-time (2 women), 8 part-time (3 women). *Degree requirements:* For master's, one foreign language, comprehensive exam, thesis or alternative. *Entrance requirements:* For master's, minimum GPA of 3.0 during previous 2 years, portfolio (MA). Additional exam requirements/recommendations for international students: Required—TOEFL. *Application deadline:* For fall admission, 7/1 priority date for domestic students, 5/1 for international students; for spring admission, 11/1 for domestic students, 10/1 for international students. Applications are processed on a rolling basis. Application fee: $40. Electronic applications accepted. *Expenses:* Tuition, state resident: full-time $5364. Tuition, nonresident: full-time $8314. *Financial support:* Research assistantships, teaching assistantships with full tuition reimbursements, unspecified assistantships available. Financial award application deadline: 3/15; financial award applicants required to submit FAFSA. *Faculty research:* Photographic documentation. *Unit head:* Brian Frink, Graduate Coordinator, 507-389-6412. *Application contact:* 507-389-2321, E-mail: grad@mnsu.edu.

Mississippi College, Graduate School, College of Arts and Sciences, School of Christian Studies and the Arts, Department of Art, Clinton, MS 39058. Offers M Ed, MA, MFA. Part-time and evening/weekend programs available. *Faculty:* 5 full-time (0 women), 3 part-time/adjunct (2 women). *Students:* 9 full-time (7 women), 11 part-time (6 women); includes 4 minority (3 African Americans, 1 Asian American or Pacific Islander), 1 international. Average age 31. In 2009, 7 master's awarded. *Degree requirements:* For master's, one foreign language, comprehensive exam, thesis (for some programs). *Entrance requirements:* For master's, GRE or NTE, minimum GPA of 2.5. Additional exam requirements/recommendations for international students: Recommended—IELTS. *Application deadline:* For fall admission, 8/15 priority date for domestic and international students. Applications are processed on a rolling basis. Application fee: $30. Electronic applications accepted. *Expenses:* Tuition: Part-time $452 per credit hour. Required fees: $101 per semester. Tuition and fees vary according to degree level, campus/location, program and student level. *Financial support:* Teaching assistantships, career-related internships or fieldwork, Federal Work-Study, scholarships/grants, and unspecified assistantships available. Support available to part-time students. Financial award application deadline: 4/1; financial award applicants required to submit FAFSA. *Unit head:* Dr. Randolph B. Miley, Chair, 601-925-3912, Fax: 601-925-3926, E-mail: rmiley@mc.edu. *Application contact:* Elnora Lewis, Secretary, 601-925-3225, Fax: 601-925-3889, E-mail: lewis09@mc.edu.

Missouri State University, Graduate College, College of Arts and Letters, Department of Art and Design, Springfield, MO 65897. Offers secondary education (MS Ed), including art. Part-time programs available. *Faculty:* 8 full-time (3 women). *Students:* 1 full-time (0 women). Average age 38. 2 applicants, 100% accepted, 1 enrolled. *Entrance requirements:* For master's, minimum GPA of 3.0, 9-12 teaching certification. Additional exam requirements/recommendations for international students: Required—TOEFL (minimum score 550 paper-based; 213 computer-based; 79 iBT). *Application deadline:* For fall admission, 7/20 priority date for domestic students, 5/1 for international students; for spring admission, 12/20 priority date for domestic students, 9/1 for international students. Applications are processed on a rolling basis. Application fee: $35 ($50 for international students). Electronic applications accepted. *Expenses:* Tuition, state resident: full-time $3852; part-time $214 per credit hour. Tuition, nonresident: full-time $7524; part-time $418 per credit hour. Required fees: $696; $172 per semester. Tuition and fees vary according to course level, course load, degree level and program. *Financial support:* Federal Work-Study and unspecified assistantships available. Financial award applicants required to submit FAFSA. *Unit head:* Wade S. Thompson, Head, 417-836-6055, E-mail: artanddesign@missouristate.edu. *Application contact:* Eric Eckert, Coordinator of Graduate Admissions and Recruitment, 417-836-5331, Fax: 417-386-6888, E-mail: ericeckert@missouristate.edu.

Montana State University, College of Graduate Studies, College of Arts and Architecture, Department of Art, Bozeman, MT 59717. Offers art (MFA). *Accreditation:* NASAD. Part-time programs available. *Faculty:* 15 full-time (6 women), 7 part-time/adjunct (4 women). *Students:* 32 full-time (19 women), 31 part-time (15 women); includes 2 minority (1 African American, 1 American Indian/Alaska Native), 3 international. Average age 30. 50 applicants, 22% accepted, 11 enrolled. In 2009, 2 master's awarded. *Degree requirements:* For master's, comprehensive exam. *Entrance requirements:* For master's, GRE General Test. Additional exam requirements/recommendations for international students: Required—TOEFL (minimum score 550 paper-based; 213 computer-based). *Application deadline:* For fall admission, 7/15 priority date for domestic students, 5/15 priority date for international students; for spring admission, 12/1 priority date for domestic students, 10/1 priority date for international students. Applications are processed on a rolling basis. Application fee: $30. Electronic applications accepted. *Expenses:* Tuition, state resident: full-time $5635; part-time $3492 per year. Tuition, nonresident: full-time $17,212; part-time $7865.10 per year. Required fees: $1441; $153.15 per credit. Tuition and fees vary according to course load and program. *Financial support:* In 2009–10, 12 students received support, including 12 teaching assistantships with partial tuition reimbursements available (averaging $7,725 per year); Federal Work-Study, scholarships/grants, health care benefits, tuition waivers (partial), and unspecified assistantships also available. Financial award application deadline: 3/1; financial award applicants required to submit FAFSA. *Faculty research:* Fine arts, encaustic, letter press, design. *Unit head:* Vaughan Judge, Head, 406-994-4501, Fax: 406-994-3680, E-mail: vaughan.judge@montana.edu. *Application contact:* Dr. Carl A. Fox, Vice Provost for Graduate Education, 406-994-4145, Fax: 406-994-7433, E-mail: gradstudy@montana.edu.

Montclair State University, The Graduate School, School of the Arts, Department of Art and Design, Montclair, NJ 07043-1624. Offers art education (MA, Certificate); art history (MA); studio arts (MA, MFA). *Accreditation:* NASAD (one or more programs are accredited). Part-time and evening/weekend programs available. *Faculty:* 26 full-time (11 women), 4 part-time/adjunct (2 women). *Students:* 30 full-time (19 women), 29 part-time (24 women). Average age 32. 53 applicants, 58% accepted, 20 enrolled. In 2009, 22 master's awarded. *Degree requirements:* For master's, project. *Entrance requirements:* For master's, GRE General Test or MAT (MA), portfolio, undergraduate degree in fine arts or equivalent, 2 letters of recommendation, teaching certificate (art education). Additional exam requirements/recommendations for international students: Required—TOEFL (minimum score 83 computer-based), or IELTS. *Application deadline:* For fall admission, 2/1 for domestic and international students. Applications are processed on a rolling basis. Application fee: $60. Electronic applications accepted. *Expenses:* Tuition, area resident: Part-time $486.74 per credit. Tuition, state resident: part-time $486.74 per credit. Tuition, nonresident: part-time $751.34 per credit. Tuition and fees vary according to degree level and program. *Financial support:* In 2009–10, 7 research assistantships with full tuition reimbursements (averaging $7,000 per year) were awarded; Federal Work-Study, scholarships/grants, and unspecified assistantships also available. Support available to part-time students. Financial award application deadline: 3/1; financial award applicants required to submit FAFSA. *Unit head:* Dr. Scott Gordley, Chairperson, 973-655-7295. *Application contact:* Amy Aiello, Director of Graduate Admissions and Operations, 973-655-5147, E-mail: graduate.school@montclair.edu.

Moore College of Art & Design, Program in Studio Art, Philadelphia, PA 19103. Offers MFA. *Degree requirements:* For master's, thesis. *Entrance requirements:* For master's, bachelor's degree in visual arts or another field with completion of 15 art history credits; minimum GPA of 3.0; on-site interview; portfolio; 3 letters of recommendation; resume.

Morehead State University, Graduate Programs, Caudill College of Arts, Humanities and Social Sciences, Department of Art and Design, Morehead, KY 40351. Offers art education (MA); graphic design (MA); studio art (MA). Part-time and evening/weekend programs available. *Faculty:* 9 full-time (3 women), 2 part-time/adjunct (1 woman). *Students:* 9 full-time (4 women), 3 part-time (2 women). Average age 31. 5 applicants, 60% accepted, 3 enrolled. In 2009, 7 master's awarded. *Degree requirements:* For master's, comprehensive exam, thesis (for some programs), oral exam during exhibition. *Entrance requirements:* For master's, GRE General Test, minimum undergraduate GPA of 3.0 in major, 2.5 overall; portfolio; bachelor's degree in art. Additional exam requirements/recommendations for international students: Required—TOEFL (minimum score 500 paper-based; 173 computer-based). *Application deadline:* For fall admission, 8/1 priority date for domestic and international students; for spring admission, 12/1 priority date for domestic and international students. Applications are processed on a rolling basis. Application fee: $30. Electronic applications accepted. *Expenses:* Tuition, state resident: full-time $6318; part-time $351 per credit hour. Tuition, nonresident: full-time $15,804; part-time $878 per credit hour. *Financial support:* In 2009–10, 3 research assistantships (averaging $10,000 per year), 2 teaching assistantships (averaging $10,000 per year) were awarded; career-related internships or fieldwork, Federal Work-Study, and unspecified assistantships also available. Financial award application deadline: 3/15; financial award applicants required to submit FAFSA. *Faculty research:* Computer art, painting, drawing, ceramics, photography. *Unit head:* Robert Franzini, Chair, 606-783-2193, Fax: 606-783-5048, E-mail: r.franzi@moreheadstate.edu. *Application contact:* Michelle Barber, Graduate Recruitment and Retention Assistant Director, 606-783-5127, Fax: 606-783-5061, E-mail: m.barber@moreheadstate.edu.

National University, Academic Affairs, College of Letters and Sciences, Department of Art and Humanities, La Jolla, CA 92037-1011. Offers creative writing (MFA); English (MA); history (MA). Part-time and evening/weekend programs available. Postbaccalaureate distance learning degree programs offered (no on-campus study). *Faculty:* 13 full-time (4 women), 24 part-time/adjunct (15 women). *Students:* 204 full-time (144 women), 499 part-time (340 women); includes 160 minority (77 African Americans, 6 American Indian/Alaska Native, 17 Asian Americans or Pacific Islanders, 60 Hispanic Americans). Average age 38. 440 applicants, 100% accepted, 280 enrolled. In 2009, 152 master's awarded. *Degree requirements:* For master's, thesis (for some programs). *Entrance requirements:* For master's, interview, minimum GPA of 2.5. Additional exam requirements/recommendations for international students: Required—TOEFL (minimum score 550 paper-based; 213 computer-based; 79 iBT), IELTS (minimum score 6). *Application deadline:* Applications are processed on a rolling basis. Application fee: $60 ($65 for international students). Electronic applications accepted. *Expenses:* Tuition: Part-time $338 per quarter hour. *Financial support:* Career-related internships or fieldwork, institutionally sponsored loans, scholarships/grants, and tuition waivers (partial) available. Support available to part-time students. Financial award application deadline: 6/30; financial award applicants required to submit FAFSA. *Unit head:* Dr. Janet Baker, Chair, 858-642-8472, Fax: 858-642-8715, E-mail: jbaker@nu.edu. *Application contact:* Dominick Giovanniello, Associate Regional Dean—San Diego, 800-NAT-UNIV, Fax: 858-541-7792, E-mail: dgiovann@nu.edu.

New Jersey City University, Graduate Studies and Continuing Education, William J. Maxwell College of Arts and Sciences, Department of Art, Jersey City, NJ 07305-1597. Offers art (MFA); art education (MA); studio art (MFA). *Accreditation:* NASAD. Part-time and evening/weekend programs available. *Faculty:* 6. *Students:* 6 full-time (3 women), 5 part-time (4 women); includes 2 minority (1 African American, 1 American Indian/Alaska Native). Average age 33. In 2009, 1 master's awarded. *Degree requirements:* For master's, thesis or alternative, exhibit. *Entrance requirements:* For master's, GRE General Test or MAT, portfolio. Additional exam requirements/recommendations for international students: Required—TOEFL. *Application deadline:* For fall admission, 8/1 priority date for domestic students; for spring admission, 12/1 for domestic students. Applications are processed on a rolling basis. Application fee: $0. *Expenses:* Tuition, area resident: Part-time $456.75 per credit. Tuition, nonresident: part-time $842.55 per credit. Required fees: $65 per term. *Financial support:* Unspecified assistantships available. *Unit head:* Dr. Herbert Rosenberg, Chairperson, 201-200-2367. *Application contact:* Dr. Herbert Rosenberg, Chairperson, 201-200-2367.

New Mexico State University, Graduate School, College of Arts and Sciences, Department of Art, Las Cruces, NM 88003-8001. Offers art history (MA); ceramics (MA, MFA); design (MA, MFA); drawing (MFA); metals (MA, MFA); painting (MFA); photography (MFA); printmaking (MA, MFA); sculpture (MA, MFA). *Faculty:* 11 full-time (6 women), 2 part-time/adjunct (1 woman). *Students:* 32 full-time (15 women); includes 8 minority (2 American Indian/Alaska Native, 6 Hispanic Americans). Average age 31. 33 applicants, 55% accepted, 7 enrolled. In 2009, 8 master's awarded. *Degree requirements:* For master's, comprehensive exam (for some programs), thesis, thesis exhibit. *Entrance requirements:* For master's, portfolio, 10-page paper (art history). *Application deadline:* For fall admission, 2/15 for domestic students; for winter admission, 10/15 for domestic students; for spring admission, 7/15 for domestic students. Application fee: $30 ($50 for international students). Electronic applications accepted. *Expenses:* Tuition, state resident: full-time $4080; part-time $223 per credit. Tuition, nonresident: full-time $14,256; part-time $647 per credit. Required fees: $1278; $639 per semester. *Financial support:* In 2009–10, 1 research assistantship (averaging $7,900 per year), 29 teaching assistantships (averaging $9,092 per year) were awarded; Federal Work-Study and health care benefits also available. Support available to part-time students. Financial award application deadline: 3/1; financial award applicants required to submit FAFSA. *Faculty research:* Painting, graphic design, sculpture, printmaking, drawing, ceramics, photography, jewelry. *Unit head:* Spencer D. Fidler, Head, 575-646-1705, Fax: 575-646-8036, E-mail: sfidler@nmsu.edu. *Application contact:* Spencer D. Fidler, Head, 575-646-1705, Fax: 575-646-8036, E-mail: sfidler@nmsu.edu.

The New School: A University, Parsons The New School for Design, Program in Fine Arts, New York, NY 10011. Offers MFA. *Faculty:* 10 full-time (6 women). *Students:* 43 full-time (19 women); includes 10 minority (2 African Americans, 4 Asian Americans or Pacific Islanders, 4 Hispanic Americans), 17 international. Average age 27. 242 applicants, 26% accepted, 22 enrolled. In 2009, 22 master's awarded. *Degree requirements:* For master's, thesis. *Entrance requirements:* For master's, portfolio. Additional exam requirements/recommendations for international students: Required—TOEFL (minimum score 580 paper-based; 237 computer-based; 92 iBT). *Application deadline:* For fall admission, 2/1 for domestic and international students. Application fee: $50. Electronic applications accepted. *Financial support:* Federal Work-Study and scholarships/grants available. Support available to part-time students. Financial award application deadline: 3/1. *Unit head:* Simone Douglas, Chair, 212-229-8942 Ext. 3812, E-mail: douglass@newschool.edu. *Application contact:* David Norris, Director of Admissions, 212-229-8989 Ext. 4023, Fax: 212-229-8975, E-mail: norrisd@newschool.edu.

New York Academy of Art, Program in Figurative Art, New York, NY 10013-2911. Offers MFA. *Degree requirements:* For master's, project. *Entrance requirements:* For master's, slide portfolio. Additional exam requirements/recommendations for international students: Required—TOEFL.

New York Institute of Technology, Graduate Division, School of Arts and Sciences, Program in Fine Arts, Old Westbury, NY 11568-8000. Offers computer graphics and animation (MFA); fine arts and technology (MFA); graphic design (MFA). Part-time and evening/weekend programs available. *Students:* 17 full-time (8 women), 15 part-time (8 women); includes 5 African Americans, 1 Asian American or Pacific Islander, 4 Hispanic Americans, 7 international. Average age 32. In 2009, 2 master's awarded. *Degree requirements:* For master's, thesis or alternative. *Entrance requirements:* Additional exam requirements/recommendations for international students: Required—TOEFL (minimum score 550 paper-based; 213 computer-based). *Application deadline:* For fall admission, 7/1 priority date for domestic students; for spring admission, 12/1 priority date for domestic students. Applications are processed on a rolling basis. Application fee: $50. Electronic applications accepted. *Expenses:* Tuition: Part-time $825 per credit. *Financial support:* Research assistantships, career-related internships or fieldwork, Federal Work-Study, institutionally sponsored loans, tuition waivers (partial), and unspecified assistantships available. Support available to part-time students. Financial award applicants required to submit FAFSA. *Unit head:* Dr. Roger Yu, Dean, 516-686-7700, Fax: 516-686-1192, E-mail: ryu@nyit.edu. *Application contact:* Dr. Jacquelyn Nealon, Vice President for Enrollment Services, 516-686-7925, Fax: 516-686-7597, E-mail: jnealon@nyit.edu.

New York Studio School of Drawing, Painting and Sculpture, Certificate Program, New York, NY 10011. Offers studio art (Certificate). *Expenses:* Tuition: Full-time $21,875; part-time $4860 per semester. Required fees: $185.

New York Studio School of Drawing, Painting and Sculpture, MFA Program, New York, NY 10011. Offers painting (MFA); sculpture (MFA). *Expenses:* Tuition: Full-time $21,875; part-time $4860 per semester. Required fees: $185.

New York University, Graduate School of Arts and Science, Institute of Fine Arts, New York, NY 10012-1019. Offers art history and archaeology (MA, PhD), including architectural studies (PhD), art history and archaeology, classical art and archaeology (PhD), curatorial studies (PhD), East and South Asian art (PhD), Near Eastern art and archaeology (PhD); MA/Diploma; PhD/Certificate. Part-time programs available. *Faculty:* 19 full-time (5 women). *Students:* 193 full-time (151 women), 86 part-time (70 women); includes 23 minority (16 Asian Americans or Pacific Islanders, 7 Hispanic Americans), 26 international. Average age 32. 318 applicants, 28% accepted, 39 enrolled. In 2009, 38 master's, 18 doctorates awarded. Terminal master's awarded for partial completion of doctoral program. *Degree requirements:* For master's, 2 foreign languages, thesis or alternative, 2 qualifying papers; for doctorate, 2 foreign languages, thesis/dissertation. *Entrance requirements:* For master's, GRE General Test; for doctorate, GRE General Test, MA. Additional exam requirements/recommendations for international students: Required—TOEFL. *Application deadline:* For fall admission, 12/18 for domestic students. Application fee: $90. *Expenses:* Tuition: Full-time $30,528; part-time $1272 per credit. Required fees: $2177. *Financial support:* Fellowships with tuition reimbursements, research assistantships with tuition reimbursements, teaching assistantships with tuition reimbursements, career-related internships or fieldwork, Federal Work-Study, institutionally sponsored loans, and tuition waivers (partial) available. Financial award application deadline: 12/18; financial award applicants required to submit FAFSA. *Unit head:* Patricia Rubin, Chair, 212-992-5800, E-mail: ifa.program@nyu.edu. *Application contact:* Priscilla Saucek, Director of Graduate Studies, 212-992-5800, Fax: 212-992-5807, E-mail: ifa.program@nyu.edu.

New York University, NYU in Madrid, Madrid, NY 10012-1019, Spain. Offers creative writing in Spanish (MFA); Spanish (PhD); Spanish and Latin American literatures and cultures (MA); Spanish language and translation (MA). *Students:* 27 full-time (23 women), 1 part-time (0 women); includes 8 minority (2 African Americans, 1 Asian American or Pacific Islander, 5 Hispanic Americans), 1 international. Average age 26. 73 applicants, 90% accepted, 27 enrolled. In 2009, 22 master's awarded. Application fee: $90. *Expenses:* Tuition: Full-time $30,528; part-time $1272 per credit. Required fees: $2177. *Unit head:* Judith Nemethy, Director,

Art/Fine Arts

New York University (continued)
212-998-8770, Fax: 212-995-4149, E-mail: nyu-in-madrid@nyu.edu. *Application contact:* Judith Nemethy, Director, 212-998-8770, Fax: 212-995-4149, E-mail: nyu-in-madrid@nyu.edu.

New York University, Steinhardt School of Culture, Education, and Human Development, Department of Art and Art Professions, Program in Studio Art, New York, NY 10003. Offers MA, MFA, Advanced Certificate. Part-time programs available. *Students:* 23 full-time (11 women), 4 part-time (all women); includes 6 minority (3 Asian Americans or Pacific Islanders, 3 Hispanic Americans), 6 international. Average age 29. 337 applicants, 3% accepted, 9 enrolled. In 2009, 23 master's awarded. *Degree requirements:* For master's, thesis (for some programs). *Entrance requirements:* For master's, portfolio, interview, presentation. Additional exam requirements/recommendations for international students: Required—TOEFL. *Application deadline:* For fall admission, 12/15 priority date for domestic and international students. Applications are processed on a rolling basis. Application fee: $75. Electronic applications accepted. *Expenses:* Tuition: Full-time $30,528; part-time $1272 per credit. Required fees: $2177. *Financial support:* Career-related internships or fieldwork, Federal Work-Study, institutionally sponsored loans, scholarships/grants, tuition waivers (partial), and unspecified assistantships available. Support available to part-time students. Financial award application deadline: 2/1; financial award applicants required to submit FAFSA. *Faculty research:* Media and culture, video art and digital media, multimedia works, multimedia works, critical theory, memory and history, performance and text. *Unit head:* John Torreano, 212-998-5700, Fax: 212-995-4320, E-mail: jt2@nyu.edu. *Application contact:* 212-998-5030, Fax: 212-995-4328, E-mail: stein.hardt.gradadmissions@nyu.edu.

New York University, Steinhardt School of Culture, Education, and Human Development, Department of Art and Art Professions, Program in Visual Culture, New York, NY 10012-1019. Offers costume studies (MA). Part-time programs available. *Students:* 30 full-time (27 women), 13 part-time (all women); includes 5 minority (2 African Americans, 1 Asian American or Pacific Islander, 2 Hispanic Americans), 11 international. Average age 28. 42 applicants, 55% accepted, 15 enrolled. In 2009, 5 master's awarded. *Degree requirements:* For master's, thesis (for some programs). *Entrance requirements:* Additional exam requirements/recommendations for international students: Required—TOEFL. *Application deadline:* For fall admission, 12/15 priority date for domestic and international students. Applications are processed on a rolling basis. Application fee: $75. Electronic applications accepted. *Expenses:* Tuition: Full-time $30,528; part-time $1272 per credit. Required fees: $2177. *Financial support:* Career-related internships or fieldwork, Federal Work-Study, institutionally sponsored loans, scholarships/grants, and tuition waivers available. Support available to part-time students. Financial award application deadline: 2/1; financial award applicants required to submit FAFSA. *Faculty research:* Textiles as material culture, contemporary visual culture and globalization, cultural theory. *Unit head:* Prof. Nancy Deihl, Director, 212-998-5762, E-mail: nbd2012@nyu.edu. *Application contact:* 212-998-5030, Fax: 212-995-4328, E-mail: steinhardt.gradadmissions@nyu.edu.

New York University, Tisch School of the Arts Asia, Singapore, NY 248923, Singapore. Offers animation and digital arts (MFA); dramatic writing (MFA); film production (MFA). *Entrance requirements:* Additional exam requirements/recommendations for international students: Required—TOEFL (minimum score 610 paper-based; 250 computer-based; 105 iBT). Electronic applications accepted. *Expenses:* Tuition: Full-time $30,528; part-time $1272 per credit. Required fees: $2177.

New York University, Tisch School of the Arts, Program in Arts Politics, New York, NY 10012-1019. Offers MA. *Faculty:* 3 full-time (2 women), 4 part-time/adjunct (3 women). *Students:* 10 full-time (9 women), 1 (woman) part-time; includes 4 minority (1 African American, 3 Asian Americans or Pacific Islanders). Average age 25. 45 applicants, 58% accepted. *Degree requirements:* For master's, thesis. *Entrance requirements:* For master's, professional resume, writing sample, statement of purpose. Additional exam requirements/recommendations for international students: Required—TOEFL, IELTS or ALI. *Application deadline:* For fall admission, 1/1 for domestic and international students. Application fee: $60. *Expenses:* Tuition: Full-time $30,528; part-time $1272 per credit. Required fees: $2177. *Financial support:* In 2009–10, 2 students received support. Federal Work-Study and scholarships/grants available. Financial award application deadline: 2/15; financial award applicants required to submit FAFSA. *Unit head:* Randy Martin, Director of the program, 212-992-8248. *Application contact:* Dan Sandford, Director of Graduate Admissions, 212-998-1918, Fax: 212-995-4060, E-mail: tisch.gradadmissions@nyu.edu.

Norfolk State University, School of Graduate Studies, School of Liberal Arts, Department of Fine Arts, Norfolk, VA 23504. Offers visual studies (MA, MFA). Part-time programs available. *Degree requirements:* For master's, thesis or alternative. *Entrance requirements:* For master's, portfolio, interview, letters of recommendation. Additional exam requirements/recommendations for international students: Required—TOEFL (minimum score 500 paper-based).

Northeastern University, College of Arts, Media and Design, Department of Art + Design, Boston, MA 02115-5096. Offers studio art (MFA). *Faculty:* 16 full-time (10 women), 18 part-time/adjunct (10 women). *Students:* 1 full-time (0 women); minority (African American). 11 applicants, 27% accepted, 1 enrolled. *Degree requirements:* For master's, thesis exhibition. *Entrance requirements:* Additional exam requirements/recommendations for international students: Required—TOEFL. *Application deadline:* For fall admission, 1/15 for domestic and international students. Application fee: $50. Electronic applications accepted. *Financial support:* In 2009–10, 1 fellowship (averaging $17,040 per year) was awarded; Federal Work-Study and tuition waivers (partial) also available. Financial award application deadline: 2/1; financial award applicants required to submit FAFSA. *Unit head:* Prof. Russell Pensyl, Chair, 617-373-7926, E-mail: r.pensyl@neu.edu. *Application contact:* Jo-Anne Dickinson, Graduate Admissions Contact, 617-373-5990, Fax: 617-373-7281, E-mail: gsas@neu.edu.

Northern Illinois University, Graduate School, College of Visual and Performing Arts, School of Art, De Kalb, IL 60115-2854. Offers MA, MFA, MS. *Accreditation:* NASAD (one or more programs are accredited). Part-time and evening/weekend programs available. *Faculty:* 36 full-time (15 women), 1 (woman) part-time/adjunct. *Students:* 50 full-time (29 women), 53 part-time (38 women); includes 13 minority (1 African American, 3 Asian Americans or Pacific Islanders, 9 Hispanic Americans), 7 international. Average age 31. 83 applicants, 45% accepted, 22 enrolled. In 2009, 32 master's awarded. *Degree requirements:* For master's, variable foreign language requirement, comprehensive exam, thesis (for some programs), show or project. *Entrance requirements:* For master's, GRE General Test, minimum GPA of 2.75, portfolio. Additional exam requirements/recommendations for international students: Required—TOEFL (minimum score 550 paper-based; 213 computer-based). *Application deadline:* For fall and spring admission, 3/1 for domestic and international students. Applications are processed on a rolling basis. Application fee: $30. Electronic applications accepted. *Expenses:* Tuition, state resident: full-time $6576; part-time $274 per credit hour. Tuition, nonresident: full-time $13,152; part-time $548 per credit hour. Required fees: $1813; $75.53 per credit hour. Part-time tuition and fees vary according to course load. *Financial support:* In 2009–10, 2 research assistantships with full tuition reimbursements, 22 teaching assistantships with full tuition reimbursements were awarded; fellowships with full tuition reimbursements, career-related internships or fieldwork, Federal Work-Study, scholarships/grants, tuition waivers (full), and staff assistantships also available. Support available to part-time students. Financial award applicants required to submit FAFSA. *Faculty research:* Art education, portfolio assessment, central European design history, relationship between modern art and industrialism. *Unit head:* Doug Boughton, Director, 815-753-7850, Fax: 815-753-7701, E-mail: dboughton@niu.edu. *Application contact:* Yale Factor, Graduate Coordinator, 815-753-3801, E-mail: yfactor@niu.edu.

Northwestern State University of Louisiana, Graduate Studies and Research, School of Creative and Performing Arts, Program in Art, Natchitoches, LA 71497. Offers fine and graphic arts (MA). *Accreditation:* NASAD. *Degree requirements:* For master's, comprehensive exam, thesis or alternative. *Entrance requirements:* For master's, GRE General Test, minimum undergraduate GPA of 2.5.

Northwestern University, The Graduate School, Judd A. and Marjorie Weinberg College of Arts and Sciences, Department of Art Theory and Practice, Evanston, IL 60208. Offers visual arts (MFA). Admissions and degrees offered through The Graduate School. *Degree requirements:* For master's, essay, exhibit. *Entrance requirements:* For master's, 20 slides of recent work. Additional exam requirements/recommendations for international students: Required—TOEFL. Electronic applications accepted.

NSCAD University, Program in Fine Arts, Halifax, NS B3J 3J6, Canada. Offers craft (MFA); design (M Des); fine and media arts (MFA). *Degree requirements:* For master's, thesis, exhibit. *Entrance requirements:* For master's, portfolio, at least 5 art history classes. Additional exam requirements/recommendations for international students: Required—Michigan English Language Assessment Battery (minimum score: 80), CanTEST (minimum score: 4.5), CAEL (minimum score: 70); Recommended—TOEFL (minimum score 575 paper-based; 233 computer-based; 90 iBT), IELTS (minimum score 6.5).

The Ohio State University, Graduate School, College of the Arts, Department of Art, Columbus, OH 43210. Offers MFA. *Accreditation:* NASAD. *Faculty:* 27. *Students:* 48 full-time (30 women); includes 4 minority (1 African American, 1 American Indian/Alaska Native, 1 Asian American or Pacific Islander, 1 Hispanic American), 7 international. Average age 30. In 2009, 31 master's awarded. *Degree requirements:* For master's, thesis, exhibit, oral exams. *Entrance requirements:* For master's, portfolio. Additional exam requirements/recommendations for international students: Recommended—TOEFL (minimum score 600 paper-based; 250 computer-based). *Application deadline:* For fall admission, 8/15 priority date for domestic students, 7/1 priority date for international students; for winter admission, 12/1 priority date for domestic students, 11/1 priority date for international students; for spring admission, 3/1 priority date for domestic students, 2/1 priority date for international students. Applications are processed on a rolling basis. Application fee: $40 ($50 for international students). Electronic applications accepted. *Expenses:* Tuition, state resident: full-time $10,683. Tuition, nonresident: full-time $25,923. Tuition and fees vary according to course load and program. *Financial support:* Fellowships, teaching assistantships, Federal Work-Study, institutionally sponsored loans, and unspecified assistantships available. Support available to part-time students. *Unit head:* Michael Mercil, Graduate Studies Committee Chair, 614-292-5072, Fax: 614-292-1674, E-mail: mercil.1@osu.edu. *Application contact:* 614-292-9444, Fax: 614-292-3895, E-mail: domestic.grad@osu.edu.

Ohio University, Graduate College, College of Fine Arts, School of Art, Athens, OH 45701-2979. Offers art history (MA); ceramics (MFA); graphic design (MFA); painting (MFA); photography (MFA); printmaking (MFA); sculpture (MFA). Part-time programs available. *Faculty:* 30 full-time (16 women), 7 part-time/adjunct (3 women). *Students:* 53 full-time (30 women), 4 part-time (all women); includes 3 minority (2 Asian Americans or Pacific Islanders, 1 Hispanic American), 4 international. 150 applicants, 33% accepted, 28 enrolled. In 2009, 22 master's awarded. *Degree requirements:* For master's, thesis. *Entrance requirements:* For master's, portfolio. Additional exam requirements/recommendations for international students: Required—TOEFL (minimum score 550 paper-based; 80 iBT) or IELTS Academic (minimum score 6.5). *Application deadline:* For fall admission, 2/1 for domestic and international students. Application fee: $50 ($55 for international students). Electronic applications accepted. *Expenses:* Tuition, state resident: full-time $7839; part-time $323 per quarter hour. Tuition, nonresident: full-time $15,831; part-time $654 per quarter hour. Required fees: $2931. *Financial support:* Teaching assistantships with full and partial tuition reimbursements, career-related internships or fieldwork, Federal Work-Study, institutionally sponsored loans, scholarships/grants, tuition waivers (partial), and unspecified assistantships available. Financial award application deadline: 2/1. *Faculty research:* Vapor fired ceramics, video installation, art theory, digital photography, mixed and interdisciplinary media work. *Unit head:* David LaPalombara, Director, 740-593-4290, Fax: 740-593-0457, E-mail: lapalomb@ohio.edu. *Application contact:* Rosemarie Basile, Chair, Graduate Programs, 740-593-4281, Fax: 740-593-0457, E-mail: basile@ohio.edu.

Oklahoma City University, Petree College of Arts and Sciences, Program in Liberal Arts, Oklahoma City, OK 73106-1402. Offers art (MLA); general studies (MLA); leadership/management (MLA); literature (MLA); mass communications (MLA); philosophy (MLA); writing (MLA). Part-time and evening/weekend programs available. *Faculty:* 23 full-time (6 women), 5 part-time/adjunct (3 women). *Students:* 50 full-time (24 women), 23 part-time (14 women); includes 6 minority (4 African Americans, 1 Asian American or Pacific Islander, 1 Hispanic American), 50 international. Average age 31. 31 applicants, 94% accepted, 15 enrolled. In 2009, 21 master's awarded. *Degree requirements:* For master's, comprehensive exam, thesis optional. *Entrance requirements:* Additional exam requirements/recommendations for international students: Required—TOEFL (minimum score 550 paper-based). *Application deadline:* For fall admission, 8/20 for domestic students; for spring admission, 1/6 for domestic students. Applications are processed on a rolling basis. Application fee: $50 ($70 for international students). *Expenses:* Tuition: Full-time $15,930; part-time $885 per hour. *Financial support:* Fellowships with partial tuition reimbursements, career-related internships or fieldwork, Federal Work-Study, and tuition waivers (partial) available. Support available to part-time students. Financial award application deadline: 8/1; financial award applicants required to submit FAFSA. *Unit head:* Dr. Regina Bennett, Director, 405-208-5207, Fax: 405-208-5451, E-mail: rbennett@okcu.edu. *Application contact:* Michelle Lockhart, Director, Admissions, 800-633-7242, Fax: 405-208-5916, E-mail: gadmissions@okcu.edu.

Otis College of Art and Design, Program in Fine Arts, Los Angeles, CA 90045-9785. Offers new genres (MFA); painting (MFA); photography (MFA); sculpture (MFA). *Accreditation:* NASAD. *Faculty:* 7 part-time/adjunct (3 women). *Students:* 19 full-time (10 women), 2 part-time (both women); includes 4 minority (1 American Indian/Alaska Native, 1 Asian American or Pacific Islander, 2 Hispanic Americans), 3 international. Average age 32. 199 applicants, 21% accepted, 10 enrolled. In 2009, 10 master's awarded. *Degree requirements:* For master's, thesis. *Entrance requirements:* For master's, portfolio. Additional exam requirements/recommendations for international students: Required—TOEFL (minimum score 600 paper-based; 250 computer-based). *Application deadline:* For fall admission, 2/1 for domestic and international students; for spring admission, 11/1 for domestic and international students. Application fee: $50. Electronic applications accepted. *Expenses:* Tuition: Full-time $33,200. Required fees: $700. *Financial support:* Career-related internships or fieldwork, Federal Work-Study, scholarships/grants, and tuition waivers (partial) available. Financial award applicants required to submit FAFSA. *Unit head:* Roy Dowell, Chair, 310-665-6893, Fax: 310-665-6998, E-mail: grads@otis.edu. *Application contact:* Information Contact, 310-665-6820, Fax: 310-665-6821, E-mail: admissions@otis.edu.

Otis College of Art and Design, Program in Public Practice, Los Angeles, CA 90045-9785. Offers MFA. *Faculty:* 6 part-time/adjunct (4 women). *Students:* 17 full-time (14 women); includes 8 minority (2 Asian Americans or Pacific Islanders, 6 Hispanic Americans), 3 international. 33 applicants, 52% accepted, 8 enrolled. *Entrance requirements:* Additional exam requirements/recommendations for international students: Required—TOEFL (minimum score 600 paper-based; 250 computer-based). *Application deadline:* For fall admission, 2/1 for domestic and international students. Application fee: $50. Electronic applications accepted. *Expenses:* Tuition: Full-time $33,200. Required fees: $700. *Unit head:* Suzanne Lacy, Chair, Graduate Studies, 310-665-6820, Fax: 310-846-2612, E-mail: cvelasco@otis.edu. *Application contact:* Information Contact, 310-665-6820, Fax: 310-665-6821, E-mail: admissions@otis.edu.

Pacific Northwest College of Art, Program in Visual Studies, Portland, OR 97209. Offers MFA.

Penn State University Park, Graduate School, College of Arts and Architecture, School of Visual Arts, State College, University Park, PA 16802-1503. Offers M Ed, MFA, MS, PhD. *Accreditation:* NASAD.

Pennsylvania Academy of the Fine Arts, Graduate School, Philadelphia, PA 19102. Offers drawing (MFA, Postbaccalaureate Certificate); painting (MFA, Postbaccalaureate Certificate); printmaking (MFA, Postbaccalaureate Certificate); sculpture (MFA, Postbaccalaureate Certificate). *Accreditation:* NASAD (one or more programs are accredited). *Degree requirements:* For master's, thesis, thesis exhibit. *Entrance requirements:* For master's, 10-20 slides of work and slide list, 3 letters of recommendation. Additional exam requirements/recommendations for international students: Required—TOEFL (minimum score 500 paper-based). Electronic applications accepted.

Pittsburg State University, Graduate School, College of Arts and Sciences, Department of Art, Pittsburg, KS 66762. Offers art education (MA); studio art (MA). *Degree requirements:* For master's, thesis or alternative. *Expenses:* Tuition, state resident: full-time $4212; part-time $176 per credit. Tuition, nonresident: full-time $11,530; part-time $480 per credit. Required fees: $940; $43 per credit. Tuition and fees vary according to course level, course load, degree level, campus/location, reciprocity agreements and student level.

Portland State University, Graduate Studies, School of Fine and Performing Arts, Department of Art, Portland, OR 97207-0751. Offers drawing (MFA); mixed media (MFA); painting (MFA); printmaking (MFA); sculpture (MFA). *Accreditation:* NASAD. *Degree requirements:* For master's, variable foreign language requirement, thesis, exhibit. *Entrance requirements:* For master's, minimum GPA of 3.0 in upper-division course work or 2.75 overall, portfolio, 3 letters of recommendation. Additional exam requirements/recommendations for international students: Required—TOEFL (minimum score 550 paper-based; 213 computer-based).

Pratt Institute, School of Art and Design, Program in Fine Arts, Brooklyn, NY 11205-3899. Offers new forms (MFA); painting and drawing (MFA); photography (MFA); printmaking (MFA); sculpture (MFA). *Accreditation:* NASAD. Part-time programs available. *Faculty:* 8 full-time (2 women), 30 part-time/adjunct (15 women). *Students:* 130 full-time (79 women), 2 part-time (both women); includes 13 minority (2 African Americans, 4 Asian Americans or Pacific Islanders, 7 Hispanic Americans), 37 international. Average age 28. 299 applicants, 60% accepted, 66 enrolled. In 2009, 82 master's awarded. *Degree requirements:* For master's, thesis, exhibit. *Entrance requirements:* For master's, portfolio, letters of recommendation. Additional exam requirements/recommendations for international students: Required—TOEFL (minimum score 550 paper-based; 213 computer-based; 79 iBT). *Application deadline:* For fall admission, 1/5 for domestic and international students; for spring admission, 10/1 for domestic and international students. Application fee: $50 ($90 for international students). Electronic applications accepted. *Expenses:* Tuition: Full-time $22,734. Required fees: $1280. *Financial support:* Career-related internships or fieldwork, Federal Work-Study, institutionally sponsored loans, scholarships/grants, health care benefits, and unspecified assistantships available. Support available to part-time students. Financial award application deadline: 2/1; financial award applicants required to submit FAFSA. *Unit head:* Donna Moran, Chairperson, 718-636-3602, E-mail: dmoran@pratt.edu. *Application contact:* Young Hah, Director of Graduate Admissions, 718-636-3683, Fax: 718-399-4242, E-mail: yhah@pratt.edu.

See Close-Up on page 119.

Purchase College, State University of New York, School of Art and Design, Purchase, NY 10577-1400. Offers MFA. *Accreditation:* NASAD. *Degree requirements:* For master's, thesis, exhibit. *Entrance requirements:* For master's, portfolio. Electronic applications accepted. *Expenses:* Tuition, state resident: full-time $8370; part-time $349 per credit. Tuition, nonresident: full-time $13,250; part-time $552 per credit. Required fees: $1515; $62.11 per credit. One-time fee: $144 full-time. Tuition and fees vary according to program.

Purdue University, Graduate School, College of Liberal Arts, Department of Visual and Performing Arts, West Lafayette, IN 47907. Offers art and design (MA); theatre (MA, MFA). *Accreditation:* NASAD; NAST. Part-time programs available. *Degree requirements:* For master's, terminal exhibit, project, or thesis. *Entrance requirements:* Additional exam requirements/recommendations for international students: Required—TOEFL. Electronic applications accepted. *Faculty research:* Design, fine arts, photography, acting, directing, theatre technology.

Queens College of the City University of New York, Division of Graduate Studies, Arts and Humanities Division, Department of Art, Program in Fine Arts, Flushing, NY 11367-1597. Offers MFA. *Faculty:* 12 full-time (6 women). *Students:* 12 full-time (7 women), 5 part-time (2 women). 24 applicants, 21% accepted, 4 enrolled. In 2009, 10 master's awarded. *Degree requirements:* For master's, art show. *Entrance requirements:* For master's, minimum GPA of 3.0, portfolio. Additional exam requirements/recommendations for international students: Required—TOEFL. *Application deadline:* For fall admission, 3/15 for domestic students; for spring admission, 10/15 for domestic students. Application fee: $125. *Expenses:* Tuition, state resident: full-time $7360; part-time $310 per credit. Tuition, nonresident: part-time $575 per credit. One-time fee: $195.25 full-time; $145.25 part-time. *Financial support:* Career-related internships or fieldwork, Federal Work-Study, institutionally sponsored loans, and tuition waivers (partial) available. Support available to part-time students. Financial award application deadline: 4/1; financial award applicants required to submit FAFSA. *Unit head:* Dr. Arthur Cohen, Graduate Advisor, 718-997-4770. *Application contact:* Mario Caruso, Director of Graduate Admissions, 718-997-5200, Fax: 718-997-5193, E-mail: graduate_admissions@qc.edu.

Radford University, College of Graduate and Professional Studies, College of Visual and Performing Arts, Department of Art, Radford, VA 24142. Offers MFA. Part-time programs available. *Faculty:* 12 full-time (5 women), 8 part-time/adjunct (6 women). *Students:* 14 full-time (8 women), 4 part-time (1 woman); includes 5 minority (1 African American, 3 Asian Americans or Pacific Islanders, 1 Hispanic American). Average age 28. 15 applicants, 67% accepted, 6 enrolled. In 2009, 6 master's awarded. *Degree requirements:* For master's, comprehensive exam. *Entrance requirements:* For master's, minimum GPA of 2.75; 2 letters of reference; statement of philosophy; BFA or commensurate collegiate course work; slides or CD of recent work. Additional exam requirements/recommendations for international students: Required—TOEFL (minimum score 550 paper-based; 213 computer-based; 79 iBT). *Application deadline:* For fall admission, 3/15 priority date for domestic students, 12/1 for international students; for spring admission, 10/1 for domestic students, 7/1 for international students. Applications are processed on a rolling basis. Application fee: $50. Electronic applications accepted. *Expenses:* Tuition, state resident: full-time $5086; part-time $211 per credit hour. Tuition, nonresident: full-time $12,608; part-time $525 per credit hour. Required fees: $2508; $105 per credit hour. *Financial support:* In 2009–10, 12 students received support, including 7 research assistantships with partial tuition reimbursements available (averaging $8,000 per year), 3 teaching assistantships with partial tuition reimbursements available (averaging $8,700 per year); career-related internships or fieldwork, Federal Work-Study, institutionally sponsored loans, scholarships/grants, and unspecified assistantships also available. Financial award application deadline: 3/1; financial award applicants required to submit FAFSA. *Unit head:* Dr. Steve S. Arbury, Chair, 540-831-5475, Fax: 540-831-6799, E-mail: sarbury@radford.edu. *Application contact:* Graduate Admissions, 540-831-5431, Fax: 540-831-6061, E-mail: gradcollege@radford.edu.

Regis University, College for Professional Studies, Program in Teacher Education, Denver, CO 80221-1099. Offers adult learning, training, and development (M Ed); curriculum, instruction, and assessment (M Ed); early childhood (M Ed); educational technology (Certificate); elementary (M Ed); ESL (M Ed); fine arts (M Ed), including arts, music; instructional technology (M Ed); professional leadership (M Ed); reading (M Ed); secondary (M Ed); self-designed (M Ed); space studies (M Ed); special education (M Ed); teacher licensure (M Ed). Program also offered in Henderson and Las Vegas (Summerlin), NV. *Accreditation:* Teacher Education Accreditation Council. Part-time and evening/weekend programs available. Postbaccalaureate distance learning degree programs offered (no on-campus study). *Degree requirements:* For master's, thesis. *Entrance requirements:* For master's, resume, minimum GPA of 2.75, criminal background check. Additional exam requirements/recommendations for international students: Required—TOEFL (minimum score 213 computer-based), TWE (minimum score 5). Electronic applications accepted. *Faculty research:* Issues of equity in the middle school classroom, professional learning communities, school reform, socialinguistic and discursive obstacles to student integration, inclusive language arts curriculum.

Rensselaer Polytechnic Institute, Graduate School, School of Humanities and Social Sciences, Department of the Arts, Program in Electronic Arts, Troy, NY 12180-3590. Offers MFA, PhD. *Faculty:* 14 full-time (8 women). *Students:* 17 full-time (6 women), 2 part-time (both women); includes 3 minority (2 Asian Americans or Pacific Islanders, 1 Hispanic American), 1 international. Average age 28. 74 applicants, 34% accepted, 9 enrolled. In 2009, 5 master's awarded. *Degree requirements:* For master's, thesis in the form of a large-scale creative project; for doctorate, comprehensive exam, dissertation or creative project and dissertation text. *Entrance requirements:* For master's, portfolio; for doctorate, MA, MM, MS or MFA; portfolio; scholarly writing sample (previous thesis or publication); evidence of research-based creative orientation. Additional exam requirements/recommendations for international students: Required—TOEFL (minimum score 570 paper-based; 230 computer-based; 89 iBT), IELTS (minimum score 6.5). *Application deadline:* For fall admission, 1/15 for domestic and international students. Applications are processed on a rolling basis. Application fee: $75. Electronic applications accepted. *Expenses:* Tuition: Full-time $38,100. *Financial support:* In 2009–10, 15 students received support, including 7 fellowships with full tuition reimbursements available (averaging $16,000 per year), 8 teaching assistantships with full tuition reimbursements available (averaging $16,000 per year); unspecified assistantships also available. Financial award application deadline: 1/15. *Faculty research:* Computer music, video art, Net art, interactivity, bio art. *Unit head:* Mary Anne Staniszewski, Acting Head, 518-276-4784, Fax: 518-276-4370, E-mail: stanim@rpi.edu. *Application contact:* Jennifer Mumby, Graduate Program Administrator, 518-276-4784, Fax: 518-276-4370, E-mail: mumbyj@rpi.edu.

Rhode Island College, School of Graduate Studies, Faculty of Arts and Sciences, Department of Art, Providence, RI 02908-1991. Offers art education (MA, MAT); media studies (MA). *Accreditation:* NASAD (one or more programs are accredited). Part-time and evening/weekend programs available. *Faculty:* 4 full-time (1 woman). *Students:* 9 full-time (5 women), 15 part-time (9 women). Average age 36. In 2009, 3 master's awarded. *Degree requirements:* For master's, thesis. *Entrance requirements:* For master's, GRE General Test or MAT, portfolio (MA), 3 letters of recommendation, interview. Additional exam requirements/recommendations for international students: Recommended—TOEFL (minimum score 550 paper-based; 213 computer-based; 79 iBT). *Application deadline:* For fall admission, 4/1 for domestic students; for spring admission, 11/1 for domestic students. Applications are processed on a rolling basis. Application fee: $50. *Expenses:* Tuition, state resident: full-time $7440; part-time $310 per credit hour. Tuition, nonresident: full-time $14,784; part-time $616 per credit hour. Required fees: $552; $20 per credit. $70 per term. *Financial support:* Teaching assistantships with full tuition reimbursements, career-related internships or fieldwork, Federal Work-Study, scholarships/grants, health care benefits, and unspecified assistantships available. Support available to part-time students. Financial award application deadline: 5/15; financial award applicants required to submit FAFSA. *Unit head:* Prof. Nancy Bockbrader, Chair, 401-456-8054. *Application contact:* Graduate Studies, 401-456-8700.

Rhode Island School of Design, Graduate Studies, Division of Fine Arts, Department of Ceramics, Providence, RI 02903-2784. Offers MFA. *Accreditation:* NASAD. *Degree requirements:* For master's, thesis, exhibit. *Entrance requirements:* For master's, portfolio. Additional exam requirements/recommendations for international students: Required—TOEFL (minimum score 580 paper-based; 237 computer-based), IELTS (minimum score 6.5).

Rhode Island School of Design, Graduate Studies, Division of Fine Arts, Department of Glass, Providence, RI 02903-2784. Offers MFA. *Accreditation:* NASAD. *Degree requirements:* For master's, thesis, exhibit. *Entrance requirements:* For master's, portfolio, 3 letters of recommendation. Additional exam requirements/recommendations for international students: Required—TOEFL (minimum score 580 paper-based; 237 computer-based), IELTS (minimum score 6.5).

Rhode Island School of Design, Graduate Studies, Division of Fine Arts, Department of Jewelry and Light Metals, Providence, RI 02903-2784. Offers MFA. *Accreditation:* NASAD. *Degree requirements:* For master's, thesis, exhibit. *Entrance requirements:* For master's, portfolio, 3 letters of recommendation. Additional exam requirements/recommendations for international students: Required—TOEFL (minimum score 580 paper-based; 237 computer-based), IELTS (minimum score 6.5).

Rhode Island School of Design, Graduate Studies, Division of Fine Arts, Department of Painting, Providence, RI 02903-2784. Offers MFA. *Accreditation:* NASAD. *Degree requirements:* For master's, thesis, exhibit. *Entrance requirements:* For master's, portfolio, 3 letters of recommendation. Additional exam requirements/recommendations for international students: Required—TOEFL (minimum score 580 paper-based; 237 computer-based), IELTS (minimum score 6.5).

Rhode Island School of Design, Graduate Studies, Division of Fine Arts, Department of Printmaking, Providence, RI 02903-2784. Offers MFA. *Entrance requirements:* For master's, portfolio, 3 letters of recommendation. Additional exam requirements/recommendations for international students: Required—TOEFL (minimum score 580 paper-based; 237 computer-based), IELTS (minimum score 6.5).

Rhode Island School of Design, Graduate Studies, Division of Fine Arts, Department of Sculpture, Providence, RI 02903-2784. Offers MFA. *Accreditation:* NASAD. *Degree requirements:* For master's, thesis, exhibit. *Entrance requirements:* For master's, portfolio, 3 letters of recommendation. Additional exam requirements/recommendations for international students: Required—TOEFL (minimum score 580 paper-based; 237 computer-based), IELTS (minimum score 6.5).

Rochester Institute of Technology, Graduate Enrollment Services, College of Imaging Arts and Sciences, School for American Crafts, Program in Ceramics, Rochester, NY 14623. Offers MFA. *Accreditation:* NASAD. Part-time programs available. *Students:* 7 full-time (6 women), 1 part-time (0 women). Average age 33. 11 applicants, 91% accepted, 5 enrolled. In 2009, 3 master's awarded. *Entrance requirements:* For master's, portfolio, minimum GPA of 3.0. Additional exam requirements/recommendations for international students: Required—TOEFL (minimum score 550 paper-based; 230 computer-based; 79 iBT), or IELTS (minimum score 6.5). *Application deadline:* For fall admission, 2/15 priority date for domestic students, 2/2 priority date for international students. Applications are processed on a rolling basis. Application fee: $50. Electronic applications accepted. *Expenses:* Tuition: Full-time $31,533; part-time $876 per credit hour. Required fees: $210. *Financial support:* In 2009–10, 6 students received support; teaching assistantships with partial tuition reimbursements available, career-related internships or fieldwork, institutionally sponsored loans, scholarships/grants, and unspecified assistantships available. Support available to part-time students. Financial award applicants required to submit FAFSA. *Unit head:* Don Arday, Interim Chair, 585-475-6114, Fax: 585-475-6447, E-mail: sac@rit.edu. *Application contact:* Diane Ellison, Assistant Vice President, Graduate Enrollment Services, 585-475-2229, Fax: 585-475-7164, E-mail: gradinfo@rit.edu.

Rochester Institute of Technology, Graduate Enrollment Services, College of Imaging Arts and Sciences, School for American Crafts, Program in Glass, Rochester, NY 14623-5603. Offers MFA. *Accreditation:* NASAD. Part-time programs available. *Students:* 6 full-time (3 women), 3 international. Average age 26. 13 applicants, 46% accepted, 2 enrolled. *Entrance requirements:* For master's, portfolio, minimum GPA of 3.0. Additional exam requirements/recommendations for international students: Required—TOEFL (minimum score 550 paper-based; 230 computer-based; 79 iBT), or IELTS (minimum score 6.5). *Application deadline:* For fall admission, 2/15 priority date for domestic and international students. Applications are processed on a rolling basis. Application fee: $50. Electronic applications accepted. *Expenses:* Tuition: Full-time $31,533; part-time $876 per credit hour. Required fees: $210. *Financial support:* In 2009–10, 6 students received support; teaching assistantships with partial tuition reimbursements available, career-related internships or fieldwork, institutionally sponsored

Art/Fine Arts

Rochester Institute of Technology (continued)
loans, scholarships/grants, and unspecified assistantships available. Support available to part-time students. Financial award application deadline: 8/30; financial award applicants required to submit FAFSA. *Unit head:* Don Arday, Interim Chair, 585-475-6114, Fax: 585-475-6447, E-mail: sac@rit.edu. *Application contact:* Diane Ellison, Assistant Vice President, Graduate Enrollment Services, 585-475-2229, Fax: 585-475-7164, E-mail: gradinfo@rit.edu.

Rochester Institute of Technology, Graduate Enrollment Services, College of Imaging Arts and Sciences, School for American Crafts, Program in Metal Crafts and Jewelry, Rochester, NY 14623-5603. Offers MFA. *Accreditation:* NASAD. Part-time programs available. *Students:* 10 full-time (7 women), 1 part-time (0 women); includes 1 American Indian/Alaska Native, 1 Hispanic American, 7 international. Average age 31. 17 applicants, 71% accepted, 4 enrolled. In 2009, 1 master's awarded. *Entrance requirements:* For master's, portfolio, minimum GPA of 3.0. Additional exam requirements/recommendations for international students: Required—TOEFL (minimum score 550 paper-based; 230 computer-based; 79 iBT), or IELTS (minimum score 6.5). *Application deadline:* For fall admission, 2/15 priority date for domestic and international students. Applications are processed on a rolling basis. Application fee: $50. Electronic applications accepted. *Expenses:* Tuition: Full-time $31,533; part-time $876 per credit hour. Required fees: $210. *Financial support:* In 2009–10, 10 students received support; teaching assistantships with partial tuition reimbursements available, career-related internships or fieldwork, institutionally sponsored loans, scholarships/grants, and unspecified assistantships available. Support available to part-time students. Financial award application deadline: 8/30; financial award applicants required to submit FAFSA. *Unit head:* Don Arday, Interim Chair, 585-475-6114, Fax: 585-475-6447, E-mail: sac@rit.edu. *Application contact:* Diane Ellison, Assistant Vice President, Graduate Enrollment Services, 585-475-2229, Fax: 585-475-7164, E-mail: gradinfo@rit.edu.

Rochester Institute of Technology, Graduate Enrollment Services, College of Imaging Arts and Sciences, School for American Crafts, Program in Woodworking and Furniture Design, Rochester, NY 14623-5603. Offers MFA. Part-time programs available. *Students:* 4 full-time (1 woman). Average age 28. 4 applicants, 100% accepted, 2 enrolled. In 2009, 3 master's awarded. *Entrance requirements:* For master's, portfolio, minimum GPA of 3.0. Additional exam requirements/recommendations for international students: Required—TOEFL (minimum score 550 paper-based; 213 computer-based; 79 iBT), or IELTS (minimum score 6.5). *Application deadline:* For fall admission, 2/15 priority date for domestic and international students. Applications are processed on a rolling basis. Application fee: $50. Electronic applications accepted. *Expenses:* Tuition: Full-time $31,533; part-time $876 per credit hour. Required fees: $210. *Financial support:* In 2009–10, 4 students received support; teaching assistantships with partial tuition reimbursements available, career-related internships or fieldwork, institutionally sponsored loans, scholarships/grants, and unspecified assistantships available. Support available to part-time students. Financial award application deadline: 8/30; financial award applicants required to submit FAFSA. *Unit head:* Don Arday, Interim Chair, 585-475-6114, Fax: 585-475-6447, E-mail: sac@rit.edu. *Application contact:* Diane Ellison, Assistant Vice President, Graduate Enrollment Services, 585-475-2229, Fax: 585-475-7164, E-mail: gradinfo@rit.edu.

Rochester Institute of Technology, Graduate Enrollment Services, College of Imaging Arts and Sciences, School of Art, Program in Fine Arts, Rochester, NY 14623. Offers fine arts studio (MST); painting (MFA); printmaking (MFA). *Accreditation:* NASAD. Part-time programs available. *Students:* 18 full-time (8 women), 4 part-time (all women); includes 1 American Indian/Alaska Native, 2 Asian Americans or Pacific Islanders, 2 Hispanic Americans, 4 international. Average age 31. 28 applicants, 61% accepted, 12 enrolled. In 2009, 7 master's awarded. *Degree requirements:* For master's, thesis (for some programs). *Entrance requirements:* For master's, portfolio, minimum GPA of 3.0. Additional exam requirements/recommendations for international students: Required—TOEFL (minimum score 550 paper-based; 213 computer-based; 79 iBT), or IELTS (minimum score 6.5). *Application deadline:* For fall admission, 2/15 priority date for domestic and international students. Applications are processed on a rolling basis. Application fee: $50. Electronic applications accepted. *Expenses:* Tuition: Full-time $31,533; part-time $876 per credit hour. Required fees: $210. *Financial support:* In 2009–10, 17 students received support; teaching assistantships, career-related internships or fieldwork, institutionally sponsored loans, scholarships/grants, and unspecified assistantships available. Support available to part-time students. Financial award application deadline: 8/30; financial award applicants required to submit FAFSA. *Unit head:* Don Arday, Administrative Chair, 585-475-7562, Fax: 585-475-6344, E-mail: facpgd@rit.edu. *Application contact:* Diane Ellison, Assistant Vice President, Graduate Enrollment Services, 585-475-2229, Fax: 585-475-7164, E-mail: gradinfo@rit.edu.

Rutgers, The State University of New Jersey, New Brunswick, Mason Gross School of the Arts, Program in Visual Arts, Piscataway, NJ 08854-8097. Offers drawing (MFA); painting (MFA); sculpture (MFA). *Degree requirements:* For master's, thesis, exhibit. *Entrance requirements:* For master's, portfolio. Additional exam requirements/recommendations for international students: Required—TOEFL (minimum score 550 paper-based; 213 computer-based). Electronic applications accepted. *Faculty research:* Media, painting, sculpture, photography, film.

San Diego State University, Graduate and Research Affairs, College of Professional Studies and Fine Arts, School of Art, Design and Art History, San Diego, CA 92182. Offers art history (MA); studio arts (MA, MFA), including applied design, environmental design, graphic design, interior design, painting and printmaking, sculpture. *Accreditation:* NASAD (one or more programs are accredited). *Degree requirements:* For master's, variable foreign language requirement, thesis. *Entrance requirements:* For master's, GRE General Test, bachelor's degree in related field, slide portfolio, typed slide information sheet, 2 letters of recommendation. Additional exam requirements/recommendations for international students: Required—TOEFL. Electronic applications accepted.

San Francisco Art Institute, Graduate Program, Department of Painting, San Francisco, CA 94133. Offers MFA, Certificate. *Accreditation:* NASAD. Part-time programs available. *Degree requirements:* For master's and Certificate, oral reviews. *Entrance requirements:* For master's and Certificate, portfolio. Additional exam requirements/recommendations for international students: Required—TOEFL (minimum score 580 paper-based; 237 computer-based). Electronic applications accepted.

San Francisco Art Institute, Graduate Program, Department of Printmaking, San Francisco, CA 94133. Offers MFA, Certificate. *Accreditation:* NASAD. Part-time programs available. *Degree requirements:* For master's and Certificate, oral reviews. *Entrance requirements:* For master's and Certificate, portfolio. Additional exam requirements/recommendations for international students: Required—TOEFL (minimum score 580 paper-based; 237 computer-based). Electronic applications accepted.

San Francisco Art Institute, Graduate Program, Department of Sculpture, San Francisco, CA 94133. Offers MFA, Certificate. *Accreditation:* NASAD. Part-time programs available. *Degree requirements:* For master's and Certificate, oral reviews. *Entrance requirements:* For master's and Certificate, portfolio. Additional exam requirements/recommendations for international students: Required—TOEFL (minimum score 580 paper-based; 237 computer-based).

San Francisco State University, Division of Graduate Studies, College of Creative Arts, Department of Art, San Francisco, CA 94132-1722. Offers art (MFA); art history (MA). *Accreditation:* NASAD (one or more programs are accredited).

San Jose State University, Graduate Studies and Research, College of Humanities and the Arts, School of Art and Design, San Jose, CA 95192-0001. Offers animation/illustration (MA); art history (MA); digital media arts (MFA); photography (MFA); pictorial arts (MFA); spatial arts (MFA). *Accreditation:* NASAD (one or more programs are accredited). *Students:* 48 full-time (27 women), 24 part-time (16 women); includes 13 minority (3 African Americans, 6 Asian Americans or Pacific Islanders, 4 Hispanic Americans), 2 international. Average age 36. 69 applicants, 23% accepted, 16 enrolled. In 2009, 17 master's awarded. *Entrance requirements:* For master's, GRE. *Application deadline:* For fall admission, 6/29 for domestic students; for spring admission, 11/30 for domestic students. Applications are processed on a rolling basis. Application fee: $59. Electronic applications accepted. *Financial support:* Applicants required to submit FAFSA. *Unit head:* John Loomis, Director, 408-924-4320, Fax: 408-924-4326. *Application contact:* John Loomis, Director, 408-924-4320, Fax: 408-924-4326.

Savannah College of Art and Design, Graduate School, Program in Metals and Jewelry, Savannah, GA 31402-3146. Offers MA, MFA. Part-time programs available. *Degree requirements:* For master's, thesis, internship. *Entrance requirements:* For master's, interview, portfolio. Additional exam requirements/recommendations for international students: Required—TOEFL (minimum score 450 paper-based; 133 computer-based). Electronic applications accepted. *Expenses:* Tuition: Full-time $28,515; part-time $627 per credit hour. One-time fee: $500. Tuition and fees vary according to course load.

Savannah College of Art and Design, Graduate School, Program in Painting, Savannah, GA 31402-3146. Offers MA, MFA. Part-time programs available. *Degree requirements:* For master's, thesis, exhibit, internships. *Entrance requirements:* For master's, interview, portfolio. Additional exam requirements/recommendations for international students: Required—TOEFL (minimum score 450 paper-based; 133 computer-based). Electronic applications accepted. *Expenses:* Tuition: Full-time $28,515; part-time $627 per credit hour. One-time fee: $500. Tuition and fees vary according to course load.

Savannah College of Art and Design, Graduate School, Program in Printmaking, Savannah, GA 31402-3146. Offers MA, MFA. Part-time programs available. *Degree requirements:* For master's, thesis. *Entrance requirements:* For master's, interview, portfolio. Additional exam requirements/recommendations for international students: Required—TOEFL (minimum score 450 paper-based; 133 computer-based). Electronic applications accepted. *Expenses:* Tuition: Full-time $28,515; part-time $627 per credit hour. One-time fee: $500. Tuition and fees vary according to course load.

Savannah College of Art and Design, Graduate School, Program in Sculpture, Savannah, GA 31402-3146. Offers MA, MFA. Part-time programs available. *Degree requirements:* For master's, thesis. *Entrance requirements:* For master's, interview, portfolio. Additional exam requirements/recommendations for international students: Required—TOEFL (minimum score 450 paper-based; 133 computer-based). Electronic applications accepted. *Expenses:* Tuition: Full-time $28,515; part-time $627 per credit hour. One-time fee: $500. Tuition and fees vary according to course load.

School of the Art Institute of Chicago, Graduate Division, Department of Art and Technology Studies, Chicago, IL 60603-3103. Offers MFA. *Entrance requirements:* Additional exam requirements/recommendations for international students: Required—TOEFL, IELTS. Electronic applications accepted.

School of the Art Institute of Chicago, Graduate Division, Department of Ceramics, Chicago, IL 60603-3103. Offers MFA. *Accreditation:* NASAD. *Entrance requirements:* Additional exam requirements/recommendations for international students: Required—TOEFL, IELTS. Electronic applications accepted.

School of the Art Institute of Chicago, Graduate Division, Department of Fiber and Material Studies, Chicago, IL 60603-3103. Offers MFA. *Accreditation:* NASAD. *Entrance requirements:* Additional exam requirements/recommendations for international students: Required—TOEFL, IELTS.

School of the Art Institute of Chicago, Graduate Division, Department of Painting and Drawing, Chicago, IL 60603-3103. Offers MFA. *Accreditation:* NASAD. *Entrance requirements:* Additional exam requirements/recommendations for international students: Required—TOEFL, IELTS.

School of the Art Institute of Chicago, Graduate Division, Department of Printmaking, Chicago, IL 60603-3103. Offers MFA. *Accreditation:* NASAD. *Entrance requirements:* Additional exam requirements/recommendations for international students: Required—TOEFL, IELTS.

School of the Art Institute of Chicago, Graduate Division, Department of Sculpture, Chicago, IL 60603-3103. Offers MFA. *Accreditation:* NASAD. *Entrance requirements:* Additional exam requirements/recommendations for international students: Required—TOEFL, IELTS.

School of the Art Institute of Chicago, Graduate Division, Program in Visual and Critical Studies, Chicago, IL 60603-3103. Offers MA.

School of the Museum of Fine Arts, Boston, Graduate Program, Boston, MA 02115. Offers MAT, MFA. *Accreditation:* NASAD (one or more programs are accredited). *Degree requirements:* For master's, exhibition thesis. *Entrance requirements:* For master's, BFA or bachelor's degree in related area, portfolio. Additional exam requirements/recommendations for international students: Required—TOEFL. *Faculty research:* Public art commissions, National Endowment for the Arts grant recipients, international exhibitions.

School of Visual Arts, Graduate Programs, Computer Art Department, New York, NY 10010-3994. Offers MFA. *Accreditation:* NASAD. *Degree requirements:* For master's, final review, project or thesis. *Entrance requirements:* For master's, portfolio. Additional exam requirements/recommendations for international students: Required—TOEFL (minimum score 550 paper-based; 213 computer-based; 79 iBT). Electronic applications accepted.

School of Visual Arts, Graduate Programs, Design Department, New York, NY 10010-3994. Offers MFA. *Accreditation:* NASAD. *Degree requirements:* For master's, final review, project or thesis. *Entrance requirements:* For master's, portfolio. Additional exam requirements/recommendations for international students: Required—TOEFL (minimum score 550 paper-based; 213 computer-based; 79 iBT). Electronic applications accepted. *Expenses:* Contact institution.

School of Visual Arts, Graduate Programs, Fine Arts Department, New York, NY 10010-3994. Offers painting (MFA); printmaking (MFA); sculpture (MFA). *Accreditation:* NASAD. *Degree requirements:* For master's, final review, project or thesis. *Entrance requirements:* For master's, portfolio. Additional exam requirements/recommendations for international students: Required—TOEFL (minimum score 550 paper-based; 213 computer-based; 79 iBT). Electronic applications accepted.

School of Visual Arts, Graduate Programs, Illustration Department, New York, NY 10010-3994. Offers MFA. *Accreditation:* NASAD. *Degree requirements:* For master's, final review, project or thesis. *Entrance requirements:* For master's, portfolio. Additional exam requirements/recommendations for international students: Required—TOEFL (minimum score 550 paper-based; 213 computer-based; 79 iBT). Electronic applications accepted.

School of Visual Arts, Graduate Programs, Program in Photography, Video and Related Media, New York, NY 10010-3994. Offers MFA. *Accreditation:* NASAD. *Degree requirements:* For master's, final review, project or thesis. *Entrance requirements:* For master's, portfolio. Additional exam requirements/recommendations for international students: Required—TOEFL (minimum score 550 paper-based; 213 computer-based; 79 iBT). Electronic applications accepted.

Seton Hall University, College of Arts and Sciences, Department of Art, Music and Design, South Orange, NJ 07079-2697. Offers museum professions (MA), including exhibition development, museum education, museum management, museum registration. Part-time and evening/weekend programs available. *Faculty:* 5 full-time (4 women), 8 part-time/adjunct (5 women). *Students:* 40 full-time (36 women), 32 part-time (26 women); includes 7 minority (2 African Americans, 1 Asian American or Pacific Islander, 4 Hispanic Americans), 1 international. Average age 28. 54 applicants, 80% accepted, 20 enrolled. In 2009, 12 master's awarded.

Degree requirements: For master's, thesis. *Entrance requirements:* For master's, GRE General Test, previous course work in art history. Additional exam requirements/recommendations for international students: Required—TOEFL. *Application deadline:* For fall admission, 7/1 priority date for domestic and international students; for spring admission, 11/1 priority date for domestic and international students. Applications are processed on a rolling basis. Application fee: $50. Electronic applications accepted. *Financial support:* Research assistantships, career-related internships or fieldwork, Federal Work-Study, and unspecified assistantships available. Financial award applicants required to submit FAFSA. *Faculty research:* History of museums, museum education, theory of museums, nineteenth century art, African-American art, Renaissance art history, museum registration, museum ethics. *Unit head:* Dr. Susan Leshnoff, Chair, 973-761-9459, Fax: 973-275-2368, E-mail: leshnosu@shu.edu. *Application contact:* Dr. Petra Chu, Director of Graduate Studies, 973-761-9460, Fax: 973-275-2368, E-mail: chupetra@shu.edu.

Southern Illinois University Carbondale, Graduate School, College of Liberal Arts, School of Art and Design, Carbondale, IL 62901-4701. Offers ceramics (MFA); drawing (MFA); fiber/weaving (MFA); glass (MFA); jewelry (MFA); metalsmithing/blacksmithing (MFA); painting (MFA); printmaking (MFA); sculpture (MFA). *Accreditation:* NASAD. *Degree requirements:* For master's, thesis or alternative. *Entrance requirements:* For master's, minimum GPA of 2.7, portfolio, slides. Additional exam requirements/recommendations for international students: Required—TOEFL. *Faculty research:* Prints/woodcuts, foundry, watercolor.

Southern Illinois University Edwardsville, Graduate Studies and Research, College of Arts and Sciences, Department of Art and Design, Program in Studio Art, Edwardsville, IL 62026-0001. Offers MFA. Part-time programs available. *Students:* 26 full-time (16 women). Average age 26. 51 applicants, 27% accepted. In 2009, 6 master's awarded. *Degree requirements:* For master's, thesis, exhibition. *Entrance requirements:* For master's, portfolio. Additional exam requirements/recommendations for international students: Required—TOEFL (minimum score 550 paper-based; 213 computer-based; 79 iBT), IELTS (minimum score 6.5). *Application deadline:* For fall admission, 2/1 for domestic and international students. Application fee: $30. Electronic applications accepted. *Expenses:* Tuition, state resident: part-time $1252.50 per semester. Tuition, nonresident: part-time $3131.25 per semester. Required fees: $586.85 per semester. Tuition and fees vary according to course load. *Financial support:* In 2009–10, 1 fellowship with full tuition reimbursement, 25 teaching assistantships with full tuition reimbursements (averaging $8,064 per year) were awarded; research assistantships with full tuition reimbursements, Federal Work-Study, institutionally sponsored loans, and unspecified assistantships also available. Support available to part-time students. Financial award application deadline: 3/1; financial award applicants required to submit FAFSA. *Unit head:* Dr. John Denhouter, Chair, 618-650-3074, E-mail: jdenhou@siue.edu. *Application contact:* Michelle Robinson, Coordinator for Graduate Recruitment, 618-650-2811, Fax: 618-650-3523, E-mail: michero@siue.edu.

Southern Methodist University, Meadows School of the Arts, Division of Art, Dallas, TX 75275. Offers studio art (MFA), including ceramics, drawing, painting, photography, printmaking, sculpture. *Accreditation:* NASAD. *Faculty:* 12 full-time (3 women), 3 part-time/adjunct (1 woman). *Students:* 9 full-time (4 women); includes 1 minority (Hispanic American), 1 international. Average age 29. 35 applicants, 20% accepted, 6 enrolled. In 2009, 4 master's awarded. *Degree requirements:* For master's, thesis or alternative, exhibit. *Entrance requirements:* For master's, BFA or equivalent, letters of recommendation, portfolio. Additional exam requirements/recommendations for international students: Required—TOEFL (minimum score 550 paper-based; 213 computer-based; 80 iBT). *Application deadline:* For fall admission, 2/15 for domestic and international students. Application fee: $75. *Financial support:* In 2009–10, 5 fellowships (averaging $32,914 per year), 5 teaching assistantships (averaging $3,000 per year) were awarded; scholarships/grants and unspecified assistantships also available. Financial award application deadline: 3/1; financial award applicants required to submit FAFSA. *Faculty research:* American stoneware, Southwestern furniture traditions, photographic apparatus and techniques, American ceramists, architecture. Total annual research expenditures: $20,000. *Unit head:* James W. Sullivan, Chair, 214-768-2489, E-mail: jsulliva@smu.edu. *Application contact:* Jean Cherry, Director of Graduate Admissions and Records, 214-768-3765, Fax: 214-768-3272, E-mail: jcherry@smu.edu.

Spring Hill College, Graduate Programs, Program in Liberal Arts, Mobile, AL 36608-1791. Offers fine arts (MLA); history and social science (MLA); leadership and ethics (MLA); literature (MLA). Part-time and evening/weekend programs available. *Faculty:* 11 full-time (4 women), 3 part-time/adjunct (2 women). *Students:* 1 (woman) full-time, 33 part-time (16 women); includes 6 minority (5 African Americans, 1 Hispanic American), 2 international. Average age 35. 27 applicants, 41% accepted, 6 enrolled. In 2009, 6 master's awarded. *Degree requirements:* For master's, capstone course, completion of program within 6 years of initial admittance. *Entrance requirements:* For master's, bachelor's degree with minimum undergraduate GPA of 3.0 or graduate/professional degree. Additional exam requirements/recommendations for international students: Required—TOEFL (minimum score 550 paper-based; 213 computer-based; 80 iBT), IELTS (minimum score 6.5). *Application deadline:* For fall admission, 8/1 priority date for domestic and international students; for spring admission, 12/1 priority date for domestic and international students. Applications are processed on a rolling basis. Application fee: $25 ($35 for international students). Electronic applications accepted. *Expenses:* Contact institution. *Financial support:* In 2009–10, 30 students received support. Career-related internships or fieldwork, institutionally sponsored loans, and scholarships/grants available. Support available to part-time students. Financial award applicants required to submit FAFSA. *Unit head:* Dr. Alexander R. Landi, Director, 251-380-3056, Fax: 251-460-2115, E-mail: landi@shc.edu. *Application contact:* Donna B. Tarasavage, Director of Marketing and Recruiting, Graduate and Continuing Studies, 251-380-3067, Fax: 251-460-2190, E-mail: dtarasavage@shc.edu.

Stanford University, School of Humanities and Sciences, Department of Art and Art History, Stanford, CA 94305-9991. Offers art history (PhD); art practice (MFA); MS/MFA. *Degree requirements:* For master's, thesis (for some programs), faculty reviews; for doctorate, 2 foreign languages, thesis/dissertation. *Entrance requirements:* For master's and doctorate, GRE General Test. Additional exam requirements/recommendations for international students: Required—TOEFL. Electronic applications accepted. *Expenses:* Tuition: Full-time $37,380; part-time $2760 per quarter. Required fees: $501.

State University of New York at New Paltz, Graduate School, School of Fine and Performing Arts, Department of Fine Arts, New Paltz, NY 12561. Offers art studio (MA); ceramics (MFA); metal (MFA); painting/drawing (MFA); printmaking (MFA); sculpture (MFA). *Accreditation:* NASAD (one or more programs are accredited). Part-time and evening/weekend programs available. *Faculty:* 16 full-time (10 women), 1 (woman) part-time/adjunct. *Students:* 41 full-time (31 women), 19 part-time (14 women); includes 5 minority (2 African Americans, 1 American Indian/Alaska Native, 1 Asian American or Pacific Islander, 1 Hispanic American), 4 international. Average age 31. 98 applicants, 35% accepted, 24 enrolled. In 2009, 26 master's awarded. *Degree requirements:* For master's, thesis, portfolio, exhibit (MFA). *Entrance requirements:* For master's, minimum GPA of 3.0, portfolio. Additional exam requirements/recommendations for international students: Required—TOEFL (minimum score 550 paper-based; 213 computer-based; 80 iBT), IELTS (minimum score 6.5). *Application deadline:* For fall admission, 2/15 priority date for domestic and international students. Applications are processed on a rolling basis. Application fee: $50. Electronic applications accepted. *Financial support:* In 2009–10, 11 students received support, including 1 fellowship (averaging $9,000 per year), 1 research assistantship with partial tuition reimbursement available (averaging $5,000 per year), 8 teaching assistantships with partial tuition reimbursements available (averaging $5,000 per year); Federal Work-Study, institutionally sponsored loans, scholarships/grants, traineeships, tuition waivers (full), and unspecified assistantships also available. Financial award application deadline: 8/1; financial award applicants required to submit FAFSA. *Unit head:* Prof. Myra Mimlitsch-Gray, Chair, 845-257-3833, E-mail: mimlitsm@newpaltz.edu. *Application contact:* Prof. Emily Puthoffe, Coordinator, 845-257-3834, E-mail: puthoffe@newpaltz.edu.

State University of New York at Oswego, Graduate Studies, College of Arts and Sciences, Department of Art, Oswego, NY 13126. Offers MA. *Accreditation:* NASAD. Part-time programs available. *Degree requirements:* For master's, exhibit, final presentation. *Entrance requirements:* For master's, slides of previous work. Additional exam requirements/recommendations for international students: Required—TOEFL (minimum score 560 paper-based; 220 computer-based). *Faculty research:* Ancient and primitive art, nineteenth century art, medieval art, Renaissance art.

Stephen F. Austin State University, Graduate School, College of Fine Arts, School of Art, Nacogdoches, TX 75962. Offers art (MA); design (MFA); drawing (MFA); painting (MFA); sculpture (MFA). *Accreditation:* NASAD. Part-time programs available. *Degree requirements:* For master's, comprehensive exam, thesis, exhibit. *Entrance requirements:* For master's, GRE General Test, portfolio. Additional exam requirements/recommendations for international students: Required—TOEFL. *Faculty research:* Printmaking, jewelry, photography, ceramics, art history.

Stony Brook University, State University of New York, Graduate School, College of Arts and Sciences, Department of Art, Program in Studio Art, Stony Brook, NY 11794. Offers MFA. *Students:* 15 full-time (11 women); includes 2 minority (1 African American, 1 Hispanic American), 2 international. Average age 32. 21 applicants, 38% accepted. In 2009, 4 master's awarded. *Degree requirements:* For master's, comprehensive exam, thesis, reading knowledge of German, French, or Italian; exhibition. *Entrance requirements:* For master's, GRE General Test, minimum undergraduate GPA of 3.0. Additional exam requirements/recommendations for international students: Required—TOEFL. *Application deadline:* For fall admission, 1/15 priority date for domestic students. Application fee: $60. *Expenses:* Tuition, state resident: full-time $8370; part-time $349 per credit. Tuition, nonresident: full-time $13,250; part-time $552 per credit. Required fees: $933. *Unit head:* Stephanie Dinkins, Director, 631-632-7254, E-mail: sdinkins@ms.cc.sunysb.edu. *Application contact:* Dr. Michele Bogart, Director, 631-632-7270.

Sul Ross State University, School of Arts and Sciences, Department of Fine Arts and Communication, Alpine, TX 79832. Offers art education (M Ed); art history (M Ed); studio art (M Ed), including ceramics, design, drawing, jewelry, painting, printmaking, sculpture, weaving. Part-time programs available. *Degree requirements:* For master's, oral or written exam. *Entrance requirements:* For master's, GRE General Test, minimum GPA of 2.5 in last 60 hours of undergraduate work. *Faculty research:* Ceramic sculpture, watercolor, wood sculpture, rock art.

Syracuse University, College of Visual and Performing Arts, Program in Ceramics, Syracuse, NY 13244. Offers MFA. *Accreditation:* NASAD. Part-time programs available. *Students:* 4 full-time (1 woman). Average age 27. 9 applicants, 22% accepted, 2 enrolled. *Degree requirements:* For master's, thesis or alternative. *Entrance requirements:* For master's, portfolio. Additional exam requirements/recommendations for international students: Required—TOEFL (minimum score 100 iBT). *Application deadline:* For fall admission, 2/1 priority date for domestic and international students. Application fee: $75. Electronic applications accepted. *Expenses:* Tuition: Full-time $26,808; part-time $1117 per credit. Required fees: $1024. *Financial support:* Fellowships with full tuition reimbursements, research assistantships with full and partial tuition reimbursements, teaching assistantships with full and partial tuition reimbursements, tuition waivers (partial) available. Financial award application deadline: 1/1; financial award applicants required to submit FAFSA. *Unit head:* Errol Willett, Chair, 315-443-3830, E-mail: eswillett@syr.edu. *Application contact:* Harriett Conti, Assistant Dean for Recruitment and Admissions, 315-443-5755, E-mail: hmconti@syr.edu.

Syracuse University, College of Visual and Performing Arts, Program in Jewelry and Metalsmithing, Syracuse, NY 13244. Offers MFA. *Students:* 2 full-time (both women). Average age 25. 4 applicants, 100% accepted, 2 enrolled. In 2009, 2 master's awarded. *Degree requirements:* For master's, thesis or alternative. *Entrance requirements:* For master's, portfolio. Additional exam requirements/recommendations for international students: Required—TOEFL (minimum score 100 iBT). *Application deadline:* For fall admission, 2/1 priority date for domestic and international students. Application fee: $75. Electronic applications accepted. *Expenses:* Tuition: Full-time $26,808; part-time $1117 per credit. Required fees: $1024. *Financial support:* Fellowships with full and partial tuition reimbursements, teaching assistantships with full and partial tuition reimbursements available. Financial award application deadline: 1/1; financial award applicants required to submit FAFSA. *Unit head:* Errol Willett, Chair, 315-443-3830, E-mail: eswillett@syr.edu. *Application contact:* Harriett Conti, Assistant Dean for Recruitment and Admissions, 315-443-5755, E-mail: hmconti@syr.edu.

Syracuse University, College of Visual and Performing Arts, Program in Painting, Syracuse, NY 13244. Offers MFA. *Students:* 9 full-time (5 women); includes 3 minority (1 Asian American or Pacific Islander, 2 Hispanic Americans). Average age 28. 22 applicants, 14% accepted, 3 enrolled. In 2009, 4 master's awarded. *Degree requirements:* For master's, thesis or alternative. *Entrance requirements:* For master's, portfolio. Additional exam requirements/recommendations for international students: Required—TOEFL (minimum score 100 iBT). *Application deadline:* For fall admission, 2/1 priority date for domestic and international students. Application fee: $75. Electronic applications accepted. *Expenses:* Tuition: Full-time $26,808; part-time $1117 per credit. Required fees: $1024. *Financial support:* Fellowships with full and partial tuition reimbursements, teaching assistantships with full and partial tuition reimbursements available. Financial award application deadline: 1/1; financial award applicants required to submit FAFSA. *Unit head:* Errol Willett, Chair, 315-443-3830, E-mail: eswillett@syr.edu. *Application contact:* Harriett Conti, Assistant Dean for Recruitment and Admissions, 315-443-5755, E-mail: hmconti@syr.edu.

Syracuse University, College of Visual and Performing Arts, Program in Printmaking, Syracuse, NY 13244. Offers MFA. *Students:* 3 full-time (1 woman). Average age 29. 8 applicants, 0% accepted, 0 enrolled. In 2009, 1 master's awarded. *Entrance requirements:* For master's, portfolio. Additional exam requirements/recommendations for international students: Required—TOEFL (minimum score 100 iBT). *Application deadline:* For fall admission, 2/1 priority date for domestic and international students. Application fee: $75. Electronic applications accepted. *Expenses:* Tuition: Full-time $26,808; part-time $1117 per credit. Required fees: $1024. *Financial support:* Fellowships with full and partial tuition reimbursements, teaching assistantships with full and partial tuition reimbursements available. Financial award application deadline: 1/1; financial award applicants required to submit FAFSA. *Unit head:* Errol Willett, Chair, 315-443-3830, E-mail: eswillett@syr.edu. *Application contact:* Harriett Conti, Assistant Dean for Recruitment and Admissions, 315-443-5755, E-mail: hmconti@syr.edu.

Syracuse University, College of Visual and Performing Arts, Program in Sculpture, Syracuse, NY 13244. Offers MFA. *Students:* 8 full-time (4 women); includes 1 minority (Asian American or Pacific Islander). Average age 28. 12 applicants, 25% accepted, 3 enrolled. In 2009, 2 master's awarded. *Degree requirements:* For master's, thesis or alternative. *Entrance requirements:* For master's, portfolio. Additional exam requirements/recommendations for international students: Required—TOEFL (minimum score 100 iBT). *Application deadline:* For fall admission, 2/1 priority date for domestic and international students. Application fee: $75. Electronic applications accepted. *Expenses:* Tuition: Full-time $26,808; part-time $1117 per credit. Required fees: $1024. *Financial support:* Fellowships with full and partial tuition reimbursements, teaching assistantships with full and partial tuition reimbursements available. Financial award application deadline: 1/1; financial award applicants required to submit FAFSA. *Unit head:* Errol Willett, Chair, 315-443-3830, E-mail: eswillett@syr.edu. *Application contact:* Harriett Conti, Assistant Dean for Recruitment and Admissions, 315-443-5755, E-mail: hmconti@syr.edu.

Temple University, Graduate School, Tyler School of Art, Department of Crafts, Philadelphia, PA 19122-6096. Offers ceramics/glass (MFA); fibers and fabric design (MFA); metals/jewelry/CAD-CAM (MFA). *Degree requirements:* For master's, essay, exhibit. *Entrance requirements:* For master's, minimum GPA of 3.0, slide portfolio, 40 credits in studio art, 12 credits in art

Art/Fine Arts

Temple University (continued)
history. Additional exam requirements/recommendations for international students: Required—TOEFL (minimum score 550 paper-based; 213 computer-based; 79 iBT). Electronic applications accepted.

Temple University, Graduate School, Tyler School of Art, Department of Graphic Arts and Design, Philadelphia, PA 19122-6096. Offers graphic and interactive design (MFA); photography (MFA); printmaking (MFA). *Degree requirements:* For master's, essay, exhibit. *Entrance requirements:* For master's, minimum GPA of 3.0; slide portfolio, 40 credits in studio art; 12 credits in art history. Additional exam requirements/recommendations for international students: Required—TOEFL (minimum score 550 paper-based; 213 computer-based; 79 iBT). Electronic applications accepted.

Temple University, Graduate School, Tyler School of Art, Department of Painting, Drawing, and Sculpture, Philadelphia, PA 19122-6096. Offers painting (MFA); sculpture (MFA). *Degree requirements:* For master's, essay, exhibit. *Entrance requirements:* For master's, minimum GPA of 3.0, slide portfolio, 40 credits in studio art, 12 credits in art history. Additional exam requirements/recommendations for international students: Required—TOEFL (minimum score 550 paper-based; 213 computer-based; 79 iBT). Electronic applications accepted.

Texas A&M University, College of Architecture, Department of Visualization, College Station, TX 77843. Offers visualization sciences (MS, PhD). *Faculty:* 13. *Students:* 51 full-time (18 women), 22 part-time (2 women); includes 13 minority (6 Asian Americans or Pacific Islanders, 7 Hispanic Americans), 13 international. In 2009, 10 master's awarded. *Expenses:* Tuition, state resident: full-time $3991; part-time $221.74 per credit hour. Tuition, nonresident: full-time $9049; part-time $502.74 per credit hour. *Unit head:* Dr. Tim McLaughlin, Department Head, 979-845-3465, E-mail: timm@viz.tamu.edu. *Application contact:* Prof. Carol LaFayette, Program Coordinator, 979-845-3465, E-mail: vizinfo@viz.tamu.edu.

Texas A&M University–Commerce, Graduate School, College of Arts and Sciences, Department of Art, Commerce, TX 75429-3011. Offers art (MA, MS); art history (MA); fine arts (MFA); studio art (MA). Part-time programs available. *Degree requirements:* For master's, comprehensive exam, thesis (for some programs). *Entrance requirements:* For master's, GRE General Test. Electronic applications accepted. *Faculty research:* Use of different art media.

Texas A&M University–Corpus Christi, Graduate Studies and Research, College of Liberal Arts, Program in Studio Arts, Corpus Christi, TX 78412-5503. Offers MA, MFA. Part-time and evening/weekend programs available. *Degree requirements:* For master's, comprehensive exam, thesis (for some programs). *Entrance requirements:* For master's, GRE General Test. Additional exam requirements/recommendations for international students: Required—TOEFL. Electronic applications accepted.

Texas A&M University–Kingsville, College of Graduate Studies, College of Arts and Sciences, Department of Art, Kingsville, TX 78363. Offers MA, MS. Part-time programs available. *Degree requirements:* For master's, comprehensive exam, thesis or alternative. *Entrance requirements:* For master's, GRE General Test, minimum GPA of 3.0. Additional exam requirements/recommendations for international students: Required—TOEFL.

Texas Christian University, College of Fine Arts, Department of Art and Art History, Fort Worth, TX 76129. Offers art history (MA); studio art (MFA). *Accreditation:* NASAD. Part-time programs available. *Degree requirements:* For master's, thesis, internship, foreign language exam. *Entrance requirements:* For master's, GRE General Test, writing sample. Additional exam requirements/recommendations for international students: Required—TOEFL. *Application deadline:* For fall admission, 3/15 for domestic students. Applications are processed on a rolling basis. Application fee: $0. *Expenses:* Tuition: Full-time $17,640; part-time $980 per credit hour. Tuition and fees vary according to program. *Financial support:* Unspecified assistantships available. Financial award application deadline: 3/1. *Unit head:* Ron Watson, Chairperson, 817-257-7643, E-mail: r.watson@tcu.edu. *Application contact:* Dr. Joseph Butler, Associate Dean, College of Fine Arts, E-mail: j.butler@tcu.edu.

Texas Southern University, College of Liberal Arts and Behavioral Sciences, Department of Fine Arts, Houston, TX 77004-4584. Offers fine arts (MA); music (MA). Part-time programs available. *Faculty:* 3 full-time (1 woman), 1 (woman) part-time/adjunct. *Students:* 2 full-time (0 women), 4 part-time (1 woman); all minorities (all African Americans). Average age 35. 2 applicants, 100% accepted, 2 enrolled. *Degree requirements:* For master's, one foreign language, comprehensive exam, recital. *Entrance requirements:* For master's, GRE General Test, minimum GPA of 2.5. Additional exam requirements/recommendations for international students: Required—TOEFL. *Application deadline:* For fall admission, 7/1 for domestic and international students; for spring admission, 11/1 for domestic and international students. Applications are processed on a rolling basis. Application fee: $50 ($75 for international students). Electronic applications accepted. *Expenses:* Tuition, state resident: full-time $1805; part-time $100 per credit hour. Tuition, nonresident: full-time $6470; part-time $343 per credit hour. Tuition and fees vary according to course level, course load and degree level. *Financial support:* Fellowships, teaching assistantships, scholarships/grants and unspecified assistantships available. Support available to part-time students. Financial award application deadline: 5/1. *Faculty research:* Music theory, choral music, composition, percussion composition, ethnic musicology. *Unit head:* Dianne F. Jemison-Pollard, Chair, 713-313-7337, Fax: 713-313-1869, E-mail: jemison_dp@tsu.edu. *Application contact:* Dr. Gregory Maddox, Interim Dean of the Graduate School, 713-313-7011 Ext. 4410, Fax: 713-639-1876, E-mail: maddox_gh@tsu.edu.

Texas Tech University, Graduate School, College of Visual and Performing Arts, Fine Arts Doctoral Program, Lubbock, TX 79409. Offers arts (PhD); music (PhD); theatre arts (PhD). *Accreditation:* NAST. *Students:* 44 full-time (18 women), 31 part-time (16 women); includes 9 minority (3 African Americans, 1 American Indian/Alaska Native, 1 Asian American or Pacific Islander, 4 Hispanic Americans), 10 international. Average age 36. 33 applicants, 30% accepted, 3 enrolled. In 2009, 10 doctorates awarded. *Degree requirements:* For doctorate, thesis/dissertation. *Entrance requirements:* For doctorate, GRE General Test. Additional exam requirements/recommendations for international students: Required—TOEFL (minimum score 550 paper-based; 213 computer-based). *Application deadline:* For fall admission, 3/1 priority date for international students; for spring admission, 11/1 priority date for international students. Applications are processed on a rolling basis. Application fee: $50 ($75 for international students). Electronic applications accepted. *Expenses:* Tuition, state resident: full-time $5100; part-time $213 per credit hour. Tuition, nonresident: full-time $11,748; part-time $490 per credit hour. Required fees: $2298; $50 per credit hour. $555 per semester. *Financial support:* Research assistantships with partial tuition reimbursements, teaching assistantships with partial tuition reimbursements available. Financial award application deadline: 4/15. *Faculty research:* Art criticism and theory, music, theatre arts; arts education; history of arts. *Unit head:* Dr. Brian D. Steele, Director, 806-742-0700, Fax: 806-742-0695, E-mail: brian.steele@ttu.edu. *Application contact:* Dr. Brian D. Steele, Director, 806-742-0700, Fax: 806-742-0695, E-mail: brian.steele@ttu.edu.

Texas Tech University, Graduate School, College of Visual and Performing Arts, School of Art, Lubbock, TX 79409. Offers art (MFA); art education (MAE); fine arts-art (PhD). *Accreditation:* NASAD (one or more programs are accredited). Part-time programs available. *Faculty:* 22 full-time (11 women). *Students:* 45 full-time (14 women), 25 part-time (20 women); includes 9 minority (1 African American, 2 American Indian/Alaska Native, 6 Hispanic Americans), 10 international. Average age 34. 91 applicants, 42% accepted, 20 enrolled. In 2009, 12 master's, 2 doctorates awarded. *Degree requirements:* For master's, thesis (for some programs); for doctorate, thesis/dissertation. *Entrance requirements:* For master's and doctorate, GRE General Test. Additional exam requirements/recommendations for international students: Required—TOEFL (minimum score 550 paper-based; 213 computer-based). *Application deadline:* For fall admission, 3/1 priority date for international students; for spring admission, 11/1 priority date for international students. Applications are processed on a rolling basis. Application fee: $50 ($75 for international students). Electronic applications accepted. *Expenses:* Tuition, state resident: full-time $5100; part-time $213 per credit hour. Tuition, nonresident: full-time $11,748; part-time $490 per credit hour. Required fees: $2298; $50 per credit hour. $555 per semester. *Financial support:* In 2009–10, 18 teaching assistantships with partial tuition reimbursements (averaging $8,730 per year) were awarded; research assistantships with partial tuition reimbursements, career-related internships or fieldwork, Federal Work-Study, and institutionally sponsored loans also available. Support available to part-time students. Financial award application deadline: 4/15; financial award applicants required to submit FAFSA. *Faculty research:* Studio, art history, art education. *Unit head:* Prof. Tina Fuentes, Director, 806-742-3825 Ext. 223, Fax: 806-742-1971, E-mail: tina.fuentes@ttu.edu. *Application contact:* Sang-Mi Yoo, Graduate Advisor, 806-742-3825 Ext. 244, Fax: 806-742-1971, E-mail: sang-mi.yoo@ttu.edu.

Texas Tech University, Graduate School, College of Visual and Performing Arts, School of Music, Lubbock, TX 79409. Offers composition (MM, DMA); conducting (DMA); fine arts-music (PhD); music education (MM Ed); music theory (MM); musicology (MM); pedagogy (MM); performance (MM, DMA); piano pedagogy (DMA). *Accreditation:* NASM. Part-time programs available. *Faculty:* 40 full-time (15 women), 1 part-time/adjunct (0 women). *Students:* 105 full-time (41 women), 28 part-time (15 women); includes 17 minority (5 African Americans, 12 Hispanic Americans), 27 international. Average age 30. 123 applicants, 60% accepted, 37 enrolled. In 2009, 19 master's, 20 doctorates awarded. *Degree requirements:* For master's, thesis or alternative; for doctorate, thesis/dissertation. *Entrance requirements:* For master's and doctorate, GRE General Test. Additional exam requirements/recommendations for international students: Required—TOEFL (minimum score 550 paper-based; 213 computer-based). *Application deadline:* For fall admission, 3/1 priority date for international students; for spring admission, 11/1 priority date for international students. Applications are processed on a rolling basis. Application fee: $50 ($75 for international students). Electronic applications accepted. *Expenses:* Tuition, state resident: full-time $5100; part-time $213 per credit hour. Tuition, nonresident: full-time $11,748; part-time $490 per credit hour. Required fees: $2298; $50 per credit hour. $555 per semester. *Financial support:* In 2009–10, 32 teaching assistantships with partial tuition reimbursements (averaging $8,206 per year) were awarded; research assistantships with partial tuition reimbursements, Federal Work-Study and institutionally sponsored loans also available. Support available to part-time students. Financial award application deadline: 4/15; financial award applicants required to submit FAFSA. *Faculty research:* Strategies for music pedagogy in grades K-12, performance practice of traditional music, role of the woman piano virtuoso, vernacular music center, voice health and culture. Total annual research expenditures: $9,083. *Unit head:* Prof. William Ballenger, Director, 806-742-2270, Fax: 806-742-2294, E-mail: william.ballenger@ttu.edu. *Application contact:* Carin Wanner, Admissions and Scholarship Coordinator, 806-742-2270 Ext. 225, Fax: 806-742-2294, E-mail: melissacarin.wanner@ttu.edu.

Texas Woman's University, Graduate School, College of Arts and Sciences, School of the Arts, Department of Visual Arts, Denton, TX 76201. Offers art (MA, MFA). *Faculty:* 13 full-time (7 women), 4 part-time/adjunct (3 women). *Students:* 24 full-time (23 women), 19 part-time (18 women); includes 10 minority (3 African Americans, 1 American Indian/Alaska Native, 1 Asian American or Pacific Islander, 5 Hispanic Americans), 3 international. Average age 38. 24 applicants, 92% accepted, 11 enrolled. In 2009, 16 master's awarded. *Degree requirements:* For master's, thesis (for some programs), exhibit (MFA), oral exam, thesis or professional paper (MA). *Entrance requirements:* For master's, GRE General Test (MFA), portfolio, interview, curriculum vitae, letter of intent. Additional exam requirements/recommendations for international students: Required—TOEFL (minimum score 550 paper-based; 213 computer-based; 79 iBT). *Application deadline:* For fall admission, 2/15 priority date for domestic students, 3/1 for international students; for spring admission, 10/16 priority date for domestic students, 7/1 for international students. Applications are processed on a rolling basis. Application fee: $50. Electronic applications accepted. *Expenses:* Tuition, state resident: full-time $3564; part-time $198 per credit hour. Tuition, nonresident: full-time $8550; part-time $475 per credit hour. Required fees: $69.26 per credit hour. Tuition and fees vary according to course load. *Financial support:* In 2009–10, 17 students received support, including 8 research assistantships (averaging $9,684 per year), 9 teaching assistantships (averaging $9,684 per year); career-related internships or fieldwork, Federal Work-Study, institutionally sponsored loans, scholarships/grants, traineeships, health care benefits, and unspecified assistantships also available. Support available to part-time students. Financial award application deadline: 3/1; financial award applicants required to submit FAFSA. *Faculty research:* Art education and electronic technology, film noir, handmade paper, one-of-a-kind art books, women in film. *Unit head:* Gary Washmon, Acting Chair, 940-898-2530, Fax: 940-898-2496, E-mail: gwashmon@twu.edu. *Application contact:* Samuel Wheeler, Assistant Director of Admissions, 940-898-3188, Fax: 940-898-3081, E-mail: wheelersr@twu.edu.

Towson University, College of Graduate Studies and Research, Program in Studio Arts, Towson, MD 21252-0001. Offers MFA. *Degree requirements:* For master's, exam. *Entrance requirements:* For master's, portfolio, minimum GPA of 3.0. Additional exam requirements/recommendations for international students: Required—TOEFL (minimum score 550 paper-based). Electronic applications accepted.

Tufts University, Graduate School of Arts and Sciences, Department of Art and Art History, Program in Studio Art, Medford, MA 02155. Offers MFA, MA/MFA, MFA/Certificate. *Faculty:* 11 full-time, 5 part-time/adjunct. *Students:* 83 full-time (54 women); includes 13 minority (3 African Americans, 2 American Indian/Alaska Native, 2 Asian Americans or Pacific Islanders, 6 Hispanic Americans), 18 international. Average age 27. 164 applicants, 57% accepted, 39 enrolled. In 2009, 20 master's awarded. *Degree requirements:* For master's, exhibit. *Entrance requirements:* For master's, portfolio. Additional exam requirements/recommendations for international students: Required—TOEFL (minimum score 550 paper-based; 213 computer-based; 80 iBT). *Application deadline:* For fall admission, 1/15 for domestic students, 12/15 for international students. Applications are processed on a rolling basis. Application fee: $75. *Expenses:* Tuition: Full-time $38,096; part-time $3962 per credit. Required fees: $686; $40 per year. Tuition and fees vary according to course level, course load, degree level, program and student level. *Financial support:* Federal Work-Study, scholarships/grants, and tuition waivers (partial) available. Financial award application deadline: 1/15; financial award applicants required to submit FAFSA. *Unit head:* Susan Clain, Dean, School of the Museum of Fine Arts, 617-267-6100, Fax: 617-424-6271. *Application contact:* David Brown, Associate Dean of Academic Affairs—Graduate programs, 617-369-6100.

Tulane University, School of Liberal Arts, Department of Art, New Orleans, LA 70118-5669. Offers art (MFA); art history (MA). *Degree requirements:* For master's, one foreign language, thesis. *Entrance requirements:* For master's, GRE General Test, minimum B average in undergraduate course work. Additional exam requirements/recommendations for international students: Required—TOEFL. Electronic applications accepted.

United Theological Seminary of the Twin Cities, Professional Program, New Brighton, MN 55112-2598. Offers advanced theological studies (Diploma); justice and peace studies (M Div, MA); leadership toward racial justice (MA, Certificate); leadership towards racial justice (M Div); Methodist studies (M Div, MA, Certificate); ministry (D Min); ministry renewal and professional development (Certificate); pastoral care and counseling (M Div, MA, MARL); religion and theology (MA); theological and religious studies (Certificate); theology and the arts (M Div, MA); urban ministry (M Div, MA, MARL); women's studies: religion, theology and ministry (MA); women's studies: religions, theology and ministry (M Div). *Accreditation:* ACIPE; ATS. Part-time and evening/weekend programs available. *Faculty:* 9 full-time (6 women), 22 part-time/adjunct (10 women). *Students:* 49 full-time (34 women), 105 part-time (68 women). Average age 47. 41 applicants, 98% accepted, 34 enrolled. In 2009, 24 first professional degrees, 5 master's, 2 doctorates, 2 other advanced degrees awarded. *Degree requirements:* For master's, thesis; for doctorate, comprehensive exam, thesis/dissertation; for M Div, integrative notebook, spiritual chronicle. *Entrance requirements:* For M Div and master's, minimum GPA of 2.75; strong analytical, reflective thinking and writing skills; vocational and academic goals compatible with those of Seminary; for doctorate, M Div or equivalent, minimum GPA of 3.0, 3 years experience in professional ministry; for other advanced degree, BA or equivalent life experience; strong analytical, reflective thinking and writing skills (Certificate); proficiency in English language, previous study of theology at a theological school, recommendation of student's denomination (Diploma). Additional exam requirements/recommendations for international students: Required—TOEFL (minimum score 550 paper-based). *Application deadline:* For fall admission, 7/1 priority date for domestic students, 11/1 priority date for international students; for winter admission, 11/1 priority date for domestic students; for spring admission, 11/15 priority date for domestic students. Applications are processed on a rolling basis. Application fee: $50. *Expenses:* Tuition: Full-time $11,502; part-time $426 per credit hour. Required fees: $295; $155 per term. One-time fee: $25. Tuition and fees vary according to course load, degree level and program. *Financial support:* In 2009–10, 120 students received support. Career-related internships or fieldwork, institutionally sponsored loans, and scholarships/grants available. Support available to part-time students. Financial award application deadline: 5/1; financial award applicants required to submit FAFSA. *Unit head:* Dr. Richard D. Weis, Dean of the Seminary, 651-255-6108 Ext. 108, Fax: 651-633-4315, E-mail: rweis@unitedseminary.edu. *Application contact:* Rev. Glen Herrington-Hall, Director of Admissions, 651-255-6107 Ext. 107, Fax: 651-633-4315, E-mail: gherrington-hall@unitedseminary.edu.

Universidad del Turabo, Graduate Programs, Programs in Education, Program in Teaching of Fine Arts, Gurabo, PR 00778-3030. Offers M Ed. *Students:* 34 full-time (23 women), 36 part-time (22 women); includes 65 Hispanic Americans. Average age 35. 18 applicants, 94% accepted, 16 enrolled. In 2009, 38 master's awarded. *Unit head:* Angela Candelario, Dean, 787-743-7979 Ext. 4126. *Application contact:* Virginia Gonzalez, Admissions Officer, 787-746-3009.

Université du Québec à Chicoutimi, Graduate Programs, Program in Fine Arts, Chicoutimi, QC G7H 2B1, Canada. Offers MA. Part-time programs available. *Degree requirements:* For master's, thesis optional. *Entrance requirements:* For master's, appropriate bachelor's degree, proficiency in French.

Université du Québec à Montréal, Graduate Programs, Program in Fine Arts, Montréal, QC H3C 3P8, Canada. Offers MA. Part-time programs available. *Degree requirements:* For master's, thesis optional. *Entrance requirements:* For master's, appropriate bachelor's degree or equivalent, proficiency in French.

Université Laval, Faculty of Architecture, Planning and Visual Arts, School of Visual Arts, Programs in Visual Arts, Québec, QC G1K 7P4, Canada. Offers graphic design and multimedia (MA); visual arts (MA). *Degree requirements:* For master's, thesis (for some programs). *Entrance requirements:* For master's, technical exam, interview, mastery of pertinent software, knowledge of French. Electronic applications accepted.

University at Albany, State University of New York, College of Arts and Sciences, Department of Art, Albany, NY 12222-0001. Offers MA, MFA. *Degree requirements:* For master's, exhibit. *Entrance requirements:* For master's, portfolio. Additional exam requirements/recommendations for international students: Required—TOEFL (minimum score 550 paper-based; 213 computer-based). *Faculty research:* Art history, sculpture, painting and drawing, photography, digital media.

University at Buffalo, the State University of New York, Graduate School, College of Arts and Sciences, Department of Visual Studies, Buffalo, NY 14260. Offers art (MFA), including fine arts; art history (MA, Certificate), including art history (MA), critical museum studies (Certificate). *Degree requirements:* For master's, thesis.

The University of Alabama, Graduate School, College of Arts and Sciences, Department of Art, Tuscaloosa, AL 35487. Offers art history (MA); studio art (MA, MFA), including ceramics, painting, photography, printmaking, sculpture. *Accreditation:* NASAD. Part-time programs available. *Faculty:* 16 full-time (8 women), 1 part-time/adjunct (0 women). *Students:* 17 full-time (10 women), 4 part-time (all women); includes 1 minority (Asian American or Pacific Islander), 1 international. Average age 31. 31 applicants, 39% accepted, 7 enrolled. In 2009, 1 degree awarded. *Degree requirements:* For master's, one foreign language, comprehensive exam (for some programs), oral exam, thesis statement, exhibit (studio art), thesis (art history). *Entrance requirements:* For master's, GRE General Test or MAT (art history), minimum GPA of 3.0, BFA or equivalent (studio art). Additional exam requirements/recommendations for international students: Required—TOEFL (minimum score 550 paper-based; 213 computer-based). *Application deadline:* For fall admission, 3/15 for domestic and international students; for spring admission, 10/15 for domestic and international students. Applications are processed on a rolling basis. Application fee: $50 ($60 for international students). Electronic applications accepted. *Expenses:* Tuition, state resident: full-time $7000. Tuition, nonresident: full-time $19,200. *Financial support:* In 2009–10, 2 fellowships with full tuition reimbursements (averaging $14,000 per year), 13 teaching assistantships with full and partial tuition reimbursements (averaging $9,206 per year) were awarded; career-related internships or fieldwork, institutionally sponsored loans, scholarships/grants, and unspecified assistantships also available. Financial award application deadline: 7/14. *Faculty research:* Nineteenth century American art history, Chinese art history, Baroque art history, twentieth century art history, Asian art history. *Unit head:* William T. Dooley, Chairperson, 205-348-1890, Fax: 205-348-0287, E-mail: wtdooley@bama.ua.edu. *Application contact:* Craig R. Wedderspoon, Graduate Coordinator, 205-348-1898, Fax: 205-348-0287, E-mail: cwedders@bama.ua.edu.

University of Alaska Fairbanks, College of Liberal Arts, Department of Art, Fairbanks, AK 99775-5640. Offers art (MFA); ceramics (MFA); computer art (MFA); drawing (MFA); Native arts (MFA); painting (MFA); photography (MFA); printmaking (MFA); sculpture (MFA). Part-time programs available. *Faculty:* 7 full-time (2 women), 4 part-time/adjunct (3 women). *Students:* 7 full-time (3 women), 2 part-time (0 women); includes 1 minority (American Indian/Alaska Native). Average age 33. 10 applicants, 30% accepted, 2 enrolled. In 2009, 2 master's awarded. *Degree requirements:* For master's, comprehensive exam, thesis, oral exam, oral defense. *Entrance requirements:* For master's, portfolio. Additional exam requirements/recommendations for international students: Required—TOEFL (minimum score 550 paper-based; 213 computer-based; 80 iBT). *Application deadline:* For fall admission, 6/1 for domestic students, 3/1 for international students; for spring admission, 10/15 for domestic students, 9/1 for international students. Applications are processed on a rolling basis. Application fee: $60. Electronic applications accepted. *Expenses:* Tuition, state resident: full-time $7584; part-time $316 per credit. Tuition, nonresident: full-time $15,504; part-time $646 per credit. Required fees: $23 per credit. $135 per semester. Tuition and fees vary according to course level, course load and reciprocity agreements. *Financial support:* In 2009–10, 1 fellowship (averaging $13,500 per year), 4 teaching assistantships (averaging $12,058 per year) were awarded; research assistantships, Federal Work-Study, scholarships/grants, health care benefits, and unspecified assistantships also available. Support available to part-time students. Financial award application deadline: 7/1; financial award applicants required to submit FAFSA. *Faculty research:* Computer art, survey of arts in Alaska; found object art, visualization and animation, painting from the wilderness. *Unit head:* Todd Sherman, Chair, 907-474-7530, Fax: 907-474-5853, E-mail: fyart@uaf.edu. *Application contact:* Todd Sherman, Chair, 907-474-7530, Fax: 907-474-5853, E-mail: fyart@uaf.edu.

University of Alberta, Faculty of Graduate Studies and Research, Department of Art and Design, Edmonton, AB T6G 2E1, Canada. Offers drawing (MFA); history of art, design, and visual culture (MA); industrial design (M Des); painting (MFA); printmaking (MFA); sculpture (MFA); visual communication design (M Des). *Faculty:* 19 full-time (7 women). *Students:* 28 full-time (16 women), 12 part-time (8 women). Average age 25. 66 applicants, 26% accepted, 12 enrolled. In 2009, 10 master's awarded. *Degree requirements:* For master's, thesis. *Entrance requirements:* For master's, portfolio (MFA and MDES). Additional exam requirements/recommendations for international students: Required—TOEFL (minimum score 550 paper-based; 213 computer-based). *Application deadline:* For fall admission, 2/1 for domestic and international students. Application fee: $0. Tuition and fees charges are reported in Canadian dollars. *Expenses:* Tuition, area resident: Full-time $4626 Canadian dollars; part-time $99.72 Canadian dollars per unit. International tuition: $8216 Canadian dollars full-time. Required fees: $3590 Canadian dollars; $99.72 Canadian dollars per unit. $215 Canadian dollars per term. *Financial support:* In 2009–10, 29 students received support, including 5 research assistantships (averaging $3,300 per year), 13 teaching assistantships (averaging $8,100 per year); scholarships/grants and unspecified assistantships also available. Financial award application deadline: 2/1. *Unit head:* Dr. Liz Ingram, Acting Chair, 780-492-3261, Fax: 780-492-7870. *Application contact:* Sharon Orescan, Administrative Assistant, 780-492-5712, Fax: 780-492-7870, E-mail: artdes@ualberta.ca.

The University of Arizona, Graduate College, College of Fine Arts, School of Art, Program in Studio Art, Tucson, AZ 85721. Offers MFA. *Accreditation:* NASAD. Part-time programs available. *Students:* 31 full-time (18 women), 5 part-time (2 women); includes 3 minority (all Hispanic Americans), 2 international. Average age 28. 118 applicants, 20% accepted, 15 enrolled. In 2009, 14 master's awarded. *Degree requirements:* For master's, thesis or alternative. *Entrance requirements:* For master's, portfolio, minimum GPA of 3.0 for last 60 units, 3 letters of recommendation, resume or curriculum vitae. Additional exam requirements/recommendations for international students: Required—TOEFL (minimum score 550 paper-based). *Application deadline:* For fall admission, 2/1 for domestic students, 12/1 for international students. Application fee: $75. *Expenses:* Tuition, state resident: full-time $9028. Tuition, nonresident: full-time $24,890. *Financial support:* In 2009–10, 2 fellowships with full and partial tuition reimbursements (averaging $10,000 per year), 15 teaching assistantships with full tuition reimbursements (averaging $5,000 per year) were awarded; career-related internships or fieldwork, Federal Work-Study, institutionally sponsored loans, scholarships/grants, and tuition waivers (full) also available. Support available to part-time students. Financial award application deadline: 4/1; financial award applicants required to submit FAFSA. *Faculty research:* Painting, photography and intermedia, sculpture, printmaking, ceramics. *Unit head:* Dr. Julie Plax, Associate Director, Academic Affairs, 520-621-7000, E-mail: jplax@email.arizona.edu. *Application contact:* Kimberly Mast, Graduate Coordinator, 520-621-8518, E-mail: kmast@email.arizona.edu.

University of Arkansas, Graduate School, J. William Fulbright College of Arts and Sciences, Department of Art, Fayetteville, AR 72701-1201. Offers MFA. *Students:* 13 full-time (5 women), 2 part-time (0 women); includes 1 minority (Asian American or Pacific Islander), 5 international. In 2009, 2 master's awarded. *Degree requirements:* For master's, exhibit or thesis. Application fee: $40 ($50 for international students). *Expenses:* Tuition, state resident: full-time $7355; part-time $356.58 per hour. Tuition, nonresident: full-time $17,401; part-time $775.17 per hour. Required fees: $1203. *Financial support:* In 2009–10, 1 research assistantship, 8 teaching assistantships were awarded; fellowships, career-related internships or fieldwork and Federal Work-Study also available. Support available to part-time students. Financial award application deadline: 4/1; financial award applicants required to submit FAFSA. *Unit head:* Lynn Jacobs, Department Chairperson, 479-575-5202, Fax: 479-575-2062, E-mail: ljacobs@uark.edu. *Application contact:* Tom Hapgood, Graduate Coordinator, 479-575-7405, Fax: 479-575-2062, E-mail: thapgoo@uark.edu.

University of Arkansas at Little Rock, Graduate School, College of Arts, Humanities, and Social Science, Department of Art, Little Rock, AR 72204-1099. Offers art education (MA); art history (MA); studio art (MA). *Accreditation:* NASAD. Part-time programs available. *Degree requirements:* For master's, 4 foreign languages, oral exam, oral defense of thesis or exhibit. *Entrance requirements:* For master's, portfolio review or term paper evaluation, minimum GPA of 2.7.

The University of British Columbia, Faculty of Arts and Faculty of Graduate Studies, Department of Art History, Visual Art, and Theory, Vancouver, BC V6T1Z2, Canada. Offers art history (MA, PhD, Diploma); critical and curatorial studies (MA); visual art (MFA). *Degree requirements:* For master's, one foreign language, thesis, final exhibition (MFA, MA in critical and curatorial studies); for doctorate, 2 foreign languages, comprehensive exam, thesis/dissertation. *Entrance requirements:* For master's, bachelor's degree with minimum B+ average (MFA, MA in critical and curatorial studies), A- (MA in art history); for doctorate, master's degree with minimum A- average. Additional exam requirements/recommendations for international students: Required—TOEFL (minimum score 600 paper-based; 250 computer-based). Electronic applications accepted. *Faculty research:* Conceptual art, Asian art, indigenous North American art, post-second war art, eighteenth and nineteenth century art, curatorial, digital art.

University of Calgary, Faculty of Graduate Studies, Faculty of Fine Arts, Department of Art, Calgary, AB T2N 1N4, Canada. Offers MA, MFA. *Degree requirements:* For master's, thesis. *Entrance requirements:* Additional exam requirements/recommendations for international students: Required—TOEFL. *Faculty research:* Painting, sculpture, drawing, photography, printmaking, new media.

University of California, Berkeley, Graduate Division, College of Letters and Science, Department of Art Practice, Berkeley, CA 94720-1500. Offers MFA. *Faculty:* 7 full-time, 12 part-time/adjunct. *Students:* 14 full-time (9 women). Average age 31. 241 applicants, 7 enrolled. In 2009, 7 master's awarded. *Entrance requirements:* For master's, GRE General Test, minimum GPA of 3.0, sample of work, 3 letters of recommendation. Additional exam requirements/recommendations for international students: Required—TOEFL (minimum score 570 paper-based; 230 computer-based). *Application deadline:* For fall admission, 12/15 for domestic students. Application fee: $70 ($90 for international students). Electronic applications accepted. *Financial support:* Fellowships, teaching assistantships, unspecified assistantships available. Financial award applicants required to submit FAFSA. *Unit head:* Prof. Hertha Wong, Chair, 501-642-2582. *Application contact:* Dee Levister, Graduate Assistant, 510-643-2582, Fax: 510-643-0884, E-mail: artgrad@berkeley.edu.

University of California, Berkeley, UC Berkeley Extension, Certificate Programs in Art and Design, Berkeley, CA 94720-1500. Offers interior design and interior architecture (Certificate); landscape architecture (Certificate); visual arts (Postbaccalaureate Certificate). *Unit head:* Diana Wu, Dean, 510-642-4181. *Application contact:* Art and Design, 415-284-1041, E-mail: visualarts@unex.berkeley.edu.

University of California, Davis, Graduate Studies, Program in Art, Davis, CA 95616. Offers MFA. *Degree requirements:* For master's, final exhibit. *Entrance requirements:* For master's, minimum GPA of 3.0, portfolio. Additional exam requirements/recommendations for international students: Required—TOEFL (minimum score 550 paper-based; 213 computer-based). Electronic applications accepted. *Faculty research:* Drawing, painting, photography, video, interactive art.

University of California, Irvine, Office of Graduate Studies, Claire Trevor School of the Arts, Department of Studio Art, Irvine, CA 92697. Offers MFA. *Students:* 33 full-time (15 women); includes 11 minority (5 Asian Americans or Pacific Islanders, 6 Hispanic Americans), 1 international. Average age 30. 100 applicants, 12% accepted, 9 enrolled. In 2009, 11 master's awarded. *Degree requirements:* For master's, thesis. *Entrance requirements:* For master's, minimum GPA of 3.0. *Application deadline:* For fall admission, 1/15 for domestic and international students. Applications are processed on a rolling basis. Application fee: $70 ($90 for international students). Electronic applications accepted. *Financial support:* Fellowships with tuition reimbursements, research assistantships with tuition reimbursements, teaching assistantships with tuition reimbursements, institutionally sponsored loans, traineeships, health care benefits, and unspecified assistantships available. Financial award application deadline: 3/1; financial award applicants required to submit FAFSA. *Faculty research:* Experimental concepts, processes relevant to contemporary issues. *Unit head:* Yong Soon Min, Chair, 949-824-5779, E-mail: ysmin@uci.edu. *Application contact:* Colleen Grigg, Administrative Assistant, 949-824-6648, Fax: 949-824-5297, E-mail: cgrigg@uci.edu.

University of California, Los Angeles, Graduate Division, School of the Arts and Architecture, Department of Art, Los Angeles, CA 90095-1615. Offers MA, MFA. Program is not accepting applications for the MA in Art for 2009-2010. *Degree requirements:* For master's, comprehensive

Art/Fine Arts

University of California, Los Angeles (continued)
exam. *Entrance requirements:* For master's, 20 slides and/or videotape, minimum GPA of 3.0. Electronic applications accepted.

University of California, Riverside, Graduate Division, Program in Visual Arts, Riverside, CA 92521-0102. Offers MFA. *Faculty:* 7 full-time (3 women), 5 part-time/adjunct (4 women). *Students:* 10 full-time (3 women); includes 1 minority (Asian American or Pacific Islander). Average age 29. 39 applicants, 18% accepted, 3 enrolled. In 2009, 4 master's awarded. *Degree requirements:* For master's, thesis. *Entrance requirements:* For master's, portfolio, minimum GPA of 3.2. Additional exam requirements/recommendations for international students: Required—TOEFL (minimum score 550 paper-based; 213 computer-based; 80 iBT). *Application deadline:* 1/5 for domestic and international students. Application fee: $70 ($85 for international students). Electronic applications accepted. *Financial support:* In 2009–10, 10 students received support, including fellowships with partial tuition reimbursements available (averaging $12,000 per year), teaching assistantships with full tuition reimbursements available (averaging $16,500 per year); career-related internships or fieldwork, institutionally sponsored loans, scholarships/grants, health care benefits, tuition waivers (partial), and unspecified assistantships also available. Financial award application deadline: 1/5; financial award applicants required to submit FAFSA. *Faculty research:* Painting, photography, sculpture, digital art, video. *Unit head:* Charles Long, Department Chair, 951-827-4634, Fax: 951-827-2385, E-mail: artdept@ucr.edu. *Application contact:* Amir Zaki, Graduate Advisor, 951-827-4634, Fax: 951-827-2385, E-mail: artdept@ucr.edu.

University of California, San Diego, Office of Graduate Studies, Department of Visual Arts, La Jolla, CA 92093. Offers MFA, PhD. *Degree requirements:* For master's, thesis, exhibit, oral exam. Electronic applications accepted. *Faculty research:* Developments within art and art theory.

University of California, Santa Barbara, Graduate Division, College of Letters and Sciences, Division of Humanities and Fine Arts, Department of Art, Santa Barbara, CA 93106-7120. Offers MFA. *Faculty:* 10 full-time (5 women), 11 part-time/adjunct (4 women). *Students:* 12 full-time (7 women). Average age 28. 54 applicants, 20% accepted, 7 enrolled. In 2009, 8 master's awarded. *Entrance requirements:* For master's, 20 slide portfolio, 3 letters of recommendation, resume/curriculum vitae. Additional exam requirements/recommendations for international students: Required—TOEFL (minimum score 550 paper-based; 213 computer-based; 80 iBT), or IELTS (minimum score 7). *Application deadline:* For fall admission, 1/4 for domestic and international students. Application fee: $70 ($90 for international students). Electronic applications accepted. *Financial support:* In 2009–10, 12 students received support, including 12 fellowships with full and partial tuition reimbursements available (averaging $11,100 per year), 12 teaching assistantships with partial tuition reimbursements available (averaging $7,300 per year); career-related internships or fieldwork, Federal Work-Study, institutionally sponsored loans, scholarships/grants, and health care benefits also available. Financial award application deadline: 1/7; financial award applicants required to submit FAFSA. *Faculty research:* Fine arts, contemporary art practice, visual arts, critical theory, interdisciplinary research. *Unit head:* Prof. Colin Gardner, Chair, 805-893-5694, E-mail: colingardner@cox.net. *Application contact:* Yumi Kinoshita, Staff Graduate Advisor, 805-893-5962, Fax: 805-893-7206, E-mail: ykinoshita@arts.ucsb.edu.

University of California, Santa Barbara, Graduate Division, College of Letters and Sciences, Division of Humanities and Fine Arts, Department of Media Arts and Technology, Santa Barbara, CA 93106-6065. Offers electronic music and sound design (MA); media arts and technology (PhD); multimedia engineering (MS); visual and spatial arts (MA). *Faculty:* 33 full-time (3 women). *Students:* 29 full-time (3 women). Average age 30. 55 applicants, 33% accepted, 8 enrolled. In 2009, 5 master's awarded. Terminal master's awarded for partial completion of doctoral program. *Degree requirements:* For master's, comprehensive exam, thesis; for doctorate, comprehensive exam, thesis/dissertation. *Entrance requirements:* For master's, GRE, portfolios; programming language and calculus-based math (expertise in 1 discipline and experience in another); 3 letters of recommendation; resume/curriculum vitae; for doctorate, GRE, portfolios; programming language and calculus-based math (expertise in 1 discipline and experience in another); 3 letters of recommendation; statement of purpose; personal achievements/contributions statement; resume/curriculum vitae; transcripts for post-secondary institutions attended. Additional exam requirements/recommendations for international students: Required—TOEFL (minimum score 550 paper-based; 213 computer-based; 80 iBT), or IELTS (minimum score 7). *Application deadline:* For fall admission, 1/15 for domestic and international students. Application fee: $70 ($90 for international students). Electronic applications accepted. *Financial support:* In 2009–10, 23 students received support, including 10 fellowships with full and partial tuition reimbursements available (averaging $4,800 per year), 6 research assistantships with full and partial tuition reimbursements available (averaging $8,300 per year), 18 teaching assistantships with partial tuition reimbursements available (averaging $7,300 per year); career-related internships or fieldwork, Federal Work-Study, institutionally sponsored loans, scholarships/grants, health care benefits, tuition waivers (full and partial), and unspecified assistantships also available. Financial award application deadline: 1/15; financial award applicants required to submit FAFSA. *Faculty research:* Electronic music and sound design: computer music and algorithmic composition, computer generated music, human-computer cooperation in music, design and synthesis of new sounds, sonic diffusion, 3D spatial sound; interactive art: installations, generative and algorithmic art, immersive art environments, computational photography; visualization; transarchitecture, multimedia signal processing, human-computer interaction, multimedia systems. *Unit head:* Prof. Matthew A. Turk, Chair, 805-893-4236, Fax: 805-893-2930, E-mail: mturk@cs.ucsb.edu. *Application contact:* Diane E. Harden, Graduate Program Assistant, 805-893-2887, Fax: 805-893-2930, E-mail: diane@mat.ucsb.edu.

University of California, Santa Cruz, Division of Graduate Studies, Division of the Arts, Program in Digital Arts and New Media, Santa Cruz, CA 95064. Offers MFA. *Entrance requirements:* Additional exam requirements/recommendations for international students: Required—TOEFL; Recommended—IELTS. Electronic applications accepted.

University of Central Florida, College of Arts and Humanities, Department of Art, Orlando, FL 32816. Offers studio art and the computer (MFA). *Faculty:* 24 full-time (5 women), 6 part-time/adjunct (2 women). *Students:* 20 full-time (14 women); includes 2 minority (both Asian Americans or Pacific Islanders). Average age 30. 20 applicants, 60% accepted, 10 enrolled. In 2009, 10 master's awarded. Application fee: $30. Electronic applications accepted. *Expenses:* Tuition, state resident: part-time $306.31 per credit hour. Tuition, nonresident: part-time $1099.01 per credit hour. Part-time tuition and fees vary according to degree level and program. *Financial support:* In 2009–10, 2 fellowships (averaging $5,300 per year), 3 research assistantships (averaging $3,200 per year), 2 teaching assistantships (averaging $6,400 per year) were awarded; scholarships/grants and unspecified assistantships also available. *Unit head:* Jack Lew, Interim Chair, 407-823-3145, Fax: 407-823-6470. *Application contact:* Jack Lew, Interim Chair, 407-823-3145, Fax: 407-823-6470.

University of Chicago, Division of the Humanities, Committee on the Visual Arts, Chicago, IL 60637-1513. Offers MFA. *Entrance requirements:* For master's, GRE General Test.

University of Cincinnati, Graduate School, College of Design, Architecture, Art, and Planning, School of Art, Program in Fine Arts, Cincinnati, OH 45221. Offers MFA. *Accreditation:* NASAD. Part-time programs available. *Degree requirements:* For master's, thesis, oral exam. *Entrance requirements:* Additional exam requirements/recommendations for international students: Required—TOEFL. Electronic applications accepted. *Faculty research:* Painting, drawing, ceramics, printmaking, sculpture.

University of Colorado at Boulder, Graduate School, College of Arts and Sciences, Department of Art and Art History, Boulder, CO 80309. Offers art history (MA), including 19th century art, contemporary art criticism, early 20th century art, Russian and Soviet art; ceramics (MFA); drawing (MFA); painting (MFA); photography and media arts (MFA); printmaking (MFA); sculpture (MFA). *Faculty:* 28 full-time (13 women). *Students:* 42 full-time (25 women), 1 (woman) part-time; includes 9 minority (1 American Indian/Alaska Native, 3 Asian Americans or Pacific Islanders, 5 Hispanic Americans), 1 international. Average age 31. 224 applicants, 6% accepted, 14 enrolled. In 2009, 17 master's awarded. *Degree requirements:* For master's, variable foreign language requirement, comprehensive exam, thesis (for some programs). *Entrance requirements:* For master's, GRE General Test, minimum undergraduate GPA of 3.0, portfolio. *Application deadline:* For fall admission, 1/15 priority date for domestic students, 12/1 for international students. Application fee: $50 ($60 for international students). *Financial support:* In 2009–10, 6 fellowships (averaging $1,713 per year), 13 research assistantships (averaging $5,087 per year) were awarded; Federal Work-Study, scholarships/grants, and tuition waivers (full) also available. Financial award application deadline: 1/15. *Faculty research:* Drawing, painting, ceramics, sculpture, photography and media arts, printmaking, Russian and Soviet art, early twentieth century art, contemporary art criticism, nineteenth century art. Total annual research expenditures: $10,586.

University of Connecticut, Graduate School, School of Fine Arts, Department of Art and Art History, Field of Studio Art, Storrs, CT 06269. Offers MFA. *Accreditation:* NASAD. *Students:* 9 full-time (6 women), 1 (woman) part-time; includes 1 minority (Asian American or Pacific Islander). Average age 28. 52 applicants, 10% accepted, 5 enrolled. In 2009, 5 master's awarded. *Entrance requirements:* Additional exam requirements/recommendations for international students: Required—TOEFL (minimum score 550 paper-based; 213 computer-based). *Application deadline:* For fall admission, 2/1 priority date for domestic and international students; for spring admission, 11/1 for domestic students, 10/1 for international students. Applications are processed on a rolling basis. Application fee: $55. Electronic applications accepted. *Expenses:* Tuition, state resident: full-time $4725; part-time $525 per credit. Tuition, nonresident: full-time $12,267; part-time $1363 per credit. Required fees: $346 per semester. Tuition and fees vary according to course load. *Financial support:* In 2009–10, 9 research assistantships with full tuition reimbursements were awarded; teaching assistantships with full tuition reimbursements, Federal Work-Study, health care benefits, and unspecified assistantships also available. Financial award application deadline: 2/1; financial award applicants required to submit FAFSA. *Unit head:* Charles Hagen, Chairperson, 860-486-2659, E-mail: chagen@finearts.sfa.uconn.edu. *Application contact:* Kelly Gillett, Administrative Assistant, 860-486-3930.

University of Dallas, Braniff Graduate School of Liberal Arts, Program in Art, Irving, TX 75062-4736. Offers MA, MFA. Part-time programs available. *Faculty:* 5 full-time (2 women). *Students:* 16 full-time (9 women), 1 (woman) part-time; includes 3 minority (1 African American, 2 Hispanic Americans). Average age 32. 16 applicants, 50% accepted, 6 enrolled. In 2009, 8 master's awarded. *Degree requirements:* For master's, exhibit, oral exam. *Entrance requirements:* For master's, GRE General Test, portfolio. Additional exam requirements/recommendations for international students: Required—TOEFL (minimum score 550 paper-based; 213 computer-based). *Application deadline:* For fall admission, 2/15 for domestic students. Applications are processed on a rolling basis. Application fee: $50. *Expenses:* Tuition: Full-time $10,080; part-time $560 per credit hour. Required fees: $50 per term. Tuition and fees vary according to program. *Financial support:* In 2009–10, 17 students received support; research assistantships, scholarships/grants available. Financial award application deadline: 2/15; financial award applicants required to submit FAFSA. *Faculty research:* Ceramics, printmaking, sculpture, art history, religious imagery and architecture. *Unit head:* Dan Hammett, Chairman, 972-721-5318, Fax: 972-721-5017, E-mail: hammett@udallas.edu. *Application contact:* Graduate Coordinator, 972-721-5106, Fax: 972-721-5280, E-mail: graduate@acad.udallas.edu.

University of Delaware, College of Arts and Sciences, Department of Art, Newark, DE 19716. Offers MA, MFA. *Degree requirements:* For master's, exposition paper final exhibition. *Entrance requirements:* For master's, portfolio of creative work. Electronic applications accepted. *Faculty research:* Painting, printmaking, ceramics, photography, sculpture.

University of Denver, Division of Arts, Humanities and Social Sciences, School of Art and Art History, Denver, CO 80208. Offers art history (MA); art history/museum studies (MA); electronic media arts and design (MFA). *Accreditation:* NASAD. Part-time programs available. *Faculty:* 16 full-time (11 women), 9 part-time/adjunct (5 women). *Students:* 15 full-time (14 women), 7 part-time (6 women); includes 1 minority (Hispanic American). Average age 29. 55 applicants, 51% accepted, 14 enrolled. In 2009, 10 master's awarded. *Degree requirements:* For master's, one foreign language, research paper. *Entrance requirements:* For master's, GRE. Additional exam requirements/recommendations for international students: Required—TOEFL. *Application deadline:* Applications are processed on a rolling basis. Application fee: $50. Electronic applications accepted. *Expenses:* Tuition: Full-time $34,596; part-time $961 per quarter hour. Required fees: $4 per quarter hour. Tuition and fees vary according to course load, campus/location and program. *Financial support:* Career-related internships or fieldwork, Federal Work-Study, institutionally sponsored loans, and scholarships/grants available. Support available to part-time students. Financial award application deadline: 3/1; financial award applicants required to submit FAFSA. *Faculty research:* Images of women in alchemical manuscripts and books, Giovanni Benedetto, Salvatore Castiglione. *Unit head:* Dr. Annette Stott, Director, 303-871-2846. *Application contact:* Dr. Annabeth Headrick, Graduate Advisor, 303-871-3574, E-mail: saah-interest@du.edu.

University of Florida, Graduate School, College of Fine Arts, School of Art and Art History, Gainesville, FL 32611. Offers art (MFA), including ceramics, creative photography, drawing, electronic intermedia, graphic design, painting, printmaking, sculpture; art education (MA); art history (MA, PhD); digital arts and sciences (MA); museology (museum studies) (MA). *Accreditation:* NASAD. *Degree requirements:* For master's, variable foreign language requirement, project or thesis (MFA). *Entrance requirements:* For master's, portfolio (MFA), writing sample (MA), GRE General Test or minimum GPA of 3.0. Additional exam requirements/recommendations for international students: Required—TOEFL (minimum score 550 paper-based; 213 computer-based). Electronic applications accepted. *Faculty research:* Studio production, art historical studies of style context.

University of Georgia, Graduate School, College of Arts and Sciences, Lamar Dodd School of Art, Program in Art, Athens, GA 30602. Offers MFA. *Accreditation:* NASAD. *Students:* 60 full-time (38 women), 10 part-time (all women); includes 11 minority (1 American Indian/Alaska Native, 5 Asian Americans or Pacific Islanders, 5 Hispanic Americans), 2 international. 220 applicants, 14% accepted, 27 enrolled. In 2009, 14 master's awarded. *Entrance requirements:* For master's, GRE General Test. *Application deadline:* For fall admission, 7/1 priority date for domestic students; for spring admission, 11/15 for domestic students. Application fee: $50. Electronic applications accepted. *Expenses:* Tuition, state resident: full-time $6000; part-time $250 per credit hour. Tuition, nonresident: full-time $20,904; part-time $871 per credit hour. Required fees: $730 per semester. *Financial support:* Fellowships, research assistantships, teaching assistantships, unspecified assistantships available. *Unit head:* Prof. Georgia Strange, Director, 706-542-1600, Fax: 706-542-0226, E-mail: strange@uga.edu. *Application contact:* Larry Millard, Graduate Coordinator, 706-542-1624, Fax: 706-542-0226, E-mail: lmillard@uga.edu.

University of Guam, Office of Graduate Studies, College of Liberal Arts and Social Sciences, Division of Fine Arts, Mangilao, GU 96923. Offers ceramics (MA); graphics (MA); painting (MA). *Degree requirements:* For master's, thesis or alternative, exhibit, final oral exam. *Entrance requirements:* For master's, GRE General Test, portfolio. Additional exam requirements/recommendations for international students: Required—TOEFL.

University of Guelph, Graduate Program Services, College of Arts, School of Fine Art and Music, Guelph, ON N1G 2W1, Canada. Offers studio art (MFA). *Degree requirements:* For master's, exhibition, support paper, oral defense. *Entrance requirements:* For master's, minimum B- average during previous 2 years of course work. Additional exam requirements/

recommendations for international students: Required—TOEFL. Electronic applications accepted. *Faculty research:* Studio practice in painting, sculpture, print, photo, drawing, video.

University of Hartford, Hartford Art School, West Hartford, CT 06117-1599. Offers MFA. *Accreditation:* NASAD. Part-time programs available. *Degree requirements:* For master's, thesis. *Entrance requirements:* For master's, portfolio, 3 letters of recommendation. Additional exam requirements/recommendations for international students: Required—TOEFL (minimum score 550 paper-based; 213 computer-based). Electronic applications accepted. *Expenses:* Contact institution.

University of Hawaii at Manoa, Graduate Division, College of Arts and Humanities, Department of Art and Art History, Honolulu, HI 96822. Offers art (MA); art history (MA); visual arts (MFA). Part-time programs available. *Faculty:* 12 full-time (5 women), 13 part-time/adjunct (6 women). *Students:* 24 full-time (16 women), 4 part-time (2 women); includes 2 minority (both Asian Americans or Pacific Islanders), 4 international. Average age 30. 46 applicants, 33% accepted, 10 enrolled. In 2009, 7 master's awarded. *Degree requirements:* For master's, thesis optional. *Entrance requirements:* For master's, GRE General Test, BFA, 18 hours of course work in art history. Additional exam requirements/recommendations for international students: Required—TOEFL (minimum score 600 paper-based; 250 computer-based; 100 iBT), IELTS (minimum score 7). *Application deadline:* For fall admission, 1/15 for domestic students, 12/15 for international students. Application fee: $60. *Expenses:* Tuition, state resident: full-time $8900; part-time $372 per credit. Tuition, nonresident: full-time $21,400; part-time $898 per credit. Required fees: $207 per semester. *Financial support:* In 2009–10, 4 students received support, including 10 fellowships (averaging $2,336 per year), 11 teaching assistantships (averaging $9,152 per year); Federal Work-Study, scholarships/grants, and tuition waivers (full and partial) also available. Financial award application deadline: 3/1; financial award applicants required to submit FAFSA. *Faculty research:* Painting, sculpture, glass, design, printmaking. Total annual research expenditures: $22,388. *Application contact:* Charles Cohan, Graduate Field Chairperson, 808-956-8251, Fax: 808-956-9043, E-mail: gradart@hawaii.edu.

University of Houston, College of Liberal Arts and Social Sciences, Department of Art, Houston, TX 77204. Offers art (MA); graphic communication (MFA); interdisciplinary practice and emerging forms (MFA); painting (MFA); photography/digital media (MFA); sculpture (MFA). *Faculty:* 10 full-time (6 women), 7 part-time/adjunct (3 women). *Students:* 35 full-time (20 women); includes 5 minority (2 African Americans, 1 Asian American or Pacific Islander, 2 Hispanic Americans), 4 international. Average age 32. 61 applicants, 31% accepted, 13 enrolled. In 2009, 12 master's awarded. *Entrance requirements:* For master's, GRE General Test, includes baccalaureate degree and portfolio. Additional exam requirements/recommendations for international students: Required—TOEFL. *Application deadline:* For fall admission, 2/1 for domestic and international students. Application fee: $25 ($75 for international students). Electronic applications accepted. *Expenses:* Tuition, state resident: full-time $7676; part-time $320 per credit hour. Tuition, nonresident: full-time $14,324; part-time $597 per credit hour. Required fees: $3034. *Financial support:* In 2009–10, 22 teaching assistantships with full tuition reimbursements (averaging $10,400 per year) were awarded; career-related internships or fieldwork, Federal Work-Study, institutionally sponsored loans, scholarships/grants, health care benefits, and unspecified assistantships also available. Support available to part-time students. Financial award application deadline: 3/10. *Faculty research:* Painting, sculpture, photography/installation/video, graphic design and typography, art history (Pre-Columbian to Surrealism). *Unit head:* Dr. John Reed, Chairperson, 713-743-3001, Fax: 713-743-2823, E-mail: jreed@uh.edu. *Application contact:* Cathy Hunt, Graduate Advisor and Instructional Assistant Professor, 713-743-2830, Fax: 713-743-2823, E-mail: chunt@uh.edu.

University of Idaho, College of Graduate Studies, College of Art and Architecture, Department of Art and Design, Moscow, ID 83844-2282. Offers art (MAT, MFA). *Accreditation:* NASAD. *Faculty:* 4 full-time. *Students:* 16 full-time, 11 part-time. In 2009, 4 master's awarded. *Degree requirements:* For master's, thesis (for some programs). *Entrance requirements:* For master's, minimum GPA of 2.8. *Application deadline:* For fall admission, 8/1 for domestic students; for spring admission, 12/15 for domestic students. Application fee: $55 ($60 for international students). *Expenses:* Tuition, state resident: full-time $6120. Tuition, nonresident: full-time $17,712. *Financial support:* Research assistantships, teaching assistantships available. Financial award application deadline: 2/15. *Faculty research:* Information design. *Unit head:* William Woolston, Chair, 208-885-7837. *Application contact:* William Woolston, Chair, 208-885-7837.

University of Illinois at Chicago, Graduate College, College of Architecture and Art, School of Art and Design, Chicago, IL 60607-7128. Offers electronic visualization (MFA); film animation (MFA); graphic design (MFA); industrial design (MFA); photography (MFA); studio arts (MFA). *Accreditation:* NASAD. *Degree requirements:* For master's, thesis, exhibit. *Entrance requirements:* For master's, MAT, portfolio. Additional exam requirements/recommendations for international students: Required—TOEFL. Electronic applications accepted.

University of Illinois at Urbana–Champaign, Graduate College, College of Fine and Applied Arts, School of Art and Design, Program in Design and Media, Champaign, IL 61820. Offers art and design (MFA), including new media; graphic design (MFA); industrial design (MFA). *Accreditation:* NASAD. *Students:* 18 full-time (9 women), 2 part-time (1 woman); includes 2 minority (both Asian Americans or Pacific Islanders), 10 international. 109 applicants, 7% accepted, 8 enrolled. In 2009, 4 master's awarded. *Entrance requirements:* For master's, minimum GPA of 3.0. Additional exam requirements/recommendations for international students: Required—TOEFL (minimum score 550 paper-based; 213 computer-based; 79 iBT). *Application deadline:* Applications are processed on a rolling basis. Application fee: $60 ($75 for international students). Electronic applications accepted. *Financial support:* Fellowships, research assistantships, teaching assistantships, tuition waivers (full and partial) available. *Unit head:* Ernest Scott, Chair, 217-333-1579, E-mail: ernscott@illinois.edu. *Application contact:* Marsha Biddle, Coordinator of Graduate Academic Affairs, 217-333-0642, Fax: 217-244-7688, E-mail: mbiddle@illinois.edu.

University of Illinois at Urbana–Champaign, Graduate College, College of Fine and Applied Arts, School of Art and Design, Program in Studio Arts, Champaign, IL 61820. Offers art and design (MFA); crafts (MFA); metals (MFA); painting (MFA); photography (MFA); sculpture (MFA). *Accreditation:* NASAD. *Students:* 22 full-time (15 women), 2 part-time (1 woman); includes 5 minority (2 American Indian/Alaska Native, 2 Asian Americans or Pacific Islanders, 1 Hispanic American), 5 international. 86 applicants, 12% accepted, 10 enrolled. In 2009, 12 master's awarded. *Entrance requirements:* For master's, minimum GPA of 3.0. Additional exam requirements/recommendations for international students: Required—TOEFL (minimum score 550 paper-based; 213 computer-based; 79 iBT). *Application deadline:* Applications are processed on a rolling basis. Application fee: $60 ($75 for international students). Electronic applications accepted. *Financial support:* Fellowships, research assistantships, teaching assistantships, tuition waivers (full and partial) available. *Unit head:* Timothy Van Laar, Chair, 217-333-6611, E-mail: tvanlaar@illinois.edu. *Application contact:* Marsha Biddle, Assistant to the Associate Director, 217-333-0642, Fax: 217-244-7688, E-mail: mbiddle@illinois.edu.

University of Indianapolis, Graduate Programs, College of Arts and Sciences, Department of Art, Indianapolis, IN 46227-3697. Offers MA. *Accreditation:* NASAD. Part-time and evening/weekend programs available. *Faculty:* 2 full-time (0 women). *Students:* 2 full-time (1 woman), 9 part-time (7 women); includes 1 minority (African American), 3 international. Average age 37. *Entrance requirements:* For master's, GRE Subject Test, 3 letters of recommendation, portfolio. Additional exam requirements/recommendations for international students: Required—TOEFL. *Application deadline:* Applications are processed on a rolling basis. Application fee: $30. *Financial support:* Federal Work-Study, scholarships/grants, and tuition waivers (full and partial) available. Support available to part-time students. Financial award application deadline: 5/1; financial award applicants required to submit FAFSA. *Unit head:* Dee Schaad, Chair, 317-788-3253, E-mail: dschaad@uindy.edu. *Application contact:* Katherine Fries, 317-788-3253, E-mail: frieskj@uindy.edu.

The University of Iowa, Graduate College, College of Liberal Arts and Sciences, School of Art and Art History, Programs in Art, Iowa City, IA 52242-1316. Offers MA, MFA. *Faculty:* 23 full-time (10 women), 7 part-time/adjunct (4 women). *Students:* 79 full-time (47 women), 9 part-time (7 women); includes 16 minority (2 African Americans, 1 American Indian/Alaska Native, 8 Asian Americans or Pacific Islanders, 5 Hispanic Americans), 7 international. Average age 30. 173 applicants, 36% accepted, 51 enrolled. In 2009, 43 master's awarded. *Degree requirements:* For master's, thesis, final exam. *Entrance requirements:* For master's, portfolio. Additional exam requirements/recommendations for international students: Required—TOEFL (minimum score 550 paper-based; 213 computer-based; 81 iBT). *Application deadline:* For fall admission, 2/1 for domestic and international students. Application fee: $50 ($75 for international students). Electronic applications accepted. *Financial support:* In 2009–10, 7 fellowships with full and partial tuition reimbursements (averaging $11,486 per year), 3 research assistantships with partial tuition reimbursements (averaging $7,993 per year), 37 teaching assistantships with partial tuition reimbursements (averaging $7,993 per year) were awarded; career-related internships or fieldwork, Federal Work-Study, institutionally sponsored loans, scholarships/grants, health care benefits, and unspecified assistantships also available. Support available to part-time students. Financial award application deadline: 2/1. *Faculty research:* Ceramics, painting and drawing, design, printmaking, photography. *Unit head:* Prof. Isabel Barbuzza, Director of Graduate Studies, 319-335-1789, Fax: 319-384-2715. *Application contact:* Laura Jorgensen, Graduate Secretary, 319-335-1758, Fax: 319-335-1774, E-mail: art@uiowa.edu.

The University of Kansas, Graduate Studies, College of Liberal Arts and Sciences, Department of Visual Art, Program in Visual Art Education, Lawrence, KS 66045. Offers MA. Part-time programs available. *Faculty:* 3 full-time (2 women). *Students:* 12 full-time (11 women), 8 part-time (all women); includes 2 minority (1 African American, 1 Asian American or Pacific Islander). Average age 26. 18 applicants, 83% accepted, 13 enrolled. In 2009, 2 master's awarded. *Degree requirements:* For master's, thesis or alternative. *Entrance requirements:* For master's, portfolio, 3 letters of recommendation, minimum GPA of 3.0. Additional exam requirements/recommendations for international students: Required—TOEFL (minimum score 570 paper-based; 230 computer-based) or IELTS (minimum score 6.5). *Application deadline:* For fall admission, 5/1 for domestic and international students; for spring admission, 10/15 for domestic and international students. Application fee: $45 ($55 for international students). Electronic applications accepted. *Expenses:* Tuition, state resident: full-time $6492; part-time $270.50 per credit hour. Tuition, nonresident: full-time $15,510; part-time $646.25 per credit hour. Required fees: $847; $70.56 per credit hour. Tuition and fees vary according to course load and program. *Financial support:* Teaching assistantships with full tuition reimbursements, Federal Work-Study, scholarships/grants, and unspecified assistantships available. Financial award application deadline: 5/1. *Faculty research:* Museum education, art educator education. *Unit head:* Prof. Dawn Marie Guernsey, Chairperson, 785-864-4401, E-mail: guernsey@ku.edu. *Application contact:* Tanya E. Hartman, Director, 785-864-2957, Fax: 785-864-4404, E-mail: thartman@ku.edu.

University of Kentucky, Graduate School, College of Fine Arts, Program in Art Studio, Lexington, KY 40506-0032. Offers MFA. *Accreditation:* NASAD. *Degree requirements:* For master's, comprehensive exam. *Entrance requirements:* For master's, GRE General Test, minimum undergraduate GPA of 2.75. Additional exam requirements/recommendations for international students: Required—TOEFL (minimum score 550 paper-based; 213 computer-based). Electronic applications accepted.

University of Lethbridge, School of Graduate Studies, Lethbridge, AB T1K 3M4, Canada. Offers accounting (MScM); addictions counseling (M Sc); agricultural biotechnology (M Sc); agricultural studies (M Sc, MA); anthropology (MA); archaeology (MA); art (MA, MFA); biochemistry (M Sc); biological sciences (M Sc); biomolecular science (PhD); biosystems and biodiversity (PhD); Canadian studies (MA); chemistry (M Sc); computer science (M Sc); computer science and geographical information science (M Sc); counseling psychology (M Ed); dramatic arts (MA); earth, space, and physical science (PhD); economics (MA); educational leadership (M Ed); English (MA); environmental science (M Sc); evolution and behavior (PhD); exercise science (M Sc); finance (MScM); French (MA); French/German (MA); French/Spanish (MA); general education (M Ed); general management (MScM); geography (M Sc, MA); German (MA); health science (M Sc); health sciences (MA); history (MA); human resource management and labour relations (MScM); individualized multidisciplinary (M Sc, MA); information systems (MScM); international management (MScM); kinesiology (M Sc, MA); management (M Sc, MA); marketing (MScM); mathematics (M Sc); music (M Mus, MA); Native American studies (MA); neuroscience (M Sc, PhD); new media (MA); nursing (M Sc); philosophy (MA); physics (M Sc); policy and strategy (MScM); political science (MA); psychology (M Sc, MA); religious studies (MA); social sciences (MA); sociology (MA); theatre and dramatic arts (MFA); theoretical and computational science (PhD); urban and regional studies (MA); women's studies (MA). Part-time and evening/weekend programs available. *Degree requirements:* For doctorate, comprehensive exam, thesis/dissertation. *Entrance requirements:* For master's, GMAT (M Sc in management), bachelor's degree in related field, minimum GPA of 3.0 during previous 20 graded semester courses, 2 years teaching or related experience (M Ed); for doctorate, master's degree, minimum graduate GPA of 3.5. Additional exam requirements/recommendations for international students: Required—TOEFL. *Faculty research:* Movement and brain plasticity, gibberellin physiology, photosynthesis, carbon cycling, molecular properties of main-group ring components.

University of Louisville, Graduate School, College of Arts and Sciences, Department of Fine Arts, Louisville, KY 40292. Offers art history (MA, PhD); creative art (MA); curatorial studies (MA). *Faculty:* 18 full-time (8 women), 3 part-time/adjunct (0 women). *Students:* 23 full-time (20 women), 13 part-time (9 women); includes 3 minority (2 African Americans, 1 Hispanic American), 2 international. Average age 38. 28 applicants, 54% accepted, 9 enrolled. In 2009, 9 master's awarded. *Degree requirements:* For master's, thesis; for doctorate, 2 foreign languages, comprehensive exam, thesis/dissertation. *Entrance requirements:* For master's and doctorate, GRE General Test. *Application deadline:* For fall admission, 1/15 for domestic and international students. Applications are processed on a rolling basis. Application fee: $50. *Financial support:* Teaching assistantships available. *Faculty research:* Art history in the periods from ancient to contemporary and various regions, 2D and 3D studio areas, intermedia, curatorial studies. *Unit head:* James T. Grubola, Chair, 502-852-0759, Fax: 502-852-6791, E-mail: grubola@louisville.edu. *Application contact:* Libby Leggett, Director, Graduate Admissions, 502-852-3101, Fax: 502-852-6536, E-mail: gradadm@louisville.edu.

University of Maryland, Baltimore County, Graduate School, College of Arts, Humanities and Social Sciences, Department of Visual Arts, Baltimore, MD 21250. Offers imaging and digital arts (MFA). *Faculty:* 24 full-time (13 women), 11 part-time/adjunct (5 women). *Students:* 18 full-time (9 women); includes 1 minority (Hispanic American), 2 international. Average age 32. 35 applicants, 23% accepted, 6 enrolled. In 2009, 7 master's awarded. *Degree requirements:* For master's, thesis, oral defense, thesis exhibition. *Entrance requirements:* For master's, minimum GPA of 3.0. Additional exam requirements/recommendations for international students: Required—TOEFL. *Application deadline:* For fall admission, 2/1 for domestic and international students. Application fee: $50. Electronic applications accepted. *Financial support:* In 2009–10, 16 students received support, including 12 research assistantships with full and partial tuition reimbursements available (averaging $14,300 per year); scholarships/grants and health care benefits also available. Financial award application deadline: 2/1. *Faculty research:* Advanced visual studies, digital imaging and interactive art, studio and computer art, video art. Total annual research expenditures: $22,500. *Unit head:* Prof. Vin Grabill, Chair, 410-455-1656, Fax: 410-455-1053, E-mail: grabill@umbc.edu. *Application contact:* Prof. Steve Bradley, Graduate Program Director, 410-455-2721, Fax: 410-455-1053, E-mail: sbradley@umbc.edu.

University of Maryland, College Park, Academic Affairs, College of Arts and Humanities, Department of Art, College Park, MD 20742. Offers MFA. *Faculty:* 16 full-time (6 women), 15 part-time/adjunct (7 women). *Students:* 16 full-time (5 women); includes 1 minority (African American), 1 international. 63 applicants, 19% accepted, 7 enrolled. In 2009, 3 master's

Art/Fine Arts

University of Maryland, College Park (continued)
awarded. *Degree requirements:* For master's, thesis, oral defense. *Entrance requirements:* For master's, minimum GPA of 3.0, portfolio, 15 slides, 3 letters of recommendation. *Application deadline:* For fall admission, 1/16 for domestic students, 2/1 for international students. Applications are processed on a rolling basis. Application fee: $60. Electronic applications accepted. *Expenses:* Tuition, area resident: Part-time $471 per credit hour. Tuition, state resident: part-time $471 per credit hour. Tuition, nonresident: part-time $1016 per credit hour. Required fees: $337.04 per term. *Financial support:* In 2009–10, 1 fellowship with partial tuition reimbursement (averaging $11,990 per year), 13 teaching assistantships with tuition reimbursements (averaging $15,571 per year) were awarded; research assistantships with tuition reimbursements, Federal Work-Study and scholarships/grants also available. Support available to part-time students. Financial award applicants required to submit FAFSA. *Faculty research:* Studio art. *Unit head:* Dr. John Ruppert, Chair, 301-405-1446, Fax: 301-314-9740, E-mail: ruppertj@umd.edu. *Application contact:* Dean of Graduate School, 301-405-0376, Fax: 301-314-9305.

University of Massachusetts Amherst, Graduate School, College of Humanities and Fine Arts, Department of Art, Programs in Art, Amherst, MA 01003. Offers art education (MA); studio art (MFA). Part-time programs available. *Students:* 20 full-time (14 women), 17 part-time (16 women); includes 3 minority (2 Asian Americans or Pacific Islanders, 1 Hispanic American), 2 international. Average age 31. 72 applicants, 26% accepted, 14 enrolled. In 2009, 12 master's awarded. *Degree requirements:* For master's, thesis (for some programs). *Entrance requirements:* For master's, portfolio. Additional exam requirements/recommendations for international students: Required—TOEFL (minimum score 530 paper-based; 213 computer-based; 80 iBT), IELTS (minimum score 6.5). *Application deadline:* For fall admission, 2/1 for domestic and international students. Applications are processed on a rolling basis. Application fee: $50 ($65 for international students). Electronic applications accepted. *Expenses:* Tuition, state resident: full-time $2640; part-time $110 per credit. Tuition, nonresident: full-time $9936; part-time $414 per credit. Tuition and fees vary according to course load. *Financial support:* In 2009–10, 1 fellowship with full tuition reimbursement (averaging $3,629 per year), 1 research assistantship with full tuition reimbursement (averaging $2,903 per year), 27 teaching assistantships with full tuition reimbursements (averaging $5,943 per year) were awarded; career-related internships or fieldwork, Federal Work-Study, scholarships/grants, traineeships, health care benefits, tuition waivers (full), and unspecified assistantships also available. Support available to part-time students. Financial award application deadline: 2/1. *Unit head:* Dr. Shona M. Macdonald, Graduate Program Director, 413-545-6937, Fax: 413-545-3929. *Application contact:* Jean M. Ames, Supervisor of Admissions, 413-545-0722, Fax: 413-577-0100, E-mail: gradadm@grad.umass.edu.

University of Massachusetts Dartmouth, Graduate School, College of Visual and Performing Arts, Program in Artisanry, North Dartmouth, MA 02747-2300. Offers ceramics (MFA, Postbaccalaureate Certificate); fibers (MFA); fibers/textiles (Postbaccalaureate Certificate); jewelry/metals (MFA, Postbaccalaureate Certificate); wood/furniture design (MFA, Postbaccalaureate Certificate). *Accreditation:* NASAD. *Faculty:* 7 full-time (4 women), 5 part-time/adjunct (3 women). *Students:* 14 full-time (12 women), 13 part-time (7 women); includes 3 minority (2 Asian Americans or Pacific Islanders, 1 Hispanic American), 3 international. Average age 29. 37 applicants, 57% accepted, 12 enrolled. In 2009, 9 master's awarded. *Degree requirements:* For master's, thesis, visual thesis. *Entrance requirements:* For master's, portfolio, interview, minimum GPA of 3.0, 3 letters of recommendation. Additional exam requirements/recommendations for international students: Required—TOEFL (minimum score 500 paper-based). *Application deadline:* For fall admission, 2/1 for domestic students, 12/1 for international students. Applications are processed on a rolling basis. Application fee: $40 ($60 for international students). Electronic applications accepted. *Expenses:* Tuition, state resident: full-time $2071; part-time $86.29 per credit. Tuition, nonresident: full-time $8099; part-time $337.46 per credit. Required fees: $9446. Tuition and fees vary according to class time, course load and reciprocity agreements. *Financial support:* In 2009–10, 2 fellowships with full tuition reimbursements (averaging $5,333 per year), 1 research assistantship with full tuition reimbursement (averaging $7,400 per year), 14 teaching assistantships with full tuition reimbursements (averaging $3,088 per year) were awarded; Federal Work-Study and unspecified assistantships also available. Support available to part-time students. Financial award application deadline: 3/1; financial award applicants required to submit FAFSA. *Faculty research:* Historic European tapestry, computerized weaving. Total annual research expenditures: $4,000. *Unit head:* Memory Holloway, Director, 508-999-8010, E-mail: mholloway@umassd.edu. *Application contact:* Elan Turcotte-Shamski, Graduate Admissions Officer, 508-999-8604, Fax: 508-999-8183, E-mail: graduate@umassd.edu.

University of Massachusetts Dartmouth, Graduate School, College of Visual and Performing Arts, Program in Fine Arts, North Dartmouth, MA 02747-2300. Offers drawing (MFA); painting (MFA); printmaking (MFA); sculpture (MFA). *Faculty:* 12 full-time (3 women), 8 part-time/adjunct (4 women). *Students:* 12 full-time (8 women), 4 part-time (3 women); includes 1 minority (Hispanic American). Average age 29. 35 applicants, 51% accepted, 7 enrolled. In 2009, 6 master's awarded. *Degree requirements:* For master's, visual thesis. *Entrance requirements:* For master's, minimum GPA of 3.0, portfolio, 3 letters of recommendation. Additional exam requirements/recommendations for international students: Required—TOEFL (minimum score 500 paper-based). *Application deadline:* For fall admission, 2/1 priority date for domestic students, 12/1 priority date for international students. Applications are processed on a rolling basis. Application fee: $40 ($60 for international students). Electronic applications accepted. *Expenses:* Tuition, state resident: full-time $2071; part-time $86.29 per credit. Tuition, nonresident: full-time $8099; part-time $337.46 per credit. Required fees: $9446. Tuition and fees vary according to class time, course load and reciprocity agreements. *Financial support:* In 2009–10, 1 fellowship with full tuition reimbursement (averaging $5,333 per year), 8 teaching assistantships with full tuition reimbursements (averaging $3,088 per year) were awarded; research assistantships, Federal Work-Study and unspecified assistantships also available. Support available to part-time students. Financial award application deadline: 3/1. Total annual research expenditures: $3,000. *Unit head:* Memory Holloway, Director, 508-999-8554, E-mail: mholloway@umassd.edu. *Application contact:* Elan Turcotte-Shamski, Graduate Admissions Officer, 508-999-8604, Fax: 508-999-8183, E-mail: graduate@umassd.edu.

University of Memphis, Graduate School, College of Communication and Fine Arts, Department of Art, Memphis, TN 38152. Offers art (Graduate Certificate); art history (MA), including Egyptian art and archaeology, general art history; ceramics (MFA); graphic design (MFA); interior design (MFA); painting (MFA); printmaking/photography (MFA); sculpture (MFA). *Accreditation:* NASAD (one or more programs are accredited). *Faculty:* 20 full-time (7 women), 4 part-time/adjunct (2 women). *Students:* 39 full-time (26 women), 10 part-time (8 women); includes 4 African Americans, 1 Asian American or Pacific Islander, 1 international. Average age 29. 44 applicants, 77% accepted, 22 enrolled. In 2009, 16 master's, 5 other advanced degrees awarded. *Degree requirements:* For master's, 2 foreign languages, comprehensive exam, thesis. *Entrance requirements:* For master's, GRE General Test or MAT, portfolio (MFA). *Application deadline:* For fall admission, 8/1 for domestic students; for spring admission, 12/1 for domestic students. Applications are processed on a rolling basis. Application fee: $35 ($60 for international students). *Expenses:* Tuition, state resident: full-time $6246; part-time $347 per credit hour. Tuition, nonresident: full-time $15,894; part-time $883 per credit hour. Required fees: $1160. Full-time tuition and fees vary according to course load, degree level and program. *Financial support:* In 2009–10, 38 students received support; research assistantships with full tuition reimbursements available, teaching assistantships with full tuition reimbursements available, Federal Work-Study, scholarships/grants, and unspecified assistantships available. Financial award application deadline: 2/15; financial award applicants required to submit FAFSA. *Faculty research:* Online collaborative learning, advanced art history studies, electronic publishing/design, studio arts, architectural studies. *Unit head:* Prof. Richard Lou, Chair, 901-678-2216, Fax: 901-678-2735, E-mail: gmyatt@memphis.edu. *Application contact:* Greely Myat, Graduate Studies Coordinator, 901-678-2650.

University of Miami, Graduate School, College of Arts and Sciences, Department of Art and Art History, Coral Gables, FL 33124. Offers art history (MA); ceramics/glass (MFA); graphic design/multimedia (MFA); painting (MFA); photography/digital imaging (MFA); printmaking (MFA); sculpture (MFA). Part-time programs available. *Degree requirements:* For master's, variable foreign language requirement, thesis, exhibit (MFA), comprehensive exam (MA). *Entrance requirements:* For master's, GRE General Test (MA), research paper (MA), slide portfolio (MFA). Additional exam requirements/recommendations for international students: Required—TOEFL. Electronic applications accepted. *Faculty research:* Installation art, public art.

University of Michigan, Horace H. Rackham School of Graduate Studies, School of Art and Design, Ann Arbor, MI 48109. Offers art and design (MFA). *Accreditation:* NASAD. *Degree requirements:* For master's, thesis, exhibit (MFA), slide lecture. *Entrance requirements:* For master's, portfolio. Additional exam requirements/recommendations for international students: Required—TOEFL, IELTS. Electronic applications accepted. *Expenses:* Tuition, state resident: full-time $17,286; part-time $1099 per credit hour. Tuition, nonresident: full-time $34,944; part-time $2080 per credit hour. Required fees: $95 per semester. Tuition and fees vary according to course load, degree level and program. *Faculty research:* Creative expression, commercial design, preparation for teaching.

University of Minnesota, Duluth, Graduate School, School of Fine Arts, Department of Art and Design, Duluth, MN 55812-2496. Offers graphic design (MFA). Part-time programs available. *Faculty:* 15 full-time (10 women), 6 part-time/adjunct (5 women). *Students:* 7 full-time (4 women), 1 part-time (0 women), 2 international. Average age 26. 11 applicants, 18% accepted, 2 enrolled. In 2009, 2 master's awarded. *Degree requirements:* For master's, final exhibit, project, supporting paper. *Entrance requirements:* For master's, minimum GPA of 3.0, writing sample, slide portfolio. Additional exam requirements/recommendations for international students: Required—TOEFL (minimum score 550 paper-based; 213 computer-based). *Application deadline:* For fall admission, 4/15 for domestic and international students; for spring admission, 11/1 for domestic and international students. Application fee: $55 ($75 for international students). *Financial support:* In 2009–10, 8 students received support, including research assistantships with full tuition reimbursements available (averaging $13,000 per year), teaching assistantships with full tuition reimbursements available (averaging $13,000 per year); career-related internships or fieldwork, institutionally sponsored loans, scholarships/grants, health care benefits, and unspecified assistantships also available. Financial award application deadline: 3/15. *Faculty research:* Motion graphics, graphic design history, interactive design, typography, education. Total annual research expenditures: $50,000. *Unit head:* Prof. Janice Kmetz, Director of Graduate Studies, 218-726-8150, E-mail: jkmetz@d.umn.edu. *Application contact:* M. J. Leone, Executive Administrative Specialist, 218-726-7523, Fax: 218-726-6970, E-mail: grad@d.umn.edu.

University of Minnesota, Twin Cities Campus, Graduate School, College of Liberal Arts, Department of Art, Minneapolis, MN 55455-0213. Offers MFA. *Faculty:* 22 full-time (9 women). *Students:* 37 full-time (21 women); includes 4 minority (1 Asian American or Pacific Islander, 3 Hispanic Americans), 4 international. Average age 26. 109 applicants, 17% accepted, 13 enrolled. In 2009, 13 master's awarded. *Degree requirements:* For master's, oral exam, supporting paper, thesis exhibit. *Entrance requirements:* For master's, portfolio, letters of recommendation, 3.0 GPA. Additional exam requirements/recommendations for international students: Required—TOEFL (minimum score 550 paper-based; 79 iBT); Recommended—IELTS (minimum score 6.5). *Application deadline:* For fall admission, 1/5 for domestic and international students. Application fee: $75 ($95 for international students). Electronic applications accepted. *Financial support:* In 2009–10, 37 students received support, including 13 fellowships (averaging $6,000 per year), 13 teaching assistantships with partial tuition reimbursements available (averaging $6,922 per year); Federal Work-Study, scholarships/grants, health care benefits, tuition waivers (partial), and unspecified assistantships also available. Financial award application deadline: 1/5; financial award applicants required to submit FAFSA. *Faculty research:* Photography as code and symbol, sculpture with an emphasis on multimedia, high-fired salt glazed and utilitarian ceramic earthenware, performance and installations contemporary theory, electronic technology and the human body. *Unit head:* Chair, 612-625-8096, Fax: 612-625-7881, E-mail: artdept@umn.edu. *Application contact:* Jan Estep, Director of Graduate Studies, 612-625-8096, Fax: 612-625-7881, E-mail: artdept@umn.edu.

University of Mississippi, Graduate School, College of Liberal Arts, Department of Art, Oxford, University, MS 38677. Offers art education (MA); art history (MA); fine arts (MFA). *Accreditation:* NASAD (one or more programs are accredited). Part-time programs available. *Students:* 9 full-time (3 women), 1 international. In 2009, 6 master's awarded. *Degree requirements:* For master's, thesis (for some programs). *Entrance requirements:* For master's, GRE General Test, minimum GPA of 3.0. Additional exam requirements/recommendations for international students: Required—TOEFL. *Application deadline:* For fall admission, 3/1 for domestic students; for spring admission, 10/1 for domestic students. Applications are processed on a rolling basis. Application fee: $25. Electronic applications accepted. *Financial support:* Fellowships, scholarships/grants and unspecified assistantships available. Financial award application deadline: 3/1; financial award applicants required to submit FAFSA. *Unit head:* Dr. Sheri Fleck Reith, Chair, 662-915-7193, Fax: 662-915-5013, E-mail: art@olemiss.edu. *Application contact:* Dr. Christy M. Wyandt, Associate Dean, 662-915-7474, Fax: 662-915-7577, E-mail: cwyandt@olemiss.edu.

University of Missouri, Graduate School, College of Arts and Sciences, Department of Art, Columbia, MO 65211. Offers MFA. *Faculty:* 13 full-time (3 women), 8 part-time/adjunct (5 women). *Students:* 15 full-time (9 women), 5 part-time (4 women); includes 1 minority (Asian American or Pacific Islander), 5 international. Average age 34. 27 applicants, 19% accepted, 4 enrolled. In 2009, 4 master's awarded. *Degree requirements:* For master's, thesis. *Entrance requirements:* For master's, GRE General Test, minimum GPA of 3.0. Additional exam requirements/recommendations for international students: Required—TOEFL (minimum score 550 paper-based; 80 iBT), IELTS (minimum score 5.5). *Application deadline:* For fall admission, 2/1 priority date for domestic students; for winter admission, 9/1 for domestic students; for spring admission, 2/1 for domestic students. Applications are processed on a rolling basis. Application fee: $45 ($60 for international students). Electronic applications accepted. *Financial support:* In 2009–10, 2 research assistantships with full tuition reimbursements, 14 teaching assistantships with full tuition reimbursements were awarded; institutionally sponsored loans, health care benefits, and unspecified assistantships also available. *Faculty research:* Painting, digital art, new media, photography, ceramics. *Unit head:* Dr. Lampo Leong, Department Chair, E-mail: leongl@missouri.edu. *Application contact:* Brenda J. Warren, 573-882-4037, E-mail: warrenb@missouri.edu.

University of Missouri–Kansas City, College of Arts and Sciences, Department of Art and Art History, Kansas City, MO 64110-2499. Offers art history (MA, PhD); studio art (MA). PhD (interdisciplinary) offered through the School of Graduate Studies. Part-time programs available. *Faculty:* 11 full-time (5 women), 6 part-time/adjunct (3 women). *Students:* 5 full-time (2 women), 36 part-time (33 women); includes 3 minority (1 African American, 1 American Indian/Alaska Native, 1 Hispanic American), 2 international. Average age 33. 21 applicants, 67% accepted, 8 enrolled. In 2009, 7 master's awarded. Terminal master's awarded for partial completion of doctoral program. *Degree requirements:* For master's, thesis, qualifying exam; for doctorate, thesis/dissertation, exams. *Entrance requirements:* For master's, good general education in the humanities. Additional exam requirements/recommendations for international students: Required—TOEFL (minimum score 550 paper-based; 213 computer-based; 80 iBT). *Application deadline:* For fall admission, 3/1 priority date for domestic and international students; for spring admission, 10/15 for domestic and international students. Applications are processed on a rolling basis. Application fee: $45 ($50 for international students). Electronic applications accepted. *Expenses:* Tuition, state resident: full-time $5378; part-time $299 per credit hour. Tuition, nonresident: full-time $13,881; part-time $771 per credit hour. Required fees: $641; $71 per credit hour. Tuition and fees vary according to course load and program. *Financial support:* In 2009–10, 7 teaching assistantships with partial tuition reimbursements (averaging

$11,750 per year) were awarded; career-related internships or fieldwork, Federal Work-Study, institutionally sponsored loans, and tuition waivers (full and partial) also available. Support available to part-time students. Financial award application deadline: 3/1; financial award applicants required to submit FAFSA. *Faculty research:* Painting, electronic media, Western and non-Western art history, photography. *Unit head:* Dr. Kati Toivanen, Chair, 816-235-6230, Fax: 816-235-5507, E-mail: toivanenk@umkc.edu. *Application contact:* Dr. Burton Dunbar, Associate Professor, 816-235-2531, Fax: 816-235-5507, E-mail: dunbarb@umkc.edu.

The University of Montana, Graduate School, School of Fine Arts, Department of Art, Missoula, MT 59812-0002. Offers fine arts (MA, MFA), including art (MA), art history (MA), ceramics (MFA), integrated arts and education (MA), media arts (MFA), painting and drawing (MFA), photography (MFA), printmaking (MFA), sculpture (MFA). *Accreditation:* NASAD (one or more programs are accredited). *Degree requirements:* For master's, thesis exhibit. *Entrance requirements:* For master's, GRE General Test, portfolio.

The University of Montana, Graduate School, School of Fine Arts, Department of Drama/Dance, Missoula, MT 59812-0002. Offers fine arts (MA, MFA), including acting (MFA), design/technology (MFA), directing (MFA), drama (MA), integrated arts and education (MA), media arts (MFA). *Accreditation:* NAST (one or more programs are accredited). *Degree requirements:* For master's, thesis or alternative. *Entrance requirements:* For master's, GRE General Test, audition, portfolio, production notebook.

University of Nebraska–Lincoln, Graduate College, College of Fine and Performing Arts, Department of Art and Art History, Lincoln, NE 68588. Offers art history (MA); studio art (MFA);). *Accreditation:* NASAD. *Degree requirements:* For master's, thesis. *Entrance requirements:* For master's, slide portfolio. Additional exam requirements/recommendations for international students: Required—TOEFL (minimum score 550 paper-based; 213 computer-based). Electronic applications accepted. *Faculty research:* Classical archaeology, contemporary art, printmaking, photography.

University of Nevada, Las Vegas, Graduate College, College of Fine Arts, Department of Art, Las Vegas, NV 89154-5013. Offers MFA. *Accreditation:* NASAD. Part-time programs available. *Faculty:* 1 full-time (0 women). *Students:* 13 full-time (8 women); includes 1 minority (Hispanic American), 1 international. Average age 33. 34 applicants, 21% accepted, 3 enrolled. In 2009, 5 master's awarded. *Degree requirements:* For master's, comprehensive exam, thesis. *Entrance requirements:* Additional exam requirements/recommendations for international students: Required—TOEFL (minimum score 550 paper-based; 213 computer-based; 80 iBT), IELTS (minimum score 7). *Application deadline:* For fall admission, 2/1 priority date for domestic and international students. Applications are processed on a rolling basis. Application fee: $60 ($95 for international students). Electronic applications accepted. *Financial support:* In 2009–10, 13 students received support, including 8 research assistantships with partial tuition reimbursements available (averaging $10,000 per year), 5 teaching assistantships with partial tuition reimbursements available (averaging $10,000 per year); institutionally sponsored loans, scholarships/grants, health care benefits, and unspecified assistantships also available. Financial award application deadline: 3/1. *Unit head:* Dr. Jeffrey Burden, Chair/ Professor, 702-895-3112, Fax: 702-895-4194, E-mail: jeff.burden@unlv.edu. *Application contact:* Graduate College Admissions Evaluator, 702-895-3320, Fax: 702-895-4180, E-mail: gradcollege@unlv.edu.

University of Nevada, Reno, Graduate School, College of Liberal Arts, Department of Fine Arts, Reno, NV 89557. Offers MFA. *Degree requirements:* For master's, thesis optional. *Entrance requirements:* For master's, minimum GPA of 2.75. Additional exam requirements/recommendations for international students: Required—TOEFL (minimum score 500 paper-based; 173 computer-based; 61 iBT), IELTS (minimum score 6). Electronic applications accepted. *Faculty research:* Ceramics; digital-media; drawing; painting; performance; photography; printmaking; sculpture; video; studio program supported by a strong emphasis in the areas of contemporary art, theory and criticism.

University of New Hampshire, Graduate School, College of Liberal Arts, Program in Painting, Durham, NH 03824. Offers MFA. Program offered in fall only. Part-time programs available. *Faculty:* 12 full-time (4 women). *Students:* 7 full-time (4 women); includes 1 minority (Asian American or Pacific Islander). Average age 33. 18 applicants, 56% accepted, 4 enrolled. In 2009, 4 master's awarded. *Degree requirements:* For master's, thesis or alternative. *Entrance requirements:* For master's, slide portfolio. Additional exam requirements/recommendations for international students: Required—TOEFL (minimum score 550 paper-based; 213 computer-based; 80 iBT). *Application deadline:* For fall admission, 2/15 priority date for domestic students, 2/15 for international students. Applications are processed on a rolling basis. Application fee: $65. Electronic applications accepted. *Expenses:* Tuition, state resident: full-time $10,380; part-time $577 per credit hour. Tuition, nonresident: full-time $24,350; part-time $1002 per credit hour. Required fees: $1550; $387.50 per semester. Tuition and fees vary according to course load and program. *Financial support:* In 2009–10, 7 students received support, including 3 research assistantships; fellowships, teaching assistantships, career-related internships or fieldwork, Federal Work-Study, and scholarships/grants also available. Support available to part-time students. Financial award application deadline: 2/15. *Unit head:* Michael McConnell, Chair, 603-862-3820. *Application contact:* Eileen Wong, Administrative Assistant, 603-862-3820, E-mail: mfa.painting@unh.edu.

University of New Mexico, Graduate School, College of Fine Arts, Department of Art and Art History, Program in Studio Arts, Albuquerque, NM 87131-2039. Offers MFA. *Faculty:* 34 full-time (22 women), 16 part-time/adjunct (8 women). *Students:* 39 full-time (28 women), 5 part-time (4 women); includes 7 minority (1 African American, 2 American Indian/Alaska Native, 1 Asian American or Pacific Islander, 3 Hispanic Americans), 4 international. Average age 32. 134 applicants, 20% accepted, 20 enrolled. In 2009, 10 master's awarded. *Degree requirements:* For master's, comprehensive exam, thesis or alternative, studio reviews, qualifying exams. *Entrance requirements:* Additional exam requirements/recommendations for international students: Required—TOEFL (minimum score 550 paper-based; 213 computer-based). *Application deadline:* For fall admission, 1/15 for domestic students. Application fee: $50. Electronic applications accepted. *Expenses:* Tuition, state resident: full-time $2099; part-time $233.20 per credit hour. Tuition, nonresident: full-time $6650. Required fees: $25 per semester. Tuition and fees vary according to course load, program and reciprocity agreements. *Financial support:* In 2009–10, 40 students received support, including 5 research assistantships with tuition reimbursements available (averaging $6,700 per year), 40 teaching assistantships with partial tuition reimbursements available (averaging $6,700 per year); Federal Work-Study, institutionally sponsored loans, scholarships/grants, health care benefits, and unspecified assistantships also available. Support available to part-time students. Financial award application deadline: 3/1; financial award applicants required to submit FAFSA. *Faculty research:* Photography, painting, drawing, printmaking, sculpture and ceramics, electronic arts, art and ecology. *Unit head:* Dr. Justine Andrews, Graduate Director, 505-277-3441, Fax: 505-277-5955, E-mail: jandrews@unm.edu. *Application contact:* Kat Heatherington, Graduate Advisor, 505-277-6672, Fax: 505-277-5955, E-mail: art255@unm.edu.

University of New Orleans, Graduate School, College of Liberal Arts, Department of Fine Arts, New Orleans, LA 70148. Offers MFA. *Accreditation:* NASAD. *Degree requirements:* For master's, thesis. *Entrance requirements:* For master's, GRE General Test, slide review. Additional exam requirements/recommendations for international students: Required—TOEFL (minimum score 550 paper-based; 213 computer-based; 79 iBT). Electronic applications accepted. *Faculty research:* Large-scale painting and sculpture, black-and-white and color photography, computer graphics.

The University of North Carolina at Chapel Hill, Graduate School, College of Arts and Sciences, Department of Art, Studio Art Program, Chapel Hill, NC 27599. Offers MFA. *Degree requirements:* For master's, variable foreign language requirement. *Entrance requirements:* For master's, minimum GPA of 3.0, portfolio. Electronic applications accepted. *Faculty research:* Environmental installation, painting, photography, mixed media, printmaking.

The University of North Carolina at Greensboro, Graduate School, College of Arts and Sciences, Department of Art, Greensboro, NC 27412-5001. Offers studio arts (MFA). *Degree requirements:* For master's, thesis (for some programs). *Entrance requirements:* For master's, GRE General Test, 39 hours of course work in studio art, 15 hours of course work in art history, portfolio. Additional exam requirements/recommendations for international students: Required—TOEFL. Electronic applications accepted.

University of North Dakota, Graduate School, College of Arts and Sciences, Department of Visual Arts, Grand Forks, ND 58202. Offers MFA. *Accreditation:* NASAD. *Degree requirements:* For master's, thesis or alternative, comprehensive evaluation, professional exhibition. *Entrance requirements:* For master's, minimum GPA of 3.0. Additional exam requirements/recommendations for international students: Required—TOEFL (minimum score 550 paper-based; 213 computer-based; 79 iBT), IELTS (minimum score 6.5). Electronic applications accepted. *Faculty research:* Ceramics, drawing, metalsmithing, printmaking, painting.

University of Northern Colorado, Graduate School, College of Performing and Visual Arts, School of Visual Arts, Greeley, CO 80639. Offers visual arts (MA). Part-time programs available. *Faculty:* 5 full-time (3 women). *Students:* 2 full-time (both women), 11 part-time (10 women); includes 1 minority (Hispanic American). Average age 40. 2 applicants, 0% accepted, 0 enrolled. In 2009, 3 master's awarded. *Degree requirements:* For master's, comprehensive exam, thesis. *Entrance requirements:* For master's, GRE General Test, portfolio, 3 letters of recommendation, minimum undergraduate GPA of 3.0. *Application deadline:* Applications are processed on a rolling basis. Application fee: $50 ($60 for international students). Electronic applications accepted. *Expenses:* Tuition, state resident: full-time $5770; part-time $320.55 per credit hour. Tuition, nonresident: full-time $13,847; part-time $769.27 per credit hour. Required fees: $948.78; $52.72 per credit. *Financial support:* In 2009–10, 2 research assistantships (averaging $3,482 per year), 1 teaching assistantship (averaging $11,396 per year) were awarded; fellowships, unspecified assistantships also available. Financial award application deadline: 3/1; financial award applicants required to submit FAFSA. *Unit head:* Dr. Dennis Morimoto, Director, 970-351-2143, Fax: 970-351-2299. *Application contact:* Linda Sisson, Graduate Student Admission Coordinator, 970-351-1807, Fax: 970-351-2371, E-mail: linda.sisson@unco.edu.

University of Northern Iowa, Graduate College, College of Humanities and Fine Arts, Department of Art, Cedar Falls, IA 50614. Offers art (MA); art education (MA). *Accreditation:* NASAD. Part-time and evening/weekend programs available. *Students:* 2 full-time (0 women), 5 part-time (4 women); includes 2 minority (both Hispanic Americans). 1 applicant, 100% accepted, 1 enrolled. In 2009, 3 master's awarded. *Degree requirements:* For master's, comprehensive exam (for some programs), thesis or alternative. *Entrance requirements:* For master's, minimum GPA of 3.0, portfolio. Additional exam requirements/recommendations for international students: Required—TOEFL (minimum score 500 paper-based; 180 computer-based; 61 iBT). *Application deadline:* For fall admission, 8/1 priority date for domestic students. Applications are processed on a rolling basis. Application fee: $30 ($50 for international students). Electronic applications accepted. *Financial support:* Career-related internships or fieldwork, Federal Work-Study, scholarships/grants, and tuition waivers (full and partial) available. Support available to part-time students. Financial award application deadline: 2/1. *Unit head:* Dr. Jeffery Byrd, Department Head/Professor, 319-273-2077, Fax: 319-273-7333, E-mail: jeffery.byrd@uni.edu. *Application contact:* Laurie S. Russell, Record Analyst, 319-273-2623, Fax: 319-273-6792, E-mail: laurie.russell@uni.edu.

University of North Texas, Robert B. Toulouse School of Graduate Studies, College of Visual Arts and Design, Department of Studio Art, Denton, TX 76203. Offers metalsmithing and jewelry (MFA), including Ceramics, Fibers, Metalsmithing & Jewelry, New Media, Photography, Printmaking, Sculpture, Watercolor. Part-time programs available. *Degree requirements:* For master's, exhibition, extended artists statement disk of 20 images from show, committee approval. *Entrance requirements:* For master's, resume, 2 letters of recommendation, portfolio of 20 works. Additional exam requirements/recommendations for international students: Recommended—TOEFL (minimum score 550 paper-based; 213 computer-based; 79 iBT). *Application deadline:* Applications are processed on a rolling basis. Application fee: $50 ($75 for international students). Electronic applications accepted. *Expenses:* Tuition, state resident: full-time $4298; part-time $239 per contact hour. Tuition, nonresident: full-time $9878; part-time $549 per contact hour. Required fees: $265 per contact hour. *Financial support:* Fellowships with partial tuition reimbursements, teaching assistantships with partial tuition reimbursements, tuition waivers and unspecified assistantships available. Financial award applicants required to submit FAFSA. *Faculty research:* Altered terrain, enameling on metal, electrical and mechanical interactivity, interactive animation, environmental conservation.

University of Notre Dame, Graduate School, College of Arts and Letters, Division of Humanities, Department of Art, Art History, and Design, Notre Dame, IN 46556. Offers art history (MA); design (MFA), including graphic design, industrial design; studio art (MFA), including ceramics, painting, photography, printmaking, sculpture. *Accreditation:* NASAD. *Degree requirements:* For master's, comprehensive exam (for some programs), thesis. *Entrance requirements:* For master's, GRE General Test, minimum GPA of 3.0. Additional exam requirements/recommendations for international students: Required—TOEFL (minimum score 600 paper-based; 250 computer-based; 80 iBT). Electronic applications accepted. *Faculty research:* Studio art practice in ceramics, printing, photography, printmaking and sculpture, graphic design and industrial design, digital imaging in design and photography, Renaissance and American art history, contemporary art theory and criticism.

University of Oklahoma, Graduate College, College of Fine Arts, School of Art and Art History, Norman, OK 73019. Offers art (MA, MFA); art history (MA, MFA); ceramics (MFA); film and video (MFA); painting (MFA); photography (MFA); printmaking (MFA); visual communications (MFA). *Faculty:* 27 full-time (11 women). *Students:* 25 full-time (13 women), 13 part-time (12 women); includes 8 minority (2 African Americans, 5 American Indian/Alaska Native, 1 Asian American or Pacific Islander), 6 international. 36 applicants, 53% accepted, 11 enrolled. In 2009, 4 master's awarded. *Degree requirements:* For master's, thesis (MA), exhibit (MFA), departmental qualifying exam. *Entrance requirements:* For master's, GRE General Test (MA), bachelor's degree in art (MFA) or art history (MA), minimum GPA of 3.0 in last 60 undergraduate hours, 3 letters of recommendation, written research paper. Additional exam requirements/recommendations for international students: Required—TOEFL (minimum score 550 paper-based; 213 computer-based). *Application deadline:* For fall admission, 2/1 priority date for domestic students, 2/1 for international students; for spring admission, 10/1 for domestic and international students. Applications are processed on a rolling basis. Application fee: $40 ($90 for international students). Electronic applications accepted. *Expenses:* Tuition, state resident: full-time $3744; part-time $156 per credit hour. Tuition, nonresident: full-time $13,577; part-time $565.70 per credit hour. Required fees: $2415; $90.10 per credit hour. *Financial support:* In 2009–10, 26 students received support, including 17 research assistantships with partial tuition reimbursements available (averaging $9,940 per year), 1 teaching assistantship with partial tuition reimbursement available (averaging $9,586 per year); career-related internships or fieldwork, Federal Work-Study, institutionally sponsored loans, scholarships/grants, health care benefits, tuition waivers (full and partial), and unspecified assistantships also available. Financial award application deadline: 4/7; financial award applicants required to submit FAFSA. *Faculty research:* Native American art history and art of the American West, contemporary and figurative sculpture, painting and print making, graphic design, media. Total annual research expenditures: $34,861. *Unit head:* Mary Jo Watson, Director, 405-325-2691, Fax: 405-325-1668, E-mail: mjwatson@ou.edu. *Application contact:* Jonathan Hils, Graduate Liaison, 405-325-2691, Fax: 405-325-1668, E-mail: hils@ou.edu.

University of Oregon, Graduate School, School of Architecture and Allied Arts, Department of Art, Eugene, OR 97403. Offers MFA. *Accreditation:* NASAD. *Degree requirements:* For master's, thesis or alternative. *Entrance requirements:* For master's, BFA or equivalent. Additional exam requirements/recommendations for international students: Required—TOEFL.

Art/Fine Arts

University of Pennsylvania, School of Design, Department of Fine Arts, Philadelphia, PA 19104. Offers MFA. *Faculty:* 3 full-time (1 woman), 2 part-time/adjunct (both women). *Students:* 41 full-time (23 women), 1 (woman) part-time; includes 12 minority (6 African Americans, 5 Asian Americans or Pacific Islanders, 1 Hispanic American), 2 international. 530 applicants, 46% accepted. In 2009, 24 master's awarded. *Entrance requirements:* For master's, slide portfolio. Additional exam requirements/recommendations for international students: Required—TOEFL. *Application deadline:* For fall admission, 1/2 priority date for domestic students. Application fee: $70. *Expenses:* Tuition: Full-time $25,660; part-time $4758 per course. Required fees: $2152; $270 per course. Tuition and fees vary according to course load, degree level and program. *Financial support:* Fellowships, teaching assistantships available. Financial award applicants required to submit FAFSA. *Faculty research:* Painting, sculpture, printmaking, combined media.

See Close-Up on page 147.

University of Regina, Faculty of Graduate Studies and Research, Faculty of Fine Arts, Department of Visual Arts, Regina, SK S4S 0A2, Canada. Offers MA, MFA. *Faculty:* 11 full-time (6 women). *Students:* 17 full-time (9 women), 5 part-time (4 women). 11 applicants, 45% accepted. In 2009, 6 master's awarded. *Degree requirements:* For master's, exhibition, support paper, oral defense. *Entrance requirements:* For master's, 20 slides of recent work, slide list, BFA or the equivalent. Additional exam requirements/recommendations for international students: Required—TOEFL (minimum score 580 paper-based; 237 computer-based; 80 iBT). *Application deadline:* For fall admission, 2/15 for domestic students. Application fee: $90 ($100 for international students). *Financial support:* In 2009–10, 7 students received support, including 3 fellowships (averaging $19,000 per year), 5 research assistantships (averaging $16,910 per year), 2 teaching assistantships (averaging $6,650 per year); scholarships/grants also available. Financial award application deadline: 6/15. *Faculty research:* Painting, sculpture, ceramics, printmaking, intermedia. *Unit head:* Dr. Carmen Robertson, Graduate Program Coordinator, 306-585-2227, Fax: 306-585-5526, E-mail: carmen.robertson@uregina.ca. *Application contact:* Dr. Carmen Robertson, Graduate Program Coordinator, 306-585-2227, Fax: 306-585-5526, E-mail: carmen.robertson@uregina.ca.

University of Rochester, The College, Arts and Sciences, Department of Art and Art History, Rochester, NY 14627. Offers visual and cultural studies (MA, PhD). Terminal master's awarded for partial completion of doctoral program. *Degree requirements:* For master's, thesis optional; for doctorate, one foreign language, thesis/dissertation, qualifying exam. *Entrance requirements:* For master's and doctorate, GRE General Test. Additional exam requirements/recommendations for international students: Required—TOEFL.

See Close-Up on page 197.

University of Saint Francis, Graduate School, Department of Art and Visual Communication, Fort Wayne, IN 46808-3994. Offers fine art (MA). *Accreditation:* NASAD. Part-time and evening/weekend programs available. *Degree requirements:* For master's, thesis, exhibit. *Entrance requirements:* For master's, minimum GPA of 3.0 in art, portfolio.

University of Saskatchewan, College of Graduate Studies and Research, College of Arts and Sciences, Department of Art and Art History, Saskatoon, SK S7N 5A2, Canada. Offers MFA. Part-time programs available. *Faculty:* 12. *Students:* 18. In 2009, 3 master's awarded. *Degree requirements:* For master's, thesis. *Entrance requirements:* Additional exam requirements/recommendations for international students: Required—TOEFL (minimum score 80 iBT); Recommended—IELTS (minimum score 6.5). *Application deadline:* For fall admission, 7/1 priority date for domestic students. Applications are processed on a rolling basis. Application fee: $75. Tuition and fees charges are reported in Canadian dollars. *Expenses:* Tuition, area resident: Full-time $3000 Canadian dollars; part-time $500 Canadian dollars per term. Required fees: $700 Canadian dollars; $100 Canadian dollars per term. *Financial support:* Fellowships, research assistantships, teaching assistantships available. Financial award application deadline: 1/31. *Unit head:* Dr. Susan Shantz, Head, 306-966-4199, Fax: 306-966-4266, E-mail: susan.shantz@usask.ca. *Application contact:* Dr. Tim Nowlin, Graduate Chair, 306-966-4200, Fax: 306-966-4266, E-mail: tim.nowlin@usask.ca.

University of South Carolina, The Graduate School, College of Arts and Sciences, Department of Art, Columbia, SC 29208. Offers art education (IMA, MA, MAT); art history (MA); art studio (MA); media arts (MMA); studio art (MFA). *Accreditation:* NASAD. *Degree requirements:* For master's, comprehensive exam (for some programs), thesis (for some programs). *Entrance requirements:* For master's, GRE General Test or MAT, portfolio. Additional exam requirements/recommendations for international students: Required—TOEFL. Electronic applications accepted. *Faculty research:* Script writing, teaching art at the elementary and secondary levels of education, history of art and architecture.

The University of South Dakota, Graduate School, College of Fine Arts, Department of Art, Vermillion, SD 57069-2390. Offers MFA. *Accreditation:* NASAD. *Degree requirements:* For master's, thesis or alternative. *Entrance requirements:* For master's, portfolio, minimum GPA of 2.7. Additional exam requirements/recommendations for international students: Required—TOEFL (minimum score 550 paper-based; 213 computer-based; 79 iBT). Electronic applications accepted.

University of Southern California, Graduate School, College of Letters, Arts and Sciences, Department of Art History, Los Angeles, CA 90089. Offers art history (MA, PhD); history of collecting and display (Graduate Certificate); visual studies (Graduate Certificate). *Faculty:* 12 full-time (9 women), 7 part-time/adjunct (5 women). *Students:* 42 full-time (34 women); includes 8 minority (7 Asian Americans or Pacific Islanders, 1 Hispanic American), 4 international. In 2009, 6 master's, 1 doctorate, 4 other advanced degrees awarded. *Degree requirements:* For doctorate, 2 foreign languages, comprehensive exam, thesis/dissertation. *Entrance requirements:* For doctorate, GRE. *Application deadline:* For fall admission, 12/1 for domestic students. Application fee: $85. *Expenses:* Tuition: Full-time $25,980; part-time $1315 per unit. Required fees: $554. One-time fee: $35 full-time. Full-time tuition and fees vary according to degree level and program. *Financial support:* In 2009–10, 8 fellowships with full tuition reimbursements (averaging $19,000 per year), 10 teaching assistantships with full tuition reimbursements (averaging $19,000 per year) were awarded; career-related internships or fieldwork, institutionally sponsored loans, scholarships/grants, health care benefits, unspecified assistantships, and cash awards for travel and research also available. Financial award application deadline: 2/1. *Faculty research:* Ancient, medieval, Renaissance, eighteenth-nineteenth century, contemporary. *Unit head:* Dr. Carolyn Malone, Professor and Chair, 213-740-4552, Fax: 213-740-8971, E-mail: cmalone@usc.edu. *Application contact:* Jeanne Herman, Academic Advisor, 213-740-9516, Fax: 213-740-8971, E-mail: jaherman@usc.edu.

University of Southern California, Graduate School, Roski School of Fine Arts, Graduate Programs in Fine Arts, Los Angeles, CA 90089. Offers painting/drawing (MFA); photography (MFA); sculpture/new genres (MFA). *Faculty:* 5 full-time (3 women), 1 part-time/adjunct (0 women). *Students:* 16 full-time (5 women); includes 2 minority (1 Asian American or Pacific Islander, 1 Hispanic American), 3 international. Average age 27. 312 applicants, 3% accepted, 8 enrolled. In 2009, 8 master's awarded. *Degree requirements:* For master's, thesis. *Entrance requirements:* For master's, portfolio and artist statement, 3 ltrs of recommendation. Additional exam requirements/recommendations for international students: Required—TOEFL (minimum score 600 paper-based; 250 computer-based; 100 iBT). *Application deadline:* For fall admission, 2/1 for domestic and international students. Application fee: $85. Electronic applications accepted. *Expenses:* Tuition: Full-time $25,980; part-time $1315 per unit. Required fees: $554. One-time fee: $35 full-time. Full-time tuition and fees vary according to degree level and program. *Financial support:* In 2009–10, 16 students received support, including 3 research assistantships (averaging $3,500 per year), 13 teaching assistantships with full tuition reimbursements available (averaging $9,500 per year); health care benefits and unspecified assistantships also available. Financial award application deadline: 2/1. *Faculty research:* Film and community growth, adolescence and transgenderism. *Unit head:* Charlie White, MFA Director, 213-743-1804, Fax: 213-743-1817. *Application contact:* Dwayne Moser, MFA Coordinator, 213-743-1804, Fax: 213-743-1817, E-mail: dmoser@usc.edu.

University of South Florida, Graduate School, College of The Arts, School of Art and Art History, Tampa, FL 33620-9951. Offers art history (MA); studio art (MFA). *Accreditation:* NASAD. Part-time programs available. *Faculty:* 20 full-time (9 women), 3 part-time/adjunct (0 women). *Students:* 38 full-time (21 women), 6 part-time (5 women); includes 7 minority (2 African Americans, 1 American Indian/Alaska Native, 1 Asian American or Pacific Islander, 3 Hispanic Americans), 2 international. Average age 32. 89 applicants, 26% accepted, 18 enrolled. In 2009, 13 master's awarded. *Degree requirements:* For master's, thesis, exhibition (MFA). *Entrance requirements:* For master's, GRE General Test (MA), minimum GPA of 3.0 in last 60 hours of coursework. *Application deadline:* For fall admission, 1/15 for domestic students, 1/2 for international students. Application fee: $30. *Financial support:* In 2009–10, 8 fellowships with full tuition reimbursements (averaging $7,000 per year), 35 teaching assistantships with full tuition reimbursements (averaging $4,600 per year) were awarded; scholarships/grants, health care benefits, and unspecified assistantships also available. Support available to part-time students. Financial award application deadline: 2/15; financial award applicants required to submit FAFSA. *Faculty research:* Contemporary art and role of the artist, identity strategies, political iconography, art practice and technology, construction of race in art. Total annual research expenditures: $52,987. *Unit head:* Prof. Wallace Wilson, Director, 813-974-2360, Fax: 813-974-9226, E-mail: wwilson2@usf.edu. *Application contact:* Gloria Ann Quigley, Academic Specialist, 813-974-9249, Fax: 813-974-9226, E-mail: gquigley@usf.edu.

The University of Tennessee, Graduate School, College of Arts and Sciences, School of Art, Knoxville, TN 37996. Offers ceramics (MFA); drawing (MFA); graphic design (MFA); inter-area studies (MFA); media arts (MFA); painting (MFA); printmaking (MFA); sculpture (MFA); watercolor (MFA). *Accreditation:* NASAD. *Degree requirements:* For master's, thesis or alternative, exhibit. *Entrance requirements:* For master's, portfolio, minimum GPA of 2.7. Additional exam requirements/recommendations for international students: Required—TOEFL. Electronic applications accepted. *Expenses:* Tuition, state resident: full-time $6826; part-time $380 per semester hour. Tuition, nonresident: full-time $21,844; part-time $1147 per semester hour. Tuition and fees vary according to program.

The University of Texas at Arlington, Graduate School, College of Liberal Arts, Department of Art and Art History, Arlington, TX 76019. Offers MFA. *Accreditation:* NASAD. Part-time and evening/weekend programs available. *Faculty:* 21 full-time (6 women). *Students:* 17 full-time (8 women), 3 part-time (2 women); includes 6 minority (1 American Indian/Alaska Native, 1 Asian American or Pacific Islander, 4 Hispanic Americans), 1 international. 18 applicants, 100% accepted, 3 enrolled. *Degree requirements:* For master's, thesis or alternative. *Entrance requirements:* For master's, minimum GPA of 3.0, 3 letters of recommendation, portfolio, resume. Additional exam requirements/recommendations for international students: Required—TOEFL (minimum score 550 paper-based; 213 computer-based). *Application deadline:* For fall admission, 6/1 for domestic students. Applications are processed on a rolling basis. Electronic applications accepted. *Financial support:* In 2009–10, 4 fellowships (averaging $2,000 per year), 2 research assistantships (averaging $9,000 per year), 12 teaching assistantships (averaging $10,000 per year) were awarded. Financial award application deadline: 5/1; financial award applicants required to submit FAFSA. *Unit head:* Dr. Robert Hower, Professor, 817-272-2891, E-mail: hower@uta.edu. *Application contact:* Dr. Nancy Palmieri, Associate Professor, 817-272-2891, E-mail: palmieri@uta.edu.

The University of Texas at Austin, Graduate School, College of Fine Arts, Department of Art and Art History, Program in Studio Art, Austin, TX 78712-1111. Offers MFA. *Accreditation:* NASAD. *Degree requirements:* For master's, thesis, oral exam. *Entrance requirements:* For master's, minimum GPA of 3.0, portfolio of 15 slides. Electronic applications accepted. *Faculty research:* Painting, sculpture, transmedia, photography, printmaking.

The University of Texas at El Paso, Graduate School, College of Liberal Arts, Department of Art, El Paso, TX 79968-0001. Offers art education (MA); studio art (MA). Part-time and evening/weekend programs available. *Students:* 12 (8 women); includes 9 minority (all Hispanic Americans), 2 international. Average age 34. In 2009, 1 master's awarded. *Degree requirements:* For master's, thesis optional. *Entrance requirements:* For master's, minimum GPA of 3.0, digital portfolio, letters of recommendation. Additional exam requirements/recommendations for international students: Required—TOEFL; Recommended—IELTS. *Application deadline:* For fall admission, 8/1 priority date for domestic students, 3/1 for international students; for spring admission, 11/1 priority date for domestic students, 9/1 for international students. Applications are processed on a rolling basis. Application fee: $45 ($80 for international students). Electronic applications accepted. *Financial support:* In 2009–10, research assistantships with partial tuition reimbursements (averaging $18,625 per year), teaching assistantships with partial tuition reimbursements (averaging $14,900 per year) were awarded; fellowships with partial tuition reimbursements, institutionally sponsored loans, scholarships/grants, health care benefits, tuition waivers (partial), and unspecified assistantships also available. Support available to part-time students. Financial award application deadline: 3/15; financial award applicants required to submit FAFSA. *Unit head:* Dr. J. Quinnan, Chair, 915-747-5181, Fax: 915-747-6749, E-mail: jquinnan@utep.edu. *Application contact:* Dr. Patricia D. Witherspoon, Dean of the Graduate School, 915-747-5491, Fax: 915-747-5788, E-mail: withersp@utep.edu.

The University of Texas at San Antonio, College of Liberal and Fine Arts, Department of Art and Art History, San Antonio, TX 78249-0617. Offers art history (MA); studio art (MFA). *Accreditation:* NASAD (one or more programs are accredited). *Faculty:* 14 full-time (6 women). *Students:* 30 full-time (19 women), 18 part-time (13 women); includes 21 minority (1 American Indian/Alaska Native, 1 Asian American or Pacific Islander, 19 Hispanic Americans), 1 international. Average age 33. 41 applicants, 66% accepted, 12 enrolled. In 2009, 13 master's awarded. *Degree requirements:* For master's, comprehensive exam (for some programs), thesis (for some programs). *Entrance requirements:* For master's, GRE General Test, portfolio, minimum GPA of 3.0 in last 60 hours, 3 letters of recommendation. Additional exam requirements/recommendations for international students: Required—TOEFL (minimum score 500 paper-based; 173 computer-based; 61 iBT), IELTS (minimum score 5). *Application deadline:* For fall admission, 7/1 for domestic students, 4/1 for international students; for spring admission, 11/1 for domestic students, 9/1 for international students. Applications are processed on a rolling basis. Application fee: $45 ($80 for international students). Electronic applications accepted. *Expenses:* Tuition, state resident: full-time $3975; part-time $221 per contact hour. Tuition, nonresident: full-time $13,947; part-time $775 per contact hour. Required fees: $1853. *Financial support:* In 2009–10, 24 students received support, including 11 research assistantships (averaging $8,357 per year), 11 teaching assistantships (averaging $4,715 per year); career-related internships or fieldwork, scholarships/grants, tuition waivers (partial), and unspecified assistantships also available. Support available to part-time students. *Faculty research:* Artistic production in media; art history and criticism, focusing on American and Hispanic art. *Unit head:* Dr. Kent T. Rush, Chair, 210-458-4362, Fax: 210-458-4356, E-mail: kent.rush@utsa.edu. *Application contact:* Dr. Kent T. Rush, Chair, 210-458-4362, Fax: 210-458-4356, E-mail: kent.rush@utsa.edu.

The University of Texas at Tyler, College of Arts and Sciences, Department of Art and Art History, Tyler, TX 75799-0001. Offers art history (MA); interdisciplinary (MAIS); studio art (MFA). *Faculty:* 7 full-time (4 women). *Students:* 9 full-time (6 women), 2 part-time (both women); includes 1 minority (Hispanic American). Average age 31. 2 applicants, 100% accepted, 1 enrolled. In 2009, 3 master's awarded. *Degree requirements:* For master's, thesis, graduate committee review. *Entrance requirements:* For master's, minimum GPA of 3.0. Additional exam requirements/recommendations for international students: Required—TOEFL (minimum score 79 computer-based). *Application deadline:* For fall admission, 8/17 priority date for domestic students, 7/1 priority date for international students; for spring admission, 12/21 priority date for domestic students, 11/1 priority date for international students. Applications are processed on a rolling basis. Application fee: $25 ($50 for international students). *Expenses:* Tuition, state resident: part-time $665 per semester hour. Tuition, nonresident: part-time $942 per semester hour. Part-time tuition and fees vary according to degree level and program. *Financial support:* Application deadline: 7/1. *Faculty research:* Classical myths in contemporary art, social issues in contemporary art, casting methods, Renaissance art. *Unit head:* Gary Hatcher, Chair, 903-566-7486, Fax: 903-566-7062, E-mail: ghatcher@mail.uttyl.edu. *Application contact:* Dr. Rachel Sailor, Program Chair, Art History, 903-566-7398, E-mail: rasailor@uttyler.edu.

The University of Texas–Pan American, College of Arts and Humanities, Department of Art, Edinburg, TX 78539. Offers MFA. Part-time programs available. *Degree requirements:* For master's, thesis, thesis show of artwork. *Entrance requirements:* For master's, bachelor's degree in fine arts, portfolio, 3 letters of reference. *Expenses:* Tuition, state resident: full-time $3630.60; part-time $201.70 per credit hour. Tuition, nonresident: full-time $8617; part-time $478.70 per credit hour. Required fees: $806.50. *Faculty research:* Creative art, ceramics, painting, sculpture, computer art.

The University of the Arts, College of Art and Design, Department of Book Arts/Printmaking, Philadelphia, PA 19102-4944. Offers MFA. *Accreditation:* NASAD. Part-time programs available. *Degree requirements:* For master's, thesis. *Entrance requirements:* For master's, portfolio. Additional exam requirements/recommendations for international students: Required—TOEFL (minimum score 550 paper-based; 213 computer-based).

See Close-Up on page 199.

The University of the Arts, College of Art and Design, Program in Ceramics, Philadelphia, PA 19102-4944. Offers MFA. Offered during summer only. *Accreditation:* NASAD. Part-time programs available. *Degree requirements:* For master's, thesis, summer residency. *Entrance requirements:* For master's, portfolio. Additional exam requirements/recommendations for international students: Required—TOEFL (minimum score 550 paper-based; 213 computer-based). Electronic applications accepted.

See Close-Up on page 199.

The University of the Arts, College of Art and Design, Program in Painting, Philadelphia, PA 19102-4944. Offers MFA. Offered during summer only. *Accreditation:* NASAD. Part-time programs available. *Degree requirements:* For master's, thesis, summer residency. *Entrance requirements:* For master's, portfolio. Additional exam requirements/recommendations for international students: Required—TOEFL (minimum score 550 paper-based; 213 computer-based).

See Close-Up on page 199.

The University of the Arts, College of Art and Design, Program in Sculpture, Philadelphia, PA 19102-4944. Offers MFA. Offered during summer only. *Accreditation:* NASAD. Part-time programs available. *Degree requirements:* For master's, thesis, summer residency. *Entrance requirements:* For master's, portfolio. Additional exam requirements/recommendations for international students: Required—TOEFL (minimum score 550 paper-based; 213 computer-based).

See Close-Up on page 199.

University of Toronto, School of Graduate Studies, Humanities Division, Department of Art, Toronto, ON M5S 1A1, Canada. Offers art history (MA, PhD); visual studies (MVS). Part-time programs available. *Degree requirements:* For master's, 2 foreign languages, language proficiency exams; for doctorate, 2 foreign languages, comprehensive exam, thesis/dissertation. *Entrance requirements:* For master's, coursework in a foreign language, 3 letters of reference, sample research paper, minimum B+ average in senior art history and/or humanities courses; for doctorate, minimum A– average in senior art history and/or humanities courses, 2 letters of reference, sample research paper.

University of Tulsa, Graduate School, College of Arts and Sciences, Department of Art, Tulsa, OK 74104-3189. Offers MA, MFA, MTA. Part-time programs available. *Faculty:* 7 full-time (4 women), 1 (woman) part-time/adjunct. *Students:* 9 full-time (5 women), 1 part-time (0 women); includes 1 minority (American Indian/Alaska Native). Average age 33. 16 applicants, 25% accepted, 1 enrolled. In 2009, 3 master's awarded. *Degree requirements:* For master's, comprehensive exam (for some programs), thesis (for some programs). *Entrance requirements:* For master's, portfolio. Additional exam requirements/recommendations for international students: Required—TOEFL (minimum score 575 paper-based; 231 computer-based; 91 iBT), IELTS (minimum score 6.5). *Application deadline:* For fall admission, 2/1 for domestic and international students. Application fee: $40. Electronic applications accepted. *Expenses:* Tuition: Full-time $16,182; part-time $899 per credit hour. Required fees: $4 per credit hour. Tuition and fees vary according to course load. *Financial support:* In 2009–10, 7 students received support, including 1 fellowship with full tuition reimbursement available (averaging $13,996 per year), 6 teaching assistantships with full and partial tuition reimbursements available (averaging $10,894 per year); research assistantships with full tuition reimbursements available, career-related internships or fieldwork, Federal Work-Study, scholarships/grants, traineeships, health care benefits, tuition waivers (full and partial), and unspecified assistantships also available. Support available to part-time students. Financial award application deadline: 2/1; financial award applicants required to submit FAFSA. *Faculty research:* Drawing, painting, printmaking, ceramics, graphic design. *Unit head:* Dr. Susan Dixon, Chairperson, 918-631-2740, Fax: 918-631-3423, E-mail: susan-dixon@utulsa.edu. *Application contact:* Prof. Whitney Forsyth, Adviser, 918-631-3700, Fax: 918-631-3423, E-mail: whitney-forsyth@utulsa.edu.

University of Utah, The Graduate School, College of Fine Arts, Department of Art and Art History, Salt Lake City, UT 84112-0380. Offers art history (MA); ceramics (MFA); community-based art education (MFA); drawing (MFA); graphic design (MFA); painting (MFA); photography/digital imaging (MFA); printmaking (MFA); sculpture/intermedia (MFA). *Faculty:* 24 full-time (11 women). *Students:* 20 full-time (15 women), 2 part-time (both women), 1 international. Average age 31. 59 applicants, 24% accepted, 9 enrolled. In 2009, 11 master's awarded. *Degree requirements:* For master's, variable foreign language requirement, comprehensive exam (for some programs), thesis or alternative, exhibit and final project paper (for MFA). *Entrance requirements:* For master's, CD portfolio (MFA), writing sample (MA), curriculum vitae, letters of recommendation. Additional exam requirements/recommendations for international students: Required—TOEFL (minimum score 575 paper-based; 183 computer-based; 75 iBT). *Application deadline:* For fall admission, 1/2 priority date for domestic and international students. Application fee: $55 ($65 for international students). Electronic applications accepted. *Expenses:* Tuition, state resident: full-time $4004; part-time $1674 per semester. Tuition, nonresident: full-time $14,134; part-time $5915 per semester. Required fees: $324 per semester. Tuition and fees vary according to course load, degree level and program. *Financial support:* In 2009–10, 2 fellowships, 6 research assistantships with partial tuition reimbursements, 34 teaching assistantships with partial tuition reimbursements were awarded; Federal Work-Study, institutionally sponsored loans, scholarships/grants, tuition waivers (partial), unspecified assistantships, and stipends also available. Financial award application deadline: 1/2; financial award applicants required to submit FAFSA. *Faculty research:* Studio art, European art history, Asian art history, Latin American art history, twentieth century/contemporary art history. Total annual research expenditures: $8,748. *Unit head:* Dr. Elizabeth A. Peterson, Chair, 801-581-7012, Fax: 801-585-6171, E-mail: elizabeth.peterson@art.utah.edu. *Application contact:* Prof. John O'Connell, Director of Graduate Studies, 801-581-8677, Fax: 801-585-6171, E-mail: j.oconnell@utah.edu.

University of Victoria, Faculty of Graduate Studies, Faculty of Fine Arts, Department of Visual Arts, Victoria, BC V8W 2Y2, Canada. Offers digital multimedia (MFA); drawing (MFA); painting (MFA); photography (MFA); sculpture (MFA); video (MFA). *Degree requirements:* For master's, exhibit, oral exam. *Entrance requirements:* For master's, portfolio, BFA. Additional exam requirements/recommendations for international students: Required—TOEFL (minimum score 575 paper-based; 233 computer-based), IELTS (minimum score 7). Electronic applications accepted.

University of Washington, Graduate School, College of Arts and Sciences, School of Art, Division of Art, Seattle, WA 98195. Offers painting and drawing (MFA); photography (MFA). *Degree requirements:* For master's, thesis, exhibit. *Entrance requirements:* For master's, BFA or equivalent academic work in art, 20 slide portfolio. Additional exam requirements/recommendations for international students: Required—TOEFL. Electronic applications accepted.

University of Waterloo, Graduate Studies, Faculty of Arts, Department of Fine Arts, Waterloo, ON N2L 3G1, Canada. Offers studio art (MFA). *Degree requirements:* For master's, thesis exhibit. *Entrance requirements:* For master's, honors degree, minimum A- average, sample of work. Additional exam requirements/recommendations for international students: Required—TOEFL, TWE. Electronic applications accepted. *Faculty research:* Ceramic sculpture, computer imaging, painting, drawing, contemporary art theory.

University of Windsor, Faculty of Graduate Studies, Faculty of Arts and Social Sciences, School of Visual Arts, Windsor, ON N9B 3P4, Canada. Offers MFA. *Degree requirements:* For master's, thesis. *Entrance requirements:* For master's, minimum B average, portfolio. Additional exam requirements/recommendations for international students: Required—TOEFL (minimum score 560 paper-based; 220 computer-based). Electronic applications accepted.

University of Wisconsin–Madison, Graduate School, School of Education, Department of Art, Madison, WI 53706-1380. Offers art (MA, MFA); art education (MA). *Accreditation:* NASAD. *Application deadline:* For fall admission, 1/10 for domestic students. Application fee: $56. Electronic applications accepted. *Expenses:* Tuition, state resident: part-time $594 per credit. Tuition, nonresident: part-time $1504 per credit. Required fees: $65 per credit. Tuition and fees vary according to course load, program and reciprocity agreements. *Financial support:* Fellowships with full tuition reimbursements, research assistantships with full tuition reimbursements, teaching assistantships with full tuition reimbursements, project assistantships available. *Unit head:* Dr. Tom Loeser, Chair, 608-262-1662. *Application contact:* Dr. Tom Loeser, Chair, 608-262-1662.

University of Wisconsin–Milwaukee, Graduate School, Peck School of the Arts, Department of Art, Milwaukee, WI 53201-0413. Offers art (MA, MFA); art education (MA, MFA, MS). Part-time programs available. *Faculty:* 22 full-time (15 women). *Students:* 20 full-time (12 women), 3 part-time (2 women); includes 1 minority (Asian American or Pacific Islander), 1 international. Average age 34. 36 applicants, 36% accepted, 8 enrolled. In 2009, 10 master's awarded. *Degree requirements:* For master's, comprehensive exam, thesis or alternative. *Entrance requirements:* For master's, portfolio. Additional exam requirements/recommendations for international students: Required—TOEFL (minimum score 550 paper-based; 79 iBT), IELTS (minimum score 6.5). *Application deadline:* For fall admission, 1/1 priority date for domestic students; for spring admission, 9/1 for domestic students. Applications are processed on a rolling basis. Application fee: $45 ($75 for international students). *Expenses:* Tuition, state resident: full-time $8800. Tuition, nonresident: full-time $20,760. Tuition and fees vary according to program and reciprocity agreements. *Financial support:* In 2009–10, 7 teaching assistantships were awarded; career-related internships or fieldwork and unspecified assistantships also available. Support available to part-time students. Financial award application deadline: 4/15. *Unit head:* Denis Sargent, Representative, 414-229-6053, E-mail: artgrado@uwm.edu. *Application contact:* General Information Contact, 414-229-4982, Fax: 414-229-6967, E-mail: gradschool@uwm.edu.

University of Wisconsin–River Falls, Outreach and Graduate Studies, College of Arts and Science, Program in Fine Arts, River Falls, WI 54022. Offers MSE.

University of Wisconsin–Superior, Graduate Division, Department of Visual Arts, Superior, WI 54880-4500. Offers art education (MA); art history (MA); art therapy (MA); studio arts (MA). Part-time programs available. *Faculty:* 7 full-time (1 woman), 1 (woman) part-time/adjunct. *Students:* 12 full-time (8 women), 18 part-time (15 women); includes 1 minority (American Indian/Alaska Native), 2 international. 14 applicants, 100% accepted. In 2009, 7 master's awarded. *Degree requirements:* For master's, comprehensive exam, exhibit. *Entrance requirements:* For master's, minimum GPA of 2.75, portfolio. *Application deadline:* For fall admission, 4/1 priority date for domestic students; for spring admission, 10/15 priority date for domestic students. Applications are processed on a rolling basis. Application fee: $45. *Financial support:* Career-related internships or fieldwork, Federal Work-Study, scholarships/grants, and tuition waivers (partial) available. Support available to part-time students. Financial award application deadline: 4/15; financial award applicants required to submit FAFSA. *Unit head:* Tim Cleary, Coordinator, 715-394-8398. *Application contact:* Sandy Wallgren, Program Assistant/Status Examiner, 715-394-8295, Fax: 715-394-8146, E-mail: gradstudy@uwsuper.edu.

Utah State University, School of Graduate Studies, College of Humanities, Arts and Social Sciences, Department of Art, Logan, UT 84322. Offers MA, MFA. *Degree requirements:* For master's, thesis, exhibit. *Entrance requirements:* For master's, GRE General Test or MAT, minimum GPA of 3.0, slide portfolio of art. Additional exam requirements/recommendations for international students: Required—TOEFL. *Faculty research:* Painting, drawing, sculpture, ceramics, photography.

Virginia Commonwealth University, Graduate School, College of Humanities and Sciences, School of Mass Communications, Program in Media, Art, and Text, Richmond, VA 23284-9005. Offers PhD. *Entrance requirements:* For doctorate, GRE, MA, MAE, or MFA in appropriate field of study (English, art history, studio art, poetry, mass communications); 3 letters of recommendation.

Virginia Commonwealth University, Graduate School, School of the Arts, Richmond, VA 23284-9005. Offers art education (MAE); art history (MA, PhD), including architectural history (MA), art history, historical studies (MA), museum studies (MA); ceramics (MFA); fibers (MFA); furniture design (MFA); glassworking (MFA); graphic design (MFA), including design/visual communications, interior environment, photography and film; jewelry/metalworking (MFA); kinetic imaging (MFA); music (MM), including education; painting (MFA); photography and film (MFA); printmaking (MFA); sculpture (MFA); theatre (MFA), including acting, costume design, directing, pedagogy, scene design/technical theater. Part-time programs available. *Entrance requirements:* For doctorate, GRE General Test.

Washington State University, Graduate School, College of Liberal Arts, Department of Fine Arts, Pullman, WA 99164. Offers ceramics (MFA); digital media (MFA); drawing (MFA); painting (MFA); photography (MFA); print making (MFA); sculpture (MFA). *Faculty:* 10. *Students:* 15 full-time (8 women); includes 2 minority (1 African American, 1 Hispanic American). Average age 29. 30 applicants, 20% accepted, 5 enrolled. In 2009, 5 master's awarded. *Degree requirements:* For master's, comprehensive exam (for some programs), thesis, exhibit, oral exam. *Entrance requirements:* For master's, GRE, Graduate School application, statement of intent indicating your area(s) of focus, the subject of your work, the concepts and issues you are exploring, and how you foresee your work evolving within the program, portfolio of no more than 15 images on CD/DVD,inventory list with the title, medium, size and approximate date of completion for each work. Additional exam requirements/recommendations for international students: Required—TOEFL (minimum score 550 paper-based; 213 computer-based), IELTS. *Application deadline:* For fall admission, 1/10 for domestic and international students. Application fee: $50. Electronic applications accepted. *Financial support:* In 2009–10, fellowships with full and partial tuition reimbursements (averaging $3,114 per year), research assistantships with full and partial tuition reimbursements (averaging $13,917 per year), teaching assistantships with full and partial tuition reimbursements (averaging $13,056 per year) were awarded; career-related internships or fieldwork, Federal Work-Study, institutionally sponsored loans, tuition waivers (partial), and unspecified assistantships also available. Financial award application deadline: 2/15; financial award applicants required to submit FAFSA. *Faculty research:* Polynesian art, museum representation, number theory. *Unit head:* Dr. Chris Watts, Interim Chair, 509-335-7107, Fax: 509-335-7742, E-mail: cjwatts@wsu.edu. *Application contact:* Graduate School Admissions, 800-GRADWSU, Fax: 509-335-1949, E-mail: gradsch@wsu.edu.

Art/Fine Arts

Washington University in St. Louis, Sam Fox School of Design and Visual Arts, Graduate School of Art, St. Louis, MO 63130-4899. Offers MFA. *Accreditation:* NASAD. *Degree requirements:* For master's, thesis, exhibition. *Entrance requirements:* For master's, portfolio, resume. Additional exam requirements/recommendations for international students: Required—TOEFL (minimum score 550 paper-based; 213 computer-based; 79 iBT). Electronic applications accepted. *Expenses:* Contact institution. *Faculty research:* New media, design, fine arts.

Wayne State University, College of Fine, Performing and Communication Arts, Department of Art and Art History, Program in Art, Detroit, MI 48202. Offers MA, MFA. *Degree requirements:* For master's, thesis (MFA). *Entrance requirements:* Additional exam requirements/recommendations for international students: Required—TOEFL (minimum score 550 paper-based; 213 computer-based); Recommended—TWE (minimum score 6). Electronic applications accepted. *Faculty research:* Painting, drawing, computer art.

Webster University, Leigh Gerdine College of Fine Arts, Department of Art, St. Louis, MO 63119-3194. Offers art (MA); arts management and leadership (MFA). Part-time programs available. *Degree requirements:* For master's, thesis. *Entrance requirements:* For master's, BA or BFA in related field, interview, portfolio. Additional exam requirements/recommendations for international students: Required—TOEFL. *Expenses:* Tuition: Part-time $565 per credit hour. Tuition and fees vary according to degree level, campus/location and program.

Western Carolina University, Graduate School, College of Fine and Performing Arts, Cullowhee, NC 28723. Offers MA Ed, MAT, MFA, MM. Part-time programs available. *Students:* 25 full-time (17 women), 12 part-time (6 women). Average age 33. 39 applicants, 46% accepted, 17 enrolled. In 2009, 13 master's awarded. *Degree requirements:* For master's, comprehensive exam, thesis optional. *Entrance requirements:* For master's, GRE, appropriate undergraduate degree, portfolio, letters of recommendation, letter of intent, live audition and/or interview. Additional exam requirements/recommendations for international students: Required—TOEFL (minimum score 550 paper-based; 270 computer-based; 79 iBT). *Application deadline:* For fall admission, 3/1 for domestic students. Applications are processed on a rolling basis. Application fee: $45. *Financial support:* In 2009–10, 15 students received support, including 3 research assistantships with full and partial tuition reimbursements available (averaging $7,000 per year), 12 teaching assistantships with full and partial tuition reimbursements available (averaging $7,417 per year); fellowships, career-related internships or fieldwork, institutionally sponsored loans, scholarships/grants, and unspecified assistantships also available. Financial award application deadline: 3/31; financial award applicants required to submit FAFSA. *Faculty research:* Vernacular cultural studies and oral history, sound mixing for television, music technology. *Unit head:* Dr. Robert Kehrberg, Dean, 828-227-7028, Fax: 828-227-7707, E-mail: rkehrberg@email.wcu.edu. *Application contact:* Admissions Specialist for Fine and Performing Arts, 828-227-7398, Fax: 828-227-7480, E-mail: gradsch@email.wcu.edu.

Western Connecticut State University, Division of Graduate Studies, School of Visual and Performing Arts, Department of Art, Danbury, CT 06810-6885. Offers illustration (MFA); painting (MFA). Part-time programs available. *Faculty:* 3 full-time (2 women), 3 part-time/adjunct (0 women). *Students:* 23 full-time (14 women); includes 1 minority (African American), 2 international. Average age 31. In 2009, 10 master's awarded. *Degree requirements:* For master's, individual exhibition of artwork, review of student's progress prior to admission to final semester, completion of program in 6 years. *Entrance requirements:* For master's, portfolio review, minimum GPA of 2.5. Additional exam requirements/recommendations for international students: Recommended—TOEFL (minimum score 550 paper-based; 213 computer-based; 79 iBT), IELTS (minimum score 6). *Application deadline:* For fall admission, 8/5 priority date for domestic students; for spring admission, 1/5 priority date for domestic students. Application fee: $50. *Expenses:* Tuition, state resident: full-time $5012; part-time $278 per credit hour. Tuition, nonresident: full-time $13,962; part-time $284 per credit hour. Required fees: $3886; $139 per credit hour. Full-time tuition and fees vary according to course load and program. Part-time tuition and fees vary according to course level, degree level and program. *Financial support:* In 2009–10, 8 students received support. Scholarships/grants available. Financial award application deadline: 5/1; financial award applicants required to submit FAFSA. *Unit head:* Margaret Grimes, Graduate Co-Coordinator, 203-837-8402, Fax: 203-837-8945, E-mail: grimesm@wcsu.edu. *Application contact:* Chris Shankle, Associate Director of Graduate Studies, 203-837-9005, Fax: 203-837-8326, E-mail: shanklec@wcsu.edu.

West Texas A&M University, College of Fine Arts and Humanities, Department of Art, Communication, and Theater, Program in Art, Canyon, TX 79016-0001. Offers MA. Part-time programs available. *Degree requirements:* For master's, comprehensive exam, thesis optional, exhibit, portfolio review. *Entrance requirements:* For master's, GRE General Test, interview, portfolio. Additional exam requirements/recommendations for international students: Required—TOEFL (minimum score 550 paper-based). Electronic applications accepted. *Faculty research:* Ceramics, graphic design, woodblock prints, art history, aesthetics, glassblowing.

West Texas A&M University, College of Fine Arts and Humanities, Department of Art, Communication, and Theater, Program in Studio Art, Canyon, TX 79016-0001. Offers MFA. Part-time programs available. *Degree requirements:* For master's, comprehensive exam, thesis optional, exhibit, portfolio review, professional paper. *Entrance requirements:* For master's, GRE General Test, interview, portfolio. Additional exam requirements/recommendations for international students: Required—TOEFL (minimum score 550 paper-based). *Faculty research:* Ceramics, printmaking, graphic design, art history, aesthetics, glass blowing.

West Virginia University, College of Creative Arts, Division of Art and Design, Morgantown, WV 26506. Offers art education (MA); art history (MA); ceramics (MFA); graphic design (MFA); painting (MFA); printmaking (MFA); sculpture (MFA); studio art (MA). *Accreditation:* NASAD. *Degree requirements:* For master's, thesis, exhibit. *Entrance requirements:* For master's, minimum GPA of 2.75, portfolio. Additional exam requirements/recommendations for international students: Required—TOEFL. *Expenses:* Contact institution. *Faculty research:* Medieval art history.

Wichita State University, Graduate School, College of Fine Arts, School of Art and Design, Wichita, KS 67260. Offers studio arts (MFA), including ceramics, painting, printmaking, sculpture. *Expenses:* Tuition, state resident: full-time $4247; part-time $235.95 per credit hour. Tuition, nonresident: full-time $11,171; part-time $620.60 per credit hour. Required fees: $34; $3.60 per credit hour. $17 per term. Tuition and fees vary according to campus/location and program. *Unit head:* Prof. Barry Badgett, Director, 316-978-3555, Fax: 316-978-5418, E-mail: barry.badgett@wichita.edu. *Application contact:* Prof. Barry Badgett, Director, 316-978-3555, Fax: 316-978-5418, E-mail: barry.badgett@wichita.edu.

William Paterson University of New Jersey, College of the Arts and Communication, Wayne, NJ 07470-8420. Offers art (MFA); music (MM); professional communication (MA). Part-time and evening/weekend programs available. *Students:* 27 full-time (11 women), 28 part-time (11 women); includes 3 minority (1 African American, 1 Asian American or Pacific Islander, 1 Hispanic American), 4 international. *Entrance requirements:* For master's, minimum GPA of 2.75. *Application deadline:* Applications are processed on a rolling basis. Application fee: $50. Electronic applications accepted. *Financial support:* In 2009–10, 3 students received support; research assistantships with full tuition reimbursements available, career-related internships or fieldwork, Federal Work-Study, and unspecified assistantships available. Support available to part-time students. Financial award application deadline: 4/1; financial award applicants required to submit FAFSA. *Unit head:* Dr. Raymond Torres-Santos, Dean, College of Arts and Communication, 973-720-2232, E-mail: torressantosr@wpunj.edu. *Application contact:* Christina Aiello, Assistant Director, Graduate Admissions, 973-720-2506, Fax: 973-720-2035, E-mail: aielloc@wpunj.edu.

Winthrop University, College of Visual and Performing Arts, Department of Art, Rock Hill, SC 29733. Offers art (MFA); art administration (MA); art education (MA). *Accreditation:* NASAD. Part-time programs available. *Degree requirements:* For master's, thesis, documented exhibit, oral exam. *Entrance requirements:* For master's, GRE General Test or MAT, PRAXIS (MA), minimum GPA of 3.0, resume, slide portfolio, teaching certificate (MA). Electronic applications accepted.

Yale University, School of Art, New Haven, CT 06520. Offers graphic design (MFA); painting/printmaking (MFA); photography (MFA); sculpture (MFA). *Faculty:* 7 full-time (3 women), 36 part-time/adjunct (12 women). *Students:* 119 full-time (62 women); includes 17 minority (4 African Americans, 6 Asian Americans or Pacific Islanders, 7 Hispanic Americans), 25 international. Average age 28. 1,266 applicants, 5% accepted, 58 enrolled. In 2009, 57 master's awarded. *Degree requirements:* For master's, thesis (for some programs). *Entrance requirements:* Additional exam requirements/recommendations for international students: Required—TOEFL (minimum score 550 paper-based; 250 computer-based; 100 iBT). *Application deadline:* For fall admission, 1/5 for domestic and international students. Application fee: $100. Electronic applications accepted. *Expenses:* Contact institution. *Financial support:* In 2009–10, 90 students received support, including 54 teaching assistantships (averaging $1,900 per year); Federal Work-Study, scholarships/grants, and unspecified assistantships also available. Financial award application deadline: 3/1; financial award applicants required to submit FAFSA. *Unit head:* Robert Storr, Dean, 203-432-2606. *Application contact:* Patricia Ann DeChiara, Director of Academic Affairs, 203-432-2600, E-mail: artschool.info@yale.edu.

York University, Faculty of Graduate Studies, Faculty of Fine Arts, Program in Visual Arts, Toronto, ON M3J 1P3, Canada. Offers MFA, PhD. *Degree requirements:* For master's, thesis. *Entrance requirements:* For master's, portfolio. Electronic applications accepted.

Art History

American University, College of Arts and Sciences, Department of Art, Program in Art History, Washington, DC 2006-8004. Offers MA. Part-time programs available. *Students:* 13 full-time (all women), 25 part-time (all women); includes 2 minority (1 Asian American or Pacific Islander, 1 Hispanic American), 1 international. Average age 26. 67 applicants, 54% accepted, 12 enrolled. In 2009, 7 master's awarded. *Degree requirements:* For master's, one foreign language, comprehensive exam, thesis or alternative. *Entrance requirements:* For master's, GRE, 24 hours of undergraduate course work in art history, portfolio. *Application deadline:* For fall admission, 2/1 priority date for domestic students; for spring admission, 10/1 for domestic students. Application fee: $80. *Expenses:* Tuition: Full-time $22,266; part-time $1237 per credit hour. Required fees: $430. Tuition and fees vary according to program. *Financial support:* Fellowships, research assistantships with tuition reimbursements, teaching assistantships with tuition reimbursements, career-related internships or fieldwork, Federal Work-Study, and institutionally sponsored loans available. Support available to part-time students. Financial award application deadline: 1/15. *Faculty research:* Renaissance, twentieth century, American, baroque, rococo. *Unit head:* Luis Silva, Chair, 202-885-1682, Fax: 202-885-1132. *Application contact:* Glenna K. Haynie, Administrative Coordinator, 202-885-1671.

American University of Puerto Rico, Program in Education, Bayamón, PR 00960-2037. Offers art history (M Ed); elementary education (4-6) (M Ed); elementary education (k-3) (M Ed); general science education (M Ed); physical education (k-12) (M Ed); special education at secondary level (transition) (M Ed). *Faculty:* 1 full-time (0 women), 22 part-time/adjunct (6 women). *Students:* 121 full-time (98 women), 64 part-time (50 women); includes all Hispanic Americans. Average age 30. 250 applicants, 80% accepted, 185 enrolled. *Entrance requirements:* For master's, EXADEP or GRE or MAT, 2 letters of recommendation, minimum GPA of 2.5. *Application deadline:* For fall admission, 8/4 for domestic students; for winter admission, 10/18 for domestic students; for spring admission, 3/22 for domestic students. Applications are processed on a rolling basis. Application fee: $50. *Application contact:* Information Contact, E-mail: oficnaadmisiones@aupr.edu.

Bard College, Program in History of the Decorative Arts, Design and Culture, Annandale-on-Hudson, NY 12504. Offers MA, PhD. Part-time programs available. *Degree requirements:* For master's, one foreign language, thesis, internship; for doctorate, 2 foreign languages, thesis/dissertation, exams. *Entrance requirements:* For master's, GRE General Test, writing sample, 3 letters of recommendation; for doctorate, GRE General Test, master's thesis or equivalent, 3 letters of recommendation. Additional exam requirements/recommendations for international students: Required—TOEFL. *Expenses:* Contact institution.

Bard Graduate Center for Studies in the Decorative Arts, Design, and Culture, Program in Decorative Arts, Design History, and Material Culture, New York, NY 10024-3602. Offers MA, PhD. Bard Graduate Center for Studies in the Decorative Arts is a unit of Bard College. Part-time programs available. *Degree requirements:* For master's, one foreign language, thesis, internship; for doctorate, 2 foreign languages, thesis/dissertation, exams. *Entrance requirements:* For master's, GRE General Test, writing sample, 3 letters of recommendation; for doctorate, GRE General Test, master's thesis or equivalent, 3 letters of recommendation. Additional exam requirements/recommendations for international students: Required—TOEFL. *Faculty research:* English craftsmen, ancient furniture, aesthetics and politics, Art Nouveau jewelry, European sculpture.

See Close-Up on page 191.

Boston University, Graduate School of Arts and Sciences, Department of Art History, Boston, MA 02215. Offers art history (MA, PhD); museum studies (Certificate). *Students:* 48 full-time (43 women), 14 part-time (13 women); includes 6 minority (5 African Americans, 1 Asian American or Pacific Islander), 7 international. Average age 31. 227 applicants, 32% accepted, 14 enrolled. In 2009, 11 master's, 6 doctorates awarded. Terminal master's awarded for partial completion of doctoral program. *Degree requirements:* For master's, one foreign language, comprehensive exam, thesis; for doctorate, 2 foreign languages, comprehensive exam, thesis/dissertation. *Entrance requirements:* For master's and doctorate, GRE General Test, 3 letters of recommendation; for Certificate, GRE General Test. Additional exam requirements/recommendations for international students: Required—TOEFL (minimum score 600 paper-based; 250 computer-based). *Application deadline:* For fall admission, 1/15 for domestic and international students; for spring admission, 10/15 for domestic and international students. Application fee: $70. *Expenses:* Tuition: Full-time $37,910; part-time $1184 per credit hour. Required fees: $386; $40 per semester. Part-time tuition and fees vary according to class time, course level, degree level and program. *Financial support:* In 2009–10, 23 students received support, including 2 fellowships (averaging $18,900 per year), 1 research assistantship (averaging $18,200 per year), 6 teaching assistantships with full tuition reimbursements available (averaging $18,200 per year); career-related internships or fieldwork, Federal Work-Study, and unspecified assistantships also available. Support available to part-time students. Financial award application deadline: 1/15; financial award applicants required to submit FAFSA. *Unit head:* Fred S. Kleiner, Chairman, 617-353-2520, Fax: 617-353-3243, E-mail: fsk@bu.edu. *Application contact:* Cheryl Crombie, Administrative Assistant, 617-353-2522, Fax: 617-353-3243, E-mail: ccrombie@bu.edu.

Bowling Green State University, Graduate College, College of Arts and Sciences, School of Art, Bowling Green, OH 43403. Offers 2-D studio art (MA, MFA); 3-D studio art (MA, MFA); art education (MA); art history (MA); computer art (MA); design (MFA); digital arts (MFA); graphics (MFA). *Accreditation:* NASAD. Part-time programs available. *Degree requirements:* For master's, thesis or alternative, final exhibit (MFA). *Entrance requirements:* For master's, GRE General Test (MA), slide portfolio (15-20 slides). Additional exam requirements/recommendations for international students: Required—TOEFL. Electronic applications accepted. *Faculty research:* Computer animation and virtual reality, Spanish still-life painting from 1600 to 1800, art and psychotherapy, Japanese wood-firing techniques in ceramics, non-toxic printmaking technologies.

Brigham Young University, Graduate Studies, College of Fine Arts and Communications, Department of Visual Arts, Provo, UT 84602-6414. Offers art education (MA); art history (MA); studio art (MFA). Art education applications accepted biennially. *Accreditation:* NASAD. *Faculty:* 24 full-time (7 women), 2 part-time/adjunct (1 woman). *Students:* 33 full-time (22 women); includes 4 minority (all Asian Americans or Pacific Islanders). Average age 26. 32 applicants, 38% accepted, 11 enrolled. In 2009, 9 master's awarded. *Degree requirements:* For master's, one foreign language, thesis (art history), selected project (MFA), curriculum project (art education). *Entrance requirements:* For master's, GRE (art history), minimum GPA of 3.0 (MFA, MA in art education), 3.3 (MA in art history), portfolio in slide form (MFA), writing samples (MA in art education, art history). Additional exam requirements/recommendations for international students: Required—TOEFL (minimum score 500 paper-based). *Application deadline:* For fall admission, 2/1 for domestic and international students. Application fee: $50. Electronic applications accepted. *Expenses:* Tuition: Full-time $5580; part-time $301 per credit hour. Tuition and fees vary according to student's religious affiliation. *Financial support:* In 2009–10, 27 students received support; research assistantships, teaching assistantships with partial tuition reimbursements available, scholarships/grants and tuition waivers (partial) available. Financial award application deadline: 2/1. *Faculty research:* Methodology-standards-assessment, medieval architecture, classical/Islamic eighteenth and nineteenth century art, Netherlandish art, contemporary art. Total annual research expenditures: $83,932. *Unit head:* Prof. Linda A. Reynolds, Chair, 801-422-4429, Fax: 801-422-0695, E-mail: sullivan@byu.edu. *Application contact:* Sharon Lyn Heelis, Secretary, 801-422-4429, Fax: 801-422-0695, E-mail: sharon_heelis@byu.edu.

Brooklyn College of the City University of New York, Division of Graduate Studies, Department of Art, Program in Art History, Brooklyn, NY 11210-2889. Offers MA, PhD. Part-time programs available. *Students:* 2 full-time (both women), 19 part-time (14 women); includes 3 minority (2 African Americans, 1 Asian American or Pacific Islander). Average age 29. 38 applicants, 79% accepted, 12 enrolled. In 2009, 4 master's awarded. *Degree requirements:* For master's, one foreign language, thesis or alternative, 2 publishable papers or thesis. *Entrance requirements:* For master's, bachelor's degree in art, minimum GPA of 3.0, portfolio, interview. Additional exam requirements/recommendations for international students: Required—TOEFL (minimum score 500 paper-based; 173 computer-based; 61 iBT). *Application deadline:* For fall admission, 3/1 priority date for domestic students, 2/1 priority date for international students; for spring admission, 11/1 priority date for domestic students, 10/1 priority date for international students. Applications are processed on a rolling basis. Application fee: $125. Electronic applications accepted. *Expenses:* Tuition, area resident: Full-time $7360; part-time $310 per credit hour. Tuition, state resident: full-time $7360; part-time $310 per credit hour. Tuition, nonresident: full-time $13,800; part-time $575 per credit hour. International tuition: $13,800 full-time. Required fees: $140.10 per semester. *Financial support:* Career-related internships or fieldwork, Federal Work-Study, institutionally sponsored loans, and scholarships/grants available. Support available to part-time students. Financial award application deadline: 5/1; financial award applicants required to submit FAFSA. *Faculty research:* Contemporary art, ancient Near East art, northern Baroque art, nineteenth century French art, Italian Renaissance art. *Unit head:* Dr. Mona Hadler, Deputy Chairperson, 718-951-5181, E-mail: mhadler@brooklyn.cuny.edu. *Application contact:* Hernan Sierra, Graduate Admissions Coordinator, 718-951-4536, Fax: 718-951-4506, E-mail: grads@brooklyn.cuny.edu.

Brown University, Graduate School, Department of History of Art and Architecture, Providence, RI 02912. Offers MA, PhD. *Degree requirements:* For master's, 2 foreign languages, thesis; for doctorate, 2 foreign languages, thesis/dissertation, oral exam. *Entrance requirements:* For master's, GRE General Test; for doctorate, GRE General Test, MA with distinction.

Brown University, Graduate School, Joukowsky Institute for Archaeology and the Ancient World, Providence, RI 02912. Offers PhD. *Degree requirements:* For doctorate, thesis/dissertation.

Bryn Mawr College, Graduate School of Arts and Sciences, Department of History of Art, Bryn Mawr, PA 19010-2899. Offers MA, PhD. Part-time programs available. *Degree requirements:* For master's, 2 foreign languages, thesis; for doctorate, 2 foreign languages, comprehensive exam, thesis/dissertation. *Entrance requirements:* For master's and doctorate, GRE General Test. Additional exam requirements/recommendations for international students: Required—TOEFL (minimum score 600 paper-based; 250 computer-based). *Expenses:* Tuition: Full-time $31,340. Required fees: $430.

California State University, Chico, Graduate School, College of Humanities and Fine Arts, Department of Art and Art History, Program in Art History, Chico, CA 95929-0722. Offers MA. *Accreditation:* NASAD. *Degree requirements:* For master's, thesis or alternative. *Entrance requirements:* For master's, 2 letters of recommendation. Additional exam requirements/recommendations for international students: Required—TOEFL (minimum score 550 paper-based; 213 computer-based; 80 iBT), IELTS (minimum score 6.5). *Application deadline:* For fall admission, 3/1 priority date for domestic students, 3/1 for international students; for spring admission, 9/15 priority date for domestic students, 9/15 for international students. Application fee: $55. *Unit head:* Dr. Cameron Crawford, Graduate Coordinator, 530-898-6860. *Application contact:* Dr. Cameron Crawford, Graduate Coordinator, 530-898-6860.

California State University, Fullerton, Graduate Studies, College of the Arts, Department of Art, Fullerton, CA 92834-9480. Offers art (MA, MFA), including ceramics (MFA), crafts, creative photography (MFA), design (MFA), drawing and painting, printmaking (MFA), sculpture; art history (MA); design (MA). *Accreditation:* NASAD (one or more programs are accredited). Part-time programs available. *Students:* 47 full-time (29 women), 38 part-time (23 women); includes 24 minority (2 African Americans, 12 Asian Americans or Pacific Islanders, 10 Hispanic Americans), 10 international. Average age 34. 76 applicants, 28% accepted, 19 enrolled. In 2009, 20 master's awarded. *Degree requirements:* For master's, project or thesis. *Entrance requirements:* For master's, minimum GPA of 2.5 in last 60 units of course work, portfolio. Application fee: $55. *Expenses:* Tuition, nonresident: full-time $11,160; part-time $373 per credit. Required fees: $1440 per term. Tuition and fees vary according to course load, degree level and program. *Financial support:* Career-related internships or fieldwork, Federal Work-Study, institutionally sponsored loans, and scholarships/grants available. Support available to part-time students. Financial award application deadline: 3/1; financial award applicants required to submit FAFSA. *Unit head:* Larry Johnson, Chair, 657-278-3471. *Application contact:* Admissions/Applications, 657-278-2371.

California State University, Long Beach, Graduate Studies, College of the Arts, Department of Art, Long Beach, CA 90840. Offers art education (MA); art history (MA); studio art (MA, MFA). *Accreditation:* NASAD. Part-time programs available. *Faculty:* 81 full-time (49 women), 1 (woman) part-time/adjunct. *Students:* 84 full-time (54 women), 44 part-time (31 women); includes 35 minority (2 American Indian/Alaska Native, 16 Asian Americans or Pacific Islanders, 17 Hispanic Americans), 5 international. Average age 34. 183 applicants, 37% accepted, 43 enrolled. *Degree requirements:* For master's, thesis (for some programs). *Entrance requirements:* For master's, minimum GPA of 3.0 in last 60 hours. *Application deadline:* For fall admission, 7/1 for domestic students; for spring admission, 12/1 for domestic students. Applications are processed on a rolling basis. Application fee: $55. Electronic applications accepted. *Expenses:* Required fees: $1802 per semester. Part-time tuition and fees vary according to course load. *Financial support:* Federal Work-Study, institutionally sponsored loans, and scholarships/grants available. Financial award application deadline: 3/2. *Unit head:* Prof. David Hadlock, Chair, 562-985-7908, Fax: 562-985-1650, E-mail: dhadlock@csulb.edu. *Application contact:* Margaret Black, Graduate Advisor, 562-985-7910, Fax: 562-985-1650.

California State University, Los Angeles, Graduate Studies, College of Arts and Letters, Department of Art, Los Angeles, CA 90032-8530. Offers art (MA), including art education, art history, art therapy, ceramics, metals, and textiles, design (MA, MFA), painting, sculpture, and graphic arts, photography; fine arts (MFA), including crafts, design (MA, MFA), studio arts. *Accreditation:* NASAD (one or more programs are accredited). Part-time and evening/weekend programs available. *Faculty:* 12 full-time (6 women), 1 part-time/adjunct (0 women). *Students:* 28 full-time (21 women), 40 part-time (28 women); includes 22 minority (1 African American, 6 Asian Americans or Pacific Islanders, 15 Hispanic Americans), 9 international. Average age 37. 30 applicants, 100% accepted, 12 enrolled. In 2009, 17 master's awarded. *Degree requirements:* For master's, comprehensive exam, project or thesis. *Entrance requirements:* For master's, portfolio. Additional exam requirements/recommendations for international students: Required—TOEFL (minimum score 500 paper-based; 173 computer-based). *Application deadline:* For fall admission, 5/1 for domestic and international students. Applications are processed on a rolling basis. Application fee: $55. Electronic applications accepted. *Financial support:* Federal Work-Study available. Support available to part-time students. Financial award application deadline: 3/1. *Faculty research:* The artist and the book, conceptual art, ceramic processes, computer graphics, architectural graphics. *Unit head:* Dr. Abbas Daneshvari, Chair, 323-343-4010, Fax: 323-343-4045, E-mail: adanesh@calstatela.edu. *Application contact:* Dr. Cheryl L. Ney, Associate Vice President for Academic Affairs and Dean of Graduate Studies, 323-343-3820, Fax: 323-343-5653, E-mail: cney@cslanet.calstatela.edu.

California State University, Northridge, Graduate Studies, College of Arts, Media, and Communication, Department of Art, Northridge, CA 91330. Offers art education (MA); art history (MA); studio art (MA, MFA); visual communications (MA, MFA). *Accreditation:* NASAD. *Faculty:* 22 full-time (12 women), 42 part-time/adjunct (16 women). *Students:* 27 full-time (21 women), 29 part-time (23 women); includes 14 minority (2 African Americans, 1 American Indian/Alaska Native, 6 Asian Americans or Pacific Islanders, 5 Hispanic Americans), 3 international. Average age 35. 84 applicants, 29% accepted, 14 enrolled. In 2009, 29 master's awarded. *Application deadline:* For fall admission, 11/30 for domestic students. Application fee: $55. *Financial support:* Application deadline: 3/1. *Unit head:* Prof. Edward Alfano, Chair, 818-677-2242, E-mail: art.dept@csun.edu. *Application contact:* Prof. Edward Alfano, Chair, 818-677-2242, E-mail: art.dept@csun.edu.

Caribbean University, Graduate School, Bayamón, PR 00960-0493. Offers administration and supervision (MA Ed); criminal justice (MA); curriculum and instruction (MA Ed), including elementary education, English education, history education, mathematics education, primary education, science education, Spanish education; education (PhD); gerontology (MSN); human resources (MBA); museology, archiving and art history (MA Ed); neonatal pediatrics (MSN); physical education (MA Ed); special education (MA Ed). *Entrance requirements:* For master's, interview, minimum GPA of 2.5.

Carleton University, Faculty of Graduate Studies, Faculty of Arts and Social Sciences, School for Studies in Art and Culture, Program in Art History: Art and its Institutions, Ottawa, ON K1S 5B6, Canada. Offers MA. *Degree requirements:* For master's, thesis. *Entrance requirements:* For master's, honors degree.

Case Western Reserve University, School of Graduate Studies, Department of Art History and Art, Program in Art History, Cleveland, OH 44106. Offers MA, PhD. MA and PhD offered jointly with the Cleveland Museum of Art. Part-time programs available. *Faculty:* 9 full-time (6 women), 11 part-time/adjunct (5 women). *Students:* 15 full-time (14 women), 6 part-time (4 women); includes 1 minority (Hispanic American). Average age 28. 19 applicants, 42% accepted, 3 enrolled. In 2009, 7 master's, 4 doctorates awarded. *Degree requirements:* For master's, one foreign language, thesis or alternative; for doctorate, 2 foreign languages, comprehensive exam, thesis/dissertation. *Entrance requirements:* For master's, GRE General Test, 2 samples of written work; for doctorate, GRE General Test, 2 samples of written work or MA thesis. Additional exam requirements/recommendations for international students: Required—TOEFL (minimum score 550 paper-based; 213 computer-based; 79 iBT). *Application deadline:* For fall admission, 2/15 priority date for domestic students. Applications are processed on a rolling basis. Application fee: $50. Electronic applications accepted. *Financial support:* Fellowships, research assistantships, teaching assistantships, career-related internships or fieldwork available. Financial award application deadline: 2/15; financial award applicants required to submit FAFSA. *Faculty research:* Greek art and architecture, Northern baroque art, Italian baroque sculpture, abstract expressionism, Indian art, nineteenth century French art, American and contemporary art. *Unit head:* Edward Olszewski, Chair, 216-368-4118, Fax: 216-368-4681, E-mail: edward.olszewski@case.edu. *Application contact:* Debby Tenenbaum, Assistant, 216-368-4118, Fax: 216-368-4681, E-mail: deborah.tenenbaum@case.edu.

Christie's Education, Program in Modern Art, Connoisseurship, and the History of the Art Market, New York, NY 10036. Offers MA. *Degree requirements:* For master's, one foreign language, thesis. *Entrance requirements:* For master's, GRE, writing sample, 3 letters of recommendation. Additional exam requirements/recommendations for international students: Required—TOEFL.

City College of the City University of New York, Graduate School, College of Liberal Arts and Science, Division of the Humanities and Arts, Department of Art, Concentrations in Art History and Museum Studies, New York, NY 10031-9198. Offers art history (MA); museum studies (MA). Part-time programs available. *Degree requirements:* For master's, one foreign language, thesis. *Entrance requirements:* For master's, minimum GPA of 3.0, portfolio, art history paper. Additional exam requirements/recommendations for international students: Required—TOEFL (minimum score 577 paper-based; 90 iBT). Electronic applications accepted. *Faculty research:* Egyptian, Greek, medieval, Romanesque, and Ottoman art.

Cleveland State University, College of Graduate Studies, College of Liberal Arts and Social Sciences, Department of Art, Cleveland, OH 44115. Offers art education (M Ed); art history (MA).

Cleveland State University, College of Graduate Studies, College of Liberal Arts and Social Sciences, Department of History, Cleveland, OH 44115. Offers art history (MA); history (MA); museum studies (MA). Part-time and evening/weekend programs available. *Degree requirements:* For master's, thesis optional. *Entrance requirements:* For master's, minimum GPA of 3.0, bachelor's degree in history. Additional exam requirements/recommendations for international students: Required—TOEFL (minimum score 525 paper-based; 197 computer-based). Electronic applications accepted. *Faculty research:* African Diaspora, social history and the city, early modern Europe, local history.

Columbia University, Graduate School of Arts and Sciences, Division of Humanities, Department of Art History and Archaeology, New York, NY 10027. Offers archaeology (M Phil, MA, PhD); art history and archaeology (M Phil, MA, PhD); modern art (MA). *Degree requirements:* For master's, 2 foreign languages, thesis; for doctorate, 3 foreign languages, thesis/dissertation. *Entrance requirements:* For master's and doctorate, GRE General Test. Additional exam requirements/recommendations for international students: Required—TOEFL.

Concordia University, School of Graduate Studies, Faculty of Fine Arts, Department of Art History, Montréal, QC H3G 1M8, Canada. Offers MA, PhD. *Degree requirements:* For master's, one foreign language, thesis. *Entrance requirements:* For master's, BFA or equivalent, minimum

Art History

Concordia University (continued)
B average in major. *Faculty research:* Ancient and modern Canadian art and architecture, Canadian decorative arts, museum studies.

Cornell University, Graduate School, Graduate Fields of Arts and Sciences, Field of History of Art, Archaeology and Visual Studies, Ithaca, NY 14853. Offers American art (PhD); ancient art and archaeology (PhD); Asian art (PhD); baroque art (PhD); medieval art (PhD); modern art (PhD); Renaissance art (PhD); Southeast Asian art (PhD); theory and criticism (PhD). *Faculty:* 23 full-time (14 women). *Students:* 20 full-time (18 women); includes 4 minority (1 African American, 1 American Indian/Alaska Native, 1 Asian American or Pacific Islander, 1 Hispanic American), 5 international. Average age 35. 73 applicants. In 2009, 3 doctorates awarded. *Degree requirements:* For doctorate, one foreign language, comprehensive exam, thesis/dissertation, general exams in 3 areas. *Entrance requirements:* For doctorate, GRE General Test, sample of written work, 3 letters of recommendation. Additional exam requirements/recommendations for international students: Required—TOEFL (minimum score 550 paper-based; 213 computer-based; 77 iBT). *Application deadline:* For fall admission, 1/15 for domestic students. Application fee: $70. Electronic applications accepted. *Expenses:* Tuition: Full-time $29,500. Required fees: $70. Full-time tuition and fees vary according to degree level, program and student level. *Financial support:* In 2009–10, 17 students received support, including 3 fellowships with full tuition reimbursements available; research assistantships with full tuition reimbursements available, teaching assistantships with full tuition reimbursements available, institutionally sponsored loans, scholarships/grants, health care benefits, tuition waivers (full and partial), and unspecified assistantships also available. Financial award applicants required to submit FAFSA. *Unit head:* Director of Graduate Studies, 607-255-4905, Fax: 607-255-0566, E-mail: art_history@cornell.edu. *Application contact:* Graduate Field Assistant, 607-255-4905, Fax: 607-255-0566, E-mail: art_history@cornell.edu.

Duke University, Graduate School, Department of Art, Art History and Visual Studies, Durham, NC 27708-0764. Offers PhD. *Faculty:* 16 full-time. *Students:* 38 full-time (33 women); includes 6 minority (2 African Americans, 1 Asian American or Pacific Islander, 3 Hispanic Americans), 10 international. 79 applicants, 19% accepted, 8 enrolled. In 2009, 3 doctorates awarded. *Degree requirements:* For doctorate, thesis/dissertation. *Entrance requirements:* For doctorate, GRE General Test. Additional exam requirements/recommendations for international students: Required—TOEFL (minimum score 550 paper-based; 213 computer-based; 83 iBT), IELTS (minimum score 7). *Application deadline:* For fall admission, 12/8 priority date for domestic and international students. Application fee: $75. Electronic applications accepted. *Financial support:* Fellowships, teaching assistantships available. Financial award application deadline: 12/8. *Unit head:* Gennifer Weisenfeld, Director of Graduate Studies, 919-684-2224, Fax: 919-684-4398, E-mail: gennifer.weisenfeld@duke.edu. *Application contact:* Thomas Steffen, Director of Admissions, 919-684-3913, E-mail: grad-admissions@duke.edu.

East Tennessee State University, School of Graduate Studies, College of Arts and Sciences, Department of Art and Design, Johnson City, TN 37614. Offers art education (MA); art history (MA); studio art (MA, MFA). *Accreditation:* NASAD. *Degree requirements:* For master's, thesis, exhibit, oral exam (MFA). *Entrance requirements:* For master's, GRE General Test, portfolio (MFA), bachelor's degree in art, minimum GPA of 3.0. Additional exam requirements/recommendations for international students: Required—TOEFL (minimum score 550 paper-based; 213 computer-based). *Faculty research:* History of sculpture, art and senior citizens, encaustic paintings, digital media in art history.

Emory University, Graduate School of Arts and Sciences, Department of Art History, Atlanta, GA 30322-1100. Offers PhD. *Degree requirements:* For doctorate, 2 foreign languages, comprehensive exam, thesis/dissertation, oral exam. *Entrance requirements:* For doctorate, GRE General Test. Electronic applications accepted.

Fashion Institute of Technology, School of Graduate Studies, Program in Art Market: Principles and Practices, New York, NY 10001-5992. Offers MA. *Accreditation:* NASAD. *Degree requirements:* For master's, one foreign language, thesis, internship. *Entrance requirements:* For master's, GRE General Test, previous course work in art history, 4 semesters of a foreign language. Additional exam requirements/recommendations for international students: Required—TOEFL (minimum score 550 paper-based; 213 computer-based). Electronic applications accepted. *Expenses:* Tuition, state resident: full-time $8198; part-time $342 per credit. Tuition, nonresident: full-time $12,972; part-time $541 per credit. Required fees: $450.

See Close-Up on page 115.

Florida State University, The Graduate School, College of Visual Arts, Theatre and Dance, Department of Art History, Tallahassee, FL 32306. Offers art history (MA, PhD); museum studies (Certificate). *Accreditation:* NASAD. Part-time programs available. *Faculty:* 10 full-time (5 women), 2 part-time/adjunct (both women). *Students:* 31 full-time (24 women), 15 part-time (12 women); includes 3 minority (1 African American, 1 Asian American or Pacific Islander, 1 Hispanic American). Average age 33. 67 applicants, 58% accepted, 19 enrolled. In 2009, 9 master's, 3 doctorates awarded. Terminal master's awarded for partial completion of doctoral program. *Degree requirements:* For master's, one foreign language, thesis (for some programs), review; for doctorate, 2 foreign languages, comprehensive exam, thesis/dissertation, review. *Entrance requirements:* For master's, GRE General Test, minimum GPA of 3.0; for doctorate, GRE General Test, minimum GPA of 3.5. Additional exam requirements/recommendations for international students: Required—TOEFL. *Application deadline:* For fall admission, 1/10 priority date for domestic and international students. Application fee: $30. Electronic applications accepted. *Expenses:* Tuition, state resident: full-time $7413. Tuition, nonresident: full-time $22,567. *Financial support:* In 2009–10, 27 students received support, including 1 fellowship with full tuition reimbursement available (averaging $18,000 per year), 21 research assistantships with full tuition reimbursements available (averaging $5,000 per year), 5 teaching assistantships with full tuition reimbursements available (averaging $14,000 per year); career-related internships or fieldwork, Federal Work-Study, institutionally sponsored loans, scholarships/grants, and unspecified assistantships also available. Financial award application deadline: 1/10; financial award applicants required to submit FAFSA. *Faculty research:* Modern art and critical theory; medieval, renaissance and Baroque art; Pre-Colombian. *Unit head:* Dr. Adam Jolles, Professor/Chair, 850-644-7066, Fax: 850-644-3259, E-mail: ajolles@fsu.edu. *Application contact:* Kathy Braun, Program Administrator/Graduate Advisor, 850-644-8201, Fax: 850-644-7065, E-mail: kbraun@fsu.edu.

George Mason University, College of Humanities and Social Sciences, Department of History and Art History, Program in Art History, Fairfax, VA 22030. Offers MA. *Faculty:* 49 full-time (19 women), 19 part-time/adjunct (10 women). *Students:* 4 full-time (3 women), 16 part-time (all women); includes 2 minority (both Hispanic Americans). Average age 32. 29 applicants, 69% accepted, 8 enrolled. In 2009, 2 master's awarded. *Degree requirements:* For master's, variable foreign language requirement, comprehensive exam, thesis optional. *Entrance requirements:* For master's, GRE, 2 letters of recommendation, resume. Additional exam requirements/recommendations for international students: Required—TOEFL. *Application deadline:* For fall admission, 4/15 priority date for domestic students; for spring admission, 11/1 for domestic students. Applications are processed on a rolling basis. Application fee: $75. Electronic applications accepted. *Expenses:* Tuition, state resident: full-time $7568; part-time $315.33 per credit hour. Tuition, nonresident: full-time $21,704; part-time $904.33 per credit hour. Required fees: $2184; $91 per credit hour. *Financial support:* In 2009–10, 1 student received support, including 1 teaching assistantship with full and partial tuition reimbursement available (averaging $2,520 per year); Federal Work-Study, scholarships/grants, unspecified assistantships, and health care benefits (full-time research or teaching assistantship recipients) also available. Support available to part-time students. Financial award application deadline: 3/1. *Faculty research:* Exhibit on Pompeii—ancient art, southeast Asia—history on Buddhist art, twentieth century Latin American interchange, Silk Road project, American art on visual imagery. Total annual research expenditures: $3.8 million. *Unit head:* Brian Platt, Graduate Director, 703-993-1250, E-mail: bplatt1@gmu.edu. *Application contact:* Mack Holt, Information Contact, 703-993-1259, E-mail: mholt@gmu.edu.

See Close-Up on page 193.

The George Washington University, Columbian College of Arts and Sciences, Department of Fine Arts and Art History, Program in Art History, Washington, DC 20052. Offers art history (MA); museum training (MA). Part-time and evening/weekend programs available. *Faculty:* 4 full-time (1 woman), 2 part-time/adjunct (0 women). *Students:* 16 full-time (15 women), 5 part-time (all women); includes 3 minority (1 Asian American or Pacific Islander, 2 Hispanic Americans). Average age 25. 70 applicants, 53% accepted, 12 enrolled. In 2009, 21 master's awarded. *Degree requirements:* For master's, one foreign language, comprehensive exam, thesis or alternative. *Entrance requirements:* For master's, GRE General Test, bachelor's degree in field, minimum GPA of 3.0. Additional exam requirements/recommendations for international students: Required—TOEFL (minimum score 550 paper-based; 213 computer-based; 80 iBT). *Application deadline:* For fall admission, 3/1 priority date for domestic students, 1/15 priority date for international students; for spring admission, 10/1 priority date for domestic students, 9/1 priority date for international students. Applications are processed on a rolling basis. Application fee: $60. Electronic applications accepted. *Financial support:* In 2009–10, 3 students received support; fellowships, teaching assistantships, career-related internships or fieldwork and Federal Work-Study available. Financial award application deadline: 1/15. *Application contact:* Information Contact, 202-994-6085, Fax: 202-994-8657, E-mail: art@gwu.edu.

Georgia State University, College of Arts and Sciences, Ernest G. Welch School of Art and Design, Program in Art History, Atlanta, GA 30302-3083. Offers MA. *Accreditation:* NASAD. *Degree requirements:* For master's, one foreign language, comprehensive exam, thesis. *Entrance requirements:* For master's, GRE General Test, writing sample. Additional exam requirements/recommendations for international students: Required—TOEFL (minimum score 550 paper-based; 213 computer-based). Electronic applications accepted. *Faculty research:* Latin American art, contemporary art, Egypt/Near East art, African American art, 19th/20th century art.

Graduate School and University Center of the City University of New York, Graduate Studies, Program in Art History, New York, NY 10016-4039. Offers architecture (PhD); graphic arts (PhD); painting (PhD); photography (PhD); sculpture (PhD). *Faculty:* 16 full-time (11 women). *Students:* 177 full-time (143 women), 10 part-time (all women); includes 14 minority (3 African Americans, 2 Asian Americans or Pacific Islanders, 9 Hispanic Americans), 18 international. Average age 34. 82 applicants, 54% accepted, 23 enrolled. In 2009, 9 doctorates awarded. *Degree requirements:* For doctorate, 2 foreign languages, thesis/dissertation. *Entrance requirements:* For doctorate, GRE General Test. Additional exam requirements/recommendations for international students: Required—TOEFL. *Application deadline:* For fall admission, 4/15 for domestic students; for spring admission, 11/15 for domestic students. Application fee: $125. Electronic applications accepted. *Financial support:* In 2009–10, 91 students received support, including 70 fellowships, 4 research assistantships, 12 teaching assistantships; career-related internships or fieldwork, Federal Work-Study, institutionally sponsored loans, and tuition waivers (full and partial) also available. Financial award application deadline: 2/1; financial award applicants required to submit FAFSA. *Unit head:* Dr. Kevin Murphy, Executive Officer, 212-817-8035, Fax: 212-817-1502, E-mail: kmurphy@gc.cuny.edu. *Application contact:* Les Gribben, Director of Admissions, 212-817-7470, Fax: 212-817-1624, E-mail: lgribben@gc.cuny.edu.

Graduate Theological Union, Graduate Programs, Berkeley, CA 94709-1212. Offers art and religion (MA, PhD, Th D); biblical languages (MA); Biblical studies (PhD, Th D); biblical studies (MA); Buddhist studies (MA); Christian spirituality (MA, PhD, Th D); cultural and historical studies of religions (MA, PhD, Th D); ethics and social theory (PhD, Th D); history (MA, PhD, Th D); homiletics (MA, PhD, Th D); interdisciplinary studies (PhD, Th D); Jewish studies (MA, PhD, Th D, Certificate); liturgical studies (MA, PhD, Th D); Near Eastern religions (PhD, Th D); Orthodox Christian studies (MA); religion and psychology (MA, PhD, Th D); religion and society/ethics and social theory (MA); systematic and philosophical theology (MA, PhD, Th D). *Accreditation:* ATS. Terminal master's awarded for partial completion of doctoral program. *Degree requirements:* For master's, one foreign language, thesis; for doctorate, one foreign language, comprehensive exam, thesis/dissertation. *Entrance requirements:* For master's, GRE General Test; for doctorate, GRE General Test, MA or M Div. Additional exam requirements/recommendations for international students: Required—TOEFL. Electronic applications accepted.

Harvard University, Graduate School of Arts and Sciences, Department of History of Art and Architecture, Cambridge, MA 02138. Offers ancient art (PhD); ancient Near Eastern art (PhD); baroque art (PhD); Byzantine art (PhD); classical art (PhD); Indian art (PhD); Islamic art (PhD); Japanese and Chinese art (PhD); medieval art (PhD); modern art (PhD); Renaissance and modern architecture (PhD); Renaissance art (PhD). *Degree requirements:* For doctorate, variable foreign language requirement, thesis/dissertation, general exams; reading exams in French, German, and Italian. *Entrance requirements:* For doctorate, GRE General Test. Additional exam requirements/recommendations for international students: Required—TOEFL. *Expenses:* Tuition: Full-time $33,696. Required fees: $1126. Full-time tuition and fees vary according to program.

Howard University, Graduate School, Division of Fine Arts, Department of Art, Program in Art History, Washington, DC 20059-0002. Offers art history (MA); history of art and visual culture (MA). *Accreditation:* NASAD. Part-time programs available. *Degree requirements:* For master's, comprehensive exam, thesis. *Entrance requirements:* For master's, GRE General Test, minimum GPA of 3.0, BA in art history or related field, portfolio.

Hunter College of the City University of New York, Graduate School, School of Arts and Sciences, Department of Art, Program in Art History, New York, NY 10021-5085. Offers MA. Part-time and evening/weekend programs available. *Faculty:* 11 full-time (6 women). *Students:* 116 part-time (102 women); includes 10 minority (2 African Americans, 8 Hispanic Americans). Average age 32. 117 applicants, 54% accepted, 28 enrolled. In 2009, 21 master's awarded. *Degree requirements:* For master's, one foreign language, comprehensive exam, thesis. *Entrance requirements:* For master's, GRE General Test, minimum 12 credits of course work in art history, reading knowledge of a foreign language (Italian, French or German), 2 letters of recommendation. Additional exam requirements/recommendations for international students: Required—TOEFL. *Application deadline:* For fall admission, 3/1 for domestic students; for spring admission, 10/1 for domestic students. Application fee: $125. *Expenses:* Tuition, state resident: full-time $7360; part-time $310 per credit. Required fees: $250 per semester. *Financial support:* Teaching assistantships, career-related internships or fieldwork, Federal Work-Study, scholarships/grants, and tuition waivers (partial) available. Support available to part-time students. Financial award application deadline: 4/15. *Faculty research:* Islamic art, Renaissance and Baroque, Impressionism, critical theory, Modernism. *Unit head:* Dr. Richard Stapleford, Graduate Adviser, 212-650-5052, E-mail: grad.arthisotryadvisor@hunter.cuny.edu. *Application contact:* William Zlata, Director for Graduate Admissions, 212-772-4482, Fax: 212-650-3336, E-mail: admissions@hunter.cuny.edu.

Illinois State University, Graduate School, College of Fine Arts, School of Art, Normal, IL 61790-2200. Offers art history (MA, MS); ceramics (MFA, MS); drawing (MFA, MS); fibers (MFA, MS); glass (MFA, MS); graphic design (MFA, MS); metals (MFA, MS); painting (MFA, MS); photography (MFA, MS); printmaking (MFA, MS); sculpture (MFA, MS). *Accreditation:* NASAD (one or more programs are accredited). *Degree requirements:* For master's, thesis or alternative, internship. *Entrance requirements:* For master's, portfolio, sample of scholarly writing. *Faculty research:* General operations support: Normal Editions Workshop for FY2007.

Indiana University Bloomington, University Graduate School, College of Arts and Sciences, Henry Radford Hope School of Fine Arts, Department of the History of Art, Bloomington, IN 47405-7000. Offers MA, PhD. *Accreditation:* NASAD. *Faculty:* 11 full-time (7 women), 1 (woman) part-time/adjunct. *Students:* 63 full-time (52 women); includes 1 minority (African

American), 6 international. Average age 31. 59 applicants, 47% accepted, 14 enrolled. In 2009, 6 master's, 4 doctorates awarded. Terminal master's awarded for partial completion of doctoral program. *Degree requirements:* For master's, one foreign language, thesis; for doctorate, 2 foreign languages, comprehensive exam, thesis/dissertation. *Entrance requirements:* For master's, GRE, writing sample, 3 letters of recommendation; for doctorate, GRE, transcript, writing samples, 3 letters of recommendation. Additional exam requirements/recommendations for international students: Required—TOEFL (minimum score 550 paper-based; 213 computer-based). *Application deadline:* For fall admission, 10/15 for domestic students; for winter admission, 12/1 for international students; for spring admission, 1/15 for domestic students. Application fee: $55 ($65 for international students). Electronic applications accepted. *Financial support:* Fellowships with full tuition reimbursements, research assistantships with full tuition reimbursements, teaching assistantships with tuition reimbursements, career-related internships or fieldwork and Federal Work-Study available. Financial award application deadline: 2/15. *Faculty research:* Art and social history, consumer culture, feminist art and theory, classical revivals. *Unit head:* Patrick McNaughton, Chair, 812-855-4924, Fax: 812-855-7498, E-mail: mcnaught@indiana.edu. *Application contact:* Fenella Jean Alice Flinn, Administrative Assistant, 812-855-9556, Fax: 812-855-7498, E-mail: fflinn@indiana.edu.

James Madison University, The Graduate School, College of Visual and Performing Arts, School of Art and Art History, Harrisonburg, VA 22807. Offers art education (MA); art history (MA); ceramics (MFA); drawing/painting (MFA); metal/jewelry (MFA); photography (MFA); printmaking (MFA); sculpture (MFA); studio art (MA); weaving/fibers (MFA). *Accreditation:* NASAD. Part-time programs available. *Faculty:* 11 full-time (6 women), 1 (woman) part-time/adjunct. *Students:* 10 full-time (8 women); includes 1 minority (African American). Average age 27. In 2009, 4 master's awarded. *Degree requirements:* For master's, thesis (for some programs). *Entrance requirements:* For master's, GRE General Test, language exam in French or German, portfolio, 3 letters of recommendation, research paper. Additional exam requirements/recommendations for international students: Required—TOEFL. *Application deadline:* For fall admission, 2/15 priority date for domestic students, 2/15 for international students; for spring admission, 10/15 priority date for domestic students, 10/15 for international students. Applications are processed on a rolling basis. Application fee: $55. Electronic applications accepted. *Expenses:* Tuition, area resident: Part-time $305 per credit hour. Tuition, state resident: part-time $305 per credit hour. Tuition, nonresident: part-time $890 per credit hour. *Financial support:* In 2009–10, 8 students received support, including 3 teaching assistantships with full tuition reimbursements available (averaging $8,664 per year); Federal Work-Study also available. Financial award application deadline: 3/1; financial award applicants required to submit FAFSA. *Unit head:* Leslie M. Bellavance, Academic Unit Head, 540-568-6216. *Application contact:* Lynette M. Bible, Director of Graduate Admissions, 540-568-6395, Fax: 540-568-7860, E-mail: biblelm@jmu.edu.

The Johns Hopkins University, Zanvyl Krieger School of Arts and Sciences, Department of History of Art, Baltimore, MD 21218. Offers MA, PhD. *Faculty:* 6 full-time (1 woman), 1 part-time/adjunct (0 women). *Students:* 16 full-time (12 women), 4 international. Average age 28. 67 applicants, 6% accepted, 4 enrolled. In 2009, 2 master's, 2 doctorates awarded. Terminal master's awarded for partial completion of doctoral program. *Degree requirements:* For master's, 2 foreign languages; for doctorate, 2 foreign languages, thesis/dissertation. *Entrance requirements:* For master's and doctorate, GRE General Test. Additional exam requirements/recommendations for international students: Required—TOEFL (minimum score 600 paper-based; 250 computer-based; 100 iBT), IELTS. *Application deadline:* For fall admission, 1/16 for domestic and international students. Application fee: $75. Electronic applications accepted. *Financial support:* In 2009–10, 14 students received support, including 6 fellowships with full tuition reimbursements available (averaging $17,500 per year), 4 research assistantships with full tuition reimbursements available (averaging $17,500 per year), 4 teaching assistantships with full tuition reimbursements available (averaging $17,500 per year). Financial award application deadline: 4/15; financial award applicants required to submit FAFSA. *Faculty research:* Modern art, Renaissance art, Medieval art, Roman art. *Unit head:* Dr. Stephen Campbell, Chair, 410-516-4928, Fax: 410-516-5188, E-mail: stephen.campbell@jhu.edu. *Application contact:* Sally Hauf, Graduate Administrative Coordinator, 410-516-7117, Fax: 410-516-5188, E-mail: arthist@jhu.edu.

Kent State University, College of the Arts, School of Art, Kent, OH 44242-0001. Offers art education (MA); art history (MA); crafts (MA, MFA), including ceramics (MA), glass, jewelry/metals, textiles/art; fine art (MA, MFA), including drawing/painting, printmaking, sculpture. *Accreditation:* NASAD (one or more programs are accredited). *Degree requirements:* For master's, one foreign language, thesis. *Entrance requirements:* For master's, undergraduate degree in proposed area of study (for fine arts and crafts programs); minimum overall GPA of 2.75 (3.0 for art major); 3 letters of recommendation; portfolio (15-20 slides for MA, 20-25 for MFA). Additional exam requirements/recommendations for international students: Required—TOEFL. Electronic applications accepted.

Lamar University, College of Graduate Studies, College of Fine Arts and Communication, Department of Art, Beaumont, TX 77710. Offers art history (MA); photography (MA); studio art (MA); visual design (MA). Part-time and evening/weekend programs available. *Faculty:* 6 full-time (3 women). *Students:* 3 full-time (1 woman), 1 (woman) part-time. Average age 45. 5 applicants, 60% accepted, 3 enrolled. *Degree requirements:* For master's, thesis. *Entrance requirements:* For master's, GRE General Test, minimum GPA of 2.5 in last 60 hours of undergraduate course work. Additional exam requirements/recommendations for international students: Required—TOEFL. *Application deadline:* For fall admission, 8/1 priority date for domestic students; for spring admission, 12/1 for domestic students. Applications are processed on a rolling basis. Application fee: $25 ($50 for international students). *Financial support:* Fellowships, career-related internships or fieldwork, Federal Work-Study, and scholarships/grants available. Financial award application deadline: 4/1. *Faculty research:* Nineteenth century academic paintings, metal casting, pigment color stability, computer-modified photography, manipulated photography. *Unit head:* Donna M. Meeks, Chair, 409-880-8141, Fax: 409-880-1799, E-mail: meeksdm@lub002.lamar.edu. *Application contact:* Debbie Piper, Coordinator of Graduate Admissions, 409-880-8356, Fax: 409-880-8414, E-mail: gradmissions@hal.lamar.edu.

Lancaster Theological Seminary, Graduate and Professional Programs, Lancaster, PA 17603-2812. Offers biblical studies (MAR); Christian education (MAR); Christianity and the arts (MAR); church history (MAR); congregational life (MAR); lay leadership (Certificate); theological studies (M Div); theology (D Min); theology and ethics (MAR). *Accreditation:* ACIPE; ATS. *Faculty:* 11 full-time (4 women), 13 part-time/adjunct (9 women). *Students:* 91 full-time (48 women), 42 part-time (33 women). *Degree requirements:* For doctorate, thesis/dissertation; for M Div, one foreign language. *Application deadline:* For fall admission, 4/1 priority date for domestic students, 1/1 for international students; for spring admission, 11/15 priority date for domestic students. Applications are processed on a rolling basis. Application fee: $50. *Expenses:* Tuition: Full-time $12,600; part-time $490 per credit. Required fees: $125 per semester. One-time fee: $3000. Tuition and fees vary according to program and student level. *Financial support:* Career-related internships or fieldwork, scholarships/grants, and tuition waivers (partial) available. Financial award application deadline: 4/15; financial award applicants required to submit FAFSA. *Unit head:* Dr. Edwin D. Aponte, Vice President of Academic Affairs and Dean of the Seminary, 717-290-8754, Fax: 717-393-0423, E-mail: eaponte@lancasterseminary.edu. *Application contact:* Virginia Whitaker-Brooks, Assistant Director of Recruitment and Admissions, 717-290-8741, Fax: 717-393-0423.

Louisiana State University and Agricultural and Mechanical College, Graduate School, College of Art and Design, School of Art, Program in Art History, Baton Rouge, LA 70803. Offers MA. *Accreditation:* NASAD. *Students:* 9 full-time (8 women), 4 part-time (3 women). Average age 29. 10 applicants, 80% accepted. In 2009, 7 master's awarded. *Degree requirements:* For master's, one foreign language, thesis. *Entrance requirements:* For master's, GRE General Test, minimum GPA of 3.0. Additional exam requirements/recommendations for international students: Required—TOEFL (minimum score 550 paper-based; 213 computer-based; 79 iBT), IELTS (minimum score 6.5). *Application deadline:* For fall admission, 1/25 priority date for domestic students, 5/15 for international students; for spring admission, 10/15 for international students. Applications are processed on a rolling basis. Application fee: $50 ($70 for international students). Electronic applications accepted. *Financial support:* In 2009–10, 2 students received support; research assistantships with partial tuition reimbursements available, teaching assistantships with partial tuition reimbursements available, career-related internships or fieldwork, Federal Work-Study, institutionally sponsored loans, scholarships/grants, traineeships, health care benefits, and unspecified assistantships available. Support available to part-time students. Financial award application deadline: 3/15. *Faculty research:* Liturgical art, Greco-Roman art, Renaissance prints, American twentieth century art, performance art. *Unit head:* Dr. Susan Ryan, Coordinator, 225-578-5411, E-mail: faryan@lsu.edu. *Application contact:* Graduate Coordinator.

Massachusetts Institute of Technology, School of Architecture and Planning, Department of Architecture, Cambridge, MA 02139-4307. Offers architecture (M Arch, PhD), including building technology (PhD), design and computation (PhD), history and theory of architecture (PhD), history and theory of art (PhD); architecture studies (SM Arch S); building technology (SMBT); visual studies (SM Vis S). *Faculty:* 35 full-time (9 women). *Students:* 221 full-time (113 women); includes 34 minority (4 African Americans, 2 American Indian/Alaska Native, 21 Asian Americans or Pacific Islanders, 7 Hispanic Americans), 81 international. Average age 28. 1,011 applicants, 14% accepted, 75 enrolled. In 2009, 71 master's, 12 doctorates awarded. *Degree requirements:* For master's, thesis; for doctorate, comprehensive exam, thesis/dissertation. *Entrance requirements:* For master's, GRE General Test (for some programs), portfolio (for some programs); for doctorate, GRE General Test (for some programs). Additional exam requirements/recommendations for international students: Required—TOEFL or IELTS. *Application deadline:* For fall admission, 12/15 for domestic and international students. Application fee: $75. Electronic applications accepted. *Expenses:* Tuition: Full-time $37,510; part-time $585 per unit. Required fees: $272. *Financial support:* In 2009–10, 211 students received support, including 153 fellowships with tuition reimbursements available (averaging $17,293 per year), 26 research assistantships with tuition reimbursements available (averaging $24,640 per year), 24 teaching assistantships with tuition reimbursements available (averaging $27,324 per year); career-related internships or fieldwork, Federal Work-Study, institutionally sponsored loans, scholarships/grants, health care benefits, and unspecified assistantships also available. *Faculty research:* Architecture and urbanism, building technology and sustainability, computation and design, history, contemporary visual art practice, theory, and criticism. Total annual research expenditures: $1.9 million. *Unit head:* Prof. Yung Ho Chang, Department Head, 617-253-7791, E-mail: arch@mit.edu. *Application contact:* Admissions Coordinator, 617-253-7387, Fax: 617-253-8993, E-mail: arch@mit.edu.

McGill University, Faculty of Graduate and Postdoctoral Studies, Faculty of Arts, Department of Art History and Communication Studies, Montréal, QC H3A 2T5, Canada. Offers MA, PhD.

Montclair State University, The Graduate School, School of the Arts, Department of Art and Design, Montclair, NJ 07043-1624. Offers art education (MA, Certificate); art history (MA); studio arts (MA, MFA). *Accreditation:* NASAD (one or more programs are accredited). Part-time and evening/weekend programs available. *Faculty:* 26 full-time (11 women), 4 part-time/adjunct (2 women). *Students:* 30 full-time (19 women), 29 part-time (24 women). Average age 32. 53 applicants, 58% accepted, 20 enrolled. In 2009, 22 master's awarded. *Degree requirements:* For master's, project. *Entrance requirements:* For master's, GRE General Test or MAT (MA), portfolio, undergraduate degree in fine arts or equivalent, 2 letters of recommendation, teaching certificate (art education). Additional exam requirements/recommendations for international students: Required—TOEFL (minimum score 83 computer-based), or IELTS. *Application deadline:* For fall admission, 2/1 for domestic and international students. Applications are processed on a rolling basis. Application fee: $60. Electronic applications accepted. *Expenses:* Tuition, area resident: Part-time $486.74 per credit. Tuition, state resident: part-time $486.74 per credit. Tuition, nonresident: part-time $751.34 per credit. Tuition and fees vary according to degree level and program. *Financial support:* In 2009–10, 7 research assistantships with full tuition reimbursements (averaging $7,000 per year) were awarded; Federal Work-Study, scholarships/grants, and unspecified assistantships also available. Support available to part-time students. Financial award application deadline: 3/1; financial award applicants required to submit FAFSA. *Unit head:* Dr. Scott Gordley, Chairperson, 973-655-7295. *Application contact:* Amy Aiello, Director of Graduate Admissions and Operations, 973-655-5147, E-mail: graduate.school@montclair.edu.

New Mexico State University, Graduate School, College of Arts and Sciences, Department of Art, Las Cruces, NM 88003-8001. Offers art history (MA); ceramics (MA, MFA); design (MA, MFA); drawing (MFA); metals (MA, MFA); painting (MFA); photography (MFA); printmaking (MA, MFA); sculpture (MA, MFA). *Faculty:* 11 full-time (6 women), 2 part-time/adjunct (1 woman). *Students:* 32 full-time (15 women); includes 8 minority (2 American Indian/Alaska Native, 6 Hispanic Americans). Average age 31. 33 applicants, 55% accepted, 7 enrolled. In 2009, 8 master's awarded. *Degree requirements:* For master's, comprehensive exam (for some programs), thesis, thesis exhibit. *Entrance requirements:* For master's, portfolio, 10-page paper (art history). *Application deadline:* For fall admission, 2/15 for domestic students; for winter admission, 10/15 for domestic students; for spring admission, 7/15 for domestic students. Application fee: $30 ($50 for international students). Electronic applications accepted. *Expenses:* Tuition, state resident: full-time $4080; part-time $223 per credit. Tuition, nonresident: full-time $14,256; part-time $647 per credit. Required fees: $1278; $639 per semester. *Financial support:* In 2009–10, 1 research assistantship (averaging $7,900 per year), 29 teaching assistantships (averaging $9,092 per year) were awarded; Federal Work-Study and health care benefits also available. Support available to part-time students. Financial award application deadline: 3/1; financial award applicants required to submit FAFSA. *Faculty research:* Painting, graphic design, sculpture, printmaking, drawing, ceramics, photography, jewelry. *Unit head:* Spencer D. Fidler, Head, 575-646-1705, Fax: 575-646-8036, E-mail: sfidler@nmsu.edu. *Application contact:* Spencer D. Fidler, Head, 575-646-1705, Fax: 575-646-8036, E-mail: sfidler@nmsu.edu.

New York University, Graduate School of Arts and Science, Institute of Fine Arts, Program in Art History and Archaeology, New York, NY 10012-1019. Offers architectural studies (PhD); art history and archaeology (MA, PhD); classical art and archaeology (PhD); curatorial studies (PhD); East and South Asian art (PhD); Near Eastern art and archaeology (PhD); MA/Diploma; PhD/Certificate. Part-time programs available. *Students:* 193 full-time (151 women), 86 part-time (70 women); includes 23 minority (16 Asian Americans or Pacific Islanders, 7 Hispanic Americans), 26 international. Average age 32. 318 applicants, 28% accepted, 39 enrolled. In 2009, 38 master's, 18 doctorates awarded. Terminal master's awarded for partial completion of doctoral program. *Degree requirements:* For master's, 2 foreign languages, thesis or alternative, 2 qualifying papers; for doctorate, 2 foreign languages, thesis/dissertation. *Entrance requirements:* For master's, GRE General Test; for doctorate, GRE General Test, MA. Additional exam requirements/recommendations for international students: Required—TOEFL. *Application deadline:* For fall admission, 12/18 for domestic students. Application fee: $90. *Expenses:* Tuition: Full-time $30,528; part-time $1272 per credit. Required fees: $2177. *Financial support:* Fellowships with tuition reimbursements, research assistantships with tuition reimbursements, teaching assistantships with tuition reimbursements, career-related internships or fieldwork, Federal Work-Study, and institutionally sponsored loans available. Financial award application deadline: 12/18; financial award applicants required to submit FAFSA. *Unit head:* Patricia Rubin, Chair, 212-992-5800, Fax: 212-992-5807, E-mail: ifa.program@nyu.edu. *Application contact:* Priscilla Saucek, Director of Graduate Studies, 212-992-5800, Fax: 212-992-5807, E-mail: ifa.program@nyu.edu.

Northwestern University, The Graduate School, Judd A. and Marjorie Weinberg College of Arts and Sciences, Department of Art History, Evanston, IL 60208. Offers PhD. Admissions and degrees offered through The Graduate School. *Degree requirements:* For doctorate, 2 foreign languages, comprehensive exam, thesis/dissertation, major and minor field exercises. *Entrance requirements:* For doctorate, GRE General Test. Additional exam requirements/

Art History

Northwestern University (continued)
recommendations for international students: Required—TOEFL. Electronic applications accepted. *Faculty research:* Modern American and European art and architecture, prehistoric and ancient art, central Asian art, medieval manuscripts and early printed books, history of museums, art of Western Africa, theory of culture.

The Ohio State University, Graduate School, College of the Arts, Department of History of Art, Columbus, OH 43210. Offers MA, PhD. *Accreditation:* NASAD. *Faculty:* 20. *Students:* 27 full-time (19 women), 15 part-time (12 women); includes 4 minority (3 Asian Americans or Pacific Islanders, 1 Hispanic American), 8 international. Average age 33. In 2009, 7 master's, 2 doctorates awarded. *Degree requirements:* For master's, one foreign language, thesis optional; for doctorate, 2 foreign languages, thesis/dissertation. *Entrance requirements:* For master's and doctorate, GRE General Test. Additional exam requirements/recommendations for international students: Recommended—TOEFL (minimum score 600 paper-based; 250 computer-based). *Application deadline:* For fall admission, 8/15 priority date for domestic students, 7/1 priority date for international students; for winter admission, 12/1 priority date for domestic students, 11/1 priority date for international students; for spring admission, 3/1 priority date for domestic students, 2/1 priority date for international students. Applications are processed on a rolling basis. Application fee: $40 ($50 for international students). Electronic applications accepted. *Expenses:* Tuition, state resident: full-time $10,683. Tuition, nonresident: full-time $25,923. Tuition and fees vary according to course load and program. *Financial support:* Fellowships, teaching assistantships, Federal Work-Study and institutionally sponsored loans available. Support available to part-time students. *Faculty research:* Western and Oriental art, African art and archaeology. *Unit head:* Judy Andrews, Graduate Studies Committee Chair, E-mail: andrews.2@osu.edu. *Application contact:* 614-688-9444, Fax: 614-292-3895, E-mail: domestic.grad@osu.edu.

Ohio University, Graduate College, College of Fine Arts, School of Art, Athens, OH 45701-2979. Offers art history (MA); ceramics (MFA); graphic design (MFA); painting (MFA); photography (MFA); printmaking (MFA); sculpture (MFA). Part-time programs available. *Faculty:* 30 full-time (16 women), 7 part-time/adjunct (3 women). *Students:* 53 full-time (30 women), 4 part-time (all women); includes 3 minority (2 Asian Americans or Pacific Islanders, 1 Hispanic American), 4 international. 150 applicants, 33% accepted, 28 enrolled. In 2009, 22 master's awarded. *Degree requirements:* For master's, thesis. *Entrance requirements:* For master's, portfolio. Additional exam requirements/recommendations for international students: Required—TOEFL (minimum score 550 paper-based; 80 iBT) or IELTS Academic (minimum score 6.5). *Application deadline:* For fall admission, 2/1 for domestic and international students. Application fee: $50 ($55 for international students). Electronic applications accepted. *Expenses:* Tuition, state resident: full-time $7839; part-time $323 per quarter hour. Tuition, nonresident: full-time $15,831; part-time $654 per quarter hour. Required fees: $2931. *Financial support:* Teaching assistantships with full and partial tuition reimbursements, career-related internships or fieldwork, Federal Work-Study, institutionally sponsored loans, scholarships/grants, tuition waivers (partial), and unspecified assistantships available. Financial award application deadline: 2/1. *Faculty research:* Vapor fired ceramics, video installation, art theory, digital photography, mixed and interdisciplinary media work. *Unit head:* David LaPalombara, Director, 740-593-4290, Fax: 740-593-0457, E-mail: lapalomb@ohio.edu. *Application contact:* Rosemarie Basile, Chair, Graduate Programs, 740-593-4281, Fax: 740-593-0457, E-mail: basile@ohio.edu.

Penn State University Park, Graduate School, College of Arts and Architecture, Department of Art History, State College, University Park, PA 16802-1503. Offers MA, PhD.

Pratt Institute, School of Art and Design, Program in Art History, Brooklyn, NY 11205-3899. Offers art history (MS); art history theory and criticism (MS); MS/MFA; MS/MS. *Accreditation:* NASAD. Part-time programs available. *Faculty:* 5 full-time (3 women), 12 part-time/adjunct (7 women). *Students:* 37 full-time (29 women), 4 part-time (3 women); includes 8 minority (4 African Americans, 2 Asian Americans or Pacific Islanders, 2 Hispanic Americans), 1 international. Average age 27. 77 applicants, 69% accepted, 17 enrolled. In 2009, 15 master's awarded. *Degree requirements:* For master's, one foreign language, thesis. *Entrance requirements:* For master's, GRE General Test, letters of recommendation, portfolio. Additional exam requirements/recommendations for international students: Required—TOEFL (minimum score 600 paper-based; 250 computer-based; 100 iBT). *Application deadline:* For fall admission, 1/5 for domestic and international students; for spring admission, 10/1 for domestic and international students. Application fee: $50 ($90 for international students). Electronic applications accepted. *Expenses:* Tuition: Full-time $22,734. Required fees: $1280. *Financial support:* Career-related internships or fieldwork, Federal Work-Study, institutionally sponsored loans, scholarships/grants, health care benefits, and unspecified assistantships available. Support available to part-time students. Financial award application deadline: 2/1; financial award applicants required to submit CSS PROFILE or FAFSA. *Faculty research:* Conservation techniques, women artists from previous centuries, art of sixteenth century Veneto, design history, nineteenth century Germany. *Unit head:* Edward DeCarbo, Chairperson, 718-636-3598, E-mail: edecarbo@pratt.edu. *Application contact:* Young Hah, Director of Graduate Admissions, 718-636-3683, Fax: 718-399-4242, E-mail: yhah@pratt.edu.

See Close-Up on page 119.

Purchase College, State University of New York, Division of Humanities, Purchase, NY 10577-1400. Offers art history (MA). *Accreditation:* NASAD. *Degree requirements:* For master's, one foreign language, thesis. *Entrance requirements:* For master's, BA or BFA, previous course work in art history. *Expenses:* Tuition, state resident: full-time $8370; part-time $349 per credit. Tuition, nonresident: full-time $13,250; part-time $552 per credit. Required fees: $1515; $62.11 per credit. One-time fee: $144 full-time. Tuition and fees vary according to program.

Queens College of the City University of New York, Division of Graduate Studies, Arts and Humanities Division, Department of Art, Program in Art History, Flushing, NY 11367-1597. Offers MA. Part-time and evening/weekend programs available. *Faculty:* 6 full-time (3 women). *Students:* 1 (woman) full-time, 20 part-time (16 women). 14 applicants, 71% accepted, 4 enrolled. In 2009, 3 master's awarded. *Degree requirements:* For master's, 2 foreign languages, thesis, qualifying exam. *Entrance requirements:* For master's, minimum GPA of 3.0. Additional exam requirements/recommendations for international students: Required—TOEFL. *Application deadline:* For fall admission, 4/1 for domestic students; for spring admission, 11/1 for domestic students. Applications are processed on a rolling basis. Application fee: $125. *Expenses:* Tuition, state resident: full-time $7360; part-time $310 per credit. Tuition, nonresident: part-time $575 per credit. One-time fee: $195.25 full-time; $145.25 part-time. *Financial support:* Career-related internships or fieldwork, Federal Work-Study, institutionally sponsored loans, and tuition waivers (partial) available. Support available to part-time students. Financial award application deadline: 4/1; financial award applicants required to submit FAFSA. *Unit head:* Dr. Barbara Lane, Head, 718-997-4820. *Application contact:* Mario Caruso, Director of Graduate Admissions, 718-997-5200, Fax: 718-997-5193, E-mail: graduate_admissions@qc.edu.

Rice University, Graduate Programs, School of Humanities, Department of Art History, Houston, TX 77251-1892. Offers PhD.

Richmond, The American International University in London, MA in Art History Program, Richmond, United Kingdom. Offers MA. Part-time programs available. *Faculty:* 1 full-time (0 women), 6 part-time/adjunct (3 women). *Students:* 10 full-time (9 women). Average age 24. 24 applicants, 83% accepted, 8 enrolled. In 2009, 8 master's awarded. *Degree requirements:* For master's, thesis. *Entrance requirements:* For master's, minimum GPA of 3.0. Additional exam requirements/recommendations for international students: Required—TOEFL, IELTS. *Application deadline:* For fall admission, 3/31 priority date for domestic and international students. Application fee: $50. Electronic applications accepted. *Expenses:* Contact institution. *Financial support:* Career-related internships or fieldwork, scholarships/grants, and tuition waivers (partial) available. Support available to part-time students. Financial award application deadline: 6/30; financial award applicants required to submit FAFSA. *Faculty research:* Archaeology of art and representation, contemporary paganisms, nineteenth century modernisms, American twentieth century art, sound media. *Unit head:* Dr. Robert Wallis, Associate Director, 44-208-332-9000, Fax: 44-208-332-1596, E-mail: ma@richmond.ac.uk. *Application contact:* Mark Kopenski, Vice President and Dean of Enrollment, 44-208-332-9000, Fax: 44-208-332-1596, E-mail: ma@richmond.ac.uk.

Rutgers, The State University of New Jersey, New Brunswick, Graduate School-New Brunswick, Program in Art History, Piscataway, NJ 08854-8097. Offers art history (MA, PhD); curatorial studies (Certificate); historic preservation (Certificate). Part-time programs available. *Degree requirements:* Terminal master's awarded for partial completion of doctoral program. *Degree requirements:* For master's, one foreign language, comprehensive exam; for doctorate, 2 foreign languages, comprehensive exam, thesis/dissertation. *Entrance requirements:* For master's and doctorate, GRE General Test, writing sample. Additional exam requirements/recommendations for international students: Required—TOEFL (minimum score 550 paper-based; 213 computer-based). Electronic applications accepted. *Faculty research:* Ancient and medieval art and architecture; Renaissance and Baroque art and architecture; modern and contemporary art and architecture; Italian studies; the arts of Asia, Africa, and the Americas.

San Diego State University, Graduate and Research Affairs, College of Professional Studies and Fine Arts, School of Art, Design and Art History, San Diego, CA 92182. Offers art history (MA); studio arts (MA, MFA), including applied design, environmental design, graphic design, interior design, painting and printmaking, sculpture. *Accreditation:* NASAD (one or more programs are accredited). *Degree requirements:* For master's, variable foreign language requirement, thesis. *Entrance requirements:* For master's, GRE General Test, bachelor's degree in related field, slide portfolio, typed slide information sheet, 2 letters of recommendation. Additional exam requirements/recommendations for international students: Required—TOEFL. Electronic applications accepted.

San Francisco Art Institute, Graduate Program, Department of History and Theory of Contemporary Art, San Francisco, CA 94133. Offers MA. *Entrance requirements:* Additional exam requirements/recommendations for international students: Required—TOEFL (minimum score 580 paper-based; 237 computer-based).

San Francisco State University, Division of Graduate Studies, College of Creative Arts, Department of Art, San Francisco, CA 94132-1722. Offers art (MFA); art history (MA). *Accreditation:* NASAD (one or more programs are accredited).

San Jose State University, Graduate Studies and Research, College of Humanities and the Arts, School of Art and Design, San Jose, CA 95192-0001. Offers animation/illustration (MA); art history (MA); digital media arts (MFA); photography (MFA); pictorial arts (MFA); spatial arts (MFA). *Accreditation:* NASAD (one or more programs are accredited). *Students:* 48 full-time (27 women), 24 part-time (16 women); includes 13 minority (3 African Americans, 6 Asian Americans or Pacific Islanders, 4 Hispanic Americans), 2 international. Average age 36. 69 applicants, 23% accepted, 16 enrolled. In 2009, 17 master's awarded. *Entrance requirements:* For master's, GRE. *Application deadline:* For fall admission, 6/29 for domestic students; for spring admission, 11/30 for domestic students. Applications are processed on a rolling basis. Application fee: $59. Electronic applications accepted. *Financial support:* Applicants required to submit FAFSA. *Unit head:* John Loomis, Director, 408-924-4320, Fax: 408-924-4326. *Application contact:* John Loomis, Director, 408-924-4320, Fax: 408-924-4326.

Savannah College of Art and Design, Graduate School, Program in Art History, Savannah, GA 31402-3146. Offers MA, MFA. Part-time programs available. *Degree requirements:* For master's, one foreign language, comprehensive exam, thesis, internship. *Entrance requirements:* For master's, art history paper, interview. Additional exam requirements/recommendations for international students: Required—TOEFL (minimum score 550 paper-based; 213 computer-based). Electronic applications accepted. *Expenses:* Tuition: Full-time $28,515; part-time $627 per credit hour. One-time fee: $500. Tuition and fees vary according to course load. *Faculty research:* Contemporary art.

School of the Art Institute of Chicago, Graduate Division, Program in Modern Art History, Theory, and Criticism, Chicago, IL 60603-3103. Offers MA, Certificate. *Accreditation:* NASAD. *Entrance requirements:* For master's, GRE. Additional exam requirements/recommendations for international students: Required—TOEFL, IELTS.

Southern Methodist University, Meadows School of the Arts, Division of Art History, Dallas, TX 75275. Offers MA. Part-time and evening/weekend programs available. *Faculty:* 8 full-time (4 women), 1 (woman) part-time/adjunct. *Students:* 12 full-time (10 women), 7 part-time (all women); includes 6 minority (1 African American, 5 Hispanic Americans), 1 international. Average age 29. 32 applicants, 25% accepted, 6 enrolled. In 2009, 4 master's awarded. *Degree requirements:* For master's, one foreign language, thesis, translation exam. *Entrance requirements:* For master's, GRE, 12 upper-level hours in art history, sample research paper. Additional exam requirements/recommendations for international students: Required—TOEFL (minimum score 550 paper-based; 213 computer-based; 80 iBT). *Application deadline:* For fall admission, 2/15 priority date for domestic and international students; for spring admission, 11/1 for domestic and international students. Application fee: $75. *Financial support:* In 2009–10, 13 students received support, including 13 teaching assistantships (averaging $3,500 per year); scholarships/grants and unspecified assistantships also available. Financial award application deadline: 3/1; financial award applicants required to submit FAFSA. *Faculty research:* American art, nineteenth and twentieth century art, classical and Byzantine art, Hispanic art, Mesoamerican art, Renaissance-Baroque. *Unit head:* Dr. Janice Bergman-Carton, Chair, 214-768-2615, E-mail: jbergman@smu.edu. *Application contact:* Joe S. Hoselton, Graduate Admissions and Records Coordinator, 214-768-3765, Fax: 214-768-3272, E-mail: hoselton@smu.edu.

State University of New York at Binghamton, Graduate School, School of Arts and Sciences, Department of Art History, Binghamton, NY 13902-6000. Offers MA, PhD. *Faculty:* 8 full-time (4 women), 2 part-time/adjunct (0 women). *Students:* 14 full-time (12 women), 22 part-time (15 women); includes 4 minority (2 Asian Americans or Pacific Islanders, 2 Hispanic Americans), 19 international. Average age 34. 33 applicants, 52% accepted, 5 enrolled. In 2009, 2 master's, 4 doctorates awarded. *Degree requirements:* For master's, one foreign language, comprehensive exam, thesis; for doctorate, 2 foreign languages, comprehensive exam, thesis/dissertation, oral exam. *Entrance requirements:* For master's and doctorate, GRE General Test, writing sample. Additional exam requirements/recommendations for international students: Required—TOEFL. *Application deadline:* For fall admission, 1/15 priority date for domestic and international students; for spring admission, 10/1 priority date for domestic and international students. Applications are processed on a rolling basis. Application fee: $60. Electronic applications accepted. *Financial support:* In 2009–10, 18 students received support, including 3 fellowships with full tuition reimbursements available (averaging $14,500 per year), 1 research assistantship with full tuition reimbursement available (averaging $14,500 per year), 13 teaching assistantships with full tuition reimbursements available (averaging $14,500 per year); career-related internships or fieldwork, Federal Work-Study, institutionally sponsored loans, scholarships/grants, health care benefits, and unspecified assistantships also available. Financial award application deadline: 2/15; financial award applicants required to submit FAFSA. *Faculty research:* History of art and architecture. *Unit head:* Dr. John Tagg, Professor and Chair, 607-777-2112, Fax: 607-777-4466, E-mail: jtagg@binghamton.edu. *Application contact:* 607-777-2112, Fax: 607-777-4466.

Stony Brook University, State University of New York, Graduate School, College of Arts and Sciences, Department of Art, Program in Art History and Criticism, Stony Brook, NY 11794. Offers MA, PhD. Part-time programs available. *Students:* 42 full-time (34 women), 4 part-time (2 women); includes 7 minority (3 African Americans, 1 American Indian/Alaska Native, 1 Asian American or Pacific Islander, 3 Hispanic Americans), 7 international. Average age 30. 67 applicants, 43% accepted. In 2009, 7 master's awarded. *Degree requirements:* For master's, comprehensive exam, thesis, reading knowledge of German or French; for doctorate, comprehensive exam, thesis/dissertation, qualifying paper, reading knowledge of German and French, qualifying examination. *Entrance requirements:* For master's, GRE General Test, minimum undergraduate GPA of 3.0; for doctorate, GRE General Test, minimum graduate GPA of 3.0. Additional exam requirements/recommendations for international students: Required—TOEFL (minimum score 550 paper-based; 213 computer-based), IELTS (minimum score 6.5). *Application deadline:* For fall admission, 1/15 for domestic students. Application fee: $60. *Expenses:* Tuition, state resident: full-time $8370; part-time $349 per credit. Tuition, nonresident: full-time $13,250; part-time $552 per credit. Required fees: $933. *Unit head:* Dr. Joseph Monteyne, Director, 631-632-7264, E-mail: jmonteyne@notes.cc.sunysb.edu. *Application contact:* Dr. Michele Bogart, Director, 631-632-7270.

Sul Ross State University, School of Arts and Sciences, Department of Fine Arts and Communication, Alpine, TX 79832. Offers art education (M Ed); art history (M Ed); studio art (M Ed), including ceramics, design, drawing, jewelry, painting, printmaking, sculpture, weaving. Part-time programs available. *Degree requirements:* For master's, oral or written exam. *Entrance requirements:* For master's, GRE General Test, minimum GPA of 2.5 in last 60 hours of undergraduate work. *Faculty research:* Ceramic sculpture, watercolor, wood sculpture, rock art.

Syracuse University, College of Arts and Sciences, Program in Art History, Syracuse, NY 13244. Offers MA. *Students:* 24 full-time (21 women), 1 part-time (0 women). Average age 25. 55 applicants, 69% accepted, 12 enrolled. In 2009, 13 master's awarded. *Degree requirements:* For master's, one foreign language, symposium presentation. *Entrance requirements:* For master's, GRE, research writing sample; second language. Additional exam requirements/recommendations for international students: Required—TOEFL (minimum score 100 iBT). *Application deadline:* For fall admission, 1/1 priority date for domestic and international students. Application fee: $75. *Expenses:* Tuition: Full-time $26,808; part-time $1117 per credit. Required fees: $1024. *Financial support:* In 2009–10, 4 fellowships were awarded; teaching assistantships. Financial award application deadline: 1/1; financial award applicants required to submit FAFSA. *Unit head:* Prof. Laurinda Dixon, Director, 315-443-4184. *Application contact:* Linda Straub, Information Contact, 315-443-4185, E-mail: ljstraub@syr.edu.

Temple University, Graduate School, Tyler School of Art, Department of Art History, Philadelphia, PA 19122-6096. Offers MA, PhD. Part-time programs available. Terminal master's awarded for partial completion of doctoral program. *Degree requirements:* For master's, 2 foreign languages, thesis, comprehensive slide exam; for doctorate, thesis/dissertation, qualifying exam. *Entrance requirements:* For master's, GRE General Test, minimum GPA of 3.0; for doctorate, MA in art history. Additional exam requirements/recommendations for international students: Required—TOEFL. Electronic applications accepted. *Faculty research:* Aegean, Greek, and Roman art; early Christian art; Medieval art and architecture; Renaissance and baroque painting, sculpture, and architecture; nineteenth and twentieth century painting and sculpture.

Texas A&M University–Commerce, Graduate School, College of Arts and Sciences, Department of Art, Commerce, TX 75429-3011. Offers art (MA, MS); art history (MA); fine arts (MFA); studio art (MA). Part-time programs available. *Degree requirements:* For master's, comprehensive exam, thesis (for some programs). *Entrance requirements:* For master's, GRE General Test. Electronic applications accepted. *Faculty research:* Use of different art media.

Texas Christian University, College of Fine Arts, Department of Art and Art History, Fort Worth, TX 76129. Offers art history (MA); studio art (MFA). *Accreditation:* NASAD. Part-time programs available. *Degree requirements:* For master's, thesis, internship, foreign language exam. *Entrance requirements:* For master's, GRE General Test, writing sample. Additional exam requirements/recommendations for international students: Required—TOEFL. *Application deadline:* For fall admission, 3/15 for domestic students. Applications are processed on a rolling basis. Application fee: $0. *Expenses:* Tuition: Full-time $17,640; part-time $980 per credit hour. Tuition and fees vary according to program. *Financial support:* Unspecified assistantships available. Financial award application deadline: 3/1. *Unit head:* Ron Watson, Chairperson, 817-257-7643, E-mail: r.watson@tcu.edu. *Application contact:* Dr. Joseph Butler, Associate Dean, College of Fine Arts, E-mail: j.butler@tcu.edu.

Tufts University, Graduate School of Arts and Sciences, Department of Art and Art History, Program in Art History, Medford, MA 02155. Offers MA. Part-time programs available. *Faculty:* 12 full-time, 2 part-time/adjunct. *Students:* 21 (19 women); includes 2 minority (both Hispanic Americans), 1 international. Average age 26. 95 applicants, 25% accepted, 11 enrolled. In 2009, 12 master's awarded. *Degree requirements:* For master's, one foreign language, thesis (for some programs). *Entrance requirements:* For master's, GRE General Test, previous course work in art history, writing sample. Additional exam requirements/recommendations for international students: Required—TOEFL (minimum score 550 paper-based; 213 computer-based; 80 iBT). *Application deadline:* For fall admission, 1/15 for domestic students, 12/15 for international students. Applications are processed on a rolling basis. Application fee: $75. Electronic applications accepted. *Expenses:* Tuition: Full-time $38,096; part-time $3962 per credit. Required fees: $686; $40 per year. Tuition and fees vary according to course level, course load, degree level, program and student level. *Financial support:* Teaching assistantships, Federal Work-Study, scholarships/grants, tuition waivers (partial), and unspecified assistantships available. Financial award application deadline: 1/15; financial award applicants required to submit FAFSA. *Unit head:* Daniel Abramson, Chair, 617-627-3567, Fax: 617-627-3890. *Application contact:* Daniel Abramson, Chair, 617-627-3567, Fax: 617-627-3890.

Tulane University, School of Liberal Arts, Department of Art, Program in Art History, New Orleans, LA 70118-5669. Offers MA. *Degree requirements:* For master's, one foreign language, thesis. *Entrance requirements:* For master's, GRE General Test, minimum B average in undergraduate course work. Additional exam requirements/recommendations for international students: Required—TOEFL. Electronic applications accepted.

Université de Montréal, Faculty of Arts and Sciences, Department of Art History and Film Studies, Montréal, QC H3C 3J7, Canada. Offers art history (MA, PhD); film studies (MA, PhD). *Degree requirements:* For master's, thesis. Electronic applications accepted. *Faculty research:* Western art from the Middle Ages, classic and modern theory, modern and contemporary art, Canadian art.

Université du Québec à Montréal, Graduate Programs, Program in Art Studies, Montréal, QC H3C 3P8, Canada. Offers art history (PhD); art studies (MA); study and practices of the arts (PhD). Part-time programs available. *Degree requirements:* For master's, thesis; for doctorate, thesis/dissertation. *Entrance requirements:* For master's, appropriate bachelor's degree or equivalent, proficiency in French; for doctorate, appropriate master's degree or equivalent, proficiency in French.

Université Laval, Faculty of Letters, Department of History, Programs in Art History, Québec, QC G1K 7P4, Canada. Offers MA, PhD. Terminal master's awarded for partial completion of doctoral program. *Degree requirements:* For master's, thesis; for doctorate, comprehensive exam, thesis/dissertation. *Entrance requirements:* For master's, English test (comprehension of written English), knowledge of French; for doctorate, English test (comprehension of written English), knowledge of French and English, knowledge of a third language. Electronic applications accepted.

University at Buffalo, the State University of New York, Graduate School, College of Arts and Sciences, Department of Visual Studies, Program in Art History, Buffalo, NY 14260. Offers art history (MA); critical museum studies (Certificate). Part-time programs available. *Degree requirements:* For master's, one foreign language, thesis, field exam. *Entrance requirements:* Additional exam requirements/recommendations for international students: Required—TOEFL (minimum score 79 iBT). Electronic applications accepted. *Faculty research:* Frank Lloyd Wright, non-Western art, Renaissance, Bronze Age Crete, American art.

The University of Alabama, Graduate School, College of Arts and Sciences, Department of Art, Tuscaloosa, AL 35487. Offers art history (MA); studio art (MA, MFA), including ceramics, painting, photography, printmaking, sculpture. *Accreditation:* NASAD. Part-time programs available. *Faculty:* 16 full-time (8 women), 1 part-time/adjunct (0 women). *Students:* 17 full-time (10 women), 4 part-time (all women); includes 1 minority (Asian American or Pacific Islander), 1 international. Average age 31. 31 applicants, 39% accepted, 7 enrolled. In 2009, 1 degree awarded. *Degree requirements:* For master's, one foreign language, comprehensive exam (for some programs), oral exam, thesis statement, exhibit (studio art), thesis (art history). *Entrance requirements:* For master's, GRE General Test or MAT (art history), minimum GPA of 3.0, BFA or equivalent (studio art). Additional exam requirements/recommendations for international students: Required—TOEFL (minimum score 550 paper-based; 213 computer-based). *Application deadline:* For fall admission, 3/15 for domestic and international students; for spring admission, 10/15 for domestic and international students. Applications are processed on a rolling basis. Application fee: $50 ($60 for international students). Electronic applications accepted. *Expenses:* Tuition, state resident: full-time $7000. Tuition, nonresident: full-time $19,200. *Financial support:* In 2009–10, 2 fellowships with full tuition reimbursements (averaging $14,000 per year), 13 teaching assistantships with full and partial tuition reimbursements (averaging $9,206 per year) were awarded; career-related internships or fieldwork, institutionally sponsored loans, scholarships/grants, and unspecified assistantships also available. Financial award application deadline: 7/14. *Faculty research:* Nineteenth century American art history, Chinese art history, Baroque art history, twentieth century art history, Asian art history. *Unit head:* William T. Dooley, Chairperson, 205-348-1890, Fax: 205-348-0287, E-mail: wtdooley@bama.ua.edu. *Application contact:* Craig R. Wedderspoon, Graduate Coordinator, 205-348-1898, Fax: 205-348-0287, E-mail: cwedders@bama.edu.

The University of Alabama at Birmingham, College of Arts and Sciences, Program in Art History, Birmingham, AL 35294. Offers MA. *Accreditation:* NASAD. *Degree requirements:* For master's, one foreign language, comprehensive exam, thesis optional. *Entrance requirements:* For master's, GRE General Test or MAT, minimum GPA of 2.75. Electronic applications accepted.

University of Alberta, Faculty of Graduate Studies and Research, Department of Art and Design, Edmonton, AB T6G 2E1, Canada. Offers drawing (MFA); history of art, design, and visual culture (MA); industrial design (M Des); painting (MFA); printmaking (MFA); sculpture (MFA); visual communication design (M Des). *Faculty:* 19 full-time (7 women). *Students:* 28 full-time (16 women), 12 part-time (8 women). Average age 25. 66 applicants, 26% accepted, 12 enrolled. In 2009, 10 master's awarded. *Degree requirements:* For master's, thesis. *Entrance requirements:* For master's, portfolio (MFA and MDES). Additional exam requirements/recommendations for international students: Required—TOEFL (minimum score 550 paper-based; 213 computer-based). *Application deadline:* For fall admission, 2/1 for domestic and international students. Application fee: $0. Tuition and fees charges are reported in Canadian dollars. *Expenses:* Tuition, area resident: Full-time $4626 Canadian dollars; part-time $99.72 Canadian dollars per unit. International tuition: $8216 Canadian dollars full-time. Required fees: $3590 Canadian dollars; $99.72 Canadian dollars per unit. $215 Canadian dollars per term. *Financial support:* In 2009–10, 29 students received support, including 5 research assistantships (averaging $3,300 per year), 13 teaching assistantships (averaging $8,100 per year); scholarships/grants and unspecified assistantships also available. Financial award application deadline: 2/1. *Unit head:* Dr. Liz Ingram, Acting Chair, 780-492-3261, Fax: 780-492-7870. *Application contact:* Sharon Orescan, Administrative Assistant, 780-492-5712, Fax: 780-492-7870, E-mail: artdes@ualberta.ca.

The University of Arizona, Graduate College, College of Fine Arts, School of Art, Program in Art History, Tucson, AZ 85721. Offers art history (MA); history and theory of art (PhD). *Accreditation:* NASAD. Part-time programs available. *Students:* 11 full-time (10 women), 5 part-time (4 women); includes 2 minority (1 Asian American or Pacific Islander, 1 Hispanic American). Average age 30. 32 applicants, 59% accepted, 11 enrolled. In 2009, 6 master's awarded. Terminal master's awarded for partial completion of doctoral program. *Degree requirements:* For master's, one foreign language, thesis; for doctorate, 2 foreign languages, comprehensive exam, thesis/dissertation. *Entrance requirements:* For master's, GRE, 3 letters of recommendation, resume or curriculum vitae, writing sample; for doctorate, GRE, 3 letters of recommendation, statement of purpose, resume or curriculum vitae, writing sample. Additional exam requirements/recommendations for international students: Required—TOEFL (minimum score 550 paper-based; 213 computer-based; 79 iBT). *Application deadline:* For fall admission, 2/1 for domestic students, 12/1 for international students; for spring admission, 10/1 for domestic students, 9/1 for international students. Application fee: $75. Electronic applications accepted. *Expenses:* Tuition, state resident: full-time $9028. Tuition, nonresident: full-time $24,890. *Financial support:* Career-related internships or fieldwork, Federal Work-Study, institutionally sponsored loans, scholarships/grants, tuition waivers (full and partial), and unspecified assistantships available. Support available to part-time students. Financial award application deadline: 4/1; financial award applicants required to submit FAFSA. *Faculty research:* American art, history of photography, Mexican art, contemporary African art. *Application contact:* Megan Bartel, Graduate Program Coordinator, 520-621-8518, Fax: 520-621-2955, E-mail: mbartel@email.arizona.edu.

University of Arkansas at Little Rock, Graduate School, College of Arts, Humanities, and Social Science, Department of Art, Little Rock, AR 72204-1099. Offers art education (MA); art history (MA); studio art (MA). *Accreditation:* NASAD. Part-time programs available. *Degree requirements:* For master's, 4 foreign languages, oral exam, oral defense of thesis or exhibit. *Entrance requirements:* For master's, portfolio review or term paper evaluation, minimum GPA of 2.7.

The University of British Columbia, Faculty of Arts and Faculty of Graduate Studies, Department of Art History, Visual Art, and Theory, Vancouver, BC V6T1Z2, Canada. Offers art history (MA, PhD, Diploma); critical and curatorial studies (MA); visual art (MFA). *Degree requirements:* For master's, one foreign language, thesis, final exhibition (MFA, MA in critical and curatorial studies); for doctorate, 2 foreign languages, comprehensive exam, thesis/dissertation. *Entrance requirements:* For master's, bachelor's degree with minimum B+ average (MFA, MA in critical and curatorial studies), A- (MA in art history); for doctorate, master's degree with minimum A- average. Additional exam requirements/recommendations for international students: Required—TOEFL (minimum score 600 paper-based; 250 computer-based). Electronic applications accepted. *Faculty research:* Conceptual art, Asian art, indigenous North American art, post-second war art, eighteenth and nineteenth century art, curatorial, digital art.

University of California, Berkeley, Graduate Division, College of Letters and Science, Department of History of Art, Berkeley, CA 94720-1500. Offers PhD. *Students:* 57 full-time (44 women). Average age 32. 146 applicants, 8 enrolled. In 2009, 10 doctorates awarded. *Degree requirements:* For doctorate, 2 foreign languages, thesis/dissertation, qualifying exam. *Entrance requirements:* For doctorate, GRE General Test, minimum GPA of 3.0, 3 letters of recommendation. Additional exam requirements/recommendations for international students: Required—TOEFL. *Application deadline:* For fall admission, 12/15 for domestic students. Application fee: $70 ($90 for international students). *Financial support:* Fellowships, research assistantships, teaching assistantships, career-related internships or fieldwork, Federal Work-Study, institutionally sponsored loans, tuition waivers (full and partial), and unspecified assistantships available. Financial award applicants required to submit FAFSA. *Faculty research:* Modernism, Italian Renaissance art and architecture, Gothic art and architecture, women artists' representations of the body, the body in ancient Greece. *Unit head:* Prof. Christopher Hallett, Chair, 510-643-7290, Fax: 510-643-2185, E-mail: ch_arthistory@ls.berkeley.edu. *Application contact:* Anna Kathleen Gazdowicz, Graduate Student Affairs Officer, 510-642-5510, Fax: 540-643-2185, E-mail: arthist_grad@berkeley.edu.

University of California, Davis, Graduate Studies, Program in Art History, Davis, CA 95616. Offers MA. *Degree requirements:* For master's, thesis. *Entrance requirements:* For master's, GRE, minimum GPA of 3.0, writing sample. Additional exam requirements/recommendations

Art History

University of California, Davis (continued)

for international students: Required—TOEFL (minimum score 550 paper-based; 213 computer-based). Electronic applications accepted.

University of California, Irvine, Office of Graduate Studies, School of Humanities, Department of Art History, Irvine, CA 92697. Offers visual studies (MA, PhD). *Students:* 41 full-time (25 women), 1 (woman) part-time; includes 5 minority (1 Asian American or Pacific Islander, 4 Hispanic Americans), 2 international. Average age 31. 91 applicants, 11% accepted, 6 enrolled. In 2009, 5 master's, 5 doctorates awarded. *Degree requirements:* For doctorate, thesis/dissertation. *Entrance requirements:* For master's, GRE, minimum GPA of 3.0; for doctorate, GRE General Test, writing sample. Additional exam requirements/recommendations for international students: Required—TOEFL (minimum score 550 paper-based; 213 computer-based). *Application deadline:* For fall admission, 12/15 for domestic and international students. Application fee: $70 ($90 for international students). Electronic applications accepted. *Financial support:* Fellowships, teaching assistantships, institutionally sponsored loans, traineeships, health care benefits, and unspecified assistantships available. Financial award application deadline: 3/1; financial award applicants required to submit FAFSA. *Faculty research:* Interdisciplinary study and research in art history, critical theory, women's studies, cultural studies, film studies. *Unit head:* James D. Herbert, Chair, 949-824-4014, E-mail: jdherb@uci.edu. *Application contact:* Jewel Wilson, Manager, 949-824-6635, Fax: 949-824-2509, E-mail: jtwilson@uci.edu.

University of California, Los Angeles, Graduate Division, College of Letters and Science, Department of Art History, Los Angeles, CA 90095. Offers MA, PhD. *Students:* 49 full-time (39 women); includes 9 minority (all Asian Americans or Pacific Islanders), 5 international. Average age 31. 93 applicants, 13% accepted, 6 enrolled. In 2009, 8 master's, 13 doctorates awarded. Terminal master's awarded for partial completion of doctoral program. *Degree requirements:* For master's, one foreign language, thesis; for doctorate, one foreign language, thesis/dissertation, oral and written qualifying exams. *Entrance requirements:* For doctorate, GRE General Test, 2 samples of research writing or thesis, minimum undergraduate GPA of 3.0, 3 letters of recommendation. *Application deadline:* For fall admission, 11/30 for domestic students. Application fee: $70 ($90 for international students). Electronic applications accepted. *Financial support:* In 2009–10, 47 fellowships with full and partial tuition reimbursements, 13 research assistantships with full and partial tuition reimbursements, 27 teaching assistantships with full and partial tuition reimbursements were awarded; Federal Work-Study, scholarships/grants, health care benefits, tuition waivers (full and partial), and unspecified assistantships also available. Financial award application deadline: 3/1; financial award applicants required to submit FAFSA. *Unit head:* Dr. Irene Bierman, Chair, 310-206-6905. *Application contact:* Department Office, 310-825-3480, E-mail: vjohnson@humnet.ucla.edu.

University of California, Riverside, Graduate Division, Department of Art History, Riverside, CA 92521-0102. Offers MA. Part-time programs available. *Faculty:* 8 full-time (4 women), 1 (woman) part-time/adjunct. *Students:* 19 full-time (18 women); includes 1 minority (Asian American or Pacific Islander). Average age 29. 38 applicants, 32% accepted, 11 enrolled. In 2009, 6 master's awarded. *Degree requirements:* For master's, one foreign language, thesis. *Entrance requirements:* For master's, GRE General Test, sample of written work, minimum GPA of 3.2. Additional exam requirements/recommendations for international students: Required—TOEFL (minimum score 550 paper-based; 213 computer-based; 80 iBT). *Application deadline:* 1/5 for domestic and international students. Application fee: $70 ($85 for international students). Electronic applications accepted. *Financial support:* In 2009–10, 19 students received support, including fellowships with full and partial tuition reimbursements available (averaging $12,000 per year), teaching assistantships with full tuition reimbursements available (averaging $16,500 per year); research assistantships with partial tuition reimbursements available, career-related internships or fieldwork, institutionally sponsored loans, scholarships/grants, tuition waivers (full and partial), and readerships also available. Financial award application deadline: 1/5; financial award applicants required to submit FAFSA. *Faculty research:* Ancient, medieval, Renaissance, seventeenth and eighteenth century art; modern European art; contemporary art and theory; modern architecture and urbanism; history of photography. *Unit head:* Dr. Malcolm Baker, Chair, 951-827-4634, Fax: 951-827-2331, E-mail: arthist@ucr.edu. *Application contact:* Dr. Elizabeth Kotz, Graduate Advisor, 951-827-4634, Fax: 951-827-2331, E-mail: arthist@ucr.edu.

University of California, Santa Barbara, Graduate Division, College of Letters and Sciences, Division of Humanities and Fine Arts, Department of History of Art and Architecture, Santa Barbara, CA 93106-7080. Offers PhD, MA/PhD. *Faculty:* 18 full-time (8 women), 2 part-time/adjunct (1 woman). *Students:* 38 full-time (34 women). Average age 30. 71 applicants, 25% accepted, 8 enrolled. In 2009, 2 doctorates awarded. Terminal master's awarded for partial completion of doctoral program. *Degree requirements:* For doctorate, 2 foreign languages, comprehensive exam, thesis/dissertation. *Entrance requirements:* For doctorate, GRE, writing sample, 3 letters of recommendation, resume/curriculum vitae. Additional exam requirements/recommendations for international students: Required—TOEFL (minimum score 550 paper-based; 213 computer-based; 80 iBT) or IELTS (minimum score 7). *Application deadline:* For fall admission, 12/15 priority date for domestic and international students. Application fee: $70 ($90 for international students). Electronic applications accepted. *Financial support:* In 2009–10, 36 students received support, including 23 fellowships with full and partial tuition reimbursements available (averaging $10,000 per year), 3 research assistantships with full and partial tuition reimbursements available (averaging $4,800 per year), 28 teaching assistantships with partial tuition reimbursements available (averaging $8,500 per year); career-related internships or fieldwork, Federal Work-Study, institutionally sponsored loans, scholarships/grants, health care benefits, and unspecified assistantships also available. Financial award application deadline: 3/2; financial award applicants required to submit FAFSA. *Faculty research:* Pre-Columbian art, Renaissance-Baroque art, architectural history, Japanese art, ancient-Medieval art. *Unit head:* Prof. Ulrich Keller, Chair, 805-893-8710. *Application contact:* Lesley Fredrickson, Graduate Program Administrator, 805-893-8710, Fax: 805-893-7117, E-mail: gd-arthist@arthistory.ucsb.edu.

University of Chicago, Division of the Humanities, Department of Art History, Chicago, IL 60637-1513. Offers AM, PhD. *Degree requirements:* For master's, variable foreign language requirement, thesis; for doctorate, variable foreign language requirement, thesis/dissertation. *Entrance requirements:* For master's and doctorate, GRE General Test.

University of Cincinnati, Graduate School, College of Design, Architecture, Art, and Planning, School of Art, Program in Art History, Cincinnati, OH 45221. Offers MA. *Accreditation:* NASAD. Part-time programs available. *Degree requirements:* For master's, one foreign language, comprehensive exam, thesis. Electronic applications accepted.

University of Colorado at Boulder, Graduate School, College of Arts and Sciences, Department of Art and Art History, Boulder, CO 80309. Offers art history (MA), including 19th century art, contemporary art criticism, early 20th century art, Russian and Soviet art; ceramics (MFA); drawing (MFA); painting (MFA); photography and media arts (MFA); printmaking (MFA); sculpture (MFA). *Faculty:* 28 full-time (13 women). *Students:* 42 full-time (25 women), 1 (woman) part-time; includes 9 minority (1 American Indian/Alaska Native, 3 Asian Americans or Pacific Islanders, 5 Hispanic Americans), 1 international. Average age 31. 224 applicants, 6% accepted, 14 enrolled. In 2009, 17 master's awarded. *Degree requirements:* For master's, variable foreign language requirement, comprehensive exam, thesis (for some programs). *Entrance requirements:* For master's, GRE General Test, minimum undergraduate GPA of 3.0, portfolio. *Application deadline:* For fall admission, 1/15 priority date for domestic students, 12/1 for international students. Application fee: $50 ($60 for international students). *Financial support:* In 2009–10, 6 fellowships (averaging $1,713 per year), 13 research assistantships (averaging $5,087 per year) were awarded; Federal Work-Study, scholarships/grants, and tuition waivers (full) also available. Financial award application deadline: 1/15. *Faculty research:* Drawing, painting, ceramics, sculpture, photography and media arts, printmaking, Russian and Soviet art, early twentieth century art, contemporary art criticism, nineteenth century art. Total annual research expenditures: $10,586.

University of Connecticut, Graduate School, School of Fine Arts, Department of Art and Art History, Field of Art History, Storrs, CT 06269. Offers MA. *Accreditation:* NASAD. *Faculty:* 18 full-time (11 women). *Students:* 7 full-time (all women), 1 international. Average age 25. 11 applicants, 36% accepted, 4 enrolled. In 2009, 4 master's awarded. *Degree requirements:* For master's, comprehensive exam. *Entrance requirements:* Additional exam requirements/recommendations for international students: Required—TOEFL (minimum score 550 paper-based; 213 computer-based). *Application deadline:* For fall admission, 2/1 priority date for domestic and international students; for spring admission, 11/1 for domestic students, 10/1 for international students. Applications are processed on a rolling basis. Application fee: $55. Electronic applications accepted. *Expenses:* Tuition, state resident: full-time $4725; part-time $525 per credit. Tuition, nonresident: full-time $12,267; part-time $1363 per credit. Required fees: $346 per semester. Tuition and fees vary according to course load. *Financial support:* In 2009–10, 7 research assistantships with full tuition reimbursements were awarded; teaching assistantships with full tuition reimbursements, Federal Work-Study, health care benefits, and unspecified assistantships also available. Financial award application deadline: 2/1; financial award applicants required to submit FAFSA. *Unit head:* Robin Greeley, Chairperson, 860-486-3365, E-mail: robin.greeley@uconn.edu. *Application contact:* Lorraine McConnell, Administrative Assistant, 860-486-8919, E-mail: lorraine.mcconnell@uconn.edu.

University of Delaware, College of Arts and Sciences, Department of Art History, Newark, DE 19716. Offers MA, PhD. Part-time programs available. *Degree requirements:* For master's, one foreign language, thesis; for doctorate, 2 foreign languages, comprehensive exam, thesis/dissertation. *Entrance requirements:* For master's and doctorate, GRE General Test, writing sample. Additional exam requirements/recommendations for international students: Required—TOEFL. Electronic applications accepted. *Faculty research:* Art of Europe and the United States, art theory, vernacular architecture, medieval manuscripts, African art and architecture.

University of Denver, Division of Arts, Humanities and Social Sciences, School of Art and Art History, Denver, CO 80208. Offers art history (MA); art history/museum studies (MA); electronic media arts and design (MFA). *Accreditation:* NASAD. Part-time programs available. *Faculty:* 16 full-time (11 women), 9 part-time/adjunct (5 women). *Students:* 15 full-time (14 women), 7 part-time (6 women); includes 1 minority (Hispanic American). Average age 29. 55 applicants, 51% accepted, 14 enrolled. In 2009, 10 master's awarded. *Degree requirements:* For master's, one foreign language, research paper. *Entrance requirements:* For master's, GRE. Additional exam requirements/recommendations for international students: Required—TOEFL. *Application deadline:* Applications are processed on a rolling basis. Application fee: $50. Electronic applications accepted. *Expenses:* Tuition: Full-time $34,596; part-time $961 per quarter hour. Required fees: $4 per quarter hour. Tuition and fees vary according to course load, campus/location and program. *Financial support:* Career-related internships or fieldwork, Federal Work-Study, institutionally sponsored loans, and scholarships/grants available. Support available to part-time students. Financial award application deadline: 3/1; financial award applicants required to submit FAFSA. *Faculty research:* Images of women in alchemical manuscripts and books, Giovanni Benedetto, Salvatore Castiglione. *Unit head:* Dr. Annette Stott, Director, 303-871-2846. *Application contact:* Dr. Annabeth Headrick, Graduate Advisor, 303-871-3574, E-mail: saah-interest@du.edu.

University of Florida, Graduate School, College of Fine Arts, School of Art and Art History, Gainesville, FL 32611. Offers art (MFA), including ceramics, creative photography, drawing, electronic intermedia, graphic design, painting, printmaking, sculpture; art education (MA); art history (MA, PhD); digital arts and sciences (MA); museology (museum studies) (MA). *Accreditation:* NASAD. *Degree requirements:* For master's, variable foreign language requirement, project or thesis (MFA). *Entrance requirements:* For master's, portfolio (MFA), writing sample (MA), GRE General Test or minimum GPA of 3.0. Additional exam requirements/recommendations for international students: Required—TOEFL (minimum score 550 paper-based; 213 computer-based). Electronic applications accepted. *Faculty research:* Studio production, art historical studies of style context.

University of Georgia, Graduate School, College of Arts and Sciences, Lamar Dodd School of Art, Program in Art History, Athens, GA 30602. Offers MA. *Accreditation:* NASAD. *Students:* 9 full-time (7 women), 2 part-time (1 woman). 27 applicants, 37% accepted, 3 enrolled. In 2009, 7 master's awarded. *Degree requirements:* For master's, one foreign language, thesis. *Entrance requirements:* For master's, GRE General Test. *Application deadline:* For fall admission, 7/1 priority date for domestic students; for spring admission, 11/15 for domestic students. Application fee: $50. Electronic applications accepted. *Expenses:* Tuition, state resident: full-time $6000; part-time $250 per credit hour. Tuition, nonresident: full-time $20,904; part-time $871 per credit hour. Required fees: $730 per semester. *Financial support:* Fellowships, research assistantships, teaching assistantships, unspecified assistantships available. *Unit head:* Prof. Georgia Strange, Director, 706-542-1600, Fax: 706-542-0226, E-mail: strange@uga.edu. *Application contact:* Dr. Janice Simon, Area Chair, 706-542-1579, Fax: 706-542-0226, E-mail: jsimon@uga.edu.

University of Hawaii at Manoa, Graduate Division, College of Arts and Humanities, Department of Art and Art History, Program in Art History, Honolulu, HI 96822. Offers MA. *Faculty:* 12 full-time (5 women), 13 part-time/adjunct (6 women). *Students:* 5 full-time (4 women), 1 part-time (0 women); includes 2 minority (both Asian Americans or Pacific Islanders), 1 international. Average age 29. 8 applicants, 63% accepted, 3 enrolled. In 2009, 2 master's awarded. *Expenses:* Tuition, state resident: full-time $8900; part-time $372 per credit. Tuition, nonresident: full-time $21,400; part-time $898 per credit. Required fees: $207 per semester. *Financial support:* In 2009–10, 1 fellowship (averaging $2,694 per year), 2 teaching assistantships (averaging $14,382 per year) were awarded. *Application contact:* Charles Cohan, Graduate Field Chairperson, 808-956-8251, Fax: 808-956-9043, E-mail: gradart@hawaii.edu.

University of Illinois at Chicago, Graduate College, College of Architecture and Art, Department of Art History, Chicago, IL 60607-7128. Offers MA, PhD. Part-time and evening/weekend programs available. Terminal master's awarded for partial completion of doctoral program. *Degree requirements:* For master's, one foreign language, thesis or alternative; for doctorate, thesis/dissertation. *Entrance requirements:* For master's, GRE General Test, minimum GPA of 2.75, 3 letters of recommendation; for doctorate, GRE General Test, M.A. in art history or equivalent, minimum GPA of 3.0. Additional exam requirements/recommendations for international students: Required—TOEFL. Electronic applications accepted. *Faculty research:* Modern painting and sculpture, history of architecture, city planning and design, history of photography.

University of Illinois at Urbana–Champaign, Graduate College, College of Fine and Applied Arts, School of Art and Design, Program in Art History, Champaign, IL 61820. Offers MA, PhD. *Accreditation:* NASAD. *Students:* 29 full-time (23 women), 2 part-time (0 women); includes 2 minority (both Asian Americans or Pacific Islanders), 6 international. 43 applicants, 7% accepted, 3 enrolled. In 2009, 9 master's, 3 doctorates awarded. *Entrance requirements:* For master's and doctorate, minimum GPA of 3.0. Additional exam requirements/recommendations for international students: Required—TOEFL (minimum score 550 paper-based; 213 computer-based; 79 iBT). *Application deadline:* Applications are processed on a rolling basis. Application fee: $60 ($75 for international students). Electronic applications accepted. *Financial support:* Fellowships, research assistantships, teaching assistantships, tuition waivers (full and partial) available. *Unit head:* Lisa Rosenthal, Chair, 217-265-5236, Fax: 217-244-7688, E-mail: lrosenth@illinois.edu. *Application contact:* Marsha Biddle, Coordinator of Graduate Academic Affairs, 217-333-0642, Fax: 217-244-7688, E-mail: mbiddle@illinois.edu.

The University of Iowa, Graduate College, College of Liberal Arts and Sciences, School of Art and Art History, Program in Art History, Iowa City, IA 52242-1316. Offers MA, PhD. *Faculty:* 11 full-time (5 women). *Students:* 13 full-time (7 women), 21 part-time (18 women); includes 2 minority (1 American Indian/Alaska Native, 1 Hispanic American), 1 international. Average age 29. 22 applicants, 59% accepted, 7 enrolled. In 2009, 2 master's, 6 doctorates awarded.

Degree requirements: For master's, one foreign language, thesis, exam; for doctorate, 2 foreign languages, comprehensive exam, thesis/dissertation, final exams. *Entrance requirements:* For master's, GRE General Test; for doctorate, GRE General Test, MA in art history. Additional exam requirements/recommendations for international students: Required—TOEFL (minimum score 550 paper-based; 213 computer-based; 81 iBT). *Application deadline:* For fall admission, 12/15 for domestic and international students. Application fee: $50 ($75 for international students). Electronic applications accepted. *Financial support:* In 2009–10, 18 students received support, including 15 fellowships with full and partial tuition reimbursements available (averaging $8,142 per year), 6 research assistantships with partial tuition reimbursements available (averaging $7,993 per year), 15 teaching assistantships with partial tuition reimbursements available (averaging $7,993 per year); career-related internships or fieldwork, Federal Work-Study, institutionally sponsored loans, scholarships/grants, health care benefits, and unspecified assistantships also available. Support available to part-time students. Financial award application deadline: 12/15. *Faculty research:* African (Oceanic), Asian, Ancient (3000 B.C.-300 A.D.), medieval, Renaissance, Baroque, eighteenth and nineteenth century European, American (includes Pre-Columbian, Native American, and African American), and Modern/Contemporary. Total annual research expenditures: $127,000. *Unit head:* Dr. Robert Bork, Division Head, 319-335-1762, Fax: 319-335-1774, E-mail: robert-bork@uiowa.edu. *Application contact:* Laura Jorgensen, Graduate Secretary, 319-335-1758, Fax: 319-335-1774, E-mail: art@uiowa.edu.

The University of Kansas, Graduate Studies, College of Liberal Arts and Sciences, History of Art Department, Lawrence, KS 66045. Offers MA, PhD. Part-time programs available. *Students:* 53 full-time (45 women), 4 part-time (3 women); includes 5 minority (1 American Indian/Alaska Native, 4 Asian Americans or Pacific Islanders), 12 international. Average age 34. 37 applicants, 57% accepted, 12 enrolled. In 2009, 8 master's, 6 doctorates awarded. Terminal master's awarded for partial completion of doctoral program. *Degree requirements:* For master's, one foreign language, comprehensive exam, thesis optional; for doctorate, 2 foreign languages, comprehensive exam, thesis/dissertation, 1 year full-time enrollment. *Entrance requirements:* For master's, GRE, minimum undergraduate GPA of 3.3, 18 credit hours of art history; for doctorate, GRE, MA in art history or related field. Additional exam requirements/recommendations for international students: Required—TOEFL, TWE (minimum score 4.5). *Application deadline:* For fall admission, 1/1 for domestic and international students; for spring admission, 10/15 for domestic and international students. Application fee: $45 ($55 for international students). Electronic applications accepted. *Expenses:* Tuition, state resident: full-time $6492; part-time $270.50 per credit hour. Tuition, nonresident: full-time $15,510; part-time $646.25 per credit hour. Required fees: $847; $70.56 per credit hour. Tuition and fees vary according to course load and program. *Financial support:* Fellowships with full tuition reimbursements, research assistantships with partial tuition reimbursements, teaching assistantships with full tuition reimbursements, scholarships/grants and unspecified assistantships available. Financial award application deadline: 1/1. *Faculty research:* American art, history of photography, African art, Asian art, European art, modern art. *Unit head:* Linda Stone-Ferrier, Chair, 785-864-4713, Fax: 785-864-5091, E-mail: lsf@ku.edu. *Application contact:* Karen Brichoux, Graduate Admissions, 785-864-4713, Fax: 785-864-5091, E-mail: arthist@ku.edu.

University of Kentucky, Graduate School, College of Fine Arts, Program in Art History, Lexington, KY 40506-0032. Offers MA. *Accreditation:* NASAD. *Degree requirements:* For master's, 2 foreign languages, comprehensive exam, thesis. *Entrance requirements:* For master's, GRE General Test, minimum undergraduate GPA of 2.75. Additional exam requirements/recommendations for international students: Required—TOEFL (minimum score 550 paper-based; 213 computer-based). Electronic applications accepted. *Faculty research:* Northern European prints and drawings, nineteenth century French painting and drawing, Roman sarcophagus sculpture, manuscript illumination, history and theory of photography.

University of Louisville, Graduate School, College of Arts and Sciences, Department of Fine Arts, Louisville, KY 40292. Offers art history (MA, PhD); creative art (MA); curatorial studies (MA). *Faculty:* 18 full-time (8 women), 3 part-time/adjunct (0 women). *Students:* 23 full-time (20 women), 13 part-time (9 women); includes 3 minority (2 African Americans, 1 Hispanic American), 2 international. Average age 38. 28 applicants, 54% accepted, 9 enrolled. In 2009, 9 master's awarded. *Degree requirements:* For master's, thesis; for doctorate, 2 foreign languages, comprehensive exam, thesis/dissertation. *Entrance requirements:* For master's and doctorate, GRE General Test. *Application deadline:* For fall admission, 1/15 for domestic and international students. Applications are processed on a rolling basis. Application fee: $50. *Financial support:* Teaching assistantships available. *Faculty research:* Art history in the periods from ancient to contemporary and various regions, 2D and 3D studio areas, intermedia, curatorial studies. *Unit head:* James T. Grubola, Chair, 502-852-0759, Fax: 502-852-6791, E-mail: grubola@louisville.edu. *Application contact:* Libby Leggett, Director, Graduate Admissions, 502-852-3101, Fax: 502-852-6536, E-mail: gradadm@louisville.edu.

University of Maryland, College Park, Academic Affairs, College of Arts and Humanities, Department of Art History and Archaeology, College Park, MD 20742. Offers art history (MA, PhD). *Faculty:* 13 full-time (7 women), 4 part-time/adjunct (3 women). *Students:* 43 full-time (35 women), 1 part-time (0 women); includes 8 minority (1 African American, 1 American Indian/Alaska Native, 6 Asian Americans or Pacific Islanders), 8 international. 101 applicants, 23% accepted, 6 enrolled. In 2009, 4 master's, 7 doctorates awarded. *Degree requirements:* For master's, one foreign language, thesis, oral exam; for doctorate, 2 foreign languages, thesis/dissertation, oral exam. *Entrance requirements:* For master's, GRE General Test, minimum GPA of 3.0, writing sample, 3 letters of recommendation. Additional exam requirements/recommendations for international students: Required—TOEFL. *Application deadline:* For fall admission, 12/10 for domestic students, 2/1 for international students. Applications are processed on a rolling basis. Application fee: $60. Electronic applications accepted. *Expenses:* Tuition, area resident: Part-time $471 per credit hour. Tuition, state resident: part-time $471 per credit hour. Tuition, nonresident: part-time $1016 per credit hour. Required fees: $337.04 per term. *Financial support:* In 2009–10, 7 fellowships with full and partial tuition reimbursements (averaging $16,986 per year), 27 teaching assistantships with tuition reimbursements (averaging $16,002 per year) were awarded; research assistantships, Federal Work-Study and scholarships/grants also available. Support available to part-time students. Financial award applicants required to submit FAFSA. *Faculty research:* Western, African, pre-Columbian, American, and East Asian art. Total annual research expenditures: $3,750. *Unit head:* Majorie Venit, Acting Chair, 301-405-1481, Fax: 301-314-9305, E-mail: venit@umd.edu. *Application contact:* Dean of Graduate School, 301-405-0376, Fax: 301-314-9305.

University of Massachusetts Amherst, Graduate School, College of Humanities and Fine Arts, Department of Art, Program in Art History, Amherst, MA 01003. Offers MA. Part-time programs available. *Students:* 14 full-time (11 women), 7 part-time (all women); includes 2 minority (1 African American, 1 Hispanic American). Average age 27. 33 applicants, 61% accepted, 12 enrolled. In 2009, 7 master's awarded. *Degree requirements:* For master's, thesis or alternative. *Entrance requirements:* For master's, GRE General Test, 7-20 page writing sample. Additional exam requirements/recommendations for international students: Required—TOEFL (minimum score 550 paper-based; 213 computer-based; 80 iBT), IELTS (minimum score 6.5). *Application deadline:* For fall admission, 1/15 for domestic and international students; for spring admission, 10/1 for domestic and international students. Applications are processed on a rolling basis. Application fee: $50 ($65 for international students). Electronic applications accepted. *Expenses:* Tuition, state resident: full-time $2640; part-time $110 per credit. Tuition, nonresident: full-time $9936; part-time $414 per credit. Tuition and fees vary according to course load. *Financial support:* In 2009–10, 4 fellowships with full tuition reimbursements (averaging $2,474 per year), 14 teaching assistantships with full tuition reimbursements (averaging $6,117 per year) were awarded; research assistantships, career-related internships or fieldwork, Federal Work-Study, scholarships/grants, traineeships, health care benefits, tuition waivers (full), and unspecified assistantships also available. Support available to part-time students. Financial award application deadline: 1/15. *Unit head:* Dr. Timothy Rohan, Graduate Program Director, 413-545-3595, Fax: 413-545-3880. *Application contact:* Jean M. Ames, Supervisor of Admissions, 413-545-0722, Fax: 413-577-0100, E-mail: gradadm@grad.umass.edu.

University of Memphis, Graduate School, College of Communication and Fine Arts, Department of Art, Memphis, TN 38152. Offers art (Graduate Certificate); art history (MA), including Egyptian art and archaeology, general art history; ceramics (MFA); graphic design (MFA); interior design (MFA); painting (MFA); printmaking/photography (MFA); sculpture (MFA). *Accreditation:* NASAD (one or more programs are accredited). *Faculty:* 20 full-time (7 women), 4 part-time/adjunct (2 women). *Students:* 39 full-time (26 women), 10 part-time (8 women); includes 4 African Americans, 1 Asian American or Pacific Islander, 1 international. Average age 29. 44 applicants, 77% accepted, 22 enrolled. In 2009, 16 master's, 5 other advanced degrees awarded. *Degree requirements:* For master's, 2 foreign languages, comprehensive exam, thesis. *Entrance requirements:* For master's, GRE General Test or MAT, portfolio (MFA). *Application deadline:* For fall admission, 8/1 for domestic students; for spring admission, 12/1 for domestic students. Applications are processed on a rolling basis. Application fee: $35 ($60 for international students). *Expenses:* Tuition, state resident: full-time $6246; part-time $347 per credit hour. Tuition, nonresident: full-time $15,894; part-time $883 per credit hour. Required fees: $1160. Full-time tuition and fees vary according to course load, degree level and program. *Financial support:* In 2009–10, 38 students received support; research assistantships with full tuition reimbursements available, teaching assistantships with full tuition reimbursements available, Federal Work-Study, scholarships/grants, and unspecified assistantships available. Financial award application deadline: 2/15; financial award applicants required to submit FAFSA. *Faculty research:* Online collaborative learning, advanced art history studies, electronic publishing/design, studio arts, architectural studies. *Unit head:* Prof. Richard Lou, Chair, 901-678-2216, Fax: 901-678-2735, E-mail: gmyatt@memphis.edu. *Application contact:* Greely Myat, Graduate Studies Coordinator, 901-678-2650.

University of Miami, Graduate School, College of Arts and Sciences, Department of Art and Art History, Coral Gables, FL 33124. Offers art history (MA); ceramics/glass (MFA); graphic design/multimedia (MFA); painting (MFA); photography/digital imaging (MFA); printmaking (MFA); sculpture (MFA). Part-time programs available. *Degree requirements:* For master's, variable foreign language requirement, thesis, exhibit (MFA), comprehensive exam (MA). *Entrance requirements:* For master's, GRE General Test (MA), research paper (MA), slide portfolio (MFA). Additional exam requirements/recommendations for international students: Required—TOEFL. Electronic applications accepted. *Faculty research:* Installation art, public art.

University of Michigan, Horace H. Rackham School of Graduate Studies, College of Literature, Science, and the Arts, Department of History of Art, Ann Arbor, MI 48109-1357. Offers PhD. *Faculty:* 18 full-time (10 women), 5 part-time/adjunct (2 women). *Students:* 35 full-time (33 women); includes 7 minority (5 Asian Americans or Pacific Islanders, 2 Hispanic Americans), 5 international. Average age 26. 92 applicants, 12% accepted, 6 enrolled. In 2009, 3 doctorates awarded. *Degree requirements:* For doctorate, 2 foreign languages, thesis/dissertation, preliminary examinations, oral defense of dissertation. *Entrance requirements:* For doctorate, GRE General Test. *Application deadline:* For fall admission, 12/12 for domestic and international students. Application fee: $65 ($75 for international students). Electronic applications accepted. *Expenses:* Tuition, state resident: full-time $17,286; part-time $1099 per credit hour. Tuition, nonresident: full-time $34,944; part-time $2080 per credit hour. Required fees: $95 per semester. Tuition and fees vary according to course load, degree level and program. *Financial support:* In 2009–10, 20 fellowships with full tuition reimbursements (averaging $18,000 per year), 1 research assistantship with full tuition reimbursement (averaging $18,000 per year), 13 teaching assistantships with full tuition reimbursements (averaging $18,000 per year) were awarded; career-related internships or fieldwork also available. Financial award application deadline: 1/1. *Faculty research:* Asian, African and African-American, ancient, medieval and Byzantine, early modern, and modern art. Total annual research expenditures: $25,000. *Unit head:* Celeste Brusati, Chair, 734-764-5400, Fax: 734-647-4121, E-mail: cbrusati@umich.edu. *Application contact:* Debbie L. Fitch, Student Services Coordinator, 734-764-5401, Fax: 734-647-4121, E-mail: dlfitch@umich.edu.

University of Michigan, Horace H. Rackham School of Graduate Studies, College of Literature, Science, and the Arts, Interdepartmental Program in Classical Art and Archaeology, Ann Arbor, MI 48109. Offers PhD. *Faculty:* 20 full-time. *Students:* 28 full-time (16 women); includes 3 minority (2 Asian Americans or Pacific Islanders, 1 Hispanic American), 4 international. Average age 28. 48 applicants, 10% accepted, 5 enrolled. In 2009, 3 doctorates awarded. *Degree requirements:* For doctorate, 4 foreign languages, comprehensive exam, thesis/dissertation, preliminary exam. *Entrance requirements:* For doctorate, GRE General Test. Additional exam requirements/recommendations for international students: Required—TOEFL (minimum score 560 paper-based; 220 computer-based). *Application deadline:* For fall admission, 1/1 for domestic and international students. Applications are processed on a rolling basis. Application fee: $60 ($75 for international students). Electronic applications accepted. *Expenses:* Tuition, state resident: full-time $17,286; part-time $1099 per credit hour. Tuition, nonresident: full-time $34,944; part-time $2080 per credit hour. Required fees: $95 per semester. Tuition and fees vary according to course load, degree level and program. *Financial support:* In 2009–10, 24 students received support, including 14 fellowships with full tuition reimbursements available (averaging $17,000 per year), 1 research assistantship with full tuition reimbursement available (averaging $16,694 per year), 8 teaching assistantships with full tuition reimbursements available (averaging $16,694 per year); career-related internships or fieldwork and health care benefits also available. Financial award application deadline: 4/15. *Faculty research:* Greek art and archaeology, roman art and archaeology, near eastern art and archaeology, archaeological theory and methodology. Total annual research expenditures: $34,240. *Unit head:* Prof. Christopher Ratte, Director, 734-936-3888, Fax: 734-763-8976, E-mail: ratte@umich.edu. *Application contact:* Alex Zwinak, Graduate Coordinator, 734-764-6323, Fax: 734-763-8976, E-mail: ipcaa.office@umich.edu.

University of Minnesota, Twin Cities Campus, Graduate School, College of Liberal Arts, Department of Art History, Minneapolis, MN 55455. Offers MA, PhD. *Faculty:* 13 full-time (5 women), 2 part-time/adjunct (both women). *Students:* 28 full-time (24 women), 7 international. Average age 26. 48 applicants, 13% accepted, 5 enrolled. In 2009, 3 master's, 4 doctorates awarded. *Degree requirements:* For master's, one foreign language, comprehensive exam, thesis; for doctorate, 2 foreign languages, comprehensive exam, thesis/dissertation. *Entrance requirements:* For master's, GRE, 3 letters of recommendation, writing sample; for doctorate, GRE, transcripts, 3 letters of recommendation, writing sample. Additional exam requirements/recommendations for international students: Required—TOEFL. *Application deadline:* For fall admission, 12/1 for domestic and international students. Application fee: $55 ($75 for international students). Electronic applications accepted. *Financial support:* In 2009–10, 22 students received support, including 9 fellowships with partial tuition reimbursements available, 2 research assistantships with full tuition reimbursements available (averaging $13,000 per year), 12 teaching assistantships with full tuition reimbursements available (averaging $13,000 per year); career-related internships or fieldwork, Federal Work-Study, institutionally sponsored loans, scholarships/grants, health care benefits, and unspecified assistantships also available. Support available to part-time students. Financial award application deadline: 6/30; financial award applicants required to submit FAFSA. *Faculty research:* Asian, Latin American, modern/contemporary, early modern, and ancient art. *Unit head:* Steven F. Ostrow, Chair, 612-624-4500, Fax: 612-626-8679, E-mail: ostro133@umn.edu. *Application contact:* Erik Farseth, Information Contact, 612-624-4500, Fax: 612-626-8679, E-mail: arthist@umn.edu.

University of Minnesota, Twin Cities Campus, Graduate School, College of Liberal Arts, Department of Classical and Near Eastern Studies, Minneapolis, MN 55455-0213. Offers ancient and medieval art and archaeology (MA, PhD); classics (MA, PhD); Greek (MA, PhD); Latin (MA, PhD); religions in antiquity (MA). Part-time programs available. *Faculty:* 22 full-time (6 women). *Students:* 24 full-time (10 women), 1 part-time (0 women), 1 international. Average age 29. 40 applicants, 20% accepted, 4 enrolled. In 2009, 5 master's awarded. Terminal master's awarded for partial completion of doctoral program. *Degree requirements:* For master's, 2 foreign languages, comprehensive exam, thesis or alternative; for doctorate, variable foreign language requirement, comprehensive exam, thesis/dissertation. *Entrance requirements:* For master's and doctorate, GRE, 3 letters of recommendation, department application, writing

Art History

University of Minnesota, Twin Cities Campus (continued)
sample, copies of transcripts, personal statement. Additional exam requirements/recommendations for international students: Required—TOEFL. *Application deadline:* For fall admission, 1/4 priority date for domestic and international students. Application fee: $50 ($75 for international students). Electronic applications accepted. *Financial support:* In 2009–10, 24 students received support, including 2 fellowships with full tuition reimbursements available (averaging $22,500 per year), 2 research assistantships with partial tuition reimbursements available (averaging $7,000 per year), 20 teaching assistantships with full tuition reimbursements available (averaging $14,000 per year); career-related internships or fieldwork, Federal Work-Study, institutionally sponsored loans, health care benefits, and tuition waivers (full and partial) also available. Support available to part-time students. Financial award application deadline: 1/4. *Faculty research:* Greek and Latin literature, religions in antiquity, ancient Near East. *Unit head:* Christopher Nappa, Chair, 612-625-624-6339, Fax: 612-624-4894, E-mail: cnappa@umn.edu. *Application contact:* Victoria H. Keller, Administrative Specialist, 612-625-8371, Fax: 612-624-4894, E-mail: kell0801@umn.edu.

University of Mississippi, Graduate School, College of Liberal Arts, Department of Art, Oxford, University, MS 38677. Offers art education (MA); art history (MA); fine arts (MFA). *Accreditation:* NASAD (one or more programs are accredited). Part-time programs available. *Students:* 9 full-time (3 women), 1 international. In 2009, 6 master's awarded. *Degree requirements:* For master's, thesis (for some programs). *Entrance requirements:* For master's, GRE General Test, minimum GPA of 3.0. Additional exam requirements/recommendations for international students: Required—TOEFL. *Application deadline:* For fall admission, 3/1 for domestic students; for spring admission, 10/1 for domestic students. Applications are processed on a rolling basis. Application fee: $25. Electronic applications accepted. *Financial support:* Fellowships, scholarships/grants and unspecified assistantships available. Financial award application deadline: 3/1; financial award applicants required to submit FAFSA. *Unit head:* Dr. Sheri Fleck Reith, Chair, 662-915-7193, Fax: 662-915-5013, E-mail: art@olemiss.edu. *Application contact:* Dr. Christy M. Wyandt, Associate Dean, 662-915-7474, Fax: 662-915-7577, E-mail: cwyandt@olemiss.edu.

University of Missouri, Graduate School, College of Arts and Sciences, Department of Art History and Archaeology, Columbia, MO 65211. Offers MA, PhD. *Faculty:* 10 full-time (5 women). *Students:* 16 full-time (14 women), 15 part-time (8 women), 3 international. Average age 31. 30 applicants, 37% accepted, 9 enrolled. In 2009, 4 master's awarded. Terminal master's awarded for partial completion of doctoral program. *Degree requirements:* For master's, 2 foreign languages, thesis; for doctorate, 2 foreign languages, thesis/dissertation. *Entrance requirements:* For master's, GRE General Test (minimum score 1000 verbal and quantitative, 4.5 analytical), minimum GPA of 3.0; min GPA of 3.3 in major field; at least 3 semesters in appropriate foreign language; for doctorate, GRE General Test, minimum GPA of 3.0; MA or equiv in art history or classical archaeology; MA thesis. Additional exam requirements/recommendations for international students: Required—TOEFL (minimum score 500 paper-based; 173 computer-based; 61 iBT), IELTS (minimum score 5.5). *Application deadline:* For fall admission, 1/18 priority date for domestic students. Applications are processed on a rolling basis. Application fee: $45 ($60 for international students). Electronic applications accepted. *Financial support:* In 2009–10, 4 fellowships with full tuition reimbursements, 13 research assistantships with full tuition reimbursements, 5 teaching assistantships with full tuition reimbursements were awarded; institutionally sponsored loans, health care benefits, and unspecified assistantships also available. *Unit head:* Dr. Anne Rufdloff Stanton, Department Chair, E-mail: stantona@missouri.edu. *Application contact:* Linda Garrison, 573-882-2757, E-mail: garrisonl@missouri.edu.

University of Missouri–Kansas City, College of Arts and Sciences, Department of Art and Art History, Kansas City, MO 64110-2499. Offers art history (MA, PhD); studio art (MA). PhD (interdisciplinary) offered through the School of Graduate Studies. Part-time programs available. *Faculty:* 11 full-time (5 women), 6 part-time/adjunct (3 women). *Students:* 5 full-time (2 women), 36 part-time (33 women); includes 3 minority (1 African American, 1 American Indian/Alaska Native, 1 Hispanic American), 2 international. Average age 33. 21 applicants, 67% accepted, 8 enrolled. In 2009, 7 master's awarded. Terminal master's awarded for partial completion of doctoral program. *Degree requirements:* For master's, thesis, qualifying exam; for doctorate, thesis/dissertation, exams. *Entrance requirements:* For master's, good general education in the humanities. Additional exam requirements/recommendations for international students: Required—TOEFL (minimum score 550 paper-based; 213 computer-based; 80 iBT). *Application deadline:* For fall admission, 3/1 priority date for domestic and international students; for spring admission, 10/15 for domestic and international students. Applications are processed on a rolling basis. Application fee: $45 ($50 for international students). Electronic applications accepted. *Expenses:* Tuition, state resident: full-time $5378; part-time $299 per credit hour. Tuition, nonresident: full-time $13,881; part-time $771 per credit hour. Required fees: $641; $71 per credit hour. Tuition and fees vary according to course load and program. *Financial support:* In 2009–10, 7 teaching assistantships with partial tuition reimbursements (averaging $11,750 per year) were awarded; career-related internships or fieldwork, Federal Work-Study, institutionally sponsored loans, and tuition waivers (full and partial) also available. Support available to part-time students. Financial award application deadline: 3/1; financial award applicants required to submit FAFSA. *Faculty research:* Painting, electronic media, Western and non-Western art history, photography. *Unit head:* Dr. Kati Toivanen, Chair, 816-235-6230, Fax: 816-235-5507, E-mail: toivanenk@umkc.edu. *Application contact:* Dr. Burton Dunbar, Associate Professor, 816-235-2531, Fax: 816-235-5507, E-mail: dunbarb@umkc.edu.

University of Nebraska–Lincoln, Graduate College, College of Fine and Performing Arts, Department of Art and Art History, Lincoln, NE 68588. Offers art history (MA); studio art (MFA);). *Accreditation:* NASAD. *Degree requirements:* For master's, thesis. *Entrance requirements:* For master's, slide portfolio. Additional exam requirements/recommendations for international students: Required—TOEFL (minimum score 550 paper-based; 213 computer-based). Electronic applications accepted. *Faculty research:* Classical archaeology, contemporary art, printmaking, photography.

University of New Mexico, Graduate School, College of Fine Arts, Department of Art and Art History, Program in Art History, Albuquerque, NM 87131-2039. Offers MA, PhD. Part-time programs available. *Students:* 22 full-time (17 women), 11 part-time (9 women); includes 9 minority (3 American Indian/Alaska Native, 6 Hispanic Americans), 7 international. Average age 38. 38 applicants, 58% accepted, 9 enrolled. In 2009, 6 master's awarded. *Degree requirements:* For master's, one foreign language, comprehensive exam (for some programs), thesis, symposium; for doctorate, 2 foreign languages, comprehensive exam, thesis/dissertation, symposium. *Entrance requirements:* Additional exam requirements/recommendations for international students: Required—TOEFL (minimum score 550 paper-based; 213 computer-based). *Application deadline:* For fall admission, 1/15 for domestic students; for spring admission, 1/15 for domestic students. Application fee: $50. Electronic applications accepted. *Expenses:* Tuition, state resident: full-time $2099; part-time $233.20 per credit hour. Tuition, nonresident: full-time $6650. Required fees: $25 per semester. Tuition and fees vary according to course load, program and reciprocity agreements. *Financial support:* In 2009–10, 15 students received support, including 2 research assistantships with tuition reimbursements available (averaging $6,700 per year), 18 teaching assistantships with partial tuition reimbursements available (averaging $6,700 per year); Federal Work-Study, institutionally sponsored loans, scholarships/grants, health care benefits, and unspecified assistantships also available. Support available to part-time students. Financial award application deadline: 3/1; financial award applicants required to submit FAFSA. *Faculty research:* Native American art, modern Latin American art, pre-Columbian art, architectural art, American art, medieval art, Spanish Colonial Art, Latin American Art, history of photography. *Unit head:* Dr. Justine Andrews, Graduate Director, 505-277-3441, Fax: 505-277-5955, E-mail: jandrews@unm.edu. *Application contact:* Kat Heatherington, Graduate Advisor, 505-277-6672, Fax: 505-277-5955, E-mail: art255@unm.edu.

The University of North Carolina at Chapel Hill, Graduate School, College of Arts and Sciences, Department of Art, Program in Art History, Chapel Hill, NC 27599. Offers MA, PhD. *Degree requirements:* For master's, one foreign language, comprehensive exam, thesis; for doctorate, one foreign language, comprehensive exam, thesis/dissertation. *Entrance requirements:* For master's and doctorate, GRE General Test, minimum GPA of 3.0.

University of North Texas, Robert B. Toulouse School of Graduate Studies, College of Visual Arts and Design, Department of Art Education and Art History, Denton, TX 76203. Offers art education (MA, PhD); art history (MA); art museum education (Certificate); arts leadership (Certificate). Part-time and evening/weekend programs available. *Degree requirements:* For master's, one foreign language, comprehensive exam (for some programs), thesis (for some programs); for doctorate, comprehensive exam, thesis/dissertation. *Entrance requirements:* For master's, GRE, writing sample, statement of purpose; for doctorate, GRE, master's degree in art education, writing sample, slides, statement of purpose. Additional exam requirements/recommendations for international students: Required—proof of English language proficiency required for non-native English speakers; Recommended—TOEFL (minimum score 550 paper-based; 213 computer-based; 79 iBT). Application fee: $50 ($75 for international students). *Expenses:* Tuition, state resident: full-time $4298; part-time $239 per contact hour. Tuition, nonresident: full-time $9878; part-time $549 per contact hour. Required fees: $265 per contact hour. *Financial support:* Fellowships with partial tuition reimbursements, research assistantships with partial tuition reimbursements, teaching assistantships with partial tuition reimbursements, Federal Work-Study, scholarships/grants, health care benefits, and unspecified assistantships available. Support available to part-time students. Financial award applicants required to submit FAFSA. *Faculty research:* Aesthetics, visual culture, arts leadership, British art, Latin American art, French art, Indian art, contemporary Arab art.

University of Notre Dame, Graduate School, College of Arts and Letters, Division of Humanities, Department of Art, Art History, and Design, Notre Dame, IN 46556. Offers art history (MA); design (MFA), including graphic design, industrial design; studio art (MFA), including ceramics, painting, photography, printmaking, sculpture. *Accreditation:* NASAD. *Degree requirements:* For master's, comprehensive exam (for some programs), thesis. *Entrance requirements:* For master's, GRE General Test, minimum GPA of 3.0. Additional exam requirements/recommendations for international students: Required—TOEFL (minimum score 600 paper-based; 250 computer-based; 80 iBT). Electronic applications accepted. *Faculty research:* Studio art practice in ceramics, printing, photography, printmaking and sculpture, graphic design and industrial design, digital imaging in design and photography, Renaissance and American art history, contemporary art theory and criticism.

University of Oklahoma, Graduate College, College of Fine Arts, School of Art and Art History, Program in Art History, Norman, OK 73019. Offers MA. *Students:* 8 full-time (5 women), 13 part-time (12 women); includes 4 minority (all American Indian/Alaska Native), 1 international. 12 applicants, 58% accepted, 3 enrolled. In 2009, 1 master's awarded. Terminal master's awarded for partial completion of doctoral program. *Degree requirements:* For master's, thesis, departmental qualifying exam, reading proficiency in French/German. *Entrance requirements:* For master's, GRE General Test, minimum GPA of 3.0, 18 undergraduate hours in art history, writing sample, 3 letters of recommendation. Additional exam requirements/recommendations for international students: Required—TOEFL (minimum score 550 paper-based; 213 computer-based). *Application deadline:* For fall admission, 2/1 priority date for domestic students, 2/1 for international students; for spring admission, 10/1 for domestic and international students. Applications are processed on a rolling basis. Application fee: $40 ($90 for international students). Electronic applications accepted. *Expenses:* Tuition, state resident: full-time $3744; part-time $156 per credit hour. Tuition, nonresident: full-time $13,577; part-time $565.70 per credit hour. Required fees: $2415; $90.10 per credit hour. *Financial support:* In 2009–10, 12 students received support. Career-related internships or fieldwork, institutionally sponsored loans, scholarships/grants, tuition waivers (partial), and unspecified assistantships available. Support available to part-time students. Financial award application deadline: 4/7; financial award applicants required to submit FAFSA. *Faculty research:* American West, Native American art, medieval, Renaissance and Baroque, contemporary art, nineteenth century art, medieval/Romanesque. *Unit head:* Mary Jo Watson, Director, 405-325-2691, Fax: 405-325-1668, E-mail: mjwatson@ou.edu. *Application contact:* Susan H. Caldwell, Assistant Director/Professor, 405-325-3252, Fax: 405-325-1668, E-mail: shcaldwell@ou.edu.

University of Oregon, Graduate School, School of Architecture and Allied Arts, Department of Art History, Eugene, OR 97403. Offers MA, PhD. *Degree requirements:* For master's, one foreign language, thesis or alternative; for doctorate, 2 foreign languages, thesis/dissertation. *Entrance requirements:* For master's, GRE General Test, minimum GPA of 3.0; for doctorate, minimum GPA of 3.0. Additional exam requirements/recommendations for international students: Required—TOEFL. *Faculty research:* Scytho-Siberian art, modern Chinese painting, European landscape painting, American architecture, German expressionist graphics.

University of Pennsylvania, School of Arts and Sciences, Graduate Group in the History of Art, Philadelphia, PA 19104. Offers AM, PhD. *Faculty:* 21 full-time (9 women), 6 part-time/adjunct (2 women). *Students:* 40 full-time (30 women), 2 part-time (1 woman); includes 2 minority (1 Asian American or Pacific Islander, 1 Hispanic American), 5 international. 189 applicants, 8% accepted, 8 enrolled. In 2009, 3 master's, 6 doctorates awarded. Terminal master's awarded for partial completion of doctoral program. *Degree requirements:* For master's, 2 foreign languages, thesis; for doctorate, 2 foreign languages, thesis/dissertation. *Entrance requirements:* For master's and doctorate, GRE, language background according to subfield of interest. Additional exam requirements/recommendations for international students: Required—TOEFL. *Application deadline:* For fall admission, 12/1 priority date for domestic students. Application fee: $70. Electronic applications accepted. *Expenses:* Tuition: Full-time $25,660; part-time $4758 per course. Required fees: $2152; $270 per course. Tuition and fees vary according to course load, degree level and program. *Financial support:* Fellowships, research assistantships, teaching assistantships, institutionally sponsored loans, scholarships/grants, traineeships, health care benefits, and unspecified assistantships available. Financial award application deadline: 12/15.

University of Pittsburgh, School of Arts and Sciences, Department of History of Art and Architecture, Pittsburgh, PA 15260. Offers MA, PhD. *Faculty:* 13 full-time (7 women). *Students:* 34 full-time (28 women), 1 (woman) part-time; includes 7 minority (all Asian Americans or Pacific Islanders). Average age 33. 51 applicants, 18% accepted, 4 enrolled. In 2009, 5 master's, 5 doctorates awarded. Terminal master's awarded for partial completion of doctoral program. *Degree requirements:* For master's, one foreign language, thesis; for doctorate, 2 foreign languages, comprehensive exam, thesis/dissertation. *Entrance requirements:* For doctorate, GRE General Test, 3 letters of recommendation, writing sample, foreign language questionnaire. Additional exam requirements/recommendations for international students: Required—TOEFL (minimum score 550 paper-based; 213 computer-based; 80 iBT). *Application deadline:* For fall admission, 1/15 for domestic and international students. Application fee: $50. Electronic applications accepted. *Expenses:* Tuition, state resident: full-time $16,402; part-time $665 per credit. Tuition, nonresident: full-time $28,694; part-time $1175 per credit. Required fees: $690; $175 per term. Tuition and fees vary according to program. *Financial support:* In 2009–10, 28 students received support, including 16 fellowships with full tuition reimbursements available (averaging $17,822 per year), 12 teaching assistantships with full tuition reimbursements available (averaging $15,675 per year); research assistantships with full tuition reimbursements available, career-related internships or fieldwork, Federal Work-Study, scholarships/grants, health care benefits, and tuition waivers (partial) also available. Financial award application deadline: 1/15. *Faculty research:* Asian, medieval, Renaissance/Baroque, modern art and architecture, contemporary. Total annual research expenditures: $10,000. *Unit head:* Dr. Kirk Savage, Chair, 412-648-2405, Fax: 412-648-2792, E-mail: ksa@pitt.edu. *Application contact:* Dr. Josh Ellenbogen, Director, Graduate Studies, 412-648-2400, Fax: 412-648-2792, E-mail: jme23@pitt.edu.

University of Rochester, The College, Arts and Sciences, Department of Art and Art History, Rochester, NY 14627. Offers visual and cultural studies (MA, PhD). Terminal master's awarded for partial completion of doctoral program. *Degree requirements:* For master's, thesis optional;

for doctorate, one foreign language, thesis/dissertation, qualifying exam. *Entrance requirements:* For master's and doctorate, GRE General Test. Additional exam requirements/recommendations for international students: Required—TOEFL.

See Close-Up on page 197.

University of St. Thomas, Graduate Studies, College of Arts and Sciences, Department of Art History, St. Paul, MN 55105-1096. Offers MA. Part-time and evening/weekend programs available. *Degree requirements:* For master's, thesis, oral exam, reading proficiency in 1 foreign language. *Entrance requirements:* For master's, bachelor's degree in art history or related field; letters of recommendation (3); writing sample. Additional exam requirements/recommendations for international students: Required—TOEFL. *Faculty research:* Pictorial narrative and theory; feminist theory and women's artistic practice; art, ritual, and popular culture; architectural history; modernism.

University of South Africa, College of Human Sciences, Pretoria, South Africa. Offers adult education (M Ed); African languages (MA, PhD); African politics (MA, PhD); Afrikaans (MA, PhD); ancient history (MA, PhD); ancient Near Eastern studies (MA, PhD); anthropology (MA, PhD); applied linguistics (MA); Arabic (MA, PhD); archaeology (MA); art history (MA); Biblical archaeology (MA); Biblical studies (M Th, D Th, PhD); Christian spirituality (M Th, D Th); church history (M Th, D Th); classical studies (MA, PhD); clinical psychology (MA); communication (MA, PhD); comparative education (M Ed, Ed D); consulting psychology (D Admin, D Com, PhD); curriculum studies (M Ed, Ed D); development studies (M Admin, MA, D Admin, PhD); didactics (M Ed, Ed D); education (M Tech); education management (M Ed, Ed D); educational psychology (M Ed); English (MA); environmental education (M Ed); French (MA, PhD); German (MA, PhD); Greek (MA); guidance and counseling (M Ed); health studies (MA, PhD), including health sciences education (MA), health services management (MA), medical and surgical nursing science (critical care general) (MA), midwifery and neonatal nursing science (MA), trauma and emergency care (MA); history (MA, PhD); history of education (Ed D); inclusive education (M Ed, Ed D); information and communications technology policy and regulation (MA); information science (MA, MIS, PhD); international politics (MA, PhD); Islamic studies (MA, PhD); Italian (MA, PhD); Judaica (MA, PhD); linguistics (MA, PhD); mathematical education (M Ed); mathematics education (MA); missiology (M Th, D Th); modern Hebrew (MA, PhD); musicology (MA, MMus, D Mus, PhD); natural science education (M Ed); New Testament (M Th, D Th); Old Testament (D Th); pastoral therapy (M Th, D Th); philosophy (MA); philosophy of education (M Ed, Ed D); politics (MA, PhD); Portuguese (MA, PhD); practical theology (M Th, D Th); psychology (MA, MS, PhD); psychology of education (M Ed, Ed D); public health (MA); religious studies (MA, D Th, PhD); Romance languages (MA); Russian (MA, PhD); Semitic languages (MA, PhD); social behavior studies in HIV/AIDS (MA); social science (mental health) (MA); social science in development studies (MA); social science in psychology (MA); social science in social work (MA); social science in sociology (MA); social work (MSW, DSW, PhD); socio-education (M Ed, Ed D); sociolinguistics (MA); sociology (MA, PhD); Spanish (MA, PhD); systematic theology (M Th, D Th); TESOL (teaching English to speakers of other languages) (MA); theological ethics (M Th, D Th); theory of literature (MA, PhD); urban ministries (D Th); urban ministry (M Th).

University of South Carolina, The Graduate School, College of Arts and Sciences, Department of Art, Program in Art History, Columbia, SC 29208. Offers MA. *Accreditation:* NASAD. Part-time programs available. *Degree requirements:* For master's, one foreign language, comprehensive exam, thesis. *Entrance requirements:* For master's, GRE General Test or MAT, writing sample. Additional exam requirements/recommendations for international students: Required—TOEFL. Electronic applications accepted. *Faculty research:* History of art and architecture.

University of Southern California, Graduate School, College of Letters, Arts and Sciences, Department of Art History, Los Angeles, CA 90089. Offers art history (MA, PhD); history of collecting and display (Graduate Certificate); visual studies (Graduate Certificate). *Faculty:* 12 full-time (9 women), 7 part-time/adjunct (5 women). *Students:* 42 full-time (34 women); includes 8 minority (7 Asian Americans or Pacific Islanders, 1 Hispanic American), 4 international. In 2009, 6 master's, 1 doctorate, 4 other advanced degrees awarded. *Degree requirements:* For doctorate, 2 foreign languages, comprehensive exam, thesis/dissertation. *Entrance requirements:* For doctorate, GRE. *Application deadline:* For fall admission, 12/1 for domestic students. Application fee: $85. *Expenses:* Tuition: Full-time $25,980; part-time $1315 per unit. Required fees: $554. One-time fee: $35 full-time. Full-time tuition and fees vary according to degree level and program. *Financial support:* In 2009–10, 8 fellowships with full tuition reimbursements (averaging $19,000 per year), 10 teaching assistantships with full tuition reimbursements (averaging $19,000 per year) were awarded; career-related internships or fieldwork, institutionally sponsored loans, scholarships/grants, health care benefits, unspecified assistantships, and cash awards for travel and research also available. Financial award application deadline: 2/1. *Faculty research:* Ancient, medieval, Renaissance, eighteenth-ninetenth century, contemporary. *Unit head:* Dr. Carolyn Malone, Professor and Chair, 213-740-4552, Fax: 213-740-8971, E-mail: cmalone@usc.edu. *Application contact:* Jeanne Herman, Academic Advisor, 213-740-9516, Fax: 213-740-8971, E-mail: jaherman@usc.edu.

University of South Florida, Graduate School, College of The Arts, School of Art and Art History, Tampa, FL 33620-9951. Offers art history (MA); studio art (MFA). *Accreditation:* NASAD. Part-time programs available. *Faculty:* 20 full-time (9 women), 3 part-time/adjunct (0 women). *Students:* 38 full-time (21 women), 6 part-time (5 women); includes 7 minority (2 African Americans, 1 American Indian/Alaska Native, 1 Asian American or Pacific Islander, 3 Hispanic Americans), 2 international. Average age 32. 89 applicants, 26% accepted, 18 enrolled. In 2009, 13 master's awarded. *Degree requirements:* For master's, thesis, exhibition (MFA). *Entrance requirements:* For master's, GRE General Test (MA), minimum GPA of 3.0 in last 60 hours of coursework. *Application deadline:* For fall admission, 1/15 for domestic students, 1/2 for international students. Application fee: $30. *Financial support:* In 2009–10, 8 fellowships with full tuition reimbursements (averaging $7,000 per year), 35 teaching assistantships with full tuition reimbursements (averaging $4,600 per year) were awarded; scholarships/grants, health care benefits, and unspecified assistantships also available. Support available to part-time students. Financial award application deadline: 2/15; financial award applicants required to submit FAFSA. *Faculty research:* Contemporary art and role of the artist, identity strategies, political iconography, art practice and technology, construction of race in art. Total annual research expenditures: $52,987. *Unit head:* Prof. Wallace Wilson, Director, 813-974-2360, Fax: 813-974-9226, E-mail: wwilson2@usf.edu. *Application contact:* Gloria Ann Quigley, Academic Specialist, 813-974-9249, Fax: 813-974-9226, E-mail: gquigley@usf.edu.

The University of Texas at Austin, Graduate School, College of Fine Arts, Department of Art and Art History, Program in Art History, Austin, TX 78712-1111. Offers MA, PhD. *Accreditation:* NASAD. Part-time programs available. *Degree requirements:* For master's, one foreign language, thesis; for doctorate, 2 foreign languages, thesis/dissertation, oral and written qualifying exam. *Entrance requirements:* For master's, GRE General Test, 2 samples of written work; for doctorate, GRE General Test, minimum GPA of 3.0, 2 samples of written work. Electronic applications accepted.

The University of Texas at San Antonio, College of Liberal and Fine Arts, Department of Art and Art History, San Antonio, TX 78249-0617. Offers art history (MA); studio art (MFA). *Accreditation:* NASAD (one or more programs are accredited). *Faculty:* 14 full-time (6 women). *Students:* 30 full-time (19 women), 18 part-time (13 women); includes 21 minority (1 American Indian/Alaska Native, 1 Asian American or Pacific Islander, 19 Hispanic Americans), 1 international. Average age 33. 41 applicants, 66% accepted, 12 enrolled. In 2009, 13 master's awarded. *Degree requirements:* For master's, comprehensive exam (for some programs), thesis (for some programs). *Entrance requirements:* For master's, GRE General Test, portfolio, minimum GPA of 3.0 in last 60 hours, 3 letters of recommendation. Additional exam requirements/recommendations for international students: Required—TOEFL (minimum score 500 paper-based; 173 computer-based; 61 iBT), IELTS (minimum score 5). *Application deadline:* For fall admission, 7/1 for domestic students, 4/1 for international students; for spring admission, 11/1 for domestic students, 9/1 for international students. Applications are processed on a rolling basis. Application fee: $45 ($80 for international students). Electronic applications accepted. *Expenses:* Tuition, state resident: full-time $3975; part-time $221 per contact hour. Tuition, nonresident: full-time $13,947; part-time $775 per contact hour. Required fees: $1853. *Financial support:* In 2009–10, 24 students received support, including 11 research assistantships (averaging $8,357 per year), 11 teaching assistantships (averaging $4,715 per year); career-related internships or fieldwork, scholarships/grants, tuition waivers (partial), and unspecified assistantships also available. Support available to part-time students. *Faculty research:* Artistic production in media; art history and criticism, focusing on American and Hispanic art. *Unit head:* Dr. Kent T. Rush, Chair, 210-458-4362, Fax: 210-458-4356, E-mail: kent.rush@utsa.edu. *Application contact:* Dr. Kent T. Rush, Chair, 210-458-4362, Fax: 210-458-4356, E-mail: kent.rush@utsa.edu.

The University of Texas at Tyler, College of Arts and Sciences, Department of Art and Art History, Tyler, TX 75799-0001. Offers art history (MA); interdisciplinary (MAIS); studio art (MFA). *Faculty:* 7 full-time (4 women). *Students:* 9 full-time (6 women), 2 part-time (both women); includes 1 minority (Hispanic American). Average age 31. 2 applicants, 100% accepted, 1 enrolled. In 2009, 3 master's awarded. *Degree requirements:* For master's, thesis, graduate committee review. *Entrance requirements:* For master's, minimum GPA of 3.0. Additional exam requirements/recommendations for international students: Required—TOEFL (minimum score 79 computer-based). *Application deadline:* For fall admission, 8/17 priority date for domestic students, 7/1 priority date for international students; for spring admission, 12/21 priority date for domestic students, 11/1 priority date for international students. Applications are processed on a rolling basis. Application fee: $25 ($50 for international students). *Expenses:* Tuition, state resident: part-time $665 per semester hour. Tuition, nonresident: part-time $942 per semester hour. Part-time tuition and fees vary according to degree level and program. *Financial support:* Application deadline: 7/1. *Faculty research:* Classical myths in contemporary art, social issues in contemporary art, casting methods, Renaissance art. *Unit head:* Gary Hatcher, Chair, 903-566-7486, Fax: 903-566-7062, E-mail: ghatcher@mail.uttyl.edu. *Application contact:* Dr. Rachel Sailor, Program Chair, Art History, 903-566-7398, E-mail: rasailor@uttyler.edu.

University of Toronto, School of Graduate Studies, Humanities Division, Department of Art, Toronto, ON M5S 1A1, Canada. Offers art history (MA, PhD); visual studies (MVS). Part-time programs available. *Degree requirements:* For master's, 2 foreign languages, language proficiency exams; for doctorate, 2 foreign languages, comprehensive exam, thesis/dissertation. *Entrance requirements:* For master's, coursework in a foreign language, 3 letters of reference, sample research paper, minimum B+ average in senior art history and/or humanities courses; for doctorate, minimum A– average in senior art history and/or humanities courses, 2 letters of reference, sample research paper.

University of Utah, The Graduate School, College of Fine Arts, Department of Art and Art History, Program in Art History, Salt Lake City, UT 84112-0380. Offers MA. Part-time programs available. *Students:* 6 full-time (all women), 1 (woman) part-time. Average age 25. 20 applicants, 35% accepted, 4 enrolled. In 2009, 1 master's awarded. *Degree requirements:* For master's, one foreign language, comprehensive exam, thesis, thesis defense. *Entrance requirements:* For master's, curriculum vitae, academic writing sample, letters of recommendation. Additional exam requirements/recommendations for international students: Required—TOEFL (minimum score 600 paper-based; 173 computer-based). *Application deadline:* For fall admission, 1/2 priority date for domestic and international students. Application fee: $55 ($65 for international students). Electronic applications accepted. *Expenses:* Tuition, state resident: full-time $4004; part-time $1674 per semester. Tuition, nonresident: full-time $14,134; part-time $5915 per semester. Required fees: $324 per semester. Tuition and fees vary according to course load, degree level and program. *Financial support:* In 2009–10, 1 fellowship, 6 teaching assistantships with partial tuition reimbursements were awarded; research assistantships with partial tuition reimbursements, Federal Work-Study, institutionally sponsored loans, scholarships/grants, tuition waivers (partial), unspecified assistantships, and stipends also available. Financial award application deadline: 1/2; financial award applicants required to submit FAFSA. *Faculty research:* Asian art, Latin American art, Baroque art, European/American art, twentieth/contemporary century art. *Unit head:* Dr. Sheila D. Muller, Director, 801-581-8677, Fax: 801-585-6171, E-mail: sheila.muller@art.utah.edu. *Application contact:* Dr. Sheila D. Muller, Director of Graduate Studies, 801-581-8677, Fax: 801-585-6171, E-mail: sheila.muller@art.utah.edu.

University of Victoria, Faculty of Graduate Studies, Faculty of Fine Arts, Department of History in Art, Victoria, BC V8W 2Y2, Canada. Offers MA, PhD. *Degree requirements:* For master's, one foreign language, thesis (for some programs), oral defense; for doctorate, 2 foreign languages, comprehensive exam, thesis/dissertation, oral defense. *Entrance requirements:* For master's, minimum B+ average in undergraduate course work; for doctorate, minimum B+ average in graduate course work. Additional exam requirements/recommendations for international students: Required—TOEFL (minimum score 575 paper-based; 233 computer-based), IELTS (minimum score 7). Electronic applications accepted. *Faculty research:* Europe, Southeast Asia, China and Islamic world, architecture of North America and the Islamic World, film.

University of Virginia, College and Graduate School of Arts and Sciences, McIntire Department of Art, Charlottesville, VA 22904-4130. Offers classical art and archaeology (MA, PhD); history of art and architecture (MA, PhD). *Degree requirements:* For master's, one foreign language, thesis, defense; for doctorate, 2 foreign languages, comprehensive exam, thesis/dissertation, defense. *Entrance requirements:* For master's and doctorate, GRE General Test, writing sample. Additional exam requirements/recommendations for international students: Recommended—TOEFL (minimum score 600 paper-based; 250 computer-based; 90 iBT), IELTS (minimum score 7). Electronic applications accepted. *Faculty research:* Classical art, renaissance art and architecture, American material culture.

University of Virginia, College and Graduate School of Arts and Sciences, Program in Art and Architectural History, Charlottesville, VA 22903. Offers MA, PhD. *Faculty:* 25 full-time (9 women), 5 part-time/adjunct (3 women). *Students:* 48 full-time (37 women), 1 (woman) part-time; includes 1 minority (African American), 1 international. Average age 31. 81 applicants, 33% accepted, 9 enrolled. In 2009, 7 master's, 7 doctorates awarded. *Degree requirements:* For master's, one foreign language, comprehensive exam, thesis; for doctorate, 2 foreign languages, thesis/dissertation, oral exam. *Entrance requirements:* For master's and doctorate, GRE, 2 letters of recommendation. *Application deadline:* For fall admission, 12/7 for domestic and international students. Applications are processed on a rolling basis. Electronic applications accepted. *Financial support:* Application deadline: 12/7. *Unit head:* Lawrence O. Goedde, Chair, 434-924-6123, Fax: 434-924-3647, E-mail: artdept@virginia.edu. *Application contact:* Daniel Ehnbom, Director of Graduate Studies, 434-924-6130, Fax: 434-924-3647, E-mail: dje6r@virginia.edu.

University of Washington, Graduate School, College of Arts and Sciences, School of Art, Division of Art History, Seattle, WA 98195. Offers MA, PhD. Terminal master's awarded for partial completion of doctoral program. *Degree requirements:* For master's, 2 foreign languages, practicum or thesis; for doctorate, 2 foreign languages, thesis/dissertation. *Entrance requirements:* For master's, GRE General Test, minimum undergraduate GPA of 3.0, undergraduate major in art history or equivalent; for doctorate, GRE General Test, MA in art history, minimum graduate GPA of 3.0. Additional exam requirements/recommendations for international students: Required—TOEFL (minimum score 580 paper-based; 237 computer-based). Electronic applications accepted. *Faculty research:* European-American (all periods), Japanese, Chinese, African, and Native American art.

University of Wisconsin–Madison, Graduate School, College of Letters and Science, Department of Art History, Madison, WI 53706-1380. Offers MA, PhD. Part-time programs available. Terminal master's awarded for partial completion of doctoral program. *Degree requirements:* For master's, one foreign language; for doctorate, 2 foreign languages, thesis/dissertation. *Entrance requirements:* For master's and doctorate, GRE. Additional exam requirements/recommendations for international students: Required—TOEFL. Electronic applica-

Art History

University of Wisconsin–Madison (continued)

tions accepted. *Expenses:* Tuition, state resident: part-time $594 per credit. Tuition, nonresident: part-time $1504 per credit. Required fees: $65 per credit. Tuition and fees vary according to course load, program and reciprocity agreements. *Faculty research:* Twentieth-century, African art, Italian Renaissance, Dutch, material culture.

University of Wisconsin–Milwaukee, Graduate School, College of Letters and Sciences, Department of Art History, Milwaukee, WI 53201-0413. Offers art history (MA); art museum studies (Certificate). Part-time programs available. *Faculty:* 9 full-time (5 women). *Students:* 14 full-time (13 women), 11 part-time (all women); includes 1 minority (African American), 1 international. Average age 29. 31 applicants, 61% accepted, 6 enrolled. In 2009, 7 master's awarded. *Degree requirements:* For master's, one foreign language, comprehensive exam, thesis or alternative. *Entrance requirements:* For master's, GRE. Additional exam requirements/recommendations for international students: Required—TOEFL (minimum score 550 paper-based; 79 iBT), IELTS (minimum score 6.5). *Application deadline:* For fall admission, 1/1 priority date for domestic students; for spring admission, 9/1 for domestic students. Applications are processed on a rolling basis. Application fee: $45 ($75 for international students). *Expenses:* Tuition, state resident: full-time $8800. Tuition, nonresident: full-time $20,760. Tuition and fees vary according to program and reciprocity agreements. *Financial support:* In 2009–10, 5 teaching assistantships were awarded; fellowships, research assistantships, career-related internships or fieldwork and unspecified assistantships also available. Support available to part-time students. Financial award application deadline: 4/15. *Faculty research:* Ancient Mediterranean art through contemporary Western art, Chinese art, Pre-Columbian art, film, theory. Total annual research expenditures: $1,035. *Unit head:* Kenneth Bendiner, Chair, 414-229-5015, Fax: 414-229-2935, E-mail: bendiner@uwm.edu. *Application contact:* Derek Counts, General Information Contact, 414-229-3466, E-mail: dbc@uwm.edu.

University of Wisconsin–Superior, Graduate Division, Department of Visual Arts, Superior, WI 54880-4500. Offers art education (MA); art history (MA); art therapy (MA); studio arts (MA). Part-time programs available. *Faculty:* 7 full-time (1 woman), 1 (woman) part-time/adjunct. *Students:* 12 full-time (8 women), 18 part-time (15 women); includes 1 minority (American Indian/Alaska Native), 2 international. 14 applicants, 100% accepted. In 2009, 7 master's awarded. *Degree requirements:* For master's, comprehensive exam, exhibit. *Entrance requirements:* For master's, minimum GPA of 2.75, portfolio. *Application deadline:* For fall admission, 4/1 priority date for domestic students; for spring admission, 10/15 priority date for domestic students. Applications are processed on a rolling basis. Application fee: $45. *Financial support:* Career-related internships or fieldwork, Federal Work-Study, scholarships/grants, and tuition waivers (partial) available. Support available to part-time students. Financial award application deadline: 4/15; financial award applicants required to submit FAFSA. *Unit head:* Tim Cleary, Coordinator, 715-394-8398. *Application contact:* Sandy Wallgren, Program Assistant/Status Examiner, 715-394-8295, Fax: 715-394-8146, E-mail: gradstudy@uwsuper.edu.

Virginia Commonwealth University, Graduate School, School of the Arts, Department of Art History, Richmond, VA 23284-9005. Offers architectural history (MA); art history (MA, PhD); historical studies (MA); museum studies (MA). *Accreditation:* NASAD. *Degree requirements:* For master's, thesis; for doctorate, comprehensive exam, thesis/dissertation. *Entrance requirements:* For master's and doctorate, GRE General Test. *Faculty research:* Modern, nineteenth century, Renaissance, American, and Medieval art.

Washington University in St. Louis, Graduate School of Arts and Sciences, Department of Art History and Archaeology, St. Louis, MO 63130-4899. Offers art history (MA, PhD); classical archaeology (MA, PhD). *Degree requirements:* For doctorate, 2 foreign languages, comprehensive exam, thesis/dissertation. *Entrance requirements:* For master's and doctorate, GRE General Test, sample of written work. Electronic applications accepted.

Wayne State University, College of Fine, Performing and Communication Arts, Department of Art and Art History, Program in Art History, Detroit, MI 48202. Offers MA. *Degree requirements:* For master's, one foreign language. *Entrance requirements:* Additional exam requirements/recommendations for international students: Required—TOEFL (minimum score 550 paper-based; 213 computer-based); Recommended—TWE (minimum score 6). Electronic applications accepted. *Faculty research:* Ancient, medieval, and nineteenth and twentieth century art history; theory and criticism.

West Virginia University, College of Creative Arts, Division of Art and Design, Morgantown, WV 26506. Offers art education (MA); art history (MA); ceramics (MFA); graphic design (MFA); painting (MFA); printmaking (MFA); sculpture (MFA); studio art (MA). *Accreditation:* NASAD. *Degree requirements:* For master's, thesis, exhibit. *Entrance requirements:* For master's, minimum GPA of 2.75, portfolio. Additional exam requirements/recommendations for international students: Required—TOEFL. *Expenses:* Contact institution. *Faculty research:* Medieval art history.

Williams College, Program in the History of Art, Williamstown, MA 01267. Offers MA. Offered jointly with Sterling and Francine Clark Art Institute. Part-time programs available. *Degree requirements:* For master's, 2 foreign languages, symposium paper and lecture. *Entrance requirements:* For master's, GRE General Test. Additional exam requirements/recommendations for international students: Required—TOEFL. Electronic applications accepted.

Yale University, Graduate School of Arts and Sciences, Department of History of Art, New Haven, CT 06520. Offers PhD. *Degree requirements:* For doctorate, 2 foreign languages, thesis/dissertation. *Entrance requirements:* For doctorate, GRE General Test.

York University, Faculty of Graduate Studies, Faculty of Fine Arts, Program in Art History, Toronto, ON M3J 1P3, Canada. Offers MA, PhD. Part-time programs available. *Degree requirements:* For master's, one foreign language, thesis or alternative. Electronic applications accepted.

Arts Administration

American University, College of Arts and Sciences, Department of Performing Arts, Program in Arts Management, Washington, DC 22016-8053. Offers MA, Certificate. Part-time and evening/weekend programs available. *Students:* 45 full-time (38 women), 30 part-time (25 women); includes 9 minority (2 African Americans, 2 Asian Americans or Pacific Islanders, 5 Hispanic Americans), 7 international. Average age 28. 86 applicants, 59% accepted, 28 enrolled. In 2009, 13 master's, 4 other advanced degrees awarded. *Degree requirements:* For master's, comprehensive exam, thesis or alternative. *Entrance requirements:* For master's, GRE, previous course work in theater, dance, music, or related field; minimum GPA of 3.0; for Certificate, bachelor's degree. Additional exam requirements/recommendations for international students: Required—TOEFL. *Application deadline:* For fall admission, 1/15 priority date for domestic students. Application fee: $80. *Expenses:* Tuition: Full-time $22,266; part-time $1237 per credit hour. Required fees: $430. Tuition and fees vary according to program. *Financial support:* Fellowships, teaching assistantships, career-related internships or fieldwork, Federal Work-Study, and institutionally sponsored loans available. Support available to part-time students. Financial award application deadline: 2/1. *Faculty research:* Arts policy, arts education.

Boston University, Metropolitan College, Program in Arts Administration, Boston, MA 02215. Offers arts administration (MS, Graduate Certificate); fundraising management (Graduate Certificate). Part-time and evening/weekend programs available. *Faculty:* 2 full-time (0 women), 14 part-time/adjunct (6 women). *Students:* 12 full-time (all women), 71 part-time (62 women); includes 6 minority (3 African Americans, 3 Hispanic Americans), 14 international. Average age 25. 128 applicants, 59% accepted, 39 enrolled. In 2009, 37 master's awarded. *Degree requirements:* For master's, internship. *Entrance requirements:* Additional exam requirements/recommendations for international students: Required—TOEFL (minimum score 590 paper-based; 213 computer-based; 84 iBT), IELTS, TWE. *Application deadline:* For fall admission, 3/31 priority date for domestic and international students; for spring admission, 11/15 priority date for domestic and international students. Applications are processed on a rolling basis. Application fee: $75. Electronic applications accepted. *Expenses:* Tuition: Full-time $37,910; part-time $1184 per credit hour. Required fees: $386; $40 per semester. Part-time tuition and fees vary according to class time, course level, degree level and program. *Financial support:* In 2009–10, 10 research assistantships were awarded; career-related internships or fieldwork and office assistantships also available. *Faculty research:* Cultural policy, artists' rights, museum practices, audience development. *Unit head:* Prof. Daniel Ranalli, Associate Professor/Director, 617-353-4064, Fax: 617-353-1230, E-mail: artsad@bu.edu. *Application contact:* Jeannie Motherwell, Program Assistant, 617-353-4064, Fax: 617-358-1230, E-mail: jmoth@bu.edu.

Carnegie Mellon University, H. John Heinz III College, Institute for the Management of Creative Enterprises and College of Fine Arts, Program in Arts Management, Pittsburgh, PA 15213-3891. Offers MAM. *Degree requirements:* For master's, internship. *Entrance requirements:* For master's, GMAT or GRE General Test, previous course work in pre-calculus and statistics. Electronic applications accepted.

Claremont Graduate University, Graduate Programs, Program in Arts Management, Claremont, CA 91711-6160. Offers MA. *Students:* 27 full-time (20 women), 3 part-time (2 women); includes 10 minority (2 African Americans, 3 Asian Americans or Pacific Islanders, 5 Hispanic Americans), 4 international. Average age 30. *Entrance requirements:* For master's, GRE General Test. Additional exam requirements/recommendations for international students: Required—TOEFL (minimum score 550 paper-based; 213 computer-based; 80 iBT). *Application deadline:* For fall admission, 2/1 priority date for domestic students. Applications are processed on a rolling basis. Application fee: $60. Electronic applications accepted. *Expenses:* Tuition: Full-time $35,046; part-time $1524 per credit. Required fees: $161 per semester. *Financial support:* Fellowships, research assistantships, teaching assistantships, Federal Work-Study, institutionally sponsored loans, and scholarships/grants available. Support available to part-time students. Financial award application deadline: 2/15; financial award applicants required to submit FAFSA. *Unit head:* Laura Zucker, Director, 909-607-9109, Fax: 909-621-8330, E-mail: laura.zucker@cgu.edu. *Application contact:* Susan Hampson, Admissions and Academic Support, 909-607-1278, Fax: 909-607-1221, E-mail: susan.hampson@cgu.edu.

The College at Brockport, State University of New York, School of Education and Human Services, Department of Public Administration, Brockport, NY 14420-2997. Offers arts administration (AGC); nonprofit management (AGC); public administration (MPA), including general public administration, health care management, nonprofit management, public safety. *Accreditation:* NASPAA. Part-time and evening/weekend programs available. *Students:* 25 full-time (18 women), 91 part-time (72 women); includes 18 minority (12 African Americans, 3 Asian Americans or Pacific Islanders, 3 Hispanic Americans). 42 applicants, 95% accepted, 33 enrolled. In 2009, 30 master's awarded. *Degree requirements:* For master's, thesis or alternative. *Entrance requirements:* For master's, GRE or minimum GPA of 3.0, letters of recommendation, statement of objectives. Additional exam requirements/recommendations for international students: Required—TOEFL (minimum score 550 paper-based; 213 computer-based; 79 iBT). *Application deadline:* For fall admission, 3/1 priority date for domestic and international students; for spring admission, 10/1 priority date for domestic and international students. Application fee: $50. Electronic applications accepted. *Expenses:* Tuition, state resident: full-time $8370; part-time $349 per credit. Tuition, nonresident: full-time $13,250; part-time $522 per credit. *Financial support:* In 2009–10, 1 fellowship with full tuition reimbursement (averaging $7,500 per year) was awarded; Federal Work-Study, scholarships/grants, and unspecified assistantships also available. Support available to part-time students. Financial award application deadline: 3/15; financial award applicants required to submit FAFSA. *Faculty research:* E-government, performance management, nonprofits and policy implementation, Medicaid and disabilities. *Unit head:* Dr. James Fatula, Chairperson, 585-395-2375, Fax: 585-395-2172, E-mail: jfatula@brockport.edu. *Application contact:* Dr. James Fatual, Chairperson, 585-395-2375, Fax: 585-395-2172, E-mail: jfatula@brockport.edu.

College of Charleston, Graduate School, School of the Arts, Program in Arts Management, Charleston, SC 29424-0001. Offers MPA, Certificate. Evening/weekend programs available. *Faculty:* 1 (woman) full-time. *Students:* 1 part-time (0 women); minority (Hispanic American). Average age 25. 2 applicants, 50% accepted, 0 enrolled. In 2009, 3 other advanced degrees awarded. *Entrance requirements:* For degree, minimum GPA of 3.0, writing sample. Additional exam requirements/recommendations for international students: Required—TOEFL. *Application deadline:* For fall admission, 4/1 for domestic students; for spring admission, 11/1 for domestic students. Application fee: $45. *Unit head:* Scott Peterson, Director, 843-953-8421, E-mail: petersons@cofc.edu. *Application contact:* Susan Hallatt, Director of Graduate Admissions, 843-953-5614, Fax: 843-953-1434, E-mail: hallatts@cofc.edu.

Columbia College Chicago, Graduate School, Department of Arts, Entertainment and Media Management, Chicago, IL 60605-1996. Offers arts, entertainment and media management (MA), including media management, music business management, performing arts management, visual arts management. Evening/weekend programs available. *Degree requirements:* For master's, thesis, internship. *Entrance requirements:* For master's, self-assessment essay. Additional exam requirements/recommendations for international students: Required—TOEFL (minimum score 550 paper-based; 213 computer-based). Electronic applications accepted. *Expenses:* Tuition: Part-time $651 per credit hour. Required fees: $651 per credit hour. $205 per semester. One-time fee: $285 part-time. Tuition and fees vary according to program.

Drexel University, Antoinette Westphal College of Media Arts and Design, Program in Arts Administration, Philadelphia, PA 19104-2875. Offers MS. *Accreditation:* NASAD. Part-time and evening/weekend programs available. *Degree requirements:* For master's, thesis, internship. *Entrance requirements:* For master's, GRE, interview, minimum GPA of 3.0, previous course work in arts and business. Additional exam requirements/recommendations for international students: Required—TOEFL. Electronic applications accepted. *Faculty research:* Evaluation of art administration structures, funding for the arts, impact of politics in the arts, computer applications.

Eastern Michigan University, Graduate School, College of Arts and Sciences, Department of Communication, Media and Theatre Arts, Program in Arts Administration, Ypsilanti, MI 48197. Offers theatre arts-arts administration (MA). Part-time and evening/weekend programs available. Postbaccalaureate distance learning degree programs offered (minimal on-campus study). *Students:* 4 full-time (3 women), 20 part-time (15 women); includes 1 minority (African American), 5 international. Average age 23. In 2009, 9 master's awarded. *Entrance requirements:* Additional exam requirements/recommendations for international students: Required—TOEFL. *Application deadline:* Applications are processed on a rolling basis. Application fee: $35. Tuition and fees vary according to course level. *Financial support:* Fellowships, research assistantships with full tuition reimbursements, teaching assistantships with full tuition reimbursements, career-related internships or fieldwork, Federal Work-Study, institutionally sponsored loans, scholarships/grants, tuition waivers (partial), and unspecified assistantships available. Support available to part-time students. Financial award applicants required to submit FAFSA. *Unit head:* Kenneth Stevens, Coordinator, 734-487-3130, Fax: 734-487-3443, E-mail: ken.stevens@emich.edu. *Application contact:* Kenneth Stevens, Coordinator, 734-487-3130, Fax: 734-487-3443, E-mail: ken.stevens@emich.edu.

Fashion Institute of Technology, School of Graduate Studies, Program in Art Market: Principles and Practices, New York, NY 10001-5992. Offers MA. *Accreditation:* NASAD. *Degree requirements:* For master's, one foreign language, thesis, internship. *Entrance requirements:* For master's, GRE General Test, previous course work in art history, 4 semesters of a foreign language. Additional exam requirements/recommendations for international students: Required—TOEFL (minimum score 550 paper-based; 213 computer-based). Electronic applications accepted. *Expenses:* Tuition, state resident: full-time $8198; part-time $342 per credit. Tuition, nonresident: full-time $12,972; part-time $541 per credit. Required fees: $450.

See Close-Up on page 115.

Florida State University, The Graduate School, College of Music, Tallahassee, FL 32306. Offers accompanying (MM); arts administration (MA); choral conducting (MM); composition (MM, DM); ethnomusicology (MM); general music (MA); instrumental accompanying (MM); instrumental conducting (MM); jazz studies (MM); music education (MM Ed, PhD); music theory (MM, PhD); music therapy (MM); musicology (MM, PhD), including ethnomusicology (PhD), historical musicology; opera (MM); performance (MM, DM); piano pedagogy (MM); piano technology (MA); vocal accompanying (MM). *Accreditation:* NASM. *Faculty:* 88 full-time, 13 part-time/adjunct. *Students:* 406 full-time (211 women); includes 98 minority (28 African Americans, 38 Asian Americans or Pacific Islanders, 32 Hispanic Americans). Average age 26. 525 applicants, 38% accepted, 145 enrolled. In 2009, 102 master's, 41 doctorates awarded. *Degree requirements:* For master's, comprehensive exam (for some programs), thesis (for some programs), departmental qualifying exam; for doctorate, comprehensive exam (for some programs), thesis/dissertation, departmental qualifying exam. *Entrance requirements:* For master's and doctorate, audition, GRE General Test or minimum GPA of 3.0. Additional exam requirements/recommendations for international students: Required—TOEFL (minimum score 550 paper-based; 213 computer-based). *Application deadline:* For fall admission, 7/1 for domestic students, 5/2 for international students; for spring admission, 11/3 for domestic students, 9/1 for international students. Applications are processed on a rolling basis. Application fee: $30. Electronic applications accepted. *Expenses:* Tuition, state resident: full-time $7413. Tuition, nonresident: full-time $22,567. *Financial support:* In 2009–10, 225 students received support, including 3 fellowships with full tuition reimbursements available (averaging $15,000 per year), 9 research assistantships with full tuition reimbursements available (averaging $4,000 per year), 173 teaching assistantships with full tuition reimbursements available (averaging $4,000 per year); career-related internships or fieldwork, Federal Work-Study, and tuition waivers (partial) also available. Support available to part-time students. Financial award application deadline: 2/28; financial award applicants required to submit FAFSA. *Unit head:* Don Gibson, Dean, 850-644-4361, Fax: 850-644-2033. *Application contact:* Dr. Seth Beckman, Senior Associate Dean for Academic Affairs/Director of Graduate Studies, 850-644-5848, Fax: 850-644-2033, E-mail: sbeckman@admin.fsu.edu.

George Mason University, College of Visual and Performing Arts, Program in Arts Management, Fairfax, VA 22030. Offers arts entrepreneurship (Certificate); arts management (MA); fund raising and development in the arts (Certificate); public relations and marketing in the arts (Certificate); special events management in the arts (Certificate). *Faculty:* 1 (woman) full-time, 3 part-time/adjunct (2 women). *Students:* 39 full-time (37 women), 48 part-time (40 women); includes 7 minority (4 African Americans, 2 Asian Americans or Pacific Islanders, 1 Hispanic American), 11 international. Average age 30. 76 applicants, 71% accepted, 37 enrolled. In 2009, 27 master's awarded. *Entrance requirements:* For master's, GRE (recommended), minimum GPA of 3.0, 2 letters of recommendation, personal interview, resume, work experience. Additional exam requirements/recommendations for international students: Required—TOEFL. *Application deadline:* For fall admission, 3/1 priority date for domestic students; for spring admission, 10/1 for domestic students. Applications are processed on a rolling basis. Application fee: $75. Electronic applications accepted. *Expenses:* Tuition, state resident: full-time $7568; part-time $315.33 per credit hour. Tuition, nonresident: full-time $21,704; part-time $904.33 per credit hour. Required fees: $2184; $91 per credit hour. *Financial support:* Application deadline: 3/1. *Faculty research:* Information technology for arts managers, special topics in arts management, directions in gallery management, arts in society, public relations/marketing strategies for art organizations. *Unit head:* William Reeder, Dean, 703-993-8624, Fax: 703-993-8883. *Application contact:* Richard Kamenitzer, Director, 703-993-9194, E-mail: rkamenit@gmu.edu.

Goucher College, Program in Arts Administration, Baltimore, MD 21204-2794. Offers MA. Part-time programs available. Postbaccalaureate distance learning degree programs offered (minimal on-campus study). *Degree requirements:* For master's, internship, major paper. *Entrance requirements:* For master's, 2 years of post-baccalaureate work experience. *Expenses:* Contact institution.

HEC Montreal, School of Business Administration, Diploma Programs in Administration, Program in Management of Cultural Organizations, Montréal, QC H3T 2A7, Canada. Offers Diploma. All courses are given in French. Part-time programs available. *Students:* 41 full-time (29 women), 144 part-time (119 women). 78 applicants, 85% accepted, 54 enrolled. In 2009, 48 Diplomas awarded. *Degree requirements:* For Diploma, one foreign language. *Entrance requirements:* For degree, 2 years of relevant work experience, 2 letters of recommendation. *Application deadline:* For fall admission, 4/15 for domestic and international students; for winter admission, 10/1 for domestic and international students. Application fee: $77 Canadian dollars. Electronic applications accepted. Tuition and fees charges are reported in Canadian dollars. *Expenses:* Tuition, area resident: Part-time $65.60 Canadian dollars per credit. Tuition, state resident: full-time $2361.60 Canadian dollars; part-time $183.36 Canadian dollars per credit. Tuition, nonresident: full-time $6601 Canadian dollars; part-time $448.13 Canadian dollars per credit. International tuition: $16,132.68 Canadian dollars full-time. Required fees: $1254.15 Canadian dollars; $28.99 Canadian dollars per course. $91.68 Canadian dollars per term. Tuition and fees vary according to degree level and program. *Financial support:* Scholarships/grants available. *Unit head:* Louise Cote, Director, 514-340-6205, Fax: 514-340-5640, E-mail: louise.cote@hec.ca. *Application contact:* Marie Deshaies, Senior Student Advisor, 514-340-6135, Fax: 514-340-6411, E-mail: marie.deshaies@hec.ca.

Montclair State University, The Graduate School, School of the Arts, Department of Theatre and Dance, Montclair, NJ 07043-1624. Offers theatre (MA), including arts management, production/stage management, theatre studies. *Accreditation:* NAST. Part-time and evening/weekend programs available. *Faculty:* 15 full-time (8 women), 37 part-time/adjunct (24 women). *Students:* 10 full-time (8 women), 15 part-time (11 women). Average age 29. 18 applicants, 56% accepted, 7 enrolled. In 2009, 7 master's awarded. *Degree requirements:* For master's, comprehensive exam, thesis or alternative. *Entrance requirements:* For master's, GRE General Test, 2 letters of recommendation. Additional exam requirements/recommendations for international students: Required—TOEFL (minimum score 83 computer-based), or IELTS. *Application deadline:* For fall admission, 6/1 for international students; for spring admission, 10/1 for international students. Applications are processed on a rolling basis. Application fee: $60. Electronic applications accepted. *Expenses:* Tuition, area resident: Part-time $486.74 per credit. Tuition, state resident: part-time $486.74 per credit. Tuition, nonresident: part-time $751.34 per credit. Tuition and fees vary according to degree level and program. *Financial support:* In 2009–10, 2 research assistantships with full tuition reimbursements (averaging $7,000 per year) were awarded; Federal Work-Study, scholarships/grants, and unspecified assistantships also available. Support available to part-time students. Financial award application deadline: 3/1; financial award applicants required to submit FAFSA. *Unit head:* Dr. Eric Diamond, Chairperson, 973-655-4217, E-mail: peterson@mail.montclair.edu. *Application contact:* Amy Aiello, Director of Graduate Admissions and Operations, 973-655-5147, E-mail: petersonj@mail.montclair.edu.

New York University, Steinhardt School of Culture, Education, and Human Development, Department of Art and Art Professions, Program in Visual Arts Administration, New York, NY 10003. Offers for-profit sector (MA); not-for-profit sector (MA). Part-time programs available. *Students:* 64 full-time (57 women), 21 part-time (20 women); includes 12 minority (3 Asian Americans or Pacific Islanders, 9 Hispanic Americans), 15 international. Average age 25. 173 applicants, 46% accepted, 45 enrolled. In 2009, 35 master's awarded. *Degree requirements:* For master's, thesis (for some programs). *Entrance requirements:* For master's, interview. Additional exam requirements/recommendations for international students: Required—TOEFL. *Application deadline:* For fall admission, 12/15 priority date for domestic and international students. Applications are processed on a rolling basis. Application fee: $75. Electronic applications accepted. *Expenses:* Tuition: Full-time $30,528; part-time $1272 per credit. Required fees: $2177. *Financial support:* Career-related internships or fieldwork, Federal Work-Study, institutionally sponsored loans, scholarships/grants, and tuition waivers (partial) available. Support available to part-time students. Financial award application deadline: 2/1; financial award applicants required to submit FAFSA. *Faculty research:* Corporate philanthropy, contemporary art and culture, public art and urban development, cultural policy, arts advocacy. *Unit head:* Sandra Lang, Head, 212-998-5723, Fax: 212-995-4320, E-mail: sandra.lang@nyu.edu. *Application contact:* 212-998-5030, Fax: 212-995-4328, E-mail: steinhardt.gradadmissions@nyu.edu.

New York University, Steinhardt School of Culture, Education, and Human Development, Department of Music and Performing Arts Professions, Program in Performing Arts Administration, New York, NY 10012-1019. Offers MA. Part-time programs available. *Students:* 31 full-time (24 women), 12 part-time (11 women); includes 7 minority (2 African Americans, 2 Asian Americans or Pacific Islanders, 3 Hispanic Americans), 13 international. Average age 27. 126 applicants, 44% accepted, 24 enrolled. In 2009, 31 master's awarded. *Degree requirements:* For master's, thesis (for some programs). *Entrance requirements:* For master's, interview. Additional exam requirements/recommendations for international students: Required—TOEFL. *Application deadline:* For fall admission, 12/15 priority date for domestic students, 12/15 for international students. Applications are processed on a rolling basis. Application fee: $75. Electronic applications accepted. *Expenses:* Tuition: Full-time $30,528; part-time $1272 per credit. Required fees: $2177. *Financial support:* Career-related internships or fieldwork, Federal Work-Study, institutionally sponsored loans, scholarships/grants, and tuition waivers (partial) available. Support available to part-time students. Financial award application deadline: 2/1; financial award applicants required to submit FAFSA. *Faculty research:* Legal dimensions of arts management, global arts management, cultural policy. *Unit head:* Prof. Brann J. Wry, Director, 212-998-5424, Fax: 212-995-4560. *Application contact:* 212-998-5030, Fax: 212-995-4328, E-mail: steinhardt.gradadmissions@nyu.edu.

New York University, Tisch School of the Arts, Program in Arts Politics, New York, NY 10012-1019. Offers MA. *Faculty:* 3 full-time (2 women), 4 part-time/adjunct (3 women). *Students:* 10 full-time (9 women), 1 (woman) part-time; includes 4 minority (1 African American, 3 Asian Americans or Pacific Islanders). Average age 25. 45 applicants, 58% accepted. *Degree requirements:* For master's, thesis. *Entrance requirements:* For master's, professional resume, writing sample, statement of purpose. Additional exam requirements/recommendations for international students: Required—TOEFL, IELTS or ALI. *Application deadline:* For fall admission, 1/1 for domestic and international students. Application fee: $60. *Expenses:* Tuition: Full-time $30,528; part-time $1272 per credit. Required fees: $2177. *Financial support:* In 2009–10, 2 students received support. Federal Work-Study and scholarships/grants available. Financial award application deadline: 2/15; financial award applicants required to submit FAFSA. *Unit head:* Randy Martin, Director of the program, 212-992-8248. *Application contact:* Dan Sandford, Director of Graduate Admissions, 212-998-1918, Fax: 212-995-4060, E-mail: tisch.gradadmissions@nyu.edu.

The Ohio State University, Graduate School, College of the Arts, Department of Art Education, Program in Arts Policy and Administration, Columbus, OH 43210. Offers MA. *Faculty:* 14. *Students:* 9 full-time (8 women), 1 (woman) part-time, 3 international. Average age 25. In 2009, 9 master's awarded. *Degree requirements:* For master's, thesis. *Entrance requirements:* For master's, GRE General Test. Additional exam requirements/recommendations for international students: Required—TOEFL (minimum score 600 paper-based; 250 computer-based). *Application deadline:* For fall admission, 8/15 priority date for domestic students, 7/1 priority date for international students; for winter admission, 12/1 priority date for domestic students, 11/1 priority date for international students; for spring admission, 3/1 priority date for domestic students, 2/1 priority date for international students. Applications are processed on a rolling basis. Application fee: $40 ($50 for international students). Electronic applications accepted. *Expenses:* Tuition, state resident: full-time $10,683. Tuition, nonresident: full-time $25,923. Tuition and fees vary according to course load and program. *Financial support:* Fellowships, career-related internships or fieldwork and unspecified assistantships available. Support available to part-time students. Financial award application deadline: 4/5; financial award applicants required to submit FAFSA. *Faculty research:* Public policy and advocacy. *Unit head:* Christine Ballengee-Morris, Graduate Studies Committee Chair, E-mail: morris.390@osu.edu. *Application contact:* 614-292-9444, Fax: 614-292-3895, E-mail: domestic.grad@osu.edu.

Pratt Institute, School of Art and Design, Program in Arts and Cultural Management, New York, NY 10011. Offers MPS. Part-time and evening/weekend programs available. *Faculty:* 1 (woman) full-time, 13 part-time/adjunct (9 women). *Students:* 59 full-time (52 women), 1 (woman) part-time; includes 11 minority (2 African Americans, 5 Asian Americans or Pacific Islanders, 4 Hispanic Americans), 17 international. Average age 28. 110 applicants, 51% accepted, 26 enrolled. In 2009, 24 master's awarded. *Degree requirements:* For master's, thesis. *Entrance requirements:* For master's, letters of recommendation, portfolio. Additional exam requirements/recommendations for international students: Required—TOEFL (minimum score 600 paper-based; 250 computer-based; 100 iBT). *Application deadline:* For fall admission, 1/5 for domestic and international students; for spring admission, 10/1 for domestic and international students. Application fee: $50 ($90 for international students). Electronic applications accepted. *Expenses:* Tuition: Full-time $22,734. Required fees: $1280. *Financial support:* Career-related internships or fieldwork, Federal Work-Study, institutionally sponsored loans, scholarships/grants, health care benefits, and unspecified assistantships available. Support available to part-time students. Financial award application deadline: 2/1; financial award applicants required to submit FAFSA. *Unit head:* Monica Shay, Director, 212-647-7560, E-mail: mshay@pratt.edu. *Application contact:* Young Hah, Director of Graduate Admissions, 718-636-3683, Fax: 718-399-4242, E-mail: yhah@pratt.edu.

Pratt Institute, School of Art and Design, Program in Design Management, New York, NY 10011. Offers MPS. Part-time programs available. *Faculty:* 2 full-time (both women), 8 part-time/adjunct (4 women). *Students:* 51 full-time (35 women); includes 8 minority (6 African Americans, 1 Asian American or Pacific Islander, 1 Hispanic American), 17 international. Average age 31. 77 applicants, 62% accepted, 26 enrolled. In 2009, 28 master's awarded. *Degree requirements:* For master's, thesis. *Entrance requirements:* For master's, letters of recommendation, portfolio. Additional exam requirements/recommendations for international students: Required—TOEFL (minimum score 600 paper-based; 250 computer-based; 100 iBT). *Application deadline:* For fall admission, 1/5 for domestic and international students; for spring admission, 10/1 for domestic and international students. Application fee: $50 ($90 for international students). Electronic applications accepted. *Expenses:* Tuition: Full-time $22,734. Required fees: $1280. *Financial support:* Career-related internships or fieldwork, Federal Work-Study, institutionally sponsored loans, scholarships/grants, health care benefits, and unspecified assistantships available. Support available to part-time students. Financial award application deadline: 2/1; financial award applicants required to submit FAFSA. *Unit head:*

Arts Administration

Pratt Institute (continued)
Mary McBride, Chairperson, 212-647-7538, E-mail: mmcb1033@pratt.edu. *Application contact:* Young Hah, Director of Graduate Admissions, 718-636-3683, Fax: 718-399-4242, E-mail: yhah@pratt.edu.

See Close-Up on page 119.

Regis University, College for Professional Studies, MA Program, Denver, CO 80221-1099. Offers criminology (MA); fine arts administration (Certificate); language and communication (MA); mediation (Certificate); psychology (MA); self-designed major (MA); social justice, peace, and reconciliation (Certificate); social science (MA); technical communication (Certificate). Program also offered in Henderson and Las Vegas (Summerlin), NV. Part-time and evening/weekend programs available. Postbaccalaureate distance learning degree programs offered (minimal on-campus study). *Degree requirements:* For master's, thesis, research project. *Entrance requirements:* For master's, resume, recommendations. Additional exam requirements/recommendations for international students: Required—TOEFL (minimum score 213 computer-based), TWE (minimum score 5). Electronic applications accepted. *Expenses:* Contact institution. *Faculty research:* Independent/nonresidential graduate study: new methods and models, adult learning and the capstone experience, Goal Setting, behavior of Adult students, Innovative Studies for Community Colleges.

Rhode Island College, School of Graduate Studies, Faculty of Arts and Sciences, Department of Art, Providence, RI 02908-1991. Offers art education (MA, MAT); media studies (MA). *Accreditation:* NASAD (one or more programs are accredited). Part-time and evening/weekend programs available. *Faculty:* 4 full-time (1 woman). *Students:* 9 full-time (5 women), 15 part-time (9 women). Average age 36. In 2009, 3 master's awarded. *Degree requirements:* For master's, thesis. *Entrance requirements:* For master's, GRE General Test or MAT, portfolio (MA), 3 letters of recommendation, interview. Additional exam requirements/recommendations for international students: Recommended—TOEFL (minimum score 550 paper-based; 213 computer-based; 79 iBT). *Application deadline:* For fall admission, 4/1 for domestic students; for spring admission, 11/1 for domestic students. Applications are processed on a rolling basis. Application fee: $50. *Expenses:* Tuition, state resident: full-time $7440; part-time $310 per credit hour. Tuition, nonresident: full-time $14,784; part-time $616 per credit hour. Required fees: $552; $20 per credit. $70 per term. *Financial support:* Teaching assistantships with full tuition reimbursements, career-related internships or fieldwork, Federal Work-Study, scholarships/grants, health care benefits, and unspecified assistantships available. Support available to part-time students. Financial award application deadline: 5/15; financial award applicants required to submit FAFSA. *Unit head:* Prof. Nancy Bockbrader, Chair, 401-456-8054. *Application contact:* Graduate Studies, 401-456-8700.

Ryerson University, School of Graduate Studies, Program in Photographic Preservation and Collections Management, Toronto, ON M5B 2K3, Canada. Offers MA.

Saint Mary's University of Minnesota, Schools of Graduate and Professional Programs, Graduate School of Business and Technology, Arts and Cultural Management Program, Winona, MN 55987-1399. Offers MA. *Unit head:* Paula Justich, Director, 612-728-5165, Fax: 612-728-5121, E-mail: pjustich@smumn.edu. *Application contact:* Yasin Alsaidi, Director of Admissions for Graduate and Professional Programs, 612-728-5207, Fax: 612-728-5121, E-mail: yalsaidi@smumn.edu.

St. Thomas University, School of Leadership Studies, Program in Art Management, Miami Gardens, FL 33054-6459. Offers MA.

Savannah College of Art and Design, Graduate School, Program in Arts Administration, Savannah, GA 31402-3146. Offers MA. Part-time programs available. *Degree requirements:* For master's, thesis. *Entrance requirements:* For master's, interview. Additional exam requirements/recommendations for international students: Required—TOEFL (minimum score 450 paper-based; 133 computer-based). *Expenses:* Tuition: Full-time $28,515; part-time $627 per credit hour. One-time fee: $500. Tuition and fees vary according to course load.

School of the Art Institute of Chicago, Graduate Division, Program in Arts Administration and Policy, Chicago, IL 60603-3103. Offers MAAAP. *Accreditation:* NASAD. *Degree requirements:* For master's, thesis, telephone interview. *Entrance requirements:* Additional exam requirements/recommendations for international students: Required—TOEFL, IELTS. *Faculty research:* Latin American artists, activist art, community-based art.

Shenandoah University, Shenandoah Conservatory, Winchester, VA 22601-5195. Offers arts administration (MS); church music (MM, Certificate); composition (MM); conducting (MM); dance (MA, MS); music education (MME, DMA); music therapy (MMT, Certificate); pedagogy (MM, DMA); performance (MM, DMA, Artist Diploma); piano accompanying (MM). *Accreditation:* NASM. *Faculty:* 39 full-time (15 women), 17 part-time/adjunct (5 women). *Students:* 72 full-time (42 women), 134 part-time (83 women); includes 40 minority (14 African Americans, 22 Asian Americans or Pacific Islanders, 4 Hispanic Americans), 16 international. Average age 35. 115 applicants, 88% accepted, 70 enrolled. In 2009, 40 master's, 5 doctorates, 9 other advanced degrees awarded. *Degree requirements:* For master's, comprehensive exam (for some programs), thesis (for some programs), internship (MS), recital (MM), research teaching project or thesis (MME), project (MA); for doctorate, comprehensive exam, thesis/dissertation (for some programs), dissertation or teaching project, recital; for other advanced degree, research project, recital. *Entrance requirements:* For master's, audition, minimum GPA of 2.5, writing sample, resume; for doctorate, audition, minimum GPA of 3.25, 2 letters of recommendation, writing sample, resume; for other advanced degree, bachelor or master's degree; minimum GPA of 2.5. Additional exam requirements/recommendations for international students: Required—TOEFL (minimum score 550 paper-based; 213 computer-based; 79 iBT), IELTS (minimum score 6.5). *Application deadline:* Applications are processed on a rolling basis. Application fee: $30. Electronic applications accepted. *Expenses:* Tuition: Full-time $11,925; part-time $695 per credit. Required fees: $400 per semester. *Financial support:* Application deadline: 3/15. *Unit head:* Dr. Laurence A. Kaptain, Dean, 540-665-4600, Fax: 540-665-5402, E-mail: lkaptain@su.edu. *Application contact:* David Anthony, Dean of Admissions, 540-665-4581, Fax: 540-665-4627, E-mail: admit@su.edu.

Southern Methodist University, Meadows School of the Arts, Division of Arts Administration, Dallas, TX 75275. Offers MA/MBA. *Faculty:* 2 full-time (both women), 1 (woman) part-time/adjunct. *Students:* 22 full-time (18 women); includes 2 minority (1 African American, 1 Asian American or Pacific Islander), 2 international. Average age 25. 18 applicants, 72% accepted, 7 enrolled. *Entrance requirements:* Additional exam requirements/recommendations for international students: Required—TOEFL (minimum score 600 paper-based; 250 computer-based; 100 iBT). *Application deadline:* For fall admission, 1/15 priority date for domestic and international students. Applications are processed on a rolling basis. Application fee: $75. Electronic applications accepted. *Unit head:* Dr. P. Gregory Warden, Interim Chair, 214-768-3425, E-mail: lhilliar@smu.edu. *Application contact:* Lynette Hilliard, Assistant Director, 214-768-3425, E-mail: ihilliar@smu.edu.

Southern Utah University, College of Performing and Visual Arts, Program in Arts Administration, Cedar City, UT 84720-2498. Offers MFA. *Faculty:* 1 full-time (0 women). *Students:* 9 full-time (4 women); includes 1 Hispanic American. Average age 26. 18 applicants, 22% accepted, 4 enrolled. In 2009, 6 master's awarded. *Entrance requirements:* For master's, GRE General Test, interview, 3 letters of recommendation, resume, minimum GPA of 3.0. *Application deadline:* For fall admission, 3/31 for domestic students. Applications are processed on a rolling basis. Application fee: $50 ($65 for international students). Electronic applications accepted. *Financial support:* In 2009–10, 10 fellowships with full tuition reimbursements (averaging $7,700 per year) were awarded. *Unit head:* Shauna Mendini, Interim Dean, 435-865-8554, Fax: 435-865-8580, E-mail: mendini_s@suu.edu. *Application contact:* Matt Neves, Director, 435-586-7873, Fax: 435-865-8657, E-mail: neves@suu.edu.

Teachers College, Columbia University, Graduate Faculty of Education, Department of Arts and Humanities, Program in Arts Administration, New York, NY 10027-6696. Offers MA. *Faculty:* 1 (woman) full-time, 2 part-time/adjunct. *Students:* 56 full-time (43 women), 13 part-time (11 women); includes 12 minority (3 African Americans, 8 Asian Americans or Pacific Islanders, 1 Hispanic American), 15 international. Average age 28. 114 applicants, 46% accepted, 30 enrolled. In 2009, 31 master's awarded. *Degree requirements:* For master's, thesis, internship. *Entrance requirements:* For master's, GRE, approximately 3 years of related experience. Additional exam requirements/recommendations for international students: Required—TOEFL. *Application deadline:* For fall admission, 1/15 priority date for domestic students. Application fee: $65. *Financial support:* Career-related internships or fieldwork, Federal Work-Study, institutionally sponsored loans, tuition waivers (partial), and unspecified assistantships available. Financial award application deadline: 2/1. *Faculty research:* Artists' career development, arts law, American culture, strategic management, international training. *Unit head:* Graeme Sullivan, Chair, 212-678-3799. *Application contact:* Graeme Sullivan, Chair, 212-678-3799.

Temple University, Graduate School, Tyler School of Art, Department of Art History, Philadelphia, PA 19122-6096. Offers MA, PhD. Part-time programs available. Terminal master's awarded for partial completion of doctoral program. *Degree requirements:* For master's, 2 foreign languages, thesis, comprehensive slide exam; for doctorate, thesis/dissertation, qualifying exam. *Entrance requirements:* For master's, GRE General Test, minimum GPA of 3.0; for doctorate, MA in art history. Additional exam requirements/recommendations for international students: Required—TOEFL. Electronic applications accepted. *Faculty research:* Aegean, Greek, and Roman art; early Christian art; Medieval art and architecture; Renaissance and baroque painting, sculpture, and architecture; nineteenth and twentieth century painting and sculpture.

Universidad del Turabo, Graduate Programs, School of Social Sciences and Humanities, Programs in Public Affairs, Program in Arts Administration, Gurabo, PR 00778-3030. Offers MPA. *Students:* 7 full-time (6 women), 1 (woman) part-time; includes 7 minority (all Hispanic Americans). Average age 32. 4 applicants, 100% accepted, 3 enrolled. In 2009, 6 master's awarded. *Unit head:* Dr. Marco A. Gil Dela Madrid, Dean, 787-743-7979. *Application contact:* Virginia Gonzalez, Admissions Officer, 787-746-3009.

The University of Akron, Graduate School, College of Creative and Professional Arts, School of Dance, Theatre, and Arts Administration, Program in Arts Administration, Akron, OH 44325. Offers MA. *Accreditation:* NASAD. *Students:* 26 full-time (22 women), 6 part-time (4 women); includes 1 minority (African American), 5 international. Average age 28. 25 applicants, 68% accepted, 12 enrolled. In 2009, 5 master's awarded. *Degree requirements:* For master's, thesis optional. *Entrance requirements:* For master's, minimum GPA of 2.75, interview. Additional exam requirements/recommendations for international students: Required—TOEFL (minimum score 550 paper-based; 213 computer-based; 79 iBT). *Application deadline:* For fall admission, 3/15 priority date for domestic and international students. Applications are processed on a rolling basis. Application fee: $30 ($40 for international students). Electronic applications accepted. *Expenses:* Tuition, state resident: full-time $6570; part-time $365 per credit hour. Tuition, nonresident: full-time $11,250; part-time $625 per credit hour. *Unit head:* Durand Pope, Coordinator, 330-972-5380, E-mail: dpope@uakron.edu. *Application contact:* Durand Pope, Coordinator, 330-972-5380, E-mail: dpope@uakron.edu.

University of Cincinnati, Graduate School, College-Conservatory of Music, Divisions of Opera, Musical Theater, Drama, and Arts Administration, Cincinnati, OH 45221. Offers arts administration (MA); directing (MFA); theater design and production (MFA); voice and opera (MM, DMA); MBA/MA. *Accreditation:* NAST (one or more programs are accredited). *Degree requirements:* For master's, final project. *Entrance requirements:* For master's, GMAT (MA), audition/interview. Additional exam requirements/recommendations for international students: Required—TOEFL (minimum score 520 paper-based; 190 computer-based). Electronic applications accepted.

University of Florida, Graduate School, Warrington College of Business Administration, Hough Graduate School of Business, Programs in Business Administration, Gainesville, FL 32611. Offers accounting (MBA); arts administration (MBA); business strategy and public policy (MBA); competitive strategy (MBA); decision and information sciences (MBA); electronic commerce (MBA); finance (MBA); general business (MBA); global management (MBA); Graham-Buffett security analysis (MBA); health administration (MBA); human resources management (MBA); international studies (MBA); Latin American business (MBA); management (MBA); marketing (MBA); sports administration (MBA); JD/MBA; MBA/MS; MBA/PhD; MBA/Pharm D; MD/MBA. *Accreditation:* AACSB. Part-time and evening/weekend programs available. Postbaccalaureate distance learning degree programs offered. *Entrance requirements:* For master's, GMAT, minimum GPA of 3.0, interview. Additional exam requirements/recommendations for international students: Required—TOEFL (minimum score 550 paper-based; 213 computer-based). Electronic applications accepted. *Faculty research:* Accounting, finance, insurance, management, real estate and urban analysis marketing.

University of New Orleans, Graduate School, College of Liberal Arts, Program in Arts Administration, New Orleans, LA 70148. Offers MA. Part-time programs available. *Degree requirements:* For master's, internship. *Entrance requirements:* For master's, GMAT, GRE General Test. Additional exam requirements/recommendations for international students: Required—TOEFL (minimum score 550 paper-based; 213 computer-based; 79 iBT). Electronic applications accepted.

University of North Carolina School of the Arts, School of Design and Production, Winston-Salem, NC 27127-2188. Offers costume design (MFA); costume technology (MFA); performance arts management (MFA); scene design (MFA); scene painting/properties (MFA); sound design (MFA); stage automation (MFA); technical direction (MFA); wig and make-up design (MFA). *Faculty:* 19 full-time (4 women), 16 part-time/adjunct (6 women). *Students:* 70 full-time (52 women); includes 10 minority (3 African Americans, 3 American Indian/Alaska Native, 3 Asian Americans or Pacific Islanders, 1 Hispanic American), 3 international. Average age 25. 86 applicants, 77% accepted, 48 enrolled. In 2009, 13 master's awarded. *Degree requirements:* For master's, thesis (for some programs), project. *Entrance requirements:* For master's, interview, portfolio. Additional exam requirements/recommendations for international students: Required—TOEFL. *Application deadline:* For fall admission, 4/1 priority date for domestic students. Applications are processed on a rolling basis. Application fee: $60 ($100 for international students). Electronic applications accepted. *Expenses:* Tuition, state resident: full-time $3797. Tuition, nonresident: full-time $15,670. Required fees: $1992. *Financial support:* In 2009–10, 47 teaching assistantships with partial tuition reimbursements (averaging $1,500 per year) were awarded; career-related internships or fieldwork, Federal Work-Study, and unspecified assistantships also available. Support available to part-time students. Financial award application deadline: 3/15; financial award applicants required to submit FAFSA. *Unit head:* Joseph A. Tilford, Dean, 336-770-3214 Ext. 103, Fax: 336-770-3213, E-mail: tilford@uncsa.edu. *Application contact:* Sheeler Lawson, Director of Admissions, 336-770-3290, Fax: 336-770-3370, E-mail: admissions@uncsa.edu.

University of Oregon, Graduate School, School of Architecture and Allied Arts, Program in Arts and Administration, Eugene, OR 97403. Offers arts management (MA, MS); media management (MA, MS). *Degree requirements:* For master's, summer internship, thesis/project. *Entrance requirements:* For master's, minimum GPA of 3.0; bachelor's degree in history, practice of visual, performing arts or other related degree. Additional exam requirements/recommendations for international students: Required—TOEFL. *Faculty research:* Museum education, arts program evaluation, community arts, information management, arts marketing.

University of Southern California, Graduate School, Roski School of Fine Arts, Graduate Programs in Public Art Studies, Los Angeles, CA 90089. Offers MPAS. *Faculty:* 2 full-time (1 woman), 5 part-time/adjunct (all women). *Students:* 27 full-time (26 women), 1 (woman) part-time; includes 10 minority (4 African Americans, 4 Asian Americans or Pacific Islanders, 2 Hispanic Americans). 46 applicants, 26% accepted, 10 enrolled. In 2009, 12 master's awarded. *Degree requirements:* For master's, thesis. *Entrance requirements:* For master's, GRE General

Test. Additional exam requirements/recommendations for international students: Required—TOEFL (minimum score 600 paper-based; 250 computer-based; 100 iBT). *Application deadline:* For fall admission, 3/1 priority date for domestic and international students. Applications are processed on a rolling basis. Application fee: $85. Electronic applications accepted. *Expenses:* Tuition: Full-time $25,980; part-time $1315 per unit. Required fees: $554. One-time fee: $35 full-time. Full-time tuition and fees vary according to degree level and program. *Financial support:* In 2009–10, 25 students received support, including 18 fellowships (averaging $2,000 per year), 6 research assistantships (averaging $3,500 per year), 1 teaching assistantship with full tuition reimbursement available (averaging $9,500 per year). Financial award application deadline: 3/1. *Unit head:* Joshua Decter, Head, 213-743-4562, Fax: 213-743-4563, E-mail: decter@usc.edu. *Application contact:* Elizabeth Lovins, Information Contact, 213-743-8540, Fax: 213-743-4563, E-mail: lovins@usc.edu.

University of Wisconsin–Madison, Graduate School, Wisconsin School of Business, Wisconsin Full-Time MBA Program, Madison, WI 53706-1380. Offers applied corporate finance (MBA); applied security analysis (MBA); arts administration (MBA); brand and product management (MBA); entrepreneurial management (MBA); marketing research (MBA); operations and technology management (MBA); real estate (MBA); risk management and insurance (MBA); strategic human resource management (MBA); strategic management in the life and engineering sciences (MBA); supply chain management (MBA). *Faculty:* 32 full-time (5 women). *Students:* 242 full-time (74 women); includes 47 minority (16 African Americans, 3 American Indian/Alaska Native, 16 Asian Americans or Pacific Islanders, 12 Hispanic Americans), 29 international. Average age 28. 526 applicants, 32% accepted, 117 enrolled. In 2009, 106 master's awarded. *Entrance requirements:* For master's, GMAT, bachelor's or equivalent degree, 2 years of work experience, letters of recommendation. Additional exam requirements/recommendations for international students: Required—TOEFL (minimum score 600 paper-based; 250 computer-based; 100 iBT), IELTS. *Application deadline:* For fall admission, 11/4 for domestic and international students; for winter admission, 2/5 for domestic and international students; for spring admission, 5/26 for domestic students, 4/5 for international students. Applications are processed on a rolling basis. Application fee: $56. Electronic applications accepted. *Expenses:* Tuition, state resident: part-time $594 per credit. Tuition, nonresident: part-time $1504 per credit. Required fees: $65 per credit. Tuition and fees vary according to course load, program and reciprocity agreements. *Financial support:* In 2009–10, 103 students received support, including 13 fellowships with full and partial tuition reimbursements available (averaging $15,000 per year), 53 research assistantships with full tuition reimbursements available (averaging $8,000 per year), 35 teaching assistantships with full tuition reimbursements available (averaging $11,000 per year); scholarships/grants, health care benefits, and unspecified assistantships also available. Financial award application deadline: 4/5; financial award applicants required to submit FAFSA. *Unit head:* Prof. Kenneth A. Kavajecz, Associate Dean of Master's Programs, 608-265-3494, Fax: 608-265-4192, E-mail: kkavajecz@bus.wisc.edu. *Application contact:* Maria Reis, Assistant Director of MBA Marketing and Recruiting, 608-262-4000, Fax: 608-265-4192, E-mail: mreis@bus.wisc.edu.

Webster University, Leigh Gerdine College of Fine Arts, Department of Art, Program in Arts Management and Leadership, St. Louis, MO 63119-3194. Offers MFA. Part-time and evening/weekend programs available. *Degree requirements:* For master's, thesis. *Entrance requirements:* For master's, GRE, BA or BFA in related field, interview. *Expenses:* Tuition: Part-time $565 per credit hour. Tuition and fees vary according to degree level, campus/location and program.

Winthrop University, College of Visual and Performing Arts, Department of Art, Rock Hill, SC 29733. Offers art (MFA); art administration (MA); art education (MA). *Accreditation:* NASAD. Part-time programs available. *Degree requirements:* For master's, thesis, documented exhibit, oral exam. *Entrance requirements:* For master's, GRE General Test or MAT, PRAXIS (MA), minimum GPA of 3.0, resume, slide portfolio, teaching certificate (MA). Electronic applications accepted.

Art Therapy

Adler School of Professional Psychology, Programs in Psychology, Chicago, IL 60601-7203. Offers art therapy (MA, Certificate); clinical hypnosis (Certificate); clinical psychology (Psy D); counseling (MA); counseling and organizational psychology (MA); forensic psychology (MA); gerontological counseling (MA); marriage and family counseling (MA); marriage and family therapy (Certificate); organizational psychology (MA); police psychology (MA); rehabilitation counseling (MA); sport and health psychology (MA); substance abuse counseling (Certificate); Psy D/Certificate; Psy D/MACAT; Psy D/MACP; Psy D/MAMFC; Psy D/MASAC. *Accreditation:* APA. Part-time and evening/weekend programs available. Postbaccalaureate distance learning degree programs offered (minimal on-campus study). *Faculty:* 41 full-time (21 women), 44 part-time/adjunct (19 women). *Students:* 551 full-time (441 women), 161 part-time (137 women). Average age 27.Terminal master's awarded for partial completion of doctoral program. *Degree requirements:* For master's, thesis or alternative, oral exam, practicum; for doctorate, thesis/dissertation, clinical exam, internship, oral exam, practicum, written qualifying exam. *Entrance requirements:* For master's, 12 semester hours in psychology, minimum GPA of 3.0; for doctorate, 18 semester hours in psychology, minimum GPA of 3.25; for Certificate, appropriate master's or doctoral degree. Additional exam requirements/recommendations for international students: Required—TOEFL (minimum score 550 paper-based; 213 computer-based; 79 iBT). *Application deadline:* For fall admission, 2/15 priority date for domestic students, 12/1 priority date for international students. Applications are processed on a rolling basis. Application fee: $50. Electronic applications accepted. *Expenses:* Tuition: Part-time $930 per credit. Required fees: $220 per term. *Financial support:* Career-related internships or fieldwork, Federal Work-Study, scholarships/grants, and tuition waivers (full and partial) available. Support available to part-time students. Financial award application deadline: 5/15; financial award applicants required to submit FAFSA. *Unit head:* Dr. Frank Gruba-McAllister, Vice President of Academic Affairs, 312-201-5900 Ext. 209, Fax: 312-201-5917. *Application contact:* Craig A. Hines, Associate Vice President of Admissions, 312-201-5900 Ext. 226, Fax: 312-201-5917, E-mail: chines@adler.edu.

See Close-Up on page 1047.

Albertus Magnus College, Program in Art Therapy, New Haven, CT 06511-1189. Offers MAAT. Part-time and evening/weekend programs available. *Faculty:* 7 full-time (6 women), 6 part-time/adjunct (4 women). *Students:* 15 full-time (all women), 31 part-time (30 women); includes 14 minority (5 African Americans, 9 Hispanic Americans). Average age 35. 12 applicants, 67% accepted, 8 enrolled. In 2009, 5 master's awarded. *Degree requirements:* For master's, thesis. *Entrance requirements:* For master's, interview, writing sample. *Application deadline:* For fall admission, 8/30 for domestic students; for spring admission, 12/30 for domestic students. Application fee: $35. *Financial support:* Available to part-time students. Application deadline: 8/17. *Unit head:* Donna Kaiser, Director, 203-773-8903, Fax: 203-773-3117. *Application contact:* Donna Kaiser, Director, 203-773-8903, Fax: 203-773-3117.

Athabasca University, Graduate Centre for Applied Psychology, Athabasca, AB T9S 3A3, Canada. Offers art therapy (MC); career counseling (MC); counseling (Advanced Certificate); counseling psychology (MC); school counseling (MC). *Faculty:* 5 full-time (2 women). *Students:* 210 part-time. Average age 35. 117 applicants, 15 enrolled. In 2009, 36 master's, 1 Advanced Certificate awarded. *Application deadline:* For fall admission, 3/1 for domestic and international students. Application fee: $80. *Expenses:* Tuition: Part-time $16,500 per degree program. Required fees: $200 per year. One-time fee: $80 part-time. *Unit head:* Dr. Trevor Gilbert, Chair, 866-242-8768, Fax: 780-675-6186, E-mail: trevorg@athabascau.ca. *Application contact:* Information Contact, 800-788-9041, Fax: 780-675-6437.

Caldwell College, Graduate Studies, Program in Counseling Psychology, Caldwell, NJ 07006-6195. Offers art therapy (MA); counseling psychology (MA); school counseling (MA). Part-time and evening/weekend programs available. *Degree requirements:* For master's, comprehensive exam, practicum. *Entrance requirements:* For master's, GRE General Test, minimum GPA of 3.0. Additional exam requirements/recommendations for international students: Required—TOEFL (minimum score 580 paper-based; 237 computer-based). Electronic applications accepted.

California Institute of Integral Studies, School of Professional Psychology, San Francisco, CA 94103. Offers clinical psychology (Psy D); community mental health (MA); drama therapy (MA); expressive arts therapy (MA); integral counseling psychology (MA); integral counseling psychology–weekend (MA); somatic psychology (MA). *Accreditation:* APA. Part-time programs available. *Students:* 639 full-time (483 women), 53 part-time (43 women); includes 148 minority (32 African Americans, 2 American Indian/Alaska Native, 62 Asian Americans or Pacific Islanders, 52 Hispanic Americans). Average age 38. 476 applicants, 71% accepted, 202 enrolled. In 2009, 136 master's, 21 doctorates awarded. *Degree requirements:* For master's, comprehensive exam; for doctorate, comprehensive exam, thesis/dissertation. *Entrance requirements:* For master's, minimum GPA of 3.0, letters of recommendation, writing sample; for doctorate, GRE, MA in psychology or social work with appropriate practical experience for advanced standing, or BA with a minimum GPA of 3.1; letters of recommendation; writing sample. Additional exam requirements/recommendations for international students: Required—TOEFL. *Application deadline:* For fall admission, 2/1 priority date for domestic and international students; for spring admission, 10/15 priority date for domestic and international students. Applications are processed on a rolling basis. Application fee: $65. Electronic applications accepted. *Expenses:* Tuition: Full-time $15,300; part-time $850 per credit hour. Required fees: $110 per semester. Tuition and fees vary according to degree level. *Financial support:* In 2009–10, 677 students received support; research assistantships with tuition reimbursements available, teaching assistantships with tuition reimbursements available, career-related internships or fieldwork, Federal Work-Study, scholarships/grants, and tuition waivers (partial) available. Support available to part-time students. Financial award application deadline: 4/15; financial award applicants required to submit FAFSA. *Faculty research:* Somatic psychology, comparative psychology, art therapy, transpersonal psychology, eco-psychology. *Application contact:* David Townes, Senior Admissions Counselor, 415-575-6152, Fax: 415-575-1268, E-mail: dtownes@ciis.edu.

California State University, Los Angeles, Graduate Studies, College of Arts and Letters, Department of Art, Los Angeles, CA 90032-8530. Offers art (MA), including art education, art history, art therapy, ceramics, metals, and textiles, design (MA, MFA), painting, sculpture, and graphic arts, photography; fine arts (MFA), including crafts, design (MA, MFA), studio arts. *Accreditation:* NASAD (one or more programs are accredited). Part-time and evening/weekend programs available. *Faculty:* 12 full-time (6 women), 1 part-time/adjunct (0 women). *Students:* 28 full-time (21 women), 40 part-time (28 women); includes 22 minority (1 African American, 6 Asian Americans or Pacific Islanders, 15 Hispanic Americans), 9 international. Average age 37. 30 applicants, 100% accepted, 12 enrolled. In 2009, 17 master's awarded. *Degree requirements:* For master's, comprehensive exam, project or thesis. *Entrance requirements:* For master's, portfolio. Additional exam requirements/recommendations for international students: Required—TOEFL (minimum score 500 paper-based; 173 computer-based). *Application deadline:* For fall admission, 5/1 for domestic and international students. Applications are processed on a rolling basis. Application fee: $55. Electronic applications accepted. *Financial support:* Federal Work-Study available. Support available to part-time students. Financial award application deadline: 3/1. *Faculty research:* The artist and the book, conceptual art, ceramic processes, computer graphics, architectural graphics. *Unit head:* Dr. Abbas Daneshvari, Chair, 323-343-4010, Fax: 323-343-4045, E-mail: adanesh@calstatela.edu. *Application contact:* Dr. Cheryl L. Ney, Associate Vice President for Academic Affairs and Dean of Graduate Studies, 323-343-3820, Fax: 323-343-5653, E-mail: cney@cslanet.calstatela.edu.

The College of New Rochelle, Graduate School, Division of Art and Communication Studies, Program in Art Therapy, New Rochelle, NY 10805-2308. Offers art therapy (MS); art therapy/counseling (MS). Part-time and evening/weekend programs available. *Degree requirements:* For master's, thesis, practicum, fieldwork. *Entrance requirements:* For master's, 12 credits in psychology, 15 credits in studio art, portfolio. *Faculty research:* Phototherapy, assessment and evaluation, developmental stages in art, creativity and mental illness.

Concordia University, School of Graduate Studies, Faculty of Fine Arts, Department of Creative Arts Therapies, Montréal, QC H3G 1M8, Canada. Offers MA.

Drexel University, College of Nursing and Health Professions, Program in Creative Arts in Therapy, Specialization in Art Therapy, Philadelphia, PA 19104-2875. Offers MA, PMC. *Accreditation:* NASAD. *Degree requirements:* For master's, comprehensive exam, thesis. *Entrance requirements:* For master's, GRE General Test or MAT, interview, minimum GPA of 2.75, portfolio. Electronic applications accepted.

Eastern Virginia Medical School, Graduate Art Therapy and Counseling Program, Norfolk, VA 23501-1980. Offers MS. *Faculty:* 3 full-time, 1 part-time/adjunct. *Degree requirements:* For master's, thesis, internship. *Entrance requirements:* For master's, 12 credit hours in psychology, including abnormal and developmental; 18 credit hours in studio art; face-to-face interview; portfolio (diverse media preferred). *Application deadline:* For fall admission, 1/15 priority date for domestic and international students. Application fee: $60. Electronic applications accepted. *Expenses:* Contact institution. *Financial support:* Institutionally sponsored loans available. *Faculty research:* Art therapy projective imagery assessment: a collection of children's drawings. *Unit head:* Abby Calisch, Director, 757-446-5895, Fax: 757-446-6179, E-mail: artthrpy@evms.edu. *Application contact:* Rose Mwayungu, Director of Enrollment for Health Professions, 757-446-7153, Fax: 757-446-8915, E-mail: mwayunra@evms.edu.

Emporia State University, School of Graduate Studies, The Teachers College, Department of Psychology, Art Therapy, Rehabilitation and Mental Health Counseling, Program in Art Therapy, Emporia, KS 66801-5087. Offers MS. *Accreditation:* NASAD. Part-time programs available. *Students:* 14 full-time (13 women), 6 part-time (all women), 2 international. 3 applicants, 100% accepted, 3 enrolled. In 2009, 4 master's awarded. *Degree requirements:* For master's, comprehensive exam or thesis, internship. *Entrance requirements:* For master's, GRE General Test or MAT, graduate essay exam, appropriate bachelor's degree. Additional exam requirements/recommendations for international students: Required—TOEFL (minimum score 520 paper-based; 133 computer-based; 68 iBT). *Application deadline:* For fall admission, 6/1 for domestic students; for spring admission, 10/1 for domestic students. Applications are processed on a rolling basis. Application fee: $30 ($75 for international students). Electronic applications accepted. *Expenses:* Tuition, state resident: full-time $4154; part-time $173 per credit hour. Tuition, nonresident: full-time $12,864; part-time $536 per credit hour. Required fees: $948; $58 per credit hour. Tuition and fees vary according to campus/location. *Financial support:* Career-related internships or fieldwork, Federal Work-Study, institutionally sponsored loans,

Art Therapy

Emporia State University (continued)
health care benefits, and unspecified assistantships available. Financial award application deadline: 3/15; financial award applicants required to submit FAFSA. *Unit head:* Dr. Brian W. Schrader, Interim Chair, 620-341-5317, E-mail: bschrade@emporia.edu. *Application contact:* Mary Sewell, Admissions Coordinator, 800-950-GRAD, Fax: 620-341-5909, E-mail: msewell@emporia.edu.

The George Washington University, Columbian College of Arts and Sciences, Program in Art Therapy, Washington, DC 20052. Offers MA. *Faculty:* 5 full-time (all women), 18 part-time/adjunct (17 women). *Students:* 48 full-time (46 women), 12 part-time (10 women); includes 14 minority (4 African Americans, 3 American Indian/Alaska Native, 4 Asian Americans or Pacific Islanders, 3 Hispanic Americans), 7 international. Average age 28. 46 applicants, 87% accepted, 25 enrolled. In 2009, 13 master's awarded. *Degree requirements:* For master's, internship, practicum paper. *Entrance requirements:* For master's, GRE General Test, interview, minimum GPA of 3.0. Additional exam requirements/recommendations for international students: Required—TOEFL (minimum score 550 paper-based; 213 computer-based; 80 iBT). *Application deadline:* For fall admission, 1/1 priority date for domestic students. Application fee: $60. *Financial support:* In 2009–10, 11 students received support; fellowships with partial tuition reimbursements available, career-related internships or fieldwork, Federal Work-Study, institutionally sponsored loans, and tuition waivers available. *Unit head:* Heidi Bardot, Director, 202-994-4148, E-mail: hbardot@gwu.edu. *Application contact:* Information Contact, 202-994-6285, Fax: 202-994-1404, E-mail: artx@gwu.edu.

Hofstra University, School of Education, Health, and Human Services, Department of Counseling, Research, Special Education and Rehabilitation, Program in Creative Arts Therapy, Hempstead, NY 11549. Offers MA. Part-time programs available. *Students:* 49 full-time (47 women), 16 part-time (all women); includes 8 minority (2 African Americans, 3 Asian Americans or Pacific Islanders, 3 Hispanic Americans), 11 international. Average age 30. 63 applicants, 71% accepted, 26 enrolled. In 2009, 30 master's awarded. *Degree requirements:* For master's, thesis optional. *Entrance requirements:* For master's, interview, portfolio, 3 letters of recommendation, 12 hours of course work in psychology, 18 hours of course work in studio art. Additional exam requirements/recommendations for international students: Required—TOEFL (minimum score 550 paper-based; 213 computer-based; 80 iBT). *Application deadline:* Applications are processed on a rolling basis. Application fee: $60. Electronic applications accepted. *Expenses:* Tuition: Full-time $16,200; part-time $900 per credit hour. Required fees: $970; $145 per term. Tuition and fees vary according to program. *Financial support:* In 2009–10, 24 students received support, including 4 fellowships with full and partial tuition reimbursements available (averaging $3,788 per year), 1 research assistantship with full and partial tuition reimbursement available (averaging $18,300 per year); career-related internships or fieldwork, Federal Work-Study, institutionally sponsored loans, scholarships/grants, tuition waivers (full and partial), and unspecified assistantships also available. Support available to part-time students. Financial award applicants required to submit FAFSA. *Faculty research:* Creativity for non-artists, medical art therapy, play and sand tray therapy, creative art therapy in schools. *Unit head:* Margaret E. Carlock-Russo, Director, 516-463-7259, Fax: 516-463-6184, E-mail: cprmec@hofstra.edu. *Application contact:* Carol Drummer, Dean of Graduate Admissions, 516-463-4876, Fax: 516-463-4664, E-mail: gradstudent@hofstra.edu.

Lesley University, Graduate School of Arts and Social Sciences, Division of Expressive Therapies, Cambridge, MA 02138-2790. Offers art (MA); dance (MA); expressive therapies (MA, PhD, CAGS); music (MA). Terminal master's awarded for partial completion of doctoral program. *Degree requirements:* For master's, internship, practicum; for doctorate, thesis/dissertation. *Entrance requirements:* For master's, art portfolio, performance DVD; for doctorate, GRE or MAT. Additional exam requirements/recommendations for international students: Required—TOEFL (minimum score 550 paper-based; 213 computer-based; 80 iBT).

Long Island University, C.W. Post Campus, School of Visual and Performing Arts, Department of Art, Brookville, NY 11548-1300. Offers art (MA); art education (MS); clinical art therapy (MA); fine art and design (MFA). Part-time and evening/weekend programs available. *Degree requirements:* For master's, thesis. Electronic applications accepted. *Faculty research:* Painting, sculpture, installation, computers, video.

Marylhurst University, Department of Art Therapy Counseling, Marylhurst, OR 97036-0261. Offers art therapy (PGC); art therapy counseling (MA); counseling (PGC). Part-time programs available. *Faculty:* 3 full-time (all women), 4 part-time/adjunct (all women). *Students:* 45 full-time (43 women), 3 part-time (all women); includes 2 minority (1 African American, 1 Asian American or Pacific Islander). Average age 32. 27 applicants, 67% accepted, 18 enrolled. In 2009, 21 master's awarded. *Degree requirements:* For master's, comprehensive exam, practicums. *Entrance requirements:* For master's, Miller Analogy Test, minimum GPA of 3.0, course work in psychology and art, slide portfolio, letters of reference, resume, autobiography, portfolio. Additional exam requirements/recommendations for international students: Required—TOEFL (minimum score 550 paper-based; 213 computer-based; 80 iBT). *Application deadline:* For fall admission, 1/31 priority date for domestic and international students. Applications are processed on a rolling basis. Application fee: $40 ($50 for international students). *Expenses:* Contact institution. *Financial support:* Scholarships/grants available. Support available to part-time students. Financial award applicants required to submit FAFSA. *Faculty research:* Scientific approaches to art therapy research, child and adolescent psychotherapy, multicultural counseling. *Unit head:* Christine Turner, Chair, 503-636-8141, Fax: 503-636-9526, E-mail: cturner@marylhurst.edu. *Application contact:* Kathleen Schneff, Admissions Specialist, 800-634-9982 Ext. 3322, Fax: 503-635-6585, E-mail: admissions@marylhurst.edu.

Marywood University, Academic Affairs, Insalaco College of Creative and Performing Arts, Art Department, Program in Art Therapy, Scranton, PA 18509-1598. Offers MA, Post Master's Certificate. *Accreditation:* NASAD. *Students:* 22 full-time (all women), 6 part-time (5 women); includes 1 minority (Asian American or Pacific Islander). Average age 30. In 2009, 3 master's awarded. *Entrance requirements:* Additional exam requirements/recommendations for international students: Required—TOEFL (minimum score 550 paper-based; 213 computer-based; 79 iBT). *Application deadline:* For fall admission, 4/1 priority date for domestic students, 3/31 priority date for international students; for spring admission, 11/1 priority date for domestic students, 8/31 priority date for international students. Applications are processed on a rolling basis. Application fee: $35. Electronic applications accepted. *Expenses:* Tuition: Part-time $715 per credit. Required fees: $270 per semester. Tuition and fees vary according to degree level, campus/location and program. *Financial support:* Career-related internships or fieldwork, scholarships/grants, and unspecified assistantships available. Support available to part-time students. Financial award application deadline: 6/30; financial award applicants required to submit FAFSA. *Faculty research:* Perspectives of leading educators in art therapy, current trends in art education. *Application contact:* Tammy Manka, Assistant Director of Graduate Admissions, 866-279-9663, E-mail: tmanka@marywood.edu.

Mount Mary College, Graduate Programs, Program in Art Therapy, Milwaukee, WI 53222-4597. Offers MS. Evening/weekend programs available. *Faculty:* 3 full-time (1 woman), 10 part-time/adjunct (all women). *Students:* 51 full-time (all women), 2 part-time (both women); includes 4 minority (3 African Americans, 1 Hispanic American), 2 international. Average age 30. 52 applicants, 67% accepted, 27 enrolled. In 2009, 20 master's awarded. *Degree requirements:* For master's, thesis or alternative, internship. *Entrance requirements:* For master's, minimum GPA of 2.75, portfolio. Additional exam requirements/recommendations for international students: Required—TOEFL (minimum score 500 paper-based; 173 computer-based). *Application deadline:* For fall admission, 3/15 for domestic and international students. Application fee: $35 ($100 for international students). Electronic applications accepted. *Expenses:* Tuition: Part-time $595 per credit. Tuition and fees vary according to program. *Financial support:* In 2009–10, 1 student received support. Career-related internships or fieldwork and Federal Work-Study available. Support available to part-time students. Financial award application deadline: 5/1; financial award applicants required to submit FAFSA. *Faculty research:* Art-based research in art therapy, consensus-group supervision, art therapy in public school programs. *Unit head:* Lynn Kapitan, Graduate Program Director, 414-256-1215, E-mail: kapitanl@mtmary.edu. *Application contact:* Lynn Kapitan, Graduate Program Director, 414-256-1215, E-mail: kapitanl@mtmary.edu.

Naropa University, Graduate Programs, Program in Transpersonal Counseling Psychology, Concentration in Art Therapy, Boulder, CO 80302-6697. Offers MA. *Degree requirements:* For master's, internships, 180 direct art contact hours of studio-based work. *Entrance requirements:* For master's, portfolio (21 slides), in-person interview, course work in psychology and art, resume, letter of interest, 3 letters of recommendation. Additional exam requirements/recommendations for international students: Required—TOEFL (minimum score 600 paper-based; 250 computer-based). Electronic applications accepted.

Nazareth College of Rochester, Graduate Studies, Department of Creative Arts Therapy, Program in Art Therapy, Rochester, NY 14618-3790. Offers MS. Part-time programs available. *Entrance requirements:* For master's, minimum GPA of 3.0, portfolio review.

New York University, Steinhardt School of Culture, Education, and Human Development, Department of Art and Art Professions, Program in Art Therapy, New York, NY 10003. Offers MA. Part-time programs available. *Students:* 39 full-time (37 women), 7 part-time (all women); includes 8 minority (2 African Americans, 4 Asian Americans or Pacific Islanders, 2 Hispanic Americans), 6 international. Average age 27. 141 applicants, 24% accepted, 23 enrolled. In 2009, 20 master's awarded. *Degree requirements:* For master's, thesis (for some programs). *Entrance requirements:* For master's, interview, portfolio. Additional exam requirements/recommendations for international students: Required—TOEFL. *Application deadline:* For fall admission, 12/15 priority date for domestic and international students. Applications are processed on a rolling basis. Application fee: $75. Electronic applications accepted. *Expenses:* Tuition: Full-time $30,528; part-time $1272 per credit. Required fees: $2177. *Financial support:* Career-related internships or fieldwork, Federal Work-Study, institutionally sponsored loans, scholarships/grants, and tuition waivers (partial) available. Support available to part-time students. Financial award application deadline: 2/1; financial award applicants required to submit FAFSA. *Faculty research:* Art therapy in non-clinical settings, international art therapy. *Unit head:* Prof. Ikuko Acosta, Director, 212-998-5726, Fax: 212-995-4320, E-mail: ia4@nyu.edu. *Application contact:* 212-998-5030, Fax: 212-995-4328, E-mail: steinhardt.gradadmissions@nyu.edu.

Notre Dame de Namur University, Division of Academic Affairs, College of Arts and Sciences, Department of Art Therapy Psychology, Belmont, CA 94002-1908. Offers art therapy (MA); marriage and family therapy (MA). Part-time programs available. *Faculty:* 2 full-time (1 woman), 8 part-time/adjunct (7 women). *Students:* 38 full-time (all women), 56 part-time (54 women); includes 17 minority (1 African American, 11 Asian Americans or Pacific Islanders, 5 Hispanic Americans). Average age 34. 33 applicants, 94% accepted, 22 enrolled. In 2009, 26 master's awarded. *Degree requirements:* For master's, thesis, oral presentation, portfolio. *Entrance requirements:* For master's, interview, minimum GPA of 2.5. Additional exam requirements/recommendations for international students: Required—TOEFL (minimum score 550 paper-based; 213 computer-based; 79 iBT). *Application deadline:* For fall admission, 8/1 priority date for domestic students; for spring admission, 12/1 priority date for domestic students. Applications are processed on a rolling basis. Application fee: $60. Electronic applications accepted. *Expenses:* Tuition: Part-time $720 per credit. Required fees: $35 per semester hour. *Financial support:* Career-related internships or fieldwork available. Support available to part-time students. Financial award applicants required to submit FAFSA. *Unit head:* Dr. Richard Carolan, Chair, 650-508-3556, Fax: 650-508-3736. *Application contact:* Candace Hallmark, Associate Director of Admissions, 650-508-3592, Fax: 650-508-3426, E-mail: grad.admit@ndnu.edu.

Ottawa University, Graduate Studies-Arizona, Program in Professional Counseling, Ottawa, KS 66067-3399. Offers Christian counseling (MA); expressive arts therapy (MA); marriage and family therapy (MA); treatment of trauma, abuse and deprivation (MA). Programs offered in Mesa, Phoenix, Tempe and West Valley, AZ. Part-time and evening/weekend programs available. Postbaccalaureate distance learning degree programs offered. *Degree requirements:* For master's, comprehensive exam, thesis or alternative, field experience, practicum. *Entrance requirements:* For master's, minimum undergraduate GPA of 3.0; course work in theories of personality, abnormal psychology, and human growth and development. Additional exam requirements/recommendations for international students: Required—TOEFL (minimum score 550 paper-based; 213 computer-based).

Pratt Institute, School of Art and Design, Programs in Creative Arts Therapy, Brooklyn, NY 11205-3899. Offers art therapy and creativity development (MPS); art therapy-special education (MPS); dance/movement therapy (MS). *Accreditation:* NASAD (one or more programs are accredited). Part-time programs available. *Faculty:* 3 full-time (all women), 19 part-time/adjunct (16 women). *Students:* 105 full-time (102 women), 4 part-time (all women); includes 19 minority (6 African Americans, 3 Asian Americans or Pacific Islanders, 10 Hispanic Americans), 6 international. Average age 30. 197 applicants, 90% accepted, 33 enrolled. In 2009, 30 master's awarded. *Degree requirements:* For master's, thesis. *Entrance requirements:* For master's, letters of recommendation, portfolio. Additional exam requirements/recommendations for international students: Required—TOEFL (minimum score 600 paper-based; 250 computer-based; 100 iBT). *Application deadline:* For fall admission, 1/5 for domestic and international students; for spring admission, 10/1 for domestic and international students. Applications are processed on a rolling basis. Application fee: $50 ($90 for international students). Electronic applications accepted. *Expenses:* Tuition: Full-time $22,734. Required fees: $1280. *Financial support:* Career-related internships or fieldwork, Federal Work-Study, institutionally sponsored loans, scholarships/grants, health care benefits, tuition waivers (full), and unspecified assistantships available. Support available to part-time students. Financial award application deadline: 2/1; financial award applicants required to submit FAFSA. *Faculty research:* Psychology and aesthetic interaction, art therapy and AIDS, art therapy and autism, art diagnosis. *Unit head:* Jean Davis, Chairperson, 718-636-3428, E-mail: jdavis@pratt.edu. *Application contact:* Young Hah, Director of Graduate Admissions, 718-636-3683, Fax: 718-399-4242, E-mail: yhah@pratt.edu.

See Close-Up on page 119.

Prescott College, Graduate Programs, Program in Counseling and Psychology, Prescott, AZ 86301. Offers adventure-based psychotherapy (MA); counseling psychology (MA); ecopsychology (MA); ecotherapy (MA); equine-assisted mental health (MA); expressive arts therapy (MA); somatic psychology (MA); student-directed independent study (MA). Part-time programs available. Postbaccalaureate distance learning degree programs offered (minimal on-campus study). *Faculty:* 3 full-time (all women), 35 part-time/adjunct (25 women). *Students:* 65 full-time (47 women), 44 part-time (39 women); includes 8 minority (2 African Americans, 2 American Indian/Alaska Native, 4 Hispanic Americans), 9 international. Average age 38. 77 applicants, 77% accepted, 40 enrolled. In 2009, 34 master's awarded. *Degree requirements:* For master's, thesis, fieldwork or internship, practicum. *Entrance requirements:* For master's, 2 letters of recommendation, resume. Additional exam requirements/recommendations for international students: Required—TOEFL (minimum score 500 paper-based; 173 computer-based). *Application deadline:* For fall admission, 4/15 priority date for domestic and international students; for spring admission, 9/15 priority date for domestic and international students. Applications are processed on a rolling basis. Application fee: $40. Electronic applications accepted. *Expenses:* Tuition: Full-time $14,712; part-time $613 per credit. Required fees: $50 per term. One-time fee: $150. Tuition and fees vary according to course load and degree level. *Financial support:* Career-related internships or fieldwork, Federal Work-Study, and scholarships/grants available. Financial award applicants required to submit FAFSA. *Unit head:* Dr. Christine Frydenborg, Chair, Fax: 928-776-5151, E-mail: csmith@prescott.edu. *Application contact:* Kerstin Alicki, Admissions Counselor, 877-412-8705, Fax: 928-277-4695, E-mail: admissions@prescott.edu.

Saint Mary-of-the-Woods College, Program in Art Therapy, Saint Mary-of-the-Woods, IN 47876. Offers MA, Post-Master's Certificate. Part-time and evening/weekend programs available.

Postbaccalaureate distance learning degree programs offered (minimal on-campus study). *Degree requirements:* For master's, thesis or project. *Entrance requirements:* For master's, minimum GPA of 2.5; for Post-Master's Certificate, 12 credit hours in abnormal and developmental psychology, 15 credit hours in studio art skills, art portfolio, interview, minimum GPA of 2.5. Electronic applications accepted.

Salve Regina University, Graduate Studies, Holistic Graduate Programs, Newport, RI 02840-4192. Offers expressive and creative arts (CAGS); holistic counseling (MA); holistic leadership (MA, CAGS); mental health (CAGS). Part-time and evening/weekend programs available. *Faculty:* 4 full-time (2 women), 9 part-time/adjunct (6 women). *Students:* 17 full-time (15 women), 73 part-time (64 women). Average age 42. 32 applicants, 81% accepted, 20 enrolled. In 2009, 7 master's, 18 other advanced degrees awarded. *Degree requirements:* For master's, internship, project. *Entrance requirements:* For master's, GMAT, GRE General Test, or MAT. Additional exam requirements/recommendations for international students: Required—TOEFL (minimum score 600 paper-based; 250 computer-based; 100 iBT), or IELTS. *Application deadline:* For fall admission, 3/15 priority date for domestic and international students; for spring admission, 9/15 priority date for domestic and international students. Applications are processed on a rolling basis. Application fee: $60. Electronic applications accepted. *Expenses:* Tuition: Part-time $395 per credit. Part-time tuition and fees vary according to degree level. *Financial support:* Career-related internships or fieldwork and Federal Work-Study available. Support available to part-time students. Financial award application deadline: 3/1; financial award applicants required to submit FAFSA. *Unit head:* Dr. Peter F. Mullen, Director, 401-341-3278, Fax: 401-341-2977, E-mail: mullenp@salve.edu. *Application contact:* Kelly Alverson, Graduate Admissions Counselor, 401-341-2153, Fax: 401-341-2973, E-mail: kelly.alverson@salve.edu.

School of the Art Institute of Chicago, Graduate Division, Program in Art Therapy, Chicago, IL 60603-3103. Offers MAAT. *Accreditation:* NASAD. *Degree requirements:* For master's, thesis, personal interview. *Entrance requirements:* Additional exam requirements/recommendations for international students: Required—TOEFL, IELTS. *Faculty research:* Migrane, ousider art, community-based practice.

School of Visual Arts, Graduate Programs, Art Therapy Department, New York, NY 10010-3994. Offers MPS. *Degree requirements:* For master's, thesis or 750 internship hours. *Entrance requirements:* For master's, portfolio, bachelor's degree with 12 credits in undergraduate psychology including child and abnormal psychology, 18 credits of studio art. Additional exam requirements/recommendations for international students: Required—TOEFL (minimum score 550 paper-based; 213 computer-based; 79 iBT). Electronic applications accepted.

Seton Hill University, Program in Art Therapy, Greensburg, PA 15601. Offers MA, Certificate. Part-time programs available. *Faculty:* 6 full-time (4 women), 4 part-time/adjunct (3 women). *Students:* 37 full-time (36 women), 14 part-time (13 women); includes 1 minority (American Indian/Alaska Native). Average age 32. 21 applicants, 81% accepted, 11 enrolled. In 2009, 4 master's awarded. *Degree requirements:* For master's, thesis or alternative. *Entrance requirements:* For master's, portfolio, 12 undergraduate credits in psychology, 15 undergraduate credits in art, minimum GPA of 3.0. Additional exam requirements/recommendations for international students: Required—TOEFL (minimum score 650 paper-based; 280 computer-based), IELTS (minimum score 7). *Application deadline:* For fall admission, 8/15 priority date for domestic students; for spring admission, 12/15 for domestic students. Applications are processed on a rolling basis. Application fee: $35. Electronic applications accepted. *Expenses:* Tuition: Full-time $12,780; part-time $710 per credit. Required fees: $300; $150 per semester. Tuition and fees vary according to course load and program. *Financial support:* Federal Work-Study, scholarships/grants, tuition waivers (partial), and unspecified assistantships available. Support available to part-time students. Financial award application deadline: 8/15; financial award applicants required to submit FAFSA. *Faculty research:* Art therapy with the deaf, art therapy with children. *Unit head:* Nina Denninger, Director, 724-830-1047, Fax: 724-830-1294, E-mail: denninger@setonhill.edu. *Application contact:* Laurel Pellis, Advisor, 724-838-4209, Fax: 724-830-1891, E-mail: lpellis@setonhill.edu.

Southern Illinois University Edwardsville, Graduate Studies and Research, College of Arts and Sciences, Department of Art and Design, Program in Art Therapy Counseling, Edwardsville, IL 62026-0001. Offers MA. Part-time programs available. *Students:* 20 full-time (18 women), 11 part-time (all women); includes 2 minority (1 African American, 1 Hispanic American), 1 international. Average age 26. 42 applicants, 21% accepted. In 2009, 8 master's awarded. *Degree requirements:* For master's, thesis or alternative, project. *Entrance requirements:* For master's, MAT, portfolio. Additional exam requirements/recommendations for international students: Required—TOEFL (minimum score 550 paper-based; 213 computer-based; 79 iBT), IELTS (minimum score 6.5). *Application deadline:* For fall admission, 2/1 for domestic and international students. Application fee: $30. Electronic applications accepted. *Expenses:* Tuition, state resident: part-time $1252.50 per semester. Tuition, nonresident: part-time $3131.25 per semester. Required fees: $586.85 per semester. Tuition and fees vary according to course load. *Financial support:* In 2009–10, 1 fellowship (averaging $8,370 per year), 18 teaching assistantships with full tuition reimbursements (averaging $8,064 per year) were awarded; research assistantships. Financial award application deadline: 3/1; financial award applicants required to submit FAFSA. *Unit head:* Dr. Patricia Klorer, Program Director, 618-650-3183, E-mail: pklorer@siue.edu. *Application contact:* Michelle Robinson, Coordinator of Graduate Recruitment, 618-650-2811, Fax: 618-650-3523, E-mail: michero@siue.edu.

Southwestern College, Program in Art Therapy/Counseling, Santa Fe, NM 87502-4788. Offers MA. Part-time and evening/weekend programs available. *Faculty:* 3 full-time (2 women), 8 part-time/adjunct (all women). *Students:* 22 full-time (20 women), 24 part-time (all women); includes 1 American Indian/Alaska Native, 1 Asian American or Pacific Islander, 4 Hispanic Americans. Average age 33. 40 applicants, 88% accepted, 31 enrolled. In 2009, 22 master's awarded. *Degree requirements:* For master's, internship. *Entrance requirements:* For master's, resume, slide portfolio, interview, 3 letters of reference. Additional exam requirements/recommendations for international students: Required—TOEFL. *Application deadline:* For fall admission, 6/1 priority date for domestic students; for winter admission, 10/15 priority date for domestic students; for spring admission, 1/30 priority date for domestic students. Applications are processed on a rolling basis. Application fee: $50. *Financial support:* In 2009–10, 35 students received support. Career-related internships or fieldwork, institutionally sponsored loans, and scholarships/grants available. Support available to part-time students. Financial award application deadline: 6/15; financial award applicants required to submit FAFSA. *Unit head:* Debbie Schroder, Chair, 505-471-5756. *Application contact:* Dru Phoenix, Director of Admissions, 505-471-5756 Ext. 26, Fax: 505-471-4071, E-mail: admissions@swc.edu.

Springfield College, Graduate Programs, Program in Art Therapy, Springfield, MA 01109-3797. Offers M Ed, MS, CAGS. Part-time programs available. *Degree requirements:* For master's, research project, final art exhibition. *Entrance requirements:* For master's, portfolio, prerequisite courses required for accreditation. Additional exam requirements/recommendations for international students: Required—TOEFL (minimum score 550 paper-based; 213 computer-based). Electronic applications accepted. *Expenses:* Tuition: Full-time $19,800; part-time $825 per credit hour. Required fees: $150. *Faculty research:* Stage development in art, psychopathology of expression, art history and art therapy.

University of Maryland, College Park, Academic Affairs, College of Education, Department of Counseling and Personnel Services, College Park, MD 20742. Offers college student personnel (M Ed, MA); college student personnel administration (PhD); community counseling (CAGS); community/career counseling (M Ed, MA); counseling and personnel services (M Ed, MA, PhD), including art therapy (M Ed), college student personnel (M Ed), counseling and personnel services (PhD), counseling psychology (M Ed), mental health counseling (M Ed), school counseling (M Ed); counseling psychology (PhD); counselor education (PhD); rehabilitation counseling (M Ed, MA, AGSC); school counseling (M Ed, MA); school psychology (M Ed, MA, PhD). *Accreditation:* ACA (one or more programs are accredited); APA (one or more programs are accredited); CORE (one or more programs are accredited); NCATE. Part-time and evening/weekend programs available. Postbaccalaureate distance learning degree programs offered (no on-campus study). *Faculty:* 34 full-time (21 women), 8 part-time/adjunct (6 women). *Students:* 152 full-time (117 women), 25 part-time (18 women); includes 67 minority (32 African Americans, 2 American Indian/Alaska Native, 20 Asian Americans or Pacific Islanders, 13 Hispanic Americans), 16 international. 319 applicants, 15% accepted, 32 enrolled. In 2009, 24 master's, 15 doctorates, 4 other advanced degrees awarded. *Degree requirements:* For master's, thesis (for some programs); for doctorate, thesis/dissertation. *Entrance requirements:* For master's, GRE General Test or MAT, minimum GPA of 3.0, 3 letters of recommendation; for doctorate, GRE General Test or MAT, minimum GPA of 3.5, 3 letters of recommendation. Additional exam requirements/recommendations for international students: Required—TOEFL. *Application deadline:* For fall admission, 12/15 for domestic and international students; for spring admission, 10/1 for domestic students, 6/1 for international students. Applications are processed on a rolling basis. Application fee: $60. Electronic applications accepted. *Expenses:* Tuition, area resident: Part-time $471 per credit hour. Tuition, state resident: part-time $471 per credit hour. Tuition, nonresident: part-time $1016 per credit hour. Required fees: $337.04 per term. *Financial support:* In 2009–10, 4 fellowships with partial tuition reimbursements (averaging $10,402 per year), 8 research assistantships (averaging $16,454 per year), 93 teaching assistantships with tuition reimbursements (averaging $16,109 per year) were awarded; career-related internships or fieldwork, Federal Work-Study, and scholarships/grants also available. Support available to part-time students. Financial award applicants required to submit FAFSA. *Faculty research:* Educational psychology, counseling, health. Total annual research expenditures: $1.5 million. *Unit head:* Dr. Dennis Kivlighan, Chair, 301-405-2858, E-mail: dennisk@umd.edu. *Application contact:* Dean of Graduate School, 301-405-0358.

University of Wisconsin–Superior, Graduate Division, Department of Visual Arts, Superior, WI 54880-4500. Offers art education (MA); art history (MA); art therapy (MA); studio arts (MA). Part-time programs available. *Faculty:* 7 full-time (1 woman), 1 (woman) part-time/adjunct. *Students:* 12 full-time (8 women), 18 part-time (15 women); includes 1 minority (American Indian/Alaska Native), 2 international. 14 applicants, 100% accepted. In 2009, 7 master's awarded. *Degree requirements:* For master's, comprehensive exam, exhibit. *Entrance requirements:* For master's, minimum GPA of 2.75, portfolio. *Application deadline:* For fall admission, 4/1 priority date for domestic students; for spring admission, 10/15 priority date for domestic students. Applications are processed on a rolling basis. Application fee: $45. *Financial support:* Career-related internships or fieldwork, Federal Work-Study, scholarships/grants, and tuition waivers (partial) available. Support available to part-time students. Financial award application deadline: 4/15; financial award applicants required to submit FAFSA. *Unit head:* Tim Cleary, Coordinator, 715-394-8398. *Application contact:* Sandy Wallgren, Program Assistant/Status Examiner, 715-394-8295, Fax: 715-394-8146, E-mail: gradstudy@uwsuper.edu.

Ursuline College, School of Graduate Studies, Program in Art Therapy Counseling, Pepper Pike, OH 44124-4398. Offers MA. Part-time programs available. *Faculty:* 4 full-time (all women), 4 part-time/adjunct (3 women). *Students:* 21 full-time (all women), 59 part-time (56 women); includes 2 minority (both African Americans). Average age 31. 40 applicants, 75% accepted, 25 enrolled. In 2009, 18 master's awarded. *Degree requirements:* For master's, thesis, 700 hour internship. *Entrance requirements:* For master's, BA in psychology, social sciences, or related field; minimum undergraduate GPA of 3.0; portfolio; work experience with human service agency. Additional exam requirements/recommendations for international students: Required—TOEFL (minimum score 500 paper-based; 173 computer-based). *Application deadline:* For fall admission, 8/1 priority date for domestic students. Applications are processed on a rolling basis. Application fee: $25. *Expenses:* Tuition: Full-time $14,544; part-time $808 per credit hour. Required fees: $230; $75 per semester. *Financial support:* In 2009–10, 9 students received support. Federal Work-Study available. Financial award application deadline: 3/1; financial award applicants required to submit FAFSA. *Faculty research:* Art therapy used with psychiatric and geriatric populations, art therapy used in treatment of chemical dependency, family therapy, child art therapy. *Unit head:* Gale Rule-Hoffman, Director, 440-646-8138, Fax: 440-684-6088. *Application contact:* Melanie Steele, Secretary, 440-646-8199, Fax: 440-684-3168, E-mail: gradsch@ursuline.edu.

Decorative Arts

Bard College, Program in History of the Decorative Arts, Design and Culture, Annandale-on-Hudson, NY 12504. Offers MA, PhD. Part-time programs available. *Degree requirements:* For master's, one foreign language, thesis, internship; for doctorate, 2 foreign languages, thesis/dissertation, exams. *Entrance requirements:* For master's, GRE General Test, writing sample, 3 letters of recommendation; for doctorate, GRE General Test, master's thesis or equivalent, 3 letters of recommendation. Additional exam requirements/recommendations for international students: Required—TOEFL. *Expenses:* Contact institution.

Bard Graduate Center for Studies in the Decorative Arts, Design, and Culture, Program in Decorative Arts, Design History, and Material Culture, New York, NY 10024-3602. Offers MA, PhD. Bard Graduate Center for Studies in the Decorative Arts is a unit of Bard College. Part-time programs available. *Degree requirements:* For master's, one foreign language, thesis, internship; for doctorate, 2 foreign languages, thesis/dissertation, exams. *Entrance requirements:* For master's, GRE General Test, writing sample, 3 letters of recommendation; for doctorate, GRE General Test, master's thesis or equivalent, 3 letters of recommendation. Additional exam requirements/recommendations for international students: Required—TOEFL. *Faculty research:* English craftsmen, ancient furniture, aesthetics and politics, Art Nouveau jewelry, European sculpture.

See Close-Up on page 191.

Corcoran College of Art and Design, Graduate Programs, Washington, DC 20006-4804. Offers art education (MAT); history of decorative arts (MA); interior design (MA). *Accreditation:* NASAD. Part-time programs available. *Entrance requirements:* Additional exam requirements/recommendations for international students: Required—TOEFL.

The New School: A University, Parsons The New School for Design, Program in the History of Decorative Arts and Design, New York, NY 10011. Offers MA. Offered jointly with the Cooper-Hewitt Museum and the Smithsonian Institution. *Accreditation:* NASAD. Part-time programs available. *Faculty:* 2 full-time (1 woman). *Students:* 59 full-time (57 women), 45 part-time (41 women); includes 9 minority (1 African American, 7 Asian Americans or Pacific Islanders, 1 Hispanic American), 8 international. Average age 33. 92 applicants, 60% accepted, 31 enrolled. In 2009, 24 master's awarded. *Degree requirements:* For master's, one foreign

Decorative Arts

The New School: A University (continued)
language, comprehensive exam or thesis project. *Entrance requirements:* For master's, sample of written work. Additional exam requirements/recommendations for international students: Required—TOEFL (minimum score 580 paper-based; 237 computer-based; 92 iBT). *Application deadline:* For fall admission, 2/1 for domestic and international students; for spring admission, 11/1 for domestic and international students. Application fee: $50. Electronic applications accepted. *Financial support:* Fellowships, research assistantships, teaching assistantships, Federal Work-Study, scholarships/grants, and tuition waivers (full and partial) available. Support available to part-time students. Financial award application deadline: 3/1; financial award applicants required to submit FAFSA. *Unit head:* Dr. Sarah E. Lawrence, Director, 212-849-8345, E-mail: lawrences@si.edu. *Application contact:* David Norris, Director of Admissions, 212-229-8989 Ext. 4023, Fax: 212-229-8975, E-mail: norrisd@newschool.edu.

Museum Studies

Arizona State University, Graduate College, College of Liberal Arts and Sciences, Division of Social Sciences, School of Human Evolution and Social Change, Tempe, AZ 85287. Offers anthropology (PhD); applied mathematics for the life and social sciences (PhD); environmental social science (PhD); museum studies in anthropology (MA); social science and health (PhD). *Degree requirements:* For master's, thesis or alternative; for doctorate, thesis/dissertation. *Entrance requirements:* For master's and doctorate, GRE.

Bard College, Center for Curatorial Studies, Annandale-on-Hudson, NY 12504. Offers MA. *Degree requirements:* For master's, thesis, exhibition. *Entrance requirements:* For master's, exhibition review, 3 letters of recommendation. Additional exam requirements/recommendations for international students: Required—TOEFL (minimum score 550 paper-based). Electronic applications accepted. *Expenses:* Contact institution. *Faculty research:* Contemporary art, history of exhibition, curatorial practice.

Baylor University, Graduate School, College of Arts and Sciences, Department of Museum Studies, Waco, TX 76798. Offers MA. *Faculty:* 6 part-time/adjunct (3 women). *Students:* 20 full-time (16 women), 1 part-time (0 women); includes 2 minority (both American Indian/Alaska Native). 13 applicants, 85% accepted. In 2009, 6 master's awarded. *Degree requirements:* For master's, thesis or alternative. *Entrance requirements:* For master's, GRE General Test. *Application deadline:* For fall admission, 4/30 priority date for domestic students. Applications are processed on a rolling basis. Application fee: $25. Electronic applications accepted. *Financial support:* In 2009–10, 3 research assistantships with partial tuition reimbursements (averaging $7,200 per year) were awarded; career-related internships or fieldwork, Federal Work-Study, institutionally sponsored loans, tuition waivers (full and partial), and unspecified assistantships also available. Support available to part-time students. Financial award application deadline: 6/1; financial award applicants required to submit FAFSA. *Faculty research:* Paleontology/archaeology, preservation. *Unit head:* Dr. Kenneth Hafertepe, Graduate Program Director, 254-710-1233, Fax: 254-710-1173, E-mail: kenneth_hafertepe@baylor.edu. *Application contact:* Marcia Cooper, Administrative Assistant, 254-710-1233, Fax: 254-710-3870, E-mail: marcia_cooper@baylor.edu.

Boston University, Graduate School of Arts and Sciences, Department of Art History, Boston, MA 02215. Offers art history (MA, PhD); museum studies (Certificate). *Students:* 48 full-time (43 women), 14 part-time (13 women); includes 6 minority (5 African Americans, 1 Asian American or Pacific Islander), 7 international. Average age 31. 227 applicants, 32% accepted, 14 enrolled. In 2009, 11 master's, 6 doctorates awarded. Terminal master's awarded for partial completion of doctoral program. *Degree requirements:* For master's, one foreign language, comprehensive exam, thesis; for doctorate, 2 foreign languages, comprehensive exam, thesis/dissertation. *Entrance requirements:* For master's and doctorate, GRE General Test, 3 letters of recommendation; for Certificate, GRE General Test. Additional exam requirements/recommendations for international students: Required—TOEFL (minimum score 600 paper-based; 250 computer-based). *Application deadline:* For fall admission, 1/15 for domestic and international students; for spring admission, 10/15 for domestic and international students. Application fee: $70. *Expenses:* Tuition: Full-time $37,910; part-time $1184 per credit hour. Required fees: $386; $40 per semester. Part-time tuition and fees vary according to class time, course level, degree level and program. *Financial support:* In 2009–10, 23 students received support, including 2 fellowships (averaging $18,900 per year), 1 research assistantship (averaging $18,200 per year), 6 teaching assistantships with full tuition reimbursements available (averaging $18,200 per year); career-related internships or fieldwork, Federal Work-Study, and unspecified assistantships also available. Support available to part-time students. Financial award application deadline: 1/15; financial award applicants required to submit FAFSA. *Unit head:* Fred S. Kleiner, Chairman, 617-353-2520, Fax: 617-353-3243, E-mail: fsk@bu.edu. *Application contact:* Cheryl Crombie, Administrative Assistant, 617-353-2522, Fax: 617-353-3243, E-mail: ccrombie@bu.edu.

Brown University, Graduate School, Department of Anthropology, Providence, RI 02912. Offers anthropology (AM, PhD); museum studies (AM). *Degree requirements:* For doctorate, one foreign language, thesis/dissertation, preliminary exam.

California College of the Arts, Graduate Programs, Program in Curatorial Practice, San Francisco, CA 94107. Offers MA. *Entrance requirements:* For master's, appropriate bachelor's degree, portfolio, resume, letters of recommendation. Additional exam requirements/recommendations for international students: Required—TOEFL (minimum score 600 paper-based; 250 computer-based). Electronic applications accepted.

California State University, Chico, Graduate School, College of Behavioral and Social Sciences, Department of Anthropology, Chico, CA 95929-0722. Offers museum studies (MA). *Students:* 14 full-time (12 women), 16 part-time (12 women); includes 3 minority (1 Asian American or Pacific Islander, 2 Hispanic Americans), 1 international. Average age 32. 37 applicants, 38% accepted, 10 enrolled. In 2009, 6 master's awarded. *Degree requirements:* For master's, thesis. *Entrance requirements:* For master's, GRE General Test, 2 letters of recommendation. Additional exam requirements/recommendations for international students: Required—TOEFL (minimum score 550 paper-based; 213 computer-based; 80 iBT), IELTS (minimum score 6.5). *Application deadline:* For fall admission, 1/15 for domestic students, 3/1 for international students. Application fee: $55. Electronic applications accepted. *Financial support:* Fellowships, career-related internships or fieldwork available. *Unit head:* Dr. William Collins, Graduate Coordinator, 530-898-4953. *Application contact:* Dr. William Collins, Graduate Coordinator, 530-898-4953.

Caribbean University, Graduate School, Bayamón, PR 00960-0493. Offers administration and supervision (MA Ed); criminal justice (MA); curriculum and instruction (MA Ed), including elementary education, English education, history education, mathematics education, primary education, science education, Spanish education; education (PhD); gerontology (MSN); human resources (MBA); museology, archiving and art history (MA Ed); neonatal pediatrics (MSN); physical education (MA Ed); special education (MA Ed). *Entrance requirements:* For master's, interview, minimum GPA of 2.5.

Case Western Reserve University, School of Graduate Studies, Department of Art History and Art, Program in Art History and Museum Studies, Cleveland, OH 44106. Offers MA, PhD. Part-time programs available. *Faculty:* 9 full-time (6 women), 11 part-time/adjunct (5 women). *Students:* 16 full-time (all women), 3 part-time (all women); includes 1 minority (Hispanic American), 1 international. Average age 28. 33 applicants, 58% accepted, 7 enrolled. In 2009, 4 master's, 1 doctorate awarded. *Degree requirements:* For master's, one foreign language, thesis or alternative; for doctorate, 2 foreign languages, thesis/dissertation. *Entrance requirements:* For master's, GRE General Test, 2 samples of written work; for doctorate, GRE General Test, 2 samples of written work or MA thesis. Additional exam requirements/recommendations for international students: Required—TOEFL (minimum score 550 paper-based; 213 computer-based; 79 iBT). *Application deadline:* For fall admission, 1/1 priority date for domestic students. Applications are processed on a rolling basis. Application fee: $50. Electronic applications accepted. *Financial support:* Fellowships, research assistantships, teaching assistantships, career-related internships or fieldwork available. Financial award application deadline: 2/15. *Faculty research:* Greek art and architecture, northern Baroque, Italian Renaissance and Baroque, abstract expressionism, Indian art, nineteenth century French art, American and contemporary art. *Unit head:* Edward Olszewski, Chair, 216-368-4118, Fax: 216-368-4681, E-mail: edward.olszewski@case.edu. *Application contact:* Debby Tenenbaum, Assistant, 216-368-4118, Fax: 216-368-4681, E-mail: deborah.tenenbaum@case.edu.

Christie's Education, Program in Modern Art, Connoisseurship, and the History of the Art Market, New York, NY 10036. Offers MA. *Degree requirements:* For master's, one foreign language, thesis. *Entrance requirements:* For master's, GRE, writing sample, 3 letters of recommendation. Additional exam requirements/recommendations for international students: Required—TOEFL.

City College of the City University of New York, Graduate School, College of Liberal Arts and Science, Division of the Humanities and Arts, Department of Art, Concentrations in Art History and Museum Studies, New York, NY 10031-9198. Offers art history (MA); museum studies (MA). Part-time programs available. *Degree requirements:* For master's, one foreign language, thesis. *Entrance requirements:* For master's, minimum GPA of 3.0, portfolio, art history paper. Additional exam requirements/recommendations for international students: Required—TOEFL (minimum score 577 paper-based; 90 iBT). Electronic applications accepted. *Faculty research:* Egyptian, Greek, medieval, Romanesque, and Ottoman art.

Claremont Graduate University, Graduate Programs, School of Arts and Humanities, Department of Cultural Studies, Claremont, CA 91711-6160. Offers Africana studies (Certificate); cultural studies (MA, PhD); media studies (MA, PhD); museum studies (MA). Part-time programs available. *Faculty:* 3 full-time (2 women). *Students:* 67 full-time (43 women), 8 part-time (6 women); includes 28 minority (14 African Americans, 1 American Indian/Alaska Native, 5 Asian Americans or Pacific Islanders, 8 Hispanic Americans), 7 international. Average age 36. In 2009, 7 master's, 3 doctorates awarded. *Entrance requirements:* For master's and doctorate, GRE General Test. Additional exam requirements/recommendations for international students: Required—TOEFL (minimum score 550 paper-based; 213 computer-based; 80 iBT). *Application deadline:* For fall admission, 2/1 priority date for domestic students. Applications are processed on a rolling basis. Application fee: $60. Electronic applications accepted. *Expenses:* Tuition: Full-time $35,046; part-time $1524 per credit. Required fees: $161 per semester. *Financial support:* Fellowships, research assistantships, Federal Work-Study, institutionally sponsored loans, and scholarships/grants available. Support available to part-time students. Financial award application deadline: 2/15; financial award applicants required to submit FAFSA. *Unit head:* Eve Oishi, Chair, 909-607-7587, E-mail: eve.oishi@cgu.edu. *Application contact:* Susan Hampson, Admissions Coordinator, 909-607-1278, Fax: 909-607-1221, E-mail: humanities@cgu.edu.

Cleveland State University, College of Graduate Studies, College of Liberal Arts and Social Sciences, Department of History, Cleveland, OH 44115. Offers art history (MA); history (MA); museum studies (MA). Part-time and evening/weekend programs available. *Degree requirements:* For master's, thesis optional. *Entrance requirements:* For master's, minimum GPA of 3.0, bachelor's degree in history. Additional exam requirements/recommendations for international students: Required—TOEFL (minimum score 525 paper-based; 197 computer-based). Electronic applications accepted. *Faculty research:* African Diaspora, social history and the city, early modern Europe, local history.

Cleveland State University, College of Graduate Studies, College of Science, Department of Biological, Geological, and Environmental Sciences, Cleveland, OH 44115. Offers biology (MS); environmental science (MS); museum studies for natural historians (MS); regulatory biology (PhD); JD/MS. Part-time programs available. Terminal master's awarded for partial completion of doctoral program. *Degree requirements:* For master's, comprehensive exam (for some programs), thesis (for some programs); for doctorate, comprehensive exam, thesis/dissertation. *Entrance requirements:* For master's, GRE General Test, 2 letters of recommendation; for doctorate, GRE General Test, 2 letters of recommendation; 1-2 page essay statement of career goals and research interests. Additional exam requirements/recommendations for international students: Required—TOEFL (minimum score 525 paper-based; 197 computer-based). Electronic applications accepted. *Faculty research:* Molecular and cell biology, immunology, urban ecology.

Duquesne University, Graduate School of Liberal Arts, Department of History, Pittsburgh, PA 15282-0001. Offers archival, museum, and editing studies (MA); history (MA). Part-time and evening/weekend programs available. *Faculty:* 6 full-time (1 woman), 3 part-time/adjunct (1 woman). *Students:* 30 full-time (21 women), 16 part-time (6 women). Average age 26. 71 applicants, 48% accepted, 21 enrolled. In 2009, 21 master's awarded. *Degree requirements:* For master's, comprehensive exam (for some programs), thesis optional. *Entrance requirements:* For master's, GRE General Test, writing sample. Additional exam requirements/recommendations for international students: Required—TOEFL. *Application deadline:* For fall admission, 8/15 for domestic students, 5/1 for international students; for spring admission, 11/1 priority date for domestic students. Applications are processed on a rolling basis. Electronic applications accepted. *Expenses:* Tuition: Part-time $851 per credit. Required fees: $81 per credit. *Financial support:* In 2009–10, 4 research assistantships with full tuition reimbursements (averaging $6,000 per year) were awarded; career-related internships or fieldwork, Federal Work-Study, scholarships/grants, tuition waivers (full and partial), and unspecified assistantships also available. Support available to part-time students. Financial award application deadline: 5/1. *Faculty research:* American studies, immigration history, local social history, applied history, Eastern European history. *Unit head:* Dr. Holly Mayer, Chair, 412-396-6470, E-mail: mayer@duq.edu. *Application contact:* Dr. Holly Mayer, Chair, 412-396-6470, E-mail: mayer@duq.edu.

Fashion Institute of Technology, School of Graduate Studies, Programs in Fashion and Textile Studies: History, Theory, and Museum Practice, New York, NY 10001-5992. Offers MA. *Accreditation:* NASAD. *Degree requirements:* For master's, one foreign language, thesis, internship. *Entrance requirements:* For master's, GRE General Test or GRE Subject Test, previous course work in art history and chemistry, 4 semesters of a foreign language. Additional exam requirements/recommendations for international students: Required—TOEFL (minimum score 550 paper-based; 213 computer-based). Electronic applications accepted. *Expenses:*

Tuition, state resident: full-time $8198; part-time $342 per credit. Tuition, nonresident: full-time $12,972; part-time $541 per credit. Required fees: $450.

See Close-Up on page 115.

Florida State University, The Graduate School, College of Visual Arts, Theatre and Dance, Department of Art History, Tallahassee, FL 32306. Offers art history (MA, PhD); museum studies (Certificate). *Accreditation:* NASAD. Part-time programs available. *Faculty:* 10 full-time (5 women), 2 part-time/adjunct (both women). *Students:* 31 full-time (24 women), 15 part-time (12 women); includes 3 minority (1 African American, 1 Asian American or Pacific Islander, 1 Hispanic American). Average age 33. 67 applicants, 58% accepted, 19 enrolled. In 2009, 9 master's, 3 doctorates awarded. Terminal master's awarded for partial completion of doctoral program. *Degree requirements:* For master's, one foreign language, thesis (for some programs), review; for doctorate, 2 foreign languages, comprehensive exam, thesis/dissertation, review. *Entrance requirements:* For master's, GRE General Test, minimum GPA of 3.0; for doctorate, GRE General Test, minimum GPA of 3.5. Additional exam requirements/recommendations for international students: Required—TOEFL. *Application deadline:* For fall admission, 1/10 priority date for domestic and international students. Application fee: $30. Electronic applications accepted. *Expenses:* Tuition, state resident: full-time $7413. Tuition, nonresident: full-time $22,567. *Financial support:* In 2009–10, 27 students received support, including 1 fellowship with full tuition reimbursement available (averaging $18,000 per year), 21 research assistantships with full tuition reimbursements available (averaging $5,000 per year), 5 teaching assistantships with full tuition reimbursements available (averaging $14,000 per year); career-related internships or fieldwork, Federal Work-Study, institutionally sponsored loans, scholarships/grants, and unspecified assistantships also available. Financial award application deadline: 1/10; financial award applicants required to submit FAFSA. *Faculty research:* Modern art and critical theory; medieval, renaissance and Baroque art; Pre-Colombian. *Unit head:* Dr. Adam Jolles, Professor/Chair, 850-644-7066, Fax: 850-644-3259, E-mail: ajolles@fsu.edu. *Application contact:* Kathy Braun, Program Administrator/Graduate Advisor, 850-644-8201, Fax: 850-644-7065, E-mail: kbraun@fsu.edu.

Florida State University, The Graduate School, College of Visual Arts, Theatre and Dance, Program in Museum Studies, Tallahassee, FL 32306. Offers Certificate. Part-time programs available. *Students:* 46 part-time (37 women); includes 5 minority (3 Asian Americans or Pacific Islanders, 2 Hispanic Americans). Average age 24. 10 applicants, 100% accepted, 10 enrolled. In 2009, 7 Certificates awarded. *Degree requirements:* For Certificate, internship. *Entrance requirements:* For degree, GRE, graduate degree or current study towards a graduate degree. *Application deadline:* For fall admission, 8/15 priority date for domestic and international students; for spring admission, 12/15 for domestic and international students. Applications are processed on a rolling basis. Application fee: $30. *Expenses:* Tuition, state resident: full-time $7413. Tuition, nonresident: full-time $22,567. *Financial support:* Career-related internships or fieldwork available. *Unit head:* Teri R. Yoo, Academic Coordinator, 850-645-4681, Fax: 850-644-7229, E-mail: tyoo@fsu.edu. *Application contact:* Teri R. Yoo, Academic Coordinator, 850-645-4681, Fax: 850-644-7229, E-mail: tyoo@fsu.edu.

The George Washington University, Columbian College of Arts and Sciences, Department of Fine Arts and Art History, Program in Art History, Washington, DC 20052. Offers art history (MA); museum training (MA). Part-time and evening/weekend programs available. *Faculty:* 4 full-time (1 woman), 2 part-time/adjunct (0 women). *Students:* 16 full-time (15 women), 5 part-time (all women); includes 3 minority (1 Asian American or Pacific Islander, 2 Hispanic Americans). Average age 25. 70 applicants, 53% accepted, 12 enrolled. In 2009, 21 master's awarded. *Degree requirements:* For master's, one foreign language, comprehensive exam, thesis or alternative. *Entrance requirements:* For master's, GRE General Test, bachelor's degree in field, minimum GPA of 3.0. Additional exam requirements/recommendations for international students: Required—TOEFL (minimum score 550 paper-based; 213 computer-based; 80 iBT). *Application deadline:* For fall admission, 3/1 priority date for domestic students, 1/15 priority date for international students; for spring admission, 10/1 priority date for domestic students, 9/1 priority date for international students. Applications are processed on a rolling basis. Application fee: $60. Electronic applications accepted. *Financial support:* In 2009–10, 3 students received support; fellowships, teaching assistantships, career-related internships or fieldwork and Federal Work-Study available. Financial award application deadline: 1/15. *Application contact:* Information Contact, 202-994-6085, Fax: 202-994-8657, E-mail: art@gwu.edu.

The George Washington University, Columbian College of Arts and Sciences, Program in Museum Studies, Washington, DC 20052. Offers MA, Certificate. Part-time and evening/weekend programs available. *Faculty:* 4 full-time (all women), 4 part-time/adjunct (all women). *Students:* 69 full-time (60 women), 63 part-time (59 women); includes 11 minority (6 African Americans, 1 American Indian/Alaska Native, 2 Asian Americans or Pacific Islanders, 2 Hispanic Americans), 4 international. Average age 28. 246 applicants, 57% accepted, 73 enrolled. In 2009, 36 master's, 39 other advanced degrees awarded. *Degree requirements:* For master's, comprehensive exam, internship. *Entrance requirements:* For master's, GRE General Test, minimum GPA of 3.0. Additional exam requirements/recommendations for international students: Required—TOEFL (minimum score 550 paper-based; 213 computer-based; 80 iBT). *Application deadline:* For fall admission, 2/1 priority date for domestic students, 1/15 priority date for international students; for spring admission, 10/15 priority date for domestic students, 9/1 priority date for international students. Applications are processed on a rolling basis. Application fee: $60. Electronic applications accepted. *Financial support:* In 2009–10, 15 students received support; fellowships with tuition reimbursements available, career-related internships or fieldwork, Federal Work-Study, institutionally sponsored loans, and tuition waivers available. Financial award application deadline: 1/15. *Unit head:* Kym S. Rice, Director, 202-994-0165, Fax: 202-994-7034, E-mail: kym@gwu.edu. *Application contact:* Information Contact, 202-994-7030, Fax: 202-994-7034, E-mail: mstd@gwu.edu.

Harvard University, Extension School, Cambridge, MA 02138-3722. Offers applied sciences (CAS); biotechnology (ALM); educational technologies (ALM); educational technology (CET); English for graduate and professional studies (DGP); environmental management (ALM, CEM); information technology (ALM); journalism (ALM); liberal arts (ALM); management (ALM, CM); mathematics for teaching (ALM); museum studies (ALM); premedical studies (Diploma); publication and communication (CPC). Part-time and evening/weekend programs available. *Degree requirements:* For master's, thesis. *Entrance requirements:* For master's, 3 completed graduate courses with grade of B or higher. Additional exam requirements/recommendations for international students: Required—TOEFL (minimum score 600 paper-based; 250 computer-based), TWE (minimum score 5). *Expenses:* Contact institution.

Indiana University–Purdue University Indianapolis, School of Liberal Arts, Department of Museum Studies, Indianapolis, IN 46202. Offers MS, Certificate. *Students:* 16 full-time (14 women), 15 part-time (all women); includes 1 minority (Hispanic American). Average age 27. 42 applicants, 40% accepted, 12 enrolled. *Entrance requirements:* For master's, GRE. *Application deadline:* For fall admission, 2/1 for domestic students; for spring admission, 10/1 for domestic students. Application fee: $55 ($65 for international students). *Financial support:* In 2009–10, 1 fellowship with partial tuition reimbursement (averaging $9,000 per year), 3 teaching assistantships (averaging $9,667 per year) were awarded. Financial award application deadline: 2/1; financial award applicants required to submit FAFSA. *Unit head:* Robert W. White, Dean, School of Liberal Arts, 317-274-8448. *Application contact:* Becky Ellis, Information Contact, 317-274-1490, E-mail: museum@iupui.edu.

John F. Kennedy University, School of Education and Liberal Arts, Department of Museum Studies, Berkeley, CA 94702. Offers museum studies (MA, Certificate), including administration, collections management, public programming. Part-time programs available. *Degree requirements:* For master's, project. *Entrance requirements:* For master's, interview. Additional exam requirements/recommendations for international students: Required—TOEFL, TWE. *Faculty research:* Emerging museum philosophies, multicultural diversity issues in museums, trends in collections management and preventive conservation, effective programming techniques and application for diverse audiences.

The Johns Hopkins University, Zanvyl Krieger School of Arts and Sciences, Advanced Academic Programs, Program in Museum Studies, Baltimore, MD 21218-2699. Offers MA. Postbaccalaureate distance learning degree programs offered (minimal on-campus study). *Faculty:* 2 full-time (both women), 21 part-time/adjunct (11 women). *Students:* 10 full-time (8 women), 134 part-time (115 women); includes 17 minority (3 African Americans, 1 American Indian/Alaska Native, 6 Asian Americans or Pacific Islanders, 7 Hispanic Americans), 5 international. Average age 34. 140 applicants, 47% accepted, 65 enrolled. Application fee: $75. *Financial support:* Scholarships/grants available. *Unit head:* Phyllis Hecht, Associate Program Chair, 202-452-1968, E-mail: phecht@jhu.edu. *Application contact:* Valana M. McMickens, Admissions Manager, 202-452-1941, Fax: 202-452-1970, E-mail: aapadmissions@jhu.edu.

New York University, Graduate School of Arts and Science, Department of History, New York, NY 10012-1019. Offers African diaspora (PhD); African history (PhD); archival management and historical editing (Advanced Certificate); Atlantic history (PhD); French studies/history (PhD); Hebrew and Judaic studies/history (PhD); history (MA, PhD), including Europe (PhD), Latin American and the Caribbean (PhD), United States (PhD), women's history (MA); Middle Eastern history (MA); Middle Eastern studies/history (PhD); public history (Advanced Certificate); world history (MA); JD/MA; MA/Advanced Certificate. Part-time programs available. *Faculty:* 43 full-time (19 women). *Students:* 141 full-time (87 women), 43 part-time (35 women); includes 33 minority (20 African Americans, 5 Asian Americans or Pacific Islanders, 8 Hispanic Americans), 32 international. Average age 30. 406 applicants, 30% accepted, 51 enrolled. In 2009, 21 master's, 10 doctorates, 4 other advanced degrees awarded. Terminal master's awarded for partial completion of doctoral program. *Degree requirements:* For master's, seminar paper; for doctorate, one foreign language, thesis/dissertation, oral and written exams; for Advanced Certificate, internship. *Entrance requirements:* For master's, GRE General Test, minimum GPA of 3.0, writing sample; for doctorate, GRE. Additional exam requirements/recommendations for international students: Required—TOEFL. *Application deadline:* For fall admission, 12/12 for domestic students. Application fee: $90. *Expenses:* Tuition: Full-time $30,528; part-time $1272 per credit. Required fees: $2177. *Financial support:* Fellowships with tuition reimbursements, research assistantships, teaching assistantships with tuition reimbursements, career-related internships or fieldwork, Federal Work-Study, institutionally sponsored loans, scholarships/grants, health care benefits, and unspecified assistantships available. Financial award application deadline: 12/12; financial award applicants required to submit FAFSA. *Faculty research:* African, East Asian, Medieval, early modern, and modern European history; U.S. history; African and African Diaspora; Latin American history; Atlantic World. *Unit head:* Joanna Waley-Cohen, Chair, 212-998-8600, Fax: 212-995-4017, E-mail: history.dept@nyu.edu. *Application contact:* Barbara Weinstein, Director of Graduate Studies, 212-998-8600, Fax: 212-995-4017, E-mail: history.dept@nyu.edu.

New York University, Graduate School of Arts and Science, Program in Museum Studies, New York, NY 10012-1019. Offers museum studies (MA, Advanced Certificate), including Africana studies (MA), Hebrew and Judaic studies (MA), Latin American and Caribbean studies (MA), Near Eastern studies (MA). Part-time and evening/weekend programs available. *Students:* 62 full-time (57 women), 23 part-time (21 women); includes 13 minority (1 African American, 2 American Indian/Alaska Native, 3 Asian Americans or Pacific Islanders, 7 Hispanic Americans), 15 international. Average age 27. 220 applicants, 52% accepted, 37 enrolled. In 2009, 37 master's awarded. *Entrance requirements:* For degree, master's degree or PhD. Additional exam requirements/recommendations for international students: Required—TOEFL. *Application deadline:* For fall admission, 2/1 for domestic students; for spring admission, 11/1 for domestic students. Application fee: $90. *Expenses:* Tuition: Full-time $30,528; part-time $1272 per credit. Required fees: $2177. *Financial support:* Application deadline: 2/1. *Faculty research:* Modern and contemporary art, history of museums and exhibitions, conservation of cultural materials, museum anthropology, ethnography. *Unit head:* Haidy Geismar, Director, 212-998-8080, Fax: 212-995-4185, E-mail: museum.studies@nyu.edu. *Application contact:* Tatiana Kamorina, Department Administrator, 212-998-8080, Fax: 212-995-4185, E-mail: museum.studies@nyu.edu.

San Francisco Art Institute, Graduate Program, Department of Exhibition and Museum Studies, San Francisco, CA 94133. Offers MA. *Entrance requirements:* Additional exam requirements/recommendations for international students: Required—TOEFL (minimum score 580 paper-based; 237 computer-based). Electronic applications accepted.

San Francisco State University, Division of Graduate Studies, College of Humanities, Museum Studies Program, San Francisco, CA 94132-1722. Offers MA. Part-time programs available.

Seton Hall University, College of Arts and Sciences, Department of Art, Music and Design, South Orange, NJ 07079-2697. Offers museum professions (MA), including exhibition development, museum education, museum management, museum registration. Part-time and evening/weekend programs available. *Faculty:* 5 full-time (4 women), 8 part-time/adjunct (5 women). *Students:* 40 full-time (36 women), 32 part-time (26 women); includes 7 minority (2 African Americans, 1 Asian American or Pacific Islander, 4 Hispanic Americans), 1 international. Average age 28. 54 applicants, 80% accepted, 20 enrolled. In 2009, 12 master's awarded. *Degree requirements:* For master's, thesis. *Entrance requirements:* For master's, GRE General Test, previous course work in art history. Additional exam requirements/recommendations for international students: Required—TOEFL. *Application deadline:* For fall admission, 7/1 priority date for domestic and international students; for spring admission, 11/1 priority date for domestic and international students. Applications are processed on a rolling basis. Application fee: $50. Electronic applications accepted. *Financial support:* Research assistantships, career-related internships or fieldwork, Federal Work-Study, and unspecified assistantships available. Financial award applicants required to submit FAFSA. *Faculty research:* History of museums, museum education, theory of museums, nineteenth century art, African-American art, Renaissance art history, museum registration, museum ethics. *Unit head:* Dr. Susan Leshnoff, Chair, 973-761-9459, Fax: 973-275-2368, E-mail: leshnosu@shu.edu. *Application contact:* Dr. Petra Chu, Director of Graduate Studies, 973-761-9460, Fax: 973-275-2368, E-mail: chupetra@shu.edu.

Southern Illinois University Edwardsville, Graduate Studies and Research, College of Arts and Sciences, Department of Historical Studies, Program in Museum Studies, Edwardsville, IL 62026-0001. Offers Postbaccalaureate Certificate. Part-time and evening/weekend programs available. *Students:* 3 full-time (all women), 7 part-time (6 women); includes 1 minority (African American). Average age 26. 12 applicants, 50% accepted. In 2009, 4 Postbaccalaureate Certificates awarded. *Entrance requirements:* Additional exam requirements/recommendations for international students: Required—TOEFL (minimum score 550 paper-based; 213 computer-based; 79 iBT), IELTS (minimum score 6.5). *Application deadline:* For fall admission, 7/23 for domestic students, 6/1 for international students; for spring admission, 12/11 for domestic students, 10/1 for international students. Applications are processed on a rolling basis. Application fee: $30. Electronic applications accepted. *Expenses:* Tuition, state resident: part-time $1252.50 per semester. Tuition, nonresident: part-time $3131.25 per semester. Required fees: $586.85 per semester. Tuition and fees vary according to course load. *Financial support:* Fellowships with full tuition reimbursements, research assistantships with full tuition reimbursements, teaching assistantships with full tuition reimbursements, career-related internships or fieldwork, Federal Work-Study, institutionally sponsored loans, scholarships/grants, traineeships, and unspecified assistantships available. Support available to part-time students. Financial award application deadline: 3/1; financial award applicants required to submit FAFSA. *Unit head:* Dr. Laura Fowler Milsk, Director, 618-650-2145, E-mail: lmilsk@siue.edu. *Application contact:* Dr. Laura Fowler Milsk, Director, 618-650-2145, E-mail: lmilsk@siue.edu.

State University of New York College at Oneonta, Graduate Education, Cooperstown Graduate Program in History Museum Studies, Cooperstown, NY 13326. Offers MA. *Students:* 31 full-time (22 women). Average age 25. 75 applicants, 20% accepted, 15 enrolled. In 2009, 16 master's awarded. *Degree requirements:* For master's, research paper or thesis. *Entrance*

Museum Studies

State University of New York College at Oneonta (continued)

requirements: For master's, GRE General Test. *Application deadline:* For fall admission, 1/10 for domestic students. Application fee: $50. *Expenses:* Contact institution. *Unit head:* Dr. Gretchen Sorin, Director, 607-547-2586, Fax: 607-547-8926, E-mail: sorings@oneonta.edu. *Application contact:* Dean, 607-436-2523, Fax: 607-436-3084, E-mail: gradoffice@oneonta.edu.

Syracuse University, College of Visual and Performing Arts, Program in Museum Studies, Syracuse, NY 13244. Offers MA. *Accreditation:* NASAD. *Students:* 23 full-time (18 women), 4 part-time (3 women). Average age 26. 27 applicants, 81% accepted, 11 enrolled. In 2009, 11 master's awarded. *Degree requirements:* For master's, thesis or alternative. *Entrance requirements:* Additional exam requirements/recommendations for international students: Required—TOEFL (minimum score 100 iBT). *Application deadline:* For fall admission, 2/1 priority date for domestic and international students. Application fee: $75. Electronic applications accepted. *Expenses:* Tuition: Full-time $26,808; part-time $1117 per credit. Required fees: $1024. *Financial support:* Fellowships with full tuition reimbursements, research assistantships with full and partial tuition reimbursements, teaching assistantships with full and partial tuition reimbursements available. Financial award application deadline: 1/1; financial award applicants required to submit FAFSA. *Unit head:* Dr. Lucinda Havenhand, Chair, 315-443-2455, Fax: 315-443-1303, E-mail: lkhavenh@syr.edu. *Application contact:* Harriett Conti, Assistant Dean for Recruitment and Admissions, 315-443-5755, E-mail: hmconti@syr.edu.

Texas Tech University, Graduate School, Program in Museum Science and Heritage Management, Lubbock, TX 79409. Offers heritage management (MS); museum science (MA). Part-time programs available. *Faculty:* 6 full-time (4 women), 1 part-time/adjunct (0 women). *Students:* 31 full-time (26 women), 7 part-time (6 women); includes 4 minority (1 African American, 3 Hispanic Americans). Average age 27. 34 applicants, 68% accepted, 14 enrolled. In 2009, 9 master's awarded. *Degree requirements:* For master's, thesis. *Entrance requirements:* For master's, GRE General Test. Additional exam requirements/recommendations for international students: Required—TOEFL (minimum score 550 paper-based; 213 computer-based). *Application deadline:* For fall admission, 3/1 priority date for international students; for spring admission, 11/1 priority date for international students. Applications are processed on a rolling basis. Application fee: $50 ($75 for international students). Electronic applications accepted. *Expenses:* Tuition, state resident: full-time $5100; part-time $213 per credit hour. Tuition, nonresident: full-time $11,748; part-time $490 per credit hour. Required fees: $2298; $50 per credit hour. $555 per semester. *Financial support:* In 2009–10, 2 research assistantships with partial tuition reimbursements (averaging $6,720 per year), 2 teaching assistantships with partial tuition reimbursements (averaging $8,018 per year) were awarded; career-related internships or fieldwork, Federal Work-Study, and institutionally sponsored loans also available. Support available to part-time students. Financial award application deadline: 4/15; financial award applicants required to submit FAFSA. *Faculty research:* Lubbock Lake Landmark; regional American fine art; museum education; Southern Plains cultural and natural heritage; natural science research. Total annual research expenditures: $48,569. *Unit head:* Dr. Eileen G. Johnson, Chair, 806-742-2442, Fax: 806-742-1136, E-mail: eileen.johnson@ttu.edu. *Application contact:* Claudia Cory, Assistant to the Director, 806-742-2442 Ext. 222, Fax: 806-742-1136, E-mail: claudia.cory@ttu.edu.

Tufts University, Graduate School of Arts and Sciences, Graduate Certificate Programs, Museum Studies Program, Medford, MA 02155. Offers Certificate. Part-time and evening/weekend programs available. *Expenses:* Contact institution.

Université de Montréal, Faculty of Arts and Sciences, Program in Museology, Montréal, QC H3C 3J7, Canada. Offers MA. Electronic applications accepted. *Faculty research:* Museum exhibits, museum education, natural science and museums, new technologies and museums.

Université du Québec à Montréal, Graduate Programs, Program in Museology, Montréal, QC H3C 3P8, Canada. Offers MA. Part-time programs available. *Entrance requirements:* For master's, appropriate bachelor's degree or equivalent and proficiency in French.

Université Laval, Faculty of Letters, Department of History, Program in Museology, Québec, QC G1K 7P4, Canada. Offers Diploma. Part-time programs available. *Entrance requirements:* For degree, English exam (comprehension of English), knowledge of French. Electronic applications accepted.

University at Buffalo, the State University of New York, Graduate School, College of Arts and Sciences, Department of Visual Studies, Program in Art History, Buffalo, NY 14260. Offers art history (MA); critical museum studies (Certificate). Part-time programs available. *Degree requirements:* For master's, one foreign language, thesis, field exam. *Entrance requirements:* Additional exam requirements/recommendations for international students: Required—TOEFL (minimum score 79 iBT). Electronic applications accepted. *Faculty research:* Frank Lloyd Wright, non-Western art, Renaissance, Bronze Age Crete, American art.

The University of British Columbia, Faculty of Arts and Faculty of Graduate Studies, Department of Art History, Visual Art, and Theory, Vancouver, BC V6T1Z2, Canada. Offers art history (MA, PhD, Diploma); critical and curatorial studies (MA); visual art (MFA). *Degree requirements:* For master's, one foreign language, thesis, final exhibition (MFA, MA in critical and curatorial studies); for doctorate, 2 foreign languages, comprehensive exam, thesis/dissertation. *Entrance requirements:* For master's, bachelor's degree with minimum B+ average (MFA, MA in critical and curatorial studies), A- (MA in art history); for doctorate, master's degree with minimum A- average. Additional exam requirements/recommendations for international students: Required—TOEFL (minimum score 600 paper-based; 250 computer-based). Electronic applications accepted. *Faculty research:* Conceptual art, Asian art, indigenous North American art, post-second war art, eighteenth and nineteenth century art, curatorial, digital art.

University of California, Riverside, Graduate Division, Department of History, Riverside, CA 92521-0102. Offers archival management (MA); historic preservation (MA); history (MA, PhD); museum curatorship (MA). Part-time programs available. Terminal master's awarded for partial completion of doctoral program. *Degree requirements:* For master's, one foreign language, comprehensive exam, internship report and oral exams, or thesis; for doctorate, 2 foreign languages, thesis/dissertation, qualifying exams, teaching experience. *Entrance requirements:* For master's, GRE General Test, minimum GPA of 3.2; for doctorate, GRE General Test, MA in history, minimum GPA of 3.2. Additional exam requirements/recommendations for international students: Required—TOEFL (minimum score 550 paper-based; 213 computer-based; 80 iBT). Electronic applications accepted. *Faculty research:* Native American history, United States, public history, Russia, Europe.

University of Central Oklahoma, College of Graduate Studies and Research, College of Liberal Arts, Department of History, Edmond, OK 73034-5209. Offers history (MA); museum studies (MA); social studies teaching (MA); Southwestern studies (MA). Part-time programs available. *Degree requirements:* For master's, thesis optional. *Entrance requirements:* Additional exam requirements/recommendations for international students: Required—TOEFL (minimum score 550 paper-based; 213 computer-based). Electronic applications accepted. *Expenses:* Tuition, state resident: full-time $4128; part-time $172 per credit hour. Tuition, nonresident: full-time $10,373; part-time $432.20 per credit hour. Required fees: $433.20; $18.05 per credit hour. *Faculty research:* China, Russia, civil war, American naval logistics.

University of Colorado at Boulder, Graduate School, Museum and Field Studies Program, Boulder, CO 80309. Offers MS. *Students:* 15 full-time (14 women), 4 part-time (2 women). Average age 30. 66 applicants, 23% accepted, 7 enrolled. In 2009, 7 master's awarded. *Degree requirements:* For master's, comprehensive exam, thesis or alternative. *Entrance requirements:* For master's, GRE General Test, GRE Subject Test, minimum undergraduate GPA of 3.0. *Application deadline:* For fall admission, 1/15 for domestic students, 12/1 for international students. Application fee: $50 ($60 for international students). *Financial support:* In 2009–10, 1 fellowship (averaging $3,000 per year), 2 research assistantships (averaging $6,584 per year) were awarded; career-related internships or fieldwork, Federal Work-Study, institutionally sponsored loans, and tuition waivers (partial) also available. Financial award application deadline: 2/1; financial award applicants required to submit FAFSA. Total annual research expenditures: $61,767.

University of Denver, Division of Arts, Humanities and Social Sciences, School of Art and Art History, Denver, CO 80208. Offers art history (MA); art history/museum studies (MA); electronic media arts and design (MFA). *Accreditation:* NASAD. Part-time programs available. *Faculty:* 16 full-time (11 women), 9 part-time/adjunct (5 women). *Students:* 15 full-time (14 women), 7 part-time (6 women); includes 1 minority (Hispanic American). Average age 29. 55 applicants, 51% accepted, 14 enrolled. In 2009, 10 master's awarded. *Degree requirements:* For master's, one foreign language, research paper. *Entrance requirements:* For master's, GRE. Additional exam requirements/recommendations for international students: Required—TOEFL. *Application deadline:* Applications are processed on a rolling basis. Application fee: $50. Electronic applications accepted. *Expenses:* Tuition: Full-time $34,596; part-time $961 per quarter hour. Required fees: $4 per quarter hour. Tuition and fees vary according to course load, campus/location and program. *Financial support:* Career-related internships or fieldwork, Federal Work-Study, institutionally sponsored loans, and scholarships/grants available. Support available to part-time students. Financial award application deadline: 3/1; financial award applicants required to submit FAFSA. *Faculty research:* Images of women in alchemical manuscripts and books, Giovanni Benedetto, Salvatore Castiglione. *Unit head:* Dr. Annette Stott, Director, 303-871-2846. *Application contact:* Dr. Annabeth Headrick, Graduate Advisor, 303-871-3574, E-mail: saah-interest@du.edu.

University of Florida, Graduate School, College of Fine Arts, School of Art and Art History, Gainesville, FL 32611. Offers art (MFA), including ceramics, creative photography, drawing, electronic intermedia, graphic design, painting, printmaking, sculpture; art education (MA); art history (MA, PhD); digital arts and sciences (MA); museology (museum studies) (MA). *Accreditation:* NASAD. *Degree requirements:* For master's, variable foreign language requirement, project or thesis (MFA). *Entrance requirements:* For master's, portfolio (MFA), writing sample (MA), GRE General Test or minimum GPA of 3.0. Additional exam requirements/recommendations for international students: Required—TOEFL (minimum score 550 paper-based; 213 computer-based). Electronic applications accepted. *Faculty research:* Studio production, art historical studies of style context.

University of Hawaii at Manoa, Graduate Division, College of Arts and Humanities, Department of American Studies, Program in Museum Studies, Honolulu, HI 96822. Offers Graduate Certificate. Part-time programs available. *Faculty:* 3 full-time (1 woman), 2 part-time/adjunct (both women). *Students:* 9 full-time (6 women), 13 part-time (9 women); includes 9 minority (8 Asian Americans or Pacific Islanders, 1 Hispanic American), 2 international. Average age 35. 10 applicants, 70% accepted, 6 enrolled. In 2009, 7 Graduate Certificates awarded. *Entrance requirements:* Additional exam requirements/recommendations for international students: Required—TOEFL (minimum score 600 paper-based; 250 computer-based; 100 iBT), IELTS (minimum score 7). *Application deadline:* For fall admission, 3/1 for domestic and international students; for spring admission, 9/1 for domestic and international students. Application fee: $60. *Expenses:* Tuition, state resident: full-time $8900; part-time $372 per credit. Tuition, nonresident: full-time $21,400; part-time $898 per credit. Required fees: $207 per semester. *Financial support:* In 2009–10, 2 students received support, including 4 fellowships (averaging $4,640 per year), 1 research assistantship (averaging $17,496 per year), 1 teaching assistantship (averaging $15,558 per year). *Application contact:* Karen Kosasa, Director, 808-956-8676, Fax: 808-956-4733, E-mail: kosasa@hawaii.edu.

The University of Kansas, Graduate Studies, College of Liberal Arts and Sciences, Museum Studies Program, Lawrence, KS 66045-7545. Offers collection conservation (Graduate Certificate); museum studies (MA). Part-time programs available. *Students:* 25 full-time (20 women), 4 part-time (all women); includes 2 minority (both Hispanic Americans), 4 international. Average age 27. 46 applicants, 52% accepted, 14 enrolled. In 2009, 11 master's awarded. *Degree requirements:* For master's, comprehensive exam. *Entrance requirements:* For master's, GRE. Additional exam requirements/recommendations for international students: Required—TOEFL. *Application deadline:* For fall admission, 1/1 priority date for domestic and international students; for spring admission, 8/15 priority date for domestic and international students. Applications are processed on a rolling basis. Application fee: $45 ($55 for international students). Electronic applications accepted. *Expenses:* Tuition, state resident: full-time $6492; part-time $270.50 per credit hour. Tuition, nonresident: full-time $15,510; part-time $646.25 per credit hour. Required fees: $847; $70.56 per credit hour. Tuition and fees vary according to course load and program. *Financial support:* Research assistantships with partial tuition reimbursements, career-related internships or fieldwork and unspecified assistantships available. *Faculty research:* Museum history, museum theory, collection studies, museum anthropology, cultural studies, history, natural history, American Studies, anthropology, and geology. *Unit head:* Dr. Marjorie Swann, Director, 785-864-4543, E-mail: museumstudies@ku.edu. *Application contact:* Sara Lundberg, Senior Administrative Associate, 785-864-4543, Fax: 785-864-5772, E-mail: saratune@ku.edu.

University of Louisville, Graduate School, College of Arts and Sciences, Department of Fine Arts, Louisville, KY 40292. Offers art history (MA, PhD); creative art (MA); curatorial studies (MA). *Faculty:* 18 full-time (8 women), 3 part-time/adjunct (0 women). *Students:* 23 full-time (20 women), 13 part-time (9 women); includes 3 minority (2 African Americans, 1 Hispanic American), 2 international. Average age 38. 28 applicants, 54% accepted, 9 enrolled. In 2009, 9 master's awarded. *Degree requirements:* For master's, thesis; for doctorate, 2 foreign languages, comprehensive exam, thesis/dissertation. *Entrance requirements:* For master's and doctorate, GRE General Test. *Application deadline:* For fall admission, 1/15 for domestic and international students. Applications are processed on a rolling basis. Application fee: $50. *Financial support:* Teaching assistantships available. *Faculty research:* Art history in the periods from ancient to contemporary and various regions, 2D and 3D studio areas, intermedia, curatorial studies. *Unit head:* James T. Grubola, Chair, 502-852-0759, Fax: 502-852-6791, E-mail: grubola@louisville.edu. *Application contact:* Libby Leggett, Director, Graduate Admissions, 502-852-3101, Fax: 502-852-6536, E-mail: gradadm@louisville.edu.

University of Manitoba, Faculty of Graduate Studies, Faculty of Arts, Department of History, Winnipeg, MB R3T 2N2, Canada. Offers archival studies (MA); history (MA, PhD). *Degree requirements:* For master's, thesis; for doctorate, one foreign language, thesis/dissertation.

University of Missouri–St. Louis, College of Arts and Sciences, Department of History, St. Louis, MO 63121. Offers history (MA); museum studies (MA, Certificate). Part-time and evening/weekend programs available. *Faculty:* 22 full-time (5 women), 7 part-time/adjunct (1 woman). *Students:* 31 full-time (21 women), 34 part-time (4 women); includes 4 minority (2 African Americans, 2 Hispanic Americans). Average age 32. 69 applicants, 58% accepted, 28 enrolled. In 2009, 39 master's, 10 other advanced degrees awarded. *Degree requirements:* For master's, thesis (for some programs). *Entrance requirements:* For master's, minimum GPA of 2.75, writing sample. Additional exam requirements/recommendations for international students: Required—TOEFL (minimum score 550 paper-based; 213 computer-based). *Application deadline:* For fall admission, 7/1 priority date for domestic and international students; for spring admission, 12/1 priority date for domestic and international students. Applications are processed on a rolling basis. Application fee: $35 ($40 for international students). Electronic applications accepted. *Expenses:* Tuition, state resident: full-time $5377; part-time $297.70 per credit hour. Tuition, nonresident: full-time $13,882; part-time $771.20 per credit hour. Required fees: $220; $12.20 per credit hour. One-time fee: $12. Tuition and fees vary according to course level, campus/location and program. *Financial support:* In 2009–10, 6 research assistantships with full and partial tuition reimbursements (averaging $7,500 per year), 5 teaching assistantships with full and partial tuition reimbursements (averaging $6,060 per year) were awarded; career-related internships or fieldwork also available. Financial award applicants required to submit FAFSA. *Faculty research:* U.S., European, East Asian, Latin American, and African history. *Unit head:* Dr. Winston Hsieh, Director of Graduate Studies,

314-516-5681, Fax: 314-516-5415, E-mail: hsiehw@umsl.edu. *Application contact:* 314-516-5458, Fax: 314-516-6996, E-mail: gradadm@umsl.edu.

University of New Hampshire, Graduate School, College of Liberal Arts, Department of History, Durham, NH 03824. Offers history (MA, PhD); museum studies (MA). Part-time programs available. *Faculty:* 24 full-time (13 women). *Students:* 32 full-time (15 women), 19 part-time (13 women); includes 3 minority (1 American Indian/Alaska Native, 2 Asian Americans or Pacific Islanders), 3 international. Average age 37. 84 applicants, 51% accepted, 17 enrolled. In 2009, 12 master's, 4 doctorates awarded. *Degree requirements:* For master's, thesis or alternative; for doctorate, 2 foreign languages, thesis/dissertation. *Entrance requirements:* For master's and doctorate, GRE General Test. Additional exam requirements/recommendations for international students: Required—TOEFL (minimum score 550 paper-based; 213 computer-based; 80 iBT). *Application deadline:* For fall admission, 6/1 priority date for domestic students, 4/15 for international students; for spring admission, 12/1 for domestic students. Applications are processed on a rolling basis. Application fee: $65. Electronic applications accepted. *Expenses:* Tuition, state resident: full-time $10,380; part-time $577 per credit hour. Tuition, nonresident: full-time $24,350; part-time $1002 per credit hour. Required fees: $1550; $387.50 per semester. Tuition and fees vary according to course load and program. *Financial support:* In 2009–10, 21 students received support, including 5 fellowships, 12 teaching assistantships; research assistantships, career-related internships or fieldwork, Federal Work-Study, scholarships/grants, and tuition waivers (full and partial) also available. Support available to part-time students. Financial award application deadline: 2/15. *Unit head:* Dr. Jan Golinski, Chairperson, 603-862-1764. *Application contact:* Susan Kilday, Administrative Assistant, 603-862-1764, E-mail: history.grad@unh.edu.

The University of North Carolina at Greensboro, Graduate School, College of Arts and Sciences, Department of History, Greensboro, NC 27412-5001. Offers historic preservation (Certificate); history (MA); museum studies (Certificate); U.S. history (PhD). Part-time programs available. *Entrance requirements:* For master's, GRE General Test. Additional exam requirements/recommendations for international students: Required—TOEFL. Electronic applications accepted. *Faculty research:* Simultaneous discovery in science, progressive social reform, Robert Mayer.

The University of North Carolina at Greensboro, Graduate School, School of Human Environmental Sciences, Department of Interior Architecture, Greensboro, NC 27412-5001. Offers historic preservation (Certificate); interior architecture (MS); museum studies (Certificate). *Degree requirements:* For master's, thesis. *Entrance requirements:* For master's, GRE General Test or MAT, bachelor's degree in interior design, interview, portfolio. Additional exam requirements/recommendations for international students: Required—TOEFL. Electronic applications accepted.

University of North Texas, Robert B. Toulouse School of Graduate Studies, College of Visual Arts and Design, Department of Art Education and Art History, Denton, TX 76203. Offers art education (MA, PhD); art history (MA); art museum education (Certificate); arts leadership (Certificate). Part-time and evening/weekend programs available. *Degree requirements:* For master's, one foreign language, comprehensive exam (for some programs), thesis (for some programs); for doctorate, comprehensive exam, thesis/dissertation. *Entrance requirements:* For master's, GRE, writing sample, statement of purpose; for doctorate, GRE, master's degree in art education, writing sample, slides, statement of purpose. Additional exam requirements/recommendations for international students: Required—proof of English language proficiency required for non-native English speakers; Recommended—TOEFL (minimum score 550 paper-based; 213 computer-based; 79 iBT). Application fee: $50 ($75 for international students). *Expenses:* Tuition, state resident: full-time $4298; part-time $239 per contact hour. Tuition, nonresident: full-time $9878; part-time $549 per contact hour. Required fees: $265 per contact hour. *Financial support:* Fellowships with partial tuition reimbursements, research assistantships with partial tuition reimbursements, teaching assistantships with partial tuition reimbursements, Federal Work-Study, scholarships/grants, health care benefits, and unspecified assistantships available. Support available to part-time students. Financial award applicants required to submit FAFSA. *Faculty research:* Aesthetics, visual culture, arts leadership, British art, Latin American art, French art, Indian art, contemporary Arab art.

University of Oklahoma, Graduate College, College of Liberal Studies, Norman, OK 73019-0390. Offers administrative leadership (MLS); integrated studies (MLS); interprofessional human and health services (MLS); museum studies (MLS). Part-time programs available. Post-baccalaureate distance learning degree programs offered (no on-campus study). *Faculty:* 15 full-time (8 women), 26 part-time/adjunct (16 women). *Students:* 17 full-time (11 women), 326 part-time (169 women); includes 71 minority (33 African Americans, 24 American Indian/Alaska Native, 4 Asian Americans or Pacific Islanders, 10 Hispanic Americans). 126 applicants, 90% accepted, 75 enrolled. In 2009, 94 master's awarded. *Degree requirements:* For master's, thesis, research project, internship. *Entrance requirements:* For master's, minimum GPA of 3.0 in last 60 hours, writing sample. Additional exam requirements/recommendations for international students: Required—TOEFL (minimum score 550 paper-based; 213 computer-based). *Application deadline:* For fall admission, 7/15 priority date for domestic students, 4/1 for international students; for spring admission, 12/1 for domestic students, 9/1 for international students. Applications are processed on a rolling basis. Application fee: $40 ($90 for international students). Electronic applications accepted. *Expenses:* Tuition, state resident: full-time $3744; part-time $156 per credit hour. Tuition, nonresident: full-time $13,577; part-time $565.70 per credit hour. Required fees: $2415; $90.10 per credit hour. *Financial support:* In 2009–10, 163 students received support. Career-related internships or fieldwork, scholarships/grants, and tuition waivers (partial) available. Support available to part-time students. Financial award applicants required to submit FAFSA. *Faculty research:* Distance education, adult learning processes, student satisfaction, administrative leadership, organizations, museum studies. *Unit head:* Dr. James Pappas, Dean and Vice President for University Outreach, 405-325-6361, Fax: 405-325-7196, E-mail: jpappas@ou.edu. *Application contact:* Dr. Julie Raadschelders, MA Program Coordinator, 405-325-1061, Fax: 405-325-9632, E-mail: jraadschelders@ou.edu.

University of South Carolina, The Graduate School, College of Arts and Sciences, Department of History, Program in Public History, Columbia, SC 29208. Offers archives (MA); historic preservation (MA); museum (MA); museum management (Certificate); MLIS/MA. *Degree requirements:* For master's, one foreign language, thesis, internship. *Entrance requirements:* For master's, GRE General Test, writing sample. Additional exam requirements/recommendations for international students: Required—TOEFL. Electronic applications accepted. *Faculty research:* Museum studies, historic preservation, archives administration.

The University of the Arts, College of Art and Design, Department of Museum Studies, Philadelphia, PA 19102-4944. Offers museum communication (MA); museum education (MA); museum exhibition planning and design (MFA). *Accreditation:* NASAD. Part-time programs available. *Degree requirements:* For master's, thesis, internship. *Entrance requirements:* For master's, portfolio. Additional exam requirements/recommendations for international students: Required—TOEFL (minimum score 550 paper-based; 213 computer-based).

See Close-Up on page 199.

University of Toronto, School of Graduate Studies, Humanities Division, Department of Art, Toronto, ON M5S 1A1, Canada. Offers art history (MA, PhD); visual studies (MVS). Part-time programs available. *Degree requirements:* For master's, 2 foreign languages, language proficiency exams; for doctorate, 2 foreign languages, comprehensive exam, thesis/dissertation. *Entrance requirements:* For master's, coursework in a foreign language, 3 letters of reference, sample research paper, minimum B+ average in senior art history and/or humanities courses; for doctorate, minimum A– average in senior art history and/or humanities courses, 2 letters of reference, sample research paper.

University of Toronto, School of Graduate Studies, Humanities Division, Program in Museum Studies, Toronto, ON M5S 1A1, Canada. Offers MM St. *Expenses:* Contact institution.

University of Washington, Graduate School, Museology Graduate Program, Seattle, WA 98195. Offers MA. *Degree requirements:* For master's, thesis or alternative. *Entrance requirements:* For master's, GRE General Test, minimum GPA of 3.0. Additional exam requirements/recommendations for international students: Required—TOEFL (minimum score 580 paper-based; 237 computer-based; 92 iBT). Electronic applications accepted. *Expenses:* Contact institution. *Faculty research:* Collection management, conservation, art history, anthropology, administration.

University of West Georgia, Graduate School, College of Arts and Sciences, Department of History, Carrollton, GA 30118. Offers history (MA); museum studies (Certificate); public history (Certificate). Part-time programs available. *Faculty:* 16 full-time (6 women). *Students:* 22 full-time (12 women), 21 part-time (11 women); includes 3 minority (1 African American, 2 Hispanic Americans). Average age 35. 23 applicants, 57% accepted, 6 enrolled. In 2009, 10 master's, 9 other advanced degrees awarded. *Degree requirements:* For master's, one foreign language, comprehensive exam, thesis or alternative. *Entrance requirements:* For master's, GRE General Test (minimum score 400 verbal, 400 quantitative, 3.5 writing), undergraduate degree in history or related social studies, minimum GPA of 2.75. *Application deadline:* For fall admission, 7/17 for domestic students; for spring admission, 11/20 for domestic students. Applications are processed on a rolling basis. Application fee: $30. Electronic applications accepted. *Expenses:* Tuition, state resident: full-time $2952; part-time $164 per semester hour. Tuition, nonresident: full-time $11,808; part-time $656 per semester hour. Required fees: $42.90 per semester hour. $307 per semester. Tuition and fees vary according to course load. *Financial support:* In 2009–10, 7 students received support, including research assistantships with full tuition reimbursements available (averaging $6,000 per year); career-related internships or fieldwork, scholarships/grants, and unspecified assistantships also available. Support available to part-time students. Financial award application deadline: 7/1; financial award applicants required to submit FAFSA. *Faculty research:* Public history, United States, Russia/Soviet Union, Africa, Europe. *Unit head:* Dr. Howard Steven Goodson, Interim Chair, 678-839-6042, E-mail: hgoodson@westga.edu. *Application contact:* Dr. Charles W. Clark, Dean, 678-839-6508, E-mail: cclark@westga.edu.

University of Wisconsin–Milwaukee, Graduate School, College of Letters and Sciences, Department of Anthropology, Milwaukee, WI 53201-0413. Offers anthropology (PhD); museum studies (Certificate). *Faculty:* 18 full-time (8 women). *Students:* 50 full-time (32 women), 44 part-time (36 women); includes 9 minority (2 African Americans, 3 American Indian/Alaska Native, 2 Asian Americans or Pacific Islanders, 2 Hispanic Americans), 2 international. Average age 33. 54 applicants, 76% accepted, 11 enrolled. In 2009, 11 master's, 1 doctorate awarded. *Degree requirements:* For master's, thesis or alternative; for doctorate, one foreign language, thesis/dissertation, departmental qualifying exam. *Entrance requirements:* For master's, GRE; for doctorate, GRE, minimum GPA of 3.0, master's degree. Additional exam requirements/recommendations for international students: Required—TOEFL (minimum score 550 paper-based; 79 iBT), IELTS (minimum score 6.5). *Application deadline:* For fall admission, 1/1 priority date for domestic students; for spring admission, 9/1 for domestic students. Applications are processed on a rolling basis. Application fee: $45 ($75 for international students). *Expenses:* Tuition, state resident: full-time $8800. Tuition, nonresident: full-time $20,760. Tuition and fees vary according to program and reciprocity agreements. *Financial support:* In 2009–10, 19 teaching assistantships were awarded; fellowships, research assistantships, career-related internships or fieldwork and unspecified assistantships also available. Support available to part-time students. Financial award application deadline: 4/15. Total annual research expenditures: $224,571. *Unit head:* J. Patrick Gray, Chair, 414-229-4822, Fax: 414-229-5848, E-mail: jpgray@uwm.edu. *Application contact:* General Information Contact, 414-229-4982, Fax: 414-229-6967, E-mail: gradschool@uwm.edu.

University of Wisconsin–Milwaukee, Graduate School, College of Letters and Sciences, Department of Art History, Milwaukee, WI 53201-0413. Offers art history (MA); art museum studies (Certificate). Part-time programs available. *Faculty:* 9 full-time (5 women). *Students:* 14 full-time (13 women), 11 part-time (all women); includes 1 minority (African American), 1 international. Average age 29. 31 applicants, 61% accepted, 6 enrolled. In 2009, 7 master's awarded. *Degree requirements:* For master's, one foreign language, comprehensive exam, thesis or alternative. *Entrance requirements:* For master's, GRE. Additional exam requirements/recommendations for international students: Required—TOEFL (minimum score 550 paper-based; 79 iBT), IELTS (minimum score 6.5). *Application deadline:* For fall admission, 1/1 priority date for domestic students; for spring admission, 9/1 for domestic students. Applications are processed on a rolling basis. Application fee: $45 ($75 for international students). *Expenses:* Tuition, state resident: full-time $8800. Tuition, nonresident: full-time $20,760. Tuition and fees vary according to program and reciprocity agreements. *Financial support:* In 2009–10, 5 teaching assistantships were awarded; fellowships, research assistantships, career-related internships or fieldwork and unspecified assistantships also available. Support available to part-time students. Financial award application deadline: 4/15. *Faculty research:* Ancient Mediterranean art through contemporary Western art, Chinese art, Pre-Columbian art, film, theory. Total annual research expenditures: $1,035. *Unit head:* Kenneth Bendiner, Chair, 414-229-5015, Fax: 414-229-2935, E-mail: bendiner@uwm.edu. *Application contact:* Derek Counts, General Information Contact, 414-229-3466, E-mail: dbc@uwm.edu.

Virginia Commonwealth University, Graduate School, School of the Arts, Department of Art History, Richmond, VA 23284-9005. Offers architectural history (MA); art history (MA, PhD); historical studies (MA); museum studies (MA). *Accreditation:* NASAD. *Degree requirements:* For master's, thesis; for doctorate, comprehensive exam, thesis/dissertation. *Entrance requirements:* For master's and doctorate, GRE General Test. *Faculty research:* Modern, nineteenth century, Renaissance, American, and Medieval art.

Western Illinois University, School of Graduate Studies, College of Fine Arts and Communication, Program in Museum Studies, Macomb, IL 61455-1390. Offers MA. Part-time programs available. *Students:* 16 full-time (14 women), 5 part-time (4 women); includes 2 minority (both Hispanic Americans). Average age 31. 12 applicants, 83% accepted. In 2009, 1 master's awarded. *Entrance requirements:* For master's, minimum GPA of 3.0. Additional exam requirements/recommendations for international students: Required—TOEFL (minimum score 600 paper-based; 250 computer-based; 100 iBT). *Application deadline:* Applications are processed on a rolling basis. Application fee: $30. Electronic applications accepted. *Expenses:* Tuition, state resident: full-time $4486; part-time $249.21 per credit hour. Tuition, nonresident: full-time $8972; part-time $498.42 per credit hour. Required fees: $72.62 per credit hour. *Financial support:* In 2009–10, 3 students received support, including 3 research assistantships with full tuition reimbursements available (averaging $7,280 per year). Financial award applicants required to submit FAFSA. *Unit head:* Ann Rowson Love, Director, 309-762-9481 Ext. 266, E-mail: a-rowsonlove@wiu.edu. *Application contact:* Evelyn Hoing, Assistant Director of Graduate Studies, 309-298-1806, Fax: 309-298-2345, E-mail: grad-office@wiu.edu.

BARD GRADUATE CENTER: DECORATIVE ARTS, DESIGN HISTORY, MATERIAL CULTURE

Programs of Study

The Bard Graduate Center (BGC) is a graduate institute affiliated with Bard College committed to the encyclopedic study of things in their historical context, drawing on methodologies and approaches from art and design history, economic history, history of technology, philosophy, anthropology, and archaeology. The project of the school is to study the cultural history of the material world.

Founded in 1993, the BGC offers M.A. and Ph.D. degrees. It is an international study and exhibition center in New York City devoted to the interdisciplinary study of the decorative arts, design history, cultural history, history and theory of museums, Renaissance and early modern studies, cultural geography, American art and culture, Asian Art, the Arts of Antiquity, eighteenth through twentieth century design and European Studies, and the material culture of New York City. Programs are designed to prepare students for careers or career advancement in museums; galleries; auction houses; government agencies; art-related education, research, publishing, and communications; and landscape and historic preservation.

There is hands-on examination of materials and objects and an extensive connection to special programs and exhibition projects with the Metropolitan Museum of Art, the New York Historical Society, the Brooklyn Museum of Art, the American Museum of Natural History, the Frick Collection, and other major cultural institutions. As part of their studies, all students undertake an internship at one of more than 250 institutions.

A semiannual interdisciplinary journal, *West 86th,* is published by the BGC and features scholarly articles about the decorative arts and their interpretation as well as book reviews. Advanced graduate students are invited to submit articles for possible publication.

Research Facilities

The Bard Graduate Center occupies a six-story town house at 18 West 86th Street and a second, newly renovated town house at 38 West 86th Street in Manhattan. The buildings' elegantly appointed rooms provide an aesthetically appropriate setting for the study of the decorative arts. Its facilities include a 40,000-volume research library; a new digital media research lab; exhibition galleries; classrooms; faculty offices; student lounges; outdoor terraces; symposium spaces; and administrative offices.

Financial Aid

The BGC offers fellowships, scholarships, and a student campus employment program. Aid is awarded on the basis of need and merit. Financial aid applications are due by January 15. About 85 percent of students receive aid.

Cost of Study

The average annual tuition for incoming full-time students in the 2009–10 academic year was $25,008 for M.A. students, based on a cost of $1042 per credit. Tuition and fees for Ph.D. students averaged $30,768 for incoming full-time students in the 2009–10 academic year; they vary for subsequent years of doctoral work. Students may contact the Office of Admissions for more detailed and updated fee schedules.

Living and Housing Costs

Bard Hall, located at 410 West 58th Street, provides housing for students, faculty members, and visiting scholars. Nine residential floors offer a variety of furnished studios and one- and two-bedroom suites with kitchens and baths. Apartments are offered year-round. For the 2009–10 academic year, the cost of a studio unit was approximately $13,300, a one-bedroom unit was $16,000, and a two-bedroom unit was $13,200 per student.

Student Group

The Bard Graduate Center accepts approximately 20–25 full-time and a limited number of part-time students into the program annually. Applications are received from many countries and from across the United States. The BGC welcomes students of all ages and backgrounds as well as working professionals.

Location

The Bard Graduate Center is located on the Upper West Side of Manhattan, near Central Park. It is situated in a landmark neighborhood conveniently served by public transportation, with easy access to the innumerable museums, libraries, auction houses, and galleries of metropolitan New York.

The College and The Center

Established by Bard College in 1993, the Bard Graduate Center is one of the many "satellite" institutions that surround the 150-year-old undergraduate liberal arts college. Others include the Jerome Levy Economics Institute of Bard College, the Milton Avery Graduate School of the Arts, and the Center for Curatorial Studies in Art and Contemporary Culture. Other graduate divisions are located in Annandale, New York.

Applying

Students are admitted to the graduate programs annually for fall admission. The application deadline for admission and financial aid is January 15. Applicants to the M.A. program must have a bachelor's degree or the equivalent; applicants to the Ph.D. program are expected to have completed a master's degree in either the decorative arts or a related field. Because of the interdisciplinary nature of the program, there are no limitations on the applicant's prior field of study. Successful applicants, however, will have had some previous study, training, or work experience in the history of art, architecture, archeology, history, the decorative arts, cultural history, or material culture studies.

Applications should include scores on the General Test of the Graduate Record Examinations (GRE), three letters of recommendation, a short resume, a sample of scholarly writing, and a statement of intent describing academic and professional objectives. International candidates must submit TOEFL scores and a Certification of Finances. An interview is required. The application fee for 2009–10 was $65.

Correspondence and Information

Office of Admissions
Bard Graduate Center: Decorative Arts, Design History, Material Culture
18 West 86th Street
New York, New York 10024
Phone: 212-501-3019
Fax: 212-501-3065
E-mail: admissions@bgc.bard.edu
Web site: http://www.bgc.bard.edu

Bard Graduate Center: Decorative Arts, Design History, and Material Culture

THE FACULTY AND THEIR RESEARCH

The BGC maintains a distinguished core of full-time faculty members, supplemented by eminent decorative arts scholars visiting from a broad range of national and international museums and institutions of higher learning.

The Bard Graduate Center Faculty

Susan Weber Soros, Iris Horowitz Professor in the History of the Decorative Arts and Director; Ph.D., Royal College of Art. Furniture studies.
Peter N. Miller, Professor and Chair of Academic Programs; Ph.D., Cambridge. European cultural history.
Kenneth Ames, Professor; Ph.D., Pennsylvania. Nineteenth century.
Jeffrey Collins, Professor; Ph.D., Yale. Eighteenth-century European art and culture.
Aaron Glass, Assistant Professor; Ph.D., NYU. Museum anthropology.
David Jaffee, Professor; Ph.D., Harvard. Landscape history and cultural geography.
Pat Kirkham, Professor; Ph.D., London. Eighteenth-, nineteenth-, and twentieth-century design history and gender studies.
Deborah L. Krohn, Associate Professor; Ph.D., Harvard. Early Modern material culture in southern Europe and museum studies.
François Louis, Associate Professor; Ph.D., Zurich. Art history of Tang and Song China, Chinese goldsmithing.
Michele Majer, Assistant Professor; M.A., NYU. Costume historian.
Andrew Morrall, Professor; Ph.D., Courtauld Institute of Art (England). Fourteenth- to eighteenth-century European arts.
Amy Ogata, Associate Professor; Ph.D., Princeton. Nineteenth- and twentieth-century design history.
Elizabeth Simpson, Professor; Ph.D., Pennsylvania. The arts of the ancient world.
Paul Stirton, Associate Professor; Ph.D. Courtauld Institute of Art (England). Design history.
Ittai Weinryb, Ph.D., Johns Hopkins. Medieval material culture.
Catherine Whalen, Assistant Professor; Ph.D., Yale. American material culture and twentieth-century design.

Visiting Faculty

Timothy Benton, M.A., Courtauld Institute of Art (England). Twentieth-century art and architecture.
Thomas Campbell, Ph.D., Courtauld Institute of Art (England). Textile historian.
Ellen Paul Denker, M.A., Delaware. American ceramics.
Stefan Heidemann, Visiting Professor, Ph.D., Free University (Berlin). Islamic art.
Timothy Husband, M.A., Institute of Fine Arts, New York. Medieval decorative arts.
Juliet Kinchin, M.A., Courtauld Institute of Art (England). Twentieth-century architecture and design.
Louis Levine, Ph.D., Pennsylvania. Jewish material culture.
Pamela Long, Ph.D., Maryland. Medieval and Renaissance technology.
Caroline Maniaque, Ph.D., Paris VIII. Architecture and urbanism.
Robert J. Moes, M.A., Michigan. The arts of Japan and Korea.
Kevin L. Stayton, M.Phil., Yale. American decorative arts.

GEORGE MASON UNIVERSITY

Department of History and Art History
Master of Arts in Art History

Program of Study

The general M.A. in Art History Program at George Mason University (GMU) offers a curriculum designed to prepare students for a variety of arts-related careers in museum or administrative positions and secondary teaching and for graduate studies at the Ph.D. level. Because it places special emphasis on new media skills, museology, and preprofessional internships, the program is unique in the region.

The Art History Program's 30-credit curriculum features required courses in art historiography and methods, history and new media, and the museum; a research seminar; and directed readings in preparation for the comprehensive exams. Students may elect courses from diverse graduate offerings, related fields, and internship opportunities. The University's joint Department of History and Art History affords students possibilities for related historical studies and training through the Center for History and New Media. Since the program began in 2006, students have gained experience from graduate internships at Dumbarton Oaks, the Textile Museum, and Christie's Auction House and through study abroad in London through the Sotheby's program.

The Department of Art and Art History's widely published faculty members teach and conduct research in many areas. Their interests and expertise range from ancient to contemporary in time periods; they span the globe to cover Europe, North and South America, Asia, and the Middle East; and they consider a full spectrum of art and artifacts. Students can expect small classes with personal attention to individual interests and career goals and the opportunity to get to know and study with one another in a small and collegial environment.

Highlights of the Master of Arts in Art History Program include training in new media as well as traditional research skills, seminar-size classes, late afternoon and evening classes, an individual tutorial class for each student, internships, and, of course, the unparalleled museum and library resources of Washington, D.C. An undergraduate art history degree is not required for admission.

Students in the program select a variety of elective courses in art history. Several specific courses in history, sociology, anthropology, and cultural studies may be included in the program. All students are required to complete a minimum of 30 semester hours of graduate-level work with a GPA of no less than 3.0. This includes 3 hours of Art History (ARTH) 600 Methods and Research in Art History; 15 hours of general elective 500- and 600-level course work in art history and related courses; 3 hours of applied learning: ARTH 593 Art History Internships or ARTH 594 The Museum; 3 hours technology/new media: HIST 696 Clio Wired: An Introduction to History and New Media or HIST 697 Creating (Art) History in New Media; 3 hours graduate research seminar: ARTH 699 Topics in Art History; 3 hours ARTH 696 Independent Directed Readings (an individualized tutorial that prepares students for the comprehensive exam); and a comprehensive exam. Students must also demonstrate reading ability in one relevant research language, to be approved by the graduate coordinator.

Students who did not major in art history as undergraduates are welcome to apply. They may be required to take up to four foundation courses (12 hours) at the undergraduate level beyond the credits required for the M.A. in art history. Full-time students generally complete the program in two years. Part-time students may take up to six years to complete the degree requirements.

Research Facilities

Students have access to the Department of Art and Art History's slide/digital image collection of 80,000 images as well as access to the University's subscription to Artstor, a digital library of more than one million images in the areas of art, architecture, the humanities, and social sciences with a set of tools to view, present, and manage images for research and pedagogical purposes.

George Mason is part of the D.C. Consortium of Universities, which also includes American University, Catholic University, Corcoran College of Art and Design, George Washington, Georgetown, and the University of Maryland. Students may enroll in courses at these universities as well as use their library facilities.

Students in the Art History Program also take full advantage of George Mason University's Center for History and New Media (CHNM). Since 1994, the Center for History and New Media has used digital media and computer technology to democratize history—to incorporate multiple voices, reach diverse audiences, and encourage popular participation in presenting and preserving the past. CHNM combines cutting-edge digital media with the latest and best historical scholarship to promote an inclusive and democratic understanding of the past as well as a broad historical literacy.

Financial Aid

At this time, student loans are the only available form of financial aid.

Cost of Study

In-state tuition is $430 per credit hour, and out-of-state tuition is $1046 per credit hour. There is a $60 graduate student fee.

Living and Housing Costs

Since GMU borders a major metropolitan area and resides in a nationally expensive county, the cost of living is relatively high. There are a variety of services available to students to locate affordable housing. Masonvale, a community of luxury apartments on the University grounds is available for graduate student housing. These apartments are unfurnished but each features unique details. One-, two-, and three-bedroom units are available. Graduate students interested in living on campus will have the opportunity to rent either a room in one of the apartments, or an entire unit to meet their housing needs while at GMU. Rental charges range from $684 to $1430 per month, per individual room, depending on amenities. Rent includes water and electricity charges; Internet, phone, and cable are not included.

Student Group

The M.A. in Art History is a new program; there are currently 20 students enrolled in course work. Some anticipate going on for the Ph.D. in art history. Several others are looking to gallery, museum work, or secondary school teaching.

In evaluating applicants to the program, faculty members examine both the liberal arts and humanities as well as the art history background of students, with the expectation that there is some prior experience in art history. They also look for evidence of writing, speaking, and research ability.

Location

Located in Fairfax, Virginia, just 15 miles from Washington, D.C., George Mason has emerged in the past decade as a major university in the state and the nation. Its development has been shaped in response to the educational needs of the northern Virginia cosmopolitan constituency. Near the D.C. metro, the University is within close reach of two major airports and the Northeast corridor via Amtrak.

Students benefit from proximity to the Library of Congress and the region's rich variety of museums, including the National Gallery of Art, the Corcoran, the Hirshhorn, the Freer-Sackler Galleries of Asian Art, the National Museum of African Art, the Phillips Collection, Dumbarton Oaks, the Textile Museum, the Renwick Gallery, the Smithsonian American Art Museum, the National Portrait Gallery, the National Museum of Women in the Arts, the Art Museum of the Americas, and the National Museum of the American Indian, among others. The D.C. area boasts major professional teams in football, basketball, baseball, and hockey and offers scores of musical and theatrical entertainments at the Kennedy Center for the Performing Arts, the Shakespeare Theater, and the Arena Stage.

The University and The Department

George Mason University's Department of History and Art History features a distinguished faculty. Five members of the Department have won Guggenheim awards; 1 was granted a MacArthur Fellowship. In addition, faculty members have received fellowships from a variety of institutions, including the National Endowment for the Humanities, the American Council of Learned Societies, the Getty Museum, the Clark Institute, DAAD, the Center for Advanced Study in the Visual Arts at the National Gallery of Art, the Fulbright Program, and the Andrew W. Mellon Foundation, and several teaching awards. George Mason art historians also have been recognized with book awards, such as the James R. Wiseman Book Award from the Archaeological Institute of America. The Art History Program offers a curriculum in ancient, medieval, early modern and modern European, American, Asian, Islamic, and Latin American art history. Affiliated with the Center for History and New Media, the program benefits from the center's international reputation for innovatively applying new technology to the study, preservation, and teaching of history and art history. Various foundations and agencies support the center's work, including the National Endowment for the Humanities and the Sloan, Kellogg, and Gould foundations.

As a relatively new institution, George Mason University is distinguished by the diversity of its campus population and programs. The residential population of undergraduates now provides a substantial collegiate feeling as do the University's Johnson Center and Fine and Performing Arts institutions.

The undergraduate and graduate degree programs in art history are located within the larger Department of History and Art History, which is part of the College of Humanities and Social Sciences within the University. The studio art programs are located in the College of Visual and Performing Arts.

Applying

For admission to the program, the applicant's undergraduate record, broadly with attention to art historical preparation, is considered. It is expected that students hold the equivalent of a minor in art history at the time of admission, although provisional admission may be granted without it. Students must also submit a resume and goals statement, two letters of academic recommendation, GRE scores, and an academic writing sample. GRE scores are waived if the student completed a bachelor's degree ten or more years ago or holds another graduate degree.

While applications are reviewed on a year-round, rolling, space-available basis, the date for spring admission is November 1 and for fall, April 15. Those interested in assistantships should apply by April 15. For further information, students should contact Ellen Wiley Todd, Graduate Director, at etodd@gmu.edu or 703-993-4374 or Sharon Bloomquist, Graduate Administrative Assistant, at 703-993-1248 or sbloomqu@gmu.edu.

Correspondence and Information

Ellen Wiley Todd, Associate Professor, Art History
M.A. Graduate Coordinator
Department of History and Art History
George Mason University
4400 University Drive, MS 3G1
Fairfax, Virginia 22030
Phone: 703-993-4374
Fax: 703-993-1251
E-mail: etodd@gmu.edu
Web site: http://historyarthistory.gmu.edu/art-history/masters/

Applicants should send materials to:
Graduate Admissions Office
MSN 3A4
George Mason University
4400 University Drive
Fairfax, Virginia 22030-4444

George Mason University

THE FACULTY AND THEIR RESEARCH

Lawrence Butler, Associate Professor; Ph.D., Pennsylvania, 1989. Medieval, Byzantine, and Islamic art history and architecture.
Robert DeCaroli, Associate Professor; Ph.D., UCLA, 1999. Asia, Southeast and South Asian art history.
Marion Deshmukh, Associate Professor; Ph.D., Columbia, 1975. Modern European and German art history, intersection between painting and politics in nineteenth- and twentieth-century Germany.
Michele Greet, Associate Professor; Ph.D., NYU, 2004. Latin American and Modern European art.
Christopher Gregg, Term Assistant Professor; Ph.D., North Carolina at Chapel Hill, 2000. Greek and Roman art.
Carol C. Mattusch, Full Professor; Ph.D., North Carolina at Chapel Hill, 1975. Greek and Roman art and archaeology.
Margaret Richardson, Term Assistant Professor; Ph.D., Virginia Commonwealth, 2005. Modern and contemporary art of Asia.
Ellen Wiley Todd, Associate Professor; Ph.D., Stanford, 1987. Art of the United States.

Memphis College *of* Art

MEMPHIS COLLEGE OF ART

Graduate Programs in Studio Practice and Art Education

Programs of Study

Memphis College of Art (MCA) is a professional center of art and design education, dedicated to preparing individuals for lives of creating, problem solving, and critical thinking. Small by choice and purpose, MCA is a cultural wellspring of creativity, nurturing and educating artists of all levels since 1936. Located within the 340-acre Overton Park, MCA offers state-of-the-art facilities, excellent faculty members, interdisciplinary programs, and cutting-edge exhibitions to the public and those pursuing B.F.A., M.F.A., or M.A. in art education and M.A.T. degrees.

As a studio-intensive program, the M.F.A. at Memphis College of Art offers a catalytic environment with the goal of developing artistic practices that contribute significantly to contemporary culture. The program offers the opportunity to focus on traditional studio practice, digital technologies, or an interdisciplinary course of study. Areas of study include, but are not limited to, painting, drawing, photography, printmaking, papermaking/book arts, sculpture, digital media, or an individually tailored program of interdisciplinary study. Studio practice is enhanced with course work in issues of history, theory, and criticism. The program consists of structured course work and independent studio practice, with the second year culminating in the M.F.A. thesis exhibition and written thesis document.

The Master of Arts in Art Education (M.A.Art.Ed.) program is designed for experienced, licensed educators who are ready to further develop their artistic, scholarly, and leadership capabilities in art education. The program explores new approaches to creating, teaching, and researching visual art processes.

The Master of Arts in Teaching (M.A.T.) art education program is designed for artists committed to the growth and development of others through the exchange of knowledge, but who are not yet certified as teachers. It is a full-time, two-year or 40-credit-hour program that integrates hands-on experience in teaching with studio preparation; ensuring students are informed by practice, current theory, and research. Upon completion of this program and obtaining passing scores on the required Praxis exams, graduates are eligible for K–12 certification in art in Tennessee and, by reciprocal agreement, most other states.

Research Facilities

All three graduate programs, graduate studios, and labs are located in the new MCA Graduate School facility in downtown Memphis. The 44,000-square-foot building houses director and faculty offices, an exhibition gallery, individual studio space, model classrooms, a teacher resource center, computer labs, and a retail store. Graduate students have 24-hour studio access for the duration of their candidacy. MCA's extensive undergraduate facilities in Rust Hall are also available to graduate students, with a shuttle service for convenient transport. Rust Hall's resources include a 4,400-square-foot shop for woodworking, metalworking, mat cutting, glass cutting, and stretcher and frame construction; large metal, clay, and sculpture studios; and a separate foundry and welding area for castings and metalwork. Printmaking, papermaking, and book arts are supported with facilities for lithography, etching, serigraphy, and other print processes; letterpresses and a bindery; and a wet room equipped with beaters, a 36-square-foot vacuum table, hydraulic press, and a pulper. The photo lab includes large- and medium-format work stations, a digital imaging area with digital cameras, slide and transparency scanners, flatbed scanners, high-resolution film printers; and a lighting studio with strobe equipment, and backgrounds. There are also facilities for non-silver and alternative photo processes including digital negative printers and a large UV-exposure unit. Four fully equipped digital labs with separate sound, animation, and shooting studios support photo, animation, and video work, and a large-format digital printing lab is available for oversized archival imaging.

Financial Aid

Aid is available for the M.F.A. and M.A.T. programs through renewable scholarships for incoming students, teaching assistantships (in the third semester only), work-study, Federal Stafford Student Loans and PLUS loans, and additional merit-based scholarship opportunities for second-year students. Students interested in government-based aid are required to complete the Free Application for Federal Student Aid (FAFSA). Applicants should contact the Financial Aid Office or the Admissions Office for forms and information. Teaching professionals in the M.A. in art education and the alternative licensure programs receive a special tuition discount and are not eligible for other institutional scholarships.

Cost of Study

Tuition and fees for the M.F.A. and M.A.T. programs for the 2010–11 academic year are $24,950. This does not include the cost of materials, supplies, and books, which is estimated at $2500. The M.A.Art.Ed. and alternative licensure programs are $500 per credit hour.

Living and Housing Costs

The estimated average cost of food and housing and miscellaneous expenses for the 2010–11 school year is $12,000. There is a large variety of affordable housing available. Student residences conveniently located within walking distance of the main campus provide living space for more than 150 students. Suite-style living (single rooms with shared common areas), shared apartments for two, and several single, efficiency apartments are available. The Office of Admissions assists students in locating a place to live and in obtaining roommate referrals.

Student Group

The student body is comprised of students who have demonstrated achievement in their field. Many have pursued careers as fine artists, graphic designers, photographers, professional weavers, surface designers, interior designers, and teachers. There are nearly equal numbers of men and women. The students in the graduate program come from all regions of the United States and from several other countries.

Location

Memphis is a great place for an aspiring artist to study. Known for blues, barbecue, and Elvis, Memphis is also home to Fortune 500 companies, an NBA team, a symphony, an opera company, a theater, a number of colleges and universities, museums, art galleries, and almost 1 million residents. Annual festivals and celebrations are popular with students. The Graduate School is located in the heart of downtown across from the National Civil Rights Museum in the South Main Arts District. Rust Hall is located in a 342-acre wooded park in midtown Memphis, adjacent to the Memphis Brooks Museum of Art, the Memphis Zoo, and a nine-hole golf course.

The College and The Programs

The College, founded in 1936, is accredited by the National Association of Schools of Art and Design and the Southern Association of Colleges and Schools. All of the College's graduate programs stress independent work toward self-defined career goals relative to the program chosen.

Applying

M.F.A. applications must be submitted by March 1 for the fall semester and November 1 for the spring semester. Graduate Education applications are accepted on a rolling basis. Application requirements include college transcripts, a portfolio with a minimum of fifteen slides (or other appropriate format), a resume, and one letter of recommendation each from a collegiate adviser or instructor and a contemporary. The applicant must also prepare a written statement of not less than 250 words describing his or her reasons for wishing to join the graduate program, life goals, and creative dreams. M.F.A. students are also asked to submit an artist statement describing the direction of their artwork. A personal interview or conference call may be required—a date and time is arranged by the Dean of Admissions after all application requirements have been met. Students are accepted for admissions in either the fall or spring semester (or summer for the graduate programs in education), based on space availability. In addition, international students must submit a minimum TOEFL score of 525 (195 on the computer-based test), certified translations of academic records, and an affidavit of support verifying ability to meet projected annual costs. Applications are available online at www.mca.edu/admissions.

Correspondence and Information

Office of Admissions, Graduate Programs
Memphis College of Art
1930 Poplar Avenue
Overton Park
Memphis, Tennessee 38104-2764
Phone: 901-272-5151
800-727-1088 (toll-free)
Fax: 901-272-5158
E-mail: info@mca.edu
Web site: http://www.mca.edu

Memphis College of Art

THE FACULTY

In addition to the regular faculty members listed below, there are guest faculty members and advisers each semester.

Nona Bolin, Professor; M.A., Memphis; M.A., Vanderbilt. Liberal studies.
Fred Burton, Professor; M.F.A., Wichita State; M.A., Kent State. Painting/drawing.
Haley Morris Cafiero, Assistant Professor; M.F.A., Arizona. Photography.
Rob Canfield, Associate Professor; Ph.D., Arizona. Liberal studies.
David Chioffi, Assistant Professor; M.A., Wesleyan. Graphic design.
Ellen Daugherty, Assistant Professor; Ph.D., Virginia. Art history.
Maritza Davila, Professor; M.F.A., Pratt. Printmaking.
Adrian Duran, Assistant Professor; Ph.D., Delaware. Art history.
Tom Lee, Associate Professor; M.F.A., Mississippi. Sculpture.
Susan Maakestad, Associate Professor; M.A., Central Washington; M.F.A., Iowa. Painting.
Remy Miller, Professor; M.F.A., Bowling Green State. Drawing.
Howard Paine, Director of M.F.A. Programs; M.F.A., Washington (St. Louis). Computer arts/design.
Joel Priddy, Assistant Professor; M.F.A., School of Visual Arts. Illustration.
Bill Price, Instructor; M.F.A., Southern Illinois. Sculpture/metals.
James Ramsey, Assistant Professor; Ph.D., Tulane. Art history.
Robert Riseling, Professor; M.A., Northern Iowa; M.F.A., Wisconsin. Painting/drawing.
Meredith Root, Assistant Professor; M.F.A., Wisconsin. Digital media.
Jennifer Sargent, Associate Professor; M.F.A., Arizona State. Surface design.
Cynthia Thompson, Associate Professor; M.F.A., Rutgers. Papermaking/book arts.
Leandra Urrutia, Assistant Professor; M.F.A., Mississippi. Sculpture.
Cathy Wilson, Director of Graduate Programs in Education; M.A.T., Ed.D., Memphis.
Jill Wissmiller, Assistant Professor; M.F.A., Northwestern. Digital media.

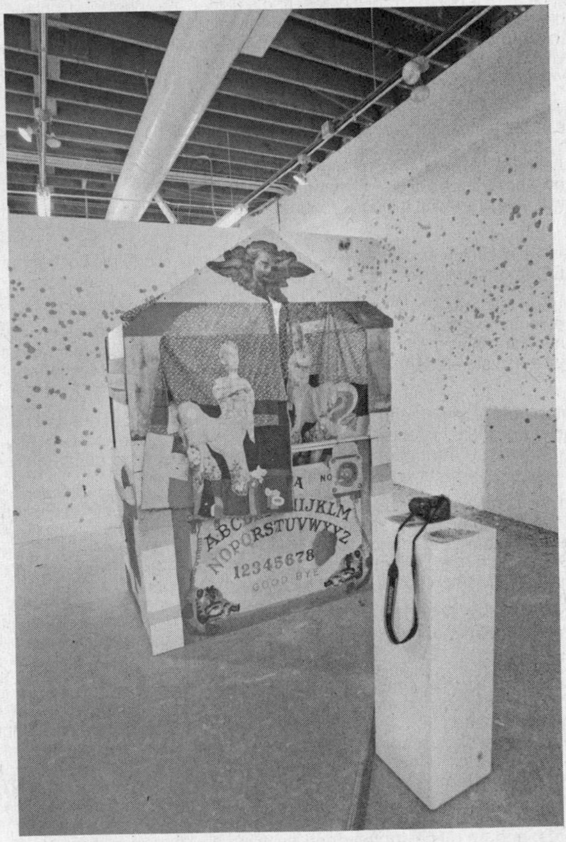

Memphis College of art offers students extensive gallery and studio facilities.

A student at work at Memphis College of Art.

UNIVERSITY OF ROCHESTER

Department of Art and Art History
Visual and Cultural Studies Program

Program of Study

The Visual and Cultural Studies Program, housed in the Department of Art and Art History, offers students the chance to earn a master's or doctoral degree by doing intensive work simultaneously in several of Rochester's humanities departments. Primary faculty members for the Visual and Cultural Studies Program teach in the Departments of Art and Art History, Anthropology, English, and Modern Languages and Cultures, all in the College of Arts and Sciences. Students take courses in those departments and may also take courses in such departments as anthropology, history, music, and philosophy. About 20 faculty members participate in the program each year, including the Visual and Cultural Studies Steering Committee, which guides the program.

An innovative graduate program with a unique emphasis on visual and cultural representation, Rochester's Visual and Cultural Studies Program provides students with an opportunity to study critically and analyze culture from a social-historical perspective. The program stresses interpretation of art, film, and media within historical and ideological frameworks. Because the main contributing faculty members work in art and art history, film and media studies, and comparative literature, students are able to relate recent developments in literary and cultural theory to visual works and investigate the interrelationships between visual texts and critical theory.

All doctoral students take eight core courses: four in visual studies and four in critical theory. In addition, they take six electives, chosen from an extensive list of courses offered by the three primary departments; when appropriate, they may substitute courses from other disciplines. All students participate in the Visual and Cultural Studies Colloquium in the fall semester of their first year of study.

Most Ph.D. students spend 3½ years completing 60 credits of course work and 30 credits of research. After this, they take a qualifying exam, based on their reading and preliminary work on their dissertation. Students serve as teaching assistants for a number of introductory courses or as research assistants.

Research Facilities

The University's libraries contain holdings of 2.5 million volumes and 16,000 periodicals. Housed within the Rush Rhees Library, the Art and Music Library includes 40,000 books and bound journals, 300 journal subscriptions and standing orders for monograph series, and a growing collection of videotapes. The Visual Resource Collection at the University consists of more than 140,000 slides and mounted pictures. The University's Memorial Art Gallery also maintains its own library of 17,000 books and bound periodicals. The Film and Media Studies Center has several thousand films and videotapes available for viewing. Students can use the film and photograph collections at the world-renowned International Museum of Photography in the George Eastman House in Rochester.

Financial Aid

The Visual and Cultural Studies Steering Committee awards graduate teaching and research assistantships to students in the program. Tuition scholarships are also offered to qualified doctoral candidates. Assistantships currently carry an annual award of up to $15,000 beyond tuition. The University also awards Sproull Fellowships and Provost's Fellowships on a competitive basis, which carry a maximum stipend of $20,000 annually for up to two years. Students can receive extra funding by assisting in studio art courses or by teaching summer school.

Cost of Study

For the most up-to-date tuition costs, please see the University's Web site at http://www.rochester.edu/college/AAH/.

Living and Housing Costs

Accommodations for graduate students are available in four University-owned projects and in off-campus housing; for a brochure, a rate sheet, an application, and off-campus housing listings, applicants should write the Housing Coordinator at the Community Living Program, 020 Gates Wing, Susan B. Anthony Halls, P.O. Box 270468, Rochester, New York 14627-0468.

Student Group

The Department accepts 5 to 7 students each year, generally all of whom are full-time. Currently, there are 27 students in residence. The diverse graduate group is equally divided between men and women, and most students are receiving some form of financial aid.

Location

Located on the south shore of Lake Ontario, Rochester is the cultural and technological center of upstate New York. More than 800,000 residents of the metropolitan area can enjoy the Memorial Art Gallery, the George Eastman House (the world's leading museum and archive of photography and motion pictures), and the University's Eastman Theatre, where concerts are given by the Rochester Philharmonic Orchestra.

The University

The University, established in 1850, is private and coeducational. Four of the University's seven schools and colleges, including the College of Arts and Science, are located on the River Campus. The School of Medicine and Dentistry and the School of Nursing are within a 5-minute walk, and the Eastman School of Music is 2 miles away in the downtown area. Graduate work is carried on in each of the University's units. There are 1,000 full-time faculty members.

Applying

The deadline for applications is January 15 for the following September; offers of admission are sent to applicants on or about March 15. The application is available online only. Along with the online application, students should submit a personal statement, three letters of recommendation, official undergraduate and graduate transcripts, a writing sample, and GRE scores. International students must also supply TOEFL scores.

Correspondence and Information

Visual and Cultural Studies Program
Department of Art and Art History
424 Morey Hall, RC Box 270456
University of Rochester
Rochester, New York 14627
Phone: 585-275-9249
E-mail: art_arthist@cc.rochester.edu
Web site: http://www.rochester.edu/college/AAH/

University of Rochester

THE FACULTY AND THEIR RESEARCH

Visual and Cultural Studies Core Faculty and Associated Faculty

Janet Berlo, Professor of Art History/Visual and Cultural Studies; Ph.D., Yale. Native American art history and museum representation of Native peoples, Plains Indians drawings, Native American women and art, textiles and American visual culture.

Douglas Crimp, Fanny Knapp Allen Professor of Art History/Visual and Cultural Studies; Ph.D., CUNY. Contemporary art and criticism, race and representation, gay studies.

Thomas DiPiero, Professor of French/Visual and Cultural Studies; Ph.D., Cornell. French prose fiction of the seventeenth and eighteenth centuries.

Paul Duro, Professor of Art History/Visual and Cultural Studies and Chair, Department of Art and Art History; Ph.D., Essex (England). Theories of imitation in European painting, institutions of art.

Robert Foster, Professor of Anthropology; Ph.D., Chicago. Social theory, nationalism, globalization, mass consumption.

Susan Gustafson, Professor of German; Ph.D., Stanford. Eighteenth-century German literature, psychoanalysis, and feminism.

Rachel Haidu, Assistant Professor of Art History; Ph.D., Columbia. Postwar American and European art, history of photography.

Rosemary Kegl, Associate Professor of English; Ph.D., Cornell. Sixteenth- and seventeenth-century English literature, contemporary Marxist and feminist theory.

John Michael, Professor of English/Visual and Cultural Studies; Ph.D., Johns Hopkins. American literature, cultural studies, and critical theory.

Greta Niu, Assistant Professor of English; Ph.D., Duke. Film studies, Asian literature.

Joan Saab, Associate Professor of Art History/Visual and Cultural Studies and Director of the Program in Visual and Cultural Studies; Ph.D., NYU. Twentieth-century American history, media and culture, urban and community studies, popular culture, cultural studies.

Jeffrey Tucker, Associate Professor of English; Ph.D., Princeton. African American literature, twentieth-century American literature, science fiction.

Sharon Willis, Professor of French/Visual and Cultural Studies; Ph.D., Cornell. Modern French literature and literary theory, critical and feminist theory, film theory and visual analysis.

UArts
The University of the Arts

UNIVERSITY OF THE ARTS

Graduate Programs

Programs of Study

University of the Arts (UArts), located on the Avenue of the Arts in Center City Philadelphia, offers graduate programs in art education; art education with a concentration in educational media; book arts/printmaking; ceramics, painting, and sculpture; industrial design; jazz studies; museum communication; museum education; museum exhibition, planning, and design; music education; teaching visual arts; postbaccalaureate certificate in crafts; postbaccalaureate teaching program (nondegree); and postbaccalaureate teaching program professional semester. The graduate programs offer an impressive combination of strengths: exceptionally accomplished faculty members, a remarkably individualized and interactive learning environment, access to outstanding facilities and resources, specialized studios, and programs of study that are both highly focused and highly flexible.

In the visual arts, programs include the Master of Arts in art education, which is designed to develop the studio, intellectual, and professional education background for educators; the Master of Arts in Teaching visual arts, which incorporates preparation for certification to teach art in grades K–12; the Master of Fine Arts in book arts/printmaking, which builds on the University's thirty-year tradition of involvement with the book and the printed image; and the Master of Fine Arts in ceramics, painting, or sculpture. These programs are designed to be completed in three years through part-time study. Also offered are the Master of Fine Arts in museum exhibition planning and design, which was developed with the support of the National Association of Museum Exhibition (NAME); the Master of Art in museum communication; the Master of Art in museum education; and the Master of Industrial Design.

In performance, the Master of Arts in Teaching in music education is a one-year-plus-summer program designed for students who have a bachelor's degree in music theory/composition, music history/literature, or other noneducation courses of study. The Master of Music in jazz studies is a one-year, 32-credit program. Designed as a finishing program in jazz performance, components of the program include advanced private instruction, hands-on internships and pedagogy study, and ensemble performances.

Research Facilities

Students use state-of-the-art digital-technology facilities, which include computer labs that support professional-level creative work, collaboration, and research. There is a dedicated Mac lab for graduate students and a wireless network throughout UArts buildings. In addition to multiple high-end graphics labs, the University hosts a New Media Center comprising two dual-platform digital laboratories that enable the integration of animation and 3-D modeling. Also available on campus are the Borowsky Center for Publication Arts; photography, film, and animation facilities with studios and darkrooms, video editing suites, and two Master Series Oxberry Animation stands; recording studios, state-of-the-art music technology MIDI studios and editing suites, and practice rooms; a bronze foundry and plaster workshop; and crafts studios and workshops for ceramics, metals, wood, glassblowing, papermaking, and fibers. Other important facilities include the digital forge 3-D printer, a bookbindery, and stone and metal welding shops.

Financial Aid

The Free Application for Federal Student Aid (FAFSA) must be filed by applicants for financial aid. Graduate teaching assistantships are available for qualified applicants. Some teaching and technical assistantships are awarded by the University of the Arts; the amounts of these awards vary.

Cost of Study

Tuition for 2010–11 is $31,900 plus applicable technology, book supplies, and activity fees.

Living and Housing Costs

There is limited University housing for graduate students.

Student Group

Students come from forty states and territories and thirty countries; about 5 percent of the total enrollment of 2,500 are international students. The graduate programs enrolled 236 students in 2009–10.

Location

The University of the Arts campus is located in the heart of Philadelphia's Avenue of the Arts, in the heart of the cultural community. The area has theaters, museums, galleries, music and dance facilities, restaurants, and shopping. Philadelphia offers a broad mix of strong cultural and educational experiences. In addition to being of historic importance, the city is also a supporter of the arts. Urban and sophisticated, it is also a series of small, close-knit neighborhoods. Fairmount Park, the largest city park in the world, provides facilities for boating, fishing, hiking, biking, picnicking, and relaxing.

The University

The University of the Arts is composed of the College of Art and Design, the College of Performing Arts, and the College of Media and Communication. The largest comprehensive educational institution of its kind in the United States, UArts prepares students for more than a hundred professional career paths in the visual, performing, and communication arts. The College of Art and Design is a professional community dedicated to the visual arts, where art is the primary and central concern. Founded in 1870 to train artists to translate the technological advances of the Industrial Revolution, it is today one of the nation's leading art colleges. The College of Performing Arts focuses on the areas of music, dance, acting, and musical theater. Founded in 1870 to educate musicians, it has expanded to offer demanding undergraduate programs of ballet, modern dance, and jazz dance as well as a program in theater arts. In 1996, the College of Media and Communication (CMAC) was founded and dedicated to the integration of art, technology, and communication. The College of Media and Communication offers undergraduate programs in writing, multimedia, and communication.

UArts sponsors a variety of activities that include social events, lectures, performances, and regular gallery and museum trips to New York City and Washington, D.C.

Applying

Required application materials include the University's Application for Graduate Study, a personal statement of intent, a nonrefundable fee of $60, official college transcripts, and at least three letters of recommendation. Portfolios must be submitted by applicants to the visual arts programs. An audition is required for applicants to the music program. International students must submit a Certification of Finance and TOEFL scores in the event the student's first language is other than English.

Applications for admission in September should be submitted by January 15 for priority consideration. Applications submitted after January 15 are considered on a space-available basis. Applications for January admission (art education, museum communications, museum education, and music only) should be submitted by the preceding November 15. Applications for the part-time M.F.A. (summer residence) should be submitted by January 1.

Correspondence and Information

Director of Admission
University of the Arts
320 South Broad Street
Philadelphia, Pennsylvania 19102
Phone: 215-717-6030
800-616-ARTS (toll-free)
Fax: 215-717-6045
E-mail: admissions@uarts.edu
Web site: http://www.uarts.edu

University of the Arts

THE FACULTY

College of Art and Design

Paul Adorno, Adjunct Assistant Professor, Art Education; M.S.Ed., Pennsylvania.
Rande Blank, Senior Lecturer, Art Education; M.Ed., Arcadia.
Joan Cohen, Adjunct Assistant Professor, Art Education; Ph.D., Temple.
Raye Cohen, Adjunct Assistant Professor Art Education; M.A., University of the Arts.
Virginia Fitzpatrick, Adjunct Associate Professor, Art Education; Ph.D., Indiana.
Diane Foxman, Senior Lecturer, Art Education; M.A., Goddard.
Arlene Gostin, Associate Professor, Art Education; M.A., Philadelphia College of Art.
Randy Granger, Associate Professor, Art Education; B.F.A., Philadelphia College of Art.
June Julian, Associate Professor, Art Education; Ed.D., NYU.
Dianne Koppisch Hricko, Adjunct Associate Professor, Art Education; B.S., SUNY.
Slavko Milekic, Professor, Art Education/Industrial Design; Ph.D., Connecticut.
Susan Rodriguez, Adjunct Professor, Art Education; M.Ed., Temple.
Pearl B. Schaeffer, Adjunct Associate Professor, Art Education; M.F.A., University of the Arts.
Barbara Suplee, Associate Professor, Art Education; Ph.D., Penn State.
Jo Ann Wright, Adjunct Assistant Professor, Art Education; B.A., Rowan.
James Green, Master Lecturer, Bookarts/Printmaking; M.L.S., Columbia.
Lois M. Johnson, Professor, Bookarts/Printmaking; M.F.A., Wisconsin–Madison.
Peter Kruty, Master Lecturer, Bookarts/Printmaking; M.A., Alabama.
Hedi Kyle, Adjunct Associate Professor, Bookarts/Printmaking; Diploma, Werkkunstschule (Wiesbaden, Germany).
Carol Moore, Associate Professor, Bookarts/Printmaking/Fine Arts in Studio Art/Museum Studies; M.F.A., Temple.
Mary Phelan, Associate Professor, Bookarts/Printmaking; M.A., Wisconsin–Madison.
Winifred Radolan, Senior Lecturer, Bookarts/Printmaking, B.S., Moore College of Art and Design.
Patricia M. Smith, Associate Professor, Bookarts/Printmaking; M.A., Philadelphia College of Art.
Lori Spencer, Associate Professor, Bookarts/Printmaking; M.F.A., University of the Arts.
Susan T. Viguers, Professor, Bookarts/Printmaking; Ph.D., Bryn Mawr.
Susan White, Senior Lecturer, Bookarts/Printmaking; M.F.A., University of the Arts.
Erin Boyle, Lecturer, Fine Arts in Studio Art, M.F.A., University of the Arts.
Gerard Brown, Senior Lecturer, Fine Arts in Studio Art; M.F.A., Art Institute of Chicago.
Tom Butter, Adjunct Professor, Fine Arts in Studio Art, M.F.A., Washington (St. Louis).
Tom Csaszar, Master Lecturer, Fine Arts in Studio Art/Museum Studies; B.F.A., Pennsylvania.
Stuart Elster, Assistant Professor, Fine Arts in Studio Art, M.F.A., Yale.
Joe Girandola, Assistant Professor, Fine Arts in Studio Art, M.F.A., Georgia.
Corin Hewitt, Adjunct Assistant, Fine Arts in Studio Art, M.F.A., Bard.
Janet Koplos, Visiting Lecturer, Fine Arts in Studio Art, M.A., Illinois State.
Sumi Maeshima, Senior Lecturer, Fine Arts in Studio Art; M.F.A., University of the Arts.
Eileen Neff, Adjunct Professor, Fine Arts in Studio Art; M.F.A., Temple.
Gerald Nichols, Professor, Fine Arts in Studio Art,; M.F.A., Pennsylvania.
Dena Shottenkirk, Adjunct Associate Professor, Fine Arts in Studio Art, Ph.D., CUNY.
Jane Bedno, Professor Emerita, Museum Studies; J.D., William and Mary.
Richard Cress, Senior Lecturer, Museum Studies; B.F.A., Virginia Commonwealth.
Karie Diethorn, Master Lecturer, Museum Studies; M.A., Delaware.
Laura H. Foster, Master Lecturer, Museum Studies; J.D., Baltimore.
Ellen Gilbert, Senior Lecturer, Museum Studies, M.B.A., Temple.
Aaron Goldblatt, Senior Lecturer, Museum Studies, M.F.A., Rutgers.
Gerry Gutierrez, Master Lecturer, Museum Studies, B.S., Oklahoma.
Sharon Ann Holt, Master Lecturer, Museum Studies; Ph.D., Pennsylvania.
Carleton Johnson, Master Lecturer, Museum Studies; B.A., Michigan.
Jeanne Maier, Senior Lecturer, Museum Studies; B.F.A., Kutztown.
Barbara McGrath, Master Lecturer, Museum Studies, B.A., Philadelphia College of Art.
William McHale, Senior Lecturer, Museum Studies; B.A., South Carolina.
Polly McKenna-Cress, Associate Professor, Museum Studies; M.F.A., University of the Arts.
Anthony Mikstiz, Master Lecturer, Museum Studies; B.Arch., Kent State.
Dorothy Miles, Lecturer, Museum Studies; M.F.A., University of the Arts.
Amy Phillips-Iversen, Lecturer, Museum Studies; M.A., University of the Arts.
Tom Porett, Professor, Museum Studies; M.S., IIT.
Victoria Prizzia, Senior Lecturer, Museum Studies; M.F.A., University of the Arts.
Keith Ragone, Master Lecturer, Museum Studies; M.F.A., School of Visual Arts.
Stephanie Reyer, Master Lecturer, Museum Studies; B.F.A., Cooper Union.
Dana Schloss, Lecturer, Museum Studies; M.F.A., University of the Arts.
Christina Schneider, Lecturer, Museum Studies; M.F.A., University of the Arts.
Helen M. Shannon, Associate Professor, Museum Studies; Ph.D., Columbia.
Elizabeth Tinker, Lecturer, Museum Studies, B.A., Bryn Mawr.
Juan Miguel Tobon, Lecturer, Museum Studies, M.S., Penn State.
Robert Vosburgh Jr., Associate Professor, Museum Studies; J.D., Temple.
Sheri Watson, Senior Lecturer, Museum Studies; M.A., Drexel.
Mira Zergani, Lecturer, Museum Studies, B.A., Temple.
Douglas Fanning, Adjunct Associate Professor, Industrial Design; M.Arch., Columbia.
Anthony Guido, Associate Professor, Industrial Design; B.S.I.D., Ohio State.
Jonas Milder, Associate Professor, Industrial Design; Design Diploma (M.I.D.), Hochschule der Kuenste (Berlin).

College of Performing Arts

Paul Arbogast, Senior Lecturer, Music, M.M., University of the Arts.
Justin Binek, Assistant Professor, Music, M.M., Western Michigan.
John Blake, Adjunct Associate Professor, Music, B.M., West Virginia State.
Robert Brosh, Adjunct Assistant Professor, Music; D.A., NYU.
Norman David, Adjunct Associate Professor, Music, D.M.A., Temple.
Mike Dawson, Senior Lecturer, Music, M.M., University of the Arts.
Marc Dicciani, Professor, Music; B.M., Philadelphia Musical Academy.
Annette DiMedio, Professor, Music; Ph.D., Bryn Mawr.
Chris Farr, Adjunct Assistant Professor, Music; M.A.T., University of the Arts.
Matt Gallagher, Assistant Professor, Music; M.M., University of the Arts.
William Garton, Senior Lecturer, Music; M.A., Glassboro State.
Richard Genovese, Adjunct Assistant Professor, Music; Certificate, Curtis.
Thomas Giacabetti, Adjunct Assistant Professor, Music.
Don Glanden, Professor, Music; M.M., Rutgers.
Marjorie Goldberg, Senior Lecturer, Music; B.M.E., Hartford (Hartt).
Orlando Haddad, Adjunct Assistant Professor, Music; M.S., Drexel.
Kevin Hanson, Senior Lecturer, Music.
Erik Johnson, Senior Lecturer, Music; B.M., Temple.
Michael Johnson, Lecturer, Music, M.M., University of the Arts.
Micah Jones, Assistant Professor, Music, M.M., University of the Arts.
Randy Kapralik, Senior Lecturer, Music, B.A., Miami (Florida).
Michael Kennedy, Senior Lecturer, Music; M.M., University of the Arts.
Ronald Kerber, Professor, Music; B.M., Philadelphia College of the Performing Arts.
Jeffrey Kern, Assistant Professor, Music; M.M., Michigan.
Tom Lawton, Senior Lecturer, Music.
Christopher Maute, Lecturer, Music; B.M., University of the Arts.
Joseph Nero, Adjunct Associate Professor, Music; Diploma, Curtis.
James Paxson, Adjunct Associate Professor, Music; B.M., Philadelphia Musical Academy.
Trudy Pitts, Adjunct Associate Professor, Music; B.M., Philadelphia Musical Academy.
Mike Pracher, Senior Lecturer, Music, M.M., University of the Arts.
Robert Quaile Jr., Senior Lecturer, Music; B.M.E., Philadelphia Musical Academy.
George Rabbai, Senior Lecturer, Music.
Thomas Rudolph, Senior Lecturer, Music; D.M.E., Widener.
Evan Solot, Professor, Music, M.M., Philadelphia Musical Academy.
Arturo Stable, Senior Lecturer, Music; M.M., University of the Arts.
John Swana, Senior Lecturer, Music.
Gerald Veasley, Master Lecturer, Music.
Dennis Wasko, Adjunct Assistant Professor, Music; B.M., Philadelphia College of the Performing Arts.

Section 4
Comparative and Interdisciplinary Arts

This section contains a directory of institutions offering graduate work in comparative and interdisciplinary arts. Additional information about programs listed in the directory may be obtained by writing directly to the dean of a graduate school or chair of a department at the address given in the directory.

For programs offering related work, see also in this book *Applied Arts and Design, Architecture, Art and Art History,* and *Performing Arts.* In another guide in this series:

Graduate Programs in Business, Education, Health, Information Studies, Law & Social Work

See *Subject Areas (Art Education)*

CONTENTS

Program Directory

Comparative and Interdisciplinary Arts 202

Comparative and Interdisciplinary Arts

Bradley University, Graduate School, Slane College of Communications and Fine Arts, Department of Art, Peoria, IL 61625-0002. Offers ceramics (MA, MFA); drawing/illustration (MA, MFA); interdisciplinary art (MA, MFA); painting (MA, MFA); photography (MA, MFA); printmaking (MA, MFA); sculpture (MA, MFA); visual communication and design (MA, MFA). *Accreditation:* NASAD. Part-time programs available. *Degree requirements:* For master's, comprehensive exam, thesis, final exhibit. *Entrance requirements:* For master's, portfolio, 2 letters of recommendation. Additional exam requirements/recommendations for international students: Required—TOEFL (minimum score 550 paper-based; 213 computer-based; 79 iBT).

Brigham Young University, Graduate Studies, College of Humanities, Department of Humanities, Classics, and Comparative Literature, Provo, UT 84602-1001. Offers comparative studies (MA). *Faculty:* 25 full-time (5 women). *Students:* 16 full-time (9 women). Average age 27. 11 applicants, 55% accepted, 6 enrolled. In 2009, 7 master's awarded. *Degree requirements:* For master's, 2 foreign languages, thesis. *Entrance requirements:* For master's, GRE, minimum GPA of 3.0 in last 60 hours. Additional exam requirements/recommendations for international students: Required—TOEFL (minimum score 580 paper-based; 85 iBT), IELTS (minimum score 7). *Application deadline:* For fall admission, 3/1 for domestic and international students. Application fee: $50. Electronic applications accepted. *Expenses:* Tuition: Full-time $5580; part-time $301 per credit hour. Tuition and fees vary according to student's religious affiliation. *Financial support:* In 2009–10, 16 students received support, including 4 research assistantships (averaging $1,875 per year), 36 teaching assistantships (averaging $2,620 per year); career-related internships or fieldwork, institutionally sponsored loans, scholarships/grants, tuition waivers (full and partial), and student instructorships also available. Support available to part-time students. *Unit head:* Dr. Michael J. Call, Chair, 801-422-2550, Fax: 801-422-0305, E-mail: michael_call@byu.edu. *Application contact:* Carolyn Hone, Graduate Secretary for Humanities and Comparative Literature, 801-422-4430, Fax: 801-422-0305, E-mail: carolyn_hone@byu.edu.

Columbia College Chicago, Graduate School, Program in Interdisciplinary Arts, Chicago, IL 60605-1996. Offers interdisciplinary arts (MA); interdisciplinary book and paper arts (MFA). Part-time and evening/weekend programs available. *Degree requirements:* For master's, thesis. *Entrance requirements:* For master's, interview, minimum GPA of 3.0, portfolio, work sample. Additional exam requirements/recommendations for international students: Required—TOEFL (minimum score 550 paper-based; 213 computer-based). Electronic applications accepted. *Expenses:* Tuition: Part-time $651 per credit hour. Required fees: $651 per credit hour. $205 per semester. One-time fee: $285 part-time. Tuition and fees vary according to program.

Florida Atlantic University, Dorothy F. Schmidt College of Arts and Letters, Department of Comparative Studies, Boca Raton, FL 33431-0991. Offers PhD. Part-time programs available. *Students:* 15 full-time (10 women), 61 part-time (43 women); includes 14 minority (6 African Americans, 3 Asian Americans or Pacific Islanders, 5 Hispanic Americans), 7 international. Average age 44. 30 applicants, 0% accepted, 0 enrolled. In 2009, 10 doctorates awarded. *Degree requirements:* For doctorate, one foreign language, comprehensive exam, thesis/dissertation. *Entrance requirements:* For doctorate, GRE, minimum GPA of 3.5, 3 references. Additional exam requirements/recommendations for international students: Required—TOEFL. *Application deadline:* For fall admission, 2/1 priority date for domestic and international students. Applications are processed on a rolling basis. Application fee: $30. *Expenses:* Tuition, state resident: full-time $7055; part-time $293.94 per credit hour. Tuition, nonresident: full-time $22,096; part-time $920.66 per credit hour. *Financial support:* Teaching assistantships with tuition reimbursements available. *Faculty research:* Arts, humanities, social sciences. *Unit head:* Dr. Emily Stockard, Interim Director, 561-297-2817, Fax: 561-297-2058, E-mail: stockard@fau.edu. *Application contact:* Dr. Emily Stockard, Interim Director, 561-297-2817, Fax: 561-297-2058, E-mail: stockard@fau.edu.

Goddard College, Graduate Division, Master of Fine Arts in Interdisciplinary Arts Program, Plainfield, VT 05667-9432. Offers MFA. Postbaccalaureate distance learning degree programs offered (minimal on-campus study). *Faculty:* 28 part-time/adjunct (20 women). *Students:* 153 full-time. Average age 42. 71 applicants, 63% accepted, 39 enrolled. *Degree requirements:* For master's, thesis. *Entrance requirements:* For master's, relevant undergraduate degree, 3 letters of recommendation, study plan and resource list, interview, portfolio, artistic resume. *Application deadline:* Applications are processed on a rolling basis. Application fee: $40. Electronic applications accepted. *Expenses:* Tuition: Part-time $7223 per semester. Part-time tuition and fees vary according to program. *Financial support:* In 2009–10, 128 students received support. Applicants required to submit FAFSA. *Unit head:* Prof. Bonnie Schock, Co-Director, 802-454-8311, Fax: 802-454-7835, E-mail: bonnie.schock@goddard.edu. *Application contact:* David DeLucca, Admissions Counselor, 800-906-8312 Ext. 248, Fax: 802-454-1029, E-mail: david.delucca@goddard.edu.

John F. Kennedy University, Graduate School of Holistic Studies, Department of Arts and Consciousness, Program in Transformative Arts, Pleasant Hill, CA 94523-4817. Offers MA. Part-time and evening/weekend programs available. *Degree requirements:* For master's, thesis or alternative. *Entrance requirements:* For master's, interview. Additional exam requirements/recommendations for international students: Required—TOEFL. *Expenses:* Contact institution.

Ohio University, Graduate College, College of Fine Arts, School of Interdisciplinary Arts, Athens, OH 45701-2979. Offers PhD. *Faculty:* 7 full-time (3 women). *Students:* 18 full-time (9 women), 9 part-time (4 women); includes 3 minority (2 African Americans, 1 American Indian/Alaska Native), 5 international. 15 applicants, 47% accepted, 6 enrolled. In 2009, 2 doctorates awarded. *Degree requirements:* For doctorate, 2 foreign languages, comprehensive exam, thesis/dissertation. *Entrance requirements:* For doctorate, GRE or MAT, master's degree. Additional exam requirements/recommendations for international students: Required—TOEFL (minimum score 575 paper-based; 91 iBT) or IELTS Academic (minimum score 7). *Application deadline:* For fall admission, 1/31 priority date for domestic and international students. Application fee: $50 ($55 for international students). Electronic applications accepted. *Expenses:* Tuition, state resident: full-time $7839; part-time $323 per quarter hour. Tuition, nonresident: full-time $15,831; part-time $654 per quarter hour. Required fees: $2931. *Financial support:* In 2009–10, teaching assistantships with tuition reimbursements (averaging $15,615 per year); Federal Work-Study and institutionally sponsored loans also available. Financial award application deadline: 1/31. *Faculty research:* Comparative studies of theater, music, and the visual arts. *Unit head:* Dr. Dora J. Wilson, Director, 740-593-9413, Fax: 740-593-0578, E-mail: wilsond@ohio.edu. *Application contact:* Brenda Llewellyn, Administrative Coordinator, 740-593-1314, E-mail: llewelb@ohio.edu.

Simon Fraser University, Graduate Studies, Faculty of Arts and Social Sciences, School for the Contemporary Arts, Burnaby, BC V5A 1S6, Canada. Offers MFA. *Degree requirements:* For master's, minimum GPA of 3.0. For master's, thesis or alternative. *Entrance requirements:* Additional exam requirements/recommendations for international students: Required—TOEFL or IELTS. *Faculty research:* Dance theory, screenplays, drawing and painting, acting, electroacoustic music.

Section 5
Film, Television, and Video

This section contains a directory of institutions offering graduate work in film, television, and video. Additional information about programs listed in the directory but not augmented by an in-depth entry may be obtained by writing directly to the dean of a graduate school or chair of a department at the address given in the directory.

For programs offering related work, see also in this book *Art and Art History* and *Communication and Media*. In the other guides in this series:

Graduate Programs in Engineering & Applied Sciences
See *Telecommunications*

Graduate Programs in Business, Education, Health, Information Studies, Law & Social Work
See *Advertising and Public Relations*

CONTENTS

Program Directories

Film, Television, and Video Production 204
Film, Television, and Video Theory and Criticism 210

Close-Ups

See:

American University—Communication 673
Art Center College of Design—Art and Design 113
Boston University—Communication 675
Columbia University—Film, Theater Arts, Visual Arts, and Writing 261
Miami International University of Art & Design—Art and Design 117

Film, Television, and Video Production

Academy of Art University, Graduate Program, School of Animation and Visual Effects, San Francisco, CA 94105-3410. Offers 2D animation (MFA); 3D animation (MFA); 3D modeling (MFA); games (MFA); visual effects (MFA). Part-time programs available. Postbaccalaureate distance learning degree programs offered (no on-campus study). *Degree requirements:* For master's, final review. *Entrance requirements:* For master's, portfolio. Electronic applications accepted.

Academy of Art University, Graduate Program, School of Motion Pictures and Television, San Francisco, CA 94105-3410. Offers MFA. Part-time programs available. Postbaccalaureate distance learning degree programs offered (no on-campus study). *Degree requirements:* For master's, final review. *Entrance requirements:* For master's, portfolio. Electronic applications accepted.

American Film Institute Conservatory, Graduate Program, Los Angeles, CA 90027-1657. Offers cinematography (MFA); directing (MFA); editing (MFA); producing (MFA); production design (MFA); screenwriting (MFA). *Degree requirements:* For master's, thesis, production of film or screenplay, portfolio piece. *Entrance requirements:* For master's, portfolio, resume, letters of recommendation, interview. Additional exam requirements/recommendations for international students: Required—TOEFL (minimum score 600 paper-based; 250 computer-based; 100 iBT). *Faculty research:* Film production, TV production.

American University, School of Communication, Film and Electronic Media Program, Washington, DC 20016-8001. Offers MFA. *Faculty:* 14 full-time (6 women). *Students:* 34 full-time (16 women), 39 part-time (19 women). 51 applicants, 73% accepted, 22 enrolled. In 2009, 141 master's awarded. *Degree requirements:* For master's, comprehensive exam, thesis or alternative. *Entrance requirements:* For master's, GRE General Test. Additional exam requirements/recommendations for international students: Required—TOEFL (minimum score 600 paper-based; 250 computer-based). *Application deadline:* For fall admission, 2/1 priority date for domestic and international students; for spring admission, 11/15 for domestic and international students. Applications are processed on a rolling basis. Application fee: $50. Electronic applications accepted. *Expenses:* Tuition: Full-time $22,266; part-time $1237 per credit hour. Required fees: $430. Tuition and fees vary according to program. *Financial support:* In 2009–10, 10 students received support, including 2 fellowships with partial tuition reimbursements available (averaging $13,000 per year), 2 research assistantships with partial tuition reimbursements available (averaging $11,000 per year), 4 teaching assistantships with partial tuition reimbursements available (averaging $11,000 per year); career-related internships or fieldwork, Federal Work-Study, institutionally sponsored loans, scholarships/grants, tuition waivers (partial), and unspecified assistantships also available. Financial award application deadline: 2/1. *Faculty research:* Documentary film production, social media, media and public policy, visual literacy, new technology. *Unit head:* Prof. John Douglass, Director, Film and Media Arts Division, 202-885-2045, Fax: 202-885-2019, E-mail: jdougla@american.edu. *Application contact:* Sharmeen Ahsan-Bracciale, Graduate Admissions Office, 202-885-2040, Fax: 202-885-2019, E-mail: sharmeen@american.edu.

American University, School of Communication, Film and Video Program, Washington, DC 20016-8001. Offers film and video (MA); producing for film and video (MA). Part-time and evening/weekend programs available. *Faculty:* 14 full-time (6 women). *Students:* 14 full-time (4 women), 29 part-time (12 women). 95 applicants, 56% accepted, 32 enrolled. In 2009, 29 master's awarded. *Degree requirements:* For master's, comprehensive exam, thesis or alternative. *Entrance requirements:* For master's, GRE General Test. Additional exam requirements/recommendations for international students: Required—TOEFL (minimum score 660 paper-based; 250 computer-based). *Application deadline:* For fall admission, 2/1 priority date for domestic and international students; for spring admission, 11/15 for domestic and international students. Applications are processed on a rolling basis. Application fee: $50. Electronic applications accepted. *Expenses:* Tuition: Full-time $22,266; part-time $1237 per credit hour. Required fees: $430. Tuition and fees vary according to program. *Financial support:* In 2009–10, 2 research assistantships with partial tuition reimbursements (averaging $11,000 per year), 4 teaching assistantships with partial tuition reimbursements (averaging $11,000 per year) were awarded; career-related internships or fieldwork, Federal Work-Study, institutionally sponsored loans, scholarships/grants, tuition waivers (partial), and unspecified assistantships also available. Financial award application deadline: 2/1. *Faculty research:* Documentary film and video production, visual literacy, Eastern European cinema, media and public policy, social media. *Unit head:* Prof. John Douglass, Director, Film and Media Arts Division, 202-885-2045, Fax: 202-885-2019, E-mail: jdougla@american.edu. *Application contact:* Sharmeen Ahsan-Bracciale, Graduate Admissions Office, 202-885-2040, Fax: 202-885-2019, E-mail: sharmeen@american.edu.

See Close-Up on page 673.

American University, School of Communication, Weekend Programs in Communication, Washington, DC 20016-8001. Offers interactive journalism (MA); news media studies (MA); producing for film and video (MA); public communication (MA). *Accreditation:* ACEJMC. Part-time and evening/weekend programs available. *Faculty:* 5 part-time/adjunct (2 women). *Students:* 112 part-time (75 women). 137 applicants, 61% accepted, 61 enrolled. In 2009, 15 master's awarded. *Degree requirements:* For master's, comprehensive exam, thesis or alternative. *Entrance requirements:* Additional exam requirements/recommendations for international students: Required—TOEFL (minimum score 600 paper-based; 250 computer-based). *Application deadline:* For fall admission, 8/1 for domestic students. Applications are processed on a rolling basis. Application fee: $50. Electronic applications accepted. *Expenses:* Tuition: Full-time $22,266; part-time $1237 per credit hour. Required fees: $430. Tuition and fees vary according to program. *Financial support:* In 2009–10, 3 fellowships (averaging $3,500 per year) were awarded; institutionally sponsored loans also available. *Unit head:* Wendell Cochran, Journalism Weekend Program Director, 202-885-2075, E-mail: cochran@american.edu. *Application contact:* Sharmeen Ahsan-Bracciale, Graduate Admissions Office, 202-885-2040, Fax: 202-885-2019, E-mail: sharmeen@american.edu.

See Close-Up on page 673.

Antioch University Midwest, Graduate Programs, Individualized Liberal and Professional Studies Program, Yellow Springs, OH 45387-1609. Offers liberal and professional studies (MA), including counseling, creative writing, education, film studies, liberal studies, management, modern literature, psychology, theatre, visual arts. Part-time and evening/weekend programs available. Postbaccalaureate distance learning degree programs offered (minimal on-campus study). *Faculty:* 1 full-time (0 women), 2 part-time/adjunct (1 woman). *Students:* 23 full-time (13 women), 41 part-time (30 women); includes 13 minority (11 African Americans, 2 Hispanic Americans). Average age 40. 21 applicants, 76% accepted, 15 enrolled. In 2009, 24 master's awarded. *Degree requirements:* For master's, thesis or alternative. *Entrance requirements:* For master's, resume, 2 letters of reference. *Application deadline:* For fall admission, 8/1 for domestic students; for winter admission, 12/1 for domestic students; for spring admission, 3/10 for domestic students. Applications are processed on a rolling basis. Application fee: $50. Electronic applications accepted. *Expenses:* Contact institution. *Financial support:* Federal Work-Study available. Financial award applicants required to submit FAFSA. *Unit head:* Dr. Jon Saari, Chair, 937-769-1879, Fax: 937-769-1807, E-mail: jsaari@antioch.edu. *Application contact:* Seth Gordon, Assistant Director of Admissions, 937-769-1800 Ext. 1825, Fax: 937-769-1804, E-mail: sgordon@antioch.edu.

Arizona State University, Graduate College, College of Liberal Arts and Sciences, Division of Humanities, Program in Film and Media Studies, Tempe, AZ 85287. Offers American media and popular culture (MAS); film analysis (MLS); screenwriting (MAS).

Art Center College of Design, Graduate Division, Broadcast Cinema Department, Pasadena, CA 91103. Offers MFA. *Accreditation:* NASAD. *Faculty:* 3 part-time/adjunct (0 women). *Students:* 14 full-time (2 women), 5 part-time (2 women); includes 4 minority (2 African Americans, 2 Hispanic Americans). Average age 29. 29 applicants, 83% accepted, 14 enrolled. In 2009, 2 master's awarded. *Degree requirements:* For master's, thesis, studio project. *Entrance requirements:* For master's, portfolio. Additional exam requirements/recommendations for international students: Required—TOEFL (minimum score 100 iBT). *Application deadline:* For fall admission, 3/1 priority date for domestic and international students; for spring admission, 10/1 priority date for domestic and international students. Applications are processed on a rolling basis. Application fee: $50 ($70 for international students). *Expenses:* Tuition: Full-time $16,737. *Financial support:* Teaching assistantships, career-related internships or fieldwork, Federal Work-Study, and scholarships/grants available. Financial award application deadline: 3/1. *Unit head:* Robert Peterson, Chair, 626-396-2274. *Application contact:* Nijo Watanabe, 626-396-4226.

See Close-Up on page 113.

The Art Institute of California–San Francisco, Master of Fine Arts Program, San Francisco, CA 94102. Offers computer animation (MFA).

Bob Jones University, Graduate Programs, Greenville, SC 29614. Offers accountancy (MS); Bible (MA); Bible translation (MA); Biblical studies (Certificate); broadcast management (MS); business administration (MBA); church history (MA, PhD); church ministries (MA); church music (MM); cinema and video production (MA); counseling (MS); curriculum and instruction (Ed D); divinity (M Div); dramatic production (MA); educational leadership (MS, Ed D, Ed S); elementary education (M Ed, MAT); English (M Ed, MA, MAT); fine arts (MA); graphic design (MA); history (M Ed, MA); illustration (MA); interpretative speech (MA); mathematics (M Ed, MAT); medical missions (Certificate); ministry (MM, D Min); multi-categorical special education (M Ed, MAT); music (M Ed); New Testament interpretation (PhD); Old Testament interpretation (PhD); orchestral instrument performance (MM); organ performance (MM); pastoral studies (MA); personnel services (MS, Ed S); piano pedagogy (MM); piano performance (MM); platform arts (MA); radio and television broadcasting (MS); rhetoric and public address (MA); secondary education (M Ed); studio art (MA); teaching Bible (MA); theology (MA, PhD); voice performance (MM); youth ministries (MA); M Div/MM.

Boston University, College of Communication, Department of Film and Television, Boston, MA 02215. Offers film production (MFA); film studies (MFA); media ventures (MS); screenwriting (MFA); television production (MS); MBA/MS. Part-time programs available. *Faculty:* 13 full-time, 27 part-time/adjunct. *Students:* 108 full-time (49 women), 5 part-time (2 women); includes 11 minority (4 African Americans, 1 American Indian/Alaska Native, 3 Asian Americans or Pacific Islanders, 3 Hispanic Americans), 19 international. Average age 27. In 2009, 16 master's awarded. *Degree requirements:* For master's, thesis. *Entrance requirements:* For master's, GRE General Test, sample of written or creative work. Additional exam requirements/recommendations for international students: Required—TOEFL (minimum score 600 paper-based; 250 computer-based; 100 iBT). *Application deadline:* For fall admission, 2/1 for domestic and international students. Application fee: $70. Electronic applications accepted. *Expenses:* Tuition: Full-time $37,910; part-time $1184 per credit hour. Required fees: $386; $40 per semester. Part-time tuition and fees vary according to class time, course level, degree level and program. *Financial support:* Teaching assistantships with partial tuition reimbursements, career-related internships or fieldwork, Federal Work-Study, institutionally sponsored loans, scholarships/grants, and unspecified assistantships available. Support available to part-time students. Financial award application deadline: 2/1; financial award applicants required to submit FAFSA. *Unit head:* Paul Schneider, Chairman, 617-353-3483, Fax: 617-353-1084, E-mail: ftvchair@bu.edu. *Application contact:* Kate Iserman, Administrator of Graduate Services, 617-353-3481, Fax: 617-358-0399, E-mail: comgrad@bu.edu.

See Close-Up on page 675.

Bowling Green State University, Graduate College, College of Arts and Sciences, Department of Theatre and Film, Bowling Green, OH 43403. Offers MA, PhD. *Accreditation:* NAST. Part-time programs available. Terminal master's awarded for partial completion of doctoral program. *Degree requirements:* For master's, thesis or alternative; for doctorate, comprehensive exam, thesis/dissertation, 9 hour research tool. *Entrance requirements:* For master's and doctorate, GRE General Test. Additional exam requirements/recommendations for international students: Required—TOEFL. Electronic applications accepted. *Faculty research:* Theatre history, dramatic theory, cultural studies, performance studies, American theatre history.

Brigham Young University, Graduate Studies, College of Fine Arts and Communications, Department of Theatre and Media Arts, Provo, UT 84602-6404. Offers MA. MA program accepts applications in odd-numbered years only. *Accreditation:* NAST. *Faculty:* 14 full-time (5 women). *Students:* 16 full-time (11 women), 2 part-time (1 woman), 1 international. Average age 32. 13 applicants, 77% accepted, 9 enrolled. In 2009, 6 master's awarded. *Degree requirements:* For master's, comprehensive exam, thesis, oral defense. *Entrance requirements:* For master's, GRE General Test, writing samples. Additional exam requirements/recommendations for international students: Required—TOEFL (minimum score 580 paper-based; 237 computer-based; 85 iBT). *Application deadline:* For fall admission, 2/1 priority date for domestic and international students. Application fee: $50. Electronic applications accepted. *Expenses:* Tuition: Full-time $5580; part-time $301 per credit hour. Tuition and fees vary according to student's religious affiliation. *Financial support:* In 2009–10, 17 students received support, including 4 research assistantships with partial tuition reimbursements available (averaging $3,500 per year), 20 teaching assistantships with partial tuition reimbursements available (averaging $3,500 per year); career-related internships or fieldwork, institutionally sponsored loans, scholarships/grants, health care benefits, tuition waivers (partial), unspecified assistantships, and administrative aides also available. Support available to part-time students. *Faculty research:* Media literacy, children's media, popular culture, theatre historiography, performance studies. *Unit head:* Dr. Rodger D. Sorensen, Department Chair, 801-422-8132, Fax: 801-422-0654, E-mail: rodger_sorensen@byu.edu. *Application contact:* Kim Poole, Secretary, 801-422-3750, Fax: 801-422-0654, E-mail: kim_poole@byu.edu.

Brooklyn College of the City University of New York, Division of Graduate Studies, Department of Television and Radio, Brooklyn, NY 11210-2889. Offers media studies (MS); television production (MFA). Part-time and evening/weekend programs available. *Students:* 11 full-time (6 women), 40 part-time (11 women); includes 17 minority (10 African Americans, 2 Asian Americans or Pacific Islanders, 5 Hispanic Americans), 17 international. Average age 31. 36 applicants, 86% accepted, 16 enrolled. In 2009, 14 master's awarded. *Degree requirements:* For master's, comprehensive exam. *Entrance requirements:* For master's, GRE General Test or MAT, 12 credits in television/radio with a minimum B average, 2 letters of recommendation. Additional exam requirements/recommendations for international students: Required—TOEFL (minimum score 580 paper-based; 237 computer-based; 92 iBT). *Application deadline:* For fall admission, 3/1 priority date for domestic students, 2/1 priority date for international students; for spring admission, 11/1 priority date for domestic students, 10/1 priority date for international students. Applications are processed on a rolling basis. Application fee: $125. Electronic applications accepted. *Expenses:* Tuition, area resident: Full-time $7360; part-time $310 per credit hour. Tuition, state resident: full-time $7360; part-time $310 per credit hour. Tuition, nonresident: full-time $13,800; part-time $575 per credit hour. International tuition: $13,800 full-time. Required fees: $140.10 per semester. *Financial support:* Career-related internships or fieldwork, Federal Work-Study, and institutionally sponsored loans available. Support available to part-time students. Financial award application deadline: 5/1; financial award applicants required to submit FAFSA. *Faculty research:* Criticism, research methods, audience behavior, policy and regulation, program history, international television and radio. *Unit head:* Dr. Fred Wasser, Chairperson, 718-951-5555, E-mail: fwasser@brooklyn.cuny.edu.

Application contact: Hernan Sierra, Graduate Admissions Coordinator, 718-951-4536, Fax: 718-951-4506, E-mail: grads@brooklyn.cuny.edu.

California College of the Arts, Graduate Programs, Programs in Fine Art, San Francisco, CA 94107. Offers ceramics (MFA); film/video/performance (MFA); glass (MFA); jewelry/metal arts (MFA); painting/drawing (MFA); photography (MFA); printmaking (MFA); sculpture (MFA); textiles (MFA); wood/furniture (MFA). *Accreditation:* NASAD. *Degree requirements:* For master's, thesis, exhibit. *Entrance requirements:* For master's, appropriate bachelor's degree, portfolio. Additional exam requirements/recommendations for international students: Required—TOEFL (minimum score 600 paper-based; 250 computer-based). Electronic applications accepted.

California Institute of the Arts, School of Film/Video, Valencia, CA 91355-2340. Offers experimental animation (MFA); film directing (MFA, Adv C); film/video (Adv C). *Entrance requirements:* For master's, portfolio. Additional exam requirements/recommendations for international students: Required—TOEFL. Electronic applications accepted. *Faculty research:* Experimental and character animation, experimental film/video, video graphics.

California State University, Fullerton, Graduate Studies, College of the Arts, Department of Theatre and Dance, Fullerton, CA 92834-9480. Offers acting (MFA); acting and directing (MA); dance (MA); directing (MFA); dramatic literature/criticism (MA); oral interpretation (MA); playwriting (MA); technical theater (MA); technical theater and design (MFA); television (MA); theatre for children (MA); theatre history (MA). *Accreditation:* NASD; NAST (one or more programs are accredited). Part-time programs available. *Students:* 15 full-time (6 women), 3 part-time (1 woman); includes 3 minority (1 African American, 2 Hispanic Americans). Average age 29. 14 applicants, 50% accepted, 7 enrolled. In 2009, 5 master's awarded. *Degree requirements:* For master's, oral and written exam, project or thesis. *Entrance requirements:* For master's, major in theatre or related field, audition or interview, minimum GPA of 2.5 in last 60 units of course work. Application fee: $55. *Expenses:* Tuition, nonresident: full-time $11,160; part-time $373 per credit. Required fees: $1440 per term. Tuition and fees vary according to course load, degree level and program. *Financial support:* Career-related internships or fieldwork, Federal Work-Study, institutionally sponsored loans, and scholarships/grants available. Support available to part-time students. Financial award application deadline: 3/1; financial award applicants required to submit FAFSA. *Unit head:* Dr. Susan Hallman, Chair, 657-278-3628. *Application contact:* Admissions/Applications, 657-278-2371.

California State University, Los Angeles, Graduate Studies, College of Arts and Letters, Department of Communication Studies, Los Angeles, CA 90032-8530. Offers speech communication (MA); television, film and theatre (MFA). Part-time and evening/weekend programs available. *Faculty:* 6 full-time (3 women), 8 part-time/adjunct (4 women). *Students:* 69 full-time (40 women), 52 part-time (38 women); includes 48 minority (18 African Americans, 9 Asian Americans or Pacific Islanders, 21 Hispanic Americans), 18 international. Average age 31. 92 applicants, 99% accepted, 34 enrolled. In 2009, 17 master's awarded. *Degree requirements:* For master's, comprehensive exam or thesis. *Entrance requirements:* For master's, minimum GPA of 2.75 in last 90 units of course work. Additional exam requirements/recommendations for international students: Required—TOEFL (minimum score 500 paper-based; 173 computer-based). *Application deadline:* For fall admission, 5/1 for domestic and international students. Applications are processed on a rolling basis. Application fee: $55. Electronic applications accepted. *Financial support:* Career-related internships or fieldwork and Federal Work-Study available. Support available to part-time students. Financial award application deadline: 3/1. *Faculty research:* Organizational, interpersonal, intercultural, and instructional communication; rhetorical theories. *Unit head:* Dr. Suzanne Regan, Chair, 323-343-4200, Fax: 323-343-6467, E-mail: sregan@calstatela.edu. *Application contact:* Dr. Cheryl L. Ney, Associate Vice President for Academic Affairs and Dean of Graduate Studies, 323-343-3820, Fax: 323-343-5653, E-mail: cney@cslanet.calstatela.edu.

California State University, Northridge, Graduate Studies, College of Arts, Media, and Communication, Department of Cinema and Television Arts, Northridge, CA 91330. Offers screenwriting (MA). *Faculty:* 2 part-time/adjunct (0 women). *Students:* 12 full-time (6 women), 25 part-time (10 women); includes 1 African American, 1 American Indian/Alaska Native, 2 Hispanic Americans, 1 international. Average age 37. 60 applicants, 40% accepted, 14 enrolled. In 2009, 16 master's awarded. *Entrance requirements:* For master's, GRE (if cumulative undergraduate GPA less than 3.0). *Unit head:* Robert Gustafson, Chair, 818-677-3192, E-mail: robert.gustafson@csun.edu. *Application contact:* Robert Gustafson, Chair, 818-677-3192, E-mail: robert.gustafson@csun.edu.

Carleton University, Faculty of Graduate Studies, Faculty of Arts and Social Sciences, School for Studies in Art and Culture, Program in Film Studies, Ottawa, ON K1S 5B6, Canada. Offers MA. *Degree requirements:* For master's, thesis. *Entrance requirements:* For master's, honors degree. Additional exam requirements/recommendations for international students: Required—TOEFL.

Carnegie Mellon University, School of Computer Science and College of Fine Arts, Program in Entertainment Technology, Pittsburgh, PA 15213-3891. Offers MET.

Central Michigan University, College of Graduate Studies, College of Communication and Fine Arts, School of Broadcasting and Cinematic Arts, Mount Pleasant, MI 48859. Offers electronic media management (MA); electronic media studies (MA); film theory and criticism (MA); media production (MA). Part-time programs available. *Degree requirements:* For master's, thesis or alternative. *Entrance requirements:* For master's, undergraduate degree in broadcasting, film studies, or an associated discipline with minimum GPA of 2.7. Electronic applications accepted. *Faculty research:* Multimedia production, film history and criticism, writing and promotions, international broadcasting and media systems, history of American broadcasting.

Chapman University, Graduate Studies, Dodge College of Film and Media Arts, Conservatory of Motion Pictures, Orange, CA 92866. Offers film and television producing (MFA); film production (MFA); film studies (MA); production design (MFA); screenwriting (MFA); JD/MFA; MBA/MFA. Part-time and evening/weekend programs available. *Faculty:* 34 full-time (7 women), 52 part-time/adjunct (16 women). *Students:* 230 full-time (86 women), 11 part-time (3 women); includes 31 minority (8 African Americans, 2 American Indian/Alaska Native, 7 Asian Americans or Pacific Islanders, 14 Hispanic Americans), 40 international. Average age 27. 342 applicants, 44% accepted, 85 enrolled. In 2009, 76 master's awarded. *Degree requirements:* For master's, thesis. *Entrance requirements:* For master's, GRE General Test, minimum undergraduate GPA of 2.5, portfolio. Additional exam requirements/recommendations for international students: Required—TOEFL (minimum score 550 paper-based). *Application deadline:* For fall admission, 3/1 priority date for domestic students. Application fee: $55. Electronic applications accepted. *Expenses:* Contact institution. *Financial support:* Fellowships, Federal Work-Study and scholarships/grants available. Financial award application deadline: 6/30; financial award applicants required to submit FAFSA. *Unit head:* Joseph Slowensky, Director, 714-744-7882, E-mail: jslowens@chapman.edu. *Application contact:* Jojo Delfin, Information Contact, 714-997-6786, E-mail: delfin@chapman.edu.

Chatham University, Program in Film and Digital Technology, Pittsburgh, PA 15232-2826. Offers emerging media (MFA). Part-time and evening/weekend programs available. *Students:* 11 full-time (7 women), 6 part-time (3 women). Average age 29. 19 applicants, 79% accepted, 13 enrolled. *Degree requirements:* For master's, thesis, capstone project. *Entrance requirements:* Additional exam requirements/recommendations for international students: Required—TOEFL (minimum score 600 paper-based; 250 computer-based; 100 iBT), IELTS (minimum score 6.5), TWE. *Application deadline:* For fall admission, 7/1 priority date for domestic students, 6/1 priority date for international students; for spring admission, 12/1 priority date for domestic students, 11/1 priority date for international students. Applications are processed on a rolling basis. Application fee: $45. Electronic applications accepted. *Financial support:* Applicants required to submit FAFSA. *Unit head:* Dr. Prajna Parasher, Director, 412-365-1182, E-mail: parasher@chatham.edu. *Application contact:* Dory Perry, Associate Director of Graduate Admissions, 412-365-2758, Fax: 412-365-1609, E-mail: gradadmissions@chatham.edu.

Columbia College Chicago, Graduate School, Department of Film and Video, Chicago, IL 60605-1996. Offers MFA. Part-time programs available. *Degree requirements:* For master's, thesis, film project. *Entrance requirements:* For master's, interview, minimum GPA of 3.0, portfolio or script. Additional exam requirements/recommendations for international students: Required—TOEFL (minimum score 550 paper-based; 213 computer-based). Electronic applications accepted. *Expenses:* Tuition: Part-time $651 per credit hour. Required fees: $651 per credit hour. $205 per semester. One-time fee: $285 part-time. Tuition and fees vary according to program.

Columbia University, School of the Arts, Film Division, New York, NY 10027. Offers directing (MFA); film studies (MA); producing (MFA); screen writing (MFA). *Degree requirements:* For master's, thesis. *Entrance requirements:* For master's, 3 letters of recommendation, writing sample, complete a scene, feature film treatment (optional visual submission). Additional exam requirements/recommendations for international students: Required—TOEFL (minimum score 600 paper-based; 250 computer-based; 100 iBT). Electronic applications accepted.

See Close-Up on page 261.

Concordia University, School of Graduate Studies, Faculty of Fine Arts, Department of Studio Arts, Montréal, QC H3G 1M8, Canada. Offers studio arts (MFA), including film production, open media, painting, photography, print media, sculpture, ceramics and fibers. *Degree requirements:* For master's, thesis or alternative. *Entrance requirements:* For master's, portfolio.

Concordia University, School of Graduate Studies, Faculty of Fine Arts, Mel Hoppenheim School of Cinema, Montréal, QC H3G 1M8, Canada. Offers film studies (MA).

Drexel University, Antoinette Westphal College of Media Arts and Design, Program in Television Management, Philadelphia, PA 19104-2875. Offers MS, MS/MBA.

Florida Atlantic University, Dorothy F. Schmidt College of Arts and Letters, School of Communication and Multimedia Studies, Boca Raton, FL 33431-0991. Offers communication studies (MA); film and video (Certificate); film studies (MA); multimedia journalism studies (MA). Part-time programs available. *Faculty:* 21 full-time (10 women), 14 part-time/adjunct (3 women). *Students:* 14 full-time (11 women), 13 part-time (8 women); includes 3 minority (1 African American, 1 Asian American or Pacific Islander, 1 Hispanic American), 3 international. Average age 28. 39 applicants, 26% accepted, 6 enrolled. In 2009, 7 master's awarded. *Degree requirements:* For master's, one foreign language, comprehensive exam (for some programs), thesis (for some programs). *Entrance requirements:* For master's, GRE General Test, minimum GPA of 3.0. *Application deadline:* For fall admission, 7/1 priority date for domestic students, 4/1 for international students; for spring admission, 11/1 for domestic students, 10/1 for international students. Applications are processed on a rolling basis. Application fee: $30. Electronic applications accepted. *Expenses:* Tuition, state resident: full-time $7055; part-time $293.94 per credit hour. Tuition, nonresident: full-time $22,096; part-time $920.66 per credit hour. *Financial support:* Teaching assistantships with partial tuition reimbursements, Federal Work-Study and institutionally sponsored loans available. Support available to part-time students. Financial award application deadline: 3/1. *Faculty research:* Cultural studies, gender studies, film, communication theory, journalism, new media. *Unit head:* Dr. Susan S. Reilly, Director, 561-297-1095, Fax: 561-297-2615, E-mail: sreilly@fau.edu. *Application contact:* Dr. Eric M. Freedman, Graduate Coordinator, 561-297-2534, Fax: 561-297-2615, E-mail: efreedma@fau.edu.

Florida State University, The Graduate School, College of Motion Picture Arts, Tallahassee, FL 32306-2350. Offers production (MFA); screen and play writing (MFA). *Faculty:* 14 full-time (3 women), 4 part-time/adjunct (1 woman). *Students:* 56 full-time (22 women); includes 16 minority (5 African Americans, 6 Asian Americans or Pacific Islanders, 5 Hispanic Americans). Average age 27. 207 applicants, 14% accepted, 30 enrolled. In 2009, 28 master's awarded. *Degree requirements:* For master's, thesis, thesis project. *Entrance requirements:* For master's, GRE General Test, minimum GPA of 3.0, film/video experience. Additional exam requirements/recommendations for international students: Required—TOEFL (minimum score 550 paper-based; 253 computer-based; 80 iBT). *Application deadline:* For fall admission, 12/1 for domestic and international students. Application fee: $30. *Expenses:* Tuition, state resident: full-time $7413. Tuition, nonresident: full-time $22,567. *Financial support:* In 2009–10, 22 students received support, including 1 fellowship with partial tuition reimbursement available (averaging $6,300 per year), 22 teaching assistantships with partial tuition reimbursements available (averaging $4,100 per year); Federal Work-Study and unspecified assistantships also available. Financial award application deadline: 1/1; financial award applicants required to submit FAFSA. *Faculty research:* Producing, screenwriting, directing, cinematography, editing. *Unit head:* Frank Patterson, Dean, 850-644-0453, Fax: 850-644-2626. *Application contact:* Sandra Howard, Assistant to Associate Dean, 850-644-4927, Fax: 850-644-2626, E-mail: showard@film.fsu.edu.

Georgia State University, College of Arts and Sciences, Department of Communication, Atlanta, GA 30302-3083. Offers film/video/digital imaging (MA); human communication and social influence (MA); mass communication (MA); moving image studies (PhD); public communication (PhD). Part-time programs available. *Degree requirements:* For master's, one foreign language, thesis or alternative; for doctorate, comprehensive exam, thesis/dissertation. *Entrance requirements:* For master's and doctorate, GRE General Test. Additional exam requirements/recommendations for international students: Required—TOEFL (minimum score 80 computer-based). Electronic applications accepted. *Faculty research:* Critical/cultural studies, rhetoric studies, film/media studies, mass communications/journalism, audience studies.

Hofstra University, School of Communication, Department of Radio/Television/Film, Hempstead, NY 11549. Offers documentary studies and production (MFA). Part-time and evening/weekend programs available. *Faculty:* 4 full-time (0 women). *Students:* 13 full-time (6 women), 5 part-time (4 women); includes 4 minority (3 Asian Americans or Pacific Islanders, 1 Hispanic American), 3 international. Average age 30. 19 applicants, 95% accepted, 9 enrolled. *Degree requirements:* For master's, thesis, thesis project. *Entrance requirements:* For master's, 2 letters of recommendation, portfolio, interview. Additional exam requirements/recommendations for international students: Required—TOEFL (minimum score 550 paper-based; 213 computer-based; 80 iBT). *Application deadline:* Applications are processed on a rolling basis. Application fee: $60. Electronic applications accepted. *Expenses:* Tuition: Full-time $16,200; part-time $900 per credit hour. Required fees: $970; $145 per term. Tuition and fees vary according to program. *Financial support:* In 2009–10, 3 students received support, including 1 fellowship with full and partial tuition reimbursement available (averaging $3,000 per year), 1 research assistantship with full and partial tuition reimbursement available (averaging $10,529 per year); Federal Work-Study, institutionally sponsored loans, scholarships/grants, tuition waivers (full and partial), and unspecified assistantships also available. Support available to part-time students. Financial award applicants required to submit FAFSA. *Faculty research:* Community and citizen's media: indigenous movements in Latin America; communication, development, and globalization; animation, feminism, and documentary; working class women; film aesthetics and theory. *Unit head:* Dr. Christine Noschese, Program Director, 516-463-7141, E-mail: sphmjs@hofstra.edu. *Application contact:* Carol Drummer, Dean of Graduate Admissions, 516-463-4876, Fax: 516-463-4664, E-mail: gradstudent@hofstra.edu.

Hollins University, Graduate Programs, Program in Screenwriting and Film Studies, Roanoke, VA 24020-1603. Offers MA, MFA. Offered during summer only. Part-time programs available. *Faculty:* 2 full-time (1 woman), 5 part-time/adjunct (3 women). *Students:* 37 full-time (22 women), 1 (woman) part-time; includes 8 minority (6 African Americans, 2 Hispanic Americans), 2 international. Average age 34. 22 applicants, 86% accepted, 13 enrolled. In 2009, 8 master's awarded. *Degree requirements:* For master's, one foreign language, comprehensive exam, thesis. *Entrance requirements:* For master's, letters of recommendation, portfolio. Additional exam requirements/recommendations for international students: Required—TOEFL (minimum

Film, Television, and Video Production

Hollins University (continued)
score 550 paper-based; 213 computer-based; 79 iBT). *Application deadline:* For fall admission, 2/15 for domestic and international students. Application fee: $40. Electronic applications accepted. *Expenses:* Tuition: Full-time $27,780; part-time $295 per contact hour. Required fees: $280; $70 per unit. Part-time tuition and fees vary according to course load and program. *Financial support:* In 2009–10, 10 students received support, including 5 fellowships (averaging $1,000 per year); Federal Work-Study and scholarships/grants also available. Support available to part-time students. Financial award application deadline: 2/15; financial award applicants required to submit FAFSA. *Faculty research:* German film, women in film, censorship, minorities in film. *Unit head:* Dr. Klaus Phillips, Director, 540-362-6308, E-mail: kphillips@hollins.edu. *Application contact:* Cathy S. Koon, Manager of Graduate Services, 540-362-6326, Fax: 540-362-6288, E-mail: ckoon@hollins.edu.

Howard University, School of Communications, Department of Radio, Television and Film, Washington, DC 20059-0002. Offers film (MFA). Part-time programs available. *Degree requirements:* For master's, thesis optional. *Entrance requirements:* For master's, GRE General Test, minimum GPA of 3.0.

Humboldt State University, Graduate Studies, College of Arts, Humanities, and Social Sciences, Department of Theatre, Film and Dance, Arcata, CA 95521-8299. Offers theatre arts (MA, MFA), including film production (MA), production (MA), scenography (MFA). *Students:* 15 full-time (9 women), 1 (woman) part-time; includes 3 minority (1 Asian American or Pacific Islander, 2 Hispanic Americans). Average age 33. 12 applicants, 42% accepted, 5 enrolled. In 2009, 3 master's awarded. *Degree requirements:* For master's, thesis or alternative, qualifying exam. *Entrance requirements:* For master's, minimum GPA of 2.5. Additional exam requirements/recommendations for international students: Required—TOEFL (minimum score 500 paper-based; 173 computer-based). *Application deadline:* For fall admission, 4/15 for domestic students. Applications are processed on a rolling basis. Application fee: $55. *Expenses:* Tuition, nonresident: full-time $8928. Required fees: $6102. Tuition and fees vary according to program. *Financial support:* Fellowships available. Financial award application deadline: 3/1; financial award applicants required to submit FAFSA. *Faculty research:* Physical theater, design, playwriting. *Unit head:* Bernadette Cheyne, Chair/Coordinator, 707-826-4606, Fax: 707-826-5494, E-mail: bmc3@humboldt.edu. *Application contact:* Bernadette Cheyne, Chair/Coordinator, 707-826-4606, Fax: 707-826-5494, E-mail: bmc3@humboldt.edu.

Loyola Marymount University, School of Film and Television, Department of Production, Program in Production (Film and Television), Los Angeles, CA 90045-8347. Offers MFA. *Faculty:* 12 full-time (3 women). *Students:* 45 full-time (14 women), 8 part-time (3 women); includes 14 minority (6 African Americans, 3 Asian Americans or Pacific Islanders, 5 Hispanic Americans), 11 international. Average age 26. 94 applicants, 66% accepted, 13 enrolled. In 2009, 5 master's awarded. *Degree requirements:* For master's, thesis, film. *Entrance requirements:* For master's, GRE General Test, creative work, 2 letters of recommendation. Additional exam requirements/recommendations for international students: Required—TOEFL (minimum score 600 paper-based; 250 computer-based; 100 iBT). *Application deadline:* For fall admission, 2/15 for domestic students. Application fee: $50. Electronic applications accepted. *Financial support:* In 2009–10, 46 students received support, including 2 research assistantships (averaging $1,200 per year); career-related internships or fieldwork and scholarships/grants also available. Support available to part-time students. Financial award application deadline: 6/1; financial award applicants required to submit FAFSA. *Unit head:* Luis Proenca, Chair, 310-338-3764, E-mail: lproenca@lmu.edu. *Application contact:* Chake H. Kouyoumjian, Associate Dean of Graduate Admissions, 310-338-2721, Fax: 310-338-6086, E-mail: ckouyoum@lmu.edu.

Marywood University, Academic Affairs, Insalaco College of Creative and Performing Arts, Department of Communication Arts, Program in Communication Arts, Scranton, PA 18509-1598. Offers interdisciplinary (MA); media management (MA); production (MA). *Students:* 12 full-time (7 women), 25 part-time (13 women); includes 5 minority (2 African Americans, 1 Asian American or Pacific Islander, 2 Hispanic Americans). Average age 33. In 2009, 11 master's awarded. *Entrance requirements:* Additional exam requirements/recommendations for international students: Required—TOEFL (minimum score 550 paper-based; 213 computer-based; 79 iBT). *Application deadline:* For fall admission, 4/1 for domestic students, 3/31 for international students; for spring admission, 11/1 for domestic students, 8/31 for international students. Applications are processed on a rolling basis. Application fee: $35. Electronic applications accepted. *Expenses:* Tuition: Part-time $715 per credit. Required fees: $270 per semester. Tuition and fees vary according to degree level, campus/location and program. *Financial support:* Career-related internships or fieldwork, scholarships/grants, and unspecified assistantships available. Support available to part-time students. Financial award application deadline: 6/30; financial award applicants required to submit FAFSA. *Application contact:* Tammy Manka, Assistant Director of Admissions, 866-279-9663, E-mail: tmanka@marywood.edu.

Massachusetts College of Art and Design, Graduate Programs, Program in Fine Arts, Boston, MA 02115-5882. Offers ceramics (MFA); design (MFA); fibers (MFA); film/video (MFA); glass (MFA); media and performing arts (MFA); metals/jewelry (MFA); painting (MFA); photography (MFA); printmaking (MFA); sculpture (MFA). *Accreditation:* NASAD. *Faculty:* 10 full-time (5 women), 8 part-time/adjunct (6 women). *Students:* 89 full-time (56 women), 12 part-time (8 women); includes 8 minority (5 Asian Americans or Pacific Islanders, 3 Hispanic Americans), 10 international. Average age 34. 295 applicants, 24% accepted, 40 enrolled. In 2009, 44 master's awarded. *Degree requirements:* For master's, thesis, exhibit. *Entrance requirements:* For master's, 12 units of course work in art history, portfolio, resume, letters of reference, interview. Additional exam requirements/recommendations for international students: Required—TOEFL (minimum score 563 paper-based; 223 computer-based; 85 iBT); Recommended—IELTS (minimum score 6.5). *Application deadline:* For fall admission, 1/15 for domestic and international students. Application fee: $75. Electronic applications accepted. *Expenses:* Tuition, state resident: full-time $18,450; part-time $615 per credit. Tuition, nonresident: full-time $18,450; part-time $615 per credit. Tuition and fees vary according to program. *Financial support:* In 2009–10, 50 research assistantships (averaging $2,000 per year), 40 teaching assistantships (averaging $2,000 per year) were awarded; career-related internships or fieldwork, Federal Work-Study, and clerical/technical assistantships ($2000) also available. Support available to part-time students. Financial award application deadline: 5/1; financial award applicants required to submit FAFSA. *Unit head:* George Creamer, Dean of Graduate Programs, 617-879-7163, Fax: 617-879-7171, E-mail: creamer@massart.edu. *Application contact:* George Creamer, Dean of Graduate Programs, 617-879-7163, Fax: 617-879-7171, E-mail: creamer@massart.edu.

Miami International University of Art & Design, Program in Film, Miami, FL 33132-1418. Offers MFA. Postbaccalaureate distance learning degree programs offered. *Application contact:* Office of Graduate Admissions, 305-428-5700.

See Close-Up on page 117.

Minneapolis College of Art and Design, Program in Visual Studies, Minneapolis, MN 55404-4347. Offers animation (MFA); comic art (MFA); drawing (MFA); filmmaking (MFA); fine arts (MFA); furniture design (MFA); graphic design (MFA); illustration (MFA); interactive media (MFA); painting (MFA); photography (MFA); printmaking (MFA); sculpture (MFA). *Accreditation:* NASAD. Part-time programs available. *Faculty:* 42 full-time (13 women). *Students:* 12 full-time (2 women), 18 part-time (8 women). Average age 27. 166 applicants, 28% accepted, 12 enrolled. In 2009, 10 master's awarded. *Degree requirements:* For master's, thesis, thesis exhibit. *Entrance requirements:* For master's, portfolio of visual artwork, resume, 3 letters of recommendation. Additional exam requirements/recommendations for international students: Required—TOEFL (minimum score 550 paper-based; 213 computer-based; 79 iBT). *Application deadline:* For fall admission, 1/15 for domestic and international students. Application fee: $50. Electronic applications accepted. *Expenses:* Tuition: Full-time $29,500; part-time $985 per credit. Required fees: $100. *Financial support:* In 2009–10, 23 students received support, including 15 teaching assistantships (averaging $6,000 per year); career-related internships or fieldwork, Federal Work-Study, scholarships/grants, and unspecified assistantships also available. Support available to part-time students. Financial award application deadline: 3/15; financial award applicants required to submit FAFSA. *Faculty research:* Visual arts: animation, comic art, drawing, filmmaking, furniture design, graphic design, illustration, interactive media, painting, photography, printmaking, sculpture. *Unit head:* Carole Fisher, Graduate Director, 612-874-3629, E-mail: carole_fisher@mcad.edu. *Application contact:* William Mullen, Vice President of Enrollment Management, 612-874-3760, Fax: 612-874-3701, E-mail: william_mullen@mcad.edu.

Montana State University, College of Graduate Studies, College of Arts and Architecture, School of Film and Photography, Program in Science and Natural History Filmmaking, Bozeman, MT 59717. Offers MFA. *Degree requirements:* For master's, comprehensive exam. *Entrance requirements:* For master's, GRE General Test. Additional exam requirements/recommendations for international students: Required—TOEFL (minimum score 550 paper-based; 213 computer-based). *Application deadline:* For fall admission, 3/1 for domestic and international students. Application fee: $50. *Expenses:* Tuition, state resident: full-time $5635; part-time $3492 per year. Tuition, nonresident: full-time $17,212; part-time $7865.10 per year. Required fees: $1441; $153.15 per credit. Tuition and fees vary according to course load and program. *Financial support:* Application deadline: 3/1. *Faculty research:* Documentary, experimental video. *Unit head:* Dr. Dennis L. Aig, Director, 406-994-6216, Fax: 406-994-6214, E-mail: daig@montana.edu. *Application contact:* Dr. Dennis L. Aig, Director, 406-994-6216, Fax: 406-994-6214, E-mail: daig@montana.edu.

New York Film Academy, Program in Filmmaking–Hollywood, Los Angeles, CA 90068. Offers acting for film (MFA); filmmaking (MFA); producing (MFA); screenwriting (MFA).

New York Film Academy, Program in Filmmaking–New York, New York, NY 10003. Offers acting for film (MFA); filmmaking (MFA); producing (MFA); screenwriting (MFA).

New York Film Academy, Program in Filmmaking–United Arab Emirates, Abu Dhabi, CA 90068, United Arab Emirates. Offers acting for film (MFA); filmmaking (MFA); producing (MFA); screenwriting (MFA).

New York University, Tisch School of the Arts Asia, Singapore, NY 248923, Singapore. Offers animation and digital arts (MFA); dramatic writing (MFA); film production (MFA). *Entrance requirements:* Additional exam requirements/recommendations for international students: Required—TOEFL (minimum score 610 paper-based; 250 computer-based; 105 iBT). Electronic applications accepted. *Expenses:* Tuition: Full-time $30,528; part-time $1272 per credit. Required fees: $2177.

New York University, Tisch School of the Arts and Graduate School of Arts and Science, Department of Cinema Studies, Program in Moving Image Archiving and Preservation, New York, NY 10012-1019. Offers MA. *Faculty:* 2 full-time, 4 part-time/adjunct. *Students:* 16 full-time (6 women), 1 (woman) part-time; includes 1 minority (Hispanic American). Average age 28. 15 applicants, 87% accepted, 7 enrolled. In 2009, 6 master's awarded. *Degree requirements:* For master's, internship. *Entrance requirements:* For master's, GRE. Additional exam requirements/recommendations for international students: Required—TOEFL, IELTS or ALI. *Application deadline:* For fall admission, 12/1 for domestic and international students. Application fee: $60. Electronic applications accepted. *Expenses:* Tuition: Full-time $30,528; part-time $1272 per credit. Required fees: $2177. *Financial support:* In 2009–10, 11 students received support, including 5 fellowships with full and partial tuition reimbursements available; tuition waivers (partial) also available. Financial award application deadline: 2/15. *Unit head:* Howard Besser, Head, 212-998-1618. *Application contact:* Dan Sandford, Director of Graduate Admissions, 212-998-1918, Fax: 212-995-4060, E-mail: tisch.gradadmissions@nyu.edu.

New York University, Tisch School of the Arts, Kanbar Institute of Film and Television, New York, NY 10012-1019. Offers MFA. *Faculty:* 19 full-time, 20 part-time/adjunct. *Students:* 111 full-time (53 women), 76 part-time (35 women); includes 67 minority (23 African Americans, 2 American Indian/Alaska Native, 36 Asian Americans or Pacific Islanders, 6 Hispanic Americans). Average age 25. 630 applicants, 9% accepted, 37 enrolled. In 2009, 30 master's awarded. *Degree requirements:* For master's, 4 films. *Entrance requirements:* For master's, portfolio. Additional exam requirements/recommendations for international students: Required—TOEFL, IELTS or ALI. *Application deadline:* For fall admission, 12/1 for domestic and international students. Application fee: $60. Electronic applications accepted. *Expenses:* Tuition: Full-time $30,528; part-time $1272 per credit. Required fees: $2177. *Financial support:* In 2009–10, 60 students received support, including 16 fellowships with full and partial tuition reimbursements available, 6 teaching assistantships with tuition reimbursements available; Federal Work-Study, institutionally sponsored loans, scholarships/grants, tuition waivers (full and partial), and unspecified assistantships also available. Financial award application deadline: 2/15; financial award applicants required to submit FAFSA. *Unit head:* John Tintori, Chair, 212-998-1780, E-mail: jt42@nyu.edu. *Application contact:* Dan Sandford, Director of Graduate Admissions, 212-998-1918, Fax: 212-995-4060, E-mail: tisch.gradadmissions@nyu.edu.

Northwestern University, The Graduate School, School of Communication, Department of Radio/Television/Film, Evanston, IL 60208. Offers MA, MFA, PhD. Admissions and degrees offered through The Graduate School. Part-time programs available. Terminal master's awarded for partial completion of doctoral program. *Degree requirements:* For master's, comprehensive exam or thesis; for doctorate, thesis/dissertation, qualifying exam. *Entrance requirements:* For master's and doctorate, GRE General Test. Additional exam requirements/recommendations for international students: Required—TOEFL. Electronic applications accepted. *Faculty research:* Art and new media, media theory and criticism, gender, media history, documentary.

Ohio University, Graduate College, College of Fine Arts, School of Film, Athens, OH 45701-2979. Offers film (MFA); film studies (MA). *Faculty:* 8 full-time (2 women), 2 part-time/adjunct (1 woman). *Students:* 48 full-time (15 women), 5 part-time (2 women); includes 5 minority (3 African Americans, 1 Asian American or Pacific Islander, 1 Hispanic American), 18 international. Average age 25. 109 applicants, 23% accepted, 16 enrolled. In 2009, 12 master's awarded. *Degree requirements:* For master's, one foreign language, thesis. *Entrance requirements:* Additional exam requirements/recommendations for international students: Required—TOEFL (minimum score 550 paper-based; 80 iBT) or IELTS Academic (minimum score 6.5). *Application deadline:* For fall admission, 2/1 for domestic and international students. Application fee: $50 ($55 for international students). Electronic applications accepted. *Expenses:* Tuition, state resident: full-time $7839; part-time $323 per quarter hour. Tuition, nonresident: full-time $15,831; part-time $654 per quarter hour. Required fees: $2931. *Financial support:* In 2009–10, 34 students received support; research assistantships with full tuition reimbursements available, teaching assistantships with full tuition reimbursements available, institutionally sponsored loans, scholarships/grants, tuition waivers (full and partial), and unspecified assistantships available. Financial award application deadline: 2/1. *Faculty research:* Scriptwriting, sound, editing, cinematography, film theory, digital post production. *Unit head:* Steven Ross, Director, 740-593-9969, Fax: 740-593-1328, E-mail: rosss2@ohio.edu. *Application contact:* Tamra LaGraff, Administrative Associate, 740-593-1323, Fax: 740-593-1328, E-mail: lagraff@ohio.edu.

Polytechnic Institute of NYU, Department of Electrical and Computer Engineering, Major in Image Processing, Brooklyn, NY 11201-2990. Offers Certificate. *Entrance requirements:* Additional exam requirements/recommendations for international students: Required—TOEFL (minimum score 550 paper-based; 213 computer-based; 80 iBT); Recommended—IELTS (minimum score 6.5). *Application deadline:* For fall admission, 7/31 priority date for domestic students, 4/30 priority date for international students; for spring admission, 12/31 priority date for domestic students, 10/30 priority date for international students. Applications are processed on a rolling basis. Application fee: $75. Electronic applications accepted. *Expenses:* Tuition: Full-time $21,492; part-time $1194 per credit hour. Required fees: $1160; $204 per course. *Financial support:* Institutionally sponsored loans, scholarships/grants, and unspecified assistantships available. Support available to part-time students. *Unit head:* Dr. Jonathan Chao, Head, 718-860-3478, Fax: 718-260-3302, E-mail: chao@poly.edu. *Application contact:* JeanCarlo

Bonilla, Director of Graduate Enrollment Management, 718-260-3182, Fax: 718-260-3624, E-mail: gradinfo@poly.edu.

Regent University, Graduate School, School of Communication and the Arts, Virginia Beach, VA 23464-9800. Offers acting (MFA); acting and directing (MFA); cinema arts/television arts (MA); communication (MA, PhD); digital media (MA); directing for cinema/TV (MA); journalism (MA); producing for cinema/TV (MA); script and screenwriting (MFA); theatre (MA). Part-time programs available. Postbaccalaureate distance learning degree programs offered (minimal on-campus study). *Faculty:* 27 full-time (3 women), 24 part-time/adjunct (8 women). *Students:* 120 full-time (65 women), 160 part-time (82 women); includes 70 minority (53 African Americans, 2 American Indian/Alaska Native, 4 Asian Americans or Pacific Islanders, 11 Hispanic Americans), 10 international. Average age 31. 221 applicants, 58% accepted, 62 enrolled. In 2009, 61 master's, 13 doctorates awarded. *Degree requirements:* For master's, thesis or alternative; for doctorate, thesis/dissertation. *Entrance requirements:* For master's, GRE General Test or MAT, minimum undergraduate GPA of 3.0, writing sample, computer literacy survey, recommendation, resume, interview, audition (MFA programs); for doctorate, GRE General Test, minimum graduate GPA of 3.0, writing sample, computer literacy survey, recommendation, interview, transcripts. Additional exam requirements/recommendations for international students: Required—TOEFL (minimum score 577 paper-based; 233 computer-based). *Application deadline:* For fall admission, 3/1 priority date for domestic students; for spring admission, 10/1 priority date for domestic students. Applications are processed on a rolling basis. Application fee: $50. Electronic applications accepted. *Expenses:* Contact institution. *Financial support:* In 2009–10, 229 students received support; fellowships with full and partial tuition reimbursements available, career-related internships or fieldwork, scholarships/grants, tuition waivers (full and partial), and unspecified assistantships available. Support available to part-time students. Financial award application deadline: 9/1; financial award applicants required to submit FAFSA. *Faculty research:* Southern gospel music, education and entertainment, celebrities and the media, journalism and ethics, C. S. Lewis. *Unit head:* Michael Patrick, Dean, 757-352-4970, Fax: 757-352-4279, E-mail: michpat@regent.edu. *Application contact:* Matthew Chadwick, Director of Admissions, 800-373-5504, Fax: 757-352-4381, E-mail: admissions@regent.edu.

Rochester Institute of Technology, Graduate Enrollment Services, College of Imaging Arts and Sciences, School of Photographic Arts and Sciences, Program in Imaging Arts, Rochester, NY 14623-5603. Offers MFA. *Accreditation:* NASAD. Part-time programs available. *Students:* 66 full-time (35 women), 17 part-time (10 women); includes 1 African American, 2 Asian Americans or Pacific Islanders, 3 Hispanic Americans, 31 international. Average age 29. 165 applicants, 36% accepted, 22 enrolled. In 2009, 23 master's awarded. *Degree requirements:* For master's, thesis, exhibit. *Entrance requirements:* For master's, portfolio, minimum GPA of 3.0. Additional exam requirements/recommendations for international students: Required—TOEFL (minimum score 550 paper-based; 213 computer-based; 79 iBT), or IELTS (minimum score 6.5). *Application deadline:* For fall admission, 2/15 priority date for domestic and international students. Applications are processed on a rolling basis. Application fee: $50. Electronic applications accepted. *Expenses:* Tuition: Full-time $31,533; part-time $876 per credit hour. Required fees: $210. *Financial support:* In 2009–10, 45 students received support; fellowships with partial tuition reimbursements available, research assistantships with partial tuition reimbursements available, teaching assistantships with partial tuition reimbursements available, career-related internships or fieldwork, institutionally sponsored loans, scholarships/grants, tuition waivers (partial), and unspecified assistantships available. Support available to part-time students. Financial award application deadline: 8/30; financial award applicants required to submit FAFSA. *Unit head:* Angela Kelly, MFA Coordinator, 585-475-2717, Fax: 585-475-5804, E-mail: spasinfo@rit.edu. *Application contact:* Diane Ellison, Assistant Vice President, Graduate Enrollment Services, 585-475-2229, Fax: 585-475-7164, E-mail: gradinfo@rit.edu.

St. Thomas University, School of Leadership Studies, Program in Electronic Media, Miami Gardens, FL 33054-6459. Offers MA.

San Diego State University, Graduate and Research Affairs, College of Professional Studies and Fine Arts, School of Theater, Television and Film, Program in Television, Film, and New Media Production, San Diego, CA 92182. Offers MA. *Entrance requirements:* For master's, GRE General Test, 3 letters of recommendation, resume, sample reel, influential book list, influential films list, hobby list. Additional exam requirements/recommendations for international students: Required—TOEFL. Electronic applications accepted. *Faculty research:* Experimental film and television programs, documentary film, television research and production.

San Francisco Art Institute, Graduate Program, Department of Film, San Francisco, CA 94133. Offers MFA, Certificate. *Accreditation:* NASAD. Part-time programs available. *Degree requirements:* For master's and Certificate, oral reviews. *Entrance requirements:* For master's and Certificate, portfolio. Additional exam requirements/recommendations for international students: Required—TOEFL (minimum score 580 paper-based; 237 computer-based). Electronic applications accepted.

San Francisco Art Institute, Graduate Program, Department of New Genres, San Francisco, CA 94133. Offers new genres (Certificate); performance/video (MFA). *Accreditation:* NASAD. Part-time programs available. *Degree requirements:* For master's and Certificate, oral reviews. *Entrance requirements:* For master's and Certificate, portfolio. Additional exam requirements/recommendations for international students: Required—TOEFL (minimum score 580 paper-based; 237 computer-based). Electronic applications accepted.

San Francisco State University, Division of Graduate Studies, College of Creative Arts, Department of Broadcast and Electronic Communication Arts, San Francisco, CA 94132-1722. Offers radio and television (MA).

San Francisco State University, Division of Graduate Studies, College of Creative Arts, Department of Cinema, San Francisco, CA 94132-1722. Offers cinema (MFA); cinema studies (MA).

San Jose State University, Graduate Studies and Research, College of Humanities and the Arts, Department of Television, Radio, Film and Theatre, San Jose, CA 95192-0001. Offers theatre arts (MA). *Accreditation:* NAST. *Students:* 8 full-time (6 women), 22 part-time (15 women); includes 8 minority (2 Asian Americans or Pacific Islanders, 6 Hispanic Americans), 1 international. Average age 35. 24 applicants, 54% accepted, 8 enrolled. In 2009, 11 master's awarded. *Degree requirements:* For master's, written exam. *Entrance requirements:* Additional exam requirements/recommendations for international students: Required—TOEFL (minimum score 570 paper-based). *Application deadline:* For fall admission, 6/29 for domestic students; for spring admission, 11/30 for domestic students. Applications are processed on a rolling basis. Application fee: $59. Electronic applications accepted. *Financial support:* Scholarships/grants available. Financial award applicants required to submit FAFSA. *Unit head:* Anne Fountain, Chair, 408-924-4567, Fax: 408-924-4574. *Application contact:* Dr. David Kahn, Graduate Advisor, 408-924-4540, E-mail: david.kahn@sjsu.edu.

San Jose State University, Graduate Studies and Research, College of Humanities and the Arts, School of Art and Design, San Jose, CA 95192-0001. Offers animation/illustration (MA); art history (MA); digital media arts (MFA); photography (MFA); pictorial arts (MFA); spatial arts (MFA). *Accreditation:* NASAD (one or more programs are accredited). *Students:* 48 full-time (27 women), 24 part-time (16 women); includes 13 minority (3 African Americans, 6 Asian Americans or Pacific Islanders, 4 Hispanic Americans), 2 international. Average age 36. 69 applicants, 23% accepted, 16 enrolled. In 2009, 17 master's awarded. *Entrance requirements:* For master's, GRE. *Application deadline:* For fall admission, 6/29 for domestic students; for spring admission, 11/30 for domestic students. Applications are processed on a rolling basis. Application fee: $59. Electronic applications accepted. *Financial support:* Applicants required to submit FAFSA. *Unit head:* John Loomis, Director, 408-924-4320, Fax: 408-924-4326. *Application contact:* John Loomis, Director, 408-924-4320, Fax: 408-924-4326.

Savannah College of Art and Design, Graduate School, Program in Animation, Savannah, GA 31402-3146. Offers MA, MFA. Part-time programs available. *Degree requirements:* For master's, thesis, internships. *Entrance requirements:* For master's, interview, portfolio. Additional exam requirements/recommendations for international students: Required—TOEFL (minimum score 450 paper-based; 133 computer-based). Electronic applications accepted. *Expenses:* Tuition: Full-time $28,515; part-time $627 per credit hour. One-time fee: $500. Tuition and fees vary according to course load.

Savannah College of Art and Design, Graduate School, Program in Film and Television, Savannah, GA 31402-3146. Offers MA, MFA. Part-time programs available. *Degree requirements:* For master's, thesis, internship. *Entrance requirements:* For master's, interview, videotape. Additional exam requirements/recommendations for international students: Required—TOEFL (minimum score 450 paper-based; 133 computer-based). Electronic applications accepted. *Expenses:* Tuition: Full-time $28,515; part-time $627 per credit hour. One-time fee: $500. Tuition and fees vary according to course load.

Savannah College of Art and Design, Graduate School, Program in Sound Design, Savannah, GA 31402-3146. Offers MA, MFA. Part-time programs available. *Degree requirements:* For master's, thesis, internships. *Entrance requirements:* For master's, interview, portfolio. Additional exam requirements/recommendations for international students: Required—TOEFL (minimum score 450 paper-based; 133 computer-based). *Expenses:* Tuition: Full-time $28,515; part-time $627 per credit hour. One-time fee: $500. Tuition and fees vary according to course load.

School of the Art Institute of Chicago, Graduate Division, Department of Film, Video, and New Media, Chicago, IL 60603-3103. Offers MFA. *Accreditation:* NASAD. *Degree requirements:* For master's, thesis exhibit. *Entrance requirements:* Additional exam requirements/recommendations for international students: Required—TOEFL, IELTS. Electronic applications accepted.

School of the Art Institute of Chicago, Graduate Division, Department of Sound, Chicago, IL 60603-3103. Offers MFA. *Entrance requirements:* Additional exam requirements/recommendations for international students: Required—TOEFL, IELTS.

School of Visual Arts, Graduate Programs, Program in Photography, Video and Related Media, New York, NY 10010-3994. Offers MFA. *Accreditation:* NASAD. *Degree requirements:* For master's, final review, project or thesis. *Entrance requirements:* For master's, portfolio. Additional exam requirements/recommendations for international students: Required—TOEFL (minimum score 550 paper-based; 213 computer-based; 79 iBT). Electronic applications accepted.

Southern Methodist University, Meadows School of the Arts, Department of Cinema and Television, Dallas, TX 75275. Offers MA, MFA. *Faculty:* 11 full-time (4 women), 4 part-time/adjunct (0 women). *Students:* 9 full-time (4 women), 1 (woman) part-time; includes 2 minority (1 American Indian/Alaska Native, 1 Hispanic American), 3 international. Average age 33. In 2009, 3 master's awarded. *Unit head:* Sean Griffin, Chair, 214-768-4356, E-mail: spgriffi@mail.smu.edu. *Application contact:* Jean Cherry, Director of Graduate Admissions and Records, 214-768-3765, Fax: 214-768-3272, E-mail: jcherry@smu.edu.

Southern Methodist University, Meadows School of the Arts, Division of Communication Arts, Dallas, TX 75275. Offers MA. Part-time and evening/weekend programs available. *Faculty:* 9 full-time (4 women), 2 part-time/adjunct (both women). *Students:* 27 full-time (19 women), 1 (woman) part-time; includes 6 minority (1 American Indian/Alaska Native, 5 Hispanic Americans), 5 international. Average age 27. 9 applicants, 78% accepted, 4 enrolled. In 2009, 6 master's awarded. *Degree requirements:* For master's, thesis or alternative. *Entrance requirements:* For master's, GRE General Test, minimum undergraduate GPA of 3.0 in major field during last 2 years. Additional exam requirements/recommendations for international students: Required—TOEFL (minimum score 550 paper-based; 213 computer-based; 80 iBT). *Application deadline:* For fall admission, 3/1 priority date for domestic and international students. Application fee: $75. *Financial support:* In 2009–10, 7 students received support, including 7 teaching assistantships (averaging $6,500 per year); research assistantships, scholarships/grants, tuition waivers (full), and unspecified assistantships also available. Financial award application deadline: 3/15. *Faculty research:* Digital sound, new technology, film and gender study, popular film and TV genres, Asian cinema. Total annual research expenditures: $10,000. *Unit head:* Rick Worland, Chair, 214-768-3708, Fax: 214-768-2784, E-mail: rworland@smu.edu. *Application contact:* Jean Cherry, Director of Graduate Admissions and Records, 214-768-3765, Fax: 214-768-3272, E-mail: jcherry@smu.edu.

Syracuse University, College of Visual and Performing Arts, Program in Film, Syracuse, NY 13244. Offers MFA. *Students:* 8 full-time (4 women); includes 1 minority (African American), 6 international. Average age 27. 28 applicants, 29% accepted, 2 enrolled. In 2009, 4 master's awarded. *Degree requirements:* For master's, thesis or alternative. *Entrance requirements:* For master's, portfolio. Additional exam requirements/recommendations for international students: Required—TOEFL (minimum score 100 iBT). *Application deadline:* For fall admission, 2/1 priority date for domestic and international students. Application fee: $75. Electronic applications accepted. *Expenses:* Tuition: Full-time $26,808; part-time $1117 per credit. Required fees: $1024. *Financial support:* Fellowships with tuition reimbursements, teaching assistantships with tuition reimbursements available. Financial award application deadline: 1/1; financial award applicants required to submit FAFSA. *Unit head:* Heath Hanlin, Chair, 315-443-1033, E-mail: hahanlin@syr.edu. *Application contact:* Harriett Conti, Assistant Dean for Recruitment and Admissions, 315-443-35755, E-mail: hmconti@syr.edu.

Syracuse University, S. I. Newhouse School of Public Communications, Program in Documentary Film and History, Syracuse, NY 13244. Offers MA. *Students:* 10 full-time (3 women), 1 part-time (0 women); includes 2 minority (1 African American, 1 Hispanic American), 2 international. Average age 27. 23 applicants, 83% accepted, 11 enrolled. In 2009, 4 master's awarded. *Entrance requirements:* For master's, GRE General Test. Additional exam requirements/recommendations for international students: Required—TOEFL (minimum score 100 iBT). *Application deadline:* For fall admission, 2/1 priority date for domestic and international students. Application fee: $45. Electronic applications accepted. *Expenses:* Tuition: Full-time $26,808; part-time $1117 per credit. Required fees: $1024. *Financial support:* Fellowships with tuition reimbursements, research assistantships with tuition reimbursements, teaching assistantships with tuition reimbursements, tuition waivers (partial) available. Financial award application deadline: 2/1. *Unit head:* Richard Breyer, Director, 315-443-9249. *Application contact:* Martha Coria, Graduate Records Office, 315-443-5749, Fax: 315-443-1834, E-mail: pcgrad@syr.edu.

Temple University, Graduate School, School of Communications and Theater, Department of Film and Media Arts, Philadelphia, PA 19122-6096. Offers MFA. Part-time programs available. *Degree requirements:* For master's, comprehensive exam, project. *Entrance requirements:* For master's, GRE General Test, minimum GPA of 3.0; exhibit. Additional exam requirements/recommendations for international students: Required—TOEFL (minimum score 550 paper-based; 213 computer-based; 79 iBT). Electronic applications accepted. *Faculty research:* Filmmaking and videography, documentary theory and practice, screenwriting, media culture studies, film studies.

Universidad Autonoma de Guadalajara, Graduate Programs, Guadalajara, Mexico. Offers administrative law and justice (LL M); advertising and corporate communications (MA); architecture (M Arch); business (MBA); computational science (MCC); education (Ed M, Ed D); English-Spanish translation (MA); fiscal law (MA); integrated management of digital animation (MA); international business (MIB); international corporate law (LL M); internet technologies (MS); labor health (MS); manufacturing systems (MMS); philosophy (MA, PhD); power electronics (MS); quality systems (MQS); renewable energy (MS); social evaluation of projects (MBA); strategic market research (MBA); teaching mathematics (MA).

Film, Television, and Video Production

The University of Alabama, Graduate School, College of Communication and Information Sciences, Department of Telecommunication and Film, Tuscaloosa, AL 35487-0152. Offers MA. *Faculty:* 8 full-time (2 women). *Students:* 7 full-time (3 women), 1 part-time (0 women), 3 international. Average age 27. 12 applicants, 25% accepted, 3 enrolled. In 2009, 5 degrees awarded. Terminal master's awarded for partial completion of doctoral program. *Degree requirements:* For master's, comprehensive exam, thesis or alternative. *Entrance requirements:* For master's, GRE, minimum GPA of 3.0. Additional exam requirements/recommendations for international students: Required—TOEFL (minimum score 600 paper-based; 79 iBT). *Application deadline:* For fall admission, 4/15 priority date for domestic students, 1/15 priority date for international students; for spring admission, 11/1 for domestic students, 10/1 priority date for international students. Applications are processed on a rolling basis. Application fee: $50 ($60 for international students). Electronic applications accepted. *Expenses:* Tuition, state resident: full-time $7000. Tuition, nonresident: full-time $19,200. *Financial support:* In 2009–10, 6 students received support, including 2 research assistantships with tuition reimbursements available (averaging $9,825 per year), 2 teaching assistantships with tuition reimbursements available (averaging $9,825 per year); institutionally sponsored loans also available. Financial award application deadline: 2/15. *Faculty research:* Entertainment theory, news and public affairs, effects of telecommunications, management, media law and policy. *Unit head:* Dr. Gary A. Copeland, Chair, 205-348-6350, Fax: 205-348-5162, E-mail: copeland@ua.edu. *Application contact:* Dr. Shuhua Zhou, Graduate Coordinator, 205-348-8653, Fax: 205-348-5162, E-mail: szhou@bama.ua.edu.

The University of British Columbia, Faculty of Arts, Creative Writing Program, Vancouver, BC V6T 1Z1, Canada. Offers creative writing (MFA); creative writing and film (MFA); creative writing and theatre (MFA). Part-time programs available. Postbaccalaureate distance learning degree programs offered (minimal on-campus study). *Degree requirements:* For master's, thesis. *Entrance requirements:* For master's, sample of written work. Additional exam requirements/recommendations for international students: Required—TOEFL (minimum score 550 paper-based; 213 computer-based). Electronic applications accepted. *Expenses:* Contact institution. *Faculty research:* Writing of fiction; poetry, creative nonfiction, plays for stage, screen, television, radio, writing for children and translation, song lyrics and libretto, new media and graphic novel.

The University of British Columbia, Faculty of Arts and Faculty of Graduate Studies, Department of Theatre and Film, Film Program, Vancouver, BC V6T 1Z2, Canada. Offers creative writing and film production (MFA); film production (MFA, Diploma); film studies (MA). *Degree requirements:* For master's, variable foreign language requirement, comprehensive exam, thesis (MA), thesis or project (MFA). *Entrance requirements:* For master's, portfolio (MFA). Additional exam requirements/recommendations for international students: Required—TOEFL (minimum score 600 paper-based; 250 computer-based). Electronic applications accepted. *Faculty research:* Film theory and violence; American and European cinema; cult cinema; Irish cinema.

University of California, Los Angeles, Graduate Division, Graduate School of Education and Information Studies, Department of Information Studies, Los Angeles, CA 90095. Offers archival studies (MLIS); informatics (MLIS); information studies (PhD); library and information science (Certificate); library studies (MLIS); moving image archive studies (MA); MBA/MLIS; MLIS/MA. *Accreditation:* ALA (one or more programs are accredited). *Faculty:* 14 full-time (8 women), 11 part-time/adjunct (10 women). *Students:* 171 full-time (125 women), 29 part-time (20 women); includes 76 minority (8 African Americans, 1 American Indian/Alaska Native, 44 Asian Americans or Pacific Islanders, 23 Hispanic Americans), 4 international. Average age 27. 214 applicants, 54% accepted, 82 enrolled. In 2009, 74 master's, 6 doctorates awarded. Terminal master's awarded for partial completion of doctoral program. *Degree requirements:* For master's, thesis or alternative, professional portfolio; for doctorate, thesis/dissertation, oral and written qualifying exams. *Entrance requirements:* For master's, GRE General Test, previous course work in computer programming and statistics; for doctorate, GRE General Test, previous course work in statistics, 2 samples of research writing in English. Additional exam requirements/recommendations for international students: Required—TOEFL (minimum score 613 paper-based; 220 computer-based; 87 iBT), IELTS (minimum score 7). *Application deadline:* For fall admission, 11/30 for domestic students, 10/30 for international students. Applications are processed on a rolling basis. Application fee: $60 ($80 for international students). Electronic applications accepted. *Financial support:* In 2009–10, 55 students received support, including 37 fellowships (averaging $15,750 per year), 12 research assistantships with partial tuition reimbursements available (averaging $28,600 per year), 6 teaching assistantships with partial tuition reimbursements available (averaging $54,040 per year); career-related internships or fieldwork, Federal Work-Study, institutionally sponsored loans, scholarships/grants, and unspecified assistantships also available. Financial award application deadline: 3/1; financial award applicants required to submit FAFSA. *Faculty research:* Multimedia, digital libraries, archives and electronic records, interface design, information technology and preservation, preservation, access. *Unit head:* Dr. Gregory H. Leazer, Associate Professor and Chair, 310-825-8799, E-mail: gleazer@ucla.edu. *Application contact:* Susan S. Abler, Student Affairs Officer, 310-825-5269, Fax: 310-206-4460, E-mail: abler@gseis.ucla.edu.

University of California, Los Angeles, Graduate Division, School of Theater, Film and Television, Department of Film, Television, and Digital Media, Los Angeles, CA 90034. Offers film and television (MA, MFA, PhD); MFA/MA. *Students:* 271 full-time (136 women); includes 76 minority (17 African Americans, 4 American Indian/Alaska Native, 26 Asian Americans or Pacific Islanders, 29 Hispanic Americans), 28 international. Average age 30. 1,043 applicants, 12% accepted, 86 enrolled. In 2009, 93 master's, 4 doctorates awarded. *Degree requirements:* For master's, comprehensive exam; for doctorate, one foreign language, thesis/dissertation, oral and written qualifying exams. *Entrance requirements:* For master's, film or TV project, animation, or script (MFA), minimum GPA of 3.0; for doctorate, GRE General Test, minimum undergraduate GPA of 3.0. Application fee: $70 ($90 for international students). Electronic applications accepted. *Financial support:* In 2009–10, 216 fellowships with full and partial tuition reimbursements, 15 research assistantships with full and partial tuition reimbursements, 138 teaching assistantships with full and partial tuition reimbursements were awarded; Federal Work-Study, institutionally sponsored loans, scholarships/grants, health care benefits, tuition waivers (full and partial), and unspecified assistantships also available. Financial award application deadline: 3/1; financial award applicants required to submit FAFSA. *Unit head:* Barbara Boyle, Chair, 310-825-7741. *Application contact:* Department Office, 310-825-7741, E-mail: info@tft.ucla.edu.

University of California, Santa Barbara, Graduate Division, College of Letters and Sciences, Division of Humanities and Fine Arts, Department of Film and Media Studies, Santa Barbara, CA 93106-4010. Offers PhD, MA/PhD. *Faculty:* 21 full-time (12 women). *Students:* 20 full-time (12 women). Average age 27. 112 applicants, 10% accepted, 5 enrolled. *Degree requirements:* For doctorate, one foreign language, comprehensive exam, thesis/dissertation. *Entrance requirements:* For doctorate, GRE, 3 letters of recommendation, statement of purpose, personal achievements/contributions statement, resume/curriculum vitae, transcripts for post-secondary institutions attended. Additional exam requirements/recommendations for international students: Required—TOEFL (minimum score 600 paper-based; 250 computer-based; 100 iBT) or IELTS (minimum score 7). *Application deadline:* For fall admission, 12/1 for domestic and international students. Application fee: $70 ($90 for international students). Electronic applications accepted. *Financial support:* In 2009–10, 20 students received support, including 10 fellowships with full and partial tuition reimbursements available (averaging $18,300 per year), 16 teaching assistantships with partial tuition reimbursements available (averaging $10,600 per year); career-related internships or fieldwork, Federal Work-Study, institutionally sponsored loans, scholarships/grants, health care benefits, tuition waivers (full and partial), and unspecified assistantships also available. Financial award application deadline: 12/1; financial award applicants required to submit FAFSA. *Faculty research:* Global media, broadcast history, cultural studies, film history and historiography, documentary film, film and ethnography, the Western and trauma and memory, classical and contemporary film theory, aesthetics, narrative, point of view, analysis, film history and theory, media studies, feminist theory, science and technology studies, contemporary art, post-colonial media theory, Asian cinemas, cinema and media of the Americas. *Unit head:* Dr. Lisa Parks, Chair, 805-893-5547, Fax: 805-893-8630, E-mail: parks@filmandmedia.ucsb.edu. *Application contact:* Melany J. Miners, Graduate Program Assistant, 805-893-8535, Fax: 805-893-8630, E-mail: mminers@filmandmedia.ucsb.edu.

University of Central Arkansas, Graduate School, College of Fine Arts and Communication, Program in Digital Filmmaking, Conway, AR 72035-0001. Offers MFA. *Accreditation:* NASAD. *Faculty:* 5 full-time (0 women). *Students:* 24 full-time (6 women), 3 part-time (0 women); includes 2 minority (1 African American, 1 Asian American or Pacific Islander), 1 international. Average age 28. 9 applicants, 89% accepted, 6 enrolled. In 2009, 1 master's awarded. *Degree requirements:* For master's, thesis. *Entrance requirements:* For master's, GRE General Test, minimum GPA of 2.7. Additional exam requirements/recommendations for international students: Required—TOEFL (minimum score 550 paper-based; 213 computer-based). *Application deadline:* For fall admission, 3/1 priority date for domestic and international students; for spring admission, 10/1 priority date for domestic and international students. Applications are processed on a rolling basis. Application fee: $25 ($50 for international students). *Expenses:* Tuition, state resident: full-time $5136; part-time $214 per credit hour. Required fees: $379.50; $127 per term. Tuition and fees vary according to course level, course load and campus/location. *Financial support:* Unspecified assistantships available. *Unit head:* Dr. Joseph Anderson, Chair, 501-450-3162, E-mail: josepha@uca.edu. *Application contact:* Brenda Herring, Admissions Assistant, 501-450-5065, Fax: 501-450-5678, E-mail: bherring@uca.edu.

University of Central Florida, College of Arts and Humanities, Division of Film and Digital Media, Orlando, FL 32816. Offers interactive entertainment (MS). *Students:* 50 full-time (5 women), 49 part-time (5 women); includes 31 minority (5 African Americans, 5 Asian Americans or Pacific Islanders, 21 Hispanic Americans), 6 international. Average age 25. 92 applicants, 64% accepted, 49 enrolled. In 2009, 31 master's awarded. Application fee: $30. *Expenses:* Tuition, state resident: part-time $306.31 per credit hour. Tuition, nonresident: part-time $1099.01 per credit hour. Part-time tuition and fees vary according to degree level and program. *Financial support:* In 2009–10, 1 student received support, including 1 fellowship with partial tuition reimbursement available (averaging $10,000 per year), 3 research assistantships (averaging $3,200 per year), 2 teaching assistantships (averaging $6,400 per year). *Unit head:* Dr. Jose Maunez-Cuadra, Interim Chair, 407-823-2121, Fax: 407-317-7094, E-mail: info@fiea.ucf.edu. *Application contact:* Dr. Jose Maunez-Cuadra, Interim Chair, 407-823-2121, Fax: 407-317-7094, E-mail: info@fiea.ucf.edu.

University of Denver, Division of Arts, Humanities and Social Sciences, Department of Mass Communications, Denver, CO 80208. Offers advertising management (MS); digital media studies (MA); mass communications (MA); public relations (MS); video production (MA). Part-time programs available. *Faculty:* 14 full-time (8 women), 4 part-time/adjunct (3 women). *Students:* 37 full-time (28 women), 32 part-time (27 women); includes 8 minority (1 African American, 2 Asian Americans or Pacific Islanders, 5 Hispanic Americans), 3 international. Average age 26. 163 applicants, 64% accepted, 45 enrolled. In 2009, 24 master's awarded. *Degree requirements:* For master's, thesis (for some programs). *Entrance requirements:* For master's, GRE General Test. Additional exam requirements/recommendations for international students: Required—TOEFL, TWE. *Application deadline:* Applications are processed on a rolling basis. Application fee: $50. Electronic applications accepted. *Expenses:* Tuition: Full-time $34,596; part-time $961 per quarter hour. Required fees: $4 per quarter hour. Tuition and fees vary according to course load, campus/location and program. *Financial support:* In 2009–10, 10 research assistantships with full and partial tuition reimbursements (averaging $14,000 per year), 5 teaching assistantships with full and partial tuition reimbursements (averaging $11,500 per year) were awarded; career-related internships or fieldwork, Federal Work-Study, institutionally sponsored loans, and scholarships/grants also available. Support available to part-time students. Financial award application deadline: 3/1; financial award applicants required to submit FAFSA. *Faculty research:* Youth and civic engagement. Total annual research expenditures: $162,000. *Unit head:* Dr. Diane Waldman, Chair, 303-871-2008. *Application contact:* Information Contact, 303-871-2008, E-mail: mcom@du.edu.

The University of Iowa, Graduate College, College of Liberal Arts and Sciences, Department of Cinema and Comparative Literature, Program in Film and Video Production, Iowa City, IA 52242-1316. Offers MA, MFA. *Degree requirements:* For master's, thesis (for some programs), exam. *Entrance requirements:* For master's, GRE General Test, minimum GPA of 3.0. Additional exam requirements/recommendations for international students: Required—TOEFL (minimum score 550 paper-based; 213 computer-based; 81 iBT). Electronic applications accepted.

University of Memphis, Graduate School, College of Communication and Fine Arts, Department of Communication, Memphis, TN 38152. Offers communication (MA); communication arts (PhD); film and video production (MA). Part-time programs available. *Faculty:* 12 full-time (6 women). *Students:* 35 full-time (21 women), 15 part-time (9 women); includes 8 minority (6 African Americans, 1 American Indian/Alaska Native, 1 Asian American or Pacific Islander), 1 international. Average age 35. 47 applicants, 66% accepted, 13 enrolled. In 2009, 6 master's, 4 doctorates awarded. *Degree requirements:* For master's, comprehensive exam, thesis or alternative; for doctorate, comprehensive exam, thesis/dissertation. *Entrance requirements:* For master's and doctorate, GRE General Test. Additional exam requirements/recommendations for international students: Required—TOEFL (minimum score 550 paper-based; 210 computer-based). *Application deadline:* For fall admission, 8/1 for domestic students. Application fee: $35 ($60 for international students). *Expenses:* Tuition, state resident: full-time $6246; part-time $347 per credit hour. Tuition, nonresident: full-time $15,894; part-time $883 per credit hour. Required fees: $1160. Full-time tuition and fees vary according to course load, degree level and program. *Financial support:* In 2009–10, 27 students received support; research assistantships with full tuition reimbursements available, teaching assistantships with full tuition reimbursements available, Federal Work-Study, scholarships/grants, and unspecified assistantships available. Financial award application deadline: 2/15; financial award applicants required to submit FAFSA. *Faculty research:* Rhetoric, media studies, applied communication (health communication). *Unit head:* Dr. Mike Leff, Chair, 901-678-2565, Fax: 901-678-4331, E-mail: m_leff@bellsouth.net. *Application contact:* Dr. Sandra Sarkela, Coordinator of Graduate Studies, 901-678-3173, Fax: 901-678-4331, E-mail: ssarkela@memphis.edu.

University of Miami, Graduate School, School of Communication, Coral Gables, FL 33124. Offers communication (PhD); communication studies (MA); film studies (MA, PhD); motion pictures (MFA), including production, producing, and screenwriting; print journalism (MA); public relations (MA); Spanish language journalism (MA); television broadcast journalism (MA). *Accreditation:* ACEJMC. Part-time programs available. *Degree requirements:* For master's, comprehensive exam (for some programs), thesis (for some programs); for doctorate, comprehensive exam, thesis/dissertation. *Entrance requirements:* For master's, GRE General Test; for doctorate, GRE General Test, master's thesis or scholarly research. Additional exam requirements/recommendations for international students: Required—TOEFL (minimum score 600 paper-based; 250 computer-based; 100 iBT). Electronic applications accepted. *Faculty research:* Communication studies, mass communication, international/interpersonal communication, film studies, journalism.

University of Nevada, Las Vegas, Graduate College, College of Fine Arts, Department of Film, Las Vegas, NV 89154-5015. Offers screenwriting (MFA). Part-time programs available. *Faculty:* 6 full-time (0 women), 7 part-time/adjunct (0 women). *Students:* 5 full-time (2 women). Average age 41. 16 applicants, 31% accepted, 5 enrolled. In 2009, 2 master's awarded. *Degree requirements:* For master's, comprehensive exam, creative project. *Entrance requirements:* Additional exam requirements/recommendations for international students: Required—TOEFL (minimum score 550 paper-based; 213 computer-based), IELTS (minimum score 7). *Application deadline:* For fall admission, 1/15 priority date for domestic and international students. Applications are processed on a rolling basis. Application fee: $60 ($95 for international students). Electronic applications accepted. *Financial support:* In 2009–10, 8 teaching assistantships with partial tuition reimbursements (averaging $10,000 per year) were awarded; institutionally sponsored loans, scholarships/grants, health care benefits, and unspecified assistantships also available. Financial award application deadline: 3/1. *Faculty research:* Filmmaking: directing, producing, cinematography, editing; screenwriting; film archiving and restoration; film study publication; literary fiction. *Unit head:* Francisco Menendez, Chair/Professor, 702-895-4223, Fax: 702-895-4395, E-mail: francisco.menendez@unlv.edu. *Application contact:* Graduate College Admissions Evaluator, 702-895-3320, Fax: 702-895-4180, E-mail: gradcollege@unlv.edu.

University of New Orleans, Graduate School, College of Liberal Arts, Department of Film, Theatre and Communication Arts, New Orleans, LA 70148. Offers film production (MFA); theatre directing (MFA); theatre performance (MFA). *Accreditation:* NAST. *Degree requirements:* For master's, comprehensive exam, thesis. *Entrance requirements:* Additional exam requirements/recommendations for international students: Required—TOEFL (minimum score 550 paper-based; 213 computer-based; 79 iBT). Electronic applications accepted. *Faculty research:* Mass communication theory, nineteenth- and twentieth-century theater history, film criticism and history.

The University of North Carolina at Greensboro, Graduate School, College of Arts and Sciences, Department of Broadcasting and Cinema, Greensboro, NC 27412-5001. Offers film and video production (MFA).

University of North Carolina School of the Arts, School of Filmmaking, Winston-Salem, NC 27127-2188. Offers film music composition (MFA). *Faculty:* 1 full-time (0 women). *Students:* 7 full-time (0 women); includes 1 minority (Asian American or Pacific Islander). Average age 25. 6 applicants, 33% accepted, 2 enrolled. In 2009, 3 master's awarded. *Entrance requirements:* For master's, audition, performance, portfolio, interview. *Application deadline:* For fall admission, 4/1 priority date for domestic students. Applications are processed on a rolling basis. Application fee: $60 ($100 for international students). *Expenses:* Tuition, state resident: full-time $3797. Tuition, nonresident: full-time $15,670. Required fees: $1992. *Financial support:* In 2009–10, fellowships (averaging $2,000 per year); career-related internships or fieldwork and Federal Work-Study also available. Support available to part-time students. Financial award application deadline: 3/15; financial award applicants required to submit FAFSA. *Unit head:* Jordan Kerner, Dean, 336-770-1330, Fax: 336-770-1339, E-mail: kernerj@uncsa.edu. *Application contact:* Sheeler Lawson, Director of Admissions, 336-770-3290, Fax: 336-770-3370, E-mail: admissions@uncsa.edu.

University of North Texas, Robert B. Toulouse School of Graduate Studies, College of Arts and Sciences, Department of Radio, Television and Film, Denton, TX 76203. Offers MA, MFA, MS. Part-time programs available. *Degree requirements:* For master's, thesis, thesis production (MFA). *Entrance requirements:* For master's, GRE General Test, 2 letters of recommendation, writing sample, goal statement (MA, MS); portfolio, 3 letters of recommendation, writing sample, goal statement (MFA). Additional exam requirements/recommendations for international students: Required—proof of English language proficiency required for non-native English speakers; Recommended—TOEFL (minimum score 550 paper-based; 213 computer-based; 79 iBT). *Application deadline:* Applications are processed on a rolling basis. Application fee: $50 ($75 for international students). Electronic applications accepted. *Expenses:* Tuition, state resident: full-time $4298; part-time $239 per contact hour. Tuition, nonresident: full-time $9878; part-time $549 per contact hour. Required fees: $265 per contact hour. *Financial support:* Fellowships, research assistantships, teaching assistantships, career-related internships or fieldwork, Federal Work-Study, and institutionally sponsored loans available. Financial award applicants required to submit FAFSA. *Faculty research:* Media law and regulation, industry studies, film and broadcasting history, documentary production, critical and cultural studies. *Application contact:* Director of Graduate Studies, 940-565-3222, Fax: 940-369-7838, E-mail: samuel.sauls@unt.edu.

University of Oklahoma, Graduate College, College of Fine Arts, School of Art and Art History, Norman, OK 73019. Offers art (MA, MFA); art history (MA, MFA); ceramics (MFA); film and video (MFA); painting (MFA); photography (MFA); printmaking (MFA); visual communications (MFA). *Faculty:* 27 full-time (11 women). *Students:* 25 full-time (13 women), 13 part-time (12 women); includes 8 minority (2 African Americans, 5 American Indian/Alaska Native, 1 Asian American or Pacific Islander), 6 international. 36 applicants, 53% accepted, 11 enrolled. In 2009, 4 master's awarded. *Degree requirements:* For master's, thesis (MA), exhibit (MFA), departmental qualifying exam. *Entrance requirements:* For master's, GRE General Test (MA), bachelor's degree in art (MFA) or art history (MA), minimum GPA of 3.0 in last 60 undergraduate hours, 3 letters of recommendation, written research paper. Additional exam requirements/recommendations for international students: Required—TOEFL (minimum score 550 paper-based; 213 computer-based). *Application deadline:* For fall admission, 2/1 priority date for domestic students, 2/1 for international students; for spring admission, 10/1 for domestic and international students. Applications are processed on a rolling basis. Application fee: $40 ($90 for international students). Electronic applications accepted. *Expenses:* Tuition, state resident: full-time $3744; part-time $156 per credit hour. Tuition, nonresident: full-time $13,577; part-time $565.70 per credit hour. Required fees: $2415; $90.10 per credit hour. *Financial support:* In 2009–10, 26 students received support, including 17 research assistantships with partial tuition reimbursements available (averaging $9,940 per year), 1 teaching assistantship with partial tuition reimbursement available (averaging $9,586 per year); career-related internships or fieldwork, Federal Work-Study, institutionally sponsored loans, scholarships/grants, health care benefits, tuition waivers (full and partial), and unspecified assistantships also available. Financial award application deadline: 4/7; financial award applicants required to submit FAFSA. *Faculty research:* Native American art history and art of the American West, contemporary and figurative sculpture, painting and print making, graphic design, media. Total annual research expenditures: $34,861. *Unit head:* Mary Jo Watson, Director, 405-325-2691, Fax: 405-325-1668, E-mail: mjwatson@ou.edu. *Application contact:* Jonathan Hils, Graduate Liaison, 405-325-2691, Fax: 405-325-1668, E-mail: hils@ou.edu.

University of Southern California, Graduate School, School of Cinematic Arts, Division of Animation and Digital Arts, Los Angeles, CA 90089. Offers MFA. *Faculty:* 8 full-time (5 women), 14 part-time/adjunct (5 women). *Students:* 43 full-time (20 women); includes 9 minority (2 African Americans, 1 American Indian/Alaska Native, 2 Asian Americans or Pacific Islanders, 4 Hispanic Americans), 12 international. In 2009, 13 master's awarded. *Degree requirements:* For master's, thesis, digital media and research. *Application deadline:* For fall admission, 12/1 for domestic and international students. Electronic applications accepted. *Expenses:* Contact institution. *Financial support:* In 2009–10, 21 students received support, including 6 fellowships with partial tuition reimbursements available; career-related internships or fieldwork, scholarships/grants, and tuition waivers (partial) also available. Financial award application deadline: 3/9; financial award applicants required to submit FAFSA. *Faculty research:* Science visualization, visual effects, experimental animation, documentary visualization, motion graphics. *Unit head:* Sheila M. Sofian, Department Chair and Associate Professor, 213-740-7595, Fax: 213-740-5869, E-mail: ssofian@cinema.usc.edu. *Application contact:* Daphne M. Sigismondi, Assistant Director, 213-740-3986, Fax: 213-740-5869, E-mail: dsigismondi@cinema.usc.edu.

University of Southern California, Graduate School, School of Cinematic Arts, Division of Film and Television Production, Los Angeles, CA 90089. Offers film and television production (MFA). *Faculty:* 34 full-time (8 women), 76 part-time/adjunct (13 women). *Students:* 341 full-time (100 women), 33 part-time (11 women); includes 105 minority (29 African Americans, 3 American Indian/Alaska Native, 32 Asian Americans or Pacific Islanders, 41 Hispanic Americans), 52 international. In 2009, 66 master's awarded. Terminal master's awarded for partial completion of doctoral program. *Degree requirements:* For master's, advanced project. *Entrance requirements:* Additional exam requirements/recommendations for international students: Required—TOEFL (minimum score 600 paper-based; 250 computer-based; 100 iBT). *Application deadline:* For fall admission, 12/1 for domestic and international students; for spring admission, 9/1 for domestic and international students. Application fee: $85. Electronic applications accepted. *Expenses:* Tuition: Full-time $25,980; part-time $1315 per unit. Required fees: $554. One-time fee: $35 full-time. Full-time tuition and fees vary according to degree level and program. *Financial support:* In 2009–10, 51 students received support, including 5 fellowships with partial tuition reimbursements available (averaging $20,000 per year), 117 teaching assistantships (averaging $3,000 per year); career-related internships or fieldwork, Federal Work-Study, institutionally sponsored loans, scholarships/grants, health care benefits, and student assistantships also available. Support available to part-time students. Financial award application deadline: 5/3; financial award applicants required to submit FAFSA. *Faculty research:* Documentary filmmaking, narrative filmmaking, initiatives related to health issues, public service announcements on social issues. Total annual research expenditures: $50,000. *Unit head:* Michael Taylor, Chair, 213-821-3113, Fax: 213-740-3395, E-mail: taylor@cinema.usc.edu. *Application contact:* Admissions Director, 213-740-8358, Fax: 213-740-4013, E-mail: admissions@cinema.usc.edu.

University of Southern California, Graduate School, School of Cinematic Arts, The Peter Stark Producing Program, Los Angeles, CA 90089. Offers motion picture producing (MFA). *Faculty:* 1 full-time (0 women), 23 part-time/adjunct (4 women). *Students:* 50 full-time (20 women); includes 8 minority (4 African Americans, 2 Asian Americans or Pacific Islanders, 2 Hispanic Americans), 12 international. 192 applicants, 13% accepted, 25 enrolled. In 2009, 25 master's awarded. *Degree requirements:* For master's, thesis, oral examination. *Entrance requirements:* For master's, GRE. Additional exam requirements/recommendations for international students: Required—TOEFL (minimum score 600 paper-based; 250 computer-based; 100 iBT), IELTS (minimum score 7). *Application deadline:* For fall admission, 12/10 for domestic and international students. Application fee: $85. Electronic applications accepted. *Expenses:* Tuition: Full-time $25,980; part-time $1315 per unit. Required fees: $554. One-time fee: $35 full-time. Full-time tuition and fees vary according to degree level and program. *Financial support:* In 2009–10, 30 students received support, including 11 fellowships (averaging $1,112 per year), 2 teaching assistantships with partial tuition reimbursements available; institutionally sponsored loans, scholarships/grants, and departmental assistantships also available. Financial award application deadline: 3/13. *Unit head:* Prof. Lawrence Turman, Assistant Director, 213-740-3304, Fax: 213-745-6652, E-mail: lturman@cinema.usc.edu. *Application contact:* Richard Shepherd, Assistant Director, 213-740-3304, Fax: 213-745-6652, E-mail: rshepherd@cinema.usc.edu.

University of Southern California, Graduate School, School of Cinematic Arts, Writing for Screen and Television Division, Los Angeles, CA 90089. Offers MFA, Graduate Certificate. *Students:* 72 full-time (34 women), 2 part-time (1 woman); includes 17 minority (7 African Americans, 7 Asian Americans or Pacific Islanders, 3 Hispanic Americans), 4 international. 238 applicants, 15% accepted, 33 enrolled. In 2009, 26 master's awarded. *Degree requirements:* For master's, thesis. *Entrance requirements:* For master's, GRE. *Application deadline:* For fall admission, 12/1 for domestic and international students. Electronic applications accepted. *Expenses:* Tuition: Full-time $25,980; part-time $1315 per unit. Required fees: $554. One-time fee: $35 full-time. Full-time tuition and fees vary according to degree level and program. *Financial support:* Fellowships with partial tuition reimbursements available. Financial award application deadline: 3/10; financial award applicants required to submit FAFSA. *Unit head:* Jack Epps, Chair, 213-740-3303, E-mail: jepps@cinema.usc.edu. *Application contact:* Kristen Wiley Davis, Program Manager, 213-740-3303, E-mail: writing@cinema.usc.edu.

The University of Texas at Austin, Graduate School, College of Communication, Department of Radio-Television-Film, Austin, TX 78712-1111. Offers film and video production (MFA); radio-television-film (MA, PhD); screenwriting (MFA). *Degree requirements:* For master's, thesis (for some programs); for doctorate, thesis/dissertation. *Entrance requirements:* For master's and doctorate, GRE General Test. Electronic applications accepted. *Faculty research:* International communication, film studies, media and culture, telecommunication and new media, gender and sexuality.

University of the Sacred Heart, Graduate Programs, Department of Communication, San Juan, PR 00914-0383. Offers contemporary culture and media (MA); digital journalism (Certificate); editing for media (MA, Certificate); public relations (MA, Certificate); publicity (MA, Certificate); scriptwriting (MA, Certificate). Part-time and evening/weekend programs available. *Degree requirements:* For master's, thesis.

University of Utah, The Graduate School, College of Fine Arts, Division of Film Studies, Salt Lake City, UT 84112-0380. Offers MFA. *Faculty:* 6 full-time (2 women), 3 part-time/adjunct (0 women). *Students:* 8 full-time (6 women), 2 part-time (both women), 1 international. Average age 31. 23 applicants, 22% accepted, 4 enrolled. In 2009, 5 master's awarded. *Degree requirements:* For master's, comprehensive exam, film or video portfolio. *Entrance requirements:* For master's, minimum GPA of 3.0. Additional exam requirements/recommendations for international students: Required—TOEFL (minimum score 500 paper-based; 173 computer-based). *Application deadline:* For fall admission, 11/30 for domestic and international students. Application fee: $55 ($65 for international students). *Expenses:* Tuition, state resident: full-time $4004; part-time $1674 per semester. Tuition, nonresident: full-time $14,134; part-time $5915 per semester. Required fees: $324 per semester. Tuition and fees vary according to course load, degree level and program. *Financial support:* In 2009–10, teaching assistantships with full and partial tuition reimbursements (averaging $8,500 per year); career-related internships or fieldwork, Federal Work-Study, institutionally sponsored loans, and health care benefits also available. Financial award application deadline: 3/1; financial award applicants required to submit FAFSA. *Faculty research:* Film history, criticism, cultural studies, production of narrative and documentary films. Total annual research expenditures: $44,826. *Unit head:* Prof. Kevin D. Hauson, Chair, 801-581-7428, Fax: 801-585-3192, E-mail: kevin.hauson@utah.edu. *Application contact:* Dr. Chris Lippard, Director of Graduate Studies, 801-585-9358, Fax: 801-585-3192, E-mail: c.lippard@utah.edu.

University of Victoria, Faculty of Graduate Studies, Faculty of Fine Arts, Department of Visual Arts, Victoria, BC V8W 2Y2, Canada. Offers digital multimedia (MFA); drawing (MFA); painting (MFA); photography (MFA); sculpture (MFA); video (MFA). *Degree requirements:* For master's, exhibit, oral exam. *Entrance requirements:* For master's, portfolio, BFA. Additional exam requirements/recommendations for international students: Required—TOEFL (minimum score 575 paper-based; 233 computer-based), IELTS (minimum score 7). Electronic applications accepted.

University of Wisconsin–Milwaukee, Graduate School, Peck School of the Arts, Program in Performing Arts, Milwaukee, WI 53201-0413. Offers dance (MFA); film (MFA); theatre (MFA). Part-time programs available. *Faculty:* 31 full-time (19 women). *Students:* 18 full-time (12 women), 2 part-time (both women); includes 4 minority (2 African Americans, 1 Asian American or Pacific Islander, 1 Hispanic American), 1 international. Average age 34. 23 applicants, 22% accepted, 3 enrolled. In 2009, 18 master's awarded. *Degree requirements:* For master's, variable foreign language requirement, comprehensive exam, thesis or alternative. *Entrance requirements:* For master's, audition, interview. Additional exam requirements/recommendations for international students: Required—TOEFL (minimum score 550 paper-based; 79 iBT), IELTS (minimum score 6.5). *Application deadline:* For fall admission, 1/1 priority date for domestic students; for spring admission, 9/1 for domestic students. Applications are processed on a rolling basis. Application fee: $45 ($75 for international students). *Expenses:* Tuition, state resident: full-time $8800. Tuition, nonresident: full-time $20,760. Tuition and fees vary according to program and reciprocity agreements. *Financial support:* In 2009–10, 15 teaching assistantships were awarded; career-related internships or fieldwork and unspecified assistantships also available. Support available to part-time students. Financial award application deadline: 4/15. *Unit head:* Simone Ferro, Representative, 414-229-4178, E-mail: sferro@uwm.edu. *Application contact:* General Information Contact, 414-229-4982, Fax: 414-229-6967, E-mail: gradschool@uwm.edu.

York University, Faculty of Graduate Studies, Faculty of Fine Arts, Program in Film, Toronto, ON M3J 1P3, Canada. Offers MA, MFA, PhD. *Degree requirements:* For master's, thesis. *Entrance requirements:* For master's, portfolio. Electronic applications accepted.

Film, Television, and Video Theory and Criticism

Boston University, College of Communication, Department of Film and Television, Boston, MA 02215. Offers film production (MFA); film studies (MFA); media ventures (MS); screenwriting (MFA); television production (MS); MBA/MS. Part-time programs available. *Faculty:* 13 full-time, 27 part-time/adjunct. *Students:* 108 full-time (49 women), 5 part-time (2 women); includes 11 minority (4 African Americans, 1 American Indian/Alaska Native, 3 Asian Americans or Pacific Islanders, 3 Hispanic Americans), 19 international. Average age 27. In 2009, 16 master's awarded. *Degree requirements:* For master's, thesis. *Entrance requirements:* For master's, GRE General Test, sample of written or creative work. Additional exam requirements/recommendations for international students: Required—TOEFL (minimum score 600 paper-based; 250 computer-based; 100 iBT). *Application deadline:* For fall admission, 2/1 for domestic and international students. Application fee: $70. Electronic applications accepted. *Expenses:* Tuition: Full-time $37,910; part-time $1184 per credit hour. Required fees: $386; $40 per semester. Part-time tuition and fees vary according to class time, course level, degree level and program. *Financial support:* Teaching assistantships with partial tuition reimbursements, career-related internships or fieldwork, Federal Work-Study, institutionally sponsored loans, scholarships/grants, and unspecified assistantships available. Support available to part-time students. Financial award application deadline: 2/1; financial award applicants required to submit FAFSA. *Unit head:* Paul Schneider, Chairman, 617-353-3483, Fax: 617-353-1084, E-mail: ftvchair@bu.edu. *Application contact:* Kate Iserman, Administrator of Graduate Services, 617-353-3481, Fax: 617-358-0399, E-mail: comgrad@bu.edu.

See Close-Up on page 675.

California College of the Arts, Graduate Programs, Program in Visual and Critical Studies, San Francisco, CA 94107. Offers MA. *Degree requirements:* For master's, thesis, exhibit. *Entrance requirements:* For master's, appropriate bachelor's degree, portfolio. Additional exam requirements/recommendations for international students: Required—TOEFL (minimum score 600 paper-based; 250 computer-based). Electronic applications accepted.

Central Michigan University, College of Graduate Studies, College of Communication and Fine Arts, School of Broadcasting and Cinematic Arts, Mount Pleasant, MI 48859. Offers electronic media management (MA); electronic media studies (MA); film theory and criticism (MA); media production (MA). Part-time programs available. *Degree requirements:* For master's, thesis or alternative. *Entrance requirements:* For master's, undergraduate degree in broadcasting, film studies, or an associated discipline with minimum GPA of 2.7. Electronic applications accepted. *Faculty research:* Multimedia production, film history and criticism, writing and promotions, international broadcasting and media systems, history of American broadcasting.

Claremont Graduate University, Graduate Programs, School of Arts and Humanities, Department of English, Claremont, CA 91711-6160. Offers American studies (MA, PhD); critical theory (MA, PhD); early modern studies (MA, PhD); English (M Phil, MA, PhD); literary theory (PhD); literature (MA, PhD); literature and creative writing (MA); literature and film (MA); MBA/MA; MBA/PhD. Part-time programs available. *Faculty:* 2 full-time (1 woman), 2 part-time/adjunct (0 women). *Students:* 83 full-time (60 women), 19 part-time (11 women); includes 17 minority (1 African American, 1 American Indian/Alaska Native, 8 Asian Americans or Pacific Islanders, 7 Hispanic Americans), 4 international. Average age 35. In 2009, 6 master's, 4 doctorates awarded. *Entrance requirements:* For master's and doctorate, GRE General Test. Additional exam requirements/recommendations for international students: Required—TOEFL (minimum score 550 paper-based; 213 computer-based; 80 iBT). *Application deadline:* For fall admission, 2/1 priority date for domestic students. Applications are processed on a rolling basis. Application fee: $60. Electronic applications accepted. *Expenses:* Tuition: Full-time $35,046; part-time $1524 per credit. Required fees: $161 per semester. *Financial support:* Fellowships, Federal Work-Study, institutionally sponsored loans, and scholarships/grants available. Support available to part-time students. Financial award application deadline: 2/15; financial award applicants required to submit FAFSA. *Faculty research:* American, comparative, and English Renaissance literature; modernism; feminist literature and theory. *Unit head:* Wendy Martin, Chair, 909-621-8612, Fax: 909-607-1221, E-mail: wendy.martin@cgu.edu. *Application contact:* Susan Hampson, Admissions Coordinator, 909-607-1278, Fax: 909-607-1221, E-mail: humanities@cgu.edu.

College of Staten Island of the City University of New York, Graduate Programs, Program in Cinema and Media Studies, Staten Island, NY 10314-6600. Offers MA. Part-time and evening/weekend programs available. *Faculty:* 3 full-time (2 women). *Students:* 1 full-time (0 women), 18 part-time (7 women); includes 1 minority (African American), 4 international. Average age 28. 31 applicants, 65% accepted, 10 enrolled. In 2009, 7 master's awarded. *Degree requirements:* For master's, comprehensive exam, original film, media or production thesis or written examination. *Entrance requirements:* For master's, 10-12 page critical writing sample on film or media topic, 3 letters of recommendation. Additional exam requirements/recommendations for international students: Required—TOEFL (minimum score 550 paper-based; 213 computer-based; 79 iBT). *Application deadline:* For fall admission, 4/15 priority date for domestic and international students; for spring admission, 11/15 for domestic and international students. Applications are processed on a rolling basis. Application fee: $125. Electronic applications accepted. *Expenses:* Tuition, state resident: full-time $7360; part-time $310 per credit. Tuition, nonresident: part-time $575 per credit. Required fees: $378; $113 per semester. *Financial support:* In 2009–10, 4 teaching assistantships (averaging $1,250 per year) were awarded; career-related internships or fieldwork, Federal Work-Study, and scholarships/grants also available. Support available to part-time students. Financial award applicants required to submit FAFSA. *Unit head:* Dr. Matthew Solomon, Coordinator/Associate Professor, 718-982-2548, E-mail: cinemamasters@mail.csi.cuny.edu. *Application contact:* Sasha Spence, Assistant Director of Graduate Recruitment and Admissions, 718-982-2699, Fax: 718-982-2500, E-mail: sasha.spence@csi.cuny.edu.

Concordia University, School of Graduate Studies, Faculty of Fine Arts, Mel Hoppenheim School of Cinema, Montréal, QC H3G 1M8, Canada. Offers film studies (MA).

Emory University, Graduate School of Arts and Sciences, Department of Film Studies, Atlanta, GA 30322-1100. Offers MA, PhD/Certificate. *Degree requirements:* For master's, comprehensive exam, thesis or alternative. *Entrance requirements:* For master's, GRE General Test, 3 letters of reference, 2 writing samples. Additional exam requirements/recommendations for international students: Required—TOEFL. Electronic applications accepted. *Faculty research:* International film history, film theory, film style, feminism and film, reception.

Emory University, Graduate School of Arts and Sciences, Department of Spanish and Portuguese, Atlanta, GA 30322-1100. Offers comparative literature (Certificate); film studies (Certificate); Spanish (PhD); women's studies (Certificate). *Degree requirements:* For doctorate, 2 foreign languages, comprehensive exam, thesis/dissertation. *Entrance requirements:* For doctorate, GRE General Test. Additional exam requirements/recommendations for international students: Required—TOEFL. Electronic applications accepted. *Faculty research:* Spanish literature, Spanish-American literature, literary theory, criticism, cultural studies.

Florida Atlantic University, Dorothy F. Schmidt College of Arts and Letters, School of Communication and Multimedia Studies, Boca Raton, FL 33431-0991. Offers communication studies (MA); film and video (Certificate); film studies (MA); multimedia journalism studies (MA). Part-time programs available. *Faculty:* 21 full-time (10 women), 14 part-time/adjunct (3 women). *Students:* 14 full-time (11 women), 13 part-time (8 women); includes 3 minority (1 African American, 1 Asian American or Pacific Islander, 1 Hispanic American), 3 international. Average age 28. 39 applicants, 26% accepted, 6 enrolled. In 2009, 7 master's awarded. *Degree requirements:* For master's, one foreign language, comprehensive exam (for some programs), thesis (for some programs). *Entrance requirements:* For master's, GRE General Test, minimum GPA of 3.0. *Application deadline:* For fall admission, 7/1 priority date for domestic students, 4/1 for international students; for spring admission, 11/1 for domestic students, 10/1 for international students. Applications are processed on a rolling basis. Application fee: $30. Electronic applications accepted. *Expenses:* Tuition, state resident: full-time $7055; part-time $293.94 per credit hour. Tuition, nonresident: full-time $22,096; part-time $920.66 per credit hour. *Financial support:* Teaching assistantships with partial tuition reimbursements, Federal Work-Study and institutionally sponsored loans available. Support available to part-time students. Financial award application deadline: 3/1. *Faculty research:* Cultural studies, gender studies, film, communication theory, journalism, new media. *Unit head:* Dr. Susan S. Reilly, Director, 561-297-1095, Fax: 561-297-2615, E-mail: sreilly@fau.edu. *Application contact:* Dr. Eric M. Freedman, Graduate Coordinator, 561-297-2534, Fax: 561-297-2615, E-mail: efreedma@fau.edu.

Hollins University, Graduate Programs, Program in Screenwriting and Film Studies, Roanoke, VA 24020-1603. Offers MA, MFA. Offered during summer only. Part-time programs available. *Faculty:* 2 full-time (1 woman), 5 part-time/adjunct (3 women). *Students:* 37 full-time (22 women), 1 (woman) part-time; includes 8 minority (6 African Americans, 2 Hispanic Americans), 2 international. Average age 34. 22 applicants, 86% accepted, 13 enrolled. In 2009, 8 master's awarded. *Degree requirements:* For master's, one foreign language, comprehensive exam, thesis. *Entrance requirements:* For master's, letters of recommendation, portfolio. Additional exam requirements/recommendations for international students: Required—TOEFL (minimum score 550 paper-based; 213 computer-based; 79 iBT). *Application deadline:* For fall admission, 2/15 for domestic and international students. Application fee: $40. Electronic applications accepted. *Expenses:* Tuition: Full-time $27,780; part-time $295 per contact hour. Required fees: $280; $70 per unit. Part-time tuition and fees vary according to course load and program. *Financial support:* In 2009–10, 10 students received support, including 5 fellowships (averaging $1,000 per year); Federal Work-Study and scholarships/grants also available. Support available to part-time students. Financial award application deadline: 2/15; financial award applicants required to submit FAFSA. *Faculty research:* German film, women in film, censorship, minorities in film. *Unit head:* Dr. Klaus Phillips, Director, 540-362-6308, E-mail: kphillips@hollins.edu. *Application contact:* Cathy S. Koon, Manager of Graduate Services, 540-362-6326, Fax: 540-362-6288, E-mail: ckoon@hollins.edu.

Indiana University Bloomington, University Graduate School, College of Arts and Sciences, Department of Communication and Culture, Bloomington, IN 47405-7000. Offers film and media studies (PhD); performance and ethnography (PhD); rhetoric and public culture (PhD). *Faculty:* 24 full-time (12 women). *Students:* 85 full-time (43 women), 1 (woman) part-time; includes 9 minority (1 African American, 1 Asian American or Pacific Islander, 7 Hispanic Americans), 9 international. Average age 32. 179 applicants, 15% accepted, 15 enrolled. In 2009, 5 master's, 11 doctorates awarded. *Degree requirements:* For master's, comprehensive exam; for doctorate, one foreign language, comprehensive exam, thesis/dissertation, student teaching. *Entrance requirements:* For master's and doctorate, GRE General Test (recommended), minimum GPA of 3.0, 3 letters of recommendation, writing sample. Additional exam requirements/recommendations for international students: Required—TOEFL (minimum score 550 paper-based; 213 computer-based). *Application deadline:* For winter admission, 1/1 for domestic students, 12/1 for international students. Application fee: $55 ($65 for international students). Electronic applications accepted. *Financial support:* In 2009–10, 65 students received support, including 4 fellowships with full tuition reimbursements available (averaging $18,000 per year), 61 teaching assistantships with full tuition reimbursements available (averaging $12,961 per year). Financial award application deadline: 4/15. *Faculty research:* Rhetoric and public culture, film and media studies, performance ethnography. *Unit head:* Prof. Gregory A. Waller, Chair, 812-855-2367, Fax: 812-855-6014, E-mail: cmcl@indiana.edu. *Application contact:* Kathy P. Teige, Graduate Secretary, 812-855-6389, Fax: 812-855-6014, E-mail: kteige@indiana.edu.

New York University, Tisch School of the Arts and Graduate School of Arts and Science, Department of Cinema Studies, New York, NY 10012-1019. Offers cinema studies (MA, PhD); moving image archiving and preservation (MA). *Faculty:* 15 full-time, 9 part-time/adjunct. *Students:* 70 full-time (36 women), 2 part-time (1 woman); includes 14 minority (1 African American, 1 American Indian/Alaska Native, 6 Asian Americans or Pacific Islanders, 6 Hispanic Americans). Average age 31. 233 applicants, 42% accepted, 49 enrolled. In 2009, 26 master's, 8 doctorates awarded. *Degree requirements:* For master's, comprehensive exam; for doctorate, one foreign language, thesis/dissertation, 3 comprehensive exams. *Entrance requirements:* For master's, GRE, sample of written work; for doctorate, GRE, master's degree, writing sample. Additional exam requirements/recommendations for international students: Required—TOEFL, IELTS or ALI. *Application deadline:* For fall admission, 12/1 for domestic and international students. Application fee: $60. Electronic applications accepted. *Expenses:* Contact institution. *Financial support:* In 2009–10, 59 students received support, including 45 fellowships with full and partial tuition reimbursements available, 10 research assistantships, 4 teaching assistantships; Federal Work-Study, institutionally sponsored loans, tuition waivers (full and partial), and unspecified assistantships also available. Support available to part-time students. Financial award application deadline: 2/15; financial award applicants required to submit FAFSA. *Faculty research:* History and aesthetics of American, European, and Third World cinemas; theory of film and the moving image; cultural studies; gay and lesbian media. *Unit head:* Dr. Richard Allen, Chair, 212-998-1600. *Application contact:* Dan Sandford, Director of Graduate Admissions, 212-998-1918, Fax: 212-995-4060, E-mail: tisch.gradadmissions@nyu.edu.

Ohio University, Graduate College, College of Fine Arts, School of Film, Athens, OH 45701-2979. Offers film (MFA); film studies (MA). *Faculty:* 8 full-time (2 women), 2 part-time/adjunct (1 woman). *Students:* 48 full-time (15 women), 5 part-time (2 women); includes 5 minority (3 African Americans, 1 Asian American or Pacific Islander, 1 Hispanic American), 18 international. Average age 25. 109 applicants, 23% accepted, 16 enrolled. In 2009, 12 master's awarded. *Degree requirements:* For master's, one foreign language, thesis. *Entrance requirements:* Additional exam requirements/recommendations for international students: Required—TOEFL (minimum score 550 paper-based; 80 iBT) or IELTS Academic (minimum score 6.5). *Application deadline:* For fall admission, 2/1 for domestic and international students. Application fee: $50 ($55 for international students). Electronic applications accepted. *Expenses:* Tuition, state resident: full-time $7839; part-time $323 per quarter hour. Tuition, nonresident: full-time $15,831; part-time $654 per quarter hour. Required fees: $2931. *Financial support:* In 2009–10, 34 students received support; research assistantships with full tuition reimbursements available, teaching assistantships with full tuition reimbursements available, institutionally sponsored loans, scholarships/grants, tuition waivers (full and partial), and unspecified assistantships available. Financial award application deadline: 2/1. *Faculty research:* Scriptwriting, sound, editing, cinematography, film theory, digital post production. *Unit head:* Steven Ross, Director, 740-593-9969, Fax: 740-593-1328, E-mail: rosss2@ohio.edu. *Application contact:* Tamra LaGraff, Administrative Associate, 740-593-1323, Fax: 740-593-1328, E-mail: lagraff@ohio.edu.

San Francisco State University, Division of Graduate Studies, College of Creative Arts, Department of Cinema, San Francisco, CA 94132-1722. Offers cinema (MFA); cinema studies (MA).

Savannah College of Art and Design, Graduate School, Program in Cinema Studies, Savannah, GA 31402-3146. Offers MA. Part-time programs available. *Degree requirements:*

For master's, thesis. *Entrance requirements:* For master's, interview. Additional exam requirements/recommendations for international students: Required—TOEFL (minimum score 450 paper-based; 133 computer-based). Electronic applications accepted. *Expenses:* Tuition: Full-time $28,515; part-time $627 per credit hour. One-time fee: $500. Tuition and fees vary according to course load.

Syracuse University, S. I. Newhouse School of Public Communications, Program in Documentary Film and History, Syracuse, NY 13244. Offers MA. *Students:* 10 full-time (3 women), 1 part-time (0 women); includes 2 minority (1 African American, 1 Hispanic American), 2 international. Average age 27. 23 applicants, 83% accepted, 11 enrolled. In 2009, 4 master's awarded. *Entrance requirements:* For master's, GRE General Test. Additional exam requirements/recommendations for international students: Required—TOEFL (minimum score 100 iBT). *Application deadline:* For fall admission, 2/1 priority date for domestic and international students. Application fee: $45. Electronic applications accepted. *Expenses:* Tuition: Full-time $26,808; part-time $1117 per credit. Required fees: $1024. *Financial support:* Fellowships with tuition reimbursements, research assistantships with tuition reimbursements, teaching assistantships with tuition reimbursements, tuition waivers (partial) available. Financial award application deadline: 2/1. *Unit head:* Richard Breyer, Director, 315-443-9249. *Application contact:* Martha Coria, Graduate Records Office, 315-443-5749, Fax: 315-443-1834, E-mail: pcgrad@syr.edu.

Université de Montréal, Faculty of Arts and Sciences, Department of Art History and Film Studies, Montréal, QC H3C 3J7, Canada. Offers art history (MA, PhD); film studies (MA, PhD). *Degree requirements:* For master's, thesis. Electronic applications accepted. *Faculty research:* Western art from the Middle Ages, classic and modern theory, modern and contemporary art, Canadian art.

Université de Montréal, Faculty of Arts and Sciences, Department of Literatures and Modern Languages, Montréal, QC H3C 3J7, Canada. Offers German literature (PhD); German studies (MA); Hispanic literature (PhD); Hispanic studies (MA); literature and cinema (PhD). Terminal master's awarded for partial completion of doctoral program. *Degree requirements:* For master's, 2 foreign languages, thesis; for doctorate, 2 foreign languages, thesis/dissertation, general exam. Electronic applications accepted.

Université Laval, Faculty of Letters, Department of Literature, Programs in Literature and Arts of the Screen and Stage, Québec, QC G1K 7P4, Canada. Offers MA, PhD. Part-time programs available. Terminal master's awarded for partial completion of doctoral program. *Degree requirements:* For master's, thesis; for doctorate, comprehensive exam, thesis/dissertation. *Entrance requirements:* For master's and doctorate, linguistics exams, knowledge of French, knowledge of a second language. Electronic applications accepted.

The University of British Columbia, Faculty of Arts and Faculty of Graduate Studies, Department of Theatre and Film, Film Program, Vancouver, BC V6T 1Z2, Canada. Offers creative writing and film production (MFA); film production (MFA, Diploma); film studies (MA). *Degree requirements:* For master's, variable foreign language requirement, comprehensive exam, thesis (MA), thesis or project (MFA). *Entrance requirements:* For master's, portfolio (MFA). Additional exam requirements/recommendations for international students: Required—TOEFL (minimum score 600 paper-based; 250 computer-based). Electronic applications accepted. *Faculty research:* Film theory and violence; American and European cinema; cult cinema; Irish cinema.

University of Chicago, Division of the Humanities, Committee on Cinema and Media Studies, Chicago, IL 60637-1513. Offers AM, PhD. *Degree requirements:* For master's, one foreign language, thesis; for doctorate, 2 foreign languages, thesis/dissertation.

The University of Iowa, Graduate College, College of Liberal Arts and Sciences, Department of Cinema and Comparative Literature, Program in Film Studies, Iowa City, IA 52242-1316. Offers MA, PhD. *Degree requirements:* For master's, thesis optional, exam; for doctorate, comprehensive exam, thesis/dissertation. *Entrance requirements:* For master's and doctorate, GRE General Test, minimum GPA of 3.0. Additional exam requirements/recommendations for international students: Required—TOEFL (minimum score 550 paper-based; 213 computer-based; 81 iBT). Electronic applications accepted.

The University of Kansas, Graduate Studies, College of Liberal Arts and Sciences, Department of Film and Media Studies, Lawrence, KS 66045. Offers MA, PhD. *Faculty:* 10 full-time (2 women). *Students:* 24 full-time (7 women), 2 part-time (0 women); includes 1 minority (Asian American or Pacific Islander), 5 international. Average age 34. 8 applicants, 100% accepted, 7 enrolled. *Degree requirements:* For master's, thesis; for doctorate, one foreign language, comprehensive exam, thesis/dissertation. *Entrance requirements:* For master's, GRE General Test, minimum GPA of 3.2; for doctorate, GRE General Test, minimum GPA of 3.5; MA in film, or related field. Additional exam requirements/recommendations for international students: Required—TOEFL. *Application deadline:* For fall admission, 2/15 for domestic and international students. *Expenses:* Tuition, state resident: full-time $6492; part-time $270.50 per credit hour. Tuition, nonresident: full-time $15,510; part-time $646.25 per credit hour. Required fees: $847; $70.56 per credit hour. Tuition and fees vary according to course load and program. *Financial support:* Teaching assistantships with full and partial tuition reimbursements available. Financial award application deadline: 1/1; financial award applicants required to submit FAFSA. *Faculty research:* Film and media theory, film and media history, East Asian cinema, Latin American cinema, film and video production. *Unit head:* Dr. Tamara L. Falicov, Chair, 785-864-1353, Fax: 785-331-2671, E-mail: tfalicov@ku.edu. *Application contact:* Dr. Michael Baskett, Associate Professor, 785-864-1384, Fax: 785-331-2671, E-mail: eiga@ku.edu.

The University of Kansas, Graduate Studies, College of Liberal Arts and Sciences, Department of Theatre and Film, Lawrence, KS 66045. Offers theatre (MA, PhD); theatre design (MFA), including scenography. *Faculty:* 15 full-time (7 women). *Students:* 17 full-time (9 women), 2 part-time (1 woman), 1 international. Average age 32. 19 applicants, 58% accepted, 4 enrolled. In 2009, 2 master's, 3 doctorates awarded. *Degree requirements:* For master's, thesis; for doctorate, one foreign language, comprehensive exam, thesis/dissertation. *Entrance requirements:* For master's, GRE General Test, minimum GPA of 3.2; for doctorate, GRE General Test, minimum GPA of 3.5; MA or MFA in theatre or related field. Additional exam requirements/recommendations for international students: Required—TOEFL. *Application deadline:* For fall admission, 1/1 priority date for domestic students, 1/1 for international students. Application fee: $45 ($55 for international students). Electronic applications accepted. *Expenses:* Tuition, state resident: full-time $6492; part-time $270.50 per credit hour. Tuition, nonresident: full-time $15,510; part-time $646.25 per credit hour. Required fees: $847; $70.56 per credit hour. Tuition and fees vary according to course load and program. *Financial support:* Fellowships with tuition reimbursements, research assistantships with full tuition reimbursements, teaching assistantships with full and partial tuition reimbursements, Federal Work-Study, scholarships/grants, and unspecified assistantships available. Financial award application deadline: 1/1. *Faculty research:* Theatre history, performance studies, scenography, theatre historiography. *Unit head:* John Staniunas, Chair, 785-864-3511, Fax: 785-864-5251, E-mail: stanj@ku.edu. *Application contact:* Dr. Henry Bial, Director of Graduate Studies, 785-864-3511, Fax: 785-864-5251, E-mail: hbial@ku.edu.

University of Miami, Graduate School, School of Communication, Coral Gables, FL 33124. Offers communication (PhD); communication studies (MA); film studies (MA, PhD); motion pictures (MFA), including production, producing, and screenwriting; print journalism (MA); public relations (MA); Spanish language journalism (MA); television broadcast journalism (MA). *Accreditation:* ACEJMC. Part-time programs available. *Degree requirements:* For master's, comprehensive exam (for some programs), thesis (for some programs); for doctorate, comprehensive exam, thesis/dissertation. *Entrance requirements:* For master's, GRE General Test; for doctorate, GRE General Test, master's thesis or scholarly research. Additional exam requirements/recommendations for international students: Required—TOEFL (minimum score 600 paper-based; 250 computer-based; 100 iBT). Electronic applications accepted. *Faculty research:* Communication studies, mass communication, international/interpersonal communication, film studies, journalism.

University of Michigan, Horace H. Rackham School of Graduate Studies, College of Literature, Science, and the Arts, Department of Screen Arts and Cultures, Ann Arbor, MI 48109. Offers PhD, Certificate. *Faculty:* 10 full-time (3 women). *Students:* 8 full-time (5 women), 1 international. Average age 28. 48 applicants, 8% accepted; 4 enrolled. In 2009, 3 other advanced degrees awarded. *Degree requirements:* For doctorate, one foreign language, comprehensive exam, thesis/dissertation; for Certificate, Certificate program: 15 credit hours (3 directed study). *Entrance requirements:* For doctorate, GRE. Additional exam requirements/recommendations for international students: Required—TOEFL. *Application deadline:* For fall admission, 12/15 for domestic and international students. Application fee: $60 ($75 for international students). Electronic applications accepted. *Expenses:* Tuition, state resident: full-time $17,286; part-time $1099 per credit hour. Tuition, nonresident: full-time $34,944; part-time $2080 per credit hour. Required fees: $95 per semester. Tuition and fees vary according to course load, degree level and program. *Financial support:* In 2009–10, 8 students received support, including 2 fellowships with full tuition reimbursements available (averaging $52,000 per year), 3 teaching assistantships with full tuition reimbursements available (averaging $52,000 per year); scholarships/grants, health care benefits, unspecified assistantships, and summer research funds also available. Financial award application deadline: 12/15; financial award applicants required to submit FAFSA. *Faculty research:* Transnational cinema, classical Hollywood cinema, silent cinema, film theory, television. *Unit head:* Prof. Markus Nornes, Chair, 734-763-1314, Fax: 734-936-1846, E-mail: amnornes@umich.edu. *Application contact:* Carrie Moore, Student Services Coordinator, 734-647-6909, Fax: 734-936-1846, E-mail: ctave@umich.edu.

University of Southern California, Graduate School, School of Cinematic Arts, Division of Critical Studies, Los Angeles, CA 90089. Offers cinema-television (MA); cinema-television (critical studies) (PhD). *Faculty:* 12 full-time (6 women), 9 part-time/adjunct (3 women). *Students:* 81 full-time (46 women), 2 part-time (both women); includes 21 minority (7 African Americans, 8 Asian Americans or Pacific Islanders, 6 Hispanic Americans), 12 international. 180 applicants, 25% accepted, 20 enrolled. In 2009, 15 master's, 9 doctorates awarded. *Degree requirements:* For master's, comprehensive exam, thesis or alternative; for doctorate, comprehensive exam, thesis/dissertation. *Entrance requirements:* For master's and doctorate, GRE. Additional exam requirements/recommendations for international students: Recommended—TOEFL (minimum score 100 iBT). *Application deadline:* For fall admission, 12/1 for domestic and international students. Application fee: $85. *Expenses:* Tuition: Full-time $25,980; part-time $1315 per unit. Required fees: $554. One-time fee: $35 full-time. Full-time tuition and fees vary according to degree level and program. *Financial support:* In 2009–10, 12 students received support, including 11 fellowships with full tuition reimbursements available (averaging $24,545 per year), 40 teaching assistantships with full tuition reimbursements available (averaging $16,863 per year); scholarships/grants also available. Financial award application deadline: 1/19. *Faculty research:* Transnational cinema; race and cultural studies; global media, television studies; digital media; feminist studies. *Unit head:* Dr. Akira Mizuta Lippit, Chair, 213-740-6919, Fax: 213-740-9471, E-mail: lippit@usc.edu. *Application contact:* Linda Overholt, Program Coordinator, 213-740-7515, Fax: 213-740-9471, E-mail: loverholt@cinema.usc.edu.

University of South Florida, Graduate School, College of Arts and Sciences, Department of Humanities and Cultural Studies, Tampa, FL 33617. Offers American studies (MA); film studies (MLA); humanities (MLA). Part-time and evening/weekend programs available. *Faculty:* 8 full-time (4 women). *Students:* 26 full-time (18 women), 14 part-time (9 women); includes 10 minority (7 African Americans, 3 Hispanic Americans). Average age 32. 24 applicants, 58% accepted, 11 enrolled. In 2009, 15 master's awarded. *Degree requirements:* For master's, comprehensive exam, thesis. *Entrance requirements:* For master's, GRE General Test, minimum GPA of 3.0 in last 60 hours, academic writing sample. Additional exam requirements/recommendations for international students: Required—TOEFL (minimum score 550 paper-based; 213 computer-based). *Application deadline:* For fall admission, 2/15 priority date for domestic students, 1/2 for international students; for spring admission, 10/15 priority date for domestic students, 6/1 for international students. Application fee: $30. *Financial support:* In 2009–10, 4 teaching assistantships with tuition reimbursements were awarded; scholarships/grants also available. Financial award application deadline: 4/4. *Faculty research:* American South, American autobiography, material culture, critical theory, cultural studies. *Unit head:* Daniel Belgrad, Chairperson, 813-974-9388, Fax: 813-974-9409, E-mail: dbelgrad@cas.usf.edu. *Application contact:* Maria Cizmic, Program Director, 813-974-9383, Fax: 813-974-9409, E-mail: mcizmic@cas.usf.edu.

University of Wisconsin–Madison, Graduate School, College of Letters and Science, Department of Communication Arts, Madison, WI 53706-1380. Offers communication science (MA, PhD); film (MA, PhD); media and cultural studies (MA, PhD); rhetoric (MA, PhD). Terminal master's awarded for partial completion of doctoral program. *Degree requirements:* For master's, one foreign language, thesis (for some programs); for doctorate, one foreign language, thesis/dissertation. *Entrance requirements:* For master's and doctorate, GRE General Test, minimum GPA of 3.5. Electronic applications accepted. *Expenses:* Tuition, state resident: part-time $594 per credit. Tuition, nonresident: part-time $1504 per credit. Required fees: $65 per credit. Tuition and fees vary according to course load, program and reciprocity agreements.

Wilfrid Laurier University, Faculty of Graduate Studies, Faculty of Arts, Department of English and Film Studies, Waterloo, ON N2L 3C5, Canada. Offers MA, PhD. *Degree requirements:* For master's, thesis optional; for doctorate, thesis/dissertation. *Entrance requirements:* For master's, honours BA or the equivalent in English, minimum B+ in English courses above first year level; for doctorate, MA in English, minimum A- average in graduate work. Additional exam requirements/recommendations for international students: Recommended—TOEFL (minimum score 230 computer-based; 89 iBT). Electronic applications accepted. *Faculty research:* Gender and genre, Canadian studies, early modern studies, postcolonial studies, nineteenth century studies.

Yale University, Graduate School of Arts and Sciences, Department of East Asian Languages and Literatures, New Haven, CT 06520. Offers East Asian languages and literatures (PhD); East Asian languages and literatures and film studies (PhD). *Degree requirements:* For doctorate, 2 foreign languages, thesis/dissertation. *Entrance requirements:* For doctorate, GRE General Test.

Yale University, Graduate School of Arts and Sciences, Department of Slavic Languages and Literatures, New Haven, CT 06520. Offers medieval Slavic literature and philology (PhD); Polish literature (PhD); Russian literature (PhD); Slavic languages and literatures and film studies (PhD). *Degree requirements:* For doctorate, 3 foreign languages, thesis/dissertation. *Entrance requirements:* For doctorate, GRE General Test.

Yale University, Graduate School of Arts and Sciences, Interdisciplinary Program in Film Studies, New Haven, CT 06520. Offers PhD.

Section 6
Performing Arts

This section contains a directory of institutions offering graduate work in performing arts, followed by an in-depth entry submitted by an institution that chose to prepare detailed a program description. Additional information about programs listed in the directory but not augmented by an in-depth entry may be obtained by writing directly to the dean of a graduate school or chair of a department at the address given in the directory.

For programs offering related work, see also in this book *Area and Cultural Studies, Art and Art History, Communication and Media,* and *Film, Television, and Video.* In another guide in this series:

Graduate Programs in Business, Education, Health, Information Studies, Law & Social Work

See *Leisure Studies and Recreation, Subject Areas (Music Education),* and *Physical Education and Kinesiology*

CONTENTS

Program Directories

Dance 214
Music 217
Theater 245
Therapies—Dance, Drama, and Music 258

Close-Up

Columbia University 261

See also:

Pratt Institute—Art and Design 119
The University of the Arts—Graduate Studies 199

Dance

Arizona State University, Graduate College, Herberger College of the Arts, Department of Dance, Tempe, AZ 85287. Offers MFA. *Degree requirements:* For master's, thesis optional.

Bennington College, Graduate Programs, MFA in Dance Program, Bennington, VT 05201. Offers MFA. Part-time programs available. *Faculty:* 3 full-time (2 women), 3 part-time/adjunct (all women). *Students:* 2 full-time (0 women); includes 1 minority (African American). Average age 37. 6 applicants, 50% accepted, 2 enrolled. *Degree requirements:* For master's, performances. *Application deadline:* For fall admission, 2/1 for domestic students. Application fee: $60. *Expenses:* Tuition: Full-time $20,950; part-time $2935 per course. One-time fee: $75. Tuition and fees vary according to program. *Financial support:* In 2009–10, 2 students received support, including 2 teaching assistantships (averaging $20,950 per year); unspecified assistantships also available. Financial award application deadline: 4/1; financial award applicants required to submit FAFSA. *Faculty research:* Exploration of relationship between emergent improvisation and complex systems. *Unit head:* Terry Creach, Associate Dean for Academic Affairs, 802-440-4406, Fax: 802-440-4876, E-mail: tcreach@bennington.edu. *Application contact:* Mary Surdam, Admissions Coordinator, 802-440-4312, Fax: 802-440-4320, E-mail: admissions@bennington.edu.

California Institute of the Arts, School of Dance, Valencia, CA 91355-2340. Offers MFA, Adv C. *Accreditation:* NASD. *Degree requirements:* For master's, thesis presentation. *Entrance requirements:* For master's, audition, video of choreography. Additional exam requirements/recommendations for international students: Required—TOEFL.

California State University, Fullerton, Graduate Studies, College of the Arts, Department of Theatre and Dance, Fullerton, CA 92834-9480. Offers acting (MFA); acting and directing (MA); dance (MA); directing (MFA); dramatic literature/criticism (MA); oral interpretation (MA); playwriting (MA); technical theater (MA); technical theater and design (MFA); television (MA); theatre for children (MA); theatre history (MA). *Accreditation:* NASD; NAST (one or more programs are accredited). Part-time programs available. *Students:* 15 full-time (6 women), 3 part-time (1 woman); includes 3 minority (1 African American, 2 Hispanic Americans). Average age 29. 14 applicants, 50% accepted, 7 enrolled. In 2009, 5 master's awarded. *Degree requirements:* For master's, oral and written exam, project or thesis. *Entrance requirements:* For master's, major in theatre or related field, audition or interview, minimum GPA of 2.5 in last 60 units of course work. Application fee: $55. *Expenses:* Tuition, nonresident: full-time $11,160; part-time $373 per credit. Required fees: $1440 per term. Tuition and fees vary according to course load, degree level and program. *Financial support:* Career-related internships or fieldwork, Federal Work-Study, institutionally sponsored loans, and scholarships/grants available. Support available to part-time students. Financial award application deadline: 3/1; financial award applicants required to submit FAFSA. *Unit head:* Dr. Susan Hallman, Chair, 657-278-3628. *Application contact:* Admissions/Applications, 657-278-2371.

California State University, Long Beach, Graduate Studies, College of the Arts, Department of Dance, Long Beach, CA 90840. Offers MA, MFA. *Accreditation:* NASD. Part-time programs available. *Faculty:* 2 full-time (both women). *Students:* 6 full-time (5 women). Average age 27. 48 applicants, 48% accepted, 4 enrolled. *Degree requirements:* For master's, thesis. *Application deadline:* Applications are processed on a rolling basis. Application fee: $5. Electronic applications accepted. *Expenses:* Required fees: $1802 per semester. Part-time tuition and fees vary according to course load. *Financial support:* Federal Work-Study, institutionally sponsored loans, scholarships/grants, and traineeships available. Financial award application deadline: 3/2. *Unit head:* Prof. Cyrus Parker-Jeannette, Chair, 562-985-4747, Fax: 562-985-7896, E-mail: cyparker@csulb.edu. *Application contact:* Dr. Colleen Dunagan, Graduate Advisor, 562-985-7040, Fax: 562-985-7896, E-mail: cdunagan@csulb.edu.

California State University, Sacramento, Graduate Studies, College of Arts and Letters, Department of Theatre and Dance, Sacramento, CA 95819. Offers MA. *Accreditation:* NAST. Part-time programs available. *Degree requirements:* For master's, thesis or alternative, writing proficiency exam. *Entrance requirements:* For master's, GRE General Test, BA in drama or equivalent, minimum GPA of 2.5 during previous 2 years of course work. Additional exam requirements/recommendations for international students: Required—TOEFL. Electronic applications accepted.

Case Western Reserve University, School of Graduate Studies, Department of Theater and Dance, Cleveland, OH 44106. Offers acting (MFA); contemporary dance (MFA); dance (MA); theater (MFA). *Degree requirements:* For master's, thesis, oral presentation and defense, portfolio, thesis concert production and presentation (MFA). *Entrance requirements:* For master's, audition, interview. Additional exam requirements/recommendations for international students: Required—TOEFL (minimum score 550 paper-based; 213 computer-based; 79 iBT). Electronic applications accepted. *Faculty research:* Playwriting; history of theater; participation in professional area theaters in performing, design, acting, coaching, and dance.

The College at Brockport, State University of New York, School of Arts, Humanities and Social Sciences, Department of Dance, Brockport, NY 14420-2997. Offers dance (MA, MFA), including choreography/performance (MA), dance education (preK-12) (MA), dance studies (MA). *Accreditation:* NASD. Part-time programs available. *Students:* 16 full-time (15 women), 6 part-time (all women); includes 7 minority (4 African Americans, 2 Asian Americans or Pacific Islanders, 1 Hispanic American). 23 applicants, 43% accepted, 6 enrolled. In 2009, 8 master's awarded. *Degree requirements:* For master's, thesis or alternative. *Entrance requirements:* For master's, local writing assessment assignment, audition/interview, minimum GPA of 3.0, letters of recommendation. Additional exam requirements/recommendations for international students: Required—TOEFL (minimum score 550 paper-based; 213 computer-based; 79 iBT). *Application deadline:* For fall admission, 4/15 priority date for domestic and international students. Application fee: $50. Electronic applications accepted. *Expenses:* Tuition, state resident: full-time $8370; part-time $349 per credit. Tuition, nonresident: full-time $13,250; part-time $522 per credit. *Financial support:* In 2009–10, 3 teaching assistantships with full tuition reimbursements (averaging $6,000 per year) were awarded; Federal Work-Study, scholarships/grants, and unspecified assistantships also available. Support available to part-time students. Financial award application deadline: 3/15; financial award applicants required to submit FAFSA. *Faculty research:* Choreography and performance, world dance and culture, dance process and theory, dance education, dance science and somatics. *Unit head:* Dr. Jacqueline Davis, Chairperson, 585-395-2153, Fax: 585-395-5134, E-mail: jdavis@brockport.edu. *Application contact:* Dr. Maura Keefe, Graduate Program Director, 585-395-5302, Fax: 585-395-5134, E-mail: mkeefe@brockport.edu.

Florida State University, The Graduate School, College of Visual Arts, Theatre and Dance, School of Dance, Tallahassee, FL 32306-2120. Offers American dance studies (MA); dance (MFA); studio and related studies (MA). *Accreditation:* NASD. *Faculty:* 15 full-time (9 women), 9 part-time/adjunct (7 women). *Students:* 33 full-time (32 women); includes 8 minority (all African Americans). Average age 28. 26 applicants, 65% accepted, 12 enrolled. In 2009, 13 master's awarded. *Degree requirements:* For master's, comprehensive exam (for some programs), thesis (for some programs), technical proficiency (MFA), 1 foreign language (MA). *Entrance requirements:* For master's, GRE General Test (MA in American dance studies), audition, writing sample (MFA, MA in dance). Additional exam requirements/recommendations for international students: Required—TOEFL (minimum score 550 paper-based; 213 computer-based). *Application deadline:* For fall admission, 1/20 priority date for domestic students, 1/21 priority date for international students; for spring admission, 11/1 priority date for domestic students, 7/1 priority date for international students. Applications are processed on a rolling basis. Application fee: $30. Electronic applications accepted. *Expenses:* Tuition, state resident: full-time $7413. Tuition, nonresident: full-time $22,567. *Financial support:* In 2009–10, 30 students received support, including 9 research assistantships with full tuition reimbursements available (averaging $5,000 per year), 21 teaching assistantships with full tuition reimbursements available (averaging $5,000 per year); fellowships with full tuition reimbursements available, scholarships/grants, health care benefits, and unspecified assistantships also available. Financial award application deadline: 6/30; financial award applicants required to submit FAFSA. *Faculty research:* Choreography, performance, dance and cultural significance, American dance history, dance technology. Total annual research expenditures: $131,959. *Unit head:* Russell Sandifer, Professor and Co-Chair, 850-644-1024, Fax: 850-644-1277, E-mail: rsandifer@fsu.edu. *Application contact:* Prof. Patricia Phillips, Co-Chair, 850-644-1024, Fax: 850-644-1277, E-mail: pphillips@fsu.edu.

George Mason University, College of Visual and Performing Arts, Program in Dance, Fairfax, VA 22030. Offers MFA. *Faculty:* 8 full-time (5 women), 7 part-time/adjunct (5 women). *Students:* Average age 35. 1 applicant. In 2009, 3 master's awarded. *Degree requirements:* For master's, choreographed performance. *Entrance requirements:* For master's, video of choreography or performance, resume, 3 letters of recommendation, curriculum vitae. *Application deadline:* For fall admission, 4/1 for domestic students. Application fee: $75. Electronic applications accepted. *Expenses:* Tuition, state resident: full-time $7568; part-time $315.33 per credit hour. Tuition, nonresident: full-time $21,704; part-time $904.33 per credit hour. Required fees: $2184; $91 per credit hour. *Financial support:* In 2009–10, 1 student received support, including 1 teaching assistantship (averaging $2,835 per year); career-related internships or fieldwork and institutionally sponsored loans also available. Support available to part-time students. Financial award application deadline: 3/1; financial award applicants required to submit FAFSA. *Faculty research:* Choreography, performance. *Unit head:* Elizabeth Price, Chair, 703-993-2137, E-mail: eprice@gmu.edu. *Application contact:* Karen Studd, Associate Professor, 703-993-3196, E-mail: kstudd@gmu.edu.

Hollins University, Graduate Programs, Program in Dance, Roanoke, VA 24020-1603. Offers MFA. Part-time programs available. *Faculty:* 2 full-time (1 woman), 2 part-time/adjunct (both women). *Students:* 21 full-time (17 women), 1 part-time (0 women); includes 4 minority (3 African Americans, 1 Asian American or Pacific Islander), 6 international. Average age 34. 80 applicants, 41% accepted, 16 enrolled. In 2009, 15 master's awarded. *Degree requirements:* For master's, thesis. *Entrance requirements:* For master's, videotape of selected works, 3 letters of recommendation, resume. Additional exam requirements/recommendations for international students: Required—TOEFL (minimum score 550 paper-based; 213 computer-based; 79 iBT). *Application deadline:* For fall admission, 12/1 for domestic and international students. Application fee: $40. Electronic applications accepted. *Expenses:* Tuition: Full-time $27,780; part-time $295 per contact hour. Required fees: $280; $70 per unit. Part-time tuition and fees vary according to course load and program. *Financial support:* In 2009–10, 22 students received support, including 22 fellowships (averaging $4,000 per year); teaching assistantships. Support available to part-time students. Financial award application deadline: 2/2. *Unit head:* Donna Faye Burchfield, Artistic Director, 540-362-6596, E-mail: dburchfield@hollins.edu. *Application contact:* Cathy S. Koon, Manager of Graduate Services, 540-362-6326, Fax: 540-362-6288, E-mail: ckoon@hollins.edu.

Mills College, Graduate Studies, Department of Dance, Oakland, CA 94613-1000. Offers dance (MA, MFA), including choreography and performance (MA). Part-time programs available. *Faculty:* 4 full-time (3 women), 5 part-time/adjunct (4 women). *Students:* 18 full-time (all women); includes 5 minority (3 African Americans, 2 Asian Americans or Pacific Islanders), 2 international. Average age 31. 38 applicants, 66% accepted, 9 enrolled. In 2009, 8 master's awarded. *Degree requirements:* For master's, comprehensive exam, thesis, performance. *Entrance requirements:* For master's, audition or tape. Additional exam requirements/recommendations for international students: Required—TOEFL. *Application deadline:* For fall admission, 2/1 priority date for domestic and international students. Applications are processed on a rolling basis. Application fee: $50. *Expenses:* Tuition: Full-time $26,326; part-time $6584 per course. Required fees: $896. One-time fee: $896 part-time. Tuition and fees vary according to program. *Financial support:* In 2009–10, 18 students received support, including 18 fellowships (averaging $7,859 per year), 9 teaching assistantships with partial tuition reimbursements available (averaging $4,753 per year); scholarships/grants and unspecified assistantships also available. Financial award application deadline: 2/1; financial award applicants required to submit FAFSA. *Faculty research:* Video and dance, modern dance technique, performance art, rhythmic analysis. *Unit head:* Sonya Delwaide, Head, 510-430-3258, E-mail: sdelwaid@mills.edu. *Application contact:* Jessica King, Graduate Admission Specialist, 510-430-3305, Fax: 510-430-2159, E-mail: grad-studies@mills.edu.

New York University, Steinhardt School of Culture, Education, and Human Development, Department of Music and Performing Arts Professions, Program in Dance Education, New York, NY 10012-1019. Offers dance education (MA), including teaching dance in higher education and the professions, teaching dance: ABT ballet pedagogy, teaching dance: all grades. Part-time programs available. *Students:* 54 full-time (45 women), 36 part-time (33 women); includes 30 minority (20 African Americans, 2 Asian Americans or Pacific Islanders, 8 Hispanic Americans), 11 international. Average age 30. 57 applicants, 84% accepted, 39 enrolled. In 2009, 32 master's awarded. *Degree requirements:* For master's, thesis (for some programs). *Entrance requirements:* For master's, audition, interview. Additional exam requirements/recommendations for international students: Required—TOEFL. *Application deadline:* For fall admission, 12/15 priority date for domestic and international students; for spring admission, 11/1 for domestic and international students. Applications are processed on a rolling basis. Application fee: $75. Electronic applications accepted. *Expenses:* Tuition: Full-time $30,528; part-time $1272 per credit. Required fees: $2177. *Financial support:* Career-related internships or fieldwork, Federal Work-Study, institutionally sponsored loans, and scholarships/grants available. Support available to part-time students. Financial award application deadline: 2/1; financial award applicants required to submit FAFSA. *Faculty research:* Dance cognition and creativity, technology in dance, development of teacher expertise, ballet pedagogy. *Unit head:* Dr. Susan Koff, Director, 212-998-5424, Fax: 212-995-4043, E-mail: sk120@nyu.edu. *Application contact:* 212-998-5030, Fax: 212-995-4328, E-mail: steinhardt.gradadmissions@nyu.edu.

New York University, Tisch School of the Arts, Department of Dance, New York, NY 10012-1019. Offers MFA. *Faculty:* 11 full-time, 16 part-time/adjunct. *Students:* 29 full-time (25 women), 1 part-time (0 women); includes 5 minority (2 African Americans, 3 Asian Americans or Pacific Islanders). Average age 27. 81 applicants, 31% accepted, 15 enrolled. In 2009, 13 master's awarded. *Entrance requirements:* For master's, audition. Additional exam requirements/recommendations for international students: Required—TOEFL, IELTS or ALI. *Application deadline:* For fall admission, 1/1 priority date for domestic students, 1/1 for international students. Application fee: $60. Electronic applications accepted. *Expenses:* Tuition: Full-time $30,528; part-time $1272 per credit. Required fees: $2177. *Financial support:* In 2009–10, 19 fellowships with full and partial tuition reimbursements were awarded; Federal Work-Study, institutionally sponsored loans, tuition waivers (partial), and unspecified assistantships also available. Financial award application deadline: 2/15; financial award applicants required to submit FAFSA. *Unit head:* Cherylyn Lavagnino, Chair, 212-998-1980, Fax: 212-995-4644. *Application contact:* Dan Sandford, Director of Graduate Admissions, 212-998-1918, Fax: 212-995-4060, E-mail: tisch.gradadmissions@nyu.edu.

New York University, Tisch School of the Arts and Graduate School of Arts and Science, Department of Performance Studies, New York, NY 10012-1019. Offers MA, PhD. *Faculty:* 12 full-time (7 women), 4 part-time/adjunct (3 women). *Students:* 63 full-time (46 women), 1 (woman) part-time; includes 16 minority (4 African Americans, 4 Asian Americans or Pacific Islanders, 8 Hispanic Americans). Average age 31. 198 applicants, 51% accepted, 54 enrolled. In 2009, 36 master's, 7 doctorates awarded. *Degree requirements:* For doctorate, one foreign language, comprehensive exam, thesis/dissertation, dissertation defense, qualifying exam. *Entrance requirements:* For master's, sample of written work; for doctorate, master's degree, writing sample. Additional exam requirements/recommendations for international students: Required—TOEFL, IELTS or ALI. *Application deadline:* For fall admission, 12/1 for domestic and international students. Application fee: $60. Electronic applications accepted. *Expenses:* Contact institution. *Financial support:* In 2009–10, 32 students received support, including 24 fellowships with full and partial tuition reimbursements available, 4 research assistantships, 4 teaching assistantships; Federal Work-Study, institutionally sponsored loans, tuition waivers (partial), and unspecified assistantships also available. Financial award application deadline: 2/15; financial award applicants required to submit CSS PROFILE or FAFSA. *Faculty research:* Performance theory, dance, folklore and festivals, postcolonial theory, anthropology and gender studies. *Unit head:* Jose Munoz, Chair, 212-998-1620, Fax: 212-995-4571, E-mail: performance.studies@nyu.edu. *Application contact:* Dan Sandford, Director of Graduate Admissions, 212-998-1918, Fax: 212-995-4060, E-mail: tisch.gradadmissions@nyu.edu.

Northern Illinois University, Graduate School, College of Visual and Performing Arts, School of Theatre and Dance, De Kalb, IL 60115-2854. Offers MFA. *Accreditation:* NAST. Part-time programs available. *Faculty:* 16 full-time (9 women). *Students:* 19 full-time (9 women), 2 part-time (1 woman); includes 2 minority (both African Americans). Average age 27. 43 applicants, 49% accepted, 19 enrolled. In 2009, 3 master's awarded. *Degree requirements:* For master's, comprehensive exam, final project and defense. *Entrance requirements:* For master's, minimum GPA of 2.75, audition or portfolio. Additional exam requirements/recommendations for international students: Required—TOEFL (minimum score 550 paper-based; 213 computer-based). *Application deadline:* For fall admission, 4/1 priority date for domestic students, 5/1 for international students; for spring admission, 10/15 priority date for domestic students, 10/1 for international students. Applications are processed on a rolling basis. Application fee: $30. Electronic applications accepted. *Expenses:* Tuition, state resident: full-time $6576; part-time $274 per credit hour. Tuition, nonresident: full-time $13,152; part-time $548 per credit hour. Required fees: $1813; $75.53 per credit hour. Part-time tuition and fees vary according to course load. *Financial support:* In 2009–10, 1 research assistantship with full tuition reimbursement, 8 teaching assistantships with full tuition reimbursements were awarded; fellowships with full tuition reimbursements, career-related internships or fieldwork, Federal Work-Study, scholarships/grants, tuition waivers (full), and staff assistantships also available. Support available to part-time students. Financial award applicants required to submit FAFSA. *Faculty research:* Theatre history, choreography, performance art spectacles, storytelling, computer visualization of the ethical space. *Unit head:* Alexander Gelman, Director, 815-753-8253, Fax: 815-753-8415, E-mail: agelman@niu.edu. *Application contact:* Terrence McClellan, Information Contact, 815-753-8257, E-mail: tmcclell@niu.edu.

The Ohio State University, Graduate School, College of the Arts, Department of Dance, Program in Dance Studies, Columbus, OH 43210. Offers PhD. *Students:* 6 full-time (5 women), 2 part-time (both women). Average age 34. *Application deadline:* Applications are processed on a rolling basis. Application fee: $40 ($50 for international students). Electronic applications accepted. *Expenses:* Tuition, state resident: full-time $10,683. Tuition, nonresident: full-time $25,923. Tuition and fees vary according to course load and program. *Unit head:* Victoria E. Uris, Graduate Studies Committee Chair, 614-292-0984, Fax: 614-292-0939, E-mail: uris.1@osu.edu. *Application contact:* Victoria E. Uris, Graduate Studies Committee Chair, 614-292-0984, Fax: 614-292-0939, E-mail: uris.1@osu.edu.

Oklahoma City University, Margaret E. Petree College of Performing Arts, Ann Lacy School of American Dance and Arts Management, Oklahoma City, OK 73106-1402. Offers dance (MFA). *Faculty:* 8 full-time (all women). *Students:* 4 full-time (all women), 1 (woman) part-time; includes 2 minority (1 African American, 1 Hispanic American). Average age 24. 10 applicants, 40% accepted, 3 enrolled. In 2009, 1 master's awarded. *Degree requirements:* For master's, thesis optional. *Entrance requirements:* For master's, minimum GPA of 3.0, audition. Additional exam requirements/recommendations for international students: Required—TOEFL (minimum score 600 paper-based). *Application deadline:* For fall admission, 3/27 for domestic students. Application fee: $50 ($70 for international students). *Expenses:* Tuition: Full-time $15,930; part-time $885 per hour. *Financial support:* Applicants required to submit FAFSA. *Unit head:* Melanie Shelley, Associate Dean, 405-208-5982, Fax: 405-208-5313, E-mail: mshelley@okcu.edu. *Application contact:* Michelle Lockhart, Director, Admissions, 405-208-5340, Fax: 405-208-5916, E-mail: gadmissions@okcu.edu.

Purchase College, State University of New York, Conservatory of Dance, Purchase, NY 10577-1400. Offers MFA. *Degree requirements:* For master's, performance. *Entrance requirements:* For master's, audition. Electronic applications accepted. *Expenses:* Tuition, state resident: full-time $8370; part-time $349 per credit. Tuition, nonresident: full-time $13,250; part-time $552 per credit. Required fees: $1515; $62.11 per credit. One-time fee: $144 full-time. Tuition and fees vary according to program.

Sam Houston State University, College of Arts and Sciences, Department of Theatre and Dance, Huntsville, TX 77341. Offers dance (MFA). *Faculty:* 3 full-time (2 women). *Students:* 6 full-time (5 women), 2 part-time (both women); includes 1 minority (African American). Average age 25. 4 applicants, 75% accepted, 3 enrolled. In 2009, 1 master's awarded. *Degree requirements:* For master's, thesis, project. *Entrance requirements:* For master's, GRE General Test. Additional exam requirements/recommendations for international students: Required—TOEFL (minimum score 550 paper-based; 213 computer-based; 79 iBT). *Application deadline:* For fall admission, 8/1 for domestic and international students; for spring admission, 12/1 for domestic and international students. Applications are processed on a rolling basis. Application fee: $20. *Expenses:* Tuition, state resident: full-time $3690; part-time $205 per credit hour. Tuition, nonresident: full-time $8676; part-time $482 per credit hour. Required fees: $1474. Tuition and fees vary according to course load and campus/location. *Financial support:* Teaching assistantships, career-related internships or fieldwork, Federal Work-Study, and institutionally sponsored loans available. Financial award application deadline: 5/31; financial award applicants required to submit FAFSA. *Unit head:* Penelope Hasekoester, Chair, 936-294-1330, Fax: 936-294-3898, E-mail: drm_pah@shsu.edu. *Application contact:* Penelope Hasekoester, Chair, 936-294-1330, Fax: 936-294-3898, E-mail: drm_pah@shsu.edu.

Sarah Lawrence College, Graduate Studies, Program in Dance, Bronxville, NY 10708-5999. Offers MFA. *Faculty:* 25 part-time/adjunct (16 women). *Students:* 10 full-time (all women); includes 1 minority (African American), 1 international. 36 applicants, 25% accepted, 5 enrolled. In 2009, 3 master's awarded. *Degree requirements:* For master's, performance. *Entrance requirements:* For master's, audition, minimum B average in undergraduate course work. *Application deadline:* For fall admission, 1/15 for domestic and international students. Application fee: $60. *Expenses:* Tuition: Part-time $1161 per credit. Required fees: $232 per semester. Part-time tuition and fees vary according to course load, program and student level. *Financial support:* In 2009–10, 10 fellowships (averaging $5,950 per year) were awarded; career-related internships or fieldwork, scholarships/grants, and health care benefits also available. Support available to part-time students. Financial award application deadline: 3/1; financial award applicants required to submit FAFSA. *Unit head:* Sara Rudner, Director, 914-395-2371. *Application contact:* Emanual Lomax, Director of Graduate Admissions, 914-395-2371, E-mail: sguma@mail.slc.edu.

Shenandoah University, Shenandoah Conservatory, Winchester, VA 22601-5195. Offers arts administration (MS); church music (MM, Certificate); composition (MM); conducting (MM); dance (MA, MS); music education (MME, DMA); music therapy (MMT, Certificate); pedagogy (MM, DMA); performance (MM, DMA, Artist Diploma); piano accompanying (MM). *Accreditation:* NASM. *Faculty:* 39 full-time (15 women), 17 part-time/adjunct (5 women). *Students:* 72 full-time (42 women), 134 part-time (83 women); includes 40 minority (14 African Americans, 22 Asian Americans or Pacific Islanders, 4 Hispanic Americans), 16 international. Average age 35. 115 applicants, 88% accepted, 70 enrolled. In 2009, 40 master's, 5 doctorates, 9 other advanced degrees awarded. *Degree requirements:* For master's, comprehensive exam (for some programs), thesis (for some programs), internship (MS), recital (MM), research teaching project or thesis (MME), project (MA); for doctorate, comprehensive exam, thesis/dissertation (for some programs), dissertation or teaching project, recital; for other advanced degree, research project, recital. *Entrance requirements:* For master's, audition, minimum GPA of 2.5, writing sample, resume; for doctorate, audition, minimum GPA of 3.25, 2 letters of recommendation, writing sample, resume; for other advanced degree, bachelor or master's degree; minimum GPA of 2.5. Additional exam requirements/recommendations for international students: Required—TOEFL (minimum score 550 paper-based; 213 computer-based; 79 iBT), IELTS (minimum score 6.5). *Application deadline:* Applications are processed on a rolling basis. Application fee: $30. Electronic applications accepted. *Expenses:* Tuition: Full-time $11,925; part-time $695 per credit. Required fees: $400 per semester. *Financial support:* Application deadline: 3/15. *Unit head:* Dr. Laurence A. Kaptain, Dean, 540-665-4600, Fax: 540-665-5402, E-mail: lkaptain@su.edu. *Application contact:* David Anthony, Dean of Admissions, 540-665-4581, Fax: 540-665-4627, E-mail: admit@su.edu.

Smith College, Graduate and Special Programs, Department of Dance, Northampton, MA 01063. Offers MFA. Part-time programs available. *Faculty:* 2 full-time (1 woman), 1 (woman) part-time/adjunct. *Students:* 8 part-time (all women); includes 1 minority (African American). Average age 27. 15 applicants, 27% accepted, 4 enrolled. In 2009, 3 master's awarded. *Degree requirements:* For master's, thesis performance. *Entrance requirements:* For master's, audition. Additional exam requirements/recommendations for international students: Required—TOEFL (minimum score 590 paper-based; 243 computer-based; 97 iBT). *Application deadline:* For fall admission, 1/15 for domestic and international students. Application fee: $60. *Financial support:* In 2009–10, 8 students received support, including 8 teaching assistantships with full tuition reimbursements available (averaging $5,955 per year); institutionally sponsored loans and scholarships/grants also available. Support available to part-time students. Financial award application deadline: 1/15; financial award applicants required to submit CSS PROFILE or FAFSA. *Unit head:* Rodger Blum, Chair, 413-585-3234, E-mail: rblum@smith.edu. *Application contact:* Susan Waltner, Graduate Student Adviser, 413-585-3236, E-mail: swaltner@smith.edu.

Southern Methodist University, Meadows School of the Arts, Division of Dance, Dallas, TX 75275. Offers MFA. *Accreditation:* NASD. *Faculty:* 9 full-time (6 women). *Students:* 4 full-time (2 women); includes 1 minority (African American), 1 international. Average age 35. *Degree requirements:* For master's, thesis or alternative, written qualifying exam. *Entrance requirements:* For master's, BA or BFA in dance, interview, professional-level experience. Additional exam requirements/recommendations for international students: Required—TOEFL (minimum score 550 paper-based; 213 computer-based; 80 iBT). *Application deadline:* For fall admission, 3/1 priority date for domestic and international students. Applications are processed on a rolling basis. Application fee: $75. *Financial support:* In 2009–10, 4 teaching assistantships (averaging $3,000 per year) were awarded; scholarships/grants and unspecified assistantships also available. Financial award application deadline: 3/1; financial award applicants required to submit FAFSA. *Faculty research:* Labanotation, dance preservation and documentation, dance history. *Unit head:* Myra Woodruff, Chair, 214-768-2718, Fax: 214-768-4540, E-mail: woodruff@smu.edu. *Application contact:* Jean Cherry, Director of Graduate Admissions and Records, 214-768-3765, Fax: 214-768-3272, E-mail: jcherry@smu.edu.

Temple University, Graduate School, Esther Boyer College of Music and Dance, Department of Dance, Philadelphia, PA 19122-6096. Offers Ed M, MFA, PhD. *Accreditation:* NASD. Part-time programs available. *Degree requirements:* For master's, thesis optional, professional project; for doctorate, thesis/dissertation. *Entrance requirements:* For master's and doctorate, minimum GPA of 3.0, audition/interview. Additional exam requirements/recommendations for international students: Required—TOEFL. Electronic applications accepted. *Faculty research:* Cultural studies, dance education, dance technology, aesthetics.

Texas Tech University, Graduate School, College of Visual and Performing Arts, Department of Theatre and Dance, Lubbock, TX 79409. Offers fine arts (PhD); theatre arts (MA, MFA), including design (MFA), performance/pedagogy (MFA), playwriting (MFA), theatre management (MFA). *Accreditation:* NAST. Part-time programs available. *Faculty:* 11 full-time (6 women). *Students:* 40 full-time (19 women), 20 part-time (10 women); includes 7 minority (3 African Americans, 1 Asian American or Pacific Islander, 3 Hispanic Americans), 3 international. Average age 34. 30 applicants, 50% accepted, 9 enrolled. In 2009, 5 master's, 2 doctorates awarded. *Degree requirements:* For master's, variable foreign language requirement, thesis; for doctorate, thesis/dissertation. *Entrance requirements:* For master's and doctorate, GRE General Test. Additional exam requirements/recommendations for international students: Required—TOEFL (minimum score 550 paper-based; 213 computer-based). *Application deadline:* For fall admission, 3/1 priority date for international students; for spring admission, 11/1 priority date for international students. Applications are processed on a rolling basis. Application fee: $50 ($75 for international students). Electronic applications accepted. *Expenses:* Tuition, state resident: full-time $5100; part-time $213 per credit hour. Tuition, nonresident: full-time $11,748; part-time $490 per credit hour. Required fees: $2298; $50 per credit hour. $555 per semester. *Financial support:* In 2009–10, 18 teaching assistantships with partial tuition reimbursements (averaging $10,564 per year) were awarded; research assistantships with partial tuition reimbursements, Federal Work-Study and institutionally sponsored loans also available. Support available to part-time students. Financial award application deadline: 4/15; financial award applicants required to submit FAFSA. *Faculty research:* New student plays program, theatre planning, dramaturgy; feminist theatre; arts administration; dance aesthetics. *Unit head:* Prof. Frederick B. Christoffel, Chair, 806-742-3601 Ext. 228, Fax: 806-742-1338, E-mail: fred.christoffel@ttu.edu. *Application contact:* Dr. James Bush, Graduate Adviser, 806-742-3601 Ext. 230, Fax: 806-742-1338, E-mail: james.bush@ttu.edu.

Texas Tech University, Graduate School, College of Visual and Performing Arts, Fine Arts Doctoral Program, Lubbock, TX 79409. Offers arts (PhD); music (PhD); theatre arts (PhD). *Accreditation:* NAST. *Students:* 44 full-time (18 women), 31 part-time (16 women); includes 9 minority (3 African Americans, 1 American Indian/Alaska Native, 1 Asian American or Pacific Islander, 4 Hispanic Americans), 10 international. Average age 36. 33 applicants, 30% accepted, 3 enrolled. In 2009, 10 doctorates awarded. *Degree requirements:* For doctorate, thesis/dissertation. *Entrance requirements:* For doctorate, GRE General Test. Additional exam requirements/recommendations for international students: Required—TOEFL (minimum score 550 paper-based; 213 computer-based). *Application deadline:* For fall admission, 3/1 priority date for international students; for spring admission, 11/1 priority date for international students. Applications are processed on a rolling basis. Application fee: $50 ($75 for international students). Electronic applications accepted. *Expenses:* Tuition, state resident: full-time $5100; part-time $213 per credit hour. Tuition, nonresident: full-time $11,748; part-time $490 per credit hour. Required fees: $2298; $50 per credit hour. $555 per semester. *Financial support:* Research assistantships with partial tuition reimbursements, teaching assistantships with partial tuition reimbursements available. Financial award application deadline: 4/15. *Faculty research:* Art criticism and theory, music, theatre arts; arts education; history of arts. *Unit head:* Dr. Brian D. Steele, Director, 806-742-0700, Fax: 806-742-0695, E-mail: brian.steele@ttu.edu. *Application contact:* Dr. Brian D. Steele, Director, 806-742-0700, Fax: 806-742-0695, E-mail: brian.steele@ttu.edu.

Texas Woman's University, Graduate School, College of Arts and Sciences, School of the Arts, Department of Dance, Denton, TX 76201. Offers MA, MFA, PhD. *Accreditation:* NASD. *Faculty:* 5 full-time (4 women). *Students:* 26 full-time (22 women), 12 part-time (10 women); includes 6 minority (2 African Americans, 2 Asian Americans or Pacific Islanders, 2 Hispanic Americans), 4 international. Average age 35. 16 applicants, 81% accepted, 9 enrolled. In 2009, 8 master's awarded. *Degree requirements:* For master's, thesis (for some programs), choreography portfolio, professional paper; for doctorate, comprehensive exam, thesis/dissertation. *Entrance requirements:* For master's, audition, 3 letters of recommendation, interview, writing sample, solo performance, resume; for doctorate, audition, portfolio, interview, 3 letters of reference, scholarly writing sample, resume, personal essay, curriculum vitae, department program application information form, sample syllabus for university-level course. Additional exam requirements/recommendations for international students: Required—TOEFL (minimum score 550 paper-based; 213 computer-based; 79 iBT). *Application deadline:* For fall admission, 2/1 priority date for domestic and international students. Applications are processed on a rolling basis. Application fee: $50. Electronic applications accepted. *Expenses:* Tuition, state resident: full-time $3564; part-time $198 per credit hour. Tuition, nonresident: full-time $8550; part-time $475 per credit hour. Required fees: $69.26 per credit hour. Tuition and fees

Dance

Texas Woman's University (continued)
vary according to course load. *Financial support:* In 2009–10, 23 students received support, including 1 fellowship (averaging $10,000 per year), 5 research assistantships (averaging $11,862 per year), 9 teaching assistantships (averaging $11,862 per year); career-related internships or fieldwork, Federal Work-Study, institutionally sponsored loans, scholarships/grants, traineeships, health care benefits, tuition waivers (partial), and unspecified assistantships also available. Support available to part-time students. Financial award application deadline: 3/1; financial award applicants required to submit FAFSA. *Faculty research:* Performance, choreography, pedagogy, somatic practices, theorizing artistic practice. *Unit head:* Dr. Penelope Hanstein, Chair, 940-898-2085, Fax: 940-898-2098, E-mail: dance@twu.edu. *Application contact:* Samuel Wheeler, Assistant Director of Admissions, 940-898-3188, Fax: 940-898-3081, E-mail: wheelersr@twu.edu.

Tulane University, School of Liberal Arts, Department of Theatre and Dance, New Orleans, LA 70118-5669. Offers design and technical production (MFA). *Entrance requirements:* For master's, GRE General Test, minimum B average in undergraduate course work. Additional exam requirements/recommendations for international students: Required—TOEFL. Electronic applications accepted. *Faculty research:* Scene design, stage management, costume design, technical direction, lighting design.

Université du Québec à Montréal, Graduate Programs, Program in Dance, Montréal, QC H3C 3P8, Canada. Offers MA. Part-time programs available. *Degree requirements:* For master's, thesis optional. *Entrance requirements:* For master's, appropriate bachelor's degree or equivalent and proficiency in French.

The University of Arizona, Graduate College, College of Fine Arts, School of Dance, Tucson, AZ 85721. Offers MFA. *Faculty:* 7. *Students:* 12 full-time (7 women); includes 3 Asian Americans or Pacific Islanders, 1 international. Average age 30. 15 applicants, 40% accepted, 6 enrolled. In 2009, 5 master's awarded. Application fee: $75. *Expenses:* Tuition, state resident: full-time $9028. Tuition, nonresident: full-time $24,890. *Financial support:* In 2009–10, 8 teaching assistantships with full tuition reimbursements (averaging $11,600 per year) were awarded. *Unit head:* Jory Hancock, Interim Dean and Director, 520-626-8030, E-mail: jory@email.arizona.edu. *Application contact:* General Information, 520-621-1301, Fax: 520-621-1307, E-mail: finearts@email.arizona.edu.

University of California, Irvine, Office of Graduate Studies, Claire Trevor School of the Arts, Department of Dance, Irvine, CA 92697. Offers MFA. *Students:* 21 full-time (18 women); includes 2 minority (1 Asian American or Pacific Islander, 1 Hispanic American), 1 international. Average age 28. 34 applicants, 32% accepted, 11 enrolled. In 2009, 12 master's awarded. *Degree requirements:* For master's, thesis. *Entrance requirements:* For master's, minimum GPA of 3.0. *Application deadline:* For fall admission, 1/15 priority date for domestic students, 1/15 for international students. Applications are processed on a rolling basis. Application fee: $70 ($90 for international students). Electronic applications accepted. *Financial support:* Fellowships, teaching assistantships, institutionally sponsored loans, traineeships, health care benefits, and unspecified assistantships available. Financial award application deadline: 3/1; financial award applicants required to submit FAFSA. *Faculty research:* Dance science, digital technology, history and theory, choreography. *Unit head:* Alan Terricciano, Chair, 949-824-5744, Fax: 949-824-4563, E-mail: aterricc@uci.edu. *Application contact:* Karen Ricketts, Department Manager, 949-824-6929, Fax: 949-824-4563, E-mail: kbricket@uci.edu.

University of California, Los Angeles, Graduate Division, School of the Arts and Architecture, Department of World Arts and Cultures, Los Angeles, CA 90095. Offers culture and performance (MA, PhD); dance (MFA). *Degree requirements:* For master's, comprehensive exam or thesis; for doctorate, one foreign language, thesis/dissertation, oral and written qualifying exams. *Entrance requirements:* For master's, minimum GPA of 3.0; for doctorate, GRE General Test, writing sample. Electronic applications accepted.

University of California, Riverside, Graduate Division, Department of Dance, Riverside, CA 92521. Offers critical dance studies (PhD); experimental choreography (MFA). *Faculty:* 8 full-time (7 women). *Students:* 33 full-time (31 women); includes 8 minority (2 African Americans, 3 Asian Americans or Pacific Islanders, 3 Hispanic Americans), 7 international. Average age 34. 32 applicants, 41% accepted, 6 enrolled. In 2009, 2 master's, 4 doctorates awarded. *Degree requirements:* For doctorate, one foreign language, thesis/dissertation, qualifying exams. *Entrance requirements:* For master's, choreographed piece (MFA); for doctorate, GRE General Test, minimum GPA of 3.2, writing sample. Additional exam requirements/recommendations for international students: Required—TOEFL (minimum score 550 paper-based; 213 computer-based; 80 iBT). *Application deadline:* For fall admission, 1/5 for domestic and international students. Application fee: $80 ($100 for international students). Electronic applications accepted. *Financial support:* In 2009–10, 13 students received support, including fellowships with full tuition reimbursements available (averaging $12,000 per year), teaching assistantships with full tuition reimbursements available (averaging $15,600 per year); research assistantships with tuition reimbursements available, career-related internships or fieldwork, Federal Work-Study, institutionally sponsored loans, tuition waivers (full and partial), and unspecified assistantships also available. Financial award application deadline: 1/5; financial award applicants required to submit FAFSA. *Faculty research:* Movement analysis, cultural postcolonial gender studies of performance, theories of dance, anthropology of dance, history and reconstruction of dance. *Unit head:* Linda Tomko, Chair, 951-827-3944, Fax: 951-827-4651, E-mail: linda.tomko@ucr.edu. *Application contact:* Anthea Kraut, Graduate Adviser, 951-827-3944, Fax: 951-827-4651, E-mail: danceadvising@ucr.edu.

University of Colorado at Boulder, Graduate School, College of Arts and Sciences, Department of Theatre and Dance, Boulder, CO 80309. Offers dance (MFA); theatre (MA, PhD). *Faculty:* 16 full-time (8 women). *Students:* 37 full-time (26 women), 9 part-time (5 women); includes 7 minority (4 African Americans, 3 Hispanic Americans), 1 international. Average age 33. 56 applicants, 32% accepted, 12 enrolled. In 2009, 6 master's, 2 doctorates awarded. Terminal master's awarded for partial completion of doctoral program. *Degree requirements:* For master's, comprehensive exam, thesis; for doctorate, one foreign language, thesis/dissertation. *Entrance requirements:* For master's, GRE General Test (MA), audition (MFA), minimum undergraduate GPA of 2.75. *Application deadline:* For fall admission, 1/15 priority date for domestic students, 12/1 for international students. Application fee: $50 ($60 for international students). *Financial support:* In 2009–10, 16 fellowships (averaging $2,499 per year), 14 research assistantships (averaging $1,463 per year) were awarded; tuition waivers (full) also available. Financial award application deadline: 1/15. *Faculty research:* Dance: performance choreography; pedagogy administration; body therapies; multi-media forms; film/video; cultural studies; non-concert forms; music; poetry/writing/literature; kinesiology; theatre: theatre history; theory and literature; theatre production; acting; directing; dramaturgy and design. Total annual research expenditures: $3,749.

University of Hawaii at Manoa, Graduate Division, College of Arts and Humanities, Department of Theatre and Dance, Honolulu, HI 96822. Offers dance (MA, MFA); theatre (MA, MFA, PhD). Part-time programs available. *Degree requirements:* For master's, one foreign language, thesis optional; for doctorate, one foreign language, comprehensive exam, thesis/dissertation. *Entrance requirements:* For master's and doctorate, GRE General Test. Additional exam requirements/recommendations for international students: Required—TOEFL (minimum score 600 paper-based; 250 computer-based; 100 iBT), IELTS (minimum score 7). *Expenses:* Tuition, state resident: full-time $8900; part-time $372 per credit. Tuition, nonresident: full-time $21,400; part-time $898 per credit. Required fees: $207 per semester. *Faculty research:* Asian theatre, feminist theatre and dance, Russian theatre, Australian theatre.

University of Illinois at Urbana–Champaign, Graduate College, College of Fine and Applied Arts, Department of Dance, Champaign, IL 61820. Offers MFA. *Accreditation:* NASD. *Faculty:* 10 full-time (8 women). *Students:* 14 full-time (11 women); includes 1 minority (Hispanic American), 1 international. 29 applicants, 14% accepted, 4 enrolled. In 2009, 2 master's awarded. *Entrance requirements:* For master's, audition, minimum GPA of 3.0. Additional exam requirements/recommendations for international students: Required—TOEFL (minimum score 550 paper-based; 213 computer-based). *Application deadline:* Applications are processed on a rolling basis. Application fee: $60 ($75 for international students). Electronic applications accepted. *Financial support:* In 2009–10, 8 fellowships, 1 research assistantship, 12 teaching assistantships were awarded; tuition waivers (full and partial) also available. *Unit head:* Jan K. Erkert, Head, 217-333-1010, Fax: 217-333-3000, E-mail: erkert@illinois.edu. *Application contact:* Cynthia C. Howard, Program Coordinator, 217-333-1011, Fax: 217-333-3000, E-mail: choward1@illinois.edu.

The University of Iowa, Graduate College, College of Liberal Arts and Sciences, Department of Dance, Iowa City, IA 52242-1316. Offers MFA. *Degree requirements:* For master's, thesis, exam. *Entrance requirements:* For master's, minimum GPA of 3.0. Additional exam requirements/recommendations for international students: Required—TOEFL (minimum score 550 paper-based; 213 computer-based; 81 iBT). Electronic applications accepted.

University of Maryland, Baltimore County, Graduate School, College of Arts, Humanities and Social Sciences, Department of Education, Program in Teaching, Baltimore, MD 21250. Offers early childhood education (MAT); elementary education (MAT); secondary education (MAT), including art, biology, chemistry, dance, earth/space science, English, foreign language, mathematics, music, physics, theatre; secondary science (MAT), including social studies. Part-time and evening/weekend programs available. *Faculty:* 24 full-time (18 women), 25 part-time/adjunct (19 women). *Students:* 52 full-time (41 women), 64 part-time (55 women); includes 20 minority (5 African Americans, 1 American Indian/Alaska Native, 10 Asian Americans or Pacific Islanders, 4 Hispanic Americans), 3 international. Average age 31. 88 applicants, 57% accepted, 39 enrolled. In 2009, 106 master's awarded. *Degree requirements:* For master's, comprehensive exam (for some programs), thesis (for some programs). *Entrance requirements:* For master's, PRAXIS I and II, minimum GPA of 3.0. Additional exam requirements/recommendations for international students: Required—TOEFL. *Application deadline:* For fall admission, 6/1 for domestic students; for spring admission, 11/1 for domestic students. Applications are processed on a rolling basis. Application fee: $50. Electronic applications accepted. *Financial support:* In 2009–10, 6 students received support, including research assistantships with full tuition reimbursements available (averaging $12,000 per year); career-related internships or fieldwork, Federal Work-Study, scholarships/grants, tuition waivers, and unspecified assistantships also available. Financial award application deadline: 3/1. *Faculty research:* STEM teacher education, culturally sensitive pedagogy, ESOL/bilingual education, early childhood education, language, literacy and culture. *Unit head:* Dr. Susan M. Blunck, Director, 410-455-2869, Fax: 410-455-3986, E-mail: blunck@umbc.edu. *Application contact:* Dr. Susan M. Blunck, Director, 410-455-2869, Fax: 410-455-3986, E-mail: blunck@umbc.edu.

University of Maryland, College Park, Academic Affairs, College of Arts and Humanities, Department of Dance, College Park, MD 20742. Offers MFA. *Faculty:* 8 full-time (6 women), 6 part-time/adjunct (5 women). *Students:* 9 full-time (7 women); includes 1 minority (African American), 1 international. 23 applicants, 22% accepted, 4 enrolled. In 2009, 3 master's awarded. *Degree requirements:* For master's, final project. *Entrance requirements:* For master's, audition/interview, video tapes/writing sample. Additional exam requirements/recommendations for international students: Required—TOEFL. *Application deadline:* For fall admission, 2/1 for domestic and international students. Applications are processed on a rolling basis. Application fee: $60. Electronic applications accepted. *Expenses:* Tuition, area resident: Part-time $471 per credit hour. Tuition, state resident: part-time $471 per credit hour. Tuition, nonresident: part-time $1016 per credit hour. Required fees: $337.04 per term. *Financial support:* In 2009–10, 1 fellowship with full tuition reimbursement (averaging $22,541 per year), 8 teaching assistantships (averaging $19,492 per year) were awarded; research assistantships, Federal Work-Study and scholarships/grants also available. *Faculty research:* Performance and choreography. *Unit head:* Daniel M. Wagner, Acting Chair, 301-405-6679, E-mail: dmwagner@umd.edu. *Application contact:* Dean of Graduate School, 301-405-0376, Fax: 301-314-9305.

University of Michigan, Horace H. Rackham School of Graduate Studies, The School of Music, Theatre, and Dance, Department of Dance, Ann Arbor, MI 48109-2217. Offers modern dance performance and choreography (MFA). Offered through the Horace H. Rackham School of Graduate Studies. *Accreditation:* NASD. *Faculty:* 10 full-time (6 women), 4 part-time/adjunct (all women). *Students:* 3 full-time (2 women). Average age 31. 13 applicants, 54% accepted. In 2009, 4 master's awarded. *Degree requirements:* For master's, thesis. *Entrance requirements:* For master's, audition. Additional exam requirements/recommendations for international students: Required—TOEFL (minimum score 600 paper-based; 250 computer-based; 100 iBT). *Application deadline:* For fall admission, 2/1 priority date for domestic and international students. Applications are processed on a rolling basis. Application fee: $60 ($75 for international students). Electronic applications accepted. *Expenses:* Tuition, state resident: full-time $17,286; part-time $1099 per credit hour. Tuition, nonresident: full-time $34,944; part-time $2080 per credit hour. Required fees: $95 per semester. Tuition and fees vary according to course load, degree level and program. *Financial support:* In 2009–10, fellowships with tuition reimbursements (averaging $5,000 per year), 4 teaching assistantships with full and partial tuition reimbursements (averaging $38,208 per year) were awarded; Federal Work-Study, institutionally sponsored loans, and scholarships/grants also available. Financial award application deadline: 2/1. *Faculty research:* Life forms software. Total annual research expenditures: $70,000. *Unit head:* Prof. Angela Kane, Chair, 734-763-5460, Fax: 734-763-5962, E-mail: atkane@umich.edu. *Application contact:* Samantha Strayer, Admin. Asst., 734-763-5460, Fax: 734-763-5962, E-mail: sstrayer@umich.edu.

University of Minnesota, Twin Cities Campus, Graduate School, College of Liberal Arts, Department of Theatre Arts and Dance, Minneapolis, MN 55455-0213. Offers design technology (MFA); theatre arts and dance (MA, PhD). *Accreditation:* NASD; NAST (one or more programs are accredited). *Faculty:* 15 full-time (6 women), 3 part-time/adjunct (2 women). *Students:* 26 full-time (17 women), 13 part-time (7 women); includes 6 minority (2 African Americans, 4 Hispanic Americans), 2 international. Average age 31. 43 applicants, 23% accepted, 9 enrolled. In 2009, 4 master's, 3 doctorates awarded. Terminal master's awarded for partial completion of doctoral program. *Degree requirements:* For master's, thesis (for some programs), final creative project (MFA), foreign language (MA); for doctorate, one foreign language, thesis/dissertation, oral defense, written exams. *Entrance requirements:* For master's, GRE General Test, minimum GPA of 3.0, audition or portfolio; for doctorate, GRE General Test, minimum GPA of 3.0, writing sample, 1 foreign language. Additional exam requirements/recommendations for international students: Required—TOEFL (minimum score 550 paper-based; 213 computer-based; 79 iBT). *Application deadline:* For fall admission, 1/15 priority date for domestic and international students. Applications are processed on a rolling basis. Application fee: $55 ($75 for international students). Electronic applications accepted. *Financial support:* In 2009–10, 30 students received support, including 3 fellowships with full tuition reimbursements available (averaging $14,000 per year), 27 teaching assistantships with full tuition reimbursements available (averaging $12,253 per year); career-related internships or fieldwork, Federal Work-Study, scholarships/grants, health care benefits, tuition waivers (partial), and unspecified assistantships also available. Financial award application deadline: 4/15; financial award applicants required to submit FAFSA. *Faculty research:* Theatre history, Eastern European theatre, performance studies, medieval studies. Total annual research expenditures: $42,506. *Unit head:* Prof. Michal Kobialka, Professor, 612-625-0048, Fax: 612-625-6334, E-mail: kobia001@umn.edu. *Application contact:* Ginni Arons, Graduate Studies Assistant, 612-625-5029, Fax: 612-625-6334, E-mail: theatre@umn.edu.

University of New Mexico, Graduate School, College of Fine Arts, Department of Theatre and Dance, Albuquerque, NM 87131-2039. Offers dramatic writing (MFA); theater and dance (MA). *Accreditation:* NASD; NAST. *Faculty:* 21 full-time (12 women), 16 part-time/adjunct (6 women). *Students:* 23 full-time (19 women), 5 part-time (4 women); includes 7 minority (1 Asian American or Pacific Islander, 6 Hispanic Americans), 2 international. Average age 31. 34 applicants, 53% accepted, 12 enrolled. In 2009, 10 master's awarded. *Degree requirements:* For master's, comprehensive exam (for some programs), thesis (for some programs). *Entrance* *requirements:* For master's, minimum GPA of 3.0, undergraduate major in theatre, dance or closely related field, 3 letters of recommendation, letter of intent. *Application deadline:* For fall admission, 4/15 for domestic students; for spring admission, 11/10 for domestic students. Application fee: $50. Electronic applications accepted. *Expenses:* Tuition, state resident: full-time $2099; part-time $233.20 per credit hour. Tuition, nonresident: full-time $6650. Required fees: $25 per semester. Tuition and fees vary according to course load, program and reciprocity agreements. *Financial support:* In 2009–10, 14 students received support, including 5 research assistantships with partial tuition reimbursements available (averaging $8,000 per year), 6 teaching assistantships with partial tuition reimbursements available (averaging $8,000 per year); Federal Work-Study, health care benefits, tuition waivers (partial), and unspecified assistantships also available. Financial award application deadline: 3/1; financial award applicants required to submit FAFSA. *Faculty research:* Theater education and outreach, choreography, dramatic writing, dance history/criticism. *Unit head:* Bill Liotta, Chair, 505-277-4332, Fax: 505-277-8921, E-mail: wliotta@unm.edu. *Application contact:* Christina Squire, Administrator II, 505-277-7362, Fax: 505-277-8921, E-mail: csquire@unm.edu.

The University of North Carolina at Charlotte, Graduate School, College of Education, Program in Teacher Education, Charlotte, NC 28223-0001. Offers art education (K-12) (MAT); dance education (K-12) (MAT); elementary education (K-6) (MAT); English as a second language (K-12) (MAT); foreign language education (K-12) (MAT); general teacher education (MAT); middle grades education (6-9) (MAT); music education (K-12) (MAT); secondary education (9-12) (MAT); special education (K-12) (MAT); theatre education (K-12) (MAT). *Faculty:* 108 full-time (64 women), 16 part-time/adjunct (12 women). *Students:* 29 full-time (20 women), 229 part-time (189 women); includes 32 minority (22 African Americans, 2 American Indian/Alaska Native, 3 Asian Americans or Pacific Islanders, 5 Hispanic Americans). Average age 32. 108 applicants, 92% accepted, 85 enrolled. In 2009, 59 master's awarded. *Entrance requirements:* For master's, GRE or MAT. Additional exam requirements/recommendations for international students: Required—TOEFL (minimum score 557 paper-based; 220 computer-based; 83 iBT). *Application deadline:* For fall admission, 7/1 for domestic students, 5/1 for international students; for spring admission, 11/1 for domestic students, 10/1 for international students. Applications are processed on a rolling basis. Application fee: $55. Electronic applications accepted. *Financial support:* In 2009–10, 5 students received support, including 1 research assistantship (averaging $18,000 per year), 3 teaching assistantships (averaging $12,183 per year); career-related internships or fieldwork, Federal Work-Study, institutionally sponsored loans, scholarships/grants, and administrative assistantship also available. Support available to part-time students. Financial award application deadline: 4/1; financial award applicants required to submit FAFSA. Total annual research expenditures: $5.1 million. *Unit head:* Dr. Kimberly J. Hartman, Coordinator, 704-687-8883, Fax: 704-687-6430, E-mail: khartman@uncc.edu. *Application contact:* Kathy B. Giddings, Director of Graduate Admissions, 704-687-5503, Fax: 704-687-3279, E-mail: gradadmn@uncc.edu.

The University of North Carolina at Greensboro, Graduate School, School of Health and Human Performance, Department of Dance, Greensboro, NC 27412-5001. Offers MA, MFA. *Accreditation:* NASD. *Degree requirements:* For master's, thesis. *Entrance requirements:* For master's, GRE General Test or MAT, audition or video (MFA). Additional exam requirements/recommendations for international students: Required—TOEFL. Electronic applications accepted. *Faculty research:* Consciousness-raising images, perspectives on ballet.

University of Oklahoma, Graduate College, College of Fine Arts, School of Dance, Norman, OK 73019. Offers MFA. Part-time programs available. *Faculty:* 18 full-time (6 women), 1 part-time/adjunct (0 women). *Students:* 8 full-time (7 women); includes 1 minority (Hispanic American), 1 international. 7 applicants, 43% accepted, 3 enrolled. In 2009, 1 master's awarded. *Degree requirements:* For master's, comprehensive exam, departmental qualifying exams, solo performance or choreography of a work. *Entrance requirements:* For master's, minimum GPA of 3.0 or equivalent experience, resume, audition, interview, 3 letters of reference, video, personal choreography. Additional exam requirements/recommendations for international students: Required—TOEFL (minimum score 550 paper-based; 213 computer-based). *Application deadline:* For fall admission, 6/1 for domestic students, 4/1 for international students; for spring admission, 11/1 for domestic students, 9/1 for international students. Applications are processed on a rolling basis. Application fee: $40 ($90 for international students). Electronic applications accepted. *Expenses:* Tuition, state resident: full-time $3744; part-time $156 per credit hour. Tuition, nonresident: full-time $13,577; part-time $565.70 per credit hour. Required fees: $2415; $90.10 per credit hour. *Financial support:* In 2009–10, 8 students received support, including 5 fellowships with full tuition reimbursements available (averaging $4,889 per year), 7 teaching assistantships with partial tuition reimbursements available (averaging $13,884 per year); health care benefits and unspecified assistantships also available. Support available to part-time students. Financial award application deadline: 3/15; financial award applicants required to submit FAFSA. *Faculty research:* Dance history, body science, teaching methods and flamenco. *Unit head:* Mary Margaret Holt, Director, 405-325-4051, Fax: 405-325-7024, E-mail: marymholt@ou.edu. *Application contact:* Jeremy Lindberg, Associate Professor, 405-325-5312, Fax: 405-325-7024, E-mail: jlindberg@ou.edu.

University of Oregon, Graduate School, School of Music, Department of Dance, Eugene, OR 97403. Offers MA, MS. *Degree requirements:* For master's, thesis or alternative. *Entrance requirements:* For master's, minimum GPA of 3.0. Additional exam requirements/recommendations for international students: Required—TOEFL. *Faculty research:* Choreography, dance history, dance pedagogy, scientific aspects of dance.

The University of Texas at Austin, Graduate School, College of Fine Arts, Department of Theatre and Dance, Austin, TX 78712-1111. Offers acting (MFA); dance (MFA); directing (MFA); drama and theatre for youth (MFA); performance as public practice (MA, MFA, PhD); playwriting (MFA); theatre technology (MFA); theatrical design (MFA). *Accreditation:* NASD. *Degree requirements:* For master's, thesis; for doctorate, variable foreign language requirement, thesis/dissertation. *Entrance requirements:* For master's and doctorate, GRE General Test.

University of Utah, The Graduate School, College of Fine Arts, Department of Ballet, Salt Lake City, UT 84112. Offers MFA. *Accreditation:* NASD. *Faculty:* 7 full-time (4 women), 1 part-time/adjunct (0 women). *Students:* 11 full-time (10 women); includes 2 minority (both Asian Americans or Pacific Islanders), 2 international. Average age 28. 17 applicants, 59% accepted, 8 enrolled. In 2009, 5 master's awarded. *Degree requirements:* For master's, one foreign language, choreography projects, performance, teaching experience with written support. *Entrance requirements:* For master's, audition, videos/DVDs of teaching and choreography. Additional exam requirements/recommendations for international students: Required—TOEFL (minimum score 500 paper-based; 173 computer-based). *Application deadline:* For fall admission, 4/1 for domestic and international students; for spring admission, 10/1 for domestic and international students. Applications are processed on a rolling basis. Application fee: $55 ($65 for international students). *Expenses:* Tuition, state resident: full-time $4004; part-time $1674 per semester. Tuition, nonresident: full-time $14,134; part-time $5915 per semester. Required fees: $324 per semester. Tuition and fees vary according to course load, degree level and program. *Financial support:* In 2009–10, 1 teaching assistantship with full and partial tuition reimbursement (averaging $5,700 per year) was awarded; Federal Work-Study, institutionally sponsored loans, and scholarships/grants also available. Financial award application deadline: 3/1; financial award applicants required to submit FAFSA. *Faculty research:* Choreography, jazz, technique, fitness and dance injuries. *Unit head:* Bené C. Arnold, Interim Chair, 801-581-8231, Fax: 801-581-5442, E-mail: bene.arnold@utah.edu. *Application contact:* Richard Wacko, Associate Professor, 801-587-3742, E-mail: richard.wacko@utah.edu.

University of Utah, The Graduate School, College of Fine Arts, Department of Modern Dance, Salt Lake City, UT 84112. Offers MA, MFA. *Accreditation:* NASD. *Faculty:* 9 full-time (6 women). *Students:* 16 full-time (15 women), 3 part-time (2 women), 4 international. Average age 28. 21 applicants, 38% accepted, 7 enrolled. In 2009, 9 master's awarded. *Degree requirements:* For master's, thesis, project, oral examination. *Entrance requirements:* For master's, audition, interview, minimum GPA of 3.0. Additional exam requirements/recommendations for international students: Required—TOEFL (minimum score 500 paper-based; 173 computer-based). *Application deadline:* For fall admission, 3/1 for domestic and international students. Applications are processed on a rolling basis. Application fee: $55 ($65 for international students). Electronic applications accepted. *Expenses:* Tuition, state resident: full-time $4004; part-time $1674 per semester. Tuition, nonresident: full-time $14,134; part-time $5915 per semester. Required fees: $324 per semester. Tuition and fees vary according to course load, degree level and program. *Financial support:* In 2009–10, 14 students received support; fellowships with full and partial tuition reimbursements available, teaching assistantships with tuition reimbursements available, Federal Work-Study, institutionally sponsored loans, scholarships/grants, health care benefits, and unspecified assistantships available. Financial award application deadline: 3/1; financial award applicants required to submit FAFSA. *Faculty research:* Choreography, teaching methods, performance, cultural studies, dance technology. Total annual research expenditures: $9,912. *Unit head:* Donna White, Chair, 801-581-7327, Fax: 801-581-5442, E-mail: d.m.white@utah.edu. *Application contact:* Steve Koester, Director of Graduate Studies, 801-581-9808, Fax: 801-581-5442, E-mail: stephen.koester@utah.edu.

University of Washington, Graduate School, College of Arts and Sciences, Program in Dance, Seattle, WA 98195. Offers MFA. *Degree requirements:* For master's, performance, project. *Entrance requirements:* For master's, 8 years of professional dance experience, resume, performance DVD or VHS tape, 3 letters of reference. Electronic applications accepted. *Faculty research:* Choreography, history, anatomy.

University of Wisconsin–Milwaukee, Graduate School, Peck School of the Arts, Program in Performing Arts, Milwaukee, WI 53201-0413. Offers dance (MFA); film (MFA); theatre (MFA). Part-time programs available. *Faculty:* 31 full-time (19 women). *Students:* 18 full-time (12 women), 2 part-time (both women); includes 4 minority (2 African Americans, 1 Asian American or Pacific Islander, 1 Hispanic American), 1 international. Average age 34. 23 applicants, 22% accepted, 3 enrolled. In 2009, 18 master's awarded. *Degree requirements:* For master's, variable foreign language requirement, comprehensive exam, thesis or alternative. *Entrance requirements:* For master's, audition, interview. Additional exam requirements/recommendations for international students: Required—TOEFL (minimum score 550 paper-based; 79 iBT), IELTS (minimum score 6.5). *Application deadline:* For fall admission, 1/1 priority date for domestic students; for spring admission, 9/1 for domestic students. Applications are processed on a rolling basis. Application fee: $45 ($75 for international students). *Expenses:* Tuition, state resident: full-time $8800. Tuition, nonresident: full-time $20,760. Tuition and fees vary according to program and reciprocity agreements. *Financial support:* In 2009–10, 15 teaching assistantships were awarded; career-related internships or fieldwork and unspecified assistantships also available. Support available to part-time students. Financial award application deadline: 4/15. *Unit head:* Simone Ferro, Representative, 414-229-4178, E-mail: sferro@uwm.edu. *Application contact:* General Information Contact, 414-229-4982, Fax: 414-229-6967, E-mail: gradschool@uwm.edu.

York University, Faculty of Graduate Studies, Faculty of Fine Arts, Program in Dance, Toronto, ON M3J 1P3, Canada. Offers MA, MFA. *Degree requirements:* For master's, thesis or alternative. Electronic applications accepted.

Music

Alabama Agricultural and Mechanical University, School of Graduate Studies, School of Education, Area in Music Education, Huntsville, AL 35811. Offers music (MS); music education (M Ed). *Accreditation:* NCATE. Part-time and evening/weekend programs available. *Degree requirements:* For master's, comprehensive exam. *Entrance requirements:* For master's, GRE General Test. Additional exam requirements/recommendations for international students: Required—TOEFL (minimum score 500 paper-based; 173 computer-based; 61 iBT). Electronic applications accepted. *Faculty research:* Jazz and black music, Alabama folk music.

Alabama State University, School of Graduate Studies, Department of Music, Montgomery, AL 36101-0271. Offers instrumental music (M Ed); vocal/choral music (M Ed). *Accreditation:* NASM. Part-time programs available. *Degree requirements:* For master's, comprehensive exam. *Entrance requirements:* For master's, GRE General Test or MAT, graduate writing competency test. Additional exam requirements/recommendations for international students: Required—TOEFL (minimum score 500 paper-based; 173 computer-based). *Faculty research:* Computer applications.

Albany State University, College of Arts and Humanities, Program in Music Education, Albany, GA 31705-2717. Offers music (M Ed). *Accreditation:* NCATE. *Degree requirements:* For master's, comprehensive exam, teaching demonstration. *Entrance requirements:* For master's, placement examination in music theory and music history. *Expenses:* Tuition, state resident: full-time $2970; part-time $162 per credit hour. Tuition, nonresident: full-time $12,168; part-time $676 per credit hour. Required fees: $962; $75 per credit hour.

Andrews University, School of Graduate Studies, College of Arts and Sciences, Department of Music, Berrien Springs, MI 49104. Offers M Mus, MA. *Accreditation:* NASM. *Faculty:* 8 full-time (5 women). *Students:* 15 full-time (12 women), 8 part-time (3 women); includes 6 minority (2 African Americans, 4 Hispanic Americans), 15 international. Average age 30. 18 applicants, 56% accepted, 3 enrolled. In 2009, 4 master's awarded. *Degree requirements:* For master's, variable foreign language requirement. *Entrance requirements:* For master's, GRE Subject Test, minimum undergraduate GPA of 2.6. Additional exam requirements/recommendations for international students: Required—TOEFL (minimum score 550 paper-based). *Application deadline:* Applications are processed on a rolling basis. Application fee: $40. *Unit head:* Dr. Carlos Flores, Chairman, 269-471-3555. *Application contact:* Carolyn Hurst, Supervisor of Graduate Admission, 800-253-2874, Fax: 269-471-6321, E-mail: graduate@andrews.edu.

Appalachian State University, Cratis D. Williams Graduate School, School of Music, Boone, NC 28608. Offers music education (MM); music performance (MM); music therapy (MMT). *Accreditation:* NASM. Part-time programs available. *Faculty:* 29 full-time (11 women), 2 part-time/adjunct (both women). *Students:* 26 full-time (17 women), 7 part-time (5 women); includes 1 minority (African American), 1 international. 24 applicants, 92% accepted, 9 enrolled. In 2009, 7 master's awarded. *Degree requirements:* For master's, comprehensive exam, thesis or alternative. *Entrance requirements:* For master's, GRE General Test, 3 letters of reference, audition. Additional exam requirements/recommendations for international students: Required—TOEFL (minimum score 550 paper-based; 230 computer-based; 79 iBT), IELTS (minimum score 6.5). *Application deadline:* For fall admission, 7/1 for domestic students, 2/1 for inter-

Music

Appalachian State University (continued)
national students; for spring admission, 11/1 for domestic students, 7/1 for international students. Applications are processed on a rolling basis. Application fee: $50. Electronic applications accepted. *Expenses:* Tuition, state resident: full-time $2960. Tuition, nonresident: full-time $14,051. Required fees: $2320. *Financial support:* In 2009–10, 16 research assistantships (averaging $8,000 per year) were awarded; fellowships, teaching assistantships, career-related internships or fieldwork, Federal Work-Study, scholarships/grants, tuition waivers (partial), and unspecified assistantships also available. Financial award application deadline: 4/1; financial award applicants required to submit FAFSA. *Faculty research:* Music of the Holocaust, Celtic folk music, early nineteenth century performance practice, hypermeter and phase rhythm, world music, music and psychoneuroimmunology. *Unit head:* Dr. William Pelto, Dean, 828-262-6446, E-mail: peltowl@appstate.edu. *Application contact:* Dr. Nancy Schneeloch-Bingham, Graduate Program Director, 828-262-6463, E-mail: schneelochna@appstate.edu.

Arizona State University, Graduate College, Herberger College of the Arts, School of Music, Tempe, AZ 85287. Offers composition (MM); music (MA, DMA); music education (MM); music therapy (MM); performance (MM). *Accreditation:* NASM. *Degree requirements:* For doctorate, thesis/dissertation. *Entrance requirements:* For master's, GRE or MAT; for doctorate, GRE.

Arkansas State University—Jonesboro, Graduate School, College of Fine Arts, Department of Music, Jonesboro, State University, AR 72467. Offers music education (MME, SCCT); performance (MM). *Accreditation:* NASM (one or more programs are accredited). Part-time programs available. *Faculty:* 14 full-time (3 women), 2 part-time/adjunct (both women). *Students:* 6 full-time (3 women), 3 part-time (1 woman); includes 1 minority (American Indian/Alaska Native). Average age 29. 3 applicants, 67% accepted, 2 enrolled. In 2009, 5 master's awarded. *Degree requirements:* For master's, 2 foreign languages, comprehensive exam, thesis or alternative; for SCCT, comprehensive exam. *Entrance requirements:* For master's, GRE General Test or MAT, university entrance exam, appropriate bachelor's degree, audition; for SCCT, GRE General Test or MAT, interview, master's degree, official transcript, immunization records. Additional exam requirements/recommendations for international students: Required—TOEFL (minimum score 550 paper-based; 213 computer-based; 79 iBT), IELTS (minimum score 6). *Application deadline:* For fall admission, 7/1 for domestic and international students; for spring admission, 11/15 for domestic students, 11/13 for international students. Applications are processed on a rolling basis. Application fee: $30 ($40 for international students). Electronic applications accepted. *Expenses:* Tuition, state resident: full-time $3744; part-time $208 per credit hour. Tuition, nonresident: full-time $9540; part-time $530 per credit hour. Required fees: $896; $47 per credit hour. $25 per term. One-time fee: $50. Tuition and fees vary according to course load and program. *Financial support:* In 2009–10, 5 students received support; teaching assistantships, career-related internships or fieldwork, scholarships/grants, and unspecified assistantships available. Financial award application deadline: 7/1; financial award applicants required to submit FAFSA. *Unit head:* Ken Hatch, Interim Chair, 870-972-2094, Fax: 870-972-3932, E-mail: khatch@astate.edu. *Application contact:* Dr. Andrew Sustich, Dean of the Graduate School, 870-972-3029, Fax: 870-972-3857, E-mail: sustich@astate.edu.

Austin Peay State University, College of Graduate Studies, College of Arts and Letters, Department of Music, Clarksville, TN 37044. Offers music education (M Mu); music performance (M Mu). *Accreditation:* NASM. Part-time programs available. *Faculty:* 16 full-time (7 women), 2 part-time/adjunct (both women). *Students:* 21 full-time (9 women), 3 part-time (1 woman); includes 4 minority (2 African Americans, 1 Asian American or Pacific Islander, 1 Hispanic American), 1 international. Average age 29. 20 applicants, 100% accepted, 10 enrolled. In 2009, 7 master's awarded. *Degree requirements:* For master's, comprehensive exam, thesis optional. *Entrance requirements:* For master's, GRE General Test, diagnostic exams, audition, bachelor's degree, 3 letters of recommendation. Additional exam requirements/recommendations for international students: Required—TOEFL (minimum score 500 paper-based; 173 computer-based). *Application deadline:* For fall admission, 7/27 priority date for domestic students; for spring admission, 12/17 priority date for domestic students. Applications are processed on a rolling basis. Application fee: $25. Electronic applications accepted. *Expenses:* Tuition, state resident: full-time $6160; part-time $608 per credit hour. Tuition, nonresident: full-time $17,080; part-time $854 per credit hour. Required fees: $1224; $61.20 per credit hour. *Financial support:* In 2009–10, 11 students received support, including 11 research assistantships with full tuition reimbursements available (averaging $5,184 per year); career-related internships or fieldwork, Federal Work-Study, institutionally sponsored loans, scholarships/grants, and unspecified assistantships also available. Support available to part-time students. Financial award application deadline: 3/1; financial award applicants required to submit FAFSA. *Unit head:* Dr. Douglas Rose, Chair, 931-221-7808, Fax: 931-221-7529, E-mail: rosed@apsu.edu. *Application contact:* Dr. Dixie Dennis, Dean, College of Graduate Studies, 931-221-7662, Fax: 931-221-7641, E-mail: dennisdi@apsu.edu.

Azusa Pacific University, School of Music, Azusa, CA 91702-7000. Offers education (M Mus); performance (M Mus). *Accreditation:* NASM. Part-time and evening/weekend programs available. *Degree requirements:* For master's, recital. *Entrance requirements:* For master's, interview, audition. Additional exam requirements/recommendations for international students: Required—TOEFL (minimum score 550 paper-based). *Faculty research:* Tribal music of northeast India, rare Motown recordings in England.

Bard College, Conservatory of Music, The Conductors Institute, Annandale-on-Hudson, NY 12504. Offers MFA. *Entrance requirements:* For master's, resume, 3 letters of recommendation.

Bard College, Conservatory of Music, Graduate Program in Vocal Arts, Annandale-on-Hudson, NY 12504. Offers MM. *Entrance requirements:* For master's, portfolio, 3 letters of recommendation, headshot, repertoire list.

Baylor University, Graduate School, School of Music, Waco, TX 76798. Offers church music (MM); collaborative piano (MM); composition (MM); conducting (MM); music history and literature (MM); music theory (MM); performance (MM); piano pedagogy and performance (MM); M Div/MM. *Accreditation:* NASM. *Students:* 16 full-time (8 women), 35 part-time (16 women); includes 4 minority (1 American Indian/Alaska Native, 3 Hispanic Americans), 8 international. In 2009, 23 master's awarded. *Degree requirements:* For master's, variable foreign language requirement, thesis (for some programs). *Entrance requirements:* For master's, GRE General Test. *Application deadline:* For fall admission, 8/1 for domestic students; for spring admission, 12/1 for domestic students. Applications are processed on a rolling basis. Application fee: $25. *Financial support:* In 2009–10, 43 teaching assistantships with full tuition reimbursements (averaging $5,990 per year) were awarded; Federal Work-Study and institutionally sponsored loans also available. *Unit head:* Dr. David Music, Graduate Program Director, 254-710-2360, Fax: 254-710-1191, E-mail: david_music@baylor.edu. *Application contact:* Melinda Coates, Administrative Assistant, 254-710-2360, Fax: 254-710-3870, E-mail: melinda_coats@baylor.edu.

Belmont University, College of Visual and Performing Arts, School of Music, Nashville, TN 37212-3757. Offers church music (MM); composition (MM); music education (MM); pedagogy (MM); performance (MM). *Accreditation:* NASM. Part-time programs available. *Degree requirements:* For master's, comprehensive exam, thesis (for some programs). *Entrance requirements:* For master's, placement exam, GRE or MAT, audition, interview, minimum GPA of 2.75. Additional exam requirements/recommendations for international students: Required—TOEFL (minimum score 500 paper-based; 173 computer-based). Electronic applications accepted.

Bennington College, Graduate Programs, MFA in Music Program, Bennington, VT 05201. Offers MFA. Part-time programs available. *Faculty:* 7 full-time (2 women), 12 part-time/adjunct (4 women). *Students:* 1 (woman) full-time. Average age 52. 3 applicants, 33% accepted, 1 enrolled. *Degree requirements:* For master's, thesis, concert performances. *Application deadline:* For fall admission, 2/1 for domestic students. Application fee: $60. *Expenses:* Tuition: Full-time $20,950; part-time $2935 per course. One-time fee: $75. Tuition and fees vary according to program. *Financial support:* In 2009–10, 1 student received support, including 1 teaching assistantship (averaging $10,475 per year). Financial award application deadline: 4/1; financial award applicants required to submit FAFSA. *Unit head:* Allen Shawn, Director, 802-440-4525, E-mail: ashawn@bennington.edu. *Application contact:* Mary Surdam, Admissions Coordinator, 802-440-4312, Fax: 802-440-4320, E-mail: admissions@bennington.edu.

Bethesda Christian University, Graduate and Professional Programs, Anaheim, CA 92801. Offers biblical studies (MA); music (MA); theology (M Div). *Entrance requirements:* For M Div and master's, interview.

Birmingham-Southern College, Program in Music, Birmingham, AL 35254. Offers MM. *Accreditation:* NASM. *Entrance requirements:* For master's, 3 letters of recommendation, audition. Additional exam requirements/recommendations for international students: Required—TOEFL.

Bob Jones University, Graduate Programs, Greenville, SC 29614. Offers accountancy (MS); Bible (MA); Bible translation (MA); Biblical studies (Certificate); broadcast management (MS); business administration (MBA); church history (MA, PhD); church ministries (MA); church music (MM); cinema and video production (MA); counseling (MS); curriculum and instruction (Ed D); divinity (M Div); dramatic production (MA); educational leadership (MS, Ed D, Ed S); elementary education (M Ed, MAT); English (M Ed, MA, MAT); fine arts (MA); graphic design (MA); history (M Ed, MA); illustration (MA); interpretative speech (MA); mathematics (M Ed, MAT); medical missions (Certificate); ministry (MM, D Min); multi-categorical special education (M Ed, MAT); music (M Ed); New Testament interpretation (PhD); Old Testament interpretation (PhD); orchestral instrument performance (MM); organ performance (MM); pastoral studies (MA); personnel services (MS, Ed S); piano pedagogy (MM); piano performance (MM); platform arts (MA); radio and television broadcasting (MS); rhetoric and public address (MA); secondary education (M Ed); studio art (MA); teaching Bible (MA); theology (MA, PhD); voice performance (MM); youth ministries (MA); M Div/MM.

Boise State University, Graduate College, College of Arts and Sciences, Department of Music, Boise, ID 83725-0399. Offers music (MM); music education (MM); pedagogy (MM); performance (MM). *Accreditation:* NASM. Part-time programs available. *Degree requirements:* For master's, thesis optional. *Entrance requirements:* For master's, minimum GPA of 3.0, performance demonstration. Electronic applications accepted. *Expenses:* Tuition, state resident: full-time $3106; part-time $209 per credit. Tuition, nonresident: part-time $284 per credit.

The Boston Conservatory, Graduate Division, Music Division, Boston, MA 02215. Offers music (MM, ADP, Certificate); music education (MM). Part-time programs available. *Degree requirements:* For master's, thesis (for some programs), recital; for other advanced degree, recital. *Entrance requirements:* For master's and other advanced degree, audition. Electronic applications accepted.

Boston University, College of Fine Arts, School of Music, Boston, MA 02215. Offers collaborative piano (MM, DMA); composition (MM, DMA); conducting (MM, Artist Diploma, Performance Diploma); historical performance (MM, DMA, Artist Diploma, Performance Diploma); music education (MM, DMA); music theory (MM); musicology (MM); opera performance (Certificate); performance (MM, DMA, Artist Diploma, Performance Diploma). *Accreditation:* NASM. Part-time programs available. *Faculty:* 36 full-time, 21 part-time/adjunct. *Students:* 279 full-time (182 women), 8 part-time (4 women); includes 28 minority (8 African Americans, 2 American Indian/Alaska Native, 14 Asian Americans or Pacific Islanders, 4 Hispanic Americans), 107 international. Average age 29. 632 applicants, 48% accepted, 110 enrolled. In 2009, 61 master's, 11 doctorates, 14 other advanced degrees awarded. *Degree requirements:* For master's, thesis; for doctorate, 2 foreign languages, thesis/dissertation. *Entrance requirements:* Additional exam requirements/recommendations for international students: Required—TOEFL. *Application deadline:* For fall admission, 1/1 priority date for domestic and international students. Application fee: $60. Electronic applications accepted. *Expenses:* Tuition: Full-time $37,910; part-time $1184 per credit hour. Required fees: $386; $40 per semester. Part-time tuition and fees vary according to class time, course level, degree level and program. *Financial support:* Fellowships, teaching assistantships available. Financial award application deadline: 1/15. *Unit head:* Robert Dodson, Director, 617-353-8789, Fax: 617-353-7455, E-mail: jfilippi@bu.edu. *Application contact:* Mark Krone, Manager, Graduate Admissions, E-mail: arts@bu.edu.

Boston University, Graduate School of Arts and Sciences, Department of Music, Boston, MA 02215. Offers composition (MA); music education (MA); music history/theory (PhD); musicology (MA, PhD). *Accreditation:* NASM. *Students:* 2 part-time (1 woman); includes 1 minority (Hispanic American). Average age 28. 19 applicants, 32% accepted, 2 enrolled. In 2009, 1 master's awarded. *Degree requirements:* For master's, 2 foreign languages, comprehensive exam, thesis; for doctorate, 2 foreign languages, comprehensive exam, thesis/dissertation. *Entrance requirements:* For master's and doctorate, GRE General Test, musical composition or research paper, 3 letters of recommendation. Additional exam requirements/recommendations for international students: Required—TOEFL (minimum score 550 paper-based; 213 computer-based). *Application deadline:* For fall admission, 3/15 for domestic and international students; for spring admission, 10/15 for domestic and international students. Application fee: $70. Electronic applications accepted. *Expenses:* Tuition: Full-time $37,910; part-time $1184 per credit hour. Required fees: $386; $40 per semester. Part-time tuition and fees vary according to class time, course level, degree level and program. *Financial support:* Federal Work-Study, scholarships/grants, and unspecified assistantships available. Support available to part-time students. Financial award application deadline: 1/15; financial award applicants required to submit FAFSA. *Unit head:* Jeremy Yudkin, Director, 617-353-3362, Fax: 617-353-7455, E-mail: yudkinj@bu.edu. *Application contact:* Jessica Smith, Administrative Coordinator, 617-353-6887, Fax: 617-353-7455, E-mail: smithj08@bu.edu.

Bowling Green State University, Graduate College, College of Musical Arts, Bowling Green, OH 43403. Offers composition (MM); contemporary music (DMA), including composition, performance; ethnomusicology (MM); music education (MM), including choral, comprehensive, instrumental; music history (MM); music theory (MM); performance (MM). *Accreditation:* NASM. Part-time programs available. *Degree requirements:* For master's, thesis or alternative, recitals; for doctorate, comprehensive exam, thesis/dissertation. *Entrance requirements:* For master's, GRE General Test, diagnostic placement exams in music history and theory, audition, interview. Additional exam requirements/recommendations for international students: Required—TOEFL. Electronic applications accepted. *Faculty research:* Ethnomusicology.

Brandeis University, Graduate School of Arts and Sciences, Department of Music, Waltham, MA 02454-9110. Offers composition and theory (MA, MFA, PhD); music and women's and gender studies (MA); musicology (MA, MFA, PhD). Part-time programs available. *Faculty:* 7 full-time (1 woman), 8 part-time/adjunct (3 women). *Students:* 46 full-time (18 women), 1 (woman) part-time; includes 2 minority (1 Asian American or Pacific Islander, 1 Hispanic American), 9 international. Average age 28. 73 applicants, 33% accepted, 15 enrolled. In 2009, 6 master's, 4 doctorates awarded. Terminal master's awarded for partial completion of doctoral program. *Degree requirements:* For master's, one foreign language, thesis or alternative; for doctorate, 2 foreign languages, comprehensive exam, thesis/dissertation. *Entrance requirements:* For master's, GRE General Test (musicology), resume, sample of work (music composition), letters of recommendation; for doctorate, GRE General Test (musicology), resume, writing sample (musicology), letters of recommendation, sample of work—recording (composition). Additional exam requirements/recommendations for international students: Required—TOEFL (minimum score 600 paper-based; 250 computer-based; 100 iBT); Recommended—IELTS (minimum score 7). *Application deadline:* For fall admission, 1/31 for domestic and international students. Application fee: $75. Electronic applications accepted. *Financial support:* In 2009–10, 23 students received support, including 24 fellowships with full tuition reimbursements available (averaging $20,000 per year), 4 teaching assistantships with partial tuition reimbursements available (averaging $3,200 per year); research assistantships, scholarships/grants, health care benefits, and tuition waivers (full and partial) also available. Support available to part-time students. Financial award application deadline: 4/15; financial award applicants required to submit FAFSA. *Faculty research:* History of theory; music of Monteverdi, Bach, Mozart, Lizst, and Wagner; compositional process; computer music. *Unit head:* Prof. Mary Ruth Ray, Chair, 781-736-3310, E-mail: ray@brandeis.edu. *Application contact:* Mark Kagan, Senior Academic Administrator, 781-736-3311, E-mail: kagan@brandeis.edu.

Brandon University, School of Music, Brandon, MB R7A 6A9, Canada. Offers composition (M Mus); music education (M Mus); performance and literature (M Mus), including piano, strings. Part-time programs available. *Faculty:* 8 full-time (4 women). *Students:* 8 full-time (4 women), 1 part-time (0 women), 2 international. Average age 25. 7 applicants, 100% accepted. In 2009, 2 master's awarded. *Degree requirements:* For master's, comprehensive exam (for some programs), thesis (for some programs). *Entrance requirements:* For master's, B Mus. Additional exam requirements/recommendations for international students: Required—TOEFL (minimum score 580 paper-based; 237 computer-based) or IELTS. *Application deadline:* For spring admission, 5/1 priority date for domestic students. Applications are processed on a rolling basis. Application fee: $60 ($125 for international students). Electronic applications accepted. *Financial support:* In 2009–10, 4 students received support, including 1 research assistantship, 3 teaching assistantships (averaging $3,250 per year). Financial award application deadline: 5/1. *Faculty research:* Composition, community music, evaluation and assessment, performance anxiety, performance injuries, philosophy of music, teacher education. *Unit head:* Dr. Michael Kim, Dean, 204-727-9633, Fax: 204-728-6839, E-mail: kimm@brandonu.ca. *Application contact:* Dr. Sheila Scott, Joint Chair of Graduate Music Department, 204-727-7435, Fax: 204-728-6839.

Brigham Young University, Graduate Studies, College of Fine Arts and Communications, School of Music, Provo, UT 84602-1001. Offers composition (MM); conducting (MM); music education (MA, MM); musicology (MA); performance (MM). *Accreditation:* NASM. *Faculty:* 44 full-time (8 women). *Students:* 56 full-time (40 women), 9 part-time (4 women); includes 4 minority (all Asian Americans or Pacific Islanders). Average age 28. 54 applicants, 57% accepted, 27 enrolled. In 2009, 25 master's awarded. *Degree requirements:* For master's, comprehensive exam (for some programs), thesis (for some programs), recital, project or composition (for some programs). *Entrance requirements:* For master's, placement exam, minimum GPA of 3.0 in last 60 hours, BM. Additional exam requirements/recommendations for international students: Required—TOEFL (minimum score 580 paper-based; 237 computer-based; 85 iBT). *Application deadline:* For fall admission, 2/1 priority date for domestic students, 1/15 priority date for international students. Application fee: $50. Electronic applications accepted. *Expenses:* Tuition: Full-time $5580; part-time $301 per credit hour. Tuition and fees vary according to student's religious affiliation. *Financial support:* In 2009–10, 56 students received support, including 39 teaching assistantships (averaging $5,000 per year); research assistantships, career-related internships or fieldwork, institutionally sponsored loans, scholarships/grants, tuition waivers (partial), and unspecified assistantships also available. Support available to part-time students. Financial award application deadline: 2/1; financial award applicants required to submit FAFSA. *Faculty research:* Louis Armstrong, rock and roll, Balinese gamelan. *Unit head:* Prof. Kory L. Katseanes, Director, 801-422-6304, Fax: 801-422-0533, E-mail: kory_katseanes@byu.edu. *Application contact:* Dr. Thomas L. Durham, Graduate Coordinator, 801-422-3226, Fax: 801-422-0533, E-mail: thomas_durham@byu.edu.

Brooklyn College of the City University of New York, Division of Graduate Studies, Conservatory of Music, Brooklyn, NY 11210-2889. Offers composition (MM); music (DMA, PhD); music education (MA); musicology (MA); performance (MM); performance practice (MA). Part-time programs available. *Students:* 1 full-time (0 women), 78 part-time (44 women); includes 15 minority (4 African Americans, 2 Asian Americans or Pacific Islanders, 9 Hispanic Americans), 14 international. Average age 28. 76 applicants, 79% accepted, 37 enrolled. In 2009, 24 master's awarded. *Degree requirements:* For master's, one foreign language, comprehensive exam, thesis. *Entrance requirements:* For master's, placement exam, 36 credits in music, audition, completed composition, writing sample. Additional exam requirements/recommendations for international students: Required—TOEFL (minimum score 550 paper-based; 213 computer-based; 79 iBT). *Application deadline:* For fall admission, 3/1 priority date for domestic students, 2/1 priority date for international students; for spring admission, 11/1 priority date for domestic students, 10/1 priority date for international students. Applications are processed on a rolling basis. Application fee: $125. Electronic applications accepted. *Expenses:* Tuition, area resident: Full-time $7360; part-time $310 per credit hour. Tuition, state resident: full-time $7360; part-time $310 per credit hour. Tuition, nonresident: full-time $13,800; part-time $575 per credit hour. International tuition: $13,800 full-time. Required fees: $140.10 per semester. *Financial support:* Career-related internships or fieldwork, Federal Work-Study, institutionally sponsored loans, and scholarships/grants available. Support available to part-time students. Financial award application deadline: 5/1; financial award applicants required to submit FAFSA. *Faculty research:* American music, computer music. *Unit head:* Dr. Bruce MacIntyre, Chairperson, 718-951-5286, E-mail: brucem@brooklyn.cuny.edu. *Application contact:* Hernan Sierra, Graduate Admissions Coordinator, 718-951-4536, Fax: 718-951-4506, E-mail: grads@brooklyn.cuny.edu.

Brooklyn College of the City University of New York, Division of Graduate Studies, Program in Performance and Interactive Media Arts, Brooklyn, NY 11210-2889. Offers MFA, CAS. *Students:* 11 full-time (7 women), 14 part-time (9 women); includes 6 minority (2 African Americans, 4 Hispanic Americans), 3 international. Average age 31. In 2009, 3 master's, 1 other advanced degree awarded. *Entrance requirements:* For master's, 2 letters of recommendation, resume, portfolio, interview; for CAS, 2 letters of recommendation. Additional exam requirements/recommendations for international students: Required—TOEFL (minimum score 500 paper-based; 173 computer-based; 61 iBT). *Application deadline:* For fall admission, 2/15 priority date for domestic students, 2/1 priority date for international students. Applications are processed on a rolling basis. Application fee: $125. Electronic applications accepted. *Expenses:* Tuition, area resident: Full-time $7360; part-time $310 per credit hour. Tuition, state resident: full-time $7360; part-time $310 per credit hour. Tuition, nonresident: full-time $13,800; part-time $575 per credit hour. International tuition: $13,800 full-time. Required fees: $140.10 per semester. *Financial support:* Application deadline: 5/1. *Unit head:* Dr. David Grubbs, Director, 718-951-4203, E-mail: dgrubbs@brooklyn.cuny.edu. *Application contact:* Hernan Sierra, Graduate Admissions Coordinator, 718-951-4536, Fax: 718-951-4506, E-mail: grads@brooklyn.cuny.edu.

Brown University, Graduate School, Department of Music, Providence, RI 02912. Offers electronic music and multimedia (PhD); ethnomusicology (PhD). *Degree requirements:* For doctorate, 2 foreign languages, comprehensive exam, thesis/dissertation, departmental qualifying exam. *Entrance requirements:* For doctorate, GRE General Test. *Faculty research:* Ethnomusicology.

Butler University, Jordan College of Fine Arts, Department of Music, Indianapolis, IN 46208-3485. Offers composition (MM); conducting (MM); music (MM); music education (MM); music history (MM); organ (MM); performance (MM). *Accreditation:* NASM. Part-time and evening/weekend programs available. *Faculty:* 14 full-time (3 women), 10 part-time/adjunct (3 women). *Students:* 20 full-time (8 women), 20 part-time (6 women), 5 international. Average age 27. 40 applicants, 48% accepted, 8 enrolled. In 2009, 10 master's awarded. *Degree requirements:* For master's, thesis (for some programs). *Entrance requirements:* For master's, GRE General Test, GRE Subject Test, audition, interview. *Application deadline:* For fall admission, 8/15 priority date for domestic students. Applications are processed on a rolling basis. Application fee: $35. Electronic applications accepted. *Financial support:* In 2009–10, 15 teaching assistantships with full tuition reimbursements (averaging $2,500 per year) were awarded; fellowships, career-related internships or fieldwork, institutionally sponsored loans, and scholarships/grants also available. Support available to part-time students. Financial award application deadline: 7/15; financial award applicants required to submit FAFSA. *Unit head:* Dr. Daniel Bolin, Head, 317-940-9988, Fax: 317-940-9658, E-mail: dbolin@butler.edu. *Application contact:* Kathy Lang, Admission Representative, 317-940-9646, Fax: 317-940-9658, E-mail: klang@butler.edu.

California Baptist University, Program in Music, Riverside, CA 92504-3206. Offers conducting (MM); music education (MM); performance (MM). *Accreditation:* NASM. Part-time programs available. *Faculty:* 4 full-time (1 woman), 1 (woman) part-time/adjunct. *Students:* 15 full-time (10 women), 4 part-time (3 women); includes 2 minority (both African Americans), 10 international. 12 applicants, 42% accepted, 4 enrolled. In 2009, 6 master's awarded. *Degree requirements:* For master's, thesis or alternative. *Entrance requirements:* For master's, minimum undergraduate GPA of 2.75; bachelor's degree in music. Additional exam requirements/recommendations for international students: Required—TOEFL (minimum score 575 paper-based; 230 computer-based; 89 iBT). *Application deadline:* For fall admission, 8/1 priority date for domestic students, 7/1 for international students; for spring admission, 12/1 priority date for domestic students, 10/15 for international students. Applications are processed on a rolling basis. Application fee: $45. Electronic applications accepted. *Expenses:* Tuition: Full-time $8352; part-time $464 per semester hour. Required fees: $125 per semester. Tuition and fees vary according to course load, campus/location and program. *Financial support:* Federal Work-Study and scholarships/grants available. Support available to part-time students. Financial award applicants required to submit FAFSA. *Unit head:* Dr. Gary Bonner, Dean, School of Music, 951-343-4251, Fax: 951-343-4570, E-mail: gbonner@calbaptist.edu. *Application contact:* Gail Ronveaux, Dean of Graduate Enrollment, 951-343-5045, Fax: 951-343-5095, E-mail: graduateadmissions@calbaptist.edu.

California Institute of the Arts, School of Music, Valencia, CA 91355-2340. Offers African music (MFA, Adv C); composition (MFA, Adv C); composition/new media (MFA, Adv C); Indonesian music (MFA, Adv C); jazz (MFA, Adv C); North Indian music (MFA, Adv C); performance (MFA, Adv C); performer/composer (MFA, Adv C); voice (MFA, Adv C); world music performance (MFA). *Accreditation:* NASM. Part-time programs available. *Degree requirements:* For master's, composition or recital. *Entrance requirements:* For master's, audition or portfolio. Additional exam requirements/recommendations for international students: Required—TOEFL. Electronic applications accepted. *Faculty research:* Music composition and twentieth century performance practice, interactive multimedia and computer music, music cognition.

California State University, Chico, Graduate School, College of Humanities and Fine Arts, Department of Music, Chico, CA 95929-0722. Offers MA. *Accreditation:* NASM. *Students:* 4 part-time (2 women). Average age 37. 3 applicants, 0% accepted, 0 enrolled. In 2009, 7 master's awarded. *Degree requirements:* For master's, thesis or alternative, recital. *Entrance requirements:* For master's, GRE General Test, departmental exam, audition tape (off-campus applicants), music scores (for composers), 2 letters of recommendation. Additional exam requirements/recommendations for international students: Required—TOEFL (minimum score 550 paper-based; 213 computer-based; 80 iBT), IELTS (minimum score 6.5). *Application deadline:* For fall admission, 3/1 priority date for domestic students, 3/1 for international students; for spring admission, 9/15 priority date for domestic students, 9/15 for international students. Applications are processed on a rolling basis. Application fee: $55. Electronic applications accepted. *Financial support:* Teaching assistantships available. *Unit head:* Dr. Warren Pinckney, Graduate Coordinator, 530-898-4795. *Application contact:* Dr. Warren Pinckney, Graduate Coordinator, 530-898-4795.

California State University, East Bay, Academic Programs and Graduate Studies, College of Letters, Arts, and Social Sciences, Department of Music, Hayward, CA 94542-3000. Offers MA. *Accreditation:* NASM. Part-time programs available. *Faculty:* 6 full-time (0 women). *Students:* 7 full-time (3 women), 18 part-time (7 women); includes 3 minority (2 Asian Americans or Pacific Islanders, 1 Hispanic American), 2 international. Average age 36. 22 applicants, 55% accepted, 10 enrolled. In 2009, 6 master's awarded. *Degree requirements:* For master's, variable foreign language requirement, comprehensive exam, project, recital, or thesis. *Entrance requirements:* For master's, minimum GPA of 3.0 in field; audition or work sample. Additional exam requirements/recommendations for international students: Required—TOEFL (minimum score 550 paper-based; 213 computer-based). *Application deadline:* For fall admission, 5/14 for domestic and international students. Application fee: $55. Electronic applications accepted. *Financial support:* Fellowships, Federal Work-Study, institutionally sponsored loans, and scholarships/grants available. Support available to part-time students. Financial award application deadline: 3/2. *Unit head:* Dr. Rafael Hernandez, Chair, 510-885-3135, E-mail: rafael.hernandez@csueastbay.edu. *Application contact:* Donna Wiley, Interim Associate Director, 510-885-2928, Fax: 510-885-4777, E-mail: donna.wiley@csueastbay.edu.

California State University, Fresno, Division of Graduate Studies, College of Arts and Humanities, Department of Music, Fresno, CA 93740-8027. Offers music (MA); music education (MA); performance (MA). *Accreditation:* NASM. Part-time programs available. *Degree requirements:* For master's, thesis or alternative. *Entrance requirements:* For master's, GRE General Test, BA in music, minimum GPA of 3.0. Additional exam requirements/recommendations for international students: Required—TOEFL. Electronic applications accepted. *Faculty research:* Technology transfer, folk art.

California State University, Fullerton, Graduate Studies, College of the Arts, Department of Music, Fullerton, CA 92834-9480. Offers music education (MA); music history and literature (MA); performance (MM); piano pedagogy (MA); theory-composition (MM). *Accreditation:* NASM. Part-time programs available. *Students:* 19 full-time (11 women), 53 part-time (31 women); includes 21 minority (1 African American, 15 Asian Americans or Pacific Islanders, 5 Hispanic Americans), 10 international. Average age 29. 68 applicants, 37% accepted, 18 enrolled. In 2009, 17 master's awarded. *Degree requirements:* For master's, comprehensive exam, project or thesis. *Entrance requirements:* For master's, audition, major in music or related field, minimum GPA of 2.5 in last 60 units of course work. Application fee: $55. *Expenses:* Tuition, nonresident: full-time $11,160; part-time $373 per credit. Required fees: $1440 per term. Tuition and fees vary according to course load, degree level and program. *Financial support:* Career-related internships or fieldwork, Federal Work-Study, institutionally sponsored loans, and scholarships/grants available. Support available to part-time students. Financial award application deadline: 3/1; financial award applicants required to submit FAFSA. *Unit head:* Dr. Marc Dickey, Chair, 657-278-3511. *Application contact:* Admissions/Applications, 657-278-2371.

California State University, Long Beach, Graduate Studies, College of the Arts, Department of Music, Long Beach, CA 90840. Offers composition (MM); conducting-choral (MM); conducting-instrumental (MM); instrument/vocal performance (MM); jazz studies (MM); music (MA); opera performance (MM). *Accreditation:* NASM. Part-time programs available. *Faculty:* 26 full-time (3 women), 35 part-time/adjunct (11 women). *Students:* 51 full-time (22 women), 30 part-time (17 women); includes 18 minority (1 African American, 8 Asian Americans or Pacific Islanders, 9 Hispanic Americans), 7 international. Average age 30. 98 applicants, 48% accepted, 34 enrolled. *Degree requirements:* For master's, thesis or alternative, departmental qualifying exam. *Application deadline:* For fall admission, 5/1 for domestic students; for spring admission, 12/1 for domestic students. Applications are processed on a rolling basis. Application fee: $55. Electronic applications accepted. *Expenses:* Required fees: $1802 per semester. Part-time tuition and fees vary according to course load. *Financial support:* Federal Work-Study, institutionally sponsored loans, and scholarships/grants available. Financial award application deadline: 3/2. *Unit head:* John A. Carnahan, Director, 562-985-4781, Fax: 562-985-2490, E-mail: jcarnaha@csulb.edu. *Application contact:* Dr. Leland Vail, Graduate Advisor, 562-985-4399, Fax: 562-985-2490, E-mail: lvail@csulb.edu.

California State University, Long Beach, Graduate Studies, College of the Arts, Department of Theatre Arts, Long Beach, CA 90840. Offers acting (MFA); design (MFA); theatre management (MFA); MBA/MFA. *Accreditation:* NAST. Part-time programs available. *Faculty:* 11 full-time (9 women). *Students:* 38 full-time (26 women), 15 part-time (10 women); includes 5 minority (4 Asian Americans or Pacific Islanders, 1 Hispanic American), 10 international. Average age 30. 24 applicants, 29% accepted, 5 enrolled. *Degree requirements:* For master's, thesis or alternative. *Application deadline:* For fall admission, 7/1 for domestic students; for spring admission, 12/1 for domestic students. Applications are processed on a rolling basis. Application

Music

California State University, Long Beach (continued)
fee: $55. Electronic applications accepted. *Expenses:* Required fees: $1802 per semester. Part-time tuition and fees vary according to course load. *Financial support:* Research assistantships, teaching assistantships, Federal Work-Study, institutionally sponsored loans, scholarships/grants, and traineeships available. Financial award application deadline: 3/2. *Unit head:* Dr. Joanne L. Gordon, Chair, 562-985-7891, Fax: 562-985-2263, E-mail: jgordon@csulb.edu. *Application contact:* Barbara Matthews, Graduate Advisor, 562-985-4042, Fax: 562-985-2263, E-mail: jmatthew@csulb.edu.

California State University, Los Angeles, Graduate Studies, College of Arts and Letters, Department of Music, Los Angeles, CA 90032-8530. Offers music composition (MM); music education (MA); musicology (MA); performance (MM). *Accreditation:* NASM. Part-time and evening/weekend programs available. *Faculty:* 13 full-time (3 women), 10 part-time/adjunct (4 women). *Students:* 32 full-time (12 women), 34 part-time (13 women); includes 25 minority (4 African Americans, 5 Asian Americans or Pacific Islanders, 16 Hispanic Americans), 8 international. Average age 37. 21 applicants, 100% accepted, 11 enrolled. In 2009, 28 master's awarded. *Degree requirements:* For master's, comprehensive exam, project or thesis. *Entrance requirements:* For master's, audition. Additional exam requirements/recommendations for international students: Required—TOEFL (minimum score 500 paper-based; 173 computer-based). *Application deadline:* For fall admission, 5/1 for domestic and international students. Applications are processed on a rolling basis. Application fee: $55. Electronic applications accepted. *Financial support:* Career-related internships or fieldwork and Federal Work-Study available. Support available to part-time students. Financial award application deadline: 3/1. *Faculty research:* Gregorian semiology, Baroque opera. *Unit head:* Dr. George DeGraffenreid, Chair, 323-343-4060, Fax: 323-343-4063, E-mail: gdegraf@calstatela.edu. *Application contact:* Dr. Cheryl L. Ney, Associate Vice President for Academic Affairs and Dean of Graduate Studies, 323-343-3820, Fax: 323-343-5653, E-mail: cney@cslanet.calstatela.edu.

California State University, Northridge, Graduate Studies, College of Arts, Media, and Communication, Department of Music, Northridge, CA 91330. Offers composition (MM); conducting (MM); music education (MA); performance (MM). *Accreditation:* NASM. *Faculty:* 22 full-time (6 women), 47 part-time/adjunct (15 women). *Students:* 29 full-time (20 women), 32 part-time (19 women); includes 16 minority (3 African Americans, 4 Asian Americans or Pacific Islanders, 9 Hispanic Americans), 10 international. Average age 29. 92 applicants, 36% accepted, 22 enrolled. In 2009, 17 master's awarded. *Degree requirements:* For master's, thesis. *Entrance requirements:* For master's, audition, GRE General Test or minimum GPA of 3.0. Additional exam requirements/recommendations for international students: Required—TOEFL. *Application deadline:* For fall admission, 11/30 for domestic students. Application fee: $55. *Financial support:* Application deadline: 3/1. *Faculty research:* Touring program. *Unit head:* Dr. Elizabeth Sellers, Chair, 816-677-4752, E-mail: elizabeth.a.sellers@csun.edu. *Application contact:* Julia Heinen, Graduate Advisor, 818-677-3168, E-mail: julia.heinen@csun.edu.

California State University, Sacramento, Graduate Studies, College of Arts and Letters, Department of Music, Sacramento, CA 95819. Offers MM. *Accreditation:* NASM. Part-time programs available. *Degree requirements:* For master's, thesis or alternative, writing proficiency exam. *Entrance requirements:* For master's, BA in music or equivalent, minimum GPA of 2.5 during previous 2 years of course work. Additional exam requirements/recommendations for international students: Required—TOEFL. Electronic applications accepted.

Campbellsville University, School of Music, Campbellsville, KY 42718-2799. Offers church music (MM); music (MA); music education (MM). *Accreditation:* NASM. Part-time programs available. *Degree requirements:* For master's, thesis (for some programs), paper or recital. *Entrance requirements:* For master's, GRE General Test or PRAXIS, minimum GPA of 2.75. Additional exam requirements/recommendations for international students: Required—TOEFL (minimum score 550 paper-based). Electronic applications accepted. *Expenses:* Tuition: Full-time $6750; part-time $375 per credit hour.

Capital University, Conservatory of Music, Columbus, OH 43209-2394. Offers music education (MM), including instrumental emphasis, Kodály emphasis. Program offered only in summer. *Accreditation:* NASM. Part-time programs available. *Degree requirements:* For master's, comprehensive exam, thesis or alternative, chamber performance exam. *Entrance requirements:* For master's, music theory exam, minimum undergraduate GPA of 3.0. Additional exam requirements/recommendations for international students: Required—TOEFL (minimum score 550 paper-based; 213 computer-based; 80 iBT). Electronic applications accepted. *Expenses:* Contact institution. *Faculty research:* Folk song research, Kodály method, performance, composition.

Cardinal Stritch University, College of Arts and Sciences, Music Department, Milwaukee, WI 53217-3985. Offers piano (MM). Part-time programs available. *Degree requirements:* For master's, comprehensive exam, recital permission audition. *Entrance requirements:* For master's, placement test in music theory and music history, 3 letters of recommendation, audition. Electronic applications accepted.

Carleton University, Faculty of Graduate Studies, Faculty of Arts and Social Sciences, School for Studies in Art and Culture, Program in Music and Culture, Ottawa, ON K1S 5B6, Canada. Offers MA.

Carnegie Mellon University, College of Fine Arts, School of Music, Pittsburgh, PA 15213-3891. Offers composition (MM); conducting (MM); instrumental performance (MM); music and technology (MS); music education (MM); vocal performance (MM). *Accreditation:* NASM. Part-time programs available. *Degree requirements:* For master's, comprehensive exam, recital. *Entrance requirements:* For master's, audition. *Faculty research:* Computer music, music history.

Case Western Reserve University, School of Graduate Studies, Department of Music, Cleveland, OH 44106. Offers early music (MA, D Mus A); music education (MA, PhD); music history (MA); musicology (PhD). *Accreditation:* NASM (one or more programs are accredited). *Faculty:* 13 full-time (5 women), 15 part-time/adjunct (8 women). *Students:* 28 full-time (14 women), 8 part-time (2 women); includes 4 minority (1 African American, 2 Asian Americans or Pacific Islanders, 1 Hispanic American), 1 international. Average age 28. 40 applicants, 38% accepted, 13 enrolled. In 2009, 9 master's awarded. *Degree requirements:* For doctorate, thesis/dissertation. *Entrance requirements:* For master's and doctorate, GRE, audition/writing sample. Additional exam requirements/recommendations for international students: Required—TOEFL (minimum score 550 paper-based; 213 computer-based; 79 iBT). *Application deadline:* For fall admission, 1/15 priority date for domestic students. Application fee: $50. Electronic applications accepted. *Financial support:* Fellowships, research assistantships, teaching assistantships, career-related internships or fieldwork and tuition waivers (full) available. Financial award application deadline: 1/15; financial award applicants required to submit FAFSA. *Faculty research:* Early music performance practices; sixteenth, seventeenth, and twentieth centuries; Mahler; wind ensemble direction; measurement/evaluation in music education. *Unit head:* Mary E. Davis, Chair, 216-368-2400, Fax: 216-368-6557, E-mail: mary.e.davis@case.edu. *Application contact:* Laura Stauffer, Admissions, 216-368-2400, Fax: 216-368-6557, E-mail: laura.stauffer@case.edu.

The Catholic University of America, The Benjamin T. Rome School of Music, Washington, DC 20064. Offers chamber music (MM); composition (MM, DMA), including concert music (DMA), stage music (MM); music (Certificate); musicology (MA, PhD), including music history (MA), music theory (MA); orchestral conducting (MM); orchestral instruments (DMA); piano pedagogy (MM, DMA); piano performance (MM); sacred music (MMSM, DMA); vocal pedagogy (MM); vocal performance (MM). *Accreditation:* NASM. Part-time programs available. *Faculty:* 17 full-time (4 women), 23 part-time/adjunct (9 women). *Students:* 45 full-time (23 women), 91 part-time (60 women); includes 25 minority (6 African Americans, 11 Asian Americans or Pacific Islanders, 8 Hispanic Americans), 25 international. Average age 33. 121 applicants, 60% accepted, 38 enrolled. In 2009, 18 master's, 13 doctorates awarded. *Degree requirements:* For master's, comprehensive exam (for some programs), thesis (for some programs); for doctorate, comprehensive exam (for some programs), thesis/dissertation (for some programs), minimum GPA of 3.0. *Entrance requirements:* For master's, theory placement test, 2 letters of recommendation, minimum undergraduate B average, BA in music, demonstration of performance proficiency; for doctorate, school qualifying exam, statement of purpose, official copies of academic transcripts, 4 letters of recommendation, audition/interview. Additional exam requirements/recommendations for international students: Required—TOEFL (minimum score 580 paper-based; 237 computer-based). *Application deadline:* For fall admission, 8/1 priority date for domestic students, 7/15 for international students; for spring admission, 12/1 priority date for domestic students, 10/15 for international students. Applications are processed on a rolling basis. Application fee: $55. Electronic applications accepted. *Expenses:* Tuition: Full-time $31,740; part-time $1245 per credit hour. Required fees: $50; $25 per semester hour. One-time fee: $425. *Financial support:* Fellowships, research assistantships, teaching assistantships, Federal Work-Study, scholarships/grants, tuition waivers (full and partial), and unspecified assistantships available. Financial award application deadline: 2/1; financial award applicants required to submit FAFSA. *Faculty research:* Composition, sacred music, orchestral instruments, piano, voice, music history and theory. *Unit head:* Murry Sidlin, Dean, 202-319-5417, Fax: 202-319-6280, E-mail: cua-music@cua.edu. *Application contact:* Julie Schwing, Director of Graduate Admissions, 202-319-5057, Fax: 202-319-6533, E-mail: cua-admissions@cua.edu.

Central Michigan University, College of Graduate Studies, College of Communication and Fine Arts, School of Music, Mount Pleasant, MI 48859. Offers conducting (MM); music composition (MM); music education (MM); music performance (MM); piano pedagogy (MM). *Accreditation:* NASM. Part-time programs available. *Degree requirements:* For master's, thesis or alternative. Electronic applications accepted. *Faculty research:* Music education, music composition, conducting, music performance, piano pedagogy.

Central Washington University, Graduate Studies and Research, College of Arts and Humanities, Department of Music, Ellensburg, WA 98926. Offers MM. *Accreditation:* NASM. *Faculty:* 20 full-time (4 women). *Students:* 13 full-time (6 women). 16 applicants, 81% accepted, 13 enrolled. In 2009, 8 master's awarded. *Degree requirements:* For master's, thesis or alternative. *Entrance requirements:* For master's, minimum GPA of 3.0. Additional exam requirements/recommendations for international students: Required—TOEFL (minimum score 550 paper-based; 213 computer-based; 79 iBT). *Application deadline:* For fall admission, 2/1 priority date for domestic students; for winter admission, 10/1 for domestic students; for spring admission, 1/1 for domestic students. Applications are processed on a rolling basis. Application fee: $50. Electronic applications accepted. *Expenses:* Tuition, state resident: full-time $7353; part-time $245 per credit. Tuition, nonresident: full-time $16,383; part-time $546 per credit. Required fees: $882. Tuition and fees vary according to degree level. *Financial support:* In 2009–10, 9 teaching assistantships with full and partial tuition reimbursements (averaging $9,145 per year) were awarded; Federal Work-Study, health care benefits, and unspecified assistantships also available. Financial award application deadline: 3/1; financial award applicants required to submit FAFSA. *Unit head:* Dr. Peter Gries, Chair, 509-963-1216, Fax: 509-963-1239, E-mail: griesp@cwu.edu. *Application contact:* Justine Eason, Admissions Program Coordinator, 509-963-3103, Fax: 509-963-1799, E-mail: masters@cwu.edu.

City College of the City University of New York, Graduate School, College of Liberal Arts and Science, Division of the Humanities and Arts, Department of Music, New York, NY 10031-9198. Offers MA. Part-time programs available. *Degree requirements:* For master's, one foreign language, thesis. *Entrance requirements:* For master's, minimum GPA of 3.0, portfolio (composition), writing samples (history and theory), audition (performance). Additional exam requirements/recommendations for international students: Required—TOEFL (minimum score 575 paper-based; 90 iBT). Electronic applications accepted. *Faculty research:* Tonal theory, American music, musicology, atonal theory, performance.

Claremont Graduate University, Graduate Programs, School of Arts and Humanities, Department of Music, Claremont, CA 91711-6160. Offers church music (MA, DCM); composition (MA, DMA); historical performance practices (MA, DMA); musicology (MA, PhD); performance (MA, DMA); MBA/PhD. Part-time programs available. *Faculty:* 3 full-time (1 woman). *Students:* 49 full-time (22 women), 1 (woman) part-time; includes 12 minority (1 African American, 4 Asian Americans or Pacific Islanders, 7 Hispanic Americans), 8 international. Average age 36. In 2009, 2 master's, 10 doctorates awarded. Terminal master's awarded for partial completion of doctoral program. *Degree requirements:* For master's, one foreign language, comprehensive exam, thesis (for some programs), oral and written qualifying exams, recitals; for doctorate, 2 foreign languages, comprehensive exam, thesis/dissertation (for some programs), oral and written qualifying exams, oral defense of dissertation, recitals. *Entrance requirements:* For master's and doctorate, GRE General Test, auditions, compositions, or papers. Additional exam requirements/recommendations for international students: Required—TOEFL (minimum score 550 paper-based; 213 computer-based; 80 iBT). *Application deadline:* For fall admission, 2/1 priority date for domestic students. Applications are processed on a rolling basis. Application fee: $60. Electronic applications accepted. *Expenses:* Tuition: Full-time $35,046; part-time $1524 per credit. Required fees: $161 per semester. *Financial support:* Fellowships, research assistantships, teaching assistantships, Federal Work-Study, institutionally sponsored loans, and scholarships/grants available. Support available to part-time students. Financial award application deadline: 2/15; financial award applicants required to submit FAFSA. *Unit head:* Robert Zappulla, Chair, 909-607-9664, Fax: 909-607-3694, E-mail: robert.zappulla@cgu.edu. *Application contact:* Sylvia Quintana, Department Secretary, 909-607-3289, Fax: 909-607-1221, E-mail: sylvia.quintana@cgu.edu.

Cleveland Institute of Music, Graduate Programs, Cleveland, OH 44106-1776. Offers MM, DMA, AD, CPS. *Accreditation:* NASM (one or more programs are accredited). *Degree requirements:* For master's, comprehensive exam, recital; for doctorate, comprehensive exam, thesis/dissertation (for some programs), final projects; for other advanced degree, recital. *Entrance requirements:* For master's, theory placement tests, audition; for doctorate, diagnostic exams, theory placement test, audition; for other advanced degree, audition. Additional exam requirements/recommendations for international students: Required—TOEFL (minimum score 550 paper-based; 213 computer-based). Electronic applications accepted.

Cleveland State University, College of Graduate Studies, College of Liberal Arts and Social Sciences, Department of Music, Cleveland, OH 44115. Offers composition (MM); music education (MM); performance (MM). *Accreditation:* NASM. Part-time and evening/weekend programs available. *Degree requirements:* For master's, comprehensive exam, thesis or recital. *Entrance requirements:* For master's, departmental assessment in music history, minimum undergraduate GPA of 2.75. Additional exam requirements/recommendations for international students: Required—TOEFL (minimum score 525 paper-based; 197 computer-based). *Faculty research:* Ethnomusicology, classical-romantic music, new performance practices, electronic music, interdisciplinary studies.

The College of Saint Rose, Graduate Studies, School of Arts and Humanities, Music Department, Program in Music, Albany, NY 12203-1419. Offers MA. *Accreditation:* NASM. *Degree requirements:* For master's, final project. *Entrance requirements:* For master's, audition, minimum undergraduate GPA of 3.0. Additional exam requirements/recommendations for international students: Required—TOEFL (minimum score 550 paper-based; 213 computer-based). Electronic applications accepted.

Colorado State University, Graduate School, College of Liberal Arts, Department of Music, Theater, and Dance, Fort Collins, CO 80523-1779. Offers music (MM). *Accreditation:* NASM. Part-time programs available. *Faculty:* 28 full-time (7 women). *Students:* 55 full-time (38 women), 69 part-time (56 women); includes 18 minority (2 African Americans, 1 American Indian/Alaska Native, 7 Asian Americans or Pacific Islanders, 8 Hispanic Americans), 14 international. Average age 30. 90 applicants, 74% accepted, 40 enrolled. In 2009, 29 master's awarded. *Degree requirements:* For master's, variable foreign language requirement, comprehensive exam (for some programs), thesis (for some programs), 2 recitals, project. *Entrance requirements:* For master's, minimum GPA of 3.0, audition, bachelor's degree, letters of recommendation. Additional exam requirements/recommendations for international students: Required—TOEFL (minimum score 550 paper-based; 213 computer-based). *Application deadline:* For fall admission, 2/15 priority date for domestic students; for spring admission, 11/15 priority date for domestic students. Applications are processed on a rolling basis. Application fee: $50. Electronic applications accepted. *Expenses:* Tuition, state resident: full-time $6434; part-time $359.10 per credit. Tuition, nonresident: full-time $18,116; part-time $1006.45 per credit. Required fees: $1496; $83 per credit. *Financial support:* In 2009–10, 26 students received support, including 26 teaching assistantships with full and partial tuition reimbursements available (averaging $6,428 per year); fellowships, research assistantships with partial tuition reimbursements available, career-related internships or fieldwork, Federal Work-Study, scholarships/grants, traineeships, and unspecified assistantships also available. Financial award application deadline: 3/1; financial award applicants required to submit FAFSA. *Faculty research:* Neurobiology, musicology, music literacy, music learning, music therapy. *Unit head:* Dr. Michael H. Thaut, Chair, 970-491-5529, Fax: 970-491-7541, E-mail: michael.thaut@colostate.edu. *Application contact:* Dr. Eric Hollenbeck, Director of Graduate Studies, 970-491-4054, Fax: 970-491-7541, E-mail: eric.hollenbeck@colostate.edu.

Columbia College Chicago, Graduate School, Program in Music Composition for the Screen, Chicago, IL 60605-1996. Offers MFA. *Expenses:* Tuition: Part-time $651 per credit hour. Required fees: $651 per credit hour. $205 per semester. One-time fee: $285 part-time. Tuition and fees vary according to program.

Columbia University, Graduate School of Arts and Sciences, Division of Humanities, Department of Music, New York, NY 10027. Offers M Phil, MA, DMA, PhD. *Degree requirements:* For master's, 2 foreign languages, thesis or alternative; for doctorate, variable foreign language requirement, thesis/dissertation. *Entrance requirements:* For master's and doctorate, GRE General Test, GRE Subject Test, sample of written work. Additional exam requirements/recommendations for international students: Required—TOEFL. *Faculty research:* Historical musicology, ethnomusicology, composition and theory.

Concordia University, School of Graduate Studies, Faculty of Fine Arts, Department of Music, Montréal, QC H3G 1M8, Canada. Offers advanced music performance studies (Diploma). *Degree requirements:* For Diploma, performance, 2 recitals.

Concordia University Chicago, College of Graduate and Innovative Programs, Program in Church Music, River Forest, IL 60305-1499. Offers MCM. *Accreditation:* NASM. Part-time programs available. *Degree requirements:* For master's, composition, recital, or thesis. *Entrance requirements:* For master's, minimum GPA of 2.9, audition. Additional exam requirements/recommendations for international students: Required—TOEFL (minimum score 550 paper-based; 195 computer-based). Electronic applications accepted. *Faculty research:* Twentieth-century sacred choral music, liturgical context of sacred music after the Council of Trent, dance and music of J.S. Bach.

Concordia University Chicago, College of Graduate and Innovative Programs, Program in Music, River Forest, IL 60305-1499. Offers MA. Part-time programs available. *Degree requirements:* For master's, composition, recital, or thesis. *Entrance requirements:* For master's, minimum GPA of 2.9, audition. Additional exam requirements/recommendations for international students: Required—TOEFL (minimum score 550 paper-based; 195 computer-based). Electronic applications accepted.

Concordia University Wisconsin, Graduate Programs, School of Arts and Sciences, Program in Church Music, Mequon, WI 53097-2402. Offers MCM. *Degree requirements:* For master's, comprehensive exam, thesis or alternative. *Entrance requirements:* For master's, minimum GPA of 3.0. Additional exam requirements/recommendations for international students: Required—TOEFL.

Conservatorio de Musica, Program in Musical Performance, San Juan, PR 00918-2199. Offers instrumental performance (Diploma); vocal performance (Diploma). *Entrance requirements:* For degree, 3 letters of recommendation, audition, degree in music, minimum GPA of 2.5.

Converse College, Carroll McDaniel Petrie School of Music, Spartanburg, SC 29302-0006. Offers instrumental performance (M Mus); music education (M Mus); piano pedagogy (M Mus); vocal performance (M Mus). *Accreditation:* NASM. Part-time and evening/weekend programs available. *Degree requirements:* For master's, variable foreign language requirement, comprehensive exam, thesis (for some programs), recitals. *Entrance requirements:* For master's, NTE (music education), audition, 3 letters of recommendation. Additional exam requirements/recommendations for international students: Required—TOEFL. Electronic applications accepted. *Faculty research:* Chamber music, opera, performance, composition, recording.

Cornell University, Graduate School, Graduate Fields of Arts and Sciences, Field of Music, Ithaca, NY 14853-0001. Offers composition (DMA); musicology (PhD); performance practice (DMA); theory of music (MA). *Faculty:* 23 full-time (8 women). *Students:* 36 full-time (13 women); includes 3 minority (1 American Indian/Alaska Native, 1 Asian American or Pacific Islander, 1 Hispanic American), 19 international. Average age 28. 139 applicants, 7% accepted, 6 enrolled. In 2009, 4 master's, 6 doctorates awarded. *Degree requirements:* For doctorate, comprehensive exam, thesis/dissertation, 1 foreign language (DMA), 2 foreign languages (PhD). *Entrance requirements:* For doctorate, GRE General Test, 2 music papers; 2 recent scores (with recording) and 1 music paper (DMA composition); 1 music paper, recording and audition (DMA performance practice). Additional exam requirements/recommendations for international students: Required—TOEFL (minimum score 600 paper-based; 250 computer-based; 77 iBT). *Application deadline:* For fall admission, 1/15 for domestic students. Application fee: $70. Electronic applications accepted. *Expenses:* Tuition: Full-time $29,500. Required fees: $70. Full-time tuition and fees vary according to degree level, program and student level. *Financial support:* In 2009–10, 32 students received support, including 5 fellowships with full tuition reimbursements available; research assistantships with full tuition reimbursements available, teaching assistantships with full tuition reimbursements available, institutionally sponsored loans, scholarships/grants, health care benefits, tuition waivers (full and partial), and unspecified assistantships also available. Financial award applicants required to submit FAFSA. *Faculty research:* Music history, music theory, performance practice, ethnomusicology, composition. *Unit head:* Director of Graduate Studies, 607-255-9078. *Application contact:* Graduate Field Assistant, 607-255-9078, E-mail: grad_music@cornell.edu.

Curtis Institute of Music, Graduate Studies, Philadelphia, PA 19103-6107. Offers opera (MM). *Accreditation:* NASM. *Entrance requirements:* For master's, audition or performance in 2 or more principal roles or 6 major scenes.

Dalhousie University, Faculty of Arts and Social Science, Department of Musicology, Halifax, NS B3H 4R2, Canada. Offers MA. *Entrance requirements:* Additional exam requirements/recommendations for international students: Required—TOEFL, IELTS, CANTEST, CAEL, or Michigan English Language Assessment Battery. *Application deadline:* For fall admission, 6/1 for domestic students, 4/1 for international students; for winter admission, 11/15 for domestic students, 8/31 for international students; for spring admission, 2/28 for domestic students, 12/31 for international students. Application fee: $70. Electronic applications accepted. *Financial support:* Scholarships/grants and health care benefits available. *Unit head:* Dr. Jennifer Bain, Graduate Coordinator, 902-494-3867, Fax: 902-494-2801, E-mail: musicgrd@dal.ca. *Application contact:* Jessica Mailhiot, Graduate Administrator, 902-494-8517, Fax: 902-494-2801, E-mail: musicgrd@dal.ca.

Dartmouth College, Arts and Sciences Graduate Programs, Department of Music, Hanover, NH 03755. Offers electro-acoustic music (AM). *Faculty:* 10 full-time (3 women), 21 part-time/adjunct (4 women). *Students:* 6 full-time (0 women). Average age 25. 18 applicants, 28% accepted, 3 enrolled. In 2009, 2 master's awarded. *Degree requirements:* For master's, thesis or alternative. *Entrance requirements:* Additional exam requirements/recommendations for international students: Required—TOEFL. *Application deadline:* For fall admission, 2/1 priority date for domestic students. Application fee: $35. *Financial support:* In 2009–10, 5 students received support, including fellowships with full tuition reimbursements available (averaging $14,370 per year); career-related internships or fieldwork, institutionally sponsored loans, and tuition waivers (full) also available. *Faculty research:* Composition and design of computer music software and related topics. *Unit head:* Michael Casey, Director, Graduate Program in Electro-Acoustic Music, 603-646-3531, Fax: 603-646-2551. *Application contact:* Catherine La Touche, Administrative Assistant, 603-646-2520, Fax: 603-646-2551.

DePaul University, School of Music, Chicago, IL 60614. Offers applied music (performance) (MM, Certificate); jazz studies (MM), including composition, performance; music composition (MM); music education (MM). *Accreditation:* NASM (one or more programs are accredited). Part-time and evening/weekend programs available. *Faculty:* 11 full-time (2 women), 50 part-time/adjunct (14 women). *Students:* 53 full-time (23 women), 65 part-time (38 women); includes 10 minority (1 African American, 3 Asian Americans or Pacific Islanders, 6 Hispanic Americans), 25 international. Average age 24. 312 applicants, 31% accepted, 50 enrolled. In 2009, 40 master's, 5 Certificates awarded. *Degree requirements:* For master's, comprehensive exam, terminal project, graduate recital for performers; for Certificate, recital (certificate). *Entrance requirements:* For master's, auditions (performance), scores (composition), bachelor's degree in music or related field, audition, minimum GPA of 3.0; for Certificate, auditions for performance majors, master's degree in performance or related field. Additional exam requirements/recommendations for international students: Required—TOEFL (minimum score 550 paper-based; 213 computer-based; 80 iBT). *Application deadline:* For fall admission, 1/15 priority date for domestic and international students. Applications are processed on a rolling basis. Application fee: $40. Electronic applications accepted. *Expenses:* Contact institution. *Financial support:* In 2009–10, 4 fellowships with partial tuition reimbursements were awarded; teaching assistantships, career-related internships or fieldwork, Federal Work-Study, scholarships/grants, and tuition waivers also available. Support available to part-time students. Financial award application deadline: 1/15. *Unit head:* Dr. Donald E. Casey, Dean, 773-325-7256, E-mail: dcasey@depaul.edu. *Application contact:* Ross Beacraft, Director of Admissions, 773-325-7444, Fax: 773-325-7429, E-mail: rbeacraf@depaul.edu.

Duke University, Graduate School, Department of Music, Durham, NC 27708. Offers music composition (AM, PhD); musicology (AM, PhD); performance practice (AM, PhD). Part-time programs available. *Faculty:* 13 full-time. *Students:* 40 full-time (20 women); includes 1 minority (Asian American or Pacific Islander), 9 international. 49 applicants, 20% accepted, 9 enrolled. In 2009, 11 master's, 6 doctorates awarded. Terminal master's awarded for partial completion of doctoral program. *Degree requirements:* For master's, 2 foreign languages; for doctorate, 3 foreign languages, thesis/dissertation. *Entrance requirements:* For master's and doctorate, GRE General Test. Additional exam requirements/recommendations for international students: Required—TOEFL (minimum score 550 paper-based; 213 computer-based; 83 iBT), IELTS (minimum score 7). *Application deadline:* For fall admission, 12/8 priority date for domestic and international students; for spring admission, 11/1 for domestic students. Application fee: $75. Electronic applications accepted. *Financial support:* Fellowships, research assistantships, teaching assistantships, Federal Work-Study available. Financial award application deadline: 12/31. *Unit head:* Philip Rupprecht, Director of Graduate Studies, Fax: 919-660-3308, E-mail: christy.reuss@duke.edu. *Application contact:* Cynthia Robertson, Associate Dean for Enrollment Services, 919-684-3913, E-mail: grad-admissions@duke.edu.

Duquesne University, Mary Pappert School of Music, Pittsburgh, PA 15282-0001. Offers music composition (MM); music education (MM); music performance (MM, AD); music technology (MM); music theory (MM); sacred music (MM). *Accreditation:* NASM. Part-time programs available. *Faculty:* 28 full-time (10 women), 73 part-time/adjunct (19 women). *Students:* 77 full-time (40 women), 16 part-time (7 women); includes 9 minority (5 African Americans, 2 Asian Americans or Pacific Islanders, 2 Hispanic Americans), 20 international. Average age 23. 95 applicants, 80% accepted, 36 enrolled. In 2009, 15 master's, 5 ADs awarded. *Degree requirements:* For master's, comprehensive exam, thesis (for some programs), recital (music performance); for AD, recital. *Entrance requirements:* For master's, audition, minimum undergraduate QPA of 3.0 in music, portfolio of original compositions, theoretical papers, or music education experience; for AD, audition. Additional exam requirements/recommendations for international students: Required—TOEFL (minimum score 550 paper-based; 213 computer-based; 79 iBT). *Application deadline:* For fall admission, 7/1 priority date for domestic and international students; for spring admission, 12/1 priority date for domestic and international students. Applications are processed on a rolling basis. Application fee: $50. Electronic applications accepted. *Expenses:* Contact institution. *Financial support:* In 2009–10, 50 students received support, including 45 fellowships with full and partial tuition reimbursements available; career-related internships or fieldwork, Federal Work-Study, institutionally sponsored loans, and tuition waivers (full and partial) also available. Support available to part-time students. Financial award application deadline: 4/1. *Faculty research:* Performance; computer-assisted instruction in music at elementary and secondary levels; electronic music; contemporary music, theory, and analysis; development of online graduate music courses. Total annual research expenditures: $8,000. *Unit head:* Dr. Edward W. Kocher, Dean, 412-396-6082, Fax: 412-396-1524, E-mail: kocher@duq.edu. *Application contact:* Peggy Eiseman, Administrative Assistant of Admissions, 412-396-5064, Fax: 412-396-5479, E-mail: eiseman@duq.edu.

East Carolina University, Graduate School, College of Fine Arts and Communication, School of Music, Greenville, NC 27858-4353. Offers music education (MM); music therapy (MM); performance (MM); theory and composition (MM). *Accreditation:* NASM. Part-time programs available. *Degree requirements:* For master's, comprehensive exam, thesis optional. *Entrance requirements:* For master's, GRE General Test or MAT. Additional exam requirements/recommendations for international students: Required—TOEFL.

Eastern Illinois University, Graduate School, College of Arts and Humanities, Department of Music, Charleston, IL 61920-3099. Offers MA. *Accreditation:* NASM. Part-time programs available. *Faculty:* 21 full-time (3 women). In 2009, 4 master's awarded. *Degree requirements:* For master's, thesis or alternative, recital. *Application deadline:* For fall admission, 3/31 priority date for domestic students. Applications are processed on a rolling basis. Application fee: $30. *Expenses:* Tuition, state resident: full-time $9434; part-time $239 per credit hour. Tuition, nonresident: full-time $23,774; part-time $717 per credit hour. Required fees: $802.63. *Financial support:* In 2009–10, research assistantships with tuition reimbursements (averaging $8,100 per year), 8 teaching assistantships with tuition reimbursements (averaging $8,100 per year) were awarded. *Unit head:* Dr. Jerry Daniels, Chairperson, 217-581-3010, Fax: 217-581-2722, E-mail: wpmelvin@eiu.edu. *Application contact:* Dr. Marilyn Coles, Coordinator, 217-581-3010, E-mail: mjcoles@eiu.edu.

Eastern Kentucky University, The Graduate School, College of Arts and Sciences, Department of Music, Richmond, KY 40475-3102. Offers choral conducting (MM); performance (MM); theory/composition (MM). *Accreditation:* NASM. Part-time programs available. *Degree requirements:* For master's, thesis optional. *Entrance requirements:* For master's, GRE General Test, minimum GPA of 2.5. *Faculty research:* Technology.

Eastern Michigan University, Graduate School, College of Arts and Sciences, Department of Communication, Media and Theatre Arts, Programs in Theatre Arts, Ypsilanti, MI 48197. Offers interpretation/performance studies (MA); theatre arts (MA). Part-time and evening/weekend programs available. Postbaccalaureate distance learning degree programs offered (minimal on-campus study). *Students:* 4 full-time (3 women), 13 part-time (7 women); includes 1 minority (African American). Average age 31. 14 applicants, 93% accepted, 6 enrolled. In 2009, 4 master's awarded. *Degree requirements:* For master's, thesis or alternative. *Entrance requirements:* Additional exam requirements/recommendations for international students: Required—TOEFL. *Application deadline:* Applications are processed on a rolling basis. Application fee: $35. Tuition and fees vary according to course level. *Financial support:* Fellowships, research assistantships with full tuition reimbursements, teaching assistantships with full tuition reimbursements, career-related internships or fieldwork, Federal Work-Study,

Music

Eastern Michigan University (continued)
institutionally sponsored loans, scholarships/grants, and unspecified assistantships available. Support available to part-time students. Financial award applicants required to submit FAFSA. *Unit head:* Kenneth Stevens, Coordinator, 734-487-3130, Fax: 734-487-3443, E-mail: ken.stevens@emich.edu. *Application contact:* Kenneth Stevens, Coordinator, 734-487-3130, Fax: 734-487-3443, E-mail: ken.stevens@emich.edu.

Eastern Michigan University, Graduate School, College of Arts and Sciences, Department of Music and Dance, Ypsilanti, MI 48197. Offers music composition (MM); music education (MM); music pedagogy (MM); music performance (MM). *Accreditation:* NASM. Part-time and evening/weekend programs available. Postbaccalaureate distance learning degree programs offered (minimal on-campus study). *Faculty:* 26 full-time (10 women). *Students:* 3 full-time (1 woman), 33 part-time (18 women); includes 5 minority (2 African Americans, 1 Asian American or Pacific Islander, 2 Hispanic Americans), 5 international. Average age 31. 25 applicants, 80% accepted, 8 enrolled. In 2009, 8 master's awarded. *Entrance requirements:* Additional exam requirements/recommendations for international students: Required—TOEFL. *Application deadline:* Applications are processed on a rolling basis. Application fee: $35. Tuition and fees vary according to course level. *Financial support:* Fellowships, research assistantships with full tuition reimbursements, teaching assistantships with full tuition reimbursements, career-related internships or fieldwork, Federal Work-Study, institutionally sponsored loans, scholarships/grants, tuition waivers (partial), and unspecified assistantships available. Support available to part-time students. Financial award applicants required to submit FAFSA. *Unit head:* Dr. David Woike, Department Head, 734-487-4380, Fax: 734-487-6939, E-mail: dwoike@emich.edu. *Application contact:* Dr. David Pierce, Coordinator of Music Advising, 734-487-4380, Fax: 734-487-6939, E-mail: david.pierce@emich.edu.

Eastern Washington University, Graduate Studies, College of Arts and Letters, Department of Music, Cheney, WA 99004-2431. Offers composition (MA); instrumental/vocal performance (MA); music education (MA); music history and literature (MA). *Accreditation:* NASM. Part-time programs available. *Degree requirements:* For master's, comprehensive exam, thesis or alternative. *Entrance requirements:* For master's, GRE General Test, minimum GPA of 3.0. *Expenses:* Tuition, state resident: full-time $7476; part-time $249 per quarter hour. Tuition, nonresident: full-time $18,030; part-time $601 per quarter hour. Required fees: $3.50 per quarter hour. $142 per quarter.

Emory University, Graduate School of Arts and Sciences, Department of Music, Atlanta, GA 30322-1100. Offers choral conducting (MM, MSM); organ performance (MM, MSM). *Accreditation:* NASM. *Degree requirements:* For master's, comprehensive exam, recital or worship service/recital. *Entrance requirements:* For master's, GRE General Test, audition, interview. Additional exam requirements/recommendations for international students: Required—TOEFL. Electronic applications accepted. *Faculty research:* 19th century criticism, Schenker, Bach Aria styles, contemporary passion music, Andriesson, cross-cultural research, organ performance.

Emporia State University, School of Graduate Studies, College of Liberal Arts and Sciences, Department of Music, Emporia, KS 66801-5087. Offers music education (MM), including instrumental, vocal; performance (MM). *Accreditation:* NASM. Part-time programs available. *Faculty:* 13 full-time (4 women), 4 part-time/adjunct (all women). *Students:* 5 full-time (3 women), 4 part-time (3 women); includes 1 minority (Asian American or Pacific Islander), 2 international. In 2009, 11 master's awarded. *Degree requirements:* For master's, comprehensive exam or thesis. *Entrance requirements:* For master's, music qualifying exam, appropriate undergraduate degree. Additional exam requirements/recommendations for international students: Required—TOEFL (minimum score 520 paper-based; 133 computer-based; 68 iBT). *Application deadline:* For fall admission, 8/15 priority date for domestic students. Applications are processed on a rolling basis. Application fee: $30 ($75 for international students). Electronic applications accepted. *Expenses:* Tuition, state resident: full-time $4154; part-time $173 per credit hour. Tuition, nonresident: full-time $12,864; part-time $536 per credit hour. Required fees: $948; $58 per credit hour. Tuition and fees vary according to campus/location. *Financial support:* In 2009–10, 1 research assistantship with full tuition reimbursement (averaging $7,059 per year), 4 teaching assistantships with full tuition reimbursements (averaging $7,059 per year) were awarded; Federal Work-Study, institutionally sponsored loans, health care benefits, and unspecified assistantships also available. Financial award application deadline: 3/15; financial award applicants required to submit FAFSA. *Unit head:* Dr. Allan D. Comstock, Interim Chair, 620-341-5431, E-mail: acomstoc@emporia.edu. *Application contact:* Dr. Andrew Houchins, Graduate Coordinator, 620-341-6089, E-mail: ahouchin@emporia.edu.

Five Towns College, Department of Music, Dix Hills, NY 11746-6055. Offers jazz/commercial music (MM); music (DMA); music education (MM). Part-time programs available. *Faculty:* 5 full-time (2 women), 11 part-time/adjunct (2 women). *Students:* 17 full-time (4 women), 38 part-time (9 women); includes 5 minority (2 African Americans, 3 Hispanic Americans), 15 international. Average age 28. *Degree requirements:* For master's, exams, major composition or capstone project, recital; for doctorate, comprehensive exam, thesis/dissertation, final oral exam. *Entrance requirements:* For master's, audition, bachelor's degree in music or music education, minimum GPA of 2.75, 36 hours of course work in performance; for doctorate, master's degree in music, minimum GPA of 3.0, 3 letters of recommendation. Additional exam requirements/recommendations for international students: Required—TOEFL (minimum score 550 paper-based; 213 computer-based; 80 iBT). *Application deadline:* Applications are processed on a rolling basis. Application fee: $50. *Expenses:* Tuition: Full-time $11,880; part-time $495 per credit. Required fees: $110 per semester. *Financial support:* Fellowships with tuition reimbursements, tuition waivers (partial) available. Financial award applicants required to submit FAFSA. *Faculty research:* Teaching methods, teaching strategies and techniques, analysis of modern music, jazz. *Unit head:* Dr. Jill Miller-Thorn, Dean of Graduate Studies, 631-656-2142, Fax: 631-656-2172, E-mail: jmillerthorn@ftc.edu. *Application contact:* Jerry Cohen, Dean of Enrollment, 631-656-2121, Fax: 631-656-2172, E-mail: jcohen@ftc.edu.

Florida Atlantic University, Dorothy F. Schmidt College of Arts and Letters, Department of Music, Boca Raton, FL 33431-0991. Offers commercial music (MA); music history/literature (MA); performance (MA). *Accreditation:* NASM. Part-time programs available. *Faculty:* 17 full-time (8 women), 20 part-time/adjunct (4 women). *Students:* 21 full-time (9 women), 15 part-time (8 women); includes 9 minority (6 African Americans, 3 Hispanic Americans), 9 international. Average age 36. 21 applicants, 81% accepted, 6 enrolled. In 2009, 7 master's awarded. *Degree requirements:* For master's, lecture/recital or thesis. *Entrance requirements:* For master's, audition, minimum GPA of 3.0 in last 60 hours of course work, placement evaluations in music history and theory. *Application deadline:* For fall admission, 7/1 priority date for domestic students, 2/15 for international students; for spring admission, 11/1 for domestic students, 7/15 for international students. Applications are processed on a rolling basis. Application fee: $30. *Expenses:* Tuition, state resident: full-time $7055; part-time $293.94 per credit hour. Tuition, nonresident: full-time $22,096; part-time $920.66 per credit hour. *Financial support:* Fellowships with partial tuition reimbursements, teaching assistantships with partial tuition reimbursements, career-related internships or fieldwork, Federal Work-Study, and scholarships/grants available. Financial award application deadline: 5/1. *Faculty research:* Classical guitar history and literature, women composers, Mozart opera, composition, performance. *Unit head:* Dr. Heather J. Coltman, Chair, 561-297-3821, Fax: 561-297-2944, E-mail: coltman@fau.edu. *Application contact:* Dr. Heather J. Coltman, Chair, 561-297-3821, Fax: 561-297-2944, E-mail: coltman@fau.edu.

Florida International University, College of Architecture and the Arts, School of Music, Miami, FL 33199. Offers music (MM); music education (MS). Part-time and evening/weekend programs available. *Faculty:* 18 full-time (5 women). *Students:* 23 full-time (11 women), 21 part-time (8 women); includes 24 minority (3 African Americans, 2 Asian Americans or Pacific Islanders, 19 Hispanic Americans), 5 international. Average age 28. 31 applicants, 52% accepted, 15 enrolled. In 2009, 12 master's awarded. *Degree requirements:* For master's, thesis (for some programs). *Entrance requirements:* For master's, GRE (depending on program), Statement of intent; 2 Letters of recommendation (must be sent to Music dept directly); departmental application; Audition, interview and/or writing sample depending on the area. Additional exam requirements/recommendations for international students: Required—TOEFL (minimum score 550 paper-based; 80 iBT). *Application deadline:* For fall admission, 6/1 for domestic students, 4/1 for international students; for spring admission, 10/1 for domestic students, 9/1 for international students. Applications are processed on a rolling basis. Application fee: $30. Electronic applications accepted. *Expenses:* Tuition, state resident: full-time $8008; part-time $4004 per year. Tuition, nonresident: full-time $20,104; part-time $10,052 per year. Required fees: $298; $149 per term. *Financial support:* Institutionally sponsored loans and scholarships/grants available. Financial award application deadline: 3/1; financial award applicants required to submit FAFSA. *Unit head:* Orlando Garcia, Chair, 305-348-3357, Fax: 305-348-4073, E-mail: orlando.garcia@fiu.edu. *Application contact:* Joel Galand, Graduate Program Director, 305-348-2896, Fax: 305-348-4073, E-mail: joel.galand@fiu.edu.

Florida State University, The Graduate School, College of Arts and Sciences, Department of English, Tallahassee, FL 32306. Offers creative writing (MFA); English (PhD), including creative writing, literature, rhetoric and composition; literature (MA); rhetoric and composition (MA). Part-time programs available. *Faculty:* 48 full-time (23 women), 6 part-time/adjunct (1 woman). *Students:* 150 full-time (90 women), 20 part-time (10 women); includes 31 minority (15 African Americans, 1 American Indian/Alaska Native, 5 Asian Americans or Pacific Islanders, 10 Hispanic Americans). Average age 30. 480 applicants, 21% accepted, 58 enrolled. In 2009, 22 master's, 14 doctorates awarded. *Degree requirements:* For master's, one foreign language, thesis or alternative; for doctorate, comprehensive exam, thesis/dissertation, 27 hours of coursework, 24 hours of dissertation work. *Entrance requirements:* For master's and doctorate, GRE General Test, GRE Subject Test (literature only), sample of written work, 3 letters of recommendation, resume. Additional exam requirements/recommendations for international students: Required—TOEFL. *Application deadline:* For fall admission, 1/1 priority date for domestic and international students. Application fee: $30. Electronic applications accepted. *Expenses:* Tuition, state resident: full-time $7413. Tuition, nonresident: full-time $22,567. *Financial support:* In 2009–10, 126 students received support, including 5 fellowships, teaching assistantships (averaging $11,375 per year); career-related internships or fieldwork, Federal Work-Study, and institutionally sponsored loans also available. Financial award application deadline: 1/1; financial award applicants required to submit FAFSA. *Faculty research:* British and Irish literature, American literature, creative writing, rhetoric and composition, multiethnic transnational literature. *Unit head:* Dr. Ralph Berry, Chairman, 850-644-4230, Fax: 850-644-0811, E-mail: rberry@fsu.edu. *Application contact:* Dr. Ralph Berry, Chairman, 850-644-4230, Fax: 850-644-0811, E-mail: rberry@fsu.edu.

Florida State University, The Graduate School, College of Music, Tallahassee, FL 32306. Offers accompanying (MM); arts administration (MA); choral conducting (MM); composition (MM, DM); ethnomusicology (MM); general music (MA); instrumental accompanying (MM); instrumental conducting (MM); jazz studies (MM); music education (MM Ed, PhD); music theory (MM, PhD); music therapy (MM); musicology (MM, PhD), including ethnomusicology (PhD), historical musicology; opera (MM); performance (MM, DM); piano pedagogy (MM); piano technology (MA); vocal accompanying (MM). *Accreditation:* NASM. *Faculty:* 88 full-time, 13 part-time/adjunct. *Students:* 406 full-time (211 women); includes 98 minority (28 African Americans, 38 Asian Americans or Pacific Islanders, 32 Hispanic Americans). Average age 26. 525 applicants, 38% accepted, 145 enrolled. In 2009, 102 master's, 41 doctorates awarded. *Degree requirements:* For master's, comprehensive exam (for some programs), thesis (for some programs), departmental qualifying exam; for doctorate, comprehensive exam (for some programs), thesis/dissertation, departmental qualifying exam. *Entrance requirements:* For master's and doctorate, audition, GRE General Test or minimum GPA of 3.0. Additional exam requirements/recommendations for international students: Required—TOEFL (minimum score 550 paper-based; 213 computer-based). *Application deadline:* For fall admission, 7/1 for domestic students, 5/2 for international students; for spring admission, 11/3 for domestic students, 9/1 for international students. Applications are processed on a rolling basis. Application fee: $30. Electronic applications accepted. *Expenses:* Tuition, state resident: full-time $7413. Tuition, nonresident: full-time $22,567. *Financial support:* In 2009–10, 225 students received support, including 3 fellowships with full tuition reimbursements available (averaging $15,000 per year), 9 research assistantships with full tuition reimbursements available (averaging $4,000 per year), 173 teaching assistantships with full tuition reimbursements available (averaging $4,000 per year); career-related internships or fieldwork, Federal Work-Study, and tuition waivers (partial) also available. Support available to part-time students. Financial award application deadline: 2/28; financial award applicants required to submit FAFSA. *Unit head:* Don Gibson, Dean, 850-644-4361, Fax: 850-644-2033. *Application contact:* Dr. Seth Beckman, Senior Associate Dean for Academic Affairs/Director of Graduate Studies, 850-644-5848, Fax: 850-644-2033, E-mail: sbeckman@admin.fsu.edu.

Fuller Theological Seminary, Graduate School of Theology, Pasadena, CA 91182. Offers Christian leadership (MACL); evangelism (MA); family life education (MA); ministry (M Div, D Min); pastoral ministry (MA); recovery ministry (MA); theology (MAT, Th M, PhD); worship music ministry (MA); worship, theology, and the arts (MA); youth, family, and culture (MA). M Div offered jointly with Denver Conservative Baptist Seminary. *Accreditation:* ACIPE; ATS (one or more programs are accredited). Part-time and evening/weekend programs available. *Degree requirements:* For doctorate, variable foreign language requirement, thesis/dissertation; for M Div, 2 foreign languages. *Entrance requirements:* For doctorate, GRE General Test. *Faculty research:* New Testament, Old Testament, systematic theology, history, practical theology.

Garrett-Evangelical Theological Seminary, Graduate and Professional Programs, Evanston, IL 60201-3298. Offers Bible and culture (PhD); Christian education (MA); Christian education and congregational studies (PhD); contemporary theology and culture (PhD); divinity (M Div); ethics, church, and society (MA); liturgical studies (PhD); ministry (D Min); music ministry (MA); pastoral care and counseling (MA); pastoral theology, personality, and culture (PhD); spiritual formation and evangelism (MA); theological studies (MTS); M Div/MSW. *Accreditation:* ACIPE; ATS (one or more programs are accredited). Part-time programs available. *Degree requirements:* For master's, thesis (for some programs); for doctorate, thesis/dissertation. *Entrance requirements:* For doctorate, GRE (PhD). Additional exam requirements/recommendations for international students: Required—TOEFL (minimum score 560 paper-based; 230 computer-based). Electronic applications accepted.

George Mason University, College of Visual and Performing Arts, Department of Music, Fairfax, VA 22030. Offers instrumental performance artist (Certificate); music (MM); music education (PhD); musical arts (DMA); piano performance artist (Certificate); vocal performance artist (Certificate). *Accreditation:* NASM. Part-time and evening/weekend programs available. *Faculty:* 23 full-time (9 women), 20 part-time/adjunct (11 women). *Students:* 21 full-time (11 women), 44 part-time (28 women); includes 11 minority (6 African Americans, 3 Asian Americans or Pacific Islanders, 2 Hispanic Americans), 1 international. Average age 30. 46 applicants, 57% accepted, 15 enrolled. In 2009, 25 master's awarded. *Degree requirements:* For master's, recital (for all except MM in music education), summer auditions, portfolios, compositions. *Entrance requirements:* For master's, 2 letters of recommendation. Additional exam requirements/recommendations for international students: Required—TOEFL. *Application deadline:* For fall admission, 4/1 priority date for domestic students; for spring admission, 11/1 priority date for domestic students. Applications are processed on a rolling basis. Application fee: $75. Electronic applications accepted. *Expenses:* Contact institution. *Financial support:* Fellowships with partial tuition reimbursements, research assistantships, teaching assistantships with partial tuition reimbursements, unspecified assistantships and health care benefits (full-time research or teaching assistantship recipients) available. Financial award application deadline: 3/1; financial award applicants required to submit FAFSA. *Faculty research:* Single or multiple instruments, music education, composition, conducting, pedagogy. Total annual research expenditures: $25,586. *Unit head:* Mark Camphouse, Interim Director, 703-993-3598, Fax: 703-993-1394, E-mail: mcamphou@gmu.edu. *Application contact:* Victoria Salmon, Graduate Studies, 703-993-4541, E-mail: vsalmon@gmu.edu.

Georgia Southern University, Jack N. Averitt College of Graduate Studies, College of Liberal Arts and Social Sciences, Department of Music, Statesboro, GA 30460. Offers MM. *Accreditation:* NASM. Part-time and evening/weekend programs available. *Students:* 13 full-time (6 women), 11 part-time (1 woman); includes 9 minority (all African Americans), 1 international. Average age 28. 9 applicants, 89% accepted, 7 enrolled. In 2009, 6 master's awarded. *Degree requirements:* For master's, comprehensive exam, recital or final project. *Entrance requirements:* For master's, minimum GPA of 2.5, audition, letters of recommendation. Additional exam requirements/recommendations for international students: Required—TOEFL (minimum score 550 paper-based; 213 computer-based; 80 iBT). *Application deadline:* For fall admission, 3/1 priority date for domestic and international students; for spring admission, 10/1 priority date for domestic students, 10/1 for international students. Applications are processed on a rolling basis. Application fee: $50. Electronic applications accepted. *Expenses:* Tuition, state resident: full-time $5040; part-time $210 per credit hour. Tuition, nonresident: full-time $20,136; part-time $839 per credit hour. Required fees: $1644. *Financial support:* In 2009–10, 23 students received support, including research assistantships with partial tuition reimbursements available (averaging $7,200 per year), teaching assistantships with partial tuition reimbursements available (averaging $7,200 per year); Federal Work-Study, scholarships/grants, tuition waivers (partial), and unspecified assistantships also available. Support available to part-time students. Financial award application deadline: 4/15; financial award applicants required to submit FAFSA. *Faculty research:* Music history and literature, technology in music, music composition, music performance, music/education. *Unit head:* Dr. Richard E. Mercier, Chair, 912-478-5396, Fax: 912-478-1295, E-mail: rmercier@georgiasouthern.edu. *Application contact:* Dr. Charles Ziglar, Coordinator for Graduate Student Recruitment, 912-478-5635, Fax: 912-478-0740, E-mail: gradadmissions@georgiasouthern.edu.

Georgia State University, College of Arts and Sciences, School of Music, Atlanta, GA 30303. Offers M Mu. *Accreditation:* NASM. Part-time and evening/weekend programs available. *Degree requirements:* For master's, comprehensive exam, thesis (for some programs), recital, exam. *Entrance requirements:* For master's, GRE General Test or MAT (music education), GRE (composition), departmental supplemental form, audition. Additional exam requirements/recommendations for international students: Required—TOEFL. Electronic applications accepted. *Faculty research:* Teaching effectiveness assessment, computer music applications, arts/arts education policy, community music, psychology of music learning.

Graduate School and University Center of the City University of New York, Graduate Studies, Program in Music, New York, NY 10016-4039. Offers DMA, PhD. *Faculty:* 62 full-time (9 women). *Students:* 199 full-time (102 women), 1 (woman) part-time; includes 19 minority (3 African Americans, 10 Asian Americans or Pacific Islanders, 6 Hispanic Americans), 40 international. Average age 35. 130 applicants, 33% accepted, 21 enrolled. In 2009, 19 doctorates awarded. *Degree requirements:* For doctorate, 2 foreign languages, thesis/dissertation. *Entrance requirements:* For doctorate, GRE General Test. Additional exam requirements/recommendations for international students: Required—TOEFL. *Application deadline:* For fall admission, 12/1 priority date for domestic students. Application fee: $125. Electronic applications accepted. *Financial support:* In 2009–10, 92 students received support, including 87 fellowships, 3 research assistantships, 6 teaching assistantships; career-related internships or fieldwork, Federal Work-Study, institutionally sponsored loans, and tuition waivers (full and partial) also available. Financial award application deadline: 2/1; financial award applicants required to submit FAFSA. *Unit head:* Dr. David W. Olan, Executive Officer, 212-817-8591, Fax: 212-817-1529, E-mail: dolan@gc.cuny.edu. *Application contact:* Les Gribben, Director of Admissions, 212-817-7470, Fax: 212-817-1624, E-mail: lgribben@gc.cuny.edu.

Gratz College, Graduate Programs, Program in Jewish Music, Melrose Park, PA 19027. Offers MA, Certificate, MA/MA. Part-time programs available. *Degree requirements:* For master's, one foreign language, comprehensive exam, recital or thesis. *Entrance requirements:* For master's, audition, interview.

Hardin-Simmons University, Graduate School, School of Music and Fine Arts, Abilene, TX 79698-0001. Offers church music (MM); music education (MM); music performance (MM); theory-composition (MM). *Accreditation:* NASM. Part-time programs available. *Faculty:* 13 full-time (3 women), 1 (woman) part-time/adjunct. *Students:* 6 full-time (2 women), 10 part-time (6 women). Average age 28. 7 applicants, 100% accepted, 3 enrolled. In 2009, 5 master's awarded. *Degree requirements:* For master's, one foreign language, comprehensive exam, thesis (for some programs). *Entrance requirements:* For master's, minimum undergraduate GPA of 3.0 in major, 2.7 overall; performance; writing sample; demonstrated knowledge in chosen area. Additional exam requirements/recommendations for international students: Required—TOEFL (minimum score 550 paper-based; 213 computer-based; 75 iBT). *Application deadline:* For fall admission, 8/15 priority date for domestic students, 4/1 for international students; for spring admission, 1/5 priority date for domestic students, 9/1 for international students. Applications are processed on a rolling basis. Application fee: $50. *Expenses:* Tuition: Full-time $11,430; part-time $635 per credit hour. Required fees: $650; $110 per semester. Tuition and fees vary according to degree level. *Financial support:* In 2009–10, 13 students received support; fellowships, career-related internships or fieldwork and scholarships/grants available. Support available to part-time students. Financial award application deadline: 6/30; financial award applicants required to submit FAFSA. *Unit head:* Dr. Leigh Anne Hunsaker, Director, 325-670-1391, Fax: 325-670-5873, E-mail: hunsaker@hsutx.edu. *Application contact:* Dr. Gary Stanlake, Dean of Graduate Studies, 325-670-1298, Fax: 325-670-1564, E-mail: gradoff@hsutx.edu.

Harvard University, Graduate School of Arts and Sciences, Department of Music, Cambridge, MA 02138. Offers composition (AM, PhD); musicology (AM); musicology and ethnomusicology (PhD); theory (AM, PhD). *Degree requirements:* For doctorate, 3 foreign languages, thesis/dissertation, composition, analytical paper. *Entrance requirements:* For master's and doctorate, GRE General Test. Additional exam requirements/recommendations for international students: Required—TOEFL. *Expenses:* Tuition: Full-time $33,696. Required fees: $1126. Full-time tuition and fees vary according to program.

Hebrew College, Program in Jewish Studies, Newton Centre, MA 02459. Offers Jewish liturgical music (Certificate); Jewish music education (Certificate); Jewish studies (MA). Part-time and evening/weekend programs available. Postbaccalaureate distance learning degree programs offered (minimal on-campus study). *Degree requirements:* For master's, one foreign language. *Entrance requirements:* For master's, GRE, interview. Additional exam requirements/recommendations for international students: Required—TOEFL.

Hebrew Union College–Jewish Institute of Religion, School of Sacred Music, New York, NY 10012-1186. Offers MSM. *Degree requirements:* For master's, one foreign language, thesis, recital. *Entrance requirements:* For master's, GRE, minimum 2 years of college-level Hebrew, bachelor's degree in music or related area, trained singing voice. Additional exam requirements/recommendations for international students: Required—TOEFL. *Expenses:* Contact institution.

Hofstra University, School of Education, Health, and Human Services, Department of Curriculum and Teaching, Program in Music Education, Hempstead, NY 11549. Offers music education (MA, MS Ed); wind conducting (MA). Part-time programs available. *Students:* 16 full-time (8 women), 25 part-time (19 women); includes 10 minority (4 African Americans, 1 Asian American or Pacific Islander, 5 Hispanic Americans). Average age 26. 24 applicants, 100% accepted, 16 enrolled. In 2009, 19 master's awarded. *Degree requirements:* For master's, one foreign language, thesis (for some programs). *Entrance requirements:* For master's, 2 letters of recommendation, teacher certification (MA). Additional exam requirements/recommendations for international students: Required—TOEFL (minimum score 550 paper-based; 213 computer-based; 80 iBT). *Application deadline:* Applications are processed on a rolling basis. Application fee: $60. Electronic applications accepted. *Expenses:* Tuition: Full-time $16,200; part-time $900 per credit hour. Required fees: $970; $145 per term. Tuition and fees vary according to program. *Financial support:* In 2009–10, 14 students received support, including 5 fellowships with full and partial tuition reimbursements available (averaging $4,290 per year), 1 research assistantship with full and partial tuition reimbursement available (averaging $500 per year); Federal Work-Study, institutionally sponsored loans, scholarships/grants, tuition waivers (full and partial), and unspecified assistantships also available. Support available to part-time students. Financial award applicants required to submit FAFSA. *Faculty research:* Creative thinking, musical thinking, curriculum design, teaching preparation. *Unit head:* Dr. Nathalie G. Robinson, Program Director, 516-463-4514, Fax: 516-463-6393, E-mail: musngr@hofstra.edu. *Application contact:* Carol Drummer, Dean of Graduate Admissions, 516-463-4876, Fax: 516-463-4664, E-mail: gradstudent@hofstra.edu.

Hollins University, Graduate Programs, Program in Liberal Studies, Roanoke, VA 24020-1603. Offers humanities (MALS); interdisciplinary studies (MALS); justice and legal studies (MALS); liberal studies (CAS); social science (MALS); visual and performing arts (MALS). Part-time and evening/weekend programs available. *Faculty:* 7 full-time (1 woman), 4 part-time/adjunct (2 women). *Students:* 23 full-time (22 women), 73 part-time (57 women); includes 15 minority (13 African Americans, 2 Asian Americans or Pacific Islanders), 4 international. Average age 39. 31 applicants, 94% accepted, 25 enrolled. In 2009, 30 master's awarded. *Degree requirements:* For master's, thesis. *Entrance requirements:* For master's, letters of recommendation, interview. Additional exam requirements/recommendations for international students: Required—TOEFL (minimum score 550 paper-based; 213 computer-based; 79 iBT). *Application deadline:* For fall admission, 7/1 priority date for domestic and international students; for spring admission, 12/10 priority date for domestic and international students. Applications are processed on a rolling basis. Application fee: $40. Electronic applications accepted. *Expenses:* Tuition: Full-time $27,780; part-time $295 per contact hour. Required fees: $280; $70 per unit. Part-time tuition and fees vary according to course load and program. *Financial support:* In 2009–10, 31 students received support, including 2 fellowships (averaging $902 per year); Federal Work-Study and scholarships/grants also available. Support available to part-time students. Financial award application deadline: 7/15; financial award applicants required to submit FAFSA. *Faculty research:* Elderly blacks, film, feminist economics, US voting patterns, Wagner, diversity. *Unit head:* Dr. Edward A. Lynch, Director, 540-362-6475, Fax: 540-362-6288, E-mail: elynch@hollins.edu. *Application contact:* Cathy S. Koon, Manager of Graduate Services, 540-362-6326, Fax: 540-362-6288, E-mail: ckoon@hollins.edu.

Holy Names University, Graduate Division, Department of Music, Oakland, CA 94619-1699. Offers Kodaly specialist certificate (Certificate); Kodaly summer certificate (Certificate); music education with Kodaly emphasis (MM); piano pedagogy (MM); piano pedagogy with Suzuki emphasis (MM); vocal pedagogy (MM). *Degree requirements:* For master's, comprehensive exam, recital. *Entrance requirements:* For master's, audition, minimum undergraduate GPA of 2.6 overall, 3.0 in major. Additional exam requirements/recommendations for international students: Required—TOEFL (minimum score 550 paper-based; 213 computer-based; 80 iBT). *Faculty research:* Performance practice with special interest in baroque, Romantic, and twentieth-century instrumental and vocal music, choral pedagogy, Hungarian music education.

Hope International University, School of Graduate and Professional Studies, Programs in Ministry, Fullerton, CA 92831-3138. Offers Christian leadership (MCM); church music (MA); church music (Korean track) (MCM); church planting (MCM); intercultural studies (MCM); worship (MCM). Part-time and evening/weekend programs available. Postbaccalaureate distance learning degree programs offered (minimal on-campus study). *Degree requirements:* For master's, thesis (for some programs), project. *Entrance requirements:* For master's, minimum GPA of 3.0, MCM program requires an undergraduate degree in music, 2 references. Additional exam requirements/recommendations for international students: Required—TOEFL (minimum score 550 paper-based; 213 computer-based; 86 iBT); Recommended—IELTS (minimum score 6.5). Electronic applications accepted. *Expenses:* Contact institution. *Faculty research:* Church dynamics, growth methodologies.

Houghton College, Greatbatch School of Music, Houghton, NY 14744. Offers collaborative performance (MMus); composition (MMus); conducting (MMus); music (MA); performance (MMus); world music with theology and intercultural studies (MA). *Accreditation:* NASM. *Faculty:* 14 full-time (5 women), 5 part-time/adjunct (2 women). *Students:* 13 full-time (8 women), 1 part-time (0 women); includes 1 minority (Asian American or Pacific Islander). Average age 24. 16 applicants, 88% accepted, 9 enrolled. *Degree requirements:* For master's, comprehensive exam (for some programs), thesis (for some programs), recitals (for some programs). *Entrance requirements:* For master's, bachelor of music or equivalent. Additional exam requirements/recommendations for international students: Required—TOEFL (minimum score 600 paper-based; 250 computer-based). *Application deadline:* Applications are processed on a rolling basis. Application fee: $40. Electronic applications accepted. *Expenses:* Tuition: Full-time $10,500. *Financial support:* Fellowships with full tuition reimbursements, unspecified assistantships available. Financial award application deadline: 3/1; financial award applicants required to submit FAFSA. *Faculty research:* Bach Studies; original compositions; professional performance; contemporary women composers; music in Christian worship. *Unit head:* Dr. Ben R. King, Director/Associate Dean, 585-567-9468, Fax: 585-567-9517, E-mail: ben.king@houghton.edu. *Application contact:* Mindy Airhart, Graduate Music Program Coordinator, 585-567-9468, Fax: 585-567-9517, E-mail: mindy.airhart@houghton.edu.

Howard University, Graduate School, Division of Fine Arts, Department of Music, Washington, DC 20059-0002. Offers applied music (MM); instrument (MM Ed); jazz studies (MM); organ (MM Ed); piano (MM Ed); voice (MM Ed). *Accreditation:* NASM. Part-time programs available. *Degree requirements:* For master's, comprehensive exam, thesis or alternative, departmental qualifying exam, recital. *Entrance requirements:* For master's, minimum GPA of 3.0, bachelor's degree in music or music education. Additional exam requirements/recommendations for international students: Required—TOEFL.

Hunter College of the City University of New York, Graduate School, School of Arts and Sciences, Department of Music, New York, NY 10021-5085. Offers music (MA); music education (MA). Part-time and evening/weekend programs available. *Faculty:* 12 full-time (3 women), 2 part-time/adjunct (1 woman). *Students:* 3 full-time (all women), 30 part-time (18 women); includes 9 minority (1 African American, 8 Asian Americans or Pacific Islanders). Average age 32. 33 applicants, 52% accepted, 12 enrolled. In 2009, 13 master's awarded. *Degree requirements:* For master's, one foreign language, thesis, composition, essay, or recital; proficiency exam. *Entrance requirements:* For master's, undergraduate major in music (minimum 24 credits) or equivalent, sample of work, research paper. Additional exam requirements/recommendations for international students: Required—TOEFL. *Application deadline:* For fall admission, 4/1 for domestic students, 2/1 for international students; for spring admission, 11/1 for domestic students, 9/1 for international students. Applications are processed on a rolling basis. Application fee: $125. *Expenses:* Tuition, state resident: full-time $7360; part-time $310 per credit. Required fees: $250 per semester. *Financial support:* In 2009–10, 4 fellowships (averaging $1,000 per year) were awarded; Federal Work-Study, tuition waivers (partial), and lesson stipends also available. Support available to part-time students. Financial award application deadline: 4/15. *Faculty research:* African and African-American music, Bach, Renaissance music, early romantic music, theory of tonal music. *Unit head:* Dr. Ruth DeFord, Department Chair, 212-772-5026, Fax: 212-772-5022, E-mail: ruth.deford@hunter.cuny.edu. *Application contact:* L. Pondie Burstein, Graduate Adviser, 212-772-5152, E-mail: huntermust@aol.com.

Illinois State University, Graduate School, College of Fine Arts, School of Music, Normal, IL 61790-2200. Offers MM, MM Ed. *Accreditation:* NASM. *Degree requirements:* For master's, thesis or alternative, performance. *Entrance requirements:* For master's, minimum GPA of 3.0 in music, 2.6 overall; auditions. *Faculty research:* Concerts on the Quad summer concert series.

Indiana State University, School of Graduate Studies, College of Arts and Sciences, Department of Music, Terre Haute, IN 47809. Offers music performance (MM). *Accreditation:* NASM. *Degree requirements:* For master's, comprehensive exam, thesis (for some programs), departmental qualifying exam. Electronic applications accepted.

Music

Indiana University Bloomington, Jacobs School of Music, Bloomington, IN 47405-7000. Offers MA, MM, MM/MLS, MME, MS, DM, DME, PhD, AD, Performance Diploma, Spec, MA/MLS. *Accreditation:* NASM (one or more programs are accredited). *Faculty:* 139 full-time (35 women), 11 part-time/adjunct (3 women). *Students:* 687 full-time (347 women), 172 part-time (85 women); includes 102 minority (21 African Americans, 3 American Indian/Alaska Native, 59 Asian Americans or Pacific Islanders, 19 Hispanic Americans), 223 international. Average age 29. 1,280 applicants, 35% accepted, 244 enrolled. In 2009, 180 master's, 52 doctorates, 58 other advanced degrees awarded. Terminal master's awarded for partial completion of doctoral program. *Degree requirements:* For master's, comprehensive exam (for some programs); for doctorate, comprehensive exam, thesis/dissertation. *Entrance requirements:* For master's and doctorate, GRE, audition, 3 letters of recommendation. Additional exam requirements/recommendations for international students: Required—TOEFL (minimum score 560 paper-based; 223 computer-based; 84 iBT). *Application deadline:* For fall admission, 12/1 for domestic and international students; for spring admission, 9/1 for domestic and international students. Applications are processed on a rolling basis. Application fee: $135 ($145 for international students). Electronic applications accepted. *Expenses:* Contact institution. *Financial support:* In 2009–10, 225 students received support, including 6 fellowships with full and partial tuition reimbursements available (averaging $17,000 per year), 85 teaching assistantships with full tuition reimbursements available (averaging $6,000 per year); research assistantships with tuition reimbursements available, Federal Work-Study, institutionally sponsored loans, scholarships/grants, health care benefits, tuition waivers (full and partial), and unspecified assistantships also available. Support available to part-time students. Financial award application deadline: 3/1; financial award applicants required to submit FAFSA. Total annual research expenditures: $8,300. *Unit head:* Gwyn Richards, Dean, 812-855-2435, E-mail: jln@indiana.edu. *Application contact:* Music Admissions, 812-855-7998, Fax: 812-856-6086, E-mail: musicadm@indiana.edu.

Indiana University Bloomington, University Graduate School, College of Arts and Sciences, Department of Communication and Culture, Bloomington, IN 47405-7000. Offers film and media studies (PhD); performance and ethnography (PhD); rhetoric and public culture (PhD). *Faculty:* 24 full-time (12 women). *Students:* 85 full-time (43 women), 1 (woman) part-time; includes 9 minority (1 African American, 1 Asian American or Pacific Islander, 7 Hispanic Americans), 9 international. Average age 32. 179 applicants, 15% accepted, 15 enrolled. In 2009, 5 master's, 11 doctorates awarded. *Degree requirements:* For master's, comprehensive exam; for doctorate, one foreign language, comprehensive exam, thesis/dissertation, student teaching. *Entrance requirements:* For master's and doctorate, GRE General Test (recommended), minimum GPA of 3.0, 3 letters of recommendation, writing sample. Additional exam requirements/recommendations for international students: Required—TOEFL (minimum score 550 paper-based; 213 computer-based). *Application deadline:* For winter admission, 1/1 for domestic students, 12/1 for international students. Application fee: $55 ($65 for international students). Electronic applications accepted. *Financial support:* In 2009–10, 65 students received support, including 4 fellowships with full tuition reimbursements available (averaging $18,000 per year), 61 teaching assistantships with full tuition reimbursements available (averaging $12,961 per year). Financial award application deadline: 4/15. *Faculty research:* Rhetoric and public culture, film and media studies, performance ethnography. *Unit head:* Prof. Gregory A. Waller, Chair, 812-855-2367, Fax: 812-855-6014, E-mail: cmcl@indiana.edu. *Application contact:* Kathy P. Teige, Graduate Secretary, 812-855-6389, Fax: 812-855-6014, E-mail: kteige@indiana.edu.

Indiana University Bloomington, University Graduate School, College of Arts and Sciences, Department of Folklore and Ethnomusicology, Bloomington, IN 47408-3890. Offers folklore (MA, PhD), including ethnomusicology. Part-time programs available. *Faculty:* 12 full-time (5 women), 11 part-time/adjunct (6 women). *Students:* 110 full-time (69 women), 5 part-time (all women); includes 24 minority (13 African Americans, 1 American Indian/Alaska Native, 5 Asian Americans or Pacific Islanders, 5 Hispanic Americans), 21 international. Average age 34. 74 applicants, 61% accepted, 17 enrolled. In 2009, 14 master's, 9 doctorates awarded. *Degree requirements:* For master's, one foreign language, comprehensive exam, thesis or alternative, project or thesis; for doctorate, 2 foreign languages, comprehensive exam, thesis/dissertation. *Entrance requirements:* For master's and doctorate, GRE General Test, minimum GPA of 3.0. Additional exam requirements/recommendations for international students: Required—TOEFL (minimum score 550 paper-based; 213 computer-based; 79 iBT). *Application deadline:* For fall admission, 1/15 for domestic students, 12/1 for international students. Application fee: $55 ($65 for international students). Electronic applications accepted. *Financial support:* In 2009–10, 38 students received support, including 9 fellowships with full tuition reimbursements available (averaging $18,000 per year), 23 research assistantships with full tuition reimbursements available (averaging $11,500 per year), 22 teaching assistantships with full tuition reimbursements available (averaging $12,500 per year); Federal Work-Study and unspecified assistantships also available. Financial award application deadline: 3/1; financial award applicants required to submit FAFSA. *Faculty research:* Narrative, performance studies, material culture, popular culture, music. *Unit head:* Dr. Portia Maultsby, Chair, 812-855-0395, Fax: 812-855-4008, E-mail: maultsby@indiana.edu. *Application contact:* Christopher Roush, Graduate Secretary, 812-855-0389, Fax: 812-855-4008, E-mail: croush@indiana.edu.

Indiana University of Pennsylvania, School of Graduate Studies and Research, College of Fine Arts, Department of Music and Music Education, Program in Music, Indiana, PA 15705-1087. Offers music education (MA); music history and literature (MA); music theory and composition (MA); performance (MA). *Accreditation:* NASM. Part-time programs available. *Faculty:* 14 full-time (6 women). *Students:* 10 full-time (4 women), 5 part-time (3 women). Average age 29. 17 applicants, 41% accepted, 4 enrolled. In 2009, 4 master's awarded. *Degree requirements:* For master's, thesis optional. *Entrance requirements:* For master's, 2 letters of recommendation, audition. Additional exam requirements/recommendations for international students: Required—TOEFL. *Application deadline:* For fall admission, 7/1 priority date for domestic students; for spring admission, 11/1 for domestic students. Applications are processed on a rolling basis. Application fee: $40. *Expenses:* Tuition, state resident: full-time $6666; part-time $370 per credit hour. Tuition, nonresident: full-time $10,666; part-time $593 per credit hour. Required fees: $813 per semester. *Financial support:* In 2009–10, 5 research assistantships with full and partial tuition reimbursements (averaging $4,906 per year) were awarded; fellowships, Federal Work-Study also available. Support available to part-time students. Financial award application deadline: 3/15; financial award applicants required to submit FAFSA. *Unit head:* Dr. Stephanie Caulder, Head, 724-357-4408, E-mail: stephanie.caulder@iup.edu. *Application contact:* Dr. Stephanie Caulder, Head, 724-357-4408, E-mail: stephanie.caulder@iup.edu.

Indiana University–Purdue University Indianapolis, School of Music, Indianapolis, IN 46202-2896. Offers music technology (MS). Part-time and evening/weekend programs available. Postbaccalaureate distance learning degree programs offered. *Students:* 11 full-time (4 women), 40 part-time (14 women); includes 9 minority (8 African Americans, 1 Asian American or Pacific Islander), 3 international. Average age 35. 24 applicants, 71% accepted, 12 enrolled. In 2009, 13 master's awarded. *Degree requirements:* For master's, internship or final project. *Entrance requirements:* For master's, audition, minimum GPA of 3.0. Additional exam requirements/recommendations for international students: Required—TOEFL. *Application deadline:* For fall admission, 4/15 priority date for domestic students, 3/15 for international students; for spring admission, 11/15 priority date for domestic students, 11/15 for international students. Applications are processed on a rolling basis. Application fee: $55 ($65 for international students). *Financial support:* Teaching assistantships with full tuition reimbursements, Federal Work-Study, institutionally sponsored loans, and scholarships/grants available. Support available to part-time students. Financial award application deadline: 11/15. *Unit head:* G. David Peters, Director, 317-278-2594. *Application contact:* G. David Peters, Director, 317-278-2594.

Indiana University South Bend, School of the Arts, South Bend, IN 46634-7111. Offers music (MM); studio teaching (MM). Part-time programs available. *Faculty:* 1 full-time (0 women). *Students:* 10 full-time (8 women), 2 part-time (1 woman); includes 1 minority (African American), 7 international. Average age 29. In 2009, 7 master's awarded. *Entrance requirements:* For master's, performance audition. *Application deadline:* For fall admission, 7/1 priority date for domestic students; for spring admission, 11/1 for domestic students. Applications are processed on a rolling basis. Application fee: $46 ($58 for international students). *Financial support:* In 2009–10, 4 fellowships (averaging $2,855 per year), 1 teaching assistantship (averaging $1,320 per year) were awarded; Federal Work-Study also available. Support available to part-time students. Financial award application deadline: 3/1; financial award applicants required to submit FAFSA. *Faculty research:* Orchestral conducting. *Unit head:* Dr. Thomas Miller, Dean, 574-520-4301, Fax: 574-520-4317, E-mail: messelst@iusb.edu. *Application contact:* Dr. Thomas Miller, Dean, 574-520-4301, Fax: 574-520-4317, E-mail: messelst@iusb.edu.

Ithaca College, Division of Graduate and Professional Studies, School of Music, Program in Music and Music Education, Ithaca, NY 14850. Offers composition (MM); conducting (MM); music education (MM, MS); performance (MM); Suzuki pedagogy (MM). *Accreditation:* NASM. Part-time programs available. *Faculty:* 58 full-time (21 women), 2 part-time/adjunct (1 woman). *Students:* 42 full-time (17 women), 2 part-time (1 woman); includes 2 minority (1 African American, 1 Hispanic American), 1 international. Average age 24. 154 applicants, 45% accepted, 25 enrolled. In 2009, 29 master's awarded. *Degree requirements:* For master's, comprehensive exam, thesis (for some programs). *Entrance requirements:* For master's, audition, minimum GPA of 3.0. Additional exam requirements/recommendations for international students: Required—TOEFL (minimum score 550 paper-based; 213 computer-based; 80 iBT). *Application deadline:* For fall admission, 3/1 for domestic and international students; for spring admission, 12/1 for domestic and international students. Applications are processed on a rolling basis. Application fee: $40. Electronic applications accepted. *Expenses:* Tuition: Full-time $18,960; part-time $632 per credit hour. *Financial support:* In 2009–10, 42 students received support, including 38 teaching assistantships (averaging $8,459 per year); career-related internships or fieldwork, Federal Work-Study, scholarships/grants, and unspecified assistantships also available. Support available to part-time students. Financial award application deadline: 4/1; financial award applicants required to submit CSS PROFILE or FAFSA. *Faculty research:* Musical performance and performance studies; musical composition; music theory and analysis; music education, teaching and learning; musical direction and conducting. *Unit head:* Dr. Timothy Johnson, Chairperson, Graduate Studies in Music, 607-274-3527, Fax: 607-274-1263, E-mail: gps@ithaca.edu. *Application contact:* Rob Gearhart, Dean, Graduate and Professional Studies, 607-274-3527, Fax: 607-274-1263, E-mail: gps@ithaca.edu.

Jacksonville State University, College of Graduate Studies and Continuing Education, College of Arts and Sciences, Department of Music, Jacksonville, AL 36265-1602. Offers MA. *Accreditation:* NASM. Part-time and evening/weekend programs available. *Degree requirements:* For master's, comprehensive exam, thesis (for some programs). *Entrance requirements:* For master's, GRE General Test or MAT. Electronic applications accepted.

James Madison University, The Graduate School, College of Visual and Performing Arts, School of Music, Doctor of Musical Arts Program, Harrisonburg, VA 22807. Offers DMA. Part-time programs available. *Students:* 22 full-time (8 women), 4 part-time (1 woman); includes 2 minority (1 African American, 1 Hispanic American), 6 international. Average age 27. *Degree requirements:* For doctorate, comprehensive exam, written and oral exams. *Entrance requirements:* For doctorate, GRE General Test, written statement of future goals (professional and educational), 3 letters of recommendation, audition. Additional exam requirements/recommendations for international students: Required—TOEFL. *Application deadline:* For fall admission, 4/1 priority date for domestic students, 4/1 for international students; for spring admission, 4/1 priority date for domestic students, 4/1 for international students. Applications are processed on a rolling basis. Application fee: $55. Electronic applications accepted. *Expenses:* Tuition, area resident: Part-time $305 per credit hour. Tuition, state resident: part-time $305 per credit hour. Tuition, nonresident: part-time $890 per credit hour. *Financial support:* In 2009–10, 6 students received support. Application deadline: 3/1. *Unit head:* Dr. Jeffrey A. Showell, Academic Unit Head, 540-568-6197. *Application contact:* Dr. Mary Jane Speare, Graduate Coordinator, 540-568-6197.

The Jewish Theological Seminary, H. L. Miller Cantorial School and College of Jewish Music, New York, NY 10027-4649. Offers MSM. *Degree requirements:* For master's, one foreign language, comprehensive exam, departmental qualifying exam, recitals. *Entrance requirements:* For master's, music aptitude test, audition, interview, 3 letters of recommendation. Additional exam requirements/recommendations for international students: Required—TOEFL. *Expenses:* Contact institution.

The Johns Hopkins University, Peabody Conservatory, Baltimore, MD 21218-2699. Offers MA, MM, DMA, AD, GPD. *Accreditation:* NASM. *Faculty:* 74 full-time (22 women), 61 part-time/adjunct (20 women). *Students:* 307 full-time (183 women), 21 part-time (15 women); includes 44 minority (13 African Americans, 24 Asian Americans or Pacific Islanders, 7 Hispanic Americans), 121 international. Average age 25. 734 applicants, 58% accepted, 184 enrolled. In 2009, 117 master's, 9 doctorates, 25 other advanced degrees awarded. *Degree requirements:* For master's, thesis (for some programs), departmental qualifying exam, recital; for doctorate, 2 foreign languages, thesis/dissertation (for some programs), departmental qualifying exam, recitals; for other advanced degree, recitals. *Entrance requirements:* For master's and other advanced degree, audition; for doctorate, audition, interview. Additional exam requirements/recommendations for international students: Required—TOEFL (minimum score 550 paper-based; 213 computer-based; 79 iBT). *Application deadline:* For fall admission, 12/1 for domestic students. Application fee: $100. *Expenses:* Contact institution. *Financial support:* In 2009–10, 293 students received support, including 61 teaching assistantships (averaging $23,738 per year); Federal Work-Study, institutionally sponsored loans, scholarships/grants, and unspecified assistantships also available. Financial award application deadline: 2/1; financial award applicants required to submit FAFSA. *Unit head:* Jeffrey Sharkey, Director, 410-234-4700, Fax: 410-659-8131. *Application contact:* David Lane, Director of Admissions, 800-368-2521, Fax: 410-659-8102, E-mail: admissions@peabody.jhu.edu.

The Juilliard School, Program in Music, New York, NY 10023-6588. Offers MM, DMA, Artist Diploma, Diploma. *Degree requirements:* For master's and other advanced degree, performance jury, recital; for doctorate, one foreign language, thesis/dissertation, performance jury, 3 recitals. *Entrance requirements:* For master's and other advanced degree, audition; for doctorate, audition, interview, dossier. Additional exam requirements/recommendations for international students: Required—TOEFL (minimum score 570 paper-based; 230 computer-based; 89 iBT). Electronic applications accepted.

Kansas State University, Graduate School, College of Arts and Sciences, Department of Music, Manhattan, KS 66506. Offers music education (MM); music education/band conducting (MM); music history and literature (MM); performance (MM); performance with pedagogy emphasis (MM); theory and composition (MM). *Accreditation:* NASM. Part-time programs available. *Faculty:* 23 full-time (8 women), 1 (woman) part-time/adjunct. *Students:* 12 applicants, 92% accepted. In 2009, 10 master's awarded. *Degree requirements:* For master's, thesis optional. *Entrance requirements:* For master's, GRE, audition (in person or recording), interview (music education). Additional exam requirements/recommendations for international students: Required—TOEFL (minimum score 600 paper-based). *Application deadline:* For fall admission, 2/1 priority date for domestic and international students; for spring admission, 8/1 priority date for domestic and international students. Applications are processed on a rolling basis. Application fee: $40 ($55 for international students). Electronic applications accepted. *Financial support:* In 2009–10, 12 teaching assistantships with full tuition reimbursements (averaging $7,500 per year) were awarded; institutionally sponsored loans, scholarships/grants, and tuition waivers (full and partial) also available. Support available to part-time students. Financial award application deadline: 3/1; financial award applicants required to submit FAFSA. *Faculty research:* Music since 1945, music by women composers, American music, opera, current performance practices. Total annual research expenditures: $12,026. *Unit head:* Dr. Gary Mortenson, Head, 785-532-3828, Fax: 785-532-7732, E-mail: garym@ksu.edu. *Application contact:* Fred Burrack, Director, 785-532-5764, Fax: 785-532-7732, E-mail: fburrack@ksu.edu.

Kent State University, College of the Arts, Hugh A. Glauser School of Music, Kent, OH 44242-0001. Offers composition (MA); conducting (MM); ethnomusicology (MA); music education (MM, PhD); musicology (MA); musicology-ethnomusicology (PhD); performance (MM); theory (MA); theory and composition (PhD). *Accreditation:* NASM. *Degree requirements:* For master's, variable foreign language requirement, comprehensive exam, 2 recitals, essay and recital, or thesis; for doctorate, variable foreign language requirement, comprehensive exam, thesis/dissertation. *Entrance requirements:* For master's, diagnostic exams in music history and theory, audition, minimum GPA of 2.75; for doctorate, diagnostic exams in music history and theory, master's thesis or scholarly paper, minimum GPA of 3.0. Additional exam requirements/recommendations for international students: Required—TOEFL. Electronic applications accepted. *Faculty research:* Music composition, performance, teaching and history.

Lamar University, College of Graduate Studies, College of Fine Arts and Communication, Department of Music, Theatre, and Dance, Beaumont, TX 77710. Offers music education (MM Ed); music performance (MM); theatre (MS). *Accreditation:* NASM (one or more programs are accredited). *Faculty:* 8 full-time (2 women). *Students:* 5 full-time (3 women), 3 part-time (2 women); includes 1 minority (African American). Average age 29. 9 applicants, 44% accepted, 4 enrolled. In 2009, 3 master's awarded. *Degree requirements:* For master's, comprehensive exam, thesis optional. *Entrance requirements:* For master's, GRE General Test, theory placement exams, audition. Additional exam requirements/recommendations for international students: Required—TOEFL. *Application deadline:* For fall admission, 8/1 for domestic students; for spring admission, 12/1 for domestic students. Applications are processed on a rolling basis. Application fee: $25 ($50 for international students). *Financial support:* In 2009–10, 4 fellowships with tuition reimbursements (averaging $2,000 per year), 2 teaching assistantships were awarded; institutionally sponsored loans and tuition waivers (partial) also available. Support available to part-time students. Financial award application deadline: 4/1. *Faculty research:* Performance: ensembles and personal. *Unit head:* Dr. L. Randolph Babin, Chair, 409-880-8144, Fax: 409-880-8143, E-mail: babinlr@hal.lamar.edu. *Application contact:* Dr. Robert M. Culbertson, Adviser, 409-880-8073, Fax: 409-880-8143, E-mail: culbertsrm@hal.lamar.edu.

Lee University, Program in Music, Cleveland, TN 37320-3450. Offers church music (MCM); music education (MM); music performance (MM). *Accreditation:* NASM. Part-time programs available. *Faculty:* 21 full-time (5 women), 14 part-time/adjunct (7 women). *Students:* 15 full-time (6 women), 20 part-time (8 women); includes 3 minority (all African Americans), 5 international. Average age 30. 9 applicants, 100% accepted, 8 enrolled. In 2009, 8 master's awarded. *Degree requirements:* For master's, variable foreign language requirement, comprehensive exam, thesis, internship. *Entrance requirements:* For master's, audition, resume, interview, minimum GPA of 2.75. Additional exam requirements/recommendations for international students: Required—TOEFL (minimum score 450 paper-based; 45 computer-based). *Application deadline:* For fall admission, 4/1 for domestic students; for spring admission, 10/1 for domestic students. Applications are processed on a rolling basis. Application fee: $25. *Expenses:* Tuition: Full-time $11,100; part-time $463 per credit. Required fees: $305. *Financial support:* Teaching assistantships, career-related internships or fieldwork, Federal Work-Study, institutionally sponsored loans, and scholarships/grants available. Financial award application deadline: 3/1; financial award applicants required to submit FAFSA. *Unit head:* Dr. Jim W. Burns, Director, 423-614-8240, Fax: 423-614-8242, E-mail: gradmusic@leeuniversity.edu. *Application contact:* Vicki Glasscock, Graduate Admissions Director, 423-614-8059, E-mail: vglasscock@leeuniversity.edu.

Long Island University, C.W. Post Campus, School of Visual and Performing Arts, Department of Music, Brookville, NY 11548-1300. Offers music (MA); music education (MS). Part-time programs available. *Degree requirements:* For master's, thesis. *Entrance requirements:* For master's, GRE General Test (MA), GRE Subject Test in music, minimum undergraduate GPA of 3.0, 2 professional and/or academic letters of recommendation, current resume. Electronic applications accepted. *Faculty research:* Performance, composing, musicology, conducting, computer-based music technology.

Longy School of Music, Conservatory at Longy, Cambridge, MA 02138. Offers chamber ensemble (Artist Diploma); collaborative piano (MM, Artist Diploma, GPD); composition (MM); Dalcroze eurhythmics (MM); early music (MM, Artist Diploma, GPD); instrumental performance (MM, Artist Diploma, GPD); modern American music (MM, GPD); opera performance (MM, GPD); organ performance (MM, Artist Diploma, GPD); piano performance (MM, Artist Diploma, GPD); vocal performance (MM, Artist Diploma, GPD). *Accreditation:* NASM. Part-time programs available. *Faculty:* 98 part-time/adjunct (52 women). *Students:* 130 full-time (91 women), 41 part-time (22 women); includes 16 minority (6 African Americans, 9 Asian Americans or Pacific Islanders, 1 Hispanic American), 46 international. Average age 28. 196 applicants, 70% accepted, 70 enrolled. In 2009, 42 master's, 21 GPDs awarded. *Degree requirements:* For master's, thesis (for some programs), recital; for other advanced degree, recital. *Entrance requirements:* For master's and other advanced degree, audition. Additional exam requirements/recommendations for international students: Required—TOEFL (minimum score 550 paper-based; 213 computer-based; 79 iBT). *Application deadline:* For fall admission, 12/1 priority date for domestic and international students; for spring admission, 11/1 for domestic and international students. Application fee: $100. Electronic applications accepted. *Expenses:* Tuition: Full-time $28,000. Required fees: $450. *Financial support:* In 2009–10, 145 students received support, including 12 teaching assistantships (averaging $3,000 per year); scholarships/grants and unspecified assistantships also available. Financial award application deadline: 3/1; financial award applicants required to submit FAFSA. *Unit head:* Karen Zorn, President, 617-876-0956, Fax: 617-876-9326, E-mail: music@longy.edu. *Application contact:* Alex Powell, Director of Admissions and Student Services, 617-876-0956 Ext. 1521, Fax: 617-876-9326, E-mail: admissions@longy.edu.

Louisiana State University and Agricultural and Mechanical College, Graduate School, College of Music and Dramatic Arts, School of Music, Baton Rouge, LA 70803. Offers music (MM, DMA, PhD); music education (PhD). *Accreditation:* NASM. Part-time programs available. *Faculty:* 50 full-time (15 women), 1 (woman) part-time/adjunct. *Students:* 155 full-time (79 women), 44 part-time (23 women); includes 21 minority (10 African Americans, 4 Asian Americans or Pacific Islanders, 7 Hispanic Americans), 37 international. Average age 29. 171 applicants, 51% accepted, 55 enrolled. In 2009, 40 master's, 16 doctorates awarded. Terminal master's awarded for partial completion of doctoral program. *Degree requirements:* For doctorate, thesis/dissertation (for some programs). *Entrance requirements:* For master's, minimum GPA of 3.0, audition/interview; for doctorate, GRE General Test, minimum GPA of 3.0, audition/interview. Additional exam requirements/recommendations for international students: Required—TOEFL (minimum score 550 paper-based; 213 computer-based; 79 iBT) or IELTS (minimum score 6.5). *Application deadline:* For fall admission, 3/15 priority date for domestic students, 5/15 for international students; for spring admission, 10/15 for international students. Applications are processed on a rolling basis. Application fee: $50 ($70 for international students). Electronic applications accepted. *Financial support:* In 2009–10, 158 students received support, including 3 fellowships (averaging $31,007 per year), 2 research assistantships with full and partial tuition reimbursements available (averaging $15,250 per year), 84 teaching assistantships with full and partial tuition reimbursements available (averaging $10,673 per year); Federal Work-Study, institutionally sponsored loans, scholarships/grants, health care benefits, tuition waivers (full and partial), and unspecified assistantships also available. Support available to part-time students. Financial award applicants required to submit FAFSA. *Faculty research:* Music education, music literature, formal and harmonic analysis, pedagogy, performance. Total annual research expenditures: $65,241. *Unit head:* Dr. Jane Cassidy, Interim Dean, 225-578-3261, Fax: 225-578-2562. *Application contact:* Dr. Lori Bade, Director of Graduate Studies, 225-578-3261, Fax: 225-578-2562, E-mail: lbade1@lsu.edu.

Loyola University New Orleans, College of Music and Fine Arts, New Orleans, LA 70118-6195. Offers music therapy (MMT); performance (MM). *Accreditation:* NASM. Part-time programs available. *Students:* 17 full-time (8 women), 4 part-time (all women); includes 5 minority (4 African Americans, 1 Hispanic American), 1 international. Average age 25. 22 applicants, 68% accepted, 11 enrolled. In 2009, 8 master's awarded. *Degree requirements:* For master's, comprehensive exam, thesis, comprehensive written and oral exams. *Entrance requirements:* For master's, performance audition, appropriate bachelor's degree, minimum GPA of 3.0, letters of recommendation, resume. Additional exam requirements/recommendations for international students: Required—TOEFL (minimum score 550 paper-based; 213 computer-based). *Application deadline:* For fall admission, 8/15 priority date for domestic and international students; for spring admission, 1/1 priority date for domestic and international students. Applications are processed on a rolling basis. Application fee: $20. Electronic applications accepted. *Expenses:* Contact institution. *Financial support:* Career-related internships or fieldwork, Federal Work-Study, institutionally sponsored loans, scholarships/grants, and unspecified assistantships available. Support available to part-time students. Financial award application deadline: 5/1; financial award applicants required to submit FAFSA. *Faculty research:* Music business, music therapy, musicology, music theory, music education. *Unit head:* Donald R. Boomgaarden, Dean, 504-865-3039, Fax: 504-865-2852, E-mail: deancmfa@loyno.edu. *Application contact:* Anthony A. Decuir, Associate Dean, 504-865-3037, Fax: 504-865-2852, E-mail: decuir@loyno.edu.

Lynchburg College, Graduate Studies, School of Communications and the Arts, Lynchburg, VA 24501-3199. Offers music (MA), including choral or instrumental conducting. Part-time and evening/weekend programs available. *Degree requirements:* For master's, comprehensive exam. *Entrance requirements:* For master's, GRE, minimum undergraduate GPA of 3.0. Additional exam requirements/recommendations for international students: Required—TOEFL. *Expenses:* Tuition: Full-time $7020; part-time $390 per credit hour.

Lynn University, Conservatory of Music, Boca Raton, FL 33431-5598. Offers composition (MM); performance (MM); professional performance (Certificate). *Accreditation:* NASM. Part-time and evening/weekend programs available. *Degree requirements:* For Certificate, performance, recitals, orchestra, chamber music. *Entrance requirements:* For master's, resume, 2 letters of recommendation, minimum undergraduate GPA of 3.0; for Certificate, bachelor's degree in music performance or equivalent, audition. Additional exam requirements/recommendations for international students: Required—TOEFL (minimum score 550 paper-based; 213 computer-based). *Application deadline:* For fall admission, 3/31 priority date for domestic and international students; for spring admission, 12/1 priority date for domestic and international students. Applications are processed on a rolling basis. Application fee: $50. *Expenses:* Tuition: Part-time $580 per credit. One-time fee: $200 part-time. Part-time tuition and fees vary according to degree level. *Financial support:* Federal Work-Study, institutionally sponsored loans, scholarships/grants, and unspecified assistantships available. Support available to part-time students. Financial award application deadline: 8/1; financial award applicants required to submit FAFSA. *Unit head:* Dr. Jon Robertson, Dean, 561-237-7702, Fax: 561-237-9002, E-mail: jrobertson@lynn.edu. *Application contact:* Dr. Larissa Baia, Assistant Director of Graduate Admissions, 561-237-7916, Fax: 561-237-7100, E-mail: admissionpm@lynn.edu.

Manhattan School of Music, Graduate Programs, New York, NY 10027-4698. Offers composition (MM, DMA); jazz (MM, DMA); music performance (MM, DMA); orchestral performance (MM). *Degree requirements:* For master's, recital; for doctorate, variable foreign language requirement, thesis/dissertation, departmental qualifying exam, recitals. *Entrance requirements:* For master's, audition, pre-screen CD, bachelor's degree; for doctorate, departmental exam, audition, interview, pre-screen CD, master's degree. Additional exam requirements/recommendations for international students: Required—TOEFL (minimum score 550 paper-based; 213 computer-based; 79 iBT). Electronic applications accepted.

Manhattan School of Music, Professional Studies Certificate Program, New York, NY 10027-4698. Offers instrumental music (CPS), including accompanying, brass, composition, guitar, orchestral performance, organ, piano, strings, voice, woodwinds; vocal music (CPS), including accompanying, brass, composition, guitar, orchestral performance, organ, piano, strings, voice, woodwinds. *Degree requirements:* For CPS, recital. *Entrance requirements:* For degree, audition, pre-screen CD. Additional exam requirements/recommendations for international students: Required—TOEFL (minimum score 550 paper-based; 213 computer-based). Electronic applications accepted.

Mansfield University of Pennsylvania, Graduate Studies, Department of Music, Mansfield, PA 16933. Offers band conducting (MA); choral conducting (MA); performance (MA). *Accreditation:* NASM. Part-time and evening/weekend programs available. *Faculty:* 7 full-time (4 women), 1 part-time/adjunct (0 women). *Students:* 9 full-time (6 women), 2 part-time (0 women), 1 international. Average age 27. In 2009, 2 master's awarded. *Degree requirements:* For master's, comprehensive exam, thesis optional. *Entrance requirements:* For master's, minimum GPA of 3.0, audition. Additional exam requirements/recommendations for international students: Required—TOEFL (minimum score 550 paper-based; 220 computer-based). *Application deadline:* For fall admission, 8/1 priority date for domestic students, 6/1 for international students; for spring admission, 11/1 priority date for domestic students, 9/1 for international students. Applications are processed on a rolling basis. Application fee: $25. Electronic applications accepted. *Expenses:* Tuition, state resident: full-time $6666; part-time $370 per credit. Tuition, nonresident: full-time $10,666; part-time $593 per credit. Required fees: $1388. *Financial support:* Career-related internships or fieldwork and unspecified assistantships available. Financial award application deadline: 5/1; financial award applicants required to submit FAFSA. *Unit head:* Dr. Shellie Gregorich, Chairperson, 570-662-4714, E-mail: sgregori@mansfield.edu. *Application contact:* Christina Hall, Assistant Director of Enrollment Services/Graduate Admissions, 570-662-4812, Fax: 570-662-4121, E-mail: chale@mansfield.edu.

Marshall University, Academic Affairs Division, College of Fine Arts, Department of Music, Huntington, WV 25755. Offers MA. *Accreditation:* NASM. Evening/weekend programs available. *Faculty:* 14 full-time (4 women), 25 part-time/adjunct (13 women). *Students:* 16 full-time (7 women), 3 part-time (1 woman); includes 2 minority (1 African American, 1 Asian American or Pacific Islander), 2 international. Average age 28. In 2009, 8 master's awarded. *Degree requirements:* For master's, thesis optional. Application fee: $40. *Unit head:* Dr. Jeffrey Pappas, Chairperson, 304-696-3117, E-mail: pappas@marshall.edu. *Application contact:* Information Contact, 304-746-1900, Fax: 304-746-1902, E-mail: services@marshall.edu.

McGill University, Faculty of Graduate and Postdoctoral Studies, Schulich School of Music, Montréal, QC H3A 2T5, Canada. Offers composition (M Mus, D Mus, PhD); music education (MA, PhD); music technology (MA, PhD); musicology (MA, PhD); performance (M Mus); performance studies (D Mus); sound recording (M Mus, PhD); theory (MA, PhD).

Memorial University of Newfoundland, School of Graduate Studies, Interdisciplinary Program in Ethnomusicology, St. John's, NL A1C 5S7, Canada. Offers MA, PhD. *Degree requirements:* For master's, thesis optional, research paper (non-thesis option); for doctorate, one foreign language, comprehensive exam, thesis/dissertation, oral defense of thesis. *Entrance requirements:* For master's, minimum B+ average with a B Mus or humanities/social sciences degree; for doctorate, MA in ethnomusicology or a related field.

Memorial University of Newfoundland, School of Graduate Studies, School of Music, St. John's, NL A1C 5S7, Canada. Offers conducting (MMus); performance pedagogy (MMus); performing (MMus). *Entrance requirements:* For master's, diagnostic exams measuring skills and knowledge in musical literacy, B Mus with first-class standing, audition (ca. 60 min. performance). Electronic applications accepted.

Mercer University, Graduate Studies, Macon Campus, School of Music, Macon, GA 31207-0003. Offers choral conducting (MM); church music (M Div, MM); collaborative piano (MM); instrumental conducting (MM); performance (MM). Part-time programs available. *Faculty:* 2 full-time (0 women). *Students:* 12 full-time (7 women), 2 part-time (both women), 3 international. Average age 29. 5 applicants, 100% accepted, 5 enrolled. In 2009, 8 master's awarded. *Degree requirements:* For master's, comprehensive exam, recitals. *Entrance requirements:* For master's, GRE, audition. Additional exam requirements/recommendations for international students: Required—TOEFL (minimum score 550 paper-based; 213 computer-based; 80 iBT).

Music

Mercer University (continued)

Application deadline: Applications are processed on a rolling basis. Application fee: $100. Electronic applications accepted. *Expenses:* Contact institution. *Financial support:* In 2009–10, 14 students received support. Tuition waivers and unspecified assistantships available. Financial award applicants required to submit FAFSA. *Faculty research:* Philosophy of church music; performance practices of the Baroque and Classical periods; organ repertoire of the High Baroque. Total annual research expenditures: $5,000. *Unit head:* Dr. Charles David Keith, Director of Graduate Studies, 478-301-4012, Fax: 478-301-5633, E-mail: keith_cd@mercer.edu. *Application contact:* Kimberly T. Beach, Enrollment Associate, 478-301-2570, Fax: 478-301-2650, E-mail: beach_kt@mercer.edu.

Meredith College, John E. Weems Graduate School, Department of Music, Raleigh, NC 27607-5298. Offers MM. *Accreditation:* NASM. Part-time and evening/weekend programs available. *Faculty:* 1 full-time (0 women), 1 (woman) part-time/adjunct. *Students:* 2 part-time (both women). Average age 47. In 2009, 1 master's awarded. *Degree requirements:* For master's, thesis optional. *Entrance requirements:* For master's, audition, interview, letters of recommendation. *Application deadline:* For fall admission, 7/1 priority date for domestic and international students; for spring admission, 11/1 priority date for domestic and international students. Applications are processed on a rolling basis. Application fee: $50. Electronic applications accepted. *Expenses:* Contact institution. *Financial support:* Institutionally sponsored loans, scholarships/grants, and tuition waivers (partial) available. Support available to part-time students. Financial award application deadline: 2/15; financial award applicants required to submit FAFSA. *Unit head:* Dr. David Lynch, Head, 919-760-8536, Fax: 919-760-2359, E-mail: lynchd@meredith.edu. *Application contact:* Dr. James Fogle, Coordinator, 919-760-8576, Fax: 919-760-2359, E-mail: foglej@meredith.edu.

Messiah College, Program in Conducting, Grantham, PA 17027. Offers choral conducting (MM); orchestral conducting (MM); wind conducting (MM). Part-time programs available. *Degree requirements:* For master's, advanced conducting project. *Application deadline:* Applications are processed on a rolling basis. Application fee: $30. Electronic applications accepted. *Expenses:* Tuition: Part-time $518 per credit hour. *Financial support:* Applicants required to submit FAFSA. *Unit head:* Dr. Bradley Genevro, Program Coordinator, 717-796-1800 Ext. 2750, Fax: 717-691-2386, E-mail: bgenevro@messiah.edu. *Application contact:* Dr. Bradley Genevro, Program Coordinator, 717-796-1800 Ext. 2750, Fax: 717-691-2386, E-mail: bgenevro@messiah.edu.

Miami University, Graduate School, School of Fine Arts, Department of Music, Oxford, OH 45056. Offers music education (MM); music performance (MM). *Accreditation:* NASM. *Students:* 21 full-time (8 women), 2 part-time (both women); includes 6 minority (3 African Americans, 1 Asian American or Pacific Islander, 2 Hispanic Americans), 1 international. *Entrance requirements:* For master's, audition, minimum undergraduate GPA of 3.0 during previous 2 years or 3.0 overall. Application fee: $50. *Expenses:* Tuition, state resident: full-time $11,280. Tuition, nonresident: full-time $24,912. Required fees: $516. *Financial support:* Fellowships with full tuition reimbursements, research assistantships, teaching assistantships, Federal Work-Study, health care benefits, tuition waivers (full), and unspecified assistantships available. Financial award application deadline: 3/1. *Unit head:* Dr. Richard Green, Chair, 513-529-3014, Fax: 513-529-3027. *Application contact:* Chair, Graduate Studies, The Department of Music, 513-529-3014, E-mail: music@muohio.edu.

Michigan State University, The Graduate School, College of Music, East Lansing, MI 48824. Offers collaborative piano (M Mus); jazz studies (M Mus); music (PhD); music composition (M Mus, DMA); music conducting (M Mus, DMA); music education (M Mus); music performance (M Mus, DMA); music theory (M Mus); music therapy (M Mus); musicology (MA); piano pedagogy (M Mus). *Accreditation:* NASM. *Faculty:* 57 full-time (14 women), 2 part-time/adjunct (0 women). *Students:* 234 full-time (120 women), 41 part-time (28 women); includes 30 minority (9 African Americans, 6 American Indian/Alaska Native, 10 Asian Americans or Pacific Islanders, 5 Hispanic Americans), 107 international. Average age 29. 378 applicants, 21% accepted. In 2009, 57 master's, 34 doctorates awarded. *Entrance requirements:* Additional exam requirements/recommendations for international students: Required—TOEFL. Electronic applications accepted. *Expenses:* Tuition, state resident: part-time $478.25 per credit hour. Tuition, nonresident: part-time $966.50 per credit hour. Part-time tuition and fees vary according to program. *Financial support:* In 2009–10, 15 research assistantships with tuition reimbursements (averaging $6,188 per year), 86 teaching assistantships with tuition reimbursements (averaging $6,110 per year) were awarded. *Unit head:* Prof. James B. Forger, Dean, 517-355-4583, Fax: 517-432-7081, E-mail: forger@msu.edu. *Application contact:* Anne Simon, Assistant to the Associate Dean for Graduate Studies and Research, 517-353-9122, Fax: 517-432-2880, E-mail: musgrad@msu.edu.

Middle Tennessee State University, College of Graduate Studies, College of Liberal Arts, School of Music, Murfreesboro, TN 37132. Offers MA. *Accreditation:* NASM. Part-time and evening/weekend programs available. Postbaccalaureate distance learning degree programs offered. *Faculty:* 16 full-time (6 women), 2 part-time/adjunct (1 woman). *Students:* 5 full-time (2 women), 23 part-time (12 women); includes 1 minority (Asian American or Pacific Islander). Average age 27. 26 applicants, 73% accepted, 19 enrolled. In 2009, 9 master's awarded. *Degree requirements:* For master's, one foreign language, comprehensive exam, thesis optional. *Entrance requirements:* For master's, GRE or MAT. Additional exam requirements/recommendations for international students: Required—TOEFL (minimum score 525 paper-based; 195 computer-based; 71 iBT) or IELTS (minimum score 6). *Application deadline:* For fall admission, 6/1 for domestic and international students. Applications are processed on a rolling basis. Application fee: $25 ($30 for international students). Electronic applications accepted. *Expenses:* Tuition, state resident: full-time $4404. Tuition, nonresident: full-time $10,956. *Financial support:* In 2009–10, 12 students received support. Institutionally sponsored loans available. Support available to part-time students. Financial award application deadline: 5/1; financial award applicants required to submit FAFSA. *Unit head:* Dr. George Riordan, Director, 615-898-2469, Fax: 615-898-5037. *Application contact:* Dr. Michael Allen, Dean and Vice Provost for Research, 615-898-2840, Fax: 615-904-8020, E-mail: mallen@mtsu.edu.

Middle Tennessee State University, College of Graduate Studies, College of Mass Communication, Department of Recording Industry, Murfreesboro, TN 37132. Offers recording arts and technologies (MFA). Part-time and evening/weekend programs available. Postbaccalaureate distance learning degree programs offered. *Faculty:* 15 full-time (1 woman). *Students:* 18 full-time (3 women), 17 part-time (2 women); includes 7 minority (all African Americans). Average age 26. 35 applicants, 31% accepted, 11 enrolled. In 2009, 7 master's awarded. *Degree requirements:* For master's, comprehensive exam, thesis optional. *Entrance requirements:* For master's, GRE. Additional exam requirements/recommendations for international students: Required—TOEFL (minimum score 525 paper-based; 195 computer-based; 71 iBT) or IELTS (minimum score 6). *Application deadline:* For fall admission, 6/1 for domestic and international students. Applications are processed on a rolling basis. Application fee: $25 ($30 for international students). *Expenses:* Tuition, state resident: full-time $4404. Tuition, nonresident: full-time $10,956. *Financial support:* In 2009–10, 4 students received support. Institutionally sponsored loans available. Support available to part-time students. Financial award application deadline: 5/1. *Faculty research:* Digital audio, music production. *Unit head:* Dr. Loren Mulraine, Chair, 615-898-2578, Fax: 615-898-5682, E-mail: lmulrain@mtsu.edu. *Application contact:* Dr. Michael Allen, Dean and Vice Provost for Research, 615-898-2840, Fax: 615-904-8020, E-mail: mallen@mtsu.edu.

Midwestern Baptist Theological Seminary, Graduate and Professional Programs, Kansas City, MO 64118-4697. Offers Biblical archaeology (MA); Biblical languages (MA); Christian education (M Div, MACE); Christian foundations—lay ministry (Graduate Certificate); collegiate ministries (M Div); counseling (MA); educational ministry (D Ed Min); international church planting (M Div); ministry (M Div, D Min); North American church planting (M Div); sacred music (MCM); urban ministry (M Div); worship leadership (M Div); youth ministry (M Div). *Accreditation:* ATS. Part-time programs available. Postbaccalaureate distance learning degree programs offered (minimal on-campus study). *Degree requirements:* For doctorate, thesis/dissertation; for M Div, 2 foreign languages. *Entrance requirements:* For doctorate, MAT. Electronic applications accepted. *Faculty research:* Ministerial studies, Biblical and theological studies, missions, counseling.

Mills College, Graduate Studies, Department of Dance, Oakland, CA 94613-1000. Offers dance (MA, MFA), including choreography and performance (MA). Part-time programs available. *Faculty:* 4 full-time (3 women), 5 part-time/adjunct (4 women). *Students:* 18 full-time (all women); includes 5 minority (3 African Americans, 2 Asian Americans or Pacific Islanders), 2 international. Average age 31. 38 applicants, 66% accepted, 9 enrolled. In 2009, 8 master's awarded. *Degree requirements:* For master's, comprehensive exam, thesis, performance. *Entrance requirements:* For master's, audition or tape. Additional exam requirements/recommendations for international students: Required—TOEFL. *Application deadline:* For fall admission, 2/1 priority date for domestic and international students. Applications are processed on a rolling basis. Application fee: $50. *Expenses:* Tuition: Full-time $26,326; part-time $6584 per course. Required fees: $896. One-time fee: $896 part-time. Tuition and fees vary according to program. *Financial support:* In 2009–10, 18 students received support, including 18 fellowships (averaging $7,859 per year), 9 teaching assistantships with partial tuition reimbursements available (averaging $4,753 per year); scholarships/grants and unspecified assistantships also available. Financial award application deadline: 2/1; financial award applicants required to submit FAFSA. *Faculty research:* Video and dance, modern dance technique, performance art, rhythmic analysis. *Unit head:* Sonya Delwaide, Head, 510-430-3258, E-mail: sdelwaid@mills.edu. *Application contact:* Jessica King, Graduate Admission Specialist, 510-430-3305, Fax: 510-430-2159, E-mail: grad-studies@mills.edu.

Mills College, Graduate Studies, Department of Music, Oakland, CA 94613-1000. Offers composition (MA); electronic music and recording media (MFA); music performance and literature (MFA). Part-time programs available. *Faculty:* 6 full-time (2 women), 5 part-time/adjunct (3 women). *Students:* 50 full-time (15 women); includes 4 minority (1 African American, 1 Asian American or Pacific Islander, 2 Hispanic Americans), 3 international. Average age 28. 74 applicants, 74% accepted, 29 enrolled. In 2009, 18 master's awarded. *Degree requirements:* For master's, variable foreign language requirement, thesis, performance or recital. *Entrance requirements:* For master's, tape. Additional exam requirements/recommendations for international students: Required—TOEFL. *Application deadline:* For fall admission, 2/1 priority date for domestic students; for spring admission, 11/1 for domestic students. Applications are processed on a rolling basis. Application fee: $50. Electronic applications accepted. *Expenses:* Tuition: Full-time $26,326; part-time $6584 per course. Required fees: $896. One-time fee: $896 part-time. Tuition and fees vary according to program. *Financial support:* In 2009–10, 45 students received support, including 45 fellowships (averaging $7,779 per year), 25 teaching assistantships with partial tuition reimbursements available (averaging $8,160 per year); scholarships/grants also available. Support available to part-time students. Financial award application deadline: 2/1; financial award applicants required to submit FAFSA. *Faculty research:* Electronic and computer music, twentieth century theory and performance practice, Mozart, music theory. Total annual research expenditures: $7,500. *Unit head:* Fred Frith, Chairperson, 510-430-2171, Fax: 510-430-3314, E-mail: grad-studies@mills.edu. *Application contact:* Jessica King, Graduate Admission Specialist, 510-430-3305, Fax: 510-430-2159, E-mail: grad-studies@mills.edu.

Minnesota State University Mankato, College of Graduate Studies, College of Arts and Humanities, Department of Music, Mankato, MN 56001. Offers MAT, MM. *Accreditation:* NASM. *Students:* 1 full-time (0 women), 8 part-time (4 women). *Degree requirements:* For master's, comprehensive exam, thesis or alternative. *Entrance requirements:* For master's, minimum GPA of 3.0 during previous 2 years, audition or test. Additional exam requirements/recommendations for international students: Required—TOEFL. *Application deadline:* For fall admission, 7/1 priority date for domestic students; for spring admission, 11/1 for domestic students. Applications are processed on a rolling basis. Application fee: $40. Electronic applications accepted. *Expenses:* Tuition, state resident: full-time $5364. Tuition, nonresident: full-time $8314. *Financial support:* Research assistantships with full tuition reimbursements, teaching assistantships with full tuition reimbursements, career-related internships or fieldwork, Federal Work-Study, and institutionally sponsored loans available. Support available to part-time students. Financial award application deadline: 3/15. *Unit head:* Dr. John Lindberg, Chairperson, 507-389-2118. *Application contact:* 507-389-2321, E-mail: grad@mnsu.edu.

Mississippi College, Graduate School, College of Arts and Sciences, School of Christian Studies and the Arts, Department of Music, Clinton, MS 39058. Offers applied music performance (MM); conducting (MM); music education (MM); music performance: organ (MM); vocal pedagogy (MM). *Accreditation:* NASM. Part-time and evening/weekend programs available. *Faculty:* 9 full-time (5 women), 5 part-time/adjunct (3 women). *Students:* 8 full-time (6 women), 7 part-time (5 women), 8 international. Average age 26. In 2009, 12 master's awarded. *Degree requirements:* For master's, comprehensive exam, recital. *Entrance requirements:* For master's, GRE, minimum GPA of 2.5. Additional exam requirements/recommendations for international students: Recommended—IELTS. *Application deadline:* For fall admission, 8/15 priority date for domestic and international students. Applications are processed on a rolling basis. Application fee: $30. Electronic applications accepted. *Expenses:* Tuition: Part-time $452 per credit hour. Required fees: $101 per semester. Tuition and fees vary according to degree level, campus/location, program and student level. *Financial support:* Teaching assistantships, Federal Work-Study, scholarships/grants, and unspecified assistantships available. Support available to part-time students. Financial award application deadline: 4/1; financial award applicants required to submit FAFSA. *Unit head:* Dr. James Meaders, Chair, 601-925-3441, Fax: 601-925-3945, E-mail: meaders@mc.edu. *Application contact:* Elnora Lewis, Secretary, 601-925-3225, Fax: 601-925-3889, E-mail: lewis09@mc.edu.

Missouri State University, Graduate College, College of Arts and Letters, Department of Music, Springfield, MO 65897. Offers music (MM), including conducting, music education, music pedagogy, music theory and composition, performance; secondary education (MS Ed), including music. *Accreditation:* NASM. Part-time programs available. *Faculty:* 24 full-time (9 women). *Students:* 13 full-time (9 women), 29 part-time (14 women); includes 1 minority (Asian American or Pacific Islander), 4 international. Average age 30. 14 applicants, 100% accepted, 8 enrolled. In 2009, 12 master's awarded. *Degree requirements:* For master's, comprehensive exam, thesis or alternative. *Entrance requirements:* For master's, GRE, interview/audition (MM), 9-12 teaching certification (MS Ed). Additional exam requirements/recommendations for international students: Required—TOEFL (minimum score 550 paper-based; 213 computer-based; 79 iBT). *Application deadline:* For fall admission, 7/20 for domestic students, 5/1 for international students; for spring admission, 12/20 for domestic students, 9/1 for international students. Applications are processed on a rolling basis. Application fee: $35 ($50 for international students). Electronic applications accepted. *Expenses:* Tuition, state resident: full-time $3852; part-time $214 per credit hour. Tuition, nonresident: full-time $7524; part-time $418 per credit hour. Required fees: $696; $172 per semester. Tuition and fees vary according to course level, course load, degree level and program. *Financial support:* In 2009–10, 10 teaching assistantships with full tuition reimbursements (averaging $7,340 per year) were awarded; Federal Work-Study, institutionally sponsored loans, scholarships/grants, tuition waivers (partial), and unspecified assistantships also available. Financial award application deadline: 3/31; financial award applicants required to submit FAFSA. *Faculty research:* Bulgarian violin literature, Ozarks fiddle music, carillon, nineteenth century piano. *Unit head:* Diane C. Strickland, Head, 417-836-4122, Fax: 417-836-7665, E-mail: music@missouristate.edu. *Application contact:* Eric Eckert, Coordinator of Graduate Admissions and Recruitment, 417-836-5331, Fax: 417-836-6888.

Montclair State University, The Graduate School, School of the Arts, Department of Music, Montclair, NJ 07043-1624. Offers music (AD); music education (MA); music therapy (MA); performance (MA, Certificate); theory/composition (MA). *Accreditation:* NASM. Part-time and evening/weekend programs available. *Faculty:* 19 full-time (7 women), 95 part-time/adjunct (41 women). *Students:* 21 full-time (11 women), 43 part-time (25 women). Average age 31. 44

applicants, 68% accepted, 21 enrolled. In 2009, 7 master's, 4 other advanced degrees awarded. *Degree requirements:* For master's, comprehensive exam, compositions, recitals, or thesis. *Entrance requirements:* For master's, GRE General Test, audition; teaching certificate (MA in music education). Additional exam requirements/recommendations for international students: Required—TOEFL (minimum score 83 computer-based), or IELTS. *Application deadline:* For fall admission, 6/1 for international students; for spring admission, 10/1 for international students. Applications are processed on a rolling basis. Application fee: $60. Electronic applications accepted. *Expenses:* Tuition, area resident: Part-time $486.74 per credit. Tuition, state resident: part-time $486.74 per credit. Tuition, nonresident: part-time $751.34 per credit. Tuition and fees vary according to degree level and program. *Financial support:* In 2009–10, 3 research assistantships with full tuition reimbursements (averaging $7,000 per year) were awarded; Federal Work-Study, scholarships/grants, and unspecified assistantships also available. Support available to part-time students. Financial award application deadline: 3/1; financial award applicants required to submit FAFSA. *Unit head:* Prof. Robert Aldridge, Chairperson, 973-655-7212. *Application contact:* Amy Aiello, Director of Graduate Admissions and Operations, 973-655-5147, Fax: 973-655-7869, E-mail: graduate.school@montclair.edu.

Morehead State University, Graduate Programs, Caudill College of Arts, Humanities and Social Sciences, Department of Music, Theatre and Dance, Morehead, KY 40351. Offers music education (MM); music performance (MM). *Accreditation:* NASM. Part-time and evening/weekend programs available. *Faculty:* 16 full-time (5 women). *Students:* 8 full-time (5 women), 12 part-time (5 women), 2 international. Average age 26. 13 applicants, 69% accepted, 7 enrolled. In 2009, 9 master's awarded. *Degree requirements:* For master's, comprehensive exam, oral and written exams. *Entrance requirements:* For master's, music entrance exam, BA in music with minimum GPA of 3.0, 2.5 overall; audition. Additional exam requirements/recommendations for international students: Required—TOEFL (minimum score 550 paper-based; 173 computer-based). *Application deadline:* For fall admission, 8/1 priority date for domestic and international students; for spring admission, 12/1 priority date for domestic and international students. Applications are processed on a rolling basis. Application fee: $30. Electronic applications accepted. *Expenses:* Tuition, state resident: full-time $6318; part-time $351 per credit hour. Tuition, nonresident: full-time $15,804; part-time $878 per credit hour. *Financial support:* In 2009–10, 9 research assistantships (averaging $10,000 per year) were awarded; career-related internships or fieldwork, Federal Work-Study, and unspecified assistantships also available. Financial award application deadline: 3/15; financial award applicants required to submit FAFSA. *Faculty research:* Musical instrument digital interface (MIDI) applications, tonal concepts of euphonium and baritone horn, digital synthesis, computer-assisted instruction in music, musical composition. *Unit head:* Dr. Curtis Hammond, Interim Department Chair, 606-783-2473, E-mail: l.hammon@moreheadstate.edu. *Application contact:* Michelle Barber, Graduate Recruitment and Retention Assistant Director, 606-783-5127, Fax: 606-783-5061, E-mail: m.barber@moreheadstate.edu.

Morgan State University, School of Graduate Studies, College of Liberal Arts, Department of Music, Baltimore, MD 21251. Offers MA. *Accreditation:* NASM. Part-time and evening/weekend programs available. *Degree requirements:* For master's, comprehensive exam, thesis. *Entrance requirements:* Additional exam requirements/recommendations for international students: Required—TOEFL (minimum score 550 paper-based; 213 computer-based).

Murray State University, College of Humanities and Fine Arts, Program in Music, Murray, KY 42071. Offers music education (MME). *Accreditation:* NASM. Part-time programs available. *Entrance requirements:* For master's, GRE General Test or MAT. Additional exam requirements/recommendations for international students: Required—TOEFL.

New England Conservatory of Music, Graduate Program in Music, Boston, MA 02115-5000. Offers MM, DMA, Diploma. *Accreditation:* NASM (one or more programs are accredited). *Degree requirements:* For master's, thesis (for some programs), recital, 3 foreign languages (vocal majors); for doctorate, one foreign language, comprehensive exam, thesis/dissertation, qualifying exams, recital. *Entrance requirements:* For master's and Diploma, audition; for doctorate, music theory and musicology exam, audition. Additional exam requirements/recommendations for international students: Required—TOEFL (minimum score 550 paper-based; 213 computer-based; 79 iBT).

New Jersey City University, Graduate Studies and Continuing Education, William J. Maxwell College of Arts and Sciences, Department of Music, Dance and Theatre, Jersey City, NJ 07305-1597. Offers music education (MA); performance (MM). *Accreditation:* NASM. Part-time and evening/weekend programs available. *Faculty:* 5. *Students:* 9 full-time (4 women), 8 part-time (2 women); includes 2 minority (both Hispanic Americans), 2 international. Average age 33. In 2009, 2 master's awarded. *Degree requirements:* For master's, thesis optional, recital. *Entrance requirements:* For master's, GRE General Test or MAT. Additional exam requirements/recommendations for international students: Required—TOEFL. *Application deadline:* For fall admission, 8/1 priority date for domestic students; for spring admission, 12/1 for domestic students. Applications are processed on a rolling basis. Application fee: $0. *Expenses:* Tuition, area resident: Part-time $456.75 per credit. Tuition, nonresident: part-time $842.55 per credit. Required fees: $65 per term. *Financial support:* Unspecified assistantships available. *Unit head:* Dr. Edward Raditz, Chairperson, 201-200-3157, E-mail: eraditz@njcu.edu. *Application contact:* Dr. Edward Raditz, Chairperson, 201-200-3157, E-mail: eraditz@njcu.edu.

New Mexico State University, Graduate School, College of Arts and Sciences, Department of Music, Las Cruces, NM 88003-8001. Offers conducting (MM); music education (MM); performance (MM). *Accreditation:* NASM. Part-time programs available. *Faculty:* 10 full-time (4 women), 1 part-time/adjunct (0 women). *Students:* 12 full-time (4 women), 11 part-time (5 women); includes 6 minority (1 African American, 5 Hispanic Americans), 6 international. Average age 32. 19 applicants, 89% accepted, 12 enrolled. In 2009, 2 master's awarded. *Degree requirements:* For master's, comprehensive exam (for some programs), thesis (for some programs), recital. *Entrance requirements:* For master's, diagnostic exam, audition, bachelor's degree or equivalent from an accredited institution. Additional exam requirements/recommendations for international students: Required—TOEFL. *Application deadline:* For fall admission, 7/1 priority date for domestic students; for spring admission, 11/1 for domestic students. Applications are processed on a rolling basis. Application fee: $30 ($50 for international students). Electronic applications accepted. *Expenses:* Contact institution. *Financial support:* In 2009–10, 13 students received support, including 5 teaching assistantships (averaging $14,220 per year); fellowships, Federal Work-Study and health care benefits also available. Support available to part-time students. Financial award application deadline: 3/1. *Faculty research:* Music education, contemporary wind band literature, performance. *Unit head:* Dr. Ken Van Winkle, Head, 575-646-2421, Fax: 575-646-8199, E-mail: kvanwink@nmsu.edu. *Application contact:* Dr. Lisa Van Winkle, Assistant Professor, 575-646-2523, Fax: 575-646-2472, E-mail: lvanwink@nmsu.edu.

New Orleans Baptist Theological Seminary, Graduate and Professional Programs, Division of Church Music Ministries, New Orleans, LA 70126-4858. Offers MMCM, DMA. *Accreditation:* NASM. *Degree requirements:* For doctorate, one foreign language, thesis/dissertation. *Entrance requirements:* For doctorate, GRE General Test.

The New School: A University, Mannes College The New School for Music, New York, NY 10024. Offers music performance and composition (MM). *Faculty:* 7 full-time (1 woman). *Students:* 173 full-time (104 women), 1 (woman) part-time; includes 13 minority (6 Asian Americans or Pacific Islanders, 7 Hispanic Americans), 92 international. Average age 25. 770 applicants, 33% accepted, 90 enrolled. In 2009, 64 master's awarded. *Degree requirements:* For master's, recital, professional performance with graduation juries. *Entrance requirements:* For master's, audition. Additional exam requirements/recommendations for international students: Required—TOEFL. *Application deadline:* For fall admission, 12/1 for domestic and international students; for spring admission, 11/1 for domestic and international students. Application fee: $100. Electronic applications accepted. *Financial support:* Federal Work-Study, scholarships/grants, and tuition waivers (full and partial) available. Financial award application deadline: 3/1; financial award applicants required to submit FAFSA. *Unit head:* Joel Lester, Dean, 212-580-0210 Ext. 4848, E-mail: lesterj@newschool.edu. *Application contact:* Georgia Schmitt, Director of Admissions, 212-580-0210 Ext. 4805, Fax: 212-580-1738, E-mail: mannesadmissions@newschool.edu.

New York University, Graduate School of Arts and Science, Department of Music, New York, NY 10012-1019. Offers composition and theory (MA, PhD); early music performance (Advanced Certificate); ethnomusicology (MA, PhD). *Students:* 44 full-time (22 women), 4 part-time (2 women); includes 3 minority (1 African American, 2 Asian Americans or Pacific Islanders), 12 international. Average age 33. 160 applicants, 4% accepted, 5 enrolled. In 2009, 1 master's, 9 doctorates awarded. Terminal master's awarded for partial completion of doctoral program. *Degree requirements:* For master's, one foreign language, thesis (for some programs), general exam; for doctorate, 2 foreign languages, thesis/dissertation, general and special exams. *Entrance requirements:* For master's, GRE General Test, bachelor's degree in liberal arts or music; for doctorate, GRE General Test, master's degree in music; for Advanced Certificate, bachelor's degree in music. Additional exam requirements/recommendations for international students: Required—TOEFL. *Application deadline:* For fall admission, 1/4 for domestic students. Application fee: $90. *Expenses:* Tuition: Full-time $30,528; part-time $1272 per credit. Required fees: $2177. *Financial support:* Fellowships with tuition reimbursements, teaching assistantships with tuition reimbursements, Federal Work-Study, institutionally sponsored loans, scholarships/grants, health care benefits, and unspecified assistantships available. Financial award application deadline: 1/4; financial award applicants required to submit FAFSA. *Faculty research:* Early music (nineteenth century), Wagner, Verdi, performance practice. *Unit head:* Michael Beckerman, Chair, 212-998-8300, Fax: 212-995-4147, E-mail: fas.music.gradadmissions@nyu.edu. *Application contact:* Elizabeth Hoffman, Director of Graduate Studies, 212-998-8300, Fax: 212-995-4147, E-mail: fas.music.gradadmissions@nuy.edu.

New York University, Steinhardt School of Culture, Education, and Human Development, Department of Music and Performing Arts Professions, Program in Music Business, New York, NY 10012-1019. Offers MA. Part-time programs available. *Students:* 64 full-time (36 women), 17 part-time (8 women); includes 16 minority (7 African Americans, 4 Asian Americans or Pacific Islanders, 5 Hispanic Americans), 21 international. Average age 25. 152 applicants, 34% accepted, 40 enrolled. In 2009, 21 master's awarded. *Degree requirements:* For master's, thesis (for some programs). *Entrance requirements:* For master's, interview. Additional exam requirements/recommendations for international students: Required—TOEFL. *Application deadline:* For fall admission, 12/15 priority date for domestic and international students. Applications are processed on a rolling basis. Application fee: $75. Electronic applications accepted. *Expenses:* Tuition: Full-time $30,528; part-time $1272 per credit. Required fees: $2177. *Financial support:* Career-related internships or fieldwork, Federal Work-Study, scholarships/grants, and tuition waivers (partial) available. Support available to part-time students. Financial award application deadline: 2/1; financial award applicants required to submit FAFSA. *Faculty research:* Strategic marketing, new technologies, intellectual property, entrepreneurship, globalization, music in video games. *Unit head:* Dr. Catherine Moore, Director, 212-998-5424, Fax: 212-998-4560, E-mail: catherine.moore@nyu.edu. *Application contact:* 212-998-5030, Fax: 212-995-4328, E-mail: steinhardt.gradadmissions@nyu.edu.

New York University, Steinhardt School of Culture, Education, and Human Development, Department of Music and Performing Arts Professions, Program in Music Performance and Composition, New York, NY 10012-1019. Offers instrumental performance (MM), including jazz instrumental performance; music theory and composition (MM, PhD), including scoring for film and multimedia (MM); piano performance (MM), including collaborative performance, solo piano; vocal pedagogy (Advanced Certificate); vocal performance (MM), including classical voice, music theatre performance; MM/Advanced Certificate. Part-time programs available. *Students:* 205 full-time (81 women), 78 part-time (37 women); includes 33 minority (7 African Americans, 14 Asian Americans or Pacific Islanders, 12 Hispanic Americans), 90 international. Average age 28. 396 applicants, 58% accepted, 133 enrolled. In 2009, 97 master's, 4 doctorates awarded. *Degree requirements:* For master's, thesis (for some programs); for doctorate, thesis/dissertation. *Entrance requirements:* For master's, audition; for doctorate, GRE General Test, audition, interview. Additional exam requirements/recommendations for international students: Required—TOEFL. *Application deadline:* For fall admission, 12/15 priority date for domestic and international students; for spring admission, 11/1 for domestic and international students. Applications are processed on a rolling basis. Application fee: $75. Electronic applications accepted. *Expenses:* Tuition: Full-time $30,528; part-time $1272 per credit. Required fees: $2177. *Financial support:* Fellowships with full and partial tuition reimbursements, Federal Work-Study, scholarships/grants, and tuition waivers (partial) available. Support available to part-time students. Financial award application deadline: 2/1; financial award applicants required to submit FAFSA. *Faculty research:* Aesthetics, performance analysis, twentieth century music, music methodologies for arts criticism and analysis. *Application contact:* 212-998-5030, Fax: 212-995-4328, E-mail: steinhardt.gradadmissions@nyu.edu.

New York University, Steinhardt School of Culture, Education, and Human Development, Department of Music and Performing Arts Professions, Program in Music Technology, New York, NY 10012-1019. Offers MM, PhD. Part-time programs available. *Students:* 45 full-time (10 women), 35 part-time (8 women); includes 16 minority (8 African Americans, 4 Asian Americans or Pacific Islanders, 4 Hispanic Americans), 26 international. Average age 30. 68 applicants, 69% accepted, 28 enrolled. In 2009, 21 master's awarded. *Degree requirements:* For master's, thesis (for some programs). *Entrance requirements:* For master's, portfolio; for doctorate, short essay, 3 letters of recommendation, master's degree. Additional exam requirements/recommendations for international students: Required—TOEFL. *Application deadline:* For fall admission, 12/15 priority date for domestic and international students; for spring admission, 11/1 for domestic and international students. Applications are processed on a rolling basis. Application fee: $75. Electronic applications accepted. *Expenses:* Tuition: Full-time $30,528; part-time $1272 per credit. Required fees: $2177. *Financial support:* Fellowships with full and partial tuition reimbursements, research assistantships with full and partial tuition reimbursements, career-related internships or fieldwork, Federal Work-Study, institutionally sponsored loans, scholarships/grants, and tuition waivers (partial) available. Support available to part-time students. Financial award application deadline: 2/1; financial award applicants required to submit FAFSA. *Faculty research:* Pattern processing in music, computer music, acoustics, music perception, interactive music systems. *Unit head:* Dr. Kenneth J. Peacock, Director, 212-998-5424, Fax: 212-995-4043. *Application contact:* 212-998-5030, Fax: 212-995-4328, E-mail: steinhardt.gradadmissions@nyu.edu.

New York University, Tisch School of the Arts, Graduate Musical Theatre Writing Program, New York, NY 10012-1019. Offers MFA. *Faculty:* 6 full-time, 14 part-time/adjunct. *Students:* 61 full-time (27 women); includes 7 minority (1 African American, 5 Asian Americans or Pacific Islanders, 1 Hispanic American). Average age 28. 60 applicants, 73% accepted, 30 enrolled. In 2009, 21 master's awarded. *Degree requirements:* For master's, full-length musical theatre work. *Entrance requirements:* For master's, interview, portfolio. Additional exam requirements/recommendations for international students: Required—TOEFL or IELTS. *Application deadline:* For fall admission, 2/1 priority date for domestic and international students. Application fee: $60. Electronic applications accepted. *Expenses:* Tuition: Full-time $30,528; part-time $1272 per credit. Required fees: $2177. *Financial support:* In 2009–10, 18 students received support; fellowships with tuition reimbursements available, career-related internships or fieldwork, Federal Work-Study, tuition waivers (partial), and unspecified assistantships available. Financial award application deadline: 2/15; financial award applicants required to submit FAFSA. *Unit head:* Sarah Schlesinger, Chair, 212-998-1830, Fax: 212-995-4873, E-mail: musical.theatre@nyu.edu. *Application contact:* Dan Sandford, Director of Graduate Admissions, 212-998-1918, Fax: 212-995-4060, E-mail: tisch.gradadmissions@nyu.edu.

The Nigerian Baptist Theological Seminary, Graduate Studies, Ogbomoso, Nigeria. Offers church music (M Div, M Th, Diploma); divinity (M Div); ministry (D Min); religious education (M Div, M Th, PhD); theological studies (MATS); theology (M Th, PhD). Part-time programs

Music

The Nigerian Baptist Theological Seminary (continued)
available. *Degree requirements:* For master's, thesis, 2 Nigerian languages; for M Div, thesis/dissertation (for some programs), 2 biblical languages; for Diploma, thesis or alternative.

Norfolk State University, School of Graduate Studies, School of Liberal Arts, Department of Music, Norfolk, VA 23504. Offers music (MM); music education (MM); performance (MM); theory and composition (MM). *Accreditation:* NASM. Part-time programs available. *Degree requirements:* For master's, thesis or alternative. *Entrance requirements:* For master's, minimum GPA of 2.7, letters of recommendation. Additional exam requirements/recommendations for international students: Required—TOEFL.

North Carolina Central University, Division of Academic Affairs, College of Liberal Arts, Department of Music, Durham, NC 27707-3129. Offers jazz studies (MM).

North Dakota State University, College of Graduate and Interdisciplinary Studies, College of Arts, Humanities and Social Sciences, Department of Music, Fargo, ND 58108. Offers M Ed, MM, DMA. *Accreditation:* NASM. *Students:* 13 full-time (5 women), 1 (woman) part-time; includes 1 Hispanic American, 2 international. In 2009, 2 master's, 5 doctorates awarded. *Degree requirements:* For master's, 2 foreign languages, comprehensive exam, thesis or alternative, recitals; for doctorate, 2 foreign languages, comprehensive exam, thesis/dissertation or alternative, recitals. *Entrance requirements:* For master's and doctorate, music history, music theory, performance audition. Additional exam requirements/recommendations for international students: Required—TOEFL (minimum score 525 paper-based; 197 computer-based; 71 iBT). *Application deadline:* Applications are processed on a rolling basis. Application fee: $45 ($60 for international students). Electronic applications accepted. *Financial support:* Fellowships with full tuition reimbursements, teaching assistantships with full tuition reimbursements, tuition waivers (partial) and unspecified assistantships available. Support available to part-time students. Financial award applicants required to submit FAFSA. *Faculty research:* Performance, conducting. *Unit head:* Dr. John Miller, Director, Division of Fine Arts, 701-231-7932, E-mail: ej.miller@ndsu.edu. *Application contact:* Dr. Jo Ann Miller, Director, Graduate Studies, 701-231-7822, E-mail: jo.miller@ndsu.edu.

Northeastern Illinois University, Graduate College, College of Arts and Sciences, Department of Music, Program in Music, Chicago, IL 60625-4699. Offers MA. Part-time and evening/weekend programs available. *Degree requirements:* For master's, comprehensive exam, thesis optional. *Entrance requirements:* For master's, departmental exam, audition, minimum GPA of 2.75. Additional exam requirements/recommendations for international students: Required—TOEFL (minimum score 550 paper-based; 213 computer-based; 80 iBT). Electronic applications accepted. *Faculty research:* World music, computers as applied instruments, vocal pedagogy, vocal interpretation, jazz repertory.

Northern Arizona University, Graduate College, College of Arts and Letters, School of Music, Flagstaff, AZ 86011. Offers choral conducting (MM); instrumental conducting (MM); instrumental performance (MM); music education (MM); musicology (MM); theory and composition (MM); vocal performance (MM). *Accreditation:* NASM. *Faculty:* 41 full-time (16 women). *Students:* 23 full-time (11 women); includes 5 minority (all Hispanic Americans), 1 international. Average age 30. 33 applicants, 70% accepted, 13 enrolled. In 2009, 10 master's awarded. *Degree requirements:* For master's, departmental exams. *Entrance requirements:* Additional exam requirements/recommendations for international students: Required—TOEFL (minimum score 550 paper-based; 213 computer-based; 80 iBT), IELTS (minimum score 7), or a bachelor's degree from an English-speaking university and demonstrated proficiency. *Application deadline:* For fall admission, 3/15 priority date for domestic students, 9/15 for international students. Applications are processed on a rolling basis. Application fee: $65. Electronic applications accepted. *Financial support:* In 2009–10, 14 teaching assistantships with partial tuition reimbursements (averaging $9,488 per year) were awarded; Federal Work-Study, health care benefits, tuition waivers (full and partial), and unspecified assistantships also available. Support available to part-time students. Financial award application deadline: 3/30; financial award applicants required to submit FAFSA. *Unit head:* Todd E. Sullivan, Chair, 928-523-3731, Fax: 928-523-2562, E-mail: todd.sullivan@nau.edu. *Application contact:* Joyce Richards, Coordinator, 928-523-3731, Fax: 928-523-2562, E-mail: joyce.richards@nau.edu.

Northern Illinois University, Graduate School, College of Visual and Performing Arts, School of Music, De Kalb, IL 60115-2854. Offers MM, Performer's Certificate. *Accreditation:* NASM. Part-time programs available. *Faculty:* 33 full-time (3 women), 14 part-time/adjunct (3 women). *Students:* 51 full-time (22 women), 51 part-time (32 women); includes 17 minority (6 African Americans, 10 Asian Americans or Pacific Islanders, 1 Hispanic American), 23 international. Average age 28. 74 applicants, 61% accepted, 27 enrolled. In 2009, 33 master's, 6 Performer's Certificates awarded. *Degree requirements:* For master's, comprehensive exam, thesis optional, recital or project; for Performer's Certificate, recitals. *Entrance requirements:* For master's, minimum GPA of 2.75, appropriate bachelor's degree, audition, interview; for Performer's Certificate, minimum GPA of 2.75 (undergraduate), 3.2 (graduate); audition. Additional exam requirements/recommendations for international students: Required—TOEFL (minimum score 550 paper-based; 213 computer-based). *Application deadline:* For fall admission, 4/1 for domestic students, 5/1 for international students; for spring admission, 11/1 for domestic students, 10/1 for international students. Applications are processed on a rolling basis. Application fee: $30. Electronic applications accepted. *Expenses:* Tuition, state resident: full-time $6576; part-time $274 per credit hour. Tuition, nonresident: full-time $13,152; part-time $548 per credit hour. Required fees: $1813; $75.53 per credit hour. Part-time tuition and fees vary according to course load. *Financial support:* In 2009–10, 5 teaching assistantships with full tuition reimbursements were awarded; fellowships with full tuition reimbursements, research assistantships with full tuition reimbursements, Federal Work-Study, scholarships/grants, tuition waivers (full), and staff assistantships also available. Support available to part-time students. Financial award applicants required to submit FAFSA. *Faculty research:* Impact of music on urban children and acquisition of language skills, music in seventeenth century Madrid, Finnish music and culture, jazz studies. *Unit head:* Dr. Paul Bauer, Director, 815-753-1551, Fax: 815-753-1759, E-mail: paulbauer@niu.edu. *Application contact:* Dr. Charles T. Blickhan, Graduate Coordinator, 815-753-0394, E-mail: blickhan@niu.edu.

Northern Kentucky University, Office of Graduate Programs, College of Arts and Sciences, Program in English, Highland Heights, KY 41099. Offers composition and rhetoric (Certificate); English (MA); professional writing (Certificate). Part-time and evening/weekend programs available. *Students:* 7 full-time (4 women), 49 part-time (36 women); includes 3 minority (2 African Americans, 1 Hispanic American). Average age 33. 49 applicants, 76% accepted, 32 enrolled. *Degree requirements:* For master's, comprehensive exam or thesis. *Entrance requirements:* For master's, minimum GPA of 3.0, two letters of reference. Additional exam requirements/recommendations for international students: Required—TOEFL (minimum score 550 paper-based; 213 computer-based; 79 iBT); Recommended—IELTS (minimum score 6.5). *Application deadline:* For fall admission, 7/1 priority date for domestic students, 6/1 priority date for international students; for spring admission, 11/1 for domestic students, 10/1 for international students. Applications are processed on a rolling basis. Application fee: $40. Electronic applications accepted. *Expenses:* Tuition, state resident: full-time $6912; part-time $384 per credit hour. Tuition, nonresident: full-time $12,150; part-time $675 per credit hour. Tuition and fees vary according to course load, program and reciprocity agreements. *Financial support:* Unspecified assistantships available. Financial award applicants required to submit FAFSA. *Faculty research:* Professional writing and new media studies, composition and rhetoric, literary studies, creative writing, cinema studies. *Unit head:* Dr. Roxanne Kent-Drury, Coordinator, 859-572-6636, E-mail: rkdrury@nku.edu. *Application contact:* Dr. Peg Griffin, Director of Graduate Programs, 859-572-6934, Fax: 859-572-6670, E-mail: griffinp@nku.edu.

Northwestern State University of Louisiana, Graduate Studies and Research, School of Creative and Performing Arts, Program in Music, Natchitoches, LA 71497. Offers MM. *Accreditation:* NASM. *Degree requirements:* For master's, comprehensive exam, thesis or alternative. *Entrance requirements:* For master's, GRE General Test, minimum undergraduate GPA of 2.5.

Northwestern University, The Graduate School, School of Communication, Department of Performance Studies, Evanston, IL 60208. Offers MA, PhD. Admissions and degrees offered through The Graduate School. Part-time programs available. Terminal master's awarded for partial completion of doctoral program. *Degree requirements:* For master's, recital; for doctorate, one foreign language, thesis/dissertation, recital. *Entrance requirements:* For master's and doctorate, GRE General Test. Additional exam requirements/recommendations for international students: Required—TOEFL. *Faculty research:* Adaptation/performance of literature, ethnography of performance, critical cultural studies, performance theory, intercultural performance, gender studies.

Northwestern University, Henry and Leigh Bienen School of Music, Department of Music Performance, Evanston, IL 60208. Offers collaborative arts (DM); conducting (MM, DM); jazz (MM); performance (MM), including string chamber music and orchestral literature; piano performance (MM, DM, CP); piano performance and collaborative arts (MM); piano performance and pedagogy (MM); string performance and pedagogy (MM); strings (MM, DM); strings, winds and percussion (CP); voice (MM, DM, CP); winds and percussion (MM, DM). *Accreditation:* NASM. *Students:* 151 full-time (57 women). 759 applicants, 22% accepted, 85 enrolled. In 2009, 61 master's, 16 doctorates, 6 other advanced degrees awarded. *Degree requirements:* For master's, recital; for doctorate, comprehensive exam, thesis/dissertation, 3 recitals; for CP, 2 recitals. *Entrance requirements:* For master's, audition, preliminary tapes in voice, flute, percussion; for doctorate, written essay exam (theory and music history), audition, preliminary tapes; for CP, audition, preliminary tapes. Additional exam requirements/recommendations for international students: Required—TOEFL (minimum score 600 paper-based; 250 computer-based; 100 iBT). *Application deadline:* For fall admission, 12/15 for domestic and international students. Application fee: $55. *Financial support:* In 2009–10, 100 students received support; teaching assistantships with partial tuition reimbursements available, career-related internships or fieldwork, Federal Work-Study, institutionally sponsored loans, scholarships/grants, tuition waivers (full and partial), and unspecified assistantships available. Financial award application deadline: 5/1; financial award applicants required to submit FAFSA. *Unit head:* Karen Brunssen, Co-chair, 847-491-7228, Fax: 847-467-2363. *Application contact:* Linda A. Garton, Assistant Dean, Music Admission and Student Affairs, 847-491-3141, Fax: 847-467-7440, E-mail: lgarton@northwestern.edu.

Northwestern University, Henry and Leigh Bienen School of Music, Department of Music Studies, Evanston, IL 60208. Offers music composition (DM); music education (MM, PhD); music theory (MM, PhD); musicology (MM, PhD). PhD admissions and degree offered through The Graduate School. *Accreditation:* NASM. *Faculty:* 20 full-time (5 women). *Students:* 34 full-time (20 women). 176 applicants, 20% accepted, 18 enrolled. In 2009, 28 master's, 7 doctorates awarded. *Degree requirements:* For doctorate, comprehensive exam, thesis/dissertation. *Entrance requirements:* For master's, portfolio or research papers; for doctorate, GRE General Test (PhD), portfolio, research papers. Additional exam requirements/recommendations for international students: Required—TOEFL (minimum score 600 paper-based; 250 computer-based; 100 iBT), TOEFL (minimum score 560 paper-based; 220 computer-based) or IELTS (minimum score 6). *Application deadline:* For fall admission, 12/15 for domestic and international students. Application fee: $55. *Financial support:* In 2009–10, 30 students received support, including 10 fellowships with full tuition reimbursements available (averaging $20,000 per year); research assistantships, teaching assistantships, Federal Work-Study, institutionally sponsored loans, scholarships/grants, tuition waivers (partial), and unspecified assistantships also available. Financial award application deadline: 5/1; financial award applicants required to submit FAFSA. *Faculty research:* Music cognition, cognitive learning, aesthetic education, computer music, technology in education. *Unit head:* Dr. Peter Webster, Chair, 847-491-1682, Fax: 847-491-5260, E-mail: pwebster@northwestern.edu. *Application contact:* Ryan O'Mealey, Associate Director, Admission and Financial Aid, 847-491-3141, Fax: 847-467-7440, E-mail: r-omealey@northwestern.edu.

Notre Dame de Namur University, Division of Academic Affairs, College of Arts and Sciences, Department of Music, Belmont, CA 94002-1908. Offers musical performance (MFA, Certificate). Part-time and evening/weekend programs available. *Faculty:* 3 full-time (2 women), 8 part-time/adjunct (4 women). *Students:* 8 full-time (6 women), 5 part-time (3 women); includes 2 minority (1 Asian American or Pacific Islander, 1 Hispanic American), 1 international. Average age 30. 6 applicants, 100% accepted, 5 enrolled. In 2009, 9 master's awarded. *Degree requirements:* For master's, exams. *Entrance requirements:* For master's, audition, appropriate bachelor's degree, minimum GPA of 2.5. Additional exam requirements/recommendations for international students: Required—TOEFL (minimum score 550 paper-based; 213 computer-based; 79 iBT). *Application deadline:* For fall admission, 8/1 priority date for domestic students; for spring admission, 12/1 priority date for domestic students. Applications are processed on a rolling basis. Application fee: $50. Electronic applications accepted. *Expenses:* Tuition: Part-time $720 per credit. Required fees: $35 per semester hour. *Financial support:* Available to part-time students. Applicants required to submit FAFSA. *Unit head:* Debra Lambert, Chair, 650-580-3694. *Application contact:* Candace Hallmark, Associate Director of Admissions, 650-508-3592, Fax: 650-508-3426, E-mail: grad.admit@ndnu.edu.

Oakland University, Graduate Study and Lifelong Learning, College of Arts and Sciences, Department of Music, Rochester, MI 48309-4401. Offers music (MM); music education (PhD). *Accreditation:* NASM. *Entrance requirements:* For master's, minimum GPA of 3.0 for unconditional admission. Additional exam requirements/recommendations for international students: Required—TOEFL (minimum score 550 paper-based; 213 computer-based). Electronic applications accepted. *Expenses:* Contact institution.

Oberlin College, Conservatory of Music, Oberlin, OH 44074-1588. Offers MM, MMT, AD. *Accreditation:* NASM. *Degree requirements:* For master's, 2 recitals. *Entrance requirements:* For master's, audition. Additional exam requirements/recommendations for international students: Required—TOEFL (minimum score 550 paper-based; 213 computer-based; 79 iBT). Electronic applications accepted.

The Ohio State University, Graduate School, College of the Arts, Department of Dance, Columbus, OH 43210. Offers choreography (MFA); dance (MA, MFA, PhD); dance and technology (MFA); dance studies (PhD); Labanotation (MFA); lighting (MFA); performance (MFA). *Accreditation:* NASD. *Faculty:* 17. *Students:* 31 full-time (23 women), 5 part-time (4 women); includes 4 minority (2 African Americans, 1 Asian American or Pacific Islander, 1 Hispanic American), 3 international. Average age 31. In 2009, 10 master's awarded. *Degree requirements:* For master's, thesis optional. *Entrance requirements:* For master's, GRE General Test (MA); for doctorate, GRE General Test. Additional exam requirements/recommendations for international students: Recommended—TOEFL (minimum score 600 paper-based; 250 computer-based). *Application deadline:* For fall admission, 8/15 priority date for domestic students, 7/1 priority date for international students; for winter admission, 12/1 priority date for domestic students, 11/1 priority date for international students; for spring admission, 3/1 priority date for domestic students, 2/1 priority date for international students. Applications are processed on a rolling basis. Application fee: $40 ($50 for international students). Electronic applications accepted. *Expenses:* Tuition, state resident: full-time $10,683. Tuition, nonresident: full-time $25,923. Tuition and fees vary according to course load and program. *Financial support:* Fellowships, teaching assistantships, Federal Work-Study and institutionally sponsored loans available. Support available to part-time students. *Unit head:* Victoria E. Uris, Graduate Studies Committee Chair, 614-292-0984, Fax: 614-292-0939, E-mail: uris.1@osu.edu. *Application contact:* 614-292-9444, Fax: 614-292-3895, E-mail: domestic.grad@osu.edu.

The Ohio State University, Graduate School, College of the Arts, School of Music, Columbus, OH 43210. Offers M Mus, MA, DMA, PhD. *Accreditation:* NASM. Part-time programs available. *Faculty:* 59. *Students:* 101 full-time (52 women), 62 part-time (33 women); includes 15 minority (7 African Americans, 2 Asian Americans or Pacific Islanders, 6 Hispanic Americans), 31 international. Average age 30. In 2009, 38 master's, 18 doctorates awarded. *Degree requirements:* For master's, thesis optional; for doctorate, 2 foreign languages, thesis/dissertation. *Entrance requirements:* For master's and doctorate, GRE General Test. Additional exam requirements/recommendations for international students: Recommended—TOEFL (minimum score 600 paper-based; 250 computer-based). *Application deadline:* For fall admission, 8/15 priority date for domestic students, 7/1 priority date for international students; for winter admission, 12/1 priority date for domestic students, 11/1 priority date for international students; for spring admission, 3/1 priority date for domestic students, 2/1 priority date for international students. Applications are processed on a rolling basis. Application fee: $40 ($50 for international students). Electronic applications accepted. *Expenses:* Tuition, state resident: full-time $10,683. Tuition, nonresident: full-time $25,923. Tuition and fees vary according to course load and program. *Financial support:* Fellowships, research assistantships, teaching assistantships, Federal Work-Study, institutionally sponsored loans, and unspecified assistantships available. Support available to part-time students. *Unit head:* Patrick Woliver, Graduate Studies Committee Chair, 614-292-7664, Fax: 614-292-1102, E-mail: woliver.1@osu.edu. *Application contact:* 614-292-9444, Fax: 614-292-3895, E-mail: domestic.grad@osu.edu.

Ohio University, Graduate College, College of Fine Arts, School of Music, Athens, OH 45701-2979. Offers accompanying (MM); composition (MM); conducting (MM); history/literature (MM); music education (MM); music therapy (MM); performance (MM, Certificate); performance/pedagogy (MM); theory (MM). *Accreditation:* NASM. Part-time and evening/weekend programs available. Postbaccalaureate distance learning degree programs offered (minimal on-campus study). *Faculty:* 35 full-time (10 women), 1 part-time/adjunct (0 women). *Students:* 42 full-time (19 women), 11 part-time (8 women); includes 5 minority (2 African Americans, 1 Asian American or Pacific Islander, 2 Hispanic Americans), 10 international. 85 applicants, 59% accepted, 22 enrolled. In 2009, 22 master's awarded. *Degree requirements:* For master's, comprehensive exam, thesis (for some programs), oral exam. *Entrance requirements:* For master's, audition, interview, portfolio, recordings (varies by program). Additional exam requirements/recommendations for international students: Required—TOEFL (minimum score 550 paper-based; 80 iBT) or IELTS Academic (minimum score 6.5). *Application deadline:* For fall admission, 1/1 priority date for domestic and international students. Application fee: $50 ($55 for international students). Electronic applications accepted. *Expenses:* Tuition, state resident: full-time $7839; part-time $323 per quarter hour. Tuition, nonresident: full-time $15,831; part-time $654 per quarter hour. Required fees: $2931. *Financial support:* In 2009–10, 35 teaching assistantships with full and partial tuition reimbursements (averaging $4,500 per year) were awarded; career-related internships or fieldwork, Federal Work-Study, institutionally sponsored loans, and tuition waivers (full and partial) also available. Financial award application deadline: 1/1. *Unit head:* Dr. W. Michael Parkinson, Director, 740-593-4244, Fax: 740-593-1429, E-mail: parkinsw@ohio.edu. *Application contact:* Dr. Richard Wetzel, Graduate Chair, 740-593-1652, Fax: 740-593-1429, E-mail: wetzel@ohio.edu.

Oklahoma City University, Margaret E. Petree College of Performing Arts, Wanda L. Bass School of Music, Oklahoma City, OK 73106-1402. Offers composition (MM); conducting (MM); musical theatre (MM); opera performance (MM); performance (MM). *Accreditation:* NASM. Part-time programs available. *Faculty:* 19 full-time (6 women), 25 part-time/adjunct (12 women). *Students:* 64 full-time (42 women), 3 part-time (2 women); includes 2 minority (1 American Indian/Alaska Native, 1 Asian American or Pacific Islander), 24 international. Average age 25. 75 applicants, 67% accepted, 25 enrolled. In 2009, 6 master's awarded. *Degree requirements:* For master's, thesis, departmental qualifying exam, recital. *Entrance requirements:* For master's, audition, bachelor's degree in music, minimum GPA of 3.0. Additional exam requirements/recommendations for international students: Required—TOEFL. *Application deadline:* For fall admission, 8/20 for domestic students; for spring admission, 1/6 for domestic students. Applications are processed on a rolling basis. Application fee: $50 ($70 for international students). *Expenses:* Tuition: Full-time $15,930; part-time $885 per hour. *Financial support:* Fellowships with partial tuition reimbursements, career-related internships or fieldwork and Federal Work-Study available. Financial award application deadline: 4/1; financial award applicants required to submit FAFSA. *Unit head:* Mark Parker, Dean, 405-208-5474, Fax: 405-208-5971, E-mail: mparker@okcu.edu. *Application contact:* Michelle Lockhart, Director, Admission, 800-633-7242, Fax: 405-208-5916, E-mail: gadmissions@okcu.edu.

Oklahoma State University, College of Arts and Sciences, Department of Music, Stillwater, OK 74078. Offers pedagogy and performance (MM). *Accreditation:* NASM. *Faculty:* 28 full-time (11 women), 6 part-time/adjunct (4 women). *Students:* 10 full-time (2 women), 3 part-time (1 woman). Average age 30. 22 applicants, 45% accepted, 5 enrolled. In 2009, 4 master's awarded. *Degree requirements:* For master's, final project, oral exam. *Entrance requirements:* For master's, GRE, audition. Additional exam requirements/recommendations for international students: Required—TOEFL (minimum score 550 paper-based; 79 iBT). *Application deadline:* For fall admission, 3/1 priority date for international students; for spring admission, 8/1 priority date for international students. Applications are processed on a rolling basis. Application fee: $40 ($75 for international students). Electronic applications accepted. *Expenses:* Tuition, state resident: full-time $3716; part-time $154.85 per credit hour. Tuition, nonresident: full-time $14,448; part-time $602 per credit hour. Required fees: $1772; $73.85 per credit hour. One-time fee: $50. Tuition and fees vary according to course load and campus/location. *Financial support:* In 2009–10, 11 teaching assistantships (averaging $8,041 per year) were awarded; career-related internships or fieldwork, Federal Work-Study, scholarships/grants, health care benefits, tuition waivers (partial), and unspecified assistantships also available. Support available to part-time students. Financial award application deadline: 3/1; financial award applicants required to submit FAFSA. *Faculty research:* Discovery and presentation of music literature of other countries, transportation of ancient music literature to modern notation. *Unit head:* Dr. Brant Adams, Head, 405-744-6133, Fax: 405-744-9324. *Application contact:* Dr. Gordon Emslie, Dean, 405-744-6368, Fax: 405-744-0355, E-mail: grad-i@okstate.edu.

Penn State University Park, Graduate School, College of Arts and Architecture, School of Music, State College, University Park, PA 16802-1503. Offers M Mus, MA, MME, DMA, PhD. *Accreditation:* NASM.

Phillips Theological Seminary, Programs in Theology, Tulsa, OK 74116. Offers administration of church agencies (M Div); campus ministry (M Div); church-related social work (M Div); college and seminary teaching (M Div); global mission work (M Div); institutional chaplaincy (M Div); ministerial vocations in Christian education (M Div); ministry (D Min), including parish ministry, pastoral counseling, practices of ministry; ministry and culture (MAMC), including Christian education, congregational leadership, history and practice of Christian spirituality, theology, ethics, and culture; ministry of music (M Div); pastoral care and counseling (M Div); pastoral ministry (M Div); theological studies (MTS). *Accreditation:* ATS. Part-time programs available. Postbaccalaureate distance learning degree programs offered (minimal on-campus study). *Degree requirements:* For master's, thesis (for some programs); for doctorate, thesis/dissertation. *Entrance requirements:* For master's, minimum GPA of 2.5; for doctorate, M Div, minimum GPA of 3.0. *Faculty research:* Biblical studies, historical studies, theology and culture, practical theology, theology and film.

Pittsburg State University, Graduate School, College of Arts and Sciences, Department of Music, Pittsburg, KS 66762. Offers instrumental music education (MM); music history/music literature (MM); performance (MM), including orchestral performance, organ, piano, voice; theory and composition (MM); vocal music education (MM). *Accreditation:* NASM. *Degree requirements:* For master's, thesis or alternative. *Expenses:* Tuition, state resident: full-time $4212; part-time $176 per credit. Tuition, nonresident: full-time $11,530; part-time $480 per credit. Required fees: $940; $43 per credit. Tuition and fees vary according to course level, course load, degree level, campus/location, reciprocity agreements and student level.

Point Park University, Conservatory of Performing Arts, Pittsburgh, PA 15222-1984. Offers theatre arts-acting (MFA). *Faculty:* 2 full-time, 1 part-time/adjunct. *Students:* 6 full-time (3 women), 1 international. Average age 41. 2 applicants, 0% accepted, 0 enrolled. *Degree requirements:* For master's, comprehensive exam (for some programs), thesis or alternative. *Entrance requirements:* For master's, interview, undergraduate degree in related field, theatre experience. Additional exam requirements/recommendations for international students: Required—TOEFL (minimum score 550 paper-based; 79 iBT). *Application deadline:* Applications are processed on a rolling basis. Application fee: $30. Electronic applications accepted. *Expenses:* Tuition: Full-time $11,880; part-time $660 per credit. Required fees: $486; $27 per credit. *Financial support:* In 2009–10, 5 students received support, including 5 teaching assistantships with full tuition reimbursements available (averaging $6,400 per year); scholarships/grants also available. Financial award application deadline: 4/15; financial award applicants required to submit FAFSA. *Unit head:* Ronald Allan-Lindblom, Dean/Artistic Producing Director, 412-392-3454, Fax: 412-392-2424, E-mail: rlindblom@pointpark.edu. *Application contact:* Lynn C. Ribar, Associate Director, Adult and Graduate Enrollment, 412-392-3908, Fax: 412-392-6164, E-mail: lribar@pointpark.edu.

Portland State University, Graduate Studies, School of Fine and Performing Arts, Department of Music, Portland, OR 97207-0751. Offers conducting (MMC); music education (MAT, MST); performance (MMP). *Accreditation:* NASM. Part-time programs available. *Degree requirements:* For master's, variable foreign language requirement, exit exam. *Entrance requirements:* For master's, GRE General Test, departmental exam, minimum GPA of 3.0 in upper-division course work or 2.75 overall. Additional exam requirements/recommendations for international students: Required—TOEFL (minimum score 550 paper-based; 213 computer-based). *Faculty research:* Composition, music analysis, music history, jazz.

Princeton University, Graduate School, Department of Music, Princeton, NJ 08544-1019. Offers composition (PhD); musicology (PhD). *Degree requirements:* For doctorate, variable foreign language requirement, thesis/dissertation. *Entrance requirements:* For doctorate, GRE General Test, sample of written work. Additional exam requirements/recommendations for international students: Required—TOEFL (minimum score 600 paper-based; 250 computer-based). Electronic applications accepted. *Faculty research:* Computer synthesis, history of Western music, comparative musicology, theory.

Purchase College, State University of New York, Conservatory of Music, Purchase, NY 10577-1400. Offers composition (MM); instrumental performance (MM); jazz studies (MM); studio composition (MM); voice and opera studies (MM). *Degree requirements:* For master's, thesis or alternative, composition, performance. *Entrance requirements:* For master's, audition. Electronic applications accepted. *Expenses:* Tuition, state resident: full-time $8370; part-time $349 per credit. Tuition, nonresident: full-time $13,250; part-time $552 per credit. Required fees: $1515; $62.11 per credit. One-time fee: $144 full-time. Tuition and fees vary according to program.

Queens College of the City University of New York, Division of Graduate Studies, Arts and Humanities Division, Aaron Copland School of Music, Flushing, NY 11367-1597. Offers MA. Part-time programs available. *Faculty:* 25 full-time (5 women). *Students:* 24 full-time (7 women), 122 part-time (45 women). 173 applicants, 49% accepted, 57 enrolled. In 2009, 36 master's awarded. *Degree requirements:* For master's, one foreign language, qualifying exams, recital. *Entrance requirements:* For master's, audition, bachelor's degree in music, minimum GPA of 3.0. Additional exam requirements/recommendations for international students: Required—TOEFL. *Application deadline:* For fall admission, 4/1 for domestic students; for spring admission, 11/1 for domestic students. Applications are processed on a rolling basis. Application fee: $125. *Expenses:* Tuition, state resident: full-time $7360; part-time $310 per credit. Tuition, nonresident: part-time $575 per credit. One-time fee: $195.25 full-time; $145.25 part-time. *Financial support:* Career-related internships or fieldwork, Federal Work-Study, institutionally sponsored loans, and tuition waivers (partial) available. Support available to part-time students. Financial award application deadline: 4/1; financial award applicants required to submit FAFSA. *Unit head:* Dr. Edward Smaldone, Chair/Director, 718-997-3800, E-mail: edward_smaldone@qc.edu. *Application contact:* Mario Caruso, Director of Graduate Admissions, 718-997-5200, Fax: 718-997-5193, E-mail: graduate_admissions@qc.edu.

Radford University, College of Graduate and Professional Studies, College of Visual and Performing Arts, Department of Music, Radford, VA 24142. Offers music (MA); music education (MS); music therapy (MS). *Accreditation:* NASM. Part-time programs available. *Faculty:* 9 full-time (2 women), 3 part-time/adjunct (1 woman). *Students:* 12 full-time (8 women), 4 part-time (all women); includes 3 minority (all African Americans), 1 international. Average age 26. 8 applicants, 88% accepted, 4 enrolled. In 2009, 5 master's awarded. *Degree requirements:* For master's, comprehensive exam, thesis or alternative. *Entrance requirements:* For master's, GRE, major field test in music or PRAXIS II (content knowledge), written diagnostics exams in music, minimum GPA of 2.75; 3 letters of reference. Additional exam requirements/recommendations for international students: Required—TOEFL (minimum score 550 paper-based; 213 computer-based; 79 iBT). *Application deadline:* For fall admission, 12/1 for international students; for spring admission, 7/1 for international students. Applications are processed on a rolling basis. Application fee: $50. Electronic applications accepted. *Expenses:* Tuition, state resident: full-time $5086; part-time $211 per credit hour. Tuition, nonresident: full-time $12,608; part-time $525 per credit hour. Required fees: $2508; $105 per credit hour. *Financial support:* In 2009–10, 10 students received support, including 3 research assistantships with partial tuition reimbursements available (averaging $8,000 per year), 8 teaching assistantships with partial tuition reimbursements available (averaging $8,700 per year); career-related internships or fieldwork, Federal Work-Study, institutionally sponsored loans, scholarships/grants, and unspecified assistantships also available. Financial award application deadline: 3/1; financial award applicants required to submit FAFSA. *Unit head:* Dr. Allen F. Wojtera, Chair, 540-831-5177, Fax: 540-831-6133, E-mail: awojtera@radford.edu. *Application contact:* Graduate Admissions, 540-831-5431, Fax: 540-831-6061, E-mail: gradcollege@radford.edu.

Regis University, College for Professional Studies, Program in Teacher Education, Denver, CO 80221-1099. Offers adult learning, training, and development (M Ed); curriculum, instruction, and assessment (M Ed); early childhood (M Ed); educational technology (Certificate); elementary (M Ed); ESL (M Ed); fine arts (M Ed), including arts, music; instructional technology (M Ed); professional leadership (M Ed); reading (M Ed); secondary (M Ed); self-designed (M Ed); space studies (M Ed); special education (M Ed); teacher licensure (M Ed). Program also offered in Henderson and Las Vegas (Summerlin), NV. *Accreditation:* Teacher Education Accreditation Council. Part-time and evening/weekend programs available. Postbaccalaureate distance learning degree programs offered (no on-campus study). *Degree requirements:* For master's, thesis. *Entrance requirements:* For master's, resume, minimum GPA of 2.75, criminal background check. Additional exam requirements/recommendations for international students: Required—TOEFL (minimum score 213 computer-based), TWE (minimum score 5). Electronic applications accepted. *Faculty research:* Issues of equity in the middle school classroom, professional learning communities, school reform, socialinguistic and discursive obstacles to student integration, inclusive language arts curriculum.

Reinhardt University, Program in Music, Waleska, GA 30183-2981. Offers conducting (MM); music education (MM); piano pedagogy (MM). *Accreditation:* NASM. *Entrance requirements:* For master's, GRE, audition (for piano pedagogy and conducting), 2 letters of reference. Additional exam requirements/recommendations for international students: Required—TOEFL. *Application deadline:* For fall admission, 5/7 for domestic and international students. Applications are processed on a rolling basis. Application fee: $25. Electronic applications accepted. *Expenses:* Tuition: Full-time $16,500; part-time $325 per credit hour. One-time fee: $100. Tuition and fees vary according to course load and program. *Financial support:* Application deadline: 5/1. *Unit head:* Dr. Paula Thomas-Lee, Graduate Program Coordinator, 770-720-5658, E-mail: ptl@reinhardt.edu. *Application contact:* Ray Schumacher, Admissions Counselor, 770-993-6971, Fax: 770-475-0263, E-mail: res@reinhardt.edu.

Rice University, Graduate Programs, Shepherd School of Music, Houston, TX 77251-1892. Offers composition (MM, DMA); conducting (MM); musicology (MM); performance (MM, DMA); theory (MM). *Faculty:* 39 full-time (11 women), 19 part-time/adjunct (6 women). *Students:* 160 full-time (79 women); includes 15 minority (3 African Americans, 11 Asian Americans or Pacific Islanders, 1 Hispanic American), 35 international. Average age 24. 700 applicants, 12%

Music

Rice University (continued)

accepted, 65 enrolled. *Degree requirements:* For master's, thesis (for some programs), 2 recitals; for doctorate, one foreign language, comprehensive exam, thesis/dissertation, 4 recitals. *Entrance requirements:* For master's, GRE General Test (musicology); for doctorate, GRE General Test. Additional exam requirements/recommendations for international students: Required—TOEFL (minimum score 600 paper-based; 250 computer-based; 100 iBT), IELTS (minimum score 7). *Application deadline:* For fall admission, 12/1 priority date for domestic and international students. Application fee: $70. *Financial support:* Fellowships with full and partial tuition reimbursements, teaching assistantships with full tuition reimbursements, scholarships/grants and tuition waivers (full and partial) available. Financial award application deadline: 1/2; financial award applicants required to submit FAFSA. *Faculty research:* Musicology, performance, theory, composition. *Unit head:* Dr. Robert Yekovich, Dean, 713-348-4854, Fax: 713-348-5317. *Application contact:* Geoffrey Scott, Director of Music Admissions, 713-348-4854.

Roosevelt University, Graduate Division, Chicago College of Performing Arts, The Music Conservatory, Chicago, IL 60605. Offers music (MM); piano pedagogy (Diploma). *Accreditation:* NASM. Part-time and evening/weekend programs available.

Rowan University, Graduate School, College of Fine and Performing Arts, Program in Music, Glassboro, NJ 08028-1701. Offers performance (MM). *Accreditation:* NASM. Part-time and evening/weekend programs available. *Students:* 6 full-time (3 women), 8 part-time (3 women). Average age 31. 5 applicants, 60% accepted, 3 enrolled. In 2009, 2 master's awarded. *Degree requirements:* For master's, thesis (for some programs). *Entrance requirements:* For master's, GRE General Test. Additional exam requirements/recommendations for international students: Required—TOEFL. *Application deadline:* Applications are processed on a rolling basis. Application fee: $50. Electronic applications accepted. *Expenses:* Tuition, state resident: full-time $10,624; part-time $590 per semester hour. Tuition, nonresident: full-time $10,624; part-time $590 per semester hour. Required fees: $2320; $125 per semester hour. *Financial support:* Career-related internships or fieldwork, scholarships/grants, health care benefits, and unspecified assistantships available. Support available to part-time students. *Unit head:* Dr. Mira Lalovic-Hand, Interim Associate Provost/Director of Graduate School, 856-256-5120, E-mail: lalovic-hand@rowan.edu. *Application contact:* Karen Haynes, Graduate Coordinator, 856-256-4052, Fax: 856-256-4436, E-mail: haynes@rowan.edu.

Rutgers, The State University of New Jersey, Newark, Graduate School, Program in Jazz History and Research, Newark, NJ 07102. Offers MA. *Entrance requirements:* For master's, GRE, minimum B average. Electronic applications accepted.

Rutgers, The State University of New Jersey, New Brunswick, Mason Gross School of the Arts, Program in Music, Piscataway, NJ 08854-8097. Offers collaborative piano (MM, DMA); conducting: choral (MM, DMA); conducting: instrumental (MM, DMA); conducting: orchestral (MM, DMA); jazz studies (MM); music (DMA, AD); music education (MM, DMA); music performance (MM). *Accreditation:* NASM. *Degree requirements:* For doctorate, one foreign language. *Entrance requirements:* For doctorate, audition. Additional exam requirements/recommendations for international students: Required—TOEFL (minimum score 550 paper-based; 213 computer-based). Electronic applications accepted. *Faculty research:* Performance, twentieth century music, jazz.

St. Cloud State University, School of Graduate Studies, College of Fine Arts and Humanities, Department of Music, St. Cloud, MN 56301-4498. Offers conducting and literature (MM); music education (MM); piano pedagogy (MM). *Accreditation:* NASM. *Faculty:* 16 full-time (7 women), 1 part-time/adjunct (0 women). *Students:* 2 full-time (1 woman), 13 part-time (5 women); includes 1 minority (Asian American or Pacific Islander), 1 international. 4 applicants, 100% accepted. In 2009, 7 master's awarded. *Degree requirements:* For master's, comprehensive exam (for some programs), thesis or alternative. *Entrance requirements:* For master's, GRE General Test, minimum GPA of 2.75. Additional exam requirements/recommendations for international students: Required—Michigan English Language Assessment Battery; Recommended—TOEFL (minimum score 550 paper-based; 213 computer-based), IELTS (minimum score 6.5). *Application deadline:* For fall admission, 6/1 priority date for domestic students, 4/1 for international students; for spring admission, 10/1 priority date for domestic students, 8/1 for international students. Applications are processed on a rolling basis. Application fee: $35. Electronic applications accepted. *Financial support:* Federal Work-Study, scholarships/grants, and unspecified assistantships available. Financial award application deadline: 3/1. *Unit head:* Dr. Mark Springer, Chairperson, 320-308-3223, Fax: 320-308-2902. *Application contact:* Linda Lou Krueger, School of Graduate Studies, 320-308-2113, Fax: 320-308-5371, E-mail: lekrueger@stcloudstate.edu.

Saint John's University, Saint John's School of Theology and Seminary, Collegeville, MN 56321. Offers divinity (M Div); liturgical music (MA); liturgical studies (MA); pastoral ministry (MA); theology (MA), including church history, liturgy, monastic studies, scripture, spirituality, systematics; M Div/MA. *Accreditation:* ATS. Part-time programs available. Postbaccalaureate distance learning degree programs offered (no on-campus study). *Degree requirements:* For master's, one foreign language, comprehensive exam (for some programs), thesis (for some programs). *Entrance requirements:* For master's, GRE General Test or MAT. Electronic applications accepted. *Faculty research:* Religious education, biblical literature.

Saint Joseph's College, Rensselaer Program of Church Music and Liturgy, Rensselaer, IN 47978. Offers church music and liturgy (MA); pastoral liturgy and music (Diploma). Offered during summer only. Part-time programs available. *Degree requirements:* For master's, thesis, research paper, service recital. *Entrance requirements:* For master's, entrance exams in music theory, conducting, keyboard, voice, and history.

St. Vladimir's Orthodox Theological Seminary, Graduate School of Theology, Crestwood, NY 10707-1699. Offers general theological studies (MA); liturgical music (MA); religious education (MA); theology (M Div, M Th, D Min); M Div/MA. MA in general theological studies, M Div offered jointly with St. Nersess Seminary. *Accreditation:* ATS. Part-time programs available. *Degree requirements:* For master's, one foreign language, thesis, fieldwork; for doctorate, thesis/dissertation, fieldwork; for M Div, one foreign language, thesis/dissertation, fieldwork. *Entrance requirements:* For doctorate, M Div, minimum GPA of 3.0. Additional exam requirements/recommendations for international students: Required—TOEFL (minimum score 250 computer-based).

Samford University, School of the Arts, Birmingham, AL 35229. Offers church music (MM); music (MME), including instrumental, vocal choral; piano pedagogy (MM). *Accreditation:* NASM. Part-time programs available. *Faculty:* 7 full-time (3 women), 4 part-time/adjunct (1 woman). *Students:* 8 full-time (4 women), 4 part-time (2 women); includes 1 minority (African American), 1 international. Average age 27. 7 applicants, 71% accepted, 5 enrolled. In 2009, 9 master's awarded. *Degree requirements:* For master's, oral exams, comprehensive exam (MME). *Entrance requirements:* For master's, GRE General Test or MAT, institutional exam, minimum GPA of 3.0. Additional exam requirements/recommendations for international students: Required—TOEFL (minimum score 550 paper-based; 213 computer-based). *Application deadline:* For fall admission, 5/1 priority date for domestic students; for spring admission, 12/1 priority date for domestic students. Applications are processed on a rolling basis. Application fee: $35. *Expenses:* Tuition: Full-time $26,660; part-time $595 per credit hour. Required fees: $110 per semester. *Financial support:* In 2009–10, 11 students received support, including research assistantships (averaging $4,000 per year); Federal Work-Study, scholarships/grants, and tuition waivers (partial) also available. Financial award application deadline: 9/1. *Faculty research:* Hymnology, choral techniques, assessment of music learning at elementary and secondary levels, piano pedagogy, special education and inclusion, learning theories. *Unit head:* Dr. Joseph H. Hopkins, Dean, 205-726-2165, E-mail: jhhopkin@samford.edu. *Application contact:* Dr. Moya Nordlund, Director, Graduate Studies, 205-726-2651, Fax: 205-726-2165, E-mail: mlnordlu@samford.edu.

Sam Houston State University, College of Arts and Sciences, School of Music, Huntsville, TX 77341. Offers music (MM); music education (MM). *Accreditation:* NASM. Part-time programs available. *Faculty:* 14 full-time (3 women), 1 part-time/adjunct (0 women). *Students:* 11 full-time (6 women), 7 part-time (4 women); includes 2 minority (both Hispanic Americans), 4 international. Average age 31. 11 applicants, 91% accepted, 9 enrolled. In 2009, 13 master's awarded. *Degree requirements:* For master's, thesis (for some programs), departmental qualifying exam. *Entrance requirements:* For master's, GRE General Test. Additional exam requirements/recommendations for international students: Required—TOEFL (minimum score 550 paper-based; 213 computer-based; 79 iBT). *Application deadline:* For fall admission, 8/1 for domestic and international students; for spring admission, 12/1 for domestic and international students. Applications are processed on a rolling basis. Application fee: $20. *Expenses:* Tuition, state resident: full-time $3690; part-time $205 per credit hour. Tuition, nonresident: full-time $8676; part-time $482 per credit hour. Required fees: $1474. Tuition and fees vary according to course load and campus/location. *Financial support:* Teaching assistantships, Federal Work-Study and scholarships/grants available. Financial award application deadline: 5/31; financial award applicants required to submit FAFSA. *Unit head:* Dr. James Bankhead, Director, 936-294-3808, Fax: 936-294-3765, E-mail: bankhead@shsu.edu. *Application contact:* Scott Plugge, Advisor, 936-294-1393, E-mail: plugge@shsu.edu.

San Diego State University, Graduate and Research Affairs, College of Professional Studies and Fine Arts, School of Music and Dance, San Diego, CA 92182. Offers composition (acoustic and electronic) (MM); conducting (MM); ethnomusicology (MA); jazz studies (MM); musicology (MA); performance (MM); piano pedagogy (MA); theory (MA). *Degree requirements:* For master's, comprehensive exam (for some programs), thesis (for some programs). *Entrance requirements:* For master's, GRE General Test, bachelor's degree in related field, 2 letters of reference. Additional exam requirements/recommendations for international students: Required—TOEFL. Electronic applications accepted.

San Francisco Conservatory of Music, Graduate Division, San Francisco, CA 94102. Offers chamber music (MM); classical guitar (MM); composition (MM); conducting (MM); keyboards (MM); orchestral instruments (MM); voice (MM). *Accreditation:* NASM. *Faculty:* 31 full-time (10 women), 69 part-time/adjunct (20 women). *Students:* 203 full-time (113 women), 5 part-time (3 women); includes 18 minority (1 African American, 11 Asian Americans or Pacific Islanders, 6 Hispanic Americans), 58 international. Average age 25. 614 applicants, 35% accepted, 118 enrolled. In 2009, 80 master's awarded. *Degree requirements:* For master's, variable foreign language requirement, 1-2 recitals, 1-3 juried performances. *Entrance requirements:* For master's, audition, recommendations. Additional exam requirements/recommendations for international students: Required—TOEFL (minimum score 500 paper-based; 173 computer-based; 61 iBT). *Application deadline:* For fall admission, 12/1 for domestic and international students; for spring admission, 10/1 for domestic and international students. Application fee: $100. Electronic applications accepted. *Expenses:* Tuition: Full-time $33,000; part-time $1460 per credit. Required fees: $198. One-time fee: $50 full-time. *Financial support:* In 2009–10, 91 students received support, including 20 fellowships (averaging $2,635 per year); Federal Work-Study, scholarships/grants, and unspecified assistantships also available. Support available to part-time students. Financial award application deadline: 2/15; financial award applicants required to submit FAFSA. *Unit head:* Mary Ellen Poole, Dean, 415-503-6212, Fax: 415-503-6299, E-mail: mep@sfcm.edu. *Application contact:* Melissa Cocco-Mitten, Director of Admissions, 415-503-6231, Fax: 415-503-6299, E-mail: admit@sfcm.edu.

San Francisco State University, Division of Graduate Studies, College of Creative Arts, School of Music and Dance, San Francisco, CA 94132-1722. Offers chamber music (MM); classical performance (MM); composition (MA); conducting (MM); music education (MA); music history (MA). *Accreditation:* NASM.

San Jose State University, Graduate Studies and Research, College of Humanities and the Arts, School of Music and Dance, San Jose, CA 95192-0001. Offers music (MA). *Accreditation:* NASM. *Students:* 13 full-time (7 women), 14 part-time (9 women); includes 7 minority (all Asian Americans or Pacific Islanders), 2 international. Average age 33. 28 applicants, 36% accepted, 6 enrolled. In 2009, 13 master's awarded. *Degree requirements:* For master's, thesis or alternative. *Entrance requirements:* For master's, minimum GPA of 3.0 in last 60 units of undergraduate coursework; 3 letters of recommendation; audition or portfolio. Additional exam requirements/recommendations for international students: Required—TOEFL (minimum score 590 paper-based; 243 computer-based; 96 iBT). *Application deadline:* For fall admission, 6/29 for domestic students; for spring admission, 11/30 for domestic students. Applications are processed on a rolling basis. Application fee: $59. Electronic applications accepted. *Financial support:* Applicants required to submit FAFSA. *Unit head:* Dr. Edward C. Harris, Director, 408-924-4677, Fax: 408-924-4773. *Application contact:* Dr. Edward C. Harris, Director, 408-924-4677, Fax: 408-924-4773.

Santa Clara University, College of Arts and Sciences, Graduate Programs in Pastoral Ministries, Program in Liturgical Music, Santa Clara, CA 95053. Offers MA. Part-time and evening/weekend programs available. *Students:* 2 part-time (1 woman); includes 1 minority (Asian American or Pacific Islander). Average age 32. *Degree requirements:* For master's, comprehensive exam, thesis (for some programs), recital. *Entrance requirements:* For master's, 3 letters of recommendation, resume. Additional exam requirements/recommendations for international students: Required—TOEFL. *Application deadline:* Applications are processed on a rolling basis. Application fee: $50. Electronic applications accepted. *Expenses:* Contact institution. *Financial support:* Fellowships, research assistantships, teaching assistantships, career-related internships or fieldwork, Federal Work-Study, and health care benefits available. Support available to part-time students. Financial award applicants required to submit FAFSA. *Unit head:* Fr. Paul Crowley, Department Chair of Religious Studies, 408-554-4542. *Application contact:* Fr. Paul Crowley, Department Chair of Religious Studies, 408-554-4542.

Savannah College of Art and Design, Graduate School, Savannah, GA 31402-3146. Offers advertising design (MA, MFA); animation (MA, MFA); architectural history (MA, MFA); architecture (M Arch); art history (MA, MFA); arts administration (MA); broadcast design (MA, MFA); cinema studies (MA); commercial photography (MA); digital photography (MA); documentary photography (MA); fashion (MA, MFA); fibers (MA, MFA); film and television (MA, MFA); furniture design (MA, MFA); graphic design (MA, MFA); historic preservation (MA, MFA); illustration (MA, MFA); illustration design (MA); industrial design (MA, MFA); interactive design and game development (MA, MFA); interior design (MA, MFA); metals and jewelry (MA, MFA); painting (MA, MFA); performing arts (MA, MFA); photography (MA, MFA); printmaking (MA, MFA); production design (MA, MFA); professional education (MA); professional writing (MFA); sculpture (MA, MFA); sequential art (MA, MFA); sound design (MA, MFA); urban design and development (MA); visual effects (MA, MFA). Part-time programs available. Postbaccalaureate distance learning degree programs offered (no on-campus study). *Degree requirements:* For master's, thesis, internship. *Entrance requirements:* For master's, interview, 3 letters of recommendation. Additional exam requirements/recommendations for international students: Required—TOEFL (minimum score 500 paper-based; 133 computer-based). Electronic applications accepted. *Expenses:* Tuition: Full-time $28,515; part-time $627 per credit hour. One-time fee: $500. Tuition and fees vary according to course load. *Faculty research:* Urban planning for diverse communities, photovoltaics-powered environmental control, computer-aided design and virtual reality, multimedia design.

School of the Art Institute of Chicago, Graduate Division, Department of Performance, Chicago, IL 60603-3103. Offers MFA. *Entrance requirements:* Additional exam requirements/recommendations for international students: Required—TOEFL, IELTS.

Seabury-Western Theological Seminary, School of Theology, Evanston, IL 60201-2976. Offers advanced theological studies (Certificate); church music and liturgy (MTS); congregational development (D Min); preaching (D Min); theological studies (MA); theology (M Div, L Th). D Min in congregational development offered in summer only. *Accreditation:* ACIPE; ATS (one or more programs are accredited). Part-time programs available. *Degree requirements:* For master's, thesis; for doctorate, thesis/dissertation; for other advanced degree, thesis (for some programs). *Entrance requirements:* For M Div and master's, interview, sample of written work. *Faculty research:* Liturgical interpretations of baptism, trinitarian theology, congregational development, post modern biblical criticism-Matthew.

Shenandoah University, Shenandoah Conservatory, Winchester, VA 22601-5195. Offers arts administration (MS); church music (MM, Certificate); composition (MM); conducting (MM); dance (MA, MS); music education (MME, DMA); music therapy (MMT, Certificate); pedagogy (MM, DMA); performance (MM, DMA, Artist Diploma); piano accompanying (MM). *Accreditation:* NASM. *Faculty:* 39 full-time (15 women), 17 part-time/adjunct (5 women). *Students:* 72 full-time (42 women), 134 part-time (83 women); includes 40 minority (14 African Americans, 22 Asian Americans or Pacific Islanders, 4 Hispanic Americans), 16 international. Average age 35. 115 applicants, 88% accepted, 70 enrolled. In 2009, 40 master's, 5 doctorates, 9 other advanced degrees awarded. *Degree requirements:* For master's, comprehensive exam (for some programs), thesis (for some programs), internship (MS), recital (MM), research teaching project or thesis (MME), project (MA); for doctorate, comprehensive exam, thesis/dissertation (for some programs), dissertation or teaching project, recital; for other advanced degree, research project, recital. *Entrance requirements:* For master's, audition, minimum GPA of 2.5, writing sample, resume; for doctorate, audition, minimum GPA of 3.25, 2 letters of recommendation, writing sample, resume; for other advanced degree, bachelor or master's degree; minimum GPA of 2.5. Additional exam requirements/recommendations for international students: Required—TOEFL (minimum score 550 paper-based; 213 computer-based; 79 iBT), IELTS (minimum score 6.5). *Application deadline:* Applications are processed on a rolling basis. Application fee: $30. Electronic applications accepted. *Expenses:* Tuition: Full-time $11,925; part-time $695 per credit. Required fees: $400 per semester. *Financial support:* Application deadline: 3/15. *Unit head:* Dr. Laurence A. Kaptain, Dean, 540-665-4600, Fax: 540-665-5402, E-mail: lkaptain@su.edu. *Application contact:* David Anthony, Dean of Admissions, 540-665-4581, Fax: 540-665-4627, E-mail: admit@su.edu.

Southeastern Baptist Theological Seminary, Graduate and Professional Programs, Wake Forest, NC 27588-1889. Offers advanced biblical studies (M Div); Christian education (M Div, MACE); Christian ethics (PhD); Christian ministry (M Div); Christian planting (M Div); church music (MACM); counseling (MACO); evangelism (PhD); language (M Div); ministry (D Min); New Testament (PhD); Old Testament (PhD); philosophy (PhD); theology (Th M, PhD); women's studies (M Div). *Accreditation:* ACIPE; ATS (one or more programs are accredited). *Degree requirements:* For master's, thesis (for some programs), oral exam; for doctorate, thesis/dissertation, fieldwork; for M Div, supervised ministry. *Entrance requirements:* For master's, Cooperative English Test, minimum GPA of 2.0, M Div or equivalent (Th M); for doctorate, GRE General Test or MAT, Cooperative English Test, M Div or equivalent, 3 years of professional experience.

Southeastern Louisiana University, College of Arts, Humanities and Social Sciences, Department of Music and Dramatic Arts, Hammond, LA 70402. Offers music (M Mus). *Accreditation:* NASM. Part-time programs available. *Faculty:* 13 full-time (1 woman), 2 part-time/adjunct (both women). *Students:* 13 full-time (3 women); includes 1 minority (African American), 4 international. Average age 25. 5 applicants, 100% accepted, 5 enrolled. In 2009, 9 master's awarded. *Degree requirements:* For master's, comprehensive exam, thesis (for some programs), recital (for some programs). *Entrance requirements:* For master's, bachelor's degree in music, senior recital. Additional exam requirements/recommendations for international students: Required—TOEFL (minimum score 500 paper-based; 173 computer-based; 61 iBT). *Application deadline:* For fall admission, 7/15 priority date for domestic students, 6/1 priority date for international students; for spring admission, 12/1 priority date for domestic students, 10/1 priority date for international students. Applications are processed on a rolling basis. Application fee: $20 ($30 for international students). Electronic applications accepted. *Expenses:* Tuition, state resident: full-time $3086; part-time $225 per credit hour. Tuition, nonresident: part-time $529 per credit hour. Required fees: $1195. Tuition and fees vary according to course level and course load. *Financial support:* In 2009–10, 12 students received support, including 12 teaching assistantships (averaging $9,171 per year); career-related internships or fieldwork, Federal Work-Study, institutionally sponsored loans, scholarships/grants, and administrative assistantships also available. Support available to part-time students. Financial award application deadline: 5/1; financial award applicants required to submit FAFSA. *Faculty research:* Music composition, pedagogical clinics, music and column editing, music theory, music performance. *Unit head:* Dr. David Evenson, Department Head, 985-549-2184, Fax: 985-549-2892, E-mail: devenson@selu.edu. *Application contact:* Sandra Meyers, Graduate Admissions Analyst, 985-549-5620, Fax: 985-549-5632, E-mail: admissions@selu.edu.

Southern Baptist Theological Seminary, School of Church Music and Worship, Louisville, KY 40280-0004. Offers church music (M Div, MCM, MM); church music and worship (DMA, DMM); worship (M Div, MAW). *Accreditation:* NASM. *Degree requirements:* For master's, comprehensive exam; for doctorate, one foreign language, thesis/dissertation. *Entrance requirements:* For doctorate, GRE General Test, MAT, auditions. Additional exam requirements/recommendations for international students: Required—TOEFL, TWE. *Faculty research:* Baptist hymnody, church music drama, keyboard literature, impact of contemporary pop culture on church music.

Southern Illinois University Carbondale, Graduate School, College of Liberal Arts, School of Music, Carbondale, IL 62901-4701. Offers composition and theory (MM); history and literature (MM); music education (MM); opera/music theater (MM); performance (MM); piano pedagogy (MM). *Accreditation:* NASM. Part-time programs available. *Degree requirements:* For master's, one foreign language, thesis or alternative. *Entrance requirements:* For master's, audition, minimum GPA of 2.7. Additional exam requirements/recommendations for international students: Required—TOEFL. *Faculty research:* Performance practices, historical research, operatic development.

Southern Illinois University Edwardsville, Graduate Studies and Research, College of Arts and Sciences, Department of Music, Program in Music, Edwardsville, IL 62026-0001. Offers music education (MM); music performance (MM). Part-time programs available. *Faculty:* 15 full-time (4 women). *Students:* 10 full-time (5 women), 24 part-time (15 women); includes 4 minority (1 African American, 2 Asian Americans or Pacific Islanders, 1 Hispanic American), 2 international. Average age 26. 18 applicants, 39% accepted. In 2009, 10 master's awarded. *Degree requirements:* For master's, one foreign language, thesis (for some programs), recital. *Entrance requirements:* Additional exam requirements/recommendations for international students: Required—TOEFL (minimum score 550 paper-based; 213 computer-based; 79 iBT), IELTS (minimum score 6.5). *Application deadline:* For fall admission, 7/23 for domestic students, 6/1 for international students; for spring admission, 12/11 for domestic students, 10/1 for international students. Applications are processed on a rolling basis. Application fee: $30. Electronic applications accepted. *Expenses:* Tuition, state resident: part-time $1252.50 per semester. Tuition, nonresident: part-time $3131.25 per semester. Required fees: $586.85 per semester. Tuition and fees vary according to course load. *Financial support:* In 2009–10, 13 teaching assistantships with full tuition reimbursements (averaging $8,064 per year) were awarded; career-related internships or fieldwork, Federal Work-Study, institutionally sponsored loans, scholarships/grants, and traineeships also available. Support available to part-time students. Financial award application deadline: 3/1; financial award applicants required to submit FAFSA. *Unit head:* Dr. Audrey Tallant, Chair, 618-650-3900, E-mail: atallan@siue.edu. *Application contact:* Dr. Darryl Coan, Director, 618-650-2012, E-mail: dcoan@siue.edu.

Southern Methodist University, Meadows School of the Arts, Division of Music, Dallas, TX 75275. Offers conducting (MM); music composition (MM); music education (MM); music history (MM); music theory (MM); performance (MM); piano performance and pedagogy (MM); sacred music (MSM). *Accreditation:* NASM. Part-time programs available. *Faculty:* 34 full-time (12 women), 39 part-time/adjunct (16 women). *Students:* 18 full-time (7 women), 78 part-time (47 women); includes 18 minority (9 African Americans, 3 Asian Americans or Pacific Islanders, 6 Hispanic Americans), 14 international. Average age 27. 148 applicants, 54% accepted, 55 enrolled. In 2009, 44 master's, 13 Certificates awarded. *Degree requirements:* For master's, variable foreign language requirement, comprehensive exam, project, recital, or thesis. *Entrance requirements:* For master's, placement exams in music history and theory, audition; bachelor's degree in music or equivalent; minimum GPA of 3.0; research paper in history, theory, education. Additional exam requirements/recommendations for international students: Required—TOEFL (minimum score 550 paper-based; 213 computer-based; 80 iBT). *Application deadline:* For fall admission, 3/1 priority date for domestic and international students; for spring admission, 11/1 for domestic and international students. Applications are processed on a rolling basis. Application fee: $75. Electronic applications accepted. *Financial support:* In 2009–10, 77 students received support, including 70 teaching assistantships with full and partial tuition reimbursements available (averaging $4,000 per year); career-related internships or fieldwork, Federal Work-Study, scholarships/grants, tuition waivers (full and partial), and unspecified assistantships also available. Financial award application deadline: 3/1; financial award applicants required to submit FAFSA. *Faculty research:* Music perception and cognition, computer-based instruction, music medicine and therapy, theoretical and historical analysis–medieval to contemporary. *Unit head:* Dr. Sam Holland, Director, 214-768-1951, Fax: 214-768-4669, E-mail: sholland@smu.edu. *Application contact:* Joe S. Hoselton, Graduate Admissions and Records Coordinator, 214-768-3765, Fax: 214-768-3272, E-mail: hoselton@smu.edu.

Southwestern Baptist Theological Seminary, School of Church Music, Fort Worth, TX 76122-0000. Offers MACM, MAWSHP, MM, DMA, PhD, SPCM. *Accreditation:* NASM. Part-time programs available. Terminal master's awarded for partial completion of doctoral program. *Degree requirements:* For master's, comprehensive exam, thesis; for doctorate, comprehensive exam, thesis/dissertation. *Entrance requirements:* For master's, audition; for doctorate, MM or equivalent. Additional exam requirements/recommendations for international students: Required—TOEFL. Electronic applications accepted.

Southwestern Oklahoma State University, College of Arts and Sciences, Department of Music, Weatherford, OK 73096-3098. Offers music education (MM); performance (MM). *Accreditation:* NASM. Part-time programs available. *Degree requirements:* For master's, comprehensive exam, recital (music performance). *Entrance requirements:* For master's, minimum GPA of 2.5. Additional exam requirements/recommendations for international students: Required—TOEFL.

Stanford University, School of Humanities and Sciences, Department of Music, Stanford, CA 94305-9991. Offers computer-based music theory and acoustics (MA, PhD); music composition (MA, DMA); music history (MA); music, science, and technology (MA); musicology (PhD). Terminal master's awarded for partial completion of doctoral program. *Degree requirements:* For master's, variable foreign language requirement, thesis or alternative, project; for doctorate, variable foreign language requirement, thesis/dissertation (for some programs), qualifying, special area, and oral exams (PhD); composition project, lecture-demonstration exams (DMA). *Entrance requirements:* For master's and doctorate, GRE General Test, departmental theory/analysis test, samples of work. Additional exam requirements/recommendations for international students: Required—TOEFL. Electronic applications accepted. *Expenses:* Tuition: Full-time $37,380; part-time $2760 per quarter. Required fees: $501.

State University of New York at Binghamton, Graduate School, School of Arts and Sciences, Department of Music, Binghamton, NY 13902-6000. Offers MA, MM. *Accreditation:* NASM. *Faculty:* 9 full-time (3 women), 27 part-time/adjunct (10 women). *Students:* 19 full-time (14 women), 4 part-time (1 woman); includes 1 minority (Hispanic American). Average age 29. 34 applicants, 44% accepted, 7 enrolled. In 2009, 10 master's awarded. *Degree requirements:* For master's, one foreign language, thesis. *Entrance requirements:* For master's, GRE General Test, GRE Subject Test. Additional exam requirements/recommendations for international students: Required—TOEFL (minimum score 550 paper-based; 213 computer-based; 80 iBT). *Application deadline:* For fall admission, 6/15 priority date for domestic and international students; for spring admission, 10/15 priority date for domestic and international students. Applications are processed on a rolling basis. Application fee: $60. Electronic applications accepted. *Financial support:* In 2009–10, 11 students received support, including 2 fellowships with full tuition reimbursements available (averaging $9,500 per year), 9 teaching assistantships with full tuition reimbursements available (averaging $9,500 per year); career-related internships or fieldwork, Federal Work-Study, institutionally sponsored loans, scholarships/grants, health care benefits, and unspecified assistantships also available. Financial award application deadline: 2/15; financial award applicants required to submit FAFSA. *Unit head:* Dr. Timothy Perry, Chairperson, 607-777-2591, E-mail: tperry@binghamton.edu. *Application contact:* Victoria Williams, Recruiting and Admissions Coordinator, 607-777-2151, Fax: 607-777-2501, E-mail: vwilliam@binghamton.edu.

State University of New York at Fredonia, Graduate Studies, School of Music, Program in Music, Fredonia, NY 14063-1136. Offers MM. *Accreditation:* NASM. Part-time and evening/weekend programs available. *Degree requirements:* For master's, thesis optional. *Expenses:* Tuition, state resident: full-time $8370; part-time $349 per credit. Tuition, nonresident: full-time $13,250; part-time $552 per credit. Required fees: $1289; $53.55 per credit.

State University of New York at New Paltz, Graduate School, School of Fine and Performing Arts, Department of Music, New Paltz, NY 12561. Offers music therapy (MS). *Accreditation:* NASM. Part-time programs available. *Faculty:* 4 full-time (2 women), 2 part-time/adjunct (0 women). *Students:* 19 full-time (16 women), 13 part-time (10 women); includes 3 minority (all Asian Americans or Pacific Islanders), 5 international. Average age 28. 10 applicants, 80% accepted, 7 enrolled. In 2009, 9 master's awarded. *Degree requirements:* For master's, thesis. *Entrance requirements:* For master's, audition, minimum GPA of 3.0. Additional exam requirements/recommendations for international students: Required—TOEFL (minimum score 550 paper-based; 213 computer-based; 80 iBT), IELTS (minimum score 6.5). *Application deadline:* For fall admission, 5/15 for domestic and international students; for spring admission, 11/15 for domestic and international students. Application fee: $50. Electronic applications accepted. *Financial support:* In 2009–10, 2 students received support, including 2 teaching assistantships with partial tuition reimbursements available (averaging $5,000 per year). Financial award application deadline: 8/1; financial award applicants required to submit FAFSA. *Unit head:* Dr. Edward Lundergan, Chair, 845-257-3121, E-mail: lunderge@newpaltz.edu. *Application contact:* Prof. Mary Boyle, Coordinator, 845-257-2709, E-mail: boylem@newpaltz.edu.

State University of New York College at Potsdam, Crane School of Music, Potsdam, NY 13676. Offers music composition (MM); music education (MM); music performance (MM). Part-time programs available. *Faculty:* 25 full-time (9 women), 5 part-time/adjunct (1 woman). *Students:* 22 full-time (10 women), 3 part-time (2 women); includes 1 minority (Asian American or Pacific Islander), 2 international. 27 applicants, 67% accepted, 18 enrolled. In 2009, 23 master's awarded. *Degree requirements:* For master's, variable foreign language requirement, thesis. *Entrance requirements:* For master's, audition, minimum GPA of 3.0. Additional exam requirements/recommendations for international students: Required—TOEFL (minimum score 550 paper-based; 213 computer-based; 80 iBT), IELTS (minimum score 6). *Application deadline:* For fall admission, 3/1 for domestic and international students. Applications are processed on a rolling basis. Application fee: $50. *Expenses:* Tuition, state resident: full-time $8370; part-time $349 per credit hour. Tuition, nonresident: full-time $13,250; part-time $552 per credit hour. Required fees: $942; $38.70 per credit hour. *Financial support:* In 2009–10, 1 student received support; teaching assistantships with full tuition reimbursements available, career-related internships or fieldwork, Federal Work-Study, scholarships/grants, and unspecified assistantships available. Support available to part-time students. Financial award application deadline: 3/1; financial award applicants required to submit FAFSA. *Unit head:* Dr. Michael R. Sitton, Dean, 315-267-2415, Fax: 315-267-2413, E-mail: sittonmr@potsdam.edu. *Application contact:* Karen Miller, Secretary, 315-267-3418, Fax: 315-267-2413, E-mail: millerkl@potsdam.edu.

Stephen F. Austin State University, Graduate School, College of Fine Arts, School of Music, Nacogdoches, TX 75962. Offers MA, MM. *Accreditation:* NASM (one or more programs are accredited). Part-time programs available. *Degree requirements:* For master's, comprehensive exam, thesis optional. *Entrance requirements:* For master's, GRE General Test, audition. Additional exam requirements/recommendations for international students: Required—TOEFL.

Music

Stephen F. Austin State University (continued)

Faculty research: Music classroom methodology, serial music, seventeenth century sacred music, vocal pedagogy, organ duet literature.

Stony Brook University, State University of New York, Graduate School, College of Arts and Sciences, Department of Music, Program in Ethnomusicology, Stony Brook, NY 11794. Offers MA, PhD. *Entrance requirements:* For master's and doctorate, GRE, 3 letters of recommendation. Additional exam requirements/recommendations for international students: Required—TOEFL. *Application deadline:* For fall admission, 1/15 for domestic students. Application fee: $60. *Expenses:* Tuition, state resident: full-time $8370; part-time $349 per credit. Tuition, nonresident: full-time $13,250; part-time $552 per credit. Required fees: $933. *Financial support:* Teaching assistantships, scholarships/grants available. *Unit head:* Judith Lochhead, Graduate Director, 631-632-7330, Fax: 631-632-7404, E-mail: judith.lochhead@stonybrook.edu. *Application contact:* Judith Lochhead, Graduate Director, 631-632-7330, Fax: 631-632-7404, E-mail: judith.lochhead@stonybrook.edu.

Stony Brook University, State University of New York, Graduate School, College of Arts and Sciences, Department of Music, Program in Music History/Theory, Stony Brook, NY 11794. Offers MA, PhD. *Students:* 41 full-time (21 women), 2 part-time (both women); includes 4 minority (1 African American, 3 Hispanic Americans), 11 international. 106 applicants, 25% accepted. In 2009, 4 master's, 5 doctorates awarded. *Degree requirements:* For doctorate, thesis/dissertation. *Entrance requirements:* For master's and doctorate, GRE General Test. Additional exam requirements/recommendations for international students: Required—TOEFL. *Application deadline:* For fall admission, 1/15 for domestic students. Application fee: $60. Electronic applications accepted. *Expenses:* Tuition, state resident: full-time $8370; part-time $349 per credit. Tuition, nonresident: full-time $13,250; part-time $552 per credit. Required fees: $933. *Unit head:* Dr. Daniel Weymouth, Chair, 631-632-7330. *Application contact:* Judith Lochhead, Director, 631-632-7330, Fax: 631-632-7404.

Stony Brook University, State University of New York, Graduate School, College of Arts and Sciences, Department of Music, Program in Music Performance, Stony Brook, NY 11794. Offers MM, DMA. *Students:* 187 full-time (110 women), 16 part-time (11 women); includes 29 minority (1 African American, 23 Asian Americans or Pacific Islanders, 5 Hispanic Americans), 77 international. 382 applicants, 22% accepted. In 2009, 10 master's, 35 doctorates awarded. *Degree requirements:* For doctorate, thesis/dissertation. *Entrance requirements:* For master's and doctorate, GRE General Test. Additional exam requirements/recommendations for international students: Required—TOEFL. *Application deadline:* For fall admission, 1/15 for domestic students. Application fee: $60. *Expenses:* Tuition, state resident: full-time $8370; part-time $349 per credit. Tuition, nonresident: full-time $13,250; part-time $552 per credit. Required fees: $933. *Unit head:* Dr. Daniel Weymouth, Chair, 631-632-7330. *Application contact:* Judith Lochhead, Director, 631-632-7330, Fax: 631-632-7404.

Syracuse University, College of Visual and Performing Arts, Program in Conducting, Syracuse, NY 13244. Offers M Mu. *Accreditation:* NASM. *Students:* 2 full-time (both women), 1 part-time (0 women); includes 1 minority (Asian American or Pacific Islander). Average age 24. 2 applicants, 50% accepted, 1 enrolled. In 2009, 1 master's awarded. *Degree requirements:* For master's, thesis or alternative. *Entrance requirements:* For master's, audition, interview. Additional exam requirements/recommendations for international students: Required—TOEFL (minimum score 100 iBT). *Application deadline:* For fall admission, 2/1 priority date for domestic and international students. Application fee: $75. Electronic applications accepted. *Expenses:* Tuition: Full-time $26,808; part-time $1117 per credit. Required fees: $1024. *Financial support:* Fellowships with full tuition reimbursements, research assistantships with full and partial tuition reimbursements, teaching assistantships with full and partial tuition reimbursements, Federal Work-Study and tuition waivers (partial) available. Financial award application deadline: 1/1; financial award applicants required to submit FAFSA. *Unit head:* Dr. Bradley Ethington, Director, 315-443-5892, E-mail: bpething@syr.edu. *Application contact:* Harriett Conti, Assistant Dean for Recruitment and Admissions, 315-443-5755, E-mail: hmconti@syr.edu.

Syracuse University, College of Visual and Performing Arts, Program in Music Composition, Syracuse, NY 13244. Offers M Mus. *Students:* 3 full-time (1 woman), 2 international. Average age 28. 8 applicants, 25% accepted, 1 enrolled. In 2009, 4 master's awarded. *Degree requirements:* For master's, thesis or alternative. *Entrance requirements:* For master's, performance recording. Additional exam requirements/recommendations for international students: Required—TOEFL (minimum score 100 iBT). *Application deadline:* For fall admission, 2/1 priority date for domestic and international students. Application fee: $75. Electronic applications accepted. *Expenses:* Tuition: Full-time $26,808; part-time $1117 per credit. Required fees: $1024. *Financial support:* Fellowships with full and partial tuition reimbursements, teaching assistantships with full and partial tuition reimbursements available. Financial award application deadline: 1/1; financial award applicants required to submit FAFSA. *Unit head:* Dr. Bradley Ethington, Chair, 315-443-5893, E-mail: bpething@syr.edu. *Application contact:* Harriett Conti, Assistant Dean for Recruitment and Admissions, 315-443-5755, E-mail: hmconti@syr.edu.

Syracuse University, College of Visual and Performing Arts, Program in Organ, Syracuse, NY 13244. Offers M Mus. *Students:* 1 full-time (0 women). Average age 25. *Degree requirements:* For master's, thesis or alternative. *Entrance requirements:* For master's, audition. Additional exam requirements/recommendations for international students: Required—TOEFL (minimum score 100 iBT). *Application deadline:* For fall admission, 2/1 priority date for domestic and international students. Application fee: $75. Electronic applications accepted. *Expenses:* Tuition: Full-time $26,808; part-time $1117 per credit. Required fees: $1024. *Financial support:* Fellowships with full and partial tuition reimbursements, teaching assistantships with full and partial tuition reimbursements available. Financial award application deadline: 1/1; financial award applicants required to submit FAFSA. *Unit head:* Dr. Bradley Ethington, Chair, 315-443-5893. *Application contact:* Harriett Conti, Assistant Dean of Recruitment and Admissions, 315-443-5755, E-mail: hmconti@syr.edu.

Syracuse University, College of Visual and Performing Arts, Program in Percussion, Syracuse, NY 13244. Offers M Mus. *Students:* 1 applicant, 100% accepted, 0 enrolled. *Degree requirements:* For master's, thesis or alternative. *Entrance requirements:* For master's, audition. Additional exam requirements/recommendations for international students: Required—TOEFL (minimum score 100 iBT). *Application deadline:* For fall admission, 2/1 priority date for domestic and international students. Application fee: $75. Electronic applications accepted. *Expenses:* Tuition: Full-time $26,808; part-time $1117 per credit. Required fees: $1024. *Financial support:* Fellowships with full and partial tuition reimbursements, teaching assistantships with full and partial tuition reimbursements available. Financial award application deadline: 1/1; financial award applicants required to submit FAFSA. *Unit head:* Dr. Bradley Ethington, Chair, 315-443-5893, E-mail: bpething@syr.edu. *Application contact:* Harriett Conti, Assistant Dean for Recruitment and Admissions, 315-443-5755, E-mail: hmconti@syr.edu.

Syracuse University, College of Visual and Performing Arts, Program in Piano, Syracuse, NY 13244. Offers M Mus. *Students:* 4 full-time (1 woman), 1 international. Average age 23. 4 applicants, 50% accepted, 2 enrolled. In 2009, 4 master's awarded. *Degree requirements:* For master's, thesis or alternative. *Entrance requirements:* For master's, audition. Additional exam requirements/recommendations for international students: Required—TOEFL (minimum score 100 iBT). *Application deadline:* For fall admission, 2/1 priority date for domestic and international students. Application fee: $75. Electronic applications accepted. *Expenses:* Tuition: Full-time $26,808; part-time $1117 per credit. Required fees: $1024. *Financial support:* Fellowships with tuition reimbursements, teaching assistantships with tuition reimbursements available. Financial award application deadline: 1/1; financial award applicants required to submit FAFSA. *Unit head:* Dr. Bradley Ethington, Chair, 315-443-5893, E-mail: bpething@syr.edu. *Application contact:* Harriett Conti, Assistant Dean for Recruitment and Admissions, 315-443-5755, E-mail: hmconti@syr.edu.

Syracuse University, College of Visual and Performing Arts, Program in Strings, Syracuse, NY 13244. Offers M Mus. *Students:* 3 full-time (1 woman), all international. Average age 28. 4 applicants, 100% accepted, 2 enrolled. In 2009, 3 master's awarded. *Degree requirements:* For master's, thesis or alternative. *Entrance requirements:* Additional exam requirements/recommendations for international students: Required—TOEFL (minimum score 100 iBT). *Application deadline:* For fall admission, 2/1 priority date for domestic and international students. Application fee: $75. Electronic applications accepted. *Expenses:* Tuition: Full-time $26,808; part-time $1117 per credit. Required fees: $1024. *Financial support:* Fellowships with full and partial tuition reimbursements, teaching assistantships with full and partial tuition reimbursements available. Financial award application deadline: 1/1. *Unit head:* Dr. Bradley Ethington, Chair, 315-443-5893, E-mail: bpething@syr.edu. *Application contact:* Harriett Conti, Assistant Dean for Recruitment and Admissions, 315-443-5755, E-mail: hmconti@syr.edu.

Syracuse University, College of Visual and Performing Arts, Program in Voice, Syracuse, NY 13244. Offers M Mus. *Students:* 1 (woman) full-time, 1 (woman) part-time, 1 international. Average age 34. 7 applicants, 71% accepted, 1 enrolled. In 2009, 2 master's awarded. *Degree requirements:* For master's, thesis or alternative. *Entrance requirements:* For master's, audition. Additional exam requirements/recommendations for international students: Required—TOEFL (minimum score 100 iBT). *Application deadline:* For fall admission, 2/1 priority date for domestic and international students. Application fee: $75. Electronic applications accepted. *Expenses:* Tuition: Full-time $26,808; part-time $1117 per credit. Required fees: $1024. *Financial support:* Fellowships with full and partial tuition reimbursements, teaching assistantships with full and partial tuition reimbursements available. Financial award application deadline: 1/1; financial award applicants required to submit FAFSA. *Unit head:* Dr. Bradley Ethington, Chair, 315-443-, E-mail: bpething@syr.edu. *Application contact:* Harriett Conti, Assistant Dean for Recruitment and Admissions, 315-443-5755, E-mail: hmconti@syr.edu.

Syracuse University, College of Visual and Performing Arts, Program in Wind Instruments, Syracuse, NY 13244. Offers M Mus. *Students:* 3 applicants, 33% accepted, 0 enrolled. *Degree requirements:* For master's, thesis or alternative. *Entrance requirements:* For master's, audition. Additional exam requirements/recommendations for international students: Required—TOEFL (minimum score 100 iBT). *Application deadline:* For fall admission, 2/1 priority date for domestic and international students. Application fee: $75. Electronic applications accepted. *Expenses:* Tuition: Full-time $26,808; part-time $1117 per credit. Required fees: $1024. *Financial support:* Fellowships with full and partial tuition reimbursements, teaching assistantships with full and partial tuition reimbursements available. Financial award application deadline: 1/1; financial award applicants required to submit FAFSA. *Unit head:* Dr. Bradley Ethington, Chair, 315-443-5893, E-mail: bpething@syr.edu. *Application contact:* Harriett Conti, Assistant Dean for Recruitment and Admissions, 315-443-5755, E-mail: hmconti@syr.edu.

Temple University, Graduate School, Esther Boyer College of Music and Dance, Department of Choral Activities, Philadelphia, PA 19122-6096. Offers MM. Part-time and evening/weekend programs available. *Entrance requirements:* Additional exam requirements/recommendations for international students: Required—TOEFL. Electronic applications accepted.

Temple University, Graduate School, Esther Boyer College of Music and Dance, Department of Instrumental Studies, Philadelphia, PA 19122-6096. Offers MM, DMA. Part-time programs available. *Entrance requirements:* Additional exam requirements/recommendations for international students: Required—TOEFL. Electronic applications accepted.

Temple University, Graduate School, Esther Boyer College of Music and Dance, Department of Music Studies, Philadelphia, PA 19122-6096. Offers composition (MM, DMA); music history (MM); music theory (MM). *Accreditation:* NASM. Part-time and evening/weekend programs available. *Degree requirements:* For master's, one foreign language, thesis (for some programs), compositions, recitals; for doctorate, one foreign language, thesis/dissertation, compositions, recitals. *Entrance requirements:* For doctorate, GRE or MAT. Additional exam requirements/recommendations for international students: Required—TOEFL. Electronic applications accepted. *Faculty research:* Computer composition, computer music synthesis, musical instrument digital interface (MIDI) applications.

Temple University, Graduate School, Esther Boyer College of Music and Dance, Department of Voice and Opera, Philadelphia, PA 19122-6096. Offers MM, DMA. *Accreditation:* NASM. Part-time and evening/weekend programs available. *Degree requirements:* For master's, compositions, recitals; for doctorate, compositions, 6 recitals. *Entrance requirements:* Additional exam requirements/recommendations for international students: Required—TOEFL. Electronic applications accepted.

Texas A&M University–Commerce, Graduate School, College of Arts and Sciences, Department of Music, Commerce, TX 75429-3011. Offers music (MA, MS); music composition (MA, MM); music education (MA, MM, MS); music literature (MA); music performance (MA, MM); music theory (MA, MM). *Accreditation:* NASM. Part-time programs available. *Degree requirements:* For master's, comprehensive exam, thesis (for some programs). *Entrance requirements:* For master's, GRE General Test. Electronic applications accepted.

Texas Christian University, AddRan College of Liberal Arts, Department of English, Fort Worth, TX 76129-0002. Offers composition (MA); English (PhD), including rhetoric and/or literature; literature (MA); rhetoric (MA); rhetoric/composition (PhD). Part-time and evening/weekend programs available. *Degree requirements:* For master's, one foreign language, thesis, candidacy exam; for doctorate, one foreign language, comprehensive exam, thesis/dissertation, 66 hours, diagnostic exam, qualifying exam. *Entrance requirements:* For master's and doctorate, GRE General Test, 30 hours of English; 12 hours of foreign language study. Additional exam requirements/recommendations for international students: Required—TOEFL. *Application deadline:* For fall admission, 1/31 for domestic and international students; for spring admission, 10/15 for domestic and international students. Application fee: $0. *Expenses:* Tuition: Full-time $17,640; part-time $980 per credit hour. Tuition and fees vary according to program. *Financial support:* In 2009–10, 28 students received support; fellowships with full tuition reimbursements available, research assistantships with full tuition reimbursements available, teaching assistantships with full tuition reimbursements available, tuition waivers (full) and unspecified assistantships available. Financial award application deadline: 3/1; financial award applicants required to submit FAFSA. *Unit head:* Dr. Brad Lucas, Chairperson, 817-257-7240. *Application contact:* Dr. Bonnie Carol Blackwell, Associate Professor/Director of Graduate Studies, 817-257-6263, E-mail: b.blackwell@tcu.edu.

Texas Christian University, College of Fine Arts, School of Music, Fort Worth, TX 76129-0002. Offers composition (DMA); conducting (M Mus, DMA); music education (MM Ed); musicology (M Mus); organ performance (M Mus); pedagogy (DMA); performance (DMA); piano (Artist Diploma); piano pedagogy (M Mus); piano performance (M Mus); string performance (M Mus); theory/composition (M Mus); vocal performance (M Mus); voice pedagogy (M Mus); wind and percussion performance (M Mus). *Accreditation:* NASM. *Degree requirements:* For master's, one foreign language, comprehensive exam, thesis (for some programs), thesis or recital; for doctorate, one foreign language, comprehensive exam, thesis/dissertation. *Entrance requirements:* For master's, GRE General Test (theory/composition, musicology), audition or composition/theory, letters of recommendation; for doctorate, GRE General Test, on site entrance exam, audition, interview. Additional exam requirements/recommendations for international students: Required—TOEFL iBT (minimum score 80; 100 for DMA). *Application deadline:* For fall admission, 1/15 for domestic and international students; for spring admission, 10/1 for domestic and international students. Application fee: $0. *Expenses:* Tuition: Full-time $17,640; part-time $980 per credit hour. Tuition and fees vary according to program. *Financial support:* Application deadline: 1/15. *Unit head:* Dr. Richard Gipson, Director, 817-257-7602. *Application contact:* Dr. Joseph Butler, Associate Dean, College of Fine Arts, E-mail: j.butler@tcu.edu.

Texas Southern University, College of Liberal Arts and Behavioral Sciences, Department of Fine Arts, Houston, TX 77004-4584. Offers fine arts (MA); music (MA). Part-time programs available. *Faculty:* 3 full-time (1 woman), 1 (woman) part-time/adjunct. *Students:* 2 full-time (0 women), 4 part-time (1 woman); all minorities (all African Americans). Average age 35. 2 applicants, 100% accepted, 2 enrolled. *Degree requirements:* For master's, one foreign language, comprehensive exam, recital. *Entrance requirements:* For master's, GRE General Test, minimum GPA of 2.5. Additional exam requirements/recommendations for international students: Required—TOEFL. *Application deadline:* For fall admission, 7/1 for domestic and international students; for spring admission, 11/1 for domestic and international students. Applications are processed on a rolling basis. Application fee: $50 ($75 for international students). Electronic applications accepted. *Expenses:* Tuition, state resident: full-time $1805; part-time $100 per credit hour. Tuition, nonresident: full-time $6470; part-time $343 per credit hour. Tuition and fees vary according to course level, course load and degree level. *Financial support:* Fellowships, teaching assistantships, scholarships/grants and unspecified assistantships available. Support available to part-time students. Financial award application deadline: 5/1. *Faculty research:* Music theory, choral music, composition, percussion composition, ethnic musicology. *Unit head:* Dianne F. Jemison-Pollard, Chair, 713-313-7337, Fax: 713-313-1869, E-mail: jemison_dp@tsu.edu. *Application contact:* Dr. Gregory Maddox, Interim Dean of the Graduate School, 713-313-7011 Ext. 4410, Fax: 713-639-1876, E-mail: maddox_gh@tsu.edu.

Texas State University–San Marcos, Graduate School, College of Fine Arts and Communication, School of Music, Program in Music Performance, San Marcos, TX 78666. Offers MM. *Accreditation:* NASM. Part-time programs available. *Faculty:* 9 full-time (3 women). *Students:* 45 full-time (25 women), 15 part-time (8 women); includes 24 minority (1 African American, 7 Asian Americans or Pacific Islanders, 16 Hispanic Americans), 7 international. Average age 28. 39 applicants, 87% accepted, 24 enrolled. In 2009, 23 master's awarded. *Degree requirements:* For master's, comprehensive exam. *Entrance requirements:* For master's, minimum GPA of 2.75 in last 60 hours of course work. Additional exam requirements/recommendations for international students: Required—TOEFL (minimum score 550 paper-based; 213 computer-based). *Application deadline:* For fall admission, 6/15 priority date for domestic students; for spring admission, 10/15 priority date for domestic students. Applications are processed on a rolling basis. Application fee: $40 ($90 for international students). Electronic applications accepted. *Expenses:* Tuition, state resident: full-time $5784; part-time $241 per credit hour. Tuition, nonresident: part-time $551 per credit hour. Required fees: $1728; $48 per credit hour. $306. Tuition and fees vary according to course load. *Financial support:* In 2009–10, 60 students received support, including 13 teaching assistantships (averaging $1,399 per year); research assistantships, career-related internships or fieldwork, Federal Work-Study, and institutionally sponsored loans also available. Support available to part-time students. Financial award application deadline: 4/1; financial award applicants required to submit FAFSA. *Unit head:* Dr. Kevin Mooney, Graduate Advisor, 512-245-2651, Fax: 512-245-8181, E-mail: km30@txstate.edu. *Application contact:* Dr. J. Michael Willoughby, Dean of Graduate School, 512-245-2581, Fax: 512-245-8365, E-mail: gradcollege@txstate.edu.

Texas State University–San Marcos, Graduate School, College of Liberal Arts, Department of English, Program in Rhetoric and Composition, San Marcos, TX 78666. Offers MA. Part-time programs available. *Faculty:* 5 full-time (3 women). *Students:* 4 full-time (3 women), 10 part-time (7 women); includes 5 minority (1 American Indian/Alaska Native, 1 Asian American or Pacific Islander, 3 Hispanic Americans). Average age 33. 9 applicants, 100% accepted, 5 enrolled. In 2009, 4 master's awarded. *Degree requirements:* For master's, comprehensive exam, thesis optional. *Entrance requirements:* For master's, minimum GPA of 3.25 in minimum of 24 hours of undergraduate English, 6 hours of a foreign language. Additional exam requirements/recommendations for international students: Required—TOEFL (minimum score 550 paper-based; 213 computer-based). *Application deadline:* For fall admission, 6/15 for domestic students, 6/1 for international students; for spring admission, 10/15 for domestic students, 10/1 for international students. Applications are processed on a rolling basis. Application fee: $40 ($90 for international students). Electronic applications accepted. *Expenses:* Tuition, state resident: full-time $5784; part-time $241 per credit hour. Tuition, nonresident: part-time $551 per credit hour. Required fees: $1728; $48 per credit hour. $306. Tuition and fees vary according to course load. *Financial support:* In 2009–10, 9 students received support, including 1 research assistantship (averaging $6,290 per year); teaching assistantships, Federal Work-Study and institutionally sponsored loans also available. Support available to part-time students. Financial award application deadline: 4/1; financial award applicants required to submit FAFSA. *Unit head:* Dr. Rebecca Jackson, Graduate Advisor, 512-245-2163, E-mail: rj10@txstate.edu. *Application contact:* Dr. J. Michael Willoughby, Dean of Graduate School, 512-245-2581, Fax: 512-245-8365, E-mail: gradcollege@txstate.edu.

Texas Tech University, Graduate School, College of Visual and Performing Arts, Department of Theatre and Dance, Lubbock, TX 79409. Offers fine arts (PhD); theatre arts (MA, MFA), including design (MFA), performance/pedagogy (MFA), playwriting (MFA), theatre management (MFA). *Accreditation:* NAST. Part-time programs available. *Faculty:* 11 full-time (6 women). *Students:* 40 full-time (19 women), 20 part-time (10 women); includes 7 minority (3 African Americans, 1 Asian American or Pacific Islander, 3 Hispanic Americans), 3 international. Average age 34. 30 applicants, 50% accepted, 9 enrolled. In 2009, 5 master's, 2 doctorates awarded. *Degree requirements:* For master's, variable foreign language requirement, thesis; for doctorate, thesis/dissertation. *Entrance requirements:* For master's and doctorate, GRE General Test. Additional exam requirements/recommendations for international students: Required—TOEFL (minimum score 550 paper-based; 213 computer-based). *Application deadline:* For fall admission, 3/1 priority date for international students; for spring admission, 11/1 priority date for international students. Applications are processed on a rolling basis. Application fee: $50 ($75 for international students). Electronic applications accepted. *Expenses:* Tuition, state resident: full-time $5100; part-time $213 per credit hour. Tuition, nonresident: full-time $11,748; part-time $490 per credit hour. Required fees: $2298; $50 per credit hour. $555 per semester. *Financial support:* In 2009–10, 18 teaching assistantships with partial tuition reimbursements (averaging $10,564 per year) were awarded; research assistantships with partial tuition reimbursements, Federal Work-Study and institutionally sponsored loans also available. Support available to part-time students. Financial award application deadline: 4/15; financial award applicants required to submit FAFSA. *Faculty research:* New student plays program, theatre planning, dramaturgy; feminist theatre; arts administration; dance aesthetics. *Unit head:* Prof. Frederick B. Christoffel, Chair, 806-742-3601 Ext. 228, Fax: 806-742-1338, E-mail: fred.christoffel@ttu.edu. *Application contact:* Dr. James Bush, Graduate Adviser, 806-742-3601 Ext. 230, Fax: 806-742-1338, E-mail: james.bush@ttu.edu.

Texas Tech University, Graduate School, College of Visual and Performing Arts, Fine Arts Doctoral Program, Lubbock, TX 79409. Offers arts (PhD); music (PhD); theatre arts (PhD). *Accreditation:* NAST. *Students:* 44 full-time (18 women), 31 part-time (16 women); includes 9 minority (3 African Americans, 1 American Indian/Alaska Native, 1 Asian American or Pacific Islander, 4 Hispanic Americans), 10 international. Average age 36. 33 applicants, 30% accepted, 3 enrolled. In 2009, 10 doctorates awarded. *Degree requirements:* For doctorate, thesis/dissertation. *Entrance requirements:* For doctorate, GRE General Test. Additional exam requirements/recommendations for international students: Required—TOEFL (minimum score 550 paper-based; 213 computer-based). *Application deadline:* For fall admission, 3/1 priority date for international students; for spring admission, 11/1 priority date for international students. Applications are processed on a rolling basis. Application fee: $50 ($75 for international students). Electronic applications accepted. *Expenses:* Tuition, state resident: full-time $5100; part-time $213 per credit hour. Tuition, nonresident: full-time $11,748; part-time $490 per credit hour. Required fees: $2298; $50 per credit hour. $555 per semester. *Financial support:* Research assistantships with partial tuition reimbursements, teaching assistantships with partial tuition reimbursements available. Financial award application deadline: 4/15. *Faculty research:* Art criticism and theory, music, theatre arts; arts education; history of arts. *Unit head:* Dr. Brian D. Steele, Director, 806-742-0700, Fax: 806-742-0695, E-mail: brian.steele@ttu.edu. *Application contact:* Dr. Brian D. Steele, Director, 806-742-0700, Fax: 806-742-0695, E-mail: brian.steele@ttu.edu.

Texas Tech University, Graduate School, College of Visual and Performing Arts, School of Music, Lubbock, TX 79409. Offers composition (MM, DMA); conducting (DMA); fine arts-music (PhD); music education (MM Ed); music theory (MM); musicology (MM); pedagogy (MM); performance (MM, DMA); piano pedagogy (DMA). *Accreditation:* NASM. Part-time programs available. *Faculty:* 40 full-time (15 women), 1 part-time/adjunct (0 women). *Students:* 105 full-time (41 women), 28 part-time (15 women); includes 17 minority (5 African Americans, 12 Hispanic Americans), 27 international. Average age 30. 123 applicants, 60% accepted, 37 enrolled. In 2009, 19 master's, 20 doctorates awarded. *Degree requirements:* For master's, thesis or alternative; for doctorate, thesis/dissertation. *Entrance requirements:* For master's and doctorate, GRE General Test. Additional exam requirements/recommendations for international students: Required—TOEFL (minimum score 550 paper-based; 213 computer-based). *Application deadline:* For fall admission, 3/1 priority date for international students; for spring admission, 11/1 priority date for international students. Applications are processed on a rolling basis. Application fee: $50 ($75 for international students). Electronic applications accepted. *Expenses:* Tuition, state resident: full-time $5100; part-time $213 per credit hour. Tuition, nonresident: full-time $11,748; part-time $490 per credit hour. Required fees: $2298; $50 per credit hour. $555 per semester. *Financial support:* In 2009–10, 32 teaching assistantships with partial tuition reimbursements (averaging $8,206 per year) were awarded; research assistantships with partial tuition reimbursements, Federal Work-Study and institutionally sponsored loans also available. Support available to part-time students. Financial award application deadline: 4/15; financial award applicants required to submit FAFSA. *Faculty research:* Strategies for music pedagogy in grades K-12, performance practice of traditional music, role of the woman piano virtuoso, vernacular music center, voice health and culture. Total annual research expenditures: $9,083. *Unit head:* Prof. William Ballenger, Director, 806-742-2270, Fax: 806-742-2294, E-mail: william.ballenger@ttu.edu. *Application contact:* Carin Wanner, Admissions and Scholarship Coordinator, 806-742-2270 Ext. 225, Fax: 806-742-2294, E-mail: melissacarin.wanner@ttu.edu.

Texas Woman's University, Graduate School, College of Arts and Sciences, School of the Arts, Department of Music and Drama, Denton, TX 76201. Offers drama (MA); music (MA). *Accreditation:* NASM. Part-time programs available. *Faculty:* 13 full-time (7 women), 4 part-time/adjunct (3 women). *Students:* 43 full-time (35 women), 31 part-time (24 women); includes 16 minority (5 African Americans, 1 American Indian/Alaska Native, 2 Asian Americans or Pacific Islanders, 8 Hispanic Americans), 11 international. Average age 31. 47 applicants, 94% accepted, 37 enrolled. In 2009, 13 master's awarded. *Degree requirements:* For master's, thesis optional, project recital. *Entrance requirements:* For master's, music history/theory placement exam. Additional exam requirements/recommendations for international students: Required—TOEFL (minimum score 550 paper-based; 213 computer-based; 79 iBT). *Application deadline:* For fall admission, 7/1 priority date for domestic students, 3/1 for international students; for spring admission, 12/1 priority date for domestic students, 7/1 for international students. Applications are processed on a rolling basis. Application fee: $50. Electronic applications accepted. *Expenses:* Tuition, state resident: full-time $3564; part-time $198 per credit hour. Tuition, nonresident: full-time $8550; part-time $475 per credit hour. Required fees: $69.26 per credit hour. Tuition and fees vary according to course load. *Financial support:* In 2009–10, 2 research assistantships (averaging $9,684 per year), 1 teaching assistantship (averaging $9,684 per year) were awarded; career-related internships or fieldwork, Federal Work-Study, institutionally sponsored loans, scholarships/grants, traineeships, health care benefits, tuition waivers (partial), and unspecified assistantships also available. Support available to part-time students. Financial award application deadline: 3/1; financial award applicants required to submit FAFSA. *Faculty research:* Musical development in early childhood, little known or neglected compositions for flute (especially by women composers), relationship of visual art to piano music, pedagogical development of the singing voice, guided imagery and music. *Unit head:* Dr. James Chenevert, Chair, 940-898-2500, Fax: 940-898-2494, E-mail: music@twu.edu. *Application contact:* Samuel Wheeler, Assistant Director of Admissions, 940-898-3188, Fax: 940-898-3081, E-mail: wheelersr@twu.edu.

Towson University, College of Graduate Studies and Research, Program in Music Performance and Composition, Towson, MD 21252-0001. Offers MM. *Accreditation:* NASM. Part-time and evening/weekend programs available. *Degree requirements:* For master's, exam. *Entrance requirements:* For master's, audition, bachelor's degree in music or music education, minimum GPA of 3.0. Electronic applications accepted.

Trinity Lutheran Seminary, Graduate and Professional Programs, Columbus, OH 43209-2334. Offers Christian education (MA); church music (MA); divinity (M Div); sacred theology (STM); theological studies (MTS); youth and family ministry (MA); MSN/MTS; MTS/JD. *Accreditation:* ACIPE; ATS. Part-time programs available. *Faculty:* 15 full-time (7 women), 10 part-time/adjunct (3 women). *Students:* 99 full-time (38 women), 44 part-time (18 women); includes 21 minority (15 African Americans, 4 Asian Americans or Pacific Islanders, 2 Hispanic Americans), 4 international. Average age 35. 71 applicants, 77% accepted, 49 enrolled. In 2009, 29 first professional degrees, 9 master's awarded. *Degree requirements:* For master's, comprehensive exam (for some programs), thesis (for some programs); for M Div, 2 foreign languages, internship. *Entrance requirements:* For master's, M Div or equivalent (STM). Additional exam requirements/recommendations for international students: Required—TOEFL (minimum score 500 paper-based; 173 computer-based; 61 iBT). *Application deadline:* For fall admission, 7/15 priority date for domestic and international students. Applications are processed on a rolling basis. Application fee: $25. *Expenses:* Tuition: Full-time $11,400; part-time $380 per semester hour. Required fees: $115 per semester. One-time fee: $150 full-time. *Financial support:* In 2009–10, 102 students received support. Career-related internships or fieldwork, Federal Work-Study, institutionally sponsored loans, and scholarships/grants available. Support available to part-time students. Financial award application deadline: 5/1; financial award applicants required to submit FAFSA. *Unit head:* Dr. James M. Childs, Interim Academic Dean, 614-235-4136, Fax: 614-384-4635, E-mail: jchilds@trinitylutheranseminary.edu. *Application contact:* Rev. Sheri L. Ayers, Director of Admissions, 614-235-4136 Ext. 4614, Fax: 866-610-8572, E-mail: sayers@trinitylutheranseminary.edu.

Troy University, Graduate School, College of Education, Program in Postsecondary Education, Troy, AL 36082. Offers adult education (M Ed); biology (M Ed); criminal justice (M Ed); english (M Ed); foundations of education (M Ed); general science (M Ed); higher education administration (M Ed); history (M Ed); instructional technology (M Ed); mathematics (M Ed); music industry (M Ed); physical fitness (M Ed); political science (M Ed); public administration (M Ed); social science (M Ed); teaching english (M Ed). Also offered through the University College. *Accreditation:* NCATE. Part-time and evening/weekend programs available. *Students:* 267 full-time (192 women), 381 part-time (293 women); includes 326 minority (309 African Americans, 4 American Indian/Alaska Native, 5 Asian Americans or Pacific Islanders, 8 Hispanic Americans). Average age 34. 343 applicants, 90% accepted. In 2009, 480 master's awarded. *Degree requirements:* For master's, comprehensive exam, thesis. *Entrance requirements:* For master's, MAT (minimum score 385), minimum GPA of 2.5. Additional exam requirements/recommendations for international students: Required—TOEFL (minimum score 523 paper-based; 193 computer-based; 70 iBT), IELTS, or ACT Compass ESL (minimum score 270 on Listening, Reading, and Grammar with no individual score below 85 and a minimum score of 8 out of 12 on writing test). *Application deadline:* Applications are processed on a rolling basis. Application fee: $50. Electronic applications accepted. *Financial support:* Available to part-time students. Applicants required to submit FAFSA. *Unit head:* Dr. Andrew Creamer, Chair, 334-670-3350, E-mail: drcreamer@troy.edu. *Application contact:* Brenda K. Campbell, Director of Graduate Admissions, 334-670-3178, Fax: 334-670-3733, E-mail: bcamp@troy.edu.

Truman State University, Graduate School, School of Arts and Letters, Program in Music, Kirksville, MO 63501-4221. Offers MA. *Accreditation:* NASM. *Degree requirements:* For master's, comprehensive exam, thesis or alternative. *Entrance requirements:* For master's, GRE General Test, minimum GPA of 3.0. Additional exam requirements/recommendations for international students: Required—TOEFL (minimum score 550 paper-based; 213 computer-based). Electronic applications accepted. *Expenses:* Tuition, state resident: part-time $291 per credit. Tuition, nonresident: part-time $499 per credit hour. Tuition and fees vary according to course load.

Tufts University, Graduate School of Arts and Sciences, Department of Music, Medford, MA 02155. Offers ethnomusicology (MA); music history and literature (MA); music theory and

Tufts University (continued)
composition (MA). Part-time programs available. *Faculty:* 11 full-time, 14 part-time/adjunct. *Students:* 15 (5 women), 4 international. 44 applicants, 34% accepted, 6 enrolled. In 2009, 13 master's awarded. *Degree requirements:* For master's, one foreign language, thesis. *Entrance requirements:* For master's, GRE General Test, writing sample or musical score. Additional exam requirements/recommendations for international students: Required—TOEFL (minimum score 550 paper-based; 213 computer-based; 80 iBT). *Application deadline:* For fall admission, 2/1 for domestic students, 12/15 for international students. Applications are processed on a rolling basis. Application fee: $75. Electronic applications accepted. *Expenses:* Tuition: Full-time $38,096; part-time $3962 per credit. Required fees: $686; $40 per year. Tuition and fees vary according to course level, course load, degree level, program and student level. *Financial support:* Teaching assistantships with full and partial tuition reimbursements, Federal Work-Study, scholarships/grants, tuition waivers (partial), and unspecified assistantships available. Financial award application deadline: 2/1; financial award applicants required to submit FAFSA. *Unit head:* Joseph Auner, Chair, 617-627-3564, Fax: 617-627-3967. *Application contact:* Information Contact, 617-628-5000.

Tulane University, School of Liberal Arts, Department of Music, New Orleans, LA 70118-5669. Offers MA, MFA. *Degree requirements:* For master's, one foreign language, thesis (for some programs), recital or composition (MA). *Entrance requirements:* For master's, GRE General Test, minimum B average in undergraduate course work. Additional exam requirements/recommendations for international students: Required—TOEFL. Electronic applications accepted. *Faculty research:* New Orleans music, composition, piano, voice, music theatre, classical guitar.

Université de Montréal, Faculty of Music, Montréal, QC H3C 3J7, Canada. Offers composition (M Mus, D Mus); musicology and ethnomusicology (MA, PhD); orchestra conducting (M Mus, D Mus); orchestral repertoire (DESS); performance interpretation (DESS); voice and instruments interpretation (M Mus, D Mus). *Degree requirements:* For doctorate, thesis/dissertation, general exam. Electronic applications accepted. *Faculty research:* Semiology, music in Creole areas, computer-assisted composition, Argentinean tango.

Université Laval, Faculty of Music, Programs in Music, Québec, QC G1K 7P4, Canada. Offers composition (M Mus); instrumental didactics (M Mus); interpretation (M Mus); music education (M Mus, PhD); musicology (M Mus, PhD). Terminal master's awarded for partial completion of doctoral program. *Degree requirements:* For master's, thesis (for some programs); for doctorate, comprehensive exam, thesis/dissertation. *Entrance requirements:* For master's, English exam, audition, knowledge of French; for doctorate, English exam, knowledge of French, third language. Electronic applications accepted.

University at Buffalo, the State University of New York, Graduate School, College of Arts and Sciences, Department of Music, Buffalo, NY 14260. Offers historical musicology and music theory (PhD); music composition (MA, PhD); music history (MA); music performance (MM); music theory (MA). Terminal master's awarded for partial completion of doctoral program. *Degree requirements:* For master's, variable foreign language requirement, comprehensive exam (for some programs), thesis optional, recitals (MM); for doctorate, variable foreign language requirement, comprehensive exam, thesis/dissertation. *Entrance requirements:* For master's, GRE General Test, audition (MM), compositions, writing sample; for doctorate, GRE General Test, compositions, writing sample. Additional exam requirements/recommendations for international students: Required—TOEFL (minimum score 550 paper-based; 213 computer-based; 79 iBT). Electronic applications accepted. *Faculty research:* Concert performance, analytical theory, musicology/history, computer composition.

The University of Akron, Graduate School, College of Creative and Professional Arts, School of Music, Program in Composition, Akron, OH 44325. Offers MM. *Students:* 1 part-time (0 women). Average age 33. 2 applicants, 50% accepted, 1 enrolled. *Degree requirements:* For master's, comprehensive exam, thesis or project. *Entrance requirements:* For master's, minimum GPA of 2.75, interview, audition, letters of recommendation. Additional exam requirements/recommendations for international students: Required—TOEFL (minimum score 550 paper-based; 213 computer-based; 79 iBT). *Application deadline:* Applications are processed on a rolling basis. Application fee: $30 ($40 for international students). Electronic applications accepted. *Expenses:* Tuition, state resident: full-time $6570; part-time $365 per credit hour. Tuition, nonresident: full-time $11,250; part-time $625 per credit hour. *Unit head:* Dr. Daniel W. McCarthy, Head, 330-972-2199, E-mail: dmccarthy@uakron.edu. *Application contact:* Dr. Daniel W. McCarthy, Head, 330-972-2199, E-mail: dmccarthy@uakron.edu.

The University of Akron, Graduate School, College of Creative and Professional Arts, School of Music, Program in Music History and Literature, Akron, OH 44325. Offers MM. *Students:* 1 (woman) full-time, 1 part-time (0 women). Average age 41. 1 applicant, 100% accepted, 1 enrolled. *Degree requirements:* For master's, comprehensive exam, thesis or project. *Entrance requirements:* For master's, minimum GPA of 2.75, interview, audition, letters of recommendation. Additional exam requirements/recommendations for international students: Required—TOEFL (minimum score 550 paper-based; 213 computer-based; 79 iBT). *Application deadline:* Applications are processed on a rolling basis. Application fee: $30 ($40 for international students). Electronic applications accepted. *Expenses:* Tuition, state resident: full-time $6570; part-time $365 per credit hour. Tuition, nonresident: full-time $11,250; part-time $625 per credit hour. *Unit head:* Dr. Brooks Toliver, Head, 330-972-5207, E-mail: brooks@uakron.edu. *Application contact:* Dr. Brooks Toliver, Head, 330-972-5207, E-mail: brooks@uakron.edu.

The University of Akron, Graduate School, College of Creative and Professional Arts, School of Music, Program in Music Technology, Akron, OH 44325. Offers MM. *Students:* 4 full-time (1 woman), 1 part-time (0 women); includes 1 minority (African American). Average age 32. 1 applicant, 100% accepted, 1 enrolled. In 2009, 1 master's awarded. *Degree requirements:* For master's, comprehensive exam, thesis or project. *Entrance requirements:* For master's, minimum GPA of 2.75, interview, audition, letters of recommendation. Additional exam requirements/recommendations for international students: Required—TOEFL (minimum score 550 paper-based; 213 computer-based; 79 iBT). *Application deadline:* Applications are processed on a rolling basis. Application fee: $30 ($40 for international students). Electronic applications accepted. *Expenses:* Tuition, state resident: full-time $6570; part-time $365 per credit hour. Tuition, nonresident: full-time $11,250; part-time $625 per credit hour. *Unit head:* V. Douglas Hicks, Head, 330-972-6356, E-mail: vhicks@uakron.edu. *Application contact:* V. Douglas Hicks, Head, 330-972-6356, E-mail: vhicks@uakron.edu.

The University of Akron, Graduate School, College of Creative and Professional Arts, School of Music, Program in Performance, Akron, OH 44325. Offers MM. *Students:* 50 full-time (33 women), 5 part-time (1 woman); includes 4 minority (all African Americans), 6 international. Average age 30. 56 applicants, 88% accepted, 25 enrolled. In 2009, 18 master's awarded. *Degree requirements:* For master's, comprehensive exam. *Entrance requirements:* For master's, minimum GPA of 2.75, interview, audition, letters of recommendation. Additional exam requirements/recommendations for international students: Required—TOEFL (minimum score 550 paper-based; 213 computer-based; 79 iBT). *Application deadline:* Applications are processed on a rolling basis. Application fee: $30 ($40 for international students). Electronic applications accepted. *Expenses:* Tuition, state resident: full-time $6570; part-time $365 per credit hour. Tuition, nonresident: full-time $11,250; part-time $625 per credit hour. *Unit head:* Dr. William Guegold, Director, 330-972-7590, E-mail: guegold@uakron.edu. *Application contact:* Dr. William Guegold, Director, 330-972-7590, E-mail: guegold@uakron.edu.

The University of Akron, Graduate School, College of Creative and Professional Arts, School of Music, Program in Theory, Akron, OH 44325. Offers MM. *Students:* 2 full-time (0 women), 2 part-time (1 woman); includes 1 minority (African American). Average age 25. 2 applicants, 50% accepted, 1 enrolled. In 2009, 1 master's awarded. *Degree requirements:* For master's, comprehensive exam, thesis or project. *Entrance requirements:* For master's, minimum GPA of 2.75, interview, letters of recommendation. Additional exam requirements/recommendations for international students: Required—TOEFL (minimum score 550 paper-based; 213 computer-based; 79 iBT). *Application deadline:* Applications are processed on a rolling basis. Application fee: $30 ($40 for international students). Electronic applications accepted. *Expenses:* Tuition, state resident: full-time $6570; part-time $365 per credit hour. Tuition, nonresident: full-time $11,250; part-time $625 per credit hour. *Unit head:* Dr. Daniel W. McCarthy, Head, 330-972-2199, E-mail: dmccarthy@uakron.edu. *Application contact:* Dr. Daniel W. McCarthy, Head, 330-972-2199, E-mail: dmccarthy@uakron.edu.

The University of Alabama, Graduate School, College of Arts and Sciences, Department of English, Tuscaloosa, AL 35487. Offers composition and rhetoric (PhD); creative writing (MFA), including fiction, poetry; literature (MA, PhD); rhetoric and composition (MA); teaching English as a second language (MATESOL). *Faculty:* 30 full-time (12 women). *Students:* 123 full-time (71 women), 12 part-time (9 women); includes 14 minority (9 African Americans, 2 American Indian/Alaska Native, 1 Asian American or Pacific Islander, 2 Hispanic Americans), 4 international. Average age 27. 339 applicants, 17% accepted, 39 enrolled. In 2009, 31 degrees awarded. *Degree requirements:* For master's, one foreign language, comprehensive exam, thesis (for some programs); for doctorate, 2 foreign languages, comprehensive exam, thesis/dissertation. *Entrance requirements:* For master's and doctorate, GRE, minimum GPA of 3.0, critical writing sample. Additional exam requirements/recommendations for international students: Required—TOEFL. *Application deadline:* For fall admission, 1/15 priority date for domestic students, 1/15 for international students. Application fee: $50 ($60 for international students). Electronic applications accepted. *Expenses:* Tuition, state resident: full-time $7000. Tuition, nonresident: full-time $19,200. *Financial support:* In 2009–10, 7 fellowships with full tuition reimbursements (averaging $15,000 per year), 1 research assistantship (averaging $11,708 per year), 106 teaching assistantships with full tuition reimbursements (averaging $11,708 per year) were awarded; career-related internships or fieldwork, scholarships/grants, health care benefits, and unspecified assistantships also available. Financial award application deadline: 1/15. *Faculty research:* Critical theory; modern, Renaissance, and African-American literature. *Unit head:* Dr. Catherine E. Davies, Director of Graduate Studies, 205-348-8499, E-mail: cdavies@bama.ua.edu. *Application contact:* Vernita W. James, Office Assistant II, 205-348-0766, Fax: 205-348-1388, E-mail: vwjames@bama.ua.edu.

The University of Alabama, Graduate School, College of Arts and Sciences, School of Music, Tuscaloosa, AL 35487. Offers arranging (MM); choral conducting (MM, DMA); composition (MM, DMA); music education (MA, PhD); music history (MM); performance (MM, DMA); theory (MM); wind conducting (MM, DMA). *Accreditation:* NASM. *Faculty:* 32 full-time (11 women). *Students:* 63 full-time (35 women), 26 part-time (11 women); includes 13 minority (5 African Americans, 5 Asian Americans or Pacific Islanders, 3 Hispanic Americans), 13 international. Average age 30. 66 applicants, 42% accepted, 22 enrolled. In 2009, 12 master's, 4 doctorates awarded. *Median time to degree:* Of those who began their doctoral program in fall 2001, 50% received their degree in 8 years or less. *Degree requirements:* For master's, comprehensive exam, thesis, oral and written exams, recital; for doctorate, comprehensive exam, thesis/dissertation, oral and written exams, recital. *Entrance requirements:* For master's and doctorate, audition. Additional exam requirements/recommendations for international students: Required—TOEFL, or IELTS. *Application deadline:* For fall admission, 2/1 priority date for domestic and international students; for winter admission, 2/1 for domestic students, 2/1 priority date for international students; for spring admission, 2/1 priority date for domestic and international students. Applications are processed on a rolling basis. Application fee: $50 ($60 for international students). Electronic applications accepted. *Expenses:* Tuition, state resident: full-time $7000. Tuition, nonresident: full-time $19,200. *Financial support:* In 2009–10, 22 students received support, including 1 fellowship with tuition reimbursement available (averaging $30,000 per year), 40 teaching assistantships with full and partial tuition reimbursements available (averaging $8,181 per year); Federal Work-Study, institutionally sponsored loans, and unspecified assistantships also available. Financial award application deadline: 7/14. *Faculty research:* Performance practice, musicology, theory, composition. *Unit head:* Charles G. Snead, Director, 205-348-7110, Fax: 205-348-1473, E-mail: ssnead@music.ua.edu. *Application contact:* Dr. Marvin Johnson, Director of Graduate Studies, 205-348-6604, Fax: 205-348-1473, E-mail: mjohnson@music.ua.edu.

University of Alaska Fairbanks, College of Liberal Arts, Department of Music, Fairbanks, AK 99775-5660. Offers conducting (MA); music education (MA); music history (MA); music theory/composition (MA); performance (MA). *Accreditation:* NASM. Part-time programs available. *Faculty:* 12 full-time (3 women), 6 part-time/adjunct (4 women). *Students:* 11 full-time (6 women), 4 part-time (2 women). Average age 36. 18 applicants, 67% accepted, 11 enrolled. In 2009, 5 master's awarded. *Degree requirements:* For master's, comprehensive exam, thesis or alternative, oral exam, oral defense. *Entrance requirements:* For master's, evaluative preliminary examination in music theory and history. Additional exam requirements/recommendations for international students: Required—TOEFL (minimum score 550 paper-based; 213 computer-based; 80 iBT). *Application deadline:* For fall admission, 6/1 for domestic students, 3/1 for international students; for spring admission, 10/15 for domestic students, 9/1 for international students. Applications are processed on a rolling basis. Application fee: $60. Electronic applications accepted. *Expenses:* Tuition, state resident: full-time $7584; part-time $316 per credit. Tuition, nonresident: full-time $15,504; part-time $646 per credit. Required fees: $23 per credit. $135 per semester. Tuition and fees vary according to course level, course load and reciprocity agreements. *Financial support:* In 2009–10, 4 teaching assistantships (averaging $12,472 per year) were awarded; fellowships, Federal Work-Study, scholarships/grants, health care benefits, and unspecified assistantships also available. Support available to part-time students. Financial award application deadline: 7/1; financial award applicants required to submit FAFSA. *Faculty research:* Symphony, opera, jazz, chamber and solo performance. *Unit head:* Dr. Eduard Zilberkant, Department Chair, 907-474-7555, Fax: 907-474-6420, E-mail: uaf.music@alaska.edu. *Application contact:* Dr. Eduard Zilberkant, Department Chair, 907-474-7555, Fax: 907-474-6420, E-mail: uaf.music@alaska.edu.

University of Alberta, Faculty of Graduate Studies and Research, Department of Music, Edmonton, AB T6G 2E1, Canada. Offers applied music (M Mus); choral conducting (M Mus); composition (M Mus); music (PhD); organ and choral conductors (D Mus); piano (D Mus). *Faculty:* 22 full-time (5 women), 12 part-time/adjunct (4 women). *Students:* 30 full-time (16 women), 20 part-time (15 women). In 2009, 10 master's, 3 doctorates awarded. *Degree requirements:* For master's, one foreign language, thesis; for doctorate, one foreign language, thesis/dissertation. *Entrance requirements:* Additional exam requirements/recommendations for international students: Required—TOEFL (minimum score 550 paper-based; 213 computer-based). *Application deadline:* For fall admission, 12/15 priority date for international students; for winter admission, 12/15 for domestic students. Applications are processed on a rolling basis. Electronic applications accepted. Tuition and fees charges are reported in Canadian dollars. *Expenses:* Tuition, area resident: Full-time $4626 Canadian dollars; part-time $99.72 Canadian dollars per unit. International tuition: $8216 Canadian dollars full-time. Required fees: $3590 Canadian dollars; $99.72 Canadian dollars per unit. $215 Canadian dollars per term. *Financial support:* In 2009–10, 8 fellowships with full tuition reimbursements (averaging $13,000 per year), 10 research assistantships with partial tuition reimbursements (averaging $4,000 per year), 10 teaching assistantships with partial tuition reimbursements (averaging $7,000 per year) were awarded; scholarships/grants also available. *Faculty research:* Classical/Indian and West African music, popular music, choral conducting, theory and composition, musicology, applied music. *Unit head:* Dr. H. Klumpenhouwer, Graduate Coordinator, 780-492-0603, Fax: 780-492-9246. *Application contact:* Information Contact, E-mail: musicgs@ualberta.ca.

The University of Arizona, Graduate College, College of Fine Arts, School of Music, Tucson, AZ 85721. Offers composition (MM, A Mus D); conducting (MM, A Mus D); music education (MM, PhD); music theory (MM, PhD); musicology (MM); performance (MM, A Mus D). *Accreditation:* NASD (one or more programs are accredited); NASM (one or more programs are accredited). Part-time programs available. *Faculty:* 42. *Students:* 117 full-time (47 women), 100 part-time (47 women); includes 4 Hispanic Americans, 49 international. Average age 32. 162 applicants, 48% accepted, 50 enrolled. In 2009, 19 master's, 15 doctorates awarded.

Degree requirements: For master's, thesis or alternative, orals; for doctorate, comprehensive exam, thesis/dissertation or alternative. *Entrance requirements:* For master's, 3 letters of recommendation; for doctorate, 3 letters of recommendation, statement of purpose. Additional exam requirements/recommendations for international students: Required—TOEFL (minimum score 550 paper-based; 213 computer-based; 79 iBT). *Application deadline:* For fall admission, 6/1 for domestic students, 12/1 for international students; for spring admission, 10/1 for domestic students, 6/1 for international students. Applications are processed on a rolling basis. Application fee: $75. Electronic applications accepted. *Expenses:* Tuition, state resident: full-time $9028. Tuition, nonresident: full-time $24,890. *Financial support:* In 2009–10, 51 teaching assistantships with full tuition reimbursements (averaging $12,473 per year) were awarded; career-related internships or fieldwork, institutionally sponsored loans, scholarships/grants, health care benefits, tuition waivers (full), and unspecified assistantships also available. Support available to part-time students. Financial award application deadline: 2/15; financial award applicants required to submit FAFSA. *Faculty research:* Music in general education, psychology of music learning, innovation in string music education, Zarzuela, Franz Liszt's work. Total annual research expenditures: $934. *Unit head:* Dr. Peter A. McAllister, Director, 520-621-7023, Fax: 520-621-1351, E-mail: pmcallis@email.arizona.edu. *Application contact:* Lyneen Elmore, 520-621-5929, Fax: 520-621-8118, E-mail: lyneen@u.arizona.edu.

The University of Arizona, Graduate College, College of Humanities, Department of English, Rhetoric, Composition and the Teaching of English Program, Tucson, AZ 85721. Offers PhD. *Students:* 8 full-time (7 women), 45 part-time (37 women); includes 3 minority (1 American Indian/Alaska Native, 2 Hispanic Americans), 2 international. Average age 34. 41 applicants, 15% accepted, 6 enrolled. In 2009, 17 doctorates awarded. *Degree requirements:* For doctorate, one foreign language, comprehensive exam, thesis/dissertation. *Entrance requirements:* For doctorate, GRE General Test, 3 letters of recommendation, writing sample. Additional exam requirements/recommendations for international students: Required—TOEFL (minimum score 550 paper-based; 213 computer-based; 79 iBT). *Application deadline:* Applications are processed on a rolling basis. Application fee: $75. Electronic applications accepted. *Expenses:* Tuition, state resident: full-time $9028. Tuition, nonresident: full-time $24,890. *Unit head:* Theresa Enos, Director, 520-621-3255, Fax: 520-621-7397, E-mail: enos@u.arizona.edu. *Application contact:* Alison Miller, Program Assistant, 520-621-7213, Fax: 520-621-7397, E-mail: admiller@u.arizona.edu.

University of Arkansas, Graduate School, J. William Fulbright College of Arts and Sciences, Department of Music, Fayetteville, AR 72701-1201. Offers MM. *Accreditation:* NASM. *Students:* 24 full-time (7 women), 7 part-time (3 women); includes 1 minority (African American), 5 international. In 2009, 14 master's awarded. *Entrance requirements:* For master's, GRE General Test. Application fee: $40 ($50 for international students). *Expenses:* Tuition, state resident: full-time $7355; part-time $356.58 per hour. Tuition, nonresident: full-time $17,401; part-time $775.17 per hour. Required fees: $1203. *Financial support:* In 2009–10, 8 research assistantships, 15 teaching assistantships were awarded; fellowships, career-related internships or fieldwork and Federal Work-Study also available. Support available to part-time students. Financial award application deadline: 4/1; financial award applicants required to submit FAFSA. *Unit head:* Dr. Ronda Mains, Department Chair, 479-575-4701, Fax: 479-575-5409, E-mail: rmains@uark.edu. *Application contact:* Dr. Stephen Gates, Graduate Coordinator, 479-575-4701, E-mail: sgates@uark.edu.

The University of British Columbia, Faculty of Arts and Faculty of Graduate Studies, School of Music, Vancouver, BC V6T 1Z2, Canada. Offers M Mus, MA, DMA, PhD. Part-time programs available. *Degree requirements:* For master's, recital (M Mus), thesis (MA); for doctorate, one foreign language, comprehensive exam, public performance or composition (DMA), dissertation (PhD). *Entrance requirements:* For master's, audition/performance (M Mus); for doctorate, audition/performance (DMA). Additional exam requirements/recommendations for international students: Required—TOEFL (minimum score 580 paper-based; 237 computer-based; 93 iBT). Electronic applications accepted. *Faculty research:* Performance, composition, opera, musicology, ethnomusicology, theory.

University of Calgary, Faculty of Graduate Studies, Faculty of Fine Arts, Department of Music, Calgary, AB T2N 1N4, Canada. Offers M Mus, MA, PhD. *Degree requirements:* For master's, one foreign language, thesis; for doctorate, 2 foreign languages, thesis/dissertation. *Entrance requirements:* For master's, audition (performance), 3 compositions. Additional exam requirements/recommendations for international students: Required—TOEFL. Electronic applications accepted. *Faculty research:* Musicology, theory and composition, performance and performance practice, teaching methodology, folk music collection and analyses.

University of California, Berkeley, Graduate Division, College of Letters and Science, Department of Music, Berkeley, CA 94720-1500. Offers composition (PhD); ethnomusicology (PhD); musicology (PhD). *Faculty:* 21 full-time, 53 part-time/adjunct. *Students:* 46 full-time (27 women). Average age 31. 190 applicants, 8 enrolled. *Degree requirements:* For doctorate, 2 foreign languages, thesis/dissertation, qualifying exam. *Entrance requirements:* For doctorate, GRE General Test, minimum GPA of 3.0, examples of work, 3 letters of recommendation. Additional exam requirements/recommendations for international students: Required—TOEFL (minimum score 570 paper-based; 230 computer-based). *Application deadline:* For fall admission, 12/15 for domestic students. Application fee: $70 ($90 for international students). *Financial support:* Fellowships with full tuition reimbursements, research assistantships, teaching assistantships with full tuition reimbursements, Federal Work-Study, institutionally sponsored loans, scholarships/grants, health care benefits, and unspecified assistantships available. Financial award applicants required to submit FAFSA. *Faculty research:* Historical musicology, music criticism, computer music. *Unit head:* Prof. Benjamin Brinner, Chair, 510-642-2678, Fax: 510-642-8480, E-mail: music@berkeley.edu. *Application contact:* Melissa Hacker, Student Affairs Officer, 510-642-2678, Fax: 510-642-8482, E-mail: melhacker@berkeley.edu.

University of California, Davis, Graduate Studies, Program in Music, Davis, CA 95616. Offers composition (MA, PhD); conducting (MA, PhD); musicology (MA, PhD). Terminal master's awarded for partial completion of doctoral program. *Degree requirements:* For master's, one foreign language, thesis; for doctorate, 2 foreign languages, thesis/dissertation. *Entrance requirements:* For master's, minimum GPA of 3.0; for doctorate, GRE, minimum GPA of 3.0. Additional exam requirements/recommendations for international students: Required—TOEFL (minimum score 550 paper-based; 213 computer-based). Electronic applications accepted.

University of California, Davis, Graduate Studies, Program in Performance Studies, Davis, CA 95616. Offers dramatic art (PhD). *Degree requirements:* For doctorate, 2 foreign languages, thesis/dissertation. *Entrance requirements:* For doctorate, GRE, minimum GPA of 3.25. Additional exam requirements/recommendations for international students: Required—TOEFL (minimum score 550 paper-based; 213 computer-based). Electronic applications accepted.

University of California, Irvine, Office of Graduate Studies, Claire Trevor School of the Arts, Department of Music, Irvine, CA 92697. Offers accompanying (MFA); choral conducting (MFA); composition and technology (MFA); guitar/lute performance (MFA); instrumental performance (MFA); jazz instrumental/composition (MFA); piano performance (MFA); vocal performance (MFA). *Students:* 20 full-time (3 women), 2 part-time (1 woman); includes 9 minority (1 African American, 1 American Indian/Alaska Native, 2 Asian Americans or Pacific Islanders, 5 Hispanic Americans), 2 international. Average age 28. 21 applicants, 67% accepted, 12 enrolled. In 2009, 13 master's awarded. *Degree requirements:* For master's, one foreign language, thesis. *Entrance requirements:* For master's, minimum GPA of 3.0. *Application deadline:* For fall admission, 1/15 priority date for domestic students, 1/15 for international students. Applications are processed on a rolling basis. Application fee: $70 ($90 for international students). Electronic applications accepted. *Financial support:* Fellowships, teaching assistantships, institutionally sponsored loans, traineeships, health care benefits, and unspecified assistantships available. Financial award application deadline: 3/1; financial award applicants required to submit FAFSA. *Faculty research:* Composition, instrumental and choral performance, African-American music, Italian baroque music and performance practice. *Unit head:* Dr. George C. Harvey, Chair, 949-824-6614, Fax: 949-824-4914, E-mail: gcharvey@uci.edu. *Application contact:* Sally L. Avila, Administrative Assistant, 949-824-6615, Fax: 949-824-4914, E-mail: slavila@uci.edu.

University of California, Los Angeles, Graduate Division, College of Letters and Science, Department of Musicology, Los Angeles, CA 90095. Offers MA, PhD. *Students:* 29 full-time (19 women); includes 3 minority (1 American Indian/Alaska Native, 2 Asian Americans or Pacific Islanders), 4 international. Average age 29. 42 applicants, 17% accepted, 5 enrolled. In 2009, 4 master's, 7 doctorates awarded. Terminal master's awarded for partial completion of doctoral program. *Degree requirements:* For master's, one foreign language, thesis; for doctorate, 2 foreign languages, thesis/dissertation, oral and written qualifying exams. *Entrance requirements:* For master's, minimum GPA of 3.0, sample of written work; for doctorate, minimum undergraduate GPA of 3.0, MA or equivalent in music, sample of written work. *Application deadline:* For fall admission, 12/1 for domestic and international students. Application fee: $70 ($90 for international students). Electronic applications accepted. *Financial support:* In 2009–10, 27 fellowships with full and partial tuition reimbursements, 6 research assistantships with full and partial tuition reimbursements, 23 teaching assistantships with full and partial tuition reimbursements were awarded; Federal Work-Study, health care benefits, tuition waivers (full and partial), and unspecified assistantships also available. Financial award application deadline: 3/1; financial award applicants required to submit FAFSA. *Unit head:* Dr. Robert Fink, Chair, 310-206-7549. *Application contact:* Department Office, 310-206-5187, E-mail: bvannost@humnet.ucla.edu.

University of California, Los Angeles, Graduate Division, School of the Arts and Architecture, Department of Ethnomusicology, Los Angeles, CA 90095. Offers MA, PhD. *Degree requirements:* For master's, one foreign language; for doctorate, 2 foreign languages, thesis/dissertation, oral and written qualifying exams. *Entrance requirements:* For master's, minimum GPA of 3.0, sample research paper, musical performance ability. Electronic applications accepted.

University of California, Los Angeles, Graduate Division, School of the Arts and Architecture, Department of Music, Los Angeles, CA 90095. Offers composition (MA, PhD); performance (MM, DMA). *Degree requirements:* For master's, one foreign language, thesis, final recital (MM), oral and written qualifying exams (MA); for doctorate, one foreign language, thesis/dissertation, oral/written qualifying exams; lecture recital (DMA); 2 foreign languages (PhD). *Entrance requirements:* For master's, departmental assessment exams, minimum GPA of 3.0, audition (MM); sample of work (MA); for doctorate, departmental assessment exams, minimum GPA of 3.0, audition (DMA); sample of work (PhD). Electronic applications accepted.

University of California, Riverside, Graduate Division, Department of Music, Riverside, CA 92521-0102. Offers composition (PhD); ethnomusicology (MA, PhD); musicology (PhD). *Faculty:* 9 full-time (2 women). *Students:* 29 full-time (11 women); includes 7 minority (3 Asian Americans or Pacific Islanders, 4 Hispanic Americans), 2 international. Average age 29. 54 applicants, 26% accepted, 5 enrolled. In 2009, 8 master's awarded. Terminal master's awarded for partial completion of doctoral program. *Degree requirements:* For master's, one foreign language, comprehensive exam, thesis (for some programs), oral exams; for doctorate, 2 foreign languages, comprehensive exam, thesis/dissertation, written and oral qualifying examination. *Entrance requirements:* For master's and doctorate, GRE General Test, minimum GPA of 3.2. Additional exam requirements/recommendations for international students: Required—TOEFL (minimum score 550 paper-based; 213 computer-based; 80 iBT). *Application deadline:* For fall admission, 5/1 for domestic and international students. Applications are processed on a rolling basis. Application fee: $70 ($85 for international students). Electronic applications accepted. *Financial support:* In 2009–10, 5 students received support, including 5 fellowships with full and partial tuition reimbursements available (averaging $12,000 per year), 2 teaching assistantships with partial tuition reimbursements available (averaging $16,500 per year); research assistantships, career-related internships or fieldwork, Federal Work-Study, institutionally sponsored loans, health care benefits, and tuition waivers (full and partial) also available. Financial award application deadline: 4/15; financial award applicants required to submit FAFSA. *Faculty research:* Composition, ethnomusicology (especially Southeast Asian and Asian-American music), cultural musicology, gender studies, performance practice. Total annual research expenditures: $60,695. *Unit head:* Dr. Deborah Wong, Chair, 951-827-3726, Fax: 951-827-4651, E-mail: deborah.wong@ucr.edu. *Application contact:* Dr. Tim Labor, Graduate Adviser, 951-827-5703, Fax: 951-827-4651, E-mail: timlabor@ucr.edu.

University of California, San Diego, Office of Graduate Studies, Department of Music, La Jolla, CA 92093. Offers MA, DMA, PhD. *Degree requirements:* For master's, thesis; for doctorate, thesis/dissertation. Electronic applications accepted. *Faculty research:* Computer music, extended instrumental techniques, comparison of brain wave resonances with musical resonances, composition, performance.

University of California, Santa Barbara, Graduate Division, College of Letters and Sciences, Division of Humanities and Fine Arts, Department of Music, Santa Barbara, CA 93106-6070. Offers brass (MM); composition (MA, PhD); conducting (MM, DMA); ethnomusicology (MA, PhD); feminist studies (PhD); keyboard (MM, DMA); musicology (MA, PhD); piano accompanying (MM); strings (MM, DMA); theory (MA, PhD); voice (MM, DMA); woodwinds (MM); MA/PhD; MM/DMA. *Faculty:* 28 full-time (6 women), 17 part-time/adjunct (6 women). *Students:* 71 full-time (34 women). Average age 30. 103 applicants, 31% accepted, 24 enrolled. In 2009, 13 master's, 11 doctorates awarded. Terminal master's awarded for partial completion of doctoral program. *Degree requirements:* For master's, variable foreign language requirement, comprehensive exam (for some programs), thesis (for some programs); for doctorate, variable foreign language requirement, comprehensive exam, thesis/dissertation. *Entrance requirements:* For master's, GRE, tape/audition, media (performance), portfolio (composition), writing sample, 3 letters of recommendation, resume/curriculum vitae; for doctorate, tape/audition (DMA), media (performance), portfolio (composition), writing sample, 3 letters of recommendation, statement of purpose, personal achievements/contributions statement, resume/curriculum vitae, transcripts for post-secondary institutions attended. Additional exam requirements/recommendations for international students: Required—TOEFL (minimum score 550 paper-based; 213 computer-based; 80 iBT) or IELTS (minimum score 7). Application fee: $70 ($90 for international students). Electronic applications accepted. *Financial support:* In 2009–10, 62 students received support, including 31 fellowships with full and partial tuition reimbursements available (averaging $7,700 per year), 2 research assistantships with full and partial tuition reimbursements available (averaging $6,200 per year), 42 teaching assistantships with partial tuition reimbursements available (averaging $8,500 per year); Federal Work-Study, institutionally sponsored loans, scholarships/grants, health care benefits, tuition waivers (full and partial), and unspecified assistantships also available. Financial award applicants required to submit FAFSA. *Faculty research:* Music theory, ethnomusicology, musicology, music performance, music composition. *Unit head:* Dr. Paul Berkowitz, Chair, Fax: 805-893-7194, E-mail: berkowit@music.ucsb.edu. *Application contact:* David L. Holmes, Student Affairs Officer, 805-893-4603, Fax: 805-893-7194, E-mail: dholmes@music.ucsb.edu.

University of California, Santa Cruz, Division of Graduate Studies, Division of the Arts, Department of Music, Santa Cruz, CA 95064. Offers music (MA, PhD); music composition (DMA). *Degree requirements:* For master's, one foreign language, thesis. *Entrance requirements:* For master's, GRE General Test. Electronic applications accepted. *Faculty research:* Western music history, new music, composition, ethnomusicology, musicology.

University of Central Arkansas, Graduate School, College of Fine Arts and Communication, Department of Music, Conway, AR 72035-0001. Offers choral conducting (MM); instrumental conducting (MM); music education (MM); music theory (MM); performance (MM). *Accreditation:* NASM. Part-time programs available. *Faculty:* 12 full-time (4 women), 1 part-time/adjunct (0 women). *Students:* 15 full-time (7 women), 2 part-time (both women); includes 4 minority (3 African Americans, 1 Asian American or Pacific Islander), 2 international. Average age 27. 10 applicants, 100% accepted, 8 enrolled. In 2009, 8 master's awarded. *Degree requirements:* For master's, comprehensive exam, thesis optional. *Entrance requirements:* For master's, GRE General Test, minimum GPA of 2.7. Additional exam requirements/recommendations for

Music

University of Central Arkansas (continued)
international students: Required—TOEFL (minimum score 550 paper-based; 213 computer-based). *Application deadline:* For fall admission, 3/1 priority date for domestic students; for spring admission, 10/1 priority date for domestic students. Applications are processed on a rolling basis. Application fee: $25 ($50 for international students). *Expenses:* Tuition, state resident: full-time $5136; part-time $214 per credit hour. Required fees: $379.50; $127 per term. Tuition and fees vary according to course level, course load and campus/location. *Financial support:* Federal Work-Study, scholarships/grants, tuition waivers (partial), and unspecified assistantships available. Financial award application deadline: 2/15; financial award applicants required to submit FAFSA. *Unit head:* Jeffrey Jarvis, Unit Head, 501-450-3163. *Application contact:* Brenda Herring, Admissions Assistant, 501-450-5065, Fax: 501-450-5678, E-mail: bherring@uca.edu.

University of Central Florida, College of Arts and Humanities, Department of Music, Orlando, FL 32816. Offers MA. *Accreditation:* NASM; NCATE. Part-time and evening/weekend programs available. *Faculty:* 28 full-time (4 women), 17 part-time/adjunct (10 women). *Students:* 17 full-time (6 women), 16 part-time (8 women); includes 3 minority (1 Asian American or Pacific Islander, 2 Hispanic Americans), 1 international. Average age 32. 25 applicants, 68% accepted, 15 enrolled. In 2009, 10 master's awarded. *Entrance requirements:* For master's, GRE General Test. Additional exam requirements/recommendations for international students: Required—TOEFL. *Application deadline:* For fall admission, 7/15 for domestic students; for spring admission, 12/1 for domestic students. Application fee: $30. Electronic applications accepted. *Expenses:* Tuition, state resident: part-time $306.31 per credit hour. Tuition, nonresident: part-time $1099.01 per credit hour. Part-time tuition and fees vary according to degree level and program. *Financial support:* In 2009–10, 7 students received support, including 1 fellowship with partial tuition reimbursement available (averaging $10,000 per year), 1 research assistantship (averaging $3,900 per year), 6 teaching assistantships with partial tuition reimbursements available (averaging $10,000 per year); career-related internships or fieldwork, Federal Work-Study, institutionally sponsored loans, tuition waivers (partial), and unspecified assistantships also available. Financial award application deadline: 3/1; financial award applicants required to submit FAFSA. *Unit head:* Jeffrey Moore, Chair, 407-823-2879, Fax: 407-823-3378, E-mail: jmmoore@mail.ucf.edu. *Application contact:* Jeffrey Moore, Chair, 407-823-2879, Fax: 407-823-3378, E-mail: jmmoore@mail.ucf.edu.

University of Central Missouri, The Graduate School, College of Arts, Humanities and Social Sciences, Warrensburg, MO 64093. Offers English (MA); history (MA); mass communication (MA); music (MA); psychology (MS); speech communication (MA); teaching english as a second language (MA); theatre (MA). Part-time programs available. *Faculty:* 82. *Students:* 60 full-time (35 women), 101 part-time (61 women); includes 11 minority (5 African Americans, 3 Asian Americans or Pacific Islanders, 3 Hispanic Americans), 17 international. Average age 30. 80 applicants, 80% accepted, 58 enrolled. In 2009, 51 master's awarded. *Entrance requirements:* Additional exam requirements/recommendations for international students: Required—TOEFL (minimum score 550 paper-based; 79 computer-based). *Application deadline:* For fall admission, 6/1 priority date for domestic students, 5/1 for international students; for spring admission, 10/1 priority date for domestic students, 10/1 for international students. Applications are processed on a rolling basis. Application fee: $30 ($75 for international students). Electronic applications accepted. *Expenses:* Tuition, area resident: Part-time $245.80 per credit hour. Tuition, nonresident: part-time $491.60 per credit hour. Required fees: $24.20 per credit hour. Full-time tuition and fees vary according to course load, degree level, campus/location and reciprocity agreements. *Financial support:* Research assistantships with full and partial tuition reimbursements, teaching assistantships with full and partial tuition reimbursements, career-related internships or fieldwork, Federal Work-Study, scholarships/grants, and administrative and laboratory assistantships available. Support available to part-time students. Financial award application deadline: 3/1; financial award applicants required to submit FAFSA. *Unit head:* Dr. Gersham Nelson, Dean, 660-543-4750, Fax: 660-543-8271, E-mail: nelson@ucmo.edu. *Application contact:* Laurie Delap, Admissions Coordinator, 660-543-4621, Fax: 660-543-4778, E-mail: gradinfo@ucmo.edu.

University of Central Oklahoma, College of Graduate Studies and Research, College of Arts, Media, and Design, Department of Music, Edmond, OK 73034-5209. Offers music education (MM); performance (MM). *Accreditation:* NASM. Part-time programs available. *Entrance requirements:* Additional exam requirements/recommendations for international students: Required—TOEFL (minimum score 550 paper-based; 213 computer-based). Electronic applications accepted. *Expenses:* Tuition, state resident: full-time $4128; part-time $172 per credit hour. Tuition, nonresident: full-time $10,373; part-time $432.20 per credit hour. Required fees: $433.20; $18.05 per credit hour. *Faculty research:* Opera/orchestral composition, western/world music, ethnomusicology, literature for librettos.

University of Chicago, Division of the Humanities, Department of Music, Chicago, IL 60637-1513. Offers AM, PhD. *Degree requirements:* For master's, 2 foreign languages, thesis; for doctorate, 3 foreign languages, thesis/dissertation. *Entrance requirements:* For master's and doctorate, GRE General Test. Additional exam requirements/recommendations for international students: Required—TOEFL.

University of Cincinnati, Graduate School, College-Conservatory of Music, Division of Composition, Musicology and Theory, Cincinnati, OH 45221. Offers composition (MM, DMA); music history (MM); music theory (MM, PhD); musicology (PhD). *Accreditation:* NASM. *Degree requirements:* For master's, variable foreign language requirement, comprehensive exam, thesis; for doctorate, variable foreign language requirement, comprehensive exam, thesis/dissertation. *Entrance requirements:* For master's and doctorate, GRE General Test, interview. Additional exam requirements/recommendations for international students: Required—TOEFL (minimum score 520 paper-based; 190 computer-based). Electronic applications accepted.

University of Cincinnati, Graduate School, College-Conservatory of Music, Division of Ensembles and Conducting, Cincinnati, OH 45221. Offers choral conducting (MM, DMA); orchestral conducting (MM, DMA); wind conducting (MM, DMA). *Accreditation:* NASM. *Degree requirements:* For master's, comprehensive exam, conducting performances; for doctorate, one foreign language, comprehensive exam, thesis/dissertation, conducting performances, lecture recital. *Entrance requirements:* For master's and doctorate, GRE General Test, audition, interview. Additional exam requirements/recommendations for international students: Required—TOEFL (minimum score 520 paper-based; 190 computer-based). Electronic applications accepted.

University of Cincinnati, Graduate School, College-Conservatory of Music, Division of Keyboard Studies, Cincinnati, OH 45221. Offers MM, DMA, AD. *Degree requirements:* For master's, comprehensive exam; for doctorate, one foreign language, comprehensive exam, thesis/dissertation. *Entrance requirements:* For master's and doctorate, GRE General Test, audition; for AD, audition. Additional exam requirements/recommendations for international students: Required—TOEFL (minimum score 520 paper-based; 190 computer-based). Electronic applications accepted.

University of Cincinnati, Graduate School, College-Conservatory of Music, Division of Performance Studies, Cincinnati, OH 45221. Offers performance (MM, DMA, AD). MM, DMA, and AD are available for every instrument. *Accreditation:* NASM. *Degree requirements:* For master's, comprehensive exam, recitals; for doctorate, one foreign language, comprehensive exam, thesis/dissertation, recitals; for AD, recitals. *Entrance requirements:* For master's and doctorate, GRE General Test, audition. Additional exam requirements/recommendations for international students: Required—TOEFL (minimum score 520 paper-based; 190 computer-based). Electronic applications accepted. *Faculty research:* Performance, guest teaching.

University of Cincinnati, Graduate School, College-Conservatory of Music, Divisions of Opera, Musical Theater, Drama, and Arts Administration, Cincinnati, OH 45221. Offers arts administration (MA); directing (MFA); theater design and production (MFA); voice and opera (MM, DMA); MBA/MA. *Accreditation:* NAST (one or more programs are accredited). *Degree requirements:* For master's, final project. *Entrance requirements:* For master's, GMAT (MA), audition/interview. Additional exam requirements/recommendations for international students: Required—TOEFL (minimum score 520 paper-based; 190 computer-based). Electronic applications accepted.

University of Colorado at Boulder, Graduate School, College of Music, Boulder, CO 80309. Offers composition (M Mus, D Mus A); conducting (M Mus); instrumental conducting and literature (D Mus A); literature and performance of choral music (D Mus A); music education (M Mus Ed, PhD); musicology (PhD); performance (M Mus, D Mus A); performance/pedagogy (M Mus, D Mus A); theory (M Mus). *Accreditation:* NASM. *Faculty:* 55 full-time (19 women). *Students:* 194 full-time (108 women), 56 part-time (30 women); includes 25 minority (3 African Americans, 1 American Indian/Alaska Native, 10 Asian Americans or Pacific Islanders, 11 Hispanic Americans), 28 international. Average age 30. 440 applicants, 32% accepted, 67 enrolled. In 2009, 53 master's, 25 doctorates awarded. Terminal master's awarded for partial completion of doctoral program. *Degree requirements:* For master's, variable foreign language requirement, comprehensive exam, thesis or alternative, recital; for doctorate, variable foreign language requirement, thesis/dissertation. *Entrance requirements:* For master's, GRE General Test, GRE Subject Test (music literature), minimum undergraduate GPA of 2.75; for doctorate, GRE General Test, GRE Subject Test, audition, sample of research. *Application deadline:* For fall admission, 3/1 priority date for domestic students, 12/1 for international students. Applications are processed on a rolling basis. Application fee: $50 ($60 for international students). *Financial support:* In 2009–10, 88 fellowships (averaging $3,325 per year), 38 research assistantships (averaging $6,550 per year) were awarded; tuition waivers (full) also available. Financial award application deadline: 3/1. Total annual research expenditures: $22,375.

University of Colorado Denver, College of Arts and Media, Program in Recording Arts, Denver, CO 80217-3364. Offers MS. *Accreditation:* NASM. Part-time and evening/weekend programs available. *Students:* 12 full-time (1 woman), 1 part-time (0 women); includes 1 minority (Hispanic American). 24 applicants, 46% accepted, 9 enrolled. In 2009, 6 master's awarded. *Degree requirements:* For master's, thesis or alternative. *Entrance requirements:* For master's, GRE General Test, minimum GPA of 2.75, portfolio, resume, interview, 3 letters of recommendation. Additional exam requirements/recommendations for international students: Required—TOEFL (minimum score 500 paper-based; 173 computer-based). *Application deadline:* For fall admission, 6/1 for domestic students; for spring admission, 11/1 for domestic students. Applications are processed on a rolling basis. Application fee: $50 ($75 for international students). Electronic applications accepted. *Financial support:* Federal Work-Study, institutionally sponsored loans, and scholarships/grants available. Support available to part-time students. Financial award application deadline: 4/1; financial award applicants required to submit FAFSA. *Unit head:* Dr. David Dynak, Dean, 303-556-2279, E-mail: david.dynak@cudenver.edu. *Application contact:* Clark Strickland, Assistant Dean for Programs and Resources, 303-556-2279, E-mail: clark.strickland@cudenver.edu.

University of Connecticut, Graduate School, School of Fine Arts, Department of Music, Storrs, CT 06269. Offers conducting (M Mus, DMA); historical musicology (MA); music (Performer's Certificate); music education (M Mus, PhD); music theory (MA); music theory and history (PhD); performance (M Mus, DMA). *Accreditation:* NASM. *Faculty:* 19 full-time (5 women). *Students:* 38 full-time (19 women), 25 part-time (12 women); includes 5 minority (1 African American, 1 American Indian/Alaska Native, 1 Asian American or Pacific Islander, 2 Hispanic Americans), 9 international. Average age 32. 60 applicants, 33% accepted, 11 enrolled. In 2009, 13 master's, 6 doctorates, 4 other advanced degrees awarded. Terminal master's awarded for partial completion of doctoral program. *Degree requirements:* For master's, comprehensive exam; for doctorate, thesis/dissertation. *Entrance requirements:* For master's, GRE General Test, GRE Subject Test, audition; for doctorate, GRE Subject Test, MAT, audition. Additional exam requirements/recommendations for international students: Required—TOEFL (minimum score 550 paper-based; 213 computer-based). *Application deadline:* For fall admission, 2/1 priority date for domestic and international students; for spring admission, 11/1 for domestic students, 10/1 for international students. Application fee: $55. *Expenses:* Tuition, state resident: full-time $4725; part-time $525 per credit. Tuition, nonresident: full-time $12,267; part-time $1363 per credit. Required fees: $346 per semester. Tuition and fees vary according to course load. *Financial support:* In 2009–10, 9 research assistantships with full tuition reimbursements, 25 teaching assistantships with full tuition reimbursements were awarded; fellowships, Federal Work-Study, health care benefits, and unspecified assistantships also available. Financial award application deadline: 2/1; financial award applicants required to submit FAFSA. *Unit head:* Karla Fox, Head, 860-486-1361, E-mail: karla.fox@uconn.edu. *Application contact:* David Maker, Associate Head, 860-486-1617, E-mail: david.maker@uconn.edu.

University of Delaware, College of Arts and Sciences, Department of Music, Newark, DE 19716. Offers composition (MM); music education (MM); performance (MM). *Accreditation:* NASM. Part-time programs available. *Entrance requirements:* For master's, audition. Additional exam requirements/recommendations for international students: Required—TOEFL. Electronic applications accepted. *Faculty research:* Teaching of music.

University of Denver, Division of Arts, Humanities and Social Sciences, Lamont School of Music, Denver, CO 80208. Offers composition (MA); conducting (MA); jazz and commercial music (Certificate); music (MM); music education (MA); music history and literature (MA); Orff-Schulwerk (MA); performance (MA); piano pedagogy (MA); Suzuki pedagogy (MA); Suzuki teaching (Certificate); theory (MA). *Accreditation:* NASM. Part-time programs available. *Faculty:* 27 full-time (9 women), 37 part-time/adjunct (16 women). *Students:* 19 full-time (8 women), 45 part-time (27 women); includes 5 minority (2 African Americans, 2 Asian Americans or Pacific Islanders, 1 Hispanic American), 6 international. Average age 28. 85 applicants, 69% accepted, 39 enrolled. In 2009, 20 master's, 2 other advanced degrees awarded. *Degree requirements:* For master's, thesis (for some programs), recital or project, 2 years language (performance, music history and literature). *Entrance requirements:* For master's, GRE General Test, music history and theory qualifying exams. Additional exam requirements/recommendations for international students: Required—TOEFL. *Application deadline:* Applications are processed on a rolling basis. Application fee: $50. Electronic applications accepted. *Expenses:* Tuition: Full-time $34,596; part-time $961 per quarter hour. Required fees: $4 per quarter hour. Tuition and fees vary according to course load, campus/location and program. *Financial support:* In 2009–10, 37 teaching assistantships with full and partial tuition reimbursements (averaging $4,500 per year) were awarded; career-related internships or fieldwork, Federal Work-Study, institutionally sponsored loans, and scholarships/grants also available. Support available to part-time students. Financial award application deadline: 4/15; financial award applicants required to submit FAFSA. *Unit head:* Joseph Docksey, Director, 303-871-6986. *Application contact:* Information Contact, 303-871-6400.

University of Florida, Graduate School, College of Fine Arts, School of Music, Gainesville, FL 32611. Offers choral conducting (MM, PhD); composition/theory (MM, PhD); ethnomusicology (PhD); instrumental conducting (MM, PhD); music (MM, PhD); music education (MM, PhD); music history and literature (MM); musicology (PhD); performance (MM); sacred music (MM). *Accreditation:* NASM. *Degree requirements:* For master's, variable foreign language requirement, thesis; for doctorate, thesis/dissertation. *Entrance requirements:* For master's and doctorate, audition, GRE General Test or minimum GPA of 3.0. Additional exam requirements/recommendations for international students: Required—TOEFL (minimum score 550 paper-based; 213 computer-based). Electronic applications accepted.

University of Georgia, Graduate School, College of Arts and Sciences, Hugh Hodgson School of Music, Athens, GA 30602. Offers MA, MM, DMA, PhD. *Accreditation:* NASM. *Faculty:* 35 full-time (9 women), 1 part-time/adjunct (0 women). *Students:* 99 full-time (47 women), 26 part-time (11 women); includes 12 minority (5 African Americans, 5 Asian Americans or Pacific Islanders, 2 Hispanic Americans), 15 international. 124 applicants, 60% accepted, 36 enrolled. In 2009, 21 master's, 16 doctorates awarded. *Degree requirements:* For master's, variable foreign language requirement, thesis (MA); for doctorate, variable foreign language requirement, thesis/dissertation. *Entrance requirements:* For master's and doctorate, GRE General Test. *Application deadline:* For fall admission, 7/1 priority date for domestic students; for spring admission, 11/15 for domestic students. Application fee: $50. Electronic applications accepted. *Expenses:* Tuition, state resident: full-time $6000; part-time $250 per credit hour. Tuition, nonresident: full-time $20,904; part-time $871 per credit hour. Required fees: $730 per semester. *Financial support:* Fellowships, research assistantships, teaching assistantships, unspecified assistantships available. *Unit head:* Dr. Donald R. Lowe, Director, 706-542-2276, Fax: 706-542-2773, E-mail: dlowe@uga.edu. *Application contact:* Dr. Kenneth M. Fischer, Graduate Coordinator, 206-542-2743, E-mail: kfischer@uga.edu.

University of Hartford, The Hartt School, West Hartford, CT 06117-1599. Offers choral conducting (MM Ed); composition (MM, DMA, Artist Diploma, Diploma); conducting (MM, DMA, Artist Diploma, Diploma), including choral (MM, Diploma), instrumental (MM, Diploma); early childhood education (MM Ed); instrumental conducting (MM Ed); Kodály (MM Ed); music (CAGS); music education (DMA, PhD); music history (MM); music theory (MM); pedagogy (MM Ed); performance (MM, MM Ed, DMA, Artist Diploma, Diploma); research (MM Ed); technology (MM Ed). Part-time programs available. *Degree requirements:* For master's, variable foreign language requirement, thesis (for some programs), recital; for doctorate, variable foreign language requirement, thesis/dissertation (for some programs), recital; for other advanced degree, recital. *Entrance requirements:* For master's, audition, letters of recommendation; for doctorate, proficiency exam, audition, interview, research paper; for other advanced degree, audition. Additional exam requirements/recommendations for international students: Required—TOEFL. Electronic applications accepted. *Expenses:* Contact institution.

University of Hawaii at Manoa, Graduate Division, College of Arts and Humanities, Department of Music, Honolulu, HI 96822. Offers M Mus, MA, PhD. *Accreditation:* NASM. Part-time programs available. *Faculty:* 17 full-time (5 women), 5 part-time/adjunct (3 women). *Students:* 34 full-time (16 women), 14 part-time (5 women); includes 14 minority (1 American Indian/Alaska Native, 13 Asian Americans or Pacific Islanders), 6 international. Average age 31. 34 applicants, 53% accepted, 12 enrolled. In 2009, 16 master's, 3 doctorates awarded. *Degree requirements:* For master's, variable foreign language requirement, thesis optional; for doctorate, variable foreign language requirement, comprehensive exam, thesis/dissertation. *Entrance requirements:* For master's, GRE General Test, diagnostic exams in acoustics theory; for doctorate, diagnostic exams in music history and theory, GRE General Test. Additional exam requirements/recommendations for international students: Required—TOEFL (minimum score 540 paper-based; 207 computer-based; 76 iBT), IELTS (minimum score 5). *Application deadline:* For fall admission, 2/1 for domestic students, 1/15 for international students; for spring admission, 9/1 for domestic students, 8/1 for international students. Application fee: $60. *Expenses:* Tuition, state resident: full-time $8900; part-time $372 per credit. Tuition, nonresident: full-time $21,400; part-time $898 per credit. Required fees: $207 per semester. *Financial support:* In 2009–10, 2 students received support, including 16 fellowships (averaging $2,192 per year), 1 research assistantship (averaging $15,558 per year), 7 teaching assistantships (averaging $15,219 per year); Federal Work-Study and tuition waivers (full) also available. *Faculty research:* Original compositions, nineteenth century German music, Korean and Indonesian music, piano/voice performance, Pacific music. *Application contact:* Lesley Wright, Graduate Field Chairperson, 808-956-7756, Fax: 808-956-9657, E-mail: wright@hawaii.edu.

University of Houston, College of Liberal Arts and Social Sciences, Moores School of Music, Houston, TX 77204. Offers MM, DMA. *Accreditation:* NASM. Part-time programs available. *Faculty:* 30 full-time (6 women), 20 part-time/adjunct (8 women). *Students:* 108 full-time (53 women), 44 part-time (23 women); includes 25 minority (6 African Americans, 1 American Indian/Alaska Native, 9 Asian Americans or Pacific Islanders, 9 Hispanic Americans), 28 international. Average age 30. 119 applicants, 50% accepted, 36 enrolled. In 2009, 43 master's, 9 doctorates awarded. *Degree requirements:* For master's, one foreign language, comprehensive exam, recital; for doctorate, one foreign language, comprehensive exam, thesis/dissertation. *Entrance requirements:* For master's, audition, resume, 3 letter of recommendation; for doctorate, Writing sample, audition, statement of purpose, resume. Additional exam requirements/recommendations for international students: Required—TOEFL (minimum score 550 paper-based; 213 computer-based; 79 iBT). *Application deadline:* For fall admission, 2/22 for domestic and international students; for spring admission, 10/13 for domestic and international students. Application fee: $0 ($75 for international students). Electronic applications accepted. *Expenses:* Tuition, state resident: full-time $7676; part-time $320 per credit hour. Tuition, nonresident: full-time $14,324; part-time $597 per credit hour. Required fees: $3034. *Financial support:* In 2009–10, 8 teaching assistantships with full tuition reimbursements (averaging $9,800 per year) were awarded; career-related internships or fieldwork, Federal Work-Study, institutionally sponsored loans, scholarships/grants, health care benefits, and unspecified assistantships also available. Support available to part-time students. Financial award application deadline: 2/1. *Faculty research:* Twentieth century music, Baroque music, history of music theory, music analysis. *Unit head:* David Ashley White, Chairperson, 713-743-3009, Fax: 713-743-3166, E-mail: daw@orpheus.music.uh.edu. *Application contact:* Douglas Goldberg, Graduate Advisor, 713-743-3314, Fax: 713-743-3166, E-mail: gradmusic@uh.edu.

University of Idaho, College of Graduate Studies, College of Letters, Arts and Social Sciences, Lionel Hampton School of Music, Moscow, ID 83844-2282. Offers M Mus, MA. *Accreditation:* NASM. *Faculty:* 21 full-time, 3 part-time/adjunct. *Students:* 17 full-time, 3 part-time. In 2009, 8 master's awarded. *Degree requirements:* For master's, one foreign language, thesis or alternative. *Entrance requirements:* For master's, minimum GPA of 2.8. *Application deadline:* For fall admission, 8/1 for domestic students; for spring admission, 12/15 for domestic students. Application fee: $55 ($60 for international students). *Expenses:* Tuition, state resident: full-time $6120. Tuition, nonresident: full-time $17,712. *Financial support:* Research assistantships, teaching assistantships available. Financial award application deadline: 2/15. *Unit head:* Dr. Kevin B. Woelfel, Director, 208-885-6231. *Application contact:* Dr. Kevin B. Woelfel, Director, 208-885-6231.

University of Illinois at Urbana–Champaign, Graduate College, College of Fine and Applied Arts, School of Music, Champaign, IL 61820. Offers music (M Mus, DMA, AD); music education (MME, Ed D, PhD); musicology (PhD). *Accreditation:* NASM. *Faculty:* 68 full-time (11 women), 6 part-time/adjunct (2 women). *Students:* 282 full-time (133 women), 94 part-time (59 women); includes 27 minority (7 African Americans, 1 American Indian/Alaska Native, 10 Asian Americans or Pacific Islanders, 9 Hispanic Americans), 136 international. 551 applicants, 39% accepted, 105 enrolled. In 2009, 69 master's, 50 doctorates awarded. *Entrance requirements:* For master's and doctorate, minimum GPA of 3.0. Additional exam requirements/recommendations for international students: Required—TOEFL (minimum score 590 paper-based; 243 computer-based). *Application deadline:* Applications are processed on a rolling basis. Application fee: $60 ($75 for international students). Electronic applications accepted. *Financial support:* In 2009–10, 29 fellowships, 9 research assistantships, 120 teaching assistantships were awarded; tuition waivers (full and partial) also available. *Unit head:* Karl Kramer, Director, 217-244-2676, Fax: 217-244-4585, E-mail: kramerk@illinois.edu. *Application contact:* Jennifer Phillips, Office Manager, 217-244-8385, Fax: 217-244-4585, E-mail: jhorn@illinois.edu.

The University of Iowa, Graduate College, College of Liberal Arts and Sciences, School of Music, Iowa City, IA 52242-1316. Offers MA, MFA, DMA, PhD. *Accreditation:* NASM. *Degree requirements:* For master's, thesis (for some programs), exam; for doctorate, comprehensive exam, thesis/dissertation. *Entrance requirements:* For master's and doctorate, minimum GPA of 3.0. Additional exam requirements/recommendations for international students: Required—TOEFL (minimum score 550 paper-based; 213 computer-based; 81 iBT). Electronic applications accepted.

The University of Kansas, Graduate Studies, School of Music, Program in Music, Lawrence, KS 66045. Offers MM, DMA, PhD. *Accreditation:* NASM. *Students:* 127 full-time (66 women), 27 part-time (12 women); includes 19 minority (3 African Americans, 1 American Indian/Alaska Native, 5 Asian Americans or Pacific Islanders, 10 Hispanic Americans), 28 international. Average age 30. 143 applicants, 56% accepted, 45 enrolled. In 2009, 19 master's, 12 doctorates awarded. *Degree requirements:* For master's, comprehensive exam (for some programs), thesis (for some programs), recitals; for doctorate, comprehensive exam, thesis/dissertation, recitals (DMA). *Entrance requirements:* For master's, KU Musicology and Music Theory diagnostic exam, minimum GPA of 3.0, audition (performance); for doctorate, GRE (PhD); KU Musicology and Music Theory diagnostic exam, minimum GPA of 3.0, audition (DMA). Additional exam requirements/recommendations for international students: Required—TOEFL or IELTS (minimum score 6). *Application deadline:* For fall admission, 12/15 priority date for domestic and international students; for spring admission, 5/15 priority date for domestic and international students. Applications are processed on a rolling basis. Application fee: $45 ($55 for international students). Electronic applications accepted. *Expenses:* Tuition, state resident: full-time $6492; part-time $270.50 per credit hour. Tuition, nonresident: full-time $15,510; part-time $646.25 per credit hour. Required fees: $847; $70.56 per credit hour. Tuition and fees vary according to course load and program. *Financial support:* Fellowships with full tuition reimbursements, research assistantships with partial tuition reimbursements, teaching assistantships with full and partial tuition reimbursements, institutionally sponsored loans, scholarships/grants, and unspecified assistantships available. Financial award application deadline: 12/15; financial award applicants required to submit FAFSA. *Faculty research:* Musicology, music theory, church music, music composition, performance. *Unit head:* Dr. Lawrence Mallett, 785-864-3436, Fax: 785-864-5866, E-mail: music@ku.edu. *Application contact:* Director of Graduate Studies, 785-864-9699, Fax: 785-864-5866, E-mail: choir@ku.edu.

University of Kentucky, Graduate School, College of Fine Arts, Program in Music, Lexington, KY 40506-0032. Offers music (PhD); music composition (MM); music education (MM); music performance (MM); music theory (MA); musical arts (DMA); musicology (MA). *Accreditation:* NASM. Part-time and evening/weekend programs available. *Degree requirements:* For master's, variable foreign language requirement, comprehensive exam, thesis (for some programs); for doctorate, variable foreign language requirement, comprehensive exam, thesis/dissertation. *Entrance requirements:* For master's, GRE General Test, minimum undergraduate GPA of 2.75; for doctorate, GRE General Test, minimum undergraduate GPA of 2.75, graduate 3.0. Additional exam requirements/recommendations for international students: Required—TOEFL (minimum score 550 paper-based; 213 computer-based). Electronic applications accepted. *Faculty research:* Musicology, music theory, jazz, music education, performance and conducting.

University of Lethbridge, School of Graduate Studies, Lethbridge, AB T1K 3M4, Canada. Offers accounting (MScM); addictions counseling (M Sc); agricultural biotechnology (M Sc); agricultural studies (M Sc, MA); anthropology (MA); archaeology (MA); art (MA, MFA); biochemistry (M Sc); biological sciences (M Sc); biomolecular science (PhD); biosystems and biodiversity (PhD); Canadian studies (MA); chemistry (M Sc); computer science (M Sc); computer science and geographical information science (M Sc); counseling psychology (M Ed); dramatic arts (MA); earth, space, and physical science (PhD); economics (MA); educational leadership (M Ed); English (MA); environmental science (M Sc); evolution and behavior (PhD); exercise science (M Sc); finance (MScM); French (MA); French/German (MA); French/Spanish (MA); general education (M Ed); general management (MScM); geography (M Sc, MA); German (MA); health science (M Sc); health sciences (MA); history (MA); human resource management and labour relations (MScM); individualized multidisciplinary (M Sc, MA); information systems (MScM); international management (MScM); kinesiology (M Sc, MA); management (M Sc, MA); marketing (MScM); mathematics (M Sc); music (M Mus, MA); Native American studies (MA); neuroscience (M Sc, PhD); new media (MA); nursing (M Sc); philosophy (MA); physics (M Sc); policy and strategy (MScM); political science (MA); psychology (M Sc, MA); religious studies (MA); social sciences (MA); sociology (MA); theatre and dramatic arts (MFA); theoretical and computational science (PhD); urban and regional studies (MA); women's studies (MA). Part-time and evening/weekend programs available. *Degree requirements:* For doctorate, comprehensive exam, thesis/dissertation. *Entrance requirements:* For master's, GMAT (M Sc in management), bachelor's degree in related field, minimum GPA of 3.0 during previous 20 graded semester courses, 2 years teaching or related experience (M Ed); for doctorate, master's degree, minimum graduate GPA of 3.5. Additional exam requirements/recommendations for international students: Required—TOEFL. *Faculty research:* Movement and brain plasticity, gibberellin physiology, photosynthesis, carbon cycling, molecular properties of main-group ring components.

University of Louisiana at Lafayette, College of the Arts, School of Music, Lafayette, LA 70504. Offers conducting (MM); pedagogy (MM); vocal and instrumental performance (MM). *Accreditation:* NASM. *Degree requirements:* For master's, thesis or alternative. *Entrance requirements:* For master's, GRE General Test, minimum GPA of 2.75. Additional exam requirements/recommendations for international students: Required—TOEFL (minimum score 550 paper-based; 213 computer-based). Electronic applications accepted. *Faculty research:* Nineteenth century American music, trumpet pedagogy, fifteenth century Renaissance polyphony, Charles Ives.

University of Louisiana at Monroe, Graduate School, College of Arts and Sciences, School of Visual and Performing Arts, Program in Music, Monroe, LA 71209-0001. Offers MM. *Accreditation:* NASM. Part-time programs available. *Faculty:* 10 full-time (3 women). *Students:* 9 full-time (2 women), 6 part-time (1 woman); includes 3 minority (1 African American, 2 Hispanic Americans), 1 international. Average age 29. In 2009, 6 master's awarded. *Degree requirements:* For master's, thesis (for some programs). *Entrance requirements:* For master's, GRE, minimum GPA of 2.5. Additional exam requirements/recommendations for international students: Required—TOEFL (minimum score 500 paper-based; 173 computer-based; 61 iBT). *Application deadline:* For fall admission, 8/24 priority date for domestic students, 7/1 for international students; for winter admission, 12/14 priority date for domestic students; for spring admission, 1/19 for domestic students, 11/1 for international students. Applications are processed on a rolling basis. Application fee: $20 ($30 for international students). Electronic applications accepted. *Expenses:* Tuition, state resident: part-time $159 per credit hour. Tuition, nonresident: part-time $159 per credit hour. Required fees: $1300 per year. Tuition and fees vary according to course load. *Financial support:* In 2009–10, 6 teaching assistantships with full tuition reimbursements (averaging $2,500 per year) were awarded; career-related internships or fieldwork, Federal Work-Study, and unspecified assistantships also available. Financial award application deadline: 4/1; financial award applicants required to submit FAFSA. *Unit head:* Dr. Mark R. Clark, Dean, 318-342-1569, Fax: 318-342-1599, E-mail: mclark@ulm.edu. *Application contact:* Dr. Mark R. Clark, Dean, 318-342-1569, Fax: 318-342-1599, E-mail: mclark@ulm.edu.

University of Louisville, Graduate School, School of Music, Louisville, KY 40292-0001. Offers music composition (MM); music education (MME); music history and literature (MM); music theory (MM); performance (MM). *Accreditation:* NASM. Part-time and evening/weekend programs available. *Faculty:* 33 full-time (10 women), 38 part-time/adjunct (10 women). *Students:* 52 full-time (17 women), 9 part-time (6 women); includes 7 minority (4 African Americans, 3 Hispanic Americans), 9 international. Average age 28. 75 applicants, 56% accepted, 28 enrolled. In 2009, 25 master's awarded. *Degree requirements:* For master's, one foreign language, thesis (for some programs), recital (performance), paper (music education), major composition (composition). *Entrance requirements:* For master's, GRE General Test, music history and theory exam, jazz exam, audition, portfolio. Additional exam requirements/recommendations for international students: Required—TOEFL (minimum score 550 paper-based; 213 computer-based; 79 iBT). *Application deadline:* For fall admission, 3/15 priority date for domestic and international students; for spring admission, 11/15 priority date for domestic and international students. Applications are processed on a rolling basis. Application fee: $50. *Financial support:* In 2009–10, 50 students received support, including 4 fellowships with full tuition reimbursements available (averaging $12,000 per year), 24 teaching assistantships with full tuition reimbursements available (averaging $12,000 per year); scholarships/grants, health care benefits, tuition waivers (full and partial), and unspecified assistantships also available. Financial award application deadline: 3/15; financial award applicants required to submit FAFSA. *Faculty research:* Performance, composition, music education, music therapy, music history. *Unit head:* Dr. Christopher Doane, Dean, 502-852-6907, Fax: 502-852-1874,

Music

University of Louisville (continued)

E-mail: doane@louisville.edu. *Application contact:* Toni Robinson, Esq., Admissions Counselor, 502-852-1623, Fax: 502-852-0520, E-mail: toni.robinson@louisville.edu.

University of Maine, Graduate School, College of Liberal Arts and Sciences, School of Performing Arts, Orono, ME 04469. Offers music (MM). Part-time programs available. *Faculty:* 12 full-time (3 women), 5 part-time/adjunct (3 women). *Students:* 8 full-time (2 women), 3 part-time (2 women), 1 international. Average age 33. 8 applicants, 75% accepted, 3 enrolled. *Entrance requirements:* For master's, GRE General Test. Additional exam requirements/recommendations for international students: Required—TOEFL. *Application deadline:* For fall admission, 2/1 priority date for domestic students. Applications are processed on a rolling basis. Application fee: $65. Electronic applications accepted. *Financial support:* In 2009–10, 4 teaching assistantships with tuition reimbursements (averaging $12,790 per year) were awarded; career-related internships or fieldwork, Federal Work-Study, institutionally sponsored loans, scholarships/grants, and tuition waivers (full and partial) also available. Support available to part-time students. Financial award application deadline: 3/1. *Unit head:* Dr. Currin Farnham, Director, 207-581-4702, Fax: 207-581-4701. *Application contact:* Scott G. Delcourt, Associate Dean of the Graduate School, 207-581-3291, Fax: 207-581-3232, E-mail: graduate@maine.edu.

University of Manitoba, Faculty of Graduate Studies, Marcel A. Desautels Faculty of Music, Winnipeg, MB R3T 2N2, Canada. Offers M Mus.

University of Maryland, Baltimore County, Graduate School, College of Arts, Humanities and Social Sciences, Department of Music, Baltimore, MD 21250. Offers American contemporary music (Postbaccalaureate Certificate). Part-time programs available. *Faculty:* 12 full-time, 7 part-time/adjunct. *Students:* 5 part-time (4 women), 1 international. Average age 24. 6 applicants, 83% accepted, 5 enrolled. In 2009, 4 Postbaccalaureate Certificates awarded. *Entrance requirements:* For degree, minimum GPA of 3.0, resume, reference letters, VHS tape of performance. *Application deadline:* For fall admission, 12/1 priority date for domestic and international students; for winter admission, 1/30 priority date for domestic and international students; for spring admission, 5/15 for domestic students, 3/1 for international students. Applications are processed on a rolling basis. Application fee: $50. *Faculty research:* Music, composition, performance, music technology, contemporary music. *Unit head:* Dr. E. Michael Richards, Chair, 410-455-3064, E-mail: emrichards@umbc.edu. *Application contact:* Dr. Anna Rubin, Director, 410-455-3190, Fax: 410-455-1181, E-mail: airubin@umbc.edu.

University of Maryland, College Park, Academic Affairs, College of Arts and Humanities, School of Music, Program in Ethnomusicology, College Park, MD 20742. Offers MA. *Students:* 25 full-time (18 women), 6 part-time (5 women); includes 4 minority (1 African American, 1 American Indian/Alaska Native, 1 Asian American or Pacific Islander, 1 Hispanic American), 10 international. 11 applicants, 36% accepted, 4 enrolled. In 2009, 1 master's awarded. *Degree requirements:* For master's, comprehensive exam, thesis optional, oral defense. *Entrance requirements:* Additional exam requirements/recommendations for international students: Required—TOEFL. *Application deadline:* For fall admission, 12/1 for domestic and international students. Application fee: $60. *Expenses:* Tuition, area resident: Part-time $471 per credit hour. Tuition, state resident: part-time $471 per credit hour. Tuition, nonresident: part-time $1016 per credit hour. Required fees: $337.04 per term. *Financial support:* In 2009–10, 2 fellowships with full and partial tuition reimbursements (averaging $12,904 per year), 12 teaching assistantships (averaging $16,740 per year) were awarded. *Unit head:* Dr. Robert Gibson, Director, 301-405-5553, Fax: 301-314-9504, E-mail: rgibson@umd.edu. *Application contact:* Dean of Graduate School, 301-405-0358, Fax: 301-314-9305.

University of Maryland, College Park, Academic Affairs, College of Arts and Humanities, School of Music, Program in Music, College Park, MD 20742. Offers M Ed, MA, MM, DMA, Ed D, PhD. *Students:* 172 full-time (110 women), 66 part-time (33 women); includes 43 minority (9 African Americans, 30 Asian Americans or Pacific Islanders, 4 Hispanic Americans), 41 international. 586 applicants, 19% accepted, 52 enrolled. In 2009, 38 master's, 29 doctorates awarded. *Entrance requirements:* Additional exam requirements/recommendations for international students: Required—TOEFL. *Application deadline:* For fall admission, 12/1 for domestic and international students. Application fee: $60. *Expenses:* Tuition, area resident: Part-time $471 per credit hour. Tuition, state resident: part-time $471 per credit hour. Tuition, nonresident: part-time $1016 per credit hour. Required fees: $337.04 per term. *Financial support:* In 2009–10, 1 fellowship with full tuition reimbursement (averaging $15,711 per year), 109 teaching assistantships (averaging $15,897 per year) were awarded. *Unit head:* Dr. Robert Gibson, Director, 301-405-5553, Fax: 301-314-9504, E-mail: rgibson@umd.edu. *Application contact:* Dean of Graduate School, 301-405-0358, Fax: 301-314-9305.

University of Massachusetts Amherst, Graduate School, College of Humanities and Fine Arts, Department of Music and Dance, Amherst, MA 01003. Offers music (MM, PhD). *Accreditation:* NASM. Part-time programs available. *Faculty:* 17 full-time (3 women). *Students:* 58 full-time (25 women), 22 part-time (8 women); includes 7 minority (2 African Americans, 3 Asian Americans or Pacific Islanders, 2 Hispanic Americans), 8 international. Average age 28. 88 applicants, 61% accepted, 25 enrolled. In 2009, 20 master's awarded. Terminal master's awarded for partial completion of doctoral program. *Degree requirements:* For master's, thesis or alternative; for doctorate, comprehensive exam, thesis/dissertation. *Entrance requirements:* For master's and doctorate, original scores, research papers, audition or tape. Additional exam requirements/recommendations for international students: Required—TOEFL (minimum score 550 paper-based; 213 computer-based; 80 iBT), IELTS (minimum score 6.5). *Application deadline:* For fall admission, 1/15 for domestic and international students; for spring admission, 10/1 for domestic and international students. Applications are processed on a rolling basis. Application fee: $50 ($65 for international students). Electronic applications accepted. *Expenses:* Tuition, state resident: full-time $2640; part-time $110 per credit. Tuition, nonresident: full-time $9936; part-time $414 per credit. Tuition and fees vary according to course load. *Financial support:* In 2009–10, 16 fellowships with full tuition reimbursements (averaging $3,856 per year), 41 teaching assistantships with full tuition reimbursements (averaging $5,489 per year) were awarded; research assistantships, career-related internships or fieldwork, Federal Work-Study, scholarships/grants, traineeships, health care benefits, tuition waivers (full), and unspecified assistantships also available. Support available to part-time students. Financial award application deadline: 1/15. *Unit head:* Dr. T. Dennis Brown, Graduate Program Director, 413-545-0311, Fax: 413-545-2092. *Application contact:* Jean M. Ames, Supervisor of Admissions, 413-545-0722, Fax: 413-577-0010, E-mail: gradadm@grad.umass.edu.

University of Massachusetts Lowell, College of Arts and Sciences, Department of Music, Lowell, MA 01854-2881. Offers music education (MM); sound recording technology (MM). *Accreditation:* NASM. Part-time programs available. *Degree requirements:* For master's, one foreign language, thesis. *Entrance requirements:* For master's, MAT, audition. Electronic applications accepted.

University of Memphis, Graduate School, College of Arts and Sciences, Department of English, Memphis, TN 38152. Offers African-American literature (Graduate Certificate); applied linguistics (PhD); composition studies (PhD); creative writing (MFA); English as a second language (MA); linguistics (MA); literary and cultural studies (PhD), including African-American literature; literature (MA); professional writing (MA, PhD); teaching English as a second language (Graduate Certificate). Part-time and evening/weekend programs available. Post-baccalaureate distance learning degree programs offered (no on-campus study). *Faculty:* 31 full-time (15 women), 2 part-time/adjunct (both women). *Students:* 98 full-time (59 women), 99 part-time (66 women); includes 36 minority (28 African Americans, 5 Asian Americans or Pacific Islanders, 3 Hispanic Americans), 7 international. Average age 34. 128 applicants, 71% accepted, 29 enrolled. In 2009, 38 master's, 4 doctorates, 21 other advanced degrees awarded. Terminal master's awarded for partial completion of doctoral program. *Degree requirements:* For master's, one foreign language, comprehensive exam, thesis optional; for doctorate, 2 foreign languages, comprehensive exam, thesis/dissertation. *Entrance requirements:* For master's, GRE; for doctorate, GRE. Additional exam requirements/recommendations for international students: Required—TOEFL. *Application deadline:* For fall admission, 7/1 for domestic students; for spring admission, 10/15 for domestic students. Applications are processed on a rolling basis. Application fee: $35 ($60 for international students). Electronic applications accepted. *Expenses:* Tuition, state resident: full-time $6246; part-time $347 per credit hour. Tuition, nonresident: full-time $15,894; part-time $883 per credit hour. Required fees: $1160. Full-time tuition and fees vary according to course load, degree level and program. *Financial support:* In 2009–10, 123 students received support; research assistantships with full tuition reimbursements available, teaching assistantships with full tuition reimbursements available, Federal Work-Study, scholarships/grants, and unspecified assistantships available. Financial award application deadline: 2/15; financial award applicants required to submit FAFSA. *Faculty research:* Applied linguistis, British and American literature, professional writing, composition studies. *Unit head:* Dr. Eric C. Link, Chair, 901-678-2651, Fax: 901-678-2226, E-mail: eclink@memphis.edu. *Application contact:* Dr. Verner D. Mitchell, Director, Graduate Studies, 901-678-3099, Fax: 901-678-2226, E-mail: vdmtchll@memphis.edu.

University of Memphis, Graduate School, College of Communication and Fine Arts, Rudi E. Scheidt School of Music, Memphis, TN 38152. Offers applied music (M Mu, DMA); composition (M Mu, DMA); conducting (M Mu, DMA); historical musicology (PhD); jazz and studio performance (M Mu); music education (M Mu, DMA); musicology (M Mu). *Accreditation:* NASM. Part-time programs available. *Faculty:* 36 full-time (7 women), 7 part-time/adjunct (4 women). *Students:* 84 full-time (34 women), 44 part-time (21 women); includes 24 minority (17 African Americans, 2 Asian Americans or Pacific Islanders, 5 Hispanic Americans), 24 international. Average age 32. 76 applicants, 87% accepted, 42 enrolled. In 2009, 13 master's, 10 doctorates awarded. Terminal master's awarded for partial completion of doctoral program. *Degree requirements:* For master's, comprehensive exam, thesis or alternative; for doctorate, one foreign language, comprehensive exam, thesis/dissertation, exam. *Entrance requirements:* For master's, GRE General Test or MAT, proficiency exam, audition; for doctorate, GRE General Test or MAT, proficiency exam, audition, master's degree. Additional exam requirements/recommendations for international students: Required—TOEFL. *Application deadline:* For fall admission, 8/1 for domestic students; for spring admission, 12/1 for domestic students. Applications are processed on a rolling basis. Application fee: $35 ($60 for international students). *Expenses:* Tuition, state resident: full-time $6246; part-time $347 per credit hour. Tuition, nonresident: full-time $15,894; part-time $883 per credit hour. Required fees: $1160. Full-time tuition and fees vary according to course load, degree level and program. *Financial support:* In 2009–10, 73 students received support; research assistantships with full and partial tuition reimbursements available, teaching assistantships with full and partial tuition reimbursements available, Federal Work-Study, scholarships/grants, and unspecified assistantships available. Financial award application deadline: 2/15; financial award applicants required to submit FAFSA. *Faculty research:* Spanish Renaissance, twentieth century music, Project OPTIMUS, composition, musical performance, regional music, performance, performance practice, composition. *Unit head:* Dr. Patricia J. Hoy, Director, 901-678-2541, Fax: 901-678-3096, E-mail: phoy@memphis.edu. *Application contact:* Dr. John Baur, Assistant Director for Graduate Admissions, 901-678-3362, Fax: 901-678-3096, E-mail: jbaur@memphis.edu.

University of Miami, Graduate School, Frost School of Music, Department of Instrumental Performance, Coral Gables, FL 33124. Offers instrumental conducting (MM, DMA); instrumental performance (MM, DMA, AD); multiple woodwinds (MM, DMA). *Accreditation:* NASM. *Degree requirements:* For master's, thesis, recital paper, recital; for doctorate, thesis/dissertation, essay, 2 research tools, 3 recitals. *Entrance requirements:* For master's and doctorate, GRE General Test, audition. Additional exam requirements/recommendations for international students: Required—TOEFL (minimum score 550 paper-based; 213 computer-based; 59 iBT). Electronic applications accepted. *Faculty research:* Performance, conducting, composition.

University of Miami, Graduate School, Frost School of Music, Department of Keyboard Performance, Coral Gables, FL 33124. Offers accompanying and chamber music (MM, DMA); keyboard performance and pedagogy (MM, DMA); piano performance (MM, DMA, AD). *Accreditation:* NASM. *Degree requirements:* For master's, thesis, recital paper, recital; for doctorate, thesis/dissertation, essay, 2 research tools, 3 recitals. *Entrance requirements:* For master's and doctorate, GRE General Test, audition. Additional exam requirements/recommendations for international students: Required—TOEFL (minimum score 555 paper-based; 213 computer-based; 59 iBT). Electronic applications accepted.

University of Miami, Graduate School, Frost School of Music, Department of Music Media and Industry, Coral Gables, FL 33124. Offers music business and entertainment industries (MM); music engineering (MS). *Accreditation:* NASM. *Degree requirements:* For master's, thesis, internship (MM), research project (MS). *Entrance requirements:* For master's, GRE General Test. Additional exam requirements/recommendations for international students: Required—TOEFL (minimum score 550 paper-based; 213 computer-based; 59 iBT). Electronic applications accepted. *Faculty research:* Recording rights and property, digital sound design, recording industry, Internet-based music industries.

University of Miami, Graduate School, Frost School of Music, Department of Musicology, Coral Gables, FL 33124. Offers MM. *Accreditation:* NASM. *Degree requirements:* For master's, thesis. *Entrance requirements:* For master's, GRE General Test. Additional exam requirements/recommendations for international students: Required—TOEFL (minimum score 550 paper-based; 213 computer-based; 59 iBT). Electronic applications accepted.

University of Miami, Graduate School, Frost School of Music, Department of Music Theory-Composition, Coral Gables, FL 33124. Offers composition (MM, DMA); electronic music (MM); media writing and production (MM); music theory (MM). *Accreditation:* NASM. *Degree requirements:* For master's, thesis; for doctorate, thesis/dissertation, essay. *Entrance requirements:* For master's and doctorate, GRE General Test, portfolio. Additional exam requirements/recommendations for international students: Required—TOEFL (minimum score 550 paper-based; 213 computer-based; 59 iBT). Electronic applications accepted. *Faculty research:* Composition, commercial music and media music.

University of Miami, Graduate School, Frost School of Music, Department of Studio Music and Jazz, Coral Gables, FL 33124. Offers jazz composition (DMA); jazz pedagogy (MM); jazz performance (MM, DMA); studio jazz writing (MM). *Accreditation:* NASM. *Degree requirements:* For master's, thesis. *Entrance requirements:* For master's and doctorate, GRE General Test, portfolio. Additional exam requirements/recommendations for international students: Required—TOEFL (minimum score 550 paper-based; 213 computer-based; 59 iBT). Electronic applications accepted. *Faculty research:* Jazz performance, jazz conducting, jjazz composition.

University of Miami, Graduate School, Frost School of Music, Department of Vocal Performance, Coral Gables, FL 33124. Offers choral conducting (MM, DMA); vocal pedagogy (DMA); vocal performance (MM, DMA, AD). *Accreditation:* NASM. *Degree requirements:* For master's, 2 foreign languages, thesis, recital paper; for doctorate, thesis/dissertation, essay. *Entrance requirements:* For master's and doctorate, GRE General Test, audition. Additional exam requirements/recommendations for international students: Required—TOEFL (minimum score 550 paper-based; 213 computer-based; 59 iBT). Electronic applications accepted. *Faculty research:* Opera, musical theatre, performance, directing, pedagogy.

University of Michigan, Horace H. Rackham School of Graduate Studies, The School of Music, Theatre, and Dance, Ann Arbor, MI 48109-2085. Offers MA, MFA, MM, A Mus D, PhD, Spec M, MBA/MM. *Accreditation:* NASM. *Faculty:* 84 full-time (25 women), 34 part-time/adjunct (10 women). *Students:* 280 full-time (145 women); includes 42 minority (18 African Americans, 2 American Indian/Alaska Native, 16 Asian Americans or Pacific Islanders, 6 Hispanic Americans), 57 international. 978 applicants, 32% accepted. In 2009, 76 master's, 29 doctorates awarded. *Entrance requirements:* For master's, audition, portfolio, interview. Additional exam requirements/recommendations for international students: Required—TOEFL (minimum score 560 paper-based; 237 computer-based). *Application deadline:* For fall admission, 12/1 for domestic and international students; for winter admission, 9/15 for domestic and international students. Applications are processed on a rolling basis. Application fee: $60 ($75 for international students). Electronic applications accepted. *Expenses:* Tuition, state resident: full-time $17,286; part-time $1099 per credit hour. Tuition, nonresident: full-time $34,944; part-time $2080 per credit hour. Required fees: $95 per semester. Tuition and fees vary according to course load, degree level and program. *Financial support:* Fellowships, teaching assistantships, career-related internships or fieldwork, Federal Work-Study, institutionally sponsored loans, and scholarships/grants available. Financial award application deadline: 2/1; financial award applicants required to submit FAFSA. *Unit head:* Christopher Kendall, Dean, 734-764-0584, Fax: 734-763-5097, E-mail: ckndll@umich.edu. *Application contact:* Laura Hoffman, Asst. Dean for Enrollment Management and Student Services, 734-734/764-0593, Fax: 734-763-5097, E-mail: lauras@umich.edu.

University of Minnesota, Duluth, Graduate School, School of Fine Arts, Department of Music, Duluth, MN 55812-2496. Offers music education (MM); performance (MM). *Accreditation:* NASM. Part-time programs available. *Degree requirements:* For master's, comprehensive exam, thesis (for some programs), recital (MM in performance). *Entrance requirements:* For master's, audition, minimum GPA of 3.0, sample of written work, interview, bachelor's degree in music, video of teaching. Additional exam requirements/recommendations for international students: Required—TOEFL (minimum score 550 paper-based; 213 computer-based). *Faculty research:* Band composition, music aesthetics, learning theory, value theory, music advocacy.

University of Minnesota, Twin Cities Campus, Graduate School, College of Liberal Arts, School of Music, Minneapolis, MN 55455-0213. Offers MA, MM, DMA, PhD. *Accreditation:* NASM. *Faculty:* 50 full-time (14 women), 15 part-time/adjunct (3 women). *Students:* 186 full-time (96 women), 26 part-time (13 women); includes 55 minority (4 African Americans, 43 Asian Americans or Pacific Islanders, 8 Hispanic Americans). Average age 25. 340 applicants, 81% accepted, 63 enrolled. In 2009, 38 master's, 27 doctorates awarded. *Degree requirements:* For master's, comprehensive exam, thesis (for some programs), foreign language (MA), recital (MM); for doctorate, comprehensive exam, thesis/dissertation (for some programs), 5 recitals (DMA); 2 foreign languages or computer languages, dissertation (PhD). *Entrance requirements:* For master's, GRE (MA); for doctorate, GRE (PhD). Additional exam requirements/recommendations for international students: Required—TOEFL (minimum score 550 paper-based; 213 computer-based; 79 iBT), IELTS (minimum score 6.5), TOEFL iBT also requires minimum of 21 in writing and 19 in reading. *Application deadline:* For fall admission, 12/15 for domestic and international students; for spring admission, 10/15 for domestic and international students. Applications are processed on a rolling basis. Application fee: $75 ($95 for international students). Electronic applications accepted. *Financial support:* In 2009–10, 175 students received support, including 56 fellowships with partial tuition reimbursements available (averaging $10,000 per year), 1 research assistantship with partial tuition reimbursement available (averaging $10,000 per year), 106 teaching assistantships with partial tuition reimbursements available (averaging $6,923 per year); Federal Work-Study, institutionally sponsored loans, scholarships/grants, health care benefits, tuition waivers (full and partial), and unspecified assistantships also available. Financial award application deadline: 2/7; financial award applicants required to submit FAFSA. *Unit head:* Dr. David Myers, Director, 612-626-1882, Fax: 612-626-2200, E-mail: musicdir@umn.edu. *Application contact:* Aaron Rosenberger, Admissions Coordinator, 612-624-2847, Fax: 612-624-8001, E-mail: mnmusic@umn.edu.

University of Mississippi, Graduate School, College of Liberal Arts, Department of Music, Oxford, University, MS 38677. Offers MM, DA. *Accreditation:* NASM. *Faculty:* 26 full-time (6 women), 7 part-time/adjunct (6 women). *Students:* 27 full-time (11 women), 11 part-time (4 women); includes 9 minority (all African Americans), 3 international. In 2009, 21 master's, 4 doctorates awarded. *Degree requirements:* For master's, thesis (for some programs); for doctorate, thesis/dissertation. *Entrance requirements:* For master's, GRE General Test, minimum GPA of 3.0; for doctorate, GRE General Test. Additional exam requirements/recommendations for international students: Required—TOEFL. *Application deadline:* For fall admission, 4/1 for domestic students; for spring admission, 10/1 for domestic students. Applications are processed on a rolling basis. Application fee: $25. Electronic applications accepted. *Financial support:* Scholarships/grants available. Financial award application deadline: 3/1; financial award applicants required to submit FAFSA. *Unit head:* Dr. Charles Gates, Chairman, 662-915-7268, Fax: 662-915-1203, E-mail: music@olemiss.edu. *Application contact:* Dr. Christy M. Wyandt, Associate Dean, 662-915-7474, Fax: 662-915-7577, E-mail: cwyandt@olemiss.edu.

University of Missouri, Graduate School, College of Arts and Sciences, School of Music, Columbia, MO 65211. Offers MA, MM. *Accreditation:* NASM. *Faculty:* 35 full-time (13 women), 13 part-time/adjunct (6 women). *Students:* 19 full-time (2 women), 24 part-time (6 women); includes 2 minority (1 American Indian/Alaska Native, 1 Asian American or Pacific Islander), 8 international. Average age 25. 48 applicants, 71% accepted, 27 enrolled. In 2009, 9 master's awarded. *Degree requirements:* For master's, 3 foreign languages, thesis. *Entrance requirements:* For master's, minimum GPA of 3.0. Additional exam requirements/recommendations for international students: Required—TOEFL (minimum score 500 paper-based; 173 computer-based; 61 iBT). *Application deadline:* For fall admission, 3/1 priority date for domestic students. Applications are processed on a rolling basis. Application fee: $45 ($60 for international students). Electronic applications accepted. *Financial support:* In 2009–10, 1 fellowship with full tuition reimbursement, 40 teaching assistantships with full tuition reimbursements were awarded; research assistantships, institutionally sponsored loans, health care benefits, and unspecified assistantships also available. *Unit head:* Dr. Robert Shay, Director, E-mail: shayr@missouri.edu. *Application contact:* Dr. Dan Willett, Associate Director, 573-882-0933, E-mail: willettd@missouri.edu.

University of Missouri–Kansas City, Conservatory of Music, Kansas City, MO 64110-2499. Offers composition (MM, DMA); conducting (MM, DMA); music (MA); music education (MME, PhD); music history and literature (MM); music theory (MM); performance (MM, DMA). PhD (interdisciplinary) offered through the School of Graduate Studies. *Accreditation:* NASM. Part-time programs available. *Faculty:* 58 full-time (24 women), 29 part-time/adjunct (13 women). *Students:* 143 full-time (65 women), 103 part-time (58 women); includes 12 minority (7 African Americans, 1 American Indian/Alaska Native, 2 Asian Americans or Pacific Islanders, 2 Hispanic Americans), 64 international. Average age 29. 267 applicants, 45% accepted, 59 enrolled. In 2009, 43 master's, 21 doctorates awarded. *Degree requirements:* For master's, variable foreign language requirement, comprehensive exam, thesis (for some programs); for doctorate, variable foreign language requirement, comprehensive exam, thesis/dissertation or alternative. *Entrance requirements:* For master's, minimum GPA of 3.0 in major, auditions (performance); for doctorate, minimum graduate GPA of 3.5, auditions (performance degrees), portfolio of compositions. Additional exam requirements/recommendations for international students: Required—TOEFL (minimum score 550 paper-based; 213 computer-based; 80 iBT). *Application deadline:* For fall admission, 1/15 priority date for domestic students, 1/15 for international students. Application fee: $45 ($50 for international students). *Expenses:* Tuition, state resident: full-time $5378; part-time $299 per credit hour. Tuition, nonresident: full-time $13,881; part-time $771 per credit hour. Required fees: $641; $71 per credit hour. Tuition and fees vary according to course load and program. *Financial support:* In 2009–10, 52 teaching assistantships with partial tuition reimbursements (averaging $8,772 per year) were awarded; career-related internships or fieldwork, Federal Work-Study, institutionally sponsored loans, scholarships/grants, tuition waivers (partial), and unspecified assistantships also available. Support available to part-time students. Financial award application deadline: 3/1; financial award applicants required to submit FAFSA. *Faculty research:* Electro-acoustic composition, affective music responses, American music theatre, Russian choral music, music therapy and Alzheimer's. Total annual research expenditures: $8,559. *Unit head:* Peter Witte, Dean, 816-235-2731, Fax: 816-235-5265, E-mail: wittep@umkc.edu. *Application contact:* James Elswick, Associate Director, 816-235-2932, Fax: 816-235-5264, E-mail: cadmissions@umkc.edu.

The University of Montana, Graduate School, School of Fine Arts, Department of Music, Missoula, MT 59812-0002. Offers music (MM), including composition/technology, music education, musical theater, performance. *Accreditation:* NASM. *Entrance requirements:* For master's, GRE General Test, GRE Subject Test, portfolio.

University of Nebraska at Omaha, Graduate Studies, College of Communication, Fine Arts and Media, Department of Music, Omaha, NE 68182. Offers MM. *Accreditation:* NASM. Part-time and evening/weekend programs available. *Faculty:* 12 full-time (3 women). *Students:* 7 full-time (4 women), 27 part-time (17 women); includes 1 minority (African American). Average age 30. 20 applicants, 80% accepted, 12 enrolled. In 2009, 13 master's awarded. *Degree requirements:* For master's, comprehensive exam, thesis (for some programs). *Entrance requirements:* For master's, departmental diagnostic exam, minimum GPA of 3.0. Additional exam requirements/recommendations for international students: Required—TOEFL (minimum score 500 paper-based; 173 computer-based; 61 iBT). *Application deadline:* For fall admission, 6/15 priority date for domestic students; for spring admission, 11/15 priority date for domestic students. Applications are processed on a rolling basis. Application fee: $45. Electronic applications accepted. *Financial support:* In 2009–10, 12 students received support; research assistantships with tuition reimbursements available, career-related internships or fieldwork, Federal Work-Study, institutionally sponsored loans, scholarships/grants, tuition waivers (partial), and unspecified assistantships available. Support available to part-time students. Financial award application deadline: 3/1; financial award applicants required to submit FAFSA. *Unit head:* Dr. Melissa Berke, Chairperson, 402-554-2251. *Application contact:* Penny Harmoney, Director, Graduate Studies, 402-554-2341, Fax: 402-554-3143, E-mail: graduate@unomaha.edu.

University of Nebraska–Lincoln, Graduate College, College of Arts and Sciences, Department of English, Lincoln, NE 68588-0333. Offers composition and rhetoric (MA, PhD); creative writing (MA, PhD); literature studies (MA, PhD). *Degree requirements:* For master's, thesis optional; for doctorate, one foreign language, comprehensive exam, thesis/dissertation. *Entrance requirements:* For master's, writing sample; for doctorate, GRE General Test, writing sample. Additional exam requirements/recommendations for international students: Required—TOEFL (minimum score 600 paper-based; 250 computer-based). Electronic applications accepted. *Faculty research:* Creative writing, composition and rhetoric, women's studies, North American literature, medieval/Renaissance studies.

University of Nebraska–Lincoln, Graduate College, College of Fine and Performing Arts, School of Music, Lincoln, NE 68588. Offers composition (MM, DMA); conducting (MM, DMA); music education (MM, PhD); music history (MM); music theory (MM); performance (MM, DMA); piano pedagogy (MM); woodwind specialties (MM). *Accreditation:* NASM. *Degree requirements:* For master's, thesis optional; for doctorate, comprehensive exam, thesis/dissertation. *Entrance requirements:* For master's and doctorate, audition. Additional exam requirements/recommendations for international students: Required—TOEFL. Electronic applications accepted. *Faculty research:* Mozart, Tchaikovsky, Josquin des Prez, practice of J.S. Bach's organ works, instructional strategies in music education.

University of Nevada, Las Vegas, Graduate College, College of Fine Arts, Department of Music, Las Vegas, NV 89154-5025. Offers music (MM); musical arts (DMA). *Accreditation:* NASM. Part-time programs available. *Faculty:* 28 full-time (8 women), 19 part-time/adjunct (5 women). *Students:* 55 full-time (22 women), 37 part-time (17 women); includes 9 minority (2 African Americans, 1 American Indian/Alaska Native, 1 Asian American or Pacific Islander, 5 Hispanic Americans), 13 international. Average age 32. 67 applicants, 79% accepted, 33 enrolled. In 2009, 26 master's, 5 doctorates awarded. *Degree requirements:* For master's, thesis optional, oral and/or written comprehensive exam; for doctorate, one foreign language, comprehensive exam, lecture-recital and document. *Entrance requirements:* Additional exam requirements/recommendations for international students: Required—TOEFL (minimum score 550 paper-based; 213 computer-based; 80 iBT), IELTS (minimum score 7). *Application deadline:* For fall admission, 5/1 priority date for domestic and international students; for spring admission, 11/15 priority date for domestic students, 10/1 for international students. Applications are processed on a rolling basis. Application fee: $60 ($95 for international students). Electronic applications accepted. *Financial support:* In 2009–10, 40 students received support, including 1 research assistantship with partial tuition reimbursement available (averaging $10,000 per year), 39 teaching assistantships with partial tuition reimbursements available (averaging $10,948 per year); institutionally sponsored loans, scholarships/grants, health care benefits, and unspecified assistantships also available. Financial award application deadline: 3/1. *Faculty research:* Richard Wagner, seventeenth-eighteenth century repertoires, reception history; commissioned opera 'Red Earth—Hunger"; music for winds and percussion; history of Las Vegas hotel bands 1940-1989; incorporation of technology into the music classroom. *Unit head:* Dr. Jonathan Good, Chair/ Professor, 702-895-3332, Fax: 702-895-4239, E-mail: janathan.good@unlv.edu. *Application contact:* Graduate College Admissions Evaluator, 702-895-3320, Fax: 702-895-4180, E-mail: gradcollege@unlv.edu.

University of Nevada, Reno, Graduate School, College of Liberal Arts, Department of Music, Reno, NV 89557. Offers MA, MM. *Accreditation:* NASM. *Degree requirements:* For master's, thesis optional. *Entrance requirements:* For master's, minimum GPA of 2.75. Additional exam requirements/recommendations for international students: Required—TOEFL (minimum score 500 paper-based; 173 computer-based; 61 iBT), IELTS (minimum score 6). Electronic applications accepted. *Faculty research:* Performance, conducting, music composition and arranging.

University of New Hampshire, Graduate School, College of Liberal Arts, Department of Music, Durham, NH 03824. Offers music education (MA); music history (MA). *Accreditation:* NASM. *Faculty:* 17 full-time (3 women). *Students:* 7 full-time (1 woman), 5 part-time (3 women); includes 1 minority (Hispanic American), 1 international. Average age 28. 9 applicants, 100% accepted, 5 enrolled. In 2009, 5 master's awarded. *Degree requirements:* For master's, one foreign language. *Entrance requirements:* For master's, audition. Additional exam requirements/recommendations for international students: Required—TOEFL (minimum score 550 paper-based; 213 computer-based; 80 iBT). *Application deadline:* For fall admission, 4/1 priority date for domestic students, 4/1 for international students; for spring admission, 12/1 for domestic students. Applications are processed on a rolling basis. Application fee: $65. Electronic applications accepted. *Expenses:* Tuition, state resident: full-time $10,380; part-time $577 per credit hour. Tuition, nonresident: full-time $24,350; part-time $1002 per credit hour. Required fees: $1550; $387.50 per semester. Tuition and fees vary according to course load and program. *Financial support:* In 2009–10, 5 students received support, including 4 teaching assistantships; fellowships, research assistantships, career-related internships or fieldwork, Federal Work-Study, scholarships/grants, and tuition waivers (full and partial) also available. Support available to part-time students. Financial award application deadline: 2/15. *Unit head:* Dr. Rob Stibler, Chairperson, 603-862-2418. *Application contact:* Alexis Zaricki, Administrative Assistant, 603-862-2418, E-mail: grad.music@unh.edu.

University of New Mexico, Graduate School, College of Fine Arts, Department of Music, Albuquerque, NM 87131-2039. Offers M Mu. *Accreditation:* NASM. Part-time programs available. *Faculty:* 34 full-time (10 women), 21 part-time/adjunct (12 women). *Students:* 51 full-time (21 women), 40 part-time (22 women); includes 15 minority (3 African Americans, 1 American Indian/Alaska Native, 1 Asian American or Pacific Islander, 10 Hispanic Americans), 19 international. Average age 30. 58 applicants, 78% accepted, 29 enrolled. In 2009, 30 master's awarded. *Degree requirements:* For master's, thesis (for some programs), oral exam, recital (for some programs). *Entrance requirements:* For master's, placement exams in music history and theory. Additional exam requirements/recommendations for international students: Required—TOEFL (minimum score 550 paper-based; 213 computer-based). *Application deadline:* For fall admission, 7/1 for domestic students, 5/1 for international students; for spring admission, 11/1 for domestic students. Application fee: $50. Electronic applications accepted. *Expenses:* Tuition, state resident: full-time $2099; part-time $233.20 per credit hour. Tuition, nonresident: full-time $6650. Required fees: $25 per semester. Tuition and fees vary according to course load, program and reciprocity agreements. *Financial support:* In 2009–10, 30 students received support, including 20 teaching assistantships with tuition reimbursements available (averaging $6,437 per year); Federal Work-Study, scholarships/grants, and unspecified assistantships also available. Support available to part-time students. Financial award application deadline: 3/1; financial award applicants required to submit FAFSA. *Faculty research:* Opera, twentieth century and contemporary music, performance, conducting. Total annual research expenditures: $3,149. *Unit head:* Dr. Steven Block, Chair, 505-277-2127, Fax: 505-277-4202,

Music

University of New Mexico (continued)
E-mail: sblock@unm.edu. *Application contact:* Colleen Sheinberg, Graduate Coordinator, 505-277-8401, Fax: 505-277-4202, E-mail: colleens@unm.edu.

University of New Orleans, Graduate School, College of Liberal Arts, Department of Music, New Orleans, LA 70148. Offers MM. *Accreditation:* NASM. Evening/weekend programs available. *Degree requirements:* For master's, recital. *Entrance requirements:* For master's, GRE General Test, audition. Additional exam requirements/recommendations for international students: Required—TOEFL (minimum score 550 paper-based; 213 computer-based; 79 iBT). Electronic applications accepted. *Faculty research:* American jazz, Czech music, Hispanic music.

The University of North Carolina at Chapel Hill, Graduate School, College of Arts and Sciences, Department of Music, Chapel Hill, NC 27599. Offers MA, PhD. Terminal master's awarded for partial completion of doctoral program. *Degree requirements:* For master's, one foreign language, thesis, theory and keyboard exams; for doctorate, 2 foreign languages, comprehensive exam, thesis/dissertation, theory and keyboard exams. *Entrance requirements:* For master's and doctorate, GRE General Test, department diagnostic exam, minimum GPA of 3.0. Additional exam requirements/recommendations for international students: Required—TOEFL. Electronic applications accepted. *Expenses:* Contact institution. *Faculty research:* Music theory, ethnomusicology, music history.

The University of North Carolina at Greensboro, Graduate School, School of Music, Greensboro, NC 27412-5001. Offers composition (MM); education (MM); music education (PhD); performance (MM, DMA). *Accreditation:* NASM. *Degree requirements:* For master's, variable foreign language requirement, thesis (for some programs), recital; for doctorate, comprehensive exam, thesis/dissertation, diagnostic exam, recital. *Entrance requirements:* For master's, GRE General Test, NTE, audition; for doctorate, GRE General Test, GRE Subject Test (music), audition. Additional exam requirements/recommendations for international students: Required—TOEFL. Electronic applications accepted.

University of North Carolina School of the Arts, School of Filmmaking, Winston-Salem, NC 27127-2188. Offers film music composition (MFA). *Faculty:* 1 full-time (0 women). *Students:* 7 full-time (0 women); includes 1 minority (Asian American or Pacific Islander). Average age 25. 6 applicants, 33% accepted, 2 enrolled. In 2009, 3 master's awarded. *Entrance requirements:* For master's, audition, performance, portfolio, interview. *Application deadline:* For fall admission, 4/1 priority date for domestic students. Applications are processed on a rolling basis. Application fee: $60 ($100 for international students). *Expenses:* Tuition, state resident: full-time $3797. Tuition, nonresident: full-time $15,670. Required fees: $1992. *Financial support:* In 2009–10, fellowships (averaging $2,000 per year); career-related internships or fieldwork and Federal Work-Study also available. Support available to part-time students. Financial award application deadline: 3/15; financial award applicants required to submit FAFSA. *Unit head:* Jordan Kerner, Dean, 336-770-1330, Fax: 336-770-1339, E-mail: kernerj@uncsa.edu. *Application contact:* Sheeler Lawson, Director of Admissions, 336-770-3290, Fax: 336-770-3370, E-mail: admissions@uncsa.edu.

University of North Carolina School of the Arts, School of Music, Winston-Salem, NC 27127-2188. Offers music performance (MM), including chamber music performance. *Faculty:* 30 full-time (9 women), 11 part-time/adjunct (3 women). *Students:* 43 full-time (20 women); includes 6 minority (3 African Americans, 1 American Indian/Alaska Native, 2 Hispanic Americans), 3 international. Average age 25. In 2009, 12 master's awarded. *Entrance requirements:* For master's, audition (music performance), interview, original score. Additional exam requirements/recommendations for international students: Required—TOEFL. *Application deadline:* For fall admission, 4/1 priority date for domestic students. Applications are processed on a rolling basis. Application fee: $60 ($100 for international students). *Expenses:* Tuition, state resident: full-time $3797. Tuition, nonresident: full-time $15,670. Required fees: $1992. *Financial support:* In 2009–10, 8 fellowships with partial tuition reimbursements (averaging $2,000 per year), 10 teaching assistantships with partial tuition reimbursements (averaging $3,000 per year) were awarded; career-related internships or fieldwork and Federal Work-Study also available. Financial award application deadline: 3/15; financial award applicants required to submit FAFSA. *Unit head:* Dr. Wade Weast, Dean, 336-770-3251, Fax: 336-770-3248, E-mail: weastw@uncsa.edu. *Application contact:* Sheeler Lawson, Director of Admissions, 336-770-3290, Fax: 336-770-3370, E-mail: admissions@uncsa.edu.

University of North Dakota, Graduate School, College of Arts and Sciences, Department of Music, Grand Forks, ND 58202. Offers music (M Mus); music education (M Mus, DMEd). *Accreditation:* NASM. Part-time programs available. *Degree requirements:* For master's, comprehensive exam, thesis or alternative. *Entrance requirements:* For master's, minimum GPA of 3.0. Additional exam requirements/recommendations for international students: Required—TOEFL (minimum score 550 paper-based; 213 computer-based; 79 iBT), IELTS (minimum score 6.5). Electronic applications accepted.

University of Northern Colorado, Graduate School, College of Performing and Visual Arts, School of Music, Greeley, CO 80639. Offers collaborative keyboard (MM); conducting (MM); instrumental performance (MM); jazz studies (MM); music conducting (DA); music education (MM, DA); music history and literature (MM, DA); music performance (DA); music theory and composition (MM, DA); vocal performance (MM). *Accreditation:* NASM; NCATE (one or more programs are accredited). Part-time programs available. *Faculty:* 30 full-time (8 women). *Students:* 76 full-time (28 women), 19 part-time (8 women); includes 3 minority (2 Asian Americans or Pacific Islanders, 1 Hispanic American), 14 international. Average age 29. 79 applicants, 82% accepted, 38 enrolled. In 2009, 22 master's, 2 doctorates awarded. *Degree requirements:* For master's, comprehensive exam, thesis or alternative; for doctorate, comprehensive exam, thesis/dissertation. *Entrance requirements:* For master's, audition; for doctorate, GRE General Test, audition, 3 letters of recommendation. *Application deadline:* Applications are processed on a rolling basis. Application fee: $50 ($60 for international students). Electronic applications accepted. *Expenses:* Tuition, state resident: full-time $5770; part-time $320.55 per credit hour. Tuition, nonresident: full-time $13,847; part-time $769.27 per credit hour. Required fees: $948.78; $52.72 per credit. *Financial support:* In 2009–10, 30 research assistantships (averaging $4,101 per year), 17 teaching assistantships (averaging $5,787 per year) were awarded; fellowships, unspecified assistantships also available. Financial award application deadline: 3/1; financial award applicants required to submit FAFSA. *Unit head:* David Caffey, Director, 970-351-2679. *Application contact:* Linda Sisson, Graduate Student Admission Coordinator, 970-351-1807, Fax: 970-351-2371, E-mail: linda.sisson@unco.edu.

University of Northern Iowa, Graduate College, College of Humanities and Fine Arts, School of Music, Program in Music, Cedar Falls, IA 50614. Offers composition (MM); conducting (MM); music (MM); music history (MM); performance (MM). *Accreditation:* NASM. *Students:* 31 full-time (21 women), 7 part-time (5 women); includes 2 minority (both Hispanic Americans), 8 international. 49 applicants, 61% accepted, 16 enrolled. In 2009, 8 master's awarded. *Degree requirements:* For master's, comprehensive exam, thesis or alternative. *Entrance requirements:* For master's, written diagnostic exam in theory, music history, expository writing skills and in the area of claimed competency, portfolio, tape recordings of compositions, in person auditions, minimum GPA of 3.0. Additional exam requirements/recommendations for international students: Required—TOEFL (minimum score 500 paper-based; 180 computer-based; 61 iBT). *Application deadline:* For fall admission, 8/1 priority date for domestic students. Applications are processed on a rolling basis. Application fee: $30 ($50 for international students). Electronic applications accepted. *Financial support:* Career-related internships or fieldwork, Federal Work-Study, and tuition waivers (full and partial) available. Support available to part-time students. Financial award application deadline: 2/1. *Unit head:* Dr. Rebecca Burkhardt, Coordinator/Professor, 319-273-4723, Fax: 319-273-7320, E-mail: rebecca.burkhardt@uni.edu. *Application contact:* Laurie S. Russell, Record Analyst, 319-273-2623, Fax: 319-273-6792, E-mail: laurie.russell@uni.edu.

University of North Texas, Robert B. Toulouse School of Graduate Studies, College of Music, Denton, TX 76203. Offers composition (MM, DMA); jazz studies (MM); music (MA); music education (MM, MME, PhD); music theory (MM, PhD); musicology (MM, PhD); performance (MM, DMA). *Accreditation:* NASM. In 2009, 82 master's awarded. Terminal master's awarded for partial completion of doctoral program. *Degree requirements:* For master's, one foreign language, comprehensive exam (for some programs), thesis (for some programs); for doctorate, one foreign language, comprehensive exam (for some programs), thesis/dissertation (for some programs). *Entrance requirements:* For master's and doctorate, audition, writing samples. Additional exam requirements/recommendations for international students: Required—proof of English language proficiency; Recommended—TOEFL (minimum score 550 paper-based; 213 computer-based). *Application deadline:* Applications are processed on a rolling basis. Application fee: $50 ($75 for international students). Electronic applications accepted. *Expenses:* Tuition, state resident: full-time $4298; part-time $239 per contact hour. Tuition, nonresident: full-time $9878; part-time $549 per contact hour. Required fees: $265 per contact hour. *Financial support:* Fellowships with partial tuition reimbursements, research assistantships, teaching assistantships with partial tuition reimbursements, career-related internships or fieldwork, Federal Work-Study, institutionally sponsored loans, and scholarships/grants available. Financial award application deadline: 4/1. *Faculty research:* Electro-acoustical music, intermedia, music and medicine, music performance. *Application contact:* Admissions and Scholarship Services, 940-367-7771, Fax: 940-565-2002.

University of Oklahoma, Graduate College, College of Fine Arts, School of Music, Norman, OK 73019-0390. Offers choral conducting (M Mus); conducting (M Mus Ed, DMA); general (M Mus Ed); instrumental (M Mus Ed); instrumental conducting (M Mus); music composition (M Mus, DMA); music education (M Mus Ed, PhD); music theory (M Mus); musicology (M Mus); organ (M Mus, DMA); piano (M Mus, DMA); voice (M Mus, DMA); wind/percussion/string (M Mus, DMA). *Accreditation:* NASM. *Faculty:* 53 full-time (16 women), 1 part-time/adjunct (0 women). *Students:* 102 full-time (60 women), 59 part-time (29 women); includes 15 minority (1 African American, 3 American Indian/Alaska Native, 9 Asian Americans or Pacific Islanders, 2 Hispanic Americans), 17 international. 88 applicants, 69% accepted, 44 enrolled. In 2009, 44 master's, 14 doctorates awarded. *Degree requirements:* For master's, variable foreign language requirement, thesis (for some programs), departmental qualifying exam, oral and preliminary exams; for doctorate, variable foreign language requirement, thesis/dissertation, departmental qualifying exam, general and oral exams. *Entrance requirements:* For master's, audition, BA in music, minimum GPA of 3.0; for doctorate, audition, minimum GPA of 3.0. Additional exam requirements/recommendations for international students: Required—TOEFL (minimum score 550 paper-based; 213 computer-based). *Application deadline:* For fall admission, 6/1 priority date for domestic students, 4/1 for international students; for spring admission, 11/1 for domestic students, 9/1 for international students. Applications are processed on a rolling basis. Application fee: $40 ($90 for international students). Electronic applications accepted. *Expenses:* Tuition, state resident: full-time $3744; part-time $156 per credit hour. Tuition, nonresident: full-time $13,577; part-time $565.70 per credit hour. Required fees: $2415; $90.10 per credit hour. *Financial support:* In 2009–10, 116 students received support, including 9 fellowships with full tuition reimbursements available (averaging $5,000 per year), 22 research assistantships with partial tuition reimbursements available (averaging $10,918 per year), 76 teaching assistantships with partial tuition reimbursements available (averaging $10,055 per year); unspecified assistantships also available. Financial award application deadline: 4/7; financial award applicants required to submit FAFSA. *Faculty research:* Piano pedagogy, vocal and instrumental performance, music education. Total annual research expenditures: $37,246. *Unit head:* Dr. Steven Curtis, Director, 405-325-2081, Fax: 405-325-7574, E-mail: scurtis@ou.edu. *Application contact:* Jan Russell, Office Assistant, 405-325-5393, Fax: 405-325-7574, E-mail: jrussell@ou.edu.

University of Oklahoma—Tulsa, Kodaly Certification Programs, Tulsa, OK 74135-2512. Offers Kodaly biography (Certificate); Kodaly concept (Certificate); Kodaly philosophy (Certificate).

University of Oregon, Graduate School, School of Music, Program in Music, Eugene, OR 97403. Offers composition (M Mus, DMA, PhD); conducting (M Mus); jazz studies (M Mus); music (MA), including music history, music theory; music history (PhD); music theory (PhD); performance (M Mus, DMA); piano pedagogy (M Mus). *Entrance requirements:* For master's, minimum GPA of 3.0, audition (performance applicants), videotape or interview (conducting applicants); for doctorate, GRE General Test, minimum GPA of 3.0, audition (performance applicants), videotape or interview (conducting applicants). Additional exam requirements/recommendations for international students: Required—TOEFL.

University of Ottawa, Faculty of Graduate and Postdoctoral Studies, Faculty of Arts, Department of Music, Ottawa, ON K1N 6N5, Canada. Offers music (M Mus, MA); orchestral studies (Certificate); piano pedagogy research (Certificate). *Degree requirements:* For master's, thesis optional. *Entrance requirements:* For master's, honors degree or equivalent, minimum B+ average. Electronic applications accepted. *Faculty research:* Performance, theory, musicology.

University of Pennsylvania, School of Arts and Sciences, Graduate Group in Music, Philadelphia, PA 19104. Offers AM, PhD. *Faculty:* 12 full-time (5 women), 4 part-time/adjunct (0 women). *Students:* 40 full-time (20 women); includes 2 minority (1 African American, 1 Hispanic American), 9 international. 118 applicants, 15% accepted, 11 enrolled. In 2009, 2 master's, 7 doctorates awarded. Terminal master's awarded for partial completion of doctoral program. *Degree requirements:* For master's, variable foreign language requirement; for doctorate, variable foreign language requirement, thesis/dissertation. *Entrance requirements:* For master's and doctorate, GRE General Test, GRE Subject Test, samples of previous work. Additional exam requirements/recommendations for international students: Required—TOEFL. *Application deadline:* For fall admission, 12/1 priority date for domestic students. Application fee: $70. Electronic applications accepted. *Expenses:* Tuition: Full-time $25,660; part-time $4758 per course. Required fees: $2152; $270 per course. Tuition and fees vary according to course load, degree level and program. *Financial support:* Institutionally sponsored loans, scholarships/grants, traineeships, health care benefits, and unspecified assistantships available. Financial award application deadline: 12/15.

University of Pittsburgh, School of Arts and Sciences, Department of Music, Pittsburgh, PA 15260. Offers composition and theory (MA, PhD); ethnomusicology (MA, PhD); historical musicology (MA, PhD). Part-time programs available. *Faculty:* 10 full-time (3 women), 1 part-time/adjunct (0 women). *Students:* 36 full-time (12 women), 4 part-time (3 women); includes 3 minority (2 African Americans, 1 Hispanic American), 15 international. Average age 30. 37 applicants, 32% accepted, 8 enrolled. In 2009, 5 master's, 7 doctorates awarded. Terminal master's awarded for partial completion of doctoral program. *Degree requirements:* For master's, comprehensive exam, thesis, 1 foreign language (historical musicology); for doctorate, one foreign language, comprehensive exam, thesis/dissertation, 2 foreign languages (historical musicology). *Entrance requirements:* For master's and doctorate, GRE General Test, samples of work, references. Additional exam requirements/recommendations for international students: Required—TOEFL (minimum score 600 paper-based; 250 computer-based). *Application deadline:* For fall admission, 1/5 for domestic and international students. Application fee: $50. Electronic applications accepted. *Expenses:* Tuition, state resident: full-time $16,402; part-time $665 per credit. Tuition, nonresident: full-time $28,694; part-time $1175 per credit. Required fees: $690; $175 per term. Tuition and fees vary according to program. *Financial support:* In 2009–10, 27 students received support, including 9 fellowships with full tuition reimbursements available (averaging $17,800 per year), 1 research assistantship with full and partial tuition reimbursement available (averaging $12,300 per year), 17 teaching assistantships with full and partial tuition reimbursements available (averaging $15,065 per year); scholarships/grants, health care benefits, tuition waivers (partial), and unspecified assistantships also available. Financial award application deadline: 1/5. *Faculty research:* Composition, ethnomusicology, historical musicology, intercultural musicology, jazz. Total annual research expenditures: $100,000. *Unit head:* Dr. Mathew Rosenblum, Chairman, 412-624-

4126, Fax: 412-624-4186, E-mail: rosenblu@pitt.edu. *Application contact:* Dr. Bell Yung, Director of Graduate Admissions, 412-624-4124, Fax: 412-624-4186, E-mail: byun@pitt.edu.

University of Pittsburgh, School of Arts and Sciences, Department of Theatre Arts, Pittsburgh, PA 15260. Offers performance pedagogy (MFA); theatre and performance studies (MA, PhD). *Accreditation:* NAST. *Faculty:* 4 full-time (1 woman). *Students:* 25 full-time (15 women); includes 1 minority (African American), 1 international. Average age 31. 71 applicants, 21% accepted, 8 enrolled. In 2009, 3 master's, 3 doctorates awarded. Terminal master's awarded for partial completion of doctoral program. *Degree requirements:* For master's, comprehensive exam; for doctorate, one foreign language, comprehensive exam, thesis/dissertation, diagnostic exams. *Entrance requirements:* For master's and doctorate, GRE General Test, samples of written work. Additional exam requirements/recommendations for international students: Required—TOEFL (minimum score 550 paper-based; 213 computer-based; 80 iBT). *Application deadline:* For fall admission, 1/15 priority date for domestic and international students. Application fee: $50. Electronic applications accepted. *Expenses:* Tuition, state resident: full-time $16,402; part-time $665 per credit. Tuition, nonresident: full-time $28,694; part-time $1175 per credit. Required fees: $690; $175 per term. Tuition and fees vary according to program. *Financial support:* In 2009–10, 21 students received support, including 1 fellowship with full tuition reimbursement available (averaging $18,200 per year), 13 research assistantships with full and partial tuition reimbursements available (averaging $12,300 per year), 17 teaching assistantships with full and partial tuition reimbursements available (averaging $15,675 per year); career-related internships or fieldwork, Federal Work-Study, institutionally sponsored loans, scholarships/grants, health care benefits, and unspecified assistantships also available. Support available to part-time students. Financial award application deadline: 1/15; financial award applicants required to submit FAFSA. *Faculty research:* American theatre, Renaissance theatre, Asian theatre, dramatic structure, performance theory. *Unit head:* Dr. Bruce McConachie, Chairman, 412-624-6156, Fax: 412-624-6338, E-mail: bamcco@pitt.edu. *Application contact:* Connie Anne Markiw, Graduate Secretary, 412-624-6568, Fax: 412-624-6338, E-mail: cam177@pitt.edu.

University of Portland, College of Arts and Sciences, Department of Performing and Fine Arts, Portland, OR 97203-5798. Offers drama (MFA), including directing; music (MA). Part-time and evening/weekend programs available. *Faculty:* 7 full-time (1 woman). *Students:* 4 full-time (3 women), 2 part-time (1 woman); includes 1 minority (African American). Average age 35. 9 applicants, 67% accepted, 4 enrolled. In 2009, 5 master's awarded. *Degree requirements:* For master's, thesis optional. *Entrance requirements:* For master's, GRE General Test, minimum GPA of 3.0, resume, 3 letters of recommendation, statement of goals, official transcripts. Additional exam requirements/recommendations for international students: Required—TOEFL (minimum score 600 paper-based; 100 iBT), IELTS (minimum score 7.5). *Application deadline:* For fall admission, 7/15 priority date for domestic and international students; for spring admission, 12/15 priority date for domestic and international students. Applications are processed on a rolling basis. Application fee: $50. *Expenses:* Tuition: Part-time $860 per semester hour. *Financial support:* Federal Work-Study, scholarships/grants, and tuition waivers (partial) available. Financial award application deadline: 3/1; financial award applicants required to submit FAFSA. *Unit head:* Dr. Kenneth Kleszynski, Head, 503-943-7294, E-mail: kkleszyn@up.edu. *Application contact:* Chris James Olinger, Administrative Assistant, 503-943-7107, Fax: 503-943-7315, E-mail: olingerc@up.edu.

University of Redlands, College of Arts and Sciences, School of Music, Redlands, CA 92373-0999. Offers MM. *Accreditation:* NASM. Part-time programs available. *Degree requirements:* For master's, comprehensive exam, thesis, 3 recitals, major conducted ensemble. *Entrance requirements:* For master's, GRE, bachelor's degree in music, minimum GPA of 2.75, audition, original scores. Additional exam requirements/recommendations for international students: Required—TOEFL (minimum score 550 paper-based). *Expenses:* Contact institution. *Faculty research:* Performance, composition.

University of Regina, Faculty of Graduate Studies and Research, Faculty of Fine Arts, Department of Music, Regina, SK S4S 0A2, Canada. Offers music (M Mus); music theory (MA); musicology (MA, PhD). *Faculty:* 10 full-time (6 women). *Students:* 3 full-time (1 woman), 2 part-time (1 woman). In 2009, 1 doctorate awarded. *Degree requirements:* For master's, thesis (for some programs), recital, oral exam; for doctorate, thesis/dissertation. *Entrance requirements:* For master's, B Mus or equivalent. Additional exam requirements/recommendations for international students: Required—TOEFL (minimum score 580 paper-based; 237 computer-based; 80 iBT). *Application deadline:* For fall admission, 3/15 for domestic students. Application fee: $90 ($100 for international students). *Financial support:* In 2009–10, 1 research assistantship (averaging $16,910 per year), 1 teaching assistantship (averaging $6,650 per year) were awarded; fellowships, scholarships/grants also available. Financial award application deadline: 6/15. *Faculty research:* Social status of eighteenth century musicians in the Habsburg Empire studies, electronic and computer music, piano performance. *Unit head:* Dr. Lynn Cavanagh, Head, 306-585-5507, Fax: 306-585-5780, E-mail: lynn.cavanagh@uregina.ca. *Application contact:* Randal Rogers, Graduate Program Coordinator, 306-585-4746, Fax: 306-585-5544, E-mail: randal.rogers@uregina.ca.

University of Rhode Island, Graduate School, College of Arts and Sciences, Department of Music, Kingston, RI 02881. Offers music education (MM); music performance (MM). *Accreditation:* NASM. Part-time programs available. *Faculty:* 14 full-time (5 women). *Students:* 9 full-time (3 women), 5 part-time (1 woman); includes 1 minority (Asian American or Pacific Islander). In 2009, 5 master's awarded. *Entrance requirements:* For master's, 2 letters of recommendation, audition. Additional exam requirements/recommendations for international students: Required—TOEFL (minimum score 550 paper-based; 213 computer-based). *Application deadline:* For fall admission, 7/15 for domestic students, 2/1 for international students; for spring admission, 7/15 for international students. Application fee: $65. Electronic applications accepted. *Expenses:* Tuition, state resident: full-time $8828; part-time $490 per credit hour. Tuition, nonresident: full-time $22,100; part-time $1228 per credit hour. Required fees: $1118; $57 per semester. Tuition and fees vary according to program. *Financial support:* In 2009–10, 3 teaching assistantships with full and partial tuition reimbursements (averaging $6,368 per year) were awarded. Financial award application deadline: 3/15; financial award applicants required to submit FAFSA. *Unit head:* Dr. Ronald T. Lee, Chair, 401-874-2431, Fax: 401-874-2772, E-mail: rlee@uri.edu. *Application contact:* Dr. Eliane Aberdam, Co-Director of Graduate Studies, 401-874-2794, Fax: 401-874-2772, E-mail: eliane@uri.edu.

University of Rochester, Eastman School of Music, Rochester, NY 14627. Offers composition (MA, MM, DMA, PhD); conducting (MM, DMA); education (MA, PhD); jazz studies/contemporary media (MM); music education (MM, DMA); musicology (MA, PhD); pedagogy of music theory (MA); performance and literature (MM, DMA); piano accompanying and chamber music (MM, DMA); theory (MA, PhD). *Accreditation:* NASM. Part-time programs available. *Degree requirements:* For master's, thesis (for some programs); for doctorate, comprehensive exam (for some programs), thesis/dissertation (for some programs). *Entrance requirements:* For master's and doctorate, GRE. *Expenses:* Contact institution.

University of Saskatchewan, College of Graduate Studies and Research, College of Arts and Sciences, Department of Music, Saskatoon, SK S7N 5A2, Canada. Offers M Mus, MA. *Faculty:* 9. *Students:* 9. In 2009, 2 master's awarded. *Degree requirements:* For master's, thesis. *Entrance requirements:* Additional exam requirements/recommendations for international students: Required—TOEFL (minimum score 80 iBT); Recommended—IELTS (minimum score 6.5). *Application deadline:* Applications are processed on a rolling basis. Application fee: $75. Electronic applications accepted. Tuition and fees charges are reported in Canadian dollars. *Expenses:* Tuition, area resident: Full-time $3000 Canadian dollars; part-time $500 Canadian dollars per term. Required fees: $700 Canadian dollars; $100 Canadian dollars per term. *Unit head:* Dr. Dean McNeill, Acting Head, 306-966-6171, Fax: 306-966-8719, E-mail: dean.mcneill@usask.ca. *Application contact:* Dr. Gregory Marion, Graduate Chair, 306-966-6171, Fax: 306-966-8719, E-mail: gregory.marion@usask.ca.

University of South Africa, College of Human Sciences, Pretoria, South Africa. Offers adult education (M Ed); African languages (MA, PhD); African politics (MA, PhD); Afrikaans (MA, PhD); ancient history (MA, PhD); ancient Near Eastern studies (MA, PhD); anthropology (MA, PhD); applied linguistics (MA); Arabic (MA, PhD); archaeology (MA); art history (MA); Biblical archaeology (MA); Biblical studies (M Th, D Th, PhD); Christian spirituality (M Th, D Th); church history (M Th, D Th); classical studies (MA, PhD); clinical psychology (MA); communication (MA, PhD); comparative education (M Ed, Ed D); consulting psychology (D Admin, D Com, PhD); curriculum studies (M Ed, Ed D); development studies (M Admin, MA, D Admin, PhD); didactics (M Ed, Ed D); education (M Tech); education management (M Ed, Ed D); educational psychology (M Ed); English (MA); environmental education (M Ed); French (MA, PhD); German (MA, PhD); Greek (MA); guidance and counseling (M Ed); health studies (MA, PhD), including health sciences education (MA), health services management (MA), medical and surgical nursing science (critical care general) (MA), midwifery and neonatal nursing science (MA), trauma and emergency care (MA); history (MA, PhD); history of education (Ed D); inclusive education (M Ed, Ed D); information and communications technology policy and regulation (MA); information science (MA, MIS, PhD); international politics (MA, PhD); Islamic studies (MA, PhD); Italian (MA, PhD); Judaica (MA, PhD); linguistics (MA, PhD); mathematical education (M Ed); mathematics education (MA); missiology (M Th, D Th); modern Hebrew (MA, PhD); musicology (MA, MMus, D Mus, PhD); natural science education (M Ed); New Testament (M Th, D Th); Old Testament (D Th); pastoral therapy (M Th, D Th); philosophy (MA); philosophy of education (M Ed, Ed D); politics (MA, PhD); Portuguese (MA, PhD); practical theology (M Th, D Th); psychology (MA, MS, PhD); psychology of education (M Ed, Ed D); public health (MA); religious studies (MA, D Th, PhD); Romance languages (MA); Russian (MA, PhD); Semitic languages (MA, PhD); social behavior studies in HIV/AIDS (MA); social science (mental health) (MA); social science in development studies (MA); social science in psychology (MA); social science in social work (MA); social science in sociology (MA); social work (MSW, DSW, PhD); socio-education (M Ed, Ed D); sociolinguistics (MA); sociology (MA, PhD); Spanish (MA, PhD); systematic theology (M Th, D Th); TESOL (teaching English to speakers of other languages) (MA); theological ethics (M Th, D Th); theory of literature (MA, PhD); urban ministries (D Th); urban ministry (M Th).

University of South Carolina, The Graduate School, School of Music, Columbia, SC 29208. Offers composition (MM, DMA); conducting (MM, DMA); jazz studies (MM); music education (MM Ed, PhD); music history (MM); music performance (Certificate); music theory (MM); opera theater (MM); performance (MM, DMA); piano pedagogy (MM, DMA). *Accreditation:* NASM (one or more programs are accredited). Part-time programs available. *Degree requirements:* For master's, 5 foreign languages, comprehensive exam, thesis (for some programs); for doctorate, one foreign language, comprehensive exam, thesis/dissertation; for Certificate, recitals. *Entrance requirements:* For master's and doctorate, GRE General Test or MAT, music diagnostic exam. Additional exam requirements/recommendations for international students: Required—TOEFL (minimum score 570 paper-based; 230 computer-based). Electronic applications accepted. *Expenses:* Contact institution. *Faculty research:* Music skills in pre-school children, evaluation of school performing ensembles.

The University of South Dakota, Graduate School, College of Fine Arts, Department of Music, Vermillion, SD 57069-2390. Offers MM. *Accreditation:* NASM. *Degree requirements:* For master's, thesis or alternative. *Entrance requirements:* For master's, minimum GPA of 2.7, audition or performance tape. Additional exam requirements/recommendations for international students: Required—TOEFL (minimum score 550 paper-based; 213 computer-based; 79 iBT). Electronic applications accepted.

University of Southern California, Graduate School, Thornton School of Music, Los Angeles, CA 90089. Offers brass performance (MM, DMA, Graduate Certificate); choral and sacred music (MM, DMA); classical guitar (MM, DMA, Graduate Certificate); composition (MM, DMA); early music (MA, DMA); harp performance (MM, DMA, Graduate Certificate); historical musicology (PhD); jazz studies (MM, DMA, Graduate Certificate); keyboard collaborative arts (MM, Graduate Certificate); music education (MM, DMA); organ performance (MM, DMA, Graduate Certificate); percussion performance (MM, DMA, Graduate Certificate); piano performance (MM, DMA, Graduate Certificate); scoring for motion pictures and television (Graduate Certificate); strings performance (MM, DMA, Graduate Certificate); studio jazz guitar (MM, DMA, Graduate Certificate); teaching music (MA); vocal arts (classical voice/opera) (MM, DMA, Graduate Certificate); woodwind performance (MM, DMA, Graduate Certificate). *Accreditation:* NASM. Part-time and evening/weekend programs available. *Faculty:* 74 full-time (14 women), 120 part-time/adjunct (29 women). *Students:* 354 full-time (155 women), 43 part-time (32 women); includes 72 minority (5 African Americans, 2 American Indian/Alaska Native, 47 Asian Americans or Pacific Islanders, 18 Hispanic Americans), 111 international. 784 applicants, 36% accepted, 145 enrolled. In 2009, 54 master's, 2 doctorates, 96 other advanced degrees awarded. Terminal master's awarded for partial completion of doctoral program. *Degree requirements:* For master's, variable foreign language requirement, comprehensive exam (for some programs), thesis (for some programs); for doctorate, variable foreign language requirement, comprehensive exam, thesis/dissertation (for some programs). *Entrance requirements:* For master's, GRE, for MA Early Music, MAT and MM in Music Education; for doctorate, GRE, for all DMA programs. Additional exam requirements/recommendations for international students: Required—TOEFL (minimum score 560 paper-based; 220 computer-based; 83 iBT). *Application deadline:* For fall admission, 12/1 for domestic and international students; for spring admission, 10/1 for domestic and international students. Application fee: $85. Electronic applications accepted. *Expenses:* Contact institution. *Financial support:* In 2009–10, 65 teaching assistantships with full tuition reimbursements (averaging $9,600 per year) were awarded; tuition waivers also available. Financial award application deadline: 12/1; financial award applicants required to submit FAFSA. *Faculty research:* Early Modern musical improvisation and composition, maternal sound stimulation of the premature infant, physiological characteristics of jazz guitarists, the musical experience of the very young child, electronic music. *Unit head:* PJ Woolston, Dean, 213-740-2311, E-mail: woolston@thornton.usc.edu. *Application contact:* Ligaya J. Jones, Admission Coordinator, 213-740-8986, E-mail: ljones@thornton.usc.edu.

University of Southern Maine, College of Arts and Sciences, Program in Music, Portland, ME 04104-9300. Offers MM. *Accreditation:* NASM.

University of Southern Mississippi, Graduate School, College of Arts and Letters, School of Music, Hattiesburg, MS 39406-0001. Offers conducting (MM); history and literature (MM); music education (MME, PhD); performance (MM); performance and pedagogy (DMA); theory and composition (MM); woodwind performance (MM). *Accreditation:* NASM. *Faculty:* 33 full-time (10 women), 2 part-time/adjunct (0 women). *Students:* 72 full-time (24 women), 24 part-time (7 women); includes 7 minority (4 African Americans, 3 Hispanic Americans), 15 international. Average age 32. 71 applicants, 73% accepted, 35 enrolled. In 2009, 26 master's, 11 doctorates awarded. Terminal master's awarded for partial completion of doctoral program. *Degree requirements:* For master's, comprehensive exam, thesis (for some programs); for doctorate, comprehensive exam, thesis/dissertation. *Entrance requirements:* For master's, GRE General Test, minimum GPA of 2.75 in last 60 hours; for doctorate, GRE General Test, minimum GPA of 3.5. Additional exam requirements/recommendations for international students: Required—TOEFL. *Application deadline:* For fall admission, 3/1 priority date for domestic students; for spring admission, 12/13 for domestic students. Applications are processed on a rolling basis. Application fee: $35. *Expenses:* Tuition, state resident: full-time $5096; part-time $284 per hour. Tuition, nonresident: full-time $13,052; part-time $726 per hour. Required fees: $402. Tuition and fees vary according to course level and course load. *Financial support:* In 2009–10, 1 fellowship with full tuition reimbursement (averaging $12,000 per year), 51 teaching assistantships with full tuition reimbursements (averaging $6,000 per year) were awarded; research assistantships, Federal Work-Study, scholarships/grants, tuition waivers (partial), and unspecified assistantships also available. Financial award application deadline: 3/15; financial award applicants required to submit FAFSA. *Faculty research:* Music theory, composition. *Unit head:* Dr. Charles Elliott, Director, 601-266-5543, Fax: 601-266-6427, E-mail: celliott@usm.edu. *Application contact:* Graduate Coordinator, 601-266-5369, Fax: 601-266-6427.

Music

University of South Florida, Graduate School, College of The Arts, School of Music, Tampa, FL 33620-9951. Offers chamber music (MM); composition (MM); conducting (MM); electro-acoustic music (MM); jazz studies (MM), including composition, performance; music education (MA, PhD); piano pedagogy (MM); theory (MM). *Accreditation:* NASM. Part-time and evening/weekend programs available. *Faculty:* 19 full-time (8 women), 10 part-time/adjunct (4 women). *Students:* 61 full-time (29 women), 28 part-time (14 women); includes 10 minority (2 African Americans, 3 Asian Americans or Pacific Islanders, 5 Hispanic Americans), 11 international. Average age 32. 81 applicants, 84% accepted, 36 enrolled. In 2009, 37 master's, 1 doctorate awarded. *Degree requirements:* For master's, comprehensive exam, thesis, 30-34 credit hours; for doctorate, comprehensive exam, thesis/dissertation. *Entrance requirements:* For master's, diagnostic exam in theory and history, audition, portfolio, minimum GPA of 3.0; for doctorate, GRE, writing samples, interview, teaching video. Additional exam requirements/recommendations for international students: Required—TOEFL (minimum score 550 paper-based; 213 computer-based). *Application deadline:* For fall admission, 2/15 priority date for domestic students, 3/15 for international students; for spring admission, 10/15 for domestic students, 6/1 for international students. Application fee: $30. *Financial support:* In 2009–10, teaching assistantships with tuition reimbursements (averaging $19,251 per year); unspecified assistantships also available. Financial award application deadline: 2/15. *Faculty research:* Education, conducting, performance, history, theory. *Unit head:* Wade Weast, Director, 813-974-2311, Fax: 813-974-8721, E-mail: wweast@usf.edu. *Application contact:* David Williams, Program Director, 813-974-2311, Fax: 813-974-8721, E-mail: davidw@usf.edu.

The University of Tennessee, Graduate School, College of Arts and Sciences, Department of Theatre, Knoxville, TN 37996. Offers costume design (MFA); lighting design (MFA); performance (MFA); scene design (MFA); theatre technology (MFA). *Degree requirements:* For master's, thesis or alternative. *Entrance requirements:* For master's, audition, minimum GPA of 2.7. Additional exam requirements/recommendations for international students: Required—TOEFL. Electronic applications accepted. *Expenses:* Tuition, state resident: full-time $6826; part-time $380 per semester hour. Tuition, nonresident: full-time $21,844; part-time $1147 per semester hour. Tuition and fees vary according to program.

The University of Tennessee, Graduate School, College of Arts and Sciences, School of Music, Knoxville, TN 37996. Offers accompanying (MM); choral conducting (MM); composition (MM); instrumental conducting (MM); jazz (MM); music education (MM); music theory (MM); musicology (MM); performance (MM); piano pedagogy and literature (MM). *Accreditation:* NASM. Part-time programs available. *Degree requirements:* For master's, thesis (for some programs). *Entrance requirements:* For master's, audition, minimum GPA of 2.7. Additional exam requirements/recommendations for international students: Required—TOEFL. Electronic applications accepted. *Expenses:* Tuition, state resident: full-time $6826; part-time $380 per semester hour. Tuition, nonresident: full-time $21,844; part-time $1147 per semester hour. Tuition and fees vary according to program.

The University of Tennessee at Chattanooga, Graduate School, College of Arts and Sciences, Department of Music, Chattanooga, TN 37403. Offers music education (MM); performance (MM). *Accreditation:* NASM. Part-time programs available. *Faculty:* 7 full-time (1 woman). *Students:* 7 full-time (4 women), 10 part-time (6 women); includes 1 minority (African American), 2 international. Average age 32. 4 applicants, 100% accepted, 4 enrolled. In 2009, 6 master's awarded. *Degree requirements:* For master's, comprehensive exam, thesis or alternative, senior recital. *Entrance requirements:* For master's, GRE General Test or MAT, bachelor's degree in music, audition for placement. Additional exam requirements/recommendations for international students: Required—TOEFL (minimum score 550 paper-based; 213 computer-based; 79 iBT), IELTS (minimum score 6). *Application deadline:* For fall admission, 8/1 priority date for domestic students, 6/1 for international students; for spring admission, 12/1 priority date for domestic students, 10/1 for international students. Applications are processed on a rolling basis. Application fee: $35. Electronic applications accepted. *Expenses:* Tuition, state resident: full-time $5404; part-time $300 per credit hour. Tuition, nonresident: full-time $16,702; part-time $928 per credit hour. Required fees: $1150; $130 per credit hour. *Financial support:* In 2009–10, 5 research assistantships with full and partial tuition reimbursements (averaging $5,500 per year) were awarded; Federal Work-Study, scholarships/grants, and unspecified assistantships also available. *Faculty research:* Music education, conducting, opera, vocal instruction, orchestras. *Unit head:* Dr. Lee Harris, Department Head, 423-425-4601, Fax: 423-425-4603, E-mail: lee-harris@utc.edu. *Application contact:* Dr. Stephanie Bellar, Dean of Graduate Studies, 423-425-4666, Fax: 423-425-5223, E-mail: stephanie-bellar@utc.edu.

The University of Texas at Arlington, Graduate School, College of Liberal Arts, Department of Music, Arlington, TX 76019. Offers education (MM); performance (MM). *Accreditation:* NASM. Part-time and evening/weekend programs available. *Faculty:* 24 full-time (9 women). *Students:* 9 full-time (3 women), 25 part-time (14 women); includes 6 minority (2 African Americans, 4 Hispanic Americans), 9 international. 13 applicants, 100% accepted, 10 enrolled. In 2009, 6 master's awarded. *Degree requirements:* For master's, comprehensive exam, thesis optional. *Entrance requirements:* For master's, GRE, 3 letters of recommendation, minimum GPA of 3.0 in last 60 hours of course work. Additional exam requirements/recommendations for international students: Required—TOEFL (minimum score 550 paper-based; 213 computer-based). *Application deadline:* For fall admission, 6/1 for domestic students. Application fee: $35 ($50 for international students). *Financial support:* In 2009–10, 2 research assistantships (averaging $6,500 per year), 5 teaching assistantships with partial tuition reimbursements (averaging $6,500 per year) were awarded; scholarships/grants also available. *Unit head:* Dr. John Burton, Chair, 817-272-3471, Fax: 817-272-3434. *Application contact:* Assistant Chair/Graduate Advisor.

The University of Texas at Austin, Graduate School, College of Fine Arts, Butler School of Music, Austin, TX 78712-1111. Offers M Music, DMA, PhD. *Accreditation:* NASM. Part-time programs available. *Degree requirements:* For master's, one foreign language, comprehensive exam, thesis (for some programs), recital (performance or composition majors); for doctorate, one foreign language, comprehensive exam, thesis/dissertation (for some programs), recital for performance or composition majors. *Entrance requirements:* For master's, GRE General Test (unless a performance or composition major), audition (performance majors); for doctorate, GRE General Test (not required for performance or composition majors), audition (performance majors). Electronic applications accepted.

The University of Texas at El Paso, Graduate School, College of Liberal Arts, Department of Music, El Paso, TX 79968-0001. Offers music education (MM); music performance (MM). *Accreditation:* NASM. Part-time and evening/weekend programs available. *Students:* 23 (7 women); includes 13 minority (1 African American, 1 American Indian/Alaska Native, 11 Hispanic Americans), 4 international. Average age 34. In 2009, 8 master's awarded. *Degree requirements:* For master's, thesis optional. *Entrance requirements:* For master's, audition, interview, letters of recommendation. Additional exam requirements/recommendations for international students: Required—TOEFL; Recommended—IELTS. *Application deadline:* For fall admission, 8/1 priority date for domestic students, 3/1 for international students; for spring admission, 11/1 priority date for domestic students, 9/1 for international students. Applications are processed on a rolling basis. Application fee: $45 ($80 for international students). Electronic applications accepted. *Financial support:* In 2009–10, research assistantships (averaging $18,625 per year), teaching assistantships with partial tuition reimbursements (averaging $14,900 per year) were awarded; fellowships with partial tuition reimbursements, institutionally sponsored loans, scholarships/grants, health care benefits, tuition waivers (partial), and unspecified assistantships also available. Support available to part-time students. Financial award application deadline: 3/15; financial award applicants required to submit FAFSA. *Unit head:* Dr. Lowell Graham, Chair, 915-747-5606, Fax: 915-747-5023, E-mail: legraham@utep.edu. *Application contact:* Dr. Patricia D. Witherspoon, Dean of the Graduate School, 915-747-5491, Fax: 915-747-5788, E-mail: withersp@utep.edu.

The University of Texas at San Antonio, College of Liberal and Fine Arts, Department of Music, San Antonio, TX 78249-0617. Offers keyboard pedagogy (Graduate Certificate); keyboard performance (Graduate Certificate); music (MM). *Accreditation:* NASM. Part-time programs available. *Faculty:* 14 full-time (7 women), 3 part-time/adjunct (0 women). *Students:* 11 full-time (6 women), 9 part-time (3 women); includes 8 minority (1 African American, 1 Asian American or Pacific Islander, 6 Hispanic Americans). Average age 29. 14 applicants, 71% accepted, 5 enrolled. In 2009, 2 master's awarded. *Degree requirements:* For master's, one foreign language, comprehensive exam (for some programs), thesis (for some programs), recital. *Entrance requirements:* For master's, GRE, audition, 3 letters of recommendation. Additional exam requirements/recommendations for international students: Required—TOEFL (minimum score 500 paper-based; 173 computer-based; 61 iBT), IELTS (minimum score 5). *Application deadline:* For fall admission, 7/1 for domestic students, 4/1 for international students; for spring admission, 11/1 for domestic students, 9/1 for international students. Applications are processed on a rolling basis. Application fee: $45 ($80 for international students). Electronic applications accepted. *Expenses:* Tuition, state resident: full-time $3975; part-time $221 per contact hour. Tuition, nonresident: full-time $13,947; part-time $775 per contact hour. Required fees: $1853. *Financial support:* In 2009–10, 9 students received support, including 9 research assistantships (averaging $8,605 per year), 2 teaching assistantships (averaging $6,000 per year); career-related internships or fieldwork, scholarships/grants, and unspecified assistantships also available. Support available to part-time students. Financial award application deadline: 3/1. *Faculty research:* Vocal singing health, rhythmic and movement therapy, implied harmonic and polyphonic structures in music, historical music of Latin America, documenting early twentieth century American choral music. Total annual research expenditures: $6,881. *Unit head:* Dr. Eugene Dowdy, Chair, 210-458-4354, E-mail: edowdy@utsa.edu. *Application contact:* Dr. Eugene Dowdy, Chair, 210-458-4354, E-mail: edowdy@utsa.edu.

The University of Texas–Pan American, College of Arts and Humanities, Department of Music, Edinburg, TX 78539. Offers ethnomusicology (M Mus); interdisciplinary studies (MAIS); music education (M Mus); performance (M Mus). Part-time programs available. *Degree requirements:* For master's, comprehensive exam, thesis optional, recital (performance). *Entrance requirements:* For master's, audition for performance area, bachelor's degree in music. *Expenses:* Tuition, state resident: full-time $3630.60; part-time $201.70 per credit hour. Tuition, nonresident: full-time $8617; part-time $478.70 per credit hour. Required fees: $806.50. *Faculty research:* Music history, instrumental pedagogy, vocal pedagogy, music education, ethnomusicology.

The University of the Arts, College of Performing Arts, School of Music, Program in Jazz Studies, Philadelphia, PA 19102-4944. Offers MM. Part-time programs available. *Degree requirements:* For master's, professional internship, recital. *Entrance requirements:* For master's, audition. Additional exam requirements/recommendations for international students: Required—TOEFL (minimum score 550 paper-based; 213 computer-based).

See Close-Up on page 199.

University of the Pacific, Conservatory of Music, Stockton, CA 95211-0197. Offers MA, MM. *Accreditation:* NASM. *Faculty:* 4 full-time (3 women), 4 part-time/adjunct (2 women). *Students:* 5 full-time (all women), 17 part-time (13 women); includes 3 minority (2 Asian Americans or Pacific Islanders, 1 Hispanic American), 5 international. Average age 29. 33 applicants, 48% accepted, 7 enrolled. In 2009, 4 master's awarded. *Entrance requirements:* For master's, GRE General Test. Additional exam requirements/recommendations for international students: Required—TOEFL (minimum score 475 paper-based; 150 computer-based). *Application deadline:* For fall admission, 3/1 priority date for domestic students; for spring admission, 10/1 priority date for domestic students. Applications are processed on a rolling basis. Application fee: $75. *Financial support:* Teaching assistantships, institutionally sponsored loans available. Support available to part-time students. Financial award application deadline: 3/1; financial award applicants required to submit FAFSA. *Unit head:* Dr. Giulio Ongaro, Dean, 209-946-2417. *Application contact:* Dr. Therese West, Chairperson, 209-946-3194.

The University of Toledo, College of Graduate Studies, College of Arts and Sciences, Department of Music, Toledo, OH 43606-3390. Offers performance (MMP). *Accreditation:* NASM. *Entrance requirements:* For master's, audition (performance), minimum A average in student teaching or teaching experience (music education). Electronic applications accepted.

University of Toronto, School of Graduate Studies, Humanities Division, Faculty of Music, Toronto, ON M5S 1A1, Canada. Offers composition (M Mus, DMA); music education (MA, PhD); musicology/theory (MA, PhD); performance (M Mus, DMA). Part-time programs available. *Degree requirements:* For master's, comprehensive exam (for some programs), oral examination (Mus M in composition), 1 foreign language (MA); for doctorate, thesis/dissertation (for some programs), recital of original works (Mus Doc), thesis (PhD). *Entrance requirements:* For master's, Bachelor of Music in area of specialization with minimum B average in final 2 years, original compositions (Mus M in composition); for doctorate, master's degree in area of specialization, minimum B+ average, at least 2 extended compositions (Mus Doc).

University of Trinity College, Faculty of Divinity, Toronto, ON M5S 1H8, Canada. Offers ministry (Diploma); ministry for church musicians (Diploma); theology (M Div, MTS, Th M, D Min, PhD, Th D, Diploma, L Th); M Div/MA. *Accreditation:* ATS. Part-time programs available. *Degree requirements:* For master's, 2 foreign languages, thesis (for some programs); for doctorate, 3 foreign languages, comprehensive exam, thesis/dissertation; for M Div, thesis/dissertation optional; for other advanced degree, thesis (for some programs). *Entrance requirements:* For M Div, interview; for master's, 1 language (modern or ancient), interview; for doctorate, 2 languages (modern and ancient). Additional exam requirements/recommendations for international students: Required—TOEFL, TWE. *Faculty research:* Interreligious dialogue, feminist theology, systematic theology, philosophy of religion, pastoral theology.

University of Utah, The Graduate School, College of Fine Arts, School of Music, Salt Lake City, UT 84112. Offers M Mus, MA, DMA, PhD. *Accreditation:* NASM. *Faculty:* 31 full-time (13 women), 25 part-time/adjunct (8 women). *Students:* 78 full-time (44 women), 41 part-time (23 women); includes 11 minority (2 American Indian/Alaska Native, 6 Asian Americans or Pacific Islanders, 3 Hispanic Americans), 17 international. Average age 32. 97 applicants, 57% accepted, 31 enrolled. In 2009, 35 master's, 1 doctorate awarded. *Degree requirements:* For master's, one foreign language, thesis (for some programs), 2 recitals, final oral exam; for doctorate, one foreign language, final oral exam, 4 recitals (DMA); thesis (PhD). *Entrance requirements:* For master's and doctorate, placement exams, minimum GPA of 3.0, audition, Bachelor's degree in Music. Additional exam requirements/recommendations for international students: Required—TOEFL (minimum score 500 paper-based; 173 computer-based; 61 iBT). *Application deadline:* For fall admission, 2/15 for domestic students, 1/15 for international students; for spring admission, 10/1 for domestic students, 9/1 for international students. Application fee: $55 ($65 for international students). *Expenses:* Tuition, state resident: full-time $4004; part-time $1674 per semester. Tuition, nonresident: full-time $14,134; part-time $5915 per semester. Required fees: $324 per semester. Tuition and fees vary according to course load, degree level and program. *Financial support:* In 2009–10, 52 students received support, including 52 teaching assistantships with full and partial tuition reimbursements available (averaging $8,250 per year); fellowships with full and partial tuition reimbursements available, research assistantships with full and partial tuition reimbursements available, health care benefits and unspecified assistantships also available. Financial award application deadline: 2/1. *Faculty research:* Music education, conducting, musicology, composition, performance. Total annual research expenditures: $17,005. *Unit head:* Dr. Robert Walzel, Director, 801-581-6762, Fax: 801-581-5683, E-mail: robert.walzel@music.utah.edu. *Application contact:* Jill Wilson, Graduate Secretary, Recruitment, 801-585-6972, Fax: 801-581-5683, E-mail: jill.wilson@utah.edu.

University of Utah, The Graduate School, College of Humanities, Department of English, Salt Lake City, UT 84112. Offers American studies (MA, PhD), including rhetoric/composition; British American literature (MA, PhD); creative writing (MA, MFA, PhD), including rhetoric/composition (MA, PhD); literature (PhD); rhetoric and composition (PhD). *Faculty:* 36 full-time (16 women). *Students:* 57 full-time (36 women), 17 part-time (13 women); includes 5 minority

(3 African Americans, 1 American Indian/Alaska Native, 1 Asian American or Pacific Islander), 2 international. Average age 33. 270 applicants, 10% accepted, 24 enrolled. In 2009, 20 master's, 8 doctorates awarded. Terminal master's awarded for partial completion of doctoral program. *Degree requirements:* For master's, one foreign language, comprehensive exam, thesis (for some programs), written exam; for doctorate, 2 foreign languages, comprehensive exam, thesis/dissertation. *Entrance requirements:* For master's and doctorate, GRE General Test, minimum GPA of 3.2. Additional exam requirements/recommendations for international students: Required—TOEFL (minimum score 650 paper-based; 280 computer-based; 115 iBT). *Application deadline:* For fall admission, 12/15 for domestic and international students. Application fee: $55 ($65 for international students). Electronic applications accepted. *Expenses:* Tuition, state resident: full-time $4004; part-time $1674 per semester. Tuition, nonresident: full-time $14,134; part-time $5915 per semester. Required fees: $324 per semester. Tuition and fees vary according to course load, degree level and program. *Financial support:* In 2009–10, 52 students received support, including 9 fellowships with full tuition reimbursements available (averaging $12,400 per year), 43 teaching assistantships with full tuition reimbursements available (averaging $12,400 per year); research assistantships, health care benefits also available. Financial award application deadline: 12/15; financial award applicants required to submit FAFSA. *Faculty research:* Poetics and modern poetry, nineteenth and twentieth century British and American literature, the American west, environmental studies, critical theory and race and gender studies. Total annual research expenditures: $45,462. *Unit head:* Prof. Vincent P. Pecora, Chair, 801-581-6168, E-mail: v.pecora@utah.edu. *Application contact:* Prof. Scott Black, Director of Graduate Studies, 801-581-5137, E-mail: scott.black@utah.edu.

University of Victoria, Faculty of Graduate Studies, Faculty of Fine Arts, School of Music, Victoria, BC V8W 2Y2, Canada. Offers composition (M Mus); musicology (MA, PhD); musicology with performance (MA); performance (M Mus). *Degree requirements:* For master's, 2 foreign languages, thesis; for doctorate, 2 foreign languages, thesis/dissertation, candidacy exam. *Entrance requirements:* For master's, theory placement test, audition or sample papers and compositions; for doctorate, audition or sample papers and compositions. Additional exam requirements/recommendations for international students: Required—TOEFL (minimum score 575 paper-based; 233 computer-based), IELTS (minimum score 7). Electronic applications accepted. *Faculty research:* Beethoven, Wagner, metrical structure in tonal music, French baroque, eighteenth century opera.

University of Virginia, College and Graduate School of Arts and Sciences, Department of Music, Charlottesville, VA 22903. Offers MA, PhD. *Faculty:* 16 full-time (4 women), 14 part-time/adjunct (5 women). *Students:* 30 full-time (14 women), 1 part-time (0 women); includes 2 minority (both Asian Americans or Pacific Islanders), 4 international. Average age 30. 51 applicants, 22% accepted, 5 enrolled. *Degree requirements:* For master's, one foreign language, article-length paper; for doctorate, one foreign language, comprehensive exam, thesis/dissertation. *Entrance requirements:* For master's and doctorate, GRE General Test, 2 writing samples or portfolio. Additional exam requirements/recommendations for international students: Required—TOEFL (minimum score 600 paper-based; 250 computer-based; 90 iBT), IELTS (minimum score 7). *Application deadline:* For fall admission, 1/2 for domestic and international students. Applications are processed on a rolling basis. Application fee: $60. Electronic applications accepted. *Financial support:* Teaching assistantships available. Financial award applicants required to submit FAFSA. *Unit head:* Kate Tamarkin, Chair, 434-924-3052, Fax: 434-924-6033, E-mail: tamarkin@virginia.edu. *Application contact:* Fred Maus, Director of Graduate Studies, 434-924-3052, Fax: 434-924-6033, E-mail: fem2x@virginia.edu.

University of Washington, Graduate School, College of Arts and Sciences, School of Music, Concentration in Choral Conducting, Seattle, WA 98195. Offers MM, DMA.

University of Washington, Graduate School, College of Arts and Sciences, School of Music, Concentration in Ethnomusicology, Seattle, WA 98195. Offers MA.

University of Washington, Graduate School, College of Arts and Sciences, School of Music, Concentration in Music History, Seattle, WA 98195. Offers MA, PhD.

University of Washington, Graduate School, College of Arts and Sciences, School of Music, Department of Choral Music, Seattle, WA 98195. Offers choral conducting (MM, DMA).

The University of Western Ontario, Faculty of Graduate Studies, Faculty of Arts and Humanities, Don Wright Faculty of Music, London, ON N6A 5B8, Canada. Offers music (M Mus, PhD); popular music and culture (MA). Part-time programs available. Terminal master's awarded for partial completion of doctoral program. *Degree requirements:* For master's, 2 foreign languages, thesis (for some programs), recital; for doctorate, 2 foreign languages, thesis/dissertation. *Entrance requirements:* For master's, honors degree in music; minimum A average in proposed area of concentration, B average overall; for doctorate, MA or equivalent. *Faculty research:* Systematic musicology, musicology, theory, music education.

University of West Georgia, Graduate School, College of Arts and Sciences, Department of Music, Carrollton, GA 30118. Offers music education (M Mus); performance (M Mus). *Accreditation:* NASM. Part-time programs available. *Faculty:* 7 full-time (3 women), 3 part-time/adjunct (2 women). *Students:* 3 full-time (2 women), 11 part-time (7 women); includes 3 minority (all African Americans). Average age 32. 4 applicants, 75% accepted, 2 enrolled. In 2009, 3 master's awarded. *Degree requirements:* For master's, comprehensive exam, thesis optional, recital (MM in performance), departmental qualifying exam. *Entrance requirements:* For master's, qualifying exam, minimum GPA of 2.5, bachelor's degree in music education or teacher certification (music education), performance evaluation. *Application deadline:* For fall admission, 7/17 for domestic students; for spring admission, 11/20 for domestic students. Applications are processed on a rolling basis. Application fee: $30. Electronic applications accepted. *Expenses:* Tuition, state resident: full-time $2952; part-time $164 per semester hour. Tuition, nonresident: full-time $11,808; part-time $656 per semester hour. Required fees: $42.90 per semester hour. $307 per semester. Tuition and fees vary according to course load. *Financial support:* In 2009–10, 2 students received support, including 2 research assistantships with full tuition reimbursements available (averaging $6,000 per year); career-related internships or fieldwork, tuition waivers (full), and unspecified assistantships also available. Support available to part-time students. Financial award application deadline: 7/1; financial award applicants required to submit FAFSA. *Faculty research:* Ethnomusicology, instrumental music/music education, jazz performance, French music, Latin American music. *Unit head:* Dr. Kevin Hibbard, Chair, 678-839-6516, Fax: 678-839-6259, E-mail: khibbard@westga.edu. *Application contact:* Dr. Charles W. Clark, Dean, 678-839-6508, E-mail: cclark@westga.edu.

University of Wisconsin–Madison, Graduate School, College of Letters and Science, School of Music, Program in Composition, Madison, WI 53706-1380. Offers MM, DMA. *Accreditation:* NASM. *Degree requirements:* For doctorate, thesis/dissertation. *Expenses:* Tuition, state resident: part-time $594 per credit. Tuition, nonresident: part-time $1504 per credit. Required fees: $65 per credit. Tuition and fees vary according to course load, program and reciprocity agreements.

University of Wisconsin–Madison, Graduate School, College of Letters and Science, School of Music, Program in Conducting, Madison, WI 53706-1380. Offers choral (MM, DMA); instrumental (MM, DMA); orchestral (MM, DMA). *Accreditation:* NASM. *Degree requirements:* For doctorate, thesis/dissertation. *Expenses:* Tuition, state resident: part-time $594 per credit. Tuition, nonresident: part-time $1504 per credit. Required fees: $65 per credit. Tuition and fees vary according to course load, program and reciprocity agreements.

University of Wisconsin–Madison, Graduate School, College of Letters and Science, School of Music, Program in Musicology and Ethnomusicology, Madison, WI 53706-1380. Offers ethnomusicology (MA, PhD); historical musicology (PhD); music history (MA). *Accreditation:* NASM. *Degree requirements:* For doctorate, 2 foreign languages, thesis/dissertation. *Entrance requirements:* For doctorate, GRE General Test. *Expenses:* Tuition, state resident: part-time $594 per credit. Tuition, nonresident: part-time $1504 per credit. Required fees: $65 per credit. Tuition and fees vary according to course load, program and reciprocity agreements.

University of Wisconsin–Madison, Graduate School, College of Letters and Science, School of Music, Program in Music Performance, Madison, WI 53706-1380. Offers MM, DMA. *Accreditation:* NASM. *Degree requirements:* For doctorate, one foreign language, thesis/dissertation. *Expenses:* Tuition, state resident: part-time $594 per credit. Tuition, nonresident: part-time $1504 per credit. Required fees: $65 per credit. Tuition and fees vary according to course load, program and reciprocity agreements.

University of Wisconsin–Madison, Graduate School, College of Letters and Science, School of Music, Program in Music Theory, Madison, WI 53706-1380. Offers MA, PhD. *Accreditation:* NASM. *Degree requirements:* For master's, thesis, 1 foreign language (MA); for doctorate, 2 foreign languages, thesis/dissertation. *Entrance requirements:* For master's, GRE General Test (MA); for doctorate, GRE General Test. *Expenses:* Tuition, state resident: part-time $594 per credit. Tuition, nonresident: part-time $1504 per credit. Required fees: $65 per credit. Tuition and fees vary according to course load, program and reciprocity agreements.

University of Wisconsin–Milwaukee, Graduate School, Peck School of the Arts, Department of Music, Milwaukee, WI 53201-0413. Offers chamber music performance (Certificate); music composition (MM); music education (MM); music history and literature (MM); opera and vocal arts (Certificate); string pedagogy (MM); MLIS/MM. *Accreditation:* NASM. Part-time programs available. *Faculty:* 24 full-time (6 women). *Students:* 38 full-time (19 women), 28 part-time (14 women); includes 3 minority (2 Asian Americans or Pacific Islanders, 1 Hispanic American), 7 international. Average age 27. 54 applicants, 72% accepted, 22 enrolled. In 2009, 22 master's awarded. *Degree requirements:* For master's, variable foreign language requirement, comprehensive exam, thesis or alternative. *Entrance requirements:* For master's, GRE General Test, GRE Subject Test, audition, interview. Additional exam requirements/recommendations for international students: Required—TOEFL (minimum score 550 paper-based; 79 iBT), IELTS (minimum score 6.5). *Application deadline:* For fall admission, 1/1 priority date for domestic students; for spring admission, 9/1 for domestic students. Applications are processed on a rolling basis. Application fee: $45 ($75 for international students). *Expenses:* Contact institution. *Financial support:* In 2009–10, 9 teaching assistantships were awarded; career-related internships or fieldwork and unspecified assistantships also available. Support available to part-time students. Financial award application deadline: 4/15. *Unit head:* Timothy Noonan, Representative, 414-229-2286, Fax: 414-229-2776, E-mail: tpnoonan@uwm.edu. *Application contact:* General Information Contact, 414-229-4982, Fax: 414-229-6967, E-mail: gradschool@uwm.edu.

University of Wyoming, College of Arts and Sciences, Department of Music, Laramie, WY 82070. Offers music education (MME); performance (MM). *Accreditation:* NASM. *Degree requirements:* For master's, comprehensive exam, thesis or alternative. *Entrance requirements:* For master's, minimum GPA of 3.0. Additional exam requirements/recommendations for international students: Required—TOEFL (minimum score 540 paper-based; 207 computer-based). Electronic applications accepted.

Virginia Commonwealth University, Graduate School, School of the Arts, Department of Music, Richmond, VA 23284-9005. Offers education (MM). *Accreditation:* NASM. *Degree requirements:* For master's, departmental qualifying exam, recital. *Entrance requirements:* For master's, department examination, audition or tapes, portfolio. *Faculty research:* Composition, conducting, education, performance.

Washington State University, Graduate School, College of Liberal Arts, School of Music and Theatre Arts, Pullman, WA 99164. Offers composition (MA); jazz (MA); music (MA); music education (MA); performance (MA). *Accreditation:* NASM. *Faculty:* 38. *Students:* 17 full-time (10 women); includes 2 minority (1 African American, 1 Hispanic American), 3 international. Average age 30. 14 applicants, 64% accepted, 5 enrolled. In 2009, 7 master's awarded. *Degree requirements:* For master's, comprehensive exam (for some programs), thesis (for some programs), oral exam. *Entrance requirements:* For master's, audition, minimum GPA of 3.0, 3 letters of recommendation, composition portfolio and recording (composition), writing sample and written philosophy (music education), writing sample (music history), in-depth audition (performance). Additional exam requirements/recommendations for international students: Required—TOEFL, IELTS. *Application deadline:* For fall admission, 1/10 priority date for domestic students, 1/10 for international students; for spring admission, 7/1 for domestic and international students. Applications are processed on a rolling basis. Application fee: $50. Electronic applications accepted. *Financial support:* In 2009–10, 1 fellowship (averaging $3,500 per year), research assistantships (averaging $13,917 per year), 11 teaching assistantships with full and partial tuition reimbursements (averaging $13,056 per year) were awarded; career-related internships or fieldwork, Federal Work-Study, institutionally sponsored loans, and tuition waivers (partial) also available. Financial award application deadline: 2/15; financial award applicants required to submit FAFSA. Total annual research expenditures: $3,000. *Unit head:* Dr. Gerald Berthiaume, Director, 509-335-2509, Fax: 509-335-4245, E-mail: berthia@wsu.edu. *Application contact:* Graduate School Admissions, 800-GRADWSU, Fax: 509-335-1949, E-mail: gradsch@wsu.edu.

Washington University in St. Louis, Graduate School of Arts and Sciences, Department of Music, St. Louis, MO 63130-4899. Offers MM, PhD. Terminal master's awarded for partial completion of doctoral program. *Degree requirements:* For master's, thesis or alternative; for doctorate, thesis/dissertation. *Entrance requirements:* For master's, GRE General Test, departmental exam; for doctorate, departmental exam, GRE General Test. Electronic applications accepted.

Wayne State University, College of Fine, Performing and Communication Arts, Department of Music, Detroit, MI 48202. Offers choral conducting (MM); composition (MM); music (MA, MM); music education (MM); orchestral studies (Certificate); performance (MM); theory (MM). *Accreditation:* NASM. *Degree requirements:* For master's, variable foreign language requirement. *Entrance requirements:* For master's, audition, interview. Additional exam requirements/recommendations for international students: Required—TOEFL (minimum score 550 paper-based; 213 computer-based); Recommended—TWE (minimum score 6). Electronic applications accepted. *Faculty research:* Teacher training, pedagogy, musicology, composition/theory, conducting/performance practice.

Webster University, Leigh Gerdine College of Fine Arts, Department of Music, St. Louis, MO 63119-3194. Offers church music (MM); composition (MM); conducting (MM); jazz studies (MM); music (MA); music education (MM); performance (MM); piano (MM). *Accreditation:* NASM. *Entrance requirements:* Additional exam requirements/recommendations for international students: Required—TOEFL. *Expenses:* Tuition: Part-time $565 per credit hour. Tuition and fees vary according to degree level, campus/location and program.

Wesleyan University, Graduate Programs, Department of Music, Middletown, CT 06459. Offers composition (MA); ethnomusicology (MA, PhD). *Faculty:* 8 full-time (2 women), 8 part-time/adjunct (0 women). *Students:* 24 full-time (8 women); includes 2 African Americans, 7 Asian Americans or Pacific Islanders, 1 Hispanic American. Average age 31. 68 applicants, 18% accepted. In 2009, 8 master's, 3 doctorates awarded. *Degree requirements:* For master's, one foreign language, thesis; for doctorate, 2 foreign languages, comprehensive exam, thesis/dissertation. *Entrance requirements:* For doctorate, MA. Additional exam requirements/recommendations for international students: Required—TOEFL. *Application deadline:* For fall admission, 1/15 for domestic and international students. Application fee: $75. Electronic applications accepted. *Financial support:* In 2009–10, 21 students received support, including 21 teaching assistantships with full tuition reimbursements available (averaging $14,000 per year). *Faculty research:* Ethnomusicology, musicology, music theory, composition, performance. *Unit head:* Dr. Eric Charry, Director of Graduate Studies/Associate Professor, 860-685-2579, Fax: 860-685-2651, E-mail: echarry@wesleyan.edu. *Application contact:* Deborah Shore, Administrative Assistant, 860-685-2598, Fax: 860-685-2651, E-mail: dshore@wesleyan.edu.

West Chester University of Pennsylvania, Office of Graduate Studies, College of Visual and Performing Arts, Department of Applied Music, West Chester, PA 19383. Offers accompanying

Music

West Chester University of Pennsylvania (continued)
(MM); performance (MM); piano pedagogy (MM, Certificate). Part-time and evening/weekend programs available. *Students:* 3 full-time (2 women), 29 part-time (15 women); includes 6 minority (3 African Americans, 2 Asian Americans or Pacific Islanders, 1 Hispanic American), 5 international. Average age 27. 23 applicants, 91% accepted, 15 enrolled. In 2009, 5 master's awarded. *Degree requirements:* For master's, comprehensive exam, thesis optional, recital. *Entrance requirements:* For master's and Certificate, GRE General Test, School of Music Graduate Admission Test (GAT), audition, interview. Additional exam requirements/recommendations for international students: Required—TOEFL (minimum score 550 paper-based; 213 computer-based; 80 iBT). *Application deadline:* For fall admission, 4/15 priority date for domestic students, 3/15 for international students; for spring admission, 10/15 for domestic students, 9/1 for international students. Applications are processed on a rolling basis. Application fee: $35. Electronic applications accepted. *Expenses:* Tuition, state resident: full-time $6666; part-time $370 per credit. Tuition, nonresident: full-time $10,666; part-time $593 per credit. Required fees: $122.56 per credit. *Financial support:* In 2009–10, 7 research assistantships with full and partial tuition reimbursements (averaging $5,000 per year) were awarded; unspecified assistantships also available. Support available to part-time students. Financial award application deadline: 2/15; financial award applicants required to submit FAFSA. *Unit head:* Dr. Chris Hanning, Interim Chair, 610-436-4178, E-mail: channing@wcupa.edu. *Application contact:* Dr. J. Bryan Burton, Graduate Coordinator, 610-436-2222, E-mail: jburton@wcupa.edu.

West Chester University of Pennsylvania, Office of Graduate Studies, College of Visual and Performing Arts, Department of Music Education, West Chester, PA 19383. Offers 21st Century music education (Certificate); Kodaly methodology (Certificate); music education (Teaching Certificate); music technology (Certificate); Orff-Schulwerk (Certificate); performance (MM), including performance; research (MM), including research; technology (MM), including technology. *Accreditation:* NASM; NCATE. Part-time and evening/weekend programs available. *Students:* 38 part-time (29 women); includes 1 minority (Asian American or Pacific Islander). Average age 28. 35 applicants, 91% accepted, 14 enrolled. In 2009, 19 master's, 5 Certificates awarded. *Degree requirements:* For master's, comprehensive exam, thesis optional, recital. *Entrance requirements:* For master's and other advanced degree, GRE General Test, School of Music Graduate Admission Test (GAT), audition, interview. Additional exam requirements/recommendations for international students: Required—TOEFL (minimum score 550 paper-based; 213 computer-based; 80 iBT). *Application deadline:* For fall admission, 4/15 priority date for domestic students, 3/15 for international students; for spring admission, 10/15 for domestic students, 9/1 for international students. Applications are processed on a rolling basis. Application fee: $35. Electronic applications accepted. *Expenses:* Tuition, state resident: full-time $6666; part-time $370 per credit. Tuition, nonresident: full-time $10,666; part-time $593 per credit. Required fees: $122.56 per credit. *Financial support:* In 2009–10, research assistantships with full and partial tuition reimbursements (averaging $5,000 per year); unspecified assistantships also available. Support available to part-time students. Financial award application deadline: 2/15; financial award applicants required to submit FAFSA. *Faculty research:* Developing music listening skills. *Unit head:* Dr. J. Bryan Burton, Chair and Graduate Coordinator, 610-436-2222, E-mail: jburton@wcupa.edu. *Application contact:* Dr. J. Bryan Burton, Chair and Graduate Coordinator, 610-436-2222, E-mail: jburton@wcupa.edu.

West Chester University of Pennsylvania, Office of Graduate Studies, College of Visual and Performing Arts, Department of Music History and Literature, West Chester, PA 19383. Offers music history (MA). Part-time and evening/weekend programs available. *Students:* 2 part-time (1 woman). Average age 29. 1 applicant, 0% accepted, 0 enrolled. In 2009, 1 master's awarded. *Degree requirements:* For master's, comprehensive exam, thesis optional. *Entrance requirements:* For master's, GRE General Test, School of Music Graduate Admission Test (GAT), audition, interview. Additional exam requirements/recommendations for international students: Required—TOEFL (minimum score 550 paper-based; 213 computer-based; 80 iBT). *Application deadline:* For fall admission, 4/15 priority date for domestic students, 3/15 for international students; for spring admission, 10/15 for domestic students, 9/1 for international students. Applications are processed on a rolling basis. Application fee: $35. Electronic applications accepted. *Expenses:* Tuition, state resident: full-time $6666; part-time $370 per credit. Tuition, nonresident: full-time $10,666; part-time $593 per credit. Required fees: $122.56 per credit. *Financial support:* In 2009–10, research assistantships with full and partial tuition reimbursements (averaging $5,000 per year); unspecified assistantships also available. Support available to part-time students. Financial award application deadline: 2/15; financial award applicants required to submit FAFSA. *Faculty research:* Musicology, eighteenth century European music. *Unit head:* Dr. Scott Balthazar, Chair, 610-436-2284, E-mail: sbalthazar@wcupa.edu. *Application contact:* Dr. J. Bryan Burton, Graduate Coordinator, 610-436-2222, E-mail: jburton@wcupa.edu.

West Chester University of Pennsylvania, Office of Graduate Studies, College of Visual and Performing Arts, Department of Music Theory and Composition, West Chester, PA 19383. Offers music: composition (MM); music: theory and composition (MM). Part-time and evening/weekend programs available. *Students:* 1 full-time (0 women), 3 part-time (0 women). Average age 33. 5 applicants, 80% accepted, 3 enrolled. In 2009, 1 master's awarded. *Degree requirements:* For master's, comprehensive exam, thesis optional. *Entrance requirements:* For master's, GRE General Test, School of Music Graduate Admission Test (GAT), audition, interview. Additional exam requirements/recommendations for international students: Required—TOEFL (minimum score 550 paper-based; 213 computer-based; 80 iBT). *Application deadline:* For fall admission, 4/15 priority date for domestic students, 3/15 for international students; for spring admission, 10/15 for domestic students, 9/1 for international students. Applications are processed on a rolling basis. Application fee: $35. Electronic applications accepted. *Expenses:* Tuition, state resident: full-time $6666; part-time $370 per credit. Tuition, nonresident: full-time $10,666; part-time $593 per credit. Required fees: $122.56 per credit. *Financial support:* In 2009–10, research assistantships with full and partial tuition reimbursements (averaging $5,000 per year); unspecified assistantships also available. Support available to part-time students. Financial award application deadline: 2/15; financial award applicants required to submit FAFSA. *Unit head:* Dr. Robert Maggio, Chair, 610-436-2646. *Application contact:* Dr. J. Bryan Burton, Graduate Coordinator, 610-436-2222, E-mail: jburton@wcupa.edu.

Western Carolina University, Graduate School, College of Fine and Performing Arts, School of Music, Cullowhee, NC 28723. Offers MM. *Accreditation:* NASM. Part-time programs available. *Students:* 5 full-time (2 women), 2 part-time (both women). Average age 30. 6 applicants, 50% accepted, 3 enrolled. In 2009, 4 master's awarded. *Degree requirements:* For master's, comprehensive exam, thesis. *Entrance requirements:* For master's, GRE, music entrance exam, appropriate undergraduate degree, live audition and/or interview. Additional exam requirements/recommendations for international students: Required—TOEFL (minimum score 550 paper-based; 270 computer-based; 79 iBT). *Application deadline:* For fall admission, 5/1 priority date for domestic students; for spring admission, 9/1 priority date for domestic students. Application fee: $45. *Financial support:* In 2009–10, 5 students received support, including 3 research assistantships with full and partial tuition reimbursements available (averaging $7,000 per year), 2 teaching assistantships with full and partial tuition reimbursements available (averaging $7,000 per year); fellowships, institutionally sponsored loans, scholarships/grants, and unspecified assistantships also available. Financial award application deadline: 3/31; financial award applicants required to submit FAFSA. *Faculty research:* Music experiences for K-12 students, marching band, sound mixing for television, music technology, choral methods, music history. *Unit head:* Dr. William Peebles, Director, 828-227-7242, Fax: 828-227-7162, E-mail: wpeebles@email.wcu.edu. *Application contact:* Admissions Specialist for School of Music, 828-227-7398, Fax: 828-227-7480, E-mail: gradsch@email.wcu.edu.

Western Illinois University, School of Graduate Studies, College of Fine Arts and Communication, School of Music, Macomb, IL 61455-1390. Offers MM. *Accreditation:* NASM. Part-time programs available. *Students:* 21 full-time (12 women), 2 part-time (1 woman); includes 2 minority (1 African American, 1 Asian American or Pacific Islander), 5 international. Average age 27. 22 applicants, 55% accepted. In 2009, 18 master's awarded. *Degree requirements:* For master's, comprehensive exam, thesis or alternative. *Entrance requirements:* For master's, audition. Additional exam requirements/recommendations for international students: Required—TOEFL (minimum score 550 paper-based; 213 computer-based; 80 iBT). *Application deadline:* Applications are processed on a rolling basis. Application fee: $30. Electronic applications accepted. *Expenses:* Tuition, state resident: full-time $4486; part-time $249.21 per credit hour. Tuition, nonresident: full-time $8972; part-time $498.42 per credit hour. Required fees: $72.62 per credit hour. *Financial support:* In 2009–10, 19 students received support, including 19 research assistantships with full tuition reimbursements available (averaging $7,280 per year). Financial award applicants required to submit FAFSA. *Unit head:* Dr. Bart Shanklin, Director, 309-298-1544. *Application contact:* Evelyn Hoing, Assistant Director of Graduate Studies, 309-298-1806, Fax: 309-298-2345, E-mail: grad-office@wiu.edu.

Western Michigan University, Graduate College, College of Fine Arts, School of Music, Kalamazoo, MI 49008. Offers composition (MM); conducting (MM); music (MA); music education (MM); music therapy (MM); performance (MM). *Accreditation:* NASM.

Western Oregon University, Graduate Programs, College of Liberal Arts and Sciences, Division of Creative Arts, Monmouth, OR 97361-1394. Offers contemporary music (MM). *Accreditation:* NASM. *Entrance requirements:* Additional exam requirements/recommendations for international students: Required—TOEFL (minimum score 550 paper-based; 213 computer-based; 79 iBT), IELTS (minimum score 6.5).

Western Washington University, Graduate School, College of Fine and Performing Arts, Department of Music, Bellingham, WA 98225-5996. Offers M Mus. *Accreditation:* NASM. Part-time programs available. *Degree requirements:* For master's, thesis. *Entrance requirements:* For master's, GRE General Test, department placement exams, audition, portfolio, minimum GPA of 3.0 in last 60 semester hours or last 90 quarter hours of course work. Additional exam requirements/recommendations for international students: Required—TOEFL (minimum score 567 paper-based; 227 computer-based). Electronic applications accepted. *Faculty research:* Baroque opera, historical music of the Silk Road, original composition, 20th century orchestral music, 13th century polyphony.

Westminster Choir College of Rider University, Graduate Programs in Music, Princeton, NJ 08540-3899. Offers choral conducting (MM); composition (MM); music education (MM, MME); organ performance (MM); piano accompanying and coaching (MM); piano pedagogy and performance (MM); piano performance (MM); sacred music (MM); vocal pedagogy and performance (MM); vocal training (MVP). Part-time programs available. *Degree requirements:* For master's, variable foreign language requirement, departmental qualifying exam. *Entrance requirements:* For master's, audition, interview, repertoire list, 2 letters of reference, resume. Additional exam requirements/recommendations for international students: Required—TOEFL (minimum score 525 paper-based; 195 computer-based). Electronic applications accepted.

West Texas A&M University, College of Fine Arts and Humanities, Department of Music and Dance, Program in Music, Canyon, TX 79016-0001. Offers MA. *Accreditation:* NASM. Part-time programs available. *Degree requirements:* For master's, comprehensive exam, thesis optional. *Entrance requirements:* For master's, GRE General Test. Additional exam requirements/recommendations for international students: Required—TOEFL (minimum score 550 paper-based). Electronic applications accepted.

West Texas A&M University, College of Fine Arts and Humanities, Department of Music and Dance, Program in Performance, Canyon, TX 79016-0001. Offers MM. *Accreditation:* NASM. Part-time programs available. *Degree requirements:* For master's, comprehensive exam, thesis optional. *Entrance requirements:* For master's, GRE General Test. Additional exam requirements/recommendations for international students: Required—TOEFL (minimum score 550 paper-based). Electronic applications accepted.

West Virginia University, College of Creative Arts, Division of Music, Morgantown, WV 26506. Offers music composition (MM, DMA); music education (MM, PhD); music history (MM); music performance (MM, DMA); music theory (MM). *Accreditation:* NASM. *Degree requirements:* For master's, comprehensive exam, thesis (for some programs), recitals; for doctorate, variable foreign language requirement, comprehensive exam, thesis/dissertation, recitals (DMA). *Entrance requirements:* For master's, GRE General Test (music history), minimum GPA of 3.0, audition; for doctorate, GRE General Test (music education), minimum GPA of 3.0, audition. Additional exam requirements/recommendations for international students: Required—TOEFL. *Faculty research:* Jazz history, seventeenth century French court music, nineteenth century composition theory.

Wichita State University, Graduate School, College of Fine Arts, School of Music, Wichita, KS 67260. Offers music (MM); music education (MME). *Accreditation:* NASM. Part-time programs available. *Expenses:* Tuition, state resident: full-time $4247; part-time $235.95 per credit hour. Tuition, nonresident: full-time $11,171; part-time $620.60 per credit hour. Required fees: $34; $3.60 per credit hour. $17 per term. Tuition and fees vary according to campus/location and program. *Unit head:* Prof. Russ Widener, Director, 316-978-6435, Fax: 316-978-3625, E-mail: russ.widener@wichita.edu. *Application contact:* Prof. Russ Widener, Director, 316-978-6435, Fax: 316-978-3625, E-mail: russ.widener@wichita.edu.

William Paterson University of New Jersey, College of the Arts and Communication, Wayne, NJ 07470-8420. Offers art (MFA); music (MM); professional communication (MA). Part-time and evening/weekend programs available. *Students:* 27 full-time (11 women), 28 part-time (11 women); includes 3 minority (1 African American, 1 Asian American or Pacific Islander, 1 Hispanic American), 4 international. *Entrance requirements:* For master's, minimum GPA of 2.75. *Application deadline:* Applications are processed on a rolling basis. Application fee: $50. Electronic applications accepted. *Financial support:* In 2009–10, 3 students received support; research assistantships with full tuition reimbursements available, career-related internships or fieldwork, Federal Work-Study, and unspecified assistantships available. Support available to part-time students. Financial award application deadline: 4/1; financial award applicants required to submit FAFSA. *Unit head:* Dr. Raymond Torres-Santos, Dean, College of Arts and Communication, 973-720-2232, E-mail: torressantosr@wpunj.edu. *Application contact:* Christina Aiello, Assistant Director, Graduate Admissions, 973-720-2506, Fax: 973-720-2035, E-mail: aielloc@wpunj.edu.

Winthrop University, College of Visual and Performing Arts, Department of Music, Rock Hill, SC 29733. Offers conducting (MM); music education (MME); performance (MM). *Accreditation:* NASM. Part-time programs available. *Degree requirements:* For master's, oral and written exams, recital (MM). *Entrance requirements:* For master's, GRE General Test, audition, minimum GPA of 3.0, 2 recitals. Electronic applications accepted.

Wright State University, School of Graduate Studies, College of Liberal Arts, Department of Music, Dayton, OH 45435. Offers music education (M Mus); performance (M Mus). *Accreditation:* NASM. Part-time programs available. *Degree requirements:* For master's, thesis or alternative, oral exam. *Entrance requirements:* For master's, theory placement test, BA in music. Additional exam requirements/recommendations for international students: Required—TOEFL. *Faculty research:* General music, current needs, role of teacher, expectations in music education.

Yale University, Graduate School of Arts and Sciences, Department of Music, New Haven, CT 06520. Offers music history (MA); music theory (MA). *Accreditation:* NASM. Terminal master's awarded for partial completion of doctoral program. *Degree requirements:* For master's, one foreign language; for doctorate, 3 foreign languages, thesis/dissertation. *Entrance requirements:* For doctorate, GRE General Test, GRE Subject Test.

Yale University, School of Music, New Haven, CT 06520. Offers MM, MMA, DMA, AD, Certificate. *Accreditation:* NASM. *Faculty:* 25 full-time (9 women), 29 part-time/adjunct (3 women). *Students:* 220 full-time (94 women); includes 31 minority (7 African Americans, 21 Asian Americans or Pacific Islanders, 3 Hispanic Americans), 91 international. Average age

24. 1,286 applicants, 10% accepted, 104 enrolled. In 2009, 79 master's, 7 doctorates, 25 other advanced degrees awarded. Terminal master's awarded for partial completion of doctoral program. *Degree requirements:* For master's, one foreign language, thesis (for some programs), recitals; for doctorate, one foreign language, thesis/dissertation, oral and written exam, recitals; for other advanced degree, one foreign language, recitals. *Entrance requirements:* For master's and other advanced degree, departmental exams, audition; for doctorate, GRE, departmental exams in history and theory of music, audition. Additional exam requirements/recommendations for international students: Required—TOEFL (minimum score 567 paper-based; 227 computer-based; 86 iBT). *Application deadline:* For fall admission, 12/1 for domestic and international students. Application fee: $100. Electronic applications accepted. *Expenses:* Contact institution. *Financial support:* In 2009–10, 220 students received support, including 220 fellowships (averaging $30,500 per year); Federal Work-Study and scholarships/grants also available. Financial award application deadline: 5/30; financial award applicants required to submit FAFSA. *Faculty research:* Performance, composition, conducting, music history and theory. *Unit head:* Robert Blocker, Dean, 203-432-4160, Fax: 203-432-7542. *Application contact:* Suzanne M. Stringer, Registrar and Financial Aid Administrator, 203-432-1962, Fax: 203-432-7448, E-mail: suzanne.stringer@yale.edu.

York University, Faculty of Graduate Studies, Faculty of Fine Arts, Program in Ethnomusicology and Musicology, Toronto, ON M3J 1P3, Canada. Offers composition (MA); musicology and ethnomusicology (MA, PhD). Part-time programs available. *Degree requirements:* For master's, one foreign language, thesis optional; for doctorate, 2 foreign languages, comprehensive exam, thesis/dissertation. *Entrance requirements:* For master's, portfolio. Electronic applications accepted.

Youngstown State University, Graduate School, College of Fine and Performing Arts, Dana School of Music, Youngstown, OH 44555-0001. Offers jazz studies (MM); music education (MM); music history and literature (MM); music theory and composition (MM); performance (MM). *Accreditation:* NASM. Part-time and evening/weekend programs available. *Degree requirements:* For master's, one foreign language, thesis optional, final qualifying exam. *Entrance requirements:* For master's, audition; GRE General Test or minimum GPA of 2.7. Additional exam requirements/recommendations for international students: Required—TOEFL. *Faculty research:* Teaching education, use of computers, conducting.

Theater

American Conservatory Theater, Program in Acting, San Francisco, CA 94108-5800. Offers MFA, Certificate. Certificate open only to applicants with undergraduate degree from a non-accredited institution. Curriculum is the same as MFA Program in Acting. *Faculty:* 17 full-time (6 women), 16 part-time/adjunct (7 women). *Students:* 34 full-time (16 women); includes 9 minority (all African Americans), 2 international. Average age 24. 320 applicants, 4% accepted, 14 enrolled. In 2009, 16 master's awarded. *Degree requirements:* For master's, thesis (for some programs), performance. *Entrance requirements:* For master's, audition, interview, bachelor's degree from an accredited institution, 2 confidential letters of recommendation. *Application deadline:* For fall admission, 1/14 for domestic students. Application fee: $75. *Expenses:* Tuition: Full-time $17,445. Required fees: $510. *Financial support:* In 2009–10, 32 students received support. Federal Work-Study, scholarships/grants, and tuition waivers (full and partial) available. Financial award application deadline: 2/16; financial award applicants required to submit FAFSA. *Unit head:* Melissa Smith, Conservatory Director, 415-439-2405, E-mail: mysmith@act-sf.org. *Application contact:* Dr. Jack F. Sharrar, Director of Academic Affairs, 415-439-2426, Fax: 415-834-3210, E-mail: jsharrar@act-sf.org.

Antioch University Midwest, Graduate Programs, Individualized Liberal and Professional Studies Program, Yellow Springs, OH 45387-1609. Offers liberal and professional studies (MA), including counseling, creative writing, education, film studies, liberal studies, management, modern literature, psychology, theatre, visual arts. Part-time and evening/weekend programs available. Postbaccalaureate distance learning degree programs offered (minimal on-campus study). *Faculty:* 1 full-time (0 women), 2 part-time/adjunct (1 woman). *Students:* 23 full-time (13 women), 41 part-time (30 women); includes 13 minority (11 African Americans, 2 Hispanic Americans). Average age 40. 21 applicants, 76% accepted, 15 enrolled. In 2009, 24 master's awarded. *Degree requirements:* For master's, thesis or alternative. *Entrance requirements:* For master's, resume, 2 letters of reference. *Application deadline:* For fall admission, 8/1 for domestic students; for winter admission, 12/1 for domestic students; for spring admission, 3/10 for domestic students. Applications are processed on a rolling basis. Application fee: $50. Electronic applications accepted. *Expenses:* Contact institution. *Financial support:* Federal Work-Study available. Financial award applicants required to submit FAFSA. *Unit head:* Dr. Jon Saari, Chair, 937-769-1879, Fax: 937-769-1807, E-mail: jsaari@antioch.edu. *Application contact:* Seth Gordon, Assistant Director of Admissions, 937-769-1800 Ext. 1825, Fax: 937-769-1804, E-mail: sgordon@antioch.edu.

Arcadia University, Graduate Studies, Department of Education, Glenside, PA 19038-3295. Offers art education (M Ed, MA Ed); biology education (MA Ed); chemistry education (MA Ed); child development (CAS); computer education (M Ed, CAS); computer education 7–12 (MA Ed); early childhood education (M Ed, CAS), including individualized (M Ed), master teacher (M Ed), research in child development (M Ed); educational leadership (M Ed, CAS); educational psychology (CAS); elementary education (M Ed, CAS); English education (MA Ed); environmental education (MA Ed, CAS); history education (MA Ed); language arts (M Ed, CAS); mathematics education (M Ed, MA Ed, CAS); music education (MA Ed); psychology (MA Ed); pupil personnel services (CAS); reading (M Ed, CAS); school library science (M Ed); science education (M Ed, CAS); secondary education (M Ed, CAS); special education (M Ed, Ed D, CAS); theater arts (MA Ed); written communication (MA Ed). *Accreditation:* NASAD. Part-time and evening/weekend programs available. Postbaccalaureate distance learning degree programs offered (minimal on-campus study). *Faculty:* 12 full-time (8 women), 38 part-time/adjunct (26 women). *Students:* 89 full-time (74 women), 622 part-time (487 women); includes 112 minority (94 African Americans, 9 Asian Americans or Pacific Islanders, 9 Hispanic Americans), 2 international. Average age 32. In 2009, 257 master's, 4 doctorates awarded. *Application deadline:* Applications are processed on a rolling basis. Application fee: $40. Electronic applications accepted. *Expenses:* Tuition: Full-time $30,450; part-time $620 per credit hour. Required fees: $165. Tuition and fees vary according to program. *Financial support:* Career-related internships or fieldwork, tuition waivers (partial), and unspecified assistantships available. *Unit head:* Dr. Steven P. Gulkus. *Application contact:* 215-572-2925, Fax: 215-572-2126, E-mail: grad@arcadia.edu.

Arizona State University, Graduate College, Herberger College of the Arts, School of Theatre and Film, Tempe, AZ 85287. Offers creative writing (playwriting) (MFA); theatre (MA, MFA, PhD). *Degree requirements:* For master's, thesis or alternative; for doctorate, thesis/dissertation. *Entrance requirements:* For master's, GRE or MAT.

Arkansas State University—Jonesboro, Graduate School, College of Communications, Department of Communication Studies, Jonesboro, State University, AR 72467. Offers communication studies and theatre arts (MA); communication studies and theatre arts education (SCCT). Part-time programs available. *Faculty:* 5 full-time (2 women). *Students:* 6 full-time (3 women), 4 part-time (2 women); includes 2 minority (both African Americans), 2 international. Average age 28. 11 applicants, 73% accepted, 5 enrolled. In 2009, 4 master's awarded. *Degree requirements:* For master's, one foreign language, comprehensive exam, thesis or alternative; for SCCT, comprehensive exam. *Entrance requirements:* For master's, GRE General Test or MAT, appropriate bachelor's degree, writing sample, letter of recommendation; for SCCT, GRE or MAT, appropriate master's degree, interview, official transcript, immunization records. Additional exam requirements/recommendations for international students: Required—TOEFL (minimum score 550 paper-based; 213 computer-based; 79 iBT), IELTS (minimum score 6). *Application deadline:* For fall admission, 7/15 for domestic students, 7/1 for international students; for spring admission, 12/1 for domestic students, 11/13 for international students. Applications are processed on a rolling basis. Application fee: $30 ($40 for international students). Electronic applications accepted. *Expenses:* Tuition, state resident: full-time $3744; part-time $208 per credit hour. Tuition, nonresident: full-time $9540; part-time $530 per credit hour. Required fees: $896; $47 per credit hour. $25 per term. One-time fee: $50. Tuition and fees vary according to course load and program. *Financial support:* In 2009–10, 6 students received support; teaching assistantships, career-related internships or fieldwork, scholarships/grants, and unspecified assistantships available. Financial award application deadline: 7/1; financial award applicants required to submit FAFSA. *Unit head:* Dr. Thomas Bagland, Chair, 870-972-3091, Fax: 870-972-3856, E-mail: tbaglan@astate.edu. *Application contact:* Dr. Andrew Sustich, Dean of the Graduate School, 870-972-3029, Fax: 870-972-3857, E-mail: sustich@astate.edu.

Arkansas State University—Jonesboro, Graduate School, College of Fine Arts, Department of Theatre, Jonesboro, State University, AR 72467. Offers communication studies and theatre arts (MA); communication studies and theatre arts education (SCCT). Part-time programs available. *Faculty:* 3 full-time (1 woman). *Students:* 2 part-time (1 woman). Average age 27. 2 applicants, 50% accepted, 1 enrolled. *Degree requirements:* For master's, one foreign language, comprehensive exam, thesis or alternative; for SCCT, comprehensive exam. *Entrance requirements:* For master's, GRE General Test or MAT, appropriate bachelor's degree, writing sample, letters of recommendation; for SCCT, GRE General Test or MAT, interview, master's degree, official transcript, immunization records. Additional exam requirements/recommendations for international students: Required—TOEFL (minimum score 550 paper-based; 213 computer-based; 79 iBT), IELTS (minimum score 6). *Application deadline:* For fall admission, 7/1 for domestic and international students; for spring admission, 11/15 for domestic students, 11/13 for international students. Applications are processed on a rolling basis. Application fee: $30 ($40 for international students). Electronic applications accepted. *Expenses:* Tuition, state resident: full-time $3744; part-time $208 per credit hour. Tuition, nonresident: full-time $9540; part-time $530 per credit hour. Required fees: $896; $47 per credit hour. $25 per term. One-time fee: $50. Tuition and fees vary according to course load and program. *Financial support:* In 2009–10, 1 student received support; teaching assistantships, career-related internships or fieldwork, scholarships/grants, and unspecified assistantships available. Financial award application deadline: 7/1; financial award applicants required to submit FAFSA. *Unit head:* Bobby Simpson, Chair, 870-972-2037, Fax: 870-972-2830, E-mail: bsimpson@astate.edu. *Application contact:* Dr. Andrew Sustich, Dean of the Graduate School, 870-972-3029, Fax: 870-972-3857, E-mail: sustich@astate.edu.

Austin College, Program in Education, Sherman, TX 75090-4400. Offers art education (MA); elementary education (MA); middle school education (MA); music education (MA); physical education and coaching (MA); secondary education (MA); theatre education (MA). Part-time programs available. *Faculty:* 5 full-time (3 women), 1 (woman) part-time/adjunct. *Students:* 29 full-time (21 women); includes 3 minority (1 Asian American or Pacific Islander, 2 Hispanic Americans). Average age 23. In 2009, 23 master's awarded. *Degree requirements:* For master's, one foreign language, thesis or alternative. *Entrance requirements:* For master's, Texas Academic Skills Program Test. *Application deadline:* For fall admission, 5/1 priority date for domestic students; for spring admission, 1/15 priority date for domestic students. Applications are processed on a rolling basis. Application fee: $35. Electronic applications accepted. *Expenses:* Tuition: Full-time $31,575. Required fees: $160. *Financial support:* Career-related internships or fieldwork, Federal Work-Study, scholarships/grants, and unspecified assistantships available. Support available to part-time students. Financial award application deadline: 4/1; financial award applicants required to submit FAFSA. *Unit head:* Dr. Barbara Sylvester, Director of Teaching Program, 903-813-2327, Fax: 903-813-2326, E-mail: bsylvester@austincollege.edu. *Application contact:* Dr. Barbara Sylvester, Director of Teaching Program, 903-813-2327, Fax: 903-813-2326, E-mail: bsylvester@austincollege.edu.

Baylor University, Graduate School, College of Arts and Sciences, Department of Theatre Arts, Waco, TX 76798. Offers directing (MFA). *Accreditation:* NAST. *Students:* 5 full-time (2 women). In 2009, 3 master's awarded. *Degree requirements:* For master's, thesis. *Entrance requirements:* For master's, GRE General Test. *Application deadline:* Applications are processed on a rolling basis. Application fee: $25. *Financial support:* Fellowships, teaching assistantships, Federal Work-Study and institutionally sponsored loans available. *Unit head:* Dr. DeAnna Toten Beard, Graduate Program Director, 254-710-6486, Fax: 254-710-1765, E-mail: deanna_toten_beard@baylor.edu. *Application contact:* Renee Cluke, Administrative Assistant, 254-710-1861, Fax: 254-710-1765, E-mail: renee_cluke@baylor.edu.

Bennington College, Graduate Programs, MA in Teaching Program, Bennington, VT 05201. Offers art education (MAT); early childhood (MAT); elementary education (MAT); English education (MAT); foreign language education (MAT); k-12 education (MAT); mathematics education (MAT); music education (MAT); science education (MAT); secondary education (MAT); social studies education (MAT); theater arts (MAT). *Faculty:* 5 part-time/adjunct (3 women). *Students:* 8 full-time (5 women), 1 part-time (0 women). Average age 28. 11 applicants, 27% accepted, 1 enrolled. In 2009, 4 master's awarded. *Degree requirements:* For master's, comprehensive exam, 1 year teaching practicum, professional portfolio. *Entrance requirements:* For master's, interview. *Application deadline:* For fall admission, 3/1 for domestic students. Application fee: $60. *Expenses:* Contact institution. *Financial support:* In 2009–10, 6 students received support, including 4 fellowships (averaging $10,475 per year); scholarships/grants and unspecified assistantships also available. Financial award application deadline: 4/1; financial award applicants required to submit FAFSA. *Unit head:* Carol Meyer, Director of Programs in Teacher Education, 802-440-4375, E-mail: cmeyer@bennington.edu. *Application contact:* Nancy Pearlman, Assistant Director of Programs in Teacher Education, 802-440-4710, Fax: 802-440-4383, E-mail: npearlman@bennington.edu.

Bob Jones University, Graduate Programs, Greenville, SC 29614. Offers accountancy (MS); Bible (MA); Bible translation (MA); Biblical studies (Certificate); broadcast management (MS); business administration (MBA); church history (MA, PhD); church ministries (MA); church music (MM); cinema and video production (MA); counseling (MS); curriculum and instruction (Ed D); divinity (M Div); dramatic production (MA); educational leadership (MS, Ed D, Ed S); elementary education (M Ed, MAT); English (M Ed, MA, MAT); fine arts (MA); graphic design (MA); history (M Ed, MA); illustration (MA); interpretative speech (MA); mathematics (M Ed, MAT); medical missions (Certificate); ministry (MM, D Min); multi-categorical special education (M Ed, MAT); music (M Ed); New Testament interpretation (PhD); Old Testament interpretation (PhD); orchestral instrument performance (MM); organ performance (MM); pastoral studies (MA); personnel services (MS, Ed S); piano pedagogy (MM); piano performance (MM); platform arts (MA); radio and television broadcasting (MS); rhetoric and public address (MA); secondary

Theater

Bob Jones University (continued)
education (M Ed); studio art (MA); teaching Bible (MA); theology (MA, PhD); voice performance (MM); youth ministries (MA); M Div/MM.

The Boston Conservatory, Graduate Division, Theater Division, Boston, MA 02215. Offers MM. Part-time programs available. *Degree requirements:* For master's, performances. *Entrance requirements:* For master's, audition. Additional exam requirements/recommendations for international students: Required—TOEFL (minimum score 580 paper-based; 237 computer-based). Electronic applications accepted.

Boston University, College of Fine Arts, School of Theatre, Boston, MA 02215. Offers costume design (MFA); costume production (MFA); directing (MFA); lighting design (MFA); scene design (MFA); technical production (MFA, Certificate); theatre crafts (Certificate); theatre education (MFA). *Faculty:* 16 full-time, 9 part-time/adjunct. *Students:* 36 full-time (18 women); includes 4 minority (all Hispanic Americans). Average age 27. 138 applicants, 28% accepted, 15 enrolled. In 2009, 7 master's awarded. *Entrance requirements:* For master's, interview, portfolio. Additional exam requirements/recommendations for international students: Required—TOEFL. *Application deadline:* For fall admission, 2/15 priority date for domestic and international students. Application fee: $60. *Expenses:* Tuition: Full-time $37,910; part-time $1184 per credit hour. Required fees: $386; $40 per semester. Part-time tuition and fees vary according to class time, course level, degree level and program. *Financial support:* Fellowships, teaching assistantships available. Financial award application deadline: 2/15. *Unit head:* Jim Petosa, Director, 617-353-3390. *Application contact:* Mark Krone, Manager, Graduate Admissions, 617-353-3350, E-mail: arts@bu.edu.

Bowling Green State University, Graduate College, College of Arts and Sciences, Department of Theatre and Film, Bowling Green, OH 43403. Offers MA, PhD. *Accreditation:* NAST. Part-time programs available. Terminal master's awarded for partial completion of doctoral program. *Degree requirements:* For master's, thesis or alternative; for doctorate, comprehensive exam, thesis/dissertation, 9 hour research tool. *Entrance requirements:* For master's and doctorate, GRE General Test. Additional exam requirements/recommendations for international students: Required—TOEFL. Electronic applications accepted. *Faculty research:* Theatre history, dramatic theory, cultural studies, performance studies, American theatre history.

Brandeis University, Graduate School of Arts and Sciences, Department of Theater Arts, Waltham, MA 02454-9110. Offers acting (MFA). *Faculty:* 10 full-time (6 women), 10 part-time/adjunct (4 women). *Students:* 25 full-time (15 women); includes 4 minority (3 African Americans, 1 Hispanic American), 3 international. Average age 26. 25 applicants, 44% accepted, 3 enrolled. In 2009, 3 master's awarded. *Entrance requirements:* For master's, curriculum vitae or resume, 2 letters of recommendation, interview and audition (acting), head shot and artistic resume. Additional exam requirements/recommendations for international students: Required—TOEFL (minimum score 600 paper-based; 250 computer-based; 100 iBT); Recommended—IELTS (minimum score 7). *Application deadline:* For fall admission, 2/15 priority date for domestic students. Applications are processed on a rolling basis. Application fee: $75. Electronic applications accepted. *Financial support:* In 2009–10, 22 students received support, including 10 fellowships with full tuition reimbursements available (averaging $10,800 per year), 8 teaching assistantships with partial tuition reimbursements available (averaging $3,200 per year); research assistantships with tuition reimbursements available, career-related internships or fieldwork, institutionally sponsored loans, scholarships/grants, and tuition waivers (full and partial) also available. Financial award application deadline: 4/15; financial award applicants required to submit FAFSA. *Faculty research:* Acting, dramatic writing, dramaturgy, movement, voice and speech, theater literature. *Unit head:* Prof. Susan Dibble, Chair, 781-736-3340, Fax: 781-736-3408, E-mail: theater@brandeis.edu. *Application contact:* Alicia Hyland, Academic Administrator, 781-736-3340, Fax: 781-736-3408, E-mail: theater@brandeis.edu.

Brigham Young University, Graduate Studies, College of Fine Arts and Communications, Department of Theatre and Media Arts, Provo, UT 84602-6404. Offers MA. MA program accepts applications in odd-numbered years only. *Accreditation:* NAST. *Faculty:* 14 full-time (5 women). *Students:* 16 full-time (11 women), 2 part-time (1 woman), 1 international. Average age 32. 13 applicants, 77% accepted, 9 enrolled. In 2009, 6 master's awarded. *Degree requirements:* For master's, comprehensive exam, thesis, oral defense. *Entrance requirements:* For master's, GRE General Test, writing samples. Additional exam requirements/recommendations for international students: Required—TOEFL (minimum score 580 paper-based; 237 computer-based; 85 iBT). *Application deadline:* For fall admission, 2/1 priority date for domestic and international students. Application fee: $50. Electronic applications accepted. *Expenses:* Tuition: Full-time $5580; part-time $301 per credit hour. Tuition and fees vary according to student's religious affiliation. *Financial support:* In 2009–10, 17 students received support, including 4 research assistantships with partial tuition reimbursements available (averaging $3,500 per year), 20 teaching assistantships with partial tuition reimbursements available (averaging $3,500 per year); career-related internships or fieldwork, institutionally sponsored loans, scholarships/grants, health care benefits, tuition waivers (partial), unspecified assistantships, and administrative aides also available. Support available to part-time students. *Faculty research:* Media literacy, children's media, popular culture, theatre historiography, performance studies. *Unit head:* Dr. Rodger D. Sorensen, Department Chair, 801-422-8132, Fax: 801-422-0654, E-mail: rodger_sorensen@byu.edu. *Application contact:* Kim Poole, Secretary, 801-422-3750, Fax: 801-422-0654, E-mail: kim_poole@byu.edu.

Brooklyn College of the City University of New York, Division of Graduate Studies, Department of Theater, Brooklyn, NY 11210-2889. Offers acting (MFA); criticism and history (MA); design and technical production (MFA); directing (MFA); dramaturgy (MFA); performing arts management (MFA); theater (PhD). Part-time programs available. *Students:* 52 full-time (39 women), 19 part-time (7 women); includes 8 minority (4 African Americans, 1 Asian American or Pacific Islander, 3 Hispanic Americans), 6 international. Average age 31. 127 applicants, 30% accepted, 34 enrolled. In 2009, 40 master's awarded. *Degree requirements:* For master's, thesis, professional residency. *Entrance requirements:* For master's, audition or interview, 18 credits in theater, 2 letters of recommendation, essay. Additional exam requirements/recommendations for international students: Required—TOEFL. *Application deadline:* For fall admission, 2/1 for domestic and international students. Application fee: $125. Electronic applications accepted. *Expenses:* Tuition, area resident: Full-time $7360; part-time $310 per credit hour. Tuition, state resident: full-time $7360; part-time $310 per credit hour. Tuition, nonresident: full-time $13,800; part-time $575 per credit hour. International tuition: $13,800 full-time. Required fees: $140.10 per semester. *Financial support:* Career-related internships or fieldwork, Federal Work-Study, institutionally sponsored loans, and scholarships/grants available. Support available to part-time students. Financial award application deadline: 5/1; financial award applicants required to submit FAFSA. *Faculty research:* Multiculturalism and the arts, art education, arts collaboration. *Unit head:* Dr. Thomas Bullard, Chairperson, 718-951-5666, Fax: 718-951-4606, E-mail: tbullard@brooklyn.cuny.edu. *Application contact:* Hernan Sierra, Graduate Admissions Coordinator, 718-951-4536, Fax: 718-951-4506, E-mail: grads@brooklyn.cuny.edu.

Brown University, Graduate School, Department of Theatre Arts and Performance Studies, Providence, RI 02912. Offers acting and directing (MFA); playwriting (MFA); theatre and performance studies (PhD). *Degree requirements:* For master's, thesis or alternative. *Entrance requirements:* For master's, GRE General Test.

California Institute of the Arts, School of Theatre, Valencia, CA 91355-2340. Offers acting (MFA, Adv C); design and technology (Adv C); directing (MFA); performing arts design and technology (MFA); theater management (MFA, Adv C); writing for performance (MFA). *Accreditation:* NAST. *Degree requirements:* For master's, thesis (for some programs), faculty review, performance or portfolio. *Entrance requirements:* For master's, audition or portfolio, interview. Additional exam requirements/recommendations for international students: Required—TOEFL. Electronic applications accepted.

California State University, Fullerton, Graduate Studies, College of the Arts, Department of Theatre and Dance, Fullerton, CA 92834-9480. Offers acting (MFA); acting and directing (MA); dance (MA); directing (MFA); dramatic literature/criticism (MA); oral interpretation (MA); playwriting (MA); technical theater (MA); technical theater and design (MFA); television (MA); theatre for children (MA); theatre history (MA). *Accreditation:* NASD; NAST (one or more programs are accredited). Part-time programs available. *Students:* 15 full-time (6 women), 3 part-time (1 woman); includes 3 minority (1 African American, 2 Hispanic Americans). Average age 29. 14 applicants, 50% accepted, 7 enrolled. In 2009, 5 master's awarded. *Degree requirements:* For master's, oral and written exam, project or thesis. *Entrance requirements:* For master's, major in theatre or related field, audition or interview, minimum GPA of 2.5 in last 60 units of course work. Application fee: $55. *Expenses:* Tuition, nonresident: full-time $11,160; part-time $373 per credit. Required fees: $1440 per term. Tuition and fees vary according to course load, degree level and program. *Financial support:* Career-related internships or fieldwork, Federal Work-Study, institutionally sponsored loans, and scholarships/grants available. Support available to part-time students. Financial award application deadline: 3/1; financial award applicants required to submit FAFSA. *Unit head:* Dr. Susan Hallman, Chair, 657-278-3628. *Application contact:* Admissions/Applications, 657-278-2371.

California State University, Long Beach, Graduate Studies, College of the Arts, Department of Theatre Arts, Long Beach, CA 90840. Offers acting (MFA); design (MFA); theatre management (MFA); MBA/MFA. *Accreditation:* NAST. Part-time programs available. *Faculty:* 11 full-time (9 women). *Students:* 38 full-time (26 women), 15 part-time (10 women); includes 5 minority (4 Asian Americans or Pacific Islanders, 1 Hispanic American), 10 international. Average age 30. 24 applicants, 29% accepted, 5 enrolled. *Degree requirements:* For master's, thesis or alternative. *Application deadline:* For fall admission, 7/1 for domestic students; for spring admission, 12/1 for domestic students. Applications are processed on a rolling basis. Application fee: $55. Electronic applications accepted. *Expenses:* Required fees: $1802 per semester. Part-time tuition and fees vary according to course load. *Financial support:* Research assistantships, teaching assistantships, Federal Work-Study, institutionally sponsored loans, scholarships/grants, and traineeships available. Financial award application deadline: 3/2. *Unit head:* Dr. Joanne L. Gordon, Chair, 562-985-7891, Fax: 562-985-2263, E-mail: jgordon@csulb.edu. *Application contact:* Barbara Matthews, Graduate Advisor, 562-985-4042, Fax: 562-985-2263, E-mail: jmatthew@csulb.edu.

California State University, Los Angeles, Graduate Studies, College of Arts and Letters, Department of Communication Studies, Los Angeles, CA 90032-8530. Offers speech communication (MA); television, film and theatre (MFA). Part-time and evening/weekend programs available. *Faculty:* 6 full-time (3 women), 8 part-time/adjunct (4 women). *Students:* 69 full-time (40 women), 52 part-time (38 women); includes 48 minority (18 African Americans, 9 Asian Americans or Pacific Islanders, 21 Hispanic Americans), 18 international. Average age 31. 92 applicants, 99% accepted, 34 enrolled. In 2009, 17 master's awarded. *Degree requirements:* For master's, comprehensive exam or thesis. *Entrance requirements:* For master's, minimum GPA of 2.75 in last 90 units of course work. Additional exam requirements/recommendations for international students: Required—TOEFL (minimum score 500 paper-based; 173 computer-based). *Application deadline:* For fall admission, 5/1 for domestic and international students. Applications are processed on a rolling basis. Application fee: $55. Electronic applications accepted. *Financial support:* Career-related internships or fieldwork and Federal Work-Study available. Support available to part-time students. Financial award application deadline: 3/1. *Faculty research:* Organizational, interpersonal, intercultural, and instructional communication; rhetorical theories. *Unit head:* Dr. Suzanne Regan, Chair, 323-343-4200, Fax: 323-343-6467, E-mail: sregan@calstatela.edu. *Application contact:* Dr. Cheryl L. Ney, Associate Vice President for Academic Affairs and Dean of Graduate Studies, 323-343-3820, Fax: 323-343-5653, E-mail: cney@cslanet.calstatela.edu.

California State University, Los Angeles, Graduate Studies, College of Arts and Letters, Department of Theater Arts and Dance, Los Angeles, CA 90032-8530. Offers theater arts (MA). Part-time and evening/weekend programs available. *Faculty:* 7 full-time (5 women), 1 part-time/adjunct (0 women). *Students:* 10 full-time (5 women), 12 part-time (8 women); includes 8 minority (2 African Americans, 2 Asian Americans or Pacific Islanders, 4 Hispanic Americans), 4 international. Average age 36. 13 applicants, 100% accepted, 10 enrolled. In 2009, 6 master's awarded. *Degree requirements:* For master's, comprehensive exam, project or thesis. *Entrance requirements:* For master's, minimum GPA of 2.5, 30 units of course work in theater. Additional exam requirements/recommendations for international students: Required—TOEFL (minimum score 500 paper-based; 173 computer-based). *Application deadline:* For fall admission, 5/1 for domestic and international students. Applications are processed on a rolling basis. Application fee: $55. Electronic applications accepted. *Financial support:* Federal Work-Study available. Support available to part-time students. Financial award application deadline: 3/1. *Faculty research:* Sondheim, Taiwanese theater, Australian theater, absurdism, dramaturgy. *Unit head:* Dr. James Hatfield, Chair, 323-343-4110, Fax: 323-343-5567, E-mail: jhatfie@calstatela.edu. *Application contact:* Dr. Cheryl L. Ney, Associate Vice President for Academic Affairs and Dean of Graduate Studies, 323-343-3820, Fax: 323-343-5653, E-mail: cney@cslanet.calstatela.edu.

California State University, Northridge, Graduate Studies, College of Arts, Media, and Communication, Department of Theatre, Northridge, CA 91330. Offers MA. *Accreditation:* NAST. *Faculty:* 9 full-time (5 women), 9 part-time/adjunct (5 women). *Students:* 6 full-time (4 women), 15 part-time (12 women); includes 3 minority (1 African American, 2 Hispanic Americans). Average age 40. 17 applicants, 47% accepted, 4 enrolled. In 2009, 1 master's awarded. *Degree requirements:* For master's, thesis. *Entrance requirements:* For master's, GRE General Test or minimum GPA of 3.0. Additional exam requirements/recommendations for international students: Required—TOEFL. *Application deadline:* For fall admission, 11/30 for domestic students. Application fee: $55. *Financial support:* Application deadline: 3/1. *Unit head:* Prof. Peter Grego, Chair, 818-677-3086, E-mail: peter.grego@csun.edu. *Application contact:* Prof. Peter Grego, Chair, 818-677-3086, E-mail: peter.grego@csun.edu.

California State University, Sacramento, Graduate Studies, College of Arts and Letters, Department of Theatre and Dance, Sacramento, CA 95819. Offers MA. *Accreditation:* NAST. Part-time programs available. *Degree requirements:* For master's, thesis or alternative, writing proficiency exam. *Entrance requirements:* For master's, GRE General Test, BA in drama or equivalent, minimum GPA of 2.5 during previous 2 years of course work. Additional exam requirements/recommendations for international students: Required—TOEFL. Electronic applications accepted.

California State University, Sacramento, Graduate Studies, College of Social Sciences and Interdisciplinary Studies, Liberal Arts Program, Sacramento, CA 95819. Offers French (MA); German (MA); Spanish (MA); theater arts (MA). *Degree requirements:* For master's, writing proficiency exam. *Entrance requirements:* Additional exam requirements/recommendations for international students: Required—TOEFL. Electronic applications accepted.

California State University, San Bernardino, Graduate Studies, College of Arts and Letters, Department of Theatre Arts, San Bernardino, CA 92407-2397. Offers theatre arts (MA); theatre education (MA); theatre for youth (MA). *Accreditation:* NAST. *Faculty:* 3 full-time (2 women). *Students:* 15 full-time (11 women), 11 part-time (7 women); includes 8 minority (3 African Americans, 1 American Indian/Alaska Native, 4 Hispanic Americans), 2 international. Average age 33. 18 applicants, 89% accepted, 11 enrolled. In 2009, 2 master's awarded. *Degree requirements:* For master's, thesis. *Entrance requirements:* For master's, writing exam. Application fee: $55. *Unit head:* Dr. Margaret Perry, Chair, 909-537-5876, E-mail: mperry@csusb.edu. *Application contact:* Olivia Rosas, Director of Admissions, 909-537-7577, Fax: 909-537-7034, E-mail: orosas@csusb.edu.

Carnegie Mellon University, College of Fine Arts, School of Drama, Pittsburgh, PA 15213-3891. Offers design (MFA); directing (MFA); dramatic writing (MFA); production technology and management (MFA). *Degree requirements:* For master's, thesis (for some programs). *Entrance requirements:* For master's, audition, portfolio review, interview. Additional exam requirements/recommendations for international students: Required—TOEFL. *Faculty research:* Developing voice and speech compact disc.

Case Western Reserve University, School of Graduate Studies, Department of Theater and Dance, Cleveland, OH 44106. Offers acting (MFA); contemporary dance (MFA); dance (MA); theater (MFA). *Degree requirements:* For master's, thesis, oral presentation and defense, portfolio, thesis concert production and presentation (MFA). *Entrance requirements:* For master's, audition, interview. Additional exam requirements/recommendations for international students: Required—TOEFL (minimum score 550 paper-based; 213 computer-based; 79 iBT). Electronic applications accepted. *Faculty research:* Playwriting; history of theater; participation in professional area theaters in performing, design, acting, coaching, and dance.

The Catholic University of America, School of Arts and Sciences, Department of Drama, Washington, DC 20064. Offers acting, directing, and playwriting (MFA); theatre education (MA); theatre history and criticism (MA). Part-time programs available. *Faculty:* 7 full-time (3 women), 7 part-time/adjunct (5 women). *Students:* 16 full-time (9 women), 15 part-time (9 women); includes 4 minority (3 African Americans, 1 American Indian/Alaska Native). Average age 30. 55 applicants, 42% accepted, 18 enrolled. In 2009, 14 master's awarded. *Degree requirements:* For master's, variable foreign language requirement, comprehensive exam. *Entrance requirements:* For master's, GRE General Test, statement of purpose, official copies of academic transcripts, three letters of recommendation, resume, writing sample. Additional exam requirements/recommendations for international students: Required—TOEFL (minimum score 580 paper-based; 237 computer-based). *Application deadline:* For fall admission, 8/1 priority date for domestic students, 7/15 for international students; for spring admission, 12/1 priority date for domestic students, 10/15 for international students. Applications are processed on a rolling basis. Application fee: $55. Electronic applications accepted. *Expenses:* Tuition: Full-time $31,740; part-time $1245 per credit hour. Required fees: $50; $25 per semester hour. One-time fee: $425. *Financial support:* Fellowships, research assistantships, teaching assistantships, Federal Work-Study, scholarships/grants, tuition waivers (full and partial), and unspecified assistantships available. Financial award application deadline: 2/1; financial award applicants required to submit FAFSA. *Faculty research:* Acting, directing, playwriting, costume design, Shakespearean stage history. *Unit head:* Gail Beach, Chair, 202-319-5351, Fax: 202-319-5359, E-mail: beach@cua.edu. *Application contact:* Julie Schwing, Director of Graduate Admissions, 202-319-5057, Fax: 202-319-6533, E-mail: cua-admissions@cua.edu.

Central Washington University, Graduate Studies and Research, College of Arts and Humanities, Department of Theatre Arts, Ellensburg, WA 98926. Offers theatre production (MA); theatre studies (MA). Part-time programs available. *Faculty:* 11 full-time (4 women). *Students:* 6 full-time (4 women), 2 part-time (both women). In 2009, 13 master's awarded. *Degree requirements:* For master's, thesis or alternative. *Entrance requirements:* For master's, minimum GPA of 3.0. Additional exam requirements/recommendations for international students: Required—TOEFL (minimum score 550 paper-based; 213 computer-based; 79 iBT). *Application deadline:* For fall admission, 4/1 for domestic students. Application fee: $50. Electronic applications accepted. *Expenses:* Tuition, state resident: full-time $7353; part-time $245 per credit. Tuition, nonresident: full-time $16,383; part-time $546 per credit. Required fees: $882. Tuition and fees vary according to degree level. *Financial support:* In 2009–10, 1 research assistantship with full and partial tuition reimbursement (averaging $9,145 per year), 4 teaching assistantships with full and partial tuition reimbursements (averaging $9,145 per year) were awarded; Federal Work-Study, health care benefits, and unspecified assistantships also available. Financial award application deadline: 3/1; financial award applicants required to submit FAFSA. *Unit head:* Prof. Scott Robinson, Chair, 509-963-1766. *Application contact:* Justine Eason, Admissions Program Coordinator, 509-963-3103, Fax: 509-963-1799, E-mail: masters@cwu.edu.

Columbia University, Graduate School of Arts and Sciences, Program in Theatre, New York, NY 10027. Offers M Phil, MA, PhD. *Degree requirements:* For master's, one foreign language, thesis, written exam; for doctorate, 2 foreign languages, thesis/dissertation. *Entrance requirements:* For master's and doctorate, GRE General Test, writing sample. Additional exam requirements/recommendations for international students: Required—TOEFL.

Columbia University, School of the Arts, Theatre Arts Division, New York, NY 10027. Offers acting (MFA); directing (MFA); dramaturgy (MFA); playwriting (MFA); stage management (MFA); theater management (MFA); JD/MFA. *Degree requirements:* For master's, thesis, 2 internships. *Entrance requirements:* For master's, 3 letters of recommendation, resume. Additional exam requirements/recommendations for international students: Required—TOEFL (minimum score 600 paper-based; 250 computer-based; 100 iBT). Electronic applications accepted.

See Close-Up on page 261.

Cornell University, Graduate School, Graduate Fields of Arts and Sciences, Field of Theatre Arts, Ithaca, NY 14853-0001. Offers drama and the theatre (PhD); theatre history (PhD); theatre theory and aesthetics (PhD). *Faculty:* 20 full-time (7 women). *Students:* 11 full-time (7 women), 4 international. Average age 33. 27 applicants, 22% accepted, 4 enrolled. In 2009, 4 doctorates awarded. *Degree requirements:* For doctorate, 2 foreign languages, comprehensive exam, thesis/dissertation. *Entrance requirements:* For doctorate, GRE General Test, sample of written work, 3 letters of recommendation. Additional exam requirements/recommendations for international students: Required—TOEFL (minimum score 600 paper-based; 250 computer-based; 77 iBT). *Application deadline:* For fall admission, 1/15 for domestic students. Application fee: $70. Electronic applications accepted. *Expenses:* Tuition: Full-time $29,500. Required fees: $70. Full-time tuition and fees vary according to degree level, program and student level. *Financial support:* In 2009–10, 8 students received support, including 4 fellowships with full tuition reimbursements available; research assistantships with full tuition reimbursements available, teaching assistantships with full tuition reimbursements available, institutionally sponsored loans, scholarships/grants, health care benefits, tuition waivers (full and partial), and unspecified assistantships also available. Financial award applicants required to submit FAFSA. *Faculty research:* Cultural studies and critical theory, seventeenth to twenty-first century European and American theater, theory of the performing arts, film history and theory, feminism and theater. *Unit head:* Director of Graduate Studies, 607-254-2757, Fax: 607-254-2733. *Application contact:* Graduate Field Assistant, 607-254-2757, Fax: 607-254-2733, E-mail: theatre_grad@cornell.edu.

Dell'Arte International School of Physical Theatre, MFA Program, Blue Lake, CA 95525. Offers ensemble based physical theatre (MFA). *Accreditation:* NAST. *Faculty:* 5 full-time (3 women), 7 part-time/adjunct (3 women). *Students:* 18 full-time (13 women); includes 2 minority (1 African American, 1 Hispanic American), 4 international. Average age 24. 42 applicants, 19% accepted, 6 enrolled. *Degree requirements:* For master's, thesis. *Entrance requirements:* For master's, undergraduate degree, audition. *Application deadline:* For winter admission, 3/4 for domestic and international students; for spring admission, 4/8 priority date for domestic and international students. Applications are processed on a rolling basis. Application fee: $50. Electronic applications accepted. *Expenses:* Tuition: Full-time $16,500. Full-time tuition and fees vary according to student level. *Financial support:* In 2009–10, 11 students received support. Career-related internships or fieldwork, institutionally sponsored loans, and scholarships/grants available. *Faculty research:* Physical theatre, international theatre, ensemble, devised. *Unit head:* Joan Schirle, Director, 707-668-5663 Ext. 11, Fax: 707-668-5665, E-mail: joans@dellarte.com. *Application contact:* Joe Krienke, Admissions Director, 707-668-5663 Ext. 27, Fax: 707-668-5665, E-mail: joe@dellarte.com.

DePaul University, The Theatre School, Chicago, IL 60614. Offers acting (MFA); arts leadership (MFA); directing (MFA). *Faculty:* 21 full-time (12 women), 21 part-time/adjunct (10 women). *Students:* 39 full-time (21 women); includes 7 minority (6 African Americans, 1 Asian American or Pacific Islander). Average age 28. 261 applicants, 8% accepted, 14 enrolled. In 2009, 14 master's awarded. *Degree requirements:* For master's, comprehensive exam, thesis. *Entrance requirements:* For master's, audition or interview. Additional exam requirements/recommendations for international students: Required—TOEFL (minimum score 550 paper-based; 213 computer-based; 80 iBT), IELTS (minimum score 6.5). *Application deadline:* For fall admission, 1/1 priority date for domestic and international students. Application fee: $25. Electronic applications accepted. *Expenses:* Contact institution. *Financial support:* In 2009–10, 39 students received support, including 39 fellowships (averaging $17,800 per year); career-related internships or fieldwork, Federal Work-Study, institutionally sponsored loans, and scholarships/grants also available. Financial award application deadline: 2/15; financial award applicants required to submit FAFSA. *Unit head:* John Culbert, Dean, 773-325-7954, Fax: 773-325-7920, E-mail: jculbert@depaul.edu. *Application contact:* Jason Beck, Director of Admissions, 773-325-7999, Fax: 773-325-7920, E-mail: jbeck1@depaul.edu.

Drew University, Caspersen School of Graduate Studies, Program in Education, Madison, NJ 07940-1493. Offers biology (MAT); chemistry (MAT); English (MAT); French (MAT); Italian (MAT); math (MAT); physics (MAT); social studies (MAT); Spanish (MAT); theatre arts (MAT). *Unit head:* Dr. Ross Danis.

Eastern Michigan University, Graduate School, College of Arts and Sciences, Department of Communication, Media and Theatre Arts, Program in Arts Administration, Ypsilanti, MI 48197. Offers theatre arts-arts administration (MA). Part-time and evening/weekend programs available. Postbaccalaureate distance learning degree programs offered (minimal on-campus study). *Students:* 4 full-time (3 women), 20 part-time (15 women); includes 1 minority (African American), 5 international. Average age 23. In 2009, 9 master's awarded. *Entrance requirements:* Additional exam requirements/recommendations for international students: Required—TOEFL. *Application deadline:* Applications are processed on a rolling basis. Application fee: $35. Tuition and fees vary according to course level. *Financial support:* Fellowships, research assistantships with full tuition reimbursements, teaching assistantships with full tuition reimbursements, career-related internships or fieldwork, Federal Work-Study, institutionally sponsored loans, scholarships/grants, tuition waivers (partial), and unspecified assistantships available. Support available to part-time students. Financial award applicants required to submit FAFSA. *Unit head:* Kenneth Stevens, Coordinator, 734-487-3130, Fax: 734-487-3443, E-mail: ken.stevens@emich.edu. *Application contact:* Kenneth Stevens, Coordinator, 734-487-3130, Fax: 734-487-3443, E-mail: ken.stevens@emich.edu.

Eastern Michigan University, Graduate School, College of Arts and Sciences, Department of Communication, Media and Theatre Arts, Program in Drama/Theatre for the Young, Ypsilanti, MI 48197. Offers MA, MFA. Part-time programs available. Postbaccalaureate distance learning degree programs offered (minimal on-campus study). *Students:* 6 full-time (4 women), 15 part-time (11 women); includes 5 minority (all African Americans), 2 international. Average age 32. In 2009, 7 master's awarded. *Degree requirements:* For master's, thesis optional. *Entrance requirements:* Additional exam requirements/recommendations for international students: Required—TOEFL. *Application deadline:* Applications are processed on a rolling basis. Application fee: $35. Tuition and fees vary according to course level. *Financial support:* Fellowships, research assistantships with full tuition reimbursements, teaching assistantships with full tuition reimbursements, career-related internships or fieldwork, Federal Work-Study, institutionally sponsored loans, scholarships/grants, tuition waivers (partial), and unspecified assistantships available. Support available to part-time students. Financial award applicants required to submit FAFSA. *Unit head:* Prof. Jessica Alexander, Coordinator, 734-487-3179, Fax: 734-487-3443, E-mail: jessica.alexander@emich.edu. *Application contact:* Graduate Coordinator.

Eastern Michigan University, Graduate School, College of Arts and Sciences, Department of Communication, Media and Theatre Arts, Programs in Theatre Arts, Ypsilanti, MI 48197. Offers interpretation/performance studies (MA); theatre arts (MA). Part-time and evening/weekend programs available. Postbaccalaureate distance learning degree programs offered (minimal on-campus study). *Students:* 4 full-time (3 women), 13 part-time (7 women); includes 1 minority (African American). Average age 31. 14 applicants, 93% accepted, 6 enrolled. In 2009, 4 master's awarded. *Degree requirements:* For master's, thesis or alternative. *Entrance requirements:* Additional exam requirements/recommendations for international students: Required—TOEFL. *Application deadline:* Applications are processed on a rolling basis. Application fee: $35. Tuition and fees vary according to course level. *Financial support:* Fellowships, research assistantships with full tuition reimbursements, teaching assistantships with full tuition reimbursements, career-related internships or fieldwork, Federal Work-Study, institutionally sponsored loans, scholarships/grants, and unspecified assistantships available. Support available to part-time students. Financial award applicants required to submit FAFSA. *Unit head:* Kenneth Stevens, Coordinator, 734-487-3130, Fax: 734-487-3443, E-mail: ken.stevens@emich.edu. *Application contact:* Kenneth Stevens, Coordinator, 734-487-3130, Fax: 734-487-3443, E-mail: ken.stevens@emich.edu.

Emerson College, Graduate Studies, School of the Arts, Department of Performing Arts, Program in Theatre Education, Boston, MA 02116-4624. Offers MA. Part-time programs available. *Faculty:* 25 full-time (12 women), 10 part-time/adjunct (8 women). *Students:* 56 full-time (47 women), 13 part-time (9 women); includes 4 minority (3 African Americans, 1 Hispanic American), 2 international. Average age 25. 61 applicants, 89% accepted, 29 enrolled. In 2009, 35 master's awarded. *Entrance requirements:* For master's, GRE General Test. Additional exam requirements/recommendations for international students: Required—TOEFL (minimum score 550 paper-based; 213 computer-based; 80 iBT), IELTS (minimum score 6.5). *Application deadline:* For fall admission, 6/1 priority date for domestic students, 5/1 priority date for international students. Applications are processed on a rolling basis. Application fee: $60 ($75 for international students). Electronic applications accepted. *Expenses:* Tuition: Full-time $22,056; part-time $919 per credit. Required fees: $120; $120 per year. One-time fee: $170 full-time. *Financial support:* In 2009–10, 27 students received support, including 1 fellowship with partial tuition reimbursement available (averaging $14,000 per year), 11 research assistantships with partial tuition reimbursements available (averaging $10,000 per year); Federal Work-Study, scholarships/grants, and unspecified assistantships also available. Financial award application deadline: 3/1; financial award applicants required to submit FAFSA. *Faculty research:* Theater. *Unit head:* Dr. Robert Colby, Graduate Program Director, 617-824-8780, E-mail: robert_colby@emerson.edu. *Application contact:* Office of Graduate Admission, 617-824-8610, Fax: 617-824-8614, E-mail: gradapp@emerson.edu.

Florida Atlantic University, Dorothy F. Schmidt College of Arts and Letters, Department of Theatre and Dance, Boca Raton, FL 33431-0991. Offers acting (MFA); design and technology (MFA). *Faculty:* 8 full-time (1 woman), 1 (woman) part-time/adjunct. *Students:* 13 full-time (8 women), 1 part-time (0 women); includes 1 minority (Hispanic American). Average age 30. 6 applicants, 67% accepted, 3 enrolled. In 2009, 4 master's awarded. *Degree requirements:* For master's, thesis, production. *Entrance requirements:* For master's, GRE General Test, minimum GPA of 3.0 during last 60 hours of undergraduate course work. *Application deadline:* For fall admission, 8/15 priority date for domestic students, 8/15 for international students. Applications are processed on a rolling basis. Application fee: $30. *Expenses:* Tuition, state resident: full-time $7055; part-time $293.94 per credit hour. Tuition, nonresident: full-time $22,096; part-time $920.66 per credit hour. *Financial support:* Fellowships, teaching assistantships with full tuition reimbursements, career-related internships or fieldwork, Federal Work-Study, and institutionally sponsored loans available. Support available to part-time students. Financial award application deadline: 3/31. *Faculty research:* Contemporary British theatre, Eastern European playwrights, Latin American drama. *Unit head:* Dr. Gvozden Kopani, Chair, 561-297-3815, Fax: 561-297-2180, E-mail: dkopani@fau.edu. *Application contact:* Dr. Emily Stockard, Associate Dean, 561-297-2817, Fax: 561-297-2744, E-mail: stockard@fau.edu.

Florida State University, The Graduate School, School of Theatre, Tallahassee, FL 32306. Offers acting (MFA); directing (MFA); lighting, costume, and scenic design (MFA); technical production (MFA); theater management (MFA); theatre (MA, MS, PhD). *Accreditation:* NAST. *Faculty:* 20 full-time (10 women). *Students:* 103 full-time (51 women), 9 part-time (6 women); includes 8 minority (3 African Americans, 1 Asian American or Pacific Islander, 4 Hispanic Americans). Average age 25. 139 applicants, 24% accepted, 27 enrolled. In 2009, 28 master's, 1 doctorate awarded. *Degree requirements:* For master's, one foreign language, comprehensive

Theater

Florida State University (continued)
exam (for some programs), thesis (for some programs); for doctorate, one foreign language, comprehensive exam, thesis/dissertation. *Entrance requirements:* For master's, GRE General Test, writing sample (MA), interview (MFA), minimum undergraduate GPA of 3.0, audition (MFA in acting), portfolio (MFA). Additional exam requirements/recommendations for international students: Required—TOEFL. *Application deadline:* For fall admission, 2/15 priority date for domestic and international students. Applications are processed on a rolling basis. Application fee: $30. Electronic applications accepted. *Expenses:* Tuition, state resident: full-time $7413. Tuition, nonresident: full-time $22,567. *Financial support:* In 2009–10, 1 fellowship with full tuition reimbursement (averaging $18,000 per year), 30 research assistantships with full tuition reimbursements (averaging $8,300 per year), 57 teaching assistantships with full tuition reimbursements (averaging $8,900 per year) were awarded; career-related internships or fieldwork, Federal Work-Study, institutionally sponsored loans, scholarships/grants, health care benefits, and unspecified assistantships also available. Financial award application deadline: 1/1; financial award applicants required to submit FAFSA. *Faculty research:* Gender theatre, performance theory, computers in theatre, dramaturgy, music theatre performance. *Unit head:* Cameron Jackson, Director, 850-644-7257, Fax: 850-644-7408, E-mail: ccjackson@admin.fsu.edu. *Application contact:* Barbara Thomas, Program Assistant, 850-644-7234, Fax: 850-644-7246, E-mail: bgthomas@admin.fsu.edu.

Fontbonne University, Graduate Programs, Department of Fine Arts, St. Louis, MO 63105-3098. Offers art (MA); fine arts (MFA); theater education (MA). Part-time and evening/weekend programs available. *Faculty:* 6 full-time (2 women), 5 part-time/adjunct (4 women). *Students:* 7 full-time (4 women), 6 part-time (5 women); includes 1 minority (African American). Average age 37. In 2009, 8 master's awarded. *Degree requirements:* For master's, thesis exhibit (MFA). *Entrance requirements:* For master's, minimum GPA of 3.0, portfolio. *Application deadline:* For fall admission, 8/1 priority date for domestic students. Applications are processed on a rolling basis. Application fee: $25. *Expenses:* Tuition: Part-time $562 per credit hour. *Financial support:* In 2009–10, teaching assistantships (averaging $2,500 per year). Support available to part-time students. Financial award application deadline: 4/1; financial award applicants required to submit FAFSA. *Unit head:* Catherine Connor-Talasek, Chairperson, 314-889-1431, Fax: 314-889-4545, E-mail: cconnor@fontbonne.edu. *Application contact:* Catherine Connor-Talasek, Chairperson, 314-889-1431, Fax: 314-889-4545, E-mail: cconnor@fontbonne.edu.

The George Washington University, Columbian College of Arts and Sciences, Department of Theatre and Dance, Washington, DC 20052. Offers classical acting (MFA); design (MFA). Part-time and evening/weekend programs available. *Faculty:* 10 full-time (6 women), 19 part-time/adjunct (14 women). *Students:* 21 full-time (13 women), 16 part-time (6 women); includes 2 minority (both African Americans), 4 international. Average age 34. 74 applicants, 39% accepted, 20 enrolled. In 2009, 12 master's awarded. *Degree requirements:* For master's, thesis. *Entrance requirements:* For master's, minimum GPA of 3.0, portfolio. Additional exam requirements/recommendations for international students: Required—TOEFL (minimum score 550 paper-based; 213 computer-based; 80 iBT). *Application deadline:* For fall admission, 8/1 priority date for domestic students; for spring admission, 10/1 priority date for domestic students. Applications are processed on a rolling basis. Application fee: $60. Electronic applications accepted. *Financial support:* In 2009–10, 2 students received support; fellowships with tuition reimbursements available, teaching assistantships with tuition reimbursements available, career-related internships or fieldwork, Federal Work-Study, and tuition waivers available. *Unit head:* Alan G. Wade, Interim Chair, 202-994-3664, E-mail: awade@gwu.edu. *Application contact:* Information Contact, 202-994-8072, E-mail: trdanews@gwu.edu.

Graduate School and University Center of the City University of New York, Graduate Studies, Program in Theatre, New York, NY 10016-4039. Offers PhD. *Faculty:* 21 full-time (4 women). *Students:* 73 full-time (41 women), 2 part-time (both women); includes 3 minority (all Hispanic Americans), 11 international. Average age 36. 52 applicants, 46% accepted, 10 enrolled. In 2009, 7 doctorates awarded. *Degree requirements:* For doctorate, 2 foreign languages, thesis/dissertation. *Entrance requirements:* For doctorate, GRE General Test, writing sample. Additional exam requirements/recommendations for international students: Required—TOEFL. *Application deadline:* For fall admission, 3/1 for domestic students. Application fee: $125. Electronic applications accepted. *Financial support:* In 2009–10, 49 students received support, including 41 fellowships, 8 research assistantships, 12 teaching assistantships; career-related internships or fieldwork, Federal Work-Study, institutionally sponsored loans, and tuition waivers (full and partial) also available. Financial award application deadline: 2/1; financial award applicants required to submit FAFSA. *Unit head:* Dr. Glenn Burger, Executive Officer, 212-817-8871, Fax: 212-817-1538, E-mail: gburger@gc.cuny.edu. *Application contact:* Les Gribben, Director of Admissions, 212-817-7470, Fax: 212-817-1624, E-mail: lgribben@gc.cuny.edu.

Hollins University, Graduate Programs, Program in Playwriting, Roanoke, VA 24020-1603. Offers MFA. Part-time programs available. *Faculty:* 1 full-time (0 women), 2 part-time/adjunct (1 woman). *Students:* 19 full-time (9 women), 1 part-time (0 women); includes 3 minority (2 African Americans, 1 Asian American or Pacific Islander), 1 international. Average age 39. 19 applicants, 95% accepted, 14 enrolled. In 2009, 1 master's awarded. *Degree requirements:* For master's, comprehensive exam, thesis. *Entrance requirements:* For master's, letters of recommendation, writing samples. Additional exam requirements/recommendations for international students: Required—TOEFL (minimum score 550 paper-based; 213 computer-based; 79 iBT). Application fee: $40. *Expenses:* Tuition: Full-time $27,780; part-time $295 per contact hour. Required fees: $280; $70 per unit. Part-time tuition and fees vary according to course load and program. *Financial support:* In 2009–10, 3 students received support, including 3 fellowships (averaging $1,000 per year). Financial award application deadline: 2/15. *Unit head:* Todd Ristau, Director, 540-362-6386, E-mail: tristau@hollins.edu. *Application contact:* Cathy S. Koon, Manager of Graduate Services, 540-362-6326, Fax: 540-362-6288, E-mail: ckoon@hollins.edu.

Humboldt State University, Graduate Studies, College of Arts, Humanities, and Social Sciences, Department of Theatre, Film and Dance, Arcata, CA 95521-8299. Offers theatre arts (MA, MFA), including film production (MA), production (MA), scenography (MFA). *Students:* 15 full-time (9 women), 1 (woman) part-time; includes 3 minority (1 Asian American or Pacific Islander, 2 Hispanic Americans). Average age 33. 12 applicants, 42% accepted, 5 enrolled. In 2009, 3 master's awarded. *Degree requirements:* For master's, thesis or alternative, qualifying exam. *Entrance requirements:* For master's, minimum GPA of 2.5. Additional exam requirements/recommendations for international students: Required—TOEFL (minimum score 500 paper-based; 173 computer-based). *Application deadline:* For fall admission, 4/15 for domestic students. Applications are processed on a rolling basis. Application fee: $55. *Expenses:* Tuition, nonresident: full-time $8928. Required fees: $6102. Tuition and fees vary according to program. *Financial support:* Fellowships available. Financial award application deadline: 3/1; financial award applicants required to submit FAFSA. *Faculty research:* Physical theater, design, playwriting. *Unit head:* Bernadette Cheyne, Chair/Coordinator, 707-826-4606, Fax: 707-826-5494, E-mail: bmc3@humboldt.edu. *Application contact:* Bernadette Cheyne, Chair/Coordinator, 707-826-4606, Fax: 707-826-5494, E-mail: bmc3@humboldt.edu.

Hunter College of the City University of New York, Graduate School, School of Arts and Sciences, Department of Theatre, New York, NY 10021-5085. Offers MA. Part-time and evening/weekend programs available. *Faculty:* 6 full-time (3 women). *Students:* 2 full-time (0 women), 35 part-time (23 women); includes 7 minority (1 African American, 1 American Indian/Alaska Native, 2 Asian Americans or Pacific Islanders, 3 Hispanic Americans). Average age 34. 16 applicants, 69% accepted, 6 enrolled. In 2009, 14 master's awarded. *Degree requirements:* For master's, comprehensive exam, thesis. *Entrance requirements:* For master's, GRE General Test. Additional exam requirements/recommendations for international students: Required—TOEFL. *Application deadline:* For fall admission, 4/1 for domestic students, 2/1 for international students; for spring admission, 11/1 for domestic students, 9/1 for international students. Application fee: $125. *Expenses:* Tuition, state resident: full-time $7360; part-time $310 per credit. Required fees: $250 per semester. *Financial support:* In 2009–10, 1 fellowship (averaging $3,000 per year), 4 teaching assistantships were awarded; research assistantships, career-related internships or fieldwork, Federal Work-Study, and tuition waivers (partial) also available. Support available to part-time students. Financial award application deadline: 4/15. *Faculty research:* Modern French mimes, acting techniques, directing, New York avant-garde theater and popular entertainment, playwriting. *Unit head:* Dr. Barbara Bosch, Chairperson, 212-772-5148/9, Fax: 212-650-3584, E-mail: bbosch@hunter.cuny.edu. *Application contact:* Mira Felner, Graduate Advisor, 212-772-4642, E-mail: theatre@hunter.cuny.edu.

Idaho State University, Office of Graduate Studies, College of Arts and Sciences, Program in Theatre and Dance, Pocatello, ID 83209-8006. Offers theatre (MA). Part-time programs available. *Faculty:* 4 full-time (2 women). *Students:* 4 full-time (3 women). Average age 31. In 2009, 3 master's awarded. *Degree requirements:* For master's, comprehensive exam, thesis optional, oral and written exam. *Entrance requirements:* For master's, GRE General Test (35th percentile or above on one of the 3 sections). Additional exam requirements/recommendations for international students: Required—TOEFL (minimum score 550 paper-based; 213 computer-based; 80 iBT). *Application deadline:* For fall admission, 7/1 for domestic students, 6/1 for international students; for spring admission, 12/1 for domestic students, 11/1 for international students. Applications are processed on a rolling basis. Application fee: $55. Electronic applications accepted. *Expenses:* Tuition, state resident: full-time $3318; part-time $297 per credit hour. Tuition, nonresident: full-time $13,120; part-time $437 per credit hour. Required fees: $2530. Tuition and fees vary according to program. *Financial support:* In 2009–10, 3 teaching assistantships with full and partial tuition reimbursements (averaging $10,841 per year) were awarded; Federal Work-Study, institutionally sponsored loans, scholarships/grants, health care benefits, tuition waivers (full and partial), and unspecified assistantships also available. Support available to part-time students. Financial award application deadline: 1/1; financial award applicants required to submit FAFSA. *Faculty research:* Theatre history, technical theatre. *Unit head:* Dr. Randy Earles, Co-Chair, 208-282-3173, Fax: 208-282-6281, E-mail: earlrand@isu.edu. *Application contact:* Tami Carson, Graduate School Technical Records Specialist, 208-282-2150, Fax: 208-282-4847, E-mail: carstami@isu.edu.

Illinois State University, Graduate School, College of Fine Arts, School of Theatre, Normal, IL 61790-2200. Offers MA, MFA, MS. *Accreditation:* NAST. Part-time programs available. *Degree requirements:* For master's, variable foreign language requirement, thesis or alternative. *Entrance requirements:* For master's, sample of written work, minimum GPA of 3.0 in last 60 hours of course work. *Faculty research:* Illinois Shakespeare festival.

Indiana University Bloomington, University Graduate School, College of Arts and Sciences, Department of Theatre and Drama, Bloomington, IN 47405-7000. Offers acting (MFA); design and technology (MFA); directing (MFA); literature (MA, PhD); playwriting (MFA); theatre and drama (MAT); theatre history (MA, PhD); theory (MA, PhD). *Accreditation:* NAST. *Faculty:* 20 full-time (4 women). *Students:* 46 full-time (19 women); includes 2 minority (both African Americans), 3 international. Average age 29. 48 applicants, 42% accepted, 19 enrolled. In 2009, 12 master's, 2 doctorates awarded. Terminal master's awarded for partial completion of doctoral program. *Degree requirements:* For master's, one foreign language, comprehensive exam, thesis; for doctorate, 2 foreign languages, comprehensive exam, thesis/dissertation, 90 credit hours. *Entrance requirements:* For master's, audition, interview, portfolio or script analysis; for doctorate, GRE General Test. Additional exam requirements/recommendations for international students: Required—TOEFL (minimum score 550 paper-based; 213 computer-based; 80 iBT). *Application deadline:* For fall admission, 1/15 priority date for domestic students, 12/1 for international students. Application fee: $55 ($65 for international students). Electronic applications accepted. *Financial support:* In 2009–10, 38 students received support, including 1 fellowship with tuition reimbursement available (averaging $15,000 per year), 18 teaching assistantships with full tuition reimbursements available (averaging $11,750 per year); research assistantships with tuition reimbursements available, career-related internships or fieldwork, Federal Work-Study, institutionally sponsored loans, scholarships/grants, health care benefits, and unspecified assistantships also available. Financial award application deadline: 3/1. *Faculty research:* American, western European, world literature; history and theory; theatrical production, design and technology; acting; directing; playwriting. *Unit head:* Jonathan R. Michaelsen, Chairperson and Professor, 812-855-4535, Fax: 812-856-0698, E-mail: theatre@indiana.edu. *Application contact:* Barb Grinder, Administrative Secretary, 812-855-4535, Fax: 812-855-0698, E-mail: bgrinder@indiana.edu.

Kansas State University, Graduate School, College of Arts and Sciences, Department of Communication Studies, Theatre and Dance, Manhattan, KS 66505. Offers rhetoric/communication (MA); theatre (MA). *Faculty:* 17 full-time (8 women), 1 (woman) part-time/adjunct. *Students:* 10 applicants, 100% accepted, 10 enrolled. In 2009, 15 master's awarded. *Degree requirements:* For master's, thesis or alternative. *Entrance requirements:* For master's, GRE General Test (recommended), minimum GPA of 3.0. Additional exam requirements/recommendations for international students: Required—TOEFL. *Application deadline:* For fall admission, 2/1 priority date for domestic and international students; for spring admission, 8/1 priority date for domestic and international students. Applications are processed on a rolling basis. Application fee: $40 ($55 for international students). Electronic applications accepted. *Financial support:* In 2009–10, 23 teaching assistantships with full tuition reimbursements (averaging $9,391 per year) were awarded; career-related internships or fieldwork, institutionally sponsored loans, and scholarships/grants also available. Support available to part-time students. Financial award application deadline: 3/1; financial award applicants required to submit FAFSA. *Faculty research:* Drama therapy, directing, costume design, scenic design, technical theatre mechanics and safety. Total annual research expenditures: $10,294. *Unit head:* Charles Griffin, Head, 785-532-6860, Fax: 785-532-3714, E-mail: charlieg@ksu.edu. *Application contact:* William Schenck-Hamlin, Director, 785-532-6861, Fax: 785-532-3714, E-mail: billsh@ksu.edu.

Kent State University, College of the Arts, School of Theatre and Dance, Kent, OH 44242-0001. Offers acting (MFA); design and technology (MFA); theatre (MA, MFA). *Accreditation:* NAST. Part-time programs available. *Degree requirements:* For master's, thesis. *Entrance requirements:* For master's, GRE General Test, minimum GPA of 2.75. Additional exam requirements/recommendations for international students: Required—TOEFL. Electronic applications accepted. *Faculty research:* Scene design, costume design, lighting design, technical direction, musical theatre.

Lamar University, College of Graduate Studies, College of Fine Arts and Communication, Department of Music, Theatre, and Dance, Beaumont, TX 77710. Offers music education (MM Ed); music performance (MM); theatre (MS). *Accreditation:* NASM (one or more programs are accredited). *Faculty:* 8 full-time (2 women). *Students:* 5 full-time (3 women), 3 part-time (2 women); includes 1 minority (African American). Average age 29. 9 applicants, 44% accepted, 4 enrolled. In 2009, 3 master's awarded. *Degree requirements:* For master's, comprehensive exam, thesis optional. *Entrance requirements:* For master's, GRE General Test, theory placement exams, audition. Additional exam requirements/recommendations for international students: Required—TOEFL. *Application deadline:* For fall admission, 8/1 for domestic students; for spring admission, 12/1 for domestic students. Applications are processed on a rolling basis. Application fee: $25 ($50 for international students). *Financial support:* In 2009–10, 4 fellowships with tuition reimbursements (averaging $2,000 per year), 2 teaching assistantships were awarded; institutionally sponsored loans and tuition waivers (partial) also available. Support available to part-time students. Financial award application deadline: 4/1. *Faculty research:* Performance: ensembles and personal. *Unit head:* Dr. L. Randolph Babin, Chair, 409-880-8144, Fax: 409-880-8143, E-mail: babinlr@hal.lamar.edu. *Application contact:* Dr. Robert M. Culbertson, Adviser, 409-880-8073, Fax: 409-880-8143, E-mail: culbertsrm@hal.lamar.edu.

Lindenwood University, Graduate Programs, School of Fine and Performing Arts, St. Charles, MO 63301-1695. Offers arts management (MA); communication arts (MA); studio art (MA, MFA); theatre (MA, MFA). Part-time programs available. *Faculty:* 15 full-time (6 women), 5 part-time/adjunct (2 women). *Students:* 31 full-time (17 women), 13 part-time (9 women);

includes 3 minority (all African Americans), 5 international. Average age 32. 6 applicants, 2 enrolled. In 2009, 9 master's awarded. *Degree requirements:* For master's, thesis (for some programs). *Entrance requirements:* For master's, audition or interview, minimum GPA of 3.0, submission of portfolio, letter of recommendation. Additional exam requirements/recommendations for international students: Required—TOEFL (minimum score 550 paper-based; 213 computer-based; 80 iBT). *Application deadline:* For fall admission, 8/27 priority date for domestic and international students; for spring admission, 1/28 priority date for domestic and international students. Applications are processed on a rolling basis. Application fee: $30 ($100 for international students). Electronic applications accepted. *Expenses:* Tuition: Full-time $12,960; part-time $370 per credit hour. Required fees: $340. One-time fee: $30 full-time. Tuition and fees vary according to course level and course load. *Financial support:* In 2009–10, 37 students received support. Career-related internships or fieldwork, institutionally sponsored loans, tuition waivers (partial), and unspecified assistantships available. Financial award application deadline: 6/30; financial award applicants required to submit FAFSA. *Unit head:* Donnell Walsh, Dean of Fine Arts, 636-949-4853, Fax: 636-949-4910, E-mail: dwalsh@lindenwood.edu. *Application contact:* Brett Barger, Dean of Evening Admissions and Extension Campuses, 636-949-4934, Fax: 636-949-4109, E-mail: adultadmissions@lindenwood.edu.

Long Island University, C.W. Post Campus, School of Visual and Performing Arts, Department of Theatre, Film, Dance and Arts Management, Brookville, NY 11548-1300. Offers interactive multimedia (MA); theatre (MA). Part-time and evening/weekend programs available. *Degree requirements:* For master's, thesis. *Entrance requirements:* For master's, placement exam. Electronic applications accepted. *Faculty research:* Playwriting, intercultural dance and theatre, translation, Suzuki, set and costume design.

Louisiana State University and Agricultural and Mechanical College, Graduate School, College of Music and Dramatic Arts, Department of Theatre, Baton Rouge, LA 70803. Offers acting (MFA); directing (MFA); theatre (PhD); theatre design/technology (MFA). *Accreditation:* NAST. *Faculty:* 15 full-time (5 women). *Students:* 22 full-time (9 women), 4 part-time (3 women), 3 international. Average age 34. 13 applicants, 23% accepted, 2 enrolled. In 2009, 6 master's awarded. *Degree requirements:* For master's, thesis; for doctorate, one foreign language, thesis/dissertation. *Entrance requirements:* For master's, GRE General Test, audition, minimum GPA of 3.0; for doctorate, GRE General Test, minimum GPA of 3.0. Additional exam requirements/recommendations for international students: Required—TOEFL (minimum score 550 paper-based; 213 computer-based; 79 iBT) or IELTS (minimum score 6.5). *Application deadline:* For fall admission, 1/25 priority date for domestic students, 5/15 for international students; for spring admission, 10/15 for international students. Applications are processed on a rolling basis. Application fee: $50 ($70 for international students). Electronic applications accepted. *Financial support:* In 2009–10, 25 students received support, including 1 fellowship with full and partial tuition reimbursement available (averaging $16,427 per year), 17 teaching assistantships with full and partial tuition reimbursements available (averaging $12,529 per year); research assistantships with full and partial tuition reimbursements available, Federal Work-Study, scholarships/grants, health care benefits, tuition waivers (full and partial), and unspecified assistantships also available. Support available to part-time students. Financial award application deadline: 6/15; financial award applicants required to submit FAFSA. *Faculty research:* Acting, American drama, arts administration, theatre history, dramatic theory/literature, black drama. *Unit head:* Dr. Michael Tick, Chair, 225-578-4174, Fax: 225-578-4135, E-mail: mtick1@lsu.edu. *Application contact:* Leigh Clemmons, Head, MFA Design/Tech, 225-578-9273, E-mail: clemons@lsu.edu.

Mary Baldwin College, Graduate Studies, Program in Shakespeare and Renaissance Literature in Performance, Staunton, VA 24401-3610. Offers acting (M Litt); directing (M Litt); Shakespeare and Renaissance literature in performance (MFA); teaching (M Litt). *Entrance requirements:* For master's, GRE (M Litt).

Massachusetts College of Art and Design, Graduate Programs, Program in Fine Arts, Boston, MA 02115-5882. Offers ceramics (MFA); design (MFA); fibers (MFA); film/video (MFA); glass (MFA); media and performing arts (MFA); metals/jewelry (MFA); painting (MFA); photography (MFA); printmaking (MFA); sculpture (MFA). *Accreditation:* NASAD. *Faculty:* 10 full-time (5 women), 8 part-time/adjunct (6 women). *Students:* 89 full-time (56 women), 12 part-time (8 women); includes 8 minority (5 Asian Americans or Pacific Islanders, 3 Hispanic Americans), 10 international. Average age 34. 295 applicants, 24% accepted, 40 enrolled. In 2009, 44 master's awarded. *Degree requirements:* For master's, thesis, exhibit. *Entrance requirements:* For master's, 12 units of course work in art history, portfolio, resume, letters of reference, interview. Additional exam requirements/recommendations for international students: Required—TOEFL (minimum score 563 paper-based; 223 computer-based; 85 iBT); Recommended—IELTS (minimum score 6.5). *Application deadline:* For fall admission, 1/15 for domestic and international students. Application fee: $75. Electronic applications accepted. *Expenses:* Tuition, state resident: full-time $18,450; part-time $615 per credit. Tuition, nonresident: full-time $18,450; part-time $615 per credit. Tuition and fees vary according to program. *Financial support:* In 2009–10, 50 research assistantships (averaging $2,000 per year), 40 teaching assistantships (averaging $2,000 per year) were awarded; career-related internships or fieldwork, Federal Work-Study, and clerical/technical assistantships ($2000) also available. Support available to part-time students. Financial award application deadline: 5/1; financial award applicants required to submit FAFSA. *Unit head:* George Creamer, Dean of Graduate Programs, 617-879-7163, Fax: 617-879-7171, E-mail: creamer@massart.edu. *Application contact:* George Creamer, Dean of Graduate Programs, 617-879-7163, Fax: 617-879-7171, E-mail: creamer@massart.edu.

Miami University, Graduate School, School of Fine Arts, Department of Theatre, Oxford, OH 45056. Offers MA. *Accreditation:* NAST. *Students:* 8 full-time (3 women); includes 1 minority (African American), 3 international. *Entrance requirements:* For master's, minimum undergraduate GPA of 3.0 during previous 2 years or 2.75 overall. Application fee: $50. *Expenses:* Tuition, state resident: full-time $11,280. Tuition, nonresident: full-time $24,912. Required fees: $516. *Financial support:* Fellowships with full tuition reimbursements, research assistantships, teaching assistantships, career-related internships or fieldwork, Federal Work-Study, health care benefits, tuition waivers (full), and unspecified assistantships available. Financial award application deadline: 3/1. *Unit head:* Dr. Elizabeth Mullenix, Chair, 513-529-3053, E-mail: mullener@muohio.edu. *Application contact:* Dr. Paul K. Jackson, Interim Director of Graduate Studies, 513-529-1406, E-mail: jacksopk@muohio.edu.

Michigan State University, The Graduate School, College of Arts and Letters, Department of Theatre, East Lansing, MI 48824. Offers MA, MFA. *Faculty:* 10 full-time (6 women). *Students:* 16 full-time (8 women), 2 part-time (both women); includes 1 minority (African American), 1 international. Average age 26. 13 applicants, 92% accepted. In 2009, 8 master's awarded. *Entrance requirements:* Additional exam requirements/recommendations for international students: Required—TOEFL. Electronic applications accepted. *Expenses:* Tuition, state resident: part-time $478.25 per credit hour. Tuition, nonresident: part-time $966.50 per credit hour. Part-time tuition and fees vary according to program. *Financial support:* In 2009–10, 16 teaching assistantships with tuition reimbursements (averaging $6,157 per year) were awarded. Total annual research expenditures: $21,431. *Unit head:* Dr. Kirk A. Domer, Acting Chairperson, 517-355-6690, Fax: 517-355-1698, E-mail: domer@msu.edu. *Application contact:* Stacey Ellen Spees, Application Contact, 517-355-6690, Fax: 517-355-1698, E-mail: theatre@msu.edu.

Minnesota State University Mankato, College of Graduate Studies, College of Arts and Humanities, Department of Theatre and Dance, Mankato, MN 56001. Offers theatre arts (MA, MFA). *Students:* 14 full-time (6 women), 4 part-time (2 women). *Degree requirements:* For master's, one foreign language, comprehensive exam, thesis. *Entrance requirements:* For master's, minimum GPA of 3.0 during previous 2 years, 3 letters of recommendation, resume of theatre work, audition. Additional exam requirements/recommendations for international students: Required—TOEFL. *Application deadline:* For fall admission, 7/1 priority date for domestic students, 5/1 for international students; for spring admission, 11/1 for domestic students, 10/1 for international students. Applications are processed on a rolling basis. Application fee: $40. Electronic applications accepted. *Expenses:* Tuition, state resident: full-time $5364. Tuition, nonresident: full-time $8314. *Financial support:* Research assistantships with full tuition reimbursements, teaching assistantships with full tuition reimbursements, career-related internships or fieldwork, Federal Work-Study, institutionally sponsored loans, and unspecified assistantships available. Support available to part-time students. Financial award application deadline: 3/15; financial award applicants required to submit FAFSA. *Unit head:* Dr. Paul Hustoles, Chairperson, 507-389-2118. *Application contact:* 507-389-2321, E-mail: grad@mnsu.edu.

Missouri State University, Graduate College, College of Arts and Letters, Department of Theatre and Dance, Springfield, MO 65897. Offers secondary education (MS Ed), including speech and theatre; theatre (MA). *Accreditation:* NAST. Part-time programs available. *Faculty:* 10 full-time (6 women). *Students:* 4 full-time (1 woman), 5 part-time (all women). Average age 30. 7 applicants, 71% accepted, 4 enrolled. In 2009, 6 master's awarded. *Degree requirements:* For master's, comprehensive exam, thesis or alternative. *Entrance requirements:* For master's, minimum GPA of 3.0 (MA), 9-12 teaching certification (MS Ed). Additional exam requirements/recommendations for international students: Required—TOEFL (minimum score 550 paper-based; 213 computer-based; 79 iBT). *Application deadline:* For fall admission, 7/20 for domestic students, 5/1 for international students; for spring admission, 12/20 for domestic students, 9/1 for international students. Applications are processed on a rolling basis. Application fee: $35 ($50 for international students). Electronic applications accepted. *Expenses:* Tuition, state resident: full-time $3852; part-time $214 per credit hour. Tuition, nonresident: full-time $7524; part-time $418 per credit hour. Required fees: $696; $172 per semester. Tuition and fees vary according to course level, course load, degree level and program. *Financial support:* In 2009–10, 3 teaching assistantships with full tuition reimbursements (averaging $7,340 per year) were awarded; Federal Work-Study, institutionally sponsored loans, scholarships/grants, and unspecified assistantships also available. Financial award application deadline: 3/31; financial award applicants required to submit FAFSA. *Unit head:* Bob Willenbrink, Department Head, 417-836-4156, Fax: 417-836-4234, E-mail: rwillenbrink@missouristate.edu. *Application contact:* Eric Eckert, Coordinator of Admissions and Recruitment, 417-836-5331, Fax: 417-836-6888, E-mail: ericeckert@missouristate.edu.

Montclair State University, The Graduate School, School of the Arts, Department of Theatre and Dance, Montclair, NJ 07043-1624. Offers theatre (MA), including arts management, production/stage management, theatre studies. *Accreditation:* NAST. Part-time and evening/weekend programs available. *Faculty:* 15 full-time (8 women), 37 part-time/adjunct (24 women). *Students:* 10 full-time (8 women), 15 part-time (11 women). Average age 29. 18 applicants, 56% accepted, 7 enrolled. In 2009, 7 master's awarded. *Degree requirements:* For master's, comprehensive exam, thesis or alternative. *Entrance requirements:* For master's, GRE General Test, 2 letters of recommendation. Additional exam requirements/recommendations for international students: Required—TOEFL (minimum score 83 computer-based), or IELTS. *Application deadline:* For fall admission, 6/1 for international students; for spring admission, 10/1 for international students. Applications are processed on a rolling basis. Application fee: $60. Electronic applications accepted. *Expenses:* Tuition, area resident: Part-time $486.74 per credit. Tuition, state resident: part-time $486.74 per credit. Tuition, nonresident: part-time $751.34 per credit. Tuition and fees vary according to degree level and program. *Financial support:* In 2009–10, 2 research assistantships with full tuition reimbursements (averaging $7,000 per year) were awarded; Federal Work-Study, scholarships/grants, and unspecified assistantships also available. Support available to part-time students. Financial award application deadline: 3/1; financial award applicants required to submit FAFSA. *Unit head:* Dr. Eric Diamond, Chairperson, 973-655-4217, E-mail: peterson@mail.montclair.edu. *Application contact:* Amy Aiello, Director of Graduate Admissions and Operations, 973-655-5147, E-mail: petersonj@mail.montclair.edu.

Naropa University, Graduate Programs, Program in Theater: Contemporary Performance, Boulder, CO 80302-6697. Offers MFA. *Degree requirements:* For master's, culminating projects and performances. *Entrance requirements:* For master's, interview, head shot, resume, 3 letters of recommendation, letter of interest. Additional exam requirements/recommendations for international students: Required—TOEFL (minimum score 600 paper-based; 250 computer-based). Electronic applications accepted.

Naropa University, Graduate Programs, Program in Theater: Lecoq-Based Actor-Created Theater, Boulder, CO 80302-6697. Offers MFA. Part-time programs available. *Degree requirements:* For master's, final student production. *Entrance requirements:* For master's, interview, head shot, 3 letters of recommendation, resume, letter of interest. Additional exam requirements/recommendations for international students: Required—TOEFL (minimum score 600 paper-based; 250 computer-based). Electronic applications accepted.

National Theatre Conservatory, Department of Acting, Denver, CO 80204-2157. Offers MFA, Certificate. *Entrance requirements:* For master's, audition/interview.

The New School: A University, The New School for Drama, New York, NY 10014. Offers acting (MFA); directing (MFA); playwriting (MFA). *Faculty:* 5 full-time (2 women), 37 part-time/adjunct (20 women). *Students:* 112 full-time (65 women), 7 part-time (4 women); includes 23 minority (14 African Americans, 9 Hispanic Americans), 14 international. Average age 27. 367 applicants, 23% accepted, 34 enrolled. In 2009, 38 master's awarded. *Degree requirements:* For master's, thesis, student involvement in theatrical production and presentation. *Entrance requirements:* For master's, audition (acting), interview (directing and playwriting). Additional exam requirements/recommendations for international students: Required—TOEFL (minimum score 600 paper-based; 250 computer-based; 100 iBT). *Application deadline:* For fall admission, 1/8 for domestic and international students. Application fee: $50. Electronic applications accepted. *Expenses:* Contact institution. *Financial support:* Federal Work-Study and scholarships/grants available. Financial award application deadline: 3/1; financial award applicants required to submit FAFSA. *Unit head:* Robert LuPone, Director, 212-229-5859 Ext. 2636, E-mail: luponer@newschool.edu. *Application contact:* Troy Menn, Director of Admissions, 212-229-5859 Ext. 2614, Fax: 212-229-5150.

New York University, Steinhardt School of Culture, Education, and Human Development, Department of Music and Performing Arts Professions, Program in Educational Theatre, New York, NY 10012-1019. Offers dual degree: educational theatre and social studies (MA); educational theatre (Ed D, PhD, Advanced Certificate); educational theatre for colleges and communities (MA); educational theatre with English 7-12 (MA); teaching educational theatre, all grades (MA). Part-time programs available. *Students:* 78 full-time (64 women), 65 part-time (43 women); includes 24 minority (10 African Americans, 1 American Indian/Alaska Native, 4 Asian Americans or Pacific Islanders, 9 Hispanic Americans), 7 international. Average age 30. 104 applicants, 84% accepted, 58 enrolled. In 2009, 74 master's, 2 doctorates awarded. *Degree requirements:* For master's, thesis (for some programs); for doctorate, thesis/dissertation. *Entrance requirements:* For master's, audition; for doctorate, GRE General Test, interview; for Advanced Certificate, master's degree. Additional exam requirements/recommendations for international students: Required—TOEFL. *Application deadline:* For fall admission, 12/15 priority date for domestic and international students; for spring admission, 11/1 for domestic and international students. Applications are processed on a rolling basis. Application fee: $75. Electronic applications accepted. *Expenses:* Tuition: Full-time $30,528; part-time $1272 per credit. Required fees: $2177. *Financial support:* Teaching assistantships with partial tuition reimbursements, career-related internships or fieldwork, Federal Work-Study, institutionally sponsored loans, and scholarships/grants available. Support available to part-time students. Financial award application deadline: 2/1; financial award applicants required to submit FAFSA. *Faculty research:* Theatre for young audiences, drama in education, applied theatre, arts education assessment, reflective praxis. *Unit head:* Dr. Philip Taylor, Director, 212-998-5424, Fax: 212-995-4043. *Application contact:* 212-998-5030, Fax: 212-995-4328, E-mail: steinhardt.gradadmissions@nyu.edu.

New York University, Tisch School of the Arts and Graduate School of Arts and Science, Department of Performance Studies, New York, NY 10012-1019. Offers MA, PhD. *Faculty:* 12

Theater

New York University (continued)
full-time (7 women), 4 part-time/adjunct (3 women). *Students:* 63 full-time (46 women), 1 (woman) part-time; includes 16 minority (4 African Americans, 4 Asian Americans or Pacific Islanders, 8 Hispanic Americans). Average age 31. 198 applicants, 51% accepted, 54 enrolled. In 2009, 36 master's, 7 doctorates awarded. *Degree requirements:* For doctorate, one foreign language, comprehensive exam, thesis/dissertation, dissertation defense, qualifying exam. *Entrance requirements:* For master's, sample of written work; for doctorate, master's degree, writing sample. Additional exam requirements/recommendations for international students: Required—TOEFL, IELTS or ALI. *Application deadline:* For fall admission, 12/1 for domestic and international students. Application fee: $60. Electronic applications accepted. *Expenses:* Contact institution. *Financial support:* In 2009–10, 32 students received support, including 24 fellowships with full and partial tuition reimbursements available, 4 research assistantships, 4 teaching assistantships; Federal Work-Study, institutionally sponsored loans, tuition waivers (partial), and unspecified assistantships also available. Financial award application deadline: 2/15; financial award applicants required to submit CSS PROFILE or FAFSA. *Faculty research:* Performance theory, dance, folklore and festivals, postcolonial theory, anthropology and gender studies. *Unit head:* Jose Munoz, Chair, 212-998-1620, Fax: 212-995-4571, E-mail: performance.studies@nyu.edu. *Application contact:* Dan Sandford, Director of Graduate Admissions, 212-998-1918, Fax: 212-995-4060, E-mail: tisch.gradadmissions@nyu.edu.

New York University, Tisch School of the Arts, Graduate Acting Program, New York, NY 10012-1019. Offers MFA. *Faculty:* 9 full-time (6 women), 11 part-time/adjunct (5 women). *Students:* 52 full-time (23 women); includes 12 minority (8 African Americans, 3 Asian Americans or Pacific Islanders, 1 Hispanic American). Average age 26. 761 applicants, 4% accepted, 18 enrolled. In 2009, 18 master's awarded. *Entrance requirements:* For master's, audition. *Application deadline:* For fall admission, 1/1 for domestic and international students. Application fee: $60. Electronic applications accepted. *Expenses:* Tuition: Full-time $30,528; part-time $1272 per credit. Required fees: $2177. *Financial support:* In 2009–10, 30 students received support, including 4 fellowships with full and partial tuition reimbursements available; Federal Work-Study, institutionally sponsored loans, scholarships/grants, tuition waivers (full and partial), and unspecified assistantships also available. Financial award application deadline: 2/15; financial award applicants required to submit FAFSA. *Unit head:* Mark Wing-Davey, Chair, 212-998-1964, Fax: 212-995-4067. *Application contact:* Dan Sandford, Director of Graduate Admissions, 212-998-1918, Fax: 212-995-4060, E-mail: tisch.gradadmissions@nyu.edu.

Northern Illinois University, Graduate School, College of Visual and Performing Arts, School of Theatre and Dance, De Kalb, IL 60115-2854. Offers MFA. *Accreditation:* NAST. Part-time programs available. *Faculty:* 16 full-time (9 women). *Students:* 19 full-time (9 women), 2 part-time (1 woman); includes 2 minority (both African Americans). Average age 27. 43 applicants, 49% accepted, 19 enrolled. In 2009, 3 master's awarded. *Degree requirements:* For master's, comprehensive exam, final project and defense. *Entrance requirements:* For master's, minimum GPA of 2.75, audition or portfolio. Additional exam requirements/recommendations for international students: Required—TOEFL (minimum score 550 paper-based; 213 computer-based). *Application deadline:* For fall admission, 4/1 priority date for domestic students, 5/1 for international students; for spring admission, 10/15 priority date for domestic students, 10/1 for international students. Applications are processed on a rolling basis. Application fee: $30. Electronic applications accepted. *Expenses:* Tuition, state resident: full-time $6576; part-time $274 per credit hour. Tuition, nonresident: full-time $13,152; part-time $548 per credit hour. Required fees: $1813; $75.53 per credit hour. Part-time tuition and fees vary according to course load. *Financial support:* In 2009–10, 1 research assistantship with full tuition reimbursement, 8 teaching assistantships with full tuition reimbursements were awarded; fellowships with full tuition reimbursements, career-related internships or fieldwork, Federal Work-Study, scholarships/grants, tuition waivers (full), and staff assistantships also available. Support available to part-time students. Financial award applicants required to submit FAFSA. *Faculty research:* Theatre history, choreography, performance art spectacles, storytelling, computer visualization of the ethical space. *Unit head:* Alexander Gelman, Director, 815-753-8253, Fax: 815-753-8415, E-mail: agelman@niu.edu. *Application contact:* Terrence McClellan, Information Contact, 815-753-8257, E-mail: tmcclell@niu.edu.

Northwestern University, The Graduate School, School of Communication, Department of Theatre, Evanston, IL 60208. Offers directing (MFA); stage design (MFA); theatre (MA). Admissions and degrees offered through The Graduate School. *Degree requirements:* For master's, thesis (MFA). *Entrance requirements:* For master's, GRE General Test. Additional exam requirements/recommendations for international students: Required—TOEFL. *Faculty research:* Critical analysis, theory and history of theatre and drama, philosophy of dance and movement, performance in multicultural contexts, storytelling, computer design process.

Northwestern University, The Graduate School, School of Communication, Interdisciplinary PhD Program in Theatre and Drama, Evanston, IL 60208. Offers PhD. Admissions and degree offered through The Graduate School. *Degree requirements:* For doctorate, thesis/dissertation, qualifying and final oral exams. *Entrance requirements:* For doctorate, GRE General Test, sample of written work. Additional exam requirements/recommendations for international students: Required—TOEFL. Electronic applications accepted. *Faculty research:* Theory and history of theatre and drama, performance theory, performance in multicultural contexts, critical analysis drama, theatre historiography.

The Ohio State University, Graduate School, College of the Arts, Department of Theatre, Columbus, OH 43210. Offers MA, MFA, PhD. *Accreditation:* NAST. *Faculty:* 22. *Students:* 39 full-time (19 women), 12 part-time (6 women); includes 8 minority (3 African Americans, 1 Asian American or Pacific Islander, 4 Hispanic Americans), 9 international. Average age 32. In 2009, 14 master's, 1 doctorate awarded. *Degree requirements:* For master's, thesis (for some programs); for doctorate, one foreign language, thesis/dissertation. *Entrance requirements:* For master's, GRE General Test (MA); for doctorate, GRE General Test. Additional exam requirements/recommendations for international students: Recommended—TOEFL (minimum score 600 paper-based; 250 computer-based). *Application deadline:* For fall admission, 8/15 priority date for domestic students, 7/1 priority date for international students; for winter admission, 12/1 priority date for domestic students, 11/1 priority date for international students; for spring admission, 3/1 priority date for domestic students, 2/1 priority date for international students. Applications are processed on a rolling basis. Application fee: $40 ($50 for international students). Electronic applications accepted. *Expenses:* Tuition, state resident: full-time $10,683. Tuition, nonresident: full-time $25,923. Tuition and fees vary according to course load and program. *Financial support:* Fellowships, teaching assistantships, Federal Work-Study and institutionally sponsored loans available. Support available to part-time students. *Unit head:* Lesley K. Ferris, Graduate Studies Committee Chair, 614-292-5821, Fax: 614-292-3222, E-mail: ferris.36@osu.edu. *Application contact:* 614-292-9444, Fax: 614-292-3895, E-mail: domestic.grad@osu.edu.

Ohio University, Graduate College, College of Fine Arts, School of Theater, Athens, OH 45701-2979. Offers MA, MFA. *Accreditation:* NAST. *Faculty:* 14 full-time (5 women), 3 part-time/adjunct (1 woman). *Students:* 57 full-time (29 women); includes 3 minority (all Hispanic Americans), 4 international. 71 applicants, 37% accepted, 25 enrolled. In 2009, 15 master's awarded. *Degree requirements:* For master's, thesis or alternative. *Entrance requirements:* For master's, minimum GPA of 3.0. Additional exam requirements/recommendations for international students: Required—TOEFL (minimum score 550 paper-based; 80 iBT) or IELTS Academic (minimum score 6.5). *Application deadline:* For fall admission, 3/15 priority date for domestic and international students. Application fee: $50 ($55 for international students). Electronic applications accepted. *Expenses:* Tuition, state resident: full-time $7839; part-time $323 per quarter hour. Tuition, nonresident: full-time $15,831; part-time $654 per quarter hour. Required fees: $2931. *Financial support:* Research assistantships with full and partial tuition reimbursements, career-related internships or fieldwork, Federal Work-Study, institutionally sponsored loans, scholarships/grants, tuition waivers (partial), and unspecified assistantships available. Financial award application deadline: 3/15; financial award applicants required to submit FAFSA. *Unit head:* William Fisher, Interim Director, 740-593-9194, Fax: 740-593-4817, E-mail: fisherw@ohio.edu. *Application contact:* Barbara M. Fiocchi, Administrative Assistant, 740-593-4818, Fax: 740-593-4817, E-mail: fiocchi@ohio.edu.

Oklahoma City University, Margaret E. Petree College of Performing Arts, School of Theatre, Oklahoma City, OK 73106-1402. Offers costume design (MA); technical theater (MA); theater (MA); theater for young audiences (MA). Part-time programs available. *Faculty:* 4 full-time (2 women), 3 part-time/adjunct (0 women). *Students:* 3 full-time (all women), 1 (woman) part-time. Average age 28. 5 applicants, 60% accepted. In 2009, 1 master's awarded. *Degree requirements:* For master's, thesis or alternative. *Entrance requirements:* For master's, interview, audition, writing sample. Additional exam requirements/recommendations for international students: Required—TOEFL (minimum score 550 paper-based; 173 computer-based; 80 iBT). *Application deadline:* For fall admission, 8/20 for domestic students; for spring admission, 1/6 for domestic students. Applications are processed on a rolling basis. Application fee: $50 ($70 for international students). *Expenses:* Tuition: Full-time $15,930; part-time $885 per hour. *Financial support:* Fellowships with partial tuition reimbursements, career-related internships or fieldwork and Federal Work-Study available. Financial award application deadline: 8/1; financial award applicants required to submit FAFSA. *Faculty research:* Translation of plays, writing plays, dramaturgical research for plays and educational outreach materials. *Unit head:* Dr. David Herendeen, Interim Director, 405-208-5003, Fax: 405-208-5129, E-mail: dchilds@okcu.edu. *Application contact:* Michelle Lockhart, Director, Admissions, 800-633-7242, Fax: 405-208-5916, E-mail: gadmissions@okcu.edu.

Oklahoma State University, College of Arts and Sciences, Department of Theatre, Stillwater, OK 74078. Offers MA. *Accreditation:* NAST. *Faculty:* 11 full-time (4 women), 1 (woman) part-time/adjunct. *Students:* 4 full-time (1 woman), 1 (woman) part-time; includes 2 minority (1 African American, 1 Hispanic American). Average age 25. 7 applicants, 71% accepted, 3 enrolled. In 2009, 1 master's awarded. *Degree requirements:* For master's, creative component or thesis. *Entrance requirements:* For master's, GRE. Additional exam requirements/recommendations for international students: Required—TOEFL (minimum score 550 paper-based; 79 iBT). *Application deadline:* For fall admission, 3/1 priority date for international students; for spring admission, 8/1 priority date for international students. Applications are processed on a rolling basis. Application fee: $40 ($75 for international students). Electronic applications accepted. *Expenses:* Tuition, state resident: full-time $3716; part-time $154.85 per credit hour. Tuition, nonresident: full-time $14,448; part-time $602 per credit hour. Required fees: $1772; $73.85 per credit hour. One-time fee: $50. Tuition and fees vary according to course load and campus/location. *Financial support:* In 2009–10, 6 teaching assistantships (averaging $11,052 per year) were awarded; career-related internships or fieldwork, Federal Work-Study, scholarships/grants, health care benefits, tuition waivers (partial), and unspecified assistantships also available. Support available to part-time students. Financial award application deadline: 3/1; financial award applicants required to submit FAFSA. *Faculty research:* Historical scene painting and scenic art, Eastern European stage design, stage direction, voice and diction for the actor, stage choreography and dance. *Unit head:* Kevin Doolen, Head, 405-744-6094, Fax: 405-744-6509. *Application contact:* Dr. Gordon Emslie, Dean, 405-744-6368, Fax: 405-744-0355, E-mail: grad-i@okstate.edu.

Pace University, Dyson College of Arts and Sciences, The Actors Studio MFA, New York, NY 10038. Offers acting (MFA); directing (MFA); playwriting (MFA). *Faculty:* 6 full-time (3 women), 10 part-time/adjunct (4 women). *Students:* 99 full-time (57 women), 3 part-time (1 woman); includes 29 minority (18 African Americans, 2 Asian Americans or Pacific Islanders, 9 Hispanic Americans), 12 international. Average age 28. 120 applicants, 59% accepted, 41 enrolled. In 2009, 25 master's awarded. *Entrance requirements:* Additional exam requirements/recommendations for international students: Required—TOEFL. *Application deadline:* For fall admission, 5/25 for domestic students. Application fee: $70. *Expenses:* Tuition: Part-time $954 per credit. Tuition and fees vary according to course load, degree level and program. *Unit head:* Andreas Manolikakis, Head, E-mail: actorsstudiomfa@pace.edu. *Application contact:* Susan Ford-Goldschein, Director of Graduate Admissions, 212-346-1531, Fax: 212-346-1585, E-mail: gradnyc@pace.edu.

Penn State University Park, Graduate School, College of Arts and Architecture, School of Theatre, State College, University Park, PA 16802-1503. Offers MFA. *Accreditation:* NAST.

Pittsburg State University, Graduate School, College of Arts and Sciences, Department of Communication, Pittsburg, KS 66762. Offers applied communication (MA); communication education (MA); theatre (MA). *Degree requirements:* For master's, thesis or alternative. *Expenses:* Tuition, state resident: full-time $4212; part-time $176 per credit. Tuition, nonresident: full-time $11,530; part-time $480 per credit. Required fees: $940; $43 per credit. Tuition and fees vary according to course level, course load, degree level, campus/location, reciprocity agreements and student level.

Point Park University, Conservatory of Performing Arts, Pittsburgh, PA 15222-1984. Offers theatre arts-acting (MFA). *Faculty:* 2 full-time, 1 part-time/adjunct. *Students:* 6 full-time (3 women), 1 international. Average age 41. 2 applicants, 0% accepted, 0 enrolled. *Degree requirements:* For master's, comprehensive exam (for some programs), thesis or alternative. *Entrance requirements:* For master's, interview, undergraduate degree in related field, theatre experience. Additional exam requirements/recommendations for international students: Required—TOEFL (minimum score 550 paper-based; 79 iBT). *Application deadline:* Applications are processed on a rolling basis. Application fee: $30. Electronic applications accepted. *Expenses:* Tuition: Full-time $11,880; part-time $660 per credit. Required fees: $486; $27 per credit. *Financial support:* In 2009–10, 5 students received support, including 5 teaching assistantships with full tuition reimbursements available (averaging $6,400 per year); scholarships/grants also available. Financial award application deadline: 4/15; financial award applicants required to submit FAFSA. *Unit head:* Ronald Allan-Lindblom, Dean/Artistic Producing Director, 412-392-3454, Fax: 412-392-2424, E-mail: rlindblom@pointpark.edu. *Application contact:* Lynn C. Ribar, Associate Director, Adult and Graduate Enrollment, 412-392-3908, Fax: 412-392-6164, E-mail: lribar@pointpark.edu.

Portland State University, Graduate Studies, School of Fine and Performing Arts, Department of Theater Arts, Portland, OR 97207-0751. Offers MA, MS, MA/MS. *Accreditation:* NAST. *Degree requirements:* For master's, variable foreign language requirement, thesis or alternative. *Entrance requirements:* For master's, minimum GPA of 3.0 in upper-division course work or 2.75 overall, 24 credits in theater arts. Additional exam requirements/recommendations for international students: Required—TOEFL (minimum score 550 paper-based; 213 computer-based). *Faculty research:* Design, acting/directing, scene/costume technology, dramatic literature, theater history.

Purchase College, State University of New York, Conservatory of Theatre Arts and Film, Purchase, NY 10577-1400. Offers theatre design (MFA); theatre technology (MFA). *Degree requirements:* For master's, thesis or alternative, performance. *Entrance requirements:* For master's, BFA, interview, portfolio. Electronic applications accepted. *Expenses:* Tuition, state resident: full-time $8370; part-time $349 per credit. Tuition, nonresident: full-time $13,250; part-time $552 per credit. Required fees: $1515; $62.11 per credit. One-time fee: $144 full-time. Tuition and fees vary according to program.

Purdue University, Graduate School, College of Liberal Arts, Department of Visual and Performing Arts, West Lafayette, IN 47907. Offers art and design (MA); theatre (MA, MFA). *Accreditation:* NASAD; NAST. Part-time programs available. *Degree requirements:* For master's, terminal exhibit, project, or thesis. *Entrance requirements:* Additional exam requirements/recommendations for international students: Required—TOEFL. Electronic applications accepted. *Faculty research:* Design, fine arts, photography, acting, directing, theatre technology.

Regent University, Graduate School, School of Communication and the Arts, Virginia Beach, VA 23464-9800. Offers acting (MFA); acting and directing (MFA); cinema arts/television arts (MA); communication (MA, PhD); digital media (MA); directing for cinema/TV (MA); journalism

(MA); producing for cinema/TV (MA); script and screenwriting (MFA); theatre (MA). Part-time programs available. Postbaccalaureate distance learning degree programs offered (minimal on-campus study). *Faculty:* 27 full-time (3 women), 24 part-time/adjunct (8 women). *Students:* 120 full-time (65 women), 160 part-time (82 women); includes 70 minority (53 African Americans, 2 American Indian/Alaska Native, 4 Asian Americans or Pacific Islanders, 11 Hispanic Americans), 10 international. Average age 31. 221 applicants, 58% accepted, 62 enrolled. In 2009, 61 master's, 13 doctorates awarded. *Degree requirements:* For master's, thesis or alternative; for doctorate, thesis/dissertation. *Entrance requirements:* For master's, GRE General Test or MAT, minimum undergraduate GPA of 3.0, writing sample, computer literacy survey, recommendation, resume, interview, audition (MFA programs); for doctorate, GRE General Test, minimum graduate GPA of 3.0, writing sample, computer literacy survey, recommendation, interview, transcripts. Additional exam requirements/recommendations for international students: Required—TOEFL (minimum score 577 paper-based; 233 computer-based). *Application deadline:* For fall admission, 3/1 priority date for domestic students; for spring admission, 10/1 priority date for domestic students. Applications are processed on a rolling basis. Application fee: $50. Electronic applications accepted. *Expenses:* Contact institution. *Financial support:* In 2009–10, 229 students received support; fellowships with full and partial tuition reimbursements available, career-related internships or fieldwork, scholarships/grants, tuition waivers (full and partial), and unspecified assistantships available. Support available to part-time students. Financial award application deadline: 9/1; financial award applicants required to submit FAFSA. *Faculty research:* Southern gospel music, education and entertainment, celebrities and the media, journalism and ethics, C. S. Lewis. *Unit head:* Michael Patrick, Dean, 757-352-4970, Fax: 757-352-4279, E-mail: michpat@regent.edu. *Application contact:* Matthew Chadwick, Director of Admissions, 800-373-5504, Fax: 757-352-4381, E-mail: admissions@regent.edu.

Rhode Island College, School of Graduate Studies, Faculty of Arts and Sciences, Department of Music, Theatre, and Dance, Providence, RI 02908-1991. Offers music education (MAT, MM Ed); theatre (MFA). Part-time and evening/weekend programs available. *Faculty:* 8 full-time (2 women), 1 (woman) part-time/adjunct. *Students:* 4 full-time (1 woman), 4 part-time (3 women). Average age 33. In 2009, 6 master's awarded. *Degree requirements:* For master's, comprehensive exam, thesis, final project (MFA). *Entrance requirements:* For master's, GRE General Test or MAT, exams in music education, theory, history and literature, audition, 3 letters of recommendation, evidence of musicianship, interview. Additional exam requirements/recommendations for international students: Recommended—TOEFL (minimum score 550 paper-based; 213 computer-based; 79 iBT). *Application deadline:* For fall admission, 4/1 for domestic students; for spring admission, 11/1 for domestic students. Applications are processed on a rolling basis. Application fee: $50. *Expenses:* Tuition, state resident: full-time $7440; part-time $310 per credit hour. Tuition, nonresident: full-time $14,784; part-time $616 per credit hour. Required fees: $552; $20 per credit. $70 per term. *Financial support:* Teaching assistantships with full tuition reimbursements, Federal Work-Study, scholarships/grants, health care benefits, and unspecified assistantships available. Support available to part-time students. Financial award application deadline: 5/15; financial award applicants required to submit FAFSA. *Unit head:* Dr. James Taylor, Chair, 401-456-8639. *Application contact:* Graduate Studies, 401-456-8700.

Roosevelt University, Graduate Division, Chicago College of Performing Arts, Theatre Conservatory, Chicago, IL 60605. Offers directing and dramaturgy (MFA); musical theatre (MFA); theatre (MA, MFA); theatre-directing (MA); theatre-performance (MFA). MA is a special 3-summer program for high school teachers only. *Degree requirements:* For master's, thesis production/performance. *Entrance requirements:* For master's, audition, interview, minimum GPA of 2.5. *Faculty research:* Brecht, Shakespeare, contemporary and new work, fully mounted theatre.

Rowan University, Graduate School, College of Fine and Performing Arts, Program in Theatre, Glassboro, NJ 08028-1701. Offers theatre (MA); theatre education (MST). *Accreditation:* NAST. Part-time and evening/weekend programs available. *Students:* 1 (woman) full-time, 1 part-time (0 women). Average age 32. In 2009, 2 master's awarded. *Degree requirements:* For master's, thesis. *Entrance requirements:* For master's, GRE General Test. Additional exam requirements/recommendations for international students: Required—TOEFL. *Application deadline:* Applications are processed on a rolling basis. Application fee: $50. Electronic applications accepted. *Expenses:* Tuition, state resident: full-time $10,624; part-time $590 per semester hour. Tuition, nonresident: full-time $10,624; part-time $590 per semester hour. Required fees: $2320; $125 per semester hour. *Financial support:* Career-related internships or fieldwork, scholarships/grants, health care benefits, and unspecified assistantships available. Support available to part-time students. *Unit head:* Dr. Mira Lalovic-Hand, Interim Associate Provost/Director of Graduate School, 856-256-5120, E-mail: lalovic-hand@rowan.edu. *Application contact:* Karen Haynes, Graduate Coordinator, 856-256-4052, Fax: 856-256-4436, E-mail: haynes@rowan.edu.

Rutgers, The State University of New Jersey, New Brunswick, Mason Gross School of the Arts, Department of Theater Arts, Piscataway, NJ 08854-8097. Offers acting (MFA); design (MFA); directing (MFA); playwriting (MFA); stage management (MFA). *Degree requirements:* For master's, thesis (for some programs), performance project. *Entrance requirements:* For master's, audition, interview, portfolio. Electronic applications accepted. *Faculty research:* Faculty of working professional.

San Diego State University, Graduate and Research Affairs, College of Professional Studies and Fine Arts, School of Theater, Television and Film, San Diego, CA 92182. Offers television, film, and new media production (MA); theatre arts (MA, MFA). *Accreditation:* NAST. Part-time programs available. *Degree requirements:* For master's, thesis. *Entrance requirements:* For master's, GRE General Test, 3 letters of recommendation, interview. Additional exam requirements/recommendations for international students: Required—TOEFL. Electronic applications accepted.

San Francisco State University, Division of Graduate Studies, College of Creative Arts, Department of Theatre Arts, San Francisco, CA 94132-1722. Offers drama (MA); theatre arts (MFA), including design/technical production, performance. *Accreditation:* NAST.

San Jose State University, Graduate Studies and Research, College of Humanities and the Arts, Department of Television, Radio, Film and Theatre, San Jose, CA 95192-0001. Offers theatre arts (MA). *Accreditation:* NAST. *Students:* 8 full-time (6 women), 22 part-time (15 women); includes 8 minority (2 Asian Americans or Pacific Islanders, 6 Hispanic Americans), 1 international. Average age 35. 24 applicants, 54% accepted, 8 enrolled. In 2009, 11 master's awarded. *Degree requirements:* For master's, written exam. *Entrance requirements:* Additional exam requirements/recommendations for international students: Required—TOEFL (minimum score 570 paper-based). *Application deadline:* For fall admission, 6/29 for domestic students; for spring admission, 11/30 for domestic students. Applications are processed on a rolling basis. Application fee: $59. Electronic applications accepted. *Financial support:* Scholarships/grants available. Financial award applicants required to submit FAFSA. *Unit head:* Anne Fountain, Chair, 408-924-4567, Fax: 408-924-4574. *Application contact:* Dr. David Kahn, Graduate Advisor, 408-924-4540, E-mail: david.kahn@sjsu.edu.

Sarah Lawrence College, Graduate Studies, Program in Theater, Bronxville, NY 10708-5999. Offers MFA. *Faculty:* 25 part-time/adjunct (8 women). *Students:* 18 full-time (14 women), 1 (woman) part-time; includes 6 minority (5 African Americans, 1 Hispanic American), 1 international. 83 applicants, 30% accepted, 8 enrolled. In 2009, 10 master's awarded. *Degree requirements:* For master's, portfolio. *Entrance requirements:* For master's, interview, minimum B average in undergraduate course work. Additional exam requirements/recommendations for international students: Required—TOEFL (minimum score 600 paper-based). *Application deadline:* For fall admission, 1/15 for domestic students. Application fee: $60. *Expenses:* Tuition: Part-time $1161 per credit. Required fees: $232 per semester. Part-time tuition and fees vary according to course load, program and student level. *Financial support:* In 2009–10, 13 fellowships (averaging $5,000 per year) were awarded; career-related internships or fieldwork, scholarships/grants, and unspecified assistantships also available. Support available to part-time students. Financial award application deadline: 3/1. *Unit head:* Christine Farrell, Interim Director, 914-395-2262. *Application contact:* Emanual Lomax, Dean of Graduate Studies, 914-395-2371, E-mail: elomax@sarahlawrence.edu.

Savannah College of Art and Design, Graduate School, Program in Production Design, Savannah, GA 31402-3146. Offers MA, MFA. Part-time programs available. *Degree requirements:* For master's, thesis. *Entrance requirements:* For master's, interview, portfolio. Additional exam requirements/recommendations for international students: Required—TOEFL (minimum score 450 paper-based; 133 computer-based). Electronic applications accepted. *Expenses:* Tuition: Full-time $28,515; part-time $627 per credit hour. One-time fee: $500. Tuition and fees vary according to course load.

Smith College, Graduate and Special Programs, Department of Theatre, Northampton, MA 01063. Offers playwriting (MFA). Part-time programs available. *Faculty:* 8 full-time (6 women). *Students:* 4 full-time (1 woman); includes 1 minority (Asian American or Pacific Islander). Average age 27. 11 applicants, 36% accepted, 3 enrolled. *Degree requirements:* For master's, one foreign language, thesis. *Entrance requirements:* Additional exam requirements/recommendations for international students: Required—TOEFL (minimum score 590 paper-based; 243 computer-based; 97 iBT). *Application deadline:* For fall admission, 4/1 for domestic students, 1/15 for international students. Application fee: $60. *Financial support:* In 2009–10, 4 students received support. Institutionally sponsored loans and scholarships/grants available. Support available to part-time students. Financial award application deadline: 1/15; financial award applicants required to submit CSS PROFILE or FAFSA. *Unit head:* Leonard Berkman, Graduate Adviser, 413-585-3206, E-mail: lberkman@smith.edu. *Application contact:* Leonard Berkman, Graduate Adviser, 413-585-3206, E-mail: lberkman@smith.edu.

Southern Illinois University Carbondale, Graduate School, College of Liberal Arts, Theater Department, Carbondale, IL 62901-4701. Offers speech/theater (PhD); theater (MFA). *Accreditation:* NAST (one or more programs are accredited). Part-time programs available. *Degree requirements:* For master's, thesis; for doctorate, thesis/dissertation. *Entrance requirements:* For master's, minimum GPA of 2.7; for doctorate, minimum GPA of 3.25. Additional exam requirements/recommendations for international students: Required—TOEFL. *Faculty research:* Scenography, theater performance, theater history, dramatic criticism, theater technology, playwriting.

Southern Methodist University, Meadows School of the Arts, Division of Theatre, Dallas, TX 75275. Offers acting (MFA); design (MFA). *Accreditation:* NAST. *Faculty:* 18 full-time (7 women), 4 part-time/adjunct (3 women). *Students:* 23 full-time (12 women); includes 6 minority (3 African Americans, 2 Asian Americans or Pacific Islanders, 1 Hispanic American). Average age 27. 24 applicants, 54% accepted, 13 enrolled. In 2009, 5 master's awarded. *Entrance requirements:* For master's, audition or interview. Additional exam requirements/recommendations for international students: Required—TOEFL (minimum score 550 paper-based; 213 computer-based; 80 iBT). *Application deadline:* For fall admission, 2/15 priority date for domestic and international students. Applications are processed on a rolling basis. Application fee: $75. Electronic applications accepted. *Financial support:* In 2009–10, 20 teaching assistantships (averaging $6,600 per year) were awarded; scholarships/grants and unspecified assistantships also available. Financial award application deadline: 3/1; financial award applicants required to submit FAFSA. *Faculty research:* European lighting techniques. *Unit head:* Cecil O'Neal, Chair, 214-768-2558, Fax: 214-768-1136, E-mail: coneal@smu.edu. *Application contact:* Joe S. Hoselton, Graduate Admissions and Records Coordinator, 214-768-3765, Fax: 214-768-3272, E-mail: hoselton@smu.edu.

Stanford University, School of Humanities and Sciences, Department of Drama, Stanford, CA 94305-9991. Offers PhD. *Degree requirements:* For doctorate, one foreign language, thesis/dissertation, qualifying exams. *Entrance requirements:* For doctorate, GRE General Test, summary of production experience. Additional exam requirements/recommendations for international students: Required—TOEFL. Electronic applications accepted. *Expenses:* Tuition: Full-time $37,380; part-time $2760 per quarter. Required fees: $501.

State University of New York at Binghamton, Graduate School, School of Arts and Sciences, Department of Theater, Binghamton, NY 13902-6000. Offers MA. *Faculty:* 12 full-time (4 women), 9 part-time/adjunct (2 women). *Students:* 6 full-time (5 women), 1 (woman) part-time, 2 international. Average age 29. 6 applicants, 100% accepted, 3 enrolled. In 2009, 2 master's awarded. *Degree requirements:* For master's, thesis. *Entrance requirements:* For master's, GRE General Test, GRE Subject Test. Additional exam requirements/recommendations for international students: Required—TOEFL (minimum score 550 paper-based; 213 computer-based; 80 iBT). *Application deadline:* For fall admission, 8/1 priority date for domestic and international students; for spring admission, 12/15 priority date for domestic and international students. Applications are processed on a rolling basis. Application fee: $60. Electronic applications accepted. *Financial support:* In 2009–10, 3 students received support, including teaching assistantships with full and partial tuition reimbursements available (averaging $9,500 per year); fellowships, career-related internships or fieldwork, Federal Work-Study, institutionally sponsored loans, scholarships/grants, health care benefits, and unspecified assistantships also available. Financial award application deadline: 2/15; financial award applicants required to submit FAFSA. *Unit head:* Dr. John E. Vestal, Chairperson, 607-777-2360, E-mail: jvestal@binghamton.edu. *Application contact:* Victoria Williams, Recruiting and Admissions Coordinator, 607-777-2151, Fax: 607-777-2501, E-mail: vwilliam@binghamton.edu.

Stony Brook University, State University of New York, Graduate School, College of Arts and Sciences, Department of Theatre Arts, Program in Dramaturgy, Stony Brook, NY 11794. Offers MFA. *Students:* 15 full-time (12 women); includes 4 minority (1 Asian American or Pacific Islander, 3 Hispanic Americans), 2 international. Average age 29. 10 applicants, 90% accepted. *Degree requirements:* For master's, one foreign language, thesis. *Entrance requirements:* For master's, GRE General Test. Additional exam requirements/recommendations for international students: Required—TOEFL. *Application deadline:* For fall admission, 1/15 for domestic students. Application fee: $60. *Expenses:* Tuition, state resident: full-time $8370; part-time $349 per credit. Tuition, nonresident: full-time $13,250; part-time $552 per credit. Required fees: $933. *Unit head:* Prof. Nick Mangano, Chair, 631-632-7300, Fax: 631-632-7258. *Application contact:* Michael Zelenak, Director of Graduate Studies, 631-632-7280.

Stony Brook University, State University of New York, Graduate School, College of Arts and Sciences, Department of Theatre Arts, Program in Theatre Arts, Stony Brook, NY 11794. Offers MA. Evening/weekend programs available. *Students:* 2 part-time (1 woman). Average age 35. 5 applicants, 100% accepted. *Degree requirements:* For master's, one foreign language, thesis. *Entrance requirements:* For master's, GRE General Test. Additional exam requirements/recommendations for international students: Required—TOEFL. *Application deadline:* For fall admission, 1/15 for domestic students. Application fee: $60. *Expenses:* Tuition, state resident: full-time $8370; part-time $349 per credit. Tuition, nonresident: full-time $13,250; part-time $552 per credit. Required fees: $933. *Unit head:* Prof. Nick Mangano, Chair, 631-632-7300, Fax: 631-632-7258. *Application contact:* Michael Zelenak, Director of Graduate Studies, 631-632-7280.

Temple University, Graduate School, School of Communications and Theater, Department of Theater, Philadelphia, PA 19122-6096. Offers acting (MFA); design (MFA); directing (MFA). *Accreditation:* NAST. Part-time programs available. *Degree requirements:* For master's, thesis (for some programs). *Entrance requirements:* For master's, minimum GPA of 3.0; audition/interview, portfolio, or samples of written work. Additional exam requirements/recommendations for international students: Required—TOEFL (minimum score 550 paper-based; 213 computer-based; 79 iBT). Electronic applications accepted.

Texas A&M University–Commerce, Graduate School, College of Arts and Sciences, Department of Communication and Theatre, Commerce, TX 75429-3011. Offers theatre (MA, MS). Part-time programs available. *Degree requirements:* For master's, comprehensive exam,

Theater

Texas A&M University–Commerce (continued)
thesis (for some programs). *Entrance requirements:* For master's, GRE General Test. Electronic applications accepted. *Faculty research:* Theater history.

Texas State University–San Marcos, Graduate School, College of Fine Arts and Communication, Department of Theatre Arts and Dance, Program in Theatre Arts, San Marcos, TX 78666. Offers MA. Part-time and evening/weekend programs available. *Faculty:* 8 full-time (5 women). *Students:* 19 full-time (13 women), 1 (woman) part-time; includes 5 minority (1 African American, 4 Hispanic Americans). Average age 31. 14 applicants, 93% accepted, 10 enrolled. In 2009, 7 master's awarded. *Degree requirements:* For master's, comprehensive exam, thesis (for some programs). *Entrance requirements:* For master's, GRE General Test, minimum GPA of 2.75 in last 60 hours of course work. Additional exam requirements/recommendations for international students: Required—TOEFL (minimum score 550 paper-based; 213 computer-based). *Application deadline:* For fall admission, 6/15 priority date for domestic students; for spring admission, 10/15 priority date for domestic students. Applications are processed on a rolling basis. Application fee: $40 ($90 for international students). Electronic applications accepted. *Expenses:* Tuition, state resident: full-time $5784; part-time $241 per credit hour. Tuition, nonresident: part-time $551 per credit hour. Required fees: $1728; $48 per credit hour. $306. Tuition and fees vary according to course load. *Financial support:* In 2009–10, 20 students received support, including 12 teaching assistantships (averaging $3,514 per year); Federal Work-Study, institutionally sponsored loans, and unspecified assistantships also available. Support available to part-time students. Financial award application deadline: 4/1; financial award applicants required to submit FAFSA. *Faculty research:* Theatre history (especially nineteenth century American theatre), stage productions, playwriting. *Unit head:* Dr. Debra Charlton, Graduate Adviser, 512-245-2147, Fax: 512-245-8440, E-mail: dc21@txstate.edu. *Application contact:* Dr. J. Michael Willoughby, Dean of Graduate School, 512-245-2581, Fax: 512-245-8365, E-mail: gradcollege@txstate.edu.

Texas Tech University, Graduate School, College of Visual and Performing Arts, Department of Theatre and Dance, Lubbock, TX 79409. Offers fine arts (PhD); theatre arts (MA, MFA), including design (MFA), performance/pedagogy (MFA), playwriting (MFA), theatre management (MFA). *Accreditation:* NAST. Part-time programs available. *Faculty:* 11 full-time (6 women). *Students:* 40 full-time (19 women), 20 part-time (10 women); includes 7 minority (3 African Americans, 1 Asian American or Pacific Islander, 3 Hispanic Americans), 3 international. Average age 34. 30 applicants, 50% accepted, 9 enrolled. In 2009, 5 master's, 2 doctorates awarded. *Degree requirements:* For master's, variable foreign language requirement, thesis; for doctorate, thesis/dissertation. *Entrance requirements:* For master's and doctorate, GRE General Test. Additional exam requirements/recommendations for international students: Required—TOEFL (minimum score 550 paper-based; 213 computer-based). *Application deadline:* For fall admission, 3/1 priority date for international students; for spring admission, 11/1 priority date for international students. Applications are processed on a rolling basis. Application fee: $50 ($75 for international students). Electronic applications accepted. *Expenses:* Tuition, state resident: full-time $5100; part-time $213 per credit hour. Tuition, nonresident: full-time $11,748; part-time $490 per credit hour. Required fees: $2298; $50 per credit hour. $555 per semester. *Financial support:* In 2009–10, 18 teaching assistantships with partial tuition reimbursements (averaging $10,564 per year) were awarded; research assistantships with partial tuition reimbursements, Federal Work-Study and institutionally sponsored loans also available. Support available to part-time students. Financial award application deadline: 4/15; financial award applicants required to submit FAFSA. *Faculty research:* New student plays program, theatre planning, dramaturgy; feminist theatre; arts administration; dance aesthetics. *Unit head:* Prof. Frederick B. Christoffel, Chair, 806-742-3601 Ext. 228, Fax: 806-742-1338, E-mail: fred.christoffel@ttu.edu. *Application contact:* Dr. James Bush, Graduate Adviser, 806-742-3601 Ext. 230, Fax: 806-742-1338, E-mail: james.bush@ttu.edu.

Texas Tech University, Graduate School, College of Visual and Performing Arts, Fine Arts Doctoral Program, Lubbock, TX 79409. Offers arts (PhD); music (PhD); theatre arts (PhD). *Accreditation:* NAST. *Students:* 44 full-time (18 women), 31 part-time (16 women); includes 9 minority (3 African Americans, 1 American Indian/Alaska Native, 1 Asian American or Pacific Islander, 4 Hispanic Americans), 10 international. Average age 36. 33 applicants, 30% accepted, 3 enrolled. In 2009, 10 doctorates awarded. *Degree requirements:* For doctorate, thesis/dissertation. *Entrance requirements:* For doctorate, GRE General Test. Additional exam requirements/recommendations for international students: Required—TOEFL (minimum score 550 paper-based; 213 computer-based). *Application deadline:* For fall admission, 3/1 priority date for international students; for spring admission, 11/1 priority date for international students. Applications are processed on a rolling basis. Application fee: $50 ($75 for international students). Electronic applications accepted. *Expenses:* Tuition, state resident: full-time $5100; part-time $213 per credit hour. Tuition, nonresident: full-time $11,748; part-time $490 per credit hour. Required fees: $2298; $50 per credit hour. $555 per semester. *Financial support:* Research assistantships with partial tuition reimbursements, teaching assistantships with partial tuition reimbursements available. Financial award application deadline: 4/15. *Faculty research:* Art criticism and theory, music, theatre arts; arts education; history of arts. *Unit head:* Dr. Brian D. Steele, Director, 806-742-0700, Fax: 806-742-0695, E-mail: brian.steele@ttu.edu. *Application contact:* Dr. Brian D. Steele, Director, 806-742-0700, Fax: 806-742-0695, E-mail: brian.steele@ttu.edu.

Texas Woman's University, Graduate School, College of Arts and Sciences, School of the Arts, Department of Music and Drama, Denton, TX 76201. Offers drama (MA); music (MA). *Accreditation:* NASM. Part-time programs available. *Faculty:* 13 full-time (7 women), 4 part-time/adjunct (3 women). *Students:* 43 full-time (35 women), 31 part-time (24 women); includes 16 minority (5 African Americans, 1 American Indian/Alaska Native, 2 Asian Americans or Pacific Islanders, 8 Hispanic Americans), 11 international. Average age 31. 47 applicants, 94% accepted, 37 enrolled. In 2009, 13 master's awarded. *Degree requirements:* For master's, thesis optional, project recital. *Entrance requirements:* For master's, music history/theory placement exam. Additional exam requirements/recommendations for international students: Required—TOEFL (minimum score 550 paper-based; 213 computer-based; 79 iBT). *Application deadline:* For fall admission, 7/1 priority date for domestic students, 3/1 for international students; for spring admission, 12/1 priority date for domestic students, 7/1 for international students. Applications are processed on a rolling basis. Application fee: $50. Electronic applications accepted. *Expenses:* Tuition, state resident: full-time $3564; part-time $198 per credit hour. Tuition, nonresident: full-time $8550; part-time $475 per credit hour. Required fees: $69.26 per credit hour. Tuition and fees vary according to course load. *Financial support:* In 2009–10, 2 research assistantships (averaging $9,684 per year), 1 teaching assistantship (averaging $9,684 per year) were awarded; career-related internships or fieldwork, Federal Work-Study, institutionally sponsored loans, scholarships/grants, traineeships, health care benefits, tuition waivers (partial), and unspecified assistantships also available. Support available to part-time students. Financial award application deadline: 3/1; financial award applicants required to submit FAFSA. *Faculty research:* Musical development in early childhood, little known or neglected compositions for flute (especially by women composers), relationship of visual art to piano music, pedagogical development of the singing voice, guided imagery and music. *Unit head:* Dr. James Chenevert, Chair, 940-898-2500, Fax: 940-898-2494, E-mail: music@twu.edu. *Application contact:* Samuel Wheeler, Assistant Director of Admissions, 940-898-3188, Fax: 940-898-3081, E-mail: wheelersr@twu.edu.

Towson University, College of Graduate Studies and Research, Program in Theatre, Towson, MD 21252-0001. Offers MFA. *Accreditation:* NAST. *Degree requirements:* For master's, thesis. *Entrance requirements:* For master's, audition or portfolio, interview, minimum GPA of 3.0. Electronic applications accepted. *Faculty research:* Playwriting, directing, entrepreneurship in the arts, movement theatre, design, drama.

Tufts University, Graduate School of Arts and Sciences, Department of Drama and Dance, Medford, MA 02155. Offers drama (MA); dramatic literature and criticism (PhD); theater history (PhD). *Faculty:* 13 full-time, 6 part-time/adjunct. *Students:* 24 (15 women); includes 2 minority (both Asian Americans or Pacific Islanders), 1 international. 31 applicants, 42% accepted, 4 enrolled. In 2009, 1 master's, 4 doctorates awarded. Terminal master's awarded for partial completion of doctoral program. *Degree requirements:* For master's, one foreign language, thesis; for doctorate, 2 foreign languages, thesis/dissertation, oral exam, written general exam. *Entrance requirements:* For master's and doctorate, GRE General Test, writing sample. Additional exam requirements/recommendations for international students: Required—TOEFL (minimum score 600 paper-based; 250 computer-based; 80 iBT). *Application deadline:* For fall admission, 1/15 for domestic students, 12/10 for international students. Applications are processed on a rolling basis. Application fee: $75. Electronic applications accepted. *Expenses:* Tuition: Full-time $38,096; part-time $3962 per credit. Required fees: $686; $40 per year. Tuition and fees vary according to course level, course load, degree level, program and student level. *Financial support:* Fellowships with full and partial tuition reimbursements, teaching assistantships with full and partial tuition reimbursements, Federal Work-Study, scholarships/grants, tuition waivers (partial), and unspecified assistantships available. Financial award application deadline: 1/15; financial award applicants required to submit FAFSA. *Unit head:* Dr. Barbara Grossman, Chair, 617-627-3524. *Application contact:* Dr. Laurence Senelick, Head, 617-627-3524.

Tulane University, School of Liberal Arts, Department of Theatre and Dance, New Orleans, LA 70118-5669. Offers design and technical production (MFA). *Entrance requirements:* For master's, GRE General Test, minimum B average in undergraduate course work. Additional exam requirements/recommendations for international students: Required—TOEFL. Electronic applications accepted. *Faculty research:* Scene design, stage management, costume design, technical direction, lighting design.

Université de Sherbrooke, Faculty of Letters and Human Sciences, Department of Letters and Communications, Sherbrooke, QC J1K 2R1, Canada. Offers comparative Canadian literature (MA, PhD); French literature (MA, PhD); linguistics (MA); theatre (MA). *Degree requirements:* For master's, thesis or alternative; for doctorate, thesis/dissertation. *Entrance requirements:* For master's, minimum GPA of 2.8; for doctorate, minimum GPA of 3.0.

Université Laval, Faculty of Letters, Department of Literature, Programs in Literature and Arts of the Screen and Stage, Québec, QC G1K 7P4, Canada. Offers MA, PhD. Part-time programs available. Terminal master's awarded for partial completion of doctoral program. *Degree requirements:* For master's, thesis; for doctorate, comprehensive exam, thesis/dissertation. *Entrance requirements:* For master's and doctorate, linguistics exams, knowledge of French, knowledge of a second language. Electronic applications accepted.

University at Albany, State University of New York, College of Arts and Sciences, Department of Theatre, Albany, NY 12222-0001. Offers MA. *Entrance requirements:* Additional exam requirements/recommendations for international students: Required—TOEFL (minimum score 550 paper-based; 213 computer-based). Electronic applications accepted.

The University of Akron, Graduate School, College of Creative and Professional Arts, School of Dance, Theatre, and Arts Administration, Program in Theatre Arts, Akron, OH 44325. Offers MA. *Students:* 2 full-time (0 women), 3 part-time (0 women); includes 1 minority (African American). Average age 37. 25 applicants, 68% accepted. In 2009, 2 master's awarded. *Degree requirements:* For master's, thesis optional. *Entrance requirements:* For master's, minimum GPA of 2.75, interview. Additional exam requirements/recommendations for international students: Required—TOEFL (minimum score 550 paper-based; 213 computer-based; 79 iBT). *Application deadline:* For fall admission, 3/15 priority date for domestic and international students. Applications are processed on a rolling basis. Application fee: $30 ($40 for international students). Electronic applications accepted. *Expenses:* Tuition, state resident: full-time $6570; part-time $365 per credit hour. Tuition, nonresident: full-time $11,250; part-time $625 per credit hour. *Unit head:* James Slowiak, Coordinator, 330-972-5909, E-mail: slowiak@uakron.edu. *Application contact:* James Slowiak, Coordinator, 330-972-5909, E-mail: slowiak@uakron.edu.

The University of Alabama, Graduate School, College of Arts and Sciences, Department of Theatre and Dance, Tuscaloosa, AL 35487. Offers acting (MFA); costume design (MFA); directing (MFA); scene design/technical production (MFA); stage management (MFA); theatre (MFA); theatre management/administration (MFA). *Accreditation:* NAST. *Faculty:* 11 full-time (2 women). *Students:* 24 full-time (9 women), 1 (woman) part-time; includes 3 minority (2 African Americans, 1 Asian American or Pacific Islander), 1 international. Average age 29. 55 applicants, 36% accepted, 18 enrolled. In 2009, 23 degrees awarded. *Degree requirements:* For master's, thesis project. *Entrance requirements:* For master's, auditions/portfolio review. *Application deadline:* For fall admission, 7/6 for domestic students, 3/1 for international students. Applications are processed on a rolling basis. Application fee: $50 ($60 for international students). Electronic applications accepted. *Expenses:* Tuition, state resident: full-time $7000. Tuition, nonresident: full-time $19,200. *Financial support:* In 2009–10, 10 research assistantships (averaging $11,508 per year), 16 teaching assistantships (averaging $11,508 per year) were awarded; Federal Work-Study and health care benefits also available. *Faculty research:* Arts management, theatre history, practice and production. *Unit head:* William Teague, Chairman and Professor, 205-348-5283, Fax: 205-348-9048, E-mail: wteague@as.ua.edu. *Application contact:* Pamela McCray, Recruiting Contact, 205-348-5283, Fax: 205-348-9048, E-mail: pmccray@bama.ua.edu.

University of Alberta, Faculty of Graduate Studies and Research, Department of Drama, Edmonton, AB T6G 2E1, Canada. Offers design (MFA); directing (MFA); drama (MA). *Faculty:* 10 full-time (3 women), 4 part-time/adjunct (3 women). *Students:* 14 full-time (7 women), 10 part-time (7 women). 30 applicants, 23% accepted. In 2009, 8 master's awarded. *Degree requirements:* For master's, one foreign language, production thesis. *Application deadline:* For winter admission, 2/15 for domestic students. Application fee: $0. Tuition and fees charges are reported in Canadian dollars. *Expenses:* Tuition, area resident: Full-time $4626 Canadian dollars; part-time $99.72 Canadian dollars per unit. International tuition: $8216 Canadian dollars full-time. Required fees: $3590 Canadian dollars; $99.72 Canadian dollars per unit. $215 Canadian dollars per term. *Financial support:* In 2009–10, 2 fellowships (averaging $13,000 per year), 9 research assistantships (averaging $6,000 per year), 9 teaching assistantships (averaging $8,000 per year) were awarded; career-related internships or fieldwork and scholarships/grants also available. Financial award application deadline: 2/15. *Faculty research:* Dramaturgy, history, theory and criticism, design. Total annual research expenditures: $54,740. *Unit head:* Dr. Lee Livingstone, Graduate Coordinator, 780-492-2274, Fax: 780-492-9156, E-mail: drama@ualberta.ca. *Application contact:* Dr. Lee Livingstone, Graduate Coordinator, 780-492-2274, Fax: 780-492-9156, E-mail: drama@ualberta.ca.

The University of Arizona, Graduate College, College of Fine Arts, School of Theatre Arts, Tucson, AZ 85721. Offers MA, MFA. *Accreditation:* NAST. *Faculty:* 14. *Students:* 10 full-time (7 women), 4 part-time (2 women), 1 international. Average age 29. 12 applicants, 33% accepted, 2 enrolled. In 2009, 6 master's awarded. *Degree requirements:* For master's, comprehensive exam (for some programs), thesis (for some programs), production monograph. *Entrance requirements:* For master's, 3 letters of recommendation, portfolio. Additional exam requirements/recommendations for international students: Required—TOEFL (minimum score 550 paper-based; 213 computer-based; 79 iBT). *Application deadline:* For fall admission, 2/15 for domestic students, 12/1 for international students. Applications are processed on a rolling basis. Application fee: $75. Electronic applications accepted. *Expenses:* Tuition, state resident: full-time $9028. Tuition, nonresident: full-time $24,890. *Financial support:* In 2009–10, 11 teaching assistantships with full tuition reimbursements (averaging $12,514 per year) were awarded; career-related internships or fieldwork, Federal Work-Study, institutionally sponsored loans, scholarships/grants, health care benefits, tuition waivers (full), and unspecified assistantships also available. Financial award application deadline: 3/1; financial award applicants required to submit FAFSA. *Faculty research:* Modern and contemporary theater, cultural studies, musical theater, women and theater. *Unit head:* Jerry Dickey, Interim Director, 520-621-8740, E-mail: jdickey@email.arizona.edu. *Application contact:* Justine M. Collins, Assistant to Director of Administration, 520-621-7007, Fax: 520-621-2412, E-mail: jcollins@email.arizona.edu.

University of Arkansas, Graduate School, J. William Fulbright College of Arts and Sciences, Department of Drama, Fayetteville, AR 72701-1201. Offers MA, MFA. *Students:* 22 full-time (10 women), 4 part-time (2 women); includes 3 minority (1 African American, 2 Hispanic Americans), 4 international. In 2009, 9 master's awarded. *Degree requirements:* For master's, thesis optional. Application fee: $40 ($50 for international students). *Expenses:* Tuition, state resident: full-time $7355; part-time $356.58 per hour. Tuition, nonresident: full-time $17,401; part-time $775.17 per hour. Required fees: $1203. *Financial support:* In 2009–10, 9 research assistantships, 12 teaching assistantships were awarded; fellowships with tuition reimbursements, career-related internships or fieldwork and Federal Work-Study also available. Support available to part-time students. Financial award application deadline: 4/1; financial award applicants required to submit FAFSA. *Unit head:* Dr. Andrew Gibbs, Department Chairperson, 479-575-2953, Fax: 479-575-7602, E-mail: dagibbs@uark.edu. *Application contact:* Dr. Andrew Gibbs, Department Chairperson, 479-575-2953, Fax: 479-575-7602, E-mail: dagibbs@uark.edu.

The University of British Columbia, Faculty of Arts, Creative Writing Program, Vancouver, BC V6T 1Z1, Canada. Offers creative writing (MFA); creative writing and film (MFA); creative writing and theatre (MFA). Part-time programs available. Postbaccalaureate distance learning degree programs offered (minimal on-campus study). *Degree requirements:* For master's, thesis. *Entrance requirements:* For master's, sample of written work. Additional exam requirements/recommendations for international students: Required—TOEFL (minimum score 550 paper-based; 213 computer-based). Electronic applications accepted. *Expenses:* Contact institution. *Faculty research:* Writing of fiction; poetry, creative nonfiction, plays for stage, screen, television, radio, writing for children and translation, song lyrics and libretto, new media and graphic novel.

The University of British Columbia, Faculty of Arts and Faculty of Graduate Studies, Department of Theatre and Film, Theatre Program, Vancouver, BC V6T 1Z2, Canada. Offers theatre (MA, PhD); theatre design (MFA); theatre directing (MFA). *Degree requirements:* For master's, variable foreign language requirement, comprehensive exam, thesis; for doctorate, 2 foreign languages, comprehensive exam, thesis/dissertation. *Entrance requirements:* For master's, portfolio (MFA); for doctorate, MA or equivalent. Additional exam requirements/recommendations for international students: Required—TOEFL score of 550 paper-based, 213 computer-based required for MFA; score of 600 paper-based, 250 computer-based required for MA and PhD programs. *Faculty research:* Devising theatre; Canadian theatre; multicultural and theatre arts; stage lighting and costume design.

University of Calgary, Faculty of Graduate Studies, Faculty of Fine Arts, Department of Drama, Calgary, AB T2N 1N4, Canada. Offers design and technical theatre (MFA); directing (MFA); playwriting (MFA); theatre studies (MFA). *Degree requirements:* For master's, thesis. *Entrance requirements:* For master's, bachelor's degree in drama, minimum GPA of 3.0, portfolio (design and playwriting). Additional exam requirements/recommendations for international students: Required—TOEFL. *Faculty research:* Popular theatre, collective creation, technical design, dramaturgy, directing styles.

University of California, Berkeley, Graduate Division, College of Letters and Science, Group in Performance Studies, Berkeley, CA 94720-1500. Offers PhD. *Faculty:* 23 full-time. *Students:* 25 full-time (17 women). Average age 30. 94 applicants, 5 enrolled. In 2009, 1 doctorate awarded. *Degree requirements:* For doctorate, one foreign language, thesis/dissertation, qualifying exam. *Entrance requirements:* For doctorate, GRE General Test, sample of critical writing, 3 letters of recommendation. Additional exam requirements/recommendations for international students: Required—TOEFL. *Application deadline:* For fall admission, 12/5 for domestic students. Application fee: $70 ($90 for international students). Electronic applications accepted. *Financial support:* Fellowships, teaching assistantships with tuition reimbursements, unspecified assistantships available. Financial award applicants required to submit FAFSA. *Faculty research:* Postcolonial performance; gender, sexuality, and performance; political performance; dramatic literature and theory; race, ethnicity, performance. *Unit head:* Prof. Shannon Jackson, Chair, 510-642-1677, E-mail: ch_dramaticart@ls.berkeley.edu. *Application contact:* Mary Ajideh, Graduate Assistant for Admission, 510-642-1677, Fax: 510-643-9956, E-mail: phdprogram@theater.berkeley.edu.

University of California, Davis, Graduate Studies, Program in Dramatic Art, Davis, CA 95616. Offers acting (MFA); dramatic art (PhD). *Entrance requirements:* For master's, minimum GPA of 3.0, portfolio. Additional exam requirements/recommendations for international students: Required—TOEFL (minimum score 550 paper-based; 213 computer-based). Electronic applications accepted. *Faculty research:* Twentieth century performance and culture.

University of California, Davis, Graduate Studies, Program in Performance Studies, Davis, CA 95616. Offers dramatic art (PhD). *Degree requirements:* For doctorate, 2 foreign languages, thesis/dissertation. *Entrance requirements:* For doctorate, GRE, minimum GPA of 3.25. Additional exam requirements/recommendations for international students: Required—TOEFL (minimum score 550 paper-based; 213 computer-based). Electronic applications accepted.

University of California, Irvine, Office of Graduate Studies, Claire Trevor School of the Arts, Department of Drama, Irvine, CA 92697. Offers acting (MFA); design and stage management (MFA); directing (MFA); drama (MFA); drama and theatre (PhD). *Students:* 70 full-time (37 women), 2 part-time (both women); includes 11 minority (6 African Americans, 2 Asian Americans or Pacific Islanders, 3 Hispanic Americans), 3 international. Average age 26. 252 applicants, 10% accepted, 22 enrolled. In 2009, 24 master's, 3 doctorates awarded. *Degree requirements:* For master's, comprehensive exam, thesis; for doctorate, one foreign language, thesis/dissertation. *Entrance requirements:* For master's, audition, interview, or portfolio; minimum GPA of 3.0; for doctorate, GRE, minimum GPA of 3.5, critical writing samples. *Application deadline:* For fall admission, 1/15 priority date for domestic students, 1/15 for international students. Applications are processed on a rolling basis. Application fee: $70 ($90 for international students). Electronic applications accepted. *Financial support:* Fellowships, teaching assistantships, institutionally sponsored loans, traineeships, health care benefits, and unspecified assistantships available. Financial award application deadline: 3/1; financial award applicants required to submit FAFSA. *Faculty research:* Costume, scenery, and lighting design; production; theatre history, literature, and criticism. *Unit head:* Dr. George C. Harvey, Chair, 949-824-6614, Fax: 949-824-4914, E-mail: gcharvey@uci.edu. *Application contact:* Felice Weis, Administrative Assistant, 949-824-6332, E-mail: fweis@uci.edu.

University of California, Los Angeles, Graduate Division, School of Theater, Film and Television, Department of Theater, Los Angeles, CA 90095. Offers theater (MA, MFA); theater and performance studies (PhD). *Accreditation:* NAST. *Students:* 83 full-time (41 women); includes 19 minority (8 African Americans, 2 American Indian/Alaska Native, 4 Asian Americans or Pacific Islanders, 5 Hispanic Americans), 5 international. Average age 28. 295 applicants, 17% accepted, 30 enrolled. In 2009, 34 master's, 3 doctorates awarded. *Degree requirements:* For master's, comprehensive exam or thesis; for doctorate, one foreign language, thesis/dissertation, oral and written exam. *Entrance requirements:* For master's, minimum GPA of 3.0, interview, portfolio, resume, script, audition; for doctorate, GRE General Test, minimum undergraduate GPA of 3.0. Application fee: $70 ($90 for international students). Electronic applications accepted. *Financial support:* In 2009–10, 50 fellowships with full and partial tuition reimbursements, 6 research assistantships with full and partial tuition reimbursements, 44 teaching assistantships with full and partial tuition reimbursements were awarded; career-related internships or fieldwork, Federal Work-Study, institutionally sponsored loans, scholarships/grants, traineeships, health care benefits, tuition waivers (full and partial), and unspecified assistantships also available. Financial award application deadline: 3/1; financial award applicants required to submit FAFSA. *Unit head:* William D. Ward, Chair, 310-825-7008. *Application contact:* Department Office, 310-825-8787, E-mail: info@tft.ucla.edu.

University of California, San Diego, Office of Graduate Studies, Department of Theatre and Dance, La Jolla, CA 92093. Offers acting (MFA); design (MFA); directing (MFA); drama and theatre (PhD); playwriting (MFA); stage management (MFA); theatre (PhD). *Degree requirements:* For master's, thesis. *Entrance requirements:* For master's, GRE General Test (directing, playwriting). Electronic applications accepted.

University of California, Santa Barbara, Graduate Division, College of Letters and Sciences, Division of Humanities and Fine Arts, Department of Theatre and Dance, Santa Barbara, CA 93106-7060. Offers theater studies (MA, PhD), including European Medieval studies (PhD), feminist studies (PhD), theater studies (PhD); MA/PhD. *Faculty:* 7 full-time (3 women), 1 (woman) part-time/adjunct. *Students:* 22 full-time (15 women). Average age 33. 22 applicants, 36% accepted, 5 enrolled. In 2009, 3 master's, 5 doctorates awarded. Terminal master's awarded for partial completion of doctoral program. *Degree requirements:* For master's, variable foreign language requirement, comprehensive exam, thesis; for doctorate, one foreign language, comprehensive exam, thesis/dissertation. *Entrance requirements:* For master's, GRE, sample of written work, 3 letters of recommendation, resume/curriculum vitae; for doctorate, GRE, sample of written work, 3 letters of recommendation, statement of purpose, personal achievements/contributions statement, resume/curriculum vitae, transcripts for post-secondary institutions attended. Additional exam requirements/recommendations for international students: Required—TOEFL (minimum score 550 paper-based; 213 computer-based; 80 iBT) or IELTS (minimum score 7). *Application deadline:* For fall admission, 1/5 for domestic and international students. Application fee: $70 ($90 for international students). Electronic applications accepted. *Financial support:* In 2009–10, 13 fellowships with full and partial tuition reimbursements (averaging $11,600 per year), 29 teaching assistantships with partial tuition reimbursements (averaging $11,500 per year) were awarded; Federal Work-Study, scholarships/grants, traineeships, health care benefits, and unspecified assistantships also available. Support available to part-time students. Financial award application deadline: 1/5; financial award applicants required to submit FAFSA. *Faculty research:* Spanish/Latin American drama, performance studies and European theatre history, East Asian and Russian studies, playwriting, Medieval theatre. *Unit head:* Prof. Simon Williams, Chair, 805-893-5515, Fax: 805-893-7029, E-mail: williams@theaterdance.ucsb.edu. *Application contact:* Mary Tench, Graduate Program Assistant, 805-893-3147, Fax: 805-893-7029, E-mail: mtench@theaterdance.ucsb.edu.

University of California, Santa Cruz, Division of Graduate Studies, Division of the Arts, Department of Theater Arts, Santa Cruz, CA 95064. Offers Certificate.

University of Central Florida, College of Arts and Humanities, Department of Theatre, Orlando, FL 32816. Offers MA, MFA. *Faculty:* 14 full-time (10 women), 3 part-time/adjunct (1 woman). *Students:* 35 full-time (23 women), 24 part-time (14 women); includes 3 minority (2 African Americans, 1 Hispanic American), 1 international. Average age 29. 20 applicants, 30% accepted, 3 enrolled. In 2009, 13 master's awarded. Application fee: $30. Electronic applications accepted. *Expenses:* Tuition, state resident: part-time $306.31 per credit hour. Tuition, nonresident: part-time $1099.01 per credit hour. Part-time tuition and fees vary according to degree level and program. *Financial support:* In 2009–10, 23 students received support, including 1 fellowship (averaging $10,000 per year), 10 research assistantships (averaging $7,700 per year), 14 teaching assistantships (averaging $6,800 per year). *Unit head:* Dr. Christopher Niess, Interim Chair, 407-823-0876, Fax: 407-823-6446, E-mail: cneiss@mail.ucf.edu. *Application contact:* Dr. Christopher Niess, Interim Chair, 407-823-0876, Fax: 407-823-6446, E-mail: cneiss@mail.ucf.edu.

University of Central Missouri, The Graduate School, College of Arts, Humanities and Social Sciences, Warrensburg, MO 64093. Offers English (MA); history (MA); mass communication (MA); music (MA); psychology (MS); speech communication (MA); teaching english as a second language (MA); theatre (MA). Part-time programs available. *Faculty:* 82. *Students:* 60 full-time (35 women), 101 part-time (61 women); includes 11 minority (5 African Americans, 3 Asian Americans or Pacific Islanders, 3 Hispanic Americans), 17 international. Average age 30. 80 applicants, 80% accepted, 58 enrolled. In 2009, 51 master's awarded. *Entrance requirements:* Additional exam requirements/recommendations for international students: Required—TOEFL (minimum score 550 paper-based; 79 computer-based). *Application deadline:* For fall admission, 6/1 priority date for domestic students, 5/1 for international students; for spring admission, 10/1 priority date for domestic students, 10/1 for international students. Applications are processed on a rolling basis. Application fee: $30 ($75 for international students). Electronic applications accepted. *Expenses:* Tuition, area resident: Part-time $245.80 per credit hour. Tuition, nonresident: part-time $491.60 per credit hour. Required fees: $24.20 per credit hour. Full-time tuition and fees vary according to course load, degree level, campus/location and reciprocity agreements. *Financial support:* Research assistantships with full and partial tuition reimbursements, teaching assistantships with full and partial tuition reimbursements, career-related internships or fieldwork, Federal Work-Study, scholarships/grants, and administrative and laboratory assistantships available. Support available to part-time students. Financial award application deadline: 3/1; financial award applicants required to submit FAFSA. *Unit head:* Dr. Gersham Nelson, Dean, 660-543-4750, Fax: 660-543-8271, E-mail: nelson@ucmo.edu. *Application contact:* Laurie Delap, Admissions Coordinator, 660-543-4621, Fax: 660-543-4778, E-mail: gradinfo@ucmo.edu.

University of Cincinnati, Graduate School, College-Conservatory of Music, Divisions of Opera, Musical Theater, Drama, and Arts Administration, Cincinnati, OH 45221. Offers arts administration (MA); directing (MFA); theater design and production (MFA); voice and opera (MM, DMA); MBA/MA. *Accreditation:* NAST (one or more programs are accredited). *Degree requirements:* For master's, final project. *Entrance requirements:* For master's, GMAT (MA), audition/interview. Additional exam requirements/recommendations for international students: Required—TOEFL (minimum score 520 paper-based; 190 computer-based). Electronic applications accepted.

University of Colorado at Boulder, Graduate School, College of Arts and Sciences, Department of Theatre and Dance, Boulder, CO 80309. Offers dance (MFA); theatre (MA, PhD). *Faculty:* 16 full-time (8 women). *Students:* 37 full-time (26 women), 9 part-time (5 women); includes 7 minority (4 African Americans, 3 Hispanic Americans), 1 international. Average age 33. 56 applicants, 32% accepted, 12 enrolled. In 2009, 6 master's, 2 doctorates awarded. Terminal master's awarded for partial completion of doctoral program. *Degree requirements:* For master's, comprehensive exam, thesis; for doctorate, one foreign language, thesis/dissertation. *Entrance requirements:* For master's, GRE General Test (MA), audition (MFA), minimum undergraduate GPA of 2.75. *Application deadline:* For fall admission, 1/15 priority date for domestic students, 12/1 for international students. Application fee: $50 ($60 for international students). *Financial support:* In 2009–10, 16 fellowships (averaging $2,499 per year), 14 research assistantships (averaging $1,463 per year) were awarded; tuition waivers (full) also available. Financial award application deadline: 1/15. *Faculty research:* Dance: performance choreography; pedagogy administration; body therapies; multi-media forms; film/video; cultural studies; non-concert forms; music; poetry/writing/literature; kinesiology; theatre: theatre history; theory and literature; theatre production; acting; directing; dramaturgy and design. Total annual research expenditures: $3,749.

University of Connecticut, Graduate School, School of Fine Arts, Department of Dramatic Arts, Storrs, CT 06269. Offers acting (MFA); costume design (MFA); lighting design (MFA); puppetry (MA, MFA); scenic design (MFA). *Faculty:* 15 full-time (4 women). *Students:* 35 full-time (16 women), 10 part-time (5 women); includes 4 minority (3 African Americans, 1 Hispanic American), 4 international. Average age 29. 25 applicants, 44% accepted, 3 enrolled. In 2009, 8 master's awarded. *Degree requirements:* For master's, comprehensive exam. *Entrance requirements:* Additional exam requirements/recommendations for international students: Required—TOEFL (minimum score 550 paper-based; 213 computer-based). *Application deadline:* For fall admission, 2/1 priority date for domestic and international students; for spring admission, 11/1 for domestic students, 10/1 for international students. Applications are processed on a rolling basis. Application fee: $55. Electronic applications accepted. *Expenses:* Tuition, state resident: full-time $4725; part-time $525 per credit. Tuition, nonresident: full-time $12,267; part-time $1363 per credit. Required fees: $346 per semester. Tuition and fees vary according to course load. *Financial support:* In 2009–10, 27 research assistantships with full tuition reimbursements, 3 teaching assistantships with full tuition reimbursements

Theater

University of Connecticut (continued)
were awarded; fellowships, Federal Work-Study, scholarships/grants, health care benefits, and unspecified assistantships also available. Financial award application deadline: 2/1; financial award applicants required to submit FAFSA. *Unit head:* Gary M. English, Head, 860-486-2281, Fax: 860-486-3110, E-mail: gary.english@uconn.edu. *Application contact:* David Alan Stern, Associate Head, 860-486-1630, Fax: 860-486-3110, E-mail: david.stern@uconn.edu.

University of Delaware, College of Arts and Sciences, Department of Theatre, Professional Theatre Training Program, Newark, DE 19716. Offers acting (MFA); stage management (MFA); technical production (MFA). Students are matriculated into program once every three years. *Entrance requirements:* For master's, audition, interview. Electronic applications accepted. *Faculty research:* Theatre training, acting, technical production, stage management.

University of Florida, Graduate School, College of Fine Arts, School of Theatre and Dance, Gainesville, FL 32611. Offers theatre (MFA). *Accreditation:* NAST. *Degree requirements:* For master's, thesis, creative project. *Entrance requirements:* For master's, audition/portfolio, bachelor's degree in theatre, interview, GRE General Test or minimum GPA of 3.0. Additional exam requirements/recommendations for international students: Required—TOEFL (minimum score 550 paper-based; 213 computer-based). Electronic applications accepted. *Faculty research:* Production, history of theatre, criticism.

University of Georgia, Graduate School, College of Arts and Sciences, Department of Theatre and Film Studies, Athens, GA 30602. Offers theatre (MFA, PhD). *Accreditation:* NAST. *Faculty:* 15 full-time (4 women), 1 part-time/adjunct (0 women). *Students:* 36 full-time (15 women), 4 part-time (all women); includes 5 minority (2 African Americans, 3 Asian Americans or Pacific Islanders), 3 international. Average age 23. 50 applicants, 60% accepted, 10 enrolled. In 2009, 17 master's, 1 doctorate awarded. *Degree requirements:* For master's, comprehensive exam, written report; for doctorate, one foreign language, comprehensive exam, thesis/dissertation. *Entrance requirements:* For master's and doctorate, GRE General Test. Additional exam requirements/recommendations for international students: Required—TOEFL (minimum score 550 paper-based). *Application deadline:* For fall admission, 7/1 for domestic students, 4/15 for international students; for winter admission, 11/15 for domestic students, 10/15 for international students; for spring admission, 5/1 for domestic students, 2/15 for international students. Application fee: $50. Electronic applications accepted. *Expenses:* Tuition, state resident: full-time $6000; part-time $250 per credit hour. Tuition, nonresident: full-time $20,904; part-time $871 per credit hour. Required fees: $730 per semester. *Financial support:* In 2009–10, research assistantships with full tuition reimbursements (averaging $10,089 per year), teaching assistantships with full tuition reimbursements (averaging $9,462 per year) were awarded; fellowships, health care benefits and unspecified assistantships also available. Financial award application deadline: 2/15. *Faculty research:* Digital media, African-American theatre, Indian theatre, history of animation, vaudeville and popular culture history. Total annual research expenditures: $375,984. *Unit head:* Dr. David Z. Saltz, Head, 706-542-2836, Fax: 706-542-2080, E-mail: saltz@uga.edu. *Application contact:* Dr. Freda Scott Giles, Graduate Coordinator, 706-542-2102, E-mail: fsgiles@uga.edu.

University of Guelph, Graduate Program Services, College of Arts, School of English and Theatre Studies, Program in Drama, Guelph, ON N1G 2W1, Canada. Offers MA. Part-time programs available. *Degree requirements:* For master's, thesis (for some programs). *Entrance requirements:* For master's, 2 letters of reference, 4 year honours undergraduate degree in English or drama. Additional exam requirements/recommendations for international students: Required—TOEFL. Electronic applications accepted. *Faculty research:* Canadian theatre, Renaissance, nineteenth and twentieth century drama and theatre, Shaw, theatre history, dramatic literature, performance theory.

University of Hawaii at Manoa, Graduate Division, College of Arts and Humanities, Department of Theatre and Dance, Honolulu, HI 96822. Offers dance (MA, MFA); theatre (MA, MFA, PhD). Part-time programs available. *Degree requirements:* For master's, one foreign language, thesis optional; for doctorate, one foreign language, comprehensive exam, thesis/dissertation. *Entrance requirements:* For master's and doctorate, GRE General Test. Additional exam requirements/recommendations for international students: Required—TOEFL (minimum score 600 paper-based; 250 computer-based; 100 iBT), IELTS (minimum score 7). *Expenses:* Tuition, state resident: full-time $8900; part-time $372 per credit. Tuition, nonresident: full-time $21,400; part-time $898 per credit. Required fees: $207 per semester. *Faculty research:* Asian theatre, feminist theatre and dance, Russian theatre, Australian theatre.

University of Houston, College of Liberal Arts and Social Sciences, School of Theatre and Dance, Houston, TX 77204. Offers MA, MFA. Part-time programs available. *Faculty:* 4 full-time (0 women), 7 part-time/adjunct (4 women). *Students:* 32 full-time (17 women), 1 (woman) part-time; includes 2 minority (1 African American, 1 Hispanic American), 1 international. Average age 28. 23 applicants, 61% accepted, 12 enrolled. In 2009, 32 master's awarded. *Degree requirements:* For master's, thesis optional. *Entrance requirements:* For master's, GRE General Test. Additional exam requirements/recommendations for international students: Required—TOEFL. Application fee: $25 ($75 for international students). Electronic applications accepted. *Expenses:* Tuition, state resident: full-time $7676; part-time $320 per credit hour. Tuition, nonresident: full-time $14,324; part-time $597 per credit hour. Required fees: $3034. *Financial support:* In 2009–10, 23 teaching assistantships with full tuition reimbursements (averaging $9,100 per year) were awarded; career-related internships or fieldwork, Federal Work-Study, institutionally sponsored loans, scholarships/grants, health care benefits, and unspecified assistantships also available. Support available to part-time students. Financial award application deadline: 2/1. *Unit head:* Steven Wallace, Chairperson, 713-743-3003, Fax: 713-749-1420, E-mail: swwallace@uh.edu. *Application contact:* Steven Wallace, Chairperson, 713-743-3003, Fax: 713-749-1420, E-mail: swwallace@uh.edu.

University of Idaho, College of Graduate Studies, College of Letters, Arts and Social Sciences, Department of Theatre and Film, Moscow, ID 83844-2282. Offers theatre arts (MFA). *Faculty:* 4 full-time, 2 part-time/adjunct. *Students:* 21 full-time (10 women). In 2009, 7 master's awarded. *Entrance requirements:* For master's, minimum GPA of 2.8. *Application deadline:* For fall admission, 8/1 for domestic students; for spring admission, 12/15 for domestic students. Application fee: $55 ($60 for international students). *Expenses:* Tuition, state resident: full-time $6120. Tuition, nonresident: full-time $17,712. *Financial support:* Research assistantships, teaching assistantships available. Financial award application deadline: 2/15. *Unit head:* Dr. Dean Fields Panttaja, Chair, 208-885-6465. *Application contact:* Dr. Dean Fields Panttaja, Chair, 208-885-6465.

University of Illinois at Urbana–Champaign, Graduate College, College of Fine and Applied Arts, Department of Theatre, Champaign, IL 61820. Offers MA, MFA, PhD. *Accreditation:* NAST. *Faculty:* 15 full-time (5 women), 3 part-time/adjunct (2 women). *Students:* 56 full-time (31 women), 4 part-time (2 women); includes 8 minority (3 African Americans, 1 American Indian/Alaska Native, 2 Asian Americans or Pacific Islanders, 2 Hispanic Americans), 7 international. 84 applicants, 29% accepted, 21 enrolled. In 2009, 21 master's awarded. *Entrance requirements:* For master's, minimum GPA of 3.0; audition, portfolio or writing sample; for doctorate, writing sample; master's degree, minimum GPA of 3.0. Additional exam requirements/recommendations for international students: Required—TOEFL (minimum score 550 paper-based; 213 computer-based). *Application deadline:* Applications are processed on a rolling basis. Application fee: $60 ($75 for international students). Electronic applications accepted. *Financial support:* In 2009–10, 6 fellowships, 4 research assistantships, 23 teaching assistantships were awarded; tuition waivers (full and partial) also available. *Unit head:* Brant Pope, Head, 217-333-2371, Fax: 217-244-1861, E-mail: brant@illinois.edu. *Application contact:* David Swinford, Admissions and Records Officer, 217-244-6189, Fax: 217-244-1861, E-mail: dswinfor@illinois.edu.

The University of Iowa, Graduate College, College of Liberal Arts and Sciences, Department of Theatre Arts, Iowa City, IA 52242-1316. Offers MFA. *Accreditation:* NAST. *Degree requirements:* For master's, thesis, exam. *Entrance requirements:* For master's, minimum GPA of 3.0. Additional exam requirements/recommendations for international students: Required—TOEFL (minimum score 550 paper-based; 213 computer-based; 81 iBT). Electronic applications accepted.

The University of Kansas, Graduate Studies, College of Liberal Arts and Sciences, Department of Theatre and Film, Lawrence, KS 66045. Offers theatre (MA, PhD); theatre design (MFA), including scenography. *Faculty:* 15 full-time (7 women). *Students:* 17 full-time (9 women), 2 part-time (1 woman), 1 international. Average age 32. 19 applicants, 58% accepted, 4 enrolled. In 2009, 2 master's, 3 doctorates awarded. *Degree requirements:* For master's, thesis; for doctorate, one foreign language, comprehensive exam, thesis/dissertation. *Entrance requirements:* For master's, GRE General Test, minimum GPA of 3.2; for doctorate, GRE General Test, minimum GPA of 3.5; MA or MFA in theatre or related field. Additional exam requirements/recommendations for international students: Required—TOEFL. *Application deadline:* For fall admission, 1/1 priority date for domestic students, 1/1 for international students. Application fee: $45 ($55 for international students). Electronic applications accepted. *Expenses:* Tuition, state resident: full-time $6492; part-time $270.50 per credit hour. Tuition, nonresident: full-time $15,510; part-time $646.25 per credit hour. Required fees: $847; $70.56 per credit hour. Tuition and fees vary according to course load and program. *Financial support:* Fellowships with tuition reimbursements, research assistantships with full tuition reimbursements, teaching assistantships with full and partial tuition reimbursements, Federal Work-Study, scholarships/grants, and unspecified assistantships available. Financial award application deadline: 1/1. *Faculty research:* Theatre history, performance studies, scenography, theatre historiography. *Unit head:* John Staniunas, Chair, 785-864-3511, Fax: 785-864-5251, E-mail: stanj@ku.edu. *Application contact:* Dr. Henry Bial, Director of Graduate Studies, 785-864-3511, Fax: 785-864-5251, E-mail: hbial@ku.edu.

University of Kentucky, Graduate School, College of Fine Arts, Program in Theatre, Lexington, KY 40506-0032. Offers MA. *Degree requirements:* For master's, comprehensive exam, thesis optional. *Entrance requirements:* For master's, GRE General Test, minimum undergraduate GPA of 2.75. Additional exam requirements/recommendations for international students: Required—TOEFL (minimum score 550 paper-based; 213 computer-based). Electronic applications accepted. *Faculty research:* Historical, critical, practical, theoretical, and experimental perspectives of acting, directing, design, performance, and dramaturgy.

University of Lethbridge, School of Graduate Studies, Lethbridge, AB T1K 3M4, Canada. Offers accounting (MScM); addictions counseling (M Sc); agricultural biotechnology (M Sc); agricultural studies (M Sc, MA); anthropology (MA); archaeology (MA); art (MA, MFA); biochemistry (M Sc); biological sciences (M Sc); biomolecular science (PhD); biosystems and biodiversity (PhD); Canadian studies (MA); chemistry (M Sc); computer science (M Sc); computer science and geographical information science (M Sc); counseling psychology (M Ed); dramatic arts (MA); earth, space, and physical science (PhD); economics (MA); educational leadership (M Ed); English (MA); environmental science (M Sc); evolution and behavior (PhD); exercise science (M Sc); finance (MScM); French (MA); French/German (MA); French/Spanish (MA); general education (M Ed); general management (MScM); geography (M Sc, MA); German (MA); health science (M Sc); health sciences (MA); history (MA); human resource management and labour relations (MScM); individualized multidisciplinary (M Sc, MA); information systems (MScM); international management (MScM); kinesiology (M Sc, MA); management (M Sc, MA); marketing (MScM); mathematics (M Sc); music (M Mus, MA); Native American studies (MA); neuroscience (M Sc, PhD); new media (MA); nursing (M Sc); philosophy (MA); physics (M Sc); policy and strategy (MScM); political science (MA); psychology (M Sc, MA); religious studies (MA); social sciences (MA); sociology (MA); theatre and dramatic arts (MFA); theoretical and computational science (PhD); urban and regional studies (MA); women's studies (MA). Part-time and evening/weekend programs available. *Degree requirements:* For doctorate, comprehensive exam, thesis/dissertation. *Entrance requirements:* For master's, GMAT (M Sc in management), bachelor's degree in related field, minimum GPA of 3.0 during previous 20 graded semester courses, 2 years teaching or related experience (M Ed); for doctorate, master's degree, minimum graduate GPA of 3.5. Additional exam requirements/recommendations for international students: Required—TOEFL. *Faculty research:* Movement and brain plasticity, gibberellin physiology, photosynthesis, carbon cycling, molecular properties of main-group ring components.

University of Louisville, Graduate School, College of Arts and Sciences, Department of Theatre Arts, Louisville, KY 40292-0001. Offers performance (MFA). *Accreditation:* NAST. *Faculty:* 6 full-time (4 women), 1 (woman) part-time/adjunct. *Students:* 15 full-time (9 women), 1 part-time (0 women); includes 7 minority (all African Americans). Average age 29. 13 applicants, 77% accepted, 9 enrolled. In 2009, 1 master's awarded. *Degree requirements:* For master's, thesis, performance project, monograph. *Entrance requirements:* For master's, GRE General Test, auditions and portfolio review. *Application deadline:* For spring admission, 4/15 priority date for domestic students. Applications are processed on a rolling basis. Application fee: $50. Electronic applications accepted. *Financial support:* In 2009–10, 15 students received support, including 12 teaching assistantships (averaging $12,000 per year); scholarships/grants and health care benefits also available. Financial award application deadline: 3/15; financial award applicants required to submit FAFSA. *Faculty research:* Speech/dialects, especially for actors of color; African diaspora theatre; community acting and creation of new works; peace studies; African American theatre. Total annual research expenditures: $10,000. *Unit head:* Dr. Russell Vandenbroucke, Chair, 502-852-8444, Fax: 502-852-7235, E-mail: r.vandenbrouke@louisville.edu. *Application contact:* Libby Leggett, Director, Graduate Admissions, 502-852-3101, Fax: 502-852-6536, E-mail: gradadm@louisville.edu.

University of Maryland, Baltimore County, Graduate School, College of Arts, Humanities and Social Sciences, Department of Education, Program in Teaching, Baltimore, MD 21250. Offers early childhood education (MAT); elementary education (MAT); secondary education (MAT), including art, biology, chemistry, dance, earth/space science, English, foreign language, mathematics, music, physics, theatre; secondary science (MAT), including social studies. Part-time and evening/weekend programs available. *Faculty:* 24 full-time (18 women), 25 part-time/adjunct (19 women). *Students:* 52 full-time (41 women), 64 part-time (55 women); includes 20 minority (5 African Americans, 1 American Indian/Alaska Native, 10 Asian Americans or Pacific Islanders, 4 Hispanic Americans), 3 international. Average age 31. 88 applicants, 57% accepted, 39 enrolled. In 2009, 106 master's awarded. *Degree requirements:* For master's, comprehensive exam (for some programs), thesis (for some programs). *Entrance requirements:* For master's, PRAXIS I and II, minimum GPA of 3.0. Additional exam requirements/recommendations for international students: Required—TOEFL. *Application deadline:* For fall admission, 6/1 for domestic students; for spring admission, 11/1 for domestic students. Applications are processed on a rolling basis. Application fee: $50. Electronic applications accepted. *Financial support:* In 2009–10, 6 students received support, including research assistantships with full tuition reimbursements available (averaging $12,000 per year); career-related internships or fieldwork, Federal Work-Study, scholarships/grants, tuition waivers, and unspecified assistantships also available. Financial award application deadline: 3/1. *Faculty research:* STEM teacher education, culturally sensitive pedagogy, ESOL/bilingual education, early childhood education, language, literacy and culture. *Unit head:* Dr. Susan M. Blunck, Director, 410-455-2869, Fax: 410-455-3986, E-mail: blunck@umbc.edu. *Application contact:* Dr. Susan M. Blunck, Director, 410-455-2869, Fax: 410-455-3986, E-mail: blunck@umbc.edu.

University of Maryland, College Park, Academic Affairs, College of Arts and Humanities, Department of Theatre, College Park, MD 20742. Offers MA, MFA, PhD. *Faculty:* 20 full-time (10 women), 2 part-time/adjunct (1 woman). *Students:* 35 full-time (21 women), 2 part-time (0 women); includes 1 minority (Asian American or Pacific Islander), 2 international. 64 applicants, 23% accepted, 8 enrolled. In 2009, 7 master's, 3 doctorates awarded. *Degree requirements:* For master's, comprehensive exam, thesis optional; for doctorate, thesis/dissertation. *Entrance requirements:* For master's, GRE General Test, minimum GPA of 3.0, writing sample, portfolio (MFA), 3 letters of recommendation; for doctorate, GRE General Test, writing sample. Additional exam requirements/recommendations for international students: Required—TOEFL. *Application* *deadline:* For fall admission, 12/15 for domestic and international students. Applications are processed on a rolling basis. Application fee: $60. Electronic applications accepted. *Expenses:* Tuition, area resident: Part-time $471 per credit hour. Tuition, state resident: part-time $471 per credit hour. Tuition, nonresident: part-time $1016 per credit hour. Required fees: $337.04 per term. *Financial support:* In 2009–10, 3 fellowships with full tuition reimbursements (averaging $19,553 per year), 26 teaching assistantships with tuition reimbursements (averaging $19,827 per year) were awarded; research assistantships with tuition reimbursements, Federal Work-Study and scholarships/grants also available. Support available to part-time students. Financial award applicants required to submit FAFSA. *Faculty research:* Theatre aesthetics, performance, history/theory, design and production. *Unit head:* Dr. Daniel M. Wagner, Chairman, 301-405-6675, Fax: 301-314-9599, E-mail: dmwagner@umd.edu. *Application contact:* Dean of Graduate School, 301-405-0376, Fax: 301-314-9305.

University of Massachusetts Amherst, Graduate School, College of Humanities and Fine Arts, Department of Theater, Amherst, MA 01003. Offers MFA. Part-time programs available. *Faculty:* 14 full-time (6 women). *Students:* 12 full-time (8 women), 2 part-time (1 woman); includes 1 minority (African American). Average age 28. 38 applicants, 16% accepted, 5 enrolled. In 2009, 7 master's awarded. *Degree requirements:* For master's, thesis. *Entrance requirements:* For master's, GRE General Test, resume of production experience, 2 critical essays or design portfolio. Additional exam requirements/recommendations for international students: Required—TOEFL (minimum score 550 paper-based; 213 computer-based; 80 iBT), IELTS (minimum score 6.5). *Application deadline:* For fall admission, 2/1 for domestic and international students. Applications are processed on a rolling basis. Application fee: $50 ($65 for international students). Electronic applications accepted. *Expenses:* Tuition, state resident: full-time $2640; part-time $110 per credit. Tuition, nonresident: full-time $9936; part-time $414 per credit. Tuition and fees vary according to course load. *Financial support:* In 2009–10, 16 teaching assistantships with full tuition reimbursements (averaging $14,062 per year) were awarded; fellowships, research assistantships, career-related internships or fieldwork, Federal Work-Study, scholarships/grants, traineeships, health care benefits, tuition waivers (full), and unspecified assistantships also available. Support available to part-time students. Financial award application deadline: 2/1. *Unit head:* Dr. Milan Dragicevich, Graduate Program Director, 413-545-3490, Fax: 413-577-0025. *Application contact:* Jean M. Ames, Supervisor of Admissions, 413-545-0722, Fax: 413-577-0010, E-mail: gradadm@grad.umass.edu.

University of Memphis, Graduate School, College of Communication and Fine Arts, Department of Theatre and Dance, Memphis, TN 38152. Offers theatre (MFA). *Accreditation:* NAST. *Faculty:* 9 full-time (3 women), 2 part-time/adjunct (both women). *Students:* 16 full-time (9 women). Average age 30. 19 applicants, 42% accepted, 8 enrolled. In 2009, 5 master's awarded. *Degree requirements:* For master's, comprehensive exam, practicum. *Entrance requirements:* For master's, minimum GPA of 3.0 in major, 2.5 overall. *Application deadline:* For fall admission, 8/1 for domestic students; for spring admission, 12/1 for domestic students. Applications are processed on a rolling basis. Application fee: $35 ($60 for international students). *Expenses:* Tuition, state resident: full-time $6246; part-time $347 per credit hour. Tuition, nonresident: full-time $15,894; part-time $883 per credit hour. Required fees: $1160. Full-time tuition and fees vary according to course load, degree level and program. *Financial support:* In 2009–10, 12 students received support; research assistantships with full tuition reimbursements available, teaching assistantships with full tuition reimbursements available, career-related internships or fieldwork, Federal Work-Study, institutionally sponsored loans, scholarships/grants, and unspecified assistantships available. Financial award application deadline: 2/15; financial award applicants required to submit FAFSA. *Faculty research:* Theatre design, production management, Lessac vocal training, movement styles, directing. *Unit head:* Prof. Robert A. Hetherington, Chair, 901-678-2523, Fax: 901-678-4331, E-mail: rhether@memphis.edu. *Application contact:* Prof. Robert A. Hetherington, Chair, 901-678-2523, Fax: 901-678-4331, E-mail: rhether@memphis.edu.

University of Michigan, Horace H. Rackham School of Graduate Studies, The School of Music, Theatre, and Dance, Department of Theatre and Drama, Ann Arbor, MI 48109. Offers design (MFA); theatre (PhD). *Faculty:* 4 full-time (2 women), 1 part-time/adjunct (0 women). In 2009, 1 doctorate awarded. *Degree requirements:* For master's, thesis; for doctorate, one foreign language, thesis/dissertation, preliminary exam, qualifying exam. *Entrance requirements:* For master's, portfolio, interview, writing sample; for doctorate, GRE General Test, writing sample, interview. Additional exam requirements/recommendations for international students: Required—TOEFL (minimum score 600 paper-based; 250 computer-based; 100 iBT). *Application deadline:* For fall admission, 1/15 for domestic students. Applications are processed on a rolling basis. Application fee: $55. Electronic applications accepted. *Expenses:* Tuition, state resident: full-time $17,286; part-time $1099 per credit hour. Tuition, nonresident: full-time $34,944; part-time $2080 per credit hour. Required fees: $95 per semester. Tuition and fees vary according to course load, degree level and program. *Financial support:* In 2009–10, fellowships (averaging $5,800 per year), 1 teaching assistantship with full and partial tuition reimbursement (averaging $38,208 per year) were awarded; career-related internships or fieldwork and scholarships/grants also available. Financial award application deadline: 2/1. *Faculty research:* Silent film, avant-garde drama, popular entertainment. Total annual research expenditures: $45,000. *Unit head:* Gregory Poggi, Chair, 734-764-5350, Fax: 734-647-2297, E-mail: theatre.info@umich.edu. *Application contact:* Dr. Leigh Woods, Head, Graduate Theatre Studies, 734-764-5350, Fax: 734-647-2297, E-mail: lawoods@umich.edu.

University of Minnesota, Twin Cities Campus, Graduate School, College of Liberal Arts, Department of Theatre Arts and Dance, Minneapolis, MN 55455-0213. Offers design technology (MFA); theatre arts and dance (MA, PhD). *Accreditation:* NASD; NAST (one or more programs are accredited). *Faculty:* 15 full-time (6 women), 3 part-time/adjunct (2 women). *Students:* 26 full-time (17 women), 13 part-time (7 women); includes 6 minority (2 African Americans, 4 Hispanic Americans), 2 international. Average age 31. 43 applicants, 23% accepted, 9 enrolled. In 2009, 4 master's, 3 doctorates awarded. Terminal master's awarded for partial completion of doctoral program. *Degree requirements:* For master's, thesis (for some programs), final creative project (MFA), foreign language (MA); for doctorate, one foreign language, thesis/dissertation, oral defense, written exams. *Entrance requirements:* For master's, GRE General Test, minimum GPA of 3.0, audition or portfolio; for doctorate, GRE General Test, minimum GPA of 3.0, writing sample, 1 foreign language. Additional exam requirements/recommendations for international students: Required—TOEFL (minimum score 550 paper-based; 213 computer-based; 79 iBT). *Application deadline:* For fall admission, 1/15 priority date for domestic and international students. Applications are processed on a rolling basis. Application fee: $55 ($75 for international students). Electronic applications accepted. *Financial support:* In 2009–10, 30 students received support, including 3 fellowships with full tuition reimbursements available (averaging $14,000 per year), 27 teaching assistantships with full tuition reimbursements available (averaging $12,253 per year); career-related internships or fieldwork, Federal Work-Study, scholarships/grants, health care benefits, tuition waivers (partial), and unspecified assistantships also available. Financial award application deadline: 4/15; financial award applicants required to submit FAFSA. *Faculty research:* Theatre history, Eastern European theatre, performance studies, medieval studies. Total annual research expenditures: $42,506. *Unit head:* Prof. Michal Kobialka, Professor, 612-625-0048, Fax: 612-625-6334, E-mail: kobia001@umn.edu. *Application contact:* Ginni Arons, Graduate Studies Assistant, 612-625-5029, Fax: 612-625-6334, E-mail: theatre@umn.edu.

University of Missouri, Graduate School, College of Arts and Sciences, Department of Theatre, Columbia, MO 65211. Offers MA, PhD. Part-time programs available. *Faculty:* 10 full-time (4 women), 21 part-time/adjunct (12 women). *Students:* 14 full-time (5 women), 11 part-time (4 women); includes 2 minority (both African Americans). Average age 38. 17 applicants, 18% accepted, 3 enrolled. In 2009, 1 master's, 1 doctorate awarded. *Degree requirements:* For doctorate, thesis/dissertation. *Entrance requirements:* For master's, GRE General Test, minimum GPA of 3.0; min GPA of 3.0 in last 60 hours; for doctorate, GRE General Test; minimum GRE scores: 600-550-5.0, minimum GPA of 3.0; min GPA of 3.0 in last 60 hours; GPA of 3.5 or better in master's program. Additional exam requirements/recommendations for international students: Required—TOEFL (minimum score 650 paper-based; 280 computer-based; 114 iBT). *Application deadline:* For fall admission, 2/1 priority date for domestic students. Applications are processed on a rolling basis. Application fee: $45 ($60 for international students). Electronic applications accepted. *Financial support:* In 2009–10, 4 fellowships with full tuition reimbursements, 1 research assistantship with full tuition reimbursement, 14 teaching assistantships with full tuition reimbursements were awarded; institutionally sponsored loans, health care benefits, and unspecified assistantships also available. *Unit head:* Dr. Clyde Ruffin, Department Chair, E-mail: ruffinc@missouri.edu. *Application contact:* Marsha Miller, Office Support Staff II, 573-882-8281, E-mail: millermt@missouri.edu.

University of Missouri–Kansas City, College of Arts and Sciences, Theatre Department, Kansas City, MO 64110-2499. Offers acting (MFA); design technology (MFA); theatre (MA). *Accreditation:* NAST. *Faculty:* 18 full-time (6 women), 8 part-time/adjunct (2 women). *Students:* 68 full-time (33 women), 16 part-time (7 women); includes 18 minority (7 African Americans, 1 American Indian/Alaska Native, 1 Asian American or Pacific Islander, 9 Hispanic Americans), 2 international. Average age 27. 63 applicants, 57% accepted, 31 enrolled. In 2009, 28 master's awarded. *Degree requirements:* For master's, thesis. *Entrance requirements:* For master's, audition or portfolio, interview. Additional exam requirements/recommendations for international students: Required—TOEFL (minimum score 550 paper-based; 213 computer-based; 80 iBT). *Application deadline:* For fall admission, 3/1 priority date for domestic and international students; for spring admission, 11/1 priority date for domestic and international students. Applications are processed on a rolling basis. Application fee: $45 ($50 for international students). Electronic applications accepted. *Expenses:* Tuition, state resident: full-time $5378; part-time $299 per credit hour. Tuition, nonresident: full-time $13,881; part-time $771 per credit hour. Required fees: $641; $71 per credit hour. Tuition and fees vary according to course load and program. *Financial support:* In 2009–10, 63 teaching assistantships with partial tuition reimbursements (averaging $10,267 per year) were awarded; career-related internships or fieldwork, Federal Work-Study, institutionally sponsored loans, and scholarships/grants also available. Financial award application deadline: 3/1; financial award applicants required to submit FAFSA. *Faculty research:* Contemporary Russian theatre, Shakespeare in performance, subtle energies in actor training, multi-channel sound, renovation of Zuni Pueblo historic Spanish mission. *Unit head:* Tom Mardikes, Chair, 816-235-2784, Fax: 816-235-6562, E-mail: mardikest@umkc.edu. *Application contact:* Cindy Stofiel, Student Affairs Representative, 816-235-6683, Fax: 816-235-6562, E-mail: stofielc@umkc.edu.

The University of Montana, Graduate School, School of Fine Arts, Department of Drama/Dance, Missoula, MT 59812-0002. Offers fine arts (MA, MFA), including acting (MFA), design/technology (MFA), directing (MFA), drama (MA), integrated arts and education (MA), media arts (MFA). *Accreditation:* NAST (one or more programs are accredited). *Degree requirements:* For master's, thesis or alternative. *Entrance requirements:* For master's, GRE General Test, audition, portfolio, production notebook.

The University of Montana, Graduate School, School of Fine Arts, Department of Music, Missoula, MT 59812-0002. Offers music (MM), including composition/technology, music education, musical theater, performance. *Accreditation:* NASM. *Entrance requirements:* For master's, GRE General Test, GRE Subject Test, portfolio.

University of Nebraska at Omaha, Graduate Studies, College of Communication, Fine Arts and Media, Department of Theatre, Omaha, NE 68182. Offers MA. Part-time programs available. *Faculty:* 6 full-time (2 women). *Students:* 9 full-time (7 women), 5 part-time (3 women); includes 2 minority (both African Americans). Average age 34. 12 applicants, 75% accepted, 7 enrolled. In 2009, 1 master's awarded. *Degree requirements:* For master's, comprehensive exam, thesis (for some programs). *Entrance requirements:* For master's, GRE General Test or MAT, minimum GPA of 3.0. Additional exam requirements/recommendations for international students: Required—TOEFL (minimum score 500 paper-based; 173 computer-based; 61 iBT). *Application deadline:* For fall admission, 7/31 priority date for domestic students; for spring admission, 12/1 priority date for domestic students. Applications are processed on a rolling basis. Application fee: $45. Electronic applications accepted. *Financial support:* In 2009–10, 9 students received support; fellowships, research assistantships with tuition reimbursements available, Federal Work-Study, institutionally sponsored loans, scholarships/grants, tuition waivers (full), and unspecified assistantships available. Support available to part-time students. Financial award application deadline: 3/1; financial award applicants required to submit FAFSA. *Unit head:* Sharon Sobel, Chairperson, 402-554-2406. *Application contact:* Dr. Cynthia Phaneuf, Student Contact, 402-554-2406.

University of Nebraska–Lincoln, Graduate College, College of Fine and Performing Arts, Johnny Carson School of Theatre and Film, Lincoln, NE 68588. Offers acting (MFA); costume (MFA); directing (MFA); stage design (MFA). *Accreditation:* NAST. *Degree requirements:* For master's, thesis. *Entrance requirements:* For master's, audition, portfolio. Additional exam requirements/recommendations for international students: Required—TOEFL (minimum score 500 paper-based; 173 computer-based). Electronic applications accepted. *Faculty research:* American theatre history, British theatre history, modern American drama, contemporary performance, Elizabethan theatre history.

University of Nevada, Las Vegas, Graduate College, College of Fine Arts, Department of Theatre, Las Vegas, NV 89154-5036. Offers theatre arts (MA, MFA). *Accreditation:* NAST. Part-time programs available. *Faculty:* 13 full-time (2 women), 4 part-time/adjunct (2 women). *Students:* 38 full-time (20 women), 5 part-time (2 women); includes 2 minority (both Hispanic Americans), 2 international. Average age 32. 33 applicants, 45% accepted, 11 enrolled. In 2009, 8 master's awarded. *Degree requirements:* For master's, thesis (for some programs), creative project, oral exam. *Entrance requirements:* Additional exam requirements/recommendations for international students: Required—TOEFL (minimum score 550 paper-based; 213 computer-based; 80 iBT), IELTS (minimum score 7). *Application deadline:* For fall admission, 6/1 priority date for domestic students, 5/1 for international students. Applications are processed on a rolling basis. Application fee: $60 ($95 for international students). Electronic applications accepted. *Financial support:* In 2009–10, 32 students received support, including 16 research assistantships with partial tuition reimbursements available (averaging $10,000 per year), 16 teaching assistantships with partial tuition reimbursements available (averaging $10,000 per year); institutionally sponsored loans, scholarships/grants, health care benefits, and unspecified assistantships also available. Financial award application deadline: 3/1. *Faculty research:* Developing a professional/academic theatre model that is sustainable, curriculum development to seamlessly integrate stage and screen acting training, integrated voice and movement training (Lugering method), costume history. *Unit head:* Brackley Frayer, Chair/Associate Professor, 702-895-3666, Fax: 702-895-0833, E-mail: brackley.frayer@unlv.edu. *Application contact:* Graduate College Admissions Evaluator, 702-895-3320, Fax: 702-895-4180, E-mail: gradcollege@unlv.edu.

University of New Mexico, Graduate School, College of Fine Arts, Department of Theatre and Dance, Albuquerque, NM 87131-2039. Offers dramatic writing (MFA); theater and dance (MA). *Accreditation:* NASD; NAST. *Faculty:* 21 full-time (12 women), 16 part-time/adjunct (6 women). *Students:* 23 full-time (19 women), 5 part-time (4 women); includes 7 minority (1 Asian American or Pacific Islander, 6 Hispanic Americans), 2 international. Average age 31. 34 applicants, 53% accepted, 12 enrolled. In 2009, 10 master's awarded. *Degree requirements:* For master's, comprehensive exam (for some programs), thesis (for some programs). *Entrance requirements:* For master's, minimum GPA of 3.0, undergraduate major in theatre, dance or closely related field, 3 letters of recommendation, letter of intent. *Application deadline:* For fall admission, 4/15 for domestic students; for spring admission, 11/10 for domestic students. Application fee: $50. Electronic applications accepted. *Expenses:* Tuition, state resident: full-time $2099; part-time $233.20 per credit hour. Tuition, nonresident: full-time $6650. Required fees: $25 per semester. Tuition and fees vary according to course load, program and reciprocity agreements. *Financial support:* In 2009–10, 14 students received support, including 5 research assistantships with partial tuition reimbursements available (averaging $8,000 per year), 6 teaching assistantships with partial tuition reimbursements available (averaging $8,000 per

Theater

University of New Mexico (continued)

year); Federal Work-Study, health care benefits, tuition waivers (partial), and unspecified assistantships also available. Financial award application deadline: 3/1; financial award applicants required to submit FAFSA. *Faculty research:* Theater education and outreach, choreography, dramatic writing, dance history/criticism. *Unit head:* Bill Liotta, Chair, 505-277-4332, Fax: 505-277-8921, E-mail: wliotta@unm.edu. *Application contact:* Christina Squire, Administrator II, 505-277-7362, Fax: 505-277-8921, E-mail: csquire@unm.edu.

University of New Orleans, Graduate School, College of Liberal Arts, Department of Film, Theatre and Communication Arts, New Orleans, LA 70148. Offers film production (MFA); theatre directing (MFA); theatre performance (MFA). *Accreditation:* NAST. *Degree requirements:* For master's, comprehensive exam, thesis. *Entrance requirements:* Additional exam requirements/recommendations for international students: Required—TOEFL (minimum score 550 paper-based; 213 computer-based; 79 iBT). Electronic applications accepted. *Faculty research:* Mass communication theory, nineteenth- and twentieth-century theater history, film criticism and history.

The University of North Carolina at Chapel Hill, Graduate School, College of Arts and Sciences, Department of Dramatic Art, Chapel Hill, NC 27599. Offers acting (MFA); costume production (MFA); technical production (MFA). *Entrance requirements:* For master's, audition or portfolio.

The University of North Carolina at Charlotte, Graduate School, College of Education, Program in Teacher Education, Charlotte, NC 28223-0001. Offers art education (K-12) (MAT); dance education (K-12) (MAT); elementary education (K-6) (MAT); English as a second language (K-12) (MAT); foreign language education (K-12) (MAT); general teacher education (MAT); middle grades education (6-9) (MAT); music education (K-12) (MAT); secondary education (9-12) (MAT); special education (K-12) (MAT); theatre education (K-12) (MAT). *Faculty:* 108 full-time (64 women), 16 part-time/adjunct (12 women). *Students:* 29 full-time (20 women), 229 part-time (189 women); includes 32 minority (22 African Americans, 2 American Indian/Alaska Native, 3 Asian Americans or Pacific Islanders, 5 Hispanic Americans). Average age 32. 108 applicants, 92% accepted, 85 enrolled. In 2009, 59 master's awarded. *Entrance requirements:* For master's, GRE or MAT. Additional exam requirements/recommendations for international students: Required—TOEFL (minimum score 557 paper-based; 220 computer-based; 83 iBT). *Application deadline:* For fall admission, 7/1 for domestic students, 5/1 for international students; for spring admission, 11/1 for domestic students, 10/1 for international students. Applications are processed on a rolling basis. Application fee: $55. Electronic applications accepted. *Financial support:* In 2009–10, 5 students received support, including 1 research assistantship (averaging $18,000 per year), 3 teaching assistantships (averaging $12,183 per year); career-related internships or fieldwork, Federal Work-Study, institutionally sponsored loans, scholarships/grants, and administrative assistantship also available. Support available to part-time students. Financial award application deadline: 4/1; financial award applicants required to submit FAFSA. Total annual research expenditures: $5.1 million. *Unit head:* Dr. Kimberly J. Hartman, Coordinator, 704-687-8883, Fax: 704-687-6430, E-mail: khartman@uncc.edu. *Application contact:* Kathy B. Giddings, Director of Graduate Admissions, 704-687-5503, Fax: 704-687-3279, E-mail: gradadmn@uncc.edu.

The University of North Carolina at Greensboro, Graduate School, College of Arts and Sciences, Department of Theater, Greensboro, NC 27412-5001. Offers acting (MFA); design (MFA); directing (MFA); theater education (M Ed); theater for youth (MFA). *Accreditation:* NAST. *Entrance requirements:* For master's, portfolio, interviews. Electronic applications accepted.

University of North Carolina School of the Arts, School of Design and Production, Winston-Salem, NC 27127-2188. Offers costume design (MFA); costume technology (MFA); performance arts management (MFA); scene design (MFA); scene painting/properties (MFA); sound design (MFA); stage automation (MFA); technical direction (MFA); wig and make-up design (MFA). *Faculty:* 19 full-time (4 women), 16 part-time/adjunct (6 women). *Students:* 70 full-time (52 women); includes 10 minority (3 African Americans, 3 American Indian/Alaska Native, 3 Asian Americans or Pacific Islanders, 1 Hispanic American), 3 international. Average age 25. 86 applicants, 77% accepted, 48 enrolled. In 2009, 13 master's awarded. *Degree requirements:* For master's, thesis (for some programs), project. *Entrance requirements:* For master's, interview, portfolio. Additional exam requirements/recommendations for international students: Required—TOEFL. *Application deadline:* For fall admission, 4/1 priority date for domestic students. Applications are processed on a rolling basis. Application fee: $60 ($100 for international students). Electronic applications accepted. *Expenses:* Tuition, state resident: full-time $3797. Tuition, nonresident: full-time $15,670. Required fees: $1992. *Financial support:* In 2009–10, 47 teaching assistantships with partial tuition reimbursements (averaging $1,500 per year) were awarded; career-related internships or fieldwork, Federal Work-Study, and unspecified assistantships also available. Support available to part-time students. Financial award application deadline: 3/15; financial award applicants required to submit FAFSA. *Unit head:* Joseph A. Tilford, Dean, 336-770-3214 Ext. 103, Fax: 336-770-3213, E-mail: tilford@uncsa.edu. *Application contact:* Sheeler Lawson, Director of Admissions, 336-770-3290, Fax: 336-770-3370, E-mail: admissions@uncsa.edu.

University of North Dakota, Graduate School, College of Arts and Sciences, Department of Theatre Arts, Grand Forks, ND 58202. Offers MA. *Accreditation:* NAST. *Degree requirements:* For master's, comprehensive exam, thesis or alternative. *Entrance requirements:* For master's, minimum GPA of 3.0. Additional exam requirements/recommendations for international students: Required—TOEFL (minimum score 550 paper-based; 213 computer-based; 79 iBT), IELTS (minimum score 6.5). Electronic applications accepted.

University of Oklahoma, Graduate College, College of Fine Arts, School of Drama, Norman, OK 73019. Offers acting (MFA); design (MFA); directing (MFA); drama (MA). *Accreditation:* NAST. *Students:* 10 full-time (4 women), 1 (woman) part-time; includes 1 minority (American Indian/Alaska Native), 1 international. 12 applicants, 33% accepted, 3 enrolled. In 2009, 4 master's awarded. *Degree requirements:* For master's, comprehensive exam, thesis (MA), departmental qualifying exam. *Entrance requirements:* For master's, BA with 36 hours in drama, auditions. Additional exam requirements/recommendations for international students: Required—TOEFL (minimum score 550 paper-based; 213 computer-based). *Application deadline:* For fall admission, 6/1 for domestic students, 4/1 for international students; for spring admission, 11/1 for domestic students, 9/1 for international students. Applications are processed on a rolling basis. Application fee: $40 ($90 for international students). Electronic applications accepted. *Expenses:* Tuition, state resident: full-time $3744; part-time $156 per credit hour. Tuition, nonresident: full-time $13,577; part-time $565.70 per credit hour. Required fees: $2415; $90.10 per credit hour. *Financial support:* In 2009–10, 2 research assistantships with partial tuition reimbursements (averaging $9,586 per year), 9 teaching assistantships with partial tuition reimbursements (averaging $9,586 per year) were awarded; unspecified assistantships also available. Financial award application deadline: 4/7; financial award applicants required to submit FAFSA. *Faculty research:* Directing, costume design, lighting design, dramaturgy. *Unit head:* Dr. Tom Orr, Director, 405-325-4021, Fax: 405-325-0400, E-mail: thorr@ou.edu. *Application contact:* Dr. Judith Pender, Graduate Liaison, 405-325-5319, Fax: 405-325-0400, E-mail: jmpender@ou.edu.

University of Oregon, Graduate School, College of Arts and Sciences, Department of Theater Arts, Eugene, OR 97403. Offers MA, MFA, MS, PhD. *Degree requirements:* For master's, variable foreign language requirement, thesis or alternative; for doctorate, variable foreign language requirement, thesis/dissertation. *Entrance requirements:* For master's and doctorate, minimum GPA of 3.0. Additional exam requirements/recommendations for international students: Required—TOEFL.

University of Ottawa, Faculty of Graduate and Postdoctoral Studies, Faculty of Arts, Department of Theatre, Ottawa, ON K1N 6N5, Canada. Offers directing for theatre (MA). Electronic applications accepted. *Faculty research:* Lamise en scéne.

University of Pittsburgh, School of Arts and Sciences, Department of Theatre Arts, Pittsburgh, PA 15260. Offers performance pedagogy (MFA); theatre and performance studies (MA, PhD). *Accreditation:* NAST. *Faculty:* 4 full-time (1 woman). *Students:* 25 full-time (15 women); includes 1 minority (African American), 1 international. Average age 31. 71 applicants, 21% accepted, 8 enrolled. In 2009, 3 master's, 3 doctorates awarded. Terminal master's awarded for partial completion of doctoral program. *Degree requirements:* For master's, comprehensive exam; for doctorate, one foreign language, comprehensive exam, thesis/dissertation, diagnostic exams. *Entrance requirements:* For master's and doctorate, GRE General Test, samples of written work. Additional exam requirements/recommendations for international students: Required—TOEFL (minimum score 550 paper-based; 213 computer-based; 80 iBT). *Application deadline:* For fall admission, 1/15 priority date for domestic and international students. Application fee: $50. Electronic applications accepted. *Expenses:* Tuition, state resident: full-time $16,402; part-time $665 per credit. Tuition, nonresident: full-time $28,694; part-time $1175 per credit. Required fees: $690; $175 per term. Tuition and fees vary according to program. *Financial support:* In 2009–10, 21 students received support, including 1 fellowship with full tuition reimbursement available (averaging $18,200 per year), 13 research assistantships with full and partial tuition reimbursements available (averaging $12,300 per year), 17 teaching assistantships with full and partial tuition reimbursements available (averaging $15,675 per year); career-related internships or fieldwork, Federal Work-Study, institutionally sponsored loans, scholarships/grants, health care benefits, and unspecified assistantships also available. Support available to part-time students. Financial award application deadline: 1/15; financial award applicants required to submit FAFSA. *Faculty research:* American theatre, Renaissance theatre, Asian theatre, dramatic structure, performance theory. *Unit head:* Dr. Bruce McConachie, Chairman, 412-624-6156, Fax: 412-624-6338, E-mail: bamcco@pitt.edu. *Application contact:* Connie Anne Markiw, Graduate Secretary, 412-624-6568, Fax: 412-624-6338, E-mail: cam177@pitt.edu.

University of Portland, College of Arts and Sciences, Department of Performing and Fine Arts, Portland, OR 97203-5798. Offers drama (MFA), including directing; music (MA). Part-time and evening/weekend programs available. *Faculty:* 7 full-time (1 woman). *Students:* 4 full-time (3 women), 2 part-time (1 woman); includes 1 minority (African American). Average age 35. 9 applicants, 67% accepted, 4 enrolled. In 2009, 5 master's awarded. *Degree requirements:* For master's, thesis optional. *Entrance requirements:* For master's, GRE General Test, minimum GPA of 3.0, resume, 3 letters of recommendation, statement of goals, official transcripts. Additional exam requirements/recommendations for international students: Required—TOEFL (minimum score 600 paper-based; 100 iBT), IELTS (minimum score 7.5). *Application deadline:* For fall admission, 7/15 priority date for domestic and international students; for spring admission, 12/15 priority date for domestic and international students. Applications are processed on a rolling basis. Application fee: $50. *Expenses:* Tuition: Part-time $860 per semester hour. *Financial support:* Federal Work-Study, scholarships/grants, and tuition waivers (partial) available. Financial award application deadline: 3/1; financial award applicants required to submit FAFSA. *Unit head:* Dr. Kenneth Kleszynski, Head, 503-943-7294, E-mail: kkleszyn@up.edu. *Application contact:* Chris James Olinger, Administrative Assistant, 503-943-7107, Fax: 503-943-7315, E-mail: olingerc@up.edu.

University of San Diego, College of Arts and Sciences, Program in Dramatic Arts, San Diego, CA 92110-2492. Offers MFA. *Faculty:* 4 full-time (3 women), 1 part-time/adjunct (0 women). *Students:* 14 full-time (6 women); includes 1 minority (African American). Average age 27. 348 applicants, 2% accepted, 7 enrolled. In 2009, 7 master's awarded. *Entrance requirements:* For master's, audition. Additional exam requirements/recommendations for international students: Required—TOEFL (minimum score 580 paper-based; 237 computer-based; 83 iBT), TWE. *Application deadline:* For fall admission, 1/3 for domestic and international students. Application fee: $55. *Expenses:* Tuition: Full-time $21,042; part-time $1169 per unit. Required fees: $224. Full-time tuition and fees vary according to course load and degree level. *Financial support:* In 2009–10, 14 students received support, including 14 fellowships with full tuition reimbursements available; career-related internships or fieldwork, Federal Work-Study, and institutionally sponsored loans also available. Financial award application deadline: 4/1; financial award applicants required to submit FAFSA. *Faculty research:* Drama, acting, instruction, voice and speech. *Unit head:* Richard Seer, Graduate Program Director, 619-260-8813, Fax: 619-231-5879. *Application contact:* Dr. John Mosby, Associate Director of Graduate Admissions, 619-260-4524, Fax: 619-260-4158, E-mail: grads@sandiego.edu.

University of Saskatchewan, College of Graduate Studies and Research, College of Arts and Sciences, Department of Drama, Saskatoon, SK S7N 5A2, Canada. Offers MA. *Faculty:* 5. *Degree requirements:* For master's, thesis. *Entrance requirements:* Additional exam requirements/recommendations for international students: Required—TOEFL (minimum score 80 iBT); Recommended—IELTS (minimum score 6.5). *Application deadline:* For fall admission, 7/1 priority date for domestic students. Applications are processed on a rolling basis. Application fee: $75. Electronic applications accepted. Tuition and fees charges are reported in Canadian dollars. *Expenses:* Tuition, area resident: Full-time $3000 Canadian dollars; part-time $500 Canadian dollars per term. Required fees: $700 Canadian dollars; $100 Canadian dollars per term. *Financial support:* Fellowships, research assistantships, teaching assistantships available. Financial award application deadline: 1/31. *Unit head:* Dr. James Guedo, Head, 306-966-5185, Fax: 306-966-8193, E-mail: dwayne.brenna@usask.ca. *Application contact:* Dr. M. Day, Graduate Chair, 306-966-5193, Fax: 306-966-8193, E-mail: moiraday@duke.usask.ca.

University of South Carolina, The Graduate School, College of Arts and Sciences, Department of Theater and Dance, Columbia, SC 29208. Offers theater (MA, MAT, MFA). IMA and MAT offered in cooperation with the College of Education. *Accreditation:* NAST (one or more programs are accredited). *Degree requirements:* For master's, comprehensive exam, thesis. *Entrance requirements:* For master's, GRE General Test, GRE or MAT (MAT), audition, interview (for MFA degree). Additional exam requirements/recommendations for international students: Required—TOEFL. Electronic applications accepted. *Faculty research:* Computer assisted design, rhetoric of science and technology, Alexander Technique, script analysis, Lessac Method.

University of South Carolina, The Graduate School, College of Education, Department of Instruction and Teacher Education, Program in Secondary Education, Columbia, SC 29208. Offers art education (IMA, MAT); business education (IMA, MAT); English (MAT); foreign language (MAT); health education (MAT); mathematics (MAT); science (IMA, MAT); secondary (Ed D); secondary education (MT, PhD); social studies (MAT); theatre and speech (MAT). IMA and MT offered jointly with the subject areas. *Accreditation:* NCATE. *Degree requirements:* For master's, comprehensive exam, thesis (for some programs), foreign language (MA); for doctorate, one foreign language, comprehensive exam, thesis/dissertation. *Entrance requirements:* For master's, GRE General Test or MAT, teaching certificate (IMA, M Ed), interview; for doctorate, GRE General Test or MAT, interview. *Faculty research:* Middle school programs, professional development, school collaboration.

The University of South Dakota, Graduate School, College of Fine Arts, Department of Theatre, Vermillion, SD 57069-2390. Offers MA, MFA. *Accreditation:* NAST. *Degree requirements:* For master's, thesis or alternative. *Entrance requirements:* For master's, GRE (MA), minimum GPA of 2.7, portfolio. Additional exam requirements/recommendations for international students: Required—TOEFL (minimum score 550 paper-based; 213 computer-based; 79 iBT). Electronic applications accepted.

University of Southern California, Graduate School, School of Theatre, Program in Acting, Los Angeles, CA 90089. Offers MFA. Postbaccalaureate distance learning degree programs offered (minimal on-campus study). *Entrance requirements:* For master's, 3 letters of recommendation, current headshot, audition. *Application deadline:* For fall admission, 1/11 for domestic students. Application fee: $85. *Expenses:* Tuition: Full-time $25,980; part-time $1315 per unit. Required fees: $554. One-time fee: $35 full-time. Full-time tuition and fees vary according to degree level and program. *Financial support:* Federal Work-Study and tuition waivers (partial) available. *Unit head:* Dr. Andrew Robinson, Director, 213-821-4163, E-mail: sotmfa@usc.edu.

Application contact: Sergio Ramirez, Director, Academic and Student Services, 213-821-4163, E-mail: sergio.ramirez@usc.edu.

University of Southern California, Graduate School, School of Theatre, Program in Dramatic Writing, Los Angeles, CA 90089. Offers MFA. *Entrance requirements:* For master's, GRE General Test, 3 letters of recommendation, play in standard Samuel French of Final Draft stage format, a synopsis of the play. *Application deadline:* For fall admission, 1/11 for domestic students. Application fee: $85. *Expenses:* Tuition: Full-time $25,980; part-time $1315 per unit. Required fees: $554. One-time fee: $35 full-time. Full-time tuition and fees vary according to degree level and program. *Financial support:* Fellowships with full tuition reimbursements, teaching assistantships with full tuition reimbursements, career-related internships or fieldwork, Federal Work-Study, and scholarships/grants available. Support available to part-time students. Financial award application deadline: 2/15; financial award applicants required to submit FAFSA. *Unit head:* Dr. Velina Hasu-Houston, Director, 213-740-2311. *Application contact:* Sergio Ramierez, Director, Academic and Student Services, 213-821-4163, E-mail: sergio.ramirez@usc.edu.

University of Southern Mississippi, Graduate School, College of Arts and Letters, Department of Theatre and Dance, Hattiesburg, MS 39406-0001. Offers theatre (MFA). *Accreditation:* NAST. Part-time programs available. *Faculty:* 8 full-time (5 women). *Students:* 12 full-time (1 woman); includes 8 minority (3 African Americans, 1 American Indian/Alaska Native, 1 Asian American or Pacific Islander, 3 Hispanic Americans). Average age 28. 23 applicants, 26% accepted, 6 enrolled. In 2009, 5 master's awarded. *Degree requirements:* For master's, comprehensive exam, thesis or alternative, creative project. *Entrance requirements:* For master's, GRE General Test, minimum GPA of 3.0. Additional exam requirements/recommendations for international students: Required—TOEFL. *Application deadline:* For fall admission, 3/1 priority date for domestic students, 3/1 for international students. Applications are processed on a rolling basis. Application fee: $35. *Expenses:* Tuition, state resident: full-time $5096; part-time $284 per hour. Tuition, nonresident: full-time $13,052; part-time $726 per hour. Required fees: $402. Tuition and fees vary according to course level and course load. *Financial support:* In 2009–10, 20 teaching assistantships with full tuition reimbursements (averaging $7,065 per year) were awarded; research assistantships, career-related internships or fieldwork, Federal Work-Study, and unspecified assistantships also available. Support available to part-time students. Financial award application deadline: 3/15; financial award applicants required to submit FAFSA. *Faculty research:* Technical design, acting. *Unit head:* Louis Rackoff, Chair, 601-266-4994, Fax: 601-266-6423. *Application contact:* Shonna Breland, Manager of Graduate Admissions, 601-266-4369, Fax: 601-266-5138, E-mail: graduatestudies@usm.edu.

The University of Tennessee, Graduate School, College of Arts and Sciences, Department of Theatre, Knoxville, TN 37996. Offers costume design (MFA); lighting design (MFA); performance (MFA); scene design (MFA); theatre technology (MFA). *Degree requirements:* For master's, thesis or alternative. *Entrance requirements:* For master's, audition, minimum GPA of 2.7. Additional exam requirements/recommendations for international students: Required—TOEFL. Electronic applications accepted. *Expenses:* Tuition, state resident: full-time $6826; part-time $380 per semester hour. Tuition, nonresident: full-time $21,844; part-time $1147 per semester hour. Tuition and fees vary according to program.

The University of Texas at Austin, Graduate School, College of Fine Arts, Department of Theatre and Dance, Austin, TX 78712-1111. Offers acting (MFA); dance (MFA); directing (MFA); drama and theatre for youth (MFA); performance as public practice (MA, MFA, PhD); playwriting (MFA); theatre technology (MFA); theatrical design (MFA). *Accreditation:* NASD. *Degree requirements:* For master's, thesis; for doctorate, variable foreign language requirement, thesis/dissertation. *Entrance requirements:* For master's and doctorate, GRE General Test.

The University of Texas–Pan American, College of Arts and Humanities, Department of Communications, Edinburg, TX 78539. Offers communication (MA); theatre (MA). *Accreditation:* NAST. Part-time and evening/weekend programs available. *Degree requirements:* For master's, comprehensive exam, thesis or alternative. *Entrance requirements:* For master's, minimum GPA of 3.0. Additional exam requirements/recommendations for international students: Required—TOEFL. *Expenses:* Tuition, state resident: full-time $3630.60; part-time $201.70 per credit hour. Tuition, nonresident: full-time $8617; part-time $478.70 per credit hour. Required fees: $806.50. *Faculty research:* Rhetorical theory, intercultural and mass communication, American theatre, multicultural theatre and drama, television and film.

University of Toronto, School of Graduate Studies, Humanities Division, Centre for the Study of Drama, Toronto, ON M5S 1A1, Canada. Offers MA, PhD. Part-time programs available. *Degree requirements:* For doctorate, one foreign language, thesis/dissertation, language examination, qualifying examination, oral examination. *Entrance requirements:* For master's, minimum B+ average, significant coursework in drama and related disciplines, resume, 2 letters of recommendation; for doctorate, minimum A- average, resumé, MA in drama; 2 letters of recommendation.

University of Victoria, Faculty of Graduate Studies, Faculty of Fine Arts, Department of Theatre, Victoria, BC V8W 2Y2, Canada. Offers design (MFA); directing (MFA); theatre history (MA). *Degree requirements:* For master's, thesis. *Entrance requirements:* Additional exam requirements/recommendations for international students: Required—TOEFL (minimum score 575 paper-based; 233 computer-based), IELTS (minimum score 7). Electronic applications accepted.

University of Virginia, College and Graduate School of Arts and Sciences, Department of Drama, Charlottesville, VA 22903. Offers MFA. *Faculty:* 18 full-time (8 women), 1 (woman) part-time/adjunct. *Students:* 17 full-time (9 women); includes 2 minority (1 African American, 1 Asian American or Pacific Islander), 1 international. Average age 27. 3 applicants, 67% accepted, 2 enrolled. In 2009, 27 master's awarded. *Degree requirements:* For master's, thesis project. *Entrance requirements:* For master's, GRE General Test, resume; 3 letters of recommendation. Additional exam requirements/recommendations for international students: Required—TOEFL (minimum score 600 paper-based; 250 computer-based; 90 iBT), IELTS (minimum score 7). *Application deadline:* For fall admission, 2/20 for domestic and international students. Applications are processed on a rolling basis. Application fee: $60. Electronic applications accepted. *Financial support:* Fellowships, teaching assistantships available. Financial award applicants required to submit FAFSA. *Faculty research:* Acting, scenic design, lighting design, technical direction, costume design/technology. *Unit head:* Tom Bloom, Chair, 434-924-3326, Fax: 434-924-1447, E-mail: drama@virginia.edu. *Application contact:* Tom Bloom, Chair, 434-924-3326, Fax: 434-924-1447, E-mail: drama@virginia.edu.

University of Washington, Graduate School, College of Arts and Sciences, School of Drama, Seattle, WA 98195. Offers acting (MFA); costume design (MFA); directing (MFA); dramatic theory (PhD); lighting design (MFA); scenic design (MFA); theatre and performance history (PhD). *Degree requirements:* For master's, thesis; for doctorate, one foreign language, comprehensive exam, thesis/dissertation. *Entrance requirements:* For master's, interview, minimum GPA of 3.0, portfolio; for doctorate, GRE General Test, minimum GPA of 3.0, writing sample. Additional exam requirements/recommendations for international students: Required—TOEFL. *Faculty research:* Semiotics, Suzuki actor training, modern American theatre, ethnic American theatre.

University of Wisconsin–Madison, Graduate School, College of Letters and Science, Department of Theatre and Drama, Madison, WI 53706-1380. Offers MA, MFA, PhD. *Accreditation:* NAST. Part-time programs available. *Degree requirements:* For master's, thesis; for doctorate, thesis/dissertation. *Entrance requirements:* For master's and doctorate, GRE. Electronic applications accepted. *Expenses:* Tuition, state resident: part-time $594 per credit. Tuition, nonresident: part-time $1504 per credit. Required fees: $65 per credit. Tuition and fees vary according to course load, program and reciprocity agreements. *Faculty research:* Theories and histories of dance, theatre and performance studies; Russian theatre and dance; postmodern performance; Holocaust drama; race and representation.

University of Wisconsin–Milwaukee, Graduate School, Peck School of the Arts, Program in Performing Arts, Milwaukee, WI 53201-0413. Offers dance (MFA); film (MFA); theatre (MFA). Part-time programs available. *Faculty:* 31 full-time (19 women). *Students:* 18 full-time (12 women), 2 part-time (both women); includes 4 minority (2 African Americans, 1 Asian American or Pacific Islander, 1 Hispanic American), 1 international. Average age 34. 23 applicants, 22% accepted, 3 enrolled. In 2009, 18 master's awarded. *Degree requirements:* For master's, variable foreign language requirement, comprehensive exam, thesis or alternative. *Entrance requirements:* For master's, audition, interview. Additional exam requirements/recommendations for international students: Required—TOEFL (minimum score 550 paper-based; 79 iBT), IELTS (minimum score 6.5). *Application deadline:* For fall admission, 1/1 priority date for domestic students; for spring admission, 9/1 for domestic students. Applications are processed on a rolling basis. Application fee: $45 ($75 for international students). *Expenses:* Tuition, state resident: full-time $8800. Tuition, nonresident: full-time $20,760. Tuition and fees vary according to program and reciprocity agreements. *Financial support:* In 2009–10, 15 teaching assistantships were awarded; career-related internships or fieldwork and unspecified assistantships also available. Support available to part-time students. Financial award application deadline: 4/15. *Unit head:* Simone Ferro, Representative, 414-229-4178, E-mail: sferro@uwm.edu. *Application contact:* General Information Contact, 414-229-4982, Fax: 414-229-6967, E-mail: gradschool@uwm.edu.

University of Wisconsin–Superior, Graduate Division, Department of Communicating Arts, Superior, WI 54880-4500. Offers mass communication (MA); speech communication (MA); theater (MA). Part-time programs available. *Faculty:* 9 full-time (3 women), 1 (woman) part-time/adjunct. *Students:* 14 full-time (9 women), 5 part-time (3 women). Average age 30. 9 applicants, 100% accepted. In 2009, 7 master's awarded. *Degree requirements:* For master's, comprehensive exam, thesis or alternative, position paper or project. *Entrance requirements:* For master's, minimum GPA of 2.75. *Application deadline:* For fall admission, 4/1 priority date for domestic students; for spring admission, 10/15 priority date for domestic students. Applications are processed on a rolling basis. Application fee: $45. *Financial support:* Career-related internships or fieldwork, Federal Work-Study, institutionally sponsored loans, scholarships/grants, and tuition waivers (partial) available. Support available to part-time students. Financial award application deadline: 4/15; financial award applicants required to submit FAFSA. *Faculty research:* Multimedia technology, ethics in journalism, diversity, electronic portfolio assessment. *Unit head:* Dr. Martha Einerson, Program Coordinator, 715-394-8477, E-mail: meinerso@uwsuper.edu. *Application contact:* Sandy Wallgren, Program Assistant/Status Examiner, 715-394-8295, Fax: 715-394-8146, E-mail: swallgr1@uwsuper.edu.

Utah State University, School of Graduate Studies, College of Humanities, Arts and Social Sciences, Department of Theatre Arts, Logan, UT 84322. Offers advanced technical practice (MFA); design (MFA); theatre arts (MA, MFA). *Degree requirements:* For master's, variable foreign language requirement, thesis (for some programs), summer internship (MFA). *Entrance requirements:* For master's, GRE General Test or MAT, portfolio (MFA), minimum GPA of 3.0, interview, BS or 20 semester credit. Additional exam requirements/recommendations for international students: Required—TOEFL. *Faculty research:* Seventeenth and eighteenth century Spanish theatre, Greek and Roman theatre, interpretation of literature for performance.

Villanova University, Graduate School of Liberal Arts and Sciences, Department of Theatre, Villanova, PA 19085-1699. Offers MA. Part-time and evening/weekend programs available. *Faculty:* 6 full-time (2 women), 2 part-time/adjunct (both women). *Students:* 24 full-time (12 women), 8 part-time (all women); includes 4 minority (2 African Americans, 2 Hispanic Americans). Average age 29. 21 applicants, 90% accepted, 10 enrolled. In 2009, 14 master's awarded. *Degree requirements:* For master's, comprehensive exam. *Entrance requirements:* For master's, GRE, minimum GPA of 3.0. Additional exam requirements/recommendations for international students: Required—TOEFL. *Application deadline:* For fall admission, 3/1 priority date for domestic and international students; for spring admission, 11/15 priority date for domestic and international students. Applications are processed on a rolling basis. Application fee: $50. Electronic applications accepted. *Expenses:* Tuition: Part-time $630 per credit. Required fees: $60 per credit. Part-time tuition and fees vary according to degree level and program. *Financial support:* Research assistantships, Federal Work-Study and scholarships/grants available. Financial award applicants required to submit FAFSA. *Unit head:* Fr. Richard Cannuli, Chairperson, 610-519-4760. *Application contact:* Dr. Adele Lindenmeyr, Dean, Graduate School of Liberal Arts and Sciences, 610-519-7093, Fax: 610-519-7096.

Virginia Commonwealth University, Graduate School, School of the Arts, Department of Theatre, Richmond, VA 23284-9005. Offers acting (MFA); costume design (MFA); directing (MFA); pedagogy (MFA); scene design/technical theater (MFA). *Accreditation:* NAST. *Degree requirements:* For master's, thesis (for some programs). *Entrance requirements:* For master's, audition, portfolio. *Faculty research:* Dramatic literature, speech.

Virginia Polytechnic Institute and State University, Graduate School, College of Liberal Arts and Human Sciences, Department of Theatre and Cinema, Blacksburg, VA 24061. Offers directing and public dialogue (MFA); stage management (MFA); theatre design and technology (MFA). *Accreditation:* NAST. *Faculty:* 17 full-time (7 women). *Students:* 13 full-time (6 women), 1 (woman) part-time. Average age 35. 30 applicants, 13% accepted, 4 enrolled. In 2009, 2 master's awarded. *Entrance requirements:* For master's, GRE, GMAT. Additional exam requirements/recommendations for international students: Required—TOEFL (minimum score 550 paper-based; 213 computer-based). *Application deadline:* For fall admission, 5/15 for international students; for spring admission, 10/15 for international students. Applications are processed on a rolling basis. Application fee: $65. Electronic applications accepted. *Expenses:* Tuition, area resident: Full-time $10,228; part-time $459 per credit hour. Tuition, nonresident: full-time $17,892; part-time $865 per credit hour. Required fees: $1966; $451 per semester. *Financial support:* In 2009–10, 9 teaching assistantships with full tuition reimbursements (averaging $11,027 per year) were awarded; career-related internships or fieldwork, Federal Work-Study, scholarships/grants, and unspecified assistantships also available. Financial award application deadline: 1/15. Total annual research expenditures: $6,520. *Unit head:* Dr. Patricia A. Raun, Dean, 540-231-5335, Fax: 540-231-7321, E-mail: praun@vt.edu. *Application contact:* Bob Leonard, Information Contact, 540-231-9299, Fax: 540-231-7321, E-mail: rhleonar@vt.edu.

Wayne State University, College of Fine, Performing and Communication Arts, Department of Theatre, Detroit, MI 48202. Offers MA, MFA, PhD. *Accreditation:* NAST. *Degree requirements:* For master's, thesis (for some programs); for doctorate, one foreign language, thesis/dissertation. *Entrance requirements:* For master's, minimum GPA of 3.0, auditions, interviews; for doctorate, GRE, MA with minimum GPA of 3.3; directing experience; recommendations; scholarly paper; statement of goals. Additional exam requirements/recommendations for international students: Required—TOEFL (minimum score 550 paper-based; 213 computer-based); Recommended—TWE (minimum score 6). Electronic applications accepted. *Faculty research:* Dramatic criticism, lighting design, acting, directing, scenography.

Western Illinois University, School of Graduate Studies, College of Fine Arts and Communication, Department of Theatre and Dance, Macomb, IL 61455-1390. Offers acting (MFA); costume design (MFA); directing (MFA); lighting design/theatre technology (MFA); scenic design (MFA). *Accreditation:* NAST. Part-time programs available. *Students:* 31 full-time (13 women), 1 part-time (0 women); includes 1 minority (Asian American or Pacific Islander), 1 international. Average age 28. 32 applicants, 25% accepted. In 2009, 9 master's awarded. *Degree requirements:* For master's, comprehensive exam, thesis or alternative, creative project, written exam. *Entrance requirements:* For master's, audition or interview. Additional exam requirements/recommendations for international students: Required—TOEFL (minimum score 550 paper-based; 213 computer-based; 80 iBT). *Application deadline:* Applications are processed on a rolling basis. Application fee: $30. Electronic applications accepted. *Expenses:* Tuition, state resident: full-time $4486; part-time $249.21 per credit hour. Tuition, nonresident: full-time $8972; part-time $498.42 per credit hour. Required fees: $72.62 per credit hour. *Financial support:* In 2009–10, 30 students received support, including 24 research assistantships with

Theater

Western Illinois University (continued)
full tuition reimbursements available (averaging $7,280 per year), 6 teaching assistantships with full tuition reimbursements available (averaging $8,400 per year). Financial award applicants required to submit FAFSA. *Unit head:* Dr. David Patrick, Chairperson, 309-298-1543. *Application contact:* Evelyn Hoing, Assistant Director of Graduate Studies, 309-298-1806, Fax: 309-298-2345, E-mail: grad-office@wiu.edu.

West Virginia University, College of Creative Arts, Division of Theatre and Dance, Morgantown, WV 26506. Offers acting (MFA); theatre design/technology (MFA). *Accreditation:* NAST. Part-time programs available. *Degree requirements:* For master's, thesis, oral defense. *Entrance requirements:* For master's, minimum GPA of 3.0, audition or portfolio. Additional exam requirements/recommendations for international students: Required—TOEFL. *Faculty research:* Professional directing, consulting, design.

Yale University, School of Drama, New Haven, CT 06520. Offers MFA, DFA, Certificate, MBA/MFA. *Degree requirements:* For master's, comprehensive exam (for some programs), thesis (for some programs); for doctorate, thesis/dissertation. *Entrance requirements:* For master's, in person audition (acting); portfolio, review (design); interview. Additional exam requirements/recommendations for international students: Required—TOEFL. Electronic applications accepted.

York University, Faculty of Graduate Studies, Faculty of Fine Arts, Program in Theatre, Toronto, ON M3J 1P3, Canada. Offers MFA. *Degree requirements:* For master's, thesis. Electronic applications accepted.

York University, Faculty of Graduate Studies, Faculty of Fine Arts, Program in Theatre Studies, Toronto, ON M3J 1P3, Canada. Offers MA, PhD.

Therapies—Dance, Drama, and Music

Antioch University New England, Graduate School, Department of Applied Psychology, Program in Dance/Movement Therapy and Counseling, Keene, NH 03431-3552. Offers M Ed, MA. *Degree requirements:* For master's, thesis, internship, practicum. *Entrance requirements:* For master's, previous course work and work experience in psychology, experience in dance or movement. Additional exam requirements/recommendations for international students: Required—TOEFL (minimum score 600 paper-based; 250 computer-based). Electronic applications accepted. *Expenses:* Contact institution. *Faculty research:* Research attitudes and needs of dance/movement therapists.

Appalachian State University, Cratis D. Williams Graduate School, School of Music, Boone, NC 28608. Offers music education (MM); music performance (MM); music therapy (MMT). *Accreditation:* NASM. Part-time programs available. *Faculty:* 29 full-time (11 women), 2 part-time/adjunct (both women). *Students:* 26 full-time (17 women), 7 part-time (5 women); includes 1 minority (African American), 1 international. 24 applicants, 92% accepted, 9 enrolled. In 2009, 7 master's awarded. *Degree requirements:* For master's, comprehensive exam, thesis or alternative. *Entrance requirements:* For master's, GRE General Test, 3 letters of reference, audition. Additional exam requirements/recommendations for international students: Required—TOEFL (minimum score 550 paper-based; 230 computer-based; 79 iBT), IELTS (minimum score 6.5). *Application deadline:* For fall admission, 7/1 for domestic students, 2/1 for international students; for spring admission, 11/1 for domestic students, 7/1 for international students. Applications are processed on a rolling basis. Application fee: $50. Electronic applications accepted. *Expenses:* Tuition, state resident: full-time $2960. Tuition, nonresident: full-time $14,051. Required fees: $2320. *Financial support:* In 2009–10, 16 research assistantships (averaging $8,000 per year) were awarded; fellowships, teaching assistantships, career-related internships or fieldwork, Federal Work-Study, scholarships/grants, tuition waivers (partial), and unspecified assistantships also available. Financial award application deadline: 4/1; financial award applicants required to submit FAFSA. *Faculty research:* Music of the Holocaust, Celtic folk music, early nineteenth century performance practice, hypermeter and phase rhythm, world music, music and psychoneuroimmunology. *Unit head:* Dr. William Pelto, Dean, 828-262-6446, E-mail: peltowl@appstate.edu. *Application contact:* Dr. Nancy Schneeloch-Bingham, Graduate Program Director, 828-262-6463, E-mail: schneelochna@appstate.edu.

Arizona State University, Graduate College, Herberger College of the Arts, School of Music, Tempe, AZ 85287. Offers composition (MM); music (MA, DMA); music education (MM); music therapy (MM); performance (MM). *Accreditation:* NASM. *Degree requirements:* For doctorate, thesis/dissertation. *Entrance requirements:* For master's, GRE or MAT; for doctorate, GRE.

California Institute of Integral Studies, School of Professional Psychology, San Francisco, CA 94103. Offers clinical psychology (Psy D); community mental health (MA); drama therapy (MA); expressive arts therapy (MA); integral counseling psychology (MA); integral counseling psychology–weekend (MA); somatic psychology (MA). *Accreditation:* APA. Part-time programs available. *Students:* 639 full-time (483 women), 53 part-time (43 women); includes 148 minority (32 African Americans, 2 American Indian/Alaska Native, 62 Asian Americans or Pacific Islanders, 52 Hispanic Americans). Average age 38. 476 applicants, 71% accepted, 202 enrolled. In 2009, 136 master's, 21 doctorates awarded. *Degree requirements:* For master's, comprehensive exam; for doctorate, comprehensive exam, thesis/dissertation. *Entrance requirements:* For master's, minimum GPA of 3.0, letters of recommendation, writing sample; for doctorate, GRE, MA in psychology or social work with appropriate practical experience for advanced standing, or BA with a minimum GPA of 3.1; letters of recommendation; writing sample. Additional exam requirements/recommendations for international students: Required—TOEFL. *Application deadline:* For fall admission, 2/1 priority date for domestic and international students; for spring admission, 10/15 priority date for domestic and international students. Applications are processed on a rolling basis. Application fee: $65. Electronic applications accepted. *Expenses:* Tuition: Full-time $15,300; part-time $850 per credit hour. Required fees: $110 per semester. Tuition and fees vary according to degree level. *Financial support:* In 2009–10, 677 students received support; research assistantships with tuition reimbursements available, teaching assistantships with tuition reimbursements available, career-related internships or fieldwork, Federal Work-Study, scholarships/grants, and tuition waivers (partial) available. Support available to part-time students. Financial award application deadline: 4/15; financial award applicants required to submit FAFSA. *Faculty research:* Somatic psychology, comparative psychology, art therapy, transpersonal psychology, eco-psychology. *Application contact:* David Townes, Senior Admissions Counselor, 415-575-6152, Fax: 415-575-1268, E-mail: dtownes@ciis.edu.

Columbia College Chicago, Graduate School, Program in Dance/Movement Therapy, Chicago, IL 60605-1996. Offers MA, Certificate. Part-time programs available. *Degree requirements:* For master's, thesis, internship. *Entrance requirements:* For master's, movement assessment, interview, minimum GPA of 3.0. Additional exam requirements/recommendations for international students: Required—TOEFL (minimum score 550 paper-based; 213 computer-based). *Expenses:* Tuition: Part-time $651 per credit hour. Required fees: $651 per credit hour. $205 per semester. One-time fee: $285 part-time. Tuition and fees vary according to program.

Drexel University, College of Nursing and Health Professions, Program in Creative Arts in Therapy, Specialization in Dance/Movement Therapy, Philadelphia, PA 19104-2875. Offers MA, PMC. Part-time programs available. *Degree requirements:* For master's, comprehensive exam, thesis. *Entrance requirements:* For master's, GRE General Test or MAT, audition, interview, minimum GPA of 2.75. Electronic applications accepted. *Faculty research:* Family nonverbal communication, early intervention, sexual abuse.

Drexel University, College of Nursing and Health Professions, Program in Creative Arts in Therapy, Specialization in Music Therapy, Philadelphia, PA 19104-2875. Offers MA, PMC. Part-time programs available. *Degree requirements:* For master's, comprehensive exam, thesis. *Entrance requirements:* For master's, GRE General Test or MAT, audition, interview, minimum GPA of 2.75. Electronic applications accepted. *Faculty research:* Early childhood intervention through creative art therapies, rhythm and dementia, music therapy and bulimia, assessment of adolescent suicide.

East Carolina University, Graduate School, College of Fine Arts and Communication, School of Music, Greenville, NC 27858-4353. Offers music education (MM); music therapy (MM); performance (MM); theory and composition (MM). *Accreditation:* NASM. Part-time programs available. *Degree requirements:* For master's, comprehensive exam, thesis optional. *Entrance requirements:* For master's, GRE General Test or MAT. Additional exam requirements/recommendations for international students: Required—TOEFL.

Florida State University, The Graduate School, College of Music, Tallahassee, FL 32306. Offers accompanying (MM); arts administration (MA); choral conducting (MM); composition (MM, DM); ethnomusicology (MM); general music (MA); instrumental accompanying (MM); instrumental conducting (MM); jazz studies (MM); music education (MM Ed, PhD); music theory (MM, PhD); music therapy (MM); musicology (MM, PhD), including ethnomusicology (PhD), historical musicology; opera (MM); performance (MM, DM); piano pedagogy (MM); piano technology (MA); vocal accompanying (MM). *Accreditation:* NASM. *Faculty:* 88 full-time, 13 part-time/adjunct. *Students:* 406 full-time (211 women); includes 98 minority (28 African Americans, 38 Asian Americans or Pacific Islanders, 32 Hispanic Americans). Average age 26. 525 applicants, 38% accepted, 145 enrolled. In 2009, 102 master's, 41 doctorates awarded. *Degree requirements:* For master's, comprehensive exam (for some programs), thesis (for some programs), departmental qualifying exam; for doctorate, comprehensive exam (for some programs), thesis/dissertation, departmental qualifying exam. *Entrance requirements:* For master's and doctorate, audition, GRE General Test or minimum GPA of 3.0. Additional exam requirements/recommendations for international students: Required—TOEFL (minimum score 550 paper-based; 213 computer-based). *Application deadline:* For fall admission, 7/1 for domestic students, 5/2 for international students; for spring admission, 11/3 for domestic students, 9/1 for international students. Applications are processed on a rolling basis. Application fee: $30. Electronic applications accepted. *Expenses:* Tuition, state resident: full-time $7413. Tuition, nonresident: full-time $22,567. *Financial support:* In 2009–10, 225 students received support, including 3 fellowships with full tuition reimbursements available (averaging $15,000 per year), 9 research assistantships with full tuition reimbursements available (averaging $4,000 per year), 173 teaching assistantships with full tuition reimbursements available (averaging $4,000 per year); career-related internships or fieldwork, Federal Work-Study, and tuition waivers (partial) also available. Support available to part-time students. Financial award application deadline: 2/28; financial award applicants required to submit FAFSA. *Unit head:* Don Gibson, Dean, 850-644-4361, Fax: 850-644-2033. *Application contact:* Dr. Seth Beckman, Senior Associate Dean for Academic Affairs/Director of Graduate Studies, 850-644-5848, Fax: 850-644-2033, E-mail: sbeckman@admin.fsu.edu.

Georgia College & State University, Graduate School, College of Health Sciences, Program in Music Therapy, Milledgeville, GA 31061. Offers MMT. Part-time and evening/weekend programs available. Postbaccalaureate distance learning degree programs offered (minimal on-campus study). *Faculty:* 3 full-time (2 women). *Students:* 5 full-time (all women), 9 part-time (7 women); includes 3 minority (2 African Americans, 1 Asian American or Pacific Islander), 1 international. Average age 27. 9 applicants, 89% accepted, 6 enrolled. In 2009, 2 master's awarded. *Degree requirements:* For master's, comprehensive exam, thesis or alternative. *Entrance requirements:* For master's, MAT or GRE, bachelor's degree in music therapy or equivalent, 2 letters of recommendation. Additional exam requirements/recommendations for international students: Recommended—TOEFL (minimum score 550 paper-based; 213 computer-based; 79 iBT). *Application deadline:* For fall admission, 7/1 for domestic students; for spring admission, 11/15 for domestic students. Applications are processed on a rolling basis. Application fee: $40 ($0 for international students). Electronic applications accepted. *Expenses:* Tuition, area resident: Part-time $241 per credit hour. Tuition, state resident: full-time $4338. Tuition, nonresident: full-time $17,352; part-time $964 per credit hour. Required fees: $609 per semester. Tuition and fees vary according to course load and campus/location. *Financial support:* In 2009–10, 1 research assistantship was awarded; career-related internships or fieldwork and unspecified assistantships also available. Support available to part-time students. Financial award application deadline: 3/1; financial award applicants required to submit FAFSA. *Unit head:* Dr. Chesley Mercado, Director, 478-445-2645, Fax: 478-445-2645, E-mail: chesley.mercado@gcsu.edu. *Application contact:* Dr. Chesley Mercado, Director, 478-445-2645, Fax: 478-445-2645, E-mail: chesley.mercado@gcsu.edu.

Immaculata University, College of Graduate Studies, Program in Music Therapy, Immaculata, PA 19345. Offers MA. *Accreditation:* NASM. Part-time and evening/weekend programs available. *Degree requirements:* For master's, comprehensive exam, thesis optional. *Entrance requirements:* For master's, GRE General Test or MAT, minimum GPA of 3.0. Additional exam requirements/recommendations for international students: Required—TOEFL. Electronic applications accepted. *Faculty research:* Biofeedback music laboratory, experimental music therapy, virtual arts therapies, sound beam.

Lesley University, Graduate School of Arts and Social Sciences, Division of Expressive Therapies, Cambridge, MA 02138-2790. Offers art (MA); dance (MA); expressive therapies (MA, PhD, CAGS); music (MA). Terminal master's awarded for partial completion of doctoral program. *Degree requirements:* For master's, internship, practicum; for doctorate, thesis/dissertation. *Entrance requirements:* For master's, art portfolio, performance DVD; for doctorate, GRE or MAT. Additional exam requirements/recommendations for international students: Required—TOEFL (minimum score 550 paper-based; 213 computer-based; 80 iBT).

Loyola University New Orleans, College of Music and Fine Arts, New Orleans, LA 70118-6195. Offers music therapy (MMT); performance (MM). *Accreditation:* NASM. Part-time programs available. *Students:* 17 full-time (8 women), 4 part-time (all women); includes 5 minority (4 African Americans, 1 Hispanic American), 1 international. Average age 25. 22 applicants, 68% accepted, 11 enrolled. In 2009, 8 master's awarded. *Degree requirements:* For master's, comprehensive exam, thesis, comprehensive written and oral exams. *Entrance requirements:* For master's, performance audition, appropriate bachelor's degree, minimum GPA of 3.0, letters of recommendation, resume. Additional exam requirements/recommendations for international students: Required—TOEFL (minimum score 550 paper-based; 213 computer-based). *Application deadline:* For fall admission, 8/15 priority date for domestic and international students; for spring admission, 1/1 priority date for domestic and international students. Applications are processed on a rolling basis. Application fee: $20. Electronic applications accepted. *Expenses:* Contact institution. *Financial support:* Career-related internships or fieldwork, Federal Work-Study, institutionally sponsored loans, scholarships/grants, and unspecified assistantships available. Support available to part-time students. Financial award application deadline: 5/1; financial award applicants required to submit FAFSA. *Faculty research:* Music business, music therapy, musicology, music theory, music education. *Unit head:* Donald R. Boomgaarden, Dean, 504-865-3039, Fax: 504-865-2852, E-mail: deancmfa@loyno.edu. *Application contact:* Anthony A. Decuir, Associate Dean, 504-865-3037, Fax: 504-865-2852, E-mail: decuir@loyno.edu.

Maryville University of Saint Louis, School of Health Professions, Program in Music Therapy, St. Louis, MO 63141-7299. Offers MMT. *Accreditation:* NASM. Part-time programs available. *Students:* 3 full-time (all women), 4 part-time (all women), 2 international. Average age 36. In 2009, 1 master's awarded. *Entrance requirements:* For master's, music audition, interview, minimum undergraduate GPA of 3.0, 3 letters of recommendation. Additional exam requirements/recommendations for international students: Required—TOEFL (minimum score 550 paper-based). *Application deadline:* Applications are processed on a rolling basis. Application fee: $40 ($60 for international students). Electronic applications accepted. *Expenses:* Tuition: Full-time $20,384; part-time $627.50 per credit hour. Required fees: $100 per semester. *Financial support:* Application deadline: 3/1. *Unit head:* Dr. Cynthia Briggs, Director, 314-529-9441, Fax: 314-529-9495, E-mail: cbriggs@maryville.edu. *Application contact:* Dr. Cynthia Briggs, Director, 314-529-9441, Fax: 314-529-9495, E-mail: cbriggs@maryville.edu.

Marywood University, Academic Affairs, Insalaco College of Creative and Performing Arts, Music, Theatre and Dance Department, Program in Music Therapy, Scranton, PA 18509-1598. Offers MMT, Certificate. *Accreditation:* NASM. *Students:* 2 full-time (1 woman). Average age 28. *Entrance requirements:* Additional exam requirements/recommendations for international students: Required—TOEFL (minimum score 550 paper-based; 213 computer-based; 79 iBT). *Application deadline:* For fall admission, 4/1 priority date for domestic students, 3/31 priority date for international students; for spring admission, 11/1 priority date for domestic students, 8/31 priority date for international students. Applications are processed on a rolling basis. Application fee: $35. Electronic applications accepted. *Expenses:* Tuition: Part-time $715 per credit. Required fees: $270 per semester. Tuition and fees vary according to degree level, campus/location and program. *Financial support:* Career-related internships or fieldwork, scholarships/grants, and unspecified assistantships available. Support available to part-time students. Financial award application deadline: 6/30; financial award applicants required to submit FAFSA. *Application contact:* Tammy Manka, Assistant Director of Graduate Admissions, 866-279-9663, E-mail: tmanka@marywood.edu.

• **Michigan State University,** The Graduate School, College of Music, East Lansing, MI 48824. Offers collaborative piano (M Mus); jazz studies (M Mus); music (PhD); music composition (M Mus, DMA); music conducting (M Mus, DMA); music education (M Mus); music performance (M Mus, DMA); music theory (M Mus); music therapy (M Mus); musicology (MA); piano pedagogy (M Mus). *Accreditation:* NASM. *Faculty:* 57 full-time (14 women), 2 part-time/adjunct (0 women). *Students:* 234 full-time (120 women), 41 part-time (28 women); includes 30 minority (9 African Americans, 6 American Indian/Alaska Native, 10 Asian Americans or Pacific Islanders, 5 Hispanic Americans), 107 international. Average age 29. 378 applicants, 21% accepted. In 2009, 57 master's, 34 doctorates awarded. *Entrance requirements:* Additional exam requirements/recommendations for international students: Required—TOEFL. Electronic applications accepted. *Expenses:* Tuition, state resident: part-time $478.25 per credit hour. Tuition, nonresident: part-time $966.50 per credit hour. Part-time tuition and fees vary according to program. *Financial support:* In 2009–10, 15 research assistantships with tuition reimbursements (averaging $6,188 per year), 86 teaching assistantships with tuition reimbursements (averaging $6,110 per year) were awarded. *Unit head:* Prof. James B. Forger, Dean, 517-355-4583, Fax: 517-432-7081, E-mail: forger@msu.edu. *Application contact:* Anne Simon, Assistant to the Associate Dean for Graduate Studies and Research, 517-353-9122, Fax: 517-432-2880, E-mail: musgrad@msu.edu.

Molloy College, Graduate Music Therapy Program, Rockville Centre, NY 11571-5002. Offers MS. *Faculty:* 2 full-time (1 woman), 2 part-time/adjunct (both women). *Students:* 9 full-time (8 women), 19 part-time (13 women); includes 2 African Americans, 4 Asian Americans or Pacific Islanders, 1 Hispanic American. Average age 32. *Application deadline:* Applications are processed on a rolling basis. *Expenses:* Tuition: Part-time $765 per credit. Required fees: $340 per semester. *Application contact:* Dr. Mary O'Shaughnessy, Interim Associate Dean/Director, 516-678-5000 Ext. 6838, Fax: 516-256-2267, E-mail: moshaughnessy@molloy.edu.

Montclair State University, The Graduate School, School of the Arts, Department of Music, Montclair, NJ 07043-1624. Offers music (AD); music education (MA); music therapy (MA); performance (MA, Certificate); theory/composition (MA). *Accreditation:* NASM. Part-time and evening/weekend programs available. *Faculty:* 19 full-time (7 women), 95 part-time/adjunct (41 women). *Students:* 21 full-time (11 women), 43 part-time (25 women). Average age 31. 44 applicants, 68% accepted, 21 enrolled. In 2009, 7 master's, 4 other advanced degrees awarded. *Degree requirements:* For master's, comprehensive exam, compositions, recitals, or thesis. *Entrance requirements:* For master's, GRE General Test, audition; teaching certificate (MA in music education). Additional exam requirements/recommendations for international students: Required—TOEFL (minimum score 83 computer-based), or IELTS. *Application deadline:* For fall admission, 6/1 for international students; for spring admission, 10/1 for international students. Applications are processed on a rolling basis. Application fee: $60. Electronic applications accepted. *Expenses:* Tuition, area resident: Part-time $486.74 per credit. Tuition, state resident: part-time $486.74 per credit. Tuition, nonresident: part-time $751.34 per credit. Tuition and fees vary according to degree level and program. *Financial support:* In 2009–10, 3 research assistantships with full tuition reimbursements (averaging $7,000 per year) were awarded; Federal Work-Study, scholarships/grants, and unspecified assistantships also available. Support available to part-time students. Financial award application deadline: 3/1; financial award applicants required to submit FAFSA. *Unit head:* Prof. Robert Aldridge, Chairperson, 973-655-7212. *Application contact:* Amy Aiello, Director of Graduate Admissions and Operations, 973-655-5147, Fax: 973-655-7869, E-mail: graduate.school@montclair.edu.

Naropa University, Graduate Programs, Program in Somatic Counseling Psychotherapy, Concentration in Dance/Movement Therapy, Boulder, CO 80302-6697. Offers MA. Part-time programs available. *Degree requirements:* For master's, comprehensive exam, thesis, internship, fieldwork, portfolio. *Entrance requirements:* For master's, in-person interview, course work in psychology and anatomy, experience in 3 forms of dance, resume, letter of interest, 3 letters of recommendation. Additional exam requirements/recommendations for international students: Required—TOEFL (minimum score 600 paper-based; 250 computer-based). Electronic applications accepted.

Nazareth College of Rochester, Graduate Studies, Department of Creative Arts Therapy, Program in Music Therapy, Rochester, NY 14618-3790. Offers MS. *Entrance requirements:* For master's, audition, minimum GPA of 3.0.

New York University, Steinhardt School of Culture, Education, and Human Development, Department of Music and Performing Arts Professions, Program in Drama Therapy, New York, NY 10012-1019. Offers MA. Part-time programs available. *Students:* 31 full-time (27 women), 11 part-time (8 women); includes 5 minority (3 African Americans, 1 American Indian/Alaska Native, 1 Hispanic American), 4 international. Average age 30. 45 applicants, 44% accepted, 17 enrolled. In 2009, 12 master's awarded. *Degree requirements:* For master's, thesis (for some programs). *Entrance requirements:* For master's, audition, interview. Additional exam requirements/recommendations for international students: Required—TOEFL. *Application deadline:* For fall admission, 12/15 priority date for domestic and international students; for spring admission, 11/1 for domestic and international students. Applications are processed on a rolling basis. Application fee: $75. Electronic applications accepted. *Expenses:* Tuition: Full-time $30,528; part-time $1272 per credit. Required fees: $2177. *Financial support:* Career-related internships or fieldwork, Federal Work-Study, institutionally sponsored loans, scholarships/grants, and tuition waivers (partial) available. Support available to part-time students. Financial award application deadline: 2/1; financial award applicants required to submit FAFSA. *Faculty research:* Meaning of role in drama, therapy, and everyday life; clinical approaches to drama therapy; trauma effects on children. *Unit head:* Dr. Robert Landy, Director, 212-998-5424. *Application contact:* 212-998-5030, Fax: 212-995-4328, E-mail: steinhardt.gradadmissions@nyu.edu.

New York University, Steinhardt School of Culture, Education, and Human Development, Department of Music and Performing Arts Professions, Program in Music Therapy, New York, NY 10012-1019. Offers MA. Part-time programs available. *Students:* 25 full-time (20 women), 20 part-time (7 women); includes 5 minority (1 African American, 2 Asian Americans or Pacific Islanders, 2 Hispanic Americans), 16 international. Average age 32. 66 applicants, 38% accepted, 17 enrolled. In 2009, 22 master's awarded. *Degree requirements:* For master's, thesis (for some programs). *Entrance requirements:* For master's, audition, interview. Additional exam requirements/recommendations for international students: Required—TOEFL. *Application deadline:* For fall admission, 12/15 priority date for domestic and international students. Applications are processed on a rolling basis. Application fee: $75. Electronic applications accepted. *Expenses:* Tuition: Full-time $30,528; part-time $1272 per credit. Required fees: $2177. *Financial support:* Career-related internships or fieldwork, Federal Work-Study, institutionally sponsored loans, scholarships/grants, and tuition waivers (partial) available. Support available to part-time students. Financial award application deadline: 2/1; financial award applicants required to submit FAFSA. *Faculty research:* Music therapy in special education, including autism and emotional disabilities, guided imagery. *Unit head:* Prof. Barbara Hesser, Director, 212-998-5424, Fax: 212-995-4043. *Application contact:* 212-998-5030, Fax: 212-995-4328, E-mail: steinhardt.gradadmissions@nyu.edu.

Ohio University, Graduate College, College of Fine Arts, School of Music, Athens, OH 45701-2979. Offers accompanying (MM); composition (MM); conducting (MM); history/literature (MM); music education (MM); music therapy (MM); performance (MM, Certificate); performance/pedagogy (MM); theory (MM). *Accreditation:* NASM. Part-time and evening/weekend programs available. Postbaccalaureate distance learning degree programs offered (minimal on-campus study). *Faculty:* 35 full-time (10 women), 1 part-time/adjunct (0 women). *Students:* 42 full-time (19 women), 11 part-time (8 women); includes 5 minority (2 African Americans, 1 Asian American or Pacific Islander, 2 Hispanic Americans), 10 international. 85 applicants, 59% accepted, 22 enrolled. In 2009, 22 master's awarded. *Degree requirements:* For master's, comprehensive exam, thesis (for some programs), oral exam. *Entrance requirements:* For master's, audition, interview, portfolio, recordings (varies by program). Additional exam requirements/recommendations for international students: Required—TOEFL (minimum score 550 paper-based; 80 iBT) or IELTS Academic (minimum score 6.5). *Application deadline:* For fall admission, 1/1 priority date for domestic and international students. Application fee: $50 ($55 for international students). Electronic applications accepted. *Expenses:* Tuition, state resident: full-time $7839; part-time $323 per quarter hour. Tuition, nonresident: full-time $15,831; part-time $654 per quarter hour. Required fees: $2931. *Financial support:* In 2009–10, 35 teaching assistantships with full and partial tuition reimbursements (averaging $4,500 per year) were awarded; career-related internships or fieldwork, Federal Work-Study, institutionally sponsored loans, and tuition waivers (full and partial) also available. Financial award application deadline: 1/1. *Unit head:* Dr. W. Michael Parkinson, Director, 740-593-4244, Fax: 740-593-1429, E-mail: parkinsw@ohio.edu. *Application contact:* Dr. Richard Wetzel, Graduate Chair, 740-593-1652, Fax: 740-593-1429, E-mail: wetzel@ohio.edu.

Pratt Institute, School of Art and Design, Programs in Creative Arts Therapy, Brooklyn, NY 11205-3899. Offers art therapy and creativity development (MPS); art therapy-special education (MPS); dance/movement therapy (MS). *Accreditation:* NASAD (one or more programs are accredited). Part-time programs available. *Faculty:* 3 full-time (all women), 19 part-time/adjunct (16 women). *Students:* 105 full-time (102 women), 4 part-time (all women); includes 19 minority (6 African Americans, 3 Asian Americans or Pacific Islanders, 10 Hispanic Americans), 6 international. Average age 30. 197 applicants, 90% accepted, 33 enrolled. In 2009, 30 master's awarded. *Degree requirements:* For master's, thesis. *Entrance requirements:* For master's, letters of recommendation, portfolio. Additional exam requirements/recommendations for international students: Required—TOEFL (minimum score 600 paper-based; 250 computer-based; 100 iBT). *Application deadline:* For fall admission, 1/5 for domestic and international students; for spring admission, 10/1 for domestic and international students. Applications are processed on a rolling basis. Application fee: $50 ($90 for international students). Electronic applications accepted. *Expenses:* Tuition: Full-time $22,734. Required fees: $1280. *Financial support:* Career-related internships or fieldwork, Federal Work-Study, institutionally sponsored loans, scholarships/grants, health care benefits, tuition waivers (full), and unspecified assistantships available. Support available to part-time students. Financial award application deadline: 2/1; financial award applicants required to submit FAFSA. *Faculty research:* Psychology and aesthetic interaction, art therapy and AIDS, art therapy and autism, art diagnosis. *Unit head:* Jean Davis, Chairperson, 718-636-3428, E-mail: jdavis@pratt.edu. *Application contact:* Young Hah, Director of Graduate Admissions, 718-636-3683, Fax: 718-399-4242, E-mail: yhah@pratt.edu.

See Close-Up on page 119.

Radford University, College of Graduate and Professional Studies, College of Visual and Performing Arts, Department of Music, Radford, VA 24142. Offers music (MA); music education (MS); music therapy (MS). *Accreditation:* NASM. Part-time programs available. *Faculty:* 9 full-time (2 women), 3 part-time/adjunct (1 woman). *Students:* 12 full-time (8 women), 4 part-time (all women); includes 3 minority (all African Americans), 1 international. Average age 26. 8 applicants, 88% accepted, 4 enrolled. In 2009, 5 master's awarded. *Degree requirements:* For master's, comprehensive exam, thesis or alternative. *Entrance requirements:* For master's, GRE, major field test in music or PRAXIS II (content knowledge), written diagnostics exams in music, minimum GPA of 2.75; 3 letters of reference. Additional exam requirements/recommendations for international students: Required—TOEFL (minimum score 550 paper-based; 213 computer-based; 79 iBT). *Application deadline:* For fall admission, 12/1 for international students; for spring admission, 7/1 for international students. Applications are processed on a rolling basis. Application fee: $50. Electronic applications accepted. *Expenses:* Tuition, state resident: full-time $5086; part-time $211 per credit hour. Tuition, nonresident: full-time $12,608; part-time $525 per credit hour. Required fees: $2508; $105 per credit hour. *Financial support:* In 2009–10, 10 students received support, including 3 research assistantships with partial tuition reimbursements available (averaging $8,000 per year), 8 teaching assistantships with partial tuition reimbursements available (averaging $8,700 per year); career-related internships or fieldwork, Federal Work-Study, institutionally sponsored loans, scholarships/grants, and unspecified assistantships also available. Financial award application deadline: 3/1; financial award applicants required to submit FAFSA. *Unit head:* Dr. Allen F. Wojtera, Chair, 540-831-5177, Fax: 540-831-6133, E-mail: awojtera@radford.edu. *Application contact:* Graduate Admissions, 540-831-5431, Fax: 540-831-6061, E-mail: gradcollege@radford.edu.

Saint Mary-of-the-Woods College, Program in Music Therapy, Saint Mary-of-the-Woods, IN 47876. Offers MA. *Accreditation:* NASM. Part-time programs available. Postbaccalaureate distance learning degree programs offered (minimal on-campus study). *Degree requirements:* For master's, thesis or alternative, qualifying exam, portfolio completion. *Entrance requirements:* For master's, diagnostic music exam, audition. Electronic applications accepted.

Shenandoah University, Shenandoah Conservatory, Winchester, VA 22601-5195. Offers arts administration (MS); church music (MM, Certificate); composition (MM); conducting (MM); dance (MA, MS); music education (MME, DMA); music therapy (MMT, Certificate); pedagogy (MM, DMA); performance (MM, DMA, Artist Diploma); piano accompanying (MM). *Accreditation:* NASM. *Faculty:* 39 full-time (15 women), 17 part-time/adjunct (5 women). *Students:* 72 full-time (42 women), 134 part-time (83 women); includes 40 minority (14 African Americans, 22 Asian Americans or Pacific Islanders, 4 Hispanic Americans), 16 international. Average age 35. 115 applicants, 88% accepted, 70 enrolled. In 2009, 40 master's, 5 doctorates, 9 other advanced degrees awarded. *Degree requirements:* For master's, comprehensive exam (for some programs), thesis (for some programs), internship (MS), recital (MM), research teaching

Therapies—Dance, Drama, and Music

Shenandoah University (continued)

project or thesis (MME), project (MA); for doctorate, comprehensive exam, thesis/dissertation (for some programs), dissertation or teaching project, recital; for other advanced degree, research project, recital. *Entrance requirements:* For master's, audition, minimum GPA of 2.5, writing sample, resume; for doctorate, audition, minimum GPA of 3.25, 2 letters of recommendation, writing sample, resume; for other advanced degree, bachelor or master's degree; minimum GPA of 2.5. Additional exam requirements/recommendations for international students: Required—TOEFL (minimum score 550 paper-based; 213 computer-based; 79 iBT), IELTS (minimum score 6.5). *Application deadline:* Applications are processed on a rolling basis. Application fee: $30. Electronic applications accepted. *Expenses:* Tuition: Full-time $11,925; part-time $695 per credit. Required fees: $400 per semester. *Financial support:* Application deadline: 3/15. *Unit head:* Dr. Laurence A. Kaptain, Dean, 540-665-4600, Fax: 540-665-5402, E-mail: lkaptain@su.edu. *Application contact:* David Anthony, Dean of Admissions, 540-665-4581, Fax: 540-665-4627, E-mail: admit@su.edu.

State University of New York at New Paltz, Graduate School, School of Fine and Performing Arts, Department of Music, New Paltz, NY 12561. Offers music therapy (MS). *Accreditation:* NASM. Part-time programs available. *Faculty:* 4 full-time (2 women), 2 part-time/adjunct (0 women). *Students:* 19 full-time (16 women), 13 part-time (10 women); includes 3 minority (all Asian Americans or Pacific Islanders), 5 international. Average age 28. 10 applicants, 80% accepted, 7 enrolled. In 2009, 9 master's awarded. *Degree requirements:* For master's, thesis. *Entrance requirements:* For master's, audition, minimum GPA of 3.0. Additional exam requirements/recommendations for international students: Required—TOEFL (minimum score 550 paper-based; 213 computer-based; 80 iBT), IELTS (minimum score 6.5). *Application deadline:* For fall admission, 5/15 for domestic and international students; for spring admission, 11/15 for domestic and international students. Application fee: $50. Electronic applications accepted. *Financial support:* In 2009–10, 2 students received support, including 2 teaching assistantships with partial tuition reimbursements available (averaging $5,000 per year). Financial award application deadline: 8/1; financial award applicants required to submit FAFSA. *Unit head:* Dr. Edward Lundergan, Chair, 845-257-3121, E-mail: lunderge@newpaltz.edu. *Application contact:* Prof. Mary Boyle, Coordinator, 845-257-2709, E-mail: boylem@newpaltz.edu.

Temple University, Graduate School, Esther Boyer College of Music and Dance, Department of Music Education and Therapy, Philadelphia, PA 19122-6096. Offers music education (MM, PhD); music therapy (MMT, PhD). *Accreditation:* NASM. Part-time and evening/weekend programs available. *Degree requirements:* For master's, thesis; for doctorate, thesis/dissertation. *Entrance requirements:* Additional exam requirements/recommendations for international students: Required—TOEFL. Electronic applications accepted. *Faculty research:* Music learning theory, guided imagery in music, computer learning theory.

The University of Kansas, Graduate Studies, School of Music, Program in Music Therapy, Lawrence, KS 66045. Offers MME. *Students:* 9 full-time (8 women), 12 part-time (11 women); includes 2 minority (both Asian Americans or Pacific Islanders), 5 international. Average age 26. 16 applicants, 38% accepted, 4 enrolled. In 2009, 3 master's awarded. *Degree requirements:* For master's, comprehensive exam, thesis or alternative. *Entrance requirements:* For master's, GRE General Test, minimum undergraduate GPA of 3.0, video, reference letters. Additional exam requirements/recommendations for international students: Required—TOEFL (minimum score 570 paper-based; 230 computer-based; 92 iBT), IELTS; Recommended—TWE. *Application deadline:* For fall admission, 2/15 priority date for domestic students, 2/15 for international students. Applications are processed on a rolling basis. Application fee: $45 ($55 for international students). Electronic applications accepted. *Expenses:* Tuition, state resident: full-time $6492; part-time $270.50 per credit hour. Tuition, nonresident: full-time $15,510; part-time $646.25 per credit hour. Required fees: $847; $70.56 per credit hour. Tuition and fees vary according to course load and program. *Financial support:* Fellowships, research assistantships with partial tuition reimbursements, teaching assistantships with full and partial tuition reimbursements, institutionally sponsored loans, scholarships/grants, and unspecified assistantships available. Financial award application deadline: 12/15; financial award applicants required to submit FAFSA. *Faculty research:* Music therapy in health, wellness, gerontology, pediatrics, early intervention, autism and hospice; Orff music therapy; influence of music on behavior. *Unit head:* Robert Walzel, Dean, 785-864-3436, Fax: 785-864-5387, E-mail: music@ku.edu. *Application contact:* Dr. James Daugherty, Director of Graduate Studies, 785-864-9637, Fax: 785-864-9640, E-mail: jdaugher@ku.edu.

University of Miami, Graduate School, Frost School of Music, Department of Music Education and Music Therapy, Coral Gables, FL 33124. Offers music education (MM, PhD, Spec M); music therapy (MM). *Accreditation:* NASM. *Degree requirements:* For master's, thesis; for doctorate, thesis/dissertation, 2 research tools; for Spec M, thesis, research project. *Entrance requirements:* For master's and doctorate, GRE General Test. Additional exam requirements/recommendations for international students: Required—TOEFL (minimum score 550 paper-based; 213 computer-based; 59 iBT). Electronic applications accepted. *Faculty research:* Motivation, quantitative research, early childhood, instrumental music, elementary music.

University of the Pacific, Conservatory of Music, Program in Music Therapy, Stockton, CA 95211-0197. Offers MA. *Faculty:* 2 full-time (both women). *Students:* 5 full-time (all women), 13 part-time (11 women); includes 3 minority (2 Asian Americans or Pacific Islanders, 1 Hispanic American), 5 international. Average age 30. 8 applicants, 38% accepted, 2 enrolled. In 2009, 1 master's awarded. *Degree requirements:* For master's, thesis (for some programs). *Entrance requirements:* For master's, GRE General Test. Additional exam requirements/recommendations for international students: Required—TOEFL (minimum score 475 paper-based; 150 computer-based). Application fee: $75. *Financial support:* Teaching assistantships, institutionally sponsored loans available. Support available to part-time students. Financial award application deadline: 3/1; financial award applicants required to submit FAFSA. *Unit head:* Dr. Therese West, Chairperson, 209-946-3194. *Application contact:* Dr. Therese West, Chairperson, 209-946-3194.

Western Michigan University, Graduate College, College of Fine Arts, School of Music, Kalamazoo, MI 49008. Offers composition (MM); conducting (MM); music (MA); music education (MM); music therapy (MM); performance (MM). *Accreditation:* NASM.

Wilfrid Laurier University, Faculty of Graduate Studies, Faculty of Music, Waterloo, ON N2L 3C5, Canada. Offers MMT. *Entrance requirements:* For master's, 4 year honours BA in music therapy with a minimum B average in final year, grade 6 RCM and grade 10 performance ability (1 year program), 4 year honours BA in an allied area (music or psychology) with a minimum B average in final year, grade 6 RCM, grade 10 performance ability (2 year program). Additional exam requirements/recommendations for international students: Required—TOEFL (minimum score 230 computer-based; 89 iBT). Electronic applications accepted.

COLUMBIA UNIVERSITY

School of the Arts
Divisions of Film, Theatre Arts, Visual Arts, and Writing

Programs of Study

The School of the Arts offers M.F.A. degrees in film (directing, producing, and screenwriting), theater arts (acting, directing, dramaturgy, playwriting, stage management, and theater management), visual arts (new genres, painting, photography, printmaking, and sculpture), and writing (fiction, nonfiction, and poetry) and an M.A. degree in film studies. The School of the Arts accepts full-time students only. In addition, the Graduate School of Arts and Sciences offers the Ph.D. degree in drama and theater arts. The M.F.A. degree programs require 60 points of completed course work. All students take a core curriculum, which provides background in the history, theory, and literature of their field, and experience an understanding of the various disciplines taught within each program. During the first two years, students focus on workshops, lectures, and seminars in their particular disciplines. Students in film and theater arts partake in production crew work. Once the 60 points of course work are completed, each student concentrates on producing a thesis and/or completing internships under research arts status. Certain concentrations within the Theatre Arts Program require two professional internships; the Film and Writing Programs recommend internships.

Research Facilities

The Film Program offers film and video production equipment, state-of-the-art digital editing facilities, a sound stage, a screening room, and a film library. The Theatre Program offers four flexible-space theaters and ten rehearsal studios. In addition, performing venues on campus may be available for student productions. Each visual arts student is assigned a private studio (24-hour access) in Watson Hall on 115th Street and Prentis Hall on 125th Street. In addition, there are various spaces on campus where students have the opportunity to exhibit. The LeRoy Neiman Center for Print Studies provides the optimum environment to expose students to techniques in the production of intaglio, lithography, serigraphy, photography, and computer imaging. The University libraries house more than 6 million books, 4 million microfilms, and more than 26 million manuscripts. The library houses several special collections related to the arts, and it includes the Avery Architecture and Fine Arts Library. Students also have access to the Performing Arts Research Center of the New York Public Library at Lincoln Center as well as the vast holdings of the Central Research Library of the New York Public Library. There are dozens of special collections throughout New York City, such as the Film Study Center of the Museum of Modern Art, the Shubert Archives, and the Collections of the Players Club. New York City offers professional theaters, museums, galleries, movie theaters, concert halls, publishing companies, bookstores, and literary readings.

Financial Aid

The School seeks to work with students in arranging to cover costs through fellowships, scholarships, loans, and work-study. University scholarships, which are awarded by each program based upon a combination of financial need and merit, are limited. During the second year, an increased number of opportunities for work and/or service fellowships become available. The Office of Financial Aid and Admissions helps qualifying students arrange for federal financial aid, working in collaboration with Columbia's Office of Student Financial Planning.

Cost of Study

Tuition and fees for the 2010–11 school year are approximately $48,800, based on full-time matriculation of 12 to 18 credits.

Living and Housing Costs

The University estimates that students need about $21,000 to cover living expenses and housing. University Apartment Housing is available to many graduate students, at rates ranging from $700 to $1500 monthly for furnished or unfurnished singles, suites, and studios to rent individually or to share. They also offer studio and one-bedroom apartments for married students.

Student Group

Columbia has an enrollment of approximately 25,500; nearly 16,000 are graduate students. The School enrolled 867 students in 2009–10: 343 students in film, 160 in theater arts, 312 in writing, and 52 in visual arts.

Location

Columbia University (including Barnard College and Teacher's College) occupies approximately eighteen square blocks in the Morningside Heights area of Manhattan. Its neighbors include Union Theological Seminary, Jewish Theological Seminary, the Manhattan School of Music, Riverside Church and the Interchurch Center, and the Cathedral of Saint John the Divine, the world's largest Gothic cathedral and home of a progressive arts program. Riverside Park and the Hudson River are a block away. The Upper West Side stretches south along Broadway for sixty blocks to Lincoln Center and beyond to the Theatre District and incorporates vital residential neighborhoods, some of the city's finest restaurants, and several theaters and museums, including the Apollo Theatre, the National Black Theatre, and City College.

The University and The School

Columbia, founded in 1754, is composed of sixteen undergraduate, graduate, and professional schools and four affiliate institutions. In the late nineteenth century, Columbia became the first university to teach theater in the United States and, in 1916, the first to teach a course in film. The School of Dramatic Arts and Painting and Sculpture was established in 1948, although the first drawing course was taught as early as 1881. These programs were joined by film, music composition, and writing in 1965 to form the School of the Arts. Columbia also offers undergraduate majors in dance, film studies, theater arts, visual arts, and writing.

Applying

Applications are accepted for the fall semester only. All deadlines are final. The application cost for fall 2010 is $110 for the online application and $150 for the paper application. The GRE is not required for application. International students are required to take the TOEFL prior to application; the minimum score required for admission is 600 on the written test, 250 on the computer-based test, and 100 on the Internet-based test.

Correspondence and Information

Admissions Office
School of the Arts
Columbia University
2960 Broadway
305 Dodge Hall, MC 1808
New York, New York 10027
Phone: 212-854-2134
E-mail: admissions-arts@columbia.edu
Web site: http://arts.columbia.edu

Columbia University

THE FACULTY

FILM
Jamal Joseph, Chair.

Full Time Professors
Ramin Bahrani
Nico Baumbach
Andrew Bienan
Hilary Brougher
Ira Deutchman
Katherine Dieckmann
Trey Ellis
Jane Gaines
Bette Gordon
Jamal Joseph
Tom Kalin
Christopher Kelly
Daniel Kleinman
Eric Mendelsohn
Evangeline Morphos
Richard Pena
Nick Proferes
Andrew Sarris
James Schamus
June Stein

Adjunct Professors
Richard Brick
Joe Cacaci
Loren-Paul Caplin
Anne Carey
John Erman
Leon Falk
Milena Jelinek
Alan Kingsberg
David Klass
Susan Korda
Christina Lazaridi
Emanuel Levy
John Lyons
David McKenna
W. Peter Miner
Stephen Molton
Bruce Ornstein
Keith Reamer
Marie Regan
John Rubin
Oren Rudavsky
Malia Scotch-Marmo
Alexandra Sichel
Ileana Solomonoff
David Sterritt
Jane Wagner
Adrienne Weiss

THEATER ARTS
Arnold Aronson, Chair.

Full Time Professors
Arnold Aronson
Anne Bogart
Steven Chaikelson
Ruth Kreshka
Brian Kulick
Kristin Linklater
Charles Mee
Gregory Mosher
Christian Parker
Andrei Serban
Nikolaus Wolcz
W. B. Worthen

Adjunct Professors
Daniel Adamian
David Auster
Leslie Ayvazian
Victoria Bailey
Gigi Bolt
Chris Boneau
Deborah Brevoort
Christopher Bruney
Sheila Callaghan
Carolyn J. Casselman
Tom Connell
Nancy Coyne
John Dias
Olympia Dukakis
Peter Entin
Robert Fried
Barry Grove
Andrea Haring
Roy Harris
Hugh Hysell
Jessica R. Jenen
Amy Kaissar
Peter Lawrence
James Leverett
Paul Libin
Ira Mont
Michael Naumann
Qui Nguyen
Eugene O'Donovan
Barney O'Hanlon
Frank Pugliese
Carol Rocamora
William Russo
Thomas Schumacher
Larry Singer
Kelly Stuart
Lucy Thurber
Livia Vanaver
Donna Walker-Kuhne
Brannon Wiles
Linda Winer
Ursula Wolcz

VISUAL ARTS
Gregory Amenoff, Chair.

Full-Time Professors
Gregory Amenoff
Sanford Biggers
Jon Kessler
Thomas Roma
Shelly Silver
Sarah Sze
Rirkrit Tiravanija
Tomas Vu Daniel
Kara Walker

Adjunct Professors
Janine Antoni
Fia Backstrom
Jackie Battenfield
Daniel Bozhkov
Ann Craven
Mark Dion
Liam Gillick
Marc Handelman
Rachel Harrison
Dana Hoey
Michael Joo
John Kelsey
Fionn Meade
John Miller
Matt Mullican
Lisi Raskin
Jerry Saltz
Collier Schorr
Dana Schutz
Amy Sillman

Visiting Graduate Critics
Jan Avgikos
Liz Deschenes
Roe Ethridge
Jason Fox
Roni Horn
Alfredo Jaar
Tom Kalin
Deborah Kass
Jutta Koether
Matvey Levenstein
Christian Marclay
Ohad Meromi
Allan McCollum
Sarah Morris
Eileen Quinlan
Eva Respini
Josh Siegal
Steven Westfall
Terry Winters
Lisa Yskavage
Andrea Zittel

WRITING
Binnie Kirshenbaum, Chair.

Full Time Professors
Donald Antrim
Josh Bell
Amy Benson
Lucie Brock-Broido
Nicholas Christopher
Stacey D'Erasmo
Timothy Donnelly
Lis Harris
Richard Howard
Michael Janeway
Margo Jefferson
Victor LaValle
Sam Lipsyte
Richard Locke
Phillip Lopate
Ben Marcus
Patricia O'Toole
Orhan Pamuk
Oliver Sacks
Michael Scammell
Gary Shteyngart
Mark Strand
Alan Ziegler

Adjunct Professors
Emily Barton
Cris Beam
Paul Beatty
Susan Bernofsky
David Bezmozgis
Mark Bibbins
Eric Chinsky
Rebecca Curtis
Jonathan Dee
David Ebershoff
Paul Elie
Rivka Galchen
Samantha Gillison
Eamon Grennan
Bob Holman
Janette Turner Hospital
Joan Houlihan
Maureen Howard
Heidi Julavits
Paul LaFarge
Sarah Manguso
Cate Marvin
Erroll McDonald
Ethan Nosowsky
Idra Novey
Stephen O'Connor
Ed Park
Mark Jude Poirier
Alice Quinn
Jim Rasenberger
Christine Schutt
Leslie T. Sharpe
Laurie Sheck
Lorin Stein
Darcey Steinke
Terese Svoboda
Benjamin Taylor
Justin Taylor
Hannah Tinti
William Wadsworth
Marjorie Welish
James Wood
John Wray
Matvei Yankelevich
Rachel Zucker

ACADEMIC AND PROFESSIONAL PROGRAMS IN THE HUMANITIES

Section 7
History

This section contains a directory of institutions offering graduate work in history, followed by an in-depth entry submitted by an institution that chose to prepare a detailed program description. Additional information about programs listed in the directory but not augmented by an in-depth entry may be obtained by writing directly to the dean of a graduate school or chair of a department at the address given in the directory.

For programs offering related work, see also in this book *Area and Cultural Studies, Architecture, Humanities, Political Science and International Affairs,* and *Sociology, Anthropology, and Archaeology.*

CONTENTS

Program Directories

History 266
History of Medicine 294
History of Science and Technology 294
Medieval and Renaissance Studies 296
Public History 299

Close-Up

Villanova University 303

History

Adams State College, The Graduate School, Department of History, Government and Philosophy, Alamosa, CO 81102. Offers history (MA).

American Public University System, AMU/APU Graduate Programs, Charles Town, WV 25414. Offers air warfare (MA Military Studies); American Revolution (MA Military Studies); business administration (MBA); Civil War (MA Military Studies); criminal justice (MA); defense management (MA Military Studies); emergency and disaster management (MA); environmental policy and management (MS); fire science management (MA); global engagement (MA); history (MA); homeland security (MA); humanities (MA); intelligence (MA Military Studies, MA Strategic Intelligence); international peace and conflict resolution (MA); international relations and conflict resolution (MA); joint warfare (MA Military Studies); land warfare international perspective (MA Military Studies); management (MA); military history (MA); military leadership (MA Military Studies); national security studies (MA); naval warfare international (MA Military Studies); naval warfare US (MA Military Studies); political science (MA); public administration (MA); public health (MA); security management (MA); space studies (MS); special ops/LIC (MA Military Studies); sports management (MA); transportation and logistics management (MA); transportation management (MA); unconventional warfare (MA Military Studies); World War II (MA Military Studies). Programs offered via distance learning only. Part-time and evening/weekend programs available. Postbaccalaureate distance learning degree programs offered (no on-campus study). *Faculty:* 10 full-time (3 women), 188 part-time/adjunct (57 women). *Students:* 340 full-time (98 women), 3,567 part-time (790 women); includes 615 minority (317 African Americans, 28 American Indian/Alaska Native, 85 Asian Americans or Pacific Islanders, 185 Hispanic Americans), 20 international. Average age 36. 2,123 applicants, 100% accepted, 893 enrolled. In 2009, 829 degrees awarded. *Degree requirements:* For master's, comprehensive exam. *Entrance requirements:* For master's, bachelor's degree or equivalent, minimum GPA of 2.7 in last 60 hours of course work. *Application deadline:* Applications are processed on a rolling basis. Application fee: $0. Electronic applications accepted. *Financial support:* Applicants required to submit FAFSA. *Faculty research:* Military history, criminal justice, management performance, national security. *Unit head:* Dr. Frank McCluskey, Provost, 877-468-6268, Fax: 304-724-3780. *Application contact:* Terry Grant, Director of Enrollment Management, 877-468-6268, Fax: 304-724-3780, E-mail: info@apus.edu.

American University, College of Arts and Sciences, Department of History, Washington, DC 20016-8038. Offers MA, PhD. Part-time and evening/weekend programs available. *Faculty:* 22 full-time (10 women), 9 part-time/adjunct (5 women). *Students:* 40 full-time (21 women), 51 part-time (29 women); includes 11 minority (6 African Americans, 2 Asian Americans or Pacific Islanders, 3 Hispanic Americans), 4 international. Average age 30. 134 applicants, 66% accepted, 25 enrolled. In 2009, 13 master's, 1 doctorate awarded. *Degree requirements:* For master's, comprehensive exam, thesis or alternative, tools of research in foreign language, methods, history or methodology; for doctorate, thesis/dissertation, tools of research, 2 seminars, 2 colloquia. *Entrance requirements:* For master's, GRE, two letters of recommendation; for doctorate, GRE, two letters of recommendation, sample of written work. Additional exam requirements/recommendations for international students: Required—TOEFL. *Application deadline:* For fall admission, 2/1 priority date for domestic students; for spring admission, 10/1 priority date for domestic students. Application fee: $80. *Expenses:* Tuition: Full-time $22,266; part-time $1237 per credit hour. Required fees: $430. Tuition and fees vary according to program. *Financial support:* In 2009–10, 20 students received support; fellowships, research assistantships with tuition reimbursements available, teaching assistantships with tuition reimbursements available, career-related internships or fieldwork, institutionally sponsored loans, tuition waivers (full and partial), and unspecified assistantships available. Financial award application deadline: 2/1. *Faculty research:* U. S. political and diplomatic history, modern European history, U. S. social and cultural history, recent U. S. history, early republic, modern Europe. *Unit head:* Dr. Robert Griffith, Chair, 202-885-2419, Fax: 202-885-6166, E-mail: bgriff@american.edu. *Application contact:* Kathleen Clowery, Director of Graduate Admissions, 202-885-3621, Fax: 202-885-1505, E-mail: clowery@american.edu.

American University of Beirut, Graduate Programs, Faculty of Arts and Sciences, Beirut, Lebanon. Offers anthropology (MA); Arabic language and literature (MA); archaeology (MA); biology (MS); chemistry (MS); computer science (MS); economics (MA); education (MA); English language (MA); English literature (MA); environmental policy planning (MSES); financial economics (MAFE); geology (MS); history (MA); mathematics (MA, MS); Middle Eastern studies (MA); philosophy (MA); physics (MS); political studies (MA); psychology (MA); public administration (MA); sociology (MA); statistics (MA, MS). Part-time programs available. *Degree requirements:* For master's, one foreign language, comprehensive exam, thesis (for some programs). *Entrance requirements:* For master's, GRE, letter of recommendation. Additional exam requirements/recommendations for international students: Required—TOEFL (minimum score 600 paper-based; 250 computer-based; 100 iBT), IELTS (minimum score 7.5). *Faculty research:* String theory and supergravity; computer graphics; algebra and number theory; popular Arabic literature; marine and freshwater biology; integrating science, math and technology.

Andrews University, School of Graduate Studies, College of Arts and Sciences, Department of History, Berrien Springs, MI 49104. Offers MA, MAT. Part-time programs available. *Faculty:* 5 full-time (3 women). *Degree requirements:* For master's, variable foreign language requirement, thesis optional. *Entrance requirements:* For master's, GRE Subject Test. *Application deadline:* Applications are processed on a rolling basis. Application fee: $40. *Financial support:* Fellowships, Federal Work-Study, institutionally sponsored loans, and unspecified assistantships available. Financial award application deadline: 6/1. *Faculty research:* American intellectual history, Civil War, American church history, modern German history. *Unit head:* Dr. Gary G. Land, Chairman, 269-471-3292. *Application contact:* Carolyn Hurst, Supervisor of Graduate Admission, 800-253-2874, Fax: 269-471-3228, E-mail: graduate@andrews.edu.

Angelo State University, College of Graduate Studies, College of Liberal and Fine Arts, Department of History, San Angelo, TX 76909. Offers MA. Part-time and evening/weekend programs available. *Faculty:* 3 full-time (0 women). *Students:* 2 full-time (1 woman), 10 part-time (6 women). Average age 38. 6 applicants, 100% accepted, 6 enrolled. In 2009, 2 master's awarded. *Degree requirements:* For master's, comprehensive exam, thesis optional. *Entrance requirements:* For master's, GRE General Test. Additional exam requirements/recommendations for international students: Required—TOEFL or IELTS. *Application deadline:* For fall admission, 7/15 priority date for domestic students, 6/10 for international students; for spring admission, 12/1 priority date for domestic students, 11/1 for international students. Applications are processed on a rolling basis. Application fee: $40 ($50 for international students). Electronic applications accepted. *Expenses:* Tuition, state resident: full-time $3396; part-time $142 per credit hour. Tuition, nonresident: full-time $10,152; part-time $423 per credit hour. Required fees: $1786; $36.25 per credit hour. $494 per semester. Full-time tuition and fees vary according to course load, degree level and program. *Financial support:* In 2009–10, 4 students received support. Federal Work-Study, scholarships/grants, and unspecified assistantships available. Support available to part-time students. Financial award application deadline: 3/1. *Unit head:* Dr. Ken Heineman, Department Head, 325-942-2113, Fax: 325-942-2057, E-mail: kenneth.heineman@angelo.edu. *Application contact:* Dr. Ken Heineman, Department Head, 325-942-2113, Fax: 325-942-2057, E-mail: kenneth.heineman@angelo.edu.

Appalachian State University, Cratis D. Williams Graduate School, Department of History, Boone, NC 28608. Offers history (MA); history education (MA); public history (MA). Part-time programs available. Postbaccalaureate distance learning degree programs offered (no on-campus study). *Faculty:* 26 full-time (8 women), 3 part-time/adjunct (1 woman). *Students:* 29 full-time (13 women), 15 part-time (3 women); includes 1 minority (African American). 33 applicants, 76% accepted, 16 enrolled. In 2009, 15 master's awarded. *Degree requirements:* For master's, one foreign language, comprehensive exam, thesis (for some programs). *Entrance requirements:* For master's, GRE General Test, 3 letters of recommendation. Additional exam requirements/recommendations for international students: Required—TOEFL (minimum score 570 paper-based; 230 computer-based; 79 iBT), IELTS (minimum score 6.5). *Application deadline:* For fall admission, 7/1 for domestic students, 2/1 for international students; for spring admission, 11/1 for domestic students, 7/1 for international students. Applications are processed on a rolling basis. Application fee: $50. Electronic applications accepted. *Expenses:* Tuition, state resident: full-time $2960. Tuition, nonresident: full-time $14,051. Required fees: $2320. *Financial support:* In 2009–10, 4 research assistantships (averaging $10,000 per year), 7 teaching assistantships (averaging $8,000 per year) were awarded; fellowships, career-related internships or fieldwork, Federal Work-Study, scholarships/grants, and unspecified assistantships also available. Financial award application deadline: 4/1; financial award applicants required to submit FAFSA. *Faculty research:* Women's history, social/cultural history, U.S. history, Latin America, medieval studies. Total annual research expenditures: $126,000. *Unit head:* Dr. Lucinda Beier, Chairperson, 828-262-2282, E-mail: beierlm@appstate.edu. *Application contact:* Dr. Lisa Holliday, Graduate Program Director, 828-262-6014, E-mail: hollidaylr@appstate.edu.

Arizona State University, Graduate College, College of Liberal Arts and Sciences, Division of Humanities, Department of History, Tempe, AZ 85287. Offers East/Southeast Asian history (MA, PhD); European history (MA, PhD); Latin American studies (MA, PhD); North American history (MA, PhD); public history (MA). *Degree requirements:* For master's, thesis or alternative; for doctorate, 2 foreign languages, thesis/dissertation. *Entrance requirements:* For master's and doctorate, GRE.

Arkansas State University—Jonesboro, Graduate School, College of Humanities and Social Sciences, Department of History, Jonesboro, State University, AR 72467. Offers history (MA); history education (MSE, SCCT); social science education (MSE). Part-time programs available. *Faculty:* 14 full-time (7 women), 2 part-time/adjunct (both women). *Students:* 13 full-time (7 women), 30 part-time (16 women); includes 5 minority (4 African Americans, 1 Hispanic American). Average age 33. 30 applicants, 90% accepted, 21 enrolled. In 2009, 14 master's, 3 other advanced degrees awarded. *Degree requirements:* For master's, comprehensive exam, thesis or alternative; for SCCT, comprehensive exam. *Entrance requirements:* For master's, GRE General Test or MAT, GMAT, appropriate bachelor's degree, letters of reference, official transcript, valid teaching certificate (for MSE), immunization records; for SCCT, GRE General Test or MAT, interview, master's degree, letters of reference, official transcript, immunization records. Additional exam requirements/recommendations for international students: Required—TOEFL (minimum score 550 paper-based; 213 computer-based; 79 iBT), IELTS (minimum score 6). *Application deadline:* For fall admission, 7/1 for domestic and international students; for spring admission, 11/15 for domestic students, 11/13 for international students. Applications are processed on a rolling basis. Application fee: $30 ($40 for international students). Electronic applications accepted. *Expenses:* Tuition, state resident: full-time $3744; part-time $208 per credit hour. Tuition, nonresident: full-time $9540; part-time $530 per credit hour. Required fees: $896; $47 per credit hour. $25 per term. One-time fee: $50. Tuition and fees vary according to course load and program. *Financial support:* In 2009–10, 10 students received support. Career-related internships or fieldwork, scholarships/grants, and unspecified assistantships available. Financial award application deadline: 7/1; financial award applicants required to submit FAFSA. *Unit head:* Dr. Gina Hogue, Chair, 870-972-3046, Fax: 870-972-2880, E-mail: ghogue@astate.edu. *Application contact:* Dr. Andrew Sustich, Dean of the Graduate School, 870-972-3029, Fax: 870-972-3857, E-mail: sustich@astate.edu.

Arkansas Tech University, Graduate College, College of Arts and Humanities, Russellville, AR 72801. Offers communication (MLA); English (M Ed, MA); fine arts (MLA); history (MA); multi-media journalism (MA); psychology (MS); social science (MLA); Spanish (MA, MLA); teaching English as a second language (MA, MLA). Part-time programs available. *Students:* 39 full-time (30 women), 80 part-time (63 women); includes 11 minority (3 African Americans, 1 American Indian/Alaska Native, 1 Asian American or Pacific Islander, 6 Hispanic Americans), 23 international. Average age 33. In 2009, 70 master's awarded. *Degree requirements:* For master's, comprehensive exam (for some programs), thesis (for some programs), project. *Entrance requirements:* For master's, GRE General Test or MAT. Additional exam requirements/recommendations for international students: Required—TOEFL (minimum score 550 paper-based; 213 computer-based; 79 iBT), IELTS (minimum score 6). *Application deadline:* For fall admission, 3/1 priority date for domestic students, 5/1 priority date for international students; for spring admission, 10/1 priority date for domestic and international students. Applications are processed on a rolling basis. Application fee: $0 ($50 for international students). Electronic applications accepted. *Expenses:* Tuition, state resident: full-time $3438; part-time $191 per hour. Tuition, nonresident: full-time $6876; part-time $382 per hour. Required fees: $482; $9 per credit hour. $140 per semester. Tuition and fees vary according to course load. *Financial support:* In 2009–10, teaching assistantships with full tuition reimbursements (averaging $4,000 per year); research assistantships, career-related internships or fieldwork, Federal Work-Study, scholarships/grants, health care benefits, and unspecified assistantships also available. Support available to part-time students. Financial award application deadline: 4/15; financial award applicants required to submit FAFSA. *Unit head:* Dr. Micheal Tarver, Dean, 479-968-0274, Fax: 479-964-0812, E-mail: mtarver@atu.edu. *Application contact:* Dr. Mary B. Gunter, Dean of Graduate College, 479-968-0398, Fax: 479-964-0542, E-mail: graduate.school@atu.edu.

Armstrong Atlantic State University, School of Graduate Studies, Program in History, Savannah, GA 31419-1997. Offers MA. Part-time and evening/weekend programs available. *Degree requirements:* For master's, one foreign language, comprehensive exam, thesis (for some programs). *Entrance requirements:* For master's, GRE General Test, minimum GPA of 3.0, letters of recommendation, BA in history or equivalent. Additional exam requirements/recommendations for international students: Required—TOEFL (minimum score 523 paper-based; 193 computer-based). Electronic applications accepted. *Faculty research:* Public history; European, Latin American, African, and United State history.

Ashland Theological Seminary, Graduate Programs, Ashland, OH 44805. Offers biblical and theological studies (MA, MAR), including New Testament (MA), Old Testament (MA); Christian ministry (MAPT); Christian studies (Diploma); clinical counseling (michigan) (MAC); clinical counsseling (Ohio) (MACC), including anabaptism, pietism; historical studies (MA), including church history; ministry (D Min); pastoral ministry (M Div); theological studies (MA). *Accreditation:* ATS. Part-time programs available. *Faculty:* 23 full-time (7 women), 74 part-time/adjunct (28 women). *Students:* 663 full-time (343 women), 124 part-time (65 women); includes 312 minority (289 African Americans, 3 American Indian/Alaska Native, 8 Asian Americans or Pacific Islanders, 12 Hispanic Americans), 25 international. Average age 43. 173 applicants, 87% accepted, 142 enrolled. In 2009, 34 first professional degrees, 102 master's, 17 doctorates, 2 other advanced degrees awarded. *Degree requirements:* For master's, 2 foreign languages, comprehensive exam (for some programs), thesis (for some programs); for doctorate, thesis/dissertation; for M Div, 2 foreign languages, comprehensive exam (for some programs). *Entrance requirements:* For M Div, minimum GPA of 2.75; for master's, minimum undergraduate GPA of 2.75; for doctorate, M Div, minimum undergraduate GPA of 3.0. Additional exam requirements/recommendations for international students: Required—TOEFL (minimum score 500 paper-based; 65 computer-based; 173 iBT). *Application deadline:* For fall admission, 8/30 for domestic students. Applications are processed on a rolling basis. Application fee: $30. Electronic applications accepted. *Expenses:* Tuition: Full-time $10,476; part-time $345 per credit hour. Required fees: $180; $15 per course. Part-time tuition and fees vary according to course load. *Financial support:* In 2009–10, 311 students received support, including 17 teaching assistantships; research assistantships, career-related internships or fieldwork, institutionally sponsored loans, scholarships/grants, and unspecified assistantships also available. Support available to part-time students. Financial award application deadline: 5/15; financial award applicants required to submit FAFSA. *Faculty research:* Semitic languages and linguistics, rhetorical and social-scientific criticism, Anabaptist studies, inner spiritual healing, African-American clergy in film and literature. *Unit head:* Dr. John C. Shultz, President, 419-289-5160, Fax: 419-289-5969, E-mail: jshultz@ashland.edu. *Application contact:* Glenn Black, Director of Enrollment Management, 419-289-5151, Fax: 419-289-5969, E-mail: gblack@ashland.edu.

Ashland University, College of Arts and Sciences, Program in American History and Government, Ashland, OH 44805-3702. Offers MAHG. Part-time programs available. *Faculty:* 5 full-time (0 women), 33 part-time/adjunct (2 women). *Students:* 57 full-time (25 women), 69 part-time (27 women); includes 7 minority (1 African American, 1 Asian American or Pacific Islander, 5 Hispanic Americans). Average age 39. 98 applicants, 72% accepted, 49 enrolled. In 2009, 5 master's awarded. *Degree requirements:* For master's, capstone project or thesis. *Entrance requirements:* For master's, minimum undergraduate GPA of 2.75, 3.0 graduate. *Application deadline:* Applications are processed on a rolling basis. Application fee: $30. Electronic applications accepted. *Expenses:* Contact institution. *Financial support:* In 2009–10, 45 students received support. Application deadline: 4/15. *Faculty research:* American founding, United States Civil War, Progressive Era. *Unit head:* Dr. Peter W. Schramm, Executive Director, Ashbrook Center, 419-289-5411, Fax: 419-289-5425, E-mail: pschramm@ashland.edu. *Application contact:* Christian A. Pascarella, Associate Director, 419-289-5411, Fax: 419-289-5425, E-mail: cpascare@ashland.edu.

Auburn University, Graduate School, College of Liberal Arts, Department of History, Auburn University, AL 36849. Offers MA, PhD. Part-time programs available. *Faculty:* 31 full-time (10 women), 2 part-time/adjunct (0 women). *Students:* 23 full-time (6 women), 33 part-time (10 women); includes 4 minority (3 African Americans, 1 Hispanic American), 1 international. Average age 34. 60 applicants, 50% accepted, 13 enrolled. In 2009, 8 master's, 9 doctorates awarded. *Degree requirements:* For master's, thesis, oral exam; for doctorate, 2 foreign languages, thesis/dissertation. *Entrance requirements:* For master's, GRE General Test; for doctorate, GRE General Test, master's degree with thesis. *Application deadline:* For fall admission, 7/7 for domestic students; for spring admission, 11/24 for domestic students. Applications are processed on a rolling basis. Application fee: $50 ($60 for international students). Electronic applications accepted. *Expenses:* Tuition, state resident: full-time $6240. Tuition, nonresident: full-time $18,720. International tuition: $18,938 full-time. Required fees: $492. Tuition and fees vary according to course load, program and reciprocity agreements. *Financial support:* Teaching assistantships, Federal Work-Study available. Support available to part-time students. Financial award application deadline: 3/15; financial award applicants required to submit FAFSA. *Unit head:* Dr. Tony Carey, Chair, 334-844-4360. *Application contact:* Dr. George Flowers, Dean of the Graduate School, 334-844-2125.

Ball State University, Graduate School, College of Sciences and Humanities, Department of History, Muncie, IN 47306-1099. Offers MA. *Faculty research:* European, British, and American history.

Baylor University, Graduate School, College of Arts and Sciences, Department of History, Waco, TX 76798. Offers MA. Part-time and evening/weekend programs available. *Students:* 15 full-time (7 women), 1 international. In 2009, 8 master's awarded. *Degree requirements:* For master's, comprehensive exam, thesis, foreign language translation exam. *Entrance requirements:* For master's, GRE General Test, 24 semester hours in history. *Application deadline:* For fall admission, 8/1 for domestic students. Applications are processed on a rolling basis. Application fee: $25. *Financial support:* Fellowships, research assistantships, Federal Work-Study and institutionally sponsored loans available. Financial award application deadline: 4/15. *Faculty research:* U. S. women's history, naval history, Chinese missions, late nineteenth century Germany, twentieth century urban U. S. *Unit head:* Dr. Barry Hankins, Graduate Program Director, 254-710-4667, Fax: 254-710-2551, E-mail: barry_hankins@baylor.edu. *Application contact:* Linda Conlon, Administrative Assistant, 254-710-6293, Fax: 254-710-3870.

Bob Jones University, Graduate Programs, Greenville, SC 29614. Offers accountancy (MS); Bible (MA); Bible translation (MA); Biblical studies (Certificate); broadcast management (MS); business administration (MBA); church history (MA, PhD); church ministries (MA); church music (MM); cinema and video production (MA); counseling (MS); curriculum and instruction (Ed D); divinity (M Div); dramatic production (MA); educational leadership (MS, Ed D, Ed S); elementary education (M Ed, MAT); English (M Ed, MA, MAT); fine arts (MA); graphic design (MA); history (M Ed, MA); illustration (MA); interpretative speech (MA); mathematics (M Ed, MAT); medical missions (Certificate); ministry (MM, D Min); multi-categorical special education (M Ed, MAT); music (M Ed); New Testament interpretation (PhD); Old Testament interpretation (PhD); orchestral instrument performance (MM); organ performance (MM); pastoral studies (MA); personnel services (MS, Ed S); piano pedagogy (MM); piano performance (MM); platform arts (MA); radio and television broadcasting (MS); rhetoric and public address (MA); secondary education (M Ed); studio art (MA); teaching Bible (MA); theology (MA, PhD); voice performance (MM); youth ministries (MA); M Div/MM.

Boise State University, Graduate College, College of Social Sciences and Public Affairs, Department of History, Boise, ID 83725-0399. Offers MA. Part-time programs available. *Degree requirements:* For master's, thesis. *Entrance requirements:* For master's, GRE General Test, minimum GPA of 3.0. Electronic applications accepted. *Expenses:* Tuition, state resident: full-time $3106; part-time $209 per credit. Tuition, nonresident: part-time $284 per credit. *Faculty research:* Public history, American social and cultural history, European history, Third World history.

Boston College, Graduate School of Arts and Sciences, Department of History, Chestnut Hill, MA 02467-3800. Offers European national studies (MA); history (MA, PhD); medieval studies (MA). *Students:* 70 full-time (38 women), 9 part-time (6 women); includes 4 minority (2 African Americans, 2 Asian Americans or Pacific Islanders), 7 international. 229 applicants, 21% accepted, 11 enrolled. In 2009, 20 master's, 7 doctorates awarded. Terminal master's awarded for partial completion of doctoral program. *Degree requirements:* For master's, one foreign language, comprehensive exam, thesis optional; for doctorate, 2 foreign languages, comprehensive exam, thesis/dissertation. *Entrance requirements:* For master's and doctorate, GRE General Test, writing sample. Additional exam requirements/recommendations for international students: Required—TOEFL (minimum score 600 paper-based; 250 computer-based; 100 iBT). *Application deadline:* For fall admission, 1/2 for domestic and international students. Application fee: $70. Electronic applications accepted. *Financial support:* In 2009–10, fellowships with full tuition reimbursements (averaging $17,000 per year), teaching assistantships with full tuition reimbursements (averaging $17,400 per year) were awarded; Federal Work-Study and scholarships/grants also available. Support available to part-time students. Financial award application deadline: 3/1; financial award applicants required to submit FAFSA. *Faculty research:* Modern and early modern European, U. S., Russian, and Soviet history; European and U. S. intellectual history. *Unit head:* Dr. Marilynn Johnson, Chairperson, 617-552-3781. *Application contact:* Dr. David Quigley, Director of Graduate Studies, 617-552-2267, E-mail: david.quigley@bc.edu.

Boston University, Graduate School of Arts and Sciences, Department of History, Boston, MA 02215. Offers MA, PhD. *Students:* 59 full-time (31 women), 13 part-time (8 women); includes 3 minority (2 African Americans, 1 Hispanic American), 6 international. Average age 31. 195 applicants, 39% accepted, 10 enrolled. In 2009, 7 master's, 1 doctorate awarded. Terminal master's awarded for partial completion of doctoral program. *Degree requirements:* For master's, one foreign language; for doctorate, 2 foreign languages, comprehensive exam, thesis/dissertation. *Entrance requirements:* For master's and doctorate, GRE General Test, 2 letters of recommendation. Additional exam requirements/recommendations for international students: Required—TOEFL (minimum score 550 paper-based; 213 computer-based). *Application deadline:* For fall admission, 1/15 for domestic and international students. Application fee: $70. Electronic applications accepted. *Expenses:* Tuition: Full-time $37,910; part-time $1184 per credit hour. Required fees: $386; $40 per semester. Part-time tuition and fees vary according to class time, course level, degree level and program. *Financial support:* In 2009–10, 28 students received support, including 5 fellowships with full tuition reimbursements available (averaging $18,900 per year), 1 research assistantship with full tuition reimbursement available (averaging $18,400 per year), 10 teaching assistantships with full tuition reimbursements available (averaging $18,400 per year); Federal Work-Study, scholarships/grants, and unspecified assistantships also available. Support available to part-time students. Financial award application deadline: 1/15; financial award applicants required to submit FAFSA. *Unit head:* Charles Dellheim, Chairman, 617-353-2550, Fax: 617-353-2556, E-mail: dellheim@bu.edu. *Application contact:* James T. Dutton, Department Administrator, 617-353-2555, Fax: 617-353-2556, E-mail: jtdutton@bu.edu.

Bowling Green State University, Graduate College, College of Arts and Sciences, Department of History, Bowling Green, OH 43403. Offers history (MA, MAT, PhD); public history (MA); MA/MA. Part-time programs available. *Degree requirements:* For master's, thesis or alternative; for doctorate, one foreign language, comprehensive exam, thesis/dissertation. *Entrance requirements:* For master's and doctorate, GRE General Test. Additional exam requirements/recommendations for international students: Required—TOEFL. Electronic applications accepted. *Faculty research:* Policy history, modern Europe, recent United States history, East Asia, Latin America.

Brandeis University, Graduate School of Arts and Sciences, Department of History, Waltham, MA 02454-9110. Offers MA, PhD. Part-time programs available. *Faculty:* 11 full-time (2 women), 3 part-time/adjunct (2 women). *Students:* 51 full-time (21 women); includes 1 minority (Hispanic American), 4 international. 117 applicants, 21% accepted, 11 enrolled. In 2009, 13 master's, 12 doctorates awarded. Terminal master's awarded for partial completion of doctoral program. *Degree requirements:* For master's, one foreign language, thesis, colloquia, seminars; for doctorate, one foreign language, comprehensive exam, thesis/dissertation, colloquia, seminars. *Entrance requirements:* For master's, GRE General Test, resume, writing sample, letters of recommendation; for doctorate, GRE General Test, resume, writing sample, letter of recommendation, statement of purpose. Additional exam requirements/recommendations for international students: Required—TOEFL (minimum score 600 paper-based; 250 computer-based; 100 iBT); Recommended—IELTS (minimum score 7.5). *Application deadline:* For fall admission, 1/15 priority date for domestic students; for spring admission, 2/1 for domestic students. Application fee: $75. Electronic applications accepted. *Financial support:* In 2009–10, 26 fellowships with full tuition reimbursements (averaging $20,000 per year), teaching assistantships (averaging $3,200 per year) were awarded; research assistantships, scholarships/grants, health care benefits, and tuition waivers (full and partial) also available. Support available to part-time students. Financial award application deadline: 4/15; financial award applicants required to submit FAFSA. *Faculty research:* American and European history, world history, regional and national history. *Unit head:* Dr. Jane Kamensky, Chair, 781-736-2275, Fax: 781-736-2273, E-mail: historia@brandeis.edu. *Application contact:* Dona DiLorenzo, Department Administrator, 781-736-2272, Fax: 781-736-2273, E-mail: delorenz@brandeis.edu.

Brock University, Faculty of Graduate Studies, Faculty of Humanities, Program in History, St. Catharines, ON L2S 3A1, Canada. Offers MA. Part-time programs available. *Degree requirements:* For master's, thesis optional. *Entrance requirements:* For master's, honors degree in history. Additional exam requirements/recommendations for international students: Required—TOEFL (minimum score 550 paper-based; 213 computer-based; 80 iBT), IELTS (minimum score 6.5), TWE (minimum score 4). Electronic applications accepted.

Brooklyn College of the City University of New York, Division of Graduate Studies, Department of History, Brooklyn, NY 11210-2889. Offers MA, PhD. Part-time and evening/weekend programs available. *Students:* 3 full-time (1 woman), 53 part-time (26 women); includes 22 minority (12 African Americans, 2 Asian Americans or Pacific Islanders, 8 Hispanic Americans), 2 international. Average age 28. 34 applicants, 85% accepted, 15 enrolled. In 2009, 11 master's awarded. *Degree requirements:* For master's, 30 credits. *Entrance requirements:* For master's, 12 credits in history, minimum GPA of 3.0 in major, 2 letters of recommendation. Additional exam requirements/recommendations for international students: Required—TOEFL (minimum score 650 paper-based; 280 computer-based; 114 iBT). *Application deadline:* For fall admission, 3/1 priority date for domestic students, 2/1 priority date for international students; for spring admission, 11/1 priority date for domestic students, 10/1 priority date for international students. Applications are processed on a rolling basis. Application fee: $125. Electronic applications accepted. *Expenses:* Tuition, area resident: Full-time $7360; part-time $310 per credit hour. Tuition, state resident: full-time $7360; part-time $310 per credit hour. Tuition, nonresident: full-time $13,800; part-time $575 per credit hour. International tuition: $13,800 full-time. Required fees: $140.10 per semester. *Financial support:* Federal Work-Study, institutionally sponsored loans, and scholarships/grants available. Support available to part-time students. Financial award application deadline: 5/1; financial award applicants required to submit FAFSA. *Faculty research:* Modern European, U. S., medieval, women's, Asian, and Caribbean history. *Unit head:* Dr. David Troyansky, Chairperson, 718-951-5303, E-mail: troyansky@brooklyn.cuny.edu. *Application contact:* Hernan Sierra, Graduate Admissions Coordinator, 718-951-4536, Fax: 718-951-4506, E-mail: grads@brooklyn.cuny.edu.

Brown University, Graduate School, Department of History, Providence, RI 02912. Offers MA, PhD. *Degree requirements:* For master's, thesis or alternative; for doctorate, variable foreign language requirement, thesis/dissertation, preliminary exam.

Buffalo State College, State University of New York, The Graduate School, Faculty of Natural and Social Sciences, Department of History and Social Studies, Buffalo, NY 14222-1095. Offers history (MA); secondary education (MS Ed), including social studies. Part-time and evening/weekend programs available. *Degree requirements:* For master's, one foreign language, thesis (for some programs), project (MS Ed). *Entrance requirements:* For master's, minimum GPA of 2.75, 30 hours in history (MA), 36 hours in history or social sciences (MS Ed). Additional exam requirements/recommendations for international students: Required—TOEFL (minimum score 550 paper-based; 213 computer-based).

Butler University, College of Liberal Arts and Sciences, Department of History, Indianapolis, IN 46208-3485. Offers MA. Part-time programs available. *Students:* 4 applicants, 0% accepted, 0 enrolled. In 2009, 3 master's awarded. *Degree requirements:* For master's, thesis or alternative. *Entrance requirements:* For master's, GRE General Test, minimum GPA of 3.25 in undergraduate major. *Application deadline:* For fall admission, 8/15 priority date for domestic students. Applications are processed on a rolling basis. Application fee: $35. Electronic applications accepted. *Financial support:* Institutionally sponsored loans available. Support available to part-time students. Financial award applicants required to submit FAFSA. *Faculty research:* Gender issues in Africa, Indiana history, transnational migration, French Revolution. *Unit head:* Dr. Scott Swanson, Head, 317-940-9680, E-mail: sswanson@butler.edu. *Application contact:* Pamela Bender, Student Services Specialist, 317-940-8100, Fax: 317-940-8250, E-mail: pbender@butler.edu.

California Polytechnic State University, San Luis Obispo, College of Liberal Arts, Department of History, San Luis Obispo, CA 93407. Offers MA. Part-time programs available. *Faculty:* 5 full-time (1 woman), 1 (woman) part-time/adjunct. *Students:* 9 full-time (4 women), 32 part-time (11 women); includes 5 minority (all Hispanic Americans), 1 international. Average age 30. 29 applicants, 83% accepted, 13 enrolled. In 2009, 5 master's awarded. *Degree requirements:* For master's, comprehensive exam (for some programs), thesis (for some programs). *Entrance requirements:* For master's, minimum GPA of 3.0 in last 90 quarter units of course work, writing sample. Additional exam requirements/recommendations for international students: Required—TOEFL (minimum score 550 paper-based; 213 computer-based), or IELTS (minimum score 6). *Application deadline:* For fall admission, 5/1 for domestic students, 11/30 for international students; for winter admission, 10/1 for domestic students, 6/30 for international students; for spring admission, 1/15 for domestic students. Applications are processed on a rolling basis. Application fee: $55. Electronic applications accepted. *Expenses:* Tuition, nonresident: full-time $11,160; part-time $248 per unit. Required fees: $7134; $1553 per quarter. *Financial support:* Federal Work-Study and scholarships/grants available. Support available to part-time students. Financial award application deadline: 3/2; financial award applicants required to submit FAFSA. *Faculty research:* American history, European history, Asian history, African history, comparative world history. *Unit head:* Dr. Tom Trice, Graduate

History

California Polytechnic State University, San Luis Obispo (continued)
Coordinator, 805-756-2724, Fax: 805-756-5055, E-mail: ttrice@calpoly.edu. *Application contact:* Dr. Tom Trice, Graduate Coordinator, 805-756-2724, Fax: 805-756-5055, E-mail: ttrice@calpoly.edu.

California State Polytechnic University, Pomona, Academic Affairs, College of Letters, Arts, and Social Sciences, Program in History, Pomona, CA 91768-2557. Offers MA. Part-time programs available. *Students:* 1 full-time (0 women), 36 part-time (18 women); includes 11 minority (3 African Americans, 1 Asian American or Pacific Islander, 7 Hispanic Americans). Average age 36. 20 applicants, 40% accepted, 6 enrolled. In 2009, 2 master's awarded. *Degree requirements:* For master's, comprehensive exam (for some programs), thesis (for some programs). *Application deadline:* For fall admission, 5/1 priority date for domestic students; for winter admission, 10/15 priority date for domestic students; for spring admission, 1/20 priority date for domestic students. Applications are processed on a rolling basis. Application fee: $55. Electronic applications accepted. *Expenses:* Tuition, nonresident: full-time $6696; part-time $248 per credit. Required fees: $5487; $3237 per term. Tuition and fees vary according to course load, degree level and program. *Unit head:* Dr. Mahmood Ibrahim, Professor, 909-869-3867, E-mail: mibrahim@csupomona.edu. *Application contact:* Dr. Mahmood Ibrahim, Professor, 909-869-3867, E-mail: mibrahim@csupomona.edu.

California State University, Bakersfield, Division of Graduate Studies, School of Humanities and Social Sciences, Program in History, Bakersfield, CA 93311. Offers MA. *Degree requirements:* For master's, comprehensive exam or thesis. *Entrance requirements:* For master's, 2 letters of recommendation. *Faculty research:* American, European, Latin American, and modern Chinese history.

California State University, Chico, Graduate School, College of Humanities and Fine Arts, Department of History, Chico, CA 95929-0722. Offers MA. Part-time programs available. *Students:* 14 full-time (4 women), 5 part-time (2 women); includes 1 minority (Hispanic American), 1 international. Average age 33. 11 applicants, 64% accepted, 7 enrolled. In 2009, 2 master's awarded. *Degree requirements:* For master's, thesis or alternative, oral exam. *Entrance requirements:* For master's, GRE General Test, 2 letters of recommendation, writing sample. Additional exam requirements/recommendations for international students: Required—TOEFL (minimum score 550 paper-based; 213 computer-based; 80 iBT), IELTS (minimum score 6.5). *Application deadline:* For fall admission, 3/1 priority date for domestic students, 3/1 for international students; for spring admission, 9/15 priority date for domestic students, 9/15 for international students. Applications are processed on a rolling basis. Application fee: $55. Electronic applications accepted. *Unit head:* Dr. Kate Transchel, Graduate Coordinator, 530-898-6417, E-mail: ktranschel@csuchico.edu. *Application contact:* Dr. Kate Transchel, Graduate Coordinator, 530-898-6417, E-mail: ktranschel@csuchico.edu.

California State University, East Bay, Academic Programs and Graduate Studies, College of Letters, Arts, and Social Sciences, Department of History, Hayward, CA 94542-3000. Offers MA. Part-time and evening/weekend programs available. *Faculty:* 9 full-time (5 women), 2 part-time/adjunct (0 women). *Students:* 30 part-time (17 women); includes 6 minority (2 Asian Americans or Pacific Islanders, 4 Hispanic Americans). Average age 40. 24 applicants, 50% accepted, 10 enrolled. In 2009, 9 master's awarded. *Degree requirements:* For master's, one foreign language, comprehensive exam, project or thesis. *Entrance requirements:* For master's, minimum GPA of 3.0 in field, 3.3 in history. Additional exam requirements/recommendations for international students: Required—TOEFL (minimum score 550 paper-based; 213 computer-based). *Application deadline:* For fall admission, 6/30 for domestic and international students; for winter admission, 10/31 for domestic students; for spring admission, 11/30 for domestic students. Applications are processed on a rolling basis. Application fee: $55. Electronic applications accepted. *Financial support:* Fellowships, teaching assistantships, career-related internships or fieldwork, Federal Work-Study, institutionally sponsored loans, and scholarships/grants available. Support available to part-time students. Financial award application deadline: 3/1; financial award applicants required to submit FAFSA. *Unit head:* Dr. Nancy Thomson, Chair, 510-885-3207, Fax: 510-885-4791. *Application contact:* Donna Wiley, Interim Associate Director, 510-885-2928, Fax: 510-885-4777, E-mail: donna.wiley@csueastbay.edu.

California State University, Fresno, Division of Graduate Studies, College of Social Sciences, Department of History, Fresno, CA 93740-8027. Offers history-teaching option (MA); history-traditional track (MA). Part-time and evening/weekend programs available. *Degree requirements:* For master's, thesis or alternative. *Entrance requirements:* For master's, GRE General Test, minimum GPA of 3.0. Additional exam requirements/recommendations for international students: Required—TOEFL. Electronic applications accepted. *Faculty research:* International education, classical art history, improving teacher quality.

California State University, Fullerton, Graduate Studies, College of Humanities and Social Sciences, Department of History, Fullerton, CA 92834-9480. Offers MA. Part-time programs available. *Students:* 19 full-time (9 women), 57 part-time (20 women); includes 21 minority (1 African American, 2 American Indian/Alaska Native, 3 Asian Americans or Pacific Islanders, 15 Hispanic Americans), 1 international. Average age 30. 52 applicants, 73% accepted, 24 enrolled. In 2009, 26 master's awarded. *Degree requirements:* For master's, comprehensive exam, project or thesis. *Entrance requirements:* For master's, undergraduate major in history or related field, minimum GPA of 3.0. Application fee: $55. *Expenses:* Tuition, nonresident: full-time $11,160; part-time $373 per credit. Required fees: $1440 per term. Tuition and fees vary according to course load, degree level and program. *Financial support:* Career-related internships or fieldwork, Federal Work-Study, institutionally sponsored loans, and scholarships/grants available. Support available to part-time students. Financial award application deadline: 3/1; financial award applicants required to submit FAFSA. *Unit head:* Dr. William Haddad, Chair, 657-278-3474. *Application contact:* Admissions/Applications, 657-278-2371.

California State University, Long Beach, Graduate Studies, College of Liberal Arts, Department of History, Long Beach, CA 90840. Offers Africa and the Middle East (MA); ancient/Medieval Europe (MA); Asia (MA); Latin America (MA); modern Europe (MA); United States (MA); world (MA). Part-time and evening/weekend programs available. *Faculty:* 9 full-time (6 women), 1 (woman) part-time/adjunct. *Students:* 10 full-time (3 women), 56 part-time (21 women); includes 19 minority (2 African Americans, 1 American Indian/Alaska Native, 4 Asian Americans or Pacific Islanders, 12 Hispanic Americans), 1 international. Average age 31. 40 applicants, 50% accepted, 11 enrolled. *Degree requirements:* For master's, one foreign language, comprehensive exam or thesis. *Application deadline:* For fall admission, 3/1 for domestic students. Applications are processed on a rolling basis. Application fee: $55. Electronic applications accepted. *Expenses:* Required fees: $1802 per semester. Part-time tuition and fees vary according to course load. *Financial support:* Research assistantships, Federal Work-Study, institutionally sponsored loans, and scholarships/grants available. Financial award application deadline: 3/2. *Faculty research:* All periods of European and American history, recent Asian and African history. *Unit head:* Dr. Nancy Quam-Wickham, Department Chair, 562-985-4431, Fax: 562-985-5431, E-mail: quamwick@csulb.edu. *Application contact:* Dr. Houri Berberian, Graduate Advisor, 562-985-4524, Fax: 562-985-4431, E-mail: hberber@csulb.edu.

California State University, Los Angeles, Graduate Studies, College of Natural and Social Sciences, Department of History, Los Angeles, CA 90032-8530. Offers MA. Part-time and evening/weekend programs available. *Faculty:* 5 full-time (3 women), 1 (woman) part-time/adjunct. *Students:* 24 full-time (9 women), 62 part-time (29 women); includes 37 minority (1 African American, 7 Asian Americans or Pacific Islanders, 29 Hispanic Americans), 4 international. Average age 34. 35 applicants, 97% accepted, 16 enrolled. In 2009, 22 master's awarded. *Degree requirements:* For master's, one foreign language, comprehensive exam or thesis. *Entrance requirements:* For master's, minimum GPA of 3.0, undergraduate major in history. Additional exam requirements/recommendations for international students: Required—TOEFL (minimum score 500 paper-based; 173 computer-based). *Application deadline:* For fall admission, 5/1 for domestic and international students. Applications are processed on a rolling basis. Application fee: $55. Electronic applications accepted. *Financial support:* Federal Work-Study available. Support available to part-time students. Financial award application deadline: 3/1. *Faculty research:* Ancient and modern Europe, the Middle East, Latin America, U.S. history–Bill of Rights. *Unit head:* Dr. Cheryl A. Koos, Chair, 323-343-2020, Fax: 323-343-6431, E-mail: ckoos@calstatela.edu. *Application contact:* Dr. Cheryl L. Ney, Associate Vice President for Academic Affairs and Dean of Graduate Studies, 323-343-3820, Fax: 323-343-5653, E-mail: cney@cslanet.calstatela.edu.

California State University, Northridge, Graduate Studies, College of Social and Behavioral Sciences, Department of History, Northridge, CA 91330. Offers MA. *Faculty:* 17 full-time (5 women), 10 part-time/adjunct (4 women). *Students:* 38 full-time (16 women), 67 part-time (38 women); includes 22 minority (4 African Americans, 1 American Indian/Alaska Native, 6 Asian Americans or Pacific Islanders, 11 Hispanic Americans). Average age 35. 74 applicants, 49% accepted, 28 enrolled. In 2009, 25 master's awarded. *Degree requirements:* For master's, one foreign language. *Entrance requirements:* For master's, GRE General Test or minimum GPA of 3.0, 2 letters of recommendation. Additional exam requirements/recommendations for international students: Required—TOEFL. *Application deadline:* For fall admission, 5/15 for domestic students; for spring admission, 11/1 for domestic students. Application fee: $55. *Financial support:* Fellowships, scholarships/grants available. Financial award application deadline: 3/1. *Unit head:* Dr. Thomas R. Maddux, Chair, 818-677-3566, E-mail: thomas.maddux@csun.edu. *Application contact:* Prof. Jeffrey Auerbach, Graduate Coordinator, 818-677-3566.

California State University, Stanislaus, College of Humanities and Social Sciences, Department of History, Turlock, CA 95382. Offers history (MA); international relations (MA); secondary school teachers (MA). Part-time programs available. *Degree requirements:* For master's, one foreign language, comprehensive exam, thesis or alternative. *Entrance requirements:* For master's, GRE General Test, minimum undergraduate GPA of 3.0. Additional exam requirements/recommendations for international students: Required—TOEFL (minimum score 550 paper-based; 213 computer-based). Electronic applications accepted. *Faculty research:* History of Ancient Greece, history and ecology of the central valley, acculturation and gender.

Cardinal Stritch University, College of Arts and Sciences, Department of History, Milwaukee, WI 53217-3985. Offers MA. Part-time programs available. *Degree requirements:* For master's, comprehensive exam, research project. *Entrance requirements:* For master's, minimum GPA of 3.0, 2 letters of recommendation. Electronic applications accepted.

Carleton University, Faculty of Graduate Studies, Faculty of Arts and Social Sciences, Department of History, Ottawa, ON K1S 5B6, Canada. Offers MA, PhD. *Degree requirements:* For master's, one foreign language, thesis; for doctorate, one foreign language, thesis/dissertation. *Entrance requirements:* For master's, honors degree; for doctorate, master's degree. Additional exam requirements/recommendations for international students: Required—TOEFL. *Faculty research:* Canadian, American, British, modern French, and modern Russian history; international, medieval, and European intellectual history; women's history.

Carnegie Mellon University, College of Humanities and Social Sciences, Department of History, Pittsburgh, PA 15213-3891. Offers African and African-American diaspora (PhD); culture and power (PhD); gender and the family (PhD); history (MA, MS); history and policy (MA); labor and politics (PhD); science, technology, medicine and environment (PhD). Part-time programs available. *Degree requirements:* For doctorate, oral and written comprehensive exams, dissertation defense. *Entrance requirements:* For doctorate, GRE General Test. Additional exam requirements/recommendations for international students: Required—TOEFL. Electronic applications accepted. *Faculty research:* Anthropology and history, African American history, technology/environment, cultural history analysis.

Case Western Reserve University, School of Graduate Studies, Department of History, Cleveland, OH 44106. Offers MA, PhD. Part-time programs available. *Faculty:* 15 full-time (6 women), 4 part-time/adjunct (1 woman). *Students:* 26 full-time (9 women), 7 part-time (2 women); includes 1 minority (Asian American or Pacific Islander), 1 international. Average age 36. 16 applicants, 56% accepted, 5 enrolled. In 2009, 2 doctorates awarded. Terminal master's awarded for partial completion of doctoral program. *Degree requirements:* For master's, thesis; for doctorate, thesis/dissertation. *Entrance requirements:* For master's and doctorate, GRE General Test, writing sample. Additional exam requirements/recommendations for international students: Required—TOEFL (minimum score 550 paper-based; 213 computer-based). *Application deadline:* For fall admission, 1/31 for domestic students. Application fee: $50. Electronic applications accepted. *Financial support:* Fellowships, research assistantships, teaching assistantships, career-related internships or fieldwork, tuition waivers (full and partial), and unspecified assistantships available. Financial award application deadline: 1/31; financial award applicants required to submit FAFSA. *Faculty research:* American social history, social policy history, history of technology and science. *Unit head:* Jonathan Sadowsky, Chair, 216-368-2622, Fax: 216-368-4681, E-mail: jonathan.sadowsky@case.edu. *Application contact:* Marissa Ross, Department Assistant, 216-368-2380, Fax: 216-368-4681, E-mail: mar14@case.edu.

The Catholic University of America, School of Arts and Sciences, Department of History, Washington, DC 20064. Offers Medieval Europe (MA, PhD); modern Europe (PhD); religion and society in the late Medieval and early modern world (MA); United States (MA); MA/JD; MSLS/MA. Part-time programs available. *Faculty:* 13 full-time (6 women), 3 part-time/adjunct (1 woman). *Students:* 14 full-time (9 women), 28 part-time (11 women); includes 1 minority (American Indian/Alaska Native), 3 international. Average age 33. 38 applicants, 50% accepted, 7 enrolled. In 2009, 8 master's, 2 doctorates awarded. *Degree requirements:* For master's, one foreign language, comprehensive exam, thesis optional; for doctorate, 2 foreign languages, comprehensive exam, thesis/dissertation, oral exams. *Entrance requirements:* For master's, GRE General Test, statement of purpose, official copies of academic transcripts, three letters of recommendation, writing sample; for doctorate, GRE General Test, MA in history, statement of purpose, official copies of academic transcripts, three letters of recommendation, writing sample. Additional exam requirements/recommendations for international students: Required—TOEFL (minimum score 580 paper-based; 237 computer-based). *Application deadline:* For fall admission, 8/1 priority date for domestic students, 7/15 for international students; for spring admission, 12/1 priority date for domestic students, 10/15 for international students. Applications are processed on a rolling basis. Application fee: $55. Electronic applications accepted. *Expenses:* Tuition: Full-time $31,740; part-time $1245 per credit hour. Required fees: $50; $25 per semester hour. One-time fee: $425. *Financial support:* Fellowships, research assistantships, teaching assistantships, Federal Work-Study, scholarships/grants, tuition waivers (full and partial), and unspecified assistantships available. Financial award application deadline: 2/1; financial award applicants required to submit FAFSA. *Faculty research:* Modern European intellectual history, history of mathematics and sciences, Renaissance, Catholic reformation, medieval women and gender. *Unit head:* Dr. Jerry Muller, Chair, 202-319-5484, Fax: 202-319-5569, E-mail: mullerj@cua.edu. *Application contact:* Julie Schwing, Director of Graduate Admissions, 202-319-5057, Fax: 202-319-6533, E-mail: cua-admissions@cua.edu.

Central Connecticut State University, School of Graduate Studies, School of Arts and Sciences, Department of History, New Britain, CT 06050-4010. Offers history (MA, Certificate); public history (MA); social studies (Certificate). Part-time and evening/weekend programs available. *Faculty:* 18 full-time (9 women), 22 part-time/adjunct (5 women). *Students:* 31 full-time (18 women), 40 part-time (20 women); includes 3 minority (1 African American, 1 American Indian/Alaska Native, 1 Hispanic American). Average age 33. 54 applicants, 39% accepted, 21 enrolled. In 2009, 11 master's, 2 other advanced degrees awarded. *Degree requirements:* For master's, comprehensive exam, thesis or alternative; for Certificate, qualifying exam. *Entrance requirements:* For master's, minimum undergraduate GPA of 3.0. Additional exam requirements/recommendations for international students: Required—TOEFL. *Application deadline:* For fall admission, 5/1 for domestic students; for spring admission, 12/1 for domestic students. Applications are processed on a rolling basis. Application fee: $50. Electronic applications accepted. *Expenses:* Tuition, area resident: Full-time $4662; part-time $440 per credit. Tuition, state resident: full-time $6994; part-time $440 per credit. Tuition, nonresident: full-time

$12,988; part-time $440 per credit. Required fees: $3606. One-time fee: $62 part-time. *Financial support:* In 2009–10, 7 students received support, including 2 research assistantships; career-related internships or fieldwork, Federal Work-Study, scholarships/grants, and unspecified assistantships also available. Support available to part-time students. Financial award application deadline: 3/1; financial award applicants required to submit FAFSA. *Faculty research:* American West, African history, Eastern Europe, modern Middle East, East Asia. *Unit head:* Dr. Glenn Sunshine, Chair, 860-832-2800. *Application contact:* Dr. Glenn Sunshine, Chair, 860-832-2800.

Central European University, Graduate Studies, Department of History, Budapest, Hungary. Offers MA, PhD. Terminal master's awarded for partial completion of doctoral program. *Degree requirements:* For master's, one foreign language, thesis; for doctorate, one foreign language, comprehensive exam, thesis/dissertation. *Entrance requirements:* For master's and doctorate, interview. Additional exam requirements/recommendations for international students: Required—TOEFL (minimum score 570 paper-based; 230 computer-based). Electronic applications accepted. *Faculty research:* Early modern intellectual history; history of ideas; contemporary historiography comparative history of empires, symbolic geography, history of cultural and religious co-existence.

Central Michigan University, College of Graduate Studies, College of Humanities and Social and Behavioral Sciences, Department of History, Mount Pleasant, MI 48859. Offers European history (Graduate Certificate); history (MA, PhD); modern history (Graduate Certificate); United States history (Graduate Certificate). Offered jointly with the University of Stratclyde, Scotland. Part-time programs available. *Degree requirements:* For master's, thesis or alternative; for doctorate, comprehensive exam, thesis/dissertation. Electronic applications accepted. *Faculty research:* Colonial and revolutionary United States history, modern European history, Latin American and transatlantic history, transnational and comparative history, United States social history.

Central Washington University, Graduate Studies and Research, College of Arts and Humanities, Department of History, Ellensburg, WA 98926. Offers MA. *Faculty:* 13 full-time (4 women). *Students:* 15 full-time (4 women), 3 part-time (1 woman); includes 1 minority (Hispanic American). 17 applicants, 71% accepted, 12 enrolled. In 2009, 8 master's awarded. *Degree requirements:* For master's, thesis or alternative. *Entrance requirements:* For master's, GRE General Test, minimum GPA of 3.0. Additional exam requirements/recommendations for international students: Required—TOEFL (minimum score 550 paper-based; 213 computer-based; 79 iBT). *Application deadline:* For fall admission, 2/1 priority date for domestic students; for winter admission, 10/1 for domestic students; for spring admission, 1/1 for domestic students. Application fee: $50. Electronic applications accepted. *Expenses:* Tuition, state resident: full-time $7353; part-time $245 per credit. Tuition, nonresident: full-time $16,383; part-time $546 per credit. Required fees: $882. Tuition and fees vary according to degree level. *Financial support:* In 2009–10, 7 teaching assistantships with partial tuition reimbursements (averaging $9,145 per year) were awarded; Federal Work-Study, health care benefits, and unspecified assistantships also available. Financial award application deadline: 3/1; financial award applicants required to submit FAFSA. *Unit head:* Dr. Karen Blair, Chair, 509-963-1655, E-mail: blairk@cwu.edu. *Application contact:* Justine Eason, Admissions Program Coordinator, 509-963-3103, Fax: 509-963-1799, E-mail: masters@cwu.edu.

Centro de Estudios Avanzados de Puerto Rico y el Caribe, Graduate Program in Puerto Rican and Caribbean Studies, Old San Juan, PR 00902-3970. Offers Puerto Rican and Caribbean history (MA, PhD); Puerto Rican and Caribbean literature (MA, PhD); Puerto Rican studies (MA). Part-time and evening/weekend programs available. *Degree requirements:* For master's, comprehensive exam, thesis; for doctorate, 2 foreign languages, comprehensive exam, thesis/dissertation. *Entrance requirements:* For master's and doctorate, interview. *Faculty research:* Literature, history, art, folklore, and culture of Puerto Rico and Caribbean countries.

Chicago State University, School of Graduate and Professional Studies, College of Arts and Sciences, Department of History, Philosophy, and Political Science, Chicago, IL 60628. Offers MA. Part-time and evening/weekend programs available. *Degree requirements:* For master's, thesis optional. *Entrance requirements:* For master's, minimum GPA of 2.75. Electronic applications accepted. *Faculty research:* Gregory the Great-use in later Middle Ages, Renaissance alchemy, Liberian wars, Waldo Frank, Sangalan oral traditions.

The Citadel, The Military College of South Carolina, Citadel Graduate College, Department of History, Charleston, SC 29409. Offers MA. Part-time and evening/weekend programs available. *Faculty:* 9 full-time (4 women). *Students:* 2 full-time (0 women), 14 part-time (3 women); includes 1 minority (Hispanic American). Average age 36. In 2009, 3 master's awarded. *Degree requirements:* For master's, comprehensive exam, thesis optional. *Entrance requirements:* For master's, GRE (minimum score of 1000 and 4-6 on the writing assessment sections) or MAT (minimum score 410), minimum undergraduate GPA of 2.5 (3.0 in major); 3 letters of recommendation; evidence of ability to conduct research and present findings. Additional exam requirements/recommendations for international students: Required—TOEFL (minimum score 550 paper-based; 213 computer-based). *Application deadline:* For fall admission, 3/1 for domestic students; for spring admission, 10/1 for domestic students. Application fee: $30. Electronic applications accepted. *Expenses:* Tuition, state resident: part-time $400 per credit hour. Tuition, nonresident: part-time $657 per credit hour. Required fees: $40 per term. *Financial support:* Fellowships, health care benefits and unspecified assistantships available. Support available to part-time students. Financial award application deadline: 7/1; financial award applicants required to submit FAFSA. *Unit head:* Dr. Keith N. Knapp, Department Head, 843-953-5073, Fax: 843-953-7020, E-mail: keith.knapp@citadel.edu. *Application contact:* Dr. Katherine H. Grenier, Director of Graduate Studies, 843-953-6935, Fax: 843-953-7020, E-mail: grenierk@citadel.edu.

City College of the City University of New York, Graduate School, College of Liberal Arts and Science, Division of the Humanities and Arts, Department of History, New York, NY 10031-9198. Offers MA. Part-time programs available. *Degree requirements:* For master's, one foreign language, comprehensive exam, thesis. *Entrance requirements:* Additional exam requirements/recommendations for international students: Required—TOEFL (minimum score 600 paper-based; 100 iBT). Electronic applications accepted. *Faculty research:* Latin American, European, Asian, urban, and architectural history.

Claremont Graduate University, Graduate Programs, School of Arts and Humanities, Department of History, Claremont, CA 91711-6160. Offers Africana history (Certificate); American studies and U.S. history (MA, PhD); archival studies (MA); early modern studies (MA, PhD); European studies (MA, PhD); oral history (MA, PhD); MBA/MA; MBA/PhD. *Faculty:* 4 full-time (2 women). *Students:* 69 full-time (31 women), 5 part-time (3 women); includes 13 minority (1 African American, 4 Asian Americans or Pacific Islanders, 8 Hispanic Americans), 2 international. Average age 36. In 2009, 10 master's, 3 doctorates awarded. Terminal master's awarded for partial completion of doctoral program. *Entrance requirements:* For master's and doctorate, GRE General Test. Additional exam requirements/recommendations for international students: Required—TOEFL (minimum score 550 paper-based; 213 computer-based; 80 iBT). *Application deadline:* For fall admission, 2/1 priority date for domestic students. Applications are processed on a rolling basis. Application fee: $60. Electronic applications accepted. *Expenses:* Tuition: Full-time $35,046; part-time $1524 per credit. Required fees: $161 per semester. *Financial support:* Fellowships, research assistantships, Federal Work-Study, institutionally sponsored loans, and scholarships/grants available. Support available to part-time students. Financial award application deadline: 2/15; financial award applicants required to submit FAFSA. *Faculty research:* Intellectual and social history, cultural studies, gender studies, Western history, Chicano history. *Unit head:* Janet Farrell Brodie, Chair, 909-621-8880, Fax: 909-621-8609, E-mail: janet.brodie@cgu.edu. *Application contact:* Susan Hampson, Admissions Coordinator, 909-607-1278, E-mail: humanities@cgu.edu.

Clark Atlanta University, School of Arts and Sciences, Department of History, Atlanta, GA 30314. Offers MA, DAH. Part-time programs available. *Faculty:* 2 full-time (0 women). *Students:* 9 part-time (5 women); includes all African Americans. Average age 37. 1 applicant, 100% accepted, 1 enrolled. *Degree requirements:* For master's, one foreign language, comprehensive exam, thesis; for doctorate, one foreign language, comprehensive exam, thesis/dissertation. *Entrance requirements:* For master's, GRE General Test, minimum GPA of 2.5. Additional exam requirements/recommendations for international students: Required—TOEFL (minimum score 550 paper-based; 173 computer-based). *Application deadline:* For fall admission, 4/1 for domestic and international students; for spring admission, 11/1 for domestic and international students. Applications are processed on a rolling basis. Application fee: $40 ($55 for international students). Electronic applications accepted. *Expenses:* Tuition: Full-time $12,240; part-time $680 per credit hour. Required fees: $710; $355 per semester. *Financial support:* Scholarships/grants and unspecified assistantships available. Financial award application deadline: 4/30; financial award applicants required to submit FAFSA. *Faculty research:* Education for public service. *Unit head:* Dr. Robert Woodrum, Chairperson, 404-880-8232, E-mail: rwoodrum@cau.edu. *Application contact:* Michelle Clark-Davis, Graduate Program Admissions, 404-880-6605, E-mail: cauadmissions@cau.edu.

Clark University, Graduate School, Department of History, Worcester, MA 01610-1477. Offers American history (MA, PhD); history (MA, CAGS); holocaust history (PhD). *Faculty:* 12 full-time (5 women), 1 part-time/adjunct (0 women). *Students:* 24 full-time (12 women), 4 international. Average age 29. 41 applicants, 32% accepted, 13 enrolled. In 2009, 4 master's awarded. *Degree requirements:* For master's, thesis, oral exam; for doctorate, thesis/dissertation. *Entrance requirements:* Additional exam requirements/recommendations for international students: Required—TOEFL. *Application deadline:* For fall admission, 1/15 priority date for domestic students. Applications are processed on a rolling basis. Application fee: $50. *Expenses:* Tuition: Full-time $34,900; part-time $4362.50 per course. *Financial support:* In 2009–10, fellowships with full and partial tuition reimbursements (averaging $11,850 per year), research assistantships with full and partial tuition reimbursements (averaging $11,850 per year), 3 teaching assistantships with full and partial tuition reimbursements (averaging $11,850 per year) were awarded; tuition waivers (full and partial) also available. *Faculty research:* American political history, comparative history, modern German and European history, Holocaust history, American family history. Total annual research expenditures: $15,000. *Unit head:* Dr. Amy Richter, Chair, 508-793-7288. *Application contact:* Diane Fenner, Academic Secretary, 508-793-7288, Fax: 508-793-8816, E-mail: history@clarku.edu.

Clemson University, Graduate School, College of Architecture, Arts, and Humanities, Department of History, Clemson, SC 29634. Offers MA. Part-time programs available. *Faculty:* 23 full-time (8 women), 2 part-time/adjunct (1 woman). *Students:* 18 full-time (4 women), 8 part-time (4 women); includes 3 minority (1 American Indian/Alaska Native, 1 Asian American or Pacific Islander, 1 Hispanic American). Average age 31. 13 applicants, 85% accepted, 8 enrolled. In 2009, 8 master's awarded. *Degree requirements:* For master's, one foreign language, thesis. *Entrance requirements:* For master's, GRE General Test. Additional exam requirements/recommendations for international students: Required—TOEFL. *Application deadline:* For fall admission, 2/20 for domestic and international students; for spring admission, 11/1 for domestic students, 9/15 for international students. Application fee: $70 ($80 for international students). Electronic applications accepted. *Expenses:* Tuition, state resident: full-time $8684; part-time $528 per credit hour. Tuition, nonresident: full-time $15,330; part-time $1078 per credit hour. Required fees: $736; $37 per semester. Part-time tuition and fees vary according to course load and program. *Financial support:* In 2009–10, 17 students received support, including 1 teaching assistantship with partial tuition reimbursement available (averaging $9,082 per year); research assistantships with partial tuition reimbursements available, career-related internships or fieldwork, institutionally sponsored loans, scholarships/grants, health care benefits, and unspecified assistantships also available. Support available to part-time students. Financial award application deadline: 2/15; financial award applicants required to submit FAFSA. *Faculty research:* American, European, British, and Third World history. Total annual research expenditures: $142,421. *Unit head:* Dr. Thomas Kuehn, Chair, 864-656-5361, Fax: 864-656-1015, E-mail: tjkuehn@clemson.edu. *Application contact:* Dr. Paul Anderson, Graduate Coordinator, 864-656-5362, Fax: 864-656-1015, E-mail: pcander@clemson.edu.

Cleveland State University, College of Graduate Studies, College of Liberal Arts and Social Sciences, Department of History, Cleveland, OH 44115. Offers art history (MA); history (MA); museum studies (MA). Part-time and evening/weekend programs available. *Degree requirements:* For master's, thesis optional. *Entrance requirements:* For master's, minimum GPA of 3.0, bachelor's degree in history. Additional exam requirements/recommendations for international students: Required—TOEFL (minimum score 525 paper-based; 197 computer-based). Electronic applications accepted. *Faculty research:* African Diaspora, social history and the city, early modern Europe, local history.

The College at Brockport, State University of New York, School of Arts, Humanities and Social Sciences, Department of History, Brockport, NY 14420-2997. Offers history (MA), including American history, American/world history, world history. Part-time and evening/weekend programs available. *Students:* 17 full-time (8 women), 31 part-time (11 women); includes 2 minority (both Hispanic Americans). 21 applicants, 76% accepted, 15 enrolled. In 2009, 16 master's awarded. *Degree requirements:* For master's, thesis or alternative. *Entrance requirements:* For master's, GRE General Test (recommended), minimum GPA of 3.0, writing sample, letters of recommendation, statement of objectives. Additional exam requirements/recommendations for international students: Required—TOEFL (minimum score 550 paper-based; 213 computer-based; 79 iBT). *Application deadline:* For fall admission, 6/1 priority date for domestic and international students; for spring admission, 11/15 priority date for domestic and international students. Application fee: $50. Electronic applications accepted. *Expenses:* Tuition, state resident: full-time $8370; part-time $349 per credit. Tuition, nonresident: full-time $13,250; part-time $522 per credit. *Financial support:* In 2009–10, 1 fellowship with tuition reimbursement (averaging $1,600 per year), 1 teaching assistantship with full tuition reimbursement (averaging $6,000 per year) were awarded; Federal Work-Study, scholarships/grants, and unspecified assistantships also available. Support available to part-time students. Financial award application deadline: 3/15; financial award applicants required to submit FAFSA. *Faculty research:* American history, women's history, European history, world history, cultural history. *Unit head:* Dr. Alison Parker, Chairperson, 585-395-5694, Fax: 585-395-2620, E-mail: jlloyd@brockport.edu. *Application contact:* Dr. Morag Martin, Graduate Director, 585-395-5690, Fax: 585-395-2620, E-mail: mmartin@brockport.edu.

College of Charleston, Graduate School, School of Humanities and Social Sciences, Program in History, Charleston, SC 29424-0001. Offers MA. Part-time and evening/weekend programs available. *Faculty:* 22 full-time (6 women), 4 part-time/adjunct (1 woman). *Students:* 20 full-time (11 women), 12 part-time (8 women); includes 3 minority (all African Americans). Average age 25. 26 applicants, 46% accepted, 8 enrolled. In 2009, 13 master's awarded. *Degree requirements:* For master's, comprehensive exam, thesis optional. *Entrance requirements:* For master's, GRE General Test or MAT, writing sample. Additional exam requirements/recommendations for international students: Required—TOEFL. *Application deadline:* For fall admission, 3/1 for domestic students; for spring admission, 10/15 for domestic students. Applications are processed on a rolling basis. Application fee: $45. Electronic applications accepted. *Financial support:* In 2009–10, research assistantships (averaging $12,400 per year); career-related internships or fieldwork, Federal Work-Study, scholarships/grants, and unspecified assistantships also available. Financial award application deadline: 6/1; financial award applicants required to submit FAFSA. *Faculty research:* Modern West Africa, labor history, Southern women's education, Native Americans, the Atlantic world. *Unit head:* Dr. William Scott Poole, Director, 843-953-4862, Fax: 843-953-6349, E-mail: poolews@cofc.edu. *Application contact:* Susan Hallatt, Director of Graduate Admissions, 843-953-5614, Fax: 843-953-1434, E-mail: hallatts@cofc.edu.

The College of Saint Rose, Graduate Studies, School of Arts and Humanities, Program in History/Political Science, Albany, NY 12203-1419. Offers MA. Part-time and evening/weekend programs available. *Degree requirements:* For master's, final paper/project, thesis or comprehensive exam. *Entrance requirements:* For master's, minimum undergraduate GPA of

History

The College of Saint Rose (continued)

3.0, 12 undergraduate credits in US history and/or political science. Additional exam requirements/recommendations for international students: Required—TOEFL (minimum score 550 paper-based; 213 computer-based). Electronic applications accepted.

College of Staten Island of the City University of New York, Graduate Programs, Program in History, Staten Island, NY 10314-6600. Offers MA. Part-time and evening/weekend programs available. *Faculty:* 4 full-time (0 women), 1 part-time/adjunct (0 women). *Students:* 2 full-time (1 woman), 17 part-time (8 women); includes 2 minority (1 African American, 1 Hispanic American), 2 international. Average age 34. 18 applicants, 50% accepted, 6 enrolled. In 2009, 4 master's awarded. *Degree requirements:* For master's, thesis. *Entrance requirements:* For master's, minimum GPA of 3.0 overall and in undergraduate history courses, 2 academic letters of recommendation, letter explaining interest. Additional exam requirements/recommendations for international students: Required—TOEFL (minimum score 550 paper-based; 213 computer-based; 79 iBT). *Application deadline:* For fall admission, 6/1 for domestic and international students; for spring admission, 12/12 for domestic students, 9/12 for international students. Applications are processed on a rolling basis. Application fee: $125. Electronic applications accepted. *Expenses:* Tuition, state resident: full-time $7360; part-time $310 per credit. Tuition, nonresident: part-time $575 per credit. Required fees: $378; $113 per semester. *Financial support:* Career-related internships or fieldwork, Federal Work-Study, and scholarships/grants available. Support available to part-time students. Financial award applicants required to submit FAFSA. *Unit head:* Dr. Sandra Gambetti, Coordinator, 718-982-2870 Ext. 2915, Fax: 718-982-2864, E-mail: historymakers@mail.csi.cuny.edu. *Application contact:* Sasha Spence, Assistant Director of Graduate Recruitment and Admissions, 718-982-2699, Fax: 718-982-2500, E-mail: sasha.spence@csi.cuny.edu.

The College of William and Mary, Faculty of Arts and Sciences, Lyon Gardiner Tyler Department of History, Williamsburg, VA 23187-8795. Offers MA, PhD. *Faculty:* 25 full-time (11 women), 5 part-time/adjunct (1 woman). *Students:* 58 full-time (34 women); includes 3 minority (2 African Americans, 1 Hispanic American), 1 international. Average age 29. 140 applicants, 25% accepted, 20 enrolled. In 2009, 13 master's, 1 doctorate awarded. Terminal master's awarded for partial completion of doctoral program. *Degree requirements:* For master's, one foreign language, comprehensive exam, thesis; for doctorate, one foreign language, comprehensive exam, thesis/dissertation. *Entrance requirements:* For master's and doctorate, GRE General Test, minimum GPA of 3.0. Additional exam requirements/recommendations for international students: Required—TOEFL. *Application deadline:* For fall admission, 12/5 for domestic and international students. Application fee: $45. Electronic applications accepted. *Expenses:* Tuition, state resident: full-time $6400; part-time $315 per credit hour. Tuition, nonresident: full-time $19,720; part-time $840 per credit hour. Required fees: $4114. *Financial support:* In 2009–10, 44 students received support, including 2 fellowships with full tuition reimbursements available (averaging $18,000 per year), 16 research assistantships with full tuition reimbursements available (averaging $18,000 per year), 10 teaching assistantships with full tuition reimbursements available (averaging $18,000 per year); career-related internships or fieldwork also available. Financial award application deadline: 12/5; financial award applicants required to submit FAFSA. *Faculty research:* Early American, U. S., and comparative history. Total annual research expenditures: $171,676. *Unit head:* Dr. Philip Daileader, Chair, 757-221-6285, Fax: 757-221-2111, E-mail: phdail@wm.edu. *Application contact:* Dr. Leisa Meyer, Director of Graduate Studies, 757-221-3737, Fax: 757-221-2111, E-mail: ldmeyer@wm.edu.

Colorado State University, Graduate School, College of Liberal Arts, Department of History, Fort Collins, CO 80523-1776. Offers MA. Part-time programs available. *Faculty:* 20 full-time (8 women). *Students:* 30 full-time (18 women), 12 part-time (4 women); includes 4 minority (1 American Indian/Alaska Native, 3 Hispanic Americans), 1 international. Average age 30. 49 applicants, 43% accepted, 14 enrolled. In 2009, 9 master's awarded. *Degree requirements:* For master's, variable foreign language requirement, comprehensive exam (for some programs), thesis (for some programs), written and oral exams. *Entrance requirements:* For master's, GRE General Test, minimum GPA of 3.0, minimum 21 credits in history, letters of recommendation. Additional exam requirements/recommendations for international students: Required—TOEFL. *Application deadline:* For fall admission, 2/1 priority date for domestic and international students; for spring admission, 11/1 for domestic and international students. Application fee: $50. Electronic applications accepted. *Expenses:* Tuition, state resident: full-time $6434; part-time $359.10 per credit. Tuition, nonresident: full-time $18,116; part-time $1006.45 per credit. Required fees: $1496; $83 per credit. *Financial support:* In 2009–10, 23 students received support, including 1 research assistantship (averaging $6,165 per year), 22 teaching assistantships with tuition reimbursements available (averaging $11,437 per year); fellowships, career-related internships or fieldwork, Federal Work-Study, institutionally sponsored loans, scholarships/grants, traineeships, and unspecified assistantships also available. Financial award application deadline: 3/1; financial award applicants required to submit FAFSA. *Faculty research:* U.S. history, world history, gender history, European history, environmental history. Total annual research expenditures: $218,185. *Unit head:* Dr. Diane Margolf, Professor and Chair, 970-491-6334, Fax: 970-491-2941, E-mail: doug.yarrington@colostate.edu. *Application contact:* Janet Ore, Graduate Studies Chair, 970-491-6334, Fax: 970-491-2941, E-mail: janet.ore@colostate.edu.

Columbia University, Graduate School of Arts and Sciences, Division of Social Sciences, Department of History, New York, NY 10027. Offers American history (M Phil, MA, PhD); history (M Phil, MA, PhD); JD/MA; JD/PhD. Part-time programs available. *Degree requirements:* For master's, one foreign language, thesis; for doctorate, variable foreign language requirement, thesis/dissertation. *Entrance requirements:* For master's and doctorate, GRE General Test, writing sample. Additional exam requirements/recommendations for international students: Required—TOEFL.

Concordia University, School of Graduate Studies, Faculty of Arts and Science, Department of History, Montréal, QC H3G 1M8, Canada. Offers MA, PhD. *Degree requirements:* For master's, one foreign language, thesis optional; for doctorate, one foreign language, comprehensive exam, thesis/dissertation. *Entrance requirements:* For master's, honors degree in history or equivalent. *Faculty research:* Canadian history, European social history, Canadian-American relations.

Converse College, School of Education and Graduate Studies, Program in Liberal Arts, Spartanburg, SC 29302-0006. Offers English (MLA); history (MLA); political science (MLA). *Degree requirements:* For master's, capstone paper. *Entrance requirements:* For master's, minimum GPA of 3.0, 2 recommendations.

Cornell University, Graduate School, Graduate Fields of Arts and Sciences, Field of History, Ithaca, NY 14853-0001. Offers African history (MA, PhD); American history (MA, PhD); ancient history (MA, PhD); early modern European history (MA, PhD); English history (MA, PhD); French history (MA, PhD); German history (MA, PhD); history of science (MA, PhD); Latin American history (MA, PhD); medieval Chinese history (MA, PhD); medieval history (MA, PhD); modern Chinese history (MA, PhD); modern European history (MA, PhD); modern Japanese history (MA, PhD); premodern Islamic history (MA, PhD); premodern Japanese history (MA, PhD); Renaissance history (MA, PhD); Russian history (MA, PhD); Southeast Asian history (MA, PhD). *Faculty:* 62 full-time (19 women). *Students:* 67 full-time (33 women); includes 10 minority (4 African Americans, 3 Asian Americans or Pacific Islanders, 3 Hispanic Americans), 24 international. Average age 31. 195 applicants, 7% accepted, 10 enrolled. In 2009, 11 master's, 3 doctorates awarded. Terminal master's awarded for partial completion of doctoral program. *Degree requirements:* For master's, thesis; for doctorate, 2 foreign languages, comprehensive exam, thesis/dissertation, 1 year of teaching experience. *Entrance requirements:* For master's and doctorate, GRE General Test, writing sample, 3 letters of recommendation. Additional exam requirements/recommendations for international students: Required—TOEFL (minimum score 550 paper-based; 213 computer-based; 77 iBT). *Application deadline:* For fall admission, 1/15 for domestic students. Application fee: $70. Electronic applications accepted. *Expenses:* Tuition: Full-time $29,500. Required fees: $70. Full-time tuition and fees vary according to degree level, program and student level. *Financial support:* In 2009–10, 54 students received support, including 8 fellowships with full tuition reimbursements available; research assistantships with full tuition reimbursements available, teaching assistantships with full tuition reimbursements available, institutionally sponsored loans, scholarships/grants, health care benefits, tuition waivers (full and partial), and unspecified assistantships also available. Financial award applicants required to submit FAFSA. *Unit head:* Director of Graduate Studies, 607-255-6738, Fax: 607-255-0469. *Application contact:* Graduate Field Assistant, 607-255-6738, Fax: 607-255-0469, E-mail: history_grad_info@cornell.edu.

Dalhousie University, Faculty of Arts and Social Science, Department of History, Halifax, NS B3H 4R2, Canada. Offers MA, PhD. *Entrance requirements:* Additional exam requirements/recommendations for international students: Required—TOEFL, IELTS, CANTEST, CAEL, or Michigan English Language Assessment Battery. *Application deadline:* For fall admission, 6/1 for domestic students, 4/1 for international students; for winter admission, 10/31 for domestic students, 8/31 for international students; for spring admission, 2/28 for domestic students, 12/31 for international students. Application fee: $70. Electronic applications accepted. *Financial support:* Career-related internships or fieldwork, scholarships/grants, and health care benefits available. *Faculty research:* African, British, Russian, Canadian and medieval history. *Unit head:* Dr. Chris Bell, Graduate Coordinator, 902-494-3586, Fax: 902-494-3349, E-mail: gradhist@dal.ca. *Application contact:* Valerie Peck, Graduate Administrator, 902-494-2011, Fax: 902-494-3349, E-mail: gradhist@dal.ca.

DePaul University, College of Liberal Arts and Sciences, Department of History, Chicago, IL 60614. Offers MA. Part-time and evening/weekend programs available. *Faculty:* 28 full-time (11 women), 7 part-time/adjunct (3 women). *Students:* 13 full-time (7 women), 16 part-time (4 women); includes 2 minority (both Hispanic Americans). Average age 32. In 2009, 6 master's awarded. *Degree requirements:* For master's, thesis optional. *Entrance requirements:* For master's, GRE General Test, bachelor's degree in social science or history, or history minor. Additional exam requirements/recommendations for international students: Required—TOEFL. *Application deadline:* 4/1 priority date for domestic and international students. Applications are processed on a rolling basis. Application fee: $25. Electronic applications accepted. *Expenses:* Tuition: Full-time $37,525; part-time $620 per credit hour. *Financial support:* In 2009–10, 3 students received support, including fellowships (averaging $7,000 per year); career-related internships or fieldwork, scholarships/grants, and tuition waivers (full) also available. Financial award application deadline: 5/1. *Faculty research:* U.S., Europe, Latin America, Asia, Africa. *Unit head:* Dr. Warren C. Schultz, Chairperson, 773-325-1561, Fax: 773-325-4764, E-mail: wschultz@depaul.edu. *Application contact:* Dr. Valentina K. Tikoff, Graduate Director, 773-325-1570, Fax: 773-325-4764, E-mail: vtikoff@depaul.edu.

Drew University, Caspersen School of Graduate Studies, Program in History and Culture, Madison, NJ 07940-1493. Offers intellectual history (MA, PhD). Part-time programs available. *Students:* 7 full-time (4 women), 1 (woman) part-time; includes 2 minority (both African Americans). Average age 33. 14 applicants, 86% accepted, 8 enrolled.Terminal master's awarded for partial completion of doctoral program. *Degree requirements:* For master's, thesis; for doctorate, one foreign language, comprehensive exam (for some programs), thesis/dissertation. *Entrance requirements:* For master's and doctorate, GRE, TOEFL, transcripts, personal statement, writing sample, recommendations. Additional exam requirements/recommendations for international students: Required—TOEFL (minimum score 585 paper-based; 240 computer-based; 95 iBT), TWE. *Application deadline:* For fall admission, 2/1 priority date for domestic students. Application fee: $35. *Expenses:* Tuition: Full-time $33,966; part-time $1887 per credit. Tuition and fees vary according to course load and program. *Financial support:* In 2009–10, 7 students received support; fellowships, career-related internships or fieldwork, Federal Work-Study, scholarships/grants, tuition waivers (full and partial), and unspecified assistantships available. Support available to part-time students. Financial award application deadline: 2/15; financial award applicants required to submit FAFSA. *Unit head:* Dr. Wyatt Evans, 973-408-3329, E-mail: wevans@drew.edu. *Application contact:* Carla J. Burns, Director of Graduate Admissions, 973-408-3110, Fax: 973-408-3242, E-mail: gradm@drew.edu.

Duke University, Graduate School, Department of History, Durham, NC 27708. Offers history (AM, PhD); Latin American studies (PhD); JD/AM; MD/PhD. *Faculty:* 37 full-time. *Students:* 56 full-time (32 women); includes 7 minority (all African Americans), 10 international. 199 applicants, 10% accepted, 5 enrolled. In 2009, 4 master's, 7 doctorates awarded. *Degree requirements:* For doctorate, 2 foreign languages, thesis/dissertation. *Entrance requirements:* For doctorate, GRE General Test. Additional exam requirements/recommendations for international students: Required—TOEFL (minimum score 550 paper-based; 213 computer-based; 83 iBT), IELTS (minimum score 7). *Application deadline:* For fall admission, 12/8 priority date for domestic and international students. Application fee: $75. Electronic applications accepted. *Financial support:* Fellowships, research assistantships, teaching assistantships, Federal Work-Study available. Financial award application deadline: 12/31. *Unit head:* Anna Krylova, Director of Graduate Studies, Fax: 919-681-5746, E-mail: rmennis@duke.edu. *Application contact:* Cynthia Robertson, Associate Dean for Enrollment Services, 919-684-3913, E-mail: grad-admissions@duke.edu.

Duquesne University, Graduate School of Liberal Arts, Department of History, Pittsburgh, PA 15282-0001. Offers archival, museum, and editing studies (MA); history (MA). Part-time and evening/weekend programs available. *Faculty:* 6 full-time (1 woman), 3 part-time/adjunct (1 woman). *Students:* 30 full-time (21 women), 16 part-time (6 women). Average age 26. 71 applicants, 48% accepted, 21 enrolled. In 2009, 21 master's awarded. *Degree requirements:* For master's, comprehensive exam (for some programs), thesis optional. *Entrance requirements:* For master's, GRE General Test, writing sample. Additional exam requirements/recommendations for international students: Required—TOEFL. *Application deadline:* For fall admission, 8/15 for domestic students, 5/1 for international students; for spring admission, 11/1 priority date for domestic students. Applications are processed on a rolling basis. Electronic applications accepted. *Expenses:* Tuition: Part-time $851 per credit. Required fees: $81 per credit. *Financial support:* In 2009–10, 4 research assistantships with full tuition reimbursements (averaging $6,000 per year) were awarded; career-related internships or fieldwork, Federal Work-Study, scholarships/grants, tuition waivers (full and partial), and unspecified assistantships also available. Support available to part-time students. Financial award application deadline: 5/1. *Faculty research:* American studies, immigration history, local social history, applied history, Eastern European history. *Unit head:* Dr. Holly Mayer, Chair, 412-396-6470, E-mail: mayer@duq.edu. *Application contact:* Dr. Holly Mayer, Chair, 412-396-6470, E-mail: mayer@duq.edu.

East Carolina University, Graduate School, Thomas Harriot College of Arts and Sciences, Department of History, Greenville, NC 27858-4353. Offers American history (MA); European history (MA); maritime history (MA). Part-time and evening/weekend programs available. *Degree requirements:* For master's, one foreign language, comprehensive exam, thesis. *Entrance requirements:* For master's, GRE General Test, GRE Subject Test. Additional exam requirements/recommendations for international students: Required—TOEFL.

Eastern Illinois University, Graduate School, College of Arts and Humanities, Department of History, Charleston, IL 61920-3099. Offers historical administration (MA); history (MA). Part-time programs available. *Faculty:* 14 full-time (2 women). In 2009, 17 master's awarded. *Application deadline:* For fall admission, 3/31 priority date for domestic students. Applications are processed on a rolling basis. Application fee: $30. *Expenses:* Tuition, state resident: full-time $9434; part-time $239 per credit hour. Tuition, nonresident: full-time $23,774; part-time $717 per credit hour. Required fees: $802.63. *Financial support:* In 2009–10, research assistantships with tuition reimbursements (averaging $8,100 per year), 9 teaching assistantships with tuition reimbursements (averaging $8,100 per year) were awarded; career-related internships or fieldwork also available. *Unit head:* Dr. Anita Shelton, Chairperson, 217-581-3310, Fax: 217-581-2722, E-mail: ashelton@eiu.edu. *Application contact:* Dr. Ed Wehrle, Graduate Coordinator, 217-581-6372, Fax: 217-581-2722, E-mail: efwehrle@eiu.edu.

Eastern Kentucky University, The Graduate School, College of Arts and Sciences, Department of History, Richmond, KY 40475-3102. Offers MA. Part-time programs available. *Degree requirements:* For master's, comprehensive exam, thesis optional. *Entrance requirements:* For master's, GRE General Test, GRE Subject Test, minimum GPA of 2.5. *Faculty research:* Twentieth-century U.S. history, Kentucky history, British history, world history, Eastern Europe.

Eastern Michigan University, Graduate School, College of Arts and Sciences, Department of History and Philosophy, Programs in History, Ypsilanti, MI 48197. Offers history (MA); state and local history (Graduate Certificate). Part-time and evening/weekend programs available. Postbaccalaureate distance learning degree programs offered (minimal on-campus study). *Students:* 8 full-time (3 women), 57 part-time (19 women); includes 3 minority (2 African Americans, 1 Asian American or Pacific Islander), 1 international. Average age 34. In 2009, 9 master's awarded. *Degree requirements:* For master's, thesis optional. *Entrance requirements:* Additional exam requirements/recommendations for international students: Required—TOEFL. *Application deadline:* Applications are processed on a rolling basis. Application fee: $35. Tuition and fees vary according to course level. *Financial support:* Fellowships, research assistantships with full tuition reimbursements, teaching assistantships with full tuition reimbursements, career-related internships or fieldwork, Federal Work-Study, institutionally sponsored loans, scholarships/grants, tuition waivers (partial), and unspecified assistantships available. Support available to part-time students. Financial award applicants required to submit FAFSA. *Application contact:* Dr. Ronald Delph, Coordinator, 734-487-0053, Fax: 734-487-6835, E-mail: rdelph@emich.edu.

Eastern Washington University, Graduate Studies, College of Social and Behavioral Sciences, Department of History, Cheney, WA 99004-2431. Offers MA. *Degree requirements:* For master's, comprehensive exam, thesis optional. *Entrance requirements:* For master's, minimum GPA of 3.0. *Expenses:* Tuition, state resident: full-time $7476; part-time $249 per quarter hour. Tuition, nonresident: full-time $18,030; part-time $601 per quarter hour. Required fees: $3.50 per quarter hour. $142 per quarter.

East Stroudsburg University of Pennsylvania, Graduate School, College of Arts and Sciences, Department of History, East Stroudsburg, PA 18301-2999. Offers M Ed, MA. Part-time and evening/weekend programs available. *Faculty:* 5 full-time (1 woman). *Students:* 9 full-time (3 women), 20 part-time (8 women); includes 2 minority (1 African American, 1 Asian American or Pacific Islander). Average age 31. In 2009, 6 master's awarded. *Degree requirements:* For master's, comprehensive exam, thesis, thesis defense. *Entrance requirements:* For master's, Commonwealth of Pennsylvania Department of Education Certification Requirements (M Ed). Additional exam requirements/recommendations for international students: Required—TOEFL (minimum score 560 paper-based; 220 computer-based; 83 iBT). *Application deadline:* For fall admission, 7/31 priority date for domestic students, 5/1 priority date for international students; for spring admission, 11/30 for domestic students, 10/1 for international students. Applications are processed on a rolling basis. Application fee: $50. *Financial support:* In 2009–10, 17 research assistantships with full and partial tuition reimbursements (averaging $1,643 per year) were awarded; Federal Work-Study and institutionally sponsored loans also available. Financial award application deadline: 3/1; financial award applicants required to submit FAFSA. *Unit head:* Dr. Lawrence Squeri, Graduate Coordinator, 570-422-3284, Fax: 570-422-3506, E-mail: lsqueri@po-box.esu.edu. *Application contact:* Kevin Quintero, Graduate Admissions Coordinator, 570-422-3890, Fax: 570-422-2711, E-mail: kquintero@po-box.esu.edu.

East Tennessee State University, School of Graduate Studies, College of Arts and Sciences, Department of History, Johnson City, TN 37614. Offers MA. Part-time and evening/weekend programs available. *Degree requirements:* For master's, comprehensive exam, thesis or alternative. *Entrance requirements:* For master's, GRE, bachelor's degree in history, minimum GPA of 3.0. Additional exam requirements/recommendations for international students: Required—TOEFL (minimum score 550 paper-based; 213 computer-based). *Faculty research:* Post-World War II German occupation, biographies of Eleanor Copenhaver Anderson and Harry M. Candill, the Miss America Pageant, encyclopedia of colonialism, the new Georgia campaign in the Pacific war.

Emory & Henry College, Graduate Programs, Emory, VA 24327-0947. Offers American history (MA Ed); organizational leadership (MOL); professional studies (M Ed); reading specialist (MA Ed). Part-time and evening/weekend programs available. *Entrance requirements:* For master's, GRE or PRAXIS I, recommendations, writing sample.

Emory University, Graduate School of Arts and Sciences, Department of History, Atlanta, GA 30322-1100. Offers PhD. *Degree requirements:* For doctorate, 2 foreign languages, comprehensive exam, thesis/dissertation. *Entrance requirements:* For doctorate, GRE General Test, minimum GPA of 3.0. Electronic applications accepted. *Faculty research:* U.S., modern Europe, early modern Europe, medieval Europe, Latin America, Africa.

Emporia State University, School of Graduate Studies, College of Liberal Arts and Sciences, Department of Social Sciences, Program in History, Emporia, KS 66801-5087. Offers American history (MA); world history (MA). Part-time programs available. *Students:* 2 full-time (both women), 15 part-time (1 woman); includes 1 minority (African American). 6 applicants, 50% accepted, 1 enrolled. In 2009, 7 master's awarded. *Degree requirements:* For master's, comprehensive exam or thesis. *Entrance requirements:* For master's, 12 credit hours in history, minimum undergraduate GPA of 2.5, writing sample. Additional exam requirements/recommendations for international students: Required—TOEFL (minimum score 520 paper-based; 133 computer-based; 68 iBT). *Application deadline:* For fall admission, 8/15 priority date for domestic students. Applications are processed on a rolling basis. Application fee: $30 ($75 for international students). Electronic applications accepted. *Expenses:* Tuition, state resident: full-time $4154; part-time $173 per credit hour. Tuition, nonresident: full-time $12,864; part-time $536 per credit hour. Required fees: $948; $58 per credit hour. Tuition and fees vary according to campus/location. *Financial support:* Federal Work-Study, institutionally sponsored loans, health care benefits, and unspecified assistantships available. Financial award application deadline: 3/15; financial award applicants required to submit FAFSA. *Faculty research:* Great Plains history. *Unit head:* Dr. Ellen Hansen, Chair, 620-341-5461, E-mail: ehansen@emporia.edu. *Application contact:* Dr. Deborah Gerish, Assistant Professor, 620-341-5579, E-mail: dgerish@emporia.edu.

Fairleigh Dickinson University, Metropolitan Campus, University College: Arts, Sciences, and Professional Studies, School of History, Political and International Studies, Program in History, Teaneck, NJ 07666-1914. Offers MA. *Students:* 2 part-time (1 woman). Average age 37. 3 applicants, 33% accepted, 1 enrolled. *Application deadline:* Applications are processed on a rolling basis. Application fee: $40. *Application contact:* Susan Brooman, University Director of Graduate Admissions, 201-692-2554, Fax: 201-692-2560, E-mail: globaleducation@fdu.edu.

Fayetteville State University, Graduate School, Department of Geography, History and Political Science, Fayetteville, NC 28301-4298. Offers history (MA); political science (MA). Part-time and evening/weekend programs available. *Faculty:* 4 full-time (0 women). *Students:* 1 full-time (0 women), 6 part-time (2 women); includes 2 minority (both African Americans). Average age 40. 1 applicant, 100% accepted, 1 enrolled. In 2009, 2 master's awarded. *Degree requirements:* For master's, comprehensive exam, internship. *Entrance requirements:* For master's, GRE General Test. *Application deadline:* For fall admission, 4/15 for domestic students; for spring admission, 10/15 for domestic students. Applications are processed on a rolling basis. Application fee: $35. Electronic applications accepted. *Unit head:* Dr. Adeguke Ademiluyi, Chairperson, 910-672-1137, E-mail: aademiluyi@uncfsu.edu. *Application contact:* Roxie Shabazz, Associate Vice-Chancellor for Enrollment Management, 910-672-1784, Fax: 910-672-2209, E-mail: rshabazz@uncfsu.edu.

Fitchburg State University, Division of Graduate and Continuing Education, Programs in History and Teaching History (Secondary Level), Fitchburg, MA 01420-2697. Offers MA, MAT, Certificate. *Accreditation:* NCATE. Part-time and evening/weekend programs available. *Students:* 2 full-time (1 woman), 26 part-time (15 women). Average age 32. 12 applicants, 100% accepted, 8 enrolled. In 2009, 8 master's awarded. *Entrance requirements:* For master's, GRE General Test or MAT, appropriate bachelor's degree, letters of recommendation, resume. Additional exam requirements/recommendations for international students: Required—TOEFL (minimum score 550 paper-based; 213 computer-based; 79 iBT). *Application deadline:* Applications are processed on a rolling basis. Application fee: $25 ($50 for international students). *Expenses:* Tuition, area resident: Part-time $150 per credit. Tuition, state resident: part-time $150 per credit. Tuition, nonresident: part-time $150 per credit. Required fees: $120 per credit. *Financial support:* In 2009–10, research assistantships with partial tuition reimbursements (averaging $5,500 per year); Federal Work-Study, scholarships/grants, and unspecified assistantships also available. Support available to part-time students. Financial award application deadline: 3/1; financial award applicants required to submit FAFSA. *Unit head:* Dr. Laura Baker, Chair, 978-665-3379, Fax: 978-665-3658, E-mail: gce@fsc.edu. *Application contact:* Director of Admissions, 978-665-3144, Fax: 978-665-4540, E-mail: admissions@fsc.edu.

Florida Agricultural and Mechanical University, Division of Graduate Studies, Research, and Continuing Education, College of Arts and Sciences, Division of History and Political Sciences, Program in Applied Social Science, Tallahassee, FL 32307-3200. Offers African American history (MASS); criminal justice (MASS); economics (MASS); history (MASS); political science (MASS); public administration (MASS); public management (MASS); social work (MASS); sociology (MASS). Part-time programs available. *Faculty:* 17 full-time (2 women). *Students:* 54 full-time (42 women), 4 part-time (2 women); includes 57 minority (all African Americans). In 2009, 14 master's awarded. *Degree requirements:* For master's, thesis optional. *Entrance requirements:* For master's, GRE General Test, minimum GPA of 3.0. *Application deadline:* For fall admission, 5/18 for domestic students, 12/18 for international students; for spring admission, 11/12 for domestic students, 5/12 for international students. Application fee: $20. *Financial support:* Fellowships, research assistantships, career-related internships or fieldwork, Federal Work-Study, and tuition waivers (full) available. Financial award application deadline: 4/1. *Faculty research:* Southern history, black history, election trends, presidential history. *Unit head:* Dr. Gary Paul, Director, 850-599-3447. *Application contact:* Dr. Chanta M. Haywood, Dean of Graduate Studies, Research, and Continuing Education, 850-599-3315, Fax: 850-599-3727.

Florida Atlantic University, Dorothy F. Schmidt College of Arts and Letters, Department of History, Boca Raton, FL 33431-0991. Offers environmental studies (Certificate); history (MA). Part-time programs available. *Faculty:* 19 full-time (8 women), 1 part-time/adjunct (0 women). *Students:* 15 full-time (4 women), 14 part-time (6 women); includes 3 minority (all Hispanic Americans), 1 international. Average age 33. 30 applicants, 40% accepted, 2 enrolled. In 2009, 13 master's awarded. *Degree requirements:* For master's, one foreign language, thesis optional. *Entrance requirements:* For master's, GRE General Test, minimum GPA of 3.0. *Application deadline:* For fall admission, 6/1 priority date for domestic students, 2/15 for international students; for spring admission, 10/15 for domestic students, 8/15 for international students. Applications are processed on a rolling basis. Application fee: $30. Electronic applications accepted. *Expenses:* Tuition, state resident: full-time $7055; part-time $293.94 per credit hour. Tuition, nonresident: full-time $22,096; part-time $920.66 per credit hour. *Financial support:* Fellowships, research assistantships, teaching assistantships with tuition reimbursements, career-related internships or fieldwork, Federal Work-Study, and tuition waivers (partial) available. Support available to part-time students. Financial award application deadline: 3/1. *Faculty research:* Twentieth century America, U.S. urban history, Florida history, history of socialism, Latin America. *Unit head:* Dr. Patricia Kollander, Chair, 561-297-3841, Fax: 561-297-2704, E-mail: kollande@fau.edu. *Application contact:* Ben Lowe, Director of Graduate Programs, 561-297-3846, Fax: 561-297-2704, E-mail: bplowe@fau.edu.

Florida Gulf Coast University, College of Arts and Sciences, Program in History, Fort Myers, FL 33965-6565. Offers MA. Part-time and evening/weekend programs available. *Faculty:* 175 full-time (74 women), 139 part-time/adjunct (64 women). *Students:* 14 full-time (3 women), 3 part-time (2 women); includes 1 minority (Hispanic American). Average age 39. 10 applicants, 60% accepted, 2 enrolled. *Entrance requirements:* Additional exam requirements/recommendations for international students: Required—TOEFL (minimum score 550 paper-based; 213 computer-based). *Application deadline:* For fall admission, 2/15 priority date for domestic students; for spring admission, 10/1 for domestic students. Applications are processed on a rolling basis. Electronic applications accepted. *Unit head:* Eric Strahorn, Head, 239-590-7214, E-mail: estraho@fgcu.edu. *Application contact:* Patricia Rice, Executive Secretary, 239-590-7196, Fax: 239-590-7200, E-mail: price@fgcu.edu.

Florida International University, College of Arts and Sciences, Department of History, Miami, FL 33199. Offers Atlantic civilization (PhD); history (MA). Part-time and evening/weekend programs available. *Faculty:* 19 full-time (10 women). *Students:* 31 full-time (15 women), 59 part-time (26 women); includes 49 minority (7 African Americans, 1 American Indian/Alaska Native, 2 Asian Americans or Pacific Islanders, 39 Hispanic Americans), 3 international. Average age 32. 45 applicants, 27% accepted, 12 enrolled. In 2009, 8 master's, 3 doctorates awarded. *Degree requirements:* For master's, one foreign language, thesis optional; for doctorate, 2 foreign languages, comprehensive exam, thesis/dissertation. *Entrance requirements:* For master's, 12 credits of history courses (non-history majors), 2 letters of recommendation; writing sample, minimum GPA of 3.25; for doctorate, GRE General Test, Two letters of recommendation, statement of purpose, CV, writing sample, Minimum of 3.25 GPA required. GRE 1120. Additional exam requirements/recommendations for international students: Required—TOEFL (minimum score 575 paper-based; 232 computer-based; 90 iBT). *Application deadline:* For fall admission, 1/15 priority date for domestic students, 1/15 for international students. Application fee: $30. Electronic applications accepted. *Expenses:* Tuition, state resident: full-time $8008; part-time $4004 per year. Tuition, nonresident: full-time $20,104; part-time $10,052 per year. Required fees: $298; $149 per term. *Financial support:* In 2009–10, 4 fellowships with partial tuition reimbursements (averaging $18,500 per year), 23 teaching assistantships with partial tuition reimbursements (averaging $18,500 per year) were awarded; institutionally sponsored loans, scholarships/grants, and unspecified assistantships also available. Financial award application deadline: 3/1; financial award applicants required to submit FAFSA. *Faculty research:* European social history, American culture, social and labor history, Latin American culture and social history, military history, Diaspora studies. *Unit head:* Dr. Kenneth Lipartito, Chair, 305-348-2328, Fax: 305-348-3561, E-mail: kenneth.lipartito@fiu.edu. *Application contact:* Dr. Gwyn Davies, Director of Graduate Studies, 305-348-2328, Fax: 305-348-3561, E-mail: daviesg@fiu.edu.

Florida State University, The Graduate School, College of Arts and Sciences, Department of History, Tallahassee, FL 32306. Offers historical administration (MA); history (MA, PhD). Part-time programs available. *Faculty:* 31 full-time (10 women). *Students:* 92 full-time (37 women), 41 part-time (15 women); includes 14 minority (7 African Americans, 1 Asian American or Pacific Islander, 6 Hispanic Americans), 3 international. Average age 26. 106 applicants, 36% accepted, 17 enrolled. In 2009, 16 master's, 3 doctorates awarded. *Degree requirements:* For master's, one foreign language, comprehensive exam (for some programs), thesis (for some programs), internships; for doctorate, one foreign language, comprehensive exam, thesis/dissertation. *Entrance requirements:* For master's, GRE General Test, minimum GPA of 3.3, minimum 18 hours of course work in history; for doctorate, GRE General Test, minimum GPA of 3.3 (undergraduate), 3.65 (graduate). Additional exam requirements/recommendations for international students: Required—TOEFL (minimum score 550 paper-based; 213 computer-based; 80 iBT). *Application deadline:* For fall admission, 1/10 for domestic students; for spring admission, 10/1 for domestic students. Applications are processed on a rolling basis. Application fee: $30. Electronic applications accepted. *Expenses:* Tuition, state resident: full-time $7413. Tuition, nonresident: full-time $22,567. *Financial support:* In 2009–10, 77 students received support, including 3 fellowships with full tuition reimbursements available (averaging $14,700 per year), 6 research assistantships with full tuition reimbursements available (averaging $9,000 per year), 24 teaching assistantships with full tuition reimbursements available (averaging $10,500 per year); Federal Work-Study, institutionally sponsored loans, scholarships/grants, and unspecified assistantships also available. Financial award application deadline: 1/10;

History

Florida State University (continued)
financial award applicants required to submit FAFSA. *Faculty research:* Southern and Caribbean studies, Napoleon and the French Revolution, modern Europe, Latin America, U. S. intellectual and cultural history. *Unit head:* Dr. Neil Jumonville, Interim Chair, 850-644-5888, Fax: 850-644-6402, E-mail: njumonville@fsu.edu. *Application contact:* Chris Pignatiello, Academic Support Assistant, 850-644-2610, Fax: 850-644-6402, E-mail: cpignatiello@fsu.edu.

Fordham University, Graduate School of Arts and Sciences, Department of History, New York, NY 10458. Offers MA, PhD. Part-time and evening/weekend programs available. *Faculty:* 32 full-time (14 women). *Students:* 19 full-time (6 women), 57 part-time (29 women); includes 11 minority (1 African American, 2 Asian Americans or Pacific Islanders, 8 Hispanic Americans), 3 international. Average age 31. 111 applicants, 48% accepted, 18 enrolled. In 2009, 3 master's, 18 doctorates awarded. Terminal master's awarded for partial completion of doctoral program. *Degree requirements:* For master's, one foreign language, thesis optional; for doctorate, 2 foreign languages, comprehensive exam, thesis/dissertation. *Entrance requirements:* For master's and doctorate, GRE General Test. Additional exam requirements/recommendations for international students: Required—TOEFL (minimum score 650 paper-based; 280 computer-based). *Application deadline:* For fall admission, 1/4 priority date for domestic students; for spring admission, 11/1 for domestic students. Application fee: $70. Electronic applications accepted. *Financial support:* In 2009–10, 23 students received support, including 2 fellowships with tuition reimbursements available (averaging $23,000 per year), 13 research assistantships with tuition reimbursements available (averaging $18,704 per year), 8 teaching assistantships with tuition reimbursements available (averaging $18,802 per year); institutionally sponsored loans, tuition waivers (full and partial), and unspecified assistantships also available. Financial award application deadline: 1/4; financial award applicants required to submit FAFSA. *Unit head:* Dr. Doran Ben-Atar, Chair, 718-817-3925, Fax: 718-817-4680. *Application contact:* Charlene Dundie, Director of Graduate Admissions, 718-817-4420, Fax: 718-817-3566, E-mail: dundie@fordham.edu.

Fort Hays State University, Graduate School, College of Arts and Sciences, Department of History, Hays, KS 67601-4099. Offers MA. *Degree requirements:* For master's, comprehensive exam, thesis or alternative. *Entrance requirements:* For master's, minimum undergraduate GPA of 3.0. Additional exam requirements/recommendations for international students: Required—TOEFL (minimum score 550 paper-based; 213 computer-based). Electronic applications accepted. *Faculty research:* Seventeenth century English legal history, Native American history, immigration history, Volga German settlement.

George Mason University, College of Humanities and Social Sciences, Department of History and Art History, Program in History, Fairfax, VA 22030. Offers MA, PhD. Evening/weekend programs available. *Faculty:* 49 full-time (19 women), 19 part-time/adjunct (10 women). *Students:* 36 full-time (21 women), 198 part-time (79 women); includes 12 minority (5 African Americans, 4 Asian Americans or Pacific Islanders, 3 Hispanic Americans), 2 international. Average age 37. 197 applicants, 63% accepted, 60 enrolled. In 2009, 37 master's, 2 doctorates awarded. *Degree requirements:* For master's, comprehensive exam, translation language exam; for doctorate, comprehensive exam, thesis/dissertation. *Entrance requirements:* For master's, GRE (waived for students who received their undergraduate degree 10 or more years ago or hold another graduate degree), 2 letters of recommendation; for doctorate, GRE, 3 letters of recommendation, writing sample, official transcripts, assistantship application. Additional exam requirements/recommendations for international students: Required—TOEFL. *Application deadline:* For fall admission, 4/15 priority date for domestic students; for spring admission, 11/1 for domestic students. Applications are processed on a rolling basis. Application fee: $75. Electronic applications accepted. *Expenses:* Tuition, state resident: full-time $7568; part-time $315.33 per credit hour. Tuition, nonresident: full-time $21,704; part-time $904.33 per credit hour. Required fees: $2184; $91 per credit hour. *Financial support:* In 2009–10, 22 students received support, including 2 fellowships with full tuition reimbursements available (averaging $18,000 per year), 9 research assistantships with full and partial tuition reimbursements available (averaging $12,083 per year), 11 teaching assistantships with full and partial tuition reimbursements available (averaging $13,981 per year); Federal Work-Study, scholarships/grants, unspecified assistantships, and health care benefits (full-time research or teaching assistantship recipients) also available. Support available to part-time students. Financial award application deadline: 3/1. *Faculty research:* History and new media, American history (digital), building digital archives in the 1930s. Total annual research expenditures: $3.8 million. *Unit head:* Brian Platt, Chair, 703-993-1253, E-mail: bplatt1@gmu.edu. *Application contact:* Ellen Todd, Art History Advisor, 703-993-4374, E-mail: etodd@gmu.edu.

Georgetown University, Graduate School of Arts and Sciences, Department of History, Washington, DC 20057-1305. Offers global history (MA); global, international and comparative history (MA); history (MA, PhD); MA/PhD; MS/MA. MA in global history offered jointly with history department at King's College London. *Degree requirements:* For master's, thesis (for some programs); for doctorate, 2 foreign languages, comprehensive exam, thesis/dissertation. *Entrance requirements:* For master's and doctorate, GRE General Test. Additional exam requirements/recommendations for international students: Required—TOEFL.

Georgetown University, Graduate School of Arts and Sciences, School of Continuing Studies, Washington, DC 20057. Offers American studies (MALS); Catholic studies (MALS); classical civilizations (MALS); ethics and the professions (MALS); human resources management (MPS); humanities (MALS); individualized study (MALS); international affairs (MALS); Islam and Muslim-Christian relations (MALS); journalism (MPS); liberal studies (DLS); literature and society (MALS); medieval and early modern European studies (MALS); public relations (MPS); real estate (MPS); religious studies (MALS); social and public policy (MALS); sports industry management (MPS); the theory and practice of American democracy (MALS); visual culture (MALS). *Entrance requirements:* Additional exam requirements/recommendations for international students: Required—TOEFL.

The George Washington University, Columbian College of Arts and Sciences, Department of History, Washington, DC 20052. Offers MA, PhD. Part-time and evening/weekend programs available. *Faculty:* 22 full-time (11 women), 26 part-time/adjunct (7 women). *Students:* 33 full-time (13 women), 34 part-time (19 women); includes 6 minority (1 African American, 2 American Indian/Alaska Native, 3 Asian Americans or Pacific Islanders), 4 international. Average age 31. 192 applicants, 33% accepted, 19 enrolled. In 2009, 18 master's, 7 doctorates awarded. Terminal master's awarded for partial completion of doctoral program. *Degree requirements:* For master's, one foreign language, comprehensive exam, thesis or alternative; for doctorate, 2 foreign languages, thesis/dissertation, general exam. *Entrance requirements:* For master's and doctorate, GRE General Test, minimum GPA of 3.0. Additional exam requirements/recommendations for international students: Required—TOEFL (minimum score 550 paper-based; 213 computer-based; 80 iBT). *Application deadline:* For fall admission, 1/15 priority date for domestic and international students; for spring admission, 10/1 priority date for domestic students, 9/1 priority date for international students. Applications are processed on a rolling basis. Application fee: $60. Electronic applications accepted. *Financial support:* In 2009–10, 28 students received support; fellowships with full tuition reimbursements available, teaching assistantships with tuition reimbursements available, career-related internships or fieldwork, Federal Work-Study, and tuition waivers available. Financial award application deadline: 1/15. *Unit head:* Tyler G. Anbinder, Chair, 202-994-6470, E-mail: anbinder@gwu.edu. *Application contact:* Information Contact, 202-994-6230, Fax: 202-994-6231, E-mail: history@www.gwu.edu.

Georgia College & State University, Graduate School, College of Arts and Sciences, Department of History, Geography and Philosophy, Milledgeville, GA 31061. Offers history (advanced studies option) (MA); history (predoctoral option) (MA); public history (MA). Part-time and evening/weekend programs available. *Faculty:* 18 full-time (3 women). *Students:* 6 full-time (5 women), 5 part-time (2 women). Average age 27. 6 applicants, 83% accepted, 3 enrolled. In 2009, 5 master's awarded. *Degree requirements:* For master's, one foreign language, comprehensive exam (for some programs), thesis optional. *Entrance requirements:* For master's, GRE, 2 letters of reference, transcript. Additional exam requirements/recommendations for international students: Recommended—TOEFL (minimum score 550 paper-based; 213 computer-based; 79 iBT). *Application deadline:* For fall admission, 7/1 for domestic students; for spring admission, 11/15 for domestic students. Applications are processed on a rolling basis. Application fee: $40. Electronic applications accepted. *Expenses:* Tuition, area resident: Part-time $241 per credit hour. Tuition, state resident: full-time $4338. Tuition, nonresident: full-time $17,352; part-time $964 per credit hour. Required fees: $609 per semester. Tuition and fees vary according to course load and campus/location. *Financial support:* In 2009–10, 6 research assistantships were awarded; unspecified assistantships also available. Support available to part-time students. Financial award applicants required to submit FAFSA. *Unit head:* Dr. John Fair, Graduate Coordinator for MA in History Program, 478-445-5215, E-mail: john.fair@gcsu.edu. *Application contact:* Dr. John Fair, Graduate Coordinator for MA in History Program, 478-445-5215, E-mail: john.fair@gcsu.edu.

Georgia Southern University, Jack N. Averitt College of Graduate Studies, College of Liberal Arts and Social Sciences, Department of History, Statesboro, GA 30460. Offers MA. Part-time programs available. *Students:* 16 full-time (6 women), 8 part-time (2 women); includes 3 minority (2 African Americans, 1 American Indian/Alaska Native). Average age 30. 4 applicants, 100% accepted, 4 enrolled. In 2009, 6 master's awarded. *Degree requirements:* For master's, one foreign language, thesis optional, terminal exams. *Entrance requirements:* For master's, GRE General Test, minimum GPA of 3.0, undergraduate major in history or equivalent, letters of reference. Additional exam requirements/recommendations for international students: Required—TOEFL (minimum score 550 paper-based; 213 computer-based; 80 iBT). *Application deadline:* For fall admission, 3/1 priority date for domestic and international students; for spring admission, 10/1 priority date for domestic students, 10/1 for international students. Applications are processed on a rolling basis. Application fee: $50. Electronic applications accepted. *Expenses:* Tuition, state resident: full-time $5040; part-time $210 per credit hour. Tuition, nonresident: full-time $20,136; part-time $839 per credit hour. Required fees: $1644. *Financial support:* In 2009–10, 17 students received support, including research assistantships with partial tuition reimbursements available (averaging $7,200 per year), teaching assistantships with partial tuition reimbursements available (averaging $7,200 per year); career-related internships or fieldwork, Federal Work-Study, scholarships/grants, tuition waivers (partial), and unspecified assistantships also available. Support available to part-time students. Financial award application deadline: 4/15; financial award applicants required to submit FAFSA. *Faculty research:* Women's/gender history, American South, military history. *Unit head:* Dr. William T. Allison, Chair, 912-478-4478, Fax: 912-478-0377, E-mail: billallison@georgiasouthern.edu. *Application contact:* Dr. Charles Ziglar, Coordinator for Graduate Student Recruitment, 912-478-5384, Fax: 912-478-0740, E-mail: gradadmissions@georgiasouthern.edu.

Georgia State University, College of Arts and Sciences, Department of History, Program in History, Atlanta, GA 30302-3083. Offers MA, PhD. Part-time and evening/weekend programs available. *Degree requirements:* For master's, one foreign language, thesis, exam; for doctorate, 2 foreign languages, thesis/dissertation, exam. *Entrance requirements:* For master's, GRE General Test; for doctorate, GRE General Test, sample of written work. Additional exam requirements/recommendations for international students: Required—TOEFL. Electronic applications accepted. *Faculty research:* World, U.S. South, cultural history, public history, labor.

Graduate School and University Center of the City University of New York, Graduate Studies, Program in History, New York, NY 10016-4039. Offers PhD. *Faculty:* 75 full-time (18 women). *Students:* 142 full-time (60 women), 2 part-time (1 woman); includes 15 minority (7 African Americans, 2 Asian Americans or Pacific Islanders, 6 Hispanic Americans), 11 international. Average age 36. 134 applicants, 40% accepted, 25 enrolled. In 2009, 11 doctorates awarded. *Degree requirements:* For doctorate, one foreign language, thesis/dissertation. *Entrance requirements:* For doctorate, GRE General Test, writing sample (15 pages). Additional exam requirements/recommendations for international students: Required—TOEFL. *Application deadline:* For fall admission, 1/15 priority date for domestic students. Application fee: $125. Electronic applications accepted. *Financial support:* In 2009–10, 86 students received support, including 90 fellowships, 12 research assistantships, 13 teaching assistantships; career-related internships or fieldwork, Federal Work-Study, institutionally sponsored loans, and tuition waivers (full and partial) also available. Financial award application deadline: 2/1; financial award applicants required to submit FAFSA. *Unit head:* Dr. Joshua Freeman, Executive Officer, 212-817-8430, Fax: 212-817-1523. *Application contact:* Les Gribben, Director of Admissions, 212-817-7470, Fax: 212-817-1624, E-mail: lgribben@gc.cuny.edu.

Hardin-Simmons University, Graduate School, Cynthia Ann Parker College of Liberal Arts, Department of History, Abilene, TX 79698-0001. Offers MA. Part-time programs available. *Faculty:* 5 full-time (2 women). *Students:* 4 part-time (1 woman). Average age 35. 1 applicant, 0% accepted, 0 enrolled. *Degree requirements:* For master's, one foreign language, comprehensive exam, thesis or alternative. *Entrance requirements:* For master's, GRE, minimum undergraduate GPA of 3.0 in history, 2.7 overall; 18 upper-level hours of course work in history; letters of recommendation; resume; writing sample. Additional exam requirements/recommendations for international students: Required—TOEFL (minimum score 550 paper-based; 213 computer-based; 75 iBT). *Application deadline:* For fall admission, 8/15 priority date for domestic students, 4/1 for international students; for spring admission, 1/5 priority date for domestic students, 9/1 for international students. Applications are processed on a rolling basis. Application fee: $50. *Expenses:* Tuition: Full-time $11,430; part-time $635 per credit hour. Required fees: $650; $110 per semester. Tuition and fees vary according to degree level. *Financial support:* In 2009–10, 2 students received support; fellowships, scholarships/grants available. Support available to part-time students. Financial award application deadline: 6/30; financial award applicants required to submit FAFSA. *Faculty research:* Vietnam, diplomatic history, Texas politics, Mexico and NAFTA, classical warfare. *Unit head:* Dr. Mark Beasley, Program Director, 325-670-1279, Fax: 325-670-1526, E-mail: mbeasley@hsutx.edu. *Application contact:* Dr. Gary Stanlake, Dean of Graduate Studies, 325-670-1298, Fax: 325-670-1564, E-mail: gradoff@hsutx.edu.

Harvard University, Graduate School of Arts and Sciences, Department of History, Cambridge, MA 02138. Offers African history (PhD); American history (PhD); ancient, medieval, early modern, and modern Europe (PhD), including Central Europe, Russia, Southeastern Europe, Western Europe; diplomatic history (PhD); East Asian history (PhD); economic and social history (PhD); intellectual history (PhD); Latin American history (PhD); Near Eastern history (PhD); oceanic history (PhD). *Degree requirements:* For doctorate, variable foreign language requirement, thesis/dissertation, oral general exam. *Entrance requirements:* For doctorate, GRE General Test, proficiency in 2 languages. Additional exam requirements/recommendations for international students: Required—TOEFL. *Expenses:* Tuition: Full-time $33,696. Required fees: $1126. Full-time tuition and fees vary according to program.

High Point University, Norcross Graduate School, High Point, NC 27262-3598. Offers business administration (MBA); educational leadership (M Ed); elementary education (M Ed); history (MA); nonprofit management (MA); special education (M Ed); sport studies (MS). *Accreditation:* ACBSP; NCATE. Part-time and evening/weekend programs available. *Degree requirements:* For master's, comprehensive exam (for some programs), thesis (for some programs). *Entrance requirements:* For master's, GMAT (MBA), GRE General Test, MAT, minimum GPA of 3.0. Additional exam requirements/recommendations for international students: Required—TOEFL (minimum score 550 paper-based). Electronic applications accepted.

Howard University, Graduate School, Department of History, Washington, DC 20059-0002. Offers African diaspora (MA, PhD); African history (MA, PhD); Latin America and the Caribbean (MA, PhD); public history (MA); United States history (MA, PhD). Part-time programs available. Terminal master's awarded for partial completion of doctoral program. *Degree requirements:* For master's, one foreign language, thesis optional; for doctorate, 2 foreign languages, comprehensive exam, thesis/dissertation. *Entrance requirements:* For master's, GRE General Test, minimum GPA of 3.0, 3 letters of recommendation; for doctorate, GRE General Test, minimum GPA of 3.5, 3 letters of recommendation. Additional exam requirements/

recommendations for international students: Required—TOEFL. Electronic applications accepted. *Faculty research:* Africa diaspora, U.S. diplomatic relations, Caribbean economic history.

Hunter College of the City University of New York, Graduate School, School of Arts and Sciences, Department of History, New York, NY 10021-5085. Offers MA. *Faculty:* 8 full-time (3 women), 2 part-time/adjunct (0 women). *Students:* 1 full-time (0 women), 51 part-time (20 women); includes 5 minority (1 African American, 1 American Indian/Alaska Native, 3 Hispanic Americans). Average age 36. 35 applicants, 66% accepted, 10 enrolled. In 2009, 15 master's awarded. *Degree requirements:* For master's, one foreign language, comprehensive exam, thesis, essay, language exam. *Entrance requirements:* For master's, GRE General Test, minimum of 18 credits in undergraduate history or related field. Additional exam requirements/recommendations for international students: Required—TOEFL. *Application deadline:* For fall admission, 4/1 for domestic students, 2/1 for international students; for spring admission, 11/1 for domestic students, 9/1 for international students. Application fee: $125. *Expenses:* Tuition, state resident: full-time $7360; part-time $310 per credit. Required fees: $250 per semester. *Financial support:* Federal Work-Study, scholarships/grants, and tuition waivers (partial) available. Support available to part-time students. *Unit head:* Dr. Barbara Welter, Chair and Graduate Advisor, 212-772-5487, E-mail: bwelter@hunter.cuny.edu. *Application contact:* William Zlata, Director for Graduate Admissions, 212-772-4482, Fax: 212-650-3336, E-mail: admissions@hunter.cuny.edu.

Idaho State University, Office of Graduate Studies, College of Arts and Sciences, Department of History, Pocatello, ID 83209-8079. Offers historical resources management (MA). Part-time programs available. *Faculty:* 7 full-time (2 women), 1 (woman) part-time/adjunct. *Students:* 6 full-time (1 woman), 4 part-time (2 women), 2 international. Average age 36. In 2009, 1 master's awarded. *Degree requirements:* For master's, comprehensive exam, thesis optional, internship. *Entrance requirements:* For master's, GRE, 3 letters of recommendation, minimum of 18 upper division history credits. Additional exam requirements/recommendations for international students: Required—TOEFL (minimum score 550 paper-based; 213 computer-based; 80 iBT). *Application deadline:* For fall admission, 7/1 for domestic students, 6/1 for international students; for spring admission, 12/1 for domestic students, 11/1 for international students. Applications are processed on a rolling basis. Application fee: $55. Electronic applications accepted. *Expenses:* Tuition, state resident: full-time $3318; part-time $297 per credit hour. Tuition, nonresident: full-time $13,120; part-time $437 per credit hour. Required fees: $2530. Tuition and fees vary according to program. *Financial support:* In 2009–10, 3 research assistantships with full and partial tuition reimbursements (averaging $8,420 per year), 3 teaching assistantships with full and partial tuition reimbursements (averaging $10,841 per year) were awarded; career-related internships or fieldwork, Federal Work-Study, institutionally sponsored loans, scholarships/grants, health care benefits, tuition waivers (full and partial), and unspecified assistantships also available. Support available to part-time students. Financial award application deadline: 1/1; financial award applicants required to submit FAFSA. *Faculty research:* Historical geographic information systems, historical and urban geography, environmental history and environmental policy, United States political history, womens' and gender history. *Unit head:* Dr. Laura Woodworth-Ney, Chairman, 208-282-2379, E-mail: woodlaur@isu.edu. *Application contact:* Tami Carson, Graduate School Technical Records Specialist, 208-282-2150, Fax: 208-282-4847, E-mail: carstami@isu.edu.

Illinois State University, Graduate School, College of Arts and Sciences, Department of History, Normal, IL 61790-2200. Offers MA, MS. *Degree requirements:* For master's, thesis or alternative. *Entrance requirements:* For master's, GRE General Test, minimum GPA of 2.6 in last 60 hours of course work.

Indiana State University, School of Graduate Studies, College of Arts and Sciences, Department of History, Terre Haute, IN 47809. Offers MA, MS. Part-time and evening/weekend programs available. *Degree requirements:* For master's, comprehensive exam (for some programs), thesis or alternative. *Entrance requirements:* For master's, equivalent of minor in geography or geology. Additional exam requirements/recommendations for international students: Required—TOEFL (minimum score 550 paper-based).

Indiana University Bloomington, University Graduate School, College of Arts and Sciences, Department of History, Bloomington, IN 47405-7000. Offers MA, MAT, PhD, MA/MLS. *Faculty:* 44 full-time (12 women), 34 part-time/adjunct (15 women). *Students:* 125 full-time (65 women), 2 part-time (1 women); includes 17 minority (7 African Americans, 1 American Indian/Alaska Native, 3 Asian Americans or Pacific Islanders, 6 Hispanic Americans), 16 international. Average age 32. 238 applicants, 15% accepted, 21 enrolled. In 2009, 16 master's, 12 doctorates awarded. Terminal master's awarded for partial completion of doctoral program. *Degree requirements:* For master's, one foreign language, thesis optional; for doctorate, one foreign language, comprehensive exam, thesis/dissertation. *Entrance requirements:* For master's and doctorate, GRE General Test. Additional exam requirements/recommendations for international students: Required—TOEFL. *Application deadline:* For fall admission, 1/2 for domestic students, 12/1 for international students. Application fee: $55 ($65 for international students). Electronic applications accepted. *Financial support:* In 2009–10, 28 fellowships with full tuition reimbursements (averaging $15,000 per year), 18 teaching assistantships with full tuition reimbursements (averaging $14,772 per year) were awarded; research assistantships with full tuition reimbursements, career-related internships or fieldwork, Federal Work-Study, institutionally sponsored loans, scholarships/grants, traineeships, health care benefits, and unspecified assistantships also available. *Faculty research:* Medieval and early modern Europe, Russia, Latin America, Middle East, Great Britain, United States, Africa and African Diaspora, Europe, eastern Europe. *Unit head:* Dr. Claude Clegg, Chairman, 812-855-3236, Fax: 812-855-3378, E-mail: cclegg@indiana.edu. *Application contact:* Mary Medley-Byers, Admissions Secretary, 812-855-8233, Fax: 812-855-3378, E-mail: histadm@indiana.edu.

Indiana University of Pennsylvania, School of Graduate Studies and Research, College of Humanities and Social Sciences, Department of History, Program in History, Indiana, PA 15705-1087. Offers MA. Part-time programs available. *Faculty:* 8 full-time (2 women). *Students:* 11 full-time (7 women). Average age 24. 21 applicants, 52% accepted, 6 enrolled. In 2009, 7 master's awarded. *Degree requirements:* For master's, thesis optional. *Entrance requirements:* For master's, GRE, 2 letters of recommendation. Additional exam requirements/recommendations for international students: Required—TOEFL. *Application deadline:* For spring admission, 11/1 for domestic students. Applications are processed on a rolling basis. Application fee: $40. *Expenses:* Tuition, state resident: full-time $6666; part-time $370 per credit hour. Tuition, nonresident: full-time $10,666; part-time $593 per credit hour. Required fees: $813 per semester. *Financial support:* In 2009–10, 5 research assistantships with full and partial tuition reimbursements (averaging $2,870 per year) were awarded; fellowships, Federal Work-Study also available. Support available to part-time students. Financial award application deadline: 3/15; financial award applicants required to submit FAFSA. *Unit head:* Dr. Werner Lippert, Graduate Coordinator, 724-357-2573, E-mail: werner.lippert@iup.edu. *Application contact:* Dr. Tami Whited, Graduate Coordinator, 724-357-2573, E-mail: twhited@iup.edu.

Indiana University–Purdue University Indianapolis, School of Liberal Arts, Department of History, Indianapolis, IN 46202-2896. Offers history (MA); public history (MA); MA/MLS. Part-time and evening/weekend programs available. *Faculty:* 14 full-time (6 women). *Students:* 24 full-time (20 women), 23 part-time (15 women), 1 international. Average age 30. 238 applicants, 15% accepted, 21 enrolled. In 2009, 11 master's awarded. *Degree requirements:* For master's, one foreign language, thesis. *Entrance requirements:* For master's, GRE General Test, minimum GPA of 3.0. *Application deadline:* For fall admission, 2/1 priority date for domestic students. Applications are processed on a rolling basis. Application fee: $55 ($65 for international students). *Financial support:* In 2009–10, 1 fellowship with full tuition reimbursement (averaging $10,000 per year), 19 teaching assistantships with full tuition reimbursements (averaging $8,612 per year) were awarded; research assistantships with full tuition reimbursements, career-related internships or fieldwork also available. *Unit head:* Robert Barrows, Chair, 317-274-2457. *Application contact:* Mary Gelzleichter, Graduate Secretary, 317-274-5840, Fax: 317-278-7800, E-mail: mgelzlei@iupui.edu.

Inter American University of Puerto Rico, Metropolitan Campus, Graduate Programs, Program in History, San Juan, PR 00919-1293. Offers American history (PhD); history (MA, PhD).

Iona College, School of Arts and Science, Program in History, New Rochelle, NY 10801-1890. Offers MA. Part-time and evening/weekend programs available. *Faculty:* 7 full-time (1 woman), 1 (woman) part-time/adjunct. *Students:* 6 full-time (2 women), 17 part-time (9 women); includes 2 minority (both Hispanic Americans), 1 international. Average age 29. 9 applicants, 100% accepted, 6 enrolled. In 2009, 7 master's awarded. *Degree requirements:* For master's, one foreign language, thesis. *Entrance requirements:* For master's, undergraduate major in history or related field, minimum GPA of 3.0. Additional exam requirements/recommendations for international students: Required—TOEFL (minimum score 550 paper-based; 213 computer-based). *Application deadline:* Applications are processed on a rolling basis. Application fee: $50. Electronic applications accepted. *Expenses:* Tuition: Part-time $830 per credit. *Financial support:* Unspecified assistantships available. Financial award application deadline: 4/15; financial award applicants required to submit FAFSA. *Faculty research:* Global studies, American diplomacy, Native Americans, foreign policy, Armenian history. *Unit head:* Dr. James Carroll, Chairman, 914-633-2694, E-mail: jcarroll@iona.edu. *Application contact:* Veronica Jarek-Prinz, Director of Graduate Admissions, 914-633-2420, Fax: 914-633-2277, E-mail: vjarekprinz@iona.edu.

Iowa State University of Science and Technology, Graduate College, College of Liberal Arts and Sciences, Department of History, Ames, IA 50011. Offers agricultural history and rural studies (PhD); history (MA); history of technology and science (MA, PhD). *Faculty:* 20 full-time (6 women). *Students:* 26 full-time (8 women), 10 part-time (5 women); includes 1 minority (Hispanic American), 2 international. 25 applicants, 84% accepted, 11 enrolled. In 2009, 6 master's, 4 doctorates awarded. *Degree requirements:* For master's, thesis or alternative; for doctorate, thesis/dissertation. *Entrance requirements:* For master's and doctorate, GRE General Test. Additional exam requirements/recommendations for international students: Required—TOEFL (minimum score 600 paper-based; 79 iBT) or IELTS (minimum score 7). *Application deadline:* For fall admission, 1/15 priority date for domestic and international students. Applications are processed on a rolling basis. Application fee: $40 ($90 for international students). Electronic applications accepted. *Expenses:* Tuition, state resident: full-time $6716. Tuition, nonresident: full-time $8908. Tuition and fees vary according to course level, course load, program and student level. *Financial support:* In 2009–10, 2 research assistantships with full and partial tuition reimbursements (averaging $13,770 per year), 19 teaching assistantships with full and partial tuition reimbursements (averaging $13,500 per year) were awarded; scholarships/grants, health care benefits, and unspecified assistantships also available. *Unit head:* Dr. Charles Dobbs, Chair, 515-294-7266, Fax: 515-294-6390, E-mail: cdobbs@iastate.edu. *Application contact:* Dr. Pamela Riney-Kehrberg, Information Contact, 515-294-1451, Fax: 515-294-6390.

Jackson State University, Graduate School, School of Liberal Arts, Department of History, Jackson, MS 39217. Offers MA. Part-time and evening/weekend programs available. *Degree requirements:* For master's, comprehensive exam, thesis or alternative. *Entrance requirements:* For master's, GRE General Test. Additional exam requirements/recommendations for international students: Required—TOEFL.

Jacksonville State University, College of Graduate Studies and Continuing Education, College of Arts and Sciences, Department of History, Jacksonville, AL 36265-1602. Offers MA. Part-time and evening/weekend programs available. *Faculty:* 11 full-time (2 women). *Students:* 5 full-time (2 women), 21 part-time (8 women); includes 3 minority (all African Americans). Average age 32. 11 applicants, 73% accepted, 8 enrolled. In 2009, 12 master's awarded. *Degree requirements:* For master's, comprehensive exam, thesis (for some programs). *Entrance requirements:* For master's, GRE General Test or MAT. *Application deadline:* Applications are processed on a rolling basis. Application fee: $30. Electronic applications accepted. *Financial support:* In 2009–10, 19 students received support. Available to part-time students. Application deadline: 4/1. *Unit head:* Dr. Harvy Jackson, Head, 256-782-5622. *Application contact:* Dr. Jean Pugliese, Associate Dean, 256-782-8278, Fax: 256-782-5321, E-mail: pugliese@jsu.edu.

James Madison University, The Graduate School, College of Arts and Letters, Department of History, Harrisonburg, VA 22807. Offers MA. Part-time programs available. *Faculty:* 20 full-time (6 women), 1 part-time/adjunct (0 women). *Students:* 24 full-time (10 women), 8 part-time (3 women). Average age 27. In 2009, 7 master's awarded. *Degree requirements:* For master's, one foreign language, comprehensive exam, thesis, reading exam in a language. *Entrance requirements:* For master's, GRE General Test, GRE Subject Test, 2 letters of recommendation. Additional exam requirements/recommendations for international students: Required—TOEFL. *Application deadline:* For fall admission, 1/15 for domestic students. Applications are processed on a rolling basis. Application fee: $55. Electronic applications accepted. *Expenses:* Tuition, area resident: Part-time $305 per credit hour. Tuition, state resident: part-time $305 per credit hour. Tuition, nonresident: part-time $890 per credit hour. *Financial support:* In 2009–10, 12 students received support, including 3 teaching assistantships with full tuition reimbursements available (averaging $8,664 per year); Federal Work-Study also available. Financial award application deadline: 3/1; financial award applicants required to submit FAFSA. *Unit head:* Dr. Michael J. Galgano, Academic Unit Head, 540-568-6132. *Application contact:* Lynette M. Bible, Director of Graduate Admissions, 540-568-6395, Fax: 540-568-7860, E-mail: biblelm@jmu.edu.

John Carroll University, Graduate School, Department of History, University Heights, OH 44118-4581. Offers MA. Part-time and evening/weekend programs available. *Degree requirements:* For master's, comprehensive exam, research essay or thesis. *Entrance requirements:* For master's, GRE General Test, minimum GPA of 2.5. Additional exam requirements/recommendations for international students: Required—TOEFL. Electronic applications accepted. *Faculty research:* Social history of Cleveland, early national Pennsylvania, modern Japanese journalism, Catholic Reformation.

The Johns Hopkins University, Zanvyl Krieger School of Arts and Sciences, Department of History, Baltimore, MD 21218-2699. Offers PhD. *Faculty:* 23 full-time (7 women). *Students:* 58 full-time (28 women); includes 2 minority (both Asian Americans or Pacific Islanders), 15 international. Average age 29. 140 applicants, 6% accepted, 7 enrolled. In 2009, 8 doctorates awarded. *Degree requirements:* For doctorate, variable foreign language requirement, comprehensive exam, thesis/dissertation. *Entrance requirements:* For doctorate, GRE General Test. Additional exam requirements/recommendations for international students: Required—TOEFL (minimum score 600 paper-based; 250 computer-based; 100 iBT), IELTS. *Application deadline:* For fall admission, 12/15 for domestic and international students. Application fee: $75. Electronic applications accepted. *Financial support:* In 2009–10, 55 students received support; fellowships with full tuition reimbursements available, research assistantships with full tuition reimbursements available, teaching assistantships with full tuition reimbursements available, Federal Work-Study and institutionally sponsored loans available. Financial award application deadline: 4/15; financial award applicants required to submit FAFSA. *Faculty research:* American, European, Latin American, East Asian history, and African history. Total annual research expenditures: $179,717. *Unit head:* Dr. William T. Rowe, Chair, 410-516-7575, Fax: 410-516-7586, E-mail: wtrowe@jhu.edu. *Application contact:* Megan B. Zeller, Senior Administrative Coordinator, 410-516-5296, Fax: 410-516-7586, E-mail: mzeller4@jhu.edu.

Kansas State University, Graduate School, College of Arts and Sciences, Department of History, Manhattan, KS 66506. Offers history (MA); security studies (MA, PhD). Part-time programs available. *Faculty:* 19 full-time (8 women), 1 part-time/adjunct (0 women). *Students:* 74 full-time (13 women), 62 part-time (14 women); includes 3 minority (1 African American, 2 Asian Americans or Pacific Islanders), 2 international. Average age 29. 86 applicants, 72% accepted, 41 enrolled. In 2009, 19 master's, 5 doctorates awarded. *Degree requirements:* For master's, thesis (for some programs); for doctorate, one foreign language, thesis/dissertation,

History

Kansas State University (continued)
qualifying exam. *Entrance requirements:* For master's, GRE General Test or MAT, minimum undergraduate GPA of 3.0; for doctorate, GRE General Test or MAT. Additional exam requirements/recommendations for international students: Required—TOEFL (minimum score 600 paper-based). *Application deadline:* For fall admission, 2/1 priority date for domestic and international students; for spring admission, 8/1 priority date for domestic and international students. Applications are processed on a rolling basis. Application fee: $40 ($55 for international students). Electronic applications accepted. *Financial support:* In 2009–10, 7 research assistantships (averaging $18,104 per year), 12 teaching assistantships with full tuition reimbursements (averaging $8,954 per year) were awarded; career-related internships or fieldwork, Federal Work-Study, institutionally sponsored loans, and scholarships/grants also available. Support available to part-time students. Financial award application deadline: 3/1; financial award applicants required to submit FAFSA. *Faculty research:* Environmental history, history of Christianity, American social history, history of war and society, history of international relations and diplomacy. Total annual research expenditures: $16,186. *Unit head:* Louise Breen, Head, 785-532-0365, Fax: 785-532-7004, E-mail: breen@ksu.edu. *Application contact:* Louise Breen, Recruiting Program Director, 785-532-0365, Fax: 785-532-7004, E-mail: breen@ksu.edu.

Kent State University, College of Arts and Sciences, Department of History, Kent, OH 44242-0001. Offers MA, PhD. Part-time programs available. *Degree requirements:* For master's, variable foreign language requirement, thesis optional; for doctorate, variable foreign language requirement, thesis/dissertation. *Entrance requirements:* For master's, GRE General Test, GRE Subject Test, minimum GPA of 2.75; for doctorate, GRE General Test, GRE Subject Test, minimum GPA of 3.0. Additional exam requirements/recommendations for international students: Required—TOEFL. Electronic applications accepted. *Faculty research:* African American, civil war, British empire, Latin America, public history.

Lakehead University, Graduate Studies, Department of History, Thunder Bay, ON P7B 5E1, Canada. Offers gerontology (MA); history (MA); women's studies (MA). Part-time programs available. *Degree requirements:* For master's, one foreign language, thesis. *Entrance requirements:* For master's, minimum B average. Additional exam requirements/recommendations for international students: Required—TOEFL. *Faculty research:* Canadian history, British history, Russian/German history, women's studies.

Lamar University, College of Graduate Studies, College of Arts and Sciences, Department of History, Beaumont, TX 77710. Offers MA. Part-time programs available. *Faculty:* 5 full-time (1 woman). *Students:* 1 (woman) full-time, 3 part-time (1 woman); includes 1 minority (African American). Average age 43. 5 applicants, 60% accepted, 0 enrolled. In 2009, 3 master's awarded. *Degree requirements:* For master's, comprehensive exam (for some programs), thesis (for some programs). *Entrance requirements:* For master's, GRE General Test, minimum GPA of 2.5 in last 60 hours of undergraduate course work. Additional exam requirements/recommendations for international students: Required—TOEFL. *Application deadline:* For fall admission, 8/1 for domestic students; for spring admission, 12/1 for domestic students. Applications are processed on a rolling basis. Application fee: $25 ($50 for international students). *Financial support:* In 2009–10, fellowships (averaging $1,000 per year), teaching assistantships (averaging $2,000 per year) were awarded. Financial award application deadline: 4/1. *Faculty research:* Old South, nineteenth century reform, twentieth century U.S., religion in America's South, Renaissance/early modern Europe. *Unit head:* Dr. John Storey, Chair, 409-880-8511, Fax: 409-880-8710, E-mail: storeyjw@hal.lamar.edu. *Application contact:* Dr. Howell H. Gwin, Graduate Adviser, 409-880-8530, Fax: 409-880-8710, E-mail: gwinhh@hal.lamar.edu.

La Salle University, School of Arts and Sciences, Program in History, Philadelphia, PA 19141-1199. Offers MA. Part-time programs available.

Laurentian University, School of Graduate Studies and Research, Programme in History, Sudbury, ON P3E 2C6, Canada. Offers European history (MA); history of Northern Ontario (MA); North American history (MA). Part-time programs available. *Degree requirements:* For master's, thesis or alternative. *Entrance requirements:* For master's, honors degree with minimum second class. *Faculty research:* Franco-Ontarian history, northern Ontarian history, Canadian social history, European social history, Franco-Canadian history.

Lehigh University, College of Arts and Sciences, Department of History, Bethlehem, PA 18015. Offers American history (PhD); British history (PhD); history (MA). Part-time programs available. *Faculty:* 14 full-time (4 women), 2 part-time/adjunct (1 woman). *Students:* 17 full-time (7 women), 17 part-time (4 women); includes 1 minority (Asian American or Pacific Islander), 1 international. Average age 32. 19 applicants, 68% accepted, 3 enrolled. In 2009, 2 master's, 3 doctorates awarded. Terminal master's awarded for partial completion of doctoral program. *Degree requirements:* For master's, thesis optional, comprehensive exam or thesis; for doctorate, comprehensive exam, thesis/dissertation. *Entrance requirements:* For master's, GRE General Test, recommendations; for doctorate, GRE General Test, recommendations, writing samples. Additional exam requirements/recommendations for international students: Required—TOEFL. *Application deadline:* For fall admission, 7/15 for domestic students; for winter admission, 1/15 priority date for domestic and international students. Applications are processed on a rolling basis. Application fee: $65. Electronic applications accepted. *Financial support:* In 2009–10, 27 students received support, including research assistantships with full tuition reimbursements available (averaging $15,600 per year), 10 teaching assistantships with full tuition reimbursements available (averaging $18,400 per year); fellowships with full tuition reimbursements available, career-related internships or fieldwork, Federal Work-Study, institutionally sponsored loans, scholarships/grants, tuition waivers (full and partial), and unspecified assistantships also available. Support available to part-time students. Financial award application deadline: 1/15. *Faculty research:* Colonial America, modern America, history of technology. *Unit head:* Dr. Stephen H. Cutcliffe, Chairman, 610-758-3360, Fax: 610-758-6554, E-mail: shc0@lehigh.edu. *Application contact:* Dr. Roger D. Simon, Graduate Coordinator, 610-758-3368, Fax: 610-758-6554, E-mail: rds2@lehigh.edu.

Lehman College of the City University of New York, Division of Arts and Humanities, Department of History, Bronx, NY 10468-1589. Offers MA. Part-time and evening/weekend programs available. *Degree requirements:* For master's, comprehensive exam, thesis. *Entrance requirements:* For master's, 18 undergraduate credits in history, minimum GPA of 2.7.

Lincoln University, School of Graduate Studies and Continuing Education, Jefferson City, MO 65102. Offers business administration (MBA), including accounting, entrepreneurship, management, public administration and policy; educational leadership (Ed S), including elementary leadership, secondary leadership, superintendency; guidance and counseling (M Ed), including community/agency counseling, elementary school, secondary school; history (MA); school administration and supervision (M Ed), including elementary school administration, secondary school administration, special education administration; school teaching (M Ed), including elementary school teaching, secondary school teaching; social science (MA), including history, political science, sociology; sociology (MA); sociology/criminal justice (MA). Part-time and evening/weekend programs available. *Students:* 52 full-time (27 women), 146 part-time (107 women); includes 40 minority (39 African Americans, 1 Asian American or Pacific Islander), 15 international. Average age 35. 76 applicants, 95% accepted, 46 enrolled. In 2009, 60 master's, 6 other advanced degrees awarded. *Degree requirements:* For master's and Ed S, comprehensive exam, thesis optional. *Entrance requirements:* For master's and Ed S, GRE, MAT or GMAT, minimum GPA of 2.75 in major, 2.5 overall; 3 letters of recommendation; minimum C average in English composition; personal statement of purpose. Additional exam requirements/recommendations for international students: Required—TOEFL (minimum score 500 paper-based; 173 computer-based; 61 iBT). *Application deadline:* For fall admission, 7/1 priority date for domestic and international students; for spring admission, 12/1 priority date for domestic and international students. Applications are processed on a rolling basis. Application fee: $20. *Expenses:* Tuition, state resident: full-time $4185; part-time $232.50 per credit hour. Tuition, nonresident: full-time $7767; part-time $431.50 per credit hour. Required fees: $270; $15 per credit hour. $20 per term. *Financial support:* Federal Work-Study and scholarships/grants available. Financial award application deadline: 4/1; financial award applicants required to submit FAFSA. *Faculty research:* Suicide prevention. *Unit head:* Dr. Linda S. Bickel, Dean, 573-681-5247, Fax: 573-681-5106, E-mail: gradschool@lincolnu.edu. *Application contact:* Irasema Steck, Administrative Assistant, 573-681-5247, Fax: 573-681-5106, E-mail: gradschool@lincolnu.edu.

Long Island University, Brooklyn Campus, Richard L. Conolly College of Liberal Arts and Sciences, Program in Social Science, Brooklyn, NY 11201-8423. Offers history (MS); United Nations studies (Certificate). Part-time and evening/weekend programs available. *Entrance requirements:* For master's, 2 letters of recommendation. Additional exam requirements/recommendations for international students: Required—TOEFL (minimum score 500 paper-based; 173 computer-based). Electronic applications accepted.

Long Island University, C.W. Post Campus, College of Liberal Arts and Sciences, Department of History, Brookville, NY 11548-1300. Offers MA. Part-time and evening/weekend programs available. *Degree requirements:* For master's, comprehensive exam or thesis. *Entrance requirements:* For master's, bachelor's degree in history, minimum GPA of 3.0. Electronic applications accepted. *Faculty research:* American slavery, women's studies, military history.

Louisiana State University and Agricultural and Mechanical College, Graduate School, College of Arts and Sciences, Department of History, Baton Rouge, LA 70803. Offers MA, PhD. Part-time programs available. *Faculty:* 29 full-time (10 women). *Students:* 51 full-time (16 women), 18 part-time (10 women); includes 4 minority (1 African American, 1 American Indian/Alaska Native, 1 Asian American or Pacific Islander, 1 Hispanic American), 2 international. Average age 31. 59 applicants, 58% accepted, 12 enrolled. In 2009, 11 master's, 1 doctorate awarded. Terminal master's awarded for partial completion of doctoral program. *Degree requirements:* For master's, thesis (for some programs), oral exam; for doctorate, one foreign language, thesis/dissertation, comprehensive written and oral exams. *Entrance requirements:* For master's and doctorate, GRE General Test, minimum GPA of 3.0. Additional exam requirements/recommendations for international students: Required—TOEFL (minimum score 550 paper-based; 213 computer-based; 79 iBT) or IELTS (minimum score 6.5). *Application deadline:* For fall admission, 1/25 priority date for domestic students, 5/15 for international students; for spring admission, 10/15 for international students. Applications are processed on a rolling basis. Application fee: $50 ($70 for international students). Electronic applications accepted. *Financial support:* In 2009–10, 53 students received support, including 1 fellowship with full tuition reimbursement available (averaging $29,011 per year), 1 research assistantship with partial tuition reimbursement available (averaging $14,310 per year), 30 teaching assistantships with partial tuition reimbursements available (averaging $12,993 per year); career-related internships or fieldwork, Federal Work-Study, institutionally sponsored loans, health care benefits, and unspecified assistantships also available. Support available to part-time students. Financial award application deadline: 1/15; financial award applicants required to submit FAFSA. *Faculty research:* U. S. South, Civil War; modern Europe, British; medieval history. Total annual research expenditures: $143,198. *Unit head:* Dr. Victor Stater, Chair, 225-578-4505, Fax: 225-578-4909, E-mail: stater@lsu.edu. *Application contact:* Dr. Victor Stater, Chair, 225-578-4505, Fax: 225-578-4909, E-mail: stater@lsu.edu.

Louisiana Tech University, Graduate School, College of Liberal Arts, Department of History, Ruston, LA 71272. Offers MA. Part-time programs available. *Degree requirements:* For master's, thesis or alternative. *Entrance requirements:* For master's, GRE General Test.

Loyola University Chicago, Graduate School, Department of History, Chicago, IL 60660. Offers history (MA, PhD); public history (MA). Part-time and evening/weekend programs available. *Faculty:* 24 full-time (9 women), 6 part-time/adjunct (3 women). *Students:* 68 full-time (32 women), 37 part-time (21 women); includes 8 minority (2 African Americans, 1 American Indian/Alaska Native, 5 Hispanic Americans). Average age 31. 138 applicants, 51% accepted, 26 enrolled. In 2009, 25 master's, 7 doctorates awarded. Terminal master's awarded for partial completion of doctoral program. *Degree requirements:* For master's, one foreign language, comprehensive exam, essay; for doctorate, 2 foreign languages, comprehensive exam, thesis/dissertation. *Entrance requirements:* For master's, GRE General Test, research paper; for doctorate, GRE General Test, seminar paper or master's thesis. Additional exam requirements/recommendations for international students: Required—TOEFL (minimum score 550 paper-based; 213 computer-based), IELTS. *Application deadline:* For fall admission, 5/1 for domestic students; for spring admission, 10/1 for domestic students. Applications are processed on a rolling basis. Application fee: $50. Electronic applications accepted. *Expenses:* Tuition: Full-time $14,220; part-time $790 per credit hour. Required fees: $60 per semester hour. Tuition and fees vary according to program. *Financial support:* In 2009–10, 24 students received support, including 11 fellowships with full tuition reimbursements available (averaging $14,500 per year), 13 teaching assistantships with full tuition reimbursements available (averaging $16,500 per year); research assistantships with full tuition reimbursements available, Federal Work-Study also available. Financial award application deadline: 1/1; financial award applicants required to submit FAFSA. *Faculty research:* Medieval and early modern Europe, U. S. public history, U. S. urban history, gender history, Britain and Ireland. *Unit head:* Dr. Timothy Gilfoyle, Chair, 773-508-2232, Fax: 773-508-2153, E-mail: tgilfoy@luc.edu. *Application contact:* Dr. Suzanne Kaufman, Director, Graduate Programs, 773-508-2233, Fax: 773-508-2153, E-mail: skaufma@luc.edu.

Lynchburg College, Graduate Studies, School of Humanities and Social Sciences, Lynchburg, VA 24501-3199. Offers English (MA); history (MA). Part-time programs available. *Degree requirements:* For master's, comprehensive exam, thesis (for some programs). *Entrance requirements:* For master's, GRE, minimum undergraduate GPA of 3.0. Additional exam requirements/recommendations for international students: Required—TOEFL. *Expenses:* Tuition: Full-time $7020; part-time $390 per credit hour.

Marquette University, Graduate School, College of Arts and Sciences, Department of History, Milwaukee, WI 53201-1881. Offers European history (MA, PhD); medieval history (MA); Renaissance and Reformation (MA); United States history (MA, PhD). Part-time programs available. *Faculty:* 23 full-time (7 women), 5 part-time/adjunct (2 women). *Students:* 32 full-time (14 women), 7 part-time (3 women); includes 1 minority (Hispanic American). Average age 30. 34 applicants, 59% accepted, 13 enrolled. In 2009, 8 master's, 8 doctorates awarded. Terminal master's awarded for partial completion of doctoral program. *Degree requirements:* For master's, comprehensive exam, thesis or alternative; for doctorate, one foreign language, thesis/dissertation, qualifying exam. *Entrance requirements:* For master's, GRE General Test, GRE Subject Test; for doctorate, GRE General Test, writing sample. Additional exam requirements/recommendations for international students: Required—TOEFL. Application fee: $40. *Financial support:* In 2009–10, 4 fellowships, 5 research assistantships, 15 teaching assistantships were awarded; Federal Work-Study, institutionally sponsored loans, scholarships/grants, and tuition waivers (full and partial) also available. Support available to part-time students. Financial award application deadline: 2/15. *Faculty research:* Social history, political history, diplomatic history, history of science, religious history. *Unit head:* James Marten, Chair, 414-288-7901, Fax: 414-288-1578. *Application contact:* Erin Fox, Assistant Director for Recruitment, 414-288-5319, Fax: 414-288-1902, E-mail: erin.fox@marquette.edu.

Marshall University, Academic Affairs Division, College of Liberal Arts, Department of History, Huntington, WV 25755. Offers MA. *Faculty:* 14 full-time (6 women), 10 part-time/adjunct (1 woman). *Students:* 16 full-time (6 women), 15 part-time (7 women); includes 1 minority (African American). Average age 33. In 2009, 10 master's awarded. *Degree requirements:* For master's, thesis optional. Application fee: $40. *Unit head:* Dr. Dan Holbrook, Interim Chair, 304-696-2417, Fax: 304-696-2957, E-mail: holbrook@marshall.edu. *Application contact:* Graduate Admissions, 304-746-1900, Fax: 304-746-1902, E-mail: services@marshall.edu.

McGill University, Faculty of Graduate and Postdoctoral Studies, Faculty of Arts, Department of History, Montréal, QC H3A 2T5, Canada. Offers history (MA, PhD); history of medicine (MA).

McMaster University, School of Graduate Studies, Faculty of Humanities, Department of History, Hamilton, ON L8S 4M2, Canada. Offers MA, PhD. Part-time programs available. *Degree requirements:* For master's, one foreign language, thesis or alternative; for doctorate, one foreign language, comprehensive exam, thesis/dissertation. *Entrance requirements:* For master's, honors BA in history, minimum B+ average. Additional exam requirements/recommendations for international students: Required—TOEFL (minimum score 580 paper-based; 237 computer-based). *Faculty research:* Canadian, European, British, U.S. history; ancient history.

Memorial University of Newfoundland, School of Graduate Studies, Department of History, St. John's, NL A1C 5S7, Canada. Offers MA, PhD. Part-time programs available. *Degree requirements:* For master's, thesis or comprehensive exam; for doctorate, one foreign language, comprehensive exam, thesis/dissertation, oral defense of thesis. *Entrance requirements:* For master's, honors degree or equivalent; for doctorate, master's degree. Electronic applications accepted. *Faculty research:* Canadian history, maritime history, Newfoundland history, social history, labor history.

Miami University, Graduate School, College of Arts and Sciences, Department of History, Oxford, OH 45056. Offers MA. Part-time programs available. *Students:* 19 full-time (13 women), 1 international. *Entrance requirements:* For master's, minimum undergraduate GPA of 3.0. Additional exam requirements/recommendations for international students: Required—TOEFL. *Application deadline:* For fall admission, 1/10 for domestic and international students. Application fee: $50. Electronic applications accepted. *Expenses:* Tuition, state resident: full-time $11,280. Tuition, nonresident: full-time $24,912. Required fees: $516. *Financial support:* Fellowships with full tuition reimbursements, research assistantships, teaching assistantships, Federal Work-Study, institutionally sponsored loans, health care benefits, tuition waivers (full), and unspecified assistantships available. Financial award application deadline: 3/1; financial award applicants required to submit FAFSA. *Unit head:* Dr. Mary Cayton, Chair, 513-529-5121, E-mail: caytonmk@muohio.edu. *Application contact:* Dr. Wietse de Boer, Director of Graduate Studies, 513-529-5146, E-mail: deboerwt@muohio.edu.

Michigan State University, The Graduate School, College of Social Science, Department of History, East Lansing, MI 48824. Offers history (MA, PhD); history-secondary school teaching (MA). *Faculty:* 48 full-time (20 women). *Students:* 71 full-time (37 women), 6 part-time (3 women); includes 15 minority (5 African Americans, 2 American Indian/Alaska Native, 1 Asian American or Pacific Islander, 7 Hispanic Americans), 11 international. Average age 30. 53 applicants, 28% accepted. In 2009, 1 master's, 14 doctorates awarded. *Entrance requirements:* Additional exam requirements/recommendations for international students: Required—TOEFL. Electronic applications accepted. *Expenses:* Tuition, state resident: part-time $478.25 per credit hour. Tuition, nonresident: part-time $966.50 per credit hour. Part-time tuition and fees vary according to program. *Financial support:* In 2009–10, 4 research assistantships with tuition reimbursements (averaging $6,061 per year), 39 teaching assistantships with tuition reimbursements (averaging $6,001 per year) were awarded. Total annual research expenditures: $130,678. *Unit head:* Dr. Keely D. Stauter-Halstead, Acting Chairperson, 517-355-7500, Fax: 517-353-5599, E-mail: stauterh@msu.edu. *Application contact:* Kelli Kolasa, Graduate Secretary, 517-355-7500, Fax: 517-353-5599, E-mail: kolasa@msu.edu.

Middle Tennessee State University, College of Graduate Studies, College of Liberal Arts, Department of History, Program in History, Murfreesboro, TN 37132. Offers MA. Part-time and evening/weekend programs available. Postbaccalaureate distance learning degree programs offered. *Students:* 3 full-time (1 woman), 62 part-time (44 women); includes 3 minority (1 African American, 1 American Indian/Alaska Native, 1 Hispanic American). 20 applicants, 80% accepted, 16 enrolled. *Degree requirements:* For master's, one foreign language, comprehensive exam, thesis. *Entrance requirements:* For master's, GRE. Additional exam requirements/recommendations for international students: Required—TOEFL (minimum score 525 paper-based; 195 computer-based; 71 iBT) or IELTS (minimum score 6). *Application deadline:* For fall admission, 6/1 for domestic and international students. Applications are processed on a rolling basis. Application fee: $25 ($30 for international students). *Expenses:* Tuition, state resident: full-time $4404. Tuition, nonresident: full-time $10,956. *Financial support:* Application deadline: 5/1. *Unit head:* Dr. Amy Sayward, Chair, 615-898-2569, Fax: 615-898-5881, E-mail: asayward@mtsu.edu. *Application contact:* Dr. Michael Allen, Dean and Vice Provost for Research, 615-898-2840, Fax: 615-904-8020, E-mail: mallen@mtsu.edu.

Midwestern State University, Graduate Studies, College of Humanities and Social Sciences, Department of History, Wichita Falls, TX 76308. Offers MA. Part-time programs available. *Degree requirements:* For master's, one foreign language. *Entrance requirements:* For master's, GRE General Test. Additional exam requirements/recommendations for international students: Required—TOEFL (minimum score 550 paper-based; 213 computer-based). Electronic applications accepted. *Expenses:* Tuition, state resident: full-time $1620; part-time $90 per credit hour. Tuition, nonresident: full-time $2160; part-time $120 per credit hour. International tuition: $7506 full-time. Required fees: $3068.80; $145.60 per credit hour. $179 per semester. *Faculty research:* Conservation, Spanish borderlands, Jacksonian era, New Deal, Texas and the Southwest.

Millersville University of Pennsylvania, College of Graduate and Professional Studies, School of Humanities and Social Sciences, Department of History, Millersville, PA 17551-0302. Offers MA. Part-time and evening/weekend programs available. *Faculty:* 12 full-time (5 women), 6 part-time/adjunct (5 women). *Students:* 6 full-time (2 women), 17 part-time (7 women). Average age 30. 13 applicants, 85% accepted, 9 enrolled. In 2009, 4 master's awarded. *Degree requirements:* For master's, thesis optional. *Entrance requirements:* For master's, GRE, 3 letters of recommendation. Additional exam requirements/recommendations for international students: Required—TOEFL (minimum score 500 paper-based; 183 computer-based; 65 iBT) or IELTS (minimum score 6). *Application deadline:* For fall admission, 1/15 priority date for domestic and international students; for winter admission, 10/1 priority date for domestic and international students; for spring admission, 10/1 priority date for domestic and international students. Applications are processed on a rolling basis. Application fee: $40 ($50 for international students). Electronic applications accepted. *Expenses:* Tuition, state resident: full-time $6666; part-time $370 per credit. Tuition, nonresident: full-time $10,666; part-time $593 per credit. Required fees: $1578.50; $76.25 per credit. One-time fee: $60 part-time. Tuition and fees vary according to course load. *Financial support:* In 2009–10, 3 students received support, including 3 research assistantships with full tuition reimbursements available (averaging $4,100 per year); institutionally sponsored loans and unspecified assistantships also available. Support available to part-time students. Financial award application deadline: 3/15; financial award applicants required to submit FAFSA. *Faculty research:* Anglo-American Puritanism, Vietnam War, Colonial Caribbean, Renaissance music, Pennsylvania history. Total annual research expenditures: $46,933. *Unit head:* Dr. Francis Bremer, Chair, 717-872-3548, Fax: 717-871-2485, E-mail: francis.bremer@millersville.edu. *Application contact:* Dr. Victor S. DeSantis, Dean of Graduate and Professional Studies, 717-872-3099, Fax: 717-872-3453, E-mail: victor.desantis@millersville.edu.

Minnesota State University Mankato, College of Graduate Studies, College of Social and Behavioral Sciences, Department of History, Mankato, MN 56001. Offers history (MA, MS); social studies (MAT). *Students:* 4 full-time (3 women), 9 part-time (1 woman). *Degree requirements:* For master's, one foreign language, comprehensive exam, thesis or alternative. *Entrance requirements:* For master's, minimum GPA of 3.0 during previous 2 years. Additional exam requirements/recommendations for international students: Required—TOEFL. *Application deadline:* For fall admission, 7/1 priority date for domestic students; for spring admission, 11/1 for domestic students. Applications are processed on a rolling basis. Application fee: $40. Electronic applications accepted. *Expenses:* Tuition, state resident: full-time $5364. Tuition, nonresident: full-time $8314. *Financial support:* Research assistantships, teaching assistantships with full tuition reimbursements, career-related internships or fieldwork, Federal Work-Study, institutionally sponsored loans, and unspecified assistantships available. Support available to part-time students. Financial award application deadline: 3/15. *Faculty research:* Charivaris, Lindbergh in the U. S., Dutch trade to South America in the seventeenth and eighteenth centuries. *Unit head:* Dr. Kathleen Gorman, Graduate Coordinator, 507-389-2720. *Application contact:* 507-389-2321, E-mail: grad@mnsu.edu.

Mississippi College, Graduate School, College of Arts and Sciences, School of Humanities and Social Sciences, Department of History, Political Science, Administration of Justice, and Paralegal Studies, Clinton, MS 39058. Offers administration of justice (MSS); history (M Ed, MA, MSS); paralegal studies (Certificate); political science (MSS); social sciences (M Ed, MSS). Part-time programs available. *Faculty:* 4 full-time (0 women), 5 part-time/adjunct (1 woman). *Students:* 10 full-time (5 women), 27 part-time (10 women); includes 8 minority (all African Americans), 1 international. Average age 32. In 2009, 12 master's awarded. *Degree requirements:* For master's, one foreign language, comprehensive exam, thesis (for some programs). *Entrance requirements:* For master's, GRE or NTE, minimum GPA of 2.5. Additional exam requirements/recommendations for international students: Recommended—IELTS. *Application deadline:* For fall admission, 8/15 priority date for domestic students. Applications are processed on a rolling basis. Application fee: $30. Electronic applications accepted. *Expenses:* Tuition: Part-time $452 per credit hour. Required fees: $101 per semester. Tuition and fees vary according to degree level, campus/location, program and student level. *Financial support:* Teaching assistantships, Federal Work-Study, scholarships/grants, and unspecified assistantships available. Support available to part-time students. Financial award application deadline: 4/1; financial award applicants required to submit FAFSA. *Unit head:* Dr. Kirk Ford, Chair, 601-925-3326, E-mail: ford@mc.edu. *Application contact:* Elnora Lewis, Secretary, 601-925-3225, Fax: 601-925-3889, E-mail: lewis09@mc.edu.

Mississippi State University, College of Arts and Sciences, Department of History, Mississippi State, MS 39762. Offers history (PhD); U. S. and European history (MA). Part-time programs available. *Faculty:* 17 full-time (6 women). *Students:* 34 full-time (13 women), 13 part-time (4 women); includes 2 minority (1 African American, 1 Asian American or Pacific Islander). Average age 32. 30 applicants, 80% accepted, 12 enrolled. In 2009, 7 master's, 2 doctorates awarded. *Degree requirements:* For master's, one foreign language, comprehensive exam, thesis optional; for doctorate, 2 foreign languages, thesis/dissertation, comprehensive oral and written exam. *Entrance requirements:* For master's, GRE (except for those with MA in history from MSU), minimum GPA of 3.0 on last two years of undergraduate courses; for doctorate, GRE, writing sample, minimum graduate GPA of 3.0. Additional exam requirements/recommendations for international students: Required—TOEFL (minimum score 475 paper-based; 153 computer-based; 53 iBT); Recommended—IELTS (minimum score 4.5). *Application deadline:* For fall admission, 4/1 for domestic students, 5/1 for international students; for spring admission, 11/1 for domestic students, 9/1 for international students. Applications are processed on a rolling basis. Application fee: $40. Electronic applications accepted. *Expenses:* Tuition, state resident: full-time $2575.50; part-time $286.25 per credit hour. Tuition, nonresident: full-time $6510; part-time $723.50 per credit hour. Tuition and fees vary according to course load. *Financial support:* In 2009–10, 2 research assistantships (averaging $9,333 per year), 26 teaching assistantships with full tuition reimbursements (averaging $11,005 per year) were awarded; Federal Work-Study, institutionally sponsored loans, scholarships/grants, and unspecified assistantships also available. Financial award application deadline: 4/1; financial award applicants required to submit FAFSA. *Faculty research:* U. S. political, diplomatic, military, social, and cultural history; modern Europe; Latin America; Asian history; African history. *Unit head:* Dr. Alan I. Marcus, Head, 662-325-3604, Fax: 662-325-1139, E-mail: aim10@msstate.edu. *Application contact:* Dr. Richard Damms, Associate Professor/Graduate Coordinator, 662-325-8821, E-mail: correspondence@history.msstate.edu.

Missouri State University, Graduate College, College of Humanities and Public Affairs, Department of History, Springfield, MO 65897. Offers history (MA); secondary education (MS Ed), including history, social science. Part-time programs available. *Faculty:* 17 full-time (4 women). *Students:* 18 full-time (7 women), 46 part-time (17 women). Average age 33. 19 applicants, 84% accepted, 15 enrolled. In 2009, 6 master's awarded. *Degree requirements:* For master's, comprehensive exam, thesis or alternative. *Entrance requirements:* For master's, minimum GPA of 2.75, 24 hours of undergraduate course work in history (MA), 9-12 teaching certification (MS Ed). Additional exam requirements/recommendations for international students: Required—TOEFL (minimum score 550 paper-based; 213 computer-based; 79 iBT). *Application deadline:* For fall admission, 7/20 priority date for domestic students, 5/1 for international students; for spring admission, 12/20 priority date for domestic students, 9/1 for international students. Applications are processed on a rolling basis. Application fee: $35 ($50 for international students). Electronic applications accepted. *Expenses:* Tuition, state resident: full-time $3852; part-time $214 per credit hour. Tuition, nonresident: full-time $7524; part-time $418 per credit hour. Required fees: $696; $172 per semester. Tuition and fees vary according to course level, course load, degree level and program. *Financial support:* In 2009–10, 5 teaching assistantships with full tuition reimbursements (averaging $7,340 per year) were awarded; Federal Work-Study, scholarships/grants, and unspecified assistantships also available. Support available to part-time students. Financial award application deadline: 3/31; financial award applicants required to submit FAFSA. *Faculty research:* U.S. history, Native American history, Latin American history, women's history, ancient Near East. *Unit head:* Thomas S. Dicke, Head, 417-836-5511, Fax: 417-836-5523, E-mail: history@missouristate.edu. *Application contact:* Eric Eckert, Coordinator of Admissions and Recruitment, 417-836-5331, Fax: 417-836-6200, E-mail: ericeckert@missouristate.edu.

Monmouth University, Graduate School, Department of History, West Long Branch, NJ 07764-1898. Offers European specialization (MA); U.S. specialization (MA); world specialization (MA). Part-time and evening/weekend programs available. *Faculty:* 13 full-time (3 women), 1 part-time/adjunct (0 women). *Students:* 3 full-time (1 woman), 59 part-time (27 women); includes 5 minority (1 Asian American or Pacific Islander, 4 Hispanic Americans). Average age 38. 31 applicants, 100% accepted, 15 enrolled. In 2009, 16 master's awarded. *Degree requirements:* For master's, comprehensive exam, thesis or alternative. *Entrance requirements:* For master's, minimum GPA of 3.0 in major, 2.5 overall. Additional exam requirements/recommendations for international students: Required—TOEFL (minimum score 550 paper-based; 213 computer-based; 79 iBT), IELTS (minimum score 5), Michigan English Language Assessment Battery (minimum score 77), Cambridge A, B, C. *Application deadline:* For fall admission, 7/15 priority date for domestic students, 6/1 for international students; for spring admission, 11/15 priority date for domestic students, 11/1 for international students. Applications are processed on a rolling basis. Application fee: $50. Electronic applications accepted. *Expenses:* Tuition: Part-time $773 per credit. Required fees: $157 per semester. *Financial support:* In 2009–10, 47 students received support, including 39 fellowships (averaging $1,270 per year), 22 research assistantships (averaging $6,668 per year); career-related internships or fieldwork, scholarships/grants, and unspecified assistantships also available. Support available to part-time students. Financial award applicants required to submit FAFSA. *Faculty research:* U.S. business; labor; British, German, and French Revolutions; Soviet Union; Africa. *Unit head:* Dr. Aaron Ansell, Director, 732-571-4495, Fax: 732-263-5112, E-mail: aansell@monmouth.edu. *Application contact:* Kevin Roane, Director, Office of Graduate Admission, 732-571-3452, Fax: 732-263-5123, E-mail: gradadm@monmouth.edu.

Montana State University, College of Graduate Studies, College of Letters and Science, Department of History, Bozeman, MT 59717. Offers MA, PhD. Part-time programs available. *Faculty:* 18 full-time (6 women), 6 part-time/adjunct (1 woman). *Students:* 7 full-time (2 women), 23 part-time (10 women); includes 2 minority (both American Indian/Alaska Native), 1 international. Average age 37. 26 applicants, 35% accepted, 8 enrolled. In 2009, 7 master's awarded. *Degree requirements:* For master's, comprehensive exam; for doctorate, comprehensive exam, thesis/dissertation. *Entrance requirements:* For master's, GRE General Test, 3 letters of recommendation; for doctorate, GRE General Test, 3 letters of recommendation, writing sample, official transcripts. Additional exam requirements/recommendations for international students: Required—TOEFL (minimum score 550 paper-based; 213 computer-based). *Application deadline:* For fall admission, 7/15 priority date for domestic students, 5/15 priority date for international students; for spring admission, 12/1 priority date for domestic students, 10/1 priority date for international students. Applications are processed on a rolling basis.

History

Montana State University (continued)

Application fee: $30. Electronic applications accepted. *Expenses:* Tuition, state resident: full-time $5635; part-time $3492 per year. Tuition, nonresident: full-time $17,212; part-time $7865.10 per year. Required fees: $1441; $153.15 per credit. Tuition and fees vary according to course load and program. *Financial support:* In 2009–10, 16 students received support, including 8 research assistantships with tuition reimbursements available (averaging $15,000 per year), 8 teaching assistantships with tuition reimbursements available (averaging $5,000 per year). Financial award application deadline: 3/1; financial award applicants required to submit FAFSA. *Faculty research:* Science, environment, technology, American west, Asian studies, Turkish history/Russian history. Total annual research expenditures: $303,183. *Unit head:* Dr. Brett Walker, Head, 406-994-4395, Fax: 406-994-6879, E-mail: bwalker@montana.edu. *Application contact:* Dr. Brett Walker, Head, 406-994-4395, Fax: 406-994-6879, E-mail: bwalker@montana.edu.

Montclair State University, The Graduate School, College of Humanities and Social Sciences, Department of History, Montclair, NJ 07043-1624. Offers social sciences (MA), including history; social studies (Certificate). Part-time and evening/weekend programs available. *Faculty:* 16 full-time (6 women), 24 part-time/adjunct (6 women). *Students:* 1 full-time (0 women), 18 part-time (7 women). Average age 32. 12 applicants, 33% accepted, 2 enrolled. In 2009, 4 master's awarded. *Degree requirements:* For master's, comprehensive exam. *Entrance requirements:* For master's, GRE General Test, 2 letters of recommendation. Additional exam requirements/recommendations for international students: Required—TOEFL (minimum score 83 computer-based), or IELTS. *Application deadline:* For fall admission, 6/1 for international students; for spring admission, 11/1 for international students. Applications are processed on a rolling basis. Application fee: $60. Electronic applications accepted. *Expenses:* Tuition, area resident: Part-time $486.74 per credit. Tuition, state resident: part-time $486.74 per credit. Tuition, nonresident: part-time $751.34 per credit. Tuition and fees vary according to degree level and program. *Financial support:* In 2009–10, 5 research assistantships with full tuition reimbursements (averaging $7,000 per year) were awarded; Federal Work-Study, scholarships/grants, and unspecified assistantships also available. Support available to part-time students. Financial award application deadline: 3/1. *Unit head:* Dr. Michael Whelan, Chairperson, 973-655-7848. *Application contact:* Amy Aiello, Director of Admissions and Operations, 973-655-5147, Fax: 973-655-7869, E-mail: graduate.school@montclair.edu.

Morgan State University, School of Graduate Studies, College of Liberal Arts, Department of History and Geography, Baltimore, MD 21251. Offers African-American studies (MA); history (MA, PhD). Part-time and evening/weekend programs available. *Degree requirements:* For master's, comprehensive exam, thesis; for doctorate, comprehensive exam, thesis/dissertation. *Entrance requirements:* For master's, minimum GPA of 2.5; for doctorate, GRE or MAT. Additional exam requirements/recommendations for international students: Required—TOEFL (minimum score 550 paper-based; 213 computer-based). *Faculty research:* Women's history, African diaspora history, urban history.

Murray State University, College of Humanities and Fine Arts, Program in History, Murray, KY 42071. Offers MA. Part-time programs available. *Degree requirements:* For master's, one foreign language, comprehensive exam, thesis (for some programs). *Entrance requirements:* For master's, GRE General Test. Additional exam requirements/recommendations for international students: Required—TOEFL.

National University, Academic Affairs, College of Letters and Sciences, Department of Art and Humanities, La Jolla, CA 92037-1011. Offers creative writing (MFA); English (MA); history (MA). Part-time and evening/weekend programs available. Postbaccalaureate distance learning degree programs offered (no on-campus study). *Faculty:* 13 full-time (4 women), 24 part-time/adjunct (15 women). *Students:* 204 full-time (144 women), 499 part-time (340 women); includes 160 minority (77 African Americans, 6 American Indian/Alaska Native, 17 Asian Americans or Pacific Islanders, 60 Hispanic Americans). Average age 38. 440 applicants, 100% accepted, 280 enrolled. In 2009, 152 master's awarded. *Degree requirements:* For master's, thesis (for some programs). *Entrance requirements:* For master's, interview, minimum GPA of 2.5. Additional exam requirements/recommendations for international students: Required—TOEFL (minimum score 550 paper-based; 213 computer-based; 79 iBT), IELTS (minimum score 6). *Application deadline:* Applications are processed on a rolling basis. Application fee: $60 ($65 for international students). Electronic applications accepted. *Expenses:* Tuition: Part-time $338 per quarter hour. *Financial support:* Career-related internships or fieldwork, institutionally sponsored loans, scholarships/grants, and tuition waivers (partial) available. Support available to part-time students. Financial award application deadline: 6/30; financial award applicants required to submit FAFSA. *Unit head:* Dr. Janet Baker, Chair, 858-642-8472, Fax: 858-642-8715, E-mail: jbaker@nu.edu. *Application contact:* Dominick Giovanniello, Associate Regional Dean—San Diego, 800-NAT-UNIV, Fax: 858-541-7792, E-mail: dgiovann@nu.edu.

Nebraska Wesleyan University, University College, Program in Historical Studies, Lincoln, NE 68504-2796. Offers MA. Part-time programs available. *Expenses:* Contact institution.

New Jersey Institute of Technology, Office of Graduate Studies, College of Science and Liberal Arts, Federated Department of History, Newark, NJ 07102. Offers MA, MAT. Part-time and evening/weekend programs available. *Entrance requirements:* For master's, GRE General Test, minimum B average in undergraduate course work. Additional exam requirements/recommendations for international students: Required—TOEFL (minimum score 550 paper-based; 213 computer-based; 79 iBT). Electronic applications accepted.

New Mexico State University, Graduate School, College of Arts and Sciences, Department of History, Las Cruces, NM 88003-8001. Offers history (MA); public history (MA). Part-time programs available. *Faculty:* 10 full-time (4 women), 2 part-time/adjunct (0 women). *Students:* 40 full-time (24 women), 12 part-time (5 women); includes 14 minority (2 American Indian/Alaska Native, 1 Asian American or Pacific Islander, 11 Hispanic Americans). Average age 32. 26 applicants, 96% accepted, 14 enrolled. In 2009, 12 master's awarded. *Degree requirements:* For master's, one foreign language, comprehensive exam, thesis (for some programs). *Entrance requirements:* For master's, 12 undergraduate history credits, writing sample. Additional exam requirements/recommendations for international students: Required—TOEFL (minimum score 530 paper-based; 71 iBT). *Application deadline:* For fall admission, 7/1 priority date for domestic students; for spring admission, 11/1 for domestic students. Applications are processed on a rolling basis. Application fee: $30 ($50 for international students). Electronic applications accepted. *Expenses:* Tuition, state resident: full-time $4080; part-time $223 per credit. Tuition, nonresident: full-time $14,256; part-time $647 per credit. Required fees: $1278; $639 per semester. *Financial support:* In 2009–10, 1 research assistantship with partial tuition reimbursement (averaging $15,800 per year), 10 teaching assistantships with partial tuition reimbursements (averaging $7,070 per year) were awarded; fellowships, career-related internships or fieldwork, Federal Work-Study, and health care benefits also available. Support available to part-time students. Financial award application deadline: 3/1. *Faculty research:* U.S. Southwestern and border history, Latin American history, U.S. women's history, European history, history of science, public history, East Asian history. *Unit head:* Dr. Jon Hunner, Head, 575-646-4601, Fax: 575-646-6096, E-mail: jhunner@nmsu.edu. *Application contact:* Dr. Andrea Orzoff, Director of Graduate Studies, 575-646-4612, Fax: 575-646-6096, E-mail: aorzoff@nmsu.edu.

The New School: A University, The New School for Social Research, Committee on Historical Studies, New York, NY 10003. Offers MA, PhD. Part-time and evening/weekend programs available. *Faculty:* 3 full-time (0 women). *Students:* 19 full-time (9 women), 5 part-time (2 women); includes 4 minority (1 African American, 1 Asian American or Pacific Islander, 2 Hispanic Americans), 4 international. Average age 28. In 2009, 1 master's awarded. Terminal master's awarded for partial completion of doctoral program. *Degree requirements:* For master's, thesis; for doctorate, comprehensive exam, thesis/dissertation, qualifying exam. *Entrance requirements:* For master's, GRE General Test; for doctorate, GRE General Test, MA. Additional exam requirements/recommendations for international students: Required—TOEFL (minimum score 600 paper-based; 250 computer-based; 100 iBT). *Application deadline:* For fall admission, 1/17 priority date for domestic and international students; for spring admission, 10/15 priority date for domestic and international students. Applications are processed on a rolling basis. Application fee: $50. Electronic applications accepted. *Financial support:* Fellowships, research assistantships, teaching assistantships, Federal Work-Study, scholarships/grants, tuition waivers (full and partial), and unspecified assistantships available. Support available to part-time students. Financial award application deadline: 3/1; financial award applicants required to submit FAFSA. *Unit head:* Dr. Oz Frankel, Chair, 212-229-5376 Ext. 4924, Fax: 212-229-5315, E-mail: frankelo@newschool.edu. *Application contact:* Robert MacDonald, Director of Admissions, 212-229-5710 Ext. 3007, Fax: 212-989-7102, E-mail: macdonar@newschool.edu.

New York University, Graduate School of Arts and Science, Department of History, New York, NY 10012-1019. Offers African diaspora (PhD); African history (PhD); archival management and historical editing (Advanced Certificate); Atlantic history (PhD); French studies/history (PhD); Hebrew and Judaic studies/history (PhD); history (MA, PhD), including Europe (PhD), Latin American and the Caribbean (PhD), United States (PhD), women's history (MA); Middle Eastern history (MA); Middle Eastern studies/history (PhD); public history (Advanced Certificate); world history (MA); JD/MA; MA/Advanced Certificate. Part-time programs available. *Faculty:* 43 full-time (19 women). *Students:* 141 full-time (87 women), 43 part-time (35 women); includes 33 minority (20 African Americans, 5 Asian Americans or Pacific Islanders, 8 Hispanic Americans), 32 international. Average age 30. 406 applicants, 30% accepted, 51 enrolled. In 2009, 21 master's, 10 doctorates, 4 other advanced degrees awarded. Terminal master's awarded for partial completion of doctoral program. *Degree requirements:* For master's, seminar paper; for doctorate, one foreign language, thesis/dissertation, oral and written exams; for Advanced Certificate, internship. *Entrance requirements:* For master's, GRE General Test, minimum GPA of 3.0, writing sample; for doctorate, GRE. Additional exam requirements/recommendations for international students: Required—TOEFL. *Application deadline:* For fall admission, 12/12 for domestic students. Application fee: $90. *Expenses:* Tuition: Full-time $30,528; part-time $1272 per credit. Required fees: $2177. *Financial support:* Fellowships with tuition reimbursements, research assistantships, teaching assistantships with tuition reimbursements, career-related internships or fieldwork, Federal Work-Study, institutionally sponsored loans, scholarships/grants, health care benefits, and unspecified assistantships available. Financial award application deadline: 12/12; financial award applicants required to submit FAFSA. *Faculty research:* African, East Asian, Medieval, early modern, and modern European history; U.S. history; African and African Diaspora; Latin American history; Atlantic World. *Unit head:* Joanna Waley-Cohen, Chair, 212-998-8600, Fax: 212-995-4017, E-mail: history.dept@nyu.edu. *Application contact:* Barbara Weinstein, Director of Graduate Studies, 212-998-8600, Fax: 212-995-4017, E-mail: history.dept@nyu.edu.

North Carolina Central University, Division of Academic Affairs, College of Liberal Arts, Department of History, Durham, NC 27707-3129. Offers MA. Part-time and evening/weekend programs available. *Degree requirements:* For master's, one foreign language, comprehensive exam, thesis. *Entrance requirements:* For master's, GRE, minimum GPA of 3.0 in major, 2.5 overall. Additional exam requirements/recommendations for international students: Required—TOEFL.

North Carolina State University, Graduate School, College of Humanities and Social Sciences, Department of History, Raleigh, NC 27695. Offers history (MA); public history (MA). Part-time and evening/weekend programs available. *Degree requirements:* For master's, thesis. *Entrance requirements:* For master's, GRE General Test. Electronic applications accepted. *Faculty research:* History of the United States, Europe, Asia Africa and the Middle East; history of science; intellectual, cultural, social, environmental and political history.

North Dakota State University, College of Graduate and Interdisciplinary Studies, College of Arts, Humanities and Social Sciences, Department of History, Fargo, ND 58108. Offers MA, MS, PhD. Part-time and evening/weekend programs available. *Faculty:* 9 full-time (1 woman), 2 part-time/adjunct (0 women). *Students:* 26 full-time (25 women), 22 part-time (19 women); includes 3 minority (1 African American, 1 American Indian/Alaska Native, 1 Hispanic American), 2 international. Average age 27. 11 applicants, 91% accepted, 10 enrolled. In 2009, 12 master's awarded. *Degree requirements:* For master's, one foreign language, comprehensive exam, thesis optional; for doctorate, 2 foreign languages, comprehensive exam, thesis/dissertation. *Entrance requirements:* For master's and doctorate, GRE General Test. Additional exam requirements/recommendations for international students: Required—TOEFL (minimum score 600 paper-based; 250 computer-based; 100 iBT). *Application deadline:* For fall admission, 2/10 priority date for domestic and international students. Applications are processed on a rolling basis. Application fee: $45 ($60 for international students). *Financial support:* In 2009–10, 9 students received support, including 1 fellowship with tuition reimbursement available (averaging $15,000 per year), 2 research assistantships with full tuition reimbursements available (averaging $9,400 per year), 4 teaching assistantships with full tuition reimbursements available (averaging $8,200 per year); career-related internships or fieldwork, Federal Work-Study, institutionally sponsored loans, and tuition waivers also available. Financial award application deadline: 3/15. *Faculty research:* Recent U. S., modern English; early modern European, North Dakota, Latin American, and Great Plains history. *Unit head:* Dr. John K. Cox, Head, 701-231-8654, Fax: 701-231-1047, E-mail: john.cox.l@ndsu.edu. *Application contact:* Dr. Jim Norris, Graduate Coordinator, 701-231-8827, Fax: 701-231-1047, E-mail: jim.norris@nodak.edu.

Northeastern Illinois University, Graduate College, College of Arts and Sciences, Department of History, Program in History, Chicago, IL 60625-4699. Offers MA. Part-time and evening/weekend programs available. *Degree requirements:* For master's, comprehensive exam, thesis optional. *Entrance requirements:* For master's, 24 undergraduate hours in history, minimum GPA of 2.75. Additional exam requirements/recommendations for international students: Required—TOEFL (minimum score 550 paper-based; 213 computer-based; 80 iBT). Electronic applications accepted. *Faculty research:* Africa; East Asia; European medieval, early-modern, and modern history; U.S. social, cultural, and intellectual history.

Northeastern University, College of Social Sciences and Humanities, Department of History, Boston, MA 02115-5096. Offers history (MA); public history (MA); world history (PhD). Part-time and evening/weekend programs available. *Faculty:* 15 full-time (6 women), 2 part-time/adjunct (0 women). *Students:* 63 full-time (42 women), 2 part-time (1 woman); includes 3 Asian Americans or Pacific Islanders, 1 Hispanic American, 5 international. 105 applicants, 53% accepted, 24 enrolled. In 2009, 19 master's, 1 doctorate awarded. Terminal master's awarded for partial completion of doctoral program. *Degree requirements:* For master's, one foreign language, thesis or alternative, project; for doctorate, thesis/dissertation. *Entrance requirements:* For master's and doctorate, GRE General Test. Additional exam requirements/recommendations for international students: Required—TOEFL. *Application deadline:* For fall admission, 2/1 for domestic students. Application fee: $50. Electronic applications accepted. *Financial support:* In 2009–10, teaching assistantships with tuition reimbursements (averaging $14,035 per year); research assistantships with tuition reimbursements, career-related internships or fieldwork, scholarships/grants, and tuition waivers (full and partial) also available. Financial award application deadline: 2/1; financial award applicants required to submit FAFSA. *Faculty research:* World history, U. S. social history. *Unit head:* Dr. Laura Frader, Chair, 617-373-2660, Fax: 617-373-2661. *Application contact:* Dr. Christina Gilmartin, Graduate Coordinator, 617-373-2660, Fax: 617-373-2661.

Northern Arizona University, Graduate College, College of Arts and Letters, Department of History, Flagstaff, AZ 86011. Offers MA, PhD. Part-time programs available. *Faculty:* 19 full-time (10 women). *Students:* 23 full-time (9 women), 5 part-time (3 women); includes 4 minority (1 African American, 2 American Indian/Alaska Native, 1 Hispanic American), 3 international. Average age 39. In 2009, 5 master's awarded. *Degree requirements:* For master's, thesis or departmental qualifying exam; for doctorate, thesis/dissertation. *Entrance requirements:* For master's and doctorate, GRE General Test. Additional exam requirements/recommendations for international students: Required—TOEFL (minimum score 550 paper-based; 213 computer-based; 80 iBT), IELTS (minimum score 7), or a bachelor's degree from an English-speaking university and demonstrated proficiency. *Application deadline:* For fall admission, 2/1 priority date for domestic students, 9/1 priority date for international students; for spring admission, 10/1 priority date for domestic students. Applications are processed on a rolling basis. Application fee: $65. Electronic applications accepted. *Financial support:* In 2009–10, 8 teaching assistantships with tuition reimbursements (averaging $11,300 per year) were awarded; Federal Work-Study, health care benefits, tuition waivers (full and partial), and unspecified assistantships also available. Support available to part-time students. Financial award application deadline: 3/30; financial award applicants required to submit FAFSA. *Faculty research:* Twentieth century U. S., U. S. trans-Mississippi West, Arizona and the Southwest, women's history, U. S. intellectual history. Total annual research expenditures: $78,000. *Unit head:* Dr. Eric Meeks, Chair, 928-523-8428, Fax: 928-523-1277, E-mail: eric.meeks@nau.edu. *Application contact:* Dr. Scott Reese, Coordinator, 928-523-9049, Fax: 928-523-1277, E-mail: scott.reese@nau.edu.

Northern Illinois University, Graduate School, College of Liberal Arts and Sciences, Department of History, De Kalb, IL 60115-2854. Offers MA, PhD. Part-time programs available. *Faculty:* 18 full-time (8 women), 2 part-time/adjunct (0 women). *Students:* 25 full-time (11 women), 38 part-time (18 women); includes 6 minority (3 African Americans, 1 American Indian/Alaska Native, 1 Asian American or Pacific Islander, 1 Hispanic American), 2 international. Average age 36. 66 applicants, 53% accepted, 18 enrolled. In 2009, 10 master's, 5 doctorates awarded. Terminal master's awarded for partial completion of doctoral program. *Degree requirements:* For master's, variable foreign language requirement, comprehensive exam, thesis optional, research seminars; for doctorate, variable foreign language requirement, thesis/dissertation, candidacy exam, dissertation defense, research seminars. *Entrance requirements:* For master's, GRE General Test, minimum GPA of 2.75; for doctorate, GRE General Test, minimum undergraduate GPA of 2.75, graduate 3.2. Additional exam requirements/recommendations for international students: Required—TOEFL (minimum score 550 paper-based; 213 computer-based). *Application deadline:* For fall admission, 6/1 for domestic students, 5/1 for international students; for spring admission, 11/1 for domestic students, 10/1 for international students. Applications are processed on a rolling basis. Application fee: $30. Electronic applications accepted. *Expenses:* Tuition, state resident: full-time $6576; part-time $274 per credit hour. Tuition, nonresident: full-time $13,152; part-time $548 per credit hour. Required fees: $1813; $75.53 per credit hour. Part-time tuition and fees vary according to course load. *Financial support:* In 2009–10, 23 teaching assistantships with full tuition reimbursements were awarded; fellowships with full tuition reimbursements, research assistantships with full tuition reimbursements, career-related internships or fieldwork, Federal Work-Study, scholarships/grants, tuition waivers (full), and unspecified assistantships also available. Support available to part-time students. Financial award applicants required to submit FAFSA. *Faculty research:* History of the Carolingian empire, world history of early modern Europe, modern Irish history, history of the Ming dynasty. *Unit head:* Dr. Beatrix Hoffman, Chair, 815-753-0851, Fax: 815-753-6302, E-mail: beatrix@niu.edu. *Application contact:* Dr. E. Taylor Atkins, Assistant Chair and Director of Graduate Studies, 815-753-6699, E-mail: etatkins@niu.edu.

Northwestern University, The Graduate School, Judd A. and Marjorie Weinberg College of Arts and Sciences, Department of History, Evanston, IL 60208. Offers PhD, JD/PhD. Admissions and degrees offered through The Graduate School. *Degree requirements:* For doctorate, variable foreign language requirement, thesis/dissertation, major and minor field exams. *Entrance requirements:* For doctorate, sample of written work. Additional exam requirements/recommendations for international students: Required—TOEFL. Electronic applications accepted. *Faculty research:* Medieval and early modern Europe, Africa, race and slavery, Atlantic history, gender.

Northwestern University, School of Continuing Studies, Program in Liberal Studies, Evanston, IL 60208. Offers American studies (MA); history (MA); religious and ethical studies (MA).

Northwest Missouri State University, Graduate School, College of Arts and Sciences, Department of History, Humanities, and Political Science, Maryville, MO 64468-6001. Offers history (MA); teaching history (MS Ed). Part-time programs available. *Faculty:* 6 full-time (2 women). *Students:* 9 full-time (7 women), 4 part-time (0 women). 8 applicants, 88% accepted, 3 enrolled. In 2009, 4 master's awarded. *Degree requirements:* For master's, comprehensive exam, thesis. *Entrance requirements:* For master's, GRE General Test, undergraduate major/minor in social studies/humanities, minimum undergraduate GPA of 2.5, writing sample. Additional exam requirements/recommendations for international students: Required—TOEFL (minimum score 550 paper-based; 213 computer-based). *Application deadline:* For fall admission, 7/1 for domestic and international students; for spring admission, 11/15 for domestic and international students. Applications are processed on a rolling basis. Application fee: $0 ($50 for international students). *Expenses:* Tuition, state resident: part-time $296.34 per credit hour. Tuition, nonresident: part-time $510.43 per credit hour. *Financial support:* In 2009–10, 2 research assistantships with full tuition reimbursements (averaging $6,000 per year) were awarded. Financial award application deadline: 4/1; financial award applicants required to submit FAFSA. *Unit head:* Dr. Richard Frucht, Chairperson, 660-562-1614. *Application contact:* Dr. Gregory Haddock, Dean of Graduate School, 660-562-1145, Fax: 660-562-1096, E-mail: gradsch@nwmissouri.edu.

Oakland University, Graduate Study and Lifelong Learning, College of Arts and Sciences, Department of History, Rochester, MI 48309-4401. Offers MA. Part-time and evening/weekend programs available. *Entrance requirements:* For master's, minimum GPA of 3.0 for unconditional admission. Additional exam requirements/recommendations for international students: Required—TOEFL (minimum score 550 paper-based; 213 computer-based). Electronic applications accepted.

The Ohio State University, Graduate School, College of Humanities, Department of History, Columbus, OH 43210. Offers MA, PhD. *Faculty:* 73. *Students:* 78 full-time (34 women), 51 part-time (16 women); includes 18 minority (11 African Americans, 3 American Indian/Alaska Native, 1 Asian American or Pacific Islander, 3 Hispanic Americans), 16 international. Average age 30. In 2009, 21 master's, 14 doctorates awarded. *Degree requirements:* For master's, thesis optional; for doctorate, variable foreign language requirement, thesis/dissertation. *Entrance requirements:* For master's and doctorate, GRE General Test. Additional exam requirements/recommendations for international students: Required—TOEFL (minimum score 600 paper-based; 250 computer-based). *Application deadline:* For fall admission, 8/15 priority date for domestic students, 7/1 priority date for international students; for winter admission, 12/1 priority date for domestic students, 11/1 priority date for international students; for spring admission, 3/1 priority date for domestic students, 2/1 priority date for international students. Applications are processed on a rolling basis. Application fee: $40 ($50 for international students). Electronic applications accepted. *Expenses:* Tuition, state resident: full-time $10,683. Tuition, nonresident: full-time $25,923. Tuition and fees vary according to course load and program. *Financial support:* Fellowships, research assistantships, teaching assistantships, Federal Work-Study, institutionally sponsored loans, and unspecified assistantships available. Support available to part-time students. *Unit head:* Paula Baker, Graduate Studies Committee Chair, E-mail: baker.973@osu.edu. *Application contact:* 614-247-9444, Fax: 614-292-3895, E-mail: domestic.grad@osu.edu.

Ohio University, Graduate College, College of Arts and Sciences, Department of History, Athens, OH 45701-2979. Offers MA, PhD. *Faculty:* 24 full-time (7 women). *Students:* 45 full-time (12 women), 4 part-time (2 women), 7 international. 55 applicants, 40% accepted, 12 enrolled. In 2009, 7 master's, 6 doctorates awarded. *Degree requirements:* For master's, one foreign language, thesis optional; for doctorate, 2 foreign languages, comprehensive exam, thesis/dissertation. *Entrance requirements:* For master's, GRE, minimum GPA of 3.0; for doctorate, GRE, minimum GPA of 3.0, MA. Additional exam requirements/recommendations for international students: Required—TOEFL (minimum score 550 paper-based; 80 iBT) or IELTS Academic (minimum score 6.5). *Application deadline:* For fall admission, 2/1 priority date for domestic and international students. Application fee: $50 ($55 for international students). Electronic applications accepted. *Expenses:* Tuition, state resident: full-time $7839; part-time $323 per quarter hour. Tuition, nonresident: full-time $15,831; part-time $654 per quarter hour. Required fees: $2931. *Financial support:* Fellowships with tuition reimbursements, teaching assistantships with tuition reimbursements, Federal Work-Study and institutionally sponsored loans available. Financial award application deadline: 2/1. *Faculty research:* U.S. foreign relations, modern Europe, Latin America, southeast Asia, U.S. women. *Unit head:* Dr. Patrick Barr-Melej, Chair, 740-591-1851, Fax: 740-593-0259, E-mail: bar-mel@ohio.edu. *Application contact:* Chester Pach, Graduate Chair, 740-593-4353, Fax: 740-593-0259, E-mail: pach@ohio.edu.

Oklahoma State University, College of Arts and Sciences, Department of History, Stillwater, OK 74078. Offers MA, PhD. *Faculty:* 24 full-time (5 women), 1 part-time/adjunct (0 women). *Students:* 15 full-time (4 women), 52 part-time (22 women); includes 7 minority (5 American Indian/Alaska Native, 2 Asian Americans or Pacific Islanders), 1 international. Average age 33. 37 applicants, 51% accepted, 11 enrolled. In 2009, 3 master's, 2 doctorates awarded. *Degree requirements:* For master's, thesis; for doctorate, comprehensive exam, thesis/dissertation. *Entrance requirements:* For master's and doctorate, GRE. Additional exam requirements/recommendations for international students: Required—TOEFL (minimum score 550 paper-based; 79 iBT). *Application deadline:* For fall admission, 3/1 priority date for international students; for spring admission, 8/1 priority date for international students. Applications are processed on a rolling basis. Application fee: $40 ($75 for international students). Electronic applications accepted. *Expenses:* Tuition, state resident: full-time $3716; part-time $154.85 per credit hour. Tuition, nonresident: full-time $14,448; part-time $602 per credit hour. Required fees: $1772; $73.85 per credit hour. One-time fee: $50. Tuition and fees vary according to course load and campus/location. *Financial support:* In 2009–10, 25 teaching assistantships (averaging $13,117 per year) were awarded; career-related internships or fieldwork, Federal Work-Study, scholarships/grants, health care benefits, tuition waivers (partial), and unspecified assistantships also available. Support available to part-time students. Financial award application deadline: 3/1; financial award applicants required to submit FAFSA. *Faculty research:* U.S. history, the American West, Native American history, modern European history, women's history. *Unit head:* Dr. Michael F. Logan, Head, 405-744-5678, Fax: 405-744-5400. *Application contact:* Dr. Gordon Emslie, Dean, 405-744-6368, Fax: 405-744-0355, E-mail: grad-i@okstate.edu.

Old Dominion University, College of Arts and Letters, Program in History, Norfolk, VA 23529. Offers MA. Part-time and evening/weekend programs available. *Faculty:* 16 full-time (7 women). *Students:* 17 full-time (10 women), 28 part-time (12 women); includes 1 minority (African American), 1 international. Average age 31. 41 applicants, 80% accepted, 20 enrolled. In 2009, 15 master's awarded. *Degree requirements:* For master's, comprehensive exam, thesis optional. *Entrance requirements:* For master's, GRE General Test, 24 credits in history with minimum GPA of 3.0. *Application deadline:* For fall admission, 6/1 for domestic students; for spring admission, 11/1 for domestic students. Applications are processed on a rolling basis. Application fee: $40. Electronic applications accepted. *Expenses:* Tuition, state resident: full-time $8112; part-time $338 per credit. Tuition, nonresident: full-time $20,256; part-time $844 per credit. Required fees: $119 per semester. One-time fee: $50. *Financial support:* In 2009–10, 1 fellowship with full tuition reimbursement (averaging $8,000 per year), 6 teaching assistantships with partial tuition reimbursements (averaging $8,000 per year) were awarded; career-related internships or fieldwork and scholarships/grants also available. Support available to part-time students. Financial award application deadline: 2/15; financial award applicants required to submit FAFSA. *Faculty research:* History: maritime, American, European, modern Asia, and Africa. *Unit head:* Dr. Ingo K. Heidbrink, Graduate Program Director, 757-683-3949, Fax: 757-683-5644, E-mail: histgpd@odu.edu. *Application contact:* Dr. Ingo K. Heidbrink, Graduate Program Director, 757-683-3949, Fax: 757-683-5644, E-mail: histgpd@odu.edu.

Oregon State University, Graduate School, College of Liberal Arts, Department of History, Corvallis, OR 97331. Offers history of science (MA, PhD). *Expenses:* Tuition, state resident: full-time $9774; part-time $362 per credit. Tuition, nonresident: full-time $15,849; part-time $587 per credit. Required fees: $1639. Full-time tuition and fees vary according to course load and program. *Unit head:* Dr. Paul L. Farber, Chair, 541-737-1273, Fax: 541-737-1257, E-mail: pfarber@oregonstate.edu. *Application contact:* Polly Jeneva, Head Adviser, 541-737-0561, Fax: 541-737-2434, E-mail: polly.jeneva@oregonstate.edu.

Penn State University Park, Graduate School, College of the Liberal Arts, Department of History, State College, University Park, PA 16802-1503. Offers MA, PhD.

Pepperdine University, Seaver College, Humanities Division, Malibu, CA 90263. Offers American studies (MA); history (MA). *Degree requirements:* For master's, oral and written exams. *Entrance requirements:* For master's, GRE General Test, undergraduate major or 15 upper-division units in history. Additional exam requirements/recommendations for international students: Required—TOEFL. *Expenses:* Tuition: Full-time $37,516; part-time $1310 per unit. Required fees: $80.

Pittsburg State University, Graduate School, College of Arts and Sciences, Department of History, Pittsburg, KS 66762. Offers MA. *Degree requirements:* For master's, thesis or alternative. *Expenses:* Tuition, state resident: full-time $4212; part-time $176 per credit. Tuition, nonresident: full-time $11,530; part-time $480 per credit. Required fees: $940; $43 per credit. Tuition and fees vary according to course level, course load, degree level, campus/location, reciprocity agreements and student level.

Pontifical Catholic University of Puerto Rico, College of Arts and Humanities, Department of History, Ponce, PR 00717-0777. Offers MA. *Entrance requirements:* For master's, GRE General Test, minimum GPA of 2.75, 2 letters of recommendation.

Pontificia Universidad Catolica Madre y Maestra, Graduate School, Santiago, Dominican Republic. Offers administration (M Adm); architecture of interiors (M Arch); architecture of tourist lodgings (M Arch); banking and financial management (M Mgmt); civil law (LL M); construction administration (ME); corporate business law (LL M); criminal procedure law (LL M); environmental engineering (ME, MEE); finance (M Mgmt); history applied to education (M Ed); human resources (EMBA); insurance (M Mgmt); international business (M Mgmt); labor law and Social Security (LL M); logistics management (ME); marketing (M Mgmt); renewable energy (ME); strategic cost management (M Mgmt). *Entrance requirements:* For master's, curriculum vitae, interview.

Portland State University, Graduate Studies, College of Liberal Arts and Sciences, Department of History, Portland, OR 97207-0751. Offers MA. Part-time programs available. *Degree requirements:* For master's, one foreign language, thesis, oral and written exams. *Entrance requirements:* For master's, GRE General Test, minimum GPA of 3.5 in upper-division history courses, 2 letters of recommendation, BA/BS in history. Additional exam requirements/recommendations for international students: Required—TOEFL (minimum score 550 paper-based; 213 computer-based). *Faculty research:* Germany and Modern Europe, early modern France and England, Mexico in the 1920's, eighteenth-century France, Reformation, U.S. cultural history.

Princeton University, Graduate School, Department of Classics, Princeton, NJ 08544-1019. Offers classical and hellenic studies (PhD); classical philosophy (PhD); history (the ancient world) (PhD); literature and philology (PhD). *Degree requirements:* For doctorate, thesis/dissertation. *Entrance requirements:* For doctorate, GRE General Test, sample of written work. Additional exam requirements/recommendations for international students: Required—TOEFL (minimum score 600 paper-based; 250 computer-based). Electronic applications accepted.

Princeton University, Graduate School, Department of History, Princeton, NJ 08544-1019. Offers history (PhD); history of science (PhD). *Degree requirements:* For doctorate, variable foreign language requirement, comprehensive exam, thesis/dissertation. *Entrance requirements:* For doctorate, GRE General Test, sample of written work. Additional exam requirements/recommendations for international students: Required—TOEFL (minimum score 600 paper-

History

Princeton University (continued)

based; 250 computer-based). Electronic applications accepted. *Faculty research:* World comparative, Europe-early modern, modern, late antique, medieval.

Providence College, Graduate Studies, Department of History, Providence, RI 02918. Offers American history (MA); European history (MA). Part-time and evening/weekend programs available. *Faculty:* 6 full-time (1 woman), 4 part-time/adjunct (1 woman). *Students:* 25 full-time (10 women), 31 part-time (16 women), 1 international. Average age 29. 19 applicants, 100% accepted. In 2009, 28 master's awarded. *Degree requirements:* For master's, comprehensive exam, thesis optional. *Entrance requirements:* Additional exam requirements/recommendations for international students: Required—TOEFL (minimum score 550 paper-based; 213 computer-based; 80 iBT). *Application deadline:* For fall admission, 8/1 priority date for domestic and international students; for spring admission, 12/31 priority date for domestic students, 12/1 priority date for international students. Applications are processed on a rolling basis. Application fee: $55. *Expenses:* Tuition: Full-time $9909; part-time $367 per credit. One-time fee: $200. Tuition and fees vary according to course load and program. *Financial support:* In 2009–10, 8 research assistantships with full tuition reimbursements (averaging $8,400 per year) were awarded; career-related internships or fieldwork, institutionally sponsored loans, and unspecified assistantships also available. Support available to part-time students. Financial award application deadline: 8/1; financial award applicants required to submit FAFSA. *Faculty research:* Modern Europe, American social and political history, modern Ireland, Rhode Island, eastern European history. *Unit head:* Dr. Paul O'Malley, Director of Graduate Program in History, 401-865-2193, Fax: 401-865-1193, E-mail: pomalley@providence.edu. *Application contact:* Phyllis S. Cardullo, Senior Administrative Coordinator, 401-865-2193, Fax: 401-865-1193, E-mail: pcardull@providence.edu.

Purdue University, Graduate School, College of Liberal Arts, Department of History, West Lafayette, IN 47907. Offers MA, PhD. Part-time programs available. *Degree requirements:* For master's, thesis optional; for doctorate, 2 foreign languages, thesis/dissertation. *Entrance requirements:* For master's and doctorate, GRE General Test, sample of written work. Additional exam requirements/recommendations for international students: Required—TOEFL. Electronic applications accepted. *Faculty research:* U.S. history, early modern and modern European history, global women's history, U.S. minority history, medieval history.

Purdue University Calumet, Graduate School, School of Liberal Arts and Social Sciences, Department of History and Political Science, Hammond, IN 46323-2094. Offers history (MA). Part-time and evening/weekend programs available. *Entrance requirements:* Additional exam requirements/recommendations for international students: Required—TOEFL. *Faculty research:* Mid-east, German history, US regional history, US social history, holocaust.

Queens College of the City University of New York, Division of Graduate Studies, Social Science Division, Department of History, Flushing, NY 11367-1597. Offers MA. Part-time and evening/weekend programs available. *Faculty:* 24 full-time (12 women). *Students:* 9 full-time (3 women), 75 part-time (33 women). 70 applicants, 59% accepted, 27 enrolled. In 2009, 15 master's awarded. *Degree requirements:* For master's, one foreign language, comprehensive exam, thesis. *Entrance requirements:* For master's, minimum GPA of 3.0. Additional exam requirements/recommendations for international students: Required—TOEFL. *Application deadline:* For fall admission, 4/1 for domestic students; for spring admission, 11/1 for domestic students. Applications are processed on a rolling basis. Application fee: $125. *Expenses:* Tuition, state resident: full-time $7360; part-time $310 per credit. Tuition, nonresident: part-time $575 per credit. One-time fee: $195.25 full-time; $145.25 part-time. *Financial support:* Career-related internships or fieldwork, Federal Work-Study, institutionally sponsored loans, and tuition waivers (partial) available. Support available to part-time students. Financial award application deadline: 4/1; financial award applicants required to submit FAFSA. *Faculty research:* Ancient, modern European, medieval, and American history. *Unit head:* Dr. Frank Warren, Chairperson, 718-997-5350, E-mail: frank_warren@qc.edu. *Application contact:* Dr. Jon Peterson, Graduate Adviser, 718-997-5350, E-mail: jon_peterson@qc.edu.

Rhode Island College, School of Graduate Studies, Faculty of Arts and Sciences, Department of History, Providence, RI 02908-1991. Offers MA. Part-time and evening/weekend programs available. *Faculty:* 7 full-time (2 women). *Students:* 3 part-time (1 woman). Average age 34. *Degree requirements:* For master's, oral exam or thesis. *Entrance requirements:* For master's, GRE General and Subject Tests or MAT, 3 letters of recommendation, interview. Additional exam requirements/recommendations for international students: Recommended—TOEFL (minimum score 550 paper-based; 213 computer-based; 79 iBT). *Application deadline:* For fall admission, 4/1 for domestic students; for spring admission, 11/1 for domestic students. Applications are processed on a rolling basis. Application fee: $50. *Expenses:* Tuition, state resident: full-time $7440; part-time $310 per credit hour. Tuition, nonresident: full-time $14,784; part-time $616 per credit hour. Required fees: $552; $20 per credit. $70 per term. *Financial support:* Teaching assistantships with full tuition reimbursements, Federal Work-Study, scholarships/grants, health care benefits, and unspecified assistantships available. Support available to part-time students. Financial award application deadline: 5/15; financial award applicants required to submit FAFSA. *Unit head:* Dr. Robert Cvornvek, Chair, 401-456-8039. *Application contact:* Graduate Studies, 401-456-8700.

Rice University, Graduate Programs, School of Humanities, Department of History, Houston, TX 77251-1892. Offers MA, PhD. *Faculty:* 15 full-time (6 women). *Students:* 35 full-time (16 women); includes 3 minority (2 African Americans, 1 Asian American or Pacific Islander), 1 international. Average age 28. 58 applicants, 10% accepted, 5 enrolled. In 2009, 4 master's, 5 doctorates awarded. Terminal master's awarded for partial completion of doctoral program. *Degree requirements:* For doctorate, variable foreign language requirement, comprehensive exam, thesis/dissertation, 4 semesters of coursework. *Entrance requirements:* For doctorate, GRE, Writing samples, letters of recommendation, personal statement, transcripts. Additional exam requirements/recommendations for international students: Required—TOEFL (minimum score 600 paper-based; 250 computer-based; 90 iBT), or IELTS (minimum score 7). *Application deadline:* For fall admission, 2/1 for domestic and international students. Application fee: $70. Electronic applications accepted. *Financial support:* In 2009–10, 9 fellowships (averaging $15,900 per year) were awarded; health care benefits and full tuition waivers, stipend for all accepted students also available. Financial award application deadline: 2/1. *Faculty research:* U. S. Southern, Caribbean, African-American, world, Latin American. *Unit head:* Paula D. Platt, Department Administrator, 713-348-3097, Fax: 713-348-5207, E-mail: pauladp@rice.edu. *Application contact:* Lisa Tate, Graduate Program Coordinator, 713-348-2288, Fax: 713-348-5207, E-mail: lisa.tate@rice.edu.

Roosevelt University, Graduate Division, College of Arts and Sciences, Department of History, Art, and Philosophy, Chicago, IL 60605. Offers history (MA). Part-time and evening/weekend programs available. *Degree requirements:* For master's, thesis or alternative. *Faculty research:* American social history, Holocaust, European history, African-American history, popular culture.

Rutgers, The State University of New Jersey, Camden, Graduate School of Arts and Sciences, Program in American and Public History, Camden, NJ 08102-1401. Offers MA. Part-time and evening/weekend programs available. *Degree requirements:* For master's, comprehensive exam. *Entrance requirements:* For master's, GRE General Test (full-time applicants), 3 letters of recommendation. Additional exam requirements/recommendations for international students: Required—TOEFL, IELTS. Electronic applications accepted. *Faculty research:* Women's history, military history, Afro-American history, urban history, history of technology.

Rutgers, The State University of New Jersey, Newark, Graduate School, Program in History, Newark, NJ 07102. Offers MA, MAT. Part-time and evening/weekend programs available. *Degree requirements:* For master's, one foreign language, comprehensive exam, thesis optional. *Entrance requirements:* For master's, GRE, minimum undergraduate B average. *Faculty research:* Global history, American history, American diplomatic and legal history, women's history, history of technology, environment and medicine.

Rutgers, The State University of New Jersey, New Brunswick, Graduate School-New Brunswick, Program in History, Piscataway, NJ 08854-8097. Offers African-American history (PhD); early American history (PhD); early modern European history (PhD); east Asian history (PhD); global and comparative history (PhD); history (PhD); history of diplomacy and foreign relations (PhD); history of technology, environment and health (PhD); history of the Atlantic cultures and African diaspora (PhD); Latin American history (PhD); medieval history (PhD); modern European history (PhD); nineteenth and twentieth century American history (PhD); women's and gender history (PhD). *Degree requirements:* For doctorate, thesis/dissertation. *Entrance requirements:* For doctorate, GRE General Test, sample of written work. Electronic applications accepted. *Faculty research:* American history, European history, Afro-American history, women's history, Latin American history.

St. Cloud State University, School of Graduate Studies, College of Social Sciences, Department of History, St. Cloud, MN 56301-4498. Offers MA, MS. Part-time programs available. *Faculty:* 12 full-time (3 women). *Students:* 11 full-time (4 women), 30 part-time (10 women); includes 1 minority (African American). 12 applicants, 75% accepted. In 2009, 7 master's awarded. *Degree requirements:* For master's, thesis or alternative. *Entrance requirements:* For master's, GRE General Test, GRE Subject Test, minimum GPA of 2.75. Additional exam requirements/recommendations for international students: Required—Michigan English Language Assessment Battery; Recommended—TOEFL (minimum score 550 paper-based; 213 computer-based), IELTS (minimum score 6.5). *Application deadline:* For fall admission, 6/1 priority date for domestic students, 4/1 for international students; for spring admission, 10/1 priority date for domestic students, 8/1 for international students. Applications are processed on a rolling basis. Application fee: $35. *Financial support:* Federal Work-Study, scholarships/grants, and unspecified assistantships available. Financial award application deadline: 3/1. *Unit head:* Dr. Peter Nayenga, Chairperson, 320-308-3165, Fax: 320-308-5198. *Application contact:* Linda Lou Krueger, School of Graduate Studies, 320-308-2113, Fax: 320-308-5371, E-mail: lekrueger@stcloudstate.edu.

St. John's University, St. John's College of Liberal Arts and Sciences, Department of History, Queens, NY 11439. Offers history (MA); modern world history (DA). Part-time and evening/weekend programs available. *Students:* 20 full-time (8 women), 27 part-time (8 women); includes 12 minority (5 African Americans, 1 Asian American or Pacific Islander, 6 Hispanic Americans), 9 international. Average age 36. 28 applicants, 57% accepted, 8 enrolled. In 2009, 8 master's, 5 doctorates awarded. *Degree requirements:* For master's, one foreign language, comprehensive exam, thesis optional; for doctorate, one foreign language, comprehensive exam, thesis/dissertation, internship, practicum. *Entrance requirements:* For master's, minimum GPA of 3.0; for doctorate, interview; minimum GPA of 3.5 in history, 3.0 overall; writing sample. Additional exam requirements/recommendations for international students: Required—TOEFL (minimum score 500 paper-based; 173 computer-based; 61 iBT), IELTS (minimum score 5.5). *Application deadline:* For fall admission, 5/1 priority date for domestic and international students; for spring admission, 11/1 priority date for domestic and international students. Applications are processed on a rolling basis. Application fee: $70. Electronic applications accepted. *Expenses:* Tuition: Full-time $16,290; part-time $905 per credit. Required fees: $300; $150 per semester. Tuition and fees vary according to program. *Financial support:* Fellowships, research assistantships, scholarships/grants available. Support available to part-time students. Financial award application deadline: 3/1; financial award applicants required to submit FAFSA. *Faculty research:* European economic history, history of East Asian culture, Irish history. *Unit head:* Dr. Mauricio Borrero, Chair, 718-990-6228, E-mail: borrerom@stjohns.edu. *Application contact:* Kathleen Davis, Director of Graduate Admission, 718-990-2790, Fax: 718-990-5686, E-mail: gradhelp@stjohns.edu.

Saint Louis University, Graduate School, College of Arts and Sciences and Graduate School, Department of History, St. Louis, MO 63103-2097. Offers MA, MA-R, PhD. Part-time programs available. *Degree requirements:* For master's, one foreign language, comprehensive exam, thesis optional, comprehensive oral exam; for doctorate, 2 foreign languages, comprehensive exam, thesis/dissertation, preliminary oral and written exams. *Entrance requirements:* For master's, GRE General Test, letters of recommendation, resume, writing sample; for doctorate, GRE General Test, letters of recommendation, resumé, writing sample, goal statement, transcripts. Additional exam requirements/recommendations for international students: Required—TOEFL (minimum score 525 paper-based; 194 computer-based). Electronic applications accepted. *Faculty research:* Medieval Europe, Crusades, Byzantine Empire, US West and Borderlands, Early Modern Europe.

Saint Mary's University, Faculty of Arts, Department of History, Halifax, NS B3H 3C3, Canada. Offers MA. Part-time programs available. *Degree requirements:* For master's, one foreign language, comprehensive exam, thesis. *Entrance requirements:* For master's, honors degree. *Application deadline:* For fall admission, 5/31 for domestic students. Applications are processed on a rolling basis. Application fee: $35. *Expenses:* Contact institution. *Financial support:* Fellowships available. *Faculty research:* Atlantic Canada, British Empire, history of science, South Africa. *Unit head:* Dr. Bill Sewell, Chair, 902-420-5756, Fax: 902-420-5141. *Application contact:* Dr. Tom Stretton, Graduate Coordinator, 902-420-5653, Fax: 902-420-5141, E-mail: historyma@smu.ca.

Salem State College, School of Graduate Studies, Program in History, Salem, MA 01970-5353. Offers MA, MAT. Part-time and evening/weekend programs available. *Students:* 10 full-time (2 women), 56 part-time (19 women); includes 1 minority (Asian American or Pacific Islander). Average age 34. 17 applicants, 94% accepted, 16 enrolled. In 2009, 29 master's awarded. *Entrance requirements:* For master's, GRE or MAT. Additional exam requirements/recommendations for international students: Required—TOEFL (minimum score 550 paper-based; 80 iBT), or IELTS (minimum score 5.5). *Application deadline:* For fall admission, 5/1 for domestic students; for spring admission, 10/1 for domestic students. Applications are processed on a rolling basis. Application fee: $50. *Expenses:* Tuition, state resident: full-time $2520; part-time $275 per credit hour. Tuition, nonresident: full-time $4140; part-time $365 per credit hour. Required fees: $2430. *Financial support:* In 2009–10, 8 students received support. Career-related internships or fieldwork, Federal Work-Study, scholarships/grants, and unspecified assistantships available. Support available to part-time students. Financial award application deadline: 5/1; financial award applicants required to submit FAFSA. *Unit head:* Bethany Jay, Program Coordinator, 978-542-6321, Fax: 978-542-7215, E-mail: bjay@salemstate.edu. *Application contact:* Dr. Lee A. Brossoit, Assistant Dean of Graduate Admissions, 978-542-6675, Fax: 978-542-7215, E-mail: lbrossoit@salemstate.edu.

Salisbury University, Graduate Division, Program in History, Salisbury, MD 21801-6837. Offers MA. Part-time programs available. *Faculty:* 8 full-time (2 women). *Students:* 3 full-time (1 woman), 8 part-time (3 women); includes 1 minority (African American). Average age 32. 4 applicants, 100% accepted, 3 enrolled. In 2009, 9 master's awarded. *Degree requirements:* For master's, comprehensive exam, thesis optional, 2 research and 3 reading seminars, final and oral exam. *Entrance requirements:* For master's, GRE General Test, minimum GPA of 3.0, 3 letters of recommendation. Additional exam requirements/recommendations for international students: Required—TOEFL (minimum score 550 paper-based; 213 computer-based). *Application deadline:* For fall admission, 5/15 for domestic students; for spring admission, 10/15 for domestic students. Application fee: $45. Electronic applications accepted. *Expenses:* Tuition, area resident: Part-time $278 per credit hour. Tuition, state resident: part-time $278 per credit hour. Tuition, nonresident: part-time $574 per credit hour. Required fees: $57 per credit hour. *Financial support:* In 2009–10, 5 students received support. Career-related internships or fieldwork and scholarships/grants available. Support available to part-time students. Financial award applicants required to submit FAFSA. *Faculty research:* History of science and technology, U. S. foreign relations, Maryland history, African-American history, medieval history. *Unit head:* Dr. Creston S. Long, Director, 410-548-5091, Fax: 410-677-5038, E-mail: cslong@salisbury.edu. *Application contact:* Mia C. Vye, Administrative Assistant II, 410-548-4499, Fax: 410-677-5038, E-mail: mcvye@salisbury.edu.

Sam Houston State University, College of Humanities and Social Sciences, Department of History, Huntsville, TX 77341. Offers MA. Part-time and evening/weekend programs available. *Faculty:* 14 full-time (5 women). *Students:* 12 full-time (5 women), 69 part-time (23 women); includes 7 minority (2 African Americans, 5 Hispanic Americans). Average age 35. 49 applicants, 78% accepted, 30 enrolled. In 2009, 13 master's awarded. *Entrance requirements:* For master's, GRE General Test. Additional exam requirements/recommendations for international students: Required—TOEFL (minimum score 550 paper-based; 213 computer-based; 79 iBT). *Application deadline:* For fall admission, 8/1 for domestic students; for spring admission, 12/1 for domestic students. Application fee: $20. *Expenses:* Tuition, state resident: full-time $3690; part-time $205 per credit hour. Tuition, nonresident: full-time $8676; part-time $482 per credit hour. Required fees: $1474. Tuition and fees vary according to course load and campus/location. *Financial support:* Teaching assistantships, Federal Work-Study and institutionally sponsored loans available. Support available to part-time students. Financial award application deadline: 5/31; financial award applicants required to submit FAFSA. *Unit head:* Dr. Terry Bilhartz, Chair, 936-294-1483, Fax: 936-294-3938, E-mail: his_tdb@shsu.edu. *Application contact:* Dr. Ken Hendrickson, Advisor, 936-294-1482, E-mail: his_keh@shsu.edu.

San Diego State University, Graduate and Research Affairs, College of Arts and Letters, Department of History, San Diego, CA 92182. Offers MA. *Degree requirements:* For master's, one foreign language. *Entrance requirements:* For master's, GRE General Test, bachelor's degree in related field. Additional exam requirements/recommendations for international students: Required—TOEFL. Electronic applications accepted. *Faculty research:* Latin American history, Filipino history.

San Francisco State University, Division of Graduate Studies, College of Behavioral and Social Sciences, Department of History, San Francisco, CA 94132-1722. Offers MA.

San Jose State University, Graduate Studies and Research, College of Social Sciences, Department of History, San Jose, CA 95192-0001. Offers history (MA); history education (MA). *Students:* 11 full-time (5 women), 53 part-time (34 women); includes 15 minority (1 African American, 7 Asian Americans or Pacific Islanders, 7 Hispanic Americans). Average age 35. 59 applicants, 34% accepted, 16 enrolled. In 2009, 10 master's awarded. *Degree requirements:* For master's, comprehensive exam, thesis or alternative. *Entrance requirements:* For master's, bachelor's degree or 15 units of course work in history, minimum GPA of 3.0. *Application deadline:* For fall admission, 2/15 for domestic students. Applications are processed on a rolling basis. Application fee: $59. Electronic applications accepted. *Financial support:* Fellowships available. Financial award applicants required to submit FAFSA. *Unit head:* Patricia Evridge Hill, Chair, 408-924-5755, Fax: 408-924-5531. *Application contact:* Libra Hilde, Graduate Advisor, 408-924-5500.

Sarah Lawrence College, Graduate Studies, Program in Women's History, Bronxville, NY 10708-5999. Offers MA. Part-time programs available. *Faculty:* 9 part-time/adjunct (8 women). *Students:* 28 full-time (26 women), 5 part-time (all women); includes 7 minority (6 African Americans, 1 Asian American or Pacific Islander), 2 international. Average age 27. 54 applicants, 63% accepted, 17 enrolled. In 2009, 12 master's awarded. *Degree requirements:* For master's, thesis. *Entrance requirements:* For master's, previous course work in history, minimum B average in undergraduate course work. Additional exam requirements/recommendations for international students: Required—TOEFL (minimum score 600 paper-based). *Application deadline:* For fall admission, 2/1 priority date for domestic students. Applications are processed on a rolling basis. Application fee: $60. *Expenses:* Tuition: Part-time $1161 per credit. Required fees: $232 per semester. Part-time tuition and fees vary according to course load, program and student level. *Financial support:* In 2009–10, 25 fellowships (averaging $5,563 per year) were awarded; career-related internships or fieldwork also available. Support available to part-time students. Financial award application deadline: 3/1; financial award applicants required to submit CSS PROFILE or FAFSA. *Unit head:* Priscilla Murolo, Director, 914-395-2405. *Application contact:* Emanual Lomax, Dean of Graduate Studies, 914-395-2371, E-mail: elomax@sarahlawrence.edu.

Seton Hall University, College of Arts and Sciences, Department of History, South Orange, NJ 07079-2697. Offers history (MA), including Catholic history, European history, global history, United States history. Part-time programs available. *Faculty:* 16 full-time (5 women). *Students:* 7 full-time (2 women), 16 part-time (5 women); includes 1 minority (African American). Average age 31. 16 applicants, 81% accepted, 8 enrolled. In 2009, 4 master's awarded. *Degree requirements:* For master's, thesis or comprehensive exam. *Entrance requirements:* For master's, GRE. Additional exam requirements/recommendations for international students: Required—TOEFL. *Application deadline:* For fall admission, 7/1 priority date for domestic and international students; for spring admission, 11/1 priority date for domestic and international students. Applications are processed on a rolling basis. Application fee: $50. Electronic applications accepted. *Financial support:* Research assistantships, career-related internships or fieldwork, Federal Work-Study, and unspecified assistantships available. Financial award applicants required to submit FAFSA. *Faculty research:* Catholic history, European history, global history, United States history, African American history. *Unit head:* Dr. Nathaniel Knight, Chair, 973-275-2984, Fax: 973-761-7798, E-mail: knightna@shu.edu. *Application contact:* Dr. Dermot Quinn, Director of Graduate Studies, 973-275-2774, Fax: 973-761-7798, E-mail: quinnder@shu.edu.

Shippensburg University of Pennsylvania, School of Graduate Studies, College of Arts and Sciences, Department of History and Philosophy, Shippensburg, PA 17257-2299. Offers applied history (MA, Certificate). Part-time and evening/weekend programs available. *Degree requirements:* For master's, thesis or internship. *Entrance requirements:* For master's, interview. Additional exam requirements/recommendations for international students: Required—TOEFL (minimum score 560 paper-based; 220 computer-based); Recommended—IELTS (minimum score 6). Electronic applications accepted.

Shippensburg University of Pennsylvania, School of Graduate Studies, College of Education and Human Services, Department of Teacher Education, Shippensburg, PA 17257-2299. Offers curriculum and instruction (M Ed), including biology, early childhood education, elementary education, English, foreign languages, geography/earth science, history, mathematics, middle school education; reading (M Ed). *Accreditation:* NCATE. Part-time and evening/weekend programs available. *Degree requirements:* For master's, comprehensive exam (for some programs), thesis optional, practicum or internship (for some programs). *Entrance requirements:* For master's, MAT (if GPA less than 2.75), interview, 3 letters of recommendation, writing sample of teaching background and future goals. Additional exam requirements/recommendations for international students: Required—TOEFL (minimum score 560 paper-based; 220 computer-based); Recommended—IELTS (minimum score 6). Electronic applications accepted.

Simmons College, College of Arts and Sciences Graduate Studies, Program in History, Boston, MA 02115. Offers MA. Part-time programs available. *Students:* 9 part-time (7 women). 4 applicants, 50% accepted, 2 enrolled. In 2009, 8 master's awarded. *Degree requirements:* For master's, thesis optional. *Application deadline:* For fall admission, 8/1 for domestic and international students; for winter admission, 12/15 for domestic and international students; for spring admission, 5/1 for domestic and international students. Applications are processed on a rolling basis. Application fee: $35. Electronic applications accepted. *Expenses:* Tuition: Part-time $925 per credit hour. Part-time tuition and fees vary according to program. *Faculty research:* Gender history, cultural history, American history, transnational history. *Unit head:* Laura Prieto, Director, 617-521-2253, E-mail: laura.prieto@simmons.edu. *Application contact:* Kristen Haack, Director, Graduate Studies Admission, 617-521-2917, Fax: 617-521-3058, E-mail: gsa@simmons.edu.

Simon Fraser University, Graduate Studies, Faculty of Arts and Social Sciences, Department of History, Burnaby, BC V5A 1S6, Canada. Offers MA, PhD. *Degree requirements:* For master's, one foreign language, thesis or alternative, project; for doctorate, one foreign language, comprehensive exam, thesis/dissertation. *Entrance requirements:* For master's, minimum GPA of 3.0; for doctorate, minimum GPA of 3.5. Additional exam requirements/recommendations for international students: Required—TOEFL or IELTS. *Faculty research:* Colonialism and imperialism, Canadian history, Middle East and Islam labor, Victorian intellect.

Slippery Rock University of Pennsylvania, Graduate Studies (Recruitment), College of Humanities, Fine and Performing Arts, Department of History, Slippery Rock, PA 16057-1383. Offers MA. Part-time and evening/weekend programs available. *Degree requirements:* For master's, comprehensive exam (for some programs), thesis (for some programs). *Entrance requirements:* For master's, GRE General Test, MAT, minimum GPA of 2.75. Additional exam requirements/recommendations for international students: Required—TOEFL (minimum score 550 paper-based; 213 computer-based). *Application deadline:* For fall admission, 3/1 priority date for domestic students, 5/1 priority date for international students; for spring admission, 11/1 priority date for domestic students, 9/1 priority date for international students. Applications are processed on a rolling basis. Application fee: $25 ($30 for international students). Electronic applications accepted. *Expenses:* Tuition, state resident: full-time $6666; part-time $370 per credit. Tuition, nonresident: full-time $10,666; part-time $593 per credit. Required fees: $2184; $182 per credit. *Financial support:* Career-related internships or fieldwork, Federal Work-Study, scholarships/grants, and unspecified assistantships available. Support available to part-time students. Financial award application deadline: 5/1; financial award applicants required to submit FAFSA. *Unit head:* Dr. Eric Tuten, Graduate Coordinator, 724-738-4913, Fax: 724-738-4762, E-mail: jeric.tuten@sru.edu. *Application contact:* Angela Piverotto, Interim Director of Graduate Studies, 724-738-2051, Fax: 724-738-2146, E-mail: graduate.admissions@sru.edu.

Smith College, Graduate and Special Programs, Department of History, Northampton, MA 01063. Offers MAT. *Faculty:* 10 full-time (5 women), 1 (woman) part-time/adjunct. *Students:* 2 full-time (1 woman). Average age 23. 3 applicants, 100% accepted, 2 enrolled. In 2009, 1 master's awarded. *Entrance requirements:* Additional exam requirements/recommendations for international students: Required—TOEFL (minimum score 590 paper-based; 243 computer-based; 97 iBT). *Application deadline:* For fall admission, 4/15 for domestic students, 1/15 for international students; for spring admission, 12/1 for domestic students. Application fee: $60. *Financial support:* In 2009–10, 2 students received support. Career-related internships or fieldwork, institutionally sponsored loans, and scholarships/grants available. Support available to part-time students. Financial award application deadline: 1/15; financial award applicants required to submit CSS PROFILE or FAFSA. *Unit head:* Serguei Glebov, Associate Professor, 413-585-3742, E-mail: sglebov@smith.edu. *Application contact:* Ruth Morgan, Administrative Assistant, 413-585-3050, Fax: 413-585-3054, E-mail: gradstdy@smith.edu.

Sonoma State University, School of Social Sciences, Department of History, Rohnert Park, CA 94928. Offers MA. Part-time programs available. *Faculty:* 6 full-time (4 women). *Students:* 7 full-time (2 women), 16 part-time (7 women); includes 1 minority (Asian American or Pacific Islander). Average age 33. 14 applicants, 79% accepted, 3 enrolled. In 2009, 4 master's awarded. *Degree requirements:* For master's, thesis or alternative. *Entrance requirements:* For master's, GRE General Test or GRE Subject Test, minimum GPA of 3.0. Additional exam requirements/recommendations for international students: Required—TOEFL (minimum score 500 paper-based; 173 computer-based). *Application deadline:* For fall admission, 11/30 for domestic students; for spring admission, 8/31 for domestic students. Application fee: $55. *Expenses:* Tuition, nonresident: full-time $11,160. Required fees: $6226. Full-time tuition and fees vary according to course load. *Financial support:* Fellowships, research assistantships, teaching assistantships, career-related internships or fieldwork and Federal Work-Study available. Financial award application deadline: 3/2; financial award applicants required to submit FAFSA. *Unit head:* Dr. Kathleen Noonan, Chair, 707-664-2959, E-mail: kathleen.noonan@sonoma.edu. *Application contact:* Elaine Sundberg, Associate Vice Provost, Academic Programs/Graduate Studies, 707-664-2215, Fax: 707-664-4060, E-mail: elaine.sundberg@sonoma.edu.

Southeastern Louisiana University, College of Arts, Humanities and Social Sciences, Department of History and Political Science, Hammond, LA 70402. Offers history (MA). Part-time programs available. *Faculty:* 11 full-time (2 women). *Students:* 4 full-time (2 women), 39 part-time (20 women); includes 4 minority (3 African Americans, 1 American Indian/Alaska Native). Average age 31. 12 applicants, 100% accepted, 10 enrolled. In 2009, 4 master's awarded. *Degree requirements:* For master's, comprehensive exam, thesis optional. *Entrance requirements:* For master's, GRE General Test (900 or better), 30 undergraduate credits in history, minimum GPA of 2.5. Additional exam requirements/recommendations for international students: Required—TOEFL (minimum score 500 paper-based; 173 computer-based; 61 iBT). *Application deadline:* For fall admission, 7/15 priority date for domestic students, 6/1 priority date for international students; for spring admission, 12/1 priority date for domestic students, 10/1 priority date for international students. Applications are processed on a rolling basis. Application fee: $20 ($30 for international students). Electronic applications accepted. *Expenses:* Tuition, state resident: full-time $3086; part-time $225 per credit hour. Tuition, nonresident: part-time $529 per credit hour. Required fees: $1195. Tuition and fees vary according to course level and course load. *Financial support:* In 2009–10, 9 students received support, including 9 teaching assistantships (averaging $9,233 per year); career-related internships or fieldwork, Federal Work-Study, institutionally sponsored loans, and administrative assistantships also available. Support available to part-time students. Financial award application deadline: 5/1; financial award applicants required to submit FAFSA. *Faculty research:* American history, British history, Southern history, public history, European history. Total annual research expenditures: $91,023. *Unit head:* Dr. William Robison, Department Head, 985-549-2109, Fax: 985-549-2012, E-mail: wrobison@selu.edu. *Application contact:* Sandra Meyers, Graduate Admissions Analyst, 985-549-5620, Fax: 985-549-5632, E-mail: admissions@selu.edu.

Southeast Missouri State University, School of Graduate Studies, Department of History, Cape Girardeau, MO 63701. Offers MA. Part-time and evening/weekend programs available. *Degree requirements:* For master's, comprehensive exam (for some programs), thesis or alternative. *Entrance requirements:* For master's, GRE, minimum undergraduate GPA of 2.75. Additional exam requirements/recommendations for international students: Required—TOEFL (minimum score 550 paper-based; 213 computer-based); Recommended—IELTS (minimum score 6). Electronic applications accepted. *Expenses:* Tuition, state resident: full-time $4266; part-time $237 per credit hour. Tuition, nonresident: full-time $7506; part-time $417 per credit hour. Required fees: $427; $427. *Faculty research:* Modern America, historic preservation, world history.

Southern Connecticut State University, School of Graduate Studies, School of Arts and Sciences, Department of History, New Haven, CT 06515-1355. Offers MA, MS, MLS/MA. Part-time and evening/weekend programs available. *Faculty:* 5 full-time. *Students:* 27 full-time (12 women), 47 part-time (23 women); includes 6 minority (2 African Americans, 2 Asian Americans or Pacific Islanders, 2 Hispanic Americans). 65 applicants, 42% accepted, 22 enrolled. In 2009, 6 master's awarded. *Degree requirements:* For master's, one foreign language, thesis. *Entrance requirements:* For master's, interview, undergraduate major or minor in history. *Application deadline:* For fall admission, 7/15 priority date for domestic students. Applications are processed on a rolling basis. Application fee: $50. Electronic applications accepted. Tuition and fees vary according to program. *Financial support:* Career-related internships or fieldwork available. Financial award application deadline: 4/15; financial award applicants required to submit FAFSA. *Unit head:* Dr. Steven Judd, Chairperson, 203-392-5605, Fax: 203-392-5670, E-mail: judds1@southernct.edu. *Application contact:* Dr. Christine Petto, Graduate Coordinator, 203-392-5612, Fax: 203-392-5670, E-mail: pettoc1@southernct.edu.

Southern Illinois University Carbondale, Graduate School, College of Liberal Arts, Department of History, Carbondale, IL 62901-4701. Offers MA, PhD. Part-time programs available. *Degree requirements:* For master's, one foreign language, research papers or thesis, written exams; for doctorate, 2 foreign languages, thesis/dissertation. *Entrance requirements:* For master's, GRE General Test, minimum GPA of 3.0; for doctorate, GRE General Test, minimum GPA of 3.25. Additional exam requirements/recommendations for international students: Required—TOEFL. *Faculty research:* American, Asian, European, and Latin American history, global history.

History

Southern Illinois University Edwardsville, Graduate Studies and Research, College of Arts and Sciences, Department of Historical Studies, Program in History, Edwardsville, IL 62026-0001. Offers MA. Part-time and evening/weekend programs available. *Students:* 16 full-time (8 women), 14 part-time (5 women); includes 3 minority (all African Americans), 1 international. Average age 26. 35 applicants, 51% accepted. In 2009, 8 master's awarded. *Degree requirements:* For master's, one foreign language, thesis (for some programs), final exam. *Entrance requirements:* For master's, GRE. Additional exam requirements/recommendations for international students: Required—TOEFL (minimum score 550 paper-based; 213 computer-based; 79 iBT), IELTS (minimum score 6.5). *Application deadline:* For fall admission, 2/28 for domestic students, 6/1 for international students; for spring admission, 10/1 for international students. Application fee: $30. Electronic applications accepted. *Expenses:* Tuition, state resident: part-time $1252.50 per semester. Tuition, nonresident: part-time $3131.25 per semester. Required fees: $586.85 per semester. Tuition and fees vary according to course load. *Financial support:* In 2009–10, 1 fellowship with full tuition reimbursement, 3 research assistantships with full tuition reimbursements (averaging $8,064 per year), 11 teaching assistantships with full tuition reimbursements (averaging $8,064 per year) were awarded; career-related internships or fieldwork, Federal Work-Study, institutionally sponsored loans, scholarships/grants, traineeships, and unspecified assistantships also available. Support available to part-time students. Financial award application deadline: 3/1; financial award applicants required to submit FAFSA. *Unit head:* Dr. Carole Frick, Director, 618-650-3237, E-mail: cfrick@siue.edu. *Application contact:* Dr. Carole Frick, Director, 618-650-3237, E-mail: cfrick@siue.edu.

Southern Methodist University, Dedman College, Clements Department of History, Dallas, TX 75275. Offers MA, PhD. Part-time programs available. *Faculty:* 22 full-time (7 women), 2 part-time/adjunct (1 woman). *Students:* 11 full-time (5 women), 20 part-time (7 women); includes 7 minority (all Hispanic Americans), 3 international. Average age 31. 21 applicants, 43% accepted, 7 enrolled. In 2009, 1 master's, 4 doctorates awarded. Terminal master's awarded for partial completion of doctoral program. *Degree requirements:* For master's, one foreign language, thesis, oral exam, thesis defense; for doctorate, one foreign language, thesis/dissertation, oral exam, dissertation defense. *Entrance requirements:* For master's and doctorate, GRE General Test, minimum GPA of 3.0, 12 undergraduate hours in advanced level history, writing sample. Additional exam requirements/recommendations for international students: Required—TOEFL. *Application deadline:* For fall admission, 2/1 priority date for domestic and international students. Applications are processed on a rolling basis. Application fee: $60. Electronic applications accepted. *Financial support:* In 2009–10, 20 students received support, including 12 fellowships with full tuition reimbursements available (averaging $16,000 per year), 1 research assistantship (averaging $30,000 per year); career-related internships or fieldwork, institutionally sponsored loans, scholarships/grants, health care benefits, and tuition waivers (full and partial) also available. Financial award application deadline: 2/1; financial award applicants required to submit FAFSA. *Faculty research:* U. S. history, European history, Latin America, Africa/Middle East, China. *Unit head:* Dr. Kathleen A. Wellman, Chair, 214-768-2970, Fax: 214-768-2404, E-mail: hist@smu.edu. *Application contact:* Dr. Sherry L. Smith, Graduate Director, 214-768-1312, Fax: 214-768-2404, E-mail: hist@smu.edu.

Southern University and Agricultural and Mechanical College, Graduate School, College of Arts and Humanities, Department of History, Baton Rouge, LA 70813. Offers social sciences (MA). Part-time programs available. *Degree requirements:* For master's, thesis. *Entrance requirements:* For master's, GRE General Test. Additional exam requirements/recommendations for international students: Required—TOEFL (minimum score 525 paper-based; 193 computer-based).

Southwestern Assemblies of God University, Thomas F. Harrison School of Graduate Studies, Program in History, Waxahachie, TX 75165-5735. Offers MA.

Spring Hill College, Graduate Programs, Program in Liberal Arts, Mobile, AL 36608-1791. Offers fine arts (MLA); history and social science (MLA); leadership and ethics (MLA); literature (MLA). Part-time and evening/weekend programs available. *Faculty:* 11 full-time (4 women), 3 part-time/adjunct (2 women). *Students:* 1 (woman) full-time, 33 part-time (16 women); includes 6 minority (5 African Americans, 1 Hispanic American), 2 international. Average age 35. 27 applicants, 41% accepted, 6 enrolled. In 2009, 6 master's awarded. *Degree requirements:* For master's, capstone course, completion of program within 6 years of initial admittance. *Entrance requirements:* For master's, bachelor's degree with minimum undergraduate GPA of 3.0 or graduate/professional degree. Additional exam requirements/recommendations for international students: Required—TOEFL (minimum score 550 paper-based; 213 computer-based; 80 iBT), IELTS (minimum score 6.5). *Application deadline:* For fall admission, 8/1 priority date for domestic and international students; for spring admission, 12/1 priority date for domestic and international students. Applications are processed on a rolling basis. Application fee: $25 ($35 for international students). Electronic applications accepted. *Expenses:* Contact institution. *Financial support:* In 2009–10, 30 students received support. Career-related internships or fieldwork, institutionally sponsored loans, and scholarships/grants available. Support available to part-time students. Financial award applicants required to submit FAFSA. *Unit head:* Dr. Alexander R. Landi, Director, 251-380-3056, Fax: 251-460-2115, E-mail: landi@shc.edu. *Application contact:* Donna B. Tarasavage, Director of Marketing and Recruiting, Graduate and Continuing Studies, 251-380-3067, Fax: 251-460-2190, E-mail: dtarasavage@shc.edu.

Stanford University, School of Humanities and Sciences, Department of History, Stanford, CA 94305-9991. Offers MA, PhD. Terminal master's awarded for partial completion of doctoral program. *Degree requirements:* For doctorate, variable foreign language requirement, thesis/dissertation, oral exam. *Entrance requirements:* For master's and doctorate, GRE General Test. Additional exam requirements/recommendations for international students: Required—TOEFL. Electronic applications accepted. *Expenses:* Tuition: Full-time $37,380; part-time $2760 per quarter. Required fees: $501.

State University of New York at Binghamton, Graduate School, School of Arts and Sciences, Department of History, Binghamton, NY 13902-6000. Offers MA, PhD. Part-time programs available. *Faculty:* 25 full-time (8 women), 2 part-time/adjunct (0 women). *Students:* 36 full-time (14 women), 61 part-time (38 women); includes 6 minority (2 Asian Americans or Pacific Islanders, 4 Hispanic Americans), 12 international. Average age 34. 81 applicants, 38% accepted, 15 enrolled. In 2009, 15 master's, 6 doctorates awarded. Terminal master's awarded for partial completion of doctoral program. *Degree requirements:* For master's, one foreign language, thesis or alternative, written exam; for doctorate, variable foreign language requirement, comprehensive exam, thesis/dissertation. *Entrance requirements:* For master's and doctorate, GRE General Test, GRE Subject Test. Additional exam requirements/recommendations for international students: Required—TOEFL (minimum score 550 paper-based; 213 computer-based; 80 iBT). *Application deadline:* For fall admission, 4/15 priority date for domestic and international students; for spring admission, 11/1 priority date for domestic and international students. Applications are processed on a rolling basis. Application fee: $60. Electronic applications accepted. *Financial support:* In 2009–10, 57 students received support, including 6 fellowships with full tuition reimbursements available (averaging $15,000 per year), 5 research assistantships with full tuition reimbursements available (averaging $15,000 per year), 41 teaching assistantships with full tuition reimbursements available (averaging $15,000 per year); career-related internships or fieldwork, Federal Work-Study, institutionally sponsored loans, scholarships/grants, health care benefits, tuition waivers (full), and unspecified assistantships also available. Financial award application deadline: 2/15; financial award applicants required to submit FAFSA. *Unit head:* Dr. Gerald Kutcher, Chairperson, 607-777-6025, E-mail: gkutcher@binghamton.edu. *Application contact:* Victoria Williams, Recruiting and Admissions Coordinator, 607-777-2151, Fax: 607-777-2501, E-mail: vwilliam@binghamton.edu.

State University of New York at Oswego, Graduate Studies, College of Arts and Sciences, Department of History, Oswego, NY 13126. Offers MA. Part-time programs available. *Degree requirements:* For master's, thesis optional. *Entrance requirements:* For master's, writing sample. Additional exam requirements/recommendations for international students: Required—TOEFL (minimum score 560 paper-based; 220 computer-based).

State University of New York College at Cortland, Graduate Studies, School of Arts and Sciences, Department of History, Cortland, NY 13045. Offers MA, MS Ed. Part-time and evening/weekend programs available. *Degree requirements:* For master's, one foreign language, comprehensive exam (for some programs), thesis (for some programs). *Entrance requirements:* For master's, GRE General Test, GRE Subject Test. Additional exam requirements/recommendations for international students: Required—TOEFL.

Stephen F. Austin State University, Graduate School, College of Liberal Arts, Department of History, Nacogdoches, TX 75962. Offers MA. Part-time and evening/weekend programs available. *Degree requirements:* For master's, comprehensive exam. *Entrance requirements:* For master's, GRE General Test. Additional exam requirements/recommendations for international students: Required—TOEFL. *Faculty research:* U.S.-Third World foreign policy, racial attitudes of antebellum Southern whites, naval warfare in World War II, demography of East Texas, medieval sermons.

Stony Brook University, State University of New York, Graduate School, College of Arts and Sciences, Department of History, Stony Brook, NY 11794. Offers MA, PhD. Evening/weekend programs available. *Faculty:* 25 full-time (12 women), 3 part-time/adjunct (2 women). *Students:* 84 full-time (34 women), 6 part-time (4 women); includes 10 minority (6 African Americans, 1 Asian American or Pacific Islander, 3 Hispanic Americans), 24 international. Average age 33. 70 applicants, 33% accepted. In 2009, 9 master's, 6 doctorates awarded. *Degree requirements:* For doctorate, thesis/dissertation. *Entrance requirements:* For master's and doctorate, GRE General Test. Additional exam requirements/recommendations for international students: Required—TOEFL. *Application deadline:* For fall admission, 1/15 for domestic students. Application fee: $60. *Expenses:* Tuition, state resident: full-time $8370; part-time $349 per credit. Tuition, nonresident: full-time $13,250; part-time $552 per credit. Required fees: $933. *Financial support:* In 2009–10, 33 teaching assistantships were awarded; fellowships, research assistantships also available. *Faculty research:* Social, cultural, and political history. Total annual research expenditures: $57,123. *Unit head:* Nancy Tomes, Chair, 631-632-7500, Fax: 631-632-7367. *Application contact:* Brooke Larson, Graduate Coordinator, 631-632-7500, Fax: 631-632-7367.

Sul Ross State University, School of Arts and Sciences, Department of Behavioral and Social Sciences, Program in History, Alpine, TX 79832. Offers MA. Part-time and evening/weekend programs available. *Degree requirements:* For master's, thesis optional. *Entrance requirements:* For master's, GRE General Test, minimum GPA of 2.5 in last 60 hours of undergraduate work. *Faculty research:* Borderland/Southwestern studies, British studies, women's history, Native American studies, local history.

Syracuse University, Maxwell School of Citizenship and Public Affairs, Program in History, Syracuse, NY 13244. Offers MA, PhD. Part-time programs available. *Students:* 38 full-time (14 women), 15 part-time (6 women); includes 3 minority (2 African Americans, 1 Asian American or Pacific Islander), 8 international. Average age 36. 50 applicants, 30% accepted, 8 enrolled. In 2009, 5 master's, 1 doctorate awarded. Terminal master's awarded for partial completion of doctoral program. *Degree requirements:* For master's, comprehensive exam, thesis or alternative; for doctorate, 2 foreign languages, comprehensive exam, thesis/dissertation. *Entrance requirements:* For master's and doctorate, GRE General Test. Additional exam requirements/recommendations for international students: Required—TOEFL (minimum score 100 iBT). *Application deadline:* For fall admission, 2/1 priority date for domestic and international students. Application fee: $75. Electronic applications accepted. *Expenses:* Tuition: Full-time $26,808; part-time $1117 per credit. Required fees: $1024. *Financial support:* Fellowships with full and partial tuition reimbursements, research assistantships with tuition reimbursements, teaching assistantships with full and partial tuition reimbursements, tuition waivers (partial) available. Financial award application deadline: 1/1; financial award applicants required to submit FAFSA. *Faculty research:* American, medieval, European, South East Asian, and Russian history. *Unit head:* Dr. Paul Hagenloh, Director of Graduate Studies, 315-443-2210, Fax: 315-443-5876, E-mail: phagenlo@syr.edu. *Application contact:* Pat Bohrer, Information Contact, 315-443-2210, E-mail: pabohrer@syr.edu.

Tarleton State University, College of Graduate Studies, College of Liberal and Fine Arts, Department of Social Sciences, Stephenville, TX 76402. Offers history (MA); political science (MA). Part-time and evening/weekend programs available. Postbaccalaureate distance learning degree programs offered (minimal on-campus study). *Degree requirements:* For master's, variable foreign language requirement, comprehensive exam, thesis optional. *Entrance requirements:* For master's, GRE General Test, minimum GPA of 3.0. Additional exam requirements/recommendations for international students: Required—TOEFL (minimum score 550 paper-based; 213 computer-based; 80 iBT). Electronic applications accepted.

Teachers College, Columbia University, Graduate Faculty of Education, Department of Arts and Humanities, Program in History and Education, New York, NY 10027-6696. Offers Ed M, MA, Ed D, PhD. *Faculty:* 1 (woman) full-time. *Students:* 1 full-time (0 women), 17 part-time (12 women); includes 6 minority (all African Americans). Average age 39. 7 applicants, 71% accepted, 3 enrolled. In 2009, 1 doctorate awarded. *Degree requirements:* For doctorate, thesis/dissertation. *Entrance requirements:* For master's, sample of historical writing (Ed M); for doctorate, sample of historical writing. *Application deadline:* For fall admission, 5/15 for domestic students; for spring admission, 12/1 for domestic students. Application fee: $65. *Financial support:* Career-related internships or fieldwork, Federal Work-Study, institutionally sponsored loans, and tuition waivers (full and partial) available. Support available to part-time students. Financial award application deadline: 2/1. *Faculty research:* History of American education. *Unit head:* Graeme Sullivan, Chair, 212-678-3799. *Application contact:* Mark E. Stearns, Associate Director of Admission, 212-678-3710, Fax: 212-678-4171.

Temple University, Graduate School, College of Liberal Arts, Department of History, Philadelphia, PA 19122-6096. Offers MA, PhD. Part-time and evening/weekend programs available. Terminal master's awarded for partial completion of doctoral program. *Degree requirements:* For doctorate, one foreign language, thesis/dissertation. *Entrance requirements:* For master's and doctorate, GRE General Test, minimum GPA of 3.0. Additional exam requirements/recommendations for international students: Required—TOEFL (minimum score 550 paper-based; 213 computer-based; 79 iBT). Electronic applications accepted. *Faculty research:* Third World; American military and diplomatic history; American social, cultural, and public history, European history.

Texas A&M International University, Office of Graduate Studies and Research, College of Arts and Sciences, Department of Social Sciences, Laredo, TX 78041-1900. Offers history (MA); political science (MA); public administration (MPA). *Faculty:* 9 full-time (3 women). *Students:* 11 full-time (4 women), 52 part-time (25 women); includes 61 minority (all Hispanic Americans), 2 international. Average age 32. 37 applicants. In 2009, 15 master's awarded. *Degree requirements:* For master's, thesis (for some programs). *Entrance requirements:* For master's, GRE General Test. Additional exam requirements/recommendations for international students: Required—TOEFL (minimum score 550 paper-based; 213 computer-based). *Application deadline:* For fall admission, 4/30 priority date for domestic students; for spring admission, 11/30 for domestic students. Applications are processed on a rolling basis. Application fee: $25. *Financial support:* In 2009–10, 14 students received support, including 2 research assistantships, 3 teaching assistantships. Financial award application deadline: 11/1. *Unit head:* Dr. Mohammed Ben-Ruwin, Chair, 956-328-2632, E-mail: mbenruwin@tamiu.edu. *Application contact:* Rosie Espinoza-Dickinson, Director of Admissions, 956-326-2200, Fax: 956-326-2199, E-mail: enroll@tamiu.edu.

Texas A&M University, College of Liberal Arts, Department of History, College Station, TX 77843. Offers MA, PhD. Part-time programs available. *Faculty:* 21. *Students:* 54 full-time (14 women), 24 part-time (5 women); includes 12 minority (4 African Americans, 8 Hispanic

Americans), 3 international. Average age 32. In 2009, 4 master's, 3 doctorates awarded. Terminal master's awarded for partial completion of doctoral program. *Degree requirements:* For master's, one foreign language, thesis optional; for doctorate, 2 foreign languages, thesis/dissertation. *Entrance requirements:* For master's and doctorate, GRE General Test. Additional exam requirements/recommendations for international students: Required—TOEFL. *Application deadline:* For fall admission, 3/1 for domestic students. Application fee: $50 ($75 for international students). *Expenses:* Tuition, state resident: full-time $3991; part-time $221.74 per credit hour. Tuition, nonresident: full-time $9049; part-time $502.74 per credit hour. *Financial support:* In 2009–10, fellowships (averaging $4,000 per year); research assistantships, teaching assistantships with partial tuition reimbursements. Financial award application deadline: 2/1. *Faculty research:* Recent U.S. history, southwest, border studies, military history, Europe. *Unit head:* Dr. Walter L. Buenger, Head, 979-845-2571, E-mail: w-buenger@tamu.edu. *Application contact:* Albert S. Broussard, Coordinator, 979-845-7130, Fax: 979-862-4314.

Texas A&M University–Commerce, Graduate School, College of Arts and Sciences, Department of History, Commerce, TX 75429-3011. Offers history (MA, MS); social sciences (M Ed, MS). Part-time programs available. *Degree requirements:* For master's, comprehensive exam, thesis (for some programs). *Entrance requirements:* For master's, GRE General Test. Electronic applications accepted. *Faculty research:* American foreign policy, colonial America, Texas politics, Medieval England.

Texas A&M University–Corpus Christi, Graduate Studies and Research, College of Liberal Arts, Corpus Christi, TX 78412-5503. Offers English (MA); history (MA); psychology (MA); public administration (MPA); studio arts (MA, MFA). Part-time and evening/weekend programs available. *Degree requirements:* For master's, comprehensive exam, thesis (for some programs). *Entrance requirements:* For master's, GRE General Test. Additional exam requirements/recommendations for international students: Required—TOEFL. Electronic applications accepted.

Texas A&M University–Kingsville, College of Graduate Studies, College of Arts and Sciences, Program in History and Political Science, Kingsville, TX 78363. Offers MA, MS. Part-time and evening/weekend programs available. *Degree requirements:* For master's, comprehensive exam, thesis or alternative. *Entrance requirements:* For master's, GRE General Test. Additional exam requirements/recommendations for international students: Required—TOEFL.

Texas Christian University, AddRan College of Liberal Arts, Department of History, Fort Worth, TX 76129-0002. Offers MA, PhD. Terminal master's awarded for partial completion of doctoral program. *Degree requirements:* For master's, thesis; for doctorate, one foreign language, comprehensive exam, thesis/dissertation, qualifying exams. *Entrance requirements:* For master's and doctorate, GRE General Test. Additional exam requirements/recommendations for international students: Required—TOEFL. *Application deadline:* For fall admission, 2/1 for domestic students; for winter admission, 2/1 for domestic students; for spring admission, 2/1 for domestic students. Applications are processed on a rolling basis. Application fee: $50. *Expenses:* Tuition: Full-time $17,640; part-time $980 per credit hour. Tuition and fees vary according to program. *Financial support:* In 2009–10, fellowships with full tuition reimbursements (averaging $15,000 per year), teaching assistantships (averaging $15,000 per year) were awarded; tuition waivers and unspecified assistantships also available. Financial award application deadline: 2/1. *Unit head:* Dr. Peter Worthing, Chairperson, 817-257-6656, Fax: 817-257-5650, E-mail: p.worthing@tcu.edu. *Application contact:* Dr. Todd Kerstetter, Director of Graduate Studies, 817-257-6736, Fax: 817-257-5650, E-mail: t.kerstetter@tcu.edu.

Texas Southern University, College of Liberal Arts and Behavioral Sciences, Department of History and Geography, Houston, TX 77004-4584. Offers history (MA). Part-time and evening/weekend programs available. *Faculty:* 5 full-time (2 women), 1 (woman) part-time/adjunct. *Students:* 1 full-time (0 women), 6 part-time (3 women); includes 6 African Americans. Average age 41. 6 applicants, 100% accepted, 5 enrolled. In 2009, 3 master's awarded. *Degree requirements:* For master's, comprehensive exam, thesis optional. *Entrance requirements:* For master's, GRE General Test, minimum GPA of 2.5. Additional exam requirements/recommendations for international students: Required—TOEFL. *Application deadline:* For fall admission, 7/1 for domestic and international students; for spring admission, 11/1 for domestic and international students. Applications are processed on a rolling basis. Application fee: $50 ($75 for international students). Electronic applications accepted. *Expenses:* Tuition, state resident: full-time $1805; part-time $100 per credit hour. Tuition, nonresident: full-time $6470; part-time $343 per credit hour. Tuition and fees vary according to course level, course load and degree level. *Financial support:* Research assistantships, teaching assistantships, scholarships/grants and unspecified assistantships available. Support available to part-time students. Financial award application deadline: 5/1. *Faculty research:* American, Colonial, African, Asian, and African-American history. *Unit head:* Dr. Ethopia Keleta, Chair, 713-313-7324, Fax: 713-313-4236, E-mail: keleta_ex@tsu.edu. *Application contact:* Dr. Gregory Maddox, Interim Dean of the Graduate School, 713-313-7011 Ext. 4410, Fax: 713-639-1876, E-mail: maddox_gh@tsu.edu.

Texas State University–San Marcos, Graduate School, College of Liberal Arts, Department of History, San Marcos, TX 78666. Offers M Ed, MA. Part-time programs available. *Faculty:* 18 full-time (7 women), 3 part-time/adjunct (1 woman). *Students:* 30 full-time (19 women), 43 part-time (20 women); includes 15 minority (1 American Indian/Alaska Native, 14 Hispanic Americans), 1 international. Average age 33. 28 applicants, 100% accepted, 24 enrolled. In 2009, 22 master's awarded. *Degree requirements:* For master's, comprehensive exam, thesis (for some programs). *Entrance requirements:* For master's, GRE General Test, minimum of 24 hours of undergraduate history with minimum GPA of 3.25; 6 hours of undergraduate foreign language; 2 letters of reference; essay. Additional exam requirements/recommendations for international students: Required—TOEFL (minimum score 550 paper-based; 213 computer-based). *Application deadline:* For fall admission, 6/15 priority date for domestic students, 6/1 for international students; for spring admission, 10/15 priority date for domestic students, 10/1 for international students. Applications are processed on a rolling basis. Application fee: $40 ($90 for international students). Electronic applications accepted. *Expenses:* Tuition, state resident: full-time $5784; part-time $241 per credit hour. Tuition, nonresident: part-time $551 per credit hour. Required fees: $1728; $48 per credit hour. $306. Tuition and fees vary according to course load. *Financial support:* In 2009–10, 38 students received support, including 24 teaching assistantships (averaging $5,192 per year); research assistantships, Federal Work-Study and institutionally sponsored loans also available. Support available to part-time students. Financial award application deadline: 4/1; financial award applicants required to submit FAFSA. *Unit head:* Dr. J. F. dela Teja, Chair, 512-245-2142, Fax: 512-245-3043. *Application contact:* Dr. Mary Brennan, Graduate Adviser, 512-245-2110, Fax: 512-245-3043, E-mail: mb18@txstate.edu.

Texas Tech University, Graduate School, College of Arts and Sciences, Department of History, Lubbock, TX 79409. Offers MA, PhD. Part-time programs available. *Faculty:* 22 full-time (6 women), 3 part-time/adjunct (1 woman). *Students:* 51 full-time (15 women), 29 part-time (12 women); includes 9 minority (2 Asian Americans or Pacific Islanders, 7 Hispanic Americans), 3 international. Average age 32. 50 applicants, 70% accepted, 16 enrolled. In 2009, 7 master's, 4 doctorates awarded. *Degree requirements:* For master's, one foreign language, thesis or alternative; for doctorate, 2 foreign languages, thesis/dissertation. *Entrance requirements:* For master's and doctorate, GRE General Test. Additional exam requirements/recommendations for international students: Required—TOEFL (minimum score 550 paper-based; 213 computer-based). *Application deadline:* For fall admission, 3/1 priority date for international students; for spring admission, 11/1 priority date for international students. Applications are processed on a rolling basis. Application fee: $50 ($75 for international students). Electronic applications accepted. *Expenses:* Tuition, state resident: full-time $5100; part-time $213 per credit hour. Tuition, nonresident: full-time $11,748; part-time $490 per credit hour. Required fees: $2298; $50 per credit hour. $555 per semester. *Financial support:* In 2009–10, 3 teaching assistantships with partial tuition reimbursements (averaging $11,867 per year) were awarded; research assistantships with partial tuition reimbursements, Federal Work-Study and institutionally sponsored loans also available. Support available to part-time students. Financial award application deadline: 4/15; financial award applicants required to submit FAFSA. *Faculty research:* History of United States Southwest/West, the borderlands, history of Vietnam War and United States military history, history of Hispanics/Latinos and other U.S. minorities, history of Europe. *Unit head:* Randy McBee, Chair, 806-742-1004, Fax: 806-742-1060, E-mail: randy.mcbee@ttu.edu. *Application contact:* Dr. Gretchen Adams, Graduate Adviser, 806-742-3744, Fax: 806-742-1060.

Texas Woman's University, Graduate School, College of Arts and Sciences, Department of History and Government, Denton, TX 76201. Offers government (MA); history (MA). Part-time and evening/weekend programs available. *Faculty:* 10 full-time (3 women), 1 (woman) part-time/adjunct. *Students:* 7 full-time (5 women), 28 part-time (23 women); includes 8 minority (4 African Americans, 1 American Indian/Alaska Native, 3 Hispanic Americans), 2 international. Average age 36. 11 applicants, 55% accepted, 6 enrolled. In 2009, 12 master's awarded. *Degree requirements:* For master's, comprehensive exam, thesis. *Entrance requirements:* For master's, GRE (waived if completed a graduate degree), minimum GPA of 3.3, writing sample/portfolio. Additional exam requirements/recommendations for international students: Required—TOEFL (minimum score 550 paper-based; 213 computer-based; 79 iBT). *Application deadline:* For fall admission, 7/1 priority date for domestic students, 3/1 for international students; for spring admission, 12/1 priority date for domestic students, 7/1 for international students. Applications are processed on a rolling basis. Application fee: $50. Electronic applications accepted. *Expenses:* Tuition, state resident: full-time $3564; part-time $198 per credit hour. Tuition, nonresident: full-time $8550; part-time $475 per credit hour. Required fees: $69.26 per credit hour. Tuition and fees vary according to course load. *Financial support:* In 2009–10, 9 students received support, including 14 research assistantships (averaging $9,684 per year), 1 teaching assistantship (averaging $9,684 per year); career-related internships or fieldwork, Federal Work-Study, institutionally sponsored loans, scholarships/grants, traineeships, health care benefits, and unspecified assistantships also available. Support available to part-time students. Financial award application deadline: 3/1; financial award applicants required to submit FAFSA. *Faculty research:* Recent American history, civil liberties, military history, legal studies, women and politics. *Unit head:* Dr. Mark Kessler, Chair, 940-898-2133, Fax: 940-898-2130, E-mail: historygov@twu.edu. *Application contact:* Samuel Wheeler, Assistant Director of Admissions, 940-898-3188, Fax: 940-898-3081, E-mail: wheelersr@twu.edu.

Trinity Western University, Faculty of Graduate Studies, Program in Interdisciplinary Humanities, Langley, BC V2Y 1Y1, Canada. Offers general humanities (MAIH); specialized (MAIH), including English, history, philosophy. Part-time and evening/weekend programs available. Postbaccalaureate distance learning degree programs offered (minimal on-campus study). *Entrance requirements:* For master's, strong undergraduate degree in Humanities or English, History or Philosophy. *Faculty research:* Literary theory, gender, medieval and early modern literature, philosophy of religion, Thomas Merton's poetics.

Troy University, Graduate School, College of Education, Program in Postsecondary Education, Troy, AL 36082. Offers adult education (M Ed); biology (M Ed); criminal justice (M Ed); english (M Ed); foundations of education (M Ed); general science (M Ed); higher education administration (M Ed); history (M Ed); instructional technology (M Ed); mathematics (M Ed); music industry (M Ed); physical fitness (M Ed); political science (M Ed); public administration (M Ed); social science (M Ed); teaching english (M Ed). Also offered through the University College. *Accreditation:* NCATE. Part-time and evening/weekend programs available. *Students:* 267 full-time (192 women), 381 part-time (293 women); includes 326 minority (309 African Americans, 4 American Indian/Alaska Native, 5 Asian Americans or Pacific Islanders, 8 Hispanic Americans). Average age 34. 343 applicants, 90% accepted. In 2009, 480 master's awarded. *Degree requirements:* For master's, comprehensive exam, thesis. *Entrance requirements:* For master's, MAT (minimum score 385), minimum GPA of 2.5. Additional exam requirements/recommendations for international students: Required—TOEFL (minimum score 523 paper-based; 193 computer-based; 70 iBT), IELTS, or ACT Compass ESL (minimum score 270 on Listening, Reading, and Grammar with no individual score below 85 and a minimum score of 8 out of 12 on writing test). *Application deadline:* Applications are processed on a rolling basis. Application fee: $50. Electronic applications accepted. *Financial support:* Available to part-time students. Applicants required to submit FAFSA. *Unit head:* Dr. Andrew Creamer, Chair, 334-670-3350, E-mail: drcreamer@troy.edu. *Application contact:* Brenda K. Campbell, Director of Graduate Admissions, 334-670-3178, Fax: 334-670-3733, E-mail: bcamp@troy.edu.

Troy University, Graduate School, College of Education, Program in Secondary Education, Troy, AL 36082. Offers 5th year biology (MS); 5th year computer science (MS); 5th year history (MS); 5th year language arts (MS); 5th year mathematics (MS); 5th year social science (MS); educationtraditional language arts (MS); traditional biology (MS); traditional computer science (MS); traditional history (MS); traditional mathematics (MS); traditional social science (MS). *Accreditation:* NCATE. Part-time and evening/weekend programs available. *Students:* 17 full-time (12 women), 25 part-time (23 women); includes 8 minority (all African Americans). Average age 27. 10 applicants, 90% accepted. In 2009, 29 master's awarded. *Degree requirements:* For master's, comprehensive exam, thesis. *Entrance requirements:* For master's, minimum GPA of 2.5. Additional exam requirements/recommendations for international students: Required—TOEFL (minimum score 523 paper-based; 193 computer-based; 70 iBT), IELTS (minimum score 6). *Application deadline:* Applications are processed on a rolling basis. Application fee: $50. Electronic applications accepted. *Financial support:* Career-related internships or fieldwork available. Support available to part-time students. Financial award applicants required to submit FAFSA. *Unit head:* Dr. Marian Parker, Coordinator, 334-670-5661, Fax: 334-670-3548, E-mail: mjparker@troy.edu. *Application contact:* Brenda K. Campbell, Director of Graduate Admissions, 334-670-3178, Fax: 334-670-3733, E-mail: bcamp@troy.edu.

Tufts University, Graduate School of Arts and Sciences, Department of History, Medford, MA 02155. Offers MA, PhD. *Faculty:* 16 full-time, 2 part-time/adjunct. *Students:* 22 full-time (16 women); includes 4 minority (2 Asian Americans or Pacific Islanders, 2 Hispanic Americans), 3 international. Average age 27. 66 applicants, 27% accepted, 11 enrolled. In 2009, 7 master's awarded. Terminal master's awarded for partial completion of doctoral program. *Degree requirements:* For master's, one foreign language; for doctorate, 2 foreign languages, thesis/dissertation. *Entrance requirements:* For master's and doctorate, GRE General Test, writing sample. Additional exam requirements/recommendations for international students: Required—TOEFL (minimum score 550 paper-based; 213 computer-based; 80 iBT). *Application deadline:* For fall admission, 1/15 for domestic students, 12/15 for international students. Applications are processed on a rolling basis. Application fee: $75. Electronic applications accepted. *Expenses:* Tuition: Full-time $38,096; part-time $3962 per credit. Required fees: $686; $40 per year. Tuition and fees vary according to course level, course load, degree level, program and student level. *Financial support:* Teaching assistantships with full and partial tuition reimbursements, Federal Work-Study, scholarships/grants, tuition waivers (partial), and unspecified assistantships available. Financial award application deadline: 1/15; financial award applicants required to submit FAFSA. *Unit head:* Howard Malchow, Chair, 617-627-3520, Fax: 617-627-3479. *Application contact:* Steve Marrone, Graduate Advisor, 617-627-3520.

Tulane University, School of Liberal Arts, Department of History, New Orleans, LA 70118-5669. Offers MA, PhD. *Degree requirements:* For master's, one foreign language, thesis; for doctorate, variable foreign language requirement, thesis/dissertation. *Entrance requirements:* For master's, GRE General Test, minimum B average in undergraduate course work; for doctorate, GRE General Test. Additional exam requirements/recommendations for international students: Required—TOEFL. Electronic applications accepted.

Union Institute & University, Master of Arts Program–Online, Montpelier, VT 05602. Offers creativity studies (MA); education (MA); health and wellness (MA); history and culture (MA); leadership, public policy, and social issues (MA); literature and writing (MA); psychology (MA). Part-time programs available. Postbaccalaureate distance learning degree programs offered (no on-campus study). *Faculty:* 3 full-time (1 woman), 16 part-time/adjunct (11 women). *Students:* 27 full-time (23 women), 113 part-time (84 women); includes 30 minority (22 African Americans, 2 American Indian/Alaska Native, 1 Asian American or Pacific Islander, 5 Hispanic

History

Union Institute & University (continued)

Americans). Average age 40. In 2009, 26 master's awarded. *Degree requirements:* For master's, thesis. *Application deadline:* Applications are processed on a rolling basis. Application fee: $50. Electronic applications accepted. *Expenses:* Contact institution. *Financial support:* Career-related internships or fieldwork and tuition waivers available. Financial award applicants required to submit FAFSA. *Unit head:* Dr. Brian Webb, Program Director, 802-828-8777, E-mail: brian.webb@tui.edu. *Application contact:* Kathleen Murphy, Interim Director of Admissions—Montpelier, 888-828-8575, E-mail: admissions@myunion.edu.

Universidad Adventista de las Antillas, EGECED Department, Mayagüez, PR 00681-0118. Offers curriculum and instruction (MA), including secondary biology, secondary history, secondary Spanish; education (MA), including ESL (elementary school level), ESL (high school level), school administration and supervision. *Degree requirements:* For master's, comprehensive exam (for some programs), thesis (for some programs). *Entrance requirements:* For master's, EXADEP or GRE General Test, recommendations. Application fee: $175. Electronic applications accepted. *Expenses:* Tuition: Full-time $3990; part-time $190 per credit. Required fees: $570; $190 per credit. $1375 per summer. *Financial support:* Fellowships, Federal Work-Study available. *Unit head:* Dr. Zilma Sepulveda, Director, 787-834-9595 Ext. 2282, Fax: 787-834-9595, E-mail: zsantiago@uaa.edu. *Application contact:* Prof. Evelyn del Valle, Admissions Department Director, 787-834-9595 Ext. 2261, Fax: 787-834-9597, E-mail: admissions@uaa.edu.

Université de Moncton, Faculty of Arts and Social Sciences, Department of History and Geography, Moncton, NB E1A 3E9, Canada. Offers history (MA). *Degree requirements:* For master's, thesis, proficiency in English and French. *Entrance requirements:* For master's, honors degree in history, minimum GPA of 2.7. Electronic applications accepted. *Faculty research:* Economic and social history (Canada, France, Acadia), sociocultural history, women's history, labor history, history of the press.

Université de Montréal, Faculty of Arts and Sciences, Department of History, Montréal, QC H3C 3J7, Canada. Offers MA, PhD. *Degree requirements:* For master's, thesis; for doctorate, thesis/dissertation, general exam. *Entrance requirements:* For doctorate, master's degree in related field. Electronic applications accepted. *Faculty research:* Preindustrial Quebec, Quebec working class, Quebec intellectual, diffusion of scientific thought, history of medicine.

Université de Sherbrooke, Faculty of Letters and Human Sciences, Department of Human Sciences, Sherbrooke, QC J1K 2R1, Canada. Offers history (MA); philosophy (MA). *Degree requirements:* For master's, thesis. *Entrance requirements:* For master's, minimum GPA of 2.75. *Faculty research:* Political, social, and urban history; history of women.

Université du Québec à Montréal, Graduate Programs, Program in History, Montréal, QC H3C 3P8, Canada. Offers MA, PhD. Part-time programs available. *Degree requirements:* For master's, thesis; for doctorate, thesis/dissertation. *Entrance requirements:* For master's, appropriate bachelor's degree or equivalent, proficiency in French; for doctorate, appropriate master's degree or equivalent, proficiency in French.

Université Laval, Faculty of Letters, Department of History, Programs in History, Québec, QC G1K 7P4, Canada. Offers MA, PhD. Terminal master's awarded for partial completion of doctoral program. *Degree requirements:* For master's, thesis (for some programs); for doctorate, comprehensive exam, thesis/dissertation. *Entrance requirements:* For master's and doctorate, English exam (comprehension of written English), knowledge of French. Electronic applications accepted.

Université Laval, Faculty of Letters, Department of Literature, Programs in Ancient Civilization, Québec, QC G1K 7P4, Canada. Offers MA, PhD. Part-time programs available. Terminal master's awarded for partial completion of doctoral program. *Degree requirements:* For master's, thesis; for doctorate, comprehensive exam, thesis/dissertation. *Entrance requirements:* For master's and doctorate, English test (comprehension of written English), knowledge of French, knowledge of an ancient language. Electronic applications accepted.

University at Albany, State University of New York, College of Arts and Sciences, Department of History, Albany, NY 12222-0001. Offers history (MA, PhD); public history (Certificate). Part-time programs available. *Degree requirements:* For master's, variable foreign language requirement, exam, research paper or thesis; for doctorate, thesis/dissertation. *Entrance requirements:* For master's, minimum GPA of 3.0; for doctorate, GRE General Test, minimum GPA of 3.0. Additional exam requirements/recommendations for international students: Required—TOEFL (minimum score 550 paper-based; 213 computer-based). Electronic applications accepted. *Faculty research:* American history (all phases); public policy; European history (Medieval to modern); Asian, African, and Latin American history.

University at Buffalo, the State University of New York, Graduate School, College of Arts and Sciences, Department of History, Buffalo, NY 14260. Offers MA, PhD. Part-time programs available. *Faculty:* 24 full-time (8 women), 11 part-time/adjunct (3 women). *Students:* 57 full-time (29 women), 12 part-time (2 women); includes 4 minority (3 African Americans, 1 Hispanic American), 6 international. Average age 29. 95 applicants. In 2009, 20 master's awarded. Terminal master's awarded for partial completion of doctoral program. *Degree requirements:* For master's, project; for doctorate, variable foreign language requirement, thesis/dissertation, general exam. *Entrance requirements:* For master's and doctorate, GRE General Test. Additional exam requirements/recommendations for international students: Required—TOEFL (minimum score 79 iBT). *Application deadline:* For fall admission, 4/1 for domestic and international students; for spring admission, 10/1 priority date for domestic students, 10/1 for international students. Application fee: $75. Electronic applications accepted. *Financial support:* In 2009–10, 25 students received support, including 5 fellowships with full tuition reimbursements available (averaging $13,000 per year), 21 teaching assistantships with full tuition reimbursements available (averaging $13,000 per year); Federal Work-Study, institutionally sponsored loans, and unspecified assistantships also available. Financial award application deadline: 1/15; financial award applicants required to submit FAFSA. *Faculty research:* Early modern and modern European social, cultural and intellectual history; American social, cultural and political history; north and south Atlantic world history; Latin America; East Asian history; women's and gender history. Total annual research expenditures: $35,000. *Unit head:* Dr. James Bono, Chair, 716-645-8423, Fax: 716-645-5954, E-mail: hischaos@buffalo.edu. *Application contact:* Dr. Patrick McDevitt, Director of Graduate Studies, 716-645-8412, Fax: 716-645-5954, E-mail: ubhistor@buffalo.edu.

The University of Akron, Graduate School, Buchtel College of Arts and Sciences, Department of History, Akron, OH 44325. Offers MA, PhD. Part-time programs available. *Faculty:* 16 full-time (6 women), 1 part-time/adjunct (0 women). *Students:* 17 full-time (7 women), 22 part-time (8 women); includes 4 minority (2 African Americans, 1 American Indian/Alaska Native, 1 Asian American or Pacific Islander), 2 international. Average age 36. 31 applicants, 61% accepted, 10 enrolled. In 2009, 6 master's, 2 doctorates awarded. *Degree requirements:* For master's, one foreign language, thesis optional, written exams, seminars; for doctorate, 2 foreign languages, comprehensive exam, thesis/dissertation, written exams, oral exams. *Entrance requirements:* For master's, GRE, minimum GPA of 3.0, writing sample, letters of recommendation, letter of intent; for doctorate, GRE, minimum GPA of 3.5, writing sample, letters of recommendation, evidence of reading knowledge in one foreign language. Additional exam requirements/recommendations for international students: Required—TOEFL (minimum score 580 paper-based; 237 computer-based; 92 iBT). *Application deadline:* For fall admission, 2/1 for domestic and international students. Application fee: $30 ($40 for international students). *Expenses:* Tuition, state resident: full-time $6570; part-time $365 per credit hour. Tuition, nonresident: full-time $11,250; part-time $625 per credit hour. *Financial support:* In 2009–10, 4 fellowships with full tuition reimbursements, 14 teaching assistantships with full tuition reimbursements were awarded; career-related internships or fieldwork, Federal Work-Study, and tuition waivers (partial) also available. Support available to part-time students. *Faculty research:* European, American, and world history. Total annual research expenditures: $144,007. *Unit head:* Dr. Michael Sheng, Chair, 330-972-7007, E-mail: whixson@uakron.edu. *Application contact:* Dr. Michael Graham, Graduate Director, 330-972-7007.

The University of Alabama, Graduate School, College of Arts and Sciences, Department of History, Tuscaloosa, AL 35487. Offers MA, PhD. *Faculty:* 26 full-time (8 women). *Students:* 43 full-time (16 women), 18 part-time (7 women); includes 5 minority (2 African Americans, 3 Hispanic Americans), 2 international. Average age 30. 69 applicants, 41% accepted, 18 enrolled. In 2009, 11 master's, 4 doctorates awarded. Terminal master's awarded for partial completion of doctoral program. *Median time to degree:* Of those who began their doctoral program in fall 2001, 67% received their degree in 8 years or less. *Degree requirements:* For master's, one foreign language, thesis optional, oral exam; for doctorate, 2 foreign languages, comprehensive exam, thesis/dissertation, oral exams, written exam. *Entrance requirements:* For master's and doctorate, GRE General Test. *Application deadline:* For fall admission, 5/1 for domestic students. Applications are processed on a rolling basis. Application fee: $50 ($60 for international students). *Expenses:* Tuition, state resident: full-time $7000. Tuition, nonresident: full-time $19,200. *Financial support:* In 2009–10, 29 students received support, including 6 fellowships with full tuition reimbursements available (averaging $10,000 per year), research assistantships (averaging $10,000 per year), 23 teaching assistantships with full tuition reimbursements available (averaging $10,200 per year); institutionally sponsored loans and unspecified assistantships also available. Financial award application deadline: 1/15. *Faculty research:* U.S., modern European, Latin American, military, and southern U.S. history. Total annual research expenditures: $3,118. *Unit head:* Dr. Michael Mendle, Chair, 205-348-7103. *Application contact:* Dr. Lisa Lindquist Dorr, Graduate Director, 205-348-1859, E-mail: ldorr@bama.ua.edu.

The University of Alabama at Birmingham, College of Arts and Sciences, Program in History, Birmingham, AL 35294. Offers MA. Part-time programs available. *Degree requirements:* For master's, variable foreign language requirement, thesis or alternative. *Entrance requirements:* For master's, GRE General Test or MAT. Electronic applications accepted. *Faculty research:* History of Europe, United States, Latin America, American South.

The University of Alabama in Huntsville, School of Graduate Studies, College of Liberal Arts, Department of History, Huntsville, AL 35899. Offers MA. Part-time and evening/weekend programs available. *Faculty:* 6 full-time (2 women). *Students:* 4 full-time (2 women), 11 part-time (6 women); includes 2 minority (both African Americans). Average age 32. 16 applicants, 69% accepted, 8 enrolled. In 2009, 4 master's awarded. *Degree requirements:* For master's, one foreign language, comprehensive exam, thesis or alternative, oral and written exams. *Entrance requirements:* For master's, GRE General Test, minimum GPA of 3.0, bachelor's degree in history or related area. Additional exam requirements/recommendations for international students: Required—TOEFL (minimum score 500 paper-based; 173 computer-based; 62 iBT). *Application deadline:* For fall admission, 7/15 for domestic students, 4/1 for international students; for spring admission, 11/30 for domestic students, 9/1 for international students. Applications are processed on a rolling basis. Application fee: $40 ($50 for international students). Electronic applications accepted. *Expenses:* Tuition, state resident: part-time $355.75 per credit hour. Tuition, nonresident: part-time $847.10 per credit hour. Required fees: $210.80 per semester. Tuition and fees vary according to course load and program. *Financial support:* In 2009–10, 5 students received support, including 1 teaching assistantship with full tuition reimbursement available (averaging $8,460 per year); career-related internships or fieldwork, Federal Work-Study, institutionally sponsored loans, scholarships/grants, health care benefits, tuition waivers (full and partial), and unspecified assistantships also available. Support available to part-time students. Financial award application deadline: 4/1; financial award applicants required to submit FAFSA. *Faculty research:* American and European history, U.S. diplomatic history, Old South, ancient and medieval history, Latin American history. *Unit head:* Dr. Andrew Dunar, Chair, 256-824-6312, Fax: 256-824-6477, E-mail: dunara@uah.edu. *Application contact:* Kathy Biggs, Graduate Studies Admissions Manager, 256-824-6199, Fax: 256-824-6405, E-mail: deangrad@uah.edu.

University of Alaska Fairbanks, College of Liberal Arts, Department of Northern Studies, Fairbanks, AK 99775-6460. Offers environmental politics and policy (MA); Northern history (MA). Part-time programs available. *Faculty:* 9 full-time (5 women), 1 part-time/adjunct (0 women). *Students:* 14 full-time (6 women), 21 part-time (15 women); includes 2 minority (1 African American, 1 American Indian/Alaska Native), 5 international. Average age 39. 19 applicants, 63% accepted, 9 enrolled. In 2009, 11 master's awarded. *Degree requirements:* For master's, comprehensive exam, thesis or alternative. *Entrance requirements:* Additional exam requirements/recommendations for international students: Required—TOEFL (minimum score 550 paper-based; 213 computer-based; 80 iBT). *Application deadline:* For fall admission, 6/1 for domestic students, 3/1 for international students; for spring admission, 10/15 for domestic students, 9/1 for international students. Applications are processed on a rolling basis. Application fee: $60. Electronic applications accepted. *Expenses:* Tuition, state resident: full-time $7584; part-time $316 per credit. Tuition, nonresident: full-time $15,504; part-time $646 per credit. Required fees: $23 per credit. $135 per semester. Tuition and fees vary according to course level, course load and reciprocity agreements. *Financial support:* In 2009–10, 3 research assistantships (averaging $7,517 per year), 11 teaching assistantships (averaging $7,671 per year) were awarded; fellowships, career-related internships or fieldwork, Federal Work-Study, scholarships/grants, health care benefits, and unspecified assistantships also available. Support available to part-time students. Financial award application deadline: 1/1; financial award applicants required to submit FAFSA. *Faculty research:* Canadian history, environmental history, Native Alaskan history and art, fetal alcohol syndrome. *Unit head:* Dr. Judith S. Kleinfeld, Co-Director, 907-474-7126, Fax: 907-474-5817, E-mail: fynors@uaf.edu. *Application contact:* Dr. Judith S. Kleinfeld, Co-Director, 907-474-7126, Fax: 907-474-5817, E-mail: fynors@uaf.edu.

University of Alberta, Faculty of Graduate Studies and Research, Department of History and Classics, Edmonton, AB T6G 2E1, Canada. Offers ancient history (PhD); classical archaeology (MA, PhD); classical literature (PhD); classics (MA); history (MA, PhD). Part-time and evening/weekend programs available. *Faculty:* 40 full-time (11 women), 30 part-time/adjunct (12 women). *Students:* 47 full-time (18 women), 31 part-time (16 women). 73 applicants, 51% accepted, 22 enrolled. In 2009, 13 master's, 6 doctorates awarded. *Degree requirements:* For master's, one foreign language, thesis (for some programs); for doctorate, one foreign language, thesis/dissertation. *Entrance requirements:* For master's, minimum B+ average; for doctorate, minimum A- average. Additional exam requirements/recommendations for international students: Required—TOEFL (minimum score 580 paper-based; 237 computer-based). *Application deadline:* For fall admission, 1/15 for domestic and international students. Electronic applications accepted. Tuition and fees charges are reported in Canadian dollars. *Expenses:* Tuition, area resident: Full-time $4626 Canadian dollars; part-time $99.72 Canadian dollars per unit. International tuition: $8216 Canadian dollars full-time. Required fees: $3590 Canadian dollars; $99.72 Canadian dollars per unit. $215 Canadian dollars per term. *Financial support:* In 2009–10, fellowships with full tuition reimbursements (averaging $20,000 per year), research assistantships with partial tuition reimbursements (averaging $10,000 per year), teaching assistantships with partial tuition reimbursements (averaging $10,000 per year) were awarded; scholarships/grants, health care benefits, and unspecified assistantships also available. Financial award application deadline: 1/15. *Faculty research:* Western Canada, classical archaeology, Britain, Eastern Europe, East Asia. Total annual research expenditures: $96,000. *Unit head:* Dr. Christopher C. Mackay, Graduate Chair, 780-492-2698, Fax: 780-492-9125. *Application contact:* Lydia A. Dugbazah, Graduate Secretary, 780-492-2698, Fax: 780-492-9125, E-mail: gradstud@ualberta.ca.

The University of Arizona, Graduate College, College of Social and Behavioral Sciences, Department of History, Tucson, AZ 85721. Offers MA, PhD. Part-time programs available. *Faculty:* 27 full-time (11 women). *Students:* 14 full-time (7 women), 62 part-time (31 women); includes 9 minority (1 American Indian/Alaska Native, 1 Asian American or Pacific Islander, 7 Hispanic Americans), 11 international. Average age 34. 91 applicants, 14% accepted, 11 enrolled. In 2009, 7 master's, 5 doctorates awarded. Terminal master's awarded for partial completion of doctoral program. *Degree requirements:* For master's, one foreign language, comprehensive exam, thesis optional; for doctorate, 2 foreign languages, comprehensive exam, thesis/dissertation. *Entrance requirements:* For master's, GRE General Test, 3 letters of recommendation, writing sample; for doctorate, GRE General Test, 3 letters of recommendation, statement of purpose, 2 writing samples. Additional exam requirements/recommendations for international students: Required—TOEFL (minimum score 550 paper-based; 213 computer-based; 79 iBT). *Application deadline:* For fall admission, 1/15 for domestic and international students. Applications are processed on a rolling basis. Application fee: $65. Electronic applications accepted. *Expenses:* Tuition, state resident: full-time $9028. Tuition, nonresident: full-time $24,890. *Financial support:* In 2009–10, 3 research assistantships with full tuition reimbursements (averaging $13,175 per year), 33 teaching assistantships with full tuition reimbursements (averaging $14,175 per year) were awarded; career-related internships or fieldwork, Federal Work-Study, institutionally sponsored loans, scholarships/grants, health care benefits, tuition waivers (full and partial), and unspecified assistantships also available. Financial award application deadline: 2/1. *Faculty research:* Latin American history, European history, U. S. history, women's history, global/environmental history. Total annual research expenditures: $202,034. *Unit head:* Dr. Kevin Gosner, Head, 520-621-1168, Fax: 520-621-2422, E-mail: kgosner@u.arizona.edu. *Application contact:* Gina M. Wasson, Information Contact, 520-621-5860, Fax: 520-621-2422, E-mail: gmus@u.arizona.edu.

University of Arkansas, Graduate School, J. William Fulbright College of Arts and Sciences, Department of History, Fayetteville, AR 72701-1201. Offers MA, PhD. Part-time programs available. *Students:* 29 full-time (11 women), 55 part-time (20 women); includes 6 minority (3 African Americans, 1 Asian American or Pacific Islander, 2 Hispanic Americans), 7 international. In 2009, 7 master's, 7 doctorates awarded. *Degree requirements:* For master's, thesis optional; for doctorate, 2 foreign languages, thesis/dissertation. *Entrance requirements:* For master's, GRE General Test; for doctorate, GRE General Test, GRE Subject Test. Application fee: $40 ($50 for international students). *Expenses:* Tuition, state resident: full-time $7355; part-time $356.58 per hour. Tuition, nonresident: full-time $17,401; part-time $775.17 per hour. Required fees: $1203. *Financial support:* In 2009–10, 8 fellowships with tuition reimbursements, 9 research assistantships, 9 teaching assistantships were awarded; career-related internships or fieldwork and Federal Work-Study also available. Support available to part-time students. Financial award application deadline: 4/1; financial award applicants required to submit FAFSA. *Unit head:* Dr. Lynda Coon, Department Chairperson, 479-575-3001, Fax: 479-575-2775, E-mail: llcoon@uark.edu. *Application contact:* Dr. Kathryn Sloan, Graduate Coordinator, 479-575-3001, Fax: 479-575-2775, E-mail: ksloan@uark.edu.

The University of British Columbia, Faculty of Arts and Faculty of Graduate Studies, Department of History, Vancouver, BC V6T 1Z1, Canada. Offers MA, PhD. Part-time programs available. *Faculty:* 34 full-time (11 women). *Students:* 75 full-time (32 women). Average age 24. 90 applicants, 27% accepted, 15 enrolled. In 2009, 10 master's, 2 doctorates awarded. *Degree requirements:* For master's, one foreign language, thesis; for doctorate, one foreign language, comprehensive exam, thesis/dissertation, four or five 3-credit courses. *Entrance requirements:* For master's, Four-year Bachelor's degree. Canadian applicants should have completed either: Honours in History with a first-class (A) standing; OR Major in History should have obtained first-class (A or A+) standing Language—appropriate to their field of study.; for doctorate, Master's degree (or equivalent) in history. Should have first-class (A) standing in graduate courses. Language—relevant to their dissertation research. Additional exam requirements/recommendations for international students: Required—TOEFL (minimum score 570 paper-based; 230 computer-based). *Application deadline:* For fall admission, 1/9 for domestic and international students. Applications are processed on a rolling basis. Application fee: $90 Canadian dollars ($150 Canadian dollars for international students). Electronic applications accepted. *Financial support:* In 2009–10, 25 students received support, including 22 fellowships with partial tuition reimbursements available (averaging $17,500 per year), 12 research assistantships with partial tuition reimbursements available (averaging $5,500 per year), 32 teaching assistantships with partial tuition reimbursements available (averaging $10,914 per year); scholarships/grants, tuition waivers (partial), and unspecified assistantships also available. Financial award application deadline: 9/21. *Faculty research:* Canadian, British, European, modern Chinese and Japanese history; international relations. *Unit head:* Dr. Daniel F. Vickers, Head, 604-827-3560, Fax: 604-822-6658, E-mail: dvickers@interchange.ubc.ca. *Application contact:* Dr. William E. French, Graduate Advisor, 604-822-5706, Fax: 604-822-6658, E-mail: wfrench@interchange.ubc.ca.

University of Calgary, Faculty of Graduate Studies, Faculty of Social Sciences, Department of History, Calgary, AB T2N 1N4, Canada. Offers MA, PhD. Part-time programs available. *Degree requirements:* For master's, one foreign language, thesis; for doctorate, one foreign language, thesis/dissertation, 3 written comprehensive exams, oral candidacy exam. *Entrance requirements:* For master's, minimum GPA of 3.4, writing sample; for doctorate, sample of written work, master's degree in history. Electronic applications accepted. *Faculty research:* Military history, Canadian history, Latin American history, gender/women's history, native history.

University of California, Berkeley, Graduate Division, College of Letters and Science, Department of History, Berkeley, CA 94720-2550. Offers PhD, MA/PhD. *Faculty:* 53 full-time (20 women). *Students:* 211 full-time (92 women); includes 41 minority (6 African Americans, 2 American Indian/Alaska Native, 20 Asian Americans or Pacific Islanders, 13 Hispanic Americans), 15 international. 372 applicants, 12% accepted, 26 enrolled. In 2009, 25 doctorates awarded. *Degree requirements:* For doctorate, variable foreign language requirement, comprehensive exam, thesis/dissertation. *Entrance requirements:* For doctorate, GRE General Test, minimum GPA of 3.0, 3 letters of recommendation, writing sample (not to exceed 10 pages). Additional exam requirements/recommendations for international students: Required—TOEFL (minimum score 570 paper-based; 230 computer-based; 68 iBT). *Application deadline:* For fall admission, 12/1 for domestic and international students. Application fee: $70 ($90 for international students). Electronic applications accepted. *Financial support:* In 2009–10, 177 students received support, including 72 fellowships with full and partial tuition reimbursements available (averaging $17,000 per year), research assistantships with partial tuition reimbursements available (averaging $3,200 per year), 119 teaching assistantships with partial tuition reimbursements available (averaging $8,300 per year); Federal Work-Study, institutionally sponsored loans, scholarships/grants, health care benefits, tuition waivers (full and partial), and unspecified assistantships also available. Financial award application deadline: 3/1; financial award applicants required to submit FAFSA. *Unit head:* Prof. Mary Elizabeth Berry, Chair, 510-642-3402, Fax: 510-643-5323, E-mail: histadm@berkeley.edu. *Application contact:* Barbara Hayashida, Graduate Admissions Coordinator, 510-642-2378, Fax: 510-643-5323, E-mail: histadm@berkeley.edu.

University of California, Berkeley, Graduate Division, College of Letters and Science, Group in Ancient History and Mediterranean Archaeology, Berkeley, CA 94720-1500. Offers MA, PhD. *Students:* 19 full-time (5 women). Average age 30. 41 applicants, 2 enrolled. In 2009, 3 master's, 2 doctorates awarded. *Degree requirements:* For master's, one foreign language, exam or thesis; for doctorate, 2 foreign languages, thesis/dissertation, qualifying exam. *Entrance requirements:* For master's and doctorate, GRE General Test, minimum GPA of 3.0, 3 letters of recommendation. Additional exam requirements/recommendations for international students: Required—TOEFL (minimum score 570 paper-based; 230 computer-based), TWE. *Application deadline:* For fall admission, 12/15 for domestic students. Application fee: $70 ($90 for international students). *Financial support:* Fellowships, research assistantships, teaching assistantships, career-related internships or fieldwork and unspecified assistantships available. *Unit head:* Prof. Andrew Stewart, Chair, 510-643-8741, E-mail: casmaadm@berkeley.edu. *Application contact:* Janet A. Yonan, Student Affairs Officer, 510-643-8741, Fax: 510-643-2959, E-mail: casmaadm@berkeley.edu.

University of California, Davis, Graduate Studies, Program in History, Davis, CA 95616. Offers MA, PhD. Terminal master's awarded for partial completion of doctoral program. *Degree requirements:* For master's, one foreign language, comprehensive exam (for some programs), thesis (for some programs); for doctorate, 2 foreign languages, thesis/dissertation. *Entrance requirements:* For master's, GRE General Test, minimum GPA of 3.0, writing sample; for doctorate, GRE General Test, master's degree, writing sample. Additional exam requirements/recommendations for international students: Required—TOEFL (minimum score 550 paper-based; 213 computer-based). Electronic applications accepted. *Faculty research:* American social, cultural, and western history; modern and early history; modern European, East Asian, and Latin American history; history of science and medicine; cross-cultural history of women.

University of California, Irvine, Office of Graduate Studies, School of Humanities, Department of History, Irvine, CA 92697. Offers MA, PhD. *Students:* 82 full-time (44 women), 6 part-time (2 women); includes 16 minority (1 African American, 7 Asian Americans or Pacific Islanders, 8 Hispanic Americans), 8 international. Average age 33. 139 applicants, 31% accepted, 12 enrolled. In 2009, 13 master's, 14 doctorates awarded. *Degree requirements:* For doctorate, thesis/dissertation. *Entrance requirements:* For master's and doctorate, GRE General Test, minimum GPA of 3.0. Additional exam requirements/recommendations for international students: Required—TOEFL (minimum score 550 paper-based; 213 computer-based). *Application deadline:* For fall admission, 1/2 priority date for domestic students, 1/2 for international students. Application fee: $70 ($90 for international students). Electronic applications accepted. *Financial support:* Fellowships, research assistantships with full tuition reimbursements, teaching assistantships, institutionally sponsored loans, traineeships, health care benefits, and unspecified assistantships available. Financial award application deadline: 3/1; financial award applicants required to submit FAFSA. *Faculty research:* European, U.S., Latin American, ancient, and East Asian history. *Unit head:* Kenneth Pomeranz, Chair, 949-824-5169, Fax: 949-824-2865, E-mail: klpomera@uci.edu. *Application contact:* Carol Roberts, Graduate Administrator, 949-824-5891, Fax: 949-824-2865, E-mail: carol@uci.edu.

University of California, Los Angeles, Graduate Division, College of Letters and Science, Department of History, Los Angeles, CA 90095. Offers MA, PhD, MLIS/MA. *Students:* 202 full-time (105 women); includes 33 minority (2 African Americans, 3 American Indian/Alaska Native, 7 Asian Americans or Pacific Islanders, 21 Hispanic Americans), 23 international. Average age 31. 314 applicants, 23% accepted, 27 enrolled. In 2009, 23 master's, 20 doctorates awarded. Terminal master's awarded for partial completion of doctoral program. *Degree requirements:* For master's, one foreign language, comprehensive exam; for doctorate, variable foreign language requirement, thesis/dissertation, oral and written qualifying exams. *Entrance requirements:* For master's, GRE General Test, minimum GPA of 3.0; for doctorate, GRE General Test, minimum undergraduate GPA of 3.0. *Application deadline:* For fall admission, 12/15 for domestic and international students. Application fee: $70 ($90 for international students). Electronic applications accepted. *Financial support:* In 2009–10, 130 fellowships with full and partial tuition reimbursements, 55 research assistantships with full and partial tuition reimbursements, 121 teaching assistantships with full and partial tuition reimbursements were awarded; Federal Work-Study, institutionally sponsored loans, scholarships/grants, health care benefits, tuition waivers (full and partial), and unspecified assistantships also available. Financial award application deadline: 3/1; financial award applicants required to submit FAFSA. *Unit head:* Dr. Edward Alpers, Chair, 310-825-1883. *Application contact:* Department Office, 310-206-2627, E-mail: gradoffice@history.ucla.edu.

University of California, Riverside, Graduate Division, Department of History, Riverside, CA 92521-0102. Offers archival management (MA); historic preservation (MA); history (MA, PhD); museum curatorship (MA). Part-time programs available. Terminal master's awarded for partial completion of doctoral program. *Degree requirements:* For master's, one foreign language, comprehensive exam, internship report and oral exams, or thesis; for doctorate, 2 foreign languages, thesis/dissertation, qualifying exams, teaching experience. *Entrance requirements:* For master's, GRE General Test, minimum GPA of 3.2; for doctorate, GRE General Test, MA in history, minimum GPA of 3.2. Additional exam requirements/recommendations for international students: Required—TOEFL (minimum score 550 paper-based; 213 computer-based; 80 iBT). Electronic applications accepted. *Faculty research:* Native American history, United States, public history, Russia, Europe.

University of California, San Diego, Office of Graduate Studies, Department of History, La Jolla, CA 92093. Offers history (MA, PhD); Judaic studies (MA); science studies (PhD). *Degree requirements:* For doctorate, thesis/dissertation. *Entrance requirements:* For master's and doctorate, GRE General Test. Electronic applications accepted.

University of California, Santa Barbara, Graduate Division, College of Letters and Sciences, Division of Humanities and Fine Arts, Department of History, Santa Barbara, CA 93106-9410. Offers feminist studies (PhD); global studies (PhD); public history (PhD); MA/PhD. *Faculty:* 40 full-time (17 women), 11 part-time/adjunct (6 women). *Students:* 120 full-time (62 women). Average age 34. 130 applicants, 38% accepted, 22 enrolled. In 2009, 9 doctorates awarded. Terminal master's awarded for partial completion of doctoral program. *Degree requirements:* For doctorate, variable foreign language requirement, comprehensive exam, thesis/dissertation. *Entrance requirements:* For doctorate, GRE, 3 letters of recommendation, resume/curriculum vitae. Additional exam requirements/recommendations for international students: Required—TOEFL (minimum score 550 paper-based; 213 computer-based; 80 iBT) or IELTS (minimum score 7). *Application deadline:* For fall admission, 12/5 for domestic and international students. Application fee: $70 ($90 for international students). Electronic applications accepted. *Financial support:* In 2009–10, 94 students received support, including 53 fellowships with full and partial tuition reimbursements available (averaging $8,600 per year), 2 research assistantships with full and partial tuition reimbursements available (averaging $7,400 per year), 70 teaching assistantships with partial tuition reimbursements available (averaging $9,400 per year); Federal Work-Study, institutionally sponsored loans, scholarships/grants, traineeships, health care benefits, tuition waivers (full and partial), and unspecified assistantships also available. Financial award application deadline: 12/5; financial award applicants required to submit FAFSA. *Faculty research:* Europe, U. S., Latin America, Africa, Middle East, East Asia. *Unit head:* Kenneth J. Moure, Chair, 805-893-2993, Fax: 805-893-8795, E-mail: moure@history.ucrb.edu. *Application contact:* Prof. Sharon Farmer, Director of Graduate Studies, 805-893-2543, Fax: 805-893-8795, E-mail: farmer@history.ucsb.edu.

University of California, Santa Cruz, Division of Graduate Studies, Division of Humanities, Department of History, Santa Cruz, CA 95064. Offers MA, PhD. *Degree requirements:* For doctorate, variable foreign language requirement, thesis/dissertation, qualifying exam. *Faculty research:* Comparative, interdisciplinary approach to history; the Americas, Asia, the Islamic world, and Europe since 1500; society history.

University of Central Arkansas, Graduate School, College of Liberal Arts, Department of History, Conway, AR 72035-0001. Offers MA. Part-time programs available. *Faculty:* 15 full-time (4 women). *Students:* 10 full-time (4 women), 11 part-time (5 women); includes 1 minority (American Indian/Alaska Native), 1 international. Average age 30. 10 applicants, 90% accepted, 9 enrolled. In 2009, 8 master's awarded. *Degree requirements:* For master's, one foreign language, comprehensive exam, thesis optional. *Entrance requirements:* For master's, GRE General Test, minimum GPA of 2.7. Additional exam requirements/recommendations for international students: Required—TOEFL (minimum score 550 paper-based; 213 computer-based). *Application deadline:* For fall admission, 3/1 priority date for domestic students; for spring admission, 10/1 priority date for domestic students. Applications are processed on a rolling basis. Application fee: $25 ($40 for international students). *Expenses:* Tuition, state resident: full-time $5136; part-time $214 per credit hour. Required fees: $379.50; $127 per term. Tuition and fees vary according to course level, course load and campus/location. *Financial support:* Federal Work-Study, scholarships/grants, and unspecified assistantships available. Financial award application deadline: 2/15; financial award applicants required to submit FAFSA. *Faculty research:* History Day, Russian culture. *Unit head:* Dr. Ken Barnes, Chairperson, 501-450-5631, Fax: 501-450-5185, E-mail: kennethb@uca.edu. *Application contact:* Brenda Herring, Admissions Assistant, 501-450-5065, Fax: 501-450-5678, E-mail: bherring@uca.edu.

University of Central Florida, College of Arts and Humanities, Department of History, Orlando, FL 32816. Offers MA. Part-time and evening/weekend programs available. *Faculty:* 27 full-time

History

University of Central Florida (continued)
(11 women), 21 part-time/adjunct (7 women). *Students:* 30 full-time (9 women), 34 part-time (12 women); includes 12 minority (2 African Americans, 2 Asian Americans or Pacific Islanders, 8 Hispanic Americans). Average age 30. 32 applicants, 78% accepted, 21 enrolled. In 2009, 3 master's awarded. *Degree requirements:* For master's, thesis, written exam. *Entrance requirements:* For master's, GRE General Test, minimum GPA of 3.0 in last 60 hours. Additional exam requirements/recommendations for international students: Required—TOEFL. *Application deadline:* For fall admission, 7/15 for domestic students; for spring admission, 12/1 for domestic students. Electronic applications accepted. *Expenses:* Tuition, state resident: part-time $306.31 per credit hour. Tuition, nonresident: part-time $1099.01 per credit hour. Part-time tuition and fees vary according to degree level and program. *Financial support:* In 2009–10, 11 students received support, including 4 fellowships with partial tuition reimbursements available (averaging $5,300 per year), 2 research assistantships with partial tuition reimbursements available (averaging $5,800 per year), 6 teaching assistantships with partial tuition reimbursements available (averaging $7,000 per year); career-related internships or fieldwork, Federal Work-Study, institutionally sponsored loans, tuition waivers (partial), and unspecified assistantships also available. Financial award application deadline: 3/1; financial award applicants required to submit FAFSA. *Unit head:* Dr. Rosalind Beiler, Chair, 407-823-6467, E-mail: beiler@mail.ucf.edu. *Application contact:* Dr. Rosalind Beiler, Chair, 407-823-6467, E-mail: beiler@mail.ucf.edu.

University of Central Missouri, The Graduate School, College of Arts, Humanities and Social Sciences, Warrensburg, MO 64093. Offers English (MA); history (MA); mass communication (MA); music (MA); psychology (MS); speech communication (MA); teaching english as a second language (MA); theatre (MA). Part-time programs available. *Faculty:* 82. *Students:* 60 full-time (35 women), 101 part-time (61 women); includes 11 minority (5 African Americans, 3 Asian Americans or Pacific Islanders, 3 Hispanic Americans), 17 international. Average age 30. 80 applicants, 80% accepted, 58 enrolled. In 2009, 51 master's awarded. *Entrance requirements:* Additional exam requirements/recommendations for international students: Required—TOEFL (minimum score 550 paper-based; 79 computer-based). *Application deadline:* For fall admission, 6/1 priority date for domestic students, 5/1 for international students; for spring admission, 10/1 priority date for domestic students, 10/1 for international students. Applications are processed on a rolling basis. Application fee: $30 ($75 for international students). Electronic applications accepted. *Expenses:* Tuition, area resident: Part-time $245.80 per credit hour. Tuition, nonresident: part-time $491.60 per credit hour. Required fees: $24.20 per credit hour. Full-time tuition and fees vary according to course load, degree level, campus/location and reciprocity agreements. *Financial support:* Research assistantships with full and partial tuition reimbursements, teaching assistantships with full and partial tuition reimbursements, career-related internships or fieldwork, Federal Work-Study, scholarships/grants, and administrative and laboratory assistantships available. Support available to part-time students. Financial award application deadline: 3/1; financial award applicants required to submit FAFSA. *Unit head:* Dr. Gersham Nelson, Dean, 660-543-4750, Fax: 660-543-8271, E-mail: nelson@ucmo.edu. *Application contact:* Laurie Delap, Admissions Coordinator, 660-543-4621, Fax: 660-543-4778, E-mail: gradinfo@ucmo.edu.

University of Central Oklahoma, College of Graduate Studies and Research, College of Liberal Arts, Department of History, Edmond, OK 73034-5209. Offers history (MA); museum studies (MA); social studies teaching (MA); Southwestern studies (MA). Part-time programs available. *Degree requirements:* For master's, thesis optional. *Entrance requirements:* Additional exam requirements/recommendations for international students: Required—TOEFL (minimum score 550 paper-based; 213 computer-based). Electronic applications accepted. *Expenses:* Tuition, state resident: full-time $4128; part-time $172 per credit hour. Tuition, nonresident: full-time $10,373; part-time $432.20 per credit hour. Required fees: $433.20; $18.05 per credit hour. *Faculty research:* China, Russia, civil war, American naval logistics.

University of Chicago, Division of Social Sciences, Department of History, Chicago, IL 60637-1513. Offers PhD. *Students:* 245. In 2009, 28 doctorates awarded. *Degree requirements:* For doctorate, variable foreign language requirement, thesis/dissertation, oral exams in 3 fields. *Entrance requirements:* For doctorate, GRE General Test. Additional exam requirements/recommendations for international students: Required—TOEFL, IELTS (minimum score 7). *Application deadline:* For fall admission, 12/10 for domestic and international students. Application fee: $55. Electronic applications accepted. *Financial support:* Fellowships, teaching assistantships, Federal Work-Study, institutionally sponsored loans, scholarships/grants, traineeships, health care benefits, and unspecified assistantships available. Financial award application deadline: 12/10. *Unit head:* Prof. Kathleen Cumings, Chair, 773-702-8397. *Application contact:* Office of the Dean of Students, 773-702-8415, E-mail: admissions@ssd.uchicago.edu.

University of Cincinnati, Graduate School, McMicken College of Arts and Sciences, Department of History, Cincinnati, OH 45221. Offers MA, PhD. Terminal master's awarded for partial completion of doctoral program. *Degree requirements:* For master's, comprehensive exam, thesis optional; for doctorate, comprehensive exam, thesis/dissertation. *Entrance requirements:* For master's, GRE General Test, BA in history; for doctorate, GRE General Test, MA in history. Additional exam requirements/recommendations for international students: Required—TOEFL (minimum score 600 paper-based). Electronic applications accepted. *Faculty research:* US cultural and social history, women's history, US and British intellectual history, modern Europe.

University of Colorado at Boulder, Graduate School, College of Arts and Sciences, Department of History, Boulder, CO 80309. Offers MA, PhD. *Faculty:* 35 full-time (14 women). *Students:* 45 full-time (19 women), 22 part-time (8 women); includes 8 minority (1 African American, 1 American Indian/Alaska Native, 2 Asian Americans or Pacific Islanders, 4 Hispanic Americans), 2 international. Average age 34. 112 applicants, 31% accepted, 14 enrolled. In 2009, 5 master's, 4 doctorates awarded. Terminal master's awarded for partial completion of doctoral program. *Degree requirements:* For master's, comprehensive exam, thesis optional; for doctorate, one foreign language, thesis/dissertation. *Entrance requirements:* For master's, GRE General Test, minimum undergraduate GPA of 2.75; for doctorate, GRE General Test. *Application deadline:* For fall admission, 1/1 priority date for domestic students, 1/1 for international students. Application fee: $50 ($60 for international students). *Financial support:* In 2009–10, 14 fellowships (averaging $12,686 per year), 24 research assistantships (averaging $9,141 per year) were awarded; tuition waivers (full) also available. *Faculty research:* History of the American West; early American history; history of women and gender; American political, social and intellectual history; early modern and modern European social history. Total annual research expenditures: $75,386.

University of Colorado at Colorado Springs, Graduate School, College of Letters, Arts and Sciences, Department of History, Colorado Springs, CO 80933-7150. Offers MA. Part-time and evening/weekend programs available. *Faculty:* 7 full-time (4 women), 4 part-time/adjunct (3 women). *Students:* 34 full-time (20 women), 15 part-time (10 women); includes 2 minority (1 African American, 1 Hispanic American). Average age 34. 34 applicants, 79% accepted, 23 enrolled. In 2009, 19 master's awarded. *Degree requirements:* For master's, portfolio of 3-4 research projects, oral exam. *Entrance requirements:* For master's, minimum GPA of 2.75, writing sample. *Application deadline:* For fall admission, 3/1 for domestic students; for spring admission, 10/15 for domestic students. Applications are processed on a rolling basis. Application fee: $60 ($75 for international students). *Expenses:* Tuition, state resident: full-time $8922; part-time $639 per credit hour. Tuition, nonresident: full-time $19,372; part-time $1154 per credit hour. Tuition and fees vary according to course level, course load, degree level, program, reciprocity agreements and student level. *Financial support:* Teaching assistantships, Federal Work-Study and scholarships/grants available. Support available to part-time students. Financial award application deadline: 3/1; financial award applicants required to submit FAFSA. *Faculty research:* U. S. to 1865, Latin America, India, medieval and modern Europe. *Unit head:* Dr. Robert E. Sackett, Chair, 719-255-4079, Fax: 719-255-4068, E-mail: rsackett@uccs.edu. *Application contact:* Dr. Debbie Scott, Administrative Assistant, 719-255-4069, Fax: 719-255-4068, E-mail: dscott@uccs.edu.

University of Colorado Denver, College of Liberal Arts and Sciences, Department of History, Denver, CO 80217-3364. Offers MA. Part-time and evening/weekend programs available. *Students:* 12 full-time (8 women), 51 part-time (22 women); includes 5 minority (1 African American, 1 American Indian/Alaska Native, 3 Hispanic Americans). 25 applicants, 56% accepted, 10 enrolled. In 2009, 13 master's awarded. *Degree requirements:* For master's, comprehensive exam, thesis. *Entrance requirements:* For master's, GRE General Test, interview, minimum GPA of 3.25. Additional exam requirements/recommendations for international students: Required—TOEFL (minimum score 525 paper-based; 197 computer-based). *Application deadline:* For fall admission, 4/1 for domestic students; for spring admission, 10/1 for domestic students. Applications are processed on a rolling basis. Application fee: $50 ($75 for international students). Electronic applications accepted. *Financial support:* Research assistantships, teaching assistantships, Federal Work-Study available. Financial award application deadline: 4/1; financial award applicants required to submit FAFSA. *Unit head:* Myra Rich, Chair, 303-556-8316, Fax: 303-556-6037, E-mail: myra.rich@ucdenver.edu. *Application contact:* Sue Sethney, Program Assistant, 303-556-4830, Fax: 303-556-6037, E-mail: sue.sethney@ucdenver.edu.

University of Connecticut, Graduate School, College of Liberal Arts and Sciences, Department of History, Storrs, CT 06269. Offers MA, PhD. *Faculty:* 39 full-time (17 women). *Students:* 53 full-time (24 women), 13 part-time (4 women); includes 9 minority (3 African Americans, 1 Asian American or Pacific Islander, 5 Hispanic Americans), 3 international. Average age 32. 110 applicants, 19% accepted, 20 enrolled. In 2009, 10 master's, 5 doctorates awarded. Terminal master's awarded for partial completion of doctoral program. *Degree requirements:* For master's, comprehensive exam; for doctorate, thesis/dissertation. *Entrance requirements:* For master's and doctorate, GRE General Test, GRE Subject Test. Additional exam requirements/recommendations for international students: Required—TOEFL (minimum score 550 paper-based; 213 computer-based). *Application deadline:* For fall admission, 2/1 priority date for domestic and international students; for spring admission, 11/1 for domestic students, 10/1 for international students. Applications are processed on a rolling basis. Application fee: $55. Electronic applications accepted. *Expenses:* Tuition, state resident: full-time $4725; part-time $525 per credit. Tuition, nonresident: full-time $12,267; part-time $1363 per credit. Required fees: $346 per semester. Tuition and fees vary according to course load. *Financial support:* In 2009–10, 1 research assistantship with full tuition reimbursement, 42 teaching assistantships with full tuition reimbursements were awarded; fellowships, Federal Work-Study, scholarships/grants, health care benefits, and unspecified assistantships also available. Financial award application deadline: 2/1; financial award applicants required to submit FAFSA. *Unit head:* Shirley A. Roe, Head, 860-486-2086, Fax: 860-486-0641, E-mail: shirley.roe@uconn.edu. *Application contact:* Shirley A. Roe, Head, 860-486-2086, Fax: 860-486-0641, E-mail: shirley.roe@uconn.edu.

University of Delaware, College of Arts and Sciences, Department of History, Hagley Program in the History of Technology and Industrialization, Newark, DE 19716. Offers MA, PhD. *Degree requirements:* For master's, thesis optional; for doctorate, comprehensive exam, thesis/dissertation. *Entrance requirements:* For master's and doctorate, interview. Electronic applications accepted.

University of Florida, Graduate School, College of Liberal Arts and Sciences, Department of History, Gainesville, FL 32611. Offers MA, PhD, JD/MA, JD/PhD. *Degree requirements:* For doctorate, thesis/dissertation. *Entrance requirements:* For master's and doctorate, GRE General Test, minimum GPA of 3.0. Additional exam requirements/recommendations for international students: Required—TOEFL (minimum score 550 paper-based; 213 computer-based). Electronic applications accepted. *Faculty research:* U.S. history, Florida studies, Latin American history, African history.

University of Georgia, Graduate School, College of Arts and Sciences, Department of History, Athens, GA 30602. Offers MA, PhD. *Faculty:* 29 full-time (8 women). *Students:* 54 full-time (21 women), 14 part-time (10 women); includes 6 minority (5 African Americans, 1 American Indian/Alaska Native), 5 international. 131 applicants, 27% accepted, 17 enrolled. In 2009, 5 master's, 7 doctorates awarded. *Degree requirements:* For master's, one foreign language, thesis; for doctorate, one foreign language, thesis/dissertation. *Entrance requirements:* For master's and doctorate, GRE General Test. *Application deadline:* For fall admission, 7/1 priority date for domestic students; for spring admission, 11/15 for domestic students. Application fee: $50. Electronic applications accepted. *Expenses:* Tuition, state resident: full-time $6000; part-time $250 per credit hour. Tuition, nonresident: full-time $20,904; part-time $871 per credit hour. Required fees: $730 per semester. *Financial support:* Fellowships, research assistantships, teaching assistantships, unspecified assistantships available. *Unit head:* Dr. Robert Antonio Pratt, Head, 706-542-2507, Fax: 706-542-2455, E-mail: rapratt@uga.edu. *Application contact:* Dr. Karl F. Friday, Graduate Coordinator, 706-542-2537, Fax: 706-542-4367, E-mail: kfriday@uga.edu.

University of Guelph, Graduate Program Services, College of Arts, Department of History, Guelph, ON N1G 2W1, Canada. Offers MA, PhD. Part-time programs available. *Degree requirements:* For master's, one foreign language, thesis (for some programs); for doctorate, one foreign language, thesis/dissertation, 3 qualifying fields. *Entrance requirements:* For master's, minimum B+ average during previous 2 years of course work; for doctorate, minimum A-average in MA. Additional exam requirements/recommendations for international students: Required—TOEFL (minimum score 550 paper-based; 219 computer-based). Electronic applications accepted. *Faculty research:* Gender and family, Scottish history, rural and urban community studies, eighteenth century England, Canadian legal and social history, modern Europe.

University of Hawaii at Manoa, Graduate Division, College of Arts and Humanities, Department of History, Honolulu, HI 96822. Offers MA, PhD. Part-time programs available. *Faculty:* 21 full-time (3 women), 12 part-time/adjunct (6 women). *Students:* 45 full-time (15 women), 16 part-time (5 women); includes 11 minority (1 American Indian/Alaska Native, 10 Asian Americans or Pacific Islanders), 8 international. Average age 32. 62 applicants, 55% accepted, 15 enrolled. In 2009, 9 master's, 4 doctorates awarded. *Degree requirements:* For master's, 2 foreign languages, thesis optional; for doctorate, 2 foreign languages, comprehensive exam, thesis/dissertation. *Entrance requirements:* For master's, GRE, minimum GPA of 3.0, writing sample; for doctorate, GRE, MA, sample of written work. Additional exam requirements/recommendations for international students: Required—TOEFL (minimum score 580 paper-based; 237 computer-based; 92 iBT), IELTS (minimum score 5). *Application deadline:* For fall admission, 1/1 for domestic and international students. Application fee: $60. *Expenses:* Tuition, state resident: full-time $8900; part-time $372 per credit. Tuition, nonresident: full-time $21,400; part-time $898 per credit. Required fees: $207 per semester. *Financial support:* In 2009–10, 1 student received support, including 14 fellowships (averaging $5,722 per year), 1 research assistantship (averaging $18,198 per year), 16 teaching assistantships (averaging $15,077 per year); scholarships/grants and tuition waivers (full) also available. Financial award application deadline: 2/1. *Faculty research:* Asian, Pacific, world, American and European history. Total annual research expenditures: $79,000. *Application contact:* James Kraft, Graduate Chair, 808-956-8358, Fax: 808-956-9600, E-mail: jkraft@hawaii.edu.

University of Houston, College of Liberal Arts and Social Sciences, Department of History, Houston, TX 77204. Offers history (MA, PhD); public history (MA). Part-time programs available. *Faculty:* 24 full-time (9 women), 2 part-time/adjunct (both women). *Students:* 57 full-time (30 women), 36 part-time (19 women); includes 15 minority (3 African Americans, 2 American Indian/Alaska Native, 1 Asian American or Pacific Islander, 9 Hispanic Americans). Average age 35. 37 applicants, 62% accepted, 14 enrolled. In 2009, 10 master's, 9 doctorates awarded. Terminal master's awarded for partial completion of doctoral program. *Degree requirements:* For master's, one foreign language, thesis (for some programs); for doctorate, one foreign language, thesis/dissertation. *Entrance requirements:* For master's, GRE General Test, minimum GPA of 3.3; for doctorate, GRE General Test, minimum GPA of 3.67. Additional exam requirements/recommendations for international students: Required—TOEFL. *Application deadline:* For fall admission, 1/15 for domestic students; for spring admission, 11/1 for domestic students. Application fee: $75 for international students. Electronic applications accepted. *Expenses:* Tuition, state resident: full-time $7676; part-time $320 per credit hour. Tuition, nonresident: full-time $14,324; part-time $597 per credit hour. Required fees: $3034. *Financial support:* In 2009–10, 1 fellowship with full tuition reimbursement (averaging $9,800 per year), 6 research assistantships with full tuition reimbursements (averaging $9,800 per year), 35 teaching assistantships with full tuition reimbursements (averaging $9,800 per year) were awarded; career-related internships or fieldwork, Federal Work-Study, institutionally sponsored loans, scholarships/grants, health care benefits, and unspecified assistantships also available. Support available to part-time students. Financial award application deadline: 2/1. *Faculty research:* U. S., Latin American, European, social, and women's history. *Unit head:* Dr. John Hart, Chairperson, 713-743-3008, Fax: 713-743-3216, E-mail: jhart@uh.edu. *Application contact:* Dr. John Hart, Chairperson, 713-743-3008, Fax: 713-743-3216, E-mail: jhart@uh.edu.

University of Houston–Clear Lake, School of Human Sciences and Humanities, Programs in Humanities and Fine Arts, Houston, TX 77058-1098. Offers history (MA); humanities (MA); literature (MA). Part-time and evening/weekend programs available. Postbaccalaureate distance learning degree programs offered (minimal on-campus study). *Degree requirements:* For master's, thesis or alternative. *Entrance requirements:* For master's, GRE General Test. Additional exam requirements/recommendations for international students: Required—TOEFL (minimum score 550 paper-based; 213 computer-based). *Faculty research:* Digital media studies, Latin American history, labor history, Chaucer evolution versus creationism debate.

University of Idaho, College of Graduate Studies, College of Letters, Arts and Social Sciences, Department of History, Moscow, ID 83844-2282. Offers MA, PhD. *Faculty:* 6 full-time, 1 part-time/adjunct. *Students:* 11 full-time, 6 part-time. In 2009, 5 master's awarded. *Degree requirements:* For doctorate, thesis/dissertation. *Entrance requirements:* For master's, minimum GPA of 2.8; for doctorate, minimum undergraduate GPA of 2.8, 3.0 graduate. *Application deadline:* For fall admission, 8/1 for domestic students; for spring admission, 12/15 for domestic students. Application fee: $55 ($60 for international students). *Expenses:* Tuition, state resident: full-time $6120. Tuition, nonresident: full-time $17,712. *Financial support:* Research assistantships, teaching assistantships available. Financial award application deadline: 2/15. *Unit head:* Dr. Richard Spence, Chair, 208-885-6253. *Application contact:* Dr. Richard Spence, Chair, 208-885-6253.

University of Illinois at Chicago, Graduate College, College of Liberal Arts and Sciences, Department of History, Chicago, IL 60607-7128. Offers MA, MAT, PhD. Part-time and evening/weekend programs available. *Degree requirements:* For master's, one foreign language, comprehensive exam; for doctorate, 2 foreign languages, comprehensive exam, thesis/dissertation. *Entrance requirements:* For master's and doctorate, GRE General Test, previous course work in a foreign language, minimum GPA of 3.0. Additional exam requirements/recommendations for international students: Required—TOEFL. Electronic applications accepted. *Faculty research:* American urban and immigration history, early modern European history, Eastern European history.

University of Illinois at Springfield, Graduate Programs, College of Liberal Arts and Sciences, Program in History, Springfield, IL 62703-5407. Offers MA. Part-time and evening/weekend programs available. *Faculty:* 9 full-time (4 women). *Students:* 17 full-time (10 women), 35 part-time (20 women); includes 9 minority (5 African Americans, 1 American Indian/Alaska Native, 3 Hispanic Americans). Average age 34. 19 applicants, 63% accepted, 10 enrolled. In 2009, 14 master's awarded. *Degree requirements:* For master's, thesis, internship, or historiography. *Entrance requirements:* For master's, BA in history or related field, minimum undergraduate GPA of 3.0, writing sample. Additional exam requirements/recommendations for international students: Required—TOEFL (minimum score 500 paper-based; 176 computer-based; 61 iBT). *Application deadline:* Applications are processed on a rolling basis. Application fee: $50 ($60 for international students). Electronic applications accepted. *Expenses:* Tuition, state resident: full-time $6390; part-time $266.25 per credit hour. Tuition, nonresident: full-time $14,226; part-time $592.75 per credit hour. Required fees: $2044; $14.36 per credit hour. $722.50 per term. *Financial support:* In 2009–10, research assistantships with full tuition reimbursements (averaging $8,109 per year), teaching assistantships with full tuition reimbursements (averaging $8,109 per year) were awarded; career-related internships or fieldwork, Federal Work-Study, scholarships/grants, health care benefits, and unspecified assistantships also available. Support available to part-time students. Financial award application deadline: 11/15; financial award applicants required to submit FAFSA. *Unit head:* Dr. Robert McGregor, Program Administrator, 217-206-7442, Fax: 217-206-6217, E-mail: mcgregor.robert@uis.edu. *Application contact:* Dr. Lynn Pardie, Office of Graduate Studies, 800-252-8533, Fax: 217-206-7623, E-mail: pardie.lynn@uis.edu.

University of Illinois at Urbana–Champaign, Graduate College, College of Liberal Arts and Sciences, Department of History, Champaign, IL 61820. Offers MA, PhD. *Faculty:* 40 full-time (16 women), 2 part-time/adjunct (1 woman). *Students:* 92 full-time (49 women), 27 part-time (13 women); includes 20 minority (12 African Americans, 5 Asian Americans or Pacific Islanders, 3 Hispanic Americans), 21 international. 246 applicants, 6% accepted, 14 enrolled. In 2009, 9 master's, 11 doctorates awarded. *Entrance requirements:* For master's, GRE General Test, minimum GPA of 3.25; writing sample; for doctorate, GRE, minimum GPA of 3.5; writing sample. Additional exam requirements/recommendations for international students: Required—TOEFL (minimum score 600 paper-based; 250 computer-based). *Application deadline:* Applications are processed on a rolling basis. Application fee: $60 ($75 for international students). Electronic applications accepted. *Financial support:* In 2009–10, 45 fellowships, 13 research assistantships, 53 teaching assistantships were awarded; tuition waivers (full and partial) also available. *Unit head:* Antoinette Burton, Chair, 217-244-2075, Fax: 217-333-2297, E-mail: aburton@illinois.edu. *Application contact:* Elaine B. Sampson, Office Manager, 217-244-2591, Fax: 217-333-2297, E-mail: esampson@illinois.edu.

University of Indianapolis, Graduate Programs, College of Arts and Sciences, Department of History and Political Science, Indianapolis, IN 46227-3697. Offers history (MA); international relations (MA). Part-time and evening/weekend programs available. *Faculty:* 5 full-time (1 woman). *Students:* 10 full-time (2 women), 17 part-time (10 women); includes 2 minority (1 African American, 1 Hispanic American), 4 international. Average age 28. *Degree requirements:* For master's, thesis optional. *Entrance requirements:* For master's, GRE Subject Test, minimum GPA of 3.0, 3 letters of recommendation. Additional exam requirements/recommendations for international students: Required—TOEFL (minimum score 550 paper-based; 213 computer-based). *Application deadline:* Applications are processed on a rolling basis. Application fee: $30. Electronic applications accepted. *Financial support:* Federal Work-Study, scholarships/grants, and tuition waivers (full and partial) available. Support available to part-time students. Financial award application deadline: 5/1; financial award applicants required to submit FAFSA. *Unit head:* Dr. Lawrence Sondhaus, Chairperson, 317-788-2196, Fax: 317-788-3480, E-mail: sondhaus@uindy.edu. *Application contact:* Dr. Lawrence Sondhaus, Chairperson, 317-788-2196, Fax: 317-788-3480, E-mail: sondhaus@uindy.edu.

The University of Iowa, Graduate College, College of Liberal Arts and Sciences, Department of History, Iowa City, IA 52242-1316. Offers MA, PhD. *Degree requirements:* For master's, thesis optional, exam; for doctorate, comprehensive exam, thesis/dissertation. *Entrance requirements:* For master's and doctorate, GRE General Test, minimum GPA of 3.0. Additional exam requirements/recommendations for international students: Required—TOEFL (minimum score 550 paper-based; 213 computer-based; 81 iBT). Electronic applications accepted.

The University of Kansas, Graduate Studies, College of Liberal Arts and Sciences, Department of History, Lawrence, KS 66045. Offers MA, PhD. Part-time programs available. *Students:* 77 full-time (25 women), 7 part-time (1 woman); includes 5 minority (3 American Indian/Alaska Native, 1 Asian American or Pacific Islander, 1 Hispanic American), 2 international. Average age 36. 74 applicants, 30% accepted, 12 enrolled. In 2009, 14 master's, 8 doctorates awarded. *Degree requirements:* For master's, variable foreign language requirement, 2 professional quality papers; for doctorate, variable foreign language requirement, comprehensive exam, thesis/dissertation. *Entrance requirements:* For master's and doctorate, GRE General Test, minimum GPA of 3.0. Additional exam requirements/recommendations for international students: Required—TOEFL. *Application deadline:* For fall admission, 12/1 for domestic students, 11/1 for international students. Application fee: $45 ($55 for international students). Electronic applications accepted. *Expenses:* Tuition, state resident: full-time $6492; part-time $270.50 per credit hour. Tuition, nonresident: full-time $15,510; part-time $646.25 per credit hour. Required fees: $847; $70.56 per credit hour. Tuition and fees vary according to course load and program. *Financial support:* In 2009–10, 6 fellowships with full tuition reimbursements, 31 teaching assistantships with full tuition reimbursements were awarded; research assistantships with full and partial tuition reimbursements, unspecified assistantships also available. Financial award application deadline: 12/1. *Faculty research:* Environment, military, early modern, East Asia, Russia/East Europe. *Unit head:* Dr. Paul Kelton, Chair, 785-864-9441, Fax: 785-864-5046, E-mail: pkelton@ku.edu. *Application contact:* Ellen Garber, Graduate Program Administrator, 785-864-9438, Fax: 785-864-5046.

University of Kentucky, Graduate School, College of Arts and Sciences, Program in History, Lexington, KY 40506-0032. Offers MA, PhD. Part-time programs available. *Degree requirements:* For master's, one foreign language, comprehensive exam, thesis optional; for doctorate, variable foreign language requirement, comprehensive exam, thesis/dissertation. *Entrance requirements:* For master's, GRE General Test, minimum undergraduate GPA of 2.75; for doctorate, GRE General Test, minimum graduate GPA of 3.0. Additional exam requirements/recommendations for international students: Required—TOEFL (minimum score 550 paper-based; 213 computer-based). Electronic applications accepted. *Faculty research:* English, British, European history; U.S. social, political and diplomatic history; U.S. early national history; U.S. Southern history; Native American and African-American history.

University of Lethbridge, School of Graduate Studies, Lethbridge, AB T1K 3M4, Canada. Offers accounting (MScM); addictions counseling (M Sc); agricultural biotechnology (M Sc); agricultural studies (M Sc, MA); anthropology (MA); archaeology (MA); art (MA, MFA); biochemistry (M Sc); biological sciences (M Sc); biomolecular science (PhD); biosystems and biodiversity (PhD); Canadian studies (MA); chemistry (M Sc); computer science (M Sc); computer science and geographical information science (M Sc); counseling psychology (M Ed); dramatic arts (MA); earth, space, and physical science (PhD); economics (MA); educational leadership (M Ed); English (MA); environmental science (M Sc); evolution and behavior (PhD); exercise science (M Sc); finance (MScM); French (MA); French/German (MA); French/Spanish (MA); general education (M Ed); general management (MScM); geography (M Sc, MA); German (MA); health science (M Sc); health sciences (MA); history (MA); human resource management and labour relations (MScM); individualized multidisciplinary (M Sc, MA); information systems (MScM); international management (MScM); kinesiology (M Sc, MA); management (M Sc, MA); marketing (MScM); mathematics (M Sc); music (M Mus, MA); Native American studies (MA); neuroscience (M Sc, PhD); new media (MA); nursing (M Sc); philosophy (MA); physics (M Sc); policy and strategy (MScM); political science (MA); psychology (M Sc, MA); religious studies (MA); social sciences (MA); sociology (MA); theatre and dramatic arts (MFA); theoretical and computational science (PhD); urban and regional studies (MA); women's studies (MA). Part-time and evening/weekend programs available. *Degree requirements:* For doctorate, comprehensive exam, thesis/dissertation. *Entrance requirements:* For master's, GMAT (M Sc in management), bachelor's degree in related field, minimum GPA of 3.0 during previous 20 graded semester courses, 2 years teaching or related experience (M Ed); for doctorate, master's degree, minimum graduate GPA of 3.5. Additional exam requirements/recommendations for international students: Required—TOEFL. *Faculty research:* Movement and brain plasticity, gibberellin physiology, photosynthesis, carbon cycling, molecular properties of main-group ring components.

University of Louisiana at Lafayette, College of Liberal Arts, Department of History and Geography, Lafayette, LA 70504. Offers history (MA). Part-time programs available. *Degree requirements:* For master's, one foreign language, thesis or alternative. *Entrance requirements:* For master's, GRE General Test, minimum GPA of 2.75. Additional exam requirements/recommendations for international students: Required—TOEFL (minimum score 550 paper-based; 213 computer-based). Electronic applications accepted.

University of Louisiana at Monroe, Graduate School, College of Arts and Sciences, Department of History, Monroe, LA 71209-0001. Offers MA. Part-time and evening/weekend programs available. *Faculty:* 8 full-time (1 woman). *Students:* 11 full-time (4 women), 6 part-time (3 women); includes 4 African Americans. Average age 38. In 2009, 5 master's awarded. *Degree requirements:* For master's, thesis (for some programs). *Entrance requirements:* For master's, GRE General Test, minimum undergraduate GPA of 2.5. Additional exam requirements/recommendations for international students: Required—TOEFL (minimum score 500 paper-based; 173 computer-based; 61 iBT). *Application deadline:* For fall admission, 8/24 priority date for domestic students, 7/1 for international students; for winter admission, 12/14 priority date for domestic students; for spring admission, 1/19 for domestic students, 11/1 for international students. Applications are processed on a rolling basis. Application fee: $20 ($30 for international students). Electronic applications accepted. *Expenses:* Tuition, state resident: part-time $159 per credit hour. Tuition, nonresident: part-time $159 per credit hour. Required fees: $1300 per year. Tuition and fees vary according to course load. *Financial support:* In 2009–10, 7 research assistantships with full tuition reimbursements (averaging $3,200 per year) were awarded; career-related internships or fieldwork, Federal Work-Study, and unspecified assistantships also available. Financial award application deadline: 4/1; financial award applicants required to submit FAFSA. *Faculty research:* Early Louisiana settlements, Soviet history, Louisiana 'Tigers" in Civil War, Anglo-American relations, U.S./East European relations. *Unit head:* Dr. Ralph W. Brown, Department Head, 318-342-1402, E-mail: rbrown@ulm.edu. *Application contact:* Dr. Ralph W. Brown, Department Head, 318-342-1402, E-mail: rbrown@ulm.edu.

University of Louisville, Graduate School, College of Arts and Sciences, Department of History, Louisville, KY 40292. Offers history (MA); public history (Certificate). Part-time programs available. *Faculty:* 17 full-time (4 women). *Students:* 8 full-time (3 women), 18 part-time (6 women); includes 3 minority (1 African American, 2 American Indian/Alaska Native). Average age 30. 25 applicants, 76% accepted, 13 enrolled. In 2009, 5 master's awarded. *Degree requirements:* For master's, one foreign language, comprehensive exam (for some programs), thesis (for some programs). *Entrance requirements:* For master's, GRE General Test. Additional exam requirements/recommendations for international students: Required—TOEFL. *Application deadline:* For fall admission, 5/15 for domestic students, 5/1 for international students; for spring admission, 12/1 for domestic students, 11/1 for international students. Applications are processed on a rolling basis. Application fee: $50. Electronic applications accepted. *Financial support:* In 2009–10, 2 students received support, including 2 teaching assistantships. Financial award applicants required to submit FAFSA. *Faculty research:* United States, British Empire, twentieth century women's history, Turkey and the Middle East, African diaspora. *Unit head:* Dr. Tracy Elaine K'Meyer, Chair, 502-852-6817, Fax: 502-852-0770, E-mail: tracyk@louisville.edu. *Application contact:* Libby Leggett, Director, Graduate Admissions, 502-852-3101, Fax: 502-852-6536, E-mail: gradadm@louisville.edu.

University of Maine, Graduate School, College of Liberal Arts and Sciences, Department of History, Orono, ME 04469. Offers MA, PhD. *Faculty:* 13 full-time (2 women), 2 part-time/adjunct (0 women). *Students:* 26 full-time (7 women), 30 part-time (13 women); includes 5 minority (3 American Indian/Alaska Native, 2 Hispanic Americans). Average age 39. 38 applicants, 66% accepted, 12 enrolled. In 2009, 4 master's, 4 doctorates awarded. Terminal master's awarded for partial completion of doctoral program. *Degree requirements:* For master's, variable foreign language requirement, thesis optional; for doctorate, one foreign language, thesis/dissertation. *Entrance requirements:* For master's and doctorate, GRE General Test. Additional exam requirements/recommendations for international students: Required—TOEFL. *Application deadline:* For fall admission, 2/1 priority date for domestic students. Applications are processed on a rolling basis. Application fee: $65. Electronic applications accepted. *Financial support:* In 2009–10, 9 teaching assistantships with tuition reimbursements (averaging $12,790 per year) were awarded; career-related internships or fieldwork, Federal Work-Study,

History

University of Maine (continued)
and tuition waivers (full and partial) also available. Support available to part-time students. Financial award application deadline: 3/1. *Faculty research:* Canadian labor and working classes; American social, cultural, and urban history. *Unit head:* Dr. Nathan Godfried, Chair, 207-581-1923, Fax: 207-581-1817. *Application contact:* Scott G. Delcourt, Associate Dean of the Graduate School, 207-581-3291, Fax: 207-581-3232, E-mail: graduate@maine.edu.

University of Manitoba, Faculty of Graduate Studies, Faculty of Arts, Department of History, Winnipeg, MB R3T 2N2, Canada. Offers archival studies (MA); history (MA, PhD). *Degree requirements:* For master's, thesis; for doctorate, one foreign language, thesis/dissertation.

University of Maryland, Baltimore County, Graduate School, College of Arts, Humanities and Social Sciences, Department of History, Baltimore, MD 21250. Offers historical studies (MA). Part-time and evening/weekend programs available. *Faculty:* 17 full-time (9 women), 12 part-time/adjunct (2 women). *Students:* 20 full-time (10 women), 57 part-time (30 women); includes 11 minority (5 African Americans, 6 Asian Americans or Pacific Islanders). Average age 33. 35 applicants, 66% accepted, 15 enrolled. In 2009, 16 master's awarded. *Degree requirements:* For master's, thesis. *Entrance requirements:* For master's, GRE General Test, minimum GPA of 3.0. Additional exam requirements/recommendations for international students: Required—TOEFL. *Application deadline:* For fall admission, 3/10 priority date for domestic students, 1/1 for international students; for spring admission, 11/1 priority date for domestic students, 5/1 for international students. Application fee: $50. Electronic applications accepted. *Financial support:* In 2009–10, 11 students received support, including 1 research assistantship with full tuition reimbursement available (averaging $11,324 per year), 9 teaching assistantships with full and partial tuition reimbursements available (averaging $11,324 per year); career-related internships or fieldwork, health care benefits, tuition waivers (partial), and unspecified assistantships also available. Financial award application deadline: 3/10; financial award applicants required to submit FAFSA. *Faculty research:* Archival administration, historical editing, U. S. history, European history, Asian History. Total annual research expenditures: $50,000. *Unit head:* Dr. Anne Sarah Rubin, Graduate Program Director, 410-455-1661, Fax: 410-455-1045, E-mail: arubin@umbc.edu. *Application contact:* Carla Ison, Administrative Assistant, 410-455-2312, Fax: 410-455-1045, E-mail: ison@umbc.edu.

University of Maryland, College Park, Academic Affairs, College of Arts and Humanities, Department of History, College Park, MD 20742. Offers MA, PhD. *Faculty:* 68 full-time (28 women), 5 part-time/adjunct (2 women). *Students:* 105 full-time (39 women), 24 part-time (10 women); includes 16 minority (8 African Americans, 3 Asian Americans or Pacific Islanders, 5 Hispanic Americans), 8 international. 218 applicants, 28% accepted, 24 enrolled. In 2009, 19 master's, 11 doctorates awarded. *Degree requirements:* For master's, comprehensive exam, thesis optional; for doctorate, one foreign language, thesis/dissertation, oral and written exams. *Entrance requirements:* For master's, GRE General Test, minimum GPA of 3.25, writing sample, 3 letters of recommendation; for doctorate, GRE General Test, minimum GPA of 3.5. Additional exam requirements/recommendations for international students: Required—TOEFL. *Application deadline:* For fall admission, 12/15 for domestic and international students. Applications are processed on a rolling basis. Application fee: $60. Electronic applications accepted. *Expenses:* Tuition, area resident: Part-time $471 per credit hour. Tuition, state resident: part-time $471 per credit hour. Tuition, nonresident: part-time $1016 per credit hour. Required fees: $337.04 per term. *Financial support:* In 2009–10, 10 fellowships with full tuition reimbursements (averaging $15,321 per year), 8 research assistantships with tuition reimbursements (averaging $17,356 per year), 52 teaching assistantships (averaging $16,916 per year) were awarded; career-related internships or fieldwork, Federal Work-Study, and scholarships/grants also available. Support available to part-time students. Financial award applicants required to submit FAFSA. *Faculty research:* Ancient, British, East Asian, Latin American, and diplomatic history; papers of Samuel Gompers; Freedman and Southern Society; Caesarea excavations; Folger Institute. Total annual research expenditures: $296,652. *Unit head:* Dr. Richard N. Price, Chair, 301-405-4260, Fax: 301-314-9652, E-mail: rnp@umd.edu. *Application contact:* Director, Graduate Admissions and Records, 301-405-0376, Fax: 301-314-9305.

University of Maryland, College Park, Academic Affairs, Program in History, Library, and Information Services, College Park, MD 20742. Offers MA/MLS. *Students:* 15 full-time (13 women), 4 part-time (all women); includes 2 minority (1 Asian American or Pacific Islander, 1 Hispanic American), 2 international. 35 applicants, 57% accepted, 6 enrolled. *Entrance requirements:* Additional exam requirements/recommendations for international students: Required—TOEFL. *Application deadline:* For fall admission, 12/15 for domestic and international students. Applications are processed on a rolling basis. Application fee: $60. Electronic applications accepted. *Expenses:* Tuition, area resident: Part-time $471 per credit hour. Tuition, state resident: part-time $471 per credit hour. Tuition, nonresident: part-time $1016 per credit hour. Required fees: $337.04 per term. *Financial support:* In 2009–10, 1 research assistantship (averaging $17,182 per year), 4 teaching assistantships (averaging $15,524 per year) were awarded; fellowships also available. Financial award applicants required to submit FAFSA. *Unit head:* Dr. Diane Barlow, Associate Dean, 301-405-2042, Fax: 301-314-9145, E-mail: dbarlow@umd.edu. *Application contact:* Dean of Graduate School, 301-405-0376, Fax: 301-314-9305.

University of Massachusetts Amherst, Graduate School, College of Humanities and Fine Arts, Department of History, Amherst, MA 01003. Offers ancient history (MA); British Empire history (MA); European (medieval and modern) history (MA, PhD); Islamic history (MA); Latin American history (MA, PhD); modern global history (MA); public history (MA); science and technology history (MA); U.S. history (MA, PhD). Part-time programs available. *Faculty:* 39 full-time (17 women). *Students:* 52 full-time (32 women), 13 part-time (6 women); includes 7 minority (4 African Americans, 1 Asian American or Pacific Islander, 2 Hispanic Americans), 3 international. Average age 33. 137 applicants, 39% accepted, 18 enrolled. In 2009, 9 master's, 2 doctorates awarded. Terminal master's awarded for partial completion of doctoral program. *Degree requirements:* For master's, one foreign language, thesis or alternative; for doctorate, one foreign language, comprehensive exam, thesis/dissertation. *Entrance requirements:* For master's and doctorate, GRE General Test, writing sample. Additional exam requirements/recommendations for international students: Required—TOEFL (minimum score 550 paper-based; 213 computer-based; 80 iBT), IELTS (minimum score 6.5). *Application deadline:* For fall admission, 1/2 for domestic and international students. Applications are processed on a rolling basis. Application fee: $50 ($65 for international students). Electronic applications accepted. *Expenses:* Tuition, state resident: full-time $2640; part-time $110 per credit. Tuition, nonresident: full-time $9936; part-time $414 per credit. Tuition and fees vary according to course load. *Financial support:* In 2009–10, 1 fellowship with full tuition reimbursement (averaging $3,973 per year), 6 research assistantships with full tuition reimbursements (averaging $6,246 per year), 36 teaching assistantships with full tuition reimbursements (averaging $12,895 per year) were awarded; career-related internships or fieldwork, Federal Work-Study, scholarships/grants, traineeships, health care benefits, tuition waivers (full), and unspecified assistantships also available. Support available to part-time students. Financial award application deadline: 1/2. *Faculty research:* Ancient and medieval history; global and comparative history; public history; history of science, technology, medicine and the environment; history of women, gender, sexuality and family. *Unit head:* Dr. Brian W. Ogilvie, Graduate Program Director, 413-545-6791, Fax: 413-545-6137. *Application contact:* Jean M. Ames, Supervisor of Admissions, 413-545-0722, Fax: 413-577-0010, E-mail: gradadm@grad.umass.edu.

University of Massachusetts Boston, Office of Graduate Studies, College of Liberal Arts, Program in History, Boston, MA 02125-3393. Offers archival methods (MA); historical archaeology (MA); history (MA). Part-time and evening/weekend programs available. *Degree requirements:* For master's, thesis, oral exam. *Entrance requirements:* For master's, minimum GPA of 2.75. *Faculty research:* European intellectual history, American labor and social history in 19th century, colonial American Revolution, Afro-American Cold War.

University of Memphis, Graduate School, College of Arts and Sciences, Department of History, Memphis, TN 38152. Offers MA, PhD. Postbaccalaureate distance learning degree programs offered (no on-campus study). *Faculty:* 22 full-time (6 women), 3 part-time/adjunct (0 women). *Students:* 61 full-time (37 women), 52 part-time (21 women); includes 18 minority (17 African Americans, 1 Hispanic American), 3 international. Average age 36. 50 applicants, 90% accepted, 15 enrolled. In 2009, 10 master's, 7 doctorates awarded. *Degree requirements:* For master's, comprehensive exam, thesis optional; for doctorate, one foreign language, comprehensive exam, thesis/dissertation, 60 credits plus 12 dissertation credits, 2 research seminars. *Entrance requirements:* For master's, GRE General Test or MAT, 18 undergraduate hours of course work in history with minimum GPA of 3.0, 2 letters of recommendation, writing sample; for doctorate, GRE General Test, GRE Subject Test, MA in history or related field, three letters of recommendation, writing sample, statement of purpose. Additional exam requirements/recommendations for international students: Required—TOEFL. *Application deadline:* For fall admission, 8/1 for domestic students; for spring admission, 12/1 for domestic students. Applications are processed on a rolling basis. Application fee: $35 ($60 for international students). Electronic applications accepted. *Expenses:* Tuition, state resident: full-time $6246; part-time $347 per credit hour. Tuition, nonresident: full-time $15,894; part-time $883 per credit hour. Required fees: $1160. Full-time tuition and fees vary according to course load, degree level and program. *Financial support:* In 2009–10, 54 students received support; research assistantships with full tuition reimbursements available, teaching assistantships with full tuition reimbursements available, career-related internships or fieldwork, Federal Work-Study, scholarships/grants, and unspecified assistantships available. Financial award application deadline: 2/15; financial award applicants required to submit FAFSA. *Faculty research:* African/African-American history, U. S. history, ancient Egyptian history, modern European history, women, gender, and family studies. *Unit head:* Dr. Janann Sherman, Chairman, 901-678-2515, Fax: 907-678-2720, E-mail: sherman@memphis.edu. *Application contact:* Dr. James M. Blythe, Coordinator of Graduate Studies, 901-678-3381, Fax: 901-678-2720, E-mail: jmblythe@memphis.edu.

University of Miami, Graduate School, College of Arts and Sciences, Department of History, Coral Gables, FL 33124. Offers MA, PhD. Part-time programs available. Terminal master's awarded for partial completion of doctoral program. *Degree requirements:* For master's, one foreign language, comprehensive exam, thesis optional; for doctorate, one foreign language, comprehensive exam, thesis/dissertation. *Entrance requirements:* For master's and doctorate, GRE General Test, GRE Subject Test. Additional exam requirements/recommendations for international students: Required—TOEFL (minimum score 550 paper-based; 213 computer-based; 59 iBT). Electronic applications accepted. *Faculty research:* Latin American, European, U.S., and public history.

University of Michigan, Horace H. Rackham School of Graduate Studies, College of Literature, Science, and the Arts, Department of History, Ann Arbor, MI 48109. Offers PhD. *Faculty:* 70 full-time (24 women), 14 part-time/adjunct (2 women). *Students:* 152 full-time (74 women); includes 32 minority (13 African Americans, 2 American Indian/Alaska Native, 9 Asian Americans or Pacific Islanders, 8 Hispanic Americans), 29 international. Average age 30. 343 applicants, 13% accepted, 20 enrolled. In 2009, 18 doctorates awarded. *Degree requirements:* For doctorate, 2 foreign languages, thesis/dissertation, oral defense of dissertation, preliminary exam. *Entrance requirements:* For doctorate, GRE General Test, writing sample. Additional exam requirements/recommendations for international students: Required—TOEFL. *Application deadline:* For fall admission, 12/1 for domestic and international students. Application fee: $65 ($75 for international students). Electronic applications accepted. *Expenses:* Tuition, state resident: full-time $17,286; part-time $1099 per credit hour. Tuition, nonresident: full-time $34,944; part-time $2080 per credit hour. Required fees: $95 per semester. Tuition and fees vary according to course load, degree level and program. *Financial support:* In 2009–10, 106 students received support, including 57 fellowships with full and partial tuition reimbursements available (averaging $19,300 per year), 1 research assistantship with full tuition reimbursement available (averaging $19,300 per year), 48 teaching assistantships with full tuition reimbursements available (averaging $19,300 per year); institutionally sponsored loans and scholarships/grants also available. Financial award application deadline: 3/1. *Faculty research:* Europe, Latin America, Africa, Asia, Middle East/Near East, United States, world/global, science/medicine/technology, and topical/thematic history. Total annual research expenditures: $101,628. *Unit head:* Prof. Geoff Eley, Chair, 734-763-2289, Fax: 734-647-4881, E-mail: ghe@umich.edu. *Application contact:* Diana Y. Denney, Graduate Programs Coordinator, 734-764-2559, Fax: 734-647-4881, E-mail: dianad@umich.edu.

University of Michigan, Horace H. Rackham School of Graduate Studies, College of Literature, Science, and the Arts, Department of Women's Studies, Ann Arbor, MI 48109. Offers English and women's studies (PhD); history and women's studies (PhD); lesbian, gay, bisexual, transgender, queer (LGBTQ) studies (Certificate); psychology and women's studies (PhD); sociology and women's studies (PhD); women's studies (Certificate). *Faculty:* 74 full-time (68 women). *Students:* 68 full-time (63 women); includes 21 minority (7 African Americans, 1 American Indian/Alaska Native, 8 Asian Americans or Pacific Islanders, 5 Hispanic Americans), 12 international. Average age 31. 119 applicants, 9% accepted, 7 enrolled. In 2009, 5 doctorates, 8 other advanced degrees awarded. *Degree requirements:* For doctorate, variable foreign language requirement, comprehensive exam (for some programs), thesis/dissertation. *Entrance requirements:* For doctorate, GRE General Test, previous undergraduate course work in women's studies. *Application deadline:* For fall admission, 12/1 for domestic and international students. Application fee: $60 ($75 for international students). Electronic applications accepted. *Expenses:* Tuition, state resident: full-time $17,286; part-time $1099 per credit hour. Tuition, nonresident: full-time $34,944; part-time $2080 per credit hour. Required fees: $95 per semester. Tuition and fees vary according to course load, degree level and program. *Financial support:* In 2009–10, 34 students received support, including 19 fellowships with full tuition reimbursements available (averaging $16,000 per year), 15 teaching assistantships with full and partial tuition reimbursements available (averaging $16,135 per year); career-related internships or fieldwork, institutionally sponsored loans, scholarships/grants, traineeships, health care benefits, and unspecified assistantships also available. *Faculty research:* Gender issues; LGBTQ studies; sexuality; women and science; global feminism. *Unit head:* Anne Herrmann, Chair, 734-763-2047, Fax: 734-647-4943, E-mail: anneh@umich.edu. *Application contact:* Aimee Germain, Graduate Program Coordinator, 734-763-2047, Fax: 734-647-4943, E-mail: wsdgradInquiry@umich.edu.

University of Michigan, Horace H. Rackham School of Graduate Studies, College of Literature, Science, and the Arts, Doctoral Program in Anthropology and History, Ann Arbor, MI 48109. Offers PhD. *Faculty:* 64 full-time (27 women). *Students:* 35 full-time (15 women); includes 7 minority (2 African Americans, 2 Asian Americans or Pacific Islanders, 3 Hispanic Americans), 15 international. Average age 32. 45 applicants, 20% accepted, 2 enrolled. In 2009, 4 doctorates awarded. *Degree requirements:* For doctorate, 2 foreign languages, thesis/dissertation, oral defense of dissertation, preliminary exam. *Entrance requirements:* For doctorate, GRE General Test, writing sample. Additional exam requirements/recommendations for international students: Required—TOEFL. *Application deadline:* For fall admission, 12/1 for domestic and international students. Application fee: $65 ($75 for international students). Electronic applications accepted. *Expenses:* Tuition, state resident: full-time $17,286; part-time $1099 per credit hour. Tuition, nonresident: full-time $34,944; part-time $2080 per credit hour. Required fees: $95 per semester. Tuition and fees vary according to course load, degree level and program. *Financial support:* In 2009–10, 29 students received support, including 14 fellowships with full and partial tuition reimbursements available (averaging $16,500 per year), 12 teaching assistantships with full tuition reimbursements available (averaging $19,300 per year); research assistantships with full tuition reimbursements available, institutionally sponsored loans and scholarships/grants also available. Financial award application deadline: 3/1. *Faculty research:* Historical anthropology. *Unit head:* Prof. Paul Christopher Johnson, Director, 734-764-1817. *Application contact:* Diana Y. Denney, Graduate Program Coordinator, 734-764-2559, Fax: 734-647-4881, E-mail: dianad@umich.edu.

University of Michigan, Horace H. Rackham School of Graduate Studies, College of Literature, Science, and the Arts, Interdepartmental Program in Greek and Roman History, Ann Arbor, MI 48109. Offers PhD, Certificate. *Faculty:* 5 full-time (1 woman), 16 part-time/adjunct (7 women).

Students: 11 full-time (5 women), 2 international. Average age 26. 20 applicants, 10% accepted, 2 enrolled. In 2009, 1 doctorate awarded. *Degree requirements:* For doctorate, 4 foreign languages, comprehensive exam, thesis/dissertation, oral defense of dissertation, dissertation prospectus, preliminary exams. *Entrance requirements:* For doctorate, GRE, knowledge of classical Greek and Latin; at least 2 years of each. Additional exam requirements/recommendations for international students: Required—TOEFL (minimum score 560 paper-based; 220 computer-based). *Application deadline:* For fall admission, 12/15 for domestic and international students. Application fee: $60 ($75 for international students). Electronic applications accepted. *Expenses:* Tuition, state resident: full-time $17,286; part-time $1099 per credit hour. Tuition, nonresident: full-time $34,944; part-time $2080 per credit hour. Required fees: $95 per semester. Tuition and fees vary according to course load, degree level and program. *Financial support:* In 2009–10, 10 students received support, including 4 fellowships with full tuition reimbursements available (averaging $16,800 per year), 7 teaching assistantships with full tuition reimbursements available (averaging $16,694 per year); career-related internships or fieldwork, Federal Work-Study, institutionally sponsored loans, scholarships/grants, traineeships, health care benefits, and unspecified assistantships also available. Financial award application deadline: 3/15. *Faculty research:* Greek history, Roman history. *Unit head:* Prof. Raymond Van Dam, Professor, 734-763-1193, E-mail: rvandam@umich.edu. *Application contact:* Michelle M. Biggs, Graduate Coordinator, 734-647-2330, Fax: 734-763-4959, E-mail: mbiggs@umich.edu.

University of Minnesota, Twin Cities Campus, Graduate School, College of Liberal Arts, Department of Classical and Near Eastern Studies, Minneapolis, MN 55455-0213. Offers ancient and medieval art and archaeology (MA, PhD); classics (MA, PhD); Greek (MA, PhD); Latin (MA, PhD); religions in antiquity (MA). Part-time programs available. *Faculty:* 22 full-time (6 women). *Students:* 24 full-time (10 women), 1 part-time (0 women), 1 international. Average age 29. 40 applicants, 20% accepted, 4 enrolled. In 2009, 5 master's awarded. Terminal master's awarded for partial completion of doctoral program. *Degree requirements:* For master's, 2 foreign languages, comprehensive exam, thesis or alternative; for doctorate, variable foreign language requirement, comprehensive exam, thesis/dissertation. *Entrance requirements:* For master's and doctorate, GRE, 3 letters of recommendation, department application, writing sample, copies of transcripts, personal statement. Additional exam requirements/recommendations for international students: Required—TOEFL. *Application deadline:* For fall admission, 1/4 priority date for domestic and international students. Application fee: $50 ($75 for international students). Electronic applications accepted. *Financial support:* In 2009–10, 24 students received support, including 2 fellowships with full tuition reimbursements available (averaging $22,500 per year), 2 research assistantships with partial tuition reimbursements available (averaging $7,000 per year), 20 teaching assistantships with full tuition reimbursements available (averaging $14,000 per year); career-related internships or fieldwork, Federal Work-Study, institutionally sponsored loans, health care benefits, and tuition waivers (full and partial) also available. Support available to part-time students. Financial award application deadline: 1/4. *Faculty research:* Greek and Latin literature, religions in antiquity, ancient Near East. *Unit head:* Christopher Nappa, Chair, 612-625-624-6339, Fax: 612-624-4894, E-mail: cnappa@umn.edu. *Application contact:* Victoria H. Keller, Administrative Specialist, 612-625-8371, Fax: 612-624-4894, E-mail: kell0801@umn.edu.

University of Minnesota, Twin Cities Campus, Graduate School, College of Liberal Arts, Department of History, Minneapolis, MN 55455-0213. Offers MA, PhD. *Faculty:* 36 full-time (20 women), 20 part-time/adjunct (11 women). *Students:* 110 full-time (46 women); includes 24 minority (6 African Americans, 1 American Indian/Alaska Native, 13 Asian Americans or Pacific Islanders, 4 Hispanic Americans). Average age 31. 233 applicants, 11% accepted, 15 enrolled. In 2009, 3 master's, 16 doctorates awarded. *Degree requirements:* For master's, one foreign language, comprehensive exam, thesis or alternative; for doctorate, 2 foreign languages, comprehensive exam, thesis/dissertation. *Entrance requirements:* For doctorate, GRE General Test, writing sample, letters of recommendation. Additional exam requirements/recommendations for international students: Required—TOEFL (minimum score 550 paper-based; 213 computer-based). *Application deadline:* For fall admission, 12/1 for domestic and international students. Application fee: $55 ($75 for international students). Electronic applications accepted. *Financial support:* In 2009–10, 24 fellowships with full tuition reimbursements (averaging $14,000 per year), 11 research assistantships with full tuition reimbursements (averaging $14,000 per year), 49 teaching assistantships with full tuition reimbursements (averaging $14,000 per year) were awarded; career-related internships or fieldwork, Federal Work-Study, scholarships/grants, health care benefits, tuition waivers (full and partial), and unspecified assistantships also available. Financial award application deadline: 12/1. *Faculty research:* Early and modern United States; medieval, early modern and modern Europe; Africa; East and South Asia; Latin America. Total annual research expenditures: $270,491. *Unit head:* Cohen Gary, Chair, 612-624-2800, Fax: 612-624-7096, E-mail: gcohen@umn.edu. *Application contact:* Anna Clark, Director of Graduate Studies, 612-624-5840, Fax: 612-624-7096, E-mail: histdgs@umn.edu.

University of Mississippi, Graduate School, College of Liberal Arts, Department of History, Oxford, University, MS 38677. Offers MA, PhD. *Faculty:* 21 full-time (7 women), 2 part-time/adjunct (1 woman). *Students:* 47 full-time (20 women), 10 part-time (5 women); includes 11 minority (9 African Americans, 2 Hispanic Americans). In 2009, 4 master's, 5 doctorates awarded. *Degree requirements:* For doctorate, thesis/dissertation. *Entrance requirements:* For master's, GRE General Test, GRE Subject Test, minimum GPA of 3.0; for doctorate, GRE General Test, GRE Subject Test. Additional exam requirements/recommendations for international students: Required—TOEFL. *Application deadline:* For fall admission, 1/15 for domestic students; for spring admission, 11/1 for domestic students. Applications are processed on a rolling basis. Application fee: $25. Electronic applications accepted. *Financial support:* Scholarships/grants available. Financial award application deadline: 3/1; financial award applicants required to submit FAFSA. *Unit head:* Dr. Joseph P. Ward, Chair, 662-915-7148, Fax: 662-915-7033, E-mail: history@olemiss.edu. *Application contact:* Dr. Joseph P. Ward, Chair, 662-915-7148, Fax: 662-915-7033, E-mail: history@olemiss.edu.

University of Missouri, Graduate School, College of Arts and Sciences, Department of History, Columbia, MO 65211. Offers MA, PhD. *Faculty:* 16 full-time (5 women), 2 part-time/adjunct (0 women). *Students:* 28 full-time (12 women), 25 part-time (7 women); includes 4 minority (3 African Americans, 1 Asian American or Pacific Islander). Average age 34. 63 applicants, 38% accepted, 9 enrolled. In 2009, 1 master's, 3 doctorates awarded. *Degree requirements:* For master's, thesis; for doctorate, 2 foreign languages, comprehensive exam, thesis/dissertation. *Entrance requirements:* For master's, GRE General Test, minimum GPA of 3.0 in last 60 hours; GPA of 3.3 in undergrad history courses and at least 18 hours in history; BA or BS degree; for doctorate, GRE General Test, minimum GPA of 3.0; MA in history strongly preferred; quality of master's thesis or research seminar paper submission. Additional exam requirements/recommendations for international students: Required—TOEFL (minimum score 500 paper-based; 173 computer-based; 61 iBT). *Application deadline:* For fall admission, 1/14 priority date for domestic students. Applications are processed on a rolling basis. Application fee: $45 ($60 for international students). Electronic applications accepted. *Financial support:* In 2009–10, 6 fellowships with full tuition reimbursements, 1 research assistantship with full tuition reimbursement, 28 teaching assistantships with full tuition reimbursements were awarded; institutionally sponsored loans, health care benefits, and unspecified assistantships also available. *Faculty research:* U.S. history, African-American history, Ancient history, Latin American history, Asian history. *Unit head:* Dr. Jonathan Sperber, Department Chair, 573-882-2068, E-mail: sperberj@missouri.edu. *Application contact:* Nancy Taube, Graduate Studies Administrator, 573-882-9461, E-mail: tauben@missouri.edu.

University of Missouri–Kansas City, College of Arts and Sciences, Department of History, Kansas City, MO 64110-2499. Offers MA, PhD. PhD (interdisciplinary) offered through the School of Graduate Studies. Part-time programs available. *Faculty:* 17 full-time (8 women), 3 part-time/adjunct (all women). *Students:* 6 full-time (3 women), 21 part-time (12 women); includes 3 minority (1 African American, 1 Asian American or Pacific Islander, 1 Hispanic American). Average age 34. 17 applicants, 71% accepted, 9 enrolled. In 2009, 8 master's awarded. *Degree requirements:* For master's, thesis optional; for doctorate, one foreign language, thesis/dissertation. *Entrance requirements:* For master's, GRE General Test, minimum GPA of 3.0, 2 writing samples, 3 letters of recommendation; for doctorate, GRE General Test. Additional exam requirements/recommendations for international students: Required—TOEFL (minimum score 550 paper-based; 213 computer-based; 80 iBT). *Application deadline:* For fall admission, 3/15 for domestic and international students; for spring admission, 10/1 priority date for domestic students, 10/1 for international students. Applications are processed on a rolling basis. Application fee: $45 ($50 for international students). Electronic applications accepted. *Expenses:* Tuition, state resident: full-time $5378; part-time $299 per credit hour. Tuition, nonresident: full-time $13,881; part-time $771 per credit hour. Required fees: $641; $71 per credit hour. Tuition and fees vary according to course load and program. *Financial support:* In 2009–10, 7 teaching assistantships with partial tuition reimbursements (averaging $14,020 per year) were awarded; career-related internships or fieldwork, Federal Work-Study, institutionally sponsored loans, and tuition waivers (full and partial) also available. Support available to part-time students. Financial award application deadline: 3/1; financial award applicants required to submit FAFSA. *Faculty research:* U.S. history, Europe, women and gender, religious studies, history of science. Total annual research expenditures: $122,933. *Unit head:* Dr. Gary Ebersole, Chair, 816-235-1631, Fax: 816-235-5723, E-mail: ebersoleg@umkc.edu. *Application contact:* Dr. Andrew Bergerson, Principal Graduate Advisor, 816-235-1631, Fax: 816-235-5723, E-mail: bergersona@umkc.edu.

The University of Montana, Graduate School, College of Arts and Sciences, Department of History, Missoula, MT 59812-0002. Offers MA, PhD. *Degree requirements:* For master's, thesis or additional course work/professional paper. *Entrance requirements:* For master's, GRE General Test. Additional exam requirements/recommendations for international students: Required—TOEFL.

University of Nebraska at Kearney, College of Graduate Study, College of Natural and Social Sciences, Department of History, Kearney, NE 68849-0001. Offers history (MA). Part-time and evening/weekend programs available. *Degree requirements:* For master's, thesis optional. *Entrance requirements:* For master's, GRE General Test, writing sample. Additional exam requirements/recommendations for international students: Required—TOEFL (minimum score 550 paper-based; 213 computer-based). Electronic applications accepted. *Faculty research:* Military history, labor history/labor and the law, state formation and nationalism, American intellectual history, Civil War and Reconstruction.

University of Nebraska at Omaha, Graduate Studies, College of Arts and Sciences, Department of History, Omaha, NE 68182. Offers MA. Part-time and evening/weekend programs available. *Faculty:* 14 full-time (5 women). *Students:* 12 full-time (6 women), 52 part-time (20 women); includes 3 minority (1 African American, 1 American Indian/Alaska Native, 1 Asian American or Pacific Islander). Average age 31. 27 applicants, 85% accepted, 18 enrolled. In 2009, 13 master's awarded. *Degree requirements:* For master's, comprehensive exam, thesis (for some programs). *Entrance requirements:* For master's, minimum GPA of 3.0, 21 hours of course work in history, 2 letters of recommendation. Additional exam requirements/recommendations for international students: Required—TOEFL (minimum score 500 paper-based; 173 computer-based; 61 iBT). *Application deadline:* For fall admission, 7/1 priority date for domestic students; for spring admission, 12/1 priority date for domestic students. Applications are processed on a rolling basis. Application fee: $45. Electronic applications accepted. *Financial support:* In 2009–10, 41 students received support; fellowships, research assistantships with tuition reimbursements available, teaching assistantships with tuition reimbursements available, Federal Work-Study, institutionally sponsored loans, scholarships/grants, tuition waivers (partial), and unspecified assistantships available. Support available to part-time students. Financial award application deadline: 3/1; financial award applicants required to submit FAFSA. *Unit head:* Dr. Bruce Garver, Chairperson, 402-554-2593. *Application contact:* Dr. Michael Tate, Student Contact, 402-554-2593.

University of Nebraska–Lincoln, Graduate College, College of Arts and Sciences, Department of History, Lincoln, NE 68588. Offers MA, PhD. *Degree requirements:* For master's, thesis optional; for doctorate, one foreign language, comprehensive exam, thesis/dissertation. *Entrance requirements:* For master's and doctorate, GRE General Test, GRE Subject Test, writing sample. Additional exam requirements/recommendations for international students: Required—TOEFL (minimum score 575 paper-based; 233 computer-based). Electronic applications accepted. *Faculty research:* Military history, indigenous peoples, German history, American history (American West society and culture).

University of Nevada, Las Vegas, Graduate College, College of Liberal Arts, Department of History, Las Vegas, NV 89154-5020. Offers MA, PhD. Part-time programs available. *Faculty:* 25 full-time (8 women). *Students:* 26 full-time (13 women), 46 part-time (21 women); includes 3 minority (1 African American, 1 Asian American or Pacific Islander, 1 Hispanic American), 1 international. Average age 40. 58 applicants, 72% accepted, 27 enrolled. In 2009, 14 master's, 3 doctorates awarded. *Degree requirements:* For master's, one foreign language, comprehensive exam (for some programs), thesis (for some programs); for doctorate, 2 foreign languages, comprehensive exam, thesis/dissertation. *Entrance requirements:* For master's, minimum overall GPA of 3.0, 3.3 in history courses; for doctorate, GRE General Test, minimum overall GPA of 3.0, 3.3 in history courses. Additional exam requirements/recommendations for international students: Required—TOEFL (minimum score 550 paper-based; 213 computer-based; 80 iBT), IELTS (minimum score 7). *Application deadline:* For fall admission, 2/1 priority date for domestic and international students; for spring admission, 11/1 priority date for domestic students, 10/1 for international students. Applications are processed on a rolling basis. Application fee: $60 ($95 for international students). Electronic applications accepted. *Financial support:* In 2009–10, 24 students received support, including 1 fellowship with full tuition reimbursement available (averaging $20,000 per year), 23 teaching assistantships with partial tuition reimbursements available (averaging $11,739 per year); institutionally sponsored loans, scholarships/grants, health care benefits, and unspecified assistantships also available. Financial award application deadline: 3/1. *Faculty research:* American West, public history, cultural history, urban history, gender and sexuality. *Unit head:* Dr. David Wrobel, Chair/ Professor, 702-895-0810, Fax: 702-895-1782, E-mail: david.wrobel@unlv.edu. *Application contact:* Graduate College Admissions Evaluator, 702-895-3320, Fax: 702-895-4180, E-mail: gradcollege@unlv.edu.

University of Nevada, Reno, Graduate School, College of Liberal Arts, Department of History, Reno, NV 89557. Offers MA, PhD. Terminal master's awarded for partial completion of doctoral program. *Degree requirements:* For master's, thesis optional; for doctorate, one foreign language, thesis/dissertation. *Entrance requirements:* For master's, GRE General Test, minimum GPA of 2.75; for doctorate, GRE General Test, minimum GPA of 3.0. Additional exam requirements/recommendations for international students: Required—TOEFL (minimum score 500 paper-based; 173 computer-based; 61 iBT), IELTS (minimum score 6). Electronic applications accepted. *Faculty research:* History of medicine, science, environmental history, western America, social/cultural history.

University of New Brunswick Fredericton, School of Graduate Studies, Faculty of Arts, Department of History, Fredericton, NB E3B 5A3, Canada. Offers MA, PhD. Part-time programs available. *Faculty:* 13 full-time (4 women), 6 part-time/adjunct (3 women). *Students:* 49 full-time (16 women), 11 part-time (7 women). In 2009, 15 master's, 3 doctorates awarded. *Degree requirements:* For master's, thesis; for doctorate, thesis/dissertation. *Entrance requirements:* For master's, minimum GPA of 3.0, resume, writing sample and/or statement of research interests; Honours degree in History or equivalent; for doctorate, minimum GPA of 3.0, statement of research interests, writing sample. Master's degree in History. Additional exam requirements/recommendations for international students: Required—TOEFL. *Application deadline:* For fall admission, 3/1 priority date for domestic students. Applications are processed on a rolling basis. Application fee: $50 Canadian dollars. Tuition and fees charges are reported in Canadian dollars. *Expenses:* Tuition, area resident: Full-time $5562 Canadian dollars; part-time $2781 Canadian dollars per year. Required fees: $49.75 Canadian dollars per term. *Financial support:* In 2009–10, 12 fellowships (averaging $13,500 per year) were awarded; scholarships/grants also available. *Faculty research:* Canadian history, colonial North America, military/international,

History

University of New Brunswick Fredericton (continued)
women's/gender history. *Unit head:* Dr. Steve Turner, Acting Director of Graduate Studies, 506-458-7433, Fax: 506-453-5068, E-mail: turner@unb.ca. *Application contact:* Elizabeth Adshade, Graduate Secretary, 506-458-7471, Fax: 506-453-5068, E-mail: eliz@unb.ca.

University of New Hampshire, Graduate School, College of Liberal Arts, Department of History, Durham, NH 03824. Offers history (MA, PhD); museum studies (MA). Part-time programs available. *Faculty:* 24 full-time (13 women). *Students:* 32 full-time (15 women), 19 part-time (13 women); includes 3 minority (1 American Indian/Alaska Native, 2 Asian Americans or Pacific Islanders), 3 international. Average age 37. 84 applicants, 51% accepted, 17 enrolled. In 2009, 12 master's, 4 doctorates awarded. *Degree requirements:* For master's, thesis or alternative; for doctorate, 2 foreign languages, thesis/dissertation. *Entrance requirements:* For master's and doctorate, GRE General Test. Additional exam requirements/recommendations for international students: Required—TOEFL (minimum score 550 paper-based; 213 computer-based; 80 iBT). *Application deadline:* For fall admission, 6/1 priority date for domestic students, 4/15 for international students; for spring admission, 12/1 for domestic students. Applications are processed on a rolling basis. Application fee: $65. Electronic applications accepted. *Expenses:* Tuition, state resident: full-time $10,380; part-time $577 per credit hour. Tuition, nonresident: full-time $24,350; part-time $1002 per credit hour. Required fees: $1550; $387.50 per semester. Tuition and fees vary according to course load and program. *Financial support:* In 2009–10, 21 students received support, including 5 fellowships, 12 teaching assistantships; research assistantships, career-related internships or fieldwork, Federal Work-Study, scholarships/grants, and tuition waivers (full and partial) also available. Support available to part-time students. Financial award application deadline: 2/15. *Unit head:* Dr. Jan Golinski, Chairperson, 603-862-1764. *Application contact:* Susan Kilday, Administrative Assistant, 603-862-1764, E-mail: history.grad@unh.edu.

University of New Mexico, Graduate School, College of Arts and Sciences, Department of History, Albuquerque, NM 87131-2039. Offers MA, PhD. Part-time programs available. *Faculty:* 23 full-time (12 women), 4 part-time/adjunct (1 woman). *Students:* 67 full-time (26 women), 34 part-time (14 women); includes 19 minority (5 American Indian/Alaska Native, 14 Hispanic Americans), 3 international. Average age 36. 84 applicants, 55% accepted, 19 enrolled. In 2009, 14 master's, 3 doctorates awarded. Terminal master's awarded for partial completion of doctoral program. *Degree requirements:* For master's, one foreign language, comprehensive exam, thesis optional; for doctorate, one foreign language, comprehensive exam, thesis/dissertation. *Entrance requirements:* For master's, GRE, BA in history or equivalent; for doctorate, MA in history or equivalent. Additional exam requirements/recommendations for international students: Required—TOEFL. *Application deadline:* For fall admission, 1/15 for domestic students; for spring admission, 10/15 for domestic students. Application fee: $50. Electronic applications accepted. *Expenses:* Tuition, state resident: full-time $2099; part-time $233.20 per credit hour. Tuition, nonresident: full-time $6650. Required fees: $25 per semester. Tuition and fees vary according to course load, program and reciprocity agreements. *Financial support:* In 2009–10, 42 students received support, including 23 teaching assistantships with full tuition reimbursements available (averaging $12,230 per year); institutionally sponsored loans, scholarships/grants, and health care benefits also available. Financial award application deadline: 1/15; financial award applicants required to submit FAFSA. *Faculty research:* American Western history, Asian history, environmental history, European history, frontiers and borderlands, gender and sexuality, Latin American history, politics and economy, race and ethnicity, religion, United States history, war and society. *Unit head:* Dr. Charlie Steen, Chair, 505-277-2451, Fax: 505-277-6023, E-mail: csteen@unm.edu. *Application contact:* Yolanda Martinez, Department Administrator, 505-277-2451, Fax: 505-277-6023, E-mail: history@unm.edu.

University of New Orleans, Graduate School, College of Liberal Arts, Department of History, New Orleans, LA 70148. Offers history (MA). *Degree requirements:* For master's, one foreign language, thesis (for some programs). *Entrance requirements:* For master's, GRE General Test. Additional exam requirements/recommendations for international students: Required—TOEFL (minimum score 550 paper-based; 213 computer-based; 79 iBT). Electronic applications accepted. *Faculty research:* Recent U.S. political, military, urban, regional, and legal history.

University of North Alabama, College of Arts and Sciences, Department of History and Political Science, Florence, AL 35632-0001. Offers MA. *Faculty:* 1 full-time (0 women), 7 part-time/adjunct (1 woman). *Students:* 5 full-time (2 women), 14 part-time (4 women); includes 1 minority (African American). Average age 38. In 2009, 2 master's awarded. *Expenses:* Tuition, state resident: full-time $5040; part-time $210 per credit hour. Tuition, nonresident: full-time $10,080; part-time $420 per credit hour. Required fees: $906. *Unit head:* Dr. Christopher Maynard, Chair, 256-765-4306, E-mail: camaynard@una.edu. *Application contact:* Kim Mauldin, Director of Admissions, 256-765-4608, Fax: 256-765-4960, E-mail: komauldin@una.edu.

The University of North Carolina at Chapel Hill, Graduate School, College of Arts and Sciences, Department of History, Chapel Hill, NC 27599. Offers MA, PhD. Terminal master's awarded for partial completion of doctoral program. *Degree requirements:* For master's, one foreign language, thesis, oral thesis defense; for doctorate, 2 foreign languages, comprehensive exam, thesis/dissertation, oral dissertation defense. *Entrance requirements:* For master's and doctorate, GRE General Test, minimum GPA of 3.0. Electronic applications accepted.

The University of North Carolina at Charlotte, Graduate School, College of Arts and Sciences, Department of History, Charlotte, NC 28223-0001. Offers MA. Part-time and evening/weekend programs available. *Faculty:* 22 full-time (7 women). *Students:* 20 full-time (12 women), 37 part-time (17 women); includes 6 minority (3 African Americans, 2 American Indian/Alaska Native, 1 Hispanic American), 1 international. Average age 29. 47 applicants, 83% accepted, 24 enrolled. In 2009, 6 master's awarded. *Degree requirements:* For master's, thesis or comprehensive exam. *Entrance requirements:* For master's, GRE General Test, minimum GPA of 3.0 in undergraduate major, 2.75 overall. Additional exam requirements/recommendations for international students: Required—TOEFL (minimum score 557 paper-based; 220 computer-based; 83 iBT). *Application deadline:* For fall admission, 7/1 for domestic students, 5/1 for international students; for spring admission, 11/1 for domestic students, 10/1 for international students. Applications are processed on a rolling basis. Application fee: $55. Electronic applications accepted. *Financial support:* In 2009–10, 11 students received support, including 1 research assistantship (averaging $7,000 per year), 10 teaching assistantships (averaging $9,139 per year); career-related internships or fieldwork, Federal Work-Study, institutionally sponsored loans, scholarships/grants, and unspecified assistantships also available. Support available to part-time students. Financial award application deadline: 4/1; financial award applicants required to submit FAFSA. *Faculty research:* Southern United States history; Latin American history; race and gender history; urban history; history of science, medicine, technology. Total annual research expenditures: $114,577. *Unit head:* Dr. Jurgen Buchenau, Chair, 704-687-4646, Fax: 704-687-3218, E-mail: jbuchenau@uncc.edu. *Application contact:* Kathy B. Giddings, Director of Graduate Admissions, 704-687-5530, Fax: 704-687-3279, E-mail: gradadm@uncc.edu.

The University of North Carolina at Greensboro, Graduate School, College of Arts and Sciences, Department of History, Greensboro, NC 27412-5001. Offers historic preservation (Certificate); history (MA); museum studies (Certificate); U.S. history (PhD). Part-time programs available. *Entrance requirements:* For master's, GRE General Test. Additional exam requirements/recommendations for international students: Required—TOEFL. Electronic applications accepted. *Faculty research:* Simultaneous discovery in science, progressive social reform, Robert Mayer.

The University of North Carolina Wilmington, College of Arts and Sciences, Department of History, Wilmington, NC 28403-3297. Offers MA. Part-time programs available. *Degree requirements:* For master's, comprehensive exam, thesis. *Entrance requirements:* For master's, GRE General Test, minimum B average in undergraduate major. Additional exam requirements/recommendations for international students: Required—TOEFL (minimum score 550 paper-based; 217 computer-based; 79 iBT), IELTS (minimum score 6.5).

University of North Dakota, Graduate School, College of Arts and Sciences, Department of History, Grand Forks, ND 58202. Offers MA, DA, PhD. *Degree requirements:* For master's, thesis, final exam; for doctorate, comprehensive exam, thesis/dissertation, final exam. *Entrance requirements:* For master's, minimum GPA of 3.0; for doctorate, minimum GPA of 3.5. Additional exam requirements/recommendations for international students: Required—TOEFL (minimum score 550 paper-based; 213 computer-based; 79 iBT), IELTS (minimum score 6.5). Electronic applications accepted. *Faculty research:* U.S. history, Latin America, Russia, modern Europe, women studies.

University of Northern British Columbia, Office of Graduate Studies, Prince George, BC V2N 4Z9, Canada. Offers business administration (Diploma); community health science (M Sc); disability management (MA); education (M Ed); first nations studies (MA); gender studies (MA); history (MA); interdisciplinary studies (MA); international studies (MA); mathematical, computer and physical sciences (M Sc); natural resources and environmental studies (M Sc, MA, MNRES, PhD); political science (MA); psychology (M Sc, PhD); social work (MSW). Part-time and evening/weekend programs available. Postbaccalaureate distance learning degree programs offered (no on-campus study). *Degree requirements:* For master's, thesis; for doctorate, thesis/dissertation. *Entrance requirements:* For master's, GRE, minimum B average in undergraduate course work; for doctorate, candidacy exam, minimum A average in graduate course work.

University of Northern Colorado, Graduate School, College of Humanities and Social Sciences, Program in History, Greeley, CO 80639. Offers MA. Part-time programs available. *Faculty:* 11 full-time (3 women). *Students:* 9 full-time (7 women), 8 part-time (3 women); includes 1 minority (Hispanic American). Average age 33. 9 applicants, 67% accepted, 5 enrolled. In 2009, 5 master's awarded. *Degree requirements:* For master's, comprehensive exam, thesis or alternative. *Entrance requirements:* For master's, GRE, 3 letters of recommendation. *Application deadline:* Applications are processed on a rolling basis. Application fee: $50 ($60 for international students). Electronic applications accepted. *Expenses:* Tuition, state resident: full-time $5770; part-time $320.55 per credit hour. Tuition, nonresident: full-time $13,847; part-time $769.27 per credit hour. Required fees: $948.78; $52.72 per credit. *Financial support:* In 2009–10, 2 teaching assistantships (averaging $8,547 per year) were awarded. Financial award application deadline: 3/1; financial award applicants required to submit FAFSA. *Unit head:* Dr. Michael Welsh, Program Coordinator, 970-351-2905, Fax: 970-351-2199. *Application contact:* Linda Sisson, Graduate Student Admission Coordinator, 970-351-1807, Fax: 970-351-2371, E-mail: linda.sisson@unco.edu.

University of Northern Colorado, Graduate School, College of Humanities and Social Sciences, School of History, Philosophy and Political Science, Greeley, CO 80639. Offers history (MA). Part-time programs available. *Faculty:* 11 full-time (3 women). *Students:* 9 full-time (7 women), 8 part-time (3 women); includes 1 minority (Hispanic American). Average age 33. 9 applicants, 67% accepted, 5 enrolled. In 2009, 5 master's awarded. *Degree requirements:* For master's, comprehensive exam, thesis or alternative. *Entrance requirements:* For master's, GRE, 3 letters of reference. *Application deadline:* Applications are processed on a rolling basis. Application fee: $50 ($60 for international students). Electronic applications accepted. *Expenses:* Tuition, state resident: full-time $5770; part-time $320.55 per credit hour. Tuition, nonresident: full-time $13,847; part-time $769.27 per credit hour. Required fees: $948.78; $52.72 per credit. *Financial support:* In 2009–10, 2 teaching assistantships (averaging $8,547 per year) were awarded; fellowships, research assistantships, unspecified assistantships also available. Financial award application deadline: 3/1; financial award applicants required to submit FAFSA. *Unit head:* Dr. Barry Rothaus, Director, 970-351-2905, Fax: 970-351-2199. *Application contact:* Linda Sisson, Graduate Student Admission Coordinator, 970-351-1807, Fax: 970-351-2371, E-mail: linda.sisson@unco.edu.

University of Northern Iowa, Graduate College, College of Social and Behavioral Sciences, Department of History, Cedar Falls, IA 50614. Offers MA. Part-time programs available. *Students:* 17 full-time (8 women), 10 part-time (7 women); includes 3 minority (2 Asian Americans or Pacific Islanders, 1 Hispanic American). 22 applicants, 59% accepted, 9 enrolled. In 2009, 5 master's awarded. *Degree requirements:* For master's, comprehensive exam (for some programs), thesis or alternative. *Entrance requirements:* For master's, minimum GPA of 3.2. Additional exam requirements/recommendations for international students: Required—TOEFL (minimum score 500 paper-based; 180 computer-based; 61 iBT). *Application deadline:* For fall admission, 8/1 priority date for domestic students. Applications are processed on a rolling basis. Application fee: $30 ($50 for international students). Electronic applications accepted. *Financial support:* Career-related internships or fieldwork, Federal Work-Study, scholarships/grants, and tuition waivers (full and partial) available. Support available to part-time students. Financial award application deadline: 2/1. *Unit head:* Dr. Robert Martin, Head, 319-273-2097, Fax: 319-273-5846, E-mail: robert.martin@uni.edu. *Application contact:* Laurie S. Russell, Record Analyst, 319-273-2623, Fax: 319-273-6792, E-mail: laurie.russell@uni.edu.

University of North Florida, College of Arts and Sciences, Department of History, Jacksonville, FL 32224. Offers European history (MA); US history (MA). Part-time programs available. *Faculty:* 13 full-time (5 women). *Students:* 19 full-time (11 women), 18 part-time (8 women); includes 1 minority (African American). Average age 37. 12 applicants, 25% accepted, 0 enrolled. In 2009, 15 master's awarded. *Degree requirements:* For master's, comprehensive exam (for some programs), thesis optional. *Entrance requirements:* For master's, GRE General Test, 3 letters of recommendation, minimum GPA of 3.0 in last 60 hours of course work. Additional exam requirements/recommendations for international students: Required—TOEFL (minimum score 500 paper-based; 173 computer-based). *Application deadline:* For fall admission, 7/1 priority date for domestic students, 5/1 for international students; for spring admission, 11/1 priority date for domestic students, 10/1 for international students. Applications are processed on a rolling basis. Application fee: $30. Electronic applications accepted. *Expenses:* Tuition, state resident: full-time $6649.20; part-time $277.05 per credit hour. Tuition, nonresident: full-time $22,970; part-time $957.08 per credit hour. Required fees: $985; $41.03 per credit hour. *Financial support:* In 2009–10, 24 students received support, including 10 teaching assistantships (averaging $4,111 per year); career-related internships or fieldwork, Federal Work-Study, and tuition waivers (partial) also available. Support available to part-time students. Financial award application deadline: 4/1; financial award applicants required to submit FAFSA. *Unit head:* Dr. Dale Clifford, 904-620-2886, Fax: 904-620-1018, E-mail: clifford@unf.edu. *Application contact:* Dr. Phil Kaplan, Graduate Coordinator, 904-620-1863, Fax: 904-620-1018, E-mail: pkaplan@unf.edu.

University of North Texas, Robert B. Toulouse School of Graduate Studies, College of Arts and Sciences, Department of History, Denton, TX 76203. Offers MA, MS, PhD. Part-time programs available. Terminal master's awarded for partial completion of doctoral program. *Degree requirements:* For master's, one foreign language, comprehensive exam, thesis or alternative; for doctorate, 2 foreign languages, comprehensive exam, thesis/dissertation. *Entrance requirements:* For master's and doctorate, GRE General Test. Additional exam requirements/recommendations for international students: Required—proof of English language proficiency required for non-native English speakers; Recommended—TOEFL (minimum score 550 paper-based; 213 computer-based). Application fee: $50 ($75 for international students). *Expenses:* Tuition, state resident: full-time $4298; part-time $239 per contact hour. Tuition, nonresident: full-time $9878; part-time $549 per contact hour. Required fees: $265 per contact hour. *Financial support:* Fellowships with tuition reimbursements, teaching assistantships, career-related internships or fieldwork, Federal Work-Study, and institutionally sponsored loans available. Financial award application deadline: 2/15. *Faculty research:* U.S. local, Texas, women's, European and military history. *Application contact:* Undergraduate and Graduate Advisor, 940-565-4284, Fax: 940-369-8838, E-mail: krj@unt.edu.

University of Notre Dame, Graduate School, College of Arts and Letters, Division of Humanities, Department of History, Notre Dame, IN 46556. Offers MA, PhD. *Degree requirements:* For doctorate, one foreign language, thesis/dissertation, candidacy exam. *Entrance requirements:* For doctorate, GRE General Test. Additional exam requirements/recommendations for international students: Required—TOEFL (minimum score 600 paper-based; 250 computer-based; 80 iBT). Electronic applications accepted. *Faculty research:* U.S., modern European and medieval history; history of European and U.S. religions; U.S. and European intellectual and cultural history; history of Central Europe.

University of Oklahoma, Graduate College, College of Arts and Sciences, Department of History, Norman, OK 73019. Offers MA, PhD. Part-time and evening/weekend programs available. *Faculty:* 37 full-time (9 women), 1 part-time/adjunct (0 women). *Students:* 37 full-time (17 women), 23 part-time (11 women); includes 11 minority (3 American Indian/Alaska Native, 3 Asian Americans or Pacific Islanders, 5 Hispanic Americans). 27 applicants, 52% accepted, 11 enrolled. In 2009, 6 master's, 5 doctorates awarded. Terminal master's awarded for partial completion of doctoral program. *Degree requirements:* For master's, one foreign language, thesis or alternative, oral and written exams; for doctorate, 2 foreign languages, thesis/dissertation, oral and written exams. *Entrance requirements:* For master's, GRE General Test, BA with 20 hours in history; for doctorate, GRE General Test. Additional exam requirements/recommendations for international students: Required—TOEFL (minimum score 550 paper-based; 213 computer-based). *Application deadline:* For fall admission, 4/1 for domestic and international students; for spring admission, 11/1 for domestic students, 9/1 for international students. Applications are processed on a rolling basis. Application fee: $40 ($90 for international students). Electronic applications accepted. *Expenses:* Tuition, state resident: full-time $3744; part-time $156 per credit hour. Tuition, nonresident: full-time $13,577; part-time $565.70 per credit hour. Required fees: $2415; $90.10 per credit hour. *Financial support:* In 2009–10, 48 students received support, including 8 fellowships with full tuition reimbursements available (averaging $4,563 per year), 5 research assistantships with partial tuition reimbursements available (averaging $16,028 per year), 30 teaching assistantships with partial tuition reimbursements available (averaging $13,922 per year); health care benefits and unspecified assistantships also available. Financial award application deadline: 1/31. *Faculty research:* Environmental, Western, Latin American and Native American history. Total annual research expenditures: $44,816. *Unit head:* Dr. Robert L. Griswold, Chair, 405-325-6002, Fax: 405-325-4503, E-mail: rgriswold@ou.edu. *Application contact:* Dr. Terry Rugeley, Professor, 405-625-6002, Fax: 405-325-4503, E-mail: trugeley@ou.edu.

University of Oregon, Graduate School, College of Arts and Sciences, Department of History, Eugene, OR 97403. Offers MA, PhD. *Degree requirements:* For master's, one foreign language, thesis or alternative, written exam; for doctorate, 2 foreign languages, thesis/dissertation, oral and written exams. *Entrance requirements:* For master's and doctorate, GRE General Test, minimum GPA of 3.0. Additional exam requirements/recommendations for international students: Required—TOEFL. *Faculty research:* U.S., European, East and Southeast Asian, Latin American, and ancient history.

University of Ottawa, Faculty of Graduate and Postdoctoral Studies, Faculty of Arts, Department of History, Ottawa, ON K1N 6N5, Canada. Offers MA, PhD. *Degree requirements:* For master's, 2 foreign languages, thesis or alternative; for doctorate, 2 foreign languages, thesis/dissertation, oral exam. *Entrance requirements:* For master's, honors degree or equivalent, minimum B average; for doctorate, master's degree, minimum B+ average. Electronic applications accepted. *Faculty research:* Canadian history.

University of Pennsylvania, School of Arts and Sciences, Graduate Group in Ancient History, Philadelphia, PA 19104. Offers AM, PhD. *Faculty:* 13 full-time (4 women), 6 part-time/adjunct (0 women). *Students:* 14 full-time (6 women), 1 (woman) part-time; includes 1 minority (Asian American or Pacific Islander), 1 international. 30 applicants, 13% accepted, 3 enrolled. In 2009, 2 master's awarded. *Degree requirements:* For doctorate, 4 foreign languages, thesis/dissertation. *Application deadline:* For fall admission, 12/1 priority date for domestic students. Application fee: $70. Electronic applications accepted. *Expenses:* Tuition: Full-time $25,660; part-time $4758 per course. Required fees: $2152; $270 per course. Tuition and fees vary according to course load, degree level and program. *Financial support:* Institutionally sponsored loans, scholarships/grants, traineeships, health care benefits, and unspecified assistantships available. Financial award application deadline: 12/15.

University of Pennsylvania, School of Arts and Sciences, Graduate Group in History, Philadelphia, PA 19104. Offers AM, PhD. *Faculty:* 58 full-time (23 women), 7 part-time/adjunct (2 women). *Students:* 109 full-time (56 women), 5 part-time (1 woman); includes 11 minority (7 African Americans, 3 Asian Americans or Pacific Islanders, 1 Hispanic American), 21 international. 423 applicants, 9% accepted, 18 enrolled. In 2009, 7 master's, 9 doctorates awarded. Terminal master's awarded for partial completion of doctoral program. *Degree requirements:* For master's, thesis; for doctorate, one foreign language, thesis/dissertation. *Entrance requirements:* For master's and doctorate, GRE General Test. Additional exam requirements/recommendations for international students: Required—TOEFL. *Application deadline:* For fall admission, 12/1 priority date for domestic students. Application fee: $70. Electronic applications accepted. *Expenses:* Tuition: Full-time $25,660; part-time $4758 per course. Required fees: $2152; $270 per course. Tuition and fees vary according to course load, degree level and program. *Financial support:* Institutionally sponsored loans, scholarships/grants, traineeships, health care benefits, and unspecified assistantships available. Financial award application deadline: 12/15.

University of Pittsburgh, School of Arts and Sciences, Department of History, Pittsburgh, PA 15260. Offers MA, PhD. Part-time programs available. *Faculty:* 24 full-time (6 women), 10 part-time/adjunct (2 women). *Students:* 41 full-time (16 women); includes 12 minority (3 African Americans, 2 Asian Americans or Pacific Islanders, 7 Hispanic Americans). 151 applicants, 11% accepted, 7 enrolled. In 2009, 7 master's, 4 doctorates awarded. Terminal master's awarded for partial completion of doctoral program. *Degree requirements:* For master's, one foreign language, oral exam, 1 seminar paper; for doctorate, 2 foreign languages, comprehensive exam, thesis/dissertation. *Entrance requirements:* For master's and doctorate, GRE General Test. Additional exam requirements/recommendations for international students: Required—TOEFL (minimum score 88 computer-based). *Application deadline:* For fall admission, 1/15 for domestic and international students. Application fee: $50. Electronic applications accepted. *Expenses:* Tuition, state resident: full-time $16,402; part-time $665 per credit. Tuition, nonresident: full-time $28,694; part-time $1175 per credit. Required fees: $690; $175 per term. Tuition and fees vary according to program. *Financial support:* In 2009–10, 5 fellowships with tuition reimbursements (averaging $13,995 per year), 24 teaching assistantships with tuition reimbursements (averaging $14,777 per year) were awarded; Federal Work-Study, scholarships/grants, and tuition waivers (full and partial) also available. Financial award application deadline: 1/15. *Faculty research:* Western Europe, Latin America, Russia, Eastern Europe, U. S., East Asia. *Unit head:* Dr. Marcus Rediker, Chairman, 412-648-7452, Fax: 412-648-9074. *Application contact:* Molly Estes, Graduate Secretary, 412-648-7454, Fax: 412-648-9074, E-mail: wid2@pitt.edu.

University of Puerto Rico, Río Piedras, College of Humanities, Department of History, San Juan, PR 00931-3300. Offers Caribbean history (PhD); history (MA); Puerto Rican history (PhD). Part-time programs available. *Degree requirements:* For master's, one foreign language, comprehensive exam, thesis; for doctorate, one foreign language, comprehensive exam, thesis/dissertation. *Entrance requirements:* For master's, PAEG or GRE, interview, minimum GPA of 3.0, 2 letters of recommendation; for doctorate, PAEG or GRE, interview, master's degree, minimum GPA of 3.0, 2 letters of recommendation.

University of Regina, Faculty of Graduate Studies and Research, Faculty of Arts, Department of History, Regina, SK S4S 0A2, Canada. Offers MA, PhD. *Faculty:* 13 full-time (2 women). *Students:* 4 full-time (2 women), 3 part-time (0 women). 3 applicants, 67% accepted. In 2009, 5 master's awarded. *Degree requirements:* For master's, thesis. *Entrance requirements:* Additional exam requirements/recommendations for international students: Required—TOEFL (minimum score 580 paper-based; 237 computer-based; 80 iBT). *Application deadline:* Applications are processed on a rolling basis. Application fee: $90 ($100 for international students). Electronic applications accepted. *Financial support:* In 2009–10, 1 fellowship (averaging $19,000 per year), 5 teaching assistantships (averaging $6,650 per year) were awarded; research assistantships, scholarships/grants also available. Financial award application deadline: 6/15. *Faculty research:* Canadian, English, United States, European, Asian, British, and Latin-American history. *Unit head:* Dr. Thomas Bredohl, Head, 306-585-4155, Fax: 306-585-4827, E-mail: thomas.bredohl@uregina.ca. *Application contact:* Dr. Philip Charrier, Graduate Program Coordinator, 306-585-4215, E-mail: philip.charrier@uregina.ca.

University of Rhode Island, Graduate School, College of Arts and Sciences, Department of History, Kingston, RI 02881. Offers MA, MA/PhD, MLIS/MA. Part-time programs available. *Faculty:* 15 full-time (9 women), 2 part-time/adjunct (1 woman). *Students:* 9 full-time (3 women), 5 part-time (1 woman). In 2009, 4 master's awarded. *Degree requirements:* For master's, comprehensive exam (for some programs), thesis optional. *Entrance requirements:* For master's, GRE, 2 letters of recommendation. Additional exam requirements/recommendations for international students: Required—TOEFL (minimum score 550 paper-based; 213 computer-based). *Application deadline:* For fall admission, 7/15 for domestic students, 2/1 for international students; for spring admission, 11/15 for domestic students, 7/15 for international students. Application fee: $65. Electronic applications accepted. *Expenses:* Tuition, state resident: full-time $8828; part-time $490 per credit hour. Tuition, nonresident: full-time $22,100; part-time $1228 per credit hour. Required fees: $1118; $57 per semester. Tuition and fees vary according to program. *Financial support:* In 2009–10, 3 teaching assistantships with full tuition reimbursements (averaging $13,894 per year) were awarded. Financial award application deadline: 2/1; financial award applicants required to submit FAFSA. Total annual research expenditures: $79,478. *Unit head:* Dr. Marie J. Schwartz, Chair, 401-874-4090, Fax: 401-874-2595, E-mail: schwartz@uri.edu. *Application contact:* Dr. Evelyn Sterne, Director of Graduate Studies, 401-874-4074, Fax: 401-874-2595, E-mail: sterne@mail.uri.edu.

University of Rochester, The College, Arts and Sciences, Department of History, Rochester, NY 14627. Offers MA, PhD. Terminal master's awarded for partial completion of doctoral program. *Degree requirements:* For master's, one foreign language, thesis or alternative; for doctorate, 2 foreign languages, thesis/dissertation, comprehensive oral exam, qualifying exam. *Entrance requirements:* For master's and doctorate, GRE General Test, sample of written work. Additional exam requirements/recommendations for international students: Required—TOEFL.

University of San Diego, College of Arts and Sciences, Department of History, San Diego, CA 92110-2492. Offers MA. Part-time and evening/weekend programs available. *Faculty:* 3 full-time (1 woman). *Students:* 6 full-time (3 women), 20 part-time (8 women); includes 7 minority (2 African Americans, 5 Hispanic Americans), 1 international. Average age 30. 26 applicants, 81% accepted, 10 enrolled. In 2009, 10 master's awarded. *Degree requirements:* For master's, thesis. *Entrance requirements:* For master's, GRE General Test, minimum GPA of 3.0. Additional exam requirements/recommendations for international students: Required—TOEFL (minimum score 580 paper-based; 237 computer-based; 83 iBT), TWE. *Application deadline:* For fall admission, 8/31 for domestic and international students; for spring admission, 11/15 for domestic and international students. Applications are processed on a rolling basis. Application fee: $45. Electronic applications accepted. *Expenses:* Tuition: Full-time $21,042; part-time $1169 per unit. Required fees: $224. Full-time tuition and fees vary according to course load and degree level. *Financial support:* In 2009–10, 18 students received support. Career-related internships or fieldwork, Federal Work-Study, institutionally sponsored loans, and unspecified assistantships available. Support available to part-time students. Financial award application deadline: 4/1; financial award applicants required to submit FAFSA. *Faculty research:* History of the American West, history of California, history of Mexico and Latin America, public history, environmental history. *Unit head:* Dr. Michael Gonzalez, Graduate Program Director, 619-260-4756, Fax: 619-260-2272, E-mail: michaelg@sandiego.edu. *Application contact:* Dr. John Mosby, Associate Director of Graduate Admissions, 619-260-4524, Fax: 619-260-4158, E-mail: grads@sandiego.edu.

University of Saskatchewan, College of Graduate Studies and Research, College of Arts and Sciences, Department of History, Saskatoon, SK S7N 5A2, Canada. Offers MA, PhD. Part-time programs available. *Faculty:* 35. *Students:* 68. In 2009, 9 master's, 3 doctorates awarded. *Degree requirements:* For master's, thesis; for doctorate, comprehensive exam (for some programs), thesis/dissertation. *Entrance requirements:* Additional exam requirements/recommendations for international students: Required—TOEFL (minimum score 80 iBT); Recommended—IELTS (minimum score 6.5). *Application deadline:* For fall admission, 7/1 priority date for domestic students. Applications are processed on a rolling basis. Application fee: $75. Electronic applications accepted. Tuition and fees charges are reported in Canadian dollars. *Expenses:* Tuition, area resident: Full-time $3000 Canadian dollars; part-time $500 Canadian dollars per term. Required fees: $700 Canadian dollars; $100 Canadian dollars per term. *Financial support:* Fellowships, research assistantships, teaching assistantships available. Financial award application deadline: 1/31. *Unit head:* Dr. Valerie Korinek, Head, 306-966-5805, Fax: 306-966-5852, E-mail: valerie.korinek@usask.ca. *Application contact:* Dr. Geoff Cunfer, Graduate Chair, 306-966-5990, Fax: 306-966-5852, E-mail: geoff.cunfer@usask.ca.

The University of Scranton, College of Graduate and Continuing Education, Department of History, Scranton, PA 18510. Offers MA. Part-time and evening/weekend programs available. *Faculty:* 11 full-time (2 women). *Students:* 7 full-time (4 women), 6 part-time (1 woman). Average age 27. In 2009, 5 master's awarded. *Degree requirements:* For master's, comprehensive exam, thesis (for some programs), capstone experience. *Entrance requirements:* For master's, minimum GPA of 2.75. Additional exam requirements/recommendations for international students: Required—TOEFL (minimum score 500 paper-based; 173 computer-based), IELTS (minimum score 5.5). *Application deadline:* Applications are processed on a rolling basis. Application fee: $0. *Financial support:* In 2009–10, 2 students received support, including 2 teaching assistantships with full tuition reimbursements available (averaging $6,600 per year); fellowships, career-related internships or fieldwork, Federal Work-Study, and unspecified assistantships also available. Support available to part-time students. Financial award application deadline: 3/1. *Faculty research:* American, European, Latin American, Russian, and Chinese history. *Unit head:* Dr. Robert W. Shaffern, Director, 570-941-4360, Fax: 570-941-7625. *Application contact:* Joseph M. Roback, Director of Admissions, 570-941-4385, Fax: 570-941-5928, E-mail: robackj2@scranton.edu.

University of South Africa, College of Human Sciences, Pretoria, South Africa. Offers adult education (M Ed); African languages (MA, PhD); African politics (MA, PhD); Afrikaans (MA, PhD); ancient history (MA, PhD); ancient Near Eastern studies (MA, PhD); anthropology (MA, PhD); applied linguistics (MA); Arabic (MA, PhD); archaeology (MA); art history (MA); Biblical archaeology (MA); Biblical studies (M Th, D Th, PhD); Christian spirituality (M Th, D Th); church history (M Th, D Th); classical studies (MA, PhD); clinical psychology (MA); communication (MA, PhD); comparative education (M Ed, Ed D); consulting psychology (D Admin, D Com, PhD); curriculum studies (M Ed, Ed D); development studies (M Admin, MA, D Admin, PhD); didactics (M Ed, Ed D); education (M Tech); education management (M Ed, Ed D); educational psychology (M Ed); English (MA); environmental education (M Ed); French (MA, PhD); German (MA, PhD); Greek (MA); guidance and counseling (M Ed); health studies (MA, PhD), including health sciences education (MA), health services management (MA), medical and surgical nursing science (critical care general) (MA), midwifery and neonatal nursing science (MA), trauma and emergency care (MA); history (MA, PhD); history of education (Ed D); inclusive education (M Ed, Ed D); information and communications technology policy and regulation (MA); information science (MA, MIS, PhD); international politics (MA, PhD); Islamic studies (MA, PhD); Italian (MA, PhD); Judaica (MA, PhD); linguistics (MA, PhD); mathematical education (M Ed); mathematics education (MA); missiology (M Th, D Th); modern Hebrew (MA, PhD); musicology (MA, MMus, D Mus, PhD); natural science education (M Ed); New Testament (M Th, D Th); Old Testament (D Th); pastoral therapy (M Th, D Th); philosophy (MA); philosophy of education (M Ed, Ed D); politics (MA, PhD); Portuguese (MA, PhD); practical theology (M Th, D Th); psychology (MA, MS, PhD); psychology of education (M Ed, Ed D); public health (MA); religious studies (MA, D Th, PhD); Romance languages (MA);

History

University of South Africa (continued)
Russian (MA, PhD); Semitic languages (MA, PhD); social behavior studies in HIV/AIDS (MA); social science (mental health) (MA); social science in development studies (MA); social science in psychology (MA); social science in social work (MA); social science in sociology (MA); social work (MSW, DSW, PhD); socio-education (M Ed, Ed D); sociolinguistics (MA); sociology (MA, PhD); Spanish (MA, PhD); systematic theology (M Th, D Th); TESOL (teaching English to speakers of other languages) (MA); theological ethics (M Th, D Th); theory of literature (MA, PhD); urban ministries (D Th); urban ministry (M Th).

University of South Alabama, Graduate School, College of Arts and Sciences, Department of History, Mobile, AL 36688-0002. Offers MA. Part-time and evening/weekend programs available. *Degree requirements:* For master's, one foreign language, comprehensive exam, thesis optional. *Entrance requirements:* For master's, GRE General Test, GRE Subject Test, 21 hours of course work in history, minimum GPA of 3.0. *Expenses:* Tuition, state resident: part-time $218 per contact hour. Required fees: $1102 per year.

University of South Carolina, The Graduate School, College of Arts and Sciences, Department of History, Columbia, SC 29208. Offers history (MA, PhD); public history (MA, Certificate), including archives (MA), historic preservation (MA), museum (MA), museum management (Certificate); MLIS/MA. IMA and MAT offered in cooperation with the College of Education. Part-time programs available. Terminal master's awarded for partial completion of doctoral program. *Degree requirements:* For master's, one foreign language, thesis; for doctorate, one foreign language, thesis/dissertation. *Entrance requirements:* For master's and doctorate, GRE General Test. Additional exam requirements/recommendations for international students: Required—TOEFL. Electronic applications accepted. *Faculty research:* U.S. history; European history; Latin American history; history of science and technology.

The University of South Dakota, Graduate School, College of Arts and Sciences, Department of History, Vermillion, SD 57069-2390. Offers MA, JD/MA. Part-time programs available. *Degree requirements:* For master's, thesis (for some programs). *Entrance requirements:* For master's, GRE General Test, minimum GPA of 2.7. Additional exam requirements/recommendations for international students: Required—TOEFL (minimum score 550 paper-based; 213 computer-based; 79 iBT). Electronic applications accepted.

University of Southern California, Graduate School, College of Letters, Arts and Sciences, Department of History, Los Angeles, CA 90089. Offers MA, PhD. MA is incidental for PhD students. *Faculty:* 30 full-time (15 women). *Students:* 63 full-time (34 women); includes 13 minority (2 African Americans, 3 Asian Americans or Pacific Islanders, 8 Hispanic Americans), 9 international. 103 applicants, 15% accepted, 9 enrolled. In 2009, 10 master's, 8 doctorates awarded. Terminal master's awarded for partial completion of doctoral program. *Degree requirements:* For master's, comprehensive exam (for some programs), thesis (for some programs); for doctorate, 2 foreign languages, comprehensive exam, thesis/dissertation, 60 units of course work. *Entrance requirements:* For master's, no admission for MA level study only; for doctorate, GRE, American BA or equivalent; minumum GPA of 3.0 or equivalent. *Application deadline:* For fall admission, 12/1 for domestic and international students. Application fee: $85. Electronic applications accepted. *Expenses:* Tuition: Full-time $25,980; part-time $1315 per unit. Required fees: $554. One-time fee: $35 full-time. Full-time tuition and fees vary according to degree level and program. *Financial support:* In 2009–10, 59 students received support, including 16 fellowships with full tuition reimbursements available (averaging $19,000 per year), 9 research assistantships with full tuition reimbursements available (averaging $19,000 per year), 28 teaching assistantships with full tuition reimbursements available (averaging $19,000 per year); scholarships/grants and health care benefits also available. Financial award application deadline: 12/1. *Faculty research:* American/United States, Latin American, European, East Asian, Middle East. *Unit head:* Prof. William J. Deverell, Director of Graduate Studies, 213-740-1657, Fax: 213-740-6999, E-mail: deverell@usc.edu. *Application contact:* Dr. Joseph A. Styles, Graduate Advisor, 213-740-1659, Fax: 213-740-6999, E-mail: styles@usc.edu.

University of Southern Mississippi, Graduate School, College of Arts and Letters, Department of History, Hattiesburg, MS 39406-0001. Offers MA, MS, PhD. Part-time programs available. *Faculty:* 18 full-time (6 women). *Students:* 31 full-time (7 women), 21 part-time (8 women), 1 international. Average age 33. 34 applicants, 56% accepted, 12 enrolled. In 2009, 10 master's, 1 doctorate awarded. *Degree requirements:* For master's, one foreign language, comprehensive exam, thesis (for some programs); for doctorate, 2 foreign languages, comprehensive exam, thesis/dissertation. *Entrance requirements:* For master's, GRE General Test, minimum GPA of 3.0 in field of study, 2.75 in last 2 years; for doctorate, GRE General Test, minimum GPA of 3.5. Additional exam requirements/recommendations for international students: Required—TOEFL. *Application deadline:* For fall admission, 3/1 priority date for domestic students, 3/1 for international students. Applications are processed on a rolling basis. Application fee: $35. *Expenses:* Tuition, state resident: full-time $5096; part-time $284 per hour. Tuition, nonresident: full-time $13,052; part-time $726 per hour. Required fees: $402. Tuition and fees vary according to course level and course load. *Financial support:* In 2009–10, 1 fellowship with full tuition reimbursement (averaging $12,000 per year), 1 research assistantship with full tuition reimbursement (averaging $12,000 per year), 20 teaching assistantships with full tuition reimbursements (averaging $9,000 per year) were awarded; Federal Work-Study, scholarships/grants, and unspecified assistantships also available. Financial award application deadline: 3/15; financial award applicants required to submit FAFSA. *Faculty research:* Civil War, civil rights, modern European history, war history. *Unit head:* Dr. Phyllis Jestice, Chair, 601-266-4333, Fax: 601-266-4334. *Application contact:* Dr. Michael Niebarg, Graduate Coordinator, 601-266-4333, Fax: 601-266-4334.

University of South Florida, Graduate School, College of Arts and Sciences, Department of History, Tampa, FL 33620-9951. Offers MA, PhD. Part-time and evening/weekend programs available. *Faculty:* 19 full-time (6 women). *Students:* 19 full-time (7 women), 32 part-time (14 women); includes 5 minority (all Hispanic Americans). Average age 32. 62 applicants, 35% accepted, 12 enrolled. In 2009, 16 master's awarded. *Degree requirements:* For master's, one foreign language, comprehensive exam, thesis optional; for doctorate, variable foreign language requirement, comprehensive exam, thesis/dissertation. *Entrance requirements:* For master's, GRE General Test (minimum score 500 verbal, 500 quantitative, 4.5 writing), minimum GPA of 3.0, 2 letters of recommendation, writing sample; for doctorate, GRE General Test (minimum score 500 verbal, 500 quantitative, 4.5 writing), minimum GPA of 3.0, MA in history or directly related field, writing sample, foreign language proficiency. Additional exam requirements/recommendations for international students: Required—TOEFL (minimum score 550 paper-based; 213 computer-based). *Application deadline:* For fall admission, 1/15 priority date for domestic students, 1/15 for international students. Applications are processed on a rolling basis. Application fee: $30. Electronic applications accepted. *Financial support:* In 2009–10, teaching assistantships with tuition reimbursements (averaging $15,000 per year); unspecified assistantships also available. Financial award application deadline: 1/15. *Faculty research:* U. S. history, European history, Latin American history, medieval history, ancient history. Total annual research expenditures: $213,413. *Unit head:* Dr. Fraser Ottanelli, Chairperson, 813-974-6209, Fax: 813-974-6228, E-mail: ottanelli@usf.edu. *Application contact:* Barbara Berglund, Program Director, 813-974-6225, Fax: 813-974-6228, E-mail: bberglun@usf.edu.

The University of Tennessee, Graduate School, College of Arts and Sciences, Department of History, Knoxville, TN 37996. Offers American history (PhD); European history (PhD); history (MA). Part-time programs available. *Degree requirements:* For master's, thesis or alternative; for doctorate, one foreign language, thesis/dissertation. *Entrance requirements:* For master's and doctorate, GRE General Test, minimum GPA of 2.7. Additional exam requirements/recommendations for international students: Required—TOEFL. Electronic applications accepted. *Expenses:* Tuition, state resident: full-time $6826; part-time $380 per semester hour. Tuition, nonresident: full-time $21,844; part-time $1147 per semester hour. Tuition and fees vary according to program.

The University of Texas at Arlington, Graduate School, College of Liberal Arts, Department of History, Arlington, TX 76019. Offers history (MA); transatlantic history (PhD). Part-time and evening/weekend programs available. *Faculty:* 21 full-time (5 women), 2 part-time/adjunct (0 women). *Students:* 38 full-time (18 women), 79 part-time (26 women); includes 15 minority (4 African Americans, 1 American Indian/Alaska Native, 3 Asian Americans or Pacific Islanders, 7 Hispanic Americans). 42 applicants, 100% accepted, 28 enrolled. In 2009, 15 master's, 2 doctorates awarded. *Degree requirements:* For master's, one foreign language, comprehensive exam (for some programs), thesis (for some programs); for doctorate, one foreign language, comprehensive exam, thesis/dissertation. *Entrance requirements:* For master's, GRE General Test, minimum GPA of 3.0 in last 60 hours, 3 letters of recommendation; for doctorate, GRE General Test, minimum graduate GPA of 3.5, 3 letters of recommendation, academic writing sample. Additional exam requirements/recommendations for international students: Required—TOEFL (minimum score 550 paper-based; 213 computer-based). *Application deadline:* For fall admission, 6/16 for domestic students. Applications are processed on a rolling basis. Application fee: $35 ($50 for international students). *Financial support:* In 2009–10, 4 fellowships with full tuition reimbursements (averaging $2,000 per year), 4 research assistantships (averaging $9,467 per year), 22 teaching assistantships (averaging $12,000 per year) were awarded; career-related internships or fieldwork also available. Financial award application deadline: 5/1; financial award applicants required to submit FAFSA. *Unit head:* Dr. Robert Fairbanks, Chair, 817-272-2861, Fax: 817-272-2852, E-mail: history@uta.edu. *Application contact:* Dr. Thomas Adam, Graduate Advisor, 817-272-2861, Fax: 817-272-2852, E-mail: adam@uta.edu.

The University of Texas at Austin, Graduate School, College of Liberal Arts, Department of History, Austin, TX 78712-1111. Offers MA, PhD. *Degree requirements:* For doctorate, thesis/dissertation. *Entrance requirements:* For master's and doctorate, GRE General Test. Electronic applications accepted. *Faculty research:* U.S., Latin American, European, African, Asian, and Middle Eastern history.

The University of Texas at Brownsville, Graduate Studies, College of Liberal Arts, Department of History, Brownsville, TX 78520-4991. Offers MAIS. Part-time and evening/weekend programs available. *Degree requirements:* For master's, comprehensive exam, thesis optional. *Entrance requirements:* For master's, GRE General Test. Additional exam requirements/recommendations for international students: Required—TOEFL.

The University of Texas at El Paso, Graduate School, College of Liberal Arts, Department of History, El Paso, TX 79968-0001. Offers border history (MA); borderlands history (PhD); history (MA). Part-time and evening/weekend programs available. *Students:* 70 (35 women); includes 50 minority (3 African Americans, 1 Asian American or Pacific Islander, 46 Hispanic Americans), 2 international. Average age 34. In 2009, 7 master's, 1 doctorate awarded. *Degree requirements:* For master's, thesis optional; for doctorate, thesis/dissertation. *Entrance requirements:* For master's, GRE, minimum GPA of 3.0, writing sample, letters of recommendation; for doctorate, GRE, Statement of Purpose, Writing Sample, Letters of Recommendation. Additional exam requirements/recommendations for international students: Required—TOEFL; Recommended—IELTS. *Application deadline:* For fall admission, 8/1 for domestic students, 3/1 for international students; for spring admission, 12/15 priority date for domestic students, 9/1 for international students. Applications are processed on a rolling basis. Application fee: $45 ($80 for international students). Electronic applications accepted. *Financial support:* In 2009–10, research assistantships with partial tuition reimbursements (averaging $21,125 per year), teaching assistantships with partial tuition reimbursements (averaging $16,900 per year) were awarded; fellowships with partial tuition reimbursements, institutionally sponsored loans, scholarships/grants, health care benefits, tuition waivers (partial), and unspecified assistantships also available. Support available to part-time students. Financial award application deadline: 3/15; financial award applicants required to submit FAFSA. *Unit head:* Dr. Paul Edison, Chair, 915-747-5508, Fax: 915-747-5948, E-mail: pedison@utep.edu. *Application contact:* Dr. Patricia D. Witherspoon, Dean of the Graduate School, 915-747-5491, Fax: 915-747-5788, E-mail: withersp@utep.edu.

The University of Texas at San Antonio, College of Liberal and Fine Arts, Department of History, San Antonio, TX 78249-0617. Offers MA. Part-time and evening/weekend programs available. *Faculty:* 11 full-time (4 women). *Students:* 24 full-time (14 women), 60 part-time (24 women); includes 31 minority (1 African American, 1 American Indian/Alaska Native, 2 Asian Americans or Pacific Islanders, 27 Hispanic Americans). Average age 34. 26 applicants, 88% accepted, 15 enrolled. In 2009, 14 master's awarded. *Degree requirements:* For master's, comprehensive exam (for some programs), thesis (for some programs). *Entrance requirements:* For master's, GRE, minimum GPA of 3.0 in last 60 hours. Additional exam requirements/recommendations for international students: Required—TOEFL (minimum score 500 paper-based; 173 computer-based; 61 iBT), IELTS (minimum score 5). *Application deadline:* For fall admission, 7/1 for domestic students, 4/1 for international students; for spring admission, 11/1 for domestic students, 9/1 for international students. Applications are processed on a rolling basis. Application fee: $45 ($80 for international students). Electronic applications accepted. *Expenses:* Tuition, state resident: full-time $3975; part-time $221 per contact hour. Tuition, nonresident: full-time $13,947; part-time $775 per contact hour. Required fees: $1853. *Financial support:* In 2009–10, 35 students received support, including 9 research assistantships (averaging $8,106 per year); career-related internships or fieldwork, scholarships/grants, tuition waivers, and unspecified assistantships also available. Total annual research expenditures: $7,537. *Unit head:* Dr. John Reynolds, Chair, 210-458-4033, Fax: 210-458-4796, E-mail: history@utsa.edu. *Application contact:* Gregg Michel, Graduate Advisor, 210-458-5701, E-mail: gregg.michel@utsa.edu.

The University of Texas at Tyler, College of Arts and Sciences, Department of History, Tyler, TX 75799-0001. Offers history (MA). Part-time and evening/weekend programs available. *Faculty:* 6 full-time (2 women). *Students:* 1 full-time (0 women), 16 part-time (6 women); includes 1 Hispanic American. Average age 38. 8 applicants, 100% accepted, 6 enrolled. In 2009, 4 master's awarded. *Degree requirements:* For master's, one foreign language, comprehensive exam, thesis optional. *Entrance requirements:* For master's, GRE General Test, minimum GPA of 3.0. Additional exam requirements/recommendations for international students: Required—TOEFL (minimum score 79 computer-based). *Application deadline:* For fall admission, 8/17 priority date for domestic students, 7/1 priority date for international students; for spring admission, 12/21 priority date for domestic students, 11/1 priority date for international students. Applications are processed on a rolling basis. Application fee: $25 ($50 for international students). Electronic applications accepted. *Expenses:* Tuition, state resident: part-time $665 per semester hour. Tuition, nonresident: part-time $942 per semester hour. Part-time tuition and fees vary according to degree level and program. *Financial support:* Federal Work-Study and unspecified assistantships available. Support available to part-time students. Financial award application deadline: 7/1; financial award applicants required to submit FAFSA. *Faculty research:* Early and modern U.S. history, early modern and modern European history. *Unit head:* Dr. Mary C. Linehan, Chair, 903-566-7395, Fax: 903-565-5700, E-mail: clinehan@uttyler.edu. *Application contact:* Dr. Patricia A. Gajda, Professor, 903-566-7440, Fax: 903-565-5700, E-mail: pgajda@uttyler.edu.

The University of Texas of the Permian Basin, Office of Graduate Studies, College of Arts and Sciences, Department of History, Odessa, TX 79762-0001. Offers MA. Part-time and evening/weekend programs available. *Degree requirements:* For master's, comprehensive exam (for some programs), thesis (for some programs). *Entrance requirements:* For master's, GRE General Test. Additional exam requirements/recommendations for international students: Required—TOEFL (minimum score 550 paper-based; 213 computer-based).

The University of Texas–Pan American, College of Arts and Humanities, Department of History, Edinburg, TX 78539. Offers MA, MAIS. Part-time and evening/weekend programs available. *Degree requirements:* For master's, comprehensive exam, thesis or alternative. *Entrance requirements:* For master's, GRE General Test, minimum GPA of 3.0. *Expenses:* Tuition, state resident: full-time $3630.60; part-time $201.70 per credit hour. Tuition, nonresident:

full-time $8617; part-time $478.70 per credit hour. Required fees: $806.50. *Faculty research:* Texas-Mexican legacy, modern America, Southwest, labor, modern Europe.

The University of Toledo, College of Graduate Studies, College of Arts and Sciences, Department of History, Toledo, OH 43606-3390. Offers MA, PhD. Part-time programs available. *Degree requirements:* For doctorate, one foreign language, thesis/dissertation, oral and written exams. *Entrance requirements:* For master's, GRE General Test, minimum GPA of 2.7; for doctorate, GRE General Test, minimum GPA of 3.0. Electronic applications accepted. *Faculty research:* U.S. diplomatic history, U.S. history, urban history, public history, European history.

University of Toronto, School of Graduate Studies, Humanities Division, Department of History, Toronto, ON M5S 1A1, Canada. Offers MA, PhD. Part-time programs available. *Degree requirements:* For master's, one foreign language, thesis or research essay, French language exam; for doctorate, comprehensive exam, thesis/dissertation, oral examination/thesis defense. *Entrance requirements:* For master's, minimum B+ average or GPA of 3.3, 6 full academic year history courses; for doctorate, MA in history, minimum A– average or GPA of 3.7.

University of Tulsa, Graduate School, College of Arts and Sciences, Department of History, Tulsa, OK 74104-3189. Offers MA, MTA, JD/MA. Part-time programs available. *Faculty:* 10 full-time (2 women), 1 (woman) part-time/adjunct. *Students:* 4 full-time (3 women), 5 part-time (2 women); includes 1 minority (American Indian/Alaska Native). Average age 35. 8 applicants, 63% accepted, 4 enrolled. In 2009, 6 master's awarded. *Degree requirements:* For master's, one foreign language, comprehensive exam or oral defense of thesis. *Entrance requirements:* For master's, GRE General Test, writing sample. Additional exam requirements/recommendations for international students: Required—TOEFL (minimum score 575 paper-based; 231 computer-based; 91 iBT), IELTS (minimum score 6.5). *Application deadline:* Applications are processed on a rolling basis. Application fee: $40. Electronic applications accepted. *Expenses:* Tuition: Full-time $16,182; part-time $899 per credit hour. Required fees: $4 per credit hour. Tuition and fees vary according to course load. *Financial support:* In 2009–10, 5 students received support, including 5 teaching assistantships with full and partial tuition reimbursements available (averaging $10,435 per year); fellowships with full and partial tuition reimbursements available, research assistantships, Federal Work-Study, scholarships/grants, health care benefits, tuition waivers (full and partial), and unspecified assistantships also available. Support available to part-time students. Financial award application deadline: 2/1; financial award applicants required to submit FAFSA. *Faculty research:* United States history, modern European history, comparative history. *Unit head:* Dr. Thomas Buoye, Chairperson, 918-631-2825, Fax: 918-631-2057, E-mail: thomas-buoye@utulsa.edu. *Application contact:* Dr. Christine Ruane, Adviser, 918-631-3814, Fax: 918-631-2057, E-mail: christine-ruane@utulsa.edu.

University of Utah, The Graduate School, College of Humanities, Department of History, Salt Lake City, UT 84112. Offers MA, MS, PhD. Part-time and evening/weekend programs available. *Faculty:* 26 full-time (7 women). *Students:* 36 full-time (16 women), 28 part-time (13 women); includes 6 minority (3 Asian Americans or Pacific Islanders, 3 Hispanic Americans), 4 international. Average age 34. 78 applicants, 35% accepted, 23 enrolled. In 2009, 13 master's, 2 doctorates awarded. Terminal master's awarded for partial completion of doctoral program. *Degree requirements:* For master's, one foreign language, comprehensive exam (for some programs), thesis (for some programs); for doctorate, 2 foreign languages, comprehensive exam, thesis/dissertation. *Entrance requirements:* For master's, GRE General Test, minimum GPA of 3.2; for doctorate, GRE General Test, minimum graduate GPA of 3.6. Additional exam requirements/recommendations for international students: Required—TOEFL (minimum score 500 paper-based; 173 computer-based). *Application deadline:* For fall admission, 1/15 for domestic and international students. Application fee: $55 ($65 for international students). Electronic applications accepted. *Expenses:* Tuition, state resident: full-time $4004; part-time $1674 per semester. Tuition, nonresident: full-time $14,134; part-time $5915 per semester. Required fees: $324 per semester. Tuition and fees vary according to course load, degree level and program. *Financial support:* In 2009–10, 13 students received support, including 3 fellowships (averaging $12,000 per year), 14 teaching assistantships with full tuition reimbursements available (averaging $11,000 per year); career-related internships or fieldwork also available. Financial award application deadline: 1/15; financial award applicants required to submit FAFSA. *Faculty research:* U. S. history, European history, Asian History, Middle East, Latin America. Total annual research expenditures: $56,210. *Unit head:* Prof. James Lehning, Chair, 801-581-5685, Fax: 801-585-0580, E-mail: jim.lehning@utah.edu. *Application contact:* Karleton Munn, Graduate Secretary, 801-581-6121, Fax: 801-585-0580, E-mail: karleton.munn@utah.edu.

University of Utah, The Graduate School, College of Humanities, Program in Middle East Studies, Salt Lake City, UT 84112. Offers anthropology (MA); Arabic (MA, PhD); Arabic and linguistics (MA, PhD); Hebrew (MA); history (MA, PhD); Persian (MA, PhD); political science (MA, PhD); Turkish (MA). *Students:* 24 full-time (8 women), 19 part-time (9 women), 13 international. Average age 33. 33 applicants, 48% accepted, 10 enrolled. In 2009, 8 master's, 2 doctorates awarded. Terminal master's awarded for partial completion of doctoral program. *Degree requirements:* For master's, 2 foreign languages, comprehensive exam, thesis optional; for doctorate, 3 foreign languages, comprehensive exam, thesis/dissertation. *Entrance requirements:* For master's, GRE General Test, minimum GPA of 3.2; for doctorate, GRE General Test, MA in Middle East studies or equivalent, minimum GPA of 3.2. Additional exam requirements/recommendations for international students: Required—TOEFL (minimum score 580 paper-based; 237 computer-based; 92 iBT). *Application deadline:* For fall admission, 1/15 priority date for domestic and international students; for spring admission, 9/15 priority date for domestic and international students. Application fee: $55 ($65 for international students). Electronic applications accepted. *Expenses:* Tuition, state resident: full-time $4004; part-time $1674 per semester. Tuition, nonresident: full-time $14,134; part-time $5915 per semester. Required fees: $324 per semester. Tuition and fees vary according to course load, degree level and program. *Financial support:* In 2009–10, 19 students received support, including 15 fellowships with full tuition reimbursements available (averaging $14,000 per year), 3 teaching assistantships with full tuition reimbursements available (averaging $12,000 per year); unspecified assistantships also available. Financial award application deadline: 1/15. *Faculty research:* Arabic linguistics; Islamic studies; Middle Eastern history; political science; Judaic studies; anthropology; Arabic, Persian, Hebrew, and Turkish language and literature. *Unit head:* Dr. Bahman Baktiari, Director, 801-581-6181, Fax: 801-581-6183, E-mail: b.baktiari@utah.edu. *Application contact:* Peter von Sivers, Director of Graduate Studies, 801-581-9028, Fax: 801-581-6183, E-mail: peter.vonsivers@utah.edu.

University of Vermont, Graduate College, College of Arts and Sciences, Department of History, Burlington, VT 05405. Offers MA. *Students:* 21 (11 women); includes 2 minority (1 American Indian/Alaska Native, 1 Asian American or Pacific Islander). 33 applicants, 55% accepted, 10 enrolled. In 2009, 10 master's awarded. *Degree requirements:* For master's, thesis. *Entrance requirements:* For master's, GRE General Test, sample project. Additional exam requirements/recommendations for international students: Required—TOEFL (minimum score 550 paper-based; 213 computer-based; 80 iBT). *Application deadline:* For fall admission, 5/1 priority date for domestic students. Applications are processed on a rolling basis. Application fee: $40. Electronic applications accepted. *Expenses:* Tuition, state resident: part-time $508 per credit hour. Tuition, nonresident: part-time $1281 per credit hour. *Financial support:* Fellowships, research assistantships, teaching assistantships, career-related internships or fieldwork available. Financial award application deadline: 3/1. *Faculty research:* American, European, and Asian history. *Unit head:* Dr. Steven Zdatny, Chair, 802-656-3180. *Application contact:* Dr. Paul Deslandes, Coordinator, 802-656-3180.

University of Victoria, Faculty of Graduate Studies, Faculty of Humanities, Department of History, Victoria, BC V8W 2Y2, Canada. Offers MA, PhD. Part-time programs available. *Degree requirements:* For master's, one foreign language, thesis; for doctorate, one foreign language, comprehensive exam, thesis/dissertation. *Entrance requirements:* Additional exam requirements/recommendations for international students: Required—TOEFL (minimum score 600 paper-based; 250 computer-based), TWE. Electronic applications accepted. *Faculty research:* Canadian social history, Canadian gender history, Canadian native history, Canadian military history, British Columbian history, Western history, medieval history, world history.

University of Virginia, College and Graduate School of Arts and Sciences, Department of History, Charlottesville, VA 22903. Offers MA, PhD, JD/MA. *Faculty:* 47 full-time (12 women), 8 part-time/adjunct (1 woman). *Students:* 118 full-time (43 women), 1 part-time (0 women); includes 5 minority (2 African Americans, 1 Asian American or Pacific Islander, 2 Hispanic Americans), 13 international. Average age 29. 216 applicants, 25% accepted, 24 enrolled. In 2009, 18 master's, 15 doctorates awarded. *Degree requirements:* For master's, one foreign language, essay; for doctorate, variable foreign language requirement, comprehensive exam, thesis/dissertation. *Entrance requirements:* For master's and doctorate, GRE General Test, 2 or more letters of recommendation. Additional exam requirements/recommendations for international students: Required—TOEFL (minimum score 600 paper-based; 250 computer-based; 90 iBT), IELTS (minimum score 7). *Application deadline:* For fall admission, 12/1 for domestic and international students. Applications are processed on a rolling basis. Application fee: $60. Electronic applications accepted. *Financial support:* Fellowships, teaching assistantships available. Financial award application deadline: 12/1; financial award applicants required to submit FAFSA. *Unit head:* Brian Owensby, Chair, 434-924-7146, Fax: 434-924-7891, E-mail: history@virginia.edu. *Application contact:* Paul Kershaw, Director of Graduate Admissions, Fax: 434-924-7891, E-mail: pjk3p@virginia.edu.

University of Washington, Graduate School, College of Arts and Sciences, Department of History, Seattle, WA 98195. Offers MA, PhD. Part-time programs available. *Degree requirements:* For master's, one foreign language, comprehensive exam, thesis optional; for doctorate, one foreign language, comprehensive exam, thesis/dissertation. *Entrance requirements:* For master's and doctorate, GRE, minimum GPA of 3.0. Additional exam requirements/recommendations for international students: Required—TOEFL. Electronic applications accepted. *Faculty research:* U.S., Asia, Europe, comparative history.

University of Waterloo, Graduate Studies, Faculty of Arts, Department of Classical Studies, Waterloo, ON N2L 3G1, Canada. Offers ancient Mediterranean cultures (MA). *Degree requirements:* For master's, one foreign language. *Faculty research:* Ancient history, philosophy, anthropology, religion, culture.

University of Waterloo, Graduate Studies, Faculty of Arts, Department of History, Waterloo, ON N2L 3G1, Canada. Offers MA, PhD. Part-time and evening/weekend programs available. *Degree requirements:* For master's, one foreign language, thesis optional; for doctorate, one foreign language, thesis/dissertation. *Entrance requirements:* For master's, honors degree, minimum B+ average, resume; for doctorate, master's degree, minimum A average, resumé, writing sample. Additional exam requirements/recommendations for international students: Required—TOEFL, TWE. Electronic applications accepted. *Faculty research:* Canadian, British, international, modern, European, and U.S. history; women's history; imperialism and slavery.

The University of Western Ontario, Faculty of Graduate Studies, Social Sciences Division, Department of History, London, ON N6A 5B8, Canada. Offers MA, PhD. Part-time programs available. *Degree requirements:* For master's, one foreign language, thesis (for some programs); for doctorate, one foreign language, thesis/dissertation. *Entrance requirements:* For master's, minimum B+ average on last 10 senior courses; for doctorate, minimum A- average on MA or last year honors degree. Additional exam requirements/recommendations for international students: Required—TOEFL. *Faculty research:* Canadian, U.S., Britain, Modern Europe, British Empire and Commonwealth Latin America.

University of West Florida, College of Arts and Sciences: Arts, Department of History, Pensacola, FL 32514-5750. Offers historic preservation (MA); history (MA); military history (MA); public history (MA). Part-time and evening/weekend programs available. *Faculty:* 5 full-time (1 woman), 1 part-time/adjunct (0 women). *Students:* 14 full-time (6 women), 23 part-time (12 women); includes 5 minority (2 African Americans, 1 American Indian/Alaska Native, 1 Asian American or Pacific Islander, 1 Hispanic American). Average age 31. 26 applicants, 73% accepted, 9 enrolled. In 2009, 10 master's awarded. *Degree requirements:* For master's, thesis or alternative. *Entrance requirements:* For master's, GRE General Test, minimum GPA of 3.0, minimum 15 hours of upper-level history courses. Additional exam requirements/recommendations for international students: Required—TOEFL (minimum score 550 paper-based; 213 computer-based). *Application deadline:* For fall admission, 6/1 for domestic students, 5/15 for international students; for spring admission, 11/1 for domestic students, 10/1 for international students. Applications are processed on a rolling basis. Application fee: $30. *Expenses:* Tuition, state resident: full-time $4982; part-time $260 per credit hour. Tuition, nonresident: full-time $20,059; part-time $919 per credit hour. Required fees: $1247; $52 per credit hour. *Financial support:* In 2009–10, 2 teaching assistantships with partial tuition reimbursements (averaging $5,000 per year) were awarded; unspecified assistantships also available. Financial award application deadline: 4/15; financial award applicants required to submit FAFSA. *Unit head:* Dr. John J. Clune, Chairperson, 850-474-2680. *Application contact:* Terry McCray, Assistant Director of Graduate Admissions, 850-473-7718, Fax: 850-473-7714, E-mail: gradadmissions@uwf.edu.

University of West Georgia, Graduate School, College of Arts and Sciences, Department of History, Carrollton, GA 30118. Offers history (MA); museum studies (Certificate); public history (Certificate). Part-time programs available. *Faculty:* 16 full-time (6 women). *Students:* 22 full-time (12 women), 21 part-time (11 women); includes 3 minority (1 African American, 2 Hispanic Americans). Average age 35. 23 applicants, 57% accepted, 6 enrolled. In 2009, 10 master's, 9 other advanced degrees awarded. *Degree requirements:* For master's, one foreign language, comprehensive exam, thesis or alternative. *Entrance requirements:* For master's, GRE General Test (minimum score 400 verbal, 400 quantitative, 3.5 writing), undergraduate degree in history or related social studies, minimum GPA of 2.75. *Application deadline:* For fall admission, 7/17 for domestic students; for spring admission, 11/20 for domestic students. Applications are processed on a rolling basis. Application fee: $30. Electronic applications accepted. *Expenses:* Tuition, state resident: full-time $2952; part-time $164 per semester hour. Tuition, nonresident: full-time $11,808; part-time $656 per semester hour. Required fees: $42.90 per semester hour. $307 per semester. Tuition and fees vary according to course load. *Financial support:* In 2009–10, 7 students received support, including research assistantships with full tuition reimbursements available (averaging $6,000 per year); career-related internships or fieldwork, scholarships/grants, and unspecified assistantships also available. Support available to part-time students. Financial award application deadline: 7/1; financial award applicants required to submit FAFSA. *Faculty research:* Public history, United States, Russia/Soviet Union, Africa, Europe. *Unit head:* Dr. Howard Steven Goodson, Interim Chair, 678-839-6042, E-mail: hgoodson@westga.edu. *Application contact:* Dr. Charles W. Clark, Dean, 678-839-6508, E-mail: cclark@westga.edu.

University of Windsor, Faculty of Graduate Studies, Faculty of Arts and Social Sciences, Department of History, Windsor, ON N9B 3P4, Canada. Offers MA. Part-time programs available. *Degree requirements:* For master's, thesis (for some programs). *Entrance requirements:* For master's, minimum B average. Additional exam requirements/recommendations for international students: Required—TOEFL (minimum score 600 paper-based; 250 computer-based). Electronic applications accepted. *Faculty research:* Gender history, social-history questions about class gender and national identity, divorce in France: 1792-1816, gender and sexuality in Western Europe during the high and later Middle Ages, U.S.-Canadian comparisons in women's history.

The University of Winnipeg, Graduate Studies, Department of History, Winnipeg, MB R3B 2E9, Canada. Offers MA. Part-time and evening/weekend programs available. *Degree requirements:* For master's, one foreign language, comprehensive exam or thesis. *Faculty research:* Canadian social history, European diplomacy, Indian history, colonial America, medieval history.

History

University of Wisconsin–Eau Claire, College of Arts and Sciences, Department of History, Eau Claire, WI 54702-4004. Offers public history (MA). Part-time programs available. *Faculty:* 12 full-time (6 women). *Students:* 12 full-time (1 woman), 20 part-time (9 women); includes 6 minority (3 American Indian/Alaska Native, 1 Asian American or Pacific Islander, 2 Hispanic Americans). Average age 32. 21 applicants, 81% accepted, 13 enrolled. In 2009, 13 master's awarded. *Degree requirements:* For master's, comprehensive exam, thesis optional, oral and written exams. *Entrance requirements:* For master's, minimum GPA of 3.15 during last 2 years, 3.3 in history, or 3.0 overall; research paper; bachelor's degree with minimum of 24 credits in history. Additional exam requirements/recommendations for international students: Required—TOEFL (minimum score 550 paper-based; 213 computer-based; 79 iBT). *Application deadline:* For fall admission, 3/1 priority date for domestic students, 6/1 priority date for international students; for spring admission, 11/1 priority date for international students. Applications are processed on a rolling basis. Application fee: $56. Electronic applications accepted. *Expenses:* Tuition, state resident: full-time $6705.90; part-time $372.55 per credit. Tuition, nonresident: full-time $16,771; part-time $931.74 per credit. Required fees: $925.50; $51.19 per credit. One-time fee: $56. *Financial support:* In 2009–10, 16 students received support, including 6 fellowships (averaging $2,000 per year); Federal Work-Study and unspecified assistantships also available. Financial award application deadline: 3/1; financial award applicants required to submit FAFSA. *Unit head:* Dr. Kate Lang, Chair, 715-836-5501, Fax: 715-836-3540, E-mail: langkh@uwec.edu. *Application contact:* Kristina Anderson, Director of Admissions, 715-836-5415, Fax: 715-836-2409, E-mail: admissions@uwec.edu.

University of Wisconsin–Madison, Graduate School, College of Letters and Science, Department of History, Madison, WI 53706-1380. Offers African history (MA, PhD); Central Asian history (MA, PhD); comparative world history (MA, PhD); East Asian history (MA, PhD); European history (MA, PhD); gender and women's history (MA, PhD); Latin American and Caribbean history (MA, PhD); Middle Eastern history (MA, PhD); South Asian history (MA, PhD); Southeast Asian history (MA, PhD); United States history (MA, PhD). Terminal master's awarded for partial completion of doctoral program. *Degree requirements:* For master's, thesis (for some programs); for doctorate, variable foreign language requirement, thesis/dissertation. *Entrance requirements:* For master's and doctorate, GRE General Test. Additional exam requirements/recommendations for international students: Required—Michigan English Language Assessment Battery or TOEFL. Electronic applications accepted. *Expenses:* Tuition, state resident: part-time $594 per credit. Tuition, nonresident: part-time $1504 per credit. Required fees: $65 per credit. Tuition and fees vary according to course load, program and reciprocity agreements. *Faculty research:* American, African, European, Asian, Latin American, and Middle Eastern history.

University of Wisconsin–Milwaukee, Graduate School, College of Letters and Sciences, Department of History, Milwaukee, WI 53201-0413. Offers global history (PhD); history (MA); modern studies (PhD); urban history (PhD); MLIS/MA. Part-time programs available. *Faculty:* 33 full-time (16 women). *Students:* 44 full-time (22 women), 41 part-time (19 women); includes 9 minority (2 African Americans, 2 American Indian/Alaska Native, 1 Asian American or Pacific Islander, 4 Hispanic Americans), 1 international. Average age 31. 74 applicants, 58% accepted, 11 enrolled. In 2009, 28 master's, 1 doctorate awarded. *Degree requirements:* For master's, comprehensive exam, thesis or alternative; for doctorate, thesis/dissertation. *Entrance requirements:* For master's and doctorate, GRE General Test. Additional exam requirements/recommendations for international students: Required—TOEFL (minimum score 550 paper-based; 79 iBT), IELTS (minimum score 6.5). *Application deadline:* For fall admission, 1/1 priority date for domestic students; for spring admission, 9/1 for domestic students. Applications are processed on a rolling basis. Application fee: $45 ($75 for international students). *Expenses:* Tuition, state resident: full-time $8800. Tuition, nonresident: full-time $20,760. Tuition and fees vary according to program and reciprocity agreements. *Financial support:* In 2009–10, 23 teaching assistantships were awarded; career-related internships or fieldwork and unspecified assistantships also available. Support available to part-time students. Financial award application deadline: 4/15. Total annual research expenditures: $7,605. *Unit head:* Joe Austin, Representative, 414-229-4361, Fax: 414-229-2435, E-mail: jaustin@uwm.edu. *Application contact:* General Information Contact, 414-229-4982, Fax: 414-229-6967, E-mail: gradschool@uwm.edu.

University of Wisconsin–Stevens Point, College of Letters and Science, Department of History, Stevens Point, WI 54481-3897. Offers MST. *Students:* 1 full-time (0 women), 3 part-time (all women); includes 1 Hispanic American. *Degree requirements:* For master's, thesis or alternative. *Application deadline:* For fall admission, 5/1 priority date for domestic students. Applications are processed on a rolling basis. Application fee: $45. *Expenses:* Tuition, state resident: full-time $7740; part-time $430 per credit hour. Tuition, nonresident: full-time $17,804; part-time $989 per credit hour. Tuition and fees vary according to course load and reciprocity agreements. *Financial support:* Federal Work-Study and unspecified assistantships available. Financial award application deadline: 5/1; financial award applicants required to submit FAFSA. *Unit head:* Dr. Greg Summers, Chair, 715-346-2334, Fax: 715-346-4489. *Application contact:* Catherine Glennon, Director of Admissions, 715-346-2441, E-mail: admiss@uwsp.edu.

University of Wyoming, College of Arts and Sciences, Department of History, Laramie, WY 82070. Offers MA, MAT. Part-time programs available. *Degree requirements:* For master's, one foreign language, thesis (for some programs). *Entrance requirements:* For master's, GRE General Test, minimum GPA of 3.0, 12 semester hours of undergraduate course work in history. Additional exam requirements/recommendations for international students: Required—TOEFL. Electronic applications accepted. *Faculty research:* American West, Native American history, nineteenth and twentieth century U.S. history, European history, Asian studies.

Utah State University, School of Graduate Studies, College of Humanities, Arts and Social Sciences, Department of History, Logan, UT 84322. Offers MA, MS. Part-time and evening/weekend programs available. *Degree requirements:* For master's, one foreign language, thesis. *Entrance requirements:* For master's, GRE General Test, minimum GPA of 3.0. Additional exam requirements/recommendations for international students: Required—TOEFL. Electronic applications accepted. *Faculty research:* U.S. race and ethnicity, early modern and modern Europe, environmental history, western regional history.

Valdosta State University, Graduate School, Department of History, Valdosta, GA 31698. Offers MA. Part-time programs available. *Degree requirements:* For master's, one foreign language, thesis optional, comprehensive written and/or oral exams. *Entrance requirements:* For master's, GRE General Test, minimum GPA of 2.5. Additional exam requirements/recommendations for international students: Required—TOEFL (minimum score 523 paper-based; 193 computer-based). Electronic applications accepted. *Faculty research:* Georgia history, U.S. history, Napoleonic France, American diplomatic history, English history.

Valparaiso University, Graduate School, Programs in Liberal Studies, Concentration in History, Valparaiso, IN 46383. Offers MALS, Post-Master's Certificate, JD/MALS. Part-time and evening/weekend programs available. *Students:* 4 full-time (1 woman), 9 part-time (5 women). Average age 31. In 2009, 4 master's awarded. *Entrance requirements:* For master's, minimum GPA of 3.0. Additional exam requirements/recommendations for international students: Required—TOEFL (minimum score 550 paper-based; 213 computer-based; 80 iBT). *Application deadline:* Applications are processed on a rolling basis. Application fee: $30 ($50 for international students). Electronic applications accepted. *Financial support:* Available to part-time students. Applicants required to submit FAFSA. *Faculty research:* Regional Chinese history, British history, Martin Luther, Latin American history, African history. *Unit head:* Dr. David L. Rowland, Dean, Graduate Studies and Continuing Education/Associate Provost, 219-464-5313, Fax: 219-464-5381, E-mail: david.rowland@valpo.edu. *Application contact:* Jamie Haney, Coordinator of Graduate Admission, 219-464-5313, Fax: 219-464-5381, E-mail: jamie.haney@valpo.edu.

Vanderbilt University, Graduate School, Department of History, Nashville, TN 37240-1001. Offers MA, MAT, PhD. *Faculty:* 43 full-time (13 women). *Students:* 49 full-time (28 women), 2 part-time (1 woman); includes 10 minority (4 African Americans, 1 American Indian/Alaska Native, 2 Asian Americans or Pacific Islanders, 3 Hispanic Americans), 8 international. Average age 31. 189 applicants, 10% accepted, 8 enrolled. In 2009, 10 master's, 3 doctorates awarded. Terminal master's awarded for partial completion of doctoral program. *Degree requirements:* For doctorate, one foreign language, comprehensive exam, thesis/dissertation, final and qualifying exams. *Entrance requirements:* For doctorate, GRE General Test, sample of written work (recommended). Additional exam requirements/recommendations for international students: Required—TOEFL (minimum score 570 paper-based; 230 computer-based; 88 iBT). *Application deadline:* For fall admission, 1/15 for domestic and international students. Application fee: $0. Electronic applications accepted. *Financial support:* Fellowships with full tuition reimbursements, teaching assistantships with full tuition reimbursements, Federal Work-Study, institutionally sponsored loans, scholarships/grants, and health care benefits available. Financial award application deadline: 1/15; financial award applicants required to submit CSS PROFILE or FAFSA. *Faculty research:* Southern American history, recent U. S. history, intellectual and cultural history, European history, Latin American history. *Unit head:* Elizabeth Lunback, Chair, 615-322-2575, Fax: 615-343-6002, E-mail: elizabeth.lunbeck@vanderbilt.edu. *Application contact:* Katherine B. Crawford, Director of Graduate Studies, 615-322-3388, Fax: 615-343-6002, E-mail: kathering.b.crawford@vanderbilt.edu.

Villanova University, Graduate School of Liberal Arts and Sciences, Department of History, Villanova, PA 19085-1699. Offers MA. Part-time and evening/weekend programs available. *Faculty:* 11 full-time (6 women). *Students:* 18 full-time (9 women), 56 part-time (28 women); includes 4 minority (3 African Americans, 1 Hispanic American), 1 international. Average age 28. 63 applicants, 90% accepted, 29 enrolled. In 2009, 26 master's awarded. *Degree requirements:* For master's, comprehensive exam, thesis optional. *Entrance requirements:* For master's, GRE General Test, minimum GPA of 3.0. Additional exam requirements/recommendations for international students: Required—TOEFL. *Application deadline:* For fall admission, 3/1 priority date for domestic and international students; for spring admission, 11/15 priority date for domestic and international students. Applications are processed on a rolling basis. Application fee: $50. Electronic applications accepted. *Expenses:* Tuition: Part-time $630 per credit. Required fees: $60 per credit. Part-time tuition and fees vary according to degree level and program. *Financial support:* Research assistantships, Federal Work-Study and scholarships/grants available. Financial award applicants required to submit FAFSA. *Unit head:* Dr. Marc Gallicchio, Chairperson, 610-519-4660. *Application contact:* Dr. Adele Lindenmeyr, Dean, Graduate School of Liberal Arts and Sciences, 610-519-7093, Fax: 610-519-7096.

See Close-Up on page 303.

Virginia Commonwealth University, Graduate School, College of Humanities and Sciences, Department of History, Richmond, VA 23284-9005. Offers MA. Part-time programs available. *Degree requirements:* For master's, thesis optional. *Entrance requirements:* For master's, GRE General Test, 30 undergraduate credits in history.

Virginia Commonwealth University, Graduate School, School of the Arts, Department of Art History, Richmond, VA 23284-9005. Offers architectural history (MA); art history (MA, PhD); historical studies (MA); museum studies (MA). *Accreditation:* NASAD. *Degree requirements:* For master's, thesis; for doctorate, comprehensive exam, thesis/dissertation. *Entrance requirements:* For master's and doctorate, GRE General Test. *Faculty research:* Modern, nineteenth century, Renaissance, American, and Medieval art.

Virginia Polytechnic Institute and State University, Graduate School, College of Liberal Arts and Human Sciences, Department of History, Blacksburg, VA 24061. Offers MA. *Faculty:* 25 full-time (7 women). *Students:* 17 full-time (6 women), 2 part-time (1 woman); includes 1 minority (American Indian/Alaska Native). Average age 28. 27 applicants, 41% accepted, 8 enrolled. In 2009, 10 master's awarded. *Entrance requirements:* For master's, GRE, GMAT. Additional exam requirements/recommendations for international students: Required—TOEFL (minimum score 550 paper-based; 213 computer-based). *Application deadline:* For fall admission, 5/15 for international students; for spring admission, 10/15 for international students. Applications are processed on a rolling basis. Application fee: $65. Electronic applications accepted. *Expenses:* Tuition, area resident: Full-time $10,228; part-time $459 per credit hour. Tuition, nonresident: full-time $17,892; part-time $865 per credit hour. Required fees: $1966; $451 per semester. *Financial support:* In 2009–10, 1 fellowship with full tuition reimbursement (averaging $18,000 per year), 13 teaching assistantships with full tuition reimbursements (averaging $12,318 per year) were awarded; career-related internships or fieldwork, Federal Work-Study, scholarships/grants, and unspecified assistantships also available. Financial award application deadline: 1/15. *Faculty research:* History of the U.S.; race, class and gender; European (area studies); history of science and technology. Total annual research expenditures: $258,207. *Unit head:* Dr. Daniel B. Thorp, Dean, 540-231-5331, Fax: 540-231-8724. *Application contact:* Amy Nelson, Information Contact, 540-231-8369, Fax: 540-231-8724, E-mail: anelson@vt.edu.

Virginia State University, School of Graduate Studies, Research, and Outreach, School of Liberal Arts and Education, Department of History, Petersburg, VA 23806-0001. Offers MA. *Degree requirements:* For master's, one foreign language, thesis (for some programs). *Entrance requirements:* For master's, GRE General Test, minimum GPA of 2.5.

Washington College, Graduate Programs, Department of History, Chestertown, MD 21620-1197. Offers MA. Part-time and evening/weekend programs available.

Washington State University, Graduate School, College of Liberal Arts, Department of History, Pullman, WA 99164. Offers early and modern European history (MA, PhD); environmental history (MA, PhD); Latin American history (MA, PhD); modern East Asia history (MA, PhD); public history (MA, PhD); US history (MA, PhD); women's history (MA, PhD); world history (MA, PhD). Part-time programs available. *Faculty:* 25. *Students:* 38 full-time (22 women), 10 part-time (4 women); includes 3 minority (1 American Indian/Alaska Native, 2 Hispanic Americans), 2 international. Average age 33. 57 applicants, 47% accepted, 10 enrolled. In 2009, 10 master's, 2 doctorates awarded. *Degree requirements:* For master's, comprehensive exam (for some programs), thesis, oral exam; for doctorate, one foreign language, comprehensive exam, thesis/dissertation, oral and written exam. *Entrance requirements:* For master's and doctorate, GRE General Test, Graduate School Application form; official transcripts from all universities attended; GRE scores; TOEFL or IELTS scores (international students only); three letters of recommendation; a statement of purpose; a writing sample, Preferred Fields of Study form; and the Language Background form. Additional exam requirements/recommendations for international students: Required—TOEFL (minimum score 550 paper-based), IELTS. *Application deadline:* For fall admission, 1/10 for domestic and international students; for spring admission, 7/1 for domestic and international students. Applications are processed on a rolling basis. Application fee: $50. Electronic applications accepted. *Financial support:* In 2009–10, 1 fellowship with partial tuition reimbursement (averaging $3,000 per year), research assistantships with full and partial tuition reimbursements (averaging $13,917 per year), 28 teaching assistantships with full and partial tuition reimbursements (averaging $13,056 per year) were awarded; career-related internships or fieldwork, Federal Work-Study, institutionally sponsored loans, scholarships/grants, and health care benefits also available. Financial award application deadline: 2/15; financial award applicants required to submit FAFSA. *Faculty research:* Public, world, environmental, women's and U. S. history. *Unit head:* Dr. Raymond Sun, Chair, 509-335-5139, Fax: 509-335-4171, E-mail: pietz@wsu.edu. *Application contact:* Graduate Studies Director, 509-335-4030, Fax: 509-335-4171, E-mail: kale@wsu.edu.

Washington State University, Graduate School, College of Liberal Arts, Program in American Studies, Pullman, WA 99164. Offers ethnic studies (MA, PhD); feminist studies (MA, PhD); history (MA, PhD); literature (MA, PhD). Part-time programs available. *Faculty:* 35. *Students:* 23 full-time (14 women), 4 part-time (2 women); includes 17 minority (5 African Americans, 4 American Indian/Alaska Native, 4 Asian Americans or Pacific Islanders, 4 Hispanic Americans), 2 international. Average age 35. 55 applicants, 7% accepted, 3 enrolled. In 2009, 1 master's,

3 doctorates awarded. *Degree requirements:* For master's, one foreign language, comprehensive exam (for some programs), thesis optional, oral exam; for doctorate, one foreign language, comprehensive exam (for some programs), thesis/dissertation, oral exam. *Entrance requirements:* For master's, GRE General Test, * Send to the Graduate School an official application form and official college transcripts sent directly from each institution attended. * Send to the American Studies program: A 3 to 5 page statement of purpose describing your areas of interest and why the program minimum GPA of 3.0, writing sample, 3 letters of recommendation; for doctorate, GRE General Test, * Send to the Graduate School an official application form and official college transcripts sent directly from each institution attended. * Send to the American Studies program: A 3 to 5 page statement of purpose describing your areas of interest and why the program minimum GPA of 3.0, writing sample, 3 letters of recommendation. Additional exam requirements/recommendations for international students: Required—TOEFL, IELTS. *Application deadline:* For fall admission, 1/10 priority date for domestic and international students; for spring admission, 7/1 priority date for domestic and international students. Applications are processed on a rolling basis. Application fee: $50. *Financial support:* In 2009–10, 1 fellowship (averaging $6,950 per year), 3 research assistantships with full and partial tuition reimbursements (averaging $14,634 per year), 17 teaching assistantships with full and partial tuition reimbursements (averaging $13,383 per year) were awarded; career-related internships or fieldwork, Federal Work-Study, institutionally sponsored loans, health care benefits, tuition waivers (partial), and teaching associateships also available. Financial award application deadline: 2/15; financial award applicants required to submit FAFSA. *Faculty research:* The American West in multicultural perspective; nineteenth century historical, literary, and cultural studies; comparative American ethnic literatures and cultures; American cultures and the environment; American rhetoric. *Unit head:* Dr. Rory J. Ong, Director, 509-335-1560, E-mail: rjong@mail.wsu.edu. *Application contact:* Graduate School Admissions, 800-GRADWSU, Fax: 509-335-1949, E-mail: gradsch@wsu.edu.

Washington State University Vancouver, Graduate Programs, Program in History, Vancouver, WA 98686. Offers MA. Part-time programs available. *Faculty:* 7. *Students:* 4 full-time (2 women), 2 part-time (1 woman); includes 1 minority (American Indian/Alaska Native), 1 international. In 2009, 1 master's awarded. *Degree requirements:* For master's, comprehensive exam (for some programs), thesis. *Entrance requirements:* For master's, GRE, minimum GPA of 3.0, writing sample, language background form, preferred field of study form, 3 letters of recommendation. Additional exam requirements/recommendations for international students: Required—TOEFL (minimum score 550 paper-based; 213 computer-based). *Application deadline:* For fall admission, 1/10 priority date for domestic students, 1/10 for international students; for spring admission, 7/1 priority date for domestic students, 7/1 for international students. Application fee: $50. *Expenses:* Tuition, state resident: full-time $4228; part-time $423 per credit. Tuition, nonresident: full-time $10,322; part-time $1032 per credit. *Financial support:* In 2009–10, research assistantships (averaging $14,634 per year), teaching assistantships with full and partial tuition reimbursements (averaging $13,383 per year) were awarded; career-related internships or fieldwork, Federal Work-Study, and unspecified assistantships also available. Financial award application deadline: 2/15. *Faculty research:* Immigration, gender, slavery, labor, public history. *Unit head:* Dr. Sue Peabody, Associate Chair of Department, 360-546-9647, E-mail: speabody@vancouver.wsu.edu. *Application contact:* Marie Loudermilk, Program Coordinator, 360-546-9640, E-mail: loudermilk@vancouver.wsu.edu.

Washington University in St. Louis, Graduate School of Arts and Sciences, Department of History, St. Louis, MO 63130-4899. Offers American history (MA, PhD); Asian history (MA, PhD); British history (MA, PhD); European history (MA, PhD); Latin American history (MA, PhD); Middle Eastern history (MA, PhD). Terminal master's awarded for partial completion of doctoral program. *Degree requirements:* For master's, one foreign language, thesis (for some programs); for doctorate, 2 foreign languages, thesis/dissertation. *Entrance requirements:* For master's and doctorate, GRE General Test. Electronic applications accepted.

Wayne State University, College of Liberal Arts and Sciences, Department of History, Detroit, MI 48202. Offers MA, PhD, JD/MA. Evening/weekend programs available. *Degree requirements:* For doctorate, 2 foreign languages, thesis/dissertation, qualifying exam in 4 fields of history. *Entrance requirements:* For master's, GRE General Test, GRE Subject Test, minimum GPA of 3.0 in history, 2.75 overall; for doctorate, GRE General Test, GRE Subject Test, minimum GPA of 3.0. Additional exam requirements/recommendations for international students: Required—TOEFL (minimum score 550 paper-based; 213 computer-based); Recommended—TWE (minimum score 6). Electronic applications accepted. *Faculty research:* Labor and social history; citizenship and governance; modern U.S. history; early modern and modern European history; African-American history.

West Chester University of Pennsylvania, Office of Graduate Studies, College of Arts and Sciences, Department of History, West Chester, PA 19383. Offers history (M Ed, MA); holocaust and genocide studies (MA, Certificate); social studies/history (Teaching Certificate). Part-time and evening/weekend programs available. *Students:* 58 part-time (30 women); includes 3 minority (1 African American, 2 Asian Americans or Pacific Islanders). Average age 28. 38 applicants, 95% accepted, 24 enrolled. In 2009, 14 master's awarded. *Degree requirements:* For master's, thesis optional. *Entrance requirements:* For master's, GMAT, statement of professional goals, writing sample, minimum GPA of 3.0 in history, three letters of recommendation. Additional exam requirements/recommendations for international students: Required—TOEFL (minimum score 550 paper-based; 213 computer-based; 80 iBT). *Application deadline:* For fall admission, 4/15 priority date for domestic students, 3/15 for international students; for spring admission, 10/15 for domestic students, 9/1 for international students. Applications are processed on a rolling basis. Application fee: $35. Electronic applications accepted. *Expenses:* Tuition, state resident: full-time $6666; part-time $370 per credit. Tuition, nonresident: full-time $10,666; part-time $593 per credit. Required fees: $122.56 per credit. *Financial support:* In 2009–10, 5 research assistantships with full and partial tuition reimbursements (averaging $5,000 per year) were awarded; unspecified assistantships also available. Support available to part-time students. Financial award application deadline: 2/15; financial award applicants required to submit FAFSA. *Faculty research:* Oral histories, siege of Leningrad. *Unit head:* Dr. Wayne Hanley, Chair, 610-436-2201, E-mail: whanley@wcupa.edu. *Application contact:* Dr. Jonathan Friedman, Director of the Holocaust/Genocide Education Center and Graduate Coordinator of Holocaust and Genocide Studies, 610-436-2972, E-mail: jfriedmans@wcupa.edu.

Western Carolina University, Graduate School, College of Arts and Sciences, Department of History, Cullowhee, NC 28723. Offers MA. Part-time and evening/weekend programs available. *Students:* 21 full-time (12 women), 11 part-time (7 women). Average age 32. 33 applicants, 85% accepted, 16 enrolled. In 2009, 3 master's awarded. *Degree requirements:* For master's, one foreign language, comprehensive exam, thesis or alternative. *Entrance requirements:* For master's, GRE General Test, appropriate undergraduate degree, 3 letters of recommendation. Additional exam requirements/recommendations for international students: Required—TOEFL (minimum score 550 paper-based; 270 computer-based; 79 iBT). *Application deadline:* For fall admission, 5/1 priority date for domestic students; for spring admission, 9/1 priority date for domestic students. Applications are processed on a rolling basis. Application fee: $45. *Financial support:* In 2009–10, 9 students received support, including 9 research assistantships with full and partial tuition reimbursements available (averaging $8,000 per year); fellowships, teaching assistantships with full and partial tuition reimbursements available, career-related internships or fieldwork, institutionally sponsored loans, scholarships/grants, and unspecified assistantships also available. Financial award application deadline: 3/31; financial award applicants required to submit FAFSA. *Faculty research:* Social and economic history of the American South, Islamic world history, German history, social and political protest, medieval social history. *Unit head:* Dr. Richard Starnes, Head, 828-227-7243, Fax: 828-227-7647, E-mail: starnes@email.wcu.edu. *Application contact:* Admissions Specialist for History, 828-227-7398, Fax: 828-227-7480, E-mail: gradsch@email.wcu.edu.

Western Connecticut State University, Division of Graduate Studies, School of Arts and Sciences, Department of History, Danbury, CT 06810-6885. Offers MA. Part-time programs available. *Faculty:* 6 full-time (2 women). *Students:* 6 full-time (2 women), 32 part-time (11 women); includes 2 minority (1 African American, 1 Asian American or Pacific Islander). Average age 38. 18 applicants, 72% accepted, 12 enrolled. In 2009, 9 master's awarded. *Degree requirements:* For master's, thesis or research project, completion of program in 6 years. *Entrance requirements:* For master's, minimum GPA of 2.5. Additional exam requirements/recommendations for international students: Recommended—TOEFL (minimum score 550 paper-based; 213 computer-based; 79 iBT), IELTS (minimum score 6). *Application deadline:* For fall admission, 8/5 priority date for domestic students; for spring admission, 1/5 priority date for domestic students. Applications are processed on a rolling basis. Application fee: $50. *Expenses:* Tuition, state resident: full-time $5012; part-time $278 per credit hour. Tuition, nonresident: full-time $13,962; part-time $284 per credit hour. Required fees: $3886; $139 per credit hour. Full-time tuition and fees vary according to course load and program. Part-time tuition and fees vary according to course level, degree level and program. *Financial support:* Application deadline: 5/1. *Unit head:* Dr. Michael Nolan, Assistant Professor, 203-837-8483, Fax: 203-837-8525, E-mail: nolanm@wcsu.edu. *Application contact:* Chris Shankle, Associate Director of Graduate Studies, 203-837-9005, Fax: 203-837-8326, E-mail: shanklec@wcsu.edu.

Western Illinois University, School of Graduate Studies, College of Arts and Sciences, Department of History, Macomb, IL 61455-1390. Offers MA. Part-time programs available. *Students:* 22 full-time (6 women), 15 part-time (1 woman); includes 2 minority (1 African American, 1 Hispanic American), 1 international. Average age 29. 20 applicants, 85% accepted. In 2009, 7 master's awarded. *Degree requirements:* For master's, thesis or alternative. *Entrance requirements:* Additional exam requirements/recommendations for international students: Required—TOEFL (minimum score 550 paper-based; 213 computer-based; 80 iBT). *Application deadline:* Applications are processed on a rolling basis. Application fee: $30. Electronic applications accepted. *Expenses:* Tuition, state resident: full-time $4486; part-time $249.21 per credit hour. Tuition, nonresident: full-time $8972; part-time $498.42 per credit hour. Required fees: $72.62 per credit hour. *Financial support:* In 2009–10, 13 students received support, including 13 research assistantships with full tuition reimbursements available (averaging $7,280 per year). Financial award applicants required to submit FAFSA. *Unit head:* Dr. Virginia Boynton, Chairperson, 309-298-1053. *Application contact:* Evelyn Hoing, Assistant Director of Graduate Studies, 309-298-1806, Fax: 309-298-2345, E-mail: grad-office@wiu.edu.

Western Kentucky University, Graduate Studies, Potter College of Arts and Letters, Department of History, Bowling Green, KY 42101. Offers MA, MA Ed. Part-time and evening/weekend programs available. Postbaccalaureate distance learning degree programs offered. *Degree requirements:* For master's, comprehensive exam, thesis optional, final exam. *Entrance requirements:* For master's, GRE General Test, minimum GPA of 2.75. Additional exam requirements/recommendations for international students: Required—TOEFL (minimum score 555 paper-based; 213 computer-based; 79 iBT). *Expenses:* Tuition, state resident: full-time $4160; part-time $416 per credit hour. Tuition, nonresident: full-time $9550; part-time $506 per credit hour. Tuition and fees vary according to campus/location and reciprocity agreements. *Faculty research:* U.S.A, Europe, China, India, Latin America.

Western Michigan University, Graduate College, College of Arts and Sciences, Department of History, Kalamazoo, MI 49008. Offers MA, PhD. *Degree requirements:* For master's, thesis optional, oral exams; for doctorate, thesis/dissertation, oral exam. *Entrance requirements:* For doctorate, GRE General Test.

Western Washington University, Graduate School, College of Humanities and Social Sciences, Department of History, Bellingham, WA 98225-5996. Offers MA. Part-time programs available. *Degree requirements:* For master's, one foreign language, comprehensive exam, thesis (for some programs). *Entrance requirements:* For master's, GRE General Test, minimum GPA of 3.0 in last 60 semester hours or last 90 quarter hours. Additional exam requirements/recommendations for international students: Required—TOEFL (minimum score 567 paper-based; 227 computer-based). Electronic applications accepted.

Westfield State College, Division of Graduate and Continuing Education, Department of History, Westfield, MA 01086. Offers M Ed. Part-time and evening/weekend programs available. *Degree requirements:* For master's, thesis. *Entrance requirements:* For master's, GRE General Test or MAT, minimum undergraduate GPA of 2.7.

West Texas A&M University, College of Education and Social Sciences, Department of History and Political Science, Program in History, Canyon, TX 79016-0001. Offers MA. Part-time and evening/weekend programs available. *Degree requirements:* For master's, comprehensive exam, thesis optional. *Entrance requirements:* For master's, GRE General Test. Additional exam requirements/recommendations for international students: Required—TOEFL (minimum score 550 paper-based). Electronic applications accepted. *Faculty research:* John B. Stetson Jr. (an American businessman in Warsaw), creation of kokugo in late Meiji Japan, canon law on cyberspace, Russian and American frontiers, Texas women of two cultures.

West Virginia University, Eberly College of Arts and Sciences, Department of History, Morgantown, WV 26506. Offers African history (MA, PhD); African-American history (MA, PhD); American history (MA, PhD); Appalachian/regional history (MA, PhD); East Asian history (MA, PhD); European history (MA, PhD); history of science and technology (MA, PhD); Latin American history (MA). Part-time programs available. *Degree requirements:* For master's, one foreign language, thesis (for some programs), oral exam, thesis defense; for doctorate, one foreign language, comprehensive exam, thesis/dissertation, dissertation defense. *Entrance requirements:* For master's, GRE General Test, minimum GPA of 3.0; for doctorate, GRE General Test. Additional exam requirements/recommendations for international students: Required—TOEFL (minimum score 550 paper-based), IELTS (minimum score 6.5). Electronic applications accepted. *Faculty research:* U.S., Appalachia, modern Europe, Africa, colonial and post-colonial societies.

Wichita State University, Graduate School, Fairmount College of Liberal Arts and Sciences, Department of History, Wichita, KS 67260. Offers MA. Part-time programs available. *Expenses:* Tuition, state resident: full-time $4247; part-time $235.95 per credit hour. Tuition, nonresident: full-time $11,171; part-time $620.60 per credit hour. Required fees: $34; $3.60 per credit hour. $17 per term. Tuition and fees vary according to campus/location and program. *Unit head:* Dr. Robert Owens, Chair, 316-978-3150, Fax: 316-978-3473, E-mail: robert.owens@wichita.edu. *Application contact:* Dr. Robert Owens, Chair, 316-978-3150, Fax: 316-978-3473, E-mail: robert.owens@wichita.edu.

Wilfrid Laurier University, Faculty of Graduate Studies, Faculty of Arts, Department of History, Waterloo, ON N2L 3C5, Canada. Offers MA, PhD. *Degree requirements:* For master's, thesis optional; for doctorate, thesis/dissertation. *Entrance requirements:* For master's, honors BA degree or the equivalent in history, minimum B+ average in undergraduate course work, exclusive of first year level courses; for doctorate, MA in history, minimum A-average. Additional exam requirements/recommendations for international students: Required—TOEFL (minimum score 230 computer-based; 89 iBT). Electronic applications accepted. *Faculty research:* Canadian, early modern European, modern European, Scottish, race/class/imperialism/slavery, British, urban and rural, science/medicine/technology, gender/women's/family, international, United States.

William Paterson University of New Jersey, College of the Humanities and Social Sciences, Wayne, NJ 07470-8420. Offers clinical and counseling psychology (MA); English (MA); history (MA); public policy and international affairs (MA); sociology (MA). Part-time and evening/weekend programs available. *Students:* 39 full-time (22 women), 123 part-time (90 women); includes 42 minority (11 African Americans, 5 Asian Americans or Pacific Islanders, 26 Hispanic Americans), 2 international. *Application deadline:* Applications are processed on a rolling basis. Application fee: $50. Electronic applications accepted. *Financial support:* In 2009–10, 13 students received support; research assistantships with full tuition reimbursements available, teaching assistantships with full tuition reimbursements available, unspecified assistantships available. Support available to part-time students. Financial award application deadline: 4/1; financial award applicants required to submit FAFSA. *Unit head:* Dr. Kara Rabbitt, Dean.

History

William Paterson University of New Jersey (continued)
College of Humanities and Social Sciences, 973-720-2180, Fax: 973-720-2955, E-mail: rabbittk@wpunj.edu. *Application contact:* Tinu Adeniran, Assistant Director, Graduate Admissions, 973-720-2764, Fax: 973-720-2035, E-mail: adenirant@wpunj.edu.

Winthrop University, College of Arts and Sciences, Department of History, Rock Hill, SC 29733. Offers MA. Part-time programs available. *Degree requirements:* For master's, one foreign language, thesis optional. *Entrance requirements:* For master's, GRE General Test or PRAXIS, 24 hours of history at the undergraduate level. Electronic applications accepted.

Worcester State College, Graduate Studies, Program in History, Worcester, MA 01602-2597. Offers M Ed. Part-time programs available. *Faculty:* 3 full-time (1 woman), 2 part-time/adjunct (0 women). *Students:* 16 part-time (5 women); includes 1 minority (Asian American or Pacific Islander). Average age 36. 11 applicants, 45% accepted, 3 enrolled. In 2009, 9 master's awarded. *Degree requirements:* For master's, comprehensive exam (for some programs), thesis optional. *Entrance requirements:* For master's, GRE General Test or MAT, 18 undergraduate credits in history, including U. S. history and Western civilizations. Additional exam requirements/recommendations for international students: Required—TOEFL (minimum score 550 paper-based; 213 computer-based; 79 iBT). *Application deadline:* Applications are processed on a rolling basis. Application fee: $30. *Expenses:* Tuition, area resident: Part-time $150 per credit. Tuition, state resident: part-time $150 per credit. Tuition, nonresident: part-time $150 per credit. Required fees: $85. *Financial support:* In 2009–10, 1 student received support, including 1 research assistantship with full tuition reimbursement available (averaging $4,800 per year); career-related internships or fieldwork, scholarships/grants, and unspecified assistantships also available. Financial award application deadline: 3/1; financial award applicants required to submit FAFSA. *Faculty research:* Labor history, Middle East politics, American-Russian relations, American–East Asian relations. *Unit head:* Dr. Charlotte Haller, Coordinator, 508-929-8046, Fax: 508-929-8155, E-mail: challer1@worcester.edu. *Application contact:* Nicole Brown, Assistant Dean of Graduate and Continuing Education, 508-929-8787, Fax: 508-929-8100, E-mail: nbrown@worcester.edu.

Wright State University, School of Graduate Studies, College of Liberal Arts, Department of History, Dayton, OH 45435. Offers MA. *Degree requirements:* For master's, thesis optional. *Entrance requirements:* For master's, GRE General Test, minimum GPA of 3.0 in history, 2.7 overall. Additional exam requirements/recommendations for international students: Required—TOEFL. *Faculty research:* U.S. religions; women's, Southern, European, and archival history.

Yale University, Graduate School of Arts and Sciences, Department of History, New Haven, CT 06520. Offers history (M Phil, MA, PhD); history of science and medicine (MA, PhD). Terminal master's awarded for partial completion of doctoral program. *Degree requirements:* For master's, one foreign language; for doctorate, 2 foreign languages, thesis/dissertation. *Entrance requirements:* For doctorate, GRE General Test.

York University, Faculty of Graduate Studies, Faculty of Arts, Program in History, Toronto, ON M3J 1P3, Canada. Offers MA, PhD. Part-time programs available. *Degree requirements:* For master's, thesis or alternative; for doctorate, one foreign language, comprehensive exam, thesis/dissertation, qualifying exam. Electronic applications accepted.

Youngstown State University, Graduate School, College of Liberal Arts and Social Sciences, Department of History, Youngstown, OH 44555-0001. Offers MA. Part-time programs available. *Degree requirements:* For master's, thesis optional, oral and written exams. *Entrance requirements:* For master's, minimum GPA of 2.75. Additional exam requirements/recommendations for international students: Required—TOEFL. *Faculty research:* Holocaust, Marxism, nineteenth- and twentieth-century United States, historic preservation, revolutionary France.

History of Medicine

McGill University, Faculty of Graduate and Postdoctoral Studies, Faculty of Arts, Department of History, Montréal, QC H3A 2T5, Canada. Offers history (MA, PhD); history of medicine (MA).

McGill University, Faculty of Graduate and Postdoctoral Studies, Faculty of Medicine, Department of Social Studies in Medicine, Montréal, QC H3A 2T5, Canada. Offers medical anthropology (MA, PhD); medical history (MA, PhD); medical sociology (MA, PhD).

Rutgers, The State University of New Jersey, New Brunswick, Graduate School-New Brunswick, Program in History, Piscataway, NJ 08854-8097. Offers African-American history (PhD); early American history (PhD); early modern European history (PhD); east Asian history (PhD); global and comparative history (PhD); history (PhD); history of diplomacy and foreign relations (PhD); history of technology, environment and health (PhD); history of the Atlantic cultures and African diaspora (PhD); Latin American history (PhD); medieval history (PhD); modern European history (PhD); nineteenth and twentieth century American history (PhD); women's and gender history (PhD). *Degree requirements:* For doctorate, thesis/dissertation. *Entrance requirements:* For doctorate, GRE General Test, sample of written work. Electronic applications accepted. *Faculty research:* American history, European history, Afro-American history, women's history, Latin American history.

University of Minnesota, Twin Cities Campus, Graduate School, Program in the History of Science, Technology and Medicine, Minneapolis, MN 55455-0213. Offers MA, PhD. Part-time programs available. *Degree requirements:* For master's, one foreign language, thesis or alternative; for doctorate, 2 foreign languages, thesis/dissertation. *Entrance requirements:* For master's and doctorate, GRE General Test. *Faculty research:* History of infectious diseases, history of public health, history of evolutionary biology, history of infertility, women in science.

Yale University, Graduate School of Arts and Sciences, Department of History, Program in the History of Science and Medicine, New Haven, CT 06520. Offers MS, PhD. *Degree requirements:* For doctorate, 2 foreign languages, thesis/dissertation. *Entrance requirements:* For doctorate, GRE General Test.

History of Science and Technology

Carnegie Mellon University, College of Humanities and Social Sciences, Department of History, Pittsburgh, PA 15213-3891. Offers African and African-American diaspora (PhD); culture and power (PhD); gender and the family (PhD); history (MA, MS); history and policy (MA); labor and politics (PhD); science, technology, medicine and environment (PhD). Part-time programs available. *Degree requirements:* For doctorate, oral and written comprehensive exams, dissertation defense. *Entrance requirements:* For doctorate, GRE General Test. Additional exam requirements/recommendations for international students: Required—TOEFL. Electronic applications accepted. *Faculty research:* Anthropology and history, African American history, technology/environment, cultural history analysis.

Cornell University, Graduate School, Graduate Fields of Arts and Sciences, Field of History, Ithaca, NY 14853-0001. Offers African history (MA, PhD); American history (MA, PhD); ancient history (MA, PhD); early modern European history (MA, PhD); English history (MA, PhD); French history (MA, PhD); German history (MA, PhD); history of science (MA, PhD); Latin American history (MA, PhD); medieval Chinese history (MA, PhD); medieval history (MA, PhD); modern Chinese history (MA, PhD); modern European history (MA, PhD); modern Japanese history (MA, PhD); premodern Islamic history (MA, PhD); premodern Japanese history (MA, PhD); Renaissance history (MA, PhD); Russian history (MA, PhD); Southeast Asian history (MA, PhD). *Faculty:* 62 full-time (19 women). *Students:* 67 full-time (33 women); includes 10 minority (4 African Americans, 3 Asian Americans or Pacific Islanders, 3 Hispanic Americans), 24 international. Average age 31. 195 applicants, 7% accepted, 10 enrolled. In 2009, 11 master's, 3 doctorates awarded. Terminal master's awarded for partial completion of doctoral program. *Degree requirements:* For master's, thesis; for doctorate, 2 foreign languages, comprehensive exam, thesis/dissertation, 1 year of teaching experience. *Entrance requirements:* For master's and doctorate, GRE General Test, writing sample, 3 letters of recommendation. Additional exam requirements/recommendations for international students: Required—TOEFL (minimum score 550 paper-based; 213 computer-based; 77 iBT). *Application deadline:* For fall admission, 1/15 for domestic students. Application fee: $70. Electronic applications accepted. *Expenses:* Tuition: Full-time $29,500. Required fees: $70. Full-time tuition and fees vary according to degree level, program and student level. *Financial support:* In 2009–10, 54 students received support, including 8 fellowships with full tuition reimbursements available; research assistantships with full tuition reimbursements available, teaching assistantships with full tuition reimbursements available, institutionally sponsored loans, scholarships/grants, health care benefits, tuition waivers (full and partial), and unspecified assistantships also available. Financial award applicants required to submit FAFSA. *Unit head:* Director of Graduate Studies, 607-255-6738, Fax: 607-255-0469. *Application contact:* Graduate Field Assistant, 607-255-6738, Fax: 607-255-0469, E-mail: history_grad_info@cornell.edu.

Cornell University, Graduate School, Graduate Fields of Arts and Sciences, Field of Science and Technology Studies, Ithaca, NY 14853-0001. Offers history and philosophy of science and technology (MA, PhD); social studies of science and technology (MA, PhD). *Faculty:* 20 full-time (10 women). *Students:* 22 full-time (15 women); includes 5 minority (1 African American, 4 Asian Americans or Pacific Islanders), 6 international. Average age 32. 32 applicants, 9% accepted, 3 enrolled. In 2009, 4 master's, 1 doctorate awarded. Terminal master's awarded for partial completion of doctoral program. *Degree requirements:* For master's, one foreign language, thesis; for doctorate, one foreign language, comprehensive exam, thesis/dissertation. *Entrance requirements:* For master's and doctorate, GRE General Test, writing sample, 3 letters of recommendation. Additional exam requirements/recommendations for international students: Required—TOEFL (minimum score 550 paper-based; 213 computer-based; 77 iBT). *Application deadline:* For fall admission, 1/10 for domestic students. Application fee: $70. Electronic applications accepted. *Expenses:* Tuition: Full-time $29,500. Required fees: $70. Full-time tuition and fees vary according to degree level, program and student level. *Financial support:* In 2009–10, 19 students received support, including 3 fellowships with full tuition reimbursements available; research assistantships with full tuition reimbursements available, teaching assistantships with full tuition reimbursements available, institutionally sponsored loans, scholarships/grants, health care benefits, tuition waivers (full and partial), and unspecified assistantships also available. Financial award applicants required to submit FAFSA. *Faculty research:* History, philosophy, sociology, politics, and policy of science and technology; gender, legal order, environment, and communication. *Unit head:* Director of Graduate Studies, 607-255-6234. *Application contact:* Graduate Field Assistant, 607-255-6234, E-mail: stsgradfield@cornell.edu.

Drexel University, College of Arts and Sciences, Department of History and Politics, Philadelphia, PA 19104-2875. Offers science, technology and society (MS). Part-time programs available. *Entrance requirements:* For master's, GRE. Additional exam requirements/recommendations for international students: Required—TOEFL. Electronic applications accepted.

Georgia Institute of Technology, Graduate Studies and Research, Ivan Allen College of Policy and International Affairs, School of History, Technology, and Society, Atlanta, GA 30332-0001. Offers history and sociology of technology and science (MS, PhD). Terminal master's awarded for partial completion of doctoral program. *Degree requirements:* For master's, research paper; for doctorate, one foreign language, comprehensive exam, thesis/dissertation. *Entrance requirements:* Additional exam requirements/recommendations for international students: Required—TOEFL. Electronic applications accepted. *Faculty research:* Industrialization, labor history, modern Europe, social history, sociology of science.

Harvard University, Graduate School of Arts and Sciences, Department of the History of Science, Cambridge, MA 02138. Offers AM, PhD. Terminal master's awarded for partial completion of doctoral program. *Degree requirements:* For master's, one foreign language; for doctorate, 2 foreign languages, thesis/dissertation. *Entrance requirements:* For master's and doctorate, GRE General Test. Additional exam requirements/recommendations for international students: Required—TOEFL. *Expenses:* Tuition: Full-time $33,696. Required fees: $1126. Full-time tuition and fees vary according to program.

Indiana University Bloomington, University Graduate School, College of Arts and Sciences, Department of History and Philosophy of Science, Bloomington, IN 47405-7000. Offers MA, PhD, MLS/MA. Part-time programs available. *Faculty:* 9 full-time (2 women). *Students:* 35 full-time (7 women), 3 part-time (0 women); includes 5 minority (1 African American, 1 Asian American or Pacific Islander, 3 Hispanic Americans), 7 international. Average age 32. 41 applicants, 78% accepted, 4 enrolled. In 2009, 9 master's awarded. Terminal master's awarded for partial completion of doctoral program. *Degree requirements:* For master's, one foreign language, thesis optional; for doctorate, 2 foreign languages, thesis/dissertation. *Entrance requirements:* For master's and doctorate, GRE General Test. Additional exam requirements/recommendations for international students: Required—TOEFL. *Application deadline:* For fall admission, 1/15 priority date for domestic students, 12/15 for international students; for spring admission, 9/1 priority date for domestic students, 9/1 for international students. Applications are processed on a rolling basis. Application fee: $55 ($65 for international students). Electronic applications accepted. *Financial support:* In 2009–10, 14 students received support, including 3 fellowships with full tuition reimbursements available (averaging $16,000 per year), 3 research assistantships with full tuition reimbursements available (averaging $13,000 per year), 14 teaching assistantships with full tuition reimbursements available (averaging $13,000 per year); Federal Work-Study, institutionally sponsored loans, scholarships/grants, health care benefits, and unspecified assistantships also available. Support available to part-time students. Financial award application deadline: 3/1; financial award applicants required to submit FAFSA. *Faculty research:* History of scientific ideas, instruments, and institutions; foundations of physics; history of philosophy of science; history and philosophy of biology; early modern science and medicine. *Unit head:* Domenico Bertoloni Meli, Chair, 812-855-8746, E-mail: dbmeli@indiana.edu. *Application contact:* Peggy Roberts, Graduate Secretary, 812-855-3622, Fax: 812-855-3631, E-mail: hpscdept@indiana.edu.

Iowa State University of Science and Technology, Graduate College, College of Liberal Arts and Sciences, Department of History, Ames, IA 50011. Offers agricultural history and rural studies (PhD); history (MA); history of technology and science (MA, PhD). *Faculty:* 20 full-time (6 women). *Students:* 26 full-time (8 women), 10 part-time (5 women); includes 1 minority (Hispanic American), 2 international. 25 applicants, 84% accepted, 11 enrolled. In 2009, 6 master's, 4 doctorates awarded. *Degree requirements:* For master's, thesis or alternative; for doctorate, thesis/dissertation. *Entrance requirements:* For master's and doctorate, GRE General Test. Additional exam requirements/recommendations for international students: Required—TOEFL (minimum score 600 paper-based; 79 iBT) or IELTS (minimum score 7). *Application deadline:* For fall admission, 1/15 priority date for domestic and international students. Applications are processed on a rolling basis. Application fee: $40 ($90 for international students). Electronic applications accepted. *Expenses:* Tuition, state resident: full-time $6716. Tuition, nonresident: full-time $8908. Tuition and fees vary according to course level, course load, program and student level. *Financial support:* In 2009–10, 2 research assistantships with full and partial tuition reimbursements (averaging $13,770 per year), 19 teaching assistantships with full and partial tuition reimbursements (averaging $13,500 per year) were awarded; scholarships/grants, health care benefits, and unspecified assistantships also available. *Unit head:* Dr. Charles Dobbs, Chair, 515-294-7266, Fax: 515-294-6390, E-mail: cdobbs@iastate.edu. *Application contact:* Dr. Pamela Riney-Kehrberg, Information Contact, 515-294-1451, Fax: 515-294-6390.

The Johns Hopkins University, Zanvyl Krieger School of Arts and Sciences, Department of the History of Science and Technology, Baltimore, MD 21218-2699. Offers MA, PhD. *Faculty:* 6 full-time (3 women), 9 part-time/adjunct (3 women). *Students:* 6 full-time (3 women), 1 part-time (0 women), 1 international. Average age 29. 23 applicants, 9% accepted, 1 enrolled. Terminal master's awarded for partial completion of doctoral program. *Degree requirements:* For master's, one foreign language, thesis; for doctorate, 2 foreign languages, thesis/dissertation. *Entrance requirements:* For doctorate, GRE General Test. Additional exam requirements/recommendations for international students: Required—TOEFL (minimum score 600 paper-based; 250 computer-based; 100 iBT), IELTS. *Application deadline:* For fall admission, 1/15 for domestic and international students. Applications are processed on a rolling basis. Application fee: $75. Electronic applications accepted. *Financial support:* In 2009–10, 7 students received support, including 3 fellowships with full tuition reimbursements available (averaging $18,500 per year), 4 teaching assistantships with full tuition reimbursements available (averaging $18,500 per year); career-related internships or fieldwork, Federal Work-Study, institutionally sponsored loans, and health care benefits also available. Financial award application deadline: 1/31; financial award applicants required to submit FAFSA. *Faculty research:* History of physical and biological sciences, history of technology, history of medicine (sixteenth-twentieth centuries), environmental science (nineteenth-twentieth century). Total annual research expenditures: $45,236. *Unit head:* Dr. Sharon Kingsland, Chair, 410-516-7505, Fax: 410-516-7502, E-mail: sharon@jhu.edu. *Application contact:* Danielle Stout, Academic Program Coordinator, 410-516-7501, Fax: 410-516-7502, E-mail: danielle@jhu.edu.

Massachusetts Institute of Technology, School of Humanities, Arts, and Social Sciences, Program in Science, Technology, and Society, Cambridge, MA 02139-4307. Offers history, anthropology, and science, technology and society (PhD). *Faculty:* 13 full-time (5 women). *Students:* 28 full-time (16 women); includes 3 minority (1 African American, 2 American Indian/Alaska Native), 7 international. Average age 30. 92 applicants, 4% accepted, 4 enrolled. In 2009, 5 doctorates awarded. *Degree requirements:* For doctorate, comprehensive exam, thesis/dissertation. *Entrance requirements:* For doctorate, GRE General Test. Additional exam requirements/recommendations for international students: Required—TOEFL (minimum score 577 paper-based; 233 computer-based; 90 iBT), IELTS (minimum score 7). *Application deadline:* For fall admission, 1/1 for domestic and international students. Application fee: $75. Electronic applications accepted. *Financial support:* In 2009–10, 26 students received support, including 19 fellowships with tuition reimbursements available (averaging $27,275 per year), 6 teaching assistantships with tuition reimbursements available (averaging $30,736 per year); research assistantships, Federal Work-Study, institutionally sponsored loans, scholarships/grants, traineeships, health care benefits, and unspecified assistantships also available. *Faculty research:* History of science, history of technology, sociology of science and technology, anthropology of science and technology, science, technology, and society. Total annual research expenditures: $543,000. *Unit head:* Prof. David A. Mindell, Director, 617-253-4062, Fax: 617-258-8118, E-mail: stsprogram@mit.edu. *Application contact:* Karen Gardner, Academic Administrator, 617-253-9759, Fax: 617-258-8118, E-mail: hasts@mit.edu.

Oregon State University, Graduate School, College of Liberal Arts, Department of History, Corvallis, OR 97331. Offers history of science (MA, PhD). *Expenses:* Tuition, state resident: full-time $9774; part-time $362 per credit. Tuition, nonresident: full-time $15,849; part-time $587 per credit. Required fees: $1639. Full-time tuition and fees vary according to course load and program. *Unit head:* Dr. Paul L. Farber, Chair, 541-737-1273, Fax: 541-737-1257, E-mail: pfarber@oregonstate.edu. *Application contact:* Polly Jeneva, Head Adviser, 541-737-0561, Fax: 541-737-2434, E-mail: polly.jeneva@oregonstate.edu.

Polytechnic Institute of NYU, Department of Humanities and Social Sciences, Major in History of Science, Brooklyn, NY 11201-2990. Offers MS. Part-time and evening/weekend programs available. *Students:* 4 applicants, 25% accepted. *Degree requirements:* For master's, comprehensive exam (for some programs), thesis (for some programs). *Entrance requirements:* Additional exam requirements/recommendations for international students: Required—TOEFL (minimum score 550 paper-based; 213 computer-based; 80 iBT); Recommended—IELTS (minimum score 6.5). *Application deadline:* For fall admission, 7/31 priority date for domestic students, 4/30 priority date for international students; for spring admission, 12/31 priority date for domestic students, 11/30 priority date for international students. Applications are processed on a rolling basis. Application fee: $75. Electronic applications accepted. *Expenses:* Tuition: Full-time $21,492; part-time $1194 per credit hour. Required fees: $1160; $204 per course. *Financial support:* Institutionally sponsored loans, scholarships/grants, and unspecified assistantships available. Support available to part-time students. *Unit head:* Prof. Teresa Feroli, Head, 718-260-3422, E-mail: tferoli@poly.edu. *Application contact:* JeanCarlo Bonilla, Director of Graduate Enrollment Management, 718-260-3182, Fax: 718-260-3624, E-mail: gradinfo@poly.edu.

Princeton University, Graduate School, Department of History, Program in History of Science, Princeton, NJ 08544-1019. Offers PhD. *Degree requirements:* For doctorate, 2 foreign languages, thesis/dissertation. *Entrance requirements:* For doctorate, GRE General Test, sample of written work, 3 letters of recommendation. Additional exam requirements/recommendations for international students: Required—TOEFL (minimum score 600 paper-based; 250 computer-based). Electronic applications accepted. *Faculty research:* Early modern science, history of modern life sciences, history of physical sciences, history of modern technology, science and medicine in European expansion and colonialism.

Rensselaer Polytechnic Institute, Graduate School, School of Humanities and Social Sciences, Department of Science and Technology Studies, Troy, NY 12180-3590. Offers design studies (MS, PhD); policy studies (MS, PhD); science studies (MS, PhD); sustainability studies (MS, PhD); technology studies (MS, PhD). Part-time programs available. *Faculty:* 16 full-time (6 women). *Students:* 21 full-time (8 women), 3 part-time (1 woman); includes 6 Asian Americans or Pacific Islanders. Average age 27. 19 applicants, 42% accepted, 5 enrolled. In 2009, 1 master's, 9 doctorates awarded. Terminal master's awarded for partial completion of doctoral program. *Degree requirements:* For master's, thesis (for some programs); for doctorate, comprehensive exam, thesis/dissertation. *Entrance requirements:* For master's and doctorate, GRE General Test. Additional exam requirements/recommendations for international students: Required—TOEFL (minimum score 600 paper-based; 250 computer-based). *Application deadline:* For fall admission, 1/15 priority date for domestic students, 1/15 for international students. Applications are processed on a rolling basis. Application fee: $75. Electronic applications accepted. *Expenses:* Tuition: Full-time $38,100. *Financial support:* In 2009–10, 22 students received support, including 5 fellowships (averaging $22,000 per year), 1 research assistantship with full tuition reimbursement available (averaging $16,500 per year), 10 teaching assistantships with full tuition reimbursements available (averaging $16,500 per year); career-related internships or fieldwork, institutionally sponsored loans, and tuition waivers (partial) also available. Financial award application deadline: 1/15. *Faculty research:* Communities and technology, social dimensions of IT and biotechnology, ethics and policy, design. Total annual research expenditures: $75,000. *Unit head:* Dr. Sharon Anderson-Gold, Chair, 518-276-8837, Fax: 518-276-2659, E-mail: anders@rpi.edu. *Application contact:* Dr. Edward J. Woodhouse, Director of Graduate Studies, 518-276-8506, Fax: 518-276-2659, E-mail: woodhouse@rpi.edu.

Rutgers, The State University of New Jersey, New Brunswick, Graduate School-New Brunswick, Program in History, Piscataway, NJ 08854-8097. Offers African-American history (PhD); early American history (PhD); early modern European history (PhD); east Asian history (PhD); global and comparative history (PhD); history (PhD); history of diplomacy and foreign relations (PhD); history of technology, environment and health (PhD); history of the Atlantic cultures and African diaspora (PhD); Latin American history (PhD); medieval history (PhD); modern European history (PhD); nineteenth and twentieth century American history (PhD); women's and gender history (PhD). *Degree requirements:* For doctorate, thesis/dissertation. *Entrance requirements:* For doctorate, GRE General Test, sample of written work. Electronic applications accepted. *Faculty research:* American history, European history, Afro-American history, women's history, Latin American history.

University of California, Berkeley, Graduate Division, College of Letters and Science, Group in Logic and the Methodology of Science, Berkeley, CA 94720-1500. Offers PhD. *Students:* 11 full-time (3 women). Average age 26. 27 applicants, 3 enrolled. In 2009, 3 doctorates awarded. *Degree requirements:* For doctorate, qualifying exam, oral defense of dissertation. *Entrance requirements:* For doctorate, GRE General Test, minimum GPA of 3.5, 3 letters of recommendation. *Application deadline:* For fall admission, 12/14 for domestic students. Application fee: $70 ($90 for international students). *Financial support:* Fellowships, research assistantships, teaching assistantships, tuition waivers (full and partial) and unspecified assistantships available. *Faculty research:* Set theory, recursion theory, theoretical computer science, philosophy of mathematics, philosophy of language. *Unit head:* Prof. Thomas Scanlon, Chair, 510-642-0665. *Application contact:* Barbara F. Waller, Student Affairs Officer, 510-642-0665, E-mail: barb@math.berkeley.edu.

University of California, San Diego, Office of Graduate Studies, Department of History, La Jolla, CA 92093. Offers history (MA, PhD); Judaic studies (MA); science studies (PhD). *Degree requirements:* For doctorate, thesis/dissertation. *Entrance requirements:* For master's and doctorate, GRE General Test. Electronic applications accepted.

University of California, San Francisco, Graduate Division, Department of History of Health Sciences, San Francisco, CA 94143. Offers MA, PhD, MD/PhD. Terminal master's awarded for partial completion of doctoral program. *Degree requirements:* For master's, 2 foreign languages, thesis; for doctorate, 2 foreign languages, thesis/dissertation. *Entrance requirements:* For master's and doctorate, GRE General Test.

University of Delaware, College of Arts and Sciences, Department of History, Hagley Program in the History of Technology and Industrialization, Newark, DE 19716. Offers MA, PhD. *Degree requirements:* For master's, thesis optional; for doctorate, comprehensive exam, thesis/dissertation. *Entrance requirements:* For master's and doctorate, interview. Electronic applications accepted.

University of Massachusetts Amherst, Graduate School, College of Humanities and Fine Arts, Department of History, Amherst, MA 01003. Offers ancient history (MA); British Empire history (MA); European (medieval and modern) history (MA, PhD); Islamic history (MA); Latin American history (MA, PhD); modern global history (MA); public history (MA); science and technology history (MA); U.S. history (MA, PhD). Part-time programs available. *Faculty:* 39 full-time (17 women). *Students:* 52 full-time (32 women), 13 part-time (6 women); includes 7 minority (4 African Americans, 1 Asian American or Pacific Islander, 2 Hispanic Americans), 3 international. Average age 33. 137 applicants, 39% accepted, 18 enrolled. In 2009, 9 master's, 2 doctorates awarded. Terminal master's awarded for partial completion of doctoral program. *Degree requirements:* For master's, one foreign language, thesis or alternative; for doctorate, one foreign language, comprehensive exam, thesis/dissertation. *Entrance requirements:* For master's and doctorate, GRE General Test, writing sample. Additional exam requirements/recommendations for international students: Required—TOEFL (minimum score 550 paper-based; 213 computer-based; 80 iBT), IELTS (minimum score 6.5). *Application deadline:* For fall admission, 1/2 for domestic and international students. Applications are processed on a rolling basis. Application fee: $50 ($65 for international students). Electronic applications accepted. *Expenses:* Tuition, state resident: full-time $2640; part-time $110 per credit. Tuition, nonresident: full-time $9936; part-time $414 per credit. Tuition and fees vary according to course load. *Financial support:* In 2009–10, 1 fellowship with full tuition reimbursement (averaging $3,973 per year), 6 research assistantships with full tuition reimbursements (averaging $6,246 per year), 36 teaching assistantships with full tuition reimbursements (averaging $12,895 per year) were awarded; career-related internships or fieldwork, Federal Work-Study, scholarships/grants, traineeships, health care benefits, tuition waivers (full), and unspecified assistantships also available. Support available to part-time students. Financial award application deadline: 1/2. *Faculty research:* Ancient and medieval history; global and comparative history; public history; history of science, technology, medicine and the environment; history of women, gender, sexuality and family. *Unit head:* Dr. Brian W. Ogilvie, Graduate Program Director, 413-545-6791, Fax: 413-545-6137. *Application contact:* Jean M. Ames, Supervisor of Admissions, 413-545-0722, Fax: 413-577-0010, E-mail: gradadm@grad.umass.edu.

University of Minnesota, Twin Cities Campus, Institute of Technology, Program in History of Science and Technology, Minneapolis, MN 55455-0213. Offers MA, PhD. Terminal master's awarded for partial completion of doctoral program. *Degree requirements:* For master's, one foreign language; for doctorate, 2 foreign languages, thesis/dissertation. *Entrance requirements:* For master's and doctorate, GRE General Test. *Faculty research:* History of physics, biology, and technology.

University of Notre Dame, Graduate School, College of Arts and Letters, Division of Humanities, Program in History and Philosophy of Science, Notre Dame, IN 46556. Offers MA, PhD. *Degree requirements:* For doctorate, 2 foreign languages, comprehensive exam, thesis/dissertation, candidacy exam. *Entrance requirements:* For doctorate, GRE General Test. Additional exam requirements/recommendations for international students: Required—TOEFL (minimum score 600 paper-based; 250 computer-based; 80 iBT). Electronic applications accepted. *Faculty research:* Philosophy of physics, science and ethics, history and philosophy of biology, history of medicine and technology, history and philosophy of economics.

University of Oklahoma, Graduate College, College of Arts and Sciences, Department of History of Science, Norman, OK 73019. Offers MA, PhD. *Faculty:* 10 full-time (3 women). *Students:* 13 full-time (4 women), 6 part-time (3 women). 13 applicants, 62% accepted, 5

History of Science and Technology

University of Oklahoma (continued)
enrolled. In 2009, 1 master's, 3 doctorates awarded. Terminal master's awarded for partial completion of doctoral program. *Degree requirements:* For master's, one foreign language, thesis (for some programs); for doctorate, 2 foreign languages, thesis/dissertation. *Entrance requirements:* For master's, GRE, minimum GPA of 3.0 in last 60 hours, 3 letters of reference, writing sample; for doctorate, GRE. Additional exam requirements/recommendations for international students: Required—TOEFL (minimum score 550 paper-based; 213 computer-based). *Application deadline:* For fall admission, 1/15 priority date for domestic students, 4/1 for international students; for spring admission, 11/1 for domestic students, 9/1 for international students. Application fee: $40 ($90 for international students). Electronic applications accepted. *Expenses:* Tuition, state resident: full-time $3744; part-time $156 per credit hour. Tuition, nonresident: full-time $13,577; part-time $565.70 per credit hour. Required fees: $2415; $90.10 per credit hour. *Financial support:* In 2009–10, 19 students received support, including 1 fellowship with full tuition reimbursement available (averaging $5,000 per year), 3 research assistantships (averaging $14,369 per year), 8 teaching assistantships with partial tuition reimbursements available (averaging $14,205 per year); institutionally sponsored loans, scholarships/grants, health care benefits, and unspecified assistantships also available. Financial award applicants required to submit FAFSA. *Faculty research:* Science and religion, medieval and early modern science, history of technology, history of science in America, natural and social sciences in the modern world. Total annual research expenditures: $18,222. *Unit head:* Steven Livesey, Professor and Department Chair, 405-325-2213, Fax: 405-325-2363, E-mail: slivesey@ou.edu. *Application contact:* Steven J. Livesy, Department Chair, 405-325-6490, Fax: 405-325-2363, E-mail: slivesey@ou.edu.

University of Pennsylvania, School of Arts and Sciences, Graduate Group in the History and Sociology of Science, Philadelphia, PA 19104. Offers AM, PhD. *Faculty:* 21 full-time (7 women), 5 part-time/adjunct (2 women). *Students:* 26 full-time (15 women), 1 (woman) part-time; includes 1 minority (Asian American or Pacific Islander), 3 international. 41 applicants, 22% accepted, 4 enrolled. In 2009, 3 master's, 4 doctorates awarded. *Degree requirements:* For master's, thesis or alternative; for doctorate, 2 foreign languages, thesis/dissertation. *Entrance requirements:* For master's and doctorate, GRE General Test. Additional exam requirements/recommendations for international students: Required—TOEFL. *Application deadline:* For fall admission, 12/1 priority date for domestic students. Application fee: $70. Electronic applications accepted. *Expenses:* Tuition: Full-time $25,660; part-time $4758 per course. Required fees: $2152; $270 per course. Tuition and fees vary according to course load, degree level and program. *Financial support:* Fellowships, research assistantships, teaching assistantships, institutionally sponsored loans, scholarships/grants, traineeships, health care benefits, and unspecified assistantships available. Financial award application deadline: 12/15.

University of Pittsburgh, School of Arts and Sciences, Department of History and Philosophy of Science, Pittsburgh, PA 15260. Offers MA, PhD. *Faculty:* 8 full-time (1 woman), 2 part-time/adjunct (0 women). *Students:* 29 full-time (9 women), 1 part-time (0 women); includes 3 minority (all Asian Americans or Pacific Islanders), 6 international. Average age 29. 57 applicants, 12% accepted, 5 enrolled. In 2009, 2 doctorates awarded. Terminal master's awarded for partial completion of doctoral program. *Degree requirements:* For master's, one foreign language, comprehensive exam; for doctorate, 2 foreign languages, comprehensive exam, thesis/dissertation. *Entrance requirements:* For master's and doctorate, GRE General Test. Additional exam requirements/recommendations for international students: Required—TOEFL (minimum score 550 paper-based; 213 computer-based). *Application deadline:* For fall admission, 1/10 for domestic and international students. Application fee: $50. Electronic applications accepted. *Expenses:* Tuition, state resident: full-time $16,402; part-time $665 per credit. Tuition, nonresident: full-time $28,694; part-time $1175 per credit. Required fees: $690; $175 per term. Tuition and fees vary according to program. *Financial support:* In 2009–10, 27 students received support, including 13 fellowships with full tuition reimbursements available, 15 teaching assistantships with full tuition reimbursements available; health care benefits also available. Financial award application deadline: 1/10. *Faculty research:* History and philosophy of biology, psychology, neuroscience; history and philosophy of physics; early modern science; rhetoric of science; philosophy of social science. *Unit head:* Dr. Sandra Mitchell, Chairman, 412-624-5896, Fax: 412-624-6825, E-mail: smitchel@pitt.edu. *Application contact:* Joann McIntyre, Graduate Admissions Secretary, 412-624-5896, Fax: 412-624-6825, E-mail: vanna@pitt.edu.

University of Toronto, School of Graduate Studies, Humanities Division, Institute for the History and Philosophy of Science and Technology, Toronto, ON M5S 1A1, Canada. Offers MA, PhD. Part-time programs available. *Degree requirements:* For master's, one foreign language, thesis optional, reading ability in French or German; for doctorate, 2 foreign languages, thesis/dissertation, reading knowledge examinations, thesis defense. *Entrance requirements:* For master's, 2 letters of reference; for doctorate, 2 letters of reference, MA in history and philosophy of science and technology, minimum A– average. Additional exam requirements/recommendations for international students: Required—TOEFL (minimum score 580 paper-based; 237 computer-based), TWE (minimum score 5).

University of Wisconsin–Madison, Graduate School, College of Letters and Science, Department of History of Science, Madison, WI 53706-1380. Offers history of medicine (MA); history of science (MA, PhD). Terminal master's awarded for partial completion of doctoral program. *Degree requirements:* For master's, thesis; for doctorate, 2 foreign languages, thesis/dissertation. *Entrance requirements:* For master's and doctorate, GRE General Test. Electronic applications accepted. *Expenses:* Tuition, state resident: part-time $594 per credit. Tuition, nonresident: part-time $1504 per credit. Required fees: $65 per credit. Tuition and fees vary according to course load, program and reciprocity agreements. *Faculty research:* History of biology, physical sciences, technology, medicine.

Virginia Polytechnic Institute and State University, Graduate School, College of Liberal Arts and Human Sciences, Program in Science and Technology Studies, Blacksburg, VA 24061. Offers MS, PhD. *Faculty:* 11 full-time (6 women). *Students:* 26 full-time (15 women), 33 part-time (13 women); includes 12 minority (7 American Indian/Alaska Native, 3 Asian Americans or Pacific Islanders, 2 Hispanic Americans). Average age 40. 22 applicants, 45% accepted, 3 enrolled. In 2009, 5 master's, 3 doctorates awarded. *Entrance requirements:* For master's and doctorate, GRE, GMAT. Additional exam requirements/recommendations for international students: Required—TOEFL (minimum score 550 paper-based; 213 computer-based). *Application deadline:* For fall admission, 5/15 for international students; for spring admission, 10/15 for international students. Applications are processed on a rolling basis. Application fee: $65. Electronic applications accepted. *Expenses:* Tuition, area resident: Full-time $10,228; part-time $459 per credit hour. Tuition, nonresident: full-time $17,892; part-time $865 per credit hour. Required fees: $1966; $451 per semester. *Financial support:* In 2009–10, 1 fellowship with full tuition reimbursement (averaging $18,240 per year), 12 teaching assistantships with full tuition reimbursements (averaging $11,722 per year) were awarded; career-related internships or fieldwork, Federal Work-Study, scholarships/grants, and unspecified assistantships also available. Financial award application deadline: 1/15. Total annual research expenditures: $259,425. *Unit head:* Dr. Skip R. Furman, Dean, 540-231-8966, Fax: 540-231-7013, E-mail: furman@vt.edu. *Application contact:* Crystal Harrell, Information Contact, 540-231-7615, Fax: 540-231-7013, E-mail: crcrigge@vt.edu.

West Virginia University, Eberly College of Arts and Sciences, Department of History, Morgantown, WV 26506. Offers African history (MA, PhD); African-American history (MA, PhD); American history (MA, PhD); Appalachian/regional history (MA, PhD); East Asian history (MA, PhD); European history (MA, PhD); history of science and technology (MA, PhD); Latin American history (MA). Part-time programs available. *Degree requirements:* For master's, one foreign language, thesis (for some programs), oral exam, thesis defense; for doctorate, one foreign language, comprehensive exam, thesis/dissertation, dissertation defense. *Entrance requirements:* For master's, GRE General Test, minimum GPA of 3.0; for doctorate, GRE General Test. Additional exam requirements/recommendations for international students: Required—TOEFL (minimum score 550 paper-based), IELTS (minimum score 6.5). Electronic applications accepted. *Faculty research:* U.S., Appalachia, modern Europe, Africa, colonial and post-colonial societies.

Yale University, Graduate School of Arts and Sciences, Department of History, Program in the History of Science and Medicine, New Haven, CT 06520. Offers MS, PhD. *Degree requirements:* For doctorate, 2 foreign languages, thesis/dissertation. *Entrance requirements:* For doctorate, GRE General Test.

Medieval and Renaissance Studies

California State University, Long Beach, Graduate Studies, College of Liberal Arts, Department of History, Long Beach, CA 90840. Offers Africa and the Middle East (MA); ancient/Medieval Europe (MA); Asia (MA); Latin America (MA); modern Europe (MA); United States (MA); world (MA). Part-time and evening/weekend programs available. *Faculty:* 9 full-time (6 women), 1 (woman) part-time/adjunct. *Students:* 10 full-time (3 women), 56 part-time (21 women); includes 19 minority (2 African Americans, 1 American Indian/Alaska Native, 4 Asian Americans or Pacific Islanders, 12 Hispanic Americans), 1 international. Average age 31. 40 applicants, 50% accepted, 11 enrolled. *Degree requirements:* For master's, one foreign language, comprehensive exam or thesis. *Application deadline:* For fall admission, 3/1 for domestic students. Applications are processed on a rolling basis. Application fee: $55. Electronic applications accepted. *Expenses:* Required fees: $1802 per semester. Part-time tuition and fees vary according to course load. *Financial support:* Research assistantships, Federal Work-Study, institutionally sponsored loans, and scholarships/grants available. Financial award application deadline: 3/2. *Faculty research:* All periods of European and American history, recent Asian and African history. *Unit head:* Dr. Nancy Quam-Wickham, Department Chair, 562-985-4431, Fax: 562-985-5431, E-mail: quamwick@csulb.edu. *Application contact:* Dr. Houri Berberian, Graduate Advisor, 562-985-4524, Fax: 562-985-4431, E-mail: hberber@csulb.edu.

The Catholic University of America, School of Arts and Sciences, Department of History, Washington, DC 20064. Offers Medieval Europe (MA, PhD); modern Europe (PhD); religion and society in the late Medieval and early modern world (MA); United States (MA); MA/JD; MSLS/MA. Part-time programs available. *Faculty:* 13 full-time (6 women), 3 part-time/adjunct (1 woman). *Students:* 14 full-time (9 women), 28 part-time (11 women); includes 1 minority (American Indian/Alaska Native), 3 international. Average age 33. 38 applicants, 50% accepted, 7 enrolled. In 2009, 8 master's, 2 doctorates awarded. *Degree requirements:* For master's, one foreign language, comprehensive exam, thesis optional; for doctorate, 2 foreign languages, comprehensive exam, thesis/dissertation, oral exams. *Entrance requirements:* For master's, GRE General Test, statement of purpose, official copies of academic transcripts, three letters of recommendation, writing sample; for doctorate, GRE General Test, MA in history, statement of purpose, official copies of academic transcripts, three letters of recommendation, writing sample. Additional exam requirements/recommendations for international students: Required—TOEFL (minimum score 580 paper-based; 237 computer-based). *Application deadline:* For fall admission, 8/1 priority date for domestic students, 7/15 for international students; for spring admission, 12/1 priority date for domestic students, 10/15 for international students. Applications are processed on a rolling basis. Application fee: $55. Electronic applications accepted. *Expenses:* Tuition: Full-time $31,740; part-time $1245 per credit hour. Required fees: $50; $25 per semester hour. One-time fee: $425. *Financial support:* Fellowships, research assistantships, teaching assistantships, Federal Work-Study, scholarships/grants, tuition waivers (full and partial), and unspecified assistantships available. Financial award application deadline: 2/1; financial award applicants required to submit FAFSA. *Faculty research:* Modern European intellectual history, history of mathematics and sciences, Renaissance, Catholic reformation, medieval women and gander. *Unit head:* Dr. Jerry Muller, Chair, 202-319-5484, Fax: 202-319-5569, E-mail: mullerj@cua.edu. *Application contact:* Julie Schwing, Director of Graduate Admissions, 202-319-5057, Fax: 202-319-6533, E-mail: cua-admissions@cua.edu.

The Catholic University of America, School of Arts and Sciences, Program in Medieval and Byzantine Studies, Washington, DC 20064. Offers MA, PhD, Certificate. Part-time programs available. *Students:* 5 full-time (0 women), 6 part-time (3 women). Average age 31. 17 applicants, 53% accepted, 2 enrolled. In 2009, 1 master's awarded. *Degree requirements:* For master's, one foreign language, comprehensive exam, thesis or alternative; for doctorate, 2 foreign languages, comprehensive exam, thesis/dissertation. *Entrance requirements:* For master's, GRE General Test, 3 letters of recommendation; for doctorate, GRE General Test, statement of purpose, official copies of academic transcripts, three letters of recommendation. Additional exam requirements/recommendations for international students: Required—TOEFL (minimum score 580 paper-based; 237 computer-based). *Application deadline:* For fall admission, 8/1 priority date for domestic students, 7/15 for international students; for spring admission, 12/1 priority date for domestic students, 10/15 for international students. Applications are processed on a rolling basis. Application fee: $55. Electronic applications accepted. *Expenses:* Tuition: Full-time $31,740; part-time $1245 per credit hour. Required fees: $50; $25 per semester hour. One-time fee: $425. *Financial support:* Fellowships, research assistantships, teaching assistantships, Federal Work-Study, scholarships/grants, tuition waivers (full and partial), and unspecified assistantships available. Financial award application deadline: 2/1; financial award applicants required to submit FAFSA. *Faculty research:* Franciscan and medieval theology, history and medieval theology, medieval institutional history, medieval political theology, early medieval history. *Unit head:* Dr. Lourdes M. Alvarez, Director, 202-319-2061, Fax: 202-319-6609, E-mail: alvarezl@cua.edu. *Application contact:* Julie Schwing, Director of Graduate Admissions, 202-319-5057, Fax: 202-319-6533, E-mail: cua-admissions@cua.edu.

Central European University, Graduate Studies, School of Social Sciences and Humanities, Budapest, Hungary. Offers economics (MA, PhD); gender studies (MA, PhD); international relations and European studies (MA, PhD); mathematics and its applications (MS, PhD); medieval studies (MA, PhD); nationalism studies (MA, PhD); philosophy (MA, PhD); political science (MA, PhD); public policy (MA, PhD); sociology and social anthropology (MA, PhD). Terminal master's awarded for partial completion of doctoral program. *Degree requirements:* For master's, one foreign language, thesis; for doctorate, one foreign language, comprehensive exam, thesis/dissertation. *Entrance requirements:* For master's, interview; for doctorate, GRE, CEU subject test, interview. Additional exam requirements/recommendations for international students: Required—TOEFL (minimum score 570 paper-based; 230 computer-based). Electronic applications accepted. *Faculty research:* Civil society, fiscal decentralization, party politics, political philosophy (especially Liberalism, theory of Democracy).

Columbia University, Graduate School of Arts and Sciences, Program in Liberal Studies, New York, NY 10027. Offers American studies (MA); East Asian studies (MA); human rights studies (MA); Islamic culture studies (MA); Jewish studies (MA); medieval studies (MA);

modern European studies (MA); South Asian studies (MA). Part-time and evening/weekend programs available. *Degree requirements:* For master's, thesis.

Cornell University, Graduate School, Graduate Fields of Arts and Sciences, Field of Archaeology, Ithaca, NY 14853-0001. Offers environmental archaeology (MA); historical archaeology (MA); Latin American archaeology (MA); medieval archaeology (MA); Mediterranean and Near Eastern archaeology (MA); Stone Age archaeology (MA). *Faculty:* 13 full-time (3 women). *Students:* 7 full-time (5 women). Average age 25. 20 applicants, 35% accepted, 4 enrolled. *Degree requirements:* For master's, one foreign language, thesis. *Entrance requirements:* For master's, GRE General Test, 3 letters of recommendation, sample of written work. Additional exam requirements/recommendations for international students: Required—TOEFL (minimum score 550 paper-based; 213 computer-based; 77 iBT). *Application deadline:* For fall admission, 1/15 for domestic students. Application fee: $70. Electronic applications accepted. *Expenses:* Tuition: Full-time $29,500. Required fees: $70. Full-time tuition and fees vary according to degree level, program and student level. *Financial support:* In 2009–10, 4 students received support; fellowships with full tuition reimbursements available, research assistantships with full tuition reimbursements available, teaching assistantships with full tuition reimbursements available, institutionally sponsored loans, scholarships/grants, health care benefits, tuition waivers (full and partial), and unspecified assistantships available. Financial award applicants required to submit FAFSA. *Faculty research:* Anatolia, Lydia, Sardis, classical and Hellenistic Greece; science in archaeology; North American Indians; Stone Age Africa; Maya trade. *Unit head:* Director of Graduate Studies, 607-255-6768, E-mail: blj7@cornell.edu. *Application contact:* Graduate Field Assistant, 607-255-6768, E-mail: dsd6@cornell.edu.

Cornell University, Graduate School, Graduate Fields of Arts and Sciences, Field of English Language and Literature, Ithaca, NY 14853-0001. Offers African-American literature (PhD); American literature after 1865 (PhD); American literature to 1865 (PhD); American studies (PhD); colonial and postcolonial literature (PhD); creative writing (MFA); cultural studies (PhD); dramatic literature (PhD); English poetry (PhD); English Renaissance to 1660 (PhD); lesbian, bisexual, and gay literature studies (PhD); literary criticism and theory (PhD); nineteenth century (PhD); Old and Middle English (PhD); prose fiction (PhD); Restoration and eighteenth century (PhD); twentieth century (PhD); women's literature (PhD); MFA/PhD. *Faculty:* 74 full-time (35 women). *Students:* 100 full-time (55 women); includes 26 minority (9 African Americans, 3 American Indian/Alaska Native, 7 Asian Americans or Pacific Islanders, 7 Hispanic Americans), 11 international. Average age 28. 890 applicants, 4% accepted, 21 enrolled. In 2009, 21 master's, 12 doctorates awarded. Terminal master's awarded for partial completion of doctoral program. *Degree requirements:* For master's, one foreign language, thesis; for doctorate, one foreign language, comprehensive exam, thesis/dissertation, teaching experience. *Entrance requirements:* For master's, GRE General Test, 3 letters of recommendation, creative writing sample; for doctorate, GRE General Test, GRE Subject Test (English), 3 letters of recommendation, writing sample. Additional exam requirements/recommendations for international students: Required—TOEFL (minimum score 600 paper-based; 250 computer-based; 77 iBT). *Application deadline:* For fall admission, 1/10 for domestic students. Application fee: $70. Electronic applications accepted. *Expenses:* Tuition: Full-time $29,500. Required fees: $70. Full-time tuition and fees vary according to degree level, program and student level. *Financial support:* In 2009–10, 96 students received support, including 13 fellowships with full tuition reimbursements available, 8 teaching assistantships with full tuition reimbursements available; research assistantships with full tuition reimbursements available, institutionally sponsored loans, scholarships/grants, health care benefits, tuition waivers (full and partial), and unspecified assistantships also available. Financial award applicants required to submit FAFSA. *Faculty research:* English and American literature, women's writing, ethnic and post-colonial literature, critical theory, medievalism. *Unit head:* Director of Graduate Studies, 607-255-7989, Fax: 607-255-6661. *Application contact:* Graduate Field Assistant, 607-255-7989, Fax: 607-255-6661, E-mail: english_grad@cornell.edu.

Cornell University, Graduate School, Graduate Fields of Arts and Sciences, Field of History, Ithaca, NY 14853-0001. Offers African history (MA, PhD); American history (MA, PhD); ancient history (MA, PhD); early modern European history (MA, PhD); English history (MA, PhD); French history (MA, PhD); German history (MA, PhD); history of science (MA, PhD); Latin American history (MA, PhD); medieval Chinese history (MA, PhD); medieval history (MA, PhD); modern Chinese history (MA, PhD); modern European history (MA, PhD); modern Japanese history (MA, PhD); premodern Islamic history (MA, PhD); premodern Japanese history (MA, PhD); Renaissance history (MA, PhD); Russian history (MA, PhD); Southeast Asian history (MA, PhD). *Faculty:* 62 full-time (19 women). *Students:* 67 full-time (33 women); includes 10 minority (4 African Americans, 3 Asian Americans or Pacific Islanders, 3 Hispanic Americans), 24 international. Average age 31. 195 applicants, 7% accepted, 10 enrolled. In 2009, 11 master's, 3 doctorates awarded. Terminal master's awarded for partial completion of doctoral program. *Degree requirements:* For master's, thesis; for doctorate, 2 foreign languages, comprehensive exam, thesis/dissertation, 1 year of teaching experience. *Entrance requirements:* For master's and doctorate, GRE General Test, writing sample, 3 letters of recommendation. Additional exam requirements/recommendations for international students: Required—TOEFL (minimum score 550 paper-based; 213 computer-based; 77 iBT). *Application deadline:* For fall admission, 1/15 for domestic students. Application fee: $70. Electronic applications accepted. *Expenses:* Tuition: Full-time $29,500. Required fees: $70. Full-time tuition and fees vary according to degree level, program and student level. *Financial support:* In 2009–10, 54 students received support, including 8 fellowships with full tuition reimbursements available; research assistantships with full tuition reimbursements available, teaching assistantships with full tuition reimbursements available, institutionally sponsored loans, scholarships/grants, health care benefits, tuition waivers (full and partial), and unspecified assistantships also available. Financial award applicants required to submit FAFSA. *Unit head:* Director of Graduate Studies, 607-255-6738, Fax: 607-255-0469. *Application contact:* Graduate Field Assistant, 607-255-6738, Fax: 607-255-0469, E-mail: history_grad_info@cornell.edu.

Cornell University, Graduate School, Graduate Fields of Arts and Sciences, Field of History of Art, Archaeology and Visual Studies, Ithaca, NY 14853. Offers American art (PhD); ancient art and archaeology (PhD); Asian art (PhD); baroque art (PhD); medieval art (PhD); modern art (PhD); Renaissance art (PhD); Southeast Asian art (PhD); theory and criticism (PhD). *Faculty:* 23 full-time (14 women). *Students:* 20 full-time (18 women); includes 4 minority (1 African American, 1 American Indian/Alaska Native, 1 Asian American or Pacific Islander, 1 Hispanic American), 5 international. Average age 35. 73 applicants. In 2009, 3 doctorates awarded. *Degree requirements:* For doctorate, one foreign language, comprehensive exam, thesis/dissertation, general exams in 3 areas. *Entrance requirements:* For doctorate, GRE General Test, sample of written work, 3 letters of recommendation. Additional exam requirements/recommendations for international students: Required—TOEFL (minimum score 550 paper-based; 213 computer-based; 77 iBT). *Application deadline:* For fall admission, 1/15 for domestic students. Application fee: $70. Electronic applications accepted. *Expenses:* Tuition: Full-time $29,500. Required fees: $70. Full-time tuition and fees vary according to degree level, program and student level. *Financial support:* In 2009–10, 17 students received support, including 3 fellowships with full tuition reimbursements available; research assistantships with full tuition reimbursements available, teaching assistantships with full tuition reimbursements available, institutionally sponsored loans, scholarships/grants, health care benefits, tuition waivers (full and partial), and unspecified assistantships also available. Financial award applicants required to submit FAFSA. *Unit head:* Director of Graduate Studies, 607-255-4905, Fax: 607-255-0566, E-mail: art_history@cornell.edu. *Application contact:* Graduate Field Assistant, 607-255-4905, Fax: 607-255-0566, E-mail: art_history@cornell.edu.

Cornell University, Graduate School, Graduate Fields of Arts and Sciences, Field of Medieval Studies, Ithaca, NY 14853-0001. Offers medieval archaeology (PhD); medieval art (PhD); medieval history (PhD); medieval literature (PhD); medieval music (PhD); medieval philology and linguistics (PhD); medieval philosophy (PhD). *Faculty:* 37 full-time (12 women). *Students:* 15 full-time (8 women), 1 international. Average age 29. 49 applicants, 10% accepted, 3 enrolled. In 2009, 3 doctorates awarded. *Degree requirements:* For doctorate, 3 foreign languages, comprehensive exam, thesis/dissertation, teaching experience. *Entrance requirements:* For doctorate, GRE General Test, 3 letters of recommendation, proficiency in Latin (recommended), 20 page writing sample on a Medieval topic. Additional exam requirements/recommendations for international students: Required—TOEFL (minimum score 600 paper-based; 250 computer-based; 77 iBT). *Application deadline:* For fall admission, 1/15 for domestic students. Application fee: $70. Electronic applications accepted. *Expenses:* Tuition: Full-time $29,500. Required fees: $70. Full-time tuition and fees vary according to degree level, program and student level. *Financial support:* In 2009–10, 14 students received support, including 3 fellowships with full tuition reimbursements available; research assistantships with full tuition reimbursements available, teaching assistantships with full tuition reimbursements available, institutionally sponsored loans, scholarships/grants, health care benefits, tuition waivers (full and partial), and unspecified assistantships also available. Financial award applicants required to submit FAFSA. *Faculty research:* Interdisciplinary study of medieval culture, languages, literatures, history, archaeology. *Unit head:* Director of Graduate Studies, 607-255-8545. *Application contact:* Graduate Field Assistant, 607-255-8545, E-mail: medievalst@cornell.edu.

Fordham University, Graduate School of Arts and Sciences, Center for Medieval Studies, New York, NY 10458. Offers MA, Certificate. Part-time and evening/weekend programs available. *Students:* 5 full-time (2 women), 18 part-time (13 women). Average age 28. 34 applicants, 59% accepted, 9 enrolled. In 2009, 5 master's awarded. *Degree requirements:* For master's, thesis. *Entrance requirements:* For master's, GRE General Test. Additional exam requirements/recommendations for international students: Required—TOEFL (minimum score 650 paper-based; 280 computer-based). *Application deadline:* For fall admission, 1/4 priority date for domestic students; for spring admission, 11/1 for domestic students. Application fee: $70. Electronic applications accepted. *Financial support:* In 2009–10, 4 students received support, including 4 research assistantships with tuition reimbursements available (averaging $17,915 per year); institutionally sponsored loans, tuition waivers (full and partial), and unspecified assistantships also available. Financial award application deadline: 1/4; financial award applicants required to submit FAFSA. *Faculty research:* Medieval literature, Medieval history, Medieval philosophy, Medieval theology, Medieval fine arts, Anglo-Norman. Total annual research expenditures: $77,440. *Unit head:* Dr. Maryanne Kowaleski, Director, 718-817-4655, E-mail: kowaleski@fordham.edu. *Application contact:* Charlene Dundie, Director of Graduate Admissions, 718-817-4420, Fax: 718-817-3566, E-mail: dundie@fordham.edu.

Georgetown University, Graduate School of Arts and Sciences, School of Continuing Studies, Washington, DC 20057. Offers American studies (MALS); Catholic studies (MALS); classical civilizations (MALS); ethics and the professions (MALS); human resources management (MPS); humanities (MALS); individualized study (MALS); international affairs (MALS); Islam and Muslim-Christian relations (MALS); journalism (MPS); liberal studies (DLS); literature and society (MALS); medieval and early modern European studies (MALS); public relations (MPS); real estate (MPS); religious studies (MALS); social and public policy (MALS); sports industry management (MPS); the theory and practice of American democracy (MALS); visual culture (MALS). *Entrance requirements:* Additional exam requirements/recommendations for international students: Required—TOEFL.

Graduate School and University Center of the City University of New York, Graduate Studies, Interdisciplinary Studies, New York, NY 10016-4039. Offers language in social context (PhD); medieval studies (PhD); public policy (MA, PhD); urban studies (MA, PhD); women's studies (MA, PhD). Terminal master's awarded for partial completion of doctoral program. *Degree requirements:* For master's, thesis; for doctorate, comprehensive exam, thesis/dissertation. *Entrance requirements:* For master's and doctorate, GRE General Test.

Harvard University, Graduate School of Arts and Sciences, Department of English and American Literature and Language, Cambridge, MA 02138. Offers critical theory (PhD); eighteenth-century literature (PhD); literature: nineteenth-century to the present (PhD); medieval literature and language (PhD); modern British and American literature (PhD); Renaissance literature (PhD). Terminal master's awarded for partial completion of doctoral program. *Degree requirements:* For doctorate, 2 foreign languages, thesis/dissertation, oral exam. *Entrance requirements:* For doctorate, GRE General Test, GRE Subject Test, writing sample. Additional exam requirements/recommendations for international students: Required—TOEFL. *Expenses:* Tuition: Full-time $33,696. Required fees: $1126. Full-time tuition and fees vary according to program. *Faculty research:* Old and Middle English language and literature, drama, creative writing, transition to Romanticism, history and theory of criticism.

Indiana University Bloomington, University Graduate School, College of Arts and Sciences, Department of Germanic Studies, Bloomington, IN 47405-7000. Offers German philology and linguistics (PhD); German studies (MA, PhD), including German (MA), German literature and culture (MA), German literature and linguistics (MA); medieval German studies (PhD); teaching German (MAT). *Faculty:* 13 full-time (4 women), 6 part-time/adjunct (2 women). *Students:* 34 full-time (19 women), 2 part-time (1 woman); includes 2 minority (1 African American, 1 Hispanic American), 9 international. Average age 30. 34 applicants, 41% accepted, 8 enrolled. In 2009, 3 master's, 2 doctorates awarded. Terminal master's awarded for partial completion of doctoral program. *Degree requirements:* For master's, one foreign language, project; for doctorate, one foreign language, comprehensive exam, thesis/dissertation. *Entrance requirements:* For master's, GRE General Test, BA in German or equivalent; for doctorate, GRE General Test, MA in German or equivalent. Additional exam requirements/recommendations for international students: Required—TOEFL. *Application deadline:* For fall admission, 1/15 priority date for domestic students, 12/15 for international students; for spring admission, 9/1 priority date for domestic students, 9/1 for international students. Applications are processed on a rolling basis. Application fee: $55 ($65 for international students). *Financial support:* In 2009–10, 8 fellowships with full and partial tuition reimbursements (averaging $20,000 per year), 1 research assistantship (averaging $13,025 per year), 20 teaching assistantships with full tuition reimbursements (averaging $13,025 per year) were awarded; Federal Work-Study, institutionally sponsored loans, scholarships/grants, and unspecified assistantships also available. Support available to part-time students. Financial award application deadline: 1/15; financial award applicants required to submit FAFSA. *Faculty research:* German and other European literature: medieval to modern/postmodern, German and culture studies, Germanic philology, literary theory, literature and the other arts. *Unit head:* William Rasch, Department Chairman, 812-855-7947, Fax: 812-855-8292, E-mail: wrasch@indiana.edu. *Application contact:* Michelle Dunbar, Graduate Secretary, 812-855-7947, E-mail: midunbar@indiana.edu.

Marquette University, Graduate School, College of Arts and Sciences, Department of History, Milwaukee, WI 53201-1881. Offers European history (MA, PhD); medieval history (MA); Renaissance and Reformation (MA); United States history (MA, PhD). Part-time programs available. *Faculty:* 23 full-time (7 women), 5 part-time/adjunct (2 women). *Students:* 32 full-time (14 women), 7 part-time (3 women); includes 1 minority (Hispanic American). Average age 30. 34 applicants, 59% accepted, 13 enrolled. In 2009, 8 master's, 8 doctorates awarded. Terminal master's awarded for partial completion of doctoral program. *Degree requirements:* For master's, comprehensive exam, thesis or alternative; for doctorate, one foreign language, thesis/dissertation, qualifying exam. *Entrance requirements:* For master's, GRE General Test, GRE Subject Test; for doctorate, GRE General Test, writing sample. Additional exam requirements/recommendations for international students: Required—TOEFL. Application fee: $40. *Financial support:* In 2009–10, 4 fellowships, 5 research assistantships, 15 teaching assistantships were awarded; Federal Work-Study, institutionally sponsored loans, scholarships/grants, and tuition waivers (full and partial) also available. Support available to part-time students. Financial award application deadline: 2/15. *Faculty research:* Social history, political history, diplomatic history, history of science, religious history. *Unit head:* James Marten, Chair, 414-288-7901, Fax: 414-288-1578. *Application contact:* Erin Fox, Assistant Director for Recruitment, 414-288-5319, Fax: 414-288-1902, E-mail: erin.fox@marquette.edu.

Rutgers, The State University of New Jersey, New Brunswick, Graduate School-New Brunswick, Program in History, Piscataway, NJ 08854-8097. Offers African-American history (PhD); early American history (PhD); early modern European history (PhD); east Asian history

Medieval and Renaissance Studies

Rutgers, The State University of New Jersey, New Brunswick (continued)
(PhD); global and comparative history (PhD); history (PhD); history of diplomacy and foreign relations (PhD); history of technology, environment and health (PhD); history of the Atlantic cultures and African diaspora (PhD); Latin American history (PhD); medieval history (PhD); modern European history (PhD); nineteenth and twentieth century American history (PhD); women's and gender history (PhD). *Degree requirements:* For doctorate, thesis/dissertation. *Entrance requirements:* For doctorate, GRE General Test, sample of written work. Electronic applications accepted. *Faculty research:* American history, European history, Afro-American history, women's history, Latin American history.

Southern Methodist University, Dedman College, Program in Medieval Studies, Dallas, TX 75275. Offers MA. Part-time programs available. *Students:* 2 part-time (0 women). Average age 29. In 2009, 3 master's awarded. *Degree requirements:* For master's, 2 foreign languages, thesis. *Entrance requirements:* For master's, GRE General Test, minimum GPA of 3.0. *Application deadline:* Applications are processed on a rolling basis. Application fee: $60. Electronic applications accepted. *Financial support:* Federal Work-Study and institutionally sponsored loans available. *Faculty research:* Byzantine culture, medieval Europe, Arthurian literature, Chaucer, Romance. *Unit head:* Dr. Bonnie Wheeler, Director, 214-768-2949, Fax: 214-768-1234, E-mail: bwheeler@smu.edu. *Application contact:* Barbara Phillips, Assistant Dean, 214-768-4202, Fax: 214-768-4235, E-mail: bphillips@smu.edu.

University of California, Santa Barbara, Graduate Division, College of Letters and Sciences, Division of Humanities and Fine Arts, Department of French and Italian, Santa Barbara, CA 93106-4140. Offers French (MA, MABL, PhD), including applied linguistics (PhD), European Medieval studies (PhD), feminist studies (PhD), French (MABL, PhD); MA/PhD. French Language Institute available during summer sessions. *Faculty:* 21 full-time (12 women). *Students:* 11 full-time (7 women). Average age 31. 16 applicants, 63% accepted, 3 enrolled. In 2009, 1 master's, 5 doctorates awarded. Terminal master's awarded for partial completion of doctoral program. *Degree requirements:* For master's, 2 foreign languages, comprehensive exam; for doctorate, 2 foreign languages, comprehensive exam, thesis/dissertation. *Entrance requirements:* For master's, GRE, sample of written work, tape of spoken French, BA or the equivalent, 3 letters of recommendation, resume/curriculum vitae; for doctorate, GRE, sample of written work, tape of spoken French, MA or the equivalent, 3 letters of recommendation, statement of purpose, personal achievements/contributions statement, resume/curriculum vitae, transcripts for post-secondary institutions attended. Additional exam requirements/recommendations for international students: Required—TOEFL (minimum score 550 paper-based; 213 computer-based; 80 iBT) or IELTS (minimum score 7). *Application deadline:* For fall admission, 5/1 for domestic and international students; for winter admission, 10/1 for domestic and international students; for spring admission, 1/15 for domestic and international students. Application fee: $70 ($90 for international students). Electronic applications accepted. *Financial support:* In 2009–10, 11 students received support, including 5 fellowships with full and partial tuition reimbursements available (averaging $8,100 per year), 11 teaching assistantships with partial tuition reimbursements available (averaging $11,400 per year); career-related internships or fieldwork, Federal Work-Study, institutionally sponsored loans, scholarships/grants, traineeships, health care benefits, tuition waivers (full and partial), and unspecified assistantships also available. Financial award applicants required to submit FAFSA. *Faculty research:* French and Francophone studies, comparative literature, second language acquisition, applied linguistics, performance studies, feminist and gender studies. Total annual research expenditures: $2,500. *Unit head:* Prof. Jon Snyder, Chair, 805-893-2220, Fax: 805-893-8826, E-mail: snyder@frit.ucsb.edu. *Application contact:* Rosa Pinter, Graduate Staff Advisor, 805-893-3398, Fax: 805-893-8826, E-mail: pinter@frit.ucsb.edu.

University of California, Santa Barbara, Graduate Division, College of Letters and Sciences, Division of Humanities and Fine Arts, Department of Religious Studies, Santa Barbara, CA 93106-3130. Offers European Medieval studies (PhD); feminist studies (PhD); global studies (PhD); religious studies (MA, PhD); MA/PhD. *Faculty:* 18 full-time (8 women), 11 part-time/adjunct (5 women). *Students:* 86 full-time (33 women). Average age 31. 151 applicants, 31% accepted, 17 enrolled. In 2009, 7 master's, 6 doctorates awarded. Terminal master's awarded for partial completion of doctoral program. *Degree requirements:* For master's, one foreign language, comprehensive exam (for some programs), thesis (for some programs); for doctorate, one foreign language, thesis/dissertation. *Entrance requirements:* For master's, GRE General Test; for doctorate, GRE General Test, MA in related field, 3 letters of recommendation, statement of purpose, personal achievements/contributions statement, resume/curriculum vitae, transcripts for post-secondary institutions attended. Additional exam requirements/recommendations for international students: Required—TOEFL (minimum score 550 paper-based; 213 computer-based; 80 iBT) or IELTS (minimum score 7). *Application deadline:* For fall admission, 12/1 for domestic and international students. Application fee: $70 ($90 for international students). Electronic applications accepted. *Financial support:* In 2009–10, 67 students received support, including 29 fellowships with full and partial tuition reimbursements available (averaging $12,600 per year), 5 research assistantships with full and partial tuition reimbursements available (averaging $7,900 per year), 46 teaching assistantships with partial tuition reimbursements available (averaging $8,400 per year); career-related internships or fieldwork, Federal Work-Study, institutionally sponsored loans, scholarships/grants, traineeships, health care benefits, tuition waivers (full and partial), and unspecified assistantships also available. Financial award application deadline: 12/1; financial award applicants required to submit FAFSA. *Faculty research:* Religion and politics, religion and violence, contemporary spirituality, religious traditions, theoretical approaches to the study of religion, area studies. *Unit head:* Prof. Catherine L. Albanese, Chair, 805-893-3564, Fax: 805-893-2059, E-mail: albanese@religion.ucsb.edu. *Application contact:* Sally J. Lombrozo, Graduate Program Assistant, 805-893-2744, Fax: 805-893-2059, E-mail: lombrozo@religion.ucsb.edu.

University of California, Santa Barbara, Graduate Division, College of Letters and Sciences, Division of Humanities and Fine Arts, Department of Spanish and Portuguese, Santa Barbara, CA 93106-4150. Offers Hispanic languages and literature (PhD), including applied linguistics, European Medieval studies, feminist studies, Hispanic languages and literature; Portuguese (MA); Spanish (MA); Spanish and Portuguese (MA); MA/PhD. Spanish Language Institute available during summer session. *Faculty:* 16 full-time (6 women). *Students:* 29 full-time (16 women). Average age 30. 46 applicants, 39% accepted, 9 enrolled. In 2009, 4 master's, 2 doctorates awarded. *Degree requirements:* For master's, 2 foreign languages, comprehensive exam (for some programs), thesis optional; for doctorate, 2 foreign languages, comprehensive exam, thesis/dissertation. *Entrance requirements:* For master's, GRE, 2 writing samples, undergraduate major in Spanish or equivalent, 3 letters of recommendation, resume/curriculum vitae; for doctorate, GRE, 2 writing samples, master's degree, 3 letters of recommendation, statement of purpose, personal achievements/contributions statement, resume/curriculum vitae, transcripts for post-secondary institutions attended. Additional exam requirements/recommendations for international students: Required—TOEFL (minimum score 550 paper-based; 213 computer-based; 80 iBT), or IELTS (minimum score 7). *Application deadline:* For fall admission, 3/1 for domestic and international students; for winter admission, 11/1 for domestic and international students; for spring admission, 2/1 for domestic and international students. Application fee: $70 ($90 for international students). Electronic applications accepted. *Financial support:* In 2009–10, 9 fellowships with full and partial tuition reimbursements (averaging $7,000 per year), 29 teaching assistantships with partial tuition reimbursements (averaging $11,500 per year) were awarded; career-related internships or fieldwork, Federal Work-Study, institutionally sponsored loans, scholarships/grants, health care benefits, tuition waivers (full and partial), and unspecified assistantships also available. Financial award application deadline: 1/7; financial award applicants required to submit FAFSA. *Faculty research:* Nineteenth century Spanish and Portuguese literature, Spanish and Spanish American literature, nineteenth and twentieth century Portuguese and Brazilian literatures, Hispanic linguistics, Catalan language and culture. *Unit head:* Prof. Francisco A. Lomeli, Chair, 805-893-5715, Fax: 805-893-8341, E-mail: lomeli@spanport.ucsb.edu. *Application contact:* Carol Conley, Graduate Program Assistant, 805-893-3162, Fax: 805-893-8341, E-mail: cconley@spanport.ucsb.edu.

University of California, Santa Barbara, Graduate Division, College of Letters and Sciences, Division of Humanities and Fine Arts, Department of Theatre and Dance, Santa Barbara, CA 93106-7060. Offers theater studies (MA, PhD), including European Medieval studies (PhD), feminist studies (PhD), theater studies (PhD); MA/PhD. *Faculty:* 7 full-time (3 women), 1 (woman) part-time/adjunct. *Students:* 22 full-time (15 women). Average age 33. 22 applicants, 36% accepted, 5 enrolled. In 2009, 3 master's, 5 doctorates awarded. Terminal master's awarded for partial completion of doctoral program. *Degree requirements:* For master's, variable foreign language requirement, comprehensive exam, thesis; for doctorate, one foreign language, comprehensive exam, thesis/dissertation. *Entrance requirements:* For master's, GRE, sample of written work, 3 letters of recommendation, resume/curriculum vitae; for doctorate, GRE, sample of written work, 3 letters of recommendation, statement of purpose, personal achievements/contributions statement, resume/curriculum vitae, transcripts for post-secondary institutions attended. Additional exam requirements/recommendations for international students: Required—TOEFL (minimum score 550 paper-based; 213 computer-based; 80 iBT) or IELTS (minimum score 7). *Application deadline:* For fall admission, 1/5 for domestic and international students. Application fee: $70 ($90 for international students). Electronic applications accepted. *Financial support:* In 2009–10, 13 fellowships with full and partial tuition reimbursements (averaging $11,600 per year), 29 teaching assistantships with partial tuition reimbursements (averaging $11,500 per year) were awarded; Federal Work-Study, scholarships/grants, traineeships, health care benefits, and unspecified assistantships also available. Support available to part-time students. Financial award application deadline: 1/5; financial award applicants required to submit FAFSA. *Faculty research:* Spanish/Latin American drama, performance studies and European theatre history, East Asian and Russian studies, playwriting, Medieval theatre. *Unit head:* Prof. Simon Williams, Chair, 805-893-5515, Fax: 805-893-7029, E-mail: williams@theaterdance.ucsb.edu. *Application contact:* Mary Tench, Graduate Program Assistant, 805-893-3147, Fax: 805-893-7029, E-mail: mtench@theaterdance.ucsb.edu.

University of Connecticut, Graduate School, College of Liberal Arts and Sciences, Field of Medieval Studies, Storrs, CT 06269. Offers MA, PhD. *Faculty:* 8 full-time (3 women). *Students:* 13 full-time (9 women), 4 part-time (1 woman); includes 1 minority (African American). Average age 30. 25 applicants, 12% accepted, 3 enrolled. In 2009, 3 master's, 1 doctorate awarded. Terminal master's awarded for partial completion of doctoral program. *Degree requirements:* For master's, comprehensive exam; for doctorate, 3 foreign languages, thesis/dissertation. *Entrance requirements:* For master's and doctorate, GRE General Test, GRE Subject Test. Additional exam requirements/recommendations for international students: Required—TOEFL (minimum score 550 paper-based; 213 computer-based). *Application deadline:* For fall admission, 2/1 priority date for domestic and international students; for spring admission, 11/1 for domestic students, 10/1 for international students. Applications are processed on a rolling basis. Application fee: $55. Electronic applications accepted. *Expenses:* Tuition, state resident: full-time $4725; part-time $525 per credit. Tuition, nonresident: full-time $12,267; part-time $1363 per credit. Required fees: $346 per semester. Tuition and fees vary according to course load. *Financial support:* In 2009–10, 13 teaching assistantships with full tuition reimbursements were awarded; fellowships, research assistantships with full tuition reimbursements, Federal Work-Study, scholarships/grants, health care benefits, and unspecified assistantships also available. Financial award application deadline: 2/1; financial award applicants required to submit FAFSA. *Unit head:* Robert Hasenfratz, Co-Director, 860-486-1525, Fax: 860-486-1530, E-mail: robert.hasenfratz@uconn.edu. *Application contact:* Robert Hasenfratz, Co-Director, 860-486-1525, Fax: 860-486-1530, E-mail: robert.hasenfratz@uconn.edu.

University of Guelph, Graduate Program Services, College of Arts, School of English and Theatre Studies, Joint Program in Literary Studies/Theatre Studies in English, Guelph, ON N1G 2W1, Canada. Offers PhD. Part-time programs available. *Degree requirements:* For doctorate, one foreign language, comprehensive exam, thesis/dissertation. *Entrance requirements:* For doctorate, MA, 3 letters of reference, writing samples, resume, minimum A- average in graduate course work. Additional exam requirements/recommendations for international students: Required—TOEFL. Electronic applications accepted. *Faculty research:* Canadian studies, Early Modern studies, Postcolonial studies, studies in gender and genre, 19th Century studies.

University of Michigan, Horace H. Rackham School of Graduate Studies, College of Literature, Science, and the Arts, Program in Medieval and Early Modern Studies, Ann Arbor, MI 48109. Offers Certificate. Interdisciplinary program offered through Departments of History, English Language and Literature, History of Art, Romance Languages and Literatures, and Near Eastern Studies. *Entrance requirements:* For degree, acceptance by Rackham Graduate School, minimum A- average grade. *Expenses:* Tuition, state resident: full-time $17,286; part-time $1099 per credit hour. Tuition, nonresident: full-time $34,944; part-time $2080 per credit hour. Required fees: $95 per semester. Tuition and fees vary according to course load, degree level and program.

University of Minnesota, Twin Cities Campus, Graduate School, College of Liberal Arts, Department of German, Scandinavian, and Dutch, Minneapolis, MN 55455-0213. Offers Germanic studies: German and Scandinavian studies track (PhD); Germanic studies: German track (MA, PhD); Germanic studies: Germanic medieval studies track (MA, PhD); Germanic studies: Scandinavian studies track (MA); Germanic studies: teaching track (MA). Part-time programs available. *Faculty:* 11 full-time (5 women), 4 part-time/adjunct (2 women). *Students:* 21 full-time (9 women), 3 part-time (1 woman); includes 2 minority (both Hispanic Americans), 3 international. 26 applicants, 42% accepted, 5 enrolled. In 2009, 4 master's, 2 doctorates awarded. Terminal master's awarded for partial completion of doctoral program. *Degree requirements:* For doctorate, 2 foreign languages, thesis/dissertation. *Entrance requirements:* For master's, GRE General Test, BA in German, Scandinavian, or equivalent; for doctorate, GRE General Test, MA in German, Scandinavian, or equivalent. Additional exam requirements/recommendations for international students: Required—TOEFL (minimum score 550 paper-based; 213 computer-based; 79 iBT). *Application deadline:* For fall admission, 12/15 for domestic and international students. Application fee: $75 ($95 for international students). Electronic applications accepted. *Financial support:* In 2009–10, 21 students received support, including 6 fellowships with full tuition reimbursements available (averaging $20,000 per year), 1 research assistantship with full tuition reimbursement available (averaging $16,000 per year), 14 teaching assistantships with full tuition reimbursements available (averaging $14,500 per year); career-related internships or fieldwork, Federal Work-Study, institutionally sponsored loans, scholarships/grants, health care benefits, and unspecified assistantships also available. Support available to part-time students. Financial award application deadline: 12/15. *Faculty research:* Cultural studies, literary theory, feminist criticism, film, Germanic philology. *Unit head:* Prof. Richard McCormick, Chair, 612-625-2080, Fax: 612-624-8297, E-mail: mccor001@umn.edu. *Application contact:* Director of Graduate Studies, 612-625-0999, Fax: 612-624-8297, E-mail: gsd@umn.edu.

University of Notre Dame, Graduate School, College of Arts and Letters, Division of Humanities, Medieval Institute, Notre Dame, IN 46556. Offers MMS, PhD. Terminal master's awarded for partial completion of doctoral program. *Degree requirements:* For master's, 3 foreign languages, comprehensive exam; for doctorate, 3 foreign languages, thesis/dissertation, candidacy exam. *Entrance requirements:* For master's and doctorate, GRE General Test. Additional exam requirements/recommendations for international students: Required—TOEFL (minimum score 600 paper-based; 250 computer-based; 80 iBT). Electronic applications accepted. *Faculty research:* Medieval history, vernacular literatures, theology, philosophy, Ambrosiana manuscripts and drawings.

University of Toronto, School of Graduate Studies, Humanities Division, Centre for Medieval Studies, Toronto, ON M5S 1A1, Canada. Offers MA, PhD. Part-time programs available. *Degree requirements:* For master's, one foreign language, 4 courses or 3 courses and a thesis; for doctorate, 3 foreign languages, thesis/dissertation, proficiency in Latin, German and French. *Entrance requirements:* For master's, letters of reference, minimum B+ average, course work in the medieval period; for doctorate, letters of reference, passing score on MA Latin examination. Additional exam requirements/recommendations for international students: Required—TOEFL (minimum score 580 paper-based; 237 computer-based), TWE (minimum score 5).

Western Michigan University, Graduate College, College of Arts and Sciences, Medieval Studies, Kalamazoo, MI 49008. Offers MA. *Degree requirements:* For master's, one foreign language, thesis optional, oral exam.

Yale University, Graduate School of Arts and Sciences, Interdisciplinary Program in Medieval Studies, New Haven, CT 06520. Offers M Phil, PhD. *Entrance requirements:* For doctorate, GRE General Test.

Yale University, Graduate School of Arts and Sciences, Program in Renaissance Studies, New Haven, CT 06520. Offers PhD. *Degree requirements:* For doctorate, 3 foreign languages. *Entrance requirements:* For doctorate, GRE General Test.

Public History

Appalachian State University, Cratis D. Williams Graduate School, Department of History, Boone, NC 28608. Offers history (MA); history education (MA); public history (MA). Part-time programs available. Postbaccalaureate distance learning degree programs offered (no on-campus study). *Faculty:* 26 full-time (8 women), 3 part-time/adjunct (1 woman). *Students:* 29 full-time (13 women), 15 part-time (3 women); includes 1 minority (African American). 33 applicants, 76% accepted, 16 enrolled. In 2009, 15 master's awarded. *Degree requirements:* For master's, one foreign language, comprehensive exam, thesis (for some programs). *Entrance requirements:* For master's, GRE General Test, 3 letters of recommendation. Additional exam requirements/recommendations for international students: Required—TOEFL (minimum score 570 paper-based; 230 computer-based; 79 iBT), IELTS (minimum score 6.5). *Application deadline:* For fall admission, 7/1 for domestic students, 2/1 for international students; for spring admission, 11/1 for domestic students, 7/1 for international students. Applications are processed on a rolling basis. Application fee: $50. Electronic applications accepted. *Expenses:* Tuition, state resident: full-time $2960. Tuition, nonresident: full-time $14,051. Required fees: $2320. *Financial support:* In 2009–10, 4 research assistantships (averaging $10,000 per year), 7 teaching assistantships (averaging $8,000 per year) were awarded; fellowships, career-related internships or fieldwork, Federal Work-Study, scholarships/grants, and unspecified assistantships also available. Financial award application deadline: 4/1; financial award applicants required to submit FAFSA. *Faculty research:* Women's history, social/cultural history, U.S. history, Latin America, medieval studies. Total annual research expenditures: $126,000. *Unit head:* Dr. Lucinda Beier, Chairperson, 828-262-2282, E-mail: beierlm@appstate.edu. *Application contact:* Dr. Lisa Holliday, Graduate Program Director, 828-262-6014, E-mail: hollidaylr@appstate.edu.

Arizona State University, Graduate College, College of Liberal Arts and Sciences, Division of Humanities, Department of History, Tempe, AZ 85287. Offers East/Southeast Asian history (MA, PhD); European history (MA, PhD); Latin American studies (MA, PhD); North American history (MA, PhD); public history (MA). *Degree requirements:* For master's, thesis or alternative; for doctorate, 2 foreign languages, thesis/dissertation. *Entrance requirements:* For master's and doctorate, GRE.

California State University, Sacramento, Graduate Studies, College of Arts and Letters, Department of History, Sacramento, CA 95819. Offers public history (MA). Part-time programs available. *Degree requirements:* For master's, thesis or alternative, writing proficiency exam. *Entrance requirements:* For master's, GRE General Test, minimum GPA of 3.25 in history, 3.0 overall during previous 2 years; BA in history or equivalent. Additional exam requirements/recommendations for international students: Required—TOEFL. Electronic applications accepted.

Eastern Illinois University, Graduate School, College of Arts and Humanities, Department of History, Charleston, IL 61920-3099. Offers historical administration (MA); history (MA). Part-time programs available. *Faculty:* 14 full-time (2 women). In 2009, 17 master's awarded. *Application deadline:* For fall admission, 3/31 priority date for domestic students. Applications are processed on a rolling basis. Application fee: $30. *Expenses:* Tuition, state resident: full-time $9434; part-time $239 per credit hour. Tuition, nonresident: full-time $23,774; part-time $717 per credit hour. Required fees: $802.63. *Financial support:* In 2009–10, research assistantships with tuition reimbursements (averaging $8,100 per year), 9 teaching assistantships with tuition reimbursements (averaging $8,100 per year) were awarded; career-related internships or fieldwork also available. *Unit head:* Dr. Anita Shelton, Chairperson, 217-581-3310, Fax: 217-581-2722, E-mail: ashelton@eiu.edu. *Application contact:* Dr. Ed Wehrle, Graduate Coordinator, 217-581-6372, Fax: 217-581-2722, E-mail: efwehrle@eiu.edu.

Florida State University, The Graduate School, College of Arts and Sciences, Department of History, Tallahassee, FL 32306. Offers historical administration (MA); history (MA, PhD). Part-time programs available. *Faculty:* 31 full-time (10 women). *Students:* 92 full-time (37 women), 41 part-time (15 women); includes 14 minority (7 African Americans, 1 Asian American or Pacific Islander, 6 Hispanic Americans), 3 international. Average age 26. 106 applicants, 36% accepted, 17 enrolled. In 2009, 16 master's, 3 doctorates awarded. *Degree requirements:* For master's, one foreign language, comprehensive exam (for some programs), thesis (for some programs), internships; for doctorate, one foreign language, comprehensive exam, thesis/dissertation. *Entrance requirements:* For master's, GRE General Test, minimum GPA of 3.3, minimum 18 hours of course work in history; for doctorate, GRE General Test, minimum GPA of 3.3 (undergraduate), 3.65 (graduate). Additional exam requirements/recommendations for international students: Required—TOEFL (minimum score 550 paper-based; 213 computer-based; 80 iBT). *Application deadline:* For fall admission, 1/10 for domestic students; for spring admission, 10/1 for domestic students. Applications are processed on a rolling basis. Application fee: $30. Electronic applications accepted. *Expenses:* Tuition, state resident: full-time $7413. Tuition, nonresident: full-time $22,567. *Financial support:* In 2009–10, 77 students received support, including 3 fellowships with full tuition reimbursements available (averaging $14,700 per year), 6 research assistantships with full tuition reimbursements available (averaging $9,000 per year), 24 teaching assistantships with full tuition reimbursements available (averaging $10,500 per year); Federal Work-Study, institutionally sponsored loans, scholarships/grants, and unspecified assistantships also available. Financial award application deadline: 1/10; financial award applicants required to submit FAFSA. *Faculty research:* Southern and Caribbean studies, Napoleon and the French Revolution, modern Europe, Latin America, U. S. intellectual and cultural history. *Unit head:* Dr. Neil Jumonville, Interim Chair, 850-644-5888, Fax: 850-644-6402, E-mail: njumonville@fsu.edu. *Application contact:* Chris Pignatiello, Academic Support Assistant, 850-644-2610, Fax: 850-644-6402, E-mail: cpignatiello@fsu.edu.

Georgia College & State University, Graduate School, College of Arts and Sciences, Department of History, Geography and Philosophy, Milledgeville, GA 31061. Offers history (advanced studies option) (MA); history (predoctoral option) (MA); public history (MA). Part-time and evening/weekend programs available. *Faculty:* 18 full-time (3 women). *Students:* 6 full-time (5 women), 5 part-time (2 women). Average age 27. 6 applicants, 83% accepted, 3 enrolled. In 2009, 5 master's awarded. *Degree requirements:* For master's, one foreign language, comprehensive exam (for some programs), thesis optional. *Entrance requirements:* For master's, GRE, 2 letters of reference, transcript. Additional exam requirements/recommendations for international students: Recommended—TOEFL (minimum score 550 paper-based; 213 computer-based; 79 iBT). *Application deadline:* For fall admission, 7/1 for domestic students; for spring admission, 11/15 for domestic students. Applications are processed on a rolling basis. Application fee: $40. Electronic applications accepted. *Expenses:* Tuition, area resident: Part-time $241 per credit hour. Tuition, state resident: full-time $4338. Tuition, nonresident: full-time $17,352; part-time $964 per credit hour. Required fees: $609 per semester. Tuition and fees vary according to course load and campus/location. *Financial support:* In 2009–10, 6 research assistantships were awarded; unspecified assistantships also available. Support available to part-time students. Financial award applicants required to submit FAFSA. *Unit head:* Dr. John Fair, Graduate Coordinator for MA in History Program, 478-445-5215, E-mail: john.fair@gcsu.edu. *Application contact:* Dr. John Fair, Graduate Coordinator for MA in History Program, 478-445-5215, E-mail: john.fair@gcsu.edu.

Indiana University–Purdue University Indianapolis, School of Liberal Arts, Department of History, Indianapolis, IN 46202-2896. Offers history (MA); public history (MA); MA/MLS. Part-time and evening/weekend programs available. *Faculty:* 14 full-time (6 women). *Students:* 24 full-time (20 women), 23 part-time (15 women), 1 international. Average age 30. 238 applicants, 15% accepted, 21 enrolled. In 2009, 11 master's awarded. *Degree requirements:* For master's, one foreign language, thesis. *Entrance requirements:* For master's, GRE General Test, minimum GPA of 3.0. *Application deadline:* For fall admission, 2/1 priority date for domestic students. Applications are processed on a rolling basis. Application fee: $55 ($65 for international students). *Financial support:* In 2009–10, 1 fellowship with full tuition reimbursement (averaging $10,000 per year), 19 teaching assistantships with full tuition reimbursements (averaging $8,612 per year) were awarded; research assistantships with full tuition reimbursements, career-related internships or fieldwork also available. *Unit head:* Robert Barrows, Chair, 317-274-2457. *Application contact:* Mary Gelzleichter, Graduate Secretary, 317-274-5840, Fax: 317-278-7800, E-mail: mgelzlei@iupui.edu.

Loyola University Chicago, Graduate School, Department of History, Chicago, IL 60660. Offers history (MA, PhD); public history (MA). Part-time and evening/weekend programs available. *Faculty:* 24 full-time (9 women), 6 part-time/adjunct (3 women). *Students:* 68 full-time (32 women), 37 part-time (21 women); includes 8 minority (2 African Americans, 1 American Indian/Alaska Native, 5 Hispanic Americans). Average age 31. 138 applicants, 51% accepted, 26 enrolled. In 2009, 25 master's, 7 doctorates awarded. Terminal master's awarded for partial completion of doctoral program. *Degree requirements:* For master's, one foreign language, comprehensive exam, essay; for doctorate, 2 foreign languages, comprehensive exam, thesis/dissertation. *Entrance requirements:* For master's, GRE General Test, research paper; for doctorate, GRE General Test, seminar paper or master's thesis. Additional exam requirements/recommendations for international students: Required—TOEFL (minimum score 550 paper-based; 213 computer-based), IELTS. *Application deadline:* For fall admission, 5/1 for domestic students; for spring admission, 10/1 for domestic students. Applications are processed on a rolling basis. Application fee: $50. Electronic applications accepted. *Expenses:* Tuition: Full-time $14,220; part-time $790 per credit hour. Required fees: $60 per semester hour. Tuition and fees vary according to program. *Financial support:* In 2009–10, 24 students received support, including 11 fellowships with full tuition reimbursements available (averaging $14,500 per year), 13 teaching assistantships with full tuition reimbursements available (averaging $16,500 per year); research assistantships with full tuition reimbursements available, Federal Work-Study also available. Financial award application deadline: 1/1; financial award applicants required to submit FAFSA. *Faculty research:* Medieval and early modern Europe, U. S. public history, U. S. urban history, gender history, Britain and Ireland. *Unit head:* Dr. Timothy Gilfoyle, Chair, 773-508-2232, Fax: 773-508-2153, E-mail: tgilfoy@luc.edu. *Application contact:* Dr. Suzanne Kaufman, Director, Graduate Programs, 773-508-2233, Fax: 773-508-2153, E-mail: skaufma@luc.edu.

Middle Tennessee State University, College of Graduate Studies, College of Liberal Arts, Department of History, Program in Public History, Murfreesboro, TN 37132. Offers MA, PhD. Part-time and evening/weekend programs available. Postbaccalaureate distance learning degree programs offered. *Students:* 20 part-time (11 women); includes 1 minority (African American). 35 applicants, 69% accepted. *Degree requirements:* For master's, one foreign language, comprehensive exam, thesis; for doctorate, comprehensive exam, thesis/dissertation. *Entrance requirements:* For master's and doctorate, GRE. Additional exam requirements/recommendations for international students: Required—TOEFL (minimum score 525 paper-based; 195 computer-based; 71 iBT) or IELTS (minimum score 6). *Application deadline:* For fall admission, 6/1 for domestic and international students. Applications are processed on a rolling basis. Application fee: $25 ($30 for international students). *Expenses:* Tuition, state resident: full-time $4404. Tuition, nonresident: full-time $10,956. *Financial support:* Application deadline: 5/1. *Unit head:* Dr. Amy Sayward, Chair, 615-898-2569, Fax: 615-898-5881, E-mail: asayward@mtsu.edu. *Application contact:* Dr. Michael Allen, Dean and Vice Provost for Research, 615-898-2840, Fax: 615-904-8020, E-mail: mallen@mtsu.edu.

New York University, Graduate School of Arts and Science, Department of History, New York, NY 10012-1019. Offers African diaspora (PhD); African history (PhD); archival management and historical editing (Advanced Certificate); Atlantic history (PhD); French studies/history (PhD); Hebrew and Judaic studies/history (PhD); history (MA, PhD), including Europe (PhD), Latin American and the Caribbean (PhD), United States (PhD), women's history (MA); Middle Eastern history (MA); Middle Eastern studies/history (PhD); public history (Advanced Certificate); world history (MA); JD/MA; MA/Advanced Certificate. Part-time programs available. *Faculty:* 43 full-time (19 women). *Students:* 141 full-time (87 women), 43 part-time (35 women); includes 33 minority (20 African Americans, 5 Asian Americans or Pacific Islanders, 8 Hispanic Americans), 32 international. Average age 30. 406 applicants, 30% accepted, 51 enrolled. In 2009, 21 master's, 10 doctorates, 4 other advanced degrees awarded. Terminal master's awarded for partial completion of doctoral program. *Degree requirements:* For master's, seminar paper; for doctorate, one foreign language, thesis/dissertation, oral and written exams; for Advanced Certificate, internship. *Entrance requirements:* For master's, GRE General Test, minimum GPA of 3.0, writing sample; for doctorate, GRE. Additional exam requirements/recommendations for international students: Required—TOEFL. *Application deadline:* For fall admission, 12/12 for domestic students. Application fee: $90. *Expenses:* Tuition: Full-time $30,528; part-time $1272 per credit. Required fees: $2177. *Financial support:* Fellowships with tuition reimbursements, research assistantships, teaching assistantships with tuition reimbursements, career-related internships or fieldwork, Federal Work-Study, institutionally sponsored loans, scholarships/grants, health care benefits, and unspecified assistantships available. Financial award application deadline: 12/12; financial award applicants required to submit FAFSA. *Faculty research:* African, East Asian, Medieval, early modern, and modern European history; U.S. history; African and African Diaspora; Latin American history; Atlantic World. *Unit head:* Joanna Waley-Cohen, Chair, 212-998-8600, Fax: 212-995-4017, E-mail: history.dept@nyu.edu. *Application contact:* Barbara Weinstein, Director of Graduate Studies, 212-998-8600, Fax: 212-995-4017, E-mail: history.dept@nyu.edu.

North Carolina State University, Graduate School, College of Humanities and Social Sciences, Department of History, Program in Public History, Raleigh, NC 27695. Offers MA. *Degree requirements:* For master's, thesis optional. *Entrance requirements:* For master's, GRE General Test. Electronic applications accepted.

Northeastern University, College of Social Sciences and Humanities, Department of History, Boston, MA 02115-5096. Offers history (MA); public history (MA); world history (PhD). Part-time

Public History

Northeastern University (continued)

and evening/weekend programs available. *Faculty:* 15 full-time (6 women), 2 part-time/adjunct (0 women). *Students:* 63 full-time (42 women), 2 part-time (1 woman); includes 3 Asian Americans or Pacific Islanders, 1 Hispanic American, 5 international. 105 applicants, 53% accepted, 24 enrolled. In 2009, 19 master's, 1 doctorate awarded. Terminal master's awarded for partial completion of doctoral program. *Degree requirements:* For master's, one foreign language, thesis or alternative, project; for doctorate, thesis/dissertation. *Entrance requirements:* For master's and doctorate, GRE General Test. Additional exam requirements/recommendations for international students: Required—TOEFL. *Application deadline:* For fall admission, 2/1 for domestic students. Application fee: $50. Electronic applications accepted. *Financial support:* In 2009–10, teaching assistantships with tuition reimbursements (averaging $14,035 per year); research assistantships with tuition reimbursements, career-related internships or fieldwork, scholarships/grants, and tuition waivers (full and partial) also available. Financial award application deadline: 2/1; financial award applicants required to submit FAFSA. *Faculty research:* World history, U. S. social history. *Unit head:* Dr. Laura Frader, Chair, 617-373-2660, Fax: 617-373-2661. *Application contact:* Dr. Christina Gilmartin, Graduate Coordinator, 617-373-2660, Fax: 617-373-2661.

Northern Kentucky University, Office of Graduate Programs, College of Arts and Sciences, Program in Public History, Highland Heights, KY 41099. Offers MA, Certificate. Part-time programs available. *Students:* 2 full-time (1 woman), 16 part-time (8 women); includes 2 minority (both African Americans). Average age 46. *Degree requirements:* For master's, comprehensive exam. *Entrance requirements:* For master's, bachelor's degree in history or related field from regionally-accredited institution with minimum undergraduate GPA of 2.5; official transcripts for all undergraduate and graduate work; 2 letters of reference. Additional exam requirements/recommendations for international students: Required—TOEFL (minimum score 550 paper-based; 213 computer-based; 79 iBT); Recommended—IELTS (minimum score 6.5). *Application deadline:* For fall admission, 8/1 priority date for domestic students, 6/1 priority date for international students; for spring admission, 12/1 priority date for domestic students, 10/1 priority date for international students. Applications are processed on a rolling basis. Application fee: $40. Electronic applications accepted. *Expenses:* Tuition, state resident: full-time $6912; part-time $384 per credit hour. Tuition, nonresident: full-time $12,150; part-time $675 per credit hour. Tuition and fees vary according to course load, program and reciprocity agreements. *Financial support:* Applicants required to submit FAFSA. *Faculty research:* Local and regional history, oral history, Appalachian history, Gilded Age and Progressive eras. *Unit head:* Dr. Rebecca Bailey, Director, 859-572-5176, E-mail: baileyr4@nku.edu. *Application contact:* Dr. Rebecca Bailey, Director of Graduate Programs, 859-572-5176, E-mail: baileyr4@nku.edu.

Rutgers, The State University of New Jersey, Camden, Graduate School of Arts and Sciences, Program in American and Public History, Camden, NJ 08102-1401. Offers MA. Part-time and evening/weekend programs available. *Degree requirements:* For master's, comprehensive exam. *Entrance requirements:* For master's, GRE General Test (full-time applicants), 3 letters of recommendation. Additional exam requirements/recommendations for international students: Required—TOEFL, IELTS. Electronic applications accepted. *Faculty research:* Women's history, military history, Afro-American history, urban history, history of technology.

Shippensburg University of Pennsylvania, School of Graduate Studies, College of Arts and Sciences, Department of History and Philosophy, Shippensburg, PA 17257-2299. Offers applied history (MA, Certificate). Part-time and evening/weekend programs available. *Degree requirements:* For master's, thesis or internship. *Entrance requirements:* For master's, interview. Additional exam requirements/recommendations for international students: Required—TOEFL (minimum score 560 paper-based; 220 computer-based); Recommended—IELTS (minimum score 6). Electronic applications accepted.

Shippensburg University of Pennsylvania, School of Graduate Studies, College of Arts and Sciences, Department of Sociology and Anthropology, Shippensburg, PA 17257-2299. Offers organizational development and leadership (MS), including business, communications, education, environmental management, higher education, historical administration, individual and organizational development, public organizations, social structures and organizations. Part-time and evening/weekend programs available. *Degree requirements:* For master's, capstone experience. *Entrance requirements:* For master's, interview (if GPA less than 2.75), resume. Additional exam requirements/recommendations for international students: Required—TOEFL (minimum score 560 paper-based; 220 computer-based); Recommended—IELTS (minimum score 6). Electronic applications accepted.

Simmons College, Graduate School of Library and Information Science and College of Arts and Sciences Graduate Studies, Program in History and Archives Management, Boston, MA 02115. Offers Certificate, MS/MA. Part-time and evening/weekend programs available. *Faculty:* 25 full-time (17 women), 34 part-time/adjunct (22 women). *Students:* 44 full-time (37 women), 207 part-time (157 women); includes 15 minority (4 African Americans, 1 American Indian/Alaska Native, 8 Asian Americans or Pacific Islanders, 2 Hispanic Americans), 4 international. Average age 30. 198 applicants, 80% accepted, 92 enrolled. *Entrance requirements:* Additional exam requirements/recommendations for international students: Required—TOEFL (minimum score 550 paper-based; 213 computer-based; 79 iBT). *Application deadline:* For fall admission, 3/1 priority date for domestic students, 3/1 for international students; for spring admission, 9/1 priority date for domestic students, 9/1 for international students. Applications are processed on a rolling basis. Application fee: $50. Electronic applications accepted. *Expenses:* Contact institution. *Financial support:* Scholarships/grants available. Financial award application deadline: 3/1; financial award applicants required to submit FAFSA. *Faculty research:* Library leadership, archives and preservation, organization, information use and users. Total annual research expenditures: $253,656. *Unit head:* Michele Cloonan, Dean of the Graduate School of Library and Information Science, 617-521-2806. *Application contact:* Sarah Petrakos, Assistant Dean, Admission and Recruitment, 617-521-2868, Fax: 617-521-3192, E-mail: gslisadm@simmons.edu.

Sonoma State University, School of Social Sciences, Program in Cultural Resources Management, Rohnert Park, CA 94928. Offers MA. Part-time programs available. *Faculty:* 3 full-time (1 woman). *Students:* 31 part-time (23 women); includes 2 minority (1 Asian American or Pacific Islander, 1 Hispanic American), 1 international. Average age 31. 25 applicants, 36% accepted, 5 enrolled. In 2009, 3 master's awarded. *Degree requirements:* For master's, thesis. *Entrance requirements:* For master's, minimum GPA of 3.0. Additional exam requirements/recommendations for international students: Required—TOEFL (minimum score 500 paper-based; 173 computer-based). *Application deadline:* For fall admission, 1/31 for domestic students. Application fee: $55. *Expenses:* Tuition, nonresident: full-time $11,160. Required fees: $6226. Full-time tuition and fees vary according to course load. *Financial support:* Career-related internships or fieldwork, scholarships/grants, traineeships, and unspecified assistantships available. Financial award application deadline: 3/2; financial award applicants required to submit FAFSA. *Unit head:* Dr. John D. Wingard, Chair, Anthropology Department, 707-664-2319, Fax: 707-664-2505, E-mail: john.wingard@sonoma.edu. *Application contact:* Margaret Purser, Coordinator, 707-664-3164, Fax: 707-664-2505, E-mail: margaret.purser@sonoma.edu.

University at Albany, State University of New York, College of Arts and Sciences, Department of History, Albany, NY 12222-0001. Offers history (MA, PhD); public history (Certificate). Part-time programs available. *Degree requirements:* For master's, variable foreign language requirement, exam, research paper or thesis; for doctorate, thesis/dissertation. *Entrance requirements:* For master's, minimum GPA of 3.0; for doctorate, GRE General Test, minimum GPA of 3.0. Additional exam requirements/recommendations for international students: Required—TOEFL (minimum score 550 paper-based; 213 computer-based). Electronic applications accepted. *Faculty research:* American history (all phases); public policy; European history (Medieval to modern); Asian, African, and Latin American history.

University of Arkansas at Little Rock, Graduate School, College of Arts, Humanities, and Social Science, Department of History, Little Rock, AR 72204-1099. Offers public history (MA). Part-time programs available. *Degree requirements:* For master's, oral exam. *Entrance requirements:* For master's, GRE General Test, minimum GPA of 3.25 in history, 2.7 overall; 18 hours of art history. *Faculty research:* Historic preservation and restoration, museum studies, archives.

The University of British Columbia, Faculty of Arts, School of Library, Archival and Information Studies, Master of Archival Studies Program, Vancouver, BC V6T 1Z1, Canada. Offers MAS. *Degree requirements:* For master's, thesis optional. *Entrance requirements:* For master's, minimum B+ average or minimum GPA of 3.3 in undergraduate upper-division courses. Additional exam requirements/recommendations for international students: Required—TOEFL (minimum score 600 paper-based; 250 computer-based; 100 iBT). Electronic applications accepted. *Faculty research:* Diplomatics, electronic record, appraisal, descriptive standards, preservation.

The University of British Columbia, Faculty of Arts, School of Library, Archival and Information Studies, PhD Program in Library, Archival and Information Studies, Vancouver, BC V6T 1Z1, Canada. Offers PhD. *Degree requirements:* For doctorate, thesis/dissertation. *Entrance requirements:* For doctorate, GRE, minimum GPA of 3.3 in MAS or MLIS (other master's degrees may be considered). Additional exam requirements/recommendations for international students: Required—TOEFL (minimum score 600 paper-based; 250 computer-based; 100 iBT). Electronic applications accepted. *Faculty research:* Computer systems/database design; library and archival management; archival description and organization; children's literature and youth services; interactive information retrieval.

University of Houston, College of Liberal Arts and Social Sciences, Department of History, Houston, TX 77204. Offers history (MA, PhD); public history (MA). Part-time programs available. *Faculty:* 24 full-time (9 women), 2 part-time/adjunct (both women). *Students:* 57 full-time (30 women), 36 part-time (19 women); includes 15 minority (3 African Americans, 2 American Indian/Alaska Native, 1 Asian American or Pacific Islander, 9 Hispanic Americans). Average age 35. 37 applicants, 62% accepted, 14 enrolled. In 2009, 10 master's, 9 doctorates awarded. Terminal master's awarded for partial completion of doctoral program. *Degree requirements:* For master's, one foreign language, thesis (for some programs); for doctorate, one foreign language, thesis/dissertation. *Entrance requirements:* For master's, GRE General Test, minimum GPA of 3.3; for doctorate, GRE General Test, minimum GPA of 3.67. Additional exam requirements/recommendations for international students: Required—TOEFL. *Application deadline:* For fall admission, 1/15 for domestic students; for spring admission, 11/1 for domestic students. Application fee: $75 for international students. Electronic applications accepted. *Expenses:* Tuition, state resident: full-time $7676; part-time $320 per credit hour. Tuition, nonresident: full-time $14,324; part-time $597 per credit hour. Required fees: $3034. *Financial support:* In 2009–10, 1 fellowship with full tuition reimbursement (averaging $9,800 per year), 6 research assistantships with full tuition reimbursements (averaging $9,800 per year), 35 teaching assistantships with full tuition reimbursements (averaging $9,800 per year) were awarded; career-related internships or fieldwork, Federal Work-Study, institutionally sponsored loans, scholarships/grants, health care benefits, and unspecified assistantships also available. Support available to part-time students. Financial award application deadline: 2/1. *Faculty research:* U. S., Latin American, European, social, and women's history. *Unit head:* Dr. John Hart, Chairperson, 713-743-3008, Fax: 713-743-3216, E-mail: jhart@uh.edu. *Application contact:* Dr. John Hart, Chairperson, 713-743-3008, Fax: 713-743-3216, E-mail: jhart@uh.edu.

University of Illinois at Springfield, Graduate Programs, College of Liberal Arts and Sciences, Program in History, Springfield, IL 62703-5407. Offers MA. Part-time and evening/weekend programs available. *Faculty:* 9 full-time (4 women). *Students:* 17 full-time (10 women), 35 part-time (20 women); includes 9 minority (5 African Americans, 1 American Indian/Alaska Native, 3 Hispanic Americans). Average age 34. 19 applicants, 63% accepted, 10 enrolled. In 2009, 14 master's awarded. *Degree requirements:* For master's, thesis, internship, or historiography. *Entrance requirements:* For master's, BA in history or related field, minimum undergraduate GPA of 3.0, writing sample. Additional exam requirements/recommendations for international students: Required—TOEFL (minimum score 500 paper-based; 176 computer-based; 61 iBT). *Application deadline:* Applications are processed on a rolling basis. Application fee: $50 ($60 for international students). Electronic applications accepted. *Expenses:* Tuition, state resident: full-time $6390; part-time $266.25 per credit hour. Tuition, nonresident: full-time $14,226; part-time $592.75 per credit hour. Required fees: $2044; $14.36 per credit hour. $722.50 per term. *Financial support:* In 2009–10, research assistantships with full tuition reimbursements (averaging $8,109 per year), teaching assistantships with full tuition reimbursements (averaging $8,109 per year) were awarded; career-related internships or fieldwork, Federal Work-Study, scholarships/grants, health care benefits, and unspecified assistantships also available. Support available to part-time students. Financial award application deadline: 11/15; financial award applicants required to submit FAFSA. *Unit head:* Dr. Robert McGregor, Program Administrator, 217-206-7442, Fax: 217-206-6217, E-mail: mcgregor.robert@uis.edu. *Application contact:* Dr. Lynn Pardie, Office of Graduate Studies, 800-252-8533, Fax: 217-206-7623, E-mail: pardie.lynn@uis.edu.

University of Louisville, Graduate School, College of Arts and Sciences, Department of History, Louisville, KY 40292. Offers history (MA); public history (Certificate). Part-time programs available. *Faculty:* 17 full-time (4 women). *Students:* 8 full-time (3 women), 18 part-time (6 women); includes 3 minority (1 African American, 2 American Indian/Alaska Native). Average age 30. 25 applicants, 76% accepted, 13 enrolled. In 2009, 5 master's awarded. *Degree requirements:* For master's, one foreign language, comprehensive exam (for some programs), thesis (for some programs). *Entrance requirements:* For master's, GRE General Test. Additional exam requirements/recommendations for international students: Required—TOEFL. *Application deadline:* For fall admission, 5/15 for domestic students, 5/1 for international students; for spring admission, 12/1 for domestic students, 11/1 for international students. Applications are processed on a rolling basis. Application fee: $50. Electronic applications accepted. *Financial support:* In 2009–10, 2 students received support, including 2 teaching assistantships. Financial award applicants required to submit FAFSA. *Faculty research:* United States, British Empire, twentieth century women's history, Turkey and the Middle East, African diaspora. *Unit head:* Dr. Tracy Elaine K'Meyer, Chair, 502-852-6817, Fax: 502-852-0770, E-mail: tracyk@louisville.edu. *Application contact:* Libby Leggett, Director, Graduate Admissions, 502-852-3101, Fax: 502-852-6536, E-mail: gradadm@louisville.edu.

University of Massachusetts Amherst, Graduate School, College of Humanities and Fine Arts, Department of History, Amherst, MA 01003. Offers ancient history (MA); British Empire history (MA); European (medieval and modern) history (MA, PhD); Islamic history (MA); Latin American history (MA, PhD); modern global history (MA); public history (MA); science and technology history (MA); U.S. history (MA, PhD). Part-time programs available. *Faculty:* 39 full-time (17 women). *Students:* 52 full-time (32 women), 13 part-time (6 women); includes 7 minority (4 African Americans, 1 Asian American or Pacific Islander, 2 Hispanic Americans), 3 international. Average age 33. 137 applicants, 39% accepted, 18 enrolled. In 2009, 9 master's, 2 doctorates awarded. Terminal master's awarded for partial completion of doctoral program. *Degree requirements:* For master's, one foreign language, thesis or alternative; for doctorate, one foreign language, comprehensive exam, thesis/dissertation. *Entrance requirements:* For master's and doctorate, GRE General Test, writing sample. Additional exam requirements/recommendations for international students: Required—TOEFL (minimum score 550 paper-based; 213 computer-based; 80 iBT), IELTS (minimum score 6.5). *Application deadline:* For fall admission, 1/2 for domestic and international students. Applications are processed on a rolling basis. Application fee: $50 ($65 for international students). Electronic applications accepted. *Expenses:* Tuition, state resident: full-time $2640; part-time $110 per credit. Tuition, nonresident: full-time $9936; part-time $414 per credit. Tuition and fees vary according to course load. *Financial support:* In 2009–10, 1 fellowship with full tuition reimbursement (averaging $3,973 per year), 6 research assistantships with full tuition reimbursements (averaging $6,246 per year), 36 teaching assistantships with full tuition reimbursements (averaging $12,895 per year),

year) were awarded; career-related internships or fieldwork, Federal Work-Study, scholarships/grants, traineeships, health care benefits, tuition waivers (full), and unspecified assistantships also available. Support available to part-time students. Financial award application deadline: 1/2. *Faculty research:* Ancient and medieval history; global and comparative history; public history; history of science, technology, medicine and the environment; history of women, gender, sexuality and family. *Unit head:* Dr. Brian W. Ogilvie, Graduate Program Director, 413-545-6791, Fax: 413-545-6137. *Application contact:* Jean M. Ames, Supervisor of Admissions, 413-545-0722, Fax: 413-577-0010, E-mail: gradadm@grad.umass.edu.

University of Massachusetts Boston, Office of Graduate Studies, College of Liberal Arts, Program in History, Boston, MA 02125-3393. Offers archival methods (MA); historical archaeology (MA); history (MA). Part-time and evening/weekend programs available. *Degree requirements:* For master's, thesis, oral exam. *Entrance requirements:* For master's, minimum GPA of 2.75. *Faculty research:* European intellectual history, American labor and social history in 19th century, colonial American Revolution, Afro-American Cold War.

University of South Carolina, The Graduate School, College of Arts and Sciences, Department of History, Program in Public History, Columbia, SC 29208. Offers archives (MA); historic preservation (MA); museum (MA); museum management (Certificate); MLIS/MA. *Degree requirements:* For master's, one foreign language, thesis, internship. *Entrance requirements:* For master's, GRE General Test, writing sample. Additional exam requirements/recommendations for international students: Required—TOEFL. Electronic applications accepted. *Faculty research:* Museum studies, historic preservation, archives administration.

The University of Texas at Austin, Graduate School, College of Liberal Arts, Department of Anthropology, Program in Folklore and Public Culture, Austin, TX 78712-1111. Offers MA, PhD. Part-time programs available. Terminal master's awarded for partial completion of doctoral program. *Degree requirements:* For master's, one foreign language, thesis, report; for doctorate, one foreign language, thesis/dissertation. *Entrance requirements:* For master's and doctorate, GRE General Test. Electronic applications accepted. *Faculty research:* Expressive culture, gender, genre, folklore and culture of British Isles, ethnography of speaking.

University of West Florida, College of Arts and Sciences: Arts, Department of History, Pensacola, FL 32514-5750. Offers historic preservation (MA); history (MA); military history (MA); public history (MA). Part-time and evening/weekend programs available. *Faculty:* 5 full-time (1 woman), 1 part-time/adjunct (0 women). *Students:* 14 full-time (6 women), 23 part-time (12 women); includes 5 minority (2 African Americans, 1 American Indian/Alaska Native, 1 Asian American or Pacific Islander, 1 Hispanic American). Average age 31. 26 applicants, 73% accepted, 9 enrolled. In 2009, 10 master's awarded. *Degree requirements:* For master's, thesis or alternative. *Entrance requirements:* For master's, GRE General Test, minimum GPA of 3.0, minimum 15 hours of upper-level history courses. Additional exam requirements/recommendations for international students: Required—TOEFL (minimum score 550 paper-based; 213 computer-based). *Application deadline:* For fall admission, 6/1 for domestic students, 5/15 for international students; for spring admission, 11/1 for domestic students, 10/1 for international students. Applications are processed on a rolling basis. Application fee: $30. *Expenses:* Tuition, state resident: full-time $4982; part-time $260 per credit hour. Tuition, nonresident: full-time $20,059; part-time $919 per credit hour. Required fees: $1247; $52 per credit hour. *Financial support:* In 2009–10, 2 teaching assistantships with partial tuition reimbursements (averaging $5,000 per year) were awarded; unspecified assistantships also available. Financial award application deadline: 4/15; financial award applicants required to submit FAFSA. *Unit head:* Dr. John J. Clune, Chairperson, 850-474-2680. *Application contact:* Terry McCray, Assistant Director of Graduate Admissions, 850-473-7718, Fax: 850-473-7714, E-mail: gradadmissions@uwf.edu.

University of West Georgia, Graduate School, College of Arts and Sciences, Department of History, Carrollton, GA 30118. Offers history (MA); museum studies (Certificate); public history (Certificate). Part-time programs available. *Faculty:* 16 full-time (6 women). *Students:* 22 full-time (12 women), 21 part-time (11 women); includes 3 minority (1 African American, 2 Hispanic Americans). Average age 35. 23 applicants, 57% accepted, 6 enrolled. In 2009, 10 master's, 9 other advanced degrees awarded. *Degree requirements:* For master's, one foreign language, comprehensive exam, thesis or alternative. *Entrance requirements:* For master's, GRE General Test (minimum score 400 verbal, 400 quantitative, 3.5 writing), undergraduate degree in history or related social studies, minimum GPA of 2.75. *Application deadline:* For fall admission, 7/17 for domestic students; for spring admission, 11/20 for domestic students. Applications are processed on a rolling basis. Application fee: $30. Electronic applications accepted. *Expenses:* Tuition, state resident: full-time $2952; part-time $164 per semester hour. Tuition, nonresident: full-time $11,808; part-time $656 per semester hour. Required fees: $42.90 per semester hour. $307 per semester. Tuition and fees vary according to course load. *Financial support:* In 2009–10, 7 students received support, including research assistantships with full tuition reimbursements available (averaging $6,000 per year); career-related internships or fieldwork, scholarships/grants, and unspecified assistantships also available. Support available to part-time students. Financial award application deadline: 7/1; financial award applicants required to submit FAFSA. *Faculty research:* Public history, United States, Russia/Soviet Union, Africa, Europe. *Unit head:* Dr. Howard Steven Goodson, Interim Chair, 678-839-6042, E-mail: hgoodson@westga.edu. *Application contact:* Dr. Charles W. Clark, Dean, 678-839-6508, E-mail: cclark@westga.edu.

Washington State University, Graduate School, College of Liberal Arts, Department of History, Pullman, WA 99164. Offers early and modern European history (MA, PhD); environmental history (MA, PhD); Latin American history (MA, PhD); modern East Asia history (MA, PhD); public history (MA, PhD); US history (MA, PhD); women's history (MA, PhD); world history (MA, PhD). Part-time programs available. *Faculty:* 25. *Students:* 38 full-time (22 women), 10 part-time (4 women); includes 3 minority (1 American Indian/Alaska Native, 2 Hispanic Americans), 2 international. Average age 33. 57 applicants, 47% accepted, 10 enrolled. In 2009, 10 master's, 2 doctorates awarded. *Degree requirements:* For master's, comprehensive exam (for some programs), thesis, oral exam; for doctorate, one foreign language, comprehensive exam, thesis/dissertation, oral and written exam. *Entrance requirements:* For master's and doctorate, GRE General Test, Graduate School Application form; official transcripts from all universities attended; GRE scores; TOEFL or IELTS scores (international students only); three letters of recommendation; a statement of purpose; a writing sample, Preferred Fields of Study form; and the Language Background form. Additional exam requirements/recommendations for international students: Required—TOEFL (minimum score 550 paper-based), IELTS. *Application deadline:* For fall admission, 1/10 for domestic and international students; for spring admission, 7/1 for domestic and international students. Applications are processed on a rolling basis. Application fee: $50. Electronic applications accepted. *Financial support:* In 2009–10, 1 fellowship with partial tuition reimbursement (averaging $3,000 per year), research assistantships with full and partial tuition reimbursements (averaging $13,917 per year), 28 teaching assistantships with full and partial tuition reimbursements (averaging $13,056 per year) were awarded; career-related internships or fieldwork, Federal Work-Study, institutionally sponsored loans, scholarships/grants, and health care benefits also available. Financial award application deadline: 2/15; financial award applicants required to submit FAFSA. *Faculty research:* Public, world, environmental, women's and U. S. history. *Unit head:* Dr. Raymond Sun, Chair, 509-335-5139, Fax: 509-335-4171, E-mail: pietz@wsu.edu. *Application contact:* Graduate Studies Director, 509-335-4030, Fax: 509-335-4171, E-mail: kale@wsu.edu.

VILLANOVA UNIVERSITY

Graduate Studies in Liberal Arts and Sciences
Department of History

Program of Study

Villanova University is one of relatively few academic institutions in the country that offers only an M.A. degree in history, rather than the M.A. and Ph.D. The program seeks to encourage students' love of history and strengthen their analytical and interpretive skills to meet diverse career goals.

Over the course of an academic year (fall and spring semesters and a summer term), twenty-three different graduate seminars are typically offered that cover a broad range of historical periods, themes, and regions. The average class size is 11 to 12 students. During the fall and spring semesters, classes meet once a week for 2 hours in the late afternoon or early evening. During the summer, classes meet one evening each week for eight weeks. The program is especially strong in European and American history, but thematic and non-Western topics are an important part of the curriculum.

Program requirements include the successful completion of ten graduate courses and a passing score on the comprehensive examination. There is no formal language requirement. Students may begin taking courses in the fall, spring, or summer sessions and may take courses on a part-time (one course per session) or full-time basis. As many as two graduate courses in related disciplines, such as literature or political science, may be taken at Villanova. Students may also transfer a maximum of 6 credits for graduate courses taken at other institutions.

Research Facilities

The University Library contains more than 780,000 volumes and 5,600 current periodicals. The Philadelphia region, with its numerous other colleges and universities, museums, historical societies, and archival collections, offers a rich cultural and institutional environment for study and research in history.

Financial Aid

The Department has graduate assistantships and tuition scholarships for 15 full-time students. Graduate assistantships are awarded on a competitive basis. The assistantship in history includes a waiver of all tuition and academic fees and a stipend of $6750 in 2010–11. A number of tuition scholarships are also available that provide a waiver of all tuition and academic fees.

In addition, the office of the director of financial aid administers the Federal Stafford Student Loan, the unsubsidized Federal Stafford Student Loan, and the Federal Supplemental Loans for Students.

Cost of Study

Graduate tuition is $650 per credit hour in 2010–11. In addition, there are a one-time application fee of $50 and a University fee of $30 each semester.

Living and Housing Costs

The area surrounding the University offers a wide selection of living quarters that are convenient to the campus, which is served by two suburban rail lines and buses. The University does not maintain accommodations for graduate students, but second-year students are eligible for positions as resident counselors in the dormitories.

Student Group

There is no typical graduate student in history at Villanova. The students comprise a large and diverse yet very congenial community. Many students enter the program directly from their undergraduate college. Others are completing graduate work in history while also engaged in careers in government service, law, business, or teaching. In any given semester, between 70 and 80 students take courses, approximately one third of whom are part-time students.

Student Outcomes

Many students continue to study toward a Ph.D. in history; recent graduates may be found in doctoral programs at Temple, Indiana Bloomington, the College of William and Mary, the University of Madrid, Brandeis, and other institutions. Other graduates pursue history-related careers in libraries, archives, or museums. Many have gone on to teaching or educational administration at the secondary or college level in places as diverse as Kuwait and West Point. Still other graduates work for government or nonprofit organizations, newspapers, or corporations.

Location

Located in the heart of the Delaware Valley's Main Line, the University occupies more than 200 handsomely landscaped acres in the town of Villanova, 12 miles west of Philadelphia. The location combines the advantages of a tranquil suburban setting with proximity to a large metropolitan city known for its outstanding historical, educational, and cultural resources.

The University

Villanova University is a private institution founded in 1842 by the Augustinian Fathers. Graduate programs were first administered separately in 1931. Currently, there are five academic units in addition to Graduate Studies: the Colleges of Arts and Sciences, Commerce and Finance, Engineering, and Nursing and the School of Law.

Applying

Applicants should have at least 18 undergraduate credits and a 3.0 average in history. The Graduate Record Examinations General Test is required for admission to the program. International applicants must take the TOEFL examination. Application deadlines are March 1 for fall admission, November 15 for spring admission, and May 1 for summer admission. The deadline is March 1 for those applying for a graduate assistantship.

Application forms and other information may be obtained from either the Department of History or the Office of Graduate Studies in the College of Liberal Arts and Sciences, Villanova University, 800 Lancaster Avenue, Villanova, Pennsylvania 19085; phone: 610-519-7090; fax: 610-519-7096; e-mail: gradinformation@villanova.edu). Online submission of applications is also possible at http://www.villanova.edu/artsci/college/academics/graduate/.

Correspondence and Information

To discuss situation, qualifications, and goals:

Dr. R. Emmet McLaughlin, Director of the History Graduate Program
Department of History
Villanova University
Villanova, Pennsylvania 19085-1696
Phone: 610-519-4660
E-mail: emmet.mclaughlin@villanova.edu
Web site: http://www.villanova.edu/artsci/history/

Villanova University

THE FACULTY AND THEIR RESEARCH

Marc Gallicchio, Professor and Chair; Ph.D., Temple, 1986. U.S. foreign relations, American political and military history.
Hibba Abugideiri, Assistant Professor; Ph.D., Georgetown, 2001. Middle East history.
Craig Bailey, Assistant Professor; Ph.D., London, 2004. History of Ireland and Britain.
Judith Ann Giesberg, Associate Professor; Ph.D., Boston College, 1997. U.S. women's history.
Christopher Haas, Associate Professor; Ph.D., Michigan, 1988. Greece, Rome, late antiquity, early Christianity history.
Lynne Ann Hartnett, Assistant Professor; Ph.D., Boston College, 2000. Russian/Soviet history, European women's history.
Jeffrey A. Johnson, Professor; Ph.D., Princeton, 1980. History of science and technology.
Maghan Keita, Professor; Ph.D., Howard, 1988. African and world history.
Catherine Kerrison, Associate Professor; Ph.D., William and Mary, 1999. Colonial and revolutionary America, U.S. women's history.
Elizabeth Kolsky, Assistant Professor; Ph.D., Columbia, 2002. South Asian history.
Adele Lindenmeyr, Professor; Ph.D., Princeton, 1980. Russia and Soviet history, environmental history.
Lawrence Little, Associate Professor; Ph.D., Ohio State, 1993. African-American history.
Timothy McCall, Assistant Professor; Ph.D., Michigan, 2005. History of Renaissance art.
R. Emmet McLaughlin, Professor; Ph.D., Yale, 1980. Renaissance and Reformation history, early modern European history.
Paul Rosier, Associate Professor; Ph.D., Rochester, 1998. Modern and Native American history.
Rev. Joseph G. Ryan, O.S.A., Assistant Professor; Ph.D., American, 1997. American history, history of medicine.
Holly Sanders, Assistant Professor; Ph.D., Princeton, 2005. History of modern Asia.
Paul R. Steege, Associate Professor; Ph.D., Chicago, 1999. Post-1945 European history.
Rebecca L. Winer, Associate Professor; Ph.D., UCLA, 1996. Medieval Europe, European women's history, Jewish history.

Section 8
Humanities

This section contains a directory of institutions offering graduate work in humanities. Additional information about programs listed in the directory may be obtained by writing directly to the dean of a graduate school or chair of a department at the address given in the directory.

For programs offering related work, see also in this book *Area and Cultural Studies, Geography, Interdisciplinary Studies, Philosophy, Political Science and International Affairs, Religious Studies,* and *Sociology, Anthropology, and Archaeology.* In another guide in this series:

Graduate Programs in Engineering & Applied Sciences
See *Management of Engineering and Technology*

CONTENTS

Program Directories

Humanities 306
Liberal Studies 310

Humanities

American Public University System, AMU/APU Graduate Programs, Charles Town, WV 25414. Offers air warfare (MA Military Studies); American Revolution (MA Military Studies); business administration (MBA); Civil War (MA Military Studies); criminal justice (MA); defense management (MA Military Studies); emergency and disaster management (MA); environmental policy and management (MS); fire science management (MA); global engagement (MA); history (MA); homeland security (MA); humanities (MA); intelligence (MA Military Studies, MA Strategic Intelligence); international peace and conflict resolution (MA); international relations and conflict resolution (MA); joint warfare (MA Military Studies); land warfare international perspective (MA Military Studies); management (MA); military history (MA); military leadership (MA Military Studies); national security studies (MA); naval warfare international (MA Military Studies); naval warfare US (MA Military Studies); political science (MA); public administration (MA); public health (MA); security management (MA); space studies (MS); special ops/LIC (MA Military Studies); sports management (MA); transportation and logistics management (MA); transportation management (MA); unconventional warfare (MA Military Studies); World War II (MA Military Studies). Programs offered via distance learning only. Part-time and evening/weekend programs available. Postbaccalaureate distance learning degree programs offered (no on-campus study). *Faculty:* 10 full-time (3 women), 188 part-time/adjunct (57 women). *Students:* 340 full-time (98 women), 3,567 part-time (790 women); includes 615 minority (317 African Americans, 28 American Indian/Alaska Native, 85 Asian Americans or Pacific Islanders, 185 Hispanic Americans), 20 international. Average age 36. 2,123 applicants, 100% accepted, 893 enrolled. In 2009, 829 degrees awarded. *Degree requirements:* For master's, comprehensive exam. *Entrance requirements:* For master's, bachelor's degree or equivalent, minimum GPA of 2.7 in last 60 hours of course work. *Application deadline:* Applications are processed on a rolling basis. Application fee: $0. Electronic applications accepted. *Financial support:* Applicants required to submit FAFSA. *Faculty research:* Military history, criminal justice, management performance, national security. *Unit head:* Dr. Frank McCluskey, Provost, 877-468-6268, Fax: 304-724-3780. *Application contact:* Terry Grant, Director of Enrollment Management, 877-468-6268, Fax: 304-724-3780, E-mail: info@apus.edu.

Arcadia University, Graduate Studies, Program in Humanities, Glenside, PA 19038-3295. Offers fine arts, theater, and music (MAH); history, philosophy, and religion (MAH); literature and language (MAH). Part-time programs available. *Faculty:* 17 full-time (5 women), 13 part-time/adjunct (10 women). *Students:* 7 full-time (3 women), 25 part-time (19 women); includes 6 minority (all African Americans), 1 international. Average age 35. In 2009, 8 master's awarded. *Degree requirements:* For master's, thesis or alternative. *Application deadline:* Applications are processed on a rolling basis. Application fee: $50. *Expenses:* Tuition: Full-time $30,450; part-time $620 per credit hour. Required fees: $165. Tuition and fees vary according to program. *Financial support:* Unspecified assistantships available. *Unit head:* Dr. Richard Wertime, Coordinator, 215-572-2963. *Application contact:* 215-572-2925, Fax: 215-572-2126, E-mail: grad@arcadia.edu.

Brigham Young University, Graduate Studies, College of Humanities, Department of Humanities, Classics, and Comparative Literature, Provo, UT 84602-1001. Offers comparative studies (MA). *Faculty:* 25 full-time (5 women). *Students:* 16 full-time (9 women). Average age 27. 11 applicants, 55% accepted, 6 enrolled. In 2009, 7 master's awarded. *Degree requirements:* For master's, 2 foreign languages, thesis. *Entrance requirements:* For master's, GRE, minimum GPA of 3.0 in last 60 hours. Additional exam requirements/recommendations for international students: Required—TOEFL (minimum score 580 paper-based; 85 iBT), IELTS (minimum score 7). *Application deadline:* For fall admission, 3/1 for domestic and international students. Application fee: $50. Electronic applications accepted. *Expenses:* Tuition: Full-time $5580; part-time $301 per credit hour. Tuition and fees vary according to student's religious affiliation. *Financial support:* In 2009–10, 16 students received support, including 4 research assistantships (averaging $1,875 per year), 36 teaching assistantships (averaging $2,620 per year); career-related internships or fieldwork, institutionally sponsored loans, scholarships/grants, tuition waivers (full and partial), and student instructorships also available. Support available to part-time students. *Unit head:* Dr. Michael J. Call, Chair, 801-422-2550, Fax: 801-422-0305, E-mail: michael_call@byu.edu. *Application contact:* Carolyn Hone, Graduate Secretary for Humanities and Comparative Literature, 801-422-4430, Fax: 801-422-0305, E-mail: carolyn_hone@byu.edu.

California Institute of Integral Studies, School of Consciousness and Transformation, San Francisco, CA 94103. Offers creative inquiry (MFA); cultural anthropology and social transformation (MA); East-West psychology (MA, PhD); integrative health studies (MA); philosophy and religion (MA, PhD), including Asian and comparative studies, philosophy, cosmology, and consciousness, women's spirituality; social and cultural anthropology (PhD); transformative leadership (MA); transformative studies (PhD); writing and consciousness (MFA). Part-time and evening/weekend programs available. Postbaccalaureate distance learning degree programs offered (minimal on-campus study). *Students:* 334 full-time (218 women), 126 part-time (77 women); includes 116 minority (40 African Americans, 4 American Indian/Alaska Native, 42 Asian Americans or Pacific Islanders, 30 Hispanic Americans). Average age 38. 265 applicants, 90% accepted, 149 enrolled. In 2009, 64 master's, 22 doctorates awarded. Terminal master's awarded for partial completion of doctoral program. *Degree requirements:* For master's, comprehensive exam (for some programs), thesis optional; for doctorate, comprehensive exam, thesis/dissertation, 1 foreign language (Asian comparative studies). *Entrance requirements:* For master's, minimum GPA of 3.0, letters of recommendation, writing sample; for doctorate, master's degree, minimum GPA of 3.0, letters of recommendation, writing sample. Additional exam requirements/recommendations for international students: Required—TOEFL. *Application deadline:* For fall admission, 2/1 priority date for domestic and international students; for spring admission, 10/15 priority date for domestic and international students. Applications are processed on a rolling basis. Application fee: $65. Electronic applications accepted. *Expenses:* Tuition: Full-time $15,300; part-time $850 per credit hour. Required fees: $110 per semester. Tuition and fees vary according to degree level. *Financial support:* In 2009–10, 330 students received support; research assistantships, teaching assistantships, career-related internships or fieldwork, Federal Work-Study, scholarships/grants, and tuition waivers (partial) available. Support available to part-time students. Financial award application deadline: 4/15; financial award applicants required to submit FAFSA. *Faculty research:* Altered states of consciousness, dreams, cosmology, postcolonial studies, integrative health studies. *Application contact:* Allyson Werner, Associate Director of Admissions, 415-575-6155, Fax: 415-575-1268.

California State University, Dominguez Hills, College of Arts and Humanities, Program in the Humanities, Carson, CA 90747-0001. Offers MA. Part-time and evening/weekend programs available. *Faculty:* 12 full-time (7 women), 6 part-time/adjunct (2 women). *Students:* 8 full-time (6 women), 40 part-time (25 women); includes 22 minority (15 African Americans, 1 American Indian/Alaska Native, 1 Asian American or Pacific Islander, 5 Hispanic Americans), 1 international. Average age 41. 34 applicants, 91% accepted, 20 enrolled. In 2009, 1 master's awarded. *Degree requirements:* For master's, thesis or alternative. *Entrance requirements:* For master's, minimum GPA of 3.0. *Application deadline:* For fall admission, 6/1 for domestic students. Applications are processed on a rolling basis. Application fee: $55. *Expenses:* Tuition, nonresident: full-time $6696; part-time $372 per unit. Required fees: $5946; $1752 per semester. *Financial support:* Institutionally sponsored loans available. Support available to part-time students. Financial award application deadline: 8/1. *Faculty research:* African American music, postmodernism, cities of antiquity, Faust, African studies. *Unit head:* Dr. Lorna Fitzsimmons, Coordinator, 310-243-3036, E-mail: lfitzsimmons@csudh.edu. *Application contact:* Dr. Gayle Ball-Parker, Director of Admissions, 310-243-3645, E-mail: gball@csudh.edu.

California State University, Dominguez Hills, College of Extended and International Education, Humanities External Degree Program, Carson, CA 90747-0001. Offers MA. Part-time and evening/weekend programs available. Postbaccalaureate distance learning degree programs offered. *Faculty:* 10 full-time (0 women), 16 part-time/adjunct (11 women). *Students:* 5 full-time (2 women), 400 part-time (213 women); includes 42 minority (9 African Americans, 3 American Indian/Alaska Native, 8 Asian Americans or Pacific Islanders, 22 Hispanic Americans). Average age 43. 161 applicants, 83% accepted, 46 enrolled. In 2009, 57 master's awarded. *Degree requirements:* For master's, thesis, advancement to candidacy essays. *Entrance requirements:* Additional exam requirements/recommendations for international students: Required—TOEFL. *Application deadline:* For fall admission, 6/1 for domestic and international students; for winter admission, 3/1 for domestic and international students; for spring admission, 11/1 for domestic and international students. Application fee: $55. *Expenses:* Contact institution. *Financial support:* Applicants required to submit FAFSA. *Faculty research:* Nineteenth and twentieth century literature, Arab history, Greek philosophy, ancient history, East Asian, Soviet cultural history, Native American history and culture, feminist studies. *Unit head:* Dr. Patricia Cherin, Coordinator, 310-243-3191, Fax: 310-516-4399, E-mail: huxonline@csudh.edu. *Application contact:* Lisa Ayers, Program Assistant, 310-243-3190, Fax: 310-516-4399, E-mail: layers@csudh.edu.

California State University, East Bay, Academic Programs and Graduate Studies, College of Education and Allied Studies, Department of Kinesiology, Hayward, CA 94542-3000. Offers humanities/cultural studies (MS). *Faculty:* 6 full-time (3 women). *Students:* 8 full-time (2 women), 35 part-time (28 women); includes 20 minority (4 African Americans, 1 American Indian/Alaska Native, 7 Asian Americans or Pacific Islanders, 8 Hispanic Americans). Average age 30. 46 applicants, 67% accepted, 19 enrolled. In 2009, 16 master's awarded. *Degree requirements:* For master's, exam or thesis. *Entrance requirements:* For master's, BA in kinesiology or related discipline, minimum major course work GPA of 3.0. Additional exam requirements/recommendations for international students: Required—TOEFL (minimum score 550 paper-based; 213 computer-based). *Application deadline:* For fall admission, 6/30 for domestic and international students. Applications are processed on a rolling basis. Application fee: $55. Electronic applications accepted. *Financial support:* Fellowships, Federal Work-Study, institutionally sponsored loans, and scholarships/grants available. Support available to part-time students. Financial award application deadline: 3/1; financial award applicants required to submit FAFSA. *Unit head:* Dr. Calvin Caplan, Graduate Coordinator, 510-885-3089, Fax: 510-885-2282, E-mail: calvin.caplan@csueastbay.edu. *Application contact:* Donna Wiley, Interim Associate Director, 510-885-2928, Fax: 510-885-4777, E-mail: donna.wiley@csueastbay.edu.

Carlow University, Humanities Division, Pittsburgh, PA 15213-3165. Offers creative writing (MFA), including fiction, nonfiction, poetry. Part-time and evening/weekend programs available. *Degree requirements:* For master's, thesis or alternative. *Entrance requirements:* For master's, minimum GPA of 3.0, resume, writing samples, 2 letters of recommendation. Additional exam requirements/recommendations for international students: Required—TOEFL (minimum score 550 paper-based; 213 computer-based). *Expenses:* Tuition: Full-time $11,250; part-time $625 per credit. Tuition and fees vary according to course load, degree level and program.

Central European University, Graduate Studies, School of Social Sciences and Humanities, Budapest, Hungary. Offers economics (MA, PhD); gender studies (MA, PhD); international relations and European studies (MA, PhD); mathematics and its applications (MS, PhD); medieval studies (MA, PhD); nationalism studies (MA, PhD); philosophy (MA, PhD); political science (MA, PhD); public policy (MA, PhD); sociology and social anthropology (MA, PhD). Terminal master's awarded for partial completion of doctoral program. *Degree requirements:* For master's, one foreign language, thesis; for doctorate, one foreign language, comprehensive exam, thesis/dissertation. *Entrance requirements:* For master's, interview; for doctorate, GRE, CEU subject test, interview. Additional exam requirements/recommendations for international students: Required—TOEFL (minimum score 570 paper-based; 230 computer-based). Electronic applications accepted. *Faculty research:* Civil society, fiscal decentralization, party politics, political philosophy (especially Liberalism, theory of Democracy).

Central Michigan University, Central Michigan University Off-Campus Programs, Program in Humanities, Mount Pleasant, MI 48859. Offers MA. Part-time and evening/weekend programs available. *Entrance requirements:* For master's, minimum GPA of 2.7 in major. Additional exam requirements/recommendations for international students: Required—TOEFL. *Application deadline:* Applications are processed on a rolling basis. Application fee: $50. Electronic applications accepted. *Financial support:* Scholarships/grants available. Support available to part-time students. Financial award applicants required to submit FAFSA. *Unit head:* Dr. Ronald Primeau, Director, 989-774-3117, Fax: 989-774-7106, E-mail: ronald.r.primeau@cmich.edu. *Application contact:* 877-268-4636, E-mail: cmuoffcampus@cmich.edu.

Central Michigan University, College of Graduate Studies, College of Humanities and Social and Behavioral Sciences, Program in Humanities, Mount Pleasant, MI 48859. Offers humanities (MA), including contemporary issues in the humanities: race, class, and gender, images and ideas of self, Native American issues in modern culture, popular culture studies, the rise of industrial society. Part-time and evening/weekend programs available. *Degree requirements:* For master's, thesis or alternative. Electronic applications accepted. *Faculty research:* Rise of industrial society; images and ideas of self; contemporary issues of race, class, and gender; popular culture; Native American issues in modern culture.

Claremont Graduate University, Graduate Programs, School of Arts and Humanities, Claremont, CA 91711-6160. Offers M Phil, MA, MFA, DCM, DMA, PhD, Certificate, MA/PhD, MBA/MA, MBA/PhD. Part-time programs available. *Faculty:* 20 full-time (9 women), 2 part-time/adjunct (0 women). *Students:* 379 full-time (210 women), 37 part-time (22 women); includes 99 minority (22 African Americans, 3 American Indian/Alaska Native, 32 Asian Americans or Pacific Islanders, 42 Hispanic Americans), 25 international. Average age 35. In 2009, 72 master's, 21 doctorates awarded. *Degree requirements:* For doctorate, 2 foreign languages, comprehensive exam, thesis/dissertation, oral and written qualifying exams, oral defense of dissertation, recitals. *Entrance requirements:* For master's and doctorate, GRE General Test. Additional exam requirements/recommendations for international students: Required—TOEFL (minimum score 550 paper-based; 213 computer-based; 80 iBT). *Application deadline:* For fall admission, 2/1 priority date for domestic students. Applications are processed on a rolling basis. Application fee: $60. Electronic applications accepted. *Expenses:* Tuition: Full-time $35,046; part-time $1524 per credit. Required fees: $161 per semester. *Financial support:* Fellowships, research assistantships, teaching assistantships, Federal Work-Study, institutionally sponsored loans, and scholarships/grants available. Support available to part-time students. Financial award application deadline: 2/15; financial award applicants required to submit FAFSA. *Unit head:* Marc Redfield, Interim Dean, 909-607-3337, Fax: 909-607-1221, E-mail: marc.redfield@cgu.edu. *Application contact:* Susan Hampson, Admissions and Academic Support, 909-607-1278, Fax: 909-607-1221, E-mail: susan.hampson@cgu.edu.

Clemson University, Graduate School, Program in International Family and Community Studies, Clemson, SC 29634. Offers PhD. *Faculty:* 6 full-time (3 women), 3 part-time/adjunct (all women). *Students:* 15 full-time (14 women), 2 part-time (1 woman); includes 2 minority (1 African American, 1 Asian American or Pacific Islander), 8 international. Average age 32. 4 applicants, 50% accepted, 2 enrolled. *Degree requirements:* For doctorate, thesis/dissertation. *Entrance requirements:* For doctorate, GRE General Test. Additional exam requirements/recommendations for international students: Required—TOEFL. *Application deadline:* Applications are processed on a rolling basis. Application fee: $70 ($80 for international students). Electronic applications accepted. *Expenses:* Contact institution. *Financial support:* In 2009–10, 14 students received support, including 3 fellowships with full and partial tuition reimbursements available (averaging $15,000 per year), 14 research assistantships with partial tuition reimbursements available (averaging $19,677 per year); career-related internships or fieldwork, institutionally sponsored loans, scholarships/grants, health care benefits, and unspecified assistantships also available. Support available to part-time students. Total annual research expenditures: $3.2 million. *Unit head:* Dr. Gary B. Melton, Director, 964-656-6271. *Application contact:* Information Contact, 861-656-3195, E-mail: gradapp@clemson.edu.

College of the Humanities and Sciences, Harrison Middleton University, Graduate Program, Tempe, AZ 85282. Offers education (MA, Ed D); humanities (MA); imaginative literature (MA);

interdisciplinary studies (DA); jurisprudence (MA); natural science (MA); philosophy and religion (MA); social science (MA). Part-time and evening/weekend programs available. Postbaccalaureate distance learning degree programs offered (no on-campus study). *Faculty:* 17 full-time (7 women), 14 part-time/adjunct (6 women). *Students:* 49 full-time (18 women). In 2009, 4 master's awarded. *Application deadline:* Applications are processed on a rolling basis. Application fee: $50. Electronic applications accepted. *Application contact:* Deborah Deacon, Dean of Graduate Studies, 877-248-6724, Fax: 800-762-1622, E-mail: ddeacon@chumsci.edu.

The Colorado College, Department of Education, Experienced Teacher Program, Colorado Springs, CO 80903-3294. Offers arts and humanities (MAT); liberal arts (MAT); Southwest studies (MAT). Programs offered during summer only. Part-time programs available. *Degree requirements:* For master's, thesis, oral exam, 50-page paper. *Application deadline:* Applications are processed on a rolling basis. Application fee: $50. *Expenses:* Contact institution. *Financial support:* Institutionally sponsored loans and half-tuition scholarships to teachers with a contract available.

Concordia University, School of Graduate Studies, Faculty of Arts and Science, Program in Humanities, Montréal, QC H3G 1M8, Canada. Offers PhD. *Degree requirements:* For doctorate, one foreign language, comprehensive exam, thesis/dissertation.

Dominican University of California, Graduate Programs, School of Arts, Humanities and Social Sciences, Program in Humanities, San Rafael, CA 94901-2298. Offers MA. Part-time programs available. *Degree requirements:* For master's, thesis or alternative. *Entrance requirements:* For master's, minimum GPA of 3.0, interview. Additional exam requirements/recommendations for international students: Required—TOEFL (minimum score 550 paper-based; 213 computer-based). Electronic applications accepted.

Drew University, Caspersen School of Graduate Studies, Program in Medical Humanities, Madison, NJ 07940-1493. Offers MMH, DMH, CMH. Part-time and evening/weekend programs available. *Students:* 14 full-time (11 women), 68 part-time (54 women); includes 12 minority (6 African Americans, 3 Asian Americans or Pacific Islanders, 3 Hispanic Americans). 20 applicants, 90% accepted, 9 enrolled. In 2009, 6 master's, 9 doctorates, 9 CMHs awarded. *Degree requirements:* For master's, thesis; for doctorate, thesis/dissertation. *Entrance requirements:* For master's and doctorate, transcripts, writing sample, personal statement, recommendations. Additional exam requirements/recommendations for international students: Required—TOEFL (minimum score 585 paper-based; 240 computer-based; 95 iBT), TWE (minimum score 4). *Application deadline:* For fall admission, 8/1 priority date for domestic students; for spring admission, 1/15 priority date for domestic students. Applications are processed on a rolling basis. Application fee: $35. *Expenses:* Contact institution. *Financial support:* In 2009–10, 38 students received support. Federal Work-Study, scholarships/grants, and tuition waivers (full and partial) available. Financial award application deadline: 2/15; financial award applicants required to submit FAFSA. *Faculty research:* Biomedical ethics, medical narrative, history of medicine, medicine and the arts. *Unit head:* Dr. Phil Scibilia, 973-408-3138, E-mail: pscibili@drew.edu. *Application contact:* Carla J. Burns, Director of Graduate Admissions, 973-408-3110, Fax: 973-408-3040, E-mail: gradm@drew.edu.

Duke University, Graduate School, Program in Humanities, Durham, NC 27708. Offers AM, JD/AM. Part-time programs available. *Students:* 9 full-time (2 women); includes 2 minority (1 African American, 1 Asian American or Pacific Islander), 1 international. 8 applicants, 100% accepted, 5 enrolled. In 2009, 2 master's awarded. *Entrance requirements:* For master's, GRE General Test. Additional exam requirements/recommendations for international students: Required—TOEFL (minimum score 550 paper-based; 213 computer-based; 83 iBT), IELTS (minimum score 7). *Application deadline:* For fall admission, 12/8 priority date for domestic and international students; for spring admission, 11/1 for domestic students. Application fee: $75. *Financial support:* Application deadline: 12/31. *Unit head:* Dr. David Bell, Director, 919-681-3252, Fax: 919-684-2277, E-mail: jgw2@duke.edu. *Application contact:* Cynthia Robertson, Associate Dean for Enrollment Services, 919-684-3913, E-mail: grad-admissions@duke.edu.

Georgetown University, Graduate School of Arts and Sciences, School of Continuing Studies, Washington, DC 20057. Offers American studies (MALS); Catholic studies (MALS); classical civilizations (MALS); ethics and the professions (MALS); human resources management (MPS); humanities (MALS); individualized study (MALS); international affairs (MALS); Islam and Muslim-Christian relations (MALS); journalism (MPS); liberal studies (DLS); literature and society (MALS); medieval and early modern European studies (MALS); public relations (MPS); real estate (MPS); religious studies (MALS); social and public policy (MALS); sports industry management (MPS); the theory and practice of American democracy (MALS); visual culture (MALS). *Entrance requirements:* Additional exam requirements/recommendations for international students: Required—TOEFL.

Hofstra University, College of Liberal Arts and Sciences, Department of Fine Arts, Art History, and Humanity, Hempstead, NY 11549. Offers comparative arts and culture (MA). Part-time programs available. *Faculty:* 5 full-time (1 woman), 3 part-time/adjunct (1 woman). *Students:* 2 full-time (both women), 8 part-time (5 women); includes 1 minority (Hispanic American), 1 international. Average age 42. 7 applicants, 100% accepted, 2 enrolled. In 2009, 1 master's awarded. *Degree requirements:* For master's, thesis. *Entrance requirements:* For master's, letter of recommendation, interview. Additional exam requirements/recommendations for international students: Required—TOEFL (minimum score 550 paper-based; 213 computer-based; 80 iBT). *Application deadline:* Applications are processed on a rolling basis. Application fee: $60. Electronic applications accepted. *Expenses:* Tuition: Full-time $16,200; part-time $900 per credit hour. Required fees: $970; $145 per term. Tuition and fees vary according to program. *Financial support:* In 2009–10, 2 students received support, including 1 fellowship with full and partial tuition reimbursement available (averaging $4,000 per year); research assistantships with full and partial tuition reimbursements available, Federal Work-Study, institutionally sponsored loans, scholarships/grants, and tuition waivers (full and partial) also available. Support available to part-time students. Financial award applicants required to submit FAFSA. *Unit head:* Prof. Alexander Mihailovic, Professor, 516-463-5435, Fax: 516-463-7082, E-mail: cllazm@hofstra.edu. *Application contact:* Carol Drummer, Dean of Graduate Admissions, 516-463-4876, Fax: 516-463-4664, E-mail: gradstudent@hofstra.edu.

Hofstra University, School of Education, Health, and Human Services, Department of Curriculum and Teaching, Program in Learning and Teaching, Hempstead, NY 11549. Offers learning and teaching (Ed D), including applied linguistics, art education, arts and humanities, early childhood education, English education, human development, math education, math, science, and technology, multicultural education, physical education, science education, social studies education, special education. Part-time and evening/weekend programs available. *Students:* 5 full-time (all women), 21 part-time (17 women); includes 2 minority (1 African American, 1 Hispanic American), 1 international. Average age 38. 22 applicants, 68% accepted, 11 enrolled. *Degree requirements:* For doctorate, comprehensive exam, thesis/dissertation. *Entrance requirements:* For doctorate, GRE, 3 letters of recommendation, interview, 2 years full-time teaching experience. Additional exam requirements/recommendations for international students: Required—TOEFL (minimum score 550 paper-based; 213 computer-based; 80 iBT). *Application deadline:* Applications are processed on a rolling basis. Application fee: $60. Electronic applications accepted. *Expenses:* Tuition: Full-time $16,200; part-time $900 per credit hour. Required fees: $970; $145 per term. Tuition and fees vary according to program. *Financial support:* In 2009–10, 24 students received support, including 20 fellowships with full and partial tuition reimbursements available (averaging $4,906 per year); research assistantships with full and partial tuition reimbursements available, Federal Work-Study, institutionally sponsored loans, scholarships/grants, and tuition waivers (full and partial) also available. Support available to part-time students. Financial award applicants required to submit FAFSA. *Faculty research:* Critical thinking, professional development, teacher quality, quantitative research. *Unit head:* Dr. Bruce A. Torff, Director, 516-463-5803, Fax: 516-463-6196, E-mail: catajs@hofstra.edu. *Application contact:* Carol Drummer, Dean of Graduate Admissions, 516-463-4876, Fax: 516-463-4664, E-mail: gradstudent@hofstra.edu.

Hollins University, Graduate Programs, Program in Liberal Studies, Roanoke, VA 24020-1603. Offers humanities (MALS); interdisciplinary studies (MALS); justice and legal studies (MALS); liberal studies (CAS); social science (MALS); visual and performing arts (MALS). Part-time and evening/weekend programs available. *Faculty:* 7 full-time (1 woman), 4 part-time/adjunct (2 women). *Students:* 23 full-time (22 women), 73 part-time (57 women); includes 15 minority (13 African Americans, 2 Asian Americans or Pacific Islanders), 4 international. Average age 39. 31 applicants, 94% accepted, 25 enrolled. In 2009, 30 master's awarded. *Degree requirements:* For master's, thesis. *Entrance requirements:* For master's, letters of recommendation, interview. Additional exam requirements/recommendations for international students: Required—TOEFL (minimum score 550 paper-based; 213 computer-based; 79 iBT). *Application deadline:* For fall admission, 7/1 priority date for domestic and international students; for spring admission, 12/10 priority date for domestic and international students. Applications are processed on a rolling basis. Application fee: $40. Electronic applications accepted. *Expenses:* Tuition: Full-time $27,780; part-time $295 per contact hour. Required fees: $280; $70 per unit. Part-time tuition and fees vary according to course load and program. *Financial support:* In 2009–10, 31 students received support, including 2 fellowships (averaging $902 per year); Federal Work-Study and scholarships/grants also available. Support available to part-time students. Financial award application deadline: 7/15; financial award applicants required to submit FAFSA. *Faculty research:* Elderly blacks, film, feminist economics, US voting patterns, Wagner, diversity. *Unit head:* Dr. Edward A. Lynch, Director, 540-362-6475, Fax: 540-362-6288, E-mail: elynch@hollins.edu. *Application contact:* Cathy S. Koon, Manager of Graduate Services, 540-362-6326, Fax: 540-362-6288, E-mail: ckoon@hollins.edu.

Hood College, Graduate School, Program in Humanities, Frederick, MD 21701-8575. Offers MA. Part-time and evening/weekend programs available. *Faculty:* 8 full-time (6 women), 5 part-time/adjunct (4 women). *Students:* 3 full-time (all women), 28 part-time (22 women); includes 2 minority (1 Asian American or Pacific Islander, 1 Hispanic American). Average age 34. 21 applicants, 86% accepted, 9 enrolled. In 2009, 10 master's awarded. *Degree requirements:* For master's, capstone/research project. *Entrance requirements:* For master's, minimum GPA of 2.75. Additional exam requirements/recommendations for international students: Required—TOEFL (minimum score 575 paper-based; 231 computer-based; 89 iBT). *Application deadline:* For fall admission, 7/15 for domestic and international students; for spring admission, 12/15 for domestic and international students. Applications are processed on a rolling basis. Application fee: $35. Electronic applications accepted. *Expenses:* Tuition: Full-time $6480; part-time $360 per credit. Required fees: $100; $50 per term. *Financial support:* Applicants required to submit FAFSA. *Unit head:* Dr. Rusty Monhollon, Director, 301-696-3690, E-mail: monhollon@hood.edu. *Application contact:* Dr. Allen P. Flora, Dean of Graduate School, 301-696-3811, Fax: 301-696-3597, E-mail: gofurther@hood.edu.

Instituto Tecnológico y de Estudios Superiores de Monterrey, Campus Central de Veracruz, Graduate Programs, Córdoba, Mexico. Offers administration (MA); administration of information technologies (MTI); computer sciences (MCC); education (MEE); educational institution administration (MAD); educational technology (MTE); electronic commerce (MCE); finance (MAF); humanistic studies (MEH); international business for Latin America (MNL); marketing (MMT); science (MCP); technology management (MTT). Part-time and evening/weekend programs available. Postbaccalaureate distance learning degree programs offered (minimal on-campus study). *Degree requirements:* For master's, thesis (for some programs). *Entrance requirements:* For master's, PAEP College Board. Electronic applications accepted.

Instituto Tecnológico y de Estudios Superiores de Monterrey, Campus Ciudad de México, Virtual University Division, Ciudad de Mexico, Mexico. Offers administration of information technologies (MA); computer sciences (MA); education (MA, PhD); educational technology (MA); environmental engineering (MA); environmental systems (MA); humanistic studies (MA); industrial engineering (MA); international business for Latin America (MA); quality systems (MA); quality systems and productivity (MA). Part-time and evening/weekend programs available. Postbaccalaureate distance learning degree programs offered (minimal on-campus study). *Entrance requirements:* For master's and doctorate, Instituto entrance exam. Additional exam requirements/recommendations for international students: Required—TOEFL.

Instituto Tecnológico y de Estudios Superiores de Monterrey, Campus Ciudad Juárez, Program in Humanistic Studies, Ciudad Juárez, Mexico. Offers MEH.

Instituto Tecnológico y de Estudios Superiores de Monterrey, Campus Estado de México, Professional and Graduate Division, Estado de Mexico, Mexico. Offers administration of information technologies (MITA); architecture (M Arch); business administration (GMBA, MBA); computer sciences (MCS, PhD); education (M Ed); educational institution administration (MAD); educational technology and innovation (PhD); electronic commerce (MEC); environmental systems (MS); finance (MAF); humanistic studies (MHS); information sciences and knowledge management (MISKM); information systems (MS); manufacturing systems (MS); marketing (MEM); quality systems and productivity (MS); science and materials engineering (PhD); telecommunications management (MTM). Part-time programs available. Postbaccalaureate distance learning degree programs offered (minimal on-campus study). *Degree requirements:* For master's, one foreign language, thesis (for some programs); for doctorate, one foreign language, thesis/dissertation. *Entrance requirements:* For master's, E-PAEP 500, interview; for doctorate, E-PAEP 500, research proposal. Additional exam requirements/recommendations for international students: Required—TOEFL (minimum score 550 paper-based). *Faculty research:* Surface treatments by plasmas, mechanical properties, robotics, graphical computing, mechatronics security protocols.

Instituto Tecnológico y de Estudios Superiores de Monterrey, Campus Irapuato, Graduate Programs, Irapuato, Mexico. Offers administration (MBA); administration of information technology (MAIT); administration of telecommunications (MAT); architecture (M Arch); computer science (MCS); education (M Ed); educational administration (MEA); educational innovation and technology (DEIT); educational technology (MET); electronic commerce (MBA); environmental administration and planning (MEAP); environmental systems (MES); finances (MBA); humanistic studies (MHS); international management for Latin American executives (MIMLAE); library and information science (MLIS); manufacturing quality management (MMQM); marketing research (MBA).

John Carroll University, Graduate School, Program in Humanities, University Heights, OH 44118-4581. Offers MA. Part-time and evening/weekend programs available. *Degree requirements:* For master's, thesis optional, comprehensive research essay. *Entrance requirements:* For master's, minimum GPA of 2.75, interview. Electronic applications accepted. *Faculty research:* Modern French history, modern American Catholic history.

Laura and Alvin Siegal College of Judaic Studies, Graduate Programs, Beachwood, OH 44122-7116. Offers humanities (MA), including Holocaust studies; religious education (MAJS), including Jewish education, Judaic studies. Part-time and evening/weekend programs available. Postbaccalaureate distance learning degree programs offered (no on-campus study). *Degree requirements:* For master's, one foreign language, thesis. *Entrance requirements:* For master's, interview.

Laurentian University, School of Graduate Studies and Research, Programme in Humanities: Interpretation and Values, Sudbury, ON P3E 2C6, Canada. Offers MA. Part-time programs available. *Faculty research:* Modern Canadian literature; aboriginal languages and cultures; relation between ethics, religion, and the arts; narrative conventions; Renaissance drama and Reformation literature, Biblical and philosophical hermeneutics.

Marshall University, Academic Affairs Division, College of Liberal Arts, Program in Humanities, Huntington, WV 25755. Offers MA. Part-time and evening/weekend programs available. *Faculty:* 2 full-time (1 woman), 2 part-time/adjunct (1 woman). *Students:* 6 full-time (3 women), 10 part-time (7 women); includes 1 minority (American Indian/Alaska Native), 1 international. Average age 38. In 2009, 3 master's awarded. *Degree requirements:* For master's, thesis, comprehensive assessment. *Entrance requirements:* For master's, GRE General Test, MAT,

Humanities

Marshall University (continued)
bachelor's degree in humanities, minimum undergraduate GPA of 3.0. Application fee: $40. *Financial support:* Applicants required to submit FAFSA. *Unit head:* Dr. Luke Eric Lassiter, Chairperson, 304-746-1923, E-mail: lassiter@marshall.edu. *Application contact:* Information Contact, 304-746-1900, Fax: 304-746-1902, E-mail: services@marshall.edu.

Marymount University, School of Arts and Sciences, Program in Humanities, Arlington, VA 22207-4299. Offers MA. Part-time and evening/weekend programs available. *Students:* 3 full-time (all women), 4 part-time (3 women); includes 1 minority (Hispanic American), 1 international. Average age 39. 3 applicants, 100% accepted, 2 enrolled. In 2009, 3 master's awarded. *Degree requirements:* For master's, thesis or alternative. *Entrance requirements:* For master's, minimum GPA of 3.0; undergraduate major or minor in art history, English, history, or philosophy; 2 letters of recommendation; interview; writing sample; essay. Additional exam requirements/recommendations for international students: Required—TOEFL (minimum score 600 paper-based; 250 computer-based; 96 iBT), IELTS (minimum score 6.5). *Application deadline:* For fall admission, 7/1 for international students; for spring admission, 10/15 for international students. Applications are processed on a rolling basis. Application fee: $40. Electronic applications accepted. *Expenses:* Tuition: Full-time $13,050; part-time $725 per credit hour. Required fees: $135; $7.50 per credit hour. *Financial support:* In 2009–10, 5 students received support; research assistantships with full and partial tuition reimbursements available, career-related internships or fieldwork, Federal Work-Study, scholarships/grants, and unspecified assistantships available. Support available to part-time students. Financial award applicants required to submit FAFSA. *Unit head:* Dr. Adam Kovach, Director of Graduate Studies, 703-526-6806, Fax: 703-284-3859, E-mail: adam.kovach@marymount.edu. *Application contact:* Francesca Reed, Director, Graduate Admissions, 703-284-5901, Fax: 703-527-3815, E-mail: grad.admissions@marymount.edu.

Massachusetts Institute of Technology, School of Humanities, Arts, and Social Sciences, Program in Writing and Humanistic Studies, Cambridge, MA 02139-4307. Offers science writing (SM). *Faculty:* 9 full-time (2 women). *Students:* 7 full-time (4 women); includes 1 minority (Hispanic American), 1 international. Average age 25. 63 applicants, 29% accepted, 7 enrolled. In 2009, 7 master's awarded. *Degree requirements:* For master's, thesis, internship. *Entrance requirements:* For master's, GRE General Test. Additional exam requirements/recommendations for international students: Required—TOEFL (minimum score 600 paper-based; 250 computer-based), IELTS (minimum score 7.5). *Application deadline:* For fall admission, 1/15 for domestic and international students. Application fee: $75. Electronic applications accepted. *Expenses:* Tuition: Full-time $37,510; part-time $585 per unit. Required fees: $272. *Financial support:* In 2009–10, 7 students received support, including 7 fellowships with tuition reimbursements available; teaching assistantships with tuition reimbursements available, career-related internships or fieldwork, Federal Work-Study, institutionally sponsored loans, scholarships/grants, health care benefits, and unspecified assistantships also available. Total annual research expenditures: $74,000. *Unit head:* Prof. James Paradis, Head of Program, 617-253-7894, Fax: 617-253-6910. *Application contact:* Science Writing Graduate Admissions, 617-253-6668, Fax: 617-452-5100, E-mail: sciwrite-www@mit.edu.

Memorial University of Newfoundland, School of Graduate Studies, Interdisciplinary Programs in Humanities, St. John's, NL A1C 5S7, Canada. Offers M Phil. *Degree requirements:* For master's, comprehensive exam, journal. *Entrance requirements:* For master's, honors bachelor's degree. Electronic applications accepted. *Faculty research:* Western language, philosophy, literature, and history.

Mount St. Mary's College, Graduate Division, Program in Humanities, Los Angeles, CA 90049-1599. Offers MA. *Faculty:* 1 (woman) full-time, 4 part-time/adjunct (2 women). *Students:* 15 full-time (11 women), 64 part-time (54 women); includes 39 minority (7 African Americans, 5 Asian Americans or Pacific Islanders, 27 Hispanic Americans). Average age 40. In 2009, 17 master's awarded. *Entrance requirements:* For master's, minimum GPA of 3.0. Additional exam requirements/recommendations for international students: Required—TOEFL (minimum score 550 iBT). *Application deadline:* For fall admission, 7/15 priority date for domestic students; for spring admission, 11/15 priority date for domestic students. *Expenses:* Tuition: Part-time $730 per unit. Part-time tuition and fees vary according to degree level and program. *Financial support:* Application deadline: 3/15. *Unit head:* Dr. Millie Kidd, Director, 213-477-2667, E-mail: mkidd@msmc.la.edu. *Application contact:* Director of Graduate Admission.

National University, Academic Affairs, College of Letters and Sciences, Department of Art and Humanities, La Jolla, CA 92037-1011. Offers creative writing (MFA); English (MA); history (MA). Part-time and evening/weekend programs available. Postbaccalaureate distance learning degree programs offered (no on-campus study). *Faculty:* 13 full-time (4 women), 24 part-time/adjunct (15 women). *Students:* 204 full-time (144 women), 499 part-time (340 women); includes 160 minority (77 African Americans, 6 American Indian/Alaska Native, 17 Asian Americans or Pacific Islanders, 60 Hispanic Americans). Average age 38. 440 applicants, 100% accepted, 280 enrolled. In 2009, 152 master's awarded. *Degree requirements:* For master's, thesis (for some programs). *Entrance requirements:* For master's, interview, minimum GPA of 2.5. Additional exam requirements/recommendations for international students: Required—TOEFL (minimum score 550 paper-based; 213 computer-based; 79 iBT), IELTS (minimum score 6). *Application deadline:* Applications are processed on a rolling basis. Application fee: $60 ($65 for international students). Electronic applications accepted. *Expenses:* Tuition: Part-time $338 per quarter hour. *Financial support:* Career-related internships or fieldwork, institutionally sponsored loans, scholarships/grants, and tuition waivers (partial) available. Support available to part-time students. Financial award application deadline: 6/30; financial award applicants required to submit FAFSA. *Unit head:* Dr. Janet Baker, Chair, 858-642-8472, Fax: 858-642-8715, E-mail: jbaker@nu.edu. *Application contact:* Dominick Giovanniello, Associate Regional Dean—San Diego, 800-NAT-UNIV, Fax: 858-541-7792, E-mail: dgiovann@nu.edu.

New York University, Graduate School of Arts and Science, Draper Interdisciplinary Program in Humanities and Social Thought, New York, NY 10012-1019. Offers humanities and social thought (MA); religion (Advanced Certificate); social theory (Advanced Certificate). Part-time programs available. *Faculty:* 6 full-time (3 women). *Students:* 104 full-time (62 women), 113 part-time (76 women); includes 35 minority (9 African Americans, 15 Asian Americans or Pacific Islanders, 11 Hispanic Americans), 11 international. Average age 27. 353 applicants, 57% accepted, 110 enrolled. In 2009, 76 master's awarded. *Degree requirements:* For master's, thesis, comprehensive exam or essay. *Entrance requirements:* For degree, master's degree. Additional exam requirements/recommendations for international students: Required—TOEFL. *Application deadline:* For fall admission, 7/1 for domestic students; for spring admission, 12/1 for domestic students. Applications are processed on a rolling basis. Application fee: $90. *Expenses:* Tuition: Full-time $30,528; part-time $1272 per credit. Required fees: $2177. *Financial support:* Teaching assistantships with tuition reimbursements, Federal Work-Study, institutionally sponsored loans, and tuition waivers (partial) available. Financial award application deadline: 7/1; financial award applicants required to submit FAFSA. *Faculty research:* Art world, gender politics, global histories, literary cultures, the city. *Unit head:* Robin Nagle, Director, 212-998-8070, Fax: 212-995-4691, E-mail: draper.program@nyu.edu. *Application contact:* Robert Dimit, Associate Director, 212-998-8070, Fax: 212-995-4691, E-mail: draper.program@nyu.edu.

Nova Southeastern University, Graduate School of Humanities and Social Sciences, Department of Multi-Disciplinary Studies, Fort Lauderdale, FL 33314-7796. Offers college student affairs (MS); cross-disciplinary studies (MA). Part-time programs available. Postbaccalaureate distance learning degree programs offered (minimal on-campus study). *Faculty:* 1 (woman) full-time. *Students:* 12 full-time (9 women), 37 part-time (32 women); includes 20 African Americans, 9 Hispanic Americans, 1 international. In 2009, 15 master's awarded. *Degree requirements:* For master's, comprehensive exam, thesis optional, portfolio. *Entrance requirements:* For master's, interview, minimum GPA of 3.0. Additional exam requirements/recommendations for international students: Required—TOEFL. *Application deadline:* For fall admission, 7/1 priority date for domestic and international students; for winter admission, 11/1 priority date for domestic and international students; for spring admission, 3/1 priority date for domestic and international students. Applications are processed on a rolling basis. Electronic applications accepted. *Financial support:* Research assistantships, career-related internships or fieldwork, Federal Work-Study, institutionally sponsored loans, and scholarships/grants available. Financial award applicants required to submit CSS PROFILE. *Unit head:* Dr. Judith McKay, Chair, 954-262-3060, Fax: 954-262-3893, E-mail: mckayj@nsu.nova.edu. *Application contact:* Marcia Arango, Student Recruitment Coordinator, 954-262-3006, Fax: 954-262-3968, E-mail: marango@nsu.nova.edu.

Old Dominion University, College of Arts and Letters, Program in Humanities, Norfolk, VA 23529. Offers MA. Part-time and evening/weekend programs available. *Faculty:* 2 full-time (1 woman). *Students:* 9 full-time (4 women), 12 part-time (10 women); includes 4 minority (1 African American, 1 Asian American or Pacific Islander, 2 Hispanic Americans), 3 international. Average age 34. 27 applicants, 96% accepted. In 2009, 8 master's awarded. *Degree requirements:* For master's, thesis optional, project. *Entrance requirements:* For master's, GRE General Test, minimum GPA of 3.0. *Application deadline:* For fall admission, 7/1 for domestic students; for spring admission, 10/1 for domestic students. Applications are processed on a rolling basis. Application fee: $40. Electronic applications accepted. *Expenses:* Tuition, state resident: full-time $8112; part-time $338 per credit. Tuition, nonresident: full-time $20,256; part-time $844 per credit. Required fees: $119 per semester. One-time fee: $50. *Financial support:* In 2009–10, 3 students received support, including 1 fellowship (averaging $4,000 per year), 2 research assistantships with tuition reimbursements available (averaging $8,000 per year); career-related internships or fieldwork, scholarships/grants, and unspecified assistantships also available. Financial award application deadline: 2/15; financial award applicants required to submit FAFSA. *Faculty research:* Media studies, communications, cultural studies, gender studies, American literature. *Unit head:* Dr. Dana Heller, Graduate Program Director, 757-683-3719, Fax: 757-683-6191, E-mail: humgpd@odu.edu. *Application contact:* Dr. Robert Wojtowicz, Associate Dean, 757-683-6077, Fax: 757-683-5746, E-mail: rwojtowi@odu.edu.

Penn State Harrisburg, Graduate School, School of Humanities, Middletown, PA 17057-4898. Offers American studies (MA). Evening/weekend programs available. *Unit head:* Dr. Kathryn Robinson, Director, 717-948-6470, E-mail: kdr12@psu.edu. *Application contact:* Robert Coffman, Director of Admissions, 717-948-6250, Fax: 717-948-6325, E-mail: ric1@psu.edu.

Pepperdine University, Seaver College, Humanities Division, Malibu, CA 90263. Offers American studies (MA); history (MA). *Degree requirements:* For master's, oral and written exams. *Entrance requirements:* For master's, GRE General Test, undergraduate major or 15 upper-division units in history. Additional exam requirements/recommendations for international students: Required—TOEFL. *Expenses:* Tuition: Full-time $37,516; part-time $1310 per unit. Required fees: $80.

Polytechnic Institute of NYU, Department of Humanities and Social Sciences, Brooklyn, NY 11201-2990. Offers environment—behavior studies (Graduate Certificate); environment-behavior studies (MS); history of science (MS); integrated digital media (MS, Graduate Certificate); technical communication (Graduate Certificate); technical writing and specialized journalism (MS). Part-time and evening/weekend programs available. *Faculty:* 7 full-time (2 women), 3 part-time/adjunct (2 women). *Students:* 27 full-time (13 women), 10 part-time (3 women); includes 6 minority (4 African Americans, 1 Asian American or Pacific Islander, 1 Hispanic American), 16 international. Average age 29. 42 applicants, 67% accepted, 19 enrolled. In 2009, 22 master's awarded. *Degree requirements:* For master's, comprehensive exam (for some programs), thesis (for some programs). *Entrance requirements:* Additional exam requirements/recommendations for international students: Required—TOEFL (minimum score 550 paper-based; 213 computer-based; 80 iBT); Recommended—IELTS (minimum score 6.5). *Application deadline:* For fall admission, 7/31 priority date for domestic students, 4/30 priority date for international students; for spring admission, 12/31 priority date for domestic students, 11/30 priority date for international students. Applications are processed on a rolling basis. Application fee: $75. Electronic applications accepted. *Expenses:* Tuition: Full-time $21,492; part-time $1194 per credit hour. Required fees: $1160; $204 per course. *Financial support:* Fellowships, research assistantships, teaching assistantships, career-related internships or fieldwork, institutionally sponsored loans, scholarships/grants, and unspecified assistantships available. Support available to part-time students. Financial award applicants required to submit FAFSA. *Faculty research:* Trade magazine journalism, technical writing, financial reporting, medical and science reporting, industrial advertising and public relations. *Unit head:* Prof. Teresa M. Feroli, Head, 718-260-3422, E-mail: tferoli@poly.edu. *Application contact:* JeanCarlo Bonilla, Director of Graduate Enrollment Management, 718-260-3182, Fax: 718-260-3624, E-mail: gradinfo@poly.edu.

Prescott College, Graduate Programs, Program in Humanities, Prescott, AZ 86301. Offers humanities (MA); student-directed independent study (MA). Part-time programs available. Postbaccalaureate distance learning degree programs offered (minimal on-campus study). *Faculty:* 2 full-time (1 woman), 49 part-time/adjunct (31 women). *Students:* 18 full-time (12 women), 37 part-time (28 women); includes 7 minority (5 African Americans, 1 American Indian/Alaska Native, 1 Asian American or Pacific Islander). Average age 40. 34 applicants, 65% accepted, 11 enrolled. In 2009, 19 master's awarded. *Degree requirements:* For master's, thesis, fieldwork or internship, practicum. *Entrance requirements:* For master's, 2 letters of recommendation, resume. Additional exam requirements/recommendations for international students: Required—TOEFL (minimum score 500 paper-based; 173 computer-based). *Application deadline:* For fall admission, 4/15 priority date for domestic and international students; for spring admission, 9/15 priority date for domestic and international students. Applications are processed on a rolling basis. Application fee: $40. Electronic applications accepted. *Expenses:* Tuition: Full-time $14,712; part-time $613 per credit. Required fees: $50 per term. One-time fee: $150. Tuition and fees vary according to course load and degree level. *Financial support:* Career-related internships or fieldwork, Federal Work-Study, and scholarships/grants available. Financial award applicants required to submit FAFSA. *Unit head:* Dr. Randall Amster, Chair, 928-350-2238, Fax: 928-776-5151, E-mail: ramster@prescott.edu. *Application contact:* Kerstin Alicki, Admissions Counselor, 877-412-8705, Fax: 928-277-4695, E-mail: admissions@prescott.edu.

St. Edward's University, New College, Program in Liberal Arts, Austin, TX 78704. Offers global issues (MLA); humanities (MLA); liberal arts (Certificate); social sciences (MLA). Part-time and evening/weekend programs available. *Students:* 3 full-time (2 women), 85 part-time (60 women); includes 21 minority (3 African Americans, 2 Asian Americans or Pacific Islanders, 16 Hispanic Americans), 1 international. Average age 34. 34 applicants, 88% accepted, 23 enrolled. In 2009, 23 master's awarded. *Degree requirements:* For master's, minimum of 24 resident hours. *Entrance requirements:* For master's, minimum GPA of 2.75 in last 60 hours of course work, interview. Additional exam requirements/recommendations for international students: Required—TOEFL (minimum score 550 paper-based; 213 computer-based; 79 iBT) or IELTS (minimum score 6). *Application deadline:* For fall admission, 7/1 for domestic and international students; for spring admission, 11/1 for domestic and international students. Applications are processed on a rolling basis. Application fee: $45 ($50 for international students). Electronic applications accepted. *Expenses:* Tuition: Full-time $14,922; part-time $829 per credit hour. Required fees: $50 per trimester. Full-time tuition and fees vary according to course load and program. *Financial support:* In 2009–10, 2 students received support. Scholarships/grants available. *Unit head:* Dr. H. Ramsey Fowler, Director, 512-448-8648, Fax: 512-448-8492, E-mail: ramseyf@stewards.edu. *Application contact:* Kay L. Arnold, Assistant Director of Admissions, 512-233-1636, Fax: 512-428-1032, E-mail: kayla@stedwards.edu.

Salve Regina University, Graduate Studies, Program in Humanities, Newport, RI 02840-4192. Offers MA, PhD, CAGS. Part-time and evening/weekend programs available. Postbaccalaureate distance learning degree programs offered (no on-campus study). *Faculty:* 7 full-time (3 women), 6 part-time/adjunct (2 women). *Students:* 10 full-time (4 women), 80 part-time (36 women); includes 6 minority (2 African Americans, 2 Asian Americans or Pacific Islanders, 2 Hispanic Americans), 1 international. Average age 47. 39 applicants, 64% accepted, 18 enrolled. In 2009, 1 master's, 7 doctorates, 1 other advanced degree awarded. *Degree* *requirements:* For master's, thesis optional; for doctorate, one foreign language, comprehensive exam, thesis/dissertation. *Entrance requirements:* For master's, GMAT, GRE General Test, or MAT; for doctorate, GRE General Test. Additional exam requirements/recommendations for international students: Required—TOEFL (minimum score 600 paper-based; 250 computer-based; 100 iBT), or IELTS. *Application deadline:* For fall admission, 3/15 priority date for domestic and international students; for spring admission, 9/15 priority date for domestic and international students. Applications are processed on a rolling basis. Application fee: $60. Electronic applications accepted. *Expenses:* Tuition: Part-time $395 per credit. Part-time tuition and fees vary according to degree level. *Financial support:* Career-related internships or fieldwork and Federal Work-Study available. Support available to part-time students. Financial award application deadline: 3/1; financial award applicants required to submit FAFSA. *Unit head:* Dr. Michael Budd, Director, 401-341-3284, E-mail: michael.budd@salve.edu. *Application contact:* Kelly Alverson, Graduate Admissions Counselor, 401-341-2153, Fax: 401-341-2973, E-mail: kelly.alverson@salve.edu.

Sam Houston State University, College of Humanities and Social Sciences, Huntsville, TX 77341. Offers English and foreign languages (MA), including English; family and consumer sciences (MS), including dietetics, family and consumer sciences; history (MA); political science (MA, MPA), including political science (MA), public administration (MPA); psychology and philosophy (MA, PhD), including clinical psychology (PhD), psychology (MA); sociology (MA); speech communication (MA). *Faculty:* 60 full-time (30 women), 1 part-time/adjunct (0 women). *Students:* 115 full-time (85 women), 167 part-time (90 women); includes 39 minority (11 African Americans, 1 American Indian/Alaska Native, 5 Asian Americans or Pacific Islanders, 22 Hispanic Americans), 9 international. Average age 30. 216 applicants, 56% accepted, 96 enrolled. In 2009, 67 master's, 4 doctorates awarded. *Entrance requirements:* For master's, GRE General Test. Additional exam requirements/recommendations for international students: Required—TOEFL (minimum score 550 paper-based; 213 computer-based; 79 iBT). *Application deadline:* For fall admission, 8/1 for domestic students; for spring admission, 12/1 for domestic students. Application fee: $20. *Expenses:* Tuition, state resident: full-time $3690; part-time $205 per credit hour. Tuition, nonresident: full-time $8676; part-time $482 per credit hour. Required fees: $1474. Tuition and fees vary according to course load and campus/location. *Unit head:* Dr. John deCastro, Dean, 936-294-2200, Fax: 936-294-2207, E-mail: jmd018@shsu.edu. *Application contact:* Dr. Kandi Tayebi, Dean of Graduate Studies and Associate Vice President for Academic Affairs, 936-294-1971, Fax: 936-294-1271, E-mail: graduate@shsu.edu.

San Francisco State University, Division of Graduate Studies, College of Humanities, Department of Humanities, San Francisco, CA 94132-1722. Offers MA. Part-time and evening/weekend programs available.

Stanford University, School of Humanities and Sciences, Department of Humanities, Stanford, CA 94305-9991. Offers MA. *Degree requirements:* For master's, one foreign language, thesis. *Entrance requirements:* For master's, GRE General Test. Additional exam requirements/recommendations for international students: Required—TOEFL. Electronic applications accepted. *Expenses:* Tuition: Full-time $37,380; part-time $2760 per quarter. Required fees: $501.

Texas Tech University, Graduate School, College of Arts and Sciences, Department of Classical and Modern Languages and Literatures, Lubbock, TX 79409. Offers applied linguistics (MA); classics (MA); German (MA); Romance language (MA); Romance languages-French (MA); Romance languages-Spanish (MA); Spanish (PhD); MBA/MA. Part-time programs available. *Faculty:* 29 full-time (11 women), 1 (woman) part-time/adjunct. *Students:* 80 full-time (45 women), 25 part-time (13 women); includes 17 minority (1 African American, 16 Hispanic Americans), 43 international. Average age 32. 72 applicants, 75% accepted, 21 enrolled. In 2009, 19 master's, 5 doctorates awarded. *Degree requirements:* For master's, thesis or alternative; for doctorate, thesis/dissertation. *Entrance requirements:* For master's and doctorate, GRE General Test. Additional exam requirements/recommendations for international students: Required—TOEFL (minimum score 550 paper-based; 213 computer-based). *Application deadline:* For fall admission, 3/1 priority date for international students; for spring admission, 11/1 priority date for international students. Applications are processed on a rolling basis. Application fee: $50 ($75 for international students). Electronic applications accepted. *Expenses:* Tuition, state resident: full-time $5100; part-time $213 per credit hour. Tuition, nonresident: full-time $11,748; part-time $490 per credit hour. Required fees: $2298; $50 per credit hour. $555 per semester. *Financial support:* In 2009–10, 19 teaching assistantships with partial tuition reimbursements (averaging $12,060 per year) were awarded; research assistantships with partial tuition reimbursements, Federal Work-Study and institutionally sponsored loans also available. Support available to part-time students. Financial award application deadline: 4/15; financial award applicants required to submit FAFSA. *Faculty research:* Literature, comparative literature, linguistics, culture, pedagogy. Total annual research expenditures: $37,015. *Unit head:* Dr. Laura Jean Beard, Interim Chair and Professor, 806-742-4355, Fax: 806-742-3306, E-mail: laura.beard@ttu.edu. *Application contact:* Liz Hildebrand, Senior Advisor, 806-742-4055, Fax: 806-742-3306, E-mail: liz.hildebrand@ttu.edu.

Tiffin University, Program in Humanities, Tiffin, OH 44883-2161. Offers MH. *Entrance requirements:* For master's, work experience. Additional exam requirements/recommendations for international students: Required—TOEFL (minimum score 550 paper-based; 213 computer-based).

Towson University, College of Graduate Studies and Research, Program in Humanities, Towson, MD 21252-0001. Offers MA. Part-time and evening/weekend programs available. *Degree requirements:* For master's, thesis or alternative. *Entrance requirements:* For master's, 2 letters of recommendation, minimum GPA of 3.0, research paper. Additional exam requirements/recommendations for international students: Required—TOEFL. Electronic applications accepted.

Trinity Western University, Faculty of Graduate Studies, Program in Interdisciplinary Humanities, Langley, BC V2Y 1Y1, Canada. Offers general humanities (MAIH); specialized (MAIH), including English, history, philosophy. Part-time and evening/weekend programs available. Postbaccalaureate distance learning degree programs offered (minimal on-campus study). *Entrance requirements:* For master's, strong undergraduate degree in Humanities or English, History or Philosophy. *Faculty research:* Literary theory, gender, medieval and early modern literature, philosophy of religion, Thomas Merton's poetics.

United Theological Seminary of the Twin Cities, Professional Program, New Brighton, MN 55112-2598. Offers advanced theological studies (Diploma); justice and peace studies (M Div, MA); leadership toward racial justice (MA, Certificate); leadership towards racial justice (M Div); Methodist studies (M Div, MA, Certificate); ministry (D Min); ministry renewal and professional development (Certificate); pastoral care and counseling (M Div, MA, MARL); religion and theology (MA); theological and religious studies (Certificate); theology and the arts (M Div, MA); urban ministry (M Div, MA, MARL); women's studies: religion, theology and ministry (MA); women's studies: religions, theology and ministry (M Div). *Accreditation:* ACIPE; ATS. Part-time and evening/weekend programs available. *Faculty:* 9 full-time (6 women), 22 part-time/adjunct (10 women). *Students:* 49 full-time (34 women), 105 part-time (68 women). Average age 47. 41 applicants, 98% accepted, 34 enrolled. In 2009, 24 first professional degrees, 5 master's, 2 doctorates, 2 other advanced degrees awarded. *Degree requirements:* For master's, thesis; for doctorate, comprehensive exam, thesis/dissertation; for M Div, integrative notebook, spiritual chronicle. *Entrance requirements:* For M Div and master's, minimum GPA of 2.75; strong analytical, reflective thinking and writing skills; vocational and academic goals compatible with those of Seminary; for doctorate, M Div or equivalent, minimum GPA of 3.0, 3 years experience in professional ministry; for other advanced degree, BA or equivalent life experience; strong analytical, reflective thinking and writing skills (Certificate); proficiency in English language, previous study of theology at a theological school, recommendation of student's denomination (Diploma). Additional exam requirements/recommendations for international students: Required—TOEFL (minimum score 550 paper-based). *Application deadline:* For fall admission, 7/1 priority date for domestic students, 11/1 priority date for international students; for winter admission, 11/1 priority date for domestic students; for spring admission, 11/15 priority date for domestic students. Applications are processed on a rolling basis. Application fee: $50. *Expenses:* Tuition: Full-time $11,502; part-time $426 per credit hour. Required fees: $295; $155 per term. One-time fee: $25. Tuition and fees vary according to course load, degree level and program. *Financial support:* In 2009–10, 120 students received support. Career-related internships or fieldwork, institutionally sponsored loans, and scholarships/grants available. Support available to part-time students. Financial award application deadline: 5/1; financial award applicants required to submit FAFSA. *Unit head:* Dr. Richard D. Weis, Dean of the Seminary, 651-255-6108 Ext. 108, Fax: 651-633-4315, E-mail: rweis@unitedseminary.edu. *Application contact:* Rev. Glen Herrington-Hall, Director of Admissions, 651-255-6107 Ext. 107, Fax: 651-633-4315, E-mail: gherrington-hall@unitedseminary.edu.

University of California, Santa Cruz, Division of Graduate Studies, Division of Humanities, Program in the History of Consciousness, Santa Cruz, CA 95064. Offers PhD. *Degree requirements:* For doctorate, one foreign language, thesis/dissertation, qualifying exam. *Entrance requirements:* Additional exam requirements/recommendations for international students: Required—TOEFL (minimum score 550 paper-based; 220 computer-based). *Faculty research:* Interdisciplinary humanities and social sciences, political theory, cultural theory, feminist studies, literary theory.

University of Chicago, Division of the Humanities, Master of Arts Program in the Humanities, Chicago, IL 60637-1513. Offers MA. MAPH students take courses from faculty members of all departments at University of Chicago. Part-time programs available. *Degree requirements:* For master's, thesis. *Entrance requirements:* For master's, GRE General Test. Additional exam requirements/recommendations for international students: Required—TOEFL (minimum score 600 paper-based; 260 computer-based). Electronic applications accepted.

University of Colorado Denver, College of Liberal Arts and Sciences, Program in Humanities, Denver, CO 80217-3364. Offers MH. Part-time and evening/weekend programs available. *Students:* 7 full-time (4 women), 48 part-time (25 women); includes 7 minority (1 African American, 3 Asian Americans or Pacific Islanders, 3 Hispanic Americans). 24 applicants, 75% accepted, 14 enrolled. In 2009, 10 master's awarded. *Degree requirements:* For master's, thesis or alternative. *Entrance requirements:* For master's, GRE or MAT, interview, minimum GPA of 2.75, writing sample. Additional exam requirements/recommendations for international students: Required—TOEFL (minimum score 525 paper-based; 197 computer-based). *Application deadline:* For fall admission, 5/15 for domestic students; for spring admission, 10/15 for domestic students. Applications are processed on a rolling basis. Application fee: $50 ($75 for international students). Electronic applications accepted. *Financial support:* Research assistantships, teaching assistantships, Federal Work-Study available. Financial award application deadline: 4/1; financial award applicants required to submit FAFSA. *Unit head:* Myra Bookman, Director, 303-556-2496, Fax: 303-556-8100, E-mail: myra.bookman@ucdenver.edu. *Application contact:* Catherine Osmundson, Program Assistant, 303-556-2305, E-mail: catherine.osmundson@ucdenver.edu.

University of Dallas, Braniff Graduate School of Liberal Arts, Program in Humanities, Irving, TX 75062-4736. Offers M Hum, MA. Part-time programs available. *Faculty:* 1 full-time (0 women), 2 part-time/adjunct (1 woman). *Students:* 33 full-time (15 women), 47 part-time (20 women); includes 9 minority (3 African Americans, 1 Asian American or Pacific Islander, 5 Hispanic Americans), 1 international. Average age 32. 34 applicants, 100% accepted, 30 enrolled. In 2009, 16 master's awarded. *Degree requirements:* For master's, one foreign language, comprehensive exam, thesis (for some programs). *Entrance requirements:* For master's, GRE General Test. Additional exam requirements/recommendations for international students: Required—TOEFL. *Application deadline:* For fall admission, 2/15 priority date for domestic students; for spring admission, 11/15 for domestic students. Applications are processed on a rolling basis. Application fee: $50. *Expenses:* Tuition: Full-time $10,080; part-time $560 per credit hour. Required fees: $50 per term. Tuition and fees vary according to program. *Financial support:* In 2009–10, 78 students received support. Scholarships/grants available. Financial award application deadline: 2/15. *Faculty research:* Classical epic poetry, scholastic poetry, Renaissance drama, nineteenth and twentieth century Continental philosophy. *Unit head:* Dr. David Sweet, Dean, 972-721-5288, Fax: 972-721-5280, E-mail: dsweet@udallas.edu. *Application contact:* Graduate Coordinator, 972-721-5106, Fax: 972-721-5280, E-mail: graduate@acad.udallas.edu.

University of Houston–Clear Lake, School of Human Sciences and Humanities, Programs in Humanities and Fine Arts, Houston, TX 77058-1098. Offers history (MA); humanities (MA); literature (MA). Part-time and evening/weekend programs available. Postbaccalaureate distance learning degree programs offered (minimal on-campus study). *Degree requirements:* For master's, thesis or alternative. *Entrance requirements:* For master's, GRE General Test. Additional exam requirements/recommendations for international students: Required—TOEFL (minimum score 550 paper-based; 213 computer-based). *Faculty research:* Digital media studies, Latin American history, labor history, Chaucer evolution versus creationism debate.

University of Louisville, Graduate School, College of Arts and Sciences, Department of Humanities, Louisville, KY 40292-0001. Offers MA, PhD, MA/JD. *Students:* 27 full-time (17 women), 47 part-time (29 women); includes 6 minority (4 African Americans, 2 Asian Americans or Pacific Islanders), 2 international. Average age 38. 27 applicants, 63% accepted, 13 enrolled. In 2009, 11 master's, 2 doctorates awarded. *Degree requirements:* For master's, one foreign language, comprehensive exam (for some programs), thesis (for some programs), internship, project; for doctorate, 2 foreign languages, thesis/dissertation, internship. *Entrance requirements:* For master's, GRE General Test; for doctorate, GRE General Test, letters of recommendation, writing sample. *Application deadline:* Applications are processed on a rolling basis. Application fee: $50. *Financial support:* Teaching assistantships, institutionally sponsored loans, scholarships/grants, and tuition waivers (partial) available. *Unit head:* Elaine O. Wise, Chair, 502-852-7149, Fax: 502-852-0078, E-mail: elaine.wise@louisville.edu. *Application contact:* Libby Leggett, Director, Graduate Admissions, 502-852-3101, Fax: 502-852-6536, E-mail: gradadm@louisville.edu.

University of South Florida, Graduate School, College of Arts and Sciences, Department of Humanities and Cultural Studies, Tampa, FL 33617. Offers American studies (MA); film studies (MLA); humanities (MLA). Part-time and evening/weekend programs available. *Faculty:* 8 full-time (4 women). *Students:* 26 full-time (18 women), 14 part-time (9 women); includes 10 minority (7 African Americans, 3 Hispanic Americans). Average age 32. 24 applicants, 58% accepted, 11 enrolled. In 2009, 15 master's awarded. *Degree requirements:* For master's, comprehensive exam, thesis. *Entrance requirements:* For master's, GRE General Test, minimum GPA of 3.0 in last 60 hours, academic writing sample. Additional exam requirements/recommendations for international students: Required—TOEFL (minimum score 550 paper-based; 213 computer-based). *Application deadline:* For fall admission, 2/15 priority date for domestic students, 1/2 for international students; for spring admission, 10/15 priority date for domestic students, 6/1 for international students. Application fee: $30. *Financial support:* In 2009–10, 4 teaching assistantships with tuition reimbursements were awarded; scholarships/grants also available. Financial award application deadline: 4/4. *Faculty research:* American South, American autobiography, material culture, critical theory, cultural studies. *Unit head:* Daniel Belgrad, Chairperson, 813-974-9388, Fax: 813-974-9409, E-mail: dbelgrad@cas.usf.edu. *Application contact:* Maria Cizmic, Program Director, 813-974-9383, Fax: 813-974-9409, E-mail: mcizmic@cas.usf.edu.

The University of Texas at Arlington, Graduate School, College of Liberal Arts, Graduate Humanities Program, Arlington, TX 76019. Offers MA. Part-time and evening/weekend programs available. *Students:* 15 part-time (7 women); includes 5 minority (2 African Americans, 2 Asian Americans or Pacific Islanders, 1 Hispanic American). 1 applicant, 100% accepted, 1 enrolled. In 2009, 1 master's awarded. *Degree requirements:* For master's, one foreign language, thesis optional. *Entrance requirements:* For master's, GRE General Test. Additional exam requirements/recommendations for international students: Required—TOEFL (minimum score 550 paper-based; 213 computer-based). *Application deadline:* For fall admission, 6/16 for domestic

Humanities

The University of Texas at Arlington (continued)

students. Applications are processed on a rolling basis. Application fee: $35 ($50 for international students). *Financial support:* In 2009–10, 1 teaching assistantship (averaging $7,500 per year) was awarded. Financial award application deadline: 6/1; financial award applicants required to submit FAFSA. *Unit head:* Dr. Susan Hekman, Graduate Advisor, 817-272-2389, Fax: 817-272-5807, E-mail: hekman@uta.edu. *Application contact:* Dr. Susan Hekman, Graduate Advisor, 817-272-2389, Fax: 817-272-5807, E-mail: hekman@uta.edu.

The University of Texas at Dallas, School of Arts and Humanities, Richardson, TX 75080. Offers arts and technology (MFA); emerging media and communications (MA); humanities (MA, MAT, PhD), including aesthetic studies, history of ideas, humanities, studies in literature; Latin American studies (MA). Part-time and evening/weekend programs available. *Faculty:* 57 full-time (19 women), 3 part-time/adjunct (1 woman). *Students:* 240 full-time (127 women), 221 part-time (115 women); includes 90 minority (30 African Americans, 5 American Indian/Alaska Native, 21 Asian Americans or Pacific Islanders, 34 Hispanic Americans), 36 international. Average age 37. 186 applicants, 70% accepted, 106 enrolled. In 2009, 57 master's, 13 doctorates awarded. *Degree requirements:* For master's, one foreign language, portfolio; for doctorate, one foreign language, thesis/dissertation. *Entrance requirements:* For master's and doctorate, minimum GPA of 3.0 in undergraduate course work in field. Additional exam requirements/recommendations for international students: Required—TOEFL (minimum score 550 paper-based; 213 computer-based). *Application deadline:* For fall admission, 7/15 for domestic students, 5/1 priority date for international students; for spring admission, 11/15 for domestic students, 9/1 priority date for international students. Applications are processed on a rolling basis. Application fee: $50 ($100 for international students). Electronic applications accepted. *Expenses:* Tuition, state resident: full-time $11,068; part-time $461 per credit hour. Tuition, nonresident: full-time $21,178; part-time $882 per credit hour. Tuition and fees vary according to course load. *Financial support:* In 2009–10, 23 research assistantships with full tuition reimbursements (averaging $10,108 per year), 92 teaching assistantships with full tuition reimbursements (averaging $10,115 per year) were awarded; fellowships, Federal Work-Study, institutionally sponsored loans, scholarships/grants, and unspecified assistantships also available. Support available to part-time students. Financial award application deadline: 4/30; financial award applicants required to submit FAFSA. *Faculty research:* Translation, science and the arts and humanities, intellectual and philosophical history, cultural studies. Total annual research expenditures: $726,917. *Unit head:* Dr. Dennis M. Kratz, Dean, 972-883-2984, Fax: 972-883-2989, E-mail: dkratz@utdallas.edu. *Application contact:* Dr. Michael Wilson, Associate Dean of Graduate Studies, 972-883-2756, Fax: 972-883-2989, E-mail: mwilson@utdallas.edu.

The University of Texas Medical Branch, Graduate School of Biomedical Sciences, Program in Medical Humanities, Galveston, TX 77555. Offers MA, PhD. *Students:* 12 full-time (9 women), 4 part-time (3 women); includes 1 minority (Asian American or Pacific Islander), 1 international. Average age 41. In 2009, 3 doctorates awarded. *Degree requirements:* For master's, thesis; for doctorate, thesis/dissertation. *Entrance requirements:* For master's and doctorate, GRE General Test, writing sample. Additional exam requirements/recommendations for international students: Required—TOEFL (minimum score 550 paper-based; 213 computer-based). Application fee: $30 ($75 for international students). Electronic applications accepted. *Financial support:* In 2009–10, fellowships (averaging $25,000 per year), research assistantships with full tuition reimbursements (averaging $25,000 per year) were awarded; institutionally sponsored loans also available. Financial award applicants required to submit FAFSA. *Unit head:* Dr. Anne Hudson Jones, Director, 409-772-2376, Fax: 409-772-5640, E-mail: ahjones@utmb.edu. *Application contact:* Donna A. Vickers, Administrative Coordinator, 409-772-9396, Fax: 409-772-5640, E-mail: davicker@utmb.edu.

University of Utah, The Graduate School, College of Humanities, Environmental Humanities Graduate Program, Salt Lake City, UT 84112-1107. Offers MA, MS. *Students:* 19 full-time (10 women), 9 part-time (5 women); includes 1 minority (Hispanic American), 1 international. Average age 30. 23 applicants, 91% accepted, 19 enrolled. In 2009, 5 master's awarded. *Degree requirements:* For master's, one foreign language, comprehensive exam (for some programs), thesis. *Entrance requirements:* For master's, GRE, B.A. or B.S. Additional exam requirements/recommendations for international students: Required—TOEFL. *Application deadline:* For spring admission, 2/1 for domestic and international students. Application fee: $55 ($65 for international students). *Expenses:* Tuition, state resident: full-time $4004; part-time $1674 per semester. Tuition, nonresident: full-time $14,134; part-time $5915 per semester. Required fees: $324 per semester. Tuition and fees vary according to course load, degree level and program. *Financial support:* In 2009–10, 12 students received support, including 12 fellowships with full tuition reimbursements available (averaging $13,000 per year); health care benefits also available. Financial award application deadline: 2/1. *Faculty research:* Environmental writing, history/philosophy of science, environmental rhetoric and communication, the nuclear American West, American environmental history, urban environmentalism. Total annual research expenditures: $1,000. *Unit head:* Dr. Robert D. Newman, Dean and Associate Vice President of Interdisciplinary Studies, 801-581-6214, Fax: 801-585-5190, E-mail: robert.newman@utah.edu. *Application contact:* Dr. Stephen Tatum, Director, 801-581-4035, Fax: 801-585-5190, E-mail: tatum@english.utah.edu.

University of West Florida, College of Arts and Sciences: Arts, Program in Interdisciplinary Humanities, Pensacola, FL 32514-5750. Offers MA. Part-time and evening/weekend programs available. *Students:* 2 part-time (1 woman). Average age 44. 1 applicant, 100% accepted. In 2009, 1 master's awarded. *Degree requirements:* For master's, thesis. *Entrance requirements:* For master's, GRE General Test, minimum GPA of 3.0 in last 60 hours. Additional exam requirements/recommendations for international students: Required—TOEFL (minimum score 550 paper-based; 213 computer-based). *Application deadline:* For fall admission, 6/1 for domestic students, 5/15 for international students; for spring admission, 11/1 for domestic students, 10/1 for international students. Applications are processed on a rolling basis. Application fee: $30. *Expenses:* Tuition, state resident: full-time $4982; part-time $260 per credit hour. Tuition, nonresident: full-time $20,059; part-time $919 per credit hour. Required fees: $1247; $52 per credit hour. *Financial support:* In 2009–10, 1 teaching assistantship with partial tuition reimbursement (averaging $3,280 per year) was awarded; unspecified assistantships also available. Financial award application deadline: 4/15; financial award applicants required to submit FAFSA. *Unit head:* Dr. Sally Ferguson, Chairperson, 850-474-2676. *Application contact:* Terry McCray, Assistant Director of Graduate Admissions, 850-473-7718, Fax: 850-473-7714, E-mail: gradadmissions@uwf.edu.

Villanova University, Graduate School of Liberal Arts and Sciences, Department of Humanities and Augustinian Tradition, Villanova, PA 19085-1699. Offers MA. Part-time and evening/weekend programs available. *Faculty:* 2 full-time (1 woman), 1 part-time/adjunct (0 women). *Students:* 4 full-time (1 woman), 8 part-time (5 women); includes 2 minority (both Asian Americans or Pacific Islanders). Average age 30. 7 applicants, 71% accepted, 4 enrolled. *Degree requirements:* For master's, comprehensive exam. *Entrance requirements:* For master's, GRE, statement of objectives. Additional exam requirements/recommendations for international students: Required—TOEFL. *Application deadline:* For fall admission, 3/1 priority date for domestic and international students; for spring admission, 11/15 priority date for domestic and international students. Applications are processed on a rolling basis. Electronic applications accepted. *Expenses:* Tuition: Part-time $630 per credit. Required fees: $60 per credit. Part-time tuition and fees vary according to degree level and program. *Financial support:* Research assistantships, Federal Work-Study available. Financial award applicants required to submit FAFSA. *Unit head:* Dr. Kevin Hughes. *Application contact:* Dr. Adele Lindenmeyr, Dean, Graduate School of Liberal Arts and Sciences, 610-519-7093, Fax: 610-519-7096.

Virginia Commonwealth University, Graduate School, College of Humanities and Sciences, Richmond, VA 23284-9005. Offers MA, MFA, MPA, MS, MURP, PhD, CASR, CCJA, CPM, CURP, Certificate, Graduate Certificate, JD/MURP, MSW/Certificate. Part-time and evening/weekend programs available.

Wright State University, School of Graduate Studies, College of Liberal Arts, Interdisciplinary Program in Humanities, Dayton, OH 45435. Offers M Hum. *Degree requirements:* For master's, thesis or alternative. *Entrance requirements:* Additional exam requirements/recommendations for international students: Required—TOEFL.

York University, Faculty of Graduate Studies, Faculty of Arts, Program in Humanities, Toronto, ON M3J 1P3, Canada. Offers MA, PhD. Part-time programs available. *Degree requirements:* For master's, thesis or alternative; for doctorate, comprehensive exam, thesis/dissertation. *Entrance requirements:* Additional exam requirements/recommendations for international students: Required—TOEFL (minimum score 600 paper-based; 250 computer-based). Electronic applications accepted.

Liberal Studies

Abilene Christian University, Graduate School, Interdisciplinary Program in the Liberal Arts, Abilene, TX 79699-9100. Offers MLA. Part-time programs available. *Students:* 4 full-time (all women), 3 part-time (1 woman); includes 1 minority (African American). 3 applicants, 100% accepted, 2 enrolled. In 2009, 2 master's awarded. *Degree requirements:* For master's, comprehensive exam, thesis or alternative. *Entrance requirements:* For master's, GRE General Test, MAT. *Application deadline:* For fall admission, 4/1 priority date for domestic students; for spring admission, 11/1 for domestic students. Applications are processed on a rolling basis. Application fee: $40. Electronic applications accepted. *Expenses:* Tuition: Full-time $11,520; part-time $640 per hour. Required fees: $1090; $53.50 per hour. $10 per term. Tuition and fees vary according to program. *Financial support:* In 2009–10, 6 students received support. Federal Work-Study available. Support available to part-time students. Financial award application deadline: 4/1; financial award applicants required to submit FAFSA. *Unit head:* Dr. David Merrell, Graduate Adviser, 325-674-2035, Fax: 325-674-6844, E-mail: merrelld@acu.edu. *Application contact:* William Horn, Graduate Admissions Counselor, 325-674-2656, Fax: 325-674-6717, E-mail: gradinfo@acu.edu.

Alaska Pacific University, Graduate Programs, Liberal Studies Department, Anchorage, AK 99508-4672. Offers self-designed study (MA).

Albertus Magnus College, Liberal Studies Program, New Haven, CT 06511-1189. Offers MALS. Part-time and evening/weekend programs available. *Degree requirements:* For master's, thesis. *Entrance requirements:* For master's, interview, writing sample.

Alvernia University, Graduate Studies, Program in Liberal Studies, Reading, PA 19607-1799. Offers MALS. Part-time and evening/weekend programs available. *Degree requirements:* For master's, thesis optional. *Entrance requirements:* For master's, MAT or GRE (alumni excluded). Electronic applications accepted.

Antioch University Midwest, Graduate Programs, Individualized Liberal and Professional Studies Program, Yellow Springs, OH 45387-1609. Offers liberal and professional studies (MA), including counseling, creative writing, education, film studies, liberal studies, management, modern literature, psychology, theatre, visual arts. Part-time and evening/weekend programs available. Postbaccalaureate distance learning degree programs offered (minimal on-campus study). *Faculty:* 1 full-time (0 women), 2 part-time/adjunct (1 woman). *Students:* 23 full-time (13 women), 41 part-time (30 women); includes 13 minority (11 African Americans, 2 Hispanic Americans). Average age 40. 21 applicants, 76% accepted, 15 enrolled. In 2009, 24 master's awarded. *Degree requirements:* For master's, thesis or alternative. *Entrance requirements:* For master's, resume, 2 letters of reference. *Application deadline:* For fall admission, 8/1 for domestic students; for winter admission, 12/1 for domestic students; for spring admission, 3/10 for domestic students. Applications are processed on a rolling basis. Application fee: $50. Electronic applications accepted. *Expenses:* Contact institution. *Financial support:* Federal Work-Study available. Financial award applicants required to submit FAFSA. *Unit head:* Dr. Jon Saari, Chair, 937-769-1879, Fax: 937-769-1807, E-mail: jsaari@antioch.edu. *Application contact:* Seth Gordon, Assistant Director of Admissions, 937-769-1800 Ext. 1825, Fax: 937-769-1804, E-mail: sgordon@antioch.edu.

Armstrong Atlantic State University, School of Graduate Studies, Program in Liberal and Professional Studies, Savannah, GA 31419-1997. Offers MALPS. Part-time programs available. *Degree requirements:* For master's, comprehensive exam, project. *Entrance requirements:* For master's, GRE, minimum GPA of 2.5, letters of recommendation. Additional exam requirements/recommendations for international students: Required—TOEFL (minimum score 523 paper-based; 193 computer-based).

Auburn University Montgomery, School of Liberal Arts, Montgomery, AL 36124-4023. Offers MLA. Part-time and evening/weekend programs available. *Faculty:* 23 full-time (10 women), 1 part-time/adjunct (0 women). *Students:* 6 full-time (4 women), 30 part-time (22 women); includes 9 minority (8 African Americans, 1 American Indian/Alaska Native). Average age 36. In 2009, 6 master's awarded. *Degree requirements:* For master's, thesis. *Entrance requirements:* For master's, GRE or MAT. *Application deadline:* Applications are processed on a rolling basis. Electronic applications accepted. *Expenses:* Tuition, state resident: full-time $2841; part-time $225 per credit hour. Tuition, nonresident: full-time $8241; part-time $675 per credit hour. Required fees: $282; $8 per hour. $45 per term. *Financial support:* In 2009–10, 2 teaching assistantships were awarded; career-related internships or fieldwork and scholarships/grants also available. Support available to part-time students. Financial award application deadline: 3/1; financial award applicants required to submit FAFSA. *Unit head:* Dr. Michael Burger, Dean, 334-244-3382, Fax: 334-244-3740, E-mail: mburger1@aum.edu. *Application contact:* Dr. Eric Sterling, Professor, 334-244-3760, Fax: 334-244-3740, E-mail: esterlin@aum.edu.

Baker University, School of Professional and Graduate Studies, Program in Liberal Arts, Baldwin City, KS 66006-0065. Offers MLA. Program also offered in Overland Park, KS. Part-time and evening/weekend programs available. *Degree requirements:* For master's, portfolio of learning. *Entrance requirements:* Additional exam requirements/recommendations for international students: Required—TOEFL (minimum score 600 paper-based; 250 computer-based).

Barry University, School of Arts and Sciences, Interdisciplinary Program, Miami Shores, FL 33161-6695. Offers MA.

Boston University, Metropolitan College, Interdisciplinary Studies, Boston, MA 02215. Offers interdisciplinary studies (MLA). Part-time and evening/weekend programs available. *Students:* 1 (woman) full-time, 17 part-time (12 women). Average age 29. 2 applicants, 100% accepted, 1 enrolled. *Degree requirements:* For master's, thesis. *Entrance requirements:* For master's, interview. Additional exam requirements/recommendations for international students: Required—TOEFL (minimum score 560 paper-based). *Application deadline:* For fall admission, 3/31 priority date for domestic and international students; for winter admission, 11/30 priority date for domestic students; for spring admission, 11/15 priority date for international students. Applications are processed on a rolling basis. Application fee: $70. Electronic applications accepted. *Expenses:* Tuition: Full-time $37,910; part-time $1184 per credit hour. Required fees: $386; $40 per semester. Part-time tuition and fees vary according to class time, course level, degree level and program. *Financial support:* Research assistantships with partial tuition reimbursements, scholarships/grants available. Support available to part-time students. *Unit head:* Prof. Daniel Ranall, Interim Chair, 617-358-0005, Fax: 617-358-1230, E-mail: dranalli@bu.edu. *Application contact:* Prof. Daniel Ranall, Interim Chair, 617-358-0005, Fax: 617-358-1230, E-mail: dranalli@bu.edu.

Bradley University, Graduate School, College of Liberal Arts and Sciences, Program in Liberal Studies, Peoria, IL 61625-0002. Offers MLS. Part-time and evening/weekend programs available. *Degree requirements:* For master's, comprehensive exam, colloquium. *Entrance requirements:* For master's, 2 letters of recommendation. Additional exam requirements/recommendations for international students: Required—TOEFL (minimum score 550 paper-based; 213 computer-based; 79 iBT). *Expenses:* Contact institution.

Brooklyn College of the City University of New York, Division of Graduate Studies, Liberal Studies Program, Brooklyn, NY 11210-2889. Offers MA. Part-time programs available. *Students:* 3 part-time (all women); includes 2 minority (1 African American, 1 Hispanic American). Average age 36. In 2009, 5 master's awarded. *Degree requirements:* For master's, thesis or alternative, final project. *Entrance requirements:* For master's, interview, 2 letters of recommendation, essay. Additional exam requirements/recommendations for international students: Required—TOEFL. *Application deadline:* For fall admission, 3/1 priority date for domestic students, 2/1 priority date for international students; for spring admission, 11/1 priority date for domestic students, 10/1 priority date for international students. Applications are processed on a rolling basis. Application fee: $125. Electronic applications accepted. *Expenses:* Tuition, area resident: Full-time $7360; part-time $310 per credit hour. Tuition, state resident: full-time $7360; part-time $310 per credit hour. Tuition, nonresident: full-time $13,800; part-time $575 per credit hour. International tuition: $13,800 full-time. Required fees: $140.10 per semester. *Financial support:* Federal Work-Study, institutionally sponsored loans, and scholarships/grants available. Support available to part-time students. Financial award application deadline: 5/1; financial award applicants required to submit FAFSA. *Faculty research:* Language acquisition, Judaic biography, ecocriticism. *Unit head:* Dr. Philip Gallagher, Director, 718-951-5252, E-mail: philipg@brooklyn.cuny.edu. *Application contact:* Hernan Sierra, Graduate Admissions Coordinator, 718-951-4536, Fax: 718-951-4506, E-mail: grads@brooklyn.cuny.edu.

Brooklyn College of the City University of New York, Division of Graduate Studies, School of Education, Program in Childhood Education, Brooklyn, NY 11210-2889. Offers bilingual education (MS Ed); liberal arts (MS Ed); mathematics (MS Ed); science/environmental education (MS Ed). Part-time and evening/weekend programs available. *Students:* 14 full-time (13 women), 245 part-time (209 women); includes 129 minority (60 African Americans, 2 American Indian/Alaska Native, 20 Asian Americans or Pacific Islanders, 47 Hispanic Americans), 6 international. Average age 30. 114 applicants, 85% accepted, 65 enrolled. In 2009, 118 master's awarded. *Entrance requirements:* For master's, LAST, interview, previous course work in education, writing sample, resume, 2 letters of recommendation. Additional exam requirements/recommendations for international students: Required—TOEFL (minimum score 500 paper-based; 173 computer-based; 61 iBT). *Application deadline:* For fall admission, 3/1 priority date for domestic students, 2/1 priority date for international students; for spring admission, 11/1 priority date for domestic students, 10/1 priority date for international students. Applications are processed on a rolling basis. Application fee: $125. Electronic applications accepted. *Expenses:* Tuition, area resident: Full-time $7360; part-time $310 per credit hour. Tuition, state resident: full-time $7360; part-time $310 per credit hour. Tuition, nonresident: full-time $13,800; part-time $575 per credit hour. International tuition: $13,800 full-time. Required fees: $140.10 per semester. *Financial support:* Career-related internships or fieldwork, Federal Work-Study, institutionally sponsored loans, and scholarships/grants available. Support available to part-time students. Financial award application deadline: 5/1; financial award applicants required to submit FAFSA. *Faculty research:* Emotional intelligence, multiculturalism, arts immersion, the Holocaust. *Unit head:* Dr. Wayne Reed, Program Head, 718-951-5214, E-mail: wreed@brooklyn.cuny.edu. *Application contact:* Hernan Sierra, Graduate Admissions Coordinator, 718-951-4536, Fax: 718-951-4506, E-mail: grads@brooklyn.cuny.edu.

California State University, Sacramento, Graduate Studies, College of Social Sciences and Interdisciplinary Studies, Liberal Arts Program, Sacramento, CA 95819. Offers French (MA); German (MA); Spanish (MA); theater arts (MA). *Degree requirements:* For master's, writing proficiency exam. *Entrance requirements:* Additional exam requirements/recommendations for international students: Required—TOEFL. Electronic applications accepted.

Cardinal Stritch University, College of Arts and Sciences, Milwaukee, WI 53217-3985. Offers MA, MM, MS. Part-time and evening/weekend programs available. *Degree requirements:* For master's, thesis.

Clark University, Graduate School, College of Professional and Continuing Education, Program in Liberal Studies, Worcester, MA 01610-1477. Offers MALA. Part-time and evening/weekend programs available. *Students:* 1 part-time (0 women). Average age 43. 1 applicant, 100% accepted, 0 enrolled. *Degree requirements:* For master's, thesis optional. *Application deadline:* Applications are processed on a rolling basis. Application fee: $50. Electronic applications accepted. *Expenses:* Tuition: Full-time $34,900; part-time $4362.50 per course. *Financial support:* Career-related internships or fieldwork available. Support available to part-time students. *Unit head:* Max E. Hess, Director of Graduate Studies, 508-793-7217, Fax: 508-793-7232. *Application contact:* Julia Parent, Director of Marketing, Communications, and Admissions, 508-793-7217, Fax: 508-793-7232, E-mail: jparent@clarku.edu.

Clayton State University, School of Graduate Studies, Program in Liberal Studies, Morrow, GA 30260-0285. Offers MALS. Part-time programs available. *Students:* 2 full-time (both women), 26 part-time (14 women); includes 13 minority (12 African Americans, 1 Asian American or Pacific Islander). Average age 41. 9 applicants, 44% accepted, 2 enrolled. In 2009, 2 master's awarded. *Degree requirements:* For master's, thesis optional. *Entrance requirements:* For master's, GRE. Additional exam requirements/recommendations for international students: Required—TOEFL (minimum score 550 paper-based; 213 computer-based; 80 iBT). *Application deadline:* For fall admission, 7/15 for domestic students, 5/1 for international students; for spring admission, 4/15 for domestic students, 2/1 for international students. Application fee: $50. Electronic applications accepted. *Expenses:* Contact institution. *Financial support:* Applicants required to submit FAFSA. *Unit head:* Dr. Wendy Burns-Ardolino, Director, 678-466-4723, Fax: 678-466-4899, E-mail: wburnsar@clayton.edu. *Application contact:* Jacqueline Person, Administrative Assistant, Master of Arts in Liberal Studies, 678-466-4723, Fax: 678-466-4899, E-mail: jacquelineperson@clayton.edu.

The College at Brockport, State University of New York, Office of the Vice Provost, Program in Liberal Studies, Brockport, NY 14420-2997. Offers MA. Part-time programs available. *Students:* 2 full-time (0 women), 20 part-time (12 women); includes 6 minority (3 African Americans, 1 Asian American or Pacific Islander, 2 Hispanic Americans). 8 applicants, 75% accepted, 6 enrolled. In 2009, 23 master's awarded. *Degree requirements:* For master's, portfolio. *Entrance requirements:* For master's, minimum GPA of 3.0, letters of recommendation. Additional exam requirements/recommendations for international students: Required—TOEFL (minimum score 550 paper-based; 213 computer-based; 79 iBT). *Application deadline:* For fall admission, 6/15 priority date for domestic and international students; for spring admission, 10/15 priority date for domestic and international students. Application fee: $50. Electronic applications accepted. *Expenses:* Tuition, state resident: full-time $8370; part-time $349 per credit. Tuition, nonresident: full-time $13,250; part-time $522 per credit. *Financial support:* Federal Work-Study, scholarships/grants, and unspecified assistantships available. Support available to part-time students. Financial award application deadline: 3/15; financial award applicants required to submit FAFSA. *Unit head:* Dr. Kalathur Rajasethupathy, Director, 585-395-2262, Fax: 585-395-2172, E-mail: kraja@brockport.edu. *Application contact:* Dr. Kalathur Rajasethupathy, Director, 585-395-2262, Fax: 585-395-2172, E-mail: kraja@brockport.edu.

College of Notre Dame of Maryland, Graduate Studies, Program in Liberal Studies, Baltimore, MD 21210-2476. Offers MA. Part-time and evening/weekend programs available. *Degree requirements:* For master's, thesis or alternative. *Entrance requirements:* For master's, minimum GPA of 3.0. Additional exam requirements/recommendations for international students: Required—TOEFL (minimum score 500 paper-based; 173 computer-based; 61 iBT). Electronic applications accepted.

College of Staten Island of the City University of New York, Graduate Programs, Program in Liberal Studies, Staten Island, NY 10314-6600. Offers MA. Evening/weekend programs available. *Faculty:* 1 full-time (0 women), 3 part-time/adjunct (0 women). *Students:* 1 full-time (0 women), 37 part-time (18 women); includes 8 minority (4 African Americans, 2 Asian Americans or Pacific Islanders, 2 Hispanic Americans), 2 international. Average age 34. 36 applicants, 75% accepted, 21 enrolled. In 2009, 10 master's awarded. *Degree requirements:* For master's, thesis. *Entrance requirements:* For master's, minimum undergraduate GPA of 3.0, interview. Additional exam requirements/recommendations for international students: Required—TOEFL (minimum score 550 paper-based; 213 computer-based; 79 iBT). *Application deadline:* For fall admission, 6/1 for domestic and international students; for spring admission, 12/12 for domestic and international students. Applications are processed on a rolling basis. Application fee: $125. Electronic applications accepted. *Expenses:* Tuition, state resident: full-time $7360; part-time $310 per credit. Tuition, nonresident: part-time $575 per credit. Required fees: $378; $113 per semester. *Financial support:* Fellowships, research assistantships, teaching assistantships, career-related internships or fieldwork, Federal Work-Study, and scholarships/grants available. Support available to part-time students. Financial award applicants required to submit FAFSA. Total annual research expenditures: $119,000. *Unit head:* Dr. David Traboulay, Coordinator, 718-982-2877, E-mail: mals@mail.csi.cuny.edu. *Application contact:* Sasha Spence, Assistant Director of Graduate Recruitment and Admissions, 718-982-2699, Fax: 718-982-2500, E-mail: sasha.spence@csi.cuny.edu.

The Colorado College, Department of Education, Experienced Teacher Program, Colorado Springs, CO 80903-3294. Offers arts and humanities (MAT); liberal arts (MAT); Southwest studies (MAT). Programs offered during summer only. Part-time programs available. *Degree requirements:* For master's, thesis, oral exam, 50-page paper. *Application deadline:* Applications are processed on a rolling basis. Application fee: $50. *Expenses:* Contact institution. *Financial support:* Institutionally sponsored loans and half-tuition scholarships to teachers with a contract available.

Columbia University, Graduate School of Arts and Sciences, Program in Liberal Studies, New York, NY 10027. Offers American studies (MA); East Asian studies (MA); human rights studies (MA); Islamic culture studies (MA); Jewish studies (MA); medieval studies (MA); modern European studies (MA); South Asian studies (MA). Part-time and evening/weekend programs available. *Degree requirements:* For master's, thesis.

Concordia University Chicago, College of Graduate and Innovative Programs, Program in Liberal Studies, River Forest, IL 60305-1499. Offers MA. *Entrance requirements:* Additional exam requirements/recommendations for international students: Required—TOEFL (minimum score 550 paper-based; 195 computer-based). Electronic applications accepted.

Converse College, School of Education and Graduate Studies, Program in Liberal Arts, Spartanburg, SC 29302-0006. Offers English (MLA); history (MLA); political science (MLA). *Degree requirements:* For master's, capstone paper. *Entrance requirements:* For master's, minimum GPA of 3.0, 2 recommendations.

Creighton University, Graduate School, College of Arts and Sciences, Program in Liberal Studies, Omaha, NE 68178-0001. Offers MLS. Part-time and evening/weekend programs available. *Faculty:* 18 full-time (5 women). *Students:* 5 full-time (3 women), 20 part-time (13 women); includes 5 minority (4 African Americans, 1 Hispanic American). Average age 32. 10 applicants, 90% accepted, 9 enrolled. In 2009, 12 master's awarded. *Degree requirements:* For master's, thesis optional. *Entrance requirements:* For master's, 3 letters of recommendation. Additional exam requirements/recommendations for international students: Required—TOEFL (minimum score 550 paper-based; 213 computer-based; 80 iBT). *Application deadline:* For fall admission, 3/1 priority date for domestic and international students; for winter admission, 12/1 priority date for domestic students, 7/1 priority date for international students; for spring admission, 4/1 priority date for domestic students, 10/1 priority date for international students. Applications are processed on a rolling basis. Application fee: $50. Electronic applications accepted. *Expenses:* Tuition: Full-time $11,700; part-time $650 per credit hour. Required fees: $126 per semester. *Financial support:* Available to part-time students. Applicants required to submit FAFSA. *Unit head:* Dr. Richard White, Professor of Philosophy, 402-280-2642, E-mail: rwhite@creighton.edu. *Application contact:* Taunya Plater, Senior Program Coordinator, 402-280-2870, Fax: 402-280-2899, E-mail: taunyaplater@creighton.edu.

Dallas Baptist University, College of Adult Education, Liberal Arts Program, Dallas, TX 75211-9299. Offers arts (MLA); Christian ministry (MLA); English (MLA); English as a second language (MLA); fine arts (MLA); history (MLA); missions (MLA); political science (MLA). Part-time and evening/weekend programs available. *Entrance requirements:* For master's, minimum GPA of 3.0. Additional exam requirements/recommendations for international students: Required—TOEFL. Electronic applications accepted. *Expenses:* Tuition: Full-time $10,674; part-time $593 per credit hour. *Faculty research:* Milton and seventeenth-century Puritans, inter-Biblical years, nineteenth-century literature, Latin American and Texas history.

Dartmouth College, Arts and Sciences Graduate Programs, Program in Liberal Studies, Hanover, NH 03755. Offers MALS. Part-time programs available. *Faculty:* 29 full-time (7 women). *Students:* 43 full-time (26 women), 25 part-time (17 women); includes 7 minority (2 African Americans, 3 Asian Americans or Pacific Islanders, 2 Hispanic Americans), 7 international. Average age 30. 82 applicants, 67% accepted, 38 enrolled. In 2009, 49 master's awarded. *Degree requirements:* For master's, thesis. *Entrance requirements:* Additional exam requirements/recommendations for international students: Required—TOEFL. *Application deadline:* For fall admission, 2/15 for domestic students; for winter admission, 7/15 for domestic students; for spring admission, 7/15 for domestic students. Application fee: $50. *Financial support:* Institutionally sponsored loans available. Financial award application deadline: 4/2. *Unit head:* Dr. Donald Pease, Chair, 603-646-3592. *Application contact:* Lauren E. Clarke, Executive Director, 603-646-3592, Fax: 603-646-3590, E-mail: lauren.e.clarke@dartmouth.edu.

Dowling College, Programs in Arts and Sciences, Oakdale, NY 11769-1999. Offers integrated math and science (MS); liberal studies (MA). Part-time and evening/weekend programs available. *Faculty:* 4 full-time (1 woman), 4 part-time/adjunct (1 woman). *Students:* 3 full-time (2 women), 9 part-time (5 women), 1 international. Average age 33. 9 applicants, 89% accepted, 2 enrolled. In 2009, 1 master's awarded. *Degree requirements:* For master's, comprehensive exam, thesis. *Entrance requirements:* For master's, minimum undergraduate GPA of 3.0, 2 letters of recommendation. Additional exam requirements/recommendations for international students: Required—TOEFL (minimum score 550 paper-based). *Application deadline:* For fall admission, 9/1 priority date for domestic students; for winter admission, 1/1 priority date for domestic students; for spring admission, 2/1 priority date for domestic students. Applications are processed on a rolling basis. Application fee: $50. Electronic applications accepted. *Expenses:* Tuition: Full-time $14,490; part-time $805 per credit. Required fees: $346 per term. *Financial support:* Federal Work-Study available. Support available to part-time students. Financial award application deadline: 6/30; financial award applicants required to submit FAFSA. *Unit head:* Dr. Paul Abramson, Dean, 631-244-3162, Fax: 631-244-1035, E-mail: abramsop@dowling.edu. *Application contact:* Glenn M. Berman, Assistant Vice President for

Liberal Studies

Dowling College (continued)
Enrollment Services/Dean of Admissions, 631-244-3357, Fax: 631-244-1059, E-mail: glenn.berman@dowling.edu.

Duke University, Graduate School, Program in Liberal Studies, Durham, NC 27708. Offers AM. Part-time and evening/weekend programs available. *Degree requirements:* For master's, thesis or alternative, final project. *Entrance requirements:* For master's, interview. Additional exam requirements/recommendations for international students: Required—IELTS (preferred) or TOEFL. Electronic applications accepted.

Duquesne University, School of Leadership and Professional Advancement, Pittsburgh, PA 15282-0001. Offers leadership (MS), including business ethics, community leadership, global leadership, information technology, leadership, liberal studies, professional administration, sports leadership. Part-time and evening/weekend programs available. Postbaccalaureate distance learning degree programs offered (no on-campus study). *Faculty:* 1 full-time (0 women), 70 part-time/adjunct (35 women). *Students:* 654 (307 women); includes 68 minority (57 African Americans, 1 American Indian/Alaska Native, 6 Asian Americans or Pacific Islanders, 4 Hispanic Americans). 161 applicants, 73% accepted, 103 enrolled. In 2009, 108 master's awarded. *Degree requirements:* For master's, capstone course. *Entrance requirements:* For master's, professional work experience, 500-word essay. Additional exam requirements/recommendations for international students: Required—TOEFL. *Application deadline:* Applications are processed on a rolling basis. Application fee: $0. Electronic applications accepted. *Expenses:* Tuition: Part-time $851 per credit. Required fees: $81 per credit. *Financial support:* Applicants required to submit FAFSA. *Unit head:* Dr. Dorothy Bassett, Dean, 412-396-2141, Fax: 412-396-4711, E-mail: bassettd@duq.edu. *Application contact:* Marianne Leister, Director of Student Services, 412-396-4933, Fax: 412-396-5072, E-mail: leister@duq.edu.

East Tennessee State University, School of Graduate Studies, Division of Cross-Disciplinary Studies, Johnson City, TN 37614. Offers liberal studies (MALS). *Entrance requirements:* For master's, GRE. Additional exam requirements/recommendations for international students: Required—TOEFL (minimum score 550 paper-based; 213 computer-based).

Excelsior College, School of Liberal Arts, Albany, NY 12203-5159. Offers liberal studies (MA). Part-time and evening/weekend programs available. Postbaccalaureate distance learning degree programs offered (no on-campus study). *Degree requirements:* For master's, thesis or alternative. Electronic applications accepted.

Florida Atlantic University, Dorothy F. Schmidt College of Arts and Letters, Program in Liberal Studies, Boca Raton, FL 33431-0991. Offers MA. *Students:* 2 full-time (1 woman), 5 part-time (3 women); includes 2 minority (1 African American, 1 Hispanic American). Average age 43. 4 applicants, 25% accepted, 1 enrolled. In 2009, 1 master's awarded. *Degree requirements:* For master's, thesis or alternative. *Entrance requirements:* For master's, GRE General Test. *Application deadline:* For fall admission, 2/1 priority date for domestic students, 2/1 for international students; for spring admission, 10/1 for domestic and international students. Applications are processed on a rolling basis. Application fee: $30. *Expenses:* Tuition, state resident: full-time $7055; part-time $293.94 per credit hour. Tuition, nonresident: full-time $22,096; part-time $920.66 per credit hour. *Unit head:* Dr. Clevis Headley, Director, 561-297-3920, E-mail: headley@fau.edu. *Application contact:* Dr. Emily Stockard, Associate Dean, 561-297-2817, Fax: 561-297-2744, E-mail: stockard@fau.edu.

Florida International University, College of Arts and Sciences, Program in Liberal Studies, Miami, FL 33199. Offers MA. Part-time and evening/weekend programs available. *Students:* 6 full-time (4 women), 14 part-time (8 women); includes 11 minority (2 African Americans, 2 Asian Americans or Pacific Islanders, 7 Hispanic Americans), 1 international. Average age 32. 10 applicants, 90% accepted, 9 enrolled. In 2009, 3 master's awarded. *Degree requirements:* For master's, thesis optional. *Entrance requirements:* For master's, minimum GPA of 3.0, two-three letters of recommendation, writing sample, cv. Additional exam requirements/recommendations for international students: Required—TOEFL (minimum score 550 paper-based; 80 iBT). *Application deadline:* For fall admission, 6/1 for domestic students, 4/1 for international students; for spring admission, 10/1 for domestic students, 9/1 for international students. Applications are processed on a rolling basis. Application fee: $30. Electronic applications accepted. *Expenses:* Tuition, state resident: full-time $8008; part-time $4004 per year. Tuition, nonresident: full-time $20,104; part-time $10,052 per year. Required fees: $298; $149 per term. *Financial support:* Institutionally sponsored loans and scholarships/grants available. Financial award application deadline: 3/1; financial award applicants required to submit FAFSA. *Unit head:* Dr. Leonard Keller, Chair, 305-348-2865, Fax: 305-348-7201, E-mail: leonard.keller@fiu.edu. *Application contact:* Dr. Kiriake Xerohemona, Graduate Program Director, 305-348-2185, Fax: 305-348-7201, E-mail: xerohemo@fiu.edu.

Fordham University, Graduate School of Arts and Sciences, Program in Humanities and Sciences, New York, NY 10458. Offers MA. Part-time and evening/weekend programs available. *Students:* 3 full-time (2 women), 18 part-time (11 women); includes 4 minority (2 African Americans, 1 American Indian/Alaska Native, 1 Hispanic American), 1 international. Average age 26. 17 applicants, 88% accepted, 8 enrolled. In 2009, 10 master's awarded. *Degree requirements:* For master's, final paper. *Entrance requirements:* Additional exam requirements/recommendations for international students: Required—TOEFL (minimum score 650 paper-based; 280 computer-based). *Application deadline:* For fall admission, 1/4 priority date for domestic students; for spring admission, 11/1 for domestic students. Application fee: $70. Electronic applications accepted. *Financial support:* In 2009–10, 1 student received support, including 1 research assistantship (averaging $18,400 per year); institutionally sponsored loans and tuition waivers (full and partial) also available. Financial award application deadline: 1/4; financial award applicants required to submit FAFSA. *Unit head:* Dr. Hugo Benavides, Director, 718-817-4407, E-mail: benavides@fordham.edu. *Application contact:* Charlene Dundie, Director of Graduate Admissions, 718-817-4420, Fax: 718-817-3566, E-mail: dundie@fordham.edu.

Fort Hays State University, Graduate School, College of Arts and Sciences, Center for Interdisciplinary Studies, Hays, KS 67601-4099. Offers liberal studies (MLS). Postbaccalaureate distance learning degree programs offered (minimal on-campus study). *Degree requirements:* For master's, comprehensive exam, thesis or alternative. *Entrance requirements:* Additional exam requirements/recommendations for international students: Required—TOEFL (minimum score 550 paper-based; 213 computer-based). Electronic applications accepted.

Georgetown University, Graduate School of Arts and Sciences, School of Continuing Studies, Washington, DC 20057. Offers American studies (MALS); Catholic studies (MALS); classical civilizations (MALS); ethics and the professions (MALS); human resources management (MPS); humanities (MALS); individualized study (MALS); international affairs (MALS); Islam and Muslim-Christian relations (MALS); journalism (MPS); liberal studies (DLS); literature and society (MALS); medieval and early modern European studies (MALS); public relations (MPS); real estate (MPS); religious studies (MALS); social and public policy (MALS); sports industry management (MPS); the theory and practice of American democracy (MALS); visual culture (MALS). *Entrance requirements:* Additional exam requirements/recommendations for international students: Required—TOEFL.

Graduate School and University Center of the City University of New York, Graduate Studies, Program in Liberal Studies, New York, NY 10016-4039. Offers MA. *Students:* 11 full-time (10 women), 97 part-time (60 women); includes 7 minority (all Hispanic Americans), 5 international. Average age 34. 60 applicants, 88% accepted, 30 enrolled. In 2009, 24 master's awarded. *Degree requirements:* For master's, thesis. *Entrance requirements:* For master's, GRE General Test. Additional exam requirements/recommendations for international students: Required—TOEFL. *Application deadline:* For fall admission, 4/15 for domestic students; for spring admission, 11/15 for domestic students. Application fee: $125. Electronic applications accepted. *Financial support:* In 2009–10, 24 students received support, including 2 fellowships; Federal Work-Study, institutionally sponsored loans, and tuition waivers (full and partial) also available. Financial award application deadline: 2/1; financial award applicants required to submit FAFSA. *Unit head:* Dr. Joseph Dauben, Executive Officer, 212-817-8481, Fax: 212-817-1525. *Application contact:* Les Gribben, Director of Admissions, 212-817-7470, Fax: 212-817-1624, E-mail: lgribben@gc.cuny.edu.

Hamline University, Graduate School of Liberal Studies, St. Paul, MN 55104-1284. Offers MALS, MFA, CALS. Part-time and evening/weekend programs available. *Faculty:* 6 full-time (4 women), 25 part-time/adjunct (18 women). *Students:* 85 full-time (59 women), 121 part-time (91 women); includes 11 minority (8 African Americans, 2 American Indian/Alaska Native, 1 Hispanic American), 1 international. Average age 36. 92 applicants, 74% accepted, 55 enrolled. In 2009, 80 master's awarded. *Degree requirements:* For master's, thesis. *Entrance requirements:* For master's, 20-page writing sample (MFA), letters of recommendation. Additional exam requirements/recommendations for international students: Required—TOEFL (minimum score 550 paper-based; 213 computer-based; 79 iBT), TWE (minimum score 5). *Application deadline:* For fall admission, 3/1 for domestic and international students; for spring admission, 9/1 for domestic and international students. Applications are processed on a rolling basis. Application fee: $0. Electronic applications accepted. *Expenses:* Contact institution. *Financial support:* In 2009–10, 6 students received support. Federal Work-Study and scholarships/grants available. Support available to part-time students. Financial award applicants required to submit FAFSA. *Unit head:* Mary Rockcastle, Dean, 651-523-2047, Fax: 651-523-2490, E-mail: mrockcastle@hamline.edu. *Application contact:* Rae A. Lenway, Director, Graduate Recruitment and Admission, 651-523-2900, Fax: 651-523-3058, E-mail: rlenway01@hamline.edu.

Harvard University, Extension School, Cambridge, MA 02138-3722. Offers applied sciences (CAS); biotechnology (ALM); educational technologies (ALM); educational technology (CET); English for graduate and professional studies (DGP); environmental management (ALM, CEM); information technology (ALM); journalism (ALM); liberal arts (ALM); management (ALM, CM); mathematics for teaching (ALM); museum studies (ALM); premedical studies (Diploma); publication and communication (CPC). Part-time and evening/weekend programs available. *Degree requirements:* For master's, thesis. *Entrance requirements:* For master's, 3 completed graduate courses with grade of B or higher. Additional exam requirements/recommendations for international students: Required—TOEFL (minimum score 600 paper-based; 250 computer-based), TWE (minimum score 5). *Expenses:* Contact institution.

Henderson State University, Graduate Studies, Ellis College of Arts and Sciences, Arkadelphia, AR 71999-0001. Offers MLA. Part-time programs available. *Faculty:* 14 full-time (6 women), 2 part-time/adjunct (1 woman). *Students:* 9 full-time (4 women), 25 part-time (18 women); includes 3 minority (all African Americans). Average age 34. 8 applicants, 100% accepted, 8 enrolled. In 2009, 8 master's awarded. *Entrance requirements:* For master's, minimum GPA of 2.7, interview. Additional exam requirements/recommendations for international students: Required—TOEFL (minimum score 550 paper-based; 213 computer-based); Recommended—IELTS (minimum score 6). *Application deadline:* For fall admission, 8/1 priority date for domestic students, 6/30 priority date for international students; for spring admission, 1/1 priority date for domestic students, 11/30 priority date for international students. Application fee: $25 ($75 for international students). Electronic applications accepted. *Expenses:* Tuition, state resident: full-time $3798; part-time $211 per credit hour. Tuition, nonresident: full-time $7596; part-time $422 per credit hour. Required fees: $903. *Financial support:* Teaching assistantships with tuition reimbursements available. *Unit head:* Dr. Clinton Atchley, MLA Director, 870-230-5276, Fax: 870-230-5144, E-mail: atchlec@hsu.edu. *Application contact:* Dr. Marck L. Beggs, Graduate Dean, 870-230-5126, Fax: 870-230-5479, E-mail: beggsm@hsu.edu.

Hollins University, Graduate Programs, Program in Liberal Studies, Roanoke, VA 24020-1603. Offers humanities (MALS); interdisciplinary studies (MALS); justice and legal studies (MALS); liberal studies (CAS); social science (MALS); visual and performing arts (MALS). Part-time and evening/weekend programs available. *Faculty:* 7 full-time (1 woman), 4 part-time/adjunct (2 women). *Students:* 23 full-time (22 women), 73 part-time (57 women); includes 15 minority (13 African Americans, 2 Asian Americans or Pacific Islanders), 4 international. Average age 39. 31 applicants, 94% accepted, 25 enrolled. In 2009, 30 master's awarded. *Degree requirements:* For master's, thesis. *Entrance requirements:* For master's, letters of recommendation, interview. Additional exam requirements/recommendations for international students: Required—TOEFL (minimum score 550 paper-based; 213 computer-based; 79 iBT). *Application deadline:* For fall admission, 7/1 priority date for domestic and international students; for spring admission, 12/10 priority date for domestic and international students. Applications are processed on a rolling basis. Application fee: $40. Electronic applications accepted. *Expenses:* Tuition: Full-time $27,780; part-time $295 per contact hour. Required fees: $280; $70 per unit. Part-time tuition and fees vary according to course load and program. *Financial support:* In 2009–10, 31 students received support, including 2 fellowships (averaging $902 per year); Federal Work-Study and scholarships/grants also available. Support available to part-time students. Financial award application deadline: 7/15; financial award applicants required to submit FAFSA. *Faculty research:* Elderly blacks, film, feminist economics, US voting patterns, Wagner, diversity. *Unit head:* Dr. Edward A. Lynch, Director, 540-362-6475, Fax: 540-362-6288, E-mail: elynch@hollins.edu. *Application contact:* Cathy S. Koon, Manager of Graduate Services, 540-362-6326, Fax: 540-362-6288, E-mail: ckoon@hollins.edu.

Houston Baptist University, College of Arts and Humanities, Program in Liberal Arts, Houston, TX 77074-3298. Offers MLA. Part-time and evening/weekend programs available. *Entrance requirements:* For master's, interview, minimum GPA of 2.5, writing sample. Additional exam requirements/recommendations for international students: Required—TOEFL (minimum score 550 paper-based; 213 computer-based).

Indiana University Kokomo, School of Arts and Sciences, Kokomo, IN 46904-9003. Offers liberal studies (MALS). *Faculty:* 32 full-time (10 women). *Students:* 2 full-time (1 woman), 12 part-time (9 women); includes 1 minority (Hispanic American). Average age 45. In 2009, 2 master's awarded. *Degree requirements:* For master's, thesis. *Entrance requirements:* For master's, minimum GPA of 3.0. Additional exam requirements/recommendations for international students: Required—TOEFL. *Application deadline:* For fall admission, 4/15 priority date for domestic students; for spring admission, 10/15 priority date for domestic students. Applications are processed on a rolling basis. Application fee: $50. *Faculty research:* Bibliography and textual studies, comparative literature, current global issues/political science. *Unit head:* Dr. Susan Sciame-Giesecke, Dean, 765-455-9258, Fax: 765-455-9566, E-mail: sgieseck@iuk.edu. *Application contact:* Dr. Susan Sciame-Giesecke, Dean, 765-455-9258, Fax: 765-455-9566, E-mail: sgieseck@iuk.edu.

Indiana University–Purdue University Fort Wayne, College of Arts and Sciences, Program in Liberal Studies, Fort Wayne, IN 46805-1499. Offers MLS. Part-time programs available. *Students:* 3 full-time (2 women), 25 part-time (15 women); includes 5 minority (4 African Americans, 1 Asian American or Pacific Islander). Average age 43. 15 applicants, 100% accepted, 9 enrolled. In 2009, 9 master's awarded. *Entrance requirements:* For master's, minimum GPA of 3.0, major or minor in related area, three letters of recommendation. Additional exam requirements/recommendations for international students: Required—TOEFL (minimum score 550 paper-based; 213 computer-based; 77 iBT). *Application deadline:* For fall admission, 8/1 for domestic students; for spring admission, 12/1 for domestic students. Applications are processed on a rolling basis. Application fee: $50. *Expenses:* Tuition, state resident: full-time $4595; part-time $255 per credit. Tuition, nonresident: full-time $10,963; part-time $609 per credit. Required fees: $528; $29.35 per credit. Tuition and fees vary according to course load. *Financial support:* Scholarships/grants available. Support available to part-time students. Financial award application deadline: 3/1; financial award applicants required to submit FAFSA. *Unit head:* Dr. Michael E. Kaufmann, Director, 260-481-6760, Fax: 260-481-6985, E-mail: kaufmann@ipfw.edu. *Application contact:* Dr. Michael E. Kaufmann, Director, 260-481-6760, Fax: 260-481-6985, E-mail: kaufmann@ipfw.edu.

Indiana University–Purdue University Indianapolis, School of Liberal Arts, Indianapolis, IN 46202-2896. Offers MA, MS, XMA, PhD, Certificate, JD/MA, MA/MA, MA/MLS, MD/MA,

MPA/MA, MSN/MA. *Students:* 36 full-time (23 women), 47 part-time (36 women); includes 12 minority (4 African Americans, 1 American Indian/Alaska Native, 4 Asian Americans or Pacific Islanders, 3 Hispanic Americans), 11 international. Average age 37. 43 applicants, 51% accepted, 20 enrolled.Application fee: $55 ($65 for international students). *Unit head:* Robert W. White, Dean, School of Liberal Arts, 317-274-8448. *Application contact:* Director of Research and Graduate Programs, 317-274-8305.

Indiana University South Bend, College of Liberal Arts and Sciences, South Bend, IN 46634-7111. Offers applied mathematics and computer science (MS); applied psychology (MA); English (MA); liberal studies (MLS). Part-time and evening/weekend programs available. *Faculty:* 79 full-time (33 women). *Students:* 27 full-time (10 women), 83 part-time (55 women); includes 17 minority (10 African Americans, 2 American Indian/Alaska Native, 2 Asian Americans or Pacific Islanders, 3 Hispanic Americans), 10 international. Average age 36. In 2009, 24 master's awarded. *Degree requirements:* For master's, thesis (for some programs). *Entrance requirements:* For master's, minimum GPA of 3.0. Additional exam requirements/recommendations for international students: Required—TOEFL. *Application deadline:* For fall admission, 7/31 priority date for domestic students, 7/1 priority date for international students; for spring admission, 3/31 priority date for domestic students, 11/1 priority date for international students. Applications are processed on a rolling basis. Application fee: $46 ($58 for international students). *Financial support:* In 2009–10, 5 students received support, including 5 teaching assistantships; Federal Work-Study also available. Support available to part-time students. *Faculty research:* Artificial intelligence, bioinformatics, English language and literature, creative writing, computer networks. Total annual research expenditures: $127,000. *Unit head:* Dr. Lynn R. Williams, Dean, 574-520-4322, Fax: 574-520-4528, E-mail: lwilliam@iusb.edu. *Application contact:* Dr. Lynn R. Williams, Dean, 574-520-4322, Fax: 574-520-4528, E-mail: lwilliam@iusb.edu.

Indiana University Southeast, Program in Liberal Studies, New Albany, IN 47150-6405. Offers MLS. *Students:* 31 part-time (24 women); includes 4 minority (all African Americans). Average age 42. In 2009, 2 master's awarded. *Degree requirements:* For master's, thesis or alternative. *Entrance requirements:* For master's, 3 letters of recommendation. Application fee: $35. *Unit head:* Dr. Sandra S. French, Director, 812-941-2393, E-mail: sfrench@ius.edu. *Application contact:* Debra Voyles, Administrative Assistant, 812-941-2604, E-mail: davoyles@ius.edu.

Jacksonville State University, College of Graduate Studies and Continuing Education, College of Arts and Sciences, Department of Liberal Studies, Jacksonville, AL 36265-1602. Offers MA. Part-time and evening/weekend programs available. *Students:* 1 full-time (0 women), 17 part-time (11 women); includes 9 minority (all African Americans). Average age 34. 8 applicants, 38% accepted, 2 enrolled. In 2009, 2 master's awarded. *Degree requirements:* For master's, comprehensive exam, thesis (for some programs). *Application deadline:* Applications are processed on a rolling basis. Application fee: $30. Electronic applications accepted. *Financial support:* In 2009–10, 16 students received support. Available to part-time students. Application deadline: 4/1. *Application contact:* Dr. Jean Pugliese, Associate Dean, 256-782-8278, Fax: 256-782-5321, E-mail: pugliese@jsu.edu.

The Johns Hopkins University, Zanvyl Krieger School of Arts and Sciences, Advanced Academic Programs, Program in Liberal Arts, Baltimore, MD 21218-2699. Offers MA, Certificate. Part-time and evening/weekend programs available. *Faculty:* 1 (woman) full-time, 9 part-time/adjunct (3 women). *Students:* 3 full-time (2 women), 93 part-time (67 women); includes 15 minority (10 African Americans, 2 Asian Americans or Pacific Islanders, 3 Hispanic Americans), 2 international. Average age 38. 38 applicants, 53% accepted, 16 enrolled. In 2009, 25 master's awarded. *Degree requirements:* For master's, thesis. *Entrance requirements:* Additional exam requirements/recommendations for international students: Required—TOEFL (minimum score 250 computer-based; 100 iBT). *Application deadline:* For fall admission, 5/31 priority date for domestic students, 4/30 priority date for international students; for spring admission, 10/31 priority date for domestic and international students. Applications are processed on a rolling basis. Application fee: $75. Electronic applications accepted. *Financial support:* Applicants required to submit FAFSA. *Unit head:* Dr. Melissa Hilbish, Associate Program Chair, 410-516-4640, E-mail: mhilbish@jhu.edu. *Application contact:* Valana M. McMickens, Admissions Manager, 202-452-1941, Fax: 202-452-1970, E-mail: aapadmissions@jhu.edu.

Kean University, College of Visual and Performing Arts, Program in Liberal Studies, Union, NJ 07083. Offers MA. Part-time and evening/weekend programs available. *Students:* 4 full-time (all women), 12 part-time (10 women); includes 9 minority (6 African Americans, 1 Asian American or Pacific Islander, 2 Hispanic Americans), 1 international. Average age 42. 7 applicants, 71% accepted, 5 enrolled. In 2009, 6 master's awarded. *Degree requirements:* For master's, comprehensive exam, thesis, final project. *Entrance requirements:* For master's, minimum GPA of 3.0, 3 letters of recommendation, interview. *Application deadline:* For fall admission, 5/1 for domestic students; for spring admission, 11/1 for domestic students. Application fee: $60 ($150 for international students). Electronic applications accepted. *Expenses:* Tuition, state resident: full-time $10,440; part-time $435 per credit. Tuition, nonresident: full-time $14,160; part-time $590 per credit. Required fees: $2642; $110 per credit. Part-time tuition and fees vary according to course load and degree level. *Financial support:* Research assistantships with full tuition reimbursements, unspecified assistantships available. *Unit head:* Dr. John C. Gruesser, Program Coordinator, 908-737-0388, E-mail: jgruesse@kean.edu. *Application contact:* Steven Koch, Pre-Admissions Coordinator, 908-737-5924, Fax: 908-737-5965, E-mail: skoch@kean.edu.

Kent State University, College of Arts and Sciences, Program in Liberal Studies, Kent, OH 44242-0001. Offers MLS. Part-time programs available. *Degree requirements:* For master's, thesis. *Entrance requirements:* For master's, minimum GPA of 2.75. Electronic applications accepted.

Lake Forest College, Graduate Program in Liberal Studies, Lake Forest, IL 60056. Offers MLS. Part-time and evening/weekend programs available. *Faculty:* 17 full-time (7 women). *Students:* 4 full-time (2 women), 42 part-time (23 women); includes 1 minority (African American), 2 international. Average age 40. 25 applicants, 60% accepted, 11 enrolled. In 2009, 7 master's awarded. *Degree requirements:* For master's, thesis optional. *Entrance requirements:* For master's, interview. Additional exam requirements/recommendations for international students: Required—TOEFL (minimum score 550 paper-based). *Application deadline:* For fall admission, 7/1 priority date for domestic students, 6/1 priority date for international students; for winter admission, 10/1 for international students; for spring admission, 11/15 priority date for domestic students, 10/1 priority date for international students. Applications are processed on a rolling basis. Application fee: $20. *Expenses:* Tuition: Full-time $12,480; part-time $2080 per course. One-time fee: $20. *Financial support:* In 2009–10, 8 students received support. Partial tuition waivers for full-time teachers available. Financial award application deadline: 7/1; financial award applicants required to submit FAFSA. *Faculty research:* Latin American film, the European Left, solid state chemistry, cast iron architecture, concepts of education in nineteenth century America. *Unit head:* Prof. D. L. LeMahieu, Director, 847-735-5133, Fax: 847-735-6291, E-mail: lemahieu@lakeforest.edu. *Application contact:* Prof. Carol Gayle, Associate Director, 847-735-5083, Fax: 847-735-6291, E-mail: gayle@lakeforest.edu.

Lock Haven University of Pennsylvania, Department of Liberal Arts, Lock Haven, PA 17745-2390. Offers MLA. *Degree requirements:* For master's, thesis. *Entrance requirements:* For master's, minimum undergraduate GPA of 3.0. Additional exam requirements/recommendations for international students: Required—TOEFL. Electronic applications accepted. *Expenses:* Tuition, state resident: full-time $6666; part-time $370 per credit hour. Tuition, nonresident: full-time $10,666; part-time $593 per credit hour. Required fees: $1988; $112 per credit hour. One-time fee: $25. Tuition and fees vary according to course load, campus/location and program.

Louisiana State University and Agricultural and Mechanical College, Graduate School, College of Arts and Sciences, Interdepartmental Program in the Liberal Arts, Baton Rouge, LA 70803. Offers MALA. Part-time and evening/weekend programs available. *Students:* 11 full-time (6 women), 8 part-time (3 women); includes 2 minority (both African Americans). Average age 35. 9 applicants, 56% accepted, 3 enrolled. In 2009, 15 master's awarded. *Degree requirements:* For master's, project or thesis. *Entrance requirements:* For master's, GRE General Test, minimum GPA of 3.0. Additional exam requirements/recommendations for international students: Required—TOEFL (minimum score 550 paper-based; 213 computer-based; 79 iBT) or IELTS (minimum score 6.5). *Application deadline:* For fall admission, 1/25 priority date for domestic students, 5/15 for international students; for spring admission, 10/15 for international students. Applications are processed on a rolling basis. Application fee: $50 ($70 for international students). Electronic applications accepted. *Financial support:* Fellowships with full tuition reimbursements, research assistantships with partial tuition reimbursements, teaching assistantships with partial tuition reimbursements, Federal Work-Study and health care benefits available. Financial award applicants required to submit FAFSA. *Unit head:* Dr. William Clark, Director, 225-578-3183, Fax: 225-578-6447. *Application contact:* Dr. Robin Roberts, Associate Dean, 225-578-8273, Fax: 225-587-6447, E-mail: rrobert@lsu.edu.

Louisiana State University in Shreveport, College of Liberal Arts, Program in Liberal Arts, Shreveport, LA 71115-2399. Offers MA. Part-time and evening/weekend programs available. *Students:* 22 full-time (14 women), 38 part-time (24 women); includes 14 minority (10 African Americans, 1 Asian American or Pacific Islander, 3 Hispanic Americans), 1 international. Average age 37. 27 applicants, 100% accepted, 21 enrolled. In 2009, 5 master's awarded. *Degree requirements:* For master's, comprehensive exam, thesis or alternative. *Entrance requirements:* For master's, interview, minimum GPA of 3.0 during final 2 years of course work, statement of purpose. Additional exam requirements/recommendations for international students: Required—TOEFL (minimum score 500 paper-based; 173 computer-based; 61 iBT). *Application deadline:* For fall admission, 6/30 for domestic and international students; for spring admission, 11/30 for domestic and international students. Applications are processed on a rolling basis. Application fee: $10 ($20 for international students). *Financial support:* In 2009–10, 3 students received support, including 3 research assistantships with partial tuition reimbursements available (averaging $30,000 per year). *Unit head:* Dr. Helen Taylor, Program Director, 318-797-5211, Fax: 318-797-5358, E-mail: helen.taylor@lsus.edu. *Application contact:* Yvonne Yarbrough, Secretary, Graduate Studies, 318-797-5247, Fax: 318-798-4120, E-mail: yyarbrou@lsus.edu.

Loyola University Maryland, Graduate Programs, College of Arts and Sciences, Program in Liberal Studies, Baltimore, MD 21210-2699. Offers MMS. Part-time and evening/weekend programs available. *Entrance requirements:* For master's, GRE General Test, GRE Subject Test (recommended). Additional exam requirements/recommendations for international students: Required—TOEFL (minimum score 550 paper-based; 213 computer-based).

Madonna University, Program in Liberal Studies, Livonia, MI 48150-1173. Offers MALS.

Manhattanville College, Graduate Programs, Humanities and Social Sciences Programs, Program in Liberal Studies, Purchase, NY 10577-2132. Offers MA. Part-time and evening/weekend programs available. *Students:* 1 (woman) full-time, 7 part-time (5 women); includes 1 African American. In 2009, 4 master's awarded. *Degree requirements:* For master's, thesis. *Entrance requirements:* For master's, interview, 2 letters of recommendation. Additional exam requirements/recommendations for international students: Required—TOEFL. *Application deadline:* Applications are processed on a rolling basis. Application fee: $70. *Financial support:* Career-related internships or fieldwork, Federal Work-Study, institutionally sponsored loans, and unspecified assistantships available. Financial award applicants required to submit FAFSA. *Unit head:* Donald Richards, Interim Dean, School of Graduate and Professional Studies, 914-323-5469, Fax: 914-694-3488, E-mail: gps@mville.edu. *Application contact:* Office of Admissions for Graduate and Professional Studies, 914-323-5418, E-mail: gps@mville.edu.

McDaniel College, Graduate and Professional Studies, Program in Liberal Studies, Westminster, MD 21157-4390. Offers MLA. Part-time and evening/weekend programs available. *Degree requirements:* For master's, final project. *Entrance requirements:* For master's, letters of reference (3). Additional exam requirements/recommendations for international students: Required—TOEFL (minimum score 213 computer-based). *Expenses:* Tuition: Part-time $325 per credit hour.

Metropolitan State University, College of Arts and Sciences, St. Paul, MN 55106-5000. Offers computer science (MS); liberal studies (MA); technical communication (MS). Part-time and evening/weekend programs available. *Entrance requirements:* For master's, minimum GPA of 2.75, resumè. Additional exam requirements/recommendations for international students: Required—TOEFL (minimum score 550 paper-based; 213 computer-based). *Expenses:* Tuition, state resident: full-time $5520; part-time $276 per credit hour. Tuition, nonresident: full-time $11,040; part-time $552 per credit hour. Required fees: $209; $10 per credit hour. Tuition and fees vary according to degree level. *Faculty research:* Computer security, software engineering, distributed systems, document design, diffusing of innovations, social issues and communication technology.

Minnesota State University Moorhead, Graduate Studies, College of Arts and Humanities, Program in Liberal Studies, Moorhead, MN 56563-0002. Offers MLA. Part-time and evening/weekend programs available. *Degree requirements:* For master's, thesis, final oral exam. *Entrance requirements:* For master's, minimum GPA of 2.75. Additional exam requirements/recommendations for international students: Required—TOEFL (minimum score 570 paper-based; 230 computer-based). Electronic applications accepted.

Mississippi College, Graduate School, Program in Liberal Studies, Clinton, MS 39058. Offers MLS. Part-time programs available. *Degree requirements:* For master's, comprehensive exam, thesis optional. *Entrance requirements:* For master's, GRE, minimum GPA of 2.5. Additional exam requirements/recommendations for international students: Recommended—IELTS. *Application deadline:* For fall admission, 8/15 priority date for domestic students. Application fee: $30. *Expenses:* Tuition: Part-time $452 per credit hour. Required fees: $101 per semester. Tuition and fees vary according to degree level, campus/location, program and student level. *Financial support:* Federal Work-Study and unspecified assistantships available. Support available to part-time students. Financial award application deadline: 4/1; financial award applicants required to submit FAFSA. *Unit head:* Dr. Debbie C. Norris, Graduate Dean, 601-925-3260, Fax: 601-925-3889, E-mail: dnorris@mc.edu. *Application contact:* Elnora Lewis, Secretary, 601-925-3225, Fax: 601-925-3889, E-mail: lewis09@mc.edu.

Monmouth University, Graduate School, Program in Liberal Arts, West Long Branch, NJ 07764-1898. Offers MA. Part-time and evening/weekend programs available. *Faculty:* 7 full-time (4 women), 1 (woman) part-time/adjunct. *Students:* 2 full-time (1 woman), 9 part-time (7 women). Average age 39. 7 applicants, 100% accepted, 4 enrolled. In 2009, 8 master's awarded. *Degree requirements:* For master's, thesis or alternative, project. *Entrance requirements:* For master's, minimum GPA of 3.0 in major, 2.5 overall. Additional exam requirements/recommendations for international students: Required—TOEFL (minimum score 550 paper-based; 213 computer-based; 79 iBT), IELTS (minimum score 5), Michigan English Language Assessment Battery (minimum score 77), Cambridge A, B, C. *Application deadline:* For fall admission, 7/15 priority date for domestic students, 6/1 for international students; for spring admission, 11/15 priority date for domestic students, 11/1 for international students. Applications are processed on a rolling basis. Application fee: $50. Electronic applications accepted. *Expenses:* Tuition: Part-time $773 per credit. Required fees: $157 per semester. *Financial support:* In 2009–10, 9 students received support, including 2 fellowships (averaging $2,100 per year); research assistantships, career-related internships or fieldwork, scholarships/grants, and unspecified assistantships also available. Support available to part-time students. Financial award applicants required to submit FAFSA. *Faculty research:* Labor history, war and society, technology, historical archeology, art and society. *Unit head:* Dr. Aaron Ansell, Director, 732-263-5451, Fax: 732-263-5192, E-mail: aansell@monmouth.edu. *Application contact:* Kevin Roane, Director, Office of Graduate Admission, 732-571-3452, Fax: 732-263-5123, E-mail: gradadm@monmouth.edu.

Liberal Studies

Nazareth College of Rochester, Graduate Studies, Department of Liberal Studies, Rochester, NY 14618-3790. Offers MA. *Entrance requirements:* For master's, minimum GPA of 3.0.

The New School: A University, The New School for Social Research, Liberal Studies Department, New York, NY 10003. Offers MA. Part-time and evening/weekend programs available. *Faculty:* 2 full-time (both women). *Students:* 22 full-time (14 women), 20 part-time (14 women); includes 8 minority (2 African Americans, 2 Asian Americans or Pacific Islanders, 4 Hispanic Americans), 10 international. Average age 29. In 2009, 16 master's awarded. *Degree requirements:* For master's, thesis. *Entrance requirements:* For master's, GRE General Test. Additional exam requirements/recommendations for international students: Required—TOEFL (minimum score 600 paper-based; 250 computer-based; 100 iBT). *Application deadline:* For fall admission, 1/17 priority date for domestic and international students; for spring admission, 10/15 priority date for domestic and international students. Applications are processed on a rolling basis. Application fee: $50. Electronic applications accepted. *Financial support:* Fellowships, research assistantships, teaching assistantships, Federal Work-Study, scholarships/grants, tuition waivers (full and partial), and unspecified assistantships available. Support available to part-time students. Financial award application deadline: 3/1; financial award applicants required to submit FAFSA. *Unit head:* Dr. James Miller, Director, 212-229-2747 Ext. 3027, E-mail: millerje@newschool.edu. *Application contact:* Robert MacDonald, Director of Admissions, 212-229-5710 Ext. 3007, Fax: 212-989-7102, E-mail: macdonar@newschool.edu.

North Carolina State University, Graduate School, College of Humanities and Social Sciences, Program in Liberal Studies, Raleigh, NC 27695. Offers MA. Part-time and evening/weekend programs available. *Degree requirements:* For master's, thesis optional. Electronic applications accepted. *Faculty research:* Humanities, social sciences, sciences.

North Central College, Graduate Programs, Department of Liberal Studies, Naperville, IL 60566-7063. Offers MALS. Part-time and evening/weekend programs available. *Degree requirements:* For master's, project. *Entrance requirements:* For master's, interview. *Expenses:* Contact institution.

Northern Arizona University, Graduate College, College of Social and Behavioral Sciences, Program in Sustainable Communities, Flagstaff, AZ 86011. Offers MA. Part-time programs available. *Faculty:* 1 (woman) full-time. *Students:* 31 full-time (21 women), 18 part-time (12 women); includes 4 minority (2 American Indian/Alaska Native, 2 Hispanic Americans). Average age 40. 42 applicants, 17% accepted, 5 enrolled. In 2009, 11 master's awarded. *Degree requirements:* For master's, thesis. *Entrance requirements:* For master's, minimum GPA of 3.0. Additional exam requirements/recommendations for international students: Required—TOEFL (minimum score 550 paper-based; 213 computer-based; 80 iBT), IELTS (minimum score 7), or a bachelor's degree from an English-speaking university and demonstrated proficiency. *Application deadline:* For fall admission, 3/15 priority date for domestic students, 9/1 priority date for international students. Applications are processed on a rolling basis. Application fee: $65. Electronic applications accepted. *Financial support:* In 2009–10, 1 research assistantship was awarded. Support available to part-time students. Financial award application deadline: 3/30. *Unit head:* Dr. Sandra Lubarsky, Director, 928-523-2382, Fax: 928-523-6777, E-mail: sandra.lubarsky@nau.edu. *Application contact:* Dr. Sandra Lubarsky, Director, 928-523-2382, Fax: 928-523-6777, E-mail: sandra.lubarsky@nau.edu.

Northern Kentucky University, Office of Graduate Programs, College of Arts and Sciences, Program in Integrative Studies, Highland Heights, KY 41099. Offers civic engagement (Certificate); integrative studies (MA). Part-time and evening/weekend programs available. Postbaccalaureate distance learning degree programs offered (no on-campus study). *Students:* 6 full-time (all women), 33 part-time (27 women); includes 7 minority (5 African Americans, 1 Asian American or Pacific Islander, 1 Hispanic American). Average age 37. 28 applicants, 68% accepted, 14 enrolled. In 2009, 10 master's awarded. *Degree requirements:* For master's, thesis optional, capstone. *Entrance requirements:* For master's, minimum GPA of 3.0, resume, 2 letters of recommendation, 1 letter of intent. Additional exam requirements/recommendations for international students: Required—TOEFL (minimum score 550 paper-based; 213 computer-based; 79 iBT); Recommended—IELTS (minimum score 6.5). *Application deadline:* For fall admission, 7/1 priority date for domestic students, 6/1 for international students; for spring admission, 12/1 priority date for domestic students, 10/1 for international students. Applications are processed on a rolling basis. Application fee: $40. Electronic applications accepted. *Expenses:* Tuition, state resident: full-time $6912; part-time $384 per credit hour. Tuition, nonresident: full-time $12,150; part-time $675 per credit hour. Tuition and fees vary according to course load, program and reciprocity agreements. *Financial support:* Unspecified assistantships available. Financial award applicants required to submit FAFSA. *Faculty research:* Medieval literature, general education and assessment. *Unit head:* Dr. Debra Meyers, Director, 859-572-5860, E-mail: meyersde@nku.edu. *Application contact:* Dr. Peg Griffin, Director of Graduate Programs, 859-572-6934, Fax: 859-572-6670, E-mail: griffinp@nku.edu.

Northwestern University, The Graduate School, Interdepartmental Programs, Interdisciplinary Program in Liberal Studies, Evanston, IL 60208. Offers MA. Admissions and degree offered through The Graduate School. Part-time and evening/weekend programs available. *Degree requirements:* For master's, thesis. *Entrance requirements:* For master's, writing sample. Additional exam requirements/recommendations for international students: Required—TOEFL. *Faculty research:* Urban and social history, literary criticism and comparative literature, women's studies, media and film criticism, philosophy.

Northwestern University, School of Continuing Studies, Program in Liberal Studies, Evanston, IL 60208. Offers American studies (MA); history (MA); religious and ethical studies (MA).

Oakland University, Graduate Study and Lifelong Learning, College of Arts and Sciences, Program in Liberal Studies, Rochester, MI 48309-4401. Offers MA. *Entrance requirements:* For master's, minimum GPA of 3.0 for unconditional admission. Additional exam requirements/recommendations for international students: Required—TOEFL (minimum score 550 paper-based; 213 computer-based). Electronic applications accepted.

Occidental College, Graduate Studies, Department of Education, Program in Elementary Education, Los Angeles, CA 90041-3314. Offers liberal studies (MAT). Part-time programs available. *Degree requirements:* For master's, comprehensive exam, graduate synthesis paper. *Entrance requirements:* For master's, GRE General Test, minimum GPA of 3.0. Additional exam requirements/recommendations for international students: Required—TOEFL (minimum score 625 paper-based; 263 computer-based). *Expenses:* Contact institution.

Ohio Dominican University, Graduate Programs, Program in Liberal Studies, Columbus, OH 43219-2099. Offers MA. Part-time and evening/weekend programs available. *Students:* 2 full-time (1 woman), 14 part-time (9 women); includes 4 minority (3 African Americans, 1 Hispanic American). Average age 32. In 2009, 4 master's awarded. *Degree requirements:* For master's, comprehensive exam or thesis. *Entrance requirements:* For master's, minimum undergraduate GPA of 3.0, 3 letters of recommendation. Additional exam requirements/recommendations for international students: Required—TOEFL (minimum score 550 paper-based; 213 computer-based). *Application deadline:* For fall admission, 7/15 priority date for domestic and international students; for spring admission, 12/15 priority date for domestic and international students. Applications are processed on a rolling basis. Application fee: $25. *Financial support:* Applicants required to submit FAFSA. *Unit head:* Jeremy Glaizer, Director, 614-251-4756, E-mail: glaizerj@ohiodominican.edu. *Application contact:* Jill M. Westerfeld, Graduate Admissions Recruiter, 614-251-4725, Fax: 614-251-4634, E-mail: westerfj@ohiodominican.edu.

Oklahoma City University, Petree College of Arts and Sciences, Program in Liberal Arts, Oklahoma City, OK 73106-1402. Offers art (MLA); general studies (MLA); leadership/management (MLA); literature (MLA); mass communications (MLA); philosophy (MLA); writing (MLA). Part-time and evening/weekend programs available. *Faculty:* 23 full-time (6 women), 5 part-time/adjunct (3 women). *Students:* 50 full-time (24 women), 23 part-time (14 women); includes 6 minority (4 African Americans, 1 Asian American or Pacific Islander, 1 Hispanic American), 50 international. Average age 31. 31 applicants, 94% accepted, 15 enrolled. In 2009, 21 master's awarded. *Degree requirements:* For master's, comprehensive exam, thesis optional. *Entrance requirements:* Additional exam requirements/recommendations for international students: Required—TOEFL (minimum score 550 paper-based). *Application deadline:* For fall admission, 8/20 for domestic students; for spring admission, 1/6 for domestic students. Applications are processed on a rolling basis. Application fee: $50 ($70 for international students). *Expenses:* Tuition: Full-time $15,930; part-time $885 per hour. *Financial support:* Fellowships with partial tuition reimbursements, career-related internships or fieldwork, Federal Work-Study, and tuition waivers (partial) available. Support available to part-time students. Financial award application deadline: 8/1; financial award applicants required to submit FAFSA. *Unit head:* Dr. Regina Bennett, Director, 405-208-5207, Fax: 405-208-5451, E-mail: rbennett@okcu.edu. *Application contact:* Michelle Lockhart, Director, Admissions, 800-633-7242, Fax: 405-208-5916, E-mail: gadmissions@okcu.edu.

Queens College of the City University of New York, Division of Graduate Studies, Social Science Division, Program in Liberal Studies, Flushing, NY 11367-1597. Offers MALS. Part-time and evening/weekend programs available. *Faculty:* 4 full-time (0 women). *Students:* 22 part-time (13 women). 23 applicants, 48% accepted, 7 enrolled. In 2009, 1 master's awarded. *Degree requirements:* For master's, thesis. *Entrance requirements:* For master's, minimum GPA of 3.0. Additional exam requirements/recommendations for international students: Required—TOEFL. *Application deadline:* For fall admission, 4/1 for domestic students; for spring admission, 11/1 for domestic students. Applications are processed on a rolling basis. Application fee: $125. *Expenses:* Tuition, state resident: full-time $7360; part-time $310 per credit. Tuition, nonresident: part-time $575 per credit. One-time fee: $195.25 full-time; $145.25 part-time. *Financial support:* Career-related internships or fieldwork, Federal Work-Study, institutionally sponsored loans, and tuition waivers (partial) available. Support available to part-time students. Financial award application deadline: 4/1; financial award applicants required to submit FAFSA. *Unit head:* Dr. Nick Jordan, Graduate Adviser, 718-997-5350. *Application contact:* Mario Caruso, Director of Graduate Admissions, 718-997-5200, Fax: 718-997-5193, E-mail: graduate_admissions@qc.edu.

Ramapo College of New Jersey, Program in Liberal Studies, Mahwah, NJ 07430. Offers MALS. Part-time and evening/weekend programs available. *Faculty:* 2 full-time (0 women), 3 part-time/adjunct (2 women). *Students:* 36 full-time (20 women); includes 8 minority (3 African Americans, 1 Asian American or Pacific Islander, 4 Hispanic Americans). Average age 42. 9 applicants, 100% accepted, 7 enrolled. In 2009, 8 master's awarded. *Degree requirements:* For master's, thesis. *Entrance requirements:* For master's, minimum undergraduate GPA of 3.0, 2 letters of recommendation. Additional exam requirements/recommendations for international students: Required—TOEFL (minimum score 550 paper-based; 213 computer-based; 90 iBT). *Application deadline:* For fall admission, 9/1 priority date for domestic and international students; for spring admission, 1/30 priority date for domestic and international students. Applications are processed on a rolling basis. Application fee: $60. Electronic applications accepted. *Expenses:* Tuition, state resident: part-time $525.30 per credit. Tuition, nonresident: part-time $675.20 per credit. Required fees: $53.55 per credit. *Financial support:* Tuition waivers (full) available. Financial award applicants required to submit FAFSA. *Faculty research:* History of science, women's studies, Native American studies, theology, genocide studies. *Unit head:* Dr. Anthony T. Padovano, Director, 201-684-7430, Fax: 201-684-7973, E-mail: apadovan@ramapo.edu. *Application contact:* Melissa C. Kupfer, MALS Secretary, 201-684-7709, Fax: 201-684-7973, E-mail: mkupfer@ramapo.edu.

Reed College, Graduate Program in Liberal Studies, Portland, OR 97202-8199. Offers MALS. Part-time and evening/weekend programs available. *Faculty:* 12 part-time/adjunct (4 women). *Students:* 37 part-time (20 women); includes 5 minority (2 African Americans, 2 Asian Americans or Pacific Islanders, 1 Hispanic American). Average age 40. 10 applicants, 50% accepted, 5 enrolled. In 2009, 8 master's awarded. *Degree requirements:* For master's, thesis, oral defense of thesis. *Entrance requirements:* For master's, interview, letters of recommendation. *Application deadline:* For fall admission, 7/1 priority date for domestic students; for spring admission, 12/1 priority date for domestic students. Applications are processed on a rolling basis. Application fee: $60. *Expenses:* Tuition: Part-time $3580 per unit. *Financial support:* In 2009–10, 4 students received support. Scholarships/grants and health care benefits available. Support available to part-time students. Financial award application deadline: 5/1; financial award applicants required to submit CSS PROFILE or FAFSA. *Unit head:* Barbara A. Amen, Director, Graduate Studies, 503-777-7259, Fax: 503-517-7345, E-mail: bamen@reed.edu. *Application contact:* Barbara A. Amen, Director, Graduate Studies, 503-777-7259, Fax: 503-517-7345, E-mail: bamen@reed.edu.

Rice University, Graduate Programs, Susanne M. Glasscock School of Continuing Studies, Houston, TX 77251-1892. Offers MLS. Part-time and evening/weekend programs available. *Faculty:* 16 full-time (3 women), 8 part-time/adjunct (5 women). *Students:* 69 part-time (47 women); includes 19 minority (6 African Americans, 4 Asian Americans or Pacific Islanders, 9 Hispanic Americans). Average age 49. 10 applicants, 80% accepted, 6 enrolled. In 2009, 21 master's awarded. *Degree requirements:* For master's, thesis or alternative, capstone paper/project. *Entrance requirements:* For master's, Bachelor's degree from accredited institution; 3.0 GPA; two letters of recommendation; personal statement; 3 writing samples; current resume. Additional exam requirements/recommendations for international students: Required—TOEFL (minimum score 600 paper-based; 250 computer-based; 90 iBT). *Application deadline:* For fall admission, 5/21 for domestic and international students; for winter admission, 10/22 for domestic and international students. Application fee: $75. *Expenses:* Contact institution. *Unit head:* Dr. Mary McIntire, Dean, Glasscock School of Continuing Studies, 713-348-4803, Fax: 713-348-5213, E-mail: mls@rice.edu. *Application contact:* Rebecca Sharp Sanchez, Assistant Director, 713-348-4767, Fax: 713-348-5213, E-mail: rksharp@rice.edu.

Rollins College, Hamilton Holt School, Program in Liberal Studies, Winter Park, FL 32789-4499. Offers MLS. Part-time and evening/weekend programs available. *Faculty:* 7 full-time (2 women), 7 part-time/adjunct (3 women). *Students:* 4 full-time (3 women), 62 part-time (45 women); includes 10 minority (3 African Americans, 1 Asian American or Pacific Islander, 6 Hispanic Americans). Average age 42. 110 applicants, 76% accepted, 49 enrolled. In 2009, 15 master's awarded. *Degree requirements:* For master's, thesis. *Entrance requirements:* For master's, GRE or MAT, interview. Additional exam requirements/recommendations for international students: Required—TOEFL. *Application deadline:* For fall admission, 12/1 for domestic students; for spring admission, 4/1 for domestic students. Applications are processed on a rolling basis. Application fee: $50. *Expenses:* Contact institution. *Financial support:* Institutionally sponsored loans and scholarships/grants available. Support available to part-time students. *Unit head:* Dr. Patricia Lancaster, Director, 407-646-2237, Fax: 407-646-2363. *Application contact:* Christian Ricaurte, Coordinator of Records and Registration, 407-646-2653, Fax: 407-646-1551, E-mail: cricaurte@rollins.edu.

Rutgers, The State University of New Jersey, Camden, Graduate School of Arts and Sciences, Program in Liberal Studies, Camden, NJ 08102-1401. Offers MALS. Part-time and evening/weekend programs available. *Degree requirements:* For master's, thesis. *Entrance requirements:* For master's, 2 letters of recommendation, writing sample. Additional exam requirements/recommendations for international students: Required—TOEFL, IELTS. Electronic applications accepted. *Faculty research:* Psychology, English, history, philosophy, religion.

Rutgers, The State University of New Jersey, Newark, Graduate School, Program in Liberal Studies, Newark, NJ 07102. Offers MALS. Part-time and evening/weekend programs available. *Degree requirements:* For master's, thesis. *Entrance requirements:* For master's, minimum B average. Electronic applications accepted.

St. Edward's University, New College, Program in Liberal Arts, Austin, TX 78704. Offers global issues (MLA); humanities (MLA); liberal arts (Certificate); social sciences (MLA). Part-time and evening/weekend programs available. *Students:* 3 full-time (2 women), 85 part-time (60 women); includes 21 minority (3 African Americans, 2 Asian Americans or Pacific Islanders, 16 Hispanic Americans), 1 international. Average age 34. 34 applicants, 88% accepted, 23 enrolled. In 2009, 23 master's awarded. *Degree requirements:* For master's, minimum of 24 resident hours. *Entrance requirements:* For master's, minimum GPA of 2.75 in last 60 hours of course work, interview. Additional exam requirements/recommendations for international students: Required—TOEFL (minimum score 550 paper-based; 213 computer-based; 79 iBT) or IELTS (minimum score 6). *Application deadline:* For fall admission, 7/1 for domestic and international students; for spring admission, 11/1 for domestic and international students. Applications are processed on a rolling basis. Application fee: $45 ($50 for international students). Electronic applications accepted. *Expenses:* Tuition: Full-time $14,922; part-time $829 per credit hour. Required fees: $50 per trimester. Full-time tuition and fees vary according to course load and program. *Financial support:* In 2009–10, 2 students received support. Scholarships/grants available. *Unit head:* Dr. H. Ramsey Fowler, Director, 512-448-8648, Fax: 512-448-8492, E-mail: ramseyf@stewards.edu. *Application contact:* Kay L. Arnold, Assistant Director of Admissions, 512-233-1636, Fax: 512-428-1032, E-mail: kayla@stedwards.edu.

St. Edward's University, School of Education, Program in Teaching, Austin, TX 78704. Offers curriculum leadership (Certificate); instructional technology (Certificate); mentoring and supervision (Certificate); sports management (Certificate); teaching (MA), including conflict resolution, initial teacher certification, liberal arts, organization development and training, sports management, teacher leadership. Part-time and evening/weekend programs available. *Students:* 5 full-time (4 women), 36 part-time (26 women); includes 10 minority (1 African American, 9 Hispanic Americans). Average age 30. 23 applicants, 70% accepted, 12 enrolled. In 2009, 9 master's awarded. *Degree requirements:* For master's, minimum of 24 resident hours. *Entrance requirements:* For master's, GRE General Test, minimum GPA of 3.0 in last 60 hours or 2.75 overall. Additional exam requirements/recommendations for international students: Required—TOEFL (minimum score 550 paper-based; 213 computer-based; 79 iBT) or IELTS (minimum score 6). *Application deadline:* For fall admission, 7/1 for domestic and international students; for spring admission, 11/1 for domestic and international students. Applications are processed on a rolling basis. Application fee: $45 ($50 for international students). Electronic applications accepted. *Expenses:* Tuition: Full-time $14,922; part-time $829 per credit hour. Required fees: $50 per trimester. Full-time tuition and fees vary according to course load and program. *Financial support:* In 2009–10, 3 students received support. Scholarships/grants available. *Unit head:* Dr. David Hollier, Director, 512-448-8666, Fax: 512-428-1372, E-mail: davidrh@stedwards.edu. *Application contact:* Kay L. Arnold, Assistant Director of Admissions, 512-233-1636, Fax: 512-428-1032, E-mail: kayla@stedwards.edu.

St. John's College, Graduate Institute in Liberal Education, Annapolis, MD 21404. Offers liberal arts (MALA). Evening/weekend programs available. *Degree requirements:* For master's, thesis optional. *Entrance requirements:* Additional exam requirements/recommendations for international students: Required—TOEFL (minimum score 650 paper-based; 250 computer-based; 112 iBT), TWE (minimum score 5).

St. John's College, Graduate Institute in Liberal Education, Program in Liberal Arts, Santa Fe, NM 87505. Offers MA. Evening/weekend programs available. *Entrance requirements:* For master's, 2 letters of recommendation. Additional exam requirements/recommendations for international students: Required—TOEFL, TWE.

St. John's University, St. John's College of Liberal Arts and Sciences, Program in Liberal Studies, Queens, NY 11439. Offers MA. Part-time and evening/weekend programs available. *Students:* 2 full-time (both women), 54 part-time (33 women); includes 15 minority (9 African Americans, 3 Asian Americans or Pacific Islanders, 3 Hispanic Americans), 2 international. Average age 35. 93 applicants, 54% accepted, 23 enrolled. In 2009, 15 master's awarded. *Degree requirements:* For master's, capstone project. *Entrance requirements:* For master's, minimum GPA of 3.0, personal essay, 2 letters of recommendation, 6 credit hours in area of concentration. Additional exam requirements/recommendations for international students: Required—TOEFL (minimum score 500 paper-based; 173 computer-based; 61 iBT), IELTS (minimum score 5.5). *Application deadline:* For fall admission, 5/1 priority date for domestic and international students; for spring admission, 11/1 priority date for domestic and international students. Applications are processed on a rolling basis. Application fee: $70. Electronic applications accepted. *Expenses:* Tuition: Full-time $16,290; part-time $905 per credit. Required fees: $300; $150 per semester. Tuition and fees vary according to program. *Financial support:* Career-related internships or fieldwork and scholarships/grants available. Support available to part-time students. *Unit head:* Fr. Jean-Pierre Ruiz, Director, 718-990-6467, E-mail: ruizj@stjohns.edu. *Application contact:* Kathleen Davis, Director of Graduate Admission, 718-990-2790, Fax: 718-990-5686, E-mail: gradhelp@stjohns.edu.

St. Norbert College, Program in Liberal Studies, De Pere, WI 54115-2099. Offers MA. Part-time programs available. *Faculty:* 2 part-time/adjunct (0 women). *Students:* 9 part-time (5 women); includes 1 minority (Hispanic American). Average age 33. 6 applicants, 100% accepted, 6 enrolled. *Degree requirements:* For master's, thesis. *Application deadline:* Applications are processed on a rolling basis. Application fee: $50. Electronic applications accepted. *Expenses:* Tuition: Part-time $390 per credit hour. *Unit head:* Dr. Howard Ebert, Director, 920-403-3956, Fax: 920-403-4086, E-mail: howard.ebert@snc.edu. *Application contact:* Program Coordinator, Fax: 920-403-4086, E-mail: deette.radant@snc.edu.

San Diego State University, Graduate and Research Affairs, College of Arts and Letters, Program in Liberal Arts and Sciences, San Diego, CA 92182. Offers MA. Part-time and evening/weekend programs available. *Degree requirements:* For master's, thesis. *Entrance requirements:* For master's, GRE General Test. Additional exam requirements/recommendations for international students: Required—TOEFL. Electronic applications accepted.

Simon Fraser University, Graduate Studies, Faculty of Arts and Social Sciences, Program in Liberal Studies, Burnaby, BC V5A 1S6, Canada. Offers MALS. Part-time and evening/weekend programs available. *Degree requirements:* For master's, thesis or alternative. *Entrance requirements:* For master's, minimum GPA of 3.0. Additional exam requirements/recommendations for international students: Required—TOEFL or IELTS. *Faculty research:* Humanities, psychology, history, women's studies, English.

Skidmore College, Liberal Studies Program, Saratoga Springs, NY 12866. Offers MA. Part-time programs available. Postbaccalaureate distance learning degree programs offered (minimal on-campus study). *Degree requirements:* For master's, thesis. Electronic applications accepted.

Southern Methodist University, Annette Caldwell Simmons School of Education and Human Development, Program in Liberal Studies, Dallas, TX 75275. Offers MLS. *Students:* 5 full-time (4 women), 175 part-time (129 women); includes 51 minority (19 African Americans, 2 American Indian/Alaska Native, 7 Asian Americans or Pacific Islanders, 23 Hispanic Americans), 3 international. Average age 39. *Unit head:* Dr. David J. Chard, Leon Simmons Endowed Dean, 214-768-7587, Fax: 214-768-1797. *Application contact:* Associate Vice President for Research and Dean of Graduate Studies.

Spring Hill College, Graduate Programs, Program in Liberal Arts, Mobile, AL 36608-1791. Offers fine arts (MLA); history and social science (MLA); leadership and ethics (MLA); literature (MLA). Part-time and evening/weekend programs available. *Faculty:* 11 full-time (4 women), 3 part-time/adjunct (2 women). *Students:* 1 (woman) full-time, 33 part-time (16 women); includes 6 minority (5 African Americans, 1 Hispanic American), 2 international. Average age 35. 27 applicants, 41% accepted, 6 enrolled. In 2009, 6 master's awarded. *Degree requirements:* For master's, capstone course, completion of program within 6 years of initial admittance. *Entrance requirements:* For master's, bachelor's degree with minimum undergraduate GPA of 3.0 or graduate/professional degree. Additional exam requirements/recommendations for international students: Required—TOEFL (minimum score 550 paper-based; 213 computer-based; 80 iBT), IELTS (minimum score 6.5). *Application deadline:* For fall admission, 8/1 priority date for domestic and international students; for spring admission, 12/1 priority date for domestic and international students. Applications are processed on a rolling basis. Application fee: $25 ($35 for international students). Electronic applications accepted. *Expenses:* Contact institution. *Financial support:* In 2009–10, 30 students received support. Career-related internships or fieldwork, institutionally sponsored loans, and scholarships/grants available. Support available to part-time students. Financial award applicants required to submit FAFSA. *Unit head:* Dr. Alexander R. Landi, Director, 251-380-3056, Fax: 251-460-2115, E-mail: landi@shc.edu. *Application contact:* Donna B. Tarasavage, Director of Marketing and Recruiting, Graduate and Continuing Studies, 251-380-3067, Fax: 251-460-2190, E-mail: dtarasavage@shc.edu.

State University of New York at Plattsburgh, School of Business and Economics, Program in Liberal Studies, Plattsburgh, NY 12901-2681. Offers MA. Part-time and evening/weekend programs available. *Faculty:* 4 full-time (1 woman), 3 part-time/adjunct (0 women). *Students:* 6 full-time (5 women), 12 part-time (5 women); includes 2 minority (1 African American, 1 Asian American or Pacific Islander). Average age 35. 11 applicants, 91% accepted, 9 enrolled. In 2009, 16 master's awarded. *Degree requirements:* For master's, thesis. *Entrance requirements:* For master's, GRE, GMAT, or MAT. Additional exam requirements/recommendations for international students: Required—TOEFL (minimum score 550 paper-based; 213 computer-based; 79 iBT). *Application deadline:* For fall admission, 2/15 priority date for domestic students; for spring admission, 10/15 priority date for domestic students. Applications are processed on a rolling basis. Application fee: $75. *Expenses:* Tuition, state resident: full-time $8370; part-time $349 per credit hour. Tuition, nonresident: full-time $13,250; part-time $552 per credit hour. Required fees: $1130. *Financial support:* Application deadline: 4/15. *Unit head:* Dr. Suzanne Catana, Coordinator, 518-792-5425, E-mail: catanasl@plattsburgh.edu. *Application contact:* Marguerite Adelman, Assistant Director, Graduate Admissions, 518-564-4723, Fax: 518-564-4722, E-mail: adelmaml@plattsburgh.edu.

State University of New York Empire State College, Graduate Studies, Program in Liberal Studies, Saratoga Springs, NY 12866-4391. Offers MA. Part-time and evening/weekend programs available. Postbaccalaureate distance learning degree programs offered (minimal on-campus study). *Degree requirements:* For master's, thesis. *Entrance requirements:* Additional exam requirements/recommendations for international students: Required—TOEFL (minimum score 600 paper-based; 250 computer-based). Electronic applications accepted.

Stony Brook University, State University of New York, School of Professional Development, Stony Brook, NY 11794. Offers biology-grade 7-12 (MAT); chemistry-grade 7-12 (MAT); coaching (Graduate Certificate); computer integrated engineering (Graduate Certificate); earth science-grade 7-12 (MAT); educational computing (Graduate Certificate); educational leadership (Advanced Certificate); English-grade 7-12 (MAT); environmental management (Graduate Certificate); environmental/occupational health and safety (Graduate Certificate); French-grade 7-12 (MAT); German-grade 7-12 (MAT); human resource management (Graduate Certificate); information systems management (Graduate Certificate); Italian-grade 7-12 (MAT); liberal studies (MA); mathematics-grade 7-12 (MAT); operation research (Graduate Certificate); physics-grade 7-12 (MAT); school administration and supervision (Graduate Certificate); school building leadership (Graduate Certificate); school district administration (Graduate Certificate); school district business leadership (Advanced Certificate); school district leadership (Graduate Certificate); social science and the professions (MPS), including environmental waste management, human resource management; social studies-grade 7-12 (MAT); Spanish-grade 7-12 (MAT); waste management (Graduate Certificate). Part-time and evening/weekend programs available. Postbaccalaureate distance learning degree programs offered. *Faculty:* 5 full-time (3 women), 131 part-time/adjunct (53 women). *Students:* 317 full-time (187 women), 1,200 part-time (773 women); includes 187 minority (77 African Americans, 2 American Indian/Alaska Native, 22 Asian Americans or Pacific Islanders, 86 Hispanic Americans), 11 international. Average age 28. In 2009, 597 master's, 234 other advanced degrees awarded. *Degree requirements:* For master's, one foreign language, thesis or alternative. *Application deadline:* Applications are processed on a rolling basis. Application fee: $62. *Expenses:* Tuition, state resident: full-time $8370; part-time $349 per credit. Tuition, nonresident: full-time $13,250; part-time $552 per credit. Required fees: $933. *Financial support:* Fellowships, research assistantships, teaching assistantships, career-related internships or fieldwork available. Support available to part-time students. *Unit head:* Dr. Paul J. Edelson, Dean, 631-632-7052, Fax: 631-632-9046, E-mail: paul.edelson@stonybrook.edu. *Application contact:* Dr. Paul J. Edelson, Dean, 631-632-7052, Fax: 631-632-9046, E-mail: paul.edelson@stonybrook.edu.

Tarleton State University, College of Graduate Studies, Program in Liberal Studies, Stephenville, TX 76402. Offers MS. Part-time and evening/weekend programs available. *Entrance requirements:* Additional exam requirements/recommendations for international students: Required—TOEFL (minimum score 550 paper-based; 213 computer-based; 80 iBT). Electronic applications accepted.

Temple University, Graduate School, College of Liberal Arts, Program in Liberal Arts, Philadelphia, PA 19122-6096. Offers MLA. Part-time and evening/weekend programs available. *Degree requirements:* For master's, thesis, qualifying paper. *Entrance requirements:* Additional exam requirements/recommendations for international students: Required—TOEFL (minimum score 550 paper-based; 213 computer-based; 79 iBT). Electronic applications accepted.

Texas Christian University, Graduate Studies, Fort Worth, TX 76129-0002. Offers MLA. Part-time and evening/weekend programs available. Postbaccalaureate distance learning degree programs offered (no on-campus study). *Entrance requirements:* Additional exam requirements/recommendations for international students: Required—TOEFL (minimum score 550 paper-based; 213 computer-based; 80 iBT). *Application deadline:* For fall admission, 8/1 for domestic students; for spring admission, 1/1 for domestic students. Applications are processed on a rolling basis. Application fee: $50. *Expenses:* Tuition: Full-time $17,640; part-time $980 per credit hour. Tuition and fees vary according to program. *Financial support:* Applicants required to submit FAFSA. *Unit head:* Dr. Bonnie Melhart, Associate Provost for Academic Affairs, 817-257-7104, E-mail: b.melhart@tcu.edu. *Application contact:* Anita Unger, Graduate Program Coordinator, 817-257-7515, E-mail: a.unger@tcu.edu.

Thomas Edison State College, Heavin School of Arts and Sciences, Program in Liberal Studies, Trenton, NJ 08608-1176. Offers MALS. Part-time programs available. Postbaccalaureate distance learning degree programs offered (no on-campus study). *Students:* 92 part-time (58 women); includes 31 minority (22 African Americans, 1 American Indian/Alaska Native, 3 Asian Americans or Pacific Islanders, 5 Hispanic Americans), 1 international. Average age 42. In 2009, 12 master's awarded. *Degree requirements:* For master's, final project. *Entrance requirements:* For master's, bachelor's degree from a regionally-accredited college or university; minimum 2 letters of recommendation; 3-5 years of related working experience; current resume. Additional exam requirements/recommendations for international students: Required—TOEFL (minimum score 550 paper-based; 213 computer-based; 79 iBT). *Application deadline:* For fall admission, 8/15 priority date for domestic and international students; for winter admission, 11/15 priority date for domestic and international students; for spring admission, 2/15 priority date for domestic and international students. Applications are processed on a rolling basis. Application fee: $75. Electronic applications accepted. *Expenses:* Tuition, area resident: Part-time $479 per credit. Tuition, state resident: part-time $479 per credit. Tuition, nonresident: part-time $479 per credit. *Financial support:* Applicants required to submit FAFSA. *Unit head:* Dr. Susan Davenport, Dean, Heavin School of Arts and Sciences, 609-984-1130, Fax: 609-984-0740, E-mail: info@tesc.edu. *Application contact:* David Hoftiezer, Director of Admissions, 888-442-8372, Fax: 609-984-8447, E-mail: admissions@tesc.edu.

Towson University, College of Graduate Studies and Research, Program in Professional Studies, Towson, MD 21252-0001. Offers MA. Part-time and evening/weekend programs available. *Degree requirements:* For master's, thesis optional, exam. *Entrance requirements:* For master's, minimum GPA of 3.0. Electronic applications accepted. *Faculty research:* History, World War II, counseling, marriage and family, human development.

Tulane University, Program in Liberal Arts, New Orleans, LA 70118-5669. Offers MLA. Part-time programs available. *Degree requirements:* For master's, thesis. *Entrance requirements:* For master's, GRE General Test, minimum B average in undergraduate course work. Additional exam requirements/recommendations for international students: Required—TOEFL.

Liberal Studies

University at Albany, State University of New York, College of Arts and Sciences, Liberal Studies Program, Albany, NY 12222-0001. Offers MA. *Entrance requirements:* Additional exam requirements/recommendations for international students: Required—TOEFL (minimum score 550 paper-based; 213 computer-based). Electronic applications accepted.

University of Arkansas at Little Rock, Graduate School, College of Arts, Humanities, and Social Science, Department of Philosophy and Liberal Studies, Little Rock, AR 72204-1099. Offers MALS. *Entrance requirements:* For master's, GRE.

University of Delaware, College of Arts and Sciences, Program in Liberal Studies, Newark, DE 19716. Offers MALS. Part-time and evening/weekend programs available. *Degree requirements:* For master's, thesis. Electronic applications accepted. *Faculty research:* British Raj, medical and scientific ethics, Jewish-American novelists, intellectual freedom.

University of Denver, University College, Denver, CO 80208. Offers applied communication (MAS, MPS, Certificate); computer information systems (MAS, Certificate); environmental policy and management (MAS, Certificate); geographic information systems (MAS, Certificate); human resource administration (MPS, Certificate); knowledge and information technologies (MAS); liberal studies (MLS, Certificate); modern languages (MLS, Certificate); organizational leadership (MPS, Certificate); security management (Certificate); technology management (MAS, Certificate), including 21st century strategic management (MAS), international markets (MAS), project management (MAS), research and development management (MAS); telecommunications (MAS, Certificate), including broadband (MAS), telecommunications management and policy (MAS), telecommunications technology (MAS), wireless networks (MAS). Part-time and evening/weekend programs available. Postbaccalaureate distance learning degree programs offered (no on-campus study). *Faculty:* 160 part-time/adjunct (64 women). *Students:* 53 full-time (25 women), 984 part-time (551 women); includes 171 minority (72 African Americans, 10 American Indian/Alaska Native, 33 Asian Americans or Pacific Islanders, 56 Hispanic Americans), 75 international. Average age 36. 537 applicants, 96% accepted, 494 enrolled. In 2009, 229 master's, 109 Certificates awarded. *Entrance requirements:* Additional exam requirements/recommendations for international students: Required—TOEFL (minimum score 550 paper-based; 213 computer-based). *Application deadline:* Applications are processed on a rolling basis. Application fee: $75. Electronic applications accepted. *Expenses:* Contact institution. *Financial support:* Applicants required to submit FAFSA. *Unit head:* Dr. James Davis, Dean, 303-871-2291, Fax: 303-871-4047, E-mail: jdavis@du.edu. *Application contact:* Information Contact, 303-871-3155.

University of Detroit Mercy, College of Liberal Arts and Education, Program in Liberal Studies, Detroit, MI 48221. Offers MALS. Part-time programs available.

The University of Findlay, Graduate and Professional Studies, College of Liberal Arts, Master of Arts Program in Liberal Studies, Findlay, OH 45840-3653. Offers MALS. Part-time and evening/weekend programs available. *Degree requirements:* For master's, thesis, cumulative project. *Entrance requirements:* For master's, minimum undergraduate GPA of 2.5 in last 64 hours of course work, 3 letters of recommendation. Additional exam requirements/recommendations for international students: Required—TOEFL (minimum score 550 paper-based; 213 computer-based; 80 iBT). Electronic applications accepted.

University of Maine, Graduate School, Program in Liberal Studies, Orono, ME 04469. Offers MA. Part-time and evening/weekend programs available. *Students:* 7 full-time (6 women), 19 part-time (15 women); includes 5 minority (3 American Indian/Alaska Native, 2 Hispanic Americans), 2 international. Average age 43. 9 applicants, 44% accepted, 3 enrolled. In 2009, 2 master's awarded. *Degree requirements:* For master's, project. *Entrance requirements:* Additional exam requirements/recommendations for international students: Required—TOEFL. *Application deadline:* For fall admission, 4/1 for domestic students; for spring admission, 11/1 for domestic students. Applications are processed on a rolling basis. Application fee: $65. Electronic applications accepted. *Financial support:* Federal Work-Study and institutionally sponsored loans available. Financial award application deadline: 3/1. *Unit head:* Amaranta Ruiz-Nelson, Coordinator, 207-581-3222, Fax: 207-581-3232, E-mail: graduate@maine.edu. *Application contact:* Amaranta Ruiz-Nelson, Coordinator, 207-581-3222, Fax: 207-581-3232, E-mail: graduate@maine.edu.

University of Memphis, Graduate School, University College, Memphis, TN 38152. Offers liberal studies (MALS); merchandising and consumer science (MS), including consumer science and education; strategic leadership (MPS). Part-time and evening/weekend programs available. *Faculty:* 3 full-time (2 women), 3 part-time/adjunct (1 woman). *Students:* 30 full-time (19 women), 122 part-time (93 women); includes 91 minority (88 African Americans, 1 American Indian/Alaska Native, 1 Asian American or Pacific Islander, 1 Hispanic American), 1 international. Average age 40. 89 applicants, 74% accepted, 8 enrolled. In 2009, 41 master's awarded. *Degree requirements:* For master's, comprehensive exam, thesis (for some programs). *Entrance requirements:* For master's, MAT, GRE General Test (MS), interview (MALS). Additional exam requirements/recommendations for international students: Required—TOEFL (minimum score 550 paper-based; 210 computer-based). *Application deadline:* For fall admission, 7/1 for domestic students, 5/1 for international students; for spring admission, 11/1 for domestic students, 9/15 for international students. Applications are processed on a rolling basis. Application fee: $35 ($60 for international students). Electronic applications accepted. *Expenses:* Tuition, state resident: full-time $6246; part-time $347 per credit hour. Tuition, nonresident: full-time $15,894; part-time $883 per credit hour. Required fees: $1160. Full-time tuition and fees vary according to course load, degree level and program. *Financial support:* In 2009–10, 123 students received support; research assistantships with full tuition reimbursements available, teaching assistantships with tuition reimbursements available, Federal Work-Study, scholarships/grants, and unspecified assistantships available. Financial award application deadline: 2/15; financial award applicants required to submit FAFSA. *Faculty research:* Media ethics, history of psychiatry, public relations. *Unit head:* Dr. Dan Lattimore, Dean, 901-678-2991. *Application contact:* Dr. Herbert McCree, Coordinator of Graduate Studies, 901-678-4171, Fax: 901-678-3363, E-mail: hmccree@memphis.edu.

University of Miami, Graduate School, College of Arts and Sciences, Program in Liberal Studies, Coral Gables, FL 33124. Offers MALS. Part-time and evening/weekend programs available. *Degree requirements:* For master's, thesis or alternative. *Entrance requirements:* For master's, minimum GPA of 3.0. Additional exam requirements/recommendations for international students: Required—TOEFL. Electronic applications accepted. *Expenses:* Contact institution.

University of Michigan–Dearborn, College of Arts, Sciences, and Letters, Master of Arts in Liberal Studies Program, Dearborn, MI 48128. Offers MA. Part-time and evening/weekend programs available. *Faculty:* 14 full-time (7 women). *Students:* 1 (woman) full-time, 24 part-time (15 women); includes 5 minority (3 African Americans, 2 Asian Americans or Pacific Islanders). Average age 42. 5 applicants, 80% accepted, 4 enrolled. In 2009, 5 master's awarded. *Degree requirements:* For master's, thesis or alternative, capstone course. *Entrance requirements:* For master's, minimum GPA of 3.0, writing sample, interview. Additional exam requirements/recommendations for international students: Required—TOEFL (minimum score 560 paper-based; 220 computer-based). *Application deadline:* For fall admission, 8/1 priority date for domestic students, 4/1 for international students; for winter admission, 12/1 priority date for domestic students, 11/1 for international students; for spring admission, 4/1 for domestic students, 3/1 for international students. Applications are processed on a rolling basis. Application fee: $60 ($75 for international students). *Expenses:* Tuition, area resident: Part-time $504.10 per credit hour. Tuition, state resident: part-time $504.10 per credit hour. Tuition, nonresident: part-time $957.90 per credit hour. *Financial support:* Scholarships/grants available. Support available to part-time students. Financial award application deadline: 4/1; financial award applicants required to submit FAFSA. *Faculty research:* History of science studies, consciousness, memory studies, early American history, environmental studies. *Unit head:* Dr. Jacqueline Vansant, Director, 313-593-5153, Fax: 313-583-6700, E-mail: jvansant@umd.umich.edu. *Application contact:* Carol Ligienza, Graduate Program Coordinator, CASL Graduate Programs, 313-593-1183, Fax: 313-583-6700, E-mail: caslgrad@umd.umich.edu.

University of Minnesota, Duluth, Graduate School, College of Liberal Arts, Department of Sociology/Anthropology, Liberal Studies Program, Duluth, MN 55812-2496. Offers MLS. Part-time and evening/weekend programs available. *Faculty research:* Nature of knowledge, cultural studies, language, literature, sociology.

University of New Hampshire, Graduate School, College of Liberal Arts, Program in Liberal Studies, Durham, NH 03824. Offers MALS. *Faculty:* 5 full-time (3 women). *Students:* 5 full-time (1 woman), 22 part-time (13 women); includes 3 minority (1 Asian American or Pacific Islander, 2 Hispanic Americans). Average age 39. 15 applicants, 87% accepted, 10 enrolled. In 2009, 2 master's awarded. *Entrance requirements:* Additional exam requirements/recommendations for international students: Required—TOEFL (minimum score 550 paper-based; 213 computer-based; 80 iBT). *Application deadline:* For fall admission, 6/1 for domestic students, 4/1 for international students; for spring admission, 12/1 for domestic students. Applications are processed on a rolling basis. Application fee: $65. Electronic applications accepted. *Expenses:* Tuition, state resident: full-time $10,380; part-time $577 per credit hour. Tuition, nonresident: full-time $24,350; part-time $1002 per credit hour. Required fees: $1550; $387.50 per semester. Tuition and fees vary according to course load and program. *Financial support:* Fellowships, research assistantships, teaching assistantships available. Financial award application deadline: 2/15. *Unit head:* Dr. Warren Brown, Chairperson, 603-862-3225, E-mail: liberal.studies@unh.edu. *Application contact:* Janis Marshall, 603-862-7150, E-mail: liberal.studies@unh.edu.

The University of North Carolina at Asheville, Graduate Studies, Asheville, NC 28804-3299. Offers MLA. Part-time and evening/weekend programs available. *Degree requirements:* For master's, thesis.

The University of North Carolina at Charlotte, Graduate School, College of Arts and Sciences, Program in Liberal Studies, Charlotte, NC 28223-0001. Offers MA. *Faculty:* 3 full-time (2 women). *Students:* 2 full-time (1 woman), 10 part-time (6 women). Average age 35. *Degree requirements:* For master's, thesis optional, comprehensive exam or project. *Entrance requirements:* For master's, GRE General Test or MAT, minimum GPA of 3.0 during previous 2 years, 2.75 overall. Additional exam requirements/recommendations for international students: Required—TOEFL (minimum score 557 paper-based; 220 computer-based; 83 iBT). *Application deadline:* For fall admission, 7/1 for domestic students, 5/1 for international students; for spring admission, 11/1 for domestic students, 10/1 for international students. Applications are processed on a rolling basis. Application fee: $55. Electronic applications accepted. *Financial support:* Career-related internships or fieldwork, Federal Work-Study, institutionally sponsored loans, scholarships/grants, and unspecified assistantships available. Support available to part-time students. Financial award application deadline: 4/1; financial award applicants required to submit FAFSA. *Unit head:* Dr. Paula Eckard, Interim Director, 704-687-4309, Fax: 704-687-4347, E-mail: pgeckard@uncc.edu. *Application contact:* Kathy B. Giddings, Director of Graduate Admissions, 704-687-5503, Fax: 704-687-3279, E-mail: gradadm@uncc.edu.

The University of North Carolina at Greensboro, Graduate School, Program in Liberal Studies, Greensboro, NC 27412-5001. Offers MALS. Electronic applications accepted.

The University of North Carolina Wilmington, College of Arts and Sciences, Interdisciplinary Program in Liberal Studies, Wilmington, NC 28403-3297. Offers MALS. Part-time programs available. *Degree requirements:* For master's, comprehensive exam, thesis or alternative, final project. *Entrance requirements:* For master's, minimum GPA of 3.0, writing sample. Additional exam requirements/recommendations for international students: Required—TOEFL (minimum score 550 paper-based; 217 computer-based; 79 iBT), IELTS (minimum score 6.5).

University of Oklahoma, Graduate College, College of Liberal Studies, Norman, OK 73019-0390. Offers administrative leadership (MLS); integrated studies (MLS); interprofessional human and health services (MLS); museum studies (MLS). Part-time programs available. Postbaccalaureate distance learning degree programs offered (no on-campus study). *Faculty:* 15 full-time (8 women), 26 part-time/adjunct (16 women). *Students:* 17 full-time (11 women), 326 part-time (169 women); includes 71 minority (33 African Americans, 24 American Indian/Alaska Native, 4 Asian Americans or Pacific Islanders, 10 Hispanic Americans). 126 applicants, 90% accepted, 75 enrolled. In 2009, 94 master's awarded. *Degree requirements:* For master's, thesis, research project, internship. *Entrance requirements:* For master's, minimum GPA of 3.0 in last 60 hours, writing sample. Additional exam requirements/recommendations for international students: Required—TOEFL (minimum score 550 paper-based; 213 computer-based). *Application deadline:* For fall admission, 7/15 priority date for domestic students, 4/1 for international students; for spring admission, 12/1 for domestic students, 9/1 for international students. Applications are processed on a rolling basis. Application fee: $40 ($90 for international students). Electronic applications accepted. *Expenses:* Tuition, state resident: full-time $3744; part-time $156 per credit hour. Tuition, nonresident: full-time $13,577; part-time $565.70 per credit hour. Required fees: $2415; $90.10 per credit hour. *Financial support:* In 2009–10, 163 students received support. Career-related internships or fieldwork, scholarships/grants, and tuition waivers (partial) available. Support available to part-time students. Financial award applicants required to submit FAFSA. *Faculty research:* Distance education, adult learning processes, student satisfaction, administrative leadership, organizations, museum studies. *Unit head:* Dr. James Pappas, Dean and Vice President for University Outreach, 405-325-6361, Fax: 405-325-7196, E-mail: jpappas@ou.edu. *Application contact:* Dr. Julie Raadschelders, MA Program Coordinator, 405-325-1061, Fax: 405-325-9632, E-mail: jraadschelders@ou.edu.

University of Pennsylvania, School of Arts and Sciences, College of Liberal and Professional Studies, Philadelphia, PA 19104. Offers environmental studies (MES); individualized study (MLA). *Students:* 98 full-time (67 women), 300 part-time (185 women); includes 23 minority (11 African Americans, 6 Asian Americans or Pacific Islanders, 6 Hispanic Americans), 30 international. 441 applicants, 50% accepted, 157 enrolled. In 2009, 175 master's awarded. *Application deadline:* For fall admission, 12/1 priority date for domestic students. Application fee: $70. Electronic applications accepted. *Expenses:* Tuition: Full-time $25,660; part-time $4758 per course. Required fees: $2152; $270 per course. Tuition and fees vary according to course load, degree level and program. *Unit head:* Dr. Kristine Billmyer, Associate Dean and Director, College of Liberal and Professional Studies, 215-898-8681, E-mail: gdasdmis@sas.upenn.edu. *Application contact:* Patricia Rea, Coordinator for Admissions, 215-573-5816, Fax: 215-573-8068, E-mail: gdasadmis@sas.upenn.edu.

University of St. Thomas, Program in Liberal Arts, Houston, TX 77006-4696. Offers MLA. Part-time and evening/weekend programs available. *Faculty:* 33 full-time (12 women), 13 part-time/adjunct (8 women). *Students:* 26 full-time (20 women), 124 part-time (84 women); includes 50 minority (13 African Americans, 6 Asian Americans or Pacific Islanders, 31 Hispanic Americans), 8 international. Average age 34. 58 applicants, 95% accepted, 48 enrolled. In 2009, 38 master's awarded. *Degree requirements:* For master's, thesis optional. *Entrance requirements:* For master's, minimum GPA of 2.5. Additional exam requirements/recommendations for international students: Required—TOEFL (minimum score 250 computer-based; 100 iBT). *Application deadline:* Applications are processed on a rolling basis. Application fee: $35. Electronic applications accepted. *Expenses:* Tuition: Full-time $14,436; part-time $802 per credit hour. Required fees: $224. *Financial support:* In 2009–10, 11 students received support. Federal Work-Study and scholarships/grants available. Support available to part-time students. Financial award application deadline: 3/1; financial award applicants required to submit FAFSA. *Unit head:* Dr. Ravi Srinivas, Dean, 713-525-6924, Fax: 713-525-6924, E-mail: srinivas@stthom.edu. *Application contact:* Kate Henderson, Program Assistant, 713-525-3556, Fax: 713-525-6924, E-mail: henderlk@stthom.edu.

University of Southern Indiana, Graduate Studies, College of Liberal Arts, Program in Liberal Studies, Evansville, IN 47712-3590. Offers MA. Part-time and evening/weekend programs available. *Faculty:* 4 full-time (1 woman). *Students:* 11 full-time (7 women), 27 part-time (22 women); includes 3 minority (2 African Americans, 1 Asian American or Pacific Islander), 1 international. Average age 38. 10 applicants, 90% accepted, 9 enrolled. In 2009, 9 master's awarded. *Entrance requirements:* For master's, minimum GPA of 2.5, resume, interview. Additional exam requirements/recommendations for international students: Required—TOEFL (minimum score 550 paper-based; 213 computer-based; 79 iBT), IELTS (minimum score 6). *Application deadline:* For fall admission, 8/15 priority date for domestic students, 3/1 priority date for international students. Applications are processed on a rolling basis. Application fee: $25. Electronic applications accepted. *Expenses:* Tuition, state resident: full-time $4592; part-time $255 per credit hour. Tuition, nonresident: full-time $9060; part-time $503 per credit hour. Required fees: $220; $22.75 per term. Tuition and fees vary according to course load and reciprocity agreements. *Financial support:* In 2009–10, 31 students received support. Federal Work-Study, scholarships/grants, tuition waivers (full and partial), and unspecified assistantships available. Financial award application deadline: 3/1; financial award applicants required to submit FAFSA. *Unit head:* Dr. Thomas M. Rivers, Director, 812-464-1753, E-mail: trivers@usi.edu. *Application contact:* Dr. Thomas M. Rivers, Director, 812-464-1753, E-mail: trivers@usi.edu.

The University of Texas at El Paso, Graduate School, College of Liberal Arts, Interdisciplinary Program in Liberal Arts, El Paso, TX 79968-0001. Offers MAIS. Part-time and evening/weekend programs available. *Students:* 12 (5 women); includes 5 minority (all Hispanic Americans), 4 international. Average age 34. In 2009, 5 master's awarded. *Entrance requirements:* For master's, GRE, minimum GPA of 3.0, letters of recommendation. Additional exam requirements/recommendations for international students: Required—TOEFL; Recommended—IELTS. *Application deadline:* For fall admission, 8/1 priority date for domestic students, 3/1 for international students; for spring admission, 11/1 priority date for domestic students, 9/1 for international students. Applications are processed on a rolling basis. Application fee: $45 ($80 for international students). Electronic applications accepted. *Financial support:* In 2009–10, research assistantships with tuition reimbursements (averaging $18,625 per year), teaching assistantships with partial tuition reimbursements (averaging $14,900 per year) were awarded; fellowships with partial tuition reimbursements, institutionally sponsored loans, scholarships/grants, health care benefits, tuition waivers (partial), and unspecified assistantships also available. Support available to part-time students. Financial award application deadline: 3/15; financial award applicants required to submit FAFSA. *Unit head:* Dr. Ronald Weber, Director, 915-747-7073, E-mail: rweber@utep.edu. *Application contact:* Dr. Patricia D. Witherspoon, Dean of the Graduate School, 915-747-5491, Fax: 915-747-5788, E-mail: withersp@utep.edu.

The University of Toledo, College of Graduate Studies, College of Arts and Sciences, Master of Liberal Studies Program, Toledo, OH 43606-3390. Offers MLS. Part-time and evening/weekend programs available. *Degree requirements:* For master's, thesis. *Entrance requirements:* For master's, interview, minimum GPA of 2.7. Electronic applications accepted.

University of Wisconsin–Milwaukee, Graduate School, College of Letters and Sciences, Interdepartmental Program in Liberal Studies, Milwaukee, WI 53201-0413. Offers MLS. *Faculty:* 10 full-time (3 women). *Students:* 7 full-time (4 women), 16 part-time (11 women); includes 4 minority (3 African Americans, 1 Hispanic American). Average age 39. 16 applicants, 100% accepted, 6 enrolled. In 2009, 12 master's awarded. *Entrance requirements:* For master's, interview, bachelor's degree. Additional exam requirements/recommendations for international students: Required—TOEFL (minimum score 600 paper-based; 79 iBT), IELTS (minimum score 7). Application fee: $45 ($75 for international students). *Expenses:* Tuition, state resident: full-time $8800. Tuition, nonresident: full-time $20,760. Tuition and fees vary according to program and reciprocity agreements. *Unit head:* Jeffrey R. Hayes, Representative, 414-229-5963, E-mail: jhayes@uwm.edu. *Application contact:* General Information Contact, 414-229-4982, Fax: 414-229-6967, E-mail: gradschool@uwm.edu.

Ursuline College, School of Graduate Studies, Program in Liberal Studies, Pepper Pike, OH 44124-4398. Offers MALS. *Faculty:* 1 part-time/adjunct (0 women). *Students:* 1 (woman) full-time, 7 part-time (6 women); includes 5 minority (all African Americans). Average age 50. *Degree requirements:* For master's, thesis. *Entrance requirements:* For master's, minimum undergraduate GPA of 3.0. Additional exam requirements/recommendations for international students: Required—TOEFL (minimum score 500 paper-based; 173 computer-based). *Application deadline:* For fall admission, 8/1 priority date for domestic students. Applications are processed on a rolling basis. Application fee: $25. Electronic applications accepted. *Expenses:* Tuition: Full-time $14,544; part-time $808 per credit hour. Required fees: $230; $75 per semester. *Financial support:* Federal Work-Study available. Financial award application deadline: 3/1; financial award applicants required to submit FAFSA. *Unit head:* Dr. Tim Kinsella, Director, 440-646-8389, Fax: 440-684-6088, E-mail: tkinsell@ursuline.edu. *Application contact:* Melanie Steele, Secretary, 440-646-8119, Fax: 440-684-6138, E-mail: gradsch@ursuline.edu.

Utica College, Liberal Studies Program, Utica, NY 13502-4892. Offers MS. Part-time and evening/weekend programs available. *Faculty:* 19 full-time (8 women). *Students:* 3 full-time (2 women), 16 part-time (14 women); includes 1 minority (Asian American or Pacific Islander), 1 international. Average age 31. In 2009, 11 master's awarded. *Degree requirements:* For master's, comprehensive exam or thesis. *Entrance requirements:* For master's, minimum GPA of 3.0. Additional exam requirements/recommendations for international students: Required—TOEFL (minimum score 525 paper-based; 195 computer-based). *Application deadline:* Applications are processed on a rolling basis. Application fee: $50. Electronic applications accepted. *Expenses:* Contact institution. *Financial support:* Career-related internships or fieldwork, scholarships/grants, tuition waivers (partial), and unspecified assistantships available. Support available to part-time students. Financial award application deadline: 3/15; financial award applicants required to submit FAFSA. *Unit head:* Dr. Lawrence Aaronson, Coordinator, 315-792-3092, E-mail: laaronson@utica.edu. *Application contact:* John D. Rowe, Director of Graduate Admissions, 315-792-3824, Fax: 315-792-3003, E-mail: jrowe@utica.edu.

Valparaiso University, Graduate School, Programs in Liberal Studies, Concentration in Human Behavior and Society, Valparaiso, IN 46383. Offers MALS, Post-Master's Certificate, JD/MALS. Part-time and evening/weekend programs available. *Students:* 4 full-time (3 women), 4 part-time (all women); includes 1 minority (African American), 3 international. Average age 32. In 2009, 7 master's awarded. *Entrance requirements:* For master's, minimum GPA of 3.0. Additional exam requirements/recommendations for international students: Required—TOEFL (minimum score 550 paper-based; 213 computer-based; 80 iBT). *Application deadline:* Applications are processed on a rolling basis. Application fee: $30 ($50 for international students). Electronic applications accepted. *Financial support:* Available to part-time students. Applicants required to submit FAFSA. *Unit head:* Dr. David L. Rowland, Dean, Graduate Studies and Continuing Education/Associate Provost, 219-464-5313, Fax: 219-464-5381, E-mail: david.rowland@valpo.edu. *Application contact:* Jamie Haney, Coordinator of Graduate Admission, 219-464-5313, Fax: 219-464-5381, E-mail: jamie.haney@valpo.edu.

Valparaiso University, Graduate School, Programs in Liberal Studies, Individualized Program, Valparaiso, IN 46383. Offers MALS, JD/MALS. Part-time and evening/weekend programs available. *Students:* 2 full-time (1 woman), 10 part-time (7 women); includes 1 minority (African American), 1 international. Average age 34. In 2009, 3 master's awarded. *Entrance requirements:* For master's, minimum GPA of 3.0. Additional exam requirements/recommendations for international students: Required—TOEFL (minimum score 550 paper-based; 213 computer-based; 80 iBT). *Application deadline:* Applications are processed on a rolling basis. Application fee: $30 ($50 for international students). Electronic applications accepted. *Financial support:* Available to part-time students. Applicants required to submit FAFSA. *Unit head:* Dr. David L. Rowland, Dean, Graduate Studies and Continuing Education/Associate Provost, 219-464-5313, Fax: 219-464-5381, E-mail: david.rowland@valpo.edu. *Application contact:* Jamie Haney, Coordinator of Graduate Admission, 219-464-5313, Fax: 219-464-5381, E-mail: jamie.haney@valpo.edu.

Vanderbilt University, Graduate School, Program in Liberal Arts and Science, Nashville, TN 37240-1001. Offers MLAS. Part-time programs available. *Students:* 71 part-time (48 women); includes 3 minority (2 African Americans, 1 Hispanic American), 2 international. Average age 45. 26 applicants, 77% accepted, 15 enrolled. In 2009, 45 master's awarded. *Degree requirements:* For master's, thesis optional. *Entrance requirements:* For master's, GRE General Test. *Application deadline:* For fall admission, 1/15 priority date for domestic students, 1/15 for international students; for spring admission, 11/15 for domestic and international students. Applications are processed on a rolling basis. Application fee: $0. *Financial support:* Institutionally sponsored loans and tuition waivers (partial) available. *Unit head:* Martin Rapisarda, Associate Dean and Director, 615-343-3140, Fax: 615-343-8453, E-mail: martin.rapisarda@vanderbilt.edu. *Application contact:* Walter B. Bieschke, Program Coordinator for Graduate Admissions, 615-343-6321, Fax: 615-343-6687, E-mail: vandygrad@vanderbilt.edu.

Villanova University, Graduate School of Liberal Arts and Sciences, Program in Liberal Studies, Villanova, PA 19085-1699. Offers MA. Part-time and evening/weekend programs available. *Faculty:* 2 full-time (0 women). *Students:* 3 full-time (2 women), 14 part-time (11 women), 1 international. Average age 39. 6 applicants, 100% accepted, 6 enrolled. In 2009, 15 master's awarded. *Degree requirements:* For master's, comprehensive exam. *Entrance requirements:* For master's, minimum GPA of 3.0. Additional exam requirements/recommendations for international students: Required—TOEFL. *Application deadline:* For fall admission, 3/1 priority date for domestic and international students; for spring admission, 11/15 priority date for domestic and international students. Applications are processed on a rolling basis. Application fee: $50. Electronic applications accepted. *Expenses:* Tuition: Part-time $630 per credit. Required fees: $60 per credit. Part-time tuition and fees vary according to degree level and program. *Financial support:* Research assistantships, Federal Work-Study available. Financial award applicants required to submit FAFSA. *Unit head:* Dr. Eugene McCarraher, Director, 610-519-4796, Fax: 610-519-4639, E-mail: eugene.mccarraher@villanova.edu. *Application contact:* Dr. Adele Lindenmeyr, Dean, Graduate School of Liberal Arts and Sciences, 610-519-7093, Fax: 610-519-7096.

Virginia Polytechnic Institute and State University, VT Online, Blacksburg, VA 24061. Offers aerospace engineering (MS); business information systems (Graduate Certificate); career and technical education (MS); computer engineering (M Eng, MS); decision support systems (Graduate Certificate); eLearning leadership (MA); electrical engineering (M Eng, MS); engineering administration (MEA); environmental politics and policy (Graduate Certificate); foundations of political analysis (Graduate Certificate); health product risk management (Graduate Certificate); information policy and society (Graduate Certificate); information security (Graduate Certificate); instructional technology (MA); liberal arts (Graduate Certificate); life sciences: health product risk management (MS); natural resources (MNR, Graduate Certificate); networking (Graduate Certificate); nonprofit and nongovernmental organization management (Graduate Certificate); ocean engineering (MS); political science (MA); security studies (Graduate Certificate); software development (Graduate Certificate).

Wake Forest University, Graduate School of Arts and Sciences, Liberal Studies Program, Winston-Salem, NC 27109. Offers MALS. Part-time programs available. *Degree requirements:* For master's, thesis. *Entrance requirements:* Additional exam requirements/recommendations for international students: Required—TOEFL (minimum score 213 computer-based; 79 iBT). Electronic applications accepted.

Washburn University, College of Arts and Sciences, Program in Liberal Studies, Topeka, KS 66621. Offers MLS. Part-time and evening/weekend programs available. *Degree requirements:* For master's, thesis, 15 seminar hours. *Entrance requirements:* For master's, minimum GPA of 3.0. Electronic applications accepted. *Faculty research:* European architecture/history, British cultural studies movement, American military strategy/history.

Wesleyan University, Graduate Liberal Studies Program, Middletown, CT 06459. Offers MALS, CAS. Part-time and evening/weekend programs available. *Students:* Average age 44. *Degree requirements:* For master's, thesis optional; for CAS, thesis. *Entrance requirements:* Additional exam requirements/recommendations for international students: Required—TOEFL. *Application deadline:* For fall admission, 9/10 for domestic students; for spring admission, 1/28 for domestic students. Applications are processed on a rolling basis. Application fee: $100. *Expenses:* Contact institution. *Financial support:* Scholarships/grants available. Support available to part-time students. *Faculty research:* Interdisciplinary studies. *Unit head:* Sheryl Culotta, Director, 860-685-3008, Fax: 860-685-2901, E-mail: sculotta@wesleyan.edu. *Application contact:* Jennifer M. Curran, Assistant Director, Admissions and Outreach, 860-685-3338, Fax: 860-685-2901, E-mail: jcurran@wesleyan.edu.

Western Illinois University, School of Graduate Studies, College of Arts and Sciences, Program in Liberal Arts and Sciences, Macomb, IL 61455-1390. Offers MLAS. Part-time programs available. *Students:* 10 full-time (6 women), 3 part-time (all women); includes 4 minority (3 African Americans, 1 Hispanic American). Average age 36. 7 applicants, 100% accepted. *Degree requirements:* For master's, thesis or alternative. *Entrance requirements:* Additional exam requirements/recommendations for international students: Required—TOEFL (minimum score 550 paper-based; 213 computer-based; 80 iBT). *Application deadline:* Applications are processed on a rolling basis. Application fee: $30. Electronic applications accepted. *Expenses:* Tuition, state resident: full-time $4486; part-time $249.21 per credit hour. Tuition, nonresident: full-time $8972; part-time $498.42 per credit hour. Required fees: $72.62 per credit hour. *Financial support:* In 2009–10, 1 student received support, including 1 research assistantship with full tuition reimbursement available (averaging $7,280 per year). Financial award applicants required to submit FAFSA. *Unit head:* Dr. Althea Alton, Program Director, 309-298-3025. *Application contact:* Evelyn Hoing, Assistant Director of Graduate Studies, 309-298-1806, Fax: 309-298-2345, E-mail: grad-office@wiu.edu.

West Virginia University, Eberly College of Arts and Sciences, Interdisciplinary Program in Liberal Studies, Morgantown, WV 26506. Offers MALS. Part-time programs available. *Degree requirements:* For master's, thesis or alternative. *Entrance requirements:* For master's, GRE General Test, minimum GPA of 3.0. Additional exam requirements/recommendations for international students: Required—TOEFL.

Wichita State University, Graduate School, Fairmount College of Liberal Arts and Sciences, Interdisciplinary Program in Liberal Studies, Wichita, KS 67260. Offers MA. Part-time programs available. *Expenses:* Tuition, state resident: full-time $4247; part-time $235.95 per credit hour. Tuition, nonresident: full-time $11,171; part-time $620.60 per credit hour. Required fees: $34; $3.60 per credit hour. $17 per term. Tuition and fees vary according to campus/location and program. *Unit head:* Dr. David Soles, Graduate Coordinator, 316-978-3125, E-mail: david.soles@wichita.edu. *Application contact:* Dr. David Soles, Graduate Coordinator, 316-978-3125, E-mail: david.soles@wichita.edu.

Widener University, College of Arts and Sciences, Program in Liberal Studies, Chester, PA 19013-5792. Offers MA. Part-time and evening/weekend programs available. *Faculty:* 4 full-time (1 woman). *Students:* 1 (woman) full-time, 13 part-time (8 women); includes 1 minority (African American). Average age 40. 3 applicants, 100% accepted. In 2009, 2 master's awarded. *Degree requirements:* For master's, thesis, project. *Entrance requirements:* For master's, interview, minimum undergraduate GPA of 3.0. *Application deadline:* Applications are processed on a rolling basis. Application fee: $25 ($300 for international students). *Expenses:* Contact institution. *Financial support:* Federal Work-Study and tuition waivers (full and partial) available. Financial award application deadline: 5/1. *Faculty research:* Contemporary analytical metaphysics, popular culture, British art, American literature, folklore. *Unit head:* Dr. Kenneth Skinner, Director, 610-499-4287, Fax: 610-499-4605, E-mail: kenneth.a.skinner@widener.edu. *Application contact:* Dr. Kenneth Skinner, Director, 610-499-4287, Fax: 610-499-4605, E-mail: kenneth.a.skinner@widener.edu.

Winthrop University, College of Arts and Sciences, Program in Liberal Arts, Rock Hill, SC 29733. Offers MLA. Part-time programs available. *Entrance requirements:* For master's, interview, minimum GPA of 3.0. Electronic applications accepted.

Section 9
Language and Literature

This section contains a directory of institutions offering graduate work in language and literature, followed by in-depth entries submitted by institutions that chose to prepare detailed program descriptions. Additional information about programs listed in the directory but not augmented by an in-depth entry may be obtained by writing directly to the dean of a graduate school or chair of a department at the address given in the directory.

For programs offering related work, see also in this book *Area and Cultural Studies, Communication and Media, Political Science and International Affairs,* and *Sociology, Anthropology, and Archaeology.* In another guide in this series:

Graduate Programs in Business, Education, Health, Information Studies, Law & Social Work

See *Special Focus* and *Subject Areas*

CONTENTS

Program Directories

Asian Languages 320
Celtic Languages 322
Chinese 322
Classics 323
Comparative Literature 330
English 336
French 369
German 380
Italian 387
Japanese 390
Near and Middle Eastern Languages 392
Portuguese 394
Romance Languages 396
Russian 398
Scandinavian Languages 400
Slavic Languages 401
Spanish 403

Close-Ups and Display

Auburn University 417
Northwestern University
English (Display) 350
Saint Louis University–Madrid Campus 419
Villanova University 421

Asian Languages

Columbia University, Graduate School of Arts and Sciences, Division of Humanities, Department of East Asian Languages and Cultures, New York, NY 10027. Offers East Asian languages and cultures (M Phil, MA, PhD); Oriental studies (M Phil, MA, PhD). *Degree requirements:* For master's, one foreign language, comprehensive exam, thesis; for doctorate, 2 foreign languages, thesis/dissertation. *Entrance requirements:* For master's and doctorate, GRE General Test. Additional exam requirements/recommendations for international students: Required—TOEFL.

Columbia University, Graduate School of Arts and Sciences, Division of Humanities, Department of Middle East Languages and Cultures, New York, NY 10027. Offers Hebrew language and literature (M Phil, MA, PhD); Middle Eastern languages and cultures (M Phil, MA, PhD); South Asian languages and cultures (M Phil, MA, PhD). Part-time programs available. *Degree requirements:* For master's, thesis, oral and written exams; for doctorate, 3 foreign languages, thesis/dissertation. *Entrance requirements:* For master's and doctorate, GRE General Test. Additional exam requirements/recommendations for international students: Required—TOEFL. *Faculty research:* Indo-Iranian, Turkish, central Asian, and Armenian studies; Arabic and ancient Semitics.

Cornell University, Graduate School, Graduate Fields of Arts and Sciences, Field of East Asian Literature, Ithaca, NY 14853-0001. Offers Asian religions (MA, PhD); Chinese linguistics (MA, PhD); Chinese philology (MA, PhD); classical Chinese literature (MA, PhD); classical Japanese literature (MA, PhD); Japanese linguistics (MA, PhD); Korean literature (MA, PhD); modern Chinese literature (MA, PhD); modern Japanese literature (MA, PhD). *Faculty:* 17 full-time (7 women). *Students:* 16 full-time (7 women); includes 4 minority (all Asian Americans or Pacific Islanders), 8 international. Average age 32. 49 applicants, 6% accepted, 2 enrolled. In 2009, 3 doctorates awarded. *Degree requirements:* For master's, 2 foreign languages, thesis, teaching experience; for doctorate, 2 foreign languages, comprehensive exam, thesis/dissertation, teaching experience. *Entrance requirements:* For master's, GRE General Test, 3 years of study in Chinese, Japanese, Korean, or Vietnamese; 3 letters of recommendation; academic writing sample; for doctorate, GRE General Test, 3 years of study in Chinese, Japanese, Korean, or Vietnamese, 3 letters of recommendation, academic writing sample. Additional exam requirements/recommendations for international students: Required—TOEFL (minimum score 600 paper-based; 250 computer-based; 77 iBT). *Application deadline:* For fall admission, 1/10 priority date for domestic students. Application fee: $70. Electronic applications accepted. *Expenses:* Tuition: Full-time $29,500. Required fees: $70. Full-time tuition and fees vary according to degree level, program and student level. *Financial support:* In 2009–10, 2 fellowships with full tuition reimbursements were awarded; research assistantships with full tuition reimbursements, teaching assistantships with full tuition reimbursements, institutionally sponsored loans, scholarships/grants, health care benefits, tuition waivers (full and partial), and unspecified assistantships also available. Financial award applicants required to submit FAFSA. *Faculty research:* Vietnamese literature; Chinese literature, drama, and film; Japanese theater and literature; popular culture in East Asia; Korean literature; Asian linguistics. *Unit head:* Director of Graduate Studies, 607-255-9099. *Application contact:* Graduate Field Assistant, 607-255-9099, E-mail: east_asian_lit@cornell.edu.

Cornell University, Graduate School, Graduate Fields of Arts and Sciences, Field of Linguistics, Ithaca, NY 14853-0001. Offers applied linguistics (MA, PhD); East Asian linguistics (MA, PhD); English linguistics (MA, PhD); general linguistics (MA, PhD); Germanic linguistics (MA, PhD); Indo-European linguistics (MA, PhD); phonetics (MA, PhD); phonological theory (MA, PhD); Romance linguistics (MA, PhD); second language acquisition (MA, PhD); semantics (MA, PhD); Slavic linguistics (MA, PhD); sociolinguistics (MA, PhD); South Asian linguistics (MA, PhD); Southeast Asian linguistics (MA, PhD); syntactic theory (MA, PhD). *Faculty:* 21 full-time (10 women). *Students:* 31 full-time (17 women), 14 international. Average age 30. 95 applicants, 12% accepted, 5 enrolled. In 2009, 5 master's, 6 doctorates awarded. Terminal master's awarded for partial completion of doctoral program. *Degree requirements:* For master's, one foreign language, thesis; for doctorate, one foreign language, comprehensive exam, thesis/dissertation. *Entrance requirements:* For master's and doctorate, GRE General Test, 2 letters of recommendation. Additional exam requirements/recommendations for international students: Required—TOEFL (minimum score 600 paper-based; 250 computer-based; 77 iBT). *Application deadline:* For fall admission, 1/15 for domestic students. Application fee: $70. Electronic applications accepted. *Expenses:* Tuition: Full-time $29,500. Required fees: $70. Full-time tuition and fees vary according to degree level, program and student level. *Financial support:* In 2009–10, 3 fellowships with full tuition reimbursements, 1 teaching assistantship with full tuition reimbursement were awarded; research assistantships with full tuition reimbursements, institutionally sponsored loans, scholarships/grants, health care benefits, tuition waivers (full and partial), and unspecified assistantships also available. Financial award applicants required to submit FAFSA. *Faculty research:* Phonology and phonetics; syntax and semantics; historical linguistics; philosophy of language; language acquisition. *Unit head:* Director of Graduate Studies, 607-255-1105. *Application contact:* Graduate Field Assistant, 607-255-1105, E-mail: lingfield@cornell.edu.

Harvard University, Graduate School of Arts and Sciences, Department of East Asian Languages and Civilizations, Cambridge, MA 02138. Offers Chinese (PhD); Japanese (PhD); Korean (PhD); Mongolian (PhD); Vietnamese (PhD). Terminal master's awarded for partial completion of doctoral program. *Degree requirements:* For doctorate, 3 foreign languages, thesis/dissertation, general exams. *Entrance requirements:* For doctorate, GRE General Test. Additional exam requirements/recommendations for international students: Required—TOEFL. *Expenses:* Tuition: Full-time $33,696. Required fees: $1126. Full-time tuition and fees vary according to program. *Faculty research:* Central Asian literature, religion, and premodern history.

Harvard University, Graduate School of Arts and Sciences, Department of Sanskrit and Indian Studies, Cambridge, MA 02138. Offers Indian philosophy (AM, PhD); Pali (AM, PhD); Sanskrit (AM, PhD); Tibetan (AM, PhD); Urdu (AM, PhD). Terminal master's awarded for partial completion of doctoral program. *Degree requirements:* For master's, 3 foreign languages; for doctorate, 3 foreign languages, thesis/dissertation. *Entrance requirements:* For master's, GRE General Test; for doctorate, GRE General Test, proficiency in French and German. Additional exam requirements/recommendations for international students: Required—TOEFL. *Expenses:* Tuition: Full-time $33,696. Required fees: $1126. Full-time tuition and fees vary according to program.

Indiana University Bloomington, University Graduate School, College of Arts and Sciences, Department of East Asian Languages and Cultures, Bloomington, IN 47405-7000. Offers Chinese (MA, PhD); East Asian languages and cultures (PhD); East Asian studies (MA); Japanese (MA, PhD); language pedagogy (MA). Part-time programs available. *Faculty:* 7 full-time (2 women). *Students:* 21 full-time (12 women), 11 part-time (8 women); includes 1 minority (Asian American or Pacific Islander), 11 international. Average age 30. 85 applicants, 38% accepted, 12 enrolled. In 2009, 6 master's, 1 doctorate awarded. *Degree requirements:* For master's, 2 foreign languages, thesis; for doctorate, 2 foreign languages, thesis/dissertation. *Entrance requirements:* Additional exam requirements/recommendations for international students: Required—TOEFL. *Application deadline:* For fall admission, 1/15 for domestic students, 12/15 for international students; for spring admission, 9/1 for domestic and international students. Applications are processed on a rolling basis. Application fee: $55 ($65 for international students). Electronic applications accepted. *Financial support:* In 2009–10, 6 fellowships with full tuition reimbursements (averaging $15,500 per year), 11 teaching assistantships with full tuition reimbursements (averaging $13,000 per year) were awarded; Federal Work-Study and tuition waivers (full) also available. Financial award application deadline: 3/1. *Faculty research:* Postwar/postmodern Japanese fiction, modern Chinese film and literature, classical Chinese literature and philosophy, Chinese and Japanese linguistics and pedagogy, East Asian politics. *Unit head:* Robert Eno, Chair, 812-855-0856, E-mail: eno@indiana.edu. *Application contact:* Edith Sarra, Director of Graduate Studies, 812-855-4031, Fax: 812-855-6402, E-mail: eserra@indiana.edu.

Naropa University, Graduate Programs, Program in Indo-Tibetan Buddhism with Language, Boulder, CO 80302-6697. Offers MA. *Degree requirements:* For master's, comprehensive exam, thesis. *Entrance requirements:* For master's, writing sample, interview (by phone or in-person), resume, letter of interest, 3 letters of recommendation. Additional exam requirements/recommendations for international students: Required—TOEFL (minimum score 600 paper-based; 250 computer-based). Electronic applications accepted.

The Ohio State University, Graduate School, College of Humanities, Department of East Asian Languages and Literatures, Columbus, OH 43210. Offers Chinese (MA, PhD); Japanese (MA, PhD). *Faculty:* 22. *Students:* 56 full-time (29 women), 11 part-time (5 women); includes 7 minority (6 Asian Americans or Pacific Islanders, 1 Hispanic American), 25 international. Average age 28. In 2009, 24 master's, 5 doctorates awarded. *Degree requirements:* For master's, thesis optional; for doctorate, thesis/dissertation. *Entrance requirements:* For master's and doctorate, GRE (if applying for financial aid). Additional exam requirements/recommendations for international students: Required—TOEFL (minimum score 577 paper-based; 233 computer-based). *Application deadline:* For fall admission, 8/15 priority date for domestic students, 7/1 priority date for international students; for winter admission, 12/1 priority date for domestic students, 11/1 priority date for international students; for spring admission, 3/1 priority date for domestic students, 2/1 priority date for international students. Applications are processed on a rolling basis. Application fee: $40 ($50 for international students). Electronic applications accepted. *Expenses:* Tuition, state resident: full-time $10,683. Tuition, nonresident: full-time $25,923. Tuition and fees vary according to course load and program. *Financial support:* Fellowships, research assistantships, teaching assistantships, Federal Work-Study, institutionally sponsored loans, and unspecified assistantships available. Support available to part-time students. *Unit head:* Mineharu Nakayama, Graduate Studies Committee Chair, 614-292-5816, Fax: 614-292-3225, E-mail: nakayama.1@osu.edu. *Application contact:* Graduate Admissions, 614-292-9444, Fax: 614-292-3895, E-mail: domestic.grad@osu.edu.

St. John's College, Graduate Institute in Liberal Education, Program in Eastern Classics, Santa Fe, NM 87505. Offers MA. Part-time and evening/weekend programs available. *Entrance requirements:* For master's, 2 letters of recommendation. Additional exam requirements/recommendations for international students: Required—TOEFL, TWE. *Expenses:* Contact institution.

Seton Hall University, College of Arts and Sciences, Department of Asian Studies, South Orange, NJ 07079-2697. Offers Asian languages (MA); Asian studies (MA); teaching Chinese language and culture (MA). Part-time and evening/weekend programs available. *Faculty:* 5 full-time (2 women), 3 part-time/adjunct (2 women). *Students:* 21 full-time (9 women), 7 part-time (6 women). Average age 30. 26 applicants, 92% accepted, 10 enrolled. In 2009, 14 master's awarded. *Degree requirements:* For master's, thesis optional. *Entrance requirements:* For master's, strong background in Asian studies or related discipline. Additional exam requirements/recommendations for international students: Required—TOEFL. *Application deadline:* For fall admission, 7/1 priority date for domestic and international students; for spring admission, 11/1 priority date for domestic and international students. Applications are processed on a rolling basis. Application fee: $50. Electronic applications accepted. *Financial support:* Teaching assistantships with full tuition reimbursements, career-related internships or fieldwork, Federal Work-Study, institutionally sponsored loans, and unspecified assistantships available. Financial award applicants required to submit FAFSA. *Faculty research:* Modern Chinese history, contemporary Chinese politics, ancient Chinese history, Hinduism, Asian business, Japanese history. *Unit head:* Dr. Edwin Pak-Wah Leung, Chair, 973-761-9464, Fax: 973-761-9596, E-mail: leungedw@shu.edu. *Application contact:* Dr. Shigeru Osuka, Director of Graduate Studies, 973-275-2712, Fax: 973-761-9596, E-mail: osukashi@shu.edu.

University of California, Berkeley, Graduate Division, College of Letters and Science, Department of South and Southeast Asian Studies, Berkeley, CA 94720-1500. Offers Hindi (MA, PhD); Indonesian (MA, PhD); Sanskrit (MA, PhD); Tamil (MA, PhD). *Faculty:* 6 full-time, 14 part-time/adjunct. *Students:* 31 full-time (14 women). Average age 34. 362 applicants, 16 enrolled. In 2009, 18 master's, 13 doctorates awarded. Terminal master's awarded for partial completion of doctoral program. *Degree requirements:* For master's, 2 foreign languages, thesis; for doctorate, 2 foreign languages, thesis/dissertation, oral qualifying exam. *Entrance requirements:* For master's and doctorate, GRE General Test, minimum GPA of 3.0, 3 letters of recommendation. *Application deadline:* For fall admission, 12/3 for domestic students. Application fee: $70 ($90 for international students). Electronic applications accepted. *Financial support:* Fellowships, research assistantships, teaching assistantships, unspecified assistantships available. *Unit head:* Prof. Alexander von Rospatt, Chair, 510-642-4564, E-mail: ch_sseas@ls.berkeley.edu. *Application contact:* Lee Amazonas, Student Affairs Officer, 510-642-4219, E-mail: casmauga@berkeley.edu.

University of California, Irvine, Office of Graduate Studies, School of Humanities, Department of East Asian Languages and Literatures, Irvine, CA 92697. Offers Chinese (MA, PhD); East Asian languages and literatures (MA, PhD); Japanese (MA, PhD). *Students:* 12 full-time (9 women); includes 2 minority (1 African American, 1 Asian American or Pacific Islander), 7 international. Average age 31. 50 applicants, 6% accepted, 2 enrolled. In 2009, 3 doctorates awarded. *Degree requirements:* For doctorate, thesis/dissertation. *Entrance requirements:* For master's, GRE, minimum GPA of 3.0; for doctorate, GRE General Test, minimum GPA of 3.0. Additional exam requirements/recommendations for international students: Required—TOEFL (minimum score 550 paper-based; 213 computer-based). *Application deadline:* For fall admission, 1/15 priority date for domestic students, 1/15 for international students. Application fee: $70 ($90 for international students). Electronic applications accepted. *Financial support:* Fellowships with tuition reimbursements, research assistantships with full tuition reimbursements, teaching assistantships with partial tuition reimbursements, institutionally sponsored loans, traineeships, health care benefits, and unspecified assistantships available. Financial award application deadline: 3/1; financial award applicants required to submit FAFSA. *Faculty research:* Chinese, Japanese, and Korean literature and culture; language and textual analysis; historical, social, and cultural dimensions of literary study. *Unit head:* Michael Fuller, Interim Chair, 949-824-2151. *Application contact:* Angie Agsalog, Graduate Staff Contact, 949-824-1601, Fax: 949-824-3248, E-mail: aagsalog@uci.edu.

University of California, Los Angeles, Graduate Division, College of Letters and Science, Department of Asian Languages and Cultures, Los Angeles, CA 90095. Offers MA, PhD. *Students:* 52 full-time (30 women); includes 14 minority (all Asian Americans or Pacific Islanders), 17 international. Average age 34. 49 applicants, 16% accepted, 4 enrolled. In 2009, 3 master's, 4 doctorates awarded. Terminal master's awarded for partial completion of doctoral program. *Degree requirements:* For master's, one foreign language, comprehensive exam or thesis; for doctorate, 2 foreign languages, thesis/dissertation, oral and written qualifying exams. *Entrance requirements:* For master's, GRE General Test, minimum GPA of 3.0, sample of written work; for doctorate, GRE General Test, minimum undergraduate GPA of 3.0, sample of research writing or thesis in English. Additional exam requirements/recommendations for international students: Required—TOEFL. *Application deadline:* For fall admission, 12/1 for domestic and international students. Application fee: $70 ($90 for international students). Electronic applications accepted. *Financial support:* In 2009–10, 36 fellowships with full and partial tuition reimbursements, 25 reimbursements, 22 research assistantships with full and partial tuition reimbursements were awarded; Federal teaching assistantships with full and partial tuition reimbursements, health care benefits, tuition Work-Study, institutionally sponsored loans, scholarships/grants, health care benefits, tuition waivers (full and partial), and unspecified assistantships also available. Financial award application deadline: 3/1; financial award applicants required to submit FAFSA. *Unit head:* Dr.

David Schaberg, Chair, 310-206-8235. *Application contact:* Department Office, 310-206-8235, E-mail: alcgen@humnet.ucla.edu.

University of California, Santa Barbara, Graduate Division, College of Letters and Sciences, Division of Humanities and Fine Arts, Department of East Asian Languages and Cultural Studies, Santa Barbara, CA 93106-7075. Offers Asian Studies (MA), including Asian Studies, East Asian language and cultural studies; Asian studies (MA), including Asian Studies, East Asian language and cultural studies; East Asian language and cultural studies (PhD); MA/PhD. *Students:* 13 full-time (8 women). Average age 27. 76 applicants, 28% accepted, 6 enrolled. In 2009, 2 master's awarded. *Degree requirements:* For master's, one foreign language, thesis or alternative; for doctorate, 2 foreign languages, thesis/dissertation. *Entrance requirements:* For master's and doctorate, GRE, 3 letters of recommendation, statement of purpose, personal achievements/contributions statement, resume/curriculum vitae, transcripts for post-secondary institutions attended. Additional exam requirements/recommendations for international students: Required—TOEFL (minimum score 550 paper-based; 213 computer-based; 80 iBT) or IELTS (minimum score 7). *Application deadline:* For fall admission, 4/1 for domestic and international students. Application fee: $70 ($90 for international students). Electronic applications accepted. *Financial support:* In 2009–10, 10 students received support, including 5 fellowships with full and partial tuition reimbursements available (averaging $11,000 per year), 10 teaching assistantships with partial tuition reimbursements available (averaging $8,200 per year); Federal Work-Study, institutionally sponsored loans, scholarships/grants, health care benefits, and unspecified assistantships also available. Financial award application deadline: 12/15; financial award applicants required to submit FAFSA. *Faculty research:* Chinese literature, Chinese film, Japanese society, Japanese literature, East Asian cultural studies. *Unit head:* Dr. William Powell, Chair, 805-893-4455, Fax: 805-893-3011, E-mail: bpowell@religion.ucsb.edu. *Application contact:* Dr. Ronald Egan, Faculty Graduate Advisor, 805-893-3770, Fax: 805-893-3011, E-mail: ronegan@eastasian.ucsb.edu.

University of California, Santa Barbara, Graduate Division, College of Letters and Sciences, Division of Humanities and Fine Arts, Program in Comparative Literature, Santa Barbara, CA 93106-4130. Offers comparative literature (PhD); East Asian literatures (PhD); feminist studies (PhD); MA/PhD. *Faculty:* 56 full-time (24 women). *Students:* 24 full-time (18 women). Average age 29. 43 applicants, 40% accepted, 5 enrolled. In 2009, 5 doctorates awarded. Terminal master's awarded for partial completion of doctoral program. *Degree requirements:* For doctorate, 2 foreign languages, comprehensive exam, thesis/dissertation. *Entrance requirements:* For doctorate, GRE. Additional exam requirements/recommendations for international students: Required—TOEFL (minimum score 550 paper-based; 213 computer-based; 80 iBT) or IELTS (minimum score 7). *Application deadline:* For fall admission, 12/15 for domestic and international students. Application fee: $70 ($90 for international students). Electronic applications accepted. *Financial support:* In 2009–10, 24 students received support, including 15 fellowships with full and partial tuition reimbursements available (averaging $6,900 per year), 1 research assistantship (averaging $10,600 per year), 18 teaching assistantships with partial tuition reimbursements available (averaging $10,400 per year); Federal Work-Study, institutionally sponsored loans, scholarships/grants, health care benefits, and tuition waivers (full and partial) also available. Financial award application deadline: 12/15; financial award applicants required to submit FAFSA. *Faculty research:* Media studies, literary theory, cultural studies, early modern and modern literature, critical theory. *Unit head:* Prof. Elisabeth Weber, Chair, 805-893-3527, Fax: 805-893-2374, E-mail: weber@gss.ucsb.edu. *Application contact:* Sierra Gray, Graduate Program Assistant, 805-893-2131, Fax: 805-893-2374, E-mail: sierra@gss.ucsb.edu.

University of Chicago, Division of the Humanities, Department of East Asian Languages and Civilizations, Chicago, IL 60637-1513. Offers AM, PhD. Terminal master's awarded for partial completion of doctoral program. *Degree requirements:* For master's, one foreign language, thesis; for doctorate, 2 foreign languages, thesis/dissertation. *Entrance requirements:* For master's and doctorate, GRE General Test. Additional exam requirements/recommendations for international students: Required—TOEFL.

University of Chicago, Division of the Humanities, Department of South Asian Languages and Civilizations, Chicago, IL 60637-1513. Offers South Asian languages and civilizations (AM, PhD), including Bengali (PhD), Hindi (PhD), Sanskrit (PhD), Tamil (PhD), Urdu (PhD). Terminal master's awarded for partial completion of doctoral program. *Degree requirements:* For master's, one foreign language, thesis; for doctorate, 2 foreign languages, thesis/dissertation. *Entrance requirements:* For master's and doctorate, GRE General Test. Additional exam requirements/recommendations for international students: Required—TOEFL.

University of Hawaii at Manoa, Graduate Division, College of Language, Linguistics and Literature, Department of East Asian Languages and Literatures, Program in Korean, Honolulu, HI 96822. Offers MA, PhD. Part-time programs available. *Faculty:* 4 full-time (1 woman), 2 part-time/adjunct (both women). *Students:* 33 full-time (19 women), 11 part-time (9 women); includes 22 minority (all Asian Americans or Pacific Islanders), 15 international. Average age 29. 32 applicants, 56% accepted, 14 enrolled. In 2009, 17 master's, 1 doctorate awarded. *Degree requirements:* For master's, 2 foreign languages, thesis optional; for doctorate, 2 foreign languages, comprehensive exam, thesis/dissertation. *Entrance requirements:* For master's and doctorate, GRE General Test. Additional exam requirements/recommendations for international students: Required—TOEFL (minimum score 560 paper-based; 220 computer-based; 83 iBT), IELTS (minimum score 5). *Application deadline:* For fall admission, 2/1 for domestic and international students; for spring admission, 9/1 for domestic and international students. Application fee: $60. *Expenses:* Tuition, state resident: full-time $8900; part-time $372 per credit. Tuition, nonresident: full-time $21,400; part-time $898 per credit. Required fees: $207 per semester. *Financial support:* In 2009–10, 2 students received support, including 9 fellowships (averaging $4,640 per year), 2 research assistantships (averaging $13,122 per year), 5 teaching assistantships (averaging $14,958 per year). Total annual research expenditures: $1.6 million. *Application contact:* Dina Yoshimi, Graduate Chair, 808-956-2069, Fax: 808-956-9515, E-mail: dinar@hawaii.edu.

University of Illinois at Urbana–Champaign, Graduate College, College of Liberal Arts and Sciences, School of Literatures, Cultures and Linguistics, Department of East Asian Languages and Cultures, Champaign, IL 61820. Offers Asian studies (MA); East Asian languages and cultures (PhD). *Faculty:* 16 full-time (6 women). *Students:* 37 full-time (32 women), 3 part-time (1 woman); includes 5 minority (1 American Indian/Alaska Native, 3 Asian Americans or Pacific Islanders, 1 Hispanic American), 28 international. 67 applicants, 16% accepted, 7 enrolled. In 2009, 7 master's, 1 doctorate awarded. *Entrance requirements:* For master's, GRE General Test, minimum GPA of 3.0; writing sample; for doctorate, GRE, minimum GPA of 3.0; writing sample. Additional exam requirements/recommendations for international students: Required—TOEFL (minimum score 103 iBT). *Application deadline:* Applications are processed on a rolling basis. Application fee: $60 ($75 for international students). Electronic applications accepted. *Financial support:* In 2009–10, 7 fellowships, 2 research assistantships, 26 teaching assistantships were awarded; tuition waivers (full and partial) also available. *Unit head:* Brian D. Ruppert, Head, 217-244-4012, Fax: 217-244-2223, E-mail: ruppert@illinois.edu. *Application contact:* Lynn Stanke, Office Support Specialist, 217-333-6269, Fax: 217-244-3050, E-mail: stanke@illinois.edu.

The University of Kansas, Graduate Studies, College of Liberal Arts and Sciences, Department of East Asian Languages and Cultures, Lawrence, KS 66045. Offers MA, MBA/MA. Part-time programs available. *Faculty:* 7. *Students:* 16 full-time (11 women), 4 part-time (1 woman); includes 2 minority (1 African American, 1 American Indian/Alaska Native), 7 international. Average age 29. 23 applicants, 52% accepted, 7 enrolled. In 2009, 3 master's awarded. *Degree requirements:* For master's, one foreign language, thesis. *Entrance requirements:* For master's, GRE, 3 letters of recommendation, writing sample. Additional exam requirements/recommendations for international students: Required—TOEFL. *Application deadline:* For fall admission, 5/1 priority date for domestic students, 5/1 for international students; for spring admission, 12/1 priority date for domestic students, 12/1 for international students. Applications are processed on a rolling basis. Application fee: $45 ($55 for international students). Electronic applications accepted. *Expenses:* Tuition, state resident: full-time $6492; part-time $270.50 per credit hour. Tuition, nonresident: full-time $15,510; part-time $646.25 per credit hour. Required fees: $847; $70.56 per credit hour. Tuition and fees vary according to course load and program. *Financial support:* Fellowships, teaching assistantships with full and partial tuition reimbursements, unspecified assistantships available. Financial award application deadline: 2/1. *Faculty research:* Gender relations in literature, ancient Chinese law, visual culture of modern Japan, Japanese language pedagogy, Chinese paleography, Korean shamanism, folklore, traditional Chinese and Japanese literature, Chinese linguistics and language pedagogy. *Unit head:* Margaret Childs, Chair and Graduate Director, 785-864-3100, E-mail: mgchilds@ku.edu. *Application contact:* Georgia Damis, Administrative Specialist, 785-864-3100, Fax: 785-864-4298, E-mail: ealc@ku.edu.

University of Michigan, Horace H. Rackham School of Graduate Studies, College of Literature, Science, and the Arts, Department of Asian Languages and Cultures, Ann Arbor, MI 48104. Offers MA, PhD. Students cannot apply directly to a terminal masters degree in this program. Masters are only awarded to PhD program students for partial completion of the degree. *Faculty:* 20 full-time (8 women). *Students:* 26 full-time (11 women); includes 4 minority (3 Asian Americans or Pacific Islanders, 1 Hispanic American). Average age 32. 58 applicants, 9% accepted, 2 enrolled. In 2009, 2 master's, 3 doctorates awarded. Terminal master's awarded for partial completion of doctoral program. *Degree requirements:* For master's, variable foreign language requirement, thesis; for doctorate, 2 foreign languages, thesis/dissertation, oral defense of dissertation, preliminary exam. *Entrance requirements:* For master's and doctorate, GRE General Test. Additional exam requirements/recommendations for international students: Required—TOEFL (minimum score 600 paper-based; 250 computer-based; 106 iBT). *Application deadline:* For fall admission, 12/15 for domestic and international students. Application fee: $75. Electronic applications accepted. *Expenses:* Tuition, state resident: full-time $17,286; part-time $1099 per credit hour. Tuition, nonresident: full-time $34,944; part-time $2080 per credit hour. Required fees: $95 per semester. Tuition and fees vary according to course load, degree level and program. *Financial support:* In 2009–10, 20 students received support, including 10 fellowships with full tuition reimbursements available (averaging $16,500 per year), 1 research assistantship with full tuition reimbursement available (averaging $16,500 per year), 9 teaching assistantships with full tuition reimbursements available (averaging $16,500 per year); Federal Work-Study and health care benefits also available. Support available to part-time students. Financial award application deadline: 12/15; financial award applicants required to submit FAFSA. *Faculty research:* Literature, linguistics, religion, music, cinema. *Unit head:* Prof. Donald Lopez, Chair, 734-764-8286, Fax: 734-647-0157, E-mail: alcgradinfo@umich.edu. *Application contact:* Nicole Baker, Graduate Program Coordinator, 734-936-3915, Fax: 734-647-0157, E-mail: nicolmba@umich.edu.

University of Minnesota, Twin Cities Campus, Graduate School, College of Liberal Arts, Department of Asian Languages and Literatures, Minneapolis, MN 55455-0213. Offers Asian literatures, cultures, and media (PhD). *Degree requirements:* For doctorate, comprehensive exam, thesis/dissertation. *Entrance requirements:* For doctorate, GRE, 3 letters of recommendation. Additional exam requirements/recommendations for international students: Required—TOEFL (minimum score 550 paper-based; 213 computer-based), IELTS (minimum score 6.5). Electronic applications accepted. *Faculty research:* Gender studies, post-colonial theory, poetics and poetic theory, film studies, post modernist thought.

University of Oregon, Graduate School, College of Arts and Sciences, Department of East Asian Languages and Literature, Eugene, OR 97403. Offers Chinese (MA, PhD); Japanese (MA, PhD). *Entrance requirements:* Additional exam requirements/recommendations for international students: Required—TOEFL. *Faculty research:* Linguistics, pedagogy.

University of Southern California, Graduate School, College of Letters, Arts and Sciences, Department of East Asian Languages and Cultures, Los Angeles, CA 90089. Offers classical Chinese literature (MA, PhD); classical Japanese literature (MA, PhD); linguistics (MA, PhD); modern Chinese literature (MA, PhD); modern Japanese literature (MA, PhD); modern Korean literature (MA, PhD). *Faculty:* 15 full-time (8 women). *Students:* 22 full-time (14 women); includes 6 minority (1 African American, 5 Asian Americans or Pacific Islanders), 10 international. 53 applicants, 21% accepted, 7 enrolled. In 2009, 5 master's, 1 doctorate awarded. *Degree requirements:* For master's, one foreign language, thesis; for doctorate, 2 foreign languages, comprehensive exam, thesis/dissertation. *Entrance requirements:* For master's and doctorate, GRE, BA in relevant field. Additional exam requirements/recommendations for international students: Required—TOEFL. *Application deadline:* For fall admission, 12/1 priority date for domestic and international students. Application fee: $85. Electronic applications accepted. *Expenses:* Tuition: Full-time $25,980; part-time $1315 per unit. Required fees: $554. One-time fee: $35 full-time. Full-time tuition and fees vary according to degree level and program. *Financial support:* In 2009–10, 18 students received support, including 4 fellowships with full tuition reimbursements available (averaging $23,650 per year), 10 teaching assistantships with partial tuition reimbursements available (averaging $18,800 per year); scholarships/grants, health care benefits, and unspecified assistantships also available. Financial award application deadline: 12/1. *Faculty research:* East Asian (Chinese, Japanese and Korean) language, literature, and culture; visual cultures and media studies with focus in East Asian visual arts; films; pre-modern Japanese, Korean and Chinese literature and cultures; modern and contemporary Chinese, Korean and Japanese literature. *Unit head:* Dominic Cheung, Chair, 213-740-3707, Fax: 213-740-9295, E-mail: dcheung@usc.edu. *Application contact:* Sherall R. Preyer, Administrative Coordinator, 213-740-3709, Fax: 213-740-9295, E-mail: preyer@college.usc.edu.

University of Southern California, Graduate School, College of Letters, Arts and Sciences, Department of Linguistics, Los Angeles, CA 90089. Offers East Asian linguistics (PhD); Hispanic linguistics (MA, PhD); linguistics (MA, PhD). *Faculty:* 21 full-time (12 women), 3 part-time/adjunct (2 women). *Students:* 46 full-time (30 women), 1 part-time (0 women); includes 6 minority (4 Asian Americans or Pacific Islanders, 2 Hispanic Americans), 24 international. 51 applicants, 35% accepted, 7 enrolled. In 2009, 11 master's, 1 doctorate awarded. *Degree requirements:* For doctorate, comprehensive exam, thesis/dissertation. *Entrance requirements:* For doctorate, GRE. Additional exam requirements/recommendations for international students: Required—TOEFL (minimum score 100 iBT). *Application deadline:* For fall admission, 12/1 priority date for domestic and international students. Application fee: $85. Electronic applications accepted. *Expenses:* Tuition: Full-time $25,980; part-time $1315 per unit. Required fees: $554. One-time fee: $35 full-time. Full-time tuition and fees vary according to degree level and program. *Financial support:* In 2009–10, 40 students received support, including 14 fellowships with full tuition reimbursements available (averaging $19,000 per year), 2 research assistantships with full tuition reimbursements available (averaging $19,000 per year), 24 teaching assistantships with full tuition reimbursements available (averaging $19,000 per year); scholarships/grants, health care benefits, and unspecified assistantships also available. *Faculty research:* Syntax, phonology, phonetics, semantics, sociolinguistics, psycholinguistics. *Unit head:* Dr. James Higginbotham, Chair, 213-740-4150, Fax: 213-740-9306, E-mail: higgy@usc.edu. *Application contact:* Dr. Joyce Perez, Student Services Advisor, 213-740-3891, Fax: 213-740-9306, E-mail: jpperez@usc.edu.

The University of Texas at Austin, Graduate School, College of Liberal Arts, Department of Asian Studies, Austin, TX 78712-1111. Offers Asian cultures and languages (MA, PhD); Asian studies (MA). Part-time programs available. *Degree requirements:* For master's, thesis; for doctorate, 3 foreign languages, thesis/dissertation. *Entrance requirements:* For master's and doctorate, GRE General Test. Electronic applications accepted. *Faculty research:* Modern Taiwanese fiction, modern Japanese literature, religious studies in South Asia during classical period.

University of Washington, Graduate School, College of Arts and Sciences, Department of Asian Languages and Literature, Seattle, WA 98195. Offers Buddhist studies (MA, PhD); Chinese language and literature (MA, PhD); Japanese language and literature (MA, PhD); Korean language and literature (MA, PhD); South Asian language and literature (MA, PhD).

Asian Languages

University of Washington (continued)
Degree requirements: For master's, 2 foreign languages, general exam, thesis or 2 research papers; for doctorate, 3 foreign languages, thesis/dissertation, general exam. *Entrance requirements:* For master's, GRE, minimum GPA of 3.0; for doctorate, GRE, master's degree in related field, minimum GPA of 3.0. Additional exam requirements/recommendations for international students: Required—TOEFL. Electronic applications accepted. *Faculty research:* Textual, linguistic, philological, and literary study of languages and literatures of Asia.

University of Wisconsin–Madison, Graduate School, College of Letters and Science, Department of Languages and Cultures of Asia, Madison, WI 53706-1380. Offers civilizations and cultures (PhD); languages and cultures of Asia (MA); languages and literatures (PhD); religions of Asia (PhD). Part-time programs available. Terminal master's awarded for partial completion of doctoral program. *Degree requirements:* For master's, one foreign language, thesis or alternative; for doctorate, 2 foreign languages, thesis/dissertation. *Entrance requirements:* For master's, minimum GPA of 3.0; for doctorate, minimum GPA of 3.25, master's degree. Electronic applications accepted. *Expenses:* Tuition, state resident: part-time $594 per credit. Tuition, nonresident: part-time $1504 per credit. Required fees: $65 per credit. Tuition and fees vary according to course load, program and reciprocity agreements. *Faculty research:* Literature, folklore, religion.

Washington University in St. Louis, Graduate School of Arts and Sciences, Department of Asian and Near Eastern Languages and Literatures, St. Louis, MO 63130-4899. Offers Chinese (MA); Chinese and comparative literature (PhD); Japanese (MA); Japanese and comparative literature (PhD). Terminal master's awarded for partial completion of doctoral program. *Degree requirements:* For master's, thesis optional; for doctorate, thesis/dissertation. *Entrance requirements:* For master's and doctorate, GRE General Test. Electronic applications accepted.

Washington University in St. Louis, Graduate School of Arts and Sciences, Program in East Asian Studies, St. Louis, MO 63130-4899. Offers East Asian studies (MA); JD/MA. PhD offered through specific departments. *Entrance requirements:* For master's, GRE General Test. Electronic applications accepted.

Yale University, Graduate School of Arts and Sciences, Department of East Asian Languages and Literatures, New Haven, CT 06520. Offers East Asian languages and literatures (PhD); East Asian languages and literatures and film studies (PhD). *Degree requirements:* For doctorate, 2 foreign languages, thesis/dissertation. *Entrance requirements:* For doctorate, GRE General Test.

Celtic Languages

Harvard University, Graduate School of Arts and Sciences, Department of Celtic Languages and Literatures, Cambridge, MA 02138. Offers Irish (PhD); Welsh (PhD). *Degree requirements:* For doctorate, thesis/dissertation, proficiency in 2 Celtic languages; reading knowledge of French, German, and Latin. *Entrance requirements:* For doctorate, GRE General Test. Additional exam requirements/recommendations for international students: Required—TOEFL. *Expenses:* Tuition: Full-time $33,696. Required fees: $1126. Full-time tuition and fees vary according to program.

Chinese

Arizona State University, Graduate College, College of Liberal Arts and Sciences, Division of Humanities, School of International Letters and Cultures, Program in Chinese, Tempe, AZ 85287. Offers MA.

Cornell University, Graduate School, Graduate Fields of Arts and Sciences, Field of East Asian Literature, Ithaca, NY 14853-0001. Offers Asian religions (MA, PhD); Chinese linguistics (MA, PhD); Chinese philology (MA, PhD); classical Chinese literature (MA, PhD); classical Japanese literature (MA, PhD); Japanese linguistics (MA, PhD); Korean literature (MA, PhD); modern Chinese literature (MA, PhD); modern Japanese literature (MA, PhD). *Faculty:* 17 full-time (7 women). *Students:* 16 full-time (7 women); includes 4 minority (all Asian Americans or Pacific Islanders), 8 international. Average age 32. 49 applicants, 6% accepted, 2 enrolled. In 2009, 3 doctorates awarded. *Degree requirements:* For master's, 2 foreign languages, thesis, teaching experience; for doctorate, 2 foreign languages, comprehensive exam, thesis/dissertation, teaching experience. *Entrance requirements:* For master's, GRE General Test, 3 years of study in Chinese, Japanese, Korean, or Vietnamese; 3 letters of recommendation; academic writing sample; for doctorate, GRE General Test, 3 years of study in Chinese, Japanese, Korean, or Vietnamese, 3 letters of recommendation, academic writing sample. Additional exam requirements/recommendations for international students: Required—TOEFL (minimum score 600 paper-based; 250 computer-based; 77 iBT). *Application deadline:* For fall admission, 1/10 priority date for domestic students. Application fee: $70. Electronic applications accepted. *Expenses:* Tuition: Full-time $29,500. Required fees: $70. Full-time tuition and fees vary according to degree level, program and student level. *Financial support:* In 2009–10, 2 fellowships with full tuition reimbursements were awarded; research assistantships with full tuition reimbursements, teaching assistantships with full tuition reimbursements, institutionally sponsored loans, scholarships/grants, health care benefits, tuition waivers (full and partial), and unspecified assistantships also available. Financial award applicants required to submit FAFSA. *Faculty research:* Vietnamese literature; Chinese literature, drama, and film; Japanese theater and literature; popular culture in East Asia; Korean literature; Asian linguistics. *Unit head:* Director of Graduate Studies, 607-255-9099. *Application contact:* Graduate Field Assistant, 607-255-9099, E-mail: east_asian_lit@cornell.edu.

Harvard University, Graduate School of Arts and Sciences, Department of East Asian Languages and Civilizations, Cambridge, MA 02138. Offers Chinese (PhD); Japanese (PhD); Korean (PhD); Mongolian (PhD); Vietnamese (PhD). Terminal master's awarded for partial completion of doctoral program. *Degree requirements:* For doctorate, 3 foreign languages, thesis/dissertation, general exams. *Entrance requirements:* For doctorate, GRE General Test. Additional exam requirements/recommendations for international students: Required—TOEFL. *Expenses:* Tuition: Full-time $33,696. Required fees: $1126. Full-time tuition and fees vary according to program. *Faculty research:* Central Asian literature, religion, and premodern history.

Indiana University Bloomington, University Graduate School, College of Arts and Sciences, Department of East Asian Languages and Cultures, Bloomington, IN 47405-7000. Offers Chinese (MA, PhD); East Asian languages and cultures (PhD); East Asian studies (MA); Japanese (MA, PhD); language pedagogy (MA). Part-time programs available. *Faculty:* 7 full-time (2 women). *Students:* 21 full-time (12 women), 11 part-time (8 women); includes 1 minority (Asian American or Pacific Islander), 11 international. Average age 30. 85 applicants, 38% accepted, 12 enrolled. In 2009, 6 master's, 1 doctorate awarded. *Degree requirements:* For master's, 2 foreign languages, thesis; for doctorate, 2 foreign languages, thesis/dissertation. *Entrance requirements:* Additional exam requirements/recommendations for international students: Required—TOEFL. *Application deadline:* For fall admission, 1/15 for domestic students, 12/15 for international students; for spring admission, 9/1 for domestic and international students. Applications are processed on a rolling basis. Application fee: $55 ($65 for international students). Electronic applications accepted. *Financial support:* In 2009–10, 6 fellowships with full tuition reimbursements (averaging $15,500 per year), 11 teaching assistantships with full tuition reimbursements (averaging $13,000 per year) were awarded; Federal Work-Study and tuition waivers (full) also available. Financial award application deadline: 3/1. *Faculty research:* Postwar/postmodern Japanese fiction, modern Chinese film and literature, classical Chinese literature and philosophy, Chinese and Japanese linguistics and pedagogy, East Asian politics. *Unit head:* Robert Eno, Chair, 812-855-0856, E-mail: eno@indiana.edu. *Application contact:* Edith Sarra, Director of Graduate Studies, 812-855-4031, Fax: 812-855-6402, E-mail: eserra@indiana.edu.

Middlebury College, Language Schools, Chinese School, Middlebury, VT 05753-6002. Offers MA. *Faculty:* 5 full-time (2 women). *Students:* 29 full-time (25 women); includes 20 minority (all Asian Americans or Pacific Islanders). Average age 34. 41 applicants, 85% accepted, 29 enrolled. In 2009, 2 master's awarded. *Degree requirements:* For master's, one foreign language, teaching practicum. *Entrance requirements:* For master's, 3 letters of recommendation, writing sample, curriculum vitae. Additional exam requirements/recommendations for international students: Required—TOEFL (minimum score 600 paper-based; 250 computer-based; 100 iBT) for Monterey option. *Application deadline:* Applications are processed on a rolling basis. Application fee: $65. Electronic applications accepted. *Financial support:* In 2009–10, 2 fellowships with full tuition reimbursements (averaging $7,000 per year) were awarded; scholarships/grants also available. Financial award applicants required to submit FAFSA. *Unit head:* Dr. Jianhua Bai, Director, 802-443-5520, Fax: 802-443-2075, E-mail: jbai@middlebury.edu. *Application contact:* Anna Sun, Coordinator, 802-443-5520, Fax: 802-443-2075, E-mail: sun@middlebury.edu.

The Ohio State University, Graduate School, College of Humanities, Department of East Asian Languages and Literatures, Columbus, OH 43210. Offers Chinese (MA, PhD); Japanese (MA, PhD). *Faculty:* 22. *Students:* 56 full-time (29 women), 11 part-time (5 women); includes 7 minority (6 Asian Americans or Pacific Islanders, 1 Hispanic American), 25 international. Average age 28. In 2009, 24 master's, 5 doctorates awarded. *Degree requirements:* For master's, thesis optional; for doctorate, thesis/dissertation. *Entrance requirements:* For master's and doctorate, GRE (if applying for financial aid). Additional exam requirements/recommendations for international students: Required—TOEFL (minimum score 577 paper-based; 233 computer-based). *Application deadline:* For fall admission, 8/15 priority date for domestic students, 7/1 priority date for international students; for winter admission, 12/1 priority date for domestic students, 11/1 priority date for international students; for spring admission, 3/1 priority date for domestic students, 2/1 priority date for international students. Applications are processed on a rolling basis. Application fee: $40 ($50 for international students). Electronic applications accepted. *Expenses:* Tuition, state resident: full-time $10,683. Tuition, nonresident: full-time $25,923. Tuition and fees vary according to course load and program. *Financial support:* Fellowships, research assistantships, teaching assistantships, Federal Work-Study, institutionally sponsored loans, and unspecified assistantships available. Support available to part-time students. *Unit head:* Mineharu Nakayama, Graduate Studies Committee Chair, 614-292-5816, Fax: 614-292-3225, E-mail: nakayama.1@osu.edu. *Application contact:* Graduate Admissions, 614-292-9444, Fax: 614-292-3895, E-mail: domestic.grad@osu.edu.

San Francisco State University, Division of Graduate Studies, College of Humanities, Department of Foreign Languages and Literatures, Program in Chinese, San Francisco, CA 94132-1722. Offers MA.

Seton Hall University, College of Arts and Sciences, Department of Asian Studies, South Orange, NJ 07079-2697. Offers Asian languages (MA); Asian studies (MA); teaching Chinese language and culture (MA). Part-time and evening/weekend programs available. *Faculty:* 5 full-time (2 women), 3 part-time/adjunct (2 women). *Students:* 21 full-time (9 women), 7 part-time (6 women). Average age 30. 26 applicants, 92% accepted, 10 enrolled. In 2009, 14 master's awarded. *Degree requirements:* For master's, thesis optional. *Entrance requirements:* For master's, strong background in Asian studies or related discipline. Additional exam requirements/recommendations for international students: Required—TOEFL. *Application deadline:* For fall admission, 7/1 priority date for domestic and international students; for spring admission, 11/1 priority date for domestic and international students. Applications are processed on a rolling basis. Application fee: $50. Electronic applications accepted. *Financial support:* Teaching assistantships with full tuition reimbursements, career-related internships or fieldwork, Federal Work-Study, institutionally sponsored loans, and unspecified assistantships available. Financial award applicants required to submit FAFSA. *Faculty research:* Modern Chinese history, contemporary Chinese politics, ancient Chinese history, Hinduism, Asian business, Japanese history. *Unit head:* Dr. Edwin Pak-Wah Leung, Chair, 973-761-9464, Fax: 973-761-9596, E-mail: leungedw@shu.edu. *Application contact:* Dr. Shigeru Osuka, Director of Graduate Studies, 973-275-2712, Fax: 973-761-9596, E-mail: osukashi@shu.edu.

Stanford University, School of Humanities and Sciences, Department of Asian Languages, Stanford, CA 94305-9991. Offers Chinese (MA, PhD); Japanese (MA, PhD). Terminal master's awarded for partial completion of doctoral program. *Degree requirements:* For master's, one foreign language, thesis or an annotated translation of a literary or historical text; for doctorate, 2 foreign languages, thesis/dissertation, field exams. *Entrance requirements:* For master's and doctorate, GRE General Test. Additional exam requirements/recommendations for international students: Required—TOEFL. Electronic applications accepted. *Expenses:* Tuition: Full-time $37,380; part-time $2760 per quarter. Required fees: $501.

Union Graduate College, School of Education, Schenectady, NY 12308-3107. Offers biology (MAT, MS); chemistry (MAT); Chinese (MAT); earth science (MAT); English (MAT); French (MAT); general science (MAT); German (MAT); Greek (MAT); languages (MAT); Latin (MAT); mathematics (MAT); mathematics and technology (MS); mentoring and teacher leadership

(AC); middle childhood extension (AC); national board certificate and teacher leadership (AC); physical science (MS); physics (MAT); social studies (MAT); Spanish (MAT). *Accreditation:* Teacher Education Accreditation Council. *Faculty:* 3 full-time (1 woman), 39 part-time/adjunct (19 women). *Students:* 46 full-time (27 women), 45 part-time (39 women); includes 5 minority (1 Asian American or Pacific Islander, 4 Hispanic Americans), 2 international. Average age 33. 66 applicants, 73% accepted, 39 enrolled. In 2009, 44 master's awarded. *Degree requirements:* For master's, thesis or project. *Entrance requirements:* For master's, minimum GPA of 3.0, letters of recommendation. Additional exam requirements/recommendations for international students: Required—TOEFL (minimum score 550 paper-based; 213 computer-based). *Application deadline:* Applications are processed on a rolling basis. Application fee: $60. Electronic applications accepted. *Expenses:* Contact institution. *Financial support:* In 2009–10, 12 research assistantships with tuition reimbursements (averaging $3,000 per year) were awarded; Federal Work-Study, scholarships/grants, health care benefits, and tuition waivers (partial) also available. Support available to part-time students. Financial award applicants required to submit FAFSA. *Faculty research:* Transformative learning, science education, National Board Certification, teacher leadership, teacher quality. *Unit head:* Dr. Patrick Allen, Dean, 518-631-9870, Fax: 518-631-9901. *Application contact:* Christine Angley, Assistant, 518-631-9871, Fax: 518-631-9903, E-mail: angleyc@uniongraduatecollege.edu.

University of Alberta, Faculty of Graduate Studies and Research, Department of East Asian Studies, Edmonton, AB T6G 2E1, Canada. Offers Chinese literature (MA); East Asian interdisciplinary studies (MA); Japanese literature (MA). Part-time programs available. *Faculty:* 7 full-time (4 women). *Students:* 4 full-time. Average age 23. 8 applicants, 50% accepted, 4 enrolled. In 2009, 3 master's awarded. *Degree requirements:* For master's, one foreign language, thesis. *Entrance requirements:* Additional exam requirements/recommendations for international students: Required—TOEFL. *Application deadline:* Applications are processed on a rolling basis. Application fee: $0. Electronic applications accepted. Tuition and fees charges are reported in Canadian dollars. *Expenses:* Tuition, area resident: Full-time $4626 Canadian dollars; part-time $99.72 Canadian dollars per unit. International tuition: $8216 Canadian dollars full-time. Required fees: $3590 Canadian dollars; $99.72 Canadian dollars per unit. $215 Canadian dollars per term. *Financial support:* In 2009–10, 4 students received support, including 3 teaching assistantships with tuition reimbursements available (averaging $10,500 per year); scholarships/grants also available. Financial award application deadline: 12/1. *Faculty research:* Classical Chinese poetry and poetics, Chinese philosophy, modern/contemporary Chinese literature, modern Japanese literature and culture, Japanese women's writing. Total annual research expenditures: $15,000. *Unit head:* Dr. Janice Brown, Chair, 780-492-3038, Fax: 780-492-7440, E-mail: janice.brown@gpu.srv.ualberta.ca. *Application contact:* Heather McDonald, Administrative Assistant, 780-492-2836, Fax: 780-492-7440, E-mail: eastasia.grad@ualberta.ca.

University of California, Berkeley, Graduate Division, College of Letters and Science, Department of East Asian Languages and Cultures, Berkeley, CA 94720-1500. Offers Chinese language (PhD); Japanese language (PhD). *Students:* 21 full-time (13 women). Average age 31. 55 applicants, 4 enrolled. In 2009, 4 doctorates awarded. *Degree requirements:* For doctorate, one foreign language, thesis/dissertation, oral qualifying exam. *Entrance requirements:* For doctorate, GRE General Test, minimum GPA of 3.0, MA thesis, 3 letters of recommendation. *Application deadline:* For fall admission, 12/8 for domestic students. Application fee: $70 ($90 for international students). Electronic applications accepted. *Financial support:* Fellowships, research assistantships, teaching assistantships, Federal Work-Study, institutionally sponsored loans, and unspecified assistantships available. Financial award applicants required to submit FAFSA. *Faculty research:* Chinese and Japanese modern and classical texts, prose, and poetry; Chinese and Japanese linguistics. *Unit head:* Prof. Alan Tansman, Chair, 510-642-3480, Fax: 510-642-6031, E-mail: ch_ealc@ls.berkeley.edu. *Application contact:* Information Contact, 510-642-3480, E-mail: ealang@berkeley.edu.

University of California, Irvine, Office of Graduate Studies, School of Humanities, Department of East Asian Languages and Literatures, Irvine, CA 92697. Offers Chinese (MA, PhD); East Asian languages and literatures (MA, PhD); Japanese (MA, PhD). *Students:* 12 full-time (9 women); includes 2 minority (1 African American, 1 Asian American or Pacific Islander), 7 international. Average age 31. 50 applicants, 6% accepted, 2 enrolled. In 2009, 3 doctorates awarded. *Degree requirements:* For doctorate, thesis/dissertation. *Entrance requirements:* For master's, GRE, minimum GPA of 3.0; for doctorate, GRE General Test, minimum GPA of 3.0. Additional exam requirements/recommendations for international students: Required—TOEFL (minimum score 550 paper-based; 213 computer-based). *Application deadline:* For fall admission, 1/15 priority date for domestic students, 1/15 for international students. Application fee: $70 ($90 for international students). Electronic applications accepted. *Financial support:* Fellowships with tuition reimbursements, research assistantships with full tuition reimbursements, teaching assistantships with partial tuition reimbursements, institutionally sponsored loans, traineeships, health care benefits, and unspecified assistantships available. Financial award application deadline: 3/1; financial award applicants required to submit FAFSA. *Faculty research:* Chinese, Japanese, and Korean literature and culture; language and textual analysis; historical, social, and cultural dimensions of literary study. *Unit head:* Michael Fuller, Interim Chair, 949-824-2151. *Application contact:* Angie Agsalog, Graduate Staff Contact, 949-824-1601, Fax: 949-824-3248, E-mail: aagsalog@uci.edu.

University of Colorado at Boulder, Graduate School, College of Arts and Sciences, Department of Asian Languages and Civilizations, Boulder, CO 80309. Offers Chinese (MA, PhD); Japanese (MA, PhD). Part-time programs available. *Faculty:* 10 full-time (6 women). *Students:* 30 full-time (19 women), 4 part-time (3 women); includes 9 minority (1 American Indian/Alaska Native, 6 Asian Americans or Pacific Islanders, 2 Hispanic Americans), 7 international. Average age 27. 30 applicants, 30% accepted, 9 enrolled. In 2009, 16 master's awarded. *Degree requirements:* For master's, comprehensive exam. *Entrance requirements:* For master's, BA in Chinese or Japanese, minimum undergraduate GPA of 3.0. Additional exam requirements/recommendations for international students: Required—TOEFL. *Application deadline:* For fall admission, 1/1 priority date for domestic students, 12/1 for international students; for spring admission, 10/1 for domestic students, 9/1 for international students. Applications are processed on a rolling basis. Application fee: $50 ($60 for international students). *Financial support:* In 2009–10, 7 fellowships (averaging $13,865 per year), 10 research assistantships (averaging $6,596 per year) were awarded; career-related internships or fieldwork and Federal Work-Study also available. Financial award application deadline: 2/1. *Faculty research:* Chinese and Japanese modern and classical literature, religions, linguistics, language pedagogy, pre-modern and contemporary fiction, sociolinguistics. Total annual research expenditures: $819,946.

University of Hawaii at Manoa, Graduate Division, College of Language, Linguistics and Literature, Department of East Asian Languages and Literatures, Program in Chinese, Honolulu, HI 96822. Offers MA, PhD. Part-time programs available. *Faculty:* 7 full-time (1 woman), 3 part-time/adjunct (1 woman). *Students:* 19 full-time (17 women), 2 part-time (1 woman); includes 3 minority (all Asian Americans or Pacific Islanders), 16 international. Average age 30. 31 applicants, 65% accepted, 7 enrolled. In 2009, 4 master's, 4 doctorates awarded. *Degree requirements:* For master's, 2 foreign languages, thesis optional; for doctorate, 2 foreign languages, comprehensive exam, thesis/dissertation. *Entrance requirements:* For master's and doctorate, GRE General Test. Additional exam requirements/recommendations for international students: Required—TOEFL (minimum score 560 paper-based; 220 computer-based; 83 iBT), IELTS (minimum score 5). *Application deadline:* For fall admission, 2/1 for domestic and international students; for spring admission, 9/1 for domestic and international students. Application fee: $50. *Expenses:* Tuition, state resident: full-time $8900; part-time $372 per credit. Tuition, nonresident: full-time $21,400; part-time $898 per credit. Required fees: $207 per semester. *Financial support:* In 2009–10, 3 fellowships (averaging $3,559 per year), 3 teaching assistantships (averaging $14,958 per year) were awarded. *Application contact:* Dina Yoshimi, Graduate Chair, 808-956-2069, Fax: 808-956-9515, E-mail: dinar@hawaii.edu.

University of Hawaii at Manoa, Graduate Division, School of Pacific and Asian Studies, Program in Asian Studies, Concentration in Chinese Studies, Honolulu, HI 96822. Offers Graduate Certificate. Part-time programs available. In 2009, 3 Graduate Certificates awarded. *Degree requirements:* For Graduate Certificate, one foreign language. *Entrance requirements:* For degree, GRE. Additional exam requirements/recommendations for international students: Required—TOEFL (minimum score 560 paper-based; 220 computer-based; 83 iBT), IELTS (minimum score 5). Application fee: $60. *Expenses:* Tuition, state resident: full-time $8900; part-time $372 per credit. Tuition, nonresident: full-time $21,400; part-time $898 per credit. Required fees: $207 per semester. Total annual research expenditures: $187,500. *Application contact:* Dr. Ricardo D. Trimillos, Graduate Field Chairperson, 808-956-0827, Fax: 808-956-2682, E-mail: rtrimil@hawaii.edu.

University of Massachusetts Amherst, Graduate School, College of Humanities and Fine Arts, Department of Languages, Literatures, and Cultures, Programs in Asian Languages and Literatures, Amherst, MA 01003. Offers Chinese (MA); Japanese (MA). Part-time programs available. *Faculty:* 8 full-time (4 women). *Students:* 17 full-time (14 women), 13 part-time (8 women); includes 7 minority (1 African American, 6 Asian Americans or Pacific Islanders), 12 international. Average age 29. 27 applicants, 74% accepted, 8 enrolled. In 2009, 9 master's awarded. *Degree requirements:* For master's, thesis, general exam. *Entrance requirements:* For master's, GRE General Test, minimum GPA of 3.0. Additional exam requirements/recommendations for international students: Required—TOEFL (minimum score 550 paper-based; 213 computer-based; 80 iBT), IELTS (minimum score 6.5). *Application deadline:* For fall admission, 2/1 for domestic and international students. Applications are processed on a rolling basis. Application fee: $50 ($65 for international students). Electronic applications accepted. *Expenses:* Tuition, state resident: full-time $2640; part-time $110 per credit. Tuition, nonresident: full-time $9936; part-time $414 per credit. Tuition and fees vary according to course load. *Financial support:* In 2009–10, 21 teaching assistantships with full tuition reimbursements (averaging $7,431 per year) were awarded; fellowships, research assistantships, career-related internships or fieldwork, Federal Work-Study, scholarships/grants, traineeships, health care benefits, tuition waivers (full), and unspecified assistantships also available. Support available to part-time students. Financial award application deadline: 2/1. *Unit head:* Dr. Amanda C. Seaman, Director, 413-545-0886, Fax: 413-545-4975. *Application contact:* Jean M. Ames, Supervisor of Admissions, 413-545-0722, Fax: 413-577-0100, E-mail: gradadm@grad.umass.edu.

University of Oregon, Graduate School, College of Arts and Sciences, Department of East Asian Languages and Literature, Eugene, OR 97403. Offers Chinese (MA, PhD); Japanese (MA, PhD). *Entrance requirements:* Additional exam requirements/recommendations for international students: Required—TOEFL. *Faculty research:* Linguistics, pedagogy.

University of Washington, Graduate School, College of Arts and Sciences, Department of Asian Languages and Literature, Seattle, WA 98195. Offers Buddhist studies (MA, PhD); Chinese language and literature (MA, PhD); Japanese language and literature (MA, PhD); Korean language and literature (MA, PhD); South Asian language and literature (MA, PhD). *Degree requirements:* For master's, 2 foreign languages, general exam, thesis or 2 research papers; for doctorate, 3 foreign languages, thesis/dissertation, general exam. *Entrance requirements:* For master's, GRE, minimum GPA of 3.0; for doctorate, GRE, master's degree in related field, minimum GPA of 3.0. Additional exam requirements/recommendations for international students: Required—TOEFL. Electronic applications accepted. *Faculty research:* Textual, linguistic, philological, and literary study of languages and literatures of Asia.

University of Wisconsin–Madison, Graduate School, College of Letters and Science, Department of East Asian Languages and Literature, Program in Chinese Literature, Madison, WI 53706-1380. Offers MA, PhD. Part-time programs available. Terminal master's awarded for partial completion of doctoral program. *Degree requirements:* For master's, one foreign language, seminars, written exam; for doctorate, 3 foreign languages, thesis/dissertation, seminars, preliminary exams, oral exam. *Entrance requirements:* For master's, bachelor's degree or equivalent in Chinese; for doctorate, master's degree or equivalent in Chinese. Electronic applications accepted. *Expenses:* Tuition, state resident: part-time $594 per credit. Tuition, nonresident: part-time $1504 per credit. Required fees: $65 per credit. Tuition and fees vary according to course load, program and reciprocity agreements. *Faculty research:* Chinese historical and modern linguistics, classical Chinese literary and cultural history, modern Chinese literary and cultural history, Chinese paleography.

Washington University in St. Louis, Graduate School of Arts and Sciences, Department of Asian and Near Eastern Languages and Literatures, St. Louis, MO 63130-4899. Offers Chinese (MA); Chinese and comparative literature (PhD); Japanese (MA); Japanese and comparative literature (PhD). Terminal master's awarded for partial completion of doctoral program. *Degree requirements:* For master's, thesis optional; for doctorate, thesis/dissertation. *Entrance requirements:* For master's and doctorate, GRE General Test. Electronic applications accepted.

Classics

Asbury University, School of Graduate and Professional Studies, Wilmore, KY 40390-1198. Offers biology: alternative certificate (MA Ed); chemistry: alternative certificate (MA Ed); English (MA Ed); English as a second language (MA Ed); ESL (MA Ed); French (MA Ed); Latin: alternative certificate (MA Ed); mathematics: alternative certificate (MA Ed); reading/writing endorsement (MA Ed); social studies (MA Ed); social work (MSW), including child and family services; Spanish (MA Ed); special education (MA Ed); special education: alternative certificate (MA Ed); teacher as leader endorsement (MA Ed). *Accreditation:* NCATE. Part-time programs available. *Faculty:* 8 full-time (7 women), 9 part-time/adjunct (4 women). *Students:* 108 part-time (87 women); includes 8 minority (4 African Americans, 2 Asian Americans or Pacific Islanders, 2 Hispanic Americans). Average age 36. 36 applicants, 86% accepted, 24 enrolled. In 2009, 20 master's awarded. *Degree requirements:* For master's, action research project, portfolio. *Entrance requirements:* For master's, PRAXIS/NTE, minimum GPA of 2.75, letters of recommendation. Additional exam requirements/recommendations for international students: Required—TOEFL (minimum score 550 paper-based). *Application deadline:* Applications are processed on a rolling basis. Application fee: $25. Electronic applications accepted. *Financial support:* Scholarships/grants and traineeships available. Financial award applicants required to submit FAFSA. *Unit head:* Dr. Bonnie J. Banker, Dean, School of Graduate and Professional Studies, 859-858-3511 Ext. 2221, Fax: 859-858-3921, E-mail: bonnie.banker@asbury.edu. *Application contact:* Lenore A. Sweigard, Graduate Program Assistant and Certification Specialist, 859-858-3511 Ext. 2502, Fax: 859-858-3921, E-mail: graded@asbury.edu.

Boston College, Graduate School of Arts and Sciences, Department of Classics, Chestnut Hill, MA 02467-3800. Offers classics (MA); Greek (MA); Latin (MA). Part-time programs

Classics

Boston College (continued)
available. *Students:* 8 full-time (6 women), 4 part-time (2 women). 16 applicants, 44% accepted, 2 enrolled. In 2009, 2 master's awarded. *Degree requirements:* For master's, one foreign language, thesis optional. *Entrance requirements:* Additional exam requirements/recommendations for international students: Required—TOEFL (minimum score 600 paper-based; 250 computer-based; 100 iBT). *Application deadline:* For fall admission, 1/2 for domestic and international students. Application fee: $70. *Financial support:* In 2009–10, teaching assistantships (averaging $8,000 per year); Federal Work-Study, scholarships/grants, and tuition waivers (full and partial) also available. Support available to part-time students. Financial award application deadline: 3/1; financial award applicants required to submit FAFSA. *Faculty research:* Classical philology, ancient history, modern Greek. *Unit head:* Dr. Gail Hoffman, Chairperson, 617-552-2236, E-mail: hoffmaga@bc.edu. *Application contact:* Dr. Gail Hoffman, Chairperson, 617-552-2236, E-mail: hoffmaga@bc.edu.

Boston University, Graduate School of Arts and Sciences, Department of Classical Studies, Boston, MA 02215. Offers MA, PhD, MA/PhD. *Faculty:* 15 full-time (7 women), 1 (woman) part-time/adjunct. *Students:* 21 full-time (7 women), 2 part-time (1 woman); includes 1 minority (Asian American or Pacific Islander). Average age 27. 48 applicants, 23% accepted, 3 enrolled. In 2009, 1 master's awarded. Terminal master's awarded for partial completion of doctoral program. *Degree requirements:* For master's, one foreign language, comprehensive exam; for doctorate, 2 foreign languages, comprehensive exam, thesis/dissertation. *Entrance requirements:* For master's, GRE General Test, 3 letters of recommendation, scholarly writing sample; for doctorate, GRE General Test, 3 letters of recommendation, scholarly writing sample, personal statement. Additional exam requirements/recommendations for international students: Required—TOEFL (minimum score 550 paper-based; 213 computer-based; 84 iBT). *Application deadline:* For fall admission, 1/15 for domestic and international students; for spring admission, 10/15 for domestic and international students. Application fee: $70. Electronic applications accepted. *Expenses:* Tuition: Full-time $37,910; part-time $1184 per credit hour. Required fees: $386; $40 per semester. Part-time tuition and fees vary according to class time, course level, degree level and program. *Financial support:* In 2009–10, 16 students received support, including 1 fellowship with full tuition reimbursement available (averaging $18,400 per year), 1 research assistantship with full tuition reimbursement available (averaging $10,000 per year), 11 teaching assistantships with full tuition reimbursements available (averaging $18,400 per year); career-related internships or fieldwork, Federal Work-Study, institutionally sponsored loans, health care benefits, and first-year scholarships also available. Support available to part-time students. Financial award application deadline: 1/15; financial award applicants required to submit FAFSA. *Faculty research:* Homer and Hesiod, tragedy and comedy, classical tradition, fifth century Athenian history, empire literature and history. *Unit head:* Dr. Loren J. Samons, Chairman, 617-353-2427, Fax: 617-353-1610, E-mail: ljs@bu.edu. *Application contact:* Stacy Fox, Department Administrator, 617-353-2426, Fax: 617-353-1610, E-mail: sfox@bu.edu.

Boston University, School of Education, Department of Curriculum and Teaching, Program in Latin and Classical Studies, Boston, MA 02215. Offers MAT. *Degree requirements:* For master's, comprehensive exam, thesis optional. *Entrance requirements:* For master's, GRE General Test or MAT. Additional exam requirements/recommendations for international students: Required—TOEFL. Electronic applications accepted. *Expenses:* Tuition: Full-time $37,910; part-time $1184 per credit hour. Required fees: $386; $40 per semester. Part-time tuition and fees vary according to class time, course level, degree level and program.

Brandeis University, Graduate School of Arts and Sciences, Department of Classical Studies, Waltham, MA 02454-9110. Offers ancient Greek and Roman studies (MA, Graduate Certificate). Part-time programs available. *Faculty:* 5 full-time (4 women). *Students:* 2 full-time (1 woman), 4 part-time (all women); includes 1 minority (American Indian/Alaska Native). 5 applicants, 100% accepted, 4 enrolled. *Degree requirements:* For master's, variable foreign language requirement, thesis. *Entrance requirements:* For master's and Graduate Certificate, 2 recommendation letters, CV or resume, statement of purpose, official transcript(s). Additional exam requirements/recommendations for international students: Required—TOEFL (minimum score 600 paper-based; 250 computer-based; 100 iBT); Recommended—IELTS (minimum score 7). *Application deadline:* Applications are processed on a rolling basis. Application fee: $75. Electronic applications accepted. *Financial support:* In 2009–10, 1 student received support, including 1 teaching assistantship with partial tuition reimbursement available (averaging $3,200 per year); scholarships/grants also available. Support available to part-time students. Financial award application deadline: 4/15; financial award applicants required to submit FAFSA. *Faculty research:* Classical archaeology, anthropology, epigraphy, Greek and Roman history, Greek and Roman art, Greek and Roman technology. *Unit head:* Dr. Ann Olga Koloski-Ostrow, Chair, Graduate Certificate Program, 781-736-2183, E-mail: aoko@brandeis.edu. *Application contact:* Heidi McAllister, Department Administrator, 781-736-2180, Fax: 781-736-2184, E-mail: hmcallister@brandeis.edu.

Brock University, Faculty of Graduate Studies, Faculty of Humanities, Program in Classics, St. Catharines, ON L2S 3A1, Canada. Offers MA. Part-time programs available. *Degree requirements:* For master's, one foreign language, major research paper or thesis. *Entrance requirements:* For master's, honors degree, 3 letters of reference, written work (no more than 20 pages). Additional exam requirements/recommendations for international students: Required—TOEFL (minimum score 550 paper-based; 213 computer-based; 80 iBT), IELTS (minimum score 6.5), TWE (minimum score 4). Electronic applications accepted.

Brown University, Graduate School, Department of Classics, Providence, RI 02912. Offers MA, PhD. *Degree requirements:* For master's, one foreign language, thesis; for doctorate, 2 foreign languages, thesis/dissertation. *Entrance requirements:* For master's and doctorate, GRE General Test. *Faculty research:* Philology, archaeology, Sanskrit.

Bryn Mawr College, Graduate School of Arts and Sciences, Department of Greek, Latin, and Classical Studies, Bryn Mawr, PA 19010-2899. Offers MA, PhD. Part-time programs available. *Degree requirements:* For master's, 2 foreign languages, thesis; for doctorate, 3 foreign languages, comprehensive exam, thesis/dissertation. *Entrance requirements:* For master's and doctorate, GRE General Test. Additional exam requirements/recommendations for international students: Required—TOEFL (minimum score 600 paper-based; 250 computer-based). *Expenses:* Tuition: Full-time $31,340. Required fees: $430.

The Catholic University of America, School of Arts and Sciences, Department of Greek and Latin, Washington, DC 20064. Offers Greek and Latin (MA, PhD); Latin (MA). Part-time programs available. *Faculty:* 5 full-time (1 woman), 1 part-time/adjunct (0 women). *Students:* 9 full-time (4 women), 9 part-time (4 women); includes 2 minority (both Asian Americans or Pacific Islanders). Average age 38. 19 applicants, 68% accepted, 6 enrolled. In 2009, 1 doctorate awarded. *Degree requirements:* For master's, one foreign language, comprehensive exam; for doctorate, 2 foreign languages, comprehensive exam, thesis/dissertation. *Entrance requirements:* For master's and doctorate, GRE General Test, essay, official copies of academic transcripts, three letters of recommendation, writing sample. Additional exam requirements/recommendations for international students: Required—TOEFL (minimum score 580 paper-based; 237 computer-based). *Application deadline:* For fall admission, 8/1 priority date for domestic students, 7/15 for international students; for spring admission, 12/1 priority date for domestic students, 10/15 for international students. Applications are processed on a rolling basis. Application fee: $55. Electronic applications accepted. *Expenses:* Tuition: Full-time $31,740; part-time $1245 per credit hour. Required fees: $50; $25 per semester hour. One-time fee: $425. *Financial support:* Fellowships, research assistantships, teaching assistantships, Federal Work-Study, scholarships/grants, tuition waivers (full and partial), and unspecified assistantships available. Financial award application deadline: 2/1; financial award applicants required to submit FAFSA. *Faculty research:* Greek and Latin history and literature; classical, late antique and patristic history and literature. *Unit head:* Dr. William E. Klingshirn, Chair, 202-319-5216, Fax: 202-319-5297, E-mail: klingshirn@cua.edu. *Application contact:* Julie Schwing, Director of Graduate Admissions, 202-319-5057, Fax: 202-319-6533, E-mail: cua-admissions@cua.edu.

Columbia University, Graduate School of Arts and Sciences, Division of Humanities, Department of Classics, New York, NY 10027. Offers M Phil, MA, PhD. *Degree requirements:* For master's, one foreign language, seminar paper; for doctorate, 3 foreign languages, thesis/dissertation. *Entrance requirements:* For master's, GRE General Test, reading knowledge of Greek or Latin; for doctorate, GRE General Test, reading knowledge of Greek and Latin. Additional exam requirements/recommendations for international students: Required—TOEFL. *Faculty research:* Greek and Latin literature, ancient philosophy.

Cornell University, Graduate School, Graduate Fields of Arts and Sciences, Field of Classics, Ithaca, NY 14853-0001. Offers ancient history (PhD); ancient philosophy (PhD); classical archaeology (PhD); classical myth (PhD); classical rhetoric (PhD); Greek and Latin language and linguistics (PhD); Greek language and literature (PhD); Indo-European linguistics (PhD); Latin language and literature (PhD); medieval and Renaissance Latin literature (PhD). *Faculty:* 28 full-time (6 women). *Students:* 19 full-time (5 women), 7 international. Average age 28. 76 applicants, 11% accepted, 2 enrolled. In 2009, 1 doctorate awarded. *Degree requirements:* For doctorate, 2 foreign languages, comprehensive exam, thesis/dissertation. *Entrance requirements:* For doctorate, GRE General Test, 3 letters of recommendation, sample of written work. Additional exam requirements/recommendations for international students: Required—TOEFL (minimum score 550 paper-based; 213 computer-based; 77 iBT). *Application deadline:* For fall admission, 1/15 for domestic students. Application fee: $70. Electronic applications accepted. *Expenses:* Tuition: Full-time $29,500. Required fees: $70. Full-time tuition and fees vary according to degree level, program and student level. *Financial support:* In 2009–10, 16 students received support, including 2 fellowships with full tuition reimbursements available; research assistantships with full tuition reimbursements available, teaching assistantships with full tuition reimbursements available, institutionally sponsored loans, scholarships/grants, health care benefits, tuition waivers (full and partial), and unspecified assistantships also available. Financial award applicants required to submit FAFSA. *Faculty research:* Greek and Roman literature, ancient philosophy, Greek and Roman archaeology, ancient history, Indo-European linguistics. *Unit head:* Director of Graduate Studies, 607-255-3354. *Application contact:* Graduate Field Assistant, 607-255-3354, E-mail: classics@cornell.edu.

Dalhousie University, Faculty of Arts and Social Science, Department of Classics, Halifax, NS B3H 4R2, Canada. Offers MA, PhD. *Entrance requirements:* Additional exam requirements/recommendations for international students: Required—TOEFL, IELTS, CANTEST, CAEL, or Michigan English Language Assessment Battery. *Application deadline:* For fall admission, 6/1 for domestic students, 4/1 for international students; for winter admission, 10/31 for domestic students, 8/31 for international students; for spring admission, 2/28 for domestic students, 12/31 for international students. Application fee: $70. Electronic applications accepted. *Financial support:* In 2009–10, 10 students received support. Career-related internships or fieldwork, scholarships/grants, and health care benefits available. *Unit head:* Dr. Wayne Hankey, Chair, 902-494-2298, Fax: 902-494-2467, E-mail: claswww@dal.ca. *Application contact:* Dr. Peter O'Brien, Graduate Coordinator, 902-494-3468, Fax: 902-494-2467, E-mail: claswww@dal.ca.

Duke University, Graduate School, Department of Classical Studies, Durham, NC 27708-0586. Offers PhD. *Faculty:* 10 full-time. *Students:* 17 full-time (7 women); includes 1 minority (Asian American or Pacific Islander), 2 international. 24 applicants, 21% accepted, 5 enrolled. In 2009, 1 doctorate awarded. *Degree requirements:* For doctorate, 2 foreign languages, thesis/dissertation. *Entrance requirements:* For doctorate, GRE General Test. Additional exam requirements/recommendations for international students: Required—TOEFL (minimum score 550 paper-based; 213 computer-based; 83 iBT), IELTS (minimum score 7). *Application deadline:* For fall admission, 12/8 priority date for domestic and international students. Application fee: $75. Electronic applications accepted. *Financial support:* Teaching assistantships, Federal Work-Study available. Financial award application deadline: 12/31. *Faculty research:* Greek Bronze Age; classical and Roman archaeology; Pompeii and Hadrian; epigraphy, papyrology, and Latin paleography. *Unit head:* Jennifer Clare Woods, Director of Graduate Studies, 919-684-6067, Fax: 919-681-4292, E-mail: cathy.puckett@duke.edu. *Application contact:* Cynthia Robertson, Associate Dean for Enfollment Services, 919-684-3913, E-mail: grad-admissions@duke.edu.

Florida State University, The Graduate School, College of Arts and Sciences, Department of Classics, Tallahassee, FL 32306-1510. Offers classical archaeology (MA); classical civilization (MA); classics (MA, PhD), including archaeology (PhD), literature and languages (PhD); Greek (MA); Greek and Latin (MA); Latin (MA). Part-time programs available. *Faculty:* 13 full-time (3 women), 1 (woman) part-time/adjunct. *Students:* 43 full-time (21 women); includes 2 Asian Americans or Pacific Islanders. Average age 24. 52 applicants, 67% accepted, 16 enrolled. In 2009, 15 master's, 1 doctorate awarded. Terminal master's awarded for partial completion of doctoral program. *Degree requirements:* For master's, one foreign language, comprehensive exam (for some programs), thesis (for some programs); for doctorate, 2 foreign languages, comprehensive exam, thesis/dissertation. *Entrance requirements:* For master's, GRE General Test, minimum GPA of 3.0; for doctorate, GRE General Test. Additional exam requirements/recommendations for international students: Required—TOEFL. *Application deadline:* For fall admission, 1/15 priority date for domestic students, 2/15 for international students. Applications are processed on a rolling basis. Application fee: $30. Electronic applications accepted. *Expenses:* Tuition, state resident: full-time $7413. Tuition, nonresident: full-time $22,567. *Financial support:* In 2009–10, 42 students received support, including 2 fellowships with full tuition reimbursements available (averaging $18,000 per year), 2 research assistantships with full tuition reimbursements available (averaging $10,000 per year), 28 teaching assistantships with full tuition reimbursements available (averaging $10,000 per year); Federal Work-Study, institutionally sponsored loans, and tuition waivers (full and partial) also available. Support available to part-time students. Financial award application deadline: 1/15; financial award applicants required to submit FAFSA. *Faculty research:* Greek and Latin literature, classical archaeology, history, Roman religion. Total annual research expenditures: $100,000. *Unit head:* Dr. Daniel J. Pullen, Chairman, 850-644-0304, Fax: 850-644-4073, E-mail: dpullen@fsu.edu. *Application contact:* Dr. Nancy de Grummond, Admissions Director, 850-644-0305, Fax: 850-644-0303, E-mail: ndegrummond@fsu.edu.

Fordham University, Graduate School of Arts and Sciences, Department of Classical Languages and Literatures, New York, NY 10458. Offers classical Greek and Latin literature (MA); classics (PhD). Part-time and evening/weekend programs available. *Faculty:* 7 full-time (1 woman). *Students:* 12 full-time (3 women), 20 part-time (6 women); includes 1 minority (Asian American or Pacific Islander), 1 international. Average age 29. 16 applicants, 50% accepted, 2 enrolled. In 2009, 1 master's awarded. Terminal master's awarded for partial completion of doctoral program. *Degree requirements:* For master's, one foreign language, comprehensive exam; for doctorate, 2 foreign languages, comprehensive exam, thesis/dissertation. *Entrance requirements:* For master's and doctorate, GRE General Test. Additional exam requirements/recommendations for international students: Required—TOEFL (minimum score 650 paper-based; 280 computer-based). *Application deadline:* For fall admission, 1/4 priority date for domestic students; for spring admission, 11/1 for domestic students. Application fee: $70. Electronic applications accepted. *Financial support:* In 2009–10, 11 students received support, including 1 fellowship with tuition reimbursement available (averaging $21,800 per year), 4 research assistantships with tuition reimbursements available (averaging $18,400 per year), 6 teaching assistantships with tuition reimbursements available (averaging $20,666 per year); Federal Work-Study, institutionally sponsored loans, scholarships/grants, tuition waivers (full and partial), and unspecified assistantships also available. Support available to part-time students. Financial award application deadline: 1/4; financial award applicants required to submit FAFSA. *Unit head:* Dr. Robert Penella, Chair, 718-817-3132, Fax: 718-817-3134, E-mail: penella@fordham.edu. *Application contact:* Charlene Dundie, Director of Graduate Admissions, 718-817-4420, Fax: 718-817-3566, E-mail: dundie@fordham.edu.

Graduate School and University Center of the City University of New York, Graduate Studies, Program in Classics, New York, NY 10016-4039. Offers MA, PhD. *Faculty:* 14 full-time (5 women). *Students:* 15 full-time (5 women), 11 part-time (2 women), 1 international. Average age 40. 11 applicants, 82% accepted, 4 enrolled. In 2009, 3 master's awarded. *Degree* *requirements:* For master's, 2 foreign languages, thesis; for doctorate, 2 foreign languages, thesis/dissertation. *Entrance requirements:* For master's and doctorate, GRE General Test. Additional exam requirements/recommendations for international students: Required—TOEFL. *Application deadline:* For fall admission, 4/15 for domestic students. Application fee: $125. Electronic applications accepted. *Financial support:* In 2009–10, 9 students received support, including 10 fellowships, 1 teaching assistantship; research assistantships, career-related internships or fieldwork, Federal Work-Study, institutionally sponsored loans, and tuition waivers (full and partial) also available. Financial award application deadline: 2/1; financial award applicants required to submit FAFSA. *Unit head:* Dr. Dee Clayman, Executive Officer, 212-817-8151, Fax: 212-817-1508. *Application contact:* Les Gribben, Director of Admissions, 212-817-7470, Fax: 212-817-1624, E-mail: lgribben@gc.cuny.edu.

Graduate School and University Center of the City University of New York, Graduate Studies, Program in Comparative Literature, New York, NY 10016-4039. Offers comparative literature (MA, PhD), including classics (PhD), German (PhD), Italian (PhD). *Faculty:* 16 full-time (3 women). *Students:* 110 full-time (70 women), 3 part-time (all women); includes 5 minority (2 Asian Americans or Pacific Islanders, 3 Hispanic Americans), 29 international. Average age 37. 51 applicants, 35% accepted, 11 enrolled. In 2009, 5 master's, 8 doctorates awarded. Terminal master's awarded for partial completion of doctoral program. *Degree requirements:* For master's, 2 foreign languages, comprehensive exam, thesis; for doctorate, 3 foreign languages, comprehensive exam, thesis/dissertation. *Entrance requirements:* For master's and doctorate, GRE General Test. Additional exam requirements/recommendations for international students: Required—TOEFL. *Application deadline:* For fall admission, 4/15 for domestic students; for spring admission, 11/15 for domestic students. Application fee: $125. Electronic applications accepted. *Financial support:* In 2009–10, 63 students received support, including 60 fellowships, 5 research assistantships, 14 teaching assistantships; career-related internships or fieldwork, Federal Work-Study, institutionally sponsored loans, and tuition waivers (full and partial) also available. Financial award application deadline: 2/1; financial award applicants required to submit FAFSA. *Unit head:* Dr. Andre Aciman, Executive Officer, 212-817-8170, Fax: 212-817-1509, E-mail: aaciman@gc.cuny.edu. *Application contact:* Les Gribben, Director of Admissions, 212-817-7470, Fax: 212-817-1624, E-mail: lgribben@gc.cuny.edu.

Harvard University, Graduate School of Arts and Sciences, Department of the Classics, Cambridge, MA 02138. Offers Byzantine Greek (PhD); classical archaeology (PhD); classical philology (PhD); classical philosophy (PhD); medieval Latin (PhD). *Degree requirements:* For doctorate, 4 foreign languages, thesis/dissertation, preliminary and special exams. *Entrance requirements:* For doctorate, GRE General Test. Additional exam requirements/recommendations for international students: Required—TOEFL. *Expenses:* Tuition: Full-time $33,696. Required fees: $1126. Full-time tuition and fees vary according to program.

Heritage Christian University, Graduate Programs, Florence, AL 35630. Offers counseling (MM); Greek (MA); ministry (MM); New Testament (MA). *Degree requirements:* For master's, practicum (MM), major research paper (MA). *Entrance requirements:* For master's, MAT or GRE, bachelor's degree in Bible from an accredited college or university, minimum GPA of 2.75, 3 letters of recommendation.

Hunter College of the City University of New York, Graduate School, School of Arts and Sciences, Department of Classical and Oriental Studies, Program in Teaching Latin, New York, NY 10021-5085. Offers MA. Part-time and evening/weekend programs available. *Faculty:* 2 full-time (1 woman). *Students:* 1 (woman) full-time, 18 part-time (10 women). Average age 30. 13 applicants, 92% accepted, 9 enrolled. In 2009, 1 master's awarded. *Degree requirements:* For master's, one foreign language, comprehensive exam. *Entrance requirements:* For master's, undergraduate major in Latin or equivalent with a minimum GPA of 3.0, 2.8 overall; interview, 2 letters of recommendation. Additional exam requirements/recommendations for international students: Required—TOEFL. *Application deadline:* For fall admission, 4/28 for domestic students; for spring admission, 11/21 for domestic students. Application fee: $125. *Expenses:* Tuition, state resident: full-time $7360; part-time $310 per credit. Required fees: $250 per semester. *Financial support:* Federal Work-Study, scholarships/grants, and tuition waivers (partial) available. Support available to part-time students. Financial award application deadline: 4/15. *Faculty research:* Late antique religion and social history, women in antiquity, Horace and lyric poetry, Roman comedy, Latin prose. *Unit head:* Dr. Ronnie Aucona, Director, 212-772-4960, E-mail: rancona@hunter.cuny.edu. *Application contact:* William Zlata, Director of Admissions, 212-772-4482, E-mail: admissions@hunter.cuny.edu.

Indiana University Bloomington, University Graduate School, College of Arts and Sciences, Department of Classical Studies, Bloomington, IN 47405. Offers MA, MAT, PhD. Part-time programs available. *Faculty:* 5 full-time (3 women). *Students:* 25 full-time (9 women), 1 (woman) part-time, 2 international. Average age 30. 35 applicants, 9% accepted, 2 enrolled. In 2009, 2 master's, 1 doctorate awarded. *Degree requirements:* For master's, 2 foreign languages, comprehensive exam; for doctorate, 3 foreign languages, thesis/dissertation. *Entrance requirements:* For master's and doctorate, GRE, minimum GPA of 3.0. Additional exam requirements/recommendations for international students: Required—TOEFL. *Application deadline:* For fall admission, 1/15 priority date for domestic students, 12/15 for international students; for spring admission, 9/1 priority date for domestic students, 9/1 for international students. Applications are processed on a rolling basis. Application fee: $55 ($65 for international students). *Financial support:* Fellowships with full tuition reimbursements, teaching assistantships with full tuition reimbursements, Federal Work-Study available. *Faculty research:* Roman literature (particularly Empire and late Latin), Greek drama, Homer, history of ideas, papyrology. *Unit head:* Prof. Matthew Christ, Chair, 812-855-6651. *Application contact:* Yvette Rollins, Graduate Secretary, 812-855-6651, E-mail: rollinsy@indiana.edu.

The Johns Hopkins University, Zanvyl Krieger School of Arts and Sciences, Department of Classics, Baltimore, MD 21218-2699. Offers PhD. *Faculty:* 5 full-time (1 woman). *Students:* 17 full-time (10 women); includes 1 minority (African American), 6 international. Average age 27. 26 applicants, 19% accepted, 3 enrolled. Terminal master's awarded for partial completion of doctoral program. *Degree requirements:* For doctorate, 4 foreign languages, thesis/dissertation. *Entrance requirements:* For doctorate, GRE General Test. Additional exam requirements/recommendations for international students: Required—TOEFL (minimum score 600 paper-based; 250 computer-based), IELTS (minimum score 7). *Application deadline:* For fall admission, 1/15 for domestic and international students. Application fee: $75. Electronic applications accepted. *Financial support:* In 2009–10, 16 students received support, including 8 fellowships with full tuition reimbursements available (averaging $17,500 per year), 1 research assistantship with full tuition reimbursement available (averaging $17,500 per year), 7 teaching assistantships with full tuition reimbursements available (averaging $17,500 per year); career-related internships or fieldwork, institutionally sponsored loans, scholarships/grants, and health care benefits also available. Financial award application deadline: 1/15. *Faculty research:* Greek culture and mythology, classical sculpture, Early Imperial Roman society. *Unit head:* Dr. Matthew Roller, Professor and Chair, 410-516-5095, Fax: 410-516-4848, E-mail: mroller@jhu.edu. *Application contact:* Ginnie Miller, Admissions Coordinator, 410-516-7556, Fax: 410-516-4848, E-mail: gmiller@jhu.edu.

Kent State University, College of Arts and Sciences, Department of Modern and Classical Language Studies, Kent, OH 44242-0001. Offers French literature (MA); French, Spanish, German and Latin pedagogy (MA); German literature (MA); Spanish literature (MA); translation (MA), including French, German, Japanese, Russian, Spanish; translation studies (PhD). Part-time and evening/weekend programs available. *Degree requirements:* For master's, one foreign language, comprehensive exam (for some programs), thesis (for some programs); for doctorate, comprehensive exam, thesis/dissertation (for some programs). *Entrance requirements:* For master's, minimum GPA of 3.0, writing sample, audio tape or CD; for doctorate, 3 recommendations. Additional exam requirements/recommendations for international students: Required—TOEFL (minimum score 197 computer-based). Electronic applications accepted. *Faculty research:* Literature, pedagogy, applied linguistics, translation studies.

Marshall University, Academic Affairs Division, College of Liberal Arts, Program in Latin, Huntington, WV 25755. Offers MA. *Faculty:* 3 full-time (2 women). *Students:* 2 full-time (1 woman). Average age 23. In 2009, 2 master's awarded. *Unit head:* Caroline Perkins, Chair, 304-696-6749, E-mail: classical-studies@marshall.edu. *Application contact:* Information Contact, 304-746-1900, Fax: 304-746-1902, E-mail: services@marshall.edu.

McMaster University, School of Graduate Studies, Faculty of Humanities, Department of Classics, Hamilton, ON L8S 4M2, Canada. Offers MA, PhD. *Degree requirements:* For master's, one foreign language, thesis or alternative; for doctorate, 2 foreign languages, comprehensive exam, thesis/dissertation. *Entrance requirements:* For master's, honors degree, minimum B+ average. Additional exam requirements/recommendations for international students: Required—TOEFL (minimum score 580 paper-based; 237 computer-based). *Faculty research:* Ancient history, art and archaeology, Latin language and literature, Greek language and literature.

Memorial University of Newfoundland, School of Graduate Studies, Department of Classics, St. John's, NL A1C 5S7, Canada. Offers MA. Part-time programs available. *Degree requirements:* For master's, one foreign language, thesis, language exam, translation exam, research essay. *Entrance requirements:* For master's, honors degree in related field, course work in Greek and Latin. Electronic applications accepted. *Faculty research:* Ancient history, historiography, literature, drama, philosophy, paleography, epigraphy, and textual criticism.

New York University, Graduate School of Arts and Science, Department of Classics, New York, NY 10012-1019. Offers classics (MA, PhD); poetics and theory (Advanced Certificate). Part-time programs available. *Faculty:* 11 full-time (3 women). *Students:* 18 full-time (8 women), 3 part-time (1 woman); includes 2 minority (1 Asian American or Pacific Islander, 1 Hispanic American), 3 international. Average age 29. 70 applicants, 17% accepted, 5 enrolled. *Degree requirements:* For master's, 4 foreign languages, exam or specialized project; for doctorate, 4 foreign languages, thesis/dissertation, exams. *Entrance requirements:* For master's, GRE General Test, knowledge of Greek and Latin history and literature, proficiency in Greek and Latin translation; for doctorate, GRE General Test. Additional exam requirements/recommendations for international students: Required—TOEFL. *Application deadline:* For fall admission, 1/4 priority date for domestic students. Application fee: $90. *Expenses:* Tuition: Full-time $30,528; part-time $1272 per credit. Required fees: $2177. *Financial support:* Fellowships with tuition reimbursements, teaching assistantships with tuition reimbursements, Federal Work-Study, institutionally sponsored loans, scholarships/grants, health care benefits, and unspecified assistantships available. Financial award application deadline: 1/4; financial award applicants required to submit FAFSA. *Faculty research:* Greek and Latin literature, Greek and Roman history, epigraphy, Greek and Roman philosophy, classical archeology. *Unit head:* David Levene, Chair, 212-998-8590, Fax: 212-995-4209, E-mail: gsas.classic@nyu.edu. *Application contact:* Markus Asper, Director of Graduate Studies, 212-998-8590, Fax: 212-995-4209, E-mail: gsas.classics@nyu.edu.

The Ohio State University, Graduate School, College of Humanities, Program in Classics, Columbus, OH 43210. Offers MA, PhD. Electronic applications accepted. *Expenses:* Tuition, state resident: full-time $10,683. Tuition, nonresident: full-time $25,923. Tuition and fees vary according to course load and program.

The Ohio State University, Graduate School, College of Humanities, Programs in Greek and Latin, Columbus, OH 43210. Offers ancient Greek (MA); Greek studies (MA, PhD); Latin studies (MA, PhD); modern Greek (MA, PhD). *Faculty:* 17. *Students:* 19 full-time (4 women), 8 part-time (3 women); includes 3 minority (1 African American, 1 Asian American or Pacific Islander, 1 Hispanic American). Average age 27. In 2009, 5 master's, 5 doctorates awarded. *Degree requirements:* For master's, 2 foreign languages; for doctorate, 2 foreign languages, thesis/dissertation. *Entrance requirements:* For master's and doctorate, GRE General Test. Additional exam requirements/recommendations for international students: Required—TOEFL (minimum score 600 paper-based; 250 computer-based). *Application deadline:* For fall admission, 8/15 priority date for domestic students, 7/1 priority date for international students; for winter admission, 12/1 priority date for domestic students, 11/1 priority date for international students; for spring admission, 3/1 priority date for domestic students, 2/1 priority date for international students. Applications are processed on a rolling basis. Application fee: $40 ($50 for international students). Electronic applications accepted. *Expenses:* Tuition, state resident: full-time $10,683. Tuition, nonresident: full-time $25,923. Tuition and fees vary according to course load and program. *Financial support:* Fellowships, teaching assistantships, Federal Work-Study and institutionally sponsored loans available. Support available to part-time students. *Unit head:* Frank Coulson, Graduate Studies Committee Chair, E-mail: coulson.1@osu.edu. *Application contact:* 614-292-9444, Fax: 614-292-3895, E-mail: domestic.grad@osu.edu.

Princeton University, Graduate School, Department of Classics, Princeton, NJ 08544-1019. Offers classical and hellenic studies (PhD); classical philosophy (PhD); history (the ancient world) (PhD); literature and philology (PhD). *Degree requirements:* For doctorate, thesis/dissertation. *Entrance requirements:* For doctorate, GRE General Test, sample of written work. Additional exam requirements/recommendations for international students: Required—TOEFL (minimum score 600 paper-based; 250 computer-based). Electronic applications accepted.

Queen's University at Kingston, School of Graduate Studies and Research, Faculty of Arts and Sciences, Department of Classics, Kingston, ON K7L 3N6, Canada. Offers classics, Greek, Latin (MA). Part-time programs available. *Degree requirements:* For master's, one foreign language, thesis (for some programs). *Entrance requirements:* For master's, 3 years of Latin, 2 years of Greek. Additional exam requirements/recommendations for international students: Required—TOEFL. Electronic applications accepted. *Faculty research:* Greek and Latin literature, Greek and Roman history, ancient philosophy, Greek archaeology.

Rutgers, The State University of New Jersey, New Brunswick, Graduate School-New Brunswick, Department of Classics, Piscataway, NJ 08854-8097. Offers classics (MA, MAT, PhD); interdisciplinary classical studies and ancient history (MA, PhD). Part-time and evening/weekend programs available. Terminal master's awarded for partial completion of doctoral program. *Degree requirements:* For master's, 3 foreign languages, comprehensive exam, thesis or alternative; for doctorate, 3 foreign languages, comprehensive exam, thesis/dissertation. *Entrance requirements:* For master's and doctorate, GRE General Test. *Faculty research:* Greek and Latin literature, Greek and Roman social and political history, mythology, religion, ancient philosophy.

San Francisco State University, Division of Graduate Studies, College of Humanities, Department of Classics, San Francisco, CA 94132-1722. Offers MA. Part-time programs available.

Stanford University, School of Humanities and Sciences, Department of Classics, Stanford, CA 94305-9991. Offers MA, PhD. *Degree requirements:* For master's, 2 foreign languages, thesis or alternative; for doctorate, 4 foreign languages, thesis/dissertation, general exams. *Entrance requirements:* For master's and doctorate, GRE General Test. Additional exam requirements/recommendations for international students: Required—TOEFL. Electronic applications accepted. *Expenses:* Tuition: Full-time $37,380; part-time $2760 per quarter. Required fees: $501.

Texas Tech University, Graduate School, College of Arts and Sciences, Department of Classical and Modern Languages and Literatures, Program in Classics, Lubbock, TX 79409. Offers MA. *Students:* 8 full-time (3 women), 2 part-time (0 women). Average age 25. 7 applicants, 71% accepted, 2 enrolled. In 2009, 2 master's awarded. *Entrance requirements:* For master's, GRE General Test. Additional exam requirements/recommendations for international students: Required—TOEFL (minimum score 550 paper-based; 213 computer-based). *Application deadline:* For fall admission, 3/1 priority date for international students; for spring admission, 11/1 priority date for international students. Applications are processed on a rolling basis. Application fee: $50 ($75 for international students). Electronic applications accepted. *Expenses:* Tuition, state resident: full-time $5100; part-time $213 per credit hour. Tuition, nonresident: full-time $11,748; part-time $490 per credit hour. Required fees: $2298;

Classics

Texas Tech University (continued)

$50 per credit hour. $555 per semester. *Financial support:* Research assistantships with partial tuition reimbursements, teaching assistantships with partial tuition reimbursements available. Financial award application deadline: 4/15. *Faculty research:* Greek and Latin language; literature and criticism; archaeology; gender and sexuality. *Unit head:* Dr. David H. J. Larmour, Professor and Graduate Advisor, 806-742-3145 Ext. 260, Fax: 806-742-3306, E-mail: david.larmour@ttu.edu. *Application contact:* Liz Hildebrand, Senior Advisor, 806-742-4055, Fax: 806-742-3306, E-mail: liz.hildebrand@ttu.edu.

Tufts University, Graduate School of Arts and Sciences, Department of Classics, Medford, MA 02155. Offers classical archaeology (MA); classics (MA). Part-time programs available. *Faculty:* 7 full-time, 4 part-time/adjunct. *Students:* 12 full-time (7 women). Average age 27. 22 applicants, 68% accepted, 5 enrolled. In 2009, 7 master's awarded. *Degree requirements:* For master's, 2 foreign languages, comprehensive exam, thesis or alternative. *Entrance requirements:* For master's, GRE General Test, writing sample. Additional exam requirements/recommendations for international students: Required—TOEFL (minimum score 550 paper-based; 213 computer-based; 80 iBT). *Application deadline:* For fall admission, 2/15 for domestic students, 12/15 for international students; for spring admission, 10/15 for domestic students, 9/15 for international students. Applications are processed on a rolling basis. Application fee: $75. Electronic applications accepted. *Expenses:* Tuition: Full-time $38,096; part-time $3962 per credit. Required fees: $686; $40 per year. Tuition and fees vary according to course level, course load, degree level, program and student level. *Financial support:* Teaching assistantships with full and partial tuition reimbursements, Federal Work-Study, scholarships/grants, tuition waivers (partial), and unspecified assistantships available. Financial award application deadline: 2/15; financial award applicants required to submit FAFSA. *Unit head:* Gregory Crane, Chair, 617-627-3213. *Application contact:* David J. Proctor, Information Contact, 617-627-3213.

Tulane University, School of Liberal Arts, Department of Classical Studies, New Orleans, LA 70118-5669. Offers MA. *Degree requirements:* For master's, 2 foreign languages, thesis or alternative. *Entrance requirements:* For master's, GRE General Test, minimum B average in undergraduate course work. Additional exam requirements/recommendations for international students: Required—TOEFL. Electronic applications accepted.

Union Graduate College, School of Education, Schenectady, NY 12308-3107. Offers biology (MAT, MS); chemistry (MAT); Chinese (MAT); earth science (MAT); English (MAT); French (MAT); general science (MAT); German (MAT); Greek (MAT); languages (MAT); Latin (MAT); mathematics (MAT); mathematics and technology (MS); mentoring and teacher leadership (AC); middle childhood extension (AC); national board certificate and teacher leadership (AC); physical science (MS); physics (MAT); social studies (MAT); Spanish (MAT). *Accreditation:* Teacher Education Accreditation Council. *Faculty:* 3 full-time (1 woman), 39 part-time/adjunct (19 women). *Students:* 46 full-time (27 women), 45 part-time (39 women); includes 5 minority (1 Asian American or Pacific Islander, 4 Hispanic Americans), 2 international. Average age 33. 66 applicants, 73% accepted, 39 enrolled. In 2009, 44 master's awarded. *Degree requirements:* For master's, thesis or project. *Entrance requirements:* For master's, minimum GPA of 3.0, letters of recommendation. Additional exam requirements/recommendations for international students: Required—TOEFL (minimum score 550 paper-based; 213 computer-based). *Application deadline:* Applications are processed on a rolling basis. Application fee: $60. Electronic applications accepted. *Expenses:* Contact institution. *Financial support:* In 2009–10, 12 research assistantships with tuition reimbursements (averaging $3,000 per year) were awarded; Federal Work-Study, scholarships/grants, health care benefits, and tuition waivers (partial) also available. Support available to part-time students. Financial award applicants required to submit FAFSA. *Faculty research:* Transformative learning, science education, National Board Certification, teacher leadership, teacher quality. *Unit head:* Dr. Patrick Allen, Dean, 518-631-9870, Fax: 518-631-9901. *Application contact:* Christine Angley, Assistant, 518-631-9871, Fax: 518-631-9903, E-mail: angleyc@uniongraduatecollege.edu.

Université de Montréal, Faculty of Arts and Sciences, Programs in Classical Studies, Montréal, QC H3C 3J7, Canada.

University at Buffalo, the State University of New York, Graduate School, College of Arts and Sciences, Department of Classics, Buffalo, NY 14260. Offers MA, PhD. Terminal master's awarded for partial completion of doctoral program. *Degree requirements:* For master's, 3 foreign languages, project; for doctorate, 4 foreign languages, thesis/dissertation, general and 2 special exams. *Entrance requirements:* For master's and doctorate, GRE General Test. Additional exam requirements/recommendations for international students: Required—TOEFL. Electronic applications accepted. *Expenses:* Contact institution. *Faculty research:* Greek and Latin literature, historiography, and epigraphy; Greek archaeology, mythology, and ancient philosophy; ancient and Roman religion and women's studies.

University at Buffalo, the State University of New York, Graduate School, Graduate School of Education, Department of Learning and Instruction, Buffalo, NY 14260. Offers biology education (Ed M, Certificate); chemistry education (Ed M, Certificate); childhood education (Ed M); childhood education with bilingual extension (Ed M); early childhood education (Ed M); earth science education (Ed M, Certificate); elementary education (Ed D, PhD); English education (Ed M, PhD, Certificate); English for speakers of other languages (Ed M); foreign and second language education (PhD); French education (Ed M, Certificate); general education (Ed M); German education (Ed M, Certificate); gifted education (online) (Certificate); Latin education (Ed M, Certificate); literary specialist (Ed M); mathematics education (Ed M, PhD, Certificate); music education (Ed M, Certificate); physics education (Ed M, Certificate); reading education (PhD); science and the public (online) (Ed M); science education (PhD); social studies education (Ed M, Certificate); Spanish education (Ed M, Certificate); special education (PhD); teaching and leading for diversity (Certificate); teaching English to speakers of other languages (Ed M). Part-time and evening/weekend programs available. Postbaccalaureate distance learning degree programs offered (no on-campus study). *Faculty:* 34 full-time (24 women), 50 part-time/adjunct (39 women). *Students:* 332 full-time (245 women), 365 part-time (272 women); includes 50 minority (18 African Americans, 4 American Indian/Alaska Native, 10 Asian Americans or Pacific Islanders, 18 Hispanic Americans), 55 international. Average age 30. 627 applicants, 78% accepted, 286 enrolled. In 2009, 255 master's, 16 doctorates, 51 other advanced degrees awarded. *Degree requirements:* For master's, comprehensive exam; for doctorate, thesis/dissertation, research analysis exam, research experience component. *Entrance requirements:* For doctorate, GRE General Test or MAT, interview, writing sample, letters of recommendation. Additional exam requirements/recommendations for international students: Required—TOEFL (minimum score 600 paper-based; 250 computer-based; 96 iBT). *Application deadline:* For fall admission, 2/1 priority date for domestic and international students; for spring admission, 11/15 priority date for domestic students, 10/1 for international students. Applications are processed on a rolling basis. Application fee: $50. Electronic applications accepted. *Financial support:* In 2009–10, 23 fellowships with full tuition reimbursements (averaging $9,000 per year), 42 research assistantships with full tuition reimbursements (averaging $10,000 per year) were awarded; teaching assistantships with full tuition reimbursements, career-related internships or fieldwork, Federal Work-Study, institutionally sponsored loans, scholarships/grants, tuition waivers (partial), and unspecified assistantships also available. Financial award application deadline: 2/28; financial award applicants required to submit FAFSA. *Faculty research:* Science assessment, foreign language teaching and learning, early learning, new literacies, gender and education. Total annual research expenditures: $1.8 million. *Unit head:* Dr. Suzanne Miller, Chair, 716-645-2455, Fax: 716-645-3161, E-mail: smiller@buffalo.edu. *Application contact:* Cathy Dimino, Admissions Assistant, 716-645-2110, Fax: 716-645-7937, E-mail: cadimino@buffalo.edu.

University of Alberta, Faculty of Graduate Studies and Research, Department of History and Classics, Edmonton, AB T6G 2E1, Canada. Offers ancient history (PhD); classical archaeology (MA, PhD); classical literature (PhD); classics (MA); history (MA, PhD). Part-time and evening/weekend programs available. *Faculty:* 40 full-time (11 women), 30 part-time/adjunct (12 women). *Students:* 47 full-time (18 women), 31 part-time (16 women). 73 applicants, 51% accepted, 22 enrolled. In 2009, 13 master's, 6 doctorates awarded. *Degree requirements:* For master's, one foreign language, thesis (for some programs); for doctorate, one foreign language, thesis/dissertation. *Entrance requirements:* For master's, minimum B+ average; for doctorate, minimum A- average. Additional exam requirements/recommendations for international students: Required—TOEFL (minimum score 580 paper-based; 237 computer-based). *Application deadline:* For fall admission, 1/15 for domestic and international students. Electronic applications accepted. Tuition and fees charges are reported in Canadian dollars. *Expenses:* Tuition, area resident: Full-time $4626 Canadian dollars; part-time $99.72 Canadian dollars per unit. International tuition: $8216 Canadian dollars full-time. Required fees: $3590 Canadian dollars; $99.72 Canadian dollars per unit. $215 Canadian dollars per term. *Financial support:* In 2009–10, fellowships with full tuition reimbursements (averaging $20,000 per year), research assistantships with partial tuition reimbursements (averaging $10,000 per year), teaching assistantships with partial tuition reimbursements (averaging $10,000 per year) were awarded; scholarships/grants, health care benefits, and unspecified assistantships also available. Financial award application deadline: 1/15. *Faculty research:* Western Canada, classical archaeology, Britain, Eastern Europe, East Asia. Total annual research expenditures: $96,000. *Unit head:* Dr. Christopher C. Mackay, Graduate Chair, 780-492-2698, Fax: 780-492-9125. *Application contact:* Lydia A. Dugbazah, Graduate Secretary, 780-492-2698, Fax: 780-492-9125, E-mail: gradstud@ualberta.ca.

The University of Arizona, Graduate College, College of Humanities, Department of Classics, Tucson, AZ 85721. Offers MA. Part-time programs available. *Faculty:* 5. *Students:* 18 full-time (7 women), 8 part-time (5 women); includes 4 minority (2 American Indian/Alaska Native, 1 Asian American or Pacific Islander, 1 Hispanic American). Average age 27. 47 applicants, 60% accepted, 12 enrolled. In 2009, 12 master's awarded. *Degree requirements:* For master's, one foreign language, comprehensive exam, thesis. *Entrance requirements:* For master's, GRE General Test (minimum combined score of 1000 verbal and quantitative), 2 letters of recommendation. Additional exam requirements/recommendations for international students: Required—TOEFL (minimum score 550 paper-based; 213 computer-based; 79 iBT). *Application deadline:* For fall admission, 2/15 for domestic students, 1/15 for international students. Applications are processed on a rolling basis. Application fee: $75. Electronic applications accepted. *Expenses:* Tuition, state resident: full-time $9028. Tuition, nonresident: full-time $24,890. *Financial support:* In 2009–10, 23 teaching assistantships with full tuition reimbursements (averaging $14,024 per year) were awarded; research assistantships with full tuition reimbursements, career-related internships or fieldwork, Federal Work-Study, institutionally sponsored loans, scholarships/grants, health care benefits, tuition waivers (full), and unspecified assistantships also available. Support available to part-time students. Financial award application deadline: 4/15. *Faculty research:* Greek and Roman archaeology, ancient Greek, modern Greek, Latin, Greek and Roman religion, women in antiquity. Total annual research expenditures: $9,645. *Unit head:* Dr. Mary Voyatzis, Head, 520-621-3446, Fax: 520-621-3678, E-mail: mev@u.arizona.edu. *Application contact:* LeeAnn Landphair, Graduate Secretary, 520-621-1396, Fax: 520-621-3678, E-mail: landphai@email.arizona.edu.

The University of British Columbia, Faculty of Arts and Faculty of Graduate Studies, Department of Classical, Near Eastern and Religious Studies, Programmes in Classics, Vancouver, BC V6T 1Z1, Canada. Offers ancient culture, religion, and ethnicity (MA); classical and near eastern archaeology (MA); classics (MA, PhD). Part-time programs available. *Degree requirements:* For master's, 2 foreign languages, thesis or comprehensive exam; for doctorate, 2 foreign languages, comprehensive exam, thesis/dissertation. *Entrance requirements:* For doctorate, MA. Additional exam requirements/recommendations for international students: Required—TOEFL (minimum score 600 paper-based; 250 computer-based), IELTS (minimum score 7.5). Electronic applications accepted. *Faculty research:* Classical archaeology, ancient historians, late antiquity, ancient prose fiction, epigraphy.

University of Calgary, Faculty of Graduate Studies, Faculty of Humanities, Department of Greek and Roman Studies, Calgary, AB T2N 1N4, Canada. Offers MA, PhD. Part-time programs available. *Degree requirements:* For master's, one foreign language; for doctorate, 2 foreign languages, comprehensive exam, thesis/dissertation. *Entrance requirements:* For master's, BA in classics or related field, knowledge of Latin and/or Greek, minimum GPA of 3.7; for doctorate, MA in classics or related field, knowledge of Latin and Greek, GPA 3.7. Additional exam requirements/recommendations for international students: Required—TOEFL. Electronic applications accepted. *Faculty research:* Greek literature, Latin literature, Greek history, Roman history, classical archaeology.

University of California, Berkeley, Graduate Division, College of Letters and Science, Department of Classics, Berkeley, CA 94720-1500. Offers classical archaeology (MA, PhD); classics (MA, PhD); Greek (MA); Latin (MA). *Faculty:* 19 full-time, 3 part-time/adjunct. *Students:* 32 full-time (17 women). Average age 29. 74 applicants, 3 enrolled. In 2009, 6 master's, 1 doctorate awarded. Terminal master's awarded for partial completion of doctoral program. *Degree requirements:* For master's, one foreign language, exams; for doctorate, 2 foreign languages, thesis/dissertation, qualifying exam. *Entrance requirements:* For master's and doctorate, GRE General Test, minimum GPA of 3.0, 3 letters of recommendation. Additional exam requirements/recommendations for international students: Required—TOEFL (minimum score 570 paper-based; 230 computer-based), TWE. *Application deadline:* For fall admission, 12/15 for domestic students. Application fee: $70 ($90 for international students). *Financial support:* Fellowships, research assistantships, teaching assistantships, Federal Work-Study, institutionally sponsored loans, and unspecified assistantships available. *Faculty research:* Greek and Latin literature, textual criticism, history, archaeology and philosophy. *Unit head:* Prof. Leslie Kurke, Chair, 510-642-4218, Fax: 510-643-2959, E-mail: ch_classics@ls.berkeley.edu. *Application contact:* Valerie Brown, Secretary, 510-642-4218, Fax: 510-643-2959, E-mail: casmaoff@berkeley.edu.

University of California, Irvine, Office of Graduate Studies, School of Humanities, Department of Classics, Irvine, CA 92697. Offers MA, PhD. *Students:* 13 full-time (5 women); includes 3 minority (all Hispanic Americans). Average age 30. 10 applicants, 50% accepted, 3 enrolled. In 2009, 3 master's, 1 doctorate awarded. Terminal master's awarded for partial completion of doctoral program. *Degree requirements:* For master's, one foreign language, thesis or alternative; for doctorate, 2 foreign languages, thesis/dissertation. *Entrance requirements:* For master's and doctorate, GRE General Test, minimum GPA of 3.0. Additional exam requirements/recommendations for international students: Required—TOEFL (minimum score 550 paper-based; 213 computer-based). *Application deadline:* For fall admission, 1/15 priority date for domestic students, 1/15 for international students. Applications are processed on a rolling basis. Application fee: $70 ($90 for international students). Electronic applications accepted. *Financial support:* Fellowships, research assistantships with full tuition reimbursements, teaching assistantships, institutionally sponsored loans, traineeships, health care benefits, and unspecified assistantships available. Financial award application deadline: 3/1; financial award applicants required to submit FAFSA. *Faculty research:* Greek literature, computer application to Greek literature, Latin literature. *Unit head:* Dana Sutton, Acting Chair, 949-824-5896, Fax: 949-824-1966, E-mail: dfsutton@uci.edu. *Application contact:* DeeDee Nunez, Department Manager, 949-824-7254, Fax: 949-824-1966, E-mail: dynunez@uci.edu.

University of California, Los Angeles, Graduate Division, College of Letters and Science, Department of Classics, Los Angeles, CA 90095. Offers classics (MA, PhD); Greek (MA); Latin (MA). *Students:* 24 full-time (10 women). Average age 29. 44 applicants, 18% accepted, 3 enrolled. In 2009, 2 master's, 1 doctorate awarded. *Degree requirements:* For master's, 2 foreign languages, comprehensive exam; for doctorate, 2 foreign languages, thesis/dissertation, oral and written qualifying exams. *Entrance requirements:* For master's, GRE General Test, minimum GPA of 3.0, sample of written work; for doctorate, GRE General Test, minimum undergraduate GPA of 3.0, sample of written work, MA in classics. *Application deadline:* For fall admission, 12/15 for domestic and international students. Application fee: $70 ($90 for international students). Electronic applications accepted. *Financial support:* In 2009–10, 22 fellowships with full and partial tuition reimbursements, 3 research assistantships with full and partial tuition reimbursements, 16 teaching assistantships with full and partial tuition reimbursements were awarded; Federal Work-Study, institutionally sponsored loans, scholarships/grants, health care benefits, tuition waivers (full and partial), and unspecified assistantships also available. Financial award application deadline: 3/1; financial award applicants required to submit FAFSA. *Faculty research:* Homeric studies, archaeology, ancient comedy, ancient philosophy, Augustan poetry. *Unit head:* Dr. John Papadopoulos, Chair, 310-825-4171. *Application contact:* Department Office, 310-206-1590, E-mail: dabugheida@humnet.ucla.edu.

University of California, Riverside, Graduate Division, Tri-Campus Program in Classics, Riverside, CA 92521-0102. Offers PhD. *Faculty:* 6 full-time (3 women). *Students:* 1 full-time (0 women). Average age 31. *Degree requirements:* For doctorate, 3 foreign languages, comprehensive exam, thesis/dissertation. *Entrance requirements:* For doctorate, GRE, MA in classics. Additional exam requirements/recommendations for international students: Required—TOEFL (minimum score 550 paper-based; 213 computer-based; 80 iBT). *Application deadline:* For fall admission, 1/5 for domestic students, 2/1 for international students; for winter admission, 9/1 for domestic students, 7/1 for international students; for spring admission, 12/1 for domestic students, 10/1 for international students. Applications are processed on a rolling basis. Application fee: $60 ($75 for international students). Electronic applications accepted. *Financial support:* Fellowships with tuition reimbursements, research assistantships, teaching assistantships with tuition reimbursements, scholarships/grants, health care benefits, tuition waivers (full and partial), and unspecified assistantships available. Financial award application deadline: 1/5; financial award applicants required to submit FAFSA. *Faculty research:* Rhetoric, Greek and Latin drama, Hellenistic poetry, Anglo-Latin literature, Greek and Latin prose. *Unit head:* Dr. Anthony E. Edwards, Professor of Classics, UC San Diego, 858-534-3143, Fax: 858-534-8686, E-mail: aedwards@ucsd.edu. *Application contact:* Dr. Andrew Zissos, Assistant Professor, 949-824-6584, Fax: 949-824-1966, E-mail: pzissos@ucr.edu.

University of California, Santa Barbara, Graduate Division, College of Letters and Sciences, Division of Humanities and Fine Arts, Department of Classics, Santa Barbara, CA 93106-3120. Offers ancient history (MA, PhD); classics (MA); literature and theory (PhD); MA/PhD. *Faculty:* 8 full-time (4 women). *Students:* 15 full-time (9 women). Average age 27. 30 applicants, 50% accepted, 4 enrolled. In 2009, 2 master's awarded. Terminal master's awarded for partial completion of doctoral program. *Degree requirements:* For master's, 3 foreign languages, comprehensive exam, thesis optional; for doctorate, 4 foreign languages, comprehensive exam, thesis/dissertation. *Entrance requirements:* For master's, GRE, BA in classics, minimum 2 years of college course work in Latin and Greek, writing sample, 3 letters of recommendation, resume/curriculum vitae; for doctorate, GRE, MA in classics, writing sample, 3 letters of recommendation, statement of purpose, personal achievements/contributions statement, resume/curriculum vitae, transcripts for post-secondary institutions attended. Additional exam requirements/recommendations for international students: Required—TOEFL (minimum score 550 paper-based; 213 computer-based; 80 iBT), or IELTS (minimum score 7). *Application deadline:* For fall admission, 12/8 priority date for domestic and international students; for winter admission, 11/1 for domestic and international students; for spring admission, 2/1 for domestic and international students. Applications are processed on a rolling basis. Application fee: $70 ($90 for international students). Electronic applications accepted. *Financial support:* In 2009–10, 15 students received support, including 5 fellowships with full and partial tuition reimbursements available (averaging $4,600 per year), 1 research assistantship with partial tuition reimbursement available (averaging $1,600 per year), 14 teaching assistantships with partial tuition reimbursements available (averaging $10,500 per year); Federal Work-Study, institutionally sponsored loans, scholarships/grants, traineeships, health care benefits, tuition waivers (partial), unspecified assistantships, and readerships also available. Financial award application deadline: 12/8; financial award applicants required to submit FAFSA. *Faculty research:* Literary theory and cultural history, gender studies, Greek and Latin literature, Greek and Roman History, drama and performance. Total annual research expenditures: $35,000. *Unit head:* Prof. Robert Morstein-Marx, Chair, 805-893-3007, Fax: 805-893-4487, E-mail: morstein@classics.ucsb.edu. *Application contact:* Prof. Frances Hahn, Graduate Advisor, 805-893-3605, Fax: 805-893-4487, E-mail: fhahn@classics.ucsb.edu.

University of Chicago, Division of the Humanities, Department of Classics, Chicago, IL 60637-1513. Offers ancient philosophy (AM, PhD); classical archaeology (AM, PhD); classical languages and literatures (AM, PhD). Terminal master's awarded for partial completion of doctoral program. *Degree requirements:* For master's, one foreign language, thesis; for doctorate, 2 foreign languages, thesis/dissertation. *Entrance requirements:* For master's and doctorate, GRE General Test. Additional exam requirements/recommendations for international students: Required—TOEFL.

University of Cincinnati, Graduate School, McMicken College of Arts and Sciences, Department of Classics, Cincinnati, OH 45221. Offers MA, PhD. Part-time programs available. Terminal master's awarded for partial completion of doctoral program. *Degree requirements:* For master's, comprehensive exam (for some programs), thesis (for some programs); for doctorate, 2 foreign languages, comprehensive exam, thesis/dissertation. *Entrance requirements:* For master's and doctorate, GRE. Additional exam requirements/recommendations for international students: Required—TOEFL. Electronic applications accepted. *Faculty research:* Archaeology (bronze age and classical), philosophy (Greek and Latin), ancient history (Greek and Roman).

University of Colorado at Boulder, Graduate School, College of Arts and Sciences, Department of Classics, Boulder, CO 80309. Offers MA, PhD. Part-time programs available. *Faculty:* 12 full-time (5 women). *Students:* 26 full-time (15 women), 2 part-time (1 woman). Average age 27. 53 applicants, 45% accepted, 15 enrolled. In 2009, 11 master's, 1 doctorate awarded. Terminal master's awarded for partial completion of doctoral program. *Degree requirements:* For master's, one foreign language, comprehensive exam, thesis or alternative, oral exam; for doctorate, 4 foreign languages, comprehensive exam, thesis/dissertation. *Entrance requirements:* For master's, minimum undergraduate GPA of 2.75; for doctorate, master's degree in classics or related field. *Application deadline:* For fall admission, 4/10 priority date for domestic students, 4/10 for international students; for spring admission, 11/1 for domestic students, 10/1 for international students. Applications are processed on a rolling basis. Application fee: $50 ($60 for international students). *Financial support:* In 2009–10, 6 fellowships with full tuition reimbursements (averaging $19,552 per year), 6 research assistantships (averaging $10,328 per year) were awarded; Federal Work-Study, scholarships/grants, tuition waivers (full), and unspecified assistantships also available. Financial award application deadline: 2/1. *Faculty research:* Roman and Greek history, Roman and Greek art and architecture, comparative literature, Greek philosophy, textual criticism, Greek and Latin poetry, Greek and Latin prose. Total annual research expenditures: $24,000.

University of Florida, Graduate School, College of Liberal Arts and Sciences, Department of Classics, Gainesville, FL 32611. Offers classical studies (MA, PhD); Latin (MA, MAT, ML). Part-time programs available. Postbaccalaureate distance learning degree programs offered. *Degree requirements:* For master's, 2 foreign languages, thesis; for doctorate, 2 foreign languages, thesis/dissertation. *Entrance requirements:* For master's, GRE General Test, minimum GPA of 3.0; for doctorate, GRE General Test, minimum GPA of 3.0, MA in classical studies. Additional exam requirements/recommendations for international students: Required—TOEFL (minimum score 550 paper-based; 213 computer-based). Electronic applications accepted. *Faculty research:* Greek, literature, epigraphy.

University of Georgia, Graduate School, College of Arts and Sciences, Department of Classics, Athens, GA 30602. Offers classical languages (MA); Greek (MA); Latin (MA). *Faculty:* 11 full-time (4 women). *Students:* 18 full-time (6 women), 4 part-time (3 women); includes 1 minority (Hispanic American). 28 applicants, 54% accepted, 9 enrolled. In 2009, 8 master's awarded. *Degree requirements:* For master's, one foreign language, thesis. *Entrance requirements:* For master's, GRE General Test. *Application deadline:* For fall admission, 7/1 priority date for domestic students; for spring admission, 11/15 for domestic students. Application fee: $50. Electronic applications accepted. *Expenses:* Tuition, state resident: full-time $6000; part-time $250 per credit hour. Tuition, nonresident: full-time $20,904; part-time $871 per credit hour. Required fees: $730 per semester. *Financial support:* Fellowships, research assistantships, teaching assistantships, unspecified assistantships available. *Unit head:* Dr. Charles Platter, Head, 706-542-9260, Fax: 706-542-8503, E-mail: cplatter@uga.edu. *Application contact:* Dr. Erika T. Hermancwicz, Graduate Coordinator, 706-542-7466, Fax: 706-542-8503, E-mail: erikat@uga.edu.

University of Illinois at Urbana–Champaign, Graduate College, College of Liberal Arts and Sciences, School of Literatures, Cultures and Linguistics, Department of the Classics, Champaign, IL 61820. Offers classical philology (PhD); classics (MA); teaching of Latin (MA). *Faculty:* 8 full-time (4 women), 1 part-time/adjunct (0 women). *Students:* 9 full-time (4 women), 7 part-time (5 women); includes 4 minority (2 Asian Americans or Pacific Islanders, 2 Hispanic Americans), 1 international. 22 applicants, 32% accepted, 2 enrolled. In 2009, 3 master's, 1 doctorate awarded. *Entrance requirements:* For master's, GRE, minimum GPA of 3.0; for doctorate, GRE, writing sample; minimum GPA of 3.0. Additional exam requirements/recommendations for international students: Required—TOEFL (minimum score 79 iBT). *Application deadline:* Applications are processed on a rolling basis. Application fee: $60 ($75 for international students). Electronic applications accepted. *Financial support:* In 2009–10, 5 fellowships, 15 teaching assistantships were awarded; research assistantships, tuition waivers (full and partial) also available. *Faculty research:* Greek and Latin language, papyrology, epigraphy, classical archaeology. *Unit head:* David Sansone, Head, 217-333-7573, Fax: 217-244-8430, E-mail: dsansone@illinois.edu. *Application contact:* Lynn Stanke, Office Support Specialist, 217-333-6269, Fax: 217-244-3050, E-mail: stanke@illinois.edu.

The University of Iowa, Graduate College, College of Liberal Arts and Sciences, Department of Classics, Iowa City, IA 52242-1316. Offers MA, PhD. *Degree requirements:* For master's, exam; for doctorate, comprehensive exam, thesis/dissertation. *Entrance requirements:* For master's and doctorate, GRE General Test, minimum GPA of 3.0. Additional exam requirements/recommendations for international students: Required—TOEFL (minimum score 550 paper-based; 213 computer-based; 81 iBT). Electronic applications accepted.

The University of Kansas, Graduate Studies, College of Liberal Arts and Sciences, Department of Classics, Lawrence, KS 66045. Offers MA. Part-time programs available. *Faculty:* 8 full-time (3 women), 3 part-time/adjunct (2 women). *Students:* 9 full-time (6 women), 2 part-time (1 woman); includes 1 minority (Hispanic American). Average age 26. 12 applicants, 58% accepted, 2 enrolled. In 2009, 4 master's awarded. *Degree requirements:* For master's, 3 foreign languages, comprehensive exam, thesis optional. *Entrance requirements:* For master's, GRE (recommended), 15 junior/senior hours of course work in Latin and/or Greek (recommended). Additional exam requirements/recommendations for international students: Required—TOEFL. *Application deadline:* For fall admission, 5/1 priority date for domestic students, 2/1 priority date for international students; for spring admission, 1/15 priority date for domestic students, 9/1 priority date for international students. Applications are processed on a rolling basis. Application fee: $45 ($55 for international students). Electronic applications accepted. *Expenses:* Tuition, state resident: full-time $6492; part-time $270.50 per credit hour. Tuition, nonresident: full-time $15,510; part-time $646.25 per credit hour. Required fees: $847; $70.56 per credit hour. Tuition and fees vary according to course load and program. *Financial support:* In 2009–10, 10 students received support; fellowships with full tuition reimbursements available, teaching assistantships with full and partial tuition reimbursements available, career-related internships or fieldwork, Federal Work-Study, scholarships/grants, traineeships, and unspecified assistantships available. Support available to part-time students. Financial award application deadline: 1/15; financial award applicants required to submit FAFSA. *Faculty research:* Greek and Roman literature, Greek cultural history, Roman cultural history, translation theory, sex and gender. *Unit head:* Pam Gordon, Chair, 785-864-3153, Fax: 785-864-5566, E-mail: pgordon@ku.edu. *Application contact:* Tara Welch, Graduate Director, 785-864-2395, Fax: 785-864-5566, E-mail: tswelch@ku.edu.

University of Kentucky, Graduate School, College of Arts and Sciences, Program in Modern and Classical Languages and Literatures, Lexington, KY 40506-0032. Offers classics (MA). Part-time programs available. *Degree requirements:* For master's, one foreign language, comprehensive exam, thesis optional. *Entrance requirements:* For master's, GRE General Test, minimum undergraduate GPA of 2.75. Additional exam requirements/recommendations for international students: Required—TOEFL (minimum score 550 paper-based; 213 computer-based). Electronic applications accepted. *Faculty research:* Erasmus, Renaissance Latin, Greek and Roman epic, Greek biography, early Christian literature, classical philosophy.

University of Manitoba, Faculty of Graduate Studies, Faculty of Arts, Department of Classics, Winnipeg, MB R3T 2N2, Canada. Offers MA. *Degree requirements:* For master's, thesis.

University of Maryland, College Park, Academic Affairs, College of Arts and Humanities, Department of Classics, College Park, MD 20742. Offers MA. *Faculty:* 6 full-time (3 women), 3 part-time/adjunct (1 woman). *Students:* 5 full-time (2 women), 3 part-time (2 women); includes 1 minority (Hispanic American). 18 applicants, 6% accepted, 1 enrolled. In 2009, 4 master's awarded. *Degree requirements:* For master's, 2 foreign languages, thesis or alternative. *Entrance requirements:* For master's, writing sample, 3 letters of recommendation. Additional exam requirements/recommendations for international students: Required—TOEFL. *Application deadline:* For fall admission, 8/15 for domestic students, 2/1 for international students; for spring admission, 11/15 for domestic students, 6/1 for international students. Applications are processed on a rolling basis. Application fee: $60. Electronic applications accepted. *Expenses:* Tuition, area resident: Part-time $471 per credit hour. Tuition, state resident: part-time $471 per credit hour. Tuition, nonresident: part-time $1016 per credit hour. Required fees: $337.04 per term. *Financial support:* In 2009–10, 5 teaching assistantships with tuition reimbursements (averaging $15,800 per year) were awarded; fellowships with full tuition reimbursements, Federal Work-Study and scholarships/grants also available. Support available to part-time students. Financial award applicants required to submit FAFSA. *Faculty research:* Latin, Greek, and Roman culture. *Unit head:* Dr. Hugh Lee, Chair, 301-405-2014, Fax: 301-314-9084, E-mail: hlee6@umd.edu. *Application contact:* Dean of Graduate School, 301-405-0376, Fax: 301-314-9305.

University of Massachusetts Amherst, Graduate School, College of Humanities and Fine Arts, Department of Classics, Amherst, MA 01003. Offers Latin and classical humanities (MAT). Part-time programs available. *Faculty:* 9 full-time (4 women). *Students:* 11 full-time (5 women), 1 (woman) part-time; includes 1 minority (Hispanic American). Average age 24. 20 applicants, 30% accepted, 6 enrolled. In 2009, 7 master's awarded. *Degree requirements:* For master's, thesis or alternative. *Entrance requirements:* For master's, GRE General Test. Additional exam requirements/recommendations for international students: Required—TOEFL (minimum score 550 paper-based; 213 computer-based; 80 iBT), IELTS (minimum score 6.5). *Application deadline:* For fall admission, 2/1 for domestic and international students. Applications are processed on a rolling basis. Application fee: $50 ($65 for international students). Electronic applications accepted. *Expenses:* Tuition, state resident: full-time $2640; part-time $110 per credit. Tuition, nonresident: full-time $9936; part-time $414 per credit. Tuition and fees vary according to course load. *Financial support:* In 2009–10, 12 teaching assistantships with full tuition reimbursements (averaging $13,663 per year) were awarded; fellowships, research assistantships, career-related internships or fieldwork, Federal Work-Study, scholarships/grants, traineeships, health care benefits, tuition waivers (full), and unspecified assistantships also available. Support available to part-time students. Financial award application deadline: 2/1. *Unit head:* Dr. Kenneth F. Kitchell, Graduate Program Director, 413-545-0512, Fax: 413-545-6995. *Application contact:* Jean M. Ames, Supervisor of Admissions, 413-545-0722, Fax: 413-577-0100, E-mail: gradadm@grad.umass.edu.

University of Michigan, Horace H. Rackham School of Graduate Studies, College of Literature, Science, and the Arts, Department of Classical Studies, Ann Arbor, MI 48109. Offers classical studies (PhD); teaching Latin (MAT). *Faculty:* 21 full-time (8 women), 10 part-time/adjunct (6 women). *Students:* 26 full-time (17 women); includes 3 minority (2 Asian Americans or Pacific Islanders, 1 Hispanic American), 1 international. Average age 27. 98 applicants, 4% accepted,

Classics

University of Michigan (continued)

3 enrolled. In 2009, 3 master's, 7 doctorates awarded. Terminal master's awarded for partial completion of doctoral program. *Degree requirements:* For master's, one foreign language, comprehensive exam; for doctorate, 4 foreign languages, thesis/dissertation, oral defense of dissertation, preliminary exams. *Entrance requirements:* For master's, GRE General Test; for doctorate, GRE General Test, minimum of 3 years of college-level Latin and 2 years of college-level Greek. Additional exam requirements/recommendations for international students: Required—TOEFL (minimum score 560 paper-based; 220 computer-based). *Application deadline:* For fall admission, 1/5 for domestic and international students. Application fee: $60 ($75 for international students). Electronic applications accepted. *Expenses:* Tuition, state resident: full-time $17,286; part-time $1099 per credit hour. Tuition, nonresident: full-time $34,944; part-time $2080 per credit hour. Required fees: $95 per semester. Tuition and fees vary according to course load, degree level and program. *Financial support:* In 2009–10, 26 students received support, including 3 fellowships with full tuition reimbursements available (averaging $18,000 per year), 15 teaching assistantships with full tuition reimbursements available (averaging $16,694 per year); career-related internships or fieldwork, Federal Work-Study, institutionally sponsored loans, scholarships/grants, traineeships, health care benefits, and unspecified assistantships also available. Financial award application deadline: 3/15. *Faculty research:* Greek and Latin literature, ancient history, papyrology, archaeology. *Unit head:* Prof. Ruth Scodel, Chair, 734-764-0360, Fax: 734-763-4959, E-mail: classics@umich.edu. *Application contact:* Michelle M. Biggs, Graduate Coordinator, 734-647-2330, Fax: 734-763-4959, E-mail: mbiggs@umich.edu.

University of Michigan, Horace H. Rackham School of Graduate Studies, College of Literature, Science, and the Arts, Interdepartmental Program in Greek and Roman History, Ann Arbor, MI 48109. Offers PhD, Certificate. *Faculty:* 5 full-time (1 woman), 16 part-time/adjunct (7 women). *Students:* 11 full-time (5 women), 2 international. Average age 26. 20 applicants, 10% accepted, 2 enrolled. In 2009, 1 doctorate awarded. *Degree requirements:* For doctorate, 4 foreign languages, comprehensive exam, thesis/dissertation, oral defense of dissertation, dissertation prospectus, preliminary exams. *Entrance requirements:* For doctorate, GRE, knowledge of classical Greek and Latin; at least 2 years of each. Additional exam requirements/recommendations for international students: Required—TOEFL (minimum score 560 paper-based; 220 computer-based). *Application deadline:* For fall admission, 12/15 for domestic and international students. Application fee: $60 ($75 for international students). Electronic applications accepted. *Expenses:* Tuition, state resident: full-time $17,286; part-time $1099 per credit hour. Tuition, nonresident: full-time $34,944; part-time $2080 per credit hour. Required fees: $95 per semester. Tuition and fees vary according to course load, degree level and program. *Financial support:* In 2009–10, 10 students received support, including 4 fellowships with full tuition reimbursements available (averaging $16,800 per year), 7 teaching assistantships with full tuition reimbursements available (averaging $16,694 per year); career-related internships or fieldwork, Federal Work-Study, institutionally sponsored loans, scholarships/grants, traineeships, health care benefits, and unspecified assistantships also available. Financial award application deadline: 3/15. *Faculty research:* Greek history, Roman history. *Unit head:* Prof. Raymond Van Dam, Professor, 734-763-1193, E-mail: rvandam@umich.edu. *Application contact:* Michelle M. Biggs, Graduate Coordinator, 734-647-2330, Fax: 734-763-4959, E-mail: mbiggs@umich.edu.

University of Minnesota, Twin Cities Campus, Graduate School, College of Liberal Arts, Department of Classical and Near Eastern Studies, Minneapolis, MN 55455-0213. Offers ancient and medieval art and archaeology (MA, PhD); classics (MA, PhD); Greek (MA, PhD); Latin (MA, PhD); religions in antiquity (MA). Part-time programs available. *Faculty:* 22 full-time (6 women). *Students:* 24 full-time (10 women), 1 part-time (0 women), 1 international. Average age 29. 40 applicants, 20% accepted, 4 enrolled. In 2009, 5 master's awarded. Terminal master's awarded for partial completion of doctoral program. *Degree requirements:* For master's, 2 foreign languages, comprehensive exam, thesis or alternative; for doctorate, variable foreign language requirement, comprehensive exam, thesis/dissertation. *Entrance requirements:* For master's and doctorate, GRE, 3 letters of recommendation, department application, writing sample, copies of transcripts, personal statement. Additional exam requirements/recommendations for international students: Required—TOEFL. *Application deadline:* For fall admission, 1/4 priority date for domestic and international students. Application fee: $50 ($75 for international students). Electronic applications accepted. *Financial support:* In 2009–10, 24 students received support, including 2 fellowships with full tuition reimbursements available (averaging $22,500 per year), 2 research assistantships with partial tuition reimbursements available (averaging $7,000 per year), 20 teaching assistantships with full tuition reimbursements available (averaging $14,000 per year); career-related internships or fieldwork, Federal Work-Study, institutionally sponsored loans, health care benefits, and tuition waivers (full and partial) also available. Support available to part-time students. Financial award application deadline: 1/4. *Faculty research:* Greek and Latin literature, religions in antiquity, ancient Near East. *Unit head:* Christopher Nappa, Chair, 612-625-624-6339, Fax: 612-624-4894, E-mail: cnappa@umn.edu. *Application contact:* Victoria H. Keller, Administrative Specialist, 612-625-8371, Fax: 612-624-4894, E-mail: kell0801@umn.edu.

University of Mississippi, Graduate School, College of Liberal Arts, Department of Classics, Oxford, University, MS 38677. Offers MA. *Faculty:* 6 full-time (3 women). In 2009, 1 master's awarded. *Degree requirements:* For master's, thesis. *Entrance requirements:* For master's, GRE General Test, minimum GPA of 3.0. Additional exam requirements/recommendations for international students: Required—TOEFL. *Application deadline:* For fall admission, 4/1 for domestic students; for spring admission, 10/1 for domestic students. Applications are processed on a rolling basis. Application fee: $25. Electronic applications accepted. *Financial support:* Scholarships/grants available. Financial award application deadline: 3/1; financial award applicants required to submit FAFSA. *Unit head:* Dr. Aileen Ajootian, Acting Chair, 662-915-1152, E-mail: ajootian@olemiss.edu. *Application contact:* Dr. Christy M. Wyandt, Associate Dean, 662-915-7474, Fax: 662-915-7577, E-mail: cwyandt@olemiss.edu.

University of Missouri, Graduate School, College of Arts and Sciences, Department of Classical Studies, Columbia, MO 65211. Offers classical languages (MA, PhD); classical studies (MA, PhD). *Faculty:* 9 full-time (2 women), 3 part-time/adjunct (1 woman). *Students:* 16 full-time (9 women), 9 part-time (2 women); includes 2 minority (both African Americans), 2 international. Average age 29. 19 applicants, 47% accepted, 6 enrolled. In 2009, 6 master's awarded. Terminal master's awarded for partial completion of doctoral program. *Degree requirements:* For master's, one foreign language; for doctorate, 2 foreign languages, comprehensive exam, thesis/dissertation. *Entrance requirements:* For master's, GRE General Test, minimum GPA of 3.0 during last 2 years; BA from accredited college/university; reading knowledge of Greek and/or Latin; for doctorate, GRE General Test, minimum GPA of 3.0; MA w a major in Greek, Latin or classics or equivalent of min 21 hours of grad work; reading knowledge of Greek, Latin, German, and French (or Italian). Additional exam requirements/recommendations for international students: Required—TOEFL (minimum score 500 paper-based; 173 computer-based; 61 iBT), IELTS (minimum score 5.5). *Application deadline:* For fall admission, 4/1 priority date for domestic students; for winter admission, 11/1 for domestic students. Applications are processed on a rolling basis. Application fee: $45 ($60 for international students). *Financial support:* In 2009–10, 4 fellowships with full tuition reimbursements, 1 research assistantship with full tuition reimbursement, 10 teaching assistantships with full tuition reimbursements were awarded; institutionally sponsored loans, traineeships, and health care benefits also available. *Unit head:* Dr. Dennis Trout, Department Chair, 573-884-8593, E-mail: troutd@missouri.edu. *Application contact:* Debbie Strodtman, Administrative Assistant, 573-882-0679, E-mail: strodtmand@missouri.edu.

University of Nebraska–Lincoln, Graduate College, College of Arts and Sciences, Department of Classics and Religious Studies, Lincoln, NE 68588. Offers MA. *Degree requirements:* For master's, thesis optional. *Entrance requirements:* For master's, GRE. Additional exam requirements/recommendations for international students: Required—TOEFL (minimum score 550 paper-based; 213 computer-based). Electronic applications accepted. *Faculty research:* Greek and Latin poetry and prose, Greek and Latin linguistics, patristics, gnosticism, religion of late antiquity.

University of New Brunswick Fredericton, School of Graduate Studies, Faculty of Arts, Department of Classics and Ancient History, Fredericton, NB E3B 5A3, Canada. Offers classics (MA). Part-time programs available. *Faculty:* 5 full-time (2 women), 4 part-time/adjunct (1 woman). *Students:* 5 full-time (3 women). *Degree requirements:* For master's, thesis. *Entrance requirements:* For master's, minimum GPA of 3.0, minimum of 18 credit hours or equivalent in either Greek or Latin. Additional exam requirements/recommendations for international students: Required—TOEFL, TWE. *Application deadline:* 1/31 for domestic and international students. Applications are processed on a rolling basis. Application fee: $50 Canadian dollars. Tuition and fees charges are reported in Canadian dollars. *Expenses:* Tuition, area resident: Full-time $5562 Canadian dollars; part-time $2781 Canadian dollars per year. Required fees: $49.75 Canadian dollars per term. *Financial support:* In 2009–10, 2 teaching assistantships were awarded. Financial award application deadline: 1/31. *Faculty research:* Roman history, silver-age Latin poetry, stamped roof tiles, Plato, early Christianity, Greek and Roman archaeology. *Unit head:* Prof. William Kerr, Director of Graduate Studies, 506-458-7507, Fax: 506-447-3072, E-mail: wkerr@unb.ca. *Application contact:* Susan Miller, Graduate Secretary, 506-453-4762, Fax: 506-447-3072, E-mail: smiller@unb.ca.

The University of North Carolina at Chapel Hill, Graduate School, College of Arts and Sciences, Department of Classics, Chapel Hill, NC 27599. Offers classical archaeology (MA, PhD); classics (MA, PhD). Terminal master's awarded for partial completion of doctoral program. *Degree requirements:* For master's, one foreign language, comprehensive exam, thesis; for doctorate, 2 foreign languages, comprehensive exam, thesis/dissertation. *Entrance requirements:* For master's and doctorate, GRE General Test, minimum GPA of 3.0. Electronic applications accepted.

The University of North Carolina at Greensboro, Graduate School, College of Arts and Sciences, Department of Classical Studies, Greensboro, NC 27412-5001. Offers Latin (M Ed). *Entrance requirements:* For master's, GRE General Test, MAT, or PRAXIS. Additional exam requirements/recommendations for international students: Required—TOEFL. Electronic applications accepted.

University of Oregon, Graduate School, College of Arts and Sciences, Department of Classics, Eugene, OR 97403. Offers classical civilization (MA); classics (MA), including Greek, Latin; Greek (MA); Latin (MA). Part-time programs available. *Degree requirements:* For master's, 2 foreign languages, thesis or alternative. *Entrance requirements:* For master's, GRE General Test, minimum GPA of 3.0. Additional exam requirements/recommendations for international students: Required—TOEFL. *Faculty research:* Roman religion, Greek philosophy, archaeology, Greek and Roman literature.

University of Ottawa, Faculty of Graduate and Postdoctoral Studies, Faculty of Arts, Department of Classics and Religious Studies, Ottawa, ON K1N 6N5, Canada. Offers classical studies (MA); religious studies (PhD). *Degree requirements:* For master's, comprehensive exam, thesis or alternative; for doctorate, comprehensive exam, thesis/dissertation. *Entrance requirements:* For master's, honors degree or equivalent, minimum B average; for doctorate, master's degree, minimum B+ average. Electronic applications accepted. *Faculty research:* Religions in Canada, including Amerindian and Inuit religions; religion and culture; late antiquity.

University of Pennsylvania, School of Arts and Sciences, Graduate Group in Classical Studies, Philadelphia, PA 19104. Offers AM, PhD. *Faculty:* 15 full-time (5 women), 4 part-time/adjunct (0 women). *Students:* 21 full-time (11 women), 2 part-time (0 women), 3 international. 69 applicants, 16% accepted, 6 enrolled. In 2009, 10 master's, 3 doctorates awarded. Terminal master's awarded for partial completion of doctoral program. *Degree requirements:* For master's, 3 foreign languages, thesis or alternative; for doctorate, 4 foreign languages, thesis/dissertation. *Entrance requirements:* For master's and doctorate, GRE General Test, undergraduate course work in classical language and history. Additional exam requirements/recommendations for international students: Required—TOEFL. *Application deadline:* For fall admission, 12/1 priority date for domestic students. Application fee: $70. Electronic applications accepted. *Expenses:* Tuition: Full-time $25,660; part-time $4758 per course. Required fees: $2152; $270 per course. Tuition and fees vary according to course load, degree level and program. *Financial support:* Institutionally sponsored loans, scholarships/grants, traineeships, health care benefits, and unspecified assistantships available. Financial award application deadline: 12/15.

University of Pittsburgh, School of Arts and Sciences, Department of Classics, Pittsburgh, PA 15260. Offers MA, PhD. *Faculty:* 7 full-time (1 woman), 4 part-time/adjunct (0 women). *Students:* 9 full-time (1 woman), 1 international. Average age 31. 17 applicants, 29% accepted, 1 enrolled. In 2009, 1 master's, 1 doctorate awarded. Terminal master's awarded for partial completion of doctoral program. *Degree requirements:* For master's, one foreign language, comprehensive exam, thesis optional; for doctorate, 2 foreign languages, comprehensive exam, thesis/dissertation. *Entrance requirements:* For master's and doctorate, GRE General Test, advanced reading knowledge of Greek and Latin. Additional exam requirements/recommendations for international students: Required—TOEFL. *Application deadline:* For fall admission, 1/16 for domestic and international students. Application fee: $50. Electronic applications accepted. *Expenses:* Tuition, state resident: full-time $16,402; part-time $665 per credit. Tuition, nonresident: full-time $28,694; part-time $1175 per credit. Required fees: $690; $175 per term. Tuition and fees vary according to program. *Financial support:* In 2009–10, 6 students received support, including 2 fellowships with full tuition reimbursements available (averaging $18,350 per year), 6 teaching assistantships with full tuition reimbursements available (averaging $15,675 per year); Federal Work-Study and health care benefits also available. Financial award application deadline: 1/16. *Faculty research:* Greek and Roman poetry, Greek drama, Greek and Roman historiography, Greek societal organization. *Unit head:* Dr. D. Mark Possanza, Chairman, 412-624-4486, Fax: 412-624-4419, E-mail: possanza@pitt.edu. *Application contact:* Dr. Andrew M. Miller, Graduate Adviser, 412-624-4485, Fax: 412-624-4419, E-mail: amm2@pitt.edu.

University of South Africa, College of Human Sciences, Pretoria, South Africa. Offers adult education (M Ed); African languages (MA, PhD); African politics (MA, PhD); Afrikaans (MA, PhD); ancient history (MA, PhD); ancient Near Eastern studies (MA, PhD); anthropology (MA, PhD); applied linguistics (MA); Arabic (MA, PhD); archaeology (MA); art history (MA); Biblical archaeology (MA); Biblical studies (M Th, D Th, PhD); Christian spirituality (M Th, D Th); church history (M Th, D Th); classical studies (MA, PhD); clinical psychology (MA); communication (MA, PhD); comparative education (M Ed, Ed D); consulting psychology (D Admin, D Com, PhD); curriculum studies (M Ed, Ed D); development studies (M Admin, MA, D Admin, PhD); didactics (M Ed, Ed D); education (M Tech); education management (M Ed, Ed D); educational psychology (M Ed); English (MA); environmental education (M Ed); French (MA, PhD); German (MA, PhD); Greek (MA); guidance and counseling (M Ed); health studies (MA, PhD), including health sciences education (MA), health services management (MA), medical and surgical nursing science (critical care general) (MA), midwifery and neonatal nursing science (MA), trauma and emergency care (MA); history (MA, PhD); history of education (Ed D); inclusive education (M Ed, Ed D); information and communications technology policy and regulation (MA); information science (MA, MIS, PhD); international politics (MA, PhD); Islamic studies (MA, PhD); Italian (MA, PhD); Judaica (MA, PhD); linguistics (MA, PhD); mathematical education (M Ed); mathematics education (MA); missiology (M Th, D Th); modern Hebrew (MA, PhD); musicology (MA, MMus, D Mus, PhD); natural science education (M Ed); New Testament (M Th, D Th); Old Testament (D Th); pastoral therapy (M Th, D Th); philosophy (MA); philosophy of education (M Ed, Ed D); politics (MA, PhD); Portuguese (MA, PhD); practical theology (M Th, D Th); psychology (MA, MS, PhD); psychology of education (M Ed, Ed D); public health (MA); religious studies (MA, D Th, PhD); Romance languages (MA); Russian (MA, PhD); Semitic languages (MA, PhD); social behavior studies in HIV/AIDS (MA); social science (mental health) (MA); social science in development studies (MA); social science in psychology (MA); social science in social work (MA); social science in sociology

(MA); social work (MSW, DSW, PhD); socio-education (M Ed, Ed D); sociolinguistics (MA); sociology (MA, PhD); Spanish (MA, PhD); systematic theology (M Th, D Th); TESOL (teaching English to speakers of other languages) (MA); theological ethics (M Th, D Th); theory of literature (MA, PhD); urban ministries (D Th); urban ministry (M Th).

University of Southern California, Graduate School, College of Letters, Arts and Sciences, Department of Classics, Los Angeles, CA 90089. Offers MA, PhD. *Faculty:* 10 full-time (3 women), 1 (woman) part-time/adjunct. *Students:* 26 full-time (11 women), 1 (woman) part-time; includes 2 minority (1 American Indian/Alaska Native, 1 Hispanic American), 5 international. 15 applicants, 40% accepted, 5 enrolled. In 2009, 3 master's, 1 doctorate awarded. Terminal master's awarded for partial completion of doctoral program. *Degree requirements:* For master's, 2 foreign languages, comprehensive exam, thesis or alternative, Greek and Latin; for doctorate, 2 foreign languages, comprehensive exam, thesis/dissertation, Greek and Latin. *Application deadline:* For fall admission, 1/15 priority date for domestic and international students. Applications are processed on a rolling basis. Application fee: $85. Electronic applications accepted. *Expenses:* Tuition: Full-time $25,980; part-time $1315 per unit. Required fees: $554. One-time fee: $35 full-time. Full-time tuition and fees vary according to degree level and program. *Financial support:* In 2009–10, 15 students received support, including 5 fellowships with full tuition reimbursements available (averaging $21,000 per year), 10 teaching assistantships with full tuition reimbursements available (averaging $19,600 per year). *Faculty research:* Roman literature, Roman history, Greek tragedy, ancient rhetoric and oratory, Greek philosophy. *Unit head:* Prof. Thomas Habinek, Professor and Chair, 213-821-5303, Fax: 213-740-7360, E-mail: habinek@usc.edu. *Application contact:* Christine Shaw, 213-740-3676, Fax: 213-740-7360, E-mail: shaw@usc.edu.

University of South Florida, Graduate School, College of Arts and Sciences, World Languages Department, Tampa, FL 33620-9951. Offers classics: Latin/Greek (MA); French (MA); linguistics (MA); linguistics: ESL (MA); Spanish (MA). Part-time and evening/weekend programs available. *Faculty:* 19 full-time (14 women), 1 part-time/adjunct (0 women). *Students:* 36 full-time (26 women), 22 part-time (16 women); includes 23 minority (5 African Americans, 3 American Indian/Alaska Native, 2 Asian Americans or Pacific Islanders, 13 Hispanic Americans), 12 international. Average age 32. 29 applicants, 52% accepted, 12 enrolled. In 2009, 18 master's awarded. *Degree requirements:* For master's, comprehensive exam, thesis. *Entrance requirements:* For master's, GRE General Test, minimum GPA of 3.0 in last 60 hours. Additional exam requirements/recommendations for international students: Required—TOEFL (minimum score 600 paper-based; 250 computer-based). *Application deadline:* For fall admission, 2/15 for domestic students, 1/2 for international students; for spring admission, 10/15 for domestic students, 6/1 for international students. Application fee: $30. Electronic applications accepted. *Financial support:* In 2009–10, teaching assistantships with tuition reimbursements (averaging $17,024 per year); tuition waivers (partial) and unspecified assistantships also available. Financial award application deadline: 6/30. *Faculty research:* Second language writing, academic literacy. Total annual research expenditures: $19,891. *Unit head:* Dr. Victor Peppard, Chairperson, 813-974-2012, Fax: 813-974-1718, E-mail: peppard@.cas.usf.edu. *Application contact:* Dr. Victor Peppard, Chairperson, 813-974-2012, Fax: 813-974-1718, E-mail: peppard@.cas.usf.edu.

The University of Texas at Austin, Graduate School, College of Liberal Arts, Department of Classics, Austin, TX 78712-1111. Offers MA, PhD. *Degree requirements:* For master's, 2 foreign languages, comprehensive exam, thesis; for doctorate, 4 foreign languages, comprehensive exam, thesis/dissertation. *Entrance requirements:* For master's, GRE General Test, proficiency in classics; for doctorate, GRE General Test, master's degree in classics. Electronic applications accepted.

University of Toronto, School of Graduate Studies, Humanities Division, Department of Classics, Toronto, ON M5S 1A1, Canada. Offers MA, PhD. Part-time programs available. *Degree requirements:* For master's, qualifying examinations, sight translation exams in Greek and Latin; for doctorate, thesis/dissertation, qualifying examinations, sight translation exams in Greek and Latin. *Entrance requirements:* For master's, minimum B+ average in final year of an undergraduate program in classics, 3–4 years of course work in Greek and Latin; for doctorate, minimum B+ average with at least one A–; MA in classics.

University of Vermont, Graduate College, College of Arts and Sciences, Department of Classics, Burlington, VT 05405. Offers Greek (MA); Greek and Latin (MAT); Latin (MA). *Students:* 6 (3 women); includes 1 minority (Hispanic American). 11 applicants, 64% accepted, 4 enrolled. In 2009, 1 master's awarded. *Degree requirements:* For master's, one foreign language, thesis. *Entrance requirements:* For master's, GRE General Test. Additional exam requirements/recommendations for international students: Required—TOEFL (minimum score 550 paper-based; 213 computer-based; 80 iBT). *Application deadline:* For fall admission, 4/1 priority date for domestic students. Applications are processed on a rolling basis. Application fee: $40. Electronic applications accepted. *Expenses:* Tuition, state resident: part-time $508 per credit hour. Tuition, nonresident: part-time $1281 per credit hour. *Financial support:* Fellowships, teaching assistantships available. Financial award application deadline: 3/1. *Faculty research:* Early Greek literature. *Unit head:* Dr. Mark Usher, Chair, 802-656-3210. *Application contact:* Jacques Bailly, Coordinator, 802-656-3210.

University of Victoria, Faculty of Graduate Studies, Faculty of Humanities, Department of Greek and Roman Studies, Victoria, BC V8W 2Y2, Canada. Offers MA, PhD. PhD offered by special arrangement. Part-time programs available. *Degree requirements:* For master's, 3 foreign languages, thesis. *Entrance requirements:* For master's, knowledge of Greek and Latin. Additional exam requirements/recommendations for international students: Required—TOEFL (minimum score 575 paper-based; 233 computer-based), IELTS (minimum score 7). Electronic applications accepted. *Faculty research:* Roman social history, Roman archaeology and technology, Roman literature, Greek literature, Homer and tragedy, Greek historiography.

University of Virginia, College and Graduate School of Arts and Sciences, Department of Classics, Charlottesville, VA 22903. Offers MA, PhD. *Faculty:* 10 full-time (3 women). *Students:* 23 full-time (11 women), 1 part-time (0 women); includes 2 minority (1 Asian American or Pacific Islander, 1 Hispanic American), 2 international. Average age 27. 63 applicants, 25% accepted, 4 enrolled. In 2009, 7 master's, 2 doctorates awarded. *Degree requirements:* For master's, one foreign language, comprehensive exam, thesis, oral exam; for doctorate, 2 foreign languages, comprehensive exam, thesis/dissertation, oral exam. *Entrance requirements:* For master's and doctorate, GRE General Test, 2 letters of recommendation. Additional exam requirements/recommendations for international students: Required—TOEFL (minimum score 600 paper-based; 250 computer-based; 90 iBT), IELTS (minimum score 7). *Application deadline:* Applications are processed on a rolling basis. Application fee: $60. Electronic applications accepted. *Financial support:* Fellowships, teaching assistantships, unspecified assistantships available. Financial award application deadline: 1/3; financial award applicants required to submit FAFSA. *Unit head:* John Miller, Chair, 434-924-3008, Fax: 434-924-3062, E-mail: classics@virginia.edu. *Application contact:* Tony Woodman, Director of Graduate Admissions, 434-924-3008, E-mail: ajw6n@virginia.edu.

University of Washington, Graduate School, College of Arts and Sciences, Department of Classics, Seattle, WA 98195. Offers MA, PhD. Part-time programs available. *Faculty:* 10 full-time (6 women). *Students:* 19 full-time (13 women), 6 part-time (1 woman); includes 4 minority (1 Asian American or Pacific Islander, 3 Hispanic Americans), 4 international. Average age 30. 75 applicants, 24% accepted, 3 enrolled. In 2009, 8 master's, 3 doctorates awarded. Terminal master's awarded for partial completion of doctoral program. *Degree requirements:* For master's, one foreign language, thesis or alternative; for doctorate, 2 foreign languages, comprehensive exam, thesis/dissertation. *Entrance requirements:* For master's, GRE, bachelor's degree in classics, Greek, or Latin; minimum GPA of 3.0; for doctorate, GRE, minimum GPA of 3.0. Additional exam requirements/recommendations for international students: Required—TOEFL. *Application deadline:* For fall admission, 1/5 for domestic students. Application fee: $50. Electronic applications accepted. *Financial support:* In 2009–10, 20 students received support, including 1 fellowship with full tuition reimbursement available (averaging $13,725 per year), 1 research assistantship with full tuition reimbursement available (averaging $13,725 per year), 15 teaching assistantships with full tuition reimbursements available (averaging $13,725 per year); Federal Work-Study, institutionally sponsored loans, and tuition waivers (partial) also available. Financial award application deadline: 3/1; financial award applicants required to submit FAFSA. *Faculty research:* Greek and Latin poetry, Greek and Roman cultural institutions, Greek and Latin historiography, Greek tragedy. *Unit head:* Alain M. Gowing, Chair, 206-543-2266, Fax: 206-543-2267, E-mail: alain@u.washington.edu. *Application contact:* Catherine Connors, Graduate Coordinator, 206-543-2266, Fax: 206-543-2267, E-mail: cconnors@u.washington.edu.

University of Washington, Graduate School, College of Arts and Sciences, Department of Philosophy, Seattle, WA 98195. Offers classics and philosophy (PhD); philosophy (MA, PhD). Terminal master's awarded for partial completion of doctoral program. *Degree requirements:* For master's, 3 papers; for doctorate, thesis/dissertation, general exam. *Entrance requirements:* For master's and doctorate, GRE, minimum GPA of 3.0. Additional exam requirements/recommendations for international students: Required—TOEFL. *Faculty research:* History and philosophy of science, epistemology, Aristotle's metaphysics, ethics and politics, causation in modern philosophy.

The University of Western Ontario, Faculty of Graduate Studies, Faculty of Arts and Humanities, Department of Classical Studies, London, ON N6A 5B8, Canada. Offers MA. Part-time programs available. *Degree requirements:* For master's, one foreign language. *Entrance requirements:* For master's, honors degree, minimum B+ average. Additional exam requirements/recommendations for international students: Required—TOEFL. *Faculty research:* Greek literature, Roman history and law, ancient sport, Byzantine literature, Bronze Age archaeology.

University of Wisconsin–Madison, Graduate School, College of Letters and Science, Department of Classics, Madison, WI 53706-1380. Offers classics (MA, PhD); Greek (MA); Latin (MA). Part-time programs available. Terminal master's awarded for partial completion of doctoral program. *Degree requirements:* For master's, 3 foreign languages, oral and written exams; for doctorate, 4 foreign languages, thesis/dissertation, written exams. *Entrance requirements:* For master's, GRE; for doctorate, master's degree. Electronic applications accepted. *Expenses:* Tuition, state resident: part-time $594 per credit. Tuition, nonresident: part-time $1504 per credit. Required fees: $65 per credit. Tuition and fees vary according to course load, program and reciprocity agreements. *Faculty research:* Greek tragedy, Latin elegy, historiography, Homer, Greek lyric poetry.

University of Wisconsin–Milwaukee, Graduate School, College of Letters and Sciences, Interdepartmental Program in Foreign Language and Literature, Milwaukee, WI 53201-0413. Offers classics and Hebrew studies (MAFLL); comparative literature (MAFLL); French and Italian (MAFLL); German (MAFLL); Slavic studies (MAFLL); translation (Certificate). Part-time programs available. *Faculty:* 37 full-time (18 women). *Students:* 32 full-time (25 women), 28 part-time (19 women); includes 5 minority (1 Asian American or Pacific Islander, 4 Hispanic Americans), 22 international. Average age 33. 54 applicants, 69% accepted, 20 enrolled. In 2009, 24 master's awarded. *Degree requirements:* For master's, 2 foreign languages, thesis or alternative. *Entrance requirements:* Additional exam requirements/recommendations for international students: Required—TOEFL (minimum score 550 paper-based; 79 iBT), IELTS (minimum score 6.5). *Application deadline:* For fall admission, 1/1 priority date for domestic students; for spring admission, 9/1 for domestic students. Applications are processed on a rolling basis. Application fee: $45 ($75 for international students). *Expenses:* Tuition, state resident: full-time $8800. Tuition, nonresident: full-time $20,760. Tuition and fees vary according to program and reciprocity agreements. *Financial support:* In 2009–10, 2 research assistantships, 21 teaching assistantships were awarded; career-related internships or fieldwork and unspecified assistantships also available. Support available to part-time students. Financial award application deadline: 4/15. Total annual research expenditures: $285,237. *Unit head:* Gabrielle Verdier, Representative, 414-229-3346, Fax: 414-229-2741, E-mail: verdier@uwm.edu. *Application contact:* General Information Contact, 414-229-4982, Fax: 414-229-6967, E-mail: gradschool@uwm.edu.

Vanderbilt University, Graduate School, Department of Classical Studies, Nashville, TN 37240-1001. Offers classics (MA); Latin (MAT). *Faculty:* 14 full-time (7 women). *Students:* 7 full-time (4 women); includes 1 minority (Hispanic American), 1 international. Average age 24. 31 applicants, 16% accepted, 3 enrolled. In 2009, 2 master's awarded. *Degree requirements:* For master's, 2 foreign languages, thesis. *Entrance requirements:* For master's, GRE General Test. Additional exam requirements/recommendations for international students: Required—TOEFL (minimum score 570 paper-based; 230 computer-based; 88 iBT). *Application deadline:* For fall admission, 1/15 for domestic and international students. Application fee: $0. Electronic applications accepted. *Financial support:* Fellowships with full and partial tuition reimbursements, teaching assistantships with full and partial tuition reimbursements, Federal Work-Study, institutionally sponsored loans, scholarships/grants, and health care benefits available. Financial award application deadline: 1/15; financial award applicants required to submit CSS PROFILE or FAFSA. *Faculty research:* Greek and Latin literature and language, Greek and Roman history, classical archaeology, philosophy, religion. *Unit head:* Barbara Tsakirgis, Chair, 615-322-2516, Fax: 615-343-7261, E-mail: barbara.tsakirgis@vanderbilt.edu. *Application contact:* Thomas McGinn, Director of Graduate Studies, 615-322-2516, Fax: 615-343-7261, E-mail: thomas.a.mcginn@vanderbilt.edu.

Washington University in St. Louis, Graduate School of Arts and Sciences, Department of Classics, St. Louis, MO 63130-4899. Offers MA. *Degree requirements:* For master's, thesis or alternative. *Entrance requirements:* For master's, GRE General Test. Electronic applications accepted.

Wayne State University, College of Liberal Arts and Sciences, Department of Classical and Modern Languages, Literatures, and Cultures, Program in Classics, Greek, and Latin, Detroit, MI 48202. Offers classics (MA); Latin (MA). *Degree requirements:* For master's, thesis optional. *Entrance requirements:* For master's, GRE, bachelor's degree in Latin, Greek, or classics; letters of recommendation; writing sample. Additional exam requirements/recommendations for international students: Required—TOEFL (minimum score 550 paper-based; 213 computer-based); Recommended—TWE (minimum score 6). Electronic applications accepted.

West Chester University of Pennsylvania, Office of Graduate Studies, College of Arts and Sciences, Department of Languages and Cultures, West Chester, PA 19383. Offers French (M Ed, MA, Teaching Certificate); German (M Ed, Teaching Certificate); Latin (M Ed, Teaching Certificate); Spanish (M Ed, MA, Teaching Certificate). Part-time and evening/weekend programs available. *Students:* 4 full-time (all women), 27 part-time (21 women); includes 6 minority (2 African Americans, 1 Asian American or Pacific Islander, 3 Hispanic Americans). Average age 33. 16 applicants, 94% accepted, 9 enrolled. In 2009, 7 master's awarded. *Degree requirements:* For master's, one foreign language, comprehensive exam, thesis optional. *Entrance requirements:* For master's, GRE or MAT, placement test. Additional exam requirements/recommendations for international students: Required—TOEFL (minimum score 550 paper-based; 213 computer-based; 80 iBT). *Application deadline:* For fall admission, 4/15 priority date for domestic students, 3/15 for international students; for spring admission, 10/15 for domestic students, 9/1 for international students. Applications are processed on a rolling basis. Application fee: $35. Electronic applications accepted. *Expenses:* Tuition, state resident: full-time $6666; part-time $370 per credit. Tuition, nonresident: full-time $10,666; part-time $593 per credit. Required fees: $122.56 per credit. *Financial support:* In 2009–10, 1 research assistantship with full and partial tuition reimbursement (averaging $5,000 per year) was awarded; unspecified assistantships also available. Support available to part-time students. Financial award application deadline: 2/15; financial award applicants required to submit FAFSA. *Faculty research:* Implementation of world languages curriculum framework. *Unit head:* Dr. Jerry Williams, Chair, 610-436-2700, Fax: 610-436-3048, E-mail: jwilliams2@wcupa.edu. *Application contact:* Dr. Rebecca Pauly, Graduate Coordinator, 610-436-2382, E-mail: rpauly@wcupa.edu.

Classics

Wilfrid Laurier University, Faculty of Graduate Studies, Faculty of Arts, Department of Archaeology and Classical Studies, Waterloo, ON N2L 3C5, Canada. Offers MA. *Degree requirements:* For master's, thesis optional. *Entrance requirements:* For master's, minimum B+ average in last two undergraduate years (exclusive of first year level courses in those years). Additional exam requirements/recommendations for international students: Required—TOEFL.

Yale University, Graduate School of Arts and Sciences, Department of Classics, New Haven, CT 06520. Offers M Phil, MA, PhD. *Degree requirements:* For doctorate, 2 foreign languages, thesis/dissertation. *Entrance requirements:* For doctorate, GRE General Test.

Comparative Literature

American University, College of Arts and Sciences, Department of Literature, Program in Literature, Washington, DC 20016-8047. Offers MA. Part-time and evening/weekend programs available. *Students:* 20 full-time (17 women), 11 part-time (9 women); includes 2 minority (1 African American, 1 Asian American or Pacific Islander), 3 international. Average age 28. 49 applicants, 76% accepted, 15 enrolled. In 2009, 8 master's awarded. *Degree requirements:* For master's, comprehensive exam, thesis or alternative. *Entrance requirements:* For master's, GRE, writing sample. Additional exam requirements/recommendations for international students: Required—TOEFL. *Application deadline:* For fall admission, 2/1 for domestic students. Application fee: $80. *Expenses:* Tuition: Full-time $22,266; part-time $1237 per credit hour. Required fees: $430. Tuition and fees vary according to program. *Financial support:* In 2009–10, 6 students received support; fellowships, research assistantships, teaching assistantships, career-related internships or fieldwork, Federal Work-Study, institutionally sponsored loans, and tuition waivers (full and partial) available. Support available to part-time students. Financial award application deadline: 2/1. *Faculty research:* British, American, African-American, and Third World literature; cinema studies; literary theory; feminist criticism. *Unit head:* Dr. Jonathon Loesberg, Chair, 202-885-2998, Fax: 202-885-2938, E-mail: jloesbe@american.edu. *Application contact:* Dr. Jonathon Loesberg, Chair, 202-885-2998, Fax: 202-885-2938, E-mail: jloesbe@american.edu.

The American University in Cairo, Graduate Studies and Research, School of Humanities and Social Sciences, Department of English and Comparative Literature, Cairo, Egypt. Offers MA. Part-time programs available. *Degree requirements:* For master's, thesis, proficiency in French or German. *Entrance requirements:* Additional exam requirements/recommendations for international students: Required—English entrance exam and/or TOEFL.

Antioch University Midwest, Graduate Programs, Individualized Liberal and Professional Studies Program, Yellow Springs, OH 45387-1609. Offers liberal and professional studies (MA), including counseling, creative writing, education, film studies, liberal studies, management, modern literature, psychology, theatre, visual arts. Part-time and evening/weekend programs available. Postbaccalaureate distance learning degree programs offered (minimal on-campus study). *Faculty:* 1 full-time (0 women), 2 part-time/adjunct (1 woman). *Students:* 23 full-time (13 women), 41 part-time (30 women); includes 13 minority (11 African Americans, 2 Hispanic Americans). Average age 40. 21 applicants, 76% accepted, 15 enrolled. In 2009, 24 master's awarded. *Degree requirements:* For master's, thesis or alternative. *Entrance requirements:* For master's, resume, 2 letters of reference. *Application deadline:* For fall admission, 8/1 for domestic students; for winter admission, 12/1 for domestic students; for spring admission, 3/10 for domestic students. Applications are processed on a rolling basis. Application fee: $50. Electronic applications accepted. *Expenses:* Contact institution. *Financial support:* Federal Work-Study available. Financial award applicants required to submit FAFSA. *Unit head:* Dr. Jon Saari, Chair, 937-769-1879, Fax: 937-769-1807, E-mail: jsaari@antioch.edu. *Application contact:* Seth Gordon, Assistant Director of Admissions, 937-769-1800 Ext. 1825, Fax: 937-769-1804, E-mail: sgordon@antioch.edu.

Arizona State University, Graduate College, College of Liberal Arts and Sciences, Division of Humanities, Department of English, Tempe, AZ 85287. Offers creative writing (MFA); English (MA, PhD), including comparative literature (MA), linguistics (MA), literature, rhetoric and composition (MA), rhetoric/composition and linguistics (PhD); teaching English to speakers of other languages (MTESOL). *Degree requirements:* For doctorate, thesis/dissertation. *Entrance requirements:* For master's and doctorate, GRE.

Brigham Young University, Graduate Studies, College of Humanities, Department of Humanities, Classics, and Comparative Literature, Provo, UT 84602-1001. Offers comparative studies (MA). *Faculty:* 25 full-time (5 women). *Students:* 16 full-time (9 women). Average age 27. 11 applicants, 55% accepted, 6 enrolled. In 2009, 7 master's awarded. *Degree requirements:* For master's, 2 foreign languages, thesis. *Entrance requirements:* For master's, GRE, minimum GPA of 3.0 in last 60 hours. Additional exam requirements/recommendations for international students: Required—TOEFL (minimum score 580 paper-based; 85 iBT), IELTS (minimum score 7). *Application deadline:* For fall admission, 3/1 for domestic and international students. Application fee: $50. Electronic applications accepted. *Expenses:* Tuition: Full-time $5580; part-time $301 per credit hour. Tuition and fees vary according to student's religious affiliation. *Financial support:* In 2009–10, 16 students received support, including 4 research assistantships (averaging $1,875 per year), 36 teaching assistantships (averaging $2,620 per year); career-related internships or fieldwork, institutionally sponsored loans, scholarships/grants, tuition waivers (full and partial), and student instructorships also available. Support available to part-time students. *Unit head:* Dr. Michael J. Call, Chair, 801-422-2550, Fax: 801-422-0305, E-mail: michael_call@byu.edu. *Application contact:* Carolyn Hone, Graduate Secretary for Humanities and Comparative Literature, 801-422-4430, Fax: 801-422-0305, E-mail: carolyn_hone@byu.edu.

Brock University, Faculty of Graduate Studies, Faculty of Humanities, Program in Studies in Comparative Literatures and Arts, St. Catharines, ON L2S 3A1, Canada. Offers MA. *Degree requirements:* For master's, thesis optional. *Entrance requirements:* For master's, honors degree. Additional exam requirements/recommendations for international students: Required—TOEFL (minimum score 550 paper-based; 213 computer-based; 80 iBT), IELTS (minimum score 6.5), TWE (minimum score 4). Electronic applications accepted.

Brown University, Graduate School, Department of Comparative Literature, Providence, RI 02912. Offers PhD. *Degree requirements:* For doctorate, 2 foreign languages, thesis/dissertation, preliminary exam. *Entrance requirements:* For doctorate, GRE General Test, GRE Subject Test.

California State University, Fullerton, Graduate Studies, College of Humanities and Social Sciences, Department of English and Comparative Literature, Fullerton, CA 92834-9480. Offers comparative literature (MA); English (MA). Part-time programs available. *Students:* 31 full-time (22 women), 58 part-time (44 women); includes 25 minority (3 African Americans, 4 Asian Americans or Pacific Islanders, 18 Hispanic Americans). Average age 29. 69 applicants, 46% accepted, 23 enrolled. In 2009, 35 master's awarded. *Degree requirements:* For master's, comprehensive exam, thesis or alternative. *Entrance requirements:* For master's, minimum GPA of 3.0 in major, 2.5 in last 60 hours. Application fee: $55. *Expenses:* Tuition, nonresident: full-time $11,160; part-time $373 per credit. Required fees: $1440 per term. Tuition and fees vary according to course load, degree level and program. *Financial support:* Career-related internships or fieldwork, Federal Work-Study, institutionally sponsored loans, and scholarships/grants available. Support available to part-time students. Financial award application deadline: 3/1; financial award applicants required to submit FAFSA. *Unit head:* Dr. Joseph Sawicki, Chair, 657-278-3163. *Application contact:* Admissions/Applications, 657-278-2371.

California State University, Northridge, Graduate Studies, College of Humanities, Department of English, Northridge, CA 91330. Offers creative writing (MA); literature (MA); rhetoric and composition theory (MA). Part-time and evening/weekend programs available. *Faculty:* 31 full-time (13 women), 66 part-time/adjunct (58 women). *Students:* 36 full-time (22 women), 130 part-time (87 women); includes 1 American Indian/Alaska Native, 16 Asian Americans or Pacific Islanders, 22 Hispanic Americans, 1 international. Average age 33. 119 applicants, 65% accepted, 42 enrolled. In 2009, 36 master's awarded. *Degree requirements:* For master's, thesis or alternative. *Entrance requirements:* For master's, writing proficiency test, GRE General Test or minimum GPA of 3.0. Additional exam requirements/recommendations for international students: Required—TOEFL. *Application deadline:* For fall admission, 11/30 for domestic students. Application fee: $55. *Financial support:* Teaching assistantships available. Financial award application deadline: 3/1. *Faculty research:* Reading improvement, professional writing, Dickens, Shaw, English as a second language. *Unit head:* Dr. George Uba, Chair, 818-677-3434, E-mail: george.uba@csun.edu. *Application contact:* Dr. Marjie Seagoe, Graduate Studies Secretary, 818-677-3433.

Carleton University, Faculty of Graduate Studies, Faculty of Arts and Social Sciences, School for Languages, Literatures, and Comparative Literary Studies, Ottawa, ON K1S 5B6, Canada. Offers cultural mediations (PhD). *Entrance requirements:* Additional exam requirements/recommendations for international students: Required—TOEFL. *Faculty research:* Literary history, theory of literature, cross-cultural studies, modernism/postmodernism, comparative Canadian literature.

Carnegie Mellon University, College of Humanities and Social Sciences, Department of English, Pittsburgh, PA 15213-3891. Offers communication planning and design (M Des); literary and cultural studies (MA, PhD); professional writing (MAPW), including editing and publishing, policy and non-profit communication, public and media relations / corporate communications, science or healthcare communication, technical writing, writing for new media, writing for print media; rhetoric (MA, PhD). Part-time programs available. Terminal master's awarded for partial completion of doctoral program. *Degree requirements:* For doctorate, 2 foreign languages, comprehensive exam, thesis/dissertation. *Entrance requirements:* For master's and doctorate, GRE General Test. Additional exam requirements/recommendations for international students: Required—TOEFL, TWE. *Faculty research:* Cognitive processes in discourse with emphasis on writing, testing, and evaluation.

Case Western Reserve University, School of Graduate Studies, Department of Modern Languages and Literatures and Department of English, Program in World Literature, Cleveland, OH 44106. Offers MA. *Faculty:* 16 full-time (11 women), 9 part-time/adjunct (6 women). *Students:* 1 (woman) part-time. 4 applicants, 50% accepted, 1 enrolled. In 2009, 1 master's awarded. *Degree requirements:* For master's, 2 foreign languages, written exam. *Entrance requirements:* For master's, GRE General Test, sample of written work. Additional exam requirements/recommendations for international students: Required—TOEFL (minimum score 550 paper-based; 213 computer-based; 79 iBT). *Application deadline:* For fall admission, 3/1 for domestic students. Applications are processed on a rolling basis. Application fee: $50. Electronic applications accepted. *Financial support:* Fellowships, career-related internships or fieldwork, institutionally sponsored loans, and tuition waivers (partial) available. Financial award application deadline: 3/1; financial award applicants required to submit FAFSA. *Faculty research:* Literary theory, literary translation, Romanticism. *Application contact:* Marie Lathers, Director, Graduate Studies (French), 216-368-3071, Fax: 216-368-2216, E-mail: mhl5@case.edu.

Claremont Graduate University, Graduate Programs, School of Arts and Humanities, Department of English, Claremont, CA 91711-6160. Offers American studies (MA, PhD); critical theory (MA, PhD); early modern studies (MA, PhD); English (M Phil, MA, PhD); literary theory (PhD); literature (MA, PhD); literature and creative writing (MA); literature and film (MA); MBA/MA; MBA/PhD. Part-time programs available. *Faculty:* 2 full-time (1 woman), 2 part-time/adjunct (0 women). *Students:* 83 full-time (60 women), 19 part-time (11 women); includes 17 minority (1 African American, 1 American Indian/Alaska Native, 8 Asian Americans or Pacific Islanders, 7 Hispanic Americans), 4 international. Average age 35. In 2009, 6 master's, 4 doctorates awarded. *Entrance requirements:* For master's and doctorate, GRE General Test. Additional exam requirements/recommendations for international students: Required—TOEFL (minimum score 550 paper-based; 213 computer-based; 80 iBT). *Application deadline:* For fall admission, 2/1 priority date for domestic students. Applications are processed on a rolling basis. Application fee: $60. Electronic applications accepted. *Expenses:* Tuition: Full-time $35,046; part-time $1524 per credit. Required fees: $161 per semester. *Financial support:* Fellowships, Federal Work-Study, institutionally sponsored loans, and scholarships/grants available. Support available to part-time students. Financial award application deadline: 2/15; financial award applicants required to submit FAFSA. *Faculty research:* American, comparative, and English Renaissance literature; modernism; feminist literature and theory. *Unit head:* Wendy Martin, Chair, 909-621-8612, Fax: 909-607-1221, E-mail: wendy.martin@cgu.edu. *Application contact:* Susan Hampson, Admissions Coordinator, 909-607-1278, Fax: 909-607-1221, E-mail: humanities@cgu.edu.

College of the Humanities and Sciences, Harrison Middleton University, Graduate Program, Tempe, AZ 85282. Offers education (MA, Ed D); humanities (MA); imaginative literature (MA); interdisciplinary studies (DA); jurisprudence (MA); natural science (MA); philosophy and religion (MA); social science (MA). Part-time and evening/weekend programs available. Postbaccalaureate distance learning degree programs offered (no on-campus study). *Faculty:* 17 full-time (7 women), 14 part-time/adjunct (6 women). *Students:* 49 full-time (18 women). In 2009, 4 master's awarded. *Application deadline:* Applications are processed on a rolling basis. Application fee: $50. Electronic applications accepted. *Application contact:* Deborah Deacon, Dean of Graduate Studies, 877-248-6724, Fax: 800-762-1622, E-mail: ddeacon@chumsci.edu.

Columbia University, Graduate School of Arts and Sciences, Division of Humanities, Department of English and Comparative Literature, New York, NY 10027. Offers comparative literature (M Phil, MA, PhD); English literature (M Phil, MA, PhD); literature-writing (M Phil, MA, PhD). Part-time programs available. *Degree requirements:* For master's, one foreign language, comprehensive exam, seminar papers; for doctorate, thesis/dissertation. *Entrance requirements:* For master's and doctorate, GRE General Test. Additional exam requirements/recommendations for international students: Required—TOEFL. *Faculty research:* Medieval through modern literature, drama, literary criticism.

Cornell University, Graduate School, Graduate Fields of Arts and Sciences, Field of Comparative Literature, Ithaca, NY 14853-0001. Offers PhD. *Faculty:* 52 full-time (20 women). *Students:* 26 full-time (18 women); includes 4 minority (3 Asian Americans or Pacific Islanders, 1 Hispanic American), 7 international. Average age 30. 87 applicants, 3% accepted, 2 enrolled.

In 2009, 7 doctorates awarded. *Degree requirements:* For doctorate, 2 foreign languages, comprehensive exam, thesis/dissertation, teaching experience. *Entrance requirements:* For doctorate, GRE General Test, proficiency in 2 foreign literatures, writing sample, 3 letters of recommendation. Additional exam requirements/recommendations for international students: Required—TOEFL (minimum score 550 paper-based; 213 computer-based; 77 iBT). *Application deadline:* For fall admission, 1/10 for domestic students. Application fee: $70. Electronic applications accepted. *Expenses:* Tuition: Full-time $29,500. Required fees: $70. Full-time tuition and fees vary according to degree level, program and student level. *Financial support:* In 2009–10, 22 students received support, including 2 fellowships with full tuition reimbursements available; research assistantships with full tuition reimbursements available, teaching assistantships with full tuition reimbursements available, institutionally sponsored loans, health care benefits, and tuition waivers (full and partial) also available. Financial award applicants required to submit FAFSA. *Faculty research:* Critical theory, European studies, Latin American studies, Asian studies. *Unit head:* Director of Graduate Studies, 607-255-4155. *Application contact:* Graduate Field Assistant, 607-255-4155, E-mail: complit@cornell.edu.

Dartmouth College, Arts and Sciences Graduate Programs, Comparative Literature Program, Hanover, NH 03755. Offers AM. *Faculty:* 23 full-time (16 women). *Students:* 8 full-time (6 women); includes 3 minority (1 African American, 2 Hispanic Americans), 5 international. Average age 24. 28 applicants, 46% accepted, 8 enrolled. In 2009, 7 master's awarded. *Degree requirements:* For master's, final paper, oral exams. *Entrance requirements:* For master's, proficiency in 2 languages. Additional exam requirements/recommendations for international students: Required—TOEFL. *Application deadline:* For fall admission, 2/1 priority date for domestic students. Application fee: $30. Electronic applications accepted. *Financial support:* In 2009–10, 4 students received support, including fellowships with full tuition reimbursements available (averaging $14,832 per year), teaching assistantships with full tuition reimbursements available (averaging $14,832 per year); career-related internships or fieldwork, institutionally sponsored loans, scholarships/grants, and tuition waivers (full) also available. Support available to part-time students. Financial award applicants required to submit CSS PROFILE. *Unit head:* Dr. Silvia Spitta, Chair, 603-646-2912. *Application contact:* Karen DeRosa, Program Administrator, 603-646-2912, Fax: 603-646-2912.

Duke University, Graduate School, Program in Literature, Durham, NC 27708. Offers PhD. *Faculty:* 24 full-time. *Students:* 48 full-time (25 women); includes 12 minority (2 African Americans, 4 Asian Americans or Pacific Islanders, 6 Hispanic Americans), 13 international. 161 applicants, 5% accepted, 5 enrolled. In 2009, 2 doctorates awarded. *Degree requirements:* For doctorate, 2 foreign languages, thesis/dissertation. *Entrance requirements:* For doctorate, GRE General Test. Additional exam requirements/recommendations for international students: Required—TOEFL (minimum score 550 paper-based; 213 computer-based; 83 iBT), IELTS (minimum score 7). *Application deadline:* For fall admission, 12/8 priority date for domestic and international students. Application fee: $75. *Financial support:* Fellowships, research assistantships, teaching assistantships, Federal Work-Study available. Financial award application deadline: 12/31. *Unit head:* Katherine Hayles, Director of Graduate Studies, 919-684-9319, Fax: 919-684-4423, E-mail: johns194@duke.edu. *Application contact:* Cynthia Robertson, Associate Dean for Enrollment Services, 919-684-3913, E-mail: grad-admissions@duke.edu.

Emory University, Graduate School of Arts and Sciences, Department of Comparative Literature, Atlanta, GA 30322-1100. Offers comparative literature (PhD); English (Certificate); French (Certificate); Middle Eastern studies (PhD); philosophy (Certificate); psychoanalytic studies (PhD); religion (PhD); Spanish (Certificate); women studies (Certificate). *Degree requirements:* For doctorate, 2 foreign languages, comprehensive exam, thesis/dissertation. *Entrance requirements:* For doctorate, GRE General Test, minimum GPA of 3.0. Additional exam requirements/recommendations for international students: Required—TOEFL. Electronic applications accepted. *Faculty research:* Literary theory, psychoanalysis trauma and testimony, literature and religion, literature and technology, literature and philosophy, politics and global culture, literature and aesthetics.

Emory University, Graduate School of Arts and Sciences, Department of Spanish and Portuguese, Atlanta, GA 30322-1100. Offers comparative literature (Certificate); film studies (Certificate); Spanish (PhD); women's studies (Certificate). *Degree requirements:* For doctorate, 2 foreign languages, comprehensive exam, thesis/dissertation. *Entrance requirements:* For doctorate, GRE General Test. Additional exam requirements/recommendations for international students: Required—TOEFL. Electronic applications accepted. *Faculty research:* Spanish literature, Spanish-American literature, literary theory, criticism, cultural studies.

Fairleigh Dickinson University, Metropolitan Campus, University College: Arts, Sciences, and Professional Studies, Department of English, Philosophy, and Humanities, Program in English and Literature, Teaneck, NJ 07666-1914. Offers MA. *Students:* 4 full-time (3 women), 6 part-time (5 women). Average age 29. 6 applicants, 100% accepted, 2 enrolled. Application fee: $40. *Application contact:* Susan Brooman, University Director of Graduate Admissions, 201-692-2554, Fax: 201-692-2560, E-mail: globaleducation@fdu.edu.

Florida Atlantic University, Dorothy F. Schmidt College of Arts and Letters, Department of Languages, Linguistics, and Comparative Literature, Boca Raton, FL 33431-0991. Offers comparative literature (MA); French (MA); linguistics (MA); Spanish (MA). Part-time programs available. *Faculty:* 23 full-time (20 women), 12 part-time/adjunct (10 women). *Students:* 20 full-time (14 women), 14 part-time (10 women); includes 16 minority (3 African Americans, 1 Asian American or Pacific Islander, 12 Hispanic Americans), 4 international. Average age 35. 35 applicants, 60% accepted, 13 enrolled. In 2009, 16 master's awarded. *Degree requirements:* For master's, one foreign language, comprehensive exam, thesis optional. *Entrance requirements:* For master's, GRE General Test, minimum GPA of 3.0. *Application deadline:* For fall admission, 7/1 priority date for domestic students, 2/15 for international students; for spring admission, 11/1 for domestic students, 7/15 for international students. Applications are processed on a rolling basis. Application fee: $30. *Expenses:* Tuition, state resident: full-time $7055; part-time $293.94 per credit hour. Tuition, nonresident: full-time $22,096; part-time $920.66 per credit hour. *Financial support:* Fellowships, research assistantships, teaching assistantships with partial tuition reimbursements, Federal Work-Study and tuition waivers (partial) available. Support available to part-time students. Financial award application deadline: 4/1. *Faculty research:* Modern European studies, modern Latin America, medieval Europe. *Unit head:* Dr. Michael Horswell, Chair, 561-297-3860, Fax: 561-297-2756, E-mail: horswell@fau.edu. *Application contact:* Dr. Emily Stockard, Associate Dean, 561-297-2817, Fax: 561-297-2744, E-mail: stockard@fau.edu.

Georgetown University, Graduate School of Arts and Sciences, School of Continuing Studies, Washington, DC 20057. Offers American studies (MALS); Catholic studies (MALS); classical civilizations (MALS); ethics and the professions (MALS); human resources management (MPS); humanities (MALS); individualized study (MALS); international affairs (MALS); Islam and Muslim-Christian relations (MALS); journalism (MPS); liberal studies (DLS); literature and society (MALS); medieval and early modern European studies (MALS); public relations (MPS); real estate (MPS); religious studies (MALS); social and public policy (MALS); sports industry management (MPS); the theory and practice of American democracy (MALS); visual culture (MALS). *Entrance requirements:* Additional exam requirements/recommendations for international students: Required—TOEFL.

Graduate School and University Center of the City University of New York, Graduate Studies, Program in Comparative Literature, New York, NY 10016-4039. Offers comparative literature (MA, PhD), including classics (PhD), German (PhD), Italian (PhD). *Faculty:* 16 full-time (3 women). *Students:* 110 full-time (70 women), 3 part-time (all women); includes 5 minority (2 Asian Americans or Pacific Islanders, 3 Hispanic Americans), 29 international. Average age 37. 51 applicants, 35% accepted, 11 enrolled. In 2009, 5 master's, 8 doctorates awarded. Terminal master's awarded for partial completion of doctoral program. *Degree requirements:* For master's, 2 foreign languages, comprehensive exam, thesis; for doctorate, 3 foreign languages, comprehensive exam, thesis/dissertation. *Entrance requirements:* For master's and doctorate, GRE General Test. Additional exam requirements/recommendations for international students: Required—TOEFL. *Application deadline:* For fall admission, 4/15 for domestic students; for spring admission, 11/15 for domestic students. Application fee: $125. Electronic applications accepted. *Financial support:* In 2009–10, 63 students received support, including 60 fellowships, 5 research assistantships, 14 teaching assistantships; career-related internships or fieldwork, Federal Work-Study, institutionally sponsored loans, and tuition waivers (full and partial) also available. Financial award application deadline: 2/1; financial award applicants required to submit FAFSA. *Unit head:* Dr. Andre Aciman, Executive Officer, 212-817-8170, Fax: 212-817-1509, E-mail: aaciman@gc.cuny.edu. *Application contact:* Les Gribben, Director of Admissions, 212-817-7470, Fax: 212-817-1624, E-mail: lgribben@gc.cuny.edu.

Harvard University, Graduate School of Arts and Sciences, Department of Comparative Literature, Cambridge, MA 02138. Offers comparative literature (PhD); oral literature (PhD). *Degree requirements:* For doctorate, 4 foreign languages, thesis/dissertation, written and oral exams. *Entrance requirements:* For doctorate, GRE General Test, GRE Subject Test (recommended), sample of written work. Additional exam requirements/recommendations for international students: Required—TOEFL. *Expenses:* Tuition: Full-time $33,696. Required fees: $1126. Full-time tuition and fees vary according to program.

Hofstra University, College of Liberal Arts and Sciences, Department of Comparative Literature and Languages, Hempstead, NY 11549. Offers applied linguistics (MA). Part-time programs available. *Faculty:* 4 full-time (0 women), 1 part-time/adjunct (0 women). *Students:* 2 full-time (1 woman), 2 part-time (both women), 2 international. Average age 27. 8 applicants, 75% accepted, 3 enrolled. In 2009, 3 master's awarded. *Degree requirements:* For master's, thesis, capstone. *Entrance requirements:* For master's, bachelor's degree in related area, interview, 2 letters of recommendation. Additional exam requirements/recommendations for international students: Required—TOEFL (minimum score 550 paper-based; 213 computer-based; 80 iBT). *Application deadline:* Applications are processed on a rolling basis. Application fee: $60. Electronic applications accepted. *Expenses:* Tuition: Full-time $16,200; part-time $900 per credit hour. Required fees: $970; $145 per term. Tuition and fees vary according to program. *Financial support:* Fellowships with full and partial tuition reimbursements, research assistantships with full and partial tuition reimbursements, Federal Work-Study, institutionally sponsored loans, scholarships/grants, tuition waivers (full and partial), and unspecified assistantships available. Support available to part-time students. Financial award applicants required to submit FAFSA. *Faculty research:* Second language acquisition, second language writing. *Unit head:* Dr. George L. Greaney, Director, 516-463-5651, E-mail: cllglg@hofstra.edu. *Application contact:* Carol Drummer, Dean of Graduate Admissions, 516-463-4876, Fax: 516-463-4664, E-mail: gradstudent@hofstra.edu.

Indiana State University, School of Graduate Studies, College of Arts and Sciences, Department of English, Terre Haute, IN 47809. Offers English teaching (MA); history (MA); literature (MA). Part-time and evening/weekend programs available. *Degree requirements:* For master's, one foreign language, thesis optional. *Entrance requirements:* For master's, minimum GPA of 2.75 in all English courses above freshman level. Additional exam requirements/recommendations for international students: Required—TOEFL (minimum score 550 paper-based). Electronic applications accepted.

Indiana University Bloomington, University Graduate School, College of Arts and Sciences, Department of Comparative Literature, Bloomington, IN 47405. Offers MA, MAT, PhD. Part-time programs available. *Faculty:* 6 full-time (3 women), 18 part-time/adjunct (11 women). *Students:* 39 full-time (29 women), 2 part-time (both women); includes 5 minority (1 African American, 1 American Indian/Alaska Native, 2 Asian Americans or Pacific Islanders, 1 Hispanic American), 13 international. Average age 31. 39 applicants, 46% accepted, 8 enrolled. In 2009, 8 master's, 4 doctorates awarded. *Degree requirements:* For master's, 2 foreign languages, comprehensive exam (for some programs), thesis (for some programs); for doctorate, 3 foreign languages, comprehensive exam, thesis/dissertation. *Entrance requirements:* For master's, GRE, proficiency in 1 foreign language, writing sample; for doctorate, GRE, proficiency in 2 foreign languages, writing sample. Additional exam requirements/recommendations for international students: Required—TOEFL (minimum score 550 paper-based; 213 computer-based; 79 iBT). *Application deadline:* For fall admission, 1/15 priority date for domestic students, 12/15 priority date for international students. Application fee: $55 ($65 for international students). Electronic applications accepted. *Financial support:* In 2009–10, 9 students received support, including 6 fellowships with full tuition reimbursements available (averaging $17,000 per year), 3 research assistantships with partial tuition reimbursements available (averaging $14,000 per year), 20 teaching assistantships with full tuition reimbursements available (averaging $11,300 per year); Federal Work-Study and unspecified assistantships also available. Financial award application deadline: 1/15. *Faculty research:* East-West literary relations, film studies, translation, medieval studies, comparative arts. *Unit head:* Eileen Julien, Chairperson, 812-855-8422, Fax: 812-855-2688, E-mail: ejulien@indiana.edu. *Application contact:* Connie Sue May, Administrative Secretary, 812-855-9602, Fax: 812-855-2688, E-mail: csmay@indiana.edu.

The Johns Hopkins University, Zanvyl Krieger School of Arts and Sciences, Humanities Center, Baltimore, MD 21218-2699. Offers PhD. Part-time programs available. *Faculty:* 7 full-time (4 women). *Students:* 16 full-time (7 women); includes 3 minority (2 Asian Americans or Pacific Islanders, 1 Hispanic American), 4 international. Average age 29. 52 applicants, 2% accepted, 1 enrolled. In 2009, 1 doctorate awarded. *Degree requirements:* For doctorate, 2 foreign languages, thesis/dissertation. *Entrance requirements:* For doctorate, GRE General Test, samples of written work. Additional exam requirements/recommendations for international students: Required—TOEFL, IELTS. *Application deadline:* For fall admission, 12/1 for domestic and international students. Application fee: $75. Electronic applications accepted. *Financial support:* In 2009–10, 14 students received support, including 7 fellowships with full tuition reimbursements available (averaging $17,500 per year), 6 teaching assistantships with full tuition reimbursements available (averaging $17,500 per year); Federal Work-Study, institutionally sponsored loans, tuition waivers (full), and unspecified assistantships also available. Financial award application deadline: 12/1. *Unit head:* Prof. Hent de Vries, Chair, 410-516-0474, Fax: 410-516-4897, E-mail: hentdevries@jhu.edu. *Application contact:* Marva Philip, Administrator, 410-516-7619, Fax: 410-516-4897, E-mail: mphilip@jhu.edu.

Kent State University, College of Arts and Sciences, Department of English, Kent, OH 44242-0001. Offers comparative literature (MA); creative writing (MFA); English (PhD); English for teachers (MA); literature and writing (MA); rhetoric and composition (PhD); teaching English as a second language (MA). Part-time programs available. Terminal master's awarded for partial completion of doctoral program. *Degree requirements:* For master's, one foreign language, thesis optional; for doctorate, one foreign language, thesis/dissertation, qualifying exams. *Entrance requirements:* For master's and doctorate, GRE General Test, writing sample, letters of recommendation. Additional exam requirements/recommendations for international students: Required—TOEFL (minimum score 600 paper-based). Electronic applications accepted. *Faculty research:* British and American literature, textual editing, rhetoric and composition, cultural studies, linguistic and critical theories.

Long Island University, Brooklyn Campus, Richard L. Conolly College of Liberal Arts and Sciences, Department of English, Brooklyn, NY 11201-8423. Offers creative writing (MFA); literature (MA); professional writing (MA); writing and rhetoric (MA). Part-time and evening/weekend programs available. *Degree requirements:* For master's, thesis or alternative. *Entrance requirements:* For master's, 2 letters of recommendation (at least 1 from a former professor or teacher). Additional exam requirements/recommendations for international students: Required—TOEFL (minimum score 550 paper-based; 173 computer-based). Electronic applications accepted.

Louisiana State University and Agricultural and Mechanical College, Graduate School, College of Arts and Sciences, Interdepartmental Program in Comparative Literature, Baton Rouge, LA 70803. Offers MA, PhD. *Students:* 13 full-time (8 women), 5 part-time (2 women); includes 2 minority (both Hispanic Americans), 3 international. Average age 36. 8 applicants, 13% accepted, 0 enrolled. In 2009, 3 master's, 1 doctorate awarded. Terminal master's awarded for partial completion of doctoral program. *Degree requirements:* For master's, 2

Comparative Literature

Louisiana State University and Agricultural and Mechanical College (continued)
foreign languages, thesis optional; for doctorate, 2 foreign languages, thesis/dissertation. *Entrance requirements:* For master's and doctorate, GRE General Test, minimum GPA of 3.0. Additional exam requirements/recommendations for international students: Required—TOEFL (minimum score 550 paper-based; 213 computer-based; 79 iBT). *Application deadline:* For fall admission, 7/1 priority date for domestic students, 5/15 for international students; for spring admission, 10/15 for international students. Applications are processed on a rolling basis. Application fee: $25. Electronic applications accepted. *Financial support:* In 2009–10, 14 students received support, including 10 teaching assistantships with full and partial tuition reimbursements available (averaging $14,021 per year); fellowships with full tuition reimbursements available, research assistantships with full and partial tuition reimbursements available, health care benefits and unspecified assistantships also available. Financial award application deadline: 3/15; financial award applicants required to submit FAFSA. *Faculty research:* World literature, Islamic studies, Dante, Foucault. *Unit head:* Dr. Greg Stone, Director, 225-578-6627, Fax: 225-578-6628, E-mail: stone@lsu.edu. *Application contact:* Dr. Greg Stone, Director, 225-578-6627, Fax: 225-578-6628, E-mail: stone@lsu.edu.

New York University, Graduate School of Arts and Science, Department of Comparative Literature, New York, NY 10012-1019. Offers MA, PhD. Part-time programs available. *Faculty:* 15 full-time (4 women). *Students:* 36 full-time (23 women), 15 part-time (9 women); includes 5 minority (1 African American, 1 Asian American or Pacific Islander, 3 Hispanic Americans), 19 international. Average age 31. 186 applicants, 9% accepted, 6 enrolled. In 2009, 10 master's, 8 doctorates awarded. *Degree requirements:* For master's, 2 foreign languages, thesis; for doctorate, 3 foreign languages, thesis/dissertation. *Entrance requirements:* For master's and doctorate, GRE General Test. Additional exam requirements/recommendations for international students: Required—TOEFL. *Application deadline:* For fall admission, 1/4 for domestic students. Application fee: $90. *Expenses:* Tuition: Full-time $30,528; part-time $1272 per credit. Required fees: $2177. *Financial support:* Fellowships with tuition reimbursements, teaching assistantships with tuition reimbursements, Federal Work-Study, institutionally sponsored loans, scholarships/grants, health care benefits, and unspecified assistantships available. Financial award application deadline: 1/4; financial award applicants required to submit FAFSA. *Faculty research:* European and non-European literature and culture, comparative poetics, cultural studies, colonial and post-colonial literature and theory, philosophical issues and literary theory. *Unit head:* Jacques Lezra, Chair, 212-998-8790, Fax: 212-995-4377, E-mail: complit.info@nyu.edu. *Application contact:* Kristin J. Ross, Director of Graduate Studies, 212-998-8790, Fax: 212-995-4377, E-mail: complit.info@nyu.edu.

Northwestern University, The Graduate School, Interdepartmental Programs, Program in Literature, Evanston, IL 60208. Offers MA. Part-time programs available. *Degree requirements:* For master's, thesis. *Entrance requirements:* For master's, writing sample. Additional exam requirements/recommendations for international students: Required—TOEFL. *Faculty research:* Sociology of literature, creative writing, women writers, modernism and post-modernism.

Northwestern University, The Graduate School, Judd A. and Marjorie Weinberg College of Arts and Sciences, Department of French and Italian, Evanston, IL 60208. Offers eighteenth-century studies (Certificate); French (PhD); French and comparative literature (PhD); Italian studies (Certificate). Admissions and degrees offered through The Graduate School. *Degree requirements:* For doctorate, one foreign language, thesis/dissertation, written and oral exams. *Entrance requirements:* For doctorate, GRE, writing sample, cassette recording. Additional exam requirements/recommendations for international students: Required—TOEFL. *Faculty research:* Francophone studies, 18th century contemporary theory.

Northwestern University, The Graduate School, Judd A. and Marjorie Weinberg College of Arts and Sciences, Program in Comparative Literary Studies, Evanston, IL 60208. Offers PhD. Admissions and degrees offered through The Graduate School. Part-time programs available. *Degree requirements:* For doctorate, 2 foreign languages, thesis/dissertation, preliminary exams. *Entrance requirements:* For doctorate, GRE General Test, sample of written work. Additional exam requirements/recommendations for international students: Required—TOEFL. *Faculty research:* The novel, modernism, post-colonial literature and theory, literature and the arts, Middle Ages and Renaissance, literature and philosophy.

Northwestern University, School of Continuing Studies, Program in Literature, Evanston, IL 60208. Offers American literature (MA); British literature (MA); comparative and world literature (MA).

Oklahoma City University, Petree College of Arts and Sciences, Program in Liberal Arts, Oklahoma City, OK 73106-1402. Offers art (MLA); general studies (MLA); leadership/management (MLA); literature (MLA); mass communications (MLA); philosophy (MLA); writing (MLA). Part-time and evening/weekend programs available. *Faculty:* 23 full-time (6 women), 5 part-time/adjunct (3 women). *Students:* 50 full-time (24 women), 23 part-time (14 women); includes 6 minority (4 African Americans, 1 Asian American or Pacific Islander, 1 Hispanic American), 50 international. Average age 31. 31 applicants, 94% accepted, 15 enrolled. In 2009, 21 master's awarded. *Degree requirements:* For master's, comprehensive exam, thesis optional. *Entrance requirements:* Additional exam requirements/recommendations for international students: Required—TOEFL (minimum score 550 paper-based). *Application deadline:* For fall admission, 8/20 for domestic students; for spring admission, 1/6 for domestic students. Applications are processed on a rolling basis. Application fee: $50 ($70 for international students). *Expenses:* Tuition: Full-time $15,930; part-time $885 per hour. *Financial support:* Fellowships with partial tuition reimbursements, career-related internships or fieldwork, Federal Work-Study, and tuition waivers (partial) available. Support available to part-time students. Financial award application deadline: 8/1; financial award applicants required to submit FAFSA. *Unit head:* Dr. Regina Bennett, Director, 405-208-5207, Fax: 405-208-5451, E-mail: rbennett@okcu.edu. *Application contact:* Michelle Lockhart, Director, Admissions, 800-633-7242, Fax: 405-208-5916, E-mail: gadmissions@okcu.edu.

Princeton University, Graduate School, Department of Comparative Literature, Princeton, NJ 08544-1019. Offers PhD. *Degree requirements:* For doctorate, variable foreign language requirement, thesis/dissertation. *Entrance requirements:* For doctorate, GRE General Test, GRE Subject Test, sample of written work. Additional exam requirements/recommendations for international students: Required—TOEFL (minimum score 600 paper-based; 250 computer-based). Electronic applications accepted.

Purdue University, Graduate School, College of Liberal Arts, Program in Comparative Literature, West Lafayette, IN 47907. Offers MA, PhD. Part-time programs available. *Degree requirements:* For master's, one foreign language; for doctorate, 2 foreign languages, thesis/dissertation. *Entrance requirements:* For master's, GRE General Test, writing sample; for doctorate, GRE General Test. Additional exam requirements/recommendations for international students: Required—TOEFL. Electronic applications accepted. *Faculty research:* Theory and criticism, philosophy and aesthetics, East Asian literature, postcolonial literature, classics.

Rutgers, The State University of New Jersey, New Brunswick, Graduate School-New Brunswick, Program in Comparative Literature, Piscataway, NJ 08854-8097. Offers MA, PhD. Part-time programs available. Terminal master's awarded for partial completion of doctoral program. *Degree requirements:* For master's, comprehensive exam; for doctorate, 3 foreign languages, thesis/dissertation, written and oral exams. *Entrance requirements:* For doctorate, GRE General Test, GRE Subject Test (recommended). Additional exam requirements/recommendations for international students: Required—TOEFL. Electronic applications accepted. *Faculty research:* Genres and periods, modern literary theory, psychoanalytic approaches to literature, literature and gender, cultural studies.

San Francisco State University, Division of Graduate Studies, College of Humanities, Department of Comparative and World Literature, San Francisco, CA 94132-1722. Offers comparative literature (MA). Part-time programs available. *Degree requirements:* For master's, one foreign language.

San Jose State University, Graduate Studies and Research, College of Humanities and the Arts, Department of English and Comparative Literature, San Jose, CA 95192-0001. Offers English (MFA); English literature (MA). *Students:* 35 full-time (21 women), 56 part-time (39 women); includes 21 minority (1 African American, 16 Asian Americans or Pacific Islanders, 4 Hispanic Americans), 3 international. Average age 34. 96 applicants, 34% accepted, 28 enrolled. In 2009, 17 master's awarded. *Degree requirements:* For master's, one foreign language, thesis or alternative. *Entrance requirements:* For master's, GRE. Additional exam requirements/recommendations for international students: Required—TOEFL. *Application deadline:* For fall admission, 6/29 for domestic students; for spring admission, 11/30 for domestic students. Applications are processed on a rolling basis. Application fee: $59. Electronic applications accepted. *Financial support:* Applicants required to submit FAFSA. *Unit head:* John Engell, Chair, 408-924-4499, Fax: 408-924-4580, E-mail: john.engell@sjsu.edu. *Application contact:* Dr. Noelle Brada-Williams, Graduate Coordinator, 408-924-4439.

Stanford University, School of Humanities and Sciences, Department of Comparative Literature, Stanford, CA 94305-9991. Offers PhD. *Degree requirements:* For doctorate, 3 foreign languages, thesis/dissertation, qualification procedures. *Entrance requirements:* For doctorate, GRE General Test, GRE Subject Test. Additional exam requirements/recommendations for international students: Required—TOEFL. Electronic applications accepted. *Expenses:* Tuition: Full-time $37,380; part-time $2760 per quarter. Required fees: $501.

Stanford University, School of Humanities and Sciences, Program in Modern Thought and Literature, Stanford, CA 94305-9991. Offers PhD. *Degree requirements:* For doctorate, 2 foreign languages, thesis/dissertation, qualifying paper, oral exam. *Entrance requirements:* For doctorate, GRE General Test. Additional exam requirements/recommendations for international students: Required—TOEFL. Electronic applications accepted. *Expenses:* Tuition: Full-time $37,380; part-time $2760 per quarter. Required fees: $501.

State University of New York at Binghamton, Graduate School, School of Arts and Sciences, Department of Comparative Literature, Binghamton, NY 13902-6000. Offers MA, PhD. Part-time programs available. *Faculty:* 9 full-time (5 women), 2 part-time/adjunct (1 woman). *Students:* 22 full-time (14 women), 42 part-time (26 women); includes 11 minority (2 African Americans, 1 American Indian/Alaska Native, 4 Asian Americans or Pacific Islanders, 4 Hispanic Americans), 25 international. Average age 35. 26 applicants, 81% accepted, 9 enrolled. In 2009, 6 master's, 2 doctorates awarded. Terminal master's awarded for partial completion of doctoral program. *Degree requirements:* For master's, 2 foreign languages, thesis or alternative, written exam; for doctorate, 3 foreign languages, comprehensive exam, thesis/dissertation. *Entrance requirements:* For master's and doctorate, GRE General Test, GRE Subject Test. Additional exam requirements/recommendations for international students: Required—TOEFL (minimum score 550 paper-based; 213 computer-based; 80 iBT). *Application deadline:* For fall admission, 2/1 priority date for domestic and international students; for spring admission, 10/15 priority date for domestic and international students. Applications are processed on a rolling basis. Application fee: $60. Electronic applications accepted. *Financial support:* In 2009–10, 22 students received support, including 1 fellowship with full tuition reimbursement available (averaging $14,500 per year), 19 teaching assistantships with full tuition reimbursements available (averaging $14,500 per year); research assistantships, career-related internships or fieldwork, Federal Work-Study, institutionally sponsored loans, scholarships/grants, health care benefits, and unspecified assistantships also available. Financial award application deadline: 2/15; financial award applicants required to submit FAFSA. *Unit head:* Dr. Gisela Brinker-Gabler, Chairperson, 607-777-2890, E-mail: gbrinker@binghamton.edu. *Application contact:* Victoria Williams, Recruiting and Admissions Coordinator, 607-777-2151, Fax: 607-777-2501, E-mail: vwilliam@binghamton.edu.

Stony Brook University, State University of New York, Graduate School, College of Arts and Sciences, Department of Comparative Literary and Cultural Studies, Stony Brook, NY 11794. Offers comparative literature (MA, PhD); cultural studies (PhD). Evening/weekend programs available. *Faculty:* 7 full-time (1 woman). *Students:* 35 full-time (21 women), 4 part-time (3 women); includes 6 minority (5 Asian Americans or Pacific Islanders, 1 Hispanic American), 17 international. Average age 30. 101 applicants, 19% accepted. In 2009, 1 master's, 1 doctorate awarded. Terminal master's awarded for partial completion of doctoral program. *Degree requirements:* For master's, 2 foreign languages, exam; for doctorate, 3 foreign languages, comprehensive exam, thesis/dissertation. *Entrance requirements:* For master's and doctorate, GRE General Test, minimum GPA of 3.5 in major, 3.0 overall. Additional exam requirements/recommendations for international students: Required—TOEFL. *Application deadline:* For fall admission, 1/15 for domestic students. Application fee: $60. *Expenses:* Tuition, state resident: full-time $8370; part-time $349 per credit. Tuition, nonresident: full-time $13,250; part-time $552 per credit. Required fees: $933. *Financial support:* In 2009–10, 24 teaching assistantships were awarded; fellowships, research assistantships also available. *Faculty research:* Literary theory, interdisciplinary studies, literary history. *Unit head:* Prof. Krin Gabbard, Chairman, 631-632-7456. *Application contact:* Dr. Kent Marks, Assistant Dean, Admissions and Records, 631-632-4723, Fax: 631-632-7243, E-mail: kmarks@notes.cc.sunysb.edu.

Université de Montréal, Faculty of Arts and Sciences, Department of Comparative Literature, Montréal, QC H3C 3J7, Canada. Offers comparative literature (MA); literature (PhD). *Degree requirements:* For master's, 2 foreign languages, thesis; for doctorate, 3 foreign languages, thesis/dissertation, general exam. *Entrance requirements:* For doctorate, MA with minimum B+ average. Electronic applications accepted.

Université de Sherbrooke, Faculty of Letters and Human Sciences, Department of Letters and Communications, Sherbrooke, QC J1K 2R1, Canada. Offers comparative Canadian literature (MA, PhD); French literature (MA, PhD); linguistics (MA); theatre (MA). *Degree requirements:* For master's, thesis or alternative; for doctorate, thesis/dissertation. *Entrance requirements:* For master's, minimum GPA of 2.8; for doctorate, minimum GPA of 3.0.

Université du Québec à Chicoutimi, Graduate Programs, Program in Literary Studies, Chicoutimi, QC G7H 2B1, Canada. Offers MA. Part-time programs available. *Degree requirements:* For master's, thesis optional. *Entrance requirements:* For master's, appropriate bachelor's degree, proficiency in French.

Université du Québec à Montréal, Graduate Programs, Program in Literary Studies, Montréal, QC H3C 3P8, Canada. Offers MA, PhD. Part-time programs available. *Degree requirements:* For master's, thesis; for doctorate, thesis/dissertation. *Entrance requirements:* For master's, appropriate bachelor's degree or equivalent, proficiency in French; for doctorate, appropriate master's degree or equivalent, proficiency in French.

Université du Québec à Montréal, Graduate Programs, Program in Semiology, Montréal, QC H3C 3P8, Canada. Offers PhD. Part-time programs available. *Degree requirements:* For doctorate, thesis/dissertation. *Entrance requirements:* For doctorate, appropriate master's degree or equivalent, proficiency in French.

Université du Québec à Rimouski, Graduate Programs, Program in Literary Studies, Rimouski, QC G5L 3A1, Canada. Offers MA, PhD. Part-time programs available. *Degree requirements:* For master's, thesis or alternative. *Entrance requirements:* For master's, appropriate bachelor's degree, proficiency in French.

Université du Québec à Trois-Rivières, Graduate Programs, Program in Literary Studies, Trois-Rivières, QC G9A 5H7, Canada. Offers MA. Part-time programs available. *Degree requirements:* For master's, thesis optional. *Entrance requirements:* For master's, appropriate bachelor's degree, proficiency in French.

Université Laval, Faculty of Letters, Department of Literature, Programs in Literary Studies, Québec, QC G1K 7P4, Canada. Offers MA, PhD. Part-time programs available. Terminal master's awarded for partial completion of doctoral program. *Degree requirements:* For master's, thesis; for doctorate, comprehensive exam, thesis/dissertation. *Entrance requirements:* For master's and doctorate, linguistics exams, knowledge of French, knowledge of a second language. Electronic applications accepted.

University at Buffalo, the State University of New York, Graduate School, College of Arts and Sciences, Department of Comparative Literature, Buffalo, NY 14260. Offers MA, PhD. Part-time programs available. *Faculty:* 7 full-time (2 women). *Students:* 35 full-time (16 women); includes 5 minority (1 African American, 2 Asian Americans or Pacific Islanders, 2 Hispanic Americans). Average age 25. 45 applicants, 56% accepted, 7 enrolled. In 2009, 4 master's, 2 doctorates awarded. Terminal master's awarded for partial completion of doctoral program. *Degree requirements:* For master's, one foreign language, exam or thesis; for doctorate, 2 foreign languages, comprehensive exam, thesis/dissertation. *Entrance requirements:* For master's and doctorate, GRE General Test, writing sample, 3 letters of recommendation. Additional exam requirements/recommendations for international students: Required—TOEFL (minimum score 550 paper-based; 213 computer-based; 79 iBT). *Application deadline:* For fall admission, 1/15 for domestic and international students. Application fee: $50. Electronic applications accepted. *Financial support:* In 2009–10, 13 students received support, including 2 fellowships with tuition reimbursements available (averaging $4,150 per year), 1 research assistantship with tuition reimbursement available (averaging $10,400 per year), 16 teaching assistantships with tuition reimbursements available (averaging $10,400 per year); Federal Work-Study, institutionally sponsored loans, and unspecified assistantships also available. Financial award application deadline: 1/15; financial award applicants required to submit FAFSA. *Faculty research:* Theory; interaction between literature and philosophy; European, Francophone, African, American, and South American literature; postmodernism; postcolonialism. *Unit head:* Dr. David Johnson, Chair, 716-645-0854, Fax: 716-645-5979, E-mail: dj@buffalo.edu. *Application contact:* Dr. Krzysztof Ziarek, Director of Graduate Studies, 716-645-0858, Fax: 716-645-5979, E-mail: kziarek@buffalo.edu.

University of Arkansas, Graduate School, Interdisciplinary Program in Comparative Literature and Cultural Studies, Fayetteville, AR 72701-1201. Offers classical studies (MA); comparative literature (PhD). *Degree requirements:* For master's, one foreign language, comprehensive exam, thesis optional; for doctorate, 2 foreign languages, comprehensive exam, thesis/dissertation. *Entrance requirements:* For master's and doctorate, GRE General Test. *Expenses:* Tuition, state resident: full-time $7355; part-time $356.58 per hour. Tuition, nonresident: full-time $17,401; part-time $775.17 per hour. Required fees: $1203. *Faculty research:* Literary and cultural theory, cultural studies, postcolonial theory, gender studies, world literature.

University of California, Berkeley, Graduate Division, College of Letters and Science, Department of Comparative Literature, Berkeley, CA 94720-1500. Offers PhD. *Students:* 70 full-time (44 women). Average age 31. 126 applicants, 10 enrolled. In 2009, 9 doctorates awarded. *Degree requirements:* For doctorate, 3 foreign languages, thesis/dissertation, qualifying exam. *Entrance requirements:* For doctorate, GRE General Test, fluency in 1 foreign language (2 preferred), minimum GPA of 3.0, writing sample, 3 letters of recommendation. *Application deadline:* For fall admission, 12/5 for domestic students. Application fee: $70 ($90 for international students). *Financial support:* Fellowships, research assistantships, teaching assistantships, institutionally sponsored loans, tuition waivers (full and partial), and unspecified assistantships available. Financial award applicants required to submit FAFSA. *Unit head:* Prof. Eric Naiman, Chair, 510-642-2712, E-mail: ch_complit@ls.berkeley.edu. *Application contact:* Erica Roberts, Student Affairs Officer, 510-642-2629, Fax: 510-642-8852, E-mail: complit@ls.berkeley.edu.

University of California, Davis, Graduate Studies, Graduate Group in Comparative Literature, Davis, CA 95616. Offers PhD. *Degree requirements:* For doctorate, 3 foreign languages, thesis/dissertation. *Entrance requirements:* For doctorate, GRE General Test, minimum GPA of 3.0. Additional exam requirements/recommendations for international students: Required—TOEFL (minimum score 550 paper-based; 213 computer-based). Electronic applications accepted. *Faculty research:* Literary criticism, literary theory, gender history and literature, genre.

University of California, Irvine, Office of Graduate Studies, School of Humanities, Department of English and Comparative Literature, Program in Comparative Literature, Irvine, CA 92697. Offers MA, PhD. *Faculty:* 9 full-time (5 women), 1 part-time/adjunct (0 women). *Students:* 48 full-time (25 women), 1 part-time (0 women); includes 15 minority (2 American Indian/Alaska Native, 10 Asian Americans or Pacific Islanders, 3 Hispanic Americans), 2 international. Average age 30. 87 applicants, 8% accepted, 4 enrolled. In 2009, 10 master's, 5 doctorates awarded. *Degree requirements:* For master's, one foreign language; for doctorate, 2 foreign languages, thesis/dissertation. *Entrance requirements:* For doctorate, GRE General Test, minimum GPA of 3.5, sample of written work, 3 letters of recommendation. Additional exam requirements/recommendations for international students: Required—TOEFL (minimum score 550 paper-based; 213 computer-based). *Application deadline:* For fall admission, 12/15 for domestic and international students. Application fee: $70 ($90 for international students). Electronic applications accepted. *Financial support:* In 2009–10, fellowships with full tuition reimbursements (averaging $1,400 per year), research assistantships with full tuition reimbursements (averaging $15,000 per year), teaching assistantships with partial tuition reimbursements (averaging $14,145 per year) were awarded; institutionally sponsored loans and tuition waivers (partial) also available. Financial award application deadline: 3/2; financial award applicants required to submit FAFSA. *Faculty research:* Critical theory, feminist studies, Asian American studies. Total annual research expenditures: $99,000. *Unit head:* Director, 949-824-6718, Fax: 949-824-2916. *Application contact:* Arielle Read, Graduate Administrator, 949-824-6718, Fax: 949-824-2916, E-mail: eclgradapp@uci.edu.

University of California, Los Angeles, Graduate Division, College of Letters and Science, Department of Comparative Literature, Los Angeles, CA 90095. Offers MA, PhD. *Students:* 44 full-time (27 women); includes 10 minority (1 African American, 8 Asian Americans or Pacific Islanders, 1 Hispanic American), 3 international. Average age 29. 73 applicants, 12% accepted, 6 enrolled. In 2009, 2 master's, 4 doctorates awarded. Terminal master's awarded for partial completion of doctoral program. *Degree requirements:* For master's, 2 foreign languages, comprehensive exam; for doctorate, 2 foreign languages, thesis/dissertation, oral and written qualifying exams. *Entrance requirements:* For master's, GRE General Test, sample of written work, previous course work in literature, minimum GPA of 3.4 in upper-division course work; for doctorate, GRE General Test, sample of written work, MA in comparative literature. *Application deadline:* For fall admission, 12/1 for domestic and international students. Application fee: $70 ($90 for international students). Electronic applications accepted. *Financial support:* In 2009–10, 43 fellowships with full and partial tuition reimbursements, 12 research assistantships with full and partial tuition reimbursements, 39 teaching assistantships with full and partial tuition reimbursements were awarded; Federal Work-Study, institutionally sponsored loans, scholarships/grants, health care benefits, tuition waivers (full and partial), and unspecified assistantships also available. Financial award application deadline: 3/1; financial award applicants required to submit FAFSA. *Unit head:* Ali Behdad, Chair, 310-267-4922. *Application contact:* Department Office, 310-825-7650, E-mail: klipp@humnet.ucla.edu.

University of California, Riverside, Graduate Division, Department of Comparative Literature and Foreign Languages, Riverside, CA 92521-0102. Offers comparative literature (MA, PhD). *Faculty:* 17 full-time (9 women), 16 part-time/adjunct (13 women). *Students:* 32 full-time (22 women); includes 7 minority (1 African American, 6 Asian Americans or Pacific Islanders), 15 international. Average age 31. 27 applicants, 30% accepted, 8 enrolled. In 2009, 2 master's, 2 doctorates awarded. Terminal master's awarded for partial completion of doctoral program. *Degree requirements:* For master's, 3 foreign languages, comprehensive exam; for doctorate, 3 foreign languages, thesis/dissertation, qualifying exams. *Entrance requirements:* For master's and doctorate, GRE General Test, minimum GPA of 3.2. Additional exam requirements/recommendations for international students: Required—TOEFL (minimum score 550 paper-based; 213 computer-based; 80 iBT). *Application deadline:* For fall admission, 1/5 for domestic students, 2/1 for international students; for winter admission, 9/1 for domestic students, 7/1 for international students; for spring admission, 12/1 for domestic students, 10/1 for international students. Applications are processed on a rolling basis. Application fee: $80 ($100 for international students). Electronic applications accepted. *Financial support:* Fellowships with partial tuition reimbursements, research assistantships, teaching assistantships with partial tuition reimbursements, career-related internships or fieldwork, Federal Work-Study, institutionally sponsored loans, and tuition waivers (full and partial) available. Financial award application deadline: 1/5; financial award applicants required to submit FAFSA. *Faculty research:* French and German Enlightenment, modern drama and theatre, contemporary critical theory, East-West comparative studies, science fiction and fantasy. *Unit head:* Dr. Thomas F. Scanlon, Chair, 951-827-1462, Fax: 951-827-2160, E-mail: thomas.scanlon@ucr.edu. *Application contact:* Dr. Marguerite Waller, Graduate Advisor, 951-827-7859, Fax: 951-827-2160, E-mail: clhsgrad@ucr.edu.

University of California, San Diego, Office of Graduate Studies, Department of Literature, Program in Comparative Literature, La Jolla, CA 92093. Offers MA, PhD. *Degree requirements:* For master's, thesis; for doctorate, thesis/dissertation. *Entrance requirements:* For master's and doctorate, GRE General Test, GRE Subject Test. Electronic applications accepted. *Faculty research:* Problems of theory and method, relationship of the humanities to the social sciences.

University of California, Santa Barbara, Graduate Division, College of Letters and Sciences, Division of Humanities and Fine Arts, Program in Comparative Literature, Santa Barbara, CA 93106-4130. Offers comparative literature (PhD); East Asian literatures (PhD); feminist studies (PhD); MA/PhD. *Faculty:* 56 full-time (24 women). *Students:* 24 full-time (18 women). Average age 29. 43 applicants, 40% accepted, 5 enrolled. In 2009, 5 doctorates awarded. Terminal master's awarded for partial completion of doctoral program. *Degree requirements:* For doctorate, 2 foreign languages, comprehensive exam, thesis/dissertation. *Entrance requirements:* For doctorate, GRE. Additional exam requirements/recommendations for international students: Required—TOEFL (minimum score 550 paper-based; 213 computer-based; 80 iBT) or IELTS (minimum score 7). *Application deadline:* For fall admission, 12/15 for domestic and international students. Application fee: $70 ($90 for international students). Electronic applications accepted. *Financial support:* In 2009–10, 24 students received support, including 15 fellowships with full and partial tuition reimbursements available (averaging $6,900 per year), 1 research assistantship (averaging $10,600 per year), 18 teaching assistantships with partial tuition reimbursements available (averaging $10,400 per year); Federal Work-Study, institutionally sponsored loans, scholarships/grants, health care benefits, and tuition waivers (full and partial) also available. Financial award application deadline: 12/15; financial award applicants required to submit FAFSA. *Faculty research:* Media studies, literary theory, cultural studies, early modern and modern literature, critical theory. *Unit head:* Prof. Elisabeth Weber, Chair, 805-893-3527, Fax: 805-893-2374, E-mail: weber@gss.ucsb.edu. *Application contact:* Sierra Gray, Graduate Program Assistant, 805-893-2131, Fax: 805-893-2374, E-mail: sierra@gss.ucsb.edu.

University of California, Santa Cruz, Division of Graduate Studies, Division of Humanities, Department of Literature, Santa Cruz, CA 95064. Offers MA, PhD. Terminal master's awarded for partial completion of doctoral program. *Degree requirements:* For master's, thesis; for doctorate, one foreign language, thesis/dissertation, qualifying exam. *Entrance requirements:* For master's, GRE General Test, writing sample, minimum GPA of 3.5; for doctorate, GRE General Test, minimum GPA of 3.5, writing sample. Electronic applications accepted. *Faculty research:* Comparative literature; German, Spanish, classical, American, and English literature.

University of Chicago, Division of the Humanities, Department of Comparative Literature, Chicago, IL 60637-1513. Offers AM, PhD. Terminal master's awarded for partial completion of doctoral program. *Degree requirements:* For master's, 2 foreign languages, thesis; for doctorate, 3 foreign languages, thesis/dissertation. *Entrance requirements:* For master's and doctorate, GRE General Test.

University of Colorado at Boulder, Graduate School, College of Arts and Sciences, Department of Comparative Literature and Humanities, Boulder, CO 80309. Offers MA, PhD. *Faculty:* 3 full-time (0 women). *Students:* 23 full-time (13 women), 4 part-time (3 women); includes 1 minority (Asian American or Pacific Islander), 4 international. Average age 33. 38 applicants, 16% accepted, 6 enrolled. In 2009, 5 master's awarded. Terminal master's awarded for partial completion of doctoral program. *Degree requirements:* For master's, 2 foreign languages, comprehensive exam, thesis or alternative; for doctorate, 3 foreign languages, comprehensive exam, thesis/dissertation. *Entrance requirements:* For master's, GRE General Test, minimum undergraduate GPA of 2.75; for doctorate, GRE General Test, MA in related field. *Application deadline:* For fall admission, 1/1 priority date for domestic students, 12/1 for international students. Applications are processed on a rolling basis. Application fee: $50 ($60 for international students). *Financial support:* In 2009–10, 2 fellowships (averaging $23,964 per year), 3 research assistantships (averaging $15,284 per year) were awarded; tuition waivers (full) also available. Financial award application deadline: 1/1. *Faculty research:* Enlightenment to modern literature; literary theory and history; philosophy and literature; popular culture studies; reception, translation and interpretation; gender and sexual orientation; nationalism. Total annual research expenditures: $23,115.

University of Connecticut, Graduate School, College of Liberal Arts and Sciences, Department of Modern and Classical Languages, Field of Comparative Literature and Cultural Studies, Storrs, CT 06269. Offers MA, PhD. *Faculty:* 24 full-time (11 women). *Students:* 13 full-time (10 women), 8 part-time (5 women); includes 2 minority (1 American Indian/Alaska Native, 1 Hispanic American), 4 international. Average age 34. 21 applicants, 19% accepted, 3 enrolled. In 2009, 4 master's, 3 doctorates awarded. Terminal master's awarded for partial completion of doctoral program. *Degree requirements:* For master's, comprehensive exam; for doctorate, thesis/dissertation. *Entrance requirements:* For master's and doctorate, GRE General Test, GRE Subject Test. Additional exam requirements/recommendations for international students: Required—TOEFL (minimum score 550 paper-based; 213 computer-based). *Application deadline:* For fall admission, 2/1 priority date for domestic and international students; for spring admission, 11/1 for domestic students, 10/1 for international students. Applications are processed on a rolling basis. Application fee: $55. Electronic applications accepted. *Expenses:* Tuition, state resident: full-time $4725; part-time $525 per credit. Tuition, nonresident: full-time $12,267; part-time $1363 per credit. Required fees: $346 per semester. Tuition and fees vary according to course load. *Financial support:* In 2009–10, 12 teaching assistantships with full tuition reimbursements were awarded; fellowships, research assistantships with full tuition reimbursements, Federal Work-Study, scholarships/grants, health care benefits, and unspecified assistantships also available. Financial award application deadline: 2/1; financial award applicants required to submit FAFSA. *Unit head:* Lucy S. McNeece, Co-Chair, 860-486-3315, E-mail: lucy.mcneece@uconn.edu. *Application contact:* Patricia Parlette-Schaff, Administrative Assistant, 860-486-3313, Fax: 860-486-4392, E-mail: patricia.parlette@uconn.edu.

University of Dallas, Braniff Graduate School of Liberal Arts, Institute of Philosophic Studies, Program in Literature, Irving, TX 75062-4736. Offers PhD. *Faculty:* 5 full-time (1 woman). *Students:* 25 full-time (10 women), 7 part-time (3 women); includes 3 minority (1 American Indian/Alaska Native, 2 Hispanic Americans). Average age 29. 24 applicants, 33% accepted, 2 enrolled. In 2009, 1 doctorate awarded. *Degree requirements:* For doctorate, 2 foreign languages, comprehensive exam, thesis/dissertation, qualifying exams. *Entrance requirements:* For doctorate, GRE General Test. Additional exam requirements/recommendations for international students: Required—TOEFL. *Application deadline:* For fall admission, 2/15 priority date for domestic students. Application fee: $50. *Expenses:* Tuition: Full-time $10,080; part-time $560 per credit hour. Required fees: $50 per term. Tuition and fees vary according to program. *Financial support:* In 2009–10, 25 students received support. Scholarships/grants available. Financial award application deadline: 2/15. *Faculty research:* Medieval studies, modern literature, Renaissance, Shakespeare. *Unit head:* Dr. Theresa Kenney, Director, 972-721-4069, Fax:

Comparative Literature

University of Dallas (continued)
972-721-4007, E-mail: tereska@udallas.edu. *Application contact:* Graduate Coordinator, 972-721-5106, Fax: 972-721-5280, E-mail: graduate@acad.udallas.edu.

University of Georgia, Graduate School, College of Arts and Sciences, Department of Comparative Literature, Athens, GA 30602. Offers MA, PhD. *Faculty:* 18 full-time (7 women). *Students:* 23 full-time (15 women), 4 part-time (3 women); includes 1 minority (Hispanic American), 7 international. 25 applicants, 40% accepted, 9 enrolled. In 2009, 7 master's, 2 doctorates awarded. *Degree requirements:* For master's, 2 foreign languages, thesis; for doctorate, one foreign language, thesis/dissertation. *Entrance requirements:* For master's and doctorate, GRE General Test. *Application deadline:* For fall admission, 7/1 priority date for domestic students; for spring admission, 11/15 for domestic students. Application fee: $50. Electronic applications accepted. *Expenses:* Tuition, state resident: full-time $6000; part-time $250 per credit hour. Tuition, nonresident: full-time $20,904; part-time $871 per credit hour. Required fees: $730 per semester. *Financial support:* Fellowships, research assistantships, teaching assistantships, unspecified assistantships available. *Unit head:* Dr. James H. McGregor, Department Co-Head, 706-542-2140, E-mail: mcgregor@uga.edu. *Application contact:* Dr. Thomas Cerbu, Graduate Coordinator, 706-542-2263, Fax: 706-542-2155, E-mail: tcerbu@uga.edu.

University of Guelph, Graduate Program Services, College of Arts, School of English and Theatre Studies, Joint Program in Literary Studies/Theatre Studies in English, Guelph, ON N1G 2W1, Canada. Offers PhD. Part-time programs available. *Degree requirements:* For doctorate, one foreign language, comprehensive exam, thesis/dissertation. *Entrance requirements:* For doctorate, MA, 3 letters of reference, writing samples, resume, minimum A- average in graduate course work. Additional exam requirements/recommendations for international students: Required—TOEFL. Electronic applications accepted. *Faculty research:* Canadian studies, Early Modern studies, Postcolonial studies, studies in gender and genre, 19th Century studies.

University of Illinois at Urbana–Champaign, Graduate College, College of Liberal Arts and Sciences, School of Literatures, Cultures and Linguistics, Program in Comparative and World Literature, Champaign, IL 61820. Offers comparative literature (MA, PhD). *Faculty:* 6 full-time (5 women), 1 (woman) part-time/adjunct. *Students:* 22 full-time (14 women), 1 (woman) part-time; includes 3 minority (2 Asian Americans or Pacific Islanders, 1 Hispanic American), 12 international. 30 applicants, 17% accepted, 1 enrolled. In 2009, 8 master's, 5 doctorates awarded. *Entrance requirements:* For master's, minimum GPA of 3.0; writing sample. Additional exam requirements/recommendations for international students: Required—TOEFL (minimum score 105 iBT). *Application deadline:* Applications are processed on a rolling basis. Application fee: $60 ($75 for international students). Electronic applications accepted. *Financial support:* In 2009–10, 9 fellowships, 1 research assistantship, 19 teaching assistantships were awarded; tuition waivers (full and partial) also available. *Unit head:* Jean-Phillipe R. Mathy, Director, 217-244-2727, Fax: 217-244-4019, E-mail: jmathy@illinois.edu. *Application contact:* Lynn Stanke, Office Support Specialist, 217-333-6269, Fax: 217-244-4019, E-mail: stanke@illinois.edu.

The University of Iowa, Graduate College, College of Liberal Arts and Sciences, Department of Cinema and Comparative Literature, Program in Comparative Literature, Iowa City, IA 52242-1316. Offers MA, PhD. *Degree requirements:* For master's, thesis optional, exam; for doctorate, comprehensive exam, thesis/dissertation. *Entrance requirements:* For master's and doctorate, GRE General Test, minimum GPA of 3.0. Additional exam requirements/recommendations for international students: Required—TOEFL (minimum score 520 paper-based; 213 computer-based; 81 iBT). Electronic applications accepted.

The University of Iowa, Graduate College, College of Liberal Arts and Sciences, Department of Cinema and Comparative Literature, Program in Comparative Literature Translation, Iowa City, IA 52242-1316. Offers MFA. *Degree requirements:* For master's, thesis, exam. *Entrance requirements:* For master's, GRE General Test, minimum GPA of 3.0. Additional exam requirements/recommendations for international students: Required—TOEFL (minimum score 550 paper-based; 213 computer-based; 81 iBT). Electronic applications accepted.

University of Maryland, College Park, Academic Affairs, College of Arts and Humanities, Department of English, Program in Comparative Literature, College Park, MD 20742. Offers MA, PhD. *Students:* 11 full-time (8 women), 4 international. 13 applicants, 15% accepted, 2 enrolled. In 2009, 1 doctorate awarded. *Degree requirements:* For master's, thesis, oral defense; for doctorate, 3 foreign languages, thesis/dissertation, comprehensive exams in 4 areas. *Entrance requirements:* For master's, GRE General Test, minimum GPA of 3.0, foreign language, writing sample, 3 letters of recommendation; for doctorate, GRE General Test, minimum GPA of 3.0, foreign language, writing sample. Additional exam requirements/recommendations for international students: Required—TOEFL. *Application deadline:* For fall admission, 1/15 for domestic and international students. Applications are processed on a rolling basis. Application fee: $60. Electronic applications accepted. *Expenses:* Tuition, area resident: Part-time $471 per credit hour. Tuition, state resident: part-time $471 per credit hour. Tuition, nonresident: part-time $1016 per credit hour. Required fees: $337.04 per term. *Financial support:* In 2009–10, 5 teaching assistantships with tuition reimbursements (averaging $17,798 per year) were awarded; fellowships, research assistantships, career-related internships or fieldwork, Federal Work-Study, and scholarships/grants also available. Support available to part-time students. Financial award applicants required to submit FAFSA. *Faculty research:* Renaissance studies, drama, modern literature, postcolonial studies, feminist scholarship. *Unit head:* Kent Cartwright, Chair of English Department, 301-405-3807, E-mail: kcartwri@umd.edu. *Application contact:* Dean of Graduate School, 301-405-0376, Fax: 301-314-9305.

University of Massachusetts Amherst, Graduate School, College of Humanities and Fine Arts, Department of Languages, Literatures, and Cultures, Program in Comparative Literature, Amherst, MA 01003. Offers MA, PhD. Part-time programs available. *Faculty:* 12 full-time (4 women). *Students:* 38 full-time (23 women), 2 part-time (0 women); includes 6 minority (all Hispanic Americans), 15 international. Average age 32. 66 applicants, 23% accepted, 9 enrolled. In 2009, 4 master's, 1 doctorate awarded. Terminal master's awarded for partial completion of doctoral program. *Degree requirements:* For master's, 2 foreign languages, thesis or alternative; for doctorate, 2 foreign languages, comprehensive exam, thesis/dissertation. *Entrance requirements:* For master's, GRE General Test; for doctorate, GRE General Test, writing samples. Additional exam requirements/recommendations for international students: Required—TOEFL (minimum score 550 paper-based; 213 computer-based; 80 iBT), IELTS (minimum score 6.5). *Application deadline:* For fall admission, 2/1 for domestic and international students. Applications are processed on a rolling basis. Application fee: $50 ($65 for international students). Electronic applications accepted. *Expenses:* Tuition, state resident: full-time $2640; part-time $110 per credit. Tuition, nonresident: full-time $9936; part-time $414 per credit. Tuition and fees vary according to course load. *Financial support:* In 2009–10, 4 research assistantships with full tuition reimbursements (averaging $5,469 per year), 22 teaching assistantships with full tuition reimbursements (averaging $11,217 per year) were awarded; fellowships, career-related internships or fieldwork, Federal Work-Study, scholarships/grants, traineeships, health care benefits, tuition waivers (full), and unspecified assistantships also available. Support available to part-time students. Financial award application deadline: 2/1. *Unit head:* Dr. William Moebius, Graduate Program Director, 413-545-0929, Fax: 413-545-0908. *Application contact:* Jean M. Ames, Supervisor of Admissions, 413-545-0722, Fax: 413-577-0100, E-mail: gradadm@grad.umass.edu.

University of Memphis, Graduate School, College of Arts and Sciences, Department of English, Memphis, TN 38152. Offers African-American literature (Graduate Certificate); applied linguistics (PhD); composition studies (PhD); creative writing (MFA); English as a second language (MA); linguistics (MA); literary and cultural studies (PhD), including African-American literature; literature (MA); professional writing (MA, PhD); teaching English as a second language (Graduate Certificate). Part-time and evening/weekend programs available. Post-baccalaureate distance learning degree programs offered (no on-campus study). *Faculty:* 31 full-time (15 women), 2 part-time/adjunct (both women). *Students:* 98 full-time (59 women), 99 part-time (66 women); includes 36 minority (28 African Americans, 5 Asian Americans or Pacific Islanders, 3 Hispanic Americans), 7 international. Average age 34. 128 applicants, 71% accepted, 29 enrolled. In 2009, 38 master's, 4 doctorates, 21 other advanced degrees awarded. Terminal master's awarded for partial completion of doctoral program. *Degree requirements:* For master's, one foreign language, comprehensive exam, thesis optional; for doctorate, 2 foreign languages, comprehensive exam, thesis/dissertation. *Entrance requirements:* For master's, GRE; for doctorate, GRE. Additional exam requirements/recommendations for international students: Required—TOEFL. *Application deadline:* For fall admission, 7/1 for domestic students; for spring admission, 10/15 for domestic students. Applications are processed on a rolling basis. Application fee: $35 ($60 for international students). Electronic applications accepted. *Expenses:* Tuition, state resident: full-time $6246; part-time $347 per credit hour. Tuition, nonresident: full-time $15,894; part-time $883 per credit hour. Required fees: $1160. Full-time tuition and fees vary according to course load, degree level and program. *Financial support:* In 2009–10, 123 students received support; research assistantships with full tuition reimbursements available, teaching assistantships with full tuition reimbursements available, Federal Work-Study, scholarships/grants, and unspecified assistantships available. Financial award application deadline: 2/15; financial award applicants required to submit FAFSA. *Faculty research:* Applied linguistis, British and American literature, professional writing, composition studies. *Unit head:* Dr. Eric C. Link, Chair, 901-678-2651, Fax: 901-678-2226, E-mail: eclink@memphis.edu. *Application contact:* Dr. Verner D. Mitchell, Director, Graduate Studies, 901-678-3099, Fax: 901-678-2226, E-mail: vdmtchll@memphis.edu.

University of Michigan, Horace H. Rackham School of Graduate Studies, College of Literature, Science, and the Arts, Department of Comparative Literature, Ann Arbor, MI 48109. Offers PhD. *Faculty:* 20 full-time (11 women). *Students:* 42 full-time (23 women); includes 2 Asian Americans or Pacific Islanders, 4 Hispanic Americans, 17 international. Average age 31. 62 applicants, 16% accepted, 6 enrolled. In 2009, 3 doctorates awarded. *Degree requirements:* For doctorate, 2 foreign languages, thesis/dissertation, oral defense of dissertation, prospectus, preliminary exam. *Entrance requirements:* For doctorate, GRE General Test. Additional exam requirements/recommendations for international students: Required—TOEFL (minimum score 560 paper-based; 220 computer-based; 84 iBT), IELTS (minimum score 6.5), TOEFL (minimum score 560 paper-based; 220 computer-based; 84 iBT) or Michigan English Language Assessment Battery. *Application deadline:* For fall admission, 12/31 for domestic and international students. Application fee: $60 ($75 for international students). Electronic applications accepted. *Expenses:* Tuition, state resident: full-time $17,286; part-time $1099 per credit hour. Tuition, nonresident: full-time $34,944; part-time $2080 per credit hour. Required fees: $95 per semester. Tuition and fees vary according to course load, degree level and program. *Financial support:* In 2009–10, 27 students received support, including 8 fellowships with full tuition reimbursements available (averaging $33,286 per year), 11 teaching assistantships with full tuition reimbursements available (averaging $33,980 per year); research assistantships, career-related internships or fieldwork, Federal Work-Study, institutionally sponsored loans, scholarships/grants, health care benefits, and unspecified assistantships also available. Support available to part-time students. Financial award application deadline: 12/31. *Faculty research:* Postcolonial theory, cultural studies, ideology of aesthetics, translation studies, comparative poetics. *Unit head:* Yopie Prins, Chair, 734-763-2351, Fax: 734-764-8503, E-mail: yprins@umich.edu. *Application contact:* Nancy E. W. Harris, Student Services Coordinator, 734-647-4894, Fax: 734-764-8503, E-mail: nwh@umich.edu.

University of Minnesota, Twin Cities Campus, Graduate School, College of Liberal Arts, Department of Cultural Studies and Comparative Literature, Program in Comparative Literature, Minneapolis, MN 55455-0213. Offers PhD. *Faculty:* 13 full-time (2 women), 6 part-time/adjunct (4 women). *Students:* 20 full-time (8 women); includes 2 minority (1 African American, 1 Asian American or Pacific Islander), 3 international. 42 applicants, 10% accepted, 3 enrolled. In 2009, 3 doctorates awarded. *Degree requirements:* For doctorate, 3 foreign languages, comprehensive exam, thesis/dissertation. *Entrance requirements:* For doctorate, GRE General Test, sample of written work. Additional exam requirements/recommendations for international students: Required—TOEFL. *Application deadline:* For fall admission, 12/10 for domestic students. Application fee: $55 ($75 for international students). *Financial support:* In 2009–10, 1 fellowship with full tuition reimbursement (averaging $22,500 per year), 18 teaching assistantships with full tuition reimbursements (averaging $13,800 per year) were awarded; research assistantships with full tuition reimbursements, Federal Work-Study, institutionally sponsored loans, health care benefits, and tuition waivers (full and partial) also available. Financial award application deadline: 12/10. *Faculty research:* Literary theory, emergent literatures, popular culture, postcolonial literature, gender and sexuality. *Unit head:* Robert I. Brown, Director of Graduate Studies, 612-624-8878, Fax: 612-626-0228, E-mail: brown004@umn.edu. *Application contact:* Robert L. Brown, Director of Graduate Studies, 612-624-8878, Fax: 612-626-0228, E-mail: brown004@umn.edu.

University of Missouri, Graduate School, College of Arts and Sciences, Department of Romance Languages and Literature, Columbia, MO 65211. Offers French (MA, PhD); literature (MA); Spanish (MA, PhD); teaching (MA). *Faculty:* 21 full-time (13 women), 19 part-time/adjunct (15 women). *Students:* 16 full-time (12 women), 26 part-time (16 women); includes 11 minority (2 African Americans, 2 Asian Americans or Pacific Islanders, 7 Hispanic Americans), 9 international. Average age 35. 28 applicants, 71% accepted, 14 enrolled. In 2009, 2 master's awarded. Terminal master's awarded for partial completion of doctoral program. *Degree requirements:* For master's, one foreign language; for doctorate, 4 foreign languages, comprehensive exam, thesis/dissertation. *Entrance requirements:* For master's, GRE General Test, minimum GPA of 3.0 in field of major; must have bachelor's degree; for doctorate, GRE General Test, minimum GPA of 3.0 in field of major; must have maser's degree. Additional exam requirements/recommendations for international students: Required—TOEFL (minimum score 500 paper-based; 173 computer-based; 61 iBT). *Application deadline:* For fall admission, 2/15 priority date for domestic students; for winter admission, 10/15 for domestic students. Applications are processed on a rolling basis. Application fee: $45 ($60 for international students). Electronic applications accepted. *Financial support:* In 2009–10, 37 teaching assistantships with full tuition reimbursements were awarded; research assistantships, institutionally sponsored loans, health care benefits, and unspecified assistantships also available. *Unit head:* Dr. Flore Zephir, Department Chair, E-mail: zephirf@missouri.edu. *Application contact:* Mary Harriss, Administrative Assistant, 573-882-5039, E-mail: harrisma@missouri.edu.

University of Nebraska–Lincoln, Graduate College, College of Arts and Sciences, Department of English, Lincoln, NE 68588-0333. Offers composition and rhetoric (MA, PhD); creative writing (MA, PhD); literature studies (MA, PhD). *Degree requirements:* For master's, thesis optional; for doctorate, one foreign language, comprehensive exam, thesis/dissertation. *Entrance requirements:* For master's, writing sample; for doctorate, GRE General Test, writing sample. Additional exam requirements/recommendations for international students: Required—TOEFL (minimum score 600 paper-based; 250 computer-based). Electronic applications accepted. *Faculty research:* Creative writing, composition and rhetoric, women's studies, North American literature, medieval/Renaissance studies.

University of New Hampshire, Graduate School, College of Liberal Arts, Department of English, Durham, NH 03824. Offers English (MFA, PhD); English education (MST); language and linguistics (MA); literature (MA); writing (MA). Part-time programs available. *Faculty:* 35 full-time (18 women). *Students:* 54 full-time (33 women), 64 part-time (40 women); includes 5 minority (1 African American, 2 American Indian/Alaska Native, 2 Hispanic Americans), 5 international. Average age 34. 279 applicants, 43% accepted, 38 enrolled. In 2009, 32 master's, 5 doctorates awarded. *Degree requirements:* For master's, one foreign language; for doctorate, 2 foreign languages, thesis/dissertation. *Entrance requirements:* For master's, GRE General Test, sample of written work; for doctorate, GRE General Test, GRE Subject Test, sample of written work. Additional exam requirements/recommendations for international students: Required—TOEFL (minimum score 550 paper-based; 213 computer-based; 80 iBT). *Application deadline:* For fall admission, 6/1 priority date for domestic students, 2/15 for international students; for spring admission, 12/1 for domestic students. Applications are processed on a rolling basis. Application fee: $65. Electronic applications accepted. *Expenses:* Tuition, state resident: full-time $10,380; part-time $577 per credit hour. Tuition, nonresident: full-time $24,350; part-time $1002 per credit hour. Required fees: $1550; $387.50 per semester. Tuition and fees vary according to course load and program. *Financial support:* In 2009–10, 57 students received support, including 4 fellowships, 46 teaching assistantships; research assistantships, career-related internships or fieldwork, Federal Work-Study, scholarships/grants, and tuition waivers (full and partial) also available. Support available to part-time students. Financial award application deadline: 2/15. *Unit head:* Dr. Andrew Merton, Chairperson, 603-862-3963. *Application contact:* Jamie Auger, Administrative Assistant, 603-862-3963, E-mail: engl.grad@unh.edu.

University of New Mexico, Graduate School, College of Arts and Sciences, Department of Foreign Languages and Literature, Albuquerque, NM 87131-2039. Offers comparative literature and cultural studies (MA); French (MA); French studies (PhD); German studies (MA). Part-time programs available. *Faculty:* 15 full-time (11 women), 8 part-time/adjunct (4 women). *Students:* 9 full-time (8 women), 4 part-time (2 women), 6 international. Average age 33. 9 applicants, 44% accepted, 3 enrolled. In 2009, 5 master's awarded. *Degree requirements:* For master's, one foreign language, thesis optional; for doctorate, 2 foreign languages, thesis/dissertation. *Entrance requirements:* Additional exam requirements/recommendations for international students: Required—TOEFL. *Application deadline:* For fall admission, 2/1 priority date for domestic students; for spring admission, 10/1 priority date for domestic students. Application fee: $50. Electronic applications accepted. *Expenses:* Tuition, state resident: full-time $2099; part-time $233.20 per credit hour. Tuition, nonresident: full-time $6650. Required fees: $25 per semester. Tuition and fees vary according to course load, program and reciprocity agreements. *Financial support:* In 2009–10, 20 teaching assistantships with tuition reimbursements (averaging $12,023 per year) were awarded; Federal Work-Study, health care benefits, and unspecified assistantships also available. Financial award application deadline: 3/1; financial award applicants required to submit FAFSA. *Faculty research:* German, Russian, Italian, Japanese, French, comparative literature, culture studies, classics. Total annual research expenditures: $4,750. *Unit head:* Dr. Natasha Kolchevska, Chair, 505-277-4771, Fax: 505-277-3599, E-mail: nakol@unm.edu. *Application contact:* Jean Aragon, Application and Graduation Advisor, 505-277-4471, Fax: 505-277-3599, E-mail: peaslee@unm.edu.

The University of North Carolina at Chapel Hill, Graduate School, College of Arts and Sciences, Curriculum in Comparative Literature, Chapel Hill, NC 27599. Offers MA, PhD. Terminal master's awarded for partial completion of doctoral program. *Degree requirements:* For master's, one foreign language, thesis, exams; for doctorate, 2 foreign languages, thesis/dissertation, exams. *Entrance requirements:* For master's and doctorate, GRE General Test, minimum GPA of 3.0. Additional exam requirements/recommendations for international students: Required—TOEFL (minimum score 600 paper-based; 250 computer-based). Electronic applications accepted. *Faculty research:* Realism, literature and medicine, Proust, literary theory, Arthurian romance.

University of Notre Dame, Graduate School, College of Arts and Letters, Division of Humanities, PhD Program in Literature, Notre Dame, IN 46556. Offers PhD. *Degree requirements:* For doctorate, 3 foreign languages, thesis/dissertation, candidacy exam. *Entrance requirements:* For doctorate, GRE General Test. Additional exam requirements/recommendations for international students: Required—TOEFL (minimum score 600 paper-based; 250 computer-based; 80 iBT). Electronic applications accepted. *Faculty research:* Interdisciplinary study of literature from a transitional and intercultural perspective; Classics, East Asian, French, German, Irish, Italian, Iberian and Latin American (Portuguese, Spanish).

University of Oregon, Graduate School, College of Arts and Sciences, Program in Comparative Literature, Eugene, OR 97403. Offers MA, PhD. Part-time programs available. Terminal master's awarded for partial completion of doctoral program. *Degree requirements:* For master's, 2 foreign languages, field exam; for doctorate, 2 foreign languages, thesis/dissertation, field exam. *Entrance requirements:* For master's, previous course work in English and literature, proficiency in 3 foreign languages, writing sample; for doctorate, previous course work in English and literature, proficiency in 2 foreign languages, writing sample. Additional exam requirements/recommendations for international students: Required—TOEFL. *Faculty research:* Critical theory, historical periods, interdisciplinary approach, Feminist studies.

University of Pennsylvania, School of Arts and Sciences, Graduate Group in Comparative Literature and Literary Theory, Philadelphia, PA 19104. Offers comparative literature (AM, PhD); literary theory (AM, PhD). *Faculty:* 60 full-time (24 women), 4 part-time/adjunct (1 woman). *Students:* 32 full-time (18 women); includes 3 minority (2 African Americans, 1 Hispanic American), 9 international. 126 applicants, 10% accepted, 8 enrolled. In 2009, 3 master's, 8 doctorates awarded. *Degree requirements:* For master's, one foreign language, thesis; for doctorate, variable foreign language requirement, thesis/dissertation. *Entrance requirements:* For master's, GRE General Test, proficiency in 1 foreign language; for doctorate, GRE General Test, master's degree in a literature field, proficiency in 1 foreign language. Additional exam requirements/recommendations for international students: Required—TOEFL. *Application deadline:* For fall admission, 12/1 priority date for domestic students. Application fee: $70. Electronic applications accepted. *Expenses:* Tuition: Full-time $25,660; part-time $4758 per course. Required fees: $2152; $270 per course. Tuition and fees vary according to course load, degree level and program. *Financial support:* Institutionally sponsored loans, scholarships/grants, traineeships, health care benefits, and unspecified assistantships available. Financial award application deadline: 12/15.

University of Puerto Rico, Río Piedras, College of Humanities, Department of Comparative Literature, San Juan, PR 00931-3300. Offers MA. Part-time programs available. *Degree requirements:* For master's, comprehensive exam, thesis. *Entrance requirements:* For master's, EXADEP, interview, minimum GPA of 3.0, letter of recommendation.

University of South Carolina, The Graduate School, College of Arts and Sciences, Department of Languages, Literatures, and Cultures, Columbia, SC 29208. Offers comparative literature (MA, PhD); foreign languages (MAT), including French, German, Spanish; French (MA); German (MA); Spanish (MA). MAT offered in cooperation with the College of Education. Part-time programs available. *Degree requirements:* For master's, one foreign language, comprehensive exam, thesis optional; for doctorate, 2 foreign languages, comprehensive exam, thesis/dissertation. *Entrance requirements:* For master's and doctorate, GRE General Test, writing sample. Additional exam requirements/recommendations for international students: Required—TOEFL (minimum score 230 computer-based; 75 iBT). Electronic applications accepted. *Faculty research:* Modern literature, linguistics, literature and culture, medieval literature, literary theory.

University of Southern California, Graduate School, College of Letters, Arts and Sciences, Department of Comparative Literature, Los Angeles, CA 90089. Offers MA, PhD. *Faculty:* 15 full-time (7 women), 1 part-time/adjunct (0 women). *Students:* 28 full-time (17 women), 1 (woman) part-time; includes 8 minority (3 African Americans, 2 Asian Americans or Pacific Islanders, 3 Hispanic Americans), 7 international. 27 applicants, 19% accepted, 1 enrolled. In 2009, 1 master's, 1 doctorate awarded. *Degree requirements:* For doctorate, 2 foreign languages, comprehensive exam, thesis/dissertation. *Entrance requirements:* For doctorate, GRE. Additional exam requirements/recommendations for international students: Required—TOEFL. *Application deadline:* For fall admission, 12/1 priority date for domestic and international students. Application fee: $85. Electronic applications accepted. *Expenses:* Tuition: Full-time $25,980; part-time $1315 per unit. Required fees: $554. One-time fee: $35 full-time. Full-time tuition and fees vary according to degree level and program. *Financial support:* In 2009–10, 26 students received support, including 7 fellowships with full tuition reimbursements available (averaging $25,000 per year), 17 teaching assistantships with full tuition reimbursements available (averaging $25,000 per year); institutionally sponsored loans, tuition waivers, and unspecified assistantships also available. Financial award applicants required to submit FAFSA. *Faculty research:* Literary theory, Japanese film and contemporary fiction, Francophone literature and cinema, Latin American and Caribbean literature, nineteenth and twentieth century British and American literature. *Application contact:* Katherine Guevarra, Administrative Assistant, 213-740-0102, Fax: 213-740-0858, E-mail: kguevarr@usc.edu.

The University of Texas at Austin, Graduate School, College of Liberal Arts, Program in Comparative Literature, Austin, TX 78712-1111. Offers MA, PhD. *Degree requirements:* For master's, 2 foreign languages, report or thesis; for doctorate, 3 foreign languages, thesis/dissertation. *Entrance requirements:* For master's and doctorate, GRE General Test. Electronic applications accepted.

The University of Texas at Dallas, School of Arts and Humanities, Richardson, TX 75080. Offers arts and technology (MFA); emerging media and communications (MA); humanities (MA, MAT, PhD), including aesthetic studies, history of ideas, humanities, studies in literature; Latin American studies (MA). Part-time and evening/weekend programs available. *Faculty:* 57 full-time (19 women), 3 part-time/adjunct (1 woman). *Students:* 240 full-time (127 women), 221 part-time (115 women); includes 90 minority (30 African Americans, 5 American Indian/Alaska Native, 21 Asian Americans or Pacific Islanders, 34 Hispanic Americans), 36 international. Average age 37. 186 applicants, 70% accepted, 106 enrolled. In 2009, 57 master's, 13 doctorates awarded. *Degree requirements:* For master's, one foreign language, portfolio; for doctorate, one foreign language, thesis/dissertation. *Entrance requirements:* For master's and doctorate, minimum GPA of 3.0 in undergraduate course work in field. Additional exam requirements/recommendations for international students: Required—TOEFL (minimum score 550 paper-based; 213 computer-based). *Application deadline:* For fall admission, 7/15 for domestic students, 5/1 priority date for international students; for spring admission, 11/15 for domestic students, 9/1 priority date for international students. Applications are processed on a rolling basis. Application fee: $50 ($100 for international students). Electronic applications accepted. *Expenses:* Tuition, state resident: full-time $11,068; part-time $461 per credit hour. Tuition, nonresident: full-time $21,178; part-time $882 per credit hour. Tuition and fees vary according to course load. *Financial support:* In 2009–10, 23 research assistantships with full tuition reimbursements (averaging $10,108 per year), 92 teaching assistantships with full tuition reimbursements (averaging $10,115 per year) were awarded; fellowships, Federal Work-Study, institutionally sponsored loans, scholarships/grants, and unspecified assistantships also available. Support available to part-time students. Financial award application deadline: 4/30; financial award applicants required to submit FAFSA. *Faculty research:* Translation, science and the arts and humanities, intellectual and philosophical history, cultural studies. Total annual research expenditures: $726,917. *Unit head:* Dr. Dennis M. Kratz, Dean, 972-883-2984, Fax: 972-883-2989, E-mail: dkratz@utdallas.edu. *Application contact:* Dr. Michael Wilson, Associate Dean of Graduate Studies, 972-883-2756, Fax: 972-883-2989, E-mail: mwilson@utdallas.edu.

University of Toronto, School of Graduate Studies, Humanities Division, Centre for Comparative Literature, Toronto, ON M5S 1A1, Canada. Offers MA, PhD. Part-time programs available. *Degree requirements:* For doctorate, thesis/dissertation. *Entrance requirements:* For master's, 2 letters of recommendation, sample of work (short essay on a literary topic preferred), resume; for doctorate, 2 letters of recommendation, sample of work (short essay on a literary topic preferred), resumé.

University of Utah, The Graduate School, College of Humanities, Department of Languages and Literature, Salt Lake City, UT 84112-1107. Offers comparative literary and cultural studies (MA, PhD); French (MA, MALP); German (MA, MALP, PhD); Spanish (MA, MALP, PhD); world languages with secondary teaching licensure (MA). *Faculty:* 35 full-time (22 women), 1 part-time/adjunct (0 women). *Students:* 30 full-time (20 women), 10 part-time (9 women); includes 8 minority (1 American Indian/Alaska Native, 2 Asian Americans or Pacific Islanders, 5 Hispanic Americans), 6 international. Average age 35. 47 applicants, 40% accepted, 18 enrolled. In 2009, 7 master's, 3 doctorates awarded. Terminal master's awarded for partial completion of doctoral program. *Degree requirements:* For master's, 2 foreign languages, comprehensive exam, thesis, standard proficiency in 2 languages other than English; for doctorate, 3 foreign languages, comprehensive exam, thesis/dissertation, standard proficiency in 2 languages other than English and language of study, advanced proficiency in 1 language other than English and language of study. *Entrance requirements:* For master's, bachelor's degree or strong undergraduate record in target languages, minimum GPA of 3.0; for doctorate, GRE, MA, advanced proficiency in a target language. Additional exam requirements/recommendations for international students: Required—TOEFL (minimum score 500 paper-based; 173 computer-based). *Application deadline:* For fall admission, 1/15 priority date for domestic students, 12/15 priority date for international students. Application fee: $55 ($65 for international students). *Expenses:* Tuition, state resident: full-time $4004; part-time $1674 per semester. Tuition, nonresident: full-time $14,134; part-time $5915 per semester. Required fees: $324 per semester. Tuition and fees vary according to course load, degree level and program. *Financial support:* In 2009–10, 21 students received support, including 21 teaching assistantships with full tuition reimbursements available (averaging $11,000 per year); health care benefits also available. Financial award application deadline: 2/1; financial award applicants required to submit FAFSA. *Faculty research:* Literary theory, linguistics, cultural studies, comparative studies. Total annual research expenditures: $22,986. *Unit head:* Dr. Christine A. Jones, Director of Graduate Studies, 801-585-3002, Fax: 801-581-7581, E-mail: cjones@hum.utah.edu. *Application contact:* Virginia Ellinwood, Academic Advisor, 801-585-9437, Fax: 801-581-7581, E-mail: v.ellinwood@mail.hum.utah.edu.

University of Washington, Graduate School, College of Arts and Sciences, Department of Comparative Literature, Seattle, WA 98195. Offers MA, PhD. Part-time programs available. Terminal master's awarded for partial completion of doctoral program. *Degree requirements:* For master's, 2 foreign languages, thesis optional; for doctorate, 3 foreign languages, thesis/dissertation. *Entrance requirements:* For master's, GRE General Test, BA in comparative literature or equivalent, minimum GPA of 3.0, proficiency in 1 foreign language; for doctorate, GRE General Test, MA in comparative literature or equivalent, minimum GPA of 3.0, proficiency in 2 foreign languages. Additional exam requirements/recommendations for international students: Required—TOEFL. Electronic applications accepted. *Faculty research:* Literature and culture from classical antiquity to twentieth-century, literary theory and criticism.

The University of Western Ontario, Faculty of Graduate Studies, Faculty of Arts and Humanities, Department of Comparative Literature, London, ON N6A 5B8, Canada. Offers comparative literature (MA, PhD); Spanish (MA). Part-time programs available. *Degree requirements:* For master's, 2 foreign languages, thesis (for some programs). *Entrance requirements:* For master's, honors degree in Spanish or equivalent, minimum B average. Additional exam requirements/recommendations for international students: Required—TOEFL, TOEFL (comparative literature). *Faculty research:* Spanish golden age, Latin-American, romance, medieval, film.

University of Wisconsin–Madison, Graduate School, College of Letters and Science, Department of Comparative Literature, Madison, WI 53706-1380. Offers MA, PhD. Part-time programs available. Terminal master's awarded for partial completion of doctoral program. *Degree requirements:* For master's, one foreign language, second-year exam; for doctorate, 3 foreign languages, thesis/dissertation, 3 preliminary exams. *Entrance requirements:* For master's, GRE General Test, writing sample; for doctorate, GRE General Test. Electronic applications accepted. *Expenses:* Tuition, state resident: part-time $594 per credit. Tuition, nonresident: part-time $1504 per credit. Required fees: $65 per credit. Tuition and fees vary according to course load, program and reciprocity agreements. *Faculty research:* Literary theory, cultural criticism, classics through early modern literature, postmodernity, gender studies.

University of Wisconsin–Madison, Graduate School, College of Letters and Science, Department of East Asian Languages and Literature, Program in Chinese Literature, Madison, WI 53706-1380. Offers MA, PhD. Part-time programs available. Terminal master's awarded for partial completion of doctoral program. *Degree requirements:* For master's, one foreign language, seminars, written exam; for doctorate, 3 foreign languages, thesis/dissertation, seminars, preliminary exams, oral exam. *Entrance requirements:* For master's, bachelor's degree or equivalent in Chinese; for doctorate, master's degree or equivalent in Chinese. Electronic

Comparative Literature

University of Wisconsin–Madison (continued)
applications accepted. *Expenses:* Tuition, state resident: part-time $594 per credit. Tuition, nonresident: part-time $1504 per credit. Required fees: $65 per credit. Tuition and fees vary according to course load, program and reciprocity agreements. *Faculty research:* Chinese historical and modern linguistics, classical Chinese literary and cultural history, modern Chinese literary and cultural history, Chinese paleography.

University of Wisconsin–Madison, Graduate School, College of Letters and Science, Department of Scandinavian Studies, Madison, WI 53706-1380. Offers area studies (MA); folklore (PhD); literature (MA, PhD); philology (PhD). Part-time programs available. *Degree requirements:* For master's, 2 foreign languages, exam; for doctorate, thesis/dissertation, exam. *Entrance requirements:* For master's, minimum GPA of 3.25; for doctorate, minimum GPA of 3.5. Electronic applications accepted. *Expenses:* Tuition, state resident: part-time $594 per credit. Tuition, nonresident: part-time $1504 per credit. Required fees: $65 per credit. Tuition and fees vary according to course load, program and reciprocity agreements. *Faculty research:* Historical fiction, Icelandic poetry, nineteenth-century literature, theater, gender studies, folklore.

University of Wisconsin–Milwaukee, Graduate School, College of Letters and Sciences, Department of English, Milwaukee, WI 53201-0413. Offers creative writing (PhD); English (MA); international technical communication (Certificate); linguistics (PhD); professional writing (PhD); professional writing and communication (Certificate); rhetoric and composition (PhD); MLIS/MA. *Faculty:* 38 full-time (19 women). *Students:* 107 full-time (64 women), 82 part-time (54 women); includes 13 minority (8 African Americans, 1 American Indian/Alaska Native, 2 Asian Americans or Pacific Islanders, 2 Hispanic Americans), 23 international. Average age 34. 193 applicants, 51% accepted, 31 enrolled. In 2009, 26 master's, 16 doctorates awarded. *Degree requirements:* For master's, thesis or alternative; for doctorate, one foreign language, thesis/dissertation. *Entrance requirements:* For master's, GRE General Test, GRE Subject Test; for doctorate, GRE. Additional exam requirements/recommendations for international students: Required—TOEFL (minimum score 550 paper-based; 79 iBT), IELTS (minimum score 6.5). *Application deadline:* For fall admission, 1/1 priority date for domestic students; for spring admission, 9/1 for domestic students. Applications are processed on a rolling basis. Application fee: $45 ($75 for international students). *Expenses:* Tuition, state resident: full-time $8800. Tuition, nonresident: full-time $20,760. Tuition and fees vary according to program and reciprocity agreements. *Financial support:* In 2009–10, 75 teaching assistantships were awarded; career-related internships or fieldwork and unspecified assistantships also available. Support available to part-time students. Financial award application deadline: 4/15. Total annual research expenditures: $41,495. *Unit head:* Tasha Oren, Representative, 414-229-4637, Fax: 414-229-2643, E-mail: tgoren@uwm.edu. *Application contact:* General Information Contact, 414-229-4982, Fax: 414-229-6967, E-mail: gradschool@uwm.edu.

University of Wisconsin–Milwaukee, Graduate School, College of Letters and Sciences, Interdepartmental Program in Foreign Language and Literature, Milwaukee, WI 53201-0413. Offers classics and Hebrew studies (MAFLL); comparative literature (MAFLL); French and Italian (MAFLL); German (MAFLL); Slavic studies (MAFLL); translation (Certificate). Part-time programs available. *Faculty:* 37 full-time (18 women). *Students:* 32 full-time (25 women), 28 part-time (19 women); includes 5 minority (1 Asian American or Pacific Islander, 4 Hispanic Americans), 22 international. Average age 33. 54 applicants, 69% accepted, 20 enrolled. In 2009, 24 master's awarded. *Degree requirements:* For master's, 2 foreign languages, thesis or alternative. *Entrance requirements:* Additional exam requirements/recommendations for international students: Required—TOEFL (minimum score 550 paper-based; 79 iBT), IELTS (minimum score 6.5). *Application deadline:* For fall admission, 1/1 priority date for domestic students; for spring admission, 9/1 for domestic students. Applications are processed on a rolling basis. Application fee: $45 ($75 for international students). *Expenses:* Tuition, state resident: full-time $8800. Tuition, nonresident: full-time $20,760. Tuition and fees vary according to program and reciprocity agreements. *Financial support:* In 2009–10, 2 research assistantships, 21 teaching assistantships were awarded; career-related internships or fieldwork and unspecified assistantships also available. Support available to part-time students. Financial award application deadline: 4/15. Total annual research expenditures: $285,237. *Unit head:* Gabrielle Verdier, Representative, 414-229-3346, Fax: 414-229-2741, E-mail: verdier@uwm.edu. *Application contact:* General Information Contact, 414-229-4982, Fax: 414-229-6967, E-mail: gradschool@uwm.edu.

Washington University in St. Louis, Graduate School of Arts and Sciences, Department of Asian and Near Eastern Languages and Literatures, St. Louis, MO 63130-4899. Offers Chinese (MA); Chinese and comparative literature (PhD); Japanese (MA); Japanese and comparative literature (PhD). Terminal master's awarded for partial completion of doctoral program. *Degree requirements:* For master's, thesis optional; for doctorate, thesis/dissertation. *Entrance requirements:* For master's and doctorate, GRE General Test. Electronic applications accepted.

Washington University in St. Louis, Graduate School of Arts and Sciences, Program in Comparative Literature, St. Louis, MO 63130-4899. Offers MA, PhD. Terminal master's awarded for partial completion of doctoral program. *Degree requirements:* For master's, thesis or alternative; for doctorate, thesis/dissertation. *Entrance requirements:* For master's and doctorate, GRE General Test. Electronic applications accepted.

Wayne State University, College of Liberal Arts and Sciences, Department of English, Program in Comparative Literature, Detroit, MI 48202. Offers MA. *Degree requirements:* For master's, one foreign language, essay or thesis. *Entrance requirements:* For master's, GRE General Test, minimum GPA of 3.25 in English, 3.0 overall. Additional exam requirements/recommendations for international students: Required—TOEFL (minimum score 550 paper-based; 213 computer-based); Recommended—TWE (minimum score 6). Electronic applications accepted.

Western Kentucky University, Graduate Studies, Potter College of Arts and Letters, Department of English, Bowling Green, KY 42101. Offers education (MA); English (MA Ed); literature (MA), including American literature, British literature, literary theory, women writers, world literature; teaching English as a second language (MA); writing (MA). Part-time and evening/weekend programs available. *Degree requirements:* For master's, comprehensive exam, thesis optional, final exam. *Entrance requirements:* For master's, GRE General Test, minimum GPA of 2.75. Additional exam requirements/recommendations for international students: Required—TOEFL (minimum score 555 paper-based; 213 computer-based; 79 iBT). *Expenses:* Tuition, state resident: full-time $4160; part-time $416 per credit hour. Tuition, nonresident: full-time $9550; part-time $506 per credit hour. Tuition and fees vary according to campus/location and reciprocity agreements. *Faculty research:* Improving writing, linking teacher knowledge and performance, Victorian women writers, Kentucky women writers, Kentucky poets.

Yale University, Graduate School of Arts and Sciences, Department of Comparative Literature, New Haven, CT 06520. Offers PhD. *Degree requirements:* For doctorate, 2 foreign languages, thesis/dissertation. *Entrance requirements:* For doctorate, GRE General Test.

English

Abilene Christian University, Graduate School, College of Arts and Sciences, Department of English, Abilene, TX 79699-9100. Offers composition/rhetoric (MA); literature (MA); writing (MA). Part-time programs available. *Faculty:* 17 part-time/adjunct (7 women). *Students:* 15 full-time (7 women), 2 part-time (both women); includes 1 minority (Hispanic American), 1 international. 10 applicants, 100% accepted, 8 enrolled. In 2009, 6 master's awarded. *Degree requirements:* For master's, one foreign language, comprehensive exam, thesis optional. *Entrance requirements:* For master's, GRE General Test. *Application deadline:* For fall admission, 4/1 priority date for domestic students; for spring admission, 11/1 for domestic students. Applications are processed on a rolling basis. Application fee: $40. Electronic applications accepted. *Expenses:* Tuition: Full-time $11,520; part-time $640 per hour. Required fees: $1090; $53.50 per hour. $10 per term. Tuition and fees vary according to program. *Financial support:* Teaching assistantships, Federal Work-Study available. Support available to part-time students. Financial award application deadline: 4/1; financial award applicants required to submit FAFSA. *Faculty research:* Feminism, Shakespearean dimensions of new literature, poetic consciousness, deconstruction myths. *Unit head:* Dr. Dana McMichael, Graduate Adviser, 325-674-2083, Fax: 325-674-2408, E-mail: dana.mcmichael@acu.edu. *Application contact:* William Horn, Graduate Admissions Counselor, 325-674-2656, Fax: 325-674-6717, E-mail: gradinfo@acu.edu.

Acadia University, Faculty of Arts, Department of English, Wolfville, NS B4P 2R6, Canada. Offers MA. *Faculty:* 15 full-time (6 women). *Students:* 5 full-time (4 women), 3 part-time (1 woman). Average age 25. 16 applicants, 50% accepted, 5 enrolled. In 2009, 3 master's awarded. *Degree requirements:* For master's, thesis. *Entrance requirements:* For master's, honors degree in English, minimum A- average. Additional exam requirements/recommendations for international students: Required—TOEFL (minimum score 630 paper-based; 267 computer-based; 93 iBT), IELTS (minimum score 6.5). *Application deadline:* For fall admission, 2/1 priority date for domestic students; for spring admission, 3/30 for domestic students. Applications are processed on a rolling basis. Application fee: $50. *Financial support:* Fellowships, teaching assistantships, scholarships/grants and unspecified assistantships available. Financial award application deadline: 2/1. *Faculty research:* Renaissance, Canadian, Medieval, Victorian, and Romantic literature. *Unit head:* Dr. Patricia Rigg, Chair, 902-585-1503, Fax: 902-585-1070, E-mail: patricia.rigg@acadiau.ca. *Application contact:* Christine Reed, Secretary, 902-585-1502, Fax: 902-585-1070, E-mail: christine.reed@acadiau.ca.

The American University in Cairo, Graduate Studies and Research, School of Humanities and Social Sciences, Department of English and Comparative Literature, Cairo, Egypt. Offers MA. Part-time programs available. *Degree requirements:* For master's, thesis, proficiency in French or German. *Entrance requirements:* Additional exam requirements/recommendations for international students: Required—English entrance exam and/or TOEFL.

American University of Beirut, Graduate Programs, Faculty of Arts and Sciences, Beirut, Lebanon. Offers anthropology (MA); Arabic language and literature (MA); archaeology (MA); biology (MS); chemistry (MS); computer science (MS); economics (MA); education (MA); English language (MA); English literature (MA); environmental policy planning (MSES); financial economics (MAFE); geology (MS); history (MA); mathematics (MA, MS); Middle Eastern studies (MA); philosophy (MA); physics (MS); political studies (MA); psychology (MA); public administration (MA); sociology (MA); statistics (MA, MS). Part-time programs available. *Degree requirements:* For master's, one foreign language, comprehensive exam, thesis (for some programs). *Entrance requirements:* For master's, GRE, letter of recommendation. Additional exam requirements/recommendations for international students: Required—TOEFL (minimum score 600 paper-based; 250 computer-based; 100 iBT), IELTS (minimum score 7.5). *Faculty research:* String theory and supergravity; computer graphics; algebra and number theory; popular Arabic literature; marine and freshwater biology; integrating science, math and technology.

Andrews University, School of Graduate Studies, College of Arts and Sciences, Department of English, Berrien Springs, MI 49104. Offers MA, MAT. Part-time programs available. *Faculty:* 10 full-time (4 women), 3 part-time/adjunct (2 women). *Students:* 12 full-time (6 women), 6 part-time (3 women); includes 4 minority (1 African American, 2 Asian Americans or Pacific Islanders, 1 Hispanic American), 3 international. Average age 34. 11 applicants, 45% accepted, 2 enrolled. In 2009, 1 master's awarded. *Degree requirements:* For master's, one foreign language, thesis optional. *Entrance requirements:* For master's, GRE Subject Test. Additional exam requirements/recommendations for international students: Required—TOEFL (minimum score 550 paper-based). *Application deadline:* For fall admission, 8/15 for domestic students. Applications are processed on a rolling basis. Application fee: $40. *Financial support:* Fellowships, research assistantships, teaching assistantships, career-related internships or fieldwork and Federal Work-Study available. *Faculty research:* Christianity and literature, Victorian literature, social linguistics, rhetoric, American literature. *Unit head:* Dr. Douglas Jones, Chairperson, 269-471-3298. *Application contact:* Carolyn Hurst, Supervisor of Graduate Admission, 800-253-2874, Fax: 269-471-6321, E-mail: graduate@andrews.edu.

Angelo State University, College of Graduate Studies, College of Liberal and Fine Arts, Department of English, San Angelo, TX 76909. Offers MA. Part-time and evening/weekend programs available. *Faculty:* 5 full-time (2 women). *Students:* 5 full-time (4 women), 8 part-time (5 women); includes 2 minority (both Hispanic Americans). Average age 26. 2 applicants, 100% accepted, 2 enrolled. In 2009, 7 master's awarded. *Degree requirements:* For master's, comprehensive exam, thesis optional. *Entrance requirements:* For master's, GRE General Test. Additional exam requirements/recommendations for international students: Required—TOEFL or IELTS. *Application deadline:* For fall admission, 7/15 priority date for domestic students, 6/10 for international students; for spring admission, 12/1 priority date for domestic students, 11/1 for international students. Applications are processed on a rolling basis. Application fee: $40 ($50 for international students). Electronic applications accepted. *Expenses:* Tuition, state resident: full-time $3396; part-time $142 per credit hour. Tuition, nonresident: full-time $10,152; part-time $423 per credit hour. Required fees: $1786; $36.25 per credit hour. $494 per semester. Full-time tuition and fees vary according to course load, degree level and program. *Financial support:* In 2009–10, 9 students received support, including 4 teaching assistantships (averaging $10,251 per year); Federal Work-Study, scholarships/grants, and unspecified assistantships also available. Support available to part-time students. Financial award application deadline: 3/1; financial award applicants required to submit FAFSA. *Unit head:* Dr. Laurence E. Musgrove, Department Head, 325-942-2273 Ext. 231, Fax: 325-942-2208, E-mail: lmusgrove@angelo.edu. *Application contact:* Dr. Terry Dalrymple, Graduate Advisor, 325-942-2252 Ext. 225, Fax: 325-942-2208, E-mail: terry.dalrymple@angelo.edu.

Appalachian State University, Cratis D. Williams Graduate School, Department of English, Boone, NC 28608. Offers English (MA); English education (MA). Part-time programs available. *Faculty:* Postbaccalaureate distance learning degree programs offered (no on-campus study). *Faculty:* 37 full-time (18 women). *Students:* 14 full-time (9 women), 14 part-time (7 women); includes 1 minority (African American), 1 international. 21 applicants, 86% accepted, 11 enrolled. In 2009, 16 master's awarded. *Degree requirements:* For master's, one foreign language, comprehensive exam, thesis (for some programs). *Entrance requirements:* For master's, GRE General Test, 3 letters of recommendation. Additional exam requirements/recommendations for international students: Required—TOEFL (minimum score 570 paper-based; 230 computer-based; 79 iBT),

IELTS (minimum score 6.5). *Application deadline:* For fall admission, 7/1 for domestic students, 2/1 for international students; for spring admission, 11/1 for domestic students, 7/1 for international students. Applications are processed on a rolling basis. Application fee: $50. Electronic applications accepted. *Expenses:* Tuition, state resident: full-time $2960. Tuition, nonresident: full-time $14,051. Required fees: $2320. *Financial support:* In 2009–10, 10 research assistantships (averaging $8,000 per year), 12 teaching assistantships (averaging $8,000 per year) were awarded; fellowships, career-related internships or fieldwork, Federal Work-Study, scholarships/grants, and unspecified assistantships also available. Financial award application deadline: 4/1; financial award applicants required to submit FAFSA. *Faculty research:* Contemporary Irish literature, Romantic psychology, cultural practices of everyday life, Gullah linguistics, Renaissance women's writing. Total annual research expenditures: $15,000. *Unit head:* Dr. James Ivory, Chair, 828-262-3098, E-mail: ivoryjm@appstate.edu. *Application contact:* Dr. Colin Ramsey, Graduate Program Director, 828-262-7390, E-mail: ramseyct@appstate.edu.

Arcadia University, Graduate Studies, Department of English, Glenside, PA 19038-3295. Offers MAE. Part-time and evening/weekend programs available. *Faculty:* 8 full-time (3 women), 2 part-time/adjunct (both women). *Students:* 23 full-time (17 women), 52 part-time (35 women); includes 4 minority (all African Americans). Average age 30. In 2009, 27 master's awarded. *Degree requirements:* For master's, thesis optional. *Application deadline:* Applications are processed on a rolling basis. Application fee: $50. *Expenses:* Tuition: Full-time $30,450; part-time $620 per credit hour. Required fees: $165. Tuition and fees vary according to program. *Financial support:* Teaching assistantships, unspecified assistantships available. *Unit head:* Dr. Joanne Weiner, Chair, 215-572-2105. *Application contact:* 215-572-2925, Fax: 215-572-2126, E-mail: grad@arcadia.edu.

Arizona State University, Graduate College, College of Liberal Arts and Sciences, Division of Humanities, Department of English, Tempe, AZ 85287. Offers creative writing (MFA); English (MA, PhD), including comparative literature (MA), linguistics (MA), literature, rhetoric and composition (MA), rhetoric/composition and linguistics (PhD); teaching English to speakers of other languages (MTESOL). *Degree requirements:* For doctorate, thesis/dissertation. *Entrance requirements:* For master's and doctorate, GRE.

Arkansas State University—Jonesboro, Graduate School, College of Humanities and Social Sciences, Department of English and Philosophy, Jonesboro, State University, AR 72467. Offers English (MA); English education (MSE, SCCT). Part-time programs available. *Faculty:* 14 full-time (4 women). *Students:* 13 full-time (9 women), 14 part-time (5 women); includes 1 minority (African American), 8 international. Average age 29. 23 applicants, 91% accepted, 14 enrolled. In 2009, 10 master's awarded. *Degree requirements:* For master's, variable foreign language requirement, comprehensive exam, thesis or alternative; for SCCT, comprehensive exam. *Entrance requirements:* For master's, GRE General Test or MAT, preliminary exam, appropriate bachelor's degree, official transcript, valid teaching certificate (for MSE), immunization records; for SCCT, GRE General Test or MAT, interview, master's degree, official transcript, immunization records. Additional exam requirements/recommendations for international students: Required—TOEFL (minimum score 550 paper-based; 213 computer-based; 79 iBT), IELTS (minimum score 6). *Application deadline:* For fall admission, 4/7 for domestic and international students; for spring admission, 11/7 for domestic and international students. Applications are processed on a rolling basis. Application fee: $30 ($40 for international students). Electronic applications accepted. *Expenses:* Tuition, state resident: full-time $3744; part-time $208 per credit hour. Tuition, nonresident: full-time $9540; part-time $530 per credit hour. Required fees: $896; $47 per credit hour. $25 per term. One-time fee: $50. Tuition and fees vary according to course load and program. *Financial support:* In 2009–10, 12 students received support; teaching assistantships, career-related internships or fieldwork, scholarships/grants, and unspecified assistantships available. Financial award application deadline: 7/1; financial award applicants required to submit FAFSA. *Unit head:* Dr. Jerry Ball, Interim Chair, 870-972-3043, Fax: 870-972-3045, E-mail: jball@astate.edu. *Application contact:* Dr. Andrew Sustich, Dean of the Graduate School, 870-972-3029, Fax: 870-972-3857, E-mail: sustich@astate.edu.

Arkansas Tech University, Graduate College, College of Arts and Humanities, Russellville, AR 72801. Offers communication (MLA); English (M Ed, MA); fine arts (MLA); history (MA); multi-media journalism (MA); psychology (MS); social science (MLA); Spanish (MA, MLA); teaching English as a second language (MA, MLA). Part-time programs available. *Students:* 39 full-time (30 women), 80 part-time (63 women); includes 11 minority (3 African Americans, 1 American Indian/Alaska Native, 1 Asian American or Pacific Islander, 6 Hispanic Americans), 23 international. Average age 33. In 2009, 70 master's awarded. *Degree requirements:* For master's, comprehensive exam (for some programs), thesis (for some programs), project. *Entrance requirements:* For master's, GRE General Test or MAT. Additional exam requirements/recommendations for international students: Required—TOEFL (minimum score 550 paper-based; 213 computer-based; 79 iBT), IELTS (minimum score 6). *Application deadline:* For fall admission, 3/1 priority date for domestic students, 5/1 priority date for international students; for spring admission, 10/1 priority date for domestic and international students. Applications are processed on a rolling basis. Application fee: $0 ($50 for international students). Electronic applications accepted. *Expenses:* Tuition, state resident: full-time $3438; part-time $191 per hour. Tuition, nonresident: full-time $6876; part-time $382 per hour. Required fees: $482; $9 per credit hour. $140 per semester. Tuition and fees vary according to course load. *Financial support:* In 2009–10, teaching assistantships with full tuition reimbursements (averaging $4,000 per year); research assistantships, career-related internships or fieldwork, Federal Work-Study, scholarships/grants, health care benefits, and unspecified assistantships also available. Support available to part-time students. Financial award application deadline: 4/15; financial award applicants required to submit FAFSA. *Unit head:* Dr. Micheal Tarver, Dean, 479-968-0274, Fax: 479-964-0812, E-mail: mtarver@atu.edu. *Application contact:* Dr. Mary B. Gunter, Dean of Graduate College, 479-968-0398, Fax: 479-964-0542, E-mail: graduate.school@atu.edu.

Asbury University, School of Graduate and Professional Studies, Wilmore, KY 40390-1198. Offers biology: alternative certificate (MA Ed); chemistry: alternative certificate (MA Ed); English (MA Ed); English as a second language (MA Ed); ESL (MA Ed); French (MA Ed); Latin: alternative certificate (MA Ed); mathematics: alternative certificate (MA Ed); reading/writing endorsement (MA Ed); social studies (MA Ed); social work (MSW), including child and family services; Spanish (MA Ed); special education (MA Ed); special education: alternative certificate (MA Ed); teacher as leader endorsement (MA Ed). *Accreditation:* NCATE. Part-time programs available. *Faculty:* 8 full-time (7 women), 9 part-time/adjunct (4 women). *Students:* 108 part-time (87 women); includes 8 minority (4 African Americans, 2 Asian Americans or Pacific Islanders, 2 Hispanic Americans). Average age 36. 36 applicants, 86% accepted, 24 enrolled. In 2009, 20 master's awarded. *Degree requirements:* For master's, action research project, portfolio. *Entrance requirements:* For master's, PRAXIS/NTE, minimum GPA of 2.75, letters of recommendation. Additional exam requirements/recommendations for international students: Required—TOEFL (minimum score 550 paper-based). *Application deadline:* Applications are processed on a rolling basis. Application fee: $25. Electronic applications accepted. *Financial support:* Scholarships/grants and traineeships available. Financial award applicants required to submit FAFSA. *Unit head:* Dr. Bonnie J. Banker, Dean, School of Graduate and Professional Studies, 859-858-3511 Ext. 2221, Fax: 859-858-3921, E-mail: bonnie.banker@asbury.edu. *Application contact:* Lenore A. Sweigard, Graduate Program Assistant and Certification Specialist, 859-858-3511 Ext. 2502, Fax: 859-858-3921, E-mail: graded@asbury.edu.

Auburn University, Graduate School, College of Liberal Arts, Department of English, Auburn University, AL 36849. Offers MA, MTPC, PhD. Part-time programs available. *Faculty:* 56 full-time (30 women), 18 part-time/adjunct (10 women). *Students:* 18 full-time (14 women), 53 part-time (37 women); includes 3 minority (all African Americans), 1 international. Average age 29. 58 applicants, 52% accepted, 20 enrolled. In 2009, 23 master's, 4 doctorates awarded. *Degree requirements:* For master's, one foreign language, thesis optional, written exam; for doctorate, 2 foreign languages, thesis/dissertation, oral and written exams. *Entrance requirements:* For master's, GRE General Test, sample of written work; for doctorate, GRE General Test, GRE Subject Test, sample of written work. *Application deadline:* For fall admission, 7/7 for domestic students; for spring admission, 11/24 for domestic students. Applications are processed on a rolling basis. Application fee: $50 ($60 for international students). Electronic applications accepted. *Expenses:* Tuition, state resident: full-time $6240. Tuition, nonresident: full-time $18,720. International tuition: $18,938 full-time. Required fees: $492. Tuition and fees vary according to course load, program and reciprocity agreements. *Financial support:* Fellowships, teaching assistantships, Federal Work-Study available. Support available to part-time students. Financial award application deadline: 3/15; financial award applicants required to submit FAFSA. *Faculty research:* English literature, American literature, linguistics, rhetoric and composition, literary theory. *Unit head:* Dr. George W. Crandell, Head, 334-844-4620. *Application contact:* Dr. George Flowers, Dean of the Graduate School, 334-844-2125.

See Close-Up on page 417.

Austin Peay State University, College of Graduate Studies, College of Arts and Letters, Department of Languages and Literature, Clarksville, TN 37044. Offers English (MA). Part-time programs available. Postbaccalaureate distance learning degree programs offered (minimal on-campus study). *Faculty:* 9 full-time (4 women). *Students:* 17 full-time (11 women), 11 part-time (6 women); includes 1 minority (Asian American or Pacific Islander), 1 international. Average age 34. 17 applicants, 100% accepted, 7 enrolled. In 2009, 6 master's awarded. *Degree requirements:* For master's, comprehensive exam, thesis optional. *Entrance requirements:* For master's, GRE General Test, 3 letters of recommendation. Additional exam requirements/recommendations for international students: Required—TOEFL (minimum score 500 paper-based; 173 computer-based). *Application deadline:* For fall admission, 7/27 priority date for domestic students; for spring admission, 12/17 priority date for domestic students. Applications are processed on a rolling basis. Application fee: $25. Electronic applications accepted. *Expenses:* Tuition, state resident: full-time $6160; part-time $608 per credit hour. Tuition, nonresident: full-time $17,080; part-time $854 per credit hour. Required fees: $1224; $61.20 per credit hour. *Financial support:* In 2009–10, 10 students received support, including 10 research assistantships with full tuition reimbursements available (averaging $5,184 per year); career-related internships or fieldwork, Federal Work-Study, institutionally sponsored loans, scholarships/grants, and unspecified assistantships also available. Support available to part-time students. Financial award application deadline: 3/1; financial award applicants required to submit FAFSA. *Faculty research:* English literature, creative writing, American literature, linguistics. *Unit head:* Dr. David Guest, Professor/Chair, 931-221-7891, Fax: 931-221-7219, E-mail: mcnabbw@apsu.edu. *Application contact:* Dr. Dixie Dennis, Dean, College of Graduate Studies, 931-221-7662, Fax: 931-221-7641, E-mail: dennisdi@apsu.edu.

Ball State University, Graduate School, College of Sciences and Humanities, Department of English, Muncie, IN 47306-1099. Offers English (MA, PhD), including composition, creative writing (MA), general (MA), literature; linguistics (MA, PhD), including applied linguistics (PhD); linguistics and teaching English to speakers of other languages (MA); teaching English to speakers of other languages (MA). *Degree requirements:* For doctorate, variable foreign language requirement, thesis/dissertation. *Entrance requirements:* For master's, GRE General Test, writing sample; for doctorate, GRE General Test, GRE Subject Test, minimum graduate GPA of 3.2, writing sample. *Faculty research:* American literature; literary editing; Medieval, Renaissance, and eighteenth century British literature; rhetoric.

Baylor University, Graduate School, College of Arts and Sciences, Department of English, Waco, TX 76798. Offers MA, PhD. Part-time programs available. *Faculty:* 19 full-time (6 women). *Students:* 24 full-time (19 women), 42 part-time (24 women); includes 2 minority (1 American Indian/Alaska Native, 1 Hispanic American), 1 international. 25 applicants, 88% accepted. In 2009, 9 master's, 5 doctorates awarded. *Degree requirements:* For master's, one foreign language, thesis; for doctorate, 2 foreign languages, thesis/dissertation. *Entrance requirements:* For master's, GRE General Test, 18 hours of upper-level course work in English; for doctorate, GRE General Test. *Application deadline:* For fall admission, 3/15 priority date for domestic students. Applications are processed on a rolling basis. Application fee: $25. Electronic applications accepted. *Financial support:* In 2009–10, 10 research assistantships, 28 teaching assistantships were awarded; fellowships, Federal Work-Study, institutionally sponsored loans, and laboratory assistantships also available. *Faculty research:* Nineteenth century British literature, Renaissance studies, American studies, Medieval studies, rhetoric and composition. Total annual research expenditures: $48,400. *Unit head:* Dr. Jay Losey, Graduate Program Director, 254-710-1768, Fax: 254-710-3894, E-mail: jay_losey@baylor.edu. *Application contact:* Lois Avey, Administrative Assistant, 254-710-1768, Fax: 254-710-3870, E-mail: lois_avey@baylor.edu.

Belmont University, College of Arts and Sciences, Department of English, Nashville, TN 37212-3757. Offers literature (MA); writing (MA). Part-time and evening/weekend programs available. *Degree requirements:* For master's, one foreign language, comprehensive exam (for some programs), thesis optional. *Entrance requirements:* For master's, GRE, letters of recommendation, writing sample. Additional exam requirements/recommendations for international students: Required—TOEFL. Electronic applications accepted. *Expenses:* Contact institution. *Faculty research:* Gender, autobiography, folklore, Shakespeare, editing.

Bemidji State University, School of Graduate Studies, College of Arts and Letters, Department of English, Bemidji, MN 56601-2699. Offers MA, MS. Part-time programs available. *Degree requirements:* For master's, one foreign language, thesis. *Entrance requirements:* For master's, letters of Rec. Additional exam requirements/recommendations for international students: Required—TOEFL. Electronic applications accepted. *Faculty research:* Creative writing; modern languages; film; electronic writing; rhetoric and composition; literary criticism.

Bennington College, Graduate Programs, The Bennington Writing Seminars, Bennington, VT 05201. Offers creative writing (MFA). Postbaccalaureate distance learning degree programs offered (minimal on-campus study). *Faculty:* 16 full-time (7 women), 6 part-time/adjunct (2 women). *Students:* 106 full-time (80 women); includes 14 minority (4 African Americans, 1 American Indian/Alaska Native, 4 Asian Americans or Pacific Islanders, 5 Hispanic Americans), 1 international. Average age 38. 158 applicants, 37% accepted, 35 enrolled. In 2009, 50 master's awarded. *Degree requirements:* For master's, thesis, collection of essays or poems, or collection of short stories and/or a novel. *Entrance requirements:* For master's, manuscript. *Application deadline:* For fall admission, 3/1 for domestic students; for spring admission, 9/1 for domestic students. Application fee: $60. *Expenses:* Contact institution. *Financial support:* In 2009–10, 11 students received support. Scholarships/grants available. Financial award application deadline: 4/1; financial award applicants required to submit FAFSA. *Unit head:* Sven Birkerts, Director, 802-440-4452, Fax: 802-440-4453, E-mail: writing@bennington.edu. *Application contact:* Victoria Clausi, Associate Director, 802-440-4454, Fax: 802-440-4453, E-mail: writing@bennington.edu.

Bob Jones University, Graduate Programs, Greenville, SC 29614. Offers accountancy (MS); Bible (MA); Bible translation (MA); Biblical studies (Certificate); broadcast management (MS); business administration (MBA); church history (MA, PhD); church ministries (MA); church music (MM); cinema and video production (MA); counseling (MS); curriculum and instruction (Ed D); divinity (M Div); dramatic production (MA); educational leadership (MS, Ed D, Ed S); elementary education (M Ed, MAT); English (M Ed, MA, MAT); fine arts (MA); graphic design (MA); history (M Ed, MA); illustration (MA); interpretative speech (MA); mathematics (M Ed, MAT); medical missions (Certificate); ministry (MM, D Min); multi-categorical special education (M Ed, MAT); music (M Ed); New Testament interpretation (PhD); Old Testament interpretation (PhD); orchestral instrument performance (MM); organ performance (MM); pastoral studies (MA); personnel services (MS, Ed S); piano pedagogy (MM); piano performance (MM); platform arts (MA); radio and television broadcasting (MS); rhetoric and public address (MA); secondary education (M Ed); studio art (MA); teaching Bible (MA); theology (MA, PhD); voice performance (MM); youth ministries (MA); M Div/MM.

Boise State University, Graduate College, College of Arts and Sciences, Department of English, Program in English, Boise, ID 83725-0399. Offers MA. Part-time programs available. *Degree requirements:* For master's, thesis. *Entrance requirements:* For master's, GRE General

English

Boise State University (continued)

Test, minimum GPA of 3.0. Electronic applications accepted. *Expenses:* Tuition, state resident: full-time $3106; part-time $209 per credit. Tuition, nonresident: part-time $284 per credit.

Boston College, Graduate School of Arts and Sciences, Department of English, Chestnut Hill, MA 02467-3800. Offers MA, PhD. *Students:* 79 full-time (53 women), 14 part-time (9 women); includes 6 minority (1 American Indian/Alaska Native, 3 Asian Americans or Pacific Islanders, 2 Hispanic Americans), 1 international. 260 applicants, 41% accepted, 30 enrolled. In 2009, 39 master's, 7 doctorates awarded. *Degree requirements:* For master's, one foreign language, thesis optional; for doctorate, 2 foreign languages, thesis/dissertation. *Entrance requirements:* For master's and doctorate, GRE General Test, GRE Subject Test. Additional exam requirements/recommendations for international students: Required—TOEFL (minimum score 600 paper-based; 250 computer-based; 100 iBT). *Application deadline:* For fall admission, 1/2 priority date for domestic students, 1/2 for international students. Application fee: $70. Electronic applications accepted. *Financial support:* In 2009–10, fellowships (averaging $17,000 per year), teaching assistantships (averaging $17,000 per year) were awarded; Federal Work-Study, scholarships/grants, and tuition waivers (full and partial) also available. Support available to part-time students. Financial award application deadline: 3/1; financial award applicants required to submit FAFSA. *Faculty research:* English and American literature, critical theory. *Unit head:* Dr. Mary Crane, Chairperson, 617-552-3701, E-mail: mary.crane@bc.edu. *Application contact:* Dr. Robert Stanton, Graduate Program Director, 617-552-3701, E-mail: robert.stanton@bc.edu.

Boston University, Graduate School of Arts and Sciences, Department of English, Boston, MA 02215. Offers creative writing (MA); English (MA, PhD). *Students:* 53 full-time (35 women), 6 part-time (5 women); includes 1 minority (Asian American or Pacific Islander), 1 international. Average age 28. 278 applicants, 7% accepted, 15 enrolled. In 2009, 8 master's, 2 doctorates awarded. Terminal master's awarded for partial completion of doctoral program. *Degree requirements:* For master's, one foreign language, thesis; for doctorate, 2 foreign languages, comprehensive exam, thesis/dissertation, qualifying/oral exam. *Entrance requirements:* For master's and doctorate, GRE General Test, GRE Subject Test, sample of written work, 2 letters of recommendation. Additional exam requirements/recommendations for international students: Required—TOEFL (minimum score 550 paper-based; 213 computer-based). *Application deadline:* For fall admission, 1/1 for domestic and international students. Application fee: $70. Electronic applications accepted. *Expenses:* Tuition: Full-time $37,910; part-time $1184 per credit hour. Required fees: $386; $40 per semester. Part-time tuition and fees vary according to class time, course level, degree level and program. *Financial support:* In 2009–10, 39 students received support, including 2 fellowships with full tuition reimbursements available (averaging $18,900 per year), 25 teaching assistantships with partial tuition reimbursements available (averaging $18,400 per year); Federal Work-Study, scholarships/grants, and unspecified assistantships also available. Financial award application deadline: 1/15; financial award applicants required to submit FAFSA. *Unit head:* William Carroll, Interim Chairman, 617-353-2509, Fax: 617-353-3653, E-mail: wcarroll@bu.edu. *Application contact:* Amanda Trainor, Administrative Assistant, 617-353-2509, Fax: 617-353-3653, E-mail: hlane@bu.edu.

Bowie State University, Graduate Programs, Program in English, Bowie, MD 20715-9465. Offers MA. Part-time and evening/weekend programs available. *Entrance requirements:* For master's, minimum GPA of 2.5, English degree. Electronic applications accepted.

Bowling Green State University, Graduate College, College of Arts and Sciences, Department of English, Program in English, Bowling Green, OH 43403. Offers English (MA, PhD); literature (MA); rhetoric and writing (PhD); scientific and technical communication (MA). Part-time programs available. *Degree requirements:* For master's, thesis or alternative; for doctorate, comprehensive exam, thesis/dissertation, foreign language or proficiency in Old English. *Entrance requirements:* For master's and doctorate, GRE General Test. Additional exam requirements/recommendations for international students: Required—TOEFL. Electronic applications accepted. *Faculty research:* Postmodern literary theory, rhetorical theory, ethnic American literature, literature and culture, composition pedagogy.

Bradley University, Graduate School, College of Liberal Arts and Sciences, Department of English, Peoria, IL 61625-0002. Offers MA. Part-time programs available. *Degree requirements:* For master's, comprehensive exam. *Entrance requirements:* For master's, writing sample, 2 letters of recommendation. Additional exam requirements/recommendations for international students: Required—TOEFL (minimum score 550 paper-based; 213 computer-based; 79 iBT).

Brandeis University, Graduate School of Arts and Sciences, Department of English and American Literature, Waltham, MA 02454-9110. Offers English (MA, PhD); English and women's and gender studies (MA). Part-time programs available. *Faculty:* 15 full-time (8 women), 7 part-time/adjunct (4 women). *Students:* 50 full-time (24 women), 2 part-time (1 woman); includes 3 minority (1 Asian American or Pacific Islander, 2 Hispanic Americans), 4 international. 154 applicants, 20% accepted, 10 enrolled. In 2009, 10 master's, 3 doctorates awarded. *Degree requirements:* For master's, one foreign language, thesis, symposium; for doctorate, 2 foreign languages, thesis/dissertation, field exam, symposium presentation, prospectus defense. *Entrance requirements:* For master's, GRE General Test, resume, sample of work, letters of recommendation; for doctorate, GRE General Test, GRE Subject Test, resume, sample of work, letters of recommendation. Additional exam requirements/recommendations for international students: Required—TOEFL (minimum score 600 paper-based; 250 computer-based; 100 iBT); Recommended—IELTS (minimum score 7). *Application deadline:* For fall admission, 1/5 for domestic students. Application fee: $75. Electronic applications accepted. *Financial support:* In 2009–10, 27 fellowships with full tuition reimbursements (averaging $20,000 per year), 4 teaching assistantships with partial tuition reimbursements (averaging $3,200 per year) were awarded; research assistantships with full tuition reimbursements, scholarships/grants, health care benefits, and tuition waivers (full and partial) also available. Financial award application deadline: 4/15; financial award applicants required to submit FAFSA. *Faculty research:* Feminist and gender theory, American literature, Anglophone literature, early modern literature, modernism. *Unit head:* Dr. John Burt, Director of Graduate Studies, 781-736-2130, Fax: 781-736-2179, E-mail: chaucer@brandeis.edu. *Application contact:* Shannon Hunt, Department Administrator, 781-736-2130, Fax: 781-736-2179, E-mail: shuntl@brandeis.edu.

Bridgewater State University, School of Graduate Studies, School of Arts and Sciences, Department of English, Bridgewater, MA 02325-0001. Offers MA, MAT. Part-time and evening/weekend programs available. *Degree requirements:* For master's, one foreign language, comprehensive exam, thesis optional. *Entrance requirements:* For master's, GRE General Test.

Brigham Young University, Graduate Studies, College of Humanities, Department of English, Provo, UT 84602-1001. Offers creative writing (MFA); literature (MA); rhetoric/composition (MA). *Faculty:* 54 full-time (18 women). *Students:* 80 full-time (53 women), 5 part-time (3 women); includes 2 minority (both Asian Americans or Pacific Islanders). Average age 25. 98 applicants, 36% accepted, 29 enrolled. In 2009, 36 master's awarded. *Degree requirements:* For master's, thesis. *Entrance requirements:* For master's, GRE General Test. Additional exam requirements/recommendations for international students: Required—TOEFL. *Application deadline:* For fall admission, 1/15 for domestic students. Application fee: $50. Electronic applications accepted. *Expenses:* Tuition: Full-time $5580; part-time $301 per credit hour. Tuition and fees vary according to student's religious affiliation. *Financial support:* In 2009–10, 79 students received support, including 10 research assistantships (averaging $3,000 per year), 62 teaching assistantships (averaging $6,000 per year); career-related internships or fieldwork, institutionally sponsored loans, scholarships/grants, and tuition waivers (partial) also available. Support available to part-time students. Financial award application deadline: 3/15. *Faculty research:* English literature, American literature, rhetoric, creative writing. *Unit head:* Prof. Ed Cutler, Head, 801-422-3581, Fax: 801-422-0221, E-mail: ed_cutler@byu.edu. *Application contact:* Lou Ann C. Crisler, Graduate Secretary, 801-422-8673, Fax: 801-422-0221, E-mail: louann_crisler@byu.edu.

Brock University, Faculty of Graduate Studies, Faculty of Humanities, Program in English, St. Catharines, ON L2S 3A1, Canada. Offers MA. Part-time programs available. *Degree requirements:* For master's, thesis optional. *Entrance requirements:* For master's, honours in English. Additional exam requirements/recommendations for international students: Required—TOEFL (minimum score 550 paper-based; 213 computer-based; 80 iBT), IELTS (minimum score 6.5), TWE (minimum score 4). Electronic applications accepted. *Faculty research:* Literary theory, Canadian literature, Milton and 17th century American literature, 19th century American literature, British Romantic literature and culture.

Brooklyn College of the City University of New York, Division of Graduate Studies, Department of English, Brooklyn, NY 11210-2889. Offers creative writing (MFA), including fiction, playwriting, poetry; English (MA, PhD). Part-time and evening/weekend programs available. *Students:* 15 full-time (12 women), 182 part-time (115 women); includes 49 minority (23 African Americans, 12 Asian Americans or Pacific Islanders, 14 Hispanic Americans), 6 international. Average age 30. 539 applicants, 27% accepted, 66 enrolled. In 2009, 51 master's awarded. *Degree requirements:* For master's, one foreign language, comprehensive exam (for some programs), thesis (for some programs). *Entrance requirements:* For master's, advanced undergraduate courses in English, 2 letters of recommendation, writing sample, statement of purpose. Additional exam requirements/recommendations for international students: Required—TOEFL. *Application deadline:* For fall admission, 3/1 priority date for domestic students, 2/1 priority date for international students; for spring admission, 11/15 priority date for domestic students, 10/15 priority date for international students. Applications are processed on a rolling basis. Application fee: $125. Electronic applications accepted. *Expenses:* Tuition, area resident: Full-time $7360; part-time $310 per credit hour. Tuition, state resident: full-time $7360; part-time $310 per credit hour. Tuition, nonresident: full-time $13,800; part-time $575 per credit hour. International tuition: $13,800 full-time. Required fees: $140.10 per semester. *Financial support:* Federal Work-Study, institutionally sponsored loans, and scholarships/grants available. Support available to part-time students. Financial award application deadline: 5/1; financial award applicants required to submit FAFSA. *Faculty research:* Cultural studies, medieval literature, Virginia Woolf. *Unit head:* Dr. Ellen Tremper, Chairperson, 718-951-5195, E-mail: etremper@brooklyn.cuny.edu. *Application contact:* Hernan Sierra, Graduate Admissions Coordinator, 718-951-4536, Fax: 718-951-4506, E-mail: grads@brooklyn.cuny.edu.

Brown University, Graduate School, Department of English, Program in Literatures and Cultures in English, Providence, RI 02912. Offers MA, PhD. *Degree requirements:* For doctorate, variable foreign language requirement, thesis/dissertation. *Entrance requirements:* For master's and doctorate, GRE General Test, GRE Subject Test.

Bucknell University, Graduate Studies, College of Arts and Sciences, Department of English, Lewisburg, PA 17837. Offers MA. Part-time programs available. *Degree requirements:* For master's, one foreign language, thesis. *Entrance requirements:* For master's, GRE General Test, GRE Subject Test, minimum GPA of 2.8. Additional exam requirements/recommendations for international students: Required—TOEFL.

Buffalo State College, State University of New York, The Graduate School, Faculty of Arts and Humanities, Department of English, Buffalo, NY 14222-1095. Offers English (MA); secondary education (MS Ed), including English. Part-time and evening/weekend programs available. *Degree requirements:* For master's, thesis or project, 1 foreign language (MS Ed). *Entrance requirements:* For master's, minimum GPA of 2.75, 36 hours in English, New York teaching certificate (MS Ed). Additional exam requirements/recommendations for international students: Required—TOEFL (minimum score 550 paper-based; 213 computer-based).

Butler University, College of Liberal Arts and Sciences, Department of English, Indianapolis, IN 46208-3485. Offers MA. Part-time and evening/weekend programs available. *Faculty:* 1 full-time (0 women), 1 (woman) part-time/adjunct. *Students:* 3 full-time (2 women), 30 part-time (19 women), 2 international. Average age 39. 11 applicants, 55% accepted, 6 enrolled. In 2009, 6 master's awarded. *Entrance requirements:* For master's, GRE General Test, GRE Subject Test. *Application deadline:* For fall admission, 8/15 priority date for domestic students. Applications are processed on a rolling basis. Application fee: $35. Electronic applications accepted. *Financial support:* Applicants required to submit FAFSA. *Faculty research:* Modern poetry, ethnic literature, liberal education, Chaucer, ethics. *Unit head:* Dr. Hilene Flanzbaum, Head, 317-940-9860, E-mail: hflanzba@butler.edu. *Application contact:* Pamela Bender, Student Services Specialist, 317-940-8100, Fax: 317-940-8250, E-mail: pbender@butler.edu.

California Baptist University, Program in English, Riverside, CA 92504-3206. Offers English pedagogy (MA); literature (MA); teaching English as a second language (TESOL) (MA). Part-time programs available. *Faculty:* 4 full-time (3 women). *Students:* 3 full-time (all women), 29 part-time (21 women); includes 3 minority (1 African American, 1 Asian American or Pacific Islander, 1 Hispanic American), 5 international. 51 applicants, 55% accepted, 12 enrolled. In 2009, 3 master's awarded. *Degree requirements:* For master's, thesis (for some programs). *Entrance requirements:* For master's, minimum undergraduate GPA of 2.75, 18 semester hours of course work in English beyond freshman level. Additional exam requirements/recommendations for international students: Required—TOEFL (minimum score 575 paper-based; 230 computer-based; 89 iBT). *Application deadline:* For fall admission, 8/1 priority date for domestic students, 7/1 for international students; for spring admission, 12/1 priority date for domestic students, 10/15 for international students. Applications are processed on a rolling basis. Application fee: $45. Electronic applications accepted. *Expenses:* Tuition: Full-time $8352; part-time $464 per semester hour. Required fees: $125 per semester. Tuition and fees vary according to course load, campus/location and program. *Financial support:* Federal Work-Study and scholarships/grants available. Support available to part-time students. Financial award applicants required to submit FAFSA. *Unit head:* Dr. Jennifer Newton, Director, 951-343-4276, Fax: 951-343-4661, E-mail: jnewton@calbaptist.edu. *Application contact:* Gail Ronveaux, Dean of Graduate Enrollment, 951-343-5045, Fax: 951-343-5095, E-mail: graduateadmissions@calbaptist.edu.

California Polytechnic State University, San Luis Obispo, College of Liberal Arts, Department of English, San Luis Obispo, CA 93407. Offers MA. Part-time programs available. *Faculty:* 4 full-time (3 women). *Students:* 20 full-time (14 women), 17 part-time (11 women); includes 4 minority (1 African American, 3 Hispanic Americans). Average age 26. 35 applicants, 66% accepted, 16 enrolled. In 2009, 6 master's awarded. *Degree requirements:* For master's, one foreign language, comprehensive exam. *Entrance requirements:* For master's, minimum GPA of 3.0 in last 90 quarter units of course work, writing sample. Additional exam requirements/recommendations for international students: Required—TOEFL (minimum score 550 paper-based; 213 computer-based), or IELTS (minimum score 6). *Application deadline:* For fall admission, 7/1 for domestic students, 11/30 for international students; for winter admission, 11/1 for domestic students, 6/30 for international students; for spring admission, 2/1 for domestic students. Applications are processed on a rolling basis. Application fee: $55. *Expenses:* Tuition, nonresident: full-time $11,160; part-time $248 per unit. Required fees: $7134; $1553 per quarter. *Financial support:* Teaching assistantships, career-related internships or fieldwork, Federal Work-Study, institutionally sponsored loans, and tutorships, writing laboratory assistantships available. Support available to part-time students. Financial award application deadline: 3/2; financial award applicants required to submit FAFSA. *Faculty research:* Feminist literary criticism, modern British novel, literary theory, Shakespeare, Victorian literature. *Unit head:* Dr. Debora Schwartz, Graduate Coordinator, 805-756-2636, Fax: 805-756-6374, E-mail: dschwart@calpoly.edu. *Application contact:* Dr. Debora Schwartz, Graduate Coordinator, 805-756-2636, Fax: 805-756-6374, E-mail: dschwart@calpoly.edu.

California State Polytechnic University, Pomona, Academic Affairs, College of Letters, Arts, and Social Sciences, Program in English, Pomona, CA 91768-2557. Offers MA. Part-time programs available. *Students:* 20 full-time (10 women), 62 part-time (48 women); includes 38 minority (3 African Americans, 1 American Indian/Alaska Native, 12 Asian Americans or Pacific Islanders, 22 Hispanic Americans), 2 international. Average age 31. 50 applicants, 76% accepted, 24 enrolled. In 2009, 31 master's awarded. *Degree requirements:* For master's, one foreign language, thesis or alternative. *Application deadline:* For fall admission, 5/1 priority date for domestic students; for winter admission, 10/15 priority date for domestic students; for spring admission, 1/20 priority date for domestic students. Applications are processed on a rolling basis. Application fee: $55. Electronic applications accepted. *Expenses:* Tuition, nonresident: full-time $6696; part-time $248 per credit. Required fees: $5487; $3237 per term. Tuition and fees vary according to course load, degree level and program. *Financial support:* In 2009–10, 2 fellowships were awarded; Federal Work-Study and institutionally sponsored loans also available. Support available to part-time students. Financial award application deadline: 3/2; financial award applicants required to submit FAFSA. *Unit head:* Dr. Karen A. Russikoff, Coordinator, 909-869-3836, E-mail: krussikoff@csupomona.edu. *Application contact:* Scott J. Duncan, Director, Admissions, 909-869-3258, Fax: 909-869-4529, E-mail: sjduncan@csupomona.edu.

California State University, Bakersfield, Division of Graduate Studies, School of Humanities and Social Sciences, Program in English, Bakersfield, CA 93311. Offers MA. *Degree requirements:* For master's, comprehensive exam or thesis. *Entrance requirements:* For master's, GRE General Test, GRE Subject Test (literature), minimum GPA of 2.5 for last 90 quarter units. Additional exam requirements/recommendations for international students: Required—TOEFL (minimum score 550 paper-based; 213 computer-based).

California State University, Chico, Graduate School, College of Humanities and Fine Arts, Department of English, Program in English, Chico, CA 95929-0722. Offers MA. *Students:* 15 full-time (10 women), 19 part-time (12 women); includes 6 minority (1 African American, 1 American Indian/Alaska Native, 4 Hispanic Americans). Average age 35. 10 applicants, 80% accepted, 7 enrolled. In 2009, 14 master's awarded. *Degree requirements:* For master's, thesis. *Entrance requirements:* For master's, GRE General Test, 2 letters of recommendation, writing sample. Additional exam requirements/recommendations for international students: Required—TOEFL (minimum score 550 paper-based; 213 computer-based; 80 iBT), IELTS (minimum score 6.5). *Application deadline:* For fall admission, 3/1 for domestic and international students; for spring admission, 9/15 for domestic and international students. Application fee: $55. *Unit head:* Dr. Rob Davidson, Graduate Coordinator, 530-898-6457. *Application contact:* Dr. Rob Davidson, Graduate Coordinator, 530-898-6457.

California State University, Dominguez Hills, College of Arts and Humanities, Department of English, Carson, CA 90747-0001. Offers English (MA); rhetoric and composition (Certificate); teaching English as a second language (Certificate). Part-time and evening/weekend programs available. *Faculty:* 13 full-time (5 women). *Students:* 23 full-time (14 women), 52 part-time (33 women); includes 34 minority (9 African Americans, 5 Asian Americans or Pacific Islanders, 20 Hispanic Americans), 3 international. Average age 39. 39 applicants, 79% accepted, 19 enrolled. In 2009, 20 master's awarded. *Degree requirements:* For master's, comprehensive exam (for some programs), thesis or alternative. *Entrance requirements:* For master's, minimum GPA of 3.0 in last 60 units. Additional exam requirements/recommendations for international students: Required—TOEFL (minimum score 550 paper-based; 213 computer-based). *Application deadline:* Applications are processed on a rolling basis. Application fee: $55. Electronic applications accepted. *Expenses:* Tuition, nonresident: full-time $6696; part-time $372 per unit. Required fees: $5946; $1752 per semester. *Faculty research:* Gender studies, transnationalism, discourse analysis, visual culture, Shakespeare. *Unit head:* Dr. Helen Oesterheld, Chair, 310-243-3322, E-mail: hoesterheld@csudh.edu. *Application contact:* 310-243-3600.

California State University, East Bay, Academic Programs and Graduate Studies, College of Letters, Arts, and Social Sciences, Department of English, Hayward, CA 94542-3000. Offers MA. Part-time programs available. *Faculty:* 12 full-time (8 women), 1 (woman) part-time/adjunct. *Students:* 26 full-time (18 women), 59 part-time (39 women); includes 29 minority (8 African Americans, 8 Asian Americans or Pacific Islanders, 13 Hispanic Americans), 10 international. Average age 36. 73 applicants, 59% accepted, 26 enrolled. In 2009, 35 master's awarded. *Degree requirements:* For master's, one foreign language, comprehensive exam, thesis optional. *Entrance requirements:* For master's, minimum GPA of 3.0 in field. Additional exam requirements/recommendations for international students: Required—TOEFL (minimum score 550 paper-based; 213 computer-based). *Application deadline:* For fall admission, 6/30 for domestic and international students; for winter admission, 10/31 for domestic students; for spring admission, 11/30 for domestic students. Applications are processed on a rolling basis. Application fee: $55. Electronic applications accepted. *Financial support:* Fellowships, teaching assistantships, career-related internships or fieldwork, Federal Work-Study, institutionally sponsored loans, and scholarships/grants available. Support available to part-time students. Financial award application deadline: 3/1; financial award applicants required to submit FAFSA. *Unit head:* Dr. E. James Murphy, Chair, 510-885-3151, Fax: 510-885-4797, E-mail: james.murphy@csueastbay.edu. *Application contact:* Donna Wiley, Interim Associate Director, 510-885-2928, Fax: 510-885-4777, E-mail: donna.wiley@csueastbay.edu.

California State University, Fresno, Division of Graduate Studies, College of Arts and Humanities, Department of English, Fresno, CA 93740-8027. Offers composition theory (MA); creative writing (MFA); literature (MA). Part-time and evening/weekend programs available. *Degree requirements:* For master's, one foreign language, thesis. *Entrance requirements:* For master's, GRE General Test, minimum GPA of 3.0, writing sample. Additional exam requirements/recommendations for international students: Required—TOEFL. Electronic applications accepted. *Faculty research:* American literature, Renaissance literature, foreign literature.

California State University, Fullerton, Graduate Studies, College of Humanities and Social Sciences, Department of English and Comparative Literature, Fullerton, CA 92834-9480. Offers comparative literature (MA); English (MA). Part-time programs available. *Students:* 31 full-time (22 women), 58 part-time (44 women); includes 25 minority (3 African Americans, 4 Asian Americans or Pacific Islanders, 18 Hispanic Americans). Average age 29. 69 applicants, 46% accepted, 23 enrolled. In 2009, 35 master's awarded. *Degree requirements:* For master's, comprehensive exam, thesis or alternative. *Entrance requirements:* For master's, minimum GPA of 3.0 in major, 2.5 in last 60 hours. Application fee: $55. *Expenses:* Tuition, nonresident: full-time $11,160; part-time $373 per credit. Required fees: $1440 per term. Tuition and fees vary according to course load, degree level and program. *Financial support:* Career-related internships or fieldwork, Federal Work-Study, institutionally sponsored loans, and scholarships/grants available. Support available to part-time students. Financial award application deadline: 3/1; financial award applicants required to submit FAFSA. *Unit head:* Dr. Joseph Sawicki, Chair, 657-278-3163. *Application contact:* Admissions/Applications, 657-278-2371.

California State University, Long Beach, Graduate Studies, College of Liberal Arts, Department of English, Long Beach, CA 90840. Offers creative writing (MFA); English (MA). Part-time programs available. *Faculty:* 28 full-time (12 women), 2 part-time/adjunct (1 woman). *Students:* 63 full-time (44 women), 106 part-time (76 women); includes 45 minority (4 African Americans, 19 Asian Americans or Pacific Islanders, 22 Hispanic Americans), 3 international. Average age 31. *Degree requirements:* For master's, one foreign language, comprehensive exam or thesis. *Entrance requirements:* For master's, GRE Subject Test, minimum GPA of 3.0 in English. *Application deadline:* For fall admission, 5/1 for domestic students. Applications are processed on a rolling basis. Application fee: $55. Electronic applications accepted. *Expenses:* Required fees: $1802 per semester. Part-time tuition and fees vary according to course load. *Financial support:* Federal Work-Study, institutionally sponsored loans, and scholarships/grants available. Financial award application deadline: 3/2. *Faculty research:* English and American literature, literary theory, linguistics, rhetoric and composition. *Unit head:* Dr. Eileen S. Klink, Chair, 562-985-4223, Fax: 562-985-2369, E-mail: eklink@csulb.edu. *Application contact:* Dr. Beth Lau, Graduate Adviser, 562-985-4252, Fax: 562-985-4223, E-mail: blau@csulb.edu.

California State University, Los Angeles, Graduate Studies, College of Arts and Letters, Department of English, Los Angeles, CA 90032-8530. Offers MA. Part-time and evening/weekend programs available. *Faculty:* 6 full-time (3 women), 4 part-time/adjunct (2 women). *Students:* 13 full-time (8 women), 62 part-time (35 women); includes 23 minority (1 African American, 5 Asian Americans or Pacific Islanders, 17 Hispanic Americans), 6 international. Average age 36. 26 applicants, 100% accepted, 8 enrolled. In 2009, 28 master's awarded. *Degree requirements:* For master's, comprehensive exam or thesis. *Entrance requirements:* Additional exam requirements/recommendations for international students: Required—TOEFL (minimum score 500 paper-based; 173 computer-based). *Application deadline:* For fall admission, 5/1 for international students. Applications are processed on a rolling basis. Application fee: $55. Electronic applications accepted. *Financial support:* Federal Work-Study available. Support available to part-time students. Financial award application deadline: 3/1. *Faculty research:* English and American literature, linguistics, composition. *Unit head:* Dr. Hema Chari, Acting Chair, 323-343-4140, Fax: 323-343-6470, E-mail: hchari@calstatela.edu. *Application contact:* Dr. Cheryl L. Ney, Associate Vice President for Academic Affairs and Dean of Graduate Studies, 323-343-3820, Fax: 323-343-5653, E-mail: cney@cslanet.calstatela.edu.

California State University, Northridge, Graduate Studies, College of Humanities, Department of English, Northridge, CA 91330. Offers creative writing (MA); literature (MA); rhetoric and composition theory (MA). Part-time and evening/weekend programs available. *Faculty:* 31 full-time (13 women), 66 part-time/adjunct (58 women). *Students:* 36 full-time (22 women), 130 part-time (87 women); includes 1 American Indian/Alaska Native, 16 Asian Americans or Pacific Islanders, 22 Hispanic Americans, 1 international. Average age 33. 119 applicants, 65% accepted, 42 enrolled. In 2009, 36 master's awarded. *Degree requirements:* For master's, thesis or alternative. *Entrance requirements:* For master's, writing proficiency test, GRE General Test or minimum GPA of 3.0. Additional exam requirements/recommendations for international students: Required—TOEFL. *Application deadline:* For fall admission, 11/30 for domestic students. Application fee: $55. *Financial support:* Teaching assistantships available. Financial award application deadline: 3/1. *Faculty research:* Reading improvement, professional writing, Dickens, Shaw, English as a second language. *Unit head:* Dr. George Uba, Chair, 818-677-3434, E-mail: george.uba@csun.edu. *Application contact:* Dr. Marjie Seagoe, Graduate Studies Secretary, 818-677-3433.

California State University, Sacramento, Graduate Studies, College of Arts and Letters, Department of English, Sacramento, CA 95819. Offers creative writing (MA); teaching English to speakers of other languages (MA). Part-time programs available. *Degree requirements:* For master's, thesis, project, or comprehensive exam; writing proficiency exam. *Entrance requirements:* For master's, portfolio (creative writing); minimum GPA of 3.0 in English, 2.75 overall during previous 2 years. Additional exam requirements/recommendations for international students: Required—TOEFL. Electronic applications accepted. *Faculty research:* Teaching composition, remedial writing.

California State University, San Bernardino, Graduate Studies, College of Arts and Letters, Department of English, San Bernardino, CA 92407-2397. Offers creative writing (MFA); English composition (MA). Part-time and evening/weekend programs available. *Faculty:* 14 full-time (7 women). *Students:* 90 full-time (57 women), 46 part-time (34 women); includes 50 minority (12 African Americans, 6 Asian Americans or Pacific Islanders, 32 Hispanic Americans), 2 international. Average age 34. 105 applicants, 61% accepted, 44 enrolled. In 2009, 19 master's awarded. *Degree requirements:* For master's, one foreign language, thesis. *Entrance requirements:* For master's, BA in English or linguistics, minimum GPA of 3.0. Additional exam requirements/recommendations for international students: Required—TOEFL. *Application deadline:* For fall admission, 8/31 priority date for domestic students. Application fee: $55. *Financial support:* Research assistantships, teaching assistantships, career-related internships or fieldwork, Federal Work-Study, institutionally sponsored loans, and writing center tutorships available. Support available to part-time students. Financial award application deadline: 3/1. *Faculty research:* Composition and literary theory, theatrical theory, creative writing, relationship between evaluating writing and teaching composition. *Unit head:* Dr. Juan Delgado, Chair, 909-537-5834, Fax: 909-537-7086, E-mail: jdelgado@csusb.edu. *Application contact:* Olivia Rosas, Director of Admissions, 909-537-7577, Fax: 909-537-7034, E-mail: orosas@csusb.edu.

California State University, San Marcos, College of Arts and Sciences, Program in Literature and Writing Studies, San Marcos, CA 92096-0001. Offers MA. Part-time and evening/weekend programs available. *Degree requirements:* For master's, one foreign language, thesis. *Entrance requirements:* For master's, GRE General Test, minimum GPA of 3.0, writing sample. *Faculty research:* Postcolonialism, feminism rhetoric, cultural studies, creative writing, critical theory.

California State University, Stanislaus, College of Humanities and Social Sciences, Department of English, Turlock, CA 95382. Offers English (MA); literature (MA); rhetoric and teaching of writing (MA); TESOL (MA, Certificate). Part-time programs available. *Degree requirements:* For master's, one foreign language, comprehensive exam, thesis. *Entrance requirements:* For master's, GRE General Test, minimum GPA of 3.0, 2 letters of reference; for Certificate, minimum GPA of 3.0, 2 letters of reference. Additional exam requirements/recommendations for international students: Required—TOEFL (minimum score 550 paper-based; 213 computer-based), TWE (minimum score 4). Electronic applications accepted. *Faculty research:* Transnational literacies, Renaissance and Medieval literature, abolition writings and slave narratives, qualitative writing.

Carleton University, Faculty of Graduate Studies, Faculty of Arts and Social Sciences, Department of English Language and Literature, Ottawa, ON K1S 5B6, Canada. Offers MA, PhD. *Degree requirements:* For master's, thesis optional. *Entrance requirements:* For master's, honors degree. Additional exam requirements/recommendations for international students: Required—TOEFL. *Faculty research:* British, Canadian, American, and Commonwealth literatures; English language and writing; literary criticism; social and historical context of literature.

Carnegie Mellon University, College of Humanities and Social Sciences, Department of English, Pittsburgh, PA 15213-3891. Offers communication planning and design (M Des); literary and cultural studies (MA, PhD); professional writing (MAPW), including editing and publishing, policy and non-profit communication, public and media relations / corporate communications, science or healthcare communication, technical writing, writing for new media, writing for print media; rhetoric (MA, PhD). Part-time programs available. Terminal master's awarded for partial completion of doctoral program. *Degree requirements:* For doctorate, 2 foreign languages, comprehensive exam, thesis/dissertation. *Entrance requirements:* For master's and doctorate, GRE General Test. Additional exam requirements/recommendations for international students: Required—TOEFL, TWE. *Faculty research:* Cognitive processes in discourse with emphasis on writing, testing, and evaluation.

Case Western Reserve University, School of Graduate Studies, Department of English, Cleveland, OH 44106. Offers MA, PhD. Part-time programs available. *Faculty:* 20 full-time (11 women), 1 (woman) part-time/adjunct. *Students:* 24 full-time (13 women), 10 part-time (9 women); includes 1 minority (African American), 2 international. Average age 32. 61 applicants, 30% accepted, 12 enrolled. In 2009, 4 master's, 2 doctorates awarded. *Degree requirements:* For master's, one foreign language, comprehensive exam, thesis or alternative, written exam; for doctorate, one foreign language, thesis/dissertation, oral and written exams. *Entrance requirements:* For master's and doctorate, GRE General Test, sample of written work. Additional exam requirements/recommendations for international students: Required—TOEFL (minimum score 550 paper-based; 213 computer-based; 79 iBT). *Application deadline:* For fall admission, 2/1 priority date for domestic students; for spring admission, 1/2 for domestic students. Applications are processed on a rolling basis. Application fee: $50. Electronic applications accepted. *Financial support:* Fellowships, research assistantships, teaching assistantships, Federal Work-Study, institutionally sponsored loans, and tuition waivers (partial) available. Financial award application deadline: 2/15; financial award applicants required to submit FAFSA. *Faculty research:* Sixteenth to twentieth century English literature, rhetorical and critical theory, women's studies, genre studies, Renaissance, America modernism, authorship. *Unit head:* Mary Grimm, Chair, 216-368-2355, Fax: 216-368-4681, E-mail: mary.grimm@case.edu. *Application contact:* Christopher Flint, Associate Professor and Graduate Director, 216-368-2362, Fax: 216-368-4367, E-mail: christopher.flint@case.edu.

English

The Catholic University of America, School of Arts and Sciences, Department of English Language and Literature, Washington, DC 20064. Offers English language and literature (MA, PhD); rhetoric (MA, PhD); MSLS/MA. Part-time programs available. *Faculty:* 13 full-time (5 women), 3 part-time/adjunct (0 women). *Students:* 20 full-time (15 women), 36 part-time (26 women), 1 international. Average age 28. 85 applicants, 52% accepted, 14 enrolled. In 2009, 10 master's, 3 doctorates awarded. *Degree requirements:* For master's, one foreign language, comprehensive exam, thesis or alternative; for doctorate, 2 foreign languages, comprehensive exam, thesis/dissertation. *Entrance requirements:* For master's, GRE General Test, 3 letters of recommendation; for doctorate, GRE General Test, statement of purpose, official copies of academic transcripts, three letters of recommendation. Additional exam requirements/recommendations for international students: Required—TOEFL (minimum score 580 paper-based; 237 computer-based). *Application deadline:* For fall admission, 8/1 priority date for domestic students, 7/15 for international students; for spring admission, 12/1 priority date for domestic students, 10/15 for international students. Applications are processed on a rolling basis. Application fee: $55. Electronic applications accepted. *Expenses:* Tuition: Full-time $31,740; part-time $1245 per credit hour. Required fees: $50; $25 per semester hour. One-time fee: $425. *Financial support:* Fellowships, research assistantships, teaching assistantships, Federal Work-Study, scholarships/grants, tuition waivers (full and partial), and unspecified assistantships available. Financial award application deadline: 2/1; financial award applicants required to submit FAFSA. *Faculty research:* Medieval literature, theory and history of rhetoric, Renaissance literature, English and literature, English and American drama. *Unit head:* Dr. Ernest Suarez, Chair, 202-319-5488, Fax: 202-319-4188, E-mail: suarez@cua.edu. *Application contact:* Julie Schwing, Director of Graduate Admissions, 202-319-5057, Fax: 202-319-6533, E-mail: cua-admissions@cua.edu.

Central Connecticut State University, School of Graduate Studies, School of Arts and Sciences, Department of English, Program in English, New Britain, CT 06050-4010. Offers MA, Certificate. Part-time and evening/weekend programs available. *Students:* 23 full-time (13 women), 29 part-time (19 women); includes 6 minority (3 African Americans, 1 Asian American or Pacific Islander, 2 Hispanic Americans). Average age 33. 42 applicants, 55% accepted, 20 enrolled. In 2009, 8 master's, 7 other advanced degrees awarded. *Degree requirements:* For master's, comprehensive exam, thesis or alternative; for Certificate, qualifying exam. *Entrance requirements:* For master's, minimum undergraduate GPA of 3.0. Additional exam requirements/recommendations for international students: Required—TOEFL. *Application deadline:* For fall admission, 7/1 for domestic students; for spring admission, 12/1 for domestic students. Applications are processed on a rolling basis. Application fee: $50. Electronic applications accepted. *Expenses:* Tuition, area resident: Full-time $4662; part-time $440 per credit. Tuition, state resident: full-time $6994; part-time $440 per credit. Tuition, nonresident: full-time $12,988; part-time $440 per credit. Required fees: $3606. One-time fee: $62 part-time.

Central Michigan University, College of Graduate Studies, College of Humanities and Social and Behavioral Sciences, Department of English Language and Literature, Mount Pleasant, MI 48859. Offers English composition and communication (MA); English language and literature (MA), including children's and young adult literature, creative writing, general concentration; teaching English to speakers of other languages (TESOL) (MA). Part-time and evening/weekend programs available. *Degree requirements:* For master's, thesis or alternative. Electronic applications accepted. *Faculty research:* Composition theory, science fiction history and bibliography, children's and young adult literature, nineteenth century American literature, applied linguistics.

Central Washington University, Graduate Studies and Research, College of Arts and Humanities, Department of English, Ellensburg, WA 98926. Offers English (MA); teaching English as a second language (MA). Part-time programs available. *Faculty:* 20 full-time (11 women). *Students:* 26 full-time (18 women), 7 part-time (2 women); includes 4 minority (2 Asian Americans or Pacific Islanders, 2 Hispanic Americans). 27 applicants, 93% accepted, 25 enrolled. In 2009, 10 master's awarded. *Degree requirements:* For master's, thesis or alternative. *Entrance requirements:* For master's, GRE General Test, minimum GPA of 3.0, writing sample. Additional exam requirements/recommendations for international students: Required—TOEFL (minimum score 550 paper-based; 213 computer-based; 79 iBT). *Application deadline:* For fall admission, 2/1 priority date for domestic students; for winter admission, 10/1 for domestic students; for spring admission, 1/1 for domestic students. Applications are processed on a rolling basis. Application fee: $50. Electronic applications accepted. *Expenses:* Tuition, state resident: full-time $7353; part-time $245 per credit. Tuition, nonresident: full-time $16,383; part-time $546 per credit. Required fees: $882. Tuition and fees vary according to degree level. *Financial support:* In 2009–10, 17 teaching assistantships with partial tuition reimbursements (averaging $9,145 per year) were awarded; research assistantships with partial tuition reimbursements, Federal Work-Study, health care benefits, and unspecified assistantships also available. Financial award application deadline: 3/1; financial award applicants required to submit FAFSA. *Unit head:* Dr. George Drake, Chair, 509-963-1546, Fax: 509-963-1561, E-mail: drakeg@cwu.edu. *Application contact:* Justine Eason, Admissions Program Coordinator, 509-963-3103, Fax: 509-963-1799, E-mail: masters@cwu.edu.

Chapman University, Graduate Studies, Wilkinson College of Humanities and Social Sciences, Department of English, Orange, CA 92866. Offers creative writing (MFA); English (MA). Part-time and evening/weekend programs available. *Faculty:* 20 full-time (8 women), 21 part-time/adjunct (8 women). *Students:* 35 full-time (18 women), 21 part-time (14 women); includes 8 minority (3 African Americans, 1 American Indian/Alaska Native, 1 Asian American or Pacific Islander, 3 Hispanic Americans). Average age 33. 55 applicants, 62% accepted, 17 enrolled. In 2009, 38 master's awarded. *Degree requirements:* For master's, comprehensive exam (for some programs), thesis (for some programs). *Entrance requirements:* For master's, GRE or MAT, minimum undergraduate GPA of 2.5. Additional exam requirements/recommendations for international students: Required—TOEFL (minimum score 550 paper-based; 213 computer-based; 80 iBT). *Application deadline:* For fall admission, 5/1 priority date for domestic students. Applications are processed on a rolling basis. Application fee: $50. Electronic applications accepted. *Expenses:* Contact institution. *Financial support:* Fellowships, Federal Work-Study and scholarships/grants available. Financial award application deadline: 3/2; financial award applicants required to submit FAFSA. *Unit head:* Dr. Patrick Fuery, Department Chair, 714-532-7789, E-mail: fuery@chapman.edu. *Application contact:* Priscilla Garcia Powers, Graduate Admission Counselor, 714-997-6711, E-mail: pgarcia@chapman.edu.

Chicago State University, School of Graduate and Professional Studies, College of Arts and Sciences, Department of English, Chicago, IL 60628. Offers creative writing (MFA); English (MA). *Degree requirements:* For master's, comprehensive exam. *Entrance requirements:* For master's, minimum GPA of 2.75.

The Citadel, The Military College of South Carolina, Citadel Graduate College, Department of English, Charleston, SC 29409. Offers MA. Part-time and evening/weekend programs available. *Faculty:* 5 full-time (1 woman). *Students:* 1 (woman) full-time, 4 part-time (3 women), 1 international. Average age 27. In 2009, 2 master's awarded. *Degree requirements:* For master's, one foreign language, comprehensive exam, thesis optional. *Entrance requirements:* For master's, GRE (minimum score 1400, 4 writing) or MAT (minimum score 403), minimum undergraduate GPA of 2.5 (3.0 in major); 2 letters of recommendation from former professors or recent supervisors; writing sample showing ability to perform literary analysis and to conduct research. Additional exam requirements/recommendations for international students: Required—TOEFL (minimum score 550 paper-based; 213 computer-based). *Application deadline:* Applications are processed on a rolling basis. Application fee: $30. Electronic applications accepted. *Expenses:* Tuition, state resident: part-time $400 per credit hour. Tuition, nonresident: part-time $657 per credit hour. Required fees: $40 per term. *Financial support:* Research assistantships, career-related internships or fieldwork, health care benefits, and unspecified assistantships available. Support available to part-time students. Financial award application deadline: 7/1; financial award applicants required to submit FAFSA. *Faculty research:* Renaissance literature; eighteenth and nineteenth century British literature; eighteenth, nineteenth, and twentieth century American literature. *Unit head:* Dr. David G. Allen, Department Head, 843-953-5134, Fax: 843-953-1881, E-mail: david.allen@citadel.edu. *Application contact:* Dr. James M. Hutchisson, Graduate Coordinator, 843-953-5139, Fax: 843-953-1881, E-mail: jim.hutchisson@citadel.edu.

City College of the City University of New York, Graduate School, College of Liberal Arts and Science, Division of the Humanities and Arts, Department of English, Program in English and American Literature, New York, NY 10031-9198. Offers MA. *Degree requirements:* For master's, one foreign language, comprehensive exam, thesis. *Entrance requirements:* For master's, minimum GPA of 3.0. Additional exam requirements/recommendations for international students: Required—TOEFL (minimum score 600 paper-based; 100 iBT). Electronic applications accepted.

Claremont Graduate University, Graduate Programs, School of Arts and Humanities, Department of English, Claremont, CA 91711-6160. Offers American studies (MA, PhD); critical theory (MA, PhD); early modern studies (MA, PhD); English (M Phil, MA, PhD); literary theory (PhD); literature (MA, PhD); literature and creative writing (MA); literature and film (MA); MBA/MA; MBA/PhD. Part-time programs available. *Faculty:* 2 full-time (1 woman), 2 part-time/adjunct (0 women). *Students:* 83 full-time (60 women), 19 part-time (11 women); includes 17 minority (1 African American, 1 American Indian/Alaska Native, 8 Asian Americans or Pacific Islanders, 7 Hispanic Americans), 4 international. Average age 35. In 2009, 6 master's, 4 doctorates awarded. *Entrance requirements:* For master's and doctorate, GRE General Test. Additional exam requirements/recommendations for international students: Required—TOEFL (minimum score 550 paper-based; 213 computer-based; 80 iBT). *Application deadline:* For fall admission, 2/1 priority date for domestic students. Applications are processed on a rolling basis. Application fee: $60. Electronic applications accepted. *Expenses:* Tuition: Full-time $35,046; part-time $1524 per credit. Required fees: $161 per semester. *Financial support:* Fellowships, Federal Work-Study, institutionally sponsored loans, and scholarships/grants available. Support available to part-time students. Financial award application deadline: 2/15; financial award applicants required to submit FAFSA. *Faculty research:* American, comparative, and English Renaissance literature; modernism; feminist literature and theory. *Unit head:* Wendy Martin, Chair, 909-621-8612, Fax: 909-607-1221, E-mail: wendy.martin@cgu.edu. *Application contact:* Susan Hampson, Admissions Coordinator, 909-607-1278, Fax: 909-607-1221, E-mail: humanities@cgu.edu.

Clarion University of Pennsylvania, Office of Research and Graduate Studies, College of Arts and Sciences, Department of English, Clarion, PA 16214. Offers MA. *Degree requirements:* For master's, thesis optional. *Entrance requirements:* For master's, GRE General Test, minimum QPA of 2.75. Additional exam requirements/recommendations for international students: Required—TOEFL (minimum score 550 paper-based; 213 computer-based; 80 iBT). Electronic applications accepted.

Clark Atlanta University, School of Arts and Sciences, Department of English, Atlanta, GA 30314. Offers MA, DAH. Part-time programs available. *Faculty:* 4 full-time (2 women). *Students:* 9 full-time (7 women), 14 part-time (10 women); all minorities (all African Americans). Average age 33. 7 applicants, 86% accepted, 0 enrolled. *Degree requirements:* For master's, one foreign language, comprehensive exam, thesis; for doctorate, 2 foreign languages, comprehensive exam, thesis/dissertation. *Entrance requirements:* For master's, GRE General Test, minimum GPA of 2.5. Additional exam requirements/recommendations for international students: Required—TOEFL (minimum score 500 paper-based; 173 computer-based). *Application deadline:* For fall admission, 4/1 for domestic and international students; for spring admission, 11/1 for domestic and international students. Applications are processed on a rolling basis. Application fee: $40 ($55 for international students). *Expenses:* Tuition: Full-time $12,240; part-time $680 per credit hour. Required fees: $710; $355 per semester. *Financial support:* Career-related internships or fieldwork, Federal Work-Study, scholarships/grants, and unspecified assistantships available. Support available to part-time students. Financial award application deadline: 4/30; financial award applicants required to submit FAFSA. *Unit head:* Dr. Alma Vineyard, Chairperson, 404-880-8067, E-mail: avineyard@cau.edu. *Application contact:* Michelle Clark-Davis, Graduate Program Admissions, 404-880-6605, E-mail: cauadmissions@cau.edu.

Clark University, Graduate School, Department of English, Worcester, MA 01610-1477. Offers MA. Part-time programs available. *Faculty:* 11 full-time (8 women), 6 part-time/adjunct (3 women). *Students:* 9 full-time (3 women), 3 part-time (2 women), 4 international. Average age 29. 14 applicants, 93% accepted, 6 enrolled. In 2009, 9 master's awarded. *Degree requirements:* For master's, thesis, oral exam. *Entrance requirements:* For master's, GRE Subject Test. Additional exam requirements/recommendations for international students: Required—TOEFL. *Application deadline:* For fall admission, 2/1 priority date for domestic students. Applications are processed on a rolling basis. Application fee: $50. *Expenses:* Tuition: Full-time $34,900; part-time $4362.50 per course. *Financial support:* In 2009–10, fellowships with tuition reimbursements (averaging $10,300 per year), research assistantships with full and partial tuition reimbursements (averaging $10,300 per year), 4 teaching assistantships with full and partial tuition reimbursements (averaging $10,300 per year) were awarded; career-related internships or fieldwork and tuition waivers (partial) also available. Support available to part-time students. Financial award application deadline: 2/15. *Faculty research:* Writings of James Fenimore Cooper, Renaissance literature, American literature, medieval literature, Victorian literature. *Unit head:* Dr. Jay Elliott, Chair, 508-793-7142. *Application contact:* Terri Rutkiewicz, Academic Secretary, 508-793-7142, Fax: 508-793-8892, E-mail: engma@clarku.edu.

Clemson University, Graduate School, College of Architecture, Arts, and Humanities, Department of English, Program in English, Clemson, SC 29634. Offers MA. *Students:* 32 full-time (24 women), 9 part-time (7 women); includes 5 minority (3 African Americans, 2 Hispanic Americans), 1 international. Average age 27. 36 applicants, 44% accepted, 8 enrolled. In 2009, 17 master's awarded. *Degree requirements:* For master's, thesis optional. *Entrance requirements:* For master's, GRE, minimum GPA of 3.0, 2 letters of recommendation. Additional exam requirements/recommendations for international students: Required—TOEFL. *Application deadline:* Applications are processed on a rolling basis. Application fee: $70 ($80 for international students). Electronic applications accepted. *Expenses:* Tuition, state resident: full-time $8684; part-time $528 per credit hour. Tuition, nonresident: full-time $15,330; part-time $1078 per credit hour. Required fees: $736; $37 per semester. Part-time tuition and fees vary according to course load and program. *Financial support:* In 2009–10, 27 students received support, including 17 teaching assistantships with partial tuition reimbursements available (averaging $13,724 per year); fellowships with full and partial tuition reimbursements available, research assistantships with partial tuition reimbursements available, career-related internships or fieldwork, institutionally sponsored loans, scholarships/grants, health care benefits, and unspecified assistantships also available. Support available to part-time students. *Unit head:* Dr. Lee Morrissey, Chair, 864-656-3151, Fax: 864-656-1345, E-mail: lmorris@clemson.edu. *Application contact:* Dr. Catherine Paul, Graduate Program Contact, 864-656-3543, Fax: 864-656-1345, E-mail: cpaul@clemson.edu.

Cleveland State University, College of Graduate Studies, College of Liberal Arts and Social Sciences, Department of English, Cleveland, OH 44115. Offers creative writing (MFA); English (MA). Part-time and evening/weekend programs available. *Degree requirements:* For master's, comprehensive exam, thesis. *Entrance requirements:* For master's, minimum GPA of 2.75, undergraduate concentration in English, writing sample, portfolio. Additional exam requirements/recommendations for international students: Required—TOEFL (525 paper-based; 197 computer-based) or IELTS (6 paper-based). Electronic applications accepted. *Faculty research:* Literary history and criticism, linguistics, literature.

The College at Brockport, State University of New York, School of Arts, Humanities and Social Sciences, Department of English, Brockport, NY 14420-2997. Offers English (MA), including creative writing, literature. Part-time programs available. *Students:* 28 full-time (17 women), 30 part-time (18 women). 15 applicants, 87% accepted, 10 enrolled. In 2009, 8 master's awarded. *Degree requirements:* For master's, thesis. *Entrance requirements:* For master's, minimum GPA of 3.0, letters of recommendation, writing sample. Additional exam requirements/recommendations for international students: Required—TOEFL (minimum score 550 paper-based; 213 computer-based; 79 iBT). *Application deadline:* For fall admission, 4/15 priority date for domestic and international students; for spring admission, 11/15 priority date for domestic and international students. Application fee: $50. Electronic applications accepted. *Expenses:* Tuition, state resident: full-time $8370; part-time $349 per credit. Tuition, nonresident: full-time $13,250; part-time $522 per credit. *Financial support:* In 2009–10, 1 fellowship with full tuition reimbursement (averaging $7,500 per year), 3 teaching assistantships with full tuition reimbursements (averaging $6,000 per year) were awarded; Federal Work-Study, scholarships/grants, and unspecified assistantships also available. Support available to part-time students. Financial award application deadline: 3/15; financial award applicants required to submit FAFSA. *Faculty research:* British and American literature, creative writing, film studies, children's literature, ancient and modern world literature. *Unit head:* Dr. J. Roger Kurtz, Chairperson, 585-395-2503, Fax: 585-395-2391, E-mail: rkurtz@brockport.edu. *Application contact:* Dr. Stefan Jurasinski, Graduate Program Director, 585-395-5714, Fax: 585-395-2391, E-mail: sjurasin@brockport.edu.

College of Charleston, Graduate School, School of Humanities and Social Sciences, Program in English, Charleston, SC 29424-0001. Offers MA. Part-time and evening/weekend programs available. *Faculty:* 29 full-time (16 women). *Students:* 17 full-time (13 women), 15 part-time (13 women); includes 1 minority (Hispanic American). Average age 27. 29 applicants, 48% accepted, 10 enrolled. In 2009, 13 master's awarded. *Degree requirements:* For master's, one foreign language, comprehensive exam, thesis optional. *Entrance requirements:* For master's, GRE General Test or MAT, minimum GPA of 2.5 overall, 3.0 in major; 2 letters of recommendation; writing sample. Additional exam requirements/recommendations for international students: Required—TOEFL. *Application deadline:* For fall admission, 6/1 for domestic students; for spring admission, 11/1 for domestic students. Application fee: $45. Electronic applications accepted. *Financial support:* In 2009–10, 5 research assistantships (averaging $12,400 per year) were awarded; fellowships, scholarships/grants and unspecified assistantships also available. Financial award application deadline: 6/1; financial award applicants required to submit FAFSA. *Unit head:* Dr. Susan Farrell, Director, 843-953-5664, Fax: 843-953-3180, E-mail: farrells@cofc.edu. *Application contact:* Susan Hallatt, Director of Graduate Admissions, 843-953-5614, Fax: 843-953-1434, E-mail: hallatts@cofc.edu.

The College of New Jersey, Graduate Division, School of Culture and Society, Department of English, Program in English, Ewing, NJ 08628. Offers MA. Part-time programs available. *Students:* 6 full-time (5 women), 25 part-time (19 women); includes 1 minority (Asian American or Pacific Islander). 42 applicants, 60% accepted. In 2009, 13 master's awarded. *Degree requirements:* For master's, comprehensive exam. *Entrance requirements:* For master's, GRE, minimum GPA of 3.0 in field or 2.75 overall. Additional exam requirements/recommendations for international students: Required—TOEFL. *Application deadline:* For fall admission, 2/1 priority date for domestic students; for spring admission, 10/1 priority date for domestic students. Application fee: $70. Electronic applications accepted. *Expenses:* Tuition, state resident: part-time $573.70 per credit. Tuition, nonresident: part-time $887.75 per credit. Required fees: $140.85 per credit. One-time fee: $10 part-time. *Financial support:* Tuition waivers (partial) and unspecified assistantships available. Financial award application deadline: 5/1; financial award applicants required to submit FAFSA. *Unit head:* Dr. Michele Lise Tarter, Coordinator. *Application contact:* Susan L. Hydro, Assistant Dean, Office of Graduate Studies, 609-771-2300, Fax: 609-637-5105, E-mail: graduate@tcnj.edu.

The College of Saint Rose, Graduate Studies, School of Arts and Humanities, Department of English, Albany, NY 12203-1419. Offers MA. Part-time and evening/weekend programs available. *Degree requirements:* For master's, thesis optional, advanced project. *Entrance requirements:* For master's, 24 credits in English, minimum undergraduate GPA of 3.2, writing sample. Additional exam requirements/recommendations for international students: Required—TOEFL (minimum score 550 paper-based; 213 computer-based). Electronic applications accepted.

College of Staten Island of the City University of New York, Graduate Programs, Program in English, Staten Island, NY 10314-6600. Offers MA. Part-time and evening/weekend programs available. *Faculty:* 5 full-time (2 women). *Students:* 5 full-time (4 women), 28 part-time (20 women); includes 4 minority (3 African Americans, 1 Hispanic American). Average age 31. 23 applicants, 52% accepted, 9 enrolled. In 2009, 8 master's awarded. *Degree requirements:* For master's, comprehensive exam, 3-hour written exam, 2 papers. *Entrance requirements:* For master's, 32 undergraduate credits in English, minimum GPA of 3.0. Additional exam requirements/recommendations for international students: Required—TOEFL (minimum score 550 paper-based; 213 computer-based; 79 iBT). *Application deadline:* Applications are processed on a rolling basis. Application fee: $125. Electronic applications accepted. *Expenses:* Tuition, state resident: full-time $7360; part-time $310 per credit. Tuition, nonresident: part-time $575 per credit. Required fees: $378; $113 per semester. *Financial support:* Career-related internships or fieldwork, Federal Work-Study, institutionally sponsored loans, scholarships/grants, and institutional work-study available. Support available to part-time students. Financial award applicants required to submit FAFSA. *Unit head:* Dr. Maryann Feola, Coordinator, 718-982-3666, Fax: 718-982-3643, E-mail: englishmasters@mail.csi.cuny.edu. *Application contact:* Sasha Spence, Assistant Director of Graduate Recruitment Admissions, 718-982-2699, Fax: 718-982-2500, E-mail: sasha.spence@csi.cuny.edu.

Colorado State University, Graduate School, College of Liberal Arts, Department of English, Fort Collins, CO 80523-1773. Offers creative writing (MFA); English (MA). Part-time programs available. *Faculty:* 32 full-time (19 women). *Students:* 96 full-time (57 women), 46 part-time (32 women); includes 10 minority (1 American Indian/Alaska Native, 2 Asian Americans or Pacific Islanders, 7 Hispanic Americans), 15 international. Average age 30. 289 applicants, 34% accepted, 36 enrolled. In 2009, 53 master's awarded. *Degree requirements:* For master's, variable foreign language requirement, thesis (for some programs), exams. *Entrance requirements:* For master's, GRE, writing sample, BA/BS with minimum GPA of 3.0, letters of recommendation. Additional exam requirements/recommendations for international students: Required—TOEFL (minimum score 550 paper-based), TOEFL paper-based score of 575 required for creative writing. *Application deadline:* For fall admission, 4/1 priority date for domestic students; for spring admission, 9/1 priority date for domestic students. Applications are processed on a rolling basis. Application fee: $50. Electronic applications accepted. *Expenses:* Tuition, state resident: full-time $6434; part-time $359.10 per credit. Tuition, nonresident: full-time $18,116; part-time $1006.45 per credit. Required fees: $1496; $83 per credit. *Financial support:* In 2009–10, 36 students received support, including 36 teaching assistantships with full tuition reimbursements available (averaging $12,564 per year); fellowships, research assistantships, career-related internships or fieldwork, Federal Work-Study, institutionally sponsored loans, scholarships/grants, traineeships, and unspecified assistantships also available. Support available to part-time students. Financial award application deadline: 5/1; financial award applicants required to submit FAFSA. *Faculty research:* Computers and writing, environmental writing, cultural studies, new historicism, performance and identity. Total annual research expenditures: $43,684. *Unit head:* Dr. Bruce Ronda, Chair, 970-491-6428, Fax: 970-491-5601, E-mail: bruce.ronda@colostate.edu. *Application contact:* Marnie Leonard, Administrative Assistant, 970-491-2403, Fax: 970-491-7541, E-mail: marnie.leonard@colostate.edu.

Columbia University, Graduate School of Arts and Sciences, Division of Humanities, Department of English and Comparative Literature, New York, NY 10027. Offers comparative literature (M Phil, MA, PhD); English literature (M Phil, MA, PhD); literature-writing (M Phil, MA, PhD). Part-time programs available. *Degree requirements:* For master's, one foreign language, comprehensive exam, seminar papers; for doctorate, thesis/dissertation. *Entrance requirements:* For master's and doctorate, GRE General Test. Additional exam requirements/recommendations for international students: Required—TOEFL. *Faculty research:* Medieval through modern literature, drama, literary criticism.

Concordia University, School of Graduate Studies, Faculty of Arts and Science, Department of English, Program in English, Montréal, QC H3G 1M8, Canada. Offers MA. *Degree requirements:* For master's, one foreign language, thesis optional. *Entrance requirements:* For master's, honors degree in English, minimum GPA of 3.3 in English literature.

Converse College, School of Education and Graduate Studies, Program in Liberal Arts, Spartanburg, SC 29302-0006. Offers English (MLA); history (MLA); political science (MLA). *Degree requirements:* For master's, capstone paper. *Entrance requirements:* For master's, minimum GPA of 3.0, 2 recommendations.

Cornell University, Graduate School, Graduate Fields of Arts and Sciences, Field of English Language and Literature, Ithaca, NY 14853-0001. Offers African-American literature (PhD); American literature after 1865 (PhD); American literature to 1865 (PhD); American studies (PhD); colonial and postcolonial literature (PhD); creative writing (MFA); cultural studies (PhD); dramatic literature (PhD); English poetry (PhD); English Renaissance to 1660 (PhD); lesbian, bisexual, and gay literature studies (PhD); literary criticism and theory (PhD); nineteenth century (PhD); Old and Middle English (PhD); prose fiction (PhD); Restoration and eighteenth century (PhD); twentieth century (PhD); women's literature (PhD); MFA/PhD. *Faculty:* 74 full-time (35 women). *Students:* 100 full-time (55 women); includes 26 minority (9 African Americans, 3 American Indian/Alaska Native, 7 Asian Americans or Pacific Islanders, 7 Hispanic Americans), 11 international. Average age 28. 890 applicants, 4% accepted, 21 enrolled. In 2009, 21 master's, 12 doctorates awarded. Terminal master's awarded for partial completion of doctoral program. *Degree requirements:* For master's, one foreign language, thesis; for doctorate, one foreign language, comprehensive exam, thesis/dissertation, teaching experience. *Entrance requirements:* For master's, GRE General Test, 3 letters of recommendation, creative writing sample; for doctorate, GRE General Test, GRE Subject Test (English), 3 letters of recommendation, writing sample. Additional exam requirements/recommendations for international students: Required—TOEFL (minimum score 600 paper-based; 250 computer-based; 77 iBT). *Application deadline:* For fall admission, 1/10 for domestic students. Application fee: $70. Electronic applications accepted. *Expenses:* Tuition: Full-time $29,500. Required fees: $70. Full-time tuition and fees vary according to degree level, program and student level. *Financial support:* In 2009–10, 96 students received support, including 13 fellowships with full tuition reimbursements available, 8 teaching assistantships with full tuition reimbursements available; research assistantships with full tuition reimbursements available, institutionally sponsored loans, scholarships/grants, health care benefits, tuition waivers (full and partial), and unspecified assistantships also available. Financial award applicants required to submit FAFSA. *Faculty research:* English and American literature, women's writing, ethnic and post-colonial literature, critical theory, medievalism. *Unit head:* Director of Graduate Studies, 607-255-7989, Fax: 607-255-6661. *Application contact:* Graduate Field Assistant, 607-255-7989, Fax: 607-255-6661, E-mail: english_grad@cornell.edu.

Cornell University, Graduate School, Graduate Fields of Arts and Sciences, Field of Linguistics, Ithaca, NY 14853-0001. Offers applied linguistics (MA, PhD); East Asian linguistics (MA, PhD); English linguistics (MA, PhD); general linguistics (MA, PhD); Germanic linguistics (MA, PhD); Indo-European linguistics (MA, PhD); phonetics (MA, PhD); phonological theory (MA, PhD); Romance linguistics (MA, PhD); second language acquisition (MA, PhD); semantics (MA, PhD); Slavic linguistics (MA, PhD); sociolinguistics (MA, PhD); South Asian linguistics (MA, PhD); Southeast Asian linguistics (MA, PhD); syntactic theory (MA, PhD). *Faculty:* 21 full-time (10 women). *Students:* 31 full-time (17 women), 14 international. Average age 30. 95 applicants, 12% accepted, 5 enrolled. In 2009, 5 master's, 6 doctorates awarded. Terminal master's awarded for partial completion of doctoral program. *Degree requirements:* For master's, one foreign language, thesis; for doctorate, one foreign language, comprehensive exam, thesis/dissertation. *Entrance requirements:* For master's and doctorate, GRE General Test, 2 letters of recommendation. Additional exam requirements/recommendations for international students: Required—TOEFL (minimum score 600 paper-based; 250 computer-based; 77 iBT). *Application deadline:* For fall admission, 1/15 for domestic students. Application fee: $70. Electronic applications accepted. *Expenses:* Tuition: Full-time $29,500. Required fees: $70. Full-time tuition and fees vary according to degree level, program and student level. *Financial support:* In 2009–10, 3 fellowships with full tuition reimbursements, 1 teaching assistantship with full tuition reimbursement were awarded; research assistantships with full tuition reimbursements, institutionally sponsored loans, scholarships/grants, health care benefits, tuition waivers (full and partial), and unspecified assistantships also available. Financial award applicants required to submit FAFSA. *Faculty research:* Phonology and phonetics; syntax and semantics; historical linguistics; philosophy of language; language acquisition. *Unit head:* Director of Graduate Studies, 607-255-1105. *Application contact:* Graduate Field Assistant, 607-255-1105, E-mail: lingfield@cornell.edu.

Creighton University, Graduate School, College of Arts and Sciences, Department of English, Omaha, NE 68178-0001. Offers creative writing (MA). Part-time programs available. *Faculty:* 17 full-time (9 women). *Students:* 12 full-time (8 women), 4 part-time (2 women); includes 1 minority (Hispanic American), 3 international. 21 applicants, 95% accepted, 13 enrolled. In 2009, 6 master's awarded. *Degree requirements:* For master's, thesis optional. *Entrance requirements:* For master's, GRE, 10-15 page writing sample, 3 letters of recommendation. Additional exam requirements/recommendations for international students: Required—TOEFL (minimum score 550 paper-based; 213 computer-based; 80 iBT). *Application deadline:* For fall admission, 3/15 priority date for domestic and international students. Application fee: $50. Electronic applications accepted. *Expenses:* Tuition: Full-time $11,700; part-time $650 per credit hour. Required fees: $126 per semester. *Financial support:* In 2009–10, 5 fellowships with full and partial tuition reimbursements (averaging $10,437 per year) were awarded; tuition waivers (partial) also available. Financial award applicants required to submit FAFSA. *Unit head:* Dr. Greg Zacharias, Director, 402-280-2729, E-mail: gregzacharias@creighton.edu. *Application contact:* Taunya Plater, Senior Program Coordinator, 402-280-2870, Fax: 402-280-2899, E-mail: taunyaplater@creighton.edu.

Dalhousie University, Faculty of Arts and Social Science, Department of English, Halifax, NS B3H 4R2, Canada. Offers MA, PhD. *Students:* 37 full-time (22 women), 1 (woman) part-time. 65 applicants, 20% accepted. *Entrance requirements:* Additional exam requirements/recommendations for international students: Required—TOEFL, IELTS, CANTEST, CAEL, or Michigan English Language Assessment Battery. *Application deadline:* For fall admission, 6/1 for domestic students, 4/1 for international students; for winter admission, 10/31 for domestic students, 8/31 for international students; for spring admission, 2/28 for domestic students, 12/31 for international students. Application fee: $70. Electronic applications accepted. *Financial support:* Career-related internships or fieldwork, scholarships/grants, and health care benefits available. *Faculty research:* Victorian, Canadian, Renaissance, eighteenth century, and modern literature. *Unit head:* Dr. Christina Luckyj, Chair, 902-494-6924, Fax: 902-494-2176, E-mail: gradengl@dal.ca. *Application contact:* Dr. Leonard Diepeveen, Graduate Coordinator, 902-494-3331, Fax: 902-494-2176, E-mail: gradengl@dal.ca.

DePaul University, College of Liberal Arts and Sciences, Department of English, Chicago, IL 60614. Offers English (MA); writing and publishing (MA); writing, rhetoric, and discourse (MA). Part-time and evening/weekend programs available. *Faculty:* 29 full-time (12 women). *Students:* 112 full-time (74 women), 77 part-time (67 women); includes 19 minority (7 African Americans, 4 Asian Americans or Pacific Islanders, 8 Hispanic Americans), 1 international. Average age 27. 95 applicants, 56% accepted. In 2009, 100 master's awarded. *Degree requirements:* For master's, written exam. *Entrance requirements:* Additional exam requirements/recommendations for international students: Required—TOEFL. *Application deadline:* For fall admission, 7/1 priority date for domestic students; for winter admission, 10/1 priority date for domestic students; for spring admission, 2/1 priority date for domestic students. Applications are processed on a rolling basis. Application fee: $40. Electronic applications accepted. *Expenses:* Tuition: Full-time $37,525; part-time $620 per credit hour. *Financial support:* In 2009–10, 2 research assistantships with full tuition reimbursements, 7 teaching assistantships with full tuition reimbursements (averaging $7,500 per year) were awarded; fellowships with partial tuition reimbursements, career-related internships or fieldwork, institutionally sponsored loans, scholarships/grants, tuition waivers (partial), and unspecified assistantships also available. Support available to part-time students. Financial award application deadline: 4/1. *Faculty*

English

DePaul University (continued)

research: Rhetoric and composition, technical writing, creative writing, linguistics, literacy theory. *Unit head:* Dr. Janet Hickey, Chairperson, 773-325-4635, E-mail: jhicke11@depaul.edu. *Application contact:* Dr. Lesley Kordecki, Director, 773-325-1786, Fax: 773-325-8607, E-mail: lkordeck@depaul.edu.

Drew University, Caspersen School of Graduate Studies, Program in Education, Madison, NJ 07940-1493. Offers biology (MAT); chemistry (MAT); English (MAT); French (MAT); Italian (MAT); math (MAT); physics (MAT); social studies (MAT); Spanish (MAT); theatre arts (MAT). *Unit head:* Dr. Ross Danis.

Duke University, Graduate School, Department of English, Durham, NC 27708. Offers PhD, JD/AM. *Faculty:* 30 full-time. *Students:* 71 full-time (38 women); includes 13 minority (8 African Americans, 1 American Indian/Alaska Native, 1 Asian American or Pacific Islander, 3 Hispanic Americans), 12 international. 394 applicants, 5% accepted, 12 enrolled. In 2009, 11 doctorates awarded. *Degree requirements:* For doctorate, 2 foreign languages, thesis/dissertation. *Entrance requirements:* For doctorate, GRE General Test. Additional exam requirements/recommendations for international students: Required—TOEFL (minimum score 550 paper-based; 213 computer-based; 83 iBT), IELTS (minimum score 7). *Application deadline:* For fall admission, 12/8 priority date for domestic and international students. Application fee: $75. Electronic applications accepted. *Financial support:* Fellowships, research assistantships, teaching assistantships, Federal Work-Study available. Financial award application deadline: 12/31. *Unit head:* Kathy Psomiades, Director of Graduate Studies, 919-684-5538, Fax: 919-66055-38, E-mail: maryscot.mullins@duke.edu. *Application contact:* Cynthia Roberston, Associate Dean for Enrollment Services, 919-684-3913, E-mail: grad-admissions@duke.edu.

Duquesne University, Graduate School of Liberal Arts, Program in English, Pittsburgh, PA 15282-0001. Offers MA, PhD. Part-time and evening/weekend programs available. *Faculty:* 17 full-time (10 women), 29 part-time/adjunct (17 women). *Students:* 61 full-time (47 women), 16 part-time (11 women), 2 international. Average age 25. 60 applicants, 43% accepted, 18 enrolled. In 2009, 11 master's, 7 doctorates awarded. *Degree requirements:* For master's, comprehensive exam, thesis or alternative; for doctorate, 2 foreign languages, comprehensive exam, thesis/dissertation. *Entrance requirements:* For master's and doctorate, GRE General Test, bachelor's degree in English, writing sample. Additional exam requirements/recommendations for international students: Required—TOEFL. *Application deadline:* For fall admission, 2/1 priority date for domestic and international students. Applications are processed on a rolling basis. Electronic applications accepted. *Expenses:* Tuition: Part-time $851 per credit. Required fees: $81 per credit. *Financial support:* In 2009–10, 22 teaching assistantships with full tuition reimbursements (averaging $13,000 per year) were awarded; research assistantships, Federal Work-Study, scholarships/grants, tuition waivers (partial), and unspecified assistantships also available. Support available to part-time students. Financial award application deadline: 5/1. *Unit head:* Dr. Magali Michael, Chair, 412-396-6420. *Application contact:* Dr. Susan Howard, Director of Graduate Studies, 412-396-6420.

East Carolina University, Graduate School, Thomas Harriot College of Arts and Sciences, Department of English, Greenville, NC 27858-4353. Offers MA. Part-time and evening/weekend programs available. *Degree requirements:* For master's, one foreign language, comprehensive exam, thesis optional. *Entrance requirements:* For master's, GRE General Test, MAT (MA Ed). Additional exam requirements/recommendations for international students: Required—TOEFL.

Eastern Illinois University, Graduate School, College of Arts and Humanities, Department of English, Charleston, IL 61920-3099. Offers MA. Part-time programs available. *Faculty:* 40 full-time (12 women). In 2009, 12 master's awarded. *Entrance requirements:* For master's, GRE General Test. *Application deadline:* For fall admission, 3/31 priority date for domestic students. Applications are processed on a rolling basis. Application fee: $30. *Expenses:* Tuition, state resident: full-time $9434; part-time $239 per credit hour. Tuition, nonresident: full-time $23,774; part-time $717 per credit hour. Required fees: $802.63. *Financial support:* In 2009–10, research assistantships (averaging $8,100 per year), 9 teaching assistantships (averaging $8,100 per year) were awarded. *Unit head:* Dr. Dana Ringuette, Chairperson, 217-581-2428, Fax: 217-581-7209, E-mail: dringuette@eiu.edu. *Application contact:* Dr. James D. Smith, Coordinator, 217-581-6290, Fax: 217-581-7209, E-mail: jdsmith3@eiu.edu.

Eastern Kentucky University, The Graduate School, College of Arts and Sciences, Department of English and Theatre, Richmond, KY 40475-3102. Offers creative writing (MFA); English (MA). Part-time and evening/weekend programs available. *Degree requirements:* For master's, thesis optional. *Entrance requirements:* For master's, GRE General Test, minimum GPA of 2.5, minor in English with 3.0 GPA. *Faculty research:* Old English, Victorian studies, women's studies, rhetoric, popular culture, novel studies.

Eastern Michigan University, Graduate School, College of Arts and Sciences, Department of English Language and Literature, Program in Children's Literature, Ypsilanti, MI 48197. Offers MA. Part-time and evening/weekend programs available. Postbaccalaureate distance learning degree programs offered (minimal on-campus study). *Students:* 5 full-time (all women), 11 part-time (all women); includes 2 minority (both African Americans), 2 international. Average age 30. In 2009, 14 master's awarded. *Entrance requirements:* Additional exam requirements/recommendations for international students: Required—TOEFL. *Application deadline:* Applications are processed on a rolling basis. Application fee: $35. Tuition and fees vary according to course level. *Financial support:* Fellowships, research assistantships with full tuition reimbursements, teaching assistantships with full tuition reimbursements, tuition waivers (partial) available. Financial award applicants required to submit FAFSA. *Unit head:* Dr. Rebecca Sipe, Department Head, 734-487-4220, Fax: 734-483-9744, E-mail: rebecca.sipe@emich.edu. *Application contact:* Dr. Annette Wannamaker, Program Advisor, 734-487-0148, Fax: 734-483-9744, E-mail: awannamak@emich.edu.

Eastern Michigan University, Graduate School, College of Arts and Sciences, Department of English Language and Literature, Program in English Linguistics, Ypsilanti, MI 48197. Offers MA. Part-time and evening/weekend programs available. Postbaccalaureate distance learning degree programs offered (minimal on-campus study). *Students:* 12 full-time (8 women), 7 part-time (4 women); includes 2 minority (1 African American, 1 Asian American or Pacific Islander), 7 international. Average age 27. In 2009, 8 master's awarded. *Degree requirements:* For master's, thesis (for some programs). *Entrance requirements:* Additional exam requirements/recommendations for international students: Required—TOEFL. *Application deadline:* Applications are processed on a rolling basis. Application fee: $35. Tuition and fees vary according to course level. *Financial support:* Fellowships with tuition reimbursements, research assistantships with full tuition reimbursements, teaching assistantships with full tuition reimbursements, career-related internships or fieldwork, Federal Work-Study, institutionally sponsored loans, scholarships/grants, tuition waivers (partial), and unspecified assistantships available. Support available to part-time students. Financial award applicants required to submit FAFSA. *Application contact:* Dr. T. Daniel Seely, Program Advisor, 734-487-0145, Fax: 734-483-9744, E-mail: tseely@emich.edu.

Eastern Michigan University, Graduate School, College of Arts and Sciences, Department of English Language and Literature, Program in Literature, Ypsilanti, MI 48197. Offers MA, Graduate Certificate. Part-time and evening/weekend programs available. Postbaccalaureate distance learning degree programs offered (minimal on-campus study). *Students:* 15 full-time (4 women), 30 part-time (15 women); includes 3 minority (2 African Americans, 1 Hispanic American), 2 international. Average age 28. In 2009, 21 master's awarded. *Entrance requirements:* Additional exam requirements/recommendations for international students: Required—TOEFL. *Application deadline:* Applications are processed on a rolling basis. Application fee: $35. Tuition and fees vary according to course level. *Financial support:* Fellowships, research assistantships with full tuition reimbursements, teaching assistantships with full tuition reimbursements, career-related internships or fieldwork, Federal Work-Study, institutionally sponsored loans, scholarships/grants, tuition waivers (partial), and unspecified assistantships available. Support available to part-time students. Financial award applicants required to submit FAFSA. *Unit head:* Dr. Rebecca Sipe, Department Head, 734-487-4220, Fax: 734-483-9744, E-mail: rebecca.sipe@emich.edu. *Application contact:* Dr. Andrea Kaston-Tange, Program Coordinator, 734-487-2296, Fax: 734-483-9744, E-mail: akastont@emich.edu.

Eastern New Mexico University, Graduate School, College of Liberal Arts and Sciences, Department of Languages and Literature, Portales, NM 88130. Offers English (MA). Part-time programs available. *Faculty:* 5 full-time (3 women). *Students:* 1 (woman) full-time, 14 part-time (13 women); includes 5 minority (1 Asian American or Pacific Islander, 4 Hispanic Americans), 1 international. Average age 31. 7 applicants, 86% accepted, 1 enrolled. In 2009, 4 master's awarded. *Degree requirements:* For master's, one foreign language, comprehensive exam, thesis. *Entrance requirements:* For master's, minimum GPA of 3.0, academic writing sample. Additional exam requirements/recommendations for international students: Required—TOEFL (minimum score 550 paper-based; 213 computer-based; 79 iBT), IELTS (minimum score 6). *Application deadline:* For fall admission, 7/20 priority date for domestic students, 6/20 priority date for international students. Applications are processed on a rolling basis. Application fee: $10. Electronic applications accepted. *Expenses:* Tuition, state resident: full-time $2922; part-time $121.75 per credit hour. Tuition, nonresident: full-time $8454; part-time $352.25 per credit hour. Required fees: $1038; $43.25 per credit hour. *Financial support:* In 2009–10, 8 research assistantships with partial tuition reimbursements (averaging $4,250 per year), 1 teaching assistantship with partial tuition reimbursement (averaging $4,250 per year) were awarded; fellowships, tuition waivers (partial) and unspecified assistantships also available. Support available to part-time students. Financial award applicants required to submit FAFSA. *Unit head:* Dr. Linda Sumption, Graduate Coordinator, 575-562-2136, E-mail: linda.sumption@emnu.edu. *Application contact:* Dr. Linda Sumption, Graduate Coordinator, 575-562-2136, E-mail: linda.sumption@emnu.edu.

Eastern Washington University, Graduate Studies, College of Arts and Letters, Department of English, Cheney, WA 99004-2431. Offers literature (MA); rhetoric, composition, and technical communication (MA); teaching English as a second language (MA). *Degree requirements:* For master's, comprehensive exam, thesis or alternative. *Entrance requirements:* For master's, GRE General Test, minimum GPA of 3.0. *Expenses:* Tuition, state resident: full-time $7476; part-time $249 per quarter hour. Tuition, nonresident: full-time $18,030; part-time $601 per quarter hour. Required fees: $3.50 per quarter hour. $142 per quarter.

East Tennessee State University, School of Graduate Studies, College of Arts and Sciences, Department of English, Johnson City, TN 37614. Offers MA. Part-time and evening/weekend programs available. *Degree requirements:* For master's, oral defense of thesis. *Entrance requirements:* For master's, GRE General Test or GRE Subject Test, minimum undergraduate GPA of 3.0 in English. Additional exam requirements/recommendations for international students: Required—TOEFL (minimum score 550 paper-based; 213 computer-based). *Faculty research:* Appalachian studies, women's studies, sports images in religion, British and American literature.

Elmhurst College, Graduate Programs, Program in English Studies, Elmhurst, IL 60126-3296. Offers MA. Part-time and evening/weekend programs available. *Faculty:* 1 (woman) full-time, 1 part-time/adjunct (0 women). *Students:* 23 part-time (17 women); includes 4 minority (3 African Americans, 1 Asian American or Pacific Islander). Average age 26. 11 applicants, 73% accepted, 7 enrolled. In 2009, 2 master's awarded. *Degree requirements:* For master's, thesis optional. *Entrance requirements:* For master's, 3 recommendations. Additional exam requirements/recommendations for international students: Required—TOEFL (minimum score 550 paper-based; 213 computer-based). *Application deadline:* Applications are processed on a rolling basis. Application fee: $25. Electronic applications accepted. *Expenses:* Contact institution. *Financial support:* In 2009–10, 5 students received support. Federal Work-Study and scholarships/grants available. Support available to part-time students. Financial award application deadline: 6/1; financial award applicants required to submit FAFSA. *Unit head:* Dr. Ted Lerud, Associate Dean of the Faculty, 630-617-3661, Fax: 630-617-6415, E-mail: gradadm@elmhurst.edu. *Application contact:* Elizabeth D. Kuebler, Director of Adult and Graduate Admission, 630-617-3069, Fax: 630-617-5501, E-mail: betsyk@elmhurst.edu.

Emory University, Graduate School of Arts and Sciences, Department of Comparative Literature, Atlanta, GA 30322-1100. Offers comparative literature (PhD); English (Certificate); French (Certificate); Middle Eastern studies (PhD); philosophy (Certificate); psychoanalytic studies (PhD); religion (PhD); Spanish (Certificate); women studies (Certificate). *Degree requirements:* For doctorate, 2 foreign languages, comprehensive exam, thesis/dissertation. *Entrance requirements:* For doctorate, GRE General Test, minimum GPA of 3.0. Additional exam requirements/recommendations for international students: Required—TOEFL. Electronic applications accepted. *Faculty research:* Literary theory, psychoanalysis trauma and testimony, literature and religion, literature and technology, literature and philosophy, politics and global culture, literature and aesthetics.

Emory University, Graduate School of Arts and Sciences, Department of English, Atlanta, GA 30322-1100. Offers PhD. *Degree requirements:* For doctorate, one foreign language, comprehensive exam, thesis/dissertation. *Entrance requirements:* For doctorate, GRE General Test, minimum GPA of 3.0. Additional exam requirements/recommendations for international students: Required—TOEFL. Electronic applications accepted. *Faculty research:* American literature, renaissance literature, twentieth century poetry, Irish literature, cultural studies.

Emporia State University, School of Graduate Studies, College of Liberal Arts and Sciences, Department of English, Modern Languages and Journalism, Emporia, KS 66801-5087. Offers English (MA); teaching English to speakers of other languages (MA). Part-time programs available. *Faculty:* 27 full-time (13 women), 2 part-time/adjunct (both women). *Students:* 6 full-time (5 women), 10 part-time (7 women); includes 3 minority (1 American Indian/Alaska Native, 2 Hispanic Americans), 1 international. 6 applicants, 67% accepted, 2 enrolled. In 2009, 11 master's awarded. *Degree requirements:* For master's, comprehensive exam or thesis. *Entrance requirements:* For master's, appropriate undergraduate degree, writing sample. Additional exam requirements/recommendations for international students: Required—TOEFL (minimum score 520 paper-based; 133 computer-based; 68 iBT). *Application deadline:* For fall admission, 8/15 priority date for domestic students. Applications are processed on a rolling basis. Application fee: $30 ($75 for international students). Electronic applications accepted. *Expenses:* Tuition, state resident: full-time $4154; part-time $173 per credit hour. Tuition, nonresident: full-time $12,864; part-time $536 per credit hour. Required fees: $948; $58 per credit hour. Tuition and fees vary according to campus/location. *Financial support:* In 2009–10, 14 teaching assistantships with full tuition reimbursements (averaging $7,610 per year) were awarded; Federal Work-Study, institutionally sponsored loans, health care benefits, and unspecified assistantships also available. Financial award application deadline: 3/15; financial award applicants required to submit FAFSA. *Unit head:* Dr. Marie Miller, Interim Chair, 620-341-5216, E-mail: mmiller@emporia.edu. *Application contact:* Dr. Mel Storm, Graduate Coordinator, 620-341-5563, E-mail: mstorm@emporia.edu.

Fairleigh Dickinson University, Metropolitan Campus, University College: Arts, Sciences, and Professional Studies, Department of English, Philosophy, and Humanities, Program in English and Literature, Teaneck, NJ 07666-1914. Offers MA. *Students:* 4 full-time (3 women), 6 part-time (5 women). Average age 29. 6 applicants, 100% accepted, 2 enrolled.Application fee: $40. *Application contact:* Susan Brooman, University Director of Graduate Admissions, 201-692-2554, Fax: 201-692-2560, E-mail: globaleducation@fdu.edu.

Fayetteville State University, Graduate School, Program in English, Fayetteville, NC 28301-4298. Offers MA. Part-time and evening/weekend programs available. *Faculty:* 4 full-time (3 women). *Students:* 5 part-time (3 women). Average age 28. *Degree requirements:* For master's, comprehensive exam, thesis, internship. *Entrance requirements:* For master's, GRE General Test. *Application deadline:* For fall admission, 4/15 for domestic students; for spring admission, 10/15 for domestic students. Applications are processed on a rolling basis. Application fee: $35. Electronic applications accepted. *Faculty research:* Online film culture; literature and pre-Raphaelite, Symbolist, and Surrealist painting; aesthetics of African-American gospel music; power of sheltered instruction. Total annual research expenditures: $19,000. *Unit head:* Dr. Edward McShane, Chairperson, 910-672-1416, E-mail: emcshane@uncfsu.edu. *Application contact:* Roxie Shabazz, Associate Vice-Chancellor for Enrollment Management, 910-672-1784, Fax: 910-672-2209, E-mail: rshabazz@uncfsu.edu.

Fitchburg State University, Division of Graduate and Continuing Education, Programs in English and Teaching English (Secondary Level), Fitchburg, MA 01420-2697. Offers MA, MAT, Certificate. *Accreditation:* NCATE. Part-time and evening/weekend programs available. *Students:* 1 full-time (0 women), 30 part-time (20 women). Average age 34. 13 applicants, 100% accepted, 10 enrolled. In 2009, 14 master's awarded. *Entrance requirements:* For master's, GRE General Test or MAT, letters of recommendation, resume. Additional exam requirements/recommendations for international students: Required—TOEFL (minimum score 550 paper-based; 213 computer-based; 79 iBT). *Application deadline:* Applications are processed on a rolling basis. Application fee: $25 ($50 for international students). *Expenses:* Tuition, area resident: Part-time $150 per credit. Tuition, state resident: part-time $150 per credit. Tuition, nonresident: part-time $150 per credit. Required fees: $120 per credit. *Financial support:* In 2009–10, research assistantships with partial tuition reimbursements (averaging $5,500 per year); Federal Work-Study, scholarships/grants, and unspecified assistantships also available. Support available to part-time students. Financial award application deadline: 3/1; financial award applicants required to submit FAFSA. *Unit head:* Dr. Chola Chisunka, Chair, 978-665-3445, Fax: 978-665-3658, E-mail: gce@fsc.edu. *Application contact:* Director of Admissions, 978-665-3144, Fax: 978-665-4540, E-mail: admissions@fsc.edu.

Florida Atlantic University, Dorothy F. Schmidt College of Arts and Letters, Department of English, Boca Raton, FL 33431-0991. Offers British and American literature (MA); creative nonfiction (MFA); creative writing (MA); fiction (MFA); multicultural literatures and literacies (MA); poetry (MFA); science fiction and fantasy (MA); teaching English (MAT). Part-time programs available. *Faculty:* 49 full-time (24 women), 17 part-time/adjunct (7 women). *Students:* 63 full-time (36 women), 28 part-time (21 women); includes 22 minority (6 African Americans, 2 American Indian/Alaska Native, 2 Asian Americans or Pacific Islanders, 12 Hispanic Americans), 1 international. Average age 31. 70 applicants, 54% accepted, 16 enrolled. In 2009, 21 master's awarded. *Degree requirements:* For master's, one foreign language, thesis. *Entrance requirements:* For master's, GRE General Test, minimum GPA of 3.0, writing samples, 2 letters of recommendation. *Application deadline:* For fall admission, 3/1 for domestic students, 2/15 for international students; for spring admission, 11/1 for domestic students, 7/15 for international students. Applications are processed on a rolling basis. Application fee: $30. Electronic applications accepted. *Expenses:* Tuition, state resident: full-time $7055; part-time $293.94 per credit hour. Tuition, nonresident: full-time $22,096; part-time $920.66 per credit hour. *Financial support:* Fellowships, teaching assistantships with partial tuition reimbursements, Federal Work-Study and tuition waivers available. Support available to part-time students. Financial award application deadline: 3/1. *Faculty research:* African-American writers, critical theory, British-American, Asian-American. *Unit head:* Dr. Wenying Xu, Chair, 561-297-2065, Fax: 561-297-3807, E-mail: wxu@fau.edu. *Application contact:* Dr. Andrew Furman, Director of Graduate Studies, 561-297-3835, Fax: 561-297-3807, E-mail: afurman@fau.edu.

Florida Gulf Coast University, College of Arts and Sciences, Program in English, Fort Myers, FL 33965-6565. Offers MA. *Faculty:* 175 full-time (74 women), 139 part-time/adjunct (64 women). *Students:* 11 full-time (5 women), 5 part-time (2 women). Average age 31. 26 applicants, 38% accepted, 4 enrolled. In 2009, 11 master's awarded. *Entrance requirements:* For master's, GRE General Test, minimum GPA of 3.0. Additional exam requirements/recommendations for international students: Required—TOEFL (minimum score 550 paper-based; 213 computer-based). *Application deadline:* For fall admission, 2/15 for domestic students. Application fee: $30. *Unit head:* Joe Wisdom, Chair, 239-590-7157, E-mail: jwisdom@fgcu.edu. *Application contact:* Patricia Rice, Executive Secretary, 239-590-7196, Fax: 239-590-7200, E-mail: price@fgcu.edu.

Florida International University, College of Arts and Sciences, Department of English, Program in English, Miami, FL 33199. Offers literature (MA). Part-time and evening/weekend programs available. *Students:* 10 full-time (8 women), 22 part-time (15 women); includes 25 minority (3 African Americans, 2 Asian Americans or Pacific Islanders, 20 Hispanic Americans). Average age 29. 16 applicants, 44% accepted, 7 enrolled. In 2009, 10 master's awarded. *Degree requirements:* For master's, thesis. *Entrance requirements:* For master's, GRE General Test, minimum GPA of 3.0, letters of recommendation/letter of intent. Additional exam requirements/recommendations for international students: Required—TOEFL (minimum score 550 paper-based; 80 iBT). *Application deadline:* For fall admission, 2/1 for domestic and international students; for spring admission, 10/1 for domestic students, 9/1 for international students. Application fee: $30. Electronic applications accepted. *Expenses:* Tuition, state resident: full-time $8008; part-time $4004 per year. Tuition, nonresident: full-time $20,104; part-time $10,052 per year. Required fees: $298; $149 per term. *Financial support:* Institutionally sponsored loans and scholarships/grants available. Financial award application deadline: 3/1; financial award applicants required to submit FAFSA. *Unit head:* Dr. James Sutton, Chair, English Department, 305-348-2874, Fax: 305-348-3878, E-mail: james.sutton@fiu.edu. *Application contact:* Dr. Asher Milbauer, Director of Graduate Studies in Literature, 305-348-2259, Fax: 305-348-3878, E-mail: milbauer@fiu.edu.

Florida State University, The Graduate School, College of Arts and Sciences, Department of English, Tallahassee, FL 32306. Offers creative writing (MFA); English (PhD), including creative writing, literature, rhetoric and composition; literature (MA); rhetoric and composition (MA). Part-time programs available. *Faculty:* 48 full-time (23 women), 6 part-time/adjunct (1 woman). *Students:* 150 full-time (90 women), 20 part-time (10 women); includes 31 minority (15 African Americans, 1 American Indian/Alaska Native, 5 Asian Americans or Pacific Islanders, 10 Hispanic Americans). Average age 30. 480 applicants, 21% accepted, 58 enrolled. In 2009, 22 master's, 14 doctorates awarded. *Degree requirements:* For master's, one foreign language, thesis or alternative; for doctorate, comprehensive exam, thesis/dissertation, 27 hours of coursework, 24 hours of dissertation work. *Entrance requirements:* For master's and doctorate, GRE General Test, GRE Subject Test (literature only), sample of written work, 3 letters of recommendation, resume. Additional exam requirements/recommendations for international students: Required—TOEFL. *Application deadline:* For fall admission, 1/1 priority date for domestic and international students. Application fee: $30. Electronic applications accepted. *Expenses:* Tuition, state resident: full-time $7413. Tuition, nonresident: full-time $22,567. *Financial support:* In 2009–10, 126 students received support, including 5 fellowships, teaching assistantships (averaging $11,375 per year); career-related internships or fieldwork, Federal Work-Study, and institutionally sponsored loans also available. Financial award application deadline: 1/1; financial award applicants required to submit FAFSA. *Faculty research:* British and Irish literature, American literature, creative writing, rhetoric and composition, multiethnic transnational literature. *Unit head:* Dr. Ralph Berry, Chairman, 850-644-4230, Fax: 850-644-0811, E-mail: rberry@fsu.edu. *Application contact:* Dr. Ralph Berry, Chairman, 850-644-4230, Fax: 850-644-0811, E-mail: rberry@fsu.edu.

Fordham University, Graduate School of Arts and Sciences, Department of English Language and Literature, New York, NY 10458. Offers MA, PhD. Part-time and evening/weekend programs available. *Faculty:* 37 full-time (23 women). *Students:* 33 full-time (26 women), 103 part-time (74 women); includes 14 minority (3 African Americans, 1 American Indian/Alaska Native, 1 Asian American or Pacific Islander, 9 Hispanic Americans), 5 international. Average age 30. 216 applicants, 36% accepted, 30 enrolled. In 2009, 10 master's, 9 doctorates awarded. Terminal master's awarded for partial completion of doctoral program. *Degree requirements:* For master's, one foreign language, comprehensive exam, thesis optional; for doctorate, 2 foreign languages, comprehensive exam, thesis/dissertation. *Entrance requirements:* For master's, GRE General Test; for doctorate, GRE General Test, GRE Subject Test. Additional exam requirements/recommendations for international students: Required—TOEFL (minimum score 650 paper-based; 280 computer-based). *Application deadline:* For fall admission, 1/4 priority date for domestic students; for spring admission, 11/1 for domestic students. Application fee: $70. Electronic applications accepted. *Financial support:* In 2009–10, 63 students received support, including 2 fellowships with tuition reimbursements available (averaging $21,900 per year), 27 research assistantships with tuition reimbursements available (averaging $18,461 per year), 34 teaching assistantships with tuition reimbursements available (averaging $14,917 per year); institutionally sponsored loans, tuition waivers (full and partial), and unspecified assistantships also available. Financial award application deadline: 1/4; financial award applicants required to submit FAFSA. *Faculty research:* Nineteenth century British and American literature, Shakespeare and early modern drama, Aesthetic theory, Old Norse, poetics of race and gender, Anglo-Norman. Total annual research expenditures: $22,000. *Unit head:* Dr. Nicola Pitchford, Chair, 718-817-4007, Fax: 718-817-4010, E-mail: pitchford@fordham.edu. *Application contact:* Charlene Dundie, Director of Graduate Admissions, 718-817-4420, Fax: 718-817-3566, E-mail: dundie@fordham.edu.

Fort Hays State University, Graduate School, College of Arts and Sciences, Department of English, Hays, KS 67601-4099. Offers MA. *Degree requirements:* For master's, comprehensive exam, thesis or alternative. *Entrance requirements:* Additional exam requirements/recommendations for international students: Required—TOEFL (minimum score 550 paper-based; 213 computer-based). Electronic applications accepted. *Faculty research:* Eisenhower and Hansen papers, Celtic literature and culture, poetry of Robert Frost.

Gannon University, School of Graduate Studies, College of Humanities, Education, and Social Sciences, School of Humanities, Program in English, Erie, PA 16541-0001. Offers MA. Part-time and evening/weekend programs available. *Students:* 8 full-time (6 women), 8 part-time (6 women), 2 international. Average age 28. 18 applicants, 89% accepted, 1 enrolled. In 2009, 7 master's awarded. *Degree requirements:* For master's, thesis. *Entrance requirements:* For master's, interview. Additional exam requirements/recommendations for international students: Required—TOEFL (minimum score 79 iBT). *Application deadline:* Applications are processed on a rolling basis. Application fee: $25. Electronic applications accepted. *Expenses:* Tuition: Full-time $13,590; part-time $755 per credit. Required fees: $524; $17 per credit. Tuition and fees vary according to course load, degree level, campus/location and program. *Financial support:* In 2009–10, 5 teaching assistantships (averaging $6,300 per year) were awarded; career-related internships or fieldwork and scholarships/grants also available. Financial award application deadline: 7/1; financial award applicants required to submit FAFSA. *Unit head:* Dr. Penelope Smith, Chair, 814-871-7748, E-mail: smith006@gannon.edu. *Application contact:* Kara Morgan, Assistant Director of Graduate Admissions, 814-871-5831, Fax: 814-871-5827, E-mail: graduate@gannon.edu.

Gardner-Webb University, Graduate School, Department of English, Boiling Springs, NC 28017. Offers English (MA); English education (MA). Part-time and evening/weekend programs available. *Faculty:* 2 full-time (both women), 1 (woman) part-time/adjunct. *Students:* 10 part-time (8 women); includes 3 minority (all African Americans). Average age 35. 4 applicants, 100% accepted, 4 enrolled. In 2009, 1 master's awarded. *Degree requirements:* For master's, comprehensive exam. *Entrance requirements:* For master's, GRE General Test, MAT, or NTE; PRAXIS, minimum GPA of 2.5. *Application deadline:* For fall admission, 8/1 priority date for domestic students. Applications are processed on a rolling basis. Application fee: $25. Electronic applications accepted. *Expenses:* Tuition: Part-time $305 per credit hour. *Financial support:* Unspecified assistantships available. *Unit head:* Dr. June Hobbs, Chair, 704-406-4412, Fax: 704-406-3921, E-mail: jhobbs@gardner-webb.edu. *Application contact:* Dr. Franki Burch, Dean, Graduate School, 704-406-4724, Fax: 704-406-4329, E-mail: gradschool@gardner-webb.edu.

George Mason University, College of Humanities and Social Sciences, Department of English, Fairfax, VA 22030. Offers creative writing (MFA); English (MA); folklore studies (Certificate); linguistics (PhD); professional writing and rhetoric (Certificate); teaching English as a second language (Certificate). *Faculty:* 82 full-time (47 women), 48 part-time/adjunct (29 women). *Students:* 72 full-time (51 women), 228 part-time (172 women); includes 39 minority (12 African Americans, 3 American Indian/Alaska Native, 20 Asian Americans or Pacific Islanders, 4 Hispanic Americans), 10 international. Average age 31. 314 applicants, 57% accepted, 86 enrolled. In 2009, 63 master's, 12 other advanced degrees awarded. *Degree requirements:* For master's, thesis (for some programs), proficiency in a foreign language by course work or translation test. *Entrance requirements:* For master's, 30 credits in graduate English courses, minimum undergraduate GPA of 3.0, 2 letters of recommendation. Additional exam requirements/recommendations for international students: Required—TOEFL. *Application deadline:* For fall admission, 3/15 priority date for domestic students; for spring admission, 10/15 for domestic students. Application fee: $75. Electronic applications accepted. *Expenses:* Tuition, state resident: full-time $7568; part-time $315.33 per credit hour. Tuition, nonresident: full-time $21,704; part-time $904.33 per credit hour. Required fees: $2184; $91 per credit hour. *Financial support:* In 2009–10, 49 students received support, including 1 fellowship with full tuition reimbursement available (averaging $18,000 per year), 3 research assistantships with full and partial tuition reimbursements available (averaging $9,443 per year), 46 teaching assistantships with full and partial tuition reimbursements available (averaging $10,509 per year); Federal Work-Study, scholarships/grants, unspecified assistantships, and health care benefits (full-time research or teaching assistantship recipients) also available. Support available to part-time students. Financial award application deadline: 3/1; financial award applicants required to submit FAFSA. *Faculty research:* Literature, professional writing and editing, writing of fiction or poetry. Total annual research expenditures: $1.2 million. *Unit head:* Robert Matz, Chair, 703-993-1170, E-mail: rmatz@gmu.edu. *Application contact:* Denise Albanese, Graduate Director, 703-993-1175, E-mail: dalbanes@gmu.edu.

Georgetown University, Graduate School of Arts and Sciences, Department of English, Washington, DC 20057. Offers British and American literature (MA). *Degree requirements:* For master's, thesis or alternative, independent study, oral exam. *Entrance requirements:* For master's, GRE General Test. Additional exam requirements/recommendations for international students: Required—TOEFL.

The George Washington University, Columbian College of Arts and Sciences, Department of English, Washington, DC 20052. Offers MA, PhD. Part-time and evening/weekend programs available. *Faculty:* 34 full-time (16 women), 22 part-time/adjunct (12 women). *Students:* 24 full-time (15 women), 26 part-time (23 women); includes 7 minority (2 African Americans, 4 Asian Americans or Pacific Islanders, 1 Hispanic American), 3 international. Average age 29. 126 applicants, 63% accepted, 16 enrolled. In 2009, 2 master's, 2 doctorates awarded. Terminal master's awarded for partial completion of doctoral program. *Degree requirements:* For master's, one foreign language, comprehensive exam, thesis or alternative; for doctorate, 2 foreign languages, thesis/dissertation, general exam. *Entrance requirements:* For master's and doctorate, GRE General Test, GRE Subject Test, minimum GPA of 3.0, writing sample. Additional exam requirements/recommendations for international students: Required—TOEFL (minimum score 550 paper-based; 213 computer-based; 80 iBT). *Application deadline:* For fall admission, 1/15 priority date for domestic and international students; for spring admission, 10/1 priority date for domestic students, 9/1 priority date for international students. Applications are processed on a rolling basis. Application fee: $60. Electronic applications accepted. *Financial support:* In 2009–10, 18 students received support; fellowships with tuition reimbursements available, teaching assistantships with tuition reimbursements available, Federal Work-Study available. Financial award application deadline: 1/15. *Unit head:* Jeffrey Jerome Cohen, Chair, 202-994-6180, E-mail: jjcohen@gwu.edu. *Application contact:* Jeffrey Jerome Cohen, Chair, 202-994-6180, E-mail: jjcohen@gwu.edu.

Georgia College & State University, Graduate School, College of Arts and Sciences, Department of English and Rhetoric, Program in English, Milledgeville, GA 31061. Offers MA. Part-time and evening/weekend programs available. *Students:* 9 full-time (5 women), 5 part-time (3 women); includes 2 minority (both African Americans). Average age 30. 10 applicants, 100% accepted, 7 enrolled. In 2009, 1 master's awarded. *Degree requirements:* For master's, one foreign language, comprehensive exam, thesis optional. *Entrance requirements:* For master's, GRE (minimum score 550 verbal, 4.5 analytical), undergraduate major in English, minimum GPA of 3.0, letters of recommendation. Additional exam requirements/

English

Georgia College & State University (continued)
recommendations for international students: Recommended—TOEFL (minimum score 550 paper-based; 213 computer-based; 79 iBT). *Application deadline:* For fall admission, 7/1 for domestic students, 4/1 priority date for international students; for spring admission, 11/15 for domestic students, 9/1 priority date for international students. Applications are processed on a rolling basis. Application fee: $40. Electronic applications accepted. *Expenses:* Tuition, area resident: Part-time $241 per credit hour. Tuition, state resident: full-time $4338. Tuition, nonresident: full-time $17,352; part-time $964 per credit hour. Required fees: $609 per semester. Tuition and fees vary according to course load and campus/location. *Financial support:* In 2009–10, 3 research assistantships with full tuition reimbursements were awarded; unspecified assistantships also available. Financial award applicants required to submit FAFSA. *Unit head:* Dr. Elaine Whitaker, Chair, Department of English and Rhetoric, 478-445-4581, E-mail: elaine.whitaker@gcsu.edu. *Application contact:* Dr. Elaine Whitaker, Chair, Department of English and Rhetoric, 478-445-4581, E-mail: elaine.whitaker@gcsu.edu.

Georgia Southern University, Jack N. Averitt College of Graduate Studies, College of Liberal Arts and Social Sciences, Department of Literature and Philosophy, Statesboro, GA 30460. Offers English (MA). Part-time programs available. *Students:* 13 full-time (11 women), 7 part-time (4 women); includes 1 minority (African American). Average age 27. 9 applicants, 100% accepted, 6 enrolled. In 2009, 9 master's awarded. *Degree requirements:* For master's, one foreign language, thesis optional, terminal exams. *Entrance requirements:* For master's, GRE General Test, minimum GPA of 3.0, letters of reference. Additional exam requirements/recommendations for international students: Required—TOEFL (minimum score 550 paper-based; 213 computer-based; 80 iBT). *Application deadline:* For fall admission, 3/1 priority date for domestic and international students; for spring admission, 10/1 priority date for domestic students, 10/1 for international students. Applications are processed on a rolling basis. Application fee: $50. Electronic applications accepted. *Expenses:* Tuition, state resident: full-time $5040; part-time $210 per credit hour. Tuition, nonresident: full-time $20,136; part-time $839 per credit hour. Required fees: $1644. *Financial support:* In 2009–10, 16 students received support, including research assistantships with partial tuition reimbursements available (averaging $7,200 per year), teaching assistantships with partial tuition reimbursements available (averaging $7,200 per year); career-related internships or fieldwork, Federal Work-Study, scholarships/grants, tuition waivers (partial), and unspecified assistantships also available. Support available to part-time students. Financial award application deadline: 4/15; financial award applicants required to submit FAFSA. *Faculty research:* The fiction of Nuguib Mahfouz and Shusako Enato, a book-length collection of essays on playwright Paula Vogel, a critical edition of math, Gregory Lewis' Tales of Wonder (1800), the dramatic works of English poet John Dryden, post modern childhoods, post modern poetries. *Unit head:* David Dudley, Chair, 912-478-5471, Fax: 912-478-0653, E-mail: dldudley@georgiasouthern.edu. *Application contact:* Dr. Charles Ziglar, Coordinator for Graduate Student Recruitment, 912-478-5635, Fax: 912-478-0740, E-mail: gradadmissions@georgiasouthern.edu.

Georgia State University, College of Arts and Sciences, Department of English, Atlanta, GA 30302-3083. Offers creative writing (MA, MFA, PhD), including fiction/poetry; English (MA, PhD); fiction (MFA); literary studies (MA, PhD); poetry (MFA); rhetoric and composition (MA, PhD). Part-time and evening/weekend programs available. *Degree requirements:* For master's, variable foreign language requirement, thesis; for doctorate, one foreign language, comprehensive exam, thesis/dissertation, second exam. *Entrance requirements:* For master's and doctorate, GRE General Test. Additional exam requirements/recommendations for international students: Required—TOEFL (minimum score 0 paper-based; 0 computer-based). Electronic applications accepted. *Faculty research:* Literature, theory, culture, rhetoric/composition, professional/technical writing.

Governors State University, College of Arts and Sciences, Program in English, University Park, IL 60466-0975. Offers MA. Part-time and evening/weekend programs available. *Degree requirements:* For master's, thesis or alternative. *Entrance requirements:* For master's, bachelor's degree in related field.

Graduate School and University Center of the City University of New York, Graduate Studies, Program in English, New York, NY 10016-4039. Offers PhD. *Faculty:* 51 full-time (13 women). *Students:* 286 full-time (176 women), 1 (woman) part-time; includes 32 minority (8 African Americans, 2 American Indian/Alaska Native, 12 Asian Americans or Pacific Islanders, 10 Hispanic Americans), 24 international. Average age 35. 241 applicants, 31% accepted, 31 enrolled. In 2009, 27 doctorates awarded. *Degree requirements:* For doctorate, 2 foreign languages, thesis/dissertation. *Entrance requirements:* For doctorate, GRE General Test, GRE Subject Test, writing sample, curriculum vitae. Additional exam requirements/recommendations for international students: Required—TOEFL. *Application deadline:* For fall admission, 1/1 for domestic students. Application fee: $125. Electronic applications accepted. *Financial support:* In 2009–10, 201 students received support, including 163 fellowships, 29 research assistantships, 27 teaching assistantships; career-related internships or fieldwork, Federal Work-Study, institutionally sponsored loans, and tuition waivers (full and partial) also available. Financial award application deadline: 2/1; financial award applicants required to submit FAFSA. *Unit head:* Dr. Steven Kruger, Executive Officer, 212-817-8352, Fax: 212-817-1518. *Application contact:* Les Gribben, Director of Admissions, 212-817-7470, Fax: 212-817-1624, E-mail: lgribben@gc.cuny.edu.

Grambling State University, School of Graduate Studies and Research, College of Education, Department of Educational Leadership, Grambling, LA 71245. Offers curriculum and instruction (Ed D); developmental education (MS, Ed D), including curriculum and instruction: reading (Ed D), English (MS), guidance and counseling (MS), higher education administration (Ed D), instructional systems and technology (Ed D), mathematics (MS), reading (MS), science (MS), student development and personnel services (Ed D); educational leadership (MS, Ed D). Part-time and evening/weekend programs available. *Faculty:* 19 full-time (12 women). *Students:* 23 full-time (18 women), 84 part-time (62 women); includes 81 minority (80 African Americans, 1 Asian American or Pacific Islander), 5 international. Average age 39. 72 applicants, 75% accepted, 39 enrolled. In 2009, 5 master's, 9 doctorates awarded. *Degree requirements:* For master's, comprehensive exam, thesis (for some programs); for doctorate, comprehensive exam, thesis/dissertation. *Entrance requirements:* For master's, GRE, minimum GPA of 2.5 on last degree; for doctorate, GRE (minimum 1000, 500 on Verbal), master's degree, minimum GPA of 3.0 on last degree. Additional exam requirements/recommendations for international students: Required—TOEFL (minimum score 500 paper-based; 173 computer-based; 61 iBT). *Application deadline:* For fall admission, 7/1 for domestic and international students; for spring admission, 12/1 for domestic and international students. Applications are processed on a rolling basis. Application fee: $20 ($30 for international students). Electronic applications accepted. *Expenses:* Tuition, state resident: full-time $2610. Tuition, nonresident: full-time $2610. *Financial support:* In 2009–10, 5 research assistantships (averaging $10,948 per year) were awarded; health care benefits, tuition waivers (full), and unspecified assistantships also available. Financial award application deadline: 5/31; financial award applicants required to submit FAFSA. *Unit head:* Dr. Olatunde Ogunyemi, Director, 318-274-6105, Fax: 318-274-2799, E-mail: ogunyemio@gram.edu. *Application contact:* Laketha Richards, Administrative Assistant III, 318-274-6105, Fax: 318-274-6249, E-mail: richardsl@gram.edu.

Grand Valley State University, College of Liberal Arts and Sciences, English Department, Allendale, MI 49401-9403. Offers MA. *Faculty:* 9 full-time (5 women), 9 part-time/adjunct (5 women). *Students:* 7 full-time (6 women), 32 part-time (18 women). Average age 33. 9 applicants, 67% accepted, 4 enrolled. In 2009, 5 master's awarded. *Entrance requirements:* Additional exam requirements/recommendations for international students: Required—TOEFL. Application fee: $30. *Expenses:* Tuition, state resident: part-time $471 per credit hour. Tuition, nonresident: part-time $646 per credit hour. Tuition and fees vary according to course level. *Financial support:* In 2009–10, 3 students received support, including 3 research assistantships with full and partial tuition reimbursements available (averaging $7,730 per year). *Faculty research:* Literary history, philosophy and literature, feminist issues in literature. *Unit head:* Dr. Jill VanAntwerp, Chair, 616-331-3405, E-mail: vanantwj@gvsu.edu. *Application contact:* Dr. Ben Lockerd, Information Contact, 616-331-3575, E-mail: lockerdb@gvsu.edu.

Hardin-Simmons University, Graduate School, Cynthia Ann Parker College of Liberal Arts, Department of English, Abilene, TX 79698-0001. Offers MA. Part-time programs available. *Faculty:* 5 full-time (1 woman), 1 part-time/adjunct (0 women). *Students:* 2 full-time (both women), 4 part-time (all women); includes 1 minority (African American). Average age 29. 1 applicant, 100% accepted, 1 enrolled. In 2009, 1 master's awarded. *Degree requirements:* For master's, one foreign language, comprehensive exam, thesis or alternative. *Entrance requirements:* For master's, minimum undergraduate GPA of 3.0 in English, 2.7 overall; writing sample; letters of recommendation; interview. Additional exam requirements/recommendations for international students: Required—TOEFL (minimum score 550 paper-based; 213 computer-based; 75 iBT). *Application deadline:* For fall admission, 8/15 priority date for domestic students, 4/1 for international students; for spring admission, 1/5 priority date for domestic students, 9/1 for international students. Applications are processed on a rolling basis. Application fee: $50. *Expenses:* Tuition: Full-time $11,430; part-time $635 per credit hour. Required fees: $650; $110 per semester. Tuition and fees vary according to degree level. *Financial support:* In 2009–10, 3 students received support, including 1 fellowship (averaging $3,000 per year); scholarships/grants also available. Support available to part-time students. Financial award application deadline: 6/30; financial award applicants required to submit FAFSA. *Faculty research:* Milton, Tennyson, American Romantic period, Derek Walcott, women's literature. *Unit head:* Dr. Laura Pogue, Program Director, 325-670-1366, Fax: 325-670-5859, E-mail: lpogue@hsutx.edu. *Application contact:* Dr. Gary Stanlake, Dean of Graduate Studies, 325-670-1298, Fax: 325-670-1564, E-mail: gradoff@hsutx.edu.

Harvard University, Extension School, Cambridge, MA 02138-3722. Offers applied sciences (CAS); biotechnology (ALM); educational technologies (ALM); educational technology (CET); English for graduate and professional studies (DGP); environmental management (ALM, CEM); information technology (ALM); journalism (ALM); liberal arts (ALM); management (ALM, CM); mathematics for teaching (ALM); museum studies (ALM); premedical studies (Diploma); publication and communication (CPC). Part-time and evening/weekend programs available. *Degree requirements:* For master's, thesis. *Entrance requirements:* For master's, 3 completed graduate courses with grade of B or higher. Additional exam requirements/recommendations for international students: Required—TOEFL (minimum score 600 paper-based; 250 computer-based), TWE (minimum score 5). *Expenses:* Contact institution.

Harvard University, Graduate School of Arts and Sciences, Department of English and American Literature and Language, Cambridge, MA 02138. Offers critical theory (PhD); eighteenth-century literature (PhD); literature: nineteenth-century to the present (PhD); medieval literature and language (PhD); modern British and American literature (PhD); Renaissance literature (PhD). Terminal master's awarded for partial completion of doctoral program. *Degree requirements:* For doctorate, 2 foreign languages, thesis/dissertation, oral exam. *Entrance requirements:* For doctorate, GRE General Test, GRE Subject Test, writing sample. Additional exam requirements/recommendations for international students: Required—TOEFL. *Expenses:* Tuition: Full-time $33,696. Required fees: $1126. Full-time tuition and fees vary according to program. *Faculty research:* Old and Middle English language and literature, drama, creative writing, transition to Romanticism, history and theory of criticism.

Heritage University, Graduate Programs in Education, Program in Professional Studies, Toppenish, WA 98948-9599. Offers bilingual education/ESL (M Ed); biology (M Ed); English and literature (M Ed); reading/literacy (M Ed); special education (M Ed). Part-time and evening/weekend programs available. *Degree requirements:* For master's, comprehensive exam (for some programs), thesis (for some programs).

Hofstra University, College of Liberal Arts and Sciences, Department of English, Hempstead, NY 11549. Offers English and creative writing (MA); English literature (MA). Part-time programs available. *Faculty:* 12 full-time (3 women), 1 part-time/adjunct (0 women). *Students:* 23 full-time (16 women), 12 part-time (9 women); includes 3 minority (1 African American, 1 Asian American or Pacific Islander, 1 Hispanic American). Average age 27. 28 applicants, 82% accepted, 14 enrolled. In 2009, 18 master's awarded. *Degree requirements:* For master's, thesis optional. *Entrance requirements:* For master's, writing sample, minimum GPA of 3.0 in literature courses. Additional exam requirements/recommendations for international students: Required—TOEFL (minimum score 550 paper-based; 213 computer-based; 80 iBT). *Application deadline:* Applications are processed on a rolling basis. Application fee: $60. Electronic applications accepted. *Expenses:* Tuition: Full-time $16,200; part-time $900 per credit hour. Required fees: $970; $145 per term. Tuition and fees vary according to program. *Financial support:* In 2009–10, 22 students received support, including 2 fellowships with full and partial tuition reimbursements available (averaging $3,250 per year), 1 research assistantship with full and partial tuition reimbursement available (averaging $21,930 per year); Federal Work-Study, institutionally sponsored loans, scholarships/grants, and tuition waivers (full and partial) also available. Support available to part-time students. Financial award applicants required to submit FAFSA. *Faculty research:* Herman Melville, disability studies, early American literature, Queer Theory, twentieth century popular culture. *Unit head:* Dr. Joseph A. Fichtelberg, Chairperson, 516-463-5455, Fax: 516-463-6395, E-mail: engjaf@hofstra.edu. *Application contact:* Carol Drummer, Dean of Graduate Admissions, 516-463-4876, Fax: 516-463-4664, E-mail: gradstudent@hofstra.edu.

Hollins University, Graduate Programs, Program in Children's Literature, Roanoke, VA 24020-1603. Offers MA, MFA. Offered during summer only. Part-time programs available. *Faculty:* 11 part-time/adjunct (7 women). *Students:* 66 full-time (62 women), 7 part-time (all women); includes 6 minority (4 African Americans, 1 American Indian/Alaska Native, 1 Hispanic American), 4 international. Average age 34. 49 applicants, 88% accepted, 25 enrolled. In 2009, 14 master's awarded. *Degree requirements:* For master's, one foreign language, comprehensive exam, thesis. *Entrance requirements:* For master's, letters of recommendation, portfolio. Additional exam requirements/recommendations for international students: Required—TOEFL (minimum score 550 paper-based; 213 computer-based; 79 iBT). *Application deadline:* For fall admission, 2/15 for domestic and international students. Application fee: $40. Electronic applications accepted. *Expenses:* Tuition: Full-time $27,780; part-time $295 per contact hour. Required fees: $280; $70 per unit. Part-time tuition and fees vary according to course load and program. *Financial support:* In 2009–10, 30 students received support, including 24 fellowships (averaging $823 per year); Federal Work-Study, scholarships/grants, and unspecified assistantships also available. Support available to part-time students. Financial award application deadline: 2/15; financial award applicants required to submit FAFSA. *Faculty research:* Fantasy, children's film, young adult fiction, gender studies, mythology and folk tales, children's poetry, picture books. *Unit head:* Amanda Cockrell, Director, 540-362-6024, Fax: 540-362-6642, E-mail: acockrell@hollins.edu. *Application contact:* Cathy S. Koon, Manager of Graduate Services, 540-362-6326, Fax: 540-362-6288, E-mail: ckoon@hollins.edu.

Howard University, Graduate School, Department of English, Washington, DC 20059-0002. Offers MA, PhD. Part-time programs available. *Degree requirements:* For master's, one foreign language, comprehensive exam, thesis; for doctorate, 2 foreign languages, comprehensive exam, thesis/dissertation, qualifying exam. *Entrance requirements:* For master's, GRE General Test, minimum GPA of 3.0; for doctorate, GRE General Test.

Humboldt State University, Graduate Studies, College of Arts, Humanities, and Social Sciences, Department of English, Arcata, CA 95521-8299. Offers English (MA), including international program, literature, teaching of writing. *Students:* 19 full-time (13 women), 6 part-time (5 women); includes 1 minority (Hispanic American). Average age 32. 20 applicants, 55% accepted, 9 enrolled. In 2009, 15 master's awarded. *Degree requirements:* For master's, one foreign language, thesis or alternative, qualifying exam. *Entrance requirements:* For master's, GRE, minimum GPA of 3.0, 3 letters of recommendation, sample of writing. Additional exam requirements/recommendations for international students: Required—TOEFL (minimum score 500 paper-based; 173 computer-based). *Application deadline:* For fall admission, 3/1 for domestic students; for spring admission, 11/1 for domestic students. Applications are processed on a rolling basis. Application fee: $55. *Expenses:* Tuition, nonresident: full-time $8928. Required fees: $6102. Tuition and fees vary according to program. *Financial support:* Teaching assistantships, career-related internships or fieldwork, Federal Work-Study, and institutionally sponsored loans available. Financial award application deadline: 3/1; financial award applicants required to submit FAFSA. *Faculty research:* Teaching of writing, literature. *Unit head:* Dr. Susan Bennett, Chair, 707-826-3758, Fax: 707-826-5939, E-mail: sgb1@humboldt.edu. *Application contact:* Dr. Michael S. Eldridge, Graduate Coordinator, 707-826-5906, Fax: 707-826-5939, E-mail: me2@humboldt.edu.

Hunter College of the City University of New York, Graduate School, School of Arts and Sciences, Department of English, Program in British and American Literature, New York, NY 10021-5085. Offers MA. Part-time and evening/weekend programs available. *Faculty:* 24 full-time (10 women), 3 part-time/adjunct (2 women). *Students:* 1 (woman) full-time, 63 part-time (41 women); includes 7 minority (4 African Americans, 1 Asian American or Pacific Islander, 2 Hispanic Americans). Average age 33. 70 applicants, 56% accepted, 19 enrolled. In 2009, 19 master's awarded. *Degree requirements:* For master's, one foreign language, comprehensive exam, thesis, essay. *Entrance requirements:* For master's, GRE General Test, minimum 18 credits of course work in English, excluding journalism and writing. Additional exam requirements/recommendations for international students: Required—TOEFL. *Application deadline:* For fall admission, 4/1 for domestic students, 2/1 for international students; for spring admission, 11/1 for domestic students, 9/1 for international students. Application fee: $125. *Expenses:* Tuition, state resident: full-time $7360; part-time $310 per credit. Required fees: $250 per semester. *Financial support:* Federal Work-Study and tuition waivers (partial) available. Support available to part-time students. Financial award application deadline: 4/15. *Unit head:* Dr. Christina Alfar, Associate Professor, 212-772-5187, E-mail: calfar@hunter.cuny.edu. *Application contact:* David Carlson, Education Adviser, 212-772-5074, E-mail: dcarlson@hunter.cuny.edu.

Idaho State University, Office of Graduate Studies, College of Arts and Sciences, Department of English, Pocatello, ID 83209-8056. Offers English (MA, DA); English and the teaching of English (PhD); TESOL (Post-Master's Certificate). Part-time programs available. *Faculty:* 20 full-time (7 women). *Students:* 29 full-time (16 women), 37 part-time (22 women); includes 4 minority (1 Asian American or Pacific Islander, 3 Hispanic Americans), 5 international. Average age 37. In 2009, 6 master's, 2 doctorates, 2 other advanced degrees awarded. *Degree requirements:* For master's, one foreign language, comprehensive exam, thesis optional; for doctorate, one foreign language, comprehensive exam, thesis/dissertation, 2 papers, 2 teaching internships; for Post-Master's Certificate, 6 credits of elective linguistics, practicum. *Entrance requirements:* For master's, GRE General Test (minimum 50th percentile verbal), general literature exam, minimum GPA of 3.0, 3 letters of recommendation, 5-page writing sample; for doctorate, GRE General Test, GRE Subject Test, minimum GPA of 3.5, writing examples, 3 letters of recommendation, master's degree in English; for Post-Master's Certificate, GRE (minimum 35th percentile on verbal section), bachelor's degree, minimum undergraduate GPA of 3.0 in last 2 years, 3 letters of recommendation, knowledge of second language. Additional exam requirements/recommendations for international students: Required—TOEFL (minimum score 550 paper-based; 213 computer-based; 80 iBT). *Application deadline:* For fall admission, 7/1 for domestic students, 6/1 for international students; for spring admission, 12/1 for domestic students, 11/1 for international students. Applications are processed on a rolling basis. Application fee: $55. Electronic applications accepted. *Expenses:* Tuition, state resident: full-time $3318; part-time $297 per credit hour. Tuition, nonresident: full-time $13,120; part-time $437 per credit hour. Required fees: $2530. Tuition and fees vary according to program. *Financial support:* In 2009–10, 7 fellowships with full and partial tuition reimbursements (averaging $12,282 per year), 2 research assistantships (averaging $9,401 per year), 9 teaching assistantships with full and partial tuition reimbursements (averaging $10,841 per year) were awarded; career-related internships or fieldwork, Federal Work-Study, institutionally sponsored loans, scholarships/grants, health care benefits, tuition waivers (full and partial), and unspecified assistantships also available. Support available to part-time students. Financial award application deadline: 1/1; financial award applicants required to submit FAFSA. *Faculty research:* American literature, Renaissance literature, composition and rhetoric, Intermountain West studies, ethics. *Unit head:* Dr. Margaret Johnson, Department Chair, 208-282-3207, Fax: 208-282-4472, E-mail: johnmarg@isu.edu. *Application contact:* Tami Carson, Graduate School Technical Records Specialist, 208-282-2150, Fax: 208-282-4847, E-mail: carstami@isu.edu.

Illinois State University, Graduate School, College of Arts and Sciences, Department of English, Program in English, Normal, IL 61790-2200. Offers English (MA, MS); English studies (PhD). *Degree requirements:* For doctorate, thesis/dissertation, 2 terms of residency. *Entrance requirements:* For master's, GRE General Test, minimum GPA of 3.0 in last 60 hours; for doctorate, GRE General Test.

Indiana State University, School of Graduate Studies, College of Arts and Sciences, Department of English, Terre Haute, IN 47809. Offers English teaching (MA); history (MA); literature (MA). Part-time and evening/weekend programs available. *Degree requirements:* For master's, one foreign language, thesis optional. *Entrance requirements:* For master's, minimum GPA of 2.75 in all English courses above freshman level. Additional exam requirements/recommendations for international students: Required—TOEFL (minimum score 550 paper-based). Electronic applications accepted.

Indiana University Bloomington, University Graduate School, College of Arts and Sciences, Department of English, Bloomington, IN 47405-7000. Offers composition, literacy, and culture (PhD); creative writing (MA, MFA), including fiction, poetry; language (MA); literature (MA, PhD); writing (MA). Part-time programs available. *Faculty:* 51 full-time (23 women). *Students:* 221 full-time (139 women), 10 part-time (5 women); includes 27 minority (7 African Americans, 11 Asian Americans or Pacific Islanders, 9 Hispanic Americans), 9 international. Average age 30. 602 applicants, 15% accepted, 47 enrolled. In 2009, 21 master's, 9 doctorates awarded. Terminal master's awarded for partial completion of doctoral program. *Degree requirements:* For master's, one foreign language, thesis (for some programs); for doctorate, 2 foreign languages, thesis/dissertation, qualifying exam. *Entrance requirements:* For master's, GRE General Test, GRE Subject Test (for all but MFA and MA in creative writing), minimum GPA of 3.5; for doctorate, GRE General Test, GRE Subject Test, minimum GPA of 3.7. Additional exam requirements/recommendations for international students: Required—TOEFL. *Application deadline:* For fall admission, 1/15 priority date for domestic students, 12/15 for international students. Application fee: $55 ($65 for international students). Electronic applications accepted. *Financial support:* In 2009–10, 15 fellowships with full and partial tuition reimbursements (averaging $15,000 per year), 152 teaching assistantships with full tuition reimbursements (averaging $15,000 per year) were awarded; research assistantships with partial tuition reimbursements, career-related internships or fieldwork and health care benefits also available. Financial award application deadline: 2/1. *Unit head:* George Hutchinson, Chair, 812-855-8225, E-mail: gbhutchi@indiana.edu. *Application contact:* Patricia Ingham, Director of Admissions, 812-855-0521, Fax: 812-855-9535, E-mail: pingham@indiana.edu.

Indiana University of Pennsylvania, School of Graduate Studies and Research, College of Humanities and Social Sciences, Department of English, Program in Composition and Teaching English to Speakers of Other Languages, Indiana, PA 15705-1087. Offers composition and teaching English to speakers of other languages (PhD); teaching English (MAT); teaching English to speakers of other languages (MA). *Faculty:* 27 full-time (15 women). *Students:* 73 full-time (48 women), 142 part-time (95 women); includes 10 minority (2 African Americans, 6 Asian Americans or Pacific Islanders, 2 Hispanic Americans), 63 international. Average age 36. 203 applicants, 36% accepted, 45 enrolled. In 2009, 20 master's, 12 doctorates awarded. *Degree requirements:* For master's, thesis optional; for doctorate, one foreign language, comprehensive exam, thesis/dissertation. *Entrance requirements:* For master's and doctorate, 2 letters of recommendation. Additional exam requirements/recommendations for international students: Required—TOEFL. *Application deadline:* For fall admission, 7/1 priority date for domestic students; for spring admission, 11/1 for domestic students. Applications are processed on a rolling basis. Application fee: $40. *Expenses:* Tuition, state resident: full-time $6666; part-time $370 per credit hour. Tuition, nonresident: full-time $10,666; part-time $593 per credit hour. Required fees: $813 per semester. *Financial support:* In 2009–10, 4 fellowships (averaging $938 per year), 22 research assistantships with full and partial tuition reimbursements (averaging $5,922 per year), 8 teaching assistantships with partial tuition reimbursements (averaging $17,498 per year) were awarded. Financial award application deadline: 3/15; financial award applicants required to submit FAFSA. *Unit head:* Dr. Ben Rafoth, Graduate Coordinator, 724-357-2272. *Application contact:* Dr. Ben Rafoth, Graduate Coordinator, 724-357-2272.

Indiana University of Pennsylvania, School of Graduate Studies and Research, College of Humanities and Social Sciences, Department of English, Program in Literature and Criticism, Indiana, PA 15705-1087. Offers generalist (MA); literature (MA); literature and criticism (PhD). *Faculty:* 31 full-time (17 women). *Students:* 60 full-time (32 women), 90 part-time (46 women); includes 5 minority (3 African Americans, 1 Asian American or Pacific Islander, 1 Hispanic American), 33 international. Average age 34. 123 applicants, 49% accepted, 37 enrolled. In 2009, 20 master's, 16 doctorates awarded. *Degree requirements:* For master's, thesis optional; for doctorate, one foreign language, comprehensive exam, thesis/dissertation. *Entrance requirements:* For master's and doctorate, 2 letters of recommendation. Additional exam requirements/recommendations for international students: Required—TOEFL. *Application deadline:* For fall admission, 7/1 priority date for domestic students; for spring admission, 11/1 for domestic students. Applications are processed on a rolling basis. Application fee: $40. *Expenses:* Tuition, state resident: full-time $6666; part-time $370 per credit hour. Tuition, nonresident: full-time $10,666; part-time $593 per credit hour. Required fees: $813 per semester. *Financial support:* In 2009–10, 7 fellowships (averaging $1,750 per year), 18 research assistantships with full and partial tuition reimbursements (averaging $6,036 per year), 9 teaching assistantships with partial tuition reimbursements (averaging $13,360 per year) were awarded. Financial award application deadline: 3/15; financial award applicants required to submit FAFSA. *Unit head:* Dr. David Downing, Graduate Coordinator, 724-357-3963, E-mail: david.downing@iup.edu. *Application contact:* Dr. David Downing, Graduate Coordinator, 724-357-3963, E-mail: david.downing@iup.edu.

Indiana University–Purdue University Fort Wayne, College of Arts and Sciences, Department of English and Linguistics, Fort Wayne, IN 46805-1499. Offers English (MA, MAT); TENL (teaching English as a new language) (Certificate). Part-time programs available. *Faculty:* 28 full-time (14 women). *Students:* 8 full-time (5 women), 23 part-time (14 women); includes 2 minority (both Asian Americans or Pacific Islanders). Average age 35. 14 applicants, 100% accepted, 14 enrolled. In 2009, 10 master's, 2 other advanced degrees awarded. *Degree requirements:* For master's, one foreign language, thesis (for some programs), teaching certificate (MAT). *Entrance requirements:* For master's, GRE General Test, minimum GPA of 3.0, major or minor in English, 3 letters of recommendation; for Certificate, bachelor's degree with minimum GPA of 2.5. Additional exam requirements/recommendations for international students: Required—TOEFL (minimum score 600 paper-based; 260 computer-based). *Application deadline:* For fall admission, 8/1 for domestic students; for spring admission, 10/15 for domestic students. Applications are processed on a rolling basis. Application fee: $50. *Expenses:* Tuition, state resident: full-time $4595; part-time $255 per credit. Tuition, nonresident: full-time $10,963; part-time $609 per credit. Required fees: $528; $29.35 per credit. Tuition and fees vary according to course load. *Financial support:* In 2009–10, 13 teaching assistantships with partial tuition reimbursements (averaging $12,740 per year) were awarded; career-related internships or fieldwork, scholarships/grants, and unspecified assistantships also available. Support available to part-time students. Financial award application deadline: 3/1; financial award applicants required to submit FAFSA. *Faculty research:* Shakespeare, three-volume novels, poetry of Nikola Vaptsarov, philanthropy. Total annual research expenditures: $52,321. *Unit head:* Dr. Hardin Aasand, Chair and Professor, 260-481-6750, Fax: 260-481-6985, E-mail: aasandh@ipfw.edu. *Application contact:* Dr. Michael Stapleton, Graduate Program Director, 260-481-6772, Fax: 260-481-6985, E-mail: stapletm@ipfw.edu.

Indiana University–Purdue University Indianapolis, School of Liberal Arts, Department of English, Indianapolis, IN 46202-2896. Offers English (MA); teaching English (MA). *Faculty:* 20 full-time (8 women). *Students:* 22 full-time (17 women), 27 part-time (19 women); includes 4 minority (1 American Indian/Alaska Native, 3 Asian Americans or Pacific Islanders), 1 international. Average age 34. 21 applicants, 90% accepted, 6 enrolled. In 2009, 10 master's awarded. *Entrance requirements:* For master's, GRE. Application fee: $55 ($65 for international students). *Financial support:* In 2009–10, 2 fellowships (averaging $10,000 per year), 12 teaching assistantships (averaging $7,103 per year) were awarded; research assistantships, career-related internships or fieldwork also available. *Unit head:* Susanmarie Harrington, Chair, 317-278-1153. *Application contact:* Susanmarie Harrington, Chair, 317-278-1153.

Indiana University South Bend, College of Liberal Arts and Sciences, South Bend, IN 46634-7111. Offers applied mathematics and computer science (MS); applied psychology (MA); English (MA); liberal studies (MLS). Part-time and evening/weekend programs available. *Faculty:* 79 full-time (33 women). *Students:* 27 full-time (10 women), 83 part-time (55 women); includes 17 minority (10 African Americans, 2 American Indian/Alaska Native, 2 Asian Americans or Pacific Islanders, 3 Hispanic Americans), 10 international. Average age 36. In 2009, 24 master's awarded. *Degree requirements:* For master's, thesis (for some programs). *Entrance requirements:* For master's, minimum GPA of 3.0. Additional exam requirements/recommendations for international students: Required—TOEFL. *Application deadline:* For fall admission, 7/31 priority date for domestic students, 7/1 priority date for international students; for spring admission, 3/31 priority date for domestic students, 11/1 priority date for international students. Applications are processed on a rolling basis. Application fee: $46 ($58 for international students). *Financial support:* In 2009–10, 5 students received support, including 5 teaching assistantships; Federal Work-Study also available. Support available to part-time students. *Faculty research:* Artificial intelligence, bioinformatics, English language and literature, creative writing, computer networks. Total annual research expenditures: $127,000. *Unit head:* Dr. Lynn R. Williams, Dean, 574-520-4322, Fax: 574-520-4528, E-mail: lwilliam@iusb.edu. *Application contact:* Dr. Lynn R. Williams, Dean, 574-520-4322, Fax: 574-520-4528, E-mail: lwilliam@iusb.edu.

Inter American University of Puerto Rico, Metropolitan Campus, Graduate Programs, Program in English, San Juan, PR 00919-1293. Offers MA.

Iona College, School of Arts and Science, Department of English, New Rochelle, NY 10801-1890. Offers MA. Part-time and evening/weekend programs available. *Faculty:* 13 full-time (7 women). *Students:* 4 full-time (3 women), 18 part-time (10 women); includes 2 minority (both African Americans). Average age 32. 7 applicants, 71% accepted, 5 enrolled. In 2009, 2 master's awarded. *Degree requirements:* For master's, one foreign language, thesis or alternative. *Entrance requirements:* For master's, minimum GPA of 3.0. Additional exam requirements/recommendations for international students: Required—TOEFL (minimum score 550 paper-based; 213 computer-based). *Application deadline:* Applications are processed on a rolling basis. Application fee: $50. Electronic applications accepted. *Expenses:* Tuition: Part-time $830 per credit. *Financial support:* Tuition waivers (partial) and unspecified assistantships available. Support available to part-time students. Financial award application deadline: 4/15; financial award applicants required to submit FAFSA. *Faculty research:* Victorian fiction, women's studies, nineteenth century American literature, Irish literature, Shakespeare. *Unit head:* Dr. Laura Shea, Chair, 914-637-2723, E-mail: lshea@iona.edu. *Application contact:* Veronica Jarek-Prinz, Director of Graduate Admissions, 914-633-2420, Fax: 914-633-2277, E-mail: vjarekprinz@iona.edu.

Iowa State University of Science and Technology, Graduate College, College of Liberal Arts and Sciences, Department of English, Ames, IA 50011. Offers creative writing (MFA); English (MA); rhetoric and professional communication (PhD). *Faculty:* 53 full-time (26 women), 8 part-time/adjunct (6 women). *Students:* 105 full-time (68 women), 25 part-time (17 women); includes 3 minority (all Hispanic Americans), 28 international. 99 applicants, 62% accepted, 39 enrolled. In 2009, 30 master's, 3 doctorates awarded. *Degree requirements:* For master's, thesis or alternative; for doctorate, thesis/dissertation. *Entrance requirements:* For master's, GRE General Test, sample of written work, resume, portfolio in creative writing; for doctorate,

English

Iowa State University of Science and Technology (continued)

GRE General Test, sample of written work, resume. Additional exam requirements/recommendations for international students: Required—TOEFL (minimum score 600 paper-based; 100 iBT) or IELTS (minimum score 7). *Application deadline:* For fall admission, 1/5 priority date for domestic and international students. Application fee: $40 ($90 for international students). Electronic applications accepted. *Expenses:* Tuition, state resident: full-time $6716. Tuition, nonresident: full-time $8908. Tuition and fees vary according to course level, course load, program and student level. *Financial support:* In 2009–10, 10 research assistantships with full and partial tuition reimbursements (averaging $18,120 per year), 84 teaching assistantships with full and partial tuition reimbursements (averaging $18,120 per year) were awarded; fellowships, scholarships/grants, health care benefits, and unspecified assistantships also available. *Faculty research:* Creative writing, literature, rhetoric, composition and professional communication, teaching English as a second language, applied linguistics. *Unit head:* Dr. Charles Kostelnick, Chair, 515-294-2477, Fax: 515-294-2125, E-mail: englgrad@iastate.edu. *Application contact:* Dr. Constance Post, Director of Graduate Education, 515-294-3175, E-mail: englgrad@iastate.edu.

Jackson State University, Graduate School, School of Liberal Arts, Department of English and Modern Foreign Languages, Jackson, MS 39217. Offers English (MA); teaching English (MAT). Part-time and evening/weekend programs available. *Degree requirements:* For master's, comprehensive exam, thesis or alternative. *Entrance requirements:* For master's, GRE General Test. Additional exam requirements/recommendations for international students: Required—TOEFL.

Jacksonville State University, College of Graduate Studies and Continuing Education, College of Arts and Sciences, Department of English, Jacksonville, AL 36265-1602. Offers MA. Part-time and evening/weekend programs available. *Faculty:* 5 full-time (2 women). *Students:* 4 full-time (all women), 15 part-time (13 women); includes 3 minority (2 African Americans, 1 Hispanic American). Average age 27. 11 applicants, 64% accepted, 7 enrolled. In 2009, 7 master's awarded. *Degree requirements:* For master's, comprehensive exam, thesis (for some programs). *Entrance requirements:* For master's, GRE General Test or MAT. *Application deadline:* Applications are processed on a rolling basis. Application fee: $30. Electronic applications accepted. *Financial support:* In 2009–10, 18 students received support. Available to part-time students. Application deadline: 4/1. *Unit head:* Dr. Robert Felgar, Head, 256-782-5413. *Application contact:* Dr. Jean Pugliese, Associate Dean, 256-782-8278, Fax: 256-782-5321, E-mail: pugliese@jsu.edu.

James Madison University, The Graduate School, College of Arts and Letters, Department of English, Harrisonburg, VA 22807. Offers MA. Part-time programs available. *Faculty:* 8 full-time (6 women). *Students:* 14 full-time (7 women), 6 part-time (all women); includes 2 minority (both African Americans). Average age 27. In 2009, 5 master's awarded. *Degree requirements:* For master's, one foreign language, thesis, reading exam in languages, formal exam based on required reading list. *Entrance requirements:* For master's, GRE General Test, GRE Subject Test, 2 letters of recommendation, writing sample. Additional exam requirements/recommendations for international students: Required—TOEFL. *Application deadline:* For fall admission, 2/10 priority date for domestic students. Applications are processed on a rolling basis. Application fee: $55. Electronic applications accepted. *Expenses:* Tuition, area resident: Part-time $305 per credit hour. Tuition, state resident: part-time $305 per credit hour. Tuition, nonresident: part-time $890 per credit hour. *Financial support:* In 2009–10, 8 students received support, including 7 teaching assistantships with full tuition reimbursements available (averaging $8,664 per year); Federal Work-Study also available. Financial award application deadline: 3/1; financial award applicants required to submit FAFSA. *Unit head:* Dr. Mark L. Parker, Academic Unit Head, 540-568-6797. *Application contact:* Lynette M. Bible, Director of Graduate Admissions, 540-568-6395, Fax: 540-568-7860, E-mail: biblelm@jmu.edu.

John Carroll University, Graduate School, Department of English, University Heights, OH 44118-4581. Offers MA. Part-time and evening/weekend programs available. *Degree requirements:* For master's, comprehensive exam, research essay or thesis. *Entrance requirements:* For master's, GRE General Test, GRE Subject Test, minimum GPA of 3.0, writing sample. Additional exam requirements/recommendations for international students: Required—TOEFL. Electronic applications accepted. *Faculty research:* Post-colonial literature, African-American literature, Renaissance poetry, Anglo-Saxon literature, American literature.

The Johns Hopkins University, Zanvyl Krieger School of Arts and Sciences, Department of English, Baltimore, MD 21218-2699. Offers English and American literature (PhD). *Faculty:* 9 full-time (3 women). *Students:* 32 full-time (16 women), 1 (woman) part-time, 3 international. Average age 28. 130 applicants, 5% accepted, 7 enrolled. In 2009, 3 doctorates awarded. *Degree requirements:* For doctorate, 2 foreign languages, comprehensive exam, thesis/dissertation, 10 seminars, 2 oral exams. *Entrance requirements:* Additional exam requirements/recommendations for international students: Required—TOEFL (minimum score 600 paper-based; 250 computer-based; 100 iBT), IELTS. *Application deadline:* For fall admission, 12/10 priority date for domestic and international students. Application fee: $75. Electronic applications accepted. *Financial support:* In 2009–10, 30 students received support, including 12 fellowships with full tuition reimbursements available (averaging $18,000 per year), 16 teaching assistantships with full tuition reimbursements available (averaging $18,000 per year); research assistantships, Federal Work-Study, institutionally sponsored loans, and unspecified assistantships also available. Financial award application deadline: 4/15; financial award applicants required to submit FAFSA. *Faculty research:* Nineteenth century British, eighteenth century, Renaissance, American, cultural studies. Total annual research expenditures: $1,859. *Unit head:* Dr. Douglas Mao, Chair, 410-516-7335, Fax: 410-516-4757, E-mail: dougmao@jhu.edu. *Application contact:* Nicole Goode, Admissions Coordinator, 410-516-4311, Fax: 410-516-4757, E-mail: ngoode@jhu.edu.

Kansas State University, Graduate School, College of Arts and Sciences, Department of English, Manhattan, KS 66506. Offers MA. Part-time programs available. *Faculty:* 28 full-time (17 women), 1 part-time/adjunct (0 women). *Students:* 58 full-time (43 women), 8 part-time (5 women); includes 1 minority (Hispanic American), 5 international. Average age 27. 47 applicants, 91% accepted, 27 enrolled. In 2009, 33 master's awarded. *Degree requirements:* For master's, one foreign language, thesis optional. *Entrance requirements:* For master's, GRE, minimum B average in English. Additional exam requirements/recommendations for international students: Required—TOEFL. *Application deadline:* For fall admission, 2/1 priority date for domestic and international students; for spring admission, 8/1 priority date for domestic and international students. Applications are processed on a rolling basis. Application fee: $40 ($55 for international students). Electronic applications accepted. *Financial support:* In 2009–10, 41 teaching assistantships with full tuition reimbursements (averaging $9,902 per year) were awarded; career-related internships or fieldwork, Federal Work-Study, institutionally sponsored loans, scholarships/grants, and tuition waivers (full) also available. Support available to part-time students. Financial award application deadline: 3/1; financial award applicants required to submit FAFSA. *Faculty research:* Cultural studies, children's literature, American literature, rhetorical and composition theory, British literature. Total annual research expenditures: $2,650. *Unit head:* Karin Westman, Head, 785-532-2190, Fax: 785-532-2192, E-mail: westmank@ksu.edu. *Application contact:* Greg Eiselein, Director, 785-532-0386, Fax: 785-532-2192, E-mail: eiselei@ksu.edu.

Kent State University, College of Arts and Sciences, Department of English, Kent, OH 44242-0001. Offers comparative literature (MA); creative writing (MFA); English (PhD); English for teachers (MA); literature and writing (MA); rhetoric and composition (PhD); teaching English as a second language (MA). Part-time programs available. Terminal master's awarded for partial completion of doctoral program. *Degree requirements:* For master's, one foreign language, thesis optional; for doctorate, one foreign language, thesis/dissertation, qualifying exams. *Entrance requirements:* For master's and doctorate, GRE General Test, writing sample, letters of recommendation. Additional exam requirements/recommendations for international students: Required—TOEFL (minimum score 600 paper-based). Electronic applications accepted. *Faculty research:* British and American literature, textual editing, rhetoric and composition, cultural studies, linguistic and critical theories.

Kutztown University of Pennsylvania, College of Liberal Arts and Sciences, Program in English, Kutztown, PA 19530-0730. Offers MA. Part-time and evening/weekend programs available. *Faculty:* 4 full-time (1 woman). *Students:* 5 full-time (3 women), 10 part-time (8 women); includes 1 minority (Hispanic American). Average age 29. 19 applicants, 53% accepted, 2 enrolled. In 2009, 9 master's awarded. *Degree requirements:* For master's, one foreign language, comprehensive exam, thesis optional. *Entrance requirements:* For master's, GRE General Test. Additional exam requirements/recommendations for international students: Required—TOEFL. *Application deadline:* For fall admission, 8/15 priority date for domestic and international students; for spring admission, 12/15 priority date for domestic and international students. Applications are processed on a rolling basis. Application fee: $35. Electronic applications accepted. *Expenses:* Tuition, state resident: full-time $6666; part-time $370 per credit. Tuition, nonresident: full-time $10,666; part-time $593 per credit. Required fees: $62 per credit. $60 per semester. *Financial support:* Career-related internships or fieldwork, Federal Work-Study, scholarships/grants, and unspecified assistantships available. Financial award application deadline: 3/1; financial award applicants required to submit FAFSA. *Faculty research:* Women science fiction writers, Joyce Cary, myth and symbol, folklore, Victorian revision modes. *Unit head:* Dr. Janice Chernekoff, Chairperson, 610-683-4353, Fax: 610-683-4355, E-mail: cherneko@kutztown.edu. *Application contact:* Kelly D. Burr, Associate Director, Graduate Admissions, 610-683-4200, Fax: 610-683-1393, E-mail: graduate@kutztown.edu.

Lakehead University, Graduate Studies, Faculty of Social Sciences and Humanities, Department of English, Thunder Bay, ON P7B 5E1, Canada. Offers English (MA); women's studies (MA). Part-time and evening/weekend programs available. *Degree requirements:* For master's, one foreign language, thesis optional. *Entrance requirements:* For master's, minimum B average. Additional exam requirements/recommendations for international students: Required—TOEFL. *Faculty research:* Rhetoric and literary studies, children's literature, nineteenth- and twentieth-century American literature, modern literature, women's studies.

Lamar University, College of Graduate Studies, College of Arts and Sciences, Department of English and Foreign Languages, Beaumont, TX 77710. Offers English (MA). Part-time and evening/weekend programs available. *Faculty:* 9 full-time (3 women). *Students:* 7 full-time (5 women), 14 part-time (12 women); includes 2 minority (1 Asian American or Pacific Islander, 1 Hispanic American). Average age 35. 16 applicants, 50% accepted, 6 enrolled. In 2009, 2 master's awarded. *Degree requirements:* For master's, one foreign language, thesis optional, practicum. *Entrance requirements:* For master's, GRE General Test, minimum GPA of 2.5 in last 60 hours of undergraduate course work. Additional exam requirements/recommendations for international students: Required—TOEFL. *Application deadline:* For fall admission, 8/1 for domestic students; for spring admission, 12/1 for domestic students. Applications are processed on a rolling basis. Application fee: $25 ($50 for international students). *Financial support:* In 2009–10, 6 students received support, including 4 teaching assistantships (averaging $8,000 per year); career-related internships or fieldwork, Federal Work-Study, and institutionally sponsored loans also available. Support available to part-time students. Financial award application deadline: 4/1. *Faculty research:* British, Renaissance, nineteenth century, and American literature; creative writing; modern literature; African-American literature. *Unit head:* Dr. Joe E. Nordgren, Chair, 409-880-8558, Fax: 409-880-8591, E-mail: nordgrenje@hal.lamar.edu. *Application contact:* Dr. James W. Westgate, Assistant Dean, 409-880-7978, E-mail: westgate@hal.lamar.edu.

La Sierra University, College of Arts and Sciences, Department of English and Communication, Riverside, CA 92515. Offers communication (MA), including public relations/advertising, theory emphasis; English (MA), including literary emphasis, writing emphasis. Part-time programs available. *Degree requirements:* For master's, one foreign language. *Entrance requirements:* For master's, GRE General Test.

Lehigh University, College of Arts and Sciences, Department of English, Bethlehem, PA 18015. Offers MA, PhD. *Faculty:* 18 full-time (10 women). *Students:* 38 full-time (23 women), 5 part-time (3 women); includes 1 minority (Asian American or Pacific Islander), 1 international. Average age 33. 35 applicants, 26% accepted, 4 enrolled. In 2009, 5 master's, 6 doctorates awarded. Terminal master's awarded for partial completion of doctoral program. *Degree requirements:* For master's, thesis; for doctorate, one foreign language, comprehensive exam, thesis/dissertation. *Entrance requirements:* For master's, GRE Subject Test (literature), GRE General Test, minimum GPA of 3.0 in undergraduate English courses; for doctorate, GRE Subject Test (literature), GRE General Test, minimum GPA of 3.5 in MA coursework. Additional exam requirements/recommendations for international students: Required—TOEFL (minimum score 620 paper-based; 260 computer-based; 96 iBT). *Application deadline:* For fall admission, 1/2 priority date for domestic and international students. Application fee: $65. Electronic applications accepted. *Financial support:* In 2009–10, 3 fellowships with full tuition reimbursements (averaging $22,000 per year), 32 teaching assistantships with full tuition reimbursements (averaging $16,900 per year) were awarded; career-related internships or fieldwork, Federal Work-Study, institutionally sponsored loans, scholarships/grants, tuition waivers (full and partial), and unspecified assistantships also available. Support available to part-time students. Financial award application deadline: 1/2. *Faculty research:* Literature and social justice, narrative theory, modernism, transatlantic study, literature and medicine. Total annual research expenditures: $6,850. *Unit head:* Dr. Barry M. Kroll, Chairperson, 610-758-3311, Fax: 610-758-6616, E-mail: bmk3@lehigh.edu. *Application contact:* Dr. Dawn Keetley, Director of Graduate Studies, 610-758-5926, Fax: 610-758-6616, E-mail: dek7@lehigh.edu.

Lehman College of the City University of New York, Division of Arts and Humanities, Department of English, Bronx, NY 10468-1589. Offers MA. *Degree requirements:* For master's, thesis. *Entrance requirements:* For master's, GRE, 18 upper-level credits in U. S. or English literature.

Long Island University, Brooklyn Campus, Richard L. Conolly College of Liberal Arts and Sciences, Department of English, Brooklyn, NY 11201-8423. Offers creative writing (MFA); literature (MA); professional writing (MA); writing and rhetoric (MA). Part-time and evening/weekend programs available. *Degree requirements:* For master's, thesis or alternative. *Entrance requirements:* For master's, 2 letters of recommendation (at least 1 from a former professor or teacher). Additional exam requirements/recommendations for international students: Required—TOEFL (minimum score 550 paper-based; 173 computer-based). Electronic applications accepted.

Long Island University, C.W. Post Campus, College of Liberal Arts and Sciences, Department of English, Brookville, NY 11548-1300. Offers English (MA); English for adolescence education (MS). Part-time and evening/weekend programs available. *Degree requirements:* For master's, comprehensive exam (for some programs), thesis (for some programs). *Entrance requirements:* For master's, minimum GPA of 3.5 in major, 3.0 overall; 21 credits of English. Electronic applications accepted. *Faculty research:* English Renaissance, Sinclair Lewis: The Early Years, puppetry archives, Irish-American Experiences: literature of memory, Henry James's anxiety of Poe's influence.

Longwood University, Office of Graduate Studies, Department of English and Modern Languages, Farmville, VA 23909. Offers 6-12 initial teaching/licensure (MA); creative writing (MA); English education and writing (MA); literature (MA). Part-time programs available. *Degree requirements:* For master's, comprehensive exam (for some programs), thesis (for some programs). *Entrance requirements:* For master's, minimum GPA of 2.75. Additional exam requirements/recommendations for international students: Required—TOEFL (minimum score 550 paper-based; 213 computer-based).

Louisiana State University and Agricultural and Mechanical College, Graduate School, College of Arts and Sciences, Department of English, Baton Rouge, LA 70803. Offers creative writing (MFA); English (MA, PhD). Part-time programs available. *Faculty:* 53 full-time (23 women). *Students:* 80 full-time (42 women), 9 part-time (6 women); includes 6 minority (2 African Americans, 1 American Indian/Alaska Native, 1 Asian American or Pacific Islander, 2 Hispanic Americans), 5 international. Average age 30. 218 applicants, 9% accepted, 18 enrolled. In 2009, 15 master's, 7 doctorates awarded. Terminal master's awarded for partial completion of doctoral program. *Degree requirements:* For master's, comprehensive exam; for doctorate, one foreign language, comprehensive exam, thesis/dissertation. *Entrance requirements:* For master's, GRE General Test, minimum GPA of 3.0; for doctorate, GRE General Test, GRE Subject Test, minimum GPA of 3.0. Additional exam requirements/recommendations for international students: Required—TOEFL (minimum score 550 paper-based; 213 computer-based; 79 iBT) or IELTS (minimum score 6.5). *Application deadline:* For fall admission, 5/15 priority date for domestic students, 5/15 for international students; for spring admission, 10/15 priority date for domestic students, 10/15 for international students. Applications are processed on a rolling basis. Application fee: $50 ($70 for international students). Electronic applications accepted. *Financial support:* In 2009–10, 82 students received support, including 1 fellowship with full tuition reimbursement available (averaging $19,109 per year), 3 research assistantships with partial tuition reimbursements available (averaging $16,333 per year), 74 teaching assistantships with partial tuition reimbursements available (averaging $16,547 per year); career-related internships or fieldwork, Federal Work-Study, traineeships, and health care benefits also available. Financial award application deadline: 2/1; financial award applicants required to submit FAFSA. *Faculty research:* American literature, British literature, cultural studies, rhetoric and composition, folklore. Total annual research expenditures: $152,193. *Unit head:* Dr. Richard Morland, Chair, 225-578-0812, Fax: 225-578-2214, E-mail: english@lsu.edu. *Application contact:* Dr. Sharon Weltman, Director of Graduate Studies, 225-578-0812, Fax: 225-578-4129, E-mail: egs@lsu.edu.

Louisiana Tech University, Graduate School, College of Liberal Arts, Department of English, Ruston, LA 71272. Offers MA. Part-time programs available. *Degree requirements:* For master's, thesis or alternative. *Entrance requirements:* For master's, GRE General Test.

Loyola Marymount University, College of Liberal Arts, Department of English, Program in English, Los Angeles, CA 90045. Offers MA. *Faculty:* 27 full-time (13 women). *Students:* 20 full-time (13 women), 8 part-time (5 women); includes 11 minority (3 African Americans, 1 American Indian/Alaska Native, 2 Asian Americans or Pacific Islanders, 5 Hispanic Americans). Average age 30. 44 applicants, 59% accepted, 12 enrolled. In 2009, 21 master's awarded. *Degree requirements:* For master's, thesis. *Entrance requirements:* For master's, GRE, 2 letters of recommendation, writing sample (10-15 pages). Additional exam requirements/recommendations for international students: Required—TOEFL (minimum score 600 paper-based; 250 computer-based; 100 iBT). *Application deadline:* For fall admission, 4/1 for domestic students. Application fee: $50. *Financial support:* In 2009–10, 22 students received support, including 6 research assistantships (averaging $1,300 per year), 8 teaching assistantships (averaging $20,500 per year); scholarships/grants and unspecified assistantships also available. Support available to part-time students. Financial award application deadline: 6/1; financial award applicants required to submit FAFSA. *Unit head:* Dr. David Killoran, Chair, 310-338-2851, Fax: 310-338-7727, E-mail: dkillora@lmu.edu. *Application contact:* Chake H. Kouyoumjian, Associate Dean of Graduate Studies, 310-338-2721, Fax: 310-338-6086, E-mail: ckouyoum@lmu.edu.

Loyola University Chicago, Graduate School, Department of English, Chicago, IL 60660. Offers MA, PhD. Part-time and evening/weekend programs available. *Faculty:* 21 full-time (8 women). *Students:* 51 full-time (30 women), 2 part-time (1 woman); includes 5 minority (2 African Americans, 1 Asian American or Pacific Islander, 2 Hispanic Americans), 1 international. Average age 30. 146 applicants, 24% accepted, 15 enrolled. In 2009, 10 master's, 7 doctorates awarded. Terminal master's awarded for partial completion of doctoral program. *Degree requirements:* For master's, comprehensive exam, thesis or alternative; for doctorate, one foreign language, comprehensive exam, thesis/dissertation. *Entrance requirements:* For master's and doctorate, GRE General Test, GRE Subject Test. Additional exam requirements/recommendations for international students: Required—TOEFL, IELTS. *Application deadline:* For fall admission, 6/1 for domestic students. Applications are processed on a rolling basis. Application fee: $50. Electronic applications accepted. *Expenses:* Tuition: Full-time $14,220; part-time $790 per credit hour. Required fees: $60 per semester hour. Tuition and fees vary according to program. *Financial support:* In 2009–10, 26 students received support, including 5 fellowships with full tuition reimbursements available (averaging $13,500 per year), research assistantships with full tuition reimbursements available (averaging $10,000 per year), 21 teaching assistantships with full tuition reimbursements available (averaging $10,000 per year); Federal Work-Study, institutionally sponsored loans, tuition waivers (partial), and unspecified assistantships also available. Support available to part-time students. Financial award application deadline: 1/15; financial award applicants required to submit FAFSA. *Faculty research:* Medieval and Renaissance studies, Romantic period, literary history and theory, American studies, modernism and postmodernism. *Unit head:* Dr. Pamela Caughie, Chair, 773-508-2240, Fax: 773-508-8696, E-mail: pcaughi@luc.edu. *Application contact:* Maureen Taylor, Graduate Program Secretary, 773-508-2255, Fax: 773-508-8696, E-mail: mtaylo3@luc.edu.

Lynchburg College, Graduate Studies, School of Humanities and Social Sciences, Lynchburg, VA 24501-3199. Offers English (MA); history (MA). Part-time programs available. *Degree requirements:* For master's, comprehensive exam, thesis (for some programs). *Entrance requirements:* For master's, GRE, minimum undergraduate GPA of 3.0. Additional exam requirements/recommendations for international students: Required—TOEFL. *Expenses:* Tuition: Full-time $7020; part-time $390 per credit hour.

Marquette University, Graduate School, College of Arts and Sciences, Department of English, Milwaukee, WI 53201-1881. Offers American literature (PhD); British and American literature (MA); British literature (PhD). Part-time programs available. *Faculty:* 35 full-time (16 women), 23 part-time/adjunct (15 women). *Students:* 46 full-time (29 women), 12 part-time (7 women); includes 3 minority (1 Asian American or Pacific Islander, 2 Hispanic Americans), 1 international. Average age 30. 77 applicants, 52% accepted, 16 enrolled. In 2009, 9 master's, 2 doctorates awarded. Terminal master's awarded for partial completion of doctoral program. *Degree requirements:* For master's, comprehensive exam, thesis or alternative; for doctorate, one foreign language, thesis/dissertation, qualifying exam. *Entrance requirements:* For master's and doctorate, GRE General Test, GRE Subject Test. Additional exam requirements/recommendations for international students: Required—TOEFL. Application fee: $40. *Financial support:* In 2009–10, 5 research assistantships, 35 teaching assistantships were awarded; Federal Work-Study, institutionally sponsored loans, scholarships/grants, and tuition waivers (full and partial) also available. Support available to part-time students. Financial award application deadline: 2/15. *Faculty research:* Discourse analysis, cultural studies, textual criticism, literary history, literary theory. *Unit head:* Dr. Tim Machan, Chair, 414-288-7179, Fax: 414-288-1578. *Application contact:* Dr. Ed Block, Director of Graduate Studies, 414-288-7260.

Marshall University, Academic Affairs Division, College of Liberal Arts, Department of English, Huntington, WV 25755. Offers MA. *Faculty:* 16 full-time (6 women), 15 part-time/adjunct (10 women). *Students:* 37 full-time (26 women), 14 part-time (11 women), 6 international. Average age 29. In 2009, 16 master's awarded. *Degree requirements:* For master's, one foreign language, thesis optional. *Entrance requirements:* For master's, GRE General Test. Application fee: $40. *Unit head:* Dr. Jane Hill, Interim Chairperson, 304-696-6638, E-mail: hillj@marshall.edu. *Application contact:* Dr. Katharine Rodier, Information Contact, 304-696-3128, Fax: 304-746-1902, E-mail: rodier@marshall.edu.

Mary Baldwin College, Graduate Studies, Program in Shakespeare and Renaissance Literature in Performance, Staunton, VA 24401-3610. Offers acting (M Litt); directing (M Litt); Shakespeare and Renaissance literature in performance (MFA); teaching (M Litt). *Entrance requirements:* For master's, GRE (M Litt).

Marygrove College, Graduate Division, Program in English, Detroit, MI 48221-2599. Offers MA.

Marymount University, School of Arts and Sciences, Program in Literature and Languages, Arlington, VA 22207-4299. Offers MA. Part-time and evening/weekend programs available. *Faculty:* 3 full-time (all women). *Students:* 1 (woman) full-time, 12 part-time (8 women); includes 4 minority (3 African Americans, 1 Hispanic American), 1 international. Average age 35. 5 applicants, 80% accepted, 3 enrolled. In 2009, 7 master's awarded. *Degree requirements:* For master's, thesis or alternative. *Entrance requirements:* For master's, 2 letters of recommendation, interview, minimum undergraduate GPA of 3.0 with major in English or other humanities discipline, writing sample. Additional exam requirements/recommendations for international students: Required—TOEFL (minimum score 600 paper-based; 250 computer-based; 96 iBT), IELTS (minimum score 6.5). *Application deadline:* For fall admission, 7/1 for international students; for spring admission, 10/15 for international students. Applications are processed on a rolling basis. Application fee: $40. Electronic applications accepted. *Expenses:* Tuition: Full-time $13,050; part-time $725 per credit hour. Required fees: $135; $7.50 per credit hour. *Financial support:* In 2009–10, 4 students received support; research assistantships with full and partial tuition reimbursements available, career-related internships or fieldwork, Federal Work-Study, scholarships/grants, and unspecified assistantships available. Support available to part-time students. Financial award applicants required to submit FAFSA. *Unit head:* Dr. Sean Hoare, Director of Graduate Studies, 703-284-3829, Fax: 703-284-3859, E-mail: sean.hoare@marymount.edu. *Application contact:* Francesca Reed, Director, Graduate Admissions, 703-284-5901, Fax: 703-527-3815, E-mail: grad.admissions@marymount.edu.

McGill University, Faculty of Graduate and Postdoctoral Studies, Faculty of Arts, Department of English, Montréal, QC H3A 2T5, Canada. Offers MA, PhD. Electronic applications accepted.

McMaster University, School of Graduate Studies, Faculty of Humanities, Department of English and Cultural Studies, Hamilton, ON L8S 4M2, Canada. Offers cultural studies and critical theory (MA); English (MA, PhD). Part-time programs available. *Degree requirements:* For master's, one foreign language, thesis; for doctorate, one foreign language, comprehensive exam, thesis/dissertation. *Entrance requirements:* For master's, honors degree, minimum B+ average in at least 6 full courses of English beyond year 1; for doctorate, MA; minimum A- average in two of three courses. Additional exam requirements/recommendations for international students: Required—TOEFL (minimum score 580 paper-based; 237 computer-based). *Faculty research:* Literary theory, feminist theory, literature of migration, Bakhting globalization.

McNeese State University, Doré School of Graduate Studies, College of Liberal Arts, Department of English and Foreign Languages, Program in English, Lake Charles, LA 70609. Offers MA. Evening/weekend programs available. *Faculty:* 15 full-time (9 women). *Students:* 7 full-time (5 women), 3 part-time (all women); includes 1 minority (Asian American or Pacific Islander). In 2009, 7 master's awarded. *Degree requirements:* For master's, one foreign language, thesis or alternative. *Entrance requirements:* For master's, GRE. *Application deadline:* For fall admission, 5/15 priority date for domestic and international students; for spring admission, 10/15 priority date for domestic and international students. Applications are processed on a rolling basis. Application fee: $20 ($30 for international students). *Expenses:* Tuition, area resident: Full-time $2556. Tuition, state resident: full-time $2556. Required fees: $1031. Tuition and fees vary according to course load. *Financial support:* Teaching assistantships available. Financial award application deadline: 5/1. *Faculty research:* Textual criticism, seventeenth century literature, American women writers, Romanticism and the origins of diplomacy. *Unit head:* Dr. Jacob D. Blevins, Head, 337-475-5325, Fax: 337-475-5327, E-mail: jblevins@mcneese.edu. *Application contact:* Dr. George F. Mead, Interim Dean of Dore' School of Graduate Studies, 337-475-5396, Fax: 337-475-5397, E-mail: admissions@mcneese.edu.

Memorial University of Newfoundland, School of Graduate Studies, Department of English Language and Literature, St. John's, NL A1C 5S7, Canada. Offers MA, PhD. *Degree requirements:* For master's, thesis optional; for doctorate, one foreign language, comprehensive exam, thesis/dissertation, oral thesis defense, minimum 3 semesters of full-time study. *Entrance requirements:* For master's, honors degree. Electronic applications accepted. *Faculty research:* American, British, Canadian, and Anglo-Irish literature; Newfoundland literature.

Mercy College, School of Liberal Arts, Program in English Literature, Dobbs Ferry, NY 10522-1189. Offers MA. Part-time and evening/weekend programs available. Postbaccalaureate distance learning degree programs offered (no on-campus study). *Students:* 5 full-time (3 women), 59 part-time (52 women); includes 10 African Americans, 1 Asian American or Pacific Islander, 7 Hispanic Americans. Average age 37. 58 applicants, 53% accepted, 22 enrolled. In 2009, 12 master's awarded. *Degree requirements:* For master's, comprehensive exam, thesis. *Entrance requirements:* For master's, 2 letters of reference; BA/BS in English with minimum GPA of 3.0, in related subject area with minor in English literature, or in another discipline demonstrating the potential to succeed in a graduate program. Additional exam requirements/recommendations for international students: Required—TOEFL (minimum score 600 paper-based; 250 computer-based; 100 iBT). *Application deadline:* For fall admission, 8/1 for international students. Applications are processed on a rolling basis. Application fee: $40. Electronic applications accepted. *Expenses:* Tuition: Full-time $13,158; part-time $731 per credit. Required fees: $500. Tuition and fees vary according to degree level and program. *Financial support:* Career-related internships or fieldwork, Federal Work-Study, scholarships/grants, and unspecified assistantships available. Support available to part-time students. Financial award applicants required to submit FAFSA. *Faculty research:* Medieval literature, poetic forms, American literature, African literature. *Unit head:* Dr. Joel N. Feimer, Program Director, 914-245-6100 Ext. 2235, E-mail: jfeimer@mercy.edu. *Application contact:* Dr. Joel N. Feimer, Program Director, 914-245-6100 Ext. 2235, E-mail: jfeimer@mercy.edu.

Miami University, Graduate School, College of Arts and Sciences, Department of English, Oxford, OH 45056. Offers MA, MAT, MTSC, PhD. Part-time programs available. *Students:* 82 full-time (52 women), 86 part-time (76 women); includes 13 minority (8 African Americans, 1 American Indian/Alaska Native, 3 Asian Americans or Pacific Islanders, 1 Hispanic American), 6 international. *Entrance requirements:* For master's, minimum undergraduate GPA of 3.0 during previous 2 years or 2.75 overall; for doctorate, minimum GPA of 2.75 (undergraduate), 3.0 (graduate). Additional exam requirements/recommendations for international students: Required—TOEFL. *Application deadline:* For fall admission, 1/15 for domestic and international students. Application fee: $50. *Expenses:* Tuition, state resident: full-time $11,280. Tuition, nonresident: full-time $24,912. Required fees: $516. *Financial support:* Fellowships with full tuition reimbursements, research assistantships with full tuition reimbursements, teaching assistantships with full tuition reimbursements, Federal Work-Study, institutionally sponsored loans, tuition waivers (full), and unspecified assistantships available. Financial award application deadline: 3/1; financial award applicants required to submit FAFSA. *Unit head:* Dr. J. Kerry Powell, Chair, 513-529-5221, Fax: 513-529-1392, E-mail: english@muohio.edu. *Application contact:* Dr. Cynthia Lewiecki-Wilson, Director of Graduate Studies, 513-529-5221, E-mail: lewiecc@muohio.edu.

Michigan State University, The Graduate School, College of Arts and Letters, Department of English, East Lansing, MI 48824. Offers English (PhD); literature in English (MA). *Faculty:* 37 full-time (15 women). *Students:* 59 full-time (42 women), 5 part-time (2 women); includes 11 minority (7 African Americans, 1 American Indian/Alaska Native, 3 Hispanic Americans), 15 international. Average age 32. 119 applicants, 11% accepted. In 2009, 1 master's, 6 doctorates awarded. *Entrance requirements:* For master's, GRE General Test, minimum GPA of 3.25, 2 years of foreign language or American Sign Language study, 3 letters of recommendation; for doctorate, GRE General Test, master's degree in English, 2 years of foreign language study, 3 letters of recommendation. Additional exam requirements/recommendations for international students: Required—TOEFL. Electronic applications accepted. *Expenses:* Tuition, state resident: part-time $478.25 per credit hour. Tuition, nonresident: part-time $966.50 per credit hour. Part-time tuition and fees vary according to program. *Financial support:* In 2009–10, 3 research assistantships with tuition reimbursements (averaging $6,056 per year), 38 teaching assistantships with tuition reimbursements (averaging $6,139 per year) were awarded. Total annual research expenditures: $1,409. *Unit head:* Dr. Stephen Carl Arch, Chairperson, 517-355-7575,

English

Michigan State University (continued)
E-mail: arch@msu.edu. *Application contact:* Jackie Campbell, Graduate Programs Secretary, 517-355-7572, Fax: 517-353-3755, E-mail: campbe29@msu.edu.

Middlebury College, Bread Loaf School of English, Middlebury, VT 05753. Offers M Litt, MA. Offered during summer only. *Faculty:* 54 full-time. *Students:* 488 full-time. Average age 30. 215 applicants, 72% accepted, 121 enrolled. In 2009, 89 master's awarded. *Entrance requirements:* For master's, Application Form, 2 Letters of Recommendation; Statement of Purpose; official transcripts both undergraduate and graduate, 10-page writing sample. *Application deadline:* Applications are processed on a rolling basis. Application fee: $55. Electronic applications accepted. *Financial support:* In 2009–10, 239 students received support, including 18 fellowships; scholarships/grants also available. Support available to part-time students. *Unit head:* Dr. James Maddox, Director, 802-443-5418, Fax: 802-443-2060, E-mail: blse@breadnet.middlebury.edu. *Application contact:* Sandra LeGault, Admissions, Bread Loaf School of English, 802-443-5053, Fax: 802-443-2060.

Middle Tennessee State University, College of Graduate Studies, College of Liberal Arts, Department of English, Murfreesboro, TN 37132. Offers MA, PhD. Part-time and evening/weekend programs available. Postbaccalaureate distance learning degree programs offered. *Faculty:* 42 full-time (24 women). *Students:* 3 full-time (2 women), 93 part-time (65 women); includes 9 minority (3 African Americans, 5 Asian Americans or Pacific Islanders, 1 Hispanic American). Average age 31. 52 applicants, 81% accepted, 42 enrolled. In 2009, 7 master's, 5 doctorates awarded. *Degree requirements:* For master's, one foreign language, comprehensive exam, thesis optional; for doctorate, one foreign language, comprehensive exam, thesis/dissertation. *Entrance requirements:* For master's and doctorate, GRE. Additional exam requirements/recommendations for international students: Required—TOEFL (minimum score 525 paper-based; 195 computer-based; 71 iBT) or IELTS (minimum score 6). *Application deadline:* For fall admission, 6/1 for domestic and international students. Applications are processed on a rolling basis. Application fee: $25 ($30 for international students). Electronic applications accepted. *Expenses:* Tuition, state resident: full-time $4404. Tuition, nonresident: full-time $10,956. *Financial support:* In 2009–10, 40 students received support. Career-related internships or fieldwork and institutionally sponsored loans available. Support available to part-time students. Financial award application deadline: 5/1; financial award applicants required to submit FAFSA. *Unit head:* Dr. Tom Strawman, Chair, 615-898-2573, Fax: 615-898-5098, E-mail: strawman@mtsu.edu. *Application contact:* Dr. Michael Allen, Dean and Vice Provost for Research, 615-898-2840, Fax: 615-904-8020, E-mail: mallen@mtsu.edu.

Midwestern State University, Graduate Studies, College of Humanities and Social Sciences, Department of English, Wichita Falls, TX 76308. Offers MA. Part-time and evening/weekend programs available. *Degree requirements:* For master's, one foreign language, thesis optional. *Entrance requirements:* For master's, GRE General Test, MAT or GMAT. Additional exam requirements/recommendations for international students: Required—TOEFL (minimum score 550 paper-based; 213 computer-based). Electronic applications accepted. *Expenses:* Tuition, state resident: full-time $1620; part-time $90 per credit hour. Tuition, nonresident: full-time $2160; part-time $120 per credit hour. International tuition: $7506 full-time. Required fees: $3068.80; $145.60 per credit hour. $179 per semester. *Faculty research:* Jung and literature, Shakespeare, Oscar Hahn, origins of language, modern American literature.

Millersville University of Pennsylvania, College of Graduate and Professional Studies, School of Humanities and Social Sciences, Department of English, Millersville, PA 17551-0302. Offers English (MA); English education (M Ed). Part-time programs available. *Faculty:* 24 full-time (13 women), 12 part-time/adjunct (8 women). *Students:* 13 full-time (9 women), 23 part-time (12 women); includes 4 minority (3 African Americans, 1 Asian American or Pacific Islander). Average age 31. 16 applicants, 94% accepted, 10 enrolled. In 2009, 11 master's awarded. *Degree requirements:* For master's, one foreign language, thesis optional. *Entrance requirements:* For master's, GRE or MAT, 3 letters of recommendation. Additional exam requirements/recommendations for international students: Required—TOEFL (minimum score 500 paper-based; 183 computer-based; 65 iBT) or IELTS (minimum score 6). *Application deadline:* For fall admission, 1/15 priority date for domestic and international students; for winter admission, 10/1 priority date for domestic and international students; for spring admission, 10/1 priority date for domestic and international students. Applications are processed on a rolling basis. Application fee: $40 ($50 for international students). Electronic applications accepted. *Expenses:* Tuition, state resident: full-time $6666; part-time $370 per credit. Tuition, nonresident: full-time $10,666; part-time $593 per credit. Required fees: $1578.50; $76.25 per credit. One-time fee: $60 part-time. Tuition and fees vary according to course load. *Financial support:* In 2009–10, 10 students received support, including 10 research assistantships with full and partial tuition reimbursements available (averaging $3,890 per year); institutionally sponsored loans and unspecified assistantships also available. Support available to part-time students. Financial award application deadline: 3/15; financial award applicants required to submit FAFSA. *Faculty research:* Comparative literatures, writing studies, linguistics, film studies, curriculum and instruction/educational pedagogy. *Unit head:* Dr. Beverly Schneller, Chair, 717-871-2342, Fax: 717-871-2446, E-mail: beverly.schneller@millersville.edu. *Application contact:* Dr. Victor S. DeSantis, Dean of Graduate and Professional Studies, 717-872-3099, Fax: 717-872-3453, E-mail: victor.desantis@millersville.edu.

Mills College, Graduate Studies, Department of English, Oakland, CA 94613-1000. Offers book art and creative writing (MFA); creative writing, poetry (MFA); creative writing, prose (MFA); English and American literature (MA). Part-time programs available. *Faculty:* 10 full-time (8 women), 16 part-time/adjunct (13 women). *Students:* 92 full-time (71 women), 5 part-time (4 women); includes 26 minority (11 African Americans, 1 American Indian/Alaska Native, 8 Asian Americans or Pacific Islanders, 6 Hispanic Americans). Average age 31. 176 applicants, 85% accepted, 42 enrolled. In 2009, 63 master's awarded. *Degree requirements:* For master's, comprehensive exam, thesis. *Entrance requirements:* For master's, manuscript, writing sample. Additional exam requirements/recommendations for international students: Required—TOEFL. *Application deadline:* For fall admission, 2/1 priority date for domestic students; for spring admission, 11/1 for domestic students. Applications are processed on a rolling basis. Application fee: $50. Electronic applications accepted. *Expenses:* Tuition: Full-time $26,326; part-time $6584 per course. Required fees: $896. One-time fee: $896 part-time. Tuition and fees vary according to program. *Financial support:* In 2009–10, 85 students received support, including 85 fellowships (averaging $7,587 per year), 35 teaching assistantships with partial tuition reimbursements available (averaging $2,667 per year); scholarships/grants also available. Support available to part-time students. Financial award application deadline: 2/1; financial award applicants required to submit FAFSA. *Faculty research:* Creative writing, African-American literature, Victorian women writers, theories of sexuality, Shakespeare. *Unit head:* Dr. Cynthia Scheinberg, Chair, 510-430-2213, E-mail: cyns@mills.edu. *Application contact:* Jessica King, Graduate Admission Specialist, 510-430-3305, Fax: 510-430-2159, E-mail: grad-studies@mills.edu.

Minnesota State University Mankato, College of Graduate Studies, College of Arts and Humanities, Department of English, Mankato, MN 56001. Offers creative writing (MFA); English (MAT); English studies (MA); literature (MA); teaching English as a second language (MA, Certificate); technical communication (MA, Certificate). Part-time programs available. *Students:* 54 full-time (34 women), 114 part-time (78 women). *Degree requirements:* For master's, one foreign language, comprehensive exam, thesis or alternative. *Entrance requirements:* For master's, minimum GPA of 3.0 during previous 2 years, writing sample (MFA). Additional exam requirements/recommendations for international students: Required—TOEFL. *Application deadline:* Applications are processed on a rolling basis. Application fee: $40. Electronic applications accepted. *Expenses:* Tuition, state resident: full-time $5364. Tuition, nonresident: full-time $8314. *Financial support:* Research assistantships with full tuition reimbursements, teaching assistantships with full tuition reimbursements, career-related internships or fieldwork, Federal Work-Study, and unspecified assistantships available. Financial award application deadline: 3/15; financial award applicants required to submit FAFSA. *Faculty research:* Keats and Christianity. *Unit head:* Dr. John Banschbach, Chairperson, 507-389-2117. *Application contact:* 507-389-2321, E-mail: grad@mnsu.edu.

Mississippi College, Graduate School, College of Arts and Sciences, School of Humanities and Social Sciences, Department of English, Clinton, MS 39058. Offers M Ed, MA. Part-time and evening/weekend programs available. *Faculty:* 8 full-time (4 women), 1 part-time/adjunct (0 women). *Students:* 5 full-time (4 women), 31 part-time (24 women); includes 6 minority (all African Americans). Average age 31. In 2009, 2 master's awarded. *Degree requirements:* For master's, one foreign language, comprehensive exam, thesis or alternative. *Entrance requirements:* For master's, GRE or NTE, minimum GPA of 2.5. Additional exam requirements/recommendations for international students: Recommended—IELTS. *Application deadline:* For fall admission, 8/15 priority date for domestic and international students. Applications are processed on a rolling basis. Application fee: $30. Electronic applications accepted. *Expenses:* Tuition: Part-time $452 per credit hour. Required fees: $101 per semester. Tuition and fees vary according to degree level, campus/location, program and student level. *Financial support:* Teaching assistantships, Federal Work-Study, tuition waivers (partial), and unspecified assistantships available. Support available to part-time students. Financial award application deadline: 4/1; financial award applicants required to submit FAFSA. *Unit head:* Dr. David Miller, Interim Chair, 601-925-3336, Fax: 601-925-3998, E-mail: dmiller@mc.edu. *Application contact:* Elnora Lewis, Secretary, 601-925-3225, Fax: 601-925-3889, E-mail: lewis09@mc.edu.

Mississippi State University, College of Arts and Sciences, Department of English, Mississippi State, MS 39762. Offers MA. Part-time programs available. *Faculty:* 21 full-time (9 women). *Students:* 26 full-time (19 women), 3 part-time (1 woman); includes 3 minority (all African Americans). Average age 26. 24 applicants, 71% accepted, 12 enrolled. In 2009, 18 master's awarded. *Degree requirements:* For master's, comprehensive exam, thesis optional, comprehensive oral or written exam. *Entrance requirements:* For master's, GRE General Test, minimum GPA of 2.75 on last two years of undergraduate courses. Additional exam requirements/recommendations for international students: Required—TOEFL (minimum score 475 paper-based; 153 computer-based; 53 iBT); Recommended—IELTS (minimum score 4.5). *Application deadline:* For fall admission, 7/1 for domestic students, 5/1 for international students; for spring admission, 11/1 for domestic students, 9/1 for international students. Applications are processed on a rolling basis. Application fee: $40. Electronic applications accepted. *Expenses:* Tuition, state resident: full-time $2575.50; part-time $286.25 per credit hour. Tuition, nonresident: full-time $6510; part-time $723.50 per credit hour. Tuition and fees vary according to course load. *Financial support:* In 2009–10, 26 teaching assistantships (averaging $9,218 per year) were awarded; Federal Work-Study, institutionally sponsored loans, scholarships/grants, and unspecified assistantships also available. Financial award applicants required to submit FAFSA. *Faculty research:* Literary criticism, linguistics, textual editing, editing *Mississippi Quarterly*, Southern literature. *Unit head:* Dr. Richard Raymond, Department Head, 662-325-3606, Fax: 662-325-3645, E-mail: rr165@msstate.edu. *Application contact:* Dr. Richard Patteson, Professor/Director of Graduate Studies, 662-325-3644, E-mail: rfp1@ra.msstate.edu.

Missouri State University, Graduate College, College of Arts and Letters, Department of English, Springfield, MO 65897. Offers English and writing (MA); secondary education (MS Ed), including English. Part-time and evening/weekend programs available. *Faculty:* 24 full-time (15 women), 3 part-time/adjunct (0 women). *Students:* 38 full-time (29 women), 56 part-time (40 women); includes 2 minority (1 African American, 1 Hispanic American), 4 international. Average age 30. 39 applicants, 97% accepted, 23 enrolled. In 2009, 43 master's awarded. *Degree requirements:* For master's, one foreign language, comprehensive exam, thesis or alternative. *Entrance requirements:* For master's, GRE (MA), minimum GPA of 3.0 (MA), 9-12 teacher certification (MS Ed). Additional exam requirements/recommendations for international students: Required—TOEFL (minimum score 550 paper-based; 213 computer-based; 79 iBT). *Application deadline:* For fall admission, 7/20 for domestic students, 5/1 for international students; for spring admission, 12/20 for domestic students, 9/1 for international students. Applications are processed on a rolling basis. Application fee: $35 ($50 for international students). Electronic applications accepted. *Expenses:* Tuition, state resident: full-time $3852; part-time $214 per credit hour. Tuition, nonresident: full-time $7524; part-time $418 per credit hour. Required fees: $696; $172 per semester. Tuition and fees vary according to course level, course load, degree level and program. *Financial support:* In 2009–10, 36 teaching assistantships with full tuition reimbursements (averaging $7,340 per year) were awarded; Federal Work-Study, institutionally sponsored loans, scholarships/grants, and unspecified assistantships also available. Support available to part-time students. Financial award application deadline: 3/31; financial award applicants required to submit FAFSA. *Faculty research:* Renaissance literature, William Blake, autobiography, Georgian theatre, TESOL. *Unit head:* Dr. W. D. Blackmon, Head, 417-836-5107, Fax: 417-836-6940, E-mail: wdblackon@missouristate.edu. *Application contact:* Eric Eckert, Coordinator of Graduate Admissions and Recruitment, 417-836-5331, Fax: 417-836-6888, E-mail: ericeckert@missouristate.edu.

Monmouth University, Graduate School, Department of English, West Long Branch, NJ 07764-1898. Offers creative writing (MA); New Jersey studies (MA); rhetoric and writing (MA). Part-time and evening/weekend programs available. *Faculty:* 11 full-time (8 women). *Students:* 7 full-time (5 women), 26 part-time (20 women); includes 2 minority (1 African American, 1 Hispanic American). Average age 35. 22 applicants, 95% accepted, 10 enrolled. In 2009, 14 master's awarded. *Degree requirements:* For master's, comprehensive exam (for some programs), thesis (for some programs). *Entrance requirements:* For master's, minimum overall GPA of 2.75, at least 15 credits in literary studies. Additional exam requirements/recommendations for international students: Required—TOEFL (minimum score 550 paper-based; 213 computer-based; 79 iBT), IELTS (minimum score 5), Michigan English Language Assessment Battery (minimum score 77), Cambridge A, B, C. *Application deadline:* For fall admission, 7/15 for domestic students, 6/1 for international students; for spring admission, 11/15 for domestic students, 11/1 for international students. Application fee: $50. *Expenses:* Tuition: Part-time $773 per credit. Required fees: $157 per semester. *Financial support:* In 2009–10, 28 students received support, including 20 fellowships (averaging $1,891 per year), 4 research assistantships (averaging $3,334 per year); career-related internships or fieldwork, scholarships/grants, and unspecified assistantships also available. Support available to part-time students. Financial award applicants required to submit FAFSA. *Faculty research:* Renaissance and medieval literature, nineteenth century American literature, eighteenth century British literature and women's studies, Old English and Middle English, African diaspora and African post-colonial literature. *Unit head:* Dr. Hiede Estes, Program Director, 732-571-7547, E-mail: hestes@monmouth.edu. *Application contact:* Kevin Roane, Director, Office of Graduate Admission, 732-571-3452, Fax: 732-263-5123, E-mail: gradadm@monmouth.edu.

Montana State University, College of Graduate Studies, College of Letters and Science, Department of English, Bozeman, MT 59717. Offers MA. Part-time programs available. *Faculty:* 16 full-time (8 women), 14 part-time/adjunct (9 women). *Students:* 10 full-time (9 women), 10 part-time (all women), 1 international. Average age 27. 21 applicants, 67% accepted, 7 enrolled. In 2009, 7 master's awarded. *Degree requirements:* For master's, comprehensive exam. *Entrance requirements:* For master's, GRE General Test, minimum GPA of 3.0, 3 recommendations. Additional exam requirements/recommendations for international students: Required—TOEFL (minimum score 550 paper-based; 213 computer-based). *Application deadline:* For fall admission, 7/15 priority date for domestic students, 5/15 for international students; for spring admission, 12/1 priority date for domestic students, 10/1 for international students. Applications are processed on a rolling basis. Application fee: $30. Electronic applications accepted. *Expenses:* Tuition, state resident: full-time $5635; part-time $3492 per year. Tuition, nonresident: full-time $17,212; part-time $7865.10 per year. Required fees: $1441; $153.15 per credit. Tuition and fees vary according to course load and program. *Financial support:* In 2009–10, 2 students received support, including 11 teaching assistantships with tuition reimbursements available (averaging $10,582 per year). Financial award application deadline: 3/1; financial award applicants required to submit FAFSA. *Faculty research:* Writing studies, writing in the disciplines, contemporary literature, Renaissance, Shakespeare, American studies, global studies, urban studies, Victorian literature, popular culture gender and sexuality studies, queer theory, English education, literacy education, literary theory. Total annual research expenditures: $10,271. *Unit head:* Dr. Linda Karell, Head, 406-994-3768, Fax: 406-994-2422, E-mail: lkarell@english.montana.edu. *Application contact:* Dr. Carl A. Fox, Vice Provost for Graduate Education, 406-994-4145, Fax: 406-994-7433, E-mail: gradstudy@montana.edu.

Montclair State University, The Graduate School, College of Humanities and Social Sciences, Department of English, Montclair, NJ 07043-1624. Offers MA, Certificate. Part-time and evening/weekend programs available. *Faculty:* 45 full-time (26 women), 56 part-time/adjunct (46 women). *Students:* 15 full-time (9 women), 57 part-time (39 women). Average age 33. 39 applicants, 64% accepted, 14 enrolled. In 2009, 10 master's awarded. *Degree requirements:* For master's, thesis. *Entrance requirements:* For master's, GRE General Test, 2 letters of recommendation. Additional exam requirements/recommendations for international students: Required—TOEFL (minimum score 83 computer-based), or IELTS. *Application deadline:* For fall admission, 4/1 for domestic and international students; for spring admission, 11/1 for domestic and international students. Applications are processed on a rolling basis. Application fee: $60. Electronic applications accepted. *Expenses:* Tuition, area resident: Part-time $486.74 per credit. Tuition, state resident: part-time $486.74 per credit. Tuition, nonresident: part-time $751.34 per credit. Tuition and fees vary according to degree level and program. *Financial support:* In 2009–10, 9 research assistantships with full tuition reimbursements (averaging $7,000 per year) were awarded; Federal Work-Study, scholarships/grants, and unspecified assistantships also available. Support available to part-time students. Financial award application deadline: 3/1; financial award applicants required to submit FAFSA. *Unit head:* Dr. Dan Bronson, Chairperson, 973-655-4274. *Application contact:* Amy Aiello, Director of Graduate Admissions and Operations, 973-655-5147, Fax: 973-655-7869, E-mail: graduate.school@montclair.edu.

Morehead State University, Graduate Programs, Caudill College of Arts, Humanities and Social Sciences, Department of English, Morehead, KY 40351. Offers English (MA). Part-time and evening/weekend programs available. *Faculty:* 8 full-time (5 women). *Students:* 9 full-time (7 women), 60 part-time (48 women); includes 6 minority (2 African Americans, 2 Asian Americans or Pacific Islanders, 2 Hispanic Americans). Average age 33. 57 applicants, 56% accepted, 21 enrolled. In 2009, 6 master's awarded. *Degree requirements:* For master's, comprehensive exam, thesis optional. *Entrance requirements:* For master's, GRE General Test, minimum GPA of 3.0 in English; undergraduate major or minor in English. Additional exam requirements/recommendations for international students: Required—TOEFL (minimum score 500 paper-based; 173 computer-based). *Application deadline:* For fall admission, 8/1 priority date for domestic and international students; for spring admission, 12/1 priority date for domestic and international students. Applications are processed on a rolling basis. Application fee: $30. Electronic applications accepted. *Expenses:* Tuition, state resident: full-time $6318; part-time $351 per credit hour. Tuition, nonresident: full-time $15,804; part-time $878 per credit hour. *Financial support:* In 2009–10, 3 teaching assistantships (averaging $10,000 per year) were awarded; career-related internships or fieldwork, Federal Work-Study, and unspecified assistantships also available. Financial award application deadline: 3/15; financial award applicants required to submit FAFSA. *Faculty research:* Nineteenth and twentieth century American literature, linguistics, Victorian literature, modern British literature, creative writing. *Unit head:* Dr. Philip Krummrich, Chair, 606-783-2185, Fax: 606-783-5346, E-mail: p.krummrich@moreheadstate.edu. *Application contact:* Michelle Barber, Graduate Recruitment and Retention Assistant Director, 606-783-5127, Fax: 606-783-5061, E-mail: m.barber@moreheadstate.edu.

Morgan State University, School of Graduate Studies, College of Liberal Arts, Department of English, Baltimore, MD 21251. Offers MA, PhD. Part-time programs available. *Degree requirements:* For master's, comprehensive exam, thesis; for doctorate, comprehensive exam, thesis/dissertation. *Entrance requirements:* For master's, GRE, minimum GPA of 2.5; for doctorate, GRE. Additional exam requirements/recommendations for international students: Required—TOEFL (minimum score 550 paper-based; 213 computer-based). *Faculty research:* African and African-American studies, nineteenth century American literature, rhetoric, women's studies, children's literature.

Mount Mary College, Graduate Programs, Program in English, Milwaukee, WI 53222-4597. Offers MA. Evening/weekend programs available. *Faculty:* 2 full-time (both women), 6 part-time/adjunct (4 women). *Students:* 27 full-time (25 women), 35 part-time (32 women); includes 13 minority (5 African Americans, 1 Asian American or Pacific Islander, 7 Hispanic Americans). Average age 39. 14 applicants, 79% accepted, 10 enrolled. In 2009, 9 master's awarded. *Degree requirements:* For master's, comprehensive exam, thesis or alternative. *Entrance requirements:* For master's, minimum GPA of 2.75. Additional exam requirements/recommendations for international students: Required—TOEFL (minimum score 500 paper-based; 173 computer-based). *Application deadline:* For fall admission, 8/1 priority date for domestic and international students; for spring admission, 12/1 priority date for domestic and international students. Applications are processed on a rolling basis. Application fee: $35 ($100 for international students). Electronic applications accepted. *Expenses:* Tuition: Part-time $595 per credit. Tuition and fees vary according to program. *Financial support:* In 2009–10, 1 student received support. Career-related internships or fieldwork and Federal Work-Study available. Support available to part-time students. Financial award application deadline: 5/1; financial award applicants required to submit FAFSA. *Unit head:* Dr. Kristi Siegel, Director, 414-258-4810 Ext. 287, E-mail: siegelkr@mtmary.edu. *Application contact:* Dr. Kristi Siegel, Director, 414-258-4810 Ext. 287, E-mail: siegelkr@mtmary.edu.

Murray State University, College of Humanities and Fine Arts, Department of English and Philosophy, Program in English, Murray, KY 42071. Offers MA. Part-time programs available. *Degree requirements:* For master's, comprehensive exam, thesis (for some programs).

National University, Academic Affairs, College of Letters and Sciences, Department of Art and Humanities, La Jolla, CA 92037-1011. Offers creative writing (MFA); English (MA); history (MA). Part-time and evening/weekend programs available. Postbaccalaureate distance learning degree programs offered (no on-campus study). *Faculty:* 13 full-time (4 women), 24 part-time/adjunct (15 women). *Students:* 204 full-time (144 women), 499 part-time (340 women); includes 160 minority (77 African Americans, 6 American Indian/Alaska Native, 17 Asian Americans or Pacific Islanders, 60 Hispanic Americans). Average age 38. 440 applicants, 100% accepted, 280 enrolled. In 2009, 152 master's awarded. *Degree requirements:* For master's, thesis (for some programs). *Entrance requirements:* For master's, interview, minimum GPA of 2.5. Additional exam requirements/recommendations for international students: Required—TOEFL (minimum score 550 paper-based; 213 computer-based; 79 iBT), IELTS (minimum score 6). *Application deadline:* Applications are processed on a rolling basis. Application fee: $60 ($65 for international students). Electronic applications accepted. *Expenses:* Tuition: Part-time $338 per quarter hour. *Financial support:* Career-related internships or fieldwork, institutionally sponsored loans, scholarships/grants, and tuition waivers (partial) available. Support available to part-time students. Financial award application deadline: 6/30; financial award applicants required to submit FAFSA. *Unit head:* Dr. Janet Baker, Chair, 858-642-8472, Fax: 858-642-8715, E-mail: jbaker@nu.edu. *Application contact:* Dominick Giovanniello, Associate Regional Dean—San Diego, 800-NAT-UNIV, Fax: 858-541-7792, E-mail: dgiovann@nu.edu.

New Mexico Highlands University, Graduate Studies, College of Arts and Sciences, Department of Humanities, Las Vegas, NM 87701. Offers English (MA), including creative writing, language, rhetoric and composition, literature. *Degree requirements:* For master's, comprehensive exam, thesis. *Entrance requirements:* For master's, minimum undergraduate GPA of 3.0. Additional exam requirements/recommendations for international students: Required—TOEFL (minimum score 540 paper-based; 207 computer-based). *Faculty research:* 20th century literature, life path writing in homeless shelters, native American philosophy, medieval intellectual and cultural history, creating pedagogical tools for teaching law.

New Mexico State University, Graduate School, College of Arts and Sciences, Department of English, Las Cruces, NM 88003-8001. Offers creative writing (MFA); English (MA); rhetoric and professional communication (PhD). Part-time programs available. *Faculty:* 26 full-time (15 women). *Students:* 81 full-time (45 women), 35 part-time (19 women); includes 23 minority (4 African Americans, 3 Asian Americans or Pacific Islanders, 16 Hispanic Americans), 7 international. Average age 32. 89 applicants, 66% accepted, 26 enrolled. In 2009, 27 master's awarded. *Degree requirements:* For master's, one foreign language, thesis (for some programs); for doctorate, comprehensive exam, thesis/dissertation, internship. *Entrance requirements:* For master's and doctorate, sample of written work. *Application deadline:* For fall admission, 2/1 for domestic and international students. Application fee: $30 ($50 for international students). Electronic applications accepted. *Expenses:* Tuition, state resident: full-time $4080; part-time $223 per credit. Tuition, nonresident: full-time $14,256; part-time $647 per credit. Required fees: $1278; $639 per semester. *Financial support:* In 2009–10, 2 research assistantships (averaging $7,900 per year), 55 teaching assistantships (averaging $15,193 per year) were awarded; fellowships, career-related internships or fieldwork, Federal Work-Study, institutionally sponsored loans, scholarships/grants, health care benefits, and unspecified assistantships also available. Financial award application deadline: 2/1; financial award applicants required to submit FAFSA. *Faculty research:* Composition research, history and theory of rhetoric, technical/professional communication, creative writing, English and American literature. *Unit head:* Dr. Monica F. Torres, Head, 575-646-2319, Fax: 575-646-7725, E-mail: mftorres@nmsu.edu. *Application contact:* Dr. Elizabeth Schirmer, Director of Graduate Studies, 575-646-1733, E-mail: eschirme@nmsu.edu.

New York University, Graduate School of Arts and Science, Department of English, Program in English and American Literature, New York, NY 10012-1019. Offers MA, PhD. *Students:* 108 full-time (68 women), 28 part-time (21 women); includes 16 minority (3 African Americans, 2 American Indian/Alaska Native, 5 Asian Americans or Pacific Islanders, 6 Hispanic Americans), 17 international. Average age 28. 564 applicants, 30% accepted, 45 enrolled. In 2009, 38 master's, 11 doctorates awarded. *Degree requirements:* For master's, one foreign language, thesis or alternative, qualifying exams, special project; for doctorate, one foreign language, thesis/dissertation. *Entrance requirements:* For master's, GRE General Test. Additional exam requirements/recommendations for international students: Required—TOEFL. *Application deadline:* For fall admission, 12/15 for domestic students. Application fee: $90. *Expenses:* Tuition: Full-time $30,528; part-time $1272 per credit. Required fees: $2177. *Financial support:* Fellowships with tuition reimbursements, teaching assistantships with tuition reimbursements, Federal Work-Study, institutionally sponsored loans, scholarships/grants, health care benefits, and unspecified assistantships available. Financial award application deadline: 12/18; financial award applicants required to submit FAFSA. *Unit head:* Phillip Harper, Chair, 212-998-8800, Fax: 212-995-4019, E-mail: gasa.english.admissions@nyu.edu. *Application contact:* Elizabeth McHenry, Director of Graduate Studies, 212-998-8800, Fax: 212-995-4019, E-mail: gsas.english.admissions@nyu.edu.

New York University, Steinhardt School of Culture, Education, and Human Development, Department of Teaching and Learning, Program in English Education, New York, NY 10012-1019. Offers secondary and college (PhD), including applied linguistics, comparative education, curriculum, literature and reading, media education; teachers of English 7-12 (MA); teachers of English language and literature in college (Advanced Certificate). *Accreditation:* Teacher Education Accreditation Council. Part-time programs available. *Students:* 36 full-time (30 women), 30 part-time (25 women); includes 11 minority (4 African Americans, 3 Asian Americans or Pacific Islanders, 4 Hispanic Americans), 2 international. Average age 26. 91 applicants, 80% accepted, 21 enrolled. In 2009, 27 master's, 6 doctorates, 1 other advanced degree awarded. *Degree requirements:* For master's, thesis (for some programs); for doctorate, thesis/dissertation. *Entrance requirements:* For doctorate, GRE General Test, interview; for Advanced Certificate, master's degree. Additional exam requirements/recommendations for international students: Required—TOEFL. *Application deadline:* For fall admission, 12/15 priority date for domestic and international students; for spring admission, 11/1 for domestic and international students. Applications are processed on a rolling basis. Application fee: $75. Electronic applications accepted. *Expenses:* Tuition: Full-time $30,528; part-time $1272 per credit. Required fees: $2177. *Financial support:* Fellowships with full and partial tuition reimbursements, teaching assistantships with full and partial tuition reimbursements, career-related internships or fieldwork, Federal Work-Study, institutionally sponsored loans, scholarships/grants, tuition waivers (partial), and unspecified assistantships available. Support available to part-time students. Financial award application deadline: 2/1; financial award applicants required to submit FAFSA. *Faculty research:* Making meaning of literature, teaching of literature, urban adolescent literacy and equity, literacy development and globalization, digital media and literacy. *Unit head:* Director, 212-998-5460, Fax: 212-995-4049. *Application contact:* 212-998-5030, Fax: 212-995-4328, E-mail: steinhardt.gradadmissions@nyu.edu.

North Carolina Agricultural and Technical State University, Graduate School, College of Arts and Sciences, Department of English, Greensboro, NC 27411. Offers English (MA); English and Afro-American literature (MA); English education (MS). Part-time and evening/weekend programs available. *Degree requirements:* For master's, comprehensive exam, qualifying exam. *Entrance requirements:* For master's, GRE General Test, minimum GPA of 3.0.

North Carolina Central University, Division of Academic Affairs, College of Liberal Arts, Department of English and Mass Communication, Durham, NC 27707-3129. Offers English (MA). Part-time and evening/weekend programs available. *Degree requirements:* For master's, one foreign language, comprehensive exam, thesis. *Entrance requirements:* For master's, GRE, minimum GPA of 3.0 in major, 2.5 overall. Additional exam requirements/recommendations for international students: Required—TOEFL. *Faculty research:* Victorian literature, African-American literature, women's studies, literature and film, twentieth-century literature.

North Carolina State University, Graduate School, College of Humanities and Social Sciences, Department of English, Program in English, Raleigh, NC 27695. Offers MA. *Degree requirements:* For master's, thesis. *Entrance requirements:* For master's, GRE General Test. Electronic applications accepted. *Faculty research:* Creative writing, linguistics, rhetoric and composition, rhetoric and technical communication, film studies.

North Dakota State University, College of Graduate and Interdisciplinary Studies, College of Arts, Humanities and Social Sciences, Department of English, Fargo, ND 58108. Offers MA, MS. Part-time programs available. *Faculty:* 12 full-time (6 women), 1 part-time/adjunct (0 women). *Students:* 21 full-time (15 women), 13 part-time (11 women), 2 international. Average age 31. 33 applicants, 61% accepted, 14 enrolled. In 2009, 11 master's awarded. *Degree requirements:* For master's, one foreign language, thesis. *Entrance requirements:* Additional exam requirements/recommendations for international students: Required—TOEFL (minimum score 600 paper-based; 250 computer-based; 100 iBT), IELTS (minimum score 7). *Application deadline:* For fall admission, 4/1 priority date for domestic students; for spring admission, 12/15 priority date for domestic students. Applications are processed on a rolling basis. Application fee: $45 ($60 for international students). Electronic applications accepted. *Financial support:* In 2009–10, 3 fellowships with full tuition reimbursements (averaging $12,150 per year), 1 research assistantship (averaging $3,000 per year), 18 teaching assistantships with full tuition reimbursements (averaging $8,100 per year) were awarded; Federal Work-Study, institutionally sponsored loans, and scholarships/grants also available. Support available to part-time students. Financial award application deadline: 5/1. *Faculty research:* American and English literature, women's studies, language attitudes, composition practices, computers and composition. *Unit head:* Dr. Dale Sullivan, Head, 701-231-7143, Fax: 701-231-1047, E-mail: dale.sullivan@ndsu.edu. *Application contact:* Dr. Dale Sullivan, Head, 701-231-7143, Fax: 701-231-1047, E-mail: dale.sullivan@ndsu.edu.

Northeastern Illinois University, Graduate College, College of Arts and Sciences, Department of English, Programs in English, Chicago, IL 60625-4699. Offers composition/writing (MA); literature (MA). Part-time and evening/weekend programs available. *Degree requirements:* For master's, comprehensive exam, thesis optional. *Entrance requirements:* For master's, 30 hours of undergraduate course work in literature and composition (literature), BA in English or approval (composition/writing), minimum GPA of 2.75. Additional exam requirements/recommendations for international students: Required—TOEFL (minimum score 550 paper-

English

Northeastern Illinois University (continued)
based; 213 computer-based; 80 iBT). Electronic applications accepted. *Faculty research:* Arthurian literature, Southern American literature, rhetoric and theories of authorship.

Northeastern State University, Graduate College, College of Liberal Arts, Department of Languages and Literature, Tahlequah, OK 74464-2399. Offers English (MA), including literature, rhetoric/composition. *Degree requirements:* For master's, thesis. *Entrance requirements:* For master's, GRE or MAT, minimum GPA of 2.5. Additional exam requirements/recommendations for international students: Required—TOEFL (minimum score 213 computer-based). Electronic applications accepted.

Northeastern University, College of Social Sciences and Humanities, Department of English, Boston, MA 02115-5096. Offers cinema studies (Certificate); English (MA, PhD); women's studies (Certificate). Part-time and evening/weekend programs available. *Faculty:* 33 full-time (22 women), 28 part-time/adjunct (22 women). *Students:* 63 full-time (42 women), 2 part-time (1 woman); includes 3 Asian Americans or Pacific Islanders, 1 Hispanic American, 5 international. 106 applicants, 40% accepted, 22 enrolled. In 2009, 6 master's, 1 doctorate awarded. *Degree requirements:* For master's, one foreign language, comprehensive exam, qualifying exams; for doctorate, 2 foreign languages, comprehensive exam, thesis/dissertation, qualifying exams. *Entrance requirements:* For master's and doctorate, GRE General Test, GRE Subject Test, sample of written work. Additional exam requirements/recommendations for international students: Required—TOEFL. *Application deadline:* For fall admission, 2/1 priority date for domestic and international students. Applications are processed on a rolling basis. Application fee: $50. Electronic applications accepted. *Financial support:* In 2009–10, 30 teaching assistantships with tuition reimbursements (averaging $15,550 per year) were awarded; fellowships with tuition reimbursements, research assistantships with tuition reimbursements, career-related internships or fieldwork, tuition waivers (full and partial), and unspecified assistantships also available. Financial award application deadline: 3/1; financial award applicants required to submit FAFSA. *Faculty research:* Literature, creative writing, composition studies, linguistics. *Unit head:* Dr. Elizabeth Dillon, Graduate Coordinator, 617-373-3692, Fax: 617-373-2509, E-mail: gradenglish@neu.edu. *Application contact:* Jo-Anne Dickinson, Admissions Contact, 617-373-5990, Fax: 617-373-7281, E-mail: gsas@neu.edu.

Northern Arizona University, Graduate College, College of Arts and Letters, Department of English, Program in English, Flagstaff, AZ 86011. Offers creative writing (MA); English education (MA); general English studies (MA); literacy, technology and professional writing (MA); literature (MA). *Faculty:* 40 full-time (24 women). *Students:* 87 full-time (59 women), 94 part-time (70 women); includes 20 minority (6 African Americans, 6 American Indian/Alaska Native, 3 Asian Americans or Pacific Islanders, 5 Hispanic Americans), 1 international. Average age 31. 99 applicants, 66% accepted, 45 enrolled. In 2009, 77 master's awarded. *Degree requirements:* For master's, thesis (for some programs), departmental qualifying exam. *Entrance requirements:* For master's, minimum GPA of 3.0 or GRE. Additional exam requirements/recommendations for international students: Required—TOEFL (minimum score 550 paper-based; 213 computer-based; 80 iBT), IELTS (minimum score 7), or a bachelor's degree from an English-speaking university and demonstrated proficiency. *Application deadline:* For fall admission, 2/15 priority date for domestic students, 9/1 priority date for international students; for winter admission, 4/15 priority date for domestic students; for spring admission, 11/15 priority date for domestic students. Applications are processed on a rolling basis. Application fee: $65. Electronic applications accepted. *Financial support:* In 2009–10, 63 teaching assistantships with partial tuition reimbursements (averaging $11,623 per year) were awarded; Federal Work-Study, scholarships/grants, health care benefits, and unspecified assistantships also available. Support available to part-time students. Financial award application deadline: 3/30; financial award applicants required to submit FAFSA. *Unit head:* Dr. Allen Woodman, Chair, 928-523-5651, Fax: 928-523-7074, E-mail: allen.woodman@nau.edu. *Application contact:* Barbara Hanks, 928-523-4911, Fax: 928-523-7074, E-mail: barbara.hanks@nau.edu.

Northern Illinois University, Graduate School, College of Liberal Arts and Sciences, Department of English, De Kalb, IL 60115-2854. Offers MA, PhD. Part-time programs available. *Faculty:* 32 full-time (13 women), 2 part-time/adjunct (both women). *Students:* 52 full-time (33 women), 76 part-time (46 women); includes 5 minority (1 African American, 1 American Indian/Alaska Native, 3 Hispanic Americans), 4 international. Average age 32. 113 applicants, 42% accepted, 32 enrolled. In 2009, 34 master's, 6 doctorates awarded. Terminal master's awarded for partial completion of doctoral program. *Degree requirements:* For master's, variable foreign language requirement, comprehensive exam, thesis optional; for doctorate, variable foreign language requirement, thesis/dissertation, candidacy exam, dissertation defense. *Entrance requirements:* For master's, GRE General Test, minimum GPA of 2.75; for doctorate, GRE General Test, minimum GPA of 2.75 (undergraduate), 3.2 (graduate). Additional exam requirements/recommendations for international students: Required—TOEFL (minimum score 550 paper-based; 213 computer-based). *Application deadline:* For fall admission, 6/1 for domestic students, 5/1 for international students; for spring admission, 11/1 for domestic students, 10/1 for international students. Applications are processed on a rolling basis. Application fee: $30. Electronic applications accepted. *Expenses:* Tuition, state resident: full-time $6576; part-time $274 per credit hour. Tuition, nonresident: full-time $13,152; part-time $548 per credit hour. Required fees: $1813; $75,53 per credit hour. Part-time tuition and fees vary according to course load. *Financial support:* In 2009–10, 62 teaching assistantships with full tuition reimbursements were awarded; fellowships with full tuition reimbursements, research assistantships with full tuition reimbursements, career-related internships or fieldwork, Federal Work-Study, scholarships/grants, tuition waivers (full), and unspecified assistantships also available. Support available to part-time students. Financial award applicants required to submit FAFSA. *Faculty research:* Nineteenth century English literature, linguistic programs, portfolio assembly, Mideast literature, old English folklore. *Unit head:* Dr. Phillip Eubanks, Chair, 815-753-0615, Fax: 815-753-0606, E-mail: eubanks@niu.edu. *Application contact:* Dr. Jeffrey Johnson, Director, Graduate Studies, 815-753-6602, E-mail: jsjohnson@niu.edu.

Northern Kentucky University, Office of Graduate Programs, College of Arts and Sciences, Program in English, Highland Heights, KY 41099. Offers composition and rhetoric (Certificate); English (MA); professional writing (Certificate). Part-time and evening/weekend programs available. *Students:* 7 full-time (4 women), 49 part-time (36 women); includes 3 minority (2 African Americans, 1 Hispanic American). Average age 33. 49 applicants, 76% accepted, 32 enrolled. *Degree requirements:* For master's, comprehensive exam or thesis. *Entrance requirements:* For master's, minimum GPA of 3.0, two letters of reference. Additional exam requirements/recommendations for international students: Required—TOEFL (minimum score 550 paper-based; 213 computer-based; 79 iBT); Recommended—IELTS (minimum score 6.5). *Application deadline:* For fall admission, 7/1 priority date for domestic students, 6/1 priority date for international students; for spring admission, 11/1 for domestic students, 10/1 for international students. Applications are processed on a rolling basis. Application fee: $40. Electronic applications accepted. *Expenses:* Tuition, state resident: full-time $6912; part-time $384 per credit hour. Tuition, nonresident: full-time $12,150; part-time $675 per credit hour. Tuition and fees vary according to course load, program and reciprocity agreements. *Financial support:* Unspecified assistantships available. Financial award applicants required to submit FAFSA. *Faculty research:* Professional writing and new media studies, composition and rhetoric, literary studies, creative writing, cinema studies. *Unit head:* Dr. Roxanne Kent-Drury, Coordinator, 859-572-6636, E-mail: rkdrury@nku.edu. *Application contact:* Dr. Peg Griffin, Director of Graduate Programs, 859-572-6934, Fax: 859-572-6670, E-mail: griffinp@nku.edu.

Northern Michigan University, College of Graduate Studies, College of Arts and Sciences, Department of English, Marquette, MI 49855-5301. Offers creative writing (MFA); literature (MA); pedagogy (MA); writing (MA). Part-time programs available. *Degree requirements:* For master's, thesis or alternative. *Entrance requirements:* For master's, minimum GPA of 2.75.

Northwestern State University of Louisiana, Graduate Studies and Research, Department of Language and Communication, Natchitoches, LA 71497. Offers English (MA). *Degree* *requirements:* For master's, one foreign language, comprehensive exam, thesis or alternative. *Entrance requirements:* For master's, GRE General Test, minimum undergraduate GPA of 2.5.

Northwestern University, The Graduate School, Judd A. and Marjorie Weinberg College of Arts and Sciences, Department of English, Evanston, IL 60208. Offers MA, PhD. Admissions and degrees offered through The Graduate School. Terminal master's awarded for partial completion of doctoral program. *Degree requirements:* For master's, thesis; for doctorate, one foreign language, thesis/dissertation, oral and written qualifying exam. *Entrance requirements:* For master's and doctorate, GRE General Test, sample of written work. Additional exam requirements/recommendations for international students: Required—TOEFL. Electronic applications accepted. *Faculty research:* Renaissance literature, theatre and drama, American literature, modern European contemporary literature, poetry, cultural history.

See Display on page 350.

Northwestern University, School of Continuing Studies, Program in Literature, Evanston, IL 60208. Offers American literature (MA); British literature (MA); comparative and world literature (MA).

Northwest Missouri State University, Graduate School, College of Arts and Sciences, Department of English, Maryville, MO 64468-6001. Offers English (MA); English with speech emphasis (MA); teaching English (option 1) (MS Ed); teaching English with speech emphasis (MS Ed). Part-time programs available. *Faculty:* 8 full-time (2 women). *Students:* 11 full-time (6 women), 4 part-time (3 women). 9 applicants, 67% accepted, 4 enrolled. In 2009, 3 master's awarded. *Degree requirements:* For master's, comprehensive exam, thesis optional. *Entrance requirements:* For master's, GRE General Test, minimum undergraduate GPA of 2.5, writing sample. Additional exam requirements/recommendations for international students: Required—TOEFL (minimum score 550 paper-based; 213 computer-based). *Application deadline:* For fall admission, 7/1 for domestic and international students; for spring admission, 11/15 for domestic and international students. Applications are processed on a rolling basis. Application fee: $0 ($50 for international students). *Expenses:* Tuition, state resident: part-time $296.34 per credit hour. Tuition, nonresident: part-time $510.43 per credit hour. *Financial support:* In 2009–10, 5 teaching assistantships with full tuition reimbursements (averaging $6,000 per year) were awarded. Financial award application deadline: 4/1; financial award applicants required to submit FAFSA. *Unit head:* Dr. Beth Richards, Chairperson, 660-562-1745. *Application contact:* Dr. Gregory Haddock, Dean of Graduate School, 660-562-1145, Fax: 660-562-1096, E-mail: gradsch@nwmissouri.edu.

Notre Dame de Namur University, Division of Academic Affairs, College of Arts and Sciences, Department of English, Belmont, CA 94002-1908. Offers English (MA); teaching English to speakers of other languages (Certificate). Part-time and evening/weekend programs available. *Faculty:* 5 full-time (2 women), 5 part-time/adjunct (3 women). *Students:* 3 full-time (all women), 15 part-time (12 women); includes 4 minority (1 Asian American or Pacific Islander, 3 Hispanic Americans), 1 international. Average age 28. 6 applicants, 100% accepted, 4 enrolled. In 2009, 10 master's awarded. *Degree requirements:* For master's, thesis optional, exam. *Entrance requirements:* For master's, minimum GPA of 2.5, writing sample. Additional exam requirements/recommendations for international students: Required—TOEFL (minimum score 550 paper-based; 213 computer-based; 79 iBT). *Application deadline:* For fall admission, 8/1 priority date for domestic students; for spring admission, 12/1 priority date for domestic students. Applications are processed on a rolling basis. Application fee: $50 ($500 for international students). Electronic applications accepted. *Expenses:* Tuition: Part-time $720 per credit. Required fees: $35 per semester hour. *Financial support:* Career-related internships or fieldwork available. Support available to part-time students. Financial award applicants required to submit FAFSA. *Unit head:* Jacqueline Berger, Director, 650-508-3730. *Application contact:* Candace Hallmark, Associate Director of Admissions, 650-508-3592, Fax: 650-508-3426, E-mail: grad.admit@ndnu.edu.

Oakland University, Graduate Study and Lifelong Learning, College of Arts and Sciences, Department of English, Rochester, MI 48309-4401. Offers MA. Part-time and evening/weekend programs available. *Entrance requirements:* For master's, minimum GPA of 3.0 for unconditional admission. Additional exam requirements/recommendations for international students: Required—TOEFL (minimum score 550 paper-based; 213 computer-based). Electronic applications accepted.

The Ohio State University, Graduate School, College of Humanities, Department of English, Columbus, OH 43210. Offers MA, MFA, PhD. *Faculty:* 100. *Students:* 126 full-time (81 women), 57 part-time (33 women); includes 25 minority (6 African Americans, 8 Asian Americans or Pacific Islanders, 11 Hispanic Americans), 9 international. Average age 29. In 2009, 36 master's, 14 doctorates awarded. *Degree requirements:* For master's, one foreign language, thesis or written exam; for doctorate, one foreign language, thesis/dissertation. *Entrance requirements:* For master's and doctorate, GRE General Test. Additional exam requirements/recommendations for international students: Required—TOEFL (minimum score 600 paper-based; 250 computer-based). *Application deadline:* For fall admission, 8/15 priority date for domestic students, 7/1 priority date for international students; for winter admission, 12/1 priority date for domestic students, 11/1 priority date for international students; for spring admission, 3/1 priority date for domestic students, 2/1 priority date for international students. Applications are processed on a rolling basis. Application fee: $40 ($50 for international students). Electronic applications accepted. *Expenses:* Tuition, state resident: full-time $10,683. Tuition, nonresident: full-time $25,923. Tuition and fees vary according to course load and program. *Financial support:* Fellowships, research assistantships, teaching assistantships, Federal Work-Study, institutionally sponsored loans, and unspecified assistantships available. Support available to part-time students. *Unit head:* Nancy Johnson, Graduate Studies Committee Chair, E-mail: johnson.112@osu.edu. *Application contact:* Graduate Admissions, 614-292-9444, Fax: 614-292-3895, E-mail: domestic.grad@osu.edu.

Ohio University, Graduate College, College of Arts and Sciences, Department of English Language and Literature, Athens, OH 45701-2979. Offers MA, PhD. Part-time programs available. *Faculty:* 36 full-time (15 women). *Students:* 71 full-time (46 women), 1 (woman) part-time; includes 5 minority (1 African American, 1 American Indian/Alaska Native, 1 Asian American or Pacific Islander, 2 Hispanic Americans), 9 international. 207 applicants, 16% accepted, 31 enrolled. In 2009, 16 master's, 6 doctorates awarded. *Degree requirements:* For master's, one foreign language, thesis or alternative; for doctorate, one foreign language, comprehensive exam, thesis/dissertation, oral exam, public lecture. *Entrance requirements:* For master's, GRE General Test, minimum GPA of 3.0, writing sample; for doctorate, GRE General Test, minimum GPA of 3.0, master's degree in English, writing sample. Additional exam requirements/recommendations for international students: Required—TOEFL (minimum score 550 paper-based; 80 iBT) or IELTS Academic (minimum score 6.5). *Application deadline:* For fall admission, 1/15 for domestic and international students. Application fee: $50 ($55 for international students). Electronic applications accepted. *Expenses:* Tuition, state resident: full-time $7839; part-time $323 per quarter hour. Tuition, nonresident: full-time $15,831; part-time $654 per quarter hour. Required fees: $2931. *Financial support:* Teaching assistantships with full tuition reimbursements, Federal Work-Study, institutionally sponsored loans, and unspecified assistantships available. Financial award application deadline: 1/15. *Faculty research:* Environmental literature, post-colonial studies, print culture, film in popular culture, computers in pedagogy. Total annual research expenditures: $54,676. *Unit head:* Dr. Joseph McLaughlin, Department Chair, 740-593-2838, Fax: 740-593-2818, E-mail: mclaughj@ohio.edu. *Application contact:* Dr. Marsha Dutton, Graduate Chair, 740-597-2752, Fax: 740-593-2832, E-mail: dutton@ohio.edu.

Oklahoma State University, College of Arts and Sciences, Department of English, Stillwater, OK 74078. Offers creative writing (MFA); English (MA, PhD). *Faculty:* 50 full-time (31 women), 2 part-time/adjunct (both women). *Students:* 15 full-time (9 women), 134 part-time (72 women); includes 15 minority (4 African Americans, 9 American Indian/Alaska Native, 1 Asian American or Pacific Islander, 1 Hispanic American), 21 international. Average age 32. 130 applicants, 49% accepted, 37 enrolled. In 2009, 15 master's, 7 doctorates awarded. *Degree requirements:* For master's, comprehensive exam, thesis; for doctorate, comprehensive exam, thesis/dissertation. *Entrance requirements:* For master's, GRE General Test, minimum GPA of 3.0, writing sample; for doctorate, GRE General Test, minimum GPA of 3.5, writing sample. Additional exam requirements/recommendations for international students: Required—TOEFL (minimum score 550 paper-based; 79 iBT). *Application deadline:* For fall admission, 3/1 priority date for international students; for spring admission, 8/1 priority date for international students. Applications are processed on a rolling basis. Application fee: $40 ($75 for international students). Electronic applications accepted. *Expenses:* Tuition, state resident: full-time $3716; part-time $154.85 per credit hour. Tuition, nonresident: full-time $14,448; part-time $602 per credit hour. Required fees: $1772; $73.85 per credit hour. One-time fee: $50. Tuition and fees vary according to course load and campus/location. *Financial support:* In 2009–10, 3 research assistantships (averaging $11,313 per year), 97 teaching assistantships (averaging $14,184 per year) were awarded; career-related internships or fieldwork, Federal Work-Study, scholarships/grants, health care benefits, tuition waivers (partial), and unspecified assistantships also available. Support available to part-time students. Financial award application deadline: 3/1; financial award applicants required to submit FAFSA. *Faculty research:* American and British novels, poetry, and autobiography; Native American languages and literature; institutional history of American film, history, and adaptations; rhetoric and theories of human communication; learning strategies of second language learners. *Unit head:* Dr. Carol Moder, Head, 405-744-9474, Fax: 405-744-6326. *Application contact:* Dr. Gordon Emslie, Dean, 405-744-6368, Fax: 405-744-0355, E-mail: grad-i@okstate.edu.

Old Dominion University, College of Arts and Letters, Doctoral Program in English, Norfolk, VA 23529. Offers PhD. Part-time and evening/weekend programs available. Postbaccalaureate distance learning degree programs offered (minimal on-campus study). *Faculty:* 17 full-time (10 women). *Students:* 15 full-time (13 women), 24 part-time (19 women); includes 6 minority (5 African Americans, 1 Hispanic American), 1 international. Average age 35. 32 applicants, 38% accepted, 6 enrolled. *Degree requirements:* For doctorate, comprehensive exam, thesis/dissertation, research competency in foreign language, statistics, or new media. *Entrance requirements:* For doctorate, GRE General Test, MA in English or related field with minimum GPA of 3.5, writing sample, resume. Additional exam requirements/recommendations for international students: Required—TOEFL. *Application deadline:* For fall admission, 2/15 for domestic students. Application fee: $40. Electronic applications accepted. *Expenses:* Tuition, state resident: full-time $8112; part-time $338 per credit. Tuition, nonresident: full-time $20,256; part-time $844 per credit. Required fees: $119 per semester. One-time fee: $50. *Financial support:* In 2009–10, 13 students received support, including 3 fellowships with full tuition reimbursements available (averaging $15,000 per year), 1 research assistantship with full tuition reimbursement available (averaging $15,000 per year), 9 teaching assistantships with full tuition reimbursements available (averaging $15,000 per year); career-related internships or fieldwork, scholarships/grants, and unspecified assistantships also available. Support available to part-time students. Financial award application deadline: 2/15; financial award applicants required to submit FAFSA. *Faculty research:* New media studies, rhetorical history and theory, digital studies, writing studies, professional writing and document design, linguistics, textual studies, literary studies. *Unit head:* Dr. Joyce Neff, Graduate Program Director, 757-683-6875, Fax: 757-683-3241, E-mail: jneff@odu.edu. *Application contact:* Dr. Robert Wojtowicz, Associate Dean, 757-683-6077, Fax: 757-683-5746, E-mail: rwojtowi@odu.edu.

Old Dominion University, College of Arts and Letters, Master's in English Program, Norfolk, VA 23529. Offers MA. Part-time and evening/weekend programs available. Postbaccalaureate distance learning degree programs offered (minimal on-campus study). *Faculty:* 17 full-time (8 women). *Students:* 20 full-time (13 women), 33 part-time (27 women); includes 16 minority (13 African Americans, 1 Asian American or Pacific Islander, 2 Hispanic Americans), 2 international. Average age 30. 56 applicants, 66% accepted, 30 enrolled. In 2009, 25 master's awarded. *Degree requirements:* For master's, comprehensive exam, thesis optional. *Entrance requirements:* For master's, GRE General Test, 24 hours in English, sample of written work. Additional exam requirements/recommendations for international students: Required—TOEFL. *Application deadline:* For fall admission, 6/1 priority date for domestic students; for winter admission, 11/1 priority date for domestic students; for spring admission, 3/1 priority date for domestic students. Applications are processed on a rolling basis. Application fee: $40. Electronic applications accepted. *Expenses:* Tuition, state resident: full-time $8112; part-time $338 per credit. Tuition, nonresident: full-time $20,256; part-time $844 per credit. Required fees: $119 per semester. One-time fee: $50. *Financial support:* In 2009–10, 3 fellowships with tuition reimbursements (averaging $15,000 per year), 3 research assistantships with partial tuition reimbursements (averaging $8,119 per year), 14 teaching assistantships with partial tuition reimbursements (averaging $12,000 per year) were awarded; career-related internships or fieldwork, scholarships/grants, and unspecified assistantships also available. Support available to part-time students. Financial award application deadline: 2/15; financial award applicants required to submit FAFSA. *Faculty research:* Literary theory, composition theory, professional writing, rhetoric, British and American literature. Total annual research expenditures: $3,451. *Unit head:* Dr. Jeffrey H. Richards, Graduate Program Director, 757-683-4032, Fax: 757-683-3241, E-mail: jhrichar@odu.edu. *Application contact:* Dr. Jeffrey H. Richards, Graduate Program Director, 757-683-4032, Fax: 757-683-3241, E-mail: jhrichar@odu.edu.

Old Dominion University, Darden College of Education, Programs in Secondary Education, Norfolk, VA 23529. Offers biology (MS Ed); chemistry (MS Ed); English (MS Ed); instructional technology (MS Ed); library science (MS Ed); secondary education (MS Ed). *Accreditation:* NCATE. Part-time and evening/weekend programs available. Postbaccalaureate distance learning degree programs offered (minimal on-campus study). *Faculty:* 20 full-time (16 women). *Students:* 74 full-time (54 women), 137 part-time (92 women); includes 41 minority (22 African Americans, 1 American Indian/Alaska Native, 11 Asian Americans or Pacific Islanders, 7 Hispanic Americans). Average age 33. 67 applicants, 79% accepted, 53 enrolled. In 2009, 131 master's awarded. *Degree requirements:* For master's, comprehensive exam, thesis. *Entrance requirements:* For master's, GRE General Test or MAT, PRAXIS I (for licensure), minimum GPA of 2.8, teaching certificate. Additional exam requirements/recommendations for international students: Required—TOEFL. *Application deadline:* For fall admission, 6/1 for domestic and international students; for winter admission, 11/1 for domestic and international students; for spring admission, 3/1 for domestic and international students. Applications are processed on a rolling basis. Application fee: $50. Electronic applications accepted. *Expenses:* Tuition, state resident: full-time $8112; part-time $338 per credit. Tuition, nonresident: full-time $20,256; part-time $844 per credit. Required fees: $119 per semester. One-time fee: $50. *Financial support:* In 2009–10, 56 students received support, including fellowships (averaging $15,000 per year), 2 research assistantships with tuition reimbursements available (averaging $9,000 per year), 3 teaching assistantships with tuition reimbursements available (averaging $12,500 per year); career-related internships or fieldwork, Federal Work-Study, institutionally sponsored loans, scholarships/grants, and tuition waivers (partial) also available. Support available to part-time students. Financial award application deadline: 2/15; financial award applicants required to submit FAFSA. *Faculty research:* Use of technology, writing project for teachers, geography teaching, reading. *Unit head:* Dr. Robert Lucking, Graduate Program Director, 757-683-5545, Fax: 757-683-5862, E-mail: rlucking@odu.edu. *Application contact:* Dr. Robert Lucking, Graduate Program Director, 757-683-5545, Fax: 757-683-5862, E-mail: rlucking@odu.edu.

Oregon State University, Graduate School, College of Liberal Arts, Department of English, Corvallis, OR 97331. Offers MA, MAIS, MFA. *Faculty:* 29 full-time (13 women), 2 part-time/adjunct (0 women). *Students:* 17 full-time (11 women), 2 part-time (both women); includes 3 minority (1 Asian American or Pacific Islander, 2 Hispanic Americans), 1 international. Average age 28. In 2009, 3 master's awarded. *Degree requirements:* For master's, one foreign language, thesis. *Entrance requirements:* For master's, minimum GPA of 3.0 in last 90 hours of course work. Additional exam requirements/recommendations for international students: Required—TOEFL. Application fee: $50. *Expenses:* Tuition, state resident: full-time $9774; part-time $362 per credit. Tuition, nonresident: full-time $15,849; part-time $587 per credit. Required fees:

English

Oregon State University (continued)
$1639. Full-time tuition and fees vary according to course load and program. *Financial support:* Fellowships, teaching assistantships, career-related internships or fieldwork, Federal Work-Study, and institutionally sponsored loans available. Support available to part-time students. Financial award application deadline: 2/1. *Faculty research:* Composition and rhetoric, American literature theory, American renaissance, gender studies, English drama. *Unit head:* Dr. Tracy Daugherty, Chair, 541-737-1634, Fax: 541-737-3589, E-mail: tdaugherty@oregonstate.edu. *Application contact:* Polly Jeneva, Head Adviser, 541-737-0561, Fax: 541-737-2434, E-mail: polly.jeneva@oregonstate.edu.

Our Lady of the Lake University of San Antonio, College of Arts and Sciences, Program in English, San Antonio, TX 78207-4689. Offers communication arts (MA); English and literature (MA); English education (MA); writing (MA). Part-time and evening/weekend programs available. *Students:* 9 full-time (5 women), 15 part-time (14 women); includes 16 minority (all Hispanic Americans). Average age 31. In 2009, 15 master's awarded. *Degree requirements:* For master's, comprehensive exam, thesis optional. *Entrance requirements:* For master's, GRE General Test or MAT, minimum GPA of 3.0 in last 60 hours, 2.5 overall. Additional exam requirements/recommendations for international students: Required—TOEFL. *Application deadline:* Applications are processed on a rolling basis. Application fee: $25 ($50 for international students). Electronic applications accepted. *Expenses:* Tuition: Full-time $12,330; part-time $685 per contact hour. Required fees: $139; $12 per contact hour. $57 per semester. Tuition and fees vary according to campus/location. *Financial support:* Research assistantships, teaching assistantships, career-related internships or fieldwork, Federal Work-Study, institutionally sponsored loans, and tuition waivers (partial) available. Financial award application deadline: 4/15. *Faculty research:* Writing theory and research, contemporary Southern literature, popular culture, poetry, literature of the Southwest. *Unit head:* Dr. Michael Lueker, Chair, 210-434-6711 Ext. 2242, E-mail: luekm@lake.ollusa.edu. *Application contact:* 210-434-6711, Fax: 210-431-4036, E-mail: gradadm@lake.ollusa.edu.

Penn State University Park, Graduate School, College of the Liberal Arts, Department of English, State College, University Park, PA 16802-1503. Offers MA, MFA, PhD.

Pittsburg State University, Graduate School, College of Arts and Sciences, Department of English, Pittsburg, KS 66762. Offers MA. *Degree requirements:* For master's, thesis or alternative. *Expenses:* Tuition, state resident: full-time $4212; part-time $176 per credit. Tuition, nonresident: full-time $11,530; part-time $480 per credit. Required fees: $940; $43 per credit. Tuition and fees vary according to course level, course load, degree level, campus/location, reciprocity agreements and student level. *Faculty research:* American fiction, American poetry, British fiction, British poetry, composition theory.

Portland State University, Graduate Studies, College of Liberal Arts and Sciences, Department of English, Portland, OR 97207-0751. Offers MA, MA/MS. Part-time and evening/weekend programs available. *Degree requirements:* For master's, one foreign language, comprehensive exam (for some programs), thesis (for some programs), oral and written exams. *Entrance requirements:* For master's, minimum GPA of 3.25 in upper-division course work and English courses or 2.75 overall, 3 letters of recommendation. Additional exam requirements/recommendations for international students: Required—TOEFL (minimum score 600 paper-based). *Faculty research:* American literature and cultural studies, Medieval and British literature, writing prose fiction and poetry, rhetoric and composition, women's literature.

Prairie View A&M University, College of Arts and Sciences, Department of Languages and Communication, Prairie View, TX 77446-0519. Offers English (MA). Part-time programs available. *Faculty:* 3 full-time (2 women). *Students:* 6 full-time (1 woman), 1 part-time (0 women); includes 4 minority (all African Americans). Average age 27. 2 applicants, 100% accepted, 2 enrolled. In 2009, 1 master's awarded. *Degree requirements:* For master's, comprehensive exam, thesis, exit exam. *Entrance requirements:* For master's, GRE General Test, bachelor's degree in English or equivalent. Additional exam requirements/recommendations for international students: Required—TOEFL. *Application deadline:* For fall admission, 7/1 for domestic students, 6/1 for international students; for winter admission, 4/1 for domestic students, 10/1 for international students; for spring admission, 3/1 for domestic students, 2/1 for international students. Application fee: $50. *Expenses:* Tuition, state resident: full-time $2200. Tuition, nonresident: full-time $5600. Required fees: $1720. Tuition and fees vary according to course load. *Financial support:* In 2009–10, 8 fellowships with tuition reimbursements (averaging $12,000 per year), 10 research assistantships with partial tuition reimbursements (averaging $15,000 per year) were awarded; teaching assistantships with partial tuition reimbursements, career-related internships or fieldwork, Federal Work-Study, institutionally sponsored loans, and tuition waivers (full and partial) also available. Support available to part-time students. Financial award application deadline: 4/1; financial award applicants required to submit FAFSA. *Faculty research:* Composition, rhetoric, technical writing, literature, communication, pedagogy in general and for literature, online teaching. *Unit head:* Dr. Dejun Liu, Head, 936-261-3731, Fax: 936-261-3209, E-mail: deliu@pvamu.edu. *Application contact:* Dr. Dejun Liu, Head, 936-261-3731, Fax: 936-261-3209, E-mail: deliu@pvamu.edu.

Princeton University, Graduate School, Department of English, Princeton, NJ 08544-1019. Offers PhD. *Degree requirements:* For doctorate, 2 foreign languages, thesis/dissertation. *Entrance requirements:* For doctorate, GRE General Test, GRE Subject Test, sample of written work. Additional exam requirements/recommendations for international students: Required—TOEFL (minimum score 600 paper-based; 250 computer-based). Electronic applications accepted.

Purdue University, Graduate School, College of Liberal Arts, Department of English, West Lafayette, IN 47907. Offers creative writing (MFA); literature (MA, PhD), including linguistics, literature and philosophy (PhD), rhetoric and composition, theory and cultural studies (PhD). Part-time programs available. *Degree requirements:* For master's, one foreign language; for doctorate, one foreign language, thesis/dissertation. *Entrance requirements:* For master's and doctorate, GRE General Test, sample of written work. Additional exam requirements/recommendations for international students: Required—TOEFL. Electronic applications accepted. *Faculty research:* Cultural studies, postmodern narrative, contemporary women writers, composition theory, slave narratives.

Purdue University Calumet, Graduate School, School of Liberal Arts and Social Sciences, Department of English and Philosophy, Hammond, IN 46323-2094. Offers English (MA). Part-time and evening/weekend programs available. Postbaccalaureate distance learning degree programs offered (minimal on-campus study). *Degree requirements:* For master's, comprehensive exam, thesis optional. *Entrance requirements:* Additional exam requirements/recommendations for international students: Required—TOEFL. Electronic applications accepted. *Faculty research:* English literature, American literature, critical theory, women's studies, historical philosophy.

Queens College of the City University of New York, Division of Graduate Studies, Arts and Humanities Division, Department of English, Flushing, NY 11367-1597. Offers creative writing (MA); English language and literature (MA). Part-time and evening/weekend programs available. *Faculty:* 53 full-time (25 women). *Students:* 2 full-time (1 woman), 118 part-time (81 women). 158 applicants, 38% accepted, 38 enrolled. In 2009, 47 master's awarded. *Degree requirements:* For master's, one foreign language, thesis (for some programs), oral exam (English language and literature). *Entrance requirements:* For master's, manuscript (creative writing), minimum GPA of 3.0. Additional exam requirements/recommendations for international students: Required—TOEFL. *Application deadline:* For fall admission, 4/1 for domestic students; for spring admission, 11/1 for domestic students. Applications are processed on a rolling basis. Application fee: $125. *Expenses:* Tuition, state resident: full-time $7360; part-time $310 per credit. Tuition, nonresident: part-time $575 per credit. One-time fee: $195.25 full-time; $145.25 part-time. *Financial support:* Career-related internships or fieldwork, Federal Work-Study, institutionally sponsored loans, and tuition waivers (partial) available. Support available to part-time students. Financial award application deadline: 4/1; financial award applicants required to submit FAFSA. *Unit head:* Dr. Nancy Comley, Chairperson, 718-997-4600, E-mail: nancy_comley@qc.edu. *Application contact:* Dr. Talia Schaffer, Graduate Adviser, 718-997-4600, E-mail: talia_schaffer@qc.edu.

Queen's University at Kingston, School of Graduate Studies and Research, Faculty of Arts and Sciences, Department of English Language and Literature, Kingston, ON K7L 3N6, Canada. Offers MA, PhD. *Degree requirements:* For master's, one foreign language, thesis optional; for doctorate, 2 foreign languages, comprehensive exam, thesis/dissertation. *Entrance requirements:* For master's, B.A.H. upper 2nd class standing, 10 full courses in English; for doctorate, M.A. upper 2nd class standing. Additional exam requirements/recommendations for international students: Required—TOEFL, TWE. *Faculty research:* Renaissance, 18th century, post colonial, Canadian, 19th century.

Radford University, College of Graduate and Professional Studies, College of Humanities and Behavioral Sciences, Department of English, Radford, VA 24142. Offers MA, MS. Part-time programs available. *Faculty:* 21 full-time (10 women), 1 (woman) part-time/adjunct. *Students:* 34 full-time (25 women), 3 part-time (all women); includes 2 minority (1 Asian American or Pacific Islander, 1 Hispanic American). Average age 28. 29 applicants, 97% accepted, 20 enrolled. In 2009, 20 master's awarded. *Degree requirements:* For master's, comprehensive exam, thesis (for some programs). *Entrance requirements:* For master's, GRE, minimum GPA of 2.75; 2 letters of reference; sample of expository writing. Additional exam requirements/recommendations for international students: Required—TOEFL (minimum score 550 paper-based; 213 computer-based; 79 iBT). *Application deadline:* For fall admission, 12/1 for international students; for spring admission, 7/1 for international students. Applications are processed on a rolling basis. Application fee: $50. Electronic applications accepted. *Expenses:* Tuition, state resident: full-time $5086; part-time $211 per credit hour. Tuition, nonresident: full-time $12,608; part-time $525 per credit hour. Required fees: $2508; $105 per credit hour. *Financial support:* In 2009–10, 20 students received support, including 2 research assistantships with partial tuition reimbursements available (averaging $8,000 per year), 16 teaching assistantships with partial tuition reimbursements available (averaging $8,700 per year); career-related internships or fieldwork, Federal Work-Study, institutionally sponsored loans, scholarships/grants, and unspecified assistantships also available. Financial award application deadline: 3/1; financial award applicants required to submit FAFSA. *Unit head:* Dr. Rosemary F. Guruswamy, Chair, 540-831-5285, Fax: 540-831-6800, E-mail: rguruswa@radford.edu. *Application contact:* Graduate Admissions, 540-831-5431, Fax: 540-831-6061, E-mail: gradcollege@radford.edu.

Rhode Island College, School of Graduate Studies, Faculty of Arts and Sciences, Department of English, Providence, RI 02908-1991. Offers creative writing (MA); English (MA). Part-time and evening/weekend programs available. *Faculty:* 9 full-time (7 women). *Students:* 3 full-time (all women), 17 part-time (11 women). Average age 35. In 2009, 6 master's awarded. *Degree requirements:* For master's, thesis (for some programs). *Entrance requirements:* For master's, GRE General Test, 3 letters of recommendation, interview. Additional exam requirements/recommendations for international students: Recommended—TOEFL (minimum score 550 paper-based; 213 computer-based; 79 iBT). *Application deadline:* For fall admission, 4/1 for domestic students; for spring admission, 11/1 for domestic students. Applications are processed on a rolling basis. Application fee: $50. *Expenses:* Tuition, state resident: full-time $7440; part-time $310 per credit hour. Tuition, nonresident: full-time $14,784; part-time $616 per credit hour. Required fees: $552; $20 per credit. $70 per term. *Financial support:* Teaching assistantships with full tuition reimbursements, career-related internships or fieldwork, Federal Work-Study, scholarships/grants, health care benefits, and unspecified assistantships available. Support available to part-time students. Financial award application deadline: 5/15; financial award applicants required to submit FAFSA. *Unit head:* Dr. Maureen Reddy, Chair, 401-456-8028. *Application contact:* Graduate Studies, 401-456-8700.

Rice University, Graduate Programs, School of Humanities, Department of English, Houston, TX 77251-1892. Offers MA, PhD. Terminal master's awarded for partial completion of doctoral program. *Degree requirements:* For master's, comprehensive exam, thesis (for some programs); for doctorate, comprehensive exam, thesis/dissertation. *Entrance requirements:* For master's and doctorate, GRE General Test, minimum GPA of 3.0. Additional exam requirements/recommendations for international students: Required—TOEFL (minimum score 600 paper-based; 250 computer-based; 90 iBT). Electronic applications accepted. *Faculty research:* Traditional periods and genres (excluding Old English), literary criticism and theory, Victorian literature, feminist literature, Renaissance literature, American literature, African-American literature.

Rivier College, School of Graduate Studies, Department of English, Nashua, NH 03060. Offers English (MA, MAT); writing and literature (MA). Part-time and evening/weekend programs available. *Faculty:* 4 full-time (2 women), 2 part-time/adjunct (both women). *Students:* 1 (woman) full-time, 9 part-time (7 women). Average age 36. 4 applicants, 50% accepted, 1 enrolled. In 2009, 4 master's awarded. *Degree requirements:* For master's, comprehensive exam (for some programs). *Entrance requirements:* For master's, GRE Subject Test. *Application deadline:* Applications are processed on a rolling basis. Application fee: $25. *Expenses:* Tuition: Part-time $447 per credit. *Financial support:* Available to part-time students. Application deadline: 2/1. *Unit head:* Dr. Brad Stull, Chairman, 603-897-8238, E-mail: bstull@rivier.edu. *Application contact:* Mathew Kittredge, Director of Graduate Admissions, 603-897-8129, Fax: 603-897-8810, E-mail: mkittredge@rivier.edu.

Roosevelt University, Graduate Division, College of Arts and Sciences, Department of Literature and Languages, Program in English, Chicago, IL 60605. Offers MA. Part-time and evening/weekend programs available. *Degree requirements:* For master's, one foreign language, thesis or alternative. *Faculty research:* Eighteenth-century Victorian literature and culture, creative writing, eighteenth through twentieth century literature, American literature and culture.

Rosemont College, Schools of Graduate and Professional Studies, Program in English and Publishing and English Literature, Rosemont, PA 19010-1699. Offers English and publishing (MA); English literature (MA). Part-time programs available. *Degree requirements:* For master's, comprehensive exam (for some programs), thesis. *Entrance requirements:* For master's, 3 letters of recommendation. Additional exam requirements/recommendations for international students: Required—TOEFL. Electronic applications accepted.

Rutgers, The State University of New Jersey, Camden, Graduate School of Arts and Sciences, Program in English, Camden, NJ 08102-1401. Offers MA. Part-time and evening/weekend programs available. *Degree requirements:* For master's, comprehensive exam, thesis optional. *Entrance requirements:* For master's, GRE General Test, 3 letters of recommendation, writing sample. Additional exam requirements/recommendations for international students: Required—TOEFL, IELTS. *Faculty research:* British literature; American literature; women's studies; literary, poetic, and rhetorical theory; creative writing.

Rutgers, The State University of New Jersey, Newark, Graduate School, Program in English, Newark, NJ 07102. Offers MA. Part-time and evening/weekend programs available. *Degree requirements:* For master's, one foreign language, comprehensive exam, thesis optional. *Entrance requirements:* For master's, GRE, minimum undergraduate B average. Electronic applications accepted. *Faculty research:* British and American literature, cultural studies, literary theory, minority literatures.

Rutgers, The State University of New Jersey, New Brunswick, Graduate School-New Brunswick, Program of Literatures in English, Piscataway, NJ 08854-8097. Offers PhD. *Degree requirements:* For doctorate, one foreign language, thesis/dissertation, qualifying exam. *Entrance requirements:* For doctorate, GRE General Test, GRE Subject Test, writing sample, 3 letters of recommendation. Additional exam requirements/recommendations for international students: Required—TOEFL. Electronic applications accepted. *Faculty research:* Medieval literature; Renaissance; African American literature; 18th century British literature; feminism, gender, and sexuality; postcolonial studies.

St. Bonaventure University, School of Graduate Studies, School of Franciscan Studies, Department of English, St. Bonaventure, NY 14778-2284. Offers MA. Part-time programs available. *Faculty:* 7 full-time (1 woman). *Students:* 10 full-time (4 women), 8 part-time (4 women), 1 international. Average age 26. 17 applicants, 82% accepted, 9 enrolled. In 2009, 5 master's awarded. *Degree requirements:* For master's, one foreign language, comprehensive exam, thesis optional. *Entrance requirements:* For master's, GRE General Test. Additional exam requirements/recommendations for international students: Required—TOEFL (minimum score 550 paper-based; 240 computer-based; 95 iBT). *Application deadline:* For fall admission, 8/1 for domestic students, 12/15 for international students; for spring admission, 10/15 priority date for domestic students, 3/15 for international students. Applications are processed on a rolling basis. Application fee: $30. *Expenses:* Tuition: Full-time $11,700; part-time $650 per credit. *Financial support:* In 2009–10, 8 fellowships (averaging $6,500 per year) were awarded; research assistantships, scholarships/grants and tuition waivers (full and partial) also available. Support available to part-time students. Financial award application deadline: 4/15; financial award applicants required to submit FAFSA. *Faculty research:* Victorian, Renaissance, American, modern British, and Romantic literature. *Unit head:* Dr. Jeff Slagle, Program Director, 716-375-2447, E-mail: jslagle@sbu.edu. *Application contact:* Bruce Campbell, Director of Graduate Admissions, 716-375-2449.

St. Cloud State University, School of Graduate Studies, College of Fine Arts and Humanities, Department of English, St. Cloud, MN 56301-4498. Offers English (MA, MS); teaching English as a second language (MA). Part-time programs available. *Faculty:* 35 full-time (16 women). *Students:* 58 full-time (42 women), 62 part-time (44 women); includes 10 minority (3 African Americans, 1 American Indian/Alaska Native, 5 Asian Americans or Pacific Islanders, 1 Hispanic American), 16 international. 30 applicants, 100% accepted. In 2009, 31 master's awarded. *Degree requirements:* For master's, thesis or alternative. *Entrance requirements:* For master's, GRE General Test, minimum GPA of 2.75. Additional exam requirements/recommendations for international students: Required—Michigan English Language Assessment Battery; Recommended—TOEFL (minimum score 550 paper-based; 213 computer-based), IELTS (minimum score 6.5). *Application deadline:* For fall admission, 6/1 priority date for domestic students, 4/1 for international students; for spring admission, 10/1 priority date for domestic students, 8/1 for international students. Applications are processed on a rolling basis. Application fee: $35. Electronic applications accepted. *Financial support:* Federal Work-Study, scholarships/grants, and unspecified assistantships available. Financial award application deadline: 3/1. *Unit head:* Dr. Robert Inkster, Chairperson, 320-308-3061, Fax: 320-308-5524. *Application contact:* Linda Lou Krueger, School of Graduate Studies, 320-308-2113, Fax: 320-308-5371, E-mail: lekrueger@stcloudstate.edu.

St. John's University, St. John's College of Liberal Arts and Sciences, Department of English, Queens, NY 11439. Offers MA, DA. Part-time and evening/weekend programs available. *Students:* 30 full-time (17 women), 50 part-time (32 women); includes 14 minority (1 African American, 5 Asian Americans or Pacific Islanders, 8 Hispanic Americans), 2 international. Average age 32. 52 applicants, 58% accepted, 25 enrolled. In 2009, 9 master's, 2 doctorates awarded. *Degree requirements:* For master's, thesis optional; for doctorate, one foreign language, comprehensive exam, thesis/dissertation, residency. *Entrance requirements:* For master's, GRE General Test, GRE Subject Test, minimum GPA of 3.0; for doctorate, GRE General Test, GRE Subject Test, interview; minimum GPA of 3.5 in literature, 3.0 overall; writing sample. Additional exam requirements/recommendations for international students: Required—TOEFL (minimum score 500 paper-based; 173 computer-based; 61 iBT), IELTS (minimum score 5.5). *Application deadline:* For fall admission, 5/1 priority date for domestic and international students; for spring admission, 11/1 priority date for domestic and international students. Applications are processed on a rolling basis. Application fee: $70. Electronic applications accepted. *Expenses:* Tuition: Full-time $16,290; part-time $905 per credit. Required fees: $300; $150 per semester. Tuition and fees vary according to program. *Financial support:* Fellowships, research assistantships, scholarships/grants available. Support available to part-time students. Financial award application deadline: 3/1; financial award applicants required to submit FAFSA. *Faculty research:* Modern comparative drama, literary theories and criticism, nineteenth and early twentieth century American literature, Chaucer, Elizabethan drama. *Unit head:* Dr. Stephen Sicari, Chair, 718-990-6390, E-mail: sicaris@stjohns.edu. *Application contact:* Kathleen Davis, Director of Graduate Admission, 718-990-2790, Fax: 718-990-5686, E-mail: gradhelp@stjohns.edu.

Saint Louis University, Graduate School, College of Arts and Sciences and Graduate School, Department of English, St. Louis, MO 63103-2097. Offers MA, MA-R, PhD. Part-time programs available. *Degree requirements:* For master's, one foreign language, comprehensive exam, thesis optional, comprehensive oral exam; for doctorate, 2 foreign languages, comprehensive exam, thesis/dissertation, preliminary oral and written exams. *Entrance requirements:* For master's, GRE General Test, GRE Subject Test, letters of recommendation, resume, writing sample, interview; for doctorate, GRE General Test, GRE Subject Test, letters of recommendation, resumé, writing sample, interview, goal statement, writing sample. Additional exam requirements/recommendations for international students: Required—TOEFL (minimum score 550 paper-based; 213 computer-based). *Faculty research:* English literature, American literature, post-colonial literature, composition, literary theory.

Saint Louis University–Madrid Campus, Graduate Programs, Master of Arts in English Program, Madrid, Spain. Offers MA. Students at the Madrid Campus may also earn a degree from the Universidad Autonoma de Madrid. Part-time programs available. *Faculty:* 67 full-time (40 women), 1 part-time/adjunct (0 women). *Students:* 7 full-time (4 women), 2 part-time (1 woman). Average age 28. 10 applicants, 90% accepted, 4 enrolled. In 2009, 5 master's awarded. *Degree requirements:* For master's, one foreign language, comprehensive exam, thesis optional. *Entrance requirements:* For master's, GRE General Test, GRE Subject Test, transcripts, 3 letters of recommendation, writing sample, personal statement, curriculum vitae. Additional exam requirements/recommendations for international students: Required—TOEFL (minimum score 550 paper-based; 80 computer-based; 80 iBT). *Application deadline:* For fall admission, 3/1 for domestic and international students; for spring admission, 11/1 for domestic and international students. Applications are processed on a rolling basis. Application fee: $40. Tuition charges are reported in euros. *Expenses:* Tuition: Full-time 7740 euros; part-time 430 euros per credit. *Financial support:* In 2009–10, 5 students received support, including 2 fellowships with partial tuition reimbursements available, 3 teaching assistantships with full and partial tuition reimbursements available (averaging $1,350 per year); career-related internships or fieldwork, scholarships/grants, health care benefits, and unspecified assistantships also available. Support available to part-time students. Financial award application deadline: 4/30; financial award applicants required to submit FAFSA. *Faculty research:* English, Irish and American literature; literary theory; translation; linguistics. *Unit head:* Dr. Anne McCabe, Language and Literature Chair, 34-91-554-58-58, Fax: 34-91-554-62-02, E-mail: mccabea@slu.edu. *Application contact:* Laura Beth Good, Admissions Counselor, (34)-91-554-58-58, Fax: 34-91-554-62-02, E-mail: graduate_admissions@madrid.slu.edu.

St. Mary's University, Graduate School, Department of English and Communication Studies, Program in English Literature and Language, San Antonio, TX 78228-8507. Offers MA. Part-time programs available. *Degree requirements:* For master's, comprehensive exam. *Entrance requirements:* For master's, GRE. Additional exam requirements/recommendations for international students: Required—TOEFL (minimum score 550 paper-based; 213 computer-based; 80 iBT). Electronic applications accepted. *Expenses:* Tuition: Full-time $8004. Required fees: $536. One-time fee: $5 full-time. Full-time tuition and fees vary according to program.

Saint Xavier University, Graduate Studies, School of Arts and Sciences, Department of English, Chicago, IL 60655-3105. Offers English (CAS); literary studies (MA); teaching of writing (MA); writing pedagogy (CAS). Part-time and evening/weekend programs available. *Entrance requirements:* For master's, MAT or GRE, minimum GPA of 3.0. *Expenses:* Tuition: Part-time $743 per credit hour. Required fees: $135 per semester.

Salem State College, School of Graduate Studies, Program in English, Salem, MA 01970-5353. Offers English (MA, MAT, MA/MAT); MA/MAT. Part-time and evening/weekend programs available. *Students:* 12 full-time (8 women), 61 part-time (47 women); includes 2 minority (1 African American, 1 Asian American or Pacific Islander). Average age 34. 14 applicants, 93% accepted, 13 enrolled. In 2009, 28 master's awarded. *Entrance requirements:* For master's, GRE or MAT. Additional exam requirements/recommendations for international students: Required—TOEFL (minimum score 550 paper-based; 80 iBT), or IELTS (minimum score 5.5). *Application deadline:* For fall admission, 5/1 for domestic students; for spring admission, 10/1 for domestic students. Applications are processed on a rolling basis. Application fee: $50. *Expenses:* Tuition, state resident: full-time $2520; part-time $275 per credit hour. Tuition, nonresident: full-time $4140; part-time $365 per credit hour. Required fees: $2430. *Financial support:* In 2009–10, 27 students received support. Career-related internships or fieldwork, Federal Work-Study, scholarships/grants, and unspecified assistantships available. Support available to part-time students. Financial award application deadline: 5/1; financial award applicants required to submit FAFSA. *Unit head:* Lisa Mulman, Coordinator, 978-542-6321, E-mail: lmulman@salemstate.edu. *Application contact:* Dr. Lee A. Brossoit, Assistant Dean of Graduate Admissions, 978-542-6673, Fax: 978-542-7215, E-mail: lbrossoit@salemstate.edu.

Salisbury University, Graduate Division, Program in English, Salisbury, MD 21801-6837. Offers composition, language and rhetoric (MA); literature (MA); teaching English to speakers of other languages (MA). Part-time and evening/weekend programs available. *Faculty:* 11 full-time (6 women). *Students:* 17 full-time (14 women), 20 part-time (14 women); includes 2 minority (both Hispanic Americans), 1 international. Average age 28. 31 applicants, 52% accepted, 2 enrolled. In 2009, 16 master's awarded. *Degree requirements:* For master's, comprehensive exam (for some programs), thesis optional. *Entrance requirements:* For master's, GRE General Test, MAT or PRAXIS, minimum GPA of 3.0, 2 letters of recommendation. Additional exam requirements/recommendations for international students: Required—TOEFL (minimum score 550 paper-based; 213 computer-based). *Application deadline:* For fall admission, 8/1 for domestic students; for spring admission, 1/1 for domestic students. Applications are processed on a rolling basis. Application fee: $45. Electronic applications accepted. *Expenses:* Tuition, area resident: Part-time $278 per credit hour. Tuition, state resident: part-time $278 per credit hour. Tuition, nonresident: part-time $574 per credit hour. Required fees: $57 per credit hour. *Financial support:* In 2009–10, 9 students received support, including 14 teaching assistantships with full tuition reimbursements available; career-related internships or fieldwork and scholarships/grants also available. Support available to part-time students. Financial award applicants required to submit FAFSA. *Faculty research:* Shakespeare, Keats, J. D. Salinger, Samuel Johnson, post-colonial theory. *Unit head:* Dr. John D. Kalb, Director, 410-543-6049, Fax: 410-548-2142, E-mail: jdkalb@salisbury.edu. *Application contact:* Dr. John D. Kalb, Director, 410-543-6049, Fax: 410-548-2142, E-mail: jdkalb@salisbury.edu.

Sam Houston State University, College of Humanities and Social Sciences, Department of English and Foreign Languages, Huntsville, TX 77341. Offers English (MA). Part-time and evening/weekend programs available. *Faculty:* 9 full-time (4 women). *Students:* 10 full-time (5 women), 30 part-time (20 women). Average age 33. 14 applicants, 86% accepted, 10 enrolled. In 2009, 13 master's awarded. *Degree requirements:* For master's, comprehensive exam, thesis optional. *Entrance requirements:* For master's, GRE General Test. Additional exam requirements/recommendations for international students: Required—TOEFL (minimum score 550 paper-based; 213 computer-based; 79 iBT). *Application deadline:* For fall admission, 8/1 for domestic students; for spring admission, 12/31 for domestic students. Applications are processed on a rolling basis. Application fee: $20. *Expenses:* Tuition, state resident: full-time $3690; part-time $205 per credit hour. Tuition, nonresident: full-time $8676; part-time $482 per credit hour. Required fees: $1474. Tuition and fees vary according to course load and campus/location. *Financial support:* Teaching assistantships, Federal Work-Study and institutionally sponsored loans available. Support available to part-time students. Financial award application deadline: 5/31; financial award applicants required to submit FAFSA. *Unit head:* Dr. Helena Halmari, Chair, 936-294-1404, Fax: 936-294-1408, E-mail: eng_shh@shsu.edu. *Application contact:* Dr. Paul Child, Advisor, 936-294-1412, E-mail: eng_pwc@shsu.edu.

San Diego State University, Graduate and Research Affairs, College of Arts and Letters, Department of English and Comparative Literature, San Diego, CA 92182. Offers creative writing (MFA); English (MA). *Degree requirements:* For master's, one foreign language, comprehensive exam (for some programs), thesis (for some programs). *Entrance requirements:* For master's, GRE General Test, minimum GPA of 2.85, writing sample, 3 letters of recommendation. Additional exam requirements/recommendations for international students: Required—TOEFL. Electronic applications accepted.

San Francisco State University, Division of Graduate Studies, College of Humanities, Department of English Language and Literature, Program in Composition, San Francisco, CA 94132-1722. Offers MA, Certificate. Part-time programs available. *Degree requirements:* For master's, comprehensive exam. *Entrance requirements:* Additional exam requirements/recommendations for international students: Required—TOEFL, TWE.

San Francisco State University, Division of Graduate Studies, College of Humanities, Department of English Language and Literature, Program in Literature, San Francisco, CA 94132-1722. Offers MA. Part-time programs available.

San Jose State University, Graduate Studies and Research, College of Humanities and the Arts, Department of English and Comparative Literature, San Jose, CA 95192-0001. Offers English (MFA); English literature (MA). *Students:* 35 full-time (21 women), 56 part-time (39 women); includes 21 minority (1 African American, 16 Asian Americans or Pacific Islanders, 4 Hispanic Americans), 3 international. Average age 34. 96 applicants, 34% accepted, 28 enrolled. In 2009, 17 master's awarded. *Degree requirements:* For master's, one foreign language, thesis or alternative. *Entrance requirements:* For master's, GRE. Additional exam requirements/recommendations for international students: Required—TOEFL. *Application deadline:* For fall admission, 6/29 for domestic students; for spring admission, 11/30 for domestic students. Applications are processed on a rolling basis. Application fee: $59. Electronic applications accepted. *Financial support:* Applicants required to submit FAFSA. *Unit head:* John Engell, Chair, 408-924-4499, Fax: 408-924-4580, E-mail: john.engell@sjsu.edu. *Application contact:* Dr. Noelle Brada-Williams, Graduate Coordinator, 408-924-4439.

Seton Hall University, College of Arts and Sciences, Department of English, South Orange, NJ 07079-2697. Offers English (MA), including literature, writing. Part-time and evening/weekend programs available. *Faculty:* 15 full-time (8 women). *Students:* 23 full-time (15 women), 20 part-time (15 women); includes 3 minority (2 African Americans, 1 Asian American or Pacific Islander), 1 international. Average age 28. 32 applicants, 91% accepted, 17 enrolled. In 2009, 11 master's awarded. *Degree requirements:* For master's, one foreign language, comprehensive exam, thesis. *Entrance requirements:* For master's, GRE, minimum of 21 undergraduate credits in English. Additional exam requirements/recommendations for international students: Required—TOEFL. *Application deadline:* For fall admission, 7/1 priority date for domestic and international students; for spring admission, 11/1 priority date for domestic and international students. Applications are processed on a rolling basis. Application fee: $50. Electronic applications accepted. *Financial support:* Teaching assistantships with full tuition reimbursements, Federal Work-Study and unspecified assistantships available. Financial award applicants required to submit FAFSA. *Faculty research:* The essay, modern poetry, the novel, medieval poetry, Renaissance drama. *Unit head:* Dr. Mary McAleer Balkun, Chair, 973-761-9387, Fax: 973-761-9596, E-mail: balkunma@shu.edu. *Application contact:* Dr. Angela Weisl, Director of Graduate Studies, 973-275-5889, Fax: 973-761-9596, E-mail: weislang@shu.edu.

Sewanee: The University of the South, Sewanee School of Letters, Sewanee, TN 37383-1000. Offers American literature and English literature (MA); creative writing (MFA). Programs offered only during the summer. Part-time programs available. *Degree requirements:* For master's, thesis (for some programs). *Entrance requirements:* For master's, writing sample, 2 letters of recommendation. Electronic applications accepted. *Expenses:* Contact institution.

Simmons College, College of Arts and Sciences Graduate Studies, Program in Children's Literature, Boston, MA 02115. Offers children's literature (MA); writing for children (MFA);

English

Simmons College (continued)
MA/MFA; MAT/MA. Part-time programs available. *Students:* 13 full-time (all women), 58 part-time (54 women); includes 1 minority (Asian American or Pacific Islander), 2 international. 86 applicants, 67% accepted, 28 enrolled. In 2009, 15 master's awarded. *Entrance requirements:* For master's, writing portfolio (for MFA). Additional exam requirements/recommendations for international students: Required—TOEFL (minimum score 600 paper-based; 250 computer-based; 100 iBT). *Application deadline:* For fall admission, 8/1 priority date for domestic and international students; for winter admission, 12/15 priority date for domestic and international students; for spring admission, 5/1 priority date for domestic and international students. Applications are processed on a rolling basis. Application fee: $35. Electronic applications accepted. *Expenses:* Contact institution. *Financial support:* Application deadline: 3/1. *Faculty research:* Reception theory, narratology, material culture. *Unit head:* Dr. Cathryn Mercier, Associate Dean/Director, Center for the Study of Children's Literature, 617-521-2541. *Application contact:* Kristen Haack, Director, Graduate Studies Admission, 617-521-2917, Fax: 617-521-3058, E-mail: gsa@simmons.edu.

Simmons College, College of Arts and Sciences Graduate Studies, Program in English, Boston, MA 02115. Offers MA, MAT/MA. Part-time programs available. *Students:* 10 full-time (8 women), 18 part-time (16 women); includes 2 minority (1 Asian American or Pacific Islander, 1 Hispanic American), 1 international. 38 applicants, 66% accepted, 13 enrolled. In 2009, 13 master's awarded. *Degree requirements:* For master's, one foreign language, thesis optional. *Entrance requirements:* For master's, analytical writing sample. Additional exam requirements/recommendations for international students: Required—TOEFL (minimum score 600 paper-based; 250 computer-based; 100 iBT). *Application deadline:* For fall admission, 8/1 priority date for domestic and international students; for winter admission, 12/15 priority date for domestic and international students; for spring admission, 5/1 priority date for domestic and international students. Applications are processed on a rolling basis. Application fee: $35. Electronic applications accepted. *Expenses:* Contact institution. *Financial support:* Application deadline: 3/1. *Faculty research:* Women in literature, native American literature, early American women's poetry. *Unit head:* Renee Bergland, Professor/Director, 617-521-2220, E-mail: renee.bergland@simmons.edu. *Application contact:* Kristen Haack, Director, Graduate Studies Admission, 617-521-2917, Fax: 617-521-3058, E-mail: gsa@simmons.edu.

Simon Fraser University, Graduate Studies, Faculty of Arts and Social Sciences, Department of English, Burnaby, BC V5A 1S6, Canada. Offers MA, PhD. Part-time programs available. *Degree requirements:* For master's, one foreign language, thesis or alternative; for doctorate, one foreign language, thesis/dissertation, field exams. *Entrance requirements:* For master's, minimum GPA of 3.0; for doctorate, minimum GPA of 3.5. Additional exam requirements/recommendations for international students: Required—TOEFL or IELTS. *Faculty research:* Literary criticism, literature and psychoanalysis, Renaissance drama and poetry, Shakespeare, Canadian and American literature.

Slippery Rock University of Pennsylvania, Graduate Studies (Recruitment), College of Humanities, Fine and Performing Arts, Department of English, Slippery Rock, PA 16057-1383. Offers literature and composition (MA); professional writing (MA). Part-time and evening/weekend programs available. *Degree requirements:* For master's, comprehensive exam (for some programs), thesis (for some programs). *Entrance requirements:* For master's, GRE General Test, MAT, minimum GPA of 2.75. *Application deadline:* For fall admission, 3/1 priority date for domestic students, 5/1 priority date for international students; for spring admission, 11/1 priority date for domestic students, 9/1 priority date for international students. Applications are processed on a rolling basis. Application fee: $25 ($30 for international students). Electronic applications accepted. *Expenses:* Tuition, state resident: full-time $6666; part-time $370 per credit. Tuition, nonresident: full-time $10,666; part-time $593 per credit. Required fees: $2184; $182 per credit. *Financial support:* Career-related internships or fieldwork, Federal Work-Study, scholarships/grants, and unspecified assistantships available. Support available to part-time students. Financial award application deadline: 5/1; financial award applicants required to submit FAFSA. *Unit head:* Dr. Joseph McCarren, Graduate Coordinator, 724-738-2868, Fax: 724-738-4829, E-mail: joseph.mccarren@sru.edu. *Application contact:* Angela Piverotto, Interim Director of Graduate Studies, 724-738-2051, Fax: 724-738-2146, E-mail: graduate.admissions@sru.edu.

Sonoma State University, School of Arts and Humanities, Department of English, Rohnert Park, CA 94928. Offers American literature (MA); creative writing (MA); English literature (MA); world literature (MA). Part-time and evening/weekend programs available. *Faculty:* 5 full-time (3 women), 2 part-time/adjunct (1 woman). *Students:* 22 full-time (14 women), 15 part-time (10 women); includes 1 minority (Asian American or Pacific Islander). Average age 34. 30 applicants, 90% accepted, 11 enrolled. In 2009, 11 master's awarded. *Degree requirements:* For master's, one foreign language, thesis or alternative. *Entrance requirements:* For master's, minimum GPA of 2.5. Additional exam requirements/recommendations for international students: Required—TOEFL (minimum score 500 paper-based; 173 computer-based). *Application deadline:* For fall admission, 11/30 priority date for domestic students. Application fee: $55. *Expenses:* Tuition, nonresident: full-time $11,160. Required fees: $6226. Full-time tuition and fees vary according to course load. *Financial support:* Teaching assistantships, career-related internships or fieldwork and Federal Work-Study available. Financial award application deadline: 3/2; financial award applicants required to submit FAFSA. *Unit head:* Dr. Thaine Stearns, Chair of Graduate Studies, 707-661-2882, E-mail: thaine.stearns@sonoma.edu. *Application contact:* Dr. Thaine Stearns, Chair of Graduate Studies, 707-661-2882, E-mail: thaine.stearns@sonoma.edu.

South Dakota State University, Graduate School, College of Arts and Science, Department of English, Brookings, SD 57007. Offers MA. Part-time programs available. *Degree requirements:* For master's, comprehensive exam (for some programs), thesis (for some programs), oral and written exams. *Entrance requirements:* For master's, minimum GPA of 2.75. Additional exam requirements/recommendations for international students: Required—TOEFL (minimum score 600 paper-based; 250 computer-based; 100 iBT). *Faculty research:* English and American literature topics, regional literature (Midwestern), women's literature, Lakota literature and culture, rhetoric and writing.

Southeastern Louisiana University, College of Arts, Humanities and Social Sciences, Department of English, Hammond, LA 70402. Offers creative writing (MA); language and literacy (MA); professional writing (MA). Part-time and evening/weekend programs available. *Faculty:* 15 full-time (7 women), 1 (woman) part-time/adjunct. *Students:* 27 full-time (15 women), 22 part-time (15 women); includes 4 minority (3 African Americans, 1 Asian American or Pacific Islander). Average age 29. 16 applicants, 94% accepted, 11 enrolled. In 2009, 12 master's awarded. *Degree requirements:* For master's, one foreign language, comprehensive exam, thesis optional. *Entrance requirements:* For master's, GRE General Test (850 or better), 24 undergraduate credit hours in English, minimum GPA of 2.5. Additional exam requirements/recommendations for international students: Required—TOEFL (minimum score 500 paper-based; 173 computer-based; 61 iBT). *Application deadline:* For fall admission, 7/15 priority date for domestic students, 6/1 priority date for international students; for spring admission, 12/1 priority date for domestic students, 10/1 priority date for international students. Applications are processed on a rolling basis. Application fee: $20 ($30 for international students). Electronic applications accepted. *Expenses:* Tuition, state resident: full-time $3086; part-time $225 per credit hour. Tuition, nonresident: part-time $529 per credit hour. Required fees: $1195. Tuition and fees vary according to course level and course load. *Financial support:* In 2009–10, 11 students received support, including 1 fellowship (averaging $13,050 per year), 9 research assistantships (averaging $8,078 per year), 1 teaching assistantship (averaging $6,700 per year); career-related internships or fieldwork, Federal Work-Study, institutionally sponsored loans, scholarships/grants, and administrative assistantships also available. Support available to part-time students. Financial award application deadline: 5/1; financial award applicants required to submit FAFSA. *Faculty research:* Composition/rhetoric, professional and technical writing, film and performance studies, literary criticism, creative writing. Total annual research expenditures: $34,307. *Unit head:* Dr. David Hanson, Department Head, 985-549-2100, Fax: 985-549-5021, E-mail: dhanson@selu.edu. *Application contact:* Sandra Meyers, Graduate Admissions Analyst, 985-549-5620, Fax: 985-549-5632, E-mail: admissions@selu.edu.

Southeast Missouri State University, School of Graduate Studies, Department of English, Cape Girardeau, MO 63701-4799. Offers English (MA); teaching English to speakers of other languages (MA). Part-time and evening/weekend programs available. Postbaccalaureate distance learning degree programs offered (no on-campus study). *Degree requirements:* For master's, comprehensive exam (for some programs), thesis or alternative. *Entrance requirements:* For master's, minimum undergraduate GPA of 2.5. Additional exam requirements/recommendations for international students: Required—TOEFL (minimum score 550 paper-based; 213 computer-based); Recommended—IELTS (minimum score 6). Electronic applications accepted. *Expenses:* Tuition, state resident: full-time $4266; part-time $237 per credit hour. Tuition, nonresident: full-time $7506; part-time $417 per credit hour. Required fees: $427; $427. *Faculty research:* Literature, writing, linguistics, education, TESOL.

Southern Connecticut State University, School of Graduate Studies, School of Arts and Sciences, Department of English, New Haven, CT 06515-1355. Offers MA, MS, MLS/MS. Part-time and evening/weekend programs available. *Faculty:* 15 full-time, 1 part-time/adjunct. *Students:* 35 full-time (21 women), 58 part-time (39 women). 46 applicants, 61% accepted, 22 enrolled. In 2009, 17 master's awarded. *Degree requirements:* For master's, one foreign language, thesis or alternative. *Entrance requirements:* For master's, interview. *Application deadline:* For fall admission, 5/1 priority date for domestic students; for spring admission, 12/1 priority date for domestic students. Applications are processed on a rolling basis. Application fee: $50. Electronic applications accepted. Tuition and fees vary according to program. *Financial support:* In 2009–10, teaching assistantships (averaging $4,800 per year). Financial award application deadline: 4/15; financial award applicants required to submit FAFSA. *Unit head:* Dr. Michael Shea, Chairperson, 203-392-6741, Fax: 203-392-6731, E-mail: sheam1@southernct.edu. *Application contact:* Dr. Ken Florey, Coordinator, 203-392-6733, Fax: 203-392-6731, E-mail: floreyk1@southernct.edu.

Southern Illinois University Carbondale, Graduate School, College of Liberal Arts, Department of English, Carbondale, IL 62901-4701. Offers composition (MA, PhD), including composition, literature, rhetoric; creative writing (MFA). *Degree requirements:* For master's, one foreign language, thesis; for doctorate, 2 foreign languages, thesis/dissertation. *Entrance requirements:* For master's, GRE General Test, GRE Subject Test, minimum GPA of 2.7; for doctorate, GRE General Test, GRE Subject Test, minimum GPA of 3.25. Additional exam requirements/recommendations for international students: Required—TOEFL. *Faculty research:* British literature, English literature, modern Continental literature, literary criticism and theory, film studies, Irish studies.

Southern Illinois University Edwardsville, Graduate Studies and Research, College of Arts and Sciences, Department of English Language and Literature, Program in American and English Literature, Edwardsville, IL 62026-0001. Offers MA, Postbaccalaureate Certificate. Part-time programs available. *Students:* 9 full-time (6 women), 15 part-time (13 women); includes 2 minority (1 African American, 1 Asian American or Pacific Islander). Average age 26. In 2009, 8 master's, 1 other advanced degree awarded. *Degree requirements:* For master's, one foreign language, thesis (for some programs), written papers, oral examination. *Entrance requirements:* Additional exam requirements/recommendations for international students: Required—TOEFL (minimum score 550 paper-based; 213 computer-based; 79 iBT), IELTS (minimum score 6.5). *Application deadline:* For fall admission, 7/23 for domestic students, 6/1 for international students; for spring admission, 12/11 for domestic students, 10/1 for international students. Applications are processed on a rolling basis. Application fee: $30. Electronic applications accepted. *Expenses:* Tuition, state resident: part-time $1252.50 per semester. Tuition, nonresident: part-time $3131.25 per semester. Required fees: $586.85 per semester. Tuition and fees vary according to course load. *Financial support:* Fellowships with full tuition reimbursements, research assistantships with full tuition reimbursements, teaching assistantships with full tuition reimbursements, Federal Work-Study, institutionally sponsored loans, scholarships/grants, and unspecified assistantships available. Support available to part-time students. Financial award application deadline: 3/1; financial award applicants required to submit FAFSA. *Unit head:* Dr. Joel Hardman, Director, 618-650-5978, E-mail: jhardma@siue.edu. *Application contact:* Dr. Joel Hardman, Director, 618-650-5978, E-mail: jhardma@siue.edu.

Southern Methodist University, Dedman College, Department of English, Dallas, TX 75275. Offers MA, PhD. *Faculty:* 41 full-time (23 women), 14 part-time/adjunct (12 women). *Students:* 12 full-time (5 women), 6 part-time (3 women), 1 international. Average age 28. 63 applicants, 16% accepted, 6 enrolled. In 2009, 5 master's awarded. Terminal master's awarded for partial completion of doctoral program. *Degree requirements:* For master's, one foreign language, comprehensive exam, thesis optional, oral exam; for doctorate, one foreign language, comprehensive exam, thesis/dissertation. *Entrance requirements:* For master's, GRE General Test, minimum GPA of 3.0; for doctorate, GRE General Test, minimum GPA of 3.5, BA in English or other appropriate field. Additional exam requirements/recommendations for international students: Required—TOEFL (minimum score 550 paper-based). *Application deadline:* For fall admission, 1/15 priority date for domestic and international students. Application fee: $75. Electronic applications accepted. *Financial support:* In 2009–10, 12 students received support, including 12 fellowships with full tuition reimbursements available (averaging $24,800 per year); health care benefits and tuition waivers (full) also available. Financial award application deadline: 1/15. *Faculty research:* British/American literature, critical theory, medieval studies, gender studies, book history. *Unit head:* Prof. Nina Schwartz, Chair, 214-768-2946, Fax: 214-768-1234, E-mail: nschwart@smu.edu. *Application contact:* Prof. Darryl Dickson-Carr, Director of Graduate Studies, 214-768-4689, Fax: 214-768-1234, E-mail: dcarr@smu.edu.

Spring Hill College, Graduate Programs, Program in Liberal Arts, Mobile, AL 36608-1791. Offers fine arts (MLA); history and social science (MLA); leadership and ethics (MLA); literature (MLA). Part-time and evening/weekend programs available. *Faculty:* 11 full-time (4 women), 3 part-time/adjunct (2 women). *Students:* 1 (woman) full-time, 33 part-time (16 women); includes 6 minority (5 African Americans, 1 Hispanic American), 2 international. Average age 35. 27 applicants, 41% accepted, 6 enrolled. In 2009, 6 master's awarded. *Degree requirements:* For master's, capstone course, completion of program within 6 years of initial admittance. *Entrance requirements:* For master's, bachelor's degree with minimum undergraduate GPA of 3.0 or graduate/professional degree. Additional exam requirements/recommendations for international students: Required—TOEFL (minimum score 550 paper-based; 213 computer-based; 80 iBT), IELTS (minimum score 6.5). *Application deadline:* For fall admission, 8/1 priority date for domestic and international students; for spring admission, 12/1 priority date for domestic and international students. Applications are processed on a rolling basis. Application fee: $25 ($35 for international students). Electronic applications accepted. *Expenses:* Contact institution. *Financial support:* In 2009–10, 30 students received support. Career-related internships or fieldwork, institutionally sponsored loans, and scholarships/grants available. Support available to part-time students. Financial award applicants required to submit FAFSA. *Unit head:* Dr. Alexander R. Landi, Director, 251-380-3056, Fax: 251-460-2115, E-mail: landi@shc.edu. *Application contact:* Donna B. Tarasavage, Director of Marketing and Recruiting, Graduate and Continuing Studies, 251-380-3067, Fax: 251-460-2190, E-mail: dtarasavage@shc.edu.

Stanford University, School of Humanities and Sciences, Department of English, Stanford, CA 94305-9991. Offers MA, PhD. Terminal master's awarded for partial completion of doctoral program. *Degree requirements:* For master's, one foreign language, thesis (for some programs); for doctorate, 2 foreign languages, thesis/dissertation, oral exam. *Entrance requirements:* For master's and doctorate, GRE General Test, GRE Subject Test. Additional exam requirements/recommendations for international students: Required—TOEFL. Electronic applications accepted. *Expenses:* Tuition: Full-time $37,380; part-time $2760 per quarter. Required fees: $501.

State University of New York at Binghamton, Graduate School, School of Arts and Sciences, Department of English, Binghamton, NY 13902-6000. Offers MA, PhD. Part-time programs available. *Faculty:* 32 full-time (16 women), 26 part-time/adjunct (14 women). *Students:* 57 full-time (27 women), 56 part-time (33 women); includes 17 minority (5 African Americans, 2 American Indian/Alaska Native, 3 Asian Americans or Pacific Islanders, 7 Hispanic Americans), 7 international. Average age 33. 108 applicants, 44% accepted, 22 enrolled. In 2009, 22 master's, 15 doctorates awarded. Terminal master's awarded for partial completion of doctoral program. *Degree requirements:* For master's, thesis (for some programs), written exam; for doctorate, one foreign language, comprehensive exam, thesis/dissertation. *Entrance requirements:* For master's and doctorate, GRE General Test, GRE Subject Test, critical writing sample. Additional exam requirements/recommendations for international students: Required—TOEFL (minimum score 550 paper-based; 213 computer-based; 80 iBT). *Application deadline:* For fall admission, 2/15 priority date for domestic and international students; for spring admission, 11/15 priority date for domestic and international students. Applications are processed on a rolling basis. Application fee: $60. Electronic applications accepted. *Financial support:* In 2009–10, 48 students received support, including 5 fellowships with full tuition reimbursements available (averaging $15,000 per year), 36 teaching assistantships with full tuition reimbursements available (averaging $15,000 per year); research assistantships, career-related internships or fieldwork, Federal Work-Study, institutionally sponsored loans, scholarships/grants, health care benefits, and unspecified assistantships also available. Financial award application deadline: 2/15; financial award applicants required to submit FAFSA. *Unit head:* Dr. Jean-Pierre Mileur, Chairperson, 607-777-2169, E-mail: jpmleur@binghamton.edu. *Application contact:* Victoria Williams, Recruiting and Admissions Coordinator, 607-777-2151, Fax: 607-777-2501, E-mail: vwilliam@binghamton.edu.

State University of New York at Fredonia, Graduate Studies, Department of English, Fredonia, NY 14063-1136. Offers MA, MS Ed. Part-time and evening/weekend programs available. *Degree requirements:* For master's, thesis optional. *Expenses:* Tuition, state resident: full-time $8370; part-time $349 per credit. Tuition, nonresident: full-time $13,250; part-time $552 per credit. Required fees: $1289; $53.55 per credit.

State University of New York at New Paltz, Graduate School, School of Liberal Arts and Sciences, Department of English, New Paltz, NY 12561. Offers MA. Part-time and evening/weekend programs available. *Faculty:* 13 full-time (5 women). *Students:* 14 full-time (4 women), 45 part-time (33 women); includes 4 minority (1 Asian American or Pacific Islander, 3 Hispanic Americans), 1 international. Average age 29. 28 applicants, 68% accepted, 17 enrolled. In 2009, 18 master's awarded. *Degree requirements:* For master's, comprehensive exam, thesis (for some programs), foreign language proficiency exam. *Entrance requirements:* For master's, minimum GPA of 3.0, 10-15 page writing sample. Additional exam requirements/recommendations for international students: Required—TOEFL (minimum score 85 iBT), IELTS (minimum score 7). *Application deadline:* For fall admission, 5/15 priority date for domestic students, 5/15 for international students; for spring admission, 11/15 for domestic and international students. Application fee: $50. Electronic applications accepted. *Financial support:* In 2009–10, 20 students received support, including 2 research assistantships with partial tuition reimbursements available (averaging $5,000 per year), 17 teaching assistantships with partial tuition reimbursements available (averaging $5,000 per year); career-related internships or fieldwork, Federal Work-Study, institutionally sponsored loans, and tuition waivers (full) also available. Financial award application deadline: 8/1; financial award applicants required to submit FAFSA. *Faculty research:* Twentieth century British literature, Hemingway and Modernism, British Modernist fiction, Faulkner and the Southern Renaissance, revisionary approaches to early twentieth-century literature. *Unit head:* Dr. Thomas Olsen, Chair, 845-257-2723, E-mail: olsent@newpaltz.edu. *Application contact:* Dr. Daniel Kempton, Coordinator, 845-257-2728, E-mail: kemptond@newpaltz.edu.

State University of New York at Oswego, Graduate Studies, College of Arts and Sciences, Department of English, Oswego, NY 13126. Offers MA. Part-time programs available. *Degree requirements:* For master's, thesis optional. *Entrance requirements:* Additional exam requirements/recommendations for international students: Required—TOEFL (minimum score 560 paper-based; 220 computer-based).

State University of New York College at Cortland, Graduate Studies, School of Arts and Sciences, Department of English, Cortland, NY 13045. Offers MA, MAT, MS Ed. Part-time and evening/weekend programs available. *Degree requirements:* For master's, one foreign language, comprehensive exam, thesis (for some programs). *Entrance requirements:* For master's, GRE General Test.

State University of New York College at Potsdam, School of Arts and Sciences, Department of English and Communication, Potsdam, NY 13676. Offers English and communication (MA). Part-time and evening/weekend programs available. *Faculty:* 5 full-time (3 women). *Students:* 4 full-time (all women), 9 part-time (7 women); includes 1 minority (African American), 1 international. 4 applicants, 75% accepted, 3 enrolled. In 2009, 5 master's awarded. *Degree requirements:* For master's, one foreign language, thesis or alternative. *Entrance requirements:* For master's, minimum GPA of 3.0 in last 60 hours of undergraduate course work. Additional exam requirements/recommendations for international students: Required—TOEFL (minimum score 550 paper-based; 213 computer-based; 80 iBT), IELTS (minimum score 6). *Application deadline:* For fall admission, 4/1 priority date for domestic and international students; for spring admission, 10/15 priority date for domestic and international students. Applications are processed on a rolling basis. Application fee: $50. *Expenses:* Tuition, state resident: full-time $8370; part-time $349 per credit hour. Tuition, nonresident: full-time $13,250; part-time $552 per credit hour. Required fees: $942; $38.70 per credit hour. *Financial support:* In 2009–10, 1 student received support; teaching assistantships with full tuition reimbursements available, Federal Work-Study and unspecified assistantships available. Support available to part-time students. Financial award application deadline: 3/1; financial award applicants required to submit FAFSA. *Unit head:* Dr. Sharmain van Blommestein, Director of Graduate Studies, 315-267-3158, Fax: 315-267-3256, E-mail: vanblos@potsdam.edu. *Application contact:* Peter Cutler, Graduate Admissions Counselor, 315-267-3154, Fax: 315-267-4802, E-mail: cutlerpj@potsdam.edu.

State University of New York College at Potsdam, School of Education and Professional Studies, Program in Secondary Education, Potsdam, NY 13676. Offers English (MST); mathematics (with grades 5-6 extension) (MST); science (MST), including biology, chemistry, earth science, physics; Social Studies (with grades 5-6 extension) (MST). *Accreditation:* NCATE. *Faculty:* 9 full-time (3 women), 3 part-time/adjunct (2 women). *Students:* 49 full-time (27 women), 6 part-time (1 woman); includes 5 minority (3 African Americans, 2 American Indian/Alaska Native), 7 international. 13 applicants, 62% accepted, 8 enrolled. In 2009, 49 master's awarded. *Degree requirements:* For master's, thesis optional, culminating experience. *Entrance requirements:* For master's, minimum GPA of 2.75 in last 60 hours of course work (3.0 for English program). Additional exam requirements/recommendations for international students: Required—TOEFL (minimum score 550 paper-based; 213 computer-based; 80 iBT), IELTS (minimum score 6). *Application deadline:* For fall admission, 4/1 priority date for domestic and international students; for spring admission, 10/15 priority date for domestic and international students. Applications are processed on a rolling basis. Application fee: $50. *Expenses:* Tuition, state resident: full-time $8370; part-time $349 per credit hour. Tuition, nonresident: full-time $13,250; part-time $552 per credit hour. Required fees: $942; $38.70 per credit hour. *Financial support:* Fellowships, teaching assistantships, career-related internships or fieldwork, Federal Work-Study, scholarships/grants, and unspecified assistantships available. Support available to part-time students. Financial award application deadline: 3/1; financial award applicants required to submit FAFSA. *Unit head:* Dr. Peter Brouwer, Chairperson, 315-267-3018, Fax: 315-267-4802, E-mail: brouweps@potsdam.edu. *Application contact:* Peter Cutler, Graduate Admissions Counselor, 315-267-3154, Fax: 315-267-4802, E-mail: cutlerpj@potsdam.edu.

Stephen F. Austin State University, Graduate School, College of Liberal Arts, Department of English and Philosophy, Nacogdoches, TX 75962. Offers English (MA). *Degree requirements:* For master's, comprehensive exam. *Entrance requirements:* For master's, GRE General Test. Additional exam requirements/recommendations for international students: Required—TOEFL. *Faculty research:* Creative writing, Latin American literature, modern American literature, modern British literature, literature for children.

Stetson University, College of Arts and Sciences, Division of Humanities, Department of English, DeLand, FL 32723. Offers MA. *Students:* 9 part-time (7 women); includes 1 minority (Asian American or Pacific Islander). Average age 28. In 2009, 4 master's awarded. *Degree requirements:* For master's, thesis. *Entrance requirements:* For master's, GRE General Test. *Application deadline:* For fall admission, 3/1 priority date for domestic students; for spring admission, 11/1 for domestic students. Applications are processed on a rolling basis. Application fee: $25. Tuition and fees vary according to course load, campus/location and program. *Unit head:* Dr. Joel Davis, Director, 386-822-7720. *Application contact:* Diana Belian, Office of Graduate Studies, 386-822-7075, Fax: 386-822-7388, E-mail: dbelian@stetson.edu.

Stony Brook University, State University of New York, Graduate School, College of Arts and Sciences, Department of Comparative Literary and Cultural Studies, Stony Brook, NY 11794. Offers comparative literature (MA, PhD); cultural studies (PhD). Evening/weekend programs available. *Faculty:* 7 full-time (1 woman). *Students:* 35 full-time (21 women), 4 part-time (3 women); includes 6 minority (5 Asian Americans or Pacific Islanders, 1 Hispanic American), 17 international. Average age 30. 101 applicants, 19% accepted. In 2009, 1 master's, 1 doctorate awarded. Terminal master's awarded for partial completion of doctoral program. *Degree requirements:* For master's, 2 foreign languages, exam; for doctorate, 3 foreign languages, comprehensive exam, thesis/dissertation. *Entrance requirements:* For master's and doctorate, GRE General Test, minimum GPA of 3.5 in major, 3.0 overall. Additional exam requirements/recommendations for international students: Required—TOEFL. *Application deadline:* For fall admission, 1/15 for domestic students. Application fee: $60. *Expenses:* Tuition, state resident: full-time $8370; part-time $349 per credit. Tuition, nonresident: full-time $13,250; part-time $552 per credit. Required fees: $933. *Financial support:* In 2009–10, 24 teaching assistantships were awarded; fellowships, research assistantships also available. *Faculty research:* Literary theory, interdisciplinary studies, literary history. *Unit head:* Prof. Krin Gabbard, Chairman, 631-632-7456. *Application contact:* Dr. Kent Marks, Assistant Dean, Admissions and Records, 631-632-4723, Fax: 631-632-7243, E-mail: kmarks@notes.cc.sunysb.edu.

Stony Brook University, State University of New York, Graduate School, College of Arts and Sciences, Department of English, Stony Brook, NY 11794. Offers composition studies (Certificate); English (MA, PhD); English education (MAT). MAT offered through the School of Professional Development. Evening/weekend programs available. *Faculty:* 25 full-time (10 women), 1 part-time/adjunct (0 women). *Students:* 77 full-time (46 women), 23 part-time (18 women); includes 12 minority (5 African Americans, 3 Asian Americans or Pacific Islanders, 4 Hispanic Americans), 5 international. Average age 32. 154 applicants, 23% accepted. In 2009, 16 master's, 7 doctorates awarded. Terminal master's awarded for partial completion of doctoral program. *Degree requirements:* For doctorate, thesis/dissertation. *Entrance requirements:* For master's and doctorate, GRE General Test. Additional exam requirements/recommendations for international students: Required—TOEFL. *Application deadline:* For fall admission, 1/15 for domestic students. Application fee: $60. *Expenses:* Tuition, state resident: full-time $8370; part-time $349 per credit. Tuition, nonresident: full-time $13,250; part-time $552 per credit. Required fees: $933. *Financial support:* In 2009–10, 42 teaching assistantships were awarded; fellowships, research assistantships also available. *Faculty research:* American literature, British literature, literary critical theory, rhetoric and composition theory, women's studies. *Unit head:* Dr. Stephen Spector, Chair, 631-632-7420, Fax: 631-632-7568. *Application contact:* Dr. Helen M. Cooper, Director, 631-632-7784, Fax: 631-632-7568, E-mail: hcooper@notes.cc.sunysb.edu.

Sul Ross State University, School of Arts and Sciences, Department of Languages and Literature, Alpine, TX 79832. Offers English (MA). Part-time and evening/weekend programs available. *Degree requirements:* For master's, thesis optional. *Entrance requirements:* For master's, GRE General Test, minimum GPA of 2.5 in last 60 hours of undergraduate work. *Faculty research:* Narrative theory, feminist literary criticism, autobiography studies, multiculturalism, biblical narrative.

Syracuse University, College of Arts and Sciences, Programs in English, Syracuse, NY 13244. Offers MA, PhD. Part-time programs available. *Students:* 30 full-time (17 women); includes 2 minority (1 African American, 1 American Indian/Alaska Native), 6 international. Average age 29. 110 applicants, 17% accepted, 7 enrolled. In 2009, 4 master's, 2 doctorates awarded. *Entrance requirements:* For master's and doctorate, GRE General Test. Additional exam requirements/recommendations for international students: Required—TOEFL (minimum score 100 iBT). *Application deadline:* For fall admission, 1/10 priority date for domestic and international students. Application fee: $75. Electronic applications accepted. *Expenses:* Tuition: Full-time $26,808; part-time $1117 per credit. Required fees: $1024. *Financial support:* Application deadline: 1/1. *Unit head:* Department Chair, 315-443-9485. *Application contact:* Terri Zollo, Information Contact, 315-443-2174, E-mail: tazollo@syr.edu.

Tarleton State University, College of Graduate Studies, College of Liberal and Fine Arts, Department of English and Languages, Stephenville, TX 76402. Offers English (MA). Part-time and evening/weekend programs available. *Degree requirements:* For master's, comprehensive exam, thesis (for some programs). *Entrance requirements:* For master's, GRE General Test, minimum GPA of 3.0. Additional exam requirements/recommendations for international students: Required—TOEFL (minimum score 550 paper-based; 213 computer-based; 80 iBT). Electronic applications accepted.

Temple University, Graduate School, College of Liberal Arts, Department of English, Philadelphia, PA 19122-6096. Offers creative writing (MA); English (MA, PhD). Part-time programs available. *Degree requirements:* For doctorate, 2 foreign languages, thesis/dissertation. *Entrance requirements:* For master's and doctorate, GRE General Test, minimum GPA of 3.0. Additional exam requirements/recommendations for international students: Required—TOEFL (minimum score 550 paper-based; 213 computer-based; 79 iBT). Electronic applications accepted. *Faculty research:* Renaissance, Victorian, Modern British, and American literature; critical theory; composition.

Tennessee State University, The School of Graduate Studies and Research, College of Arts and Sciences, Department of Languages, Literature, and Philosophy, Nashville, TN 37209-1561. Offers English (MA). *Degree requirements:* For master's, thesis optional. *Entrance requirements:* For master's, GRE General Test or MAT. Electronic applications accepted. *Faculty research:* American literature, British literature, Anglo/Saxon literature, cultural/women's studies.

Tennessee Technological University, Graduate School, College of Arts and Sciences, Department of English, Cookeville, TN 38505. Offers MA. Part-time programs available. *Faculty:* 23 full-time (8 women). *Students:* 6 full-time (4 women), 8 part-time (5 women). Average age 28. 11 applicants, 55% accepted, 5 enrolled. In 2009, 9 master's awarded. *Degree requirements:* For master's, comprehensive exam, thesis or alternative. *Entrance requirements:* For master's, GRE General Test. Additional exam requirements/recommendations for international students: Required—TOEFL (minimum score 550 paper-based; 79 iBT), IELTS (minimum score 5.5). *Application deadline:* For fall admission, 8/1 for domestic students, 5/1 for international students; for spring admission, 11/1 for domestic students, 10/1 for international students. Application fee: $25 ($30 for international students). Electronic applications accepted. *Expenses:* Tuition, state resident: full-time $7034; part-time $368 per credit hour. *Financial support:* In 2009–10, research assistantships (averaging $4,000 per year), 9 teaching assistantships (averaging $6,750 per year) were awarded; fellowships also available. Financial award application deadline: 4/1. *Unit head:* Dr. Homer Kemp, Interim Chairperson, 931-372-3343, Fax: 931-372-6142. *Application contact:* Shelia K. Kendrick, Coordinator of Graduate Studies, 931-372-3808, Fax: 931-372-3497, E-mail: skendrick@tntech.edu.

English

Texas A&M International University, Office of Graduate Studies and Research, College of Arts and Sciences, Department of Language and Literature, Laredo, TX 78041-1900. Offers English (MA); Hispanic studies (PhD); Spanish (MA). *Faculty:* 6 full-time (3 women). *Students:* 4 full-time (3 women), 49 part-time (33 women); includes 46 minority (all Hispanic Americans), 1 international. Average age 34. 26 applicants. In 2009, 3 master's awarded. *Entrance requirements:* For master's, GRE General Test. Additional exam requirements/recommendations for international students: Required—TOEFL (minimum score 550 paper-based; 213 computer-based). *Application deadline:* For fall admission, 4/30 priority date for domestic students; for spring admission, 11/30 for domestic students. Applications are processed on a rolling basis. Application fee: $25. *Financial support:* In 2009–10, 12 students received support, including 1 fellowship, 1 research assistantship, 6 teaching assistantships. Financial award application deadline: 11/1. *Unit head:* Dr. Manuel Broncano, Chair, 956-326-2470, E-mail: manuel.broncano@tamiu.edu. *Application contact:* Rosie Espinoza-Dickinson, Director of Admissions, 956-326-2200, Fax: 956-326-2199, E-mail: enroll@tamiu.edu.

Texas A&M University, College of Liberal Arts, Department of English, College Station, TX 77843. Offers MA, PhD. *Faculty:* 33. *Students:* 94 full-time (60 women), 17 part-time (12 women); includes 11 minority (3 African Americans, 1 Asian American or Pacific Islander, 7 Hispanic Americans), 28 international. Average age 24. In 2009, 12 master's, 12 doctorates awarded. Terminal master's awarded for partial completion of doctoral program. *Degree requirements:* For master's, one foreign language, thesis optional; for doctorate, 2 foreign languages, thesis/dissertation. *Entrance requirements:* For master's and doctorate, GRE General Test, sample of written work. Additional exam requirements/recommendations for international students: Required—TOEFL. *Application deadline:* For fall admission, 2/1 priority date for domestic and international students; for spring admission, 10/1 priority date for domestic and international students. Applications are processed on a rolling basis. Application fee: $50 ($75 for international students). Electronic applications accepted. *Expenses:* Tuition, state resident: full-time $3991; part-time $221.74 per credit hour. Tuition, nonresident: full-time $9049; part-time $502.74 per credit hour. *Financial support:* In 2009–10, fellowships with partial tuition reimbursements (averaging $10,000 per year), research assistantships with partial tuition reimbursements (averaging $12,000 per year), teaching assistantships with partial tuition reimbursements (averaging $12,000 per year) were awarded; career-related internships or fieldwork, Federal Work-Study, institutionally sponsored loans, scholarships/grants, and unspecified assistantships also available. Financial award application deadline: 4/1. *Faculty research:* American, Renaissance, Medieval, textual studies, discourse studies. *Unit head:* Dr. Jimmie Killingworth, Head, 979-845-3890, E-mail: killingworth@tamu.edu. *Application contact:* Howard Marchitello, Director of Graduate Programs, 979-845-9836, Fax: 979-862-2292, E-mail: info-grad@english.tamu.edu.

Texas A&M University–Commerce, Graduate School, College of Arts and Sciences, Department of Literature and Languages, Commerce, TX 75429-3011. Offers college teaching of English (PhD); English (MA, MS); Spanish (MA). Part-time programs available. Terminal master's awarded for partial completion of doctoral program. *Degree requirements:* For master's, comprehensive exam, thesis (for some programs); for doctorate, one foreign language, thesis/dissertation, departmental qualifying exam. *Entrance requirements:* For master's and doctorate, GRE General Test. Electronic applications accepted. *Faculty research:* Latino literature, American film studies, ethnographic research, Willa Carter.

Texas A&M University–Corpus Christi, Graduate Studies and Research, College of Liberal Arts, Program in English, Corpus Christi, TX 78412-5503. Offers MA. Part-time and evening/weekend programs available. *Degree requirements:* For master's, comprehensive exam, thesis (for some programs). *Entrance requirements:* For master's, GRE General Test. Additional exam requirements/recommendations for international students: Required—TOEFL. Electronic applications accepted.

Texas A&M University–Kingsville, College of Graduate Studies, College of Arts and Sciences, Department of Language and Literature, Kingsville, TX 78363. Offers English (MA, MS); Spanish (MA). Part-time and evening/weekend programs available. *Degree requirements:* For master's, comprehensive exam, thesis or alternative. *Entrance requirements:* For master's, GRE General Test, minimum GPA of 3.0. Additional exam requirements/recommendations for international students: Required—TOEFL. *Faculty research:* Linguistics, culture, Spanish American literature, Spanish peninsular literature, American literature.

Texas A&M University–Texarkana, Graduate Studies and Research, College of Education and Liberal Arts, Texarkana, TX 75505-5518. Offers adult education (MS); curriculum and instruction (M Ed); education (MS); educational administration (M Ed); English (MA); instructional technology (MS); interdisciplinary studies (MA, MS); special education (MS). Part-time and evening/weekend programs available. *Degree requirements:* For master's, comprehensive exam (for some programs), thesis optional. *Entrance requirements:* For master's, minimum GPA of 2.5 on last 60 hours of bachelor's degree. Additional exam requirements/recommendations for international students: Required—TOEFL. Electronic applications accepted.

Texas Christian University, AddRan College of Liberal Arts, Department of English, Fort Worth, TX 76129-0002. Offers composition (MA); English (PhD), including rhetoric and/or literature; literature (MA); rhetoric (MA); rhetoric/composition (PhD). Part-time and evening/weekend programs available. *Degree requirements:* For master's, one foreign language, thesis, candidacy exam; for doctorate, one foreign language, comprehensive exam, thesis/dissertation, 66 hours, diagnostic exam, qualifying exam. *Entrance requirements:* For master's and doctorate, GRE General Test, 30 hours of English; 12 hours of foreign language study. Additional exam requirements/recommendations for international students: Required—TOEFL. *Application deadline:* For fall admission, 1/31 for domestic and international students; for spring admission, 10/15 for domestic and international students. Application fee: $0. *Expenses:* Tuition: Full-time $17,640; part-time $980 per credit hour. Tuition and fees vary according to program. *Financial support:* In 2009–10, 28 students received support; fellowships with full tuition reimbursements available, research assistantships with full tuition reimbursements available, teaching assistantships with full tuition reimbursements available, tuition waivers (full) and unspecified assistantships available. Financial award application deadline: 3/1; financial award applicants required to submit FAFSA. *Unit head:* Dr. Brad Lucas, Chairperson, 817-257-7240. *Application contact:* Dr. Bonnie Carol Blackwell, Associate Professor/Director of Graduate Studies, 817-257-6263, E-mail: b.blackwell@tcu.edu.

Texas Southern University, College of Liberal Arts and Behavioral Sciences, Department of English, Houston, TX 77004-4584. Offers MA. Part-time programs available. *Faculty:* 6 full-time (2 women). *Students:* 3 full-time (all women), 8 part-time (5 women); includes 8 African Americans, 1 Asian American or Pacific Islander. Average age 32. 4 applicants, 100% accepted, 3 enrolled. In 2009, 1 master's awarded. *Degree requirements:* For master's, one foreign language, comprehensive exam, thesis. *Entrance requirements:* For master's, GRE General Test, minimum GPA of 2.5. Additional exam requirements/recommendations for international students: Required—TOEFL. *Application deadline:* For fall admission, 7/1 priority date for domestic students, 7/1 for international students; for spring admission, 11/1 for domestic and international students. Applications are processed on a rolling basis. Application fee: $50 ($75 for international students). Electronic applications accepted. *Expenses:* Tuition, state resident: full-time $1805; part-time $100 per credit hour. Tuition, nonresident: full-time $6470; part-time $343 per credit hour. Tuition and fees vary according to course level, course load and degree level. *Financial support:* In 2009–10, 1 teaching assistantship (averaging $4,050 per year) was awarded; fellowships, scholarships/grants and unspecified assistantships also available. Support available to part-time students. Financial award application deadline: 5/1. *Faculty research:* Linguistics, teaching of English, African-American literature, African literature, developmental English. *Unit head:* Dr. Rhonda Saldivar, Interim Chair, 713-313-7536, Fax: 713-313-7538, E-mail: saldivar_rx@tsu.edu. *Application contact:* Dr. Gregory Maddox, Interim Dean of the Graduate School, 713-313-7011 Ext. 4410, Fax: 713-639-1876, E-mail: maddox_gh@tsu.edu.

Texas State University–San Marcos, Graduate School, College of Liberal Arts, Department of English, Program in Literature, San Marcos, TX 78666. Offers MA. Part-time and evening/weekend programs available. *Faculty:* 32 full-time (15 women). *Students:* 36 full-time (26 women), 50 part-time (33 women); includes 15 minority (3 African Americans, 2 American Indian/Alaska Native, 1 Asian American or Pacific Islander, 9 Hispanic Americans). Average age 31. 47 applicants, 91% accepted, 24 enrolled. In 2009, 20 master's awarded. *Degree requirements:* For master's, comprehensive exam, thesis optional. *Entrance requirements:* For master's, minimum GPA of 2.75 in last 60 hours, 24 undergraduate hours of course work in English (12 advanced) with minimum GPA of 3.25, 6 hours of course work in foreign language. Additional exam requirements/recommendations for international students: Required—TOEFL (minimum score 550 paper-based; 213 computer-based). *Application deadline:* For fall admission, 6/15 priority date for domestic students, 6/1 for international students; for spring admission, 10/15 priority date for domestic students, 10/1 for international students. Applications are processed on a rolling basis. Application fee: $40 ($90 for international students). Electronic applications accepted. *Expenses:* Tuition, state resident: full-time $5784; part-time $241 per credit hour. Tuition, nonresident: part-time $551 per credit hour. Required fees: $1728; $48 per credit hour. $306. Tuition and fees vary according to course load. *Financial support:* In 2009–10, 70 students received support, including 4 research assistantships (averaging $5,608 per year), 15 teaching assistantships (averaging $5,535 per year); Federal Work-Study and institutionally sponsored loans also available. Support available to part-time students. Financial award application deadline: 4/1; financial award applicants required to submit FAFSA. *Unit head:* Dr. Paul Cohen, Acting Graduate Adviser, 512-245-2163, Fax: 512-245-8546, E-mail: pc06@txstate.edu. *Application contact:* Dr. J. Michael Willoughby, Dean of Graduate School, 512-245-2581, Fax: 512-245-8365, E-mail: gradcollege@txstate.edu.

Texas Tech University, Graduate School, College of Arts and Sciences, Department of English, Lubbock, TX 79409. Offers English (MA, PhD); technical communication (MA); technical communication and rhetoric (PhD). Part-time programs available. *Faculty:* 38 full-time (15 women), 2 part-time/adjunct (both women). *Students:* 101 full-time (62 women), 94 part-time (58 women); includes 14 minority (4 African Americans, 2 American Indian/Alaska Native, 2 Asian Americans or Pacific Islanders, 6 Hispanic Americans), 15 international. Average age 35. 208 applicants, 31% accepted, 45 enrolled. In 2009, 30 master's, 10 doctorates awarded. *Degree requirements:* For master's, one foreign language, thesis (for some programs); for doctorate, thesis/dissertation. *Entrance requirements:* For master's and doctorate, GRE General Test. Additional exam requirements/recommendations for international students: Required—TOEFL (minimum score 550 paper-based; 213 computer-based). *Application deadline:* For fall admission, 3/1 priority date for international students; for spring admission, 11/1 priority date for international students. Applications are processed on a rolling basis. Application fee: $50 ($75 for international students). Electronic applications accepted. *Expenses:* Tuition, state resident: full-time $5100; part-time $213 per credit hour. Tuition, nonresident: full-time $11,748; part-time $490 per credit hour. Required fees: $2298; $50 per credit hour. $555 per semester. *Financial support:* In 2009–10, 8 research assistantships with partial tuition reimbursements (averaging $19,712 per year), 9 teaching assistantships with partial tuition reimbursements (averaging $14,010 per year) were awarded; Federal Work-Study and institutionally sponsored loans also available. Support available to part-time students. Financial award application deadline: 4/15; financial award applicants required to submit FAFSA. *Faculty research:* Computers and writing; technical communication and rhetoric; creative writing; nineteenth century studies; literature of social justice and the environment. *Unit head:* Dr. Sam Dragga, Chair, 806-742-2501, Fax: 806-742-0989, E-mail: sam.dragga@ttu.edu. *Application contact:* Dr. Brian McFadden, Director of Graduate Studies, 806-742-2501, Fax: 806-742-0989, E-mail: english.gradadvisor@ttu.edu.

Texas Woman's University, Graduate School, College of Arts and Sciences, Department of English, Speech, and Foreign Languages, Denton, TX 76201. Offers English (MA); rhetoric (PhD). Part-time programs available. *Faculty:* 16 full-time (10 women). *Students:* 9 full-time (8 women), 50 part-time (43 women); includes 11 minority (4 African Americans, 1 American Indian/Alaska Native, 2 Asian Americans or Pacific Islanders, 4 Hispanic Americans). Average age 38. 12 applicants, 75% accepted, 5 enrolled. In 2009, 4 master's, 5 doctorates awarded. *Degree requirements:* For master's, comprehensive exam, thesis; for doctorate, comprehensive exam, thesis/dissertation. *Entrance requirements:* For master's, GRE General Test (minimum score 500 verbal, 350 quantitative), 3 letters of reference, interview, minimum GPA of 3.0; for doctorate, GRE General Test, writing sample, 3 letters of reference, interview, minimum GPA of 3.0 on previous upper-division and graduate work. Additional exam requirements/recommendations for international students: Recommended—TOEFL (minimum score 600 paper-based; 213 computer-based; 79 iBT). *Application deadline:* For fall admission, 7/1 priority date for domestic students, 3/1 for international students; for spring admission, 12/1 priority date for domestic students, 7/1 for international students. Applications are processed on a rolling basis. Application fee: $50. Electronic applications accepted. *Expenses:* Tuition, state resident: full-time $3564; part-time $198 per credit hour. Tuition, nonresident: full-time $8550; part-time $475 per credit hour. Required fees: $69.26 per credit hour. Tuition and fees vary according to course load. *Financial support:* In 2009–10, 24 students received support, including 6 research assistantships (averaging $10,746 per year), 15 teaching assistantships (averaging $10,746 per year); career-related internships or fieldwork, Federal Work-Study, institutionally sponsored loans, scholarships/grants, traineeships, health care benefits, and unspecified assistantships also available. Support available to part-time students. Financial award application deadline: 3/1; financial award applicants required to submit FAFSA. *Faculty research:* British and American literature, rhetoric: historical and applied, composition studies and technology, literary theory and criticism, women's literature and feminist rhetoric. *Unit head:* Dr. Genevieve West, Chair, 940-898-2324, Fax: 940-898-2297, E-mail: engspfl@twu.edu. *Application contact:* Samuel Wheeler, Assistant Director of Admissions, 940-898-3188, Fax: 940-898-3081, E-mail: wheelersr@twu.edu.

Trinity College, Graduate Programs, Department of English, Hartford, CT 06106-3100. Offers MA. Part-time and evening/weekend programs available. *Faculty:* 4 full-time (3 women), 2 part-time/adjunct (0 women). *Students:* 38 part-time (21 women); includes 1 Hispanic American. Average age 38. In 2009, 7 master's awarded. *Degree requirements:* For master's, thesis. *Entrance requirements:* For master's, minimum GPA of 3.0. *Application deadline:* For fall admission, 4/15 for domestic students; for spring admission, 11/15 for domestic students. Application fee: $50. *Expenses:* Tuition: Part-time $1700 per course. One-time fee: $75 full-time. *Financial support:* Fellowships, tuition waivers (full) available. Support available to part-time students. Financial award application deadline: 4/1. *Unit head:* Dr. Milla Riggio, Graduate Director, 860-297-2467. *Application contact:* Nicola Dawkins, Graduate Studies Administrative Assistant, 860-297-2151, Fax: 860-297-5179, E-mail: nicola.dawkins@trincoll.edu.

Trinity Western University, Faculty of Graduate Studies, Program in Interdisciplinary Humanities, Langley, BC V2Y 1Y1, Canada. Offers general humanities (MAIH); specialized (MAIH), including English, history, philosophy. Part-time and evening/weekend programs available. Postbaccalaureate distance learning degree programs offered (minimal on-campus study). *Entrance requirements:* For master's, strong undergraduate degree in Humanities or English, History or Philosophy. *Faculty research:* Literary theory, gender, medieval and early modern literature, philosophy of religion, Thomas Merton's poetics.

Truman State University, Graduate School, School of Arts and Letters, Program in English, Kirksville, MO 63501-4221. Offers MA. *Degree requirements:* For master's, thesis. *Entrance requirements:* For master's, GRE General Test, minimum GPA of 3.0. Additional exam requirements/recommendations for international students: Required—TOEFL (minimum score 550 paper-based; 213 computer-based). Electronic applications accepted. *Expenses:* Tuition, state resident: part-time $291 per credit. Tuition, nonresident: part-time $499 per credit hour. Tuition and fees vary according to course load.

Tufts University, Graduate School of Arts and Sciences, Department of English, Medford, MA 02155. Offers MA, PhD. *Faculty:* 19 full-time, 28 part-time/adjunct. *Students:* 63 full-time (39 women); includes 6 minority (3 African Americans, 3 Hispanic Americans), 6 international. Average age 27. 137 applicants, 18% accepted, 9 enrolled. In 2009, 3 master's, 5 doctorates awarded. Terminal master's awarded for partial completion of doctoral program. *Degree* *requirements:* For master's, one foreign language, thesis; for doctorate, 2 foreign languages, thesis/dissertation. *Entrance requirements:* For master's and doctorate, GRE General Test, GRE Subject Test, writing sample. Additional exam requirements/recommendations for international students: Required—TOEFL (minimum score 550 paper-based; 213 computer-based; 80 iBT). *Application deadline:* For fall admission, 1/15 for domestic students, 12/15 for international students. Applications are processed on a rolling basis. Application fee: $75. Electronic applications accepted. *Expenses:* Tuition: Full-time $38,096; part-time $3962 per credit. Required fees: $686; $40 per year. Tuition and fees vary according to course level, course load, degree level, program and student level. *Financial support:* Fellowships with full tuition reimbursements, teaching assistantships with full tuition reimbursements, Federal Work-Study, scholarships/grants, tuition waivers (full and partial), and unspecified assistantships available. Financial award application deadline: 2/15; financial award applicants required to submit FAFSA. *Unit head:* Dr. Lee Edelman, Chair, 617-627-3459. *Application contact:* Judith Haber, Graduate Advisor, 617-627-3459.

Tulane University, School of Liberal Arts, Department of English, New Orleans, LA 70118-5669. Offers MA, PhD. *Degree requirements:* For master's, one foreign language, thesis or alternative; for doctorate, 2 foreign languages, thesis/dissertation. *Entrance requirements:* For master's, GRE General Test, minimum B average in undergraduate course work; for doctorate, GRE General Test. Additional exam requirements/recommendations for international students: Required—TOEFL. Electronic applications accepted.

Universidad de las Américas–Puebla, Division of Graduate Studies, School of Humanities, Program in Literature, Puebla, Mexico. Offers MA. Part-time and evening/weekend programs available. *Degree requirements:* For master's, one foreign language, thesis. *Entrance requirements:* Additional exam requirements/recommendations for international students: Required—TOEFL. *Faculty research:* Women in literature, Mexican and Hispanic literature.

Université de Montréal, Faculty of Arts and Sciences, Department of English Studies, Montréal, QC H3C 3J7, Canada. Offers MA, PhD. *Degree requirements:* For doctorate, thesis/dissertation, general exam. *Entrance requirements:* For master's, BA in English with minimum B+ average; for doctorate, MA in English with minimum B+ average. Electronic applications accepted. *Faculty research:* British, Canadian, and American literature.

Université Laval, Faculty of Letters, Department of Literature, Programs in Ancient Civilization, Québec, QC G1K 7P4, Canada. Offers MA, PhD. Part-time programs available. Terminal master's awarded for partial completion of doctoral program. *Degree requirements:* For master's, thesis; for doctorate, comprehensive exam, thesis/dissertation. *Entrance requirements:* For master's and doctorate, English test (comprehension of written English), knowledge of French, knowledge of an ancient language. Electronic applications accepted.

Université Laval, Faculty of Letters, Department of Literature, Programs in English Literatures, Québec, QC G1K 7P4, Canada. Offers MA, PhD. Part-time programs available. Terminal master's awarded for partial completion of doctoral program. *Degree requirements:* For master's, thesis (for some programs); for doctorate, comprehensive exam, thesis/dissertation. *Entrance requirements:* For master's, French exam, knowledge of English; for doctorate, French exam, knowledge of English, knowledge of a third language. Electronic applications accepted.

University at Albany, State University of New York, College of Arts and Sciences, Department of English, Albany, NY 12222-0001. Offers MA, PhD. *Degree requirements:* For master's, one foreign language; for doctorate, one foreign language, comprehensive exam, thesis/dissertation, residency. *Entrance requirements:* For master's and doctorate, GRE General Test, GRE Subject Test. Additional exam requirements/recommendations for international students: Required—TOEFL (minimum score 550 paper-based; 213 computer-based). Electronic applications accepted. *Faculty research:* Women playwrights; critical literary theory; poetry and poetics; media history, writing and reporting; creative non-fiction.

University at Buffalo, the State University of New York, Graduate School, College of Arts and Sciences, Department of English, Buffalo, NY 14260. Offers MA, PhD. Part-time programs available. *Faculty:* 44 full-time (18 women). *Students:* 151 full-time (80 women), 22 part-time (10 women). Average age 29. 326 applicants, 26% accepted. In 2009, 24 master's, 15 doctorates awarded. Terminal master's awarded for partial completion of doctoral program. *Degree requirements:* For master's, thesis or alternative; for doctorate, thesis/dissertation, departmental qualifying exam. *Entrance requirements:* For master's and doctorate, GRE General Test, sample of written work. Additional exam requirements/recommendations for international students: Required—TOEFL (minimum score 79 iBT). *Application deadline:* For fall admission, 12/15 for domestic and international students. Application fee: $75. Electronic applications accepted. *Financial support:* In 2009–10, 80 students received support, including 12 fellowships with full tuition reimbursements available (averaging $16,400 per year), 65 teaching assistantships with full tuition reimbursements available (averaging $13,900 per year); research assistantships, career-related internships or fieldwork, Federal Work-Study, institutionally sponsored loans, and unspecified assistantships also available. Financial award application deadline: 12/15; financial award applicants required to submit FAFSA. *Faculty research:* Psychoanalysis, early modern British literature, poetics, nineteenth century American literature. Total annual research expenditures: $38,000. *Unit head:* Dr. Cristanne Miller, Chair, 716-645-0674, Fax: 716-645-5980, E-mail: ccmiller@.buffalo.edu. *Application contact:* Dr. Graham Hammill, Director of Graduate Admissions, 716-645-2575, Fax: 716-645-5980, E-mail: eng-grad@buffalo.edu.

The University of Akron, Graduate School, Buchtel College of Arts and Sciences, Department of English, Akron, OH 44325. Offers composition (MA); creative writing (MFA); literature (MA). Part-time programs available. *Faculty:* 18 full-time (5 women). *Students:* 48 full-time (24 women), 45 part-time (31 women); includes 6 minority (4 African Americans, 1 Asian American or Pacific Islander, 1 Hispanic American), 1 international. Average age 32. 37 applicants, 89% accepted, 16 enrolled. In 2009, 20 master's awarded. *Degree requirements:* For master's, thesis optional. *Entrance requirements:* For master's, BA in English, minimum GPA of 2.75, writing portfolio, letters of recommendation. Additional exam requirements/recommendations for international students: Required—TOEFL (minimum score 580 paper-based; 237 computer-based; 92 iBT). *Application deadline:* Applications are processed on a rolling basis. Application fee: $30 ($40 for international students). Electronic applications accepted. *Expenses:* Tuition, state resident: full-time $6570; part-time $365 per credit hour. Tuition, nonresident: full-time $11,250; part-time $625 per credit hour. *Financial support:* In 2009–10, 5 research assistantships with full tuition reimbursements, 23 teaching assistantships with full tuition reimbursements were awarded. *Faculty research:* British and American literary studies, literary theory, creative writing, applied linguistics. Total annual research expenditures: $1,332. *Unit head:* Dr. Michael Schuldiner, Chair, 330-972-8556, E-mail: schuldi@uakron.edu. *Application contact:* Dr. Hillary Nunn, Director of Graduate Studies, 330-972-7601, E-mail: nunn@uakron.edu.

The University of Alabama, Graduate School, College of Arts and Sciences, Department of English, Tuscaloosa, AL 35487. Offers composition and rhetoric (PhD); creative writing (MFA), including fiction, poetry; literature (MA, PhD); rhetoric and composition (MA); teaching English as a second language (MATESOL). *Faculty:* 30 full-time (12 women). *Students:* 123 full-time (71 women), 12 part-time (9 women); includes 14 minority (9 African Americans, 2 American Indian/Alaska Native, 1 Asian American or Pacific Islander, 2 Hispanic Americans), 4 international. Average age 27. 339 applicants, 17% accepted, 39 enrolled. In 2009, 31 degrees awarded. *Degree requirements:* For master's, one foreign language, comprehensive exam, thesis (for some programs); for doctorate, 2 foreign languages, comprehensive exam, thesis/dissertation. *Entrance requirements:* For master's and doctorate, GRE, minimum GPA of 3.0, critical writing sample. Additional exam requirements/recommendations for international students: Required—TOEFL. *Application deadline:* For fall admission, 1/15 priority date for domestic students, 1/15 for international students. Application fee: $50 ($60 for international students). Electronic applications accepted. *Expenses:* Tuition, state resident: full-time $7000. Tuition, nonresident: full-time $19,200. *Financial support:* In 2009–10, 7 fellowships with full tuition reimbursements (averaging $15,000 per year), 1 research assistantship (averaging $11,708 per year), 106 teaching assistantships with full tuition reimbursements (averaging $11,708 per year) were awarded; career-related internships or fieldwork, scholarships/grants, health care benefits, and unspecified assistantships also available. Financial award application deadline: 1/15. *Faculty research:* Critical theory; modern, Renaissance, and African-American literature. *Unit head:* Dr. Catherine E. Davies, Director of Graduate Studies, 205-348-8499, E-mail: cdavies@bama.ua.edu. *Application contact:* Vernita W. James, Office Assistant II, 205-348-0766, Fax: 205-348-1388, E-mail: vwjames@bama.ua.edu.

The University of Alabama at Birmingham, College of Arts and Sciences, Program in English, Birmingham, AL 35294. Offers MA. *Degree requirements:* For master's, one foreign language, comprehensive exam, thesis optional. *Entrance requirements:* For master's, GRE General Test or MAT, minimum GPA of 2.75. Electronic applications accepted.

The University of Alabama in Huntsville, School of Graduate Studies, College of Liberal Arts, Department of English, Huntsville, AL 35899. Offers English (MA); teaching of English to speakers of other languages (Certificate); technical communications (Certificate). Part-time and evening/weekend programs available. *Faculty:* 14 full-time (9 women). *Students:* 14 full-time (9 women), 39 part-time (31 women); includes 11 minority (8 African Americans, 1 American Indian/Alaska Native, 2 Hispanic Americans). Average age 33. 28 applicants, 86% accepted, 17 enrolled. In 2009, 23 master's, 1 other advanced degree awarded. *Degree requirements:* For master's, one foreign language, comprehensive exam, thesis or alternative, oral and written exams. *Entrance requirements:* For master's and Certificate, GRE General Test, minimum GPA of 3.0. Additional exam requirements/recommendations for international students: Required—TOEFL (minimum score 500 paper-based; 173 computer-based; 62 iBT). *Application deadline:* For fall admission, 7/15 for domestic students, 4/1 for international students; for spring admission, 11/30 for domestic students, 9/1 for international students. Applications are processed on a rolling basis. Application fee: $40 ($50 for international students). Electronic applications accepted. *Expenses:* Tuition, state resident: part-time $355.75 per credit hour. Tuition, nonresident: part-time $847.10 per credit hour. Required fees: $210.80 per semester. Tuition and fees vary according to course load and program. *Financial support:* In 2009–10, 9 students received support, including 4 teaching assistantships with full and partial tuition reimbursements available (averaging $8,460 per year); career-related internships or fieldwork, Federal Work-Study, institutionally sponsored loans, scholarships/grants, health care benefits, tuition waivers, and unspecified assistantships also available. Support available to part-time students. Financial award application deadline: 4/1; financial award applicants required to submit FAFSA. *Faculty research:* American and British literature, linguistics, technical writing, women's studies, rhetoric. *Unit head:* Dr. Rose Norman, Chair, 256-824-6320, Fax: 256-824-6949, E-mail: normanr@uah.edu. *Application contact:* Kathy Biggs, Graduate Studies Admissions Manager, 256-824-6199, Fax: 256-824-6405, E-mail: deangrad@uah.edu.

University of Alaska Anchorage, College of Arts and Sciences, Department of English, Anchorage, AK 99508. Offers MA. Part-time programs available. *Degree requirements:* For master's, comprehensive exam, thesis or alternative. *Entrance requirements:* For master's, GRE General Test, GRE Subject Test, portfolio, minimum GPA of 3.5, writing sample. Additional exam requirements/recommendations for international students: Required—TOEFL (minimum score 550 paper-based; 213 computer-based). *Faculty research:* The rhetoric of essays, American and American Indian literature, linguistics, Shakespeare, literature of war.

University of Alaska Fairbanks, College of Liberal Arts, Department of English, Fairbanks, AK 99775-5720. Offers creative writing (MFA); literature (MA); MA/MFA. Part-time programs available. *Faculty:* 15 full-time (6 women), 6 part-time/adjunct (5 women). *Students:* 33 full-time (14 women), 11 part-time (8 women); includes 5 minority (2 American Indian/Alaska Native, 2 Asian Americans or Pacific Islanders, 1 Hispanic American). Average age 42. 50 applicants, 30% accepted, 9 enrolled. In 2009, 6 master's awarded. *Degree requirements:* For master's, comprehensive exam, thesis or alternative, oral exams, oral defense. *Entrance requirements:* For master's, GRE General Test, academic writing sample. Additional exam requirements/recommendations for international students: Required—TOEFL (minimum score 550 paper-based; 213 computer-based; 80 iBT). *Application deadline:* For fall admission, 6/1 for domestic students, 3/1 for international students; for spring admission, 10/15 for domestic students, 9/1 for international students. Applications are processed on a rolling basis. Application fee: $60. Electronic applications accepted. *Expenses:* Tuition, state resident: full-time $7584; part-time $316 per credit. Tuition, nonresident: full-time $15,504; part-time $646 per credit. Required fees: $23 per credit. $135 per semester. Tuition and fees vary according to course level, course load and reciprocity agreements. *Financial support:* In 2009–10, 1 research assistantship (averaging $13,330 per year), 26 teaching assistantships (averaging $11,844 per year) were awarded; fellowships, Federal Work-Study, scholarships/grants, health care benefits, and unspecified assistantships also available. Support available to part-time students. Financial award application deadline: 7/1; financial award applicants required to submit FAFSA. *Faculty research:* Traditional Alaskan native literature, British literature, pedagogy, American literature, rhetoric/composition history. *Unit head:* Dr. Cooper Burns, Department Chair, 907-474-7193, Fax: 907-474-5247, E-mail: faengl@uaf.edu. *Application contact:* Dr. Cooper Burns, Department Chair, 907-474-7193, Fax: 907-474-5247, E-mail: faengl@uaf.edu.

University of Alberta, Faculty of Graduate Studies and Research, Department of English and Film Studies, Edmonton, AB T6G 2E1, Canada. Offers English (MA, PhD). Part-time and evening/weekend programs available. *Faculty:* 54 full-time (20 women), 1 part-time/adjunct (0 women). *Students:* 84 full-time (27 women), 27 part-time (12 women). Average age 33. 107 applicants, 68% accepted, 34 enrolled. In 2009, 8 master's, 12 doctorates awarded. *Degree requirements:* For master's, one foreign language, thesis optional; for doctorate, 2 foreign languages, thesis/dissertation. *Entrance requirements:* For master's, honors BA or equivalent; for doctorate, honors BA and MA. Additional exam requirements/recommendations for international students: Required—TOEFL (minimum score 600 paper-based). *Application deadline:* For fall admission, 1/7 for domestic students. Electronic applications accepted. Tuition and fees charges are reported in Canadian dollars. *Expenses:* Tuition, area resident: Full-time $4626 Canadian dollars; part-time $99.72 Canadian dollars per unit. International tuition: $8216 Canadian dollars full-time. Required fees: $3590 Canadian dollars; $99.72 Canadian dollars per unit. $215 Canadian dollars per term. *Financial support:* In 2009–10, 76 students received support, including 33 fellowships, 20 research assistantships, 23 teaching assistantships; scholarships/grants and unspecified assistantships also available. Financial award application deadline: 1/7. *Faculty research:* Women's writing, postcolonial theory, Victorian literature, Renaissance literature, Canadian literature. *Unit head:* Prof. H. Zwicker, Graduate Coordinator, 780-492-4701, Fax: 780-492-8142. *Application contact:* Kim Brown, Department Office, 780-492-4701, Fax: 780-492-8142, E-mail: englgrad@mails.arts.ualberta.ca.

The University of Arizona, Graduate College, College of Humanities, Department of English, Tucson, AZ 85721. Offers creative writing (MFA); English (MA, PhD); English language/linguistics (MA), including ESL; rhetoric, composition and the teaching of English (MA, PhD). Part-time programs available. *Faculty:* 44. *Students:* 81 full-time (54 women), 112 part-time (72 women); includes 13 minority (2 African Americans, 2 American Indian/Alaska Native, 2 Asian Americans or Pacific Islanders, 7 Hispanic Americans), 10 international. Average age 34. 482 applicants, 21% accepted, 53 enrolled. In 2009, 41 master's, 25 doctorates awarded. Terminal master's awarded for partial completion of doctoral program. *Degree requirements:* For master's, one foreign language, comprehensive exam; for doctorate, one foreign language, comprehensive exam, thesis/dissertation, preliminary and qualifying exams. *Entrance requirements:* For master's, GRE General Test, GRE Subject Test, bachelor's degree in English, minimum major GPA of 3.5, writing sample; for doctorate, GRE General Test, GRE Subject Test (literature), bachelor's degree in English, minimum major GPA of 3.5, statement of purpose, writing sample. Additional exam requirements/recommendations for international students: Required—TOEFL (minimum score 550 paper-based; 213 computer-based; 79 iBT). *Application deadline:* For fall admission, 1/9 for domestic students, 12/10 for international students. Applications are processed on a rolling basis. Application fee: $75. Electronic applications accepted. *Expenses:* Tuition, state resident: full-time $9028. Tuition, nonresident: full-time $24,890. *Financial support:* In 2009–10, 1 research assistantship with full tuition reimbursement (averaging $16,916 per year), 122

English

The University of Arizona (continued)
teaching assistantships with full tuition reimbursements (averaging $15,130 per year) were awarded; career-related internships or fieldwork, scholarships/grants, health care benefits, tuition waivers (full and partial), and unspecified assistantships also available. *Faculty research:* Literature, women's studies, Southwestern literature, feminist theory. Total annual research expenditures: $129,807. *Unit head:* Dr. Jun Liu, Department Head, 520-621-3287, E-mail: junliu@email.arizona.edu. *Application contact:* Marcia Marma, Graduate Secretary, 520-621-1358, Fax: 520-621-7397, E-mail: mmarma@u.arizona.edu.

University of Arkansas, Graduate School, J. William Fulbright College of Arts and Sciences, Department of English, Program in English, Fayetteville, AR 72701-1201. Offers MA, PhD. *Students:* 26 full-time (14 women), 48 part-time (31 women); includes 5 minority (3 American Indian/Alaska Native, 2 Hispanic Americans), 5 international. In 2009, 16 master's, 5 doctorates awarded. *Degree requirements:* For master's, thesis; for doctorate, thesis/dissertation. *Entrance requirements:* For master's, GRE General Test; for doctorate, GRE General Test, GRE Subject Test. Application fee: $40 ($50 for international students). *Expenses:* Tuition, state resident: full-time $7355; part-time $356.58 per hour. Tuition, nonresident: full-time $17,401; part-time $775.17 per hour. Required fees: $1203. *Financial support:* In 2009–10, 10 fellowships with tuition reimbursements, 43 teaching assistantships were awarded; research assistantships, career-related internships or fieldwork and Federal Work-Study also available. Support available to part-time students. Financial award application deadline: 4/1; financial award applicants required to submit FAFSA. *Faculty research:* Creative writing, seventeenth century literature, twentieth century literature, American literature. *Unit head:* Dr. Joseph Candido, Department Chairperson, 479-575-4301, Fax: 479-575-5919, E-mail: candido@uark.edu. *Application contact:* Dr. Bill Quinn, Graduate Coordinator, 479-575-4301, Fax: 479-575-5919, E-mail: wquinn@uark.edu.

The University of British Columbia, Faculty of Arts and Faculty of Graduate Studies, Department of English, Vancouver, BC V6T 1Z1, Canada. Offers MA, PhD. *Degree requirements:* For master's, thesis or alternative; for doctorate, one foreign language, comprehensive exam, thesis/dissertation. *Entrance requirements:* For doctorate, MA. Additional exam requirements/recommendations for international students: Required—TOEFL (minimum score 615 paper-based; 258 computer-based; 104 iBT), IELTS (minimum score 8). Electronic applications accepted. *Faculty research:* English, American, Canadian, and Commonwealth post-colonial literature; English language; rhetoric.

The University of British Columbia, Faculty of Arts, School of Library, Archival and Information Studies, Master of Arts Program in Children's Literature, Vancouver, BC V6T 1Z1, Canada. Offers MA. Part-time programs available. *Degree requirements:* For master's, thesis. *Entrance requirements:* For master's, minimum GPA of 3.3 in undergraduate upper-division courses. Additional exam requirements/recommendations for international students: Required—TOEFL (minimum score 600 paper-based; 250 computer-based; 100 iBT). Electronic applications accepted. *Faculty research:* Children's and young adult literature; children's and young adult public library services; Canadian children's and young adult literature; publishing for youth.

University of Calgary, Faculty of Graduate Studies, Faculty of Humanities, Department of English, Calgary, AB T2N 1N4, Canada. Offers MA, PhD. Part-time programs available. *Degree requirements:* For master's, one foreign language, comprehensive exam (for some programs), thesis; for doctorate, one foreign language, thesis/dissertation, candidacy exam. *Entrance requirements:* Additional exam requirements/recommendations for international students: Required—TOEFL (minimum score 600 paper-based; 250 computer-based). Electronic applications accepted. *Faculty research:* Various national and period literatures, creative writing, literary theory, gender and women's studies, postcolonial literatures.

University of California, Berkeley, Graduate Division, College of Letters and Science, Department of English, Berkeley, CA 94720-1500. Offers PhD. *Students:* 133 full-time (73 women). Average age 30. 466 applicants, 22 enrolled. In 2009, 21 doctorates awarded. *Degree requirements:* For doctorate, 2 foreign languages, thesis/dissertation, qualifying exam. *Entrance requirements:* For doctorate, GRE General Test, GRE Subject Test, minimum GPA of 3.0, writing sample, 3 letters of recommendation. *Application deadline:* For fall admission, 12/10 for domestic students. Application fee: $70 ($90 for international students). *Financial support:* Fellowships, research assistantships, teaching assistantships, Federal Work-Study, institutionally sponsored loans, scholarships/grants, tuition waivers (partial), and unspecified assistantships available. Financial award applicants required to submit FAFSA. *Unit head:* Prof. Samuel Otter, Chair, 510-642-3877, E-mail: ch_english@ls.berkeley.edu. *Application contact:* Doreen L. Barton, Graduate Assistant, 510-642-4005, Fax: 510-642-8738, E-mail: dlbarton@berkeley.edu.

University of California, Davis, Graduate Studies, Program in English, Davis, CA 95616. Offers creative writing (MA); English (MA, PhD). Terminal master's awarded for partial completion of doctoral program. *Degree requirements:* For master's, one foreign language, thesis optional; for doctorate, 2 foreign languages, thesis/dissertation. *Entrance requirements:* For master's and doctorate, GRE General Test, GRE Subject Test, minimum GPA of 3.0, writing sample. Additional exam requirements/recommendations for international students: Required—TOEFL (minimum score 550 paper-based; 213 computer-based). Electronic applications accepted. *Faculty research:* Feminist theory, ethnic literature, literary theory, history of literature, literature of nature.

University of California, Irvine, Office of Graduate Studies, School of Humanities, Department of English and Comparative Literature, English Summer Program, Irvine, CA 92697. Offers MA. Offered during summer only. *Faculty:* 8 full-time (2 women). *Students:* 17 full-time (12 women); includes 3 minority (all Hispanic Americans). Average age 31. 18 applicants, 94% accepted, 17 enrolled. In 2009, 34 master's awarded. *Degree requirements:* For master's, thesis. *Entrance requirements:* For master's, GRE General Test, GRE Subject Test, writing sample, 3 letters of recommendation. *Application deadline:* For fall admission, 3/15 priority date for domestic students. Application fee: $70 ($90 for international students). Electronic applications accepted. *Expenses:* Contact institution. *Financial support:* Institutionally sponsored loans available. Financial award application deadline: 3/2; financial award applicants required to submit FAFSA. *Faculty research:* Shakespeare, American multiculturalism, literary theory. *Unit head:* Dr. Richard Kroll, Director, 949-824-2557, Fax: 949-824-2916, E-mail: rwkroll@uci.edu. *Application contact:* Kitty Roos, Graduate Administrator, 949-824-6714, Fax: 949-824-2916, E-mail: kroos@uci.edu.

University of California, Irvine, Office of Graduate Studies, School of Humanities, Department of English and Comparative Literature, Program in English, Irvine, CA 92697. Offers English (MA); English and American literature (PhD). *Faculty:* 21 full-time (9 women), 2 part-time/adjunct (1 woman). *Students:* 85 full-time (39 women), 1 part-time (0 women); includes 17 minority (1 African American, 10 Asian Americans or Pacific Islanders, 6 Hispanic Americans), 1 international. Average age 30. 201 applicants, 9% accepted, 10 enrolled. In 2009, 34 master's, 13 doctorates awarded. Terminal master's awarded for partial completion of doctoral program. *Degree requirements:* For master's, one foreign language, comprehensive exam; for doctorate, 2 foreign languages, comprehensive exam, thesis/dissertation. *Entrance requirements:* For doctorate, GRE General Test, GRE Subject Test, minimum GPA of 3.5, sample of written work, 3 letters of recommendation. Additional exam requirements/recommendations for international students: Required—TOEFL (minimum score 550 paper-based; 213 computer-based). *Application deadline:* For fall admission, 12/1 for domestic and international students. Application fee: $70 ($90 for international students). Electronic applications accepted. *Financial support:* In 2009–10, 75 students received support, including 30 fellowships with full tuition reimbursements available (averaging $14,000 per year), 3 research assistantships (averaging $15,000 per year), 41 teaching assistantships with partial tuition reimbursements available (averaging $14,145 per year); institutionally sponsored loans, health care benefits, tuition waivers (full and partial), and unspecified assistantships also available. Financial award application deadline: 3/2; financial award applicants required to submit FAFSA. *Faculty research:* Critical theory, literary history, cultural studies. *Unit head:* Chair, 949-824-4857, Fax: 949-824-2916. *Application contact:* Nancy Benay, Graduate Administrator, 949-824-4857, Fax: 949-824-2916, E-mail: ndbenay@uci.edu.

University of California, Los Angeles, Graduate Division, College of Letters and Science, Department of English, Los Angeles, CA 90095. Offers MA, PhD. *Students:* 95 full-time (59 women); includes 21 minority (6 African Americans, 6 Asian Americans or Pacific Islanders, 9 Hispanic Americans), 2 international. Average age 29. 328 applicants, 9% accepted, 9 enrolled. In 2009, 12 master's, 18 doctorates awarded. Terminal master's awarded for partial completion of doctoral program. *Degree requirements:* For master's, comprehensive exam or thesis; for doctorate, 2 foreign languages, thesis/dissertation, oral and written qualifying exams. *Entrance requirements:* For master's, GRE General Test, GRE Subject Test (literature), minimum GPA of 3.0, sample of written work; for doctorate, GRE General Test, GRE Subject Test (literature), minimum GPA of 3.5 (undergraduate), 3.7 (graduate), sample of written work. *Application deadline:* For fall admission, 12/15 for domestic and international students. Application fee: $70 ($90 for international students). Electronic applications accepted. *Financial support:* In 2009–10, 66 fellowships with full and partial tuition reimbursements, 28 research assistantships with full and partial tuition reimbursements, 76 teaching assistantships with full and partial tuition reimbursements were awarded; Federal Work-Study, institutionally sponsored loans, scholarships/grants, health care benefits, tuition waivers (full and partial), and unspecified assistantships also available. Financial award application deadline: 3/1; financial award applicants required to submit FAFSA. *Unit head:* Dr. Rafael Perez-Torrez, Chair, 310-206-5887. *Application contact:* Department Office, 310-825-3927, E-mail: graduate@english.ucla.edu.

University of California, Riverside, Graduate Division, Department of English, Riverside, CA 92521-0102. Offers MA, PhD. *Degree requirements:* For master's, one foreign language, comprehensive exam; for doctorate, 2 foreign languages, thesis/dissertation, qualifying exams. *Entrance requirements:* For master's and doctorate, GRE General Test, minimum GPA of 3.5. Additional exam requirements/recommendations for international students: Required—TOEFL (minimum score 550 paper-based; 213 computer-based; 80 iBT). Electronic applications accepted. *Faculty research:* Critical theory, cultural and film studies, lesbian and gay studies, minority and feminist discourses, rhetoric and composition.

University of California, San Diego, Office of Graduate Studies, Department of Literature, Program in Literatures in English, La Jolla, CA 92093. Offers MA. *Degree requirements:* For master's, thesis. *Entrance requirements:* For master's, GRE General Test, GRE Subject Test. Electronic applications accepted.

University of California, Santa Barbara, Graduate Division, College of Letters and Sciences, Division of Humanities and Fine Arts, Department of English, Santa Barbara, CA 93106-3170. Offers English (PhD); feminist studies (PhD); global studies (PhD); MA/PhD. *Faculty:* 26 full-time (13 women), 17 part-time/adjunct (12 women). *Students:* 81 full-time (43 women). Average age 30. 151 applicants, 19% accepted, 13 enrolled. In 2009, 12 doctorates awarded. Terminal master's awarded for partial completion of doctoral program. *Degree requirements:* For doctorate, one foreign language, comprehensive exam, thesis/dissertation. *Entrance requirements:* For doctorate, GRE General Test, GRE Subject Test (literature), sample of written work, 3 letters of recommendation, resume/curriculum vitae. Additional exam requirements/recommendations for international students: Required—TOEFL (minimum score 550 paper-based; 213 computer-based; 80 iBT) or IELTS (minimum score 7). *Application deadline:* For fall admission, 12/15 for domestic and international students. Application fee: $70 ($90 for international students). Electronic applications accepted. *Financial support:* In 2009–10, 70 students received support, including 32 fellowships with full and partial tuition reimbursements available (averaging $10,800 per year), 6 research assistantships with full and partial tuition reimbursements available (averaging $4,200 per year), 54 teaching assistantships with partial tuition reimbursements available (averaging $10,800 per year); Federal Work-Study, institutionally sponsored loans, scholarships/grants, health care benefits, tuition waivers (full and partial), and unspecified assistantships also available. Financial award application deadline: 12/15; financial award applicants required to submit FAFSA. *Faculty research:* Renaissance literature, eighteenth century literature, American literature, race and ethnic studies, literature and theory of technology/media/information. *Unit head:* Prof. Alan Liu, Chair, 805-893-3478, Fax: 805-893-4622, E-mail: ayliu@english.ucsb.edu. *Application contact:* Chelsea Houdyshell, Staff Graduate Advisor, 805-893-2639, Fax: 805-893-4622, E-mail: chelsea@english.ucsb.edu.

University of California, Santa Cruz, Division of Graduate Studies, Division of Humanities, Department of Literature, Santa Cruz, CA 95064. Offers MA, PhD. Terminal master's awarded for partial completion of doctoral program. *Degree requirements:* For master's, thesis; for doctorate, one foreign language, thesis/dissertation, qualifying exam. *Entrance requirements:* For master's, GRE General Test, writing sample, minimum GPA of 3.5; for doctorate, GRE General Test, minimum GPA of 3.5, writing sample. Electronic applications accepted. *Faculty research:* Comparative literature; German, Spanish, classical, American, and English literature.

University of Central Arkansas, Graduate School, College of Liberal Arts, Department of English, Conway, AR 72035-0001. Offers MA. Part-time programs available. *Faculty:* 17 full-time (2 women). *Students:* 10 full-time (2 women), 13 part-time (11 women); includes 2 minority (1 African American, 1 American Indian/Alaska Native). Average age 32. 8 applicants, 100% accepted, 6 enrolled. In 2009, 5 master's awarded. *Degree requirements:* For master's, comprehensive exam, thesis optional. *Entrance requirements:* For master's, GRE General Test, minimum GPA of 2.7. Additional exam requirements/recommendations for international students: Required—TOEFL (minimum score 550 paper-based; 213 computer-based). *Application deadline:* For fall admission, 3/1 priority date for domestic and international students; for spring admission, 10/1 priority date for domestic and international students. Applications are processed on a rolling basis. Application fee: $25 ($50 for international students). *Expenses:* Tuition, state resident: full-time $5136; part-time $214 per credit hour. Required fees: $379.50; $127 per term. Tuition and fees vary according to course level, course load and campus/location. *Financial support:* Federal Work-Study, scholarships/grants, and unspecified assistantships available. Financial award application deadline: 2/15; financial award applicants required to submit FAFSA. *Faculty research:* Writing project. *Unit head:* Dr. Jay Ruud, Chairperson, 501-450-5100, Fax: 501-450-5102, E-mail: jruud@uca.edu. *Application contact:* Brenda Herring, Admissions Assistant, 501-450-5065, Fax: 501-450-5678, E-mail: bherring@uca.edu.

University of Central Florida, College of Arts and Humanities, Department of English, Program in English, Orlando, FL 32816. Offers creative writing (MFA); English (MA). *Students:* 44 full-time (30 women), 47 part-time (33 women); includes 14 minority (6 African Americans, 2 Asian Americans or Pacific Islanders, 6 Hispanic Americans). Average age 30. 87 applicants, 52% accepted, 35 enrolled. In 2009, 21 master's awarded. Application fee: $30. Electronic applications accepted. *Expenses:* Tuition, state resident: part-time $306.31 per credit hour. Tuition, nonresident: part-time $1099.01 per credit hour. Part-time tuition and fees vary according to degree level and program. *Financial support:* In 2009–10, 8 fellowships with partial tuition reimbursements (averaging $3,600 per year), 2 research assistantships with partial tuition reimbursements (averaging $10,200 per year), 20 teaching assistantships with partial tuition reimbursements (averaging $7,600 per year) were awarded.

University of Central Missouri, The Graduate School, College of Arts, Humanities and Social Sciences, Warrensburg, MO 64093. Offers English (MA); history (MA); mass communication (MA); music (MA); psychology (MS); speech communication (MA); teaching english as a second language (MA); theatre (MA). Part-time programs available. *Faculty:* 82. *Students:* 60 full-time (35 women), 101 part-time (61 women); includes 11 minority (5 African Americans, 3 Asian Americans or Pacific Islanders, 3 Hispanic Americans), 17 international. Average age 30. 80 applicants, 80% accepted, 58 enrolled. In 2009, 51 master's awarded. *Entrance requirements:* Additional exam requirements/recommendations for international students: Required—TOEFL (minimum score 550 paper-based; 79 computer-based). *Application deadline:* For fall admission, 6/1 priority date for domestic students, 5/1 for international students; for spring admission, 10/1 priority date for domestic students, 10/1 for international students.

Applications are processed on a rolling basis. Application fee: $30 ($75 for international students). Electronic applications accepted. *Expenses:* Tuition, area resident: Part-time $245.80 per credit hour. Tuition, nonresident: part-time $491.60 per credit hour. Required fees: $24.20 per credit hour. Full-time tuition and fees vary according to course load, degree level, campus/location and reciprocity agreements. *Financial support:* Research assistantships with full and partial tuition reimbursements, teaching assistantships with full and partial tuition reimbursements, career-related internships or fieldwork, Federal Work-Study, scholarships/grants, and administrative and laboratory assistantships available. Support available to part-time students. Financial award application deadline: 3/1; financial award applicants required to submit FAFSA. *Unit head:* Dr. Gersham Nelson, Dean, 660-543-4750, Fax: 660-543-8271, E-mail: nelson@ucmo.edu. *Application contact:* Laurie Delap, Admissions Coordinator, 660-543-4621, Fax: 660-543-4778, E-mail: gradinfo@ucmo.edu.

University of Central Oklahoma, College of Graduate Studies and Research, College of Liberal Arts, Department of English, Edmond, OK 73034-5209. Offers composition skills (MA); contemporary literature (MA); creative writing (MA); teaching English as a second language (MA); traditional studies (MA). Part-time programs available. *Degree requirements:* For master's, one foreign language. *Entrance requirements:* For master's, 24 hours of course work in English language and literature. Additional exam requirements/recommendations for international students: Required—TOEFL (minimum score 550 paper-based; 213 computer-based). Electronic applications accepted. *Expenses:* Tuition, state resident: full-time $4128; part-time $172 per credit hour. Tuition, nonresident: full-time $10,373; part-time $432.20 per credit hour. Required fees: $433.20; $18.05 per credit hour. *Faculty research:* John Milton, Harriet Beecher Stowe.

University of Chicago, Division of the Humanities, Department of English Language and Literature, Chicago, IL 60637-1513. Offers AM, PhD. *Degree requirements:* For master's, one foreign language, thesis; for doctorate, 2 foreign languages, thesis/dissertation. *Entrance requirements:* For master's and doctorate, GRE General Test, GRE Subject Test (English). Additional exam requirements/recommendations for international students: Required—TOEFL.

University of Cincinnati, Graduate School, McMicken College of Arts and Sciences, Department of English, Cincinnati, OH 45221. Offers MA, MAT, PhD. Part-time programs available. Terminal master's awarded for partial completion of doctoral program. *Degree requirements:* For master's, one foreign language, thesis (for some programs); for doctorate, 2 foreign languages, thesis/dissertation. *Entrance requirements:* For master's, GRE General Test, letters of recommendation (3), writing samples; for doctorate, GRE General Test, GRE Subject Test, letters of recommendation (3), writing samples. Additional exam requirements/recommendations for international students: Required—TOEFL. Electronic applications accepted. *Faculty research:* Literature/theory, creative writing, composition, professional writing/editing, linguistics.

University of Colorado at Boulder, Graduate School, College of Arts and Sciences, Department of English, Boulder, CO 80309. Offers literature (MA, PhD), including creative writing (MA). Part-time programs available. *Faculty:* 48 full-time (26 women). *Students:* 96 full-time (58 women), 22 part-time (14 women); includes 14 minority (6 African Americans, 1 American Indian/Alaska Native, 1 Asian American or Pacific Islander, 6 Hispanic Americans), 2 international. Average age 32. 334 applicants, 11% accepted, 32 enrolled. In 2009, 32 master's, 2 doctorates awarded. *Degree requirements:* For master's, one foreign language, comprehensive exam, thesis or alternative; for doctorate, 2 foreign languages, comprehensive exam, thesis/dissertation. *Entrance requirements:* For master's, GRE General Test, GRE Subject Test, minimum undergraduate GPA of 3.0; for doctorate, GRE General Test, GRE Subject Test. *Application deadline:* For fall admission, 1/1 for domestic students, 12/1 for international students. Application fee: $50 ($60 for international students). *Financial support:* In 2009–10, 22 fellowships (averaging $3,976 per year), 42 research assistantships (averaging $11,068 per year) were awarded; Federal Work-Study and tuition waivers (full) also available. Financial award application deadline: 1/1; financial award applicants required to submit FAFSA. *Faculty research:* Creative writing, literature, language, critical theory. Total annual research expenditures: $9,912.

University of Colorado at Boulder, Graduate School, College of Arts and Sciences, Department of Spanish and Portuguese, Boulder, CO 80309. Offers Hispanic linguistics (MA); medieval/early modern Hispanic literatures (PhD); Spanish and Spanish American literatures (MA, PhD). Part-time programs available. *Faculty:* 14 full-time (5 women). *Students:* 38 full-time (19 women), 7 part-time (5 women); includes 11 minority (all Hispanic Americans), 17 international. Average age 31. 52 applicants, 35% accepted, 12 enrolled. In 2009, 5 master's, 3 doctorates awarded. Terminal master's awarded for partial completion of doctoral program. *Degree requirements:* For master's, one foreign language, comprehensive exam, thesis or alternative; for doctorate, 2 foreign languages, thesis/dissertation. *Entrance requirements:* For master's, minimum undergraduate GPA of 2.75. *Application deadline:* For fall admission, 12/15 priority date for domestic students, 12/15 for international students. Applications are processed on a rolling basis. Application fee: $50 ($60 for international students). *Financial support:* In 2009–10, 7 fellowships with full tuition reimbursements (averaging $3,436 per year), 19 research assistantships (averaging $12,128 per year) were awarded; tuition waivers (full) also available. Financial award application deadline: 12/15. *Faculty research:* Spanish peninsular and Spanish-American literatures; Hispanic linguistics; medieval, Golden Age, eighteenth and nineteenth century literatures.

University of Colorado Denver, College of Liberal Arts and Sciences, Department of English, Denver, CO 80217-3364. Offers applied linguistics (MA); English studies (MA); literature (MA); teaching English to speakers of other languages (Certificate); teaching of writing (MA). Part-time and evening/weekend programs available. *Students:* 12 full-time (9 women), 47 part-time (28 women); includes 3 minority (1 Asian American or Pacific Islander, 2 Hispanic Americans), 2 international. 36 applicants, 78% accepted, 19 enrolled. In 2009, 19 master's awarded. *Degree requirements:* For master's, thesis optional. *Entrance requirements:* For master's, GRE General Test, minimum GPA of 3.0. Additional exam requirements/recommendations for international students: Required—TOEFL (minimum score 550 paper-based). *Application deadline:* For fall admission, 5/25 for domestic students; for spring admission, 10/25 for domestic students. Applications are processed on a rolling basis. Application fee: $50 ($75 for international students). Electronic applications accepted. *Financial support:* Research assistantships, teaching assistantships, Federal Work-Study available. Financial award application deadline: 4/1; financial award applicants required to submit FAFSA. *Unit head:* Prof. Nancy Ciccone, Chair, 303-556-8395, Fax: 303-556-2959, E-mail: nancy.ciccone@ucdenver.edu. *Application contact:* Prof. Ian Ying, Program Advisor, 303-556-6728, Fax: 303-556-2959, E-mail: hongguang.ying@ucdenver.edu.

University of Connecticut, Graduate School, College of Liberal Arts and Sciences, Department of English, Storrs, CT 06269. Offers MA, PhD. *Faculty:* 61 full-time (32 women). *Students:* 72 full-time (52 women), 19 part-time (8 women); includes 5 minority (1 African American, 1 American Indian/Alaska Native, 3 Hispanic Americans), 3 international. Average age 34. 224 applicants, 8% accepted, 16 enrolled. In 2009, 19 master's, 7 doctorates awarded. Terminal master's awarded for partial completion of doctoral program. *Degree requirements:* For master's, comprehensive exam; for doctorate, thesis/dissertation. *Entrance requirements:* For master's and doctorate, GRE General Test, GRE Subject Test. Additional exam requirements/recommendations for international students: Required—TOEFL (minimum score 550 paper-based; 213 computer-based). *Application deadline:* For fall admission, 2/1 priority date for domestic and international students; for spring admission, 11/1 for domestic students, 10/1 for international students. Applications are processed on a rolling basis. Application fee: $55. Electronic applications accepted. *Expenses:* Tuition, state resident: full-time $4725; part-time $525 per credit. Tuition, nonresident: full-time $12,267; part-time $1363 per credit. Required fees: $346 per semester. Tuition and fees vary according to course load. *Financial support:* In 2009–10, 1 research assistantship with full tuition reimbursement, 71 teaching assistantships with full tuition reimbursements were awarded; fellowships, Federal Work-Study, scholarships/grants, health care benefits, and unspecified assistantships also available. Financial award application deadline: 2/1; financial award applicants required to submit FAFSA. *Unit head:* Robert Tilton, Head, 860-486-2141, Fax: 860-486-1530, E-mail: robert.tilton@uconn.edu. *Application contact:* Mary Udal, Administrative Assistant, 860-486-2329, Fax: 860-486-1530, E-mail: mary.udal@uconn.edu.

University of Dallas, Braniff Graduate School of Liberal Arts, Department of English, Irving, TX 75062-4736. Offers English literature (MA, MENG). Part-time programs available. *Faculty:* 16 full-time (5 women). *Students:* 20 full-time (10 women), 10 part-time (4 women); includes 1 minority (Hispanic American), 1 international. Average age 25. 22 applicants, 95% accepted, 20 enrolled. In 2009, 12 master's awarded. *Degree requirements:* For master's, one foreign language. *Entrance requirements:* For master's, GRE General Test. *Application deadline:* For fall admission, 2/15 priority date for domestic students; for spring admission, 11/15 for domestic students. Applications are processed on a rolling basis. Application fee: $50. *Expenses:* Tuition: Full-time $10,080; part-time $560 per credit hour. Required fees: $50 per term. Tuition and fees vary according to program. *Financial support:* In 2009–10, 29 students received support. Scholarships/grants available. Financial award application deadline: 2/15. *Faculty research:* Modern literature, Renaissance, Shakespeare, medieval studies. *Unit head:* Dr. Theresa Kenney, Chair, 972-721-4069, Fax: 972-721-4007, E-mail: teresaka@udallas.edu. *Application contact:* Graduate Coordinator, 972-721-5106, Fax: 972-721-5280, E-mail: graduate@acad.udallas.edu.

University of Dayton, Graduate School, College of Arts and Sciences, Department of English, Dayton, OH 45469-1300. Offers MA. Part-time and evening/weekend programs available. *Faculty:* 18 full-time (7 women). *Students:* 24 full-time (20 women), 15 part-time (13 women); includes 6 minority (4 African Americans, 1 Asian American or Pacific Islander, 1 Hispanic American). Average age 29. 31 applicants, 81% accepted, 14 enrolled. In 2009, 12 master's awarded. *Degree requirements:* For master's, thesis optional. *Entrance requirements:* For master's, minimum GPA of 3.0, 24 upper level credit hours of course work in English. Additional exam requirements/recommendations for international students: Required—TOEFL (minimum score 550 paper-based; 213 computer-based; 80 iBT). *Application deadline:* For fall admission, 4/4 priority date for domestic students, 3/1 priority date for international students; for winter admission, 7/1 priority date for international students; for spring admission, 1/1 priority date for international students. Applications are processed on a rolling basis. Application fee: $0 ($50 for international students). Electronic applications accepted. *Expenses:* Tuition: Full-time $8412; part-time $701 per credit hour. Required fees: $325; $65 per course. $25 per semester. Tuition and fees vary according to course load, degree level and program. *Financial support:* In 2009–10, 13 teaching assistantships with full tuition reimbursements (averaging $9,891 per year) were awarded; institutionally sponsored loans, health care benefits, and unspecified assistantships also available. Financial award applicants required to submit FAFSA. *Faculty research:* Religion and literature, rhetoric and composition, teaching literature and writing and creative writing. Total annual research expenditures: $6,000. *Unit head:* Dr. Sheila Hughes, Chair, 937-229-3434, Fax: 937-229-3563, E-mail: sheila.hughes@notes.udayton.edu. *Application contact:* Graduate Admissions, 937-229-4411, Fax: 937-229-4729, E-mail: gradadmission@udayton.edu.

University of Delaware, College of Arts and Sciences, Department of English, Newark, DE 19716. Offers English and American literature (MA, PhD); MA/PhD. Terminal master's awarded for partial completion of doctoral program. *Degree requirements:* For master's, one foreign language, thesis optional; for doctorate, 2 foreign languages, comprehensive exam, thesis/dissertation, specialty exam. *Entrance requirements:* For master's and doctorate, GRE General Test, GRE Subject Test. Additional exam requirements/recommendations for international students: Required—TOEFL (minimum score 550 paper-based; 213 computer-based). Electronic applications accepted. *Faculty research:* Significant strengths in American literature and culture, material cultural studies, Renaissance studies, archival studies.

University of Denver, Division of Arts, Humanities and Social Sciences, Department of English, Denver, CO 80208. Offers MA, PhD. Part-time programs available. *Faculty:* 18 full-time (7 women), 1 (woman) part-time/adjunct. *Students:* 37 full-time (22 women), 6 part-time (5 women); includes 2 minority (1 African American, 1 Asian American or Pacific Islander), 1 international. Average age 33. 164 applicants, 14% accepted, 15 enrolled. In 2009, 3 master's, 9 doctorates awarded. *Degree requirements:* For master's, one foreign language, thesis; for doctorate, 2 foreign languages, thesis/dissertation. *Entrance requirements:* For master's and doctorate, GRE General Test, GRE Subject Test. Additional exam requirements/recommendations for international students: Required—TOEFL. *Application deadline:* Applications are processed on a rolling basis. Application fee: $50. Electronic applications accepted. *Expenses:* Tuition: Full-time $34,596; part-time $961 per quarter hour. Required fees: $4 per quarter hour. Tuition and fees vary according to course load, campus/location and program. *Financial support:* In 2009–10, 33 teaching assistantships with full and partial tuition reimbursements (averaging $14,200 per year) were awarded; Federal Work-Study, institutionally sponsored loans, and scholarships/grants also available. Support available to part-time students. Financial award application deadline: 2/1; financial award applicants required to submit FAFSA. *Faculty research:* Cultural studies, creative nonfiction, eighteenth century colonial literature, multicultural literature, Cervantes. *Unit head:* Dr. Ann Dobyns, Chair, 303-871-2266. *Application contact:* Information Contact, 303-871-2266, E-mail: kheeps@du.edu.

University of Florida, Graduate School, College of Liberal Arts and Sciences, Department of English, Gainesville, FL 32611. Offers creative writing (MFA); English (MA, PhD). *Degree requirements:* For master's, variable foreign language requirement, thesis or alternative; for doctorate, thesis/dissertation. *Entrance requirements:* For master's and doctorate, GRE General Test, minimum GPA of 3.0. Additional exam requirements/recommendations for international students: Required—TOEFL (minimum score 550 paper-based; 213 computer-based). Electronic applications accepted.

University of Georgia, Graduate School, College of Arts and Sciences, Department of English, Athens, GA 30602. Offers creative writing (MFA, PhD); English (MA, MAT, PhD). *Faculty:* 35 full-time (13 women), 2 part-time/adjunct (0 women). *Students:* 77 full-time (45 women), 26 part-time (15 women); includes 7 minority (all African Americans), 1 international. 241 applicants, 33% accepted, 26 enrolled. In 2009, 17 master's, 14 doctorates awarded. *Degree requirements:* For master's, one foreign language, thesis (MA); for doctorate, 2 foreign languages, thesis/dissertation. *Entrance requirements:* For master's and doctorate, GRE General Test. Additional exam requirements/recommendations for international students: Required—TWE. *Application deadline:* For fall admission, 7/1 priority date for domestic students; for spring admission, 11/15 for domestic students. Application fee: $50. Electronic applications accepted. *Expenses:* Tuition, state resident: full-time $6000; part-time $250 per credit hour. Tuition, nonresident: full-time $20,904; part-time $871 per credit hour. Required fees: $730 per semester. *Financial support:* Fellowships, research assistantships, teaching assistantships, unspecified assistantships available. *Unit head:* Dr. Doug Anderson, Head, 706-543-2248, Fax: 706-542-2181, E-mail: anderson@uga.edu. *Application contact:* Dr. Kris Boudreau, Graduate Coordinator, 706-542-2197, E-mail: boudreau@uga.edu.

University of Guam, Office of Graduate Studies, College of Liberal Arts and Social Sciences, Department of English, Mangilao, GU 96923. Offers MA. *Entrance requirements:* For master's, GRE. Additional exam requirements/recommendations for international students: Required—TOEFL.

University of Guelph, Graduate Program Services, College of Arts, School of English and Theatre Studies, Program in English, Guelph, ON N1G 2W1, Canada. Offers MA. Part-time programs available. *Degree requirements:* For master's, thesis (for some programs). *Entrance requirements:* For master's, letters of reference, 4-year honours undergraduate degree in English or drama. Additional exam requirements/recommendations for international students: Required—TOEFL. Electronic applications accepted. *Faculty research:* Post-colonial literature, Canadian literature, children's literature, Scottish literature, American literature, cultural studies.

English

University of Hawaii at Manoa, Graduate Division, College of Language, Linguistics and Literature, Department of English, Honolulu, HI 96822. Offers MA, PhD. Part-time programs available. *Faculty:* 51 full-time (19 women), 8 part-time/adjunct (7 women). *Students:* 61 full-time (40 women), 29 part-time (20 women); includes 33 minority (30 Asian Americans or Pacific Islanders, 3 Hispanic Americans), 13 international. Average age 31. 109 applicants, 25% accepted, 20 enrolled. In 2009, 25 master's, 6 doctorates awarded. *Degree requirements:* For master's, 2 foreign languages, thesis optional; for doctorate, 2 foreign languages, comprehensive exam, thesis/dissertation. *Entrance requirements:* For master's, GRE General Test; for doctorate, GRE General Test, GRE Subject Test. Additional exam requirements/recommendations for international students: Required—TOEFL (minimum score 600 paper-based; 250 computer-based; 100 iBT), IELTS (minimum score 7). Application fee: $60. *Expenses:* Tuition, state resident: full-time $8900; part-time $372 per credit. Tuition, nonresident: full-time $21,400; part-time $898 per credit. Required fees: $207 per semester. *Financial support:* In 2009–10, 2 students received support, including 16 fellowships (averaging $2,614 per year), 1 research assistantship (averaging $17,496 per year), 33 teaching assistantships (averaging $12,012 per year); tuition waivers (full) also available. Financial award application deadline: 3/1. *Faculty research:* British and American literature, creative writing, cultural studies, rhetoric and composition. Total annual research expenditures: $54,000. *Application contact:* Laura Lyons, Graduate Chair, 808-956-8956, Fax: 808-956-3083, E-mail: lelyons@hawaii.edu.

University of Houston–Clear Lake, School of Human Sciences and Humanities, Programs in Humanities and Fine Arts, Houston, TX 77058-1098. Offers history (MA); humanities (MA); literature (MA). Part-time and evening/weekend programs available. Postbaccalaureate distance learning degree programs offered (minimal on-campus study). *Degree requirements:* For master's, thesis or alternative. *Entrance requirements:* For master's, GRE General Test. Additional exam requirements/recommendations for international students: Required—TOEFL (minimum score 550 paper-based; 213 computer-based). *Faculty research:* Digital media studies, Latin American history, labor history, Chaucer evolution versus creationism debate.

University of Houston–Downtown, College of Humanities and Social Sciences, Department of English, Houston, TX 77002. Offers professional writing and technical communication (MS). Part-time and evening/weekend programs available. *Faculty:* 5 full-time (3 women). *Students:* 4 full-time (all women), 18 part-time (14 women); includes 9 minority (7 African Americans, 1 Asian American or Pacific Islander, 1 Hispanic American). Average age 37. 5 applicants, 80% accepted, 4 enrolled. In 2009, 4 master's awarded. *Degree requirements:* For master's, thesis optional, graduation portfolio with oral defense. *Entrance requirements:* For master's, GRE (including Analytical Writing section), personal application statement, resume, writing sample, 3 letters of recommendation. Additional exam requirements/recommendations for international students: Required—TOEFL (minimum score 600 paper-based; 250 computer-based; 86 iBT). *Application deadline:* For fall admission, 5/1 for domestic and international students; for spring admission, 11/1 for domestic and international students. Application fee: $35 ($60 for international students). Electronic applications accepted. *Expenses:* Tuition, state resident: full-time $3150; part-time $175 per credit hour. Tuition, nonresident: full-time $7506; part-time $417 per credit hour. Required fees: $908; $322 per term. *Financial support:* Applicants required to submit FAFSA. *Faculty research:* Environmental rhetoric, instructional design, usability, assessment, presentation slides. *Unit head:* Dr. Robert Jarrett, Chair, 713-221-8013, Fax: 713-226-5205, E-mail: jarrettr@uhd.edu. *Application contact:* Dr. Michelle Moosally, Coordinator of MS in Professional Writing and Technical Communication and Professor, Department of English, 713-221-8013, Fax: 713-226-5205, E-mail: mspwtc@uhd.edu.

University of Idaho, College of Graduate Studies, College of Letters, Arts and Social Sciences, Department of English, Program in English, Moscow, ID 83844-2282. Offers MA, MAT. *Students:* 13 full-time, 4 part-time. In 2009, 8 master's awarded. *Entrance requirements:* For master's, minimum GPA of 2.8. *Application deadline:* For fall admission, 8/1 for domestic students; for spring admission, 12/15 for domestic students. Application fee: $55 ($60 for international students). *Expenses:* Tuition, state resident: full-time $6120. Tuition, nonresident: full-time $17,712. *Financial support:* Research assistantships, teaching assistantships available. Financial award application deadline: 2/15. *Unit head:* Dr. Gary Williams, Chair, 208-883-6156. *Application contact:* Dr. Gary Williams, Chair, 208-883-6156.

University of Illinois at Chicago, Graduate College, College of Liberal Arts and Sciences, Department of English, Chicago, IL 60607-7128. Offers English (MA, PhD), including creative writing (PhD), English education (MA), English studies, writing (MA); linguistics (MA), including teaching English to speakers of other languages/applied linguistics. Part-time and evening/weekend programs available. *Degree requirements:* For doctorate, variable foreign language requirement, thesis/dissertation, written and oral exams. *Entrance requirements:* For master's, GRE General Test, GRE Subject Test; for doctorate, GRE General Test, GRE Subject Test, minimum GPA of 2.0. Additional exam requirements/recommendations for international students: Required—TOEFL. Electronic applications accepted. *Faculty research:* Literary history and theory.

University of Illinois at Springfield, Graduate Programs, College of Liberal Arts and Sciences, Program in English, Springfield, IL 62703-5407. Offers MA. Part-time and evening/weekend programs available. *Faculty:* 9 full-time (6 women), 1 part-time/adjunct (0 women). *Students:* 3 full-time (1 woman), 19 part-time (17 women); includes 2 minority (1 African American, 1 Asian American or Pacific Islander). Average age 35. 14 applicants, 43% accepted, 2 enrolled. In 2009, 9 master's awarded. *Degree requirements:* For master's, comprehensive exam, thesis, or project. *Entrance requirements:* For master's, GRE General Test, analytical writing sample, two letters of recommendation. Additional exam requirements/recommendations for international students: Required—TOEFL (minimum score 500 paper-based; 176 computer-based; 61 iBT). *Application deadline:* Applications are processed on a rolling basis. Application fee: $50 ($60 for international students). Electronic applications accepted. *Expenses:* Tuition, state resident: full-time $6390; part-time $266.25 per credit hour. Tuition, nonresident: full-time $14,226; part-time $592.75 per credit hour. Required fees: $2044; $14.36 per credit hour. $722.50 per term. *Financial support:* In 2009–10, research assistantships (averaging $8,109 per year), teaching assistantships (averaging $8,109 per year) were awarded; career-related internships or fieldwork, Federal Work-Study, scholarships/grants, health care benefits, and unspecified assistantships also available. Support available to part-time students. Financial award application deadline: 11/15; financial award applicants required to submit FAFSA. *Unit head:* Dr. Terry Bodenhorn, Interim Program Administrator, 217-206-7435, Fax: 217-206-6217, E-mail: bodenhorn.terry@uis.edu. *Application contact:* Dr. Lynn Pardie, Office of Graduate Studies, 800-252-8533, Fax: 217-206-7623, E-mail: pardie.lynn@uis.edu.

University of Illinois at Urbana–Champaign, Graduate College, College of Liberal Arts and Sciences, Department of English, Champaign, IL 61820. Offers creative writing (MFA); English (MA, PhD). *Faculty:* 52 full-time (22 women), 2 part-time/adjunct (1 woman). *Students:* 101 full-time (63 women), 58 part-time (40 women); includes 22 minority (3 African Americans, 8 Asian Americans or Pacific Islanders, 11 Hispanic Americans), 12 international. 310 applicants, 18% accepted, 29 enrolled. In 2009, 19 master's, 14 doctorates awarded. *Entrance requirements:* For master's, GRE General Test, GRE Subject Test, minimum GPA of 3.0; writing sample. Additional exam requirements/recommendations for international students: Required—TOEFL (minimum score 550 paper-based; 213 computer-based). *Application deadline:* Applications are processed on a rolling basis. Application fee: $60 ($75 for international students). Electronic applications accepted. *Financial support:* In 2009–10, 64 fellowships, 22 research assistantships, 132 teaching assistantships were awarded; tuition waivers (full and partial) also available. *Faculty research:* English and American literature, cultural studies and critical theory. *Unit head:* Curtis Perry, Head, 217-333-2391, Fax: 217-333-4321, E-mail: cperry@illinois.edu. *Application contact:* Stephanie J. Shockey, Office Support Specialist, 217-333-3646, Fax: 217-333-4321, E-mail: shockey@illinois.edu.

University of Indianapolis, Graduate Programs, College of Arts and Sciences, Department of English Language and Literature, Indianapolis, IN 46227-3697. Offers English (MA). Part-time and evening/weekend programs available. *Faculty:* 2 full-time (both women), 1 (woman) part-time/adjunct. *Students:* 4 full-time (all women), 10 part-time (all women); includes 2 minority (both African Americans). Average age 34. *Entrance requirements:* For master's, GRE Subject Test, minimum GPA of 2.5. Additional exam requirements/recommendations for international students: Required—TOEFL (minimum score 550 paper-based; 213 computer-based). *Application deadline:* Applications are processed on a rolling basis. Application fee: $30. Electronic applications accepted. *Financial support:* Federal Work-Study, scholarships/grants, and tuition waivers (full and partial) available. Support available to part-time students. Financial award application deadline: 5/1; financial award applicants required to submit FAFSA. *Unit head:* Dr. William R. Dynes, Chair, 317-788-2072, Fax: 317-788-3480. *Application contact:* Dr. William R. Dynes, Chair, 317-788-2072, Fax: 317-788-3480.

The University of Iowa, Graduate College, College of Liberal Arts and Sciences, Department of English, Iowa City, IA 52242-1316. Offers English (PhD); literary criticism (PhD); literary history (PhD); literary studies (MA); nonfiction writing (MFA); rhetorical theory and stylistics (PhD); writer's workshop (MFA); JD/PhD. *Degree requirements:* For master's, thesis (for some programs), exam; for doctorate, comprehensive exam, thesis/dissertation. *Entrance requirements:* For master's and doctorate, GRE General Test, minimum GPA of 3.0. Additional exam requirements/recommendations for international students: Required—TOEFL (minimum score 640 paper-based; 273 computer-based; 111 iBT). Electronic applications accepted.

The University of Kansas, Graduate Studies, College of Liberal Arts and Sciences, Department of English, Lawrence, KS 66045. Offers creative writing (MFA); English (MA, PhD). Part-time programs available. *Faculty:* 39 full-time (18 women). *Students:* 72 full-time (49 women), 10 part-time (6 women); includes 9 minority (6 African Americans, 3 Hispanic Americans), 4 international. Average age 32. 173 applicants, 34% accepted, 27 enrolled. In 2009, 7 master's, 10 doctorates awarded. *Degree requirements:* For master's, one foreign language, comprehensive exam (for some programs), thesis or alternative; for doctorate, 2 foreign languages, comprehensive exam, thesis/dissertation. *Entrance requirements:* For master's and doctorate, GRE General Test, minimum GPA of 3.3. Additional exam requirements/recommendations for international students: Required—TOEFL. *Application deadline:* For fall admission, 12/31 for domestic and international students. Application fee: $45 ($55 for international students). Electronic applications accepted. *Expenses:* Tuition, state resident: full-time $6492; part-time $270.50 per credit hour. Tuition, nonresident: full-time $15,510; part-time $646.25 per credit hour. Required fees: $847; $70.56 per credit hour. Tuition and fees vary according to course load and program. *Financial support:* Fellowships with full tuition reimbursements, research assistantships, teaching assistantships with full and partial tuition reimbursements, unspecified assistantships available. Financial award application deadline: 12/31. *Faculty research:* African-American literature, twentieth century American literature, Renaissance literature, creative writing. *Unit head:* Marta Caminero-Santangelo, Chair, 785-864-4520, E-mail: camsan@ku.edu. *Application contact:* Joseph Harrington, Director of Graduate Studies, 785-864-4520, E-mail: jharring@ku.edu.

University of Kentucky, Graduate School, College of Arts and Sciences, Program in English, Lexington, KY 40506-0032. Offers MA, PhD. *Degree requirements:* For master's, one foreign language, comprehensive exam, thesis optional; for doctorate, one foreign language, comprehensive exam, thesis/dissertation. *Entrance requirements:* For master's, GRE General Test, minimum undergraduate GPA of 2.75; for doctorate, GRE General Test, minimum graduate GPA of 3.0. Additional exam requirements/recommendations for international students: Required—TOEFL (minimum score 550 paper-based; 213 computer-based). Electronic applications accepted.

University of Lethbridge, School of Graduate Studies, Lethbridge, AB T1K 3M4, Canada. Offers accounting (MScM); addictions counseling (M Sc); agricultural biotechnology (M Sc); agricultural studies (M Sc, MA); anthropology (MA); archaeology (MA); art (MA, MFA); biochemistry (M Sc); biological sciences (M Sc); biomolecular science (PhD); biosystems and biodiversity (PhD); Canadian studies (MA); chemistry (M Sc); computer science (M Sc); computer science and geographical information science (M Sc); counseling psychology (M Ed); dramatic arts (MA); earth, space, and physical science (PhD); economics (MA); educational leadership (M Ed); English (MA); environmental science (M Sc); evolution and behavior (PhD); exercise science (M Sc); finance (MScM); French (MA); French/German (MA); French/Spanish (MA); general education (M Ed); general management (MScM); geography (M Sc, MA); German (MA); health science (M Sc); health sciences (MA); history (MA); human resource management and labour relations (MScM); individualized multidisciplinary (M Sc, MA); information systems (MScM); international management (MScM); kinesiology (M Sc, MA); management (M Sc, MA); marketing (MScM); mathematics (M Sc); music (M Mus, MA); Native American studies (MA); neuroscience (M Sc, PhD); new media (MA); nursing (M Sc); philosophy (MA); physics (M Sc); policy and strategy (MScM); political science (MA); psychology (M Sc, MA); religious studies (MA); social sciences (MA); sociology (MA); theatre and dramatic arts (MFA); theoretical and computational science (PhD); urban and regional studies (MA); women's studies (MA). Part-time and evening/weekend programs available. *Degree requirements:* For doctorate, comprehensive exam, thesis/dissertation. *Entrance requirements:* For master's, GMAT (M Sc in management), bachelor's degree in related field, minimum GPA of 3.0 during previous 20 graded semester courses, 2 years teaching or related experience (M Ed); for doctorate, master's degree, minimum graduate GPA of 3.5. Additional exam requirements/recommendations for international students: Required—TOEFL. *Faculty research:* Movement and brain plasticity, gibberellin physiology, photosynthesis, carbon cycling, molecular properties of main-group ring components.

University of Louisiana at Lafayette, College of Liberal Arts, Department of English, Lafayette, LA 70504. Offers British and American literature (MA), including creative writing, folklore, rhetoric; creative writing (PhD); literature (PhD); rhetoric (PhD). Part-time programs available. *Degree requirements:* Terminal master's awarded for partial completion of doctoral program. *Degree requirements:* For master's, one foreign language, thesis or alternative; for doctorate, 2 foreign languages, comprehensive exam, thesis/dissertation. *Entrance requirements:* For master's, GRE General Test, minimum GPA of 2.75; for doctorate, GRE General Test, minimum GPA of 3.0. Additional exam requirements/recommendations for international students: Required—TOEFL (minimum score 550 paper-based; 213 computer-based). Electronic applications accepted. *Faculty research:* Composition theory, Southern literature, medieval literature.

University of Louisiana at Monroe, Graduate School, College of Arts and Sciences, Department of English, Monroe, LA 71209-0001. Offers MA. Part-time and evening/weekend programs available. *Faculty:* 13 full-time (4 women). *Students:* 9 full-time (7 women), 1 (woman) part-time; includes 1 minority (Asian American or Pacific Islander). Average age 30. In 2009, 2 master's awarded. *Degree requirements:* For master's, one foreign language, thesis (for some programs). *Entrance requirements:* For master's, GRE General Test (minimum score 900 verbal and quantitative), minimum GPA of 3.0. Additional exam requirements/recommendations for international students: Required—TOEFL (minimum score 500 paper-based; 173 computer-based; 61 iBT), or Michigan English Language Assessment Battery. *Application deadline:* For fall admission, 8/24 priority date for domestic students, 7/1 for international students; for winter admission, 12/14 priority date for domestic students; for spring admission, 1/19 for domestic students, 11/1 for international students. Applications are processed on a rolling basis. Application fee: $20 ($30 for international students). Electronic applications accepted. *Expenses:* Tuition, state resident: part-time $159 per credit hour. Tuition, nonresident: part-time $159 per credit hour. Required fees: $1300 per year. Tuition and fees vary according to course load. *Financial support:* In 2009–10, 8 teaching assistantships with full tuition reimbursements (averaging $3,000 per year) were awarded; career-related internships or fieldwork, Federal Work-Study, institutionally sponsored loans, and unspecified assistantships also available. Financial award application deadline: 4/1; financial award applicants required to submit FAFSA. *Faculty research:* Creative writing, American literature, British literature, multicultural literature, literary theory. *Unit head:* Dr. Fleming J. McClelland, Interim Head, 318-342-1485, Fax: 318-342-1491, E-mail: mcclelland@ulm.edu. *Application contact:* Dr. Julia Guernsey-Shaw, Information Contact, 318-342-1496, E-mail: shaw@ulm.edu.

University of Louisville, Graduate School, College of Arts and Sciences, Department of English, Louisville, KY 40292. Offers English (MA), including creative writing, literature, rhetoric and composition (MA, PhD); English rhetoric and composition (PhD), including rhetoric and composition (MA, PhD). Part-time programs available. *Faculty:* 40 full-time (24 women). *Students:* 71 full-time (41 women), 29 part-time (20 women); includes 12 minority (7 African Americans, 1 American Indian/Alaska Native, 2 Asian Americans or Pacific Islanders, 2 Hispanic Americans), 5 international. Average age 30. 82 applicants, 65% accepted, 22 enrolled. In 2009, 22 master's, 7 doctorates awarded. *Degree requirements:* For master's, one foreign language, thesis or alternative, thesis or culminating project; for doctorate, 2 foreign languages, comprehensive exam, thesis/dissertation. *Entrance requirements:* For master's, GRE General Test, 2 academic letters of recommendation; for doctorate, GRE General Test, 15-20 page critical writing sample, 1000-word statement of professional goals, 3 academic letters of recommendation, application for graduate teaching assistantship (resume plus statement of teaching philosophy), transcripts of all college work. Additional exam requirements/recommendations for international students: Required—TOEFL (minimum score 600 paper-based; 210 computer-based; 100 iBT). *Application deadline:* For fall admission, 1/5 for domestic and international students. Applications are processed on a rolling basis. Application fee: $50. Electronic applications accepted. *Financial support:* Fellowships, teaching assistantships, health care benefits and unspecified assistantships available. Financial award application deadline: 1/5. *Faculty research:* American and English literatures and cultures, rhetoric and composition, critical theory and cultural studies, creative writing. Total annual research expenditures: $278,898. *Unit head:* Dr. Susan Griffin, Chair, 502-852-6801, Fax: 502-852-4182, E-mail: smgriff01@louisville.edu. *Application contact:* Libby Leggett, Director, Graduate Admissions, 502-852-3101, Fax: 502-852-6536, E-mail: gradadm@louisville.edu.

University of Maine, Graduate School, College of Liberal Arts and Sciences, Department of English, Orono, ME 04469. Offers MA. Part-time and evening/weekend programs available. *Faculty:* 19 full-time (8 women), 21 part-time/adjunct (12 women). *Students:* 28 full-time (19 women), 5 part-time (4 women). Average age 29. 46 applicants, 63% accepted, 13 enrolled. In 2009, 21 master's awarded. *Degree requirements:* For master's, one foreign language, thesis optional. *Entrance requirements:* For master's, GRE General Test, minimum GPA of 3.0. Additional exam requirements/recommendations for international students: Required—TOEFL. *Application deadline:* For fall admission, 2/1 priority date for domestic students. Applications are processed on a rolling basis. Application fee: $65. Electronic applications accepted. *Financial support:* In 2009–10, 21 teaching assistantships with tuition reimbursements (averaging $12,790 per year) were awarded; Federal Work-Study and tuition waivers (full and partial) also available. Financial award application deadline: 3/1. *Faculty research:* Contemporary poetics, contemporary criticism, composition theory and pedagogy, feminist approaches to literature. *Unit head:* Dr. Naomi Jacobs, Chair, 207-581-3822, Fax: 207-581-1604. *Application contact:* Scott G. Delcourt, Associate Dean of the Graduate School, 207-581-3291, Fax: 207-581-3232, E-mail: graduate@maine.edu.

University of Manitoba, Faculty of Graduate Studies, Faculty of Arts, Department of English, Film, and Theatre, Winnipeg, MB R3T 2N2, Canada. Offers English (MA, PhD). *Degree requirements:* For master's, one foreign language, thesis; for doctorate, one foreign language, thesis/dissertation.

University of Maryland, College Park, Academic Affairs, College of Arts and Humanities, Department of English, Program in English Language and Literature, College Park, MD 20742. Offers MA, PhD. *Students:* 142 full-time (98 women), 19 part-time (9 women); includes 26 minority (20 African Americans, 1 Asian American or Pacific Islander, 5 Hispanic Americans), 5 international. 283 applicants, 31% accepted, 29 enrolled. In 2009, 16 master's, 10 doctorates awarded. *Degree requirements:* For master's, thesis optional; for doctorate, one foreign language, thesis/dissertation, oral and written exams. *Entrance requirements:* For master's, GRE General Test, minimum GPA of 3.5, writing sample, 3 letters of recommendation; for doctorate, GRE General Test, minimum GPA of 3.7, writing sample. Additional exam requirements/recommendations for international students: Required—TOEFL. *Application deadline:* For fall admission, 12/8 for domestic and international students. Applications are processed on a rolling basis. Application fee: $60. Electronic applications accepted. *Expenses:* Tuition, area resident: Part-time $471 per credit hour. Tuition, state resident: part-time $471 per credit hour. Tuition, nonresident: part-time $1016 per credit hour. Required fees: $337.04 per term. *Financial support:* In 2009–10, 15 fellowships (averaging $16,536 per year), 1 research assistantship (averaging $25,360 per year), 75 teaching assistantships (averaging $16,714 per year) were awarded. Financial award applicants required to submit FAFSA. *Unit head:* Kent Cartwright, Chair, 301-405-3807, Fax: 301-314-7539, E-mail: kcartwri@umd.edu. *Application contact:* Dean of Graduate School, 301-405-0376, Fax: 301-314-9305.

University of Massachusetts Amherst, Graduate School, College of Humanities and Fine Arts, Department of English, Amherst, MA 01003. Offers creative writing (MFA); English and American literature (MA, PhD). Part-time programs available. *Faculty:* 47 full-time (23 women). *Students:* 115 full-time (65 women), 88 part-time (54 women); includes 27 minority (10 African Americans, 2 American Indian/Alaska Native, 7 Asian Americans or Pacific Islanders, 8 Hispanic Americans), 7 international. Average age 30. 864 applicants, 14% accepted, 49 enrolled. In 2009, 29 master's, 8 doctorates awarded. Terminal master's awarded for partial completion of doctoral program. *Degree requirements:* For master's, one foreign language, thesis optional; for doctorate, one foreign language, comprehensive exam, thesis/dissertation. *Entrance requirements:* For master's, GRE General Test, GRE Subject Test (MA), writing sample (MFA); for doctorate, GRE General Test, GRE Subject Test. Additional exam requirements/recommendations for international students: Required—TOEFL (minimum score 550 paper-based; 213 computer-based; 80 iBT), IELTS (minimum score 6.5). *Application deadline:* For fall admission, 12/1 for domestic and international students. Applications are processed on a rolling basis. Application fee: $50 ($65 for international students). Electronic applications accepted. *Expenses:* Tuition, state resident: full-time $2640; part-time $110 per credit. Tuition, nonresident: full-time $9936; part-time $414 per credit. Tuition and fees vary according to course load. *Financial support:* In 2009–10, 8 fellowships with full tuition reimbursements (averaging $4,868 per year), 5 research assistantships with full tuition reimbursements (averaging $8,729 per year), 48 teaching assistantships with full tuition reimbursements (averaging $8,846 per year) were awarded; career-related internships or fieldwork, Federal Work-Study, scholarships/grants, traineeships, health care benefits, tuition waivers (full), and unspecified assistantships also available. Support available to part-time students. Financial award application deadline: 12/1. *Unit head:* Dr. Joseph F. Bartolomeo, Department Head, 413-545-2575, Fax: 413-545-3880. *Application contact:* Jean M. Ames, Supervisor of Admissions, 413-545-0722, Fax: 413-577-0010, E-mail: gradadm@grad.umass.edu.

University of Massachusetts Boston, Office of Graduate Studies, College of Liberal Arts, Program in English, Boston, MA 02125-3393. Offers MA. Part-time and evening/weekend programs available. *Degree requirements:* For master's, one foreign language, final project. *Entrance requirements:* For master's, minimum GPA of 2.75. *Faculty research:* Working class literature, women writers, British fiction, composition theory, modern American literature.

University of Memphis, Graduate School, College of Arts and Sciences, Department of English, Memphis, TN 38152. Offers African-American literature (Graduate Certificate); applied linguistics (PhD); composition studies (PhD); creative writing (MFA); English as a second language (MA); linguistics (MA); literary and cultural studies (PhD), including African-American literature; literature (MA); professional writing (MA, PhD); teaching English as a second language (Graduate Certificate). Part-time and evening/weekend programs available. Post-baccalaureate distance learning degree programs offered (no on-campus study). *Faculty:* 31 full-time (15 women), 2 part-time/adjunct (both women). *Students:* 98 full-time (59 women), 99 part-time (66 women); includes 36 minority (28 African Americans, 5 Asian Americans or Pacific Islanders, 3 Hispanic Americans), 7 international. Average age 34. 128 applicants, 71% accepted, 29 enrolled. In 2009, 38 master's, 4 doctorates, 21 other advanced degrees awarded. Terminal master's awarded for partial completion of doctoral program. *Degree requirements:* For master's, one foreign language, comprehensive exam, thesis optional; for doctorate, 2 foreign languages, comprehensive exam, thesis/dissertation. *Entrance requirements:* For master's, GRE; for doctorate, GRE. Additional exam requirements/recommendations for international students: Required—TOEFL. *Application deadline:* For fall admission, 7/1 for domestic students; for spring admission, 10/15 for domestic students. Applications are processed on a rolling basis. Application fee: $35 ($60 for international students). Electronic applications accepted. *Expenses:* Tuition, state resident: full-time $6246; part-time $347 per credit hour. Tuition, nonresident: full-time $15,894; part-time $883 per credit hour. Required fees: $1160. Full-time tuition and fees vary according to course load, degree level and program. *Financial support:* In 2009–10, 123 students received support; research assistantships with full tuition reimbursements available, teaching assistantships with full tuition reimbursements available, Federal Work-Study, scholarships/grants, and unspecified assistantships available. Financial award application deadline: 2/15; financial award applicants required to submit FAFSA. *Faculty research:* Applied linguistics, British and American literature, professional writing, composition studies. *Unit head:* Dr. Eric C. Link, Chair, 901-678-2651, Fax: 901-678-2226, E-mail: eclink@memphis.edu. *Application contact:* Dr. Verner D. Mitchell, Director, Graduate Studies, 901-678-3099, Fax: 901-678-2226, E-mail: vdmtchll@memphis.edu.

University of Miami, Graduate School, College of Arts and Sciences, Department of English, Coral Gables, FL 33124. Offers creative writing (MFA); English (MA, PhD). Part-time programs available. Terminal master's awarded for partial completion of doctoral program. *Degree requirements:* For master's, one foreign language, thesis optional; for doctorate, one foreign language, thesis/dissertation. *Entrance requirements:* For master's and doctorate, GRE General Test. Electronic applications accepted. *Faculty research:* Anglo-Irish literature, feminist criticism and theory, Caribbean literature, early modern literature and culture, postcolonial and ethnic studies.

University of Michigan, Horace H. Rackham School of Graduate Studies, College of Literature, Science, and the Arts, Department of English Language and Literature, Ann Arbor, MI 48109. Offers creative writing (MFA); English and education (PhD); English and women's studies (PhD); English language and literature (PhD). *Faculty:* 53 full-time (30 women). *Students:* 73 full-time (46 women); includes 7 minority (1 African American, 5 Asian Americans or Pacific Islanders, 1 Hispanic American), 5 international. 354 applicants, 9% accepted, 11 enrolled. In 2009, 12 doctorates awarded. *Degree requirements:* For doctorate, 2 foreign languages, comprehensive exam, thesis/dissertation, oral defense of dissertation, preliminary exam. *Entrance requirements:* For doctorate, GRE General Test, GRE Subject Test, writing sample. Additional exam requirements/recommendations for international students: Required—TOEFL (minimum score 620 paper-based; 260 computer-based; 106 iBT). *Application deadline:* For fall admission, 12/15 for domestic and international students. Application fee: $60 ($75 for international students). Electronic applications accepted. *Expenses:* Tuition, state resident: full-time $17,286; part-time $1099 per credit hour. Tuition, nonresident: full-time $34,944; part-time $2080 per credit hour. Required fees: $95 per semester. Tuition and fees vary according to course load, degree level and program. *Financial support:* Fellowships with full tuition reimbursements, teaching assistantships with full tuition reimbursements, health care benefits and summer funding available. *Faculty research:* Post colonialism, modernism, early modern, American, British. *Unit head:* Dr. Sara Blair, Graduate Chair, 734-936-2274. *Application contact:* Graduate Admissions Office, 734-936-2274, Fax: 734-763-3128, E-mail: grad.eng.admis@um.cc.umich.edu.

University of Michigan, Horace H. Rackham School of Graduate Studies, College of Literature, Science, and the Arts, Department of Women's Studies, Ann Arbor, MI 48109. Offers English and women's studies (PhD); history and women's studies (PhD); lesbian, gay, bisexual, transgender, queer (LGBTQ) studies (Certificate); psychology and women's studies (PhD); sociology and women's studies (PhD); women's studies (Certificate). *Faculty:* 74 full-time (68 women). *Students:* 68 full-time (63 women); includes 21 minority (7 African Americans, 1 American Indian/Alaska Native, 8 Asian Americans or Pacific Islanders, 5 Hispanic Americans), 12 international. Average age 31. 119 applicants, 9% accepted, 7 enrolled. In 2009, 5 doctorates, 8 other advanced degrees awarded. *Degree requirements:* For doctorate, variable foreign language requirement, comprehensive exam (for some programs), thesis/dissertation. *Entrance requirements:* For doctorate, GRE General Test, previous undergraduate course work in women's studies. *Application deadline:* For fall admission, 12/1 for domestic and international students. Application fee: $60 ($75 for international students). Electronic applications accepted. *Expenses:* Tuition, state resident: full-time $17,286; part-time $1099 per credit hour. Tuition, nonresident: full-time $34,944; part-time $2080 per credit hour. Required fees: $95 per semester. Tuition and fees vary according to course load, degree level and program. *Financial support:* In 2009–10, 34 students received support, including 19 fellowships with full tuition reimbursements available (averaging $16,000 per year), 15 teaching assistantships with full and partial tuition reimbursements available (averaging $16,135 per year); career-related internships or fieldwork, institutionally sponsored loans, scholarships/grants, traineeships, health care benefits, and unspecified assistantships also available. *Faculty research:* Gender issues; LGBTQ studies; sexuality; women and science; global feminism. *Unit head:* Anne Herrmann, Chair, 734-763-2047, Fax: 734-647-4943, E-mail: anneh@umich.edu. *Application contact:* Aimee Germain, Graduate Program Coordinator, 734-763-2047, Fax: 734-647-4943, E-mail: wsdgradInquiry@umich.edu.

University of Michigan–Flint, College of Arts and Sciences, Program in English, Flint, MI 48502-1950. Offers MA. Part-time programs available. *Faculty:* 11 full-time (6 women). *Students:* 8 full-time (7 women), 48 part-time (33 women); includes 8 minority (3 African Americans, 1 American Indian/Alaska Native, 4 Hispanic Americans). Average age 36. 31 applicants, 87% accepted, 16 enrolled. In 2009, 7 master's awarded. *Entrance requirements:* Additional exam requirements/recommendations for international students: Required—TOEFL (minimum score 550 paper-based; 220 computer-based), IELTS (minimum score 6.5). *Application deadline:* For fall admission, 8/1 priority date for domestic students, 5/1 priority date for international students; for winter admission, 11/15 priority date for domestic students, 9/15 priority date for international students; for spring admission, 3/15 priority date for domestic students, 1/15 priority date for international students. Application fee: $55. *Expenses:* Contact institution. *Financial support:* Federal Work-Study, scholarships/grants, and unspecified assistantships available. Support available to part-time students. Financial award application deadline: 6/1; financial award applicants required to submit FAFSA. *Unit head:* Dr. Tom Foster, Program Director, 810-762-3285, E-mail: tfos@umflint.edu. *Application contact:* Bradley T. Maki, Director of Graduate Admissions, 810-762-3171, Fax: 810-766-6789, E-mail: bmaki@umflint.edu.

University of Minnesota, Duluth, Graduate School, College of Liberal Arts, Department of English, Duluth, MN 55812-2496. Offers MA. Part-time programs available. *Degree requirements:* For master's, one foreign language, comprehensive exam, 2 extended papers or projects. *Entrance requirements:* For master's, GRE General Test, minimum GPA of 3.0. Additional exam requirements/recommendations for international students: Required—TOEFL (minimum score 213 computer-based). *Faculty research:* British cultural studies, Irish literature, American studies, linguistics, information design.

University of Minnesota, Twin Cities Campus, Graduate School, College of Liberal Arts, Department of English, Minneapolis, MN 55455-0213. Offers MA, MFA, PhD. *Faculty:* 40 full-time (22 women), 12 part-time/adjunct (4 women). *Students:* 128 full-time (75 women); includes 10 minority (2 African Americans, 1 American Indian/Alaska Native, 5 Asian Americans or Pacific Islanders, 2 Hispanic Americans), 15 international. 561 applicants, 8% accepted, 26 enrolled. In 2009, 1 master's, 12 doctorates awarded. Terminal master's awarded for partial completion of doctoral program. *Degree requirements:* For master's, one foreign language, thesis or alternative; for doctorate, 2 foreign languages, thesis/dissertation. *Entrance requirements:* For master's and doctorate, GRE General Test. Additional exam requirements/recommendations for international students: Required—TOEFL (minimum score 620 paper-based; 96 iBT). *Application deadline:* For fall admission, 12/20 for domestic and international students. Application fee: $75 ($95 for international students). Electronic applications accepted. *Financial support:* In 2009–10, 17 fellowships with full tuition reimbursements (averaging $19,250 per year), 1 research assistantship with full tuition reimbursement (averaging $13,845

English

University of Minnesota, Twin Cities Campus (continued)
per year), 93 teaching assistantships with full tuition reimbursements (averaging $13,845 per year) were awarded. Financial award application deadline: 12/20. *Faculty research:* British and American literature, medieval and early modern literature, postcolonial literature, feminist studies in literature, creative writing, cultural studies. *Unit head:* Geoffrey Sirc, Chair, 612-625-3363, Fax: 612-626-1659, E-mail: sirc@umn.edu. *Application contact:* Madelon Sprengnether, Director of Graduate Studies, 612-625-3882, Fax: 612-624-8228, E-mail: spren001@umn.edu.

University of Mississippi, Graduate School, College of Liberal Arts, Department of English, Oxford, University, MS 38677. Offers MA, MFA, PhD. *Faculty:* 54 full-time (21 women), 24 part-time/adjunct (13 women). *Students:* 53 full-time (26 women), 11 part-time (9 women); includes 6 minority (4 African Americans, 1 Asian American or Pacific Islander, 1 Hispanic American), 1 international. In 2009, 4 master's, 13 doctorates awarded. *Degree requirements:* For master's, one foreign language, thesis; for doctorate, 2 foreign languages, thesis/dissertation. *Entrance requirements:* For master's, GRE General Test, minimum GPA of 3.0; for doctorate, GRE General Test. Additional exam requirements/recommendations for international students: Required—TOEFL. *Application deadline:* For fall admission, 2/1 for domestic students; for spring admission, 10/1 for domestic students. Applications are processed on a rolling basis. Application fee: $25. *Financial support:* Scholarships/grants available. Financial award application deadline: 3/1; financial award applicants required to submit FAFSA. *Unit head:* Dr. Ivo Kamps, Chairman, 662-915-7439, Fax: 662-915-5787, E-mail: engl@olemiss.edu. *Application contact:* Dr. Christy M. Wyandt, Associate Dean, 662-915-7474, Fax: 662-915-7577, E-mail: cwyandt@olemiss.edu.

University of Missouri, Graduate School, College of Arts and Sciences, Department of English, Columbia, MO 65211. Offers MA, PhD. *Faculty:* 58 full-time (36 women), 14 part-time/adjunct (7 women). *Students:* 67 full-time (38 women), 35 part-time (18 women); includes 10 minority (5 African Americans, 1 Asian American or Pacific Islander, 4 Hispanic Americans), 6 international. Average age 32. 163 applicants, 14% accepted, 21 enrolled. In 2009, 3 master's, 6 doctorates awarded. Terminal master's awarded for partial completion of doctoral program. *Degree requirements:* For doctorate, 2 foreign languages, comprehensive exam, thesis/dissertation. *Entrance requirements:* For master's, GRE General Test, minimum GPA of 3.0; for doctorate, GRE General Test, minimum GPA of 3.0; MA in English or equivalent. Additional exam requirements/recommendations for international students: Required—TOEFL (minimum score 500 paper-based; 173 computer-based; 61 iBT). *Application deadline:* For fall admission, 1/15 priority date for domestic students. Applications are processed on a rolling basis. Application fee: $45 ($60 for international students). *Financial support:* In 2009–10, 42 fellowships with full tuition reimbursements, 3 research assistantships with full tuition reimbursements, 47 teaching assistantships with full tuition reimbursements were awarded; institutionally sponsored loans, health care benefits, and unspecified assistantships also available. *Unit head:* Dr. Pat Okker, Department Chair, 573-882-6066, E-mail: okkerp@missouri.edu. *Application contact:* Vickie Thorp, Secretary Sr, 573-882-4676, E-mail: thorpv@missouri.edu.

University of Missouri–Kansas City, College of Arts and Sciences, Department of English, Kansas City, MO 64110-2499. Offers creative writing and media arts (MFA); English (MA, PhD). PhD (interdisciplinary) offered through the School of Graduate Studies. Part-time and evening/weekend programs available. *Faculty:* 22 full-time (15 women), 18 part-time/adjunct (11 women). *Students:* 10 full-time (6 women), 39 part-time (22 women); includes 5 minority (4 African Americans, 1 Asian American or Pacific Islander). Average age 31. 38 applicants, 63% accepted, 12 enrolled. In 2009, 13 master's awarded. *Degree requirements:* For master's, one foreign language; for doctorate, 2 foreign languages, comprehensive exam, thesis/dissertation. *Entrance requirements:* For master's, GRE General Test, 3 letters of recommendation. Additional exam requirements/recommendations for international students: Required—TOEFL (minimum score 550 paper-based; 213 computer-based; 80 iBT). *Application deadline:* For fall admission, 1/15 for domestic students, 1/15 priority date for international students. Applications are processed on a rolling basis. Application fee: $45 ($50 for international students). Electronic applications accepted. *Expenses:* Tuition, state resident: full-time $5378; part-time $299 per credit hour. Tuition, nonresident: full-time $13,881; part-time $771 per credit hour. Required fees: $641; $71 per credit hour. Tuition and fees vary according to course load and program. *Financial support:* In 2009–10, 15 teaching assistantships (averaging $12,180 per year) were awarded; career-related internships or fieldwork, Federal Work-Study, and institutionally sponsored loans also available. Support available to part-time students. Financial award application deadline: 3/1; financial award applicants required to submit FAFSA. *Faculty research:* Creative writing: poetry and prose, computational linguistics, rhetoric and composition, African-American and British literature, print culture. Total annual research expenditures: $105,946. *Unit head:* Dr. Jeff Rydberg-Cox, Co-Chair, 816-235-2560, Fax: 816-235-1308, E-mail: rydbergcoxj@umkc.edu. *Application contact:* Dr. Joan Dean, Director of Graduate Studies, 816-235-2555, E-mail: deanj@umkc.edu.

University of Missouri–St. Louis, College of Arts and Sciences, Department of English, St. Louis, MO 63121. Offers American literature (MA); creative writing (MFA); English (MA); English literature (MA); linguistics (MA); teaching of writing (Graduate Certificate). Part-time and evening/weekend programs available. *Faculty:* 21 full-time (11 women), 2 part-time/adjunct (1 woman). *Students:* 32 full-time (15 women), 97 part-time (62 women); includes 10 minority (5 African Americans, 2 American Indian/Alaska Native, 2 Asian Americans or Pacific Islanders, 1 Hispanic American), 1 international. Average age 31. 114 applicants, 46% accepted, 36 enrolled. In 2009, 28 master's, 1 other advanced degree awarded. *Degree requirements:* For master's, thesis optional. *Entrance requirements:* For master's, writing sample. Additional exam requirements/recommendations for international students: Required—TOEFL (minimum score 550 paper-based; 213 computer-based). *Application deadline:* For fall admission, 7/1 priority date for domestic and international students; for spring admission, 12/1 priority date for domestic and international students. Applications are processed on a rolling basis. Application fee: $35 ($40 for international students). Electronic applications accepted. *Expenses:* Tuition, state resident: full-time $5377; part-time $297.70 per credit hour. Tuition, nonresident: full-time $13,882; part-time $771.20 per credit hour. Required fees: $220; $12.20 per credit hour. One-time fee: $12. Tuition and fees vary according to course level, campus/location and program. *Financial support:* In 2009–10, 4 research assistantships (averaging $5,500 per year), 7 teaching assistantships with full and partial tuition reimbursements (averaging $9,000 per year) were awarded. Financial award applicants required to submit FAFSA. *Faculty research:* Victorian literature, Shakespeare and Renaissance literature, eighteenth century literature, composition theory. *Unit head:* Dr. Frank Grady, Director of Graduate Studies, 314-516-5541, Fax: 314-516-5781, E-mail: fgrady@umsl.edu. *Application contact:* 314-516-5458, Fax: 314-516-5310, E-mail: gradadm@umsl.edu.

The University of Montana, Graduate School, College of Arts and Sciences, Department of English, Program in Literature, Missoula, MT 59812-0002. Offers MA. *Degree requirements:* For master's, thesis optional. *Entrance requirements:* For master's, GRE General Test, sample of written work. Additional exam requirements/recommendations for international students: Required—TOEFL. *Faculty research:* Literary history, cultural studies, criticism and theory, Western studies.

University of Montevallo, College of Arts and Sciences, Department of English, Montevallo, AL 35115. Offers English literature (MA). Part-time programs available. *Students:* 8 full-time (6 women), 7 part-time (4 women); includes 2 minority (1 African American, 1 Asian American or Pacific Islander). In 2009, 7 master's awarded. *Degree requirements:* For master's, comprehensive exam, thesis optional. *Entrance requirements:* For master's, GRE General Test, MAT, minimum undergraduate GPA of 2.75 in last 60 hours or 2.5 overall, bachelor's degree in English or equivalent. Additional exam requirements/recommendations for international students: Required—TOEFL (minimum score 550 paper-based; 213 computer-based). *Application deadline:* For fall admission, 7/15 for domestic students; for spring admission, 11/15 for domestic students. Application fee: $25. *Expenses:* Tuition, state resident: full-time $5592; part-time $233 per credit. Tuition, nonresident: full-time $11,184; part-time $466 per credit hour. Required fees: $482; $241 per semester. One-time fee: $25 part-time. *Financial support:* Federal Work-Study, scholarships/grants, and unspecified assistantships available. *Unit head:* Dr. Jim Murphy, Chair, 205-665-6420, E-mail: murphyj@montevallo.edu. *Application contact:* Dr. Jim Murphy, Chair, 205-665-6420, E-mail: murphyj@montevallo.edu.

University of Nebraska at Kearney, College of Graduate Study, College of Fine Arts and Humanities, Department of English, Kearney, NE 68849-0001. Offers creative writing (MA); literature (MA). Part-time and evening/weekend programs available. *Degree requirements:* For master's, thesis optional. *Entrance requirements:* For master's, GRE General Test. Additional exam requirements/recommendations for international students: Required—TOEFL (minimum score 550 paper-based; 213 computer-based). Electronic applications accepted. *Faculty research:* Narrative theory, popular culture, western and plains literature, women's studies, media studies.

University of Nebraska at Omaha, Graduate Studies, College of Arts and Sciences, Department of English, Omaha, NE 68182. Offers advanced writing (Certificate); English (MA); teaching English to speakers of other languages (Certificate); technical communication (Certificate). Part-time and evening/weekend programs available. *Faculty:* 20 full-time (10 women). *Students:* 11 full-time (4 women), 59 part-time (43 women); includes 2 minority (1 African American, 1 Asian American or Pacific Islander), 3 international. Average age 32. 40 applicants, 68% accepted, 17 enrolled. In 2009, 13 master's, 8 other advanced degrees awarded. *Degree requirements:* For master's, comprehensive exam, thesis (for some programs). *Entrance requirements:* For master's, minimum GPA of 3.0, 3 letters of recommendation, writing sample. Additional exam requirements/recommendations for international students: Required—TOEFL (minimum score 600 paper-based; 250 computer-based; 100 iBT). *Application deadline:* For fall admission, 8/1 priority date for domestic students; for spring admission, 12/1 priority date for domestic students. Applications are processed on a rolling basis. Application fee: $45. Electronic applications accepted. *Financial support:* In 2009–10, 34 students received support; fellowships, teaching assistantships with tuition reimbursements available, Federal Work-Study, institutionally sponsored loans, scholarships/grants, tuition waivers (partial), and unspecified assistantships available. Support available to part-time students. Financial award application deadline: 3/1; financial award applicants required to submit FAFSA. *Unit head:* Dr. Susan Maher, Chairperson, 402-554-3636. *Application contact:* Dr. Joan Latchaw, Student Contact, 402-554-3636.

University of Nebraska–Lincoln, Graduate College, College of Arts and Sciences, Department of English, Lincoln, NE 68588-0333. Offers composition and rhetoric (MA, PhD); creative writing (MA, PhD); literature studies (MA, PhD). *Degree requirements:* For master's, thesis optional; for doctorate, one foreign language, comprehensive exam, thesis/dissertation. *Entrance requirements:* For master's, writing sample; for doctorate, GRE General Test, writing sample. Additional exam requirements/recommendations for international students: Required—TOEFL (minimum score 600 paper-based; 250 computer-based). Electronic applications accepted. *Faculty research:* Creative writing, composition and rhetoric, women's studies, North American literature, medieval/Renaissance studies.

University of Nevada, Las Vegas, Graduate College, College of Liberal Arts, Department of English, Las Vegas, NV 89154-5011. Offers creative writing (MFA); English (MA, PhD). Part-time programs available. *Faculty:* 32 full-time (12 women), 5 part-time/adjunct (0 women). *Students:* 66 full-time (31 women), 21 part-time (14 women); includes 7 minority (1 Asian American or Pacific Islander, 6 Hispanic Americans), 4 international. Average age 36. 170 applicants, 19% accepted, 23 enrolled. In 2009, 21 master's, 5 doctorates awarded. *Degree requirements:* For master's, one foreign language, comprehensive exam, thesis (for some programs); for doctorate, 2 foreign languages, comprehensive exam, thesis/dissertation. *Entrance requirements:* For master's, GRE General Test (verbal); for doctorate, GRE General Test (Verbal and Subject). Additional exam requirements/recommendations for international students: Required—TOEFL (minimum score 550 paper-based; 213 computer-based; 80 iBT), IELTS (minimum score 7). *Application deadline:* For fall admission, 2/15 priority date for domestic and international students. Applications are processed on a rolling basis. Application fee: $60 ($95 for international students). Electronic applications accepted. *Financial support:* In 2009–10, 68 students received support, including 1 fellowship with full tuition reimbursement available (averaging $20,000 per year), 12 research assistantships with partial tuition reimbursements available (averaging $13,782 per year), 55 teaching assistantships with partial tuition reimbursements available (averaging $11,127 per year); institutionally sponsored loans, scholarships/grants, health care benefits, and unspecified assistantships also available. Financial award application deadline: 3/1. *Faculty research:* Contemporary poetry and fiction, Renaissance literature and Renaissance studies, Post-Structuralist literary theory and criticism, business and professional writing, nineteenth and twentieth century British and American literature. *Unit head:* Dr. Richard Harp, Chair/ Professor, 702-895-0919, Fax: 702-895-4801, E-mail: richard.harp@unlv.edu. *Application contact:* Graduate College Admissions Evaluator, 702-895-3320, Fax: 702-895-4180, E-mail: gradcollege@unlv.edu.

University of Nevada, Reno, Graduate School, College of Liberal Arts, Department of English, Reno, NV 89557. Offers MA, MATE, PhD. Terminal master's awarded for partial completion of doctoral program. *Degree requirements:* For master's, variable foreign language requirement, thesis optional; for doctorate, variable foreign language requirement, thesis/dissertation. *Entrance requirements:* For master's, GRE General Test, minimum GPA of 2.75; for doctorate, GRE General Test, minimum GPA of 3.0. Additional exam requirements/recommendations for international students: Required—TOEFL (minimum score 500 paper-based; 173 computer-based; 61 iBT), IELTS (minimum score 6). Electronic applications accepted. *Faculty research:* Translating Persian/Iraqi literature, Shakespearean literature, modern American literature, composition and rhetoric.

University of New Brunswick Fredericton, School of Graduate Studies, Faculty of Arts, Department of English, Fredericton, NB E3B 5A3, Canada. Offers MA, PhD. Part-time programs available. *Faculty:* 15 full-time (7 women), 1 (woman) part-time/adjunct. *Students:* 44 full-time (20 women), 3 part-time (0 women). Average age 25. 62 applicants, 53% accepted, 15 enrolled. In 2009, 10 master's awarded. *Degree requirements:* For master's, thesis, 18 credit hours; for doctorate, one foreign language, comprehensive exam, thesis/dissertation. *Entrance requirements:* For master's, BA with minimum GPA of 3.6, honors English (preferred); for doctorate, minimum GPA of 3.7; MA in English. Additional exam requirements/recommendations for international students: Required—TOEFL (minimum score 550 paper-based). *Application deadline:* 1/31 priority date for domestic and international students. Applications are processed on a rolling basis. Application fee: $50 Canadian dollars. Tuition and fees charges are reported in Canadian dollars. *Expenses:* Tuition, area resident: Full-time $5562 Canadian dollars; part-time $2781 Canadian dollars per year. Required fees: $49.75 Canadian dollars per term. *Financial support:* In 2009–10, 13 research assistantships with full tuition reimbursements (averaging $10,750 per year), 13 teaching assistantships with full tuition reimbursements (averaging $4,000 per year) were awarded; health care benefits also available. Financial award application deadline: 1/31. *Faculty research:* Creative writing, Canadian literature, post-Colonial literature, early Modern literature, scholarly editing and textual studies. *Unit head:* Dr. Edith Snook, Director of Graduate Studies, 506-458-7397, Fax: 506-453-5069, E-mail: esnook@unb.ca. *Application contact:* Theresa Keenan, Graduate Secretary, 506-451-6809, Fax: 506-453-5069, E-mail: tkeenan@unb.ca.

University of New Hampshire, Graduate School, College of Liberal Arts, Department of English, Durham, NH 03824. Offers English (MFA, PhD); English education (MST); language and linguistics (MA); literature (MA); writing (MA). Part-time programs available. *Faculty:* 35 full-time (18 women). *Students:* 54 full-time (33 women), 64 part-time (40 women); includes 5 minority (1 African American, 2 American Indian/Alaska Native, 2 Hispanic Americans), 5 international. Average age 34. 279 applicants, 43% accepted, 38 enrolled. In 2009, 32 master's, 5 doctorates awarded. *Degree requirements:* For master's, one foreign language; for doctorate, 2 foreign languages, thesis/dissertation. *Entrance requirements:* For master's, GRE General Test, sample of written work; for doctorate, GRE General Test, GRE Subject Test, sample of written work. Additional exam requirements/recommendations for international students: Required—TOEFL (minimum score 550 paper-based; 213 computer-based; 80 iBT). *Application deadline:* For fall admission, 6/1 priority date for domestic students, 2/15 for international students; for spring admission, 12/1 for domestic students. Applications are processed on a rolling basis. Application fee: $65. Electronic applications accepted. *Expenses:* Tuition, state resident: full-time $10,380; part-time $577 per credit hour. Tuition, nonresident: full-time $24,350; part-time $1002 per credit hour. Required fees: $1550; $387.50 per semester. Tuition and fees vary according to course load and program. *Financial support:* In 2009–10, 57 students received support, including 4 fellowships, 46 teaching assistantships; research assistantships, career-related internships or fieldwork, Federal Work-Study, scholarships/grants, and tuition waivers (full and partial) also available. Support available to part-time students. Financial award application deadline: 2/15. *Unit head:* Dr. Andrew Merton, Chairperson, 603-862-3963. *Application contact:* Jamie Auger, Administrative Assistant, 603-862-3963, E-mail: engl.grad@unh.edu.

University of New Mexico, Graduate School, College of Arts and Sciences, Department of English, Program in English, Albuquerque, NM 87131-2039. Offers MA, PhD. *Faculty:* 38 full-time (22 women), 31 part-time/adjunct (20 women). *Students:* 50 full-time (37 women), 19 part-time (14 women); includes 7 minority (1 African American, 2 American Indian/Alaska Native, 4 Hispanic Americans), 1 international. Average age 34. 65 applicants, 51% accepted, 18 enrolled. In 2009, 8 master's, 10 doctorates awarded. *Degree requirements:* For master's, one foreign language, comprehensive exam (for some programs), thesis (for some programs), portfolio; for doctorate, 2 foreign languages, comprehensive exam, thesis/dissertation. *Entrance requirements:* For master's, GRE General Test; for doctorate, GRE General Test, GRE Subject Test (literature). *Application deadline:* For fall admission, 1/15 for domestic and international students. Application fee: $50. Electronic applications accepted. *Expenses:* Tuition, state resident: full-time $2099; part-time $233.20 per credit hour. Tuition, nonresident: full-time $6650. Required fees: $25 per semester. Tuition and fees vary according to course load, program and reciprocity agreements. *Financial support:* In 2009–10, 75 teaching assistantships with full tuition reimbursements were awarded; health care benefits also available. *Faculty research:* American literature, Native American literature, Chicano literature, British and Irish literature, rhetoric and writing. *Unit head:* Dr. Gail Turley Houston, Chair, 505-277-6347, Fax: 505-277-0021, E-mail: ghouston@unm.edu. *Application contact:* N. Ezra Meier, Graduate Advisor, 505-277-4437, Fax: 505-277-0021, E-mail: nezra@unm.edu.

University of New Orleans, Graduate School, College of Liberal Arts, Department of English, Program in English, New Orleans, LA 70148. Offers MA. Part-time and evening/weekend programs available. *Degree requirements:* For master's, one foreign language, thesis (for some programs). *Entrance requirements:* For master's, GRE General Test. Additional exam requirements/recommendations for international students: Required—TOEFL (minimum score 550 paper-based; 213 computer-based; 79 iBT). Electronic applications accepted.

University of North Alabama, College of Arts and Sciences, Department of English, Florence, AL 35632-0001. Offers MAEN. Part-time and evening/weekend programs available. *Faculty:* 1 full-time (0 women), 9 part-time/adjunct (5 women). *Students:* 8 full-time (5 women), 16 part-time (15 women); includes 3 minority (all Asian Americans or Pacific Islanders). Average age 32. In 2009, 7 master's awarded. *Application deadline:* For fall admission, 7/1 priority date for domestic students; for spring admission, 12/1 for domestic students. Applications are processed on a rolling basis. Application fee: $25. Electronic applications accepted. *Expenses:* Tuition, state resident: full-time $5040; part-time $210 per credit hour. Tuition, nonresident: full-time $10,080; part-time $420 per credit hour. Required fees: $906. *Unit head:* Dr. Ronald Smith, Chair, 256-765-4238, Fax: 256-765-4239, E-mail: resmith@una.edu. *Application contact:* Kim Mauldin, Director of Admissions, 256-765-4608, Fax: 256-765-4960, E-mail: komauldin@una.edu.

The University of North Carolina at Chapel Hill, Graduate School, College of Arts and Sciences, Department of English, Chapel Hill, NC 27599. Offers MA, PhD. *Degree requirements:* For master's, one foreign language, comprehensive exam, thesis; for doctorate, 2 foreign languages, comprehensive exam, thesis/dissertation. *Entrance requirements:* For master's and doctorate, GRE General Test, GRE Subject Test, minimum GPA of 3.0 for last 2 undergraduate years, writing sample. Additional exam requirements/recommendations for international students: Required—TOEFL. Electronic applications accepted. *Faculty research:* African American, Southern, period studies, genre studies, critical theory/culture studies.

The University of North Carolina at Charlotte, Graduate School, College of Arts and Sciences, Department of English, Charlotte, NC 28223-0001. Offers English (MA); English education (MA). Part-time and evening/weekend programs available. *Faculty:* 35 full-time (20 women). *Students:* 37 full-time (25 women), 52 part-time (38 women); includes 11 minority (7 African Americans, 3 Asian Americans or Pacific Islanders, 1 Hispanic American), 1 international. Average age 28. 57 applicants, 84% accepted, 35 enrolled. In 2009, 13 master's awarded. *Degree requirements:* For master's, comprehensive exam, thesis optional. *Entrance requirements:* For master's, GRE General Test, minimum undergraduate GPA of 3.0 in major, 2.75 overall. Additional exam requirements/recommendations for international students: Required—TOEFL (minimum score 557 paper-based; 220 computer-based; 83 iBT). *Application deadline:* For fall admission, 7/15 for domestic students, 5/1 for international students; for spring admission, 11/15 for domestic students, 10/1 for international students. Applications are processed on a rolling basis. Application fee: $55. Electronic applications accepted. *Financial support:* In 2009–10, 14 students received support, including 14 teaching assistantships (averaging $7,571 per year); career-related internships or fieldwork, institutionally sponsored loans, scholarships/grants, and unspecified assistantships also available. Support available to part-time students. Financial award application deadline: 4/1; financial award applicants required to submit FAFSA. *Faculty research:* English as a second language (ESL), composition theory and pedagogy, children's literature, technical and professional writing, English for specific purposes (ESP). Total annual research expenditures: $154,437. *Unit head:* Dr. Malin Pereira, Chair, 704-687-2299, Fax: 704-687-3961, E-mail: mpereira@uncc.edu. *Application contact:* Kathy B. Giddings, Director of Graduate Admissions, 704-687-5503, Fax: 704-687-3279, E-mail: gradadm@uncc.edu.

The University of North Carolina at Greensboro, Graduate School, College of Arts and Sciences, Department of English, Program in English, Greensboro, NC 27412-5001. Offers American literature (PhD); English (M Ed, MA); English literature (PhD); rhetoric and composition (PhD). *Degree requirements:* For master's, comprehensive exam, thesis or alternative; for doctorate, variable foreign language requirement, thesis/dissertation, preliminary exam. *Entrance requirements:* For master's, GRE General Test, GRE Subject Test, minimum GPA of 3.0; for doctorate, GRE General Test, GRE Subject Test, critical writing sample, minimum GPA of 3.0. Additional exam requirements/recommendations for international students: Required—TOEFL. Electronic applications accepted.

The University of North Carolina Wilmington, College of Arts and Sciences, Department of English, Wilmington, NC 28403-3297. Offers MA. *Degree requirements:* For master's, comprehensive exam, thesis. *Entrance requirements:* For master's, GRE General Test, minimum B average in undergraduate major. Additional exam requirements/recommendations for international students: Required—TOEFL (minimum score 550 paper-based; 217 computer-based; 79 iBT), IELTS (minimum score 6.5).

University of North Dakota, Graduate School, College of Arts and Sciences, Department of English, Grand Forks, ND 58202. Offers MA, PhD. *Degree requirements:* For master's, one foreign language, comprehensive exam, thesis or alternative; for doctorate, one foreign language, comprehensive exam, thesis/dissertation. *Entrance requirements:* For master's and doctorate, GRE General Test, minimum GPA of 3.0. Additional exam requirements/recommendations for international students: Required—TOEFL (minimum score 550 paper-based; 213 computer-based; 79 iBT), IELTS (minimum score 6.5). Electronic applications accepted. *Faculty research:* Creative writing, rhetorical theory, cinema, American literature, European literature.

University of Northern Colorado, Graduate School, College of Humanities and Social Sciences, School of English Language and Literature, Program in English, Greeley, CO 80639. Offers MA. Part-time programs available. *Faculty:* 9 full-time (4 women). *Students:* 18 full-time (11 women), 9 part-time (4 women); includes 3 minority (1 Asian American or Pacific Islander, 2 Hispanic Americans). Average age 31. 19 applicants, 95% accepted, 7 enrolled. In 2009, 5 master's awarded. *Degree requirements:* For master's, comprehensive exam. *Entrance requirements:* For master's, GRE General Test, 2 letters of recommendation. *Application deadline:* Applications are processed on a rolling basis. Application fee: $50 ($60 for international students). Electronic applications accepted. *Expenses:* Tuition, state resident: full-time $5770; part-time $320.55 per credit hour. Tuition, nonresident: full-time $13,847; part-time $769.27 per credit hour. Required fees: $948.78; $52.72 per credit. *Financial support:* In 2009–10, 6 research assistantships (averaging $5,009 per year), 16 teaching assistantships (averaging $9,169 per year) were awarded; unspecified assistantships also available. Financial award application deadline: 3/1; financial award applicants required to submit FAFSA. *Unit head:* Dr. Marcus Embry, Program Coordinator, 970-351-2971, Fax: 970-351-3378. *Application contact:* Linda Sisson, Graduate Student Admission Coordinator, 970-351-1807, Fax: 970-351-2371, E-mail: linda.sisson@unco.edu.

University of Northern Iowa, Graduate College, College of Humanities and Fine Arts, Department of English Language and Literature, Cedar Falls, IA 50614. Offers English (MA); teaching English to speakers of other languages (MA). Part-time and evening/weekend programs available. *Students:* 34 full-time (24 women), 33 part-time (27 women); includes 4 minority (2 African Americans, 1 Asian American or Pacific Islander, 1 Hispanic American), 8 international. 45 applicants, 64% accepted, 16 enrolled. In 2009, 29 master's awarded. *Degree requirements:* For master's, one foreign language, comprehensive exam, thesis or alternative, portfolio. *Entrance requirements:* For master's, minimum GPA of 3.0. Additional exam requirements/recommendations for international students: Required—TOEFL (minimum score 600 paper-based; 250 computer-based; 100 iBT). *Application deadline:* For fall admission, 8/1 priority date for domestic students. Applications are processed on a rolling basis. Application fee: $30 ($50 for international students). Electronic applications accepted. *Financial support:* Career-related internships or fieldwork, Federal Work-Study, scholarships/grants, and tuition waivers (full and partial) available. Support available to part-time students. Financial award application deadline: 2/1. *Unit head:* Dr. Jeffrey S. Copeland, Head, 319-273-3855, Fax: 319-273-5807, E-mail: jeffrey.copeland@uni.edu. *Application contact:* Laurie S. Russell, Record Analyst, 319-273-2623, Fax: 319-273-6792, E-mail: laurie.russell@uni.edu.

University of North Florida, College of Arts and Sciences, Department of English, Jacksonville, FL 32224. Offers MA. Part-time and evening/weekend programs available. *Faculty:* 15 full-time (7 women). *Students:* 17 full-time (11 women), 45 part-time (35 women); includes 4 minority (1 African American, 2 Asian Americans or Pacific Islanders, 1 Hispanic American), 1 international. Average age 30. 27 applicants, 26% accepted, 4 enrolled. In 2009, 33 master's awarded. *Degree requirements:* For master's, comprehensive exam, thesis optional. *Entrance requirements:* For master's, GRE General Test, minimum GPA of 3.0 in last 60 hours, writing sample. Additional exam requirements/recommendations for international students: Required—TOEFL (minimum score 500 paper-based; 173 computer-based). *Application deadline:* For fall admission, 7/1 priority date for domestic students, 5/1 for international students; for spring admission, 11/1 priority date for domestic students, 10/1 for international students. Applications are processed on a rolling basis. Application fee: $30. Electronic applications accepted. *Expenses:* Tuition, state resident: full-time $6649.20; part-time $277.05 per credit hour. Tuition, nonresident: full-time $22,970; part-time $957.08 per credit hour. Required fees: $985; $41.03 per credit hour. *Financial support:* In 2009–10, 39 students received support, including 1 teaching assistantship (averaging $2,000 per year); research assistantships, Federal Work-Study and tuition waivers (partial) also available. Support available to part-time students. Financial award application deadline: 4/1; financial award applicants required to submit FAFSA. *Faculty research:* Genre, period, and individual author studies in British, American, and world literature; literary criticism and theory—psychological, new historical and cultural, deconstructive, feminist, narrative, mythic; film and popular culture; online poetry publishing. *Unit head:* Dr. Samuel A. Kimball, Chair, 904-620-2273, Fax: 904-620-3940, E-mail: skimball@unf.edu. *Application contact:* Dr. Jason Mauro, Graduate Coordinator, 904-620-2273, Fax: 904-620-3940, E-mail: jmauro@unf.edu.

University of North Texas, Robert B. Toulouse School of Graduate Studies, College of Arts and Sciences, Department of English, Denton, TX 76203. Offers creative writing (MA); English (MA, PhD). Terminal master's awarded for partial completion of doctoral program. *Degree requirements:* For master's, one foreign language, comprehensive exam, thesis optional; for doctorate, one foreign language, comprehensive exam, thesis/dissertation. *Entrance requirements:* For master's, GRE General Test, minimum GPA of 3.0, personal statement, current curriculum vitae/resume, writing sample (for creative writing program); for doctorate, GRE General Test, minimum GPA of 3.5, 3 letters of recommendation, personal statement, writing sample. Additional exam requirements/recommendations for international students: Required—proof of English language proficiency required for non-native English speakers; Recommended—TOEFL (minimum score 550 paper-based; 213 computer-based; 79 iBT). Application fee: $50 ($75 for international students). *Expenses:* Tuition, state resident: full-time $4298; part-time $239 per contact hour. Tuition, nonresident: full-time $9878; part-time $549 per contact hour. Required fees: $265 per contact hour. *Financial support:* Fellowships with full tuition reimbursements, teaching assistantships with partial tuition reimbursements, career-related internships or fieldwork, Federal Work-Study, institutionally sponsored loans, scholarships/grants, health care benefits, and unspecified assistantships available. Financial award application deadline: 4/1; financial award applicants required to submit FAFSA. *Faculty research:* Creative writing, British and American literature, composition and rhetoric. *Application contact:* Chair of Graduate Studies, 940-565-2114, Fax: 940-565-4355.

University of Notre Dame, Graduate School, College of Arts and Letters, Division of Humanities, Department of English, Notre Dame, IN 46556. Offers creative writing (MFA); English (MA, PhD). *Degree requirements:* For doctorate, one foreign language, thesis/dissertation, candidacy exam. *Entrance requirements:* For master's, GRE General Test, minimum GPA of 3.0; for doctorate, GRE General Test, GRE Subject Test, minimum GPA of 3.0. Additional exam requirements/recommendations for international students: Required—TOEFL (minimum score 600 paper-based; 250 computer-based; 80 iBT). Electronic applications accepted. *Faculty research:* Early modern studies (medieval/Renaissance), modern British studies (18th-20th centuries), American Studies, literature and philosophy, Irish studies.

University of Oklahoma, Graduate College, College of Arts and Sciences, Department of English, Norman, OK 73019. Offers MA, PhD. Part-time programs available. *Faculty:* 34 full-time (15 women). *Students:* 43 full-time (24 women), 14 part-time (13 women); includes 8 minority (1 African American, 6 American Indian/Alaska Native, 1 Hispanic American), 5 international. 38 applicants, 50% accepted, 13 enrolled. In 2009, 8 master's, 5 doctorates awarded. *Degree requirements:* For master's, one foreign language, thesis or alternative, qualifying exam; for doctorate, 2 foreign languages, thesis/dissertation, qualifying exam. *Entrance requirements:* For master's, GRE General Test, minimum GPA of 3.0, BA with 27 hours of course work in English or 15 hours of upper-level courses; for doctorate, GRE General Test, GRE Subject Test (English literature), minimum graduate GPA of 3.5. Additional exam requirements/recommendations for international students: Required—TOEFL (minimum score 550 paper-based; 213 computer-based). *Application deadline:* For fall admission, 4/1 priority date for domestic students, 4/1 for international students; for spring admission, 11/1 for domestic students, 9/1 for international students. Applications are processed on a rolling basis. Application fee: $40 ($90 for international students). Electronic applications accepted. *Expenses:* Tuition, state resident: full-time $3744; part-time $156 per credit hour. Tuition, nonresident: full-time $13,577; part-time $565.70 per credit hour. Required fees: $2415; $90.10 per credit hour. *Financial support:* In 2009–10, 55 students received support, including 1 fellowship with full tuition reimbursement available (averaging $2,500 per year), 2 research assistantships with partial tuition reimbursements available (averaging $12,009 per year), 45 teaching assistantships with partial tuition reimbursements available (averaging $12,215 per year); scholarships/

English

University of Oklahoma (continued)
grants, health care benefits, and unspecified assistantships also available. Financial award application deadline: 3/1; financial award applicants required to submit FAFSA. *Faculty research:* Composition, rhetoric and literacy, Native American studies, literary theory, transnational studies, modern and contemporary studies. Total annual research expenditures: $16,528. *Unit head:* David Mair, Chair, 405-325-4661, Fax: 405-325-0831, E-mail: dmair@ou.edu. *Application contact:* Timothy S. Murphy, Graduate Liaison, 405-325-6250, Fax: 405-325-0831, E-mail: tmurphy@ou.edu.

University of Oregon, Graduate School, College of Arts and Sciences, Department of English, Eugene, OR 97403. Offers MA, PhD. Terminal master's awarded for partial completion of doctoral program. *Degree requirements:* For master's, one foreign language; for doctorate, 2 foreign languages, thesis/dissertation. *Entrance requirements:* For master's, GRE General Test; for doctorate, GRE Subject Test (English literature), minimum GPA of 3.5. Additional exam requirements/recommendations for international students: Required—TOEFL. *Faculty research:* Old and Middle English, women writers, critical theory, literature and the environment, rhetoric and composition.

University of Ottawa, Faculty of Graduate and Postdoctoral Studies, Faculty of Arts, Department of English, Ottawa, ON K1N 6N5, Canada. Offers MA, PhD. Part-time and evening/weekend programs available. *Degree requirements:* For master's, one foreign language, thesis optional; for doctorate, 2 foreign languages, comprehensive exam, thesis/dissertation. *Entrance requirements:* For master's, honors degree or equivalent, minimum B average; for doctorate, master's degree, minimum B+ average. Electronic applications accepted. *Faculty research:* Anglo-Saxon and medieval literature.

University of Pennsylvania, School of Arts and Sciences, Graduate Group in English, Philadelphia, PA 19104. Offers AM, PhD. *Faculty:* 43 full-time (20 women), 5 part-time/adjunct (1 woman). *Students:* 83 full-time (58 women), 2 part-time (0 women); includes 12 minority (4 African Americans, 7 Asian Americans or Pacific Islanders, 1 Hispanic American), 11 international. 579 applicants, 5% accepted, 20 enrolled. In 2009, 10 master's, 6 doctorates awarded. Terminal master's awarded for partial completion of doctoral program. *Degree requirements:* For master's, one foreign language; for doctorate, 2 foreign languages, thesis/dissertation, oral and written qualifying exams. *Entrance requirements:* For master's, GRE General Test, GRE Subject Test, sample of written work; for doctorate, GRE General Test, GRE Subject Test. Additional exam requirements/recommendations for international students: Required—TOEFL. *Application deadline:* For fall admission, 12/1 priority date for domestic students. Application fee: $70. Electronic applications accepted. *Expenses:* Tuition: Full-time $25,660; part-time $4758 per course. Required fees: $2152; $270 per course. Tuition and fees vary according to course load, degree level and program. *Financial support:* Fellowships, teaching assistantships, institutionally sponsored loans, scholarships/grants, traineeships, health care benefits, and unspecified assistantships available. Financial award application deadline: 12/15. *Faculty research:* Renaissance literature and intellectual theory, feminist studies, literary theory.

University of Pittsburgh, School of Arts and Sciences, Department of English, Pittsburgh, PA 15260. Offers cultural and critical studies (PhD); English (MA); writing (MFA). Part-time programs available. *Faculty:* 53 full-time (25 women). *Students:* 170 full-time (106 women), 37 part-time (33 women); includes 21 minority (8 African Americans, 1 American Indian/Alaska Native, 6 Asian Americans or Pacific Islanders, 6 Hispanic Americans), 5 international. Average age 23. 410 applicants, 12% accepted, 19 enrolled. In 2009, 22 master's, 10 doctorates awarded. *Degree requirements:* For master's, one foreign language; for doctorate, 2 foreign languages, comprehensive exam, thesis/dissertation. *Entrance requirements:* For master's and doctorate, GRE General Test, writing sample. Additional exam requirements/recommendations for international students: Required—TOEFL (minimum score 550 paper-based; 213 computer-based; 80 iBT). *Application deadline:* For fall admission, 12/10 for domestic and international students. Application fee: $50. *Expenses:* Tuition, state resident: full-time $16,402; part-time $665 per credit. Tuition, nonresident: full-time $28,694; part-time $1175 per credit. Required fees: $690; $175 per term. Tuition and fees vary according to program. *Financial support:* In 2009–10, 100 students received support, including 19 fellowships with full tuition reimbursements available (averaging $17,822 per year), 5 research assistantships with full and partial tuition reimbursements available (averaging $12,300 per year), 64 teaching assistantships with full tuition reimbursements available (averaging $15,065 per year); Federal Work-Study, tuition waivers (full and partial), and unspecified assistantships also available. Financial award application deadline: 12/12. *Faculty research:* Cultural studies, literary history and theory, film, composition. *Unit head:* Dr. John Twyning, Chairman, 412-624-6509, Fax: 412-624-6639, E-mail: twyning@pitt.edu. *Application contact:* Michelle Delie, Graduate Administrator, 412-624-6549, Fax: 412-624-6639, E-mail: mid29@pitt.edu.

University of Puerto Rico, Mayagüez Campus, Graduate Studies, College of Arts and Sciences, Department of English, Mayagüez, PR 00681-9000. Offers English education (MA). Part-time programs available. *Degree requirements:* For master's, comprehensive exam, thesis optional. *Entrance requirements:* For master's, course work in linguistics or language, American literature, British literature, and structure/grammar or syntax. *Faculty research:* Teaching English as a second language, linguistics, American literature, British literature.

University of Puerto Rico, Río Piedras, College of Humanities, Department of English, San Juan, PR 00931-3300. Offers Caribbean linguistics (PhD); Caribbean literature (PhD); English (MA). Part-time programs available. *Degree requirements:* For master's, one foreign language, comprehensive exam, thesis; for doctorate, residency. *Entrance requirements:* For master's, PAEG or GRE, interview, minimum GPA of 3.0, 2 letters of recommendation; for doctorate, PAEG or GRE, minimum GPA of 3.0, 3 letters of recommendation, interview.

University of Regina, Faculty of Graduate Studies and Research, Faculty of Arts, Department of English, Regina, SK S4S 0A2, Canada. Offers MA, PhD. Part-time programs available. *Faculty:* 23 full-time (10 women). *Students:* 7 full-time (6 women), 10 part-time (7 women). 18 applicants, 44% accepted. In 2009, 10 degrees awarded. *Degree requirements:* For master's, thesis optional; for doctorate, thesis/dissertation. *Entrance requirements:* For master's, writing sample. Additional exam requirements/recommendations for international students: Required—TOEFL (minimum score 580 paper-based; 237 computer-based; 80 iBT). *Application deadline:* For fall admission, 3/15 for international students. Application fee: $90 ($100 for international students). Electronic applications accepted. *Financial support:* In 2009–10, 5 fellowships (averaging $19,000 per year), 4 teaching assistantships (averaging $6,650 per year) were awarded; research assistantships, scholarships/grants also available. Financial award application deadline: 6/15. *Faculty research:* British, American, Canadian and post-colonial literature. *Unit head:* Dr. Dorothy Lane, Head, 306-585-4465, Fax: 306-585-5429, E-mail: dorothy.lane@uregina.ca. *Application contact:* Dr. Jeanne Shami, Graduate Program Coordinator, 306-585-4432, Fax: 306-585-4299, E-mail: jeanne.shami@uregina.ca.

University of Rhode Island, Graduate School, College of Arts and Sciences, Department of English, Kingston, RI 02881. Offers MA, PhD, MLIS/MA. Part-time programs available. *Faculty:* 21 full-time (13 women), 3 part-time/adjunct (2 women). *Students:* 43 full-time (30 women), 29 part-time (15 women); includes 1 minority (American Indian/Alaska Native), 5 international. In 2009, 6 master's, 3 doctorates awarded. *Degree requirements:* For master's, comprehensive exam (for some programs), thesis optional; for doctorate, comprehensive exam, thesis/dissertation. *Entrance requirements:* For master's, 3 letters of recommendation, writing sample; for doctorate, GRE, 3 letters of recommendation, writing sample. Additional exam requirements/recommendations for international students: Required—TOEFL (minimum score 550 paper-based; 213 computer-based; 91 iBT). *Application deadline:* For fall admission, 1/15 for domestic and international students. Application fee: $65. Electronic applications accepted. *Expenses:* Tuition, state resident: full-time $8828; part-time $490 per credit hour. Tuition, nonresident: full-time $22,100; part-time $1228 per credit hour. Required fees: $1118; $57 per semester. Tuition and fees vary according to program. *Financial support:* In 2009–10, 28 teaching assistantships with full tuition reimbursements (averaging $14,428 per year) were awarded. Financial award application deadline: 1/15; financial award applicants required to submit FAFSA. *Unit head:* Dr. Stephen Barber, Chair, 401-874-9088, Fax: 401-874-2580, E-mail: engchair@gmail.com. *Application contact:* Dr. Ryan S. Trimm, Director of Graduate Studies, 401-874-4685, Fax: 401-874-2580, E-mail: enggradir@gmail.com.

University of Rochester, The College, Arts and Sciences, Department of English, Rochester, NY 14627. Offers MA, PhD. Terminal master's awarded for partial completion of doctoral program. *Degree requirements:* For doctorate, one foreign language, thesis/dissertation, qualifying exam. *Entrance requirements:* For master's and doctorate, GRE General Test. Additional exam requirements/recommendations for international students: Required—TOEFL.

University of St. Thomas, Graduate Studies, College of Arts and Sciences, Graduate Program in English, St. Paul, MN 55105-1096. Offers MA. Part-time and evening/weekend programs available. *Degree requirements:* For master's, essay. *Entrance requirements:* For master's, minimum GPA of 3.0, previous course work in literature, sample of written work. Additional exam requirements/recommendations for international students: Required—TOEFL. *Expenses:* Contact institution. *Faculty research:* Multicultural literature, literature and theory, regional writers.

University of Saskatchewan, College of Graduate Studies and Research, College of Arts and Sciences, Department of English, Saskatoon, SK S7N 5A2, Canada. Offers MA, PhD. *Faculty:* 33. *Students:* 47. In 2009, 6 master's awarded. *Degree requirements:* For master's, one foreign language, thesis; for doctorate, one foreign language, comprehensive exam (for some programs), thesis/dissertation. *Entrance requirements:* Additional exam requirements/recommendations for international students: Required—TOEFL (minimum score 80 iBT); Recommended—IELTS (minimum score 6.5). *Application deadline:* For fall admission, 7/1 priority date for domestic students. Applications are processed on a rolling basis. Application fee: $75. Electronic applications accepted. Tuition and fees charges are reported in Canadian dollars. *Expenses:* Tuition, area resident: Full-time $3000 Canadian dollars; part-time $500 Canadian dollars per term. Required fees: $700 Canadian dollars; $100 Canadian dollars per term. *Financial support:* Fellowships, research assistantships, teaching assistantships available. Financial award application deadline: 1/31. *Unit head:* Dr. Douglas Thorpe, Head, 306-966-5500, Fax: 306-966-5951, E-mail: doug.thorpe@usask.ca. *Application contact:* Dr. Lisa Varga, Graduate Chair, 306-966-5500, Fax: 306-966-5951, E-mail: lisa.varga@usask.ca.

University of South Africa, College of Human Sciences, Pretoria, South Africa. Offers adult education (M Ed); African languages (MA, PhD); African politics (MA, PhD); Afrikaans (MA, PhD); ancient history (MA, PhD); ancient Near Eastern studies (MA, PhD); anthropology (MA, PhD); applied linguistics (MA); Arabic (MA, PhD); archaeology (MA); art history (MA); Biblical archaeology (MA); Biblical studies (M Th, D Th, PhD); Christian spirituality (M Th, D Th); church history (M Th, D Th); classical studies (MA, PhD); clinical psychology (MA); communication (MA, PhD); comparative education (M Ed, Ed D); consulting psychology (D Admin, D Com, PhD); curriculum studies (M Ed, Ed D); development studies (M Admin, MA, D Admin, PhD); didactics (M Ed, Ed D); education (M Tech); education management (M Ed, Ed D); educational psychology (M Ed); English (MA); environmental education (M Ed); French (MA, PhD); German (MA, PhD); Greek (MA); guidance and counseling (M Ed); health studies (MA, PhD), including health sciences education (MA), health services management (MA), medical and surgical nursing science (critical care general) (MA), midwifery and neonatal nursing science (MA), trauma and emergency care (MA); history (MA, PhD); history of education (Ed D); inclusive education (M Ed, Ed D); information and communications technology policy and regulation (MA); information science (MA, MIS, PhD); international politics (MA, PhD); Islamic studies (MA, PhD); Italian (MA, PhD); Judaica (MA, PhD); linguistics (MA, PhD); mathematical education (M Ed); mathematics education (MA); missiology (M Th, D Th); modern Hebrew (MA, PhD); musicology (MA, MMus, D Mus, PhD); natural science education (M Ed); New Testament (M Th, D Th); Old Testament (D Th); pastoral therapy (M Th, D Th); philosophy (MA); philosophy of education (M Ed, Ed D); politics (MA, PhD); Portuguese (MA, PhD); practical theology (M Th, D Th); psychology (MA, MS, PhD); psychology of education (M Ed, Ed D); public health (MA); religious studies (MA, D Th, PhD); Romance languages (MA); Russian (MA, PhD); Semitic languages (MA, PhD); social behavior studies in HIV/AIDS (MA); social science (mental health) (MA); social science in development studies (MA); social science in psychology (MA); social science in social work (MA); social science in sociology (MA); social work (MSW, DSW, PhD); socio-education (M Ed, Ed D); sociolinguistics (MA); sociology (MA, PhD); Spanish (MA, PhD); systematic theology (M Th, D Th); TESOL (teaching English to speakers of other languages) (MA); theological ethics (M Th, D Th); theory of literature (MA, PhD); urban ministries (D Th); urban ministry (M Th).

University of South Alabama, Graduate School, College of Arts and Sciences, Department of English, Mobile, AL 36688-0002. Offers MA. Part-time and evening/weekend programs available. *Degree requirements:* For master's, one foreign language, comprehensive exam, thesis optional. *Entrance requirements:* For master's, GRE General Test, BA in English or 40 hours of course work in English, minimum GPA of 3.0. *Expenses:* Tuition, state resident: part-time $218 per contact hour. Required fees: $1102 per year.

University of South Carolina, The Graduate School, College of Arts and Sciences, Department of English Language and Literature, Columbia, SC 29208. Offers creative writing (MFA); English (MA, PhD); English education (MAT); MLIS/MA. MAT offered in cooperation with the College of Education. Part-time programs available. *Degree requirements:* For master's, one foreign language, comprehensive exam, thesis; for doctorate, 2 foreign languages, comprehensive exam, thesis/dissertation. *Entrance requirements:* For master's, GRE General Test (MFA), GRE Subject Test (MA, MAT), sample of written work; for doctorate, GRE General Test, GRE Subject Test, sample of written work. Additional exam requirements/recommendations for international students: Required—TOEFL. Electronic applications accepted. *Faculty research:* American literature, British literature, composition and rhetoric, linguistics, speech communication.

The University of South Dakota, Graduate School, College of Arts and Sciences, Department of English, Vermillion, SD 57069-2390. Offers MA, PhD. *Degree requirements:* For master's, comprehensive exam (for some programs), thesis (for some programs); for doctorate, comprehensive exam, thesis/dissertation. *Entrance requirements:* For master's, minimum GPA of 3.0, writing sample; for doctorate, GRE, minimum GPA of 3.0, writing sample. Additional exam requirements/recommendations for international students: Required—TOEFL (minimum score 620 paper-based; 260 computer-based; 105 iBT). Electronic applications accepted.

University of Southern California, Graduate School, College of Letters, Arts and Sciences, Department of English, Los Angeles, CA 90089. Offers English (MA, PhD); literature and creative writing (PhD). *Faculty:* 37 full-time (18 women), 12 part-time/adjunct (5 women). *Students:* 110 full-time (68 women), 3 part-time (1 woman); includes 20 minority (1 African American, 1 American Indian/Alaska Native, 6 Asian Americans or Pacific Islanders, 12 Hispanic Americans), 9 international. 90 applicants, 16% accepted, 12 enrolled. In 2009, 5 master's, 21 doctorates awarded. Terminal master's awarded for partial completion of doctoral program. *Degree requirements:* For doctorate, one foreign language, comprehensive exam, thesis/dissertation. *Entrance requirements:* For doctorate, GRE General Test, GRE Subject Test (English literature). Additional exam requirements/recommendations for international students: Required—TOEFL. *Application deadline:* For fall admission, 12/1 for domestic and international students. Application fee: $85. Electronic applications accepted. *Expenses:* Tuition: Full-time $25,980; part-time $1315 per unit. Required fees: $554. One-time fee: $35 full-time. Full-time tuition and fees vary according to degree level and program. *Financial support:* In 2009–10, 11 students received support, including 14 fellowships with full tuition reimbursements available (averaging $21,000 per year), 2 research assistantships with full tuition reimbursements available (averaging $19,500 per year), 30 teaching assistantships with full tuition reimbursements available (averaging $21,000 per year); scholarships/grants, health care benefits, tuition waivers, and unspecified assistantships also available. *Faculty research:* Creative writing and literature; early modern studies; gender and sexuality; narrative studies; poetry and poetics; media, film, and popular culture; studies in race and minority literature. *Unit head:* Dr. Margaret Russett, Chair, 213-740-3737, Fax: 213-741-0377, E-mail: russett@

usc.edu. *Application contact:* Flora Ruiz, Graduate Coordinator of Student Affairs, 213-740-3725, Fax: 213-741-0377, E-mail: fruiz@usc.edu.

University of Southern Mississippi, Graduate School, College of Arts and Letters, Department of English, Hattiesburg, MS 39406-0001. Offers MA, PhD. *Faculty:* 26 full-time (13 women), 1 part-time/adjunct (0 women). *Students:* 61 full-time (28 women), 22 part-time (19 women); includes 4 minority (2 African Americans, 1 American Indian/Alaska Native, 1 Hispanic American), 3 international. Average age 33. 77 applicants, 69% accepted, 22 enrolled. In 2009, 12 master's, 9 doctorates awarded. *Degree requirements:* For master's, one foreign language, comprehensive exam, thesis; for doctorate, 2 foreign languages, comprehensive exam, thesis/dissertation. *Entrance requirements:* For master's, GRE General Test, minimum GPA of 3.0 in field of study, 2.75 in last 2 years; for doctorate, GRE General Test, minimum GPA of 3.5. Additional exam requirements/recommendations for international students: Required—TOEFL. *Application deadline:* For fall admission, 3/15 priority date for domestic students, 3/15 for international students. Application fee: $35. Electronic applications accepted. *Expenses:* Tuition, state resident: full-time $5096; part-time $284 per hour. Tuition, nonresident: full-time $13,052; part-time $726 per hour. Required fees: $402. Tuition and fees vary according to course level and course load. *Financial support:* In 2009–10, 1 fellowship (averaging $14,000 per year), 2 research assistantships with full tuition reimbursements (averaging $10,000 per year), 44 teaching assistantships with full tuition reimbursements (averaging $10,000 per year) were awarded; Federal Work-Study, institutionally sponsored loans, scholarships/grants, and unspecified assistantships also available. Financial award application deadline: 3/15; financial award applicants required to submit FAFSA. *Faculty research:* English and American literature, critical theory and cultural studies, creative writing. *Unit head:* Dr. W. Michael Mays, Chair, 601-266-4319, Fax: 601-266-5757, E-mail: michael.mays@usm.edu. *Application contact:* Dr. Jameela Lares, Graduate Coordinator, 601-266-4320, Fax: 601-266-5757.

University of South Florida, Graduate School, College of Arts and Sciences, Department of English, Tampa, FL 33620-9951. Offers MA, MFA, PhD. Part-time and evening/weekend programs available. *Faculty:* 24 full-time (13 women), 2 part-time/adjunct (1 woman). *Students:* 81 full-time (51 women), 39 part-time (28 women); includes 10 minority (1 African American, 2 American Indian/Alaska Native, 1 Asian American or Pacific Islander, 6 Hispanic Americans), 6 international. Average age 32. 127 applicants, 31% accepted, 26 enrolled. In 2009, 19 master's, 5 doctorates awarded. *Degree requirements:* For master's, comprehensive exam, thesis (for some programs); for doctorate, comprehensive exam, thesis/dissertation. *Entrance requirements:* For master's, GRE General Test, minimum GPA of 3.5; for doctorate, GRE General Test, minimum GPA of 3.7. Additional exam requirements/recommendations for international students: Required—TOEFL (minimum score 550 paper-based; 213 computer-based). *Application deadline:* For fall admission, 2/1 for domestic students, 1/2 for international students. Applications are processed on a rolling basis. Application fee: $30. Electronic applications accepted. *Financial support:* In 2009–10, teaching assistantships with tuition reimbursements (averaging $25,071 per year); unspecified assistantships also available. Financial award application deadline: 6/30; financial award applicants required to submit FAFSA. *Faculty research:* British and American literature, rhetoric and composition. Total annual research expenditures: $94,250. *Unit head:* Hunt Hawkins, Chairperson, 813-974-9420, Fax: 813-974-2270, E-mail: hhawkins@cas.usf.edu. *Application contact:* Dr. Laura Runge, Director, 813-974-9469, Fax: 813-974-2270, E-mail: runge@chuma.cas.usf.edu.

The University of Tennessee, Graduate School, College of Arts and Sciences, Department of English, Knoxville, TN 37996. Offers MA, PhD. Part-time programs available. *Degree requirements:* For master's, one foreign language, thesis or alternative; for doctorate, one foreign language, thesis/dissertation. *Entrance requirements:* For master's, GRE General Test, minimum GPA of 2.7; for doctorate, GRE General Test, GRE Subject Test, minimum GPA of 2.7. Additional exam requirements/recommendations for international students: Required—TOEFL. Electronic applications accepted. *Expenses:* Tuition, state resident: full-time $6826; part-time $380 per semester hour. Tuition, nonresident: full-time $21,844; part-time $1147 per semester hour. Tuition and fees vary according to program.

The University of Tennessee at Chattanooga, Graduate School, College of Arts and Sciences, Department of English, Chattanooga, TN 37403. Offers creative writing (MA); literary study (MA); rhetoric and writing (MA, Graduate Certificate). Part-time and evening/weekend programs available. *Faculty:* 12 full-time (7 women). *Students:* 11 full-time (10 women), 28 part-time (13 women); includes 2 minority (both African Americans). Average age 32. 27 applicants, 81% accepted, 11 enrolled. In 2009, 15 master's awarded. *Degree requirements:* For master's, one foreign language, comprehensive exam, thesis. *Entrance requirements:* For master's, GRE General Test or GRE Subject Test in literature, minimum GPA of 3.0 in English. Additional exam requirements/recommendations for international students: Required—TOEFL (minimum score 550 paper-based; 213 computer-based; 79 iBT), IELTS (minimum score 6). *Application deadline:* For fall admission, 8/1 priority date for domestic students, 6/1 for international students; for spring admission, 12/1 priority date for domestic students, 10/1 for international students. Applications are processed on a rolling basis. Application fee: $35. Electronic applications accepted. *Expenses:* Tuition, state resident: full-time $5404; part-time $300 per credit hour. Tuition, nonresident: full-time $16,702; part-time $928 per credit hour. Required fees: $1150; $130 per credit hour. *Financial support:* In 2009–10, 6 research assistantships with full and partial tuition reimbursements (averaging $5,500 per year) were awarded; career-related internships or fieldwork, scholarships/grants, and unspecified assistantships also available. Support available to part-time students. *Faculty research:* Technical writing, African-American literature, Milton, creative writing and poetry, American modernism and gender theory. Total annual research expenditures: $74,953. *Unit head:* Dr. Verbie Prevost, Head, 423-425-4238, Fax: 423-785-2282, E-mail: verbie-prevost@utc.edu. *Application contact:* Dr. Stephanie Bellar, Dean of Graduate Studies, 423-425-4666, Fax: 423-425-5223, E-mail: stephanie-bellar@utc.edu.

The University of Texas at Arlington, Graduate School, College of Liberal Arts, Department of English, Arlington, TX 76019. Offers English (MA); literature (PhD). Part-time and evening/weekend programs available. *Faculty:* 19 full-time (9 women). *Students:* 10 full-time (6 women), 100 part-time (69 women); includes 17 minority (8 African Americans, 5 Asian Americans or Pacific Islanders, 4 Hispanic Americans), 2 international. 36 applicants, 97% accepted, 15 enrolled. In 2009, 12 master's, 3 doctorates awarded. *Degree requirements:* For master's, thesis or comprehensive exam; for doctorate, one foreign language, comprehensive exam, thesis/dissertation. *Entrance requirements:* For master's, GRE General Test, minimum 5-page writing sample, minimum GPA of 3.0, 3 letters of recommendation; for doctorate, GRE General Test, minimum graduate GPA of 3.5, writing sample, 3 letters of recommendation. Additional exam requirements/recommendations for international students: Required—TOEFL (minimum score 550 paper-based; 213 computer-based). *Application deadline:* For fall admission, 6/16 for domestic students. Applications are processed on a rolling basis. Application fee: $35 ($50 for international students). *Financial support:* In 2009–10, 4 fellowships (averaging $2,000 per year) were awarded; scholarships/grants also available. Financial award application deadline: 5/1; financial award applicants required to submit FAFSA. *Faculty research:* Rhetoric composition, American literature, British literature, cultural studies, women's studies. *Unit head:* Dr. Wendy Faris, Chair, 817-272-2692, Fax: 817-272-2718, E-mail: wbfaris@uta.edu. *Application contact:* Dr. Tim Morris, Associate Chair for Graduate Studies, 817-272-2739, E-mail: morris@uta.edu.

The University of Texas at Austin, Graduate School, College of Liberal Arts, Department of English, Austin, TX 78712-1111. Offers creative writing (MA); English (MA, PhD). Part-time programs available. Terminal master's awarded for partial completion of doctoral program. *Degree requirements:* For master's, 2 foreign languages; for doctorate, variable foreign language requirement. *Entrance requirements:* For master's and doctorate, GRE General Test. Electronic applications accepted.

The University of Texas at Brownsville, Graduate Studies, College of Liberal Arts, Department of English, Brownsville, TX 78520-4991. Offers English (MA); interdisciplinary studies (MAIS). Part-time and evening/weekend programs available. *Degree requirements:* For master's, comprehensive exam or thesis. *Entrance requirements:* For master's, GRE General Test. Additional exam requirements/recommendations for international students: Required—TOEFL. *Faculty research:* Sandra Cisneros, Nathaniel Hawthorne, Rodolfo Araya, Isabel Allende, linguistics.

The University of Texas at El Paso, Graduate School, College of Liberal Arts, Department of English, El Paso, TX 79968-0001. Offers bilingual professional writing (Certificate); English and American literature (MA); rhetoric and composition (PhD); rhetoric and writing studies (MA); teaching English (MAT). Part-time and evening/weekend programs available. *Degree requirements:* For master's, thesis optional. *Entrance requirements:* For master's, GRE General Test, minimum GPA of 3.0. Additional exam requirements/recommendations for international students: Required—TOEFL. Electronic applications accepted. *Faculty research:* Literature, creative writing, literary theory.

The University of Texas at San Antonio, College of Liberal and Fine Arts, Department of English, Classics and Philosophy, San Antonio, TX 78249-0617. Offers English (MA, PhD). Part-time and evening/weekend programs available. *Faculty:* 16 full-time (12 women), 1 (woman) part-time/adjunct. *Students:* 39 full-time (30 women), 46 part-time (36 women); includes 26 minority (3 African Americans, 1 Asian American or Pacific Islander, 22 Hispanic Americans), 2 international. Average age 33. 52 applicants, 67% accepted, 27 enrolled. In 2009, 17 master's, 5 doctorates awarded. *Degree requirements:* For master's, comprehensive exam (for some programs), thesis (for some programs); for doctorate, comprehensive exam, thesis/dissertation. *Entrance requirements:* For master's, GRE General Test, minimum GPA of 3.3 on all upper division English courses; for doctorate, GRE General Test. Additional exam requirements/recommendations for international students: Required—TOEFL (minimum score 500 paper-based; 173 computer-based; 61 iBT), IELTS (minimum score 5). *Application deadline:* For fall admission, 7/1 for domestic students, 4/1 for international students; for spring admission, 11/1 for domestic students, 9/1 for international students. Applications are processed on a rolling basis. Application fee: $45 ($80 for international students). Electronic applications accepted. *Expenses:* Tuition, state resident: full-time $3975; part-time $221 per contact hour. Tuition, nonresident: full-time $13,947; part-time $775 per contact hour. Required fees: $1853. *Financial support:* In 2009–10, 22 students received support, including 17 research assistantships (averaging $10,673 per year), 14 teaching assistantships (averaging $6,428 per year); career-related internships or fieldwork, institutionally sponsored loans, scholarships/grants, and unspecified assistantships also available. Support available to part-time students. *Faculty research:* History of English, principles of linguistics. Total annual research expenditures: $32,801. *Unit head:* Dr. Bernadette Andrea, Chair, 210-458-5130, Fax: 210-458-5366, E-mail: bandrea@utsa.edu. *Application contact:* Dr. Dorothy A. Flannagan, Dean of the Graduate School, 210-458-4330, Fax: 210-458-4332, E-mail: dorothy.flannagan@utsa.edu.

The University of Texas at Tyler, College of Arts and Sciences, Department of Literature and Languages, Tyler, TX 75799-0001. Offers English (MA); interdisciplinary studies (MAIS). Part-time and evening/weekend programs available. *Faculty:* 12 full-time (7 women). *Students:* 6 full-time (3 women), 19 part-time (16 women); includes 1 minority (Hispanic American). Average age 34. 9 applicants, 100% accepted, 5 enrolled. In 2009, 2 master's awarded. *Degree requirements:* For master's, one foreign language, comprehensive exam, thesis optional. *Entrance requirements:* For master's, GRE General Test, minimum GPA of 3.0; four semesters or the equivalent of one foreign language. Additional exam requirements/recommendations for international students: Required—TOEFL (minimum score 79 computer-based). *Application deadline:* For fall admission, 8/17 priority date for domestic students, 7/1 priority date for international students; for spring admission, 12/21 priority date for domestic students, 11/1 priority date for international students. Applications are processed on a rolling basis. Application fee: $25 ($50 for international students). Electronic applications accepted. *Expenses:* Tuition, state resident: part-time $665 per semester hour. Tuition, nonresident: part-time $942 per semester hour. Part-time tuition and fees vary according to degree level and program. *Financial support:* In 2009–10, fellowships with full and partial tuition reimbursements (averaging $1,000 per year), 1 research assistantship with full and partial tuition reimbursement (averaging $6,000 per year) were awarded; teaching assistantships with full and partial tuition reimbursements, Federal Work-Study, institutionally sponsored loans, scholarships/grants, tuition waivers, and unspecified assistantships also available. Financial award application deadline: 7/1; financial award applicants required to submit FAFSA. *Faculty research:* Medieval and Tudor drama, Shakespeare, British Romanticism, British and Irish modernism, American realism, Greek drama, nineteenth century American literature. *Unit head:* Dr. Hui Wu, Chair, 903-566-7289, Fax: 903-565-5700, E-mail: hui_wu@uttyler.edu. *Application contact:* Dr. Hui Wu, Chair, 903-566-7289, Fax: 903-565-5700, E-mail: hui_wu@uttyler.edu.

The University of Texas of the Permian Basin, Office of Graduate Studies, College of Arts and Sciences, Department of Literature and Languages, Program in English, Odessa, TX 79762-0001. Offers MA. Part-time and evening/weekend programs available. *Degree requirements:* For master's, comprehensive exam (for some programs), thesis (for some programs). *Entrance requirements:* For master's, GRE General Test. Additional exam requirements/recommendations for international students: Required—TOEFL (minimum score 550 paper-based; 213 computer-based).

The University of Texas–Pan American, College of Arts and Humanities, Department of English, Edinburg, TX 78539. Offers English (MA, MAIS); English as a second language (MA). Part-time and evening/weekend programs available. *Degree requirements:* For master's, comprehensive exam, thesis optional. *Entrance requirements:* For master's, GRE General Test, minimum GPA of 3.0. *Expenses:* Tuition, state resident: full-time $3630.60; part-time $201.70 per credit hour. Tuition, nonresident: full-time $8617; part-time $478.70 per credit hour. Required fees: $806.50. *Faculty research:* Oral vs. literary culture, Borderland literature, Mexican-American literature, topics in British and American literature, discourse analysis.

University of the District of Columbia, College of Arts and Sciences, Department of English, Program in English Composition and Rhetoric, Washington, DC 20008-1175. Offers MA. *Students:* 1 (woman) full-time, 7 part-time (4 women); all minorities (7 African Americans, 1 Asian American or Pacific Islander). Average age 31. 5 applicants, 80% accepted, 3 enrolled. *Degree requirements:* For master's, comprehensive exam. *Entrance requirements:* For master's, writing proficiency exam. *Application deadline:* For fall admission, 6/15 priority date for domestic students; for spring admission, 11/1 for domestic students. Applications are processed on a rolling basis. Application fee: $20. *Expenses:* Tuition, state resident: full-time $7580. Tuition, nonresident: full-time $14,580. Required fees: $620. *Unit head:* Dr. Chester Wright, Chair/Professor, 202-274-5137. *Application contact:* Ann Marie Waterman, Associate Vice President of Admission, Recruitment and Financial Aid, 202-274-6069.

The University of Toledo, College of Graduate Studies, College of Arts and Sciences, Department of English Language and Literature, Toledo, OH 43606-3390. Offers English as a second language (MA); literature (MA); teaching of writing (Certificate). Part-time programs available. *Degree requirements:* For master's, one foreign language. *Entrance requirements:* For master's, minimum GPA of 2.7. Electronic applications accepted. *Faculty research:* Literary criticism, linguistics, creative writing, folklore and cultural studies.

University of Toronto, School of Graduate Studies, Humanities Division, Department of English, Toronto, ON M5S 1A1, Canada. Offers MA, PhD. Part-time programs available. *Degree requirements:* For master's, thesis optional; for doctorate, 2 foreign languages, thesis/dissertation. *Entrance requirements:* For master's, minimum B+ average, 2 letters of reference, portfolio (creative writing program); for doctorate, minimum A– average, 2 letters of reference, writing sample.

University of Tulsa, Graduate School, College of Arts and Sciences, Department of English Language and Literature, Tulsa, OK 74104-3189. Offers MA, MTA, PhD, JD/MA. Part-time and evening/weekend programs available. *Faculty:* 13 full-time (6 women), 1 (woman) part-time/adjunct. *Students:* 39 full-time (25 women), 10 part-time (5 women), 6 international. Average age 29. 56 applicants, 71% accepted, 16 enrolled. In 2009, 11 master's, 6 doctorates awarded.

English

University of Tulsa (continued)

Degree requirements: For master's, independent research project; for doctorate, one foreign language, comprehensive exam, thesis/dissertation. *Entrance requirements:* For master's and doctorate, GRE General Test. Additional exam requirements/recommendations for international students: Required—TOEFL (minimum score 575 paper-based; 231 computer-based; 91 iBT), IELTS (minimum score 6.5). *Application deadline:* For fall admission, 2/1 priority date for domestic students. Applications are processed on a rolling basis. Application fee: $40. Electronic applications accepted. *Expenses:* Tuition: Full-time $16,182; part-time $899 per credit hour. Required fees: $4 per credit hour. Tuition and fees vary according to course load. *Financial support:* In 2009–10, 43 students received support, including 14 fellowships with full and partial tuition reimbursements available (averaging $5,732 per year), 2 research assistantships with full and partial tuition reimbursements available (averaging $10,067 per year), 34 teaching assistantships with full and partial tuition reimbursements available (averaging $11,172 per year); Federal Work-Study, scholarships/grants, health care benefits, tuition waivers (full and partial), and unspecified assistantships also available. Support available to part-time students. Financial award application deadline: 2/1; financial award applicants required to submit FAFSA. *Faculty research:* Twentieth century literature; modern and contemporary British, Irish, and American literatures; Victorian literature; American studies; cultural and gender studies; African American literature; women's literature. Total annual research expenditures: $83,535. *Unit head:* Dr. Lars Engle, Chairperson, 918-631-2807, Fax: 918-631-3033, E-mail: lars-engle@utulsa.edu. *Application contact:* Dr. Laura Stevens, Advisor, 918-631-2859, Fax: 918-631-3033, E-mail: laura-stevens@utulsa.edu.

University of Utah, The Graduate School, College of Humanities, Department of English, Salt Lake City, UT 84112. Offers American studies (MA, PhD), including rhetoric/composition; British American literature (MA, PhD); creative writing (MA, MFA, PhD), including rhetoric/composition (MA, PhD); literature (PhD); rhetoric and composition (PhD). *Faculty:* 36 full-time (16 women). *Students:* 57 full-time (36 women), 17 part-time (13 women); includes 5 minority (3 African Americans, 1 American Indian/Alaska Native, 1 Asian American or Pacific Islander), 2 international. Average age 33. 270 applicants, 10% accepted, 24 enrolled. In 2009, 20 master's, 8 doctorates awarded. Terminal master's awarded for partial completion of doctoral program. *Degree requirements:* For master's, one foreign language, comprehensive exam, thesis (for some programs), written exam; for doctorate, 2 foreign languages, comprehensive exam, thesis/dissertation. *Entrance requirements:* For master's and doctorate, GRE General Test, minimum GPA of 3.2. Additional exam requirements/recommendations for international students: Required—TOEFL (minimum score 650 paper-based; 280 computer-based; 115 iBT). *Application deadline:* For fall admission, 12/15 for domestic and international students. Application fee: $55 ($65 for international students). Electronic applications accepted. *Expenses:* Tuition, state resident: full-time $4004; part-time $1674 per semester. Tuition, nonresident: full-time $14,134; part-time $5915 per semester. Required fees: $324 per semester. Tuition and fees vary according to course load, degree level and program. *Financial support:* In 2009–10, 52 students received support, including 9 fellowships with full tuition reimbursements available (averaging $12,400 per year), 43 teaching assistantships with full tuition reimbursements available (averaging $12,400 per year); research assistantships, health care benefits also available. Financial award application deadline: 12/15; financial award applicants required to submit FAFSA. *Faculty research:* Poetics and modern poetry, nineteenth and twentieth century British and American literature, the American west, environmental studies, critical theory and race and gender studies. Total annual research expenditures: $45,462. *Unit head:* Prof. Vincent P. Pecora, Chair, 801-581-6168, E-mail: v.pecora@utah.edu. *Application contact:* Prof. Scott Black, Director of Graduate Studies, 801-581-5137, E-mail: scott.black@utah.edu.

University of Vermont, Graduate College, College of Arts and Sciences, Department of English, Burlington, VT 05405. Offers MA. *Students:* 37 (21 women); includes 3 minority (1 African American, 1 American Indian/Alaska Native, 1 Asian American or Pacific Islander). 75 applicants, 85% accepted, 16 enrolled. In 2009, 13 master's awarded. *Degree requirements:* For master's, one foreign language, thesis. *Entrance requirements:* For master's, GRE General Test, writing sample. Additional exam requirements/recommendations for international students: Required—TOEFL (minimum score 550 paper-based; 213 computer-based; 80 iBT). *Application deadline:* For fall admission, 2/15 priority date for domestic students. Applications are processed on a rolling basis. Application fee: $40. Electronic applications accepted. *Expenses:* Tuition, state resident: part-time $508 per credit hour. Tuition, nonresident: part-time $1281 per credit hour. *Financial support:* Fellowships, teaching assistantships available. Financial award application deadline: 3/1. *Unit head:* Dr. LoKangaka Losambe, Chair, 802-656-3056. *Application contact:* Dr. Todd McGowan, Coordinator, 802-656-3056.

University of Victoria, Faculty of Graduate Studies, Faculty of Humanities, Department of English, Victoria, BC V8W 2Y2, Canada. Offers MA, PhD. Part-time programs available. *Degree requirements:* For master's, one foreign language, thesis (for some programs); for doctorate, 2 foreign languages, comprehensive exam, thesis/dissertation, candidacy exam. *Entrance requirements:* For master's, minimum A- average in last 2 years of undergraduate course work, writing sample, resume; for doctorate, minimum A- average in graduate course work, writing sample, resumé. Additional exam requirements/recommendations for international students: Required—TOEFL (minimum score 630 paper-based; 267 computer-based). Electronic applications accepted. *Faculty research:* Critical theory, nineteenth century literature, postcolonialism/multiculturalism, medieval and Renaissance literature, cultural theory.

University of Virginia, College and Graduate School of Arts and Sciences, Department of English Language and Literature, Program in English, Charlottesville, VA 22903. Offers MA, PhD. *Students:* 141 full-time (83 women), 1 (woman) part-time; includes 11 minority (6 African Americans, 3 Asian Americans or Pacific Islanders, 2 Hispanic Americans), 6 international. Average age 29. 463 applicants, 15% accepted, 33 enrolled. In 2009, 35 master's, 14 doctorates awarded. *Degree requirements:* For master's, one foreign language, oral exam or thesis; for doctorate, 2 foreign languages, comprehensive exam, thesis/dissertation. *Entrance requirements:* For master's, GRE General Test, GRE Subject Test, 3 letters of recommendation, 2 writing samples; for doctorate, GRE General Test, GRE Subject Test, 3 letters of recommendation; 2 writing samples. Additional exam requirements/recommendations for international students: Required—TOEFL (minimum score 600 paper-based; 250 computer-based; 90 iBT), IELTS (minimum score 7). *Application deadline:* For fall admission, 1/2 for domestic and international students. Applications are processed on a rolling basis. Application fee: $60. Electronic applications accepted. *Financial support:* Fellowships, teaching assistantships available. Financial award applicants required to submit FAFSA. *Unit head:* Cynthia Wall, Chair, 434-924-7105, Fax: 434-924-1478, E-mail: wall@virginia.edu. *Application contact:* J. Paul Hunter, Director of Graduate Admissions, Fax: 434-924-1478, E-mail: jph7f@virginia.edu.

University of Virginia, Curry School of Education, Department of Curriculum, Instruction, and Special Education, Program in Curriculum and Instruction, Charlottesville, VA 22903. Offers curriculum and instruction (M Ed, Ed S); elementary (M Ed, Ed D); English (M Ed, Ed D); foreign language (M Ed); mathematics (M Ed, Ed D); reading (M Ed, Ed D, Ed S); science (Ed D); social studies (M Ed). *Students:* 12 full-time (8 women), 30 part-time (24 women); includes 2 minority (1 Asian American or Pacific Islander, 1 Hispanic American), 1 international. Average age 36. 55 applicants, 69% accepted, 26 enrolled. In 2009, 247 master's, 14 doctorates, 10 other advanced degrees awarded. *Degree requirements:* For master's, comprehensive exam (for some programs); for doctorate, comprehensive exam, thesis/dissertation; for Ed S, comprehensive exam. *Entrance requirements:* For master's, doctorate, and Ed S, GRE General Test, 2 letters of recommendation. Additional exam requirements/recommendations for international students: Required—TOEFL (minimum score 600 paper-based; 250 computer-based; 90 iBT), IELTS (minimum score 7). *Application deadline:* Applications are processed on a rolling basis. Application fee: $60. Electronic applications accepted. *Financial support:* Fellowships with tuition reimbursements, research assistantships with tuition reimbursements, teaching assistantships with tuition reimbursements available. Financial award application deadline: 1/5; financial award applicants required to submit FAFSA.

University of Washington, Graduate School, College of Arts and Sciences, Department of English, Seattle, WA 98195. Offers creative writing (MFA); English as a second language (MAT); English literature and language (MA, MAT, PhD). Part-time programs available. Terminal master's awarded for partial completion of doctoral program. *Degree requirements:* For master's, one foreign language, thesis (for some programs); for doctorate, one foreign language, thesis/dissertation. *Entrance requirements:* For master's, GRE General Test, GRE Subject Test (MA and MAT in English), minimum GPA of 3.0; for doctorate, GRE General Test, GRE Subject Test. Additional exam requirements/recommendations for international students: Required—TOEFL. Electronic applications accepted. *Faculty research:* English and American literature, critical theory, creative writing, language theory.

University of Waterloo, Graduate Studies, Faculty of Arts, Department of English, Language and Literature, Waterloo, ON N2L 3G1, Canada. Offers English language and literature (PhD); literary studies (MA); rhetoric and communication design (MA). Part-time programs available. *Degree requirements:* For master's, one foreign language, thesis optional; for doctorate, 2 foreign languages, thesis/dissertation. *Entrance requirements:* For master's, honors degree, minimum B+ average; for doctorate, master's degree, minimum A- average. Additional exam requirements/recommendations for international students: Required—TOEFL, TWE. Electronic applications accepted. *Faculty research:* Shakespeare, American literature, rhetoric, Romantics, moderns.

The University of Western Ontario, Faculty of Graduate Studies, Faculty of Arts and Humanities, Department of English, London, ON N6A 5B8, Canada. Offers Canadian literature (MA); English (PhD); English literature (MA). *Degree requirements:* For master's, one foreign language, thesis or alternative; for doctorate, 2 foreign languages, thesis/dissertation, qualifying exam. *Entrance requirements:* For master's, minimum A average in appropriate field; for doctorate, MA or equivalent, minimum A average. Additional exam requirements/recommendations for international students: Required—TOEFL (minimum score 630 paper-based; 267 computer-based). *Faculty research:* Renaissance, nineteenth-century, modern, and postcolonial literature.

University of West Florida, College of Arts and Sciences: Arts, Department of English and Foreign Languages, Pensacola, FL 32514-5750. Offers creative writing (MA); literature (MA). Part-time and evening/weekend programs available. *Faculty:* 5 full-time (2 women). *Students:* 12 full-time (8 women), 31 part-time (19 women); includes 4 minority (2 African Americans, 2 American Indian/Alaska Native). Average age 32. 24 applicants, 79% accepted, 10 enrolled. In 2009, 1 master's awarded. *Degree requirements:* For master's, thesis. *Entrance requirements:* For master's, GRE General Test, minimum GPA of 3.0. Additional exam requirements/recommendations for international students: Required—TOEFL (minimum score 550 paper-based; 213 computer-based). *Application deadline:* For fall admission, 6/1 for domestic students, 5/15 for international students; for spring admission, 11/1 for domestic students, 10/1 for international students. Applications are processed on a rolling basis. Application fee: $30. *Expenses:* Tuition, state resident: full-time $4982; part-time $260 per credit hour. Tuition, nonresident: full-time $20,059; part-time $919 per credit hour. Required fees: $1247; $52 per credit hour. *Financial support:* In 2009–10, 4 research assistantships with partial tuition reimbursements (averaging $3,280 per year), 12 teaching assistantships with partial tuition reimbursements (averaging $5,884 per year) were awarded; unspecified assistantships also available. Financial award application deadline: 4/15; financial award applicants required to submit FAFSA. *Faculty research:* Faulkner, Shakespeare, American humor, women's studies, poetry. *Unit head:* Dr. Bob Yeager, Chairperson, 850-474-2923. *Application contact:* Terry McCray, Assistant Director of Graduate Admissions, 850-473-7718, Fax: 850-473-7714, E-mail: gradadmissions@uwf.edu.

University of West Georgia, Graduate School, College of Arts and Sciences, Department of English and Philosophy, Carrollton, GA 30118. Offers English (MA). Part-time and evening/weekend programs available. *Faculty:* 20 full-time (11 women). *Students:* 2 full-time (both women), 23 part-time (12 women); includes 2 minority (both African Americans). Average age 32. 11 applicants, 64% accepted, 2 enrolled. In 2009, 5 master's awarded. *Degree requirements:* For master's, one foreign language, comprehensive exam, thesis optional. *Entrance requirements:* For master's, GRE General Test, NTE, undergraduate degree in English, minimum GPA of 3.2. *Application deadline:* For fall admission, 7/17 for domestic students; for spring admission, 11/20 for domestic students. Application fee: $30. Electronic applications accepted. *Expenses:* Tuition, state resident: full-time $2952; part-time $164 per semester hour. Tuition, nonresident: full-time $11,808; part-time $656 per semester hour. Required fees: $42.90 per semester hour. $307 per semester. Tuition and fees vary according to course load. *Financial support:* In 2009–10, 10 students received support, including 10 research assistantships with full tuition reimbursements available (averaging $4,000 per year); career-related internships or fieldwork and unspecified assistantships also available. Support available to part-time students. Financial award application deadline: 7/1; financial award applicants required to submit FAFSA. *Unit head:* Dr. Randy J. Hendricks, Chair, 678-839-6512, Fax: 678-839-4849, E-mail: rhendricl@westga.edu. *Application contact:* Dr. Charles W. Clark, Dean, 678-839-6508, E-mail: cclark@westga.edu.

University of Windsor, Faculty of Graduate Studies, Faculty of Arts and Social Sciences, Department of English Language, Literature and Creative Writing, Windsor, ON N9B 3P4, Canada. Offers English: creative writing and language and literature (MA); English: language and literature (MA). Part-time programs available. *Degree requirements:* For master's, thesis. *Entrance requirements:* For master's, minimum B average, portfolio. Additional exam requirements/recommendations for international students: Required—TOEFL (minimum score 600 paper-based; 250 computer-based). Electronic applications accepted. *Faculty research:* Use of gender-related terms in popular culture; international and Aboriginal literatures: expression of cultural identity; critical analysis of authors: Pope, Munroe, Lady Morgan, Orwell, Thomas; the 'feminine" voice in literature and contemporary culture.

University of Wisconsin–Eau Claire, College of Arts and Sciences, Program in English, Eau Claire, WI 54702-4004. Offers MA. Part-time programs available. *Faculty:* 23 full-time (15 women). *Students:* 4 full-time (3 women), 16 part-time (9 women); includes 2 minority (1 Asian American or Pacific Islander, 1 Hispanic American). Average age 30. 13 applicants, 77% accepted, 6 enrolled. In 2009, 4 master's awarded. *Degree requirements:* For master's, thesis, oral defense with thesis. *Entrance requirements:* For master's, minimum GPA of 3.25 in English, 3.0 overall; bachelor's degree with minimum of 24 credits in English. Additional exam requirements/recommendations for international students: Required—TOEFL (minimum score 550 paper-based; 213 computer-based; 79 iBT). *Application deadline:* For fall admission, 7/1 priority date for domestic students, 6/1 priority date for international students; for spring admission, 12/1 priority date for domestic students, 11/1 priority date for international students. Applications are processed on a rolling basis. Application fee: $56. Electronic applications accepted. *Expenses:* Tuition, state resident: full-time $6705.90; part-time $372.55 per credit. Tuition, nonresident: full-time $16,771; part-time $931.74 per credit. Required fees: $925.50; $51.19 per credit. One-time fee: $56. *Financial support:* In 2009–10, 14 students received support, including 2 fellowships (averaging $3,500 per year); Federal Work-Study and unspecified assistantships also available. Financial award application deadline: 3/1; financial award applicants required to submit FAFSA. *Unit head:* Dr. Jack Bushnell, Chair, 715-836-2639, Fax: 715-836-5996, E-mail: bushnejp@uwec.edu. *Application contact:* Kristina Anderson, Director of Admissions, 715-836-5415, Fax: 715-836-2409, E-mail: admissions@uwec.edu.

University of Wisconsin–Eau Claire, College of Education and Human Sciences, Program in Secondary Education, Eau Claire, WI 54702-4004. Offers English (MST); professional development (MEPD), including library science, professional educator. Part-time and evening/weekend programs available. Postbaccalaureate distance learning degree programs offered. *Faculty:* 13 full-time (8 women). *Students:* 3 full-time (2 women), 9 part-time (5 women); includes 1 minority (African American). Average age 31. 8 applicants, 50% accepted, 3 enrolled. In 2009, 14 master's awarded. *Degree requirements:* For master's, thesis optional, oral exam, portfolio, written exam. *Entrance requirements:* For master's, certification to teach, minimum GPA of 2.75. Additional exam requirements/recommendations for international students: Required—TOEFL (minimum score 550 paper-based; 213 computer-based; 79 iBT). *Application deadline:* For fall admission, 7/1 priority date for domestic students, 6/1 priority date for international students; for spring admission, 12/1 priority date for domestic students, 11/1 priority date for international students. Applications are processed on a rolling basis. Application fee: $56. Electronic applications accepted. *Expenses:* Tuition, state resident: full-time $6705.90; part-time $372.55 per credit. Tuition, nonresident: full-time $16,771; part-time $931.74 per credit. Required fees: $925.50; $51.19 per credit. One-time fee: $56. *Financial support:* In 2009–10, 6 students received support, including 4 fellowships (averaging $3,125 per year); Federal Work-Study and unspecified assistantships also available. Financial award application deadline: 3/1; financial award applicants required to submit FAFSA. *Unit head:* Dr. Dwight Watson, Chair, 715-836-2013, Fax: 715-836-4868, E-mail: watsondc@uwec.edu. *Application contact:* Kristina Anderson, Director of Admissions, 715-836-5415, Fax: 715-836-2409, E-mail: admissions@uwec.edu.

University of Wisconsin–Madison, Graduate School, College of Letters and Science, Department of English, Madison, WI 53706-1380. Offers applied English linguistics (MA); composition and rhetoric (PhD); creative writing (MFA); English language and linguistics (PhD); literary studies (MA, PhD). *Degree requirements:* For doctorate, thesis/dissertation. *Expenses:* Tuition, state resident: part-time $594 per credit. Tuition, nonresident: part-time $1504 per credit. Required fees: $65 per credit. Tuition and fees vary according to course load, program and reciprocity agreements.

University of Wisconsin–Milwaukee, Graduate School, College of Letters and Sciences, Department of English, Milwaukee, WI 53201-0413. Offers creative writing (PhD); English (MA); international technical communication (Certificate); linguistics (PhD); professional writing (PhD); professional writing and communication (Certificate); rhetoric and composition (PhD); MLIS/MA. *Faculty:* 38 full-time (19 women). *Students:* 107 full-time (64 women), 82 part-time (54 women); includes 13 minority (8 African Americans, 1 American Indian/Alaska Native, 2 Asian Americans or Pacific Islanders, 2 Hispanic Americans), 23 international. Average age 34. 193 applicants, 51% accepted, 31 enrolled. In 2009, 26 master's, 16 doctorates awarded. *Degree requirements:* For master's, thesis or alternative; for doctorate, one foreign language, thesis/dissertation. *Entrance requirements:* For master's, GRE General Test, GRE Subject Test; for doctorate, GRE. Additional exam requirements/recommendations for international students: Required—TOEFL (minimum score 550 paper-based; 79 iBT), IELTS (minimum score 6.5). *Application deadline:* For fall admission, 1/1 priority date for domestic students; for spring admission, 9/1 for domestic students. Applications are processed on a rolling basis. Application fee: $45 ($75 for international students). *Expenses:* Tuition, state resident: full-time $8800. Tuition, nonresident: full-time $20,760. Tuition and fees vary according to program and reciprocity agreements. *Financial support:* In 2009–10, 75 teaching assistantships were awarded; career-related internships or fieldwork and unspecified assistantships also available. Support available to part-time students. Financial award application deadline: 4/15. Total annual research expenditures: $41,495. *Unit head:* Tasha Oren, Representative, 414-229-4637, Fax: 414-229-2643, E-mail: tgoren@uwm.edu. *Application contact:* General Information Contact, 414-229-4982, Fax: 414-229-6967, E-mail: gradschool@uwm.edu.

University of Wisconsin–Oshkosh, The Office of Graduate Studies, College of Letters and Science, Department of English, Oshkosh, WI 54901. Offers MA. Part-time programs available. *Degree requirements:* For master's, thesis or alternative. *Entrance requirements:* For master's, GRE. Additional exam requirements/recommendations for international students: Required—TOEFL (minimum score 550 paper-based; 213 computer-based; 79 iBT). Electronic applications accepted.

University of Wisconsin–Stevens Point, College of Letters and Science, Department of English, Stevens Point, WI 54481-3897. Offers MST. *Students:* 1 full-time (0 women), 6 part-time (4 women). *Degree requirements:* For master's, thesis or alternative. *Application deadline:* For fall admission, 5/1 priority date for domestic students. Applications are processed on a rolling basis. Application fee: $45. *Expenses:* Tuition, state resident: full-time $7740; part-time $430 per credit hour. Tuition, nonresident: full-time $17,804; part-time $989 per credit hour. Tuition and fees vary according to course load and reciprocity agreements. *Financial support:* Federal Work-Study and unspecified assistantships available. Financial award application deadline: 5/1; financial award applicants required to submit FAFSA. *Unit head:* Dr. Michael Williams, Chair, 715-346-4757, Fax: 715-346-4215. *Application contact:* Catherine Glennon, Director of Admissions, 715-346-2441, E-mail: admiss@uwsp.edu.

University of Wyoming, College of Arts and Sciences, Department of English, Laramie, WY 82070. Offers creative writing (MFA); English (MA). Part-time programs available. *Degree requirements:* For master's, thesis or alternative, internship. *Entrance requirements:* For master's, GRE General Test, minimum GPA of 3.0. Electronic applications accepted. *Faculty research:* Literature and theory, creative writing, English as a second language, ethnic and women's studies, composition.

Utah State University, School of Graduate Studies, College of Humanities, Arts and Social Sciences, Department of English, Logan, UT 84322. Offers American studies (MA, MS), including folklore, western American literature and culture; English (MA, MS), including literature and writing, technical writing. Part-time and evening/weekend programs available. *Degree requirements:* For master's, thesis or alternative. *Entrance requirements:* For master's, GRE General Test or MAT, minimum GPA of 3.0, recommendation letters, writing samples. Additional exam requirements/recommendations for international students: Required—TOEFL. *Faculty research:* Scottish enlightenment, material culture, composition theory, creative nonfiction, literary criticism.

Valdosta State University, Graduate School, Department of English, Valdosta, GA 31698. Offers MA. Part-time programs available. *Degree requirements:* For master's, one foreign language, thesis, comprehensive written and/or oral exams. *Entrance requirements:* For master's, GRE General Test, minimum GPA of 3.0. Additional exam requirements/recommendations for international students: Required—TOEFL (minimum score 523 paper-based; 193 computer-based). Electronic applications accepted. *Faculty research:* American literature.

Valparaiso University, Graduate School, Programs in Liberal Studies, Concentration in English, Valparaiso, IN 46383. Offers MALS, Post-Master's Certificate, JD/MALS. Part-time and evening/weekend programs available. *Students:* 4 full-time (3 women), 4 part-time (all women); includes 1 minority (African American), 2 international. Average age 34. In 2009, 6 master's awarded. *Entrance requirements:* For master's, minimum GPA of 3.0. Additional exam requirements/recommendations for international students: Required—TOEFL (minimum score 550 paper-based; 213 computer-based; 80 iBT). *Application deadline:* Applications are processed on a rolling basis. Application fee: $30 ($50 for international students). Electronic applications accepted. *Financial support:* Available to part-time students. Applicants required to submit FAFSA. *Unit head:* Dr. David L. Rowland, Dean, Graduate Studies and Continuing Education/Associate Provost, 219-464-5313, Fax: 219-464-5381, E-mail: david.rowland@valpo.edu. *Application contact:* Jamie Haney, Coordinator of Graduate Admission, 219-464-5313, Fax: 219-464-5381, E-mail: jamie.haney@valpo.edu.

Vanderbilt University, Graduate School, Department of English, Nashville, TN 37240-1001. Offers MA, MAT, PhD. *Faculty:* 43 full-time (25 women). *Students:* 36 full-time (25 women), 1 part-time (0 women); includes 10 minority (4 African Americans, 1 American Indian/Alaska Native, 3 Asian Americans or Pacific Islanders, 2 Hispanic Americans), 1 international. Average age 29. 420 applicants, 4% accepted, 8 enrolled. In 2009, 7 master's, 11 doctorates awarded. *Degree requirements:* For master's, thesis; for doctorate, one foreign language, comprehensive exam, thesis/dissertation, final and qualifying exams. *Entrance requirements:* For master's and doctorate, GRE General Test, sample of written work. Additional exam requirements/recommendations for international students: Required—TOEFL (minimum score 570 paper-based; 230 computer-based; 88 iBT). *Application deadline:* For fall admission, 1/15 for domestic and international students. Application fee: $0. Electronic applications accepted. *Financial support:* Fellowships with full and partial tuition reimbursements, research assistantships with full and partial tuition reimbursements, teaching assistantships with full tuition reimbursements, Federal Work-Study, institutionally sponsored loans, scholarships/grants, and health care benefits available. Financial award application deadline: 1/15; financial award applicants required to submit CSS PROFILE or FAFSA. *Faculty research:* British, American, and Anglophone literature, film, cultural studies, and literary theory. *Unit head:* Jay Clayton, Chair, 615-322-2542, Fax: 615-343-8028, E-mail: jay.clayton@vanderbilt.edu. *Application contact:* Kathryn Schwarz, Director of Graduate Studies, 615-322-2541, Fax: 615-343-8028, E-mail: kathryn.schwarz@vanderbilt.edu.

Villanova University, Graduate School of Liberal Arts and Sciences, Department of English, Villanova, PA 19085-1699. Offers MA. Part-time and evening/weekend programs available. *Faculty:* 7 full-time (5 women). *Students:* 26 full-time (15 women), 24 part-time (16 women); includes 4 minority (3 Asian Americans or Pacific Islanders, 1 Hispanic American). Average age 28. 37 applicants, 57% accepted, 8 enrolled. In 2009, 21 master's awarded. *Degree requirements:* For master's, comprehensive exam, thesis optional. *Entrance requirements:* For master's, GRE General Test, GRE Subject Test, minimum GPA of 3.0, writing sample. Additional exam requirements/recommendations for international students: Required—TOEFL. *Application deadline:* For fall admission, 3/1 priority date for domestic and international students; for spring admission, 11/15 priority date for domestic and international students. Applications are processed on a rolling basis. Application fee: $50. Electronic applications accepted. *Expenses:* Tuition: Part-time $630 per credit. Required fees: $60 per credit. Part-time tuition and fees vary according to degree level and program. *Financial support:* Research assistantships, Federal Work-Study, scholarships/grants, and unspecified assistantships available. Financial award applicants required to submit FAFSA. *Unit head:* Dr. Evan Radcliffe, Chairperson, 610-519-4630. *Application contact:* Dr. Adele Lindenmeyr, Dean, Graduate School of Liberal Arts and Sciences, 610-519-7093, Fax: 610-519-7096.

See Close-Up on page 421.

Virginia Commonwealth University, Graduate School, College of Humanities and Sciences, Department of English, Program in English, Richmond, VA 23284-9005. Offers literature (MA); writing and rhetoric (MA).

Virginia Polytechnic Institute and State University, Graduate School, College of Liberal Arts and Human Sciences, Department of English, Blacksburg, VA 24061. Offers creative writing (MFA); English (MA); rhetoric and writing (PhD). *Entrance requirements:* Additional exam requirements/recommendations for international students: Required—TOEFL. *Application deadline:* For fall admission, 5/15 for international students; for spring admission, 10/15 for international students. Applications are processed on a rolling basis. Application fee: $65. Electronic applications accepted. *Expenses:* Tuition, area resident: Full-time $10,228; part-time $459 per credit hour. Tuition, nonresident: full-time $17,892; part-time $865 per credit hour. Required fees: $1966; $451 per semester. *Financial support:* Teaching assistantships with full tuition reimbursements, career-related internships or fieldwork, Federal Work-Study, scholarships/grants, and unspecified assistantships available. *Faculty research:* Critical theory, feminist criticism, textual editing, literary histor. *Unit head:* Dr. Carolyn D. Rude, Dean, 540-231-5152, Fax: 540-231-5692, E-mail: carolynr@vt.edu. *Application contact:* Dr. Carolyn D. Rude, Dean, 540-231-5152, Fax: 540-231-5692, E-mail: carolynr@vt.edu.

Virginia State University, School of Graduate Studies, Research, and Outreach, School of Liberal Arts and Education, Department of Languages and Literature, Petersburg, VA 23806-0001. Offers English (MA). Part-time and evening/weekend programs available. *Degree requirements:* For master's, one foreign language, thesis (for some programs). *Entrance requirements:* For master's, GRE General Test. *Faculty research:* Writing and learning instruction, high-risk students, twentieth-century literature.

Wake Forest University, Graduate School of Arts and Sciences, Department of English, Winston-Salem, NC 27109. Offers MA. Part-time programs available. *Degree requirements:* For master's, one foreign language, thesis. *Entrance requirements:* For master's, GRE General Test, writing sample. Additional exam requirements/recommendations for international students: Required—TOEFL (minimum score 213 computer-based; 79 iBT). Electronic applications accepted. *Faculty research:* Modern and contemporary poetry, feminist criticism and theory, Irish literature, British Commonwealth literature, medieval poetry.

Washington College, Graduate Programs, Department of English, Chestertown, MD 21620-1197. Offers MA. Part-time and evening/weekend programs available.

Washington State University, Graduate School, College of Liberal Arts, Department of English, Pullman, WA 99164. Offers composition (MA); English (MA, PhD); teaching of English (MA). *Faculty:* 32. *Students:* 48 full-time (26 women), 5 part-time (4 women); includes 7 minority (4 African Americans, 3 American Indian/Alaska Native), 4 international. Average age 32. 105 applicants, 26% accepted, 10 enrolled. In 2009, 11 master's, 6 doctorates awarded. *Degree requirements:* For master's, one foreign language, comprehensive exam (for some programs), thesis (for some programs), oral exam; for doctorate, 2 foreign languages, comprehensive exam, thesis/dissertation, oral exam, written exam. *Entrance requirements:* For master's and doctorate, GRE General Test, GRE Subject Test, Requirements for admission include official transcripts; official GRE scores; TOEFL or IELTS (international students only); writing sample (approximately 10 pages); three letters of recommendation; statement of purpose (approximately 500 words); undergraduate major in English or other appropriate discipline. Additional exam requirements/recommendations for international students: Required—TOEFL, IELTS. *Application deadline:* For fall admission, 1/10 priority date for domestic students, 1/10 for international students. Applications are processed on a rolling basis. Application fee: $50. *Financial support:* In 2009–10, 48 students received support, including 1 fellowship (averaging $2,000 per year), 2 research assistantships with full and partial tuition reimbursements available (averaging $13,917 per year), 44 teaching assistantships with full and partial tuition reimbursements available (averaging $13,056 per year); career-related internships or fieldwork, Federal Work-Study, institutionally sponsored loans, scholarships/grants, health care benefits, and tuition waivers (partial) also available. Financial award application deadline: 2/10; financial award applicants required to submit FAFSA. *Faculty research:* Nationalism and gender in the American West, slavery and exploitation in nineteenth century Britain, photography and the color line, D. H. Lawrence and Mexico, social movement cultures and the arts. Total annual research expenditures: $5,000. *Unit head:* Dr. William Hamlin, Director, 509-335-7398, Fax: 509-335-2582, E-mail: whamlin@wsu.edu. *Application contact:* Graduate School Admissions, 800-GRADWSU, Fax: 509-335-1949, E-mail: gradsch@wsu.edu.

Washington State University, Graduate School, College of Liberal Arts, Program in American Studies, Pullman, WA 99164. Offers ethnic studies (MA, PhD); feminist studies (MA, PhD); history (MA, PhD); literature (MA, PhD). Part-time programs available. *Faculty:* 35. *Students:* 23 full-time (14 women), 4 part-time (2 women); includes 17 minority (5 African Americans, 4 American Indian/Alaska Native, 4 Asian Americans or Pacific Islanders, 4 Hispanic Americans), 2 international. Average age 35. 55 applicants, 7% accepted, 3 enrolled. In 2009, 1 master's, 3 doctorates awarded. *Degree requirements:* For master's, one foreign language, comprehensive exam (for some programs), thesis optional, oral exam; for doctorate, one foreign language, comprehensive exam (for some programs), thesis/dissertation, oral exam. *Entrance requirements:* For master's, GRE General Test, * Send to the Graduate School an official application form and official college transcripts sent directly from each institution attended. * Send to the American Studies program: A 3 to 5 page statement of purpose describing your areas of interest and why the program minimum GPA of 3.0, writing sample, 3 letters of recommendation; for doctorate, GRE General Test, * Send to the Graduate School an official application form and official college transcripts sent directly from each institution attended. * Send to the American Studies program: A 3 to 5 page statement of purpose describing your areas of interest and why the program minimum GPA of 3.0, writing sample, 3 letters of recommendation. Additional exam requirements/recommendations for international students: Required—TOEFL, IELTS. *Application deadline:* For fall admission, 1/10 priority date for

English

Washington State University (continued)
domestic and international students; for spring admission, 7/1 priority date for domestic and international students. Applications are processed on a rolling basis. Application fee: $50. *Financial support:* In 2009–10, 1 fellowship (averaging $6,950 per year), 3 research assistantships with full and partial tuition reimbursements (averaging $14,634 per year), 17 teaching assistantships with full and partial tuition reimbursements (averaging $13,383 per year) were awarded; career-related internships or fieldwork, Federal Work-Study, institutionally sponsored loans, health care benefits, tuition waivers (partial), and teaching associateships also available. Financial award application deadline: 2/15; financial award applicants required to submit FAFSA. *Faculty research:* The American West in multicultural perspective; nineteenth century historical, literary, and cultural studies; comparative American ethnic literatures and cultures; American cultures and the environment; American rhetoric. *Unit head:* Dr. Rory J. Ong, Director, 509-335-1560, E-mail: rjong@mail.wsu.edu. *Application contact:* Graduate School Admissions, 800-GRADWSU, Fax: 509-335-1949, E-mail: gradsch@wsu.edu.

Washington University in St. Louis, Graduate School of Arts and Sciences, Department of English and American Literature, St. Louis, MO 63130-4899. Offers English and American literature (MA, PhD); writing (MFAW). Terminal master's awarded for partial completion of doctoral program. *Degree requirements:* For master's, thesis or written exam; for doctorate, 2 foreign languages, thesis/dissertation. *Entrance requirements:* For master's and doctorate, GRE General Test, sample of written work. Electronic applications accepted.

Wayne State University, College of Liberal Arts and Sciences, Department of English, Detroit, MI 48202. Offers comparative literature (MA); English (MA, PhD). *Degree requirements:* For master's, one foreign language, essay or thesis; for doctorate, one foreign language, thesis/dissertation. *Entrance requirements:* For master's, GRE General Test, minimum GPA of 3.25 in English, 3.0 overall; references; for doctorate, GRE General Test, GRE Subject Test, statement of purpose, references, sample essay. Additional exam requirements/recommendations for international students: Required—TOEFL (minimum score 550 paper-based; 213 computer-based); Recommended—TWE (minimum score 6). Electronic applications accepted. *Faculty research:* English and American literature, cultural studies, composition, linguistics, film.

Weber State University, College of Arts and Humanities, Program in English, Ogden, UT 84408-1001. Offers MENG. Part-time and evening/weekend programs available. *Degree requirements:* For master's, one foreign language, additional course hours, thesis or research project. *Entrance requirements:* For master's, MAT or GRE, 3 letters of recommendation. *Faculty research:* Victoria literature, Middle East women writers, Irish literature (Seamus Heanes).

West Chester University of Pennsylvania, Office of Graduate Studies, College of Arts and Sciences, Department of English, West Chester, PA 19383. Offers English (MA, Teaching Certificate); TESL (MA, Certificate). Part-time and evening/weekend programs available. *Students:* 15 full-time (8 women), 104 part-time (75 women); includes 16 minority (6 African Americans, 10 Asian Americans or Pacific Islanders), 3 international. Average age 31. 91 applicants, 98% accepted, 54 enrolled. In 2009, 32 master's, 2 other advanced degrees awarded. *Degree requirements:* For master's, thesis optional. *Entrance requirements:* For master's, minimum GPA of 2.8, 3 letters of recommendation, writing sample, interview, 1 foreign language (TESL programs); for other advanced degree, goals statement; one foreign language (for TESL programs). Additional exam requirements/recommendations for international students: Required—TOEFL (minimum score 550 paper-based; 213 computer-based; 80 iBT). *Application deadline:* For fall admission, 4/15 priority date for domestic students, 3/15 for international students; for spring admission, 10/15 for domestic students, 9/1 for international students. Applications are processed on a rolling basis. Application fee: $35. Electronic applications accepted. *Expenses:* Tuition, state resident: full-time $6666; part-time $370 per credit. Tuition, nonresident: full-time $10,666; part-time $593 per credit. Required fees: $122.56 per credit. *Financial support:* In 2009–10, 12 research assistantships with full and partial tuition reimbursements (averaging $5,000 per year) were awarded; unspecified assistantships also available. Support available to part-time students. Financial award application deadline: 2/15; financial award applicants required to submit FAFSA. *Faculty research:* William Smith, Sara Winnemucca Hopkins, literacy practices for students at risk. *Unit head:* Dr. Anne Herzog, Chair, 610-436-2822, E-mail: aherzog@wcupa.edu. *Application contact:* Dr. Carolyn Sorisio, Graduate Coordinator, 610-436-2745, E-mail: kfitts@wcupa.edu.

Western Carolina University, Graduate School, College of Arts and Sciences, Department of English, Cullowhee, NC 28723. Offers English (MA); teaching English as a second language or foreign language (MA). Part-time and evening/weekend programs available. *Students:* 24 full-time (15 women), 14 part-time (12 women). Average age 30. 25 applicants, 88% accepted, 14 enrolled. In 2009, 7 master's awarded. *Degree requirements:* For master's, one foreign language, comprehensive exam, thesis (for some programs). *Entrance requirements:* For master's, GRE General Test, appropriate undergraduate degree, writing sample, 3 letters of recommendation. Additional exam requirements/recommendations for international students: Required—TOEFL (minimum score 550 paper-based; 270 computer-based; 79 iBT). *Application deadline:* For fall admission, 5/1 priority date for domestic students; for spring admission, 9/1 priority date for domestic students. Applications are processed on a rolling basis. Application fee: $45. *Financial support:* In 2009–10, 13 students received support, including 7 research assistantships with full and partial tuition reimbursements available (averaging $7,429 per year), 5 teaching assistantships with full and partial tuition reimbursements available (averaging $7,500 per year); fellowships with full and partial tuition reimbursements available, career-related internships or fieldwork, institutionally sponsored loans, scholarships/grants, and unspecified assistantships also available. Financial award application deadline: 3/31; financial award applicants required to submit FAFSA. *Faculty research:* TESOL, language assessment, applied linguistics, poetry, folk and fairy tales, post World War II British literature, Appalachian and southern literature. *Unit head:* Dr. Elizabeth Addison, Head, 828-227-7264, Fax: 828-227-7266, E-mail: addisson@email.wcu.edu. *Application contact:* Admission Specialist for Department of English, 828-227-7398, Fax: 828-227-7480, E-mail: gradsch@email.wcu.edu.

Western Connecticut State University, Division of Graduate Studies, School of Arts and Sciences, Department of English, Danbury, CT 06810-6885. Offers English (MA); literature option (MA); TESOL option (MA); writing option (MA). Part-time programs available. *Faculty:* 4 full-time (3 women), 1 part-time/adjunct (0 women). *Students:* 3 full-time (2 women), 33 part-time (24 women); includes 5 minority (2 African Americans, 3 Hispanic Americans). Average age 40. 15 applicants, 73% accepted, 7 enrolled. In 2009, 6 master's awarded. *Degree requirements:* For master's, thesis (writing option), completion of program in 6 years. *Entrance requirements:* For master's, minimum GPA of 2.5, writing sample. Additional exam requirements/recommendations for international students: Recommended—TOEFL (minimum score 550 paper-based; 213 computer-based; 79 iBT), IELTS (minimum score 6). *Application deadline:* For fall admission, 8/5 priority date for domestic students; for spring admission, 1/5 priority date for domestic students. Applications are processed on a rolling basis. Application fee: $50. *Expenses:* Tuition, state resident: full-time $5012; part-time $278 per credit hour. Tuition, nonresident: full-time $13,962; part-time $284 per credit hour. Required fees: $3886; $139 per credit hour. Full-time tuition and fees vary according to course load and program. Part-time tuition and fees vary according to course level, degree level and program. *Financial support:* Application deadline: 5/1. *Unit head:* Dr. Shouhua Qi, Co-Coordinator, 203-837-9048, Fax: 203-837-8525, E-mail: qis@wcsu.edu. *Application contact:* Chris Shankle, Associate Director of Graduate Studies, 203-837-9005, Fax: 203-837-8326, E-mail: shanklec@wcsu.edu.

Western Illinois University, School of Graduate Studies, College of Arts and Sciences, Department of English and Journalism, Macomb, IL 61455-1390. Offers English (MA, Certificate). Part-time programs available. *Students:* 13 full-time (7 women), 23 part-time (16 women); includes 2 minority (1 African American, 1 Hispanic American), 1 international. Average age 30. 15 applicants, 60% accepted. In 2009, 10 master's awarded. *Degree requirements:* For master's, thesis or alternative. *Entrance requirements:* Additional exam requirements/recommendations for international students: Required—TOEFL (minimum score 575 paper-based; 230 computer-based; 88 iBT). *Application deadline:* Applications are processed on a rolling basis. Application fee: $30. Electronic applications accepted. *Expenses:* Tuition, state resident: full-time $4486; part-time $249.21 per credit hour. Tuition, nonresident: full-time $8972; part-time $498.42 per credit hour. Required fees: $72.62 per credit hour. *Financial support:* In 2009–10, 17 students received support, including 9 research assistantships with full tuition reimbursements available (averaging $7,280 per year), 8 teaching assistantships with full tuition reimbursements available (averaging $8,400 per year). Financial award applicants required to submit FAFSA. *Unit head:* Dr. Mohammad Siddiqi, Chairperson, 309-298-1103. *Application contact:* Evelyn Hoing, Assistant Director of Graduate Studies, 309-298-1806, Fax: 309-298-2345, E-mail: grad-office@wiu.edu.

Western Kentucky University, Graduate Studies, Potter College of Arts and Letters, Department of English, Bowling Green, KY 42101. Offers education (MA); English (MA Ed); literature (MA), including American literature, British literature, literary theory, women writers, world literature; teaching English as a second language (MA); writing (MA). Part-time and evening/weekend programs available. *Degree requirements:* For master's, comprehensive exam, thesis optional, final exam. *Entrance requirements:* For master's, GRE General Test, minimum GPA of 2.75. Additional exam requirements/recommendations for international students: Required—TOEFL (minimum score 555 paper-based; 213 computer-based; 79 iBT). *Expenses:* Tuition, state resident: full-time $4160; part-time $416 per credit hour. Tuition, nonresident: full-time $9550; part-time $506 per credit hour. Tuition and fees vary according to campus/location and reciprocity agreements. *Faculty research:* Improving writing, linking teacher knowledge and performance, Victorian women writers, Kentucky women writers, Kentucky poets.

Western Michigan University, Graduate College, College of Arts and Sciences, Department of English, Kalamazoo, MI 49008. Offers creative writing (MFA, PhD); English (MA, PhD); English education (MA, PhD). *Degree requirements:* For master's, oral exams; for doctorate, one foreign language, thesis/dissertation, oral exam, written exams. *Entrance requirements:* For master's and doctorate, GRE General Test, GRE Subject Test.

Western Washington University, Graduate School, College of Humanities and Social Sciences, Department of English, Bellingham, WA 98225-5996. Offers MA. Part-time programs available. *Degree requirements:* For master's, one foreign language, comprehensive exam, thesis (for some programs). *Entrance requirements:* For master's, GRE General Test, writing sample, minimum GPA of 3.0 in last 60 semester hours or last 90 quarter hours of course work. Additional exam requirements/recommendations for international students: Required—TOEFL (minimum score 567 paper-based; 227 computer-based). Electronic applications accepted. *Faculty research:* Literature and technology, film, composition and rhetoric, technical writing, critical and cultural theory.

Westfield State College, Division of Graduate and Continuing Education, Department of English, Westfield, MA 01086. Offers MA. Part-time and evening/weekend programs available. *Degree requirements:* For master's, one foreign language, thesis. *Entrance requirements:* For master's, GRE General Test, MAT, minimum undergraduate GPA of 2.7, undergraduate course work in English.

West Texas A&M University, College of Fine Arts and Humanities, Department of English and Modern Languages, Canyon, TX 79016-0001. Offers English (MA). Part-time and evening/weekend programs available. *Degree requirements:* For master's, comprehensive exam, thesis optional. *Entrance requirements:* For master's, GRE General Test. Additional exam requirements/recommendations for international students: Required—TOEFL (minimum score 550 paper-based). Electronic applications accepted. *Faculty research:* Medieval studies, composition theory, literary criticism, Evelyn Scott, transformation of literacy in computer mediated communication.

West Virginia University, Eberly College of Arts and Sciences, Department of English, Morgantown, WV 26506. Offers creative writing (MFA); English (MA, PhD); literary/cultural studies (MA, PhD); writing (MA). Part-time and evening/weekend programs available. *Degree requirements:* For master's, one foreign language, thesis optional; for doctorate, one foreign language, thesis/dissertation, preliminary exam. *Entrance requirements:* For master's, GRE General Test, minimum GPA of 3.0; for doctorate, GRE General Test, GRE Subject Test, minimum GPA of 3.0. Additional exam requirements/recommendations for international students: Required—TOEFL. Electronic applications accepted. *Faculty research:* American studies, gender studies, media studies, cultural studies.

Wichita State University, Graduate School, Fairmount College of Liberal Arts and Sciences, Department of English, Wichita, KS 67260. Offers creative writing (MFA); English (MA). Part-time and evening/weekend programs available. *Entrance requirements:* For master's, writing sample (MFA). *Expenses:* Tuition, state resident: full-time $4247; part-time $235.95 per credit hour. Tuition, nonresident: full-time $11,171; part-time $620.60 per credit hour. Required fees: $34; $3.60 per credit hour. $17 per term. Tuition and fees vary according to campus/location and program. *Unit head:* Dr. Donald Wineke, Chair, 316-978-3130, Fax: 316-978-3548, E-mail: donald.wineke@wichita.edu. *Application contact:* Dr. Donald Wineke, Chair, 316-978-3130, Fax: 316-978-3548, E-mail: donald.wineke@wichita.edu.

Wilfrid Laurier University, Faculty of Graduate Studies, Faculty of Arts, Department of English and Film Studies, Waterloo, ON N2L 3C5, Canada. Offers MA, PhD. *Degree requirements:* For master's, thesis optional; for doctorate, thesis/dissertation. *Entrance requirements:* For master's, honours BA or the equivalent in English, minimum B+ in English courses above first year level; for doctorate, MA in English, minimum A- average in graduate work. Additional exam requirements/recommendations for international students: Recommended—TOEFL (minimum score 230 computer-based; 89 iBT). Electronic applications accepted. *Faculty research:* Gender and genre, Canadian studies, early modern studies, postcolonial studies, nineteenth century studies.

William Paterson University of New Jersey, College of the Humanities and Social Sciences, Wayne, NJ 07470-8420. Offers clinical and counseling psychology (MA); English (MA); history (MA); public policy and international affairs (MA); sociology (MA). Part-time and evening/weekend programs available. *Students:* 39 full-time (22 women), 123 part-time (90 women); includes 42 minority (11 African Americans, 5 Asian Americans or Pacific Islanders, 26 Hispanic Americans), 2 international. *Application deadline:* Applications are processed on a rolling basis. Application fee: $50. Electronic applications accepted. *Financial support:* In 2009–10, 13 students received support; research assistantships with full tuition reimbursements available, teaching assistantships with full tuition reimbursements available, unspecified assistantships available. Support available to part-time students. Financial award application deadline: 4/1; financial award applicants required to submit FAFSA. *Unit head:* Dr. Kara Rabbitt, Dean, College of Humanities and Social Sciences, 973-720-2180, Fax: 973-720-2955, E-mail: rabbittk@wpunj.edu. *Application contact:* Tinu Adeniran, Assistant Director, Graduate Admissions, 973-720-2764, Fax: 973-720-2035, E-mail: adenirant@wpunj.edu.

Winona State University, College of Liberal Arts, Department of English, Winona, MN 55987-5838. Offers MA, MS. Part-time programs available. *Degree requirements:* For master's, thesis or alternative.

Winthrop University, College of Arts and Sciences, Department of English, Rock Hill, SC 29733. Offers MA. Part-time and evening/weekend programs available. *Degree requirements:* For master's, one foreign language, thesis optional. *Entrance requirements:* For master's, GRE General Test, MAT or PRAXIS, 24 undergraduate hours of course work in English. Electronic applications accepted.

Wright State University, School of Graduate Studies, College of Liberal Arts, Department of English Language and Literatures, Dayton, OH 45435. Offers composition and rhetoric (MA); English (MA); literature (MA); teaching English to speakers of other languages (MA). *Degree* *requirements:* For master's, thesis optional, portfolio. *Entrance requirements:* For master's, 20 hours in upper-level English. Additional exam requirements/recommendations for international students: Required—TOEFL. *Faculty research:* American literature, world literature in English, applied linguistics, writing theory and pedagogy.

Xavier University, College of Arts and Sciences, Department of English, Cincinnati, OH 45207. Offers MA. Part-time and evening/weekend programs available. *Faculty:* 5 full-time (2 women). *Students:* 2 full-time (both women), 17 part-time (16 women), 1 international. Average age 31. 19 applicants, 53% accepted, 5 enrolled. In 2009, 6 master's awarded. *Degree requirements:* For master's, one foreign language, comprehensive exam, thesis optional. *Entrance requirements:* For master's, GRE, 2 letters of recommendation, writing sample, minimum GPA of 3.2. Additional exam requirements/recommendations for international students: Required—TOEFL (minimum score 550 paper-based; 213 computer-based; 79 iBT). *Application deadline:* Applications are processed on a rolling basis. Application fee: $35. Electronic applications accepted. *Expenses:* Tuition: Part-time $697 per credit hour. One-time fee: $35 part-time. *Financial support:* In 2009–10, 3 students received support. Tuition waivers (partial) and unspecified assistantships available. Financial award applicants required to submit FAFSA. *Faculty research:* British literature, American literature, linguistics, literary theory, composition studies. *Unit head:* Dr. Stephen Yandell, Chair, 513-745-3598, Fax: 513-745-3065, E-mail: yandell@xavier.edu. *Application contact:* Dr. Stephen Yandell, Chair, 513-745-3598, Fax: 513-745-3065, E-mail: yandell@xavier.edu.

Yale University, Graduate School of Arts and Sciences, Department of English Language and Literature, New Haven, CT 06520. Offers MA, PhD. Terminal master's awarded for partial completion of doctoral program. *Degree requirements:* For master's, 2 foreign languages; for doctorate, 3 foreign languages, thesis/dissertation. *Entrance requirements:* For master's and doctorate, GRE General Test, GRE Subject Test.

York University, Faculty of Graduate Studies, Faculty of Arts, Program in English, Toronto, ON M3J 1P3, Canada. Offers MA, PhD. Part-time programs available. *Degree requirements:* For master's, thesis or alternative; for doctorate, one foreign language, comprehensive exam, thesis/dissertation. Electronic applications accepted.

Youngstown State University, Graduate School, College of Liberal Arts and Social Sciences, Department of English, Youngstown, OH 44555-0001. Offers MA. Part-time programs available. *Degree requirements:* For master's, portfolio. *Entrance requirements:* For master's, bachelor's degree in English, minimum GPA of 2.7. Additional exam requirements/recommendations for international students: Required—TOEFL. *Faculty research:* Technical communications, multicultural literacy, children's literature, women's literature, film study, linguistics.

French

American University, College of Arts and Sciences, Department of Language and Foreign Studies, Program in French, Washington, DC 20016-8045. Offers translation (Certificate). Part-time and evening/weekend programs available. *Students:* 2 full-time (both women), 1 (woman) part-time; includes 1 minority (African American), 1 international. Average age 29. In 2009, 1 Certificate awarded. *Entrance requirements:* For degree, bachelor's degree in French or evidence of French proficiency plus BA in any field. Additional exam requirements/recommendations for international students: Required—TOEFL. *Application deadline:* For fall admission, 2/1 for domestic students; for spring admission, 10/1 for domestic students. Application fee: $50. *Expenses:* Tuition: Full-time $22,266; part-time $1237 per credit hour. Required fees: $430. Tuition and fees vary according to program. *Financial support:* Fellowships, career-related internships or fieldwork, Federal Work-Study, and institutionally sponsored loans available. Financial award application deadline: 2/1. *Faculty research:* Literature, language, modern French politics, contemporary French society, the civilization of Quebec, business French and translation studies.

Arizona State University, Graduate College, College of Liberal Arts and Sciences, Division of Humanities, School of International Letters and Cultures, Program in French, Tempe, AZ 85287. Offers MA. *Degree requirements:* For master's, thesis or alternative. *Entrance requirements:* For master's, GRE.

Asbury University, School of Graduate and Professional Studies, Wilmore, KY 40390-1198. Offers biology: alternative certificate (MA Ed); chemistry: alternative certificate (MA Ed); English (MA Ed); English as a second language (MA Ed); ESL (MA Ed); French (MA Ed); Latin: alternative certificate (MA Ed); mathematics: alternative certificate (MA Ed); reading/writing endorsement (MA Ed); social studies (MA Ed); social work (MSW), including child and family services; Spanish (MA Ed); special education (MA Ed); special education: alternative certificate (MA Ed); teacher as leader endorsement (MA Ed). *Accreditation:* NCATE. Part-time programs available. *Faculty:* 8 full-time (7 women), 9 part-time/adjunct (4 women). *Students:* 108 part-time (87 women); includes 8 minority (4 African Americans, 2 Asian Americans or Pacific Islanders, 2 Hispanic Americans). Average age 36. 36 applicants, 86% accepted, 24 enrolled. In 2009, 20 master's awarded. *Degree requirements:* For master's, action research project, portfolio. *Entrance requirements:* For master's, PRAXIS/NTE, minimum GPA of 2.75, letters of recommendation. Additional exam requirements/recommendations for international students: Required—TOEFL (minimum score 550 paper-based). *Application deadline:* Applications are processed on a rolling basis. Application fee: $25. Electronic applications accepted. *Financial support:* Scholarships/grants and traineeships available. Financial award applicants required to submit FAFSA. *Unit head:* Dr. Bonnie J. Banker, Dean, School of Graduate and Professional Studies, 859-858-3511 Ext. 2221, Fax: 859-858-3921, E-mail: bonnie.banker@asbury.edu. *Application contact:* Lenore A. Sweigard, Graduate Program Assistant and Certification Specialist, 859-858-3511 Ext. 2502, Fax: 859-858-3921, E-mail: graded@asbury.edu.

Bennington College, Graduate Programs, MA in Teaching a Second Language Program, Bennington, VT 05201. Offers education (MATSL); foreign language education (MATSL); French (MATSL); Spanish (MATSL). Part-time programs available. *Faculty:* 1 full-time (0 women), 3 part-time/adjunct (2 women). *Students:* 16 part-time (14 women); includes 3 minority (1 African American, 2 Hispanic Americans). Average age 37. 16 applicants, 63% accepted, 9 enrolled. In 2009, 6 master's awarded. *Degree requirements:* For master's, one foreign language, 2 major projects and presentations. *Entrance requirements:* For master's, Oral Proficiency Interview (OPI). Additional exam requirements/recommendations for international students: Required—TOEFL (minimum score 577 paper-based; 233 computer-based; 91 iBT). *Application deadline:* For spring admission, 4/1 priority date for domestic and international students. Applications are processed on a rolling basis. Application fee: $60. *Expenses:* Contact institution. *Financial support:* In 2009–10, 1 student received support. Scholarships/grants available. Financial award application deadline: 4/1; financial award applicants required to submit FAFSA. *Faculty research:* Acquisition, evaluation, assessment, conceptual teaching and learning content-driven communication, applied linguistics. *Unit head:* Carol Meyer, Director, 802-440-4375, E-mail: cmeyer@bennington.edu. *Application contact:* Nancy Pearlman, Assistant Director, 802-440-4710, E-mail: matsl@bennington.edu.

Boston College, Graduate School of Arts and Sciences, Department of Romance Languages and Literatures, Chestnut Hill, MA 02467-3800. Offers French (MA, PhD); Italian (MA); medieval language (PhD); Spanish (MA, PhD). Part-time programs available. *Students:* 43 full-time (39 women), 4 part-time (3 women); includes 5 minority (2 Asian Americans or Pacific Islanders, 3 Hispanic Americans), 9 international. 65 applicants, 35% accepted, 11 enrolled. In 2009, 2 master's, 9 doctorates awarded. Terminal master's awarded for partial completion of doctoral program. *Degree requirements:* For master's, one foreign language; for doctorate, 2 foreign languages, thesis/dissertation. *Entrance requirements:* Additional exam requirements/recommendations for international students: Required—TOEFL (minimum score 600 paper-based; 250 computer-based; 100 iBT). *Application deadline:* For fall admission, 1/2 for domestic and international students. Application fee: $75. Electronic applications accepted. *Financial support:* In 2009–10, fellowships with full tuition reimbursements (averaging $16,000 per year), teaching assistantships with full tuition reimbursements (averaging $16,300 per year) were awarded; Federal Work-Study and unspecified assistantships also available. Support available to part-time students. Financial award application deadline: 3/1; financial award applicants required to submit FAFSA. *Faculty research:* Spanish-American literature, philology, medieval French romance and troubadour/trouvere lyrics, Golden Age Peninsular literature, secondary language acquisition and pedagogy. *Unit head:* Dr. Dwayne Carpenter, Chairperson, 617-552-3828, E-mail: dwayne.carpenter@bc.edu. *Application contact:* Dr. Dwayne Carpenter, Chairperson, 617-552-3828, E-mail: dwayne.carpenter@bc.edu.

Boston University, Graduate School of Arts and Sciences, Department of Romance Studies, Boston, MA 02215. Offers French language and literature (MA, PhD); Hispanic language and literatures (MA, PhD). *Students:* 45 full-time (37 women), 5 part-time (3 women); includes 4 minority (all Hispanic Americans), 15 international. Average age 31. 50 applicants, 58% accepted, 12 enrolled. In 2009, 2 master's, 4 doctorates awarded. Terminal master's awarded for partial completion of doctoral program. *Degree requirements:* For master's, one foreign language, comprehensive exam; for doctorate, 2 foreign languages, comprehensive exam, thesis/dissertation. *Entrance requirements:* For master's and doctorate, GRE General Test, sample of written work, 3 letters of recommendation. Additional exam requirements/recommendations for international students: Required—TOEFL (minimum score 550 paper-based; 213 computer-based). *Application deadline:* For fall admission, 4/15 for domestic and international students; for spring admission, 10/15 for domestic and international students. Application fee: $70. Electronic applications accepted. *Expenses:* Tuition: Full-time $37,910; part-time $1184 per credit hour. Required fees: $386; $40 per semester. Part-time tuition and fees vary according to class time, course level, degree level and program. *Financial support:* In 2009–10, 48 students received support, including 2 fellowships with full tuition reimbursements available (averaging $18,900 per year), 35 teaching assistantships with full tuition reimbursements available (averaging $18,400 per year); research assistantships, Federal Work-Study and scholarships/grants also available. Support available to part-time students. Financial award application deadline: 1/15; financial award applicants required to submit FAFSA. *Unit head:* James Iffland, Chairman, 617-353-6225, Fax: 617-353-6246, E-mail: Iffland@bu.edu. *Application contact:* Sharo Gineo, Administrative Assistant, 617-353-2641, Fax: 617-353-6246, E-mail: sdow@bu.edu.

Bowling Green State University, Graduate College, College of Arts and Sciences, Department of Romance and Classical Studies, Program in French, Bowling Green, OH 43403. Offers French (MA); French education (MAT). Part-time programs available. *Degree requirements:* For master's, one foreign language, thesis or alternative. *Entrance requirements:* For master's, GRE General Test. Additional exam requirements/recommendations for international students: Required—TOEFL. Electronic applications accepted. *Faculty research:* Francophone literature, French cinema, business French, nineteenth and twentieth century literature.

Brigham Young University, Graduate Studies, College of Humanities, Department of French and Italian, Provo, UT 84602. Offers French studies (MA). *Faculty:* 11 full-time (1 woman). *Students:* 3 full-time (2 women), 6 part-time (4 women); includes 1 minority (Hispanic American). Average age 28. 3 applicants, 67% accepted, 2 enrolled. In 2009, 5 master's awarded. *Degree requirements:* For master's, one foreign language, thesis. *Entrance requirements:* For master's, GRE General Test, BA in French. Additional exam requirements/recommendations for international students: Required—TOEFL. *Application deadline:* For fall admission, 2/28 for domestic and international students. Application fee: $50. Electronic applications accepted. *Expenses:* Tuition: Full-time $5580; part-time $301 per credit hour. Tuition and fees vary according to student's religious affiliation. *Financial support:* In 2009–10, 9 students received support, including 2 teaching assistantships (averaging $8,480 per year); research assistantships, career-related internships or fieldwork, institutionally sponsored loans, scholarships/grants, and tuition waivers (full and partial) also available. Support available to part-time students. *Faculty research:* Francophone studies, medieval literature, Provençal literature, existentialism, second language acquisition. *Unit head:* Dr. Corry L. Cropper, Department Chair, 801-422-4484, Fax: 801-422-0260, E-mail: corrycropper@gmail.com. *Application contact:* Dr. Anca M. Sprenger, Graduate Coordinator, 801-422-2306, Fax: 801-422-0260, E-mail: anca_sprenger@byu.edu.

Brooklyn College of the City University of New York, Division of Graduate Studies, Department of Modern Languages and Literature, Brooklyn, NY 11210-2889. Offers French (MA); modern languages and literature (PhD); Spanish (MA). *Students:* 24 part-time (16 women); includes 16 minority (8 African Americans, 8 Hispanic Americans), 5 international. Average age 41. 10 applicants, 80% accepted, 6 enrolled. In 2009, 13 master's awarded. *Degree requirements:* For master's, comprehensive exam or research paper. *Entrance requirements:* For master's, 18 credits in advanced courses in Spanish, 2 letters of recommendation. Additional exam requirements/recommendations for international students: Required—TOEFL (minimum score 500 paper-based; 173 computer-based; 61 iBT). *Application deadline:* For fall admission, 8/14 for domestic students, 6/14 priority date for international students; for spring admission, 1/15 for domestic students, 12/15 priority date for international students. Applications are processed on a rolling basis. Application fee: $125. Electronic applications accepted. *Expenses:* Tuition, area resident: Full-time $7360; part-time $310 per credit hour. Tuition, state resident: full-time $7360; part-time $310 per credit hour. Tuition, nonresident: full-time $13,800; part-time $575 per credit hour. International tuition: $13,800 full-time. Required fees: $140.10 per semester. *Financial support:* Federal Work-Study, institutionally sponsored loans, and scholarships/grants available. Support available to part-time students. Financial award application deadline: 5/1; financial award applicants required to submit FAFSA. *Faculty research:* Latin American contemporary novel, Caribbean female contemporary literature, nineteenth and twentieth century Spanish novel, twentieth century Mexican poetry. *Unit head:* Dr. Luigi Bonafinni, Chairperson, 718-951-5451, E-mail: luigi@brooklyn.cuny.edu. *Application contact:* Hernan Sierra, Graduate Admissions Coordinator, 718-951-4536, Fax: 718-951-4506, E-mail: grads@brooklyn.cuny.edu.

Brown University, Graduate School, Department of French Studies, Providence, RI 02912. Offers PhD, MA/PhD. *Degree requirements:* For doctorate, variable foreign language requirement, thesis/dissertation, preliminary exam.

Bryn Mawr College, Graduate School of Arts and Sciences, Department of French, Bryn Mawr, PA 19010-2899. Offers MA, PhD. Part-time programs available. *Degree requirements:* For master's, one foreign language, thesis. *Entrance requirements:* For master's, GRE General Test. Additional exam requirements/recommendations for international students: Required—TOEFL (minimum score 600 paper-based; 250 computer-based). *Expenses:* Tuition: Full-time $31,340. Required fees: $430.

French

California State University, Fullerton, Graduate Studies, College of Humanities and Social Sciences, Department of Modern Languages and Literatures, Fullerton, CA 92834-9480. Offers French (MA); German (MA); Spanish (MA); teaching English to speakers of other languages (MS). Part-time programs available. *Students:* 40 full-time (30 women), 63 part-time (47 women); includes 49 minority (1 African American, 14 Asian Americans or Pacific Islanders, 34 Hispanic Americans), 20 international. Average age 33. 101 applicants, 52% accepted, 29 enrolled. In 2009, 37 master's awarded. *Degree requirements:* For master's, comprehensive exam, thesis or alternative. *Entrance requirements:* For master's, minimum GPA of 2.5 in last 60 hours of course work, undergraduate major in a language. Application fee: $55. *Expenses:* Tuition, nonresident: full-time $11,160; part-time $373 per credit. Required fees: $1440 per term. Tuition and fees vary according to course load, degree level and program. *Financial support:* Career-related internships or fieldwork, Federal Work-Study, institutionally sponsored loans, and scholarships/grants available. Support available to part-time students. Financial award application deadline: 3/1; financial award applicants required to submit FAFSA. *Unit head:* Dr. Janet Eyring, Chair, 657-278-3534. *Application contact:* Admissions/Applications, 657-278-2371.

California State University, Long Beach, Graduate Studies, College of Liberal Arts, Department of Romance, German, and Russian Languages and Literature, Program in French and Francophone Studies, Long Beach, CA 90840. Offers MA. Part-time programs available. *Students:* 7 full-time (4 women), 9 part-time (8 women); includes 4 minority (3 Asian Americans or Pacific Islanders, 1 Hispanic American). Average age 35. 9 applicants, 67% accepted, 4 enrolled. *Degree requirements:* For master's, one foreign language, comprehensive exam, thesis optional. *Entrance requirements:* For master's, BA in French. *Application deadline:* For fall admission, 7/1 for domestic students. Applications are processed on a rolling basis. Application fee: $55. Electronic applications accepted. *Expenses:* Required fees: $1802 per semester. Part-time tuition and fees vary according to course load. *Financial support:* Federal Work-Study, institutionally sponsored loans, and scholarships/grants available. Financial award application deadline: 3/2. *Faculty research:* Eighteenth century encyclopedism, development of the novel, Chanson de Roland. *Unit head:* Dr. Clorinda Donato, Graduate Advisor, 562-985-4318, Fax: 562-985-4259, E-mail: cdonato@csulb.edu. *Application contact:* Dr. Clorinda Donato, Graduate Advisor, 562-985-4318, Fax: 562-985-4259, E-mail: cdonato@csulb.edu.

California State University, Los Angeles, Graduate Studies, College of Arts and Letters, Department of Modern Languages and Literatures, Los Angeles, CA 90032-8530. Offers French (MA); Spanish (MA). Part-time and evening/weekend programs available. *Faculty:* 4 full-time (3 women), 3 part-time/adjunct (2 women). *Students:* 19 full-time (10 women), 36 part-time (30 women); includes 38 minority (2 Asian Americans or Pacific Islanders, 36 Hispanic Americans), 4 international. Average age 39. 12 applicants, 100% accepted, 4 enrolled. In 2009, 5 master's awarded. *Degree requirements:* For master's, comprehensive exam. *Entrance requirements:* Additional exam requirements/recommendations for international students: Required—TOEFL (minimum score 500 paper-based; 173 computer-based). *Application deadline:* For fall admission, 5/1 for domestic and international students. Applications are processed on a rolling basis. Application fee: $55. Electronic applications accepted. *Financial support:* Federal Work-Study available. Support available to part-time students. Financial award application deadline: 3/1. *Faculty research:* French literature, language teaching and methodology, Spanish poetry, Spanish-American fiction and poetry. *Unit head:* Dr. Sachiko Matsunaga, Chair, 323-343-4230, Fax: 323-343-4234, E-mail: smatsun@calstatela.edu. *Application contact:* Dr. Cheryl L. Ney, Associate Vice President for Academic Affairs and Dean of Graduate Studies, 323-343-3820, Fax: 323-343-5653, E-mail: cney@cslanet.calstatela.edu.

California State University, Sacramento, Graduate Studies, College of Social Sciences and Interdisciplinary Studies, Liberal Arts Program, Sacramento, CA 95819. Offers French (MA); German (MA); Spanish (MA); theater arts (MA). *Degree requirements:* For master's, writing proficiency exam. *Entrance requirements:* Additional exam requirements/recommendations for international students: Required—TOEFL. Electronic applications accepted.

Carleton University, Faculty of Graduate Studies, Faculty of Arts and Social Sciences, Department of French, Ottawa, ON K1S 5B6, Canada. Offers MA. *Degree requirements:* For master's, thesis optional. *Entrance requirements:* For master's, honors degree. *Faculty research:* French, French Canadian and Acadian literatures and linguistics, Francophone studies, rhetorical studies.

Case Western Reserve University, School of Graduate Studies, Department of Modern Languages and Literatures, Program in French, Cleveland, OH 44106. Offers MA. Part-time programs available. *Faculty:* 6 full-time (3 women), 13 part-time/adjunct (9 women). *Students:* 1 applicant, 100% accepted.Terminal master's awarded for partial completion of doctoral program. *Degree requirements:* For master's, one foreign language, thesis or alternative. *Entrance requirements:* For master's, GRE General Test, writing sample. Additional exam requirements/recommendations for international students: Required—TOEFL (minimum score 550 paper-based; 213 computer-based; 79 iBT). *Application deadline:* For fall admission, 3/1 priority date for domestic students. Applications are processed on a rolling basis. Application fee: $50. Electronic applications accepted. *Financial support:* Fellowships, tuition waivers (full) available. Financial award application deadline: 3/1; financial award applicants required to submit FAFSA. *Faculty research:* Eighteenth and nineteenth century literature (novel, poetry, drama), literary theory, women's studies, cultural criticism. *Application contact:* Marie Lathers, Director, Graduate Studies (French), 216-368-3071, Fax: 216-368-2216, E-mail: mhl5@case.edu.

Central Connecticut State University, School of Graduate Studies, School of Arts and Sciences, Department of Modern Languages, Program in Modern Language, New Britain, CT 06050-4010. Offers French (MA, Certificate); German (Certificate); Italian (Certificate); modern language (MA); Spanish language and Hispanic culture (MA). Part-time and evening/weekend programs available. *Students:* 2 full-time (1 woman), 40 part-time (35 women); includes 14 minority (all Hispanic Americans). Average age 38. 16 applicants, 69% accepted, 9 enrolled. In 2009, 9 master's awarded. *Degree requirements:* For master's, one foreign language, comprehensive exam, thesis or alternative; for Certificate, qualifying exam. *Entrance requirements:* For master's, minimum undergraduate GPA of 2.7, 24 credits of undergraduate courses in either Italian or Spanish. Additional exam requirements/recommendations for international students: Required—TOEFL. *Application deadline:* For fall admission, 7/1 for domestic students; for spring admission, 12/1 for domestic students. Applications are processed on a rolling basis. Application fee: $50. Electronic applications accepted. *Expenses:* Tuition, area resident: Full-time $4662; part-time $440 per credit. Tuition, state resident: full-time $6994; part-time $440 per credit. Tuition, nonresident: full-time $12,988; part-time $440 per credit. Required fees: $3606. One-time fee: $62 part-time. *Faculty research:* Twentieth century French theater, seventeenth century French literature, French Middle Ages.

Cleveland State University, College of Graduate Studies, College of Liberal Arts and Social Sciences, Department of Modern Languages, Cleveland, OH 44115. Offers French (M Ed); Spanish (M Ed, MA), including language and linguistics (MA), Latin American studies (MA), peninsular studies (MA), Spanish (MA). Part-time and evening/weekend programs available. *Degree requirements:* For master's, one foreign language, comprehensive exam, thesis optional, study abroad. *Entrance requirements:* For master's, undergraduate major in Spanish or equivalent, essay in Spanish, writing sample. Additional exam requirements/recommendations for international students: Required—TOEFL (minimum score 525 paper-based; 197 computer-based). Electronic applications accepted. *Faculty research:* Second language acquisition, sociolinguistics, contemporary Spanish novel, Arabic diaspora in Latin America, border literature.

Columbia University, Graduate School of Arts and Sciences, Division of Humanities, Department of French and Romance Philology, New York, NY 10027. Offers French and Romance philology (M Phil, PhD); Romance languages (MA). Part-time programs available. *Degree requirements:* For master's, one foreign language, thesis, written exam; for doctorate, 2 foreign languages, thesis/dissertation. *Entrance requirements:* For master's and doctorate, GRE General Test, knowledge of Latin, writing sample. Additional exam requirements/recommendations for international students: Required—TOEFL. *Faculty research:* Theory of literature, literary semiotics, poetics.

Columbia University, Graduate School of Arts and Sciences, Program in French Cultural Studies, New York, NY 10027. Offers MA. Program offered in Paris, France. *Expenses:* Contact institution.

Concordia University, School of Graduate Studies, Faculty of Arts and Science, Department of Études Françaises, Montréal, QC H3G 1M8, Canada. Offers écriture (Certificate); anglais-français en langue et techniques de localisation (Certificate); littératures francophones et résonances médiatiques (MA); traductologie (MA); translation (Diploma). *Degree requirements:* For other advanced degree, one foreign language.

Cornell University, Graduate School, Graduate Fields of Arts and Sciences, Field of Romance Studies, Ithaca, NY 14853-0001. Offers French linguistics (PhD); French literature (PhD); Hispanic literature (PhD); Italian linguistics (PhD); Italian literature (PhD); Romance linguistics (PhD); Spanish linguistics (PhD). *Faculty:* 42 full-time (19 women). *Students:* 54 full-time (27 women); includes 9 minority (all Hispanic Americans), 17 international. Average age 30. 78 applicants, 17% accepted, 10 enrolled. In 2009, 7 doctorates awarded. *Degree requirements:* For doctorate, 2 foreign languages, comprehensive exam, thesis/dissertation. *Entrance requirements:* For doctorate, GRE General Test, sample of written work, 3 letters of recommendation. Additional exam requirements/recommendations for international students: Required—TOEFL (minimum score 550 paper-based; 213 computer-based; 77 iBT). *Application deadline:* For fall admission, 1/15 for domestic students. Application fee: $70. Electronic applications accepted. *Expenses:* Tuition: Full-time $29,500. Required fees: $70. Full-time tuition and fees vary according to degree level, program and student level. *Financial support:* In 2009–10, 46 students received support, including 8 fellowships with full tuition reimbursements available, 2 teaching assistantships with full tuition reimbursements available; research assistantships with full tuition reimbursements available, institutionally sponsored loans, scholarships/grants, health care benefits, tuition waivers (full and partial), and unspecified assistantships also available. Financial award applicants required to submit FAFSA. *Faculty research:* Literary theory, Hispanic studies, French studies, gender studies. *Unit head:* Director of Graduate Studies, 607-255-8222. *Application contact:* Graduate Field Assistant, 607-255-4246, E-mail: romance_studies@cornell.edu.

Dalhousie University, Faculty of Arts and Social Science, Department of French, Halifax, NS B3H 4R2, Canada. Offers MA, PhD. *Entrance requirements:* Additional exam requirements/recommendations for international students: Required—TOEFL, IELTS, CANTEST, CAEL, or Michigan English Language Assessment Battery. *Application deadline:* For fall admission, 6/1 for domestic students, 4/1 for international students; for winter admission, 10/31 for domestic students, 8/31 for international students; for spring admission, 2/28 for domestic students, 12/31 for international students. Application fee: $70. Electronic applications accepted. *Financial support:* Career-related internships or fieldwork, scholarships/grants, and health care benefits available. *Faculty research:* Literature, linguistics, French civilization, French and Francophone literature of all periods, translation and cultural studies. *Unit head:* Dr. Vittorio Frigerio, Chair, 902-494-6805, Fax: 902-494-1626, E-mail: french@dal.ca. *Application contact:* Dr. Raymond Mopoho, Graduate Coordinator, 902-494-2018, Fax: 902-494-1626, E-mail: french@dal.ca.

Drew University, Caspersen School of Graduate Studies, Program in Education, Madison, NJ 07940-1493. Offers biology (MAT); chemistry (MAT); English (MAT); French (MAT); Italian (MAT); math (MAT); physics (MAT); social studies (MAT); Spanish (MAT); theatre arts (MAT). *Unit head:* Dr. Ross Danis.

Duke University, Graduate School, Department of Romance Studies, Durham, NC 27708. Offers French (PhD); Spanish (PhD); JD/AM. *Faculty:* 29 full-time. *Students:* 42 full-time (28 women); includes 10 minority (1 African American, 9 Hispanic Americans), 15 international. 54 applicants, 22% accepted, 3 enrolled. In 2009, 6 doctorates awarded. *Degree requirements:* For doctorate, 2 foreign languages, thesis/dissertation. *Entrance requirements:* For doctorate, GRE General Test. Additional exam requirements/recommendations for international students: Required—TOEFL (minimum score 550 paper-based; 213 computer-based; 83 iBT), IELTS (minimum score 7). *Application deadline:* For fall admission, 12/8 priority date for domestic and international students. Application fee: $75. Electronic applications accepted. *Financial support:* Fellowships, research assistantships, teaching assistantships, Federal Work-Study available. Financial award application deadline: 12/31. *Unit head:* Esther Gabara, Director of Graduate Studies, 919-660-3100. *Application contact:* Esther Gabara, Director of Graduate Studies, 919-660-3100.

Eastern Michigan University, Graduate School, College of Arts and Sciences, Department of World Languages, Programs in Foreign Languages, Ypsilanti, MI 48197. Offers French (MA); German (MA); German for business (Graduate Certificate); Hispanic language and cultures (Graduate Certificate); Japanese business practices (Graduate Certificate); Spanish (MA). Part-time and evening/weekend programs available. Postbaccalaureate distance learning degree programs offered (minimal on-campus study). *Students:* 1 full-time (0 women), 15 part-time (14 women); includes 4 minority (1 African American, 3 Hispanic Americans), 1 international. Average age 39. In 2009, 6 master's awarded. *Degree requirements:* For master's, one foreign language, thesis optional. *Entrance requirements:* Additional exam requirements/recommendations for international students: Required—TOEFL. *Application deadline:* Applications are processed on a rolling basis. Application fee: $35. Tuition and fees vary according to course level. *Financial support:* Fellowships, research assistantships with full tuition reimbursements, teaching assistantships with full tuition reimbursements, career-related internships or fieldwork, Federal Work-Study, institutionally sponsored loans, scholarships/grants, tuition waivers (partial), and unspecified assistantships available. Support available to part-time students. Financial award applicants required to submit FAFSA. *Application contact:* Dr. Genevieve Peden, Program Advisor, 734-487-2283, Fax: 734-487-3411, E-mail: gpeden@emich.edu.

Emory University, Graduate School of Arts and Sciences, Department of Comparative Literature, Atlanta, GA 30322-1100. Offers comparative literature (PhD); English (Certificate); French (Certificate); Middle Eastern studies (PhD); philosophy (Certificate); psychoanalytic studies (PhD); religion (PhD); Spanish (Certificate); women studies (Certificate). *Degree requirements:* For doctorate, 2 foreign languages, comprehensive exam, thesis/dissertation. *Entrance requirements:* For doctorate, GRE General Test, minimum GPA of 3.0. Additional exam requirements/recommendations for international students: Required—TOEFL. Electronic applications accepted. *Faculty research:* Literary theory, psychoanalysis trauma and testimony, literature and religion, literature and technology, literature and philosophy, politics and global culture, literature and aesthetics.

Emory University, Graduate School of Arts and Sciences, Department of French and Italian, Atlanta, GA 30322-1100. Offers French (PhD); French and educational studies (PhD). *Degree requirements:* For doctorate, one foreign language, comprehensive exam, thesis/dissertation. *Entrance requirements:* For doctorate, GRE General Test. Electronic applications accepted. *Faculty research:* French literature through multidisciplinary critical approaches, second language acquisition theory.

Florida Atlantic University, Dorothy F. Schmidt College of Arts and Letters, Department of Languages, Linguistics, and Comparative Literature, Boca Raton, FL 33431-0991. Offers comparative literature (MA); French (MA); linguistics (MA); Spanish (MA). Part-time programs available. *Faculty:* 23 full-time (20 women), 12 part-time/adjunct (10 women). *Students:* 20 full-time (14 women), 14 part-time (10 women); includes 16 minority (3 African Americans, 1 Asian American or Pacific Islander, 12 Hispanic Americans), 4 international. Average age 35. 35 applicants, 60% accepted, 13 enrolled. In 2009, 16 master's awarded. *Degree requirements:* For master's, one foreign language, comprehensive exam, thesis optional. *Entrance requirements:* For master's, GRE General Test, minimum GPA of 3.0. *Application deadline:* For fall admission, 7/1 priority date for domestic students, 2/15 for international students; for spring admission, 11/1 for domestic students, 7/15 for international students. Applications are processed on a rolling basis. Application fee: $30. *Expenses:* Tuition, state resident: full-time $7055; part-time $293.94 per credit hour. Tuition, nonresident: full-time $22,096; part-time $920.66 per credit hour. *Financial support:* Fellowships, research assistantships, teaching assistantships with partial tuition reimbursements, Federal Work-Study and tuition waivers (partial) available. Support available to part-time students. Financial award application deadline: 4/1. *Faculty research:* Modern European studies, modern Latin America, medieval Europe. *Unit head:* Dr. Michael Horswell, Chair, 561-297-3860, Fax: 561-297-2756, E-mail: horswell@fau.edu. *Application contact:* Dr. Emily Stockard, Associate Dean, 561-297-2817, Fax: 561-297-2744, E-mail: stockard@fau.edu.

Florida State University, The Graduate School, College of Arts and Sciences, Department of Modern Languages, Program in French, Tallahassee, FL 32306. Offers MA, PhD. *Faculty:* 9 full-time (4 women). *Students:* 19 full-time (17 women); includes 4 minority (2 African Americans, 2 Asian Americans or Pacific Islanders). Average age 25. 22 applicants, 64% accepted, 12 enrolled. In 2009, 2 degrees awarded. Terminal master's awarded for partial completion of doctoral program. *Degree requirements:* For master's, thesis optional; for doctorate, thesis/dissertation, reading knowledge of French and 2 other languages. *Entrance requirements:* For master's and doctorate, GRE General Test or minimum GPA of 3.0. Additional exam requirements/recommendations for international students: Required—TOEFL (minimum score 550 paper-based; 213 computer-based). *Application deadline:* For fall admission, 2/1 for domestic and international students. Applications are processed on a rolling basis. Application fee: $30. Electronic applications accepted. *Expenses:* Tuition, state resident: full-time $7413. Tuition, nonresident: full-time $22,567. *Financial support:* In 2009–10, 1 fellowship with partial tuition reimbursement (averaging $16,500 per year), research assistantships with partial tuition reimbursements (averaging $9,500 per year), 18 teaching assistantships with partial tuition reimbursements (averaging $10,200 per year) were awarded. Financial award application deadline: 1/15; financial award applicants required to submit FAFSA. *Faculty research:* Twentieth century European novel, Renaissance and Middle Ages literature, second language acquisition. *Application contact:* Wendy E. Pigott, Graduate Academic Coordinator, 850-644-8397, Fax: 850-644-0524, E-mail: wpigott@fsu.edu.

Georgia State University, College of Arts and Sciences, Department of Modern and Classical Languages, Program in French, Atlanta, GA 30302-3083. Offers MA. Part-time and evening/weekend programs available. *Degree requirements:* For master's, one foreign language, thesis or alternative, general exam. *Entrance requirements:* For master's, GRE General Test. Additional exam requirements/recommendations for international students: Required—TOEFL. Electronic applications accepted. *Faculty research:* French literature of the sixteenth-, eighteenth-, nineteenth-, and twentieth-centuries.

Georgia State University, College of Arts and Sciences, Department of Modern and Classical Languages, Program in Translation and Interpretation, Atlanta, GA 30302-3083. Offers French (Certificate); German (Certificate); Spanish (Certificate). Electronic applications accepted.

Graduate School and University Center of the City University of New York, Graduate Studies, Program in French, New York, NY 10016-4039. Offers PhD. *Faculty:* 20 full-time (11 women). *Students:* 46 full-time (34 women), 5 international. Average age 37. 21 applicants, 67% accepted, 7 enrolled. In 2009, 6 doctorates awarded. *Degree requirements:* For doctorate, 2 foreign languages, thesis/dissertation. *Entrance requirements:* For doctorate, GRE General Test. Additional exam requirements/recommendations for international students: Required—TOEFL. *Application deadline:* For fall admission, 1/15 for domestic students. Application fee: $125. Electronic applications accepted. *Financial support:* In 2009–10, 35 students received support, including 28 fellowships, 5 research assistantships, 6 teaching assistantships; career-related internships or fieldwork, Federal Work-Study, institutionally sponsored loans, and tuition waivers (full and partial) also available. Financial award application deadline: 2/1; financial award applicants required to submit FAFSA. *Unit head:* Dr. Francesca Sautman, Executive Officer, 212-817-8366, Fax: 212-817-1520, E-mail: fsautman@gc.cuny.edu. *Application contact:* Les Gribben, Director of Admissions, 212-817-7470, Fax: 212-817-1624, E-mail: lgribben@gc.cuny.edu.

Harvard University, Graduate School of Arts and Sciences, Department of Romance Languages and Literatures, Cambridge, MA 02138. Offers French (AM, PhD); Italian (AM, PhD); Portuguese (AM, PhD); Spanish (AM, PhD). Terminal master's awarded for partial completion of doctoral program. *Degree requirements:* For master's, 2 foreign languages; for doctorate, 2 foreign languages, thesis/dissertation. *Entrance requirements:* For master's and doctorate, GRE General Test, sample of written work. Additional exam requirements/recommendations for international students: Required—TOEFL. *Expenses:* Tuition: Full-time $33,696. Required fees: $1126. Full-time tuition and fees vary according to program.

Hofstra University, School of Education, Health, and Human Services, Department of Curriculum and Teaching, Program in Foreign Language Education, Hempstead, NY 11549. Offers foreign language and TESOL (MS Ed); foreign language education (MA, MS Ed), including French, German, Russian, Spanish. Part-time and evening/weekend programs available. *Students:* 4 full-time (all women), 3 part-time (1 woman); includes 2 minority (both Hispanic Americans). Average age 29. 9 applicants, 67% accepted, 3 enrolled. In 2009, 2 master's awarded. *Degree requirements:* For master's, one foreign language. *Entrance requirements:* For master's, 2 letters of recommendation, teacher certification (MA). Additional exam requirements/recommendations for international students: Required—TOEFL (minimum score 550 paper-based; 213 computer-based; 80 iBT). *Application deadline:* Applications are processed on a rolling basis. Application fee: $60. Electronic applications accepted. *Expenses:* Tuition: Full-time $16,200; part-time $900 per credit hour. Required fees: $970; $145 per term. Tuition and fees vary according to program. *Financial support:* In 2009–10, 6 students received support, including 2 fellowships with full and partial tuition reimbursements available (averaging $2,878 per year); research assistantships with full and partial tuition reimbursements available, Federal Work-Study, institutionally sponsored loans, scholarships/grants, tuition waivers (full and partial), and unspecified assistantships also available. Support available to part-time students. Financial award applicants required to submit FAFSA. *Faculty research:* First language acquisition and second language learning; theory and practice in language teaching; technology and language teaching and learning; language and colonialism. *Unit head:* Dr. Mustapha Masrour, Program Director, 516-463-6033, Fax: 516-463-6266, E-mail: lalmzm@hofstra.edu. *Application contact:* Carol Drummer, Dean of Graduate Admissions, 516-463-4876, Fax: 516-463-4664, E-mail: gradstudent@hofstra.edu.

Howard University, Graduate School, Department of Modern Languages and Literatures, Washington, DC 20059-0002. Offers French (MA); Spanish (MA). Part-time programs available. *Degree requirements:* For master's, one foreign language, comprehensive exam, thesis. *Entrance requirements:* For master's, GRE General Test, writing samples in English and French or Spanish. *Faculty research:* African literature in French, Spanish linguistics, Spanish Peninsular literature, Spanish sociolinguistics.

Hunter College of the City University of New York, Graduate School, School of Arts and Sciences, Department of Romance Languages, Program in French, New York, NY 10021-5085. Offers French (MA); French education (MA). Part-time and evening/weekend programs available. *Faculty:* 3 full-time (1 woman). *Students:* 4 part-time (1 woman). Average age 32. 8 applicants, 50% accepted, 1 enrolled. In 2009, 2 master's awarded. *Degree requirements:* For master's, 2 foreign languages, comprehensive exam, thesis optional. *Entrance requirements:* For master's, GRE General Test, GRE Subject Test, ability to read, speak, and write French; interview. Additional exam requirements/recommendations for international students: Required—TOEFL. *Application deadline:* For fall admission, 4/1 for domestic students, 2/1 for international students; for spring admission, 11/1 for domestic students, 9/1 for international students. Application fee: $125. *Expenses:* Tuition, state resident: full-time $7360; part-time $310 per credit. Required fees: $250 per semester. *Financial support:* Fellowships, Federal Work-Study, scholarships/grants, and tuition waivers (partial) available. Support available to part-time students. Financial award application deadline: 4/15. *Faculty research:* Contemporary French theater, Villiers-dell Isle-Adam, Voltaire, medieval folklore, fin-de-siécle. *Unit head:* Prof. Marlene Barloum, Graduate Advisor, 212-650-3511, E-mail: mbarloum@hunter.cuny.edu. *Application contact:* William Zlata, Director for Graduate Admissions, 212-772-4482, Fax: 212-650-3336, E-mail: admissions@hunter.cuny.edu.

Illinois State University, Graduate School, College of Arts and Sciences, Department of Foreign Languages, Literatures and Cultures, Normal, IL 61790-2200. Offers French (MA); French and German (MA); French and Spanish (MA); German (MA); German and Spanish (MA); Spanish (MA). *Degree requirements:* For master's, variable foreign language requirement, comprehensive exam, 1 term of residency. *Entrance requirements:* For master's, GRE General Test, minimum GPA of 2.8 in last 60 hours of course work.

Indiana University Bloomington, University Graduate School, College of Arts and Sciences, Department of French and Italian, Bloomington, IN 47405-7000. Offers French (MA, PhD), including French instruction (MA), French linguistics, French literature; Italian (MA, PhD). Part-time programs available. *Faculty:* 19 full-time (7 women). *Students:* 69 full-time (42 women), 5 part-time (4 women); includes 3 minority (1 American Indian/Alaska Native, 1 Asian American or Pacific Islander, 1 Hispanic American), 28 international. Average age 30. 48 applicants, 63% accepted, 15 enrolled. In 2009, 12 master's, 2 doctorates awarded. Terminal master's awarded for partial completion of doctoral program. *Degree requirements:* For master's, one foreign language, comprehensive exam, thesis optional; for doctorate, 2 foreign languages, comprehensive exam, thesis/dissertation. *Entrance requirements:* For master's and doctorate, GRE General Test. Additional exam requirements/recommendations for international students: Required—TOEFL (minimum score 550 paper-based; 213 computer-based; 79 iBT). *Application deadline:* For fall admission, 1/15 priority date for domestic students, 12/1 priority date for international students; for spring admission, 9/1 priority date for domestic and international students. Application fee: $55 ($65 for international students). Electronic applications accepted. *Financial support:* In 2009–10, 4 fellowships with partial tuition reimbursements (averaging $15,000 per year), 5 research assistantships with partial tuition reimbursements (averaging $13,025 per year), 39 teaching assistantships with partial tuition reimbursements (averaging $13,025 per year) were awarded. Financial award application deadline: 1/15. *Faculty research:* All periods of French and Italian literature and various areas of French linguistics, including the novel and political theory, literature and fine arts, literary theory, postcolonialism, French-Creole studies, French literature of Africa and its Diaspora, humanism, medieval folklore and mythology, humor in medieval and Renaissance literature, cinema Old Occitan and Old French, emigration, second language acquisition, syntax, sociolinguistics, phonology, lexicography. *Unit head:* Prof. Emanuel Mickel, Interim Chairman, 812-855-5458, Fax: 812-855-8877, E-mail: fritchr@indiana.edu. *Application contact:* Jocelyn Karlan, Secretary, 812-855-1088, Fax: 812-855-8877, E-mail: fritgs@indiana.edu.

The Johns Hopkins University, Zanvyl Krieger School of Arts and Sciences, Department of German and Romance Languages and Literatures, Baltimore, MD 21218-2699. Offers French (PhD); German (PhD); Italian (PhD); romance languages (PhD); Spanish (PhD). *Faculty:* 31 full-time (20 women), 1 part-time/adjunct (0 women). *Students:* 49 full-time (30 women); includes 4 minority (all Hispanic Americans), 21 international. Average age 30. 51 applicants, 37% accepted, 19 enrolled. In 2009, 5 doctorates awarded. *Degree requirements:* For doctorate, 2 foreign languages, thesis/dissertation. *Entrance requirements:* For doctorate, GRE General Test. Additional exam requirements/recommendations for international students: Required—TOEFL (minimum score 600 paper-based; 250 computer-based; 100 iBT), IELTS. *Application deadline:* For fall admission, 12/30 for domestic and international students. Application fee: $75. Electronic applications accepted. *Financial support:* In 2009–10, 40 fellowships with full tuition reimbursements (averaging $17,000 per year), 2 research assistantships with full tuition reimbursements (averaging $17,000 per year), 19 teaching assistantships with full tuition reimbursements (averaging $17,000 per year) were awarded; institutionally sponsored loans also available. *Faculty research:* Nineteenth century French prose and poetry, genetic theory and criticism; twentieth century Latin American literature and film; Medieval and Renaissance Italian literature; Gender and Queer Theory in German literature; the ideology of baroque and neobaroque aesthetics. *Unit head:* Dr. William Egginton, Chair, 410-516-7510, Fax: 410-516-5358, E-mail: egginton@jhu.edu. *Application contact:* Rebecca Swisdak, Graduate Administrative Coordinator, 410-516-7227, Fax: 410-516-5358, E-mail: rswisdak@jhu.edu.

Kansas State University, Graduate School, College of Arts and Sciences, Department of Modern Languages, Manhattan, KS 66506. Offers French (MA); German (MA); Spanish (MA). Part-time and evening/weekend programs available. Postbaccalaureate distance learning degree programs offered (minimal on-campus study). *Faculty:* 17 full-time (9 women). *Students:* 15 full-time (6 women), 15 part-time (13 women); includes 5 minority (1 Asian American or Pacific Islander, 4 Hispanic Americans), 10 international. Average age 32. 20 applicants, 75% accepted, 10 enrolled. In 2009, 6 master's awarded. *Degree requirements:* For master's, thesis optional. *Entrance requirements:* For master's, teaching certificate. Additional exam requirements/recommendations for international students: Required—TOEFL (minimum score 560 paper-based). *Application deadline:* For fall admission, 2/1 priority date for domestic and international students; for spring admission, 8/1 priority date for domestic and international students. Applications are processed on a rolling basis. Application fee: $40 ($55 for international students). Electronic applications accepted. *Financial support:* In 2009–10, 16 teaching assistantships with full tuition reimbursements (averaging $8,914 per year) were awarded; Federal Work-Study, institutionally sponsored loans, and scholarships/grants also available. Support available to part-time students. Financial award application deadline: 3/1; financial award applicants required to submit FAFSA. *Faculty research:* Second language acquisitions; Chicano literature; Francophone literature; cultural studies; German, French, Spanish, and Spanish-American literature from the Middle Ages to the modern era. *Unit head:* Robert Corum, Head, 785-532-1987, Fax: 785-532-7004, E-mail: corum@ksu.edu. *Application contact:* Claire Dehon, Director, 785-532-1929, Fax: 785-532-7004, E-mail: dehoncl@ksu.edu.

Kent State University, College of Arts and Sciences, Department of Modern and Classical Language Studies, Kent, OH 44242-0001. Offers French literature (MA); French, Spanish, German and Latin pedagogy (MA); German literature (MA); Spanish literature (MA); translation (MA), including French, German, Japanese, Russian, Spanish; translation studies (PhD). Part-time and evening/weekend programs available. *Degree requirements:* For master's, one foreign language, comprehensive exam (for some programs), thesis (for some programs); for doctorate, comprehensive exam, thesis/dissertation (for some programs). *Entrance requirements:* For master's, minimum GPA of 3.0, writing sample, audio tape or CD; for doctorate, 3 recommendations. Additional exam requirements/recommendations for international students: Required—TOEFL (minimum score 197 computer-based). Electronic applications accepted. *Faculty research:* Literature, pedagogy, applied linguistics, translation studies.

Louisiana State University and Agricultural and Mechanical College, Graduate School, College of Arts and Sciences, Department of French Studies, Baton Rouge, LA 70803. Offers French literature and linguistics (MA, PhD). *Faculty:* 16 full-time (6 women). *Students:* 23 full-time (15 women), 3 part-time (2 women); includes 1 minority (Hispanic American), 3 international. Average age 29. 18 applicants, 78% accepted, 7 enrolled. In 2009, 3 master's, 2 doctorates awarded. Terminal master's awarded for partial completion of doctoral program. *Degree requirements:* For master's, thesis optional; for doctorate, 2 foreign languages, thesis/dissertation. *Entrance requirements:* For master's and doctorate, GRE General Test, minimum GPA of 3.0. Additional exam requirements/recommendations for international students: Required—TOEFL (minimum score 550 paper-based; 213 computer-based; 79 iBT) or IELTS (minimum score 6.5). *Application deadline:* For fall admission, 1/25 priority date for domestic students, 5/15 for international students; for spring admission, 10/15 for international students. Applications are processed on a rolling basis. Application fee: $50 ($70 for international students). Electronic applications accepted. *Financial support:* In 2009–10, 24 students received support, including 1 fellowship with full tuition reimbursement available (averaging $18,409 per year), 5 research assistantships with partial tuition reimbursements available (averaging $15,500 per year), 14 teaching assistantships with partial tuition reimbursements available (averaging

French

Louisiana State University and Agricultural and Mechanical College (continued)
$18,045 per year); career-related internships or fieldwork, Federal Work-Study, institutionally sponsored loans, health care benefits, tuition waivers (full), and unspecified assistantships also available. Support available to part-time students. Financial award application deadline: 7/1; financial award applicants required to submit FAFSA. *Faculty research:* French literature of all periods, modern critical theory, linguistics, cinema, Francophonia. Total annual research expenditures: $63,973. *Unit head:* Dr. Greg Stone, Chair, 225-578-6627, Fax: 225-578-6628, E-mail: stone@lsu.edu. *Application contact:* Dr. Alexandre Lupin, Adviser, 225-578-6627, Fax: 225-578-6628, E-mail: frleup@lsu.edu.

McGill University, Faculty of Graduate and Postdoctoral Studies, Faculty of Arts, Department of French Language and Literature, Montréal, QC H3A 2T5, Canada. Offers MA, PhD.

McMaster University, School of Graduate Studies, Faculty of Humanities, Department of French, Hamilton, ON L8S 4M2, Canada. Offers MA. Part-time and evening/weekend programs available. *Degree requirements:* For master's, thesis or alternative. *Entrance requirements:* For master's, honors degree in French, minimum B+ average. Additional exam requirements/recommendations for international students: Required—TOEFL (minimum score 580 paper-based; 237 computer-based). *Faculty research:* Medieval literature, eighteenth- and nineteenth-century literature, twentieth-century French and Francophone literature, linguistics.

Memorial University of Newfoundland, School of Graduate Studies, Department of French and Spanish, St. John's, NL A1C 5S7, Canada. Offers French studies (MA). Part-time programs available. *Degree requirements:* For master's, one foreign language, thesis. *Entrance requirements:* For master's, honors degree (minimum 2nd class standing). Electronic applications accepted. *Faculty research:* French and French-Canadian literature, literary theory, linguistics, philosophy, translation, Francophone culture.

Miami University, Graduate School, College of Arts and Sciences, Department of French and Italian, Oxford, OH 45056. Offers French (MA). Part-time programs available. *Students:* 6 full-time (2 women), 2 international. *Entrance requirements:* For master's, GRE General Test (recommended), minimum undergraduate GPA of 3.0 during previous 2 years or 2.75 overall. Additional exam requirements/recommendations for international students: Required—TOEFL. Application fee: $50. *Expenses:* Tuition, state resident: full-time $11,280. Tuition, nonresident: full-time $24,912. Required fees: $516. *Financial support:* Fellowships with full tuition reimbursements, research assistantships, teaching assistantships, Federal Work-Study, health care benefits, tuition waivers (full), and unspecified assistantships available. Financial award application deadline: 3/1; financial award applicants required to submit FAFSA. *Unit head:* Dr. Jonathan Strauss, Chair, 513-529-7508, E-mail: strausja@muohio.edu. *Application contact:* Dr. Elisabeth Hodges, Graduate Director, 513-529-5809, E-mail: hodgesed@muohio.edu.

Michigan State University, The Graduate School, College of Arts and Letters, Department of French, Classics, and Italian, East Lansing, MI 48824. Offers French (MA); French language and literature (PhD). *Faculty:* 10 full-time (4 women). *Students:* 13 full-time (10 women), 1 (woman) part-time; includes 2 minority (both African Americans), 4 international. Average age 32. 10 applicants, 30% accepted. In 2009, 3 master's, 2 doctorates awarded. *Entrance requirements:* Additional exam requirements/recommendations for international students: Required—TOEFL. Electronic applications accepted. *Expenses:* Tuition, state resident: part-time $478.25 per credit hour. Tuition, nonresident: part-time $966.50 per credit hour. Part-time tuition and fees vary according to program. *Financial support:* In 2009–10, 1 research assistantship with tuition reimbursement (averaging $6,334 per year), 9 teaching assistantships with tuition reimbursements (averaging $5,934 per year) were awarded. *Unit head:* Dr. Anna Norris, Acting Chairperson, 517-432-8305, Fax: 517-432-6130, E-mail: norrisa@msu.edu. *Application contact:* Information, 517-355-8351, Fax: 517-432-6130.

Middlebury College, Language Schools, French School, Middlebury, VT 05753-6002. Offers MA, DML. *Faculty:* 32 full-time (12 women). *Students:* 100 full-time (80 women); includes 17 minority (3 African Americans, 2 American Indian/Alaska Native, 3 Asian Americans or Pacific Islanders, 9 Hispanic Americans). Average age 30. 166 applicants, 78% accepted, 100 enrolled. In 2009, 45 master's, 2 doctorates awarded. *Degree requirements:* For master's, one foreign language; for doctorate, 2 foreign languages, comprehensive exam, thesis/dissertation, residence abroad, teaching experience. *Entrance requirements:* For master's, 3 letters of recommendation, writing sample; for doctorate, 1st and 2nd language placement exam, 3 letters of recommendation, writing sample. *Application deadline:* Applications are processed on a rolling basis. Application fee: $65. Electronic applications accepted. *Financial support:* Scholarships/grants available. Financial award applicants required to submit FAFSA. *Unit head:* Dr. Aline Germain-Rutherford, Director, 802-443-5526, Fax: 802-443-2075. *Application contact:* Sheila Schwaneflugel, Coordinator, 802-443-5526, Fax: 802-443-2075, E-mail: keim@middlebury.edu.

Millersville University of Pennsylvania, College of Graduate and Professional Studies, School of Humanities and Social Sciences, Department of Foreign Languages, Program in French, Millersville, PA 17551-0302. Offers M Ed, MA. Part-time programs available. *Faculty:* 8 full-time (4 women), 7 part-time/adjunct (6 women). *Students:* 1 part-time (0 women). Average age 24. 1 applicant, 100% accepted, 1 enrolled. In 2009, 3 master's awarded. *Degree requirements:* For master's, comprehensive exam, thesis optional. *Entrance requirements:* For master's, 3 letters of recommendation. Additional exam requirements/recommendations for international students: Required—TOEFL (minimum score 500 paper-based; 183 computer-based; 65 iBT) or IELTS (minimum score 6). *Application deadline:* For fall admission, 1/15 priority date for domestic and international students; for winter admission, 10/1 priority date for domestic and international students; for spring admission, 10/1 priority date for domestic and international students. Applications are processed on a rolling basis. Application fee: $40 ($50 for international students). Electronic applications accepted. *Expenses:* Tuition, state resident: full-time $6666; part-time $370 per credit. Tuition, nonresident: full-time $10,666; part-time $593 per credit. Required fees: $1578.50; $76.25 per credit. One-time fee: $60 part-time. Tuition and fees vary according to course load. *Financial support:* Research assistantships, institutionally sponsored loans and unspecified assistantships available. Support available to part-time students. Financial award application deadline: 3/15; financial award applicants required to submit FAFSA. *Unit head:* Dr. Christine M. Gaudry-Hudson, Coordinator of Foreign Language Graduate Program, 717-872-3663, E-mail: christine.gaudry-hudson@millersville.edu. *Application contact:* Dr. Victor S. DeSantis, Dean of Graduate Studies, 717-872-3099, Fax: 717-872-3453, E-mail: victor.desantis@millersville.edu.

Minnesota State University Mankato, College of Graduate Studies, College of Arts and Humanities, Department of Modern Languages, Program in French, Mankato, MN 56001. Offers MAT, MS. *Students:* 1 (woman) full-time. *Degree requirements:* For master's, one foreign language, comprehensive exam, thesis or alternative. *Entrance requirements:* For master's, minimum GPA of 3.0 during previous 2 years. Additional exam requirements/recommendations for international students: Required—TOEFL. *Application deadline:* For fall admission, 7/1 priority date for domestic students; for spring admission, 11/1 for domestic students. Applications are processed on a rolling basis. Application fee: $40. Electronic applications accepted. *Expenses:* Tuition, state resident: full-time $5364. Tuition, nonresident: full-time $8314. *Financial support:* Research assistantships, teaching assistantships with full tuition reimbursements, unspecified assistantships available. Financial award application deadline: 3/15; financial award applicants required to submit FAFSA. *Unit head:* Dr. John Janc, Graduate Coordinator, 507-389-1817. *Application contact:* 507-389-2321, E-mail: grad@mnsu.edu.

Mississippi State University, College of Arts and Sciences, Department of Foreign Languages, Mississippi State, MS 39762. Offers foreign language (MA), including French, German, Spanish. Part-time programs available. *Faculty:* 8 full-time (3 women). *Students:* 9 full-time (7 women), 2 part-time (1 woman); includes 1 minority (Hispanic American), 3 international. Average age 31. 5 applicants, 100% accepted, 3 enrolled. In 2009, 5 master's awarded. *Degree requirements:* For master's, one foreign language, comprehensive exam (for some programs), thesis optional, comprehensive oral or written exam. *Entrance requirements:* For master's, minimum GPA of 2.75 on last two years of undergraduate courses. Additional exam requirements/recommendations for international students: Required—TOEFL (minimum score 525 paper-based). *Application deadline:* For fall admission, 7/1 for domestic students, 5/1 for international students; for spring admission, 11/1 for domestic students, 9/1 for international students. Applications are processed on a rolling basis. Application fee: $40. Electronic applications accepted. *Expenses:* Tuition, state resident: full-time $2575.50; part-time $286.25 per credit hour. Tuition, nonresident: full-time $6510; part-time $723.50 per credit hour. Tuition and fees vary according to course load. *Financial support:* In 2009–10, 7 teaching assistantships with full tuition reimbursements (averaging $8,766 per year) were awarded; Federal Work-Study, institutionally sponsored loans, and unspecified assistantships also available. Financial award application deadline: 4/1; financial award applicants required to submit FAFSA. *Faculty research:* French, German, Spanish literature from medieval era to present; gender and cultural studies in French; Spanish American literature; foreign language methodology; linguistics. *Unit head:* Dr. Jack Jordan, Professor/Head, 662-325-3480, Fax: 662-325-8209, E-mail: jordan@ra.msstate.edu. *Application contact:* Dr. Edward T. Potter, Assistant Professor/Graduate Coordinator, 662-325-2399, Fax: 662-325-8209, E-mail: ep75@.msstate.edu.

Montclair State University, The Graduate School, College of Education and Human Services, Department of Curriculum and Teaching, Montclair, NJ 07043-1624. Offers education (M Ed); educational technology (M Ed); learning disabled teacher consultant (Certificate); school library media specialist (Certificate); teaching (MAT, Certificate), including art (MAT), biological science (MAT), early childhood education (P-3) (MAT), earth science (MAT), elementary education (K-8) (MAT), English (MAT), French (MAT), health and physical education (MAT), health education (MAT), home economics (MAT), mathematics (MAT), music (MAT), physical education (MAT), physical science (MAT), social studies (MAT), Spanish (MAT), teacher of ESL (MAT), teacher of students with disabilities (MAT). Part-time and evening/weekend programs available. *Faculty:* 17 full-time (12 women), 29 part-time/adjunct (21 women). *Students:* 124 full-time (63 women), 174 part-time (126 women). Average age 31. 112 applicants, 69% accepted, 59 enrolled. In 2009, 179 master's, 2 other advanced degrees awarded. *Degree requirements:* For master's, comprehensive exam, field experience. *Entrance requirements:* For master's, GRE, 2 letters of recommendation. Additional exam requirements/recommendations for international students: Required—TOEFL (minimum score 83 computer-based), or IELTS. *Application deadline:* For fall admission, 2/15 for domestic and international students; for spring admission, 9/15 for domestic and international students. Applications are processed on a rolling basis. Application fee: $60. Electronic applications accepted. *Expenses:* Tuition, area resident: Part-time $486.74 per credit. Tuition, state resident: part-time $486.74 per credit. Tuition, nonresident: part-time $751.34 per credit. Tuition and fees vary according to degree level and program. *Financial support:* In 2009–10, 12 research assistantships with full tuition reimbursements (averaging $7,000 per year) were awarded; Federal Work-Study, scholarships/grants, and unspecified assistantships also available. Support available to part-time students. Financial award application deadline: 3/1; financial award applicants required to submit FAFSA. *Unit head:* Dr. David Schwarzer, Chairperson, 973-655-5187. *Application contact:* Amy Aiello, Director of Graduate Admissions and Operations, 973-655-5147, Fax: 973-655-7869, E-mail: graduate.school@montclair.edu.

Montclair State University, The Graduate School, College of Humanities and Social Sciences, Department of French, German and Russian, Montclair, NJ 07043-1624. Offers French (MA, Certificate), including French literature (MA), French studies (MA). Part-time and evening/weekend programs available. *Faculty:* 8 full-time (5 women), 19 part-time/adjunct (13 women). *Students:* 5 full-time (2 women), 14 part-time (11 women). Average age 37. 6 applicants, 33% accepted, 2 enrolled. In 2009, 2 master's awarded. *Degree requirements:* For master's, comprehensive exam, thesis optional. *Entrance requirements:* For master's, GRE General Test, 24 credits of undergraduate course work in French, 2 letters of recommendation. Additional exam requirements/recommendations for international students: Required—TOEFL (minimum score 83 computer-based), or IELTS. *Application deadline:* For fall admission, 6/1 for international students; for spring admission, 11/1 for international students. Applications are processed on a rolling basis. Application fee: $60. Electronic applications accepted. *Expenses:* Tuition, area resident: Part-time $486.74 per credit. Tuition, state resident: part-time $486.74 per credit. Tuition, nonresident: part-time $751.34 per credit. Tuition and fees vary according to degree level and program. *Financial support:* In 2009–10, 1 research assistantship with full tuition reimbursement (averaging $7,000 per year) was awarded; Federal Work-Study, scholarships/grants, and unspecified assistantships also available. Support available to part-time students. Financial award application deadline: 3/1; financial award applicants required to submit FAFSA. *Unit head:* Dr. Lois Oppenheim, Chairperson, 973-655-4283. *Application contact:* Amy Aiello, Director of Graduate Admissions and Operations, 973-655-5147, Fax: 973-655-7869, E-mail: graduate.school@montclair.edu.

New York University, Graduate School of Arts and Science, Center for French Civilization and Culture, Department of French, New York, NY 10012-1019. Offers French (PhD); French language and civilization (MA); French literature (MA); Romance languages and literatures (MA). Part-time programs available. *Faculty:* 18 full-time (7 women), 2 part-time/adjunct (both women). *Students:* 58 full-time (37 women), 6 part-time (3 women); includes 5 minority (1 African American, 3 Asian Americans or Pacific Islanders, 1 Hispanic American), 19 international. Average age 30. 49 applicants, 49% accepted, 15 enrolled. In 2009, 20 master's, 4 doctorates awarded. Terminal master's awarded for partial completion of doctoral program. *Degree requirements:* For master's, one foreign language, thesis (for some programs); for doctorate, one foreign language, thesis/dissertation. *Entrance requirements:* For master's and doctorate, GRE General Test, proficiency in French. Additional exam requirements/recommendations for international students: Required—TOEFL. *Application deadline:* For fall admission, 1/4 for domestic students; for spring admission, 11/1 for domestic students. Application fee: $90. *Expenses:* Tuition: Full-time $30,528; part-time $1272 per credit. Required fees: $2177. *Financial support:* Fellowships with tuition reimbursements, teaching assistantships with tuition reimbursements, Federal Work-Study, institutionally sponsored loans, scholarships/grants, traineeships, health care benefits, unspecified assistantships, and instructorships available. Financial award application deadline: 1/4; financial award applicants required to submit FAFSA. *Faculty research:* French and Francophone literature, literary theory, and history; rhetoric and poetics; cultural history; theater and cinema. *Unit head:* Judith Miller, Chair, 212-998-8700, Fax: 212-995-3539, E-mail: french.grad@nyu.edu. *Application contact:* Brett Underhill, Graduate Secretary, 212-998-8700, Fax: 212-995-3539, E-mail: french.grad@nyu.edu.

New York University, Graduate School of Arts and Science, Center for French Civilization and Culture, Institute of French Studies, New York, NY 10012-1019. Offers French civilization (PhD); French studies (MA, PhD, Advanced Certificate); French studies and anthropology (PhD); French studies and history (PhD); French studies and journalism (MA); French studies and sociology (PhD); JD/MA; MBA/MA. Part-time programs available. *Students:* 37 full-time (31 women), 6 part-time (4 women); includes 4 minority (2 African Americans, 2 Asian Americans or Pacific Islanders), 8 international. Average age 29. 51 applicants, 65% accepted, 14 enrolled. In 2009, 9 master's, 1 doctorate, 2 other advanced degrees awarded. Terminal master's awarded for partial completion of doctoral program. *Degree requirements:* For master's, one foreign language, comprehensive exam; for doctorate, one foreign language, thesis/dissertation, qualifying exam. *Entrance requirements:* For master's and doctorate, GRE General Test, knowledge of French. Additional exam requirements/recommendations for international students: Required—TOEFL. *Application deadline:* For fall admission, 1/4 for domestic students. Application fee: $90. *Expenses:* Tuition: Full-time $30,528; part-time $1272 per credit. Required fees: $2177. *Financial support:* Fellowships with tuition reimbursements, teaching assistantships with tuition reimbursements, Federal Work-Study, institutionally sponsored loans, scholarships/grants, health care benefits, and unspecified assistantships available. Financial award application deadline: 1/4; financial award applicants required to submit FAFSA. *Faculty research:* Contemporary French society, politics, economy, and culture; French history since 1789; French cultural studies, French colonialism and the post-colonial world; France and the European community. *Unit head:* Edward Berenson, Director, 212-988-8740, Fax: 212-995-

4142, E-mail: institute.french@nyu.edu. *Application contact:* Herrick Chapman, Director of Graduate Studies, 212-988-8740, Fax: 212-995-4142, E-mail: institute.french@nyu.edu.

New York University, NYU in Paris, Paris, NY 10012-1019, France. Offers teaching French as a foreign language (MA). *Students:* 7 full-time (6 women), 2 part-time (both women); includes 1 Asian American or Pacific Islander, 1 Hispanic American. Average age 29. 13 applicants, 85% accepted, 7 enrolled. In 2009, 20 master's awarded. Application fee: $90. *Expenses:* Tuition: Full-time $30,528; part-time $1272 per credit. Required fees: $2177. *Unit head:* Henriette Goldwyn, Acting Director, 212-998-7625, Fax: 212-995-4667, E-mail: nyuparis@nyu.edu. *Application contact:* Henriette Goldwyn, Acting Director, 212-998-7625, Fax: 212-995-4667, E-mail: nyuparis@nyu.edu.

North Carolina State University, Graduate School, College of Humanities and Social Sciences, Department of Foreign Languages and Literatures, Program in French Language and Literature, Raleigh, NC 27695. Offers MA. *Degree requirements:* For master's, thesis optional. *Entrance requirements:* For master's, fluency in French. Electronic applications accepted. *Faculty research:* 19th-century visual culture, translation, cinema, modern theater, linguistics.

Northern Illinois University, Graduate School, College of Liberal Arts and Sciences, Department of Foreign Languages and Literatures, De Kalb, IL 60115-2854. Offers French (MA); Spanish (MA). Part-time programs available. *Faculty:* 25 full-time (11 women). *Students:* 4 full-time (2 women), 18 part-time (9 women); includes 7 minority (all Hispanic Americans), 2 international. Average age 31. 10 applicants, 60% accepted, 4 enrolled. In 2009, 9 master's awarded. *Degree requirements:* For master's, one foreign language, comprehensive exam, thesis or alternative, language proficiency exam. *Entrance requirements:* For master's, GRE General Test, interview, minimum GPA of 2.75, undergraduate major in French or Spanish. Additional exam requirements/recommendations for international students: Required—TOEFL (minimum score 550 paper-based; 213 computer-based). *Application deadline:* For fall admission, 6/1 for domestic students, 5/1 for international students; for spring admission, 11/1 for domestic students, 10/1 for international students. Applications are processed on a rolling basis. Application fee: $30. Electronic applications accepted. *Expenses:* Tuition, state resident: full-time $6576; part-time $274 per credit hour. Tuition, nonresident: full-time $13,152; part-time $548 per credit hour. Required fees: $1813; $75.53 per credit hour. Part-time tuition and fees vary according to course load. *Financial support:* In 2009–10, 13 teaching assistantships with full tuition reimbursements were awarded; fellowships with full tuition reimbursements, research assistantships with full tuition reimbursements, career-related internships or fieldwork, Federal Work-Study, scholarships/grants, tuition waivers (full), and unspecified assistantships also available. Support available to part-time students. Financial award applicants required to submit FAFSA. *Faculty research:* Francophone women writers, prosodies of French and Italian, early Spanish drama, business German, history of Burmese literature. *Unit head:* Anne Birbeck, Chair, 815-753-1259, Fax: 815-753-5989, E-mail: annie@niu.edu. *Application contact:* Graduate School Office, 815-753-0395, E-mail: gradsch@niu.edu.

Northwestern University, The Graduate School, Judd A. and Marjorie Weinberg College of Arts and Sciences, Department of French and Italian, Evanston, IL 60208. Offers eighteenth-century studies (Certificate); French (PhD); French and comparative literature (PhD); Italian studies (Certificate). Admissions and degrees offered through The Graduate School. *Degree requirements:* For doctorate, one foreign language, thesis/dissertation, written and oral exams. *Entrance requirements:* For doctorate, GRE, writing sample, cassette recording. Additional exam requirements/recommendations for international students: Required—TOEFL. *Faculty research:* Francophone studies, 18th century contemporary theory.

The Ohio State University, Graduate School, College of Humanities, Department of French and Italian, Columbus, OH 43210. Offers French (MA, PhD); Italian (MA). *Faculty:* 20. *Students:* 29 full-time (19 women), 12 part-time (8 women), 7 international. Average age 32. In 2009, 7 master's, 1 doctorate awarded. *Degree requirements:* For master's, variable foreign language requirement, thesis optional; for doctorate, variable foreign language requirement, thesis/dissertation. *Entrance requirements:* For master's and doctorate, GRE General Test. Additional exam requirements/recommendations for international students: Required—TOEFL. *Application deadline:* For fall admission, 8/15 priority date for domestic students, 7/1 priority date for international students; for winter admission, 12/1 priority date for domestic students, 11/1 priority date for international students; for spring admission, 3/1 priority date for domestic students, 2/1 priority date for international students. Applications are processed on a rolling basis. Application fee: $40 ($50 for international students). Electronic applications accepted. *Expenses:* Tuition, state resident: full-time $10,683. Tuition, nonresident: full-time $25,923. Tuition and fees vary according to course load and program. *Financial support:* Fellowships, research assistantships, teaching assistantships, Federal Work-Study, institutionally sponsored loans, and unspecified assistantships available. Support available to part-time students. *Faculty research:* Italian and Romance linguistics. *Unit head:* Jennifer Willging, Graduate Studies Committee Chair, E-mail: willging.1@osu.edu. *Application contact:* 614-292-9444, Fax: 614-292-3895, E-mail: domestic.grad@osu.edu.

Ohio University, Graduate College, College of Arts and Sciences, Department of Modern Languages, Athens, OH 45701-2979. Offers French (MA); Spanish (MA). Part-time programs available. *Faculty:* 18 full-time (8 women), 2 part-time/adjunct (both women). *Students:* 29 full-time (25 women), 1 (woman) part-time; includes 4 minority (1 African American, 3 Hispanic Americans), 6 international. 19 applicants, 79% accepted, 14 enrolled. In 2009, 10 master's awarded. *Degree requirements:* For master's, 2 foreign languages, comprehensive exam, thesis optional. *Entrance requirements:* For master's, oral and written samples. Additional exam requirements/recommendations for international students: Required—TOEFL (minimum score 550 paper-based; 80 iBT) or IELTS Academic (minimum score 6.5). *Application deadline:* For fall admission, 1/15 priority date for domestic and international students. Application fee: $50 ($55 for international students). Electronic applications accepted. *Expenses:* Tuition, state resident: full-time $7839; part-time $323 per quarter hour. Tuition, nonresident: full-time $15,831; part-time $654 per quarter hour. Required fees: $2931. *Financial support:* In 2009–10, teaching assistantships with tuition reimbursements (averaging $10,300 per year); Federal Work-Study, institutionally sponsored loans, and tuition waivers (partial) also available. Financial award application deadline: 1/15. *Faculty research:* French and Spanish language and literature. *Unit head:* Dr. Betsy Partyka, Chair, 740-593-2764, Fax: 740-593-0729, E-mail: partyka@ohio.edu. *Application contact:* Dr. Thomas Franz, Graduate Chair, 740-593-2762, Fax: 740-593-0729, E-mail: franz@ohio.edu.

Penn State University Park, Graduate School, College of the Liberal Arts, Department of French, State College, University Park, PA 16802-1503. Offers MA, PhD.

Portland State University, Graduate Studies, College of Liberal Arts and Sciences, Department of Foreign Languages and Literatures, Portland, OR 97207-0751. Offers foreign literature and language (MA); French (MA); German (MA); Japanese (MA); Spanish (MA). Part-time programs available. *Degree requirements:* For master's, one foreign language, thesis (for some programs). *Entrance requirements:* Additional exam requirements/recommendations for international students: Required—TOEFL (minimum score 550 paper-based; 213 computer-based). *Faculty research:* Foreign language pedagogy, applied and social linguistics, literary history and criticism.

Princeton University, Graduate School, Department of French and Italian, Princeton, NJ 08544-1019. Offers French language and literature (PhD). *Degree requirements:* For doctorate, variable foreign language requirement, thesis/dissertation. *Entrance requirements:* For doctorate, GRE General Test, sample of written work. Additional exam requirements/recommendations for international students: Required—TOEFL (minimum score 600 paper-based; 250 computer-based). Electronic applications accepted.

Purdue University, Graduate School, College of Liberal Arts, Department of Foreign Languages and Literatures, West Lafayette, IN 47907. Offers French (MA, MAT, PhD), including French (MA, PhD), French education (MAT); German (MA, MAT, PhD), including German (MA, PhD), German education (MAT); Spanish (MA, MAT, PhD), including Spanish (MA, PhD), Spanish education (MAT). Terminal master's awarded for partial completion of doctoral program. *Degree requirements:* For master's, one foreign language; for doctorate, 2 foreign languages, thesis/dissertation. *Entrance requirements:* For master's, GRE, sample recording of English and language of study; for doctorate, GRE, writing sample, sample recording of English and language of study. Additional exam requirements/recommendations for international students: Required—TOEFL. Electronic applications accepted. *Faculty research:* Linguistics, semiotics, literary criticism, pedagogy.

Queens College of the City University of New York, Division of Graduate Studies, Arts and Humanities Division, Department of European Languages and Literatures, Program in French, Flushing, NY 11367-1597. Offers MA. Part-time and evening/weekend programs available. *Faculty:* 5 full-time (1 woman). *Students:* 3 part-time (all women). 5 applicants, 20% accepted, 1 enrolled. In 2009, 4 master's awarded. *Degree requirements:* For master's, 2 foreign languages, comprehensive exam, thesis or alternative. *Entrance requirements:* For master's, minimum GPA of 3.0. Additional exam requirements/recommendations for international students: Required—TOEFL. *Application deadline:* For fall admission, 4/1 for domestic students; for spring admission, 11/1 for domestic students. Applications are processed on a rolling basis. Application fee: $125. *Expenses:* Tuition, state resident: full-time $7360; part-time $310 per credit. Tuition, nonresident: part-time $575 per credit. One-time fee: $195.25 full-time; $145.25 part-time. *Financial support:* Career-related internships or fieldwork, Federal Work-Study, institutionally sponsored loans, and tuition waivers (partial) available. Support available to part-time students. Financial award application deadline: 4/1; financial award applicants required to submit FAFSA. *Unit head:* Dr. Joseph Sungolowsky, Graduate Adviser, 718-997-5980. *Application contact:* Mario Caruso, Director of Graduate Admissions, 718-997-5200, Fax: 718-997-5193, E-mail: graduate_admissions@qc.edu.

Queen's University at Kingston, School of Graduate Studies and Research, Faculty of Arts and Sciences, Department of French Studies, Kingston, ON K7L 3N6, Canada. Offers MA, PhD. Part-time programs available. *Degree requirements:* For master's, thesis or 4 credits and oral exam; for doctorate, one foreign language, comprehensive exam, thesis/dissertation. *Entrance requirements:* For master's, minimum B+ average; for doctorate, minimum 80% average. Additional exam requirements/recommendations for international students: Required—TOEFL (minimum score 550 paper-based; 213 computer-based). Electronic applications accepted. *Faculty research:* Reception of Quebec literature in English Canada, autobiography and postcolonialism, irony in women's writing, critical editions of renaissance authors, aspectual systems and grammatical categories.

Rider University, Department of Graduate Education, Leadership and Counseling, Teacher Certification Program, Lawrenceville, NJ 08648-3001. Offers business education (Certificate); elementary education (Certificate); English as a second language (Certificate); English education (Certificate); mathematics education (Certificate); preschool to grade 3 (Certificate); science education (Certificate); social studies education (Certificate); world languages (Certificate), including French, German, Spanish. Part-time programs available. *Degree requirements:* For Certificate, internship, professional portfolio. *Entrance requirements:* For degree, PRAXIS, resume. Additional exam requirements/recommendations for international students: Required—TOEFL (minimum score 550 paper-based; 213 computer-based). Electronic applications accepted. *Faculty research:* Conceptual foundations for optimal development of creativity; creative theory, cognitive processes in mathematics learning, teacher collaboration.

Rutgers, The State University of New Jersey, New Brunswick, Graduate School-New Brunswick, Program in French, Piscataway, NJ 08854-8097. Offers French (MA, PhD); French studies (MAT). Part-time and evening/weekend programs available. Terminal master's awarded for partial completion of doctoral program. *Degree requirements:* For master's, one foreign language, written and oral exams (MA); for doctorate, 3 foreign languages, thesis/dissertation, qualifying exam. *Entrance requirements:* For master's and doctorate, GRE General Test. *Faculty research:* Literatures in French, literary history and theory, rhetoric and poetics.

Saint Louis University, Graduate School, College of Arts and Sciences and Graduate School, Department of Modern and Classical Languages, St. Louis, MO 63103-2097. Offers French (MA); Spanish (MA). Part-time programs available. *Degree requirements:* For master's, one foreign language, comprehensive exam, thesis/dissertation (Spanish). *Entrance requirements:* For master's, GRE General Test or MAT, letters of recommendation, resume, interview. Additional exam requirements/recommendations for international students: Required—TOEFL (minimum score 525 paper-based; 194 computer-based). Electronic applications accepted. *Faculty research:* Culture studies, literature studies, foreign language acquisition.

San Francisco State University, Division of Graduate Studies, College of Humanities, Department of Foreign Languages and Literatures, Program in French, San Francisco, CA 94132-1722. Offers MA.

San Jose State University, Graduate Studies and Research, College of Humanities and the Arts, Department of Foreign Languages, Program in French, San Jose, CA 95192-0001. Offers MA. *Degree requirements:* For master's, 2 foreign languages, thesis or comprehensive written and oral exam. *Entrance requirements:* Additional exam requirements/recommendations for international students: Required—TOEFL (minimum score 580 paper-based). *Application deadline:* For fall admission, 6/29 for domestic students; for spring admission, 11/30 for domestic students. Applications are processed on a rolling basis. Application fee: $59. Electronic applications accepted. *Financial support:* Fellowships, scholarships/grants available. Financial award applicants required to submit FAFSA. *Unit head:* Dr. Danielle Trudeau, Graduate Advisor, 408-924-4594, E-mail: danielle.trudeau@sjsu.edu. *Application contact:* Dr. Danielle Trudeau, Graduate Advisor, 408-924-4594, E-mail: danielle.trudeau@sjsu.edu.

Simon Fraser University, Graduate Studies, Faculty of Arts and Social Sciences, Department of French, Burnaby, BC V5A 1S6, Canada. Offers MA. *Degree requirements:* For master's, one foreign language, thesis or alternative. *Entrance requirements:* For master's, minimum GPA of 3.0. Additional exam requirements/recommendations for international students: Required—TOEFL or IELTS. *Faculty research:* French linguistics, Creole linguistics, French literature of the Middle Ages and Ancient Régime, modern and contemporary French literature, French Canadian language and literature.

Smith College, Graduate and Special Programs, Department of French Language and Literature, Northampton, MA 01063. Offers MAT. Part-time programs available. *Faculty:* 9 full-time (7 women). *Students:* 1 applicant, 100% accepted, 0 enrolled. *Degree requirements:* For master's, one foreign language. *Entrance requirements:* Additional exam requirements/recommendations for international students: Required—TOEFL (minimum score 590 paper-based; 243 computer-based; 97 iBT). *Application deadline:* For fall admission, 4/1 for domestic students, 1/15 for international students; for spring admission, 12/1 for domestic students. Application fee: $60. *Financial support:* Career-related internships or fieldwork, institutionally sponsored loans, and scholarships/grants available. Support available to part-time students. Financial award application deadline: 1/15; financial award applicants required to submit CSS PROFILE or FAFSA. *Unit head:* Mary Ellen Birkett, Chair, 413-585-3351, E-mail: mbirkett@smith.edu. *Application contact:* Ruth Morgan, Administrative Assistant, 413-585-3050, Fax: 413-585-3054, E-mail: gradstdy@smith.edu.

Stanford University, School of Humanities and Sciences, Department of French and Italian, Stanford, CA 94305-9991. Offers French (MA, PhD); Italian (MA, PhD). Terminal master's awarded for partial completion of doctoral program. *Degree requirements:* For master's, one foreign language, written exam; for doctorate, 2 foreign languages, thesis/dissertation, oral exam. *Entrance requirements:* For master's and doctorate, GRE General Test. Additional exam requirements/recommendations for international students: Required—TOEFL. Electronic applications accepted. *Expenses:* Tuition: Full-time $37,380; part-time $2760 per quarter. Required fees: $501.

French

State University of New York at Binghamton, Graduate School, School of Arts and Sciences, Department of Romance Languages and Literatures, Program in French, Binghamton, NY 13902-6000. Offers MA. *Students:* 1 (woman) part-time. Average age 24. 5 applicants, 100% accepted, 0 enrolled. *Degree requirements:* For master's, one foreign language, comprehensive exam, thesis or alternative. *Entrance requirements:* For master's, GRE General Test, GRE Subject Test. Additional exam requirements/recommendations for international students: Required—TOEFL (minimum score 550 paper-based; 213 computer-based; 80 iBT). *Application deadline:* For fall admission, 2/15 priority date for domestic and international students; for spring admission, 11/15 priority date for domestic and international students. Applications are processed on a rolling basis. Application fee: $60. Electronic applications accepted. *Financial support:* Fellowships, research assistantships, teaching assistantships, career-related internships or fieldwork, Federal Work-Study, institutionally sponsored loans, and unspecified assistantships available. Support available to part-time students. Financial award application deadline: 2/15. *Unit head:* Dr. Antonio Sobejano-Moran, Chairperson, 607-777-4635, E-mail: antobianco@msn.com. *Application contact:* Victoria Williams, Recruiting and Admissions Coordinator, 607-777-2151, Fax: 607-777-2501, E-mail: vwilliam@binghamton.edu.

Stony Brook University, State University of New York, Graduate School, College of Arts and Sciences, Department of European Languages, Literatures, and Cultures, Program in French, Stony Brook, NY 11794. Offers Romance languages (MA). Evening/weekend programs available. *Degree requirements:* For master's, one foreign language. *Entrance requirements:* For master's, GRE General Test. Additional exam requirements/recommendations for international students: Required—TOEFL. *Application deadline:* For fall admission, 1/15 for domestic students. Application fee: $60. *Expenses:* Tuition, state resident: full-time $8370; part-time $349 per credit. Tuition, nonresident: full-time $13,250; part-time $552 per credit. Required fees: $933. *Unit head:* Prosper Sanou, Coordinator, 631-632-7440, E-mail: prosper.sanou@stonybrook.edu. *Application contact:* Dr. Andrea Fedi, Director of Graduate Studies, 631-632-7438, Fax: 631-632-9612.

Syracuse University, College of Arts and Sciences, Program in French and Francophone Studies, Syracuse, NY 13244. Offers MA. Part-time programs available. *Students:* 8 full-time (6 women), 3 international. Average age 24. 9 applicants, 67% accepted, 6 enrolled. In 2009, 3 master's awarded. *Degree requirements:* For master's, comprehensive exam (for some programs), thesis or alternative. *Entrance requirements:* For master's, GRE General Test. Additional exam requirements/recommendations for international students: Required—TOEFL (minimum score 100 iBT). *Application deadline:* For fall admission, 1/10 priority date for domestic and international students. Application fee: $75. Electronic applications accepted. *Expenses:* Tuition: Full-time $26,808; part-time $1117 per credit. Required fees: $1024. *Financial support:* Fellowships with full tuition reimbursements, teaching assistantships with full tuition reimbursements, tuition waivers (partial) available. Financial award application deadline: 1/1; financial award applicants required to submit FAFSA. *Unit head:* Dr. Jean Jonassaint, Director, 315-443-5906, E-mail: jjonassa@syr.edu. *Application contact:* Karen Ames, Information Contact, 315-443-3022, E-mail: koames@syr.edu.

Texas Tech University, Graduate School, College of Arts and Sciences, Department of Classical and Modern Languages and Literatures, Program in Romance Languages-French, Lubbock, TX 79409. Offers MA. *Students:* 14 full-time (7 women), 2 part-time (both women); includes 4 minority (all Hispanic Americans), 7 international. Average age 31. 23 applicants, 78% accepted, 10 enrolled. In 2009, 5 master's awarded. *Entrance requirements:* For master's, GRE General Test. Additional exam requirements/recommendations for international students: Required—TOEFL (minimum score 550 paper-based; 213 computer-based). *Application deadline:* For fall admission, 3/1 priority date for international students; for spring admission, 11/1 priority date for international students. Applications are processed on a rolling basis. Application fee: $50 ($75 for international students). Electronic applications accepted. *Expenses:* Tuition, state resident: full-time $5100; part-time $213 per credit hour. Tuition, nonresident: full-time $11,748; part-time $490 per credit hour. Required fees: $2298; $50 per credit hour. $555 per semester. *Financial support:* Application deadline: 4/15. *Faculty research:* French and Francophone literature, French cinema, French and Francophone culture, business French. *Unit head:* Dr. Diane Wood, Professor and Graduate Advisor of French, 806-742-3145 Ext. 258, Fax: 806-742-3306, E-mail: diane.wood@ttu.edu. *Application contact:* Liz Hildebrand, Senior Advisor, 806-742-4055, Fax: 806-742-3306, E-mail: liz.hildebrand@ttu.edu.

Tufts University, Graduate School of Arts and Sciences, Program in French, Medford, MA 02155. Offers MA. Part-time programs available. *Faculty:* 19 full-time, 42 part-time/adjunct. *Students:* 5 (3 women); includes 3 minority (2 African Americans, 1 Asian American or Pacific Islander). 7 applicants, 86% accepted, 3 enrolled. In 2009, 1 master's awarded. *Degree requirements:* For master's, one foreign language. *Entrance requirements:* For master's, GRE General Test, writing sample. Additional exam requirements/recommendations for international students: Required—TOEFL (minimum score 550 paper-based; 213 computer-based; 80 iBT). *Application deadline:* For fall admission, 2/15 for domestic students, 12/15 for international students; for spring admission, 10/15 for domestic students, 9/15 for international students. Applications are processed on a rolling basis. Application fee: $75. Electronic applications accepted. *Expenses:* Tuition: Full-time $38,096; part-time $3962 per credit. Required fees: $686; $40 per year. Tuition and fees vary according to course level, course load, degree level, program and student level. *Financial support:* Federal Work-Study, scholarships/grants, and tuition waivers (partial) available. Support available to part-time students. Financial award application deadline: 2/15; financial award applicants required to submit FAFSA. *Unit head:* Jose Mazzotti, Chair, 617-627-3289. *Application contact:* Jose Mazzotti, Chair, 617-627-3289.

Tulane University, School of Liberal Arts, Department of French and Italian, New Orleans, LA 70118-5669. Offers French (MA, PhD). *Degree requirements:* For master's, one foreign language, thesis or alternative; for doctorate, 2 foreign languages, thesis/dissertation. *Entrance requirements:* For master's, GRE General Test, minimum B average in undergraduate course work; for doctorate, GRE General Test. Additional exam requirements/recommendations for international students: Required—TOEFL. Electronic applications accepted.

Université de Moncton, Faculty of Arts and Social Sciences, Department of French Studies, Moncton, NB E1A 3E9, Canada. Offers MA, PhD. Part-time programs available. Terminal master's awarded for partial completion of doctoral program. *Degree requirements:* For master's, thesis, proficiency in French; for doctorate, thesis/dissertation, proficiency in French. *Entrance requirements:* For master's, honors degree in French; for doctorate, MA in French. Electronic applications accepted. *Faculty research:* Language, linguistics, literature, ethnology, Acadian studies.

Université de Montréal, Faculty of Arts and Sciences, Department of French Literature, Montréal, QC H3C 3J7, Canada. Offers MA, PhD. *Degree requirements:* For master's, one foreign language, thesis; for doctorate, one foreign language, thesis/dissertation, general exam. Electronic applications accepted. *Faculty research:* Literary history, literary genres, critical edition, creative writing, Quebecois literature.

Université de Sherbrooke, Faculty of Letters and Human Sciences, Department of Letters and Communications, Sherbrooke, QC J1K 2R1, Canada. Offers comparative Canadian literature (MA, PhD); French literature (MA, PhD); linguistics (MA); theatre (MA). *Degree requirements:* For master's, thesis or alternative; for doctorate, thesis/dissertation. *Entrance requirements:* For master's, minimum GPA of 2.8; for doctorate, minimum GPA of 3.0.

Université du Québec à Chicoutimi, Graduate Programs, Program in Didactics of French-Mother Tongue, Chicoutimi, QC G7H 2B1, Canada. Offers Diploma. Part-time programs available. *Entrance requirements:* For degree, appropriate bachelor's degree, proficiency in French.

University at Albany, State University of New York, College of Arts and Sciences, Department of Languages, Literatures, and Cultures, Program in French, Albany, NY 12222-0001. Offers MA, PhD. *Degree requirements:* For master's, one foreign language; for doctorate, thesis/dissertation.

University at Buffalo, the State University of New York, Graduate School, College of Arts and Sciences, Department of Romance Languages and Literatures, Buffalo, NY 14260. Offers French (MA, PhD); Spanish (MA, PhD). Part-time programs available. *Students:* Average age 31. Terminal master's awarded for partial completion of doctoral program. *Degree requirements:* For master's, one foreign language, project, thesis; for doctorate, 2 foreign languages, thesis/dissertation. *Entrance requirements:* For master's and doctorate, GRE. Additional exam requirements/recommendations for international students: Required—TOEFL (minimum score 550 paper-based; 213 computer-based; 79 iBT). *Application deadline:* For fall admission, 1/15 priority date for domestic students, 1/15 for international students. Applications are processed on a rolling basis. Application fee: $75. Electronic applications accepted. *Financial support:* In 2009–10, fellowships with full tuition reimbursements (averaging $6,000 per year), teaching assistantships with full tuition reimbursements (averaging $13,000 per year) were awarded; Federal Work-Study and institutionally sponsored loans also available. Financial award application deadline: 2/28; financial award applicants required to submit FAFSA. *Faculty research:* Romance linguistics, cultural studies, literary studies, literature and philosophy. *Unit head:* Dr. David Castillo, Chair, 716-645-0869, Fax: 716-645-5981, E-mail: dc63@buffalo.edu. *Application contact:* Dr. Justin Read, Director of Graduate Studies, 716-645-0878, Fax: 716-645-5981, E-mail: jread2@buffalo.edu.

University at Buffalo, the State University of New York, Graduate School, Graduate School of Education, Department of Learning and Instruction, Buffalo, NY 14260. Offers biology education (Ed M, Certificate); chemistry education (Ed M, Certificate); childhood education (Ed M); childhood education with bilingual extension (Ed M); early childhood education (Ed M); earth science education (Ed M, Certificate); elementary education (Ed D, PhD); English education (Ed M, PhD, Certificate); English for speakers of other languages (Ed M); foreign and second language education (PhD); French education (Ed M, Certificate); general education (Ed M); German education (Ed M, Certificate); gifted education (online) (Certificate); Latin education (Ed M, Certificate); literary specialist (Ed M); mathematics education (Ed M, PhD, Certificate); music education (Ed M, Certificate); physics education (Ed M, Certificate); reading education (PhD); science and the public (online) (Ed M); science education (PhD); social studies education (Ed M, Certificate); Spanish education (Ed M, Certificate); special education (PhD); teaching and leading for diversity (Certificate); teaching English to speakers of other languages (Ed M). Part-time and evening/weekend programs available. Postbaccalaureate distance learning degree programs offered (no on-campus study). *Faculty:* 34 full-time (24 women), 50 part-time/adjunct (39 women). *Students:* 332 full-time (245 women), 365 part-time (272 women); includes 50 minority (18 African Americans, 4 American Indian/Alaska Native, 10 Asian Americans or Pacific Islanders, 18 Hispanic Americans), 55 international. Average age 30. 627 applicants, 78% accepted, 286 enrolled. In 2009, 255 master's, 16 doctorates, 51 other advanced degrees awarded. *Degree requirements:* For master's, comprehensive exam; for doctorate, thesis/dissertation, research analysis exam, research experience component. *Entrance requirements:* For doctorate, GRE General Test or MAT, interview, writing sample, letters of recommendation. Additional exam requirements/recommendations for international students: Required—TOEFL (minimum score 600 paper-based; 250 computer-based; 96 iBT). *Application deadline:* For fall admission, 2/1 priority date for domestic and international students; for spring admission, 11/15 priority date for domestic students, 10/1 for international students. Applications are processed on a rolling basis. Application fee: $50. Electronic applications accepted. *Financial support:* In 2009–10, 23 fellowships with full tuition reimbursements (averaging $9,000 per year), 42 research assistantships with full tuition reimbursements (averaging $10,000 per year) were awarded; teaching assistantships with full tuition reimbursements, career-related internships or fieldwork, Federal Work-Study, institutionally sponsored loans, scholarships/grants, tuition waivers (partial), and unspecified assistantships also available. Financial award application deadline: 2/28; financial award applicants required to submit FAFSA. *Faculty research:* Science assessment, foreign language teaching and learning, early learning, new literacies, gender and education. Total annual research expenditures: $1.8 million. *Unit head:* Dr. Suzanne Miller, Chair, 716-645-2455, Fax: 716-645-3161, E-mail: smiller@buffalo.edu. *Application contact:* Cathy Dimino, Admissions Assistant, 716-645-2110, Fax: 716-645-7937, E-mail: cadimino@buffalo.edu.

The University of Alabama, Graduate School, College of Arts and Sciences, Department of Modern Languages and Classics, Tuscaloosa, AL 35487. Offers French (MA, PhD); French and Spanish (PhD); German (MA); Romance languages (MA, PhD); Spanish (MA, PhD). Part-time programs available. *Faculty:* 22 full-time (11 women). *Students:* 46 full-time (31 women), 8 part-time (6 women); includes 7 minority (4 African Americans, 3 Hispanic Americans), 16 international. Average age 31. 31 applicants, 42% accepted, 11 enrolled. In 2009, 12 master's, 5 doctorates awarded. *Median time to degree:* Of those who began their doctoral program in fall 2001, 40% received their degree in 8 years or less. *Degree requirements:* For master's, comprehensive exam, thesis optional; for doctorate, one foreign language, thesis/dissertation, preliminary exam. *Entrance requirements:* For master's and doctorate, minimum GPA of 3.0, writing sample. Additional exam requirements/recommendations for international students: Required—TOEFL or IELTS. *Application deadline:* For fall admission, 7/6 priority date for domestic students, 1/15 priority date for international students; for spring admission, 12/6 priority date for domestic students, 6/1 priority date for international students. Applications are processed on a rolling basis. Application fee: $50 ($60 for international students). Electronic applications accepted. *Expenses:* Tuition, state resident: full-time $7000. Tuition, nonresident: full-time $19,200. *Financial support:* In 2009–10, 7 students received support, including 1 fellowship, research assistantships with full tuition reimbursements available (averaging $10,291 per year), 6 teaching assistantships with full tuition reimbursements available (averaging $10,291 per year); career-related internships or fieldwork, Federal Work-Study, institutionally sponsored loans, and scholarships/grants also available. Financial award application deadline: 7/14. *Faculty research:* Non-English literature, linguistics, culture, film. *Unit head:* Dr. Michael Picone, Chair and Professor, 205-348-5054, Fax: 205-348-2042, E-mail: mpicone@bama.ua.edu. *Application contact:* Dr. K. Barbara Fischer, Graduate Director and Associate Professor, 205-348-8465, Fax: 205-348-2042, E-mail: bfischer@bama.ua.edu.

University of Alberta, Faculty of Graduate Studies and Research, Department of Modern Languages and Cultural Studies, Edmonton, AB T6G 2E1, Canada. Offers applied linguistics (Germanic, Romance, Slavic) (MA); French language, literatures and linguistics (PhD); French language, literatures, and linguistics (MA); Germanic languages, literatures and linguistics (PhD); Germanic languages, literatures, and linguistics (MA); Italian studies (MA); Slavic languages and literatures (Russian, Ukrainian) (MA, PhD); Slavic linguistics (Russian, Ukrainian) (MA, PhD); Spanish and Latin American studies (MA, PhD); Ukrainian folklore (MA, PhD). Part-time programs available. *Faculty:* 33 full-time (15 women), 2 part-time/adjunct (1 woman). *Students:* 39 full-time (29 women), 13 part-time (12 women). 300 applicants, 10% accepted. In 2009, 12 master's, 2 doctorates awarded. *Degree requirements:* For master's, one foreign language, thesis; for doctorate, 2 foreign languages, comprehensive exam, thesis/dissertation. *Entrance requirements:* For master's and doctorate, 1 language other than English. Additional exam requirements/recommendations for international students: Required—Michigan English Language Assessment Battery or TOEFL (minimum score 550 paper-based; 213 computer-based). *Application deadline:* For fall admission, 7/1 for domestic and international students; for winter admission, 11/1 for domestic and international students; for spring admission, 3/1 for domestic students. Applications are processed on a rolling basis. Electronic applications accepted. Tuition and fees charges are reported in Canadian dollars. *Expenses:* Tuition, area resident: Full-time $4626 Canadian dollars; part-time $99.72 Canadian dollars per unit. International tuition: $8216 Canadian dollars full-time. Required fees: $3590 Canadian dollars; $99.72 Canadian dollars per unit. $215 Canadian dollars per term. *Financial support:* In 2009–10, 2 fellowships with full and partial tuition reimbursements (averaging $18,000 per year), 23 research assistantships with full and partial tuition reimbursements (averaging $10,450 per year), 21 teaching assistantships with full and partial tuition reimbursements (averaging $12,572 per year) were awarded; scholarships/grants also available. Support available to part-time students. Financial award application deadline: 3/31. *Faculty research:* Russian/Ukrainian studies; German studies; contemporary Latin American, French and Francophone studies; Italian studies. *Unit head:* Dr. Don Bruce, Chair, 780-492-3273, Fax: 780-492-9106. *Application contact:* Jane Wilson, Graduate Programs Secretary, 780-492-3273, Fax: 780-492-9106, E-mail: mlcsgrad@ualberta.ca.

The University of Arizona, Graduate College, College of Humanities, Department of French and Italian, Tucson, AZ 85721. Offers French (MA). Part-time programs available. *Faculty:* 13. *Students:* 2 full-time (1 woman), 8 part-time (5 women); includes 3 minority (2 African Americans, 1 Hispanic American), 6 international. Average age 38. 7 applicants, 29% accepted, 2 enrolled. In 2009, 1 master's awarded. *Entrance requirements:* For master's, 3 letters of reference, writing sample in French, audio recording. Additional exam requirements/recommendations for international students: Required—TOEFL (minimum score 550 paper-based; 213 computer-based; 79 iBT). *Application deadline:* For fall admission, 12/15 for domestic and international students. Applications are processed on a rolling basis. Application fee: $75. Electronic applications accepted. *Expenses:* Tuition, state resident: full-time $9028. Tuition, nonresident: full-time $24,890. *Financial support:* In 2009–10, 2 research assistantships (averaging $14,542 per year), 10 teaching assistantships with full tuition reimbursements (averaging $15,017 per year) were awarded; Federal Work-Study, institutionally sponsored loans, scholarships/grants, health care benefits, tuition waivers (partial), and unspecified assistantships also available. *Faculty research:* French literature (history, criticism, and theory), Francophone literature and culture, second language acquisition and teaching. *Unit head:* Dr. Irene d'Almeda, Department Head, 520-621-7349, Fax: 520-626-8022, E-mail: dalmedia@email.arizona.edu. *Application contact:* Dava Jondall, Graduate Secretary, 520-621-5345, Fax: 520-626-8022, E-mail: roman@email.arizona.edu.

University of Arkansas, Graduate School, J. William Fulbright College of Arts and Sciences, Department of Foreign Languages, Program in French, Fayetteville, AR 72701-1201. Offers MA. *Students:* 6 full-time (5 women), 1 (woman) part-time; includes 1 minority (Hispanic American), 1 international. 8 applicants, 88% accepted. In 2009, 2 master's awarded. *Degree requirements:* For master's, variable foreign language requirement. Application fee: $40 ($50 for international students). *Expenses:* Tuition, state resident: full-time $7355; part-time $356.58 per hour. Tuition, nonresident: full-time $17,401; part-time $775.17 per hour. Required fees: $1203. *Financial support:* In 2009–10, 6 teaching assistantships were awarded; fellowships, research assistantships, career-related internships or fieldwork and Federal Work-Study also available. Support available to part-time students. Financial award application deadline: 4/1; financial award applicants required to submit FAFSA. *Unit head:* Dr. Joan Turner, Department Chair, 479-575-2951, Fax: 479-575-6795, E-mail: joant@uark.edu. *Application contact:* Dr. Nancy Arenberg, Graduate Coordinator, 479-575-2951, Fax: 479-575-6795, E-mail: arenberg@uark.edu.

The University of British Columbia, Faculty of Arts and Faculty of Graduate Studies, Department of French, Hispanic and Italian Studies, Vancouver, BC V6T 1Z1, Canada. Offers French (MA, PhD); Hispanic studies (MA, PhD). Part-time programs available. *Degree requirements:* For master's, thesis optional; for doctorate, 2 foreign languages, comprehensive exam, thesis/dissertation. *Entrance requirements:* For doctorate, MA. Additional exam requirements/recommendations for international students: Required—TOEFL (minimum score 550 paper-based; 213 computer-based; 80 iBT). Electronic applications accepted. *Faculty research:* Medieval and Renaissance literature, modern literature, romance philology and linguistics, cultural studies, women's literature.

University of California, Berkeley, Graduate Division, College of Letters and Science, Department of French, Berkeley, CA 94720-1500. Offers PhD. *Students:* 31 full-time (22 women). Average age 29. 42 applicants, 5 enrolled. In 2009, 2 doctorates awarded. *Degree requirements:* For doctorate, one foreign language, thesis/dissertation, qualifying exam. *Entrance requirements:* For doctorate, minimum GPA of 3.0, 3 letters of recommendation. *Application deadline:* For fall admission, 12/15 for domestic students. Application fee: $70 ($90 for international students). *Financial support:* Fellowships, research assistantships, teaching assistantships, unspecified assistantships available. *Unit head:* Michael Lucey, Chair, 510-642-2712, Fax: 510-642-8852, E-mail: ch_french@ls.berkeley.edu. *Application contact:* Dr. Susan M. Dennehy, Graduate Student Affairs Officer, 510-642-2714, Fax: 510-642-8852, E-mail: frenchga@berkeley.edu.

University of California, Berkeley, Graduate Division, College of Letters and Science, Group in Romance Languages and Literature, Berkeley, CA 94720-1500. Offers French (PhD); Italian (PhD); Spanish (PhD). *Faculty:* 16 full-time. *Students:* 15 full-time (8 women). Average age 33. 34 applicants, 1 enrolled. In 2009, 4 doctorates awarded. *Degree requirements:* For doctorate, thesis/dissertation, qualifying exam. *Entrance requirements:* For doctorate, GRE General Test, minimum GPA of 3.0, 3 letters of recommendation. Additional exam requirements/recommendations for international students: Required—TOEFL (minimum score 570 paper-based; 230 computer-based). *Application deadline:* For fall admission, 12/15 for domestic students. Application fee: $70 ($90 for international students). *Financial support:* Fellowships with full tuition reimbursements, teaching assistantships with partial tuition reimbursements, health care benefits and unspecified assistantships available. Financial award applicants required to submit FAFSA. *Unit head:* Jose Rabasa, Chair, 510-642-2105, E-mail: jrabasa@berkeley.edu. *Application contact:* Jose Rabasa, Chair, 510-642-2105, E-mail: jrabasa@berkeley.edu.

University of California, Davis, Graduate Studies, Program in French, Davis, CA 95616. Offers PhD. Part-time programs available. *Degree requirements:* For doctorate, thesis/dissertation. *Entrance requirements:* For doctorate, GRE General Test, minimum GPA of 3.0. Additional exam requirements/recommendations for international students: Required—TOEFL (minimum score 550 paper-based; 213 computer-based). Electronic applications accepted. *Faculty research:* Art and art criticism, Francophone literature, travel narrative, colonial and postcolonial studies and romance linguistics.

University of California, Irvine, Office of Graduate Studies, School of Humanities, Department of French and Italian, Irvine, CA 92697. Offers French (MA, PhD). *Students:* 6 full-time (4 women), 1 international. Average age 32. 8 applicants, 75% accepted, 2 enrolled. In 2009, 2 master's, 2 doctorates awarded. *Degree requirements:* For doctorate, thesis/dissertation. *Entrance requirements:* For master's and doctorate, GRE General Test, minimum GPA of 3.0. Additional exam requirements/recommendations for international students: Required—TOEFL (minimum score 550 paper-based; 213 computer-based). *Application deadline:* For fall admission, 1/15 for domestic and international students. Applications are processed on a rolling basis. Application fee: $70 ($90 for international students). Electronic applications accepted. *Financial support:* Fellowships, research assistantships with full tuition reimbursements, teaching assistantships, institutionally sponsored loans, traineeships, health care benefits, and unspecified assistantships available. Financial award application deadline: 3/1; financial award applicants required to submit FAFSA. *Faculty research:* Montaigne, psychoanalysis, feminism and the problem of repression, aesthetics of nationalism and the limits of culture. *Unit head:* David Carroll, Chair, 949-824-4940, Fax: 949-824-1031, E-mail: dcarroll@uci.edu. *Application contact:* Lin Xi, Administrative Assistant, 949-824-6407, Fax: 949-824-1031, E-mail: lxi@uci.edu.

University of California, Los Angeles, Graduate Division, College of Letters and Science, Department of French and Francophone Studies, Los Angeles, CA 90034. Offers MA, PhD. *Students:* 28 full-time (22 women); includes 2 minority (1 African American, 1 Hispanic American), 2 international. Average age 30. 19 applicants, 53% accepted, 5 enrolled. In 2009, 1 master's, 4 doctorates awarded. Terminal master's awarded for partial completion of doctoral program. *Degree requirements:* For master's, one foreign language, comprehensive exam; for doctorate, 2 foreign languages, thesis/dissertation, oral and written qualifying exams. *Entrance requirements:* For master's, GRE General Test, minimum GPA of 3.0, sample of written work in French; for doctorate, GRE General Test, MA in French or equivalent; minimum undergraduate GPA of 3.0; sample of written work in French. *Application deadline:* For fall admission, 12/15 for domestic and international students. Application fee: $70 ($90 for international students). Electronic applications accepted. *Financial support:* In 2009–10, 18 fellowships with full and partial tuition reimbursements, 7 research assistantships with full and partial tuition reimbursements, 13 teaching assistantships with full and partial tuition reimbursements were awarded; Federal Work-Study, institutionally sponsored loans, health care benefits, tuition waivers (full and partial), and unspecified assistantships also available. Financial award applicants required to submit FAFSA. *Unit head:* Dr. Dominic Thomas, Chair, 310-794-8923. *Application contact:* Department Office, 310-825-1145, E-mail: allen@humnet.ucla.edu.

University of California, San Diego, Office of Graduate Studies, Department of Literature, Program in French Literature, La Jolla, CA 92093. Offers MA. *Degree requirements:* For master's, thesis. *Entrance requirements:* For master's, GRE General Test, GRE Subject Test. Electronic applications accepted.

University of California, Santa Barbara, Graduate Division, College of Letters and Sciences, Division of Humanities and Fine Arts, Department of French and Italian, Santa Barbara, CA 93106-4140. Offers French (MA, MABL, PhD), including applied linguistics (PhD), European Medieval studies (PhD), feminist studies (PhD), French (MABL, PhD); MA/PhD. French Language Institute available during summer sessions. *Faculty:* 21 full-time (12 women). *Students:* 11 full-time (7 women). Average age 31. 16 applicants, 63% accepted, 3 enrolled. In 2009, 1 master's, 5 doctorates awarded. Terminal master's awarded for partial completion of doctoral program. *Degree requirements:* For master's, 2 foreign languages, comprehensive exam; for doctorate, 2 foreign languages, comprehensive exam, thesis/dissertation. *Entrance requirements:* For master's, GRE, sample of written work, tape of spoken French, BA or the equivalent, 3 letters of recommendation, resume/curriculum vitae; for doctorate, GRE, sample of written work, tape of spoken French, MA or the equivalent, 3 letters of recommendation, statement of purpose, personal achievements/contributions statement, resume/curriculum vitae, transcripts for post-secondary institutions attended. Additional exam requirements/recommendations for international students: Required—TOEFL (minimum score 550 paper-based; 213 computer-based; 80 iBT) or IELTS (minimum score 7). *Application deadline:* For fall admission, 5/1 for domestic and international students; for winter admission, 10/1 for domestic and international students; for spring admission, 1/15 for domestic and international students. Application fee: $70 ($90 for international students). Electronic applications accepted. *Financial support:* In 2009–10, 11 students received support, including 5 fellowships with full and partial tuition reimbursements available (averaging $8,100 per year), 11 teaching assistantships with partial tuition reimbursements available (averaging $11,400 per year); career-related internships or fieldwork, Federal Work-Study, institutionally sponsored loans, scholarships/grants, traineeships, health care benefits, tuition waivers (full and partial), and unspecified assistantships also available. Financial award applicants required to submit FAFSA. *Faculty research:* French and Francophone studies, comparative literature, second language acquisition, applied linguistics, performance studies, feminist and gender studies. Total annual research expenditures: $2,500. *Unit head:* Prof. Jon Snyder, Chair, 805-893-2220, Fax: 805-893-8826, E-mail: snyder@frit.ucsb.edu. *Application contact:* Rosa Pinter, Graduate Staff Advisor, 805-893-3398, Fax: 805-893-8826, E-mail: pinter@frit.ucsb.edu.

University of California, Santa Barbara, Summer Sessions, Santa Barbara, CA 93106-2010. Offers French (MA); Spanish (MA). In 2009, 17 master's awarded. *Degree requirements:* For master's, comprehensive exam (for some programs). *Entrance requirements:* For master's, GRE, 3 letters of recommendation, resume/curriculum vitae. Additional exam requirements/recommendations for international students: Required—TOEFL (minimum score 550 paper-based; 213 computer-based; 80 iBT) or IELTS (minimum score 7). Application fee: $70 ($90 for international students). Electronic applications accepted. *Expenses:* Contact institution. *Financial support:* Scholarships/grants available. Financial award applicants required to submit FAFSA. *Unit head:* Dr. Loy Lytle, Dean of Summer Sessions, 805-893-2706, Fax: 805-893-7306, E-mail: low.lytle@els.ucsb.edu. *Application contact:* Program Manager, 805-893-7053, Fax: 805-893-7306, E-mail: language.institutes@summersessions.ucsb.edu.

University of Chicago, Division of the Humanities, Department of Romance Languages and Literatures, Chicago, IL 60637-1513. Offers French (AM, PhD); Italian (AM, PhD); Spanish (AM, PhD). Terminal master's awarded for partial completion of doctoral program. *Degree requirements:* For master's, 2 foreign languages, thesis; for doctorate, 3 foreign languages, thesis/dissertation. *Entrance requirements:* For master's and doctorate, GRE General Test, GRE Subject Test. Additional exam requirements/recommendations for international students: Required—TOEFL.

University of Cincinnati, Graduate School, McMicken College of Arts and Sciences, Department of Romance Languages and Literature, Program in French, Cincinnati, OH 45221. Offers MA, PhD. Terminal master's awarded for partial completion of doctoral program. *Degree requirements:* For master's, thesis optional; for doctorate, 2 foreign languages, thesis/dissertation. *Entrance requirements:* For master's, minimum GPA of 3.0. Electronic applications accepted.

University of Colorado at Boulder, Graduate School, College of Arts and Sciences, Department of French and Italian, Boulder, CO 80309. Offers French (MA, PhD). *Faculty:* 12 full-time (7 women). *Students:* 15 full-time (12 women), 9 part-time (7 women); includes 1 minority (Asian American or Pacific Islander), 5 international. Average age 34. 15 applicants, 33% accepted, 4 enrolled. In 2009, 5 master's, 4 doctorates awarded. Terminal master's awarded for partial completion of doctoral program. *Degree requirements:* For master's, 2 foreign languages, comprehensive exam, thesis or alternative; for doctorate, 3 foreign languages, thesis/dissertation. *Entrance requirements:* For master's, GRE General Test, minimum undergraduate GPA of 3.0; for doctorate, GRE General Test. *Application deadline:* For fall admission, 2/1 priority date for domestic students, 1/1 for international students. Applications are processed on a rolling basis. Application fee: $50 ($60 for international students). *Financial support:* In 2009–10, 3 fellowships (averaging $1,709 per year), 20 research assistantships (averaging $13,790 per year) were awarded; tuition waivers (full) also available. Financial award application deadline: 2/1. *Faculty research:* All periods of French literature from the Middle Ages to the present (including Francophone literature, cultural studies and literary theory). Total annual research expenditures: $2,879.

University of Connecticut, Graduate School, College of Liberal Arts and Sciences, Department of Modern and Classical Languages, Field of French, Storrs, CT 06269. Offers MA, PhD. *Faculty:* 7 full-time (6 women). *Students:* 12 full-time (7 women), 3 part-time (all women); includes 1 minority (Hispanic American), 9 international. Average age 31. 6 applicants, 50% accepted, 2 enrolled. In 2009, 2 master's awarded. Terminal master's awarded for partial completion of doctoral program. *Degree requirements:* For master's, comprehensive exam; for doctorate, thesis/dissertation. *Entrance requirements:* For master's and doctorate, GRE General Test, GRE Subject Test. Additional exam requirements/recommendations for international students: Required—TOEFL (minimum score 550 paper-based; 213 computer-based). *Application deadline:* For fall admission, 2/1 priority date for domestic and international students; for spring admission, 11/1 for domestic students, 10/1 for international students. Applications are processed on a rolling basis. Application fee: $55. Electronic applications accepted. *Expenses:* Tuition, state resident: full-time $4725; part-time $525 per credit. Tuition, nonresident: full-time $12,267; part-time $1363 per credit. Required fees: $346 per semester. Tuition and fees vary according to course load. *Financial support:* In 2009–10, 12 teaching assistantships with full tuition reimbursements were awarded; fellowships, research assistantships with full tuition reimbursements, Federal Work-Study, scholarships/grants, health care benefits, and unspecified assistantships also available. Financial award application deadline: 2/1; financial award applicants required to submit FAFSA. *Unit head:* Roger Celestin, Co-Chair, 860-486-3091, E-mail: roger.celestin@uconn.edu. *Application contact:* Anne Berthelot, Graduate Advisor, 860-486-3173, E-mail: anne.berthlot@uconn.edu.

University of Delaware, College of Arts and Sciences, Department of Foreign Languages and Literatures, Newark, DE 19716. Offers foreign languages and literatures (MA), including French, German, Spanish; foreign languages pedagogy (MA), including French, German, Spanish. *Degree requirements:* For master's, one foreign language, comprehensive exam, thesis optional. *Entrance requirements:* For master's, GRE General Test, letters of recom-

French

University of Delaware (continued)
mendation, writing sample. Additional exam requirements/recommendations for international students: Required—TOEFL. Electronic applications accepted. *Faculty research:* Medieval to Modern French and Spanish literature, Twentieth Century German, French, Spanish literature by women, computer-assisted instruction.

University of Florida, Graduate School, College of Liberal Arts and Sciences, Department of Romance Languages and Literatures, Program in French, Gainesville, FL 32611. Offers MA, PhD. *Degree requirements:* For master's, thesis optional; for doctorate, one foreign language, thesis/dissertation. *Entrance requirements:* For master's and doctorate, GRE General Test, minimum GPA of 3.0. Additional exam requirements/recommendations for international students: Required—TOEFL (minimum score 550 paper-based; 213 computer-based). Electronic applications accepted. *Faculty research:* Medieval, sixteenth, seventeenth, nineteenth, and twentieth century French literature.

University of Georgia, Graduate School, College of Arts and Sciences, Department of Romance Languages, Program in French, Athens, GA 30602. Offers MA. *Students:* 4 full-time (all women), 2 part-time (1 woman); includes 1 minority (African American). 8 applicants, 63% accepted, 4 enrolled. In 2009, 2 master's awarded. *Degree requirements:* For master's, one foreign language, thesis (MA). *Entrance requirements:* For master's, GRE General Test. *Application deadline:* For fall admission, 7/1 priority date for domestic students; for spring admission, 11/15 for domestic students. Application fee: $50. Electronic applications accepted. *Expenses:* Tuition, state resident: full-time $6000; part-time $250 per credit hour. Tuition, nonresident: full-time $20,904; part-time $871 per credit hour. Required fees: $730 per semester. *Financial support:* Fellowships, research assistantships, teaching assistantships, unspecified assistantships available. *Unit head:* Dr. Nina Hellerstein, Department Head, 706-542-3122, E-mail: hellerst@uga.edu. *Application contact:* Dr. Catherine M. Jones, Graduate Coordinator, 706-542-3159, Fax: 706-542-3287, E-mail: cmjones@uga.edu.

University of Guelph, Graduate Program Services, College of Arts, School of Languages and Literatures, Guelph, ON N1G 2W1, Canada. Offers European studies (MA); French studies (MA). *Entrance requirements:* For master's, honours BA or equivalent. Electronic applications accepted. *Faculty research:* Sociolinguistics, poetics and politics of literature, language acquisition.

University of Hawaii at Manoa, Graduate Division, College of Language, Linguistics and Literature, Department of Languages and Literatures of Europe and the Americas, Program in French, Honolulu, HI 96822. Offers MA. Part-time programs available. *Students:* 13 full-time (9 women), 3 part-time (all women); includes 7 minority (1 African American, 1 American Indian/Alaska Native, 4 Asian Americans or Pacific Islanders, 1 Hispanic American). Average age 33. 11 applicants, 64% accepted, 6 enrolled. In 2009, 3 master's awarded. *Degree requirements:* For master's, one foreign language, thesis optional. *Entrance requirements:* Additional exam requirements/recommendations for international students: Required—TOEFL (minimum score 580 paper-based; 237 computer-based; 92 iBT), IELTS (minimum score 5). *Application deadline:* For fall admission, 3/1 for domestic students, 2/1 for international students; for spring admission, 9/1 for domestic students, 8/15 for international students. Application fee: $60. *Expenses:* Tuition, state resident: full-time $8900; part-time $372 per credit. Tuition, nonresident: full-time $21,400; part-time $898 per credit. Required fees: $207 per semester. *Financial support:* In 2009–10, 1 fellowship (averaging $1,333 per year), 10 teaching assistantships (averaging $14,382 per year) were awarded. *Application contact:* Robert Ball, Information Contact, 808-956-4187, Fax: 808-956-9536, E-mail: rball@hawaii.edu.

University of Illinois at Chicago, Graduate College, College of Liberal Arts and Sciences, Department of Spanish, French, Italian and Portuguese, Program in French, Chicago, IL 60607-7128. Offers MA. Part-time programs available. *Degree requirements:* For master's, one foreign language, thesis optional, exam. *Entrance requirements:* For master's, minimum GPA of 2.75. Additional exam requirements/recommendations for international students: Required—TOEFL. Electronic applications accepted. *Faculty research:* French civilization, feminist theory, French theater, sociology of literature, narrative theory.

University of Illinois at Urbana–Champaign, Graduate College, College of Liberal Arts and Sciences, School of Literatures, Cultures and Linguistics, Department of French, Champaign, IL 61820. Offers MA, PhD. *Faculty:* 13 full-time (6 women). *Students:* 22 full-time (14 women), 6 part-time (4 women); includes 2 minority (1 African American, 1 Asian American or Pacific Islander), 9 international. 35 applicants, 26% accepted, 5 enrolled. In 2009, 5 master's, 1 doctorate awarded. *Entrance requirements:* For master's, GRE, minimum GPA of 3.0, 2 writing samples in French; for doctorate, GRE, minimum GPA of 3.5, 2 writing samples in French. Additional exam requirements/recommendations for international students: Required—TOEFL (minimum score 550 paper-based; 213 computer-based; 79 iBT), or IELTS (minimum score 6.5). *Application deadline:* Applications are processed on a rolling basis. Application fee: $60 ($75 for international students). Electronic applications accepted. *Financial support:* In 2009–10, 7 fellowships, 2 research assistantships, 31 teaching assistantships were awarded; tuition waivers (full and partial) also available. *Unit head:* Karen L. Fresco, Head, 217-244-2716, Fax: 217-244-2223, E-mail: kfresco@illinois.edu. *Application contact:* Lynn Stanke, Office Support Specialist, 217-333-6269, Fax: 217-244-3050, E-mail: stanke@illinois.edu.

The University of Iowa, Graduate College, College of Liberal Arts and Sciences, Department of French and Italian, Iowa City, IA 52242-1316. Offers French (MA, PhD). *Degree requirements:* For master's, thesis optional, exam; for doctorate, comprehensive exam, thesis/dissertation. *Entrance requirements:* For master's and doctorate, GRE General Test, minimum GPA of 3.0. Additional exam requirements/recommendations for international students: Required—TOEFL (minimum score 550 paper-based; 213 computer-based; 81 iBT). Electronic applications accepted.

The University of Kansas, Graduate Studies, College of Liberal Arts and Sciences, Department of French and Italian, Lawrence, KS 66045-7590. Offers French (MA, PhD). Part-time programs available. *Faculty:* 11 full-time (6 women), 1 (woman) part-time/adjunct. *Students:* 25 full-time (18 women), 3 international. Average age 33. 10 applicants, 90% accepted, 3 enrolled. In 2009, 4 master's awarded. *Degree requirements:* For master's, one foreign language, comprehensive exam, thesis optional; for doctorate, 2 foreign languages, comprehensive exam, thesis/dissertation. *Entrance requirements:* For master's and doctorate, GRE. Additional exam requirements/recommendations for international students: Required—TOEFL, IELTS. *Application deadline:* For fall admission, 1/15 priority date for domestic and international students. Applications are processed on a rolling basis. Application fee: $45 ($55 for international students). Electronic applications accepted. *Expenses:* Tuition, state resident: full-time $6492; part-time $270.50 per credit hour. Tuition, nonresident: full-time $15,510; part-time $646.25 per credit hour. Required fees: $847; $70.56 per credit hour. Tuition and fees vary according to course load and program. *Financial support:* Fellowships, teaching assistantships with full tuition reimbursements, unspecified assistantships available. Financial award applicants required to submit FAFSA. *Faculty research:* French literature and cultural studies; Francophone literature, film. *Unit head:* Van Kelly, Chair, 785-864-4056, Fax: 785-864-5179, E-mail: vkelly@ku.edu. *Application contact:* Bruce Hayes, Associate Professor, 785-864-9028, E-mail: bhayes@ku.edu.

University of Kentucky, Graduate School, College of Arts and Sciences, Program in French, Lexington, KY 40506-0032. Offers MA. *Degree requirements:* For master's, one foreign language, comprehensive exam. *Entrance requirements:* For master's, GRE General Test, minimum undergraduate GPA of 2.75. Additional exam requirements/recommendations for international students: Required—TOEFL (minimum score 550 paper-based; 213 computer-based). Electronic applications accepted. *Faculty research:* The fables of Marie DeFrance, Rabelais and reading; the family romance in eighteenth century narrative; women of Dada and surrealism; postcolonialism; postmodernism.

University of Lethbridge, School of Graduate Studies, Lethbridge, AB T1K 3M4, Canada. Offers accounting (MScM); addictions counseling (M Sc); agricultural biotechnology (M Sc); agricultural studies (M Sc, MA); anthropology (MA); archaeology (MA); art (MA, MFA); biochemistry (M Sc); biological sciences (M Sc); biomolecular science (PhD); biosystems and biodiversity (PhD); Canadian studies (MA); chemistry (M Sc); computer science (M Sc); computer science and geographical information science (M Sc); counseling psychology (M Ed); dramatic arts (MA); earth, space, and physical science (PhD); economics (MA); educational leadership (M Ed); English (MA); environmental science (M Sc); evolution and behavior (PhD); exercise science (M Sc); finance (MScM); French (MA); French/German (MA); French/Spanish (MA); general education (M Ed); general management (MScM); geography (M Sc, MA); German (MA); health science (M Sc); health sciences (MA); history (MA); human resource management and labour relations (MScM); individualized multidisciplinary (M Sc, MA); information systems (MScM); international management (MScM); kinesiology (M Sc, MA); management (M Sc, MA); marketing (MScM); mathematics (M Sc); music (M Mus, MA); Native American studies (MA); neuroscience (M Sc, PhD); new media (MA); nursing (M Sc); philosophy (MA); physics (M Sc); policy and strategy (MScM); political science (MA); psychology (M Sc, MA); religious studies (MA); social sciences (MA); sociology (MA); theatre and dramatic arts (MFA); theoretical and computational science (PhD); urban and regional studies (MA); women's studies (MA). Part-time and evening/weekend programs available. *Degree requirements:* For doctorate, comprehensive exam, thesis/dissertation. *Entrance requirements:* For master's, GMAT (M Sc in management), bachelor's degree in related field, minimum GPA of 3.0 during previous 20 graded semester courses, 2 years teaching or related experience (M Ed); for doctorate, master's degree, minimum graduate GPA of 3.5. Additional exam requirements/recommendations for international students: Required—TOEFL. *Faculty research:* Movement and brain plasticity, gibberellin physiology, photosynthesis, carbon cycling, molecular properties of main-group ring components.

University of Louisiana at Lafayette, College of Liberal Arts, Department of Modern Languages, Program in Francophone Studies, Lafayette, LA 70504. Offers PhD. *Degree requirements:* For doctorate, 2 foreign languages, comprehensive exam, thesis/dissertation. *Entrance requirements:* For doctorate, GRE General Test, minimum GPA of 2.75. Additional exam requirements/recommendations for international students: Required—TOEFL (minimum score 550 paper-based; 213 computer-based). Electronic applications accepted. *Faculty research:* Louisiana folklore, eighteenth century French literature, contemporary criticism.

University of Louisiana at Lafayette, College of Liberal Arts, Department of Modern Languages, Program in French, Lafayette, LA 70504. Offers MA. Part-time programs available. *Degree requirements:* For master's, 2 foreign languages, thesis or alternative. *Entrance requirements:* For master's, GRE General Test, minimum GPA of 2.75. Additional exam requirements/recommendations for international students: Required—TOEFL (minimum score 550 paper-based; 213 computer-based). Electronic applications accepted. *Faculty research:* Louisiana studies, nineteenth century French literature, Francophone studies.

University of Louisville, Graduate School, College of Arts and Sciences, Department of Classical and Modern Languages, Louisville, KY 40292-0001. Offers French (MA); Spanish (MA). *Faculty:* 14 full-time (8 women). *Students:* 13 full-time (9 women), 19 part-time (10 women); includes 7 minority (3 African Americans, 4 Hispanic Americans), 1 international. Average age 30. 18 applicants, 72% accepted, 8 enrolled. In 2009, 13 master's awarded. *Degree requirements:* For master's, one foreign language, thesis optional. *Entrance requirements:* For master's, GRE General Test. *Application deadline:* Applications are processed on a rolling basis. Application fee: $50. *Financial support:* In 2009–10, 9 students received support, including 8 teaching assistantships with full tuition reimbursements available (averaging $12,000 per year); fellowships also available. *Unit head:* Dr. Mary Makris, Acting Chair, 502-852-0491, Fax: 502-852-8885, E-mail: mmakris@louisville.edu. *Application contact:* Libby Leggett, Director, Graduate Admissions, 502-852-3101, Fax: 502-852-6536, E-mail: gradadm@louisville.edu.

University of Maine, Graduate School, College of Liberal Arts and Sciences, Department of Modern Languages and Classics, Orono, ME 04469. Offers French (MA, MAT). Part-time programs available. *Faculty:* 9 full-time (6 women), 7 part-time/adjunct (5 women). *Students:* 5 full-time (3 women), 2 part-time (1 woman); includes 1 minority (African American). Average age 31. 6 applicants, 83% accepted, 4 enrolled. In 2009, 9 master's awarded. *Degree requirements:* For master's, one foreign language, thesis (for some programs). *Entrance requirements:* For master's, GRE General Test. Additional exam requirements/recommendations for international students: Required—TOEFL. *Application deadline:* For fall admission, 2/1 priority date for domestic students. Applications are processed on a rolling basis. Application fee: $60. Electronic applications accepted. *Financial support:* In 2009–10, 3 teaching assistantships with tuition reimbursements (averaging $12,790 per year) were awarded; Federal Work-Study, tuition waivers (full and partial), and instructorships also available. Financial award application deadline: 3/1. *Faculty research:* Narratology, poetics, Quebec literature, theater, women's studies. *Unit head:* Dr. Jane Smith, Chair, 207-581-2079, Fax: 207-581-1832. *Application contact:* Scott G. Delcourt, Associate Dean of the Graduate School, 207-581-3291, Fax: 207-581-3232, E-mail: graduate@maine.edu.

University of Manitoba, Faculty of Graduate Studies, Faculty of Arts, Department of French, Spanish and Italian, Winnipeg, MB R3T 2N2, Canada. Offers French (MA, PhD). *Degree requirements:* For master's, one foreign language, thesis; for doctorate, 2 foreign languages, thesis/dissertation.

University of Maryland, College Park, Academic Affairs, College of Arts and Humanities, School of Languages, Literature, and Cultures, Modern French Studies Program, College Park, MD 20742. Offers PhD. *Students:* 14 full-time (13 women); includes 1 minority (African American), 8 international. 14 applicants, 36% accepted, 3 enrolled. In 2009, 2 doctorates awarded. *Entrance requirements:* Additional exam requirements/recommendations for international students: Required—TOEFL. *Application deadline:* For fall admission, 1/15 for domestic and international students. Application fee: $60. *Expenses:* Tuition, area resident: Part-time $471 per credit hour. Tuition, state resident: part-time $471 per credit hour. Tuition, nonresident: part-time $1016 per credit hour. Required fees: $337.04 per term. *Financial support:* In 2009–10, 2 fellowships (averaging $13,900 per year), 7 teaching assistantships (averaging $17,926 per year) were awarded. *Unit head:* Carol Mossman, Director, 301-405-4025, Fax: 301-314-9928, E-mail: cmossman@umd.edu. *Application contact:* Dean of Graduate School, 301-405-0358, Fax: 301-314-9305.

University of Maryland, College Park, Academic Affairs, College of Arts and Humanities, School of Languages, Literature, and Cultures, Program in French Language and Literature, College Park, MD 20742. Offers MA. *Students:* 9 full-time (8 women), 3 part-time (all women); includes 1 minority (Asian American or Pacific Islander), 1 international. 15 applicants, 47% accepted, 5 enrolled. In 2009, 3 master's awarded. *Degree requirements:* For master's, one foreign language, comprehensive exam, thesis or alternative. *Entrance requirements:* For master's, GRE General Test, GRE Subject Test, minimum GPA of 3.0, 3 letters of recommendation. Additional exam requirements/recommendations for international students: Required—TOEFL. *Application deadline:* For fall admission, 1/15 for domestic and international students. Applications are processed on a rolling basis. Application fee: $60. Electronic applications accepted. *Expenses:* Tuition, area resident: Part-time $471 per credit hour. Tuition, state resident: part-time $471 per credit hour. Tuition, nonresident: part-time $1016 per credit hour. Required fees: $337.04 per term. *Financial support:* In 2009–10, 2 fellowships with full and partial tuition reimbursements (averaging $12,799 per year), 7 teaching assistantships with tuition reimbursements (averaging $17,990 per year) were awarded; Federal Work-Study also available. Support available to part-time students. Financial award applicants required to submit FAFSA. *Unit head:* Carol Mossman, Director, School of Languages, Literatures and Cultures, 301-405-6464, E-mail: cmossman@umd.edu. *Application contact:* Dean of Graduate School, 301-405-0358, Fax: 301-314-9305.

University of Maryland, College Park, Academic Affairs, College of Arts and Humanities, School of Languages, Literature, and Cultures, Program in Second Language Acquisition and Application, College Park, MD 20742. Offers French (MA); German (MA); Japanese (MA); Russian (MA); second language instruction (PhD); second language learning (PhD); second language measurement and assessment (PhD); second language use (PhD); Spanish (MA). *Students:* 12 full-time (10 women), 5 part-time (3 women); includes 2 minority (both Asian Americans or Pacific Islanders), 5 international. 47 applicants, 15% accepted, 3 enrolled. In 2009, 7 master's awarded. *Entrance requirements:* For master's, BA or BS in related field, demonstrated language competency, 3 letters of reference. *Application deadline:* For fall admission, 1/15 for domestic and international students; for spring admission, 6/1 for domestic and international students. Applications are processed on a rolling basis. Application fee: $60. Electronic applications accepted. *Expenses:* Tuition, area resident: Part-time $471 per credit hour. Tuition, state resident: part-time $471 per credit hour. Tuition, nonresident: part-time $1016 per credit hour. Required fees: $337.04 per term. *Financial support:* In 2009–10, 2 fellowships with full and partial tuition reimbursements (averaging $13,928 per year), 4 research assistantships (averaging $21,457 per year), 6 teaching assistantships (averaging $20,933 per year) were awarded. *Faculty research:* Second language acquisition, pedagogical perspectives, technological applications, language use in professional contexts. *Unit head:* Carol Mossman, Director, School of Languages, Literatures, and Cultures, 301-405-4025, E-mail: cmossman@umd.edu. *Application contact:* Dean of Graduate School, 301-405-0376, Fax: 301-314-9305.

University of Massachusetts Amherst, Graduate School, College of Humanities and Fine Arts, Department of Languages, Literatures, and Cultures, Program in French and Francophone Studies, Amherst, MA 01003. Offers French (MA, MAT). Part-time programs available. *Faculty:* 7 full-time (4 women). *Students:* 7 full-time (5 women), 3 part-time (1 woman), 1 international. Average age 34. 10 applicants, 80% accepted, 2 enrolled. In 2009, 4 master's awarded. *Degree requirements:* For master's, thesis or alternative. *Entrance requirements:* For master's, GRE General Test. Additional exam requirements/recommendations for international students: Required—TOEFL (minimum score 550 paper-based; 213 computer-based; 80 iBT), IELTS (minimum score 6.5). *Application deadline:* For fall admission, 2/1 for domestic and international students; for spring admission, 10/1 for domestic and international students. Applications are processed on a rolling basis. Application fee: $50 ($65 for international students). Electronic applications accepted. *Expenses:* Tuition, state resident: full-time $2640; part-time $110 per credit. Tuition, nonresident: full-time $9936; part-time $414 per credit. Tuition and fees vary according to course load. *Financial support:* In 2009–10, 17 teaching assistantships with full tuition reimbursements (averaging $12,253 per year) were awarded; fellowships, research assistantships, career-related internships or fieldwork, Federal Work-Study, scholarships/grants, traineeships, health care benefits, tuition waivers (full), and unspecified assistantships also available. Support available to part-time students. Financial award application deadline: 2/1. *Unit head:* Dr. Luke P. Bouvier, Graduate Program Director, 413-545-2314, Fax: 412-545-4778. *Application contact:* Jean M. Ames, Supervisor of Admissions, 413-545-0722, Fax: 413-577-0100, E-mail: gradadm@grad.umass.edu.

University of Memphis, Graduate School, College of Arts and Sciences, Department of Foreign Languages and Literatures, Memphis, TN 38152. Offers French (MA); Spanish (MA). Part-time programs available. *Faculty:* 12 full-time (5 women), 1 part-time/adjunct (0 women). *Students:* 14 full-time (10 women), 5 part-time (all women); includes 5 minority (2 African Americans, 1 American Indian/Alaska Native, 2 Hispanic Americans), 2 international. Average age 34. 12 applicants, 92% accepted, 5 enrolled. In 2009, 7 master's awarded. *Degree requirements:* For master's, 2 foreign languages, comprehensive exam. *Entrance requirements:* For master's, GRE, interview in language of concentration (French/Spanish). Additional exam requirements/recommendations for international students: Required—TOEFL (minimum score 79 iBT). *Application deadline:* For fall admission, 3/15 for domestic students, 2/15 for international students; for spring admission, 10/30 for domestic students, 10/5 for international students. Applications are processed on a rolling basis. Application fee: $35 ($60 for international students). Electronic applications accepted. *Expenses:* Tuition, state resident: full-time $6246; part-time $347 per credit hour. Tuition, nonresident: full-time $15,894; part-time $883 per credit hour. Required fees: $1160. Full-time tuition and fees vary according to course load, degree level and program. *Financial support:* In 2009–10, 11 students received support; research assistantships with full tuition reimbursements available, teaching assistantships with full tuition reimbursements available, Federal Work-Study, scholarships/grants, and unspecified assistantships available. Financial award application deadline: 2/15; financial award applicants required to submit FAFSA. *Faculty research:* Latin American studies, Brazilian culture and literature, Modernity and Postmodernity, Hispanic studies, French studies, French and Hispanic culture and literature, Hispanic linguistics, applied linguistics. *Unit head:* Dr. Ralph Albanese, Professor and Chair, 901-678-2507, E-mail: ralbanes@memphis.edu. *Application contact:* Dr. Fernando Burgos, Professor and Coordinator of Graduate Studies, 901-678-3158, E-mail: fburgos@memphis.edu.

University of Miami, Graduate School, College of Arts and Sciences, Department of Modern Languages and Literatures, Coral Gables, FL 33124. Offers romance studies (PhD), including French, Spanish. *Degree requirements:* For doctorate, 2 foreign languages, thesis/dissertation, area exam, qualifying exam. *Entrance requirements:* For doctorate, 1 writing sample in English and 1 writing sample in French or Spanish, minimum GPA of 3.0, oral interview, letters of recommendation. Additional exam requirements/recommendations for international students: Required—TOEFL (minimum score 550 paper-based; 213 computer-based; 59 iBT). Electronic applications accepted. *Faculty research:* Transatlantic studies, Caribbean studies, comparative literature, gender theory, cultural studies.

University of Michigan, Horace H. Rackham School of Graduate Studies, College of Literature, Science, and the Arts, Department of Romance Languages and Literatures, Program in French, Ann Arbor, MI 48109. Offers PhD. *Faculty:* 8 full-time (4 women). *Students:* 17 full-time (9 women); includes 2 African Americans, 2 Hispanic Americans. Average age 31. 26 applicants, 19% accepted, 2 enrolled. In 2009, 2 doctorates awarded. *Degree requirements:* For doctorate, 2 foreign languages, thesis/dissertation, oral defense of dissertation, preliminary exams. *Entrance requirements:* For doctorate, GRE General Test. Additional exam requirements/recommendations for international students: Required—TOEFL or Michigan English Language Assessment Battery. *Application deadline:* For fall admission, 1/1 for domestic and international students. Application fee: $60. Electronic applications accepted. *Expenses:* Tuition, state resident: full-time $17,286; part-time $1099 per credit hour. Tuition, nonresident: full-time $34,944; part-time $2080 per credit hour. Required fees: $95 per semester. Tuition and fees vary according to course load, degree level and program. *Financial support:* In 2009–10, 2 fellowships with full tuition reimbursements (averaging $20,000 per year), 13 teaching assistantships with full tuition reimbursements (averaging $20,000 per year) were awarded; institutionally sponsored loans, scholarships/grants, and unspecified assistantships also available. Financial award application deadline: 1/1. *Faculty research:* Comparative Romance studies, medieval and early modern studies, postcolonial and minority literatures, culture and materiality, reflection on the nature and function of scholarship. *Unit head:* Dr. Michele Hannoosh, Chair, 734-764-5344, Fax: 734-764-8163. *Application contact:* Annette Herbert, Graduate Assistant, 734-764-8164, Fax: 734-764-8163, E-mail: rll-admissions@umich.edu.

University of Minnesota, Twin Cities Campus, Graduate School, College of Liberal Arts, Department of French and Italian, Minneapolis, MN 55455-0213. Offers French (MA, PhD). Part-time programs available. *Degree requirements:* For master's, one foreign language, comprehensive exam, thesis optional; for doctorate, one foreign language, thesis/dissertation, individualized exam on topic areas. *Entrance requirements:* For master's and doctorate, GRE, minimum GPA of 3.25 (recommended). Additional exam requirements/recommendations for international students: Required—TOEFL (minimum score 550 paper-based; 213 computer-based). Electronic applications accepted. *Faculty research:* Francophone literature, cultural studies, feminism, critical theory, medieval studies.

University of Mississippi, Graduate School, College of Liberal Arts, Department of Modern Languages, Oxford, University, MS 38677. Offers French (MA); German (MA); Spanish (MA). *Faculty:* 50 full-time (30 women). *Students:* 43 full-time (31 women), 16 part-time (11 women); includes 12 minority (7 African Americans, 5 Hispanic Americans), 11 international. In 2009, 12 master's awarded. *Degree requirements:* For master's, thesis (for some programs). *Entrance requirements:* For master's, GRE General Test, minimum GPA of 3.0. Additional exam requirements/recommendations for international students: Required—TOEFL. *Application deadline:* For fall admission, 2/1 for domestic students; for spring admission, 10/1 for domestic students. Applications are processed on a rolling basis. Application fee: $25. Electronic applications accepted. *Financial support:* Scholarships/grants available. Financial award application deadline: 3/1; financial award applicants required to submit FAFSA. *Unit head:* Dr. Donald L. Dyer, Chair, 662-915-7298, Fax: 662-915-1086, E-mail: mlangs@olemiss.edu. *Application contact:* Dr. Christy M. Wyandt, Associate Dean, 662-915-7474, Fax: 662-915-7577, E-mail: cwyandt@olemiss.edu.

University of Missouri, Graduate School, College of Arts and Sciences, Department of Romance Languages and Literature, Program in French, Columbia, MO 65211. Offers MA, PhD. *Degree requirements:* For master's, one foreign language; for doctorate, 4 foreign languages, thesis/dissertation. *Entrance requirements:* For master's and doctorate, GRE General Test, minimum GPA of 3.0. Additional exam requirements/recommendations for international students: Required—TOEFL (minimum score 500 paper-based; 173 computer-based; 61 iBT).

The University of Montana, Graduate School, College of Arts and Sciences, Department of Modern and Classical Languages and Literatures, Missoula, MT 59812-0002. Offers French (MA); German (MA); Spanish (MA). *Degree requirements:* For master's, one foreign language. *Entrance requirements:* For master's, GRE General Test. Additional exam requirements/recommendations for international students: Required—TOEFL.

University of Nebraska–Lincoln, Graduate College, College of Arts and Sciences, Department of Modern Languages and Literatures, Lincoln, NE 68588. Offers French (MA, PhD); German (MA, PhD); Spanish (MA, PhD). *Degree requirements:* For master's, thesis optional; for doctorate, comprehensive exam, thesis/dissertation. *Entrance requirements:* For master's and doctorate, writing sample in target language. Additional exam requirements/recommendations for international students: Required—TOEFL (minimum score 550 paper-based; 213 computer-based). Electronic applications accepted. *Faculty research:* French, German, and Spanish language, literature, and culture.

University of Nevada, Reno, Graduate School, College of Liberal Arts, Department of Foreign Languages and Literatures, Reno, NV 89557. Offers French (MA); German (MA); Spanish (MA). *Degree requirements:* For master's, one foreign language, thesis optional. *Entrance requirements:* For master's, GRE General Test, minimum GPA of 2.75. Additional exam requirements/recommendations for international students: Required—TOEFL (minimum score 500 paper-based; 173 computer-based; 61 iBT), IELTS (minimum score 6). *Faculty research:* Thirteenth century mysticism, contemporary Spanish and Latin American poetry and theater, French interrelation between narration and photography, exile literature and Holocaust.

University of New Mexico, Graduate School, College of Arts and Sciences, Department of Foreign Languages and Literature, Albuquerque, NM 87131-2039. Offers comparative literature and cultural studies (MA); French (MA); French studies (PhD); German studies (MA). Part-time programs available. *Faculty:* 15 full-time (11 women), 8 part-time/adjunct (4 women). *Students:* 9 full-time (8 women), 4 part-time (2 women), 6 international. Average age 33. 9 applicants, 44% accepted, 3 enrolled. In 2009, 5 master's awarded. *Degree requirements:* For master's, one foreign language, thesis optional; for doctorate, 2 foreign languages, thesis/dissertation. *Entrance requirements:* Additional exam requirements/recommendations for international students: Required—TOEFL. *Application deadline:* For fall admission, 2/1 priority date for domestic students; for spring admission, 10/1 priority date for domestic students. Application fee: $50. Electronic applications accepted. *Expenses:* Tuition, state resident: full-time $2099; part-time $233.20 per credit hour. Tuition, nonresident: full-time $6650. Required fees: $25 per semester. Tuition and fees vary according to course load, program and reciprocity agreements. *Financial support:* In 2009–10, 20 teaching assistantships with tuition reimbursements (averaging $12,023 per year) were awarded; Federal Work-Study, health care benefits, and unspecified assistantships also available. Financial award application deadline: 3/1; financial award applicants required to submit FAFSA. *Faculty research:* German, Russian, Italian, Japanese, French, comparative literature, culture studies, classics. Total annual research expenditures: $4,750. *Unit head:* Dr. Natasha Kolchevska, Chair, 505-277-4771, Fax: 505-277-3599, E-mail: nakol@unm.edu. *Application contact:* Jean Aragon, Application and Graduation Advisor, 505-277-4471, Fax: 505-277-3599, E-mail: peaslee@unm.edu.

The University of North Carolina at Chapel Hill, Graduate School, College of Arts and Sciences, Department of Romance Languages, Chapel Hill, NC 27599. Offers French (MA, PhD); Italian (MA, PhD); Portuguese (MA, PhD); Romance languages (MA, PhD); Romance philology (MA, PhD); Spanish (MA, PhD). *Degree requirements:* For master's, one foreign language, comprehensive exam, thesis; for doctorate, 2 foreign languages, comprehensive exam, thesis/dissertation. *Entrance requirements:* For master's and doctorate, GRE General Test, minimum GPA of 3.0. Additional exam requirements/recommendations for international students: Required—TOEFL (minimum score 550 paper-based; 213 computer-based). Electronic applications accepted.

The University of North Carolina at Greensboro, Graduate School, College of Arts and Sciences, Department of Romance Languages, Program in French, Greensboro, NC 27412-5001. Offers MA. *Degree requirements:* For master's, one foreign language, comprehensive exam, thesis or alternative. *Entrance requirements:* For master's, GRE General Test, 3-5 minute tape demonstrating foreign language proficiency, composition in French, sample paper in English. Additional exam requirements/recommendations for international students: Required—TOEFL. Electronic applications accepted.

University of Northern Iowa, Graduate College, College of Humanities and Fine Arts, Department of Modern Languages, Program in French, Cedar Falls, IA 50614. Offers French (MA); teaching English to speakers of other languages/French (MA). Part-time and evening/weekend programs available. *Students:* 3 full-time (2 women), 3 part-time (2 women); includes 1 minority (Hispanic American), 2 international. 3 applicants, 67% accepted, 1 enrolled. In 2009, 5 master's awarded. *Degree requirements:* For master's, one foreign language, comprehensive exam, thesis or alternative. *Entrance requirements:* For master's, minimum GPA of 3.0, valid teaching license, documentation of successful teaching experience. Additional exam requirements/recommendations for international students: Required—TOEFL (minimum score 600 paper-based; 250 computer-based; 100 iBT). *Application deadline:* For fall admission, 8/1 priority date for domestic students. Applications are processed on a rolling basis. Application fee: $30 ($50 for international students). Electronic applications accepted. *Financial support:* Career-related internships or fieldwork, Federal Work-Study, and tuition waivers (full and partial) available. Support available to part-time students. Financial award application deadline: 2/1. *Unit head:* Dr. Anne Lair, Coordinator, 319-273-2183, Fax: 319-273-2848, E-mail: anne.lair@uni.edu. *Application contact:* Laurie S. Russell, Record Analyst, 319-273-2623, Fax: 319-273-6792, E-mail: laurie.russell@uni.edu.

University of North Texas, Robert B. Toulouse School of Graduate Studies, College of Arts and Sciences, Department of Foreign Languages and Literatures, Denton, TX 76203. Offers French (MA); Spanish (MA). Part-time programs available. *Degree requirements:* For master's, 2 foreign languages, comprehensive exam, thesis optional. *Entrance requirements:* For master's, GRE General Test, minimum undergraduate GPA of 3.0, curriculum vitae, 250-word essay in French or Spanish, 12 advanced credits in French or Spanish. Additional exam requirements/recommendations for international students: Recommended—TOEFL (minimum score 550 paper-based; 213 computer-based; 79 iBT). Application fee: $50 ($75 for international students). *Expenses:* Tuition, state resident: full-time $4298; part-time $239 per contact hour. Tuition, nonresident: full-time $9878; part-time $549 per contact hour. Required fees: $265 per contact hour. *Financial support:* Fellowships, teaching assistantships, career-related internships or fieldwork, Federal Work-Study, and institutionally sponsored loans available. Financial award

French

University of North Texas (continued)
application deadline: 4/1; financial award applicants required to submit FAFSA. *Faculty research:* Literature of Austria, France, Germany, Latin America, Spain; culture/civilization; applied linguistics. *Unit head:* Chair. *Application contact:* Chair.

University of Notre Dame, Graduate School, College of Arts and Letters, Division of Humanities, Department of Romance Languages and Literatures, Notre Dame, IN 46556. Offers French and Francophone studies (MA); Iberian and Latin American studies (MA); Italian studies (MA); Romance literatures (MA). *Degree requirements:* For master's, 2 foreign languages, comprehensive exam, thesis optional. *Entrance requirements:* For master's, GRE General Test, BA in target language. Additional exam requirements/recommendations for international students: Required—TOEFL (minimum score 600 paper-based; 250 computer-based; 80 iBT). Electronic applications accepted. *Faculty research:* Literature of discovery and exploration, modern literature, literary criticism, medieval literature, feminist critical theory.

University of Oklahoma, Graduate College, College of Arts and Sciences, Department of Modern Languages, Program in French, Norman, OK 73019. Offers MA, PhD, MBA/MA. Part-time programs available. *Students:* 11 full-time (9 women), 1 part-time (0 women); includes 2 minority (1 African American, 1 Hispanic American), 5 international. 6 applicants, 67% accepted, 3 enrolled. In 2009, 2 master's awarded. *Degree requirements:* For master's, 2 foreign languages, comprehensive exam, thesis optional, departmental qualifying exam; for doctorate, 3 foreign languages, comprehensive exam, thesis/dissertation, departmental qualifying exam. *Entrance requirements:* For master's, BA in French or equivalent, minimum GPA of 3.0 in last 60 hours, 3 letters of recommendation. Additional exam requirements/recommendations for international students: Required—TOEFL (minimum score 550 paper-based; 213 computer-based). *Application deadline:* For fall admission, 6/1 priority date for domestic students, 4/1 for international students; for spring admission, 11/1 for domestic students, 9/1 for international students. Applications are processed on a rolling basis. Application fee: $40 ($90 for international students). Electronic applications accepted. *Expenses:* Tuition, state resident: full-time $3744; part-time $156 per credit hour. Tuition, nonresident: full-time $13,577; part-time $565.70 per credit hour. Required fees: $2415; $90.10 per credit hour. *Financial support:* In 2009–10, 11 students received support. Scholarships/grants, health care benefits, and unspecified assistantships available. Financial award applicants required to submit FAFSA. *Faculty research:* French and Francophone literature and cultural studies, history of medicine, critical theory, food and culture, European culture and identity. *Unit head:* Dr. Pamela Genova, Chair, 405-325-6181, Fax: 405-325-0103, E-mail: genova@ou.edu. *Application contact:* Dr. Logan E. Whalen, Graduate Liaison, 405-325-5088, Fax: 405-325-0103, E-mail: mlllgradinfo@ou.edu.

University of Oregon, Graduate School, College of Arts and Sciences, Department of Romance Languages, Program in French, Eugene, OR 97403. Offers MA. Part-time programs available. *Degree requirements:* For master's, one foreign language. *Entrance requirements:* For master's, GRE General Test, minimum GPA of 3.0. Additional exam requirements/recommendations for international students: Required—TOEFL.

University of Ottawa, Faculty of Graduate and Postdoctoral Studies, Faculty of Arts, Department of Lettres Françaises, Ottawa, ON K1N 6N5, Canada. Offers MA, PhD. *Degree requirements:* For master's, thesis or alternative; for doctorate, thesis/dissertation, oral exam. *Entrance requirements:* For master's, honors degree or equivalent, minimum B average; for doctorate, master's degree, minimum B+ average. Electronic applications accepted. *Faculty research:* Littérature française, du Moyen-Âge à nos jours; littérature québécoise, des origines au XXe siècle; création littéraire.

University of Pennsylvania, School of Arts and Sciences, Graduate Group in Romance Languages, Philadelphia, PA 19104. Offers French (AM, PhD); Italian (AM, PhD); Spanish (AM, PhD). *Faculty:* 60 full-time (24 women), 4 part-time/adjunct (1 woman). *Students:* 60 full-time (38 women), 2 part-time (both women); includes 7 minority (1 American Indian/Alaska Native, 6 Hispanic Americans), 17 international. 101 applicants, 26% accepted, 13 enrolled. In 2009, 12 master's, 7 doctorates awarded. Terminal master's awarded for partial completion of doctoral program. *Degree requirements:* For master's, one foreign language, thesis or alternative; for doctorate, 2 foreign languages, thesis/dissertation. *Entrance requirements:* For master's and doctorate, GRE General Test. Additional exam requirements/recommendations for international students: Required—TOEFL. *Application deadline:* For fall admission, 12/1 priority date for domestic students. Application fee: $70. Electronic applications accepted. *Expenses:* Tuition: Full-time $25,660; part-time $4758 per course. Required fees: $2152; $270 per course. Tuition and fees vary according to course load, degree level and program. *Financial support:* In 2009–10, 23 fellowships, 2 research assistantships, 39 teaching assistantships were awarded; institutionally sponsored loans, scholarships/grants, traineeships, health care benefits, and unspecified assistantships also available. Financial award application deadline: 12/15. *Faculty research:* Literary theory and criticism, cultural studies, history of Romance literatures, gender studies.

University of Pittsburgh, School of Arts and Sciences, Department of French and Italian, Program in French, Pittsburgh, PA 15260. Offers MA, PhD. Part-time programs available. *Faculty:* 7 full-time (5 women). *Students:* 19 full-time (9 women), 4 international. Average age 30. 23 applicants, 35% accepted, 3 enrolled. In 2009, 3 master's, 3 doctorates awarded. Terminal master's awarded for partial completion of doctoral program. *Degree requirements:* For master's, one foreign language, comprehensive exam, seminar paper; for doctorate, one foreign language, comprehensive exam, thesis/dissertation, dissertation defense. *Entrance requirements:* For master's, GRE General Test, phone interview, 2 writing samples (French and English); for doctorate, GRE General Test, phone interview, 2 writing samples (French and English), personal essay. Additional exam requirements/recommendations for international students: Required—TOEFL (minimum score 554 paper-based; 213 computer-based; 80 iBT). *Application deadline:* For fall admission, 1/10 priority date for domestic and international students. Application fee: $50. Electronic applications accepted. *Expenses:* Tuition, state resident: full-time $16,402; part-time $665 per credit. Tuition, nonresident: full-time $28,694; part-time $1175 per credit. Required fees: $690; $175 per term. Tuition and fees vary according to program. *Financial support:* In 2009–10, 16 students received support, including 4 fellowships with full tuition reimbursements available (averaging $17,822 per year), 12 teaching assistantships with full tuition reimbursements available (averaging $15,065 per year); career-related internships or fieldwork, Federal Work-Study, institutionally sponsored loans, scholarships/grants, traineeships, health care benefits, tuition waivers (partial), unspecified assistantships, and summer research stipends also available. Support available to part-time students. Financial award application deadline: 1/10; financial award applicants required to submit FAFSA. *Faculty research:* Literature and politics, constructs of the French nation, literary and cultural theory, French linguistics, gender and sexuality, French literature and culture of all periods. Total annual research expenditures: $34,000. *Unit head:* Dr. Dennis Looney, Chairman, 412-624-5220, Fax: 412-624-6263, E-mail: looney@pitt.edu. *Application contact:* Prof. Todd Reeser, Graduate Director, 412-624-6224, Fax: 412-624-6263, E-mail: reeser@pitt.edu.

University of Regina, Faculty of Graduate Studies and Research, Faculty of Arts, Department of French, Regina, SK S4S 0A2, Canada. Offers MA. *Faculty:* 5 full-time (1 woman), 1 part-time/adjunct (0 women). *Students:* 1 full-time (0 women). 2 applicants, 100% accepted. In 2009, 1 master's awarded. *Degree requirements:* For master's, thesis, 2 seminar presentations. *Entrance requirements:* Additional exam requirements/recommendations for international students: Required—TOEFL (minimum score 580 paper-based; 237 computer-based; 80 iBT). *Application deadline:* Applications are processed on a rolling basis. Application fee: $90 ($100 for international students). Electronic applications accepted. *Financial support:* Fellowships, research assistantships, teaching assistantships, scholarships/grants available. Financial award application deadline: 6/15. *Faculty research:* Literature of the sixteenth through twentieth centuries in France, French Canadian literature, literary criticism, translation, history of ideas. *Unit head:* Dr. Emmanuel Aito, Graduate Program Coordinator, 306-585-4323, Fax: 306-585-4827, E-mail: emmanuel.aito@uregina.ca. *Application contact:* Dr. Emmanuel Aito, Graduate Program Coordinator, 306-585-4323, Fax: 306-585-4827, E-mail: emmanuel.aito@uregina.ca.

University of Saskatchewan, College of Graduate Studies and Research, College of Arts and Sciences, Department of Languages and Linguistics, Saskatoon, SK S7N 5A2, Canada. Offers MA. *Faculty:* 10. *Degree requirements:* For master's, 2 foreign languages, thesis. *Entrance requirements:* Additional exam requirements/recommendations for international students: Required—TOEFL (minimum score 80 iBT); Recommended—IELTS (minimum score 6.5). *Application deadline:* For fall admission, 7/1 priority date for domestic students. Applications are processed on a rolling basis. Application fee: $75. Electronic applications accepted. Tuition and fees charges are reported in Canadian dollars. *Expenses:* Tuition, area resident: Full-time $3000 Canadian dollars; part-time $500 Canadian dollars per term. Required fees: $700 Canadian dollars; $100 Canadian dollars per term. *Financial support:* Fellowships, research assistantships, teaching assistantships available. Financial award application deadline: 1/31. *Unit head:* Dr. Richard Julien, Head, 306-966-6920, Fax: 306-966-5782, E-mail: richard.julien@usask.ca. *Application contact:* Dr. Alex Sokalski, Graduate Chair, 306-966-5648, Fax: 306-966-5782.

University of South Africa, College of Human Sciences, Pretoria, South Africa. Offers adult education (M Ed); African languages (MA, PhD); African politics (MA, PhD); Afrikaans (MA, PhD); ancient history (MA, PhD); ancient Near Eastern studies (MA, PhD); anthropology (MA, PhD); applied linguistics (MA); Arabic (MA, PhD); archaeology (MA); art history (MA); Biblical archaeology (MA); Biblical studies (M Th, D Th, PhD); Christian spirituality (M Th, D Th); church history (M Th, D Th); classical studies (MA, PhD); clinical psychology (MA); communication (MA, PhD); comparative education (M Ed, Ed D); consulting psychology (D Admin, D Com, PhD); curriculum studies (M Ed, Ed D); development studies (M Admin, MA, D Admin, PhD); didactics (M Ed, Ed D); education (M Tech); education management (M Ed, Ed D); educational psychology (M Ed); English (MA); environmental education (M Ed); French (MA, PhD); German (MA, PhD); Greek (MA); guidance and counseling (M Ed); health studies (MA, PhD), including health sciences education (MA), health services management (MA), medical and surgical nursing science (critical care general) (MA), midwifery and neonatal nursing science (MA), trauma and emergency care (MA); history (MA, PhD); history of education (Ed D); inclusive education (M Ed, Ed D); information and communications technology policy and regulation (MA); information science (MA, MIS, PhD); international politics (MA, PhD); Islamic studies (MA, PhD); Italian (MA, PhD); Judaica (MA, PhD); linguistics (MA, PhD); mathematical education (M Ed); mathematics education (MA); missiology (M Th, D Th); modern Hebrew (MA, PhD); musicology (MA, MMus, D Mus, PhD); natural science education (M Ed); New Testament (M Th, D Th); Old Testament (D Th); pastoral therapy (M Th, D Th); philosophy (MA); philosophy of education (M Ed, Ed D); politics (MA, PhD); Portuguese (MA, PhD); practical theology (M Th, D Th); psychology (MA, MS, PhD); psychology of education (M Ed, Ed D); public health (MA); religious studies (MA, D Th, PhD); Romance languages (MA); Russian (MA, PhD); Semitic languages (MA, PhD); social behavior studies in HIV/AIDS (MA); social science (mental health) (MA); social science in development studies (MA); social science in psychology (MA); social science in social work (MA); social science in sociology (MA); social work (MSW, DSW, PhD); socio-education (M Ed, Ed D); sociolinguistics (MA); sociology (MA, PhD); Spanish (MA, PhD); systematic theology (M Th, D Th); TESOL (teaching English to speakers of other languages) (MA); theological ethics (M Th, D Th); theory of literature (MA, PhD); urban ministries (D Th); urban ministry (M Th).

University of South Carolina, The Graduate School, College of Arts and Sciences, Department of Languages, Literatures, and Cultures, Columbia, SC 29208. Offers comparative literature (MA, PhD); foreign languages (MAT), including French, German, Spanish; French (MA); German (MA); Spanish (MA). MAT offered in cooperation with the College of Education. Part-time programs available. *Degree requirements:* For master's, one foreign language, comprehensive exam, thesis optional; for doctorate, 2 foreign languages, comprehensive exam, thesis/dissertation. *Entrance requirements:* For master's and doctorate, GRE General Test, writing sample. Additional exam requirements/recommendations for international students: Required—TOEFL (minimum score 230 computer-based; 75 iBT). Electronic applications accepted. *Faculty research:* Modern literature, linguistics, literature and culture, medieval literature, literary theory.

University of South Florida, Graduate School, College of Arts and Sciences, World Languages Department, Tampa, FL 33620-9951. Offers classics: Latin/Greek (MA); French (MA); linguistics (MA); linguistics: ESL (MA); Spanish (MA). Part-time and evening/weekend programs available. *Faculty:* 19 full-time (14 women), 1 part-time/adjunct (0 women). *Students:* 36 full-time (26 women), 22 part-time (16 women); includes 23 minority (5 African Americans, 3 American Indian/Alaska Native, 2 Asian Americans or Pacific Islanders, 13 Hispanic Americans), 12 international. Average age 32. 29 applicants, 52% accepted, 12 enrolled. In 2009, 18 master's awarded. *Degree requirements:* For master's, comprehensive exam, thesis. *Entrance requirements:* For master's, GRE General Test, minimum GPA of 3.0 in last 60 hours. Additional exam requirements/recommendations for international students: Required—TOEFL (minimum score 600 paper-based; 250 computer-based). *Application deadline:* For fall admission, 2/15 for domestic students, 1/2 for international students; for spring admission, 10/15 for domestic students, 6/1 for international students. Application fee: $30. Electronic applications accepted. *Financial support:* In 2009–10, teaching assistantships with tuition reimbursements (averaging $17,024 per year); tuition waivers (partial) and unspecified assistantships also available. Financial award application deadline: 6/30. *Faculty research:* Second language writing, academic literacy. Total annual research expenditures: $19,891. *Unit head:* Dr. Victor Peppard, Chairperson, 813-974-2012, Fax: 813-974-1718, E-mail: peppard@.cas.usf.edu. *Application contact:* Dr. Victor Peppard, Chairperson, 813-974-2012, Fax: 813-974-1718, E-mail: peppard@.cas.usf.edu.

The University of Tennessee, Graduate School, College of Arts and Sciences, Department of Modern Foreign Languages and Literatures, Program in French, Knoxville, TN 37996. Offers MA. *Degree requirements:* For master's, one foreign language, thesis or alternative. *Entrance requirements:* For master's, minimum GPA of 2.7. Additional exam requirements/recommendations for international students: Required—TOEFL. Electronic applications accepted. *Expenses:* Tuition, state resident: full-time $6826; part-time $380 per semester hour. Tuition, nonresident: full-time $21,844; part-time $1147 per semester hour. Tuition and fees vary according to program.

The University of Tennessee, Graduate School, College of Arts and Sciences, Department of Modern Foreign Languages and Literatures, Program in Modern Foreign Languages, Knoxville, TN 37996. Offers applied linguistics (PhD); French (PhD); German (PhD); Italian (PhD); Portuguese (PhD); Russian (PhD); Spanish (PhD). *Degree requirements:* For doctorate, 2 foreign languages, thesis/dissertation. *Entrance requirements:* For doctorate, minimum GPA of 2.7. Additional exam requirements/recommendations for international students: Required—TOEFL. Electronic applications accepted. *Expenses:* Tuition, state resident: full-time $6826; part-time $380 per semester hour. Tuition, nonresident: full-time $21,844; part-time $1147 per semester hour. Tuition and fees vary according to program.

The University of Texas at Arlington, Graduate School, College of Liberal Arts, Department of Modern Languages, Arlington, TX 76019. Offers French (MA); Spanish (MA). Part-time and evening/weekend programs available. *Degree requirements:* For master's, 2 foreign languages, comprehensive exam, thesis optional. *Entrance requirements:* For master's, GRE General Test, minimum GPA of 3.0, 3 letters of recommendation. Additional exam requirements/recommendations for international students: Required—TOEFL (minimum score 550 paper-based; 213 computer-based).

The University of Texas at Austin, Graduate School, College of Liberal Arts, Department of French and Italian, Austin, TX 78712-1111. Offers French (MA, PhD); French linguistics (MA, PhD); Italian studies (MA, PhD); Romance linguistics (MA, PhD). Part-time programs available. *Degree requirements:* For master's, one foreign language, thesis; for doctorate, 2 foreign languages, thesis/dissertation. *Entrance requirements:* For master's, GRE General Test, minimum GPA of 3.0, bachelor's degree in French or equivalent; for doctorate, GRE General Test, minimum GPA of 3.0, master's degree in French. Additional exam requirements/

recommendations for international students: Required—TOEFL. Electronic applications accepted. *Faculty research:* Nineteenth-century Italian literature, Italian Renaissance, twentieth-century French literature, Francophone literature, fifteenth-century literature and culture.

The University of Toledo, College of Graduate Studies, College of Arts and Sciences, Department of Foreign Languages, Toledo, OH 43606-3390. Offers French (MA); German (MA); Spanish (MA). Part-time programs available. *Degree requirements:* For master's, one foreign language, comprehensive reading exam in 1 additional foreign language. Electronic applications accepted.

University of Toronto, School of Graduate Studies, Humanities Division, Department of French, Toronto, ON M5S 1A1, Canada. Offers French language and literature (MA, PhD). Part-time programs available. *Degree requirements:* For master's, research essay; for doctorate, one foreign language, thesis/dissertation, field exam. *Entrance requirements:* For master's, 2 letters of reference, writing sample, minimum B+ average overall and in French, undergraduate major in French; for doctorate, 7 courses in French language and literature, minimum A- average, writing sample.

University of Utah, The Graduate School, College of Humanities, Department of Languages and Literature, Salt Lake City, UT 84112-1107. Offers comparative literary and cultural studies (MA, PhD); French (MA, MALP); German (MA, MALP, PhD); Spanish (MA, MALP, PhD); world languages with secondary teaching licensure (MA). *Faculty:* 35 full-time (22 women), 1 part-time/adjunct (0 women). *Students:* 30 full-time (20 women), 10 part-time (9 women); includes 8 minority (1 American Indian/Alaska Native, 2 Asian Americans or Pacific Islanders, 5 Hispanic Americans), 6 international. Average age 35. 47 applicants, 40% accepted, 18 enrolled. In 2009, 7 master's, 3 doctorates awarded. Terminal master's awarded for partial completion of doctoral program. *Degree requirements:* For master's, 2 foreign languages, comprehensive exam, thesis, standard proficiency in 2 languages other than English; for doctorate, 3 foreign languages, comprehensive exam, thesis/dissertation, standard proficiency in 2 languages other than English and language of study, advanced proficiency in 1 language other than English and language of study. *Entrance requirements:* For master's, bachelor's degree or strong undergraduate record in target languages, minimum GPA of 3.0; for doctorate, GRE, MA, advanced proficiency in a target language. Additional exam requirements/recommendations for international students: Required—TOEFL (minimum score 500 paper-based; 173 computer-based). *Application deadline:* For fall admission, 1/15 priority date for domestic students, 12/15 priority date for international students. Application fee: $55 ($65 for international students). *Expenses:* Tuition, state resident: full-time $4004; part-time $1674 per semester. Tuition, nonresident: full-time $14,134; part-time $5915 per semester. Required fees: $324 per semester. Tuition and fees vary according to course load, degree level and program. *Financial support:* In 2009–10, 21 students received support, including 21 teaching assistantships with full tuition reimbursements available (averaging $11,000 per year); health care benefits also available. Financial award application deadline: 2/1; financial award applicants required to submit FAFSA. *Faculty research:* Literary theory, linguistics, cultural studies, comparative studies. Total annual research expenditures: $22,986. *Unit head:* Dr. Christine A. Jones, Director of Graduate Studies, 801-585-3002, Fax: 801-581-7581, E-mail: cjones@hum.utah.edu. *Application contact:* Virginia Ellinwood, Academic Advisor, 801-585-9437, Fax: 801-581-7581, E-mail: v.ellinwood@mail.hum.utah.edu.

University of Vermont, Graduate College, College of Arts and Sciences, Department of Romance Languages, Burlington, VT 05405. Offers French (MA). *Students:* 3 (1 woman); includes 1 minority (American Indian/Alaska Native). In 2009, 3 master's awarded. *Degree requirements:* For master's, one foreign language. *Entrance requirements:* For master's, GRE General Test. Additional exam requirements/recommendations for international students: Required—TOEFL (minimum score 550 paper-based; 213 computer-based; 80 iBT). *Application deadline:* For fall admission, 8/1 priority date for domestic students. Applications are processed on a rolling basis. Application fee: $40. Electronic applications accepted. *Expenses:* Tuition, state resident: part-time $508 per credit hour. Tuition, nonresident: part-time $1281 per credit hour. *Financial support:* Fellowships, teaching assistantships available. Financial award application deadline: 3/1. *Faculty research:* French, French-Canadian, and French-African literature. *Unit head:* Dr. G. Nunley, Chairperson, 802-656-3196. *Application contact:* Dr. Gretchen VanSlyke, Coordinator, 802-656-3196.

University of Victoria, Faculty of Graduate Studies, Faculty of Humanities, Department of French, Victoria, BC V8W 2Y2, Canada. Offers literature (MA); teaching emphasis (MA). Part-time and evening/weekend programs available. *Degree requirements:* For master's, 2 foreign languages, thesis optional. *Entrance requirements:* For master's, BA in French. Additional exam requirements/recommendations for international students: Required—TOEFL (minimum score 575 paper-based; 233 computer-based), IELTS (minimum score 7). Electronic applications accepted. *Faculty research:* French-Canadian literature, stylistics, comparative literature, Francophone literature.

University of Virginia, College and Graduate School of Arts and Sciences, Department of French, Charlottesville, VA 22903. Offers MA, PhD. *Faculty:* 14 full-time (10 women), 2 part-time/adjunct (both women). *Students:* 33 full-time (24 women), 1 (woman) part-time; includes 1 minority (Asian American or Pacific Islander), 4 international. Average age 29. 32 applicants, 56% accepted, 9 enrolled. In 2009, 4 master's, 2 doctorates awarded. *Degree requirements:* For master's, one foreign language, comprehensive exam; for doctorate, one foreign language, comprehensive exam, thesis/dissertation. *Entrance requirements:* For master's and doctorate, GRE General Test, minimum GPA of 3.0 in major and overall; 2 letters of recommendation; writing sample. Additional exam requirements/recommendations for international students: Required—TOEFL (minimum score 600 paper-based; 250 computer-based; 90 iBT), IELTS (minimum score 7). *Application deadline:* For fall admission, 12/1 for domestic and international students. Applications are processed on a rolling basis. Application fee: $60. Electronic applications accepted. *Financial support:* Fellowships, teaching assistantships available. Financial award applicants required to submit FAFSA. *Unit head:* Cheryl Krueger, 434-924-7158, Fax: 434-924-7157, E-mail: cherylkrueger@virginia.edu. *Application contact:* Claire Lyu, Director of Graduate Studies, 434-924-7158, Fax: 434-924-7157, E-mail: cl9t@virginia.edu.

University of Washington, Graduate School, College of Arts and Sciences, Department of Romance Languages and Literature, Division of French and Italian Studies, Seattle, WA 98195. Offers French (MA, PhD); Italian (MA). Terminal master's awarded for partial completion of doctoral program. *Degree requirements:* For master's, 2 foreign languages, exam; for doctorate, 3 foreign languages, thesis/dissertation, exam. *Entrance requirements:* For master's and doctorate, GRE General Test, minimum GPA of 3.0. Additional exam requirements/recommendations for international students: Required—TOEFL. Electronic applications accepted. *Faculty research:* Interdisciplinary studies, literary theory and criticism, film, major periods of French and Italian literature, Francophonie.

University of Waterloo, Graduate Studies, Faculty of Arts, Department of French Studies, Waterloo, ON N2L 3G1, Canada. Offers French (MA, PhD). Part-time programs available. *Entrance requirements:* For master's, honors degree, minimum B average, course work and assignments in French, resume. Additional exam requirements/recommendations for international students: Required—TOEFL, TWE. Electronic applications accepted. *Faculty research:* French and Quebec literature: Middle Ages through twentieth century, phonology of Acadian dialect, computerized scholarly editions of medieval and Renaissance texts.

The University of Western Ontario, Faculty of Graduate Studies, Faculty of Arts and Humanities, Department of French, London, ON N6A 5B8, Canada. Offers Canadian literature (MA); French (MA, PhD). MA (Canadian literature) offered in cooperation with Department of English. *Degree requirements:* For master's, thesis or alternative; for doctorate, one foreign language, thesis/dissertation. *Entrance requirements:* For master's, minimum B average, honors degree, 2 years of teaching experience (MAT); for doctorate, MA or equivalent, minimum B average in French. Additional exam requirements/recommendations for international students: Required—TOEFL. Electronic applications accepted.

University of Wisconsin–Madison, Graduate School, College of Letters and Science, Department of French and Italian, Program in French, Madison, WI 53706-1380. Offers MA, PhD. Part-time programs available. *Degree requirements:* For master's, one foreign language; for doctorate, one foreign language, thesis/dissertation. *Entrance requirements:* For master's and doctorate, GRE. Electronic applications accepted. *Expenses:* Tuition, state resident: part-time $594 per credit. Tuition, nonresident: part-time $1504 per credit. Required fees: $65 per credit. Tuition and fees vary according to course load, program and reciprocity agreements. *Faculty research:* Francophone literature; French literature, culture, linguistics, and language pedagogy.

University of Wisconsin–Madison, Graduate School, College of Letters and Science, Department of French and Italian, Program in French Studies, Madison, WI 53706-1380. Offers MFS, Certificate. Part-time programs available. *Degree requirements:* For master's, one foreign language, thesis, internship; for Certificate, one foreign language, internship. *Entrance requirements:* For master's, GRE. Electronic applications accepted. *Expenses:* Tuition, state resident: part-time $594 per credit. Tuition, nonresident: part-time $1504 per credit. Required fees: $65 per credit. Tuition and fees vary according to course load, program and reciprocity agreements. *Faculty research:* International development, European citizenship, French and business, foreign language education, agricultural economics.

University of Wisconsin–Milwaukee, Graduate School, College of Letters and Sciences, Interdepartmental Program in Foreign Language and Literature, Milwaukee, WI 53201-0413. Offers classics and Hebrew studies (MAFLL); comparative literature (MAFLL); French and Italian (MAFLL); German (MAFLL); Slavic studies (MAFLL); translation (Certificate). Part-time programs available. *Faculty:* 37 full-time (18 women). *Students:* 32 full-time (25 women), 28 part-time (19 women); includes 5 minority (1 Asian American or Pacific Islander, 4 Hispanic Americans), 22 international. Average age 33. 54 applicants, 69% accepted, 20 enrolled. In 2009, 24 master's awarded. *Degree requirements:* For master's, 2 foreign languages, thesis or alternative. *Entrance requirements:* Additional exam requirements/recommendations for international students: Required—TOEFL (minimum score 550 paper-based; 79 iBT), IELTS (minimum score 6.5). *Application deadline:* For fall admission, 1/1 priority date for domestic students; for spring admission, 9/1 for domestic students. Applications are processed on a rolling basis. Application fee: $45 ($75 for international students). *Expenses:* Tuition, state resident: full-time $8800. Tuition, nonresident: full-time $20,760. Tuition and fees vary according to program and reciprocity agreements. *Financial support:* In 2009–10, 2 research assistantships, 21 teaching assistantships were awarded; career-related internships or fieldwork and unspecified assistantships also available. Support available to part-time students. Financial award application deadline: 4/15. Total annual research expenditures: $285,237. *Unit head:* Gabrielle Verdier, Representative, 414-229-3346, Fax: 414-229-2741, E-mail: verdier@uwm.edu. *Application contact:* General Information Contact, 414-229-4982, Fax: 414-229-6967, E-mail: gradschool@uwm.edu.

University of Wyoming, College of Arts and Sciences, Department of Modern and Classical Languages, Program in French, Laramie, WY 82070. Offers MA. Part-time programs available. *Degree requirements:* For master's, one foreign language, thesis or alternative. *Entrance requirements:* For master's, GRE General Test, minimum GPA of 3.0. *Faculty research:* Poetry, Asian literature, medieval literature, nineteenth- and twentieth century literature.

Vanderbilt University, Graduate School, Department of French and Italian, Nashville, TN 37240-1001. Offers French (MA, MAT, PhD). *Faculty:* 21 full-time (15 women). *Students:* 10 full-time (5 women); includes 1 minority (Hispanic American), 2 international. Average age 29. 41 applicants, 17% accepted, 2 enrolled.Terminal master's awarded for partial completion of doctoral program. *Degree requirements:* For master's, one foreign language, comprehensive exam; for doctorate, 2 foreign languages, comprehensive exam, thesis/dissertation, final and qualifying exams. *Entrance requirements:* For master's and doctorate, GRE General Test. Additional exam requirements/recommendations for international students: Required—TOEFL (minimum score 570 paper-based; 230 computer-based; 88 iBT). *Application deadline:* For fall admission, 1/15 for domestic and international students. Application fee: $0. Electronic applications accepted. *Financial support:* Fellowships with full and partial tuition reimbursements, teaching assistantships with full and partial tuition reimbursements, career-related internships or fieldwork, Federal Work-Study, institutionally sponsored loans, scholarships/grants, and health care benefits available. Financial award application deadline: 1/15; financial award applicants required to submit CSS PROFILE or FAFSA. *Faculty research:* Baudelaire, Rabelais, voyage literature, postcolonial literature, medieval epic. *Unit head:* Lynn Ramey, Chair, 615-322-6900, Fax: 615-343-6909, E-mail: lynn.ramey@vanderbilt.edu. *Application contact:* Robert Barsky, Director of Graduate Studies, 615-322-6900, Fax: 615-343-6909, E-mail: robert.barsky@vanderbilt.edu.

Washington University in St. Louis, Graduate School of Arts and Sciences, Department of Romance Languages and Literatures, Program in French, St. Louis, MO 63130-4899. Offers MA, PhD. Terminal master's awarded for partial completion of doctoral program. *Degree requirements:* For master's, thesis or alternative; for doctorate, thesis/dissertation. *Entrance requirements:* For master's and doctorate, GRE General Test. Electronic applications accepted.

Wayne State University, College of Liberal Arts and Sciences, Department of Classical and Modern Languages, Literatures, and Cultures, Program in French, Detroit, MI 48202. Offers MA. *Degree requirements:* For master's, one foreign language, thesis optional. *Entrance requirements:* For master's, GRE General Test, minimum GPA of 3.0. Additional exam requirements/recommendations for international students: Required—TOEFL (minimum score 550 paper-based; 213 computer-based); Recommended—TWE (minimum score 6). Electronic applications accepted. *Faculty research:* Renaissance lyric, eighteenth century theatre and poetry, Quebecois literature, nineteenth century prose, twentieth century novel and criticism.

West Chester University of Pennsylvania, Office of Graduate Studies, College of Arts and Sciences, Department of Languages and Cultures, West Chester, PA 19383. Offers French (M Ed, MA, Teaching Certificate); German (M Ed, Teaching Certificate); Latin (M Ed, Teaching Certificate); Spanish (M Ed, MA, Teaching Certificate). Part-time and evening/weekend programs available. *Students:* 4 full-time (all women), 27 part-time (21 women); includes 6 minority (2 African Americans, 1 Asian American or Pacific Islander, 3 Hispanic Americans). Average age 33. 16 applicants, 94% accepted, 9 enrolled. In 2009, 7 master's awarded. *Degree requirements:* For master's, one foreign language, comprehensive exam, thesis optional. *Entrance requirements:* For master's, GRE or MAT, placement test. Additional exam requirements/recommendations for international students: Required—TOEFL (minimum score 550 paper-based; 213 computer-based; 80 iBT). *Application deadline:* For fall admission, 4/15 priority date for domestic students, 3/15 for international students; for spring admission, 10/15 for domestic students, 9/1 for international students. Applications are processed on a rolling basis. Application fee: $35. Electronic applications accepted. *Expenses:* Tuition, state resident: full-time $6666; part-time $370 per credit. Tuition, nonresident: full-time $10,666; part-time $593 per credit. Required fees: $122.56 per credit. *Financial support:* In 2009–10, 1 research assistantship with full and partial tuition reimbursement (averaging $5,000 per year) was awarded; unspecified assistantships also available. Support available to part-time students. Financial award application deadline: 2/15; financial award applicants required to submit FAFSA. *Faculty research:* Implementation of world languages curriculum framework. *Unit head:* Dr. Jerry Williams, Chair, 610-436-2700, Fax: 610-436-3048, E-mail: jwilliams2@wcupa.edu. *Application contact:* Dr. Rebecca Pauly, Graduate Coordinator, 610-436-2382, E-mail: rpauly@wcupa.edu.

West Virginia University, Eberly College of Arts and Sciences, Department of Foreign Languages, Morgantown, WV 26506. Offers French (MA); linguistics (MA); Spanish (MA); teaching English to speakers of other languages (MA). Part-time programs available. *Degree requirements:* For master's, one foreign language, comprehensive exam (for some programs),

French

West Virginia University (continued)
thesis optional. *Entrance requirements:* For master's, minimum GPA of 3.0. Electronic applications accepted. *Faculty research:* French, German, and Spanish literature; foreign language pedagogy; English as a second language; cultural studies; linguistics.

Yale University, Graduate School of Arts and Sciences, Department of French, New Haven, CT 06520. Offers M Phil, MA, PhD. *Degree requirements:* For doctorate, 3 foreign languages, thesis/dissertation. *Entrance requirements:* For doctorate, GRE General Test.

York University, Faculty of Graduate Studies, Glendon College, Program in French Studies, Toronto, ON M3J 1P3, Canada. Offers MA. *Degree requirements:* For master's, thesis or alternative. Electronic applications accepted.

German

Arizona State University, Graduate College, College of Liberal Arts and Sciences, Division of Humanities, School of International Letters and Cultures, Program in German, Tempe, AZ 85287. Offers MA. *Degree requirements:* For master's, thesis or alternative. *Entrance requirements:* For master's, GRE.

Bowling Green State University, Graduate College, College of Arts and Sciences, Department of German, Russian, and East Asian Languages, Bowling Green, OH 43403. Offers German (MA, MAT); MA/MA. Part-time programs available. *Degree requirements:* For master's, one foreign language, thesis or alternative. *Entrance requirements:* For master's, GRE General Test. Additional exam requirements/recommendations for international students: Required—TOEFL. Electronic applications accepted.

Brigham Young University, Graduate Studies, College of Humanities, Department of Germanic and Slavic Languages, Provo, UT 84602. Offers German studies (MA). *Faculty:* 15 full-time (4 women). *Students:* 7 full-time (5 women), 1 part-time (0 women). Average age 22. 3 applicants, 100% accepted, 2 enrolled. In 2009, 1 master's awarded. *Degree requirements:* For master's, 2 foreign languages, comprehensive exam, thesis. *Entrance requirements:* For master's, GRE General Test, bachelor's degree in German or related field. Additional exam requirements/recommendations for international students: Required—TOEFL (minimum score 213 computer-based). *Application deadline:* For fall admission, 2/1 priority date for domestic and international students. Application fee: $50. Electronic applications accepted. *Expenses:* Tuition: Full-time $5580; part-time $301 per credit hour. Tuition and fees vary according to student's religious affiliation. *Financial support:* In 2009–10, 4 students received support, including 6 teaching assistantships with full and partial tuition reimbursements available (averaging $8,580 per year); career-related internships or fieldwork, institutionally sponsored loans, scholarships/grants, tuition waivers (full and partial), and unspecified assistantships also available. Support available to part-time students. Financial award application deadline: 3/15. *Faculty research:* Second language acquisition, modern German literature, critical theory, German women authors, German dialects, German cinema, German drama. Total annual research expenditures: $4,450. *Unit head:* Dr. Michelle Stott James, Chair, 801-422-4923, Fax: 801-422-0268, E-mail: michelle_james@byu.edu. *Application contact:* AnnMarie Hamar, Secretary to the Chair, 801-422-4923, Fax: 801-422-0268, E-mail: annmarie_hamar@byu.edu.

Brown University, Graduate School, Department of German Studies, Providence, RI 02912. Offers PhD, MA/PhD. *Degree requirements:* For doctorate, 2 foreign languages, thesis/dissertation, preliminary exam. *Entrance requirements:* For doctorate, GRE General Test.

California State University, Fullerton, Graduate Studies, College of Humanities and Social Sciences, Department of Modern Languages and Literatures, Fullerton, CA 92834-9480. Offers French (MA); German (MA); Spanish (MA); teaching English to speakers of other languages (MS). Part-time programs available. *Students:* 40 full-time (30 women), 63 part-time (47 women); includes 49 minority (1 African American, 14 Asian Americans or Pacific Islanders, 34 Hispanic Americans), 20 international. Average age 33. 101 applicants, 52% accepted, 29 enrolled. In 2009, 37 master's awarded. *Degree requirements:* For master's, comprehensive exam, thesis or alternative. *Entrance requirements:* For master's, minimum GPA of 2.5 in last 60 hours of course work, undergraduate major in a language. Application fee: $55. *Expenses:* Tuition, nonresident: full-time $11,160; part-time $373 per credit. Required fees: $1440 per term. Tuition and fees vary according to course load, degree level and program. *Financial support:* Career-related internships or fieldwork, Federal Work-Study, institutionally sponsored loans, and scholarships/grants available. Support available to part-time students. Financial award application deadline: 3/1; financial award applicants required to submit FAFSA. *Unit head:* Dr. Janet Eyring, Chair, 657-278-3534. *Application contact:* Admissions/Applications, 657-278-2371.

California State University, Long Beach, Graduate Studies, College of Liberal Arts, Department of Romance, German, and Russian Languages and Literature, Program in German, Long Beach, CA 90840. Offers MA. Part-time programs available. *Students:* 11 full-time (5 women), 7 part-time (5 women); includes 1 minority (Asian American or Pacific Islander), 3 international. Average age 31. 5 applicants, 80% accepted, 4 enrolled. *Degree requirements:* For master's, one foreign language, comprehensive exam or thesis. *Application deadline:* For fall admission, 7/1 for domestic students. Applications are processed on a rolling basis. Application fee: $55. Electronic applications accepted. *Expenses:* Required fees: $1802 per semester. Part-time tuition and fees vary according to course load. *Financial support:* Federal Work-Study, institutionally sponsored loans, and scholarships/grants available. Financial award application deadline: 3/2. *Faculty research:* Contemporary German society, baroque, Goethe, Wagner. *Unit head:* Dr. Lisa Vollendorf, Chair, 562-985-4318, Fax: 562-985-4259, E-mail: lvollend@csulb.edu. *Application contact:* Dr. Jeffrey High, Graduate Advisor, 562-985-5381, Fax: 562-985-2463, E-mail: jhigh@csulb.edu.

California State University, Sacramento, Graduate Studies, College of Social Sciences and Interdisciplinary Studies, Liberal Arts Program, Sacramento, CA 95819. Offers French (MA); German (MA); Spanish (MA); theater arts (MA). *Degree requirements:* For master's, writing proficiency exam. *Entrance requirements:* Additional exam requirements/recommendations for international students: Required—TOEFL. Electronic applications accepted.

Central Connecticut State University, School of Graduate Studies, School of Arts and Sciences, Department of Modern Languages, Program in Modern Language, New Britain, CT 06050-4010. Offers French (MA, Certificate); German (Certificate); Italian (Certificate); modern language (MA); Spanish language and Hispanic culture (MA). Part-time and evening/weekend programs available. *Students:* 2 full-time (1 woman), 40 part-time (35 women); includes 14 minority (all Hispanic Americans). Average age 38. 16 applicants, 69% accepted, 9 enrolled. In 2009, 9 master's awarded. *Degree requirements:* For master's, one foreign language, comprehensive exam, thesis or alternative; for Certificate, qualifying exam. *Entrance requirements:* For master's, minimum undergraduate GPA of 2.7, 24 credits of undergraduate courses in either Italian or Spanish. Additional exam requirements/recommendations for international students: Required—TOEFL. *Application deadline:* For fall admission, 7/1 for domestic students; for spring admission, 12/1 for domestic students. Applications are processed on a rolling basis. Application fee: $50. Electronic applications accepted. *Expenses:* Tuition, area resident: Full-time $4662; part-time $440 per credit. Tuition, state resident: full-time $6994; part-time $440 per credit. Tuition, nonresident: full-time $12,988; part-time $440 per credit. Required fees: $3606. One-time fee: $62 part-time. *Faculty research:* Twentieth century French theater, seventeenth century French literature, French Middle Ages.

Columbia University, Graduate School of Arts and Sciences, Division of Humanities, Department of Germanic Languages, New York, NY 10027. Offers M Phil, MA, PhD. Part-time programs available. *Degree requirements:* For master's, one foreign language, written exam; for doctorate, 2 foreign languages, thesis/dissertation. *Entrance requirements:* For master's and doctorate, GRE General Test, GRE Subject Test, sample of written work. Additional exam requirements/recommendations for international students: Required—TOEFL. *Faculty research:* German language and literature, comparative literature.

Cornell University, Graduate School, Graduate Fields of Arts and Sciences, Field of Germanic Studies, Ithaca, NY 14853-0001. Offers German area studies (MA, PhD); German intellectual history (MA, PhD); Germanic linguistics (MA, PhD); Germanic literature (MA, PhD); old Norse (MA, PhD). *Faculty:* 21 full-time (10 women). *Students:* 15 full-time (9 women); includes 2 minority (1 American Indian/Alaska Native, 1 Hispanic American), 6 international. Average age 28. 32 applicants, 19% accepted, 3 enrolled. In 2009, 4 master's, 3 doctorates awarded. Terminal master's awarded for partial completion of doctoral program. *Degree requirements:* For master's, one foreign language, thesis; for doctorate, 2 foreign languages, comprehensive exam, thesis/dissertation. *Entrance requirements:* For master's and doctorate, GRE General Test, fluency in German, writing sample, 2 letters of recommendation. Additional exam requirements/recommendations for international students: Required—TOEFL (minimum score 550 paper-based; 213 computer-based; 77 iBT). *Application deadline:* For fall admission, 1/15 for domestic students. Application fee: $70. Electronic applications accepted. *Expenses:* Tuition: Full-time $29,500. Required fees: $70. Full-time tuition and fees vary according to degree level, program and student level. *Financial support:* In 2009–10, 15 students received support, including 2 fellowships with full tuition reimbursements available, 1 teaching assistantship with full tuition reimbursement available; research assistantships with full tuition reimbursements available, institutionally sponsored loans, scholarships/grants, health care benefits, tuition waivers (full and partial), and unspecified assistantships also available. Financial award applicants required to submit FAFSA. *Faculty research:* Women's studies, minority literature, literature and intellectual history, theater and film studies, continental philosophy. *Unit head:* Director of Graduate Studies, 607-255-4047. *Application contact:* Graduate Field Assistant, 607-255-4047, E-mail: germanic_studies@cornell.edu.

Cornell University, Graduate School, Graduate Fields of Arts and Sciences, Field of Linguistics, Ithaca, NY 14853-0001. Offers applied linguistics (MA, PhD); East Asian linguistics (MA, PhD); English linguistics (MA, PhD); general linguistics (MA, PhD); Germanic linguistics (MA, PhD); Indo-European linguistics (MA, PhD); phonetics (MA, PhD); phonological theory (MA, PhD); Romance linguistics (MA, PhD); second language acquisition (MA, PhD); semantics (MA, PhD); Slavic linguistics (MA, PhD); sociolinguistics (MA, PhD); South Asian linguistics (MA, PhD); Southeast Asian linguistics (MA, PhD); syntactic theory (MA, PhD). *Faculty:* 21 full-time (10 women). *Students:* 31 full-time (17 women), 14 international. Average age 30. 95 applicants, 12% accepted, 5 enrolled. In 2009, 5 master's, 6 doctorates awarded. Terminal master's awarded for partial completion of doctoral program. *Degree requirements:* For master's, one foreign language, thesis; for doctorate, one foreign language, comprehensive exam, thesis/dissertation. *Entrance requirements:* For master's and doctorate, GRE General Test, 2 letters of recommendation. Additional exam requirements/recommendations for international students: Required—TOEFL (minimum score 600 paper-based; 250 computer-based; 77 iBT). *Application deadline:* For fall admission, 1/15 for domestic students. Application fee: $70. Electronic applications accepted. *Expenses:* Tuition: Full-time $29,500. Required fees: $70. Full-time tuition and fees vary according to degree level, program and student level. *Financial support:* In 2009–10, 3 fellowships with full tuition reimbursements, 1 teaching assistantship with full tuition reimbursement were awarded; research assistantships with full tuition reimbursements, institutionally sponsored loans, scholarships/grants, health care benefits, tuition waivers (full and partial), and unspecified assistantships also available. Financial award applicants required to submit FAFSA. *Faculty research:* Phonology and phonetics; syntax and semantics; historical linguistics; philosophy of language; language acquisition. *Unit head:* Director of Graduate Studies, 607-255-1105. *Application contact:* Graduate Field Assistant, 607-255-1105, E-mail: lingfield@cornell.edu.

Dalhousie University, Faculty of Arts and Social Science, Department of German, Halifax, NS B3H 4R2, Canada. Offers MA. *Entrance requirements:* Additional exam requirements/recommendations for international students: Required—TOEFL, IELTS, CANTEST, CAEL, or Michigan English Language Assessment Battery. *Application deadline:* For fall admission, 6/1 for domestic students, 4/1 for international students; for winter admission, 10/31 for domestic students, 8/31 for international students; for spring admission, 2/28 for domestic students, 12/31 for international students. Application fee: $70. Electronic applications accepted. *Financial support:* Career-related internships or fieldwork, scholarships/grants, and health care benefits available. *Faculty research:* Baroque age in Germany, literature and philosophy of German idealism, twentieth century German culture, aesthetics, reception of the Islamic Orient, reception of Greek and Roman antiquity, realism and ornament. *Unit head:* Dr. Jane Curran, Chair, 902-494-1091, Fax: 902-494-2719, E-mail: german@dal.ca. *Application contact:* Annett Gaudig, Administrative Secretary, 902-494-2161, Fax: 902-494-2719, E-mail: german@dal.ca.

Duke University, Graduate School, Interdisciplinary Program in German Studies, Durham, NC 27708-0256. Offers PhD. Part-time programs available. *Faculty:* 16 full-time. *Students:* 16 full-time (12 women); includes 2 minority (1 African American, 1 Hispanic American), 5 international. 12 applicants, 75% accepted, 7 enrolled. *Degree requirements:* For doctorate, thesis/dissertation. *Entrance requirements:* For doctorate, GRE General Test. Additional exam requirements/recommendations for international students: Required—TOEFL (minimum score 550 paper-based; 213 computer-based; 83 iBT), IELTS (minimum score 7). *Application deadline:* For fall admission, 12/8 priority date for domestic and international students. Application fee: $75. Electronic applications accepted. *Financial support:* Fellowships, research assistantships, teaching assistantships, Federal Work-Study available. Financial award application deadline: 12/31. *Unit head:* Thomas Pfau, Director of Graduate Studies, 919-681-3098, Fax: 919-660-3104, E-mail: sarah.gray@duke.edu. *Application contact:* Cynthia Robertson, Associate Dean for Enrollment Services, 919-684-3913, E-mail: grad-admissions@duke.edu.

Eastern Michigan University, Graduate School, College of Arts and Sciences, Department of World Languages, Programs in Foreign Languages, Ypsilanti, MI 48197. Offers French (MA); German (MA); German for business (Graduate Certificate); Hispanic language and cultures (Graduate Certificate); Japanese business practices (Graduate Certificate); Spanish (MA). Part-time and evening/weekend programs available. Postbaccalaureate distance learning degree programs offered (minimal on-campus study). *Students:* 1 full-time (0 women), 15 part-time (14 women); includes 4 minority (1 African American, 3 Hispanic Americans), 1 international. Average age 39. In 2009, 6 master's awarded. *Degree requirements:* For master's, one foreign language, thesis optional. *Entrance requirements:* Additional exam requirements/recommendations for international students: Required—TOEFL. *Application deadline:* Applications are processed on a rolling basis. Application fee: $35. Tuition and fees vary according to course level. *Financial support:* Fellowships, research assistantships with full tuition reimbursements, teaching assistantships with full tuition reimbursements, career-related internships or fieldwork, Federal Work-Study, institutionally sponsored loans, scholarships/grants, tuition waivers (partial), and unspecified assistantships available. Support available to part-time students. Financial award applicants required to submit FAFSA. *Application contact:* Dr. Genevieve Peden, Program Advisor, 734-487-2283, Fax: 734-487-3411, E-mail: gpeden@emich.edu.

Florida State University, The Graduate School, College of Arts and Sciences, Department of Modern Languages, Program in German, Tallahassee, FL 32306. Offers MA. *Faculty:* 3 full-time (1 woman), 1 part-time/adjunct (0 women). *Students:* 5 full-time (3 women), 1 (woman) part-time. Average age 25. 3 applicants, 100% accepted, 3 enrolled. In 2009, 1 master's awarded. *Degree requirements:* For master's, thesis optional. *Entrance requirements:* For master's, GRE General Test or minimum GPA of 3.0. Additional exam requirements/recommendations for international students: Required—TOEFL (minimum score 550 paper-based; 213 computer-based). *Application deadline:* For fall admission, 2/1 for domestic students. Application fee: $30. Electronic applications accepted. *Expenses:* Tuition, state resident: full-time $7413. Tuition, nonresident: full-time $22,567. *Financial support:* In 2009–10, 4 students received support, including research assistantships (averaging $12,000 per year), 5 teaching assistantships with partial tuition reimbursements available (averaging $10,200 per year). Financial award application deadline: 2/1; financial award applicants required to submit FAFSA. *Unit head:* Dr. Christian Weber, Divisional Coordinator, 850-644-8194, Fax: 850-644-0524, E-mail: eweber@fsu.edu. *Application contact:* Wendy E. Pigott, Graduate Academic Coordinator, 850-644-8397, Fax: 850-644-0524, E-mail: wpigott@fsu.edu.

Georgetown University, Graduate School of Arts and Sciences, BMW Center for German and European Studies, Washington, DC 20057. Offers MA, MA/JD, MA/PhD. *Degree requirements:* For master's, 2 foreign languages, comprehensive exam. *Entrance requirements:* For master's, GRE General Test. Additional exam requirements/recommendations for international students: Required—TOEFL. *Faculty research:* Trans-Atlantic relations, European Union, German and European Studies.

Georgetown University, Graduate School of Arts and Sciences, Department of German, Washington, DC 20057. Offers MA, MS, PhD, MA/PhD. *Degree requirements:* For master's, 2 foreign languages, research project; for doctorate, 3 foreign languages, thesis/dissertation. *Entrance requirements:* For master's, GRE General Test. Additional exam requirements/recommendations for international students: Required—TOEFL.

Georgia State University, College of Arts and Sciences, Department of Modern and Classical Languages, Program in German, Atlanta, GA 30302-3083. Offers MA. Evening/weekend programs available. *Degree requirements:* For master's, one foreign language, thesis or alternative, general exam. *Entrance requirements:* For master's, GRE General Test. Additional exam requirements/recommendations for international students: Required—TOEFL. Electronic applications accepted. *Faculty research:* Medieval and twentieth-century German literature.

Georgia State University, College of Arts and Sciences, Department of Modern and Classical Languages, Program in Translation and Interpretation, Atlanta, GA 30302-3083. Offers French (Certificate); German (Certificate); Spanish (Certificate). Electronic applications accepted.

Graduate School and University Center of the City University of New York, Graduate Studies, Program in Comparative Literature, New York, NY 10016-4039. Offers comparative literature (MA, PhD), including classics (PhD), German (PhD), Italian (PhD). *Faculty:* 16 full-time (3 women). *Students:* 110 full-time (70 women), 3 part-time (all women); includes 5 minority (2 Asian Americans or Pacific Islanders, 3 Hispanic Americans), 29 international. Average age 37. 51 applicants, 35% accepted, 11 enrolled. In 2009, 5 master's, 8 doctorates awarded. Terminal master's awarded for partial completion of doctoral program. *Degree requirements:* For master's, 2 foreign languages, comprehensive exam, thesis; for doctorate, 3 foreign languages, comprehensive exam, thesis/dissertation. *Entrance requirements:* For master's and doctorate, GRE General Test. Additional exam requirements/recommendations for international students: Required—TOEFL. *Application deadline:* For fall admission, 4/15 for domestic students; for spring admission, 11/15 for domestic students. Application fee: $125. Electronic applications accepted. *Financial support:* In 2009–10, 63 students received support, including 60 fellowships, 5 research assistantships, 14 teaching assistantships; career-related internships or fieldwork, Federal Work-Study, institutionally sponsored loans, and tuition waivers (full and partial) also available. Financial award application deadline: 2/1; financial award applicants required to submit FAFSA. *Unit head:* Dr. Andre Aciman, Executive Officer, 212-817-8170, Fax: 212-817-1509, E-mail: aaciman@gc.cuny.edu. *Application contact:* Les Gribben, Director of Admissions, 212-817-7470, Fax: 212-817-1624, E-mail: lgribben@gc.cuny.edu.

Graduate School and University Center of the City University of New York, Graduate Studies, Program in Germanic Languages and Literatures, New York, NY 10016-4039. Offers MA, PhD. *Faculty:* 11 full-time (4 women). *Students:* 1 (woman) full-time. Average age 34. In 2009, 2 doctorates awarded. *Degree requirements:* For master's, one foreign language, thesis; for doctorate, 2 foreign languages, thesis/dissertation. *Entrance requirements:* For master's and doctorate, GRE General Test. *Financial support:* Fellowships, research assistantships, teaching assistantships, career-related internships or fieldwork, Federal Work-Study, institutionally sponsored loans, and tuition waivers (full and partial) available. Financial award application deadline: 2/1; financial award applicants required to submit FAFSA. *Unit head:* Dr. Tamara Evans, Coordinator, 718-997-5790, Fax: 212-817-1509. *Application contact:* Les Gribben, Director of Admissions, 212-817-7470, Fax: 212-817-1624, E-mail: lgribben@gc.cuny.edu.

Harvard University, Graduate School of Arts and Sciences, Department of Germanic Languages and Literatures, Cambridge, MA 02138. Offers German (PhD); Scandinavian (PhD). Terminal master's awarded for partial completion of doctoral program. *Degree requirements:* For doctorate, 2 foreign languages, thesis/dissertation, exams. *Entrance requirements:* For doctorate, GRE General Test, German writing sample. Additional exam requirements/recommendations for international students: Required—TOEFL. *Expenses:* Tuition: Full-time $33,696. Required fees: $1126. Full-time tuition and fees vary according to program.

Hofstra University, School of Education, Health, and Human Services, Department of Curriculum and Teaching, Program in Foreign Language Education, Hempstead, NY 11549. Offers foreign language and TESOL (MS Ed); foreign language education (MA, MS Ed), including French, German, Russian, Spanish. Part-time and evening/weekend programs available. *Students:* 4 full-time (all women), 3 part-time (1 woman); includes 2 minority (both Hispanic Americans). Average age 29. 9 applicants, 67% accepted, 3 enrolled. In 2009, 2 master's awarded. *Degree requirements:* For master's, one foreign language. *Entrance requirements:* For master's, 2 letters of recommendation, teacher certification (MA). Additional exam requirements/recommendations for international students: Required—TOEFL (minimum score 550 paper-based; 213 computer-based; 80 iBT). *Application deadline:* Applications are processed on a rolling basis. Application fee: $60. Electronic applications accepted. *Expenses:* Tuition: Full-time $16,200; part-time $900 per credit hour. Required fees: $970; $145 per term. Tuition and fees vary according to program. *Financial support:* In 2009–10, 6 students received support, including 2 fellowships with full and partial tuition reimbursements available (averaging $2,878 per year); research assistantships with full and partial tuition reimbursements available, Federal Work-Study, institutionally sponsored loans, scholarships/grants, tuition waivers (full and partial), and unspecified assistantships also available. Support available to part-time students. Financial award applicants required to submit FAFSA. *Faculty research:* First language acquisition and second language learning; theory and practice in language teaching; technology and language teaching and learning; language and colonialism. *Unit head:* Dr. Mustapha Masrour, Program Director, 516-463-6033, Fax: 516-463-6266, E-mail: lalmzm@hofstra.edu. *Application contact:* Carol Drummer, Dean of Graduate Admissions, 516-463-4876, Fax: 516-463-4664, E-mail: gradstudent@hofstra.edu.

Illinois State University, Graduate School, College of Arts and Sciences, Department of Foreign Languages, Literatures and Cultures, Normal, IL 61790-2200. Offers French (MA); French and German (MA); French and Spanish (MA); German (MA); German and Spanish (MA); Spanish (MA). *Degree requirements:* For master's, variable foreign language requirement, comprehensive exam, 1 term of residency. *Entrance requirements:* For master's, GRE General Test, minimum GPA of 2.8 in last 60 hours of course work.

Indiana University Bloomington, University Graduate School, College of Arts and Sciences, Department of Germanic Studies, Bloomington, IN 47405-7000. Offers German philology and linguistics (PhD); German studies (MA, PhD), including German (MA), German literature and culture (MA), German literature and linguistics (MA); medieval German studies (PhD); teaching German (MAT). *Faculty:* 13 full-time (4 women), 6 part-time/adjunct (2 women). *Students:* 34 full-time (19 women), 2 part-time (1 woman); includes 2 minority (1 African American, 1 Hispanic American), 9 international. Average age 30. 34 applicants, 41% accepted, 8 enrolled. In 2009, 3 master's, 2 doctorates awarded. Terminal master's awarded for partial completion of doctoral program. *Degree requirements:* For master's, one foreign language, project; for doctorate, one foreign language, comprehensive exam, thesis/dissertation. *Entrance requirements:* For master's, GRE General Test, BA in German or equivalent; for doctorate, GRE General Test, MA in German or equivalent. Additional exam requirements/recommendations for international students: Required—TOEFL. *Application deadline:* For fall admission, 1/15 priority date for domestic students, 12/15 for international students; for spring admission, 9/1 priority date for domestic students, 9/1 for international students. Applications are processed on a rolling basis. Application fee: $55 ($65 for international students). *Financial support:* In 2009–10, 8 fellowships with full and partial tuition reimbursements (averaging $20,000 per year), 1 research assistantship (averaging $13,025 per year), 20 teaching assistantships with full tuition reimbursements (averaging $13,025 per year) were awarded; Federal Work-Study, institutionally sponsored loans, scholarships/grants, and unspecified assistantships also available. Support available to part-time students. Financial award application deadline: 1/15; financial award applicants required to submit FAFSA. *Faculty research:* German and other European literature: medieval to modern/postmodern, German and culture studies, Germanic philology, literary theory, literature and the other arts. *Unit head:* William Rasch, Department Chairman, 812-855-7947, Fax: 812-855-8292, E-mail: wrasch@indiana.edu. *Application contact:* Michelle Dunbar, Graduate Secretary, 812-855-7947, E-mail: midunbar@indiana.edu.

The Johns Hopkins University, Zanvyl Krieger School of Arts and Sciences, Department of German and Romance Languages and Literatures, Baltimore, MD 21218-2699. Offers French (PhD); German (PhD); Italian (PhD); romance languages (PhD); Spanish (PhD). *Faculty:* 31 full-time (20 women), 1 part-time/adjunct (0 women). *Students:* 49 full-time (30 women); includes 4 minority (all Hispanic Americans), 21 international. Average age 30. 51 applicants, 37% accepted, 19 enrolled. In 2009, 5 doctorates awarded. *Degree requirements:* For doctorate, 2 foreign languages, thesis/dissertation. *Entrance requirements:* For doctorate, GRE General Test. Additional exam requirements/recommendations for international students: Required—TOEFL (minimum score 600 paper-based; 250 computer-based; 100 iBT), IELTS. *Application deadline:* For fall admission, 12/30 for domestic and international students. Application fee: $75. Electronic applications accepted. *Financial support:* In 2009–10, 40 fellowships with full tuition reimbursements (averaging $17,000 per year), 2 research assistantships with full tuition reimbursements (averaging $17,000 per year), 19 teaching assistantships with full tuition reimbursements (averaging $17,000 per year) were awarded; institutionally sponsored loans also available. *Faculty research:* Nineteenth century French prose and poetry, genetic theory and criticism; twentieth century Latin American literature and film; Medieval and Renaissance Italian literature; Gender and Queer Theory in German literature; the ideology of baroque and neobaroque aesthetics. *Unit head:* Dr. William Egginton, Chair, 410-516-7510, Fax: 410-516-5358, E-mail: egginton@jhu.edu. *Application contact:* Rebecca Swisdak, Graduate Administrative Coordinator, 410-516-7227, Fax: 410-516-5358, E-mail: rswisdak@jhu.edu.

Kansas State University, Graduate School, College of Arts and Sciences, Department of Modern Languages, Manhattan, KS 66506. Offers French (MA); German (MA); Spanish (MA). Part-time and evening/weekend programs available. Postbaccalaureate distance learning degree programs offered (minimal on-campus study). *Faculty:* 17 full-time (9 women). *Students:* 15 full-time (6 women), 15 part-time (13 women); includes 5 minority (1 Asian American or Pacific Islander, 4 Hispanic Americans), 10 international. Average age 32. 20 applicants, 75% accepted, 10 enrolled. In 2009, 6 master's awarded. *Degree requirements:* For master's, thesis optional. *Entrance requirements:* For master's, teaching certificate. Additional exam requirements/recommendations for international students: Required—TOEFL (minimum score 560 paper-based). *Application deadline:* For fall admission, 2/1 priority date for domestic and international students; for spring admission, 8/1 priority date for domestic and international students. Applications are processed on a rolling basis. Application fee: $40 ($55 for international students). Electronic applications accepted. *Financial support:* In 2009–10, 16 teaching assistantships with full tuition reimbursements (averaging $8,914 per year) were awarded; Federal Work-Study, institutionally sponsored loans, and scholarships/grants also available. Support available to part-time students. Financial award application deadline: 3/1; financial award applicants required to submit FAFSA. *Faculty research:* Second language acquisitions; Chicano literature; Francophone literature; cultural studies; German, French, Spanish, and Spanish-American literature from the Middle Ages to the modern era. *Unit head:* Robert Corum, Head, 785-532-1987, Fax: 785-532-7004, E-mail: corum@ksu.edu. *Application contact:* Claire Dehon, Director, 785-532-1929, Fax: 785-532-7004, E-mail: dehoncl@ksu.edu.

Kent State University, College of Arts and Sciences, Department of Modern and Classical Language Studies, Kent, OH 44242-0001. Offers French literature (MA); French, Spanish, German and Latin pedagogy (MA); German literature (MA); Spanish literature (MA); translation (MA), including French, German, Japanese, Russian, Spanish; translation studies (PhD). Part-time and evening/weekend programs available. *Degree requirements:* For master's, one foreign language, comprehensive exam (for some programs), thesis (for some programs); for doctorate, comprehensive exam, thesis/dissertation (for some programs). *Entrance requirements:* For master's, minimum GPA of 3.0, writing sample, audio tape or CD; for doctorate, 3 recommendations. Additional exam requirements/recommendations for international students: Required—TOEFL (minimum score 197 computer-based). Electronic applications accepted. *Faculty research:* Literature, pedagogy, applied linguistics, translation studies.

McGill University, Faculty of Graduate and Postdoctoral Studies, Faculty of Arts, Department of German Studies, Montréal, QC H3A 2T5, Canada. Offers MA, PhD.

Memorial University of Newfoundland, School of Graduate Studies, Department of German and Russian, St. John's, NL A1C 5S7, Canada. Offers German language and literature (M Phil, MA). Part-time programs available. *Degree requirements:* For master's, one foreign language, thesis (for some programs), comprehensive exam (M Phil). *Entrance requirements:* For master's, honors degree (minimum 2nd class standing). Electronic applications accepted. *Faculty research:* German literature from the Middle Ages to the twentieth century, German studies.

Michigan State University, The Graduate School, College of Arts and Letters, Department of Linguistics and Germanic, Slavic, Asian, and African Languages, East Lansing, MI 48824. Offers German studies (MA, PhD); linguistics (MA, PhD); teaching English to speakers of other languages (MA). Part-time and evening/weekend programs available. *Faculty:* 30 full-time (16 women). *Students:* 78 full-time (46 women), 20 part-time (13 women); includes 8 minority (2 African Americans, 3 American Indian/Alaska Native, 2 Asian Americans or Pacific Islanders, 1 Hispanic American), 51 international. Average age 30. 149 applicants, 38% accepted. In 2009, 24 master's awarded. *Entrance requirements:* For master's, GRE General Test, minimum GPA of 3.2 in last 2 undergraduate years, 2 years of college-level foreign language, 3 letters of recommendation, portfolio (German studies); for doctorate, GRE General Test, minimum graduate GPA of 3.5, 3 letters of recommendation, master's degree or sufficient graduate course work in linguistics or language of study, master's thesis or major research paper. Additional exam requirements/recommendations for international students: Required—TOEFL. Electronic applications accepted. *Expenses:* Tuition, state resident: part-time $478.25 per credit hour. Tuition, nonresident: part-time $966.50 per credit hour. Part-time tuition and fees

German

Michigan State University (continued)

vary according to program. *Financial support:* In 2009–10, 7 research assistantships with tuition reimbursements (averaging $6,071 per year), 31 teaching assistantships with tuition reimbursements (averaging $5,986 per year) were awarded. Total annual research expenditures: $351,012. *Unit head:* Dr. David K. Prestel, Chairperson, 517-353-0740, Fax: 517-432-2736, E-mail: prestel@msu.edu. *Application contact:* Julie Delgado, Graduate Studies Secretary, 517-353-0740, Fax: 517-432-2736, E-mail: delgadof@msu.edu.

Middlebury College, Language Schools, German School, Middlebury, VT 05753-6002. Offers MA, DML. *Faculty:* 6 full-time (3 women). *Students:* 33 full-time (20 women); includes 2 minority (both Hispanic Americans). Average age 33. 51 applicants, 84% accepted, 33 enrolled. In 2009, 11 master's awarded. *Degree requirements:* For master's, one foreign language; for doctorate, 2 foreign languages, comprehensive exam, thesis/dissertation, residence abroad, teaching experience. *Entrance requirements:* For master's, placement exam, 3 letters of recommendation. *Application deadline:* Applications are processed on a rolling basis. Application fee: $65. Electronic applications accepted. *Financial support:* Scholarships/grants available. Financial award applicants required to submit FAFSA. *Unit head:* Dr. Doris Kirchner, Director, 802-443-5203, Fax: 802-443-2075, E-mail: dkirchner@middlebury.edu. *Application contact:* Christina Ellison, Coordinator, 802-443-5203, Fax: 802-443-2075, E-mail: ccartwri@middlebury.edu.

Millersville University of Pennsylvania, College of Graduate and Professional Studies, School of Humanities and Social Sciences, Department of Foreign Languages, Program in German, Millersville, PA 17551-0302. Offers M Ed, MA. Part-time programs available. *Faculty:* 8 full-time (4 women), 7 part-time/adjunct (6 women). *Students:* 2 part-time (1 woman). Average age 26. In 2009, 2 master's awarded. *Degree requirements:* For master's, comprehensive exam, thesis optional. *Entrance requirements:* For master's, 3 letters of recommendation. Additional exam requirements/recommendations for international students: Required—TOEFL (minimum score 550 paper-based; 183 computer-based; 65 iBT) or IELTS (minimum score 6). *Application deadline:* For fall admission, 1/15 priority date for domestic and international students; for winter admission, 10/1 priority date for domestic and international students; for spring admission, 10/1 priority date for domestic and international students. Applications are processed on a rolling basis. Application fee: $40 ($50 for international students). Electronic applications accepted. *Expenses:* Tuition, state resident: full-time $6666; part-time $370 per credit. Tuition, nonresident: full-time $10,666; part-time $593 per credit. Required fees: $1578.50; $76.25 per credit. One-time fee: $60 part-time. Tuition and fees vary according to course load. *Financial support:* Research assistantships, institutionally sponsored loans and unspecified assistantships available. Support available to part-time students. Financial award application deadline: 3/15; financial award applicants required to submit FAFSA. *Unit head:* Dr. Christine M. Gaudry-Hudson, Coordinator of Foreign Language Graduate Program, 717-872-3663, E-mail: christine.gaudry-hudson@millersville.edu. *Application contact:* Dr. Victor S. DeSantis, Dean of Graduate and Professional Studies, 717-872-3099, Fax: 717-872-3453, E-mail: victor.desantis@millersville.edu.

Mississippi State University, College of Arts and Sciences, Department of Foreign Languages, Mississippi State, MS 39762. Offers foreign language (MA), including French, German, Spanish. Part-time programs available. *Faculty:* 8 full-time (3 women). *Students:* 9 full-time (7 women), 2 part-time (1 woman); includes 1 minority (Hispanic American), 3 international. Average age 31. 5 applicants, 100% accepted, 3 enrolled. In 2009, 5 master's awarded. *Degree requirements:* For master's, one foreign language, comprehensive exam (for some programs), thesis optional, comprehensive oral or written exam. *Entrance requirements:* For master's, minimum GPA of 2.75 on last two years of undergraduate courses. Additional exam requirements/recommendations for international students: Required—TOEFL (minimum score 525 paper-based). *Application deadline:* For fall admission, 7/1 for domestic students, 5/1 for international students; for spring admission, 11/1 for domestic students, 9/1 for international students. Applications are processed on a rolling basis. Application fee: $40. Electronic applications accepted. *Expenses:* Tuition, state resident: full-time $2575.50; part-time $286.25 per credit hour. Tuition, nonresident: full-time $6510; part-time $723.50 per credit hour. Tuition and fees vary according to course load. *Financial support:* In 2009–10, 7 teaching assistantships with full tuition reimbursements (averaging $8,766 per year) were awarded; Federal Work-Study, institutionally sponsored loans, and unspecified assistantships also available. Financial award application deadline: 4/1; financial award applicants required to submit FAFSA. *Faculty research:* French, German, Spanish literature from medieval era to present; gender and cultural studies in French; Spanish American literature; foreign language methodology; linguistics. *Unit head:* Dr. Jack Jordan, Professor/Head, 662-325-3480, Fax: 662-325-8209, E-mail: jordan@ra.msstate.edu. *Application contact:* Dr. Edward T. Potter, Assistant Professor/Graduate Coordinator, 662-325-2399, Fax: 662-325-8209, E-mail: ep75@.msstate.edu.

New York University, Graduate School of Arts and Science, Department of German, New York, NY 10012-1019. Offers German studies and critical thought (MA, PhD). Part-time programs available. *Faculty:* 8 full-time (5 women), 5 part-time/adjunct (0 women). *Students:* 25 full-time (13 women); includes 1 minority (African American), 13 international. Average age 34. 21 applicants, 24% accepted, 3 enrolled. In 2009, 4 doctorates awarded. Terminal master's awarded for partial completion of doctoral program. *Degree requirements:* For master's, one foreign language, thesis; for doctorate, 2 foreign languages, thesis/dissertation. *Entrance requirements:* For master's, GRE Subject Test; for doctorate, GRE Subject Test, sample of written work. Additional exam requirements/recommendations for international students: Required—TOEFL. *Application deadline:* For fall admission, 1/4 priority date for domestic students. Application fee: $90. *Expenses:* Tuition: Full-time $30,528; part-time $1272 per credit. Required fees: $2177. *Financial support:* Fellowships with tuition reimbursements, teaching assistantships with tuition reimbursements, Federal Work-Study, institutionally sponsored loans, scholarships/grants, health care benefits, and unspecified assistantships available. Financial award application deadline: 1/4; financial award applicants required to submit FAFSA. *Faculty research:* Eighteenth- to twentieth-century literature, culture and critical thought, film and visual culture, philosophy, critical theory. *Unit head:* Paul Fleming, Chair, 212-998-8650, Fax: 212-995-4823, E-mail: german.dept@nyu.edu. *Application contact:* Lindsay O'Connor, Department Administrator.

Northwestern University, The Graduate School, Judd A. and Marjorie Weinberg College of Arts and Sciences, Program in German Literature and Critical Thought, Evanston, IL 60208. Offers PhD. Admissions and degrees offered through The Graduate School. *Degree requirements:* For doctorate, one foreign language, thesis/dissertation. *Entrance requirements:* For doctorate, GRE General Test. Additional exam requirements/recommendations for international students: Required—TOEFL. Electronic applications accepted. *Faculty research:* Eighteenth through twentieth century German literature, comparative literature, theory, philosophy, language pedagogy.

The Ohio State University, Graduate School, College of Humanities, Department of Germanic Languages and Literatures, Columbus, OH 43210. Offers MA, PhD. *Faculty:* 16. *Students:* 15 full-time (9 women), 9 part-time (5 women); includes 1 minority (African American), 6 international. Average age 28. In 2009, 5 master's awarded. *Degree requirements:* For master's, one foreign language, thesis optional; for doctorate, 2 foreign languages, thesis/dissertation. *Entrance requirements:* For master's and doctorate, GRE General Test. Additional exam requirements/recommendations for international students: Required—TOEFL (minimum score 600 paper-based; 250 computer-based). *Application deadline:* For fall admission, 8/15 priority date for domestic students, 7/1 priority date for international students; for winter admission, 12/1 priority date for domestic students, 11/1 priority date for international students; for spring admission, 3/1 priority date for domestic students, 2/1 priority date for international students. Applications are processed on a rolling basis. Application fee: $40 ($50 for international students). Electronic applications accepted. *Expenses:* Tuition, state resident: full-time $10,683. Tuition, nonresident: full-time $25,923. Tuition and fees vary according to course load and program. *Financial support:* Fellowships, research assistantships, teaching assistantships, Federal Work-Study and institutionally sponsored loans available. Support available to part-time students. *Faculty research:* German literature, Germanic philology, linguistics. *Unit head:* Barbara Becker-Cantarino, Graduate Studies Committee Chair, E-mail: becker-cantarino.1@osu.edu. *Application contact:* 614-292-9444, Fax: 614-292-3895, E-mail: domestic.grad@osu.edu.

Penn State University Park, Graduate School, College of the Liberal Arts, Department of Germanic and Slavic Languages and Literatures, State College, University Park, PA 16802-1503. Offers German (MA, PhD). *Faculty research:* Literature, literary theory, culture, language pedagogy.

Portland State University, Graduate Studies, College of Liberal Arts and Sciences, Department of Foreign Languages and Literatures, Portland, OR 97207-0751. Offers foreign literature and language (MA); French (MA); German (MA); Japanese (MA); Spanish (MA). Part-time programs available. *Degree requirements:* For master's, one foreign language, thesis (for some programs). *Entrance requirements:* Additional exam requirements/recommendations for international students: Required—TOEFL (minimum score 550 paper-based; 213 computer-based). *Faculty research:* Foreign language pedagogy, applied and social linguistics, literary history and criticism.

Princeton University, Graduate School, Department of German, Princeton, NJ 08544-1019. Offers PhD. *Degree requirements:* For doctorate, 2 foreign languages, thesis/dissertation. *Entrance requirements:* For doctorate, GRE General Test. Additional exam requirements/recommendations for international students: Required—TOEFL (minimum score 600 paper-based; 250 computer-based). Electronic applications accepted.

Purdue University, Graduate School, College of Liberal Arts, Department of Foreign Languages and Literatures, West Lafayette, IN 47907. Offers French (MA, MAT, PhD), including French (MA, PhD), French education (MAT); German (MA, MAT, PhD), including German (MA, PhD), German education (MAT); Spanish (MA, MAT, PhD), including Spanish (MA, PhD), Spanish education (MAT). Terminal master's awarded for partial completion of doctoral program. *Degree requirements:* For master's, one foreign language; for doctorate, 2 foreign languages, thesis/dissertation. *Entrance requirements:* For master's, GRE, sample recording of English and language of study; for doctorate, GRE, writing sample, sample recording of English and language of study. Additional exam requirements/recommendations for international students: Required—TOEFL. Electronic applications accepted. *Faculty research:* Linguistics, semiotics, literary criticism, pedagogy.

Queen's University at Kingston, School of Graduate Studies and Research, Faculty of Arts and Sciences, Department of German Language and Literature, Kingston, ON K7L 3N6, Canada. Offers MA, PhD. Part-time programs available. *Degree requirements:* For master's, thesis optional; for doctorate, one foreign language, comprehensive exam, thesis/dissertation. *Entrance requirements:* For master's, 7 German courses, honors bachelor's degree in German; for doctorate, MA or equivalent in German. Additional exam requirements/recommendations for international students: Required—TOEFL. Electronic applications accepted. *Faculty research:* Goethe and Weimar classicism, Romanticism, nineteenth- and twentieth-century German literature.

Rider University, Department of Graduate Education, Leadership and Counseling, Teacher Certification Program, Lawrenceville, NJ 08648-3001. Offers business education (Certificate); elementary education (Certificate); English as a second language (Certificate); English education (Certificate); mathematics education (Certificate); preschool to grade 3 (Certificate); science education (Certificate); social studies education (Certificate); world languages (Certificate), including French, German, Spanish. Part-time programs available. *Degree requirements:* For Certificate, internship, professional portfolio. *Entrance requirements:* For degree, PRAXIS, resume. Additional exam requirements/recommendations for international students: Required—TOEFL (minimum score 550 paper-based; 213 computer-based). Electronic applications accepted. *Faculty research:* Conceptual foundations for optimal development of creativity; creative theory, cognitive processes in mathematics learning, teacher collaboration.

Rutgers, The State University of New Jersey, New Brunswick, Graduate School-New Brunswick, Program in German, Piscataway, NJ 08854-8097. Offers German (MAT, PhD); German literature (MA, PhD). Part-time and evening/weekend programs available. Terminal master's awarded for partial completion of doctoral program. *Degree requirements:* For master's, one foreign language, comprehensive exam, thesis or alternative; for doctorate, 2 foreign languages, comprehensive exam, thesis/dissertation. *Entrance requirements:* For master's and doctorate, GRE General Test. Additional exam requirements/recommendations for international students: Required—TOEFL. Electronic applications accepted. *Faculty research:* Literature and ideology; early German novella; narrative structures, mythology, psychology, and realist literature; German-American cultural history; literary theory and aesthetics; German film.

San Francisco State University, Division of Graduate Studies, College of Humanities, Department of Foreign Languages and Literatures, Program in German, San Francisco, CA 94132-1722. Offers MA.

Stanford University, School of Humanities and Sciences, Department of German Studies, Stanford, CA 94305-9991. Offers MA, PhD. *Degree requirements:* For master's, one foreign language, oral exam; for doctorate, 2 foreign languages, thesis/dissertation, oral exam, qualifying paper and exam. *Entrance requirements:* For master's and doctorate, GRE General Test. Additional exam requirements/recommendations for international students: Required—TOEFL. Electronic applications accepted. *Expenses:* Tuition: Full-time $37,380; part-time $2760 per quarter. Required fees: $501.

Texas Tech University, Graduate School, College of Arts and Sciences, Department of Classical and Modern Languages and Literatures, Program in German, Lubbock, TX 79409. Offers MA. *Students:* 3 full-time (2 women), 4 part-time (1 woman), 4 international. Average age 34. 5 applicants, 80% accepted, 1 enrolled. In 2009, 4 master's awarded. *Entrance requirements:* For master's, GRE General Test. Additional exam requirements/recommendations for international students: Required—TOEFL (minimum score 550 paper-based; 213 computer-based). *Application deadline:* For fall admission, 3/1 priority date for international students; for spring admission, 11/1 priority date for international students. Applications are processed on a rolling basis. Application fee: $50 ($75 for international students). Electronic applications accepted. *Expenses:* Tuition, state resident: full-time $5100; part-time $213 per credit hour. Tuition, nonresident: full-time $11,748; part-time $490 per credit hour. Required fees: $2298; $50 per credit hour. $555 per semester. *Financial support:* Research assistantships with partial tuition reimbursements, teaching assistantships with partial tuition reimbursements available. Financial award application deadline: 4/15. *Faculty research:* Contemporary German literature, Goethe, business German, German culture, foreign language reading. *Unit head:* Dr. Charles A. Grair, Advisor/Associate Professor, 806-742-3145 Ext. 275, Fax: 806-742-3306, E-mail: charles.grair@ttu.edu. *Application contact:* Liz Hildebrand, Senior Advisor, 806-742-4055, Fax: 806-742-3306, E-mail: liz.hildebrand@ttu.edu.

Tufts University, Graduate School of Arts and Sciences, Department of Russian and German, Medford, MA 02155. Offers German (MA). Part-time programs available. *Faculty:* 28 full-time, 16 part-time/adjunct. *Students:* 3 (all women). 5 applicants, 80% accepted, 2 enrolled. In 2009, 4 master's awarded. *Degree requirements:* For master's, one foreign language, oral and written exam. *Entrance requirements:* Additional exam requirements/recommendations for international students: Required—TOEFL (minimum score 550 paper-based; 213 computer-based; 80 iBT). *Application deadline:* For fall admission, 3/1 for domestic students, 12/15 for international students; for spring admission, 10/15 for domestic students, 9/15 for international students. Applications are processed on a rolling basis. Application fee: $75. Electronic applications accepted. *Expenses:* Tuition: Full-time $38,096; part-time $3962 per credit. Required fees: $686; $40 per year. Tuition and fees vary according to course level, course load, degree level, program and student level. *Financial support:* Federal Work-Study, scholarships/grants, and tuition waivers (partial) available. Support available to part-time students. Financial award application deadline: 3/1; financial award applicants required to submit FAFSA. *Unit head:* Hosea Hirata, Chair, 617-627-3442, Fax: 617-627-3945. *Application contact:* Hosea Hirata, Chair, 617-627-3442, Fax: 617-627-3945.

Université de Montréal, Faculty of Arts and Sciences, Department of Literatures and Modern Languages, Program in German Studies, Montréal, QC H3C 3J7, Canada. Offers MA. *Degree requirements:* For master's, 2 foreign languages, thesis. Electronic applications accepted.

University at Buffalo, the State University of New York, Graduate School, Graduate School of Education, Department of Learning and Instruction, Buffalo, NY 14260. Offers biology education (Ed M, Certificate); chemistry education (Ed M, Certificate); childhood education (Ed M); childhood education with bilingual extension (Ed M); early childhood education (Ed M); earth science education (Ed M, Certificate); elementary education (Ed D, PhD); English education (Ed M, PhD, Certificate); English for speakers of other languages (Ed M); foreign and second language education (PhD); French education (Ed M, Certificate); general education (Ed M); German education (Ed M, Certificate); gifted education (online) (Certificate); Latin education (Ed M, Certificate); literary specialist (Ed M); mathematics education (Ed M, PhD, Certificate); music education (Ed M, Certificate); physics education (Ed M, Certificate); reading education (PhD); science and the public (online) (Ed M); science education (PhD); social studies education (Ed M, Certificate); Spanish education (Ed M, Certificate); special education (PhD); teaching and leading for diversity (Certificate); teaching English to speakers of other languages (Ed M). Part-time and evening/weekend programs available. Postbaccalaureate distance learning degree programs offered (no on-campus study). *Faculty:* 34 full-time (24 women), 50 part-time/adjunct (39 women). *Students:* 332 full-time (245 women), 365 part-time (272 women); includes 50 minority (18 African Americans, 4 American Indian/Alaska Native, 10 Asian Americans or Pacific Islanders, 18 Hispanic Americans), 55 international. Average age 30. 627 applicants, 78% accepted, 286 enrolled. In 2009, 255 master's, 16 doctorates, 51 other advanced degrees awarded. *Degree requirements:* For master's, comprehensive exam; for doctorate, thesis/dissertation, research analysis exam, research experience component. *Entrance requirements:* For doctorate, GRE General Test or MAT, interview, writing sample, letters of recommendation. Additional exam requirements/recommendations for international students: Required—TOEFL (minimum score 600 paper-based; 250 computer-based; 96 iBT). *Application deadline:* For fall admission, 2/1 priority date for domestic and international students; for spring admission, 11/15 priority date for domestic students, 10/1 for international students. Applications are processed on a rolling basis. Application fee: $50. Electronic applications accepted. *Financial support:* In 2009–10, 23 fellowships with full tuition reimbursements (averaging $9,000 per year), 42 research assistantships with full tuition reimbursements (averaging $10,000 per year) were awarded; teaching assistantships with full tuition reimbursements, career-related internships or fieldwork, Federal Work-Study, institutionally sponsored loans, scholarships/grants, tuition waivers (partial), and unspecified assistantships also available. Financial award application deadline: 2/28; financial award applicants required to submit FAFSA. *Faculty research:* Science assessment, foreign language teaching and learning, early learning, new literacies, gender and education. Total annual research expenditures: $1.8 million. *Unit head:* Dr. Suzanne Miller, Chair, 716-645-2455, Fax: 716-645-3161, E-mail: smiller@buffalo.edu. *Application contact:* Cathy Dimino, Admissions Assistant, 716-645-2110, Fax: 716-645-7937, E-mail: cadimino@buffalo.edu.

The University of Alabama, Graduate School, College of Arts and Sciences, Department of Modern Languages and Classics, Tuscaloosa, AL 35487. Offers French (MA, PhD); French and Spanish (PhD); German (MA); Romance languages (MA, PhD); Spanish (MA, PhD). Part-time programs available. *Faculty:* 22 full-time (11 women). *Students:* 46 full-time (31 women), 8 part-time (6 women); includes 7 minority (4 African Americans, 3 Hispanic Americans), 16 international. Average age 31. 31 applicants, 42% accepted, 11 enrolled. In 2009, 12 master's, 5 doctorates awarded. *Median time to degree:* Of those who began their doctoral program in fall 2001, 40% received their degree in 8 years or less. *Degree requirements:* For master's, comprehensive exam, thesis optional; for doctorate, one foreign language, thesis/dissertation, preliminary exam. *Entrance requirements:* For master's and doctorate, minimum GPA of 3.0, writing sample. Additional exam requirements/recommendations for international students: Required—TOEFL or IELTS. *Application deadline:* For fall admission, 7/6 priority date for domestic students, 1/15 priority date for international students; for spring admission, 12/6 priority date for domestic students, 6/1 priority date for international students. Applications are processed on a rolling basis. Application fee: $50 ($60 for international students). Electronic applications accepted. *Expenses:* Tuition, state resident: full-time $7000. Tuition, nonresident: full-time $19,200. *Financial support:* In 2009–10, 7 students received support, including 1 fellowship, research assistantships with full tuition reimbursements available (averaging $10,291 per year), 6 teaching assistantships with full tuition reimbursements available (averaging $10,291 per year); career-related internships or fieldwork, Federal Work-Study, institutionally sponsored loans, and scholarships/grants also available. Financial award application deadline: 7/14. *Faculty research:* Non-English literature, linguistics, culture, film. *Unit head:* Dr. Michael Picone, Chair and Professor, 205-348-5054, Fax: 205-348-2042, E-mail: mpicone@bama.ua.edu. *Application contact:* Dr. K. Barbara Fischer, Graduate Director and Associate Professor, 205-348-8465, Fax: 205-348-2042, E-mail: bfischer@bama.ua.edu.

University of Alberta, Faculty of Graduate Studies and Research, Department of Modern Languages and Cultural Studies, Edmonton, AB T6G 2E1, Canada. Offers applied linguistics (Germanic, Romance, Slavic) (MA); French language, literatures and linguistics (PhD); French language, literatures, and linguistics (MA); Germanic languages, literatures and linguistics (PhD); Germanic languages, literatures, and linguistics (MA); Italian studies (MA); Slavic languages and literatures (Russian, Ukrainian) (MA, PhD); Slavic linguistics (Russian, Ukrainian) (MA, PhD); Spanish and Latin American studies (MA, PhD); Ukrainian folklore (MA, PhD). Part-time programs available. *Faculty:* 33 full-time (15 women), 2 part-time/adjunct (1 woman). *Students:* 39 full-time (29 women), 13 part-time (12 women). 300 applicants, 10% accepted. In 2009, 12 master's, 2 doctorates awarded. *Degree requirements:* For master's, one foreign language, thesis; for doctorate, 2 foreign languages, comprehensive exam, thesis/dissertation. *Entrance requirements:* For master's and doctorate, 1 language other than English. Additional exam requirements/recommendations for international students: Required—Michigan English Language Assessment Battery or TOEFL (minimum score 550 paper-based; 213 computer-based). *Application deadline:* For fall admission, 7/1 for domestic and international students; for winter admission, 11/1 for domestic and international students; for spring admission, 3/1 for domestic students. Applications are processed on a rolling basis. Electronic applications accepted. Tuition and fees charges are reported in Canadian dollars. *Expenses:* Tuition, area resident: Full-time $4626 Canadian dollars; part-time $99.72 Canadian dollars per unit. International tuition: $8216 Canadian dollars full-time. Required fees: $3590 Canadian dollars; $99.72 Canadian dollars per unit. $215 Canadian dollars per term. *Financial support:* In 2009–10, 2 fellowships with full and partial tuition reimbursements (averaging $18,000 per year), 23 research assistantships with full and partial tuition reimbursements (averaging $10,450 per year), 21 teaching assistantships with full and partial tuition reimbursements (averaging $12,572 per year) were awarded; scholarships/grants also available. Support available to part-time students. Financial award application deadline: 3/31. *Faculty research:* Russian/Ukrainian studies; German studies; contemporary Latin American, French and Francophone studies; Italian studies. *Unit head:* Dr. Don Bruce, Chair, 780-492-3273, Fax: 780-492-9106. *Application contact:* Jane Wilson, Graduate Programs Secretary, 780-492-3273, Fax: 780-492-9106, E-mail: mlcsgrad@ualberta.ca.

The University of Arizona, Graduate College, College of Humanities, Department of German Studies, Tucson, AZ 85721. Offers German (MA). *Faculty:* 7. *Students:* 17 full-time (11 women), 2 part-time (1 woman); includes 1 minority (Asian American or Pacific Islander). Average age 29. 10 applicants, 70% accepted, 5 enrolled. In 2009, 1 master's awarded. *Degree requirements:* For master's, one foreign language, comprehensive exam, oral exam. *Entrance requirements:* For master's, minimum major GPA of 3.3, 3 letters of recommendation, audio sample, curriculum vitae. Additional exam requirements/recommendations for international students: Required—TOEFL (minimum score 550 paper-based; 213 computer-based; 79 iBT). *Application deadline:* For fall admission, 2/1 for domestic students, 12/1 for international students; for spring admission, 10/1 for domestic students, 6/1 for international students. Applications are processed on a rolling basis. Application fee: $75. Electronic applications accepted. *Expenses:* Tuition, state resident: full-time $9028. Tuition, nonresident: full-time $24,890. *Financial support:* In 2009–10, 17 teaching assistantships with full tuition reimbursements (averaging $15,004 per year) were awarded; Federal Work-Study, institutionally sponsored loans, scholarships/grants, health care benefits, tuition waivers (partial), and unspecified assistantships also available. Financial award application deadline: 3/1. *Faculty research:* Literature, language, and foreign language pedagogy; computer-assisted text analysis. *Unit head:* Dr. Mary Wildner-Bassett, Head, 520-621-1799, Fax: 520-626-8268, E-mail: wildnerb@u.arizona.edu. *Application contact:* Susanna Ruiz, Information Contact, 520-626-8123, Fax: 520-626-8268, E-mail: ruizs@u.arizona.edu.

University of Arkansas, Graduate School, J. William Fulbright College of Arts and Sciences, Department of Foreign Languages, Program in German, Fayetteville, AR 72701-1201. Offers MA. *Students:* 4 full-time (3 women), 1 (woman) part-time, 1 international. In 2009, 2 master's awarded. *Degree requirements:* For master's, variable foreign language requirement. Application fee: $40 ($50 for international students). *Expenses:* Tuition, state resident: full-time $7355; part-time $356.58 per hour. Tuition, nonresident: full-time $17,401; part-time $775.17 per hour. Required fees: $1203. *Financial support:* In 2009–10, 2 teaching assistantships were awarded; fellowships, research assistantships, career-related internships or fieldwork and Federal Work-Study also available. Support available to part-time students. Financial award application deadline: 4/1; financial award applicants required to submit FAFSA. *Unit head:* Dr. Joan Turner, Graduate Coordinator, 479-575-2951, Fax: 479-575-6795, E-mail: joant@uark.edu. *Application contact:* Dr. Jennifer Hoyer, Graduate Coordinator, 479-575-5938, E-mail: jhoyer@uark.edu.

The University of British Columbia, Faculty of Arts and Faculty of Graduate Studies, Department of Central, Eastern and Northern European Studies, Vancouver, BC V6T2Z1, Canada. Offers Germanic studies (MA, PhD). Part-time programs available. *Degree requirements:* For master's, one foreign language, thesis optional, exam; for doctorate, comprehensive exam, thesis/dissertation. *Entrance requirements:* For master's, BA in German; for doctorate, MA in German. Additional exam requirements/recommendations for international students: Required—TOEFL (minimum score 550 paper-based; 213 computer-based). Electronic applications accepted. *Faculty research:* Second language acquisition, media theory, performance theory, gender studies, cultural studies.

University of Calgary, Faculty of Graduate Studies, Faculty of Humanities, Department of Germanic, Slavic and East Asian Studies, Calgary, AB T2N 1N4, Canada. Offers German (MA). Part-time programs available. *Degree requirements:* For master's, one foreign language, thesis. *Entrance requirements:* Additional exam requirements/recommendations for international students: Required—TOEFL. Electronic applications accepted. *Faculty research:* German language and linguistics, second language acquisition, medieval and early modern literature and culture, twentieth century German literature.

University of California, Berkeley, Graduate Division, College of Letters and Science, Department of German, Berkeley, CA 94720-1500. Offers PhD. *Students:* 35 full-time (16 women). Average age 31. 25 applicants, 4 enrolled. *Degree requirements:* For doctorate, 2 foreign languages, thesis/dissertation, qualifying exam. *Entrance requirements:* For doctorate, GRE General Test, minimum GPA of 3.0, writing sample, 3 letters of recommendation. *Application deadline:* For fall admission, 12/15 for domestic students. Application fee: $70 ($90 for international students). Electronic applications accepted. *Financial support:* Fellowships, research assistantships, teaching assistantships, Federal Work-Study, tuition waivers (full and partial), and unspecified assistantships available. *Faculty research:* German literature/culture, film, Germanic linguistics, second-language acquisition. *Unit head:* Niklaus Largier, Chair, 510-643-2004, Fax: 510-643-3243, E-mail: ch_german@ls.berkeley.edu. *Application contact:* Elisabeth Lamoureaux, Graduate Assistant for Admissions, 510-643-2004, Fax: 510-642-3243, E-mail: germanga@berkeley.edu.

University of California, Davis, Graduate Studies, Program in German, Davis, CA 95616. Offers MA, PhD. Terminal master's awarded for partial completion of doctoral program. *Degree requirements:* For master's, comprehensive exam (for some programs), thesis (for some programs); for doctorate, thesis/dissertation. *Entrance requirements:* For master's, GRE; for doctorate, GRE, master's degree or equivalent. Additional exam requirements/recommendations for international students: Required—TOEFL (minimum score 550 paper-based; 213 computer-based). Electronic applications accepted. *Faculty research:* Sixteenth to twentieth century medieval literature, critical theory, women's studies.

University of California, Irvine, Office of Graduate Studies, School of Humanities, Department of German, Irvine, CA 92697. Offers MA, PhD. *Students:* 8 full-time (5 women); includes 1 minority (Asian American or Pacific Islander), 1 international. Average age 34. 17 applicants, 47% accepted. In 2009, 1 doctorate awarded. *Degree requirements:* For doctorate, thesis/dissertation. *Entrance requirements:* For master's and doctorate, GRE General Test, minimum GPA of 3.0. Additional exam requirements/recommendations for international students: Required—TOEFL (minimum score 550 paper-based; 213 computer-based). *Application deadline:* For fall admission, 1/15 priority date for domestic students, 1/15 for international students. Applications are processed on a rolling basis. Application fee: $70 ($90 for international students). Electronic applications accepted. *Financial support:* In 2009–10, fellowships (averaging $15,738 per year), teaching assistantships with partial tuition reimbursements (averaging $13,594 per year) were awarded; institutionally sponsored loans, traineeships, health care benefits, and unspecified assistantships also available. Financial award application deadline: 3/1; financial award applicants required to submit FAFSA. *Faculty research:* Goethe yearbook, fin de si?cle theory, Thomas Mann. *Unit head:* Jens Rieckmann, Chair, 949-824-6406, Fax: 949-824-6416, E-mail: jrieckma@uci.edu. *Application contact:* Karen Lowe, Manager, 949-824-4942, Fax: 949-824-6416, E-mail: kilowe@uci.edu.

University of California, Los Angeles, Graduate Division, College of Letters and Science, Department of Germanic Languages, Program in Germanic Languages, Los Angeles, CA 90095. Offers MA, PhD. *Students:* 16 full-time (10 women); includes 3 minority (2 Asian Americans or Pacific Islanders, 1 Hispanic American), 3 international. Average age 34. 9 applicants, 56% accepted, 5 enrolled. In 2009, 3 master's awarded. Terminal master's awarded for partial completion of doctoral program. *Degree requirements:* For master's, one foreign language, comprehensive exam or thesis; for doctorate, 2 foreign languages, oral and written qualifying exams. *Entrance requirements:* For master's, GRE General Test, BA in German, minimum GPA of 3.0, sample of written work; for doctorate, GRE General Test, minimum undergraduate GPA of 3.0, MA in German or equivalent, sample of written work. *Application deadline:* For fall admission, 12/15 for domestic and international students. Application fee: $70 ($90 for international students). Electronic applications accepted. *Financial support:* In 2009–10, 6 fellowships with full and partial tuition reimbursements, 4 research assistantships with full and partial tuition reimbursements, 7 teaching assistantships with full and partial tuition reimbursements were awarded; Federal Work-Study, health care benefits, tuition waivers (full and partial), and unspecified assistantships also available. Financial award applicants required to submit FAFSA. *Unit head:* Dr. James A. Schultz, Chair, 310-825-5194. *Application contact:* Department Office, 310-825-3955, E-mail: allen@humnet.ucla.edu.

University of California, San Diego, Office of Graduate Studies, Department of Literature, Program in German Literature, La Jolla, CA 92093. Offers MA. *Degree requirements:* For master's, thesis. *Entrance requirements:* For master's, GRE General Test, GRE Subject Test. Electronic applications accepted.

University of California, Santa Barbara, Graduate Division, College of Letters and Sciences, Division of Humanities and Fine Arts, Department of Germanic, Slavic, and Semitic Studies, Santa Barbara, CA 93106-4130. Offers Germanic languages and literature (MA, PhD), including applied linguistics (PhD), feminist studies (PhD); MA/PhD. *Faculty:* 7 full-time (4 women).

German

University of California, Santa Barbara (continued)
Students: 2 full-time (0 women). Average age 31. 6 applicants, 50% accepted, 1 enrolled. In 2009, 1 master's awarded. Terminal master's awarded for partial completion of doctoral program. *Degree requirements:* For master's, 2 foreign languages, comprehensive exam, thesis; for doctorate, 3 foreign languages, comprehensive exam, thesis/dissertation. *Entrance requirements:* For master's and doctorate, GRE. Additional exam requirements/recommendations for international students: Required—TOEFL (minimum score 550 paper-based; 213 computer-based; 80 iBT), or IELTS (minimum score 7). *Application deadline:* For fall admission, 12/31 priority date for domestic students, 5/1 priority date for international students; for winter admission, 11/1 priority date for domestic and international students; for spring admission, 2/1 priority date for domestic and international students. Applications are processed on a rolling basis. Application fee: $70 ($90 for international students). Electronic applications accepted. *Financial support:* In 2009–10, 2 students received support, including 2 fellowships with full and partial tuition reimbursements available (averaging $10,100 per year), 1 teaching assistantship with partial tuition reimbursement available (averaging $11,600 per year); Federal Work-Study, institutionally sponsored loans, scholarships/grants, health care benefits, and tuition waivers (full and partial) also available. Financial award application deadline: 12/31; financial award applicants required to submit FAFSA. *Faculty research:* Critical theory, media technology, psychoanalysis, German romanticism, Goethe. *Unit head:* Prof. Elisabeth Weber, Chair, 805-893-3527, Fax: 805-893-2374, E-mail: weber@gss.ucsb.edu. *Application contact:* Sierra Gray, Graduate Program Assistant, 805-893-2131, Fax: 805-893-2374, E-mail: sierra@gss.ucsb.edu.

University of Chicago, Division of the Humanities, Department of Germanic Languages and Literatures, Chicago, IL 60637-1513. Offers AM, PhD. Terminal master's awarded for partial completion of doctoral program. *Degree requirements:* For master's, one foreign language, thesis; for doctorate, 2 foreign languages, thesis/dissertation. *Entrance requirements:* For master's and doctorate, GRE General Test. Additional exam requirements/recommendations for international students: Required—TOEFL.

University of Cincinnati, Graduate School, McMicken College of Arts and Sciences, Department of German Studies, Cincinnati, OH 45221. Offers MA, PhD. Part-time programs available. Terminal master's awarded for partial completion of doctoral program. *Degree requirements:* For master's, one foreign language, thesis or alternative; for doctorate, 3 foreign languages, thesis/dissertation. *Entrance requirements:* For master's, GRE General Test; for doctorate, GRE General Test, MA in German or equivalent. Additional exam requirements/recommendations for international students: Required—TOEFL (minimum score 560 paper-based). Electronic applications accepted. *Faculty research:* German literary culture, language and linguistics, medieval and early modern, German-Jewish literature, 20th and 21st century German literature and film.

University of Colorado at Boulder, Graduate School, College of Arts and Sciences, Department of Germanic and Slavic Languages and Literature, Boulder, CO 80309. Offers German (MA). Part-time programs available. *Faculty:* 12 full-time (4 women). *Students:* 12 full-time (8 women); includes 1 minority (African American), 3 international. Average age 26. 14 applicants, 29% accepted, 4 enrolled. In 2009, 3 master's awarded. *Degree requirements:* For master's, 2 foreign languages, comprehensive exam, thesis or alternative. *Entrance requirements:* For master's, minimum undergraduate GPA of 2.75. *Application deadline:* For fall admission, 2/1 priority date for domestic students, 12/1 for international students; for spring admission, 9/15 for domestic and international students. Application fee: $50 ($60 for international students). *Financial support:* In 2009–10, 3 fellowships (averaging $11,333 per year), 2 research assistantships (averaging $7,752 per year) were awarded; Federal Work-Study, institutionally sponsored loans, and scholarships/grants also available. Financial award application deadline: 2/1. *Faculty research:* Eighteenth, nineteenth, and twentieth century literature, culture and thought; intellectual history; film; philosophy; social and political theory; German, Scandinavian and comparative literature. Total annual research expenditures: $3,481.

University of Connecticut, Graduate School, College of Liberal Arts and Sciences, Department of Modern and Classical Languages, Field of German, Storrs, CT 06269. Offers MA, PhD. *Faculty:* 5 full-time (3 women). *Students:* 11 full-time (8 women), 9 international. Average age 29. 10 applicants, 30% accepted, 1 enrolled. In 2009, 5 master's awarded. Terminal master's awarded for partial completion of doctoral program. *Degree requirements:* For master's, comprehensive exam; for doctorate, thesis/dissertation. *Entrance requirements:* For master's and doctorate, GRE General Test. Additional exam requirements/recommendations for international students: Required—TOEFL (minimum score 550 paper-based; 213 computer-based). *Application deadline:* For fall admission, 2/1 priority date for domestic and international students; for spring admission, 11/1 for domestic students, 10/1 for international students. Applications are processed on a rolling basis. Application fee: $55. Electronic applications accepted. *Expenses:* Tuition, state resident: full-time $4725; part-time $525 per credit. Tuition, nonresident: full-time $12,267; part-time $1363 per credit. Required fees: $346 per semester. Tuition and fees vary according to course load. *Financial support:* In 2009–10, 1 research assistantship with full tuition reimbursement, 10 teaching assistantships with full tuition reimbursements were awarded; fellowships, Federal Work-Study, scholarships/grants, health care benefits, and unspecified assistantships also available. Financial award application deadline: 2/1; financial award applicants required to submit FAFSA. *Unit head:* Friedmann Weidauer, Chair, 860-486-1533, E-mail: freidmann.weidauer@uconn.edu. *Application contact:* Patricia Parlette-Schaff, Administrative Assistant, 860-486-3313, Fax: 860-486-4392, E-mail: patricia.parlette@uconn.edu.

University of Delaware, College of Arts and Sciences, Department of Foreign Languages and Literatures, Newark, DE 19716. Offers foreign languages and literatures (MA), including French, German, Spanish; foreign languages pedagogy (MA), including French, German, Spanish. *Degree requirements:* For master's, one foreign language, comprehensive exam, thesis optional. *Entrance requirements:* For master's, GRE General Test, letters of recommendation, writing sample. Additional exam requirements/recommendations for international students: Required—TOEFL. Electronic applications accepted. *Faculty research:* Medieval to Modern French and Spanish literature, Twentieth Century German, French, Spanish literature by women, computer-assisted instruction.

University of Florida, Graduate School, College of Liberal Arts and Sciences, Department of Germanic and Slavic Studies, Gainesville, FL 32611. Offers German (MA, PhD). *Degree requirements:* For master's, thesis or alternative; for doctorate, thesis/dissertation. *Entrance requirements:* For master's and doctorate, GRE General Test, minimum GPA of 3.0. Additional exam requirements/recommendations for international students: Required—TOEFL (minimum score 550 paper-based; 213 computer-based). Electronic applications accepted. *Faculty research:* Literature and language, film and media.

University of Georgia, Graduate School, College of Arts and Sciences, Department of Germanic and Slavic Studies, Athens, GA 30602. Offers German (MA). *Faculty:* 9 full-time (5 women). *Students:* 10 full-time (8 women), 1 part-time (0 women), 5 international. 15 applicants, 67% accepted, 8 enrolled. In 2009, 5 master's awarded. *Degree requirements:* For master's, one foreign language, thesis. *Entrance requirements:* For master's, GRE General Test. *Application deadline:* For fall admission, 7/1 priority date for domestic students; for spring admission, 11/15 for domestic students. Application fee: $50. Electronic applications accepted. *Expenses:* Tuition, state resident: full-time $6000; part-time $250 per credit hour. Tuition, nonresident: full-time $20,904; part-time $871 per credit hour. Required fees: $730 per semester. *Financial support:* Fellowships, research assistantships, teaching assistantships, unspecified assistantships available. *Unit head:* Dr. Martin H. Kagel, Head, 706-542-2446, Fax: 706-583-0349, E-mail: mkagel@uga.edu. *Application contact:* Dr. Alexander Sager, Graduate Advisor, 706-542-6211, Fax: 706-542-2459, E-mail: asager@uga.edu.

University of Illinois at Chicago, Graduate College, College of Liberal Arts and Sciences, Department of Germanic Studies, Chicago, IL 60607-7128. Offers MA, PhD. Part-time programs available. Terminal master's awarded for partial completion of doctoral program. *Degree requirements:* For master's, thesis optional, exam; for doctorate, 2 foreign languages, thesis/dissertation. *Entrance requirements:* For master's and doctorate, GRE General Test, minimum GPA of 2.75. Additional exam requirements/recommendations for international students: Required—TOEFL. Electronic applications accepted. *Faculty research:* German literature.

University of Illinois at Urbana–Champaign, Graduate College, College of Liberal Arts and Sciences, School of Literatures, Cultures and Linguistics, Department of Germanic Languages and Literatures, Champaign, IL 61820. Offers German (MA, PhD). *Faculty:* 9 full-time (7 women), 1 (woman) part-time/adjunct. *Students:* 18 full-time (11 women), 4 international. 14 applicants, 64% accepted, 4 enrolled. In 2009, 7 master's, 1 doctorate awarded. *Entrance requirements:* For master's and doctorate, minimum GPA of 3.0; writing sample. Additional exam requirements/recommendations for international students: Required—TOEFL (minimum score 79 iBT). *Application deadline:* Applications are processed on a rolling basis. Application fee: $60 ($75 for international students). Electronic applications accepted. *Financial support:* In 2009–10, 4 fellowships, 1 research assistantship, 25 teaching assistantships were awarded; tuition waivers (full and partial) also available. *Unit head:* Mara Wade, Head, 217-333-9383, Fax: 217-244-2223, E-mail: mwade@illinois.edu. *Application contact:* Lynn Stanke, Office Support Specialist, 217-333-6269, Fax: 217-244-3050, E-mail: stanke@illinois.edu.

The University of Iowa, Graduate College, College of Liberal Arts and Sciences, Department of German, Iowa City, IA 52242-1316. Offers MA, PhD. *Degree requirements:* For master's, thesis optional, exam; for doctorate, comprehensive exam, thesis/dissertation. *Entrance requirements:* For master's and doctorate, GRE General Test, minimum GPA of 3.0. Additional exam requirements/recommendations for international students: Required—TOEFL (minimum score 600 paper-based; 250 computer-based; 100 iBT). Electronic applications accepted.

The University of Kansas, Graduate Studies, College of Liberal Arts and Sciences, Department of Germanic Languages and Literatures, Lawrence, KS 66045. Offers German (MA, PhD). Part-time programs available. *Students:* 20 full-time (14 women); includes 1 minority (Asian American or Pacific Islander), 5 international. Average age 34. 7 applicants, 71% accepted, 3 enrolled. In 2009, 3 master's, 1 doctorate awarded. *Degree requirements:* For master's, one foreign language, comprehensive exam, thesis optional, final oral exam; for doctorate, 2 foreign languages, comprehensive exam, thesis/dissertation, final oral exam. *Entrance requirements:* For master's, GRE, undergraduate major in German or equivalent; for doctorate, GRE, MA in German. Additional exam requirements/recommendations for international students: Required—TOEFL. *Application deadline:* For fall admission, 1/15 priority date for domestic and international students. Applications are processed on a rolling basis. Application fee: $45 ($55 for international students). Electronic applications accepted. *Expenses:* Tuition, state resident: full-time $6492; part-time $270.50 per credit hour. Tuition, nonresident: full-time $15,510; part-time $646.25 per credit hour. Required fees: $847; $70.56 per credit hour. Tuition and fees vary according to course load and program. *Financial support:* Fellowships, research assistantships with full tuition reimbursements, teaching assistantships with full tuition reimbursements, Federal Work-Study, institutionally sponsored loans, and unspecified assistantships available. Support available to part-time students. Financial award application deadline: 1/30; financial award applicants required to submit FAFSA. *Faculty research:* Humanism, eighteenth to twentieth century literature, Germanic linguistics, German-American studies, German applied linguistics, German philology. *Unit head:* William Keel, Chair, 785-864-4803, Fax: 785-864-4298, E-mail: wkeel@ku.edu. *Application contact:* Leonie Marx, Graduate Director, 785-864-4803, Fax: 785-864-4298, E-mail: marx@ku.edu.

University of Kentucky, Graduate School, College of Arts and Sciences, Program in German, Lexington, KY 40506-0032. Offers MA. *Degree requirements:* For master's, one foreign language, comprehensive exam, thesis optional. *Entrance requirements:* For master's, GRE General Test, minimum undergraduate GPA of 2.75. Additional exam requirements/recommendations for international students: Required—TOEFL (minimum score 550 paper-based; 213 computer-based). Electronic applications accepted. *Faculty research:* Medieval studies, literature from Enlightenment to present, literary theory, intellectual history, gender studies.

University of Lethbridge, School of Graduate Studies, Lethbridge, AB T1K 3M4, Canada. Offers accounting (MScM); addictions counseling (M Sc); agricultural biotechnology (M Sc); agricultural studies (M Sc, MA); anthropology (MA); archaeology (MA); art (MA, MFA); biochemistry (M Sc); biological sciences (M Sc); biomolecular science (PhD); biosystems and biodiversity (PhD); Canadian studies (MA); chemistry (M Sc); computer science (M Sc); computer science and geographical information science (M Sc); counseling psychology (M Ed); dramatic arts (MA); earth, space, and physical science (PhD); economics (MA); educational leadership (M Ed); English (MA); environmental science (M Sc); evolution and behavior (PhD); exercise science (M Sc); finance (MScM); French (MA); French/German (MA); French/Spanish (MA); general education (M Ed); general management (MScM); geography (M Sc, MA); German (MA); health science (M Sc); health sciences (MA); history (MA); human resource management and labour relations (MScM); individualized multidisciplinary (M Sc, MA); information systems (MScM); international management (MScM); kinesiology (M Sc, MA); management (M Sc, MA); marketing (MScM); mathematics (M Sc); music (M Mus, MA); Native American studies (MA); neuroscience (M Sc, PhD); new media (MA); nursing (M Sc); philosophy (MA); physics (M Sc); policy and strategy (MScM); political science (MA); psychology (M Sc, MA); religious studies (MA); social sciences (MA); sociology (MA); theatre and dramatic arts (MFA); theoretical and computational science (PhD); urban and regional studies (MA); women's studies (MA). Part-time and evening/weekend programs available. *Degree requirements:* For doctorate, comprehensive exam, thesis/dissertation. *Entrance requirements:* For master's, GMAT (M Sc in management), bachelor's degree in related field, minimum GPA of 3.0 during previous 20 graded semester courses, 2 years teaching or related experience (M Ed); for doctorate, master's degree, minimum graduate GPA of 3.5. Additional exam requirements/recommendations for international students: Required—TOEFL. *Faculty research:* Movement and brain plasticity, gibberellin physiology, photosynthesis, carbon cycling, molecular properties of main-group ring components.

University of Manitoba, Faculty of Graduate Studies, Faculty of Arts, Department of German and Slavic Studies, Winnipeg, MB R3T 2N2, Canada. Offers German language and literature (MA); Slavic languages and literatures (MA). *Degree requirements:* For master's, one foreign language, thesis or alternative.

University of Maryland, College Park, Academic Affairs, College of Arts and Humanities, School of Languages, Literature, and Cultures, Department of Germanic Studies, College Park, MD 20742. Offers Germanic language and literature (MA, PhD). *Students:* 14 full-time (13 women), 6 international. 9 applicants, 78% accepted, 2 enrolled. In 2009, 1 doctorate awarded. *Degree requirements:* For master's, one foreign language, thesis optional, exams; for doctorate, 2 foreign languages, comprehensive exam, thesis/dissertation, reading exam, oral defense. *Entrance requirements:* For master's, GRE General Test, writing sample, 3 letters of recommendation; for doctorate, GRE General Test, MA in German or related discipline. Additional exam requirements/recommendations for international students: Required—TOEFL. *Application deadline:* For fall admission, 1/15 for domestic and international students; for spring admission, 10/15 for domestic students, 6/1 for international students. Applications are processed on a rolling basis. Application fee: $60. Electronic applications accepted. *Expenses:* Tuition, area resident: Part-time $471 per credit hour. Tuition, state resident: part-time $471 per credit hour. Tuition, nonresident: part-time $1016 per credit hour. Required fees: $337.04 per term. *Financial support:* In 2009–10, 1 fellowship with partial tuition reimbursement (averaging $7,504 per year), 9 teaching assistantships with tuition reimbursements (averaging $17,713 per year) were awarded; career-related internships or fieldwork, Federal Work-Study, and scholarships/grants also available. Support available to part-time students. Financial award applicants required to submit FAFSA. *Faculty research:* Language pedagogy, Germanic philology, medieval culture. *Unit head:* Carol Mossman, Director, School of Languages, Literatures and Cultures, 301-405-4025, E-mail: cmossman@umd.edu. *Application contact:* Dean of Graduate School, 301-405-0358, Fax: 301-314-9305.

University of Maryland, College Park, Academic Affairs, College of Arts and Humanities, School of Languages, Literature, and Cultures, Program in Second Language Acquisition and Application, College Park, MD 20742. Offers French (MA); German (MA); Japanese (MA); Russian (MA); second language instruction (PhD); second language learning (PhD); second language measurement and assessment (PhD); second language use (PhD); Spanish (MA). *Students:* 12 full-time (10 women), 5 part-time (3 women); includes 2 minority (both Asian Americans or Pacific Islanders), 5 international. 47 applicants, 15% accepted, 3 enrolled. In 2009, 7 master's awarded. *Entrance requirements:* For master's, BA or BS in related field, demonstrated language competency, 3 letters of reference. *Application deadline:* For fall admission, 1/15 for domestic and international students; for spring admission, 6/1 for domestic and international students. Applications are processed on a rolling basis. Application fee: $60. Electronic applications accepted. *Expenses:* Tuition, area resident: Part-time $471 per credit hour. Tuition, state resident: part-time $471 per credit hour. Tuition, nonresident: part-time $1016 per credit hour. Required fees: $337.04 per term. *Financial support:* In 2009–10, 2 fellowships with full and partial tuition reimbursements (averaging $13,928 per year), 4 research assistantships (averaging $21,457 per year), 6 teaching assistantships (averaging $20,933 per year) were awarded. *Faculty research:* Second language acquisition, pedagogical perspectives, technological applications, language use in professional contexts. *Unit head:* Carol Mossman, Director, School of Languages, Literatures, and Cultures, 301-405-4025, E-mail: cmossman@umd.edu. *Application contact:* Dean of Graduate School, 301-405-0376, Fax: 301-314-9305.

University of Massachusetts Amherst, Graduate School, College of Humanities and Fine Arts, Department of Languages, Literatures, and Cultures, Programs in German and Scandinavian Studies, Amherst, MA 01003. Offers MA, PhD. Part-time programs available. *Faculty:* 8 full-time (3 women). *Students:* 18 full-time (14 women), 8 part-time (6 women); includes 4 minority (1 African American, 2 Asian Americans or Pacific Islanders, 1 Hispanic American), 4 international. Average age 33. 10 applicants, 70% accepted, 2 enrolled. In 2009, 1 master's, 4 doctorates awarded. Terminal master's awarded for partial completion of doctoral program. *Degree requirements:* For master's, thesis or alternative; for doctorate, one foreign language, comprehensive exam, thesis/dissertation. *Entrance requirements:* For master's and doctorate, writing sample in English and German. Additional exam requirements/recommendations for international students: Required—TOEFL (minimum score 550 paper-based; 213 computer-based; 80 iBT), IELTS (minimum score 6.5). *Application deadline:* For fall admission, 2/1 for domestic and international students; for spring admission, 10/1 for domestic and international students. Applications are processed on a rolling basis. Application fee: $50 ($65 for international students). Electronic applications accepted. *Expenses:* Tuition, state resident: full-time $2640; part-time $110 per credit. Tuition, nonresident: full-time $9936; part-time $414 per credit. Tuition and fees vary according to course load. *Financial support:* In 2009–10, 1 research assistantship with full tuition reimbursement (averaging $14,516 per year), 14 teaching assistantships with full tuition reimbursements (averaging $10,942 per year) were awarded; fellowships, career-related internships or fieldwork, Federal Work-Study, scholarships/grants, traineeships, health care benefits, tuition waivers (full), and unspecified assistantships also available. Support available to part-time students. Financial award application deadline: 2/1. *Unit head:* Dr. Jonathan S. Skolnik, Graduate Program Director, 413-545-6686, Fax: 413-545-6695. *Application contact:* Jean M. Ames, Supervisor of Admissions, 413-545-0722, Fax: 413-577-0010, E-mail: gradadm@grad.umass.edu.

University of Michigan, Horace H. Rackham School of Graduate Studies, College of Literature, Science, and the Arts, Department of Germanic Languages and Literatures, Ann Arbor, MI 48109. Offers German (AM, PhD). *Faculty:* 10 full-time (5 women), 5 part-time/adjunct (2 women). *Students:* 16 full-time (9 women); includes 1 Hispanic American, 3 international. Average age 27. 22 applicants, 45% accepted, 4 enrolled. In 2009, 2 doctorates awarded. *Degree requirements:* For doctorate, one foreign language, comprehensive exam, thesis/dissertation, oral defense of dissertation, preliminary exam. *Entrance requirements:* For doctorate, GRE General Test. Additional exam requirements/recommendations for international students: Required—TOEFL (minimum score 560 paper-based; 220 computer-based). *Application deadline:* For fall and winter admission, 1/10 priority date for domestic and international students. Application fee: $65 ($75 for international students). Electronic applications accepted. *Expenses:* Tuition, state resident: full-time $17,286; part-time $1099 per credit hour. Tuition, nonresident: full-time $34,944; part-time $2080 per credit hour. Required fees: $95 per semester. Tuition and fees vary according to course load, degree level and program. *Financial support:* In 2009–10, 8 students received support, including 7 fellowships with full tuition reimbursements available (averaging $16,000 per year), 5 teaching assistantships with full tuition reimbursements available (averaging $16,000 per year); research assistantships, scholarships/grants and tuition waivers (full) also available. Financial award application deadline: 3/15. *Faculty research:* German history, German literature, literary theory, film, political and social theory. *Unit head:* Dr. Scott Spector, Chair, 734-764-8018, Fax: 734-763-6557, E-mail: spec@umich.edu. *Application contact:* Katherine Ballentine, Student Services Coordinator, 734-936-0150, Fax: 734-763-6557, E-mail: kecollin@umich.edu.

University of Minnesota, Twin Cities Campus, Graduate School, College of Liberal Arts, Department of German, Scandinavian, and Dutch, Minneapolis, MN 55455-0213. Offers Germanic studies: German and Scandinavian studies track (PhD); Germanic studies: German track (MA, PhD); Germanic studies: Germanic medieval studies track (MA, PhD); Germanic studies: Scandinavian studies track (MA); Germanic studies: teaching track (MA). Part-time programs available. *Faculty:* 11 full-time (5 women), 4 part-time/adjunct (2 women). *Students:* 21 full-time (9 women), 3 part-time (1 woman); includes 2 minority (both Hispanic Americans), 3 international. 26 applicants, 42% accepted, 5 enrolled. In 2009, 4 master's, 2 doctorates awarded. Terminal master's awarded for partial completion of doctoral program. *Degree requirements:* For doctorate, 2 foreign languages, thesis/dissertation. *Entrance requirements:* For master's, GRE General Test, BA in German, Scandinavian, or equivalent; for doctorate, GRE General Test, MA in German, Scandinavian, or equivalent. Additional exam requirements/recommendations for international students: Required—TOEFL (minimum score 550 paper-based; 213 computer-based; 79 iBT). *Application deadline:* For fall admission, 12/15 for domestic and international students. Application fee: $75 ($95 for international students). Electronic applications accepted. *Financial support:* In 2009–10, 21 students received support, including 6 fellowships with full tuition reimbursements available (averaging $20,000 per year), 1 research assistantship with full tuition reimbursement available (averaging $16,000 per year), 14 teaching assistantships with full tuition reimbursements available (averaging $14,500 per year); career-related internships or fieldwork, Federal Work-Study, institutionally sponsored loans, scholarships/grants, health care benefits, and unspecified assistantships also available. Support available to part-time students. Financial award application deadline: 12/15. *Faculty research:* Cultural studies, literary theory, feminist criticism, film, Germanic philology. *Unit head:* Prof. Richard McCormick, Chair, 612-625-2080, Fax: 612-624-8297, E-mail: mccor001@umn.edu. *Application contact:* Director of Graduate Studies, 612-625-0999, Fax: 612-624-8297, E-mail: gsd@umn.edu.

University of Mississippi, Graduate School, College of Liberal Arts, Department of Modern Languages, Oxford, University, MS 38677. Offers French (MA); German (MA); Spanish (MA). *Faculty:* 50 full-time (30 women). *Students:* 43 full-time (31 women), 16 part-time (11 women); includes 12 minority (7 African Americans, 5 Hispanic Americans), 11 international. In 2009, 12 master's awarded. *Degree requirements:* For master's, thesis (for some programs). *Entrance requirements:* For master's, GRE General Test, minimum GPA of 3.0. Additional exam requirements/recommendations for international students: Required—TOEFL. *Application deadline:* For fall admission, 2/1 for domestic students; for spring admission, 10/1 for domestic students. Applications are processed on a rolling basis. Application fee: $25. Electronic applications accepted. *Financial support:* Scholarships/grants available. Financial award application deadline: 3/1; financial award applicants required to submit FAFSA. *Unit head:* Dr. Donald L. Dyer, Chair, 662-915-7298, Fax: 662-915-1086, E-mail: mlangs@olemiss.edu. *Application contact:* Dr. Christy M. Wyandt, Associate Dean, 662-915-7474, Fax: 662-915-7577, E-mail: cwyandt@olemiss.edu.

University of Missouri, Graduate School, College of Arts and Sciences, Department of German and Russian Studies, Columbia, MO 65211. Offers German (MA). *Faculty:* 16 full-time (7 women), 3 part-time/adjunct (1 woman). *Students:* 16 full-time (11 women), 7 international. Average age 29. 10 applicants, 80% accepted, 6 enrolled. In 2009, 5 master's awarded. *Entrance requirements:* For master's, GRE General Test, minimum GPA of 3.0. Additional exam requirements/recommendations for international students: Required—TOEFL (minimum score 500 paper-based; 173 computer-based; 61 iBT). *Application deadline:* For fall admission, 3/1 priority date for domestic students. Applications are processed on a rolling basis. Application fee: $45 ($60 for international students). Electronic applications accepted. *Financial support:* In 2009–10, 18 teaching assistantships with full tuition reimbursements were awarded; institutionally sponsored loans, health care benefits, and unspecified assistantships also available. *Unit head:* Dr. Carsten Strathausen, Department Chair, E-mail: strathaussenc@missouri.edu. *Application contact:* Jennifer Arnold, 573-882-4328, E-mail: arnoldj@missouri.edu.

The University of Montana, Graduate School, College of Arts and Sciences, Department of Modern and Classical Languages and Literatures, Missoula, MT 59812-0002. Offers French (MA); German (MA); Spanish (MA). *Degree requirements:* For master's, one foreign language. *Entrance requirements:* For master's, GRE General Test. Additional exam requirements/recommendations for international students: Required—TOEFL.

University of Nebraska–Lincoln, Graduate College, College of Arts and Sciences, Department of Modern Languages and Literatures, Lincoln, NE 68588. Offers French (MA, PhD); German (MA, PhD); Spanish (MA, PhD). *Degree requirements:* For master's, thesis optional; for doctorate, comprehensive exam, thesis/dissertation. *Entrance requirements:* For master's and doctorate, writing sample in target language. Additional exam requirements/recommendations for international students: Required—TOEFL (minimum score 550 paper-based; 213 computer-based). Electronic applications accepted. *Faculty research:* French, German, and Spanish language, literature, and culture.

University of Nevada, Reno, Graduate School, College of Liberal Arts, Department of Foreign Languages and Literatures, Reno, NV 89557. Offers French (MA); German (MA); Spanish (MA). *Degree requirements:* For master's, one foreign language, thesis optional. *Entrance requirements:* For master's, GRE General Test, minimum GPA of 2.75. Additional exam requirements/recommendations for international students: Required—TOEFL (minimum score 500 paper-based; 173 computer-based; 61 iBT), IELTS (minimum score 6). *Faculty research:* Thirteenth century mysticism, contemporary Spanish and Latin American poetry and theater, French interrelation between narration and photography, exile literature and Holocaust.

University of New Mexico, Graduate School, College of Arts and Sciences, Department of Foreign Languages and Literature, Albuquerque, NM 87131-2039. Offers comparative literature and cultural studies (MA); French (MA); French studies (PhD); German studies (MA). Part-time programs available. *Faculty:* 15 full-time (11 women), 8 part-time/adjunct (4 women). *Students:* 9 full-time (8 women), 4 part-time (2 women), 6 international. Average age 33. 9 applicants, 44% accepted, 3 enrolled. In 2009, 5 master's awarded. *Degree requirements:* For master's, one foreign language, thesis optional; for doctorate, 2 foreign languages, thesis/dissertation. *Entrance requirements:* Additional exam requirements/recommendations for international students: Required—TOEFL. *Application deadline:* For fall admission, 2/1 priority date for domestic students; for spring admission, 10/1 priority date for domestic students. Application fee: $50. Electronic applications accepted. *Expenses:* Tuition, state resident: full-time $2099; part-time $233.20 per credit hour. Tuition, nonresident: full-time $6650. Required fees: $25 per semester. Tuition and fees vary according to course load, program and reciprocity agreements. *Financial support:* In 2009–10, 20 teaching assistantships with tuition reimbursements (averaging $12,023 per year) were awarded; Federal Work-Study, health care benefits, and unspecified assistantships also available. Financial award application deadline: 3/1; financial award applicants required to submit FAFSA. *Faculty research:* German, Russian, Italian, Japanese, French, comparative literature, culture studies, classics. Total annual research expenditures: $4,750. *Unit head:* Dr. Natasha Kolchevska, Chair, 505-277-4771, Fax: 505-277-3599, E-mail: nakol@unm.edu. *Application contact:* Jean Aragon, Application and Graduation Advisor, 505-277-4471, Fax: 505-277-3599, E-mail: peaslee@unm.edu.

The University of North Carolina at Chapel Hill, Graduate School, College of Arts and Sciences, Department of Germanic Languages, Chapel Hill, NC 27599. Offers literature and linguistics (MA, PhD). Part-time programs available. Terminal master's awarded for partial completion of doctoral program. *Degree requirements:* For master's, comprehensive exam, thesis; for doctorate, one foreign language, comprehensive exam, thesis/dissertation. *Entrance requirements:* For master's and doctorate, GRE General Test, minimum GPA of 3.0. *Faculty research:* Gender and sexuality, literature and politics, German and Jewish culture, medieval through modern literature, Germanic linguistics.

University of Northern Iowa, Graduate College, College of Humanities and Fine Arts, Department of Modern Languages, Program in German, Cedar Falls, IA 50614. Offers German (MA); teaching English to speakers of other languages/German (MA). Part-time and evening/weekend programs available. *Students:* 4 full-time (all women), 1 part-time (0 women), 2 international. 3 applicants, 67% accepted, 2 enrolled. In 2009, 4 master's awarded. *Degree requirements:* For master's, one foreign language, comprehensive exam, thesis or alternative. *Entrance requirements:* For master's, minimum GPA of 3.0, valid teaching license, documentation of successful teaching experience. Additional exam requirements/recommendations for international students: Required—TOEFL (minimum score 600 paper-based; 250 computer-based; 100 iBT). *Application deadline:* For fall admission, 8/1 priority date for domestic students. Applications are processed on a rolling basis. Application fee: $30 ($50 for international students). *Financial support:* Career-related internships or fieldwork, Federal Work-Study, and tuition waivers (full and partial) available. Support available to part-time students. Financial award application deadline: 2/1. *Unit head:* Dr. Samuel L. Gladden, Interim Department Head/Professor, 319-273-5437, Fax: 319-273-2848, E-mail: samuel.gladden@uni.edu. *Application contact:* Laurie S. Russell, Record Analyst, 319-273-2623, Fax: 319-273-6792, E-mail: laurie.russell@uni.edu.

University of Oklahoma, Graduate College, College of Arts and Sciences, Department of Modern Languages, Program in German, Norman, OK 73019. Offers MA, MBA/MA. Part-time programs available. *Students:* 6 full-time (4 women). 2 applicants, 50% accepted, 1 enrolled. In 2009, 2 master's awarded. *Degree requirements:* For master's, 2 foreign languages, comprehensive exam, thesis optional, departmental qualifying exam. *Entrance requirements:* For master's, BA with 25 hours in German or equivalent, minimum GPA of 3.0 in last 60 hours, 3 letters of recommendation. Additional exam requirements/recommendations for international students: Required—TOEFL (minimum score 550 paper-based; 213 computer-based). *Application deadline:* For fall admission, 6/1 priority date for domestic students, 4/1 for international students; for spring admission, 11/1 for domestic students, 9/1 for international students. Applications are processed on a rolling basis. Application fee: $40 ($90 for international students). Electronic applications accepted. *Expenses:* Tuition, state resident: full-time $3744; part-time $156 per credit hour. Tuition, nonresident: full-time $13,577; part-time $565.70 per credit hour. Required fees: $2415; $90.10 per credit hour. *Financial support:* In 2009–10, 4 students received support. Scholarships/grants, health care benefits, and unspecified assistantships available. Financial award applicants required to submit FAFSA. *Faculty research:* Film studies, German literature and culture studies, fin-de-siecle Austria, Arthurian romance, the Goethe era. *Unit head:* Dr. Pamela Genova, Chair, 405-325-6181, Fax: 405-325-0103, E-mail: genova@ou.edu. *Application contact:* Dr. Logan E. Whalen, Graduate Liaison, 405-325-5088, Fax: 405-325-0103, E-mail: mlllgradinfo@ou.edu.

University of Oregon, Graduate School, College of Arts and Sciences, Department of Germanic Languages and Literatures, Eugene, OR 97403. Offers MA, PhD. *Degree requirements:* For master's, 2 foreign languages, thesis or alternative; for doctorate, 3 foreign languages, thesis/dissertation. *Entrance requirements:* For master's and doctorate, minimum GPA of 3.0. Additional exam requirements/recommendations for international students: Required—TOEFL. *Faculty*

German

University of Oregon (continued)
research: Medieval language and literature, eighteenth to twentieth century literature and philosophy, literary theory, feminist literature and theory, psychoanalysis and literature.

University of Pennsylvania, School of Arts and Sciences, Graduate Group in Germanic Languages, Philadelphia, PA 19104. Offers AM, PhD. *Faculty:* 24 full-time (7 women), 8 part-time/adjunct (2 women). *Students:* 16 full-time (9 women), 1 part-time (0 women); includes 1 minority (African American), 1 international. 17 applicants, 24% accepted, 2 enrolled. In 2009, 3 master's, 5 doctorates awarded. Terminal master's awarded for partial completion of doctoral program. *Degree requirements:* For master's, one foreign language, thesis or alternative; for doctorate, one foreign language, comprehensive exam, thesis/dissertation. *Entrance requirements:* For master's and doctorate, GRE General Test. *Application deadline:* For fall admission, 12/1 priority date for domestic students. Application fee: $70. *Expenses:* Tuition: Full-time $25,660; part-time $4758 per course. Required fees: $2152; $270 per course. Tuition and fees vary according to course load, degree level and program. *Financial support:* Fellowships, teaching assistantships, institutionally sponsored loans, scholarships/grants, traineeships, health care benefits, and unspecified assistantships available. Financial award application deadline: 12/15.

University of Pittsburgh, School of Arts and Sciences, Department of German, Pittsburgh, PA 15260. Offers MA, PhD. Part-time programs available. *Faculty:* 6 full-time (3 women), 5 part-time/adjunct (1 woman). *Students:* 9 full-time (5 women), 3 part-time (all women). Average age 32. 14 applicants, 36% accepted, 5 enrolled. In 2009, 3 master's, 1 doctorate awarded. Terminal master's awarded for partial completion of doctoral program. *Degree requirements:* For master's, one foreign language, comprehensive exam (for some programs), thesis; for doctorate, one foreign language, comprehensive exam, thesis/dissertation. *Entrance requirements:* For master's, bachelor's degree in German, minimum GPA of 3.0 or equivalent; for doctorate, MA. Additional exam requirements/recommendations for international students: Required—TOEFL. *Application deadline:* For spring admission, 1/5 priority date for domestic and international students. Application fee: $50. Electronic applications accepted. *Expenses:* Tuition, state resident: full-time $16,402; part-time $665 per credit. Tuition, nonresident: full-time $28,694; part-time $1175 per credit. Required fees: $690; $175 per term. Tuition and fees vary according to program. *Financial support:* In 2009–10, 9 students received support, including fellowships with tuition reimbursements available (averaging $15,675 per year), teaching assistantships with tuition reimbursements available (averaging $15,065 per year); scholarships/grants and health care benefits also available. Financial award application deadline: 1/15. *Faculty research:* Age of Goethe, German film, postwar culture, German-Jewish culture, literature and philosophy. *Unit head:* Dr. John B. Lyon, Chair, 412-624-5839, Fax: 412-624-6318, E-mail: jblyon@pitt.edu. *Application contact:* Dr. Clark S. Muenzer, Graduate Director, 412-624-5840, Fax: 412-624-6318, E-mail: muenzer@pitt.edu.

University of Saskatchewan, College of Graduate Studies and Research, College of Arts and Sciences, Department of Languages and Linguistics, Saskatoon, SK S7N 5A2, Canada. Offers MA. *Faculty:* 10. *Degree requirements:* For master's, 2 foreign languages, thesis. *Entrance requirements:* Additional exam requirements/recommendations for international students: Required—TOEFL (minimum score 80 iBT); Recommended—IELTS (minimum score 6.5). *Application deadline:* For fall admission, 7/1 priority date for domestic students. Applications are processed on a rolling basis. Application fee: $75. Electronic applications accepted. Tuition and fees charges are reported in Canadian dollars. *Expenses:* Tuition, area resident: Full-time $3000 Canadian dollars; part-time $500 Canadian dollars per term. Required fees: $700 Canadian dollars; $100 Canadian dollars per term. *Financial support:* Fellowships, research assistantships, teaching assistantships available. Financial award application deadline: 1/31. *Unit head:* Dr. Richard Julien, Head, 306-966-6920, Fax: 306-966-5782, E-mail: richard.julien@usask.ca. *Application contact:* Dr. Alex Sokalski, Graduate Chair, 306-966-5648, Fax: 306-966-5782.

University of South Africa, College of Human Sciences, Pretoria, South Africa. Offers adult education (M Ed); African languages (MA, PhD); African politics (MA, PhD); Afrikaans (MA, PhD); ancient history (MA, PhD); ancient Near Eastern studies (MA, PhD); anthropology (MA, PhD); applied linguistics (MA); Arabic (MA, PhD); archaeology (MA); art history (MA); Biblical archaeology (MA); Biblical studies (M Th, D Th, PhD); Christian spirituality (M Th, D Th); church history (M Th, D Th); classical studies (MA, PhD); clinical psychology (MA); communication (MA, PhD); comparative education (M Ed, Ed D); consulting psychology (D Admin, D Com, PhD); curriculum studies (M Ed, Ed D); development studies (M Admin, MA, D Admin, PhD); didactics (M Ed, Ed D); education (M Tech); education management (M Ed, Ed D); educational psychology (M Ed); English (MA); environmental education (M Ed); French (MA, PhD); German (MA, PhD); Greek (MA); guidance and counseling (M Ed); health studies (MA, PhD), including health sciences education (MA), health services management (MA), medical and surgical nursing science (critical care general) (MA), midwifery and neonatal nursing science (MA), trauma and emergency care (MA); history (MA, PhD); history of education (Ed D); inclusive education (M Ed, Ed D); information and communications technology policy and regulation (MA); information science (MA, MIS, PhD); international politics (MA, PhD); Islamic studies (MA, PhD); Italian (MA, PhD); Judaica (MA, PhD); linguistics (MA, PhD); mathematical education (M Ed); mathematics education (MA); missiology (M Th, D Th); modern Hebrew (MA, PhD); musicology (MA, MMus, D Mus, PhD); natural science education (M Ed); New Testament (M Th, D Th); Old Testament (D Th); pastoral therapy (M Th, D Th); philosophy (MA); philosophy of education (M Ed, Ed D); politics (MA, PhD); Portuguese (MA, PhD); practical theology (M Th, D Th); psychology (MA, MS, PhD); psychology of education (M Ed, Ed D); public health (MA); religious studies (MA, D Th, PhD); Romance languages (MA); Russian (MA, PhD); Semitic languages (MA, PhD); social behavior studies in HIV/AIDS (MA); social science (mental health) (MA); social science in development studies (MA); social science in psychology (MA); social science in social work (MA); social science in sociology (MA); social work (MSW, DSW, PhD); socio-education (M Ed, Ed D); sociolinguistics (MA); sociology (MA, PhD); Spanish (MA, PhD); systematic theology (M Th, D Th); TESOL (teaching English to speakers of other languages) (MA); theological ethics (M Th, D Th); theory of literature (MA, PhD); urban ministries (D Th); urban ministry (M Th).

University of South Carolina, The Graduate School, College of Arts and Sciences, Department of Languages, Literatures, and Cultures, Columbia, SC 29208. Offers comparative literature (MA, PhD); foreign languages (MAT), including French, German, Spanish; French (MA); German (MA); Spanish (MA). MAT offered in cooperation with the College of Education. Part-time programs available. *Degree requirements:* For master's, one foreign language, comprehensive exam, thesis optional; for doctorate, 2 foreign languages, comprehensive exam, thesis/dissertation. *Entrance requirements:* For master's and doctorate, GRE General Test, writing sample. Additional exam requirements/recommendations for international students: Required—TOEFL (minimum score 230 computer-based; 75 iBT). Electronic applications accepted. *Faculty research:* Modern literature, linguistics, literature and culture, medieval literature, literary theory.

The University of Tennessee, Graduate School, College of Arts and Sciences, Department of Modern Foreign Languages and Literatures, Program in German, Knoxville, TN 37996. Offers MA. Part-time programs available. *Degree requirements:* For master's, one foreign language, thesis or alternative. *Entrance requirements:* For master's, minimum GPA of 2.7. Additional exam requirements/recommendations for international students: Required—TOEFL. Electronic applications accepted. *Expenses:* Tuition, state resident: full-time $6826; part-time $380 per semester hour. Tuition, nonresident: full-time $21,844; part-time $1147 per semester hour. Tuition and fees vary according to program.

The University of Tennessee, Graduate School, College of Arts and Sciences, Department of Modern Foreign Languages and Literatures, Program in Modern Foreign Languages, Knoxville, TN 37996. Offers applied linguistics (PhD); French (PhD); German (PhD); Italian (PhD); Portuguese (PhD); Russian (PhD); Spanish (PhD). *Degree requirements:* For doctorate, 2 foreign languages, thesis/dissertation. *Entrance requirements:* For doctorate, minimum GPA of 2.7. Additional exam requirements/recommendations for international students: Required—TOEFL. Electronic applications accepted. *Expenses:* Tuition, state resident: full-time $6826; part-time $380 per semester hour. Tuition, nonresident: full-time $21,844; part-time $1147 per semester hour. Tuition and fees vary according to program.

The University of Texas at Austin, Graduate School, College of Liberal Arts, Department of Germanic Studies, Austin, TX 78712-1111. Offers MA, PhD. *Degree requirements:* For master's, one foreign language, thesis or alternative; for doctorate, 2 foreign languages, thesis/dissertation. *Entrance requirements:* For master's and doctorate, GRE General Test. *Faculty research:* Germanic languages and culture (German, Austrian, Swiss, Dutch, Danish, Norwegian, Swedish, Yiddish), language pedagogy and linguistics.

The University of Toledo, College of Graduate Studies, College of Arts and Sciences, Department of Foreign Languages, Toledo, OH 43606-3390. Offers French (MA); German (MA); Spanish (MA). Part-time programs available. *Degree requirements:* For master's, one foreign language, comprehensive reading exam in 1 additional foreign language. Electronic applications accepted.

University of Toronto, School of Graduate Studies, Humanities Division, Department of Germanic Languages and Literatures, Toronto, ON M5S 1A1, Canada. Offers MA, PhD. Part-time programs available. *Degree requirements:* For master's, thesis optional, German language competence exam; for doctorate, thesis/dissertation, qualifying exam, thesis defense. *Entrance requirements:* For master's, 7 two-semester courses in German language and literature, 3 letters of recommendation; for doctorate, MA in German, minimum A– average, 3 letters of recommendation, writing sample, resumé.

University of Utah, The Graduate School, College of Humanities, Department of Languages and Literature, Salt Lake City, UT 84112-1107. Offers comparative literary and cultural studies (MA, PhD); French (MA, MALP); German (MA, MALP, PhD); Spanish (MA, MALP, PhD); world languages with secondary teaching licensure (MA). *Faculty:* 35 full-time (22 women), 1 part-time/adjunct (0 women). *Students:* 30 full-time (20 women), 10 part-time (9 women); includes 8 minority (1 American Indian/Alaska Native, 2 Asian Americans or Pacific Islanders, 5 Hispanic Americans), 6 international. Average age 35. 47 applicants, 40% accepted, 18 enrolled. In 2009, 7 master's, 3 doctorates awarded. Terminal master's awarded for partial completion of doctoral program. *Degree requirements:* For master's, 2 foreign languages, comprehensive exam, thesis, standard proficiency in 2 languages other than English; for doctorate, 3 foreign languages, comprehensive exam, thesis/dissertation, standard proficiency in 2 languages other than English and language of study, advanced proficiency in 1 language other than English and language of study. *Entrance requirements:* For master's, bachelor's degree or strong undergraduate record in target languages, minimum GPA of 3.0; for doctorate, GRE, MA, advanced proficiency in a target language. Additional exam requirements/recommendations for international students: Required—TOEFL (minimum score 500 paper-based; 173 computer-based). *Application deadline:* For fall admission, 1/15 priority date for domestic students, 12/15 priority date for international students. Application fee: $55 ($65 for international students). *Expenses:* Tuition, state resident: full-time $4004; part-time $1674 per semester. Tuition, nonresident: full-time $14,134; part-time $5915 per semester. Required fees: $324 per semester. Tuition and fees vary according to course load, degree level and program. *Financial support:* In 2009–10, 21 students received support, including 21 teaching assistantships with full tuition reimbursements available (averaging $11,000 per year); health care benefits also available. Financial award application deadline: 2/1; financial award applicants required to submit FAFSA. *Faculty research:* Literary theory, linguistics, cultural studies, comparative studies. Total annual research expenditures: $22,986. *Unit head:* Dr. Christine A. Jones, Director of Graduate Studies, 801-585-3002, Fax: 801-581-7581, E-mail: cjones@hum.utah.edu. *Application contact:* Virginia Ellinwood, Academic Advisor, 801-585-9437, Fax: 801-581-7581, E-mail: v.ellinwood@mail.hum.utah.edu.

University of Vermont, Graduate College, College of Arts and Sciences, Department of German and Russian, Burlington, VT 05405. Offers German (MA). *Students:* 2 (1 woman). 4 applicants, 100% accepted, 1 enrolled. *Degree requirements:* For master's, one foreign language, thesis. *Entrance requirements:* For master's, GRE General Test. Additional exam requirements/recommendations for international students: Required—TOEFL (minimum score 550 paper-based; 213 computer-based; 80 iBT). *Application deadline:* For fall admission, 4/1 priority date for domestic students. Applications are processed on a rolling basis. Application fee: $40. Electronic applications accepted. *Expenses:* Tuition, state resident: part-time $508 per credit hour. Tuition, nonresident: part-time $1281 per credit hour. *Financial support:* Fellowships, teaching assistantships available. Financial award application deadline: 3/1. *Faculty research:* Medieval and eighteenth and nineteenth century literature, folklore. *Unit head:* Dr. W. Mieder, Chairperson, 802-656-3430. *Application contact:* Dr. D. Scrase, Coordinator, 802-656-3430.

University of Victoria, Faculty of Graduate Studies, Faculty of Humanities, Department of Germanic and Slavic Studies, Victoria, BC V8W 2Y2, Canada. Offers German studies (MA). Part-time programs available. *Degree requirements:* For master's, 2 foreign languages, oral defense of thesis. *Entrance requirements:* For master's, BA in German, minimum B+ average in undergraduate course work. Additional exam requirements/recommendations for international students: Required—TOEFL (minimum score 575 paper-based; 233 computer-based), IELTS (minimum score 7). Electronic applications accepted. *Faculty research:* Nineteenth and twentieth century German literature, literature and music, language acquisition, eighteenth and twentieth century drama and theater, military history.

University of Virginia, College and Graduate School of Arts and Sciences, Department of Germanic Languages and Literatures, Charlottesville, VA 22903. Offers German (MA, PhD). *Faculty:* 11 full-time (5 women), 2 part-time/adjunct (0 women). *Students:* 13 full-time (7 women), 1 part-time (0 women), 5 international. Average age 29. 10 applicants, 80% accepted, 3 enrolled. In 2009, 2 master's, 1 doctorate awarded. *Degree requirements:* For master's, one foreign language, comprehensive exam, thesis; for doctorate, one foreign language, comprehensive exam, thesis/dissertation. *Entrance requirements:* For master's, GRE General Test, 3 letters of recommendation, critical writing sample; for doctorate, GRE General Test, 3 letters of recommendation; critical writing sample. Additional exam requirements/recommendations for international students: Required—TOEFL (minimum score 600 paper-based; 250 computer-based; 90 iBT), IELTS (minimum score 7). *Application deadline:* For fall admission, 1/15 for domestic and international students. Applications are processed on a rolling basis. Application fee: $60. Electronic applications accepted. *Financial support:* Applicants required to submit FAFSA. *Unit head:* Grossman Jeffrey, Chair, 434-924-3530, Fax: 434-924-6700, E-mail: germandepartment@virginia.edu. *Application contact:* Benjamin Bennett, Director of Graduate Admissions, 434-924-6695, Fax: 434-924-6700, E-mail: bkb@virginia.edu.

University of Washington, Graduate School, College of Arts and Sciences, Department of Germanics, Seattle, WA 98195. Offers MA, PhD. Part-time programs available. Terminal master's awarded for partial completion of doctoral program. *Degree requirements:* For master's, one foreign language, 2 research papers; for doctorate, 2 foreign languages, thesis/dissertation, 3 research papers. *Entrance requirements:* For master's and doctorate, GRE, minimum GPA of 3.0. Additional exam requirements/recommendations for international students: Required—TOEFL. Electronic applications accepted. *Faculty research:* Modern German literature, Germanic linguistics and philology, language pedagogy, literary theory, cinema studies.

University of Waterloo, Graduate Studies, Faculty of Arts, Department of Germanic and Slavic Studies, Waterloo, ON N2L 3G1, Canada. Offers German (MA, PhD); Russian (MA). Part-time and evening/weekend programs available. *Degree requirements:* For master's, one foreign language, thesis optional; for doctorate, 2 foreign languages, comprehensive exam, thesis/dissertation. *Entrance requirements:* For master's, honors degree, minimum B average; for doctorate, master's degree, minimum B average. Additional exam requirements/recommendations for international students: Required—TOEFL, TWE. Electronic applications accepted. *Faculty research:* Medieval theatre; history and literature; German and Russian literary relations; seventeenth, eighteenth, nineteenth, and twentieth century German literature.

University of Wisconsin–Madison, Graduate School, College of Letters and Science, Department of German, Madison, WI 53706-1380. Offers MA, PhD. Part-time programs available. Terminal master's awarded for partial completion of doctoral program. *Degree requirements:* For master's, one foreign language, comprehensive exam, thesis optional; for doctorate, 2 foreign languages, comprehensive exam, thesis/dissertation. *Entrance requirements:* For master's and doctorate, GRE. Electronic applications accepted. *Expenses:* Tuition, state resident: part-time $594 per credit. Tuition, nonresident: part-time $1504 per credit. Required fees: $65 per credit. Tuition and fees vary according to course load, program and reciprocity agreements. *Faculty research:* Literature, culture/linguistics, film, Dutch.

University of Wisconsin–Milwaukee, Graduate School, College of Letters and Sciences, Interdepartmental Program in Foreign Language and Literature, Milwaukee, WI 53201-0413. Offers classics and Hebrew studies (MAFLL); comparative literature (MAFLL); French and Italian (MAFLL); German (MAFLL); Slavic studies (MAFLL); translation (Certificate). Part-time programs available. *Faculty:* 37 full-time (18 women). *Students:* 32 full-time (25 women), 28 part-time (19 women); includes 5 minority (1 Asian American or Pacific Islander, 4 Hispanic Americans), 22 international. Average age 33. 54 applicants, 69% accepted, 20 enrolled. In 2009, 24 master's awarded. *Degree requirements:* For master's, 2 foreign languages, thesis or alternative. *Entrance requirements:* Additional exam requirements/recommendations for international students: Required—TOEFL (minimum score 550 paper-based; 79 iBT), IELTS (minimum score 6.5). *Application deadline:* For fall admission, 1/1 priority date for domestic students; for spring admission, 9/1 for domestic students. Applications are processed on a rolling basis. Application fee: $45 ($75 for international students). *Expenses:* Tuition, state resident: full-time $8800. Tuition, nonresident: full-time $20,760. Tuition and fees vary according to program and reciprocity agreements. *Financial support:* In 2009–10, 2 research assistantships, 21 teaching assistantships were awarded; career-related internships or fieldwork and unspecified assistantships also available. Support available to part-time students. Financial award application deadline: 4/15. Total annual research expenditures: $285,237. *Unit head:* Gabrielle Verdier, Representative, 414-229-3346, Fax: 414-229-2741, E-mail: verdier@uwm.edu. *Application contact:* General Information Contact, 414-229-4982, Fax: 414-229-6967, E-mail: gradschool@uwm.edu.

University of Wyoming, College of Arts and Sciences, Department of Modern and Classical Languages, Program in German, Laramie, WY 82070. Offers MA. Part-time programs available. *Degree requirements:* For master's, one foreign language, thesis or alternative. *Entrance requirements:* For master's, GRE General Test, minimum GPA of 3.0. *Faculty research:* East German literature, German literature, theatre, poetry.

Vanderbilt University, Graduate School, Department of Germanic and Slavic Languages, Nashville, TN 37240-1001. Offers German (MA, MAT, PhD). *Faculty:* 11 full-time (5 women). *Students:* 20 full-time (13 women); includes 3 minority (1 African American, 1 Asian American or Pacific Islander, 1 Hispanic American), 7 international. Average age 32. 22 applicants, 32% accepted, 5 enrolled. In 2009, 2 master's, 1 doctorate awarded. Terminal master's awarded for partial completion of doctoral program. *Degree requirements:* For master's, one foreign language, comprehensive exam; for doctorate, 2 foreign languages, comprehensive exam, thesis/dissertation, qualifying and final exams. *Entrance requirements:* For master's and doctorate, GRE General Test, sample of written work. Additional exam requirements/recommendations for international students: Required—TOEFL (minimum score 570 paper-based; 230 computer-based; 88 iBT). *Application deadline:* For fall admission, 1/15 for domestic and international students. Application fee: $0. Electronic applications accepted. *Financial support:* Fellowships with full and partial tuition reimbursements, teaching assistantships with full and partial tuition reimbursements, career-related internships or fieldwork, Federal Work-Study, institutionally sponsored loans, scholarships/grants, and health care benefits available. Financial award application deadline: 1/15; financial award applicants required to submit CSS PROFILE or FAFSA. *Faculty research:* 1750 to present, Middle Ages, Baroque, language pedagogy, linguistics. *Unit head:* Barbara Hahn, Acting Chair, 615-322-2611, Fax: 615-343-7258, E-mail: barbara.hahn@vanderbilt.edu. *Application contact:* Meike Werner, Director of Graduate Studies, 615-322-2611, Fax: 615-343-7258, E-mail: meike.werner@vanderbilt.edu.

Washington University in St. Louis, Graduate School of Arts and Sciences, Department of Germanic Languages and Literature, St. Louis, MO 63130-4899. Offers MA, PhD. Terminal master's awarded for partial completion of doctoral program. *Degree requirements:* For master's, thesis optional; for doctorate, thesis/dissertation. *Entrance requirements:* For master's and doctorate, GRE General Test, sample of written work. Electronic applications accepted.

Wayne State University, College of Liberal Arts and Sciences, Department of Classical and Modern Languages, Literatures, and Cultures, Program in German and Slavic Studies, Detroit, MI 48202. Offers German (MA); language learning (MA); modern languages (PhD); Russian (MA). *Degree requirements:* For master's, one foreign language, thesis or alternative; for doctorate, 2 foreign languages, thesis/dissertation. *Entrance requirements:* For master's and doctorate, minimum GPA of 3.0. Additional exam requirements/recommendations for international students: Required—TOEFL (minimum score 550 paper-based; 213 computer-based); Recommended—TWE (minimum score 6). Electronic applications accepted. *Faculty research:* Exile and Holocaust, minority literature, gender studies, fairytale studies, sociolinguistics.

West Chester University of Pennsylvania, Office of Graduate Studies, College of Arts and Sciences, Department of Languages and Cultures, West Chester, PA 19383. Offers French (M Ed, MA, Teaching Certificate); German (M Ed, Teaching Certificate); Latin (M Ed, Teaching Certificate); Spanish (M Ed, MA, Teaching Certificate). Part-time and evening/weekend programs available. *Students:* 4 full-time (all women), 27 part-time (21 women); includes 6 minority (2 African Americans, 1 Asian American or Pacific Islander, 3 Hispanic Americans). Average age 33. 16 applicants, 94% accepted, 9 enrolled. In 2009, 7 master's awarded. *Degree requirements:* For master's, one foreign language, comprehensive exam, thesis optional. *Entrance requirements:* For master's, GRE or MAT, placement test. Additional exam requirements/recommendations for international students: Required—TOEFL (minimum score 550 paper-based; 213 computer-based; 80 iBT). *Application deadline:* For fall admission, 4/15 priority date for domestic students, 3/15 for international students; for spring admission, 10/15 for domestic students, 9/1 for international students. Applications are processed on a rolling basis. Application fee: $35. Electronic applications accepted. *Expenses:* Tuition, state resident: full-time $6666; part-time $370 per credit. Tuition, nonresident: full-time $10,666; part-time $593 per credit. Required fees: $122.56 per credit. *Financial support:* In 2009–10, 1 research assistantship with full and partial tuition reimbursement (averaging $5,000 per year) was awarded; unspecified assistantships also available. Support available to part-time students. Financial award application deadline: 2/15; financial award applicants required to submit FAFSA. *Faculty research:* Implementation of world languages curriculum framework. *Unit head:* Dr. Jerry Williams, Chair, 610-436-2700, Fax: 610-436-3048, E-mail: jwilliams2@wcupa.edu. *Application contact:* Dr. Rebecca Pauly, Graduate Coordinator, 610-436-2382, E-mail: rpauly@wcupa.edu.

Yale University, Graduate School of Arts and Sciences, Department of German, New Haven, CT 06520. Offers PhD. Terminal master's awarded for partial completion of doctoral program. *Degree requirements:* For doctorate, 3 foreign languages, thesis/dissertation. *Entrance requirements:* For doctorate, GRE General Test.

Italian

Boston College, Graduate School of Arts and Sciences, Department of Romance Languages and Literatures, Chestnut Hill, MA 02467-3800. Offers French (MA, PhD); Italian (MA); medieval language (PhD); Spanish (MA, PhD). Part-time programs available. *Students:* 43 full-time (39 women), 4 part-time (3 women); includes 5 minority (2 Asian Americans or Pacific Islanders, 3 Hispanic Americans), 9 international. 65 applicants, 35% accepted, 11 enrolled. In 2009, 2 master's, 9 doctorates awarded. Terminal master's awarded for partial completion of doctoral program. *Degree requirements:* For master's, one foreign language; for doctorate, 2 foreign languages, thesis/dissertation. *Entrance requirements:* Additional exam requirements/recommendations for international students: Required—TOEFL (minimum score 600 paper-based; 250 computer-based; 100 iBT). *Application deadline:* For fall admission, 1/2 for domestic and international students. Application fee: $75. Electronic applications accepted. *Financial support:* In 2009–10, fellowships with full tuition reimbursements (averaging $16,000 per year), teaching assistantships with full tuition reimbursements (averaging $16,300 per year) were awarded; Federal Work-Study and unspecified assistantships also available. Support available to part-time students. Financial award application deadline: 3/1; financial award applicants required to submit FAFSA. *Faculty research:* Spanish-American literature, philology, medieval French romance and troubadour/trouvere lyrics, Golden Age Peninsular literature, secondary language acquisition and pedagogy. *Unit head:* Dr. Dwayne Carpenter, Chairperson, 617-552-3828, E-mail: dwayne.carpenter@bc.edu. *Application contact:* Dr. Dwayne Carpenter, Chairperson, 617-552-3828, E-mail: dwayne.carpenter@bc.edu.

Brown University, Graduate School, Department of Italian Studies, Providence, RI 02912. Offers PhD, MA/PhD. Terminal master's awarded for partial completion of doctoral program. *Degree requirements:* For doctorate, 2 foreign languages, thesis/dissertation, preliminary exam.

Central Connecticut State University, School of Graduate Studies, School of Arts and Sciences, Department of Modern Languages, Program in Modern Language, New Britain, CT 06050-4010. Offers French (MA, Certificate); German (Certificate); Italian (Certificate); modern language (MA); Spanish language and Hispanic culture (MA). Part-time and evening/weekend programs available. *Students:* 2 full-time (1 woman), 40 part-time (35 women); includes 14 minority (all Hispanic Americans). Average age 38. 16 applicants, 69% accepted, 9 enrolled. In 2009, 9 master's awarded. *Degree requirements:* For master's, one foreign language, comprehensive exam, thesis or alternative; for Certificate, qualifying exam. *Entrance requirements:* For master's, minimum undergraduate GPA of 2.7, 24 credits of undergraduate courses in either Italian or Spanish. Additional exam requirements/recommendations for international students: Required—TOEFL. *Application deadline:* For fall admission, 7/1 for domestic students; for spring admission, 12/1 for domestic students. Applications are processed on a rolling basis. Application fee: $50. Electronic applications accepted. *Expenses:* Tuition, area resident: Full-time $4662; part-time $440 per credit. Tuition, state resident: full-time $6994; part-time $440 per credit. Tuition, nonresident: full-time $12,988; part-time $440 per credit. Required fees: $3606. One-time fee: $62 part-time. *Faculty research:* Twentieth century French theater, seventeenth century French literature, French Middle Ages.

Columbia University, Graduate School of Arts and Sciences, Division of Humanities, Department of Italian, New York, NY 10027. Offers M Phil, MA, PhD. Part-time programs available. *Degree requirements:* For master's, one foreign language, oral and written exams; for doctorate, 2 foreign languages, thesis/dissertation. *Entrance requirements:* For master's and doctorate, GRE General Test, writing sample. Additional exam requirements/recommendations for international students: Required—TOEFL. *Faculty research:* Medieval and Renaissance Italian literature; Italian poetry, prose, and theater; modern and contemporary Italian literature.

Cornell University, Graduate School, Graduate Fields of Arts and Sciences, Field of Romance Studies, Ithaca, NY 14853-0001. Offers French linguistics (PhD); French literature (PhD); Hispanic literature (PhD); Italian linguistics (PhD); Italian literature (PhD); Romance linguistics (PhD); Spanish linguistics (PhD). *Faculty:* 42 full-time (19 women). *Students:* 54 full-time (27 women); includes 9 minority (all Hispanic Americans), 17 international. Average age 30. 78 applicants, 17% accepted, 10 enrolled. In 2009, 7 doctorates awarded. *Degree requirements:* For doctorate, 2 foreign languages, comprehensive exam, thesis/dissertation. *Entrance requirements:* For doctorate, GRE General Test, sample of written work, 3 letters of recommendation. Additional exam requirements/recommendations for international students: Required—TOEFL (minimum score 550 paper-based; 213 computer-based; 77 iBT). *Application deadline:* For fall admission, 1/15 for domestic students. Application fee: $70. Electronic applications accepted. *Expenses:* Tuition: Full-time $29,500. Required fees: $70. Full-time tuition and fees vary according to degree level, program and student level. *Financial support:* In 2009–10, 46 students received support, including 8 fellowships with full tuition reimbursements available, 2 teaching assistantships with full tuition reimbursements available; research assistantships with full tuition reimbursements available, institutionally sponsored loans, scholarships/grants, health care benefits, tuition waivers (full and partial), and unspecified assistantships also available. Financial award applicants required to submit FAFSA. *Faculty research:* Literary theory, Hispanic studies, French studies, gender studies. *Unit head:* Director of Graduate Studies, 607-255-8222. *Application contact:* Graduate Field Assistant, 607-255-4246, E-mail: romance_studies@cornell.edu.

Drew University, Caspersen School of Graduate Studies, Program in Education, Madison, NJ 07940-1493. Offers biology (MAT); chemistry (MAT); English (MAT); French (MAT); Italian (MAT); math (MAT); physics (MAT); social studies (MAT); Spanish (MAT); theatre arts (MAT). *Unit head:* Dr. Ross Danis.

Florida State University, The Graduate School, College of Arts and Sciences, Department of Modern Languages, Program in Italian Studies, Tallahassee, FL 32306. Offers MA. *Faculty:* 6 full-time (2 women), 2 part-time/adjunct (1 woman). *Students:* 9 full-time (8 women); includes 2 minority (both Hispanic Americans). Average age 24. 9 applicants, 100% accepted, 5 enrolled. *Entrance requirements:* For master's, GRE General Test or minimum GPA of 3.0. Additional exam requirements/recommendations for international students: Required—TOEFL (minimum score 550 paper-based; 213 computer-based). *Application deadline:* For fall admission, 2/1 for domestic and international students. Applications are processed on a rolling basis. Application fee: $30. Electronic applications accepted. *Expenses:* Tuition, state resident: full-time $7413. Tuition, nonresident: full-time $22,567. *Financial support:* In 2009–10, 9 teaching assistantships with partial tuition reimbursements (averaging $10,200 per year) were awarded. Financial award application deadline: 2/15. *Unit head:* Dr. Mark Pietralunga, Coordinator, 850-644-8392, Fax: 850-644-0524, E-mail: mpietral@fsu.edu. *Application contact:* Wendy E. Pigott, Graduate Academic Coordinator, 850-644-8397, Fax: 850-644-0524, E-mail: wpigott@fsu.edu.

Graduate School and University Center of the City University of New York, Graduate Studies, Program in Comparative Literature, New York, NY 10016-4039. Offers comparative literature (MA, PhD), including classics (PhD), German (PhD), Italian (PhD). *Faculty:* 16 full-time (3 women). *Students:* 110 full-time (70 women), 3 part-time (all women); includes 5 minority (2 Asian Americans or Pacific Islanders, 3 Hispanic Americans), 29 international.

Italian

Graduate School and University Center of the City University of New York (continued)

Average age 37. 51 applicants, 35% accepted, 11 enrolled. In 2009, 5 master's, 8 doctorates awarded. Terminal master's awarded for partial completion of doctoral program. *Degree requirements:* For master's, 2 foreign languages, comprehensive exam, thesis; for doctorate, 3 foreign languages, comprehensive exam, thesis/dissertation. *Entrance requirements:* For master's and doctorate, GRE General Test. Additional exam requirements/recommendations for international students: Required—TOEFL. *Application deadline:* For fall admission, 4/15 for domestic students; for spring admission, 11/15 for domestic students. Application fee: $125. Electronic applications accepted. *Financial support:* In 2009–10, 63 students received support, including 60 fellowships, 5 research assistantships, 14 teaching assistantships; career-related internships or fieldwork, Federal Work-Study, institutionally sponsored loans, and tuition waivers (full and partial) also available. Financial award application deadline: 2/1; financial award applicants required to submit FAFSA. *Unit head:* Dr. Andre Aciman, Executive Officer, 212-817-8170, Fax: 212-817-1509, E-mail: aaciman@gc.cuny.edu. *Application contact:* Les Gribben, Director of Admissions, 212-817-7470, Fax: 212-817-1624, E-mail: lgribben@gc.cuny.edu.

Harvard University, Graduate School of Arts and Sciences, Department of Romance Languages and Literatures, Cambridge, MA 02138. Offers French (AM, PhD); Italian (AM, PhD); Portuguese (AM, PhD); Spanish (AM, PhD). Terminal master's awarded for partial completion of doctoral program. *Degree requirements:* For master's, 2 foreign languages; for doctorate, 2 foreign languages, thesis/dissertation. *Entrance requirements:* For master's and doctorate, GRE General Test, sample of written work. Additional exam requirements/recommendations for international students: Required—TOEFL. *Expenses:* Tuition: Full-time $33,696. Required fees: $1126. Full-time tuition and fees vary according to program.

Hunter College of the City University of New York, Graduate School, School of Arts and Sciences, Department of Romance Languages, Program in Italian, New York, NY 10021-5085. Offers Italian (MA); Italian education (MA). *Faculty:* 2 full-time (both women). *Students:* 6 part-time (4 women); includes 1 minority (Hispanic American). Average age 31. 7 applicants, 86% accepted, 4 enrolled. In 2009, 2 master's awarded. *Degree requirements:* For master's, 2 foreign languages, comprehensive exam, thesis optional. *Entrance requirements:* For master's, GRE General Test, GRE Subject Test, ability to read, speak, and write Italian; interview. Additional exam requirements/recommendations for international students: Required—TOEFL. *Application deadline:* For fall admission, 4/1 for domestic students, 2/1 for international students; for spring admission, 11/1 for domestic students, 9/1 for international students. Application fee: $125. *Expenses:* Tuition, state resident: full-time $7360; part-time $310 per credit. Required fees: $250 per semester. *Financial support:* Federal Work-Study, scholarships/grants, and tuition waivers (partial) available. Support available to part-time students. Financial award application deadline: 4/15. *Faculty research:* Dante, Middle Ages, Renaissance, contemporary Italian novel and poetry, late Renaissance and baroque. *Unit head:* Dr. Paolo Fasoli, Graduate Co-Adviser, 212-772-5129, Fax: 212-772-5094, E-mail: pfasoli@hunter.cuny.edu. *Application contact:* William Zlata, Director for Graduate Admissions, 212-772-4482, Fax: 212-650-3336, E-mail: admissions@hunter.cuny.edu.

Indiana University Bloomington, University Graduate School, College of Arts and Sciences, Department of French and Italian, Bloomington, IN 47405-7000. Offers French (MA, PhD), including French instruction (MA), French linguistics, French literature; Italian (MA, PhD). Part-time programs available. *Faculty:* 19 full-time (7 women). *Students:* 69 full-time (42 women), 5 part-time (4 women); includes 3 minority (1 American Indian/Alaska Native, 1 Asian American or Pacific Islander, 1 Hispanic American), 28 international. Average age 30. 48 applicants, 63% accepted, 15 enrolled. In 2009, 12 master's, 2 doctorates awarded. Terminal master's awarded for partial completion of doctoral program. *Degree requirements:* For master's, one foreign language, comprehensive exam, thesis optional; for doctorate, 2 foreign languages, comprehensive exam, thesis/dissertation. *Entrance requirements:* For master's and doctorate, GRE General Test. Additional exam requirements/recommendations for international students: Required—TOEFL (minimum score 550 paper-based; 213 computer-based; 79 iBT). *Application deadline:* For fall admission, 1/15 priority date for domestic students, 12/1 priority date for international students; for spring admission, 9/1 priority date for domestic and international students. Application fee: $55 ($65 for international students). Electronic applications accepted. *Financial support:* In 2009–10, 4 fellowships with partial tuition reimbursements (averaging $15,000 per year), 5 research assistantships with partial tuition reimbursements (averaging $13,025 per year), 39 teaching assistantships with partial tuition reimbursements (averaging $13,025 per year) were awarded. Financial award application deadline: 1/15. *Faculty research:* All periods of French and Italian literature and various areas of French linguistics, including the novel and political theory, literature and fine arts, literary theory, postcolonialism, French-Creole studies, French literature of Africa and its Diaspora, humanism, medieval folklore and mythology, humor in medieval and Renaissance literature, cinema Old Occitan and Old French, emigration, second language acquisition, syntax, sociolinguistics, phonology, lexicography. *Unit head:* Prof. Emanuel Mickel, Interim Chairman, 812-855-5458, Fax: 812-855-8877, E-mail: fritchr@indiana.edu. *Application contact:* Jocelyn Karlan, Secretary, 812-855-1088, Fax: 812-855-8877, E-mail: fritgs@indiana.edu.

Iona College, School of Arts and Science, Program in Foreign Languages, New Rochelle, NY 10801-1890. Offers Italian (MA); Spanish (MA). Part-time and evening/weekend programs available. *Faculty:* 4 full-time (2 women), 1 part-time/adjunct (0 women). *Students:* 14 part-time (13 women); includes 1 minority (Hispanic American). Average age 35. 4 applicants, 75% accepted, 2 enrolled. In 2009, 10 master's awarded. *Degree requirements:* For master's, thesis or alternative. *Entrance requirements:* For master's, minimum GPA of 3.0. Additional exam requirements/recommendations for international students: Required—TOEFL (minimum score 550 paper-based; 213 computer-based). *Application deadline:* Applications are processed on a rolling basis. Application fee: $50. Electronic applications accepted. *Expenses:* Tuition: Part-time $830 per credit. *Financial support:* Unspecified assistantships available. Support available to part-time students. Financial award application deadline: 4/15; financial award applicants required to submit FAFSA. *Faculty research:* Contemporary Spanish literature, linguistics, language acquisition, female Hispanic literature, Latina authors. *Unit head:* Dr. Victoria E. Ketz, Chair, 914-637-2738, E-mail: vketz@iona.edu. *Application contact:* Veronica Jarek-Prinz, Director of Graduate Admissions, 914-633-2420, Fax: 914-633-2277, E-mail: vjarekprinz@iona.edu.

The Johns Hopkins University, Zanvyl Krieger School of Arts and Sciences, Department of German and Romance Languages and Literatures, Baltimore, MD 21218-2699. Offers French (PhD); German (PhD); Italian (PhD); romance languages (PhD); Spanish (PhD). *Faculty:* 31 full-time (20 women), 1 part-time/adjunct (0 women). *Students:* 49 full-time (30 women); includes 4 minority (all Hispanic Americans), 21 international. Average age 30. 51 applicants, 37% accepted, 19 enrolled. In 2009, 5 doctorates awarded. *Degree requirements:* For doctorate, 2 foreign languages, thesis/dissertation. *Entrance requirements:* For doctorate, GRE General Test. Additional exam requirements/recommendations for international students: Required—TOEFL (minimum score 600 paper-based; 250 computer-based; 100 iBT), IELTS. *Application deadline:* For fall admission, 12/30 for domestic and international students. Application fee: $75. Electronic applications accepted. *Financial support:* In 2009–10, 40 fellowships with full tuition reimbursements (averaging $17,000 per year), 2 research assistantships with full tuition reimbursements (averaging $17,000 per year), 19 teaching assistantships with full tuition reimbursements (averaging $17,000 per year) were awarded; institutionally sponsored loans also available. *Faculty research:* Nineteenth century French prose and poetry, genetic theory and criticism; twentieth century Latin American literature and film; Medieval and Renaissance Italian literature; Gender and Queer Theory in German literature; the ideology of baroque and neobaroque aesthetics. *Unit head:* Dr. William Egginton, Chair, 410-516-7510, Fax: 410-516-5358, E-mail: egginton@jhu.edu. *Application contact:* Rebecca Swisdak, Graduate Administrative Coordinator, 410-516-7227, Fax: 410-516-5358, E-mail: rswisdak@jhu.edu.

McGill University, Faculty of Graduate and Postdoctoral Studies, Faculty of Arts, Department of Italian Studies, Montréal, QC H3A 2T5, Canada. Offers MA, PhD.

Middlebury College, Language Schools, Italian School, Middlebury, VT 05753-6002. Offers MA, DML. *Faculty:* 17 full-time (5 women). *Students:* 63 full-time (50 women); includes 3 minority (all Hispanic Americans). Average age 35. 99 applicants, 91% accepted, 63 enrolled. In 2009, 24 master's, 1 doctorate awarded. *Degree requirements:* For master's, one foreign language; for doctorate, 2 foreign languages, comprehensive exam, thesis/dissertation, residence abroad, teaching experience. *Entrance requirements:* For master's, placement exam, 3 letters of recommendation, writing sample. *Application deadline:* Applications are processed on a rolling basis. Application fee: $65. Electronic applications accepted. *Financial support:* Scholarships/grants available. *Unit head:* Dr. Antonio Vitti, Director, 802-443-5727, Fax: 802-443-2075, E-mail: acvitti@middlebury.edu. *Application contact:* Kara Gennarelli, Coordinator, 802-443-5727, Fax: 802-443-2075, E-mail: kgennar@middlebury.edu.

Montclair State University, The Graduate School, College of Humanities and Social Sciences, Department of Spanish and Italian, Montclair, NJ 07043-1624. Offers Italian (Certificate); Spanish (MA, Certificate); translating and interpreting Spanish (Certificate). Part-time and evening/weekend programs available. *Faculty:* 20 full-time (12 women), 24 part-time/adjunct (16 women). *Students:* 2 full-time (1 woman), 21 part-time (17 women). Average age 33. 9 applicants, 56% accepted, 4 enrolled. In 2009, 10 master's awarded. *Degree requirements:* For master's, comprehensive exam, thesis or alternative. *Entrance requirements:* For master's, GRE General Test, 2 letters of recommendation. Additional exam requirements/recommendations for international students: Required—TOEFL (minimum score 83 computer-based), or IELTS. *Application deadline:* For fall admission, 6/1 for international students; for spring admission, 11/1 for international students. Applications are processed on a rolling basis. Application fee: $60. Electronic applications accepted. *Expenses:* Tuition, area resident: Part-time $486.74 per credit. Tuition, state resident: part-time $486.74 per credit. Tuition, nonresident: part-time $751.34 per credit. Tuition and fees vary according to degree level and program. *Financial support:* In 2009–10, 1 research assistantship with full tuition reimbursement (averaging $7,000 per year) was awarded; Federal Work-Study, scholarships/grants, and unspecified assistantships also available. Support available to part-time students. Financial award application deadline: 3/1; financial award applicants required to submit FAFSA. *Unit head:* Dr. Linda Gould Levine, Chairperson, 973-655-7506. *Application contact:* Amy Aiello, Director of Graduate Admissions and Operations, 973-655-5147, Fax: 973-655-7869, E-mail: graduate.school@montclair.edu.

New York University, Graduate School of Arts and Science, Department of Italian Studies, New York, NY 10012-1019. Offers Italian (MA, PhD); Italian studies (MA). Part-time programs available. *Faculty:* 6 full-time (3 women). *Students:* 36 full-time (27 women), 2 part-time (1 woman); includes 2 minority (both Hispanic Americans), 16 international. Average age 29. 50 applicants, 48% accepted, 13 enrolled. In 2009, 6 master's, 3 doctorates awarded. Terminal master's awarded for partial completion of doctoral program. *Degree requirements:* For master's, one foreign language, thesis; for doctorate, 3 foreign languages, thesis/dissertation. *Entrance requirements:* For master's, GRE General Test, sample of written work; for doctorate, GRE General Test. Additional exam requirements/recommendations for international students: Required—TOEFL. *Application deadline:* For fall admission, 1/4 priority date for domestic students. Application fee: $90. *Expenses:* Tuition: Full-time $30,528; part-time $1272 per credit. Required fees: $2177. *Financial support:* Fellowships with tuition reimbursements, teaching assistantships with tuition reimbursements, Federal Work-Study, institutionally sponsored loans, scholarships/grants, and unspecified assistantships available. Financial award application deadline: 1/4; financial award applicants required to submit FAFSA. *Faculty research:* Dante, early modern literature, fascism and culture, contemporary literature, feminist theory. *Unit head:* Ruth Ben-Ghiat, Chairman, 212-998-8730, Fax: 212-995-4012, E-mail: italian.dept@nyu.edu. *Application contact:* Maria Luisa Ardizzone, Director of Graduate Studies, 212-998-8730, Fax: 212-995-4012, E-mail: italian.dept@nyu.edu.

Northwestern University, The Graduate School, Judd A. and Marjorie Weinberg College of Arts and Sciences, Department of French and Italian, Evanston, IL 60208. Offers eighteenth-century studies (Certificate); French (PhD); French and comparative literature (PhD); Italian studies (Certificate). Admissions and degrees offered through The Graduate School. *Degree requirements:* For doctorate, one foreign language, thesis/dissertation, written and oral exams. *Entrance requirements:* For doctorate, GRE, writing sample, cassette recording. Additional exam requirements/recommendations for international students: Required—TOEFL. *Faculty research:* Francophone studies, 18th century contemporary theory.

The Ohio State University, Graduate School, College of Humanities, Department of French and Italian, Columbus, OH 43210. Offers French (MA, PhD); Italian (MA). *Faculty:* 20. *Students:* 29 full-time (19 women), 12 part-time (8 women), 7 international. Average age 32. In 2009, 7 master's, 1 doctorate awarded. *Degree requirements:* For master's, variable foreign language requirement, thesis optional; for doctorate, variable foreign language requirement, thesis/dissertation. *Entrance requirements:* For master's and doctorate, GRE General Test. Additional exam requirements/recommendations for international students: Required—TOEFL. *Application deadline:* For fall admission, 8/15 priority date for domestic students, 7/1 priority date for international students; for winter admission, 12/1 priority date for domestic students, 11/1 priority date for international students; for spring admission, 3/1 priority date for domestic students, 2/1 priority date for international students. Applications are processed on a rolling basis. Application fee: $40 ($50 for international students). Electronic applications accepted. *Expenses:* Tuition, state resident: full-time $10,683. Tuition, nonresident: full-time $25,923. Tuition and fees vary according to course load and program. *Financial support:* Fellowships, research assistantships, teaching assistantships, Federal Work-Study, institutionally sponsored loans, and unspecified assistantships available. Support available to part-time students. *Faculty research:* Italian and Romance linguistics. *Unit head:* Jennifer Willging, Graduate Studies Committee Chair, E-mail: willging.1@osu.edu. *Application contact:* 614-292-9444, Fax: 614-292-3895, E-mail: domestic.grad@osu.edu.

Queens College of the City University of New York, Division of Graduate Studies, Arts and Humanities Division, Department of European Languages and Literatures, Program in Italian, Flushing, NY 11367-1597. Offers MA. Part-time and evening/weekend programs available. *Faculty:* 8 full-time (4 women). *Students:* 5 part-time (4 women). 5 applicants, 60% accepted, 1 enrolled. *Degree requirements:* For master's, 2 foreign languages, comprehensive exam, thesis or alternative. *Entrance requirements:* For master's, minimum GPA of 3.0. Additional exam requirements/recommendations for international students: Required—TOEFL. *Application deadline:* For fall admission, 4/1 for domestic students; for spring admission, 11/1 for domestic students. Applications are processed on a rolling basis. Application fee: $125. *Expenses:* Tuition, state resident: full-time $7360; part-time $310 per credit. Tuition, nonresident: part-time $575 per credit. One-time fee: $195.25 full-time; $145.25 part-time. *Financial support:* Career-related internships or fieldwork, Federal Work-Study, institutionally sponsored loans, and tuition waivers (partial) available. Support available to part-time students. Financial award application deadline: 4/1; financial award applicants required to submit FAFSA. *Application contact:* Mario Caruso, Director of Graduate Admissions, 718-997-5200, Fax: 718-997-5193, E-mail: graduate_admissions@qc.edu.

Rutgers, The State University of New Jersey, New Brunswick, Graduate School-New Brunswick, Program in Italian, Piscataway, NJ 08854-8097. Offers Italian (MA, PhD); Italian literature and literary criticism (MA); language, literature and culture (MAT). Part-time and evening/weekend programs available. Terminal master's awarded for partial completion of doctoral program. *Degree requirements:* For master's, one foreign language, comprehensive exam (for some programs), thesis optional; for doctorate, 2 foreign languages, thesis/dissertation, qualifying exam. *Entrance requirements:* For master's and doctorate, GRE General Test. Additional exam requirements/recommendations for international students: Required—TOEFL. *Faculty research:* Literature.

San Francisco State University, Division of Graduate Studies, College of Humanities, Department of Foreign Languages and Literatures, Program in Italian, San Francisco, CA 94132-1722. Offers MA.

Stanford University, School of Humanities and Sciences, Department of French and Italian, Stanford, CA 94305-9991. Offers French (MA, PhD); Italian (MA, PhD). Terminal master's awarded for partial completion of doctoral program. *Degree requirements:* For master's, one foreign language, written exam; for doctorate, 2 foreign languages, thesis/dissertation, oral exam. *Entrance requirements:* For master's and doctorate, GRE General Test. Additional exam requirements/recommendations for international students: Required—TOEFL. Electronic applications accepted. *Expenses:* Tuition: Full-time $37,380; part-time $2760 per quarter. Required fees: $501.

State University of New York at Binghamton, Graduate School, School of Arts and Sciences, Department of Romance Languages and Literatures, Program in Italian, Binghamton, NY 13902-6000. Offers MA. *Students:* 2 full-time (both women), 1 (woman) part-time. Average age 28. 1 applicant, 100% accepted, 1 enrolled. In 2009, 1 master's awarded. *Degree requirements:* For master's, one foreign language, comprehensive exam, thesis or alternative. *Entrance requirements:* For master's, GRE General Test, GRE Subject Test. Additional exam requirements/recommendations for international students: Required—TOEFL (minimum score 550 paper-based; 213 computer-based; 80 iBT). *Application deadline:* For fall admission, 2/15 priority date for domestic and international students; for spring admission, 11/15 priority date for domestic and international students. Applications are processed on a rolling basis. Application fee: $60. Electronic applications accepted. *Financial support:* Fellowships, research assistantships, teaching assistantships, career-related internships or fieldwork, Federal Work-Study, institutionally sponsored loans, scholarships/grants, health care benefits, and unspecified assistantships available. Financial award application deadline: 2/15; financial award applicants required to submit FAFSA. *Unit head:* Dr. Antonio Sobejano-Moran, Chairperson, 607-777-4635, E-mail: antobianco@msn.com. *Application contact:* Victoria Williams, Recruiting and Admissions Coordinator, 607-777-2151, Fax: 607-777-2501, E-mail: vwilliam@binghamton.edu.

Stony Brook University, State University of New York, Graduate School, College of Arts and Sciences, Department of European Languages, Literatures, and Cultures, Program in Italian, Stony Brook, NY 11794. Offers MA. Evening/weekend programs available. *Degree requirements:* For master's, one foreign language. *Entrance requirements:* For master's, GRE General Test. Additional exam requirements/recommendations for international students: Required—TOEFL. *Application deadline:* For fall admission, 1/15 for domestic students. Application fee: $60. *Expenses:* Tuition, state resident: full-time $8370; part-time $349 per credit. Tuition, nonresident: full-time $13,250; part-time $552 per credit. Required fees: $933. *Unit head:* Charles Franco, Coordinator, 631-632-1494, E-mail: charles.franco@stonybrook.edu. *Application contact:* Dr. Andrea Fedi, Director of Graduate Studies, 631-632-7438, Fax: 631-632-9612.

University at Albany, State University of New York, College of Arts and Sciences, Department of Languages, Literatures, and Cultures, Program in Italian, Albany, NY 12222-0001. Offers MA.

University of Alberta, Faculty of Graduate Studies and Research, Department of Modern Languages and Cultural Studies, Edmonton, AB T6G 2E1, Canada. Offers applied linguistics (Germanic, Romance, Slavic) (MA); French language, literatures and linguistics (PhD); French language, literatures, and linguistics (MA); Germanic languages, literatures and linguistics (PhD); Germanic languages, literatures, and linguistics (MA); Italian studies (MA); Slavic languages and literatures (Russian, Ukrainian) (MA, PhD); Slavic linguistics (Russian, Ukrainian) (MA, PhD); Spanish and Latin American studies (MA, PhD); Ukrainian folklore (MA, PhD). Part-time programs available. *Faculty:* 33 full-time (15 women), 2 part-time/adjunct (1 woman). *Students:* 39 full-time (29 women), 13 part-time (12 women). 300 applicants, 10% accepted. In 2009, 12 master's, 2 doctorates awarded. *Degree requirements:* For master's, one foreign language, thesis; for doctorate, 2 foreign languages, comprehensive exam, thesis/dissertation. *Entrance requirements:* For master's and doctorate, 1 language other than English. Additional exam requirements/recommendations for international students: Required—Michigan English Language Assessment Battery or TOEFL (minimum score 550 paper-based; 213 computer-based). *Application deadline:* For fall admission, 7/1 for domestic and international students; for winter admission, 11/1 for domestic and international students; for spring admission, 3/1 for domestic students. Applications are processed on a rolling basis. Electronic applications accepted. Tuition and fees charges are reported in Canadian dollars. *Expenses:* Tuition, area resident: Full-time $4626 Canadian dollars; part-time $99.72 Canadian dollars per unit. International tuition: $8216 Canadian dollars full-time. Required fees: $3590 Canadian dollars; $99.72 Canadian dollars per unit. $215 Canadian dollars per term. *Financial support:* In 2009–10, 2 fellowships with full and partial tuition reimbursements (averaging $18,000 per year), 23 research assistantships with full and partial tuition reimbursements (averaging $10,450 per year), 21 teaching assistantships with full and partial tuition reimbursements (averaging $12,572 per year) were awarded; scholarships/grants also available. Support available to part-time students. Financial award application deadline: 3/31. *Faculty research:* Russian/Ukrainian studies; German studies; contemporary Latin American, French and Francophone studies; Italian studies. *Unit head:* Dr. Don Bruce, Chair, 780-492-3273, Fax: 780-492-9106. *Application contact:* Jane Wilson, Graduate Programs Secretary, 780-492-3273, Fax: 780-492-9106, E-mail: mlcsgrad@ualberta.ca.

University of California, Berkeley, Graduate Division, College of Letters and Science, Department of Italian Studies, Berkeley, CA 94720-1500. Offers PhD. *Faculty:* 9 full-time. *Students:* 26 full-time (18 women). Average age 30. 31 applicants, 6 enrolled. *Degree requirements:* For doctorate, one foreign language, thesis/dissertation, oral and written qualifying exams. *Entrance requirements:* For doctorate, GRE General Test, minimum GPA of 3.0, 3 letters of recommendation. Additional exam requirements/recommendations for international students: Required—TOEFL (minimum score 570 paper-based; 230 computer-based). *Application deadline:* For fall admission, 12/19 for domestic students. Application fee: $70 ($90 for international students). *Financial support:* Fellowships, research assistantships, teaching assistantships, scholarships/grants and unspecified assistantships available. Financial award applicants required to submit FAFSA. *Faculty research:* Literature and culture of Italy in Middle Ages and the Renaissance, literature and culture of Italy in nineteenth and twentieth centuries, Italian film studies, interdisciplinary cultural studies. *Unit head:* Prof. Barbara Spackman, Chair, 510-642-2704, E-mail: issa@berkeley.edu. *Application contact:* Sandy Jones, Student Affairs Officer, 510-642-9051, Fax: 510-643-6220, E-mail: issag@berkeley.edu.

University of California, Berkeley, Graduate Division, College of Letters and Science, Group in Romance Languages and Literature, Berkeley, CA 94720-1500. Offers French (PhD); Italian (PhD); Spanish (PhD). *Faculty:* 16 full-time. *Students:* 15 full-time (8 women). Average age 33. 34 applicants, 1 enrolled. In 2009, 4 doctorates awarded. *Degree requirements:* For doctorate, thesis/dissertation, qualifying exam. *Entrance requirements:* For doctorate, GRE General Test, minimum GPA of 3.0, 3 letters of recommendation. Additional exam requirements/recommendations for international students: Required—TOEFL (minimum score 570 paper-based; 230 computer-based). *Application deadline:* For fall admission, 12/15 for domestic students. Application fee: $70 ($90 for international students). *Financial support:* Fellowships with full tuition reimbursements, teaching assistantships with partial tuition reimbursements, health care benefits and unspecified assistantships available. Financial award applicants required to submit FAFSA. *Unit head:* Jose Rabasa, Chair, 510-642-2105, E-mail: jrabasa@berkeley.edu. *Application contact:* Jose Rabasa, Chair, 510-642-2105, E-mail: jrabasa@berkeley.edu.

University of California, Los Angeles, Graduate Division, College of Letters and Science, Department of Italian, Los Angeles, CA 90095. Offers MA, PhD. *Students:* 21 full-time (16 women); includes 2 minority (both Hispanic Americans), 2 international. Average age 31. In 2009, 6 master's, 3 doctorates awarded. Terminal master's awarded for partial completion of doctoral program. *Degree requirements:* For master's, one foreign language, comprehensive exam or thesis; for doctorate, 2 foreign languages, thesis/dissertation, oral and written qualifying exams. *Entrance requirements:* For master's, GRE General Test, minimum GPA of 3.0, sample of written work; for doctorate, GRE General Test, minimum undergraduate GPA of 3.0, sample of written work; statement of purpose. *Application deadline:* For fall admission, 12/15 for domestic and international students. Application fee: $70 ($90 for international students). Electronic applications accepted. *Financial support:* In 2009–10, 20 fellowships with full and partial tuition reimbursements, 5 research assistantships with full and partial tuition reimbursements, 17 teaching assistantships with full and partial tuition reimbursements were awarded; Federal Work-Study, institutionally sponsored loans, health care benefits, tuition waivers (full and partial), and unspecified assistantships also available. Financial award application deadline: 3/1. *Unit head:* Edward A. Alpers, Chair, 310-825-1883. *Application contact:* Department Office, 310-825-1940, E-mail: allen@humnet.ucla.edu.

University of Chicago, Division of the Humanities, Department of Romance Languages and Literatures, Chicago, IL 60637-1513. Offers French (AM, PhD); Italian (AM, PhD); Spanish (AM, PhD). Terminal master's awarded for partial completion of doctoral program. *Degree requirements:* For master's, 2 foreign languages, thesis; for doctorate, 3 foreign languages, thesis/dissertation. *Entrance requirements:* For master's and doctorate, GRE General Test, GRE Subject Test. Additional exam requirements/recommendations for international students: Required—TOEFL.

University of Connecticut, Graduate School, College of Liberal Arts and Sciences, Department of Modern and Classical Languages, Field of Italian, Storrs, CT 06269. Offers MA, PhD. *Faculty:* 3 full-time (1 woman). *Students:* 7 full-time (5 women), 4 part-time (2 women); includes 1 minority (Asian American or Pacific Islander), 5 international. Average age 37. 6 applicants, 33% accepted, 2 enrolled. In 2009, 1 master's awarded. Terminal master's awarded for partial completion of doctoral program. *Degree requirements:* For master's, comprehensive exam; for doctorate, thesis/dissertation. *Entrance requirements:* For master's, GRE General Test. Additional exam requirements/recommendations for international students: Required—TOEFL (minimum score 550 paper-based; 213 computer-based). *Application deadline:* For fall admission, 2/1 priority date for domestic and international students; for spring admission, 11/1 for domestic students, 10/1 for international students. Applications are processed on a rolling basis. Application fee: $55. Electronic applications accepted. *Expenses:* Tuition, state resident: full-time $4725; part-time $525 per credit. Tuition, nonresident: full-time $12,267; part-time $1363 per credit. Required fees: $346 per semester. Tuition and fees vary according to course load. *Financial support:* In 2009–10, 7 teaching assistantships with full tuition reimbursements were awarded; fellowships, Federal Work-Study, scholarships/grants, health care benefits, and unspecified assistantships also available. Financial award application deadline: 2/1; financial award applicants required to submit FAFSA. *Unit head:* Franco Masciandaro, Section Head, 860-486-3275, E-mail: franco.masciandaro@uconn.edu. *Application contact:* Patricia Parlette-Schaff, Administrative Assistant, 860-486-3313, Fax: 860-486-4392, E-mail: patricia.parlette@uconn.edu.

University of Illinois at Urbana–Champaign, Graduate College, College of Liberal Arts and Sciences, School of Literatures, Cultures and Linguistics, Department of Spanish, Italian and Portuguese, Champaign, IL 61820. Offers Italian (MA, PhD); Portuguese (MA, PhD); Spanish (MA, PhD). *Faculty:* 18 full-time (11 women). *Students:* 46 full-time (35 women), 10 part-time (7 women); includes 15 minority (1 Asian American or Pacific Islander, 14 Hispanic Americans), 28 international. 46 applicants, 41% accepted, 12 enrolled. In 2009, 7 master's, 11 doctorates awarded. *Entrance requirements:* For master's, GRE General Test, minimum GPA of 3.0; writing sample; for doctorate, GRE, minimum GPA of 3.0; writing sample. Additional exam requirements/recommendations for international students: Required—TOEFL (minimum score 88 iBT). *Application deadline:* Applications are processed on a rolling basis. Application fee: $60 ($75 for international students). Electronic applications accepted. *Financial support:* In 2009–10, 10 fellowships, 3 research assistantships, 51 teaching assistantships were awarded; tuition waivers (full and partial) also available. *Unit head:* Diane Musumeci, Head, 217-333-3390, Fax: 217-244-8430, E-mail: musumeci@illinois.edu. *Application contact:* Lynn Stanke, Office Support Specialist, 217-333-6269, Fax: 217-244-3050, E-mail: stanke@illinois.edu.

University of Massachusetts Amherst, Graduate School, College of Humanities and Fine Arts, Department of Languages, Literatures, and Cultures, Program in Italian Studies, Amherst, MA 01003. Offers MAT. Part-time programs available. *Faculty:* 2 full-time (0 women). *Students:* 6 full-time (4 women), 2 international. Average age 35. 6 applicants, 50% accepted, 3 enrolled. *Degree requirements:* For master's, thesis or alternative. *Entrance requirements:* For master's, GRE General Test. Additional exam requirements/recommendations for international students: Required—TOEFL (minimum score 550 paper-based; 213 computer-based; 80 iBT), IELTS (minimum score 6.5). *Application deadline:* For fall admission, 2/1 for domestic and international students. Applications are processed on a rolling basis. Application fee: $50 ($65 for international students). Electronic applications accepted. *Expenses:* Tuition, state resident: full-time $2640; part-time $110 per credit. Tuition, nonresident: full-time $9936; part-time $414 per credit. Tuition and fees vary according to course load. *Financial support:* Career-related internships or fieldwork, Federal Work-Study, scholarships/grants, traineeships, health care benefits, tuition waivers (full), and unspecified assistantships available. Support available to part-time students. Financial award application deadline: 2/1. *Unit head:* Dr. Roberto Ludovico, Graduate Program Director, 413-545-2314, Fax: 413-545-4778. *Application contact:* Jean M. Ames, Supervisor of Admissions, 413-545-0722, Fax: 413-577-0010, E-mail: gradadm@grad.umass.edu.

The University of North Carolina at Chapel Hill, Graduate School, College of Arts and Sciences, Department of Romance Languages, Chapel Hill, NC 27599. Offers French (MA, PhD); Italian (MA, PhD); Portuguese (MA, PhD); Romance languages (MA, PhD); Romance philology (MA, PhD); Spanish (MA, PhD). *Degree requirements:* For master's, one foreign language, comprehensive exam, thesis; for doctorate, 2 foreign languages, comprehensive exam, thesis/dissertation. *Entrance requirements:* For master's and doctorate, GRE General Test, minimum GPA of 3.0. Additional exam requirements/recommendations for international students: Required—TOEFL (minimum score 550 paper-based; 213 computer-based). Electronic applications accepted.

University of Notre Dame, Graduate School, College of Arts and Letters, Division of Humanities, Department of Romance Languages and Literatures, Notre Dame, IN 46556. Offers French and Francophone studies (MA); Iberian and Latin American studies (MA); Italian studies (MA); Romance literatures (MA). *Degree requirements:* For master's, 2 foreign languages, comprehensive exam, thesis optional. *Entrance requirements:* For master's, GRE General Test, BA in target language. Additional exam requirements/recommendations for international students: Required—TOEFL (minimum score 600 paper-based; 250 computer-based; 80 iBT). Electronic applications accepted. *Faculty research:* Literature of discovery and exploration, modern literature, literary criticism, medieval literature, feminist critical theory.

University of Oregon, Graduate School, College of Arts and Sciences, Department of Romance Languages, Program in Italian, Eugene, OR 97403. Offers MA. Part-time programs available. *Degree requirements:* For master's, variable foreign language requirement. *Entrance requirements:* For master's, GRE General Test, minimum GPA of 3.0. Additional exam requirements/recommendations for international students: Required—TOEFL.

University of Pennsylvania, School of Arts and Sciences, Graduate Group in Romance Languages, Philadelphia, PA 19104. Offers French (AM, PhD); Italian (AM, PhD); Spanish (AM, PhD). *Faculty:* 60 full-time (24 women), 4 part-time/adjunct (1 woman). *Students:* 60 full-time (38 women), 2 part-time (both women); includes 7 minority (1 American Indian/Alaska Native, 6 Hispanic Americans), 17 international. 101 applicants, 26% accepted, 13 enrolled. In 2009, 12 master's, 7 doctorates awarded. Terminal master's awarded for partial completion of doctoral program. *Degree requirements:* For master's, one foreign language, thesis or alternative; for doctorate, 2 foreign languages, thesis/dissertation. *Entrance requirements:* For master's and doctorate, GRE General Test. Additional exam requirements/recommendations for international students: Required—TOEFL. *Application deadline:* For fall admission, 12/1 priority date for domestic students. Application fee: $70. Electronic applications accepted. *Expenses:* Tuition: Full-time $25,660; part-time $4758 per course. Required fees: $2152; $270 per course. Tuition and fees vary according to course load, degree level and program. *Financial*

Italian

University of Pennsylvania (continued)
support: In 2009–10, 23 fellowships, 2 research assistantships, 39 teaching assistantships were awarded; institutionally sponsored loans, scholarships/grants, traineeships, health care benefits, and unspecified assistantships also available. Financial award application deadline: 12/15. *Faculty research:* Literary theory and criticism, cultural studies, history of Romance literatures, gender studies.

University of Pittsburgh, School of Arts and Sciences, Department of French and Italian, Program in Italian, Pittsburgh, PA 15260. Offers MA. Part-time programs available. *Faculty:* 4 full-time (3 women). *Students:* 5 full-time (2 women); includes 1 minority (Hispanic American), 1 international. Average age 29. 10 applicants, 60% accepted, 1 enrolled. In 2009, 1 master's awarded. *Degree requirements:* For master's, 2 foreign languages, comprehensive exam, seminar paper. *Entrance requirements:* For master's, minimum GPA of 3.0, writing sample. Additional exam requirements/recommendations for international students: Required—TOEFL (minimum score 554 paper-based; 213 computer-based; 80 iBT). *Application deadline:* For fall admission, 2/1 priority date for domestic students, 2/1 for international students. Application fee: $50. *Expenses:* Tuition, state resident: full-time $16,402; part-time $665 per credit. Tuition, nonresident: full-time $28,694; part-time $1175 per credit. Required fees: $690; $175 per term. Tuition and fees vary according to program. *Financial support:* In 2009–10, 5 students received support, including 5 teaching assistantships with full tuition reimbursements available (averaging $15,065 per year); institutionally sponsored loans, scholarships/grants, health care benefits, and tuition waivers (partial) also available. Support available to part-time students. Financial award application deadline: 2/1; financial award applicants required to submit FAFSA. *Faculty research:* Dante and his reception, Humanism and Renaissance studies, seventeenth and eighteenth century Italian literature and culture, Italian theater, Holocaust literature and film, images of Southern Italy in European literature. *Unit head:* Dr. Dennis Looney, Chairman, 412-624-5220, Fax: 412-624-6263, E-mail: looney@pitt.edu. *Application contact:* Prof. Francesca Savoia, Graduate Director, 412-624-6265, Fax: 412-624-6263, E-mail: savoia@pitt.edu.

University of South Africa, College of Human Sciences, Pretoria, South Africa. Offers adult education (M Ed); African languages (MA, PhD); African politics (MA, PhD); Afrikaans (MA, PhD); ancient history (MA, PhD); ancient Near Eastern studies (MA, PhD); anthropology (MA, PhD); applied linguistics (MA); Arabic (MA, PhD); archaeology (MA); art history (MA); Biblical archaeology (MA); Biblical studies (M Th, D Th, PhD); Christian spirituality (M Th, D Th); church history (M Th, D Th); classical studies (MA, PhD); clinical psychology (MA); communication (MA, PhD); comparative education (M Ed, Ed D); consulting psychology (D Admin, D Com, PhD); curriculum studies (M Ed, Ed D); development studies (M Admin, MA, D Admin, PhD); didactics (M Ed, Ed D); education (M Tech); education management (M Ed, Ed D); educational psychology (M Ed); English (MA); environmental education (M Ed); French (MA, PhD); German (MA, PhD); Greek (MA); guidance and counseling (M Ed); health studies (MA, PhD), including health sciences education (MA), health services management (MA), medical and surgical nursing science (critical care general) (MA), midwifery and neonatal nursing science (MA), trauma and emergency care (MA); history (MA, PhD); history of education (Ed D); inclusive education (M Ed, Ed D); information and communications technology policy and regulation (MA); information science (MA, MIS, PhD); international politics (MA, PhD); Islamic studies (MA, PhD); Italian (MA, PhD); Judaica (MA, PhD); linguistics (MA, PhD); mathematical education (M Ed); mathematics education (MA); missiology (M Th, D Th); modern Hebrew (MA, PhD); musicology (MA, MMus, D Mus, PhD); natural science education (M Ed); New Testament (M Th, D Th); Old Testament (D Th); pastoral therapy (M Th, D Th); philosophy (MA); philosophy of education (M Ed, Ed D); politics (MA, PhD); Portuguese (MA, PhD); practical theology (M Th, D Th); psychology (MA, MS, PhD); psychology of education (M Ed, Ed D); public health (MA); religious studies (MA, D Th, PhD); Romance languages (MA); Russian (MA, PhD); Semitic languages (MA, PhD); social behavior studies in HIV/AIDS (MA); social science (mental health) (MA); social science in development studies (MA); social science in psychology (MA); social science in social work (MA); social science in sociology (MA); social work (MSW, DSW, PhD); socio-education (M Ed, Ed D); sociolinguistics (MA); sociology (MA, PhD); Spanish (MA, PhD); systematic theology (M Th, D Th); TESOL (teaching English to speakers of other languages) (MA); theological ethics (M Th, D Th); theory of literature (MA, PhD); urban ministries (D Th); urban ministry (M Th).

The University of Tennessee, Graduate School, College of Arts and Sciences, Department of Modern Foreign Languages and Literatures, Program in Modern Foreign Languages, Knoxville, TN 37996. Offers applied linguistics (PhD); French (PhD); German (PhD); Italian (PhD); Portuguese (PhD); Russian (PhD); Spanish (PhD). *Degree requirements:* For doctorate, 2 foreign languages, thesis/dissertation. *Entrance requirements:* For doctorate, minimum GPA of 2.7. Additional exam requirements/recommendations for international students: Required—TOEFL. Electronic applications accepted. *Expenses:* Tuition, state resident: full-time $6826; part-time $380 per semester hour. Tuition, nonresident: full-time $21,844; part-time $1147 per semester hour. Tuition and fees vary according to program.

The University of Texas at Austin, Graduate School, College of Liberal Arts, Department of French and Italian, Austin, TX 78712-1111. Offers French (MA, PhD); French linguistics (MA, PhD); Italian studies (MA, PhD); Romance linguistics (MA, PhD). Part-time programs available. *Degree requirements:* For master's, one foreign language, thesis; for doctorate, 2 foreign languages, thesis/dissertation. *Entrance requirements:* For master's, GRE General Test, minimum GPA of 3.0, bachelor's degree in French or equivalent; for doctorate, GRE General Test, minimum GPA of 3.0, master's degree in French. Additional exam requirements/recommendations for international students: Required—TOEFL. Electronic applications accepted. *Faculty research:* Nineteenth-century Italian literature, Italian Renaissance, twentieth-century French literature, Francophone literature, fifteenth-century literature and culture.

University of Toronto, School of Graduate Studies, Humanities Division, Department of Italian Studies, Toronto, ON M5S 1A1, Canada. Offers MA, PhD. Part-time programs available. *Degree requirements:* For doctorate, 2 foreign languages, comprehensive exam, thesis/dissertation, oral defense, language exam(s). *Entrance requirements:* For master's, minimum B average in last 2 years in Italian; minimum B average in final year, overall; 2 letters of recommendation; for doctorate, MA in Italian, minimum A– average.

University of Victoria, Faculty of Graduate Studies, Faculty of Humanities, Department of Hispanic and Italian Studies, Victoria, BC V8W 2Y2, Canada. Offers Hispanic and Italian studies (MA); Hispanic studies (MA). *Degree requirements:* For master's, one foreign language, comprehensive exam, thesis (for some programs). *Entrance requirements:* For master's, undergraduate major in Hispanic studies, minimum B+ average. Additional exam requirements/recommendations for international students: Required—TOEFL (minimum score 575 paper-based; 233 computer-based), IELTS (minimum score 7). Electronic applications accepted. *Faculty research:* Medieval/Renaissance Spanish and Italian literature, Golden Age literature, Latin American literature.

University of Virginia, College and Graduate School of Arts and Sciences, Department of Spanish, Italian and Portuguese, Program in Italian, Charlottesville, VA 22903. Offers MA. *Students:* 5 full-time (4 women), 4 international. Average age 28. 2 applicants, 100% accepted, 1 enrolled. In 2009, 5 master's awarded. *Degree requirements:* For master's, one foreign language, comprehensive exam, thesis. *Entrance requirements:* For master's, GRE General Test, BA in Italian, 2 letters of recommendation. Additional exam requirements/recommendations for international students: Required—TOEFL (minimum score 600 paper-based; 250 computer-based; 90 iBT), IELTS (minimum score 7). *Application deadline:* For fall admission, 12/1 for domestic and international students. Applications are processed on a rolling basis. Application fee: $60. Electronic applications accepted. *Financial support:* Teaching assistantships available. Financial award applicants required to submit FAFSA. *Application contact:* Enrico Cesaretti, Director of Graduate Studies, 434-924-7159, E-mail: sipinfo@virginia.edu.

University of Washington, Graduate School, College of Arts and Sciences, Department of Romance Languages and Literature, Division of French and Italian Studies, Seattle, WA 98195. Offers French (MA, PhD); Italian (MA). Terminal master's awarded for partial completion of doctoral program. *Degree requirements:* For master's, 2 foreign languages, exam; for doctorate, 3 foreign languages, thesis/dissertation, exam. *Entrance requirements:* For master's and doctorate, GRE General Test, minimum GPA of 3.0. Additional exam requirements/recommendations for international students: Required—TOEFL. Electronic applications accepted. *Faculty research:* Interdisciplinary studies, literary theory and criticism, film, major periods of French and Italian literature, Francophonie.

University of Wisconsin–Madison, Graduate School, College of Letters and Science, Department of French and Italian, Program in Italian, Madison, WI 53706-1380. Offers MA, PhD. Part-time programs available. *Degree requirements:* For master's, one foreign language; for doctorate, 2 foreign languages, thesis/dissertation. *Entrance requirements:* For master's and doctorate, GRE. Electronic applications accepted. *Expenses:* Tuition, state resident: part-time $594 per credit. Tuition, nonresident: part-time $1504 per credit. Required fees: $65 per credit. Tuition and fees vary according to course load, program and reciprocity agreements. *Faculty research:* Italian literature, culture, linguistics, cinema, and language.

University of Wisconsin–Milwaukee, Graduate School, College of Letters and Sciences, Interdepartmental Program in Foreign Language and Literature, Milwaukee, WI 53201-0413. Offers classics and Hebrew studies (MAFLL); comparative literature (MAFLL); French and Italian (MAFLL); German (MAFLL); Slavic studies (MAFLL); translation (Certificate). Part-time programs available. *Faculty:* 37 full-time (18 women). *Students:* 32 full-time (25 women), 28 part-time (19 women); includes 5 minority (1 Asian American or Pacific Islander, 4 Hispanic Americans), 22 international. Average age 33. 54 applicants, 69% accepted, 20 enrolled. In 2009, 24 master's awarded. *Degree requirements:* For master's, 2 foreign languages, thesis or alternative. *Entrance requirements:* Additional exam requirements/recommendations for international students: Required—TOEFL (minimum score 550 paper-based; 79 iBT), IELTS (minimum score 6.5). *Application deadline:* For fall admission, 1/1 priority date for domestic students; for spring admission, 9/1 for domestic students. Applications are processed on a rolling basis. Application fee: $45 ($75 for international students). *Expenses:* Tuition, state resident: full-time $8800. Tuition, nonresident: full-time $20,760. Tuition and fees vary according to program and reciprocity agreements. *Financial support:* In 2009–10, 2 research assistantships, 21 teaching assistantships were awarded; career-related internships or fieldwork and unspecified assistantships also available. Support available to part-time students. Financial award application deadline: 4/15. Total annual research expenditures: $285,237. *Unit head:* Gabrielle Verdier, Representative, 414-229-3346, Fax: 414-229-2741, E-mail: verdier@uwm.edu. *Application contact:* General Information Contact, 414-229-4982, Fax: 414-229-6967, E-mail: gradschool@uwm.edu.

Wayne State University, College of Liberal Arts and Sciences, Department of Classical and Modern Languages, Literatures, and Cultures, Program in Italian, Detroit, MI 48202. Offers MA. *Degree requirements:* For master's, one foreign language, thesis optional. *Entrance requirements:* For master's, GRE General Test, minimum GPA of 3.0. Additional exam requirements/recommendations for international students: Required—TOEFL (minimum score 550 paper-based; 213 computer-based); Recommended—TWE (minimum score 6). Electronic applications accepted. *Faculty research:* Renaissance lyric, modern theatre, Dante and Bocaccio, modern novel.

Yale University, Graduate School of Arts and Sciences, Department of Italian Language and Literature, New Haven, CT 06520. Offers PhD. *Degree requirements:* For doctorate, 3 foreign languages, thesis/dissertation. *Entrance requirements:* For doctorate, GRE General Test.

Japanese

Arizona State University, Graduate College, College of Liberal Arts and Sciences, Division of Humanities, School of International Letters and Cultures, Program in Japanese, Tempe, AZ 85287. Offers MA.

Cornell University, Graduate School, Graduate Fields of Arts and Sciences, Field of East Asian Literature, Ithaca, NY 14853-0001. Offers Asian religions (MA, PhD); Chinese linguistics (MA, PhD); Chinese philology (MA, PhD); classical Chinese literature (MA, PhD); classical Japanese literature (MA, PhD); Japanese linguistics (MA, PhD); Korean literature (MA, PhD); modern Chinese literature (MA, PhD); modern Japanese literature (MA, PhD). *Faculty:* 17 full-time (7 women). *Students:* 16 full-time (11 women); includes 4 minority (all Asian Americans or Pacific Islanders), 8 international. Average age 32. 49 applicants, 6% accepted, 2 enrolled. In 2009, 3 doctorates awarded. *Degree requirements:* For master's, 2 foreign languages, thesis, teaching experience; for doctorate, 2 foreign languages, comprehensive exam, thesis/dissertation, teaching experience. *Entrance requirements:* For master's, GRE General Test, 3 years of study in Chinese, Japanese, Korean, or Vietnamese; 3 letters of recommendation; academic writing sample; for doctorate, GRE General Test, 3 years of study in Chinese, Japanese, Korean, or Vietnamese, 3 letters of recommendation, academic writing sample. Additional exam requirements/recommendations for international students: Required—TOEFL (minimum score 600 paper-based; 250 computer-based; 77 iBT). *Application deadline:* For fall admission, 1/10 priority date for domestic students. Application fee: $70. Electronic applications accepted. *Expenses:* Tuition: Full-time $29,500. Required fees: $70. Full-time tuition and fees vary according to degree level, program and student level. *Financial support:* In 2009–10, 2 fellowships with full tuition reimbursements were awarded; research assistantships with full tuition reimbursements, teaching assistantships with full tuition reimbursements, institutionally sponsored loans, scholarships/grants, health care benefits, tuition waivers (full and partial), and unspecified assistantships also available. Financial award applicants required to submit FAFSA. *Faculty research:* Vietnamese literature; Chinese literature, drama, and film; Japanese theater and literature; popular culture in East Asia; Korean literature; Asian linguistics. *Unit head:* Director of Graduate Studies, 607-255-9099. *Application contact:* Graduate Field Assistant, 607-255-9099, E-mail: east_asian_lit@cornell.edu.

Eastern Michigan University, Graduate School, College of Arts and Sciences, Department of World Languages, Programs in Foreign Languages, Ypsilanti, MI 48197. Offers French (MA); German (MA); German for business (Graduate Certificate); Hispanic language and cultures (Graduate Certificate); Japanese business practices (Graduate Certificate); Spanish (MA). Part-time and evening/weekend programs available. Postbaccalaureate distance learning degree programs offered (minimal on-campus study). *Students:* 1 full-time (0 women), 15 part-time (14 women); includes 4 minority (1 African American, 3 Hispanic Americans), 1 international. Average age 39. In 2009, 6 master's awarded. *Degree requirements:* For master's, one foreign language, thesis optional. *Entrance requirements:* Additional exam requirements/

recommendations for international students: Required—TOEFL. *Application deadline:* Applications are processed on a rolling basis. Application fee: $35. Tuition and fees vary according to course level. *Financial support:* Fellowships, research assistantships with full tuition reimbursements, teaching assistantships with full tuition reimbursements, career-related internships or fieldwork, Federal Work-Study, institutionally sponsored loans, scholarships/grants, tuition waivers (partial), and unspecified assistantships available. Support available to part-time students. Financial award applicants required to submit FAFSA. *Application contact:* Dr. Genevieve Peden, Program Advisor, 734-487-2283, Fax: 734-487-3411, E-mail: gpeden@emich.edu.

Harvard University, Graduate School of Arts and Sciences, Department of East Asian Languages and Civilizations, Cambridge, MA 02138. Offers Chinese (PhD); Japanese (PhD); Korean (PhD); Mongolian (PhD); Vietnamese (PhD). Terminal master's awarded for partial completion of doctoral program. *Degree requirements:* For doctorate, 3 foreign languages, thesis/dissertation, general exams. *Entrance requirements:* For doctorate, GRE General Test. Additional exam requirements/recommendations for international students: Required—TOEFL. *Expenses:* Tuition: Full-time $33,696. Required fees: $1126. Full-time tuition and fees vary according to program. *Faculty research:* Central Asian literature, religion, and premodern history.

Indiana University Bloomington, University Graduate School, College of Arts and Sciences, Department of East Asian Languages and Cultures, Bloomington, IN 47405-7000. Offers Chinese (MA, PhD); East Asian languages and cultures (PhD); East Asian studies (MA); Japanese (MA, PhD); language pedagogy (MA). Part-time programs available. *Faculty:* 7 full-time (2 women). *Students:* 21 full-time (12 women), 11 part-time (8 women); includes 1 minority (Asian American or Pacific Islander), 11 international. Average age 30. 85 applicants, 38% accepted, 12 enrolled. In 2009, 6 master's, 1 doctorate awarded. *Degree requirements:* For master's, 2 foreign languages, thesis; for doctorate, 2 foreign languages, thesis/dissertation. *Entrance requirements:* Additional exam requirements/recommendations for international students: Required—TOEFL. *Application deadline:* For fall admission, 1/15 for domestic students, 12/15 for international students; for spring admission, 9/1 for domestic and international students. Applications are processed on a rolling basis. Application fee: $55 ($65 for international students). Electronic applications accepted. *Financial support:* In 2009–10, 6 fellowships with full tuition reimbursements (averaging $15,500 per year), 11 teaching assistantships with full tuition reimbursements (averaging $13,000 per year) were awarded; Federal Work-Study and tuition waivers (full) also available. Financial award application deadline: 3/1. *Faculty research:* Postwar/postmodern Japanese fiction, modern Chinese film and literature, classical Chinese literature and philosophy, Chinese and Japanese linguistics and pedagogy, East Asian politics. *Unit head:* Robert Eno, Chair, 812-855-0856, E-mail: eno@indiana.edu. *Application contact:* Edith Sarra, Director of Graduate Studies, 812-855-4031, Fax: 812-855-6402, E-mail: eserra@indiana.edu.

Kent State University, College of Arts and Sciences, Department of Modern and Classical Language Studies, Kent, OH 44242-0001. Offers French literature (MA); French, Spanish, German and Latin pedagogy (MA); German literature (MA); Spanish literature (MA); translation (MA), including French, German, Japanese, Russian, Spanish; translation studies (PhD). Part-time and evening/weekend programs available. *Degree requirements:* For master's, one foreign language, comprehensive exam (for some programs), thesis (for some programs); for doctorate, comprehensive exam, thesis/dissertation (for some programs). *Entrance requirements:* For master's, minimum GPA of 3.0, writing sample, audio tape or CD; for doctorate, 3 recommendations. Additional exam requirements/recommendations for international students: Required—TOEFL (minimum score 197 computer-based). Electronic applications accepted. *Faculty research:* Literature, pedagogy, applied linguistics, translation studies.

The Ohio State University, Graduate School, College of Humanities, Department of East Asian Languages and Literatures, Program in Japanese, Columbus, OH 43210. Offers MA, PhD. Electronic applications accepted. *Expenses:* Tuition, state resident: full-time $10,683. Tuition, nonresident: full-time $25,923. Tuition and fees vary according to course load and program.

Portland State University, Graduate Studies, College of Liberal Arts and Sciences, Department of Foreign Languages and Literatures, Portland, OR 97207-0751. Offers foreign literature and language (MA); French (MA); German (MA); Japanese (MA); Spanish (MA). Part-time programs available. *Degree requirements:* For master's, one foreign language, thesis (for some programs). *Entrance requirements:* Additional exam requirements/recommendations for international students: Required—TOEFL (minimum score 550 paper-based; 213 computer-based). *Faculty research:* Foreign language pedagogy, applied and social linguistics, literary history and criticism.

San Francisco State University, Division of Graduate Studies, College of Humanities, Department of Foreign Languages and Literatures, Program in Japanese, San Francisco, CA 94132-1722. Offers MA.

Soka University of America, Graduate School, Aliso Viejo, CA 92656. Offers teaching Japanese as a foreign language (Certificate). Evening/weekend programs available. *Entrance requirements:* For degree, bachelor's degree with minimum GPA of 3.0, proficiency in Japanese. Additional exam requirements/recommendations for international students: Required—TOEFL (minimum score 600 paper-based; 100 iBT).

Stanford University, School of Humanities and Sciences, Department of Asian Languages, Stanford, CA 94305-9991. Offers Chinese (MA, PhD); Japanese (MA, PhD). Terminal master's awarded for partial completion of doctoral program. *Degree requirements:* For master's, one foreign language, thesis or an annotated translation of a literary or historical text; for doctorate, 2 foreign languages, thesis/dissertation, field exams. *Entrance requirements:* For master's and doctorate, GRE General Test. Additional exam requirements/recommendations for international students: Required—TOEFL. Electronic applications accepted. *Expenses:* Tuition: Full-time $37,380; part-time $2760 per quarter. Required fees: $501.

University of Alberta, Faculty of Graduate Studies and Research, Department of East Asian Studies, Edmonton, AB T6G 2E1, Canada. Offers Chinese literature (MA); East Asian interdisciplinary studies (MA); Japanese literature (MA). Part-time programs available. *Faculty:* 7 full-time (4 women). *Students:* 4 full-time. Average age 23. 8 applicants, 50% accepted, 4 enrolled. In 2009, 3 master's awarded. *Degree requirements:* For master's, one foreign language, thesis. *Entrance requirements:* Additional exam requirements/recommendations for international students: Required—TOEFL. *Application deadline:* Applications are processed on a rolling basis. Application fee: $0. Electronic applications accepted. Tuition and fees charges are reported in Canadian dollars. *Expenses:* Tuition, area resident: Full-time $4626 Canadian dollars; part-time $99.72 Canadian dollars per unit. International tuition: $8216 Canadian dollars full-time. Required fees: $3590 Canadian dollars; $99.72 Canadian dollars per unit. $215 Canadian dollars per term. *Financial support:* In 2009–10, 4 students received support, including 3 teaching assistantships with tuition reimbursements available (averaging $10,500 per year); scholarships/grants also available. Financial award application deadline: 12/1. *Faculty research:* Classical Chinese poetry and poetics, Chinese philosophy, modern/contemporary Chinese literature, modern Japanese literature and culture, Japanese women's writing. Total annual research expenditures: $15,000. *Unit head:* Dr. Janice Brown, Chair, 780-492-3038, Fax: 780-492-7440, E-mail: janice.brown@gpu.srv.ualberta.ca. *Application contact:* Heather McDonald, Administrative Assistant, 780-492-2836, Fax: 780-492-7440, E-mail: eastasia.grad@ualberta.ca.

University of California, Berkeley, Graduate Division, College of Letters and Science, Department of East Asian Languages and Cultures, Berkeley, CA 94720-1500. Offers Chinese language (PhD); Japanese language (PhD). *Students:* 21 full-time (13 women). Average age 31. 55 applicants, 4 enrolled. In 2009, 4 doctorates awarded. *Degree requirements:* For doctorate, one foreign language, thesis/dissertation, oral qualifying exam. *Entrance requirements:* For doctorate, GRE General Test, minimum GPA of 3.0, MA thesis, 3 letters of recommendation. *Application deadline:* For fall admission, 12/8 for domestic students. Application fee: $70 ($90 for international students). Electronic applications accepted. *Financial support:* Fellowships, research assistantships, teaching assistantships, Federal Work-Study, institutionally sponsored loans, and unspecified assistantships available. Financial award applicants required to submit FAFSA. *Faculty research:* Chinese and Japanese modern and classical texts, prose, and poetry; Chinese and Japanese linguistics. *Unit head:* Prof. Alan Tansman, Chair, 510-642-3480, Fax: 510-642-6031, E-mail: ch_ealc@ls.berkeley.edu. *Application contact:* Information Contact, 510-642-3480, E-mail: ealang@berkeley.edu.

University of California, Irvine, Office of Graduate Studies, School of Humanities, Department of East Asian Languages and Literatures, Irvine, CA 92697. Offers Chinese (MA, PhD); East Asian languages and literatures (MA, PhD); Japanese (MA, PhD). *Students:* 12 full-time (9 women); includes 2 minority (1 African American, 1 Asian American or Pacific Islander), 7 international. Average age 31. 50 applicants, 6% accepted, 2 enrolled. In 2009, 3 doctorates awarded. *Degree requirements:* For doctorate, thesis/dissertation. *Entrance requirements:* For master's, GRE, minimum GPA of 3.0; for doctorate, GRE General Test, minimum GPA of 3.0. Additional exam requirements/recommendations for international students: Required—TOEFL (minimum score 550 paper-based; 213 computer-based). *Application deadline:* For fall admission, 1/15 priority date for domestic students, 1/15 for international students. Application fee: $70 ($90 for international students). Electronic applications accepted. *Financial support:* Fellowships with tuition reimbursements, research assistantships with full tuition reimbursements, teaching assistantships with partial tuition reimbursements, institutionally sponsored loans, traineeships, health care benefits, and unspecified assistantships available. Financial award application deadline: 3/1; financial award applicants required to submit FAFSA. *Faculty research:* Chinese, Japanese, and Korean literature and culture; language and textual analysis; historical, social, and cultural dimensions of literary study. *Unit head:* Michael Fuller, Interim Chair, 949-824-2151. *Application contact:* Angie Agsalog, Graduate Staff Contact, 949-824-1601, Fax: 949-824-3248, E-mail: aagsalog@uci.edu.

University of Colorado at Boulder, Graduate School, College of Arts and Sciences, Department of Asian Languages and Civilizations, Boulder, CO 80309. Offers Chinese (MA, PhD); Japanese (MA, PhD). Part-time programs available. *Faculty:* 10 full-time (6 women). *Students:* 30 full-time (19 women), 4 part-time (3 women); includes 9 minority (1 American Indian/Alaska Native, 6 Asian Americans or Pacific Islanders, 2 Hispanic Americans), 7 international. Average age 27. 30 applicants, 30% accepted, 9 enrolled. In 2009, 16 master's awarded. *Degree requirements:* For master's, comprehensive exam. *Entrance requirements:* For master's, BA in Chinese or Japanese, minimum undergraduate GPA of 3.0. Additional exam requirements/recommendations for international students: Required—TOEFL. *Application deadline:* For fall admission, 1/1 priority date for domestic students, 12/1 for international students; for spring admission, 10/1 for domestic students, 9/1 for international students. Applications are processed on a rolling basis. Application fee: $50 ($60 for international students). *Financial support:* In 2009–10, 7 fellowships (averaging $13,865 per year), 10 research assistantships (averaging $6,596 per year) were awarded; career-related internships or fieldwork and Federal Work-Study also available. Financial award application deadline: 2/1. *Faculty research:* Chinese and Japanese modern and classical literature, religions, linguistics, language pedagogy, premodern and contemporary fiction, sociolinguistics. Total annual research expenditures: $819,946.

University of Hawaii at Manoa, Graduate Division, College of Language, Linguistics and Literature, Department of East Asian Languages and Literatures, Program in Japanese, Honolulu, HI 96822. Offers MA, PhD. Part-time programs available. *Faculty:* 14 full-time (7 women), 4 part-time/adjunct (2 women). *Students:* 36 full-time (26 women), 8 part-time (3 women); includes 16 minority (all Asian Americans or Pacific Islanders), 12 international. Average age 30. 28 applicants, 39% accepted, 5 enrolled. In 2009, 6 master's, 4 doctorates awarded. *Degree requirements:* For master's, 2 foreign languages, thesis optional; for doctorate, 2 foreign languages, comprehensive exam, thesis/dissertation. *Entrance requirements:* For master's and doctorate, GRE General Test. Additional exam requirements/recommendations for international students: Required—TOEFL (minimum score 560 paper-based; 220 computer-based; 83 iBT), IELTS (minimum score 5). *Application deadline:* For fall admission, 2/1 for domestic and international students; for spring admission, 9/1 for domestic and international students. Application fee: $60. *Expenses:* Tuition, state resident: full-time $8900; part-time $372 per credit. Tuition, nonresident: full-time $21,400; part-time $898 per credit. Required fees: $207 per semester. *Financial support:* In 2009–10, 1 student received support, including 8 fellowships (averaging $4,450 per year), 2 research assistantships (averaging $18,210 per year), 9 teaching assistantships (averaging $14,638 per year). Total annual research expenditures: $5,000. *Application contact:* Dina Yoshimi, Graduate Chair, 808-956-2069, Fax: 808-956-9515, E-mail: dinar@hawaii.edu.

University of Hawaii at Manoa, Graduate Division, School of Pacific and Asian Studies, Program in Asian Studies, Concentration in Japanese Studies, Honolulu, HI 96822. Offers Graduate Certificate. Part-time programs available. In 2009, 3 Graduate Certificates awarded. *Degree requirements:* For Graduate Certificate, one foreign language. *Entrance requirements:* For degree, GRE. Additional exam requirements/recommendations for international students: Required—TOEFL (minimum score 560 paper-based; 220 computer-based; 83 iBT), IELTS (minimum score 5). Application fee: $60. *Expenses:* Tuition, state resident: full-time $8900; part-time $372 per credit. Tuition, nonresident: full-time $21,400; part-time $898 per credit. Required fees: $207 per semester. Total annual research expenditures: $649,000. *Application contact:* Robert Huey, Director, 808-956-2664, Fax: 808-956-2666, E-mail: huey@hawaii.edu.

University of Maryland, College Park, Academic Affairs, College of Arts and Humanities, School of Languages, Literature, and Cultures, Program in Second Language Acquisition and Application, College Park, MD 20742. Offers French (MA); German (MA); Japanese (MA); Russian (MA); second language instruction (PhD); second language learning (PhD); second language measurement and assessment (PhD); second language use (PhD); Spanish (MA). *Students:* 12 full-time (10 women), 5 part-time (3 women); includes 2 minority (both Asian Americans or Pacific Islanders), 5 international. 47 applicants, 15% accepted, 3 enrolled. In 2009, 7 master's awarded. *Entrance requirements:* For master's, BA or BS in related field, demonstrated language competency, 3 letters of reference. *Application deadline:* For fall admission, 1/15 for domestic and international students; for spring admission, 6/1 for domestic and international students. Applications are processed on a rolling basis. Application fee: $60. Electronic applications accepted. *Expenses:* Tuition, area resident: Part-time $471 per credit hour. Tuition, state resident: part-time $471 per credit hour. Tuition, nonresident: part-time $1016 per credit hour. Required fees: $337.04 per term. *Financial support:* In 2009–10, 2 fellowships with full and partial tuition reimbursements (averaging $13,928 per year), 4 research assistantships (averaging $21,457 per year), 6 teaching assistantships (averaging $20,933 per year) were awarded. *Faculty research:* Second language acquisition, pedagogical perspectives, technological applications, language use in professional contexts. *Unit head:* Carol Mossman, Director, School of Languages, Literatures, and Cultures, 301-405-4025, E-mail: cmossman@umd.edu. *Application contact:* Dean of Graduate School, 301-405-0376, Fax: 301-314-9305.

University of Massachusetts Amherst, Graduate School, College of Humanities and Fine Arts, Department of Languages, Literatures, and Cultures, Programs in Asian Languages and Literatures, Amherst, MA 01003. Offers Chinese (MA); Japanese (MA). Part-time programs available. *Faculty:* 8 full-time (4 women). *Students:* 17 full-time (14 women), 13 part-time (8 women); includes 7 minority (1 African American, 6 Asian Americans or Pacific Islanders), 12 international. Average age 29. 27 applicants, 74% accepted, 8 enrolled. In 2009, 9 master's awarded. *Degree requirements:* For master's, thesis, general exam. *Entrance requirements:* For master's, GRE General Test, minimum GPA of 3.0. Additional exam requirements/recommendations for international students: Required—TOEFL (minimum score 550 paper-based; 213 computer-based; 80 iBT), IELTS (minimum score 6.5). *Application deadline:* For fall admission, 2/1 for domestic and international students. Applications are processed on a rolling basis. Application fee: $50 ($65 for international students). Electronic applications

Japanese

University of Massachusetts Amherst (continued)

accepted. *Expenses:* Tuition, state resident: full-time $2640; part-time $110 per credit. Tuition, nonresident: full-time $9936; part-time $414 per credit. Tuition and fees vary according to course load. *Financial support:* In 2009–10, 21 teaching assistantships with full tuition reimbursements (averaging $7,431 per year) were awarded; fellowships, research assistantships, career-related internships or fieldwork, Federal Work-Study, scholarships/grants, traineeships, health care benefits, tuition waivers (full), and unspecified assistantships also available. Support available to part-time students. Financial award application deadline: 2/1. *Unit head:* Dr. Amanda C. Seaman, Director, 413-545-0886, Fax: 413-545-4975. *Application contact:* Jean M. Ames, Supervisor of Admissions, 413-545-0722, Fax: 413-577-0100, E-mail: gradadm@grad.umass.edu.

University of Oregon, Graduate School, College of Arts and Sciences, Department of East Asian Languages and Literature, Eugene, OR 97403. Offers Chinese (MA, PhD); Japanese (MA, PhD). *Entrance requirements:* Additional exam requirements/recommendations for international students: Required—TOEFL. *Faculty research:* Linguistics, pedagogy.

University of Washington, Graduate School, College of Arts and Sciences, Department of Asian Languages and Literature, Seattle, WA 98195. Offers Buddhist studies (MA, PhD); Chinese language and literature (MA, PhD); Japanese language and literature (MA, PhD); Korean language and literature (MA, PhD); South Asian language and literature (MA, PhD). *Degree requirements:* For master's, 2 foreign languages, general exam, thesis or 2 research papers; for doctorate, 3 foreign languages, thesis/dissertation, general exam. *Entrance requirements:* For master's, GRE, minimum GPA of 3.0; for doctorate, GRE, master's degree in related field, minimum GPA of 3.0. Additional exam requirements/recommendations for international students: Required—TOEFL. Electronic applications accepted. *Faculty research:* Textual, linguistic, philological, and literary study of languages and literatures of Asia.

University of Washington, Graduate School, College of Engineering, Department of Human Centered Design and Engineering, Seattle, WA 98195-2315. Offers interdisciplinary Japanese (MSE); user-centered design (MS, PhD). Part-time and evening/weekend programs available. *Faculty:* 12 full-time (7 women), 6 part-time/adjunct (2 women). *Students:* 53 full-time (33 women), 56 part-time (28 women); includes 20 minority (4 African Americans, 13 Asian Americans or Pacific Islanders, 3 Hispanic Americans), 10 international. Average age 34. 109 applicants, 69% accepted, 55 enrolled. In 2009, 28 master's, 1 doctorate awarded. *Degree requirements:* For master's, thesis or alternative; for doctorate, comprehensive exam, thesis/dissertation. *Entrance requirements:* For master's and doctorate, GRE General Test, minimum GPA of 3.0. Additional exam requirements/recommendations for international students: Required—TOEFL (minimum score 580 paper-based; 237 computer-based; 70 iBT). *Application deadline:* For fall admission, 2/1 for domestic students, 11/15 priority date for international students. Applications are processed on a rolling basis. Application fee: $65. Electronic applications accepted. *Financial support:* In 2009–10, 1 student received support, including 15 research assistantships with full tuition reimbursements available (averaging $14,400 per year), 16 teaching assistantships with full tuition reimbursements available (averaging $14,400 per year); fellowships with full tuition reimbursements available, career-related internships or fieldwork, institutionally sponsored loans, and tuition waivers (full) also available. Financial award application deadline: 2/28; financial award applicants required to submit FAFSA. *Faculty research:* Human-computer interaction, communication design, user interface design and usability, new media design, comprehension processes. Total annual research expenditures: $1.5 million. *Unit head:* Dr. Jan Spyridakis, Professor and Chair, 206-685-1557, Fax: 206-543-8858, E-mail: jansp@u.washington.edu. *Application contact:* Gian Bruno, Academic Counselor, 206-543-1798, Fax: 206-543-8858, E-mail: gbruno@u.washington.edu.

University of Wisconsin–Madison, Graduate School, College of Letters and Science, Department of East Asian Languages and Literature, Program in Japanese Linguistics, Madison, WI 53706-1380. Offers MA, PhD. Part-time programs available. Terminal master's awarded for partial completion of doctoral program. *Degree requirements:* For master's, one foreign language, seminars, written exam; for doctorate, 3 foreign languages, thesis/dissertation, seminars, preliminary exams, oral exam. *Entrance requirements:* For master's, GRE General Test, bachelor's degree or equivalent in Japanese; for doctorate, GRE General Test, master's degree or equivalent in Japanese. Electronic applications accepted. *Expenses:* Tuition, state resident: part-time $594 per credit. Tuition, nonresident: part-time $1504 per credit. Required fees: $65 per credit. Tuition and fees vary according to course load, program and reciprocity agreements. *Faculty research:* Modern and historical Japanese linguistics, modern Japanese fiction and poetry, classical Japanese literature, language pedagogy.

Washington University in St. Louis, Graduate School of Arts and Sciences, Department of Asian and Near Eastern Languages and Literatures, St. Louis, MO 63130-4899. Offers Chinese (MA); Chinese and comparative literature (PhD); Japanese (MA); Japanese and comparative literature (PhD). Terminal master's awarded for partial completion of doctoral program. *Degree requirements:* For master's, thesis optional; for doctorate, thesis/dissertation. *Entrance requirements:* For master's and doctorate, GRE General Test. Electronic applications accepted.

Near and Middle Eastern Languages

The American University in Cairo, Graduate Studies and Research, School of Humanities and Social Sciences, Department of Arabic Studies, Cairo, Egypt. Offers Arab language and literature (MA); Islamic art and architecture (MA); Islamic studies (Diploma); Middle East studies (MA, Diploma); Middle Eastern history (MA). Part-time programs available. *Degree requirements:* For master's, thesis optional, proficiency in French or German. *Entrance requirements:* Additional exam requirements/recommendations for international students: Required—English entrance exam and/or TOEFL. Electronic applications accepted. *Faculty research:* History of early Islam, Ayubbid, and Mamluk periods; nineteenth- and twentieth-century Middle East Islamic jurisprudence; contemporary Arabic literary criticism.

American University of Beirut, Graduate Programs, Faculty of Arts and Sciences, Beirut, Lebanon. Offers anthropology (MA); Arabic language and literature (MA); archaeology (MA); biology (MS); chemistry (MS); computer science (MS); economics (MA); education (MA); English language (MA); English literature (MA); environmental policy planning (MSES); financial economics (MAFE); geology (MS); history (MA); mathematics (MA, MS); Middle Eastern studies (MA); philosophy (MA); physics (MS); political studies (MA); psychology (MA); public administration (MA); sociology (MA); statistics (MA, MS). Part-time programs available. *Degree requirements:* For master's, one foreign language, comprehensive exam, thesis (for some programs). *Entrance requirements:* For master's, GRE, letter of recommendation. Additional exam requirements/recommendations for international students: Required—TOEFL (minimum score 600 paper-based; 250 computer-based; 100 iBT), IELTS (minimum score 7.5). *Faculty research:* String theory and supergravity; computer graphics; algebra and number theory; popular Arabic literature; marine and freshwater biology; integrating science, math and technology.

Brandeis University, Graduate School of Arts and Sciences, Department of Near Eastern and Judaic Studies, Waltham, MA 02454-9110. Offers Near Eastern and Judaic studies (MA, PhD); Near Eastern and Judaic studies and sociology (PhD); Near Eastern and Judaic studies and women's and gender studies (MA); teaching of Hebrew (MAT). Part-time programs available. *Faculty:* 26 full-time (11 women), 4 part-time/adjunct (1 woman). *Students:* 62 full-time (30 women), 1 part-time (0 women); includes 2 minority (1 African American, 1 Hispanic American), 7 international. Average age 33. 88 applicants, 67% accepted, 28 enrolled. In 2009, 10 master's, 6 doctorates awarded. Terminal master's awarded for partial completion of doctoral program. *Degree requirements:* For master's, one foreign language, comprehensive exam, thesis or alternative; for doctorate, 3 foreign languages, comprehensive exam, thesis/dissertation. *Entrance requirements:* For master's, GRE General Test (recommended), letters of recommendation; for doctorate, GRE General Test (recommended), letters of recommendation, transcripts, statement of purpose. Additional exam requirements/recommendations for international students: Required—TOEFL (minimum score 600 paper-based; 250 computer-based; 100 iBT); Recommended—IELTS (minimum score 7). *Application deadline:* For fall admission, 1/15 priority date for domestic and international students. Applications are processed on a rolling basis. Application fee: $75. Electronic applications accepted. *Financial support:* In 2009–10, 17 students received support, including 14 fellowships with full tuition reimbursements available (averaging $20,000 per year), 3 teaching assistantships with partial tuition reimbursements available (averaging $3,200 per year); research assistantships with full and partial tuition reimbursements available, scholarships/grants, health care benefits, and tuition waivers (full and partial) also available. Support available to part-time students. Financial award application deadline: 4/15; financial award applicants required to submit FAFSA. *Faculty research:* Ancient Near East and Bible, philosophy, history, modern Middle East, Islamic studies. *Unit head:* Dr. David Wright, Chair, 781-736-2954, Fax: 781-736-2070, E-mail: wright@brandeis.edu. *Application contact:* Joanne Arnish, Department Administrator, 781-736-2950, Fax: 781-736-2070, E-mail: arnish@brandeis.edu.

The Catholic University of America, School of Arts and Sciences, Department of Semitic and Egyptian Languages and Literature, Washington, DC 20064. Offers Ancient Near East (Biblical Hebrew/Aramaic) (MA); ancient Near East (Biblical Hebrew/Aramaic) (PhD); Arabic (PhD); Christian Near East (Biblical Hebrew/Aramaic) (MA); Coptic (MA, PhD); Syriac (MA). Part-time programs available. *Faculty:* 3 full-time (0 women), 2 part-time/adjunct (1 woman). *Students:* 14 full-time (5 women), 17 part-time (3 women); includes 4 minority (2 African Americans, 2 Asian Americans or Pacific Islanders), 4 international. Average age 36. 17 applicants, 88% accepted, 9 enrolled. In 2009, 2 master's, 1 doctorate awarded. *Degree requirements:* For master's, one foreign language, comprehensive exam; for doctorate, 2 foreign languages, comprehensive exam, thesis/dissertation. *Entrance requirements:* For master's, GRE General Test, 3 letters of recommendation; for doctorate, GRE General Test, statement of purpose, official copies of academic transcripts, three letters of recommendation. Additional exam requirements/recommendations for international students: Required—TOEFL (minimum score 580 paper-based; 237 computer-based). *Application deadline:* For fall admission, 8/1 priority date for domestic students, 7/15 for international students; for spring admission, 12/1 priority date for domestic students, 10/15 for international students. Applications are processed on a rolling basis. Application fee: $55. Electronic applications accepted. *Expenses:* Tuition: Full-time $31,740; part-time $1245 per credit hour. Required fees: $50; $25 per semester hour. One-time fee: $425. *Financial support:* Fellowships, research assistantships, teaching assistantships, Federal Work-Study, scholarships/grants, tuition waivers (full and partial), and unspecified assistantships available. Financial award application deadline: 2/1; financial award applicants required to submit FAFSA. *Faculty research:* Christian history and literature of the Near East, Biblical Hebrew, Arabic Christianity, Coptic, and Syriac. *Unit head:* Rev. Sidney H. Griffith, Chair, 202-319-5084, Fax: 202-319-4735, E-mail: griffith@cua.edu. *Application contact:* Julie Schwing, Director of Graduate Admissions, 202-319-5057, Fax: 202-319-6533, E-mail: cua-admissions@cua.edu.

Columbia University, Graduate School of Arts and Sciences, Division of Humanities, Department of Middle East Languages and Cultures, New York, NY 10027. Offers Hebrew language and literature (M Phil, MA, PhD); Middle Eastern languages and cultures (M Phil, MA, PhD); South Asian languages and cultures (M Phil, MA, PhD). Part-time programs available. *Degree requirements:* For master's, thesis, oral and written exams; for doctorate, 3 foreign languages, thesis/dissertation. *Entrance requirements:* For master's and doctorate, GRE General Test. Additional exam requirements/recommendations for international students: Required—TOEFL. *Faculty research:* Indo-Iranian, Turkish, central Asian, and Armenian studies; Arabic and ancient Semitics.

Georgetown University, Graduate School of Arts and Sciences, Department of Arabic and Islamic Studies, Washington, DC 20057. Offers Arabic area studies (PhD); Islamic studies (MA, PhD); linguistics (MA, PhD). *Degree requirements:* For master's, comprehensive exam, research project; for doctorate, one foreign language, comprehensive exam, thesis/dissertation. *Entrance requirements:* Additional exam requirements/recommendations for international students: Required—TOEFL.

Harvard University, Graduate School of Arts and Sciences, Department of Near Eastern Languages and Civilizations, Cambridge, MA 02138. Offers Akkadian and Sumerian (AM, PhD); Arabic (AM, PhD); Armenian (AM, PhD); biblical history (AM, PhD); Hebrew (AM, PhD); Indo-Muslim culture (AM, PhD); Iranian (AM, PhD); Jewish history and literature (AM, PhD); Persian (AM, PhD); Semitic philology (AM, PhD); Syro-Palestinian archaeology (AM, PhD); Turkish (AM, PhD). *Degree requirements:* For doctorate, variable foreign language requirement, thesis/dissertation, general exams. *Entrance requirements:* For master's, GRE General Test; for doctorate, GRE General Test, proficiency in a Near Eastern language. Additional exam requirements/recommendations for international students: Required—TOEFL. *Expenses:* Tuition: Full-time $33,696. Required fees: $1126. Full-time tuition and fees vary according to program.

Hebrew Union College–Jewish Institute of Religion, School of Graduate Studies, Program in Hebrew Letters, New York, NY 10012-1186. Offers DHL. *Degree requirements:* For doctorate, one foreign language, thesis/dissertation. *Entrance requirements:* For doctorate, GRE. Additional exam requirements/recommendations for international students: Required—TOEFL. *Expenses:* Contact institution. *Faculty research:* Philosophy and theology, Bible, Hebrew, pastoral care, history and Rabbinics.

Indiana University Bloomington, University Graduate School, College of Arts and Sciences, Department of Near Eastern Languages and Cultures, Bloomington, IN 47405-7000. Offers MA, PhD. Part-time programs available. *Faculty:* 5 full-time (2 women). *Students:* 46 full-time (19 women), 5 part-time (2 women); includes 2 minority (1 Asian American or Pacific Islander, 1 Hispanic American), 24 international. Average age 33. 52 applicants, 46% accepted, 11 enrolled. In 2009, 7 master's awarded. Terminal master's awarded for partial completion of doctoral program. *Degree requirements:* For master's, 2 foreign languages, thesis or alternative; for doctorate, 3 foreign languages, thesis/dissertation. *Entrance requirements:* For master's and doctorate, GRE General Test. Additional exam requirements/recommendations for international students: Required—TOEFL. *Application deadline:* For fall admission, 1/15 priority date for domestic students, 12/15 for international students; for spring admission, 9/1 priority date for domestic students, 9/1 for international students. Applications are processed on a rolling basis. Application fee: $55 ($65 for international students). *Financial support:* In 2009–10, 2 fellowships with full and partial tuition reimbursements (averaging $15,000 per year), 1 research assistantship with full and partial tuition reimbursement (averaging $15,900 per year), 11 teaching assistantships with full and partial tuition reimbursements (averaging $11,520 per year) were awarded; Federal Work-Study, institutionally sponsored loans, tuition waivers (full and partial), and unspecified assistantships also available. Financial award application deadline: 3/1; financial award applicants required to submit FAFSA. *Faculty research:* Classical and modern Arabic literature and linguistics, Biblical and modern Hebrew studies, Persian language and literature, Islamic civilization, Iranian history and language. *Unit head:* Dr. Nazif Shahrani, Chair, 812-855-4858. *Application contact:* Elaine Wright, Administrative Secretary, 812-855-5993.

The Ohio State University, Graduate School, College of Humanities, Department of Near Eastern Languages and Cultures, Columbus, OH 43210. Offers MA, PhD. *Faculty:* 19. *Students:* 21 full-time (8 women), 1 part-time (0 women); includes 2 minority (1 African American, 1 Asian American or Pacific Islander). Average age 28. In 2009, 3 master's awarded. *Degree requirements:* For master's, thesis optional. *Entrance requirements:* For master's and doctorate, GRE General Test. Additional exam requirements/recommendations for international students: Required—TOEFL (minimum score 600 paper-based; 250 computer-based). *Application deadline:* For fall admission, 8/15 priority date for domestic students, 7/1 priority date for international students; for winter admission, 12/1 priority date for domestic students, 11/1 priority date for international students; for spring admission, 3/1 priority date for domestic students, 2/1 priority date for international students. Applications are processed on a rolling basis. Application fee: $40 ($50 for international students). Electronic applications accepted. *Expenses:* Tuition, state resident: full-time $10,683. Tuition, nonresident: full-time $25,923. Tuition and fees vary according to course load and program. *Financial support:* Fellowships, research assistantships, teaching assistantships, Federal Work-Study and institutionally sponsored loans available. Support available to part-time students. *Unit head:* Sam Meier, Graduate Studies Committee Chair, E-mail: meier.3@osu.edu. *Application contact:* 614-292-9444, Fax: 614-292-3895, E-mail: domestic.grad@osu.edu.

Oral Roberts University, School of Theology and Missions, Tulsa, OK 74171. Offers biblical literature (MA), including advanced languages, Judaic-Christian studies; Christian counseling (MA), including marriage and family therapy; divinity (M Div); missions (MA); practical theology (MA); theological/historical studies (MA); theology (D Min). *Accreditation:* ATS; NASM. Part-time programs available. Postbaccalaureate distance learning degree programs offered (minimal on-campus study). *Degree requirements:* For master's, thesis (for some programs), practicum/internship; for doctorate, thesis/dissertation, applied research project; for M Div, one foreign language, field experience. *Entrance requirements:* For M Div and master's, GRE General Test or MAT, minimum GPA of 2.5; for doctorate, M Div, minimum GPA of 3.0, 3 years of full-time ministry experience. Additional exam requirements/recommendations for international students: Required—TOEFL (minimum score 550 paper-based; 213 computer-based; 79 iBT). Electronic applications accepted.

University of California, Los Angeles, Graduate Division, College of Letters and Science, Department of Near Eastern Languages and Cultures, Los Angeles, CA 90034. Offers MA, PhD. *Students:* 43 full-time (21 women); includes 2 minority (both Hispanic Americans), 2 international. Average age 29. 60 applicants, 23% accepted, 6 enrolled. In 2009, 9 master's, 2 doctorates awarded. *Degree requirements:* For master's, one foreign language, comprehensive exam; for doctorate, 2 foreign languages, thesis/dissertation, oral and written qualifying exams. *Entrance requirements:* For master's and doctorate, GRE General Test, minimum GPA of 3.25, sample of written work (recommended). Additional exam requirements/recommendations for international students: Required—TOEFL. *Application deadline:* For fall admission, 12/1 for domestic and international students. Application fee: $70 ($90 for international students). Electronic applications accepted. *Financial support:* In 2009–10, 30 fellowships with full and partial tuition reimbursements, 24 research assistantships with full and partial tuition reimbursements, 22 teaching assistantships with full and partial tuition reimbursements were awarded; Federal Work-Study, institutionally sponsored loans, scholarships/grants, health care benefits, tuition waivers (full and partial), and unspecified assistantships also available. Financial award application deadline: 3/1; financial award applicants required to submit FAFSA. *Unit head:* Dr. Elizabeth Carter, Chair, 310-206-5474. *Application contact:* Department Office, 310-825-4165, E-mail: nreast@humnet.ucla.edu.

University of Chicago, Division of the Humanities, Department of Near Eastern Languages and Civilizations, Chicago, IL 60637-1513. Offers AM, PhD. Terminal master's awarded for partial completion of doctoral program. *Degree requirements:* For master's, one foreign language, comprehensive exam, thesis; for doctorate, 2 foreign languages, comprehensive exam, thesis/dissertation. *Entrance requirements:* For master's and doctorate, GRE General Test. Additional exam requirements/recommendations for international students: Required—TOEFL.

University of Maryland, College Park, Academic Affairs, College of Arts and Humanities, The Arabic Flagship Program, College Park, MD 20742. Offers Graduate Certificate. *Students:* 10 full-time (2 women), 4 part-time (1 woman); includes 2 minority (1 African American, 1 Asian American or Pacific Islander). 72 applicants, 25% accepted, 6 enrolled. *Application deadline:* For fall admission, 1/14 for domestic and international students. *Expenses:* Tuition, area resident: Part-time $471 per credit hour. Tuition, state resident: part-time $471 per credit hour. Tuition, nonresident: part-time $1016 per credit hour. Required fees: $337.04 per term. *Unit head:* Ridha Krizi, Graduate Flagship Program Coordinator, 301-405-7492, E-mail: rkrizi@umd.edu. *Application contact:* Dean of Graduate School, 301-405-0376, Fax: 301-314-9305.

University of Maryland, College Park, Academic Affairs, College of Arts and Humanities, The Persian Flagship Program, College Park, MD 20742. Offers MPS, Graduate Certificate. *Students:* 11 full-time (3 women), 1 part-time (0 women); includes 2 Asian Americans or Pacific Islanders. 24 applicants, 92% accepted, 12 enrolled. In 2009, 5 master's awarded. *Application deadline:* For fall admission, 3/15 for domestic and international students. Applications are processed on a rolling basis. Application fee: $60. Electronic applications accepted. *Expenses:* Tuition, area resident: Part-time $471 per credit hour. Tuition, state resident: part-time $471 per credit hour. Tuition, nonresident: part-time $1016 per credit hour. Required fees: $337.04 per term. *Financial support:* In 2009–10, 1 fellowship with partial tuition reimbursement (averaging $10,000 per year) was awarded. *Unit head:* Dr. Ahmad Karimi-Hakkak, Professor and Director of the Center for Persian Studies, 301-405-3147, E-mail: karimi@umd.edu. *Application contact:* Dean of Graduate School, 301-405-0376, Fax: 301-314-9305.

University of Michigan, Horace H. Rackham School of Graduate Studies, College of Literature, Science, and the Arts, Department of Near Eastern Studies, Ann Arbor, MI 48109. Offers ancient Near Eastern studies (AM, PhD); Arabic for professional purposes (AM); Arabic language and literature (AM, PhD); Armenian studies (AM, PhD); Christianity in late antiquity (AM, PhD); Egyptology (AM, PhD); Hebrew Bible and ancient Israel (AM, PhD); Hebrew literature (AM, PhD); Islamic studies (AM, PhD); Jewish cultural studies (AM, PhD); Jewish mysticism (AM, PhD); Persian and Iranian studies (AM, PhD); Rabbinic literature (AM, PhD); Second Temple Judaism (AM, PhD); teaching of Arabic as a foreign language (AM); Turkish studies (AM, PhD). Part-time programs available. *Faculty:* 23 full-time (5 women), 15 part-time/adjunct (6 women). *Students:* 47 full-time (23 women), 1 part-time (0 women); includes 1 minority (Hispanic American), 8 international. Average age 31. 99 applicants, 15% accepted, 8 enrolled. In 2009, 4 master's, 4 doctorates awarded. Terminal master's awarded for partial completion of doctoral program. *Degree requirements:* For master's, 2 foreign languages; for doctorate, 4 foreign languages, comprehensive exam, thesis/dissertation. *Entrance requirements:* For master's, GRE General Test; for doctorate, GRE General Test, master's degree. Additional exam requirements/recommendations for international students: Required—TOEFL (minimum score 560 paper-based; 220 computer-based; 84 iBT). *Application deadline:* For fall admission, 12/15 for domestic and international students. Application fee: $60 ($75 for international students). Electronic applications accepted. *Expenses:* Tuition, state resident: full-time $17,286; part-time $1099 per credit hour. Tuition, nonresident: full-time $34,944; part-time $2080 per credit hour. Required fees: $95 per semester. Tuition and fees vary according to course load, degree level and program. *Financial support:* In 2009–10, 43 students received support, including 21 fellowships with full tuition reimbursements available (averaging $16,694 per year), research assistantships with tuition reimbursements available (averaging $16,694 per year), 22 teaching assistantships with full tuition reimbursements available (averaging $16,694 per year); scholarships/grants, health care benefits, unspecified assistantships, and spring/summer stipends also available. *Faculty research:* Middle and Near Eastern literatures, languages, cultures from ancient times to the present. *Unit head:* Prof. Michael Bonner, Chair, 734-764-0314, Fax: 734-936-2679, E-mail: mbonner@umich.edu. *Application contact:* Angela Beskow, Student Services Assistant, 734-763-4539, Fax: 734-936-2679, E-mail: aradjews@umich.edu.

University of South Africa, College of Human Sciences, Pretoria, South Africa. Offers adult education (M Ed); African languages (MA, PhD); African politics (MA, PhD); Afrikaans (MA, PhD); ancient history (MA, PhD); ancient Near Eastern studies (MA, PhD); anthropology (MA, PhD); applied linguistics (MA); Arabic (MA, PhD); archaeology (MA); art history (MA); Biblical archaeology (MA); Biblical studies (M Th, D Th, PhD); Christian spirituality (M Th, D Th); church history (M Th, D Th); classical studies (MA, PhD); clinical psychology (MA); communication (MA, PhD); comparative education (M Ed, Ed D); consulting psychology (D Admin, D Com, PhD); curriculum studies (M Ed, Ed D); development studies (M Admin, MA, D Admin, PhD); didactics (M Ed, Ed D); education (M Tech); education management (M Ed, Ed D); educational psychology (M Ed); English (MA); environmental education (M Ed); French (MA, PhD); German (MA, PhD); Greek (MA); guidance and counseling (M Ed); health studies (MA, PhD), including health sciences education (MA), health services management (MA), medical and surgical nursing science (critical care general) (MA), midwifery and neonatal nursing science (MA), trauma and emergency care (MA); history (MA, PhD); history of education (Ed D); inclusive education (M Ed, Ed D); information and communications technology policy and regulation (MA); information science (MA, MIS, PhD); international politics (MA, PhD); Islamic studies (MA, PhD); Italian (MA, PhD); Judaica (MA, PhD); linguistics (MA, PhD); mathematical education (M Ed); mathematics education (MA); missiology (M Th, D Th); modern Hebrew (MA, PhD); musicology (MA, MMus, D Mus, PhD); natural science education (M Ed); New Testament (M Th, D Th); Old Testament (D Th); pastoral therapy (M Th, D Th); philosophy (MA); philosophy of education (M Ed, Ed D); politics (MA, PhD); Portuguese (MA, PhD); practical theology (M Th, D Th); psychology (MA, MS, PhD); psychology of education (M Ed, Ed D); public health (MA); religious studies (MA, D Th, PhD); Romance languages (MA); Russian (MA, PhD); Semitic languages (MA, PhD); social behavior studies in HIV/AIDS (MA); social science (mental health) (MA); social science in development studies (MA); social science in psychology (MA); social science in social work (MA); social science in sociology (MA); social work (MSW, DSW, PhD); socio-education (M Ed, Ed D); sociolinguistics (MA); sociology (MA, PhD); Spanish (MA, PhD); systematic theology (M Th, D Th); TESOL (teaching English to speakers of other languages) (MA); theological ethics (M Th, D Th); theory of literature (MA, PhD); urban ministries (D Th); urban ministry (M Th).

The University of Texas at Austin, Graduate School, College of Liberal Arts, Department of Middle Eastern Studies, Austin, TX 78712-1111. Offers Arabic (MA, PhD); Hebrew (MA). *Degree requirements:* For master's, one foreign language, comprehensive exam, thesis; for doctorate, 2 foreign languages, comprehensive exam, thesis/dissertation. *Entrance requirements:* For master's and doctorate, GRE General Test. Additional exam requirements/recommendations for international students: Required—TOEFL. Electronic applications accepted. *Faculty research:* Islamic studies, Persian language and literature, Hebrew language, Jewish studies, Arabic literature and language.

University of Utah, The Graduate School, College of Humanities, Program in Middle East Studies, Salt Lake City, UT 84112. Offers anthropology (MA); Arabic (MA, PhD); Arabic and linguistics (MA, PhD); Hebrew (MA); history (MA, PhD); Persian (MA, PhD); political science (MA, PhD); Turkish (MA). *Students:* 24 full-time (8 women), 19 part-time (9 women), 13 international. Average age 33. 33 applicants, 48% accepted, 10 enrolled. In 2009, 8 master's, 2 doctorates awarded. Terminal master's awarded for partial completion of doctoral program. *Degree requirements:* For master's, 2 foreign languages, comprehensive exam, thesis optional; for doctorate, 3 foreign languages, comprehensive exam, thesis/dissertation. *Entrance requirements:* For master's, GRE General Test, minimum GPA of 3.2; for doctorate, GRE General Test, MA in Middle East studies or equivalent, minimum GPA of 3.2. Additional exam requirements/recommendations for international students: Required—TOEFL (minimum score 580 paper-based; 237 computer-based; 92 iBT). *Application deadline:* For fall admission, 1/15 priority date for domestic and international students; for spring admission, 9/15 priority date for domestic and international students. Application fee: $55 ($65 for international students). Electronic applications accepted. *Expenses:* Tuition, state resident: full-time $4004; part-time $1674 per semester. Tuition, nonresident: full-time $14,134; part-time $5915 per semester. Required fees: $324 per semester. Tuition and fees vary according to course load, degree level and program. *Financial support:* In 2009–10, 19 students received support, including 15 fellowships with full tuition reimbursements available (averaging $14,000 per year), 3 teaching assistantships with full tuition reimbursements available (averaging $12,000 per year); unspecified assistantships also available. Financial award application deadline: 1/15. *Faculty research:* Arabic linguistics; Islamic studies; Middle Eastern history; political science; Judaic studies; anthropology; Arabic, Persian, Hebrew, and Turkish language and literature. *Unit head:* Dr. Bahman Baktiari, Director, 801-581-6181, Fax: 801-581-6183, E-mail: b.baktiari@utah.edu. *Application contact:* Peter von Sivers, Director of Graduate Studies, 801-581-9028, Fax: 801-581-6183, E-mail: peter.vonsivers@utah.edu.

University of Wisconsin–Madison, Graduate School, College of Letters and Science, Department of Hebrew and Semitic Studies, Madison, WI 53706-1380. Offers MA, PhD. Terminal master's awarded for partial completion of doctoral program. *Degree requirements:* For master's, 2 foreign languages; for doctorate, thesis/dissertation. *Entrance requirements:* For master's and doctorate, GRE. Electronic applications accepted. *Expenses:* Tuition, state resident: part-time $594 per credit. Tuition, nonresident: part-time $1504 per credit. Required fees: $65 per credit. Tuition and fees vary according to course load, program and reciprocity agreements. *Faculty research:* Biblical language and literature, Northwest Semitic languages.

Yale University, Graduate School of Arts and Sciences, Department of Near Eastern Languages and Civilizations, New Haven, CT 06520. Offers Arabic and Islamic studies (MA, PhD); archaeology of the ancient Near East (MA, PhD); Assyriology (MA, PhD); Egyptology (MA, PhD); Graeco-Arabic studies (MA, PhD); Northwest Semitic, Bible, comparative Semitics (MA, PhD). *Degree requirements:* For doctorate, 2 foreign languages, thesis/dissertation. *Entrance requirements:* For doctorate, GRE General Test.

Portuguese

Brigham Young University, Graduate Studies, College of Humanities, Department of Spanish and Portuguese, Provo, UT 84602. Offers hispanic literature (MA); Portuguese linguistics (MA); Portuguese literature (MA); Spanish linguistics (MA); Spanish teaching (MA). Part-time programs available. *Faculty:* 32 full-time (5 women). *Students:* 18 full-time (7 women), 21 part-time (10 women); includes 5 minority (all Hispanic Americans), 9 international. Average age 30. 25 applicants, 56% accepted, 14 enrolled. In 2009, 17 master's awarded. *Degree requirements:* For master's, one foreign language, comprehensive exam, thesis, 1 semester of teaching. *Entrance requirements:* For master's, minimum GPA of 3.5 in Spanish or Portuguese, 3.3 overall. Additional exam requirements/recommendations for international students: Required—TOEFL (minimum score 580 paper-based; 237 computer-based). *Application deadline:* For fall admission, 2/1 for domestic and international students. Application fee: $50. Electronic applications accepted. *Expenses:* Tuition: Full-time $5580; part-time $301 per credit hour. Tuition and fees vary according to student's religious affiliation. *Financial support:* In 2009–10, 39 students received support, including 39 teaching assistantships with partial tuition reimbursements available (averaging $8,787 per year); institutionally sponsored loans, scholarships/grants, tuition waivers (partial), and unspecified assistantships also available. Support available to part-time students. Financial award application deadline: 7/1. *Faculty research:* Mexican prose; Latin American theater, literature, phonetics, and phonology; pedagogy; classical Portuguese literature; Peninsular prose and theater. *Unit head:* Dr. Alvin F. Sherman, Chair, 801-422-3107, Fax: 801-422-0628, E-mail: alvin_sherman@byu.edu. *Application contact:* Arwen T. Wyatt, Graduate Secretary, 801-422-2196, Fax: 801-422-0628, E-mail: arwen_wyatt@byu.edu.

Emory University, Graduate School of Arts and Sciences, Department of Spanish and Portuguese, Atlanta, GA 30322-1100. Offers comparative literature (Certificate); film studies (Certificate); Spanish (PhD); women's studies (Certificate). *Degree requirements:* For doctorate, 2 foreign languages, comprehensive exam, thesis/dissertation. *Entrance requirements:* For doctorate, GRE General Test. Additional exam requirements/recommendations for international students: Required—TOEFL. Electronic applications accepted. *Faculty research:* Spanish literature, Spanish-American literature, literary theory, criticism, cultural studies.

Harvard University, Graduate School of Arts and Sciences, Department of Romance Languages and Literatures, Cambridge, MA 02138. Offers French (AM, PhD); Italian (AM, PhD); Portuguese (AM, PhD); Spanish (AM, PhD). Terminal master's awarded for partial completion of doctoral program. *Degree requirements:* For master's, 2 foreign languages; for doctorate, 2 foreign languages, thesis/dissertation. *Entrance requirements:* For master's and doctorate, GRE General Test, sample of written work. Additional exam requirements/recommendations for international students: Required—TOEFL. *Expenses:* Tuition: Full-time $33,696. Required fees: $1126. Full-time tuition and fees vary according to program.

Indiana University Bloomington, University Graduate School, College of Arts and Sciences, Department of Spanish and Portuguese, Bloomington, IN 47405-7000. Offers Hispanic linguistics (MA, PhD); Hispanic literature (MA); Luso-Brazilian literature (MA); Luso-Brazilian studies (PhD); Spanish literatures (PhD); teaching Spanish (MAT). *Faculty:* 18 full-time (10 women). *Students:* 84 full-time (47 women), 2 part-time (0 women); includes 17 minority (1 Asian American or Pacific Islander, 16 Hispanic Americans), 18 international. Average age 30. 55 applicants, 62% accepted, 15 enrolled. In 2009, 10 master's, 4 doctorates awarded. *Degree requirements:* For master's, one foreign language; for doctorate, 3 foreign languages, thesis/dissertation. *Entrance requirements:* For master's, GRE General Test, GRE Subject Test, bachelor's degree in Portuguese or Spanish, minimum GPA of 3.25; for doctorate, GRE General Test, GRE Subject Test, master's degree in Portuguese or Spanish, minimum GPA of 3.25. Additional exam requirements/recommendations for international students: Required—TOEFL. *Application deadline:* For fall admission, 1/15 priority date for domestic students, 12/15 for international students; for spring admission, 9/1 for domestic and international students. Application fee: $55 ($65 for international students). *Financial support:* In 2009–10, 1 fellowship with full tuition reimbursement (averaging $15,000 per year); 72 teaching assistantships with full tuition reimbursements (averaging $14,790 per year) were awarded; research assistantships, Federal Work-Study also available. Financial award application deadline: 1/15. *Faculty research:* Spanish-American literature, Spanish peninsular literature, Luso-Brazilian studies, Catalan studies. *Unit head:* Josep Miguel Sobrer, Chair, 812-855-8498. *Application contact:* Steven Wagschal, Student Contact, 812-855-9194, E-mail: swagscha@indiana.edu.

Michigan State University, The Graduate School, College of Arts and Letters, Department of Spanish and Portuguese, East Lansing, MI 48824. Offers applied Spanish linguistics (MA); Hispanic cultural studies (PhD); Hispanic literatures (MA). *Faculty:* 14 full-time (7 women). *Students:* 26 full-time (17 women), 3 part-time (2 women); includes 10 minority (1 African American, 1 Asian American or Pacific Islander, 8 Hispanic Americans), 6 international. Average age 31. 23 applicants, 39% accepted. In 2009, 4 master's, 6 doctorates awarded. *Entrance requirements:* Additional exam requirements/recommendations for international students: Required—TOEFL. Electronic applications accepted. *Expenses:* Tuition, state resident: part-time $478.25 per credit hour. Tuition, nonresident: part-time $966.50 per credit hour. Part-time tuition and fees vary according to program. *Financial support:* In 2009–10, 20 teaching assistantships with tuition reimbursements (averaging $6,017 per year) were awarded. *Unit head:* Dr. Douglas Noverr, Acting Chairperson, 517-353-4939, Fax: 517-432-3844, E-mail: noverr@msu.edu. *Application contact:* Victoria Reynaga, Graduate Secretary, 517-355-8350, Fax: 517-432-3844, E-mail: reynagav@cal.msu.edu.

New York University, Graduate School of Arts and Science, Department of Spanish and Portuguese Languages and Literatures, New York, NY 10012-1019. Offers Portuguese (MA, PhD); Spanish (PhD); Spanish and Latin American literatures and cultures (MA); Spanish language and translation (MA). Part-time programs available. *Students:* 105 full-time (66 women), 5 part-time (4 women); includes 41 minority (5 African Americans, 4 Asian Americans or Pacific Islanders, 32 Hispanic Americans), 40 international. Average age 31. 193 applicants, 48% accepted, 50 enrolled. In 2009, 34 master's, 5 doctorates awarded. *Degree requirements:* For master's, 2 foreign languages, thesis; for doctorate, 2 foreign languages, thesis/dissertation. *Entrance requirements:* For master's, GRE General Test; for doctorate, GRE General Test, master's degree. Additional exam requirements/recommendations for international students: Required—TOEFL. *Application deadline:* For fall admission, 1/4 priority date for domestic students. Application fee: $90. *Expenses:* Tuition: Full-time $30,528; part-time $1272 per credit. Required fees: $2177. *Financial support:* Fellowships with tuition reimbursements, teaching assistantships with tuition reimbursements, career-related internships or fieldwork, Federal Work-Study, institutionally sponsored loans, scholarships/grants, health care benefits, and unspecified assistantships available. Financial award application deadline: 1/4; financial award applicants required to submit FAFSA. *Faculty research:* Gender and sexuality, transatlantic studies, literacy and cultural theories, colonial and post colonial studies, autobiography and modern subjectivities. *Unit head:* Sibylle Fischer, Chair, 212-998-8770, Fax: 212-995-4149, E-mail: spanish.portuguese.info@nyu.edu. *Application contact:* Jo Labanyi, Director of Graduate Studies, 212-998-8770, Fax: 212-995-4149, E-mail: spanish.portuguese.info@nyu.edu.

The Ohio State University, Graduate School, College of Humanities, Department of Spanish and Portuguese, Columbus, OH 43210. Offers MA, PhD. *Faculty:* 22. *Students:* 51 full-time (35 women), 16 part-time (11 women); includes 10 minority (all Hispanic Americans), 17 international. Average age 30. In 2009, 6 master's, 3 doctorates awarded. *Degree requirements:* For master's, thesis optional; for doctorate, thesis/dissertation. *Entrance requirements:* For master's and doctorate, GRE General Test. Additional exam requirements/recommendations for international students: Required—TOEFL (minimum score 600 paper-based; 250 computer-based). *Application deadline:* For fall admission, 8/15 priority date for domestic students, 7/1 priority date for international students; for winter admission, 12/1 priority date for domestic students, 11/1 priority date for international students; for spring admission, 3/1 priority date for domestic students, 2/1 priority date for international students. Applications are processed on a rolling basis. Application fee: $40 ($50 for international students). Electronic applications accepted. *Expenses:* Tuition, state resident: full-time $10,683. Tuition, nonresident: full-time $25,923. Tuition and fees vary according to course load and program. *Financial support:* Fellowships, research assistantships, teaching assistantships, Federal Work-Study, institutionally sponsored loans, and unspecified assistantships available. Support available to part-time students. *Unit head:* Laura Podalsky, Graduate Studies Committee Chair, E-mail: podalsky.1@osu.edu. *Application contact:* 614-292-9444, Fax: 614-292-3895, E-mail: domestic.grad@osu.edu.

Princeton University, Graduate School, Department of Spanish and Portuguese Languages and Cultures, Princeton, NJ 08544-1019. Offers PhD. *Degree requirements:* For doctorate, variable foreign language requirement, thesis/dissertation. *Entrance requirements:* For doctorate, GRE General Test, sample of written work. Additional exam requirements/recommendations for international students: Required—TOEFL (minimum score 600 paper-based; 250 computer-based). Electronic applications accepted.

Tulane University, School of Liberal Arts, Department of Spanish and Portuguese, New Orleans, LA 70118-5669. Offers Portuguese (MA); Spanish (MA); Spanish and Portuguese (PhD). *Degree requirements:* For master's, 2 foreign languages; for doctorate, 2 foreign languages, thesis/dissertation. *Entrance requirements:* For master's, GRE General Test, minimum B average in undergraduate course work; for doctorate, GRE General Test. Additional exam requirements/recommendations for international students: Required—TOEFL. Electronic applications accepted.

University of California, Los Angeles, Graduate Division, College of Letters and Science, Department of Spanish and Portuguese, Program in Portuguese, Los Angeles, CA 90095. Offers MA. *Students:* 4 applicants, 0% accepted, 0 enrolled. In 2009, 1 master's awarded. *Degree requirements:* For master's, one foreign language, comprehensive exam or thesis. *Entrance requirements:* For master's, GRE General Test, minimum GPA of 3.0, sample of written work (recommended). *Application deadline:* For fall admission, 12/31 for domestic and international students. Application fee: $70 ($90 for international students). Electronic applications accepted. *Financial support:* In 2009–10, 1 fellowship with full and partial tuition reimbursement, 1 research assistantship with full and partial tuition reimbursement, 1 teaching assistantship with full and partial tuition reimbursement were awarded; Federal Work-Study, scholarships/grants, health care benefits, tuition waivers (full and partial), and unspecified assistantships also available. Financial award applicants required to submit FAFSA. *Unit head:* Dr. Maarten Van Delden, Chair, 310-825-1220. *Application contact:* Department Office, 310-825-1036, E-mail: peinado@humnet.ucla.edu.

University of California, Santa Barbara, Graduate Division, College of Letters and Sciences, Division of Humanities and Fine Arts, Department of Spanish and Portuguese, Santa Barbara, CA 93106-4150. Offers Hispanic languages and literature (PhD), including applied linguistics, European Medieval studies, feminist studies, Hispanic languages and literature; Portuguese (MA); Spanish (MA); Spanish and Portuguese (MA); MA/PhD. Spanish Language Institute available during summer session. *Faculty:* 16 full-time (6 women). *Students:* 29 full-time (16 women). Average age 30. 46 applicants, 39% accepted, 9 enrolled. In 2009, 4 master's, 2 doctorates awarded. *Degree requirements:* For master's, 2 foreign languages, comprehensive exam (for some programs), thesis optional; for doctorate, 2 foreign languages, comprehensive exam, thesis/dissertation. *Entrance requirements:* For master's, GRE, 2 writing samples, undergraduate major in Spanish or equivalent, 3 letters of recommendation, resume/curriculum vitae; for doctorate, GRE, 2 writing samples, master's degree, 3 letters of recommendation, statement of purpose, personal achievements/contributions statement, resume/curriculum vitae, transcripts for post-secondary institutions attended. Additional exam requirements/recommendations for international students: Required—TOEFL (minimum score 550 paper-based; 213 computer-based; 80 iBT), or IELTS (minimum score 7). *Application deadline:* For fall admission, 3/1 for domestic and international students; for winter admission, 11/1 for domestic and international students; for spring admission, 2/1 for domestic and international students. Application fee: $70 ($90 for international students). Electronic applications accepted. *Financial support:* In 2009–10, 9 fellowships with full and partial tuition reimbursements (averaging $7,000 per year), 29 teaching assistantships with partial tuition reimbursements (averaging $11,500 per year) were awarded; career-related internships or fieldwork, Federal Work-Study, institutionally sponsored loans, scholarships/grants, health care benefits, tuition waivers (full and partial), and unspecified assistantships also available. Financial award application deadline: 1/7; financial award applicants required to submit FAFSA. *Faculty research:* Nineteenth century Spanish and Portuguese literature, Spanish and Spanish American literature, nineteenth and twentieth century Portuguese and Brazilian literatures, Hispanic linguistics, Catalan language and culture. *Unit head:* Prof. Francisco A. Lomeli, Chair, 805-893-5715, Fax: 805-893-8341, E-mail: lomeli@spanport.ucsb.edu. *Application contact:* Carol Conley, Graduate Program Assistant, 805-893-3162, Fax: 805-893-8341, E-mail: cconley@spanport.ucsb.edu.

University of Illinois at Urbana–Champaign, Graduate College, College of Liberal Arts and Sciences, School of Literatures, Cultures and Linguistics, Department of Spanish, Italian and Portuguese, Champaign, IL 61820. Offers Italian (MA, PhD); Portuguese (MA, PhD); Spanish (MA, PhD). *Faculty:* 18 full-time (11 women). *Students:* 46 full-time (35 women), 10 part-time (7 women); includes 15 minority (1 Asian American or Pacific Islander, 14 Hispanic Americans), 28 international. 46 applicants, 41% accepted, 12 enrolled. In 2009, 7 master's, 11 doctorates awarded. *Entrance requirements:* For master's, GRE General Test, minimum GPA of 3.0; writing sample; for doctorate, GRE, minimum GPA of 3.0; writing sample. Additional exam requirements/recommendations for international students: Required—TOEFL (minimum score 88 iBT). *Application deadline:* Applications are processed on a rolling basis. Application fee: $60 ($75 for international students). Electronic applications accepted. *Financial support:* In 2009–10, 10 fellowships, 3 research assistantships, 51 teaching assistantships were awarded; tuition waivers (full and partial) also available. *Unit head:* Diane Musumeci, Head, 217-333-3390, Fax: 217-244-8430, E-mail: musumeci@illinois.edu. *Application contact:* Lynn Stanke, Office Support Specialist, 217-333-6269, Fax: 217-244-3050, E-mail: stanke@illinois.edu.

University of Maryland, College Park, Academic Affairs, College of Arts and Humanities, School of Languages, Literature, and Cultures, Department of Spanish and Portuguese, College Park, MD 20742. Offers MA, PhD. *Students:* 31 full-time (25 women), 4 part-time (2 women); includes 7 minority (1 Asian American or Pacific Islander, 6 Hispanic Americans), 19 international. 51 applicants, 33% accepted, 8 enrolled. In 2009, 6 master's, 2 doctorates awarded. *Degree requirements:* For master's, comprehensive exam, thesis optional, scholarly paper; for doctorate, 2 foreign languages, thesis/dissertation. *Entrance requirements:* For master's, minimum GPA of 3.0, interview, sample research paper, minimum of 12 credits in upper-level literature, 3 letters of recommendation; for doctorate, minimum GPA of 3.0, interview, sample research paper, minimum of 12 credits in upper-level literature. Additional exam requirements/recommendations for international students: Required—TOEFL. *Application deadline:* For fall admission, 1/7 for domestic and international students. Applications are processed on a rolling basis. Application fee: $60. Electronic applications accepted. *Expenses:* Tuition, area resident: Part-time $471 per credit hour. Tuition, state resident: part-time $471 per credit hour. Tuition, nonresident: part-time $1016 per credit hour. Required fees: $337.04 per term. *Financial support:* In 2009–10, 4 fellowships with partial tuition reimbursements (averaging $8,873 per year), 20 teaching assistantships with tuition reimbursements (averaging $18,776 per year) were awarded; Federal Work-Study also available. Support available to part-time students. Financial award applicants required to submit FAFSA. *Unit head:* Carol Mossman, Director, School of Languages, Literatures, and Cultures, 301-405-4025, E-mail: cmossman@umd.edu. *Application contact:* Dean of Graduate School, 301-405-0358, Fax: 301-314-9305.

University of Massachusetts Amherst, Graduate School, College of Humanities and Fine Arts, Department of Languages, Literatures, and Cultures, Programs in Hispanic Literatures,

Cultures and Linguistics, Amherst, MA 01003. Offers Hispanic literatures, cultures and linguistics (MA, PhD); teaching Spanish (MAT). Part-time programs available. *Faculty:* 11 full-time (5 women). *Students:* 22 full-time (18 women), 30 part-time (18 women); includes 14 minority (1 Asian American or Pacific Islander, 13 Hispanic Americans), 19 international. Average age 34. In 2009, 4 master's, 1 doctorate awarded. Terminal master's awarded for partial completion of doctoral program. *Degree requirements:* For master's, one foreign language, thesis or alternative; for doctorate, 2 foreign languages, comprehensive exam, thesis/dissertation. *Entrance requirements:* For master's and doctorate, GRE General Test, sample academic term paper. Additional exam requirements/recommendations for international students: Required—TOEFL (minimum score 550 paper-based; 213 computer-based; 80 iBT), IELTS (minimum score 6.5). *Application deadline:* For fall admission, 2/1 for domestic and international students. Applications are processed on a rolling basis. Application fee: $50 ($65 for international students). Electronic applications accepted. *Expenses:* Tuition, state resident: full-time $2640; part-time $110 per credit. Tuition, nonresident: full-time $9936; part-time $414 per credit. Tuition and fees vary according to course load. *Financial support:* In 2009–10, 36 teaching assistantships with full tuition reimbursements (averaging $14,427 per year) were awarded; fellowships, research assistantships, career-related internships or fieldwork, Federal Work-Study, scholarships/grants, traineeships, health care benefits, tuition waivers (full), and unspecified assistantships also available. Support available to part-time students. Financial award application deadline: 2/1. *Unit head:* Dr. Frank C. Fagundes, Graduate Program Director, 413-545-0544, Fax: 413-545-3178. *Application contact:* Jean M. Ames, Supervisor of Admissions, 413-545-0722, Fax: 413-577-0010, E-mail: gradadm@grad.umass.edu.

University of Massachusetts Dartmouth, Graduate School, College of Arts and Sciences, Department of Portuguese, North Dartmouth, MA 02747-2300. Offers Luso-Afro-Brazilian studies (PhD); Portuguese (MA). Part-time programs available. *Faculty:* 6 full-time (2 women), 2 part-time/adjunct (0 women). *Students:* 9 full-time (7 women), 11 part-time (7 women); includes 4 minority (1 African American, 3 Hispanic Americans), 4 international. Average age 36. 12 applicants, 83% accepted, 5 enrolled. In 2009, 2 master's awarded. *Degree requirements:* For master's, comprehensive exam (for some programs). *Entrance requirements:* For master's, GRE (recommended), 10 page writing sample; for doctorate, GRE. Additional exam requirements/recommendations for international students: Required—TOEFL (minimum score 500 paper-based). *Application deadline:* For fall admission, 4/20 priority date for domestic students, 2/20 priority date for international students; for spring admission, 11/15 priority date for domestic students, 9/15 priority date for international students. Applications are processed on a rolling basis. Application fee: $40 ($60 for international students). Electronic applications accepted. *Expenses:* Tuition, state resident: full-time $2071; part-time $86.29 per credit. Tuition, nonresident: full-time $8099; part-time $337.46 per credit. Required fees: $9446. Tuition and fees vary according to class time, course load and reciprocity agreements. *Financial support:* In 2009–10, 2 research assistantships with full tuition reimbursements (averaging $18,558 per year), 8 teaching assistantships with full tuition reimbursements (averaging $15,000 per year) were awarded. Financial award application deadline: 3/1; financial award applicants required to submit FAFSA. *Faculty research:* Translation studies, ethnicity and migration, literature in Luso-Afro-Brazilian studies, anaphoric direct objects in Portuguese. *Unit head:* Victor J. Mendes, Director, Graduate Studies, 508-999-8338, Fax: 508-999-9272, E-mail: vmendes@umassd.edu. *Application contact:* Elan Turcotte-Shamski, Graduate Admissions Officer, 508-999-8604, Fax: 508-999-8183, E-mail: graduate@umassd.edu.

University of Minnesota, Twin Cities Campus, Graduate School, College of Liberal Arts, Department of Spanish and Portuguese Studies, Minneapolis, MN 55455-0213. Offers Hispanic and Lusophone literatures, cultures and linguistics (PhD); Hispanic linguistics (MA); Hispanic literature (MA); Lusophone literature (MA). *Faculty:* 12 full-time (6 women), 3 part-time/adjunct (2 women). *Students:* 48 full-time (32 women); includes 18 minority (3 African Americans, 15 Hispanic Americans). Average age 30. 44 applicants, 25% accepted, 6 enrolled. In 2009, 4 master's, 2 doctorates awarded. *Degree requirements:* For master's, 2 foreign languages, comprehensive exam, thesis or alternative; for doctorate, 2 foreign languages, comprehensive exam, thesis/dissertation. *Entrance requirements:* For master's and doctorate, GRE General Test, samples of written work, 3 letters of recommendation, voice sample, statement of purpose. Additional exam requirements/recommendations for international students: Required—TOEFL (minimum score 550 paper-based; 213 computer-based; 79 iBT). *Application deadline:* For fall admission, 1/5 for domestic and international students. Application fee: $55 ($75 for international students). Electronic applications accepted. *Financial support:* In 2009–10, 1 fellowship with full tuition reimbursement (averaging $22,500 per year), 2 research assistantships with full tuition reimbursements (averaging $14,442 per year), 27 teaching assistantships with full tuition reimbursements (averaging $14,442 per year) were awarded; career-related internships or fieldwork and Federal Work-Study also available. Financial award application deadline: 1/5. *Faculty research:* Sociohistorical approaches to literature and culture, feminist studies, literary theory, ideologies and literature, pragmatics and sociolinguistics. *Unit head:* Ana Paula Ferreira, Department Chair, 612-625-3834, Fax: 612-625-3549, E-mail: apferrei@umn.edu. *Application contact:* Nan Nelson, Student Services: Graduate Program Assistant, 612-626-7809, Fax: 612-625-3549, E-mail: nelso789@.umn.edu.

University of New Mexico, Graduate School, College of Arts and Sciences, Department of Spanish and Portuguese, Albuquerque, NM 87131-2039. Offers Portuguese (MA); Spanish (MA); Spanish and Portuguese (PhD). Part-time programs available. *Faculty:* 11 full-time (9 women), 2 part-time/adjunct (0 women). *Students:* 53 full-time (40 women), 13 part-time (8 women); includes 32 minority (1 African American, 31 Hispanic Americans), 20 international. Average age 35. 47 applicants, 60% accepted, 18 enrolled. In 2009, 10 master's, 5 doctorates awarded. *Degree requirements:* For master's, one foreign language, comprehensive exam, thesis optional; for doctorate, one foreign language, comprehensive exam, thesis/dissertation. *Entrance requirements:* For master's, GRE, BA in Spanish or Portuguese, 3 letters of recommendation, letter of intent; for doctorate, GRE, 3 letters of recommendation, letter of intent, sample research paper. Additional exam requirements/recommendations for international students: Required—TOEFL (minimum score 550 paper-based; 213 computer-based). *Application deadline:* For fall admission, 1/15 priority date for domestic students; for spring admission, 11/15 for domestic students. Application fee: $50. Electronic applications accepted. *Expenses:* Tuition, state resident: full-time $2099; part-time $233.20 per credit hour. Tuition, nonresident: full-time $6650. Required fees: $25 per semester. Tuition and fees vary according to course load, program and reciprocity agreements. *Financial support:* In 2009–10, 30 students received support, including 30 teaching assistantships with full tuition reimbursements available (averaging $15,000 per year); Federal Work-Study, institutionally sponsored loans, scholarships/grants, health care benefits, tuition waivers (full), and unspecified assistantships also available. Support available to part-time students. Financial award application deadline: 3/1; financial award applicants required to submit FAFSA. *Faculty research:* Languages and literatures from the Iberian Peninsula, Latin America and the American Southwest. *Unit head:* Dr. Enrique Lamadrid, Chair, 505-277-5907, Fax: 505-277-3885, E-mail: lamadrid@unm.edu. *Application contact:* Martha Hurd, Graduate Administration Assistant, 505-277-2974, E-mail: marthah@unm.edu.

The University of North Carolina at Chapel Hill, Graduate School, College of Arts and Sciences, Department of Romance Languages, Chapel Hill, NC 27599. Offers French (MA, PhD); Italian (MA, PhD); Portuguese (MA, PhD); Romance languages (MA, PhD); Romance philology (MA, PhD); Spanish (MA, PhD). *Degree requirements:* For master's, one foreign language, comprehensive exam, thesis; for doctorate, 2 foreign languages, comprehensive exam, thesis/dissertation. *Entrance requirements:* For master's and doctorate, GRE General Test, minimum GPA of 3.0. Additional exam requirements/recommendations for international students: Required—TOEFL (minimum score 550 paper-based; 213 computer-based). Electronic applications accepted.

University of South Africa, College of Human Sciences, Pretoria, South Africa. Offers adult education (M Ed); African languages (MA, PhD); African politics (MA, PhD); Afrikaans (MA, PhD); ancient history (MA, PhD); ancient Near Eastern studies (MA, PhD); anthropology (MA, PhD); applied linguistics (MA); Arabic (MA, PhD); archaeology (MA); art history (MA); Biblical archaeology (MA); Biblical studies (M Th, D Th, PhD); Christian spirituality (M Th, D Th); church history (M Th, D Th); classical studies (MA, PhD); clinical psychology (MA); communication (MA, PhD); comparative education (M Ed, Ed D); consulting psychology (D Admin, D Com, PhD); curriculum studies (M Ed, Ed D); development studies (M Admin, MA, D Admin, PhD); didactics (M Ed, Ed D); education (M Tech); education management (M Ed, Ed D); educational psychology (M Ed); English (MA); environmental education (M Ed); French (MA, PhD); German (MA, PhD); Greek (MA); guidance and counseling (M Ed); health studies (MA, PhD), including health sciences education (MA), health services management (MA), medical and surgical nursing science (critical care general) (MA), midwifery and neonatal nursing science (MA), trauma and emergency care (MA); history (MA, PhD); history of education (Ed D); inclusive education (M Ed, Ed D); information and communications technology policy and regulation (MA); information science (MA, MIS, PhD); international politics (MA, PhD); Islamic studies (MA, PhD); Italian (MA, PhD); Judaica (MA, PhD); linguistics (MA, PhD); mathematical education (M Ed); mathematics education (MA); missiology (M Th, D Th); modern Hebrew (MA, PhD); musicology (MA, MMus, D Mus, PhD); natural science education (M Ed); New Testament (M Th, D Th); Old Testament (D Th); pastoral therapy (M Th, D Th); philosophy (MA); philosophy of education (M Ed, Ed D); politics (MA, PhD); Portuguese (MA, PhD); practical theology (M Th, D Th); psychology (MA, MS, PhD); psychology of education (M Ed, Ed D); public health (MA); religious studies (MA, D Th, PhD); Romance languages (MA); Russian (MA, PhD); Semitic languages (MA, PhD); social behavior studies in HIV/AIDS (MA); social science (mental health) (MA); social science in development studies (MA); social science in psychology (MA); social science in social work (MA); social science in sociology (MA); social work (MSW, DSW, PhD); socio-education (M Ed, Ed D); sociolinguistics (MA); sociology (MA, PhD); Spanish (MA, PhD); systematic theology (M Th, D Th); TESOL (teaching English to speakers of other languages) (MA); theological ethics (M Th, D Th); theory of literature (MA, PhD); urban ministries (D Th); urban ministry (M Th).

The University of Tennessee, Graduate School, College of Arts and Sciences, Department of Modern Foreign Languages and Literatures, Program in Modern Foreign Languages, Knoxville, TN 37996. Offers applied linguistics (PhD); French (PhD); German (PhD); Italian (PhD); Portuguese (PhD); Russian (PhD); Spanish (PhD). *Degree requirements:* For doctorate, 2 foreign languages, thesis/dissertation. *Entrance requirements:* For doctorate, minimum GPA of 2.7. Additional exam requirements/recommendations for international students: Required—TOEFL. Electronic applications accepted. *Expenses:* Tuition, state resident: full-time $6826; part-time $380 per semester hour. Tuition, nonresident: full-time $21,844; part-time $1147 per semester hour. Tuition and fees vary according to program.

The University of Texas at Austin, Graduate School, College of Liberal Arts, Department of Spanish and Portuguese, Austin, TX 78712-1111. Offers Hispanic linguistics (MA, PhD); Hispanic literature (MA, PhD); Luso-Brazilian literature (MA, PhD). *Degree requirements:* For master's, 2 foreign languages, thesis or alternative; for doctorate, 3 foreign languages, thesis/dissertation. *Entrance requirements:* For master's and doctorate, GRE General Test. Electronic applications accepted.

University of Toronto, School of Graduate Studies, Humanities Division, Department of Spanish and Portuguese, Toronto, ON M5S 1A1, Canada. Offers MA, PhD. Part-time programs available. *Degree requirements:* For doctorate, thesis/dissertation. *Entrance requirements:* For master's, minimum B average in final year, 2 letters of reference; for doctorate, minimum A– average, 2 letters of reference, writing sample. Additional exam requirements/recommendations for international students: Required—TOEFL, Michigan English Language Assessment Battery, IELTS or COPE.

University of Washington, Graduate School, College of Arts and Sciences, Department of Romance Languages and Literature, Division of Spanish and Portuguese Studies, Seattle, WA 98195. Offers Hispanic literary and cultural studies (MA). *Degree requirements:* For master's, 2 foreign languages, thesis optional, exam. *Entrance requirements:* For master's, GRE General Test, minimum GPA of 3.0. Additional exam requirements/recommendations for international students: Required—TOEFL. Electronic applications accepted. *Faculty research:* Medieval through modern Spanish literature and film, Latin American literature, poetry and essay, pan-Hispanic ballad, Hispanic cultural studies, second language acquisition and applied linguistics.

University of Wisconsin–Madison, Graduate School, College of Letters and Science, Department of Spanish and Portuguese, Program in Portuguese, Madison, WI 53706-1380. Offers MA, PhD. *Degree requirements:* For master's, one foreign language; for doctorate, 2 foreign languages, thesis/dissertation. *Entrance requirements:* For master's, GRE (recommended), minimum GPA of 3.25 in Spanish or Portuguese; for doctorate, GRE (recommended), minimum graduate GPA of 3.4. Additional exam requirements/recommendations for international students: Required—TOEFL. Electronic applications accepted. *Expenses:* Tuition, state resident: part-time $594 per credit. Tuition, nonresident: part-time $1504 per credit. Required fees: $65 per credit. Tuition and fees vary according to course load, program and reciprocity agreements. *Faculty research:* Portuguese and Brazilian literature.

Vanderbilt University, Graduate School, Department of Spanish and Portuguese, Nashville, TN 37240-1001. Offers Portuguese (MA); Spanish (MA, MAT, PhD); Spanish and Portuguese (PhD). *Faculty:* 14 full-time (6 women). *Students:* 30 full-time (16 women), 1 part-time (0 women); includes 3 minority (1 African American, 1 American Indian/Alaska Native, 1 Hispanic American), 13 international. Average age 31. 66 applicants, 12% accepted, 7 enrolled. In 2009, 4 doctorates awarded. *Degree requirements:* For master's, one foreign language, thesis; for doctorate, 2 foreign languages, thesis/dissertation, final and qualifying exams. *Entrance requirements:* For master's, GRE General Test; for doctorate, GRE General Test, writing sample in Spanish. Additional exam requirements/recommendations for international students: Required—TOEFL (minimum score 570 paper-based; 230 computer-based; 88 iBT). *Application deadline:* For fall admission, 1/15 for domestic and international students. Application fee: $0. Electronic applications accepted. *Financial support:* Fellowships with full and partial tuition reimbursements, teaching assistantships with full tuition reimbursements, Federal Work-Study, institutionally sponsored loans, and health care benefits available. Financial award application deadline: 1/15; financial award applicants required to submit CSS PROFILE or FAFSA. *Faculty research:* Spanish, Portuguese, and Latin American literatures; foreign language pedagogy; Renaissance and Baroque poetry; nineteenth century Spanish novel. *Unit head:* Cathy L. Jrade, Chair, 615-322-6930, Fax: 615-343-7260, E-mail: cathy.l.jrade@vanderbilt.edu. *Application contact:* Christina Karageorgou-Bastea, Director of Graduate Studies, 615-322-6930, Fax: 615-343-7260, E-mail: christina.karageorgou@vanderbilt.edu.

Yale University, Graduate School of Arts and Sciences, Department of Spanish and Portuguese, New Haven, CT 06520. Offers Latin American literature (PhD); Luso-Brazilian and Spanish/Spanish American literatures (PhD); Spanish peninsular literature (PhD). Terminal master's awarded for partial completion of doctoral program. *Degree requirements:* For doctorate, 3 foreign languages, thesis/dissertation. *Entrance requirements:* For doctorate, GRE General Test.

Romance Languages

Appalachian State University, Cratis D. Williams Graduate School, Department of Foreign Languages and Literatures, Boone, NC 28608. Offers romance languages (MA), including Spanish or French teaching. Part-time programs available. Postbaccalaureate distance learning degree programs offered (no on-campus study). *Faculty:* 15 full-time (8 women). *Students:* 3 full-time (1 woman), 16 part-time (13 women); includes 4 minority (1 African American, 3 Hispanic Americans). 13 applicants, 92% accepted, 7 enrolled. In 2009, 8 master's awarded. *Degree requirements:* For master's, one foreign language, comprehensive exam, thesis optional. *Entrance requirements:* For master's, GRE General Test, 3 letters of recommendation. Additional exam requirements/recommendations for international students: Required—TOEFL (minimum score 570 paper-based; 230 computer-based; 79 iBT), or IELTS (minimum score 6.5). *Application deadline:* For fall admission, 7/1 for domestic students, 2/1 for international students; for spring admission, 11/1 for domestic students, 7/1 for international students. Applications are processed on a rolling basis. Application fee: $50. Electronic applications accepted. *Expenses:* Tuition, state resident: full-time $2960. Tuition, nonresident: full-time $14,051. Required fees: $2320. *Financial support:* In 2009–10, 2 research assistantships (averaging $7,000 per year) were awarded; fellowships, teaching assistantships, career-related internships or fieldwork and unspecified assistantships also available. Financial award application deadline: 4/1; financial award applicants required to submit FAFSA. *Faculty research:* French and Spanish literature, Latin American culture, teaching foreign languages. Total annual research expenditures: $35,000. *Unit head:* Dr. Richard Carp, Chairperson, 828-262-3096, Fax: 828-262-3095, E-mail: carprm@appstate.edu. *Application contact:* Dr. Beverly Moser, Graduate Coordinator, 828-262-2929, E-mail: moserba@appstate.edu.

Boston University, Graduate School of Arts and Sciences, Department of Romance Studies, Boston, MA 02215. Offers French language and literature (MA, PhD); Hispanic language and literatures (MA, PhD). *Students:* 45 full-time (37 women), 5 part-time (3 women); includes 4 minority (all Hispanic Americans), 15 international. Average age 31. 50 applicants, 58% accepted, 12 enrolled. In 2009, 2 master's, 4 doctorates awarded. Terminal master's awarded for partial completion of doctoral program. *Degree requirements:* For master's, one foreign language, comprehensive exam; for doctorate, 2 foreign languages, comprehensive exam, thesis/dissertation. *Entrance requirements:* For master's and doctorate, GRE General Test, sample of written work, 3 letters of recommendation. Additional exam requirements/recommendations for international students: Required—TOEFL (minimum score 550 paper-based; 213 computer-based). *Application deadline:* For fall admission, 4/15 for domestic and international students; for spring admission, 10/15 for domestic and international students. Application fee: $70. Electronic applications accepted. *Expenses:* Tuition: Full-time $37,910; part-time $1184 per credit hour. Required fees: $386; $40 per semester. Part-time tuition and fees vary according to class time, course level, degree level and program. *Financial support:* In 2009–10, 48 students received support, including 2 fellowships with full tuition reimbursements available (averaging $18,900 per year), 35 teaching assistantships with full tuition reimbursements available (averaging $18,400 per year); research assistantships, Federal Work-Study and scholarships/grants also available. Support available to part-time students. Financial award application deadline: 1/15; financial award applicants required to submit FAFSA. *Unit head:* James Iffland, Chairman, 617-353-6225, Fax: 617-353-6246, E-mail: Iffland@bu.edu. *Application contact:* Sharo Gineo, Administrative Assistant, 617-353-2641, Fax: 617-353-6246, E-mail: sdow@bu.edu.

Clark Atlanta University, School of Arts and Sciences, Department of Foreign Languages, Atlanta, GA 30314. Offers Romance languages (MA, DAH). Part-time programs available. *Faculty:* 3 full-time (0 women), 1 part-time/adjunct (0 women). *Students:* 1 (woman) full-time; minority (African American). Average age 34. *Degree requirements:* For master's, one foreign language, thesis; for doctorate, 2 foreign languages, comprehensive exam, thesis/dissertation. *Entrance requirements:* For master's, GRE General Test, minimum GPA of 2.5. Additional exam requirements/recommendations for international students: Required—TOEFL (minimum score 500 paper-based; 173 computer-based). *Application deadline:* For fall admission, 4/1 for domestic and international students; for spring admission, 11/1 for domestic and international students. Applications are processed on a rolling basis. Application fee: $40 ($55 for international students). *Expenses:* Tuition: Full-time $12,240; part-time $680 per credit hour. Required fees: $710; $355 per semester. *Financial support:* Scholarships/grants and unspecified assistantships available. Financial award application deadline: 4/30; financial award applicants required to submit FAFSA. *Unit head:* Dr. Laurent Monye, Chairperson, 404-880-8547, E-mail: lmonye@cau.edu. *Application contact:* Michelle Clark-Davis, Graduate Program Admissions, 404-880-6605, E-mail: cauadmissions@cau.edu.

Columbia University, Graduate School of Arts and Sciences, Division of Humanities, Department of French and Romance Philology, New York, NY 10027. Offers French and Romance philology (M Phil, PhD); Romance languages (MA). Part-time programs available. *Degree requirements:* For master's, one foreign language, thesis, written exam; for doctorate, 2 foreign languages, thesis/dissertation. *Entrance requirements:* For master's and doctorate, GRE General Test, knowledge of Latin, writing sample. Additional exam requirements/recommendations for international students: Required—TOEFL. *Faculty research:* Theory of literature, literary semiotics, poetics.

Cornell University, Graduate School, Graduate Fields of Arts and Sciences, Field of Linguistics, Ithaca, NY 14853-0001. Offers applied linguistics (MA, PhD); East Asian linguistics (MA, PhD); English linguistics (MA, PhD); general linguistics (MA, PhD); Germanic linguistics (MA, PhD); Indo-European linguistics (MA, PhD); phonetics (MA, PhD); phonological theory (MA, PhD); Romance linguistics (MA, PhD); second language acquisition (MA, PhD); semantics (MA, PhD); Slavic linguistics (MA, PhD); sociolinguistics (MA, PhD); South Asian linguistics (MA, PhD); Southeast Asian linguistics (MA, PhD); syntactic theory (MA, PhD). *Faculty:* 21 full-time (10 women). *Students:* 31 full-time (17 women), 14 international. Average age 30. 95 applicants, 12% accepted, 5 enrolled. In 2009, 5 master's, 6 doctorates awarded. Terminal master's awarded for partial completion of doctoral program. *Degree requirements:* For master's, one foreign language, thesis; for doctorate, one foreign language, comprehensive exam, thesis/dissertation. *Entrance requirements:* For master's and doctorate, GRE General Test, 2 letters of recommendation. Additional exam requirements/recommendations for international students: Required—TOEFL (minimum score 600 paper-based; 250 computer-based; 77 iBT). *Application deadline:* For fall admission, 1/15 for domestic students. Application fee: $70. Electronic applications accepted. *Expenses:* Tuition: Full-time $29,500. Required fees: $70. Full-time tuition and fees vary according to degree level, program and student level. *Financial support:* In 2009–10, 3 fellowships with full tuition reimbursements, 1 teaching assistantship with full tuition reimbursement were awarded; research assistantships with full tuition reimbursements, institutionally sponsored loans, scholarships/grants, health care benefits, tuition waivers (full and partial), and unspecified assistantships also available. Financial award applicants required to submit FAFSA. *Faculty research:* Phonology and phonetics; syntax and semantics; historical linguistics; philosophy of language; language acquisition. *Unit head:* Director of Graduate Studies, 607-255-1105. *Application contact:* Graduate Field Assistant, 607-255-1105, E-mail: lingfield@cornell.edu.

Cornell University, Graduate School, Graduate Fields of Arts and Sciences, Field of Romance Studies, Ithaca, NY 14853-0001. Offers French linguistics (PhD); French literature (PhD); Hispanic literature (PhD); Italian linguistics (PhD); Italian literature (PhD); Romance linguistics (PhD); Spanish linguistics (PhD). *Faculty:* 42 full-time (19 women). *Students:* 54 full-time (27 women); includes 9 minority (all Hispanic Americans), 17 international. Average age 30. 78 applicants, 17% accepted, 10 enrolled. In 2009, 7 doctorates awarded. *Degree requirements:* For doctorate, 2 foreign languages, comprehensive exam, thesis/dissertation. *Entrance requirements:* For doctorate, GRE General Test, sample of written work, 3 letters of recommendation. Additional exam requirements/recommendations for international students: Required—TOEFL (minimum score 550 paper-based; 213 computer-based; 77 iBT). *Application deadline:* For fall admission, 1/15 for domestic students. Application fee: $70. Electronic applications accepted. *Expenses:* Tuition: Full-time $29,500. Required fees: $70. Full-time tuition and fees vary according to degree level, program and student level. *Financial support:* In 2009–10, 46 students received support, including 8 fellowships with full tuition reimbursements available, 2 teaching assistantships with full tuition reimbursements available; research assistantships with full tuition reimbursements available, institutionally sponsored loans, scholarships/grants, health care benefits, tuition waivers (full and partial), and unspecified assistantships also available. Financial award applicants required to submit FAFSA. *Faculty research:* Literary theory, Hispanic studies, French studies, gender studies. *Unit head:* Director of Graduate Studies, 607-255-8222. *Application contact:* Graduate Field Assistant, 607-255-4246, E-mail: romance_studies@cornell.edu.

Hunter College of the City University of New York, Graduate School, School of Arts and Sciences, Department of Romance Languages, New York, NY 10021-5085. Offers French (MA), including French, French education; Italian (MA), including Italian, Italian education; Spanish (MA), including Spanish, Spanish education. Part-time and evening/weekend programs available. *Faculty:* 8 full-time (5 women). *Students:* 1 (woman) full-time, 22 part-time (16 women); includes 10 minority (all Hispanic Americans). Average age 33. 27 applicants, 81% accepted, 12 enrolled. In 2009, 10 master's awarded. *Degree requirements:* For master's, 2 foreign languages, comprehensive exam, thesis optional. *Entrance requirements:* For master's, GRE General Test, GRE Subject Test, interview, proficiency in chosen language. Additional exam requirements/recommendations for international students: Required—TOEFL. *Application deadline:* For fall admission, 4/1 for domestic students, 2/1 for international students; for spring admission, 11/1 for domestic students, 9/1 for international students. Application fee: $125. *Expenses:* Tuition, state resident: full-time $7360; part-time $310 per credit. Required fees: $250 per semester. *Financial support:* Fellowships, Federal Work-Study, scholarships/grants, and tuition waivers (partial) available. Support available to part-time students. Financial award application deadline: 4/15. *Unit head:* Dr. Giuseppe Carlo DiScipio, Chair, 212-772-5108, Fax: 212-772-5094, E-mail: gdiscipi@hunter.cuny.edu. *Application contact:* William Zlata, Director for Graduate Admissions, 212-772-4482, Fax: 212-650-3336, E-mail: admissions@hunter.cuny.edu.

The Johns Hopkins University, Zanvyl Krieger School of Arts and Sciences, Department of German and Romance Languages and Literatures, Baltimore, MD 21218-2699. Offers French (PhD); German (PhD); Italian (PhD); romance languages (PhD); Spanish (PhD). *Faculty:* 31 full-time (20 women), 1 part-time/adjunct (0 women). *Students:* 49 full-time (30 women); includes 4 minority (all Hispanic Americans), 21 international. Average age 30. 51 applicants, 37% accepted, 19 enrolled. In 2009, 5 doctorates awarded. *Degree requirements:* For doctorate, 2 foreign languages, thesis/dissertation. *Entrance requirements:* For doctorate, GRE General Test. Additional exam requirements/recommendations for international students: Required—TOEFL (minimum score 600 paper-based; 250 computer-based; 100 iBT), IELTS. *Application deadline:* For fall admission, 12/30 for domestic and international students. Application fee: $75. Electronic applications accepted. *Financial support:* In 2009–10, 40 fellowships with full tuition reimbursements (averaging $17,000 per year), 2 research assistantships with full tuition reimbursements (averaging $17,000 per year), 19 teaching assistantships with full tuition reimbursements (averaging $17,000 per year) were awarded; institutionally sponsored loans also available. *Faculty research:* Nineteenth century French prose and poetry, genetic theory and criticism; twentieth century Latin American literature and film; Medieval and Renaissance Italian literature; Gender and Queer Theory in German literature; the ideology of baroque and neobaroque aesthetics. *Unit head:* Dr. William Egginton, Chair, 410-516-7510, Fax: 410-516-5358, E-mail: egginton@jhu.edu. *Application contact:* Rebecca Swisdak, Graduate Administrative Coordinator, 410-516-7227, Fax: 410-516-5358, E-mail: rswisdak@jhu.edu.

Michigan State University, The Graduate School, College of Arts and Letters, Department of French, Classics, and Italian, East Lansing, MI 48824. Offers French (MA); French language and literature (PhD). *Faculty:* 10 full-time (4 women). *Students:* 13 full-time (10 women), 1 (woman) part-time; includes 2 minority (both African Americans), 4 international. Average age 32. 10 applicants, 30% accepted. In 2009, 3 master's, 2 doctorates awarded. *Entrance requirements:* Additional exam requirements/recommendations for international students: Required—TOEFL. Electronic applications accepted. *Expenses:* Tuition, state resident: part-time $478.25 per credit hour. Tuition, nonresident: part-time $966.50 per credit hour. Part-time tuition and fees vary according to program. *Financial support:* In 2009–10, 1 research assistantship with tuition reimbursement (averaging $6,334 per year), 9 teaching assistantships with tuition reimbursements (averaging $5,934 per year) were awarded. *Unit head:* Dr. Anna Norris, Acting Chairperson, 517-432-8305, Fax: 517-432-6130, E-mail: norrisa@msu.edu. *Application contact:* Information, 517-355-8351, Fax: 517-432-6130.

New York University, Graduate School of Arts and Science, Center for French Civilization and Culture, Department of French, New York, NY 10012-1019. Offers French (PhD); French language and civilization (MA); French literature (MA); Romance languages and literatures (MA). Part-time programs available. *Faculty:* 18 full-time (7 women), 2 part-time/adjunct (both women). *Students:* 58 full-time (37 women), 6 part-time (3 women); includes 5 minority (1 African American, 3 Asian Americans or Pacific Islanders, 1 Hispanic American), 19 international. Average age 30. 49 applicants, 49% accepted, 15 enrolled. In 2009, 20 master's, 4 doctorates awarded. Terminal master's awarded for partial completion of doctoral program. *Degree requirements:* For master's, one foreign language, thesis (for some programs); for doctorate, one foreign language, thesis/dissertation. *Entrance requirements:* For master's and doctorate, GRE General Test, proficiency in French. Additional exam requirements/recommendations for international students: Required—TOEFL. *Application deadline:* For fall admission, 1/4 for domestic students; for spring admission, 11/1 for domestic students. Application fee: $90. *Expenses:* Tuition: Full-time $30,528; part-time $1272 per credit. Required fees: $2177. *Financial support:* Fellowships with tuition reimbursements, teaching assistantships with tuition reimbursements, Federal Work-Study, institutionally sponsored loans, scholarships/grants, traineeships, health care benefits, unspecified assistantships, and instructorships available. Financial award application deadline: 1/4; financial award applicants required to submit FAFSA. *Faculty research:* French and Francophone literature, literary theory, and history; rhetoric and poetics; cultural history; theater and cinema. *Unit head:* Judith Miller, Chair, 212-998-8700, Fax: 212-995-3539, E-mail: french.grad@nyu.edu. *Application contact:* Brett Underhill, Graduate Secretary, 212-998-8700, Fax: 212-995-3539, E-mail: french.grad@nyu.edu.

New York University, Graduate School of Arts and Science, Department of Spanish and Portuguese Languages and Literatures, New York, NY 10012-1019. Offers Portuguese (MA, PhD); Spanish (PhD); Spanish and Latin American literatures and cultures (MA); Spanish language and translation (MA). Part-time programs available. *Students:* 105 full-time (66 women), 5 part-time (4 women); includes 41 minority (5 African Americans, 4 Asian Americans or Pacific Islanders, 32 Hispanic Americans), 40 international. Average age 31. 193 applicants, 48% accepted, 50 enrolled. In 2009, 34 master's, 5 doctorates awarded. *Degree requirements:* For master's, 2 foreign languages, thesis; for doctorate, 2 foreign languages, thesis/dissertation. *Entrance requirements:* For master's, GRE General Test; for doctorate, GRE General Test, master's degree. Additional exam requirements/recommendations for international students: Required—TOEFL. *Application deadline:* For fall admission, 1/4 priority date for domestic students. Application fee: $90. *Expenses:* Tuition: Full-time $30,528; part-time $1272 per credit. Required fees: $2177. *Financial support:* Fellowships with tuition reimbursements, teaching assistantships with tuition reimbursements, career-related internships or fieldwork, Federal Work-Study, institutionally sponsored loans, scholarships/grants, health care benefits and unspecified assistantships available. Financial award application deadline: 1/4; financial award applicants required to submit FAFSA. *Faculty research:* Gender and sexuality, transatlantic studies, literacy and cultural theories, colonial and post colonial studies, autobiography and modern subjectivities. *Unit head:* Sibylle Fischer, Chair, 212-998-8770, Fax: 212-995-4149, E-mail: spanish.portuguese.info@nyu.edu. *Application contact:* Jo Labanyi, Director of Graduate Studies, 212-998-8770, Fax: 212-995-4149, E-mail: spanish.portuguese.info@nyu.edu.

Northern Illinois University, Graduate School, College of Liberal Arts and Sciences, Department of Foreign Languages and Literatures, De Kalb, IL 60115-2854. Offers French (MA); Spanish (MA). Part-time programs available. *Faculty:* 25 full-time (11 women). *Students:* 4 full-time (2 women), 18 part-time (9 women); includes 7 minority (all Hispanic Americans), 2 international. Average age 31. 10 applicants, 60% accepted, 4 enrolled. In 2009, 9 master's awarded. *Degree requirements:* For master's, one foreign language, comprehensive exam, thesis or alternative, language proficiency exam. *Entrance requirements:* For master's, GRE General Test, interview, minimum GPA of 2.75, undergraduate major in French or Spanish. Additional exam requirements/recommendations for international students: Required—TOEFL (minimum score 550 paper-based; 213 computer-based). *Application deadline:* For fall admission, 6/1 for domestic students, 5/1 for international students; for spring admission, 11/1 for domestic students, 10/1 for international students. Applications are processed on a rolling basis. Application fee: $30. Electronic applications accepted. *Expenses:* Tuition, state resident: full-time $6576; part-time $274 per credit hour. Tuition, nonresident: full-time $13,152; part-time $548 per credit hour. Required fees: $1813; $75.53 per credit hour. Part-time tuition and fees vary according to course load. *Financial support:* In 2009–10, 13 teaching assistantships with full tuition reimbursements were awarded; fellowships with full tuition reimbursements, research assistantships with full tuition reimbursements, career-related internships or fieldwork, Federal Work-Study, scholarships/grants, tuition waivers (full), and unspecified assistantships also available. Support available to part-time students. Financial award applicants required to submit FAFSA. *Faculty research:* Francophone women writers, prosodies of French and Italian, early Spanish drama, business German, history of Burmese literature. *Unit head:* Anne Birbeck, Chair, 815-753-1259, Fax: 815-753-5989, E-mail: annie@niu.edu. *Application contact:* Graduate School Office, 815-753-0395, E-mail: gradsch@niu.edu.

Queens College of the City University of New York, Division of Graduate Studies, Arts and Humanities Division, Department of European Languages and Literatures, Flushing, NY 11367-1597. Offers French (MA); Italian (MA). Part-time and evening/weekend programs available. *Faculty:* 13 full-time (5 women). *Students:* 8 part-time (7 women). 10 applicants, 40% accepted, 2 enrolled. In 2009, 4 master's awarded. *Degree requirements:* For master's, 2 foreign languages, comprehensive exam, thesis or alternative. *Entrance requirements:* For master's, minimum GPA of 3.0. Additional exam requirements/recommendations for international students: Required—TOEFL. *Application deadline:* For fall admission, 4/1 for domestic students; for spring admission, 11/1 for domestic students. Applications are processed on a rolling basis. Application fee: $125. *Expenses:* Tuition, state resident: full-time $7360; part-time $310 per credit. Tuition, nonresident: part-time $575 per credit. One-time fee: $195.25 full-time; $145.25 part-time. *Financial support:* Career-related internships or fieldwork, Federal Work-Study, institutionally sponsored loans, and tuition waivers (partial) available. Support available to part-time students. Financial award application deadline: 4/1; financial award applicants required to submit FAFSA. *Unit head:* Dr. Royal Brown, Chairperson, 718-997-5980, E-mail: royal_brown@qc.edu. *Application contact:* Mario Caruso, Director of Graduate Admissions, 718-997-5200, Fax: 718-997-5193, E-mail: graduate_admissions@qc.edu.

San Diego State University, Graduate and Research Affairs, College of Arts and Letters, Department of European Studies, San Diego, CA 92182. Offers MA. *Degree requirements:* For master's, one foreign language. *Entrance requirements:* For master's, GRE General Test. Additional exam requirements/recommendations for international students: Required—TOEFL. Electronic applications accepted.

Stony Brook University, State University of New York, Graduate School, College of Arts and Sciences, Department of European Languages, Literatures, and Cultures, Program in French, Stony Brook, NY 11794. Offers Romance languages (MA). Evening/weekend programs available. *Degree requirements:* For master's, one foreign language. *Entrance requirements:* For master's, GRE General Test. Additional exam requirements/recommendations for international students: Required—TOEFL. *Application deadline:* For fall admission, 1/15 for domestic students. Application fee: $60. *Expenses:* Tuition, state resident: full-time $8370; part-time $349 per credit. Tuition, nonresident: full-time $13,250; part-time $552 per credit. Required fees: $933. *Unit head:* Prosper Sanou, Coordinator, 631-632-7440, E-mail: prosper.sanou@stonybrook.edu. *Application contact:* Dr. Andrea Fedi, Director of Graduate Studies, 631-632-7438, Fax: 631-632-9612.

Texas Tech University, Graduate School, College of Arts and Sciences, Department of Classical and Modern Languages and Literatures, Lubbock, TX 79409. Offers applied linguistics (MA); classics (MA); German (MA); Romance language (MA); Romance languages-French (MA); Romance languages-Spanish (MA); Spanish (PhD); MBA/MA. Part-time programs available. *Faculty:* 29 full-time (11 women), 1 (woman) part-time/adjunct. *Students:* 80 full-time (45 women), 25 part-time (13 women); includes 17 minority (1 African American, 16 Hispanic Americans), 43 international. Average age 32. 72 applicants, 75% accepted, 21 enrolled. In 2009, 19 master's, 5 doctorates awarded. *Degree requirements:* For master's, thesis or alternative; for doctorate, thesis/dissertation. *Entrance requirements:* For master's and doctorate, GRE General Test. Additional exam requirements/recommendations for international students: Required—TOEFL (minimum score 550 paper-based; 213 computer-based). *Application deadline:* For fall admission, 3/1 priority date for international students; for spring admission, 11/1 priority date for international students. Applications are processed on a rolling basis. Application fee: $50 ($75 for international students). Electronic applications accepted. *Expenses:* Tuition, state resident: full-time $5100; part-time $213 per credit hour. Tuition, nonresident: full-time $11,748; part-time $490 per credit hour. Required fees: $2298; $50 per credit hour. $555 per semester. *Financial support:* In 2009–10, 19 teaching assistantships with partial tuition reimbursements (averaging $12,060 per year) were awarded; research assistantships with partial tuition reimbursements, Federal Work-Study and institutionally sponsored loans also available. Support available to part-time students. Financial award application deadline: 4/15; financial award applicants required to submit FAFSA. *Faculty research:* Literature, comparative literature, linguistics, culture, pedagogy. Total annual research expenditures: $37,015. *Unit head:* Dr. Laura Jean Beard, Interim Chair and Professor, 806-742-4355, Fax: 806-742-3306, E-mail: laura.beard@ttu.edu. *Application contact:* Liz Hildebrand, Senior Advisor, 806-742-4055, Fax: 806-742-3306, E-mail: liz.hildebrand@ttu.edu.

University at Buffalo, the State University of New York, Graduate School, College of Arts and Sciences, Department of Romance Languages and Literatures, Buffalo, NY 14260. Offers French (MA, PhD); Spanish (MA, PhD). Part-time programs available. *Students:* Average age 31. Terminal master's awarded for partial completion of doctoral program. *Degree requirements:* For master's, one foreign language, project, thesis; for doctorate, 2 foreign languages, thesis/dissertation. *Entrance requirements:* For master's and doctorate, GRE. Additional exam requirements/recommendations for international students: Required—TOEFL (minimum score 550 paper-based; 213 computer-based; 79 iBT). *Application deadline:* For fall admission, 1/15 priority date for domestic students, 1/15 for international students. Applications are processed on a rolling basis. Application fee: $75. Electronic applications accepted. *Financial support:* In 2009–10, fellowships with full tuition reimbursements (averaging $6,000 per year), teaching assistantships with full tuition reimbursements (averaging $13,000 per year) were awarded; Federal Work-Study and institutionally sponsored loans also available. Financial award application deadline: 2/28; financial award applicants required to submit FAFSA. *Faculty research:* Romance linguistics, cultural studies, literary studies, literature and philosophy. *Unit head:* Dr. David Castillo, Chair, 716-645-0869, Fax: 716-645-5981, E-mail: dc63@buffalo.edu. *Application contact:* Dr. Justin Read, Director of Graduate Studies, 716-645-0878, Fax: 716-645-5981, E-mail: jread2@buffalo.edu.

The University of Alabama, Graduate School, College of Arts and Sciences, Department of Modern Languages and Classics, Tuscaloosa, AL 35487. Offers French (MA, PhD); French and Spanish (PhD); German (MA); Romance languages (MA, PhD); Spanish (MA, PhD). Part-time programs available. *Faculty:* 22 full-time (11 women). *Students:* 46 full-time (31 women), 8 part-time (6 women); includes 7 minority (4 African Americans, 3 Hispanic Americans), 16 international. Average age 31. 31 applicants, 42% accepted, 11 enrolled. In 2009, 12 master's, 5 doctorates awarded. *Median time to degree:* Of those who began their doctoral program in fall 2001, 40% received their degree in 8 years or less. *Degree requirements:* For master's, comprehensive exam, thesis optional; for doctorate, one foreign language, thesis/dissertation, preliminary exam. *Entrance requirements:* For master's and doctorate, minimum GPA of 3.0, writing sample. Additional exam requirements/recommendations for international students: Required—TOEFL or IELTS. *Application deadline:* For fall admission, 7/6 priority date for domestic students, 1/15 priority date for international students; for spring admission, 12/6 priority date for domestic students, 6/1 priority date for international students. Applications are processed on a rolling basis. Application fee: $50 ($60 for international students). Electronic applications accepted. *Expenses:* Tuition, state resident: full-time $7000. Tuition, nonresident: full-time $19,200. *Financial support:* In 2009–10, 7 students received support, including 1 fellowship, research assistantships with full tuition reimbursements available (averaging $10,291 per year), 6 teaching assistantships with full tuition reimbursements available (averaging $10,291 per year); career-related internships or fieldwork, Federal Work-Study, institutionally sponsored loans, and scholarships/grants also available. Financial award application deadline: 7/14. *Faculty research:* Non-English literature, linguistics, culture, film. *Unit head:* Dr. Michael Picone, Chair and Professor, 205-348-5054, Fax: 205-348-2042, E-mail: mpicone@bama.ua.edu. *Application contact:* Dr. K. Barbara Fischer, Graduate Director and Associate Professor, 205-348-8465, Fax: 205-348-2042, E-mail: bfischer@bama.ua.edu.

University of California, Berkeley, Graduate Division, College of Letters and Science, Group in Romance Languages and Literature, Berkeley, CA 94720-1500. Offers French (PhD); Italian (PhD); Spanish (PhD). *Faculty:* 16 full-time. *Students:* 15 full-time (8 women). Average age 33. 34 applicants, 1 enrolled. In 2009, 4 doctorates awarded. *Degree requirements:* For doctorate, thesis/dissertation, qualifying exam. *Entrance requirements:* For doctorate, GRE General Test, minimum GPA of 3.0, 3 letters of recommendation. Additional exam requirements/recommendations for international students: Required—TOEFL (minimum score 570 paper-based; 230 computer-based). *Application deadline:* For fall admission, 12/15 for domestic students. Application fee: $70 ($90 for international students). *Financial support:* Fellowships with full tuition reimbursements, teaching assistantships with partial tuition reimbursements, health care benefits and unspecified assistantships available. Financial award applicants required to submit FAFSA. *Unit head:* Jose Rabasa, Chair, 510-642-2105, E-mail: jrabasa@berkeley.edu. *Application contact:* Jose Rabasa, Chair, 510-642-2105, E-mail: jrabasa@berkeley.edu.

University of Chicago, Division of the Humanities, Department of Romance Languages and Literatures, Chicago, IL 60637-1513. Offers French (AM, PhD); Italian (AM, PhD); Spanish (AM, PhD). Terminal master's awarded for partial completion of doctoral program. *Degree requirements:* For master's, 2 foreign languages, thesis; for doctorate, 3 foreign languages, thesis/dissertation. *Entrance requirements:* For master's and doctorate, GRE General Test, GRE Subject Test. Additional exam requirements/recommendations for international students: Required—TOEFL.

University of Cincinnati, Graduate School, McMicken College of Arts and Sciences, Department of Romance Languages and Literature, Cincinnati, OH 45221. Offers French (MA, PhD); Romance languages and literatures (PhD); Spanish (MA, PhD). Terminal master's awarded for partial completion of doctoral program. *Degree requirements:* For master's, 2 foreign languages, comprehensive exam, thesis optional; for doctorate, 3 foreign languages, comprehensive exam, thesis/dissertation. *Entrance requirements:* For master's, minimum GPA of 3.0; for doctorate, MA or equivalent in French or Spanish language and literature. Additional exam requirements/recommendations for international students: Required—TOEFL (minimum score 520 paper-based; 190 computer-based). Electronic applications accepted. *Faculty research:* Teaching methods in Spanish, Spanish theater, Old French, Francophone studies, poetry.

University of Georgia, Graduate School, College of Arts and Sciences, Department of Romance Languages, Program in Romance Languages, Athens, GA 30602. Offers MA, PhD. *Students:* 34 full-time (22 women), 8 part-time (6 women). 37 applicants, 41% accepted, 13 enrolled. In 2009, 3 master's, 2 doctorates awarded. *Degree requirements:* For master's, one foreign language, thesis (MA); for doctorate, one foreign language, thesis/dissertation. *Entrance requirements:* For master's and doctorate, GRE General Test. *Application deadline:* For fall admission, 7/1 priority date for domestic students; for spring admission, 11/15 for domestic students. Application fee: $50. Electronic applications accepted. *Expenses:* Tuition, state resident: full-time $6000; part-time $250 per credit hour. Tuition, nonresident: full-time $20,904; part-time $871 per credit hour. Required fees: $730 per semester. *Financial support:* Fellowships, research assistantships, teaching assistantships, unspecified assistantships available. *Unit head:* Dr. Nina Hellerstein, Department Head, 706-542-3122, E-mail: hellerst@uga.edu. *Application contact:* Dr. Catherine M. Jones, Graduate Coordinator, 706-542-3159, Fax: 706-542-3287, E-mail: cmjones@uga.edu.

University of Miami, Graduate School, College of Arts and Sciences, Department of Modern Languages and Literatures, Coral Gables, FL 33124. Offers romance studies (PhD), including French, Spanish. *Degree requirements:* For doctorate, 2 foreign languages, thesis/dissertation, area exam, qualifying exam. *Entrance requirements:* For doctorate, 1 writing sample in English and 1 writing sample in French or Spanish, minimum GPA of 3.0, oral interview, letters of recommendation. Additional exam requirements/recommendations for international students: Required—TOEFL (minimum score 550 paper-based; 213 computer-based; 59 iBT). Electronic applications accepted. *Faculty research:* Transatlantic studies, Caribbean studies, comparative literature, gender theory, cultural studies.

University of Michigan, Horace H. Rackham School of Graduate Studies, College of Literature, Science, and the Arts, Department of Linguistics, Ann Arbor, MI 48109. Offers linguistics (PhD); linguistics and Romance languages and literatures (PhD). *Faculty:* 16 full-time (7 women), 2 part-time/adjunct (both women). *Students:* 29 full-time (15 women); includes 5 minority (1 African American, 3 Asian Americans or Pacific Islanders, 1 Hispanic American), 12 international. Average age 30. 100 applicants, 8% accepted, 5 enrolled. In 2009, 1 doctorate awarded. *Degree requirements:* For doctorate, 2 foreign languages, thesis/dissertation, oral defense of dissertation. *Entrance requirements:* For doctorate, GRE General Test. Additional exam requirements/recommendations for international students: Required—TOEFL (minimum score 620 paper-based; 260 computer-based; 95 iBT), or Michigan English Language Assessment Battery. *Application deadline:* For fall admission, 12/15 for domestic and international students. Application fee: $60 ($75 for international students). Electronic applications accepted. *Expenses:* Tuition, state resident: full-time $17,286; part-time $1099 per credit hour. Tuition, nonresident: full-time $34,944; part-time $2080 per credit hour. Required fees: $95 per semester. Tuition and fees vary according to course load, degree level and program. *Financial support:* In 2009–10, 25 students received support, including 12 fellowships with full tuition reimbursements available (averaging $16,800 per year), 3 research assistantships with full tuition reimbursements available, 16 teaching assistantships with full tuition reimbursements available (averaging $16,694 per year); health care benefits also available. Financial award application deadline: 12/15. *Faculty research:* Broad-based approach to linguistics as a cognitive and social science including theoretical, experimental and computational approaches. Total annual research expenditures: $21,856. *Unit head:* Patrice Speeter Beddor, Professor and Chair, Linguistics, 734-764-0353, Fax: 734-936-3406, E-mail: linguistics@umich.edu. *Application contact:* Sylvia Suttor, Student Services Assistant Senior, 734-764-5355, Fax: 734-763-6557, E-mail: ssuttor@umich.edu.

University of Michigan, Horace H. Rackham School of Graduate Studies, College of Literature, Science, and the Arts, Department of Romance Languages and Literatures, Ann Arbor, MI 48109. Offers French (PhD); Romance linguistics (PhD); Spanish (PhD). *Faculty:* 28 full-time (13 women), 2 part-time/adjunct (1 woman). *Students:* 75 full-time (42 women); includes 2 African Americans, 1 Asian American or Pacific Islander, 26 Hispanic Americans. Average age 30. 73 applicants, 25% accepted, 8 enrolled. In 2009, 3 doctorates awarded. *Degree requirements:* For doctorate, 2 foreign languages, thesis/dissertation, oral defense of dissertation, preliminary exams. *Entrance requirements:* For doctorate, GRE General Test. Additional exam requirements/recommendations for international students: Required—TOEFL or Michigan

Romance Languages

University of Michigan (continued)
English Language Assessment Battery. *Application deadline:* For fall admission, 1/1 for domestic and international students. Application fee: $60. Electronic applications accepted. *Expenses:* Tuition, state resident: full-time $17,286; part-time $1099 per credit hour. Tuition, nonresident: full-time $34,944; part-time $2080 per credit hour. Required fees: $95 per semester. Tuition and fees vary according to course load, degree level and program. *Financial support:* In 2009–10, 1 teaching assistantship with full tuition reimbursement was awarded; fellowships with full tuition reimbursements, institutionally sponsored loans, scholarships/grants, and unspecified assistantships also available. Financial award application deadline: 1/1. *Faculty research:* Comparative Romance studies, medieval and early modern studies, postcolonial and minority literatures, culture and materiality, reflection on the nature and function of scholarship. *Unit head:* Dr. Michele Hannoosh, Chair, 734-764-5344, Fax: 734-764-8163. *Application contact:* Annette Herbert, Graduate Assistant, 734-764-8164, Fax: 734-764-8163, E-mail: rll-admissions@umich.edu.

University of Missouri, Graduate School, College of Arts and Sciences, Department of Romance Languages and Literature, Columbia, MO 65211. Offers French (MA, PhD); literature (MA); Spanish (MA, PhD); teaching (MA). *Faculty:* 21 full-time (13 women), 19 part-time/adjunct (15 women). *Students:* 16 full-time (12 women), 26 part-time (16 women); includes 11 minority (2 African Americans, 2 Asian Americans or Pacific Islanders, 7 Hispanic Americans), 9 international. Average age 35. 28 applicants, 71% accepted, 14 enrolled. In 2009, 2 master's awarded. Terminal master's awarded for partial completion of doctoral program. *Degree requirements:* For master's, one foreign language; for doctorate, 4 foreign languages, comprehensive exam, thesis/dissertation. *Entrance requirements:* For master's, GRE General Test, minimum GPA of 3.0 in field of major; must have bachelor's degree; for doctorate, GRE General Test, minimum GPA of 3.0 in field of major; must have maser's degree. Additional exam requirements/recommendations for international students: Required—TOEFL (minimum score 500 paper-based; 173 computer-based; 61 iBT). *Application deadline:* For fall admission, 2/15 priority date for domestic students; for winter admission, 10/15 for domestic students. Applications are processed on a rolling basis. Application fee: $45 ($60 for international students). Electronic applications accepted. *Financial support:* In 2009–10, 37 teaching assistantships with full tuition reimbursements were awarded; research assistantships, institutionally sponsored loans, health care benefits, and unspecified assistantships also available. *Unit head:* Dr. Flore Zephir, Department Chair, E-mail: zephirf@missouri.edu. *Application contact:* Mary Harriss, Administrative Assistant, 573-882-5039, E-mail: harrisma@missouri.edu.

University of Missouri–Kansas City, College of Arts and Sciences, Department of Foreign Languages and Literatures, Kansas City, MO 64110-2499. Offers Romance languages and literatures (MA). Part-time programs available. *Faculty:* 11 full-time (5 women), 18 part-time/adjunct (12 women). *Students:* 1 (woman) full-time, 28 part-time (20 women); includes 6 minority (all Hispanic Americans). Average age 35. 4 applicants, 100% accepted, 4 enrolled. In 2009, 11 master's awarded. *Degree requirements:* For master's, 2 foreign languages. *Entrance requirements:* For master's, GRE General Test, minimum GPA of 2.75, 2 letters of recommendation. Additional exam requirements/recommendations for international students: Required—TOEFL (minimum score 550 paper-based; 213 computer-based; 80 iBT). *Application deadline:* For fall admission, 4/1 priority date for domestic and international students; for spring admission, 11/1 priority date for domestic and international students. Applications are processed on a rolling basis. Application fee: $45 ($50 for international students). Electronic applications accepted. *Expenses:* Tuition, state resident: full-time $5378; part-time $299 per credit hour. Tuition, nonresident: full-time $13,881; part-time $771 per credit hour. Required fees: $641; $71 per credit hour. Tuition and fees vary according to course load and program. *Financial support:* Federal Work-Study, institutionally sponsored loans, and tuition waivers (full and partial) available. Support available to part-time students. Financial award application deadline: 3/1; financial award applicants required to submit FAFSA. *Faculty research:* Literary analyses; psychology and literature; narrative techniques, poetic structure, and style; literature, politics, and society (especially Latin America). *Unit head:* Dr. Kathy Krause, Chair, 816-235-1340, Fax: 816-235-1312, E-mail: krausek@umkc.edu. *Application contact:* Dr. Nacer Khelouz, Graduate Advisor/Assistant Professor, 816-235-1311, Fax: 816-235-1312, E-mail: admit@umkc.edu.

University of New Orleans, Graduate School, College of Liberal Arts, Department of Foreign Languages, New Orleans, LA 70148. Offers MA. Part-time and evening/weekend programs available. *Degree requirements:* For master's, one foreign language, thesis optional. *Entrance requirements:* For master's, GRE General Test, minimum B average. Additional exam requirements/recommendations for international students: Required—TOEFL (minimum score 550 paper-based; 213 computer-based; 79 iBT). Electronic applications accepted. *Faculty research:* Translation studies, Michelet, Scève, Spanish canzoniero, theories of representation.

The University of North Carolina at Chapel Hill, Graduate School, College of Arts and Sciences, Department of Romance Languages, Chapel Hill, NC 27599. Offers French (MA, PhD); Italian (MA, PhD); Portuguese (MA, PhD); Romance languages (MA, PhD); Romance philology (MA, PhD); Spanish (MA, PhD). *Degree requirements:* For master's, one foreign language, comprehensive exam, thesis; for doctorate, 2 foreign languages, comprehensive exam, thesis/dissertation. *Entrance requirements:* For master's and doctorate, GRE General Test, minimum GPA of 3.0. Additional exam requirements/recommendations for international students: Required—TOEFL (minimum score 550 paper-based; 213 computer-based). Electronic applications accepted.

University of Notre Dame, Graduate School, College of Arts and Letters, Division of Humanities, Department of Romance Languages and Literatures, Notre Dame, IN 46556. Offers French and Francophone studies (MA); Iberian and Latin American studies (MA); Italian studies (MA); Romance literatures (MA). *Degree requirements:* For master's, 2 foreign languages, comprehensive exam, thesis optional. *Entrance requirements:* For master's, GRE General Test, BA in target language. Additional exam requirements/recommendations for international students: Required—TOEFL (minimum score 600 paper-based; 250 computer-based; 80 iBT). Electronic applications accepted. *Faculty research:* Literature of discovery and exploration, modern literature, literary criticism, medieval literature, feminist critical theory.

University of Oregon, Graduate School, College of Arts and Sciences, Department of Romance Languages, Program in Romance Languages, Eugene, OR 97403. Offers MA, PhD. Part-time programs available. *Degree requirements:* For master's, 2 foreign languages; for doctorate, 2 foreign languages, thesis/dissertation. *Entrance requirements:* For master's and doctorate, GRE General Test, minimum GPA of 3.0. Additional exam requirements/recommendations for international students: Required—TOEFL.

University of Pennsylvania, School of Arts and Sciences, Graduate Group in Romance Languages, Philadelphia, PA 19104. Offers French (AM, PhD); Italian (AM, PhD); Spanish (AM, PhD). *Faculty:* 60 full-time (24 women), 4 part-time/adjunct (1 woman). *Students:* 60 full-time (38 women), 2 part-time (both women); includes 7 minority (1 American Indian/Alaska Native, 6 Hispanic Americans), 17 international. 101 applicants, 26% accepted, 13 enrolled. In 2009, 12 master's, 7 doctorates awarded. Terminal master's awarded for partial completion of doctoral program. *Degree requirements:* For master's, one foreign language, thesis or alternative; for doctorate, 2 foreign languages, thesis/dissertation. *Entrance requirements:* For master's and doctorate, GRE General Test. Additional exam requirements/recommendations for international students: Required—TOEFL. *Application deadline:* For fall admission, 12/1 priority date for domestic students. Application fee: $70. Electronic applications accepted. *Expenses:* Tuition: Full-time $25,660; part-time $4758 per course. Required fees: $2152; $270 per course. Tuition and fees vary according to course load, degree level and program. *Financial support:* In 2009–10, 23 fellowships, 2 research assistantships, 39 teaching assistantships were awarded; institutionally sponsored loans, scholarships/grants, traineeships, health care benefits, and unspecified assistantships also available. Financial award application deadline: 12/15. *Faculty research:* Literary theory and criticism, cultural studies, history of Romance literatures, gender studies.

University of South Africa, College of Human Sciences, Pretoria, South Africa. Offers adult education (M Ed); African languages (MA, PhD); African politics (MA, PhD); Afrikaans (MA, PhD); ancient history (MA, PhD); ancient Near Eastern studies (MA, PhD); anthropology (MA, PhD); applied linguistics (MA); Arabic (MA, PhD); archaeology (MA); art history (MA); Biblical archaeology (MA); Biblical studies (M Th, D Th, PhD); Christian spirituality (M Th, D Th); church history (M Th, D Th); classical studies (MA, PhD); clinical psychology (MA); communication (MA, PhD); comparative education (M Ed, Ed D); consulting psychology (D Admin, D Com, PhD); curriculum studies (M Ed, Ed D); development studies (M Admin, MA, D Admin, PhD); didactics (M Ed, Ed D); education (M Tech); education management (M Ed, Ed D); educational psychology (M Ed); English (MA); environmental education (M Ed); French (MA, PhD); German (MA, PhD); Greek (MA); guidance and counseling (M Ed); health studies (MA, PhD), including health sciences education (MA), health services management (MA), medical and surgical nursing science (critical care general) (MA), midwifery and neonatal nursing science (MA), trauma and emergency care (MA); history (MA, PhD); history of education (Ed D); inclusive education (M Ed, Ed D); information and communications technology policy and regulation (MA); information science (MA, MIS, PhD); international politics (MA, PhD); Islamic studies (MA, PhD); Italian (MA, PhD); Judaica (MA, PhD); linguistics (MA, PhD); mathematical education (M Ed); mathematics education (MA); missiology (M Th, D Th); modern Hebrew (MA, PhD); musicology (MA, MMus, D Mus, PhD); natural science education (M Ed); New Testament (M Th, D Th); Old Testament (D Th); pastoral therapy (M Th, D Th); philosophy (MA); philosophy of education (M Ed, Ed D); politics (MA, PhD); Portuguese (MA, PhD); practical theology (M Th, D Th); psychology (MA, MS, PhD); psychology of education (M Ed, Ed D); public health (MA); religious studies (MA, D Th, PhD); Romance languages (MA); Russian (MA, PhD); Semitic languages (MA, PhD); social behavior studies in HIV/AIDS (MA); social science (mental health) (MA); social science in development studies (MA); social science in psychology (MA); social science in social work (MA); social science in sociology (MA); social work (MSW, DSW, PhD); socio-education (M Ed, Ed D); sociolinguistics (MA); sociology (MA, PhD); Spanish (MA, PhD); systematic theology (M Th, D Th); TESOL (teaching English to speakers of other languages) (MA); theological ethics (M Th, D Th); theory of literature (MA, PhD); urban ministries (D Th); urban ministry (M Th).

The University of Texas at Austin, Graduate School, College of Liberal Arts, Department of French and Italian, Austin, TX 78712-1111. Offers French (MA, PhD); French linguistics (MA, PhD); Italian studies (MA, PhD); Romance linguistics (MA, PhD). Part-time programs available. *Degree requirements:* For master's, one foreign language, thesis; for doctorate, 2 foreign languages, thesis/dissertation. *Entrance requirements:* For master's, GRE General Test, minimum GPA of 3.0, bachelor's degree in French or equivalent; for doctorate, GRE General Test, minimum GPA of 3.0, master's degree in French. Additional exam requirements/recommendations for international students: Required—TOEFL. Electronic applications accepted. *Faculty research:* Nineteenth-century Italian literature, Italian Renaissance, twentieth-century French literature, Francophone literature, fifteenth-century literature and culture.

University of Virginia, College and Graduate School of Arts and Sciences, Department of Spanish, Italian and Portuguese, Charlottesville, VA 22903. Offers Italian (MA); Spanish (MA, PhD). *Faculty:* 22 full-time (10 women), 1 part-time/adjunct (0 women). *Students:* 52 full-time (39 women), 6 part-time (5 women); includes 9 minority (1 Asian American or Pacific Islander, 8 Hispanic Americans), 10 international. Average age 28. 50 applicants, 40% accepted, 13 enrolled. In 2009, 13 master's, 7 doctorates awarded. *Degree requirements:* For master's, comprehensive exam, thesis; for doctorate, one foreign language, comprehensive exam, thesis/dissertation. *Entrance requirements:* For master's and doctorate, GRE General Test, GRE Subject Test, 2 letters of recommendation. Additional exam requirements/recommendations for international students: Required—TOEFL (minimum score 600 paper-based; 250 computer-based; 90 iBT), IELTS (minimum score 7). *Application deadline:* For fall admission, 12/1 for domestic and international students. Applications are processed on a rolling basis. Application fee: $60. Electronic applications accepted. *Financial support:* Fellowships, teaching assistantships available. Financial award applicants required to submit FAFSA. *Unit head:* Maria-Ines Lagos, Chair, 434-924-7159, Fax: 434-924-7160, E-mail: sipinfo@virginia.edu. *Application contact:* Maria-Ines Lagos, Chair, 434-924-7159, Fax: 434-924-7160, E-mail: sipinfo@virginia.edu.

University of Washington, Graduate School, College of Arts and Sciences, Department of Romance Languages and Literature, Seattle, WA 98195. Offers French and Italian studies (MA, PhD), including French, Italian (MA); Spanish and Portuguese (MA), including Hispanic literary and cultural studies. Terminal master's awarded for partial completion of doctoral program. *Degree requirements:* For master's, 2 foreign languages, thesis optional, exam; for doctorate, 3 foreign languages, thesis/dissertation, exams. *Entrance requirements:* For master's and doctorate, GRE General Test, minimum GPA of 3.0. Additional exam requirements/recommendations for international students: Required—TOEFL. Electronic applications accepted.

Washington University in St. Louis, Graduate School of Arts and Sciences, Department of Romance Languages and Literatures, St. Louis, MO 63130-4899. Offers French (MA, PhD); Spanish (MA, PhD). Terminal master's awarded for partial completion of doctoral program. *Degree requirements:* For master's, thesis or alternative; for doctorate, thesis/dissertation. *Entrance requirements:* For master's and doctorate, GRE General Test. Electronic applications accepted.

Russian

American University, College of Arts and Sciences, Department of Language and Foreign Studies, Program in Russian, Washington, DC 20016-8045. Offers translation (Certificate). Part-time and evening/weekend programs available. *Students:* 5 part-time (3 women). Average age 35. In 2009, 2 Certificates awarded. *Entrance requirements:* For degree, bachelor's degree in Russian or evidence of Russian proficiency plus a BA. Additional exam requirements/recommendations for international students: Required—TOEFL. *Application deadline:* For fall admission, 2/1 for domestic students; for spring admission, 10/1 for domestic students. Application fee: $50. *Expenses:* Tuition: Full-time $22,266; part-time $1237 per credit hour. Required fees: $430. Tuition and fees vary according to program. *Financial support:* Fellowships, career-related internships or fieldwork, Federal Work-Study, and institutionally sponsored loans available. Financial award application deadline: 2/1. *Faculty research:* Culture, literature, and area studies; technology-assisted language instruction; linguistics.

Boston College, Graduate School of Arts and Sciences, Department of Slavic and Eastern Languages, Program in Russian and Slavic Languages and Literature, Chestnut Hill, MA 02467-3800. Offers MA, MA/JD, MBA/MA. Part-time programs available. *Degree requirements:* For master's, 3 foreign languages, comprehensive exam, thesis or alternative. *Entrance* *requirements:* Additional exam requirements/recommendations for international students: Required—TOEFL (minimum score 600 paper-based; 250 computer-based; 100 iBT). *Application deadline:* For fall admission, 1/15 for domestic students. Application fee: $75. Electronic applications accepted. *Financial support:* Teaching assistantships, Federal Work-Study available. Support available to part-time students. Financial award application deadline: 3/1; financial award applicants required to submit FAFSA. *Faculty research:* Structural analysis of language, poetry and semiotic systems. *Unit head:* Dr. Maxin Shrayer, Chairperson, 617-552-3910. *Application contact:* Dr. Maxin Shrayer, Chairperson, 617-552-3910.

Brown University, Graduate School, Department of Slavic Languages, Providence, RI 02912. Offers Russian language and literature (AM); Slavic languages (AM); Slavic studies (PhD). *Degree requirements:* For master's, one foreign language; for doctorate, 2 foreign languages, thesis/dissertation, preliminary exam.

Columbia University, Graduate School of Arts and Sciences, Division of Humanities, Department of Slavic Languages, New York, NY 10027. Offers Russian literature (M Phil, MA, PhD); Slavic languages (M Phil, MA, PhD). *Degree requirements:* For master's, one foreign language, thesis; for doctorate, 2 foreign languages, thesis/dissertation. *Entrance requirements:* For master's and doctorate, GRE General Test. Additional exam requirements/recommendations for international students: Required—TOEFL. *Faculty research:* Polish, Serbo-Croatian, Czechoslovakian, medieval and modern Russian literature.

Harvard University, Graduate School of Arts and Sciences, Department of Slavic Languages and Literatures, Cambridge, MA 02138. Offers Polish (PhD); Russian (PhD); Serbo-Croatian (PhD); Slavic philology (PhD); Ukrainian (PhD). *Degree requirements:* For doctorate, 4 foreign languages, thesis/dissertation. *Entrance requirements:* For doctorate, GRE General Test, writing sample. Additional exam requirements/recommendations for international students: Required—TOEFL. *Expenses:* Tuition: Full-time $33,696. Required fees: $1126. Full-time tuition and fees vary according to program.

Hofstra University, School of Education, Health, and Human Services, Department of Curriculum and Teaching, Program in Foreign Language Education, Hempstead, NY 11549. Offers foreign language and TESOL (MS Ed); foreign language education (MA, MS Ed), including French, German, Russian, Spanish. Part-time and evening/weekend programs available. *Students:* 4 full-time (all women), 3 part-time (1 woman); includes 2 minority (both Hispanic Americans). Average age 29. 9 applicants, 67% accepted, 3 enrolled. In 2009, 2 master's awarded. *Degree requirements:* For master's, one foreign language. *Entrance requirements:* For master's, 2 letters of recommendation, teacher certification (MA). Additional exam requirements/recommendations for international students: Required—TOEFL (minimum score 550 paper-based; 213 computer-based; 80 iBT). *Application deadline:* Applications are processed on a rolling basis. Application fee: $60. Electronic applications accepted. *Expenses:* Tuition: Full-time $16,200; part-time $900 per credit hour. Required fees: $970; $145 per term. Tuition and fees vary according to program. *Financial support:* In 2009–10, 6 students received support, including 2 fellowships with full and partial tuition reimbursements available (averaging $2,878 per year); research assistantships with full and partial tuition reimbursements available, Federal Work-Study, institutionally sponsored loans, scholarships/grants, tuition waivers (full and partial), and unspecified assistantships also available. Support available to part-time students. Financial award applicants required to submit FAFSA. *Faculty research:* First language acquisition and second language learning; theory and practice in language teaching; technology and language teaching and learning; language and colonialism. *Unit head:* Dr. Mustapha Masrour, Program Director, 516-463-6033, Fax: 516-463-6266, E-mail: lalmzm@hofstra.edu. *Application contact:* Carol Drummer, Dean of Graduate Admissions, 516-463-4876, Fax: 516-463-4664, E-mail: gradstudent@hofstra.edu.

Kent State University, College of Arts and Sciences, Department of Modern and Classical Language Studies, Kent, OH 44242-0001. Offers French literature (MA); French, Spanish, German and Latin pedagogy (MA); German literature (MA); Spanish literature (MA); translation (MA), including French, German, Japanese, Russian, Spanish; translation studies (PhD). Part-time and evening/weekend programs available. *Degree requirements:* For master's, one foreign language, comprehensive exam (for some programs), thesis (for some programs); for doctorate, comprehensive exam, thesis/dissertation (for some programs). *Entrance requirements:* For master's, minimum GPA of 3.0, writing sample, audio tape or CD; for doctorate, 3 recommendations. Additional exam requirements/recommendations for international students: Required—TOEFL (minimum score 197 computer-based). Electronic applications accepted. *Faculty research:* Literature, pedagogy, applied linguistics, translation studies.

McGill University, Faculty of Graduate and Postdoctoral Studies, Faculty of Arts, Department of Russian and Slavic Studies, Montréal, QC H3A 2T5, Canada. Offers Russian literature (MA, PhD).

Middlebury College, Language Schools, Russian School, Middlebury, VT 05753-6002. Offers MA, DML. *Faculty:* 8 full-time (4 women). *Students:* 16 full-time (12 women). Average age 33. 43 applicants, 60% accepted, 16 enrolled. In 2009, 6 master's awarded. *Degree requirements:* For master's, one foreign language; for doctorate, 2 foreign languages, comprehensive exam, thesis/dissertation. *Entrance requirements:* For master's, placement exam, 3 letters of recommendation, writing sample. *Application deadline:* Applications are processed on a rolling basis. Application fee: $65. Electronic applications accepted. *Financial support:* Scholarships/grants available. *Unit head:* Dr. Benjamin Rifkin, Director, 802-443-5230, Fax: 802-443-2075, E-mail: brifkin@middlebury.edu. *Application contact:* John Stokes, Coordinator, 802-443-5230, Fax: 802-443-2075, E-mail: jstokes@middlebury.edu.

New York University, Graduate School of Arts and Science, Department of Russian and Slavic Studies, New York, NY 10012-1019. Offers Russian literature (MA); Slavic literature (MA). Part-time programs available. *Faculty:* 8 full-time (3 women). *Students:* 9 full-time (2 women), 5 part-time (2 women), 2 international. Average age 27. 20 applicants, 95% accepted, 11 enrolled. In 2009, 2 master's awarded. *Degree requirements:* For master's, one foreign language, comprehensive exam, thesis. *Entrance requirements:* For master's, GRE General Test, minimum 3 years of undergraduate Russian or equivalent. Additional exam requirements/recommendations for international students: Required—TOEFL. *Application deadline:* For fall admission, 4/15 for domestic students; for spring admission, 11/1 for domestic students. Application fee: $90. *Expenses:* Tuition: Full-time $30,528; part-time $1272 per credit. Required fees: $2177. *Financial support:* Career-related internships or fieldwork, Federal Work-Study and institutionally sponsored loans available. Financial award application deadline: 4/15; financial award applicants required to submit FAFSA. *Faculty research:* Modern Russian literature and art, contemporary Russian and East European literature, literary theory, Slavic linguistics, Russian journalism. *Unit head:* Yanni Katsanisein, Chair, 212-998-8670, Fax: 212-995-4604, E-mail: gsas.russian.and.slavic@nyu.edu. *Application contact:* Anne Lounsbery, Director of Graduate Studies, 212-998-8670, Fax: 212-995-4604, E-mail: gsas.russian.and.slavic@nyu.edu.

Princeton University, Graduate School, Department of Slavic Languages and Literatures, Princeton, NJ 08544-1019. Offers Russian and Slavic linguistics (PhD); Russian literature (PhD). *Degree requirements:* For doctorate, variable foreign language requirement, thesis/dissertation. *Entrance requirements:* For doctorate, GRE General Test. Additional exam requirements/recommendations for international students: Required—TOEFL (minimum score 600 paper-based; 250 computer-based). Electronic applications accepted.

Stanford University, School of Humanities and Sciences, Department of Slavic Languages and Literatures, Stanford, CA 94305-9991. Offers Russian (MA); Slavic languages and literatures (PhD). Terminal master's awarded for partial completion of doctoral program. *Degree requirements:* For master's, one foreign language, thesis or alternative; for doctorate, 3 foreign languages, thesis/dissertation. *Entrance requirements:* For master's and doctorate, GRE General Test. Additional exam requirements/recommendations for international students: Required—TOEFL. Electronic applications accepted. *Expenses:* Tuition: Full-time $37,380; part-time $2760 per quarter. Required fees: $501.

University at Albany, State University of New York, College of Arts and Sciences, Department of Languages, Literatures, and Cultures, Program in Russian, Albany, NY 12222-0001. Offers Russian (MA); Russian translation (Certificate). *Faculty research:* Translation, phonology and morphology of modern Russian.

The University of Arizona, Graduate College, College of Humanities, Department of Russian and Slavic Studies, Tucson, AZ 85721. Offers Russian (MA). Part-time programs available. *Faculty:* 7. *Students:* 9 full-time (5 women), 6 part-time (3 women), 5 international. Average age 28. 15 applicants, 73% accepted, 7 enrolled. In 2009, 6 master's awarded. *Degree requirements:* For master's, one foreign language, comprehensive exam (for some programs), thesis (for some programs). *Entrance requirements:* For master's, 3 letters of recommendation, audio sample. Additional exam requirements/recommendations for international students: Required—TOEFL (minimum score 550 paper-based; 213 computer-based; 79 iBT). *Application deadline:* For fall admission, 4/1 for domestic students, 12/1 for international students; for spring admission, 10/1 for domestic students, 6/1 for international students. Applications are processed on a rolling basis. Application fee: $75. Electronic applications accepted. *Expenses:* Tuition, state resident: full-time $9028. Tuition, nonresident: full-time $24,890. *Financial support:* In 2009–10, 10 teaching assistantships with full tuition reimbursements (averaging $13,989 per year) were awarded; Federal Work-Study, scholarships/grants, health care benefits, tuition waivers (full), and unspecified assistantships also available. *Faculty research:* Russian literature, language/pedagogy, linguistics, Russian culture. *Unit head:* Dr. Teresa Polowy, Department Head, 520-621-7341, Fax: 520-626-4007, E-mail: tpolowy@email.arizona.edu. *Application contact:* Judi Greil, Graduate Coordinator, 520-621-3702, Fax: 520-626-4007, E-mail: greilj@u.arizona.edu.

University of California, Berkeley, Graduate Division, College of Letters and Science, Department of Slavic Languages and Literatures, Berkeley, CA 94720-1500. Offers Czech (PhD), including Czech linguistics, Czech literature; Polish (PhD), including Polish linguistics, Polish literature; Russian (PhD), including Russian linguistics, Russian literature; Serbo-Croatian (PhD), including Serbo-Croatian linguistics, Serbo-Croatian literature. *Faculty:* 15 full-time. *Students:* 22 full-time (17 women). Average age 30. 32 applicants, 2 enrolled. In 2009, 1 doctorate awarded. Terminal master's awarded for partial completion of doctoral program. *Degree requirements:* For doctorate, thesis/dissertation, oral and written exams. *Entrance requirements:* For doctorate, GRE General Test, minimum GPA of 3.0, 3 letters of recommendation. Additional exam requirements/recommendations for international students: Required—TOEFL (minimum score 570 paper-based; 230 computer-based). *Application deadline:* For fall admission, 12/15 for domestic students. Application fee: $70 ($90 for international students). Electronic applications accepted. *Financial support:* Fellowships, research assistantships, teaching assistantships, unspecified assistantships available. Financial award applicants required to submit FAFSA. *Unit head:* David Frick, Chair, 510-642-2979, E-mail: ch_slavic@ls.berkeley.edu. *Application contact:* Sandy Jones, Student Affairs Officer, 510-642-9051, Fax: 510-643-6220, E-mail: issag@berkeley.edu.

University of Michigan, Horace H. Rackham School of Graduate Studies, College of Literature, Science, and the Arts, Department of Slavic Languages and Literatures, Ann Arbor, MI 48109-1275. Offers Russian (AM); Slavic languages and literatures (PhD). Terminal master's awarded for partial completion of doctoral program. *Degree requirements:* For master's, 2 foreign languages, comprehensive exam; for doctorate, 3 foreign languages, comprehensive exam, thesis/dissertation, oral defense of dissertation, preliminary exam. *Entrance requirements:* For master's, GRE General Test, 3rd-year foreign language proficiency; for doctorate, GRE General Test. Additional exam requirements/recommendations for international students: Required—TOEFL (minimum score 560 paper-based; 220 computer-based). Electronic applications accepted. *Expenses:* Tuition, state resident: full-time $17,286; part-time $1099 per credit hour. Tuition, nonresident: full-time $34,944; part-time $2080 per credit hour. Required fees: $95 per semester. Tuition and fees vary according to course load, degree level and program. *Faculty research:* Russian literature (all periods), Polish literature, South Slavic literatures, Czech literature, Ukrainian literature.

The University of North Carolina at Chapel Hill, Graduate School, College of Arts and Sciences, Department of Slavic Languages and Literatures, Chapel Hill, NC 27599. Offers Polish literature (PhD); Russian literature (MA, PhD); Serbo-Croatian literature (PhD); Slavic linguistics (MA, PhD). Part-time programs available. Terminal master's awarded for partial completion of doctoral program. *Degree requirements:* For master's, 2 foreign languages, comprehensive exam, thesis; for doctorate, 4 foreign languages, comprehensive exam, thesis/dissertation. *Entrance requirements:* For master's and doctorate, GRE General Test, minimum GPA of 3.0. Electronic applications accepted. *Faculty research:* Russian cultural studies, literary translation, sociolinguistics, cognitive linguistics, émigré literature.

University of Oregon, Graduate School, College of Arts and Sciences, Program in Russian and East European Studies, Eugene, OR 97403. Offers MA. Part-time programs available. *Degree requirements:* For master's, 2 foreign languages, thesis. *Entrance requirements:* For master's, GRE General Test (recommended), minimum GPA of 3.0. Additional exam requirements/recommendations for international students: Required—TOEFL. *Faculty research:* L. N. Tolstoy's middle years, Russian folklore in eighteenth century contexts, Bulgarian syntax, medieval Bulgarian texts, contemporary Russian culture film.

University of South Africa, College of Human Sciences, Pretoria, South Africa. Offers adult education (M Ed); African languages (MA, PhD); African politics (MA, PhD); Afrikaans (MA, PhD); ancient history (MA, PhD); ancient Near Eastern studies (MA, PhD); anthropology (MA, PhD); applied linguistics (MA); Arabic (MA, PhD); archaeology (MA); art history (MA); Biblical archaeology (MA); Biblical studies (M Th, D Th, PhD); Christian spirituality (M Th, D Th); church history (M Th, D Th); classical studies (MA, PhD); clinical psychology (MA); communication (MA, PhD); comparative education (M Ed, Ed D); consulting psychology (D Admin, D Com, PhD); curriculum studies (M Ed, Ed D); development studies (M Admin, MA, D Admin, PhD); didactics (M Ed, Ed D); education (M Tech); education management (M Ed, Ed D); educational psychology (M Ed); English (MA); environmental education (M Ed); French (MA, PhD); German (MA, PhD); Greek (MA); guidance and counseling (M Ed); health studies (MA, PhD), including health sciences education (MA), health services management (MA), medical and surgical nursing science (critical care general) (MA), midwifery and neonatal nursing science (MA), trauma and emergency care (MA); history (MA, PhD); history of education (Ed D); inclusive education (M Ed, Ed D); information and communications technology policy and regulation (MA); information science (MA, MIS, PhD); international politics (MA, PhD); Islamic studies (MA, PhD); Italian (MA, PhD); Judaica (MA, PhD); linguistics (MA, PhD); mathematical education (M Ed); mathematics education (MA); missiology (M Th, D Th); modern Hebrew (MA, PhD); musicology (MA, MMus, D Mus, PhD); natural science education (M Ed); New Testament (M Th, D Th); Old Testament (D Th); pastoral therapy (M Th, D Th); philosophy (MA); philosophy of education (M Ed, Ed D); politics (MA, PhD); Portuguese (MA, PhD); practical theology (M Th, D Th); psychology (MA, MS, PhD); psychology of education (M Ed, Ed D); public health (MA); religious studies (MA, D Th, PhD); Romance languages (MA); Russian (MA, PhD); Semitic languages (MA, PhD); social behavior studies in HIV/AIDS (MA); social science (mental health) (MA); social science in development studies (MA); social science in psychology (MA); social science in social work (MA); social science in sociology (MA); social work (MSW, DSW, PhD); socio-education (M Ed, Ed D); sociolinguistics (MA); sociology (MA, PhD); Spanish (MA, PhD); systematic theology (M Th, D Th); TESOL (teaching English to speakers of other languages) (MA); theological ethics (M Th, D Th); theory of literature (MA, PhD); urban ministries (D Th); urban ministry (M Th).

The University of Tennessee, Graduate School, College of Arts and Sciences, Department of Modern Foreign Languages and Literatures, Program in Modern Foreign Languages, Knoxville, TN 37996. Offers applied linguistics (PhD); French (PhD); German (PhD); Italian (PhD); Portuguese (PhD); Russian (PhD); Spanish (PhD). *Degree requirements:* For doctorate, 2

Russian

The University of Tennessee (continued)

foreign languages, thesis/dissertation. *Entrance requirements:* For doctorate, minimum GPA of 2.7. Additional exam requirements/recommendations for international students: Required—TOEFL. Electronic applications accepted. *Expenses:* Tuition, state resident: full-time $6826; part-time $380 per semester hour. Tuition, nonresident: full-time $21,844; part-time $1147 per semester hour. Tuition and fees vary according to program.

University of Washington, Graduate School, College of Arts and Sciences, Department of Slavic Languages and Literatures, Seattle, WA 98195. Offers Russian literature (MA, PhD); Slavic linguistics (MA, PhD). *Degree requirements:* For master's, 2 foreign languages, thesis optional; for doctorate, 3 foreign languages, thesis/dissertation. *Entrance requirements:* For master's and doctorate, GRE General Test, minimum GPA of 3.0. Additional exam requirements/recommendations for international students: Required—TOEFL. Electronic applications accepted. *Faculty research:* Modern and medieval East European languages and literatures, comparative literature, Russian folk literature, Slavic literary theory and criticism, computerized morphology of Russian.

University of Waterloo, Graduate Studies, Faculty of Arts, Department of Germanic and Slavic Studies, Waterloo, ON N2L 3G1, Canada. Offers German (MA, PhD); Russian (MA). Part-time and evening/weekend programs available. *Degree requirements:* For master's, one foreign language, thesis optional; for doctorate, 2 foreign languages, comprehensive exam, thesis/dissertation. *Entrance requirements:* For master's, honors degree, minimum B average; for doctorate, master's degree, minimum B average. Additional exam requirements/recommendations for international students: Required—TOEFL, TWE. Electronic applications accepted. *Faculty research:* Medieval theatre; history and literature; German and Russian literary relations; seventeenth, eighteenth, nineteenth, and twentieth century German literature.

Wayne State University, College of Liberal Arts and Sciences, Department of Classical and Modern Languages, Literatures, and Cultures, Program in German and Slavic Studies, Detroit, MI 48202. Offers German (MA); language learning (MA); modern languages (PhD); Russian (MA). *Degree requirements:* For master's, one foreign language, thesis or alternative; for doctorate, 2 foreign languages, thesis/dissertation. *Entrance requirements:* For master's and doctorate, minimum GPA of 3.0. Additional exam requirements/recommendations for international students: Required—TOEFL (minimum score 550 paper-based; 213 computer-based); Recommended—TWE (minimum score 6). Electronic applications accepted. *Faculty research:* Exile and Holocaust, minority literature, gender studies, fairytale studies, sociolinguistics.

Yale University, Graduate School of Arts and Sciences, Department of Slavic Languages and Literatures, New Haven, CT 06520. Offers medieval Slavic literature and philology (PhD); Polish literature (PhD); Russian literature (PhD); Slavic languages and literatures and film studies (PhD). *Degree requirements:* For doctorate, 3 foreign languages, thesis/dissertation. *Entrance requirements:* For doctorate, GRE General Test.

Scandinavian Languages

Cornell University, Graduate School, Graduate Fields of Arts and Sciences, Field of Germanic Studies, Ithaca, NY 14853-0001. Offers German area studies (MA, PhD); German intellectual history (MA, PhD); Germanic linguistics (MA, PhD); Germanic literature (MA, PhD); old Norse (MA, PhD). *Faculty:* 21 full-time (10 women). *Students:* 15 full-time (9 women); includes 2 minority (1 American Indian/Alaska Native, 1 Hispanic American), 6 international. Average age 28. 32 applicants, 19% accepted, 3 enrolled. In 2009, 4 master's, 3 doctorates awarded. Terminal master's awarded for partial completion of doctoral program. *Degree requirements:* For master's, one foreign language, thesis; for doctorate, 2 foreign languages, comprehensive exam, thesis/dissertation. *Entrance requirements:* For master's and doctorate, GRE General Test, fluency in German, writing sample, 2 letters of recommendation. Additional exam requirements/recommendations for international students: Required—TOEFL (minimum score 550 paper-based; 213 computer-based; 77 iBT). *Application deadline:* For fall admission, 1/15 for domestic students. Application fee: $70. Electronic applications accepted. *Expenses:* Tuition: Full-time $29,500. Required fees: $70. Full-time tuition and fees vary according to degree level, program and student level. *Financial support:* In 2009–10, 15 students received support, including 2 fellowships with full tuition reimbursements available, 1 teaching assistantship with full tuition reimbursement available; research assistantships with full tuition reimbursements available, institutionally sponsored loans, scholarships/grants, health care benefits, tuition waivers (full and partial), and unspecified assistantships also available. Financial award applicants required to submit FAFSA. *Faculty research:* Women's studies, minority literature, literature and intellectual history, theater and film studies, continental philosophy. *Unit head:* Director of Graduate Studies, 607-255-4047. *Application contact:* Graduate Field Assistant, 607-255-4047, E-mail: germanic_studies@cornell.edu.

Harvard University, Graduate School of Arts and Sciences, Department of Germanic Languages and Literatures, Cambridge, MA 02138. Offers German (PhD); Scandinavian (PhD). Terminal master's awarded for partial completion of doctoral program. *Degree requirements:* For doctorate, 2 foreign languages, thesis/dissertation, exams. *Entrance requirements:* For doctorate, GRE General Test, German writing sample. Additional exam requirements/recommendations for international students: Required—TOEFL. *Expenses:* Tuition: Full-time $33,696. Required fees: $1126. Full-time tuition and fees vary according to program.

University of California, Berkeley, Graduate Division, College of Letters and Science, Department of Scandinavian Languages and Literatures, Berkeley, CA 94720-1500. Offers PhD. *Faculty:* 6 full-time. *Students:* 13 full-time (6 women). Average age 33. 4 applicants, 1 enrolled. In 2009, 1 doctorate awarded. *Degree requirements:* For doctorate, 2 foreign languages, thesis/dissertation, 3 field papers, qualifying exam. *Entrance requirements:* For doctorate, GRE General Test, minimum GPA of 3.0, MA in Scandinavian language or equivalent, 3 letters of recommendation. Additional exam requirements/recommendations for international students: Required—TOEFL (minimum score 570 paper-based; 230 computer-based). *Application deadline:* For fall admission, 12/15 for domestic students. Application fee: $70 ($90 for international students). *Financial support:* Fellowships, teaching assistantships, unspecified assistantships available. *Faculty research:* Modern literatures, old Norse language and literatures, folklore, film. *Unit head:* Prof. Linda Haverty Rugg, Chair, 510-642-4484, E-mail: ch_scandinavian@ls.berkeley.edu. *Application contact:* Sandy Jones, Student Affairs Officer, 510-642-9051, Fax: 510-643-6220, E-mail: issag@berkeley.edu.

University of California, Los Angeles, Graduate Division, College of Letters and Science, Department of Germanic Languages, Program in Scandinavian, Los Angeles, CA 90095. Offers MA. *Students:* 1 (woman) full-time. Average age 26. 2 applicants, 50% accepted, 0 enrolled. *Degree requirements:* For master's, one foreign language, comprehensive exam. *Entrance requirements:* For master's, GRE General Test, sample of written work. *Application deadline:* For fall admission, 12/15 for domestic and international students. Application fee: $70 ($90 for international students). Electronic applications accepted. *Financial support:* In 2009–10, 1 fellowship with full and partial tuition reimbursement was awarded; research assistantships with full and partial tuition reimbursements, teaching assistantships with full and partial tuition reimbursements, Federal Work-Study, institutionally sponsored loans, and health care benefits also available. Financial award application deadline: 3/1; financial award applicants required to submit FAFSA. *Unit head:* Timothy Tangherlini, Vice Chair, 310-825-7611. *Application contact:* Department Office, 310-825-6828, E-mail: allen@humnet.ucla.edu.

University of Massachusetts Amherst, Graduate School, College of Humanities and Fine Arts, Department of Languages, Literatures, and Cultures, Programs in German and Scandinavian Studies, Amherst, MA 01003. Offers MA, PhD. Part-time programs available. *Faculty:* 8 full-time (3 women). *Students:* 18 full-time (14 women), 8 part-time (6 women); includes 4 minority (1 African American, 2 Asian Americans or Pacific Islanders, 1 Hispanic American), 4 international. Average age 33. 10 applicants, 70% accepted, 2 enrolled. In 2009, 1 master's, 4 doctorates awarded. Terminal master's awarded for partial completion of doctoral program. *Degree requirements:* For master's, thesis or alternative; for doctorate, one foreign language, comprehensive exam, thesis/dissertation. *Entrance requirements:* For master's and doctorate, writing sample in English and German. Additional exam requirements/recommendations for international students: Required—TOEFL (minimum score 550 paper-based; 213 computer-based; 80 iBT), IELTS (minimum score 6.5). *Application deadline:* For fall admission, 2/1 for domestic and international students; for spring admission, 10/1 for domestic and international students. Applications are processed on a rolling basis. Application fee: $50 ($65 for international students). Electronic applications accepted. *Expenses:* Tuition, state resident: full-time $2640; part-time $110 per credit. Tuition, nonresident: full-time $9936; part-time $414 per credit. Tuition and fees vary according to course load. *Financial support:* In 2009–10, 1 research assistantship with full tuition reimbursement (averaging $14,516 per year), 14 teaching assistantships with full tuition reimbursements (averaging $10,942 per year) were awarded; fellowships, career-related internships or fieldwork, Federal Work-Study, scholarships/grants, traineeships, health care benefits, tuition waivers (full), and unspecified assistantships also available. Support available to part-time students. Financial award application deadline: 2/1. *Unit head:* Dr. Jonathan S. Skolnik, Graduate Program Director, 413-545-6686, Fax: 413-545-6695. *Application contact:* Jean M. Ames, Supervisor of Admissions, 413-545-0722, Fax: 413-577-0010, E-mail: gradadm@grad.umass.edu.

University of Minnesota, Twin Cities Campus, Graduate School, College of Liberal Arts, Department of German, Scandinavian, and Dutch, Minneapolis, MN 55455-0213. Offers Germanic studies: German and Scandinavian studies track (PhD); Germanic studies: German track (MA, PhD); Germanic studies: Germanic medieval studies track (MA, PhD); Germanic studies: Scandinavian studies track (MA); Germanic studies: teaching track (MA). Part-time programs available. *Faculty:* 11 full-time (5 women), 4 part-time/adjunct (2 women). *Students:* 21 full-time (9 women), 3 part-time (1 woman); includes 2 minority (both Hispanic Americans), 3 international. 26 applicants, 42% accepted, 5 enrolled. In 2009, 4 master's, 2 doctorates awarded. Terminal master's awarded for partial completion of doctoral program. *Degree requirements:* For doctorate, 2 foreign languages, thesis/dissertation. *Entrance requirements:* For master's, GRE General Test, BA in German, Scandinavian, or equivalent; for doctorate, GRE General Test, MA in German, Scandinavian, or equivalent. Additional exam requirements/recommendations for international students: Required—TOEFL (minimum score 550 paper-based; 213 computer-based; 79 iBT). *Application deadline:* For fall admission, 12/15 for domestic and international students. Application fee: $75 ($95 for international students). Electronic applications accepted. *Financial support:* In 2009–10, 21 students received support, including 6 fellowships with full tuition reimbursements available (averaging $20,000 per year), 1 research assistantship with full tuition reimbursement available (averaging $16,000 per year), 14 teaching assistantships with full tuition reimbursements available (averaging $14,500 per year); career-related internships or fieldwork, Federal Work-Study, institutionally sponsored loans, scholarships/grants, health care benefits, and unspecified assistantships also available. Support available to part-time students. Financial award application deadline: 12/15. *Faculty research:* Cultural studies, literary theory, feminist criticism, film, Germanic philology. *Unit head:* Prof. Richard McCormick, Chair, 612-625-2080, Fax: 612-624-8297, E-mail: mccor001@umn.edu. *Application contact:* Director of Graduate Studies, 612-625-0999, Fax: 612-624-8297, E-mail: gsd@umn.edu.

University of Washington, Graduate School, College of Arts and Sciences, Department of Scandinavian Studies, Seattle, WA 98195. Offers MA, PhD. *Degree requirements:* For master's, one foreign language, comprehensive exam, thesis optional; for doctorate, 2 foreign languages, comprehensive exam, thesis/dissertation. *Entrance requirements:* For master's, GRE, BA in Scandinavian or equivalent, minimum GPA of 3.0; for doctorate, GRE, master's degree, minimum GPA of 3.0. Additional exam requirements/recommendations for international students: Required—TOEFL. *Faculty research:* Scandinavian folklore, history, and politics; medieval to modern Scandinavian literature; Scandinavian fiction, poetry, drama, literary history, and theory.

University of Wisconsin–Madison, Graduate School, College of Letters and Science, Department of Scandinavian Studies, Madison, WI 53706-1380. Offers area studies (MA); folklore (PhD); literature (MA, PhD); philology (PhD). Part-time programs available. *Degree requirements:* For master's, 2 foreign languages, exam; for doctorate, thesis/dissertation, exam. *Entrance requirements:* For master's, minimum GPA of 3.25; for doctorate, minimum GPA of 3.5. Electronic applications accepted. *Expenses:* Tuition, state resident: part-time $594 per credit. Tuition, nonresident: part-time $1504 per credit. Required fees: $65 per credit. Tuition and fees vary according to course load, program and reciprocity agreements. *Faculty research:* Historical fiction, Icelandic poetry, nineteenth-century literature, theater, gender studies, folklore.

Slavic Languages

Boston College, Graduate School of Arts and Sciences, Department of Slavic and Eastern Languages, Program in Russian and Slavic Languages and Literature, Chestnut Hill, MA 02467-3800. Offers MA, MA/JD, MBA/MA. Part-time programs available. *Degree requirements:* For master's, 3 foreign languages, comprehensive exam, thesis or alternative. *Entrance requirements:* Additional exam requirements/recommendations for international students: Required—TOEFL (minimum score 600 paper-based; 250 computer-based; 100 iBT). *Application deadline:* For fall admission, 1/15 for domestic students. Application fee: $75. Electronic applications accepted. *Financial support:* Teaching assistantships, Federal Work-Study available. Support available to part-time students. Financial award application deadline: 3/1; financial award applicants required to submit FAFSA. *Faculty research:* Structural analysis of language, poetry and semiotic systems. *Unit head:* Dr. Maxin Shrayer, Chairperson, 617-552-3910. *Application contact:* Dr. Maxin Shrayer, Chairperson, 617-552-3910.

Brown University, Graduate School, Department of Slavic Languages, Providence, RI 02912. Offers Russian language and literature (AM); Slavic languages (AM); Slavic studies (PhD). *Degree requirements:* For master's, one foreign language; for doctorate, 2 foreign languages, thesis/dissertation, preliminary exam.

Columbia University, Graduate School of Arts and Sciences, Division of Humanities, Department of Slavic Languages, New York, NY 10027. Offers Russian literature (M Phil, MA, PhD); Slavic languages (M Phil, MA, PhD). *Degree requirements:* For master's, one foreign language, thesis; for doctorate, 2 foreign languages, thesis/dissertation. *Entrance requirements:* For master's and doctorate, GRE General Test. Additional exam requirements/recommendations for international students: Required—TOEFL. *Faculty research:* Polish, Serbo-Croatian, Czechoslovakian, medieval and modern Russian literature.

Cornell University, Graduate School, Graduate Fields of Arts and Sciences, Field of Linguistics, Ithaca, NY 14853-0001. Offers applied linguistics (MA, PhD); East Asian linguistics (MA, PhD); English linguistics (MA, PhD); general linguistics (MA, PhD); Germanic linguistics (MA, PhD); Indo-European linguistics (MA, PhD); phonetics (MA, PhD); phonological theory (MA, PhD); Romance linguistics (MA, PhD); second language acquisition (MA, PhD); semantics (MA, PhD); Slavic linguistics (MA, PhD); sociolinguistics (MA, PhD); South Asian linguistics (MA, PhD); Southeast Asian linguistics (MA, PhD); syntactic theory (MA, PhD). *Faculty:* 21 full-time (10 women). *Students:* 31 full-time (17 women), 14 international. Average age 30. 95 applicants, 12% accepted, 5 enrolled. In 2009, 5 master's, 6 doctorates awarded. Terminal master's awarded for partial completion of doctoral program. *Degree requirements:* For master's, one foreign language, thesis; for doctorate, one foreign language, comprehensive exam, thesis/dissertation. *Entrance requirements:* For master's and doctorate, GRE General Test, 2 letters of recommendation. Additional exam requirements/recommendations for international students: Required—TOEFL (minimum score 600 paper-based; 250 computer-based; 77 iBT). *Application deadline:* For fall admission, 1/15 for domestic students. Application fee: $70. Electronic applications accepted. *Expenses:* Tuition: Full-time $29,500. Required fees: $70. Full-time tuition and fees vary according to degree level, program and student level. *Financial support:* In 2009–10, 3 fellowships with full tuition reimbursements, 1 teaching assistantship with full tuition reimbursement were awarded; research assistantships with full tuition reimbursements, institutionally sponsored loans, scholarships/grants, health care benefits, tuition waivers (full and partial), and unspecified assistantships also available. Financial award applicants required to submit FAFSA. *Faculty research:* Phonology and phonetics; syntax and semantics; historical linguistics; philosophy of language; language acquisition. *Unit head:* Director of Graduate Studies, 607-255-1105. *Application contact:* Graduate Field Assistant, 607-255-1105, E-mail: lingfield@cornell.edu.

Duke University, Graduate School, Department of Slavic Languages and Literatures, Durham, NC 27708. Offers AM. Part-time programs available. *Faculty:* 7 full-time. *Students:* 1 (woman) full-time. 8 applicants, 63% accepted, 1 enrolled. In 2009, 1 master's awarded. *Entrance requirements:* For master's, GRE General Test. Additional exam requirements/recommendations for international students: Required—TOEFL (minimum score 550 paper-based; 213 computer-based; 83 iBT), IELTS (minimum score 7). *Application deadline:* For fall admission, 12/8 priority date for domestic and international students. Application fee: $75. Electronic applications accepted. *Financial support:* Application deadline: 12/31. *Unit head:* Jehanne Gheith, Director of Graduate Studies, 919-660-3147, Fax: 919-660-3141, E-mail: bhayes@duke.edu. *Application contact:* Cynthia Robertson, Associate Dean for Enrollment Services, 919-684-3913, E-mail: grad-admissions@duke.edu.

Florida State University, The Graduate School, College of Arts and Sciences, Department of Modern Languages, Program in Slavic Languages/Russian, Tallahassee, FL 32306. Offers Slavic languages and literatures (MA). *Faculty:* 3 full-time (2 women). *Students:* 4 full-time (all women); includes 2 minority (both Asian Americans or Pacific Islanders). Average age 24. 4 applicants, 50% accepted, 1 enrolled. *Degree requirements:* For master's, thesis optional. *Entrance requirements:* For master's, GRE General Test or minimum GPA of 3.0. Additional exam requirements/recommendations for international students: Required—TOEFL (minimum score 550 paper-based; 213 computer-based). *Application deadline:* For fall admission, 2/1 for domestic and international students. Applications are processed on a rolling basis. Application fee: $30. Electronic applications accepted. *Expenses:* Tuition, state resident: full-time $7413. Tuition, nonresident: full-time $22,567. *Financial support:* In 2009–10, 3 students received support, including 4 teaching assistantships with partial tuition reimbursements available (averaging $10,200 per year); fellowships, institutionally sponsored loans also available. Financial award application deadline: 2/1; financial award applicants required to submit FAFSA. *Faculty research:* Contemporary literature, emigré literature, Old Russian word formation, political rhetoric, structure of modern Russian. Total annual research expenditures: $4,500. *Unit head:* Dr. Robert Romanchuk, Divisional Coordinator, 850-644-8198, Fax: 850-644-0524, E-mail: rromanch@fsu.edu. *Application contact:* Wendy E. Pigott, Graduate Academic Coordinator, 850-644-8397, Fax: 850-644-0524, E-mail: wpigott@fsu.edu.

Harvard University, Graduate School of Arts and Sciences, Department of Slavic Languages and Literatures, Cambridge, MA 02138. Offers Polish (PhD); Russian (PhD); Serbo-Croatian (PhD); Slavic philology (PhD); Ukrainian (PhD). *Degree requirements:* For doctorate, 4 foreign languages, thesis/dissertation. *Entrance requirements:* For doctorate, GRE General Test, writing sample. Additional exam requirements/recommendations for international students: Required—TOEFL. *Expenses:* Tuition: Full-time $33,696. Required fees: $1126. Full-time tuition and fees vary according to program.

Indiana University Bloomington, University Graduate School, College of Arts and Sciences, Department of Slavic Languages and Literatures, Bloomington, IN 47405. Offers MA, MAT, PhD. Part-time programs available. *Faculty:* 8 full-time (3 women). *Students:* 13 full-time (10 women), 3 international. Average age 29. 15 applicants, 80% accepted, 4 enrolled. In 2009, 1 master's awarded. Terminal master's awarded for partial completion of doctoral program. *Degree requirements:* For master's, variable foreign language requirement; for doctorate, variable foreign language requirement, comprehensive exam, thesis/dissertation. *Entrance requirements:* For master's, GRE General Test. Additional exam requirements/recommendations for international students: Required—TOEFL. *Application deadline:* Applications are processed on a rolling basis. Application fee: $55 ($65 for international students). *Financial support:* In 2009–10, 1 fellowship with full tuition reimbursement, 5 teaching assistantships with full tuition reimbursements were awarded; research assistantships with full tuition reimbursements. Financial award application deadline: 2/1. *Faculty research:* Russian stress, Slavic accentology and morphophonemics, Eastern European literature, Bible translation. *Unit head:* Dr. Steven Franks, Chair, 812-855-9906, E-mail: feldstei@indiana.edu. *Application contact:* Tricia Wall, Summer Program and Student Services Assistant, 812-855-2608, Fax: 812-855-2107.

New York University, Graduate School of Arts and Science, Department of Russian and Slavic Studies, New York, NY 10012-1019. Offers Russian literature (MA); Slavic literature (MA). Part-time programs available. *Faculty:* 8 full-time (3 women). *Students:* 9 full-time (2 women), 5 part-time (2 women), 2 international. Average age 27. 20 applicants, 95% accepted, 11 enrolled. In 2009, 2 master's awarded. *Degree requirements:* For master's, one foreign language, comprehensive exam, thesis. *Entrance requirements:* For master's, GRE General Test, minimum 3 years of undergraduate Russian or equivalent. Additional exam requirements/recommendations for international students: Required—TOEFL. *Application deadline:* For fall admission, 4/15 for domestic students; for spring admission, 11/1 for domestic students. Application fee: $90. *Expenses:* Tuition: Full-time $30,528; part-time $1272 per credit. Required fees: $2177. *Financial support:* Career-related internships or fieldwork, Federal Work-Study, and institutionally sponsored loans available. Financial award application deadline: 4/15; financial award applicants required to submit FAFSA. *Faculty research:* Modern Russian literature and art, contemporary Russian and East European literature, literary theory, Slavic linguistics, Russian journalism. *Unit head:* Yanni Katsanisein, Chair, 212-998-8670, Fax: 212-995-4604, E-mail: gsas.russian.and.slavic@nyu.edu. *Application contact:* Anne Lounsbery, Director of Graduate Studies, 212-998-8670, Fax: 212-995-4604, E-mail: gsas.russian.and.slavic@nyu.edu.

Northwestern University, The Graduate School, Judd A. and Marjorie Weinberg College of Arts and Sciences, Department of Slavic Languages and Literature, Evanston, IL 60208. Offers PhD. Admissions and degrees offered through The Graduate School. Part-time programs available. *Degree requirements:* For doctorate, 3 foreign languages, thesis/dissertation. *Entrance requirements:* For doctorate, GRE General Test. Additional exam requirements/recommendations for international students: Required—TOEFL. *Faculty research:* Russian poetry and prose, nineteenth- through twentieth-centuries, translation and Russian culture, Russian intellectual history, Slavic literature and nationalism, Polish poetry.

The Ohio State University, Graduate School, College of Humanities, Department of Slavic and East European Languages and Literatures, Columbus, OH 43210. Offers Slavic and East European studies (MA); Slavic languages and literatures (MA, PhD). *Faculty:* 13. *Students:* 21 full-time (8 women), 9 part-time (6 women); includes 1 minority (Asian American or Pacific Islander), 6 international. Average age 30. In 2009, 6 master's, 3 doctorates awarded. *Degree requirements:* For master's, variable foreign language requirement, thesis optional; for doctorate, variable foreign language requirement, thesis/dissertation. *Entrance requirements:* For master's and doctorate, GRE General Test. Additional exam requirements/recommendations for international students: Required—TOEFL (minimum score 600 paper-based; 250 computer-based). *Application deadline:* For fall admission, 8/15 priority date for domestic students, 7/1 priority date for international students; for winter admission, 12/1 priority date for domestic students, 11/1 priority date for international students; for spring admission, 3/1 priority date for domestic students, 2/1 priority date for international students. Applications are processed on a rolling basis. Application fee: $40 ($50 for international students). Electronic applications accepted. *Expenses:* Tuition, state resident: full-time $10,683. Tuition, nonresident: full-time $25,923. Tuition and fees vary according to course load and program. *Financial support:* Fellowships, research assistantships, teaching assistantships, Federal Work-Study and institutionally sponsored loans available. Support available to part-time students. *Faculty research:* Polish literature. *Unit head:* Angela Brintlinger, Graduate Studies Committee Chair, E-mail: brintlinger.3@osu.edu. *Application contact:* 614-292-9444, Fax: 614-292-3895, E-mail: domestic.grad@osu.edu.

Princeton University, Graduate School, Department of Slavic Languages and Literatures, Princeton, NJ 08544-1019. Offers Russian and Slavic linguistics (PhD); Russian literature (PhD). *Degree requirements:* For doctorate, variable foreign language requirement, thesis/dissertation. *Entrance requirements:* For doctorate, GRE General Test. Additional exam requirements/recommendations for international students: Required—TOEFL (minimum score 600 paper-based; 250 computer-based). Electronic applications accepted.

Stanford University, School of Humanities and Sciences, Department of Slavic Languages and Literatures, Stanford, CA 94305-9991. Offers Russian (MA); Slavic languages and literatures (PhD). Terminal master's awarded for partial completion of doctoral program. *Degree requirements:* For master's, one foreign language, thesis or alternative; for doctorate, 3 foreign languages, thesis/dissertation. *Entrance requirements:* For master's and doctorate, GRE General Test. Additional exam requirements/recommendations for international students: Required—TOEFL. Electronic applications accepted. *Expenses:* Tuition: Full-time $37,380; part-time $2760 per quarter. Required fees: $501.

University of Alberta, Faculty of Graduate Studies and Research, Department of Modern Languages and Cultural Studies, Edmonton, AB T6G 2E1, Canada. Offers applied linguistics (Germanic, Romance, Slavic) (MA); French language, literatures and linguistics (PhD); French language, literatures, and linguistics (MA); Germanic languages, literatures and linguistics (PhD); Germanic languages, literatures, and linguistics (MA); Italian studies (MA); Slavic languages and literatures (Russian, Ukrainian) (MA, PhD); Slavic linguistics (Russian, Ukrainian) (MA, PhD); Spanish and Latin American studies (MA, PhD); Ukrainian folklore (MA, PhD). Part-time programs available. *Faculty:* 33 full-time (15 women), 2 part-time/adjunct (1 woman). *Students:* 39 full-time (29 women), 13 part-time (12 women). 300 applicants, 10% accepted. In 2009, 12 master's, 2 doctorates awarded. *Degree requirements:* For master's, one foreign language, thesis; for doctorate, 2 foreign languages, comprehensive exam, thesis/dissertation. *Entrance requirements:* For master's and doctorate, 1 language other than English. Additional exam requirements/recommendations for international students: Required—Michigan English Language Assessment Battery or TOEFL (minimum score 550 paper-based; 213 computer-based). *Application deadline:* For fall admission, 7/1 for domestic and international students; for winter admission, 11/1 for domestic and international students; for spring admission, 3/1 for domestic students. Applications are processed on a rolling basis. Electronic applications accepted. Tuition and fees charges are reported in Canadian dollars. *Expenses:* Tuition, area resident: Full-time $4626 Canadian dollars; part-time $99.72 Canadian dollars per unit. International tuition: $8216 Canadian dollars full-time. Required fees: $3590 Canadian dollars; $99.72 Canadian dollars per unit. $215 Canadian dollars per term. *Financial support:* In 2009–10, 2 fellowships with full and partial tuition reimbursements (averaging $18,000 per year), 23 research assistantships with full and partial tuition reimbursements (averaging $10,450 per year), 21 teaching assistantships with full and partial tuition reimbursements (averaging $12,572 per year) were awarded; scholarships/grants also available. Support available to part-time students. Financial award application deadline: 3/31. *Faculty research:* Russian/Ukrainian studies; German studies; contemporary Latin American, French and Francophone studies; Italian studies. *Unit head:* Dr. Don Bruce, Chair, 780-492-3273, Fax: 780-492-9106. *Application contact:* Jane Wilson, Graduate Programs Secretary, 780-492-3273, Fax: 780-492-9106, E-mail: mlcsgrad@ualberta.ca.

University of California, Berkeley, Graduate Division, College of Letters and Science, Department of Slavic Languages and Literatures, Berkeley, CA 94720-1500. Offers Czech (PhD), including Czech linguistics, Czech literature; Polish (PhD), including Polish linguistics, Polish literature; Russian (PhD), including Russian linguistics, Russian literature; Serbo-Croatian (PhD), including Serbo-Croatian linguistics, Serbo-Croatian literature. *Faculty:* 15 full-time. *Students:* 22 full-time (17 women). Average age 30. 32 applicants, 2 enrolled. In 2009, 1 doctorate awarded. Terminal master's awarded for partial completion of doctoral program. *Degree requirements:* For doctorate, thesis/dissertation, oral and written exams. *Entrance requirements:* For doctorate, GRE General Test, minimum GPA of 3.0, 3 letters of recommendation. Additional exam requirements/recommendations for international students: Required—TOEFL (minimum score 570 paper-based; 230 computer-based). *Application deadline:* For fall admission, 12/15 for domestic students. Application fee: $70 ($90 for international students). Electronic applications accepted. *Financial support:* Fellowships, research assistantships, teaching assistantships, unspecified assistantships available. Financial award applicants required to submit FAFSA. *Unit head:* David Frick, Chair, 510-642-2979, E-mail:

Slavic Languages

University of California, Berkeley (continued)
ch_slavic@ls.berkeley.edu. *Application contact:* Sandy Jones, Student Affairs Officer, 510-642-9051, Fax: 510-643-6220, E-mail: issag@berkeley.edu.

University of California, Los Angeles, Graduate Division, College of Letters and Science, Department of Slavic Languages and Literatures, Los Angeles, CA 90095. Offers MA, PhD. *Students:* 13 full-time (7 women); includes 2 minority (1 American Indian/Alaska Native, 1 Hispanic American). Average age 28. 14 applicants, 36% accepted, 1 enrolled. In 2009, 3 master's awarded. Terminal master's awarded for partial completion of doctoral program. *Degree requirements:* For master's, 2 foreign languages, comprehensive exam; for doctorate, 2 foreign languages, thesis/dissertation, oral and written qualifying exams. *Entrance requirements:* For master's, GRE General Test, minimum GPA of 3.0, sample of written work; for doctorate, GRE General Test, minimum undergraduate GPA of 3.0, proficiency in French and German, sample of written work. *Application deadline:* For fall admission, 1/15 for domestic and international students. Application fee: $70 ($90 for international students). Electronic applications accepted. *Financial support:* In 2009–10, 10 fellowships with full and partial tuition reimbursements, 5 research assistantships with full and partial tuition reimbursements, 7 teaching assistantships with full and partial tuition reimbursements were awarded; Federal Work-Study, institutionally sponsored loans, scholarships/grants, health care benefits, tuition waivers (full and partial), and unspecified assistantships also available. Financial award application deadline: 3/1; financial award applicants required to submit FAFSA. *Unit head:* Dr. David MacFadyen, Chair, 310-825-9212. *Application contact:* Department Office, 310-825-3856, E-mail: slavic@humnet.ucla.edu.

University of Chicago, Division of the Humanities, Department of Slavic Languages and Literatures, Chicago, IL 60637-1513. Offers AM, PhD. Terminal master's awarded for partial completion of doctoral program. *Degree requirements:* For master's, one foreign language; for doctorate, 2 foreign languages, thesis/dissertation. *Entrance requirements:* For master's and doctorate, GRE General Test. Additional exam requirements/recommendations for international students: Required—TOEFL.

University of Illinois at Urbana–Champaign, Graduate College, College of Liberal Arts and Sciences, School of Literatures, Cultures and Linguistics, Department of Slavic Languages and Literatures, Champaign, IL 61820. Offers MA, PhD. *Faculty:* 6 full-time (1 woman), 1 part-time/adjunct (0 women). *Students:* 11 full-time (10 women), 2 part-time (1 woman); includes 2 minority (both Asian Americans or Pacific Islanders), 5 international. 20 applicants, 40% accepted, 6 enrolled. In 2009, 1 master's, 1 doctorate awarded. *Entrance requirements:* For master's and doctorate, GRE, minimum GPA of 3.0; writing sample. Additional exam requirements/recommendations for international students: Required—TOEFL (minimum score 79 iBT). *Application deadline:* Applications are processed on a rolling basis. Application fee: $60 ($75 for international students). Electronic applications accepted. *Financial support:* In 2009–10, 9 fellowships, 2 research assistantships, 6 teaching assistantships were awarded; tuition waivers (full and partial) also available. *Unit head:* Lilya Kaganovsky, Co-Acting Head, 217-333-6157, Fax: 217-333-7310, E-mail: lilya@illinois.edu. *Application contact:* Lynn Stanke, Office Support Specialist, 217-333-6269, Fax: 217-244-3050, E-mail: stanke@illinois.edu.

The University of Kansas, Graduate Studies, College of Liberal Arts and Sciences, Department of Slavic Languages and Literatures, Lawrence, KS 66045. Offers MA, PhD. Part-time programs available. *Students:* 12 full-time (11 women), 2 part-time (1 woman), 1 international. Average age 29. 13 applicants, 69% accepted, 4 enrolled. In 2009, 1 master's, 1 doctorate awarded. Terminal master's awarded for partial completion of doctoral program. *Degree requirements:* For master's, one foreign language, comprehensive exam, thesis or alternative; for doctorate, 3 foreign languages, comprehensive exam, thesis/dissertation, 2nd Slavic language. *Entrance requirements:* For master's, GRE, BA in Slavic languages and literatures or the equivalent; for doctorate, GRE, MA in Slavic languages and literatures. Additional exam requirements/recommendations for international students: Required—TOEFL. *Application deadline:* For winter admission, 1/31 priority date for domestic and international students. Applications are processed on a rolling basis. Application fee: $45 ($55 for international students). Electronic applications accepted. *Expenses:* Tuition, state resident: full-time $6492; part-time $270.50 per credit hour. Tuition, nonresident: full-time $15,510; part-time $646.25 per credit hour. Required fees: $847; $70.56 per credit hour. Tuition and fees vary according to course load and program. *Financial support:* Fellowships with tuition reimbursements, teaching assistantships with full and partial tuition reimbursements, Federal Work-Study, institutionally sponsored loans, scholarships/grants, and unspecified assistantships available. Financial award application deadline: 1/31. *Faculty research:* Russian and south Slavic linguistics, Polish and Russian literature, folklore, Russian intellectual history. *Unit head:* Prof. Marc L. Greenberg, Chair, 785-864-3313, Fax: 785-864-4298, E-mail: mlg@ku.edu. *Application contact:* Prof. Maria Carlson, Graduate Director, 785-864-3313, Fax: 785-864-4298, E-mail: mcarlson@ku.edu.

University of Manitoba, Faculty of Graduate Studies, Faculty of Arts, Department of German and Slavic Studies, Winnipeg, MB R3T 2N2, Canada. Offers German language and literature (MA); Slavic languages and literatures (MA). *Degree requirements:* For master's, one foreign language, thesis or alternative.

University of Michigan, Horace H. Rackham School of Graduate Studies, College of Literature, Science, and the Arts, Department of Slavic Languages and Literatures, Ann Arbor, MI 48109-1275. Offers Russian (AM); Slavic languages and literatures (PhD). Terminal master's awarded for partial completion of doctoral program. *Degree requirements:* For master's, 2 foreign languages, comprehensive exam; for doctorate, 3 foreign languages, comprehensive exam, thesis/dissertation, oral defense of dissertation, preliminary exam. *Entrance requirements:* For master's, GRE General Test, 3rd-year foreign language proficiency; for doctorate, GRE General Test. Additional exam requirements/recommendations for international students: Required—TOEFL (minimum score 560 paper-based; 220 computer-based). Electronic applications accepted. *Expenses:* Tuition, state resident: full-time $17,286; part-time $1099 per credit hour. Tuition, nonresident: full-time $34,944; part-time $2080 per credit hour. Required fees: $95 per semester. Tuition and fees vary according to course load, degree level and program. *Faculty research:* Russian literature (all periods), Polish literature, South Slavic literatures, Czech literature, Ukrainian literature.

The University of North Carolina at Chapel Hill, Graduate School, College of Arts and Sciences, Department of Slavic Languages and Literatures, Chapel Hill, NC 27599. Offers Polish literature (PhD); Russian literature (MA, PhD); Serbo-Croatian literature (PhD); Slavic linguistics (MA, PhD). Part-time programs available. Terminal master's awarded for partial completion of doctoral program. *Degree requirements:* For master's, 2 foreign languages, comprehensive exam, thesis; for doctorate, 4 foreign languages, comprehensive exam, thesis/dissertation. *Entrance requirements:* For master's and doctorate, GRE General Test, minimum GPA of 3.0. Electronic applications accepted. *Faculty research:* Russian cultural studies, literary translation, sociolinguistics, cognitive linguistics, émigré literature.

University of Pittsburgh, School of Arts and Sciences, Department of Slavic Languages and Literatures, Pittsburgh, PA 15260. Offers MA, PhD. Part-time programs available. *Faculty:* 7 full-time (3 women), 1 part-time/adjunct (0 women). *Students:* 11 full-time (9 women), 2 international. Average age 28. 20 applicants, 25% accepted, 2 enrolled. In 2009, 2 master's, 1 doctorate awarded. Terminal master's awarded for partial completion of doctoral program. *Degree requirements:* For master's, 2 foreign languages, comprehensive exam; for doctorate, 3 foreign languages, comprehensive exam, thesis/dissertation. *Entrance requirements:* For master's and doctorate, GRE General Test. Additional exam requirements/recommendations for international students: Required—TOEFL. *Application deadline:* For fall admission, 1/15 priority date for domestic and international students. Application fee: $40. Electronic applications accepted. *Expenses:* Tuition, state resident: full-time $16,402; part-time $665 per credit. Tuition, nonresident: full-time $28,694; part-time $1175 per credit. Required fees: $690; $175 per term. Tuition and fees vary according to program. *Financial support:* In 2009–10, 10 students received support, including 5 fellowships with full tuition reimbursements available (averaging $16,000 per year), 6 teaching assistantships with full tuition reimbursements available (averaging $15,065 per year); Federal Work-Study, scholarships/grants, and traineeships also available. Support available to part-time students. Financial award application deadline: 1/15. *Faculty research:* Contemporary Russian literature and culture, Russian cinema. *Unit head:* Prof. David J. Birnbaum, Chair, 412-624-5906, Fax: 412-624-9714, E-mail: djbpitt@pitt.edu. *Application contact:* Christine Metil, Administrator, 412-624-5906, Fax: 412-624-9714, E-mail: metil+@pitt.edu.

University of Southern California, Graduate School, College of Letters, Arts and Sciences, Department of Slavic Languages and Literatures, Los Angeles, CA 90089. Offers MA, PhD. *Faculty:* 7 full-time (2 women). *Students:* 9 full-time (8 women), 5 international. 13 applicants, 38% accepted, 2 enrolled. In 2009, 4 master's, 2 doctorates awarded. *Degree requirements:* For master's, one foreign language, comprehensive exam, thesis or alternative, 30 units; for doctorate, 3 foreign languages, comprehensive exam, thesis/dissertation. *Entrance requirements:* For master's, GRE, BA in Russian/Russian Literature or equivalent; for doctorate, GRE, MA in Russian or equivalent. *Application deadline:* For fall admission, 12/1 priority date for domestic and international students. Applications are processed on a rolling basis. Application fee: $85. Electronic applications accepted. *Expenses:* Tuition: Full-time $25,980; part-time $1315 per unit. Required fees: $554. One-time fee: $35 full-time. Full-time tuition and fees vary according to degree level and program. *Financial support:* In 2009–10, 9 students received support, including 4 fellowships with full tuition reimbursements available (averaging $21,000 per year), 5 teaching assistantships with full tuition reimbursements available (averaging $19,600 per year); scholarships/grants, health care benefits, and unspecified assistantships also available. Financial award application deadline: 12/1. *Faculty research:* Russian avant-garde art, intertextuality in Russian literature, 18th century Russian culture, Russian poetry, Russian music history, Russian philosophy. *Unit head:* Dr. Thomas J. Seifrid, Professor/Chair, 213-740-2740, Fax: 213-740-8550, E-mail: seifrid@usc.edu. *Application contact:* Susan Kechekian, Administrative Assistant, 213-740-2735, Fax: 213-740-8550, E-mail: susan@usc.edu.

The University of Texas at Austin, Graduate School, College of Liberal Arts, Department of Slavic and Eurasian Studies, Austin, TX 78712-1111. Offers Slavic languages (MA, PhD). *Degree requirements:* For master's, 2 foreign languages, thesis; for doctorate, 3 foreign languages, thesis/dissertation. *Entrance requirements:* For master's and doctorate, GRE General Test. Electronic applications accepted. *Faculty research:* Slavic linguistics; applied linguistics; Russian, Czech, and Slavic literature and culture.

University of Toronto, School of Graduate Studies, Humanities Division, Department of Slavic Languages and Literatures, Toronto, ON M5S 1A1, Canada. Offers MA, PhD. Part-time programs available. *Degree requirements:* For doctorate, comprehensive exam, thesis/dissertation. *Entrance requirements:* For master's, BA in related area; minimum A– average in Slavic courses taken in final year, writing sample, 2 letters of recommendation; for doctorate, MA in Slavic languages and literatures, minimum A– average, writing sample, 2 letters of recommendation.

University of Virginia, College and Graduate School of Arts and Sciences, Department of Slavic Languages and Literatures, Charlottesville, VA 22903. Offers MA, PhD. *Faculty:* 8 full-time (4 women). *Students:* 13 full-time (10 women), 2 part-time (both women), 2 international. Average age 27. 8 applicants, 88% accepted, 5 enrolled. In 2009, 5 master's, 1 doctorate awarded. *Degree requirements:* For master's, one foreign language, comprehensive exam, thesis (for some programs); for doctorate, one foreign language, comprehensive exam, thesis/dissertation. *Entrance requirements:* For master's, GRE General Test, 2 letters of recommendation, writing sample in English; for doctorate, GRE General Test, 2 letters of recommendation; writing sample in English. Additional exam requirements/recommendations for international students: Required—TOEFL (minimum score 600 paper-based; 250 computer-based; 90 iBT), IELTS (minimum score 7). *Application deadline:* Applications are processed on a rolling basis. Application fee: $60. Electronic applications accepted. *Financial support:* Teaching assistantships available. Financial award application deadline: 1/15; financial award applicants required to submit FAFSA. *Unit head:* Julian W. Connolly, Chair, 434-924-3548, Fax: 434-982-2744, E-mail: slavic@virginia.edu. *Application contact:* Karen Ryan, Director of Graduate Studies, 434-924-3548, Fax: 434-982-2744, E-mail: klr8p@virginia.edu.

University of Washington, Graduate School, College of Arts and Sciences, Department of Slavic Languages and Literatures, Seattle, WA 98195. Offers Russian literature (MA, PhD); Slavic linguistics (MA, PhD). *Degree requirements:* For master's, 2 foreign languages, thesis optional; for doctorate, 3 foreign languages, thesis/dissertation. *Entrance requirements:* For master's and doctorate, GRE General Test, minimum GPA of 3.0. Additional exam requirements/recommendations for international students: Required—TOEFL. Electronic applications accepted. *Faculty research:* Modern and medieval East European languages and literatures, comparative literature, Russian folk literature, Slavic literary theory and criticism, computerized morphology of Russian.

University of Wisconsin–Madison, Graduate School, College of Letters and Science, Department of Slavic Languages and Literature, Madison, WI 53706-1380. Offers MA, PhD. Part-time programs available. Terminal master's awarded for partial completion of doctoral program. *Degree requirements:* For doctorate, thesis/dissertation. *Entrance requirements:* For master's and doctorate, GRE General Test. Additional exam requirements/recommendations for international students: Required—TOEFL. Electronic applications accepted. *Expenses:* Tuition, state resident: part-time $594 per credit. Tuition, nonresident: part-time $1504 per credit. Required fees: $65 per credit. Tuition and fees vary according to course load, program and reciprocity agreements. *Faculty research:* Polish literature, linguistics, South Slavic literature, second language acquisition, nineteenth and twentieth-century Russian literature.

University of Wisconsin–Milwaukee, Graduate School, College of Letters and Sciences, Interdepartmental Program in Foreign Language and Literature, Milwaukee, WI 53201-0413. Offers classics and Hebrew studies (MAFLL); comparative literature (MAFLL); French and Italian (MAFLL); German (MAFLL); Slavic studies (MAFLL); translation (Certificate). Part-time programs available. *Faculty:* 37 full-time (18 women). *Students:* 32 full-time (25 women), 28 part-time (19 women); includes 5 minority (1 Asian American or Pacific Islander, 4 Hispanic Americans), 22 international. Average age 33. 54 applicants, 69% accepted, 20 enrolled. In 2009, 24 master's awarded. *Degree requirements:* For master's, 2 foreign languages, thesis or alternative. *Entrance requirements:* Additional exam requirements/recommendations for international students: Required—TOEFL (minimum score 550 paper-based; 79 iBT), IELTS (minimum score 6.5). *Application deadline:* For fall admission, 1/1 priority date for domestic students; for spring admission, 9/1 for domestic students. Applications are processed on a rolling basis. Application fee: $45 ($75 for international students). *Expenses:* Tuition, state resident: full-time $8800. Tuition, nonresident: full-time $20,760. Tuition and fees vary according to program and reciprocity agreements. *Financial support:* In 2009–10, 2 research assistantships, 21 teaching assistantships were awarded; career-related internships or fieldwork and unspecified assistantships also available. Support available to part-time students. Financial award application deadline: 4/15. Total annual research expenditures: $285,237. *Unit head:* Gabrielle Verdier, Representative, 414-229-3346, Fax: 414-229-2741, E-mail: verdier@uwm.edu. *Application contact:* General Information Contact, 414-229-4982, Fax: 414-229-6967, E-mail: gradschool@uwm.edu.

Yale University, Graduate School of Arts and Sciences, Department of Slavic Languages and Literatures, New Haven, CT 06520. Offers medieval Slavic literature and philology (PhD); Polish literature (PhD); Russian literature (PhD); Slavic languages and literatures and film studies (PhD). *Degree requirements:* For doctorate, 3 foreign languages, thesis/dissertation. *Entrance requirements:* For doctorate, GRE General Test.

Spanish

American University, College of Arts and Sciences, Department of Language and Foreign Studies, Program in Spanish: Latin American Studies, Washington, DC 20016-8045. Offers Spanish: Latin American studies (MA); translation (Certificate). Part-time and evening/weekend programs available. *Students:* 11 full-time (9 women), 8 part-time (4 women); includes 8 minority (3 African Americans, 5 Hispanic Americans). Average age 26. 23 applicants, 87% accepted, 7 enrolled. In 2009, 11 master's, 7 other advanced degrees awarded. *Degree requirements:* For master's, one foreign language, comprehensive exam, thesis or alternative, research. *Entrance requirements:* For master's, GRE, bachelor's degree in language or equivalent, essay in Spanish, minimum GPA of 3.2; for Certificate, bachelor's degree in Spanish or BA in any field plus Spanish proficiency. Additional exam requirements/recommendations for international students: Required—TOEFL. *Application deadline:* For fall admission, 2/1 for domestic students; for spring admission, 10/1 for domestic students. Application fee: $80. *Expenses:* Tuition: Full-time $22,266; part-time $1237 per credit hour. Required fees: $430. Tuition and fees vary according to program. *Financial support:* Fellowships, career-related internships or fieldwork, Federal Work-Study, and institutionally sponsored loans available. Financial award application deadline: 2/1. *Faculty research:* Latin American culture, literature, and history; computer-aided instruction.

Arizona State University, Graduate College, College of Liberal Arts and Sciences, Division of Humanities, School of International Letters and Cultures, Program in Spanish, Tempe, AZ 85287. Offers MA, PhD. *Degree requirements:* For master's, thesis or alternative; for doctorate, thesis/dissertation. *Entrance requirements:* For master's and doctorate, GRE.

Arkansas Tech University, Graduate College, College of Arts and Humanities, Russellville, AR 72801. Offers communication (MLA); English (M Ed, MA); fine arts (MLA); history (MA); multi-media journalism (MA); psychology (MS); social science (MLA); Spanish (MA, MLA); teaching English as a second language (MA, MLA). Part-time programs available. *Students:* 39 full-time (30 women), 80 part-time (63 women); includes 11 minority (3 African Americans, 1 American Indian/Alaska Native, 1 Asian American or Pacific Islander, 6 Hispanic Americans), 23 international. Average age 33. In 2009, 70 master's awarded. *Degree requirements:* For master's, comprehensive exam (for some programs), thesis (for some programs), project. *Entrance requirements:* For master's, GRE General Test or MAT. Additional exam requirements/recommendations for international students: Required—TOEFL (minimum score 550 paper-based; 213 computer-based; 79 iBT), IELTS (minimum score 6). *Application deadline:* For fall admission, 3/1 priority date for domestic students, 5/1 priority date for international students; for spring admission, 10/1 priority date for domestic and international students. Applications are processed on a rolling basis. Application fee: $0 ($50 for international students). Electronic applications accepted. *Expenses:* Tuition, state resident: full-time $3438; part-time $191 per hour. Tuition, nonresident: full-time $6876; part-time $382 per hour. Required fees: $482; $9 per credit hour. $140 per semester. Tuition and fees vary according to course load. *Financial support:* In 2009–10, teaching assistantships with full tuition reimbursements (averaging $4,000 per year); research assistantships, career-related internships or fieldwork, Federal Work-Study, scholarships/grants, health care benefits, and unspecified assistantships also available. Support available to part-time students. Financial award application deadline: 4/15; financial award applicants required to submit FAFSA. *Unit head:* Dr. Micheal Tarver, Dean, 479-968-0274, Fax: 479-964-0812, E-mail: mtarver@atu.edu. *Application contact:* Dr. Mary B. Gunter, Dean of Graduate College, 479-968-0398, Fax: 479-964-0542, E-mail: graduate.school@atu.edu.

Asbury University, School of Graduate and Professional Studies, Wilmore, KY 40390-1198. Offers biology: alternative certificate (MA Ed); chemistry: alternative certificate (MA Ed); English (MA Ed); English as a second language (MA Ed); ESL (MA Ed); French (MA Ed); Latin: alternative certificate (MA Ed); mathematics: alternative certificate (MA Ed); reading/writing endorsement (MA Ed); social studies (MA Ed); social work (MSW), including child and family services; Spanish (MA Ed); special education (MA Ed); special education: alternative certificate (MA Ed); teacher as leader endorsement (MA Ed). *Accreditation:* NCATE. Part-time programs available. *Faculty:* 8 full-time (7 women), 9 part-time/adjunct (4 women). *Students:* 108 part-time (87 women); includes 8 minority (4 African Americans, 2 Asian Americans or Pacific Islanders, 2 Hispanic Americans). Average age 36. 36 applicants, 86% accepted, 24 enrolled. In 2009, 20 master's awarded. *Degree requirements:* For master's, action research project, portfolio. *Entrance requirements:* For master's, PRAXIS/NTE, minimum GPA of 2.75, letters of recommendation. Additional exam requirements/recommendations for international students: Required—TOEFL (minimum score 550 paper-based). *Application deadline:* Applications are processed on a rolling basis. Application fee: $25. Electronic applications accepted. *Financial support:* Scholarships/grants and traineeships available. Financial award applicants required to submit FAFSA. *Unit head:* Dr. Bonnie J. Banker, Dean, School of Graduate and Professional Studies, 859-858-3511 Ext. 2221, Fax: 859-858-3921, E-mail: bonnie.banker@asbury.edu. *Application contact:* Lenore A. Sweigard, Graduate Program Assistant and Certification Specialist, 859-858-3511 Ext. 2502, Fax: 859-858-3921, E-mail: graded@asbury.edu.

Auburn University, Graduate School, College of Liberal Arts, Department of Foreign Languages and Literatures, Auburn University, AL 36849. Offers Spanish (MA, MHS). Part-time programs available. *Faculty:* 32 full-time (20 women), 8 part-time/adjunct (6 women). *Students:* 14 full-time (9 women), 16 part-time (14 women); includes 6 minority (1 African American, 1 Asian American or Pacific Islander, 4 Hispanic Americans), 1 international. Average age 28. 13 applicants, 100% accepted, 13 enrolled. In 2009, 10 master's awarded. *Degree requirements:* For master's, one foreign language, comprehensive exam, thesis (for some programs). *Entrance requirements:* For master's, GRE General Test. *Application deadline:* For fall admission, 7/7 for domestic students; for spring admission, 11/24 for domestic students. Applications are processed on a rolling basis. Application fee: $50 ($60 for international students). Electronic applications accepted. *Expenses:* Tuition, state resident: full-time $6240. Tuition, nonresident: full-time $18,720. International tuition: $18,938 full-time. Required fees: $492. Tuition and fees vary according to course load, program and reciprocity agreements. *Financial support:* Fellowships, teaching assistantships, Federal Work-Study available. Support available to part-time students. Financial award application deadline: 3/15; financial award applicants required to submit FAFSA. *Unit head:* Dr. Robert G. Weigel, Chair, 334-844-4345, Fax: 334-844-6378. *Application contact:* Dr. George Flowers, Dean of the Graduate School, 334-844-2125.

Baylor University, Graduate School, College of Arts and Sciences, Department of Modern Foreign Languages, Waco, TX 76798. Offers Spanish (MA). *Students:* 8 full-time (7 women); includes 2 minority (both Hispanic Americans). In 2009, 1 master's awarded. *Entrance requirements:* For master's, GRE General Test. *Application deadline:* Applications are processed on a rolling basis. Application fee: $25. *Unit head:* Dr. Baudelio Garza, Graduate Program Director, 254-710-3711, Fax: 254-710-3799, E-mail: baudelio_garza@baylor.edu. *Application contact:* Ann Westbrook, Administrative Assistant, 254-710-6027, Fax: 254-710-3870, E-mail: ann_westbrook@baylor.edu.

Bennington College, Graduate Programs, MA in Teaching a Second Language Program, Bennington, VT 05201. Offers education (MATSL); foreign language education (MATSL); French (MATSL); Spanish (MATSL). Part-time programs available. *Faculty:* 1 full-time (0 women), 3 part-time/adjunct (2 women). *Students:* 16 part-time (14 women); includes 3 minority (1 African American, 2 Hispanic Americans). Average age 37. 16 applicants, 63% accepted, 9 enrolled. In 2009, 6 master's awarded. *Degree requirements:* For master's, one foreign language, 2 major projects and presentations. *Entrance requirements:* For master's, Oral Proficiency Interview (OPI). Additional exam requirements/recommendations for international students: Required—TOEFL (minimum score 577 paper-based; 233 computer-based; 91 iBT). *Application deadline:* For spring admission, 4/1 priority date for domestic and international students. Applications are processed on a rolling basis. Application fee: $60. *Expenses:* Contact institution. *Financial support:* In 2009–10, 1 student received support. Scholarships/grants available. Financial award application deadline: 4/1; financial award applicants required to submit FAFSA. *Faculty research:* Acquisition, evaluation, assessment, conceptual teaching and learning content-driven communication, applied linguistics. *Unit head:* Carol Meyer, Director, 802-440-4375, E-mail: cmeyer@bennington.edu. *Application contact:* Nancy Pearlman, Assistant Director, 802-440-4710, E-mail: matsl@bennington.edu.

Boston College, Graduate School of Arts and Sciences, Department of Romance Languages and Literatures, Chestnut Hill, MA 02467-3800. Offers French (MA, PhD); Italian (MA); medieval language (PhD); Spanish (MA, PhD). Part-time programs available. *Students:* 43 full-time (39 women), 4 part-time (3 women); includes 5 minority (2 Asian Americans or Pacific Islanders, 3 Hispanic Americans), 9 international. 65 applicants, 35% accepted, 11 enrolled. In 2009, 2 master's, 9 doctorates awarded. Terminal master's awarded for partial completion of doctoral program. *Degree requirements:* For master's, one foreign language; for doctorate, 2 foreign languages, thesis/dissertation. *Entrance requirements:* Additional exam requirements/recommendations for international students: Required—TOEFL (minimum score 600 paper-based; 250 computer-based; 100 iBT). *Application deadline:* For fall admission, 1/2 for domestic and international students. Application fee: $75. Electronic applications accepted. *Financial support:* In 2009–10, fellowships with full tuition reimbursements (averaging $16,000 per year), teaching assistantships with full tuition reimbursements (averaging $16,300 per year) were awarded; Federal Work-Study and unspecified assistantships also available. Support available to part-time students. Financial award application deadline: 3/1; financial award applicants required to submit FAFSA. *Faculty research:* Spanish-American literature, philology, medieval French romance and troubadour/trouvere lyrics, Golden Age Peninsular literature, secondary language acquisition and pedagogy. *Unit head:* Dr. Dwayne Carpenter, Chairperson, 617-552-3828, E-mail: dwayne.carpenter@bc.edu. *Application contact:* Dr. Dwayne Carpenter, Chairperson, 617-552-3828, E-mail: dwayne.carpenter@bc.edu.

Boston University, Graduate School of Arts and Sciences, Department of Romance Studies, Boston, MA 02215. Offers French language and literature (MA, PhD); Hispanic language and literatures (MA, PhD). *Students:* 45 full-time (37 women), 5 part-time (3 women); includes 4 minority (all Hispanic Americans), 15 international. Average age 31. 50 applicants, 58% accepted, 12 enrolled. In 2009, 2 master's, 4 doctorates awarded. Terminal master's awarded for partial completion of doctoral program. *Degree requirements:* For master's, one foreign language, comprehensive exam; for doctorate, 2 foreign languages, comprehensive exam, thesis/dissertation. *Entrance requirements:* For master's and doctorate, GRE General Test, sample of written work, 3 letters of recommendation. Additional exam requirements/recommendations for international students: Required—TOEFL (minimum score 550 paper-based; 213 computer-based). *Application deadline:* For fall admission, 4/15 for domestic and international students; for spring admission, 10/15 for domestic and international students. Application fee: $70. Electronic applications accepted. *Expenses:* Tuition: Full-time $37,910; part-time $1184 per credit hour. Required fees: $386; $40 per semester. Part-time tuition and fees vary according to class time, course level, degree level and program. *Financial support:* In 2009–10, 48 students received support, including 2 fellowships with full tuition reimbursements available (averaging $18,900 per year), 35 teaching assistantships with full tuition reimbursements available (averaging $18,400 per year); research assistantships, Federal Work-Study and scholarships/grants also available. Support available to part-time students. Financial award application deadline: 1/15; financial award applicants required to submit FAFSA. *Unit head:* James Iffland, Chairman, 617-353-6225, Fax: 617-353-6246, E-mail: Iffland@bu.edu. *Application contact:* Sharo Gineo, Administrative Assistant, 617-353-2641, Fax: 617-353-6246, E-mail: sdow@bu.edu.

Bowling Green State University, Graduate College, College of Arts and Sciences, Department of Romance and Classical Studies, Program in Spanish, Bowling Green, OH 43403. Offers Spanish (MA); Spanish education (MAT). Part-time programs available. *Degree requirements:* For master's, one foreign language, thesis or alternative. *Entrance requirements:* For master's, GRE General Test. Additional exam requirements/recommendations for international students: Required—TOEFL. Electronic applications accepted. *Faculty research:* U.S. Latino literature and culture, Latin American film and popular culture, applied linguistics, Spanish popular culture.

Brigham Young University, Graduate Studies, College of Humanities, Department of Spanish and Portuguese, Provo, UT 84602. Offers hispanic literature (MA); Portuguese linguistics (MA); Portuguese literature (MA); Spanish linguistics (MA); Spanish teaching (MA). Part-time programs available. *Faculty:* 32 full-time (5 women). *Students:* 18 full-time (7 women), 21 part-time (10 women); includes 5 minority (all Hispanic Americans), 9 international. Average age 30. 25 applicants, 56% accepted, 14 enrolled. In 2009, 17 master's awarded. *Degree requirements:* For master's, one foreign language, comprehensive exam, thesis, 1 semester of teaching. *Entrance requirements:* For master's, minimum GPA of 3.5 in Spanish or Portuguese, 3.3 overall. Additional exam requirements/recommendations for international students: Required—TOEFL (minimum score 580 paper-based; 237 computer-based). *Application deadline:* For fall admission, 2/1 for domestic and international students. Application fee: $50. Electronic applications accepted. *Expenses:* Tuition: Full-time $5580; part-time $301 per credit hour. Tuition and fees vary according to student's religious affiliation. *Financial support:* In 2009–10, 39 students received support, including 39 teaching assistantships with partial tuition reimbursements available (averaging $8,787 per year); institutionally sponsored loans, scholarships/grants, tuition waivers (partial), and unspecified assistantships also available. Support available to part-time students. Financial award application deadline: 7/1. *Faculty research:* Mexican prose; Latin American theater, literature, phonetics, and phonology; pedagogy; classical Portuguese literature; Peninsular prose and theater. *Unit head:* Dr. Alvin F. Sherman, Chair, 801-422-3107, Fax: 801-422-0628, E-mail: alvin_sherman@byu.edu. *Application contact:* Arwen T. Wyatt, Graduate Secretary, 801-422-2196, Fax: 801-422-0628, E-mail: arwen_wyatt@byu.edu.

Brooklyn College of the City University of New York, Division of Graduate Studies, Department of Modern Languages and Literature, Brooklyn, NY 11210-2889. Offers French (MA); modern languages and literature (PhD); Spanish (MA). *Students:* 24 part-time (16 women); includes 16 minority (8 African Americans, 8 Hispanic Americans), 5 international. Average age 41. 10 applicants, 80% accepted, 6 enrolled. In 2009, 13 master's awarded. *Degree requirements:* For master's, comprehensive exam or research paper. *Entrance requirements:* For master's, 18 credits in advanced courses in Spanish, 2 letters of recommendation. Additional exam requirements/recommendations for international students: Required—TOEFL (minimum score 500 paper-based; 173 computer-based; 61 iBT). *Application deadline:* For fall admission, 8/14 for domestic students, 6/14 priority date for international students; for spring admission, 1/15 for domestic students, 12/15 priority date for international students. Applications are processed on a rolling basis. Application fee: $125. Electronic applications accepted. *Expenses:* Tuition, area resident: Full-time $7360; part-time $310 per credit hour. Tuition, state resident: full-time $7360; part-time $310 per credit hour. Tuition, nonresident: full-time $13,800; part-time $575 per credit hour. International tuition: $13,800 full-time. Required fees: $140.10 per semester. *Financial support:* Federal Work-Study, institutionally sponsored loans, and scholarships/grants available. Support available to part-time students. Financial award application deadline: 5/1; financial award applicants required to submit FAFSA. *Faculty research:* Latin American contemporary novel, Caribbean female

Spanish

Brooklyn College of the City University of New York (continued)
contemporary literature, nineteenth and twentieth century Spanish novel, twentieth century Mexican poetry. *Unit head:* Dr. Luigi Bonafinni, Chairperson, 718-951-5451, E-mail: luigi@brooklyn.cuny.edu. *Application contact:* Hernan Sierra, Graduate Admissions Coordinator, 718-951-4536, Fax: 718-951-4506, E-mail: grads@brooklyn.cuny.edu.

California State University, Bakersfield, Division of Graduate Studies, School of Humanities and Social Sciences, Program in Spanish, Bakersfield, CA 93311. Offers MA. *Degree requirements:* For master's, capstone course.

California State University, Fresno, Division of Graduate Studies, College of Arts and Humanities, Department of Modern and Classical Languages and Literatures, Fresno, CA 93740-8027. Offers Spanish (MA). Part-time programs available. *Degree requirements:* For master's, one foreign language, thesis or alternative. *Entrance requirements:* For master's, GRE General Test, BA in Spanish, minimum GPA of 3.0. Additional exam requirements/recommendations for international students: Required—TOEFL. Electronic applications accepted.

California State University, Fullerton, Graduate Studies, College of Humanities and Social Sciences, Department of Modern Languages and Literatures, Fullerton, CA 92834-9480. Offers French (MA); German (MA); Spanish (MA); teaching English to speakers of other languages (MS). Part-time programs available. *Students:* 40 full-time (30 women), 63 part-time (47 women); includes 49 minority (1 African American, 14 Asian Americans or Pacific Islanders, 34 Hispanic Americans), 20 international. Average age 33. 101 applicants, 52% accepted, 29 enrolled. In 2009, 37 master's awarded. *Degree requirements:* For master's, comprehensive exam, thesis or alternative. *Entrance requirements:* For master's, minimum GPA of 2.5 in last 60 hours of course work, undergraduate major in a language. Application fee: $55. *Expenses:* Tuition, nonresident: full-time $11,160; part-time $373 per credit. Required fees: $1440 per term. Tuition and fees vary according to course load, degree level and program. *Financial support:* Career-related internships or fieldwork, Federal Work-Study, institutionally sponsored loans, and scholarships/grants available. Support available to part-time students. Financial award application deadline: 3/1; financial award applicants required to submit FAFSA. *Unit head:* Dr. Janet Eyring, Chair, 657-278-3534. *Application contact:* Admissions/Applications, 657-278-2371.

California State University, Long Beach, Graduate Studies, College of Liberal Arts, Department of Romance, German, and Russian Languages and Literature, Program in Spanish, Long Beach, CA 90840. Offers MA. Part-time programs available. *Students:* 12 full-time (10 women), 32 part-time (25 women); includes 32 minority (2 American Indian/Alaska Native, 1 Asian American or Pacific Islander, 29 Hispanic Americans), 2 international. Average age 32. 24 applicants, 54% accepted, 10 enrolled. *Degree requirements:* For master's, one foreign language, thesis or alternative, research paper. *Entrance requirements:* For master's, BA in Spanish. *Application deadline:* For fall admission, 7/1 for domestic students. Applications are processed on a rolling basis. Application fee: $55. Electronic applications accepted. *Expenses:* Required fees: $1802 per semester. Part-time tuition and fees vary according to course load. *Financial support:* Federal Work-Study, institutionally sponsored loans, and scholarships/grants available. Financial award application deadline: 3/2. *Faculty research:* Literary translation, literature and politics, women writers, Latin American poetry, Latin American theatre. *Unit head:* Dr. Lisa Vollendorf, Chair, 562-985-4318, Fax: 562-985-4259, E-mail: lvollend@csulb.edu. *Application contact:* Dr. Bonnie Gasior, Program Director, 562-985-4318, Fax: 562-985-4259, E-mail: bgasior@csulb.edu.

California State University, Los Angeles, Graduate Studies, College of Arts and Letters, Department of Modern Languages and Literatures, Los Angeles, CA 90032-8530. Offers French (MA); Spanish (MA). Part-time and evening/weekend programs available. *Faculty:* 4 full-time (3 women), 3 part-time/adjunct (2 women). *Students:* 19 full-time (10 women), 36 part-time (30 women); includes 38 minority (2 Asian Americans or Pacific Islanders, 36 Hispanic Americans), 4 international. Average age 39. 12 applicants, 100% accepted, 4 enrolled. In 2009, 5 master's awarded. *Degree requirements:* For master's, comprehensive exam. *Entrance requirements:* Additional exam requirements/recommendations for international students: Required—TOEFL (minimum score 500 paper-based; 173 computer-based). *Application deadline:* For fall admission, 5/1 for domestic and international students. Applications are processed on a rolling basis. Application fee: $55. Electronic applications accepted. *Financial support:* Federal Work-Study available. Support available to part-time students. Financial award application deadline: 3/1. *Faculty research:* French literature, language teaching and methodology, Spanish poetry, Spanish-American fiction and poetry. *Unit head:* Dr. Sachiko Matsunaga, Chair, 323-343-4230, Fax: 323-343-4234, E-mail: smatsun@calstatela.edu. *Application contact:* Dr. Cheryl L. Ney, Associate Vice President for Academic Affairs and Dean of Graduate Studies, 323-343-3820, Fax: 323-343-5653, E-mail: cney@cslanet.calstatela.edu.

California State University, Northridge, Graduate Studies, College of Humanities, Department of Modern and Classical Languages and Literatures, Northridge, CA 91330. Offers Spanish (MA). Part-time and evening/weekend programs available. *Faculty:* 11 full-time (4 women), 20 part-time/adjunct (17 women). *Students:* 11 full-time (10 women), 22 part-time (12 women); includes 1 African American, 1 Asian American or Pacific Islander, 28 Hispanic Americans. Average age 36. 20 applicants, 50% accepted, 4 enrolled. In 2009, 3 master's awarded. *Degree requirements:* For master's, one foreign language. *Entrance requirements:* For master's, GRE General Test or minimum GPA of 3.0. Additional exam requirements/recommendations for international students: Required—TOEFL. *Application deadline:* For fall admission, 11/30 for domestic students. Application fee: $55. *Financial support:* Application deadline: 3/1. *Unit head:* Dr. Brian Castronovo, Chair, 818-677-3467, E-mail: brian.castronovo@csun.edu. *Application contact:* Dr. Brian Castronovo, Chair, 818-677-3467, E-mail: brian.castronovo@csun.edu.

California State University, Sacramento, Graduate Studies, College of Social Sciences and Interdisciplinary Studies, Liberal Arts Program, Sacramento, CA 95819. Offers French (MA); German (MA); Spanish (MA); theater arts (MA). *Degree requirements:* For master's, writing proficiency exam. *Entrance requirements:* Additional exam requirements/recommendations for international students: Required—TOEFL. Electronic applications accepted.

California State University, San Bernardino, Graduate Studies, College of Arts and Letters, Department of World Languages and Literatures, San Bernardino, CA 92407-2397. Offers Spanish (MA). Part-time and evening/weekend programs available. *Faculty:* 4 full-time (2 women), 1 part-time/adjunct (0 women). *Students:* 24 full-time (16 women), 24 part-time (17 women); includes 36 minority (3 African Americans, 33 Hispanic Americans), 3 international. Average age 34. 31 applicants, 81% accepted, 14 enrolled. In 2009, 5 master's awarded. *Degree requirements:* For master's, comprehensive exam, advancement to candidacy. *Application deadline:* Applications are processed on a rolling basis. Application fee: $55. *Financial support:* Career-related internships or fieldwork, Federal Work-Study, and institutionally sponsored loans available. Support available to part-time students. *Unit head:* Terri Nelson, Chair, 909-537-5849, Fax: 909-537-7091, E-mail: tnelson@csusb.edu. *Application contact:* Olivia Rosas, Director of Admissions, 909-537-7577, Fax: 909-537-7034, E-mail: orosas@csusb.edu.

California State University, San Marcos, College of Arts and Sciences, Program in World Languages, San Marcos, CA 92096-0001. Offers Spanish (MA). Part-time and evening/weekend programs available. *Degree requirements:* For master's, 2 foreign languages, exam. *Entrance requirements:* For master's, GRE General Test, minimum GPA of 2.5, minimum GPA of 3.0 in upper division Spanish courses. Electronic applications accepted. *Faculty research:* Applied linguistics, golden age Spanish literature, Latin American literature, poetry, Chicano studies.

The Catholic University of America, School of Arts and Sciences, Department of Modern Languages and Literatures, Washington, DC 20064. Offers Spanish (MA, PhD). Part-time programs available. *Faculty:* 12 full-time (7 women), 14 part-time/adjunct (12 women). *Students:* 7 full-time (5 women), 12 part-time (10 women); includes 5 minority (all Hispanic Americans), 4 international. Average age 36. 18 applicants, 61% accepted, 3 enrolled. In 2009, 1 master's awarded. *Degree requirements:* For master's, comprehensive exam, thesis or alternative; for doctorate, one foreign language, comprehensive exam, thesis/dissertation. *Entrance requirements:* For master's and doctorate, GRE General Test, statement of purpose, official copies of academic transcripts, three letters of recommendation. Additional exam requirements/recommendations for international students: Required—TOEFL (minimum score 580 paper-based; 237 computer-based). *Application deadline:* For fall admission, 8/1 priority date for domestic students, 7/15 for international students; for spring admission, 12/1 priority date for domestic students, 10/15 for international students. Applications are processed on a rolling basis. Application fee: $55. Electronic applications accepted. *Expenses:* Tuition: Full-time $31,740; part-time $1245 per credit hour. Required fees: $50; $25 per semester hour. One-time fee: $425. *Financial support:* Fellowships, research assistantships, teaching assistantships, Federal Work-Study, scholarships/grants, tuition waivers (full and partial), and unspecified assistantships available. Financial award application deadline: 2/1; financial award applicants required to submit FAFSA. *Faculty research:* Arthurian literature and medieval lyric, eighteenth-twentieth century Spanish literature, Latin American literature, German literature, seventeenth century French literature. *Unit head:* Dr. Joan T. Grimbert, Chair, 202-319-5240, Fax: 202-319-6077, E-mail: grimbert@cua.edu. *Application contact:* Julie Schwing, Director of Graduate Admissions, 202-319-5057, Fax: 202-319-6533, E-mail: cua-admissions@cua.edu.

Central Connecticut State University, School of Graduate Studies, School of Arts and Sciences, Department of Modern Languages, Program in Modern Language, New Britain, CT 06050-4010. Offers French (MA, Certificate); German (Certificate); Italian (Certificate); modern language (MA); Spanish language and Hispanic culture (MA). Part-time and evening/weekend programs available. *Students:* 2 full-time (1 woman), 40 part-time (35 women); includes 14 minority (all Hispanic Americans). Average age 38. 16 applicants, 69% accepted, 9 enrolled. In 2009, 9 master's awarded. *Degree requirements:* For master's, one foreign language, comprehensive exam, thesis or alternative; for Certificate, qualifying exam. *Entrance requirements:* For master's, minimum undergraduate GPA of 2.7, 24 credits of undergraduate courses in either Italian or Spanish. Additional exam requirements/recommendations for international students: Required—TOEFL. *Application deadline:* For fall admission, 7/1 for domestic students; for spring admission, 12/1 for domestic students. Applications are processed on a rolling basis. Application fee: $50. Electronic applications accepted. *Expenses:* Tuition, area resident: Full-time $4662; part-time $440 per credit. Tuition, state resident: full-time $6994; part-time $440 per credit. Tuition, nonresident: full-time $12,988; part-time $440 per credit. Required fees: $3606. One-time fee: $62 part-time. *Faculty research:* Twentieth century French theater, seventeenth century French literature, French Middle Ages.

Central Connecticut State University, School of Graduate Studies, School of Arts and Sciences, Department of Modern Languages, Program in Spanish, New Britain, CT 06050-4010. Offers MS, Certificate. Part-time and evening/weekend programs available. *Students:* 3 full-time (all women), 7 part-time (5 women); includes 3 minority (all Hispanic Americans). Average age 29. 8 applicants, 100% accepted, 6 enrolled. In 2009, 1 master's, 2 other advanced degrees awarded. *Degree requirements:* For master's, one foreign language, comprehensive exam, thesis or alternative; for Certificate, qualifying exam. *Entrance requirements:* For master's, minimum undergraduate GPA of 2.7, 24 credits of undergraduate courses in either Italian or Spanish. Additional exam requirements/recommendations for international students: Required—TOEFL. *Application deadline:* For fall admission, 7/1 for domestic students; for spring admission, 12/1 for domestic students. Applications are processed on a rolling basis. Application fee: $50. Electronic applications accepted. *Expenses:* Tuition, area resident: Full-time $4662; part-time $440 per credit. Tuition, state resident: full-time $6994; part-time $440 per credit. Tuition, nonresident: full-time $12,988; part-time $440 per credit. Required fees: $3606. One-time fee: $62 part-time. *Faculty research:* Linguistics, nineteenth to twentieth century Spanish literature, Spanish Golden Age prose/drama.

Central Michigan University, College of Graduate Studies, College of Humanities and Social and Behavioral Sciences, Department of Foreign Languages, Literatures, and Cultures, Mount Pleasant, MI 48859. Offers Spanish (MA). Part-time programs available. *Degree requirements:* For master's, thesis or alternative. Electronic applications accepted.

City College of the City University of New York, Graduate School, College of Liberal Arts and Science, Division of the Humanities and Arts, Department of Foreign Languages, New York, NY 10031-9198. Offers Spanish (MA). *Degree requirements:* For master's, one foreign language, comprehensive exam, thesis or alternative. *Entrance requirements:* For master's, minimum GPA of 3.0. Additional exam requirements/recommendations for international students: Required—TOEFL (minimum score 500 paper-based; 61 iBT). Electronic applications accepted.

Cleveland State University, College of Graduate Studies, College of Liberal Arts and Social Sciences, Department of Modern Languages, Cleveland, OH 44115. Offers French (M Ed); Spanish (M Ed, MA), including language and linguistics (MA), Latin American studies (MA), peninsular studies (MA), Spanish (MA). Part-time and evening/weekend programs available. *Degree requirements:* For master's, one foreign language, comprehensive exam, thesis optional, study abroad. *Entrance requirements:* For master's, undergraduate major in Spanish or equivalent, essay in Spanish, writing sample. Additional exam requirements/recommendations for international students: Required—TOEFL (minimum score 525 paper-based; 197 computer-based). Electronic applications accepted. *Faculty research:* Second language acquisition, sociolinguistics, contemporary Spanish novel, Arabic diaspora in Latin America, border literature.

Columbia University, Graduate School of Arts and Sciences, Division of Humanities, Department of Spanish and Portuguese, New York, NY 10027. Offers M Phil, MA, PhD. Part-time programs available. *Degree requirements:* For master's, one foreign language, written exam; for doctorate, 3 foreign languages, thesis/dissertation. *Entrance requirements:* For master's and doctorate, GRE General Test, GRE Subject Test, sample of written work. Additional exam requirements/recommendations for international students: Required—TOEFL. *Faculty research:* Literary theory and criticism, Spain's Golden Age: sixteenth- and seventeenth-centuries, contemporary Spanish American literature.

Cornell University, Graduate School, Graduate Fields of Arts and Sciences, Field of Romance Studies, Ithaca, NY 14853-0001. Offers French linguistics (PhD); French literature (PhD); Hispanic literature (PhD); Italian linguistics (PhD); Italian literature (PhD); Romance linguistics (PhD); Spanish linguistics (PhD). *Faculty:* 42 full-time (19 women). *Students:* 54 full-time (27 women); includes 9 minority (all Hispanic Americans), 17 international. Average age 30. 78 applicants, 17% accepted, 10 enrolled. In 2009, 7 doctorates awarded. *Degree requirements:* For doctorate, 2 foreign languages, comprehensive exam, thesis/dissertation. *Entrance requirements:* For doctorate, GRE General Test, sample of written work, 3 letters of recommendation. Additional exam requirements/recommendations for international students: Required—TOEFL (minimum score 550 paper-based; 213 computer-based; 77 iBT). *Application deadline:* For fall admission, 1/15 for domestic students. Application fee: $70. Electronic applications accepted. *Expenses:* Tuition: Full-time $29,500. Required fees: $70. Full-time tuition and fees vary according to degree level, program and student level. *Financial support:* In 2009–10, 46 students received support, including 8 fellowships with full tuition reimbursements available, 2 teaching assistantships with full tuition reimbursements available; research assistantships with full tuition reimbursements available, institutionally sponsored loans, scholarships/grants, health care benefits, tuition waivers (full and partial), and unspecified assistantships also available. Financial award applicants required to submit FAFSA. *Faculty research:* Literary theory, Hispanic studies, French studies, gender studies. *Unit head:* Director of Graduate Studies, 607-255-8222. *Application contact:* Graduate Field Assistant, 607-255-4246, E-mail: romance_studies@cornell.edu.

Drew University, Caspersen School of Graduate Studies, Program in Education, Madison, NJ 07940-1493. Offers biology (MAT); chemistry (MAT); English (MAT); French (MAT); Italian

(MAT); math (MAT); physics (MAT); social studies (MAT); Spanish (MAT); theatre arts (MAT). *Unit head:* Dr. Ross Danis.

Duke University, Graduate School, Department of Romance Studies, Durham, NC 27708. Offers French (PhD); Spanish (PhD); JD/AM. *Faculty:* 29 full-time. *Students:* 42 full-time (28 women); includes 10 minority (1 African American, 9 Hispanic Americans), 15 international. 54 applicants, 22% accepted, 3 enrolled. In 2009, 6 doctorates awarded. *Degree requirements:* For doctorate, 2 foreign languages, thesis/dissertation. *Entrance requirements:* For doctorate, GRE General Test. Additional exam requirements/recommendations for international students: Required—TOEFL (minimum score 550 paper-based; 213 computer-based; 83 iBT), IELTS (minimum score 7). *Application deadline:* For fall admission, 12/8 priority date for domestic and international students. Application fee: $75. Electronic applications accepted. *Financial support:* Fellowships, research assistantships, teaching assistantships, Federal Work-Study available. Financial award application deadline: 12/31. *Unit head:* Esther Gabara, Director of Graduate Studies, 919-660-3100. *Application contact:* Esther Gabara, Director of Graduate Studies, 919-660-3100.

Eastern Michigan University, Graduate School, College of Arts and Sciences, Department of World Languages, Programs in Foreign Languages, Ypsilanti, MI 48197. Offers French (MA); German (MA); German for business (Graduate Certificate); Hispanic language and cultures (Graduate Certificate); Japanese business practices (Graduate Certificate); Spanish (MA). Part-time and evening/weekend programs available. Postbaccalaureate distance learning degree programs offered (minimal on-campus study). *Students:* 1 full-time (0 women), 15 part-time (14 women); includes 4 minority (1 African American, 3 Hispanic Americans), 1 international. Average age 39. In 2009, 6 master's awarded. *Degree requirements:* For master's, one foreign language, thesis optional. *Entrance requirements:* Additional exam requirements/recommendations for international students: Required—TOEFL. *Application deadline:* Applications are processed on a rolling basis. Application fee: $35. Tuition and fees vary according to course level. *Financial support:* Fellowships, research assistantships with full tuition reimbursements, teaching assistantships with full tuition reimbursements, career-related internships or fieldwork, Federal Work-Study, institutionally sponsored loans, scholarships/grants, tuition waivers (partial), and unspecified assistantships available. Support available to part-time students. Financial award applicants required to submit FAFSA. *Application contact:* Dr. Genevieve Peden, Program Advisor, 734-487-2283, Fax: 734-487-3411, E-mail: gpeden@emich.edu.

Emory University, Graduate School of Arts and Sciences, Department of Comparative Literature, Atlanta, GA 30322-1100. Offers comparative literature (PhD); English (Certificate); French (Certificate); Middle Eastern studies (PhD); philosophy (Certificate); psychoanalytic studies (PhD); religion (PhD); Spanish (Certificate); women studies (Certificate). *Degree requirements:* For doctorate, 2 foreign languages, comprehensive exam, thesis/dissertation. *Entrance requirements:* For doctorate, GRE General Test, minimum GPA of 3.0. Additional exam requirements/recommendations for international students: Required—TOEFL. Electronic applications accepted. *Faculty research:* Literary theory, psychoanalysis trauma and testimony, literature and religion, literature and technology, literature and philosophy, politics and global culture, literature and aesthetics.

Emory University, Graduate School of Arts and Sciences, Department of Spanish and Portuguese, Atlanta, GA 30322-1100. Offers comparative literature (Certificate); film studies (Certificate); Spanish (PhD); women's studies (Certificate). *Degree requirements:* For doctorate, 2 foreign languages, comprehensive exam, thesis/dissertation. *Entrance requirements:* For doctorate, GRE General Test. Additional exam requirements/recommendations for international students: Required—TOEFL. Electronic applications accepted. *Faculty research:* Spanish literature, Spanish-American literature, literary theory, criticism, cultural studies.

Florida Atlantic University, Dorothy F. Schmidt College of Arts and Letters, Department of Languages, Linguistics, and Comparative Literature, Boca Raton, FL 33431-0991. Offers comparative literature (MA); French (MA); linguistics (MA); Spanish (MA). Part-time programs available. *Faculty:* 23 full-time (20 women), 12 part-time/adjunct (10 women). *Students:* 20 full-time (14 women), 14 part-time (10 women); includes 16 minority (3 African Americans, 1 Asian American or Pacific Islander, 12 Hispanic Americans), 4 international. Average age 35. 35 applicants, 60% accepted, 13 enrolled. In 2009, 16 master's awarded. *Degree requirements:* For master's, one foreign language, comprehensive exam, thesis optional. *Entrance requirements:* For master's, GRE General Test, minimum GPA of 3.0. *Application deadline:* For fall admission, 7/1 priority date for domestic students, 2/15 for international students; for spring admission, 11/1 for domestic students, 7/15 for international students. Applications are processed on a rolling basis. Application fee: $30. *Expenses:* Tuition, state resident: full-time $7055; part-time $293.94 per credit hour. Tuition, nonresident: full-time $22,096; part-time $920.66 per credit hour. *Financial support:* Fellowships, research assistantships, teaching assistantships with partial tuition reimbursements, Federal Work-Study and tuition waivers (partial) available. Support available to part-time students. Financial award application deadline: 4/1. *Faculty research:* Modern European studies, modern Latin America, medieval Europe. *Unit head:* Dr. Michael Horswell, Chair, 561-297-3860, Fax: 561-297-2756, E-mail: horswell@fau.edu. *Application contact:* Dr. Emily Stockard, Associate Dean, 561-297-2817, Fax: 561-297-2744, E-mail: stockard@fau.edu.

Florida International University, College of Arts and Sciences, Department of Modern Languages, Miami, FL 33199. Offers Spanish (MA, PhD). Fall admissions only for PhD program. Part-time and evening/weekend programs available. *Faculty:* 21 full-time (13 women). *Students:* 24 full-time (18 women), 34 part-time (27 women); includes 52 minority (1 Asian American or Pacific Islander, 51 Hispanic Americans), 2 international. Average age 36. 23 applicants, 30% accepted, 7 enrolled. In 2009, 7 master's awarded. *Degree requirements:* For master's, 2 foreign languages, comprehensive exam, thesis or 6 elective credits; for doctorate, 3 foreign languages, comprehensive exam, thesis/dissertation. *Entrance requirements:* For master's, minimum GPA of 3.0, resume, writing sample in Spanish (6-7 pages minimum), 2 letters of recommendation; for doctorate, GRE General Test (minimum score of 1120) or EXADEP (minimum score of 500), minimum GPA of 3.0, letter of intent, resume, writing sample in Spanish (15 pages minimum), 2 letters of recommendation. Additional exam requirements/recommendations for international students: Required—TOEFL (minimum score 550 paper-based; 80 iBT). *Application deadline:* For fall admission, 3/15 for domestic and international students. Application fee: $30. Electronic applications accepted. *Expenses:* Tuition, state resident: full-time $8008; part-time $4004 per year. Tuition, nonresident: full-time $20,104; part-time $10,052 per year. Required fees: $298; $149 per term. *Financial support:* In 2009–10, 13 students received support, including 2 fellowships with partial tuition reimbursements available, 13 teaching assistantships with full tuition reimbursements available; institutionally sponsored loans, scholarships/grants, and health care benefits also available. Financial award application deadline: 3/1; financial award applicants required to submit FAFSA. *Faculty research:* Peninsular Spanish literature, Spanish-American literature, cultural studies, film studies, bilingualism. *Unit head:* Dr. Pascale Becel, Chair, 305-348-2851, Fax: 305-348-1085, E-mail: modlang@fiu.edu. *Application contact:* Nanett Rojas, Assistant Director of Graduate Admissions, 305-348-7442, Fax: 305-348-7441, E-mail: gradadm@fiu.edu.

Florida State University, The Graduate School, College of Arts and Sciences, Department of Modern Languages, Program in Spanish, Tallahassee, FL 32306. Offers MA, PhD. *Faculty:* 13 full-time (6 women), 1 part-time/adjunct (0 women). *Students:* 37 full-time (26 women), 2 part-time (1 woman); includes 2 African Americans, 1 American Indian/Alaska Native, 10 Hispanic Americans. Average age 25. 41 applicants, 71% accepted, 20 enrolled. In 2009, 1 master's, 2 doctorates awarded. Terminal master's awarded for partial completion of doctoral program. *Degree requirements:* For master's, thesis optional; for doctorate, 2 foreign languages, thesis/dissertation. *Entrance requirements:* For master's and doctorate, GRE General Test or minimum GPA of 3.0. Additional exam requirements/recommendations for international students: Required—TOEFL (minimum score 550 paper-based; 213 computer-based). *Application deadline:* For fall admission, 2/1 for domestic and international students. Applications are processed on a rolling basis. Application fee: $30. Electronic applications accepted. *Expenses:* Tuition, state resident: full-time $7413. Tuition, nonresident: full-time $22,567. *Financial support:* In 2009–10, fellowships with partial tuition reimbursements (averaging $14,000 per year), research assistantships with partial tuition reimbursements (averaging $12,000 per year), 37 teaching assistantships with partial tuition reimbursements (averaging $11,200 per year) were awarded. Financial award application deadline: 2/1; financial award applicants required to submit FAFSA. *Faculty research:* Latin American theater, Hispanic literature of the United States, twentieth century Latin American poetry, Spanish American colonial. *Unit head:* Dr. Gretchen Sunderman, Divisional Coordinator and Professor, 850-644-8186, Fax: 850-644-0524, E-mail: gsunderman@fsu.edu. *Application contact:* Wendy E. Pigott, Graduate Academic Coordinator, 850-644-8397, Fax: 850-644-0524, E-mail: wpigott@fsu.edu.

Framingham State College, Division of Graduate and Continuing Education, Program in Spanish, Framingham, MA 01701-9101. Offers M Ed.

Georgetown University, Graduate School of Arts and Sciences, Department of Spanish and Portuguese, Washington, DC 20057. Offers Spanish (MS, PhD), including Hispanic literature, Spanish linguistics, Spanish literature; MS/PhD. *Degree requirements:* For master's, one foreign language, research project; for doctorate, 3 foreign languages, thesis/dissertation. *Entrance requirements:* Additional exam requirements/recommendations for international students: Required—TOEFL.

Georgia Southern University, Jack N. Averitt College of Graduate Studies, College of Liberal Arts and Social Sciences, Department of Foreign Languages, Statesboro, GA 30460. Offers Spanish (MA). Part-time and evening/weekend programs available. *Students:* 6 full-time (3 women), 8 part-time (7 women); includes 1 minority (African American), 1 international. Average age 28. 8 applicants, 100% accepted, 6 enrolled. In 2009, 5 master's awarded. *Degree requirements:* For master's, one foreign language, thesis optional. *Entrance requirements:* For master's, GRE, minimum GPA of 3.0, letters of reference. Additional exam requirements/recommendations for international students: Required—TOEFL (minimum score 550 paper-based; 213 computer-based; 80 iBT). *Application deadline:* For fall admission, 3/1 priority date for domestic and international students; for spring admission, 10/1 priority date for domestic students, 10/1 for international students. Applications are processed on a rolling basis. Application fee: $50. Electronic applications accepted. *Expenses:* Tuition, state resident: full-time $5040; part-time $210 per credit hour. Tuition, nonresident: full-time $20,136; part-time $839 per credit hour. Required fees: $1644. *Financial support:* In 2009–10, 10 students received support, including research assistantships with partial tuition reimbursements available (averaging $7,200 per year), teaching assistantships with partial tuition reimbursements available (averaging $7,200 per year); career-related internships or fieldwork, Federal Work-Study, scholarships/grants, tuition waivers (partial), and unspecified assistantships also available. Support available to part-time students. Financial award application deadline: 4/15; financial award applicants required to submit FAFSA. *Unit head:* Dr. Eric Kartchner, Chair, 912-478-5281, Fax: 912-478-0652, E-mail: forlangs@georgiasouthern.edu. *Application contact:* Dr. Charles Ziglar, Coordinator for Graduate Student Recruitment, 912-478-5635, Fax: 912-478-0740, E-mail: gradadmissions@georgiasouthern.edu.

Georgia State University, College of Arts and Sciences, Department of Modern and Classical Languages, Program in Spanish, Atlanta, GA 30302-3083. Offers MA. Evening/weekend programs available. *Degree requirements:* For master's, one foreign language, thesis or alternative, general exam. *Entrance requirements:* For master's, GRE General Test. Additional exam requirements/recommendations for international students: Required—TOEFL. Electronic applications accepted. *Faculty research:* Spanish and Latin-American literature.

Georgia State University, College of Arts and Sciences, Department of Modern and Classical Languages, Program in Translation and Interpretation, Atlanta, GA 30302-3083. Offers French (Certificate); German (Certificate); Spanish (Certificate). Electronic applications accepted.

Graduate School and University Center of the City University of New York, Graduate Studies, Program in Hispanic and Luso-Brazilian Literatures and Languages, New York, NY 10016-4039. Offers PhD. *Faculty:* 23 full-time (8 women). *Students:* 108 full-time (71 women), 8 part-time (6 women); includes 50 minority (1 Asian American or Pacific Islander, 49 Hispanic Americans), 32 international. Average age 40. 33 applicants, 67% accepted, 13 enrolled. In 2009, 6 doctorates awarded. *Degree requirements:* For doctorate, 2 foreign languages, thesis/dissertation. *Entrance requirements:* For doctorate, GRE General Test. Additional exam requirements/recommendations for international students: Required—TOEFL. *Application deadline:* For fall admission, 1/15 priority date for domestic students; for spring admission, 11/15 for domestic students. Application fee: $125. Electronic applications accepted. *Financial support:* In 2009–10, 68 students received support, including 64 fellowships, 2 research assistantships, 9 teaching assistantships; career-related internships or fieldwork, Federal Work-Study, institutionally sponsored loans, and tuition waivers (full and partial) also available. Financial award application deadline: 2/1; financial award applicants required to submit FAFSA. *Unit head:* Dr. Lia Schwartz, Executive Officer, 212-817-8411, Fax: 212-817-1522, E-mail: lschwartz@gc.cuny.edu. *Application contact:* Dr. Lia Schwartz, Executive Officer, 212-817-8411, Fax: 212-817-1522, E-mail: lschwartz@gc.cuny.edu.

Harvard University, Graduate School of Arts and Sciences, Department of Romance Languages and Literatures, Cambridge, MA 02138. Offers French (AM, PhD); Italian (AM, PhD); Portuguese (AM, PhD); Spanish (AM, PhD). Terminal master's awarded for partial completion of doctoral program. *Degree requirements:* For master's, 2 foreign languages; for doctorate, 2 foreign languages, thesis/dissertation. *Entrance requirements:* For master's and doctorate, GRE General Test, sample of written work. Additional exam requirements/recommendations for international students: Required—TOEFL. *Expenses:* Tuition: Full-time $33,696. Required fees: $1126. Full-time tuition and fees vary according to program.

Hofstra University, College of Liberal Arts and Sciences, Department of Romance Languages and Literatures, Hempstead, NY 11549. Offers Spanish (MA). *Accreditation:* NCATE. Part-time and evening/weekend programs available. *Faculty:* 4 full-time (2 women), 1 (woman) part-time/adjunct. *Students:* 2 full-time (both women), 4 part-time (all women); includes 3 minority (all Hispanic Americans). Average age 31. 3 applicants, 100% accepted, 1 enrolled. In 2009, 3 master's awarded. *Degree requirements:* For master's, one foreign language, thesis. *Entrance requirements:* Additional exam requirements/recommendations for international students: Required—TOEFL (minimum score 550 paper-based; 213 computer-based; 80 iBT). *Application deadline:* Applications are processed on a rolling basis. Application fee: $60. Electronic applications accepted. *Expenses:* Tuition: Full-time $16,200; part-time $900 per credit hour. Required fees: $970; $145 per term. Tuition and fees vary according to program. *Financial support:* In 2009–10, 13 fellowships with full and partial tuition reimbursements (averaging $2,667 per year) were awarded; research assistantships with full and partial tuition reimbursements, career-related internships or fieldwork, Federal Work-Study, institutionally sponsored loans, scholarships/grants, and tuition waivers (full and partial) also available. Support available to part-time students. Financial award applicants required to submit FAFSA. *Faculty research:* Contemporary Spanish and Spanish American cultural studies; Spanish linguistics and history of the Spanish language; Latin American poetry; colonial Latin America, postcolonial studies, and decolonization theories, Spanish theater. *Unit head:* Dr. Benita Sampedro, Chairperson, 516-463-4521, Fax: 516-463-2310, E-mail: benita.sampedro@hofstra.edu. *Application contact:* Carol Drummer, Dean of Graduate Admissions, 516-463-4876, Fax: 516-463-4664, E-mail: gradstudent@hofstra.edu.

Hofstra University, School of Education, Health, and Human Services, Department of Curriculum and Teaching, Program in Foreign Language Education, Hempstead, NY 11549. Offers foreign language and TESOL (MS Ed); foreign language education (MA, MS Ed), including French, German, Russian, Spanish. Part-time and evening/weekend programs available. *Students:* 4 full-time (all women), 3 part-time (1 woman); includes 2 minority (both Hispanic Americans). Average age 29. 9 applicants, 67% accepted, 3 enrolled. In 2009, 2 master's awarded. *Degree requirements:* For master's, one foreign language. *Entrance*

Spanish

Hofstra University (continued)
requirements: For master's, 2 letters of recommendation, teacher certification (MA). Additional exam requirements/recommendations for international students: Required—TOEFL (minimum score 550 paper-based; 213 computer-based; 80 iBT). *Application deadline:* Applications are processed on a rolling basis. Application fee: $60. Electronic applications accepted. *Expenses:* Tuition: Full-time $16,200; part-time $900 per credit hour. Required fees: $970; $145 per term. Tuition and fees vary according to program. *Financial support:* In 2009–10, 6 students received support, including 2 fellowships with full and partial tuition reimbursements available (averaging $2,878 per year); research assistantships with full and partial tuition reimbursements available, Federal Work-Study, institutionally sponsored loans, scholarships/grants, tuition waivers (full and partial), and unspecified assistantships also available. Support available to part-time students. Financial award applicants required to submit FAFSA. *Faculty research:* First language acquisition and second language learning; theory and practice in language teaching; technology and language teaching and learning; language and colonialism. *Unit head:* Dr. Mustapha Masrour, Program Director, 516-463-6033, Fax: 516-463-6266, E-mail: lalmzm@hofstra.edu. *Application contact:* Carol Drummer, Dean of Graduate Admissions, 516-463-4876, Fax: 516-463-4664, E-mail: gradstudent@hofstra.edu.

Howard University, Graduate School, Department of Modern Languages and Literatures, Washington, DC 20059-0002. Offers French (MA); Spanish (MA). Part-time programs available. *Degree requirements:* For master's, one foreign language, comprehensive exam, thesis. *Entrance requirements:* For master's, GRE General Test, writing samples in English and French or Spanish. *Faculty research:* African literature in French, Spanish linguistics, Spanish Peninsular literature, Spanish sociolinguistics.

Hunter College of the City University of New York, Graduate School, School of Arts and Sciences, Department of Romance Languages, Program in Spanish, New York, NY 10021-5085. Offers Spanish (MA); Spanish education (MA). Part-time and evening/weekend programs available. *Faculty:* 4 full-time (3 women). *Students:* 1 (woman) full-time, 12 part-time (11 women); includes 9 minority (all Hispanic Americans). Average age 35. 12 applicants, 100% accepted, 7 enrolled. In 2009, 6 master's awarded. *Degree requirements:* For master's, 2 foreign languages, comprehensive exam, thesis optional. *Entrance requirements:* For master's, GRE General Test, GRE Subject Test, ability to read, speak, and write Spanish; interview. Additional exam requirements/recommendations for international students: Required—TOEFL. *Application deadline:* For fall admission, 4/1 for domestic students, 2/1 for international students; for spring admission, 11/1 for domestic students, 9/1 for international students. Application fee: $125. *Expenses:* Tuition, state resident: full-time $7360; part-time $310 per credit. Required fees: $250 per semester. *Financial support:* Federal Work-Study and tuition waivers (partial) available. Support available to part-time students. Financial award application deadline: 4/15. *Faculty research:* Galician studies, contemporary Spanish poetry, Lope de Vega, comparative Hispanic literatures, contemporary Hispanic poetry. *Unit head:* Dr. James O. Pellier, Graduate Advisor, 212-772-5625, E-mail: jpellice@hunter.cuny.edu. *Application contact:* William Zlata, Director for Graduate Admissions, 212-772-4482, Fax: 212-650-3336, E-mail: admissions@hunter.cuny.edu.

Illinois State University, Graduate School, College of Arts and Sciences, Department of Foreign Languages, Literatures and Cultures, Normal, IL 61790-2200. Offers French (MA); French and German (MA); French and Spanish (MA); German (MA); German and Spanish (MA); Spanish (MA). *Degree requirements:* For master's, variable foreign language requirement, comprehensive exam, 1 term of residency. *Entrance requirements:* For master's, GRE General Test, minimum GPA of 2.8 in last 60 hours of course work.

Indiana University Bloomington, University Graduate School, College of Arts and Sciences, Department of Spanish and Portuguese, Bloomington, IN 47405-7000. Offers Hispanic linguistics (MA, PhD); Hispanic literature (MA); Luso-Brazilian literature (MA); Luso-Brazilian studies (PhD); Spanish literatures (PhD); teaching Spanish (MAT). *Faculty:* 18 full-time (10 women). *Students:* 84 full-time (47 women), 2 part-time (0 women); includes 17 minority (1 Asian American or Pacific Islander, 16 Hispanic Americans), 18 international. Average age 30. 55 applicants, 62% accepted, 15 enrolled. In 2009, 10 master's, 4 doctorates awarded. *Degree requirements:* For master's, one foreign language; for doctorate, 3 foreign languages, thesis/dissertation. *Entrance requirements:* For master's, GRE General Test, GRE Subject Test, bachelor's degree in Portuguese or Spanish, minimum GPA of 3.25; for doctorate, GRE General Test, GRE Subject Test, master's degree in Portuguese or Spanish, minimum GPA of 3.25. Additional exam requirements/recommendations for international students: Required—TOEFL. *Application deadline:* For fall admission, 1/15 priority date for domestic students, 12/15 for international students; for spring admission, 9/1 for domestic and international students. Application fee: $55 ($65 for international students). *Financial support:* In 2009–10, 1 fellowship with full tuition reimbursement (averaging $15,000 per year), 72 teaching assistantships with full tuition reimbursements (averaging $14,790 per year) were awarded; research assistantships, Federal Work-Study also available. Financial award application deadline: 1/15. *Faculty research:* Spanish-American literature, Spanish peninsular literature, Luso-Brazilian studies, Catalan studies. *Unit head:* Josep Miguel Sobrer, Chair, 812-855-8498. *Application contact:* Steven Wagschal, Student Contact, 812-855-9194, E-mail: swagscha@indiana.edu.

Inter American University of Puerto Rico, Metropolitan Campus, Graduate Programs, Program in Spanish, San Juan, PR 00919-1293. Offers MA. Part-time and evening/weekend programs available. *Degree requirements:* For master's, one foreign language, comprehensive exam. *Entrance requirements:* For master's, GRE or EXADEP, interview, minimum GPA of 2.5, 6 credits each of Spanish literature and Hispanic-American literature. Electronic applications accepted.

Inter American University of Puerto Rico, Ponce Campus, Graduate School, Mercedita, PR 00715-1602. Offers accounting (MBA); biology (M Ed); chemistry (M Ed); criminal justice (MA); elementary education (M Ed); English as a Second Language (M Ed); finance (MBA); history (M Ed); human resources (MBA); marketing (MBA); mathematics (M Ed); Spanish (M Ed). *Entrance requirements:* For master's, minimum GPA of 2.5.

Iona College, School of Arts and Science, Program in Foreign Languages, New Rochelle, NY 10801-1890. Offers Italian (MA); Spanish (MA). Part-time and evening/weekend programs available. *Faculty:* 4 full-time (2 women), 1 part-time/adjunct (0 women). *Students:* 14 part-time (13 women); includes 1 minority (Hispanic American). Average age 35. 4 applicants, 75% accepted, 2 enrolled. In 2009, 10 master's awarded. *Degree requirements:* For master's, thesis or alternative. *Entrance requirements:* For master's, minimum GPA of 3.0. Additional exam requirements/recommendations for international students: Required—TOEFL (minimum score 550 paper-based; 213 computer-based). *Application deadline:* Applications are processed on a rolling basis. Application fee: $50. Electronic applications accepted. *Expenses:* Tuition: Part-time $830 per credit. *Financial support:* Unspecified assistantships available. Support available to part-time students. Financial award application deadline: 4/15; financial award applicants required to submit FAFSA. *Faculty research:* Contemporary Spanish literature, linguistics, language acquisition, female Hispanic literature, Latina authors. *Unit head:* Dr. Victoria E. Ketz, Chair, 914-637-2738, E-mail: vketz@iona.edu. *Application contact:* Veronica Jarek-Prinz, Director of Graduate Admissions, 914-633-2420, Fax: 914-633-2277, E-mail: vjarekprinz@iona.edu.

The Johns Hopkins University, Zanvyl Krieger School of Arts and Sciences, Department of German and Romance Languages and Literatures, Baltimore, MD 21218-2699. Offers French (PhD); German (PhD); Italian (PhD); romance languages (PhD); Spanish (PhD). *Faculty:* 31 full-time (20 women), 1 part-time/adjunct (0 women). *Students:* 49 full-time (30 women); includes 4 minority (all Hispanic Americans), 21 international. Average age 30. 51 applicants, 37% accepted, 19 enrolled. In 2009, 5 doctorates awarded. *Degree requirements:* For doctorate, 2 foreign languages, thesis/dissertation. *Entrance requirements:* For doctorate, GRE General Test. Additional exam requirements/recommendations for international students: Required—TOEFL (minimum score 600 paper-based; 250 computer-based; 100 iBT), IELTS. *Application deadline:* For fall admission, 12/30 for domestic and international students. Application fee: $75. Electronic applications accepted. *Financial support:* In 2009–10, 40 fellowships with full tuition reimbursements (averaging $17,000 per year), 2 research assistantships with full tuition reimbursements (averaging $17,000 per year), 19 teaching assistantships with full tuition reimbursements (averaging $17,000 per year) were awarded; institutionally sponsored loans also available. *Faculty research:* Nineteenth century French prose and poetry, genetic theory and criticism; twentieth century Latin American literature and film; Medieval and Renaissance Italian literature; Gender and Queer Theory in German literature; the ideology of baroque and neobaroque aesthetics. *Unit head:* Dr. William Egginton, Chair, 410-516-7510, Fax: 410-516-5358, E-mail: egginton@jhu.edu. *Application contact:* Rebecca Swisdak, Graduate Administrative Coordinator, 410-516-7227, Fax: 410-516-5358, E-mail: rswisdak@jhu.edu.

Kansas State University, Graduate School, College of Arts and Sciences, Department of Modern Languages, Manhattan, KS 66506. Offers French (MA); German (MA); Spanish (MA). Part-time and evening/weekend programs available. Postbaccalaureate distance learning degree programs offered (minimal on-campus study). *Faculty:* 17 full-time (9 women). *Students:* 15 full-time (6 women), 15 part-time (13 women); includes 5 minority (1 Asian American or Pacific Islander, 4 Hispanic Americans), 10 international. Average age 32. 20 applicants, 75% accepted, 10 enrolled. In 2009, 6 master's awarded. *Degree requirements:* For master's, thesis optional. *Entrance requirements:* For master's, teaching certificate. Additional exam requirements/recommendations for international students: Required—TOEFL (minimum score 560 paper-based). *Application deadline:* For fall admission, 2/1 priority date for domestic and international students; for spring admission, 8/1 priority date for domestic and international students. Applications are processed on a rolling basis. Application fee: $40 ($55 for international students). Electronic applications accepted. *Financial support:* In 2009–10, 16 teaching assistantships with full tuition reimbursements (averaging $8,914 per year) were awarded; Federal Work-Study, institutionally sponsored loans, and scholarships/grants also available. Support available to part-time students. Financial award application deadline: 3/1; financial award applicants required to submit FAFSA. *Faculty research:* Second language acquisitions; Chicano literature; Francophone literature; cultural studies; German, French, Spanish, and Spanish-American literature from the Middle Ages to the modern era. *Unit head:* Robert Corum, Head, 785-532-1987, Fax: 785-532-7004, E-mail: corum@ksu.edu. *Application contact:* Claire Dehon, Director, 785-532-1929, Fax: 785-532-7004, E-mail: dehoncl@ksu.edu.

Kean University, College of Education, Program in Instruction and Curriculum, Union, NJ 07083. Offers bilingual/bicultural education (MA); classroom instruction (MA); earth science (MA); mathematics/science/computer education (MA); teaching (MA); teaching English as a second language (MA); world languages (Spanish) (MA). *Accreditation:* NCATE. Part-time and evening/weekend programs available. *Faculty:* 16 full-time (7 women). *Students:* 45 full-time (34 women), 131 part-time (104 women); includes 60 minority (11 African Americans, 6 Asian Americans or Pacific Islanders, 43 Hispanic Americans), 6 international. Average age 33. 64 applicants, 94% accepted, 46 enrolled. In 2009, 58 master's awarded. *Entrance requirements:* For master's, GRE General Test or MAT, PRAXIS, minimum GPA of 3.0, 2 letters of recommendation, interview, teacher certification (for some programs). *Application deadline:* For fall admission, 5/1 for domestic students; for spring admission, 11/1 for domestic students. Application fee: $60 ($150 for international students). Electronic applications accepted. *Expenses:* Tuition, state resident: full-time $10,440; part-time $435 per credit. Tuition, nonresident: full-time $14,160; part-time $590 per credit. Required fees: $2642; $110 per credit. Part-time tuition and fees vary according to course load and degree level. *Financial support:* In 2009–10, 1 research assistantship with full tuition reimbursement (averaging $3,263 per year) was awarded; unspecified assistantships also available. *Unit head:* Dr. Thomas Walsh, Program Coordinator, 908-737-4296, E-mail: twalsh@kean.edu. *Application contact:* Ann-Marie Kay, Assistant Director of Graduate Admissions, 908-737-5922, Fax: 908-737-5965, E-mail: akay@kean.edu.

Kent State University, College of Arts and Sciences, Department of Modern and Classical Language Studies, Kent, OH 44242-0001. Offers French literature (MA); French, Spanish, German and Latin pedagogy (MA); German literature (MA); Spanish literature (MA); translation (MA), including French, German, Japanese, Russian, Spanish; translation studies (PhD). Part-time and evening/weekend programs available. *Degree requirements:* For master's, one foreign language, comprehensive exam (for some programs), thesis (for some programs); for doctorate, comprehensive exam, thesis/dissertation (for some programs). *Entrance requirements:* For master's, minimum GPA of 3.0, writing sample, audio tape or CD; for doctorate, 3 recommendations. Additional exam requirements/recommendations for international students: Required—TOEFL (minimum score 197 computer-based). Electronic applications accepted. *Faculty research:* Literature, pedagogy, applied linguistics, translation studies.

Lehman College of the City University of New York, Division of Arts and Humanities, Department of Languages and Literatures, Bronx, NY 10468-1589. Offers Spanish (MA). Part-time and evening/weekend programs available. *Degree requirements:* For master's, one foreign language.

Long Island University, C.W. Post Campus, College of Liberal Arts and Sciences, Department of Foreign Languages, Brookville, NY 11548-1300. Offers Spanish (MA); Spanish education (MS). Part-time programs available. *Degree requirements:* For master's, 2 foreign languages, comprehensive exam, thesis or alternative. *Entrance requirements:* For master's, 24 credits of undergraduate course work in Spanish. Electronic applications accepted. *Faculty research:* Making of a superhero, dialogue in the 19th century novel, nicknames, Menendez Pidal and Spanish School of Philology, women writers of Latin America.

Loyola University Chicago, Graduate School, Department of Modern Languages and Literatures, Chicago, IL 60660. Offers Spanish (MA). Part-time and evening/weekend programs available. *Faculty:* 6 full-time (4 women), 1 part-time/adjunct (0 women). *Students:* 15 full-time (9 women), 6 part-time (5 women); includes 4 minority (all Hispanic Americans), 1 international. Average age 31. 13 applicants, 92% accepted, 5 enrolled. In 2009, 10 master's awarded. *Degree requirements:* For master's, 2 foreign languages, comprehensive exam, thesis or alternative. *Entrance requirements:* Additional exam requirements/recommendations for international students: Required—TOEFL. *Application deadline:* For fall admission, 2/10 for domestic students; for spring admission, 12/4 for domestic students. Application fee: $50. *Expenses:* Tuition: Full-time $14,220; part-time $790 per credit hour. Required fees: $60 per semester hour. Tuition and fees vary according to program. *Financial support:* In 2009–10, 6 students received support, including 3 teaching assistantships with full tuition reimbursements available (averaging $16,000 per year); unspecified assistantships also available. Financial award applicants required to submit FAFSA. *Faculty research:* Linguistics, Latin American contemporary narrative, Latin American culture and civilization, Hispanic women's studies, twentieth century peninsular writing, Golden Age, Don Quixote. *Unit head:* Dr. Wiley Feinstein, Chair, 773-508-2868, Fax: 773-508-2893, E-mail: wfeinst@luc.edu. *Application contact:* Dr. Olympia B. Gonzalez, Graduate Program Director, 773-508-2872, E-mail: ogonzal@luc.edu.

Marquette University, Graduate School, College of Arts and Sciences, Department of Foreign Languages and Literatures, Milwaukee, WI 53201-1881. Offers Spanish (MA, MAT). Part-time programs available. *Faculty:* 33 full-time (21 women), 7 part-time/adjunct (5 women). *Students:* 7 full-time (4 women), 4 part-time (all women); includes 3 minority (all Hispanic Americans), 2 international. Average age 29. 10 applicants, 80% accepted, 5 enrolled. In 2009, 6 master's awarded. *Degree requirements:* For master's, one foreign language, comprehensive exam or thesis. *Entrance requirements:* Additional exam requirements/recommendations for international students: Required—TOEFL. Application fee: $40. *Financial support:* In 2009–10, 5 research assistantships were awarded; teaching assistantships, Federal Work-Study, institutionally sponsored loans, scholarships/grants, and tuition waivers (full and partial) also available. Support available to part-time students. Financial award application deadline: 2/15. *Faculty research:* Magic realism, African-Hispanic literature, women studies, Hispanic linguistics. *Unit head:* Dr. Belen Castaneda, Chair, 414-288-7063, Fax: 414-288-1578. *Application contact:* Dr. Armando Gonzales-Percz, Director of Graduate Studies, 414-288-7268, Fax: 414-288-1578.

Marshall University, Academic Affairs Division, College of Liberal Arts, Program in Spanish, Huntington, WV 25755. Offers MA. *Faculty:* 5 full-time (3 women). *Students:* 2 full-time (1 woman), 4 part-time (3 women); includes 2 minority (1 American Indian/Alaska Native, 1 Hispanic American). Average age 36. *Unit head:* Dr. Maria Carmen Riddel, Department Chair, 304-696-2742, E-mail: riddelm@marshall.edu. *Application contact:* Graduate Admissions, 304-746-1900, Fax: 304-746-1902, E-mail: services@marshall.edu.

Michigan State University, The Graduate School, College of Arts and Letters, Department of Spanish and Portuguese, East Lansing, MI 48824. Offers applied Spanish linguistics (MA); Hispanic cultural studies (PhD); Hispanic literatures (MA). *Faculty:* 14 full-time (7 women). *Students:* 26 full-time (17 women), 3 part-time (2 women); includes 10 minority (1 African American, 1 Asian American or Pacific Islander, 8 Hispanic Americans), 6 international. Average age 31. 23 applicants, 39% accepted. In 2009, 4 master's, 6 doctorates awarded. *Entrance requirements:* Additional exam requirements/recommendations for international students: Required—TOEFL. Electronic applications accepted. *Expenses:* Tuition, state resident: part-time $478.25 per credit hour. Tuition, nonresident: part-time $966.50 per credit hour. Part-time tuition and fees vary according to program. *Financial support:* In 2009–10, 20 teaching assistantships with tuition reimbursements (averaging $6,017 per year) were awarded. *Unit head:* Dr. Douglas Noverr, Acting Chairperson, 517-353-4939, Fax: 517-432-3844, E-mail: noverr@msu.edu. *Application contact:* Victoria Reynaga, Graduate Secretary, 517-355-8350, Fax: 517-432-3844, E-mail: reynagav@cal.msu.edu.

Middlebury College, Language Schools, Spanish School, Middlebury, VT 05753-6002. Offers MA, DML. *Faculty:* 34 full-time (14 women). *Students:* 192 full-time (136 women); includes 41 minority (3 African Americans, 1 American Indian/Alaska Native, 2 Asian Americans or Pacific Islanders, 35 Hispanic Americans). Average age 30. 295 applicants, 84% accepted. In 2009, 78 master's awarded. *Degree requirements:* For master's, one foreign language; for doctorate, 2 foreign languages, comprehensive exam, thesis/dissertation, residence abroad, teaching experience. *Entrance requirements:* For master's, placement exam, 3 letters of recommendation, writing sample. Application fee: $65. Electronic applications accepted. *Financial support:* Scholarships/grants available. *Unit head:* Dr. Jacobo Sefami, Director, 802-443-5539, Fax: 802-443-2075, E-mail: jsefami@middlebury.edu. *Application contact:* Audrey LaRock, Coordinator, 802-443-5539, Fax: 802-443-2075, E-mail: larock@middlebury.edu.

Millersville University of Pennsylvania, College of Graduate and Professional Studies, School of Humanities and Social Sciences, Department of Foreign Languages, Program in Spanish, Millersville, PA 17551-0302. Offers M Ed, MA. Part-time programs available. *Faculty:* 8 full-time (4 women), 7 part-time/adjunct (6 women). *Students:* 1 (woman) full-time, 3 part-time (2 women); includes 2 minority (1 Asian American or Pacific Islander, 1 Hispanic American). Average age 35. 1 applicant, 100% accepted, 1 enrolled. In 2009, 2 master's awarded. *Degree requirements:* For master's, comprehensive exam, thesis optional. *Entrance requirements:* For master's, writing sample, 3 letters of recommendation. Additional exam requirements/recommendations for international students: Required—TOEFL (minimum score 500 paper-based; 183 computer-based; 65 iBT) or IELTS (minimum score 6). *Application deadline:* For fall admission, 1/15 priority date for domestic and international students; for winter admission, 10/1 priority date for domestic and international students; for spring admission, 10/1 priority date for domestic and international students. Applications are processed on a rolling basis. Application fee: $40 ($50 for international students). Electronic applications accepted. *Expenses:* Tuition, state resident: full-time $6666; part-time $370 per credit. Tuition, nonresident: full-time $10,666; part-time $593 per credit. Required fees: $1578.50; $76.25 per credit. One-time fee: $60 part-time. Tuition and fees vary according to course load. *Financial support:* In 2009–10, 1 student received support, including 1 research assistantship with full tuition reimbursement available (averaging $5,000 per year); institutionally sponsored loans and unspecified assistantships also available. Support available to part-time students. Financial award application deadline: 3/15; financial award applicants required to submit FAFSA. *Unit head:* Dr. Christine M. Gaudry-Hudson, Coordinator of Foreign Language Graduate Program, 717-872-3663, E-mail: christine.gaudry-hudson@millersville.edu. *Application contact:* Dr. Victor S. DeSantis, Dean of Graduate and Professional Studies, 717-872-3099, Fax: 717-872-3453, E-mail: victor.desantis@millersville.edu.

Minnesota State University Mankato, College of Graduate Studies, College of Arts and Humanities, Department of Modern Languages, Program in Spanish, Mankato, MN 56001. Offers MAT, MS. *Students:* 4 full-time (2 women), 8 part-time (2 women). *Degree requirements:* For master's, one foreign language, comprehensive exam, thesis. *Entrance requirements:* For master's, minimum GPA of 3.0 during previous 2 years. *Application deadline:* For fall admission, 7/1 priority date for domestic students; for spring admission, 11/1 for domestic students. Applications are processed on a rolling basis. Application fee: $40. Electronic applications accepted. *Expenses:* Tuition, state resident: full-time $5364. Tuition, nonresident: full-time $8314. *Financial support:* Research assistantships with full tuition reimbursements, teaching assistantships with full tuition reimbursements, career-related internships or fieldwork, Federal Work-Study, institutionally sponsored loans, and unspecified assistantships available. Support available to part-time students. Financial award application deadline: 3/15. *Unit head:* Dr. Enrique Torner, Graduate Coordinator, 507-389-5519. *Application contact:* 507-389-2321, E-mail: grad@mnsu.edu.

Mississippi State University, College of Arts and Sciences, Department of Foreign Languages, Mississippi State, MS 39762. Offers foreign language (MA), including French, German, Spanish. Part-time programs available. *Faculty:* 8 full-time (3 women). *Students:* 9 full-time (7 women), 2 part-time (1 woman); includes 1 minority (Hispanic American), 3 international. Average age 31. 5 applicants, 100% accepted, 3 enrolled. In 2009, 5 master's awarded. *Degree requirements:* For master's, one foreign language, comprehensive exam (for some programs), thesis optional, comprehensive oral or written exam. *Entrance requirements:* For master's, minimum GPA of 2.75 on last two years of undergraduate courses. Additional exam requirements/recommendations for international students: Required—TOEFL (minimum score 525 paper-based). *Application deadline:* For fall admission, 7/1 for domestic students, 5/1 for international students; for spring admission, 11/1 for domestic students, 9/1 for international students. Applications are processed on a rolling basis. Application fee: $40. Electronic applications accepted. *Expenses:* Tuition, state resident: full-time $2575.50; part-time $286.25 per credit hour. Tuition, nonresident: full-time $6510; part-time $723.50 per credit hour. Tuition and fees vary according to course load. *Financial support:* In 2009–10, 7 teaching assistantships with full tuition reimbursements (averaging $8,766 per year) were awarded; Federal Work-Study, institutionally sponsored loans, and unspecified assistantships also available. Financial award application deadline: 4/1; financial award applicants required to submit FAFSA. *Faculty research:* French, German, Spanish literature from medieval era to present; gender and cultural studies in French; Spanish American literature; foreign language methodology; linguistics. *Unit head:* Dr. Jack Jordan, Professor/Head, 662-325-3480, Fax: 662-325-8209, E-mail: jordan@ra.msstate.edu. *Application contact:* Dr. Edward T. Potter, Assistant Professor/Graduate Coordinator, 662-325-2399, Fax: 662-325-8209, E-mail: ep75@.msstate.edu.

Missouri State University, Graduate College, College of Arts and Letters, Department of Modern and Classical Languages, Springfield, MO 65897. Offers secondary education (MS Ed), including Spanish. Part-time programs available. *Faculty:* 4 full-time (1 woman). *Students:* 1 (woman) full-time, 3 part-time (2 women); includes 1 minority (Hispanic American). Average age 37. In 2009, 1 master's awarded. *Entrance requirements:* For master's, grades 9-12 teaching certification. Additional exam requirements/recommendations for international students: Required—TOEFL (minimum score 550 paper-based; 213 computer-based; 79 iBT), IELTS (minimum score 6). *Application deadline:* For fall admission, 7/20 priority date for domestic students, 5/1 for international students; for spring admission, 12/20 priority date for domestic students, 9/1 for international students. Applications are processed on a rolling basis. Application fee: $35 ($50 for international students). Electronic applications accepted. *Expenses:* Tuition, state resident: full-time $3852; part-time $214 per credit hour. Tuition, nonresident: full-time $7524; part-time $418 per credit hour. Required fees: $696; $172 per semester. Tuition and fees vary according to course level, course load, degree level and program. *Financial support:* Federal Work-Study, scholarships/grants, and unspecified assistantships available. Financial award applicants required to submit FAFSA. *Unit head:* Dr. Madeleine Kernen, Head, 417-836-7626, E-mail: mcl@missouristate.edu. *Application contact:* Eric Eckert, Coordinator of Admissions and Recruitment, 417-836-5331, Fax: 417-836-6888, E-mail: ericeckert@missouristate.edu.

Montclair State University, The Graduate School, College of Education and Human Services, Department of Curriculum and Teaching, Montclair, NJ 07043-1624. Offers education (M Ed); educational technology (M Ed); learning disabled teacher consultant (Certificate); school library media specialist (Certificate); teaching (MAT, Certificate), including art (MAT), biological science (MAT), early childhood education (P-3) (MAT), earth science (MAT), elementary education (K-8) (MAT), English (MAT), French (MAT), health and physical education (MAT), health education (MAT), home economics (MAT), mathematics (MAT), music (MAT), physical education (MAT), physical science (MAT), social studies (MAT), Spanish (MAT), teacher of ESL (MAT), teacher of students with disabilities (MAT). Part-time and evening/weekend programs available. *Faculty:* 17 full-time (12 women), 29 part-time/adjunct (21 women). *Students:* 124 full-time (63 women), 174 part-time (126 women). Average age 31. 112 applicants, 69% accepted, 59 enrolled. In 2009, 179 master's, 2 other advanced degrees awarded. *Degree requirements:* For master's, comprehensive exam, field experience. *Entrance requirements:* For master's, GRE, 2 letters of recommendation. Additional exam requirements/recommendations for international students: Required—TOEFL (minimum score 83 computer-based), or IELTS. *Application deadline:* For fall admission, 2/15 for domestic and international students; for spring admission, 9/15 for domestic and international students. Applications are processed on a rolling basis. Application fee: $60. Electronic applications accepted. *Expenses:* Tuition, area resident: Part-time $486.74 per credit. Tuition, state resident: part-time $486.74 per credit. Tuition, nonresident: part-time $751.34 per credit. Tuition and fees vary according to degree level and program. *Financial support:* In 2009–10, 12 research assistantships with full tuition reimbursements (averaging $7,000 per year) were awarded; Federal Work-Study, scholarships/grants, and unspecified assistantships also available. Support available to part-time students. Financial award application deadline: 3/1; financial award applicants required to submit FAFSA. *Unit head:* Dr. David Schwarzer, Chairperson, 973-655-5187. *Application contact:* Amy Aiello, Director of Graduate Admissions and Operations, 973-655-5147, Fax: 973-655-7869, E-mail: graduate.school@montclair.edu.

Montclair State University, The Graduate School, College of Humanities and Social Sciences, Department of Spanish and Italian, Montclair, NJ 07043-1624. Offers Italian (Certificate); Spanish (MA, Certificate); translating and interpreting Spanish (Certificate). Part-time and evening/weekend programs available. *Faculty:* 20 full-time (12 women), 24 part-time/adjunct (16 women). *Students:* 2 full-time (1 woman), 21 part-time (17 women). Average age 33. 9 applicants, 56% accepted, 4 enrolled. In 2009, 10 master's awarded. *Degree requirements:* For master's, comprehensive exam, thesis or alternative. *Entrance requirements:* For master's, GRE General Test, 2 letters of recommendation. Additional exam requirements/recommendations for international students: Required—TOEFL (minimum score 83 computer-based), or IELTS. *Application deadline:* For fall admission, 6/1 for international students; for spring admission, 11/1 for international students. Applications are processed on a rolling basis. Application fee: $60. Electronic applications accepted. *Expenses:* Tuition, area resident: Part-time $486.74 per credit. Tuition, state resident: part-time $486.74 per credit. Tuition, nonresident: part-time $751.34 per credit. Tuition and fees vary according to degree level and program. *Financial support:* In 2009–10, 1 research assistantship with full tuition reimbursement (averaging $7,000 per year) was awarded; Federal Work-Study, scholarships/grants, and unspecified assistantships also available. Support available to part-time students. Financial award application deadline: 3/1; financial award applicants required to submit FAFSA. *Unit head:* Dr. Linda Gould Levine, Chairperson, 973-655-7506. *Application contact:* Amy Aiello, Director of Graduate Admissions and Operations, 973-655-5147, Fax: 973-655-7869, E-mail: graduate.school@montclair.edu.

New Mexico State University, Graduate School, College of Arts and Sciences, Department of Languages and Linguistics, Las Cruces, NM 88003-8001. Offers Spanish (MA). Part-time programs available. *Faculty:* 11 full-time (4 women). *Students:* 23 full-time (14 women), 7 part-time (4 women); includes 16 minority (all Hispanic Americans), 9 international. Average age 35. 49 applicants, 94% accepted, 22 enrolled. In 2009, 3 master's awarded. *Degree requirements:* For master's, one foreign language, comprehensive exam, thesis optional, oral and written exams. *Entrance requirements:* For master's, sample of written work in Spanish, cassette tape in Spanish, 3 letters of reference. *Application deadline:* For fall admission, 2/15 for domestic students; for spring admission, 10/12 for domestic students. Applications are processed on a rolling basis. Application fee: $30 ($50 for international students). Electronic applications accepted. *Expenses:* Tuition, state resident: full-time $4080; part-time $223 per credit. Tuition, nonresident: full-time $14,256; part-time $647 per credit. Required fees: $1278; $639 per semester. *Financial support:* In 2009–10, 19 teaching assistantships (averaging $13,384 per year) were awarded; research assistantships, Federal Work-Study, institutionally sponsored loans, scholarships/grants, health care benefits, and unspecified assistantships also available. Support available to part-time students. Financial award application deadline: 3/1. *Faculty research:* Spanish-American literature, U.S. Hispanic and Chicano literature and border culture, Hispanic linguistics, French and German literature and linguistics. *Unit head:* Dr. Richard Rundell, Head, 575-646-3408, Fax: 575-646-7876, E-mail: rrundell@nmsu.edu. *Application contact:* Dr. Richard Rundell, Head, 575-646-3408, Fax: 575-646-7876, E-mail: rrundell@nmsu.edu.

New York University, Graduate School of Arts and Science, Department of Spanish and Portuguese Languages and Literatures, New York, NY 10012-1019. Offers Portuguese (MA, PhD); Spanish (PhD); Spanish and Latin American literatures and cultures (MA); Spanish language and translation (MA). Part-time programs available. *Students:* 105 full-time (66 women), 5 part-time (4 women); includes 41 minority (5 African Americans, 4 Asian Americans or Pacific Islanders, 32 Hispanic Americans), 40 international. Average age 31. 193 applicants, 48% accepted, 50 enrolled. In 2009, 34 master's, 5 doctorates awarded. *Degree requirements:* For master's, 2 foreign languages, thesis; for doctorate, 2 foreign languages, thesis/dissertation. *Entrance requirements:* For master's, GRE General Test; for doctorate, GRE General Test, master's degree. Additional exam requirements/recommendations for international students: Required—TOEFL. *Application deadline:* For fall admission, 1/4 priority date for domestic students. Application fee: $90. *Expenses:* Tuition: Full-time $30,528; part-time $1272 per credit. Required fees: $2177. *Financial support:* Fellowships with tuition reimbursements, teaching assistantships with tuition reimbursements, career-related internships or fieldwork, Federal Work-Study, institutionally sponsored loans, scholarships/grants, health care benefits, and unspecified assistantships available. Financial award application deadline: 1/4; financial award applicants required to submit FAFSA. *Faculty research:* Gender and sexuality, transatlantic studies, literacy and cultural theories, colonial and post colonial studies, autobiography and modern subjectivities. *Unit head:* Sibylle Fischer, Chair, 212-998-8770, Fax: 212-995-4149, E-mail: spanish.portuguese.info@nyu.edu. *Application contact:* Jo Labanyi, Director of Graduate Studies, 212-998-8770, Fax: 212-995-4149, E-mail: spanish.portuguese.info@nyu.edu.

New York University, NYU in Madrid, Madrid, NY 10012-1019, Spain. Offers creative writing in Spanish (MFA); Spanish (PhD); Spanish and Latin American literatures and cultures (MA); Spanish language and translation (MA). *Students:* 27 full-time (23 women), 1 part-time (0 women); includes 8 minority (2 African Americans, 1 Asian American or Pacific Islander, 5 Hispanic Americans), 1 international. Average age 26. 73 applicants, 90% accepted, 27 enrolled. In 2009, 22 master's awarded. Application fee: $90. *Expenses:* Tuition: Full-time $30,528; part-time $1272 per credit. Required fees: $2177. *Unit head:* Judith Nemethy, Director, 212-998-8770, Fax: 212-995-4149, E-mail: nyu-in-madrid@nyu.edu. *Application contact:* Judith Nemethy, Director, 212-998-8770, Fax: 212-995-4149, E-mail: nyu-in-madrid@nyu.edu.

North Carolina State University, Graduate School, College of Humanities and Social Sciences, Department of Foreign Languages and Literatures, Program in Spanish Language and Literature, Raleigh, NC 27695. Offers MA. *Degree requirements:* For master's, thesis optional.

Spanish

North Carolina State University (continued)

Entrance requirements: For master's, fluency in Spanish. Electronic applications accepted. *Faculty research:* Applied linguistics, technology-assisted language instruction, Latin-American literature and culture, 20th and 21st Century Spanish narrative and film, children's literature.

Northern Arizona University, Graduate College, College of Arts and Letters, Department of Modern Languages, Flagstaff, AZ 86011. Offers Spanish teaching (MAT); Spanish teaching/Spanish education (MAT). *Faculty:* 23 full-time (16 women). *Students:* 12 full-time (7 women), 1 (woman) part-time; includes 4 minority (all Hispanic Americans), 2 international. Average age 30. 5 applicants, 100% accepted, 4 enrolled. *Degree requirements:* For master's, thesis optional. *Entrance requirements:* For master's, BA in Spanish or other foreign language, or minimum GPA of 3.0. Additional exam requirements/recommendations for international students: Required—TOEFL (minimum score 550 paper-based; 213 computer-based; 80 iBT), IELTS (minimum score 7), or a bachelor's degree from an English-speaking university and demonstrated proficiency. *Application deadline:* For fall admission, 4/21 priority date for domestic students, 9/21 priority date for international students; for spring admission, 10/21 priority date for domestic students. Applications are processed on a rolling basis. Application fee: $65. Electronic applications accepted. *Financial support:* Teaching assistantships, tuition waivers (full and partial) available. Financial award application deadline: 3/30. *Unit head:* Joseph Collentine, Chair, 928-523-5334, Fax: 928-523-0963, E-mail: j.collentine@nau.edu. *Application contact:* Cecilia Ojeda, Coordinator, 928-523-5988, Fax: 928-523-0963, E-mail: cecilia.ojeda@nau.edu.

Northern Illinois University, Graduate School, College of Liberal Arts and Sciences, Department of Foreign Languages and Literatures, De Kalb, IL 60115-2854. Offers French (MA); Spanish (MA). Part-time programs available. *Faculty:* 25 full-time (11 women). *Students:* 4 full-time (2 women), 18 part-time (9 women); includes 7 minority (all Hispanic Americans), 2 international. Average age 31. 10 applicants, 60% accepted, 4 enrolled. In 2009, 9 master's awarded. *Degree requirements:* For master's, one foreign language, comprehensive exam, thesis or alternative, language proficiency exam. *Entrance requirements:* For master's, GRE General Test, interview, minimum GPA of 2.75, undergraduate major in French or Spanish. Additional exam requirements/recommendations for international students: Required—TOEFL (minimum score 550 paper-based; 213 computer-based). *Application deadline:* For fall admission, 6/1 for domestic students, 5/1 for international students; for spring admission, 11/1 for domestic students, 10/1 for international students. Applications are processed on a rolling basis. Application fee: $30. Electronic applications accepted. *Expenses:* Tuition, state resident: full-time $6576; part-time $274 per credit hour. Tuition, nonresident: full-time $13,152; part-time $548 per credit hour. Required fees: $1813; $75.53 per credit hour. Part-time tuition and fees vary according to course load. *Financial support:* In 2009–10, 13 teaching assistantships with full tuition reimbursements were awarded; fellowships with full tuition reimbursements, research assistantships with full tuition reimbursements, career-related internships or fieldwork, Federal Work-Study, scholarships/grants, tuition waivers (full), and unspecified assistantships also available. Support available to part-time students. Financial award applicants required to submit FAFSA. *Faculty research:* Francophone women writers, prosodies of French and Italian, early Spanish drama, business German, history of Burmese literature. *Unit head:* Anne Birbeck, Chair, 815-753-1259, Fax: 815-753-5989, E-mail: annie@niu.edu. *Application contact:* Graduate School Office, 815-753-0395, E-mail: gradsch@niu.edu.

Nova Southeastern University, Fischler School of Education and Human Services, Graduate Teacher Education Program, Fort Lauderdale, FL 33314-7796. Offers athletic administration (MS); brain research (MS, Ed S); charter school education/leadership (MS); cognitive and behavioral disabilities (MS); computer science education (MS); computer science education (K-12) (MS); curriculum and teaching (Ed S); curriculum, instruction and technology (MS); curriculum, instruction, management and administration (Ed S); early childhood education (MS); early literacy and reading (Ed S); early literacy education (MS); education technology (MS); educational leadership (administration K–12) (MS, Ed S); educational media (Ed S); educational media (K-12) (MS); elementary education (MS, Ed S), including ESOL endorsement (MS); English education (MS, Ed S); environmental education (MS); exceptional student education (MS), including ESOL endorsement; gifted education (MS, Ed S); interdisciplinary arts education (MS); management and administration of educational programs (MS); mathematics (MS); mathematics education (Ed S); multicultural early intervention (MS); pre-kindergarten/primary (MS); preschool education (MS); reading (MS); reading and TESOL (MS); reading education (Ed S); science (MS); science education (Ed S); secondary education (MS); social studies (MS, Ed S); Spanish language (MS); special education and reading (MS); teaching and learning (MA, MS), including curriculum and instruction (MA), elementary mathematics (MA), elementary reading (MA), K-12 technology integration (MA); teaching English to speakers of other languages (MS, Ed S); technology management and administration (Ed S); urban studies education (MS). Part-time and evening/weekend programs available. Postbaccalaureate distance learning degree programs offered (minimal on-campus study). *Faculty:* 72 full-time (43 women), 385 part-time/adjunct (252 women). *Students:* 196 full-time (175 women), 1,304 part-time (1,128 women); includes 594 minority (471 African Americans, 5 American Indian/Alaska Native, 18 Asian Americans or Pacific Islanders, 100 Hispanic Americans). Average age 37. 2,610 applicants, 72% accepted, 1352 enrolled. In 2009, 836 other advanced degrees awarded. *Degree requirements:* For master's and Ed S, thesis, practicum, internship. *Entrance requirements:* For master's, MAT, GRE, CLAST, CBEST, PRAXIS I, General Knowledge Test, minimum GPA of 2.5; for Ed S, MAT or GRE, master's degree, teaching certificate, minimum GPA of 3.0. Additional exam requirements/recommendations for international students: Required—TSE (recommended, minimum score 50); Recommended—TOEFL (minimum score 550 paper-based; 213 computer-based; 80 iBT), IELTS (minimum score 6). *Application deadline:* For fall admission, 9/25 priority date for domestic and international students; for winter admission, 2/23 priority date for domestic and international students; for spring admission, 4/25 priority date for domestic and international students. Applications are processed on a rolling basis. Application fee: $50. Electronic applications accepted. *Financial support:* Federal Work-Study available. Support available to part-time students. Financial award application deadline: 4/15; financial award applicants required to submit FAFSA. *Faculty research:* School effectiveness, critical thinking, leadership skills acquisition, child education, multicultural education. *Unit head:* Dr. Ronald Kern, Dean of Academic Affairs, 800-986-3223 Ext. 7809, Fax: 954-262-3606, E-mail: rk429@nsu.nova.edu. *Application contact:* Dr. Jennifer Quinones Nottingham, Dean of Student Affairs, 800-986-3223 Ext. 1559.

The Ohio State University, Graduate School, College of Humanities, Department of Spanish and Portuguese, Columbus, OH 43210. Offers MA, PhD. *Faculty:* 22. *Students:* 51 full-time (35 women), 16 part-time (11 women); includes 10 minority (all Hispanic Americans), 17 international. Average age 30. In 2009, 6 master's, 3 doctorates awarded. *Degree requirements:* For master's, thesis optional; for doctorate, thesis/dissertation. *Entrance requirements:* For master's and doctorate, GRE General Test. Additional exam requirements/recommendations for international students: Required—TOEFL (minimum score 600 paper-based; 250 computer-based). *Application deadline:* For fall admission, 8/15 priority date for domestic students, 7/1 priority date for international students; for winter admission, 12/1 priority date for domestic students, 11/1 priority date for international students; for spring admission, 3/1 priority date for domestic students, 2/1 priority date for international students. Applications are processed on a rolling basis. Application fee: $40 ($50 for international students). Electronic applications accepted. *Expenses:* Tuition, state resident: full-time $10,683. Tuition, nonresident: full-time $25,923. Tuition and fees vary according to course load and program. *Financial support:* Fellowships, research assistantships, teaching assistantships, Federal Work-Study, institutionally sponsored loans, and unspecified assistantships available. Support available to part-time students. *Unit head:* Laura Podalsky, Graduate Studies Committee Chair, E-mail: podalsky.1@osu.edu. *Application contact:* 614-292-9444, Fax: 614-292-3895, E-mail: domestic.grad@osu.edu.

Ohio University, Graduate College, College of Arts and Sciences, Department of Modern Languages, Athens, OH 45701-2979. Offers French (MA); Spanish (MA). Part-time programs available. *Faculty:* 18 full-time (8 women), 2 part-time/adjunct (both women). *Students:* 29 full-time (25 women), 1 (woman) part-time; includes 4 minority (1 African American, 3 Hispanic Americans), 6 international. 19 applicants, 79% accepted, 14 enrolled. In 2009, 10 master's awarded. *Degree requirements:* For master's, 2 foreign languages, comprehensive exam, thesis optional. *Entrance requirements:* For master's, oral and written samples. Additional exam requirements/recommendations for international students: Required—TOEFL (minimum score 550 paper-based; 80 iBT) or IELTS Academic (minimum score 6.5). *Application deadline:* For fall admission, 1/15 priority date for domestic and international students. Application fee: $50 ($55 for international students). Electronic applications accepted. *Expenses:* Tuition, state resident: full-time $7839; part-time $323 per quarter hour. Tuition, nonresident: full-time $15,831; part-time $654 per quarter hour. Required fees: $2931. *Financial support:* In 2009–10, teaching assistantships with tuition reimbursements (averaging $10,300 per year); Federal Work-Study, institutionally sponsored loans, and tuition waivers (partial) also available. Financial award application deadline: 1/15. *Faculty research:* French and Spanish language and literature. *Unit head:* Dr. Betsy Partyka, Chair, 740-593-2764, Fax: 740-593-0729, E-mail: partyka@ohio.edu. *Application contact:* Dr. Thomas Franz, Graduate Chair, 740-593-2762, Fax: 740-593-0729, E-mail: franz@ohio.edu.

Penn State University Park, Graduate School, College of the Liberal Arts, Department of Spanish, Italian, and Portuguese, State College, University Park, PA 16802-1503. Offers MA, PhD. *Unit head:* Dr. William R. Blue, Interim Head, 814-865-4252, Fax: 814-863-7944, E-mail: wrb10@psu.edu. *Application contact:* Carol Toscano, Information Contact, 814-865-1016, E-mail: clt4@psu.edu.

Pontifical Catholic University of Puerto Rico, College of Arts and Humanities, Department of Hispanic Studies, Ponce, PR 00717-0777. Offers grammar and writing (Professional Certificate); Hispanic studies (MA). Part-time and evening/weekend programs available. *Degree requirements:* For master's, variable foreign language requirement, comprehensive exam, thesis or alternative. *Entrance requirements:* For master's, GRE General Test, 2 letters of recommendation, interview, minimum GPA of 2.75. Electronic applications accepted.

Portland State University, Graduate Studies, College of Liberal Arts and Sciences, Department of Foreign Languages and Literatures, Portland, OR 97207-0751. Offers foreign literature and language (MA); French (MA); German (MA); Japanese (MA); Spanish (MA). Part-time programs available. *Degree requirements:* For master's, one foreign language, thesis (for some programs). *Entrance requirements:* Additional exam requirements/recommendations for international students: Required—TOEFL (minimum score 550 paper-based; 213 computer-based). *Faculty research:* Foreign language pedagogy, applied and social linguistics, literary history and criticism.

Princeton University, Graduate School, Department of Spanish and Portuguese Languages and Cultures, Princeton, NJ 08544-1019. Offers PhD. *Degree requirements:* For doctorate, variable foreign language requirement, thesis/dissertation. *Entrance requirements:* For doctorate, GRE General Test, sample of written work. Additional exam requirements/recommendations for international students: Required—TOEFL (minimum score 600 paper-based; 250 computer-based). Electronic applications accepted.

Purdue University, Graduate School, College of Liberal Arts, Department of Foreign Languages and Literatures, West Lafayette, IN 47907. Offers French (MA, MAT, PhD), including French (MA, PhD), French education (MAT); German (MA, MAT, PhD), including German (MA, PhD), German education (MAT); Spanish (MA, MAT, PhD), including Spanish (MA, PhD), Spanish education (MAT). Terminal master's awarded for partial completion of doctoral program. *Degree requirements:* For master's, one foreign language; for doctorate, 2 foreign languages, thesis/dissertation. *Entrance requirements:* For master's, GRE, sample recording of English and language of study; for doctorate, GRE, writing sample, sample recording of English and language of study. Additional exam requirements/recommendations for international students: Required—TOEFL. Electronic applications accepted. *Faculty research:* Linguistics, semiotics, literary criticism, pedagogy.

Queens College of the City University of New York, Division of Graduate Studies, Arts and Humanities Division, Department of Hispanic Languages and Literatures, Program in Spanish, Flushing, NY 11367-1597. Offers MA. Part-time and evening/weekend programs available. *Faculty:* 10 full-time (6 women). *Students:* 16 part-time (12 women). 25 applicants, 36% accepted, 5 enrolled. In 2009, 5 master's awarded. *Degree requirements:* For master's, 2 foreign languages, comprehensive exam, thesis or alternative. *Entrance requirements:* For master's, minimum GPA of 3.0. Additional exam requirements/recommendations for international students: Required—TOEFL. *Application deadline:* For fall admission, 4/1 for domestic students; for spring admission, 11/1 for domestic students. Applications are processed on a rolling basis. Application fee: $125. *Expenses:* Tuition, state resident: full-time $7360; part-time $310 per credit. Tuition, nonresident: part-time $575 per credit. One-time fee: $195.25 full-time; $145.25 part-time. *Financial support:* Career-related internships or fieldwork, Federal Work-Study, institutionally sponsored loans, and tuition waivers (partial) available. Support available to part-time students. Financial award application deadline: 4/1; financial award applicants required to submit FAFSA. *Unit head:* Dr. Irma Llorens, Graduate Adviser, 718-997-5649. *Application contact:* Mario Caruso, Director of Graduate Admissions, 718-997-5200, Fax: 718-997-5193, E-mail: graduate_admissions@qc.edu.

Queen's University at Kingston, School of Graduate Studies and Research, Faculty of Arts and Sciences, Department of Spanish and Italian, Kingston, ON K7L 3N6, Canada. Offers Spanish language and literature (MA). Part-time programs available. *Degree requirements:* For master's, one foreign language, thesis. *Entrance requirements:* Additional exam requirements/recommendations for international students: Required—TOEFL. Electronic applications accepted. *Faculty research:* Golden Age, nineteenth- and twentieth-century Peninsular novel, literary theory, colonial Latin America, nineteenth-and-twentieth century Latin America.

Rider University, Department of Graduate Education, Leadership and Counseling, Teacher Certification Program, Lawrenceville, NJ 08648-3001. Offers business education (Certificate); elementary education (Certificate); English as a second language (Certificate); English education (Certificate); mathematics education (Certificate); preschool to grade 3 (Certificate); science education (Certificate); social studies education (Certificate); world languages (Certificate), including French, German, Spanish. Part-time programs available. *Degree requirements:* For Certificate, internship, professional portfolio. *Entrance requirements:* For degree, PRAXIS, resume. Additional exam requirements/recommendations for international students: Required—TOEFL (minimum score 550 paper-based; 213 computer-based). Electronic applications accepted. *Faculty research:* Conceptual foundations for optimal development of creativity; creative theory, cognitive processes in mathematics learning, teacher collaboration.

Roosevelt University, Graduate Division, College of Arts and Sciences, Department of Literature and Languages, Program in Spanish, Chicago, IL 60605. Offers MA. Part-time and evening/weekend programs available. *Degree requirements:* For master's, variable foreign language requirement, thesis or alternative. *Entrance requirements:* For master's, BA in Spanish or the equivalent. *Faculty research:* Latin American narrative, feminism, Hispanic cultures, twentieth century Hispanic literature, Latino studies.

Rutgers, The State University of New Jersey, New Brunswick, Graduate School-New Brunswick, Program in Spanish, Piscataway, NJ 08854-8097. Offers bilingualism and second language acquisition (MA, PhD); Spanish (MA, MAT, PhD); Spanish literature (MA, PhD); translation (MA). Part-time programs available. *Degree requirements:* For master's, comprehensive exam (for some programs), thesis (for some programs); for doctorate, 2 foreign languages, comprehensive exam, thesis/dissertation. *Entrance requirements:* For master's and doctorate, GRE General Test. Additional exam requirements/recommendations for international students: Required—TOEFL. Electronic applications accepted. *Faculty research:* Hispanic literature, Luso-Brazilian literature, Spanish linguistics, Spanish translation.

St. John's University, St. John's College of Liberal Arts and Sciences, Department of Languages and Literatures, Queens, NY 11439. Offers languages and literatures (Adv C); Spanish (MA). Part-time and evening/weekend programs available. *Students:* 4 full-time (1 woman), 5 part-time (3 women); includes 3 minority (1 African American, 2 Hispanic Americans), 2 international. Average age 31. 12 applicants, 75% accepted, 4 enrolled. In 2009, 5 master's awarded. *Degree requirements:* For master's, thesis optional. *Entrance requirements:* For master's, 24 credits of undergraduate course work in languages (18 credits in Spanish), minimum GPA of 3.0. Additional exam requirements/recommendations for international students: Required—TOEFL (minimum score 500 paper-based; 173 computer-based; 61 iBT), IELTS (minimum score 5.5). *Application deadline:* For fall admission, 5/1 priority date for domestic and international students; for spring admission, 11/1 priority date for domestic and international students. Applications are processed on a rolling basis. Application fee: $70. Electronic applications accepted. *Expenses:* Tuition: Full-time $16,290; part-time $905 per credit. Required fees: $300; $150 per semester. Tuition and fees vary according to program. *Financial support:* Research assistantships, scholarships/grants available. Support available to part-time students. Financial award application deadline: 3/1; financial award applicants required to submit FAFSA. *Unit head:* Dr. Herbert Pierson, Chair, 718-990-5211, E-mail: piersonh@stjohns.edu. *Application contact:* Kathleen Davis, Director of Graduate Admission, 718-990-2790, Fax: 718-990-5686, E-mail: gradhelp@stjohns.edu.

Saint Louis University, Graduate School, College of Arts and Sciences and Graduate School, Department of Modern and Classical Languages, St. Louis, MO 63103-2097. Offers French (MA); Spanish (MA). Part-time programs available. *Degree requirements:* For master's, one foreign language, comprehensive exam, thesis/dissertation (Spanish). *Entrance requirements:* For master's, GRE General Test or MAT, letters of recommendation, resume, interview. Additional exam requirements/recommendations for international students: Required—TOEFL (minimum score 525 paper-based; 194 computer-based). Electronic applications accepted. *Faculty research:* Culture studies, literature studies, foreign language acquisition.

Saint Louis University–Madrid Campus, Graduate Programs, Master of Arts in Spanish Program, Madrid, Spain. Offers Spanish language and literature (MA). Part-time programs available. *Faculty:* 6 full-time (4 women), 4 part-time/adjunct (3 women). *Students:* 21 full-time (16 women), 6 part-time (5 women). Average age 28. 15 applicants, 87% accepted, 10 enrolled. In 2009, 6 master's awarded. *Degree requirements:* For master's, one foreign language, comprehensive exam, thesis optional. *Entrance requirements:* For master's, GRE General Test or MAT, 3 letters of recommendation, curriculum vitae, writing sample, interview. *Application deadline:* For fall admission, 5/30 for domestic and international students; for spring admission, 10/30 for domestic and international students. Applications are processed on a rolling basis. Application fee: $40. Tuition charges are reported in euros. *Expenses:* Tuition: Full-time 7740 euros; part-time 430 euros per credit. *Financial support:* In 2009–10, 6 students received support, including 6 fellowships with partial tuition reimbursements available; career-related internships or fieldwork, scholarships/grants, health care benefits, and unspecified assistantships also available. Support available to part-time students. Financial award application deadline: 4/1; financial award applicants required to submit FAFSA. *Faculty research:* Spanish and Latin American literature, linguistics, cultural studies, gender studies. *Unit head:* Dr. Anne McCabe, Language and Literature Chair, 34-91-554-58-58, Fax: 34-91-554-62-02, E-mail: mccabea@slu.edu. *Application contact:* Diego RodrÝguez-Vila, Admissions Counselor, (34)-91-554-58-58, Fax: 34-91-554-62-02, E-mail: graduate_admissions@madrid.slu.edu.

See Close-Up on page 419.

Salem State College, School of Graduate Studies, Program in Spanish, Salem, MA 01970-5353. Offers MAT. Part-time and evening/weekend programs available. *Students:* 28 part-time (22 women); includes 1 minority (African American). Average age 32. 3 applicants, 100% accepted, 3 enrolled. In 2009, 9 master's awarded. *Entrance requirements:* For master's, GRE or MAT. Additional exam requirements/recommendations for international students: Required—TOEFL (minimum score 550 paper-based; 80 iBT), or IELTS (minimum score 5.5). *Application deadline:* For fall admission, 5/1 for domestic students; for spring admission, 10/1 for domestic students. Applications are processed on a rolling basis. Application fee: $50. *Expenses:* Tuition, state resident: full-time $2520; part-time $275 per credit hour. Tuition, nonresident: full-time $4140; part-time $365 per credit hour. Required fees: $2430. *Financial support:* In 2009–10, 4 students received support. Career-related internships or fieldwork, Federal Work-Study, scholarships/grants, and unspecified assistantships available. Support available to part-time students. Financial award application deadline: 5/1; financial award applicants required to submit FAFSA. *Unit head:* Kristine Doll, Program Coordinator, 978-542-6321, E-mail: kdoll@salemstate.edu. *Application contact:* Dr. Lee A. Brossoit, Assistant Dean of Graduate Admissions, 978-542-6675, Fax: 978-542-7215, E-mail: lbrossoit@salemstate.edu.

San Diego State University, Graduate and Research Affairs, College of Arts and Letters, Department of Spanish and Portuguese Languages and Literatures, San Diego, CA 92182. Offers Spanish (MA). *Degree requirements:* For master's, one foreign language. *Entrance requirements:* For master's, GRE General Test, 3 letters of reference. Additional exam requirements/recommendations for international students: Required—TOEFL. Electronic applications accepted. *Faculty research:* New strategies for teaching foreign languages.

San Francisco State University, Division of Graduate Studies, College of Humanities, Department of Foreign Languages and Literatures, Program in Spanish, San Francisco, CA 94132-1722. Offers MA. Part-time programs available. Electronic applications accepted.

San Jose State University, Graduate Studies and Research, College of Humanities and the Arts, Department of Foreign Languages, Program in Spanish, San Jose, CA 95192-0001. Offers MA. *Degree requirements:* For master's, 2 foreign languages, thesis or comprehensive exam. *Application deadline:* For fall admission, 6/29 for domestic students; for spring admission, 11/30 for domestic students. Applications are processed on a rolling basis. Application fee: $59. Electronic applications accepted. *Financial support:* Fellowships, scholarships/grants available. Financial award applicants required to submit FAFSA. *Unit head:* Juan Antonio Sempere, Graduate Advisor, 408-924-4592, E-mail: jsempere@email.sjsu.edu. *Application contact:* Juan Antonio Sempere, Graduate Advisor, 408-924-4592, E-mail: jsempere@email.sjsu.edu.

Simmons College, College of Arts and Sciences Graduate Studies, Program in Spanish, Boston, MA 02115. Offers MA, MAT/MA. Part-time programs available. *Students:* 4 part-time (3 women); includes 2 minority (both Hispanic Americans). In 2009, 4 master's awarded. *Degree requirements:* For master's, one foreign language, thesis optional. *Entrance requirements:* For master's, analytical writing samples in Spanish. Additional exam requirements/recommendations for international students: Required—TOEFL (minimum score 600 paper-based; 250 computer-based; 100 iBT). *Application deadline:* For fall admission, 8/1 priority date for domestic and international students; for winter admission, 12/15 priority date for domestic and international students; for spring admission, 5/1 priority date for domestic and international students. Applications are processed on a rolling basis. Application fee: $35. Electronic applications accepted. *Expenses:* Tuition: Part-time $925 per credit hour. Part-time tuition and fees vary according to program. *Financial support:* Application deadline: 3/1. *Faculty research:* Medieval and Golden Age Spanish literature, the changing roles of Latinos in the U. S., Latin-American women's fiction, post-dictatorship narratives in the Southern Cone. *Unit head:* Dr. Raquel Maria Halty, Professor/Director, 617-521-2182, Fax: 617-521-3090, E-mail: raquel.halty@simmons.edu. *Application contact:* Kristen Haack, Director, Graduate Studies Admission, 617-521-2917, Fax: 617-521-3058, E-mail: gsa@simmons.edu.

Stanford University, School of Humanities and Sciences, Department of Spanish and Portuguese, Stanford, CA 94305-9991. Offers Spanish (MA, PhD). Terminal master's awarded for partial completion of doctoral program. *Degree requirements:* For master's, 2 foreign languages; for doctorate, 3 foreign languages, thesis/dissertation, oral exam. *Entrance requirements:* For master's and doctorate, GRE General Test. Additional exam requirements/recommendations for international students: Required—TOEFL. Electronic applications accepted. *Expenses:* Tuition: Full-time $37,380; part-time $2760 per quarter. Required fees: $501.

State University of New York at Binghamton, Graduate School, School of Arts and Sciences, Department of Romance Languages and Literatures, Program in Spanish, Binghamton, NY 13902-6000. Offers Spanish (MA); translation (Certificate). *Students:* 2 full-time (1 woman), 2 part-time (both women). Average age 38. 1 applicant, 0% accepted, 0 enrolled. In 2009, 5 master's awarded. *Degree requirements:* For master's, one foreign language, comprehensive exam, thesis or alternative. *Entrance requirements:* For master's, GRE General Test, GRE Subject Test. Additional exam requirements/recommendations for international students: Required—TOEFL (minimum score 550 paper-based; 213 computer-based; 80 iBT). *Application deadline:* For fall admission, 2/15 priority date for domestic and international students; for spring admission, 11/15 priority date for domestic and international students. Applications are processed on a rolling basis. Application fee: $60. Electronic applications accepted. *Financial support:* Fellowships, research assistantships, teaching assistantships, career-related internships or fieldwork, Federal Work-Study, institutionally sponsored loans, scholarships/grants, health care benefits, and unspecified assistantships available. Financial award application deadline: 2/15; financial award applicants required to submit FAFSA. *Unit head:* Dr. Antonio Sobejano-Moran, Chairperson, 607-777-4635, E-mail: antobianco@msn.com. *Application contact:* Victoria Williams, Recruiting and Admissions Coordinator, 607-777-2151, Fax: 607-777-2501, E-mail: vwilliam@binghamton.edu.

Syracuse University, College of Arts and Sciences, Program in Spanish Language, Literature and Culture, Syracuse, NY 13244. Offers MA. Part-time programs available. *Students:* 8 full-time (6 women), 3 part-time (2 women); includes 4 minority (all Hispanic Americans), 1 international. Average age 29. 10 applicants, 60% accepted, 5 enrolled. In 2009, 4 master's awarded. *Degree requirements:* For master's, comprehensive exam (for some programs), thesis or alternative. *Entrance requirements:* For master's, GRE General Test. Additional exam requirements/recommendations for international students: Required—TOEFL (minimum score 100 iBT). *Application deadline:* For fall admission, 2/1 priority date for domestic and international students. Application fee: $75. Electronic applications accepted. *Expenses:* Tuition: Full-time $26,808; part-time $1117 per credit. Required fees: $1024. *Financial support:* Fellowships with full tuition reimbursements, teaching assistantships with full tuition reimbursements, tuition waivers (partial) available. Financial award application deadline: 1/1; financial award applicants required to submit FAFSA. *Unit head:* Dr. Alicia Rios, Graduate Director, 315-443-5379, Fax: 315-443-5376, E-mail: abrios@syr.edu. *Application contact:* Karen Ames, Information Contact, 315-443-3022, E-mail: koames@syr.edu.

Temple University, Graduate School, College of Liberal Arts, Department of Spanish and Portuguese, Philadelphia, PA 19122-6096. Offers Spanish (MA, PhD). Part-time and evening/weekend programs available. Terminal master's awarded for partial completion of doctoral program. *Degree requirements:* For master's, one foreign language; for doctorate, 2 foreign languages, thesis/dissertation. *Entrance requirements:* For master's and doctorate, GRE General Test, minimum GPA of 3.0. Additional exam requirements/recommendations for international students: Required—TOEFL (minimum score 550 paper-based; 213 computer-based; 79 iBT). Electronic applications accepted. *Faculty research:* Spanish American literature, Spanish Peninsular literature, Hispanic linguistics.

Texas A&M International University, Office of Graduate Studies and Research, College of Arts and Sciences, Department of Language and Literature, Laredo, TX 78041-1900. Offers English (MA); Hispanic studies (PhD); Spanish (MA). *Faculty:* 6 full-time (3 women). *Students:* 4 full-time (3 women), 49 part-time (33 women); includes 46 minority (all Hispanic Americans), 1 international. Average age 34. 26 applicants. In 2009, 3 master's awarded. *Entrance requirements:* For master's, GRE General Test. Additional exam requirements/recommendations for international students: Required—TOEFL (minimum score 550 paper-based; 213 computer-based). *Application deadline:* For fall admission, 4/30 priority date for domestic students; for spring admission, 11/30 for domestic students. Applications are processed on a rolling basis. Application fee: $25. *Financial support:* In 2009–10, 12 students received support, including 1 fellowship, 1 research assistantship, 6 teaching assistantships. Financial award application deadline: 11/1. *Unit head:* Dr. Manuel Broncano, Chair, 956-326-2470, E-mail: manuel.broncano@tamiu.edu. *Application contact:* Rosie Espinoza-Dickinson, Director of Admissions, 956-326-2200, Fax: 956-326-2199, E-mail: enroll@tamiu.edu.

Texas A&M University, College of Liberal Arts, Department of Hispanic Studies, College Station, TX 77843. Offers MA, PhD. *Faculty:* 10. *Students:* 26 full-time (10 women), 11 part-time (10 women); includes 17 minority (all Hispanic Americans), 6 international. In 2009, 3 master's awarded. *Expenses:* Tuition, state resident: full-time $3991; part-time $221.74 per credit hour. Tuition, nonresident: full-time $9049; part-time $502.74 per credit hour. *Unit head:* Larry Mitchell, Head, 979-845-2164, E-mail: j-mitchell@tamu.edu. *Application contact:* Dr., Associate Dean.

Texas A&M University–Commerce, Graduate School, College of Arts and Sciences, Department of Literature and Languages, Commerce, TX 75429-3011. Offers college teaching of English (PhD); English (MA, MS); Spanish (MA). Part-time programs available. Terminal master's awarded for partial completion of doctoral program. *Degree requirements:* For master's, comprehensive exam, thesis (for some programs); for doctorate, one foreign language, thesis/dissertation, departmental qualifying exam. *Entrance requirements:* For master's and doctorate, GRE General Test. Electronic applications accepted. *Faculty research:* Latino literature, American film studies, ethnographic research, Willa Carter.

Texas A&M University–Kingsville, College of Graduate Studies, College of Arts and Sciences, Department of Language and Literature, Kingsville, TX 78363. Offers English (MA, MS); Spanish (MA). Part-time and evening/weekend programs available. *Degree requirements:* For master's, comprehensive exam, thesis or alternative. *Entrance requirements:* For master's, GRE General Test, minimum GPA of 3.0. Additional exam requirements/recommendations for international students: Required—TOEFL. *Faculty research:* Linguistics, culture, Spanish American literature, Spanish peninsular literature, American literature.

Texas State University–San Marcos, Graduate School, College of Liberal Arts, Department of Modern Languages, Program in Spanish, San Marcos, TX 78666. Offers MA. Part-time and evening/weekend programs available. *Faculty:* 8 full-time (6 women). *Students:* 26 full-time (17 women), 15 part-time (12 women); includes 22 minority (all Hispanic Americans), 4 international. Average age 34. 24 applicants, 100% accepted, 19 enrolled. In 2009, 6 master's awarded. *Degree requirements:* For master's, one foreign language, comprehensive exam, internship (MAT), thesis (MA). *Entrance requirements:* For master's, minimum GPA of 3.0 in last 12 undergraduate hours of advanced Spanish with 6 hours in literature. Additional exam requirements/recommendations for international students: Required—TOEFL (minimum score 550 paper-based; 213 computer-based). *Application deadline:* For fall admission, 6/15 priority date for domestic students, 6/1 for international students; for spring admission, 10/15 priority date for domestic students, 10/1 for international students. Applications are processed on a rolling basis. Application fee: $40 ($90 for international students). Electronic applications accepted. *Expenses:* Tuition, state resident: full-time $5784; part-time $241 per credit hour. Tuition, nonresident: part-time $551 per credit hour. Required fees: $1728; $48 per credit hour. $306. Tuition and fees vary according to course load. *Financial support:* In 2009–10, 16 students received support, including 7 teaching assistantships (averaging $5,751 per year); research assistantships, career-related internships or fieldwork, Federal Work-Study, and institutionally sponsored loans also available. Support available to part-time students. Financial award application deadline: 4/1; financial award applicants required to submit FAFSA. *Faculty research:* Hispanic literature, linguistics, literary theory, computer-assisted language instruction, Hispanic philology. *Unit head:* Dr. Catherine Jaffe, Advisor, 512-245-2360, Fax: 512-245-8298, E-mail: cj10@txstate.edu. *Application contact:* Dr. J. Michael Willoughby, Dean of Graduate School, 512-245-2581, Fax: 512-245-8365, E-mail: gradcollege@txstate.edu.

Spanish

Texas Tech University, Graduate School, College of Arts and Sciences, Department of Classical and Modern Languages and Literatures, Program in Romance Languages-Spanish, Lubbock, TX 79409. Offers MA. Part-time programs available. *Students:* 6 full-time (5 women), 3 part-time (2 women); includes 4 minority (1 African American, 3 Hispanic Americans). Average age 27. In 2009, 3 master's awarded. *Degree requirements:* For master's, one foreign language, thesis optional. *Entrance requirements:* For master's, GRE General Test. Additional exam requirements/recommendations for international students: Required—TOEFL (minimum score 550 paper-based; 213 computer-based). *Application deadline:* For fall admission, 3/1 priority date for international students; for spring admission, 11/1 priority date for international students. Applications are processed on a rolling basis. Application fee: $50 ($75 for international students). Electronic applications accepted. *Expenses:* Tuition, state resident: full-time $5100; part-time $213 per credit hour. Tuition, nonresident: full-time $11,748; part-time $490 per credit hour. Required fees: $2298; $50 per credit hour. $555 per semester. *Financial support:* Research assistantships with partial tuition reimbursements, teaching assistantships with partial tuition reimbursements available. Financial award application deadline: 4/15. *Faculty research:* Peninsular literature, Latin-American literature, Portuguese language and literature, Spanish linguistics. *Unit head:* Dr. Jorge Zamora, Professor and Graduate Advisor of Spanish, 806-742-3145 Ext. 281, Fax: 806-742-3306, E-mail: jorge.zamora@ttu.edu. *Application contact:* Dr. Carmen Pereira-Muro, Graduate Admissions Officer, E-mail: carmen.pereira@ttu.edu.

Texas Tech University, Graduate School, College of Arts and Sciences, Department of Classical and Modern Languages and Literatures, Program in Spanish, Lubbock, TX 79409. Offers PhD. Part-time programs available. *Students:* 27 full-time (13 women), 10 part-time (6 women); includes 9 minority (all Hispanic Americans), 18 international. Average age 37. 15 applicants, 80% accepted, 4 enrolled. In 2009, 5 doctorates awarded. *Degree requirements:* For doctorate, one foreign language, comprehensive exam, thesis/dissertation. *Entrance requirements:* For doctorate, GRE General Test. Additional exam requirements/recommendations for international students: Required—TOEFL (minimum score 550 paper-based; 213 computer-based). *Application deadline:* For fall admission, 3/1 priority date for international students; for spring admission, 11/1 priority date for international students. Applications are processed on a rolling basis. Application fee: $50 ($75 for international students). Electronic applications accepted. *Expenses:* Tuition, state resident: full-time $5100; part-time $213 per credit hour. Tuition, nonresident: full-time $11,748; part-time $490 per credit hour. Required fees: $2298; $50 per credit hour. $555 per semester. *Financial support:* Research assistantships with partial tuition reimbursements, teaching assistantships with partial tuition reimbursements, Federal Work-Study and institutionally sponsored loans available. Support available to part-time students. Financial award application deadline: 4/15. *Unit head:* Dr. Jorge Zamora, Professor/Advisor, 806-742-3145 Ext. 243, Fax: 806-742-3306, E-mail: jorge.zamora@ttu.edu. *Application contact:* Dr. Carmen Pereira-Muro, Graduate Admissions Officer, 806-742-4055, Fax: 806-742-3306, E-mail: liz.hildebrand@ttu.edu.

Tulane University, School of Liberal Arts, Department of Spanish and Portuguese, New Orleans, LA 70118-5669. Offers Portuguese (MA); Spanish (MA); Spanish and Portuguese (PhD). *Degree requirements:* For master's, 2 foreign languages; for doctorate, 2 foreign languages, thesis/dissertation. *Entrance requirements:* For master's, GRE General Test, minimum B average in undergraduate course work; for doctorate, GRE General Test. Additional exam requirements/recommendations for international students: Required—TOEFL. Electronic applications accepted.

Universidad Adventista de las Antillas, EGECED Department, Mayagüez, PR 00681-0118. Offers curriculum and instruction (MA), including secondary biology, secondary history, secondary Spanish; education (MA), including ESL (elementary school level), ESL (high school level), school administration and supervision. *Degree requirements:* For master's, comprehensive exam (for some programs), thesis (for some programs). *Entrance requirements:* For master's, EXADEP or GRE General Test, recommendations. Application fee: $175. Electronic applications accepted. *Expenses:* Tuition: Full-time $3990; part-time $190 per credit. Required fees: $570; $190 per credit. $1375 per summer. *Financial support:* Fellowships, Federal Work-Study available. *Unit head:* Dr. Zilma Sepulveda, Director, 787-834-9595 Ext. 2282, Fax: 787-834-9595, E-mail: zsantiago@uaa.edu. *Application contact:* Prof. Evelyn del Valle, Admissions Department Director, 787-834-9595 Ext. 2261, Fax: 787-834-9597, E-mail: admissions@uaa.edu.

Universidad Autonoma de Guadalajara, Graduate Programs, Guadalajara, Mexico. Offers administrative law and justice (LL M); advertising and corporate communications (MA); architecture (M Arch); business (MBA); computational science (MCC); education (Ed M, Ed D); English-Spanish translation (MA); fiscal law (MA); integrated management of digital animation (MA); international business (MIB); international corporate law (LL M); internet technologies (MS); labor health (MS); manufacturing systems (MMS); philosophy (MA, PhD); power electronics (MS); quality systems (MQS); renewable energy (MS); social evaluation of projects (MBA); strategic market research (MBA); teaching mathematics (MA).

Université de Montréal, Faculty of Arts and Sciences, Department of Literatures and Modern Languages, Program in Hispanic Studies, Montréal, QC H3C 3J7, Canada. Offers MA. *Degree requirements:* For master's, 2 foreign languages, thesis. Electronic applications accepted. *Faculty research:* Spanish literature and culture, Latin American literature and culture.

Université Laval, Faculty of Letters, Department of Literature, Programs in Spanish Literatures, Québec, QC G1K 7P4, Canada. Offers MA, PhD. Part-time programs available. Terminal master's awarded for partial completion of doctoral program. *Degree requirements:* For master's, thesis; for doctorate, comprehensive exam, thesis/dissertation. *Entrance requirements:* For master's and doctorate, linguistics exams, knowledge of French and Spanish. Electronic applications accepted.

University at Albany, State University of New York, College of Arts and Sciences, Department of Languages, Literatures, and Cultures, Program in Spanish, Albany, NY 12222-0001. Offers MA, PhD. *Degree requirements:* For doctorate, thesis/dissertation. *Entrance requirements:* For doctorate, GRE General Test.

University at Buffalo, the State University of New York, Graduate School, College of Arts and Sciences, Department of Romance Languages and Literatures, Buffalo, NY 14260. Offers French (MA, PhD); Spanish (MA, PhD). Part-time programs available. *Students:* Average age 31. Terminal master's awarded for partial completion of doctoral program. *Degree requirements:* For master's, one foreign language, project, thesis; for doctorate, 2 foreign languages, thesis/dissertation. *Entrance requirements:* For master's and doctorate, GRE. Additional exam requirements/recommendations for international students: Required—TOEFL (minimum score 550 paper-based; 213 computer-based; 79 iBT). *Application deadline:* For fall admission, 1/15 priority date for domestic students, 1/15 for international students. Applications are processed on a rolling basis. Application fee: $75. Electronic applications accepted. *Financial support:* In 2009–10, fellowships with full tuition reimbursements (averaging $6,000 per year), teaching assistantships with full tuition reimbursements (averaging $13,000 per year) were awarded; Federal Work-Study and institutionally sponsored loans also available. Financial award application deadline: 2/28; financial award applicants required to submit FAFSA. *Faculty research:* Romance linguistics, cultural studies, literary studies, literature and philosophy. *Unit head:* Dr. David Castillo, Chair, 716-645-0869, Fax: 716-645-5981, E-mail: dc63@buffalo.edu. *Application contact:* Dr. Justin Read, Director of Graduate Studies, 716-645-0878, Fax: 716-645-5981, E-mail: jread2@buffalo.edu.

University at Buffalo, the State University of New York, Graduate School, Graduate School of Education, Department of Learning and Instruction, Buffalo, NY 14260. Offers biology education (Ed M, Certificate); chemistry education (Ed M, Certificate); childhood education (Ed M); childhood education with bilingual extension (Ed M); early childhood education (Ed M); earth science education (Ed M, Certificate); elementary education (Ed D, PhD); English education (Ed M, PhD, Certificate); English for speakers of other languages (Ed M); foreign and second language education (PhD); French education (Ed M, Certificate); general education (Ed M); German education (Ed M, Certificate); gifted education (online) (Certificate); Latin education (Ed M, Certificate); literary specialist (Ed M); mathematics education (Ed M, PhD, Certificate); music education (Ed M, Certificate); physics education (Ed M, Certificate); reading education (PhD); science and the public (online) (Ed M); science education (PhD); social studies education (Ed M, Certificate); Spanish education (Ed M, Certificate); special education (PhD); teaching and leading for diversity (Certificate); teaching English to speakers of other languages (Ed M). Part-time and evening/weekend programs available. Postbaccalaureate distance learning degree programs offered (no on-campus study). *Faculty:* 34 full-time (24 women), 50 part-time/adjunct (39 women). *Students:* 332 full-time (245 women), 365 part-time (272 women); includes 50 minority (18 African Americans, 4 American Indian/Alaska Native, 10 Asian Americans or Pacific Islanders, 18 Hispanic Americans), 55 international. Average age 30. 627 applicants, 78% accepted, 286 enrolled. In 2009, 255 master's, 16 doctorates, 51 other advanced degrees awarded. *Degree requirements:* For master's, comprehensive exam; for doctorate, thesis/dissertation, research analysis exam, research experience component. *Entrance requirements:* For doctorate, GRE General Test or MAT, interview, writing sample, letters of recommendation. Additional exam requirements/recommendations for international students: Required—TOEFL (minimum score 600 paper-based; 250 computer-based; 96 iBT). *Application deadline:* For fall admission, 2/1 priority date for domestic and international students; for spring admission, 11/15 priority date for domestic students, 10/1 for international students. Applications are processed on a rolling basis. Application fee: $50. Electronic applications accepted. *Financial support:* In 2009–10, 23 fellowships with full tuition reimbursements (averaging $9,000 per year), 42 research assistantships with full tuition reimbursements (averaging $10,000 per year) were awarded; teaching assistantships with full tuition reimbursements, career-related internships or fieldwork, Federal Work-Study, institutionally sponsored loans, scholarships/grants, tuition waivers (partial), and unspecified assistantships also available. Financial award application deadline: 2/28; financial award applicants required to submit FAFSA. *Faculty research:* Science assessment, foreign language teaching and learning, early learning, new literacies, gender and education. Total annual research expenditures: $1.8 million. *Unit head:* Dr. Suzanne Miller, Chair, 716-645-2455, Fax: 716-645-3161, E-mail: smiller@buffalo.edu. *Application contact:* Cathy Dimino, Admissions Assistant, 716-645-2110, Fax: 716-645-7937, E-mail: cadimino@buffalo.edu.

The University of Akron, Graduate School, Buchtel College of Arts and Sciences, Department of Modern Languages, Program in Spanish, Akron, OH 44325. Offers MA. Part-time and evening/weekend programs available. *Faculty:* 5 full-time (4 women). *Students:* 4 full-time (3 women), 2 part-time (both women); includes 3 minority (all Hispanic Americans). Average age 29. 11 applicants, 91% accepted, 5 enrolled. In 2009, 2 master's awarded. *Degree requirements:* For master's, one foreign language, comprehensive exam, thesis optional, oral exam, essay, research paper. *Entrance requirements:* For master's, interview, minimum GPA of 3.0, proficiency in Spanish, letters of recommendation. Additional exam requirements/recommendations for international students: Required—TOEFL (minimum score 550 paper-based; 213 computer-based; 79 iBT). *Application deadline:* Applications are processed on a rolling basis. Application fee: $30 ($40 for international students). Electronic applications accepted. *Expenses:* Tuition, state resident: full-time $6570; part-time $365 per credit hour. Tuition, nonresident: full-time $11,250; part-time $625 per credit hour. *Financial support:* Research assistantships with full tuition reimbursements, teaching assistantships with full tuition reimbursements, institutionally sponsored loans available. *Unit head:* Dr. Parizad Dejbord-Sawan, Director of Graduate Studies, 330-972-7824, E-mail: parizad@uakron.edu. *Application contact:* Dr. Parizad Dejbord-Sawan, Director of Graduate Studies, 330-972-7824, E-mail: parizad@uakron.edu.

The University of Alabama, Graduate School, College of Arts and Sciences, Department of Modern Languages and Classics, Tuscaloosa, AL 35487. Offers French (MA, PhD); French and Spanish (PhD); German (MA); Romance languages (MA, PhD); Spanish (MA, PhD). Part-time programs available. *Faculty:* 22 full-time (11 women). *Students:* 46 full-time (31 women), 8 part-time (6 women); includes 7 minority (4 African Americans, 3 Hispanic Americans), 16 international. Average age 31. 31 applicants, 42% accepted, 11 enrolled. In 2009, 12 master's, 5 doctorates awarded. *Median time to degree:* Of those who began their doctoral program in fall 2001, 40% received their degree in 8 years or less. *Degree requirements:* For master's, comprehensive exam, thesis optional; for doctorate, one foreign language, thesis/dissertation, preliminary exam. *Entrance requirements:* For master's and doctorate, minimum GPA of 3.0, writing sample. Additional exam requirements/recommendations for international students: Required—TOEFL or IELTS. *Application deadline:* For fall admission, 7/6 priority date for domestic students, 1/15 priority date for international students; for spring admission, 12/6 priority date for domestic students, 6/1 priority date for international students. Applications are processed on a rolling basis. Application fee: $50 ($60 for international students). Electronic applications accepted. *Expenses:* Tuition, state resident: full-time $7000. Tuition, nonresident: full-time $19,200. *Financial support:* In 2009–10, 7 students received support, including 1 fellowship, research assistantships with full tuition reimbursements available (averaging $10,291 per year), 6 teaching assistantships with full tuition reimbursements available (averaging $10,291 per year); career-related internships or fieldwork, Federal Work-Study, institutionally sponsored loans, and scholarships/grants also available. Financial award application deadline: 7/14. *Faculty research:* Non-English literature, linguistics, culture, film. *Unit head:* Dr. Michael Picone, Chair and Professor, 205-348-5054, Fax: 205-348-2042, E-mail: mpicone@bama.ua.edu. *Application contact:* Dr. K. Barbara Fischer, Graduate Director and Associate Professor, 205-348-8465, Fax: 205-348-2042, E-mail: bfischer@bama.ua.edu.

The University of Arizona, Graduate College, College of Humanities, Department of Spanish and Portuguese, Tucson, AZ 85721. Offers Spanish (MA, PhD). *Faculty:* 20. *Students:* 19 full-time (12 women), 48 part-time (31 women); includes 22 minority (1 Asian American or Pacific Islander, 21 Hispanic Americans), 29 international. Average age 36. 36 applicants, 28% accepted, 7 enrolled. In 2009, 6 master's, 11 doctorates awarded. Terminal master's awarded for partial completion of doctoral program. *Degree requirements:* For master's, one foreign language, comprehensive exam, thesis optional; for doctorate, 3 foreign languages, comprehensive exam, thesis/dissertation. *Entrance requirements:* For master's, GRE General Test, minimum GPA of 3.3, writing sample, 3 letters of recommendation, audio sample; for doctorate, GRE General Test, minimum GPA of 3.4, 3 letters of recommendation, statement of purpose, writing sample, audio sample. Additional exam requirements/recommendations for international students: Required—TOEFL (minimum score 550 paper-based; 213 computer-based; 79 iBT). *Application deadline:* For fall admission, 2/15 for domestic and international students; for spring admission, 8/1 for domestic and international students. Application fee: $75. Electronic applications accepted. *Expenses:* Tuition, state resident: full-time $9028. Tuition, nonresident: full-time $24,890. *Financial support:* In 2009–10, 72 teaching assistantships with full tuition reimbursements (averaging $15,555 per year) were awarded; institutionally sponsored loans, scholarships/grants, health care benefits, tuition waivers (full), and unspecified assistantships also available. Financial award application deadline: 2/15. *Faculty research:* Spanish and Latin American literature and linguistics, literary theory. Total annual research expenditures: $5,243. *Unit head:* Dr. Malcolm A. Compitello, Head, 520-621-3123, E-mail: compitel@email.arizona.edu. *Application contact:* Isela Gonzales, Administrative Assistant, 520-621-3125, Fax: 520-621-6104, E-mail: iselag@email.arizona.edu.

University of Arkansas, Graduate School, J. William Fulbright College of Arts and Sciences, Department of Foreign Languages, Program in Spanish, Fayetteville, AR 72701-1201. Offers MA. *Faculty:* 6 full-time (4 women). *Students:* 13 full-time (7 women), 4 part-time (2 women); includes 2 minority (both Hispanic Americans), 8 international. In 2009, 4 master's awarded. *Degree requirements:* For master's, one foreign language, comprehensive exam, thesis optional. *Entrance requirements:* Additional exam requirements/recommendations for international students: Required—TOEFL (minimum score 550 paper-based; 213 computer-based), IELTS (minimum score 6.5). *Application deadline:* For fall admission, 1/15 priority date for domestic students; for spring admission, 9/15 priority date for domestic students. Application fee: $40 ($50 for international students). Electronic applications accepted. *Expenses:* Tuition, state resident: full-time $7355; part-time $356.58 per hour. Tuition, nonresident: full-time $17,401; part-time $775.17 per hour. Required fees: $1203. *Financial support:* In 2009–10, fellowships with tuition reimbursements (averaging $2,178 per year), 13 teaching assistantships (averaging $8,200 per year) were awarded; research assistantships, career-related internships or fieldwork and Federal Work-Study also available. Support available to part-time students. Financial award application deadline: 1/15; financial award applicants required to submit FAFSA. *Faculty research:* Medieval and Golden Age poetry, colonial Latin America, contemporary Latin America. *Unit head:* Dr. Joan Turner, Department Chair, 479-575-2951, Fax: 479-575-6795, E-mail: joant@uark.edu. *Application contact:* Dr. M. Reina Ruiz, Graduate Coordinator, 479-575-6590, E-mail: rruiz@uark.edu.

University of California, Berkeley, Graduate Division, College of Letters and Science, Department of Hispanic Languages and Literature, Berkeley, CA 94720-1500. Offers PhD. *Faculty:* 16 full-time (6 women). *Students:* 42 full-time (23 women). Average age 33. 56 applicants, 4 enrolled. In 2009, 8 doctorates awarded. *Degree requirements:* For doctorate, thesis/dissertation, qualifying exam. *Entrance requirements:* For doctorate, GRE General Test, minimum GPA of 3.0, 3 letters of recommendation. Additional exam requirements/recommendations for international students: Required—TOEFL (minimum score 570 paper-based; 230 computer-based). *Application deadline:* For fall admission, 12/15 for domestic students. Application fee: $70 ($90 for international students). *Financial support:* Fellowships with full tuition reimbursements, research assistantships, teaching assistantships with partial tuition reimbursements, unspecified assistantships available. Financial award applicants required to submit FAFSA. *Unit head:* Prof. Michael Mascuch, Chair, 510-642-0471, E-mail: ch_spanport@ls.berkeley.edu. *Application contact:* Veronica Lopez, Student Affairs Officer, 510-642-8037, E-mail: spanga@berkeley.edu.

University of California, Berkeley, Graduate Division, College of Letters and Science, Group in Romance Languages and Literature, Berkeley, CA 94720-1500. Offers French (PhD); Italian (PhD); Spanish (PhD). *Faculty:* 16 full-time. *Students:* 15 full-time (8 women). Average age 33. 34 applicants, 1 enrolled. In 2009, 4 doctorates awarded. *Degree requirements:* For doctorate, thesis/dissertation, qualifying exam. *Entrance requirements:* For doctorate, GRE General Test, minimum GPA of 3.0, 3 letters of recommendation. Additional exam requirements/recommendations for international students: Required—TOEFL (minimum score 570 paper-based; 230 computer-based). *Application deadline:* For fall admission, 12/15 for domestic students. Application fee: $70 ($90 for international students). *Financial support:* Fellowships with full tuition reimbursements, teaching assistantships with partial tuition reimbursements, health care benefits and unspecified assistantships available. Financial award applicants required to submit FAFSA. *Unit head:* Jose Rabasa, Chair, 510-642-2105, E-mail: jrabasa@berkeley.edu. *Application contact:* Jose Rabasa, Chair, 510-642-2105, E-mail: jrabasa@berkeley.edu.

University of California, Davis, Graduate Studies, Program in Spanish, Davis, CA 95616. Offers MA, PhD. Terminal master's awarded for partial completion of doctoral program. *Degree requirements:* For master's, comprehensive exam (for some programs), thesis (for some programs); for doctorate, 2 foreign languages, thesis/dissertation. *Entrance requirements:* For master's, GRE General Test, minimum GPA of 3.0; for doctorate, GRE General Test, master's degree, minimum GPA of 3.0. Additional exam requirements/recommendations for international students: Required—TOEFL (minimum score 550 paper-based; 213 computer-based). *Faculty research:* Medieval Spanish language and literature, Spanish linguistics, Latin American literature, nineteenth century Peninsular literature.

University of California, Irvine, Office of Graduate Studies, School of Humanities, Department of Spanish and Portuguese, Irvine, CA 92697. Offers Spanish (MA, MAT, PhD). *Students:* 39 full-time (19 women), 3 part-time (2 women); includes 29 minority (1 Asian American or Pacific Islander, 28 Hispanic Americans). Average age 32. 57 applicants, 30% accepted, 8 enrolled. In 2009, 2 master's, 7 doctorates awarded. *Degree requirements:* For doctorate, thesis/dissertation. *Entrance requirements:* For master's and doctorate, GRE General Test, minimum GPA of 3.0. Additional exam requirements/recommendations for international students: Required—TOEFL (minimum score 550 paper-based; 213 computer-based). *Application deadline:* For fall admission, 1/2 priority date for domestic students, 1/2 for international students. Applications are processed on a rolling basis. Application fee: $70 ($90 for international students). Electronic applications accepted. *Financial support:* Fellowships, teaching assistantships, institutionally sponsored loans, traineeships, health care benefits, and unspecified assistantships available. Financial award application deadline: 3/1; financial award applicants required to submit FAFSA. *Faculty research:* Latin American literature, Spanish literature, Spanish linguistics in Creole studies, Hispanic literature in the U.S., Luso-Brazilian literature. *Unit head:* Ana Paula Ferreira, Chair, 949-824-7265, Fax: 949-824-2803, E-mail: apferrei@uci.edu. *Application contact:* Linda T. Le, Graduate Coordinator, 949-824-8793, Fax: 949-824-2803, E-mail: ttle@uci.edu.

University of California, Los Angeles, Graduate Division, College of Letters and Science, Department of Spanish and Portuguese, Program in Spanish, Los Angeles, CA 90095. Offers MA. *Students:* 6 full-time (3 women); includes 1 minority (Hispanic American), 1 international. Average age 29. 32 applicants, 13% accepted, 3 enrolled. In 2009, 1 master's awarded. Terminal master's awarded for partial completion of doctoral program. *Degree requirements:* For master's, one foreign language, comprehensive exam or thesis. *Entrance requirements:* For master's, GRE General Test, minimum GPA of 3.0, sample of written work (recommended). *Application deadline:* For fall admission, 12/31 for domestic and international students. Application fee: $70 ($90 for international students). Electronic applications accepted. *Financial support:* In 2009–10, 4 fellowships with full and partial tuition reimbursements, 1 research assistantship with full and partial tuition reimbursement, 2 teaching assistantships with full and partial tuition reimbursements were awarded; Federal Work-Study, scholarships/grants, health care benefits, tuition waivers (full and partial), and unspecified assistantships also available. Financial award application deadline: 3/1; financial award applicants required to submit FAFSA. *Unit head:* Dr. Maarten Van Delden, Chair, 310-825-1220. *Application contact:* Department Office, 310-825-1036, E-mail: peinado@humnet.ucla.edu.

University of California, Riverside, Graduate Division, Department of Hispanic Studies, Riverside, CA 92521-0102. Offers Spanish (MA, PhD). Terminal master's awarded for partial completion of doctoral program. *Degree requirements:* For master's, one foreign language, comprehensive exam; for doctorate, one foreign language, thesis/dissertation, qualifying exams, 1 quarter of teaching experience. *Entrance requirements:* For master's and doctorate, GRE General Test, minimum GPA of 3.2. Additional exam requirements/recommendations for international students: Required—TOEFL (minimum score 550 paper-based; 213 computer-based; 80 iBT). Electronic applications accepted. *Faculty research:* Spanish literature of sixteenth, seventeenth and twentieth century; pre-Columbian and colonial Latin American literature; nineteenth and twentieth century Latin American literature.

University of California, San Diego, Office of Graduate Studies, Department of Literature, Program in Spanish Literature, La Jolla, CA 92093. Offers MA. *Degree requirements:* For master's, thesis. *Entrance requirements:* For master's, GRE General Test, GRE Subject Test. Electronic applications accepted.

University of California, Santa Barbara, Graduate Division, College of Letters and Sciences, Division of Humanities and Fine Arts, Department of Spanish and Portuguese, Santa Barbara, CA 93106-4150. Offers Hispanic languages and literature (PhD), including applied linguistics, European Medieval studies, feminist studies, Hispanic languages and literature; Portuguese (MA); Spanish (MA); Spanish and Portuguese (MA); MA/PhD. Spanish Language Institute available during summer session. *Faculty:* 16 full-time (6 women). *Students:* 29 full-time (16 women). Average age 30. 46 applicants, 39% accepted, 9 enrolled. In 2009, 4 master's, 2 doctorates awarded. *Degree requirements:* For master's, 2 foreign languages, comprehensive exam (for some programs), thesis optional; for doctorate, 2 foreign languages, comprehensive exam, thesis/dissertation. *Entrance requirements:* For master's, GRE, 2 writing samples, undergraduate major in Spanish or equivalent, 3 letters of recommendation, resume/curriculum vitae; for doctorate, GRE, 2 writing samples, master's degree, 3 letters of recommendation, statement of purpose, personal achievements/contributions statement, resume/curriculum vitae, transcripts for post-secondary institutions attended. Additional exam requirements/recommendations for international students: Required—TOEFL (minimum score 550 paper-based; 213 computer-based; 80 iBT), or IELTS (minimum score 7). *Application deadline:* For fall admission, 3/1 for domestic and international students; for winter admission, 11/1 for domestic and international students; for spring admission, 2/1 for domestic and international students. Application fee: $70 ($90 for international students). Electronic applications accepted. *Financial support:* In 2009–10, 9 fellowships with full and partial tuition reimbursements (averaging $7,000 per year), 29 teaching assistantships with partial tuition reimbursements (averaging $11,500 per year) were awarded; career-related internships or fieldwork, Federal Work-Study, institutionally sponsored loans, scholarships/grants, health care benefits, tuition waivers (full and partial), and unspecified assistantships also available. Financial award application deadline: 1/7; financial award applicants required to submit FAFSA. *Faculty research:* Nineteenth century Spanish and Portuguese literature, Spanish and Spanish American literature, nineteenth and twentieth century Portuguese and Brazilian literatures, Hispanic linguistics, Catalan language and culture. *Unit head:* Prof. Francisco A. Lomeli, Chair, 805-893-5715, Fax: 805-893-8341, E-mail: lomeli@spanport.ucsb.edu. *Application contact:* Carol Conley, Graduate Program Assistant, 805-893-3162, Fax: 805-893-8341, E-mail: cconley@spanport.ucsb.edu.

University of California, Santa Barbara, Summer Sessions, Santa Barbara, CA 93106-2010. Offers French (MA); Spanish (MA). In 2009, 17 master's awarded. *Degree requirements:* For master's, comprehensive exam (for some programs). *Entrance requirements:* For master's, GRE, 3 letters of recommendation, resume/curriculum vitae. Additional exam requirements/recommendations for international students: Required—TOEFL (minimum score 550 paper-based; 213 computer-based; 80 iBT) or IELTS (minimum score 7). Application fee: $70 ($90 for international students). Electronic applications accepted. *Expenses:* Contact institution. *Financial support:* Scholarships/grants available. Financial award applicants required to submit FAFSA. *Unit head:* Dr. Loy Lytle, Dean of Summer Sessions, 805-893-2706, Fax: 805-893-7306, E-mail: low.lytle@els.ucsb.edu. *Application contact:* Program Manager, 805-893-7053, Fax: 805-893-7306, E-mail: language.institutes@summersessions.ucsb.edu.

University of Central Florida, College of Arts and Humanities, Department of Modern Languages and Literatures, Program in Spanish, Orlando, FL 32816. Offers MA. Part-time and evening/weekend programs available. *Students:* 7 full-time (4 women), 16 part-time (12 women); includes 18 minority (1 African American, 17 Hispanic Americans), 1 international. Average age 36. 14 applicants, 93% accepted, 9 enrolled. In 2009, 5 master's awarded. *Degree requirements:* For master's, one foreign language, comprehensive exam, thesis or alternative. *Entrance requirements:* For master's, GRE General Test, minimum GPA of 3.0 in last 60 hours. Additional exam requirements/recommendations for international students: Required—TOEFL. *Application deadline:* For fall admission, 6/1 for domestic students; for spring admission, 12/1 for domestic students. Application fee: $30. Electronic applications accepted. *Expenses:* Tuition, state resident: part-time $306.31 per credit hour. Tuition, nonresident: part-time $1099.01 per credit hour. Part-time tuition and fees vary according to degree level and program. *Financial support:* In 2009–10, 5 students received support, including 4 teaching assistantships with partial tuition reimbursements available (averaging $7,900 per year); career-related internships or fieldwork, Federal Work-Study, institutionally sponsored loans, tuition waivers (partial), and unspecified assistantships also available. Financial award application deadline: 3/1; financial award applicants required to submit FAFSA.

University of Chicago, Division of the Humanities, Department of Romance Languages and Literatures, Chicago, IL 60637-1513. Offers French (AM, PhD); Italian (AM, PhD); Spanish (AM, PhD). Terminal master's awarded for partial completion of doctoral program. *Degree requirements:* For master's, 2 foreign languages, thesis; for doctorate, 3 foreign languages, thesis/dissertation. *Entrance requirements:* For master's and doctorate, GRE General Test, GRE Subject Test. Additional exam requirements/recommendations for international students: Required—TOEFL.

University of Cincinnati, Graduate School, McMicken College of Arts and Sciences, Department of Romance Languages and Literature, Program in Spanish, Cincinnati, OH 45221. Offers MA, PhD. Terminal master's awarded for partial completion of doctoral program. *Degree requirements:* For master's, thesis optional; for doctorate, 2 foreign languages, thesis/dissertation. *Entrance requirements:* For master's, minimum GPA of 3.0. Electronic applications accepted. *Faculty research:* Applied linguistics, Spanish essay, Latin American culture, women's studies, poetry.

University of Colorado at Boulder, Graduate School, College of Arts and Sciences, Department of Spanish and Portuguese, Boulder, CO 80309. Offers Hispanic linguistics (MA); medieval/early modern Hispanic literatures (PhD); Spanish and Spanish American literatures (MA, PhD). Part-time programs available. *Faculty:* 14 full-time (5 women). *Students:* 38 full-time (19 women), 7 part-time (5 women); includes 11 minority (all Hispanic Americans), 17 international. Average age 31. 52 applicants, 35% accepted, 12 enrolled. In 2009, 5 master's, 3 doctorates awarded. Terminal master's awarded for partial completion of doctoral program. *Degree requirements:* For master's, one foreign language, comprehensive exam, thesis or alternative; for doctorate, 2 foreign languages, thesis/dissertation. *Entrance requirements:* For master's, minimum undergraduate GPA of 2.75. *Application deadline:* For fall admission, 12/15 priority date for domestic students, 12/15 for international students. Applications are processed on a rolling basis. Application fee: $50 ($60 for international students). *Financial support:* In 2009–10, 7 fellowships with full tuition reimbursements (averaging $3,436 per year), 19 research assistantships (averaging $12,128 per year) were awarded; tuition waivers (full) also available. Financial award application deadline: 12/15. *Faculty research:* Spanish peninsular and Spanish-American literatures; Hispanic linguistics; medieval, Golden Age, eighteenth and nineteenth century literatures.

University of Colorado Denver, College of Liberal Arts and Sciences, Department of Modern Languages, Denver, CO 80217-3364. Offers Spanish (MA). *Students:* 5 full-time (4 women), 22 part-time (18 women); includes 11 minority (all Hispanic Americans). 8 applicants, 100% accepted, 7 enrolled. In 2009, 4 master's awarded. *Entrance requirements:* For master's, GRE, minimum undergraduate GPA of 2.5, 3.0 in all Spanish courses. Additional exam requirements/recommendations for international students: Required—TOEFL. Application fee: $50. *Unit head:* Dr. Diane Dansereau, Chair, 303-556-2760, E-mail: diane.dansereau@ucdenver.edu. *Application contact:* Dr. Charles Ferguson, Associate Dean of Student Affairs, 303-556-4350, Fax: 303-556-4681, E-mail: charles.ferguson@ucdenver.edu.

University of Connecticut, Graduate School, College of Liberal Arts and Sciences, Department of Modern and Classical Languages, Field of Spanish, Storrs, CT 06269. Offers MA, PhD. *Faculty:* 10 full-time (5 women). *Students:* 18 full-time (11 women), 5 part-time (2 women); includes 8 minority (all Hispanic Americans), 6 international. Average age 34. 27 applicants, 30% accepted, 5 enrolled. In 2009, 2 master's, 2 doctorates awarded. Terminal master's awarded for partial completion of doctoral program. *Degree requirements:* For master's, one foreign language, comprehensive exam; for doctorate, 2 foreign languages, thesis/dissertation. *Entrance requirements:* For master's and doctorate, GRE General Test, GRE Subject Test. Additional exam requirements/recommendations for international students: Required—TOEFL (minimum score 550 paper-based; 213 computer-based). *Application deadline:* For fall admission, 2/1 priority date for domestic and international students; for spring admission, 11/1 for domestic students, 10/1 for international students. Applications are processed on a rolling basis. Application fee: $55. Electronic applications accepted. *Expenses:* Tuition, state resident: full-time $4725; part-time $525 per credit. Tuition, nonresident: full-time $12,267; part-time $1363 per credit. Required fees: $346 per semester. Tuition and fees vary according to course load. *Financial support:* In 2009–10, 16 teaching assistantships with full tuition reimbursements were awarded; fellowships, research assistantships, Federal Work-Study, scholarships/grants, health care benefits, and unspecified assistantships also available. Financial award application deadline: 2/1; financial award applicants required to submit FAFSA. *Unit head:* Miguel Gomes, Professor, 860-486-3288, E-mail: miguel.gomes@uconn.edu. *Application contact:* Patricia Parlette-Schaff, Administrative Assistant, 860-486-3313, Fax: 860-486-4392, E-mail: patricia.parlette@uconn.edu.

Spanish

University of Delaware, College of Arts and Sciences, Department of Foreign Languages and Literatures, Newark, DE 19716. Offers foreign languages and literatures (MA), including French, German, Spanish; foreign languages pedagogy (MA), including French, German, Spanish. *Degree requirements:* For master's, one foreign language, comprehensive exam, thesis optional. *Entrance requirements:* For master's, GRE General Test, letters of recommendation, writing sample. Additional exam requirements/recommendations for international students: Required—TOEFL. Electronic applications accepted. *Faculty research:* Medieval to Modern French and Spanish literature, Twentieth Century German, French, Spanish literature by women, computer-assisted instruction.

University of Florida, Graduate School, College of Liberal Arts and Sciences, Department of Romance Languages and Literatures, Program in Spanish, Gainesville, FL 32611. Offers MA, PhD. *Degree requirements:* For master's, one foreign language, thesis optional; for doctorate, one foreign language, thesis/dissertation. *Entrance requirements:* For master's and doctorate, GRE General Test, minimum GPA of 3.0. Additional exam requirements/recommendations for international students: Required—TOEFL (minimum score 550 paper-based; 213 computer-based). Electronic applications accepted. *Faculty research:* Peninsular literature, Latin American literature, Hispanic linguistics.

University of Georgia, Graduate School, College of Arts and Sciences, Department of Romance Languages, Program in Spanish, Athens, GA 30602. Offers MA. *Students:* 12 full-time (7 women), 2 part-time (both women); includes 3 minority (all Hispanic Americans), 2 international. 26 applicants, 38% accepted, 6 enrolled. In 2009, 9 master's awarded. *Degree requirements:* For master's, one foreign language, thesis (MA). *Entrance requirements:* For master's, GRE General Test. *Application deadline:* For fall admission, 7/1 priority date for domestic students; for spring admission, 11/15 for domestic students. Application fee: $50. Electronic applications accepted. *Expenses:* Tuition, state resident: full-time $6000; part-time $250 per credit hour. Tuition, nonresident: full-time $20,904; part-time $871 per credit hour. Required fees: $730 per semester. *Financial support:* Fellowships, research assistantships, teaching assistantships, unspecified assistantships available. *Unit head:* Dr. Nina Hellerstein, Interim Head, 706-542-3162, E-mail: hellerst@uga.edu. *Application contact:* Dr. Catherine M. Jones, Graduate Coordinator, 706-542-3159, E-mail: cmjones@uga.edu.

University of Hawaii at Manoa, Graduate Division, College of Language, Linguistics and Literature, Department of Languages and Literatures of Europe and the Americas, Program in Spanish, Honolulu, HI 96822. Offers MA. Part-time programs available. *Faculty:* 2 full-time (1 woman), 4 part-time/adjunct (2 women). *Students:* 15 full-time (13 women); includes 10 minority (2 Asian Americans or Pacific Islanders, 8 Hispanic Americans). Average age 31. 8 applicants, 88% accepted, 6 enrolled. In 2009, 6 master's awarded. *Degree requirements:* For master's, one foreign language, thesis optional. *Entrance requirements:* For master's, GRE General Test. Additional exam requirements/recommendations for international students: Required—TOEFL (minimum score 580 paper-based; 237 computer-based; 92 iBT), IELTS (minimum score 5). *Application deadline:* For fall admission, 3/1 for domestic students, 2/1 for international students; for spring admission, 9/1 for domestic students, 8/15 for international students. Application fee: $60. *Expenses:* Tuition, state resident: full-time $8900; part-time $372 per credit. Tuition, nonresident: full-time $21,400; part-time $898 per credit. Required fees: $207 per semester. *Financial support:* In 2009–10, 1 student received support, including 3 fellowships (averaging $3,505 per year), 11 teaching assistantships (averaging $14,382 per year). *Application contact:* Robert Ball, Graduate Chair, 808-956-4187, Fax: 808-956-9536, E-mail: rball@hawaii.edu.

University of Houston, College of Liberal Arts and Social Sciences, Department of Modern and Classical Languages, Houston, TX 77204. Offers MA. *Degree requirements:* For master's, one foreign language, thesis optional. *Entrance requirements:* For master's, GRE General Test. Additional exam requirements/recommendations for international students: Required—TOEFL. *Expenses:* Tuition, state resident: full-time $7676; part-time $320 per credit hour. Tuition, nonresident: full-time $14,324; part-time $597 per credit hour. Required fees: $3034. *Financial support:* Career-related internships or fieldwork, Federal Work-Study, institutionally sponsored loans, scholarships/grants, health care benefits, and unspecified assistantships available. Support available to part-time students. Financial award applicants required to submit FAFSA. *Unit head:* Dr. Hildegard Glass, Chairperson, 713-743-8350, Fax: 713-743-2693, E-mail: hfglass@uh.edu. *Application contact:* Dr. Hildegard Glass, Chairperson, 713-743-8350, Fax: 713-743-2693, E-mail: hfglass@uh.edu.

University of Illinois at Chicago, Graduate College, College of Liberal Arts and Sciences, Department of Spanish, French, Italian and Portuguese, Program in Hispanic Studies, Chicago, IL 60607-7128. Offers Hispanic linguistics (MA, PhD); Hispanic literary and cultural studies (MA, PhD). Part-time programs available. Terminal master's awarded for partial completion of doctoral program. *Degree requirements:* For master's, one foreign language, departmental qualifying exam. *Entrance requirements:* For master's, GRE General Test, minimum GPA of 2.75, undergraduate major in Spanish. Additional exam requirements/recommendations for international students: Required—TOEFL. Electronic applications accepted.

University of Illinois at Urbana–Champaign, Graduate College, College of Liberal Arts and Sciences, School of Literatures, Cultures and Linguistics, Department of Spanish, Italian and Portuguese, Champaign, IL 61820. Offers Italian (MA, PhD); Portuguese (MA, PhD); Spanish (MA, PhD). *Faculty:* 18 full-time (11 women). *Students:* 46 full-time (35 women), 10 part-time (7 women); includes 15 minority (1 Asian American or Pacific Islander, 14 Hispanic Americans), 28 international. 46 applicants, 41% accepted, 12 enrolled. In 2009, 7 master's, 11 doctorates awarded. *Entrance requirements:* For master's, GRE General Test, minimum GPA of 3.0; writing sample; for doctorate, GRE, minimum GPA of 3.0; writing sample. Additional exam requirements/recommendations for international students: Required—TOEFL (minimum score 88 iBT). *Application deadline:* Applications are processed on a rolling basis. Application fee: $60 ($75 for international students). Electronic applications accepted. *Financial support:* In 2009–10, 10 fellowships, 3 research assistantships, 51 teaching assistantships were awarded; tuition waivers (full and partial) also available. *Unit head:* Diane Musumeci, Head, 217-333-3390, Fax: 217-244-8430, E-mail: musumeci@illinois.edu. *Application contact:* Lynn Stanke, Office Support Specialist, 217-333-6269, Fax: 217-244-3050, E-mail: stanke@illinois.edu.

The University of Iowa, Graduate College, College of Liberal Arts and Sciences, Department of Spanish and Portuguese, Iowa City, IA 52242-1316. Offers Spanish (MA, PhD). *Degree requirements:* For master's, thesis optional, exam; for doctorate, comprehensive exam, thesis/dissertation. *Entrance requirements:* For master's and doctorate, GRE General Test, minimum GPA of 3.0. Additional exam requirements/recommendations for international students: Required—TOEFL (minimum score 600 paper-based; 250 computer-based; 100 iBT). Electronic applications accepted.

The University of Kansas, Graduate Studies, College of Liberal Arts and Sciences, Department of Spanish and Portuguese, Lawrence, KS 66045. Offers Spanish (MA, PhD). *Faculty:* 16 full-time (8 women). *Students:* 36 full-time (20 women); includes 4 minority (all Hispanic Americans), 8 international. Average age 29. 36 applicants, 44% accepted, 11 enrolled. In 2009, 4 master's, 3 doctorates awarded. *Degree requirements:* For master's, 2 foreign languages; for doctorate, 3 foreign languages, thesis/dissertation. *Entrance requirements:* Additional exam requirements/recommendations for international students: Required—TOEFL. *Application deadline:* For fall admission, 5/15 priority date for domestic students, 12/15 priority date for international students; for spring admission, 10/15 priority date for domestic students, 5/15 priority date for international students. Applications are processed on a rolling basis. Application fee: $45 ($55 for international students). Electronic applications accepted. *Expenses:* Tuition, state resident: full-time $6492; part-time $270.50 per credit hour. Tuition, nonresident: full-time $15,510; part-time $646.25 per credit hour. Required fees: $847; $70.56 per credit hour. Tuition and fees vary according to course load and program. *Financial support:* Fellowships with tuition reimbursements, research assistantships, teaching assistantships with full and partial tuition reimbursements, unspecified assistantships available. Financial award application deadline: 1/15. *Faculty research:* Latin American literary and cultural studies; medieval, early modern and contemporary Spanish literary and cultural studies. *Unit head:* Dr. Jill Kuhnheim, Chair, 785-864-3851, Fax: 785-864-4298, E-mail: spanport@ku.edu. *Application contact:* Rhonda Cook, Graduate Coordinator, 785-864-3851, Fax: 785-864-4298, E-mail: rcook@ku.edu.

University of Lethbridge, School of Graduate Studies, Lethbridge, AB T1K 3M4, Canada. Offers accounting (MScM); addictions counseling (M Sc); agricultural biotechnology (M Sc); agricultural studies (M Sc, MA); anthropology (MA); archaeology (MA); art (MA, MFA); biochemistry (M Sc); biological sciences (M Sc); biomolecular science (PhD); biosystems and biodiversity (PhD); Canadian studies (MA); chemistry (M Sc); computer science (M Sc); computer science and geographical information science (M Sc); counseling psychology (M Ed); dramatic arts (MA); earth, space, and physical science (PhD); economics (MA); educational leadership (M Ed); English (MA); environmental science (M Sc); evolution and behavior (PhD); exercise science (M Sc); finance (MScM); French (MA); French/German (MA); French/Spanish (MA); general education (M Ed); general management (MScM); geography (M Sc, MA); German (MA); health science (M Sc); health sciences (MA); history (MA); human resource management and labour relations (MScM); individualized multidisciplinary (M Sc, MA); information systems (MScM); international management (MScM); kinesiology (M Sc, MA); management (M Sc, MA); marketing (MScM); mathematics (M Sc); music (M Mus, MA); Native American studies (MA); neuroscience (M Sc, PhD); new media (MA); nursing (M Sc); philosophy (MA); physics (M Sc); policy and strategy (MScM); political science (MA); psychology (M Sc, MA); religious studies (MA); social sciences (MA); sociology (MA); theatre and dramatic arts (MFA); theoretical and computational science (PhD); urban and regional studies (MA); women's studies (MA). Part-time and evening/weekend programs available. *Degree requirements:* For doctorate, comprehensive exam, thesis/dissertation. *Entrance requirements:* For master's, GMAT (M Sc in management), bachelor's degree in related field, minimum GPA of 3.0 during previous 20 graded semester courses, 2 years teaching or related experience (M Ed); for doctorate, master's degree, minimum graduate GPA of 3.5. Additional exam requirements/recommendations for international students: Required—TOEFL. *Faculty research:* Movement and brain plasticity, gibberellin physiology, photosynthesis, carbon cycling, molecular properties of main-group ring components.

University of Louisville, Graduate School, College of Arts and Sciences, Department of Classical and Modern Languages, Louisville, KY 40292-0001. Offers French (MA); Spanish (MA). *Faculty:* 14 full-time (8 women). *Students:* 13 full-time (9 women), 19 part-time (10 women); includes 7 minority (3 African Americans, 4 Hispanic Americans), 1 international. Average age 30. 18 applicants, 72% accepted, 8 enrolled. In 2009, 13 master's awarded. *Degree requirements:* For master's, one foreign language, thesis optional. *Entrance requirements:* For master's, GRE General Test. *Application deadline:* Applications are processed on a rolling basis. Application fee: $50. *Financial support:* In 2009–10, 9 students received support, including 8 teaching assistantships with full tuition reimbursements available (averaging $12,000 per year); fellowships also available. *Unit head:* Dr. Mary Makris, Acting Chair, 502-852-0491, Fax: 502-852-8885, E-mail: mmakris@louisville.edu. *Application contact:* Libby Leggett, Director, Graduate Admissions, 502-852-3101, Fax: 502-852-6536, E-mail: gradadm@louisville.edu.

University of Maryland, College Park, Academic Affairs, College of Arts and Humanities, School of Languages, Literature, and Cultures, Department of Spanish and Portuguese, College Park, MD 20742. Offers MA, PhD. *Students:* 31 full-time (25 women), 4 part-time (2 women); includes 7 minority (1 Asian American or Pacific Islander, 6 Hispanic Americans), 19 international. 51 applicants, 33% accepted, 8 enrolled. In 2009, 6 master's, 2 doctorates awarded. *Degree requirements:* For master's, comprehensive exam, thesis optional, scholarly paper; for doctorate, 2 foreign languages, thesis/dissertation. *Entrance requirements:* For master's, minimum GPA of 3.0, interview, sample research paper, minimum of 12 credits in upper-level literature, 3 letters of recommendation; for doctorate, minimum GPA of 3.0, interview, sample research paper, minimum of 12 credits in upper-level literature. Additional exam requirements/recommendations for international students: Required—TOEFL. *Application deadline:* For fall admission, 1/7 for domestic and international students. Applications are processed on a rolling basis. Application fee: $60. Electronic applications accepted. *Expenses:* Tuition, area resident: Part-time $471 per credit hour. Tuition, state resident: part-time $471 per credit hour. Tuition, nonresident: part-time $1016 per credit hour. Required fees: $337.04 per term. *Financial support:* In 2009–10, 4 fellowships with partial tuition reimbursements (averaging $8,873 per year), 20 teaching assistantships with tuition reimbursements (averaging $18,776 per year) were awarded; Federal Work-Study also available. Support available to part-time students. Financial award applicants required to submit FAFSA. *Unit head:* Carol Mossman, Director, School of Languages, Literatures, and Cultures, 301-405-4025, E-mail: cmossman@umd.edu. *Application contact:* Dean of Graduate School, 301-405-0358, Fax: 301-314-9305.

University of Maryland, College Park, Academic Affairs, College of Arts and Humanities, School of Languages, Literature, and Cultures, Program in Second Language Acquisition and Applicatión, College Park, MD 20742. Offers French (MA); German (MA); Japanese (MA); Russian (MA); second language instruction (PhD); second language learning (PhD); second language measurement and assessment (PhD); second language use (PhD); Spanish (MA). *Students:* 12 full-time (10 women), 5 part-time (3 women); includes 2 minority (both Asian Americans or Pacific Islanders), 5 international. 47 applicants, 15% accepted, 3 enrolled. In 2009, 7 master's awarded. *Entrance requirements:* For master's, BA or BS in related field, demonstrated language competency, 3 letters of reference. *Application deadline:* For fall admission, 1/15 for domestic and international students; for spring admission, 6/1 for domestic and international students. Applications are processed on a rolling basis. Application fee: $60. Electronic applications accepted. *Expenses:* Tuition, area resident: Part-time $471 per credit hour. Tuition, state resident: part-time $471 per credit hour. Tuition, nonresident: part-time $1016 per credit hour. Required fees: $337.04 per term. *Financial support:* In 2009–10, 2 fellowships with full and partial tuition reimbursements (averaging $13,928 per year), 4 research assistantships (averaging $21,457 per year), 6 teaching assistantships (averaging $20,933 per year) were awarded. *Faculty research:* Second language acquisition, pedagogical perspectives, technological applications, language use in professional contexts. *Unit head:* Carol Mossman, Director, School of Languages, Literatures, and Cultures, 301-405-4025, E-mail: cmossman@umd.edu. *Application contact:* Dean of Graduate School, 301-405-0376, Fax: 301-314-9305.

University of Massachusetts Amherst, Graduate School, College of Humanities and Fine Arts, Department of Languages, Literatures, and Cultures, Programs in Hispanic Literatures, Cultures and Linguistics, Amherst, MA 01003. Offers Hispanic literatures, cultures and linguistics (MA, PhD); teaching Spanish (MAT). Part-time programs available. *Faculty:* 11 full-time (5 women). *Students:* 22 full-time (18 women), 30 part-time (18 women); includes 14 minority (1 Asian American or Pacific Islander, 13 Hispanic Americans), 19 international. Average age 34. In 2009, 4 master's, 1 doctorate awarded. Terminal master's awarded for partial completion of doctoral program. *Degree requirements:* For master's, one foreign language, thesis or alternative; for doctorate, 2 foreign languages, comprehensive exam, thesis/dissertation. *Entrance requirements:* For master's and doctorate, GRE General Test, sample academic term paper. Additional exam requirements/recommendations for international students: Required—TOEFL (minimum score 550 paper-based; 213 computer-based; 80 iBT), IELTS (minimum score 6.5). *Application deadline:* For fall admission, 2/1 for domestic and international students. Applications are processed on a rolling basis. Application fee: $50 ($65 for international students). Electronic applications accepted. *Expenses:* Tuition, state resident: full-time $2640; part-time $110 per credit. Tuition, nonresident: full-time $9936; part-time $414 per credit. Tuition and fees vary according to course load. *Financial support:* In 2009–10, 36 teaching assistantships with full tuition reimbursements (averaging $14,427 per year) were awarded; fellowships, research assistantships, career-related internships or fieldwork, Federal Work-Study, scholarships/grants, traineeships, health care benefits, tuition waivers (full), and unspecified assistantships also available. Support available to part-time students. Financial award application deadline: 2/1. *Unit head:* Dr. Frank C. Fagundes, Graduate Program Director, 413-545-0544, Fax:

413-545-3178. *Application contact:* Jean M. Ames, Supervisor of Admissions, 413-545-0722, Fax: 413-577-0010, E-mail: gradadm@grad.umass.edu.

University of Memphis, Graduate School, College of Arts and Sciences, Department of Foreign Languages and Literatures, Memphis, TN 38152. Offers French (MA); Spanish (MA). Part-time programs available. *Faculty:* 12 full-time (5 women), 1 part-time/adjunct (0 women). *Students:* 14 full-time (10 women), 5 part-time (all women); includes 5 minority (2 African Americans, 1 American Indian/Alaska Native, 2 Hispanic Americans), 2 international. Average age 34. 12 applicants, 92% accepted, 5 enrolled. In 2009, 7 master's awarded. *Degree requirements:* For master's, 2 foreign languages, comprehensive exam. *Entrance requirements:* For master's, GRE, interview in language of concentration (French/Spanish). Additional exam requirements/recommendations for international students: Required—TOEFL (minimum score 79 iBT). *Application deadline:* For fall admission, 3/15 for domestic students, 2/15 for international students; for spring admission, 10/30 for domestic students, 10/5 for international students. Applications are processed on a rolling basis. Application fee: $35 ($60 for international students). Electronic applications accepted. *Expenses:* Tuition, state resident: full-time $6246; part-time $347 per credit hour. Tuition, nonresident: full-time $15,894; part-time $883 per credit hour. Required fees: $1160. Full-time tuition and fees vary according to course load, degree level and program. *Financial support:* In 2009–10, 11 students received support; research assistantships with full tuition reimbursements available, teaching assistantships with full tuition reimbursements available, Federal Work-Study, scholarships/grants, and unspecified assistantships available. Financial award application deadline: 2/15; financial award applicants required to submit FAFSA. *Faculty research:* Latin American studies, Brazilian culture and literature, Modernity and Postmodernity, Hispanic studies, French studies, French and Hispanic culture and literature, Hispanic linguistics, applied linguistics. *Unit head:* Dr. Ralph Albanese, Professor and Chair, 901-678-2507, E-mail: ralbanes@memphis.edu. *Application contact:* Dr. Fernando Burgos, Professor and Coordinator of Graduate Studies, 901-678-3158, E-mail: fburgos@memphis.edu.

University of Miami, Graduate School, College of Arts and Sciences, Department of Modern Languages and Literatures, Coral Gables, FL 33124. Offers romance studies (PhD), including French, Spanish. *Degree requirements:* For doctorate, 2 foreign languages, thesis/dissertation, area exam, qualifying exam. *Entrance requirements:* For doctorate, 1 writing sample in English and 1 writing sample in French or Spanish, minimum GPA of 3.0, oral interview, letters of recommendation. Additional exam requirements/recommendations for international students: Required—TOEFL (minimum score 550 paper-based; 213 computer-based; 59 iBT). Electronic applications accepted. *Faculty research:* Transatlantic studies, Caribbean studies, comparative literature, gender theory, cultural studies.

University of Miami, Graduate School, School of Communication, Coral Gables, FL 33124. Offers communication (PhD); communication studies (MA); film studies (MA, PhD); motion pictures (MFA), including production, producing, and screenwriting; print journalism (MA); public relations (MA); Spanish language journalism (MA); television broadcast journalism (MA). *Accreditation:* ACEJMC. Part-time programs available. *Degree requirements:* For master's, comprehensive exam (for some programs), thesis (for some programs); for doctorate, comprehensive exam, thesis/dissertation. *Entrance requirements:* For master's, GRE General Test; for doctorate, GRE General Test, master's thesis or scholarly research. Additional exam requirements/recommendations for international students: Required—TOEFL (minimum score 600 paper-based; 250 computer-based; 100 iBT). Electronic applications accepted. *Faculty research:* Communication studies, mass communication, international/interpersonal communication, film studies, journalism.

University of Michigan, Horace H. Rackham School of Graduate Studies, College of Literature, Science, and the Arts, Department of Romance Languages and Literatures, Program in Spanish, Ann Arbor, MI 48109. Offers PhD. *Faculty:* 17 full-time (6 women). *Students:* 42 full-time (23 women); includes 1 Asian American or Pacific Islander, 24 Hispanic Americans. Average age 30. 44 applicants, 25% accepted, 5 enrolled. In 2009, 1 doctorate awarded. *Degree requirements:* For doctorate, 2 foreign languages, thesis/dissertation, oral defense of dissertation, preliminary exams. *Entrance requirements:* For doctorate, GRE General Test. Additional exam requirements/recommendations for international students: Required—TOEFL or Michigan English Language Assessment Battery. *Application deadline:* For fall admission, 1/1 for domestic and international students. Application fee: $60. Electronic applications accepted. *Expenses:* Tuition, state resident: full-time $17,286; part-time $1099 per credit hour. Tuition, nonresident: full-time $34,944; part-time $2080 per credit hour. Required fees: $95 per semester. Tuition and fees vary according to course load, degree level and program. *Financial support:* In 2009–10, 16 students received support, including 6 fellowships with full tuition reimbursements available (averaging $20,000 per year), 31 teaching assistantships with full tuition reimbursements available (averaging $20,000 per year); institutionally sponsored loans, scholarships/grants, and unspecified assistantships also available. Financial award application deadline: 1/1. *Faculty research:* Comparative Romance studies, medieval and early modern studies, postcolonial and minority literatures, culture and materiality, reflection in the nature and function of scholarship. *Unit head:* Dr. Michele Hannoosh, Chair, 734-764-5344, Fax: 734-764-8163. *Application contact:* Annette Herbert, Graduate Assistant, 734-764-8164, Fax: 734-764-8163, E-mail: rll-admissions@umich.edu.

University of Minnesota, Twin Cities Campus, Graduate School, College of Liberal Arts, Department of Spanish and Portuguese Studies, Minneapolis, MN 55455-0213. Offers Hispanic and Lusophone literatures, cultures and linguistics (PhD); Hispanic linguistics (MA); Hispanic literature (MA); Lusophone literature (MA). *Faculty:* 12 full-time (6 women), 3 part-time/adjunct (2 women). *Students:* 48 full-time (32 women); includes 18 minority (3 African Americans, 15 Hispanic Americans). Average age 30. 44 applicants, 25% accepted, 6 enrolled. In 2009, 4 master's, 2 doctorates awarded. *Degree requirements:* For master's, 2 foreign languages, comprehensive exam, thesis or alternative; for doctorate, 2 foreign languages, comprehensive exam, thesis/dissertation. *Entrance requirements:* For master's and doctorate, GRE General Test, samples of written work, 3 letters of recommendation, voice sample, statement of purpose. Additional exam requirements/recommendations for international students: Required—TOEFL (minimum score 550 paper-based; 213 computer-based; 79 iBT). *Application deadline:* For fall admission, 1/5 for domestic and international students. Application fee: $55 ($75 for international students). Electronic applications accepted. *Financial support:* In 2009–10, 1 fellowship with full tuition reimbursement (averaging $22,500 per year), 2 research assistantships with full tuition reimbursements (averaging $14,442 per year), 27 teaching assistantships with full tuition reimbursements (averaging $14,442 per year) were awarded; career-related internships or fieldwork and Federal Work-Study also available. Financial award application deadline: 1/5. *Faculty research:* Sociohistorical approaches to literature and culture, feminist studies, literary theory, ideologies and literature, pragmatics and sociolinguistics. *Unit head:* Ana Paula Ferreira, Department Chair, 612-625-3834, Fax: 612-625-3549, E-mail: apferrei@umn.edu. *Application contact:* Nan Nelson, Student Services: Graduate Program Assistant, 612-626-7809, Fax: 612-625-3549, E-mail: nelso789@.umn.edu.

University of Mississippi, Graduate School, College of Liberal Arts, Department of Modern Languages, Oxford, University, MS 38677. Offers French (MA); German (MA); Spanish (MA). *Faculty:* 50 full-time (30 women). *Students:* 43 full-time (31 women), 16 part-time (11 women); includes 12 minority (7 African Americans, 5 Hispanic Americans), 11 international. In 2009, 12 master's awarded. *Degree requirements:* For master's, thesis (for some programs). *Entrance requirements:* For master's, GRE General Test, minimum GPA of 3.0. Additional exam requirements/recommendations for international students: Required—TOEFL. *Application deadline:* For fall admission, 2/1 for domestic students; for spring admission, 10/1 for domestic students. Applications are processed on a rolling basis. Application fee: $25. Electronic applications accepted. *Financial support:* Scholarships/grants available. Financial award application deadline: 3/1; financial award applicants required to submit FAFSA. *Unit head:* Dr. Donald L. Dyer, Chair, 662-915-7298, Fax: 662-915-1086, E-mail: mlangs@olemiss.edu. *Application contact:* Dr. Christy M. Wyandt, Associate Dean, 662-915-7474, Fax: 662-915-7577, E-mail: cwyandt@olemiss.edu.

University of Missouri, Graduate School, College of Arts and Sciences, Department of Romance Languages and Literature, Program in Spanish, Columbia, MO 65211. Offers MA, PhD. *Degree requirements:* For master's, one foreign language; for doctorate, 4 foreign languages, thesis/dissertation. *Entrance requirements:* For master's and doctorate, GRE General Test, minimum GPA of 3.0. Additional exam requirements/recommendations for international students: Required—TOEFL (minimum score 500 paper-based; 173 computer-based).

The University of Montana, Graduate School, College of Arts and Sciences, Department of Modern and Classical Languages and Literatures, Missoula, MT 59812-0002. Offers French (MA); German (MA); Spanish (MA). *Degree requirements:* For master's, one foreign language. *Entrance requirements:* For master's, GRE General Test. Additional exam requirements/recommendations for international students: Required—TOEFL.

University of Nebraska–Lincoln, Graduate College, College of Arts and Sciences, Department of Modern Languages and Literatures, Lincoln, NE 68588. Offers French (MA, PhD); German (MA, PhD); Spanish (MA, PhD). *Degree requirements:* For master's, thesis optional; for doctorate, comprehensive exam, thesis/dissertation. *Entrance requirements:* For master's and doctorate, writing sample in target language. Additional exam requirements/recommendations for international students: Required—TOEFL (minimum score 550 paper-based; 213 computer-based). Electronic applications accepted. *Faculty research:* French, German, and Spanish language, literature, and culture.

University of Nevada, Las Vegas, Graduate College, College of Liberal Arts, Department of Foreign Languages, Las Vegas, NV 89154-5047. Offers Hispanic studies (MA); Spanish translation (Certificate). Part-time programs available. *Faculty:* 5 full-time (4 women). *Students:* 2 full-time (both women), 10 part-time (6 women); includes 8 minority (1 Asian American or Pacific Islander, 7 Hispanic Americans). Average age 41. 8 applicants, 63% accepted, 3 enrolled. In 2009, 5 master's, 1 other advanced degree awarded. *Degree requirements:* For master's and Certificate, one foreign language, comprehensive exam. *Entrance requirements:* Additional exam requirements/recommendations for international students: Required—TOEFL (minimum score 550 paper-based; 213 computer-based; 80 iBT), IELTS (minimum score 7). *Application deadline:* For fall admission, 8/1 priority date for domestic students, 5/1 for international students; for spring admission, 12/1 priority date for domestic students, 10/1 for international students. Applications are processed on a rolling basis. Application fee: $60 ($95 for international students). Electronic applications accepted. *Financial support:* In 2009–10, 2 students received support, including 2 teaching assistantships with partial tuition reimbursements available (averaging $10,000 per year); institutionally sponsored loans, scholarships/grants, health care benefits, and unspecified assistantships also available. Financial award application deadline: 3/1. *Faculty research:* Second language acquisition/Romance languages, Old French, sociolinguistics/Romance languages, Spanish poetry of the twenties and thirties, post-Spanish Civil War women's fiction. *Unit head:* Dr. Ralph Buechler, Chair/Associate Professor, 702-895-3546, Fax: 702-895-3431, E-mail: ralph.buechler@unlv.edu. *Application contact:* Graduate College Admissions Evaluator, 702-895-3320, Fax: 702-895-4180, E-mail: gradcollege@unlv.edu.

University of Nevada, Reno, Graduate School, College of Liberal Arts, Department of Foreign Languages and Literatures, Reno, NV 89557. Offers French (MA); German (MA); Spanish (MA). *Degree requirements:* For master's, one foreign language, thesis optional. *Entrance requirements:* For master's, GRE General Test, minimum GPA of 2.75. Additional exam requirements/recommendations for international students: Required—TOEFL (minimum score 500 paper-based; 173 computer-based; 61 iBT), IELTS (minimum score 6). *Faculty research:* Thirteenth century mysticism, contemporary Spanish and Latin American poetry and theater, French interrelation between narration and photography, exile literature and Holocaust.

University of New Hampshire, Graduate School, College of Liberal Arts, Program in Spanish, Durham, NH 03824. Offers MA. *Faculty:* 9 full-time (6 women). *Students:* 6 full-time (all women), 12 part-time (10 women); includes 3 minority (all Hispanic Americans), 1 international. Average age 35. 7 applicants, 86% accepted, 4 enrolled. In 2009, 9 master's awarded. *Degree requirements:* For master's, one foreign language, thesis or alternative. *Entrance requirements:* Additional exam requirements/recommendations for international students: Required—TOEFL (minimum score 550 paper-based; 213 computer-based; 80 iBT). *Application deadline:* For fall admission, 6/1 priority date for domestic students, 4/1 for international students; for spring admission, 12/1 priority date for domestic students. Applications are processed on a rolling basis. Application fee: $65. Electronic applications accepted. *Expenses:* Tuition, state resident: full-time $10,380; part-time $577 per credit hour. Tuition, nonresident: full-time $24,350; part-time $1002 per credit hour. Required fees: $1550; $387.50 per semester. Tuition and fees vary according to course load and program. *Financial support:* In 2009–10, 4 students received support, including 4 teaching assistantships; fellowships, research assistantships, career-related internships or fieldwork, Federal Work-Study, scholarships/grants, and tuition waivers (full and partial) also available. Support available to part-time students. Financial award application deadline: 2/15. *Unit head:* Dr. Piero Garofalo, Chairperson, 603-862-4005. *Application contact:* Holly Harris, Administrative Assistant, 603-862-3121, E-mail: spanish.master@unh.edu.

University of New Mexico, Graduate School, College of Arts and Sciences, Department of Spanish and Portuguese, Albuquerque, NM 87131-2039. Offers Portuguese (MA); Spanish (MA); Spanish and Portuguese (PhD). Part-time programs available. *Faculty:* 11 full-time (9 women), 2 part-time/adjunct (0 women). *Students:* 53 full-time (40 women), 13 part-time (8 women); includes 32 minority (1 African American, 31 Hispanic Americans), 20 international. Average age 35. 47 applicants, 60% accepted, 18 enrolled. In 2009, 10 master's, 5 doctorates awarded. *Degree requirements:* For master's, one foreign language, comprehensive exam, thesis optional; for doctorate, one foreign language, comprehensive exam, thesis/dissertation. *Entrance requirements:* For master's, GRE, BA in Spanish or Portuguese, 3 letters of recommendation, letter of intent; for doctorate, GRE, 3 letters of recommendation, letter of intent, sample research paper. Additional exam requirements/recommendations for international students: Required—TOEFL (minimum score 550 paper-based; 213 computer-based). *Application deadline:* For fall admission, 1/15 priority date for domestic students; for spring admission, 11/15 for domestic students. Application fee: $50. Electronic applications accepted. *Expenses:* Tuition, state resident: full-time $2099; part-time $233.20 per credit hour. Tuition, nonresident: full-time $6650. Required fees: $25 per semester. Tuition and fees vary according to course load, program and reciprocity agreements. *Financial support:* In 2009–10, 30 students received support, including 30 teaching assistantships with full tuition reimbursements available (averaging $15,000 per year); Federal Work-Study, institutionally sponsored loans, scholarships/grants, health care benefits, tuition waivers (full), and unspecified assistantships also available. Support available to part-time students. Financial award application deadline: 3/1; financial award applicants required to submit FAFSA. *Faculty research:* Languages and literatures from the Iberian Peninsula, Latin America and the American Southwest. *Unit head:* Dr. Enrique Lamadrid, Chair, 505-277-5907, Fax: 505-277-3885, E-mail: lamadrid@unm.edu. *Application contact:* Martha Hurd, Graduate Administration Assistant, 505-277-2974, E-mail: marthah@unm.edu.

The University of North Carolina at Chapel Hill, Graduate School, College of Arts and Sciences, Department of Romance Languages, Chapel Hill, NC 27599. Offers French (MA, PhD); Italian (MA, PhD); Portuguese (MA, PhD); Romance languages (MA, PhD); Romance philology (MA, PhD); Spanish (MA, PhD). *Degree requirements:* For master's, one foreign language, comprehensive exam, thesis; for doctorate, 2 foreign languages, comprehensive exam, thesis/dissertation. *Entrance requirements:* For master's and doctorate, GRE General Test, minimum GPA of 3.0. Additional exam requirements/recommendations for international students: Required—TOEFL (minimum score 550 paper-based; 213 computer-based). Electronic applications accepted.

The University of North Carolina at Charlotte, Graduate School, College of Arts and Sciences, Department of Languages and Culture Studies, Charlotte, NC 28223-0001. Offers Latin American studies (MA); Spanish (MA). Part-time and evening/weekend programs available.

Spanish

The University of North Carolina at Charlotte (continued)
Faculty: 21 full-time (11 women). *Students:* 10 full-time (8 women), 12 part-time (10 women); includes 5 minority (2 African Americans, 3 Hispanic Americans). Average age 27. 15 applicants, 87% accepted, 9 enrolled. In 2009, 7 master's awarded. *Degree requirements:* For master's, thesis optional. *Entrance requirements:* For master's, GRE, 3 letters of reference, minimum GPA of 2.75. Additional exam requirements/recommendations for international students: Required—TOEFL (minimum score 557 paper-based; 220 computer-based; 83 iBT). *Application deadline:* For fall admission, 7/15 for domestic students, 5/1 for international students; for spring admission, 11/15 for domestic students, 10/1 for international students. Applications are processed on a rolling basis. Application fee: $55. Electronic applications accepted. *Financial support:* In 2009–10, 9 students received support, including 8 teaching assistantships (averaging $3,750 per year); career-related internships or fieldwork, Federal Work-Study, institutionally sponsored loans, scholarships/grants, and administrative assistantship also available. Support available to part-time students. Financial award application deadline: 4/1; financial award applicants required to submit FAFSA. *Faculty research:* Twentieth and twenty-first century Spanish literature, Central American literature, Caribbean literature, Mexican literature, literature of the Southern Cone. Total annual research expenditures: $53,920. *Unit head:* Robert L. Reimer, Chair, 704-687-8767, Fax: 704-687-3496, E-mail: rcreimer@uncc.edu. *Application contact:* Kathy B. Giddings, Director of Graduate Admissions, 704-687-5503, Fax: 704-687-3279, E-mail: gradadm@uncc.edu.

The University of North Carolina at Greensboro, Graduate School, College of Arts and Sciences, Department of Romance Languages, Program in Spanish, Greensboro, NC 27412-5001. Offers advanced Spanish language and Hispanic cultural studies (Certificate); Spanish (MA). *Degree requirements:* For master's, one foreign language, comprehensive exam, thesis or alternative. *Entrance requirements:* For master's, GRE General Test, 3-5 minute tape demonstrating foreign language proficiency, composition in Spanish, sample paper in English. Additional exam requirements/recommendations for international students: Required—TOEFL. Electronic applications accepted.

University of Northern Colorado, Graduate School, College of Humanities and Social Sciences, School of Modern Languages and Cultural Studies, Program in Foreign Languages, Greeley, CO 80639. Offers Spanish/teaching (MA). Part-time programs available. *Faculty:* 12 full-time (6 women). *Students:* 1 part-time (0 women), all international. Average age 50. 1 applicant, 100% accepted, 0 enrolled. In 2009, 4 master's awarded. *Degree requirements:* For master's, comprehensive exam, thesis or alternative. *Entrance requirements:* For master's, minimum undergraduate GPA of 3.0, BA in Spanish, 1 year of secondary teaching. *Application deadline:* Applications are processed on a rolling basis. Application fee: $50 ($60 for international students). Electronic applications accepted. *Expenses:* Tuition, state resident: full-time $5770; part-time $320.55 per credit hour. Tuition, nonresident: full-time $13,847; part-time $769.27 per credit hour. Required fees: $948.78; $52.72 per credit. *Financial support:* In 2009–10, 1 teaching assistantship (averaging $11,969 per year) was awarded; fellowships, research assistantships, unspecified assistantships also available. Financial award application deadline: 3/1; financial award applicants required to submit FAFSA. *Unit head:* Dr. Joy Landeira, Program Coordinator, 970-351-2221, Fax: 970-351-1571. *Application contact:* Linda Sisson, Graduate Student Admission Coordinator, 970-351-1807, Fax: 970-351-2371, E-mail: linda.sisson@unco.edu.

University of Northern Iowa, Graduate College, College of Humanities and Fine Arts, Department of Modern Languages, Program in Spanish, Cedar Falls, IA 50614. Offers Spanish (MA); teaching English to speakers of other languages/Spanish (MA). Part-time and evening/weekend programs available. *Students:* 6 full-time (4 women), 11 part-time (9 women); includes 2 minority (both Hispanic Americans), 3 international. 8 applicants, 63% accepted, 1 enrolled. In 2009, 10 master's awarded. *Degree requirements:* For master's, one foreign language, comprehensive exam, thesis or alternative. *Entrance requirements:* For master's, minimum GPA of 3.0, valid teaching license, documentation of successful teaching experience. Additional exam requirements/recommendations for international students: Required—TOEFL (minimum score 600 paper-based; 250 computer-based; 100 iBT). *Application deadline:* For fall admission, 8/1 priority date for domestic students. Applications are processed on a rolling basis. Application fee: $30 ($50 for international students). Electronic applications accepted. *Financial support:* Career-related internships or fieldwork, Federal Work-Study, and tuition waivers (full and partial) available. Support available to part-time students. Financial award application deadline: 2/1. *Unit head:* Dr. Samuel L. Gladden, Interim Department Head/Associate Professor, 319-273-5437, Fax: 319-273-2848, E-mail: samuel.gladden@uni.edu. *Application contact:* Laurie S. Russell, Record Analyst, 319-273-2623, Fax: 319-273-6792, E-mail: laurie.russell@uni.edu.

University of North Texas, Robert B. Toulouse School of Graduate Studies, College of Arts and Sciences, Department of Foreign Languages and Literatures, Denton, TX 76203. Offers French (MA); Spanish (MA). Part-time programs available. *Degree requirements:* For master's, 2 foreign languages, comprehensive exam, thesis optional. *Entrance requirements:* For master's, GRE General Test, minimum undergraduate GPA of 3.0, curriculum vitae, 250-word essay in French or Spanish, 12 advanced credits in French or Spanish. Additional exam requirements/recommendations for international students: Recommended—TOEFL (minimum score 550 paper-based; 213 computer-based; 79 iBT). Application fee: $50 ($75 for international students). *Expenses:* Tuition, state resident: full-time $4298; part-time $239 per contact hour. Tuition, nonresident: full-time $9878; part-time $549 per contact hour. Required fees: $265 per contact hour. *Financial support:* Fellowships, teaching assistantships, career-related internships or fieldwork, Federal Work-Study, and institutionally sponsored loans available. Financial award application deadline: 4/1; financial award applicants required to submit FAFSA. *Faculty research:* Literature of Austria, France, Germany, Latin America, Spain; culture/civilization; applied linguistics. *Unit head:* Chair. *Application contact:* Chair.

University of Notre Dame, Graduate School, College of Arts and Letters, Division of Humanities, Department of Romance Languages and Literatures, Notre Dame, IN 46556. Offers French and Francophone studies (MA); Iberian and Latin American studies (MA); Italian studies (MA); Romance literatures (MA). *Degree requirements:* For master's, 2 foreign languages, comprehensive exam, thesis optional. *Entrance requirements:* For master's, GRE General Test, BA in target language. Additional exam requirements/recommendations for international students: Required—TOEFL (minimum score 600 paper-based; 250 computer-based; 80 iBT). Electronic applications accepted. *Faculty research:* Literature of discovery and exploration, modern literature, literary criticism, medieval literature, feminist critical theory.

University of Oklahoma, Graduate College, College of Arts and Sciences, Department of Modern Languages, Program in Spanish, Norman, OK 73019. Offers MA, PhD, MBA/MA. Part-time programs available. *Students:* 18 full-time (11 women), 2 part-time (both women); includes 6 minority (all Hispanic Americans), 3 international. 10 applicants, 60% accepted, 4 enrolled. In 2009, 4 master's, 1 doctorate awarded. *Degree requirements:* For master's, one foreign language, comprehensive exam, thesis optional, departmental qualifying exam; for doctorate, 2 foreign languages, comprehensive exam, thesis/dissertation, departmental qualifying exam. *Entrance requirements:* For master's, BA in Spanish literature, minimum GPA of 3.0 in last 60 hours, 3 letters of recommendation; for doctorate, MA in Spanish, 3 letters of recommendation, minimum graduate GPA of 3.5. Additional exam requirements/recommendations for international students: Required—TOEFL (minimum score 550 paper-based; 213 computer-based). *Application deadline:* For fall admission, 4/1 for domestic and international students; for spring admission, 10/1 for domestic students, 9/1 for international students. Application fee: $40 ($90 for international students). Electronic applications accepted. *Expenses:* Tuition, state resident: full-time $3744; part-time $156 per credit hour. Tuition, nonresident: full-time $13,577; part-time $565.70 per credit hour. Required fees: $2415; $90.10 per credit hour. *Financial support:* In 2009–10, 19 students received support. Scholarships/grants, health care benefits, and unspecified assistantships available. Financial award applicants required to submit FAFSA. *Faculty research:* Spanish and Latin American literatures, twentieth century literature of Latin American social issues, women writers, medieval and early modern intellectual history, Golden Age drama. *Unit head:* Dr. Pamela Genova, Chairperson, 405-325-6181, Fax: 405-325-0103, E-mail: pgenova@ou.edu. *Application contact:* Dr. Logan E. Whalen, Graduate Liaison, 405-325-5088, Fax: 405-325-0103, E-mail: mlllgradinfo@ou.edu.

University of Oregon, Graduate School, College of Arts and Sciences, Department of Romance Languages, Program in Spanish, Eugene, OR 97403. Offers MA. Part-time programs available. *Degree requirements:* For master's, one foreign language. *Entrance requirements:* For master's, GRE General Test, minimum GPA of 3.0. Additional exam requirements/recommendations for international students: Required—TOEFL.

University of Ottawa, Faculty of Graduate and Postdoctoral Studies, Faculty of Arts, Department of Modern Languages and Literatures, Ottawa, ON K1N 6N5, Canada. Offers Spanish (MA, PhD). Part-time and evening/weekend programs available. *Degree requirements:* For master's, one foreign language, thesis or alternative; for doctorate, one foreign language, comprehensive exam, thesis/dissertation. *Entrance requirements:* For master's, BA with honors in Spanish, minimum B average; for doctorate, MA in Spanish or equivalent, minimum B average. Electronic applications accepted. *Faculty research:* Spanish American literature, Mexican literature and film studies, Spanish golden age literature, twentieth century Spanish literature, Hispanic linguistics with special emphasis on linguistic theory.

University of Pennsylvania, School of Arts and Sciences, Graduate Group in Romance Languages, Philadelphia, PA 19104. Offers French (AM, PhD); Italian (AM, PhD); Spanish (AM, PhD). *Faculty:* 60 full-time (24 women), 4 part-time/adjunct (1 woman). *Students:* 60 full-time (38 women), 2 part-time (both women); includes 7 minority (1 American Indian/Alaska Native, 6 Hispanic Americans), 17 international. 101 applicants, 26% accepted, 13 enrolled. In 2009, 12 master's, 7 doctorates awarded. Terminal master's awarded for partial completion of doctoral program. *Degree requirements:* For master's, one foreign language, thesis or alternative; for doctorate, 2 foreign languages, thesis/dissertation. *Entrance requirements:* For master's and doctorate, GRE General Test. Additional exam requirements/recommendations for international students: Required—TOEFL. *Application deadline:* For fall admission, 12/1 priority date for domestic students. Application fee: $70. Electronic applications accepted. *Expenses:* Tuition: Full-time $25,660; part-time $4758 per course. Required fees: $2152; $270 per course. Tuition and fees vary according to course load, degree level and program. *Financial support:* In 2009–10, 23 fellowships, 2 research assistantships, 39 teaching assistantships were awarded; institutionally sponsored loans, scholarships/grants, traineeships, health care benefits, and unspecified assistantships also available. Financial award application deadline: 12/15. *Faculty research:* Literary theory and criticism, cultural studies, history of Romance literatures, gender studies.

University of Pittsburgh, School of Arts and Sciences, Department of Hispanic Languages and Literatures, Pittsburgh, PA 15260. Offers MA, PhD. Part-time programs available. *Faculty:* 9 full-time (1 woman). *Students:* 39 full-time (22 women); includes 13 minority (2 African Americans, 2 Asian Americans or Pacific Islanders, 9 Hispanic Americans), 20 international. Average age 33. 82 applicants, 34% accepted, 8 enrolled. In 2009, 6 master's, 3 doctorates awarded. Terminal master's awarded for partial completion of doctoral program. *Degree requirements:* For master's, one foreign language, comprehensive exam (for some programs), thesis or alternative, research paper; for doctorate, 2 foreign languages, comprehensive exam, thesis/dissertation. *Entrance requirements:* Additional exam requirements/recommendations for international students: Required—TOEFL (minimum score 550 paper-based; 213 computer-based; 80 iBT). *Application deadline:* For fall admission, 1/15 priority date for domestic and international students. Application fee: $50. Electronic applications accepted. *Expenses:* Tuition, state resident: full-time $16,402; part-time $665 per credit. Tuition, nonresident: full-time $28,694; part-time $1175 per credit. Required fees: $690; $175 per term. Tuition and fees vary according to program. *Financial support:* In 2009–10, 35 students received support, including 7 fellowships with full tuition reimbursements available (averaging $17,927 per year), 26 teaching assistantships with full tuition reimbursements available (averaging $15,065 per year); scholarships/grants, health care benefits, and tuition waivers (partial) also available. Financial award application deadline: 1/15. *Faculty research:* Latin American, Luso-Brazilian, and peninsular literature; cultural theory; cultural studies; race, ethnicity, and post-colonial studies; gender and sexuality studies. *Unit head:* Dr. Elizabeth Monasterios, Chair, 412-624-5226, Fax: 412-624-8505, E-mail: elm15@pitt.edu. *Application contact:* Dr. Daniel Balderston, Director of Graduate Studies, 412-628-0279, Fax: 412-624-8505, E-mail: dbalder@pitt.edu.

University of Pittsburgh, School of Arts and Sciences, Program in Hispanic Linguistics, Pittsburgh, PA 15260. Offers MA, PhD. Part-time programs available. *Faculty:* 1 (woman) full-time, 1 (woman) part-time/adjunct. *Students:* 5 full-time (4 women); includes 1 minority (Hispanic American), 2 international. Average age 30. 6 applicants, 17% accepted, 1 enrolled. In 2009, 1 master's awarded. Terminal master's awarded for partial completion of doctoral program. *Degree requirements:* For master's, one foreign language, thesis; for doctorate, 2 foreign languages, comprehensive exam, thesis/dissertation. *Entrance requirements:* For master's, GRE General Test; for doctorate, GRE General Test, MA in linguistics. Additional exam requirements/recommendations for international students: Required—TOEFL (minimum score 600 paper-based; 250 computer-based). *Application deadline:* For fall admission, 12/15 for domestic and international students. Applications are processed on a rolling basis. Application fee: $50. Electronic applications accepted. *Expenses:* Tuition, state resident: full-time $16,402; part-time $665 per credit. Tuition, nonresident: full-time $28,694; part-time $1175 per credit. Required fees: $690; $175 per term. Tuition and fees vary according to program. *Financial support:* In 2009–10, 5 students received support, including 2 fellowships (averaging $15,675 per year), 3 teaching assistantships with tuition reimbursements available (averaging $15,065 per year); Federal Work-Study, scholarships/grants, health care benefits, and unspecified assistantships also available. Support available to part-time students. Financial award application deadline: 12/15. *Faculty research:* Hispanic linguistics. *Unit head:* Dr. Alan Juffs, Chair, 412-624-5900, Fax: 412-624-6130, E-mail: juffs@pitt.edu. *Application contact:* Patricia C. Cochran, Graduate Secretary, 412-624-5900, Fax: 412-624-6130, E-mail: lingpitt@pitt.edu.

University of Rhode Island, Graduate School, College of Arts and Sciences, Department of Modern and Classical Languages and Literatures, Kingston, RI 02881. Offers Spanish (MA). Part-time programs available. *Faculty:* 7 full-time (3 women). *Students:* 4 full-time (all women), 9 part-time (8 women); includes 4 minority (all Hispanic Americans), 1 international. In 2009, 4 master's awarded. *Degree requirements:* For master's, one foreign language, comprehensive exam, thesis optional. *Entrance requirements:* For master's, 2 letters of recommendation. Additional exam requirements/recommendations for international students: Required—TOEFL (minimum score 550 paper-based; 213 computer-based). *Application deadline:* For fall admission, 7/15 for domestic students, 2/1 for international students; for spring admission, 11/15 for domestic students, 7/15 for international students. Application fee: $65. Electronic applications accepted. *Expenses:* Tuition, state resident: full-time $8828; part-time $490 per credit hour. Tuition, nonresident: full-time $22,100; part-time $1228 per credit hour. Required fees: $1118; $57 per semester. Tuition and fees vary according to program. *Financial support:* In 2009–10, 3 teaching assistantships with full and partial tuition reimbursements (averaging $11,578 per year) were awarded. Financial award application deadline: 7/15; financial award applicants required to submit FAFSA. *Unit head:* Dr. Joseph Morello, Head, 401-874-4699, Fax: 401-874-4694, E-mail: morello@uri.edu. *Application contact:* Dr. Clement White, Director of Graduate Studies, 401-874-5472, Fax: 401-874-4694, E-mail: clement@uri.edu.

University of South Africa, College of Human Sciences, Pretoria, South Africa. Offers adult education (M Ed); African languages (MA, PhD); African politics (MA, PhD); Afrikaans (MA, PhD); ancient history (MA, PhD); ancient Near Eastern studies (MA, PhD); anthropology (MA, PhD); applied linguistics (MA); Arabic (MA, PhD); archaeology (MA); art history (MA); Biblical archaeology (MA); Biblical studies (M Th, D Th, PhD); Christian spirituality (M Th, D Th); church history (M Th, D Th); classical studies (MA, PhD); clinical psychology (MA); communication (MA, PhD); comparative education (M Ed, Ed D); consulting psychology (D Admin, D Com, PhD); curriculum studies (M Ed, Ed D); development studies (M Admin, MA, D Admin, PhD); didactics (M Ed, Ed D); education (M Tech); education management (M Ed, Ed D);

educational psychology (M Ed); English (MA); environmental education (M Ed); French (MA, PhD); German (MA, PhD); Greek (MA); guidance and counseling (M Ed); health studies (MA, PhD), including health sciences education (MA), health services management (MA), medical and surgical nursing science (critical care general) (MA), midwifery and neonatal nursing science (MA), trauma and emergency care (MA); history (MA, PhD); history of education (Ed D); inclusive education (M Ed, Ed D); information and communications technology policy and regulation (MA); information science (MA, MIS, PhD); international politics (MA, PhD); Islamic studies (MA, PhD); Italian (MA, PhD); Judaica (MA, PhD); linguistics (MA, PhD); mathematical education (M Ed); mathematics education (MA); missiology (M Th, D Th); modern Hebrew (MA, PhD); musicology (MA, MMus, D Mus, PhD); natural science education (M Ed); New Testament (M Th, D Th); Old Testament (D Th); pastoral therapy (M Th, D Th); philosophy (MA); philosophy of education (M Ed, Ed D); politics (MA, PhD); Portuguese (MA, PhD); practical theology (M Th, D Th); psychology (MA, MS, PhD); psychology of education (M Ed, Ed D); public health (MA); religious studies (MA, D Th, PhD); Romance languages (MA); Russian (MA, PhD); Semitic languages (MA, PhD); social behavior studies in HIV/AIDS (MA); social science (mental health) (MA); social science in development studies (MA); social science in psychology (MA); social science in social work (MA); social science in sociology (MA); social work (MSW, DSW, PhD); socio-education (M Ed, Ed D); sociolinguistics (MA); sociology (MA, PhD); Spanish (MA, PhD); systematic theology (M Th, D Th); TESOL (teaching English to speakers of other languages) (MA); theological ethics (M Th, D Th); theory of literature (MA, PhD); urban ministries (D Th); urban ministry (M Th).

University of South Carolina, The Graduate School, College of Arts and Sciences, Department of Languages, Literatures, and Cultures, Columbia, SC 29208. Offers comparative literature (MA, PhD); foreign languages (MAT), including French, German, Spanish; French (MA); German (MA); Spanish (MA). MAT offered in cooperation with the College of Education. Part-time programs available. *Degree requirements:* For master's, one foreign language, comprehensive exam, thesis optional; for doctorate, 2 foreign languages, comprehensive exam, thesis/dissertation. *Entrance requirements:* For master's and doctorate, GRE General Test, writing sample. Additional exam requirements/recommendations for international students: Required—TOEFL (minimum score 230 computer-based; 75 iBT). Electronic applications accepted. *Faculty research:* Modern literature, linguistics, literature and culture, medieval literature, literary theory.

University of South Florida, Graduate School, College of Arts and Sciences, World Languages Department, Tampa, FL 33620-9951. Offers classics: Latin/Greek (MA); French (MA); linguistics (MA); linguistics: ESL (MA); Spanish (MA). Part-time and evening/weekend programs available. *Faculty:* 19 full-time (14 women), 1 part-time/adjunct (0 women). *Students:* 36 full-time (26 women), 22 part-time (16 women); includes 23 minority (5 African Americans, 3 American Indian/Alaska Native, 2 Asian Americans or Pacific Islanders, 13 Hispanic Americans), 12 international. Average age 32. 29 applicants, 52% accepted, 12 enrolled. In 2009, 18 master's awarded. *Degree requirements:* For master's, comprehensive exam, thesis. *Entrance requirements:* For master's, GRE General Test, minimum GPA of 3.0 in last 60 hours. Additional exam requirements/recommendations for international students: Required—TOEFL (minimum score 600 paper-based; 250 computer-based). *Application deadline:* For fall admission, 2/15 for domestic students, 1/2 for international students; for spring admission, 10/15 for domestic students, 6/1 for international students. Application fee: $30. Electronic applications accepted. *Financial support:* In 2009–10, teaching assistantships with tuition reimbursements (averaging $17,024 per year); tuition waivers (partial) and unspecified assistantships also available. Financial award application deadline: 6/30. *Faculty research:* Second language writing, academic literacy. Total annual research expenditures: $19,891. *Unit head:* Dr. Victor Peppard, Chairperson, 813-974-2012, Fax: 813-974-1718, E-mail: peppard@.cas.usf.edu. *Application contact:* Dr. Victor Peppard, Chairperson, 813-974-2012, Fax: 813-974-1718, E-mail: peppard@.cas.usf.edu.

The University of Tennessee, Graduate School, College of Arts and Sciences, Department of Modern Foreign Languages and Literatures, Program in Modern Foreign Languages, Knoxville, TN 37996. Offers applied linguistics (PhD); French (PhD); German (PhD); Italian (PhD); Portuguese (PhD); Russian (PhD); Spanish (PhD). *Degree requirements:* For doctorate, 2 foreign languages, thesis/dissertation. *Entrance requirements:* For doctorate, minimum GPA of 2.7. Additional exam requirements/recommendations for international students: Required—TOEFL. Electronic applications accepted. *Expenses:* Tuition, state resident: full-time $6826; part-time $380 per semester hour. Tuition, nonresident: full-time $21,844; part-time $1147 per semester hour. Tuition and fees vary according to program.

The University of Tennessee, Graduate School, College of Arts and Sciences, Department of Modern Foreign Languages and Literatures, Program in Spanish, Knoxville, TN 37996. Offers MA. *Degree requirements:* For master's, one foreign language, thesis or alternative. *Entrance requirements:* For master's, minimum GPA of 2.7. Additional exam requirements/recommendations for international students: Required—TOEFL. Electronic applications accepted. *Expenses:* Tuition, state resident: full-time $6826; part-time $380 per semester hour. Tuition, nonresident: full-time $21,844; part-time $1147 per semester hour. Tuition and fees vary according to program.

The University of Texas at Arlington, Graduate School, College of Liberal Arts, Department of Modern Languages, Arlington, TX 76019. Offers French (MA); Spanish (MA). Part-time and evening/weekend programs available. *Degree requirements:* For master's, 2 foreign languages, comprehensive exam, thesis optional. *Entrance requirements:* For master's, GRE General Test, minimum GPA of 3.0, 3 letters of recommendation. Additional exam requirements/recommendations for international students: Required—TOEFL (minimum score 550 paper-based; 213 computer-based).

The University of Texas at Austin, Graduate School, College of Liberal Arts, Department of Spanish and Portuguese, Austin, TX 78712-1111. Offers Hispanic linguistics (MA, PhD); Hispanic literature (MA, PhD); Luso-Brazilian literature (MA, PhD). *Degree requirements:* For master's, 2 foreign languages, thesis or alternative; for doctorate, 3 foreign languages, thesis/dissertation. *Entrance requirements:* For master's and doctorate, GRE General Test. Electronic applications accepted.

The University of Texas at Brownsville, Graduate Studies, College of Liberal Arts, Department of Modern Languages, Brownsville, TX 78520-4991. Offers interdisciplinary studies (MAIS); Spanish (MA). Part-time and evening/weekend programs available. *Degree requirements:* For master's, comprehensive exam, thesis optional. *Entrance requirements:* For master's, GRE General Test, letters of recommendation, interview. Additional exam requirements/recommendations for international students: Required—TOEFL. *Faculty research:* Children's literature, Hispanic folklore, translation.

The University of Texas at El Paso, Graduate School, College of Liberal Arts, Department of Creative Writing, El Paso, TX 79968-0001. Offers creative writing (on-line) (MFA); creative writing in English (MFA); creative writing in Spanish (MFA). Part-time and evening/weekend programs available. Postbaccalaureate distance learning degree programs offered (no on-campus study). *Students:* 47 (25 women); includes 21 minority (1 African American, 20 Hispanic Americans), 13 international. Average age 34. In 2009, 7 master's awarded. *Degree requirements:* For master's, thesis. *Entrance requirements:* For master's, Minimum GPA of 3.0, Letters of Recommendation, Writing Sample. Additional exam requirements/recommendations for international students: Required—TOEFL; Recommended—IELTS. *Application deadline:* For fall admission, 8/1 priority date for domestic students, 3/1 for international students; for spring admission, 11/1 for domestic students, 9/1 for international students. Applications are processed on a rolling basis. Application fee: $45 ($80 for international students). Electronic applications accepted. *Financial support:* In 2009–10, research assistantships (averaging $18,625 per year), teaching assistantships with partial tuition reimbursements (averaging $14,900 per year) were awarded; fellowships with partial tuition reimbursements, institutionally sponsored loans, scholarships/grants, health care benefits, tuition waivers (partial), and unspecified assistantships also available. Support available to part-time students. Financial award application deadline: 3/15; financial award applicants required to submit FAFSA. *Unit head:* Dr. Johnny Payne, Chair, 915-747-5713, Fax: 915-747-5523, E-mail: jpayne@utep.edu. *Application contact:* Dr. Patricia D. Witherspoon, Dean of the Graduate School, 915-747-5491, Fax: 915-747-5788, E-mail: withersp@utep.edu.

The University of Texas at El Paso, Graduate School, College of Liberal Arts, Department of Languages and Linguistics, El Paso, TX 79968-0001. Offers linguistics (MA); Spanish (MA); teaching English to speakers of other languages (Certificate). Part-time and evening/weekend programs available. *Students:* 28 (12 women); includes 15 minority (all Hispanic Americans), 4 international. Average age 34. In 2009, 10 master's awarded. *Degree requirements:* For master's, thesis optional. *Entrance requirements:* For master's, GRE General Test, departmental exam, minimum GPA of 3.0, letters of recommendation. Additional exam requirements/recommendations for international students: Required—TOEFL; Recommended—IELTS. *Application deadline:* For fall admission, 8/1 for domestic students, 3/1 for international students; for spring admission, 11/1 for domestic students, 9/1 for international students. Applications are processed on a rolling basis. Application fee: $45 ($80 for international students). Electronic applications accepted. *Financial support:* In 2009–10, research assistantships with partial tuition reimbursements (averaging $18,625 per year), teaching assistantships with partial tuition reimbursements (averaging $14,900 per year) were awarded; fellowships with partial tuition reimbursements, institutionally sponsored loans, scholarships/grants, health care benefits, tuition waivers (partial), and unspecified assistantships also available. Support available to part-time students. Financial award application deadline: 3/15; financial award applicants required to submit FAFSA. *Unit head:* Dr. Kirsten F. Nigro, Chair, 915-747-5767, Fax: 915-747-5292, E-mail: kfnigro@utep.edu. *Application contact:* Dr. Patricia D. Witherspoon, Dean of the Graduate School, 915-747-5491, Fax: 915-747-5788, E-mail: withersp@utep.edu.

The University of Texas at San Antonio, College of Liberal and Fine Arts, Department of Modern Languages and Literatures, San Antonio, TX 78249-0617. Offers Spanish (MA). Part-time and evening/weekend programs available. *Faculty:* 4 full-time (1 woman), 1 (woman) part-time/adjunct. *Students:* 8 full-time (7 women), 27 part-time (23 women); includes 32 minority (2 African Americans, 30 Hispanic Americans). Average age 37. 18 applicants, 78% accepted, 8 enrolled. In 2009, 7 master's awarded. *Degree requirements:* For master's, one foreign language, comprehensive exam (for some programs), thesis (for some programs). *Entrance requirements:* For master's, GRE, minimum GPA of 3.0, sample of written and spoken work. Additional exam requirements/recommendations for international students: Required—TOEFL (minimum score 500 paper-based; 173 computer-based; 61 iBT), IELTS (minimum score 5). *Application deadline:* For fall admission, 7/1 for domestic students, 4/1 for international students; for spring admission, 11/1 for domestic students, 9/1 for international students. Applications are processed on a rolling basis. Application fee: $45 ($80 for international students). Electronic applications accepted. *Expenses:* Tuition, state resident: full-time $3975; part-time $221 per contact hour. Tuition, nonresident: full-time $13,947; part-time $775 per contact hour. Required fees: $1853. *Financial support:* In 2009–10, 14 students received support, including 1 research assistantship (averaging $7,904 per year), 6 teaching assistantships (averaging $4,655 per year); career-related internships or fieldwork, institutionally sponsored loans, scholarships/grants, tuition waivers, and unspecified assistantships also available. Support available to part-time students. *Unit head:* Dr. Ritva M. Nummikoski, Chair, 210-458-4373, Fax: 210-458-5672, E-mail: mnummikoski@utsa.edu. *Application contact:* Santiago Daydi-Tolson, Graduate Advisor, 210-458-5186, E-mail: santiago.dayditolson@utsa.edu.

The University of Texas of the Permian Basin, Office of Graduate Studies, College of Arts and Sciences, Department of Literature and Languages, Odessa, TX 79762-0001. Offers English (MA); Spanish (MA). *Degree requirements:* For master's, comprehensive exam (for some programs), thesis (for some programs). *Entrance requirements:* For master's, GRE General Test. Additional exam requirements/recommendations for international students: Required—TOEFL (minimum score 550 paper-based; 213 computer-based).

The University of Texas–Pan American, College of Arts and Humanities, Department of Modern Languages and Literatures, Edinburg, TX 78539. Offers Spanish (MA). Part-time programs available. *Degree requirements:* For master's, comprehensive exam, thesis or alternative. *Entrance requirements:* For master's, GRE General Test, minimum GPA of 3.0. *Expenses:* Tuition, state resident: full-time $3630.60; part-time $201.70 per credit hour. Tuition, nonresident: full-time $8617; part-time $478.70 per credit hour. Required fees: $806.50. *Faculty research:* Latin American literature, women's literature, Caribbean literature, Latina/o studies, sociolinguistics, applied linguistics, creative writing.

The University of Toledo, College of Graduate Studies, College of Arts and Sciences, Department of Foreign Languages, Toledo, OH 43606-3390. Offers French (MA); German (MA); Spanish (MA). Part-time programs available. *Degree requirements:* For master's, one foreign language, comprehensive reading exam in 1 additional foreign language. Electronic applications accepted.

University of Toronto, School of Graduate Studies, Humanities Division, Department of Spanish and Portuguese, Toronto, ON M5S 1A1, Canada. Offers MA, PhD. Part-time programs available. *Degree requirements:* For doctorate, thesis/dissertation. *Entrance requirements:* For master's, minimum B average in final year, 2 letters of reference; for doctorate, minimum A– average, 2 letters of reference, writing sample. Additional exam requirements/recommendations for international students: Required—TOEFL, Michigan English Language Assessment Battery, IELTS or COPE.

University of Utah, The Graduate School, College of Humanities, Department of Languages and Literature, Salt Lake City, UT 84112-1107. Offers comparative literary and cultural studies (MA, PhD); French (MA, MALP); German (MA, MALP, PhD); Spanish (MA, MALP, PhD); world languages with secondary teaching licensure (MA). *Faculty:* 35 full-time (22 women), 1 part-time/adjunct (0 women). *Students:* 30 full-time (20 women), 10 part-time (9 women); includes 8 minority (1 American Indian/Alaska Native, 2 Asian Americans or Pacific Islanders, 5 Hispanic Americans), 6 international. Average age 35. 47 applicants, 40% accepted, 18 enrolled. In 2009, 7 master's, 3 doctorates awarded. Terminal master's awarded for partial completion of doctoral program. *Degree requirements:* For master's, 2 foreign languages, comprehensive exam, thesis, standard proficiency in 2 languages other than English; for doctorate, 3 foreign languages, comprehensive exam, thesis/dissertation, standard proficiency in 2 languages other than English and language of study, advanced proficiency in 1 language other than English and language of study. *Entrance requirements:* For master's, bachelor's degree or strong undergraduate record in target languages, minimum GPA of 3.0; for doctorate, GRE, MA, advanced proficiency in a target language. Additional exam requirements/recommendations for international students: Required—TOEFL (minimum score 500 paper-based; 173 computer-based). *Application deadline:* For fall admission, 1/15 priority date for domestic students, 12/15 priority date for international students. Application fee: $55 ($65 for international students). *Expenses:* Tuition, state resident: full-time $4004; part-time $1674 per semester. Tuition, nonresident: full-time $14,134; part-time $5915 per semester. Required fees: $324 per semester. Tuition and fees vary according to course load, degree level and program. *Financial support:* In 2009–10, 21 students received support, including 21 teaching assistantships with full tuition reimbursements available (averaging $11,000 per year); health care benefits also available. Financial award application deadline: 2/1; financial award applicants required to submit FAFSA. *Faculty research:* Literary theory, linguistics, cultural studies, comparative studies. Total annual research expenditures: $22,986. *Unit head:* Dr. Christine A. Jones, Director of Graduate Studies, 801-585-3002, Fax: 801-581-7581, E-mail: cjones@hum.utah.edu. *Application contact:* Virginia Ellinwood, Academic Advisor, 801-585-9437, Fax: 801-581-7581, E-mail: v.ellinwood@mail.hum.utah.edu.

University of Virginia, College and Graduate School of Arts and Sciences, Department of Spanish, Italian and Portuguese, Program in Spanish, Charlottesville, VA 22903. Offers MA, PhD. *Students:* 47 full-time (35 women), 6 part-time (5 women); includes 9 minority (1 Asian American or Pacific Islander, 8 Hispanic Americans), 6 international. Average age 28. 48

Spanish

University of Virginia (continued)
applicants, 38% accepted, 12 enrolled. In 2009, 8 master's, 7 doctorates awarded. *Degree requirements:* For master's, one foreign language, comprehensive exam, thesis; for doctorate, 2 foreign languages, comprehensive exam, thesis/dissertation. *Entrance requirements:* For master's, GRE General Test, GRE Subject Test, 2 letters of recommendation; for doctorate, GRE General Test, GRE Subject Test, 2 letters of recommendation, writing sample. Additional exam requirements/recommendations for international students: Required—TOEFL (minimum score 600 paper-based; 250 computer-based; 90 iBT), IELTS (minimum score 7). *Application deadline:* For fall admission, 12/1 for domestic and international students. Applications are processed on a rolling basis. Application fee: $60. Electronic applications accepted. *Financial support:* Fellowships, teaching assistantships available. Financial award applicants required to submit FAFSA. *Application contact:* David Gies, Director of Graduate Studies, 434-924-7159, Fax: 434-924-7160, E-mail: sipinfo@virginia.edu.

University of Washington, Graduate School, College of Arts and Sciences, Department of Romance Languages and Literature, Division of Spanish and Portuguese Studies, Seattle, WA 98195. Offers Hispanic literary and cultural studies (MA). *Degree requirements:* For master's, 2 foreign languages, thesis optional, exam. *Entrance requirements:* For master's, GRE General Test, minimum GPA of 3.0. Additional exam requirements/recommendations for international students: Required—TOEFL. Electronic applications accepted. *Faculty research:* Medieval through modern Spanish literature and film, Latin American literature, poetry and essay, pan-Hispanic ballad, Hispanic cultural studies, second language acquisition and applied linguistics.

The University of Western Ontario, Faculty of Graduate Studies, Faculty of Arts and Humanities, Department of Comparative Literature, London, ON N6A 5B8, Canada. Offers comparative literature (MA, PhD); Spanish (MA). Part-time programs available. *Degree requirements:* For master's, 2 foreign languages, thesis (for some programs). *Entrance requirements:* For master's, honors degree in Spanish or equivalent, minimum B average. Additional exam requirements/recommendations for international students: Required—TOEFL, TOEFL (comparative literature). *Faculty research:* Spanish golden age, Latin-American, romance, medieval, film.

University of Wisconsin–Madison, Graduate School, College of Letters and Science, Department of Spanish and Portuguese, Program in Spanish, Madison, WI 53706-1380. Offers MA, PhD. *Degree requirements:* For master's, one foreign language; for doctorate, 2 foreign languages, thesis/dissertation. *Entrance requirements:* For master's, GRE (recommended), minimum GPA of 3.25 in Spanish or Portuguese; for doctorate, GRE (recommended), minimum graduate GPA of 3.4, writing sample. Additional exam requirements/recommendations for international students: Required—TOEFL. Electronic applications accepted. *Expenses:* Tuition, state resident: part-time $594 per credit. Tuition, nonresident: part-time $1504 per credit. Required fees: $65 per credit. Tuition and fees vary according to course load, program and reciprocity agreements. *Faculty research:* Hispanic linguistics, Spanish and Spanish-American literature.

University of Wisconsin–Milwaukee, Graduate School, College of Letters and Sciences, Department of Spanish, Milwaukee, WI 53201-0413. Offers Spanish (MA); translation (Certificate). *Faculty:* 7 full-time (3 women). *Students:* Average age 29. 13 applicants, 85% accepted, 3 enrolled. In 2009, 1 master's awarded. *Entrance requirements:* For master's, bachelor's degree. *Expenses:* Tuition, state resident: full-time $8800. Tuition, nonresident: full-time $20,760. Tuition and fees vary according to program and reciprocity agreements. *Financial support:* In 2009–10, 18 teaching assistantships were awarded. *Faculty research:* Sociolinguistics, Spanish American literature, Spanish literature, Hispanic culture, Hispanic historiography. Total annual research expenditures: $4,590. *Unit head:* Jeffrey Oxford, Chair, 414-229-4257, E-mail: oxford@uwm.edu. *Application contact:* General Information Contact, 414-229-4982, Fax: 414-229-6967, E-mail: gradschool@uwm.edu.

University of Wyoming, College of Arts and Sciences, Department of Modern and Classical Languages, Program in Spanish, Laramie, WY 82070. Offers MA. Part-time programs available. *Degree requirements:* For master's, one foreign language, thesis or alternative. *Entrance requirements:* For master's, GRE General Test, minimum GPA of 3.0. *Faculty research:* Peninsular literature, Latin American literature, theatre, science and literature, linguistics.

Vanderbilt University, Graduate School, Department of Spanish and Portuguese, Nashville, TN 37240-1001. Offers Portuguese (MA); Spanish (MA, MAT, PhD); Spanish and Portuguese (PhD). *Faculty:* 14 full-time (6 women). *Students:* 30 full-time (16 women), 1 part-time (0 women); includes 3 minority (1 African American, 1 American Indian/Alaska Native, 1 Hispanic American), 13 international. Average age 31. 66 applicants, 12% accepted, 7 enrolled. In 2009, 4 doctorates awarded. *Degree requirements:* For master's, one foreign language, thesis; for doctorate, 2 foreign languages, thesis/dissertation, final and qualifying exams. *Entrance requirements:* For master's, GRE General Test; for doctorate, GRE General Test, writing sample in Spanish. Additional exam requirements/recommendations for international students: Required—TOEFL (minimum score 570 paper-based; 230 computer-based; 88 iBT). *Application deadline:* For fall admission, 1/15 for domestic and international students. Application fee: $0. Electronic applications accepted. *Financial support:* Fellowships with full and partial tuition reimbursements, teaching assistantships with full tuition reimbursements, Federal Work-Study, institutionally sponsored loans, and health care benefits available. Financial award application deadline: 1/15; financial award applicants required to submit CSS PROFILE or FAFSA. *Faculty research:* Spanish, Portuguese, and Latin American literatures; foreign language pedagogy; Renaissance and Baroque poetry; nineteenth century Spanish novel. *Unit head:* Cathy L. Jrade, Chair, 615-322-6930, Fax: 615-343-7260, E-mail: cathy.l.jrade@vanderbilt.edu. *Application contact:* Christina Karageorgou-Bastea, Director of Graduate Studies, 615-322-6930, Fax: 615-343-7260, E-mail: christina.karageorgou@vanderbilt.edu.

Washington State University, Graduate School, College of Liberal Arts, Department of Foreign Languages and Cultures, Pullman, WA 99164. Offers foreign languages with emphasis in Spanish (MA). *Faculty:* 7. *Students:* 11 full-time (7 women); includes 4 minority (all Hispanic Americans), 2 international. Average age 28. 21 applicants, 48% accepted, 4 enrolled. In 2009, 3 master's awarded. *Degree requirements:* For master's, comprehensive exam (for some programs), thesis (for some programs), 4 written exams, oral exam, master's paper. *Entrance requirements:* For master's, Graduate School application, three current letters of recommendation,all original transcripts including an official English translation, TOEFL Exam Score, two writing samples, letter of application stating qualifications and personal goals, brief (3-5 min.) tape recordings of two informal dialogues between yourself and a native speaker. Additional exam requirements/recommendations for international students: Required—TOEFL (minimum score 550 paper-based). *Application deadline:* For fall admission, 1/1 priority date for domestic and international students; for spring admission, 7/1 priority date for domestic students, 7/1 for international students. Application fee: $50. Electronic applications accepted. *Financial support:* In 2009–10, fellowships (averaging $2,200 per year), teaching assistantships with full and partial tuition reimbursements (averaging $13,056 per year) were awarded; career-related internships or fieldwork, Federal Work-Study, institutionally sponsored loans, scholarships/grants, and health care benefits also available. Financial award application deadline: 2/15; financial award applicants required to submit FAFSA. *Faculty research:* Spanish and Latin American literature, film, and culture; pedagogy; computer-aided instruction. Total annual research expenditures: $98,000. *Unit head:* Dr. Eloy Gonzalez, Chair, 509-335-2756, Fax: 509-335-3708, E-mail: eloygonz@wsunix.wsu.edu. *Application contact:* Graduate School Admissions, 800-GRADWSU, Fax: 509-335-1949, E-mail: gradsch@wsu.edu.

Washington University in St. Louis, Graduate School of Arts and Sciences, Department of Romance Languages and Literatures, Program in Spanish, St. Louis, MO 63130-4899. Offers MA, PhD. Terminal master's awarded for partial completion of doctoral program. *Degree requirements:* For master's, thesis or alternative; for doctorate, thesis/dissertation. *Entrance requirements:* For master's and doctorate, GRE General Test. Electronic applications accepted.

Wayne State University, College of Liberal Arts and Sciences, Department of Classical and Modern Languages, Literatures, and Cultures, Program in Spanish, Detroit, MI 48202. Offers MA. *Degree requirements:* For master's, one foreign language, thesis optional. *Entrance requirements:* For master's, GRE General Test, minimum GPA of 3.0. Additional exam requirements/recommendations for international students: Required—TOEFL (minimum score 550 paper-based; 213 computer-based); Recommended—TWE (minimum score 6). Electronic applications accepted. *Faculty research:* Drama of the Golden Age, eighteenth century humanism, Romanticism, twentieth century essay.

West Chester University of Pennsylvania, Office of Graduate Studies, College of Arts and Sciences, Department of Languages and Cultures, West Chester, PA 19383. Offers French (M Ed, MA, Teaching Certificate); German (M Ed, Teaching Certificate); Latin (M Ed, Teaching Certificate); Spanish (M Ed, MA, Teaching Certificate). Part-time and evening/weekend programs available. *Students:* 4 full-time (all women), 27 part-time (21 women); includes 6 minority (2 African Americans, 1 Asian American or Pacific Islander, 3 Hispanic Americans). Average age 33. 16 applicants, 94% accepted, 9 enrolled. In 2009, 7 master's awarded. *Degree requirements:* For master's, one foreign language, comprehensive exam, thesis optional. *Entrance requirements:* For master's, GRE or MAT, placement test. Additional exam requirements/recommendations for international students: Required—TOEFL (minimum score 550 paper-based; 213 computer-based; 80 iBT). *Application deadline:* For fall admission, 4/15 priority date for domestic students, 3/15 for international students; for spring admission, 10/15 for domestic students, 9/1 for international students. Applications are processed on a rolling basis. Application fee: $35. Electronic applications accepted. *Expenses:* Tuition, state resident: full-time $6666; part-time $370 per credit. Tuition, nonresident: full-time $10,666; part-time $593 per credit. Required fees: $122.56 per credit. *Financial support:* In 2009–10, 1 research assistantship with full and partial tuition reimbursement (averaging $5,000 per year) was awarded; unspecified assistantships also available. Support available to part-time students. Financial award application deadline: 2/15; financial award applicants required to submit FAFSA. *Faculty research:* Implementation of world languages curriculum framework. *Unit head:* Dr. Jerry Williams, Chair, 610-436-2700, Fax: 610-436-3048, E-mail: jwilliams2@wcupa.edu. *Application contact:* Dr. Rebecca Pauly, Graduate Coordinator, 610-436-2382, E-mail: rpauly@wcupa.edu.

Western Michigan University, Graduate College, College of Arts and Sciences, Department of Foreign Languages and Literatures, Kalamazoo, MI 49008. Offers Spanish (MA, PhD). *Degree requirements:* For master's, oral exam.

West Virginia University, Eberly College of Arts and Sciences, Department of Foreign Languages, Morgantown, WV 26506. Offers French (MA); linguistics (MA); Spanish (MA); teaching English to speakers of other languages (MA). Part-time programs available. *Degree requirements:* For master's, one foreign language, comprehensive exam (for some programs), thesis optional. *Entrance requirements:* For master's, minimum GPA of 3.0. Electronic applications accepted. *Faculty research:* French, German, and Spanish literature; foreign language pedagogy; English as a second language; cultural studies; linguistics.

Wichita State University, Graduate School, Fairmount College of Liberal Arts and Sciences, Department of Modern and Classical Languages and Literatures, Wichita, KS 67260. Offers Spanish (MA). Part-time programs available. *Expenses:* Tuition, state resident: full-time $4247; part-time $235.95 per credit hour. Tuition, nonresident: full-time $11,171; part-time $620.60 per credit hour. Required fees: $34; $3.60 per credit hour. $17 per term. Tuition and fees vary according to campus/location and program. *Unit head:* Dr. Wilson Baldridge, Chair, 316-978-3180, Fax: 316-978-3293, E-mail: wilson.baldridge@wichita.edu. *Application contact:* Dr. Wilson Baldridge, Chair, 316-978-3180, Fax: 316-978-3293, E-mail: wilson.baldridge@wichita.edu.

Winthrop University, College of Arts and Sciences, Program in Spanish, Rock Hill, SC 29733. Offers MA. Part-time programs available. *Entrance requirements:* For master's, GRE General Test and PRAXIS, minimum GPA of 3.0, 24 hours of undergraduate Spanish, or interview. Electronic applications accepted.

Worcester State College, Graduate Studies, Program in Spanish, Worcester, MA 01602-2597. Offers M Ed. Part-time programs available. *Faculty:* 3 full-time (2 women). *Students:* 11 part-time (9 women); includes 1 minority (Hispanic American). Average age 32. 9 applicants, 100% accepted, 0 enrolled. In 2009, 1 master's awarded. *Degree requirements:* For master's, comprehensive exam (for some programs), thesis optional. *Entrance requirements:* Additional exam requirements/recommendations for international students: Required—TOEFL (minimum score 550 paper-based; 213 computer-based; 79 iBT). *Application deadline:* Applications are processed on a rolling basis. Application fee: $30. *Expenses:* Tuition, area resident: Part-time $150 per credit. Tuition, state resident: part-time $150 per credit. Tuition, nonresident: part-time $150 per credit. Required fees: $85. *Financial support:* Career-related internships or fieldwork, scholarships/grants, and unspecified assistantships available. Financial award application deadline: 3/1; financial award applicants required to submit FAFSA. *Unit head:* Dr. Juan Orbe, Head, 508-929-8704, Fax: 508-929-8174, E-mail: jorbe@worcester.edu. *Application contact:* Nicole Brown, Assistant Dean of Graduate and Continuing Education, 508-929-8787, Fax: 508-929-8100, E-mail: nbrown@worcester.edu.

Yale University, Graduate School of Arts and Sciences, Department of Spanish and Portuguese, New Haven, CT 06520. Offers Latin American literature (PhD); Luso-Brazilian and Spanish/Spanish American literatures (PhD); Spanish peninsular literature (PhD). Terminal master's awarded for partial completion of doctoral program. *Degree requirements:* For doctorate, 3 foreign languages, thesis/dissertation. *Entrance requirements:* For doctorate, GRE General Test.

AUBURN UNIVERSITY

College of Liberal Arts
Department of English

Programs of Study

Programs of study in the Department of English at Auburn University lead to the Master of Arts (M.A.), the Master of Technical and Professional Communication (M.T.P.C.), and the Doctorate (Ph.D.) degrees. There is also a non-degree option. The Department offers a wide range of courses in American, British, and comparative literatures; literary theory; creative writing; linguistics; rhetoric and composition; and technical and professional communication. The Department seeks to enroll 6 to 8 new Ph.D. students and 12 to 15 new master's level students each year. More than 70 students are currently enrolled in the graduate programs, about half of whom are Ph.D. students.

Functioning both as a terminal degree and as preparation for doctoral study, the master's degree in English at Auburn is designed to develop and professionalize students within a subdiscipline in English studies and to bring their writing and research skills to an advanced level while providing them with experience as university-level teachers. Minimum requirements are ten courses. Students must also demonstrate reading ability in a foreign language. Students can focus course work in any of the above listed areas or combine courses from several areas to create an individualized program of study. Two courses from another department may be approved as a minor within this degree program. In addition to course work, students must pass an oral exit examination based on a portfolio of selected course papers.

The M.T.P.C. prepares students for careers as professional writers, technical editors and communicators, and teachers of technical and professional communication, as well as for doctoral work-study. Students take four required courses, three electives in English, and three courses in a coordinated minor field. Students must also pass a comprehensive exam and submit a portfolio of work.

Auburn's Ph.D. program ranks ninth nationally among low-cost schools with low student-faculty ratios and high graduate placement rates in the online Guide to Graduate Programs (sponsored by the Alfred P. Sloan Foundation and the Burroughs Wellcome Fund). The program prepares students to become scholars and to teach in higher education. It requires a minimum of sixteen courses beyond the B.A. or seven courses beyond the M.A. Working in consultation with their advisory committees, doctoral students balance broad preparation with the development of three specialized areas for their written and oral examinations. These areas include topics in literature (e.g., major authors, literary genres and periods, critical theory) and language (e.g., composition, linguistics, stylistics, rhetoric). Doctoral students must demonstrate a reading knowledge of two or extensive knowledge of one foreign language. The Ph.D. program requires candidates to write and defend a dissertation.

Research Facilities

The University and the English Department offer graduate students ready access to current technologies. Draughon Library, a member of the Association of Research Libraries, is a leader in computer-assisted research tools and facilities. It houses nearly 3 million volumes and has nearly 3 million items on microform, including full and current collections in English studies. Additionally, the library receives over 35,000 current periodicals, many of which are available online, and provides access to more than 200 databases.

Financial Aid

All students admitted to graduate degree programs in English are offered financial aid in the form of a renewable graduate teaching assistantship. The current stipend is $13,528 for M.A. and M.T.P.C. students and $14,212 for Ph.D. students. The teaching assistantship additionally covers tuition except for a small matriculation fee each semester. Each year, 5 highly ranked entering students receive an additional fellowship. Minority doctoral students are eligible for a renewable financial aid package of approximately $20,000 per year.

Entering master's level graduate assistants co-teach two sections with experienced instructors. Returning graduate assistants typically teach three sections of introductory composition yearly. Doctoral level graduate assistants may request to teach world literature. The Department also offers support for professional travel.

Living and Housing Costs

Room and board for an individual cost approximately $7500 annually. There is a variety of affordable housing from which to choose, including rental apartments, duplexes, and town houses.

Student Outcomes

Recent graduates of the master's programs have advanced to doctoral or other professional programs at Auburn and other colleges and universities, including Cornell, Emory, Florida, Georgia, North Carolina, Pittsburgh, South Carolina, Texas, Tufts, and Wisconsin; others have entered law or divinity school, or have begun careers in teaching, editing, professional and technical writing, and program administration in the U.S. and abroad. Ninety percent of M.T.P.C. graduates obtain suitable positions within three months of graduation. Recent graduates of the Ph.D. program have found tenure-track positions at Furman University, Gonzaga University, Gainesville State College, Huntington College, Middle Tennessee State, Saint Louis University, Seton Hall, Oregon State University, Stephen F. Austin State University, the University of West Georgia, and the University of Wisconsin–Eau Claire. Some Ph.D. graduates have also established successful careers in software development, editing, and humanities administration.

Location

The University is located in Auburn, Alabama, 60 miles from Montgomery, home of the Alabama Shakespeare Festival and the Civil Rights Memorial, and 120 miles from both Birmingham and Atlanta. All three cities are easily accessible by interstate highways, with Atlanta's Hartsfield-Jackson International Airport just 1½ hours away by car or shuttle. Gulf Coast beaches are about 4 hours away by car. Although the area has a population of more than 100,000, Auburn affords the security, seclusion, and clean air of a small town in rural surroundings. There are many recreational opportunities.

The University and The Department

Chartered in 1856 as a private college, Auburn University is now Alabama's public land-grant institution and the largest university in the state, enrolling almost 24,000 students, including more than 3,000 graduate students. Auburn operates on the semester system. English is the largest single department in the University. Among its graduate faculty are 5 named chairs. The Department plays a vital role in the University's core curriculum, teaching writing and world literature courses to every Auburn student. The Department sponsors conferences and colloquia, lectures, readings, and discussion groups; and is home to three professional journals: *Southern Humanities Review, IEEE Transactions in Professional Communication, and Literary Imagination: Review of the Association of Literary Scholars and Critics,* which is published by Oxford University Press. Each spring, the English Graduate Association sponsors a research colloquium.

Applying

Graduate students matriculate in the fall semester, when graduate assistantship appointments begin. Review of applications begins in January; initial offers of admission are made in late winter or early spring. Successful applicants present strong undergraduate preparation, competitive GRE scores, and cogent writing samples and statements of purpose. Applications and information requests can be processed online through the Department's Web site from links on http://media.cla.auburn.eud/english/gs/index.cfm.

Correspondence and Information

Coordinator of Graduate Studies
Department of English
9030 Haley Center
Auburn University
Auburn, Alabama 36849-5203

Phone: 334-844-4620
Fax: 334-844-9027
E-mail: gradenglish@auburn.edu
Web site: http://www.auburn.edu/english/gs/

Auburn University

THE FACULTY AND THEIR RESEARCH

Chantel Acevedo, Assistant Professor; M.F.A., Miami (Florida), 1999. Fiction.
Paula R. Backscheider, Professor and West Point Stevens–H. M. Philpott Eminent Scholar in English; Ph.D., Purdue, 1972. Restoration and eighteenth-century literature, the novel and novel theory, feminist criticism and theory.
Craig Bertolet, Associate Professor; Ph.D., Penn State, 1995. Medieval literature.
Jon Bolton, Professor; Ph.D., Maryland, 1996. Twentieth-century British literature, Irish studies.
Peter Campion, Assistant Professor; M.A., Boston College, 2000. Poetry.
Alicia Carroll, Associate Professor; Ph.D., CUNY Graduate Center, 1995. Nineteenth-century British fiction, green studies.
Miriam Marty Clark, Associate Professor; Ph.D., North Carolina at Chapel Hill, 1986. Twentieth-century literature, the short story, poetry.
George W. Crandell, Professor; Ph.D., Texas, 1985. Twentieth-century American literature, bibliography, textual criticism, Tennessee Williams.
Jeremy M. Downes, Associate Professor; Ph.D., Wisconsin, 1991. Poetry, poetics, poetry writing, the epic.
Emily Friedman, Assistant Professor; Ph.D., Missouri, 2009. Eighteenth-century British literature and culture, the novel, history of the book, textual criticism.
R. James Goldstein, Professor; Ph.D., Virginia, 1987. Medieval literature, critical theory.
Christopher Keirstead, Associate Professor; Ph.D., Delaware, 1999. Nineteenth-century British literature and culture, travel writing.
Dan Latimer, Professor; Ph.D., Michigan, 1972. Criticism, comparative literature, modernism, symbolism.
Jo Mackiewicz, Associate Professor; Ph.D., Georgetown, 2001. Technical and professional communication, applied linguistics.
Margaret Marshall, Professor; Ph.D., Michigan, 1991. Nineteenth-century American rhetoric and public discourse, composition theory and pedagogy, history of American education.
Susanna Morris, Assistant Professor; Ph.D., Emory, 2007. African American literature.
Erich Nunn, Assistant Professor; Ph.D., Virginia, 2009. American studies, the U.S. South, cultural studies, critical theory.
Constance C. Relihan, Professor; Ph.D., Minnesota, 1989. Renaissance literature, prose fiction before 1700, Shakespeare, early women writers.
Anya Riehl, Associate Professor; Ph.D., Illinois at Chicago, 2007. Early modern British literature.
Kevin Roozen, Associate Professor; Ph.D., Illinois at Urbana-Champaign, 2005. Composition and rhetoric, literacy studies.
Derek Ross, Assistant Professor; Ph.D., Texas Tech, 2009. Environmental rhetoric, research methodology and pedagogy in composition.
James Emmett Ryan, Associate Professor; Ph.D., North Carolina at Chapel Hill, 1999. Nineteenth-century American literature, religion and literature.
Robin Sabino, Associate Professor; Ph.D., Pennsylvania, 1990. Sociolinguistics, ESL, phonetics/phonology, grammatical theory.
Tricia Serviss, Associate Professor; Ph.D., Syracuse, 2010. Composition and rhetoric.
Michelle A. Sidler, Associate Professor; Ph.D., Purdue, 1998. Composition and rhetoric, literary theory.
Marc Silverstein, Hollifield Associate Professor of English Literature; Ph.D., Brown, 1989. Contemporary drama, critical theory, drama as a genre, postmodernism.
Sunny Stalter, Assistant Professor; Ph.D., Rutgers, 2007. Twentieth-century American literature, modernism, American studies.
Isabelle Thompson, Professor; Ed.D., Duke, 1982. Composition and rhetoric, technical communication.
Joanne Tong, Assistant Professor; Ph.D., UCLA, 2005. British Romanticism.
Judy Troy, Professor and Alumni Writer in Residence; M.A., Indiana, 1981. Fiction writing, the short story, twentieth-century American fiction.
Donald R. Wehrs, Professor; Ph.D., Virginia, 1986. The novel, eighteenth-century British literature, critical theory.
Stewart Whittemore, Assistant Professor; Ph.D., Michigan State, 2008. Rhetoric, technical and professional communication.
Chad Wickman, Assistant Professor; Ph.D., Kent State, 2009. Rhetoric of science and technology, workplace literacy.
Hilary E. Wyss, Associate Professor; Ph.D., North Carolina at Chapel Hill, 1998. Early American literature, Native American literature, American studies.
Susan Youngblood, Assistant Professor; Ph.D., Texas Tech, 2008. Technical communication and rhetoric, risk communication.
Matt Zarnowiecki, Assistant Professor; Ph.D., Columbia, 2007. Early modern British literature.

SAINT LOUIS UNIVERSITY–MADRID CAMPUS

Master's in Spanish Language and Literature and Master's in English

Programs of Study

Two programs of study are offered: Master of Arts degree in Spanish and the dual-degree Master's in English. Both programs are accredited by the North Central Association of Schools and Colleges (NCA). The M.A. in English, offered jointly with the Universidad Autónoma de Madrid (UAM), is also recognized as *Formación Permanente del Profesorado* (8 Apartado de la Resolución de 27 de April de 1997, B.O.E. de 25 de Mayo) for English teachers in Spain.

The Master of Arts degree program in Spanish is specifically designed for students interested in pursuing concentrated studies in a combination of Spanish language and Hispanic cultures and literature. The curriculum is suited to those individuals planning, or already engaged in, professional careers such as teaching or international affairs. The program also prepares students who wish to continue study in a Ph.D. degree program in Spanish or a related field.

Students who choose to enroll in the program at the Madrid Campus have the opportunity to immerse themselves in Spanish culture, taking with them not only a graduate degree and a stronger knowledge of Spanish language and literature, but also the experience of studying a language in its native country. Participants perfect their oral and written Spanish communication skills and broaden their knowledge of the rich Spanish literature and culture as they study with Ph.D. faculty members, all of whom are native Spanish speakers.

The program may be completed during a series of five-week summer sessions (usually three, four, or five summers). It may also be completed through attending classes during the traditional academic year, complemented by a summer or two. If students choose to spend three summers in Madrid, each summer they take two M.A. courses, each worth 3 credits, and two *Cursos de Perfeccionamiento* or optional M.A. courses, each worth 2 credits. Throughout their program, a full-time faculty member serves as their adviser. During their last session, students take the final written and oral exams.

Cursos de Perfeccionamiento, designed for secondary school teachers of Spanish, are in-service language and literature classes that allow students to earn from 2 to 8 credits by taking from one to four enrichment courses.

Saint Louis University's master's degree in English can be earned at both its Madrid and St. Louis campuses. Those students pursuing the degree in Spain meet the same admissions requirements and follow the same program as those pursuing the degree in the U.S. This dual-degree program seeks primarily to engage students in a disciplined study of texts drawn from the full experience of English and American literature. Giving due recognition to the history of the English literary tradition as it has unfolded from the Middle Ages to the present, the M.A. in English also alerts students to the exciting developments in the realm of literary theory and offers them opportunities for exploring the interpretation of English literature with the writings of other cultures and with issues raised in other fields.

Classes are taught by American and European Ph.D. faculty members from both Saint Louis University and the Universidad Autónoma de Madrid, providing a unique, international perspective on British, North American, and Anglophone literature. The individualized course of study allows students to select ten graduate seminars from such areas as the traditional periods and genres of literature in English, literary theory, linguistics, the teaching of writing, and translation.

Students completing the one- to two-year program (30 credits in the U.S. system, 70 in the European [ECTS]) earn a Master of Arts in English from Saint Louis University and a *Máster en Estudios Culturales y Anglo-norteamericanos* from the Universidad Autónoma de Madrid.

Courses in Madrid are offered on a trimester basis (October-December, January-March, April-June), to accommodate the European academic calendar. Students also take two seminars during a six-week summer session in St. Louis, Missouri. At the conclusion of their course work, students take a 1-hour oral examination on a reading list, which they have a hand in shaping.

Research Facilities

The resources of the Madrid Campus Library are bilingual in nature and designed primarily to meet the needs of the students studying at this campus. The 9,000 books and 60 journals that compose its collection respond to specific bibliographies that supplement courses offered. Furthermore, the Madrid Campus Library offers students and faculty members access to all electronic resources available at the University's main campus in St. Louis, Missouri, via the SLU proxy server and to other electronic research aids via the Pius XII library in St. Louis, Missouri.

In addition, M.A. students may request reading privileges at all libraries in Madrid and Europe, including Spain's National Library *(Biblioteca Nacional),* the country's foremost research library; the Center of North American Studies Library; the British Studies Information Center; and the British Council Library. Interlibrary loan facilities are also available, with exceptionally fast access to current periodicals via the British Library (UK) Document Supply Service as well as several Spanish research libraries.

The UAM libraries support both a B.A. and a Ph.D. program in English language and literature. The libraries of the Universidad Autónoma de Madrid contain more than 500,000 books and 4,500 periodical subscriptions. The UAM's online services provide direct links to databases, information resources, electronic journals, and catalogs of other university libraries in Madrid and around the world.

Financial Aid

U.S. citizens may apply U.S. federal financial aid to their studies at Saint Louis University–Madrid Campus. All students are eligible to apply for work-study grants. Awards are made only after a student gains full admission to the program.

Cost of Study

Costs for the 2010–11 academic year are €445 per credit hour. Students may enroll on a full-time or part-time basis.

Living and Housing Costs

During the traditional academic year, most graduate students choose to rent apartments near the campus. While prices vary according to apartment size and neighborhood, two-bedroom apartments usually start at €1000 per month in Madrid. Students may also take part in the Madrid campus residential housing program, which allows them to live in a Spanish household. Costs range from €575 to €765 per month, depending on board plan and kitchen privileges, and other factors.

During the summer, housing is available for individuals in University-run shared apartments. For couples and families, arrangements can be made to live in private apartments.

Student Group

Students enrolled in the graduate programs at the Madrid Campus come from across the United States and Europe. During the academic year, the campus hosts up to 20 graduate students; during the summer session, up to 60 students.

Location

Madrid, Spain's capital, with a population of more than 4 million, is politically, culturally, and geographically the heart of Spain. The campus is located in the university quarter of Madrid, overlooking the Sierra de Guatarrama Mountains, only 20 minutes by metro from Puerta del Sol. Surrounded by other private Spanish universities, the campus' location facilitates interaction between the University's Spanish, international, and American students.

M.A. in English students also pursue courses during the summer in the St. Louis campus of Saint Louis University, an architecturally rich urban campus located in the center of the city. The Universidad Autónoma de Madrid's spacious campus, located in Cantoblanco, is a few kilometers north of Madrid and is easily accessible via public transport.

The University

Saint Louis University is a Catholic, Jesuit university and leading research institution. Founded in 1818, the University strives to foster the intellectual and spiritual growth of its students through a broad array of undergraduate, graduate, and professional degree programs on campuses in St. Louis, Missouri, and Madrid, Spain. The Madrid Campus was the first American university program in Spain and the first free-standing campus in Europe operated by a U.S.-based university.

Applying

Spanish Language and Literature: Applications are evaluated for evidence of preparation for advanced study of language and literature and the likelihood of academic success. Applicants need to submit a classified (degree-seeking) application (included in the application packet and available online), an application fee of US$40, Graduate Record Examinations (GRE) General Test or Miller Analogies Test scores, official transcripts of all academic work completed in undergraduate, graduate, and/or professional schools, three letters of recommendation (forms are included in the application packet and are available online), a biographical goal statement of 500 words that addresses the applicant's intellectual and professional goals, a writing sample, and a curriculum vitae.

To be considered for October admission, candidates must submit materials by March 1; for January, by December 1; and for April, by February 1.

Students should make arrangements to take the Graduate Record Examinations (GRE) or Miller Analogies Test as soon as possible and have the score reports sent directly to Saint Louis University. All other materials should be sent directly to the Madrid Campus.

Cursos candidates must submit an online application as a visiting U.S. student for the second summer session, an application fee of $45 (payable online), and official transcripts of all academic work completed. Though not required, it is highly recommended that students submit at least one letter of recommendation from their department chair, principal, or other professional contact. To be considered for summer admission, all documents must be received by Saint Louis University–Madrid Campus by April 30.

English: Applications are reviewed by faculty members from both Saint Louis University and the Universidad Autónoma de Madrid. Candidates are evaluated for evidence of preparation for advanced study of literature and the likelihood of academic success.

Applicants should hold a B.A. or *Licenciatura* in English or the equivalent, with an excellent academic record. Saint Louis University's Graduate School of Arts and Sciences also requires evidence of competence or successful study of a classical or modern foreign language. Native speakers of a language other than English fulfill this requirement automatically. Candidates must submit an application, undergraduate academic transcripts, three letters of recommendation, Graduate Record Examinations (GRE) scores (both general and subject tests), a current CV, a 500-word statement of purpose, a writing sample, and a $40 application fee.

To be considered for October admission, candidates must submit materials by March 1; for January, by December 1; and for April, by February 1.

Correspondence and Information

Graduate Admissions
Saint Louis University–Madrid Campus
Avenida del Valle, 34
28003 Madrid, España
Phone: 34-91-554-5858
Fax: 34-91-554-6202
E-mail: graduate_admissions@madrid.slu.edu
Web site: http://spain.slu.edu

Saint Louis University–Madrid Campus

THE FACULTY AND THEIR RESEARCH

Master's in Spanish Language and Literature

Aitor Bikandi, Ph.D., Cincinnati. Nineteenth- and twentieth-century peninsular narrative, cultural studies, peninsular film.
Xelo Candel, Ph.D., Universidad de Valencia. Twentieth-century Latin American and peninsular poetry, golden age poetry, cultural studies.
Angeles Encinar, Ph.D., Washington (St. Louis). Nineteenth- and twentieth-century peninsular narrative, twentieth-century Latin American narrative, women's narrative.
Cristina Matute, Ph.D., Universidad Autónoma de Madrid. History of Spanish grammar, Spanish phonetics and phonology, linguistics.
Alicia Ramos, Ph.D., Northwestern. Twentieth-century peninsular narrative, twentieth-century peninsular thought, medieval literature, survey of Hispanic narrative and film.
Rafael Reig, Ph.D., SUNY at Stony Brook. Nineteenth- and twentieth-century peninsular narrative, creative writing.
Maria Teresa Rodriguez, Ph.D., Universidad Autónoma de Madrid. History of Spanish grammar, Spanish phonetics and phonology, linguistics.

Master's Program in English

Sara van den Berg, Chair, Department of English; Ph.D., Yale. Ben Jonson, Milton, seventeenth-century literature, psychoanalytic theory, medicine and the humanities.
Stephen Casmier, Ph.D., Université de Nice-Sophia Antipolis (France). African American literature, theory and expressive culture, African literature, twentieth-century American literature.
Anne Day Dewey, Ph.D., Stanford. American poetry, twentieth-century American literature, women's poetry.
Anthony Hasler, Ph.D., Cambridge. Chaucer, medieval literature, late medieval/early modern British literature, drama.
Georgia Johnston, Ph.D., Rutgers. Twentieth-century British literature, autobiography, creative writing (poetry).
Matthew Kineen, Ph.D., Wisconsin. Theory of genres, comparative literature.
María Lozano, Program Director; Ph.D., Universidad de Zaragoza (Spain). Twentieth-century American literature.
Anne McCabe, Ph.D., Aston (England). Systemic functional linguistics, contrastive rhetoric, text linguistics/analysis, teaching writing, English for academic purposes, teacher development.
Janice McIntire-Strasburg, Ph.D., Nevada. Computers and writing, Mark Twain, American literature, Native American literature.
Eulalia Piñero, Ph.D., Universidad Complutense de Madrid (Spain). Ethnic American literaturas.
Esteban Pujals, Ph.D., Universidad Complutense de Madrid (Spain). Twentieth-century American poetry.
Julia Salmerón, Ph.D., Hull (England). Gender studies, twentieth-century British literature.
Pilar Somacarrera, Ph.D., Universidad de Salamanca (Spain). Canadian literature, postcolonial literaturas.
Maura Tarnoff, Ph.D., Virginia. Renaissance literature.
Paul Vita, Chair, Department of English (Madrid Campus); Ph.D., Columbia. Nineteenth-century British literature and narrative theory.

VILLANOVA UNIVERSITY

Graduate Program in English Language and Literature

Program of Study

Villanova has been granting its master's degree in English language and literature for more than half a century. Villanova weds this sense of history with a keen awareness of the contemporary, interdisciplinary spirit of literary study. The curriculum balances a traditional, historical understanding of literary periods with newer, theoretically based considerations of writing and reading. This range of approaches provides students with expertise in much of the literature written in English, highly refined interpretive skills, and familiarity with the major intellectual currents shaping the discipline of literary study today.

All courses are conducted as small seminars, with a maximum enrollment of 15 students. Course work provides a broad range of study in a variety of areas, and the thesis or field exam provides focus within a particular field. The thesis offers an opportunity for sustained critical examination of a work, author, or topic, while the field examination is taken on a list of works compiled in consultation with the student's adviser within a field of the student's choosing.

To satisfy the requirements for the master's degree, students must complete a minimum of 30 credits, including successful completion of a thesis or an oral/written field examination. Students are expected to take at least one course in British literature before 1800 and another in American literature before 1900. An average grade of at least a B must be maintained to remain in the program. Students usually complete the curriculum in two years, taking two or three courses each semester, but may pursue their studies on a part-time basis, in which case they are allowed a period of six years to earn the degree.

At all stages, the program is deeply committed to the individual student's development and maturation as a literary scholar. Upon matriculation, each student is assigned an adviser, who assists in planning the individual course of study. After successful completion of 9 credits, the student may request an adviser with particular expertise in the student's area of interest.

Research Facilities

The Falvey Memorial Library at Villanova University houses more than 600,000 volumes and 3,000 periodicals. An interlibrary loan system operates with the efficiency of e-mail. Special holdings include the McGarrity and Worthington collections, major resources of literature and periodicals about Irish history, Irish-American relations, and writings by and about James Joyce. The library is located in the middle of the campus and includes numerous public-use computer stations that are equipped with sophisticated search engines and data-retrieval mechanisms.

Financial Aid

Applicants may compete for full financial awards, including tuition remission and a yearly stipend of approximately $13,000, which are renewable for a second year. Tuition scholarships (tuition remission without a stipend) are also offered and are renewable for the second year. The work these awards require ranges from helping individual faculty members with research materials to assisting in the University Writing and Learning Center.

Since classes in the master's program meet in the evenings, students without financial aid are often able to support their graduate study through daytime employment outside the University.

Cost of Study

Fees and expenses for graduate students in 2009–10 were $50 for the application fee, $585 per credit for tuition, and $30 per semester for general University fees.

Living and Housing Costs

A variety of affordable housing possibilities are available near the Villanova University campus. Housing costs vary in accordance with the option chosen. Villanova University does not provide on-campus housing for graduate students.

Student Group

There are usually about 50 students matriculated in the program, and the ratio of men to women is approximately 2:3. While some graduate students are dedicated to becoming professors of English, others are seeking the master's because they want to learn more about the discipline in order to decide whether a Ph.D. is right for them, they wish to advance their careers as teachers of secondary school, or they simply love literature and want to immerse themselves in it. Some students come directly from undergraduate programs, while others have pursued other careers and are returning to school to pursue a lifelong ambition.

Student Outcomes

In recent years, recipients of the master's degree in English from Villanova have been admitted to highly competitive Ph.D. programs, including Harvard, Johns Hopkins, Ohio State, Penn State, Princeton, Rutgers, UCLA, and the Universities of Kansas, Maryland, North Carolina, Pennsylvania, and Wisconsin. Others have elected to use the degree to pursue teaching positions at the excellent secondary schools adjacent to the University. Still others have chosen to pursue careers in publishing and other fields, including business and law, which demand the verbal acumen and analytical rigor Villanova's program cultivates.

Location

Villanova is situated on the historic Main Line, in a beautiful western suburb of Philadelphia. Philadelphia offers a wide variety of museums, libraries, concerts, and other cultural opportunities. Home to the greatest variety of eighteenth-century buildings in America, the city is also enjoying a renaissance in modern architecture, restaurants, and the performing arts. By car or train, the campus is only 30 minutes from downtown. It is 2 minutes from the Blue Route (Route 476) and 5 minutes from the Pennsylvania Turnpike, the Schuylkill Expressway, and Route 202. With ample parking and mass transit stops right on campus grounds, students can travel easily to and from the campus by car, bus, or train.

The University and The Department

Founded in 1842 by the friars of the Order of St. Augustine, Villanova is a comprehensive Roman Catholic institution that welcomes students of all faiths. Roughly 10,000 students attend the University, including 6,000 undergraduates and 4,000 graduate students. The Department of English at Villanova includes a number of distinguished critics, whose scholarship has earned them national and international recognition. They are well acquainted with the methods and values of current scholarship in English literature, and they seek equally to deepen the student's acquaintance with these critical discourses and develop each student's individual critical sensibility.

Applying

Villanova typically requires that applicants have at least 18 undergraduate credits and a 3.0 average in English. However, the University occasionally accepts applications from candidates who majored in related fields.

Applicants should submit the following materials: three letters of recommendation (at least two of which should be from former professors), a writing sample of approximately ten pages, a one-page personal statement, the application for admission, the nonrefundable application fee, all official postsecondary transcripts, and GRE scores; all should be sent to the Graduate Studies Office, College of Liberal Arts and Sciences, Villanova University, 800 Lancaster Avenue, Villanova, Pennsylvania 19085-1699. Application forms are available online at Villanova's Graduate School Web site. The deadline for receipt of applications for the fall semester is March 1 and for the spring semester, November 15.

Correspondence and Information

Director of Graduate Studies
Department of English
Villanova University
Villanova, Pennsylvania 19085

Phone: 610-519-7826
Fax: 610-519-6913
E-mail: gradinfo@email.villanova.edu
Web site: www.gradenglish.villanova.edu

Villanova University

THE FACULTY AND THEIR RESEARCH

Chiji Akoma, Associate Professor; Ph.D., SUNY at Binghamton. Postcolonial literature.
Michael Berthold, Associate Professor; Ph.D., Harvard. Nineteenth-century American literature, slave narrative, American Gothic.
Cristina Maria Cervone, Assistant Professor; Ph.D., Virginia. Medieval studies, poetics, history of the English language.
Charles L. Cherry, Professor; Ph.D., North Carolina. British Romanticism, madness and imagination, history of ideas.
Alice A. Dailey, Assistant Professor; Ph.D., UCLA. Renaissance literature.
Heather Hicks, Associate Professor; Ph.D., Duke. Post–World War II American fiction, postmodern theory, contemporary cultural studies.
Karyn L. Hollis, Associate Professor; Ph.D., USC. Composition studies.
Crystal J. Lucky, Associate Professor; Ph.D., Pennsylvania. African American literature, nineteenth-century African American church history, literary pedagogy.
Jean Lutes, Associate Professor; Ph.D., Wisconsin–Madison. Modern American fiction.
Hugh Ormsby-Lennon, Associate Professor; Ph.D., Pennsylvania. Augustan literature, eighteenth-century cultural studies, eighteenth-century Anglo-Irish literature, literary theory.
Megan Quigley, Assistant Professor; Ph.D., Yale. British and Irish Modernism.
Evan Radcliffe, Associate Professor; Ph.D., Cornell. British Romanticism, the French Revolution controversy, historicism.
Jill Rappaport, Assistant Professor; Ph.D., Virginia. Victorian literature and cultural history.
Lisa Sewell, Associate Professor; Ph.D., Tufts. Contemporary American poetry, poetics.
Lauren E. Shohet, Associate Professor; Ph.D., Brown. Renaissance and seventeenth-century literature, cultural studies, literary theory, gender studies.
Deborah A. Thomas, Professor; Ph.D., Rochester. Victorian literature and culture, Dickens, Thackeray, nineteenth-century British women's writing.

Section 10
Linguistic Studies

This section contains a directory of institutions offering graduate work in linguistic studies, followed by an in-depth entry submitted by an institution that chose to prepare a detailed program description. Additional information about programs listed in the directory but not augmented by an in-depth entry may be obtained by writing directly to the dean of a graduate school or chair of a department at the address given in the directory.

For programs offering related work, see also in this book *Area and Cultural Studies, Language and Literature,* and *Sociology, Anthropology, and Archaeology.*

CONTENTS

Program Directories

Linguistics 424
Translation and Interpretation 435

Close-Up

Monterey Institute of International Studies 437

Linguistics

Arizona State University, Graduate College, College of Liberal Arts and Sciences, Division of Humanities, Department of English, Tempe, AZ 85287. Offers creative writing (MFA); English (MA, PhD), including comparative literature (MA), linguistics (MA), literature, rhetoric and composition (MA), rhetoric/composition and linguistics (PhD); teaching English to speakers of other languages (MTESOL). *Degree requirements:* For doctorate, thesis/dissertation. *Entrance requirements:* For master's and doctorate, GRE.

Ball State University, Graduate School, College of Sciences and Humanities, Department of English, Program in Linguistics, Muncie, IN 47306-1099. Offers applied linguistics (PhD). *Faculty research:* Descriptive and theoretical linguistics.

Biola University, School of Intercultural Studies, La Mirada, CA 90639-0001. Offers applied linguistics (MA); intercultural education (PhD); intercultural studies (MAICS); missiology (D Miss); missions (MA); teaching English to speakers of other languages (MA, Certificate). Part-time and evening/weekend programs available. Terminal master's awarded for partial completion of doctoral program. *Degree requirements:* For master's, one foreign language, comprehensive exam; for doctorate, one foreign language, comprehensive exam, thesis/dissertation. *Entrance requirements:* For master's, minimum undergraduate GPA of 3.0; for doctorate, MA, 3 years of ministry experience, minimum graduate GPA of 3.3. Additional exam requirements/recommendations for international students: Required—TOEFL (minimum score 550 paper-based; 213 computer-based). Electronic applications accepted.

Boston College, Graduate School of Arts and Sciences, Department of Slavic and Eastern Languages, Program in Linguistics, Chestnut Hill, MA 02467-3800. Offers MA, MA/JD, MBA/MA. Part-time programs available. *Degree requirements:* For master's, 3 foreign languages, comprehensive exam, thesis or alternative. *Application deadline:* For fall admission, 1/15 for domestic students. Application fee: $75. Electronic applications accepted. *Financial support:* Application deadline: 3/1. *Unit head:* Dr. Maxin Shrayer, Chairperson, 617-552-3910. *Application contact:* Dr. Maxin Shrayer, Chairperson, 617-552-3910.

Boston University, Graduate School of Arts and Sciences, Program in Applied Linguistics, Boston, MA 02215. Offers MA, PhD. Part-time programs available. *Faculty:* 17 full-time (9 women). *Students:* 19 full-time (14 women), 13 part-time (10 women); includes 2 minority (1 African American, 1 Hispanic American), 5 international. Average age 35. 43 applicants, 9% accepted, 1 enrolled. In 2009, 5 master's awarded. Terminal master's awarded for partial completion of doctoral program. *Degree requirements:* For master's, one foreign language, project; for doctorate, 2 foreign languages, thesis/dissertation, 1 book review, 2 research papers, oral exam. *Entrance requirements:* For master's and doctorate, GRE General Test. Additional exam requirements/recommendations for international students: Required—TOEFL. *Application deadline:* For fall admission, 1/15 priority date for domestic and international students. Applications are processed on a rolling basis. Application fee: $60. Electronic applications accepted. *Expenses:* Tuition: Full-time $37,910; part-time $1184 per credit hour. Required fees: $386; $40 per semester. Part-time tuition and fees vary according to class time, course level, degree level and program. *Financial support:* In 2009–10, 16 students received support, including 2 teaching assistantships with full tuition reimbursements available (averaging $18,400 per year); Federal Work-Study, scholarships/grants, and unspecified assistantships also available. Financial award applicants required to submit FAFSA. *Faculty research:* Psycholinguistics, sociolinguistics, neurolinguistics, language acquisition, American Sign Language. Total annual research expenditures: $900,000. *Unit head:* M. Catherine O'Connor, Director, 617-353-3318, Fax: 617-358-2353, E-mail: mco@bu.edu. *Application contact:* Kathryn Franich, Program Assistant, 617-353-6197, Fax: 617-353-2353, E-mail: linguist@bu.edu.

Brandeis University, Graduate School of Arts and Sciences, Program in Computational Linguistics, Waltham, MA 02454-9110. Offers MA. Part-time programs available. *Faculty:* 6 full-time (2 women), 1 part-time/adjunct (0 women). *Students:* 8 full-time (2 women), 1 part-time (0 women), 3 international. 14 applicants, 86% accepted, 8 enrolled. In 2009, 1 master's awarded. *Degree requirements:* For master's, thesis. *Entrance requirements:* For master's, statement of purpose, 2 letters of recommendation, official transcripts, resume or curriculum vitae. Additional exam requirements/recommendations for international students: Required—TOEFL (minimum score 650 paper-based; 250 computer-based; 100 iBT); Recommended—IELTS (minimum score 7). *Application deadline:* Applications are processed on a rolling basis. Application fee: $75. Electronic applications accepted. *Financial support:* In 2009–10, 3 teaching assistantships with partial tuition reimbursements (averaging $3,200 per year) were awarded; institutionally sponsored loans and scholarships/grants also available. Financial award application deadline: 4/15; financial award applicants required to submit FAFSA. *Faculty research:* Computer science (artificial intelligence, theory of computation, and programming methods), language and linguistics (phonology, syntax, semantics, and pragmatics). *Unit head:* Dr. James Pustejovsky, Program Chair, 781-736-2701, Fax: 781-736-2741, E-mail: jamesp@brandeis.edu. *Application contact:* David F. Cotter, Graduate School of Arts and Sciences, 781-736-3410, Fax: 781-736-3412, E-mail: gradschool@brandeis.edu.

Brigham Young University, Graduate Studies, College of Humanities, Department of Linguistics and English Language, Provo, UT 84602. Offers general linguistics (MA); teaching English as a second language (MA, Certificate). Part-time programs available. *Faculty:* 20 full-time (4 women). *Students:* 97 full-time (69 women); includes 33 minority (1 African American, 29 Asian Americans or Pacific Islanders, 3 Hispanic Americans). Average age 30. 69 applicants, 78% accepted, 49 enrolled. In 2009, 11 master's, 32 other advanced degrees awarded. *Degree requirements:* For master's, 2 foreign languages, thesis. *Entrance requirements:* For master's, GRE General Test, minimum GPA of 3.6 in last 60 hours of course work. Additional exam requirements/recommendations for international students: Required—TOEFL (minimum score 580 paper-based; 237 computer-based; 90 iBT), TWE. *Application deadline:* 1/15 for domestic and international students. Application fee: $50. Electronic applications accepted. *Expenses:* Tuition: Full-time $5580; part-time $301 per credit hour. Tuition and fees vary according to student's religious affiliation. *Financial support:* In 2009–10, 51 students received support, including 52 research assistantships with partial tuition reimbursements available (averaging $2,763 per year), 28 teaching assistantships with partial tuition reimbursements available (averaging $1,704 per year); fellowships with partial tuition reimbursements available, career-related internships or fieldwork, institutionally sponsored loans, scholarships/grants, tuition waivers (partial), unspecified assistantships, and student instructorships also available. Support available to part-time students. Financial award application deadline: 3/28. *Faculty research:* TESOL, second language acquisition, computational linguistics, semiotics and semantics, computer-assisted language instruction. Total annual research expenditures: $261,058. *Unit head:* Dr. William G. Eggington, Chair, 801-422-2937, Fax: 801-422-0906, E-mail: bill_eggington@byu.edu. *Application contact:* LoriAnn Spear, Secretary, 801-422-2937, Fax: 801-422-0906, E-mail: phyllis_daniel@byu.edu.

Brown University, Graduate School, Department of Cognitive and Linguistic Sciences, Providence, RI 02912. Offers cognitive science (Sc M, PhD); linguistics (AM, PhD). *Degree requirements:* For master's, one foreign language, thesis or alternative; for doctorate, 2 foreign languages, thesis/dissertation.

California State University, Fresno, Division of Graduate Studies, College of Arts and Humanities, Department of Linguistics, Fresno, CA 93740-8027. Offers linguistics (MA), including Teaching English as a second language. Part-time and evening/weekend programs available. *Degree requirements:* For master's, comprehensive exam. *Entrance requirements:* For master's, GRE General Test, minimum GPA of 3.0. Additional exam requirements/recommendations for international students: Required—TOEFL. Electronic applications accepted. *Faculty research:* Communication systems, bilingual education, animal communication, conflict resolution, literacy programs.

California State University, Fullerton, Graduate Studies, College of Humanities and Social Sciences, Program in Linguistics, Fullerton, CA 92834-9480. Offers analysis of specific language structures (MA); anthropological linguistics (MA); applied linguistics (MA); communication and semantics (MA); disorders of communication (MA); experimental phonetics (MA). Part-time programs available. *Students:* 20 full-time (10 women), 8 part-time (5 women); includes 5 minority (1 Asian American or Pacific Islander, 4 Hispanic Americans), 11 international. Average age 31. 21 applicants, 71% accepted, 8 enrolled. In 2009, 3 master's awarded. *Degree requirements:* For master's, one foreign language, thesis or alternative, project. *Entrance requirements:* For master's, minimum GPA of 3.0, undergraduate major in linguistics or related field. Application fee: $55. *Expenses:* Tuition, nonresident: full-time $11,160; part-time $373 per credit. Required fees: $1440 per term. Tuition and fees vary according to course load, degree level and program. *Financial support:* Career-related internships or fieldwork, Federal Work-Study, institutionally sponsored loans, and scholarships/grants available. Support available to part-time students. Financial award application deadline: 3/1; financial award applicants required to submit FAFSA. *Unit head:* Dr. Franz Muller-Gotama, Adviser, 657-278-2441. *Application contact:* Admissions/Applications, 657-278-2371.

California State University, Long Beach, Graduate Studies, College of Liberal Arts, Department of Linguistics, Long Beach, CA 90840. Offers general linguistics (MA); language and culture (MA); special concentration (MA); teaching English as a second language (MA). Part-time and evening/weekend programs available. *Faculty:* 12 full-time (10 women), 1 part-time/adjunct (0 women). *Students:* 33 full-time (23 women), 36 part-time (24 women); includes 20 minority (1 African American, 10 Asian Americans or Pacific Islanders, 9 Hispanic Americans), 20 international. Average age 31. 47 applicants, 62% accepted, 15 enrolled. *Degree requirements:* For master's, one foreign language, comprehensive exam, thesis optional. *Application deadline:* For fall admission, 5/1 for domestic students. Applications are processed on a rolling basis. Application fee: $55. Electronic applications accepted. *Expenses:* Required fees: $1802 per semester. Part-time tuition and fees vary according to course load. *Financial support:* Teaching assistantships, career-related internships or fieldwork, Federal Work-Study, institutionally sponsored loans, and scholarships/grants available. Financial award application deadline: 3/2. *Faculty research:* Pedagogy of language instruction, role of language in society, Khmer language instruction. *Unit head:* Dr. Malcolm Awadajin Finney, Chair, 562-985-7425, Fax: 562-985-2593, E-mail: mfinney@csulb.edu. *Application contact:* Dr. Xiaoping Liang, Graduate Advisor, 562-985-8509, Fax: 562-985-5792, E-mail: xliang@csulb.edu.

California State University, Northridge, Graduate Studies, College of Humanities, Linguistics Program, Northridge, CA 91330. Offers MA. Part-time and evening/weekend programs available. *Faculty:* 1 (woman) part-time/adjunct. *Students:* 24 full-time (19 women), 21 part-time (20 women); includes 38 minority (16 Asian Americans or Pacific Islanders, 22 Hispanic Americans), 7 international. Average age 34. 53 applicants, 66% accepted, 20 enrolled. In 2009, 9 master's awarded. *Degree requirements:* For master's, one foreign language, comprehensive exam, thesis, or project. *Entrance requirements:* For master's, GRE General Test or minimum GPA of 3.0. Additional exam requirements/recommendations for international students: Required—TOEFL (minimum score 563 paper-based; 223 computer-based; 85 iBT). *Application deadline:* For fall admission, 11/30 for domestic students. Application fee: $55. *Financial support:* Application deadline: 3/1. *Faculty research:* Ethnography of communication, stylistics, natural language processing, linguistics and humor, Otomanguean phonology and reconstruction. *Unit head:* Dr. Evelyn McClave, Coordinator, 818-677-5019, E-mail: emcclave@csun.edu. *Application contact:* Dr. Evelyn McClave, Coordinator, 818-677-5019, E-mail: emcclave@csun.edu.

Carleton University, Faculty of Graduate Studies, Faculty of Arts and Social Sciences, School of Linguistics and Applied Language Studies, Ottawa, ON K1S 5B6, Canada. Offers applied language studies (MA). *Degree requirements:* For master's, thesis optional. *Entrance requirements:* For master's, honors degree. Additional exam requirements/recommendations for international students: Required—TOEFL or CAEL. *Faculty research:* Language learning, acquisition and use of first and/or second languages in a variety of professional and academic contexts.

Carnegie Mellon University, College of Humanities and Social Sciences, Department of Modern Languages, Pittsburgh, PA 15213-3891. Offers second language acquisition (PhD). *Degree requirements:* For doctorate, one foreign language, comprehensive exam, thesis/dissertation. *Entrance requirements:* For doctorate, GRE General Test. Additional exam requirements/recommendations for international students: Required—TOEFL.

Case Western Reserve University, School of Graduate Studies, Department of Cognitive Science, Cleveland, OH 44106. Offers cognitive linguistics (MA). Part-time programs available. *Faculty:* 6 full-time (2 women), 2 part-time/adjunct (1 woman). *Students:* 2 full-time (1 woman), 4 part-time (2 women). Average age 32. 6 applicants, 100% accepted, 1 enrolled. *Degree requirements:* For master's, thesis. *Entrance requirements:* For master's, GRE, recommendations. Additional exam requirements/recommendations for international students: Required—TOEFL (minimum score 550 paper-based; 213 computer-based; 79 iBT). *Application deadline:* For fall admission, 5/1 priority date for domestic students. Application fee: $50. Electronic applications accepted. *Faculty research:* Integrated, trans-disciplinary research into human higher-order cognition with emphases including the workings of the human mind in design, art, and technology, the interaction of brain and culture in development and evolution, the origins of human higher-order cognition. *Unit head:* Dr. Todd Oakley, Chair, 216-368-4753, E-mail: cogsci@case.edu. *Application contact:* Dr. Todd Oakley, Co-Director of Admission, 216-368-4753, E-mail: coglingadmission@case.edu.

Cleveland State University, College of Graduate Studies, College of Liberal Arts and Social Sciences, Department of Modern Languages, Cleveland, OH 44115. Offers French (M Ed); Spanish (M Ed, MA), including language and linguistics (MA), Latin American studies (MA), peninsular studies (MA), Spanish (MA). Part-time and evening/weekend programs available. *Degree requirements:* For master's, one foreign language, comprehensive exam, thesis optional, study abroad. *Entrance requirements:* For master's, undergraduate major in Spanish or equivalent, essay in Spanish, writing sample. Additional exam requirements/recommendations for international students: Required—TOEFL (minimum score 525 paper-based; 197 computer-based). Electronic applications accepted. *Faculty research:* Second language acquisition, sociolinguistics, contemporary Spanish novel, Arabic diaspora in Latin America, border literature.

Concordia University, School of Graduate Studies, Faculty of Arts and Science, Department of Education, Program in Applied Linguistics, Montréal, QC H3G 1M8, Canada. Offers applied linguistics (MA); teaching English as a second language (Certificate).

Cornell University, Graduate School, Graduate Fields of Arts and Sciences, Field of Asian Studies, Ithaca, NY 14853-0001. Offers East Asian linguistics (MA); East Asian studies (MA); South Asian linguistics (MA); South Asian studies (MA); Southeast Asian linguistics (MA); Southeast Asian studies (MA). *Faculty:* 59 full-time (21 women). *Students:* 7 full-time (1 woman); includes 3 minority (all Asian Americans or Pacific Islanders), 1 international. Average age 31. 51 applicants, 24% accepted. In 2009, 5 master's awarded. *Degree requirements:* For master's, one foreign language, thesis. *Entrance requirements:* For master's, GRE General Test, 3 letters of recommendation. Additional exam requirements/recommendations for international students: Required—TOEFL (minimum score 550 paper-based; 213 computer-based; 77 iBT). *Application deadline:* Applications are processed on a rolling basis. Application fee: $70. Electronic applications accepted. *Expenses:* Tuition: Full-time $29,500. Required fees: $70. Full-time tuition and fees vary according to degree level, program and student level. *Financial support:* In 2009–10, 5 students received support, including 1 fellowship with full tuition reimbursement available, 2 research assistantships with full tuition reimbursements available, teaching assistantships with full tuition reimbursements available, institutionally sponsored loans, scholarships/grants, health care benefits, tuition waivers (full and partial), and unspecified assistantships also available. Financial award applicants required to submit

FAFSA. *Faculty research:* East Asian studies, South Asian studies, Southeast Asian studies. *Unit head:* Director of Graduate Studies, 607-255-9099, Fax: 607-255-1345. *Application contact:* Graduate Field Assistant, 607-255-9099, Fax: 607-255-1345, E-mail: asian@cornell.edu.

Cornell University, Graduate School, Graduate Fields of Arts and Sciences, Field of Linguistics, Ithaca, NY 14853-0001. Offers applied linguistics (MA, PhD); East Asian linguistics (MA, PhD); English linguistics (MA, PhD); general linguistics (MA, PhD); Germanic linguistics (MA, PhD); Indo-European linguistics (MA, PhD); phonetics (MA, PhD); phonological theory (MA, PhD); Romance linguistics (MA, PhD); second language acquisition (MA, PhD); semantics (MA, PhD); Slavic linguistics (MA, PhD); sociolinguistics (MA, PhD); South Asian linguistics (MA, PhD); Southeast Asian linguistics (MA, PhD); syntactic theory (MA, PhD). *Faculty:* 21 full-time (10 women). *Students:* 31 full-time (17 women), 14 international. Average age 30. 95 applicants, 12% accepted, 5 enrolled. In 2009, 5 master's, 6 doctorates awarded. Terminal master's awarded for partial completion of doctoral program. *Degree requirements:* For master's, one foreign language, thesis; for doctorate, one foreign language, comprehensive exam, thesis/dissertation. *Entrance requirements:* For master's and doctorate, GRE General Test, 2 letters of recommendation. Additional exam requirements/recommendations for international students: Required—TOEFL (minimum score 600 paper-based; 250 computer-based; 77 iBT). *Application deadline:* For fall admission, 1/15 for domestic students. Application fee: $70. Electronic applications accepted. *Expenses:* Tuition: Full-time $29,500. Required fees: $70. Full-time tuition and fees vary according to degree level, program and student level. *Financial support:* In 2009–10, 3 fellowships with full tuition reimbursements, 1 teaching assistantship with full tuition reimbursement were awarded; research assistantships with full tuition reimbursements, institutionally sponsored loans, scholarships/grants, health care benefits, tuition waivers (full and partial), and unspecified assistantships also available. Financial award applicants required to submit FAFSA. *Faculty research:* Phonology and phonetics; syntax and semantics; historical linguistics; philosophy of language; language acquisition. *Unit head:* Director of Graduate Studies, 607-255-1105. *Application contact:* Graduate Field Assistant, 607-255-1105, E-mail: lingfield@cornell.edu.

Eastern Michigan University, Graduate School, College of Arts and Sciences, Department of English Language and Literature, Program in English Linguistics, Ypsilanti, MI 48197. Offers MA. Part-time and evening/weekend programs available. Postbaccalaureate distance learning degree programs offered (minimal on-campus study). *Students:* 12 full-time (8 women), 7 part-time (4 women); includes 2 minority (1 African American, 1 Asian American or Pacific Islander), 7 international. Average age 27. In 2009, 8 master's awarded. *Degree requirements:* For master's, thesis (for some programs). *Entrance requirements:* Additional exam requirements/recommendations for international students: Required—TOEFL. *Application deadline:* Applications are processed on a rolling basis. Application fee: $35. Tuition and fees vary according to course level. *Financial support:* Fellowships with tuition reimbursements, research assistantships with full tuition reimbursements, teaching assistantships with full tuition reimbursements, career-related internships or fieldwork, Federal Work-Study, institutionally sponsored loans, scholarships/grants, tuition waivers (partial), and unspecified assistantships available. Support available to part-time students. Financial award applicants required to submit FAFSA. *Application contact:* Dr. T. Daniel Seely, Program Advisor, 734-487-0145, Fax: 734-483-9744, E-mail: tseely@emich.edu.

Florida Atlantic University, Dorothy F. Schmidt College of Arts and Letters, Department of Languages, Linguistics, and Comparative Literature, Boca Raton, FL 33431-0991. Offers comparative literature (MA); French (MA); linguistics (MA); Spanish (MA). Part-time programs available. *Faculty:* 23 full-time (20 women), 12 part-time/adjunct (10 women). *Students:* 20 full-time (14 women), 14 part-time (10 women); includes 16 minority (3 African Americans, 1 Asian American or Pacific Islander, 12 Hispanic Americans), 4 international. Average age 35. 35 applicants, 60% accepted, 13 enrolled. In 2009, 16 master's awarded. *Degree requirements:* For master's, one foreign language, comprehensive exam, thesis optional. *Entrance requirements:* For master's, GRE General Test, minimum GPA of 3.0. *Application deadline:* For fall admission, 7/1 priority date for domestic students, 2/15 for international students; for spring admission, 11/1 for domestic students, 7/15 for international students. Applications are processed on a rolling basis. Application fee: $30. *Expenses:* Tuition, state resident: full-time $7055; part-time $293.94 per credit hour. Tuition, nonresident: full-time $22,096; part-time $920.66 per credit hour. *Financial support:* Fellowships, research assistantships, teaching assistantships with partial tuition reimbursements, Federal Work-Study and tuition waivers (partial) available. Support available to part-time students. Financial award application deadline: 4/1. *Faculty research:* Modern European studies, modern Latin America, medieval Europe. *Unit head:* Dr. Michael Horswell, Chair, 561-297-3860, Fax: 561-297-2756, E-mail: horswell@fau.edu. *Application contact:* Dr. Emily Stockard, Associate Dean, 561-297-2817, Fax: 561-297-2744, E-mail: stockard@fau.edu.

Florida International University, College of Arts and Sciences, Department of English, Program in Linguistics, Miami, FL 33199. Offers MA. Part-time and evening/weekend programs available. *Students:* 10 full-time (7 women), 10 part-time (8 women); includes 13 minority (1 African American, 2 Asian Americans or Pacific Islanders, 10 Hispanic Americans), 2 international. Average age 28. 20 applicants, 55% accepted, 10 enrolled. In 2009, 8 master's awarded. *Degree requirements:* For master's, thesis or alternative. *Entrance requirements:* For master's, minimum GPA of 3.0, letter of intent, two letters of recommendation. Additional exam requirements/recommendations for international students: Required—TOEFL (minimum score 550 paper-based; 80 iBT). *Application deadline:* For fall admission, 3/1 for domestic and international students; for spring admission, 10/1 for domestic students, 9/1 for international students. Application fee: $30. Electronic applications accepted. *Expenses:* Tuition, state resident: full-time $8008; part-time $4004 per year. Tuition, nonresident: full-time $20,104; part-time $10,052 per year. Required fees: $298; $149 per term. *Financial support:* Institutionally sponsored loans and scholarships/grants available. Financial award application deadline: 3/1; financial award applicants required to submit FAFSA. *Unit head:* Dr. James Sutton, Chair, English Department, 305-348-2874, Fax: 305-348-3878, E-mail: james.sutton@fiu.edu. *Application contact:* Dr. Feryal Yavas, Director, 305-348-3935, Fax: 305-348-3878, E-mail: yavas@fiu.edu.

Gallaudet University, The Graduate School, Department of Linguistics, Washington, DC 20002-3625. Offers MA, PhD. Part-time programs available. *Degree requirements:* For master's, thesis optional. *Entrance requirements:* For master's, GRE General Test or MAT. Electronic applications accepted.

George Mason University, College of Humanities and Social Sciences, Department of English, Fairfax, VA 22030. Offers creative writing (MFA); English (MA); folklore studies (Certificate); linguistics (PhD); professional writing and rhetoric (Certificate); teaching English as a second language (Certificate). *Faculty:* 82 full-time (47 women), 48 part-time/adjunct (29 women). *Students:* 72 full-time (51 women), 228 part-time (172 women); includes 39 minority (12 African Americans, 3 American Indian/Alaska Native, 20 Asian Americans or Pacific Islanders, 4 Hispanic Americans), 10 international. Average age 31. 314 applicants, 57% accepted, 86 enrolled. In 2009, 63 master's, 12 other advanced degrees awarded. *Degree requirements:* For master's, thesis (for some programs), proficiency in a foreign language by course work or translation test. *Entrance requirements:* For master's, 30 credits in graduate English courses, minimum undergraduate GPA of 3.0, 2 letters of recommendation. Additional exam requirements/recommendations for international students: Required—TOEFL. *Application deadline:* For fall admission, 3/15 priority date for domestic students; for spring admission, 10/15 for domestic students. Application fee: $75. Electronic applications accepted. *Expenses:* Tuition, state resident: full-time $7568; part-time $315.33 per credit hour. Tuition, nonresident: full-time $21,704; part-time $904.33 per credit hour. Required fees: $2184; $91 per credit hour. *Financial support:* In 2009–10, 49 students received support, including 1 fellowship with full tuition reimbursement available (averaging $18,000 per year), 3 research assistantships with full and partial tuition reimbursements available (averaging $9,443 per year), 46 teaching assistantships with full and partial tuition reimbursements available (averaging $10,509 per year); Federal Work-Study, scholarships/grants, unspecified assistantships, and health care benefits (full-time research or teaching assistantship recipients) also available. Support available to part-time students. Financial award application deadline: 3/1; financial award applicants required to submit FAFSA. *Faculty research:* Literature, professional writing and editing, writing of fiction or poetry. Total annual research expenditures: $1.2 million. *Unit head:* Robert Matz, Chair, 703-993-1170, E-mail: rmatz@gmu.edu. *Application contact:* Denise Albanese, Graduate Director, 703-993-1175, E-mail: dalbanes@gmu.edu.

Georgetown University, Graduate School of Arts and Sciences, Department of Linguistics, Washington, DC 20057. Offers bilingual education (Certificate); language and communication (MA); linguistics (MS, PhD), including applied linguistics, computational linguistics, sociolinguistics, theoretical linguistics; teaching English as a second language (MAT, Certificate); teaching English as a second language and bilingual education (MAT). Terminal master's awarded for partial completion of doctoral program. *Degree requirements:* For master's, one foreign language, comprehensive exam, optional research project; for doctorate, 2 foreign languages, comprehensive exam, thesis/dissertation. *Entrance requirements:* For master's and doctorate, 18 undergraduate credits in a foreign language. Additional exam requirements/recommendations for international students: Required—TOEFL.

Georgia State University, College of Arts and Sciences, Department of Applied Linguistics and English as a Second Language, Atlanta, GA 30302-3083. Offers applied linguistics (MA, PhD). Part-time programs available. *Degree requirements:* For master's, one foreign language, portfolio; for doctorate, one foreign language, comprehensive exam, thesis/dissertation, qualifying paper. *Entrance requirements:* For master's, GRE General Test; for doctorate, GRE. Additional exam requirements/recommendations for international students: Required—TOEFL (minimum score 600 paper-based; 250 computer-based; 97 iBT), TWE (minimum score 5). Electronic applications accepted. *Faculty research:* Native language and second language, second language literacy, intercultural communication, classroom-centered research, learning styles/strategies.

Graduate Institute of Applied Linguistics, Graduate Programs, Dallas, TX 75236. Offers applied linguistics (MA, Certificate); language development (MA). Part-time programs available. *Degree requirements:* For master's, one foreign language, comprehensive exam (for some programs), thesis (for some programs). *Entrance requirements:* For master's, GRE. Additional exam requirements/recommendations for international students: Required—TOEFL (minimum score 577 paper-based; 233 computer-based; 90 iBT). Electronic applications accepted. *Faculty research:* Minority languages, endangered languages, language documentation.

Graduate School and University Center of the City University of New York, Graduate Studies, Program in Anthropology, New York, NY 10016-4039. Offers anthropological linguistics (PhD); archaeology (PhD); cultural anthropology (PhD); physical anthropology (PhD). *Faculty:* 39 full-time (14 women). *Students:* 166 full-time (95 women), 1 (woman) part-time; includes 40 minority (13 African Americans, 1 American Indian/Alaska Native, 9 Asian Americans or Pacific Islanders, 17 Hispanic Americans), 25 international. Average age 33. 165 applicants, 27% accepted, 22 enrolled. In 2009, 13 doctorates awarded. *Degree requirements:* For doctorate, one foreign language, thesis/dissertation. *Entrance requirements:* For doctorate, GRE General Test. Additional exam requirements/recommendations for international students: Required—TOEFL. *Application deadline:* For fall admission, 1/8 priority date for domestic students. Application fee: $125. Electronic applications accepted. *Financial support:* In 2009–10, 111 students received support, including 88 fellowships, 16 research assistantships, 10 teaching assistantships; career-related internships or fieldwork, Federal Work-Study, institutionally sponsored loans, and tuition waivers (full and partial) also available. Financial award application deadline: 2/1; financial award applicants required to submit FAFSA. *Unit head:* Dr. Louise Lennihan, Executive Officer, 212-817-8006, Fax: 212-817-1501, E-mail: anthro@gc.cuny.edu. *Application contact:* Information Contact, 212-817-8005, Fax: 212-817-1501, E-mail: anthro@gc.cuny.edu.

Graduate School and University Center of the City University of New York, Graduate Studies, Program in Linguistics, New York, NY 10016-4039. Offers MA, PhD. *Faculty:* 20 full-time (5 women). *Students:* 82 full-time (59 women), 14 part-time (10 women); includes 15 minority (2 African Americans, 5 American Indian/Alaska Native, 4 Asian Americans or Pacific Islanders, 4 Hispanic Americans), 27 international. Average age 34. 68 applicants, 59% accepted, 20 enrolled. In 2009, 4 master's, 12 doctorates awarded. Terminal master's awarded for partial completion of doctoral program. *Degree requirements:* For master's, one foreign language, thesis; for doctorate, 2 foreign languages, thesis/dissertation. *Entrance requirements:* For master's and doctorate, GRE General Test. Additional exam requirements/recommendations for international students: Required—TOEFL. *Application deadline:* For fall admission, 1/15 for domestic students. Application fee: $125. Electronic applications accepted. *Financial support:* In 2009–10, 43 students received support, including 49 fellowships, 2 research assistantships; teaching assistantships, career-related internships or fieldwork, Federal Work-Study, institutionally sponsored loans, and tuition waivers (full and partial) also available. Financial award application deadline: 2/1; financial award applicants required to submit FAFSA. *Unit head:* Dr. Gita Martohardjono, Executive Officer, 212-817-8501, Fax: 212-817-1526. *Application contact:* Les Gribben, Director of Admissions, 212-817-7470, Fax: 212-817-1624, E-mail: lgribben@gc.cuny.edu.

Harvard University, Graduate School of Arts and Sciences, Department of Linguistics, Cambridge, MA 02138. Offers descriptive linguistics (PhD); historical linguistics (PhD); theoretical linguistics (PhD). *Degree requirements:* For doctorate, 4 foreign languages, thesis/dissertation, field exam, Indo-European language exam, research paper. *Entrance requirements:* For doctorate, GRE General Test. Additional exam requirements/recommendations for international students: Required—TOEFL. *Expenses:* Tuition: Full-time $33,696. Required fees: $1126. Full-time tuition and fees vary according to program.

Hofstra University, College of Liberal Arts and Sciences, Department of Comparative Literature and Languages, Hempstead, NY 11549. Offers applied linguistics (MA). Part-time programs available. *Faculty:* 4 full-time (0 women), 1 part-time/adjunct (0 women). *Students:* 2 full-time (1 woman), 2 part-time (both women), 2 international. Average age 27. 8 applicants, 75% accepted, 3 enrolled. In 2009, 3 master's awarded. *Degree requirements:* For master's, thesis, capstone. *Entrance requirements:* For master's, bachelor's degree in related area, interview, 2 letters of recommendation. Additional exam requirements/recommendations for international students: Required—TOEFL (minimum score 550 paper-based; 213 computer-based; 80 iBT). *Application deadline:* Applications are processed on a rolling basis. Application fee: $60. Electronic applications accepted. *Expenses:* Tuition: Full-time $16,200; part-time $900 per credit hour. Required fees: $970; $145 per term. Tuition and fees vary according to program. *Financial support:* Fellowships with full and partial tuition reimbursements, research assistantships with full and partial tuition reimbursements, Federal Work-Study, institutionally sponsored loans, scholarships/grants, tuition waivers (full and partial), and unspecified assistantships available. Support available to part-time students. Financial award applicants required to submit FAFSA. *Faculty research:* Second language acquisition, second language writing. *Unit head:* Dr. George L. Greaney, Director, 516-463-5651, E-mail: cllglg@hofstra.edu. *Application contact:* Carol Drummer, Dean of Graduate Admissions, 516-463-4876, Fax: 516-463-4664, E-mail: gradstudent@hofstra.edu.

Hofstra University, School of Education, Health, and Human Services, Department of Curriculum and Teaching, Program in Learning and Teaching, Hempstead, NY 11549. Offers learning and teaching (Ed D), including applied linguistics, art education, arts and humanities, early childhood education, English education, human development, math education, math, science, and technology, multicultural education, physical education, science education, social studies education, special education. Part-time and evening/weekend programs available. *Students:* 5 full-time (all women), 21 part-time (17 women); includes 2 minority (1 African American, 1 Hispanic American), 1 international. Average age 38. 22 applicants, 68% accepted, 11 enrolled. *Degree requirements:* For doctorate, comprehensive exam, thesis/dissertation. *Entrance requirements:* For doctorate, GRE, 3 letters of recommendation, interview, 2 years full-time teaching experience. Additional exam requirements/recommendations for inter-

Linguistics

Hofstra University (continued)

national students: Required—TOEFL (minimum score 550 paper-based; 213 computer-based; 80 iBT). *Application deadline:* Applications are processed on a rolling basis. Application fee: $60. Electronic applications accepted. *Expenses:* Tuition: Full-time $16,200; part-time $900 per credit hour. Required fees: $970; $145 per term. Tuition and fees vary according to program. *Financial support:* In 2009–10, 24 students received support, including 20 fellowships with full and partial tuition reimbursements available (averaging $4,906 per year); research assistantships with full and partial tuition reimbursements available, Federal Work-Study, institutionally sponsored loans, scholarships/grants, and tuition waivers (full and partial) also available. Support available to part-time students. Financial award applicants required to submit FAFSA. *Faculty research:* Critical thinking, professional development, teacher quality, quantitative research. *Unit head:* Dr. Bruce A. Torff, Director, 516-463-5803, Fax: 516-463-6196, E-mail: catajs@hofstra.edu. *Application contact:* Carol Drummer, Dean of Graduate Admissions, 516-463-4876, Fax: 516-463-4664, E-mail: gradstudent@hofstra.edu.

Indiana State University, School of Graduate Studies, College of Arts and Sciences, Department of Languages, Literatures, and Linguistics, Terre Haute, IN 47809. Offers linguistics/teaching English as a second language (MA); TESL/TEFL (CAS). *Degree requirements:* For master's, comprehensive exam. Electronic applications accepted.

Indiana University Bloomington, University Graduate School, College of Arts and Sciences, Department of French and Italian, Bloomington, IN 47405-7000. Offers French (MA, PhD), including French instruction (MA), French linguistics, French literature; Italian (MA, PhD). Part-time programs available. *Faculty:* 19 full-time (7 women). *Students:* 69 full-time (42 women), 5 part-time (4 women); includes 3 minority (1 American Indian/Alaska Native, 1 Asian American or Pacific Islander, 1 Hispanic American), 28 international. Average age 30. 48 applicants, 63% accepted, 15 enrolled. In 2009, 12 master's, 2 doctorates awarded. Terminal master's awarded for partial completion of doctoral program. *Degree requirements:* For master's, one foreign language, comprehensive exam, thesis optional; for doctorate, 2 foreign languages, comprehensive exam, thesis/dissertation. *Entrance requirements:* For master's and doctorate, GRE General Test. Additional exam requirements/recommendations for international students: Required—TOEFL (minimum score 550 paper-based; 213 computer-based; 79 iBT). *Application deadline:* For fall admission, 1/15 priority date for domestic students, 12/1 priority date for international students; for spring admission, 9/1 priority date for domestic and international students. Application fee: $55 ($65 for international students). Electronic applications accepted. *Financial support:* In 2009–10, 4 fellowships with partial tuition reimbursements (averaging $15,000 per year), 5 research assistantships with partial tuition reimbursements (averaging $13,025 per year), 39 teaching assistantships with partial tuition reimbursements (averaging $13,025 per year) were awarded. Financial award application deadline: 1/15. *Faculty research:* All periods of French and Italian literature and various areas of French linguistics, including the novel and political theory, literature and fine arts, literary theory, postcolonialism, French-Creole studies, French literature of Africa and its Diaspora, humanism, medieval folklore and mythology, humor in medieval and Renaissance literature, cinema Old Occitan and Old French, emigration, second language acquisition, syntax, sociolinguistics, phonology, lexicography. *Unit head:* Prof. Emanuel Mickel, Interim Chairman, 812-855-5458, Fax: 812-855-8877, E-mail: fritchr@indiana.edu. *Application contact:* Jocelyn Karlan, Secretary, 812-855-1088, Fax: 812-855-8877, E-mail: fritgs@indiana.edu.

Indiana University Bloomington, University Graduate School, College of Arts and Sciences, Department of Germanic Studies, Bloomington, IN 47405-7000. Offers German philology and linguistics (PhD); German studies (MA, PhD), including German (MA), German literature and culture (MA), German literature and linguistics (MA); medieval German studies (PhD); teaching German (MAT). *Faculty:* 13 full-time (4 women), 6 part-time/adjunct (2 women). *Students:* 34 full-time (19 women), 2 part-time (1 woman); includes 2 minority (1 African American, 1 Hispanic American), 9 international. Average age 30. 34 applicants, 41% accepted, 8 enrolled. In 2009, 3 master's, 2 doctorates awarded. Terminal master's awarded for partial completion of doctoral program. *Degree requirements:* For master's, one foreign language, project; for doctorate, one foreign language, comprehensive exam, thesis/dissertation. *Entrance requirements:* For master's, GRE General Test, BA in German or equivalent; for doctorate, GRE General Test, MA in German or equivalent. Additional exam requirements/recommendations for international students: Required—TOEFL. *Application deadline:* For fall admission, 1/15 priority date for domestic students, 12/15 for international students; for spring admission, 9/1 priority date for domestic students, 9/1 for international students. Applications are processed on a rolling basis. Application fee: $55 ($65 for international students). *Financial support:* In 2009–10, 8 fellowships with full and partial tuition reimbursements (averaging $20,000 per year), 1 research assistantship (averaging $13,025 per year), 20 teaching assistantships with full tuition reimbursements (averaging $13,025 per year) were awarded; Federal Work-Study, institutionally sponsored loans, scholarships/grants, and unspecified assistantships also available. Support available to part-time students. Financial award application deadline: 1/15; financial award applicants required to submit FAFSA. *Faculty research:* German and other European literature: medieval to modern/postmodern, German and culture studies, Germanic philology, literary theory, literature and the other arts. *Unit head:* William Rasch, Department Chairman, 812-855-7947, Fax: 812-855-8292, E-mail: wrasch@indiana.edu. *Application contact:* Michelle Dunbar, Graduate Secretary, 812-855-7947, E-mail: midunbar@indiana.edu.

Indiana University Bloomington, University Graduate School, College of Arts and Sciences, Department of Linguistics, Bloomington, IN 47405-7000. Offers African languages and linguistics (PhD); computational linguistics (MA, PhD); linguistics (MA, PhD). *Faculty:* 10 full-time (1 woman), 18 part-time/adjunct (7 women). *Students:* 81 full-time (45 women), 1 part-time (0 women); includes 7 minority (3 African Americans, 2 Asian Americans or Pacific Islanders, 2 Hispanic Americans), 32 international. Average age 32. 69 applicants, 43% accepted, 14 enrolled. In 2009, 8 master's, 8 doctorates awarded. Terminal master's awarded for partial completion of doctoral program. *Degree requirements:* For master's, one foreign language, thesis optional; for doctorate, one foreign language, comprehensive exam, thesis/dissertation, proficiency in research tool appropriate to research area. *Entrance requirements:* For master's and doctorate, GRE General Test. Additional exam requirements/recommendations for international students: Required—TOEFL (minimum score 580 paper-based; 237 computer-based). *Application deadline:* For fall admission, 1/15 priority date for domestic students, 12/1 priority date for international students. Application fee: $55 ($65 for international students). Electronic applications accepted. *Financial support:* In 2009–10, 29 students received support, including 10 fellowships with full tuition reimbursements available (averaging $15,000 per year), 8 research assistantships with full tuition reimbursements available (averaging $12,750 per year), 24 teaching assistantships with full tuition reimbursements available (averaging $12,750 per year); unspecified assistantships also available. *Faculty research:* African linguistics and language, semantics, phonology, syntactic theory, historical linguistics, phonetics-phonology, syntax, sociolinguistics, computational linguistics. Total annual research expenditures: $100,000. *Unit head:* Dr. Stuart Davis, Chair, 812-855-6456, Fax: 812-855-5363, E-mail: davis@indiana.edu. *Application contact:* Marilyn Estep, Secretary, 812-855-6456, Fax: 812-855-5363, E-mail: estepm@indiana.edu.

Indiana University of Pennsylvania, School of Graduate Studies and Research, College of Humanities and Social Sciences, Department of English, Indiana, PA 15705-1087. Offers composition and teaching English to speakers of other languages (MA, MAT, PhD), including composition and teaching English to speakers of other languages (PhD), teaching English (MAT), teaching English to speakers of other languages (MA); literature and criticism (MA, PhD), including generalist (MA), literature (MA), literature and criticism (PhD); rhetoric and linguistics (PhD). Part-time programs available. *Faculty:* 31 full-time (17 women). *Students:* 133 full-time (80 women), 235 part-time (141 women); includes 15 minority (5 African Americans, 7 Asian Americans or Pacific Islanders, 3 Hispanic Americans), 98 international. Average age 35. 326 applicants, 41% accepted, 82 enrolled. In 2009, 40 master's, 28 doctorates awarded. *Degree requirements:* For master's, thesis optional; for doctorate, one foreign language, comprehensive exam, thesis/dissertation. *Entrance requirements:* For master's and doctorate, 2 letters of recommendation. Additional exam requirements/recommendations for international students: Required—TOEFL. *Application deadline:* For fall admission, 7/1 priority date for domestic students; for spring admission, 11/1 for domestic students. Applications are processed on a rolling basis. Application fee: $40. *Expenses:* Tuition, state resident: full-time $6666; part-time $370 per credit hour. Tuition, nonresident: full-time $10,666; part-time $593 per credit hour. Required fees: $813 per semester. *Financial support:* In 2009–10, 11 fellowships (averaging $1,455 per year), 40 research assistantships with full and partial tuition reimbursements (averaging $5,973 per year), 17 teaching assistantships with partial tuition reimbursements (averaging $15,308 per year) were awarded. Financial award application deadline: 3/15; financial award applicants required to submit FAFSA. *Unit head:* Dr. Gail I. Berlin, Chairperson, 724-357-2261, E-mail: ivy@iup.edu. *Application contact:* Dr. Gail I. Berlin, Chairperson, 724-357-2261, E-mail: ivy@iup.edu.

Instituto Tecnologico de Santo Domingo, Graduate School, Santo Domingo, Dominican Republic. Offers applied linguistics (MA); construction administration (M Mgmt); corporate finance (M Mgmt); education (M Ed); engineering (M Eng), including data telecommunications, industrial engineering, logistics and supply chain, maintenance engineering, sanitary and environmental engineering, structural engineering; environmental science (M En S), including environmental education, environmental management, marine and coastal ecosystems, natural resources management; family therapy (MA); food science and technology (MS); human development (MA); human resources administration (M Mgmt); international business (M Mgmt); labor risks (M Mgmt); management (M Mgmt); marketing (M Mgmt); mathematics (MS); organizational development (M Mgmt); planning and taxation (M Mgmt); psychology (MA); social science (M Ed); upper management (M Mgmt). *Entrance requirements:* For master's, birth certificate, minimum GPA of 2.0.

Louisiana State University and Agricultural and Mechanical College, Graduate School, College of Arts and Sciences, Interdepartmental Program in Linguistics, Baton Rouge, LA 70803. Offers MA, PhD. *Students:* 14 full-time (12 women), 4 part-time (1 woman); includes 1 African American, 7 international. Average age 31. 20 applicants, 40% accepted, 2 enrolled. In 2009, 1 master's, 3 doctorates awarded. Terminal master's awarded for partial completion of doctoral program. *Degree requirements:* For master's, one foreign language, thesis or alternative; for doctorate, one foreign language, thesis/dissertation. *Entrance requirements:* For master's, GRE General Test, minimum GPA of 3.0; for doctorate, GRE General Test. Additional exam requirements/recommendations for international students: Required—TOEFL (minimum score 550 paper-based; 213 computer-based; 79 iBT) or IELTS (minimum score 6.5). *Application deadline:* For fall admission, 1/25 priority date for domestic students, 5/15 for international students; for spring admission, 10/15 for international students. Applications are processed on a rolling basis. Application fee: $50 ($70 for international students). Electronic applications accepted. *Financial support:* In 2009–10, 11 students received support, including 1 fellowship with full and partial tuition reimbursement available (averaging $19,243 per year), 1 research assistantship with partial tuition reimbursement available (averaging $12,000 per year), 8 teaching assistantships with partial tuition reimbursements available (averaging $10,687 per year); health care benefits also available. Financial award application deadline: 5/1; financial award applicants required to submit FAFSA. *Faculty research:* Neurolinguistics, speech science, English as a second language, Hispanic linguistics, anthropological linguistics. *Unit head:* Dr. Michael Hegarty, Associate Professor of English and Linguistics, 225-578-3021, Fax: 225-578-4129, E-mail: mhegar1@lsu.edu. *Application contact:* Dr. Michael Hegarty, Associate Professor of English and Linguistics, 225-578-3021, Fax: 225-578-4129, E-mail: mhegar1@lsu.edu.

Massachusetts Institute of Technology, School of Humanities, Arts, and Social Sciences, Department of Linguistics and Philosophy, Linguistics Section, Cambridge, MA 02139-4307. Offers PhD. *Faculty:* 13 full-time (4 women). *Students:* 36 full-time (15 women); includes 1 minority (Asian American or Pacific Islander), 25 international. Average age 28. 142 applicants, 10% accepted, 7 enrolled. In 2009, 7 doctorates awarded. *Degree requirements:* For doctorate, one foreign language, comprehensive exam, thesis/dissertation. *Entrance requirements:* Additional exam requirements/recommendations for international students: Required—TOEFL (minimum score 577 paper-based; 233 computer-based; 90 iBT), IELTS (minimum score 6.5). *Application deadline:* For fall admission, 1/2 for domestic and international students. Application fee: $75. Electronic applications accepted. *Expenses:* Tuition: Full-time $37,510; part-time $585 per unit. Required fees: $272. *Financial support:* In 2009–10, 19 fellowships with tuition reimbursements (averaging $30,718 per year), 14 research assistantships with tuition reimbursements (averaging $30,974 per year) were awarded; teaching assistantships with tuition reimbursements, Federal Work-Study, institutionally sponsored loans, scholarships/grants, health care benefits, and unspecified assistantships also available. *Unit head:* Prof. Irene Heim, Department Head and Linguistics Chair, 617-253-4141, Fax: 617-253-5017. *Application contact:* Graduate Admissions, 617-253-4141, Fax: 617-253-5017, E-mail: lp-admissions@mit.edu.

McGill University, Faculty of Graduate and Postdoctoral Studies, Faculty of Arts, Department of Linguistics, Montréal, QC H3A 2T5, Canada. Offers language acquisition (PhD); linguistics (MA, PhD).

Memorial University of Newfoundland, School of Graduate Studies, Department of Linguistics, St. John's, NL A1C 5S7, Canada. Offers MA, PhD. *Degree requirements:* For master's, one foreign language, thesis or comprehensive exam; for doctorate, 2 foreign languages, comprehensive exam, thesis/dissertation, oral defense of thesis. *Entrance requirements:* For master's, BA in linguistics; for doctorate, master's degree in linguistics. Electronic applications accepted. *Faculty research:* Aboriginal languages of eastern North America, historical/comparative linguistics, languages and dialects of Newfoundland and Labrador.

Michigan State University, The Graduate School, College of Arts and Letters, Department of Linguistics and Germanic, Slavic, Asian, and African Languages, East Lansing, MI 48824. Offers German studies (MA, PhD); linguistics (MA, PhD); teaching English to speakers of other languages (MA). Part-time and evening/weekend programs available. *Faculty:* 30 full-time (16 women). *Students:* 78 full-time (46 women), 20 part-time (13 women); includes 8 minority (2 African Americans, 3 American Indian/Alaska Native, 2 Asian Americans or Pacific Islanders, 1 Hispanic American), 51 international. Average age 30. 149 applicants, 38% accepted. In 2009, 24 master's awarded. *Entrance requirements:* For master's, GRE General Test, minimum GPA of 3.2 in last 2 undergraduate years, 2 years of college-level foreign language, 3 letters of recommendation, portfolio (German studies); for doctorate, GRE General Test, minimum graduate GPA of 3.5, 3 letters of recommendation, master's degree or sufficient graduate course work in linguistics or language of study, master's thesis or major research paper. Additional exam requirements/recommendations for international students: Required—TOEFL. Electronic applications accepted. *Expenses:* Tuition, state resident: part-time $478.25 per credit hour. Tuition, nonresident: part-time $966.50 per credit hour. Part-time tuition and fees vary according to program. *Financial support:* In 2009–10, 7 research assistantships with tuition reimbursements (averaging $6,071 per year), 31 teaching assistantships with tuition reimbursements (averaging $5,986 per year) were awarded. Total annual research expenditures: $351,012. *Unit head:* Dr. David K. Prestel, Chairperson, 517-353-0740, Fax: 517-432-2736, E-mail: prestel@msu.edu. *Application contact:* Julie Delgado, Graduate Studies Secretary, 517-353-0740, Fax: 517-432-2736, E-mail: delgadof@msu.edu.

Michigan State University, The Graduate School, College of Arts and Letters, Department of Spanish and Portuguese, East Lansing, MI 48824. Offers applied Spanish linguistics (MA); Hispanic cultural studies (PhD); Hispanic literatures (MA). *Faculty:* 14 full-time (7 women). *Students:* 26 full-time (17 women), 3 part-time (2 women); includes 10 minority (1 African American, 1 Asian American or Pacific Islander, 8 Hispanic Americans), 6 international. Average age 31. 23 applicants, 39% accepted. In 2009, 4 master's, 6 doctorates awarded. *Entrance requirements:* Additional exam requirements/recommendations for international students: Required—TOEFL. Electronic applications accepted. *Expenses:* Tuition, state resident: part-time $478.25 per credit hour. Tuition, nonresident: part-time $966.50 per credit hour. Part-time tuition and fees vary according to program. *Financial support:* In 2009–10, 20 teaching assistantships with tuition reimbursements (averaging $6,017 per year) were awarded. *Unit head:* Dr. Douglas Noverr, Acting Chairperson, 517-353-4939, Fax: 517-432-3844, E-mail: noverr@msu.edu. *Application contact:* Victoria Reynaga, Graduate Secretary, 517-355-8350, Fax: 517-432-3844, E-mail: reynagav@cal.msu.edu.

Midwestern Baptist Theological Seminary, Graduate and Professional Programs, Kansas City, MO 64118-4697. Offers Biblical archaeology (MA); Biblical languages (MA); Christian education (M Div, MACE); Christian foundations—lay ministry (Graduate Certificate); collegiate ministries (M Div); counseling (MA); educational ministry (D Ed Min); international church planting (M Div); ministry (M Div, D Min); North American church planting (M Div); sacred music (MCM); urban ministry (M Div); worship leadership (M Div); youth ministry (M Div). *Accreditation:* ATS. Part-time programs available. Postbaccalaureate distance learning degree programs offered (minimal on-campus study). *Degree requirements:* For doctorate, thesis/dissertation; for M Div, 2 foreign languages. *Entrance requirements:* For doctorate, MAT. Electronic applications accepted. *Faculty research:* Ministerial studies, Biblical and theological studies, missions, counseling.

Montclair State University, The Graduate School, College of Humanities and Social Sciences, Department of Linguistics, Montclair, NJ 07043-1624. Offers applied linguistics (MA); teacher of English as a second language (Certificate). Part-time and evening/weekend programs available. *Faculty:* 6 full-time (5 women), 18 part-time/adjunct (17 women). *Students:* 8 full-time (6 women), 26 part-time (24 women). Average age 36. 20 applicants, 55% accepted, 8 enrolled. In 2009, 17 master's, 6 other advanced degrees awarded. *Degree requirements:* For master's, comprehensive exam. *Entrance requirements:* For master's, GRE General Test, 2 letters of recommendation. Additional exam requirements/recommendations for international students: Required—TOEFL (minimum score 83 computer-based), or IELTS. *Application deadline:* For fall admission, 6/1 for international students; for spring admission, 10/1 for international students. Applications are processed on a rolling basis. Application fee: $60. Electronic applications accepted. *Expenses:* Tuition, area resident: Part-time $486.74 per credit. Tuition, state resident: part-time $486.74 per credit. Tuition, nonresident: part-time $751.34 per credit. Tuition and fees vary according to degree level and program. *Financial support:* In 2009–10, 1 research assistantship with full tuition reimbursement (averaging $7,000 per year) was awarded; Federal Work-Study, scholarships/grants, and unspecified assistantships also available. Support available to part-time students. Financial award application deadline: 3/1; financial award applicants required to submit FAFSA. *Unit head:* Dr. Eileen Fitzpatrick, Chairperson, 973-655-4480. *Application contact:* Amy Aiello, Director of Graduate Admissions and Operations, 973-655-5147, E-mail: graduate.school@montclair.edu.

New York University, Graduate School of Arts and Science, Department of Linguistics, New York, NY 10012-1019. Offers MA, PhD. Part-time programs available. *Faculty:* 8 full-time (2 women). *Students:* 44 full-time (21 women); includes 4 minority (2 African Americans, 1 Asian American or Pacific Islander, 1 Hispanic American), 15 international. Average age 30. 106 applicants, 19% accepted, 12 enrolled. In 2009, 2 master's, 5 doctorates awarded. Terminal master's awarded for partial completion of doctoral program. *Degree requirements:* For master's, one foreign language, comprehensive exam, thesis optional; for doctorate, one foreign language, thesis/dissertation, 2 publishable papers. *Entrance requirements:* For master's and doctorate, GRE General Test. Additional exam requirements/recommendations for international students: Required—TOEFL. *Application deadline:* For fall admission, 1/4 priority date for domestic students. Application fee: $90. *Expenses:* Tuition: Full-time $30,528; part-time $1272 per credit. Required fees: $2177. *Financial support:* Fellowships with tuition reimbursements, teaching assistantships with tuition reimbursements, Federal Work-Study, institutionally sponsored loans, scholarships/grants, health care benefits, and unspecified assistantships available. Financial award application deadline: 1/4; financial award applicants required to submit FAFSA. *Faculty research:* Phonology, syntax, sociolinguistics, cognitive science. *Unit head:* Alec Marantz, Chairman, 212-998-7950, Fax: 212-995-4707, E-mail: linguistics@nyu.edu. *Application contact:* Lisa Davidson, Director of Graduate Studies, 212-998-7950, Fax: 212-995-4707, E-mail: linguistics@nyu.edu.

New York University, Steinhardt School of Culture, Education, and Human Development, Department of Teaching and Learning, Program in English Education, New York, NY 10012-1019. Offers secondary and college (PhD), including applied linguistics, comparative education, curriculum, literature and reading, media education; teachers of English 7-12 (MA); teachers of English language and literature in college (Advanced Certificate). *Accreditation:* Teacher Education Accreditation Council. Part-time programs available. *Students:* 36 full-time (30 women), 30 part-time (25 women); includes 11 minority (4 African Americans, 3 Asian Americans or Pacific Islanders, 4 Hispanic Americans), 2 international. Average age 26. 91 applicants, 80% accepted, 21 enrolled. In 2009, 27 master's, 6 doctorates, 1 other advanced degree awarded. *Degree requirements:* For master's, thesis (for some programs); for doctorate, thesis/dissertation. *Entrance requirements:* For doctorate, GRE General Test, interview; for Advanced Certificate, master's degree. Additional exam requirements/recommendations for international students: Required—TOEFL. *Application deadline:* For fall admission, 12/15 priority date for domestic and international students; for spring admission, 11/1 for domestic and international students. Applications are processed on a rolling basis. Application fee: $75. Electronic applications accepted. *Expenses:* Tuition: Full-time $30,528; part-time $1272 per credit. Required fees: $2177. *Financial support:* Fellowships with full and partial tuition reimbursements, teaching assistantships with full and partial tuition reimbursements, career-related internships or fieldwork, Federal Work-Study, institutionally sponsored loans, scholarships/grants, tuition waivers (partial), and unspecified assistantships available. Support available to part-time students. Financial award application deadline: 2/1; financial award applicants required to submit FAFSA. *Faculty research:* Making meaning of literature, teaching of literature, urban adolescent literacy and equity, literacy development and globalization, digital media and literacy. *Unit head:* Director, 212-998-5460, Fax: 212-995-4049. *Application contact:* 212-998-5030, Fax: 212-995-4328, E-mail: steinhardt.gradadmissions@nyu.edu.

Northeastern Illinois University, Graduate College, College of Arts and Sciences, Department of Linguistics, Program in Linguistics, Chicago, IL 60625-4699. Offers MA. Part-time and evening/weekend programs available. *Degree requirements:* For master's, one foreign language, comprehensive exam, thesis optional. *Entrance requirements:* For master's, 9 undergraduate hours in a foreign language or equivalent, minimum GPA of 2.75. Additional exam requirements/recommendations for international students: Required—TOEFL (minimum score 550 paper-based; 213 computer-based; 80 iBT). Electronic applications accepted. *Faculty research:* Acquisition of literacy, Mayan language, Rotuman language, English as a second language methodology, Farsi language.

Northern Arizona University, Graduate College, College of Arts and Letters, Department of English, Programs in Teaching English as a Second Language/Applied Linguistics, Flagstaff, AZ 86011. Offers applied linguistics (PhD); teaching English as a second language (MA, Certificate). *Faculty:* 40 full-time (24 women). *Students:* 48 full-time (30 women), 7 part-time (4 women); includes 1 minority (Asian American or Pacific Islander), 17 international. Average age 35. 73 applicants, 71% accepted, 26 enrolled. In 2009, 32 master's, 9 doctorates awarded. *Degree requirements:* For master's, comprehensive exam, thesis optional, departmental qualifying exam; for doctorate, comprehensive exam, thesis/dissertation, departmental qualifying exam. *Entrance requirements:* For master's, minimum GPA of 3.0 or GRE General Test; for doctorate, GRE General Test. Additional exam requirements/recommendations for international students: Required—TOEFL (minimum score 570 paper-based; 230 computer-based; 89 iBT), IELTS (minimum score 7.5), or a bachelor's degree from an English-speaking university and demonstrated proficiency. *Application deadline:* For fall admission, 2/15 priority date for domestic students, 9/1 for international students; for spring admission, 11/15 priority date for domestic students. Applications are processed on a rolling basis. Application fee: $65. Electronic applications accepted. *Financial support:* In 2009–10, 63 teaching assistantships with partial tuition reimbursements (averaging $11,623 per year) were awarded; Federal Work-Study, scholarships/grants, health care benefits, tuition waivers, and unspecified assistantships also available. Support available to part-time students. Financial award application deadline: 3/30; financial award applicants required to submit FAFSA. *Unit head:* Dr. Fredricka Louise Stoller, Coordinator, 928-523-6272, Fax: 928-523-7074, E-mail: fredricka.stoller@nau.edu. *Application contact:* Barbara Hanks, Secretary, 928-523-4911, Fax: 928-523-7074, E-mail: barbara.hanks@nau.edu.

Northwestern University, The Graduate School, Judd A. and Marjorie Weinberg College of Arts and Sciences, Department of Linguistics, Evanston, IL 60208. Offers MA, PhD, JD/PhD. Admissions and degrees offered through The Graduate School. Part-time programs available. Terminal master's awarded for partial completion of doctoral program. *Degree requirements:* For master's, one foreign language, thesis; for doctorate, 2 foreign languages, thesis/dissertation, 2 qualifying papers. *Entrance requirements:* For master's and doctorate, GRE General Test. Additional exam requirements/recommendations for international students: Required—TOEFL. Electronic applications accepted. *Faculty research:* Theoretical linguistics, empirical approaches to the study of language, language and cognition.

Oakland University, Graduate Study and Lifelong Learning, College of Arts and Sciences, Department of Linguistics, Rochester, MI 48309-4401. Offers linguistics (MA); teaching English as a second language (Certificate). Part-time and evening/weekend programs available. *Entrance requirements:* For master's, minimum GPA of 3.0 for unconditional admission. Additional exam requirements/recommendations for international students: Required—TOEFL (minimum score 550 paper-based; 213 computer-based).

The Ohio State University, Graduate School, College of Humanities, Department of Linguistics, Columbus, OH 43210. Offers MA, PhD. *Faculty:* 16. *Students:* 31 full-time (18 women), 19 part-time (10 women); includes 5 minority (2 African Americans, 2 Asian Americans or Pacific Islanders, 1 Hispanic American), 16 international. Average age 28. In 2009, 9 master's, 5 doctorates awarded. *Degree requirements:* For master's, one foreign language, exam or thesis; for doctorate, 2 foreign languages, thesis/dissertation, exam. *Entrance requirements:* For master's and doctorate, GRE General Test. Additional exam requirements/recommendations for international students: Required—TOEFL (minimum score 600 paper-based; 250 computer-based). *Application deadline:* For fall admission, 8/15 priority date for domestic students, 7/1 priority date for international students; for winter admission, 12/1 priority date for domestic students, 11/1 priority date for international students; for spring admission, 3/1 priority date for domestic students, 2/1 priority date for international students. Applications are processed on a rolling basis. Application fee: $40 ($50 for international students). Electronic applications accepted. *Expenses:* Tuition, state resident: full-time $10,683. Tuition, nonresident: full-time $25,923. Tuition and fees vary according to course load and program. *Financial support:* Fellowships, research assistantships, teaching assistantships, Federal Work-Study and institutionally sponsored loans available. Support available to part-time students. *Faculty research:* Experimental phonetics, nonlinear phonology, process morphology (synchronically and diachronically), syntactic theory (GB, GPSG, HPSG, Categorical Grammar, Relational Grammar), Montague semantics. *Unit head:* Peter Culicover, Graduate Studies Committee Chair, 614-292-4052, Fax: 614-292-4273, E-mail: culicover.1@osu.edu. *Application contact:* 614-292-9444, Fax: 614-292-3895, E-mail: domestic.grad@osu.edu.

Ohio University, Graduate College, College of Arts and Sciences, Department of Linguistics, Athens, OH 45701-2979. Offers applied linguistics/TESOL (MA). Part-time programs available. *Faculty:* 9 full-time (3 women), 5 part-time/adjunct (3 women). *Students:* 37 full-time (27 women), 3 part-time (2 women); includes 2 minority (1 Asian American or Pacific Islander, 1 Hispanic American), 24 international. 53 applicants, 62% accepted, 16 enrolled. In 2009, 20 master's awarded. *Degree requirements:* For master's, one foreign language, thesis or alternative. *Entrance requirements:* For master's, minimum GPA of 3.0. Additional exam requirements/recommendations for international students: Required—TOEFL (minimum score 600 paper-based; 100 iBT) or IELTS Academic (minimum score 7). *Application deadline:* For fall admission, 2/15 priority date for domestic and international students. Application fee: $50 ($55 for international students). Electronic applications accepted. *Expenses:* Tuition, state resident: full-time $7839; part-time $323 per quarter hour. Tuition, nonresident: full-time $15,831; part-time $654 per quarter hour. Required fees: $2931. *Financial support:* In 2009–10, 2 fellowships with tuition reimbursements were awarded; research assistantships with tuition reimbursements, teaching assistantships with tuition reimbursements, Federal Work-Study, institutionally sponsored loans, tuition waivers (partial), and unspecified assistantships also available. Financial award application deadline: 2/15. *Faculty research:* Syntax, language learning, language teaching, computers for teaching, sociolinguistics. *Unit head:* Dr. Chris Thompson, Chair, E-mail: thompsoc@ohio.edu. *Application contact:* Dr. Hiroyuki Oshita, Graduate Chair, 740-593-4570, Fax: 740-593-2967, E-mail: oshita@ohio.edu.

Old Dominion University, College of Arts and Letters, Program in Applied Linguistics, Norfolk, VA 23529. Offers MA. Part-time programs available. *Faculty:* 4 full-time (all women). *Students:* 15 full-time (9 women), 11 part-time (9 women); includes 3 minority (1 African American, 1 Asian American or Pacific Islander, 1 Hispanic American), 5 international. Average age 31. 18 applicants, 78% accepted, 10 enrolled. In 2009, 8 master's awarded. *Degree requirements:* For master's, one foreign language, comprehensive exam, thesis optional. *Entrance requirements:* For master's, GRE General Test, sample of written work, 12 hours in English, minimum B average. Additional exam requirements/recommendations for international students: Required—TOEFL (minimum score 570 paper-based; 213 computer-based; 80 iBT). *Application deadline:* For fall admission, 6/1 priority date for domestic students, 4/15 priority date for international students; for spring admission, 11/1 priority date for domestic students, 10/1 priority date for international students. Applications are processed on a rolling basis. Application fee: $50. Electronic applications accepted. *Expenses:* Tuition, state resident: full-time $8112; part-time $338 per credit. Tuition, nonresident: full-time $20,256; part-time $844 per credit. Required fees: $119 per semester. One-time fee: $50. *Financial support:* In 2009–10, 7 students received support, including 1 research assistantship with partial tuition reimbursement available (averaging $8,000 per year), 3 teaching assistantships with partial tuition reimbursements available (averaging $8,000 per year); career-related internships or fieldwork, institutionally sponsored loans, and unspecified assistantships also available. Financial award application deadline: 2/15. *Faculty research:* Discourse analysis, phonology, syntax, first and second language acquisition, gender, sociolinguistics. *Unit head:* Dr. Joanne Scheibman, Graduate Program Director, 757-683-3879, Fax: 757-683-3241, E-mail: lingpd@odu.edu. *Application contact:* Dr. Robert Wojtowicz, Associate Dean, 757-683-6077, Fax: 757-683-5746, E-mail: rwojtowi@odu.edu.

Penn State University Park, Graduate School, College of the Liberal Arts, Department of Linguistics and Applied Language Studies, State College, University Park, PA 16802-1503. Offers MA, PhD. *Unit head:* Dr. Joan Kelly Hall, Head, 814-865-7365, Fax: 814-865-7944, E-mail: jkh11@psu.edu. *Application contact:* Cynthia E. Nicosia, Director, Graduate Enrollment Services, 814-865-1795, Fax: 814-865-4627, E-mail: cey1@psu.edu.

Purdue University, Graduate School, College of Liberal Arts, Department of English, West Lafayette, IN 47907. Offers creative writing (MFA); literature (MA, PhD), including linguistics, literature and philosophy (PhD), rhetoric and composition, theory and cultural studies (PhD). Part-time programs available. *Degree requirements:* For master's, one foreign language; for doctorate, one foreign language, thesis/dissertation. *Entrance requirements:* For master's and doctorate, GRE General Test, sample of written work. Additional exam requirements/recommendations for international students: Required—TOEFL. Electronic applications accepted. *Faculty research:* Cultural studies, postmodern narrative, contemporary women writers, composition theory, slave narratives.

Purdue University, Graduate School, College of Liberal Arts, Department of Speech, Language, and Hearing Sciences, West Lafayette, IN 47907. Offers audiology (MS, Au D, PhD); linguistics (MS, PhD); speech and hearing science (MS, PhD); speech-language pathology (MS, PhD). *Accreditation:* ASHA. *Degree requirements:* For master's, thesis optional; for doctorate, thesis/dissertation. *Entrance requirements:* For master's and doctorate, GRE. Additional exam requirements/recommendations for international students: Required—TOEFL. Electronic applica-

Linguistics

Purdue University (continued)
tions accepted. *Faculty research:* Psychoacoustics, speech perception, speech physiology, stuttering, child language.

Purdue University, Graduate School, College of Liberal Arts, Program in Linguistics, West Lafayette, IN 47907. Offers MS, PhD. *Entrance requirements:* For master's and doctorate, GRE, minimum GPA of 3.4. Additional exam requirements/recommendations for international students: Required—TOEFL. Electronic applications accepted. *Faculty research:* Sign languages, sociolinguistics and African American English, computational linguistics, indigenous languages, theoretical linguistics.

Queens College of the City University of New York, Division of Graduate Studies, Arts and Humanities Division, Department of Linguistics and Communication Disorders, Program in Applied Linguistics, Flushing, NY 11367-1597. Offers MA. Part-time and evening/weekend programs available. *Faculty:* 8 full-time (5 women). *Students:* 1 (woman) full-time, 6 part-time (all women). 18 applicants, 33% accepted, 4 enrolled. In 2009, 4 master's awarded. *Degree requirements:* For master's, thesis optional. *Entrance requirements:* For master's, minimum GPA of 3.0. Additional exam requirements/recommendations for international students: Required—TOEFL. *Application deadline:* For fall admission, 4/1 for domestic students; for spring admission, 11/1 for domestic students. Applications are processed on a rolling basis. Application fee: $125. *Expenses:* Tuition, state resident: full-time $7360; part-time $310 per credit. Tuition, nonresident: part-time $575 per credit. One-time fee: $195.25 full-time; $145.25 part-time. *Financial support:* Career-related internships or fieldwork, Federal Work-Study, institutionally sponsored loans, and tuition waivers (partial) available. Support available to part-time students. Financial award application deadline: 4/1; financial award applicants required to submit FAFSA. *Unit head:* Dr. Robert M. Vago, Chairperson, 718-997-2875. *Application contact:* Mario Caruso, Director of Graduate Admissions, 718-997-5200, Fax: 718-997-5193, E-mail: graduate_admissions@qc.edu.

Rice University, Graduate Programs, School of Humanities, Department of Linguistics, Houston, TX 77251-1892. Offers MA, PhD. *Faculty:* 8 full-time (4 women). *Students:* 28 full-time (18 women); includes 1 minority (Hispanic American), 14 international. Average age 30. 52 applicants, 12% accepted, 3 enrolled. In 2009, 2 master's, 1 doctorate awarded. Terminal master's awarded for partial completion of doctoral program. *Degree requirements:* For master's, one foreign language, thesis; for doctorate, 2 foreign languages, thesis/dissertation, 3 research papers. *Entrance requirements:* For master's and doctorate, GRE General Test, minimum GPA of 3.0. Additional exam requirements/recommendations for international students: Required—TOEFL (minimum score 600 paper-based; 250 computer-based; 90 iBT). *Application deadline:* For fall admission, 2/1 priority date for domestic and international students. Applications are processed on a rolling basis. Application fee: $70. Electronic applications accepted. *Financial support:* In 2009–10, 18 students received support, including 15 fellowships with full and partial tuition reimbursements available (averaging $15,900 per year); scholarships/grants, tuition waivers (full and partial), and unspecified assistantships also available. Financial award application deadline: 2/1. *Faculty research:* Typology, fieldwork and language description, cognitive grammar, historical linguistics, corpus linguistics. *Unit head:* Dr. Nancy Niedzielski, Chair, 713-348-6299, Fax: 713-348-4718, E-mail: niedz@rice.edu. *Application contact:* Rita F. Riley, Department Coordinator, 713-348-6010, Fax: 713-348-4718, E-mail: ling@rice.edu.

Rutgers, The State University of New Jersey, New Brunswick, Graduate School-New Brunswick, Department of Linguistics, Piscataway, NJ 08854-8097. Offers PhD. *Degree requirements:* For doctorate, thesis/dissertation, 2 qualifying papers. *Entrance requirements:* For doctorate, GRE General Test, 3 letters of recommendation, writing sample. Electronic applications accepted. *Faculty research:* Theoretical linguistics, syntax, semantics, phonology, computational linguistics, phoenetics.

San Diego State University, Graduate and Research Affairs, College of Arts and Letters, Department of Linguistics and Oriental Languages, San Diego, CA 92182. Offers applied linguistics and English as a second language (CAL); computational linguistics (MA); English as a second language/applied linguistics (MA); general linguistics (MA). *Degree requirements:* For master's, one foreign language, comprehensive exam, thesis optional. *Entrance requirements:* For master's, GRE General Test, 2 letters of recommendation. Additional exam requirements/recommendations for international students: Required—TOEFL (minimum score 570 paper-based). Electronic applications accepted. *Faculty research:* Cross-cultural linguistic studies of semantics.

San Francisco State University, Division of Graduate Studies, College of Humanities, Department of English Language and Literature, Program in Linguistics, San Francisco, CA 94132-1722. Offers MA. Part-time programs available. *Degree requirements:* For master's, 2 foreign languages, thesis (for some programs). *Faculty research:* Mental lexicon, endangered languages, language and gender, linguistics, discourse analysis.

San Jose State University, Graduate Studies and Research, College of Humanities and the Arts, Department of Linguistics and Language Development, San Jose, CA 95192-0001. Offers computational linguistics (Certificate); linguistics (MA); teaching English to speakers of other languages (MA, Certificate). *Students:* 44 full-time (28 women), 55 part-time (44 women); includes 35 minority (25 Asian Americans or Pacific Islanders, 10 Hispanic Americans), 18 international. Average age 38. 101 applicants, 58% accepted, 26 enrolled. In 2009, 38 master's awarded. *Entrance requirements:* Additional exam requirements/recommendations for international students: Required—TOEFL (minimum score 570 paper-based; 230 computer-based). *Application deadline:* For fall admission, 6/29 for domestic students; for spring admission, 11/30 for domestic students. Applications are processed on a rolling basis. Application fee: $59. Electronic applications accepted. *Financial support:* Applicants required to submit FAFSA. *Unit head:* Dr. Manjari Ohala, Chair, 408-924-4413, Fax: 408-924-4703. *Application contact:* Dr. Manjari Ohala, Chair, 408-924-4413, Fax: 408-924-4703.

Simon Fraser University, Graduate Studies, Faculty of Arts and Social Sciences, Department of Linguistics, Burnaby, BC V5A 1S6, Canada. Offers MA, PhD. *Degree requirements:* For master's, one foreign language, thesis; for doctorate, 2 foreign languages, thesis/dissertation. *Entrance requirements:* For master's, minimum GPA of 3.0; for doctorate, minimum GPA of 3.5. Additional exam requirements/recommendations for international students: Required—TOEFL or IELTS. *Faculty research:* History of linguistics, syntactic theory, relational grammar, experimental phonetics, pragmatics.

Southern Illinois University Carbondale, Graduate School, College of Liberal Arts, Department of Applied Linguistics, Carbondale, IL 62901-4701. Offers applied linguistics (MA); teaching English to speakers of other languages (MA). *Degree requirements:* For master's, one foreign language, thesis. *Entrance requirements:* For master's, minimum GPA of 3.0. Additional exam requirements/recommendations for international students: Required—TOEFL. *Faculty research:* Theory and methods, second language acquisition, pidgin and Creole languages, cognitive grammar.

Stanford University, School of Humanities and Sciences, Department of Linguistics, Stanford, CA 94305-9991. Offers MA, PhD. *Degree requirements:* For master's, one foreign language, thesis; for doctorate, 2 foreign languages, thesis/dissertation, oral exam, qualifying papers. *Entrance requirements:* For master's and doctorate, GRE General Test. Additional exam requirements/recommendations for international students: Required—TOEFL. Electronic applications accepted. *Expenses:* Tuition: Full-time $37,380; part-time $2760 per quarter. Required fees: $501.

Stony Brook University, State University of New York, Graduate School, College of Arts and Sciences, Department of Linguistics, Program in Linguistics, Stony Brook, NY 11794. Offers MA, PhD. *Faculty:* 10 full-time (5 women). *Students:* 25 full-time (19 women), 2 part-time (both women); includes 1 Asian American or Pacific Islander, 16 international. Average age 31. 43 applicants, 23% accepted. In 2009, 2 master's, 4 doctorates awarded. *Application deadline:* For fall admission, 1/15 for domestic students. Application fee: $60. *Expenses:* Tuition, state resident: full-time $8370; part-time $349 per credit. Tuition, nonresident: full-time $13,250; part-time $552 per credit. Required fees: $933. *Financial support:* Fellowships, research assistantships, teaching assistantships available. *Unit head:* Dr. Robert Hoberman, Chair, 631-632-7774, Fax: 631-632-9789. *Application contact:* Michelle Carbone, 631-632-7774, Fax: 631-632-9789.

Syracuse University, College of Arts and Sciences, Program in Linguistic Studies, Syracuse, NY 13244. Offers MA. Part-time programs available. *Students:* 14 full-time (11 women), 5 part-time (all women), 9 international. Average age 25. 31 applicants, 65% accepted, 10 enrolled. In 2009, 7 master's awarded. *Degree requirements:* For master's, comprehensive exam, thesis or alternative. *Entrance requirements:* For master's, GRE General Test. Additional exam requirements/recommendations for international students: Required—TOEFL (minimum score 100 iBT). *Application deadline:* For fall admission, 1/10 priority date for domestic and international students. Application fee: $75. Electronic applications accepted. *Expenses:* Tuition: Full-time $26,808; part-time $1117 per credit. Required fees: $1024. *Financial support:* Fellowships with full tuition reimbursements, teaching assistantships with full tuition reimbursements, tuition waivers (partial) available. Financial award application deadline: 1/1; financial award applicants required to submit FAFSA. *Unit head:* Dr. Tej Bhatia, Graduate Program Coordinator, 315-443-2175, Fax: 315-443-5376. *Application contact:* Barbara Moon, Recruiting Contact, 315-443-5906, E-mail: bamoon@syr.edu.

Teachers College, Columbia University, Graduate Faculty of Education, Department of Arts and Humanities, Program in Applied Linguistics, New York, NY 10027-6696. Offers Ed M, MA, Ed D. Part-time and evening/weekend programs available. *Faculty:* 4 full-time (3 women). *Students:* 10 full-time (8 women), 55 part-time (46 women); includes 17 minority (1 African American, 16 Asian Americans or Pacific Islanders), 14 international. Average age 34. 73 applicants, 47% accepted, 14 enrolled. In 2009, 23 master's, 9 doctorates awarded. Terminal master's awarded for partial completion of doctoral program. *Degree requirements:* For doctorate, variable foreign language requirement, thesis/dissertation. *Application deadline:* For fall admission, 5/15 for domestic students; for spring admission, 12/1 for domestic students. Application fee: $65. *Financial support:* Fellowships, research assistantships, teaching assistantships, career-related internships or fieldwork, Federal Work-Study, institutionally sponsored loans, and tuition waivers (full and partial) available. Support available to part-time students. Financial award application deadline: 2/1. *Faculty research:* Linguistics applied to education and other professions, sociolinguistics and second language acquisition, rude speech and social rules of speaking. *Unit head:* Graeme Sullivan, Chair, 212-678-3799. *Application contact:* Mark E. Stearns, Associate Director of Admission, 212-678-3710, Fax: 212-678-4171.

Temple University, Health Sciences Center and Graduate School, College of Health Professions, Department of Communication Sciences, Program in Linguistics, Philadelphia, PA 19122-6096. Offers MA. Part-time and evening/weekend programs available. *Degree requirements:* For master's, comprehensive exam. *Entrance requirements:* For master's, GRE General Test, minimum GPA of 3.0. Additional exam requirements/recommendations for international students: Required—TOEFL (minimum score 550 paper-based; 213 computer-based; 79 iBT). Electronic applications accepted. *Faculty research:* Generative syntax, generative phonology, formal semantics, sociolinguistics.

Texas Tech University, Graduate School, College of Arts and Sciences, Department of Classical and Modern Languages and Literatures, MA in Applied Linguistics Program, Lubbock, TX 79409. Offers MA. *Students:* 22 full-time (15 women), 4 part-time (2 women), 14 international. Average age 31. 22 applicants, 68% accepted, 4 enrolled. In 2009, 5 master's awarded. *Entrance requirements:* Additional exam requirements/recommendations for international students: Required—TOEFL (minimum score 550 paper-based; 213 computer-based). *Application deadline:* For fall admission, 3/1 priority date for international students; for spring admission, 11/1 priority date for international students. Application fee: $50 ($75 for international students). *Expenses:* Tuition, state resident: full-time $5100; part-time $213 per credit hour. Tuition, nonresident: full-time $11,748; part-time $490 per credit hour. Required fees: $2298; $50 per credit hour. $555 per semester. *Financial support:* Research assistantships available. *Faculty research:* Second language acquisition; second language instruction; language processing; assessment; general linguistics. *Unit head:* Dr. Bill VanPatten, Director and Professor, 860-742-3145 Ext. 232, Fax: 860-742-3306, E-mail: bill.vanpatten@ttu.edu. *Application contact:* Liz Hildebrand, Senior Advisor, 806-742-4055, Fax: 806-742-3306, E-mail: liz.hildebrand@ttu.edu.

Trinity Western University, Faculty of Graduate Studies, Program in Linguistics, Langley, BC V2Y 1Y1, Canada. Offers MA. *Degree requirements:* For master's, essay (for non-thesis students). *Entrance requirements:* For master's, minimum GPA of 2.7, 3.0 in last two years; 12 seminar hours; linguistic prerequisites; 1 foreign language. Additional exam requirements/recommendations for international students: Required—TOEFL (minimum score 600 paper-based; 250 computer-based). Electronic applications accepted. *Expenses:* Contact institution. *Faculty research:* Syntax, phonology, tone, historical and comparative, discourse analysis.

Universidad de las Américas–Puebla, Division of Graduate Studies, School of Humanities, Program in Applied Linguistics, Puebla, Mexico. Offers linguistics (MA). Part-time and evening/weekend programs available. *Degree requirements:* For master's, one foreign language, thesis. *Entrance requirements:* Additional exam requirements/recommendations for international students: Required—TOEFL. *Faculty research:* English linguistics, teaching English to speakers of other languages.

Université de Montréal, Faculty of Arts and Sciences, Department of Linguistics and Translation, Montréal, QC H3C 3J7, Canada. Offers linguistics and translation (MA, PhD, DESS). *Degree requirements:* For master's, thesis, general exam; for doctorate, thesis/dissertation, general exam. Electronic applications accepted.

Université de Sherbrooke, Faculty of Letters and Human Sciences, Department of Letters and Communications, Sherbrooke, QC J1K 2R1, Canada. Offers comparative Canadian literature (MA, PhD); French literature (MA, PhD); linguistics (MA); theatre (MA). *Degree requirements:* For master's, thesis or alternative; for doctorate, thesis/dissertation. *Entrance requirements:* For master's, minimum GPA of 2.8; for doctorate, minimum GPA of 3.0.

Université du Québec à Chicoutimi, Graduate Programs, Program in Linguistics, Chicoutimi, QC G7H 2B1, Canada. Offers MA. Part-time programs available. *Degree requirements:* For master's, thesis. *Entrance requirements:* For master's, appropriate bachelor's degree, proficiency in French.

Université du Québec à Montréal, Graduate Programs, Program in Linguistics, Montréal, QC H3C 3P8, Canada. Offers MA, PhD. Part-time programs available. *Degree requirements:* For master's, thesis optional; for doctorate, thesis/dissertation. *Entrance requirements:* For master's, appropriate bachelor's degree or equivalent, proficiency in French; for doctorate, appropriate master's degree or equivalent, proficiency in French.

Université Laval, Faculty of Letters, Department of Languages, Linguistics and Translations, Programs in Linguistics, Québec, QC G1K 7P4, Canada. Offers MA, PhD. Terminal master's awarded for partial completion of doctoral program. *Degree requirements:* For master's, thesis (for some programs); for doctorate, comprehensive exam, thesis/dissertation. *Entrance requirements:* For master's, English test (comprehension of written English), knowledge of French; for doctorate, English exam (comprehension of written English), knowledge of French. Electronic applications accepted.

University at Buffalo, the State University of New York, Graduate School, College of Arts and Sciences, Department of Linguistics, Buffalo, NY 14260. Offers MA, PhD. *Faculty:* 15 full-time (5 women), 2 part-time/adjunct (1 woman). *Students:* 51 full-time (23 women), 5 part-time (2 women); includes 3 minority (1 American Indian/Alaska Native, 2 Asian Americans or Pacific Islanders), 27 international. Average age 30. 58 applicants, 76% accepted, 18 enrolled. In 2009, 15 master's, 6 doctorates awarded. Terminal master's awarded for partial completion of doctoral program. *Degree requirements:* For master's, exam, project, or thesis; for doctorate, thesis/dissertation, qualifying paper. *Entrance requirements:* For master's and doctorate, GRE General Test. Additional exam requirements/recommendations for international students: Required—TOEFL (minimum score 600 paper-based; 250 computer-based; 100 iBT). *Application deadline:* For fall admission, 4/1 for domestic students, 3/1 for international students. Application fee: $50. Electronic applications accepted. *Financial support:* In 2009–10, 24 students received support, including 4 fellowships with full tuition reimbursements available (averaging $4,500 per year), 2 research assistantships with full tuition reimbursements available (averaging $11,400 per year), 18 teaching assistantships with full tuition reimbursements available (averaging $13,300 per year); scholarships/grants and unspecified assistantships also available. Financial award application deadline: 1/15; financial award applicants required to submit FAFSA. *Faculty research:* Cognitive linguistics, cross-linguistic studies, psycholinguistics, syntax, semantics. *Unit head:* Dr. Karin Michelson, Chair, 716-645-2177, Fax: 716-645-3825, E-mail: kmich@buffalo.edu. *Application contact:* Jodi L. Reiner, Secretary, 716-645-3794 Ext. 785, Fax: 716-645-3825, E-mail: jlreiner@buffalo.edu.

University of Alaska Fairbanks, College of Liberal Arts, Program in Linguistics, Fairbanks, AK 99775-6280. Offers applied linguistics (MA), including language documentation, second language acquisition teacher education. Part-time programs available. *Faculty:* 3 full-time (1 woman), 1 (woman) part-time/adjunct. *Students:* 3 full-time (2 women), 25 part-time (23 women); includes 18 minority (17 American Indian/Alaska Native, 1 Asian American or Pacific Islander), 1 international. Average age 44. 6 applicants, 50% accepted, 2 enrolled. *Degree requirements:* For master's, comprehensive exam, thesis or alternative. *Entrance requirements:* Additional exam requirements/recommendations for international students: Required—TOEFL (minimum score 550 paper-based; 213 computer-based; 80 iBT). *Application deadline:* For fall admission, 6/1 for domestic students, 3/1 for international students; for spring admission, 10/15 for domestic students, 9/1 for international students. Application fee: $60. *Expenses:* Tuition, state resident: full-time $7584; part-time $316 per credit. Tuition, nonresident: full-time $15,504; part-time $646 per credit. Required fees: $23 per credit. $135 per semester. Tuition and fees vary according to course level, course load and reciprocity agreements. *Financial support:* In 2009–10, 2 research assistantships (averaging $25,033 per year), 1 teaching assistantship (averaging $9,354 per year) were awarded; fellowships, career-related internships or fieldwork, Federal Work-Study, scholarships/grants, health care benefits, and unspecified assistantships also available. Support available to part-time students. Financial award application deadline: 7/1; financial award applicants required to submit FAFSA. *Faculty research:* Second language acquisition/teaching, INUPIAQ, Athabaskan languages, language maintenance and shift, phonology, morphology. *Unit head:* Dr. Siri Tuttle, Program Head, 907-474-7876, Fax: 907-474-6586, E-mail: ffamb@uaf.edu. *Application contact:* Dr. Siri Tuttle, Program Head, 907-474-7876, Fax: 907-474-6586, E-mail: ffamb@uaf.edu.

University of Alberta, Faculty of Graduate Studies and Research, Department of Linguistics, Edmonton, AB T6G 2E1, Canada. Offers experimental linguistics (M Sc, PhD). *Faculty:* 9 full-time (2 women), 4 part-time/adjunct (all women). *Students:* 21 full-time (12 women), 2 part-time (1 woman). Average age 30. In 2009, 3 master's, 3 doctorates awarded. *Degree requirements:* For master's, thesis (for some programs); for doctorate, thesis/dissertation. *Entrance requirements:* For master's, BA in linguistics; for doctorate, M Sc or MA in linguistics. Additional exam requirements/recommendations for international students: Required—TOEFL. *Application deadline:* For fall admission, 2/1 priority date for domestic and international students. Applications are processed on a rolling basis. Application fee: $0. Tuition and fees charges are reported in Canadian dollars. *Expenses:* Tuition, area resident: Full-time $4626 Canadian dollars; part-time $99.72 Canadian dollars per unit. International tuition: $8216 Canadian dollars full-time. Required fees: $3590 Canadian dollars; $99.72 Canadian dollars per unit. $215 Canadian dollars per term. *Financial support:* In 2009–10, 11 students received support, including 1 fellowship (averaging $30,000 per year), research assistantships (averaging $10,000 per year), teaching assistantships (averaging $10,000 per year); scholarships/grants and unspecified assistantships also available. Financial award application deadline: 3/1. *Faculty research:* Experimental phonetics, psycholinguistics, phonology, endangered languages, language acquisition. *Unit head:* Dr. John Newman, Chair, 780-492-3459, Fax: 403-492-0806, E-mail: john.newman@ualberta.ca. *Application contact:* Debra Elliot, Department Administrator, 403-492-3459, Fax: 403-492-0806, E-mail: linggrad@ualberta.ca.

University of Alberta, Faculty of Graduate Studies and Research, Department of Modern Languages and Cultural Studies, Edmonton, AB T6G 2E1, Canada. Offers applied linguistics (Germanic, Romance, Slavic) (MA); French language, literatures and linguistics (PhD); French language, literatures, and linguistics (MA); Germanic languages, literatures and linguistics (PhD); Germanic languages, literatures, and linguistics (MA); Italian studies (MA); Slavic languages and literatures (Russian, Ukrainian) (MA, PhD); Slavic linguistics (Russian, Ukrainian) (MA, PhD); Spanish and Latin American studies (MA, PhD); Ukrainian folklore (MA, PhD). Part-time programs available. *Faculty:* 33 full-time (15 women), 2 part-time/adjunct (1 woman). *Students:* 39 full-time (29 women), 13 part-time (12 women). 300 applicants, 10% accepted. In 2009, 12 master's, 2 doctorates awarded. *Degree requirements:* For master's, one foreign language, thesis; for doctorate, 2 foreign languages, comprehensive exam, thesis/dissertation. *Entrance requirements:* For master's and doctorate, 1 language other than English. Additional exam requirements/recommendations for international students: Required—Michigan English Language Assessment Battery or TOEFL (minimum score 550 paper-based; 213 computer-based). *Application deadline:* For fall admission, 7/1 for domestic and international students; for winter admission, 11/1 for domestic and international students; for spring admission, 3/1 for domestic students. Applications are processed on a rolling basis. Electronic applications accepted. Tuition and fees charges are reported in Canadian dollars. *Expenses:* Tuition, area resident: Full-time $4626 Canadian dollars; part-time $99.72 Canadian dollars per unit. International tuition: $8216 Canadian dollars full-time. Required fees: $3590 Canadian dollars; $99.72 Canadian dollars per unit. $215 Canadian dollars per term. *Financial support:* In 2009–10, 2 fellowships with full and partial tuition reimbursements (averaging $18,000 per year), 23 research assistantships with full and partial tuition reimbursements (averaging $10,450 per year), 21 teaching assistantships with full and partial tuition reimbursements (averaging $12,572 per year) were awarded; scholarships/grants also available. Support available to part-time students. Financial award application deadline: 3/31. *Faculty research:* Russian/Ukrainian studies; German studies; contemporary Latin American, French and Francophone studies; Italian studies. *Unit head:* Dr. Don Bruce, Chair, 780-492-3273, Fax: 780-492-9106. *Application contact:* Jane Wilson, Graduate Programs Secretary, 780-492-3273, Fax: 780-492-9106, E-mail: mlcsgrad@ualberta.ca.

The University of Arizona, Graduate College, College of Social and Behavioral Sciences, Department of Linguistics, Tucson, AZ 85721. Offers human language technology (MS); linguistics and anthropology (PhD); Native American linguistics (MA); theoretical linguistics (PhD). PhD in linguistics and anthropology offered jointly with Department of Anthropology. *Faculty:* 16 full-time (10 women). *Students:* 21 full-time (11 women), 23 part-time (10 women); includes 4 minority (1 African American, 3 American Indian/Alaska Native), 13 international. Average age 33. 82 applicants, 10% accepted, 2 enrolled. In 2009, 3 master's, 5 doctorates awarded. Terminal master's awarded for partial completion of doctoral program. *Degree requirements:* For master's, one foreign language, thesis; for doctorate, one foreign language, comprehensive exam, thesis/dissertation. *Entrance requirements:* For master's, GRE General Test, 3 letters of recommendation writing sample, resume; for doctorate, GRE General Test, 3 letters of recommendation, statement of purpose, writing sample, resume. Additional exam requirements/recommendations for international students: Required—TOEFL (minimum score 550 paper-based; 213 computer-based; 79 iBT). *Application deadline:* Applications are processed on a rolling basis. Application fee: $65. Electronic applications accepted. *Expenses:* Tuition, state resident: full-time $9028. Tuition, nonresident: full-time $24,890. *Financial support:* In 2009–10, 9 research assistantships with full tuition reimbursements (averaging $14,800 per year), 15 teaching assistantships with full tuition reimbursements (averaging $15,065 per year) were awarded; career-related internships or fieldwork, institutionally sponsored loans, scholarships/grants, health care benefits, tuition waivers (full and partial), and unspecified assistantships also available. Support available to part-time students. Financial award application deadline: 4/15. *Faculty research:* Semantic, syntactic, morphological, and phonological theories of natural languages; native languages of the American Southwest, psycholinguistics and computational linguistics. Total annual research expenditures: $234,017. *Unit head:* Dr. Michael Hammond, Head, 520-621-5759, Fax: 520-626-9014, E-mail: hammond@u.arizona.edu. *Application contact:* Jennifer Columbus, Information Contact, 520-621-2113, Fax: 520-626-9014, E-mail: jennife2@email.arizona.edu.

The University of Arizona, Graduate College, College of Social and Behavioral Sciences, Program in Human Language Technology, Tucson, AZ 85721. Offers MS. *Students:* 1 (woman) full-time, all international. Average age 25. 6 applicants, 33% accepted. In 2009, 5 master's awarded. *Expenses:* Tuition, state resident: full-time $9028. Tuition, nonresident: full-time $24,890. *Unit head:* Dr. Sandiway Fong, Program Coordinator, 520-626-6146, E-mail: sadc@email.arizona.edu. *Application contact:* Jennifer Columbus, Information Contact, 520-621-2113, Fax: 520-626-9014, E-mail: jennife2@email.arizona.edu.

The University of British Columbia, Faculty of Arts and Faculty of Graduate Studies, Department of Linguistics, Vancouver, BC V6T 1Z1, Canada. Offers MA, PhD. Part-time programs available. *Degree requirements:* For master's, one foreign language, thesis optional; for doctorate, 2 foreign languages, thesis/dissertation, 2 qualifying papers. *Entrance requirements:* Additional exam requirements/recommendations for international students: Required—TOEFL (minimum score 550 paper-based; 213 computer-based). Electronic applications accepted. *Faculty research:* Linguistic theory (phonology, syntax, semantics), Native American languages, African languages, first language acquisition, experimental phonetics.

University of Calgary, Faculty of Graduate Studies, Faculty of Social Sciences, Department of Linguistics, Calgary, AB T2N 1N4, Canada. Offers MA, PhD. *Degree requirements:* For master's, one foreign language, thesis; for doctorate, one foreign language, comprehensive exam, thesis/dissertation. *Entrance requirements:* For doctorate, MA. Additional exam requirements/recommendations for international students: Required—TOEFL (minimum score 560 paper-based; 220 computer-based). Electronic applications accepted. *Faculty research:* Theoretical linguistics, historical linguistics, language acquisition, Amerindian.

University of California, Berkeley, Graduate Division, College of Letters and Science, Department of Linguistics, Berkeley, CA 94720-1500. Offers PhD. *Students:* 46 full-time (24 women). Average age 29. 143 applicants, 11 enrolled. *Degree requirements:* For doctorate, thesis/dissertation, qualifying exam. *Entrance requirements:* For doctorate, GRE General Test, minimum GPA of 3.0, 3 letters of recommendation. *Application deadline:* For fall admission, 12/15 for domestic students. Application fee: $70 ($90 for international students). *Financial support:* Fellowships, teaching assistantships, unspecified assistantships available. *Unit head:* Prof. Sharon Inkelas, Chair, 510-643-7224, E-mail: linginfo@berkeley.edu. *Application contact:* Belén Flores, Student Affairs Officer, 510-643-7224, Fax: 510-643-5688, E-mail: linginfo@berkeley.edu.

University of California, Davis, Graduate Studies, Graduate Group in Linguistics, Davis, CA 95616. Offers applied linguistics (MA, PhD); linguistics (MA). *Degree requirements:* For master's, one foreign language, comprehensive exam (for some programs), thesis (for some programs); for doctorate, thesis/dissertation. *Entrance requirements:* For master's and doctorate, GRE General Test, minimum GPA of 3.0. Additional exam requirements/recommendations for international students: Required—TOEFL (minimum score 550 paper-based; 213 computer-based). Electronic applications accepted. *Faculty research:* Grammatical analysis and theory, sociolinguistics, historical linguistics, Romance linguistics, neurolinguistics.

University of California, Los Angeles, Graduate Division, College of Letters and Science, Department of Applied Linguistics and Teaching English as a Second Language, Program in Applied Linguistics, Los Angeles, CA 90095. Offers PhD. *Students:* 46 full-time (35 women); includes 8 minority (1 African American, 3 Asian Americans or Pacific Islanders, 4 Hispanic Americans), 21 international. Average age 34. 75 applicants, 15% accepted, 7 enrolled. In 2009, 11 doctorates awarded. *Degree requirements:* For doctorate, one foreign language, thesis/dissertation, oral and written qualifying exams. *Entrance requirements:* For doctorate, GRE General Test, MA in relevant field, thesis or related research paper. *Application deadline:* For fall admission, 12/15 for domestic students. Application fee: $70 ($90 for international students). Electronic applications accepted. *Financial support:* In 2009–10, 33 fellowships with full and partial tuition reimbursements, 17 research assistantships with full and partial tuition reimbursements, 28 teaching assistantships with full and partial tuition reimbursements were awarded; Federal Work-Study, institutionally sponsored loans, scholarships/grants, and tuition waivers (full and partial) also available. Financial award application deadline: 3/1; financial award applicants required to submit FAFSA. *Unit head:* Dr. Olga Yokoyama, Chair, 310-825-4631. *Application contact:* Department Office, 310-825-4631, Fax: 310-206-4118, E-mail: lyn@humnet.ucla.edu.

University of California, Los Angeles, Graduate Division, College of Letters and Science, Department of Linguistics, Los Angeles, CA 90095. Offers MA, PhD. *Students:* 33 full-time (17 women); includes 1 minority (Asian American or Pacific Islander), 11 international. Average age 26. 149 applicants, 10% accepted, 8 enrolled. In 2009, 5 master's, 3 doctorates awarded. Terminal master's awarded for partial completion of doctoral program. *Degree requirements:* For master's, one foreign language, comprehensive exam or thesis; for doctorate, thesis/dissertation, oral and written qualifying exams. *Entrance requirements:* For master's, GRE General Test, minimum GPA of 3.0, sample of written work; for doctorate, GRE General Test, minimum undergraduate GPA of 3.0, sample of written work; statement of purpose. *Application deadline:* For fall admission, 12/15 for domestic and international students. Application fee: $70 ($90 for international students). Electronic applications accepted. *Financial support:* In 2009–10, 28 fellowships with full and partial tuition reimbursements, 11 research assistantships with full and partial tuition reimbursements, 18 teaching assistantships with full and partial tuition reimbursements were awarded; Federal Work-Study, institutionally sponsored loans, scholarships/grants, health care benefits, tuition waivers (full and partial), and unspecified assistantships also available. Financial award application deadline: 3/1; financial award applicants required to submit FAFSA. *Faculty research:* Phonetics, nonlinear phonology, formal syntax, formal semantics, natural language processing. *Unit head:* Dr. Anoop Mahajan, Chair, 310-825-7968. *Application contact:* Department Office, 310-825-0634, E-mail: linguist@humnet.ucla.edu.

University of California, San Diego, Office of Graduate Studies, Department of Linguistics, La Jolla, CA 92093. Offers PhD. *Degree requirements:* For doctorate, thesis/dissertation. *Entrance requirements:* For doctorate, GRE General Test. Electronic applications accepted.

University of California, San Diego, Office of Graduate Studies, Interdisciplinary Program in Cognitive Science, La Jolla, CA 92093. Offers cognitive science/anthropology (PhD); cognitive science/communication (PhD); cognitive science/computer science and engineering (PhD); cognitive science/linguistics (PhD); cognitive science/neuroscience (PhD); cognitive science/philosophy (PhD); cognitive science/psychology (PhD); cognitive science/sociology (PhD). Admissions offered through affiliated departments. *Degree requirements:* For doctorate, thesis/dissertation. *Entrance requirements:* For doctorate, GRE General Test, acceptance into one of the eight participating departments. *Faculty research:* Language and cognition, philosophy of mind, visual perception, biological anthropology, sociolinguistics.

University of California, Santa Barbara, Graduate Division, College of Letters and Sciences, Division of Humanities and Fine Arts, Department of French and Italian, Santa Barbara, CA 93106-4140. Offers French (MA, MABL, PhD), including applied linguistics (PhD), European Medieval studies (PhD), feminist studies (PhD), French (MABL, PhD); MA/PhD. French Language Institute available during summer sessions. *Faculty:* 21 full-time (12 women). *Students:* 11 full-time (7 women). Average age 31. 16 applicants, 63% accepted, 3 enrolled. In 2009, 1 master's, 5 doctorates awarded. Terminal master's awarded for partial completion of doctoral

Linguistics

University of California, Santa Barbara (continued)
program. *Degree requirements:* For master's, 2 foreign languages, comprehensive exam; for doctorate, 2 foreign languages, comprehensive exam, thesis/dissertation. *Entrance requirements:* For master's, GRE, sample of written work, tape of spoken French, BA or the equivalent, 3 letters of recommendation, resume/curriculum vitae; for doctorate, GRE, sample of written work, tape of spoken French, MA or the equivalent, 3 letters of recommendation, statement of purpose, personal achievements/contributions statement, resume/curriculum vitae, transcripts for post-secondary institutions attended. Additional exam requirements/recommendations for international students: Required—TOEFL (minimum score 550 paper-based; 213 computer-based; 80 iBT) or IELTS (minimum score 7). *Application deadline:* For fall admission, 5/1 for domestic and international students; for winter admission, 10/1 for domestic and international students; for spring admission, 1/15 for domestic and international students. Application fee: $70 ($90 for international students). Electronic applications accepted. *Financial support:* In 2009–10, 11 students received support, including 5 fellowships with full and partial tuition reimbursements available (averaging $8,100 per year), 11 teaching assistantships with partial tuition reimbursements available (averaging $11,400 per year); career-related internships or fieldwork, Federal Work-Study, institutionally sponsored loans, scholarships/grants, traineeships, health care benefits, tuition waivers (full and partial), and unspecified assistantships also available. Financial award applicants required to submit FAFSA. *Faculty research:* French and Francophone studies, comparative literature, second language acquisition, applied linguistics, performance studies, feminist and gender studies. Total annual research expenditures: $2,500. *Unit head:* Prof. Jon Snyder, Chair, 805-893-2220, Fax: 805-893-8826, E-mail: snyder@frit.ucsb.edu. *Application contact:* Rosa Pinter, Graduate Staff Advisor, 805-893-3398, Fax: 805-893-8826, E-mail: pinter@frit.ucsb.edu.

University of California, Santa Barbara, Graduate Division, College of Letters and Sciences, Division of Humanities and Fine Arts, Department of Germanic, Slavic, and Semitic Studies, Santa Barbara, CA 93106-4130. Offers Germanic languages and literature (MA, PhD), including applied linguistics (PhD), feminist studies (PhD); MA/PhD. *Faculty:* 7 full-time (4 women). *Students:* 2 full-time (0 women). Average age 31. 6 applicants, 50% accepted, 1 enrolled. In 2009, 1 master's awarded. Terminal master's awarded for partial completion of doctoral program. *Degree requirements:* For master's, 2 foreign languages, comprehensive exam, thesis; for doctorate, 3 foreign languages, comprehensive exam, thesis/dissertation. *Entrance requirements:* For master's and doctorate, GRE. Additional exam requirements/recommendations for international students: Required—TOEFL (minimum score 550 paper-based; 213 computer-based; 80 iBT), or IELTS (minimum score 7). *Application deadline:* For fall admission, 12/31 priority date for domestic students, 5/1 priority date for international students; for winter admission, 11/1 priority date for domestic and international students; for spring admission, 2/1 priority date for domestic and international students. Applications are processed on a rolling basis. Application fee: $70 ($90 for international students). Electronic applications accepted. *Financial support:* In 2009–10, 2 students received support, including 2 fellowships with full and partial tuition reimbursements available (averaging $10,100 per year), 1 teaching assistantship with partial tuition reimbursement available (averaging $11,600 per year); Federal Work-Study, institutionally sponsored loans, scholarships/grants, health care benefits, and tuition waivers (full and partial) also available. Financial award application deadline: 12/31; financial award applicants required to submit FAFSA. *Faculty research:* Critical theory, media technology, psychoanalysis, German romanticism, Goethe. *Unit head:* Prof. Elisabeth Weber, Chair, 805-893-3527, Fax: 805-893-2374, E-mail: weber@gss.ucsb.edu. *Application contact:* Sierra Gray, Graduate Program Assistant, 805-893-2131, Fax: 805-893-2374, E-mail: sierra@gss.ucsb.edu.

University of California, Santa Barbara, Graduate Division, College of Letters and Sciences, Division of Humanities and Fine Arts, Department of Linguistics, Santa Barbara, CA 93106-3100. Offers applied linguistics (PhD); cognitive science (PhD); human development (PhD); language, interaction, and social organizations (PhD); MA/PhD. *Faculty:* 23 full-time (12 women). *Students:* 25 full-time (14 women). Average age 32. 63 applicants, 17% accepted, 5 enrolled. In 2009, 5 doctorates awarded. *Degree requirements:* For doctorate, one foreign language, comprehensive exam, thesis/dissertation. *Entrance requirements:* For doctorate, GRE, 3 letters of recommendation, resume/curriculum vitae. Additional exam requirements/recommendations for international students: Required—TOEFL (minimum score 550 paper-based; 213 computer-based; 80 iBT), or IELTS (minimum score 7). *Application deadline:* For fall admission, 12/1 priority date for domestic and international students. Application fee: $70 ($90 for international students). Electronic applications accepted. *Financial support:* In 2009–10, 24 students received support, including 19 fellowships with full and partial tuition reimbursements available (averaging $12,400 per year), 1 research assistantship with full and partial tuition reimbursement available (averaging $3,000 per year), 13 teaching assistantships with partial tuition reimbursements available (averaging $5,600 per year); Federal Work-Study, institutionally sponsored loans, scholarships/grants, health care benefits, and unspecified assistantships also available. Financial award application deadline: 12/1; financial award applicants required to submit FAFSA. *Faculty research:* Language, race and subcultural identities among California teenagers; language acquisition, psycholinguistics; language documentation, fieldwork; syntax of nominalization in 5 Tibeto-Burman languages; perceptual correlates of syllable weight. *Unit head:* Prof. Patricia M. Clancy, Chair, 805-893-8658, Fax: 805-893-7769, E-mail: pclancy@linguistics.ucsb.edu. *Application contact:* Mary Rae Staton, Graduate Program Assistant, 805-893-3776, Fax: 805-893-7769, E-mail: staton@linguistics.ucsb.edu.

University of California, Santa Barbara, Graduate Division, College of Letters and Sciences, Division of Humanities and Fine Arts, Department of Spanish and Portuguese, Santa Barbara, CA 93106-4150. Offers Hispanic languages and literature (PhD), including applied linguistics, European Medieval studies, feminist studies, Hispanic languages and literature; Portuguese (MA); Spanish (MA); Spanish and Portuguese (MA); MA/PhD. Spanish Language Institute available during summer session. *Faculty:* 16 full-time (6 women). *Students:* 29 full-time (16 women). Average age 30. 46 applicants, 39% accepted, 9 enrolled. In 2009, 4 master's, 2 doctorates awarded. *Degree requirements:* For master's, 2 foreign languages, comprehensive exam (for some programs), thesis optional; for doctorate, 2 foreign languages, comprehensive exam, thesis/dissertation. *Entrance requirements:* For master's, GRE, 2 writing samples, undergraduate major in Spanish or equivalent, 3 letters of recommendation, resume/curriculum vitae; for doctorate, GRE, 2 writing samples, master's degree, 3 letters of recommendation, statement of purpose, personal achievements/contributions statement, resume/curriculum vitae, transcripts for post-secondary institutions attended. Additional exam requirements/recommendations for international students: Required—TOEFL (minimum score 550 paper-based; 213 computer-based; 80 iBT), or IELTS (minimum score 7). *Application deadline:* For fall admission, 3/1 for domestic and international students; for winter admission, 11/1 for domestic and international students; for spring admission, 2/1 for domestic and international students. Application fee: $70 ($90 for international students). Electronic applications accepted. *Financial support:* In 2009–10, 9 fellowships with full and partial tuition reimbursements (averaging $7,000 per year), 29 teaching assistantships with partial tuition reimbursements (averaging $11,500 per year) were awarded; career-related internships or fieldwork, Federal Work-Study, institutionally sponsored loans, scholarships/grants, health care benefits, tuition waivers (full and partial), and unspecified assistantships also available. Financial award application deadline: 1/7; financial award applicants required to submit FAFSA. *Faculty research:* Nineteenth century Spanish and Portuguese literature, Spanish and Spanish American literature, nineteenth and twentieth century Portuguese and Brazilian literatures, Hispanic linguistics, Catalan language and culture. *Unit head:* Prof. Francisco A. Lomeli, Chair, 805-893-5715, Fax: 805-893-8341, E-mail: lomeli@spanport.ucsb.edu. *Application contact:* Carol Conley, Graduate Program Assistant, 805-893-3162, Fax: 805-893-8341, E-mail: cconley@spanport.ucsb.edu.

University of California, Santa Cruz, Division of Graduate Studies, Division of Humanities, Linguistics Research Center, Santa Cruz, CA 95064. Offers MA, PhD. Terminal master's awarded for partial completion of doctoral program. *Degree requirements:* For master's, one foreign language, research paper; for doctorate, one foreign language, thesis/dissertation, qualifying exam. *Entrance requirements:* For master's and doctorate, GRE General Test. *Faculty research:* Phonological, morphological, syntactic, and semantic theory; computational linguistics.

University of Chicago, Division of the Humanities, Department of Linguistics, Chicago, IL 60637-1513. Offers anthropology and linguistics (PhD); linguistics (AM, PhD). Terminal master's awarded for partial completion of doctoral program. *Degree requirements:* For master's, one foreign language, thesis; for doctorate, 2 foreign languages, thesis/dissertation. *Entrance requirements:* For master's and doctorate, GRE General Test. Additional exam requirements/recommendations for international students: Required—TOEFL.

University of Colorado at Boulder, Graduate School, College of Arts and Sciences, Department of Linguistics, Boulder, CO 80309. Offers MA, PhD. Part-time programs available. *Faculty:* 9 full-time (6 women). *Students:* 60 full-time (33 women), 15 part-time (10 women); includes 9 minority (4 American Indian/Alaska Native, 3 Asian Americans or Pacific Islanders, 2 Hispanic Americans), 6 international. Average age 33. 104 applicants, 30% accepted, 18 enrolled. In 2009, 19 master's, 3 doctorates awarded. Terminal master's awarded for partial completion of doctoral program. *Degree requirements:* For master's, comprehensive exam, thesis optional; for doctorate, one foreign language, thesis/dissertation. *Entrance requirements:* For master's, GRE General Test, minimum undergraduate GPA of 2.75; for doctorate, GRE General Test. *Application deadline:* For fall admission, 1/15 priority date for domestic students, 12/1 for international students. Applications are processed on a rolling basis. Application fee: $50 ($60 for international students). *Financial support:* In 2009–10, 9 fellowships (averaging $1,617 per year), 22 research assistantships (averaging $9,385 per year) were awarded; Federal Work-Study and tuition waivers (full) also available. Financial award application deadline: 1/15. *Faculty research:* Synchronic linguistics, discourse analysis, language acquisition, diachronic linguistics, lexicography, American Indian linguistics, psycholinguistics, African linguistics. Total annual research expenditures: $819,883.

University of Colorado Denver, College of Liberal Arts and Sciences, Department of English, Denver, CO 80217-3364. Offers applied linguistics (MA); English studies (MA); literature (MA); teaching English to speakers of other languages (Certificate); teaching of writing (MA). Part-time and evening/weekend programs available. *Students:* 12 full-time (9 women), 47 part-time (28 women); includes 3 minority (1 Asian American or Pacific Islander, 2 Hispanic Americans), 2 international. 36 applicants, 78% accepted, 19 enrolled. In 2009, 19 master's awarded. *Degree requirements:* For master's, thesis optional. *Entrance requirements:* For master's, GRE General Test, minimum GPA of 3.0. Additional exam requirements/recommendations for international students: Required—TOEFL (minimum score 550 paper-based). *Application deadline:* For fall admission, 5/25 for domestic students; for spring admission, 10/25 for domestic students. Applications are processed on a rolling basis. Application fee: $50 ($75 for international students). Electronic applications accepted. *Financial support:* Research assistantships, teaching assistantships, Federal Work-Study available. Financial award application deadline: 4/1; financial award applicants required to submit FAFSA. *Unit head:* Prof. Nancy Ciccone, Chair, 303-556-8395, Fax: 303-556-2959, E-mail: nancy.ciccone@ucdenver.edu. *Application contact:* Prof. Ian Ying, Program Advisor, 303-556-6728, Fax: 303-556-2959, E-mail: hongguang.ying@ucdenver.edu.

University of Connecticut, Graduate School, College of Liberal Arts and Sciences, Department of Linguistics, Storrs, CT 06269. Offers MA, PhD. *Faculty:* 9 full-time (3 women). *Students:* 30 full-time (17 women), 9 part-time (5 women), 27 international. Average age 32. 56 applicants, 13% accepted, 4 enrolled. In 2009, 4 master's, 1 doctorate awarded. *Degree requirements:* For doctorate, thesis/dissertation. *Entrance requirements:* For doctorate, GRE General Test. Additional exam requirements/recommendations for international students: Required—TOEFL (minimum score 550 paper-based; 213 computer-based). *Application deadline:* For fall admission, 2/1 priority date for domestic and international students; for spring admission, 11/1 for domestic students, 10/1 for international students. Applications are processed on a rolling basis. Application fee: $55. Electronic applications accepted. *Expenses:* Tuition, state resident: full-time $4725; part-time $525 per credit. Tuition, nonresident: full-time $12,267; part-time $1363 per credit. Required fees: $346 per semester. Tuition and fees vary according to course load. *Financial support:* In 2009–10, 12 research assistantships with full tuition reimbursements, 17 teaching assistantships with full tuition reimbursements were awarded; fellowships, Federal Work-Study, scholarships/grants, health care benefits, and unspecified assistantships also available. Financial award application deadline: 2/1; financial award applicants required to submit FAFSA. *Unit head:* William Snyder, Head, 860-486-0157, Fax: 860-486-0197, E-mail: william.snyder@uconn.edu. *Application contact:* Hendrikus Van Der Hulst, Chairperson, 860-486-0152, Fax: 860-486-0197, E-mail: harry.van.der.hulst@uconn.edu.

University of Delaware, College of Arts and Sciences, Department of Linguistics, Newark, DE 19716. Offers MA, PhD. *Degree requirements:* For doctorate, one foreign language, comprehensive exam, thesis/dissertation, publishable research papers. *Entrance requirements:* For master's, GRE General Test; for doctorate, GRE General Test, writing sample. Additional exam requirements/recommendations for international students: Required—TOEFL (minimum score 600 paper-based; 250 computer-based). Electronic applications accepted. *Faculty research:* East Asian, Austronesian and Romance languages, phonology, phonetics, syntax, cognitive science, semantics, psycholinguistics, language acquisition, endangered languages.

University of Florida, Graduate School, College of Liberal Arts and Sciences, Program in Linguistics, Gainesville, FL 32611. Offers linguistics (MA, PhD); teaching English as a second language (Certificate). *Degree requirements:* For master's, one foreign language, comprehensive exam, thesis optional; for doctorate, 2 foreign languages, thesis/dissertation, qualifying exam. *Entrance requirements:* For master's and doctorate, GRE General Test, minimum GPA of 3.0. Additional exam requirements/recommendations for international students: Required—TOEFL (minimum score 550 paper-based; 213 computer-based). Electronic applications accepted. *Faculty research:* Theoretical, applied, and descriptive linguistics.

University of Georgia, Graduate School, College of Arts and Sciences, Program in Linguistics, Athens, GA 30602. Offers MA, PhD. *Students:* 35 full-time (19 women), 17 part-time (9 women); includes 7 minority (2 African Americans, 5 Hispanic Americans), 5 international. 36 applicants, 67% accepted, 16 enrolled. In 2009, 4 master's, 3 doctorates awarded. *Degree requirements:* For master's, one foreign language, thesis; for doctorate, 2 foreign languages, comprehensive exam, thesis/dissertation. *Entrance requirements:* For master's and doctorate, GRE General Test. *Application deadline:* For fall admission, 7/1 priority date for domestic students; for spring admission, 11/15 for domestic students. Application fee: $50. Electronic applications accepted. *Expenses:* Contact institution. *Financial support:* In 2009–10, 3 fellowships, 7 research assistantships, 8 teaching assistantships were awarded; Federal Work-Study and institutionally sponsored loans also available. Financial award application deadline: 2/15. *Faculty research:* Applied linguistics, English linguistics, dialectology, lexicography, discourse analysis. *Unit head:* Dr. Jared Stephen Klein, Director, 706-542-9261, Fax: 706-542-2897, E-mail: jklein@uga.edu. *Application contact:* Dr. Don R. McCreary, Graduate Coordinator, 706-542-2231, E-mail: mccreary@uga.edu.

University of Hawaii at Manoa, Graduate Division, College of Language, Linguistics and Literature, Department of Linguistics, Honolulu, HI 96822. Offers MA, PhD. Part-time programs available. *Faculty:* 27 full-time (9 women), 13 part-time/adjunct (6 women). *Students:* 64 full-time (37 women), 5 part-time (4 women); includes 13 minority (2 American Indian/Alaska Native, 10 Asian Americans or Pacific Islanders, 1 Hispanic American), 29 international. Average age 29. 57 applicants, 44% accepted, 10 enrolled. In 2009, 9 master's, 3 doctorates awarded. Terminal master's awarded for partial completion of doctoral program. *Degree requirements:* For master's, 2 foreign languages, thesis optional; for doctorate, 2 foreign languages, comprehensive exam, thesis/dissertation. *Entrance requirements:* For master's and doctorate, GRE General Test. Additional exam requirements/recommendations for international students: Required—TOEFL (minimum score 600 paper-based; 250 computer-based; 100 iBT), IELTS (minimum score 7). *Application deadline:* For fall admission, 1/10 for domestic and international students; for spring admission, 9/1 for domestic and international students.

Applications are processed on a rolling basis. Application fee: $60. *Expenses:* Tuition, state resident: full-time $8900; part-time $372 per credit. Tuition, nonresident: full-time $21,400; part-time $898 per credit. Required fees: $207 per semester. *Financial support:* In 2009–10, 1 student received support, including 18 fellowships (averaging $4,602 per year), 4 research assistantships (averaging $10,943 per year), 22 teaching assistantships (averaging $14,474 per year); career-related internships or fieldwork, Federal Work-Study, scholarships/grants, and tuition waivers (full and partial) also available. Support available to part-time students. Financial award application deadline: 3/1. *Faculty research:* Languages of the Pacific and Asia. Total annual research expenditures: $139,000. *Application contact:* Patricia Donegan, Graduate Chair, 808-956-8602, Fax: 808-956-9166, E-mail: donegan@hawaii.edu.

University of Houston, College of Liberal Arts and Social Sciences, Department of English, Houston, TX 77204. Offers applied English linguistics (MA); creative writing and literature (MA, PhD); English (MFA, PhD). *Faculty:* 25 full-time (10 women), 6 part-time/adjunct (2 women). *Students:* 93 full-time (45 women), 44 part-time (36 women); includes 25 minority (3 African Americans, 1 American Indian/Alaska Native, 13 Asian Americans or Pacific Islanders, 8 Hispanic Americans), 4 international. Average age 32. 357 applicants, 13% accepted, 34 enrolled. In 2009, 21 master's, 8 doctorates awarded. *Degree requirements:* For master's, one foreign language, comprehensive exam (for some programs), thesis (MFA); for doctorate, one foreign language, comprehensive exam, thesis/dissertation. *Entrance requirements:* For master's, GRE General Test, minimum GPA of 3.0 in last 60 hours of course work; for doctorate, GRE General Test, GRE Subject Test (literature), writing sample. Additional exam requirements/recommendations for international students: Required—TOEFL (minimum score 550 paper-based; 79 iBT). *Application deadline:* For fall admission, 1/15 for domestic and international students. Application fee: $50 ($75 for international students). Electronic applications accepted. *Expenses:* Tuition, state resident: full-time $7676; part-time $320 per credit hour. Tuition, nonresident: full-time $14,324; part-time $597 per credit hour. Required fees: $3034. *Financial support:* In 2009–10, 1 fellowship with full tuition reimbursement (averaging $7,100 per year), teaching assistantships with full tuition reimbursements (averaging $12,000 per year) were awarded; career-related internships or fieldwork, Federal Work-Study, institutionally sponsored loans, scholarships/grants, health care benefits, and unspecified assistantships also available. Support available to part-time students. Financial award application deadline: 2/1. *Unit head:* Wyman Henderson, Chairperson, 713-743-3004, Fax: 713-743-3215, E-mail: whh@uh.edu. *Application contact:* Julie Kofford, Academic Advisor, 713-743-3004, E-mail: jkofford@central.uh.edu.

University of Illinois at Chicago, Graduate College, College of Liberal Arts and Sciences, Department of English, Program in Linguistics, Chicago, IL 60607-7128. Offers teaching English to speakers of other languages/applied linguistics (MA). Part-time programs available. *Degree requirements:* For master's, one foreign language, comprehensive exam, thesis (for some programs). *Entrance requirements:* For master's, minimum GPA of 3.0. Additional exam requirements/recommendations for international students: Required—TOEFL. Electronic applications accepted. *Faculty research:* Second language acquisition, methodology of second language teaching, lexicography, language, sex and gender.

University of Illinois at Urbana–Champaign, Graduate College, College of Liberal Arts and Sciences, School of Literatures, Cultures and Linguistics, Department of Linguistics, Champaign, IL 61820. Offers linguistics (MA, PhD); teaching of English as a second language (MA). *Faculty:* 16 full-time (5 women). *Students:* 65 full-time (40 women), 45 part-time (36 women); includes 9 minority (1 African American, 6 Asian Americans or Pacific Islanders, 2 Hispanic Americans), 64 international. 219 applicants, 22% accepted, 35 enrolled. In 2009, 32 master's, 7 doctorates awarded. *Entrance requirements:* For master's, GRE, minimum GPA of 3.0; writing sample; for doctorate, GRE, minimum GPA of 3.5; writing sample. Additional exam requirements/recommendations for international students: Required—TOEFL (minimum score 88 iBT). *Application deadline:* Applications are processed on a rolling basis. Application fee: $60 ($75 for international students). Electronic applications accepted. *Financial support:* In 2009–10, 17 fellowships, 22 research assistantships, 74 teaching assistantships were awarded; tuition waivers (full and partial) also available. *Unit head:* Hye Suk James Yoon, Acting Head, 217-244-3055, E-mail: jyoon@illinois.edu. *Application contact:* Lynn Stanke, Office Support Specialist, 217-333-6269, Fax: 217-244-3050, E-mail: stanke@illinois.edu.

The University of Iowa, Graduate College, College of Liberal Arts and Sciences, Department of Linguistics, Iowa City, IA 52242-1316. Offers linguistics (MA, PhD); linguistics with TESL (MA). Linguistics with TESL option offered as part of dual degree that begins at undergraduate level. *Degree requirements:* For master's, thesis optional, exam; for doctorate, comprehensive exam, thesis/dissertation. *Entrance requirements:* For master's and doctorate, GRE General Test, minimum GPA of 3.0. Additional exam requirements/recommendations for international students: Required—TOEFL (minimum score 550 paper-based; 213 computer-based; 81 iBT). Electronic applications accepted.

The University of Kansas, Graduate Studies, College of Liberal Arts and Sciences, Department of Linguistics, Lawrence, KS 66045. Offers MA, PhD. *Faculty:* 8 full-time (3 women), 1 (woman) part-time/adjunct. *Students:* 32 full-time (14 women), 4 part-time (1 woman), 22 international. Average age 32. 41 applicants, 51% accepted, 7 enrolled. In 2009, 3 master's, 4 doctorates awarded. Terminal master's awarded for partial completion of doctoral program. *Degree requirements:* For master's, one foreign language, thesis or alternative; for doctorate, one foreign language, thesis/dissertation. *Entrance requirements:* For master's, GRE General Test, curriculum vitae, 3 letters of recommendation; for doctorate, GRE General Test, CV, statement of purpose, 3 letters of recommendation. Additional exam requirements/recommendations for international students: Required—TOEFL. *Application deadline:* For fall admission, 1/1 for domestic and international students. Application fee: $45 ($55 for international students). Electronic applications accepted. *Expenses:* Tuition, state resident: full-time $6492; part-time $270.50 per credit hour. Tuition, nonresident: full-time $15,510; part-time $646.25 per credit hour. Required fees: $847; $70.56 per credit hour. Tuition and fees vary according to course load and program. *Financial support:* Fellowships with full and partial tuition reimbursements, research assistantships with full and partial tuition reimbursements, teaching assistantships with full and partial tuition reimbursements, scholarships/grants and teaching assistantships available. Financial award application deadline: 1/1. *Faculty research:* Phonetics, phonology, syntax, psycholinguistics, neurolinguistics, first and second language acquisition. *Unit head:* Dr. Allard Jongman, Chair, 785-864-3450, Fax: 785-864-5724, E-mail: liguistics@ku.edu. *Application contact:* Corinna Johnson, Department Secretary, 785-864-3450, Fax: 785-864-5724, E-mail: linguistics@ku.edu.

University of Manitoba, Faculty of Graduate Studies, Faculty of Arts, Department of Linguistics, Winnipeg, MB R3T 2N2, Canada. Offers MA, PhD.

University of Maryland, Baltimore County, Graduate School, College of Arts, Humanities and Social Sciences, Department of Modern Languages and Linguistics, Program in Intercultural Communication, Baltimore, MD 21250. Offers MA. Part-time and evening/weekend programs available. *Faculty:* 18 full-time (6 women), 3 part-time/adjunct (2 women). *Students:* 14 full-time (10 women), 29 part-time (20 women); includes 4 minority (1 African American, 3 Hispanic Americans), 14 international. 30 applicants, 57% accepted, 13 enrolled. In 2009, 7 master's awarded. *Degree requirements:* For master's, one foreign language, comprehensive exam (for some programs), thesis (for some programs). *Entrance requirements:* For master's, GRE General Test, minimum GPA of 3.0, 3 letters of recommendation, self-evaluation and statement of support, resume. Additional exam requirements/recommendations for international students: Required—TOEFL (minimum score 213 computer-based). *Application deadline:* For fall admission, 1/31 for domestic and international students. Application fee: $45. Electronic applications accepted. *Financial support:* In 2009–10, 8 students received support, including 5 teaching assistantships with full tuition reimbursements available (averaging $11,324 per year); tuition waivers also available. Financial award applicants required to submit FAFSA. *Faculty research:* Comparative television research–cross-cultural; cultural studies; social developments in Latin America; intercultural communication; French civilization and cultural studies; language, gender and sexuality; sociolinguistics; African linguistics; immigrants in U.S. and Latin American societies. *Unit head:* Dr. Edward Larkey, Director, 410-455-2104, Fax: 410-455-1025, E-mail: larkey@umbc.edu. *Application contact:* Dr. Edward Larkey, Director, 410-455-2104, Fax: 410-455-1025, E-mail: larkey@umbc.edu.

University of Maryland, College Park, Academic Affairs, College of Arts and Humanities, Department of Linguistics, College Park, MD 20742. Offers MA, PhD. *Faculty:* 22 full-time (8 women). *Students:* 39 full-time (17 women), 1 (woman) part-time; includes 3 minority (1 African American, 1 Asian American or Pacific Islander, 1 Hispanic American), 17 international. 108 applicants, 11% accepted, 8 enrolled. In 2009, 5 doctorates awarded. *Degree requirements:* For master's, thesis or alternative; for doctorate, thesis/dissertation. *Entrance requirements:* For master's, GRE General Test, minimum GPA of 3.0, sample of work, 3 letters of recommendation; for doctorate, GRE General Test, minimum GPA of 3.0, sample of work. Additional exam requirements/recommendations for international students: Required—TOEFL. *Application deadline:* For fall admission, 5/15 for domestic students, 2/1 for international students. Applications are processed on a rolling basis. Application fee: $60. Electronic applications accepted. *Expenses:* Tuition, area resident: Part-time $471 per credit hour. Tuition, state resident: part-time $471 per credit hour. Tuition, nonresident: part-time $1016 per credit hour. Required fees: $337.04 per term. *Financial support:* In 2009–10, 21 fellowships with full and partial tuition reimbursements (averaging $11,731 per year), 2 research assistantships with tuition reimbursements (averaging $22,341 per year), 28 teaching assistantships with tuition reimbursements (averaging $17,213 per year) were awarded; Federal Work-Study and scholarships/grants also available. Support available to part-time students. Financial award applicants required to submit FAFSA. *Faculty research:* Psycholinguistics, computational linguistics. Total annual research expenditures: $751,644. *Unit head:* Dr. Norbert Hornstein, Chairman, 301-405-7002, Fax: 301-314-7104, E-mail: nhorste@umd.edu. *Application contact:* Dean of Graduate School, 301-405-0376, Fax: 301-314-9305.

University of Massachusetts Amherst, Graduate School, College of Humanities and Fine Arts, Department of Linguistics, Amherst, MA 01003. Offers MA, PhD. Part-time programs available. *Faculty:* 16 full-time (8 women). *Students:* 31 full-time (18 women), 8 part-time (5 women); includes 1 minority (American Indian/Alaska Native), 16 international. Average age 28. 126 applicants, 14% accepted, 8 enrolled. In 2009, 2 master's, 8 doctorates awarded. Terminal master's awarded for partial completion of doctoral program. *Degree requirements:* For master's, thesis or alternative; for doctorate, comprehensive exam, thesis/dissertation. *Entrance requirements:* For master's and doctorate, GRE General Test. Additional exam requirements/recommendations for international students: Required—TOEFL (minimum score 550 paper-based; 213 computer-based; 80 iBT), IELTS (minimum score 6.5). *Application deadline:* For fall admission, 1/15 for domestic and international students. Applications are processed on a rolling basis. Application fee: $50 ($65 for international students). Electronic applications accepted. *Expenses:* Tuition, state resident: full-time $2640; part-time $110 per credit. Tuition, nonresident: full-time $9936; part-time $414 per credit. Tuition and fees vary according to course load. *Financial support:* In 2009–10, 16 research assistantships with full tuition reimbursements (averaging $8,866 per year), 27 teaching assistantships with full tuition reimbursements (averaging $12,855 per year) were awarded; fellowships, career-related internships or fieldwork, Federal Work-Study, scholarships/grants, traineeships, health care benefits, tuition waivers (full), and unspecified assistantships also available. Support available to part-time students. Financial award application deadline: 1/15. *Unit head:* Dr. Joseph V. Pater, Graduate Program Director, 413-545-0885, Fax: 413-545-2792. *Application contact:* Jean M. Ames, Supervisor of Admissions, 413-545-0722, Fax: 413-577-0010, E-mail: gradadm@grad.umass.edu.

University of Massachusetts Boston, Office of Graduate Studies, College of Liberal Arts, Program in Applied Linguistics, Boston, MA 02125-3393. Offers bilingual education (MA); English as a second language (MA); foreign language pedagogy (MA). Part-time and evening/weekend programs available. *Degree requirements:* For master's, one foreign language, comprehensive exam. *Entrance requirements:* For master's, minimum GPA of 2.75. *Faculty research:* Multicultural theory and curriculum development, foreign language pedagogy, language and culture, applied psycholinguistics, bilingual education.

University of Memphis, Graduate School, College of Arts and Sciences, Department of English, Memphis, TN 38152. Offers African-American literature (Graduate Certificate); applied linguistics (PhD); composition studies (PhD); creative writing (MFA); English as a second language (MA); linguistics (MA); literary and cultural studies (PhD), including African-American literature; literature (MA); professional writing (MA, PhD); teaching English as a second language (Graduate Certificate). Part-time and evening/weekend programs available. Postbaccalaureate distance learning degree programs offered (no on-campus study). *Faculty:* 31 full-time (15 women), 2 part-time/adjunct (both women). *Students:* 98 full-time (59 women), 99 part-time (66 women); includes 36 minority (28 African Americans, 5 Asian Americans or Pacific Islanders, 3 Hispanic Americans), 7 international. Average age 34. 128 applicants, 71% accepted, 29 enrolled. In 2009, 38 master's, 4 doctorates, 21 other advanced degrees awarded. Terminal master's awarded for partial completion of doctoral program. *Degree requirements:* For master's, one foreign language, comprehensive exam, thesis optional; for doctorate, 2 foreign languages, comprehensive exam, thesis/dissertation. *Entrance requirements:* For master's, GRE; for doctorate, GRE. Additional exam requirements/recommendations for international students: Required—TOEFL. *Application deadline:* For fall admission, 7/1 for domestic students; for spring admission, 10/15 for domestic students. Applications are processed on a rolling basis. Application fee: $35 ($60 for international students). Electronic applications accepted. *Expenses:* Tuition, state resident: full-time $6246; part-time $347 per credit hour. Tuition, nonresident: full-time $15,894; part-time $883 per credit hour. Required fees: $1160. Full-time tuition and fees vary according to course load, degree level and program. *Financial support:* In 2009–10, 123 students received support; research assistantships with full tuition reimbursements available, teaching assistantships with full tuition reimbursements available, Federal Work-Study, scholarships/grants, and unspecified assistantships available. Financial award application deadline: 2/15; financial award applicants required to submit FAFSA. *Faculty research:* Applied linguistis, British and American literature, professional writing, composition studies. *Unit head:* Dr. Eric C. Link, Chair, 901-678-2651, Fax: 901-678-2226, E-mail: eclink@memphis.edu. *Application contact:* Dr. Verner D. Mitchell, Director, Graduate Studies, 901-678-3099, Fax: 901-678-2226, E-mail: vdmtchll@memphis.edu.

University of Michigan, Horace H. Rackham School of Graduate Studies, College of Literature, Science, and the Arts, Department of Linguistics, Ann Arbor, MI 48109. Offers linguistics (PhD); linguistics and Romance languages and literatures (PhD). *Faculty:* 16 full-time (7 women), 2 part-time/adjunct (both women). *Students:* 29 full-time (15 women); includes 5 minority (1 African American, 3 Asian Americans or Pacific Islanders, 1 Hispanic American), 12 international. Average age 30. 100 applicants, 8% accepted, 5 enrolled. In 2009, 1 doctorate awarded. *Degree requirements:* For doctorate, 2 foreign languages, thesis/dissertation, oral defense of dissertation. *Entrance requirements:* For doctorate, GRE General Test. Additional exam requirements/recommendations for international students: Required—TOEFL (minimum score 620 paper-based; 260 computer-based; 95 iBT), or Michigan English Language Assessment Battery. *Application deadline:* For fall admission, 12/15 for domestic and international students. Application fee: $60 ($75 for international students). Electronic applications accepted. *Expenses:* Tuition, state resident: full-time $17,286; part-time $1099 per credit hour. Tuition, nonresident: full-time $34,944; part-time $2080 per credit hour. Required fees: $95 per semester. Tuition and fees vary according to course load, degree level and program. *Financial support:* In 2009–10, 25 students received support, including 12 fellowships with full tuition reimbursements available (averaging $16,800 per year), 3 research assistantships with full tuition reimbursements available, 16 teaching assistantships with full tuition reimbursements available (averaging $16,694 per year); health care benefits also available. Financial award application deadline: 12/15. *Faculty research:* Broad-based approach to linguistics as a cognitive and social science including theoretical, experimental and computational approaches. Total annual research expenditures: $21,856. *Unit head:* Patrice Speeter Beddor, Professor and Chair, Linguistics, 734-764-0353, Fax: 734-936-3406, E-mail: linguistics@umich.edu. *Application*

Linguistics

University of Michigan (continued)
contact: Sylvia Suttor, Student Services Assistant Senior, 734-764-5355, Fax: 734-763-6557, E-mail: ssuttor@umich.edu.

University of Michigan, Horace H. Rackham School of Graduate Studies, College of Literature, Science, and the Arts, Department of Romance Languages and Literatures, Ann Arbor, MI 48109. Offers French (PhD); Romance linguistics (PhD); Spanish (PhD). *Faculty:* 28 full-time (13 women), 2 part-time/adjunct (1 woman). *Students:* 75 full-time (42 women); includes 2 African Americans, 1 Asian American or Pacific Islander, 26 Hispanic Americans. Average age 30. 73 applicants, 25% accepted, 8 enrolled. In 2009, 3 doctorates awarded. *Degree requirements:* For doctorate, 2 foreign languages, thesis/dissertation, oral defense of dissertation, preliminary exams. *Entrance requirements:* For doctorate, GRE General Test. Additional exam requirements/recommendations for international students: Required—TOEFL or Michigan English Language Assessment Battery. *Application deadline:* For fall admission, 1/1 for domestic and international students. Application fee: $60. Electronic applications accepted. *Expenses:* Tuition, state resident: full-time $17,286; part-time $1099 per credit hour. Tuition, nonresident: full-time $34,944; part-time $2080 per credit hour. Required fees: $95 per semester. Tuition and fees vary according to course load, degree level and program. *Financial support:* In 2009–10, 1 teaching assistantship with full tuition reimbursement was awarded; fellowships with full tuition reimbursements, institutionally sponsored loans, scholarships/grants, and unspecified assistantships also available. Financial award application deadline: 1/1. *Faculty research:* Comparative Romance studies, medieval and early modern studies, postcolonial and minority literatures, culture and materiality, reflection on the nature and function of scholarship. *Unit head:* Dr. Michele Hannoosh, Chair, 734-764-5344, Fax: 734-764-8163. *Application contact:* Annette Herbert, Graduate Assistant, 734-764-8164, Fax: 734-764-8163, E-mail: rll-admissions@umich.edu.

University of Minnesota, Twin Cities Campus, Graduate School, College of Liberal Arts, Institute of Linguistics, English as a Second Language, and Slavic Languages and Literatures (ILES), Program in Linguistics, Minneapolis, MN 55455-0213. Offers MA, PhD. *Faculty:* 6 full-time (3 women), 16 part-time/adjunct (7 women). *Students:* 21 full-time (12 women), 4 part-time (2 women); includes 2 minority (1 African American, 1 American Indian/Alaska Native), 5 international. Average age 33. 29 applicants, 31% accepted, 3 enrolled. In 2009, 5 master's, 4 doctorates awarded. Terminal master's awarded for partial completion of doctoral program. *Degree requirements:* For master's, one foreign language, comprehensive exam, thesis; for doctorate, 2 foreign languages, comprehensive exam, thesis/dissertation. *Entrance requirements:* For master's and doctorate, GRE General Test, 3 letters of recommendation, unit questionnaire. Additional exam requirements/recommendations for international students: Required—TOEFL (minimum score 550 paper-based; 213 computer-based; 79 iBT). *Application deadline:* For fall admission, 3/15 priority date for domestic and international students. Applications are processed on a rolling basis. Application fee: $75 ($95 for international students). Electronic applications accepted. *Financial support:* In 2009–10, 13 students received support, including 3 fellowships with full tuition reimbursements available (averaging $22,000 per year), 1 research assistantship with partial tuition reimbursement available (averaging $6,923 per year), 13 teaching assistantships with full and partial tuition reimbursements available (averaging $13,846 per year); Federal Work-Study, traineeships, and unspecified assistantships also available. Financial award application deadline: 1/15; financial award applicants required to submit FAFSA. *Faculty research:* Pragmatics and language processing, syntactic theory, language policy and planning, contact linguistics, language and cognition. *Unit head:* Dr. Jeanette Gundel, Professor and Head, 612-624-7564, Fax: 612-624-4579, E-mail: gunde003@umn.edu. *Application contact:* Dr. Jeanette Gundel, Professor and Head, 612-624-7564, Fax: 612-624-4579, E-mail: gunde003@umn.edu.

University of Missouri–St. Louis, College of Arts and Sciences, Department of English, St. Louis, MO 63121. Offers American literature (MA); creative writing (MFA); English (MA); English literature (MA); linguistics (MA); teaching of writing (Graduate Certificate). Part-time and evening/weekend programs available. *Faculty:* 21 full-time (11 women), 2 part-time/adjunct (1 woman). *Students:* 32 full-time (15 women), 97 part-time (62 women); includes 10 minority (5 African Americans, 2 American Indian/Alaska Native, 2 Asian Americans or Pacific Islanders, 1 Hispanic American), 1 international. Average age 31. 114 applicants, 46% accepted, 36 enrolled. In 2009, 28 master's, 1 other advanced degree awarded. *Degree requirements:* For master's, thesis optional. *Entrance requirements:* For master's, writing sample. Additional exam requirements/recommendations for international students: Required—TOEFL (minimum score 550 paper-based; 213 computer-based). *Application deadline:* For fall admission, 7/1 priority date for domestic and international students; for spring admission, 12/1 priority date for domestic and international students. Applications are processed on a rolling basis. Application fee: $35 ($40 for international students). Electronic applications accepted. *Expenses:* Tuition, state resident: full-time $5377; part-time $297.70 per credit hour. Tuition, nonresident: full-time $13,882; part-time $771.20 per credit hour. Required fees: $220; $12.20 per credit hour. One-time fee: $12. Tuition and fees vary according to course level, campus/location and program. *Financial support:* In 2009–10, 4 research assistantships (averaging $5,500 per year), 7 teaching assistantships with full and partial tuition reimbursements (averaging $9,000 per year) were awarded. Financial award applicants required to submit FAFSA. *Faculty research:* Victorian literature, Shakespeare and Renaissance literature, eighteenth century literature, composition theory. *Unit head:* Dr. Frank Grady, Director of Graduate Studies, 314-516-5541, Fax: 314-516-5781, E-mail: fgrady@umsl.edu. *Application contact:* 314-516-5458, Fax: 314-516-5310, E-mail: gradadm@umsl.edu.

The University of Montana, Graduate School, College of Arts and Sciences, Department of Anthropology, Missoula, MT 59812-0002. Offers anthropology (MA); cultural heritage (MA); cultural heritage studies (PhD); forensic anthropology (MA); historical anthropology (PhD); linguistics (MA). *Degree requirements:* For master's, thesis (for some programs). *Entrance requirements:* For master's, GRE General Test. Additional exam requirements/recommendations for international students: Required—TOEFL. *Faculty research:* Historical preservation, plateau-plains archaeology and ethnohistory.

The University of Montana, Graduate School, College of Arts and Sciences, Program in Linguistics, Missoula, MT 59812-0002. Offers MA. *Entrance requirements:* For master's, GRE General Test. Additional exam requirements/recommendations for international students: Required—TOEFL.

University of New Hampshire, Graduate School, College of Liberal Arts, Department of English, Durham, NH 03824. Offers English (MFA, PhD); English education (MST); language and linguistics (MA); literature (MA); writing (MA). Part-time programs available. *Faculty:* 35 full-time (18 women). *Students:* 54 full-time (33 women), 64 part-time (40 women); includes 5 minority (1 African American, 2 American Indian/Alaska Native, 2 Hispanic Americans), 5 international. Average age 34. 279 applicants, 43% accepted, 38 enrolled. In 2009, 32 master's, 5 doctorates awarded. *Degree requirements:* For master's, one foreign language; for doctorate, 2 foreign languages, thesis/dissertation. *Entrance requirements:* For master's, GRE General Test, sample of written work; for doctorate, GRE General Test, GRE Subject Test, sample of written work. Additional exam requirements/recommendations for international students: Required—TOEFL (minimum score 550 paper-based; 213 computer-based; 80 iBT). *Application deadline:* For fall admission, 6/1 priority date for domestic students, 2/15 for international students; for spring admission, 12/1 for domestic students. Applications are processed on a rolling basis. Application fee: $65. Electronic applications accepted. *Expenses:* Tuition, state resident: full-time $10,380; part-time $577 per credit hour. Tuition, nonresident: full-time $24,350; part-time $1002 per credit hour. Required fees: $1550; $387.50 per semester. Tuition and fees vary according to course load and program. *Financial support:* In 2009–10, 57 students received support, including 4 fellowships, 46 teaching assistantships; research assistantships, career-related internships or fieldwork, Federal Work-Study, scholarships/grants, and tuition waivers (full and partial) also available. Support available to part-time students. Financial award application deadline: 2/15. *Unit head:* Dr. Andrew Merton, Chairperson, 603-862-3963. *Application contact:* Jamie Auger, Administrative Assistant, 603-862-3963, E-mail: engl.grad@unh.edu.

University of New Mexico, Graduate School, College of Arts and Sciences, Department of Linguistics, Albuquerque, NM 87131-2039. Offers MA, PhD. Part-time programs available. *Faculty:* 12 full-time (10 women), 3 part-time/adjunct (all women). *Students:* 30 full-time (16 women), 10 part-time (6 women); includes 4 minority (1 African American, 2 American Indian/Alaska Native, 1 Asian American or Pacific Islander), 15 international. Average age 35. 45 applicants, 44% accepted, 6 enrolled. In 2009, 5 master's, 4 doctorates awarded. Terminal master's awarded for partial completion of doctoral program. *Degree requirements:* For master's, comprehensive exam, thesis optional; for doctorate, 2 foreign languages, comprehensive exam, thesis/dissertation. *Entrance requirements:* For master's, minimum GPA of 3.0, 3 letters of recommendation, letter of intent; for doctorate, MA in linguistics or equivalent, paper of publishable quality, 3 letters of recommendation, letter of intent. Additional exam requirements/recommendations for international students: Required—TOEFL (minimum score 520 paper-based; 190 computer-based; 68 iBT), IELTS. *Application deadline:* For fall admission, 12/15 priority date for domestic and international students; for spring admission, 10/31 for domestic students, 10/1 for international students. Application fee: $50. Electronic applications accepted. *Expenses:* Tuition, state resident: full-time $2099; part-time $233.20 per credit hour. Tuition, nonresident: full-time $6650. Required fees: $25 per semester. Tuition and fees vary according to course load, program and reciprocity agreements. *Financial support:* In 2009–10, 11 students received support, including 1 fellowship with full tuition reimbursement available (averaging $15,460 per year), 6 teaching assistantships with full and partial tuition reimbursements available (averaging $6,860 per year); research assistantships, Federal Work-Study, health care benefits, and tuition waivers (full and partial) also available. Financial award application deadline: 1/15; financial award applicants required to submit FAFSA. *Faculty research:* American Sign Language, functional/cognitive linguistics, sociolinguistics, Spanish linguistics, Native American linguistics, signed language linguistics, language processing, Navajo/Dine Language, Spanish linguistics, typology, discourse, language acquisition. Total annual research expenditures: $37,817. *Unit head:* Dr. Sherman Wilcox, Chair, 505-277-6353, Fax: 505-277-6355, E-mail: wilcox@unm.edu. *Application contact:* Jessica Slocum, Administrative Assistant III, 505-277-6353, Fax: 505-277-6355, E-mail: jslocum@unm.edu.

University of New Mexico, Graduate School, College of Education, Department of Language, Literacy and Sociocultural Studies, Program in Educational Linguistics, Albuquerque, NM 87131-2039. Offers PhD. Part-time programs available. *Students:* 4 full-time (3 women), 9 part-time (7 women); includes 3 minority (1 Asian American or Pacific Islander, 2 Hispanic Americans), 5 international. Average age 46. 5 applicants, 0% accepted, 0 enrolled. *Degree requirements:* For doctorate, comprehensive exam, thesis/dissertation. *Entrance requirements:* For doctorate, masters in linguistics, or complementary field recommended. Additional exam requirements/recommendations for international students: Required—TOEFL (minimum score 550 paper-based; 213 computer-based; 79 iBT). *Application deadline:* For fall admission, 12/1 for domestic and international students. Application fee: $50. Electronic applications accepted. *Expenses:* Tuition, state resident: full-time $2099; part-time $233.20 per credit hour. Tuition, nonresident: full-time $6650. Required fees: $25 per semester. Tuition and fees vary according to course load, program and reciprocity agreements. *Financial support:* In 2009–10, 3 students received support, including 3 teaching assistantships with tuition reimbursements available (averaging $5,074 per year); fellowships with tuition reimbursements available, career-related internships or fieldwork, institutionally sponsored loans, scholarships/grants, and unspecified assistantships also available. Support available to part-time students. Financial award application deadline: 1/15; financial award applicants required to submit FAFSA. *Faculty research:* Bilingualism, language maintenance and loss, bilingual deaf education, Spanish dialectical studies, English as a second language, writing/composition, Native American language issues, language and thought, language policy studies, global English issues, assessment. *Unit head:* Dr. Lois Meyer, Graduate Director, 505-277-7244, Fax: 505-277-8362, E-mail: lsmeyer@unm.edu. *Application contact:* Mary Gurule Vernon, Program Administrator, 505-277-5282, Fax: 505-277-8362, E-mail: mgurule2@unm.edu.

The University of North Carolina at Chapel Hill, Graduate School, College of Arts and Sciences, Department of Germanic Languages, Chapel Hill, NC 27599. Offers literature and linguistics (MA, PhD). Part-time programs available. Terminal master's awarded for partial completion of doctoral program. *Degree requirements:* For master's, comprehensive exam, thesis; for doctorate, one foreign language, comprehensive exam, thesis/dissertation. *Entrance requirements:* For master's and doctorate, GRE General Test, minimum GPA of 3.0. *Faculty research:* Gender and sexuality, literature and politics, German and Jewish culture, medieval through modern literature, Germanic linguistics.

The University of North Carolina at Chapel Hill, Graduate School, College of Arts and Sciences, Department of Linguistics, Chapel Hill, NC 27599. Offers MA, PhD. Terminal master's awarded for partial completion of doctoral program. *Degree requirements:* For master's, one foreign language, comprehensive exam, thesis; for doctorate, 2 foreign languages, comprehensive exam, thesis/dissertation. *Entrance requirements:* For master's and doctorate, GRE General Test, minimum GPA of 3.0. Additional exam requirements/recommendations for international students: Required—TOEFL (minimum score 550 paper-based; 213 computer-based). Electronic applications accepted. *Faculty research:* Phonetics, phonology, syntax, historical linguistics, Indo-European.

University of North Dakota, Graduate School, College of Arts and Sciences, Program in Linguistics, Grand Forks, ND 58202. Offers MA. *Degree requirements:* For master's, one foreign language, thesis, final examination. *Entrance requirements:* For master's, minimum GPA of 3.0. Additional exam requirements/recommendations for international students: Required—TOEFL (minimum score 550 paper-based; 213 computer-based; 79 iBT), IELTS (minimum score 6.5). Electronic applications accepted. *Faculty research:* Practice-based field studies.

University of Oregon, Graduate School, College of Arts and Sciences, Department of Linguistics, Eugene, OR 97403. Offers MA, PhD. Terminal master's awarded for partial completion of doctoral program. *Degree requirements:* For master's, 2 foreign languages; for doctorate, thesis/dissertation. *Entrance requirements:* For master's and doctorate, GRE General Test, minimum GPA of 3.0. Additional exam requirements/recommendations for international students: Required—TOEFL. *Faculty research:* Functional syntax, discourse, empirical methods.

University of Ottawa, Faculty of Graduate and Postdoctoral Studies, Faculty of Arts, Department of Linguistics, Ottawa, ON K1N 6N5, Canada. Offers MA, PhD. *Degree requirements:* For master's, one foreign language, thesis or alternative; for doctorate, 2 foreign languages, comprehensive exam, thesis/dissertation. *Entrance requirements:* For master's, honors degree or equivalent, minimum B average; for doctorate, master's degree, minimum B+ average. Electronic applications accepted. *Faculty research:* Empirical linguistics, formal linguistics.

University of Pennsylvania, Graduate School of Education, Division of Language in Education, Programs in Teaching English to Speakers of Other Languages and Intercultural Communication, Philadelphia, PA 19104. Offers educational linguistics (PhD); intercultural communication (MS Ed); teaching English to speakers of other languages (MS Ed). Part-time programs available. Postbaccalaureate distance learning degree programs offered (minimal on-campus study). *Students:* 82 full-time (71 women), 23 part-time (17 women); includes 3 minority (2 African Americans, 1 Asian American or Pacific Islander), 82 international. 117 applicants, 82% accepted, 61 enrolled. In 2009, 51 master's awarded. Terminal master's awarded for partial completion of doctoral program. *Degree requirements:* For master's, comprehensive exam, thesis (for some programs); for doctorate, one foreign language, thesis/dissertation, preliminary exam. *Entrance requirements:* For master's and doctorate, GRE General Test or MAT. Additional exam requirements/recommendations for international students: Required—TOEFL. *Application deadline:* For fall admission, 12/15 priority date for domestic students. Applications are processed on a rolling basis. Application fee: $70. Electronic applications accepted. *Expenses:* Contact institution. *Financial support:* Fellowships, research assistantships, institutionally sponsored loans, scholarships/grants, traineeships, health care benefits, and unspecified assistantships available. *Faculty research:* Second language acquisition, social linguistics, English as a second language.

University of Pennsylvania, School of Arts and Sciences, Graduate Group in Linguistics, Philadelphia, PA 19104. Offers AM, PhD. *Faculty:* 22 full-time (4 women). *Students:* 35 full-time (21 women), 6 international. 137 applicants, 8% accepted, 5 enrolled. In 2009, 1 master's, 5 doctorates awarded. Terminal master's awarded for partial completion of doctoral program. *Degree requirements:* For master's, thesis; for doctorate, 2 foreign languages, thesis/dissertation. *Entrance requirements:* For master's and doctorate, GRE General Test. Additional exam requirements/recommendations for international students: Required—TOEFL. *Application deadline:* For fall admission, 12/1 priority date for domestic students. Application fee: $70. Electronic applications accepted. *Expenses:* Tuition: Full-time $25,660; part-time $4758 per course. Required fees: $2152; $270 per course. Tuition and fees vary according to course load, degree level and program. *Financial support:* Fellowships, research assistantships, teaching assistantships, institutionally sponsored loans, scholarships/grants, traineeships, health care benefits, and unspecified assistantships available. Financial award application deadline: 12/15.

University of Pittsburgh, School of Arts and Sciences, Department of Linguistics, Pittsburgh, PA 15260. Offers applied linguistics (PhD); linguistics (MA); sociolinguistics (PhD). Part-time programs available. *Faculty:* 8 full-time (3 women), 2 part-time/adjunct (1 woman). *Students:* 28 full-time (21 women), 1 (woman) part-time; includes 3 minority (all African Americans), 7 international. Average age 30. 71 applicants, 18% accepted, 2 enrolled. In 2009, 7 master's, 1 doctorate awarded. Terminal master's awarded for partial completion of doctoral program. *Degree requirements:* For master's, one foreign language, thesis; for doctorate, 2 foreign languages, comprehensive exam, thesis/dissertation. *Entrance requirements:* For master's, GRE General Test; for doctorate, GRE General Test, MA in linguistics. Additional exam requirements/recommendations for international students: Required—TOEFL (minimum score 600 paper-based; 250 computer-based). *Application deadline:* For fall admission, 12/15 priority date for domestic and international students. Applications are processed on a rolling basis. Application fee: $50. Electronic applications accepted. *Expenses:* Tuition, state resident: full-time $16,402; part-time $665 per credit. Tuition, nonresident: full-time $28,694; part-time $1175 per credit. Required fees: $690; $175 per term. Tuition and fees vary according to program. *Financial support:* In 2009–10, 6 fellowships with full and partial tuition reimbursements (averaging $15,000 per year), 4 research assistantships with full and partial tuition reimbursements (averaging $12,300 per year), 12 teaching assistantships with full and partial tuition reimbursements (averaging $15,065 per year) were awarded; Federal Work-Study, scholarships/grants, health care benefits, and unspecified assistantships also available. Support available to part-time students. *Faculty research:* Second language acquisition, applied linguistics, sociolinguistics, language contact. Total annual research expenditures: $279,685. *Unit head:* Dr. Alan Juffs, Chair, 412-624-5900, Fax: 412-624-6130, E-mail: juffs@pitt.edu. *Application contact:* Patricia C. Cochran, Graduate Secretary, 412-624-5900, Fax: 412-624-6130, E-mail: lingpitt@pitt.edu.

University of Puerto Rico, Río Piedras, College of Humanities, Department of Hispanic Studies, San Juan, PR 00931-3300. Offers Hispanic studies (MA); Latin American literature (PhD); Puerto Rican literature (PhD); Spanish linguistics (PhD); Spanish literature (PhD). Part-time programs available. *Degree requirements:* For master's, one foreign language, comprehensive exam, thesis; for doctorate, one foreign language, comprehensive exam, thesis/dissertation. *Entrance requirements:* For master's, PAEG or GRE, interview, minimum GPA of 3.0, letter of recommendation (2); for doctorate, PAEG or GRE, interview, master's degree, minimum GPA of 3.0, letter of recommendation (2). *Faculty research:* Poetry of Luis Palés Matos, short stories in Puerto Rico, language in the social process, 'Decima Popular', Anglicism.

University of Puerto Rico, Río Piedras, College of Humanities, Department of Linguistics, San Juan, PR 00931-3300. Offers MA. Part-time programs available. *Degree requirements:* For master's, one foreign language, comprehensive exam, thesis. *Entrance requirements:* For master's, PAEG or GRE, interview, minimum GPA of 3.0, letter of recommendation (2).

University of Regina, Faculty of Graduate Studies and Research, Faculty of Arts, Program in Linguistics, Regina, SK S4S 0A2, Canada. Offers MA. Offered as special case program. Part-time programs available. *Faculty:* 4 full-time (0 women). *Degree requirements:* For master's, thesis. *Entrance requirements:* Additional exam requirements/recommendations for international students: Required—TOEFL (minimum score 580 paper-based; 237 computer-based). *Application deadline:* Applications are processed on a rolling basis. Application fee: $90 ($100 for international students). Electronic applications accepted. *Financial support:* Fellowships, research assistantships, teaching assistantships, scholarships/grants available. Financial award application deadline: 6/15. *Faculty research:* Phonology, morphology, syntax, semantics, Amerindian linguistics. *Unit head:* Dr. Arok Wolvengrey, Program Coordinator, 790-790-5950 Ext. 3310, E-mail: awolvengrey@firstnations.university.ca. *Application contact:* Dr. Arok Wolvengrey, Program Coordinator, 790-790-5950 Ext. 3310, E-mail: awolvengrey@firstnations.university.ca.

University of South Africa, College of Human Sciences, Pretoria, South Africa. Offers adult education (M Ed); African languages (MA, PhD); African politics (MA, PhD); Afrikaans (MA, PhD); ancient history (MA, PhD); ancient Near Eastern studies (MA, PhD); anthropology (MA, PhD); applied linguistics (MA); Arabic (MA, PhD); archaeology (MA); art history (MA); Biblical archaeology (MA); Biblical studies (M Th, D Th, PhD); Christian spirituality (M Th, D Th); church history (M Th, D Th); classical studies (MA, PhD); clinical psychology (MA); communication (MA, PhD); comparative education (M Ed, Ed D); consulting psychology (D Admin, D Com, PhD); curriculum studies (M Ed, Ed D); development studies (M Admin, MA, D Admin, PhD); didactics (M Ed, Ed D); education (M Tech); education management (M Ed, Ed D); educational psychology (M Ed); English (MA); environmental education (M Ed); French (MA, PhD); German (MA, PhD); Greek (MA); guidance and counseling (M Ed); health studies (MA, PhD), including health sciences education (MA), health services management (MA), medical and surgical nursing science (critical care general) (MA), midwifery and neonatal nursing science (MA), trauma and emergency care (MA); history (MA, PhD); history of education (Ed D); inclusive education (M Ed, Ed D); information and communications technology policy and regulation (MA); information science (MA, MIS, PhD); international politics (MA, PhD); Islamic studies (MA, PhD); Italian (MA, PhD); Judaica (MA, PhD); linguistics (MA, PhD); mathematical education (M Ed); mathematics education (MA); missiology (M Th, D Th); modern Hebrew (MA, PhD); musicology (MA, MMus, D Mus, PhD); natural science education (M Ed); New Testament (M Th, D Th); Old Testament (D Th); pastoral therapy (M Th, D Th); philosophy (MA); philosophy of education (M Ed, Ed D); politics (MA, PhD); Portuguese (MA, PhD); practical theology (M Th, D Th); psychology (MA, MS, PhD); psychology of education (M Ed, Ed D); public health (MA); religious studies (MA, D Th, PhD); Romance languages (MA); Russian (MA, PhD); Semitic languages (MA, PhD); social behavior studies in HIV/AIDS (MA); social science (mental health) (MA); social science in development studies (MA); social science in psychology (MA); social science in social work (MA); social science in sociology (MA); social work (MSW, DSW, PhD); socio-education (M Ed, Ed D); sociolinguistics (MA); sociology (MA, PhD); Spanish (MA, PhD); systematic theology (M Th, D Th); TESOL (teaching English to speakers of other languages) (MA); theological ethics (M Th, D Th); theory of literature (MA, PhD); urban ministries (D Th); urban ministry (M Th).

University of South Carolina, The Graduate School, College of Arts and Sciences, Linguistics Program, Columbia, SC 29208. Offers linguistics (MA, PhD); teaching English to speakers of other languages (Certificate). Part-time programs available. Terminal master's awarded for partial completion of doctoral program. *Degree requirements:* For master's, one foreign language, comprehensive exam, thesis optional; for doctorate, 3 foreign languages, comprehensive exam, thesis/dissertation. *Entrance requirements:* For master's and Certificate, GRE General Test, minimum GPA of 3.0; for doctorate, GRE General Test, minimum GPA of 3.5. Additional exam requirements/recommendations for international students: Required—TOEFL. Electronic applications accepted. *Faculty research:* Second language acquisition, sociolinguistics, syntax, historical linguistics and phonology.

University of Southern California, Graduate School, College of Letters, Arts and Sciences, Department of East Asian Languages and Cultures, Los Angeles, CA 90089. Offers classical Chinese literature (MA, PhD); classical Japanese literature (MA, PhD); linguistics (MA, PhD); modern Chinese literature (MA, PhD); modern Japanese literature (MA, PhD); modern Korean literature (MA, PhD). *Faculty:* 15 full-time (8 women). *Students:* 22 full-time (14 women); includes 6 minority (1 African American, 5 Asian Americans or Pacific Islanders), 10 international. 53 applicants, 21% accepted, 7 enrolled. In 2009, 5 master's, 1 doctorate awarded. *Degree requirements:* For master's, one foreign language, thesis; for doctorate, 2 foreign languages, comprehensive exam, thesis/dissertation. *Entrance requirements:* For master's and doctorate, GRE, BA in relevant field. Additional exam requirements/recommendations for international students: Required—TOEFL. *Application deadline:* For fall admission, 12/1 priority date for domestic and international students. Application fee: $85. Electronic applications accepted. *Expenses:* Tuition: Full-time $25,980; part-time $1315 per unit. Required fees: $554. One-time fee: $35 full-time. Full-time tuition and fees vary according to degree level and program. *Financial support:* In 2009–10, 18 students received support, including 4 fellowships with full tuition reimbursements available (averaging $23,650 per year), 10 teaching assistantships with partial tuition reimbursements available (averaging $18,800 per year); scholarships/grants, health care benefits, and unspecified assistantships also available. Financial award application deadline: 12/1. *Faculty research:* East Asian (Chinese, Japanese and Korean) language, literature, and culture; visual cultures and media studies with focus in East Asian visual arts; films; pre-modern Japanese, Korean and Chinese literature and cultures; modern and contemporary Chinese, Korean and Japanese literature. *Unit head:* Dominic Cheung, Chair, 213-740-3707, Fax: 213-740-9295, E-mail: dcheung@usc.edu. *Application contact:* Sherall R. Preyer, Administrative Coordinator, 213-740-3709, Fax: 213-740-9295, E-mail: preyer@college.usc.edu.

University of Southern California, Graduate School, College of Letters, Arts and Sciences, Department of Linguistics, Los Angeles, CA 90089. Offers East Asian linguistics (PhD); Hispanic linguistics (MA, PhD); linguistics (MA, PhD). *Faculty:* 21 full-time (12 women), 3 part-time/adjunct (2 women). *Students:* 46 full-time (30 women), 1 part-time (0 women); includes 6 minority (4 Asian Americans or Pacific Islanders, 2 Hispanic Americans), 24 international. 51 applicants, 35% accepted, 7 enrolled. In 2009, 11 master's, 1 doctorate awarded. *Degree requirements:* For doctorate, comprehensive exam, thesis/dissertation. *Entrance requirements:* For doctorate, GRE. Additional exam requirements/recommendations for international students: Required—TOEFL (minimum score 100 iBT). *Application deadline:* For fall admission, 12/1 priority date for domestic and international students. Application fee: $85. Electronic applications accepted. *Expenses:* Tuition: Full-time $25,980; part-time $1315 per unit. Required fees: $554. One-time fee: $35 full-time. Full-time tuition and fees vary according to degree level and program. *Financial support:* In 2009–10, 40 students received support, including 14 fellowships with full tuition reimbursements available (averaging $19,000 per year), 2 research assistantships with full tuition reimbursements available (averaging $19,000 per year), 24 teaching assistantships with full tuition reimbursements available (averaging $19,000 per year); scholarships/grants, health care benefits, and unspecified assistantships also available. *Faculty research:* Syntax, phonology, phonetics, semantics, sociolinguistics, psycholinguistics. *Unit head:* Dr. James Higginbotham, Chair, 213-740-4150, Fax: 213-740-9306, E-mail: higgy@usc.edu. *Application contact:* Dr. Joyce Perez, Student Services Advisor, 213-740-3891, Fax: 213-740-9306, E-mail: jpperez@usc.edu.

University of South Florida, Graduate School, College of Arts and Sciences, World Languages Department, Tampa, FL 33620-9951. Offers classics: Latin/Greek (MA); French (MA); linguistics (MA); linguistics: ESL (MA); Spanish (MA). Part-time and evening/weekend programs available. *Faculty:* 19 full-time (14 women), 1 part-time/adjunct (0 women). *Students:* 36 full-time (26 women), 22 part-time (16 women); includes 23 minority (5 African Americans, 3 American Indian/Alaska Native, 2 Asian Americans or Pacific Islanders, 13 Hispanic Americans), 12 international. Average age 32. 29 applicants, 52% accepted, 12 enrolled. In 2009, 18 master's awarded. *Degree requirements:* For master's, comprehensive exam, thesis. *Entrance requirements:* For master's, GRE General Test, minimum GPA of 3.0 in last 60 hours. Additional exam requirements/recommendations for international students: Required—TOEFL (minimum score 600 paper-based; 250 computer-based). *Application deadline:* For fall admission, 2/15 for domestic students, 1/2 for international students; for spring admission, 10/15 for domestic students, 6/1 for international students. Application fee: $30. Electronic applications accepted. *Financial support:* In 2009–10, teaching assistantships with tuition reimbursements (averaging $17,024 per year); tuition waivers (partial) and unspecified assistantships also available. Financial award application deadline: 6/30. *Faculty research:* Second language writing, academic literacy. Total annual research expenditures: $19,891. *Unit head:* Dr. Victor Peppard, Chairperson, 813-974-2012, Fax: 813-974-1718, E-mail: peppard@.cas.usf.edu. *Application contact:* Dr. Victor Peppard, Chairperson, 813-974-2012, Fax: 813-974-1718, E-mail: peppard@.cas.usf.edu.

The University of Tennessee, Graduate School, College of Arts and Sciences, Department of Modern Foreign Languages and Literatures, Program in Modern Foreign Languages, Knoxville, TN 37996. Offers applied linguistics (PhD); French (PhD); German (PhD); Italian (PhD); Portuguese (PhD); Russian (PhD); Spanish (PhD). *Degree requirements:* For doctorate, 2 foreign languages, thesis/dissertation. *Entrance requirements:* For doctorate, minimum GPA of 2.7. Additional exam requirements/recommendations for international students: Required—TOEFL. Electronic applications accepted. *Expenses:* Tuition, state resident: full-time $6826; part-time $380 per semester hour. Tuition, nonresident: full-time $21,844; part-time $1147 per semester hour. Tuition and fees vary according to program.

The University of Texas at Arlington, Graduate School, College of Liberal Arts, Department of Linguistics and TESOL, Program in Linguistics, Arlington, TX 76019. Offers MA, PhD. Part-time and evening/weekend programs available. *Faculty:* 5 full-time (3 women), 2 part-time/adjunct (0 women). *Students:* 28 full-time (14 women), 31 part-time (15 women); includes 9 minority (2 African Americans, 4 Asian Americans or Pacific Islanders, 3 Hispanic Americans), 12 international. 31 applicants, 100% accepted, 11 enrolled. In 2009, 3 master's, 7 doctorates awarded. Terminal master's awarded for partial completion of doctoral program. *Degree requirements:* For master's, one foreign language, comprehensive exam (for some programs), thesis optional; for doctorate, 2 foreign languages, comprehensive exam, thesis/dissertation, qualifying exam, dissertation proposal defense, professional development. *Entrance requirements:* For master's, GRE General Test, minimum undergraduate GPA of 3.0, 9 credits of undergraduate foundation courses; for doctorate, GRE General Test, 30 hours of graduate work in linguistics or a related discipline, minimum GPA of 3.5. Additional exam requirements/recommendations for international students: Required—TOEFL (minimum score 550 paper-based; 213 computer-based). *Application deadline:* For fall admission, 6/16 for domestic students. Applications are processed on a rolling basis. Application fee: $35 ($50 for international students). *Financial support:* In 2009–10, 52 students received support, including 10 fellowships (averaging $1,000 per year), 1 research assistantship, 4 teaching assistantships; career-related internships or fieldwork and institutionally sponsored loans also available. Financial award application deadline: 3/1; financial award applicants required to submit FAFSA. *Faculty research:* Field linguistics, discourse analysis, text linguistics, phonology, teaching English as a second language. *Unit head:* Dr. Jerrold Edmondson, Chair, 817-272-3133, Fax: 817-272-2731, E-mail: jerry@uta.edu. *Application contact:* Dr. Laurel Stvan, Graduate Advisor, 817-272-3133, Fax: 817-272-2731.

The University of Texas at Austin, Graduate School, College of Liberal Arts, Department of French and Italian, Austin, TX 78712-1111. Offers French (MA, PhD); French linguistics (MA, PhD); Italian studies (MA, PhD); Romance linguistics (MA, PhD). Part-time programs available. *Degree requirements:* For master's, one foreign language, thesis; for doctorate, 2 foreign languages, thesis/dissertation. *Entrance requirements:* For master's, GRE General Test,

Linguistics

The University of Texas at Austin (continued)

minimum GPA of 3.0, bachelor's degree in French or equivalent; for doctorate, GRE General Test, minimum GPA of 3.0, master's degree in French. Additional exam requirements/recommendations for international students: Required—TOEFL. Electronic applications accepted. *Faculty research:* Nineteenth-century Italian literature, Italian Renaissance, twentieth-century French literature, Francophone literature, fifteenth-century literature and culture.

The University of Texas at Austin, Graduate School, College of Liberal Arts, Department of Linguistics, Austin, TX 78712-1111. Offers MA, PhD. *Degree requirements:* For master's, one foreign language, thesis; for doctorate, 2 foreign languages, thesis/dissertation. *Entrance requirements:* For master's and doctorate, GRE General Test. Electronic applications accepted. *Faculty research:* Theoretical linguistics, sociolinguistics, documentary and descriptive linguistics, computational linguistics.

The University of Texas at El Paso, Graduate School, College of Liberal Arts, Department of Languages and Linguistics, El Paso, TX 79968-0001. Offers linguistics (MA); Spanish (MA); teaching English to speakers of other languages (Certificate). Part-time and evening/weekend programs available. *Students:* 28 (12 women); includes 15 minority (all Hispanic Americans), 4 international. Average age 34. In 2009, 10 master's awarded. *Degree requirements:* For master's, thesis optional. *Entrance requirements:* For master's, GRE General Test, departmental exam, minimum GPA of 3.0, letters of recommendation. Additional exam requirements/recommendations for international students: Required—TOEFL; Recommended—IELTS. *Application deadline:* For fall admission, 8/1 for domestic students, 3/1 for international students; for spring admission, 11/1 for domestic students, 9/1 for international students. Applications are processed on a rolling basis. Application fee: $45 ($80 for international students). Electronic applications accepted. *Financial support:* In 2009–10, research assistantships with partial tuition reimbursements (averaging $18,625 per year), teaching assistantships with partial tuition reimbursements (averaging $14,900 per year) were awarded; fellowships with partial tuition reimbursements, institutionally sponsored loans, scholarships/grants, health care benefits, tuition waivers (partial), and unspecified assistantships also available. Support available to part-time students. Financial award application deadline: 3/15; financial award applicants required to submit FAFSA. *Unit head:* Dr. Kirsten F. Nigro, Chair, 915-747-5767, Fax: 915-747-5292, E-mail: kfnigro@utep.edu. *Application contact:* Dr. Patricia D. Witherspoon, Dean of the Graduate School, 915-747-5491, Fax: 915-747-5788, E-mail: withersp@utep.edu.

University of Toronto, School of Graduate Studies, Humanities Division, Department of Linguistics, Toronto, ON M5S 1A1, Canada. Offers MA, PhD. Part-time programs available. *Degree requirements:* For master's, 2 foreign languages; for doctorate, thesis/dissertation, oral thesis proposal. *Entrance requirements:* For master's, BA in linguistics; for doctorate, MA in linguistics.

University of Utah, The Graduate School, College of Humanities, Department of Linguistics, Salt Lake City, UT 84112-0492. Offers applied linguistics (MA, PhD); linguistics (MA, PhD). *Faculty:* 10 full-time (4 women), 1 part-time/adjunct (0 women). *Students:* 24 full-time (14 women), 12 part-time (8 women); includes 3 minority (1 Asian American or Pacific Islander, 2 Hispanic Americans), 11 international. Average age 34. 44 applicants, 25% accepted, 11 enrolled. In 2009, 14 master's, 1 doctorate awarded. *Degree requirements:* For master's, 2 foreign languages, comprehensive exam; for doctorate, 2 foreign languages, comprehensive exam, thesis/dissertation. *Entrance requirements:* For master's and doctorate, GRE General Test, minimum undergraduate GPA of 3.0. Additional exam requirements/recommendations for international students: Required—TOEFL (minimum score 600 paper-based; 250 computer-based; 100 iBT). *Application deadline:* For fall admission, 12/15 for domestic students, 11/30 for international students. Application fee: $55 ($65 for international students). Electronic applications accepted. *Expenses:* Tuition, state resident: full-time $4004; part-time $1674 per semester. Tuition, nonresident: full-time $14,134; part-time $5915 per semester. Required fees: $324 per semester. Tuition and fees vary according to course load, degree level and program. *Financial support:* In 2009–10, 2 students received support, including 1 fellowship with full tuition reimbursement available (averaging $6,000 per year), 7 research assistantships with full tuition reimbursements available (averaging $11,500 per year), 13 teaching assistantships with full and partial tuition reimbursements available (averaging $11,500 per year); scholarships/grants, tuition waivers (partial), and unspecified assistantships also available. Financial award application deadline: 2/1; financial award applicants required to submit FAFSA. *Faculty research:* American Indian languages, applied linguistics phonology, sociolinguistics, syntax. Total annual research expenditures: $13,562. *Unit head:* Dr. Edward Rubin, Chair, 801-581-8047, Fax: 801-585-7351, E-mail: erubin@linguistics.utah.edu. *Application contact:* Kate Lythgoe, Executive Secretary, 801-581-8047, Fax: 801-585-7351, E-mail: kate.lythgoe@linguistics.utah.edu.

University of Utah, The Graduate School, College of Humanities, Program in Middle East Studies, Salt Lake City, UT 84112. Offers anthropology (MA); Arabic (MA, PhD); Arabic and linguistics (MA, PhD); Hebrew (MA); history (MA, PhD); Persian (MA, PhD); political science (MA, PhD); Turkish (MA). *Students:* 24 full-time (8 women), 19 part-time (9 women), 13 international. Average age 33. 33 applicants, 48% accepted, 10 enrolled. In 2009, 8 master's, 2 doctorates awarded. Terminal master's awarded for partial completion of doctoral program. *Degree requirements:* For master's, 2 foreign languages, comprehensive exam, thesis optional; for doctorate, 3 foreign languages, comprehensive exam, thesis/dissertation. *Entrance requirements:* For master's, GRE General Test, minimum GPA of 3.2; for doctorate, GRE General Test, MA in Middle East studies or equivalent, minimum GPA of 3.2. Additional exam requirements/recommendations for international students: Required—TOEFL (minimum score 580 paper-based; 237 computer-based; 92 iBT). *Application deadline:* For fall admission, 1/15 priority date for domestic and international students; for spring admission, 9/15 priority date for domestic and international students. Application fee: $55 ($65 for international students). Electronic applications accepted. *Expenses:* Tuition, state resident: full-time $4004; part-time $1674 per semester. Tuition, nonresident: full-time $14,134; part-time $5915 per semester. Required fees: $324 per semester. Tuition and fees vary according to course load, degree level and program. *Financial support:* In 2009–10, 19 students received support, including 15 fellowships with full tuition reimbursements available (averaging $14,000 per year), 3 teaching assistantships with full tuition reimbursements available (averaging $12,000 per year); unspecified assistantships also available. Financial award application deadline: 1/15. *Faculty research:* Arabic linguistics; Islamic studies; Middle Eastern history; political science; Judaic studies; anthropology; Arabic, Persian, Hebrew, and Turkish language and literature. *Unit head:* Dr. Bahman Baktiari, Director, 801-581-6181, Fax: 801-581-6183, E-mail: b.baktiari@utah.edu. *Application contact:* Peter von Sivers, Director of Graduate Studies, 801-581-9028, Fax: 801-581-6183, E-mail: peter.vonsivers@utah.edu.

University of Victoria, Faculty of Graduate Studies, Faculty of Humanities, Department of Linguistics, Victoria, BC V8W 2Y2, Canada. Offers applied linguistics (MA); linguistics (MA, PhD). Part-time programs available. *Degree requirements:* For master's, one foreign language, thesis, colloquium; for doctorate, 2 foreign languages, comprehensive exam, thesis/dissertation, candidacy exam. *Entrance requirements:* For master's, GRE; for doctorate, GRE, sample of written work. Additional exam requirements/recommendations for international students: Required—TOEFL. Electronic applications accepted. *Faculty research:* Grammatical theory, syntactic analysis, morphology, Western Amerindian languages, Salishan, applied linguistics.

University of Virginia, College and Graduate School of Arts and Sciences, Program in Linguistics, Charlottesville, VA 22903. Offers MA. *Students:* 6 full-time (4 women); includes 1 minority (Hispanic American), 1 international. Average age 24. 15 applicants, 67% accepted, 4 enrolled. In 2009, 9 master's awarded. *Degree requirements:* For master's, one foreign language, comprehensive exam, thesis optional, reading knowledge of French or German. *Entrance requirements:* For master's, GRE General Test. Additional exam requirements/recommendations for international students: Required—TOEFL (minimum score 600 paper-based; 250 computer-based; 90 iBT), IELTS (minimum score 7). *Application deadline:* For fall admission, 2/15 for domestic and international students. Applications are processed on a rolling basis. Application fee: $60. Electronic applications accepted. *Financial support:* Teaching assistantships available. Financial award applicants required to submit FAFSA. *Unit head:* Lise Dobrin, E-mail: ld4n@virginia.edu. *Application contact:* Lise Dobrin, E-mail: ld4n@virginia.edu.

University of Washington, Graduate School, College of Arts and Sciences, Department of Linguistics, Seattle, WA 98195. Offers computational linguistics (MA); linguistics (MA, PhD); Romance linguistics (MA, PhD). Part-time programs available. Terminal master's awarded for partial completion of doctoral program. *Degree requirements:* For master's, one foreign language, thesis; for doctorate, 2 foreign languages, thesis/dissertation. *Entrance requirements:* For master's, GRE General Test, minimum GPA of 3.0; for doctorate, GRE, minimum GPA of 3.0. Additional exam requirements/recommendations for international students: Required—TOEFL. Electronic applications accepted. *Faculty research:* Syntax, phonology, semantics, phonetics, sociolinguistics.

University of Washington, Graduate School, College of Arts and Sciences, Department of Slavic Languages and Literatures, Seattle, WA 98195. Offers Russian literature (MA, PhD); Slavic linguistics (MA, PhD). *Degree requirements:* For master's, 2 foreign languages, thesis optional; for doctorate, 3 foreign languages, thesis/dissertation. *Entrance requirements:* For master's and doctorate, GRE General Test, minimum GPA of 3.0. Additional exam requirements/recommendations for international students: Required—TOEFL. Electronic applications accepted. *Faculty research:* Modern and medieval East European languages and literatures, comparative literature, Russian folk literature, Slavic literary theory and criticism, computerized morphology of Russian.

University of Wisconsin–Madison, Graduate School, College of Letters and Science, Department of East Asian Languages and Literature, Program in Japanese Linguistics, Madison, WI 53706-1380. Offers MA, PhD. Part-time programs available. Terminal master's awarded for partial completion of doctoral program. *Degree requirements:* For master's, one foreign language, seminars, written exam; for doctorate, 3 foreign languages, thesis/dissertation, seminars, preliminary exams, oral exam. *Entrance requirements:* For master's, GRE General Test, bachelor's degree or equivalent in Japanese; for doctorate, GRE General Test, master's degree or equivalent in Japanese. Electronic applications accepted. *Expenses:* Tuition, state resident: part-time $594 per credit. Tuition, nonresident: part-time $1504 per credit. Required fees: $65 per credit. Tuition and fees vary according to course load, program and reciprocity agreements. *Faculty research:* Modern and historical Japanese linguistics, modern Japanese fiction and poetry, classical Japanese literature, language pedagogy.

University of Wisconsin–Madison, Graduate School, College of Letters and Science, Department of English, Madison, WI 53706-1380. Offers applied English linguistics (MA); composition and rhetoric (PhD); creative writing (MFA); English language and linguistics (PhD); literary studies (MA, PhD). *Degree requirements:* For doctorate, thesis/dissertation. *Expenses:* Tuition, state resident: part-time $594 per credit. Tuition, nonresident: part-time $1504 per credit. Required fees: $65 per credit. Tuition and fees vary according to course load, program and reciprocity agreements.

University of Wisconsin–Madison, Graduate School, College of Letters and Science, Department of Linguistics, Madison, WI 53706-1380. Offers MA, PhD. Part-time programs available. Terminal master's awarded for partial completion of doctoral program. *Degree requirements:* For master's, 2 foreign languages; for doctorate, 3 foreign languages, thesis/dissertation. Electronic applications accepted. *Expenses:* Tuition, state resident: part-time $594 per credit. Tuition, nonresident: part-time $1504 per credit. Required fees: $65 per credit. Tuition and fees vary according to course load, program and reciprocity agreements. *Faculty research:* Formal linguistics, acoustic phonetics, American studies, Indo-European linguistics.

University of Wisconsin–Milwaukee, Graduate School, College of Letters and Sciences, Department of English, Milwaukee, WI 53201-0413. Offers creative writing (PhD); English (MA); international technical communication (Certificate); linguistics (PhD); professional writing (PhD); professional writing and communication (Certificate); rhetoric and composition (PhD); MLIS/MA. *Faculty:* 38 full-time (19 women). *Students:* 107 full-time (64 women), 82 part-time (54 women); includes 13 minority (8 African Americans, 1 American Indian/Alaska Native, 2 Asian Americans or Pacific Islanders, 2 Hispanic Americans), 23 international. Average age 34. 193 applicants, 51% accepted, 31 enrolled. In 2009, 26 master's, 16 doctorates awarded. *Degree requirements:* For master's, thesis or alternative; for doctorate, one foreign language, thesis/dissertation. *Entrance requirements:* For master's, GRE General Test, GRE Subject Test; for doctorate, GRE. Additional exam requirements/recommendations for international students: Required—TOEFL (minimum score 550 paper-based; 79 iBT), IELTS (minimum score 6.5). *Application deadline:* For fall admission, 1/1 priority date for domestic students; for spring admission, 9/1 for domestic students. Applications are processed on a rolling basis. Application fee: $45 ($75 for international students). *Expenses:* Tuition, state resident: full-time $8800. Tuition, nonresident: full-time $20,760. Tuition and fees vary according to program and reciprocity agreements. *Financial support:* In 2009–10, 75 teaching assistantships were awarded; career-related internships or fieldwork and unspecified assistantships also available. Support available to part-time students. Financial award application deadline: 4/15. Total annual research expenditures: $41,495. *Unit head:* Tasha Oren, Representative, 414-229-4637, Fax: 414-229-2643, E-mail: tgoren@uwm.edu. *Application contact:* General Information Contact, 414-229-4982, Fax: 414-229-6967, E-mail: gradschool@uwm.edu.

Wayne State University, College of Liberal Arts and Sciences, Interdisciplinary Program in Linguistics, Detroit, MI 48202. Offers MA. *Degree requirements:* For master's, one foreign language, thesis. *Entrance requirements:* Additional exam requirements/recommendations for international students: Required—TOEFL (minimum score 550 paper-based; 213 computer-based); Recommended—TWE (minimum score 6). Electronic applications accepted. *Faculty research:* Formal linguistics, psycholinguistics, sociolinguistics, historical linguistics, language acquisition.

West Virginia University, Eberly College of Arts and Sciences, Department of Foreign Languages, Morgantown, WV 26506. Offers French (MA); linguistics (MA); Spanish (MA); teaching English to speakers of other languages (MA). Part-time programs available. *Degree requirements:* For master's, one foreign language, comprehensive exam (for some programs), thesis optional. *Entrance requirements:* For master's, minimum GPA of 3.0. Electronic applications accepted. *Faculty research:* French, German, and Spanish literature; foreign language pedagogy; English as a second language; cultural studies; linguistics.

Yale University, Graduate School of Arts and Sciences, Department of Linguistics, New Haven, CT 06520. Offers PhD. *Degree requirements:* For doctorate, 2 foreign languages, thesis/dissertation. *Entrance requirements:* For doctorate, GRE General Test.

York University, Faculty of Graduate Studies, Faculty of Arts, Program in Theoretical and Applied Linguistics, Toronto, ON M3J 1P3, Canada. Offers MA, PhD. *Degree requirements:* For master's, thesis.

Translation and Interpretation

American University, College of Arts and Sciences, Department of Language and Foreign Studies, Program in French, Washington, DC 20016-8045. Offers translation (Certificate). Part-time and evening/weekend programs available. *Students:* 2 full-time (both women), 1 (woman) part-time; includes 1 minority (African American), 1 international. Average age 29. In 2009, 1 Certificate awarded. *Entrance requirements:* For degree, bachelor's degree in French or evidence of French proficiency plus BA in any field. Additional exam requirements/recommendations for international students: Required—TOEFL. *Application deadline:* For fall admission, 2/1 for domestic students; for spring admission, 10/1 for domestic students. Application fee: $50. *Expenses:* Tuition: Full-time $22,266; part-time $1237 per credit hour. Required fees: $430. Tuition and fees vary according to program. *Financial support:* Fellowships, career-related internships or fieldwork, Federal Work-Study, and institutionally sponsored loans available. Financial award application deadline: 2/1. *Faculty research:* Literature, language, modern French politics, contemporary French society, the civilization of Quebec, business French and translation studies.

American University, College of Arts and Sciences, Department of Language and Foreign Studies, Program in Russian, Washington, DC 20016-8045. Offers translation (Certificate). Part-time and evening/weekend programs available. *Students:* 5 part-time (3 women). Average age 35. In 2009, 2 Certificates awarded. *Entrance requirements:* For degree, bachelor's degree in Russian or evidence of Russian proficiency plus a BA. Additional exam requirements/recommendations for international students: Required—TOEFL. *Application deadline:* For fall admission, 2/1 for domestic students; for spring admission, 10/1 for domestic students. Application fee: $50. *Expenses:* Tuition: Full-time $22,266; part-time $1237 per credit hour. Required fees: $430. Tuition and fees vary according to program. *Financial support:* Fellowships, career-related internships or fieldwork, Federal Work-Study, and institutionally sponsored loans available. Financial award application deadline: 2/1. *Faculty research:* Culture, literature, and area studies; technology-assisted language instruction; linguistics.

American University, College of Arts and Sciences, Department of Language and Foreign Studies, Program in Spanish: Latin American Studies, Washington, DC 20016-8045. Offers Spanish: Latin American studies (MA); translation (Certificate). Part-time and evening/weekend programs available. *Students:* 11 full-time (9 women), 8 part-time (4 women); includes 8 minority (3 African Americans, 5 Hispanic Americans). Average age 26. 23 applicants, 87% accepted, 7 enrolled. In 2009, 11 master's, 7 other advanced degrees awarded. *Degree requirements:* For master's, one foreign language, comprehensive exam, thesis or alternative, research. *Entrance requirements:* For master's, GRE, bachelor's degree in language or equivalent, essay in Spanish, minimum GPA of 3.2; for Certificate, bachelor's degree in Spanish or BA in any field plus Spanish proficiency. Additional exam requirements/recommendations for international students: Required—TOEFL. *Application deadline:* For fall admission, 2/1 for domestic students; for spring admission, 10/1 for domestic students. Application fee: $80. *Expenses:* Tuition: Full-time $22,266; part-time $1237 per credit hour. Required fees: $430. Tuition and fees vary according to program. *Financial support:* Fellowships, career-related internships or fieldwork, Federal Work-Study, and institutionally sponsored loans available. Financial award application deadline: 2/1. *Faculty research:* Latin American culture, literature, and history; computer-aided instruction.

American University of Sharjah, Graduate Programs, Sharjah, United Arab Emirates. Offers business (EMBA, GEMPA, MBA); chemical engineering (MS Ch E); civil engineering (MSCE); computer engineering (MS); electrical engineering (MSEE); mechanical engineering (MSME); mechatronics engineering (MS); public administration (MPA); teaching English to speakers of other languages (MA); translation and interpreting (MA); urban planning (MUP). Part-time and evening/weekend programs available. *Faculty:* 59 full-time (4 women), 5 part-time/adjunct (1 woman). *Students:* 101 full-time (44 women), 218 part-time (95 women). Average age 27. 184 applicants, 83% accepted, 92 enrolled. In 2009, 97 master's awarded. *Entrance requirements:* For master's, GMAT (MBA). Additional exam requirements/recommendations for international students: Required—TOEFL (minimum score 550 paper-based; 213 computer-based; 80 iBT), TWE (minimum score 5). *Application deadline:* For fall admission, 7/30 priority date for domestic students, 7/15 priority date for international students; for spring admission, 12/31 priority date for domestic students, 12/16 for international students. Applications are processed on a rolling basis. Application fee: $300. Electronic applications accepted. Tuition charges are reported in United Arab Emirates dirhams. *Expenses:* Tuition: Part-time 3250 United Arab Emirates dirhams per credit hour. *Financial support:* In 2009–10, 63 students received support, including 28 research assistantships with tuition reimbursements available, 35 teaching assistantships with tuition reimbursements available. *Faculty research:* Chemical engineering, civil engineering, computer engineering, electrical engineering, linguistics, translation. *Unit head:* Ghada S. Sami, Admissions Manager, 971-65151006 Ext. 1006, Fax: 971-65151020, E-mail: graduateadmission@aus.edu. *Application contact:* Ghada S. Sami, Admissions Manager, 971-65151006 Ext. 1006, Fax: 971-65151020, E-mail: graduateadmission@aus.edu.

Babel University School of Translation, Program in Translation, Honolulu, HI 96815-1302. Offers MS. Part-time and evening/weekend programs available. Postbaccalaureate distance learning degree programs offered (no on-campus study). *Degree requirements:* For master's, comprehensive exam, thesis. *Entrance requirements:* For master's, translation exam. Additional exam requirements/recommendations for international students: Recommended—TOEFL (minimum score 550 paper-based).

College of Charleston, Graduate School, School of Languages, Cultures, and World Affairs, Program in Healthcare and Medical Interpreting, Charleston, SC 29424-0001. Offers Certificate. *Faculty:* 4 full-time (1 woman). *Students:* 1 applicant, 100% accepted, 0 enrolled. In 2009, 2 Certificates awarded. *Entrance requirements:* For degree, language exam, minimum GPA of 3.0. Additional exam requirements/recommendations for international students: Required—TOEFL. *Application deadline:* For fall admission, 6/15 for domestic students; for spring admission, 11/1 for domestic students. Application fee: $50. *Expenses:* Contact institution. *Unit head:* Dr. Gladys Matthews, Director, 843-953-5718, E-mail: matthewsg@cofc.edu. *Application contact:* Susan Hallatt, Director of Graduate Admissions, 843-953-5614, Fax: 843-953-1434, E-mail: hallatts@cofc.edu.

Concordia University, School of Graduate Studies, Faculty of Arts and Science, Department of Études Françaises, Montréal, QC H3G 1M8, Canada. Offers écriture (Certificate); anglais-français en langue et techniques de localisation (Certificate); littératures francophones et résonances médiatiques (MA); traductologie (MA); translation (Diploma). *Degree requirements:* For other advanced degree, one foreign language.

Drew University, Caspersen School of Graduate Studies, Program in Poetry, Madison, NJ 07940-1493. Offers poetry (MFA); poetry in translation (MFA). *Students:* 24 full-time (19 women); includes 4 minority (1 African American, 3 Hispanic Americans). Average age 36. 12 applicants, 92% accepted, 8 enrolled. *Degree requirements:* For master's, thesis. *Entrance requirements:* For master's, transcripts, writing sample, recommendations. *Application deadline:* For fall admission, 5/1 priority date for domestic students; for spring admission, 12/1 priority date for domestic students. Applications are processed on a rolling basis. Application fee: $35. *Expenses:* Contact institution. *Financial support:* In 2009–10, 23 students received support. Federal Work-Study, scholarships/grants, and tuition waivers (partial) available. Financial award applicants required to submit FAFSA. *Unit head:* Anne Marie Macari, 973-408-3016, E-mail: amacari@drew.edu. *Application contact:* Carla J. Burns, Director of Graduate Admissions, 973-408-3110, Fax: 973-408-3242, E-mail: gradm@drew.edu.

Georgia State University, College of Arts and Sciences, Department of Modern and Classical Languages, Program in Translation and Interpretation, Atlanta, GA 30302-3083. Offers French (Certificate); German (Certificate); Spanish (Certificate). Electronic applications accepted.

Kent State University, College of Arts and Sciences, Department of Modern and Classical Language Studies, Kent, OH 44242-0001. Offers French literature (MA); French, Spanish, German and Latin pedagogy (MA); German literature (MA); Spanish literature (MA); translation (MA), including French, German, Japanese, Russian, Spanish; translation studies (PhD). Part-time and evening/weekend programs available. *Degree requirements:* For master's, one foreign language, comprehensive exam (for some programs), thesis (for some programs); for doctorate, comprehensive exam, thesis/dissertation (for some programs). *Entrance requirements:* For master's, minimum GPA of 3.0, writing sample, audio tape or CD; for doctorate, 3 recommendations. Additional exam requirements/recommendations for international students: Required—TOEFL (minimum score 197 computer-based). Electronic applications accepted. *Faculty research:* Literature, pedagogy, applied linguistics, translation studies.

Marygrove College, Graduate Division, Program in Modern Language Translation, Detroit, MI 48221-2599. Offers Certificate.

Montclair State University, The Graduate School, College of Humanities and Social Sciences, Department of Spanish and Italian, Montclair, NJ 07043-1624. Offers Italian (Certificate); Spanish (MA, Certificate); translating and interpreting Spanish (Certificate). Part-time and evening/weekend programs available. *Faculty:* 20 full-time (12 women), 24 part-time/adjunct (16 women). *Students:* 2 full-time (1 woman), 21 part-time (17 women). Average age 33. 9 applicants, 56% accepted, 4 enrolled. In 2009, 10 master's awarded. *Degree requirements:* For master's, comprehensive exam, thesis or alternative. *Entrance requirements:* For master's, GRE General Test, 2 letters of recommendation. Additional exam requirements/recommendations for international students: Required—TOEFL (minimum score 83 computer-based), or IELTS. *Application deadline:* For fall admission, 6/1 for international students; for spring admission, 11/1 for international students. Applications are processed on a rolling basis. Application fee: $60. Electronic applications accepted. *Expenses:* Tuition, area resident: Part-time $486.74 per credit. Tuition, state resident: part-time $486.74 per credit. Tuition, nonresident: part-time $751.34 per credit. Tuition and fees vary according to degree level and program. *Financial support:* In 2009–10, 1 research assistantship with full tuition reimbursement (averaging $7,000 per year) was awarded; Federal Work-Study, scholarships/grants, and unspecified assistantships also available. Support available to part-time students. Financial award application deadline: 3/1; financial award applicants required to submit FAFSA. *Unit head:* Dr. Linda Gould Levine, Chairperson, 973-655-7506. *Application contact:* Amy Aiello, Director of Graduate Admissions and Operations, 973-655-5147, Fax: 973-655-7869, E-mail: graduate.school@montclair.edu.

Monterey Institute of International Studies, Graduate School of Translation, Interpretation and Language Education, Program in Translation and Interpretation, Monterey, CA 93940-2691. Offers conference interpretation (MA); translation (MA); translation and interpretation (MA); translation and localization management (MA). *Students:* 199 full-time (141 women), 1 (woman) part-time; includes 33 minority (2 African Americans, 15 Asian Americans or Pacific Islanders, 16 Hispanic Americans), 118 international. Average age 28. In 2009, 71 master's awarded. *Degree requirements:* For master's, one foreign language, thesis or alternative, exams. *Entrance requirements:* For master's, minimum GPA of 3.0, proficiency in a foreign language. Additional exam requirements/recommendations for international students: Required—TOEFL (minimum score 600 paper-based; 250 computer-based; 100 iBT). *Application deadline:* For fall admission, 3/15 priority date for domestic and international students; for spring admission, 10/1 priority date for domestic and international students. Applications are processed on a rolling basis. Application fee: $50. Electronic applications accepted. *Expenses:* Tuition: Full-time $31,000; part-time $1500 per credit. Required fees: $56. *Financial support:* Career-related internships or fieldwork, Federal Work-Study, institutionally sponsored loans, scholarships/grants, tuition waivers (partial), and unspecified assistantships available. Support available to part-time students. Financial award application deadline: 3/15; financial award applicants required to submit FAFSA. *Faculty research:* Assessment and testing in translation and interpretation, translation and interpretation pedagogy and curricula, integration of translation technology, language policy and planning. *Application contact:* 831-647-4123, Fax: 831-647-6405, E-mail: admit@miis.edu.

See Close-Up on page 437.

New York University, NYU in Madrid, Madrid, NY 10012-1019, Spain. Offers creative writing in Spanish (MFA); Spanish (PhD); Spanish and Latin American literatures and cultures (MA); Spanish language and translation (MA). *Students:* 27 full-time (23 women), 1 part-time (0 women); includes 8 minority (2 African Americans, 1 Asian American or Pacific Islander, 5 Hispanic Americans), 1 international. Average age 26. 73 applicants, 90% accepted, 27 enrolled. In 2009, 22 master's awarded. Application fee: $90. *Expenses:* Tuition: Full-time $30,528; part-time $1272 per credit. Required fees: $2177. *Unit head:* Judith Nemethy, Director, 212-998-8770, Fax: 212-995-4149, E-mail: nyu-in-madrid@nyu.edu. *Application contact:* Judith Nemethy, Director, 212-998-8770, Fax: 212-995-4149, E-mail: nyu-in-madrid@nyu.edu.

New York University, School of Continuing and Professional Studies, Division of Liberal Studies and Allied Arts, New York, NY 10012-1019. Offers translation (MS). *Expenses:* Tuition: Full-time $30,528; part-time $1272 per credit. Required fees: $2177.

Rutgers, The State University of New Jersey, New Brunswick, Graduate School-New Brunswick, Program in Spanish, Piscataway, NJ 08854-8097. Offers bilingualism and second language acquisition (MA, PhD); Spanish (MA, MAT, PhD); Spanish literature (MA, PhD); translation (MA). Part-time programs available. *Degree requirements:* For master's, comprehensive exam (for some programs), thesis (for some programs); for doctorate, 2 foreign languages, comprehensive exam, thesis/dissertation. *Entrance requirements:* For master's and doctorate, GRE General Test. Additional exam requirements/recommendations for international students: Required—TOEFL. Electronic applications accepted. *Faculty research:* Hispanic literature, Luso-Brazilian literature, Spanish linguistics, Spanish translation.

State University of New York at Binghamton, Graduate School, School of Arts and Sciences, Department of Romance Languages and Literatures, Program in Spanish, Binghamton, NY 13902-6000. Offers Spanish (MA); translation (Certificate). *Students:* 2 full-time (1 woman), 2 part-time (both women). Average age 38. 1 applicant, 0% accepted, 0 enrolled. In 2009, 5 master's awarded. *Degree requirements:* For master's, one foreign language, comprehensive exam, thesis or alternative. *Entrance requirements:* For master's, GRE General Test, GRE Subject Test. Additional exam requirements/recommendations for international students: Required—TOEFL (minimum score 550 paper-based; 213 computer-based; 80 iBT). *Application deadline:* For fall admission, 2/15 priority date for domestic and international students; for spring admission, 11/15 priority date for domestic and international students. Applications are processed on a rolling basis. Application fee: $60. Electronic applications accepted. *Financial support:* Fellowships, research assistantships, teaching assistantships, career-related internships or fieldwork, Federal Work-Study, institutionally sponsored loans, scholarships/grants, health care benefits, and unspecified assistantships available. Financial award application deadline: 2/15; financial award applicants required to submit FAFSA. *Unit head:* Dr. Antonio Sobejano-Moran, Chairperson, 607-777-4635, E-mail: antobianco@msn.com. *Application contact:* Victoria Williams, Recruiting and Admissions Coordinator, 607-777-2151, Fax: 607-777-2501, E-mail: vwilliam@binghamton.edu.

State University of New York at Binghamton, Graduate School, School of Arts and Sciences, Translation Research and Instruction Program, Binghamton, NY 13902-6000. Offers Certificate. Part-time programs available. *Faculty:* 1 (woman) part-time/adjunct. *Students:* 14 full-time (9 women), 10 part-time (4 women); includes 3 minority (1 African American, 2 Hispanic Americans), 13 international. Average age 36. 16 applicants, 31% accepted, 2 enrolled. In 2009, 4 Certificates awarded. *Entrance requirements:* For degree, GRE General Test. Additional exam requirements/recommendations for international students: Required—

Translation and Interpretation

State University of New York at Binghamton (continued)
TOEFL (minimum score 550 paper-based; 213 computer-based; 80 iBT). *Application deadline:* For fall admission, 1/15 priority date for domestic and international students; for spring admission, 10/15 priority date for domestic and international students. Applications are processed on a rolling basis. Application fee: $60. Electronic applications accepted. *Financial support:* In 2009–10, 6 students received support, including 2 research assistantships with full tuition reimbursements available (averaging $14,500 per year), 3 teaching assistantships with full tuition reimbursements available (averaging $14,500 per year). Financial award application deadline: 2/15. *Unit head:* Dr. Marilyn Gaddis Rose, Director, 607-777-6726, E-mail: mgrose@binghamton.edu. *Application contact:* Victoria Williams, Recruiting and Admissions Coordinator, 607-777-2151, Fax: 607-777-2501, E-mail: vwilliam@binghamton.edu.

Universidad Autonoma de Guadalajara, Graduate Programs, Guadalajara, Mexico. Offers administrative law and justice (LL M); advertising and corporate communications (MA); architecture (M Arch); business (MBA); computational science (MCC); education (Ed M, Ed D); English-Spanish translation (MA); fiscal law (MA); integrated management of digital animation (MA); international business (MIB); international corporate law (LL M); internet technologies (MS); labor health (MS); manufacturing systems (MMS); philosophy (MA, PhD); power electronics (MS); quality systems (MQS); renewable energy (MS); social evaluation of projects (MBA); strategic market research (MBA); teaching mathematics (MA).

Université de Montréal, Faculty of Arts and Sciences, Department of Linguistics and Translation, Montréal, QC H3C 3J7, Canada. Offers linguistics and translation (MA, PhD, DESS). *Degree requirements:* For master's, thesis, general exam; for doctorate, thesis/dissertation, general exam. Electronic applications accepted.

Université Laval, Faculty of Letters, Department of Languages, Linguistics and Translations, Programs in Terminology and Translation, Québec, QC G1K 7P4, Canada. Offers MA, Diploma. Part-time programs available. *Degree requirements:* For master's, thesis (for some programs). *Entrance requirements:* For master's and Diploma, knowledge of French and English. Electronic applications accepted.

University at Albany, State University of New York, College of Arts and Sciences, Department of Languages, Literatures, and Cultures, Program in Russian, Albany, NY 12222-0001. Offers Russian (MA); Russian translation (Certificate). *Faculty research:* Translation, phonology and morphology of modern Russian.

University of Arkansas, Graduate School, J. William Fulbright College of Arts and Sciences, Department of English, Program in Translation, Fayetteville, AR 72701-1201. Offers MFA. *Students:* 1 (woman) full-time, 3 part-time (1 woman). *Degree requirements:* For master's, thesis. Application fee: $40 ($50 for international students). *Expenses:* Tuition, state resident: full-time $7355; part-time $356.58 per hour. Tuition, nonresident: full-time $17,401; part-time $775.17 per hour. Required fees: $1203. *Financial support:* In 2009–10, 2 teaching assistantships were awarded; fellowships, research assistantships, career-related internships or fieldwork and Federal Work-Study also available. Support available to part-time students. Financial award application deadline: 4/1; financial award applicants required to submit FAFSA. *Unit head:* Dr. Geoffrey Brock, Interim Director, 479-575-4301, Fax: 479-575-5919, E-mail: mfa@uark.edu. *Application contact:* Dr. Geoffrey Brock, Interim Director, 479-575-4301, Fax: 479-575-5919, E-mail: mfa@uark.edu.

University of Denver, University College, Denver, CO 80208. Offers applied communication (MAS, MPS, Certificate); computer information systems (MAS, Certificate); environmental policy and management (MAS, Certificate); geographic information systems (MAS, Certificate); human resource administration (MPS, Certificate); knowledge and information technologies (MAS); liberal studies (MLS, Certificate); modern languages (MLS, Certificate); organizational leadership (MPS, Certificate); security management (Certificate); technology management (MAS, Certificate), including 21st century strategic management (MAS), international markets (MAS), project management (MAS), research and development management (MAS); telecommunications (MAS, Certificate), including broadband (MAS), telecommunications management and policy (MAS), telecommunications technology (MAS), wireless networks (MAS). Part-time and evening/weekend programs available. Postbaccalaureate distance learning degree programs offered (no on-campus study). *Faculty:* 160 part-time/adjunct (64 women). *Students:* 53 full-time (25 women), 984 part-time (551 women); includes 171 minority (72 African Americans, 10 American Indian/Alaska Native, 33 Asian Americans or Pacific Islanders, 56 Hispanic Americans), 75 international. Average age 36. 537 applicants, 96% accepted, 494 enrolled. In 2009, 229 master's, 109 Certificates awarded. *Entrance requirements:* Additional exam requirements/recommendations for international students: Required—TOEFL (minimum score 550 paper-based; 213 computer-based). *Application deadline:* Applications are processed on a rolling basis. Application fee: $75. Electronic applications accepted. *Expenses:* Contact institution. *Financial support:* Applicants required to submit FAFSA. *Unit head:* Dr. James Davis, Dean, 303-871-2291, Fax: 303-871-4047, E-mail: jdavis@du.edu. *Application contact:* Information Contact, 303-871-3155.

The University of Iowa, Graduate College, College of Liberal Arts and Sciences, Department of Cinema and Comparative Literature, Program in Comparative Literature Translation, Iowa City, IA 52242-1316. Offers MFA. *Degree requirements:* For master's, thesis, exam. *Entrance requirements:* For master's, GRE General Test, minimum GPA of 3.0. Additional exam requirements/recommendations for international students: Required—TOEFL (minimum score 550 paper-based; 213 computer-based; 81 iBT). Electronic applications accepted.

University of Nevada, Las Vegas, Graduate College, College of Liberal Arts, Department of Foreign Languages, Las Vegas, NV 89154-5047. Offers Hispanic studies (MA); Spanish translation (Certificate). Part-time programs available. *Faculty:* 5 full-time (4 women). *Students:* 2 full-time (both women), 10 part-time (6 women); includes 8 minority (1 Asian American or Pacific Islander, 7 Hispanic Americans). Average age 41. 8 applicants, 63% accepted, 3 enrolled. In 2009, 5 master's, 1 other advanced degree awarded. *Degree requirements:* For master's and Certificate, one foreign language, comprehensive exam. *Entrance requirements:* Additional exam requirements/recommendations for international students: Required—TOEFL (minimum score 550 paper-based; 213 computer-based; 80 iBT), IELTS (minimum score 7). *Application deadline:* For fall admission, 8/1 priority date for domestic students, 5/1 for international students; for spring admission, 12/1 priority date for domestic students, 10/1 for international students. Applications are processed on a rolling basis. Application fee: $60 ($95 for international students). Electronic applications accepted. *Financial support:* In 2009–10, 2 students received support, including 2 teaching assistantships with partial tuition reimbursements available (averaging $10,000 per year); institutionally sponsored loans, scholarships/grants, health care benefits, and unspecified assistantships also available. Financial award application deadline: 3/1. *Faculty research:* Second language acquisition/Romance languages, Old French, sociolinguistics/Romance languages, Spanish poetry of the twenties and thirties, post-Spanish Civil War women's fiction. *Unit head:* Dr. Ralph Buechler, Chair/Associate Professor, 702-895-3546, Fax: 702-895-3431, E-mail: ralph.buechler@unlv.edu. *Application contact:* Graduate College Admissions Evaluator, 702-895-3320, Fax: 702-895-4180, E-mail: gradcollege@unlv.edu.

University of North Florida, College of Education and Human Services, Department of Exceptional Student and Deaf Education, Jacksonville, FL 32224. Offers American sign language/English interpreting (M Ed); applied behavior analysis (M Ed); deaf education (M Ed); disability services (M Ed); exceptional student education (M Ed). *Accreditation:* NCATE. Part-time and evening/weekend programs available. *Faculty:* 11 full-time (9 women). *Students:* 34 full-time (all women), 33 part-time (28 women); includes 8 minority (2 African Americans, 3 Asian Americans or Pacific Islanders, 3 Hispanic Americans). Average age 31. 23 applicants, 61% accepted, 8 enrolled. In 2009, 34 master's awarded. *Entrance requirements:* For master's, GRE General Test, minimum GPA of 3.0 in last 60 hours, interview, 3 letters of recommendation. Additional exam requirements/recommendations for international students: Required—TOEFL (minimum score 500 paper-based; 173 computer-based). *Application deadline:* For fall admission, 7/1 priority date for domestic students, 5/1 for international students; for spring admission, 11/1 priority date for domestic students, 10/1 for international students. Applications are processed on a rolling basis. Application fee: $30. Electronic applications accepted. *Expenses:* Tuition, state resident: full-time $6649.20; part-time $277.05 per credit hour. Tuition, nonresident: full-time $22,970; part-time $957.08 per credit hour. Required fees: $985; $41.03 per credit hour. *Financial support:* In 2009–10, 40 students received support; research assistantships, teaching assistantships, career-related internships or fieldwork, Federal Work-Study, and tuition waivers (partial) available. Support available to part-time students. Financial award application deadline: 4/1; financial award applicants required to submit FAFSA. *Faculty research:* Transition, integrating technology into teacher education, written language development, professional school development, learning strategies. Total annual research expenditures: $1 million. *Unit head:* Dr. Karen Patterson, Chair, 904-620-2930, Fax: 904-620-3895, E-mail: karen.patterson@unf.edu. *Application contact:* Kiersten Jarvis, Graduate Admissions Coordinator, 904-620-2530, Fax: 904-620-1135, E-mail: kiersten.jarvis@unf.edu.

University of Ottawa, Faculty of Graduate and Postdoctoral Studies, Faculty of Arts, Institute of Canadian Studies, Ottawa, ON K1N 6N5, Canada. Offers economics (PhD); English (PhD); geography (PhD); history (PhD); lettres Françaises (PhD); linguistics (PhD); philosophy (PhD); political science (PhD); psychology (PhD); religious studies (PhD); translation studies (PhD). *Degree requirements:* For doctorate, comprehensive exam, thesis/dissertation.

University of Ottawa, Faculty of Graduate and Postdoctoral Studies, Faculty of Arts, School of Translation and Interpretation, Ottawa, ON K1N 6N5, Canada. Offers interpreting (MA); Spanish translation (MA); translation (MA); translation studies (PhD). *Degree requirements:* For master's, one foreign language, thesis or alternative, research paper; for doctorate, thesis/dissertation, doctoral exam. *Entrance requirements:* For master's, school-administered exam, honors degree or equivalent, minimum B average; for doctorate, master's degree, minimum B+ average. Electronic applications accepted. *Faculty research:* Theory of translation, Spanish translation, conference interpreting, legal translation, translation-oriented lexicology and terminology.

University of Puerto Rico, Río Piedras, College of Humanities, Program in Translation, San Juan, PR 00931-3300. Offers MA, Certificate. Part-time and evening/weekend programs available. *Degree requirements:* For master's, 2 foreign languages, comprehensive exam, thesis. *Entrance requirements:* For master's, PAEG, minimum GPA of 3.0, graduate-level knowledge of 2 languages (English, French, or Spanish), letter of recommendation.

University of Wisconsin–Milwaukee, Graduate School, College of Letters and Sciences, Department of Spanish, Milwaukee, WI 53201-0413. Offers Spanish (MA); translation (Certificate). *Faculty:* 7 full-time (3 women). *Students:* Average age 29. 13 applicants, 85% accepted, 3 enrolled. In 2009, 1 master's awarded. *Entrance requirements:* For master's, bachelor's degree. *Expenses:* Tuition, state resident: full-time $8800. Tuition, nonresident: full-time $20,760. Tuition and fees vary according to program and reciprocity agreements. *Financial support:* In 2009–10, 18 teaching assistantships were awarded. *Faculty research:* Sociolinguistics, Spanish American literature, Spanish literature, Hispanic culture, Hispanic historiography. Total annual research expenditures: $4,590. *Unit head:* Jeffrey Oxford, Chair, 414-229-4257, E-mail: oxford@uwm.edu. *Application contact:* General Information Contact, 414-229-4982, Fax: 414-229-6967, E-mail: gradschool@uwm.edu.

University of Wisconsin–Milwaukee, Graduate School, College of Letters and Sciences, Interdepartmental Program in Foreign Language and Literature, Milwaukee, WI 53201-0413. Offers classics and Hebrew studies (MAFLL); comparative literature (MAFLL); French and Italian (MAFLL); German (MAFLL); Slavic studies (MAFLL); translation (Certificate). Part-time programs available. *Faculty:* 37 full-time (18 women). *Students:* 32 full-time (25 women), 28 part-time (19 women); includes 5 minority (1 Asian American or Pacific Islander, 4 Hispanic Americans), 22 international. Average age 33. 54 applicants, 69% accepted, 20 enrolled. In 2009, 24 master's awarded. *Degree requirements:* For master's, 2 foreign languages, thesis or alternative. *Entrance requirements:* Additional exam requirements/recommendations for international students: Required—TOEFL (minimum score 550 paper-based; 79 iBT), IELTS (minimum score 6.5). *Application deadline:* For fall admission, 1/1 priority date for domestic students; for spring admission, 9/1 for domestic students. Applications are processed on a rolling basis. Application fee: $45 ($75 for international students). *Expenses:* Tuition, state resident: full-time $8800. Tuition, nonresident: full-time $20,760. Tuition and fees vary according to program and reciprocity agreements. *Financial support:* In 2009–10, 2 research assistantships, 21 teaching assistantships were awarded; career-related internships or fieldwork and unspecified assistantships also available. Support available to part-time students. Financial award application deadline: 4/15. Total annual research expenditures: $285,237. *Unit head:* Gabrielle Verdier, Representative, 414-229-3346, Fax: 414-229-2741, E-mail: verdier@uwm.edu. *Application contact:* General Information Contact, 414-229-4982, Fax: 414-229-6967, E-mail: gradschool@uwm.edu.

York University, Faculty of Graduate Studies, Glendon College, Program in Translation, Toronto, ON M3J 1P3, Canada. Offers MA. *Degree requirements:* For master's, thesis or alternative. *Entrance requirements:* For master's, professional translating experience. Electronic applications accepted.

Monterey Institute of International Studies
A Graduate School of Middlebury College

MONTEREY INSTITUTE OF INTERNATIONAL STUDIES

Translation and Interpretation

Programs of Study

The Graduate School of Translation, Interpretation, and Language Education (GSTILE) offers Master of Arts degrees in four areas: translation and interpretation (M.A.T.I.), conference interpretation (M.A.C.I.), translation (M.A.T.), and translation and localization management (M.A.T.L.M.). Each is designed to be a four-semester, 60-credit program. Students must demonstrate fluency in English and one or more of the following languages: Chinese, French, German, Japanese, Korean, Russian, or Spanish. Requirements for the advanced-entry, one-year Master of Arts degree programs are either two or more years of professional experience or a graduate degree in translation and interpretation. Nondegree certificates are offered in court or medical interpreting (Spanish only) and in the teaching of translation and interpretation.

In the first semester, all students take the same required courses: Basic Translation and Introduction to Interpretation. All students then specialize based on their degree program and career interests. M.A.T.L.M. students may take interpretation as an elective. Accounting and computer-assisted translation courses are part of the curriculum during the first semester.

The M.A.T.I. program is a balanced mix of translation and consecutive interpretation courses, while the M.A.T. program concentrates on written, sight, and computer-assisted translation. The M.A.C.I. program focuses on consecutive and simultaneous interpretation, while the M.A.T.L.M. program incorporates business courses offered through the Institute's International M.B.A. program in addition to translation technology courses. The Monterey Institute offers a variety of practicum and other courses that provide unique opportunities for interpreters-in-training to hone their skills. Translation students gain valuable training in project management, software localization, and specialized terminology in other courses.

The Translation and Interpretation program is a member of the Conférence Internationale Permanente d'Instituts Universitaires de Traducteurs et Interprètes (CIUTI) and participates in exchanges with CIUTI schools worldwide. Students may opt for a year of overseas study to consolidate their languages. The School's faculty members—experienced translators, interpreters, and educators—are dedicated to excellence and outstanding performance as both professors and working professionals. They are committed to helping students develop their analytical skills, cultural literacy, conduct, competence, and professional integrity needed to become superior professionals.

Research Facilities

Innovative and challenging curricula at the Institute require appropriate facilities and cutting-edge technology. Classrooms vary in size from large halls where plenary sessions with simultaneous interpretation can be held to smaller classrooms and labs befitting seminar-style classes for 5 to 15 students.

State-of-the-art multimedia and interpreting labs simulate professional environments. Interpretation students have access to three facilities that are equipped for simultaneous interpretation: a conference room with eight booths that conform to ISO specifications and two labs with twelve booths each. The Irvine Auditorium, site of international conferences, multilingual courses, and guest presentations, has four simultaneous interpreting booths and a seating capacity of 275.

Brahler and Gentner portable interpreting equipment transforms any classroom into a multilingual seminar, giving students further opportunities to provide and practice interpretation for Institute classes and events. To keep pace with the dynamic localization industry, the M.A.T.L.M. program teaches computer-assisted translation and develops partnerships with high-technology firms. M.A.T.L.M. students also work in a multimedia, computer-assisted translation and interpretation laboratory, where video is distributed from cable, satellite broadcasts, or the Internet, and localized versions of software and translation tools are available. A unique speech bank makes speeches in all GSTILE working languages available for student practice via the Internet.

The William Tell Coleman Library includes 95,000 volumes, more than 500 print periodicals, over 50 online databases, more than 400 academic journals, about thirty-five newspapers, and approximately 15,000 electronic books. One third of the collection is in languages other than English.

The Max Kade Language and Technology Center is a fully equipped language-learning center. It provides multimedia classrooms and conference rooms with state-of-the-art technology, including a multimedia resource center and the campus Teaching and Learning Collaborative.

In addition to numerous computer labs, the campus is fully networked utilizing the latest wireless standards. Every student is encouraged, for flexibility, to have a personal laptop computer adapted for wireless connectivity.

Financial Aid

Candidates with a minimum grade point average of 3.0 on a 4.0 scale (or equivalent) are invited to compete for merit scholarships; amounts range from $4000 to $15,000 per year. Scholarships are renewable for a second year depending upon the recipient's program and academic performance. Veterans of military service or orphans/dependants of veterans may be eligible for veteran's benefits. Other scholarships may be awarded by outside foundations.

Under the Federal Stafford Loan program, students may borrow up to $8500 in subsidized loans, or $20,500 in unsubsidized loans less any subsidized amount. Graduate PLUS Loans cover the cost of attendance minus other financial aid resources. The Federal Work-Study Program allows students to work up to $3000 per academic year, working a maximum of 20 hours per week.

Cost of Study

Tuition and fees for 2010–11 are $32,056.

Living and Housing Costs

The estimated variable expenses for books, supplies, housing, food, local transportation, personal expenses, and health insurance is $17,792.

Student Group

Institute enrollment is approximately 800. About one third of the students are from outside the United States, representing more than sixty countries. More than 90 percent of students from the U.S. have worked or studied abroad. Students speak more than fifty languages on campus. Language classes are regularly offered in English, Spanish, Arabic, French, Russian, Japanese, Chinese (Mandarin), and German. Other languages are offered by request.

Student Outcomes

GSTILE is one of the few translation and interpretation schools in the world to have a resident director of career management. Every winter, seventy to eighty employers participate in the Job and Internship Fair, and ten to twelve more recruit Translation and Interpretation students on campus outside the fair. About 100 employers post jobs with the GSTILE career manager each year on a continuous basis. International and U.S. employers are in business, educational, government, nonprofit, and translation and interpretation agency sectors. About one third of all 1,400 translation and interpretation alumni are freelancers seeking contracts from all work sectors.

Of those seeking employment in the class of 2008, 80 percent found translation, interpretation, project management, and translation and interpretation teaching jobs with employers or launched independent contracting businesses within three months of graduation. More than 75 percent of the last three graduating classes had translation- and/or interpretation-related internships or summer jobs while students; most were paid. Selected employers in the last three years include Apple Computer; Bank for International Settlements (Switzerland); Bank of Korea; Bureau of International Recycling (Belgium); Chinese Times (San Francisco); Citigroup Asset Management (Japan); Daiwa Institute of Research (Japan); Eriksen, Inc. (Brooklyn, New York); Foreign Broadcast Information Service (Washington, D.C.); Honda Kaihatsu Kogyo (U.S.); Inter-American Investment Corporation (Washington, D.C.); Korean Ministry of Forestry and Agriculture; Lionbridge Technologies (U.S.); Lucile Packard Children's Hospital (Stanford, California); Microsoft Asia (Japan); Monterey County Office of Education; Nikon Research (U.S.); Samsung Electronics; SAP (Germany); Sun Microsystems (San Jose, California); Toyota Techno Service Corporation (Japan); and the Yuda Institute of Business Technology (China).

Many of the School's alumni provide freelance and staff translation and interpretation for international organizations, including the United Nations Secretariat, UN Criminal Tribunals, Free Trade Area of the Americas, International Civil Aviation Organization, and the World Intellectual Property Organization, in addition to governments worldwide. More information can be found at http://faculty.miis.edu/gsticareers.

Location

The Monterey Institute is situated in one of the most spectacular natural environments in the world. The Monterey Peninsula is 130 miles south of San Francisco on California's central coast, surrounded by ocean and mountains. Silicon Valley is only a short drive away. With a population of 100,000, the area combines a variety of rich cultural resources and agricultural activities.

The Institute

Opened in 1955 with summer classes in language and culture, the Monterey Institute of Foreign Studies was the first institute dedicated to the then-revolutionary concept that a living language should be taught as such: French in French, German in German, etc. Full-year degree programs began in 1961. By 1979, the Institute had grown to international distinction and was renamed the Monterey Institute of International Studies.

In December 2005, the Institute became an affiliate of Middlebury College, one of the world's premier colleges, located in Middlebury, Vermont. Middlebury College is renowned for its international programs, its summer language schools, and schools abroad (currently in China, France, Germany, Italy, Russia, Spain, Argentina, Brazil, Chile, Mexico, and Uruguay). The affiliation between Middlebury College and the Monterey Institute gives these two prestigious institutions further enriched curriculum and a bicoastal presence as well as a unique opportunity, through their extensive international programs and networks, to build greater global connections. Students at the Monterey Institute are pioneering partners, with members of the administration and faculty on both campuses, in building this international venture.

Applying

Applicants to the master's programs in translation and interpretation must have a U.S. bachelor's degree or the equivalent. Application may be made at any time, provided it is received at least two months prior to the applicant's proposed semester of enrollment or three months in advance for international students residing in their home countries.

Students should visit the Monterey Institute's Web site for complete information on admission requirements and the deadlines for scholarship and financial aid.

Correspondence and Information

Admissions Office
Monterey Institute of International Studies
460 Pierce Street
Monterey, California 93940
Phone: 831-647-4123
800-824-7235 (toll-free within the U.S.)
Fax: 831-647-6405
E-mail: admit@miis.edu
Web site: http://www.miis.edu

Monterey Institute of International Studies

THE FACULTY AND THEIR RESEARCH

Program Chairs

Jacolyn Harmer, Program Chair for Translation and Interpretation; M.A., Monterey Institute; Commission of the European Union Stage (Brussels); DEA (Diplome d'Etudes Approfondies) candidate, Geneva (ETI). Simultaneous and consecutive interpretation and translation of German, French, Spanish, and English.

Barry Olsen, Program Chair of Conference Interpretation; M.A., Monterey Institute. Simultaneous and consecutive interpretation, translation of English and Spanish.

Muegge Uwe, Program Chair for Translation and Localization Management; M.A., Monterey Institute; M.A., Oregon. Computer-assisted translation, machine translation, terminology management, controlled language.

Professors

Christiane Abel, Professor; M.A., Monterey Institute; M.B.A., Graduate School of Business, Marseilles (France). Simultaneous and consecutive interpretation and translation of French and English.

John Balcom, Professor; Ph.D., Washington (St. Louis). Translation of Chinese and English.

Chuanyun Bao, Professor; United Nations Translators and Interpreters diploma. Simultaneous and consecutive translation of Chinese and English.

Laura Burain, Associate Professor; M.A., Monterey Institute. Simultaneous and consecutive interpretation and translation of Chinese and English.

Marcol Celesia, Professor; M.A., Universidad del Salvador. Simultaneous and consecutive interpretation and translation of Spanish and English.

Wallace Chen, Assistant Professor; Ph.D., Manchester (UK). Interpreting and translation of Chinese and English, corpus-based translation studies.

Yoonji Choi, Assistant Professor; M.A., Monterey Institute. Translation, software localization, simultaneous and consecutive interpretation of Korean and English.

Carl Fehlandt, Associate Professor; M.A., Monterey Institute. Translation of Spanish and English.

Michael Gillen, Associate Professor; M.B.A., Monterey Institute. Translation of Russian and English.

Andrea Hoffman-Miller, Associate Professor and German Language Coordinator; M.A., Monterey Institute. Simultaneous and consecutive interpretation and translation of German and English.

Julie Johnson, Associate Professor; M.A., Monterey Institute. Simultaneous and consecutive interpretation and translation of French and English.

Rosa Kavenoki, Associate Professor and Russian Program Coordinator; M.A., St. Petersburg State Pedagogical University. Simultaneous and consecutive interpretation and translation of Russian and English.

Holly Mikkelson, Associate Professor; M.A., Monterey Institute. Translation and interpretation of Spanish and English, court and medical interpreting.

Tanya Pound, Assistant Professor; M.A., Toronto. Translation of Japanese and English.

Xiaojing Shi, Associate Professor; M.A., Hawaii. Simultaneous and consecutive interpretation and translation of Chinese and English.

Miryoung Sohn, Assistant Professor and Korean Language Coordinator; M.A., Hankuk University (Korea). Simultaneous and consecutive interpration and translation of Korean and English.

Kayoko Takeda, Assistant Professor and Japanese Language Coordinator; Ph.D., Universitat Rovira I Virgili (Spain); M.A., Monterey Institute. Simultaneous and consecutive interpretation and translation of Japanese and English.

Zinan Ye, Associate Professor; M.A., University of the Pacific. Translation of Chinese and English.

Section 11
Philosophy and Ethics

This section contains a directory of institutions offering graduate work in philosophy and ethics. Additional information about programs listed in the directory but not augmented by an in-depth entry may be obtained by writing directly to the dean of a graduate school or chair of a department at the address given in the directory.

For programs offering related work, see also in this book *Area and Cultural Studies, History, Humanities, Religious Studies,* and *Social Sciences.*

CONTENTS

Program Directories

Ethics 440
Philosophy 442

Close-Up

See:

American University—International Service 849

Ethics

American University, College of Arts and Sciences, Department of Philosophy and Religion, Washington, DC 22016-8056. Offers ethics, peace, and global affairs (MA); philosophy (MA), including history of philosophy, philosophy and social policy. Part-time and evening/weekend programs available. *Faculty:* 11 full-time (6 women), 9 part-time/adjunct (4 women). *Students:* 8 full-time (4 women), 2 part-time (0 women); includes 2 minority (1 African American, 1 Asian American or Pacific Islander). Average age 26. 46 applicants, 61% accepted, 4 enrolled. In 2009, 10 master's awarded. *Degree requirements:* For master's, one foreign language, comprehensive exam, thesis (for some programs). *Entrance requirements:* For master's, GRE, writing sample. Additional exam requirements/recommendations for international students: Required—TOEFL. *Application deadline:* For fall admission, 2/1 for domestic students; for spring admission, 10/1 for domestic students. Application fee: $80. *Expenses:* Tuition: Full-time $22,266; part-time $1237 per credit hour. Required fees: $430. Tuition and fees vary according to program. *Financial support:* Fellowships, teaching assistantships, Federal Work-Study and institutionally sponsored loans available. Support available to part-time students. Financial award application deadline: 2/1. *Faculty research:* Oriental religion, classical and medieval philosophy, philosophy of law and ethics, comparative religion, philosophy of science. *Unit head:* Dr. Amy Oliver, Chair, 202-885-2140. *Application contact:* Kathleen Clowery, Director, Graduate Admissions, 202-885-3621, Fax: 202-885-1505.

American University, School of International Service, Washington, DC 20016-8071. Offers comparative and regional studies (Certificate); cross-cultural communication (Certificate); development management (MS); ethics, peace, and global affairs (MA); European studies (Certificate); global environmental policy (MA, Certificate); international affairs (MA), including comparative and regional studies, environmental policy, international economic policy, international politics, natural resources and sustainable development, U.S. foreign policy; international communication (MA, Certificate); international development (MA, Certificate); international development management (Certificate); international economic policy (Certificate); international economic relations (Certificate); international media (MA); international peace and conflict resolution (MA, Certificate); international relations (PhD); international service (MIS); peace building (Certificate); the Americas (Certificate); United States foreign policy (Certificate); JD/MA. Part-time and evening/weekend programs available. *Faculty:* 98 full-time (42 women), 48 part-time/adjunct (13 women). *Students:* 565 full-time (349 women), 329 part-time (189 women); includes 128 minority (44 African Americans, 2 American Indian/Alaska Native, 37 Asian Americans or Pacific Islanders, 45 Hispanic Americans), 102 international. Average age 27. 2,034 applicants, 63% accepted, 344 enrolled. In 2009, 326 master's, 6 doctorates, 9 other advanced degrees awarded. Terminal master's awarded for partial completion of doctoral program. *Degree requirements:* For master's, one foreign language, comprehensive exam, thesis or alternative; for doctorate, one foreign language, comprehensive exam, thesis/dissertation, research practicum; for Certificate, minimum 15 credit hours related course work. *Entrance requirements:* For master's, GRE; 24 credits of course work in related social sciences, minimum GPA of 3.5, 2 letters of recommendation, bachelor's degree, resume; for doctorate, GRE, 2 letters of recommendation, 24 credits in related social sciences; for Certificate, bachelor's degree. Additional exam requirements/recommendations for international students: Required—TOEFL (minimum score 600 paper-based; 250 computer-based; 100 iBT). *Application deadline:* For fall admission, 1/15 priority date for domestic students; for spring admission, 10/1 priority date for domestic students. Applications are processed on a rolling basis. Application fee: $50. *Expenses:* Tuition: Full-time $22,266; part-time $1237 per credit hour. Required fees: $430. Tuition and fees vary according to program. *Financial support:* Career-related internships or fieldwork, Federal Work-Study, and institutionally sponsored loans available. Financial award application deadline: 1/15. *Faculty research:* International intellectual property, international environmental issues, international law and legal order, international telecommunications/technology, international sustainable development. *Unit head:* Dr. Louis W. Goodman, Dean, 202-885-1600, Fax: 202-885-2494. *Application contact:* Yasmin Quianzon, Director of Graduate Admissions and Financial Aid, 202-885-2496, Fax: 202-885-1109.

See Close-Up on page 849.

Azusa Pacific University, Haggard School of Theology, Program in Religion: Theology and Ethics, Azusa, CA 91702-7000. Offers MAR.

Biola University, Talbot School of Theology, La Mirada, CA 90639-0001. Offers Bible exposition (MA); biblical and theological studies (MA); Christian education (MACE); Christian ministry and leadership (MA); divinity (M Div); education (PhD); ministry (MA Min); New Testament (MA); Old Testament (MA); philosophy of religion and ethics (MA); spiritual formation (MA); spiritual formation and soul care (MA); theology (MA, Th M, D Min). *Accreditation:* ATS. Part-time and evening/weekend programs available. *Degree requirements:* For master's, variable foreign language requirement, thesis or alternative; for doctorate, variable foreign language requirement, thesis/dissertation; for M Div, thesis/dissertation or alternative. *Entrance requirements:* For M Div, minimum GPA of 2.6; for master's, minimum undergraduate GPA of 3.0; for doctorate, minimum GPA of 3.25. Additional exam requirements/recommendations for international students: Required—TOEFL (minimum score 550 paper-based; 213 computer-based). *Faculty research:* Moral development; biological, medical, and social ethics; ancient Near Eastern historical philosophy.

Chicago Theological Seminary, Graduate and Professional Programs, Chicago, IL 60637-1507. Offers preaching (D Min); religion and health (D Min); religious studies (MA); spirituality and spiritual direction (D Min); theology (M Div); theology, ethics and the human sciences (PhD); M Div/MSW. *Accreditation:* ACIPE; ATS. Part-time programs available. *Degree requirements:* For master's, thesis; for doctorate, 2 foreign languages, comprehensive exam, thesis/dissertation; for M Div, thesis/dissertation. *Entrance requirements:* For doctorate, GRE General Test. Additional exam requirements/recommendations for international students: Required—TOEFL (minimum score 217 computer-based). *Faculty research:* Bible, culture and hermeneutics, theology, gender and sexuality, black faith and life, spirituality and psychology, practical theology.

Claremont Graduate University, Graduate Programs, School of Religion, Claremont, CA 91711-6160. Offers Hebrew Bible (MA, PhD); history of Christianity and religions of North America (MA, PhD); New Testament (MA, PhD); philosophy of religion and theology (MA, PhD); theology, ethics and culture (MA, PhD); women's studies in religion (MA, PhD); MA/PhD; MBA/PhD. Part-time programs available. *Faculty:* 7 full-time (2 women), 2 part-time/adjunct (0 women). *Students:* 223 full-time (90 women), 7 part-time (4 women); includes 37 minority (14 African Americans, 11 Asian Americans or Pacific Islanders, 12 Hispanic Americans), 23 international. Average age 37. In 2009, 10 master's, 14 doctorates awarded. Terminal master's awarded for partial completion of doctoral program. *Entrance requirements:* For master's and doctorate, GRE General Test. Additional exam requirements/recommendations for international students: Required—TOEFL (minimum score 550 paper-based; 213 computer-based; 80 iBT). *Application deadline:* For fall admission, 2/1 priority date for domestic students. Applications are processed on a rolling basis. Application fee: $60. Electronic applications accepted. *Expenses:* Tuition: Full-time $35,046; part-time $1524 per credit. Required fees: $161 per semester. *Financial support:* Fellowships, research assistantships, teaching assistantships, Federal Work-Study, institutionally sponsored loans, and scholarships/grants available. Support available to part-time students. Financial award application deadline: 2/15; financial award applicants required to submit FAFSA. *Unit head:* Anselm Min, Dean, 909-607-3214, Fax: 909-621-9587, E-mail: anselm.min@cgu.edu. *Application contact:* Brent Smith, Recruiter, 909-607-2653, Fax: 909-607-9587, E-mail: brent.smith@cgu.edu.

Claremont School of Theology, Graduate and Professional Programs, Program in Religion, Claremont, CA 91711-3199. Offers practical theology (PhD), including religious education, spiritual care and counseling; religion (PhD), including Hebrew Bible, New Testament and Christian origins, process studies, religion, ethics, and society; religion and theology (MA); religious education (MARE). *Accreditation:* ACIPE; ATS. Terminal master's awarded for partial completion of doctoral program. *Degree requirements:* For master's, thesis; for doctorate, 2 foreign languages, thesis/dissertation. *Entrance requirements:* For doctorate, GRE General Test. Additional exam requirements/recommendations for international students: Required—TOEFL (minimum score 250 computer-based). Electronic applications accepted.

Columbia University, Graduate School of Business, MBA Program, New York, NY 10027. Offers accounting (MBA); decision, risk, and operations (MBA); entrepreneurship (MBA); finance and economics (MBA); healthcare and pharmaceutical management (MBA); human resource management (MBA); international business (MBA); leadership and ethics (MBA); management (MBA); marketing (MBA); media (MBA); private equity (MBA); real estate (MBA); social enterprise (MBA); value investing (MBA); DDS/MBA; JD/MBA; MBA/MIA; MBA/MPH; MBA/MS; MD/MBA. *Faculty:* 149 full-time (23 women), 134 part-time/adjunct (16 women). *Students:* 1,293 full-time (435 women); includes 235 minority (65 African Americans, 4 American Indian/Alaska Native, 135 Asian Americans or Pacific Islanders, 31 Hispanic Americans), 417 international. Average age 28. 6,885 applicants, 15% accepted, 737 enrolled. In 2009, 696 master's awarded. *Entrance requirements:* For master's, GMAT, 2 letters of recommendation. Additional exam requirements/recommendations for international students: Required—TOEFL. *Application deadline:* For fall admission, 4/14 for domestic students, 3/3 for international students; for spring admission, 10/7 for domestic and international students. Applications are processed on a rolling basis. Application fee: $250. Electronic applications accepted. *Expenses:* Contact institution. *Financial support:* In 2009–10, 358 students received support, including 101 fellowships (averaging $23,250 per year); research assistantships, teaching assistantships, career-related internships or fieldwork, institutionally sponsored loans, and scholarships/grants also available. Financial award application deadline: 3/1; financial award applicants required to submit CSS PROFILE or FAFSA. *Faculty research:* Human decision making and behavioral research; real estate market and mortgage defaults; financial crisis and corporate governance; international business; security analysis and accounting. *Unit head:* Prof. Amir Ziv, Vice Dean of Students and the MBA Program, 212-854-3485, Fax: 212-932-0545, E-mail: az50@columbia.edu. *Application contact:* Mary J. Miller, Assistant Dean of Admissions, 212-854-1961, Fax: 212-662-6754, E-mail: apply@gsb.columbia.edu.

Duquesne University, School of Leadership and Professional Advancement, Pittsburgh, PA 15282-0001. Offers leadership (MS), including business ethics, community leadership, global leadership, information technology, leadership, liberal studies, professional administration, sports leadership. Part-time and evening/weekend programs available. Postbaccalaureate distance learning degree programs offered (no on-campus study). *Faculty:* 1 full-time (0 women), 70 part-time/adjunct (35 women). *Students:* 654 (307 women); includes 68 minority (57 African Americans, 1 American Indian/Alaska Native, 6 Asian Americans or Pacific Islanders, 4 Hispanic Americans). 161 applicants, 73% accepted, 103 enrolled. In 2009, 108 master's awarded. *Degree requirements:* For master's, capstone course. *Entrance requirements:* For master's, professional work experience, 500-word essay. Additional exam requirements/recommendations for international students: Required—TOEFL. *Application deadline:* Applications are processed on a rolling basis. Application fee: $0. Electronic applications accepted. *Expenses:* Tuition: Part-time $851 per credit. Required fees: $81 per credit. *Financial support:* Applicants required to submit FAFSA. *Unit head:* Dr. Dorothy Bassett, Dean, 412-396-2141, Fax: 412-396-4711, E-mail: bassettd@duq.edu. *Application contact:* Marianne Leister, Director of Student Services, 412-396-4933, Fax: 412-396-5072, E-mail: leister@duq.edu.

Emory University, Candler School of Theology, Atlanta, GA 30322. Offers formation and witness (M Div); leadership in church and community (M Div); religion and race (M Div); religion, health and science (M Div); scripture and interpretation (M Div); society and personality (M Div); theology (MTS, Th M, Th D); theology and ethics (M Div); theology and the arts (M Div); traditions of the church (M Div); women and religion (M Div); JD/M Div; JD/MTS; M Div/MBA; M Div/MPH; MBA/MTS; MTS/MPH. *Accreditation:* ACIPE; ATS. Part-time programs available. *Degree requirements:* For master's, thesis optional; for doctorate, thesis/dissertation; for M Div, thesis/dissertation optional. *Entrance requirements:* For M Div, minimum undergraduate GPA of 2.75; for master's, minimum undergraduate GPA of 3.0; for doctorate, GRE, M Div, 8 units of course work in clinical pastoral education. Additional exam requirements/recommendations for international students: Required—TOEFL (minimum score 600 paper-based; 250 computer-based; 95 iBT). Electronic applications accepted. *Expenses:* Contact institution. *Faculty research:* Biblical studies, church history, ministry practice, pastoral care and ethics.

Fordham University, Graduate School of Arts and Sciences, Center for Ethics Education Program, New York, NY 10458. Offers ethics and society (MA); health care ethics (Certificate). Part-time programs available. *Students:* 4 full-time (2 women), 4 part-time (2 women), 1 international. 9 applicants, 100% accepted, 8 enrolled. *Entrance requirements:* Additional exam requirements/recommendations for international students: Required—TOEFL. *Application deadline:* For fall admission, 1/4 priority date for domestic students; for spring admission, 10/31 for domestic students. Application fee: $65. Electronic applications accepted. *Financial support:* In 2009–10, 1 student received support. Federal Work-Study, institutionally sponsored loans, scholarships/grants, tuition waivers (partial), and unspecified assistantships available. Financial award application deadline: 1/4. Total annual research expenditures: $49,033. *Unit head:* Dr. Celia Fisher, Director, 718-817-3793, Fax: 212-759-2009, E-mail: fisher@fordham.edu. *Application contact:* Charlene Dundie, Director of Graduate Admissions, 718-817-4420, Fax: 718-817-3566, E-mail: dundie@fordham.edu.

Freed-Hardeman University, Program in Business Administration, Henderson, TN 38340-2399. Offers accounting (MBA); corporate responsibility (MBA); leadership (MBA). *Accreditation:* ACBSP. Part-time and evening/weekend programs available. Postbaccalaureate distance learning degree programs offered (no on-campus study). *Entrance requirements:* For master's, GMAT. Additional exam requirements/recommendations for international students: Required—TOEFL (minimum score 500 paper-based; 173 computer-based).

Georgetown University, Graduate School of Arts and Sciences, School of Continuing Studies, Washington, DC 20057. Offers American studies (MALS); Catholic studies (MALS); classical civilizations (MALS); ethics and the professions (MALS); human resources management (MPS); humanities (MALS); individualized study (MALS); international affairs (MALS); Islam and Muslim-Christian relations (MALS); journalism (MPS); liberal studies (DLS); literature and society (MALS); medieval and early modern European studies (MALS); public relations (MPS); real estate (MPS); religious studies (MALS); social and public policy (MALS); sports industry management (MPS); the theory and practice of American democracy (MALS); visual culture (MALS). *Entrance requirements:* Additional exam requirements/recommendations for international students: Required—TOEFL.

Graduate Theological Union, Graduate Programs, Berkeley, CA 94709-1212. Offers art and religion (MA, PhD, Th D); biblical languages (MA); Biblical studies (PhD, Th D); biblical studies (MA); Buddhist studies (MA); Christian spirituality (MA, PhD, Th D); cultural and historical studies of religions (MA, PhD, Th D); ethics and social theory (PhD, Th D); history (MA, PhD, Th D); homiletics (MA, PhD, Th D); interdisciplinary studies (PhD, Th D); Jewish studies (MA, PhD, Th D, Certificate); liturgical studies (MA, PhD, Th D); Near Eastern religions (PhD, Th D); Orthodox Christian studies (MA); religion and psychology (MA, PhD, Th D); religion and society/ethics and social theory (MA); systematic and philosophical theology (MA, PhD, Th D). *Accreditation:* ATS. Terminal master's awarded for partial completion of doctoral program. *Degree requirements:* For master's, one foreign language, thesis; for doctorate, one foreign language, comprehensive exam, thesis/dissertation. *Entrance requirements:* For master's, GRE General Test; for doctorate, GRE General Test, MA or M Div. Additional exam requirements/recommendations for international students: Required—TOEFL. Electronic applications accepted.

Lancaster Theological Seminary, Graduate and Professional Programs, Lancaster, PA 17603-2812. Offers biblical studies (MAR); Christian education (MAR); Christianity and the arts (MAR); church history (MAR); congregational life (MAR); lay leadership (Certificate); theological studies (M Div); theology (D Min); theology and ethics (MAR). *Accreditation:* ACIPE; ATS. *Faculty:* 11 full-time (4 women), 13 part-time/adjunct (9 women). *Students:* 91 full-time (48 women), 42 part-time (33 women). *Degree requirements:* For doctorate, thesis/dissertation; for M Div, one foreign language. *Application deadline:* For fall admission, 4/1 priority date for domestic students, 1/1 for international students; for spring admission, 11/15 priority date for domestic students. Applications are processed on a rolling basis. Application fee: $50. *Expenses:* Tuition: Full-time $12,600; part-time $490 per credit. Required fees: $125 per semester. One-time fee: $3000. Tuition and fees vary according to program and student level. *Financial support:* Career-related internships or fieldwork, scholarships/grants, and tuition waivers (partial) available. Financial award application deadline: 4/15; financial award applicants required to submit FAFSA. *Unit head:* Dr. Edwin D. Aponte, Vice President of Academic Affairs and Dean of the Seminary, 717-290-8754, Fax: 717-393-0423, E-mail: eaponte@lancasterseminary.edu. *Application contact:* Virginia Whitaker-Brooks, Assistant Director of Recruitment and Admissions, 717-290-8741, Fax: 717-393-0423.

Lutheran Theological Seminary, Graduate and Professional Programs, Saskatoon, SK S7N 0X3, Canada. Offers Biblical studies (MTS); church history (MTS); ethics/church and society (MTS); history of Christianity (STM); New Testament (STM); Old Testament (STM); pastoral studies (STM); pastoral theology (MTS); systematic theology (MTS); systematic theology and philosophy of religion (STM); theology (M Div, D Div). *Accreditation:* ATS. Part-time programs available. *Degree requirements:* For master's, thesis; for M Div, Greek, Hebrew.

Marquette University, Graduate School, College of Arts and Sciences, Department of Philosophy, Milwaukee, WI 53201-1881. Offers ancient philosophy (MA, PhD); British empiricism and analytic philosophy (MA, PhD); Christian philosophy (MA, PhD); early modern European philosophy (MA, PhD); ethics (MA, PhD); German philosophy (MA, PhD); medieval philosophy (MA, PhD); phenomenology and existentialism (MA, PhD); philosophy of religion (MA, PhD); social and applied philosophy (MA). Part-time programs available. *Faculty:* 25 full-time (5 women), 17 part-time/adjunct (3 women). *Students:* 53 full-time (12 women), 14 part-time (1 woman); includes 5 minority (1 African American, 2 Asian Americans or Pacific Islanders, 2 Hispanic Americans), 6 international. Average age 31. 120 applicants, 66% accepted, 19 enrolled. In 2009, 10 master's, 2 doctorates awarded. Terminal master's awarded for partial completion of doctoral program. *Degree requirements:* For master's, one foreign language, comprehensive exam, thesis; for doctorate, 2 foreign languages, thesis/dissertation, qualifying exams. *Entrance requirements:* For master's and doctorate, GRE General Test. Additional exam requirements/recommendations for international students: Required—TOEFL. Application fee: $40. *Financial support:* In 2009–10, 10 research assistantships, 12 teaching assistantships were awarded; Federal Work-Study, institutionally sponsored loans, scholarships/grants, and tuition waivers (full and partial) also available. Support available to part-time students. Financial award application deadline: 2/15. *Faculty research:* Aristotle, Augustine, Descartes, Hegel, Heidegger. *Unit head:* Dr. John Jones, Chair, 414-288-6857, Fax: 414-288-1578. *Application contact:* Dr. Owen Goldin, Director of Graduate Studies, 414-288-5949, Fax: 414-288-1578.

Marquette University, Graduate School, College of Arts and Sciences, Department of Theology, Milwaukee, WI 53201-1881. Offers ethics (PhD); historical theology (MA, PhD); religious studies (PhD), including scriptural theology (MA, PhD); systematic theology (MA, PhD); theology (MA), including scriptural theology (MA, PhD); theology and society (PhD). Part-time programs available. *Faculty:* 32 full-time (7 women), 22 part-time/adjunct (4 women). *Students:* 73 full-time (17 women), 44 part-time (14 women); includes 6 minority (2 African Americans, 2 Asian Americans or Pacific Islanders, 2 Hispanic Americans), 4 international. Average age 35. 154 applicants, 48% accepted, 20 enrolled. In 2009, 11 master's, 9 doctorates awarded. Terminal master's awarded for partial completion of doctoral program. *Degree requirements:* For master's, one foreign language, comprehensive exam, thesis or alternative; for doctorate, 2 foreign languages, thesis/dissertation, qualifying exam. *Entrance requirements:* For master's and doctorate, GRE General Test. Additional exam requirements/recommendations for international students: Required—TOEFL. Application fee: $40. *Financial support:* In 2009–10, 5 fellowships, 5 research assistantships, 14 teaching assistantships were awarded; Federal Work-Study, institutionally sponsored loans, scholarships/grants, and tuition waivers (full and partial) also available. Support available to part-time students. Financial award application deadline: 2/15. *Faculty research:* Old Testament theology, New Testament theology, church history, Christian ethics. *Unit head:* Rev. John Laurance, Acting Chair, 414-288-7170, Fax: 414-288-5548. *Application contact:* Dr. Christine Hinze, Director of Graduate Studies, 414-288-6802.

Northwestern University, School of Continuing Studies, Program in Liberal Studies, Evanston, IL 60208. Offers American studies (MA); history (MA); religious and ethical studies (MA).

Phillips Theological Seminary, Programs in Theology, Tulsa, OK 74116. Offers administration of church agencies (M Div); campus ministry (M Div); church-related social work (M Div); college and seminary teaching (M Div); global mission work (M Div); institutional chaplaincy (M Div); ministerial vocations in Christian education (M Div); ministry (D Min), including parish ministry, pastoral counseling, practices of ministry; ministry and culture (MAMC), including Christian education, congregational leadership, history and practice of Christian spirituality, theology, ethics, and culture; ministry of music (M Div); pastoral care and counseling (M Div); pastoral ministry (M Div); theological studies (MTS). *Accreditation:* ATS. Part-time programs available. Postbaccalaureate distance learning degree programs offered (minimal on-campus study). *Degree requirements:* For master's, thesis (for some programs); for doctorate, thesis/dissertation. *Entrance requirements:* For master's, minimum GPA of 2.5; for doctorate, M Div, minimum GPA of 3.0. *Faculty research:* Biblical studies, historical studies, theology and culture, practical theology, theology and film.

St. Edward's University, School of Management and Business, Program in Organizational Leadership and Ethics, Austin, TX 78704. Offers MS. Part-time and evening/weekend programs available. *Students:* 45 part-time (34 women); includes 17 minority (4 African Americans, 13 Hispanic Americans). Average age 38. 24 applicants, 88% accepted, 20 enrolled. In 2009, 20 master's awarded. *Degree requirements:* For master's, minimum of 24 hours in residence. *Entrance requirements:* For master's, GMAT or GRE General Test, minimum GPA of 2.75 in last 60 hours of course work. Additional exam requirements/recommendations for international students: Required—TOEFL (minimum score 550 paper-based; 213 computer-based; 79 iBT) or IELTS (minimum score 6). *Application deadline:* For fall admission, 7/1 for domestic and international students; for spring admission, 11/1 for domestic and international students. Applications are processed on a rolling basis. Application fee: $45 ($50 for international students). Electronic applications accepted. *Expenses:* Tuition: Full-time $14,922; part-time $829 per credit hour. Required fees: $50 per trimester. Full-time tuition and fees vary according to course load and program. *Financial support:* Scholarships/grants available. *Faculty research:* Business ethics. *Unit head:* Dr. Tom Sechrest, Director, 512-637-1954, Fax: 512-448-8492, E-mail: thomasl@stedwards.edu. *Application contact:* Benjamin Jimenez, Graduate Admissions Coordinator, 512-233-1694, Fax: 512-428-1032, E-mail: benjij@stedwards.edu.

Southeastern Baptist Theological Seminary, Graduate and Professional Programs, Wake Forest, NC 27588-1889. Offers advanced biblical studies (M Div); Christian education (M Div, MACE); Christian ethics (PhD); Christian ministry (M Div); Christian planting (M Div); church music (MACM); counseling (MACO); evangelism (PhD); language (M Div); ministry (D Min); New Testament (PhD); Old Testament (PhD); philosophy (PhD); theology (Th M, PhD); women's studies (M Div). *Accreditation:* ACIPE; ATS (one or more programs are accredited). *Degree requirements:* For master's, thesis (for some programs), oral exam; for doctorate, thesis/dissertation, fieldwork; for M Div, supervised ministry. *Entrance requirements:* For master's, Cooperative English Test, minimum GPA of 2.0, M Div or equivalent (Th M); for doctorate, GRE General Test or MAT, Cooperative English Test, M Div or equivalent, 3 years of professional experience.

Spring Hill College, Graduate Programs, Program in Liberal Arts, Mobile, AL 36608-1791. Offers fine arts (MLA); history and social science (MLA); leadership and ethics (MLA); literature (MLA). Part-time and evening/weekend programs available. *Faculty:* 11 full-time (4 women), 3 part-time/adjunct (2 women). *Students:* 1 (woman) full-time, 33 part-time (16 women); includes 6 minority (5 African Americans, 1 Hispanic American), 2 international. Average age 35. 27 applicants, 41% accepted, 6 enrolled. In 2009, 6 master's awarded. *Degree requirements:* For master's, capstone course, completion of program within 6 years of initial admittance. *Entrance requirements:* For master's, bachelor's degree with minimum undergraduate GPA of 3.0 or graduate/professional degree. Additional exam requirements/recommendations for international students: Required—TOEFL (minimum score 550 paper-based; 213 computer-based; 80 iBT), IELTS (minimum score 6.5). *Application deadline:* For fall admission, 8/1 priority date for domestic and international students; for spring admission, 12/1 priority date for domestic and international students. Applications are processed on a rolling basis. Application fee: $25 ($35 for international students). Electronic applications accepted. *Expenses:* Contact institution. *Financial support:* In 2009–10, 30 students received support. Career-related internships or fieldwork, institutionally sponsored loans, and scholarships/grants available. Support available to part-time students. Financial award applicants required to submit FAFSA. *Unit head:* Dr. Alexander R. Landi, Director, 251-380-3056, Fax: 251-460-2115, E-mail: landi@shc.edu. *Application contact:* Donna B. Tarasavage, Director of Marketing and Recruiting, Graduate and Continuing Studies, 251-380-3067, Fax: 251-460-2190, E-mail: dtarasavage@shc.edu.

Suffolk University, College of Arts and Sciences, Program in Ethics and Public Policy, Boston, MA 02108-2770. Offers MS. Part-time and evening/weekend programs available. *Faculty:* 2 full-time (0 women). *Students:* 7 full-time (3 women), 10 part-time (5 women), 10 international. Average age 26. 27 applicants, 74% accepted, 10 enrolled. In 2009, 1 master's awarded. *Degree requirements:* For master's, internship or thesis. *Entrance requirements:* For master's, GRE General Test, MAT, GMAT, statement of professional goals, official transcripts, 2 letters of recommendation, resume. Additional exam requirements/recommendations for international students: Required—TOEFL (minimum score 550 paper-based; 213 computer-based; 80 iBT). *Application deadline:* For fall and spring admission, 6/15 priority date for domestic and international students. Applications are processed on a rolling basis. Application fee: $50. Electronic applications accepted. *Expenses:* Contact institution. *Financial support:* In 2009–10, 15 students received support, including 134 fellowships (averaging $3,665 per year); career-related internships or fieldwork, Federal Work-Study, institutionally sponsored loans, and unspecified assistantships also available. Support available to part-time students. Financial award application deadline: 4/1; financial award applicants required to submit FAFSA. *Faculty research:* History of philosophy, ethics, political philosophy, continental philosophy and phenomenology, applied ethics. *Unit head:* Dr. Greg Fried, Chair of Philosophy Department, 617-573-8109, E-mail: gfried@suffolk.edu. *Application contact:* Judith Reynolds, Director of Graduate Admissions, 617-573-8302, Fax: 617-305-1733, E-mail: grad.admission@suffolk.edu.

Université de Sherbrooke, Faculty of Theology, Ethics and Philosophy, Sherbrooke, QC J1K 2R1, Canada. Offers applied ethics (Diploma); human science of religions (MA); intercultural training (Diploma); philosophy (MA, PhD); spiritual anthropology (Diploma); theology (MA, PhD, Diploma). Part-time and evening/weekend programs available. Postbaccalaureate distance learning degree programs offered. Terminal master's awarded for partial completion of doctoral program. *Entrance requirements:* For master's, bachelor's degree in related discipline; for doctorate, master's degree in related discipline. *Faculty research:* Faith and culture interrelation.

Université du Québec à Chicoutimi, Graduate Programs, Program in Ethics, Chicoutimi, QC G7H 2B1, Canada. Offers Diploma. *Entrance requirements:* For degree, appropriate bachelor's degree, proficiency in French.

Université du Québec à Rimouski, Graduate Programs, Program in Ethics, Rimouski, QC G5L 3A1, Canada. Offers MA, Diploma. Part-time programs available. *Degree requirements:* For master's, thesis. *Entrance requirements:* For master's, appropriate bachelor's degree, proficiency in French.

Université Laval, Faculty of Theology and Religious Sciences, Program in Applied Ethics, Québec, QC G1K 7P4, Canada. Offers DESS. Part-time programs available. *Entrance requirements:* For degree, knowledge of French. Electronic applications accepted.

University of Baltimore, Graduate School, The Yale Gordon College of Liberal Arts, Program in Legal and Ethical Studies, Baltimore, MD 21201-5779. Offers MA. Part-time and evening/weekend programs available. *Degree requirements:* For master's, thesis optional. *Entrance requirements:* For master's, minimum GPA of 3.0. Additional exam requirements/recommendations for international students: Required—TOEFL (minimum score 550 paper-based; 213 computer-based). Electronic applications accepted. *Faculty research:* Morality in law and economics, religion in lawmaking, comparative legal history, law and social change, critical issues in constitutional law, theories of justice.

University of Nevada, Las Vegas, Graduate College, College of Liberal Arts, Department of Political Science, Program in Ethics and Policy Studies, Las Vegas, NV 89154-5029. Offers MA. Part-time programs available. *Faculty:* 2 full-time (0 women), 2 part-time/adjunct (both women). *Students:* 9 part-time (2 women); includes 6 minority (1 African American, 1 American Indian/Alaska Native, 2 Asian Americans or Pacific Islanders, 2 Hispanic Americans). Average age 35. 1 applicant, 0% accepted, 0 enrolled. In 2009, 1 master's awarded. *Degree requirements:* For master's, thesis. *Entrance requirements:* For master's, GRE General Test. Additional exam requirements/recommendations for international students: Required—TOEFL (minimum score 550 paper-based; 213 computer-based; 80 iBT), IELTS (minimum score 7). *Application deadline:* For fall admission, 2/1 priority date for domestic and international students; for spring admission, 10/1 priority date for domestic and international students. Applications are processed on a rolling basis. Application fee: $60 ($95 for international students). Electronic applications accepted. *Financial support:* Institutionally sponsored loans, scholarships/grants, health care benefits, and unspecified assistantships available. Financial award application deadline: 3/1. *Faculty research:* Immigration and crime policy, ancient and contemporary political theory. *Unit head:* Dr. Mehran Tamadonfar, Chair/ Associate Professor, 702-895-5258, Fax: 702-895-1065, E-mail: mehram.tamadonfar@unlv.edu. *Application contact:* Graduate College Admissions Evaluator, 702-895-3320, Fax: 702-895-4180, E-mail: gradcollege@unlv.edu.

University of North Florida, College of Arts and Sciences, Department of Philosophy, Jacksonville, FL 32224. Offers applied ethics (Graduate Certificate); practical philosophy and applied ethics (MA). Part-time and evening/weekend programs available. *Faculty:* 11 full-time (3 women). *Students:* 11 full-time (5 women), 6 part-time (3 women); includes 3 minority (1 African American, 2 Asian Americans or Pacific Islanders). Average age 33. 12 applicants, 50% accepted, 6 enrolled. In 2009, 3 master's awarded. *Entrance requirements:* For master's, GRE General Test, minimum GPA of 3.0 in last 60 hours, 3 letters of recommendation, writing sample. Additional exam requirements/recommendations for international students: Required—TOEFL (minimum score 500 paper-based). *Application deadline:* For fall admission, 4/15 priority date for domestic students, 3/1 for international students. Applications are processed on a rolling basis. Application fee: $30. Electronic applications accepted. *Expenses:* Tuition, state resident: full-time $6649.20; part-time $277.05 per credit hour. Tuition, nonresident: full-time $22,970; part-time $957.08 per credit hour. Required fees: $985; $41.03 per credit hour. *Financial support:* In 2009–10, 14 students received support, including 3 teaching assistantships (averaging $4,222 per year). Financial award application deadline: 4/1; financial award applicants required to submit FAFSA. *Faculty research:* Late modern philosophy, pragmatism, religion and American culture, hermeneutics, philosophy of mind. Total annual research expenditures: $27,108. *Unit head:* Dr. Hans Herbert Koegler, 904-620-1330, Fax: 904-620-1840, E-mail: hkoegler@unf.edu. *Application contact:* Dr. Andrew Buchwalter, Graduate Coordinator, 904-620-1155, Fax: 904-620-1840, E-mail: abuchwal@unf.edu.

University of Pennsylvania, Wharton School, Legal Studies and Business Ethics Department, Philadelphia, PA 19104. Offers MBA, PhD. *Expenses:* Tuition: Full-time $25,660; part-time

Ethics

University of Pennsylvania (continued)
$4758 per course. Required fees: $2152; $270 per course. Tuition and fees vary according to course load, degree level and program.

University of South Africa, College of Human Sciences, Pretoria, South Africa. Offers adult education (M Ed); African languages (MA, PhD); African politics (MA, PhD); Afrikaans (MA, PhD); ancient history (MA, PhD); ancient Near Eastern studies (MA, PhD); anthropology (MA, PhD); applied linguistics (MA); Arabic (MA, PhD); archaeology (MA); art history (MA); Biblical archaeology (MA); Biblical studies (M Th, D Th, PhD); Christian spirituality (M Th, D Th); church history (M Th, D Th); classical studies (MA, PhD); clinical psychology (MA); communication (MA, PhD); comparative education (M Ed, Ed D); consulting psychology (D Admin, D Com, PhD); curriculum studies (M Ed, Ed D); development studies (M Admin, MA, D Admin, PhD); didactics (M Ed, Ed D); education (M Tech); education management (M Ed, Ed D); educational psychology (M Ed); English (MA); environmental education (M Ed); French (MA, PhD); German (MA, PhD); Greek (MA); guidance and counseling (M Ed); health studies (MA, PhD), including health sciences education (MA), health services management (MA), medical and surgical nursing science (critical care general) (MA), midwifery and neonatal nursing science (MA), trauma and emergency care (MA); history (MA, PhD); history of education (Ed D); inclusive education (M Ed, Ed D); information and communications technology policy and regulation (MA); information science (MA, MIS, PhD); international politics (MA, PhD); Islamic studies (MA, PhD); Italian (MA, PhD); Judaica (MA, PhD); linguistics (MA, PhD); mathematical education (M Ed); mathematics education (MA); missiology (M Th, D Th); modern Hebrew (MA, PhD); musicology (MA, MMus, D Mus, PhD); natural science education (M Ed); New Testament (M Th, D Th); Old Testament (D Th); pastoral therapy (M Th, D Th); philosophy (MA); philosophy of education (M Ed, Ed D); politics (MA, PhD); Portuguese (MA, PhD); practical theology (M Th, D Th); psychology (MA, MS, PhD); psychology of education (M Ed, Ed D); public health (MA); religious studies (MA, D Th, PhD); Romance languages (MA); Russian (MA, PhD); Semitic languages (MA, PhD); social behavior studies in HIV/AIDS (MA); social science (mental health) (MA); social science in development studies (MA); social science in psychology (MA); social science in social work (MA); social science in sociology (MA); social work (MSW, DSW, PhD); socio-education (M Ed, Ed D); sociolinguistics (MA); sociology (MA, PhD); Spanish (MA, PhD); systematic theology (M Th, D Th); TESOL (teaching English to speakers of other languages) (MA); theological ethics (M Th, D Th); theory of literature (MA, PhD); urban ministries (D Th); urban ministry (M Th).

Valparaiso University, Graduate School, Programs in Liberal Studies, Concentration in Ethics and Values, Valparaiso, IN 46383. Offers MALS, Post-Master's Certificate, JD/MALS. Part-time and evening/weekend programs available. *Students:* 2 part-time (both women); both minorities (both Hispanic Americans). Average age 49. *Entrance requirements:* For master's, minimum GPA of 3.0. Additional exam requirements/recommendations for international students: Required—TOEFL (minimum score 550 paper-based; 213 computer-based; 80 iBT). *Application deadline:* Applications are processed on a rolling basis. Application fee: $30 ($50 for international students). Electronic applications accepted. *Financial support:* Available to part-time students. Applicants required to submit FAFSA. *Unit head:* Dr. David L. Rowland, Dean, Graduate Studies and Continuing Education/Associate Provost, 219-464-5313, Fax: 219-464-5381, E-mail: david.rowland@valpo.edu. *Application contact:* Jamie Haney, Coordinator of Graduate Admission, 219-464-5313, Fax: 219-464-5381, E-mail: jamie.haney@valpo.edu.

Warner Pacific College, Graduate Programs, Portland, OR 97215-4099. Offers biblical and theological studies (MA); biblical studies (M Rel); education (M Ed); management/organizational leadership (MS); pastoral ministries (M Rel); religion and ethics (M Rel); teaching (MA); theology (M Rel). Part-time programs available. *Degree requirements:* For master's, thesis or alternative, presentation of defense. *Entrance requirements:* For master's, interview, minimum GPA of 2.5, letters of recommendations. *Faculty research:* New Testament studies, nineteenth-century Wesleyan theology, preaching and church growth, Christian ethics.

West Chester University of Pennsylvania, Office of Graduate Studies, College of Arts and Sciences, Department of Philosophy, West Chester, PA 19383. Offers business ethics (Certificate); healthcare ethics (Certificate); philosophy: applied ethics (MA); philosophy: general (MA). Part-time and evening/weekend programs available. *Students:* 2 full-time (1 woman), 18 part-time (9 women); includes 2 minority (1 African American, 1 Hispanic American). Average age 29. 17 applicants, 88% accepted, 9 enrolled. In 2009, 6 master's awarded. *Degree requirements:* For master's, thesis or comprehensive exam. *Entrance requirements:* For master's, GRE or writing sample, three letters of reference. Additional exam requirements/recommendations for international students: Required—TOEFL (minimum score 550 paper-based; 213 computer-based; 80 iBT). *Application deadline:* For fall admission, 4/15 priority date for domestic students, 3/15 for international students; for spring admission, 10/15 for domestic students, 9/1 for international students. Applications are processed on a rolling basis. Application fee: $35. Electronic applications accepted. *Expenses:* Tuition, state resident: full-time $6666; part-time $370 per credit. Tuition, nonresident: full-time $10,666; part-time $593 per credit. Required fees: $122.56 per credit. *Financial support:* In 2009–10, 4 research assistantships with full and partial tuition reimbursements (averaging $5,000 per year) were awarded; unspecified assistantships also available. Support available to part-time students. Financial award application deadline: 2/15; financial award applicants required to submit FAFSA. *Faculty research:* International studies. *Unit head:* Dr. Joan Woolfrey, Chair, 610-436-1004, E-mail: jwoolfrey@wcupa.edu. *Application contact:* Dr. Helen Daley Schroepfer, Graduate Coordinator, 610-436-2429, E-mail: hschroepfer@wcupa.edu.

Wilfrid Laurier University, Waterloo Lutheran Seminary, Waterloo, ON N2L 3C5, Canada. Offers Christian ethics (M Th); divinity (M Div); homiletics (M Th); ministry (D Min); pastoral counseling (M Th); spirituality in a health care setting (Diploma); theological studies (MTS); theology (Diploma); M Div/MTS/MSW. *Accreditation:* ATS. Part-time programs available. *Degree requirements:* For master's, one foreign language, thesis (for some programs); for doctorate, thesis/dissertation; for M Div, one foreign language, thesis/dissertation. *Entrance requirements:* For M Div, denominational endorsement; for master's, M Div, 2 units of clinical pastoral education (M Th); for doctorate, M Div, 3 years of ministry experience, proficiency in a foreign language, basic training in clinical pastoral education. Additional exam requirements/recommendations for international students: Required—TOEFL (minimum score 573 paper-based; 230 computer-based; 89 iBT), IELTS (minimum score 7). Electronic applications accepted. *Expenses:* Contact institution. *Faculty research:* Biblical study, church history, systematic theology.

Philosophy

American University, College of Arts and Sciences, Department of Philosophy and Religion, Washington, DC 22016-8056. Offers ethics, peace, and global affairs (MA); philosophy (MA), including history of philosophy, philosophy and social policy. Part-time and evening/weekend programs available. *Faculty:* 11 full-time (6 women), 9 part-time/adjunct (4 women). *Students:* 8 full-time (4 women), 2 part-time (0 women); includes 2 minority (1 African American, 1 Asian American or Pacific Islander). Average age 26. 46 applicants, 61% accepted, 4 enrolled. In 2009, 10 master's awarded. *Degree requirements:* For master's, one foreign language, comprehensive exam, thesis (for some programs). *Entrance requirements:* For master's, GRE, writing sample. Additional exam requirements/recommendations for international students: Required—TOEFL. *Application deadline:* For fall admission, 2/1 for domestic students; for spring admission, 10/1 for domestic students. Application fee: $80. *Expenses:* Tuition: Full-time $22,266; part-time $1237 per credit hour. Required fees: $430. Tuition and fees vary according to program. *Financial support:* Fellowships, teaching assistantships, Federal Work-Study and institutionally sponsored loans available. Support available to part-time students. Financial award application deadline: 2/1. *Faculty research:* Oriental religion, classical and medieval philosophy, philosophy of law and ethics, comparative religion, philosophy of science. *Unit head:* Dr. Amy Oliver, Chair, 202-885-2140. *Application contact:* Kathleen Clowery, Director, Graduate Admissions, 202-885-3621, Fax: 202-885-1505.

American University of Beirut, Graduate Programs, Faculty of Arts and Sciences, Beirut, Lebanon. Offers anthropology (MA); Arabic language and literature (MA); archaeology (MA); biology (MS); chemistry (MS); computer science (MS); economics (MA); education (MA); English language (MA); English literature (MA); environmental policy planning (MSES); financial economics (MAFE); geology (MS); history (MA); mathematics (MA, MS); Middle Eastern studies (MA); philosophy (MA); physics (MS); political studies (MA); psychology (MA); public administration (MA); sociology (MA); statistics (MA, MS). Part-time programs available. *Degree requirements:* For master's, one foreign language, comprehensive exam, thesis (for some programs). *Entrance requirements:* For master's, GRE, letter of recommendation. Additional exam requirements/recommendations for international students: Required—TOEFL (minimum score 600 paper-based; 250 computer-based; 100 iBT), IELTS (minimum score 7.5). *Faculty research:* String theory and supergravity; computer graphics; algebra and number theory; popular Arabic literature; marine and freshwater biology; integrating science, math and technology.

Arizona State University, Graduate College, College of Liberal Arts and Sciences, Division of Humanities, Department of Philosophy, Tempe, AZ 85287. Offers MA, PhD. *Degree requirements:* For master's, thesis. *Entrance requirements:* For master's, GRE.

Baylor University, Graduate School, College of Arts and Sciences, Department of Philosophy, Waco, TX 76798. Offers MA, PhD. *Students:* 26 full-time (5 women), 3 part-time (0 women), 2 international. In 2009, 5 master's, 7 doctorates awarded. *Degree requirements:* For master's, one foreign language, thesis or alternative. *Entrance requirements:* For master's, GRE General Test. Additional exam requirements/recommendations for international students: Required—TOEFL. *Application deadline:* Applications are processed on a rolling basis. Application fee: $25. *Financial support:* Teaching assistantships, Federal Work-Study, institutionally sponsored loans, and unspecified assistantships available. *Unit head:* Dr. Bob Roberts, Graduate Program Director, 254-710-6363, Fax: 254-710-3838, E-mail: robert_roberts@baylor.edu. *Application contact:* Marilyn McKinney, Administrative Assistant, 254-710-4237, Fax: 254-710-3870, E-mail: marilyn_mckinney@baylor.edu.

Boston College, Graduate School of Arts and Sciences, Department of Philosophy, Chestnut Hill, MA 02467-3800. Offers MA, PhD. *Students:* 114 full-time (23 women), 12 part-time (5 women); includes 10 minority (2 African Americans, 4 Asian Americans or Pacific Islanders, 4 Hispanic Americans), 20 international. 234 applicants, 44% accepted, 28 enrolled. In 2009, 18 master's, 6 doctorates awarded. Terminal master's awarded for partial completion of doctoral program. *Degree requirements:* For master's, one foreign language, thesis optional; for doctorate, 2 foreign languages, thesis/dissertation. *Entrance requirements:* For master's and doctorate, GRE General Test. Additional exam requirements/recommendations for international students: Required—TOEFL (minimum score 600 paper-based; 250 computer-based; 100 iBT). *Application deadline:* For fall admission, 1/2 for domestic and international students. Application fee: $70. *Financial support:* In 2009–10, fellowships with full tuition reimbursements (averaging $18,000 per year), teaching assistantships with full tuition reimbursements (averaging $17,000 per year) were awarded; Federal Work-Study and scholarships/grants also available. Support available to part-time students. Financial award application deadline: 3/1; financial award applicants required to submit FAFSA. *Faculty research:* History of philosophy, metaphysics, ethics. *Unit head:* Dr. Patrick Byrne, Chairperson, 617-552-3856, E-mail: patrick.byrne@bc.edu. *Application contact:* Dr. Gary Gurtler, Graduate Program Director, 617-552-3872, E-mail: gary.gurtler@bc.edu.

Boston University, Graduate School of Arts and Sciences, Department of Philosophy, Boston, MA 02215. Offers MA, PhD, JD/MA. *Students:* 58 full-time (21 women), 2 part-time (1 woman); includes 1 minority (Asian American or Pacific Islander), 16 international. Average age 29. 268 applicants, 13% accepted, 17 enrolled. In 2009, 22 master's, 7 doctorates awarded. Terminal master's awarded for partial completion of doctoral program. *Degree requirements:* For master's, one foreign language, thesis; for doctorate, one foreign language, comprehensive exam, thesis/dissertation. *Entrance requirements:* For master's and doctorate, GRE General Test, sample of written work, 3 letters of recommendation. Additional exam requirements/recommendations for international students: Required—TOEFL (minimum score 600 paper-based; 250 computer-based). *Application deadline:* For fall admission, 1/15 for domestic and international students. Application fee: $70. Electronic applications accepted. *Expenses:* Tuition: Full-time $37,910; part-time $1184 per credit hour. Required fees: $386; $40 per semester. Part-time tuition and fees vary according to class time, course level, degree level and program. *Financial support:* In 2009–10, 11 fellowships with full tuition reimbursements (averaging $18,900 per year), 2 research assistantships (averaging $18,400 per year), 18 teaching assistantships with full tuition reimbursements (averaging $18,400 per year) were awarded; Federal Work-Study and scholarships/grants also available. Financial award application deadline: 1/15; financial award applicants required to submit FAFSA. *Unit head:* Dr. Daniel Dahlstrom, Chairman, 617-353-4583, Fax: 617-353-6805, E-mail: dahlstro@bu.edu. *Application contact:* Lesley Moreau, Senior Program Coordinator, 617-353-2571, Fax: 617-353-6805, E-mail: casphilo@bu.edu.

Bowling Green State University, Graduate College, College of Arts and Sciences, Department of Philosophy, Bowling Green, OH 43403. Offers applied philosophy (PhD); institutional theory and history (PhD); philosophy (MA). Part-time programs available. Terminal master's awarded for partial completion of doctoral program. *Degree requirements:* For master's, thesis or alternative; for doctorate, comprehensive exam, thesis/dissertation, foreign language or research tool. *Entrance requirements:* For master's and doctorate, GRE General Test. Additional exam requirements/recommendations for international students: Required—TOEFL. Electronic applications accepted. *Faculty research:* Moral philosophy and ethics, political and social philosophy, decision theory, applied ethics, public policy.

Brandeis University, Graduate School of Arts and Sciences, Department of Philosophy, Waltham, MA 02454-9110. Offers MA. Part-time programs available. *Faculty:* 11 full-time (4 women), 2 part-time/adjunct (both women). *Students:* 17 full-time (2 women); includes 1 African American, 3 international. 92 applicants, 48% accepted, 17 enrolled. *Degree requirements:* For master's, thesis. *Entrance requirements:* For master's, GRE, official transcript(s), 3 recommendation letters, CV or resume, statement of purpose, writing sample. Additional exam requirements/recommendations for international students: Required—TOEFL (minimum score 600 paper-based; 250 computer-based; 100 iBT); Recommended—IELTS (minimum score 7). *Application deadline:* For fall admission, 3/15 priority date for domestic students. Applications are processed on a rolling basis. Application fee: $75. Electronic applications accepted. *Financial support:* In 2009–10, 27 teaching assistantships with partial tuition reimbursements (averaging $3,200 per year) were awarded; scholarships/grants also available.

Financial award application deadline: 4/15; financial award applicants required to submit FAFSA. *Faculty research:* Metaphysics and epistemology, ethics, social and political philosophy, philosophy of language, logic, philosophy of mind and cognitive science, early modern philosophy, aesthetics, the philosophy of law. *Unit head:* Prof. Andreas Teuber, Chair, 781-736-2788, Fax: 781-736-8562, E-mail: teuber@brandeis.edu. *Application contact:* Julie Seeger, Department Administrator, 781-736-2789, Fax: 781-736-8562, E-mail: jseeger@brandeis.edu.

Brock University, Faculty of Graduate Studies, Faculty of Humanities, Program in Philosophy, St. Catharines, ON L2S 3A1, Canada. Offers MA. Part-time programs available. *Degree requirements:* For master's, thesis optional. *Entrance requirements:* For master's, honors BA in philosophy. Additional exam requirements/recommendations for international students: Required—TOEFL (minimum score 550 paper-based; 213 computer-based; 80 iBT), IELTS (minimum score 6.5), TWE (minimum score 4). Electronic applications accepted. *Faculty research:* Contemporary continental philosophy, Chinese and comparative philosophy, Indian philosophy, ethics.

Brown University, Graduate School, Department of Philosophy, Providence, RI 02912. Offers MA, PhD. *Degree requirements:* For master's, thesis or alternative; for doctorate, variable foreign language requirement, thesis/dissertation. *Entrance requirements:* For master's and doctorate, GRE General Test.

California Institute of Integral Studies, School of Consciousness and Transformation, San Francisco, CA 94103. Offers creative inquiry (MFA); cultural anthropology and social transformation (MA); East-West psychology (MA, PhD); integrative health studies (MA); philosophy and religion (MA, PhD), including Asian and comparative studies, philosophy, cosmology, and consciousness, women's spirituality; social and cultural anthropology (PhD); transformative leadership (MA); transformative studies (PhD); writing and consciousness (MFA). Part-time and evening/weekend programs available. Postbaccalaureate distance learning degree programs offered (minimal on-campus study). *Students:* 334 full-time (218 women), 126 part-time (77 women); includes 116 minority (40 African Americans, 4 American Indian/Alaska Native, 42 Asian Americans or Pacific Islanders, 30 Hispanic Americans). Average age 38. 265 applicants, 90% accepted, 149 enrolled. In 2009, 64 master's, 22 doctorates awarded. Terminal master's awarded for partial completion of doctoral program. *Degree requirements:* For master's, comprehensive exam (for some programs), thesis optional; for doctorate, comprehensive exam, thesis/dissertation, 1 foreign language (Asian comparative studies). *Entrance requirements:* For master's, minimum GPA of 3.0, letters of recommendation, writing sample; for doctorate, master's degree, minimum GPA of 3.0, letters of recommendation, writing sample. Additional exam requirements/recommendations for international students: Required—TOEFL. *Application deadline:* For fall admission, 2/1 priority date for domestic and international students; for spring admission, 10/15 priority date for domestic and international students. Applications are processed on a rolling basis. Application fee: $65. Electronic applications accepted. *Expenses:* Tuition: Full-time $15,300; part-time $850 per credit hour. Required fees: $110 per semester. Tuition and fees vary according to degree level. *Financial support:* In 2009–10, 330 students received support; research assistantships, teaching assistantships, career-related internships or fieldwork, Federal Work-Study, scholarships/grants, and tuition waivers (partial) available. Support available to part-time students. Financial award application deadline: 4/15; financial award applicants required to submit FAFSA. *Faculty research:* Altered states of consciousness, dreams, cosmology, postcolonial studies, integrative health studies. *Application contact:* Allyson Werner, Associate Director of Admissions, 415-575-6155, Fax: 415-575-1268.

California State University, Long Beach, Graduate Studies, College of Liberal Arts, Department of Philosophy, Long Beach, CA 90840. Offers MA. Part-time programs available. *Faculty:* 5 full-time (1 woman). *Students:* 4 full-time (0 women), 15 part-time (2 women); includes 6 minority (1 African American, 1 American Indian/Alaska Native, 1 Asian American or Pacific Islander, 3 Hispanic Americans). Average age 35. 31 applicants, 32% accepted, 2 enrolled. *Degree requirements:* For master's, comprehensive exam or thesis. *Application deadline:* For fall admission, 7/1 for domestic students. Applications are processed on a rolling basis. Application fee: $55. Electronic applications accepted. *Expenses:* Required fees: $1802 per semester. Part-time tuition and fees vary according to course load. *Financial support:* Federal Work-Study, institutionally sponsored loans, and scholarships/grants available. Financial award application deadline: 3/2. *Faculty research:* Philosophy of science, ethics. *Unit head:* Dr. Martin Herman, Interim Chair, 562-985-4331, Fax: 562-985-7135, E-mail: mherman@csulb.edu. *Application contact:* Dr. Cory Wright, Graduate Advisor, 562-985-4245, Fax: 562-985-4331, E-mail: cdwright@csulb.edu.

California State University, Los Angeles, Graduate Studies, College of Arts and Letters, Department of Philosophy, Los Angeles, CA 90032-8530. Offers MA. Part-time and evening/weekend programs available. *Faculty:* 4 full-time (1 woman), 1 part-time/adjunct (0 women). *Students:* 19 full-time (4 women), 33 part-time (8 women); includes 14 minority (1 African American, 1 American Indian/Alaska Native, 3 Asian Americans or Pacific Islanders, 9 Hispanic Americans), 1 international. Average age 35. 24 applicants, 100% accepted, 12 enrolled. In 2009, 13 master's awarded. *Degree requirements:* For master's, comprehensive exam. *Entrance requirements:* Additional exam requirements/recommendations for international students: Required—TOEFL (minimum score 500 paper-based; 173 computer-based). *Application deadline:* For fall admission, 5/1 for domestic and international students. Applications are processed on a rolling basis. Application fee: $55. Electronic applications accepted. *Financial support:* Career-related internships or fieldwork and Federal Work-Study available. Support available to part-time students. Financial award application deadline: 3/1. *Faculty research:* Aesthetics, philosophy of language, ethics, philosophy of science, history of philosophy. *Unit head:* Dr. Kayley Vernallis, Chair, 323-343-4180, Fax: 323-343-4193, E-mail: kvernal@calstatela.edu. *Application contact:* Dr. Cheryl L. Ney, Associate Vice President for Academic Affairs and Dean of Graduate Studies, 323-343-3820, Fax: 323-343-5653, E-mail: cney@cslanet.calstatela.edu.

Carleton University, Faculty of Graduate Studies, Faculty of Arts and Social Sciences, Department of Philosophy, Ottawa, ON K1S 5B6, Canada. Offers MA. *Degree requirements:* For master's, thesis optional. *Entrance requirements:* For master's, honors degree. Additional exam requirements/recommendations for international students: Required—TOEFL. *Faculty research:* Application of philosophical theory to issues of current concern, history of philosophy, contemporary philosophy in North America and Europe.

Carnegie Mellon University, College of Humanities and Social Sciences, Department of Philosophy, Pittsburgh, PA 15213-3891. Offers logic and computation (MS); logic, computation and methodology (PhD); philosophy (MA). Part-time programs available. *Degree requirements:* For master's, thesis; for doctorate, comprehensive exam, thesis/dissertation. *Entrance requirements:* For master's and doctorate, GRE General Test. Additional exam requirements/recommendations for international students: Required—TOEFL. Electronic applications accepted. *Faculty research:* Philosophy of science, artificial intelligence.

The Catholic University of America, School of Philosophy, Washington, DC 20064. Offers MA, PhD, Ph L, MA/JD. Part-time programs available. *Faculty:* 20 full-time (5 women), 3 part-time/adjunct (1 woman). *Students:* 43 full-time (5 women), 73 part-time (18 women); includes 5 minority (1 African American, 1 Asian American or Pacific Islander, 3 Hispanic Americans), 13 international. Average age 32. 100 applicants, 48% accepted, 22 enrolled. In 2009, 12 master's, 6 doctorates awarded. *Degree requirements:* For master's, one foreign language, thesis, oral exam; for doctorate, 2 foreign languages, comprehensive exam, thesis/dissertation, oral exam. *Entrance requirements:* For master's and doctorate, GRE General Test, statement of purpose, official copies of academic transcripts, three letters of recommendation. Additional exam requirements/recommendations for international students: Required—TOEFL (minimum score 580 paper-based; 237 computer-based). *Application deadline:* For fall admission, 8/1 priority date for domestic students, 7/15 for international students; for spring admission, 12/1 priority date for domestic students, 10/15 for international students. Applications are processed on a rolling basis. Application fee: $55. Electronic applications accepted. *Expenses:* Tuition: Full-time $31,740; part-time $1245 per credit hour. Required fees: $50; $25 per semester hour. One-time fee: $425. *Financial support:* Fellowships, research assistantships, teaching assistantships, Federal Work-Study, scholarships/grants, tuition waivers (full and partial), and unspecified assistantships available. Financial award application deadline: 2/1; financial award applicants required to submit FAFSA. *Faculty research:* Ancient philosophy, modern philosophy, metaphysics, ethics, phenomenology. Total annual research expenditures: $57,792. *Unit head:* Rev. Kurt J. Pritzl, Dean, 202-319-5259, Fax: 202-319-4731, E-mail: pritzl@cua.edu. *Application contact:* Julie Schwing, Director of Graduate Admissions, 202-319-5057, Fax: 202-319-6533, E-mail: cua-admissions@cua.edu.

Central European University, Graduate Studies, School of Social Sciences and Humanities, Budapest, Hungary. Offers economics (MA, PhD); gender studies (MA, PhD); international relations and European studies (MA, PhD); mathematics and its applications (MS, PhD); medieval studies (MA, PhD); nationalism studies (MA, PhD); philosophy (MA, PhD); political science (MA, PhD); public policy (MA, PhD); sociology and social anthropology (MA, PhD). Terminal master's awarded for partial completion of doctoral program. *Degree requirements:* For master's, one foreign language, thesis; for doctorate, one foreign language, comprehensive exam, thesis/dissertation. *Entrance requirements:* For master's, interview; for doctorate, GRE, CEU subject test, interview. Additional exam requirements/recommendations for international students: Required—TOEFL (minimum score 570 paper-based; 230 computer-based). Electronic applications accepted. *Faculty research:* Civil society, fiscal decentralization, party politics, political philosophy (especially Liberalism, theory of Democracy).

Claremont Graduate University, Graduate Programs, School of Arts and Humanities, Department of Philosophy, Claremont, CA 91711-6160. Offers MA, PhD, MA/PhD, MBA/MA, MBA/PhD. Part-time programs available. *Faculty:* 3 full-time (1 woman). *Students:* 37 full-time (10 women), 3 part-time (1 woman); includes 11 minority (2 African Americans, 1 American Indian/Alaska Native, 4 Asian Americans or Pacific Islanders, 4 Hispanic Americans). Average age 37. In 2009, 3 master's, 1 doctorate awarded. *Degree requirements:* For doctorate, research folio. *Entrance requirements:* For master's and doctorate, GRE General Test. Additional exam requirements/recommendations for international students: Required—TOEFL (minimum score 550 paper-based; 213 computer-based; 80 iBT). *Application deadline:* For fall admission, 2/1 priority date for domestic students. Applications are processed on a rolling basis. Application fee: $60. Electronic applications accepted. *Expenses:* Tuition: Full-time $35,046; part-time $1524 per credit. Required fees: $161 per semester. *Financial support:* Fellowships, research assistantships, Federal Work-Study, institutionally sponsored loans, and scholarships/grants available. Support available to part-time students. Financial award application deadline: 2/15; financial award applicants required to submit FAFSA. *Faculty research:* Ancient philosophy, philosophy of science, probability theory, philosophical logic, philosophy of logic. *Unit head:* Charles Young, Chair, 909-607-3926, Fax: 909-607-1221, E-mail: charles.young@cgu.edu. *Application contact:* Susan Hampson, Admissions Coordinator, 909-607-1278, Fax: 909-607-1221, E-mail: humanities@cgu.edu.

Cleveland State University, College of Graduate Studies, College of Liberal Arts and Social Sciences, Department of Philosophy, Cleveland, OH 44115. Offers bioethics (MA, Certificate), including bioethics (MA); philosophy (MA), including philosophy. Part-time and evening/weekend programs available. *Degree requirements:* For master's, comprehensive exam, thesis optional. *Entrance requirements:* For master's, minimum GPA of 2.75. Additional exam requirements/recommendations for international students: Required—TOEFL (minimum score 525 paper-based; 197 computer-based). *Faculty research:* Ethics, history of philosophy, bio-ethics, social and political philosophy.

Collège Dominicain de Philosophie et de Théologie, Graduate Programs, Faculty of Philosophy, Ottawa, ON K1R 7G3, Canada. Offers MA Ph, PhD. *Faculty:* 5 full-time (0 women), 2 part-time/adjunct (0 women). *Students:* 31 full-time (7 women); includes 5 minority (3 African Americans, 2 Asian Americans or Pacific Islanders), 4 international. Average age 38. 16 applicants, 88% accepted, 7 enrolled. In 2009, 4 master's awarded. *Degree requirements:* For master's, thesis; for doctorate, 2 foreign languages, thesis/dissertation, candidacy exam. *Entrance requirements:* For master's, honors degree in philosophy, minimum B average in undergraduate course work; for doctorate, master's degree in philosophy, minimum A average in graduate course work. *Application deadline:* For fall admission, 6/1 priority date for domestic students, 3/1 priority date for international students; for winter admission, 11/20 priority date for domestic students, 10/16 priority date for international students. Applications are processed on a rolling basis. Application fee: $40. Tuition and fees charges are reported in Canadian dollars. *Expenses:* Tuition: Full-time $3560 Canadian dollars; part-time $130 Canadian dollars per credit. Required fees: $125 Canadian dollars; $105 Canadian dollars per year. *Financial support:* In 2009–10, 8 research assistantships (averaging $5,000 per year), 1 teaching assistantship (averaging $8,000 per year) were awarded. Financial award application deadline: 10/15. *Faculty research:* Ethics, philosophy of Kant. *Unit head:* Eduardo Andujar, Dean of the Faculty, 613-233-5696 Ext. 330, Fax: 613-233-6064, E-mail: eduardo.andujar@collegedominicain.ca. *Application contact:* Francis Peddle, Master of Studies, 613-233-3696 Ext. 325, Fax: 613-233-6064, E-mail: francis.peddle@collegedominicain.ca.

College of the Humanities and Sciences, Harrison Middleton University, Graduate Program, Tempe, AZ 85282. Offers education (MA, Ed D); humanities (MA); imaginative literature (MA); interdisciplinary studies (DA); jurisprudence (MA); natural science (MA); philosophy and religion (MA); social science (MA). Part-time and evening/weekend programs available. Postbaccalaureate distance learning degree programs offered (no on-campus study). *Faculty:* 17 full-time (7 women), 14 part-time/adjunct (6 women). *Students:* 49 full-time (18 women). In 2009, 4 master's awarded. *Application deadline:* Applications are processed on a rolling basis. Application fee: $50. Electronic applications accepted. *Application contact:* Deborah Deacon, Dean of Graduate Studies, 877-248-6724, Fax: 800-762-1622, E-mail: ddeacon@chumsci.edu.

Colorado State University, Graduate School, College of Liberal Arts, Department of Philosophy, Fort Collins, CO 80523-1781. Offers MA. Part-time programs available. *Faculty:* 13 full-time (3 women), 1 part-time/adjunct (0 women). *Students:* 15 full-time (2 women), 8 part-time (2 women); includes 1 minority (Hispanic American), 1 international. Average age 29. 27 applicants, 63% accepted, 9 enrolled. In 2009, 7 master's awarded. *Degree requirements:* For master's, variable foreign language requirement, comprehensive exam (for some programs), thesis (for some programs). *Entrance requirements:* For master's, GRE General Test, minimum GPA of 3.25, 3 letters of recommendation, writing sample. Additional exam requirements/recommendations for international students: Required—TOEFL. *Application deadline:* For fall admission, 2/15 priority date for domestic and international students; for spring admission, 8/1 priority date for domestic and international students. Applications are processed on a rolling basis. Application fee: $50. Electronic applications accepted. *Expenses:* Tuition, state resident: full-time $6434; part-time $359.10 per credit. Tuition, nonresident: full-time $18,116; part-time $1006.45 per credit. Required fees: $1496; $83 per credit. *Financial support:* In 2009–10, 13 students received support, including 13 teaching assistantships with full tuition reimbursements available (averaging $12,330 per year); fellowships, research assistantships, career-related internships or fieldwork, Federal Work-Study, institutionally sponsored loans, scholarships/grants, traineeships, and unspecified assistantships also available. Support available to part-time students. Financial award application deadline: 3/1; financial award applicants required to submit FAFSA. *Faculty research:* Animal ethics, environmental ethics, history of philosophy, comparative philosophy, epistemology. Total annual research expenditures: $10,000. *Unit head:* Dr. Jane E. Kneller, Chair, 970-491-7614, Fax: 970-491-4900, E-mail: jane.kneller@colostate.edu. *Application contact:* Dr. Michael Losonsky, Graduate Studies Coordinator, 970-491-6734, Fax: 970-491-4900, E-mail: losonsky@lamar.colostate.edu.

Columbia University, Graduate School of Arts and Sciences, Division of Humanities, Department of Philosophy, New York, NY 10027. Offers M Phil, MA, PhD, JD/MA, JD/PhD. Part-time programs available. *Degree requirements:* For master's, one foreign language; for doctorate, 2 foreign languages, thesis/dissertation. *Entrance requirements:* For master's and doctorate, GRE General Test, writing sample. Additional exam requirements/recommendations for international students: Required—TOEFL.

Philosophy

Columbia University, Graduate School of Arts and Sciences, Division of Natural Sciences, Department of Physics, Program in Philosophical Foundations of Physics, New York, NY 10027. Offers MA.

Concordia University, School of Graduate Studies, Faculty of Arts and Science, Department of Philosophy, Montréal, QC H3G 1M8, Canada. Offers MA. *Degree requirements:* For master's, comprehensive exam, thesis or alternative. *Entrance requirements:* For master's, honors degree in philosophy or equivalent. *Faculty research:* Anglo-American analytic thought, Continental thought, pragmatic thought.

Cornell University, Graduate School, Graduate Fields of Arts and Sciences, Field of Philosophy, Ithaca, NY 14853-0001. Offers PhD. *Faculty:* 25 full-time (8 women). *Students:* 43 full-time (11 women); includes 4 minority (2 African Americans, 2 Hispanic Americans), 20 international. Average age 30. 302 applicants, 5% accepted, 5 enrolled. In 2009, 5 doctorates awarded. *Degree requirements:* For doctorate, comprehensive exam, thesis/dissertation, teaching experience. *Entrance requirements:* For doctorate, sample of written work in philosophy, 2 letters of recommendation. Additional exam requirements/recommendations for international students: Required—TOEFL (minimum score 550 paper-based; 213 computer-based; 77 iBT). *Application deadline:* For fall admission, 1/15 for domestic students. Application fee: $70. Electronic applications accepted. *Expenses:* Tuition: Full-time $29,500. Required fees: $70. Full-time tuition and fees vary according to degree level, program and student level. *Financial support:* In 2009–10, 34 students received support, including 5 fellowships with full tuition reimbursements available; research assistantships with full tuition reimbursements available, teaching assistantships with full tuition reimbursements available, institutionally sponsored loans, scholarships/grants, health care benefits, tuition waivers (full and partial), and unspecified assistantships also available. Financial award applicants required to submit FAFSA. *Unit head:* Director of Graduate Studies, 607-255-3687, Fax: 607-255-8177. *Application contact:* Graduate Field Assistant, 607-255-3687, Fax: 607-255-8177, E-mail: philosophy@cornell.edu.

Dalhousie University, Faculty of Arts and Social Science, Department of Philosophy, Halifax, NS B3H 4R2, Canada. Offers MA, PhD. *Entrance requirements:* For doctorate, MA in philosophy. Additional exam requirements/recommendations for international students: Required—TOEFL, IELTS, CANTEST, CAEL, or Michigan English Language Assessment Battery. *Application deadline:* For fall admission, 6/1 for domestic students, 4/1 for international students; for winter admission, 10/31 for domestic students, 8/31 for international students; for spring admission, 2/28 for domestic students, 12/31 for international students. Application fee: $70. Electronic applications accepted. *Financial support:* Career-related internships or fieldwork, scholarships/grants, and health care benefits available. *Faculty research:* Ethical and political philosophy; epistemology; philosophy of language, history, and logic; bioethics; feminist theory. *Unit head:* Dr. Micheal Hymers, Grad Coordinator, 902-494-3810, Fax: 902-494-3518, E-mail: dalphil@dal.ca. *Application contact:* Laurie Finlay, Graduate Administrator, 902-494-3548, Fax: 902-494-3518, E-mail: laurie.finlay@dal.ca.

DePaul University, College of Liberal Arts and Sciences, Department of Philosophy, Chicago, IL 60604-2287. Offers MA, PhD. Part-time and evening/weekend programs available. *Faculty:* 21 full-time (8 women). *Students:* 18 full-time (7 women), 28 part-time (13 women); includes 2 minority (1 African American, 1 Hispanic American), 7 international. Average age 29. 157 applicants, 4% accepted, 6 enrolled. In 2009, 6 master's, 2 doctorates awarded. Terminal master's awarded for partial completion of doctoral program. *Degree requirements:* For master's, one foreign language, thesis optional; for doctorate, 2 foreign languages, thesis/dissertation, oral exam, 28 courses in philosophy. *Entrance requirements:* For master's, GRE General Test, sample of written work, BA, two letters of recommendation; for doctorate, GRE General Test, MA in philosophy, sample of written work, two letters of recommendation. Additional exam requirements/recommendations for international students: Required—TOEFL. *Application deadline:* For fall admission, 12/15 for domestic students; for winter admission, 12/15 for domestic students. Applications are processed on a rolling basis. Application fee: $40. Electronic applications accepted. *Expenses:* Tuition: Full-time $37,525; part-time $620 per credit hour. *Financial support:* In 2009–10, 12 fellowships with full tuition reimbursements (averaging $18,000 per year), 24 teaching assistantships with full tuition reimbursements (averaging $15,500 per year) were awarded; tuition waivers (partial) also available. Financial award application deadline: 12/15. *Faculty research:* German idealism, contemporary Continental philosophy, social and political philosophy, critical race theory, Renaissance and early modern philosophy. *Unit head:* Richard A. Lee, Chair, 773-325-4502, Fax: 773-325-7268, E-mail: rlee17@depaul.edu. *Application contact:* Avery M. Goldman, Director of Recruitment, 773-325-4811, Fax: 773-325-7268, E-mail: agoldman@depaul.edu.

Dominican School of Philosophy and Theology, Graduate Programs, Department of Philosophy, Berkeley, CA 94708. Offers MA, MA/MA. Part-time programs available. *Degree requirements:* For master's, one foreign language, thesis. *Entrance requirements:* For master's, GRE General Test, minimum GPA of 3.0. Additional exam requirements/recommendations for international students: Required—TOEFL (minimum score 550 paper-based; 68 computer-based). *Faculty research:* Pre-modernism philosophy, philosophy and science, human suffering, philosophy of language, classical philosophy.

Duke University, Graduate School, Department of Philosophy, Durham, NC 27708. Offers AM, PhD, JD/AM. *Faculty:* 14 full-time. *Students:* 30 full-time (11 women); includes 6 minority (1 American Indian/Alaska Native, 2 Asian Americans or Pacific Islanders, 3 Hispanic Americans), 5 international. 119 applicants, 11% accepted, 7 enrolled. In 2009, 4 master's, 7 doctorates awarded. *Degree requirements:* For doctorate, one foreign language, thesis/dissertation. *Entrance requirements:* For doctorate, GRE General Test. Additional exam requirements/recommendations for international students: Required—TOEFL (minimum score 550 paper-based; 213 computer-based; 83 iBT), IELTS (minimum score 7). *Application deadline:* For fall admission, 12/8 priority date for domestic and international students. Application fee: $75. Electronic applications accepted. *Financial support:* Fellowships, research assistantships, teaching assistantships, Federal Work-Study available. Financial award application deadline: 12/31. *Unit head:* Karen Neander, Director of Graduate Studies, 919-660-3050, Fax: 919-660-3060, E-mail: rjjc77@duke.edu. *Application contact:* Cynthia Robertson, Associate Dean for Enrollment Services, 919-684-3913, E-mail: grad-admissions@duke.edu.

Duquesne University, Graduate School of Liberal Arts, Department of Philosophy, Pittsburgh, PA 15282-0001. Offers MA, PhD. Part-time and evening/weekend programs available. *Faculty:* 10 full-time (3 women), 4 part-time/adjunct (2 women). *Students:* 95 full-time (25 women), 14 part-time (2 women); includes 2 minority (1 African American, 1 Hispanic American), 11 international. Average age 32. 127 applicants, 40% accepted, 29 enrolled. In 2009, 18 master's, 3 doctorates awarded. Terminal master's awarded for partial completion of doctoral program. *Degree requirements:* For master's, one foreign language; for doctorate, 2 foreign languages, comprehensive exam, thesis/dissertation. *Entrance requirements:* For master's, GRE General Test, bachelor's degree in philosophy, minimum GPA of 3.5; for doctorate, GRE General Test, master's degree in philosophy, minimum GPA of 3.75. Additional exam requirements/recommendations for international students: Required—TOEFL. *Application deadline:* For fall admission, 2/15 for domestic and international students. Electronic applications accepted. *Expenses:* Tuition: Part-time $851 per credit. Required fees: $81 per credit. *Financial support:* In 2009–10, 3 research assistantships with full tuition reimbursements (averaging $5,000 per year), 12 teaching assistantships with full tuition reimbursements (averaging $10,000 per year) were awarded; Federal Work-Study, scholarships/grants, tuition waivers (partial), and unspecified assistantships also available. Financial award application deadline: 5/1. *Faculty research:* Phenomenology, twentieth century Continental philosophy, history of philosophy. *Unit head:* Dr. James Swindal, Chair, 412-396-6572, E-mail: swiindalj@duq.edu. *Application contact:* Dr. James Swindal, Chair, 412-396-6572, E-mail: swindalj@duq.edu.

Emory University, Graduate School of Arts and Sciences, Department of Comparative Literature, Atlanta, GA 30322-1100. Offers comparative literature (PhD); English (Certificate); French (Certificate); Middle Eastern studies (PhD); philosophy (Certificate); psychoanalytic studies (PhD); religion (PhD); Spanish (Certificate); women studies (Certificate). *Degree requirements:* For doctorate, 2 foreign languages, comprehensive exam, thesis/dissertation. *Entrance requirements:* For doctorate, GRE General Test, minimum GPA of 3.0. Additional exam requirements/recommendations for international students: Required—TOEFL. Electronic applications accepted. *Faculty research:* Literary theory, psychoanalysis trauma and testimony, literature and religion, literature and technology, literature and philosophy, politics and global culture, literature and aesthetics.

Emory University, Graduate School of Arts and Sciences, Department of Philosophy, Atlanta, GA 30322-1100. Offers PhD. *Degree requirements:* For doctorate, 2 foreign languages, comprehensive exam, thesis/dissertation. *Entrance requirements:* For doctorate, GRE General Test, minimum GPA of 3.0. Additional exam requirements/recommendations for international students: Required—TOEFL. Electronic applications accepted. *Faculty research:* History of philosophy, German idealism, twentieth century Continental philosophy, ethics, social theory.

Florida State University, The Graduate School, College of Arts and Sciences, Department of Philosophy, Tallahassee, FL 32306-1500. Offers history and philosophy of science (MA); philosophy (MA, PhD). *Faculty:* 14 full-time (2 women), 2 part-time/adjunct (1 woman). *Students:* 42 full-time (12 women), 4 part-time (1 woman); includes 3 minority (1 African American, 2 Hispanic Americans), 1 international. Average age 24. 78 applicants, 17% accepted, 6 enrolled. In 2009, 7 master's, 4 doctorates awarded. Terminal master's awarded for partial completion of doctoral program. *Degree requirements:* For master's, one foreign language, comprehensive exam (for some programs), thesis (for some programs); for doctorate, one foreign language, thesis/dissertation. *Entrance requirements:* For master's and doctorate, GRE General Test. Additional exam requirements/recommendations for international students: Required—TOEFL (minimum score 550 paper-based; 213 computer-based; 80 iBT). *Application deadline:* For fall admission, 1/3 priority date for domestic and international students. Applications are processed on a rolling basis. Application fee: $30. Electronic applications accepted. *Expenses:* Tuition, state resident: full-time $7413. Tuition, nonresident: full-time $22,567. *Financial support:* In 2009–10, 1 student received support, including 2 fellowships with partial tuition reimbursements available (averaging $20,000 per year), 2 research assistantships with partial tuition reimbursements available (averaging $5,000 per year), 35 teaching assistantships with partial tuition reimbursements available (averaging $12,000 per year); Federal Work-Study, scholarships/grants, and health care benefits also available. Financial award application deadline: 1/3; financial award applicants required to submit FAFSA. *Faculty research:* Philosophy of biology, Greek philosophy, ethics, action theory, philosophy of mind. *Unit head:* Dr. John Piers Rawling, Chairman, 850-644-1483, Fax: 850-644-3832, E-mail: prawling@fsu.edu. *Application contact:* Rachel A. Baker, Academic Support Assistant, 850-644-1483, Fax: 850-644-3832, E-mail: rar04c@fsu.edu.

Fordham University, Graduate School of Arts and Sciences, Department of Philosophy, New York, NY 10458. Offers philosophical resources (MA); philosophy (MA, PhD). Part-time and evening/weekend programs available. *Faculty:* 31 full-time (10 women). *Students:* 26 full-time (5 women), 51 part-time (6 women); includes 1 minority (Asian American or Pacific Islander), 3 international. Average age 30. 195 applicants, 16% accepted, 14 enrolled. In 2009, 16 master's, 7 doctorates awarded. Terminal master's awarded for partial completion of doctoral program. *Degree requirements:* For master's, one foreign language, comprehensive exam; for doctorate, 2 foreign languages, comprehensive exam, thesis/dissertation. *Entrance requirements:* For master's and doctorate, GRE General Test. Additional exam requirements/recommendations for international students: Required—TOEFL (minimum score 650 paper-based; 280 computer-based). *Application deadline:* For fall admission, 1/4 priority date for domestic students; for spring admission, 11/1 for domestic students. Application fee: $70. Electronic applications accepted. *Financial support:* In 2009–10, 45 students received support, including 2 fellowships with tuition reimbursements available (averaging $21,175 per year), 20 research assistantships with tuition reimbursements available (averaging $17,782 per year), 23 teaching assistantships with tuition reimbursements available (averaging $15,293 per year); institutionally sponsored loans, tuition waivers (full and partial), and unspecified assistantships also available. Support available to part-time students. Financial award application deadline: 1/4. *Faculty research:* Contemporary continental philosophy (including German idealism), philosophy of religion, medieval philosophy, ethics, epistemology. *Unit head:* Dr. John Drummond, Chair, 718-817-3270, Fax: 718-817-3300, E-mail: drummond@fordham.edu. *Application contact:* Charlene Dundie, Director of Graduate Admissions, 718-817-4420, Fax: 718-817-3566, E-mail: dundie@fordham.edu.

Franciscan University of Steubenville, Graduate Programs, Department of Philosophy, Steubenville, OH 43952-1763. Offers MA. Part-time programs available. *Degree requirements:* For master's, one foreign language, thesis. *Entrance requirements:* For master's, minimum undergraduate GPA of 3.0.

George Mason University, College of Humanities and Social Sciences, Department of Philosophy, Fairfax, VA 22030. Offers philosophy (MA); professional ethics (Certificate). *Faculty:* 10 full-time (3 women), 8 part-time/adjunct (1 woman). *Students:* 6 full-time (2 women), 20 part-time (6 women); includes 1 minority (African American), 1 international. Average age 36. 14 applicants, 86% accepted, 8 enrolled. In 2009, 7 master's awarded. *Entrance requirements:* For master's, 3 letters of recommendation, current transcript, expanded goals statement, writing sample, resume. Additional exam requirements/recommendations for international students: Required—TOEFL. *Application deadline:* For fall admission, 4/15 priority date for domestic students; for spring admission, 11/1 for domestic students. Applications are processed on a rolling basis. Application fee: $75. Electronic applications accepted. *Expenses:* Tuition, state resident: full-time $7568; part-time $315.33 per credit hour. Tuition, nonresident: full-time $21,704; part-time $904.33 per credit hour. Required fees: $2184; $91 per credit hour. *Financial support:* In 2009–10, 1 student received support, including 1 teaching assistantship (averaging $7,500 per year); Federal Work-Study, scholarships/grants, unspecified assistantships, and health care benefits (full-time research or teaching assistantship recipients) also available. Support available to part-time students. Financial award application deadline: 3/1. *Faculty research:* Cultural studies, political theory philosophy, social and political philosophy, feminist theory, analytical and continental philosophy, philosophy of science. *Unit head:* Ted Kinnaman, Chair/Associate Professor, 703-993-4328, E-mail: tkinnama@gmu.edu. *Application contact:* Rose Cherubin, Graduate Coordinator, 703-993-1332, E-mail: rcherubi@gmu.edu.

Georgetown University, Graduate School of Arts and Sciences, Department of Philosophy, Washington, DC 20057. Offers bioethics (MA); philosophy (PhD); JD/MA; JD/PhD; MD/PhD. *Degree requirements:* For master's, thesis or alternative; for doctorate, 2 foreign languages, comprehensive exam, thesis/dissertation. *Entrance requirements:* For master's and doctorate, GRE General Test. Additional exam requirements/recommendations for international students: Required—TOEFL.

The George Washington University, Columbian College of Arts and Sciences, Trachtenberg School of Public Policy and Public Administration, Washington, DC 20052. Offers public administration (MPA), including budget and public finance, federal policy, politics, and management, international development management, managing public organizations, managing state and local governments, nonprofit management, policy analysis and evaluation, public administration, public-private policy and management; public policy (MA, MPP), including environmental and resource policy (MA), philosophy and social policy (MA), women's studies (MA); public policy and administration (PhD); JD/MPP; MPA/JD; PhD/MPP. Part-time and evening/weekend programs available. *Faculty:* 35 full-time (12 women), 19 part-time/adjunct (10 women). *Students:* 187 full-time (114 women), 232 part-time (151 women); includes 62 minority (15 African Americans, 3 American Indian/Alaska Native, 29 Asian Americans or Pacific Islanders, 15 Hispanic Americans), 23 international. Average age 26. 913 applicants, 56% accepted, 186 enrolled. In 2009, 106 master's, 9 doctorates awarded. *Degree requirements:* For doctorate, thesis/dissertation, general exam. *Entrance requirements:* For master's, GRE General Test, minimum GPA of 3.0; for doctorate, GRE General Test, interview, minimum GPA of 3.0. Additional exam requirements/recommendations for international students: Required—TOEFL (minimum score 600 paper-based; 250 computer-based; 100 iBT). *Application deadline:*

For fall admission, 1/15 priority date for domestic and international students; for spring admission, 10/1 priority date for domestic students, 9/1 priority date for international students. Applications are processed on a rolling basis. Application fee: $60. Electronic applications accepted. *Financial support:* In 2009–10, 87 students received support; fellowships, research assistantships, teaching assistantships, institutionally sponsored loans available. Financial award application deadline: 1/15. *Unit head:* Dr. Kathyrn E. Newcomer, Director, 202-994-3959, Fax: 202-994-3959, E-mail: newcomer@gwu.edu. *Application contact:* Information Contact, 202-994-6295, Fax: 202-994-6295, E-mail: tspppa@gwu.edu.

The George Washington University, Columbian College of Arts and Sciences, Trachtenberg School of Public Policy and Public Administration, Interdisciplinary Programs in Public Policy, Program in Philosophy and Social Policy, Washington, DC 20052. Offers MA. *Students:* 13 full-time (7 women), 10 part-time (5 women); includes 3 minority (all African Americans), 2 international. Average age 26. 15 applicants, 87% accepted, 8 enrolled. In 2009, 5 master's awarded. *Degree requirements:* For master's, comprehensive exam, thesis or alternative. *Entrance requirements:* For master's, GRE General Test, interview, minimum GPA of 3.0. Additional exam requirements/recommendations for international students: Required—TOEFL (minimum score 600 paper-based; 250 computer-based; 100 iBT). *Application deadline:* For fall admission, 4/1 priority date for domestic and international students; for spring admission, 10/1 priority date for domestic students, 9/1 priority date for international students. Applications are processed on a rolling basis. Application fee: $60. Electronic applications accepted. *Financial support:* In 2009–10, 2 students received support; fellowships with tuition reimbursements available, Federal Work-Study and institutionally sponsored loans available. Financial award application deadline: 1/15. *Unit head:* Dr. William B. Griffith, Chair and Academic Director, 202-994-8684, E-mail: wbg@gwu.edu. *Application contact:* Information Contact, 202-994-6265, Fax: 202-994-8683, E-mail: philosop@gwu.edu.

Georgia State University, College of Arts and Sciences, Department of Philosophy, Atlanta, GA 30302-4089. Offers MA, MA/JD. Part-time programs available. *Degree requirements:* For master's, thesis. *Entrance requirements:* For master's, GRE General Test, sample of written work. Additional exam requirements/recommendations for international students: Required—TOEFL. Electronic applications accepted. *Faculty research:* Ethics, ancient philosophy, German philosophy, philosophy of mind/neurophilosophy.

Gonzaga University, College of Arts and Sciences, Program in Philosophy, Spokane, WA 99258. Offers MA. Part-time programs available. *Faculty:* 21 full-time (3 women). *Students:* 4 full-time (0 women), 7 part-time (4 women). Average age 29. 21 applicants, 62% accepted, 11 enrolled. In 2009, 4 master's awarded. *Degree requirements:* For master's, comprehensive exam. *Entrance requirements:* For master's, GRE General Test or MAT, minimum GPA of 3.0. Additional exam requirements/recommendations for international students: Required—TOEFL. *Application deadline:* For fall admission, 7/20 priority date for domestic students; for spring admission, 11/1 for domestic students. Applications are processed on a rolling basis. Application fee: $50. Tuition and fees vary according to course level, course load, degree level, campus/location and program. *Financial support:* Application deadline: 3/1. *Unit head:* Dr. Rosemary Volbrecht, Chairperson, 509-328-4220, E-mail: volbrecht@calvin.gonzaga.edu. *Application contact:* Dr. Theodore DiMaria, Director of Graduate Studies in Philosophy, 509-313-6762, E-mail: dimaria@gonzaga.edu.

Graduate School and University Center of the City University of New York, Graduate Studies, Program in Philosophy, New York, NY 10016-4039. Offers MA, PhD. *Faculty:* 30 full-time (8 women). *Students:* 127 full-time (37 women), 6 part-time (1 woman); includes 3 minority (1 African American, 1 Asian American or Pacific Islander, 1 Hispanic American), 31 international. Average age 34. 154 applicants, 18% accepted, 13 enrolled. In 2009, 1 master's, 10 doctorates awarded. Terminal master's awarded for partial completion of doctoral program. *Degree requirements:* For master's, thesis; for doctorate, one foreign language, comprehensive exam, thesis/dissertation. *Entrance requirements:* For master's, GRE General Test; for doctorate, GRE General Test, 3 letters of recommendation, writing sample. Additional exam requirements/recommendations for international students: Required—TOEFL. *Application deadline:* For fall admission, 1/15 for domestic students. Application fee: $125. Electronic applications accepted. *Financial support:* In 2009–10, 81 students received support, including 60 fellowships, 5 research assistantships, 9 teaching assistantships; career-related internships or fieldwork, Federal Work-Study, institutionally sponsored loans, and tuition waivers (full and partial) also available. Financial award application deadline: 2/1. *Unit head:* Dr. Iakovos Vasiliou, Executive Officer, 212-817-8616, Fax: 212-817-1530. *Application contact:* Les Gribben, Director of Admissions, 212-817-7470, Fax: 212-817-1624, E-mail: lgribben@gc.cuny.edu.

Harvard University, Graduate School of Arts and Sciences, Department of Philosophy, Cambridge, MA 02138. Offers classical philosophy (PhD); philosophy (PhD). *Degree requirements:* For doctorate, 2 foreign languages, thesis/dissertation, final exams. *Entrance requirements:* For doctorate, GRE General Test. Additional exam requirements/recommendations for international students: Required—TOEFL. *Expenses:* Tuition: Full-time $33,696. Required fees: $1126. Full-time tuition and fees vary according to program.

Harvard University, Graduate School of Arts and Sciences, Department of Sanskrit and Indian Studies, Cambridge, MA 02138. Offers Indian philosophy (AM, PhD); Pali (AM, PhD); Sanskrit (AM, PhD); Tibetan (AM, PhD); Urdu (AM, PhD). Terminal master's awarded for partial completion of doctoral program. *Degree requirements:* For master's, 3 foreign languages; for doctorate, 3 foreign languages, thesis/dissertation. *Entrance requirements:* For master's, GRE General Test; for doctorate, GRE General Test, proficiency in French and German. Additional exam requirements/recommendations for international students: Required—TOEFL. *Expenses:* Tuition: Full-time $33,696. Required fees: $1126. Full-time tuition and fees vary according to program.

Harvard University, Graduate School of Arts and Sciences, Department of the Classics, Cambridge, MA 02138. Offers Byzantine Greek (PhD); classical archaeology (PhD); classical philology (PhD); classical philosophy (PhD); medieval Latin (PhD). *Degree requirements:* For doctorate, 4 foreign languages, thesis/dissertation, preliminary and special exams. *Entrance requirements:* For doctorate, GRE General Test. Additional exam requirements/recommendations for international students: Required—TOEFL. *Expenses:* Tuition: Full-time $33,696. Required fees: $1126. Full-time tuition and fees vary according to program.

Howard University, Graduate School, Department of Philosophy, Washington, DC 20059-0002. Offers MA. Part-time programs available. *Degree requirements:* For master's, one foreign language, comprehensive exam, thesis. *Entrance requirements:* For master's, GRE General Test. Additional exam requirements/recommendations for international students: Required—TOEFL. *Faculty research:* African and African-American philosophy, social and political philosophy, ethics, philosophy of culture, applied philosophy.

Indiana University Bloomington, University Graduate School, College of Arts and Sciences, Department of Philosophy, Bloomington, IN 47405-7000. Offers MA, PhD. *Faculty:* 17 full-time (5 women). *Students:* 37 full-time (6 women); includes 3 minority (1 Asian American or Pacific Islander, 2 Hispanic Americans), 4 international. Average age 31. 131 applicants, 9% accepted, 4 enrolled. In 2009, 3 master's, 5 doctorates awarded. Terminal master's awarded for partial completion of doctoral program. *Degree requirements:* For master's, thesis; for doctorate, comprehensive exam, thesis/dissertation, qualifying paper. *Entrance requirements:* For master's and doctorate, GRE General Test, writing sample. Additional exam requirements/recommendations for international students: Required—TOEFL. *Application deadline:* For fall admission, 1/15 priority date for domestic students, 12/15 for international students; for spring admission, 9/1 priority date for domestic students, 9/1 for international students. Applications are processed on a rolling basis. Application fee: $55 ($65 for international students). Electronic applications accepted. *Financial support:* In 2009–10, 32 students received support, including 5 fellowships with partial tuition reimbursements available (averaging $16,000 per year), 27 teaching assistantships with partial tuition reimbursements available (averaging $15,000 per year); research assistantships. Financial award application deadline: 4/15. *Faculty research:* Algebraic logic, cognitive science, history of modern philosophy, ancient and Jewish philosophy, medieval logic and semantics, epistemology, ethics, history, philosophy of mind, philosophy of language. *Unit head:* Timothy W. O'Connor, Chair and Professor, 812-855-1093, Fax: 812-855-3777, E-mail: toconnor@indiana.edu. *Application contact:* Linda J. Harl, Department Secretary, 812-855-9503, Fax: 812-855-3777, E-mail: lharl@indiana.edu.

Indiana University–Purdue University Indianapolis, School of Liberal Arts, Department of Philosophy, Indianapolis, IN 46202-2896. Offers American philosophy (Certificate); bioethics (Certificate); philosophy (MA); JD/MA; MD/MA. Part-time programs available. *Faculty:* 13 full-time (2 women), 1 part-time/adjunct (0 women). *Students:* 3 full-time (0 women), 15 part-time (7 women); includes 1 minority (Hispanic American). Average age 32. 7 applicants, 14% accepted, 0 enrolled. *Degree requirements:* For master's, thesis optional. *Entrance requirements:* For master's, GRE. Additional exam requirements/recommendations for international students: Required—TOEFL. *Application deadline:* For fall admission, 3/1 priority date for domestic and international students; for spring admission, 11/15 for domestic and international students. Applications are processed on a rolling basis. Application fee: $55 ($65 for international students). Electronic applications accepted. *Financial support:* In 2009–10, 6 students received support, including 1 fellowship (averaging $1,000 per year), 4 teaching assistantships (averaging $4,330 per year); research assistantships with full tuition reimbursements available. Financial award application deadline: 1/15; financial award applicants required to submit FAFSA. *Faculty research:* American philosophy, Peirce bioethics, metaphysics, ethical theory. *Unit head:* Dr. John Tilley, Associate Professor and Chair, 317-274-4690, Fax: 317-278-4579, E-mail: jtilley@iupui.edu. *Application contact:* Dr. Jason Thomas Eberl, Assistant Professor and Graduate Co-Director, 317-278-9239, Fax: 317-278-4579, E-mail: jeberl@iupui.edu.

Institute for Christian Studies, Graduate Programs, Toronto, ON M5T 1R4, Canada. Offers education (M Phil F, PhD); history of philosophy (M Phil F, PhD); philosophical aesthetics (M Phil F, PhD); philosophy of religion (M Phil F, PhD); political theory (M Phil F, PhD); systematic philosophy (M Phil F, PhD); theology (M Phil F, PhD); worldview studies (MWS). Part-time programs available. Postbaccalaureate distance learning degree programs offered (minimal on-campus study). *Degree requirements:* For master's, one foreign language, thesis; for doctorate, 2 foreign languages, thesis/dissertation. *Entrance requirements:* For master's and doctorate, philosophy background. Additional exam requirements/recommendations for international students: Required—TOEFL (minimum score 600 paper-based; 250 computer-based). *Faculty research:* Human rights, anthropology of self, medieval discourse, gender and body, post-modern thought; biblical hermeneutics, creational aesthetics, ecumenism, epistemology, political theory and public policy, relational psychotherapy.

The Johns Hopkins University, Zanvyl Krieger School of Arts and Sciences, Department of Philosophy, Baltimore, MD 21218-2699. Offers MA, PhD. *Faculty:* 10 full-time (3 women). *Students:* 23 full-time (4 women); includes 2 minority (both Asian Americans or Pacific Islanders), 8 international. Average age 32. 96 applicants, 7% accepted, 4 enrolled. In 2009, 1 master's, 4 doctorates awarded. *Degree requirements:* For doctorate, thesis/dissertation. *Entrance requirements:* For master's and doctorate, GRE General Test. Additional exam requirements/recommendations for international students: Required—TOEFL. *Application deadline:* For fall admission, 1/15 for domestic students. Application fee: $65. Electronic applications accepted. *Financial support:* In 2009–10, 9 fellowships with partial tuition reimbursements (averaging $17,500 per year), 1 research assistantship with partial tuition reimbursement (averaging $12,000 per year), 15 teaching assistantships with tuition reimbursements (averaging $17,500 per year) were awarded; Federal Work-Study also available. Financial award application deadline: 1/15; financial award applicants required to submit FAFSA. *Faculty research:* Historical and analytical research on range of philosophical topics. Total annual research expenditures: $198,561. *Unit head:* Dr. Richard Bett, Acting Chair and Graduate Advisor, Professor, 410-516-6863, Fax: 410-516-6848, E-mail: rbett1@jhu.edu. *Application contact:* Alicia V. Burley, Academic Program Coordinator, 410-516-7524, Fax: 410-516-6848, E-mail: aburley1@jhu.edu.

Kent State University, College of Arts and Sciences, Department of Philosophy, Kent, OH 44242-0001. Offers MA. Part-time programs available. *Degree requirements:* For master's, thesis optional. *Entrance requirements:* For master's, GRE, minimum GPA of 3.0. Electronic applications accepted.

Louisiana State University and Agricultural and Mechanical College, Graduate School, College of Arts and Sciences, Department of Philosophy and Religious Studies, Baton Rouge, LA 70803. Offers philosophy (MA). Part-time programs available. *Faculty:* 18 full-time (4 women). *Students:* 11 full-time (2 women), 3 part-time (1 woman); includes 1 minority (Asian American or Pacific Islander). Average age 26. 14 applicants, 100% accepted, 9 enrolled. In 2009, 7 master's awarded. *Degree requirements:* For master's, one foreign language, thesis (for some programs). *Entrance requirements:* For master's, GRE General Test, minimum GPA of 3.0. Additional exam requirements/recommendations for international students: Required—TOEFL (minimum score 550 paper-based; 213 computer-based; 79 iBT) or IELTS (minimum score 6.5). *Application deadline:* For fall admission, 4/25 priority date for domestic students, 5/15 for international students; for spring admission, 10/15 for international students. Applications are processed on a rolling basis. Application fee: $50 ($70 for international students). Electronic applications accepted. *Financial support:* In 2009–10, 8 students received support, including 5 teaching assistantships with partial tuition reimbursements available (averaging $10,500 per year); fellowships, research assistantships with partial tuition reimbursements available, Federal Work-Study, institutionally sponsored loans, scholarships/grants, health care benefits, and unspecified assistantships also available. Support available to part-time students. Financial award applicants required to submit FAFSA. *Faculty research:* Analytic philosophy, continental philosophy, history of philosophy, philosophy and religion, existential value theory. Total annual research expenditures: $47,850. *Unit head:* Dr. Mary Sirridge, Chair, 225-578-2278, Fax: 225-578-4897, E-mail: pisirr@lsu.edu. *Application contact:* Dr. Greg Schufrieder, Professor, 225-578-2276, Fax: 225-578-4897, E-mail: gschufr@lsu.edu.

Loyola Marymount University, College of Liberal Arts, Department of Philosophy, Program in Philosophy, Los Angeles, CA 90045. Offers MA. *Faculty:* 19 full-time (4 women). *Students:* 23 full-time (6 women), 2 part-time (0 women); includes 5 minority (2 African Americans, 2 Asian Americans or Pacific Islanders, 1 Hispanic American), 1 international. Average age 27. 26 applicants, 73% accepted, 7 enrolled. In 2009, 4 master's awarded. *Degree requirements:* For master's, one foreign language, comprehensive exam. *Entrance requirements:* For master's, GRE General Test, writing sample (10-15 pages), 2 letters of recommendation. Additional exam requirements/recommendations for international students: Required—TOEFL (minimum score 600 paper-based; 250 computer-based; 100 iBT). *Application deadline:* For fall admission, 3/15 for domestic students; for spring admission, 11/1 for domestic students. Application fee: $50. *Financial support:* In 2009–10, 25 students received support, including 6 research assistantships (averaging $1,100 per year), 6 teaching assistantships (averaging $2,500 per year); unspecified assistantships also available. Financial award application deadline: 6/1; financial award applicants required to submit FAFSA. *Unit head:* Dr. Mark D. Morelli, Graduate Director, 310-338-7384, E-mail: mmorelli@lmu.edu. *Application contact:* Chake H. Kouyoumjian, Associate Dean of Graduate Studies, 310-338-2721, Fax: 310-338-6086, E-mail: ckouyoum@lmu.edu.

Loyola University Chicago, Graduate School, Department of Philosophy, Chicago, IL 60660. Offers MA, PhD. Part-time and evening/weekend programs available. *Faculty:* 26 full-time (7 women), 2 part-time/adjunct (0 women). *Students:* 89 full-time (20 women), 11 part-time (4 women); includes 11 minority (1 African American, 6 Asian Americans or Pacific Islanders, 4 Hispanic Americans), 11 international. Average age 33. 174 applicants, 15% accepted, 15 enrolled. In 2009, 16 master's, 11 doctorates awarded. Terminal master's awarded for partial completion of doctoral program. *Degree requirements:* For master's, comprehensive exam (for some programs), thesis (for some programs), oral exam; for doctorate, one foreign language, thesis/dissertation, oral exam. *Entrance requirements:* For master's and doctorate, GRE General Test. Additional exam requirements/recommendations for international students: Required—TOEFL. *Application deadline:* For fall admission, 1/15 priority date for domestic and inter-

Philosophy

Loyola University Chicago (continued)
national students. Application fee: $50. Electronic applications accepted. *Expenses:* Tuition: Full-time $14,220; part-time $790 per credit hour. Required fees: $60 per semester hour. Tuition and fees vary according to program. *Financial support:* In 2009–10, 21 students received support, including 4 fellowships with full tuition reimbursements available (averaging $20,000 per year), 4 research assistantships with full tuition reimbursements available (averaging $18,000 per year), 13 teaching assistantships with full tuition reimbursements available (averaging $18,000 per year); institutionally sponsored loans and health care benefits also available. Financial award application deadline: 1/15; financial award applicants required to submit FAFSA. *Faculty research:* Social philosophy, ethics, medical ethics, analytic philosophy, contemporary Continental philosophy. *Unit head:* Dr. Paul Moser, Chair, 773-508-8481, Fax: 773-508-3292, E-mail: acutrof@luc.edu. *Application contact:* Dr. Andrew Cutrofello, Graduate Program Director, 773-508-8481, Fax: 773-508-2292, E-mail: acutrof@luc.edu.

Marquette University, Graduate School, College of Arts and Sciences, Department of Philosophy, Milwaukee, WI 53201-1881. Offers ancient philosophy (MA, PhD); British empiricism and analytic philosophy (MA, PhD); Christian philosophy (MA, PhD); early modern European philosophy (MA, PhD); ethics (MA, PhD); German philosophy (MA, PhD); medieval philosophy (MA, PhD); phenomenology and existentialism (MA, PhD); philosophy of religion (MA, PhD); social and applied philosophy (MA). Part-time programs available. *Faculty:* 25 full-time (5 women), 17 part-time/adjunct (3 women). *Students:* 53 full-time (12 women), 14 part-time (1 woman); includes 5 minority (1 African American, 2 Asian Americans or Pacific Islanders, 2 Hispanic Americans), 6 international. Average age 31. 120 applicants, 66% accepted, 19 enrolled. In 2009, 10 master's, 2 doctorates awarded. Terminal master's awarded for partial completion of doctoral program. *Degree requirements:* For master's, one foreign language, comprehensive exam, thesis; for doctorate, 2 foreign languages, thesis/dissertation, qualifying exams. *Entrance requirements:* For master's and doctorate, GRE General Test. Additional exam requirements/recommendations for international students: Required—TOEFL. Application fee: $40. *Financial support:* In 2009–10, 10 research assistantships, 12 teaching assistantships were awarded; Federal Work-Study, institutionally sponsored loans, scholarships/grants, and tuition waivers (full and partial) also available. Support available to part-time students. Financial award application deadline: 2/15. *Faculty research:* Aristotle, Augustine, Descartes, Hegel, Heidegger. *Unit head:* Dr. John Jones, Chair, 414-288-6857, Fax: 414-288-1578. *Application contact:* Dr. Owen Goldin, Director of Graduate Studies, 414-288-5949, Fax: 414-288-1578.

Massachusetts Institute of Technology, School of Humanities, Arts, and Social Sciences, Department of Linguistics and Philosophy, Philosophy Section, Cambridge, MA 02139-4307. Offers PhD. *Faculty:* 13 full-time (3 women). *Students:* 30 full-time (12 women), 11 international. Average age 27. 231 applicants, 3% accepted, 3 enrolled. In 2009, 5 doctorates awarded. *Degree requirements:* For doctorate, comprehensive exam, thesis/dissertation. *Entrance requirements:* Additional exam requirements/recommendations for international students: Required—TOEFL (minimum score 577 paper-based; 233 computer-based; 90 iBT), IELTS (minimum score 6.5). *Application deadline:* For fall admission, 1/2 for domestic and international students. Application fee: $75. Electronic applications accepted. *Expenses:* Tuition: Full-time $37,510; part-time $585 per unit. Required fees: $272. *Financial support:* In 2009–10, 12 fellowships with tuition reimbursements (averaging $33,112 per year), 3 research assistantships with tuition reimbursements (averaging $30,403 per year), 10 teaching assistantships with tuition reimbursements (averaging $31,099 per year) were awarded; Federal Work-Study, institutionally sponsored loans, scholarships/grants, health care benefits, and unspecified assistantships also available. *Faculty research:* Metaphysics, philosophy of mind, philosophy of language, ethics, feminist philosophy. *Unit head:* Prof. Richard Holton, Chair, 617-253-4141. *Application contact:* Graduate Admissions, 617-253-4141, Fax: 617-253-5017, E-mail: lp-admissions@mit.edu.

McGill University, Faculty of Graduate and Postdoctoral Studies, Faculty of Arts, Department of Philosophy, Montréal, QC H3A 2T5, Canada. Offers bioethics (MA); philosophy (PhD).

McMaster University, School of Graduate Studies, Faculty of Humanities, Department of Philosophy, Hamilton, ON L8S 4M2, Canada. Offers MA, PhD. Part-time programs available. *Degree requirements:* For master's, thesis; for doctorate, one foreign language, thesis/dissertation. *Entrance requirements:* For master's, honors degree in philosophy; minimum average B+; for doctorate, master's degree in philosophy. Additional exam requirements/recommendations for international students: Required—TOEFL (minimum score 580 paper-based; 237 computer-based). *Faculty research:* Twentieth-century European philosophy, twentieth-century Anglo-American philosophy, political philosophy, ethics, argumentation.

Memorial University of Newfoundland, School of Graduate Studies, Department of Philosophy, St. John's, NL A1C 5S7, Canada. Offers MA. Part-time programs available. *Degree requirements:* For master's, thesis. *Entrance requirements:* For master's, first-class undergraduate degree in philosophy. Electronic applications accepted. *Faculty research:* History of philosophy, philosophy of science, phenomenology and existentialism, contemporary metaphysics.

Miami University, Graduate School, College of Arts and Sciences, Department of Philosophy, Oxford, OH 45056. Offers MA. *Students:* 8 full-time (5 women). *Entrance requirements:* For master's, minimum undergraduate GPA of 3.0 during previous 2 years or 2.75 overall. Additional exam requirements/recommendations for international students: Required—TOEFL. *Application deadline:* For fall admission, 2/15 for domestic and international students. Application fee: $50. Electronic applications accepted. *Expenses:* Tuition, state resident: full-time $11,280. Tuition, nonresident: full-time $24,912. Required fees: $516. *Financial support:* Fellowships with full tuition reimbursements, research assistantships, teaching assistantships, Federal Work-Study, institutionally sponsored loans, health care benefits, tuition waivers (full), and unspecified assistantships available. Financial award application deadline: 3/1; financial award applicants required to submit FAFSA. *Unit head:* Dr. William McKenna, Chair, 513-529-2440, Fax: 513-529-4731, E-mail: mckennwr@muohio.edu. *Application contact:* Dr. Elaine Miller, Director of the Graduate Program, 513-529-2440, Fax: 513-529-4731, E-mail: millerep@muohio.edu.

Michigan State University, The Graduate School, College of Arts and Letters, Department of Philosophy, East Lansing, MI 48824. Offers MA, PhD. *Faculty:* 16 full-time (5 women). *Students:* 38 full-time (16 women), 6 part-time (3 women); includes 7 minority (3 African Americans, 1 American Indian/Alaska Native, 1 Asian American or Pacific Islander, 2 Hispanic Americans), 6 international. Average age 33. 45 applicants, 27% accepted. In 2009, 2 master's, 3 doctorates awarded. *Entrance requirements:* Additional exam requirements/recommendations for international students: Required—TOEFL. Electronic applications accepted. *Expenses:* Tuition, state resident: part-time $478.25 per credit hour. Tuition, nonresident: part-time $966.50 per credit hour. Part-time tuition and fees vary according to program. *Financial support:* In 2009–10, 3 research assistantships with tuition reimbursements (averaging $6,152 per year), 21 teaching assistantships with tuition reimbursements (averaging $6,323 per year) were awarded. Total annual research expenditures: $8,355. *Unit head:* Dr. Richard T. Peterson, Chairperson, 517-355-4490, Fax: 517-432-1320, E-mail: petrsnrt@msu.edu. *Application contact:* Jill Perez, Graduate Secretary, 517-355-4490, Fax: 517-432-1320, E-mail: perezji@msu.edu.

Montclair State University, The Graduate School, College of Education and Human Services, Center of Pedagogy, Montclair, NJ 07043-1624. Offers pedagogy and philosophy (Ed D). Part-time programs available. *Students:* 8 full-time (5 women), 16 part-time (7 women). Average age 37. 5 applicants, 40% accepted, 2 enrolled. In 2009, 2 doctorates awarded. *Degree requirements:* For doctorate, thesis/dissertation. *Entrance requirements:* For doctorate, GRE, 3 letters of recommendation. Additional exam requirements/recommendations for international students: Required—TOEFL, or IELTS. *Application deadline:* For fall admission, 2/1 for domestic students, 11/15 for international students. Application fee: $60. Electronic applications accepted. *Expenses:* Tuition, area resident: Part-time $486.74 per credit. Tuition, state resident: part-time $486.74 per credit. Tuition, nonresident: part-time $751.34 per credit. Tuition and fees vary according to degree level and program. *Financial support:* In 2009–10, 4 teaching assistantships (averaging $10,000 per year) were awarded; Federal Work-Study, institutionally sponsored loans, scholarships/grants, and unspecified assistantships also available. Support available to part-time students. Financial award application deadline: 3/1; financial award applicants required to submit FAFSA. *Unit head:* Jennifer Robinson, Director, 973-655-4262. *Application contact:* Amy Aiello, Director of Graduate Admissions and Operations, 973-655-5147, Fax: 973-655-7869, E-mail: graduate.school@montclair.edu.

Montclair State University, The Graduate School, College of Education and Human Services, Department of Educational Foundations, Montclair, NJ 07043-1624. Offers critical thinking (M Ed); philosophy for children (M Ed). Part-time and evening/weekend programs available. *Faculty:* 11 full-time (5 women), 21 part-time/adjunct (10 women). *Students:* 5 part-time (all women). Average age 38. 2 applicants, 100% accepted, 2 enrolled. *Degree requirements:* For master's, comprehensive exam, field experience. *Entrance requirements:* For master's, GRE or MAT, 2 letters of recommendation, teaching certificate. Additional exam requirements/recommendations for international students: Required—TOEFL (minimum score 83 computer-based), or IELTS. *Application deadline:* For fall admission, 2/1 for domestic students, 2/15 for international students; for spring admission, 10/15 for domestic and international students. Applications are processed on a rolling basis. Application fee: $60. Electronic applications accepted. *Expenses:* Tuition, area resident: Part-time $486.74 per credit. Tuition, state resident: part-time $486.74 per credit. Tuition, nonresident: part-time $751.34 per credit. Tuition and fees vary according to degree level and program. *Financial support:* In 2009–10, 5 research assistantships with full tuition reimbursements (averaging $7,000 per year) were awarded; Federal Work-Study and scholarships/grants also available. Support available to part-time students. Financial award application deadline: 3/1; financial award applicants required to submit FAFSA. *Unit head:* Dr. Jeremy Price, Chairperson, 973-655-7039. *Application contact:* Amy Aiello, Director of Graduate Admissions and Operations, 973-655-5147, Fax: 973-655-7869, E-mail: graduate.school@montclair.edu.

The New School: A University, The New School for Social Research, Department of Philosophy, New York, NY 10003. Offers MA, DS Sc, PhD. Part-time and evening/weekend programs available. *Faculty:* 11 full-time (4 women). *Students:* 150 full-time (45 women), 40 part-time (10 women); includes 14 minority (4 Asian Americans or Pacific Islanders, 10 Hispanic Americans), 45 international. Average age 31. 201 applicants, 61% accepted, 35 enrolled. In 2009, 17 master's, 12 doctorates awarded. Terminal master's awarded for partial completion of doctoral program. *Degree requirements:* For master's, one foreign language, exam or thesis; for doctorate, 2 foreign languages, comprehensive exam, thesis/dissertation, qualifying exam. *Entrance requirements:* For master's, GRE General Test; for doctorate, GRE General Test, MA. Additional exam requirements/recommendations for international students: Required—TOEFL (minimum score 600 paper-based; 250 computer-based; 100 iBT). *Application deadline:* For fall admission, 1/17 priority date for domestic and international students; for spring admission, 10/15 priority date for domestic and international students. Applications are processed on a rolling basis. Application fee: $50. Electronic applications accepted. *Financial support:* Fellowships, research assistantships, teaching assistantships, Federal Work-Study, scholarships/grants, tuition waivers (full and partial), and unspecified assistantships available. Support available to part-time students. Financial award application deadline: 3/1; financial award applicants required to submit FAFSA. *Faculty research:* Continental philosophy, history of philosophy, political philosophy, aesthetics, pragmatism. *Unit head:* Dr. Simon Critchley, Chair, 212-229-5707 Ext. 3075, E-mail: critchls@newschool.edu. *Application contact:* Robert MacDonald, Director of Admissions, 212-229-5710 Ext. 3007, Fax: 212-989-7102, E-mail: macdonar@newschool.edu.

New York University, Graduate School of Arts and Science, Department of Philosophy, New York, NY 10012-1019. Offers MA, PhD, JD/MA, JD/PhD, MD/MA. Part-time programs available. *Faculty:* 16 full-time (1 woman). *Students:* 40 full-time (9 women), 6 part-time (0 women); includes 2 minority (both Asian Americans or Pacific Islanders), 15 international. Average age 28. 324 applicants, 3% accepted, 6 enrolled. In 2009, 3 master's, 7 doctorates awarded. *Degree requirements:* For master's, thesis or alternative; for doctorate, one foreign language, thesis/dissertation. *Entrance requirements:* For master's and doctorate, GRE General Test, sample of written work. Additional exam requirements/recommendations for international students: Required—TOEFL. *Application deadline:* For fall admission, 1/4 for domestic students. Application fee: $90. *Expenses:* Tuition: Full-time $30,528; part-time $1272 per credit. Required fees: $2177. *Financial support:* Fellowships with tuition reimbursements, teaching assistantships with tuition reimbursements, Federal Work-Study, institutionally sponsored loans, scholarships/grants, health care benefits, and unspecified assistantships available. Financial award application deadline: 1/4; financial award applicants required to submit FAFSA. *Faculty research:* Philosophy of mind and language, metaphysics, ethics and political philosophy. *Unit head:* Stephen Schiffer, Chair, 212-998-8320, Fax: 212-995-4179, E-mail: philosophy@nyu.edu. *Application contact:* Sharon Street, Director of Graduate Studies, 212-998-8320, Fax: 212-995-4179, E-mail: philosophy@nyu.edu.

Northern Illinois University, Graduate School, College of Liberal Arts and Sciences, Department of Philosophy, De Kalb, IL 60115-2854. Offers MA. Part-time programs available. *Faculty:* 12 full-time (2 women), 1 part-time/adjunct (0 women). *Students:* 22 full-time (3 women), 8 part-time (1 woman); includes 4 minority (2 African Americans, 1 Asian American or Pacific Islander, 1 Hispanic American), 2 international. Average age 26. 125 applicants, 30% accepted, 14 enrolled. In 2009, 16 master's awarded. *Degree requirements:* For master's, comprehensive exam, thesis optional. *Entrance requirements:* For master's, GRE General Test, minimum GPA of 2.75, writing sample, major or minor in philosophy. Additional exam requirements/recommendations for international students: Required—TOEFL (minimum score 550 paper-based; 213 computer-based). *Application deadline:* For fall admission, 3/1 priority date for domestic students, 5/1 for international students; for spring admission, 11/1 for domestic students, 10/1 for international students. Applications are processed on a rolling basis. Application fee: $30. Electronic applications accepted. *Expenses:* Tuition, state resident: full-time $6576; part-time $274 per credit hour. Tuition, nonresident: full-time $13,152; part-time $548 per credit hour. Required fees: $1813; $75.53 per credit hour. Part-time tuition and fees vary according to course load. *Financial support:* In 2009–10, 14 teaching assistantships with full tuition reimbursements were awarded; fellowships with full tuition reimbursements, research assistantships with full tuition reimbursements, Federal Work-Study, scholarships/grants, tuition waivers (full), and unspecified assistantships also available. Support available to part-time students. Financial award applicants required to submit FAFSA. *Faculty research:* Epistemology, philosophy of biology, animal rights, philosophy of war, international ethics. *Unit head:* Dr. David J. Buller, Chair, 815-753-6299, Fax: 815-753-6302, E-mail: buller@niu.edu. *Application contact:* Dr. David Buller, Graduate Director, 815-753-6411, E-mail: askPhilosophy@niu.edu.

Northwestern University, The Graduate School, Judd A. and Marjorie Weinberg College of Arts and Sciences, Department of Philosophy, Evanston, IL 60208. Offers PhD. Admissions and degrees offered through The Graduate School. *Degree requirements:* For doctorate, 2 foreign languages, thesis/dissertation. *Entrance requirements:* For doctorate, GRE General Test, sample of written work. Additional exam requirements/recommendations for international students: Required—TOEFL. Electronic applications accepted. *Faculty research:* Phenomenology, philosophy of science, history of philosophy, ethics, social and political philosophy, epistemology.

The Ohio State University, Graduate School, College of Humanities, Department of Philosophy, Columbus, OH 43210. Offers MA, PhD. *Faculty:* 26. *Students:* 13 full-time (3 women), 24 part-time (5 women); includes 1 minority (Asian American or Pacific Islander), 5 international. Average age 29. In 2009, 5 master's, 2 doctorates awarded. *Degree requirements:* For master's, thesis optional; for doctorate, thesis/dissertation. *Entrance requirements:* For master's and doctorate, GRE General Test. Additional exam requirements/recommendations for international students: Required—TOEFL (minimum score 600 paper-based; 250 computer-based). *Application deadline:* For fall admission, 8/15 priority date for domestic students, 7/1 priority date for international students; for winter admission, 12/1 priority date for domestic students, 11/1 priority date for international students; for spring admission, 3/1 priority date for domestic students, 2/1 priority date for international students. Applications are processed on a rolling basis. Application fee: $40 ($50 for international students). Electronic applications accepted. *Expenses:* Tuition, state resident: full-time $10,683. Tuition, nonresident: full-time $25,923. Tuition and fees vary according to course load and program. *Financial support:* Fellowships, research assistantships, teaching assistantships, Federal Work-Study, institutionally sponsored loans, and unspecified assistantships available. Support available to part-time students. *Unit head:* Ben Caplan, Graduate Studies Committee Chair, 614-292-7914, Fax: 614-292-7502, E-mail: caplan.16@osu.edu. *Application contact:* 614-292-9444, Fax: 614-292-3895, E-mail: domestic.grad@osu.edu.

Ohio University, Graduate College, College of Arts and Sciences, Department of Philosophy, Athens, OH 45701-2979. Offers MA. Part-time programs available. *Faculty:* 8 full-time (2 women), 2 part-time/adjunct (1 woman). *Students:* 9 full-time (2 women), 3 part-time (1 woman). Average age 27. 18 applicants, 44% accepted, 4 enrolled. In 2009, 4 master's awarded. *Degree requirements:* For master's, thesis. *Entrance requirements:* For master's, 28 hours in philosophy including logic, ancient and modern; minimum GPA of 3.0, writing sample of philosophical writing. Additional exam requirements/recommendations for international students: Required—TOEFL (minimum score 550 paper-based; 80 iBT) or IELTS Academic (minimum score 6.5). *Application deadline:* For fall admission, 3/1 priority date for domestic and international students; for winter admission, 4/1 for domestic and international students; for spring admission, 9/1 for domestic and international students. Applications are processed on a rolling basis. Application fee: $50 ($55 for international students). Electronic applications accepted. *Expenses:* Tuition, state resident: full-time $7839; part-time $323 per quarter hour. Tuition, nonresident: full-time $15,831; part-time $654 per quarter hour. Required fees: $2931. *Financial support:* Teaching assistantships with tuition reimbursements, Federal Work-Study, institutionally sponsored loans, tuition waivers (partial), and unspecified assistantships available. Financial award application deadline: 3/1. *Faculty research:* Ethics, phenomenology, applied ethics, Aristotle, Kant, epistemology. *Unit head:* Dr. Arthur Zucker, Chair, 740-593-4588, E-mail: philosophy.department@ohio.edu. *Application contact:* Dr. John W. Bender, Graduate Chair, 740-593-4599, Fax: 740-593-4597, E-mail: bender@ohio.edu.

Oklahoma City University, Petree College of Arts and Sciences, Program in Liberal Arts, Oklahoma City, OK 73106-1402. Offers art (MLA); general studies (MLA); leadership/management (MLA); literature (MLA); mass communications (MLA); philosophy (MLA); writing (MLA). Part-time and evening/weekend programs available. *Faculty:* 23 full-time (6 women), 5 part-time/adjunct (3 women). *Students:* 50 full-time (24 women), 23 part-time (14 women); includes 6 minority (4 African Americans, 1 Asian American or Pacific Islander, 1 Hispanic American), 50 international. Average age 31. 31 applicants, 94% accepted, 15 enrolled. In 2009, 21 master's awarded. *Degree requirements:* For master's, comprehensive exam, thesis optional. *Entrance requirements:* Additional exam requirements/recommendations for international students: Required—TOEFL (minimum score 550 paper-based). *Application deadline:* For fall admission, 8/20 for domestic students; for spring admission, 1/6 for domestic students. Applications are processed on a rolling basis. Application fee: $50 ($70 for international students). *Expenses:* Tuition: Full-time $15,930; part-time $885 per hour. *Financial support:* Fellowships with partial tuition reimbursements, career-related internships or fieldwork, Federal Work-Study, and tuition waivers (partial) available. Support available to part-time students. Financial award application deadline: 8/1; financial award applicants required to submit FAFSA. *Unit head:* Dr. Regina Bennett, Director, 405-208-5207, Fax: 405-208-5451, E-mail: rbennett@okcu.edu. *Application contact:* Michelle Lockhart, Director, Admissions, 800-633-7242, Fax: 405-208-5916, E-mail: gadmissions@okcu.edu.

Oklahoma State University, College of Arts and Sciences, Department of Philosophy, Stillwater, OK 74078. Offers MA. *Faculty:* 15 full-time (7 women), 2 part-time/adjunct (0 women). *Students:* 8 full-time (0 women), 5 part-time (1 woman); includes 2 minority (1 African American, 1 American Indian/Alaska Native), 1 international. Average age 28. 16 applicants, 69% accepted, 8 enrolled. In 2009, 6 master's awarded. *Degree requirements:* For master's, comprehensive exam, thesis. *Entrance requirements:* For master's, GRE, 2 letters of recommendation. Additional exam requirements/recommendations for international students: Required—TOEFL (minimum score 550 paper-based; 79 iBT). *Application deadline:* For fall admission, 3/1 priority date for international students; for spring admission, 8/1 priority date for international students. Applications are processed on a rolling basis. Application fee: $40 ($75 for international students). Electronic applications accepted. *Expenses:* Tuition, state resident: full-time $3716; part-time $154.85 per credit hour. Tuition, nonresident: full-time $14,448; part-time $602 per credit hour. Required fees: $1772; $73.85 per credit hour. One-time fee: $50. Tuition and fees vary according to course load and campus/location. *Financial support:* In 2009–10, 9 teaching assistantships (averaging $12,347 per year) were awarded; career-related internships or fieldwork, Federal Work-Study, scholarships/grants, health care benefits, tuition waivers (partial), and unspecified assistantships also available. Support available to part-time students. Financial award application deadline: 3/1; financial award applicants required to submit FAFSA. *Faculty research:* Theoretical and applied ethics, history and philosophy of science, east/west comparative philosophy, social/political/legal philosophy, truth and theory of knowledge. *Unit head:* Dr. Doren Recker, Head, 405-744-0487, Fax: 405-744-4635. *Application contact:* Dr. Gordon Emslie, Dean, 405-744-6368, Fax: 405-744-0355, E-mail: grad-i@okstate.edu.

Penn State University Park, Graduate School, College of the Liberal Arts, Department of Philosophy, State College, University Park, PA 16802-1503. Offers MA, PhD. *Unit head:* Dr. Shannon W. Sullivan, Head, 814-865-1618, Fax: 814-865-0119, E-mail: sws10@psu.edu. *Application contact:* Dr. Shannon W. Sullivan, Head, 814-865-1618, Fax: 814-865-0119, E-mail: sws10@psu.edu.

Princeton University, Graduate School, Department of Classics, Princeton, NJ 08544-1019. Offers classical and hellenic studies (PhD); classical philosophy (PhD); history (the ancient world) (PhD); literature and philology (PhD). *Degree requirements:* For doctorate, thesis/dissertation. *Entrance requirements:* For doctorate, GRE General Test, sample of written work. Additional exam requirements/recommendations for international students: Required—TOEFL (minimum score 600 paper-based; 250 computer-based). Electronic applications accepted.

Princeton University, Graduate School, Department of Philosophy, Princeton, NJ 08544-1019. Offers classical philosophy (PhD); philosophy (PhD); philosophy of science (PhD). *Degree requirements:* For doctorate, variable foreign language requirement, thesis/dissertation. *Entrance requirements:* For doctorate, GRE General Test, sample of written work. Additional exam requirements/recommendations for international students: Required—TOEFL (minimum score 600 paper-based; 250 computer-based). Electronic applications accepted.

Princeton University, Graduate School, Department of Politics, Princeton, NJ 08544-1019. Offers political philosophy (PhD); politics (PhD). *Degree requirements:* For doctorate, comprehensive exam, thesis/dissertation, teaching experience. *Entrance requirements:* For doctorate, GRE General Test, sample of written work, letters of recommendation. Additional exam requirements/recommendations for international students: Required—TOEFL (minimum score 600 paper-based; 250 computer-based). Electronic applications accepted. *Faculty research:* American politics, comparative politics, formal and quantitative methods, international relations, public law, political theory.

Purdue University, Graduate School, College of Liberal Arts, Department of Philosophy, West Lafayette, IN 47907. Offers MA, PhD. Part-time programs available. Terminal master's awarded for partial completion of doctoral program. *Degree requirements:* For master's, thesis optional; for doctorate, one foreign language, thesis/dissertation. *Entrance requirements:* For master's and doctorate, GRE General Test. Additional exam requirements/recommendations for international students: Required—TOEFL. Electronic applications accepted. *Faculty research:* Continental philosophy, ethics and social philosophy, analytic philosophy, history of philosophy, logic.

Queen's University at Kingston, School of Graduate Studies and Research, Faculty of Arts and Sciences, Department of Philosophy, Kingston, ON K7L 3N6, Canada. Offers MA, PhD. Part-time programs available. *Degree requirements:* For master's, thesis; for doctorate, comprehensive exam, thesis/dissertation. *Entrance requirements:* Additional exam requirements/recommendations for international students: Required—TOEFL. Electronic applications accepted. *Faculty research:* Ethics, social and political philosophy, philosophy of language, epistemology, metaphysics.

Regis College, Graduate and Professional Programs, Toronto, ON M4Y 2R5, Canada. Offers eastern Christian studies (Certificate); Ignatian studies (Diploma); Lonergan studies (Diploma); ministry (D Min); ministry and spirituality (MAMS); philosophical studies (Diploma); retreat direction (Certificate); sacred theology (STB, STM, STD, STL); spiritual direction (Diploma); spiritual theology (Diploma); theological studies (MTS, Diploma); theology (M Div, MA, Th M, PhD, Th D); M Div/MA. *Accreditation:* ATS (one or more programs are accredited). *Faculty:* 13 full-time (3 women), 6 part-time/adjunct (1 woman). *Students:* 86 full-time (28 women), 130 part-time (80 women); includes 39 minority (9 African Americans, 1 American Indian/Alaska Native, 27 Asian Americans or Pacific Islanders, 2 Hispanic Americans), 51 international. Average age 46. 116 applicants, 83% accepted, 67 enrolled. In 2009, 13 first professional degrees, 12 master's, 3 doctorates, 40 other advanced degrees awarded. Terminal master's awarded for partial completion of doctoral program. *Degree requirements:* For master's, 2 foreign languages, thesis; for doctorate, 3 foreign languages, comprehensive exam, thesis/dissertation; for first professional degree, comprehensive exam. *Entrance requirements:* For first professional degree and other advanced degree, minimum GPA of 3.0; for master's, minimum GPA of 3.3; for doctorate, minimum GPA of 3.7. Additional exam requirements/recommendations for international students: Required—TOEFL (minimum score 580 paper-based; 237 computer-based; 93 iBT), TWE (minimum score 5). *Application deadline:* For fall admission, 3/15 priority date for domestic and international students; for winter admission, 12/1 for domestic and international students; for spring admission, 3/15 for domestic and international students. Applications are processed on a rolling basis. Application fee: $25. *Financial support:* In 2009–10, 61 students received support. Career-related internships or fieldwork and scholarships/grants available. Support available to part-time students. Financial award application deadline: 3/15. *Unit head:* Dr. Gordon Rixon, Dean, 416-922-5474 Ext. 225, Fax: 416-922-2898, E-mail: gordon.rixon@utoronto.ca. *Application contact:* Elaine Chu, Registrar, 416-922-5474 Ext. 226, Fax: 416-922-2898, E-mail: regis.registrar@utoronto.ca.

Rice University, Graduate Programs, School of Humanities, Department of Philosophy, Houston, TX 77251-1892. Offers MA, PhD. *Faculty:* 11 full-time (2 women), 1 part-time/adjunct (0 women). *Students:* 29 full-time (7 women); includes 3 minority (2 Asian Americans or Pacific Islanders, 1 Hispanic American), 4 international. Average age 24. 78 applicants, 17% accepted, 5 enrolled. In 2009, 4 master's, 5 doctorates awarded. Terminal master's awarded for partial completion of doctoral program. *Degree requirements:* For master's, one foreign language; for doctorate, one foreign language, comprehensive exam, thesis/dissertation. *Entrance requirements:* For master's and doctorate, GRE General Test, minimum GPA of 3.0. Additional exam requirements/recommendations for international students: Required—TOEFL (minimum score 600 paper-based; 250 computer-based; 90 iBT). *Application deadline:* For fall admission, 2/1 priority date for domestic and international students. Applications are processed on a rolling basis. Application fee: $35. Electronic applications accepted. *Financial support:* In 2009–10, 27 students received support, including 24 fellowships (averaging $15,900 per year), 3 teaching assistantships (averaging $5,000 per year); Federal Work-Study and tuition waivers (full and partial) also available. Financial award applicants required to submit FAFSA. *Faculty research:* Metaphysics, philosophy of law, philosophy of science, medical ethics, philosophy of language. *Unit head:* Steven G. Crowell, Chairman, 713-348-2719, Fax: 713-348-5847, E-mail: crowell@rice.edu. *Application contact:* Minranda Robinson-Davis, Department Coordinator, 713-348-4994, Fax: 713-348-5847, E-mail: mrd@rice.edu.

Rutgers, The State University of New Jersey, New Brunswick, Graduate School-New Brunswick, Program in Philosophy, Piscataway, NJ 08854-8097. Offers PhD. *Degree requirements:* For doctorate, comprehensive exam, thesis/dissertation. *Entrance requirements:* For doctorate, GRE General Test, writing sample. Electronic applications accepted. *Faculty research:* Philosophy of mind, epistemology, philosophy of language, philosophy of science, metaphysics.

St. John's University, St. John's College of Liberal Arts and Sciences, Department of Philosophy, Queens, NY 11439. Offers MA. Part-time and evening/weekend programs available. *Entrance requirements:* Additional exam requirements/recommendations for international students: Required—TOEFL (minimum score 500 paper-based; 173 computer-based; 61 iBT), IELTS (minimum score 5.5). *Application deadline:* For fall admission, 5/1 priority date for domestic and international students; for spring admission, 11/1 priority date for domestic and international students. *Expenses:* Tuition: Full-time $16,290; part-time $905 per credit. Required fees: $300; $150 per semester. Tuition and fees vary according to program. *Financial support:* Career-related internships or fieldwork and scholarships/grants available. Support available to part-time students. *Unit head:* Dr. Paul Gaffney, Chair, 718-990-5256, E-mail: gaffneyp@stjohns.edu. *Application contact:* Kathleen Davis, Director of Graduate Admission, 718-990-2790, Fax: 718-990-5686, E-mail: gradhelp@stjohns.edu.

Saint Louis University, Graduate School, College of Arts and Sciences and Graduate School, Department of Philosophy, St. Louis, MO 63103-2097. Offers MA, MA-R, PhD. Part-time programs available. *Degree requirements:* For master's, one foreign language, thesis, comprehensive oral and written exams; for doctorate, 2 foreign languages, thesis/dissertation, preliminary exams, comprehensive oral and written exams. *Entrance requirements:* For master's, GRE General Test, letters of recommendation, resume, writing sample, interview; for doctorate, GRE General Test, letters of recommendation, resumé, writing sample, interview, goal statement, transcripts. Additional exam requirements/recommendations for international students: Required—TOEFL (minimum score 550 paper-based; 213 computer-based). Electronic applications accepted. *Faculty research:* Medieval philosophy, philosophy of religion, political philosophy, ethics, epistemology.

Saint Mary's University, Faculty of Arts, Department of Philosophy, Halifax, NS B3H 3C3, Canada. Offers MA. *Faculty:* 6. *Degree requirements:* For master's, thesis. *Entrance requirements:* For master's, 3 letters of recommendation, 2 samples of written work. Additional exam requirements/recommendations for international students: Required—TOEFL. *Application deadline:* For fall admission, 3/15 for domestic students. Applications are processed on a rolling basis. Application fee: $35. *Financial support:* Fellowships, teaching assistantships available. *Faculty research:* History of philosophy, analytic philosophy, ethics, social philosophy, logic. *Unit head:* Dr. John E. MacKinnon, Chairperson, 902-420-5820, E-mail: john.mackinnon@smu.ca. *Application contact:* Dr. Chris MacDonald, Graduate Coordinator, 902-420-5820, E-mail: chris.macdonald@smu.ca.

San Diego State University, Graduate and Research Affairs, College of Arts and Letters, Department of Philosophy, San Diego, CA 92182. Offers MA. Part-time programs available. *Entrance requirements:* For master's, GRE General Test. Additional exam requirements/recommendations for international students: Required—TOEFL. Electronic applications accepted. *Faculty research:* Ancient philosophy, modern philosophy, philosophy of technology, logic, philosophy of mind.

San Francisco State University, Division of Graduate Studies, College of Humanities, Department of Philosophy, San Francisco, CA 94132-1722. Offers philosophy (MA); teaching critical thinking (Certificate). Part-time programs available.

San Jose State University, Graduate Studies and Research, College of Humanities and the Arts, Department of Philosophy, San Jose, CA 95192-0001. Offers MA. *Students:* 11 full-time (3 women), 19 part-time (5 women); includes 10 minority (7 Asian Americans or Pacific Islanders, 3 Hispanic Americans), 1 international. Average age 33. 31 applicants, 35% accepted, 6 enrolled. In 2009, 18 master's awarded. *Degree requirements:* For master's, one foreign language, thesis or alternative. *Application deadline:* For fall admission, 6/29 for domestic students; for spring admission, 11/30 for domestic students. Applications are processed on a

Philosophy

San Jose State University (continued)

rolling basis. Application fee: $59. Electronic applications accepted. *Financial support:* Applicants required to submit FAFSA. *Unit head:* Dr. Rita C. Manning, Chair, 408-924-4470, Fax: 408-924-4527. *Application contact:* Dr. Rita C. Manning, Chair, 408-924-4470, Fax: 408-924-4527.

Simon Fraser University, Graduate Studies, Faculty of Arts and Social Sciences, Department of Philosophy, Burnaby, BC V5A 1S6, Canada. Offers MA, PhD. Terminal master's awarded for partial completion of doctoral program. *Degree requirements:* For master's, thesis or alternative; for doctorate, thesis/dissertation. *Entrance requirements:* For master's, minimum GPA of 3.33; for doctorate, minimum GPA of 3.67. Additional exam requirements/recommendations for international students: Required—TOEFL or IELTS. Electronic applications accepted. *Faculty research:* Epistemology, philosophy of mind, philosophy of science, value theory, logic.

Southeastern Baptist Theological Seminary, Graduate and Professional Programs, Wake Forest, NC 27588-1889. Offers advanced biblical studies (M Div); Christian education (M Div, MACE); Christian ethics (PhD); Christian ministry (M Div); Christian planting (M Div); church music (MACM); counseling (MACO); evangelism (PhD); language (M Div); ministry (D Min); New Testament (PhD); Old Testament (PhD); philosophy (PhD); theology (Th M, PhD); women's studies (M Div). *Accreditation:* ACIPE; ATS (one or more programs are accredited). *Degree requirements:* For master's, thesis (for some programs), oral exam; for doctorate, thesis/dissertation, fieldwork; for M Div, supervised ministry. *Entrance requirements:* For master's, Cooperative English Test, minimum GPA of 2.0, M Div or equivalent (Th M); for doctorate, GRE General Test or MAT, Cooperative English Test, M Div or equivalent, 3 years of professional experience.

Southern Baptist Theological Seminary, School of Theology, Louisville, KY 40280-0004. Offers biblical and theological studies (M Div); biblical counseling (M Div, MA, D Min); biblical spirituality (D Min); Christian ministry (M Div); expository preaching (D Min); pastoral studies (M Div); theological studies (MA); theology (Th M, PhD); theology and arts (MA); theology and law (MA); worldview and apologetics (M Div). *Accreditation:* ATS. Part-time and evening/weekend programs available. Postbaccalaureate distance learning degree programs offered (minimal on-campus study). *Degree requirements:* For master's, 2 foreign languages, thesis; for doctorate, 4 foreign languages, thesis/dissertation; for M Div, 2 foreign languages. *Entrance requirements:* For master's, GRE General Test, MAT, M Div; for doctorate, GRE General Test, MAT, interview, M Div, field essay. Additional exam requirements/recommendations for international students: Required—TOEFL, TWE. *Faculty research:* Biblical studies, contemporary theology, church history, pastoral care, ministry/missions studies.

Southern Evangelical Seminary, Veritas Graduate School of Apologetics and Counter-Cult Ministry, Matthews, NC 28105. Offers apologetics (MA, D Min, PhD, Certificate); Islamic studies (MA); Jewish studies (MA); philosophy (MA); religion (MA). Part-time and evening/weekend programs available. Postbaccalaureate distance learning degree programs offered (minimal on-campus study). *Degree requirements:* For master's, thesis optional; for doctorate, comprehensive exam (for some programs), thesis/dissertation. *Entrance requirements:* Additional exam requirements/recommendations for international students: Required—TOEFL (minimum score 600 paper-based; 250 computer-based).

Southern Illinois University Carbondale, Graduate School, College of Liberal Arts, Department of Philosophy, Carbondale, IL 62901-4701. Offers MA, PhD. *Degree requirements:* For master's, one foreign language, thesis; for doctorate, 2 foreign languages, thesis/dissertation. *Entrance requirements:* For master's, GRE General Test, minimum GPA of 2.7; for doctorate, GRE General Test, minimum GPA of 3.25. Additional exam requirements/recommendations for international students: Required—TOEFL. *Faculty research:* Continental philosophy, American philosophy, philosophy of mind, Asian philosophy.

Stanford University, School of Humanities and Sciences, Department of Philosophy, Stanford, CA 94305-9991. Offers MA, PhD. Terminal master's awarded for partial completion of doctoral program. *Degree requirements:* For master's, oral exam; for doctorate, thesis/dissertation, oral exam. *Entrance requirements:* For master's and doctorate, GRE General Test. Additional exam requirements/recommendations for international students: Required—TOEFL. Electronic applications accepted. *Expenses:* Tuition: Full-time $37,380; part-time $2760 per quarter. Required fees: $501.

State University of New York at Binghamton, Graduate School, School of Arts and Sciences, Department of Philosophy, Binghamton, NY 13902-6000. Offers MA, PhD. *Faculty:* 14 full-time (4 women), 4 part-time/adjunct (0 women). *Students:* 1 (woman) part-time. Average age 23. 1 applicant, 0% accepted, 0 enrolled. In 2009, 2 master's awarded. *Degree requirements:* For master's, 2 foreign languages, thesis or alternative; for doctorate, thesis/dissertation. *Entrance requirements:* For master's and doctorate, GRE General Test, GRE Subject Test. Additional exam requirements/recommendations for international students: Required—TOEFL (minimum score 550 paper-based; 213 computer-based; 80 iBT). *Application deadline:* Applications are processed on a rolling basis. Application fee: $60. Electronic applications accepted. *Financial support:* Career-related internships or fieldwork, Federal Work-Study, institutionally sponsored loans, scholarships/grants, health care benefits, and unspecified assistantships available. Financial award application deadline: 2/15; financial award applicants required to submit FAFSA. *Unit head:* Dr. Max Pensky, Chairperson, 607-777-4163, E-mail: mpensky@binghamton.edu. *Application contact:* Victoria Williams, Recruiting and Admissions Coordinator, 607-777-2151, Fax: 607-777-2501, E-mail: vwilliam@binghamton.edu.

State University of New York at Binghamton, Graduate School, School of Arts and Sciences, Philosophy, Interpretation and Culture Program, Binghamton, NY 13902-6000. Offers MA, PhD. *Students:* 12 full-time (4 women), 37 part-time (19 women); includes 15 minority (6 African Americans, 2 Asian Americans or Pacific Islanders, 7 Hispanic Americans), 17 international. Average age 35. 34 applicants, 35% accepted, 4 enrolled. In 2009, 2 master's, 1 doctorate awarded. Application fee: $60. *Financial support:* In 2009–10, 21 students received support, including 5 fellowships with full tuition reimbursements available (averaging $14,500 per year), 1 research assistantship with full tuition reimbursement available (averaging $14,500 per year), 11 teaching assistantships with full tuition reimbursements available (averaging $14,500 per year); career-related internships or fieldwork, Federal Work-Study, institutionally sponsored loans, scholarships/grants, health care benefits, and unspecified assistantships also available. Financial award application deadline: 2/15; financial award applicants required to submit FAFSA. *Unit head:* Dr. Joshua Price, Director, 607-777-2348, E-mail: jmprice@binghamton.edu. *Application contact:* Victoria Williams, Recruiting and Admissions Coordinator, 607-777-2151, Fax: 607-777-2501, E-mail: vwilliam@binghamton.edu.

State University of New York at Binghamton, Graduate School, School of Arts and Sciences, Program in Social, Political, Ethical and Legal Philosophy, Binghamton, NY 13902-6000. Offers MA, PhD. *Students:* 23 full-time (12 women), 15 part-time (4 women); includes 8 minority (3 African Americans, 1 American Indian/Alaska Native, 2 Asian Americans or Pacific Islanders, 2 Hispanic Americans), 7 international. Average age 29. 48 applicants, 40% accepted, 11 enrolled. In 2009, 5 master's, 1 doctorate awarded. Application fee: $60. *Unit head:* Dr. Bat-Ami Bar-On, Chairperson, 607-777-6198, E-mail: ami@binghamton.edu. *Application contact:* Victoria Williams, Recruiting and Admissions Coordinator, 607-777-2151, Fax: 607-777-2501, E-mail: vwilliam@binghamton.edu.

Stony Brook University, State University of New York, Graduate School, College of Arts and Sciences, Department of Philosophy, Stony Brook, NY 11794. Offers MA, PhD. Evening/weekend programs available. *Faculty:* 23 full-time (6 women). *Students:* 94 full-time (35 women), 14 part-time (5 women); includes 15 minority (2 African Americans, 1 American Indian/Alaska Native, 2 Asian Americans or Pacific Islanders, 10 Hispanic Americans), 17 international. Average age 29. 254 applicants, 19% accepted. In 2009, 23 master's, 9 doctorates awarded. *Degree requirements:* For doctorate, one foreign language, thesis/dissertation. *Entrance requirements:* For master's and doctorate, GRE General Test. Additional exam requirements/recommendations for international students: Required—TOEFL. *Application deadline:* For fall admission, 1/15 for domestic students. Application fee: $60. *Expenses:* Tuition, state resident: full-time $8370; part-time $349 per credit. Tuition, nonresident: full-time $13,250; part-time $552 per credit. Required fees: $933. *Financial support:* In 2009–10, 42 teaching assistantships were awarded; fellowships, research assistantships also available. *Faculty research:* Philosophy of science, philosophy of language, analytical philosophy, phenomenology, structuralism. *Unit head:* Dr. Robert Crease, Chair, 631-632-7590, Fax: 631-632-7522. *Application contact:* Dr. Harvey Cormier, Director of Graduate Studies, 631-632-7312, Fax: 631-632-7522, E-mail: harvey.cormier@notes.cc.sunysb.edu.

Syracuse University, College of Arts and Sciences, Program in Philosophy, Syracuse, NY 13244. Offers MA, PhD. Part-time and evening/weekend programs available. *Students:* 39 full-time (8 women), 7 part-time (1 woman); includes 5 minority (3 Asian Americans or Pacific Islanders, 2 Hispanic Americans), 7 international. Average age 30. 120 applicants, 13% accepted, 6 enrolled. In 2009, 4 master's, 3 doctorates awarded. Terminal master's awarded for partial completion of doctoral program. *Degree requirements:* For master's, thesis or alternative; for doctorate, thesis/dissertation. *Entrance requirements:* For master's and doctorate, GRE, writing sample. Additional exam requirements/recommendations for international students: Required—TOEFL. *Application deadline:* For fall admission, 1/15 priority date for domestic and international students. Application fee: $75. Electronic applications accepted. *Expenses:* Tuition: Full-time $26,808; part-time $1117 per credit. Required fees: $1024. *Financial support:* In 2009–10, 25 students received support; fellowships with full and partial tuition reimbursements available, research assistantships, teaching assistantships with full tuition reimbursements available, tuition waivers (partial) available. Financial award application deadline: 1/1; financial award applicants required to submit FAFSA. *Faculty research:* Ethics, metaphysics, epistemology, philosophy of language. *Unit head:* Dr. Thomas McKay, Graduate Studies Director, 315-443-2536, Fax: 315-443-5675. *Application contact:* Lisa Farnsworth, Information Contact, 315-443-2245, E-mail: lfarmswo@syr.edu.

Temple University, Graduate School, College of Liberal Arts, Department of Philosophy, Philadelphia, PA 19122-6096. Offers MA, PhD. Part-time programs available. Terminal master's awarded for partial completion of doctoral program. *Degree requirements:* For master's, thesis or alternative; for doctorate, one foreign language, thesis/dissertation. *Entrance requirements:* For master's and doctorate, GRE General Test. Additional exam requirements/recommendations for international students: Required—TOEFL (minimum score 550 paper-based; 213 computer-based; 79 iBT). Electronic applications accepted. *Faculty research:* Philosophy of mind, aesthetics, philosophy of science, nineteenth century German philosophy, phenomenology.

Texas A&M University, College of Liberal Arts, Department of Philosophy and Humanities, College Station, TX 77843. Offers philosophy (MA, PhD). Part-time programs available. *Faculty:* 13. *Students:* 23 full-time (7 women), 3 part-time (0 women); includes 4 minority (1 American Indian/Alaska Native, 3 Hispanic Americans), 1 international. Average age 27. In 2009, 6 master's awarded. Terminal master's awarded for partial completion of doctoral program. *Degree requirements:* For master's, thesis optional; for doctorate, comprehensive exam, thesis/dissertation. *Entrance requirements:* For master's, GRE General Test, letter of recommendation, resume, writing sample; for doctorate, GRE General Test, letters of recommendation, resume, writing sample. *Application deadline:* For fall admission, 1/15 for domestic students, 3/1 for international students; for winter admission, 8/1 for international students; for spring admission, 10/15 priority date for domestic students. Application fee: $50 ($75 for international students). Electronic applications accepted. *Expenses:* Tuition, state resident: full-time $3991; part-time $221.74 per credit hour. Tuition, nonresident: full-time $9049; part-time $502.74 per credit hour. *Financial support:* In 2009–10, fellowships with partial tuition reimbursements (averaging $16,000 per year), research assistantships with partial tuition reimbursements (averaging $15,000 per year), teaching assistantships with partial tuition reimbursements (averaging $9,000 per year) were awarded; career-related internships or fieldwork, institutionally sponsored loans, scholarships/grants, and unspecified assistantships also available. Financial award application deadline: 1/15; financial award applicants required to submit FAFSA. *Faculty research:* American philosophy, applied ethics, philosophy of mind, philosophy of religion, history and philosophy of logic. *Unit head:* Dr. Daniel Conway, Head, 979-845-5696, E-mail: conway@tamu.edu. *Application contact:* Dr., Graduate Advisor, 979-845-7133, E-mail: philstaff@www-phil.tamu.edu.

Texas Tech University, Graduate School, College of Arts and Sciences, Department of Philosophy, Lubbock, TX 79409. Offers MA. Part-time programs available. *Faculty:* 7 full-time (2 women). *Students:* 18 full-time (1 woman), 1 (woman) part-time; includes 3 minority (all Hispanic Americans), 2 international. Average age 27. 27 applicants, 59% accepted, 7 enrolled. In 2009, 7 master's awarded. *Degree requirements:* For master's, thesis or alternative. *Entrance requirements:* For master's, GRE General Test. Additional exam requirements/recommendations for international students: Required—TOEFL (minimum score 550 paper-based; 213 computer-based). *Application deadline:* For fall admission, 3/1 priority date for international students; for spring admission, 11/1 priority date for international students. Applications are processed on a rolling basis. Application fee: $50 ($75 for international students). Electronic applications accepted. *Expenses:* Tuition, state resident: full-time $5100; part-time $213 per credit hour. Tuition, nonresident: full-time $11,748; part-time $490 per credit hour. Required fees: $2298; $50 per credit hour. $555 per semester. *Financial support:* In 2009–10, 11 teaching assistantships with partial tuition reimbursements (averaging $16,343 per year) were awarded; research assistantships with partial tuition reimbursements, Federal Work-Study and institutionally sponsored loans also available. Support available to part-time students. Financial award application deadline: 4/15; financial award applicants required to submit FAFSA. *Faculty research:* Aesthetics, ethics, history of philosophy, philosophy of mind, philosophy of science. *Unit head:* Dr. Mark O. Webb, Chair, 806-742-3275 Ext. 323, Fax: 806-742-0730, E-mail: mark.webb@ttu.edu. *Application contact:* Dr. Daniel O. Nathan, Director of Graduate Studies, 806-742-0373 Ext. 340, Fax: 806-742-0730, E-mail: daniel.nathan@ttu.edu.

Trinity Western University, Faculty of Graduate Studies, Program in Interdisciplinary Humanities, Langley, BC V2Y 1Y1, Canada. Offers general humanities (MAIH); specialized (MAIH), including English, history, philosophy. Part-time and evening/weekend programs available. Postbaccalaureate distance learning degree programs offered (minimal on-campus study). *Entrance requirements:* For master's, strong undergraduate degree in Humanities or English, History or Philosophy. *Faculty research:* Literary theory, gender, medieval and early modern literature, philosophy of religion, Thomas Merton's poetics.

Tufts University, Graduate School of Arts and Sciences, Department of Philosophy, Medford, MA 02155. Offers MA. *Faculty:* 14 full-time, 4 part-time/adjunct. *Students:* 29 full-time (9 women); includes 4 minority (1 African American, 3 Asian Americans or Pacific Islanders), 4 international. Average age 27. 165 applicants, 16% accepted, 11 enrolled. In 2009, 14 master's awarded. *Degree requirements:* For master's, one foreign language, comprehensive exam, departmental qualifying exam. *Entrance requirements:* For master's, GRE General Test, writing sample. Additional exam requirements/recommendations for international students: Required—TOEFL (minimum score 550 paper-based; 213 computer-based; 80 iBT). *Application deadline:* For fall admission, 1/15 for domestic students, 12/15 for international students; for spring admission, 9/15 for domestic and international students. Applications are processed on a rolling basis. Application fee: $75. Electronic applications accepted. *Expenses:* Tuition: Full-time $38,096; part-time $3962 per credit. Required fees: $686; $40 per year. Tuition and fees vary according to course level, course load, degree level, program and student level. *Financial support:* Teaching assistantships with full and partial tuition reimbursements, Federal Work-Study, scholarships/grants, tuition waivers (partial), and unspecified assistantships available. Financial award application deadline: 1/15; financial award applicants required to submit FAFSA. *Unit head:* Nancy Bauer, Chair, 617-627-3230. *Application contact:* Avner Baz, Graduate Advisor, 617-627-3230.

Tulane University, School of Liberal Arts, Department of Philosophy, New Orleans, LA 70118-5669. Offers MA, PhD. *Degree requirements:* For master's, thesis or alternative; for doctorate, one foreign language, thesis/dissertation. *Entrance requirements:* For master's,

GRE General Test, minimum B average in undergraduate course work; for doctorate, GRE General Test. Additional exam requirements/recommendations for international students: Required—TOEFL. Electronic applications accepted.

Universidad Autonoma de Guadalajara, Graduate Programs, Guadalajara, Mexico. Offers administrative law and justice (LL M); advertising and corporate communications (MA); architecture (M Arch); business (MBA); computational science (MCC); education (Ed M, Ed D); English-Spanish translation (MA); fiscal law (MA); integrated management of digital animation (MA); international business (MIB); international corporate law (LL M); internet technologies (MS); labor health (MS); manufacturing systems (MMS); philosophy (MA, PhD); power electronics (MS); quality systems (MQS); renewable energy (MS); social evaluation of projects (MBA); strategic market research (MBA); teaching mathematics (MA).

Université de Montréal, Faculty of Arts and Sciences, Department of Philosophy, Montréal, QC H3C 3J7, Canada. Offers MA, PhD. *Degree requirements:* For master's, 2 foreign languages, thesis; for doctorate, thesis/dissertation, general exam. Electronic applications accepted. *Faculty research:* Ancient and modern philosophy; logic and philosophy of language, ethics, and politics; contemporary Continental philosophy.

Université de Sherbrooke, Faculty of Letters and Human Sciences, Department of Human Sciences, Sherbrooke, QC J1K 2R1, Canada. Offers history (MA); philosophy (MA). *Degree requirements:* For master's, thesis. *Entrance requirements:* For master's, minimum GPA of 2.75. *Faculty research:* Political, social, and urban history; history of women.

Université de Sherbrooke, Faculty of Theology, Ethics and Philosophy, Sherbrooke, QC J1K 2R1, Canada. Offers applied ethics (Diploma); human science of religions (MA); intercultural training (Diploma); philosophy (MA, PhD); spiritual anthropology (Diploma); theology (MA, PhD, Diploma). Part-time and evening/weekend programs available. Postbaccalaureate distance learning degree programs offered. Terminal master's awarded for partial completion of doctoral program. *Entrance requirements:* For master's, bachelor's degree in related discipline; for doctorate, master's degree in related discipline. *Faculty research:* Faith and culture interrelation.

Université du Québec à Montréal, Graduate Programs, Program in Philosophy, Montréal, QC H3C 3P8, Canada. Offers MA, PhD. Part-time programs available. *Degree requirements:* For master's, thesis; for doctorate, thesis/dissertation. *Entrance requirements:* For master's, appropriate bachelor's degree or equivalent, proficiency in French; for doctorate, appropriate master's degree or equivalent, proficiency in French.

Université du Québec à Trois-Rivières, Graduate Programs, Program in Philosophy, Trois-Rivières, QC G9A 5H7, Canada. Offers MA, PhD. Part-time programs available. *Degree requirements:* For master's, thesis; for doctorate, thesis/dissertation. *Entrance requirements:* For master's, appropriate bachelor's degree, proficiency in French; for doctorate, appropriate master's degree, proficiency in French.

Université Laval, Faculty of Philosophy, Programs in Philosophy, Québec, QC G1K 7P4, Canada. Offers MA, PhD. Terminal master's awarded for partial completion of doctoral program. *Degree requirements:* For master's, thesis; for doctorate, comprehensive exam, thesis/dissertation. *Entrance requirements:* For master's and doctorate, French exam. Electronic applications accepted.

University at Albany, State University of New York, College of Arts and Sciences, Department of Philosophy, Albany, NY 12222-0001. Offers MA, PhD. *Degree requirements:* For master's, one foreign language, thesis; for doctorate, thesis/dissertation. *Entrance requirements:* For master's and doctorate, GRE General Test. Additional exam requirements/recommendations for international students: Required—TOEFL (minimum score 550 paper-based; 213 computer-based). Electronic applications accepted. *Faculty research:* Philosophical logic, ethics, ancient philosophy/metaphysics, aesthetics, biomedical ethics.

University at Buffalo, the State University of New York, Graduate School, College of Arts and Sciences, Department of Philosophy, Buffalo, NY 14260. Offers MA, PhD. *Faculty:* 17 full-time (1 woman), 2 part-time/adjunct (1 woman). *Students:* 42 full-time (5 women), 9 part-time (2 women); includes 5 minority (2 African Americans, 2 Asian Americans or Pacific Islanders, 1 Hispanic American), 4 international. Average age 31. 59 applicants, 58% accepted, 16 enrolled. In 2009, 3 master's, 10 doctorates awarded. Terminal master's awarded for partial completion of doctoral program. *Degree requirements:* For master's, variable foreign language requirement, thesis or alternative; for doctorate, variable foreign language requirement, comprehensive exam, thesis/dissertation. *Entrance requirements:* For master's, GRE General Test, minimum GPA of 2.67; for doctorate, GRE General Test, minimum GPA of 3.0. Additional exam requirements/recommendations for international students: Required—TOEFL (minimum score 550 paper-based; 213 computer-based; 79 iBT). *Application deadline:* For fall admission, 12/15 for domestic and international students; for spring admission, 10/1 for international students. Applications are processed on a rolling basis. Application fee: $75. Electronic applications accepted. *Financial support:* In 2009–10, 8 fellowships with full tuition reimbursements (averaging $4,000 per year), 21 teaching assistantships with full tuition reimbursements (averaging $13,250 per year) were awarded; research assistantships, Federal Work-Study, institutionally sponsored loans, tuition waivers (partial), and unspecified assistantships also available. Financial award application deadline: 2/1; financial award applicants required to submit FAFSA. *Faculty research:* Logic, metaphysics (historical and contemporary), aesthetics, epistemology, ethics (historical and contemporary), ontology. Total annual research expenditures: $3.7 million. *Unit head:* Dr. John Kearns, Chair, 716-645-8481, Fax: 716-645-6139, E-mail: kearns@acsu.buffalo.edu. *Application contact:* David Hershenov, Director of Graduate Studies, 716-645-0151, Fax: 716-645-6139, E-mail: dh25@buffalo.edu.

University of Alberta, Faculty of Graduate Studies and Research, Department of Philosophy, Edmonton, AB T6G 2E1, Canada. Offers MA, PhD. Part-time programs available. *Faculty:* 13 full-time (2 women), 1 part-time/adjunct (0 women). *Students:* 22 full-time (7 women), 10 part-time (5 women). 54 applicants, 52% accepted, 7 enrolled. In 2009, 5 master's, 2 doctorates awarded. *Degree requirements:* For master's, thesis; for doctorate, thesis/dissertation. *Entrance requirements:* Additional exam requirements/recommendations for international students: Required—TOEFL (minimum score 550 paper-based; 213 computer-based). *Application deadline:* For fall admission, 1/15 priority date for domestic and international students. Applications are processed on a rolling basis. Electronic applications accepted. Tuition and fees charges are reported in Canadian dollars. *Expenses:* Tuition, area resident: Full-time $4626 Canadian dollars; part-time $99.72 Canadian dollars per unit. International tuition: $8216 Canadian dollars full-time. Required fees: $3590 Canadian dollars; $99.72 Canadian dollars per unit. $215 Canadian dollars per term. *Financial support:* In 2009–10, 19 students received support, including 3 fellowships with full tuition reimbursements available (averaging $20,000 per year), 1 research assistantship (averaging $10,320 per year), 12 teaching assistantships with partial tuition reimbursements available (averaging $15,479 per year); scholarships/grants also available. Financial award application deadline: 1/15. *Faculty research:* Philosophy of science, cognitive science, social and political philosophy, philosophy of language and logic, environmental aesthetics. Total annual research expenditures: $88,250. *Unit head:* Dr. Bruce A. Hunter, Chair, 780-492-4102, Fax: 780-492-9160. *Application contact:* Anita Theroux, Administrative Assistant, 780-492-4102, Fax: 780-492-9160, E-mail: gsphil.dept@ualberta.ca.

The University of Arizona, Graduate College, College of Social and Behavioral Sciences, Department of Philosophy, Tucson, AZ 85721. Offers MA, PhD, JD/PhD. Part-time programs available. *Faculty:* 20. *Students:* 5 full-time (1 woman), 47 part-time (12 women); includes 1 minority (Hispanic American), 11 international. Average age 31. 160 applicants, 5% accepted, 8 enrolled. In 2009, 1 master's, 1 doctorate awarded. Terminal master's awarded for partial completion of doctoral program. *Degree requirements:* For master's, exams, qualifying paper; for doctorate, thesis/dissertation, preliminary exams. *Entrance requirements:* For doctorate, GRE General Test, 3 letters of recommendation, writing sample. Additional exam requirements/recommendations for international students: Required—TOEFL (minimum score 550 paper-based; 213 computer-based; 79 iBT). *Application deadline:* For fall admission, 1/2 for domestic and international students. Applications are processed on a rolling basis. Application fee: $65. Electronic applications accepted. *Expenses:* Tuition, state resident: full-time $9028. Tuition, nonresident: full-time $24,890. *Financial support:* In 2009–10, 43 teaching assistantships with full tuition reimbursements (averaging $14,786 per year) were awarded; research assistantships, scholarships/grants, health care benefits, tuition waivers (full), and unspecified assistantships also available. Financial award application deadline: 1/15. *Faculty research:* Law, social, and political philosophy; epistemology; philosophy of mind; cognitive science. *Unit head:* Dr. J. Christopher Maloney, Head, 520-621-3120. *Application contact:* Debbie Jackson, Program Coordinator, 520-621-5045, Fax: 520-621-9559, E-mail: debbiej@email.arizona.edu.

University of Arkansas, Graduate School, J. William Fulbright College of Arts and Sciences, Department of Philosophy, Fayetteville, AR 72701-1201. Offers MA, PhD. Part-time programs available. *Students:* 12 full-time (3 women), 16 part-time (2 women); includes 1 minority (Hispanic American), 2 international. In 2009, 8 master's, 1 doctorate awarded. *Degree requirements:* For master's, thesis; for doctorate, 2 foreign languages, thesis/dissertation. Application fee: $40 ($50 for international students). *Expenses:* Tuition, state resident: full-time $7355; part-time $356.58 per hour. Tuition, nonresident: full-time $17,401; part-time $775.17 per hour. Required fees: $1203. *Financial support:* In 2009–10, 1 research assistantship, 10 teaching assistantships were awarded; fellowships with tuition reimbursements, career-related internships or fieldwork and Federal Work-Study also available. Support available to part-time students. Financial award application deadline: 4/1; financial award applicants required to submit FAFSA. *Unit head:* Dr. Thomas Senor, Department Chairperson, 479-575-3551, Fax: 479-575-2642, E-mail: senor@uark.edu. *Application contact:* Dr. Jack Lyons, Graduate Coordinator, 479-575-5825, E-mail: jclyons@uark.edu.

The University of British Columbia, Faculty of Arts and Faculty of Graduate Studies, Department of Philosophy, Vancouver, BC V6T 1Z1, Canada. Offers MA, PhD. *Accreditation:* NCATE. Part-time programs available. *Degree requirements:* For master's, thesis (for some programs); for doctorate, comprehensive exam, thesis/dissertation. *Entrance requirements:* For master's, bachelor's degree with minimum average of 76% or minimum GPA of 3.0 in 3rd- and 4th-year coursework; 3 credits in formal logic; 6 credits at the upper-level in the history of philosophy and in metaphysics, epistemology, or philosophy; 3 credits at the upper-level in ethics or value theory; for doctorate, MA, honors BA with first class standing, or BA with first class standing in philosophy. Additional exam requirements/recommendations for international students: Required—TOEFL (minimum score 600 paper-based; 250 computer-based), IELTS (minimum score 6.5), Michigan English Language Assessment Battery: minimum overall score of 81. Electronic applications accepted. *Faculty research:* Ethics and applied ethics, metaphysics and epistemology, history of philosophy, philosophy of science, philosophy of biology.

University of Calgary, Faculty of Graduate Studies, Faculty of Humanities, Department of Philosophy, Calgary, AB T2N 1N4, Canada. Offers MA, PhD. Part-time programs available. *Degree requirements:* For master's, comprehensive exam (for some programs), thesis (for some programs); for doctorate, thesis/dissertation, candidacy exam. *Entrance requirements:* Additional exam requirements/recommendations for international students: Required—TOEFL (minimum score 550 paper-based; 213 computer-based). Electronic applications accepted. *Faculty research:* Ethics and political philosophy, metaphysics, philosophy of mind, philosophy of language.

University of California, Berkeley, Graduate Division, College of Letters and Science, Department of Philosophy, Berkeley, CA 94720-1500. Offers PhD. *Students:* 46 full-time (16 women). Average age 29. 298 applicants, 6 enrolled. In 2009, 1 doctorate awarded. *Degree requirements:* For doctorate, thesis/dissertation, qualifying exam. *Entrance requirements:* For doctorate, GRE General Test, minimum GPA of 3.0, writing sample, 3 letters of recommendation. *Application deadline:* For fall admission, 1/6 for domestic students. Application fee: $70 ($90 for international students). *Financial support:* Fellowships, research assistantships, teaching assistantships, unspecified assistantships available. *Unit head:* Prof. R. Jay Wallace, Chair, 510-642-2722, E-mail: phildept@berkeley.edu. *Application contact:* Information Contact, 510-642-2722, E-mail: phildept@berkeley.edu.

University of California, Davis, Graduate Studies, Program in Philosophy, Davis, CA 95616. Offers MA, PhD. Terminal master's awarded for partial completion of doctoral program. *Degree requirements:* For doctorate, thesis/dissertation. *Entrance requirements:* For master's and doctorate, GRE General Test, minimum GPA of 3.0. Additional exam requirements/recommendations for international students: Required—TOEFL (minimum score 550 paper-based; 213 computer-based). Electronic applications accepted. *Faculty research:* Moral and political philosophy, philosophy of language, metaphysics, philosophy of science, history of philosophy.

University of California, Irvine, Office of Graduate Studies, School of Humanities, Department of Philosophy, Irvine, CA 92697. Offers MA, PhD. *Students:* 33 full-time (7 women); includes 4 minority (all Hispanic Americans), 2 international. Average age 30. 82 applicants, 17% accepted, 7 enrolled. In 2009, 11 master's, 1 doctorate awarded. *Degree requirements:* For master's, thesis; for doctorate, thesis/dissertation. *Entrance requirements:* For master's and doctorate, GRE General Test, minimum GPA of 3.0. Additional exam requirements/recommendations for international students: Required—TOEFL (minimum score 550 paper-based; 213 computer-based). *Application deadline:* For fall admission, 1/15 priority date for domestic students, 1/15 for international students. Applications are processed on a rolling basis. Application fee: $70 ($90 for international students). Electronic applications accepted. *Financial support:* In 2009–10, teaching assistantships with partial tuition reimbursements (averaging $13,595 per year); fellowships with tuition reimbursements, institutionally sponsored loans, traineeships, health care benefits, and unspecified assistantships also available. Financial award application deadline: 3/1; financial award applicants required to submit FAFSA. *Faculty research:* Philosophy of action and decision theory, philosophy of language, philosophy of mathematics, virtue ethics, modern and contemporary Continental philosophy. *Unit head:* Nicholas White, Chair, 949-824-3289, Fax: 949-824-6520, E-mail: npwhite@uci.edu. *Application contact:* Astrid Doolaege, Graduate Coordinator, 949-824-6526, Fax: 949-824-6520, E-mail: amboetel@uci.edu.

University of California, Irvine, Office of Graduate Studies, School of Social Sciences, Department of Logic and Philosophy of Science, Irvine, CA 92697. Offers philosophy (PhD). *Students:* 21 full-time (2 women); includes 1 Hispanic American, 2 international. Average age 28. 53 applicants, 15% accepted, 2 enrolled. In 2009, 2 doctorates awarded. *Entrance requirements:* For doctorate, GRE, minimum GPA of 3.0. Additional exam requirements/recommendations for international students: Required—TOEFL (minimum score 550 paper-based; 213 computer-based). *Application deadline:* For fall admission, 1/15 for domestic and international students. Application fee: $70 ($90 for international students). *Financial support:* Fellowships, research assistantships with full tuition reimbursements, teaching assistantships, institutionally sponsored loans, traineeships, health care benefits, and unspecified assistantships available. Financial award application deadline: 3/1. *Unit head:* Dr. Jeffrey Barrett, Chair, 949-824-6491, E-mail: jabarret@uci.edu. *Application contact:* Diane Enriquez, Graduate Counselor, 949-824-5924, Fax: 949-824-3548, E-mail: dmvargas@uci.edu.

University of California, Los Angeles, Graduate Division, College of Letters and Science, Department of Philosophy, Los Angeles, CA 90095. Offers MA, PhD. *Students:* 54 full-time (19 women); includes 6 minority (3 Asian Americans or Pacific Islanders, 3 Hispanic Americans), 3 international. Average age 30. 152 applicants, 9% accepted, 6 enrolled. In 2009, 14 master's, 3 doctorates awarded. Terminal master's awarded for partial completion of doctoral program. *Degree requirements:* For master's, one foreign language, comprehensive exam; for doctorate, one foreign language, thesis/dissertation, oral and written qualifying exams, teaching experience. *Entrance requirements:* For master's, GRE General Test, minimum GPA of 3.0, sample of written work; for doctorate, GRE General Test, minimum undergraduate GPA of 3.0, sample of written work. Additional exam requirements/recommendations for international students: Required—TOEFL. *Application deadline:* For fall admission, 1/10 for domestic and international students. Application fee: $70 ($90 for international students). Electronic applications accepted. *Financial support:* In 2009–10, 35 fellowships with full and partial tuition reimburse-

Philosophy

University of California, Los Angeles (continued)
ments, 7 research assistantships with full and partial tuition reimbursements, 45 teaching assistantships with full and partial tuition reimbursements were awarded; Federal Work-Study, institutionally sponsored loans, scholarships/grants, health care benefits, tuition waivers (full and partial), and unspecified assistantships also available. Financial award application deadline: 3/1; financial award applicants required to submit FAFSA. *Unit head:* Dr. John Carriero, Chair, 310-825-4641. *Application contact:* Department Office, 310-206-1356, E-mail: alaven@humnet.ucla.edu.

University of California, Riverside, Graduate Division, Department of Philosophy, Riverside, CA 92521-0102. Offers MA, PhD. Terminal master's awarded for partial completion of doctoral program. *Degree requirements:* For master's, logic exam, professional paper; for doctorate, one foreign language, thesis/dissertation, logic exam, proposition papers, qualifying exams. *Entrance requirements:* For master's, GRE General Test, minimum GPA of 3.2; for doctorate, GRE General Test, master's degree in philosophy, minimum GPA of 3.2. Additional exam requirements/recommendations for international students: Required—TOEFL (minimum score 550 paper-based; 213 computer-based; 80 iBT). Electronic applications accepted. *Faculty research:* Moral philosophy, philosophy of science, history of philosophy, philosophy of language, Continental philosophy.

University of California, San Diego, Office of Graduate Studies, Department of Philosophy, La Jolla, CA 92093. Offers philosophy (PhD); science studies (PhD). *Degree requirements:* For doctorate, thesis/dissertation. *Entrance requirements:* For doctorate, GRE General Test, GRE Subject Test. Electronic applications accepted.

University of California, San Diego, Office of Graduate Studies, Interdisciplinary Program in Cognitive Science, La Jolla, CA 92093. Offers cognitive science/anthropology (PhD); cognitive science/communication (PhD); cognitive science/computer science and engineering (PhD); cognitive science/linguistics (PhD); cognitive science/neuroscience (PhD); cognitive science/philosophy (PhD); cognitive science/psychology (PhD); cognitive science/sociology (PhD). Admissions offered through affiliated departments. *Degree requirements:* For doctorate, thesis/dissertation. *Entrance requirements:* For doctorate, GRE General Test, acceptance into one of the eight participating departments. *Faculty research:* Language and cognition, philosophy of mind, visual perception, biological anthropology, sociolinguistics.

University of California, Santa Barbara, Graduate Division, College of Letters and Sciences, Division of Humanities and Fine Arts, Department of Philosophy, Santa Barbara, CA 93106-6070. Offers PhD, MA/PhD. *Faculty:* 11 full-time (1 woman). *Students:* 33 full-time (3 women). Average age 29. 83 applicants, 23% accepted, 5 enrolled. In 2009, 3 doctorates awarded. Terminal master's awarded for partial completion of doctoral program. *Degree requirements:* For doctorate, comprehensive exam (for some programs), thesis/dissertation. *Entrance requirements:* For doctorate, GRE, writing sample, 3 letters of recommendation, resume/curriculum vitae. Additional exam requirements/recommendations for international students: Required—TOEFL (minimum score 550 paper-based; 213 computer-based; 80 iBT) or IELTS (minimum score 7). *Application deadline:* For fall admission, 5/1 for domestic and international students; for winter admission, 11/1 for domestic and international students; for spring admission, 2/1 for domestic and international students. Application fee: $70 ($90 for international students). Electronic applications accepted. *Financial support:* In 2009–10, 8 fellowships with full and partial tuition reimbursements (averaging $13,200 per year), 30 teaching assistantships with partial tuition reimbursements (averaging $10,700 per year) were awarded; Federal Work-Study, institutionally sponsored loans, scholarships/grants, health care benefits, tuition waivers (full and partial), and unspecified assistantships also available. Financial award application deadline: 1/15; financial award applicants required to submit FAFSA. *Faculty research:* Epistemology, philosophy of language, philosophy of mind, philosophy of logic, metaphysics. *Unit head:* Prof. Voula Tsouna, Chair, 805-893-3122, Fax: 805-893-8221, E-mail: vtsouna@philosophy.ucsb.edu. *Application contact:* Marsha Bonney, Graduate Program Assistant, 805-893-3122, Fax: 805-893-8221, E-mail: mbonney@philosophy.ucsb.edu.

University of California, Santa Cruz, Division of Graduate Studies, Division of Humanities, Department of Philosophy, Santa Cruz, CA 95064. Offers MA, PhD. *Degree requirements:* For doctorate, thesis/dissertation, qualifying exam. *Entrance requirements:* For master's, GRE, 3 letters of recommendation; for doctorate, GRE, official transcripts, 3 letters of recommendation. Additional exam requirements/recommendations for international students: Required—TOEFL.

University of Chicago, Division of the Humanities, Department of Philosophy, Chicago, IL 60637-1513. Offers ancient philosophy (AM, PhD); philosophy (AM, PhD). Terminal master's awarded for partial completion of doctoral program. *Degree requirements:* For master's, thesis; for doctorate, one foreign language, thesis/dissertation. *Entrance requirements:* For master's and doctorate, GRE General Test. Additional exam requirements/recommendations for international students: Required—TOEFL.

University of Cincinnati, Graduate School, McMicken College of Arts and Sciences, Department of Philosophy, Cincinnati, OH 45221. Offers MA, PhD. Terminal master's awarded for partial completion of doctoral program. *Degree requirements:* For master's, thesis; for doctorate, one foreign language, comprehensive exam, thesis/dissertation. *Entrance requirements:* For master's and doctorate, GRE General Test, BA in philosophy or equivalent experience. Additional exam requirements/recommendations for international students: Required—TOEFL (minimum score 240 computer-based). Electronic applications accepted.

University of Colorado at Boulder, Graduate School, College of Arts and Sciences, Department of Philosophy, Boulder, CO 80309. Offers MA, PhD. *Faculty:* 23 full-time (5 women). *Students:* 47 full-time (12 women), 7 part-time (4 women); includes 6 minority (3 Asian Americans or Pacific Islanders, 3 Hispanic Americans). Average age 29. 216 applicants, 9% accepted, 16 enrolled. In 2009, 13 master's, 8 doctorates awarded. Terminal master's awarded for partial completion of doctoral program. *Degree requirements:* For master's, comprehensive exam, thesis; for doctorate, one foreign language, thesis/dissertation, logic and qualifying papers, oral exam. *Entrance requirements:* For master's, GRE General Test, writing sample, minimum undergraduate GPA of 2.75; for doctorate, GRE General Test. *Application deadline:* For fall admission, 1/15 priority date for domestic students, 12/1 for international students. Applications are processed on a rolling basis. Application fee: $50 ($60 for international students). *Financial support:* In 2009–10, 15 fellowships (averaging $4,522 per year), 23 research assistantships (averaging $5,071 per year) were awarded; Federal Work-Study, institutionally sponsored loans, and tuition waivers (full) also available. Financial award application deadline: 1/17. *Faculty research:* Metaphysics and epistemology, classical philosophy, philosophy of science, moral and political philosophy. Total annual research expenditures: $8,000.

University of Connecticut, Graduate School, College of Liberal Arts and Sciences, Department of Philosophy, Storrs, CT 06269. Offers MA, PhD. *Faculty:* 15 full-time (4 women). *Students:* 25 full-time (4 women), 6 part-time (1 woman); includes 3 minority (1 African American, 1 Asian American or Pacific Islander, 1 Hispanic American), 4 international. Average age 31. 70 applicants, 10% accepted, 3 enrolled. In 2009, 4 master's, 7 doctorates awarded. Terminal master's awarded for partial completion of doctoral program. *Degree requirements:* For master's, comprehensive exam; for doctorate, 2 foreign languages, thesis/dissertation. *Entrance requirements:* For master's and doctorate, GRE General Test. Additional exam requirements/recommendations for international students: Required—TOEFL (minimum score 550 paper-based; 213 computer-based). *Application deadline:* For fall admission, 2/1 priority date for domestic and international students; for spring admission, 11/1 for domestic students, 10/1 for international students. Applications are processed on a rolling basis. Application fee: $55. Electronic applications accepted. *Expenses:* Tuition, state resident: full-time $4725; part-time $525 per credit. Tuition, nonresident: full-time $12,267; part-time $1363 per credit. Required fees: $346 per semester. Tuition and fees vary according to course load. *Financial support:* In 2009–10, 3 research assistantships with full tuition reimbursements, 19 teaching assistantships with full tuition reimbursements were awarded; fellowships, Federal Work-Study, scholarships/grants, health care benefits, and unspecified assistantships also available. Financial award application deadline: 2/1; financial award applicants required to submit FAFSA. *Unit head:* Crawford L. Elder, Head, 860-486-4416, Fax: 860-486-0387, E-mail: crawford.elder@uconn.edu. *Application contact:* Samuel C. Wheeler, Chairperson, 860-486-3592, Fax: 860-486-0387, E-mail: samuel.wheeler@uconn.edu.

University of Dallas, Braniff Graduate School of Liberal Arts, Institute of Philosophic Studies, Doctoral Program in Philosophy, Irving, TX 75062-4736. Offers PhD. *Faculty:* 5 full-time (1 woman). *Students:* 17 full-time (2 women), 3 part-time (1 woman); includes 1 minority (African American). Average age 31. 16 applicants, 50% accepted, 3 enrolled. In 2009, 3 doctorates awarded. *Degree requirements:* For doctorate, 2 foreign languages, comprehensive exam, thesis/dissertation, qualifying exams. *Entrance requirements:* For doctorate, GRE General Test. *Application deadline:* For fall admission, 2/15 priority date for domestic students. Application fee: $50. *Expenses:* Tuition: Full-time $10,080; part-time $560 per credit hour. Required fees: $50 per term. Tuition and fees vary according to program. *Financial support:* In 2009–10, 14 students received support. Scholarships/grants available. Financial award application deadline: 2/15. *Faculty research:* Aesthetics, postmodernism, Hegel, ethics, Aristotle. *Unit head:* Dr. Lance Simmons, Chair, 972-721-5274, Fax: 972-721-4005, E-mail: simmons@udallas.edu. *Application contact:* Graduate Coordinator, 972-721-5106, Fax: 972-721-5280, E-mail: graduate@acad.udallas.edu.

University of Dallas, Braniff Graduate School of Liberal Arts, Master's Program in Philosophy, Irving, TX 75062-4736. Offers MA. *Faculty:* 9 full-time (0 women). *Students:* 12 full-time (2 women), 5 part-time (0 women); includes 4 minority (2 Asian Americans or Pacific Islanders, 2 Hispanic Americans). Average age 26. 14 applicants, 93% accepted, 12 enrolled. In 2009, 4 master's awarded. *Degree requirements:* For master's, one foreign language, comprehensive exam, thesis. *Entrance requirements:* For master's, GRE General Test. Additional exam requirements/recommendations for international students: Required—TOEFL. *Application deadline:* For fall admission, 2/15 priority date for domestic students; for spring admission, 11/15 for domestic students. Applications are processed on a rolling basis. Application fee: $50. *Expenses:* Tuition: Full-time $10,080; part-time $560 per credit hour. Required fees: $50 per term. Tuition and fees vary according to program. *Financial support:* In 2009–10, 16 students received support. Scholarships/grants available. Financial award application deadline: 2/15. *Faculty research:* Aesthetics, postmodernism, Hegel, ethics, Aristotle. *Unit head:* Dr. Lance Simmons, Chair, 972-721-5274, Fax: 972-721-4005, E-mail: simmons@udallas.edu. *Application contact:* Graduate Coordinator, 972-721-5106, Fax: 972-721-5280, E-mail: graduate@acad.udallas.edu.

University of Florida, Graduate School, College of Liberal Arts and Sciences, Department of Philosophy, Gainesville, FL 32611. Offers MA, PhD. *Degree requirements:* For master's, thesis or alternative; for doctorate, thesis/dissertation. *Entrance requirements:* For master's and doctorate, GRE General Test, minimum GPA of 3.0. Additional exam requirements/recommendations for international students: Required—TOEFL (minimum score 550 paper-based; 213 computer-based). Electronic applications accepted. *Faculty research:* History of philosophy, ethics, philosophy of the mind, philosophy of science, philosophy of language.

University of Georgia, Graduate School, College of Arts and Sciences, Department of Philosophy, Athens, GA 30602. Offers MA, PhD. Part-time programs available. *Faculty:* 13 full-time (6 women). *Students:* 26 full-time (3 women), 6 part-time (1 woman); includes 2 minority (both Hispanic Americans). 25 applicants, 48% accepted, 9 enrolled. In 2009, 1 master's, 1 doctorate awarded. *Degree requirements:* For master's, one foreign language, thesis; for doctorate, one foreign language, thesis/dissertation. *Entrance requirements:* For master's and doctorate, GRE General Test. Additional exam requirements/recommendations for international students: Required—TOEFL. *Application deadline:* For fall admission, 1/1 priority date for domestic and international students; for spring admission, 11/15 for domestic students. Application fee: $50. Electronic applications accepted. *Expenses:* Tuition, state resident: full-time $6000; part-time $250 per credit hour. Tuition, nonresident: full-time $20,904; part-time $871 per credit hour. Required fees: $730 per semester. *Financial support:* In 2009–10, 19 students received support, including 4 teaching assistantships with partial tuition reimbursements available (averaging $13,342 per year); unspecified assistantships also available. Financial award application deadline: 1/1. *Unit head:* Dr. Victoria M. Davion, Head, 706-542-2823, Fax: 706-542-2839, E-mail: vdavion@uga.edu. *Application contact:* Dr. Elizabeth Brient, Graduate Coordinator, 706-583-0668, Fax: 706-542-2839, E-mail: ebrient@uga.edu.

University of Guelph, Graduate Program Services, College of Arts, Department of Philosophy, Guelph, ON N1G 2W1, Canada. Offers MA, PhD. Part-time programs available. *Degree requirements:* For master's, thesis (for some programs); for doctorate, one foreign language, thesis/dissertation. *Entrance requirements:* For master's, minimum B- average during previous 2 years of course work; for doctorate, minimum B average. Additional exam requirements/recommendations for international students: Required—TOEFL (minimum score 550 paper-based; 213 computer-based). Electronic applications accepted. *Faculty research:* Philosophy of science, ethics, modern philosophy, social philosophy, Continental philosophy.

University of Hawaii at Manoa, Graduate Division, College of Arts and Humanities, Department of Philosophy, Honolulu, HI 96822. Offers MA, PhD. Part-time programs available. *Faculty:* 12 full-time (3 women), 3 part-time/adjunct (0 women). *Students:* 37 full-time (12 women), 9 part-time (2 women); includes 7 minority (1 American Indian/Alaska Native, 6 Asian Americans or Pacific Islanders), 7 international. Average age 29. 43 applicants, 40% accepted, 8 enrolled. In 2009, 8 master's, 2 doctorates awarded. *Degree requirements:* For master's, variable foreign language requirement, thesis optional, culminating exam; for doctorate, variable foreign language requirement, comprehensive exam, thesis/dissertation, final oral presentation. *Entrance requirements:* For master's and doctorate, GRE General Test. Additional exam requirements/recommendations for international students: Required—TOEFL (minimum score 600 paper-based; 250 computer-based; 100 iBT), IELTS (minimum score 7). *Application deadline:* For fall admission, 2/1 for domestic students, 1/15 for international students; for spring admission, 9/1 for domestic students, 8/1 for international students. Applications are processed on a rolling basis. Application fee: $60. *Expenses:* Tuition, state resident: full-time $8900; part-time $372 per credit. Tuition, nonresident: full-time $21,400; part-time $898 per credit. Required fees: $207 per semester. *Financial support:* In 2009–10, 2 students received support, including 15 fellowships (averaging $2,705 per year), 1 research assistantship (averaging $21,288 per year), 9 teaching assistantships (averaging $15,562 per year); Federal Work-Study and tuition waivers (full and partial) also available. Financial award application deadline: 3/1. *Faculty research:* Renaissance philosophy, Indian philosophy, logic, ethics, philosophy of science, philosophy of mathematics, Chinese philosophy. Total annual research expenditures: $158,000. *Application contact:* Ron Bontekoe, Graduate Chair, 808-956-8410, Fax: 808-956-9228, E-mail: bontekoe@hawaii.edu.

University of Houston, College of Liberal Arts and Social Sciences, Department of Philosophy, Houston, TX 77204. Offers MA. *Faculty:* 8 full-time (2 women), 1 part-time/adjunct (0 women). *Students:* 15 full-time (0 women), 8 part-time (2 women); includes 4 minority (1 Asian American or Pacific Islander, 3 Hispanic Americans). Average age 27. 60 applicants, 82% accepted, 12 enrolled. In 2009, 15 master's awarded. *Degree requirements:* For master's, thesis or additional course requirements. *Entrance requirements:* For master's, GRE General Test, minimum of 18 hours of course work in philosophy; 3.3 GPA in last 60 hours. Additional exam requirements/recommendations for international students: Required—TOEFL (minimum score 550 paper-based; 79 iBT). *Application deadline:* For fall admission, 3/15 for domestic students, 4/1 for international students. Applications are processed on a rolling basis. Application fee: $40. Electronic applications accepted. *Expenses:* Tuition, state resident: full-time $7676; part-time $320 per credit hour. Tuition, nonresident: full-time $14,324; part-time $597 per credit hour. Required fees: $3034. *Financial support:* In 2009–10, 9 teaching assistantships with full tuition reimbursements (averaging $10,400 per year) were awarded; career-related internships or fieldwork, Federal Work-Study, institutionally sponsored loans, scholarships/grants, health care benefits, and unspecified assistantships also available. Support available to part-time students. Financial award application deadline: 3/10. *Faculty research:* Skepticism, nominalism, history of philosophy, cognitive science. *Unit head:* Dr. David Phillips, Chairperson, 713-743-3209, Fax: 713-743-5162, E-mail: dphillips@uh.edu. *Application contact:* Dr. James Garson, Professor, 713-743-3205, E-mail: jgarson@uh.edu.

University of Illinois at Chicago, Graduate College, College of Liberal Arts and Sciences, Department of Philosophy, Chicago, IL 60607-7128. Offers MA, PhD. Terminal master's awarded for partial completion of doctoral program. *Degree requirements:* For doctorate, thesis/dissertation, preliminary exams. *Entrance requirements:* For master's and doctorate, minimum GPA of 2.75. Additional exam requirements/recommendations for international students: Required—TOEFL. Electronic applications accepted. *Faculty research:* Philosophy of science, philosophy of language, epistemology and metaphysics, ethics, aesthetics.

University of Illinois at Urbana–Champaign, Graduate College, College of Liberal Arts and Sciences, Department of Philosophy, Champaign, IL 61820. Offers MA, PhD, PhD/JD. *Faculty:* 12 full-time (2 women), 2 part-time/adjunct (0 women). *Students:* 30 full-time (1 woman), 3 part-time (1 woman); includes 2 minority (1 Asian American or Pacific Islander, 1 Hispanic American), 1 international. 59 applicants, 7% accepted, 3 enrolled. In 2009, 10 master's, 1 doctorate awarded. *Entrance requirements:* For doctorate, GRE, minimum GPA of 3.0; writing sample. Additional exam requirements/recommendations for international students: Required—TOEFL (minimum score 600 paper-based; 100 iBT). *Application deadline:* Applications are processed on a rolling basis. Application fee: $60 ($75 for international students). Electronic applications accepted. *Financial support:* In 2009–10, 8 fellowships, 33 teaching assistantships were awarded; research assistantships, tuition waivers (full and partial) also available. *Unit head:* Robert C. Cummins, Chair, 217-333-2889, Fax: 217-244-8355, E-mail: rcummins@illinois.edu. *Application contact:* Peggy Wells, Office Support Specialist, 217-244-2646, Fax: 217-244-8355, E-mail: pwells@illinois.edu.

The University of Iowa, Graduate College, College of Liberal Arts and Sciences, Department of Philosophy, Iowa City, IA 52242-1316. Offers MA, PhD, JD/MA. *Degree requirements:* For master's, thesis optional, exam; for doctorate, comprehensive exam, thesis/dissertation. *Entrance requirements:* For master's, GRE General Test or LSAT, minimum GPA of 3.0; for doctorate, GRE General Test, minimum GPA of 3.0. Additional exam requirements/recommendations for international students: Required—TOEFL (minimum score 550 paper-based; 213 computer-based; 81 iBT). Electronic applications accepted.

The University of Kansas, Graduate Studies, College of Liberal Arts and Sciences, Department of Philosophy, Lawrence, KS 66045. Offers MA, PhD, JD/MA. *Faculty:* 12 full-time (2 women). *Students:* 37 full-time (8 women), 3 part-time (1 woman), 2 international. Average age 32. 21 applicants, 67% accepted, 6 enrolled. In 2009, 4 master's, 4 doctorates awarded. Terminal master's awarded for partial completion of doctoral program. *Degree requirements:* For master's, comprehensive exam, thesis or alternative; for doctorate, one foreign language, comprehensive exam, thesis/dissertation. *Entrance requirements:* For master's and doctorate, GRE. Additional exam requirements/recommendations for international students: Required—TOEFL. *Application deadline:* For fall admission, 2/1 priority date for domestic students, 6/15 for international students. Applications are processed on a rolling basis. Application fee: $45 ($55 for international students). Electronic applications accepted. *Expenses:* Tuition, state resident: full-time $6492; part-time $270.50 per credit hour. Tuition, nonresident: full-time $15,510; part-time $646.25 per credit hour. Required fees: $847; $70.56 per credit hour. Tuition and fees vary according to course load and program. *Financial support:* Fellowships, teaching assistantships with full tuition reimbursements available. Financial award application deadline: 1/5. *Faculty research:* Theoretical and applied ethics, social and political philosophy, history of philosophy, analytic philosophy, philosophy of mind and language. *Unit head:* Prof. Ben Eggleston, Chair, 785-864-2332, Fax: 785-864-4298, E-mail: eggleston@ku.edu. *Application contact:* Prof. Dale Dorsey, Director of Graduate Studies, 785-864-2139, Fax: 785-864-4298, E-mail: ddorsey@ku.edu.

University of Kentucky, Graduate School, College of Arts and Sciences, Program in Philosophy, Lexington, KY 40506-0032. Offers MA, PhD. *Degree requirements:* For master's, one foreign language, comprehensive exam, thesis; for doctorate, one foreign language, comprehensive exam, thesis/dissertation. *Entrance requirements:* For master's, GRE General Test, minimum undergraduate GPA of 2.75; for doctorate, GRE General Test, minimum graduate GPA of 3.0. Additional exam requirements/recommendations for international students: Required—TOEFL (minimum score 550 paper-based; 213 computer-based). Electronic applications accepted. *Faculty research:* History of philosophy, history and philosophy of science, ethics, social and political philosophy.

University of Lethbridge, School of Graduate Studies, Lethbridge, AB T1K 3M4, Canada. Offers accounting (MScM); addictions counseling (M Sc); agricultural biotechnology (M Sc); agricultural studies (M Sc, MA); anthropology (MA); archaeology (MA); art (MA, MFA); biochemistry (M Sc); biological sciences (M Sc); biomolecular science (PhD); biosystems and biodiversity (PhD); Canadian studies (MA); chemistry (M Sc); computer science (M Sc); computer science and geographical information science (M Sc); counseling psychology (M Ed); dramatic arts (MA); earth, space, and physical science (PhD); economics (MA); educational leadership (M Ed); English (MA); environmental science (M Sc); evolution and behavior (PhD); exercise science (M Sc); finance (MScM); French (MA); French/German (MA); French/Spanish (MA); general education (M Ed); general management (MScM); geography (M Sc, MA); German (MA); health science (M Sc); health sciences (MA); history (MA); human resource management and labour relations (MScM); individualized multidisciplinary (M Sc, MA); information systems (MScM); international management (MScM); kinesiology (M Sc, MA); management (M Sc, MA); marketing (MScM); mathematics (M Sc); music (M Mus, MA); Native American studies (MA); neuroscience (M Sc, PhD); new media (MA); nursing (M Sc); philosophy (MA); physics (M Sc); policy and strategy (MScM); political science (MA); psychology (M Sc, MA); religious studies (MA); social sciences (MA); sociology (MA); theatre and dramatic arts (MFA); theoretical and computational science (PhD); urban and regional studies (MA); women's studies (MA). Part-time and evening/weekend programs available. *Degree requirements:* For doctorate, comprehensive exam, thesis/dissertation. *Entrance requirements:* For master's, GMAT (M Sc in management), bachelor's degree in related field, minimum GPA of 3.0 during previous 20 graded semester courses, 2 years teaching or related experience (M Ed); for doctorate, master's degree, minimum graduate GPA of 3.5. Additional exam requirements/recommendations for international students: Required—TOEFL. *Faculty research:* Movement and brain plasticity, gibberellin physiology, photosynthesis, carbon cycling, molecular properties of main-group ring components.

University of Louisville, Graduate School, College of Arts and Sciences, Department of Philosophy, Louisville, KY 40292-0001. Offers MA. *Degree requirements:* For master's, one foreign language, thesis or alternative. *Entrance requirements:* For master's, GRE General Test. *Application deadline:* Applications are processed on a rolling basis. Application fee: $50. *Unit head:* Dr. Robert Kimball, Chair, 502-852-0488, Fax: 502-852-0459, E-mail: robert.kimball@louisville.edu. *Application contact:* Libby Leggett, Director, Graduate Admissions, 502-852-3101, Fax: 502-852-6536, E-mail: gradadm@louisville.edu.

University of Manitoba, Faculty of Graduate Studies, Faculty of Arts, Department of Philosophy, Winnipeg, MB R3T 2N2, Canada. Offers MA. *Degree requirements:* For master's, variable foreign language requirement, thesis or alternative.

University of Maryland, College Park, Academic Affairs, College of Arts and Humanities, Department of Philosophy, College Park, MD 20742. Offers MA, PhD. *Faculty:* 25 full-time (8 women), 4 part-time/adjunct (1 woman). *Students:* 34 full-time (6 women), 3 part-time (1 woman); includes 4 minority (2 Asian Americans or Pacific Islanders, 2 Hispanic Americans), 8 international. 157 applicants, 3% accepted, 5 enrolled. In 2009, 2 master's, 8 doctorates awarded. *Degree requirements:* For master's, thesis optional; for doctorate, thesis/dissertation, 2 semesters of undergraduate teaching, qualification in symbolic logic. *Entrance requirements:* For master's, GRE General Test, minimum GPA of 3.0, philosophy paper, writing sample, 3 letters of recommendation; for doctorate, GRE General Test, minimum GPA of 3.0, philosophy paper, writing sample. *Application deadline:* For fall admission, 1/3 for domestic and international students. Applications are processed on a rolling basis. Application fee: $60. Electronic applications accepted. *Expenses:* Tuition, area resident: Part-time $471 per credit hour. Tuition, state resident: part-time $471 per credit hour. Tuition, nonresident: part-time $1016 per credit hour. Required fees: $337.04 per term. *Financial support:* In 2009–10, 30 teaching assistantships with tuition reimbursements (averaging $17,175 per year) were awarded; fellowships, research assistantships with tuition reimbursements, Federal Work-Study and scholarships/grants also available. Support available to part-time students. Financial award applicants required to submit FAFSA. *Faculty research:* Contemporary British and American philosophy, the relationship between philosophy and other disciplines, ethical and conceptual issues in public policy. Total annual research expenditures: $154,936. *Unit head:* John Horty, Chair, 301-405-5689, E-mail: horty@umd.edu. *Application contact:* Dean of Graduate School, 301-405-0376, Fax: 301-314-9305.

University of Massachusetts Amherst, Graduate School, College of Humanities and Fine Arts, Department of Philosophy, Amherst, MA 01003. Offers MA, PhD. Part-time programs available. *Faculty:* 16 full-time (4 women). *Students:* 22 full-time (6 women), 17 part-time (2 women); includes 1 minority (African American), 7 international. Average age 29. 125 applicants, 18% accepted, 7 enrolled. In 2009, 8 doctorates awarded. Terminal master's awarded for partial completion of doctoral program. *Degree requirements:* For master's, thesis optional; for doctorate, comprehensive exam, thesis/dissertation. *Entrance requirements:* For master's and doctorate, GRE General Test, writing sample, 3 letters of recommendation. Additional exam requirements/recommendations for international students: Required—TOEFL (minimum score 550 paper-based; 213 computer-based; 80 iBT), IELTS (minimum score 6.5). *Application deadline:* For fall admission, 1/2 for domestic and international students. Applications are processed on a rolling basis. Application fee: $50 ($65 for international students). Electronic applications accepted. *Expenses:* Tuition, state resident: full-time $2640; part-time $110 per credit. Tuition, nonresident: full-time $9936; part-time $414 per credit. Tuition and fees vary according to course load. *Financial support:* In 2009–10, 1 fellowship with full tuition reimbursement (averaging $3,275 per year), 1 research assistantship with full tuition reimbursement (averaging $3,629 per year), 25 teaching assistantships with full tuition reimbursements (averaging $11,595 per year) were awarded; career-related internships or fieldwork, Federal Work-Study, scholarships/grants, traineeships, health care benefits, tuition waivers (full), and unspecified assistantships also available. Support available to part-time students. Financial award application deadline: 1/2. *Unit head:* Dr. Fred A. Feldman, Graduate Program Director, 413-545-2330, Fax: 413-577-3800. *Application contact:* Jean M. Ames, Supervisor of Admissions, 413-545-0722, Fax: 413-577-0010, E-mail: gradadm@grad.umass.edu.

University of Memphis, Graduate School, College of Arts and Sciences, Department of Philosophy, Memphis, TN 38152. Offers MA, PhD. Part-time programs available. *Faculty:* 9 full-time (3 women), 1 part-time/adjunct (0 women). *Students:* 29 full-time (13 women), 5 part-time (4 women); includes 11 minority (8 African Americans, 2 Asian Americans or Pacific Islanders, 1 Hispanic American), 7 international. Average age 30. 78 applicants, 27% accepted, 20 enrolled. In 2009, 14 master's, 2 doctorates awarded. Terminal master's awarded for partial completion of doctoral program. *Degree requirements:* For master's, thesis optional, 2 written comprehensive exams; for doctorate, 2 foreign languages, thesis/dissertation, area and qualifying exams. *Entrance requirements:* For master's, GRE General Test, minimum GPA of 2.5, 18 hours of undergraduate course work in philosophy; for doctorate, GRE General Test, minimum GPA of 3.0, bachelor's degree in philosophy. *Application deadline:* For fall admission, 2/1 for domestic students. Application fee: $35 ($60 for international students). Electronic applications accepted. *Expenses:* Tuition, state resident: full-time $6246; part-time $347 per credit hour. Tuition, nonresident: full-time $15,894; part-time $883 per credit hour. Required fees: $1160. Full-time tuition and fees vary according to course load, degree level and program. *Financial support:* In 2009–10, 9 students received support; fellowships with full tuition reimbursements available, research assistantships with full tuition reimbursements available, teaching assistantships with full tuition reimbursements available, Federal Work-Study, scholarships/grants, tuition waivers (full), and unspecified assistantships available. Financial award application deadline: 2/15; financial award applicants required to submit FAFSA. *Faculty research:* Continental philosophy, ethics, analytic philosophy, feminist theory, Africana philosophy. *Unit head:* Dr. Deborah Tollefsen, Chair, 901-678-2535, Fax: 901-678-4365, E-mail: dtollfsn@memphis.edu. *Application contact:* Dr. Mary Beth Mader, Coordinator of Admission, 901-678-4526.

University of Miami, Graduate School, College of Arts and Sciences, Department of Philosophy, Coral Gables, FL 33124. Offers MA, PhD. Part-time programs available. Terminal master's awarded for partial completion of doctoral program. *Degree requirements:* For master's, thesis or alternative; for doctorate, comprehensive exam, thesis/dissertation. *Entrance requirements:* For master's, GRE General Test; for doctorate, GRE General Test, minimum GPA of 3.0, 3 letters of recommendation, writing sample. Additional exam requirements/recommendations for international students: Required—TOEFL. Electronic applications accepted. *Faculty research:* Ethics, epistemology, pragmatism, philosophy of science, metaphysics.

University of Michigan, Horace H. Rackham School of Graduate Studies, College of Literature, Science, and the Arts, Department of Philosophy, Ann Arbor, MI 48109. Offers AM, PhD. *Faculty:* 20 full-time (4 women), 2 part-time/adjunct (0 women). *Students:* 36 full-time (7 women); includes 1 American Indian/Alaska Native, 3 Asian Americans or Pacific Islanders, 1 Hispanic American, 9 international. Average age 28. 207 applicants, 11% accepted, 3 enrolled. In 2009, 9 master's, 10 doctorates awarded. Terminal master's awarded for partial completion of doctoral program. *Degree requirements:* For doctorate, one foreign language, thesis/dissertation, oral defense of dissertation. *Entrance requirements:* For master's and doctorate, GRE General Test, 3 letters of recommendation, writing sample. Additional exam requirements/recommendations for international students: Required—TOEFL. *Application deadline:* For fall admission, 1/15 for domestic and international students. Application fee: $60 ($75 for international students). Electronic applications accepted. *Expenses:* Tuition, state resident: full-time $17,286; part-time $1099 per credit hour. Tuition, nonresident: full-time $34,944; part-time $2080 per credit hour. Required fees: $95 per semester. Tuition and fees vary according to course load, degree level and program. *Financial support:* In 2009–10, 35 students received support, including fellowships with full tuition reimbursements available (averaging $16,800 per year), teaching assistantships with full tuition reimbursements available (averaging $16,800 per year); health care benefits also available. Financial award application deadline: 1/15. *Faculty research:* Ethics, metaphysics, philosophy of language and mind, political and social philosophy, philosophy of science. *Unit head:* James M. Joyce, Chair, 734-764-6285, Fax: 734-763-8071, E-mail: jjoyce@umich.edu. *Application contact:* Linda Shultes, Graduate Program Coordinator, 734-764-3260, Fax: 734-763-8071, E-mail: phil-admissions@umich.edu.

University of Minnesota, Twin Cities Campus, Graduate School, College of Liberal Arts, Department of Philosophy, Minneapolis, MN 55455-0213. Offers MA, PhD. Part-time programs available. *Faculty:* 17 full-time (5 women), 6 part-time/adjunct (3 women). *Students:* 27 full-time (12 women), 3 part-time (1 woman); includes 5 minority (4 Asian Americans or Pacific Islanders, 1 Hispanic American), 4 international. 67 applicants, 9% accepted, 4 enrolled. In 2009, 9 master's, 4 doctorates awarded. Terminal master's awarded for partial completion of doctoral program. *Degree requirements:* For master's, comprehensive exam, thesis and oral exam or 3 papers and oral exam; for doctorate, comprehensive exam, thesis/dissertation, first two years coursework=written exam; 3 paper plus dept review=oral prelim; thesis proposal. *Entrance requirements:* For master's and doctorate, GRE. Additional exam requirements/recommendations for international students: Required—TOEFL, TOEFL (minimum score 550 paper-based; 213 computer-based) or IELTS (minimum score 6.5) or Michigan English Language Assessment Battery (minimum score 80). *Application deadline:* For fall admission, 12/13 for domestic and international students. Application fee: $75 ($95 for international students). Electronic applications accepted. *Financial support:* In 2009–10, 15 fellowships with full tuition reimbursements (averaging $3,500 per year), 28 teaching assistantships with full tuition reimbursements (averaging $14,000 per year) were awarded; research assistantships with full tuition reimburse-

Philosophy

University of Minnesota, Twin Cities Campus (continued)

ments, Federal Work-Study, institutionally sponsored loans, scholarships/grants, health care benefits, and unspecified assistantships also available. Support available to part-time students. Financial award application deadline: 11/31. *Faculty research:* Philosophy of science; ethics and social/political philosophy; logic, language, and mind. Total annual research expenditures: $60,000. *Unit head:* Prof. Geoffrey Hellman, Chair, 612-625-7573, Fax: 612-626-8380. *Application contact:* Prof. Peter Hanks, Professor, 612-624-6415, Fax: 612-626-8380, E-mail: phanks@umn.edu.

University of Mississippi, Graduate School, College of Liberal Arts, Department of Philosophy and Religions, Oxford, University, MS 38677. Offers philosophy (MA). *Faculty:* 9 full-time (3 women), 3 part-time/adjunct (2 women). *Students:* 7 full-time (1 woman), 3 part-time (0 women); includes 1 minority (African American). In 2009, 4 master's awarded. *Degree requirements:* For master's, thesis. *Entrance requirements:* For master's, GRE General Test, minimum GPA of 3.0. Additional exam requirements/recommendations for international students: Required—TOEFL. *Application deadline:* For fall admission, 4/1 for domestic students; for spring admission, 10/1 for domestic students. Applications are processed on a rolling basis. Application fee: $25. Electronic applications accepted. *Financial support:* Scholarships/grants available. Financial award application deadline: 3/1; financial award applicants required to submit FAFSA. *Unit head:* Dr. William Lawhead, Chair, 662-915-7020, Fax: 662-915-5654, E-mail: wlawhead@olemiss.edu. *Application contact:* Dr. Christy M. Wyandt, Associate Dean, 662-915-7474, Fax: 662-915-7577, E-mail: cwyandt@olemiss.edu.

University of Missouri, Graduate School, College of Arts and Sciences, Department of Philosophy, Columbia, MO 65211. Offers MA, PhD. *Faculty:* 14 full-time (2 women), 4 part-time/adjunct (1 woman). *Students:* 22 full-time (5 women), 6 part-time (0 women); includes 2 minority (1 American Indian/Alaska Native, 1 Asian American or Pacific Islander), 6 international. Average age 28. 45 applicants, 58% accepted, 7 enrolled. In 2009, 7 master's, 1 doctorate awarded. Terminal master's awarded for partial completion of doctoral program. *Degree requirements:* For doctorate, one foreign language, comprehensive exam, thesis/dissertation. *Entrance requirements:* For master's, GRE General Test (minimum score 650 verbal, 700 quantitative), minimum GPA of 3.0; average GPA in major = 3.9; for doctorate, GRE General Test; average GRE scores: 650 verbal, 700 quantitative, minimum GPA of 3.0; average GPA in major = 3.9. Additional exam requirements/recommendations for international students: Required—TOEFL (minimum score 500 paper-based; 173 computer-based; 61 iBT). *Application deadline:* For fall admission, 1/15 priority date for domestic students. Applications are processed on a rolling basis. Application fee: $45 ($60 for international students). Electronic applications accepted. *Financial support:* In 2009–10, 3 fellowships with full tuition reimbursements, 1 research assistantship with full tuition reimbursement, 22 teaching assistantships with full tuition reimbursements were awarded; institutionally sponsored loans, health care benefits, and unspecified assistantships also available. Financial award application deadline: 2/1. *Faculty research:* Epistemology, political philosophy, philosophy of biology, decision/game/rational choice theory, ethics, philosophy of mind and psychology, Indian philosophy, metaphysics, and action theory. *Unit head:* Dr. Andrew Melnyk, Department Chair, E-mail: melnyka@missouri.edu. *Application contact:* Jonni Paxton, Administrative Assistant, 573-882-2871, E-mail: paxtonj@missouri.edu.

University of Missouri–St. Louis, College of Arts and Sciences, Department of Philosophy, St. Louis, MO 63121. Offers MA. *Faculty:* 10 full-time (3 women), 4 part-time/adjunct (0 women). *Students:* 18 full-time (3 women), 10 part-time (2 women); includes 2 minority (both Asian Americans or Pacific Islanders). Average age 28. 44 applicants, 73% accepted, 14 enrolled. In 2009, 11 master's awarded. *Entrance requirements:* For master's, writing sample, 3 letters of recommendation. Additional exam requirements/recommendations for international students: Required—TOEFL (minimum score 550 paper-based; 213 computer-based). *Application deadline:* For fall admission, 7/1 priority date for domestic and international students; for spring admission, 12/1 priority date for domestic and international students. Applications are processed on a rolling basis. Application fee: $35 ($40 for international students). Electronic applications accepted. *Expenses:* Tuition, state resident: full-time $5377; part-time $297.70 per credit hour. Tuition, nonresident: full-time $13,882; part-time $771.20 per credit hour. Required fees: $220; $12.20 per credit hour. One-time fee: $12. Tuition and fees vary according to course level, campus/location and program. *Financial support:* In 2009–10, 17 teaching assistantships with full and partial tuition reimbursements (averaging $5,585 per year) were awarded. Financial award applicants required to submit FAFSA. *Faculty research:* Ethics, philosophy and history of science, philosophical social science, aesthetics. *Unit head:* Dr. Eric Wiland, Graduate Program Director, 314-516-5631, Fax: 314-516-5816, E-mail: wiland@umsl.edu. *Application contact:* 314-516-5458, Fax: 314-516-6996, E-mail: gradadm@umsl.edu.

The University of Montana, Graduate School, College of Arts and Sciences, Department of Philosophy, Missoula, MT 59812-0002. Offers MA. *Degree requirements:* For master's, thesis or additional course work/professional paper. *Entrance requirements:* For master's, GRE General Test. Additional exam requirements/recommendations for international students: Required—TOEFL (minimum score 525 paper-based; 197 computer-based). *Faculty research:* Philosophy of law, natural science, feminism, and technology; environmental, business, and medical ethics.

University of Nebraska–Lincoln, Graduate College, College of Arts and Sciences, Department of Philosophy, Lincoln, NE 68588. Offers MA, PhD. *Degree requirements:* For master's, thesis optional; for doctorate, comprehensive exam, thesis/dissertation. *Entrance requirements:* For master's and doctorate, GRE General Test, writing sample. Additional exam requirements/recommendations for international students: Required—TOEFL (minimum score 600 paper-based; 250 computer-based). Electronic applications accepted. *Faculty research:* Ethics, epistemology, metaphysics, cognitive science, history of philosophy.

University of Nevada, Reno, Graduate School, College of Liberal Arts, Department of Philosophy, Reno, NV 89557. Offers MA. *Degree requirements:* For master's, thesis optional. *Entrance requirements:* For master's, GRE General Test, minimum GPA of 2.75. Additional exam requirements/recommendations for international students: Required—TOEFL (minimum score 500 paper-based; 173 computer-based; 61 iBT), IELTS (minimum score 6). Electronic applications accepted. *Faculty research:* Ancient philosophy (Aristotle), ethics, political theory, violence, Continental philosophy.

University of New Brunswick Fredericton, School of Graduate Studies, Policy Studies Program, Fredericton, NB E3B 5A3, Canada. Offers people, property and alternative dispute resolution (M Phil); philosophy politics and economics (M Phil); sustainable development (M Phil). Part-time programs available. *Faculty:* 6 full-time (2 women), 13 part-time/adjunct (2 women). *Students:* 8 full-time (3 women), 5 part-time (3 women). In 2009, 7 master's awarded. *Degree requirements:* For master's, thesis, report. *Entrance requirements:* For master's, minimum GPA of 3.5, BA; BA Honours. Additional exam requirements/recommendations for international students: Required—TOEFL (minimum score 600 paper-based; 250 computer-based; 100 iBT), TWE (minimum score 4), or IELTS (minimum score 7). Application fee: $50 Canadian dollars. Tuition and fees charges are reported in Canadian dollars. *Expenses:* Tuition, area resident: Full-time $5562 Canadian dollars; part-time $2781 Canadian dollars per year. Required fees: $49.75 Canadian dollars per term. *Financial support:* In 2009–10, 5 research assistantships (averaging $5,600 per year), 2 teaching assistantships (averaging $4,400 per year) were awarded. *Unit head:* Dr. Linda Eyre, Dean of Graduate Studies, 506-447-3044, Fax: 506-453-4817, E-mail: gradidst@unb.ca. *Application contact:* Janet Amurault, Graduate Secretary, 506-458-7558, Fax: 506-453-4817, E-mail: jamiraul@unb.ca.

University of New Mexico, Graduate School, College of Arts and Sciences, Department of Philosophy, Albuquerque, NM 87131-2039. Offers MA, PhD. Part-time programs available. *Faculty:* 12 full-time (2 women), 2 part-time/adjunct (0 women). *Students:* 24 full-time (5 women), 19 part-time (7 women); includes 6 minority (1 American Indian/Alaska Native, 2 Asian Americans or Pacific Islanders, 3 Hispanic Americans), 4 international. Average age 32. 61 applicants, 39% accepted, 13 enrolled. In 2009, 2 master's awarded. Terminal master's awarded for partial completion of doctoral program. *Degree requirements:* For master's, thesis (for some programs); for doctorate, one foreign language, comprehensive exam, thesis/dissertation. *Entrance requirements:* For master's and doctorate, GRE. Additional exam requirements/recommendations for international students: Required—TOEFL. *Application deadline:* For fall admission, 1/31 for domestic and international students; for spring admission, 11/1 for domestic and international students. Application fee: $50. Electronic applications accepted. *Expenses:* Tuition, state resident: full-time $2099; part-time $233.20 per credit hour. Tuition, nonresident: full-time $6650. Required fees: $25 per semester. Tuition and fees vary according to course load, program and reciprocity agreements. *Financial support:* In 2009–10, 10 students received support, including 1 fellowship with tuition reimbursement available (averaging $15,600 per year), 13 teaching assistantships with tuition reimbursements available (averaging $15,600 per year). Financial award application deadline: 1/31; financial award applicants required to submit FAFSA. *Faculty research:* History of modern philosophy, ethics, philosophy of art and literature, Indian philosophy, continental philosophy. Total annual research expenditures: $10,103. *Unit head:* Dr. John Bussanich, Chair, 505-277-8938, Fax: 505-277-6362, E-mail: john.bussanich@gmail.edu. *Application contact:* Shannon Kindilien, Administrative Assistant II, 505-277-2405, Fax: 505-277-6362, E-mail: thinker@unm.edu.

The University of North Carolina at Chapel Hill, Graduate School, College of Arts and Sciences, Department of Philosophy, Chapel Hill, NC 27599. Offers MA, PhD. *Degree requirements:* For master's, comprehensive exam, thesis; for doctorate, comprehensive exam, thesis/dissertation. *Entrance requirements:* For master's and doctorate, GRE General Test, minimum GPA of 3.0.

University of North Florida, College of Arts and Sciences, Department of Philosophy, Jacksonville, FL 32224. Offers applied ethics (Graduate Certificate); practical philosophy and applied ethics (MA). Part-time and evening/weekend programs available. *Faculty:* 11 full-time (3 women). *Students:* 11 full-time (5 women), 6 part-time (3 women); includes 3 minority (1 African American, 2 Asian Americans or Pacific Islanders). Average age 33. 12 applicants, 50% accepted, 6 enrolled. In 2009, 3 master's awarded. *Entrance requirements:* For master's, GRE General Test, minimum GPA of 3.0 in last 60 hours, 3 letters of recommendation, writing sample. Additional exam requirements/recommendations for international students: Required—TOEFL (minimum score 500 paper-based). *Application deadline:* For fall admission, 4/15 priority date for domestic students, 3/1 for international students. Applications are processed on a rolling basis. Application fee: $30. Electronic applications accepted. *Expenses:* Tuition, state resident: full-time $6649.20; part-time $277.05 per credit hour. Tuition, nonresident: full-time $22,970; part-time $957.08 per credit hour. Required fees: $985; $41.03 per credit hour. *Financial support:* In 2009–10, 14 students received support, including 3 teaching assistantships (averaging $4,222 per year). Financial award application deadline: 4/1; financial award applicants required to submit FAFSA. *Faculty research:* Late modern philosophy, pragmatism, religion and American culture, hermeneutics, philosophy of mind. Total annual research expenditures: $27,108. *Unit head:* Dr. Hans Herbert Koegler, 904-620-1330, Fax: 904-620-1840, E-mail: hkoegler@unf.edu. *Application contact:* Dr. Andrew Buchwalter, Graduate Coordinator, 904-620-1155, Fax: 904-620-1840, E-mail: abuchwal@unf.edu.

University of North Texas, Robert B. Toulouse School of Graduate Studies, College of Arts and Sciences, Department of Philosophy and Religion Studies, Denton, TX 76203. Offers philosophy (MA, PhD). *Degree requirements:* For master's, one foreign language, thesis or alternative; for doctorate, one foreign language, comprehensive exam, thesis/dissertation. *Entrance requirements:* For master's, GRE General Test. Additional exam requirements/recommendations for international students: Required—proof of English language proficiency required for non-native English speakers; Recommended—TOEFL (minimum score 550 paper-based; 213 computer-based; 79 iBT). Application fee: $50 ($75 for international students). *Expenses:* Tuition, state resident: full-time $4298; part-time $239 per contact hour. Tuition, nonresident: full-time $9878; part-time $549 per contact hour. Required fees: $265 per contact hour. *Financial support:* Application deadline: 4/1. *Application contact:* Associate Dean, 940-565-2383, Fax: 940-565-2141.

University of Notre Dame, Graduate School, College of Arts and Letters, Division of Humanities, Department of Philosophy, Notre Dame, IN 46556. Offers PhD. *Degree requirements:* For doctorate, 2 foreign languages, thesis/dissertation, candidacy exam. *Entrance requirements:* For doctorate, GRE General Test. Additional exam requirements/recommendations for international students: Required—TOEFL (minimum score 600 paper-based; 250 computer-based; 80 iBT). Electronic applications accepted. *Faculty research:* History of philosophy, ethics, philosophy of science and logic, philosophy of religion, Continental philosophy, metaphysics.

University of Oklahoma, Graduate College, College of Arts and Sciences, Department of Philosophy, Norman, OK 73019. Offers MA, PhD. Evening/weekend programs available. *Faculty:* 15 full-time (4 women). *Students:* 27 full-time (3 women), 9 part-time (2 women); includes 2 minority (1 American Indian/Alaska Native, 1 Asian American or Pacific Islander). 28 applicants, 57% accepted, 6 enrolled. In 2009, 3 master's awarded. Terminal master's awarded for partial completion of doctoral program. *Degree requirements:* For master's, thesis optional; for doctorate, thesis/dissertation, oral and written exams. *Entrance requirements:* For master's and doctorate, GRE General Test, 3 letters of recommendation, writing sample. Additional exam requirements/recommendations for international students: Required—TOEFL (minimum score 550 paper-based; 213 computer-based). *Application deadline:* For fall admission, 2/1 priority date for domestic and international students; for spring admission, 11/1 for domestic students, 9/1 for international students. Applications are processed on a rolling basis. Application fee: $40 ($90 for international students). Electronic applications accepted. *Expenses:* Tuition, state resident: full-time $3744; part-time $156 per credit hour. Tuition, nonresident: full-time $13,577; part-time $565.70 per credit hour. Required fees: $2415; $90.10 per credit hour. *Financial support:* In 2009–10, 30 students received support, including 2 fellowships (averaging $5,000 per year), 3 research assistantships with partial tuition reimbursements available (averaging $12,943 per year), 20 teaching assistantships with partial tuition reimbursements available (averaging $12,746 per year); health care benefits and unspecified assistantships also available. Financial award application deadline: 2/28; financial award applicants required to submit FAFSA. *Faculty research:* Metaphysics, epistemology, aesthetics, ethics, Chinese philosophy. *Unit head:* Dr. Hugh Benson, Chair, 405-325-6324, Fax: 405-325-2660, E-mail: hbenson@ou.edu. *Application contact:* Wayne Riggs, Director of Graduate Studies, 405-325-6324, Fax: 405-325-2660, E-mail: wriggs@ou.edu.

University of Oregon, Graduate School, College of Arts and Sciences, Department of Philosophy, Eugene, OR 97403. Offers MA, PhD. Terminal master's awarded for partial completion of doctoral program. *Degree requirements:* For master's, one foreign language, thesis or alternative; for doctorate, one foreign language, thesis/dissertation. *Entrance requirements:* For master's and doctorate, GRE General Test. Additional exam requirements/recommendations for international students: Required—TOEFL. *Faculty research:* Social and political philosophy, feminist philosophy, American philosophy, aesthetics, philosophy of mind.

University of Ottawa, Faculty of Graduate and Postdoctoral Studies, Faculty of Arts, Department of Philosophy, Ottawa, ON K1N 6N5, Canada. Offers MA, PhD. *Degree requirements:* For master's, thesis or alternative; for doctorate, comprehensive exam, thesis/dissertation. *Entrance requirements:* For master's, honors degree or equivalent, minimum B average; for doctorate, master's degree, minimum B+ average. Electronic applications accepted. *Faculty research:* History of philosophy (ancient, medieval, modern and contemporary); metaphysics/epistemology; value theory: political philosophy, ethics.

University of Pennsylvania, School of Arts and Sciences, Graduate Group in Philosophy, Philadelphia, PA 19104. Offers AM, PhD, JD/PhD. *Faculty:* 16 full-time (6 women), 2 part-time/adjunct (0 women). *Students:* 31 full-time (10 women), 8 international. 125 applicants, 10% accepted, 5 enrolled. In 2009, 3 master's, 6 doctorates awarded. Terminal master's awarded for partial completion of doctoral program. *Degree requirements:* For master's, thesis; for doctorate, thesis/dissertation, 1 year of teaching experience. *Application deadline:* For fall admission, 12/1 priority date for domestic students. Application fee: $70. Electronic applications accepted. *Expenses:* Tuition: Full-time $25,660; part-time $4758 per course. Required fees: $2152; $270 per course. Tuition and fees vary according to course load, degree level and program. *Financial support:* Fellowships, teaching assistantships, institutionally sponsored loans, scholarships/grants, traineeships, health care benefits, and unspecified assistantships available. Financial award application deadline: 12/15.

University of Pittsburgh, School of Arts and Sciences, Department of History and Philosophy of Science, Pittsburgh, PA 15260. Offers MA, PhD. *Faculty:* 8 full-time (1 woman), 2 part-time/adjunct (0 women). *Students:* 29 full-time (9 women), 1 part-time (0 women); includes 3 minority (all Asian Americans or Pacific Islanders), 6 international. Average age 29. 57 applicants, 12% accepted, 5 enrolled. In 2009, 2 doctorates awarded. Terminal master's awarded for partial completion of doctoral program. *Degree requirements:* For master's, one foreign language, comprehensive exam; for doctorate, 2 foreign languages, comprehensive exam, thesis/dissertation. *Entrance requirements:* For master's and doctorate, GRE General Test. Additional exam requirements/recommendations for international students: Required—TOEFL (minimum score 550 paper-based; 213 computer-based). *Application deadline:* For fall admission, 1/10 for domestic and international students. Application fee: $50. Electronic applications accepted. *Expenses:* Tuition, state resident: full-time $16,402; part-time $665 per credit. Tuition, nonresident: full-time $28,694; part-time $1175 per credit. Required fees: $690; $175 per term. Tuition and fees vary according to program. *Financial support:* In 2009–10, 27 students received support, including 13 fellowships with full tuition reimbursements available, 15 teaching assistantships with full tuition reimbursements available; health care benefits also available. Financial award application deadline: 1/10. *Faculty research:* History and philosophy of biology, psychology, neuroscience; history and philosophy of physics; early modern science; rhetoric of science; philosophy of social science. *Unit head:* Dr. Sandra Mitchell, Chairman, 412-624-5896, Fax: 412-624-6825, E-mail: smitchel@pitt.edu. *Application contact:* Joann McIntyre, Graduate Admissions Secretary, 412-624-5896, Fax: 412-624-6825, E-mail: vanna@pitt.edu.

University of Pittsburgh, School of Arts and Sciences, Department of Philosophy, Pittsburgh, PA 15260. Offers MA, PhD. *Faculty:* 15 full-time (1 woman). *Students:* 67 full-time (16 women); includes 8 minority (2 African Americans, 1 American Indian/Alaska Native, 5 Asian Americans or Pacific Islanders), 21 international. 207 applicants, 9% accepted, 7 enrolled. In 2009, 3 master's awarded. Terminal master's awarded for partial completion of doctoral program. *Degree requirements:* For master's, one foreign language; for doctorate, one foreign language, thesis/dissertation. *Entrance requirements:* For master's and doctorate, GRE General Test. Additional exam requirements/recommendations for international students: Required—TOEFL (minimum score 550 paper-based; 213 computer-based; 79 iBT), IELTS (minimum score 6.5). *Application deadline:* For fall admission, 1/10 for domestic and international students. Application fee: $50. Electronic applications accepted. *Expenses:* Tuition, state resident: full-time $16,402; part-time $665 per credit. Tuition, nonresident: full-time $28,694; part-time $1175 per credit. Required fees: $690; $175 per term. Tuition and fees vary according to program. *Financial support:* In 2009–10, 50 students received support, including 15 fellowships with full tuition reimbursements available (averaging $24,049 per year), 2 research assistantships with full tuition reimbursements available (averaging $15,675 per year), 33 teaching assistantships with full tuition reimbursements available (averaging $15,675 per year); Federal Work-Study, scholarships/grants, health care benefits, and tuition waivers (full and partial) also available. Financial award application deadline: 1/10. *Faculty research:* Metaphysics and epistemology, ethics, philosophy of science, history of philosophy, logic. *Unit head:* Dr. Thomas Ricketts, Chairman, 412-624-5768, Fax: 412-624-5377, E-mail: ricketts@pitt.edu. *Application contact:* Dr. Thomas Ricketts, Chairman, 412-624-5768, Fax: 412-624-5377, E-mail: ricketts@pitt.edu.

University of Puerto Rico, Río Piedras, College of Humanities, Department of Philosophy, San Juan, PR 00931-3300. Offers MA. Part-time programs available. *Degree requirements:* For master's, one foreign language, comprehensive exam, thesis. *Entrance requirements:* For master's, PAEG or GRE, interview, minimum GPA of 3.0, letter of recommendation (2).

University of Regina, Faculty of Graduate Studies and Research, Faculty of Arts, Department of Philosophy, Regina, SK S4S 0A2, Canada. Offers philosophy (MA); social and political thought (MA). *Faculty:* 9 full-time (3 women). *Students:* 1 (woman) full-time, 2 part-time (0 women). 2 applicants, 50% accepted. *Degree requirements:* For master's, thesis. *Entrance requirements:* Additional exam requirements/recommendations for international students: Required—TOEFL (minimum score 580 paper-based; 237 computer-based; 80 iBT). *Application deadline:* Applications are processed on a rolling basis. Application fee: $90 ($100 for international students). Electronic applications accepted. *Financial support:* Fellowships, research assistantships, teaching assistantships, scholarships/grants available. Financial award application deadline: 6/15. *Faculty research:* History of philosophy, ethics, aesthetics, metaphysics, epistemology. *Unit head:* Dr. Eldon Soifer, Head, 306-585-4301, Fax: 306-585-4827, E-mail: eldon.soifer@uregina.ca. *Application contact:* Dr. Eldon Soifer, Head, 306-585-4301, Fax: 306-585-4827, E-mail: eldon.soifer@uregina.ca.

University of Regina, Faculty of Graduate Studies and Research, Faculty of Arts, Program in Social and Political Thought, Regina, SK S4S 0A2, Canada. Offers MA. *Faculty:* 9 full-time (3 women). *Students:* 2 full-time (1 woman), 3 part-time (1 woman). 2 applicants, 100% accepted. In 2009, 2 master's awarded. *Degree requirements:* For master's, thesis. *Entrance requirements:* Additional exam requirements/recommendations for international students: Required—TOEFL (minimum score 580 paper-based; 237 computer-based; 80 iBT). *Application deadline:* For fall admission, 3/15 for domestic students. Application fee: $90 ($100 for international students). Electronic applications accepted. *Financial support:* In 2009–10, 1 fellowship (averaging $19,000 per year) was awarded; research assistantships, teaching assistantships. *Unit head:* Dr. Shadia Drury, Program Coordinator, 306-585-4073, E-mail: shadia.drury@uregina.ca. *Application contact:* Dr. Shadia Drury, Program Coordinator, 306-585-4073, E-mail: shadia.drury@uregina.ca.

University of Rochester, The College, Arts and Sciences, Department of Philosophy, Rochester, NY 14627. Offers MA, PhD. Terminal master's awarded for partial completion of doctoral program. *Degree requirements:* For doctorate, thesis/dissertation, qualifying exam. *Entrance requirements:* For master's, GRE General Test; for doctorate, GRE General Test, sample of written work. Additional exam requirements/recommendations for international students: Required—TOEFL.

University of St. Thomas, Center for Thomistic Studies, Houston, TX 77006-4696. Offers philosophy (MA, PhD). Part-time programs available. *Faculty:* 6 full-time (1 woman). *Students:* 8 full-time (1 woman), 19 part-time (3 women); includes 5 minority (2 Asian Americans or Pacific Islanders, 3 Hispanic Americans), 3 international. Average age 33. 5 applicants, 100% accepted, 4 enrolled. In 2009, 2 doctorates awarded. Terminal master's awarded for partial completion of doctoral program. *Degree requirements:* For master's, one foreign language, comprehensive exam, thesis (for some programs); for doctorate, 2 foreign languages, comprehensive exam, thesis/dissertation, MA level Latin exam (completed prior to 3rd semester of study). *Entrance requirements:* For master's, minimum GPA of 3.0, minimum 18 hours of undergraduate course work in philosophy, 3 letters of recommendation from professional educators qualified to evaluate the applicant's academic background, writing sample; for doctorate, MA in philosophy. *Application deadline:* Applications are processed on a rolling basis. Application fee: $35. Electronic applications accepted. *Expenses:* Tuition: Full-time $14,436; part-time $802 per credit hour. Required fees: $224. *Financial support:* In 2009–10, 14 students received support. Federal Work-Study, scholarships/grants, and unspecified assistantships available. Support available to part-time students. Financial award application deadline: 3/1; financial award applicants required to submit FAFSA. *Unit head:* Dr. Mary Catherine Sommers, Director, 713-525-3591, Fax: 713-942-3464, E-mail: sommers@stthom.edu. *Application contact:* Valerie Hall, Administrative Assistant II, 713-525-3591, Fax: 713-942-3464, E-mail: butlerp@stthom.edu.

University of Saskatchewan, College of Graduate Studies and Research, College of Arts and Sciences, Department of Philosophy, Saskatoon, SK S7N 5A2, Canada. Offers MA. *Faculty:* 14. *Students:* 15. In 2009, 3 master's awarded. *Degree requirements:* For master's, thesis. *Entrance requirements:* Additional exam requirements/recommendations for international students: Required—TOEFL (minimum score 80 iBT); Recommended—IELTS (minimum score 6.5). *Application deadline:* For fall admission, 7/1 priority date for domestic students. Applications are processed on a rolling basis. Application fee: $75. Electronic applications accepted. Tuition and fees charges are reported in Canadian dollars. *Expenses:* Tuition, area resident: Full-time $3000 Canadian dollars; part-time $500 Canadian dollars per term. Required fees: $700 Canadian dollars; $100 Canadian dollars per term. *Financial support:* Fellowships, research assistantships, teaching assistantships available. Financial award application deadline: 1/31. *Unit head:* Dr. Sarah Hoffman, Head, 306-966-6382, Fax: 306-966-2567, E-mail: sarah.hoffman@usask.ca. *Application contact:* Dr. Karl Pfeifer, Graduate Chair, 306-966-6387, Fax: 306-966-2567, E-mail: karl.pfeifer@usask.ca.

University of South Africa, College of Human Sciences, Pretoria, South Africa. Offers adult education (M Ed); African languages (MA, PhD); African politics (MA, PhD); Afrikaans (MA, PhD); ancient history (MA, PhD); ancient Near Eastern studies (MA, PhD); anthropology (MA, PhD); applied linguistics (MA); Arabic (MA, PhD); archaeology (MA); art history (MA); Biblical archaeology (MA); Biblical studies (M Th, D Th, PhD); Christian spirituality (M Th, D Th); church history (M Th, D Th); classical studies (MA, PhD); clinical psychology (MA); communication (MA, PhD); comparative education (M Ed, Ed D); consulting psychology (D Admin, D Com, PhD); curriculum studies (M Ed, Ed D); development studies (M Admin, MA, D Admin, PhD); didactics (M Ed, Ed D); education (M Tech); education management (M Ed, Ed D); educational psychology (M Ed); English (MA); environmental education (M Ed); French (MA, PhD); German (MA, PhD); Greek (MA); guidance and counseling (M Ed); health studies (MA, PhD), including health sciences education (MA), health services management (MA), medical and surgical nursing science (critical care general) (MA), midwifery and neonatal nursing science (MA), trauma and emergency care (MA); history (MA, PhD); history of education (Ed D); inclusive education (M Ed, Ed D); information and communications technology policy and regulation (MA); information science (MA, MIS, PhD); international politics (MA, PhD); Islamic studies (MA, PhD); Italian (MA, PhD); Judaica (MA, PhD); linguistics (MA, PhD); mathematical education (M Ed); mathematics education (MA); missiology (M Th, D Th); modern Hebrew (MA, PhD); musicology (MA, MMus, D Mus, PhD); natural science education (M Ed); New Testament (M Th, D Th); Old Testament (D Th); pastoral therapy (M Th, D Th); philosophy (MA); philosophy of education (M Ed, Ed D); politics (MA, PhD); Portuguese (MA, PhD); practical theology (M Th, D Th); psychology (MA, MS, PhD); psychology of education (M Ed, Ed D); public health (MA); religious studies (MA, D Th, PhD); Romance languages (MA); Russian (MA, PhD); Semitic languages (MA, PhD); social behavior studies in HIV/AIDS (MA); social science (mental health) (MA); social science in development studies (MA); social science in psychology (MA); social science in social work (MA); social science in sociology (MA); social work (MSW, DSW, PhD); socio-education (M Ed, Ed D); sociolinguistics (MA); sociology (MA, PhD); Spanish (MA, PhD); systematic theology (M Th, D Th); TESOL (teaching English to speakers of other languages) (MA); theological ethics (M Th, D Th); theory of literature (MA, PhD); urban ministries (D Th); urban ministry (M Th).

University of South Carolina, The Graduate School, College of Arts and Sciences, Department of Philosophy, Columbia, SC 29208. Offers MA, PhD. Part-time programs available. *Degree requirements:* For master's, one foreign language, comprehensive exam, thesis optional; for doctorate, one foreign language, comprehensive exam, thesis/dissertation, candidacy exam. *Entrance requirements:* For master's and doctorate, GRE General Test, 18 hours in philosophy, 3 letters of recommendation, writing sample. Additional exam requirements/recommendations for international students: Required—TOEFL (minimum score 590 paper-based; 243 computer-based). Electronic applications accepted. *Faculty research:* History of philosophy, ethics, philosophy of science, social philosophy.

University of Southern California, Graduate School, College of Letters, Arts and Sciences, School of Philosophy, Los Angeles, CA 90089. Offers MA, PhD, MA/JD. *Faculty:* 20 full-time (3 women). *Students:* 38 full-time (10 women); includes 4 minority (all Asian Americans or Pacific Islanders), 14 international. 95 applicants, 22% accepted, 6 enrolled. In 2009, 5 doctorates awarded. *Degree requirements:* For doctorate, one foreign language, thesis/dissertation, area exam, qualifying exam. *Entrance requirements:* For doctorate, GRE. *Application deadline:* For fall admission, 12/15 priority date for domestic students, 12/1 priority date for international students. Application fee: $85. Electronic applications accepted. *Expenses:* Tuition: Full-time $25,980; part-time $1315 per unit. Required fees: $554. One-time fee: $35 full-time. Full-time tuition and fees vary according to degree level and program. *Financial support:* In 2009–10, 32 students received support, including 10 fellowships with full tuition reimbursements available (averaging $19,000 per year), 1 research assistantship with full tuition reimbursement available (averaging $19,500 per year), 21 teaching assistantships with full tuition reimbursements available (averaging $19,500 per year). Financial award application deadline: 1/1; financial award applicants required to submit FAFSA. *Faculty research:* Philosophy of language, ethics-metaethics, philosophy of law, early Modern philosophy, epistemology. *Unit head:* Dr. Scott Soames, Director, 213-740-4084, Fax: 213-740-5174, E-mail: soames@usc.edu. *Application contact:* Cynthia Lugo, Administrative Assistant, 213-740-4084, Fax: 213-740-5174, E-mail: clugo@usc.edu.

University of Southern Mississippi, Graduate School, College of Arts and Letters, Department of Philosophy and Religion, Hattiesburg, MS 39406-0001. Offers philosophy (MA). Part-time programs available. *Faculty:* 6 full-time (2 women), 1 (woman) part-time/adjunct. *Students:* 7 full-time (1 woman), 1 (woman) part-time; includes 1 minority (Hispanic American). Average age 31. 3 applicants, 100% accepted, 1 enrolled. In 2009, 4 master's awarded. *Degree requirements:* For master's, one foreign language, comprehensive exam, thesis. *Entrance requirements:* For master's, GRE General Test, minimum GPA of 3.0 in philosophy, 2.75 last 60 hours. Additional exam requirements/recommendations for international students: Required—TOEFL. *Application deadline:* For fall admission, 3/1 for domestic and international students. Applications are processed on a rolling basis. Application fee: $35. *Expenses:* Tuition, state resident: full-time $5096; part-time $284 per hour. Tuition, nonresident: full-time $13,052; part-time $726 per hour. Required fees: $402. Tuition and fees vary according to course level and course load. *Financial support:* In 2009–10, 6 teaching assistantships with full tuition reimbursements (averaging $6,000 per year) were awarded; research assistantships, Federal Work-Study, scholarships/grants, and unspecified assistantships also available. Financial award application deadline: 3/15; financial award applicants required to submit FAFSA. *Faculty research:* Philosophy of religion, American philosophy, Oriental philosophy, philosophy of medicine. *Unit head:* Dr. David Holley, Chair, 601-266-4518, Fax: 601-266-5800. *Application contact:* Dr. Paula Smithka, Graduate Coordinator, 601-266-4518, Fax: 601-266-5800.

University of South Florida, Graduate School, College of Arts and Sciences, Department of Philosophy, Tampa, FL 33620-9951. Offers MA, PhD. Part-time and evening/weekend programs available. *Faculty:* 12 full-time (4 women). *Students:* 43 full-time (12 women), 27 part-time (3 women); includes 11 minority (1 African American, 1 Asian American or Pacific Islander, 9 Hispanic Americans), 4 international. Average age 32. 50 applicants, 40% accepted, 12 enrolled. In 2009, 19 master's, 24 doctorates awarded. Terminal master's awarded for partial completion of doctoral program. *Degree requirements:* For master's, one foreign language, comprehensive exam, thesis or alternative; for doctorate, 2 foreign languages, comprehensive exam, thesis/dissertation. *Entrance requirements:* For master's, GRE General Test, minimum GPA of 3.0 in last 60 hours, references; for doctorate, GRE General Test, writing sample, statement of purpose, references. Additional exam requirements/recommendations for international students: Required—TOEFL (minimum score 550 paper-based; 213 computer-based). *Application deadline:* For fall admission, 2/15 for domestic and international students; for spring admission, 10/15 for domestic students, 8/1 for international students. Application fee: $30. Electronic applications accepted. *Financial support:* In 2009–10, 34 students received support, including teaching assistantships with tuition reimbursements available (averaging $11,943 per year); unspecified assistantships also available. Financial award application deadline: 1/2. *Faculty research:* Ancient philosophy, social philosophy, ethics, continental philosophy, philosophy of science. Total annual research expenditures: $71,276. *Unit head:* Dr.

Philosophy

University of South Florida (continued)
Roger Ariew, Chairperson, 813-974-8207, Fax: 813-974-5914, E-mail: rariew@cas.usf.edu. *Application contact:* Alex Levine, Director, 813-974-5508, Fax: 813-974-5914, E-mail: alevine@cas.usf.edu.

The University of Tennessee, Graduate School, College of Arts and Sciences, Department of Philosophy, Knoxville, TN 37996. Offers medical ethics (MA, PhD); philosophy (MA, PhD); religious studies (MA). Part-time programs available. *Degree requirements:* For master's, thesis or alternative; for doctorate, one foreign language, thesis/dissertation. *Entrance requirements:* For master's and doctorate, GRE General Test, minimum GPA of 2.7. Additional exam requirements/recommendations for international students: Required—TOEFL. Electronic applications accepted. *Expenses:* Tuition, state resident: full-time $6826; part-time $380 per semester hour. Tuition, nonresident: full-time $21,844; part-time $1147 per semester hour. Tuition and fees vary according to program.

The University of Texas at Austin, Graduate School, College of Liberal Arts, Department of Philosophy, Austin, TX 78712-1111. Offers PhD. Part-time programs available. Terminal master's awarded for partial completion of doctoral program. *Degree requirements:* For doctorate, one foreign language, thesis/dissertation. *Entrance requirements:* For doctorate, GRE General Test. Electronic applications accepted. *Faculty research:* Ancient philosophy, cognitive science, continental philosophy, history and philosophy of science.

The University of Texas at El Paso, Graduate School, College of Liberal Arts, Department of Philosophy, El Paso, TX 79968-0001. Offers MA. *Degree requirements:* For master's, thesis, oral examination. *Entrance requirements:* For master's, GRE, 2 letters of recommendation.

The University of Toledo, College of Graduate Studies, College of Arts and Sciences, Department of Philosophy, Toledo, OH 43606-3390. Offers MA. Part-time programs available. *Degree requirements:* For master's, exam. Electronic applications accepted. *Faculty research:* History of philosophy, ethics, social/political philosophy, philosophy of science, European philosophy.

University of Toronto, School of Graduate Studies, Humanities Division, Department of Philosophy, Toronto, ON M5S 1A1, Canada. Offers MA, PhD. Part-time programs available. *Degree requirements:* For doctorate, one foreign language, thesis/dissertation. *Entrance requirements:* For master's, GRE, 6 courses in philosophy; minimum A– average in philosophy courses, B overall; 2 letters of reference; writing sample; for doctorate, GRE, MA in philosophy, minimum A– average, 2 letters of reference, writing sample. Additional exam requirements/recommendations for international students: Required—TOEFL (minimum score 600 paper-based), TWE (minimum score 5).

University of Utah, The Graduate School, College of Humanities, Department of Philosophy, Salt Lake City, UT 84112. Offers MA, MS, PhD. Part-time programs available. *Faculty:* 19 full-time (7 women). *Students:* 25 full-time (8 women), 8 part-time (3 women); includes 2 minority (1 African American, 1 Asian American or Pacific Islander), 2 international. Average age 33. 37 applicants, 59% accepted, 10 enrolled. In 2009, 2 master's, 2 doctorates awarded. *Degree requirements:* For master's, comprehensive exam, thesis or alternative; for doctorate, thesis/dissertation, qualifying oral exam. *Entrance requirements:* For master's, GRE General Test, minimum undergraduate GPA of 3.0; for doctorate, GRE General Test. Additional exam requirements/recommendations for international students: Required—TOEFL (minimum score 650 paper-based). *Application deadline:* For fall admission, 1/15 priority date for domestic students, 12/15 priority date for international students. Applications are processed on a rolling basis. Application fee: $55 ($65 for international students). Electronic applications accepted. *Expenses:* Tuition, state resident: full-time $4004; part-time $1674 per semester. Tuition, nonresident: full-time $14,134; part-time $5915 per semester. Required fees: $324 per semester. Tuition and fees vary according to course load, degree level and program. *Financial support:* In 2009–10, 1 student received support, including 1 fellowship with full tuition reimbursement available (averaging $11,000 per year), 15 teaching assistantships with full tuition reimbursements available (averaging $11,000 per year); research assistantships, Federal Work-Study, institutionally sponsored loans, scholarships/grants, health care benefits, and unspecified assistantships also available. Financial award application deadline: 2/15; financial award applicants required to submit FAFSA. *Faculty research:* Philosophy of biology, philosophy of science, applied ethics, practical reasoning, political philosophy, philosophy of cognitive science. Total annual research expenditures: $35,126. *Unit head:* Dr. Stephen Matthew Downes, Chair, 801-581-6094, Fax: 801-585-5195, E-mail: s.downes@.utah.edu. *Application contact:* Shannon Agnes Borcherds, Academic Coordinator, 801-581-8162, Fax: 801-585-5195, E-mail: shannon.borcherds@utah.edu.

University of Victoria, Faculty of Graduate Studies, Faculty of Humanities, Department of Philosophy, Victoria, BC V8W 2Y2, Canada. Offers MA. Part-time and evening/weekend programs available. *Degree requirements:* For master's, thesis. *Entrance requirements:* For master's, writing sample. Additional exam requirements/recommendations for international students: Required—TOEFL (minimum score 575 paper-based; 233 computer-based), IELTS (minimum score 7). *Faculty research:* Ethics, metaphysics, philosophy of mind, history of philosophy, political philosophy.

University of Virginia, College and Graduate School of Arts and Sciences, Department of Philosophy, Charlottesville, VA 22903. Offers MA, PhD, JD/MA. *Faculty:* 16 full-time (4 women). *Students:* 30 full-time (6 women), 1 part-time (0 women), 3 international. Average age 29. 145 applicants, 6% accepted, 4 enrolled. In 2009, 3 master's, 2 doctorates awarded. *Degree requirements:* For master's, 2 papers; for doctorate, thesis/dissertation, 2 papers. *Entrance requirements:* For master's, GRE General Test, GRE Subject Test, 3 letters of recommendation, writing sample; for doctorate, GRE General Test, GRE Subject Test, 3 letters of recommendation; writing sample. Additional exam requirements/recommendations for international students: Required—TOEFL (minimum score 600 paper-based; 250 computer-based; 90 iBT), IELTS. *Application deadline:* For fall admission, 1/5 for domestic and international students. Applications are processed on a rolling basis. Application fee: $60. Electronic applications accepted. *Financial support:* Fellowships, teaching assistantships available. Financial award applicants required to submit FAFSA. *Unit head:* Jorge Secada, Chair, 434-924-7701, Fax: 434-924-6927, E-mail: jes2f@virginia.edu. *Application contact:* Mitch Green, Director of Graduate Admissions, 434-924-7701, Fax: 434-924-6927, E-mail: msg6m@virginia.edu.

University of Washington, Graduate School, College of Arts and Sciences, Department of Philosophy, Seattle, WA 98195. Offers classics and philosophy (PhD); philosophy (MA, PhD). Terminal master's awarded for partial completion of doctoral program. *Degree requirements:* For master's, 3 papers; for doctorate, thesis/dissertation, general exam. *Entrance requirements:* For master's and doctorate, GRE, minimum GPA of 3.0. Additional exam requirements/recommendations for international students: Required—TOEFL. *Faculty research:* History and philosophy of science, epistemology, Aristotle's metaphysics, ethics and politics, causation in modern philosophy.

University of Waterloo, Graduate Studies, Faculty of Arts, Department of Philosophy, Waterloo, ON N2L 3G1, Canada. Offers MA, PhD. *Degree requirements:* For master's, thesis or alternative; for doctorate, one foreign language, thesis/dissertation. *Entrance requirements:* For master's, honors degree, minimum B+ average, writing sample, resume; for doctorate, master's degree, minimum A- average, resumé. Additional exam requirements/recommendations for international students: Required—TOEFL, TWE. Electronic applications accepted. *Faculty research:* Logic, ethics, social/political, cognitive science, philosophy of science.

The University of Western Ontario, Faculty of Graduate Studies, Faculty of Arts and Humanities, Department of Philosophy, London, ON N6A 5B8, Canada. Offers MA, PhD. *Degree requirements:* For master's, 1 competency exam; for doctorate, comprehensive exam, thesis/dissertation, 2 competency exams. *Entrance requirements:* For master's, honors degree. Additional exam requirements/recommendations for international students: Required—TOEFL (minimum score 600 paper-based; 250 computer-based). Electronic applications accepted. *Faculty research:* Philosophy of science, history of philosophy, philosophy of law, ethics, epistemology.

University of Windsor, Faculty of Graduate Studies, Faculty of Arts and Social Sciences, Department of Philosophy, Windsor, ON N9B 3P4, Canada. Offers MA. Part-time programs available. *Degree requirements:* For master's, thesis. *Entrance requirements:* For master's, minimum B average. Additional exam requirements/recommendations for international students: Required—TOEFL (minimum score 600 paper-based; 250 computer-based). Electronic applications accepted. *Faculty research:* Informal logic, contemporary Continental philosophy, epistemology.

University of Wisconsin–Madison, Graduate School, College of Letters and Science, Department of Philosophy, Madison, WI 53706-1380. Offers MA, PhD. Part-time programs available. Terminal master's awarded for partial completion of doctoral program. *Degree requirements:* For master's, thesis, preliminary exams; for doctorate, thesis/dissertation, preliminary exams. *Entrance requirements:* For doctorate, GRE, BA in philosophy or related area. Additional exam requirements/recommendations for international students: Required—TOEFL. Electronic applications accepted. *Expenses:* Tuition, state resident: part-time $594 per credit. Tuition, nonresident: part-time $1504 per credit. Required fees: $65 per credit. Tuition and fees vary according to course load, program and reciprocity agreements. *Faculty research:* History of philosophy, logic, philosophy of science, philosophy of mind, metaphysics.

University of Wisconsin–Milwaukee, Graduate School, College of Letters and Sciences, Department of Philosophy, Milwaukee, WI 53201-0413. Offers MA. Part-time programs available. *Faculty:* 15 full-time (4 women). *Students:* 21 full-time (4 women), 2 part-time (1 woman); includes 3 minority (1 American Indian/Alaska Native, 2 Asian Americans or Pacific Islanders), 2 international. Average age 28. 106 applicants, 24% accepted, 7 enrolled. In 2009, 10 master's awarded. *Degree requirements:* For master's, thesis or alternative. *Entrance requirements:* For master's, GRE General Test. Additional exam requirements/recommendations for international students: Required—TOEFL (minimum score 550 paper-based; 79 iBT), IELTS (minimum score 6.5). *Application deadline:* For fall admission, 1/1 priority date for domestic students; for spring admission, 9/1 for domestic students. Applications are processed on a rolling basis. Application fee: $45 ($75 for international students). *Expenses:* Tuition, state resident: full-time $8800. Tuition, nonresident: full-time $20,760. Tuition and fees vary according to program and reciprocity agreements. *Financial support:* In 2009–10, 18 teaching assistantships were awarded; career-related internships or fieldwork and unspecified assistantships also available. Support available to part-time students. Financial award application deadline: 4/15. Total annual research expenditures: $7,229. *Unit head:* Richard J. Tierney, Chair, 414-229-4736, Fax: 414-229-5022, E-mail: rtierney@uwm.edu. *Application contact:* Carla Bagnoli, General Information Contact, 414-229-5215, Fax: 414-229-6967, E-mail: cbagnoli@uwm.edu.

University of Wyoming, College of Arts and Sciences, Department of Philosophy, Laramie, WY 82070. Offers MA. Part-time programs available. *Degree requirements:* For master's, thesis, logic proficiency, first-year paper. *Entrance requirements:* For master's, GRE General Test, minimum GPA of 3.0. Additional exam requirements/recommendations for international students: Required—TOEFL (minimum score 525 paper-based; 197 computer-based). Electronic applications accepted. *Faculty research:* Philosophy of science, political and ethical theory, philosophy of language, epistemology, philosophy of mind, early modern philosophy.

Vanderbilt University, Graduate School, Department of Philosophy, Nashville, TN 37240-1001. Offers MA, PhD. *Faculty:* 21 full-time (8 women). *Students:* 45 full-time (21 women), 1 part-time (0 women); includes 4 minority (1 African American, 1 American Indian/Alaska Native, 2 Hispanic Americans), 3 international. Average age 31. 159 applicants, 6% accepted, 5 enrolled. In 2009, 4 master's, 6 doctorates awarded. Terminal master's awarded for partial completion of doctoral program. *Degree requirements:* For doctorate, one foreign language, comprehensive exam, thesis/dissertation, final and qualifying exams. *Entrance requirements:* For doctorate, GRE General Test, writing sample. Additional exam requirements/recommendations for international students: Required—TOEFL (minimum score 570 paper-based; 230 computer-based; 88 iBT). *Application deadline:* For fall admission, 1/15 for domestic and international students. Application fee: $0. Electronic applications accepted. *Financial support:* Fellowships with full tuition reimbursements, teaching assistantships with full tuition reimbursements, Federal Work-Study, institutionally sponsored loans, scholarships/grants, and health care benefits available. Financial award application deadline: 1/15; financial award applicants required to submit CSS PROFILE or FAFSA. *Faculty research:* Ancient, medieval, and modern philosophy; philosophy of science; ethics; philosophy of language; philosophy of religion. *Unit head:* Jeffrey Tlumak, Chair, 615-322-2637, Fax: 615-343-7259, E-mail: jeffrey.tlumak@vanderbilt.edu. *Application contact:* Robert Talisse, Director of Graduate Studies, 615-322-2637, Fax: 615-343-7259, E-mail: robert.talisse@vanderbilt.edu.

Villanova University, Graduate School of Liberal Arts and Sciences, Department of Philosophy, Villanova, PA 19085-1699. Offers PhD. Part-time and evening/weekend programs available. *Faculty:* 6 full-time (2 women). *Students:* 53 full-time (19 women); includes 3 minority (1 Asian American or Pacific Islander, 2 Hispanic Americans), 4 international. Average age 30. 127 applicants, 5% accepted, 6 enrolled. In 2009, 3 doctorates awarded. *Degree requirements:* For doctorate, 2 foreign languages, comprehensive exam, thesis/dissertation. *Entrance requirements:* For doctorate, GRE General Test, GRE Subject Test, minimum GPA of 3.5. Additional exam requirements/recommendations for international students: Required—TOEFL. *Application deadline:* For fall admission, 2/1 priority date for domestic and international students. Applications are processed on a rolling basis. Application fee: $50. Electronic applications accepted. *Expenses:* Tuition: Part-time $630 per credit. Required fees: $60 per credit. Part-time tuition and fees vary according to degree level and program. *Financial support:* Research assistantships, teaching assistantships, Federal Work-Study available. Financial award applicants required to submit FAFSA. *Unit head:* Dr. Walter Brogan, Chairman, 610-519-4690. *Application contact:* Dr. Adele Lindenmeyr, Dean, Graduate School of Liberal Arts and Sciences, 610-519-7093, Fax: 610-519-7096.

Virginia Polytechnic Institute and State University, Graduate School, College of Liberal Arts and Human Sciences, Department of Philosophy, Blacksburg, VA 24061. Offers MA. *Faculty:* 11 full-time (1 woman), 1 (woman) part-time/adjunct. *Students:* 22 full-time (3 women); includes 1 minority (American Indian/Alaska Native), 1 international. Average age 26. 59 applicants, 59% accepted, 8 enrolled. In 2009, 11 master's awarded. *Entrance requirements:* For master's, GRE, GMAT. Additional exam requirements/recommendations for international students: Required—TOEFL (minimum score 550 paper-based; 213 computer-based). *Application deadline:* For fall admission, 5/15 for international students; for spring admission, 10/15 for international students. Applications are processed on a rolling basis. Application fee: $65. Electronic applications accepted. *Expenses:* Tuition, area resident: Full-time $10,228; part-time $459 per credit hour. Tuition, nonresident: full-time $17,892; part-time $865 per credit hour. Required fees: $1966; $451 per semester. *Financial support:* In 2009–10, 8 teaching assistantships with full tuition reimbursements (averaging $10,438 per year) were awarded; career-related internships or fieldwork, Federal Work-Study, scholarships/grants, and unspecified assistantships also available. Financial award application deadline: 1/15. *Faculty research:* History of philosophy, ethics, history and philosophy of science and philosophy. Total annual research expenditures: $35,432. *Unit head:* Dr. James Klagge, Dean, 540-231-8487, Fax: 540-231-6367, E-mail: jklagge@vt.edu. *Application contact:* William Fitzpatrick, Information Contact, 540-231-7543, Fax: 540-231-6367, E-mail: william.fitzpatrick@vt.edu.

Washington State University, Graduate School, College of Liberal Arts, Department of Philosophy, Pullman, WA 99164. Offers MA. *Faculty:* 7. *Students:* 9 full-time (3 women); includes 1 minority (African American). 15 applicants, 73% accepted, 3 enrolled. In 2009, 5 master's awarded. *Degree requirements:* For master's, comprehensive exam (for some programs), thesis (for some programs). *Entrance requirements:* For master's, GRE, minimum GPA of 3.0, 3 letters of recommendation, writing sample. Additional exam requirements/recommendations for international students: Required—TOEFL, IELTS. *Application deadline:*

For fall admission, 1/10 for domestic and international students; for spring admission, 7/1 for domestic and international students. Application fee: $50. *Financial support:* In 2009–10, 7 teaching assistantships with tuition reimbursements (averaging $13,056 per year) were awarded. *Faculty research:* Philosophy of language and mind, philosophy of race and ethnicity, social and political philosophy. *Unit head:* Dr. David L. Shier, Chair, 509-335-1415, E-mail: shier@wsu.edu. *Application contact:* Graduate School Admissions, 800-GRADWSU, Fax: 509-335-1949, E-mail: gradsch@wsu.edu.

Washington University in St. Louis, Graduate School of Arts and Sciences, Department of Philosophy, St. Louis, MO 63130-4899. Offers philosophy (MA, PhD); philosophy/neuroscience/psychology (PhD). Terminal master's awarded for partial completion of doctoral program. *Degree requirements:* For master's, thesis optional; for doctorate, thesis/dissertation. *Entrance requirements:* For master's and doctorate, GRE General Test, sample of written work. Electronic applications accepted.

Wayne State University, College of Liberal Arts and Sciences, Department of Philosophy, Detroit, MI 48202. Offers MA, PhD. Terminal master's awarded for partial completion of doctoral program. *Degree requirements:* For master's, thesis; for doctorate, one foreign language, thesis/dissertation. *Entrance requirements:* For master's, GRE General Test or minimum GPA of 3.0; for doctorate, undergraduate GPA of at least 3.0. Additional exam requirements/recommendations for international students: Required—TOEFL (minimum score 550 paper-based; 213 computer-based); Recommended—TWE (minimum score 6). Electronic applications accepted. *Faculty research:* Metaphysics; ancient philosophy; philosophy of art; ethics; philosophy of science.

West Chester University of Pennsylvania, Office of Graduate Studies, College of Arts and Sciences, Department of Philosophy, West Chester, PA 19383. Offers business ethics (Certificate); healthcare ethics (Certificate); philosophy: applied ethics (MA); philosophy: general (MA). Part-time and evening/weekend programs available. *Students:* 2 full-time (1 woman), 18 part-time (9 women); includes 2 minority (1 African American, 1 Hispanic American). Average age 29. 17 applicants, 88% accepted, 9 enrolled. In 2009, 6 master's awarded. *Degree requirements:* For master's, thesis or comprehensive exam. *Entrance requirements:* For master's, GRE or writing sample, three letters of reference. Additional exam requirements/recommendations for international students: Required—TOEFL (minimum score 550 paper-based; 213 computer-based; 80 iBT). *Application deadline:* For fall admission, 4/15 priority date for domestic students, 3/15 for international students; for spring admission, 10/15 for domestic students, 9/1 for international students. Applications are processed on a rolling basis. Application fee: $35. Electronic applications accepted. *Expenses:* Tuition, state resident: full-time $6666; part-time $370 per credit. Tuition, nonresident: full-time $10,666; part-time $593 per credit. Required fees: $122.56 per credit. *Financial support:* In 2009–10, 4 research assistantships with full and partial tuition reimbursements (averaging $5,000 per year) were awarded; unspecified assistantships also available. Support available to part-time students. Financial award application deadline: 2/15; financial award applicants required to submit FAFSA. *Faculty research:* International studies. *Unit head:* Dr. Joan Woolfrey, Chair, 610-436-1004, E-mail: jwoolfrey@wcupa.edu. *Application contact:* Dr. Helen Daley Schroepfer, Graduate Coordinator, 610-436-2429, E-mail: hschroepfer@wcupa.edu.

Western Michigan University, Graduate College, College of Arts and Sciences, Department of Philosophy, Kalamazoo, MI 49008. Offers MA. *Degree requirements:* For master's, thesis optional.

Wilfrid Laurier University, Faculty of Graduate Studies, Faculty of Arts, Department of Philosophy, Waterloo, ON N2L 3C5, Canada. Offers MA. *Entrance requirements:* For master's, Honours BA in philosophy or equivalent with a minimum B+ in philosophy and in final year. Additional exam requirements/recommendations for international students: Required—TOEFL (minimum score 230 computer-based; 89 iBT). Electronic applications accepted. *Faculty research:* Self, agency, community.

Yale University, Graduate School of Arts and Sciences, Department of Philosophy, New Haven, CT 06520. Offers PhD. *Degree requirements:* For doctorate, 2 foreign languages, thesis/dissertation. *Entrance requirements:* For doctorate, GRE General Test.

York University, Faculty of Graduate Studies, Faculty of Arts, Program in Philosophy, Toronto, ON M3J 1P3, Canada. Offers MA, PhD. Part-time programs available. *Degree requirements:* For master's, thesis or alternative; for doctorate, one foreign language, thesis/dissertation. Electronic applications accepted.

Section 12
Religious Studies

This section contains a directory of institutions offering graduate work in religious studies, followed by in-depth entries submitted by institutions that chose to prepare detailed program descriptions. Additional information about programs listed in the directory but not augmented by an in-depth entry may be obtained by writing directly to the dean of a graduate school or chair of a department at the address given in the directory.

For programs offering related work, see also in this book *Area and Cultural Studies, History, Humanities,* and *Philosophy.* In another guide in this series:

Graduate Programs in Business, Education, Health, Information Studies, Law & Social Work

See *Subject Areas (Religious Education)*

CONTENTS

Program Directories

Missions and Missiology 458
Pastoral Ministry and Counseling 461
Religion 475
Theology 487

Close-Ups and Display

The Jewish Theological Seminary
Graduate Studies 511
Rabbinical Studies 513
St. Mary's Seminary and University
Theology (Display) 503
Villanova University 515

See also:

Argosy University, Sarasota—Psychology and Behavioral Sciences 1075

Missions and Missiology

Abilene Christian University, Graduate School, College of Biblical Studies, Graduate School of Theology, Program in Missions, Abilene, TX 79699-9100. Offers MA. Part-time programs available. *Students:* 3 full-time (2 women), 4 part-time (0 women); includes 2 minority (1 African American, 1 Hispanic American), 1 international. 7 applicants, 86% accepted, 3 enrolled. In 2009, 3 master's awarded. *Entrance requirements:* For master's, GRE, MAT. *Application deadline:* For fall admission, 4/1 priority date for domestic students; for spring admission, 11/1 for domestic students. Applications are processed on a rolling basis. Application fee: $40. Electronic applications accepted. *Expenses:* Tuition: Full-time $11,520; part-time $640 per hour. Required fees: $1090; $53.50 per hour. $10 per term. Tuition and fees vary according to program. *Financial support:* In 2009–10, 4 students received support; teaching assistantships, career-related internships or fieldwork available. Financial award application deadline: 4/1; financial award applicants required to submit FAFSA. *Faculty research:* Animism, contextualization, missions education. *Unit head:* Dr. Chris Flanders, Graduate Adviser, 325-674-3742, Fax: 325-674-6180, E-mail: clf03c@acu.edu. *Application contact:* William Horn, Graduate Admissions Counselor, 325-674-2656, Fax: 325-674-6717, E-mail: gradinfo@acu.edu.

Alliance Theological Seminary, Graduate and Professional Programs, Nyack, NY 10960. Offers Christian ministry (MPS); counseling (MA); intercultural studies (MA); missions (MPS); New Testament (MA); Old Testament (MA); theology (M Div); urban ministry (MPS). *Accreditation:* ATS. Part-time programs available. *Degree requirements:* For master's, comprehensive exam (for some programs), thesis optional, internships; for M Div, 2 foreign languages, internship. *Entrance requirements:* Proficiency in New Testament Greek, minimum GPA of 2.5 (undergraduate). Additional exam requirements/recommendations for international students: Required—TOEFL (minimum score 550 paper-based; 213 computer-based).

Ambrose University College, Ambrose Seminary, Calgary, AB T2P 3T5, Canada. Offers biblical/theological studies (MA); Chinese ministries (Certificate); Christian studies (M Div, MA, Diploma); foundations for ministry (Certificate); intercultural ministries (M Div, MA, Certificate, Diploma); leadership and ministry (MA, Certificate, Diploma). *Accreditation:* ATS (one or more programs are accredited). Part-time programs available. *Faculty:* 7 full-time (0 women), 24 part-time/adjunct (2 women). *Students:* 44 full-time (15 women), 107 part-time (49 women). Average age 41. *Degree requirements:* For master's, 2 foreign languages, internship; for M Div, one foreign language, internship. *Entrance requirements:* For master's, bachelor's degree. Additional exam requirements/recommendations for international students: Required—TOEFL or IELTS. *Application deadline:* For fall admission, 7/31 priority date for domestic students, 3/1 priority date for international students; for winter admission, 11/30 priority date for domestic students, 6/1 priority date for international students. Applications are processed on a rolling basis. Application fee: $50. Electronic applications accepted. *Expenses:* Tuition: Full-time $6000; part-time $299 per credit hour. Required fees: $306; $17 per credit hour. *Financial support:* Career-related internships or fieldwork and scholarships/grants available. Support available to part-time students. Financial award application deadline: 3/30. *Faculty research:* Evangelicalism and sociology, missiological trends, chaplaincy, intertestamental studies, postmodernism. *Unit head:* Dr. Paul Spilsbury, Vice-President of Academic Affairs, 403-410-2000 Ext. 6905, Fax: 403-571-2556, E-mail: pspilsbury@ambrose.edu. *Application contact:* Dr. Paul Spilsbury, Vice-President of Academic Affairs, 403-410-2000 Ext. 6905, Fax: 403-571-2556, E-mail: pspilsbury@ambrose.edu.

Anderson University, School of Theology, Anderson, IN 46012-3495. Offers missions (MA); theology (M Div, MTS, D Min). *Accreditation:* ACIPE; ATS. Part-time programs available. *Degree requirements:* For master's, one foreign language, thesis, integrative senior seminar; for doctorate, thesis/dissertation; for M Div, thesis/dissertation (for some programs). *Faculty research:* Small-church/bivocational ministry, women in ministry.

Asbury Theological Seminary, Graduate and Professional Programs, Wilmore, KY 40390-1199. Offers MA, MAC, MACE, MACL, MAPC, MAYM, Th M, D Miss, PhD, Certificate. *Accreditation:* ATS. Part-time programs available. Postbaccalaureate distance learning degree programs offered (minimal on-campus study). *Faculty:* 64 full-time (11 women), 74 part-time/adjunct (14 women). *Students:* 760 full-time (226 women), 768 part-time (279 women); includes 155 minority (85 African Americans, 13 American Indian/Alaska Native, 25 Asian Americans or Pacific Islanders, 32 Hispanic Americans), 141 international. Average age 25. 765 applicants, 75% accepted, 364 enrolled. In 2009, 95 master's, 15 doctorates, 38 other advanced degrees awarded. Terminal master's awarded for partial completion of doctoral program. *Degree requirements:* For master's, thesis (for some programs); for doctorate, thesis/dissertation, qualifying exam. *Entrance requirements:* For master's, minimum GPA of 2.75; for doctorate, minimum GPA of 3.0. Additional exam requirements/recommendations for international students: Required—TOEFL, IELTS. *Application deadline:* Applications are processed on a rolling basis. Application fee: $50. Electronic applications accepted. *Financial support:* In 2009–10, 1,317 students received support. Career-related internships or fieldwork, Federal Work-Study, institutionally sponsored loans, and scholarships/grants available. Support available to part-time students. Financial award applicants required to submit FAFSA. *Unit head:* Dr. Leslie A. Andrews, Provost, 859-858-2206, Fax: 859-858-2025, E-mail: leslie.andrews@asburyseminary.edu. *Application contact:* Kevin Bush, Vice President of Enrollment Management, 859-858-2211, Fax: 859-858-2287, E-mail: admissions.office@asburyseminary.edu.

Assemblies of God Theological Seminary, Graduate and Professional Programs, Springfield, MO 65802. Offers Christian ministries (MA); counseling (MA); divinity (M Div); intercultural ministry (MA); intercultural studies (D Miss, PhD); relief and development (D Miss); theological studies (MA); women in leadership (D Min). *Accreditation:* ATS. Part-time and evening/weekend programs available. Postbaccalaureate distance learning degree programs offered (minimal on-campus study). *Faculty:* 12 full-time (3 women); 23 part-time/adjunct (5 women). *Students:* 195 full-time (70 women), 221 part-time (53 women); includes 48 minority (10 African Americans, 6 American Indian/Alaska Native, 16 Asian Americans or Pacific Islanders, 16 Hispanic Americans), 9 international. Average age 36. 109 applicants, 76% accepted, 62 enrolled. In 2009, 46 first professional degrees, 65 master's, 14 doctorates awarded. *Degree requirements:* For master's, analytical reflection paper, comprehensive exam or field education research project; for doctorate, thesis/dissertation; for M Div, one foreign language, analytical reflection paper or field education research project. *Entrance requirements:* For M Div, minimum GPA of 2.5; for master's, minimum GPA of 2.5; for doctorate, minimum GPA of 3.0. Additional exam requirements/recommendations for international students: Required—TOEFL (minimum score 550 paper-based; 213 computer-based; 80 iBT). *Application deadline:* For fall admission, 7/1 priority date for domestic students, 6/1 priority date for international students; for spring admission, 12/1 priority date for domestic students, 11/1 priority date for international students. Applications are processed on a rolling basis. Application fee: $75. Electronic applications accepted. *Financial support:* Career-related internships or fieldwork, Federal Work-Study, and scholarships/grants available. Support available to part-time students. Financial award application deadline: 7/15; financial award applicants required to submit FAFSA. *Unit head:* Stephen Lim, Academic Dean, 417-268-1000, Fax: 417-268-1001, E-mail: slim@agts.edu. *Application contact:* Stephen Lim, Academic Dean, 417-268-1000, Fax: 417-268-1001, E-mail: slim@agts.edu.

Associated Mennonite Biblical Seminary, Graduate and Professional Programs, Elkhart, IN 46517-1999. Offers Christian formation (MA); divinity (M Div); mission and evangelism (MA); peace studies (MA); theological studies (MA, Certificate). *Accreditation:* ACIPE; ATS. Part-time programs available. *Degree requirements:* For master's, comprehensive exam, thesis optional; for M Div, integration paper. *Entrance requirements:* For M Div, master's, and Certificate, 3 letters of reference. Additional exam requirements/recommendations for international students: Required—TOEFL (minimum score 550 paper-based; 213 computer-based). Electronic applications accepted. *Faculty research:* Biblical studies, theology, church history, church leadership.

Baptist Bible College of Pennsylvania, Baptist Bible Seminary, Clarks Summit, PA 18411-1297. Offers biblical studies (PhD); church planting (M Div); global missions (M Div); military chaplaincy (M Div); ministry (M Min, D Min); pastor of church education (M Div); pastor of outreach (M Div); pastoral counseling (M Div); pastoral leadership (M Div); theology (M Div, Th M); youth pastor (M Div). Part-time and evening/weekend programs available. Postbaccalaureate distance learning degree programs offered (minimal on-campus study). Terminal master's awarded for partial completion of doctoral program. *Degree requirements:* For master's, 2 foreign languages, thesis; for doctorate, 2 foreign languages, comprehensive exam (for some programs), thesis/dissertation, oral exam; for M Div, 2 foreign languages, thesis/dissertation, oral exam. *Entrance requirements:* For doctorate, Greek and Hebrew entrance exams (PhD). Electronic applications accepted.

Bethel Seminary, Graduate and Professional Programs, St. Paul, MN 55112-6998. Offers applied ministry (MA); biblical studies (MATS, Certificate); children's and family ministry (MACFM); Christian education (MACE); Christian thought (M Div, MACT); church leadership (D Min); community ministry leadership (MA, Certificate); congregation and family care (D Min); global and contextual studies (MA, MATS); historical studies (MATS); lay ministry (Certificate); marriage and family studies (M Div, MATS); marriage and family therapy (MAMFT, Certificate); ministry leadership (Certificate); pastoral care and counseling (MATS); pastoral ministries (M Div); spiritual formation (Certificate); theological studies (MATS, Certificate); transformational leadership (MATL, Certificate); youth ministries (MACE). *Accreditation:* ACIPE; ATS (one or more programs are accredited). Part-time and evening/weekend programs available. Postbaccalaureate distance learning degree programs offered (minimal on-campus study). *Faculty:* 26 full-time (3 women), 76 part-time/adjunct (30 women). *Students:* 725 full-time (269 women), 300 part-time (104 women); includes 204 minority (115 African Americans, 1 American Indian/Alaska Native, 65 Asian Americans or Pacific Islanders, 23 Hispanic Americans), 13 international. Average age 37. 516 applicants, 78% accepted, 261 enrolled. In 2009, 50 first professional degrees, 100 master's, 6 doctorates awarded. *Degree requirements:* For master's, variable foreign language requirement, thesis (for some programs); for doctorate, thesis/dissertation; for M Div, one foreign language. *Entrance requirements:* For M Div and master's, letters of reference, transcripts, personal statement; for doctorate, M Div, letters of reference, organizational support. Additional exam requirements/recommendations for international students: Required—TOEFL (minimum score 550 paper-based; 213 computer-based; 87 iBT). *Application deadline:* For fall admission, 8/1 priority date for domestic students, 3/1 for international students; for winter admission, 12/1 priority date for domestic students; for spring admission, 3/1 priority date for domestic students. Applications are processed on a rolling basis. Application fee: $20. Electronic applications accepted. *Financial support:* In 2009–10, 847 students received support, including 18 teaching assistantships; career-related internships or fieldwork, Federal Work-Study, scholarships/grants, and tuition waivers (full) also available. Financial award application deadline: 7/15; financial award applicants required to submit FAFSA. *Faculty research:* Nature of theology, ethics, Biblical commentaries, nature of God, science and theology. *Unit head:* Dr. David Ridder, Vice President and Dean, 651-638-6553. *Application contact:* Joseph V. Dworak, Director of Admissions, 651-638-6288, Fax: 651-638-6002, E-mail: j-dworak@bethel.edu.

Biblical Theological Seminary, Graduate and Professional Programs, Hatfield, PA 19440-2499. Offers advanced missional leadership (D Min); advanced pastoral studies (Certificate); biblical counseling (Certificate); biblical studies (MA, Certificate); counseling (MA); ministry (MA); missional theology (MA); theology (M Div); youth ministry (Certificate). *Accreditation:* ATS. Part-time programs available. Postbaccalaureate distance learning degree programs offered. *Degree requirements:* For M Div, thesis/dissertation. *Entrance requirements:* Additional exam requirements/recommendations for international students: Required—TOEFL (minimum score 550 paper-based; 213 computer-based). *Application deadline:* Applications are processed on a rolling basis. Application fee: $30. *Expenses:* Tuition: Full-time $14,000; part-time $441 per credit hour. *Financial support:* Career-related internships or fieldwork, institutionally sponsored loans, and scholarships/grants available. Support available to part-time students. Financial award application deadline: 5/15. *Faculty research:* Old Testament narrative, Old Testament historiography, Hebrew syntax, parables, addictions. *Application contact:* Rev. Darryl John Lang, Director of Recruitment and Student Life, 215-368-5000 Ext. 147, Fax: 215-368-7002, E-mail: dlang@biblical.edu.

Biola University, School of Intercultural Studies, La Mirada, CA 90639-0001. Offers applied linguistics (MA); intercultural education (PhD); intercultural studies (MAICS); missiology (D Miss); missions (MA); teaching English to speakers of other languages (MA, Certificate). Part-time and evening/weekend programs available. Terminal master's awarded for partial completion of doctoral program. *Degree requirements:* For master's, one foreign language, comprehensive exam; for doctorate, one foreign language, comprehensive exam, thesis/dissertation. *Entrance requirements:* For master's, minimum undergraduate GPA of 3.0; for doctorate, MA, 3 years of ministry experience, minimum graduate GPA of 3.3. Additional exam requirements/recommendations for international students: Required—TOEFL (minimum score 550 paper-based; 213 computer-based). Electronic applications accepted.

Briercrest Seminary, Graduate Programs, Program in Christian Ministries, Caronport, SK S0H 0S0, Canada. Offers leadership (MA); marriage and family counseling (MA); missions (MA); pastoral counseling (MA); worship (MA); youth and family ministry (MA). Part-time programs available. *Degree requirements:* For master's, comprehensive exam, thesis optional. *Entrance requirements:* Additional exam requirements/recommendations for international students: Required—TOEFL (minimum score 550 paper-based; 213 computer-based).

Calvin Theological Seminary, Graduate and Professional Programs, Grand Rapids, MI 49546-4387. Offers Bible and theology (MA); divinity (M Div), including ancient near eastern languages and literature, contextual ministry, evangelism and teaching, history of Christianity, new church development, New Testament, Old Testament, pastoral care and leadership, preaching and worship, theological studies, youth and family ministries; educational ministry (MA); historical theology (PhD); missions and evangelism (MA); pastoral care (MA); philosophical and moral theology (PhD); systematic theology (PhD); theological studies (MTS); theology (Th M); worship (MA); youth and family ministries (MA). *Accreditation:* ACIPE; ATS. Part-time programs available. *Faculty:* 28 full-time (2 women), 20 part-time/adjunct (7 women). *Students:* 203 full-time (39 women), 48 part-time (19 women); includes 28 minority (10 African Americans, 13 Asian Americans or Pacific Islanders, 5 Hispanic Americans), 69 international. Average age 31. 152 applicants, 89% accepted, 98 enrolled. In 2009, 45 first professional degrees, 42 master's, 6 doctorates awarded. *Degree requirements:* For master's, thesis (for some programs); for doctorate, 4 foreign languages, comprehensive exam, thesis/dissertation; for M Div, 2 foreign languages. *Entrance requirements:* For doctorate, GRE General Test, Hebrew, Greek, and a modern foreign language. Additional exam requirements/recommendations for international students: Required—TOEFL (minimum score 550 paper-based; 213 computer-based), TWE (minimum score 4). *Application deadline:* For fall admission, 3/1 priority date for domestic and international students. Applications are processed on a rolling basis. Application fee: $25. Electronic applications accepted. *Expenses:* Tuition: Full-time $11,814; part-time $358 per semester hour. Tuition and fees vary according to degree level. *Financial support:* In 2009–10, 187 students received support, including 4 fellowships with full tuition reimbursements available (averaging $8,405 per year), 4 teaching assistantships with full tuition reimbursements available (averaging $5,760 per year); career-related internships or fieldwork, institutionally sponsored loans, scholarships/grants, and tuition waivers (full) also available. Support available to part-time students. Financial award application deadline: 3/1; financial award applicants required to submit FAFSA. *Faculty research:* Recent Trinity theory, Christian anthropology, Proverbs, reformed confessions, Paul's view of law. *Unit head:* Dr. Cornelius Plantinga, Head, 616-957-6024, Fax: 616-957-6536, E-mail: sempres@calvinseminary.edu. *Application contact:* Rev. Gregory Janke, Director of Admissions, 616-957-7035, Fax: 616-957-6101, E-mail: gjanke@calvinseminary.edu.

Catholic Theological Union at Chicago, Graduate and Professional Programs, Chicago, IL 60615-5698. Offers biblical spirituality (Certificate); cross-cultural ministries (D Min); cross-cultural missions (Certificate); divinity (M Div); liturgical studies (Certificate); liturgy (D Min); pastoral studies (MAPS, Certificate); spiritual formation (Certificate); spirituality (D Min); theology (MA); M Div/MA; M Div/MSW; M Div/PhD. *Accreditation:* ACIPE; ATS (one or more programs are accredited). Part-time and evening/weekend programs available. *Degree requirements:* For master's, one foreign language, comprehensive exam (for some programs), thesis (for some programs); for doctorate, thesis/dissertation. *Entrance requirements:* For doctorate, master's degree, 5 years of active ministry. *Faculty research:* Doctrine, sacraments, ethics, Bible.

Central Baptist Theological Seminary, Graduate and Professional Programs, Shawnee, KS 66226. Offers missional church studies (MA); theological studies (MA); theology (M Div, Diploma). *Accreditation:* ACIPE; ATS (one or more programs are accredited). Part-time programs available. *Degree requirements:* For master's, thesis optional, MMPI, Myers-Briggs, Enneagram; for M Div, thesis/dissertation optional. *Entrance requirements:* For master's, accredited bachelor's degree with minimum GPA of 2.3. Additional exam requirements/recommendations for international students: Required—TOEFL (minimum score 547 paper-based; 210 computer-based; 77 iBT). Electronic applications accepted.

Columbia International University, Columbia Biblical Seminary and School of Missions, Columbia, SC 29230-3122. Offers academic ministries (M Div); bible exposition (M Div, MABE); biblical studies (Certificate); counseling ministries (Certificate); divinity (M Div); educational ministries (M Div, MAEM, Certificate); intercultural studies (M Div, MAIS, Certificate); leadership (D Min); leadership for evangelism/mobilization (MALM); member care (D Min); ministry (Certificate); missions (D Min); pastoral counseling and spiritual formation (M Div, MAPS); preaching (D Min); theology (MA). *Accreditation:* ATS (one or more programs are accredited). Part-time and evening/weekend programs available. *Degree requirements:* For master's, integrative seminar; for doctorate, comprehensive exam, thesis/dissertation; for M Div, internship. *Entrance requirements:* For master's, minimum GPA of 2.7; for doctorate, 3 years of ministerial experience, M Div. Additional exam requirements/recommendations for international students: Required—TOEFL. Electronic applications accepted.

Dallas Baptist University, College of Adult Education, Liberal Arts Program, Dallas, TX 75211-9299. Offers arts (MLA); Christian ministry (MLA); English (MLA); English as a second language (MLA); fine arts (MLA); history (MLA); missions (MLA); political science (MLA). Part-time and evening/weekend programs available. *Entrance requirements:* For master's, minimum GPA of 3.0. Additional exam requirements/recommendations for international students: Required—TOEFL. Electronic applications accepted. *Expenses:* Tuition: Full-time $10,674; part-time $593 per credit hour. *Faculty research:* Milton and seventeenth-century Puritans, inter-Biblical years, nineteenth-century literature, Latin American and Texas history.

Dallas Baptist University, College of Adult Education, Professional Development Program, Dallas, TX 75211-9299. Offers accounting (MA); church leadership (MA); counseling (MA); criminal justice (MA); English as a second language (MA); finance (MA); higher education (MA); leadership studies (MA); management (MA); management information systems (MA); marketing (MA); missions (MA). Part-time and evening/weekend programs available. *Entrance requirements:* For master's, minimum GPA of 3.0. Additional exam requirements/recommendations for international students: Required—TOEFL, IELTS. *Expenses:* Tuition: Full-time $10,674; part-time $593 per credit hour.

Dallas Baptist University, Gary Cook School of Leadership, Program in Christian Education, Dallas, TX 75211-9299. Offers adult ministry (MA); business ministry (MA); childhood ministry (MA); collegiate ministry (MA); communication ministry (MA); counseling ministry (MA); education ministry (MA); general ministry (MA); missions ministry (MA); student ministry (MA); worship ministry (MA). Part-time and evening/weekend programs available. *Entrance requirements:* For master's, minimum GPA of 3.0. Additional exam requirements/recommendations for international students: Required—TOEFL. Electronic applications accepted. *Expenses:* Tuition: Full-time $10,674; part-time $593 per credit hour.

Dallas Baptist University, Gary Cook School of Leadership, Program in Global Leadership, Dallas, TX 75211-9299. Offers business communication (MA); Christian education/missions (MA); ESL (MA); general studies (MA); global studies (MA); international business (MA); missions (MA); worship/missions (MA). Part-time and evening/weekend programs available. *Entrance requirements:* For master's, minimum GPA of 3.0. Additional exam requirements/recommendations for international students: Required—TOEFL, IELTS. *Expenses:* Tuition: Full-time $10,674; part-time $593 per credit hour.

Dallas Theological Seminary, Graduate Programs, Dallas, TX 75204-6499. Offers academic ministries (Th M); Bible translation (Th M); biblical and theological studies (CGS); biblical counseling (MA, Th M); biblical exegesis and linguistics (MA); biblical exposition (PhD); biblical studies (MA); Christian education (MA, D Min); cross-cultural ministries (MA, Th M); educational leadership (Th M); evangelism and discipleship (Th M); interdisciplinary studies (Th M); media and communication (MA); media arts in ministry (Th M); ministry (D Min); New Testament studies (Th M, PhD); Old Testament studies (PhD); parachurch ministries (Th M); pastoral ministries (Th M); sacred theology (STM); theological studies (PhD); women's ministry (Th M). *Accreditation:* ATS (one or more programs are accredited). Part-time and evening/weekend programs available. *Degree requirements:* For master's, variable foreign language requirement, thesis (for some programs); for doctorate, 2 foreign languages, thesis/dissertation. *Entrance requirements:* Additional exam requirements/recommendations for international students: Required—TOEFL, TWE. Electronic applications accepted.

Eastern University, Palmer Theological Seminary, Program in Renewal of the Church for Mission, St. Davids, PA 19087-3696. Offers D Min. *Degree requirements:* For doctorate, thesis/dissertation.

Emmanuel School of Religion, Graduate and Professional Programs, Johnson City, TN 37601-9438. Offers Christian care and counseling (M Div); Christian doctrine (MAR); Christian education (M Div); church history (MAR); ministry (D Min); New Testament (MAR); Old Testament (MAR); urban ministry (M Div); world missions (M Div). *Accreditation:* ACIPE; ATS. Part-time programs available. *Faculty:* 10 full-time (2 women), 5 part-time/adjunct (0 women). *Students:* 108 full-time (27 women), 48 part-time (13 women). Average age 32. *Degree requirements:* For master's, 2 foreign languages, thesis; for M Div, 2 foreign languages, thesis/dissertation or alternative. *Entrance requirements:* For doctorate, GRE General Test, Minnesota Multiphasic Personality Inventory, M Div or equivalent. *Application deadline:* For fall admission, 8/1 priority date for domestic students. Applications are processed on a rolling basis. Application fee: $25. *Expenses:* Tuition: Full-time $7800; part-time $325 per credit hour. Required fees: $137.50 per semester. One-time fee: $240. Tuition and fees vary according to course load. *Financial support:* Teaching assistantships with partial tuition reimbursements, career-related internships or fieldwork, institutionally sponsored loans, scholarships/grants, and tuition waivers (partial) available. Support available to part-time students. Financial award application deadline: 4/1; financial award applicants required to submit FAFSA. *Faculty research:* Theology of Old Testament prophets, spiritual formation for Christian leaders, history of African churches and religions, social world of early Christianity, lay pastoral counseling. Total annual research expenditures: $12,000. *Unit head:* Dr. Rollin A. Ramsaran, Dean and Professor of New Testament, 423-461-1524, Fax: 423-926-6198, E-mail: ramsaranr@esr.edu. *Application contact:* Shelley Gasser, Administrative Assistant for Admissions, 423-461-1535, Fax: 423-926-6198, E-mail: gassers@esr.edu.

Evangelical Theological Seminary, Graduate and Professional Programs, Myerstown, PA 17067-1212. Offers Biblical studies (MAR); congregational ministry (M Div); global and contextual studies (M Div, MAR); historical and theological studies (MAR); interdisciplinary studies (MAR); marriage and family counseling (M Div); marriage and family therapy (MA); New Testament (MAR); Old Testament (MAR); spiritual formation (MAR); teaching ministry (M Div); youth ministry (M Div). *Accreditation:* ATS (one or more programs are accredited). Part-time programs available. Postbaccalaureate distance learning degree programs offered (minimal on-campus study). *Degree requirements:* For master's, 2 foreign languages; for M Div, 2 foreign languages, ministry internship. *Entrance requirements:* For M Div and master's, minimum GPA of 2.5. Additional exam requirements/recommendations for international students: Required—TOEFL (minimum score 550 paper-based; 213 computer-based). *Faculty research:* Literary form and structure within the Hebrew and Greek scriptures, Wesley studies, esoteric biblical languages, the Mosaic law and the Christian, ethics.

Fuller Theological Seminary, Graduate School of Theology, Pasadena, CA 91182. Offers Christian leadership (MACL); evangelism (MA); family life education (MA); ministry (M Div, D Min); pastoral ministry (MA); recovery ministry (MA); theology (MAT, Th M, PhD); worship music ministry (MA); worship, theology, and the arts (MA); youth, family, and culture (MA). M Div offered jointly with Denver Conservative Baptist Seminary. *Accreditation:* ACIPE; ATS (one or more programs are accredited). Part-time and evening/weekend programs available. *Degree requirements:* For doctorate, variable foreign language requirement, thesis/dissertation; for M Div, 2 foreign languages. *Entrance requirements:* For doctorate, GRE General Test. *Faculty research:* New Testament, Old Testament, systematic theology, history, practical theology.

Fuller Theological Seminary, School of Intercultural Studies, Program in Global Ministries, Pasadena, CA 91182. Offers global leadership (MA); global ministries (D Min); global ministry (Korean language) (D Min). *Degree requirements:* For doctorate, one foreign language, thesis/dissertation. *Entrance requirements:* For doctorate, qualifying exam.

Fuller Theological Seminary, School of Intercultural Studies, Program in Intercultural Studies, Pasadena, CA 91182. Offers cross-cultural studies (MA); intercultural studies (MA, Th M, PhD); intercultural studies (Korean language) (MA). *Degree requirements:* For master's, one foreign language, thesis optional; for doctorate, one foreign language, thesis/dissertation. *Entrance requirements:* For doctorate, qualifying exam, minimum GPA of 3.7, Th M and MA degrees from Graduate School of World Mission. Additional exam requirements/recommendations for international students: Required—TOEFL.

Fuller Theological Seminary, School of Intercultural Studies, Program in Missiology, Pasadena, CA 91182. Offers missiology (D Miss); missiology (Korean language) (Th M). *Degree requirements:* For doctorate, one foreign language, thesis/dissertation. *Entrance requirements:* For doctorate, qualifying exam, minimum GPA of 3.4 (D Miss), 3.7 (PhD), Th M and MA degrees from Graduate School of World Mission. Additional exam requirements/recommendations for international students: Required—TOEFL.

Gardner-Webb University, School of Divinity, Boiling Springs, NC 28017. Offers biblical studies (M Div); Christian education and formation (M Div); ministry (D Min); missiology (M Div); pastoral care and counseling (M Div); pastoral studies (M Div); M Div/MA; M Div/MBA. *Accreditation:* ACIPE; ATS. Part-time programs available. *Degree requirements:* For M Div, 2 foreign languages. *Entrance requirements:* For M Div, minimum GPA of 2.0; for doctorate, minimum GPA of 2.75. *Application deadline:* For fall admission, 8/1 priority date for domestic students; for spring admission, 12/15 priority date for domestic students. Applications are processed on a rolling basis. Application fee: $25. *Expenses:* Contact institution. *Financial support:* Fellowships, institutionally sponsored loans and unspecified assistantships available. Support available to part-time students. Financial award application deadline: 5/15. *Faculty research:* Jewish Christian dialogue, Islam. *Unit head:* Dr. Robert W. Canoy, Dean, 704-406-4400, Fax: 704-406-3935, E-mail: rcanoy@gardner-webb.edu. *Application contact:* Jeremy Fern, Director of Admissions, 704-406-3205, Fax: 704-406-3935, E-mail: jfern@gardner-webb.edu.

George Fox University, George Fox Evangelical Seminary, Newberg, OR 97132-2697. Offers Biblical studies (M Div); chaplaincy (M Div); Christian earth keeping (M Div); ministry (D Min), including global missional leadership, leadership and spiritual formation, semiotics and future studies; ministry leadership (MA); pastoral studies (M Div); spiritual formation (M Div, MA); spiritual formation and discipleship (Certificate); theological studies (MA). *Accreditation:* ACIPE; ATS. Part-time programs available. Postbaccalaureate distance learning degree programs offered (minimal on-campus study). *Faculty:* 7 full-time (2 women), 16 part-time/adjunct (8 women). *Students:* 50 full-time (16 women), 292 part-time (88 women); includes 25 minority (6 African Americans, 2 American Indian/Alaska Native, 13 Asian Americans or Pacific Islanders, 4 Hispanic Americans), 5 international. Average age 41. 152 applicants, 88% accepted, 86 enrolled. In 2009, 14 first professional degrees, 8 master's, 12 doctorates, 4 other advanced degrees awarded. *Degree requirements:* For master's, variable foreign language requirement, thesis optional, internship; for doctorate, comprehensive exam (for some programs), thesis/dissertation, internship. *Entrance requirements:* For master's, resume, admission statement, three references (one pastoral, one academic or professional, one personal), one official transcript from each college or university attended; for doctorate, resume, 3 references (1 professional, 1 academic, 1 personal). Additional exam requirements/recommendations for international students: Required—TOEFL (minimum score 577 paper-based; 233 computer-based; 90 iBT). *Application deadline:* For fall admission, 7/1 for domestic and international students; for winter admission, 11/1 for domestic and international students; for spring admission, 4/1 for domestic and international students. Applications are processed on a rolling basis. Application fee: $40. Electronic applications accepted. *Expenses:* Contact institution. *Financial support:* Career-related internships or fieldwork and scholarships/grants available. Financial award application deadline: 5/1; financial award applicants required to submit FAFSA. *Unit head:* Dr. Chuck Conniry, Vice President/Dean, 503-554-6152, E-mail: cconniry@georgefox.edu. *Application contact:* Sheila Bartlett, Admissions Counselor, 800-631-0921, Fax: 503-554-6122, E-mail: seminary@georgefox.edu.

Global University, Graduate School of Theology, Springfield, MO 65804. Offers biblical studies (MA); divinity (M Div); ministerial studies (MA), including education, leadership, missions, New Testament, Old Testament. Part-time and evening/weekend programs available. Postbaccalaureate distance learning degree programs offered (no on-campus study). *Degree requirements:* For master's, thesis (for some programs). *Entrance requirements:* For M Div, minimum undergraduate GPA of 3.0; for master's, minimum undergraduate GPA of 3.0, 15 undergraduate credit hours of course work in Bible or theology. Electronic applications accepted. *Faculty research:* Higher education, cross-cultural missions.

Gordon-Conwell Theological Seminary, Graduate and Professional Programs, South Hamilton, MA 01982. Offers Biblical languages (MABL); church history (MACH); counseling (MACO); ministry (D Min); missions/evangelism (MAME); New Testament (MANT); Old Testament (MAOT); religion (MAR); theology (M Div, MATH, Th M, Th D). *Accreditation:* ACIPE; ATS (one or more programs are accredited). Part-time and evening/weekend programs available. *Degree requirements:* For master's, one foreign language, thesis optional; for doctorate, 2 foreign languages, thesis/dissertation; for M Div, 2 foreign languages. *Entrance requirements:* For M Div and master's, minimum GPA of 2.5; for doctorate, minimum GPA of 3.0.

Grace Theological Seminary, Graduate and Professional Programs, Winona Lake, IN 46590-9907. Offers biblical studies (Certificate); camp administration (MA); counseling (M Div); exegetical studies (MA); intercultural studies (M Div, MA); local church studies (MA); pastoral studies (M Div); theological studies (MA); theology (D Min, Diploma). Part-time programs available. Postbaccalaureate distance learning degree programs offered (no on-campus study). *Degree requirements:* For master's, thesis optional; for doctorate, 2 foreign languages, thesis/dissertation; for M Div, 2 foreign languages, thesis/dissertation optional. *Entrance requirements:* For M Div and master's, MAT, minimum GPA of 2.5. Electronic applications accepted. *Faculty research:* Biblical theology, language, and church ministries.

Grand Rapids Theological Seminary of Cornerstone University, Graduate Programs, Grand Rapids, MI 49525-5897. Offers biblical counseling (MA); Biblical counseling (M Div); chaplaincy (M Div); Christian education (M Div, MA); intercultural studies (M Div, MA); New Testament (MA, Th M); Old Testament (MA, Th M); pastoral studies (M Div); systematic theology (MA); theology (Th M). *Accreditation:* ATS. Part-time programs available. Postbaccalaureate distance learning degree programs offered (minimal on-campus study). *Entrance requirements:*

Missions and Missiology

Grand Rapids Theological Seminary of Cornerstone University (continued)
Additional exam requirements/recommendations for international students: Required—TOEFL (minimum score 577 paper-based; 233 computer-based; 90 iBT). Electronic applications accepted.

Hope International University, School of Graduate and Professional Studies, Programs in Ministry, Fullerton, CA 92831-3138. Offers Christian leadership (MCM); church music (MA); church music (Korean track) (MCM); church planting (MCM); intercultural studies (MCM); worship (MCM). Part-time and evening/weekend programs available. Postbaccalaureate distance learning degree programs offered (minimal on-campus study). *Degree requirements:* For master's, thesis (for some programs), project. *Entrance requirements:* For master's, minimum GPA of 3.0, MCM program requires an undergraduate degree in music, 2 references. Additional exam requirements/recommendations for international students: Required—TOEFL (minimum score 550 paper-based; 213 computer-based; 86 iBT); Recommended—IELTS (minimum score 6.5). Electronic applications accepted. *Expenses:* Contact institution. *Faculty research:* Church dynamics, growth methodologies.

Knox Theological Seminary, Graduate Programs, Program in Evangelism, Fort Lauderdale, FL 33308. Offers ME. Part-time and evening/weekend programs available. *Entrance requirements:* Additional exam requirements/recommendations for international students: Required—TOEFL, TWE (minimum score 5).

Luther Rice University, Graduate Programs, Lithonia, GA 30038-2454. Offers Bible/theology (M Div); Christian education (M Div); Christian studies (MA); church ministry (D Min); counseling (M Div); discipleship counseling (MA); ministry (M Div, MA); missions/evangelism (M Div). Part-time programs available. Postbaccalaureate distance learning degree programs offered (no on-campus study). *Degree requirements:* For doctorate, thesis/dissertation. *Entrance requirements:* Additional exam requirements/recommendations for international students: Required—TOEFL (minimum score 500 paper-based; 173 computer-based).

Mennonite Brethren Biblical Seminary, School of Theology, Program in Intercultural Mission, Fresno, CA 93727-5097. Offers MA.

Midwestern Baptist Theological Seminary, Graduate and Professional Programs, Kansas City, MO 64118-4697. Offers Biblical archaeology (MA); Biblical languages (MA); Christian education (M Div, MACE); Christian foundations—lay ministry (Graduate Certificate); collegiate ministries (M Div); counseling (MA); educational ministry (D Ed Min); international church planting (M Div); ministry (M Div, D Min); North American church planting (M Div); sacred music (MCM); urban ministry (M Div); worship leadership (M Div); youth ministry (M Div). *Accreditation:* ATS. Part-time programs available. Postbaccalaureate distance learning degree programs offered (minimal on-campus study). *Degree requirements:* For doctorate, thesis/dissertation; for M Div, 2 foreign languages. *Entrance requirements:* For doctorate, MAT. Electronic applications accepted. *Faculty research:* Ministerial studies, Biblical and theological studies, missions, counseling.

Nazarene Theological Seminary, Graduate and Professional Programs, Kansas City, MO 64131-1263. Offers Christian education (MA); intercultural studies (MA); theological studies (MA); theology (M Div, D Min). *Accreditation:* ACIPE; ATS. Part-time programs available. *Faculty:* 19 full-time (3 women), 12 part-time/adjunct (2 women). *Students:* 136 full-time (32 women), 118 part-time (32 women); includes 21 minority (5 African Americans, 1 American Indian/Alaska Native, 7 Asian Americans or Pacific Islanders, 8 Hispanic Americans), 14 international. Average age 31. 129 applicants, 77% accepted, 71 enrolled. In 2009, 40 first professional degrees, 22 master's, 2 doctorates awarded. *Degree requirements:* For master's, comprehensive exam (for some programs), thesis (for some programs); for doctorate, thesis/dissertation. *Entrance requirements:* Additional exam requirements/recommendations for international students: Required—TOEFL. *Application deadline:* For fall admission, 3/1 priority date for domestic and international students; for spring admission, 10/1 priority date for domestic and international students. Applications are processed on a rolling basis. Application fee: $25 ($200 for international students). Electronic applications accepted. *Financial support:* In 2009–10, 235 students received support, including 15 teaching assistantships (averaging $1,400 per year); institutionally sponsored loans and scholarships/grants also available. Support available to part-time students. Financial award application deadline: 3/1; financial award applicants required to submit FAFSA. *Unit head:* Dr. Roger L. Hahn, Dean of the Faculty, 816-268-5412, Fax: 816-268-5500, E-mail: rlhahn@nts.edu. *Application contact:* Jay A. Sandbloom, Director of Admissions, 816-268-5451, Fax: 816-268-5500, E-mail: jasandbloom@nts.edu.

Northwest Nazarene University, Graduate Studies, Program in Religion, Nampa, ID 83686-5897. Offers Christian education (MA); missional leadership (MA); pastoral ministry (MA); religion (M Div); spiritual formation (MA). Part-time and evening/weekend programs available. Postbaccalaureate distance learning degree programs offered (no on-campus study). Electronic applications accepted.

Northwest University, College of Ministry, Kirkland, WA 98033. Offers ministry (MA); missional leadership (MA); theology and culture (MA). *Faculty:* 11 full-time (1 woman), 12 part-time/adjunct (2 women). *Students:* 16 full-time (3 women), 24 part-time (7 women); includes 3 minority (all African Americans). 39 applicants, 97% accepted, 22 enrolled. *Entrance requirements:* Additional exam requirements/recommendations for international students: Required—TOEFL (minimum score 550 paper-based). Application fee: $75. *Unit head:* Dr. Kent Ingle, Dean, 425-889-5253, E-mail: kent.ingle@northwestu.edu. *Application contact:* Roy Rowland, Director of Graduate and Professional Studies Enrollment, 425-889-7787, Fax: 425-803-3059, E-mail: gpse@northwestu.edu.

Oral Roberts University, School of Theology and Missions, Tulsa, OK 74171. Offers biblical literature (MA), including advanced languages, Judaic-Christian studies; Christian counseling (MA), including marriage and family therapy; divinity (M Div); missions (MA); practical theology (MA); theological/historical studies (MA); theology (D Min). *Accreditation:* ATS; NASM. Part-time programs available. Postbaccalaureate distance learning degree programs offered (minimal on-campus study). *Degree requirements:* For master's, thesis (for some programs), practicum/internship; for doctorate, thesis/dissertation, applied research project; for M Div, one foreign language, field experience. *Entrance requirements:* For M Div and master's, GRE General Test or MAT, minimum GPA of 2.5; for doctorate, M Div, minimum GPA of 3.0, 3 years of full-time ministry experience. Additional exam requirements/recommendations for international students: Required—TOEFL (minimum score 550 paper-based; 213 computer-based; 79 iBT). Electronic applications accepted.

Phillips Theological Seminary, Programs in Theology, Tulsa, OK 74116. Offers administration of church agencies (M Div); campus ministry (M Div); church-related social work (M Div); college and seminary teaching (M Div); global mission work (M Div); institutional chaplaincy (M Div); ministerial vocations in Christian education (M Div); ministry (D Min), including parish ministry, pastoral counseling, practices of ministry; ministry and culture (MAMC), including Christian education, congregational leadership, history and practice of Christian spirituality, theology, ethics, and culture; ministry of music (M Div); pastoral care and counseling (M Div); pastoral ministry (M Div); theological studies (MTS). *Accreditation:* ATS. Part-time programs available. Postbaccalaureate distance learning degree programs offered (minimal on-campus study). *Degree requirements:* For master's, thesis (for some programs); for doctorate, thesis/dissertation. *Entrance requirements:* For master's, minimum GPA of 2.5; for doctorate, M Div, minimum GPA of 3.0. *Faculty research:* Biblical studies, historical studies, theology and culture, practical theology, theology and film.

Providence College and Theological Seminary, Theological Seminary, Otterburne, MB R0A 1G0, Canada. Offers children's ministry (Certificate); Christian studies (MA, Certificate); counseling (MA); cross-cultural discipleship (Certificate); divinity (M Div); educational studies (MA), including counseling psychology, educational ministries, student development, teaching English to speakers of other languages, training teachers of English to speakers of other languages; global studies (MA); lay counseling (Diploma); ministry (D Min); teaching English to speakers of other languages (Certificate); theological studies (MA); training teacher of English to speakers of other languages (Certificate); youth ministry (Certificate). *Accreditation:* ATS. Part-time programs available. *Degree requirements:* For master's, variable foreign language requirement, thesis (for some programs); for doctorate, thesis/dissertation; for M Div, 2 foreign languages, comprehensive exam, thesis/dissertation (for some programs). *Entrance requirements:* Additional exam requirements/recommendations for international students: Recommended—TOEFL (minimum score 550 paper-based; 213 computer-based). *Faculty research:* Studies in Isaiah, theology of sin.

Reformed Theological Seminary–Jackson Campus, Graduate and Professional Programs, Jackson, MS 39209-3099. Offers Bible, theology, and missions (Certificate); biblical studies (MA); Christian education (M Div, MA); counseling (M Div); divinity (M Div, Diploma); marriage and family therapy (MA); ministry (D Min); missions (M Div, MA, D Min); New Testament (Th M); Old Testament (Th M); theological studies (MA); theology (Th M); M Div/MA. *Accreditation:* AAMFT/COAMFTE (one or more programs are accredited); ATS (one or more programs are accredited). *Degree requirements:* For master's, thesis (for some programs), fieldwork; for doctorate, 2 foreign languages, thesis/dissertation; for M Div, 2 foreign languages, thesis/dissertation (for some programs). *Entrance requirements:* For M Div and master's, minimum GPA of 2.6; for doctorate, minimum GPA of 3.0. Additional exam requirements/recommendations for international students: Required—TOEFL.

Regent University, Graduate School, School of Divinity, Virginia Beach, VA 23464-9800. Offers Biblical studies (MA); leadership and renewal (D Min); missiology (M Div, MA); practical theology (M Div, MA); renewal studies (PhD); M Div/M Ed; M Div/MA; M Div/MBA; M Ed/MA; MBA/MA. *Accreditation:* ACIPE; ATS. Part-time programs available. Postbaccalaureate distance learning degree programs offered (minimal on-campus study). *Faculty:* 19 full-time (4 women), 28 part-time/adjunct (5 women). *Students:* 108 full-time (53 women), 436 part-time (171 women); includes 244 minority (214 African Americans, 2 American Indian/Alaska Native, 13 Asian Americans or Pacific Islanders, 15 Hispanic Americans), 19 international. Average age 40. 349 applicants, 63% accepted, 97 enrolled. In 2009, 31 first professional degrees, 39 master's, 5 doctorates awarded. *Degree requirements:* For master's, comprehensive exam, thesis or alternative, internship; for doctorate, thesis/dissertation or alternative; for M Div, internship. *Entrance requirements:* For M Div, GRE General Test or MAT, minimum undergraduate GPA of 3.0, minimum 3 years of ministry experience, transcripts, recommendations; for master's, GRE General Test or MAT, minimum undergraduate GPA of 2.75, writing sample, clergy recommendation; for doctorate, M Div or theological master's degree; minimum graduate GPA of 3.5 (PhD), 3.0 (D Min); recommendations; writing sample; transcripts. Additional exam requirements/recommendations for international students: Required—TOEFL (minimum score 577 paper-based; 233 computer-based). *Application deadline:* For fall admission, 5/1 priority date for domestic students. Applications are processed on a rolling basis. Application fee: $50. Electronic applications accepted. *Expenses:* Contact institution. *Financial support:* In 2009–10, 401 students received support; fellowships with full and partial tuition reimbursements available, career-related internships or fieldwork, scholarships/grants, tuition waivers (full and partial), and unspecified assistantships available. Support available to part-time students. Financial award application deadline: 9/1; financial award applicants required to submit FAFSA. *Faculty research:* Greek and Hebrew, theology, spiritual formation, global missions and world Christianity, women's studies. *Unit head:* Dr. Michael Palmer, Dean, 757-352-4406, Fax: 757-352-4597, E-mail: mpalmer@regent.edu. *Application contact:* Matthew Chadwick, Director of Admissions, 800-373-5504, Fax: 757-352-4381, E-mail: admissions@regent.edu.

Rochester College, Center for Missional Leadership, Rochester Hills, MI 48307-2764. Offers MRE.

Saint Paul University, Faculty of Human Sciences, Program in Mission and Interreligious Studies, Ottawa, ON K1S 1C4, Canada. Offers MA. *Degree requirements:* For master's, one foreign language, thesis. *Entrance requirements:* For master's, honors BA in mission, minimum B average. *Faculty research:* Theology of mission; mission and sociology; history of mission; faith, religion, and culture; world religions; practice of mission; religious anthropology; sociocultural anthropology.

Simpson University, A.W. Tozer Theological Seminary, Redding, CA 96003-8606. Offers intellectual leadership (MA); ministry (M Div). Part-time and evening/weekend programs available. Postbaccalaureate distance learning degree programs offered (minimal on-campus study). *Faculty:* 17 part-time/adjunct (1 woman). *Students:* 35 full-time (10 women), 22 part-time (4 women); includes 1 minority (Asian American or Pacific Islander), 1 international. Average age 38. 22 applicants, 73% accepted, 16 enrolled. In 2009, 5 master's awarded. *Degree requirements:* For master's, student portfolio. *Entrance requirements:* For master's, GRE General Test (if undergraduate GPA less than 2.5), 2 letters of reference, Christian Experience statement. Additional exam requirements/recommendations for international students: Required—TOEFL. *Application deadline:* For fall admission, 9/4 priority date for domestic students, 9/4 for international students; for spring admission, 1/8 priority date for domestic students, 1/8 for international students. Applications are processed on a rolling basis. Application fee: $25. Electronic applications accepted. *Expenses:* Contact institution. *Financial support:* Scholarships/grants available. Support available to part-time students. Financial award application deadline: 3/20; financial award applicants required to submit FAFSA. *Unit head:* Dr. Sarah Sumner, Dean, 530-226-4144, Fax: 530-226-4871, E-mail: ssumner@simpsonu.edu. *Application contact:* Becky Durben, Enrollment Advisor, 530-226-4771, Fax: 530-226-4861, E-mail: rdurben@simpsonu.edu.

Southeastern Baptist Theological Seminary, Graduate and Professional Programs, Wake Forest, NC 27588-1889. Offers advanced biblical studies (M Div); Christian education (M Div, MACE); Christian ethics (PhD); Christian ministry (M Div); Christian planting (M Div); church music (MACM); counseling (MACO); evangelism (PhD); language (M Div); ministry (D Min); New Testament (PhD); Old Testament (PhD); philosophy (PhD); theology (Th M, PhD); women's studies (M Div). *Accreditation:* ACIPE; ATS (one or more programs are accredited). *Degree requirements:* For master's, thesis (for some programs), oral exam; for doctorate, thesis/dissertation, fieldwork; for M Div, supervised ministry. *Entrance requirements:* For master's, Cooperative English Test, minimum GPA of 2.0, M Div or equivalent (Th M); for doctorate, GRE General Test or MAT, Cooperative English Test, M Div or equivalent, 3 years of professional experience.

Southern Adventist University, School of Religion, Collegedale, TN 37315-0370. Offers Biblical and theological studies (MA); church leadership and management (M Min); church ministry and homiletics (M Min); evangelism and world mission (M Min); religious studies (MA). Part-time programs available. *Faculty:* 5 full-time (0 women). *Students:* 1 (woman) full-time, 1 part-time (0 women); includes 1 minority (African American). Average age 36. 2 applicants, 100% accepted, 2 enrolled. In 2009, 6 master's awarded. *Degree requirements:* For master's, comprehensive exam, thesis (for some programs). *Entrance requirements:* For master's, GRE. Additional exam requirements/recommendations for international students: Required—TOEFL (minimum score 600 paper-based; 250 computer-based). *Application deadline:* For spring admission, 5/1 priority date for domestic students, 4/30 for international students. Applications are processed on a rolling basis. Application fee: $25. *Expenses:* Tuition: Full-time $13,149; part-time $487 per credit hour. *Financial support:* Tuition waivers (full) available. Support available to part-time students. Financial award application deadline: 4/1; financial award applicants required to submit FAFSA. *Faculty research:* Biblical archaeology. *Unit head:* Dr. Greg A. King, Dean, 423-236-2975, Fax: 423-236-1976, E-mail: gking@southern.edu. *Application contact:* Susan L. Brown, Administrative Assistant, 423-236-2977, Fax: 423-236-1977, E-mail: sbrown@southern.edu.

Southern Baptist Theological Seminary, Billy Graham School of Missions, Evangelism and Church Growth, Louisville, KY 40280-0004. Offers Christian mission/world religion (PhD); evangelism/church growth (PhD); ministry (D Min); missiology (MA, D Miss); missions, evangelism and church growth (M Div); religion (Th M); theological studies (MA). *Accreditation:*

ATS. Part-time and evening/weekend programs available. Postbaccalaureate distance learning degree programs offered (minimal on-campus study). *Faculty:* 12 full-time (0 women). *Students:* 608. In 2009, 27 first professional degrees, 4 master's, 3 doctorates awarded. *Degree requirements:* For master's and M Div, 2 foreign languages; for doctorate, 4 foreign languages, thesis/dissertation. *Entrance requirements:* For doctorate, GRE General Test, MAT, M Div. Additional exam requirements/recommendations for international students: Required—TOEFL, TWE. *Application deadline:* For fall admission, 8/1 priority date for domestic students; for spring admission, 1/2 for domestic students. Applications are processed on a rolling basis. Application fee: $35. *Faculty research:* Assimilation of church congregants, effective methodologies of evangelism, expectations of church members, spiritual warfare literature, formative church discipline. *Unit head:* Dr. Chuck Lawless, Dean, 800-626-5525, E-mail: clawless@sbts.edu. *Application contact:* Chuck Haddox, Director of Admissions, 800-626-5525 Ext. 4617, E-mail: chaddox@sbts.edu.

Southern Evangelical Seminary, Graduate School of Ministry and Missions, Matthews, NC 28105. Offers apologetics (Certificate); Christian education (MA); church ministry (MA, Certificate); divinity (Certificate), including apologetics (M Div, Certificate); Islamic studies (Certificate); theology (M Div), including apologetics (M Div, Certificate), Biblical studies; youth ministry (MA). Part-time and evening/weekend programs available. Postbaccalaureate distance learning degree programs offered. *Degree requirements:* For master's, thesis (for some programs); for M Div, one foreign language. *Entrance requirements:* Additional exam requirements/recommendations for international students: Required—TOEFL (minimum score 600 paper-based; 250 computer-based).

Southwestern Assemblies of God University, Thomas F. Harrison School of Graduate Studies, Program in Theological Studies, Waxahachie, TX 75165-5735. Offers Bible and theology (MS); Biblical studies (M Div); counseling (M Div); cross cultural missions (M Div); practical theology (M Div); theological studies (M Div). Postbaccalaureate distance learning degree programs offered. *Degree requirements:* For master's, comprehensive written and oral exams. *Entrance requirements:* For master's, GRE General Test, minimum GPA of 2.5. Electronic applications accepted.

Southwestern Christian University, Program in Ministry, Bethany, OK 73008-0340. Offers church planting (M Min); church revitalization and renewal (M Min); intercultural studies (M Min); leadership (M Min); life coaching (M Min); pastoral ministries (M Min); work place ministries (M Min). Part-time programs available. *Degree requirements:* For master's, thesis. *Entrance requirements:* For master's, minimum GPA of 2.5. Additional exam requirements/recommendations for international students: Required—TOEFL (minimum score 500 paper-based). Electronic applications accepted.

Taylor College and Seminary, Graduate and Professional Programs, Edmonton, AB T6J 4T3, Canada. Offers Christian studies (Diploma); intercultural studies (MA, Diploma), including intercultural studies (Diploma), TESOL; theology (M Div, MTS). *Accreditation:* ATS. Part-time programs available. Postbaccalaureate distance learning degree programs offered (minimal on-campus study). *Faculty:* 5 full-time (0 women), 5 part-time/adjunct (1 woman). *Students:* 13 full-time (4 women), 52 part-time (24 women); includes 18 minority (2 African Americans, 1 American Indian/Alaska Native, 15 Asian Americans or Pacific Islanders). Average age 38. 40 applicants, 73% accepted, 20 enrolled. In 2009, 11 first professional degrees awarded. *Degree requirements:* For master's, thesis optional. *Entrance requirements:* Additional exam requirements/recommendations for international students: Required—TOEFL (minimum score 550 paper-based; 80 iBT), IELTS (minimum score 6.5). *Application deadline:* For fall admission, 9/1 priority date for domestic and international students. Applications are processed on a rolling basis. Application fee: $35 ($70 for international students). *Financial support:* In 2009–10, 16 students received support. Career-related internships or fieldwork and scholarships/grants available. Financial award application deadline: 8/1. *Faculty research:* Biblical studies, administration and organization, world religions, ethics, missiology. *Unit head:* Dr. Joost Pikkert, Academic Dean, 780-431-5243, Fax: 780-436-9416, E-mail: joost.pikkert@taylor-edu.ca. *Application contact:* Craig Weston, Registrar and Director of Enrolment Services, 780-431-5208, Fax: 780-436-9416, E-mail: craig.weston@taylor-edu.ca.

Trinity International University, Trinity Evangelical Divinity School, Deerfield, IL 60015-1284. Offers Biblical and Near Eastern archaeology and languages (MA); Christian studies (MA, Certificate); Christian thought (MA); church history (MA, Th M); congregational ministry: pastor-teacher (M Div); congregational ministry: team ministry (M Div); counseling ministries (MA); counseling psychology (MA); cross-cultural ministry (M Div); educational studies (PhD); evangelism (MA); history of Christianity in America (MA); intercultural studies (MA, PhD); leadership and ministry management (D Min); military chaplaincy (D Min); ministry (MA); mission and evangelism (Th M); missions and evangelism (D Min); New Testament (MA, Th M); Old Testament (Th M); Old Testament and Semitic languages (MA); pastoral care (M Div); pastoral care and counseling (D Min); pastoral counseling and psychology (Th M); pastoral theology (Th M); philosophy of religion (MA); preaching (D Min); religion (MA); research ministry (M Div); systematic theology (Th M); theological studies (PhD); urban ministry (MA). *Accreditation:* ATS (one or more programs are accredited). Part-time programs available. Postbaccalaureate distance learning degree programs offered (minimal on-campus study). *Degree requirements:* For master's, comprehensive exam, thesis, fieldwork; for doctorate, comprehensive exam (for some programs), thesis/dissertation; for M Div, 2 foreign languages, fieldwork; for Certificate, comprehensive exam, integrative papers. *Entrance requirements:* For M Div, GRE, MAT; for master's, GRE, MAT, minimum cumulative undergraduate GPA of 3.0; for doctorate, GRE, minimum cumulative graduate GPA of 3.2; for Certificate, GRE, MAT, minimum undergraduate GPA of 2.5. Additional exam requirements/recommendations for international students: Required—TOEFL (minimum score 580 paper-based; 237 computer-based), TWE (minimum score 4). Electronic applications accepted.

Trinity School for Ministry, Graduate Programs, Ambridge, PA 15003-2397. Offers Anglican studies (Diploma); basic Christian studies (Diploma); divinity (M Div); ministry (D Min); mission and evangelism (MAME, Diploma); religion (MAR); youth ministry (Diploma). *Accreditation:* ATS (one or more programs are accredited). Part-time programs available. *Degree requirements:* For master's, thesis optional; for doctorate, thesis/dissertation; for M Div, thesis/dissertation optional, Greek and Hebrew. *Entrance requirements:* Additional exam requirements/recommendations for international students: Required—TOEFL. *Faculty research:* Pauline Epistles, contemporary theology, history of Anglican liturgy, book of Ruth, biblical theology.

Tyndale University College & Seminary, Graduate Programs, Toronto, ON M2M 4B3, Canada. Offers Biblical studies (M Div); Christian foundations (MTS); Christian studies (Diploma); counseling (M Div); educational ministry (M Div); missions (M Div, Diploma); pastoral and Chinese ministry (M Div); pastoral ministry (M Div); Pentecostal studies (MTS); spiritual formation (M Div, Diploma); theological studies (M Div); theology (Th M); worship and liturgy (M Div, MTS); youth and family ministry (M Div). *Accreditation:* ATS. Part-time programs available. Postbaccalaureate distance learning degree programs offered (no on-campus study). *Degree requirements:* For M Div, one foreign language, thesis/dissertation optional. *Entrance requirements:* For M Div, master's, and Diploma, minimum C+ average in undergraduate course work. Additional exam requirements/recommendations for international students: Required—TOEFL (minimum score 570 paper-based; 230 computer-based), TWE (minimum score 5). Electronic applications accepted. *Faculty research:* Canadian church history, Chinese church history, Old Testament, counseling ministries (narrative therapy), world religions.

University of South Africa, College of Human Sciences, Pretoria, South Africa. Offers adult education (M Ed); African languages (MA, PhD); African politics (MA, PhD); Afrikaans (MA, PhD); ancient history (MA, PhD); ancient Near Eastern studies (MA, PhD); anthropology (MA, PhD); applied linguistics (MA); Arabic (MA, PhD); archaeology (MA); art history (MA); Biblical archaeology (MA); Biblical studies (M Th, D Th, PhD); Christian spirituality (M Th, D Th); church history (M Th, D Th); classical studies (MA, PhD); clinical psychology (MA); communication (MA, PhD); comparative education (M Ed, Ed D); consulting psychology (D Admin, D Com, PhD); curriculum studies (M Ed, Ed D); development studies (M Admin, MA, D Admin, PhD); didactics (M Ed, Ed D); education (M Tech); education management (M Ed, Ed D); educational psychology (M Ed); English (MA); environmental education (M Ed); French (MA, PhD); German (MA, PhD); Greek (MA); guidance and counseling (M Ed); health studies (MA, PhD), including health sciences education (MA), health services management (MA), medical and surgical nursing science (critical care general) (MA), midwifery and neonatal nursing science (MA), trauma and emergency care (MA); history (MA, PhD); history of education (Ed D); inclusive education (M Ed, Ed D); information and communications technology policy and regulation (MA); information science (MA, MIS, PhD); international politics (MA, PhD); Islamic studies (MA, PhD); Italian (MA, PhD); Judaica (MA, PhD); linguistics (MA, PhD); mathematical education (M Ed); mathematics education (MA); missiology (M Th, D Th); modern Hebrew (MA, PhD); musicology (MA, MMus, D Mus, PhD); natural science education (M Ed); New Testament (M Th, D Th); Old Testament (D Th); pastoral therapy (M Th, D Th); philosophy (MA); philosophy of education (M Ed, Ed D); politics (MA, PhD); Portuguese (MA, PhD); practical theology (M Th, D Th); psychology (MA, MS, PhD); psychology of education (M Ed, Ed D); public health (MA); religious studies (MA, D Th, PhD); Romance languages (MA); Russian (MA, PhD); Semitic languages (MA, PhD); social behavior studies in HIV/AIDS (MA); social science (mental health) (MA); social science in development studies (MA); social science in psychology (MA); social science in social work (MA); social science in sociology (MA); social work (MSW, DSW, PhD); socio-education (M Ed, Ed D); sociolinguistics (MA); sociology (MA, PhD); Spanish (MA, PhD); systematic theology (M Th, D Th); TESOL (teaching English to speakers of other languages) (MA); theological ethics (M Th, D Th); theory of literature (MA, PhD); urban ministries (D Th); urban ministry (M Th).

Wesley Biblical Seminary, Graduate Programs, Jackson, MS 39206. Offers apologetics (MA); Biblical studies (MA); Christian studies (MA); evangelism (M Div); family life ministry (M Div); honors research (M Div); missions (M Div); pastoral ministry (M Div); teaching (M Div); theological studies (MA). *Accreditation:* ATS. Part-time programs available. *Faculty:* 11 full-time (2 women), 5 part-time/adjunct (0 women). *Students:* 43 full-time (5 women), 89 part-time (33 women). *Degree requirements:* For master's, thesis. *Entrance requirements:* Additional exam requirements/recommendations for international students: Required—TOEFL. *Application deadline:* For fall admission, 7/1 priority date for domestic students; for spring admission, 12/1 priority date for domestic students. Applications are processed on a rolling basis. Application fee: $40. Electronic applications accepted. *Expenses:* Tuition: Full-time $8000; part-time $320 per credit hour. Required fees: $310; $160 per semester. Tuition and fees vary according to course load, campus/location and program. *Financial support:* Scholarships/grants available. Support available to part-time students. *Faculty research:* Patristics, missiology, culture, hermeneutics. *Unit head:* Dr. Ray R. Easley, Vice President for Academic Affairs, 601-366-8880 Ext. 112, Fax: 601-366-8832. *Application contact:* Laura McMillan, Assistant to the Vice President for Business and Student Development, 601-366-8880 Ext. 110, Fax: 601-366-8832, E-mail: admissions@wbs.edu.

Westminster Theological Seminary, Graduate and Professional Programs, Philadelphia, PA 19118. Offers apologetics (Th M); Biblical and urban studies (Certificate); Biblical counseling (MA); biblical studies (MAR); Christian studies (Certificate); church history (Th M); counseling (M Div); general studies (M Div, MAR); hermeneutics and Bible interpretations (PhD); historical and theological studies (PhD); historical theology (Th M); New Testament (Th M); Old Testament (Th M); pastoral counseling (D Min); pastoral ministry (M Div, D Min); systematic theology (Th M); theological studies (MAR); urban missions (M Div, MA, MAR, D Min). *Accreditation:* ATS. Part-time programs available. Terminal master's awarded for partial completion of doctoral program. *Degree requirements:* For master's, thesis (for some programs); for doctorate, 4 foreign languages, comprehensive exam (for some programs), thesis/dissertation; for M Div, 2 foreign languages. *Entrance requirements:* For doctorate, GRE General Test. Additional exam requirements/recommendations for international students: Required—TOEFL, TWE.

Wheaton College, Graduate School, Department of Intercultural Studies, Wheaton, IL 60187-5593. Offers evangelism (MA); intercultural studies (MA); intercultural studies/teaching English as a second language (MA); missions (MA); teaching English as a second language (Certificate). Part-time programs available. *Degree requirements:* For master's, thesis or alternative. *Entrance requirements:* For master's, GRE General Test, MAT. Electronic applications accepted.

Pastoral Ministry and Counseling

Abilene Christian University, Graduate School, College of Biblical Studies, Graduate School of Theology, Program in Ministry, Abilene, TX 79699-9100. Offers D Min. Part-time programs available. *Students:* 18 part-time (0 women), 1 international. 7 applicants, 86% accepted, 5 enrolled. In 2009, 5 doctorates awarded. *Degree requirements:* For doctorate, one foreign language, thesis/dissertation. *Entrance requirements:* For doctorate, GRE, MAT. *Application deadline:* For fall admission, 4/1 priority date for domestic students; for spring admission, 11/1 for domestic students. Applications are processed on a rolling basis. Application fee: $40. *Expenses:* Tuition: Full-time $11,520; part-time $640 per hour. Required fees: $1090; $53.50 per hour. $10 per term. Tuition and fees vary according to program. *Financial support:* In 2009–10, 4 students received support. Application deadline: 4/1. *Faculty research:* Church growth, ministry evaluation, leadership. *Unit head:* Dr. Charles Siburt, Graduate Adviser, 325-674-3732, Fax: 325-674-6716, E-mail: siburt@bible.acu.edu. *Application contact:* William Horn, Graduate Admissions Counselor, 325-674-2656, Fax: 325-674-6717, E-mail: gradinfo@acu.edu.

Abilene Christian University, Graduate School, College of Biblical Studies, Graduate School of Theology, Programs in Christian Ministry, Abilene, TX 79699-9100. Offers MACM. Part-time programs available. *Students:* 8 full-time (4 women), 36 part-time (8 women); includes 3 minority (1 American Indian/Alaska Native, 2 Hispanic Americans), 5 international. 27 applicants, 52% accepted, 9 enrolled. In 2009, 19 master's awarded. *Degree requirements:* For master's, comprehensive exam. *Entrance requirements:* For master's, GRE General Test or MAT. *Application deadline:* For fall admission, 4/1 priority date for domestic students; for spring admission, 11/1 for domestic students. Applications are processed on a rolling basis. Application fee: $40. Electronic applications accepted. *Expenses:* Tuition: Full-time $11,520; part-time $640 per hour. Required fees: $1090; $53.50 per hour. $10 per term. Tuition and fees vary according to program. *Financial support:* In 2009–10, 25 students received support. Application deadline: 4/1. *Faculty research:* Program innovation, instruments for educational evaluation. *Unit head:* Dr. Tim Sensing, Graduate Advisor, 325-674-3792, Fax: 325-674-6180, E-mail: sensingt@acu.edu. *Application contact:* William Horn, Graduate Admissions Counselor, 325-674-2656, Fax: 325-674-6717, E-mail: gradinfo@acu.edu.

Pastoral Ministry and Counseling

Alliance Theological Seminary, Graduate and Professional Programs, Nyack, NY 10960. Offers Christian ministry (MPS); counseling (MA); intercultural studies (MA); missions (MPS); New Testament (MA); Old Testament (MA); theology (M Div); urban ministry (MPS). *Accreditation:* ATS. Part-time programs available. *Degree requirements:* For master's, comprehensive exam (for some programs), thesis optional, internships; for M Div, 2 foreign languages, internship. *Entrance requirements:* Proficiency in New Testament Greek, minimum GPA of 2.5 (undergraduate). Additional exam requirements/recommendations for international students: Required—TOEFL (minimum score 550 paper-based; 213 computer-based).

American Baptist Seminary of the West, Graduate and Professional Programs, Berkeley, CA 94704-3029. Offers community leadership (MA); theology (M Div, MA). *Accreditation:* ACIPE; ATS (one or more programs are accredited). Part-time and evening/weekend programs available. *Faculty:* 6 full-time (4 women), 7 part-time/adjunct (2 women). *Students:* 25 full-time (9 women), 38 part-time (23 women); includes 50 minority (44 African Americans, 6 Asian Americans or Pacific Islanders), 13 international. *Entrance requirements:* For M Div, minimum GPA of 2.5; for master's, minimum GPA of 3.0. Additional exam requirements/recommendations for international students: Required—TOEFL (minimum score 550 paper-based; 250 computer-based). *Application deadline:* For fall admission, 4/15 priority date for domestic students, 4/15 for international students. Applications are processed on a rolling basis. Application fee: $25. Electronic applications accepted. *Expenses:* Tuition: Full-time $13,390; part-time $515 per credit. Required fees: $480; $515 per credit. $240 per semester. One-time fee: $250. *Financial support:* Career-related internships or fieldwork, institutionally sponsored loans, scholarships/grants, tuition waivers (partial), and tuition discount available. Support available to part-time students. Financial award application deadline: 4/15; financial award applicants required to submit FAFSA. *Unit head:* Dr. Paul M. Martin, President, 510-841-1905 Ext. 224, Fax: 510-841-2446, E-mail: pmartin@absw.edu. *Application contact:* Rev. Michelle M. Holmes, Vice President, 510-841-1905 Ext. 225, Fax: 510-841-2446, E-mail: mmholmes@absw.edu.

Amridge University, Graduate and Professional Programs, Montgomery, AL 36117. Offers behavioral leadership and management (MA); biblical studies (MA, PhD); family therapy (D Min); leadership and management (MS); marriage and family therapy (M Div, MA, PhD); ministerial leadership (M Div, MS); pastoral counseling (M Div, MS); practical theology (MA); professional counseling (M Div, MA); theology (M Div, D Min). *Accreditation:* ATS. Part-time and evening/weekend programs available. Postbaccalaureate distance learning degree programs offered (no on-campus study). *Faculty:* 44 full-time (9 women), 18 part-time/adjunct (7 women). *Students:* 175 full-time (95 women), 192 part-time (93 women); includes 182 minority (172 African Americans, 1 American Indian/Alaska Native, 1 Asian American or Pacific Islander, 8 Hispanic Americans). Average age 35. *Degree requirements:* For master's, one foreign language, comprehensive exam (for some programs), thesis (for some programs); for doctorate, comprehensive exam (for some programs), thesis/dissertation; for M Div, comprehensive exam (for some programs). *Entrance requirements:* For M Div, master's, and doctorate, GRE General Test or MAT. Additional exam requirements/recommendations for international students: Required—TOEFL. *Application deadline:* For fall admission, 9/1 priority date for domestic students; for spring admission, 1/1 priority date for domestic students. Applications are processed on a rolling basis. Application fee: $75. Electronic applications accepted. *Expenses:* Tuition: Full-time $10,080; part-time $560 per semester hour. Required fees: $600 per term. *Financial support:* Federal Work-Study and scholarships/grants available. Support available to part-time students. Financial award applicants required to submit FAFSA. *Faculty research:* Homiletics, hermeneutics, ancient Near Eastern history. *Unit head:* Director of Enrollment Management, 800-351-4040 Ext. 7513, Fax: 334-387-3878. *Application contact:* Ora Davis, Admissions Officer, 334-387-3877 Ext. 7524, Fax: 334-387-3878, E-mail: admissions@amridgeuniversity.edu.

Anderson University, School of Christian Ministry, Anderson, SC 29621-4035. Offers M Min. Postbaccalaureate distance learning degree programs offered. *Degree requirements:* For master's, capstone course, ministry project. *Entrance requirements:* For master's, 3 references.

Andrews University, School of Graduate Studies, Seventh-day Adventist Theological Seminary, Berrien Springs, MI 49104. Offers ministry (M Div, D Min); pastoral ministry (MA); religious education (MA, Ed D, PhD, Ed S); theology (M Th, Th D); youth ministry (MA). *Accreditation:* ATS. *Faculty:* 35 full-time (3 women), 1 (woman) part-time/adjunct. *Students:* 390 full-time (63 women), 581 part-time (69 women); includes 381 minority (196 African Americans, 2 American Indian/Alaska Native, 50 Asian Americans or Pacific Islanders, 133 Hispanic Americans), 279 international. Average age 47. 468 applicants, 59% accepted, 77 enrolled. In 2009, 96 first professional degrees, 27 master's, 28 doctorates awarded. *Degree requirements:* For master's, thesis optional; for doctorate, variable foreign language requirement, thesis/dissertation; for M Div, one foreign language, thesis/dissertation optional. *Entrance requirements:* For master's, GRE Subject Test, minimum GPA of 2.0. Additional exam requirements/recommendations for international students: Required—TOEFL (minimum score 550 paper-based). *Application deadline:* Applications are processed on a rolling basis. Application fee: $40. *Financial support:* Fellowships, research assistantships, teaching assistantships, career-related internships or fieldwork, Federal Work-Study, and institutionally sponsored loans available. *Unit head:* Dr. Denis Fortin, Dean, 269-471-3537. *Application contact:* Carolyn Hurst, Director, 800-253-2874, Fax: 269-471-6321.

Anna Maria College, Graduate Division, Program in Pastoral Ministry, Paxton, MA 01612. Offers MA. Part-time and evening/weekend programs available. *Degree requirements:* For master's, pastoral project. *Entrance requirements:* For master's, interview. Additional exam requirements/recommendations for international students: Required—TOEFL (minimum score 500 paper-based). Electronic applications accepted.

Appalachian Bible College, Graduate School, Bradley, WV 25818. Offers ministry (MA). Postbaccalaureate distance learning degree programs offered (no on-campus study). *Entrance requirements:* For master's, ABHE Bible Content Exam, bachelor's degree, 3 references, minimum undergraduate cumulative GPA of 2.75. Additional exam requirements/recommendations for international students: Required—TOEFL (minimum score 550 paper-based; 213 computer-based).

Aquinas Institute of Theology, Graduate and Professional Programs, St. Louis, MO 63108. Offers biblical studies (Certificate); health care mission (MAHCM); ministry (M Div); pastoral care (Certificate); pastoral ministry (MAPM); pastoral studies (MAPS); preaching (D Min); spiritual direction (Certificate); theology (M Div, MA); Thomistic studies (Certificate); M Div/MA; MAPS/MSW. *Accreditation:* ATS (one or more programs are accredited). Part-time and evening/weekend programs available. Postbaccalaureate distance learning degree programs offered (minimal on-campus study). *Faculty:* 17 full-time (10 women), 4 part-time/adjunct (2 women). *Students:* 65 full-time (21 women), 179 part-time (108 women); includes 37 minority (16 African Americans, 1 American Indian/Alaska Native, 8 Asian Americans or Pacific Islanders, 12 Hispanic Americans), 7 international. Average age 41. 39 applicants, 87% accepted, 27 enrolled. In 2009, 31 master's, 11 doctorates awarded. *Degree requirements:* For master's, one foreign language, comprehensive exam, thesis or major paper; for doctorate, thesis/dissertation. *Entrance requirements:* For M Div, master's, and Certificate, MAT; for doctorate, 3 years of ministerial experience, 6 hours of graduate course work in homiletics, M Div or the equivalent, minimum GPA of 3.0. Additional exam requirements/recommendations for international students: Required—TOEFL. *Application deadline:* For fall admission, 3/15 priority date for domestic and international students; for spring admission, 11/15 priority date for domestic and international students. Applications are processed on a rolling basis. Application fee: $50. *Expenses:* Tuition: Full-time $14,784; part-time $616 per credit hour. Required fees: $195 per semester. *Financial support:* Career-related internships or fieldwork, scholarships/grants, health care benefits, and tuition waivers (partial) available. Support available to part-time students. Financial award application deadline: 3/15; financial award applicants required to submit CSS PROFILE or FAFSA. *Faculty research:* Theology of preaching, hermeneutics, lay ecclesial ministry, pastoral and practical theology. *Unit head:* Fr. Gregory Heille, Academic Dean, 314-256-8800, Fax: 314-256-8888, E-mail: heille@ai.edu. *Application contact:* David Werthmann, Director of Admissions, 314-256-8806, Fax: 314-256-8888, E-mail: admissions@ai.edu.

Argosy University, Sarasota, College of Psychology and Behavioral Sciences, Sarasota, FL 34235. Offers community counseling (MA); counseling psychology (Ed D); counselor education and supervision (Ed D); forensic psychology (MA); marriage and family therapy (MA); mental health counseling (MA); pastoral community counseling (Ed D).

See Close-Up on page 1075.

Asbury Theological Seminary, Graduate and Professional Programs, Wilmore, KY 40390-1199. Offers MA, MAC, MACE, MACL, MAPC, MAYM, Th M, D Miss, PhD, Certificate. *Accreditation:* ATS. Part-time programs available. Postbaccalaureate distance learning degree programs offered (minimal on-campus study). *Faculty:* 64 full-time (11 women), 74 part-time/adjunct (14 women). *Students:* 760 full-time (226 women), 768 part-time (279 women); includes 155 minority (85 African Americans, 13 American Indian/Alaska Native, 25 Asian Americans or Pacific Islanders, 32 Hispanic Americans), 141 international. Average age 25. 765 applicants, 75% accepted, 364 enrolled. In 2009, 95 master's, 15 doctorates, 38 other advanced degrees awarded. Terminal master's awarded for partial completion of doctoral program. *Degree requirements:* For master's, thesis (for some programs); for doctorate, thesis/dissertation, qualifying exam. *Entrance requirements:* For master's, minimum GPA of 2.75; for doctorate, minimum GPA of 3.0. Additional exam requirements/recommendations for international students: Required—TOEFL, IELTS. *Application deadline:* Applications are processed on a rolling basis. Application fee: $50. Electronic applications accepted. *Financial support:* In 2009–10, 1,317 students received support. Career-related internships or fieldwork, Federal Work-Study, institutionally sponsored loans, and scholarships/grants available. Support available to part-time students. Financial award applicants required to submit FAFSA. *Unit head:* Dr. Leslie A. Andrews, Provost, 859-858-2206, Fax: 859-858-2025, E-mail: leslie.andrews@asburyseminary.edu. *Application contact:* Kevin Bush, Vice President of Enrollment Management, 859-858-2211, Fax: 859-858-2287, E-mail: admissions.office@asburyseminary.edu.

Ashland Theological Seminary, Graduate Programs, Ashland, OH 44805. Offers biblical and theological studies (MA, MAR), including New Testament (MA), Old Testament (MA); Christian ministry (MAPT); Christian studies (Diploma); clinical counseling (michigan) (MAC); clinical counsseling (Ohio) (MACC), including anabaptism, pietism; historical studies (MA), including church history; ministry (D Min); pastoral ministry (M Div); theological studies (MA). *Accreditation:* ATS. Part-time programs available. *Faculty:* 23 full-time (7 women), 74 part-time/adjunct (28 women). *Students:* 663 full-time (343 women), 124 part-time (65 women); includes 312 minority (289 African Americans, 3 American Indian/Alaska Native, 8 Asian Americans or Pacific Islanders, 12 Hispanic Americans), 25 international. Average age 43. 173 applicants, 87% accepted, 142 enrolled. In 2009, 34 first professional degrees, 102 master's, 17 doctorates, 2 other advanced degrees awarded. *Degree requirements:* For master's, 2 foreign languages, comprehensive exam (for some programs), thesis (for some programs); for doctorate, thesis/dissertation; for M Div, 2 foreign languages, comprehensive exam (for some programs). *Entrance requirements:* For M Div, minimum GPA of 2.75; for master's, minimum undergraduate GPA of 2.75; for doctorate, M Div, minimum undergraduate GPA of 3.0. Additional exam requirements/recommendations for international students: Required—TOEFL (minimum score 500 paper-based; 65 computer-based; 173 iBT). *Application deadline:* For fall admission, 8/30 for domestic students. Applications are processed on a rolling basis. Application fee: $30. Electronic applications accepted. *Expenses:* Tuition: Full-time $10,476; part-time $345 per credit hour. Required fees: $180; $15 per course. Part-time tuition and fees vary according to course load. *Financial support:* In 2009–10, 311 students received support, including 17 teaching assistantships; research assistantships, career-related internships or fieldwork, institutionally sponsored loans, scholarships/grants, and unspecified assistantships also available. Support available to part-time students. Financial award application deadline: 5/15; financial award applicants required to submit FAFSA. *Faculty research:* Semitic languages and linguistics, rhetorical and social-scientific criticism, Anabaptist studies, inner spiritual healing, African-American clergy in film and literature. *Unit head:* Dr. John C. Shultz, President, 419-289-5160, Fax: 419-289-5969, E-mail: jshultz@ashland.edu. *Application contact:* Glenn Black, Director of Enrollment Management, 419-289-5151, Fax: 419-289-5969, E-mail: gblack@ashland.edu.

Assemblies of God Theological Seminary, Graduate and Professional Programs, Springfield, MO 65802. Offers Christian ministries (MA); counseling (MA); divinity (M Div); intercultural ministry (MA); intercultural studies (D Miss, PhD); relief and development (D Miss); theological studies (MA); women in leadership (D Min). *Accreditation:* ATS. Part-time and evening/weekend programs available. Postbaccalaureate distance learning degree programs offered (minimal on-campus study). *Faculty:* 12 full-time (3 women), 23 part-time/adjunct (5 women). *Students:* 195 full-time (70 women), 221 part-time (53 women); includes 48 minority (10 African Americans, 6 American Indian/Alaska Native, 16 Asian Americans or Pacific Islanders, 16 Hispanic Americans), 9 international. Average age 36. 109 applicants, 76% accepted, 62 enrolled. In 2009, 46 first professional degrees, 65 master's, 14 doctorates awarded. *Degree requirements:* For master's, analytical reflection paper, comprehensive exam or field education research project; for doctorate, thesis/dissertation; for M Div, one foreign language, analytical reflection paper or field education research project. *Entrance requirements:* For M Div, minimum GPA of 2.5; for master's, minimum GPA of 2.5; for doctorate, minimum GPA of 3.0. Additional exam requirements/recommendations for international students: Required—TOEFL (minimum score 550 paper-based; 213 computer-based; 80 iBT). *Application deadline:* For fall admission, 7/1 priority date for domestic students, 6/1 priority date for international students; for spring admission, 12/1 priority date for domestic students, 11/1 priority date for international students. Applications are processed on a rolling basis. Application fee: $75. Electronic applications accepted. *Financial support:* Career-related internships or fieldwork, Federal Work-Study, and scholarships/grants available. Support available to part-time students. Financial award application deadline: 7/15; financial award applicants required to submit FAFSA. *Unit head:* Stephen Lim, Academic Dean, 417-268-1000, Fax: 417-268-1001, E-mail: slim@agts.edu. *Application contact:* Stephen Lim, Academic Dean, 417-268-1000, Fax: 417-268-1001, E-mail: slim@agts.edu.

The Athenaeum of Ohio, Graduate Programs, Cincinnati, OH 45230-5900. Offers biblical studies (MABS); divinity (M Div); lay ministry (Certificate); pastoral counseling (MAPC); pastoral ministry (MA); theology (MA Th); M Div/MA Th; M Div/MABS; M Div/MAPC. *Accreditation:* ATS (one or more programs are accredited). Part-time and evening/weekend programs available. *Degree requirements:* For master's, one foreign language, comprehensive exam (for some programs), thesis optional; for M Div, comprehensive exam.

Atlantic School of Theology, Graduate and Professional Programs, Halifax, NS B3H 3B5, Canada. Offers ministry (M Div); theological studies (Graduate Certificate). *Accreditation:* ATS. Part-time programs available. Postbaccalaureate distance learning degree programs offered (minimal on-campus study). *Faculty:* 6 full-time, 7 part-time/adjunct. *Students:* 50 full-time (31 women), 75 part-time (38 women). In 2009, 14 first professional degrees, 4 master's awarded. *Degree requirements:* For master's, thesis. *Entrance requirements:* For M Div, master's, and Graduate Certificate, minimum B average in undergraduate course work. *Application deadline:* For fall admission, 2/28 priority date for domestic students. Applications are processed on a rolling basis. Application fee: $40. Tuition charges are reported in Canadian dollars. *Expenses:* Tuition: Full-time $5210 Canadian dollars; part-time $521 Canadian dollars per credit. *Financial support:* Career-related internships or fieldwork available. Support available to part-time students. Financial award application deadline: 9/30. *Faculty research:* Ethics and biology; death, dying and pastoral care; theology and the economy; adult education; John and anti-Judaism. *Unit head:* Rev. Dr. David MacLachlan, Academic Dean, 902-496-7941, Fax: 902-492-4048. *Application contact:* Cynthia Thomson, Registrar, 902-425-3691, Fax: 902-492-4048, E-mail: registrar@astheology.ns.ca.

Austin Presbyterian Theological Seminary, Graduate and Professional Programs, Austin, TX 78705-5797. Offers divinity (M Div); ministry (D Min); theological studies (MA); M Div/MATS; M Div/MSSW. *Accreditation:* ACIPE; ATS. Part-time programs available. *Degree requirements:* For doctorate, thesis/dissertation; for M Div, Greek, Hebrew. *Entrance requirements:* References. Additional exam requirements/recommendations for international students: Required—TOEFL (minimum score 550 paper-based; 213 computer-based; 79 iBT).

Faculty research: Mystical theology, religious pluralism, narrative preaching, social ethics, pastoral care and healing.

Ave Maria University, Graduate Programs, Ave Maria, FL 34142. Offers pastoral theology (MTS); theology (MA, PhD). Terminal master's awarded for partial completion of doctoral program. *Degree requirements:* For master's, one foreign language, thesis; for doctorate, 3 foreign languages, comprehensive exam, thesis/dissertation. *Entrance requirements:* For master's, GRE; for doctorate, GRE, M Div or equivalent; MA or MTS in religion, theology, or philosophy; bachelor's degree with strong background in religion, theology, and/or philosophy.

Ave Maria University, Institute for Pastoral Theology, Ave Maria, FL 34142. Offers MTS. Part-time and evening/weekend programs available.

Azusa Pacific University, Haggard School of Theology, Program in Divinity, Azusa, CA 91702-7000. Offers M Div.

Azusa Pacific University, Haggard School of Theology, Program in Ministry Management, Azusa, CA 91702-7000. Offers MAMM.

Azusa Pacific University, Haggard School of Theology, Program in Pastoral Studies, Azusa, CA 91702-7000. Offers MAPS.

Azusa Pacific University, Haggard School of Theology, Program in Worship Leadership, Azusa, CA 91702-7000. Offers MAWL.

Bakke Graduate University, Programs in Pastoral Ministry and Business, Seattle, WA 98104. Offers business (MBA); global urban ministry (MA); social and civic entrepreneurship (MA); transformational leadership for the global city (D Min). Part-time programs available. Postbaccalaureate distance learning degree programs offered (minimal on-campus study). *Faculty:* 7 full-time (2 women), 30 part-time/adjunct (4 women). *Students:* 84 full-time (24 women), 284 part-time (74 women); includes 199 minority (99 African Americans, 1 American Indian/Alaska Native, 90 Asian Americans or Pacific Islanders, 9 Hispanic Americans). Average age 38. 41 applicants, 98% accepted, 25 enrolled. In 2009, 11 master's, 37 doctorates awarded. *Degree requirements:* For master's, thesis; for doctorate, thesis/dissertation. *Entrance requirements:* For master's, 2 years of ministry experience, BA in Biblical studies or theology; for doctorate, 3 years of ministry experience, M Div. Additional exam requirements/recommendations for international students: Required—TOEFL (minimum score 60 computer-based). *Application deadline:* For fall admission, 7/1 priority date for domestic students; for winter admission, 12/1 for domestic students; for spring admission, 3/15 for domestic students. Applications are processed on a rolling basis. Application fee: $75 ($25 for international students). Electronic applications accepted. *Expenses:* Tuition: Full-time $8000; part-time $2000 per course. Required fees: $175; $50 per course. *Financial support:* In 2009–10, 140 students received support. Scholarships/grants and tuition waivers (partial) available. Financial award applicants required to submit FAFSA. *Faculty research:* Theological systems, church management, worship. *Unit head:* Dr. Gwen Dewey, Academic Dean, 206-264-9100 Ext. 119, Fax: 206-264-8828, E-mail: gwend@bgu.edu. *Application contact:* Lauren Geiser, Assistant Registrar, 206-246-9100 Ext. 110, Fax: 206-264-8828, E-mail: laureng@bgu.edu.

Baptist Bible College, Graduate School of Theology, Springfield, MO 65803-3498. Offers biblical counseling (MA); biblical studies (MA); church ministry (MA); intercultural studies (MA); theology (M Div). Part-time programs available. *Degree requirements:* For master's, 2 foreign languages, thesis (for some programs); for M Div, 2 foreign languages, thesis/dissertation (for some programs). *Entrance requirements:* For master's, outcomes test. Electronic applications accepted.

Baptist Bible College of Pennsylvania, Baptist Bible Seminary, Clarks Summit, PA 18411-1297. Offers biblical studies (PhD); church planting (M Div); global missions (M Div); military chaplaincy (M Div); ministry (M Min, D Min); pastor of church education (M Div); pastor of outreach (M Div); pastoral counseling (M Div); pastoral leadership (M Div); theology (M Div, Th M); youth pastor (M Div). Part-time and evening/weekend programs available. Postbaccalaureate distance learning degree programs offered (minimal on-campus study). Terminal master's awarded for partial completion of doctoral program. *Degree requirements:* For master's, 2 foreign languages, thesis; for doctorate, 2 foreign languages, comprehensive exam (for some programs), thesis/dissertation, oral exam; for M Div, 2 foreign languages, thesis/dissertation, oral exam. *Entrance requirements:* For doctorate, Greek and Hebrew entrance exams (PhD). Electronic applications accepted.

Baptist Bible College of Pennsylvania, Graduate School, Clarks Summit, PA 18411-1297. Offers Bible (MA); biblical ministries (MS); Christian school education (MS); counseling (MS). Part-time and evening/weekend programs available. Postbaccalaureate distance learning degree programs offered (no on-campus study). *Faculty:* 2 full-time (0 women), 1 part-time/adjunct (0 women). *Students:* 12 full-time (7 women), 61 part-time (40 women); includes 3 minority (all African Americans), 1 international. Average age 31. In 2009, 13 master's awarded. *Entrance requirements:* Additional exam requirements/recommendations for international students: Required—TOEFL (minimum score 500 paper-based; 173 computer-based). *Application deadline:* Applications are processed on a rolling basis. Application fee: $30. *Financial support:* In 2009–10, 43 students received support. Institutionally sponsored loans and scholarships/grants available. Financial award application deadline: 8/20; financial award applicants required to submit FAFSA. *Unit head:* Dr. James Lytle, Provost, 570-586-2400 Ext. 9222, Fax: 570-586-1753. *Application contact:* Drew Whipple, Assitant Director of Enrollment, 570-585-9370, Fax: 570-585-9299, E-mail: gradadmissions@bbc.edu.

Baptist Theological Seminary at Richmond, Graduate and Professional Programs, Richmond, VA 23227. Offers biblical interpretation (M Div); Christian education (M Div); theology (D Min); youth and student ministries (M Div); M Div/MS; M Div/MSW. *Accreditation:* ATS. Part-time programs available. Postbaccalaureate distance learning degree programs offered (minimal on-campus study). *Faculty:* 8 full-time (2 women), 9 part-time/adjunct (3 women). *Students:* 59 full-time (33 women), 30 part-time (17 women); includes 9 minority (all African Americans), 3 international. Average age 46. In 2009, 29 first professional degrees, 6 doctorates awarded. *Degree requirements:* For doctorate, one foreign language, comprehensive exam, thesis/dissertation, field study, independent study; for M Div, one foreign language, comprehensive exam (for some programs), thesis/dissertation optional, mission immersion experience, internship. *Entrance requirements:* For doctorate, MAT, M Div, 3 years of full-time ministry experience. Additional exam requirements/recommendations for international students: Required—TOEFL (minimum score 550 paper-based; 213 computer-based). *Application deadline:* For fall admission, 8/1 priority date for domestic students, 5/1 priority date for international students; for winter admission, 12/1 priority date for domestic students, 9/1 priority date for international students; for spring admission, 1/1 priority date for domestic students, 10/1 priority date for international students. Applications are processed on a rolling basis. Application fee: $35. *Financial support:* In 2009–10, 16 teaching assistantships (averaging $1,650 per year) were awarded; scholarships/grants and tuition waivers (partial) also available. Financial award application deadline: 2/1. *Faculty research:* New Testament studies, Old Testament studies, pastoral care, church history, theology. *Unit head:* Dr. Ronald W. Crawford, President, 804-204-1201, Fax: 804-355-8182, E-mail: rcrawford@btsr.edu. *Application contact:* Tiffany Kellogg Pittman, Director of Admissions, 804-204-1208, Fax: 804-355-8182, E-mail: admissions@btsr.edu.

Barry University, School of Arts and Sciences, Department of Theology and Philosophy, Miami Shores, FL 33161-6695. Offers ministry (D Min); pastoral ministry for Hispanics (MA); pastoral theology (MA); practical theology (MA). *Accreditation:* ATS. Part-time and evening/weekend programs available. *Degree requirements:* For master's, comprehensive exam, thesis optional; for doctorate, thesis/dissertation. *Entrance requirements:* For master's, GRE General Test or MAT, minimum GPA of 3.0. Electronic applications accepted. *Faculty research:* Fundamental morals, bioethics, social ethics, liturgical and sacramental theology, biblical studies.

Bethany Theological Seminary, Graduate and Professional Programs, Richmond, IN 47374-4019. Offers biblical studies (MA Th); ministry studies (M Div); peace studies (M Div, MA Th); theological studies (MA Th, CATS); youth ministry (M Div). *Accreditation:* ACIPE; ATS. Part-time programs available. Postbaccalaureate distance learning degree programs offered (minimal on-campus study). *Degree requirements:* For master's, thesis. *Entrance requirements:* For M Div, letters of reference, minimum GPA of 2.75; for master's, letters of reference, minimum GPA of 3.0. Additional exam requirements/recommendations for international students: Required—TOEFL (minimum score 550 paper-based; 218 computer-based).

Bethel College, Division of Graduate Studies, Program in Christian Ministries, Mishawaka, IN 46545-5591. Offers M Min. Part-time and evening/weekend programs available. *Faculty:* 8 part-time/adjunct (0 women). *Students:* 15 full-time (3 women), 46 part-time (11 women); includes 8 minority (all African Americans), 3 international. 36 applicants, 97% accepted, 27 enrolled. In 2009, 17 master's awarded. *Degree requirements:* For master's, thesis or alternative. *Entrance requirements:* Additional exam requirements/recommendations for international students: Required—TOEFL (minimum score 540 paper-based; 207 computer-based). *Application deadline:* For fall admission, 5/1 for international students; for spring admission, 10/1 for international students. Applications are processed on a rolling basis. Application fee: $25. Electronic applications accepted. *Financial support:* Career-related internships or fieldwork available. Financial award applicants required to submit FAFSA. *Unit head:* Dr. Gene Carpenter, Director, 574-257-3332, E-mail: carpeng@bethelcollege.edu. *Application contact:* Dr. John Dendiu, Advisor, 574-257-2675, Fax: 574-257-3385, E-mail: dendiuj@bethelcollege.edu.

Bethel Seminary, Graduate and Professional Programs, St. Paul, MN 55112-6998. Offers applied ministry (MA); biblical studies (MATS, Certificate); children's and family ministry (MACFM); Christian education (MACE); Christian thought (M Div, MACT); church leadership (D Min); community ministry leadership (MA, Certificate); congregation and family care (D Min); global and contextual studies (MA, MATS); historical studies (MATS); lay ministry (Certificate); marriage and family studies (M Div, MATS); marriage and family therapy (MAMFT, Certificate); ministry leadership (Certificate); pastoral care and counseling (MATS); pastoral ministries (M Div); spiritual formation (Certificate); theological studies (MATS, Certificate); transformational leadership (MATL, Certificate); youth ministries (MACE). *Accreditation:* ACIPE; ATS (one or more programs are accredited). Part-time and evening/weekend programs available. Postbaccalaureate distance learning degree programs offered (minimal on-campus study). *Faculty:* 26 full-time (3 women), 76 part-time/adjunct (30 women). *Students:* 725 full-time (269 women), 300 part-time (104 women); includes 204 minority (115 African Americans, 1 American Indian/Alaska Native, 65 Asian Americans or Pacific Islanders, 23 Hispanic Americans), 13 international. Average age 37. 516 applicants, 78% accepted, 261 enrolled. In 2009, 50 first professional degrees, 100 master's, 6 doctorates awarded. *Degree requirements:* For master's, variable foreign language requirement, thesis (for some programs); for doctorate, thesis/dissertation; for M Div, one foreign language. *Entrance requirements:* For M Div and master's, letters of reference, transcripts, personal statement; for doctorate, M Div, letters of reference, organizational support. Additional exam requirements/recommendations for international students: Required—TOEFL (minimum score 550 paper-based; 213 computer-based; 87 iBT). *Application deadline:* For fall admission, 8/1 priority date for domestic students, 3/1 for international students; for winter admission, 12/1 priority date for domestic students; for spring admission, 3/1 priority date for domestic students. Applications are processed on a rolling basis. Application fee: $20. Electronic applications accepted. *Financial support:* In 2009–10, 847 students received support, including 18 teaching assistantships; career-related internships or fieldwork, Federal Work-Study, scholarships/grants, and tuition waivers (full) also available. Financial award application deadline: 7/15; financial award applicants required to submit FAFSA. *Faculty research:* Nature of theology, ethics, Biblical commentaries, nature of God, science and theology. *Unit head:* Dr. David Ridder, Vice President and Dean, 651-638-6553. *Application contact:* Joseph V. Dworak, Director of Admissions, 651-638-6288, Fax: 651-638-6002, E-mail: j-dworak@bethel.edu.

Biblical Theological Seminary, Graduate and Professional Programs, Hatfield, PA 19440-2499. Offers advanced missional leadership (D Min); advanced pastoral studies (Certificate); biblical counseling (Certificate); biblical studies (MA, Certificate); counseling (MA); ministry (MA); missional theology (MA); theology (M Div); youth ministry (Certificate). *Accreditation:* ATS. Part-time programs available. Postbaccalaureate distance learning degree programs offered. *Degree requirements:* For M Div, thesis/dissertation. *Entrance requirements:* Additional exam requirements/recommendations for international students: Required—TOEFL (minimum score 550 paper-based; 213 computer-based). *Application deadline:* Applications are processed on a rolling basis. Application fee: $30. *Expenses:* Tuition: Full-time $14,000; part-time $441 per credit hour. *Financial support:* Career-related internships or fieldwork, institutionally sponsored loans, and scholarships/grants available. Support available to part-time students. Financial award application deadline: 5/15. *Faculty research:* Old Testament narrative, Old Testament historiography, Hebrew syntax, parables, addictions. *Application contact:* Rev. Darryl John Lang, Director of Recruitment and Student Life, 215-368-5000 Ext. 147, Fax: 215-368-7002, E-mail: dlang@biblical.edu.

Bob Jones University, Graduate Programs, Greenville, SC 29614. Offers accountancy (MS); Bible (MA); Bible translation (MA); Biblical studies (Certificate); broadcast management (MS); business administration (MBA); church history (MA, PhD); church ministries (MA); church music (MM); cinema and video production (MA); counseling (MS); curriculum and instruction (Ed D); divinity (M Div); dramatic production (MA); educational leadership (MS, Ed D, Ed S); elementary education (M Ed, MAT); English (M Ed, MA, MAT); fine arts (MA); graphic design (MA); history (M Ed, MA); illustration (MA); interpretative speech (MA); mathematics (M Ed, MAT); medical missions (Certificate); ministry (MM, D Min); multi-categorical special education (M Ed, MAT); music (M Ed); New Testament interpretation (PhD); Old Testament interpretation (PhD); orchestral instrument performance (MM); organ performance (MM); pastoral studies (MA); personnel services (MS, Ed S); piano pedagogy (MM); piano performance (MM); platform arts (MA); radio and television broadcasting (MS); rhetoric and public address (MA); secondary education (M Ed); studio art (MA); teaching Bible (MA); theology (MA, PhD); voice performance (MM); youth ministries (MA); M Div/MM.

Boston College, Graduate School of Arts and Sciences, School of Theology and Ministry, Chestnut Hill, MA 02467-3800. Offers church leadership (MA); divinity (M Div); pastoral ministry (MA), including Hispanic ministry, liturgy and worship, pastoral care and counseling, spirituality; religious education (MA, PhD); sacred theology (STD, STL); social justice/social ministry (MA); spiritual direction (MA); theological studies (MTS); theology (Th M, PhD); youth ministry (MA); MA/MA; MS/MA; MSW/MA. Part-time programs available. *Degree requirements:* For doctorate, one foreign language, thesis/dissertation. *Entrance requirements:* For doctorate, GRE. Additional exam requirements/recommendations for international students: Required—TOEFL (minimum score 550 paper-based; 213 computer-based). Electronic applications accepted. *Faculty research:* Philosophy and practice of religious education, pastoral psychology, liturgical and spiritual theology, spiritual formation for the practice of ministry.

Briercrest Seminary, Graduate Programs, Program in Christian Ministries, Caronport, SK S0H 0S0, Canada. Offers leadership (MA); marriage and family counseling (MA); missions (MA); pastoral counseling (MA); worship (MA); youth and family ministry (MA). Part-time programs available. *Degree requirements:* For master's, comprehensive exam, thesis optional. *Entrance requirements:* Additional exam requirements/recommendations for international students: Required—TOEFL (minimum score 550 paper-based; 213 computer-based).

Briercrest Seminary, Graduate Programs, Program in Theology, Caronport, SK S0H 0S0, Canada. Offers Biblical studies (M Div); leadership and management (M Div); New Testament (MATS); Old Testament (MATS); pastoral counseling (M Div); pastoral ministry (M Div); theological studies (M Div); theology (MATS); worship (M Div); youth and family ministry (M Div). *Accreditation:* ATS. Part-time programs available. *Degree requirements:* For master's, comprehensive exam, thesis optional. *Entrance requirements:* Additional exam requirements/

Pastoral Ministry and Counseling

Briercrest Seminary (continued)
recommendations for international students: Required—TOEFL (minimum score 550 paper-based; 213 computer-based).

Caldwell College, Graduate Studies, Program in Pastoral Ministry, Caldwell, NJ 07006-6195. Offers MA. Part-time and evening/weekend programs available. *Degree requirements:* For master's, thesis. *Entrance requirements:* For master's, minimum GPA of 3.0, 2 years of ministry experience. Additional exam requirements/recommendations for international students: Required—TOEFL (minimum score 580 paper-based; 237 computer-based). Electronic applications accepted.

California Baptist University, Program in Counseling Ministry, Riverside, CA 92504-3206. Offers MA. Part-time programs available. *Faculty:* 2 full-time (1 woman). *Students:* 7 part-time (6 women); includes 3 minority (all Hispanic Americans). 7 applicants, 57% accepted, 4 enrolled. In 2009, 6 master's awarded. *Degree requirements:* For master's, thesis or alternative. *Entrance requirements:* For master's, Minnesota Multiphasic Personality Inventory-2, Meyers-Briggs Type Indicator, minimum undergraduate GPA of 2.75. Additional exam requirements/recommendations for international students: Required—TOEFL (minimum score 575 paper-based; 230 computer-based; 89 iBT). *Application deadline:* For fall admission, 8/1 priority date for domestic students, 7/1 for international students; for spring admission, 12/1 priority date for domestic students, 10/15 for international students. Applications are processed on a rolling basis. Application fee: $45. Electronic applications accepted. *Expenses:* Contact institution. *Financial support:* Federal Work-Study and scholarships/grants available. Support available to part-time students. Financial award applicants required to submit FAFSA. *Unit head:* Dr. Nathan Lewis, Director, 951-343-4348, Fax: 951-343-4569, E-mail: nlewis@calbaptist.edu. *Application contact:* Gail Ronveaux, Dean of Graduate Enrollment, 951-343-5045, Fax: 951-343-5095, E-mail: graduateadmissions@calbaptist.edu.

California Baptist University, Program in Counseling Psychology, Riverside, CA 92504-3206. Offers professional counseling (MS); professional ministry (MS). Part-time programs available. *Faculty:* 10 full-time (6 women), 4 part-time/adjunct (1 woman). *Students:* 112 full-time (88 women), 43 part-time (39 women); includes 70 minority (20 African Americans, 1 American Indian/Alaska Native, 9 Asian Americans or Pacific Islanders, 40 Hispanic Americans), 2 international. 97 applicants, 55% accepted, 51 enrolled. In 2009, 49 master's awarded. *Degree requirements:* For master's, comprehensive exam, 24 hours (individual) or 50 hours (group) psychotherapy, 300 hours of field work. *Entrance requirements:* For master's, Minnesota Multiphasic Personality Inventory, Myers-Briggs Type Indicator, course work in developmental psychology, theories of personality, and statistics; minimum undergraduate GPA of 2.75. Additional exam requirements/recommendations for international students: Required—TOEFL (minimum score 575 paper-based; 230 computer-based; 89 iBT). *Application deadline:* For fall admission, 9/1 for domestic students, 7/1 for international students; for spring admission, 1/3 for domestic students, 10/15 for international students. Applications are processed on a rolling basis. Application fee: $45. Electronic applications accepted. *Expenses:* Contact institution. *Financial support:* Career-related internships or fieldwork, Federal Work-Study, and scholarships/grants available. Support available to part-time students. Financial award applicants required to submit FAFSA. *Unit head:* Dr. Mischa Routon, Director, 951-343-4206, Fax: 951-343-4569, E-mail: mrouton@calbaptist.edu. *Application contact:* Gail Ronveaux, Dean of Graduate Enrollment, 951-343-5045, Fax: 951-343-5095, E-mail: graduateadmissions@calbaptist.edu.

Calvary Bible College and Theological Seminary, Calvary Theological Seminary, Kansas City, MO 64147-1341. Offers Bible and theology (MS); Biblical counseling (MA); Biblical studies (MA); Christian ministry (MA); Christian studies (MS); Christian theology (MA); New Testament (MA); Old Testament (MA); pastoral studies (M Div). Part-time and evening/weekend programs available. *Faculty:* 4 full-time (0 women), 2 part-time/adjunct (0 women). *Students:* 20 full-time (7 women), 38 part-time (8 women); includes 4 African Americans, 4 Asian Americans or Pacific Islanders, 2 Hispanic Americans, 1 international. Average age 40. 27 applicants, 96% accepted, 20 enrolled. In 2009, 18 master's awarded. *Degree requirements:* For master's, one foreign language, comprehensive exam, thesis; for M Div, 2 foreign languages, comprehensive exam, thesis/dissertation. *Entrance requirements:* For M Div and master's, minimum GPA of 2.5, 50 semester hours of course work in liberal arts, BA or BS, doctrine agreement. Additional exam requirements/recommendations for international students: Required—TOEFL (minimum score 550 paper-based; 213 computer-based). *Application deadline:* For fall admission, 7/15 priority date for domestic and international students; for spring admission, 12/1 priority date for domestic and international students. Application fee: $25. *Expenses:* Tuition: Full-time $5400; part-time $300 per credit hour. Required fees: $267 per semester. *Financial support:* Scholarships/grants available. Financial award application deadline: 11/5. *Unit head:* Dr. Thomas Baurain, Academic Dean, 816-322-0110 Ext. 1502, Fax: 816-331-4474, E-mail: thomas.baurain@calvary.edu. *Application contact:* Bob Crank, Director of Admissions, 800-326-3960 Ext. 1326, Fax: 816-331-4474, E-mail: admissions@calvary.edu.

Calvin Theological Seminary, Graduate and Professional Programs, Grand Rapids, MI 49546-4387. Offers Bible and theology (MA); divinity (M Div), including ancient near eastern languages and literature, contextual ministry, evangelism and teaching, history of Christianity, new church development, New Testament, Old Testament, pastoral care and leadership, preaching and worship, theological studies, youth and family ministries; educational ministry (MA); historical theology (PhD); missions and evangelism (MA); pastoral care (MA); philosophical and moral theology (PhD); systematic theology (PhD); theological studies (MTS); theology (Th M); worship (MA); youth and family ministries (MA). *Accreditation:* ACIPE; ATS. Part-time programs available. *Faculty:* 28 full-time (2 women), 20 part-time/adjunct (7 women). *Students:* 203 full-time (39 women), 48 part-time (19 women); includes 28 minority (10 African Americans, 13 Asian Americans or Pacific Islanders, 5 Hispanic Americans), 69 international. Average age 31. 152 applicants, 89% accepted, 98 enrolled. In 2009, 45 first professional degrees, 42 master's, 6 doctorates awarded. *Degree requirements:* For master's, thesis (for some programs); for doctorate, 4 foreign languages, comprehensive exam, thesis/dissertation; for M Div, 2 foreign languages. *Entrance requirements:* For doctorate, GRE General Test, Hebrew, Greek, and a modern foreign language. Additional exam requirements/recommendations for international students: Required—TOEFL (minimum score 550 paper-based; 213 computer-based), TWE (minimum score 4). *Application deadline:* For fall admission, 3/1 priority date for domestic and international students. Applications are processed on a rolling basis. Application fee: $25. Electronic applications accepted. *Expenses:* Tuition: Full-time $11,814; part-time $358 per semester hour. Tuition and fees vary according to degree level. *Financial support:* In 2009–10, 187 students received support, including 4 fellowships with full tuition reimbursements available (averaging $8,405 per year), 4 teaching assistantships with full tuition reimbursements available (averaging $5,760 per year); career-related internships or fieldwork, institutionally sponsored loans, scholarships/grants, and tuition waivers (full) also available. Support available to part-time students. Financial award application deadline: 3/1; financial award applicants required to submit FAFSA. *Faculty research:* Recent Trinity theory, Christian anthropology, Proverbs, reformed confessions, Paul's view of law. *Unit head:* Dr. Cornelius Plantinga, Head, 616-957-6024, Fax: 616-957-6536, E-mail: sempres@calvinseminary.edu. *Application contact:* Rev. Gregory Janke, Director of Admissions, 616-957-7035, Fax: 616-957-6101, E-mail: gjanke@calvinseminary.edu.

Capital Bible Seminary, Graduate and Professional Programs, Lanham, MD 20706-3599. Offers biblical studies (MA, Certificate); Christian counseling (MA); Christian counseling and discipleship (Certificate); ministry leadership (MA); theology (M Div, Th M). *Accreditation:* ATS (one or more programs are accredited). Part-time and evening/weekend programs available. *Degree requirements:* For master's, 2 foreign languages, comprehensive exam, thesis (for some programs); for M Div, 2 foreign languages, comprehensive exam. *Entrance requirements:* For M Div and master's, GRE General Test, Greek exam for those with 2 years of Greek, proficiency exam in theology, previous course work in Biblical studies. Additional exam requirements/recommendations for international students: Required—TOEFL (minimum score 550 paper-based; 213 computer-based). *Faculty research:* Dead Sea Scrolls, spiritual gifts, hermeneutics.

Cardinal Stritch University, College of Arts and Sciences, Department of Religious Studies, Milwaukee, WI 53217-3985. Offers lay ministries (MA); ministry (MA); religious studies (MA). Part-time and evening/weekend programs available. *Degree requirements:* For master's, comprehensive exam, thesis, faculty recommendation, research project. *Entrance requirements:* For master's, interview, minimum GPA of 2.75.

Carolina Evangelical Divinity School, Ministry Program, High Point, NC 27265. Offers D Min. *Degree requirements:* For doctorate, project. *Entrance requirements:* For doctorate, MAT, M Div or equivalent, minimum GPA of 3.0 on all previous graduate study, 3 years of ministry experience.

Catholic Theological Union at Chicago, Graduate and Professional Programs, Chicago, IL 60615-5698. Offers biblical spirituality (Certificate); cross-cultural ministries (D Min); cross-cultural missions (Certificate); divinity (M Div); liturgical studies (Certificate); liturgy (D Min); pastoral studies (MAPS, Certificate); spiritual formation (Certificate); spirituality (D Min); theology (MA); M Div/MA; M Div/MSW; M Div/PhD. *Accreditation:* ACIPE; ATS (one or more programs are accredited). Part-time and evening/weekend programs available. *Degree requirements:* For master's, one foreign language, comprehensive exam (for some programs), thesis (for some programs); for doctorate, thesis/dissertation. *Entrance requirements:* For doctorate, master's degree, 5 years of active ministry. *Faculty research:* Doctrine, sacraments, ethics, Bible.

The Catholic University of America, School of Theology and Religious Studies, Washington, DC 20064. Offers Biblical studies (STB, MA, PhD, STL); Catholic educational leadership (MA); church history (PhD); Hispanic pastoral leadership (Certificate); Hispanic/Latino ministry (M Div); historical theology (STB, STD); history of religions (Hinduism/Islam) (MA, PhD); liturgical studies/sacramental theology (MA, PhD, STD, STL); moral theology/ethics (STB, MA, PhD, STD, STL); pastoral studies (M Div, Certificate); religion and culture (PhD); religious education/catechetics (MA, MRE, PhD); spirituality (STB, PhD, STD, STL); systematic and historical theology (MA, PhD, STD, STL). *Accreditation:* ATS (one or more programs are accredited). Part-time programs available. *Faculty:* 40 full-time (6 women), 10 part-time/adjunct (2 women). *Students:* 169 full-time (26 women), 225 part-time (57 women); includes 33 minority (10 African Americans, 1 American Indian/Alaska Native, 9 Asian Americans or Pacific Islanders, 13 Hispanic Americans), 73 international. Average age 36. 226 applicants, 72% accepted, 75 enrolled. In 2009, 9 first professional degrees, 14 master's, 26 doctorates awarded. *Degree requirements:* For master's, variable foreign language requirement, comprehensive exam, thesis (for some programs); for doctorate, variable foreign language requirement, comprehensive exam, thesis/dissertation; for first professional degree, comprehensive exam. *Entrance requirements:* For first professional degree and master's, GRE General Test, statement of purpose, official copies of academic transcripts, three letters of recommendation; for doctorate, GRE General Test, 3 letters of recommendation. Additional exam requirements/recommendations for international students: Required—TOEFL (minimum score 580 paper-based; 237 computer-based). *Application deadline:* For fall admission, 8/1 priority date for domestic students, 7/15 for international students; for spring admission, 12/1 priority date for domestic students, 10/15 for international students. Applications are processed on a rolling basis. Application fee: $55. Electronic applications accepted. *Expenses:* Tuition: Full-time $31,740; part-time $1245 per credit hour. Required fees: $50; $25 per semester hour. One-time fee: $425. *Financial support:* Fellowships, research assistantships, teaching assistantships, Federal Work-Study, scholarships/grants, tuition waivers (full and partial), and unspecified assistantships available. Financial award application deadline: 2/1; financial award applicants required to submit FAFSA. *Faculty research:* Historical and systematic theology, religious education and catechetics, moral theology and ethics, Biblical studies, liturgical studies and sacramental theology. Total annual research expenditures: $66,740. *Unit head:* Msgr. Kevin W. Irwin, Dean, 202-319-5683, Fax: 202-319-4967, E-mail: irwin@cua.edu. *Application contact:* Julie Schwing, Director of Graduate Admissions, 202-319-5057, Fax: 202-319-6533, E-mail: cua-admissions@cua.edu.

Chaminade University of Honolulu, Graduate Services, Program in Pastoral Leadership, Honolulu, HI 96816-1578. Offers MAPL. Part-time and evening/weekend programs available. Postbaccalaureate distance learning degree programs offered (minimal on-campus study). *Degree requirements:* For master's, internship or thesis. *Entrance requirements:* For master's, 2 letters of recommendation. Additional exam requirements/recommendations for international students: Required—TOEFL (minimum score 550 paper-based). Electronic applications accepted.

Chaminade University of Honolulu, Graduate Services, Program in Pastoral Theology, Honolulu, HI 96816-1578. Offers MPT. Part-time and evening/weekend programs available. Postbaccalaureate distance learning degree programs offered. *Degree requirements:* For master's, capstone course. *Entrance requirements:* For master's, 2 letters of recommendation. Additional exam requirements/recommendations for international students: Required—TOEFL (minimum score 550 paper-based). Electronic applications accepted.

Chicago Theological Seminary, Graduate and Professional Programs, Chicago, IL 60637-1507. Offers preaching (D Min); religion and health (D Min); religious studies (MA); spirituality and spiritual direction (D Min); theology (M Div); theology, ethics and the human sciences (PhD); M Div/MSW. *Accreditation:* ACIPE; ATS. Part-time programs available. *Degree requirements:* For master's, thesis; for doctorate, 2 foreign languages, comprehensive exam, thesis/dissertation; for M Div, thesis/dissertation. *Entrance requirements:* For doctorate, GRE General Test. Additional exam requirements/recommendations for international students: Required—TOEFL (minimum score 217 computer-based). *Faculty research:* Bible, culture and hermeneutics, theology, gender and sexuality, black faith and life, spirituality and psychology, practical theology.

Christian Theological Seminary, Graduate and Professional Programs, Indianapolis, IN 46208-3301. Offers educational and arts ministries (MA); marriage and family therapy (MA); pastoral care and counseling (D Min); psychotherapy and faith (MA); theological studies (MTS); theology (M Div). *Accreditation:* AAMFT/COAMFTE (one or more programs are accredited); ACIPE; ATS. Part-time programs available. *Faculty:* 18 full-time (8 women), 18 part-time/adjunct (4 women). *Students:* 152 full-time (98 women), 53 part-time (28 women); includes 73 minority (53 African Americans, 1 American Indian/Alaska Native, 4 Asian Americans or Pacific Islanders, 15 Hispanic Americans), 2 international. Average age 41. 120 applicants, 86% accepted, 71 enrolled. In 2009, 31 first professional degrees, 22 master's, 3 doctorates awarded. Terminal master's awarded for partial completion of doctoral program. *Degree requirements:* For master's, comprehensive exam (for some programs), thesis (for some programs); for doctorate, comprehensive exam, thesis/dissertation; for M Div, comprehensive exam, thesis/dissertation (for some programs), missionary and cross-cultural experience. *Entrance requirements:* For master's, GRE General Test, MAT; for doctorate, M Div or BD. *Application deadline:* For fall admission, 7/15 for domestic and international students; for spring admission, 11/15 for domestic and international students. Applications are processed on a rolling basis. Application fee: $30. Electronic applications accepted. *Expenses:* Tuition: Full-time $9310; part-time $490 per credit hour. Required fees: $180; $160 per semester. Tuition and fees vary according to course load. *Financial support:* In 2009–10, 187 students received support, including 12 teaching assistantships (averaging $350 per year); career-related internships or fieldwork, Federal Work-Study, scholarships/grants, and tuition waivers (full and partial) also available. Support available to part-time students. Financial award application deadline: 4/1; financial award applicants required to submit FAFSA. *Faculty research:* Faith formation, peer learning post graduation. *Unit head:* Dr. Edward L. Wheeler, President, 317-931-2304, Fax: 317-923-1961, E-mail: wheeler@cts.edu. *Application contact:* Rev. Mary Harris, Associate Dean for Student Services, 317-931-2300, Fax: 317-923-1961, E-mail: mharris@cts.edu.

Pastoral Ministry and Counseling

Christ the King Seminary, Graduate and Professional Programs, East Aurora, NY 14052. Offers divinity (M Div); pastoral ministry (MA); pastoral studies (Certificate); theology (MA). *Accreditation:* ATS. Part-time and evening/weekend programs available. *Degree requirements:* For master's, comprehensive exam, thesis; for M Div, comprehensive exam. *Entrance requirements:* For M Div and master's, previous course work in philosophy and religious studies.

Church of God Theological Seminary, Graduate and Professional Programs, Cleveland, TN 37320-3330. Offers counseling (MA); discipleship and Christian formations (MA); ministry (D Min); theology (M Div). *Accreditation:* ACIPE. Part-time programs available. *Degree requirements:* For M Div, 2 foreign languages, thesis/dissertation, internship. *Faculty research:* Biblical exegesis.

Cincinnati Christian University, Graduate School, Program in Counseling, Cincinnati, OH 45204-3200. Offers MAC. *Degree requirements:* For master's, thesis or alternative, integration paper. *Entrance requirements:* For master's, GRE General Test, interview, minimum undergraduate GPA of 3.0. Additional exam requirements/recommendations for international students: Required—TOEFL. Electronic applications accepted. *Expenses:* Contact institution.

Claremont School of Theology, Graduate and Professional Programs, Program in Ministry, Claremont, CA 91711-3199. Offers D Min. *Accreditation:* ACIPE. *Degree requirements:* For doctorate, thesis/dissertation. *Entrance requirements:* For doctorate, GRE General Test. Additional exam requirements/recommendations for international students: Required—TOEFL (minimum score 230 computer-based). Electronic applications accepted.

Claremont School of Theology, Graduate and Professional Programs, Program in Religion, Claremont, CA 91711-3199. Offers practical theology (PhD), including religious education, spiritual care and counseling; religion (PhD), including Hebrew Bible, New Testament and Christian origins, process studies, religion, ethics, and society; religion and theology (MA); religious education (MARE). *Accreditation:* ACIPE; ATS. Terminal master's awarded for partial completion of doctoral program. *Degree requirements:* For master's, thesis; for doctorate, 2 foreign languages, thesis/dissertation. *Entrance requirements:* For doctorate, GRE General Test. Additional exam requirements/recommendations for international students: Required—TOEFL (minimum score 250 computer-based). Electronic applications accepted.

College of Mount St. Joseph, Graduate Program in Religious Studies, Cincinnati, OH 45233-1670. Offers religious education (Certificate); spiritual and pastoral care (MA, Certificate); spiritual direction (Certificate). Part-time and evening/weekend programs available. *Faculty:* 4 full-time (2 women). *Students:* 25 part-time (20 women); includes 1 minority (African American). Average age 49. 5 applicants, 100% accepted, 3 enrolled. In 2009, 9 master's awarded. *Degree requirements:* For master's, comprehensive exam, integrating project. *Entrance requirements:* For master's, 3 letters of recommendation, interview, minimum GPA of 3.0. Additional exam requirements/recommendations for international students: Required—TOEFL (minimum score 560 paper-based; 220 computer-based; 83 iBT). *Application deadline:* Applications are processed on a rolling basis. Application fee: $50. Electronic applications accepted. *Expenses:* Tuition: Part-time $500 per hour. Required fees: $200 per year. Tuition and fees vary according to degree level and program. *Financial support:* In 2009–10, 20 students received support. Scholarships/grants available. Financial award applicants required to submit FAFSA. *Faculty research:* Contextual/cultural/systematic theology, historical/spiritual theology, business/economics ethics, social justice, Biblical/cultural/pastoral theology. *Unit head:* Dr. John Trokan, Chair of Religious/Pastoral Studies, 513-244-4272, Fax: 513-244-4222, E-mail: john_trokan@mail.msj.edu. *Application contact:* Marilyn Hoskins, Assistant Director of Graduate Recruitment, 513-244-4723, Fax: 513-244-4629, E-mail: marilyn_hoskins@mail.msj.edu.

Columbia International University, Columbia Biblical Seminary and School of Missions, Columbia, SC 29230-3122. Offers academic ministries (M Div); bible exposition (M Div, MABE); biblical studies (Certificate); counseling ministries (Certificate); divinity (M Div); educational ministries (M Div, MAEM, Certificate); intercultural studies (M Div, MAIS, Certificate); leadership (D Min); leadership for evangelism/mobilization (MALM); member care (D Min); ministry (Certificate); missions (D Min); pastoral counseling and spiritual formation (M Div, MAPS); preaching (D Min); theology (MA). *Accreditation:* ATS (one or more programs are accredited). Part-time and evening/weekend programs available. *Degree requirements:* For master's, integrative seminar; for doctorate, comprehensive exam, thesis/dissertation; for M Div, internship. *Entrance requirements:* For master's, minimum GPA of 2.7; for doctorate, 3 years of ministerial experience, M Div. Additional exam requirements/recommendations for international students: Required—TOEFL. Electronic applications accepted.

Concordia University, Nebraska, Graduate Programs in Education, Program in Family Life Ministry, Seward, NE 68434-1599. Offers MS. Part-time and evening/weekend programs available. *Degree requirements:* For master's, thesis or alternative. *Entrance requirements:* For master's, GRE, MAT, or NTE, minimum GPA of 3.0, BS in education or equivalent.

Concordia University, St. Paul, College of Vocation and Ministry, St. Paul, MN 55104-5494. Offers Christian education (Certificate); Christian outreach (MA); christian outreach (Certificate). Evening/weekend programs available. Postbaccalaureate distance learning degree programs offered (minimal on-campus study). *Faculty:* 4 full-time (0 women), 2 part-time/adjunct (1 woman). *Students:* 14 full-time (8 women), 4 part-time (2 women); includes 1 minority (Asian American or Pacific Islander). Average age 38. In 2009, 5 master's, 10 other advanced degrees awarded. *Application deadline:* Applications are processed on a rolling basis. Application fee: $50. Electronic applications accepted. *Financial support:* Applicants required to submit FAFSA. *Unit head:* Dr. David Lumpp, Dean, 651-641-8217, E-mail: lumpp@csp.edu. *Application contact:* Kimberly Craig, Director of Graduate and Cohort Admission, 651-603-6223, Fax: 651-603-6320, E-mail: craig@csp.edu.

Corban University, Graduate School, Program in Counseling, Salem, OR 97301-9392. Offers MA. *Degree requirements:* For master's, internship, practicum.

The Criswell College, Graduate School of the Bible, Dallas, TX 75246-1537. Offers biblical studies (M Div); Christian leadership (MA); counseling (MA); Jewish studies (MA); ministry (MA); theological and biblical studies (MA). Part-time programs available. *Degree requirements:* For master's, 2 foreign languages, thesis optional; for M Div, 2 foreign languages, thesis/dissertation optional. *Entrance requirements:* For M Div and master's, GRE General Test, minimum GPA of 2.5. Electronic applications accepted. *Faculty research:* Emphasis on biblical languages (Hebrew and Greek), expository preaching and evangelism in the local church.

Dallas Baptist University, College of Adult Education, Professional Development Program, Dallas, TX 75211-9299. Offers accounting (MA); church leadership (MA); counseling (MA); criminal justice (MA); English as a second language (MA); finance (MA); higher education (MA); leadership studies (MA); management (MA); management information systems (MA); marketing (MA); missions (MA). Part-time and evening/weekend programs available. *Entrance requirements:* For master's, minimum GPA of 3.0. Additional exam requirements/recommendations for international students: Required—TOEFL, IELTS. *Expenses:* Tuition: Full-time $10,674; part-time $593 per credit hour.

Dallas Baptist University, Gary Cook School of Leadership, Program in Christian Education, Dallas, TX 75211-9299. Offers adult ministry (MA); business ministry (MA); childhood ministry (MA); collegiate ministry (MA); communication ministry (MA); counseling ministry (MA); education ministry (MA); general ministry (MA); missions ministry (MA); student ministry (MA); worship ministry (MA). Part-time and evening/weekend programs available. *Entrance requirements:* For master's, minimum GPA of 3.0. Additional exam requirements/recommendations for international students: Required—TOEFL. Electronic applications accepted. *Expenses:* Tuition: Full-time $10,674; part-time $593 per credit hour.

Dallas Baptist University, Gary Cook School of Leadership, Program in Christian Education: Childhood Ministry, Dallas, TX 75211-9299. Offers MA. Part-time and evening/weekend programs available. *Entrance requirements:* For master's, minimum GPA of 3.0. Additional exam requirements/recommendations for international students: Required—TOEFL, IELTS. *Expenses:* Tuition: Full-time $10,674; part-time $593 per credit hour.

Dallas Baptist University, Gary Cook School of Leadership, Program in Christian Education: Student Ministry, Dallas, TX 75211-9299. Offers MA. Part-time and evening/weekend programs available. *Entrance requirements:* For master's, minimum GPA of 3.0. Additional exam requirements/recommendations for international students: Required—TOEFL, IELTS. *Expenses:* Tuition: Full-time $10,674; part-time $593 per credit hour.

Dallas Baptist University, Gary Cook School of Leadership, Program in Global Leadership, Dallas, TX 75211-9299. Offers business communication (MA); Christian education/missions (MA); ESL (MA); general studies (MA); global studies (MA); international business (MA); missions (MA); worship/missions (MA). Part-time and evening/weekend programs available. *Entrance requirements:* For master's, minimum GPA of 3.0. Additional exam requirements/recommendations for international students: Required—TOEFL, IELTS. *Expenses:* Tuition: Full-time $10,674; part-time $593 per credit hour.

Dallas Baptist University, Gary Cook School of Leadership, Program in Worship Leadership, Dallas, TX 75211-9299. Offers MA. Part-time and evening/weekend programs available. *Entrance requirements:* For master's, minimum GPA of 3.0. Additional exam requirements/recommendations for international students: Required—TOEFL, IELTS. *Expenses:* Tuition: Full-time $10,674; part-time $593 per credit hour.

Dallas Theological Seminary, Graduate Programs, Dallas, TX 75204-6499. Offers academic ministries (Th M); Bible translation (Th M); biblical and theological studies (CGS); biblical counseling (MA, Th M); biblical exegesis and linguistics (MA); biblical exposition (PhD); biblical studies (MA); Christian education (MA, D Min); cross-cultural ministries (MA, Th M); educational leadership (Th M); evangelism and discipleship (Th M); interdisciplinary studies (Th M); media and communication (MA); media arts in ministry (Th M); ministry (D Min); New Testament studies (Th M, PhD); Old Testament studies (PhD); parachurch ministries (Th M); pastoral ministries (Th M); sacred theology (STM); theological studies (PhD); women's ministry (Th M). *Accreditation:* ATS (one or more programs are accredited). Part-time and evening/weekend programs available. *Degree requirements:* For master's, variable foreign language requirement, thesis (for some programs); for doctorate, 2 foreign languages, thesis/dissertation. *Entrance requirements:* Additional exam requirements/recommendations for international students: Required—TOEFL, TWE. Electronic applications accepted.

Denver Seminary, Graduate and Professional Programs, Littleton, CO 80120. Offers apologetics (Certificate); biblical studies (MA); Christian formation and soul care (MA, Certificate); Christian studies (MA, Certificate); church and parachurch leadership (D Min); counseling licensure (MA); counseling ministry (MA); intercultural ministry (Certificate); leadership (MA, Certificate); marriage and family counseling (D Min); pastoral ministry (D Min); philosophy of religion (MA); spiritual guidance (Certificate); theology (M Div, Certificate); worship (Certificate); youth and family ministry (MA). *Accreditation:* ACA; ACIPE; ATS (one or more programs are accredited). Part-time and evening/weekend programs available. Postbaccalaureate distance learning degree programs offered. *Degree requirements:* For master's, 2 foreign languages, thesis (for some programs); for doctorate, 2 foreign languages, thesis/dissertation; for M Div, 2 foreign languages. *Entrance requirements:* For M Div, minimum undergraduate GPA of 2.5; for master's, minimum undergraduate GPA of 3.0; for doctorate, M Div, 3 years of ministry experience. Additional exam requirements/recommendations for international students: Required—TOEFL (minimum score 575 paper-based; 233 computer-based; 90 iBT). Electronic applications accepted.

Dominican University, School of Leadership and Continuing Studies, River Forest, IL 60305-1099. Offers family ministry (MA); organizational leadership (MSOL). Part-time and evening/weekend programs available. *Faculty:* 12 part-time/adjunct (7 women). *Students:* 5 full-time (2 women), 59 part-time (38 women); includes 18 minority (14 African Americans, 1 American Indian/Alaska Native, 1 Asian American or Pacific Islander, 2 Hispanic Americans). Average age 42. In 2009, 15 master's awarded. *Entrance requirements:* Additional exam requirements/recommendations for international students: Required—TOEFL (minimum score 550 paper-based; 213 computer-based; 79 iBT). *Application deadline:* Applications are processed on a rolling basis. Application fee: $25. *Expenses:* Contact institution. *Unit head:* Dr. Bryan J. Watkins, Executive Director, 708-714-9001, E-mail: bwatkins@dom.edu. *Application contact:* Monica Halloran, Associate Director of Academic Advising, 708-714-9007, Fax: 708-714-9126, E-mail: mhallora@dom.edu.

Eastern Mennonite University, Eastern Mennonite Seminary, Harrisonburg, VA 22802-2462. Offers church leadership (MA); divinity (M Div); ministry studies (Certificate); online theological studies (Certificate); religion (MA); theological studies (Certificate). *Accreditation:* ATS. Part-time programs available. *Faculty:* 11 full-time (2 women), 8 part-time/adjunct (3 women). *Students:* 45 full-time (20 women), 81 part-time (33 women); includes 9 minority (5 African Americans, 4 Hispanic Americans), 6 international. In 2009, 13 first professional degrees, 9 master's awarded. *Degree requirements:* For master's, thesis (for some programs); for M Div, thesis/dissertation (for some programs), supervised field education. *Entrance requirements:* For M Div and master's, minimum GPA of 2.5. Additional exam requirements/recommendations for international students: Required—TOEFL (minimum score 550 paper-based; 213 computer-based). *Application deadline:* For fall admission, 6/15 priority date for domestic and international students; for winter admission, 11/15 priority date for domestic and international students; for spring admission, 3/15 priority date for domestic and international students. Applications are processed on a rolling basis. Application fee: $25. *Expenses:* Contact institution. *Financial support:* Application deadline: 6/30. *Faculty research:* Spiritual direction and culture of call, leadership coaching: an approach to leadership in a culture of call, clarity of call in the probationary process for United Methodist clergy in Virginia, EMS women's experiences of culture of call efforts, practices of excellent and fruitful Mennonite pastoral ministry. *Unit head:* Dr. Ervin R. Stutzman, Dean, 540-432-4261, Fax: 540-432-4444, E-mail: stutzerv@emu.edu. *Application contact:* Don A. Yoder, Director of Seminary and Graduate Admissions, 540-432-4257, Fax: 540-432-4598, E-mail: yoderda@emu.edu.

Eastern Mennonite University, Program in Counseling, Harrisonburg, VA 22802-2462. Offers MA, M Div/MA. *Accreditation:* ACA (one or more programs are accredited); ACIPE. Part-time programs available. *Faculty:* 3 full-time (2 women), 1 part-time/adjunct (0 women). *Students:* 30 full-time (23 women), 10 part-time (8 women); includes 3 minority (1 African American, 2 Hispanic Americans). Average age 38. In 2009, 20 master's awarded. *Degree requirements:* For master's, practicum, internship. *Entrance requirements:* For master's, minimum GPA of 3.0. Additional exam requirements/recommendations for international students: Required—TOEFL (minimum score 550 paper-based). *Application deadline:* For fall admission, 3/1 for domestic students. Application fee: $25. *Expenses:* Contact institution. *Financial support:* Scholarships/grants available. Financial award application deadline: 6/30; financial award applicants required to submit FAFSA. *Faculty research:* Career and gender, empathy and consciousness, pastoral counseling, education models. *Unit head:* Dr. P. David Glanzer, Professor of Counselor Education, 540-432-4244, Fax: 540-432-4444, E-mail: glanzerd@emu.edu. *Application contact:* Brenda C. Fairweather, Administrative Assistant, 540-432-4243, Fax: 540-432-4444, E-mail: fairweat@emu.edu.

Eastern University, Palmer Theological Seminary, Program in Ministry, St. Davids, PA 19087-3696. Offers marriage and family (D Min). Part-time programs available. *Degree requirements:* For doctorate, thesis/dissertation. *Entrance requirements:* For doctorate, 3 years of experience, involvement in ministry, church endorsement. *Expenses:* Contact institution.

Ecumenical Theological Seminary, Program in Ministry, Detroit, MI 48201. Offers D Min. *Accreditation:* ACIPE.

Emmanuel School of Religion, Graduate and Professional Programs, Johnson City, TN 37601-9438. Offers Christian care and counseling (M Div); Christian doctrine (MAR); Christian education (M Div); church history (MAR); ministry (D Min); New Testament (MAR); Old Testament

Pastoral Ministry and Counseling

Emmanuel School of Religion (continued)
(MAR); urban ministry (M Div); world missions (M Div). *Accreditation:* ACIPE; ATS. Part-time programs available. *Faculty:* 10 full-time (2 women), 5 part-time/adjunct (0 women). *Students:* 108 full-time (27 women), 48 part-time (13 women). Average age 32. *Degree requirements:* For master's, 2 foreign languages, thesis; for M Div, 2 foreign languages, thesis/dissertation or alternative. *Entrance requirements:* For doctorate, GRE General Test, Minnesota Multiphasic Personality Inventory, M Div or equivalent. *Application deadline:* For fall admission, 8/1 priority date for domestic students. Applications are processed on a rolling basis. Application fee: $25. *Expenses:* Tuition: Full-time $7800; part-time $325 per credit hour. Required fees: $137.50 per semester. One-time fee: $240. Tuition and fees vary according to course load. *Financial support:* Teaching assistantships with partial tuition reimbursements, career-related internships or fieldwork, institutionally sponsored loans, scholarships/grants, and tuition waivers (partial) available. Support available to part-time students. Financial award application deadline: 4/1; financial award applicants required to submit FAFSA. *Faculty research:* Theology of Old Testament prophets, spiritual formation for Christian leaders, history of African churches and religions, social world of early Christianity, lay pastoral counseling. Total annual research expenditures: $12,000. *Unit head:* Dr. Rollin A. Ramsaran, Dean and Professor of New Testament, 423-461-1524, Fax: 423-926-6198, E-mail: ramsaranr@esr.edu. *Application contact:* Shelley Gasser, Administrative Assistant for Admissions, 423-461-1535, Fax: 423-926-6198, E-mail: gassers@esr.edu.

Evangelical Theological Seminary, Graduate and Professional Programs, Myerstown, PA 17067-1212. Offers Biblical studies (MAR); congregational ministry (M Div); global and contextual studies (M Div, MAR); historical and theological studies (MAR); interdisciplinary studies (MAR); marriage and family counseling (M Div); marriage and family therapy (MA); New Testament (MAR); Old Testament (MAR); spiritual formation (MAR); teaching ministry (M Div); youth ministry (M Div). *Accreditation:* ATS (one or more programs are accredited). Part-time programs available. Postbaccalaureate distance learning degree programs offered (minimal on-campus study). *Degree requirements:* For master's, 2 foreign languages; for M Div, 2 foreign languages, ministry internship. *Entrance requirements:* For M Div and master's, minimum GPA of 2.5. Additional exam requirements/recommendations for international students: Required—TOEFL (minimum score 550 paper-based; 213 computer-based). *Faculty research:* Literary form and structure within the Hebrew and Greek scriptures, Wesley studies, esoteric biblical languages, the Mosaic law and the Christian, ethics.

Faith Baptist Bible College and Theological Seminary, Graduate Program, Ankeny, IA 50023. Offers biblical studies (MA); pastoral studies (M Div); pastoral training (MA); religion (MA); theological studies (MA). Part-time programs available. *Faculty:* 4 full-time (0 women), 4 part-time/adjunct (0 women). *Students:* 31 full-time (6 women), 35 part-time (8 women); includes 2 minority (1 African American, 1 Asian American or Pacific Islander), 2 international. Average age 29. In 2009, 9 first professional degrees, 12 master's awarded. *Degree requirements:* For master's, thesis or alternative; for M Div, 2 foreign languages. *Entrance requirements:* Additional exam requirements/recommendations for international students: Required—TOEFL (minimum score 550 paper-based; 197 computer-based). *Application deadline:* For fall admission, 8/1 priority date for domestic students, 8/1 for international students; for spring admission, 12/15 for domestic and international students. Applications are processed on a rolling basis. Application fee: $25. *Financial support:* Career-related internships or fieldwork and scholarships/grants available. Support available to part-time students. Financial award application deadline: 3/1; financial award applicants required to submit FAFSA. *Faculty research:* Baptist theology, American church history. *Unit head:* Dr. Ernest Schmidt, Dean of Seminary, 515-964-0601, E-mail: schmidte@faith.edu. *Application contact:* Patrick Odle, Vice President of Enrollment, 888-FAITH4U, Fax: 515-964-1638, E-mail: odlep@faith.edu.

Fordham University, Graduate School of Religion and Religious Education, New York, NY 10458. Offers pastoral counseling and spiritual care (MA); pastoral ministry/spirituality/pastoral counseling (D Min); religion and religious education (MA); religious education (MS, PhD, PD); spiritual direction (Certificate). Part-time programs available. Terminal master's awarded for partial completion of doctoral program. *Degree requirements:* For master's, research paper; for doctorate, comprehensive exam, thesis/dissertation. *Entrance requirements:* For doctorate, MAT. Electronic applications accepted. *Expenses:* Contact institution. *Faculty research:* Spirituality and spiritual direction, pastoral care and counseling, adult family and community, growth and young adult.

Freed-Hardeman University, School of Biblical Studies, Program in Ministry, Henderson, TN 38340-2399. Offers M Min. Part-time programs available. *Degree requirements:* For master's, comprehensive exam, internship. *Entrance requirements:* For master's, GRE General Test or MAT. Additional exam requirements/recommendations for international students: Required—TOEFL (minimum score 500 paper-based; 173 computer-based).

Fuller Theological Seminary, Graduate School of Theology, Pasadena, CA 91182. Offers Christian leadership (MACL); evangelism (MA); family life education (MA); ministry (M Div, D Min); pastoral ministry (MA); recovery ministry (MA); theology (MAT, Th M, PhD); worship music ministry (MA); worship, theology, and the arts (MA); youth, family, and culture (MA). M Div offered jointly with Denver Conservative Baptist Seminary. *Accreditation:* ACIPE; ATS (one or more programs are accredited). Part-time and evening/weekend programs available. *Degree requirements:* For doctorate, variable foreign language requirement, thesis/dissertation; for M Div, 2 foreign languages. *Entrance requirements:* For doctorate, GRE General Test. *Faculty research:* New Testament, Old Testament, systematic theology, history, practical theology.

Gannon University, School of Graduate Studies, College of Humanities, Education, and Social Sciences, School of Humanities, Program in Pastoral Studies, Erie, PA 16541-0001. Offers MA, Certificate. Part-time and evening/weekend programs available. *Students:* 2 full-time (both women), 8 part-time (4 women). Average age 41. 3 applicants, 67% accepted, 0 enrolled. In 2009, 1 master's awarded. *Degree requirements:* For master's, comprehensive exam, thesis or alternative, research project, internship and written evaluation. *Entrance requirements:* For master's, interview; minimum 10 credits of course work in philosophy, religious studies, or theology. Additional exam requirements/recommendations for international students: Required—TOEFL (minimum score 79 iBT). *Application deadline:* Applications are processed on a rolling basis. Application fee: $25. Electronic applications accepted. *Expenses:* Tuition: Full-time $13,590; part-time $755 per credit. Required fees: $524; $17 per credit. Tuition and fees vary according to course load, degree level, campus/location and program. *Financial support:* Career-related internships or fieldwork, scholarships/grants, and unspecified assistantships available. Financial award application deadline: 7/1; financial award applicants required to submit FAFSA. *Unit head:* Dr. Mary Anne Rivera, Director, 814-871-5646, E-mail: rivera006@gannon.edu. *Application contact:* Kara Morgan, Assistant Director of Graduate Admissions, 814-871-5831, Fax: 814-871-5827, E-mail: graduate@gannon.edu.

Gardner-Webb University, School of Divinity, Boiling Springs, NC 28017. Offers biblical studies (M Div); Christian education and formation (M Div); ministry (D Min); missiology (M Div); pastoral care and counseling (M Div); pastoral studies (M Div); M Div/MA; M Div/MBA. *Accreditation:* ACIPE; ATS. Part-time programs available. *Degree requirements:* For M Div, 2 foreign languages. *Entrance requirements:* For M Div, minimum GPA of 2.0; for doctorate, minimum GPA of 2.75. *Application deadline:* For fall admission, 8/1 priority date for domestic students; for spring admission, 12/15 priority date for domestic students. Applications are processed on a rolling basis. Application fee: $25. *Expenses:* Contact institution. *Financial support:* Fellowships, institutionally sponsored loans and unspecified assistantships available. Support available to part-time students. Financial award application deadline: 5/15. *Faculty research:* Jewish Christian dialogue, Islam. *Unit head:* Dr. Robert W. Canoy, Dean, 704-406-4400, Fax: 704-406-3935, E-mail: rcanoy@gardner-webb.edu. *Application contact:* Jeremy Fern, Director of Admissions, 704-406-3205, Fax: 704-406-3935, E-mail: jfern@gardner-webb.edu.

Garrett-Evangelical Theological Seminary, Graduate and Professional Programs, Evanston, IL 60201-3298. Offers Bible and culture (PhD); Christian education (MA); Christian education and congregational studies (PhD); contemporary theology and culture (PhD); divinity (M Div); ethics, church, and society (MA); liturgical studies (PhD); ministry (D Min); music ministry (MA); pastoral care and counseling (MA); pastoral theology, personality, and culture (PhD); spiritual formation and evangelism (MA); theological studies (MTS); M Div/MSW. *Accreditation:* ACIPE; ATS (one or more programs are accredited). Part-time programs available. *Degree requirements:* For master's, thesis (for some programs); for doctorate, thesis/dissertation. *Entrance requirements:* For doctorate, GRE (PhD). Additional exam requirements/recommendations for international students: Required—TOEFL (minimum score 560 paper-based; 230 computer-based). Electronic applications accepted.

General Theological Seminary, Graduate and Professional Programs, New York, NY 10011-4977. Offers Anglican studies (STM, Th D, Certificate); ascetical theology (Certificate); biblical studies (Certificate); congregational development (Certificate); divinity (M Div); historical and theological studies (Certificate); spiritual direction (MASD, STM, Certificate); theology (MA). *Accreditation:* ACIPE; ATS. Part-time and evening/weekend programs available. Terminal master's awarded for partial completion of doctoral program. *Degree requirements:* For master's, thesis; for doctorate, 2 foreign languages, thesis/dissertation. *Entrance requirements:* For M Div, GRE General Test, bishop's endorsement; for master's, GRE General Test; for doctorate, GRE, M Div or MA. Additional exam requirements/recommendations for international students: Required—TOEFL. *Faculty research:* Liturgy, New Testament, ethics, history, ecumenical relations.

George Fox University, George Fox Evangelical Seminary, Newberg, OR 97132-2697. Offers Biblical studies (M Div); chaplaincy (M Div); Christian earth keeping (M Div); ministry (D Min), including global missional leadership, leadership and spiritual formation, semiotics and future studies; ministry leadership (MA); pastoral studies (M Div); spiritual formation (M Div, MA); spiritual formation and discipleship (Certificate); theological studies (MA). *Accreditation:* ACIPE; ATS. Part-time programs available. Postbaccalaureate distance learning degree programs offered (minimal on-campus study). *Faculty:* 7 full-time (2 women), 16 part-time/adjunct (8 women). *Students:* 50 full-time (16 women), 292 part-time (88 women); includes 25 minority (6 African Americans, 2 American Indian/Alaska Native, 13 Asian Americans or Pacific Islanders, 4 Hispanic Americans), 5 international. Average age 41. 152 applicants, 88% accepted, 86 enrolled. In 2009, 14 first professional degrees, 8 master's, 12 doctorates, 4 other advanced degrees awarded. *Degree requirements:* For master's, variable foreign language requirement, thesis optional, internship; for doctorate, comprehensive exam (for some programs), thesis/dissertation, internship. *Entrance requirements:* For master's, resume, admission statement, three references (one pastoral, one academic or professional, one personal), one official transcript from each college or university attended; for doctorate, resume, 3 references (1 professional, 1 academic, 1 personal). Additional exam requirements/recommendations for international students: Required—TOEFL (minimum score 577 paper-based; 233 computer-based; 90 iBT). *Application deadline:* For fall admission, 7/1 for domestic and international students; for winter admission, 11/1 for domestic and international students; for spring admission, 4/1 for domestic and international students. Applications are processed on a rolling basis. Application fee: $40. Electronic applications accepted. *Expenses:* Contact institution. *Financial support:* Career-related internships or fieldwork and scholarships/grants available. Financial award application deadline: 5/1; financial award applicants required to submit FAFSA. *Unit head:* Dr. Chuck Conniry, Vice President/Dean, 503-554-6152, E-mail: cconniry@georgefox.edu. *Application contact:* Sheila Bartlett, Admissions Counselor, 800-631-0921, Fax: 503-554-6122, E-mail: seminary@georgefox.edu.

Georgian Court University, School of Arts and Humanities, Lakewood, NJ 08701-2697. Offers Catholic school leadership (Certificate); parish business management (Certificate); pastoral administration (Certificate); pastoral ministry (Certificate); religious education (Certificate); theology (MA, Certificate). Part-time and evening/weekend programs available. *Faculty:* 3 full-time (2 women), 1 (woman) part-time/adjunct. *Students:* 57 part-time (39 women); includes 8 minority (3 African Americans, 1 Asian American or Pacific Islander, 4 Hispanic Americans). Average age 52. 20 applicants, 100% accepted, 14 enrolled. In 2009, 6 master's awarded. *Degree requirements:* For master's, thesis (for some programs). *Entrance requirements:* For master's, 3 letters of recommendation. Additional exam requirements/recommendations for international students: Required—TOEFL (minimum score 550 paper-based; 213 computer-based). *Application deadline:* For fall admission, 8/1 priority date for domestic students, 4/1 for international students; for spring admission, 1/1 priority date for domestic students, 7/1 for international students. Applications are processed on a rolling basis. Application fee: $40. Electronic applications accepted. *Expenses:* Tuition: Full-time $12,510; part-time $695 per credit. Required fees: $416 per year. Tuition and fees vary according to campus/location. *Financial support:* Scholarships/grants, health care benefits, and unspecified assistantships available. Financial award application deadline: 4/15; financial award applicants required to submit FAFSA. *Unit head:* Dr. Linda James, Dean, 732-987-2617, Fax: 732-987-2007. *Application contact:* Eugene Soltys, Director of Graduate Admissions, 732-987-2770, Fax: 732-987-2084, E-mail: graduateadmissions@georgian.edu.

Golden Gate Baptist Theological Seminary, Graduate and Professional Programs, Mill Valley, CA 94941-3197. Offers divinity (M Div); early childhood education (Certificate); education leadership (MAEL, Diploma); ministry (D Min); theological studies (MTS); theology (Th M); youth ministry (Certificate). *Accreditation:* ACIPE; ATS (one or more programs are accredited). Part-time and evening/weekend programs available. *Degree requirements:* For master's, thesis (for some programs); for doctorate, 2 foreign languages, thesis/dissertation; for M Div, 2 foreign languages. *Entrance requirements:* For doctorate, MAT. Additional exam requirements/recommendations for international students: Required—TOEFL (minimum score 550 paper-based; 213 computer-based). Electronic applications accepted.

Gonzaga University, College of Arts and Sciences, Department of Religious Studies, Spokane, WA 99258. Offers pastoral ministry (MA); religious studies (MA); spirituality (MA). *Faculty:* 21 full-time (7 women), 1 part-time/adjunct (0 women). *Students:* 8 full-time (2 women), 33 part-time (20 women); includes 4 minority (1 Asian American or Pacific Islander, 3 Hispanic Americans), 1 international. Average age 43. 15 applicants, 87% accepted, 13 enrolled. In 2009, 7 master's awarded. *Degree requirements:* For master's, comprehensive exam. *Entrance requirements:* For master's, GRE General Test or MAT, minimum GPA of 3.0. Additional exam requirements/recommendations for international students: Required—TOEFL. *Application deadline:* For fall admission, 7/20 priority date for domestic students; for spring admission, 11/1 for domestic students. Applications are processed on a rolling basis. Application fee: $50. Tuition and fees vary according to course level, course load, degree level, campus/location and program. *Financial support:* Application deadline: 3/1. *Unit head:* Dr. Ron Large, Chairperson, 509-328-4220 Ext. 6782, E-mail: jennings@gonzaga.edu. *Application contact:* Dr. Ron Large, Chairperson, 509-328-4220 Ext. 6782, E-mail: jennings@gonzaga.edu.

Gordon-Conwell Theological Seminary, Graduate and Professional Programs, South Hamilton, MA 01982. Offers Biblical languages (MABL); church history (MACH); counseling (MACO); ministry (D Min); missions/evangelism (MAME); New Testament (MANT); Old Testament (MAOT); religion (MAR); theology (M Div, MATH, Th M, Th D). *Accreditation:* ACIPE; ATS (one or more programs are accredited). Part-time and evening/weekend programs available. *Degree requirements:* For master's, one foreign language, thesis optional; for doctorate, 2 foreign languages, thesis/dissertation; for M Div, 2 foreign languages. *Entrance requirements:* For M Div and master's, minimum GPA of 2.5; for doctorate, minimum GPA of 3.0.

Graceland University, Community of Christ Seminary, Independence, MO 64050. Offers Christian ministry (MACM); religion (MAR). Part-time programs available. Postbaccalaureate distance learning degree programs offered (minimal on-campus study). *Faculty:* 3 full-time (2 women), 8 part-time/adjunct (4 women). *Students:* 6 full-time (3 women), 14 part-time (7 women), 1 international. Average age 39. 13 applicants, 85% accepted, 11 enrolled. In 2009, 7 master's awarded. *Degree requirements:* For master's, thesis optional, portfolio or thesis

(MAR), practicum (MACM). *Entrance requirements:* For master's, minimum cumulative GPA of 3.0. Additional exam requirements/recommendations for international students: Required—TOEFL. *Application deadline:* For fall admission, 8/15 priority date for domestic students; for winter admission, 10/15 priority date for domestic students; for spring admission, 4/15 priority date for domestic students. Applications are processed on a rolling basis. Application fee: $50. *Expenses:* Contact institution. *Financial support:* Scholarships/grants available. Financial award application deadline: 12/15; financial award applicants required to submit FAFSA. *Faculty research:* Theology, scripture. *Unit head:* Dr. Don H. Compier, Dean, 800-833-0524 Ext. 4900, Fax: 816-833-2990, E-mail: dcompier@graceland.edu. *Application contact:* Judy K. Luffman, Executive Assistant, 816-833-0524 Ext. 4508, Fax: 816-833-2990, E-mail: luffman@graceland.edu.

Grace Theological Seminary, Graduate and Professional Programs, Winona Lake, IN 46590-9907. Offers biblical studies (Certificate); camp administration (MA); counseling (M Div); exegetical studies (MA); intercultural studies (M Div, MA); local church studies (MA); pastoral studies (M Div); theological studies (MA); theology (D Min, Diploma). Part-time programs available. Postbaccalaureate distance learning degree programs offered (no on-campus study). *Degree requirements:* For master's, thesis optional; for doctorate, 2 foreign languages, thesis/dissertation; for M Div, 2 foreign languages, thesis/dissertation optional. *Entrance requirements:* For M Div and master's, MAT, minimum GPA of 2.5. Electronic applications accepted. *Faculty research:* Biblical theology, language, and church ministries.

Grace University, College of Graduate Studies, Counseling Program, Omaha, NE 68108. Offers MA. *Entrance requirements:* For master's, minimum undergraduate GPA of 3.0.

Grand Rapids Theological Seminary of Cornerstone University, Graduate Programs, Grand Rapids, MI 49525-5897. Offers biblical counseling (MA); Biblical counseling (M Div); chaplaincy (M Div); Christian education (M Div, MA); intercultural studies (M Div, MA); New Testament (MA, Th M); Old Testament (MA, Th M); pastoral studies (M Div); systematic theology (MA); theology (Th M). *Accreditation:* ATS. Part-time programs available. Postbaccalaureate distance learning degree programs offered (minimal on-campus study). *Entrance requirements:* Additional exam requirements/recommendations for international students: Required—TOEFL (minimum score 577 paper-based; 233 computer-based; 90 iBT). Electronic applications accepted.

Greenville College, Program in Leadership and Ministry, Greenville, IL 62246-0159. Offers MA. Part-time programs available. *Degree requirements:* For master's, 6 hours of research/practicum in applied ministry. *Entrance requirements:* For master's, 1 year of work experience in Christian ministry, interview. Additional exam requirements/recommendations for international students: Required—TOEFL (minimum score 525 paper-based; 197 computer-based). Electronic applications accepted.

Hampton University, Graduate College, Department of Education, Program in Counseling, Hampton, VA 23668. Offers college student development (MA); community agency counseling (MA); pastoral counseling (MA); school counseling (MA). *Accreditation:* NCATE. Part-time and evening/weekend programs available. *Entrance requirements:* For master's, GRE General Test.

Harding University, College of Bible and Religion, Master of Ministry Program, Searcy, AR 72149-0001. Offers M Min. Part-time and evening/weekend programs available. Postbaccalaureate distance learning degree programs offered. *Faculty:* 7 part-time/adjunct (0 women). *Students:* 3 full-time (1 woman), 38 part-time (1 woman); includes 2 African Americans, 2 Hispanic Americans, 2 international. Average age 37. 19 applicants, 100% accepted, 19 enrolled. In 2009, 7 master's awarded. *Degree requirements:* For master's, 3 practica (1 hour each), portfolio, capstone project. *Entrance requirements:* For master's, 16 hours course work in Bible, minimum GPA of 2.75. *Application deadline:* For fall admission, 8/1 priority date for domestic and international students; for spring admission, 12/1 priority date for domestic students, 12/15 priority date for international students. Applications are processed on a rolling basis. Application fee: $25. Electronic applications accepted. *Expenses:* Tuition: Full-time $9720; part-time $540 per credit hour. Required fees: $22 per credit hour. Tuition and fees vary according to course load and program. *Financial support:* In 2009–10, 37 students received support. Scholarships/grants and unspecified assistantships available. *Unit head:* Dr. Bill Richardson, Director/Associate Professor, 501-279-4252, Fax: 501-279-4081, E-mail: mmin@harding.edu. *Application contact:* Debbie Stewart, Information Contact, 501-279-4252, E-mail: dstewart@harding.edu.

Harding University Graduate School of Religion, Graduate Programs, Memphis, TN 38117-5499. Offers Christian ministry (MA); counseling (MA); ministry (M Div, D Min); religion (MA). *Accreditation:* ATS. Part-time programs available. Postbaccalaureate distance learning degree programs offered (minimal on-campus study). *Degree requirements:* For master's, variable foreign language requirement, thesis (for some programs); for doctorate, one foreign language, thesis/dissertation; for M Div, 2 foreign languages, thesis/dissertation optional. *Entrance requirements:* For M Div, GRE General Test (for graduates of non-accredited schools), minimum GPA of 2.5; for master's, minimum GPA of 2.7; for doctorate, minimum GPA of 3.0. Additional exam requirements/recommendations for international students: Required—TOEFL (minimum score 550 paper-based; 213 computer-based; 79 iBT). Electronic applications accepted.

Hardin-Simmons University, Graduate School, Logsdon School of Theology, Logsdon Seminary, Seminary Program in Family Ministry, Abilene, TX 79698-0001. Offers MA. Part-time programs available. *Faculty:* 3 full-time (1 woman). *Students:* 14 full-time (6 women), 8 part-time (4 women); includes 2 minority (1 African American, 1 Hispanic American). Average age 30. 4 applicants, 100% accepted, 2 enrolled. In 2009, 2 master's awarded. *Degree requirements:* For master's, comprehensive exam, clinical experience, project. *Entrance requirements:* For master's, minimum undergraduate GPA of 3.0 in major, 2.7 overall; 6 hours each of course work in psychology and Old and New Testament; interview; writing sample; references. Additional exam requirements/recommendations for international students: Required—TOEFL (minimum score 555 paper-based; 213 computer-based; 75 iBT). *Application deadline:* For fall admission, 8/15 priority date for domestic students, 4/1 for international students; for spring admission, 1/5 priority date for domestic students, 9/1 for international students. Applications are processed on a rolling basis. Application fee: $50. *Expenses:* Tuition: Full-time $11,430; part-time $635 per credit hour. Required fees: $650; $110 per semester. Tuition and fees vary according to degree level. *Financial support:* In 2009–10, 19 students received support; fellowships, career-related internships or fieldwork and scholarships/grants available. Support available to part-time students. Financial award application deadline: 6/30; financial award applicants required to submit FAFSA. *Unit head:* Dr. Randall Maurer, Director, 325-670-1599, Fax: 325-670-1406, E-mail: rmaurer@hsutx.edu. *Application contact:* Dr. Gary Stanlake, Dean of Graduate Studies, 325-670-1298, Fax: 325-670-1564, E-mail: gradoff@hsutx.edu.

Hardin-Simmons University, Graduate School, Logsdon School of Theology, Logsdon Seminary, Seminary Program in Ministry, Abilene, TX 79698-0001. Offers D Min. Part-time programs available. *Faculty:* 6 full-time (0 women). *Students:* 9 part-time (0 women); includes 1 minority (Hispanic American). Average age 42. 9 applicants, 100% accepted, 4 enrolled. *Degree requirements:* For doctorate, ministry project. *Entrance requirements:* For doctorate, GRE or MAT, M Div or equivalent, minimum graduate GPA of 3.0, minimum 3 years ministry experience, active current ministry involvement, interview, 4 letters of recommendation, church endorsement. *Application deadline:* For fall admission, 4/30 for domestic students. Application fee: $50. *Expenses:* Tuition: Full-time $11,430; part-time $635 per credit hour. Required fees: $650; $110 per semester. Tuition and fees vary according to degree level. *Financial support:* In 2009–10, 8 students received support. Application deadline: 6/30. *Unit head:* Dr. Larry Baker, Director, 325-671-2110, E-mail: lbaker@hsutx.edu. *Application contact:* Dr. Gary Stanlake, Dean of Graduate Studies, 325-670-1298, Fax: 325-670-1564, E-mail: gradoff@hsutx.edu.

Hartford Seminary, Graduate Programs, Hartford, CT 06105-2279. Offers black ministry (Certificate); Islamic studies (MA); ministerios Hispanos (Certificate); ministry (D Min); religious studies (MA); women's leadership institute (Certificate). *Accreditation:* ATS (one or more programs are accredited). Part-time and evening/weekend programs available. Postbaccalaureate distance learning degree programs offered (no on-campus study). *Degree requirements:* For master's, thesis optional, oral exam; for doctorate, thesis/dissertation, oral exam. *Entrance requirements:* For doctorate, experience in ministry, M Div. Additional exam requirements/recommendations for international students: Required—TOEFL (minimum score 550 paper-based; 213 computer-based; 80 iBT). *Faculty research:* Liturgy and social justice, professional leadership in ministry, congregational studies, Christian-Muslim relations, American religion.

Heritage Baptist College and Heritage Theological Seminary, Program in Theological Studies, Cambridge, ON N3C 3T2, Canada. Offers chaplaincy (M Div); counselling (M Div); general (M Div); ministry (D Min); pastoral (M Div); research (M Div); theological studies (MA, Certificate). *Accreditation:* ATS.

Heritage Christian University, Graduate Programs, Florence, AL 35630. Offers counseling (MM); Greek (MA); ministry (MM); New Testament (MA). *Degree requirements:* For master's, practicum (MM), major research paper (MA). *Entrance requirements:* For master's, MAT or GRE, bachelor's degree in Bible from an accredited college or university, minimum GPA of 2.75, 3 letters of recommendation.

Hillsdale Free Will Baptist College, Department of Bible Studies, Moore, OK 73160-1208. Offers ministry (MA). Part-time and evening/weekend programs available. *Degree requirements:* For master's, thesis optional. *Entrance requirements:* Additional exam requirements/recommendations for international students: Recommended—TOEFL (minimum score 500 paper-based).

Holmes Institute, Graduate Program, Burbank, CA 91505. Offers consciousness studies (MS). Postbaccalaureate distance learning degree programs offered. *Faculty:* 50 part-time/adjunct (35 women). *Students:* 113 part-time (85 women). Average age 40. 16 applicants, 100% accepted, 16 enrolled. *Degree requirements:* For master's, comprehensive exam, 2 spiritual retreats per year, internship (1 per term), 2 spiritual conferences. *Entrance requirements:* For master's, 3 letters of recommendation, interview. *Application deadline:* Applications are processed on a rolling basis. Application fee: $300. *Expenses:* Required fees: $6177 per year. *Unit head:* Rev. Dr. Lynn Connolly, Director of Education, 720-279-8990, Fax: 303-526-0913, E-mail: lconnolly@religiousscience.org. *Application contact:* Maureen Thurston, Administrative Registrar, 720-279-8992, Fax: 303-526-0913, E-mail: mthurston@religiousscience.org.

Holy Names University, Graduate Division, Department of Counseling Psychology, Oakland, CA 94619-1699. Offers counseling psychology (MA); forensic psychology (MA, Certificate); pastoral counseling (MA, Certificate). Part-time and evening/weekend programs available. *Degree requirements:* For master's, comprehensive paper, seminars. *Entrance requirements:* For master's, minimum undergraduate GPA of 2.6 overall, 3.0 in major. Additional exam requirements/recommendations for international students: Required—TOEFL (minimum score 550 paper-based; 213 computer-based; 80 iBT). *Faculty research:* Cognitive psychology, anger management, grief and grief counseling, post-modernism and psychotherapy, spirituality and psychology.

Holy Names University, Graduate Division, Program in Pastoral Ministries, Oakland, CA 94619-1699. Offers MA, Certificate. Part-time programs available. Postbaccalaureate distance learning degree programs offered (no on-campus study). *Degree requirements:* For master's, ministry project. *Entrance requirements:* Additional exam requirements/recommendations for international students: Required—TOEFL (minimum score 550 paper-based; 213 computer-based; 80 iBT). *Faculty research:* Ethics, cross-cultural management, faith development through liturgy, multi-cultural community building.

Houston Baptist University, College of Education and Behavioral Sciences, Program in Christian Counseling, Houston, TX 77074-3298. Offers MACC. *Degree requirements:* For master's, comprehensive exam. *Entrance requirements:* For master's, GRE General Test, minimum GPA of 3.0. Additional exam requirements/recommendations for international students: Required—TOEFL (minimum score 550 paper-based; 213 computer-based).

Houston Graduate School of Theology, Graduate School, Houston, TX 77092. Offers counseling (MA); pastoral ministry (M Div, D Min); theology (MA). *Accreditation:* ATS (one or more programs are accredited). Part-time and evening/weekend programs available. *Degree requirements:* For master's, thesis (for some programs); for doctorate, thesis/dissertation; for M Div, thesis/dissertation optional. *Entrance requirements:* For doctorate, GRE General Test or MAT, M Div or equivalent. Additional exam requirements/recommendations for international students: Required—TOEFL (minimum score 550 paper-based; 213 computer-based). *Faculty research:* Hermeneutics, spirituality, religion of Eastern Europe.

Howard Payne University, Program in Youth Ministry, Brownwood, TX 76801-2715. Offers MA. *Degree requirements:* For master's, internship. *Entrance requirements:* For master's, baccalaureate degree, 3 references, interview.

Huntington University, Graduate School, Huntington, IN 46750-1299. Offers counseling (MA), including licensed mental health counselor; education (M Ed); youth ministry leadership (MA). Part-time programs available. Postbaccalaureate distance learning degree programs offered (minimal on-campus study). *Faculty:* 2 full-time (0 women), 36 part-time/adjunct (12 women). *Students:* 57 full-time (31 women), 87 part-time (58 women); includes 9 minority (8 African Americans, 1 Hispanic American), 1 international. Average age 33. 50 applicants, 92% accepted, 27 enrolled. In 2009, 4 master's awarded. *Degree requirements:* For master's, thesis. *Entrance requirements:* For master's, GRE (for counseling and education students only). Additional exam requirements/recommendations for international students: Required—TOEFL. *Application deadline:* For fall admission, 7/1 priority date for domestic students, 5/1 priority date for international students; for winter admission, 10/1 priority date for domestic students, 9/1 priority date for international students; for spring admission, 11/30 priority date for domestic students, 10/30 priority date for international students. Applications are processed on a rolling basis. Application fee: $20. Electronic applications accepted. *Expenses:* Tuition: Part-time $370 per credit hour. Part-time tuition and fees vary according to program. *Financial support:* In 2009–10, 53 students received support. Scholarships/grants and unspecified assistantships available. Support available to part-time students. Financial award application deadline: 8/1; financial award applicants required to submit FAFSA. *Faculty research:* Leadership, educational technology trends, evangelism, youth ministry, mental health. *Unit head:* Dr. Steven Holtrop, Associate Dean for Graduate and Adult Studies, 260-359-4166, Fax: 260-359-4126, E-mail: sholtrop@huntington.edu. *Application contact:* Lori Garde, Program Coordinator, 260-359-4039, Fax: 260-359-4126, E-mail: lgarde@huntington.edu.

Iliff School of Theology, Graduate and Professional Programs, Denver, CO 80210-4798. Offers biblical studies (MA); church history (MA); religion (MA); religion and social change (MA); specialized ministry (MASM), including justice and peace, pastoral theology and care, religions leadership; theology (M Div, MTS, D Min, PhD), including Biblical studies (PhD), religion and psychological studies (PhD), religion and social change (PhD), theology, philosophy and culture (PhD); theology/ethics (MA). *Accreditation:* ACIPE; ATS. Part-time and evening/weekend programs available. *Degree requirements:* For master's, one foreign language, thesis (for some programs); for doctorate, 2 foreign languages, comprehensive exam, thesis/dissertation; for M Div, thesis/dissertation optional. *Entrance requirements:* For M Div, minimum GPA of 2.75, references; for master's, minimum GPA of 3.0, writing sample, references; for doctorate, GRE General Test, minimum GPA of 3.0, writing sample, letters of recommendation. Additional exam requirements/recommendations for international students: Required—TOEFL (minimum score 550 paper-based). Electronic applications accepted. *Faculty research:* Pastoral care, history, church music, contemporary church, biblical studies.

Pastoral Ministry and Counseling

Indiana Wesleyan University, College of Graduate Studies, Wesley Seminary, Program in Ministry, Marion, IN 46953-4974. Offers ministerial leadership (MA); youth ministries (MA). Part-time programs available. Postbaccalaureate distance learning degree programs offered (minimal on-campus study). *Degree requirements:* For master's, one foreign language, capstone practicum and/or project. *Entrance requirements:* Additional exam requirements/recommendations for international students: Required—TOEFL. Electronic applications accepted. *Expenses:* Contact institution. *Faculty research:* History of worship innovation, history of New Testament afterlife traditions, second century mantanism, cross-cultural ministry, church health and growth, leadership in Christian organizations, managing change in the church, effective youth ministry, women in ministry, biblical hermeneutics.

Institute of Transpersonal Psychology, Low-Residency Programs, Palo Alto, CA 94303. Offers counseling psychology (online) (MA); spiritual guidance (MA); women's spirituality (MA). Postbaccalaureate distance learning degree programs offered (minimal on-campus study).

Inter American University of Puerto Rico, Metropolitan Campus, Graduate Programs, Program in Pastoral Theology, San Juan, PR 00919-1293. Offers PhD.

International Baptist College, Program in Ministry, Chandler, AZ 85286. Offers M Min, D Min.

Iona College, School of Arts and Science, Department of Family and Pastoral Counseling, New Rochelle, NY 10801-1890. Offers family counseling (MS, Certificate); pastoral counseling (MS). Part-time and evening/weekend programs available. *Faculty:* 4 full-time (0 women), 3 part-time/adjunct (all women). *Students:* 29 full-time (23 women), 12 part-time (11 women); includes 14 minority (7 African Americans, 7 Hispanic Americans). Average age 33. 38 applicants, 58% accepted, 14 enrolled. In 2009, 15 master's awarded. *Degree requirements:* For master's, thesis, project. *Entrance requirements:* For master's, draw-a-person test, sentence completion test, interview, minimum GPA of 3.0. *Application deadline:* Applications are processed on a rolling basis. Application fee: $50. Electronic applications accepted. *Expenses:* Contact institution. *Financial support:* Career-related internships or fieldwork, tuition waivers (partial), and unspecified assistantships available. Support available to part-time students. Financial award application deadline: 4/15; financial award applicants required to submit FAFSA. *Faculty research:* Marriage counseling. *Unit head:* Dr. Robert Burns, Chair, 914-633-2418, E-mail: rburns@iona.edu. *Application contact:* Veronica Jarek-Prinz, Director of Graduate Admissions, 914-633-2420, Fax: 914-633-2277, E-mail: vjarekprinz@iona.edu.

Jewish University of America, Graduate School, Abrams Institute of Pastoral Counseling, Skokie, IL 60077-3248. Offers counseling (MA); pastoral counseling (MPC, DPC). *Degree requirements:* For master's, thesis optional; for doctorate, one foreign language, thesis/dissertation. *Entrance requirements:* For master's and doctorate, interview.

John Brown University, Graduate Studies Division of Christian Ministry, Siloam Springs, AR 72761-2121. Offers leadership and ethics (MA); ministry leadership (MA); pastoral counseling (MA); youth ministry (MA). Part-time and evening/weekend programs available. *Faculty:* 3 full-time (0 women), 2 part-time/adjunct (1 woman). *Students:* 35 part-time (18 women); includes 1 minority (African American), 1 international. Average age 37. 32 applicants, 81% accepted, 26 enrolled. In 2009, 2 master's awarded. *Entrance requirements:* For master's, GRE General Test, MAT, minimum GPA of 3.0. Additional exam requirements/recommendations for international students: Required—TOEFL (minimum score 550 paper-based; 173 computer-based). *Application deadline:* For fall admission, 8/11 priority date for domestic students; for spring admission, 1/12 priority date for domestic students. Applications are processed on a rolling basis. Application fee: $35 ($100 for international students). Electronic applications accepted. *Expenses:* Tuition: Full-time $8100; part-time $450 per credit. *Financial support:* Application deadline: 3/1. *Unit head:* Dr. Dan Lambert, Director, 479-524-7264, Fax: 479-238-8574, E-mail: dlambert@jbu.edu. *Application contact:* Dr. Jason Lanker, Assistant Professor, 479-524-7375, E-mail: jlanker@jbu.edu.

Knox Theological Seminary, Graduate Programs, Program in Ministry, Fort Lauderdale, FL 33308. Offers D Min. Part-time programs available. *Degree requirements:* For doctorate, thesis/dissertation. *Entrance requirements:* For doctorate, M Div or equivalent. Additional exam requirements/recommendations for international students: Required—TOEFL, TWE (minimum score 5).

Lancaster Bible College & Graduate School, Graduate School, Lancaster, PA 17601-5036. Offers Bible (MA); consulting resource teacher (M Ed); counseling (MA); ministry (MA); school counseling (M Ed). Part-time and evening/weekend programs available. *Degree requirements:* For master's, comprehensive exam (for some programs), thesis (for some programs). *Entrance requirements:* For master's, bachelor's degree with a minimum of 30 credits of course work in Bible, minimum undergraduate GPA of 3.0, interview. Additional exam requirements/recommendations for international students: Required—TOEFL.

La Salle University, School of Arts and Sciences, Program in Theological, Pastoral and Liturgical Studies, Philadelphia, PA 19141-1199. Offers pastoral studies (MA); religion (MA); theological studies (MA). Part-time and evening/weekend programs available. *Entrance requirements:* For master's, 26 credits in humanistic subjects, religion, theology, or ministry-related work.

La Sierra University, School of Religion, Riverside, CA 92515. Offers pastoral ministry (M Div); religion (MA); religious education (MA); religious studies (MA). *Accreditation:* ATS. Part-time programs available. *Degree requirements:* For master's, one foreign language, thesis or alternative. *Entrance requirements:* For master's, GRE General Test, minimum GPA of 3.0.

Liberty University, College of Arts and Sciences, Lynchburg, VA 24502. Offers counseling (MA); nursing (MSN); pastoral care and counseling (PhD); professional counseling (PhD). *Accreditation:* AACN. Part-time programs available. Postbaccalaureate distance learning degree programs offered (minimal on-campus study). *Degree requirements:* For master's, comprehensive exam (for some programs); for doctorate, comprehensive exam, thesis/dissertation. *Entrance requirements:* For master's, GRE General Test (MSN), minimum undergraduate GPA of 3.0; for doctorate, GRE General Test, minimum master's GPA of 3.25. Additional exam requirements/recommendations for international students: Required—TOEFL (minimum score 600 paper-based; 250 computer-based). Electronic applications accepted. *Expenses:* Tuition: Full-time $7110; part-time $415 per credit hour. Required fees: $150 per semester. Tuition and fees vary according to course load, degree level, campus/location and program. *Faculty research:* God concept and adult attachment, building marital strength, image of God and gender, breastfeeding behavior among adolescent mothers, osteoporosis.

Lincoln Christian Seminary, Graduate and Professional Programs, Lincoln, IL 62656-2167. Offers Bible and theology (MA); Christian ministries (MA); counseling (MA); divinity (M Div); leadership ministry (D Min); religious education (MRE). *Accreditation:* ACIPE; ATS. Part-time programs available. *Degree requirements:* For master's, 2 foreign languages, thesis; for doctorate, thesis/dissertation; for M Div, 2 foreign languages. *Entrance requirements:* For M Div and master's, minimum GPA of 2.5; for doctorate, M Div or equivalent. Additional exam requirements/recommendations for international students: Required—TOEFL (minimum score 550 paper-based; 213 computer-based). Electronic applications accepted.

Loma Linda University, Faculty of Religion, Program in Clinical Ministry, Loma Linda, CA 92350. Offers MA, Certificate. *Degree requirements:* For master's, comprehensive exam, thesis optional. *Entrance requirements:* For master's, minimum GPA of 3.0. Additional exam requirements/recommendations for international students: Required—TOEFL. Electronic applications accepted.

Loras College, Graduate Division, Program in Theology and Ministry, Dubuque, IA 52004-0178. Offers ministry (MA); theology (MA). Part-time and evening/weekend programs available. *Degree requirements:* For master's, comprehensive exam (for some programs), thesis (for some programs). *Entrance requirements:* For master's, bachelor's degree or undergraduate minor in religious studies or equivalent, minimum undergraduate GPA of 2.75.

Loyola Marymount University, College of Liberal Arts, Department of Theological Studies, Program in Pastoral Theology, Los Angeles, CA 90045-8400. Offers MA. Part-time and evening/weekend programs available. *Faculty:* 24 full-time (5 women). *Students:* 18 full-time (10 women), 38 part-time (24 women); includes 28 minority (12 Asian Americans or Pacific Islanders, 16 Hispanic Americans), 2 international. Average age 43. 45 applicants, 62% accepted, 25 enrolled. In 2009, 5 master's awarded. *Degree requirements:* For master's, comprehensive exam, thesis or alternative. *Entrance requirements:* For master's, GRE General Test or MAT (recommended), 2 letters of recommendation. Additional exam requirements/recommendations for international students: Required—TOEFL (minimum score 600 paper-based; 250 computer-based; 100 iBT). *Application deadline:* For fall admission, 3/1 priority date for domestic students. Application fee: $50. Electronic applications accepted. *Financial support:* In 2009–10, 49 students received support. Scholarships/grants and unspecified assistantships available. Support available to part-time students. Financial award application deadline: 6/1; financial award applicants required to submit FAFSA. Total annual research expenditures: $84,937. *Unit head:* Dr. Michael P. Horan, Graduate Director, 310-338-2755, E-mail: mhoran@lmu.edu. *Application contact:* Chake H. Kouyoumjian, Associate Dean of Graduate Studies, 310-338-2721, Fax: 310-338-6086, E-mail: ckouyoum@lmu.edu.

Loyola University Chicago, Institute of Pastoral Studies, Program in Pastoral Counseling, Chicago, IL 60660. Offers pastoral care and counseling (MA); pastoral counseling (MA, Certificate). *Accreditation:* ACIPE. Part-time programs available. *Faculty:* 6 full-time (2 women), 12 part-time/adjunct (7 women). *Students:* 30 full-time (19 women), 20 part-time (14 women); includes 7 minority (2 African Americans, 3 Asian Americans or Pacific Islanders, 2 Hispanic Americans), 7 international. Average age 42. 31 applicants, 74% accepted, 18 enrolled. In 2009, 31 master's awarded. *Degree requirements:* For master's, thesis or alternative, integration project. *Application deadline:* For fall admission, 2/15 priority date for domestic students. Applications are processed on a rolling basis. Application fee: $50. Electronic applications accepted. *Expenses:* Tuition: Full-time $14,220; part-time $790 per credit hour. Required fees: $60 per semester hour. Tuition and fees vary according to program. *Financial support:* In 2009–10, 7 students received support. Career-related internships or fieldwork, Federal Work-Study, and institutionally sponsored loans available. Support available to part-time students. Financial award application deadline: 3/1; financial award applicants required to submit FAFSA. *Faculty research:* Pastoral psychotherapy, enrichment outcome, marriage and family therapy, marriage and family spirituality, gender and ethnicity issues, theological anthropology. *Unit head:* Dr. Paul R. Giblin, Associate Professor, 312-915-7483, Fax: 312-915-7410, E-mail: pgibli@luc.edu. *Application contact:* Dr. Paul R. Giblin, Associate Professor, 312-915-7483, Fax: 312-915-7410, E-mail: pgibli@luc.edu.

Loyola University Chicago, Institute of Pastoral Studies, Program in Pastoral Studies, Chicago, IL 60660. Offers MA. *Accreditation:* ACIPE. *Faculty:* 6 full-time (2 women). *Students:* 30 full-time (18 women), 60 part-time (44 women); includes 4 minority (all African Americans), 3 international. Average age 45. 42 applicants, 83% accepted, 30 enrolled. In 2009, 19 master's awarded. *Application deadline:* For fall admission, 8/1 priority date for domestic students; for spring admission, 12/1 for domestic students. Applications are processed on a rolling basis. Application fee: $50. *Expenses:* Tuition: Full-time $14,220; part-time $790 per credit hour. Required fees: $60 per semester hour. Tuition and fees vary according to program. *Financial support:* Career-related internships or fieldwork, Federal Work-Study, institutionally sponsored loans, and scholarships/grants available. Support available to part-time students. Financial award application deadline: 3/1. *Unit head:* Dr. Peter Gilmour, Director, 312-915-7400, Fax: 312-915-7410, E-mail: pgilmou@luc.edu. *Application contact:* Randy Gibbons, Administrative Assistant, 312-915-7450, Fax: 312-915-7410, E-mail: rgibbon@luc.edu.

Loyola University Maryland, Graduate Programs, College of Arts and Sciences, Department of Pastoral Counseling, Program in Pastoral Counseling, Baltimore, MD 21210-2699. Offers MS, PhD, CAS. Part-time and evening/weekend programs available. *Entrance requirements:* For master's, doctorate, and CAS, GRE General Test, GRE Subject Test (recommended). Additional exam requirements/recommendations for international students: Required—TOEFL (minimum score 550 paper-based; 213 computer-based).

Loyola University Maryland, Graduate Programs, College of Arts and Sciences, Department of Pastoral Counseling, Program in Spiritual and Pastoral Care, Baltimore, MD 21210-2699. Offers MA. Part-time and evening/weekend programs available. *Entrance requirements:* For master's, GRE General Test, GRE Subject Test (recommended). Additional exam requirements/recommendations for international students: Required—TOEFL (minimum score 550 paper-based; 213 computer-based).

Lutheran School of Theology at Chicago, Graduate and Professional Programs, Chicago, IL 60615-5199. Offers ministry (MAM, D Min); theological studies (MATS, PhD); theology (M Div, Th M). *Accreditation:* ACIPE; ATS (one or more programs are accredited). Part-time programs available. *Faculty:* 20 full-time (6 women), 18 part-time/adjunct (5 women). *Students:* 214 full-time (103 women), 88 part-time (52 women). Terminal master's awarded for partial completion of doctoral program. *Degree requirements:* For master's, variable foreign language requirement; for doctorate, variable foreign language requirement, comprehensive exam, thesis/dissertation; for M Div, 2 foreign languages. *Entrance requirements:* For master's, GRE (Th M), M Div or equivalent (Th M); for doctorate, GRE, M Div or equivalent, 3 years of professional experience (D Min). Additional exam requirements/recommendations for international students: Required—TOEFL (Th M). *Application deadline:* Applications are processed on a rolling basis. Application fee: $50. *Expenses:* Tuition: Full-time $11,997; part-time $1333 per course. Required fees: $35 per semester. Tuition and fees vary according to degree level and program. *Financial support:* Career-related internships or fieldwork and scholarships/grants available. Support available to part-time students. *Unit head:* Michael Shelley, Dean, 773-256-0722, Fax: 773-256-0782, E-mail: mshelley@lstc.edu. *Application contact:* Dorothy C. Dominiak, Director of Admissions and Financial Aid, 773-256-0726, Fax: 773-256-0782, E-mail: ddominia@lstc.edu.

Lutheran Theological Seminary, Graduate and Professional Programs, Saskatoon, SK S7N 0X3, Canada. Offers Biblical studies (MTS); church history (MTS); ethics/church and society (MTS); history of Christianity (STM); New Testament (STM); Old Testament (STM); pastoral studies (STM); pastoral theology (MTS); systematic theology (MTS); systematic theology and philosophy of religion (STM); theology (M Div, D Div). *Accreditation:* ATS. Part-time programs available. *Degree requirements:* For master's, thesis; for M Div, Greek, Hebrew.

Lutheran Theological Seminary at Gettysburg, Graduate and Professional Programs, Gettysburg, PA 17325-1795. Offers divinity (M Div); ministerial studies (MAMS); outdoor ministry (MAR); parish ministry (D Min); theology (STM). *Accreditation:* ACIPE; ATS (one or more programs are accredited). Part-time programs available. Postbaccalaureate distance learning degree programs offered (no on-campus study). *Degree requirements:* For master's, thesis (for some programs); for M Div, one foreign language. Electronic applications accepted.

The Lutheran Theological Seminary at Philadelphia, Graduate School, Philadelphia, PA 19119-1794. Offers divinity (M Div); ministry (D Min); religion (MAR); social ministry (Certificate); theology (STM). *Accreditation:* ACIPE; ATS. Part-time and evening/weekend programs available. *Degree requirements:* For master's, one foreign language, comprehensive exam (for some programs), thesis (for some programs); for doctorate, thesis/dissertation; for M Div, 2 foreign languages. *Entrance requirements:* For M Div and master's, minimum undergraduate GPA of 2.8; for doctorate, minimum first professional GPA of 3.0. Additional exam requirements/recommendations for international students: Required—TOEFL (minimum score 550 paper-based; 213 computer-based), TWE. Electronic applications accepted.

Luther Rice University, Graduate Programs, Lithonia, GA 30038-2454. Offers Bible/theology (M Div); Christian education (M Div); Christian studies (MA); church ministry (D Min); counseling

(M Div); discipleship counseling (MA); ministry (M Div, MA); missions/evangelism (M Div). Part-time programs available. Postbaccalaureate distance learning degree programs offered (no on-campus study). *Degree requirements:* For doctorate, thesis/dissertation. *Entrance requirements:* Additional exam requirements/recommendations for international students: Required—TOEFL (minimum score 500 paper-based; 173 computer-based).

Madonna University, Program in Religious Studies, Livonia, MI 48150-1173. Offers pastoral ministry (MA).

Maple Springs Baptist Bible College and Seminary, Graduate and Professional Programs, Capitol Heights, MD 20743. Offers biblical studies (MA, Certificate); Christian counseling (MA); church administration (MA); divinity (M Div); ministry (D Min); religious education (MRE).

Maranatha Baptist Bible College, Program in Biblical Counseling, Watertown, WI 53094. Offers MA. Part-time programs available. *Expenses:* Tuition: Full-time $4000; part-time $250 per credit. Required fees: $21 per credit.

Martin University, Graduate School of Urban Ministry, Indianapolis, IN 46218-3867. Offers urban ministry studies (MA). Part-time and evening/weekend programs available. *Degree requirements:* For master's, Greek, oral and written comprehensive exam or thesis. *Faculty research:* How to bridge the gap between black theology and the black church.

Marymount University, School of Education and Human Services, Program in Pastoral Counseling, Arlington, VA 22207-4299. Offers pastoral and spiritual care (MA); pastoral counseling (MA, Certificate). Part-time and evening/weekend programs available. *Students:* 6 full-time (5 women), 18 part-time (17 women); includes 5 minority (all African Americans), 1 international. Average age 40. 9 applicants, 89% accepted, 4 enrolled. In 2009, 1 master's awarded. *Degree requirements:* For master's, thesis or alternative. *Entrance requirements:* For master's, GRE, 2 letters of recommendation, interview, resume; for Certificate, master's degree in counseling. Additional exam requirements/recommendations for international students: Required—TOEFL (minimum score 600 paper-based; 250 computer-based; 96 iBT), IELTS (minimum score 6.5). *Application deadline:* For fall admission, 1/15 for domestic and international students; for spring admission, 10/5 for domestic and international students. Applications are processed on a rolling basis. Application fee: $40. Electronic applications accepted. *Expenses:* Tuition: Full-time $13,050; part-time $725 per credit hour. Required fees: $135; $7.50 per credit hour. *Financial support:* In 2009–10, 2 students received support; research assistantships with full tuition reimbursements available, career-related internships or fieldwork, Federal Work-Study, scholarships/grants, and unspecified assistantships available. Support available to part-time students. Financial award applicants required to submit FAFSA. *Unit head:* Dr. Lisa Jackson-Cherry, Chair, 703-284-1633, Fax: 703-284-5708, E-mail: lisa.jackson-cherry@marymount.edu. *Application contact:* Francesca Reed, Director, Graduate Admissions, 703-284-5901, Fax: 703-527-3815, E-mail: grad.admissions@marymount.edu.

The Master's College and Seminary, The Master's Seminary, Santa Clarita, CA 91321-1200. Offers biblical counseling (MABC); New Testament (Th D); Old Testament (Th D); preaching (D Min); theology (M Div, M Th, Th D). Part-time programs available. *Degree requirements:* For master's, 2 foreign languages, thesis; for doctorate, 4 foreign languages, thesis/dissertation; for M Div, 2 foreign languages, thesis/dissertation. *Entrance requirements:* For M Div, minimum 2 years of college; for master's, minimum GPA of 2.75; for doctorate, Th M, minimum GPA of 3.5. Additional exam requirements/recommendations for international students: Required—TOEFL (minimum score 550 paper-based).

McCormick Theological Seminary, Graduate and Professional Programs, Chicago, IL 60615. Offers ministry (D Min); theological studies (MATS, Certificate); theology (M Div); M Div/MSW. *Accreditation:* ACIPE; ATS (one or more programs are accredited). Part-time and evening/weekend programs available. *Degree requirements:* For master's, thesis (for some programs); for doctorate, thesis/dissertation. *Entrance requirements:* For M Div and master's, minimum GPA of 3.0; for doctorate, M Div, minimum 3 years in pastorate. *Faculty research:* Faith formation, families, biblical literature, Dead Sea scrolls, women in antiquity.

McMaster University, McMaster Divinity College, Hamilton, ON L8S 4M2, Canada. Offers biblical studies (M Div); Biblical studies (MA, MTS, Diploma); Christian interpretation/history (M Div, MA, MTS, Diploma); Christian ministry (M Div, MA, MTS, Diploma); Christian Studies (Certificate); Christian theology (PhD). Affiliated with the Toronto School of Theology. *Accreditation:* ATS. Part-time programs available. *Degree requirements:* For master's, one foreign language, thesis optional; for doctorate, 3 foreign languages, comprehensive exam, thesis/dissertation; for other advanced degree, 2 foreign languages, thesis. *Entrance requirements:* For master's, minimum B average in undergraduate course work, 3 letters of reference; for doctorate, minimum B+ average in bachelor's and master's, appropriate modern/ancient language, interview; for other advanced degree, 6 units of related Biblical language, minimum B+ average in undergraduate course work, minimum 15 units of course work in related area of study, 3 letters of recommendation. Additional exam requirements/recommendations for international students: Required—TOEFL (minimum score 550 paper-based; 237 computer-based). *Faculty research:* Ethics, Biblical studies, language studies, church history, Christian ministry.

Meadville Lombard Theological School, Graduate and Professional Programs, Chicago, IL 60637-1602. Offers divinity (M Div); ministry (D Min); religion (MA); M Div/MSW. *Accreditation:* ACIPE; ATS. Part-time programs available. Postbaccalaureate distance learning degree programs offered (minimal on-campus study). *Entrance requirements:* For M Div and master's, bachelor's degree; for doctorate, bachelor's and masters degrees, 3 years of ministry.

Mennonite Brethren Biblical Seminary, School of Theology, Program in Christian Ministry, Fresno, CA 93727-5097. Offers MA. Part-time programs available. Postbaccalaureate distance learning degree programs offered (minimal on-campus study). *Entrance requirements:* Additional exam requirements/recommendations for international students: Required—TOEFL (minimum score 550 paper-based; 213 computer-based).

Mid-America Christian University, Program in Counseling, Oklahoma City, OK 73170-4504. Offers marital and family therapy (MS); pastoral/spiritual direction (MS); professional counselor (MS). *Entrance requirements:* For master's, MAT, bachelor's degree from a regionally accredited college or university, minimum overall cumulative GPA of 2.75 of bachelor course work. Additional exam requirements/recommendations for international students: Required—TOEFL (minimum score 550 paper-based; 213 computer-based).

Midwestern Baptist Theological Seminary, Graduate and Professional Programs, Kansas City, MO 64118-4697. Offers Biblical archaeology (MA); Biblical languages (MA); Christian education (M Div, MACE); Christian foundations—lay ministry (Graduate Certificate); collegiate ministries (M Div); counseling (MA); educational ministry (D Ed Min); international church planting (M Div); ministry (M Div, D Min); North American church planting (M Div); sacred music (MCM); urban ministry (M Div); worship leadership (M Div); youth ministry (M Div). *Accreditation:* ATS. Part-time programs available. Postbaccalaureate distance learning degree programs offered (minimal on-campus study). *Degree requirements:* For doctorate, thesis/dissertation; for M Div, 2 foreign languages. *Entrance requirements:* For doctorate, MAT. Electronic applications accepted. *Faculty research:* Ministerial studies, Biblical and theological studies, missions, counseling.

Missouri Baptist University, Graduate Programs, St. Louis, MO 63141-8660. Offers business administration (MBA); Christian ministries (MACM); counseling (MAC); education (MSE); education administration (MEA); educational leadership (MSE, Ed S); teaching (MAT).

Moody Bible Institute, Graduate School, Chicago, IL 60610-3284. Offers biblical studies (MABS, Graduate Certificate); intercultural studies (MAIS, Graduate Certificate); ministry (M Div, M Min); spiritual formation and discipleship (MASF, Graduate Certificate); urban studies (MA, Graduate Certificate). Part-time programs available. *Degree requirements:* For master's, 2 foreign languages, fieldwork (MABS); colloquium, field research project (MA Min). *Entrance requirements:* For master's, 30 hours in Bible/theology, 2 years of ministry experience (MA Min).

Mount Marty College, Graduate Studies Division, Yankton, SD 57078-3724. Offers business administration (MBA); nurse anesthesia (MS); pastoral ministries (MPM). *Accreditation:* AANA/CANAEP (one or more programs are accredited). *Degree requirements:* For master's, thesis or alternative. *Entrance requirements:* For master's, GRE General Test, minimum GPA of 3.0. Electronic applications accepted. *Faculty research:* Clinical anesthesia, professional characteristics, motivations of applicants.

Mount Mary College, Graduate Programs, Program in Community Counseling, Milwaukee, WI 53222-4597. Offers community counseling (MS); pastoral counseling (MS); school counseling (MS). Part-time and evening/weekend programs available. *Faculty:* 2 full-time (both women), 8 part-time/adjunct (4 women). *Students:* 69 full-time (68 women), 23 part-time (all women); includes 25 minority (21 African Americans, 1 American Indian/Alaska Native, 3 Hispanic Americans). Average age 34. 68 applicants, 56% accepted, 28 enrolled. In 2009, 20 master's awarded. *Degree requirements:* For master's, comprehensive exam, thesis or alternative. *Entrance requirements:* For master's, minimum GPA of 3.0. Additional exam requirements/recommendations for international students: Required—TOEFL (minimum score 500 paper-based; 173 computer-based). *Application deadline:* For fall admission, 8/1 priority date for domestic and international students; for spring admission, 12/1 priority date for domestic and international students. Application fee: $35 ($100 for international students). *Expenses:* Tuition: Part-time $595 per credit. Tuition and fees vary according to program. *Financial support:* Career-related internships or fieldwork and Federal Work-Study available. Support available to part-time students. Financial award application deadline: 5/1; financial award applicants required to submit FAFSA. *Faculty research:* Cognitive behavioral interventions for depression, eating disorders and compliance. *Unit head:* Carrie King, Graduate Program Director, 414-258-4810 Ext. 318, E-mail: kingc@mtmary.edu. *Application contact:* Carrie King, Graduate Program Director, 414-258-4810 Ext. 318, E-mail: kingc@mtmary.edu.

Neumann University, Program in Pastoral Counseling, Aston, PA 19014-1298. Offers pastoral counseling (MS, CAS); spiritual direction (CSD). Part-time and evening/weekend programs available. *Faculty:* 3 full-time (2 women), 7 part-time/adjunct (5 women). *Students:* 10 full-time (4 women), 89 part-time (66 women); includes 14 minority (6 African Americans, 1 American Indian/Alaska Native, 4 Asian Americans or Pacific Islanders, 3 Hispanic Americans). Average age 49. 50 applicants, 100% accepted, 45 enrolled. In 2009, 23 master's awarded. *Degree requirements:* For master's, clinical case study. *Entrance requirements:* Additional exam requirements/recommendations for international students: Required—TOEFL. *Application deadline:* Applications are processed on a rolling basis. Application fee: $50. Electronic applications accepted. *Expenses:* Tuition: Full-time $10,260; part-time $570 per credit hour. *Financial support:* In 2009–10, 8 students received support. Available to part-time students. Application deadline: 3/15. *Faculty research:* Development of an integrated model of religion/psychology for remediation and prevention of emotional disturbance. *Unit head:* Dr. Leonard DiPaul, Executive Director, 610-558-5220, Fax: 610-459-1370, E-mail: dipall@neumann.edu. *Application contact:* Kittie D. Pain, Associate Director of Admissions, Graduate and Adult Programs, 610-558-5613, Fax: 610-558-5652, E-mail: paink@neumann.edu.

New Brunswick Theological Seminary, Graduate and Professional Programs, Program in Metro-Urban Ministry, New Brunswick, NJ 08901-1196. Offers theological studies (D Min). Part-time programs available. *Degree requirements:* For doctorate, thesis/dissertation. *Entrance requirements:* For doctorate, M Div. *Faculty research:* Urban-land use planning, theology of the city.

New Orleans Baptist Theological Seminary, Graduate and Professional Programs, Division of Pastoral Ministries, New Orleans, LA 70126-4858. Offers M Div, MAMFC, D Min, PhD. *Accreditation:* ACIPE. *Degree requirements:* For doctorate, thesis/dissertation; for M Div, project report. *Entrance requirements:* For master's and doctorate, GRE General Test.

The Nigerian Baptist Theological Seminary, Graduate Studies, Ogbomoso, Nigeria. Offers church music (M Div, M Th, Diploma); divinity (M Div); ministry (D Min); religious education (M Div, M Th, PhD); theological studies (MATS); theology (M Th, PhD). Part-time programs available. *Degree requirements:* For master's, thesis, 2 Nigerian languages; for M Div, thesis/dissertation (for some programs), 2 biblical languages; for Diploma, thesis or alternative.

Northern Baptist Theological Seminary, Graduate and Professional Programs, Lombard, IL 60148-5698. Offers Biblical studies (MA); Christian ministries (MACM); divinity (M Div); ministry (D Min); New Testament (MA); Old Testament (MA); pastoral care and counseling (MA). *Accreditation:* ATS. Part-time programs available. *Faculty:* 5 full-time (0 women), 30 part-time/adjunct (5 women). *Students:* 42 full-time (6 women), 95 part-time (45 women); includes 67 minority (51 African Americans, 12 Asian Americans or Pacific Islanders, 4 Hispanic Americans), 3 international. *Degree requirements:* For doctorate, thesis/dissertation; for M Div, field experience. *Entrance requirements:* For master's, official transcripts, letter of reference from pastor, autobiographical statement (400 words or more); for doctorate, 3 years in the ministry post-M Div, 3 letters of reference. Additional exam requirements/recommendations for international students: Required—TOEFL (minimum score 550 paper-based; 213 computer-based). *Application deadline:* Applications are processed on a rolling basis. Application fee: $35. Electronic applications accepted. *Expenses:* Tuition: Full-time $15,800; part-time $2640 per trimester. Required fees: $115 per trimester. One-time fee: $300. Tuition and fees vary according to course load. *Financial support:* Career-related internships or fieldwork and scholarships/grants available. Support available to part-time students. Financial award application deadline: 9/1. *Faculty research:* Theology, worship studies, church history, evangelism, Bible. *Unit head:* Alistair Brown, Chief Academic Officer, 630-620-2101, Fax: 630-620-2190. *Application contact:* Greg Henson, Executive Director of External Relations, 630-620-2180, Fax: 630-620-2190, E-mail: admissions@seminary.edu.

North Greenville University, T. Walter Brashier Graduate School, Greer, SC 29651. Offers Christian ministry (MCM); human resources (MBA). Part-time and evening/weekend programs available. Postbaccalaureate distance learning degree programs offered (no on-campus study). *Faculty:* 4 full-time (1 woman), 16 part-time/adjunct (1 woman). *Students:* 69 full-time (29 women), 104 part-time (33 women); includes 30 minority (27 African Americans, 3 Hispanic Americans), 2 international. Average age 32. 180 applicants, 98% accepted, 173 enrolled. In 2009, 34 master's awarded. *Degree requirements:* For master's, comprehensive exam (for some programs), thesis or alternative, capstone course. *Entrance requirements:* For master's, GMAT, GRE, minimum GPA of 2.25 overall, 2.5 in major. Additional exam requirements/recommendations for international students: Required—TOEFL (minimum score 550 paper-based; 213 computer-based). *Application deadline:* For fall admission, 8/1 for domestic students, 6/1 for international students; for winter admission, 1/1 for domestic students, 10/1 for international students; for spring admission, 3/1 for domestic students, 1/1 for international students. Applications are processed on a rolling basis. Application fee: $30. Electronic applications accepted. *Financial support:* In 2009–10, 86 students received support. Federal Work-Study, institutionally sponsored loans, scholarships/grants, and tuition waivers (partial) available. Support available to part-time students. Financial award applicants required to submit FAFSA. *Faculty research:* Organizational behavior, church growth, homiletics, human resources, business strategy. *Unit head:* Dr. Joseph Samuel Isgett, Vice President for Graduate Studies, 864-877-3052, Fax: 864-877-1653, E-mail: sisgett@ngu.edu. *Application contact:* Tawana P. Scott, Director of Graduate Enrollment, 864-877-1598, Fax: 864-877-1653, E-mail: tscott@ngu.edu.

North Park Theological Seminary, Graduate and Professional Programs, Program in Christian Ministry, Chicago, IL 60625-4895. Offers MACM, MA/MBA, MA/MM.

North Park Theological Seminary, Graduate and Professional Programs, Program in Christian Studies, Chicago, IL 60625-4895. Offers adult ministry (Certificate); camping and retreat ministry (Certificate); children and family ministry (Certificate); Christian formation-all ages (Certificate); Christian spirituality (Certificate); faith and health (Certificate); justice ministry

Pastoral Ministry and Counseling

North Park Theological Seminary (continued)
(Certificate); leadership and administration (Certificate); spiritual direction (Certificate); youth ministry (Certificate). *Accreditation:* ACIPE. Part-time programs available. *Entrance requirements:* For degree, minimum GPA of 2.5. Additional exam requirements/recommendations for international students: Required—TOEFL.

Northwest Nazarene University, Graduate Studies, Program in Religion, Nampa, ID 83686-5897. Offers Christian education (MA); missional leadership (MA); pastoral ministry (MA); religion (M Div); spiritual formation (MA). Part-time and evening/weekend programs available. Postbaccalaureate distance learning degree programs offered (no on-campus study). Electronic applications accepted.

Northwest University, College of Ministry, Kirkland, WA 98033. Offers ministry (MA); missional leadership (MA); theology and culture (MA). *Faculty:* 11 full-time (1 woman), 12 part-time/adjunct (2 women). *Students:* 16 full-time (3 women), 24 part-time (7 women); includes 3 minority (all African Americans). 39 applicants, 97% accepted, 22 enrolled. *Entrance requirements:* Additional exam requirements/recommendations for international students: Required—TOEFL (minimum score 550 paper-based). Application fee: $75. *Unit head:* Dr. Kent Ingle, Dean, 425-889-5253, E-mail: kent.ingle@northwestu.edu. *Application contact:* Roy Rowland, Director of Graduate and Professional Studies Enrollment, 425-889-7787, Fax: 425-803-3059, E-mail: gpse@northwestu.edu.

Notre Dame College, Graduate Studies, South Euclid, OH 44121-4293. Offers accounting (Certificate); creative critical thinking (M Ed); financial services management (Certificate); information systems (Certificate); learning disabilities (M Ed); management (Certificate); paralegal (Certificate); pastoral ministry (Certificate); reading (M Ed); teacher education (Certificate). Part-time and evening/weekend programs available. *Degree requirements:* For master's, thesis. *Entrance requirements:* For master's, GRE General Test, MAT, minimum GPA of 2.75, valid teaching certificate. *Faculty research:* Cognitive psychology, teaching critical thinking in the classroom.

Oakwood University, Program in Pastoral Studies, Huntsville, AL 35896. Offers MA. *Entrance requirements:* For master's, Biblical Literacy Entrance Test (BLET), minimum cumulative GPA of 2.5, 2 letters of recommendation, current resume, 3 years of pastoral or local church leadership experience. Additional exam requirements/recommendations for international students: Required—TOEFL (minimum score 500 paper-based; 173 computer-based).

Oblate School of Theology, Graduate and Professional Programs, San Antonio, TX 78216-6693. Offers divinity (M Div); Hispanic ministry (D Min); pastoral ministry (MAP Min); pastoral studies (Certificate); spirituality (MA Sp); supervision (D Min), including clinical pastoral education, general supervision; theology (MA Th); M Div/MA Th. *Accreditation:* ACIPE; ATS (one or more programs are accredited). Part-time programs available. *Faculty:* 22 full-time (7 women), 7 part-time/adjunct (1 woman). *Students:* 91 full-time (5 women), 76 part-time (43 women); includes 69 minority (5 African Americans, 1 American Indian/Alaska Native, 15 Asian Americans or Pacific Islanders, 48 Hispanic Americans), 35 international. Average age 39. 29 applicants, 100% accepted, 29 enrolled. In 2009, 8 first professional degrees, 11 master's, 4 doctorates awarded. *Degree requirements:* For master's, thesis (for some programs), practicum; for doctorate, paper, practicum; for M Div, one foreign language, seminar. *Entrance requirements:* For M Div, MAT, interview, course work in philosophy and theology; for master's, MAT, interview, course work in theology or religious studies, minimum GPA of 2.5; for doctorate, M Div. Additional exam requirements/recommendations for international students: Required—TOEFL (minimum score 197 computer-based; 71 iBT). *Application deadline:* For fall admission, 6/15 priority date for domestic and international students; for spring admission, 12/30 for domestic and international students. Applications are processed on a rolling basis. Application fee: $45. *Expenses:* Tuition: Full-time $11,960; part-time $460 per credit. Required fees: $175 per semester. Tuition and fees vary according to course level, course load and degree level. *Financial support:* Scholarships/grants available. Support available to part-time students. Financial award application deadline: 8/1; financial award applicants required to submit FAFSA. *Unit head:* Sr. Elaine Brothers, Academic Dean, 210-341-1366, Fax: 214-341-4519, E-mail: ebrothers@ost.edu. *Application contact:* James Oberhausen, Director of Admission/Registrar, 210-341-1366 Ext. 212, Fax: 210-341-4519, E-mail: registrar@ost.edu.

Oklahoma Christian University, Graduate School of Theology, Oklahoma City, OK 73136-1100. Offers family life ministry (MA); ministry (M Div, MA); youth ministry (MA). Part-time programs available. Postbaccalaureate distance learning degree programs offered (minimal on-campus study). *Degree requirements:* For master's, one foreign language, comprehensive exam, field experience; for M Div, 2 foreign languages, comprehensive exam, field experience. *Entrance requirements:* For M Div and master's, minimum undergraduate GPA of 3.0. Additional exam requirements/recommendations for international students: Required—TOEFL (minimum score 550 paper-based; 213 computer-based). Electronic applications accepted. *Faculty research:* Early marriage adjustment, new religions, Ethiopic language, church health, Hebrew rhetoric.

Oral Roberts University, School of Theology and Missions, Tulsa, OK 74171. Offers biblical literature (MA), including advanced languages, Judaic-Christian studies; Christian counseling (MA), including marriage and family therapy; divinity (M Div); missions (MA); practical theology (MA); theological/historical studies (MA); theology (D Min). *Accreditation:* ATS; NASM. Part-time programs available. Postbaccalaureate distance learning degree programs offered (minimal on-campus study). *Degree requirements:* For master's, thesis (for some programs), practicum/internship; for doctorate, thesis/dissertation, applied research project; for M Div, one foreign language, field experience. *Entrance requirements:* For M Div and master's, GRE General Test or MAT, minimum GPA of 2.5; for doctorate, M Div, minimum GPA of 3.0, 3 years of full-time ministry experience. Additional exam requirements/recommendations for international students: Required—TOEFL (minimum score 550 paper-based; 213 computer-based; 79 iBT). Electronic applications accepted.

Ottawa University, Graduate Studies-Arizona, Program in Professional Counseling, Ottawa, KS 66067-3399. Offers Christian counseling (MA); expressive arts therapy (MA); marriage and family therapy (MA); treatment of trauma, abuse and deprivation (MA). Programs offered in Mesa, Phoenix, Tempe and West Valley, AZ. Part-time and evening/weekend programs available. Postbaccalaureate distance learning degree programs offered. *Degree requirements:* For master's, comprehensive exam, thesis or alternative, field experience, practicum. *Entrance requirements:* For master's, minimum undergraduate GPA of 3.0; course work in theories of personality, abnormal psychology, and human growth and development. Additional exam requirements/recommendations for international students: Required—TOEFL (minimum score 550 paper-based; 213 computer-based).

Philadelphia Biblical University, Department of Christian Counseling, Langhorne, PA 19047-2990. Offers Christian counseling (MSCC). Part-time and evening/weekend programs available. *Faculty:* 2 full-time (0 women), 8 part-time/adjunct (7 women). *Students:* 3 full-time (all women), 110 part-time (76 women); includes 45 minority (40 African Americans, 2 Asian Americans or Pacific Islanders, 3 Hispanic Americans), 2 international. Average age 37. 77 applicants, 45% accepted, 29 enrolled. In 2009, 38 master's awarded. *Entrance requirements:* Additional exam requirements/recommendations for international students: Required—TOEFL (minimum score 550 paper-based; 213 computer-based). *Application deadline:* Applications are processed on a rolling basis. Application fee: $25. Electronic applications accepted. *Expenses:* Tuition: Full-time $10,350; part-time $575 per credit. Required fees: $10; $10 per year. Tuition and fees vary according to program. *Financial support:* In 2009–10, 31 students received support. Scholarships/grants available. Support available to part-time students. Financial award applicants required to submit FAFSA. *Unit head:* Dr. Jeff Black, Chair, 215-702-4546, E-mail: dcheyney@pbu.edu. *Application contact:* Gwen Dorsey, Enrollment Counselor, Graduate Counseling, 800-572-2472, Fax: 215-702-4248, E-mail: gdorsey@pbu.edu.

Phillips Theological Seminary, Programs in Theology, Doctor of Ministry Program, Tulsa, OK 74116. Offers parish ministry (D Min); pastoral counseling (D Min); practices of ministry (D Min). *Accreditation:* ATS. Part-time programs available. *Degree requirements:* For doctorate, thesis/dissertation. *Entrance requirements:* For doctorate, M Div, minimum GPA of 3.0, 3 years of post-M Div pastoral experience. *Expenses:* Contact institution. *Faculty research:* Politics and theology, media and theology, ecology and theology.

Phoenix Seminary, Graduate Programs, Scottsdale, AZ 85254. Offers biblical communication (M Div); biblical leadership (MA); biblical studies (Graduate Diploma); Christian counseling (Graduate Diploma); counseling and family (M Div); intercultural studies (Graduate Diploma); leadership development (M Div, Graduate Diploma); ministry (D Min); professional counseling (MA); women's studies (Graduate Diploma). *Accreditation:* ATS (one or more programs are accredited). Part-time and evening/weekend programs available. *Faculty:* 5 full-time (0 women), 5 part-time/adjunct (0 women). *Students:* 26 full-time (8 women), 151 part-time (39 women); includes 34 minority (18 African Americans, 2 American Indian/Alaska Native, 5 Asian Americans or Pacific Islanders, 9 Hispanic Americans), 1 international. 41 applicants, 90% accepted, 30 enrolled. In 2009, 21 master's, 2 doctorates, 12 other advanced degrees awarded. *Degree requirements:* For master's, 2 foreign languages, comprehensive exam; for doctorate, 2 foreign languages, thesis/dissertation. *Entrance requirements:* For master's, undergraduate degree with minimum GPA of 2.5; for doctorate, M Div (94 hours) with minimum GPA of 3.0. Additional exam requirements/recommendations for international students: Required—TOEFL (minimum score 587 paper-based; 240 computer-based; 92 iBT), TWE (minimum score 4.5). *Application deadline:* For fall admission, 7/1 for domestic students; for spring admission, 11/1 for domestic students. Applications are processed on a rolling basis. Application fee: $90. *Expenses:* Tuition: Full-time $9420; part-time $410 per credit hour. Required fees: $60 per semester. Tuition and fees vary according to course load and degree level. *Financial support:* Institutionally sponsored loans and scholarships/grants available. Support available to part-time students. Financial award application deadline: 6/1; financial award applicants required to submit FAFSA. *Application contact:* Roma Royer, Director of Admissions and Academic Services, 602-850-8000 Ext. 111, Fax: 602-850-8080, E-mail: rroyer@ps.edu.

Providence College and Theological Seminary, Theological Seminary, Otterburne, MB R0A 1G0, Canada. Offers children's ministry (Certificate); Christian studies (MA, Certificate); counseling (MA); cross-cultural discipleship (Certificate); divinity (M Div); educational studies (MA), including counseling psychology, educational ministries, student development, teaching English to speakers of other languages, training teachers of English to speakers of other languages; global studies (MA); lay counseling (Diploma); ministry (D Min); teaching English to speakers of other languages (Certificate); theological studies (MA); training teacher of English to speakers of other languages (Certificate); youth ministry (Certificate). *Accreditation:* ATS. Part-time programs available. *Degree requirements:* For master's, variable foreign language requirement, thesis (for some programs); for doctorate, thesis/dissertation; for M Div, 2 foreign languages, comprehensive exam, thesis/dissertation (for some programs). *Entrance requirements:* Additional exam requirements/recommendations for international students: Recommended—TOEFL (minimum score 550 paper-based; 213 computer-based). *Faculty research:* Studies in Isaiah, theology of sin.

Reformed Theological Seminary–Charlotte Campus, Graduate and Professional Programs, Charlotte, NC 28226-6318. Offers biblical studies (MA); ministry (D Min); pastoral ministry (M Div); theological studies (MA). Part-time programs available. *Degree requirements:* For master's, comprehensive exam; for doctorate, thesis/dissertation; for M Div, 2 foreign languages, comprehensive exam. *Entrance requirements:* For master's, minimum GPA of 2.6; for doctorate, minimum GPA of 3.0. Additional exam requirements/recommendations for international students: Required—TOEFL (minimum score 550 paper-based; 213 computer-based). Electronic applications accepted.

Reformed Theological Seminary–Jackson Campus, Graduate and Professional Programs, Jackson, MS 39209-3099. Offers Bible, theology, and missions (Certificate); biblical studies (MA); Christian education (M Div, MA); counseling (M Div); divinity (M Div, Diploma); marriage and family therapy (MA); ministry (D Min); missions (M Div, MA, D Min); New Testament (Th M); Old Testament (Th M); theological studies (MA); theology (Th M); M Div/MA. *Accreditation:* AAMFT/COAMFTE (one or more programs are accredited); ATS (one or more programs are accredited). *Degree requirements:* For master's, thesis (for some programs), fieldwork; for doctorate, 2 foreign languages, thesis/dissertation; for M Div, 2 foreign languages, thesis/dissertation (for some programs). *Entrance requirements:* For M Div and master's, minimum GPA of 2.6; for doctorate, minimum GPA of 3.0. Additional exam requirements/recommendations for international students: Required—TOEFL.

Reformed Theological Seminary–Orlando Campus, Graduate Program, Oviedo, FL 32765-7197. Offers biblical studies (MA); counseling (MA); ministry (D Min); reformation studies (Th M); theological studies (MA); theology (M Div); MA/Certificate. Part-time programs available. Postbaccalaureate distance learning degree programs offered (minimal on-campus study). *Entrance requirements:* For M Div and master's, minimum GPA of 2.6. Electronic applications accepted.

Regent University, Graduate School, School of Divinity, Virginia Beach, VA 23464-9800. Offers Biblical studies (MA); leadership and renewal (D Min); missiology (M Div, MA); practical theology (M Div, MA); renewal studies (PhD); M Div/M Ed; M Div/MA; M Div/MBA; M Ed/MA; MBA/MA. *Accreditation:* ACIPE; ATS. Part-time programs available. Postbaccalaureate distance learning degree programs offered (minimal on-campus study). *Faculty:* 19 full-time (4 women), 28 part-time/adjunct (5 women). *Students:* 108 full-time (53 women), 436 part-time (171 women); includes 244 minority (214 African Americans, 2 American Indian/Alaska Native, 13 Asian Americans or Pacific Islanders, 15 Hispanic Americans), 19 international. Average age 40. 349 applicants, 63% accepted, 97 enrolled. In 2009, 31 first professional degrees, 39 master's, 5 doctorates awarded. *Degree requirements:* For master's, comprehensive exam, thesis or alternative, internship; for doctorate, thesis/dissertation or alternative; for M Div, internship. *Entrance requirements:* For M Div, GRE General Test or MAT, minimum undergraduate GPA of 3.0, minimum 3 years of ministry experience, transcripts, recommendations; for master's, GRE General Test or MAT, minimum undergraduate GPA of 2.75, writing sample, clergy recommendation; for doctorate, M Div or theological master's degree; minimum graduate GPA of 3.5 (PhD), 3.0 (D Min); recommendations; writing sample; transcripts. Additional exam requirements/recommendations for international students: Required—TOEFL (minimum score 577 paper-based; 233 computer-based). *Application deadline:* For fall admission, 5/1 priority date for domestic students. Applications are processed on a rolling basis. Application fee: $50. Electronic applications accepted. *Expenses:* Contact institution. *Financial support:* In 2009–10, 401 students received support; fellowships with full and partial tuition reimbursements available, career-related internships or fieldwork, scholarships/grants, tuition waivers (full and partial), and unspecified assistantships available. Support available to part-time students. Financial award application deadline: 9/1; financial award applicants required to submit FAFSA. *Faculty research:* Greek and Hebrew, theology, spiritual formation, global missions and world Christianity, women's studies. *Unit head:* Dr. Michael Palmer, Dean, 757-352-4406, Fax: 757-352-4597, E-mail: mpalmer@regent.edu. *Application contact:* Matthew Chadwick, Director of Admissions, 800-373-5504, Fax: 757-352-4381, E-mail: admissions@regent.edu.

Regis College, Graduate and Professional Programs, Toronto, ON M4Y 2R5, Canada. Offers eastern Christian studies (Certificate); Ignatian studies (Diploma); Lonergan studies (Diploma); ministry (D Min); ministry and spirituality (MAMS); philosophical studies (Diploma); retreat direction (Certificate); sacred theology (STB, STM, STD, STL); spiritual direction (Diploma); spiritual theology (Diploma); theological studies (MTS, Diploma); theology (M Div, MA, Th M, PhD, Th D); M Div/MA. *Accreditation:* ATS (one or more programs are accredited). *Faculty:* 13 full-time (3 women), 6 part-time/adjunct (1 woman). *Students:* 86 full-time (28 women), 130 part-time (80 women); includes 39 minority (9 African Americans, 1 American Indian/Alaska Native, 27 Asian Americans or Pacific Islanders, 2 Hispanic Americans), 51 international. Average age 46. 116 applicants, 83% accepted, 67 enrolled. In 2009, 13 first professional degrees, 12 master's, 3 doctorates, 40 other advanced degrees awarded. Terminal master's awarded for partial completion of doctoral program. *Degree requirements:* For master's, 2 foreign languages, thesis; for doctorate, 3 foreign languages, comprehensive exam, thesis/dissertation; for first professional degree, comprehensive exam. *Entrance requirements:* For first professional degree and other advanced degree, minimum GPA of 3.0; for master's, minimum GPA of 3.3; for doctorate, minimum GPA of 3.7. Additional exam requirements/recommendations for international students: Required—TOEFL (minimum score 580 paper-based; 237 computer-based; 93 iBT), TWE (minimum score 5). *Application deadline:* For fall admission, 3/15 priority date for domestic and international students; for winter admission, 12/1 for domestic and international students; for spring admission, 3/15 for domestic and international students. Applications are processed on a rolling basis. Application fee: $25. *Financial support:* In 2009–10, 61 students received support. Career-related internships or fieldwork and scholarships/grants available. Support available to part-time students. Financial award application deadline: 3/15. *Unit head:* Dr. Gordon Rixon, Dean, 416-922-5474 Ext. 225, Fax: 416-922-2898, E-mail: gordon.rixon@utoronto.ca. *Application contact:* Elaine Chu, Registrar, 416-922-5474 Ext. 226, Fax: 416-922-2898, E-mail: regis.registrar@utoronto.ca.

Roberts Wesleyan College, Division of Social Sciences, Rochester, NY 14624-1997. Offers counseling in ministry (MA); school counseling (MS); school psychology (MS).

Sacred Heart Major Seminary, School of Theology, Detroit, MI 48206-1799. Offers pastoral studies (MAPS); theology (M Div, MA). *Accreditation:* ACIPE; ATS. Part-time and evening/weekend programs available. *Degree requirements:* For master's, one foreign language, thesis optional, integrating project; for M Div, integrating seminar. *Entrance requirements:* For M Div and master's, GRE, previous course work in philosophy and theology. *Faculty research:* Local church history, patristics, spirituality, religious education.

St. Ambrose University, College of Arts and Sciences, Program in Pastoral Theology, Davenport, IA 52803-2898. Offers MP Th. Part-time programs available. *Faculty:* 2 full-time (1 woman), 1 part-time/adjunct (0 women). *Students:* 20 part-time (9 women). Average age 42. 20 applicants, 100% accepted, 20 enrolled. In 2009, 2 master's awarded. *Degree requirements:* For master's, integration project. *Entrance requirements:* For master's, minimum GPA of 2.6, prior pastoral experience, 9 credits of course work in theology. Additional exam requirements/recommendations for international students: Required—TOEFL. *Application deadline:* For fall admission, 8/15 priority date for domestic students; for winter admission, 12/15 priority date for domestic students; for spring admission, 1/1 priority date for domestic students. Applications are processed on a rolling basis. Application fee: $25. Electronic applications accepted. *Expenses:* Contact institution. *Financial support:* Career-related internships or fieldwork, scholarships/grants, and tuition waivers (partial) available. Financial award application deadline: 8/15; financial award applicants required to submit FAFSA. *Faculty research:* Theological education, ecclesiology, spirituality and liturgy, medical ethics. *Unit head:* Dr. Corinne M. Winter, Director, 563-333-6442, Fax: 563-333-6243, E-mail: wintercorinnem@sau.edu. *Application contact:* Dr. Corinne M. Winter, Director, 563-333-6442, Fax: 563-333-6243, E-mail: wintercorinnem@sau.edu.

St. Augustine's Seminary of Toronto, Graduate and Professional Programs, Scarborough, ON M1M 1M3, Canada. Offers divinity (M Div); lay ministry (Diploma); religious education (MRE); theological studies (MTS, Diploma). *Accreditation:* ATS. Part-time and evening/weekend programs available. *Degree requirements:* For M Div, comprehensive exam (for some programs), thesis/dissertation optional, field education. *Entrance requirements:* Course work in philosophy. Additional exam requirements/recommendations for international students: Required—TOEFL (minimum score 580 paper-based; 237 computer-based), TWE (minimum score 5).

Saint Bernard's School of Theology and Ministry, Graduate and Professional Programs, Rochester, NY 14618. Offers pastoral studies (MA, Certificate); theological studies (MA); theology (M Div). *Accreditation:* ATS (one or more programs are accredited). Part-time and evening/weekend programs available. *Faculty:* 3 full-time (2 women), 8 part-time/adjunct (3 women). *Students:* 2 full-time (1 woman), 125 part-time (58 women); includes 5 minority (2 African Americans, 1 Asian American or Pacific Islander, 2 Hispanic Americans). Average age 50. 42 applicants, 100% accepted, 42 enrolled. In 2009, 7 first professional degrees, 23 master's awarded. *Degree requirements:* For master's, variable foreign language requirement, thesis (for some programs). *Entrance requirements:* For M Div, minimum GPA of 2.0; for master's, minimum GPA of 2.5. *Application deadline:* Applications are processed on a rolling basis. Application fee: $75. *Expenses:* Tuition: Part-time $1464 per course. Required fees: $30 per semester. *Financial support:* In 2009–10, 33 students received support; fellowships, research assistantships, teaching assistantships, career-related internships or fieldwork, scholarships/grants, and tuition waivers (partial) available. Support available to part-time students. Financial award application deadline: 4/15; financial award applicants required to submit FAFSA. *Unit head:* Dr. Patricia Schoelles, President, 585-271-3657 Ext. 276, Fax: 585-271-2045, E-mail: pschoelles@stbernards.edu. *Application contact:* Laura Smith, Director of Admissions and Financial Aid, 585-271-3657 Ext. 289, Fax: 585-271-2045, E-mail: admissions@stbernards.edu.

Saint Francis Seminary, Graduate and Professional Programs, St. Francis, WI 53235-3795. Offers M Div, MAPS. *Accreditation:* ACIPE; ATS. Part-time programs available. *Degree requirements:* For master's, comprehensive exam; for M Div, thesis/dissertation. *Entrance requirements:* For M Div and master's, Otis IQ Test, Terman Concept Mastery Test, interview. Additional exam requirements/recommendations for international students: Required—TOEFL (minimum score 550 paper-based).

St. John's Seminary, Graduate and Professional Programs, Camarillo, CA 93012-2598. Offers divinity (M Div); pastoral ministry (MAPM); theology (MA). *Accreditation:* ATS. Part-time programs available. *Faculty:* 21 full-time (4 women), 6 part-time/adjunct (1 woman). *Students:* 81 full-time (5 women), 10 part-time (4 women); includes 45 minority (18 Asian Americans or Pacific Islanders, 27 Hispanic Americans), 19 international. Average age 34. 37 applicants, 86% accepted, 32 enrolled. In 2009, 13 first professional degrees, 1 master's awarded. *Degree requirements:* For master's, comprehensive exam (for some programs), thesis optional, comprehensive integration paper (MAPM); for M Div, parish internship. *Entrance requirements:* For M Div, GRE General Test, bishop's approbation; for master's, GRE General Test, minimum GPA of 3.5 (MA), 2.5 (MAPM). Additional exam requirements/recommendations for international students: Required—TOEFL (minimum score 550 paper-based; 213 computer-based; 79 iBT). *Application deadline:* For fall admission, 7/15 priority date for domestic students. Applications are processed on a rolling basis. Application fee: $0. Electronic applications accepted. *Expenses:* Tuition: Full-time $13,250; part-time $442 per unit. One-time fee: $4446.52 full-time; $25 part-time. Full-time tuition and fees vary according to course load and program. *Faculty research:* Biblical studies, moral theology, historical studies, systematic theology, spiritual theology. *Unit head:* Rev. Richard Benson, Academic Dean, 805-482-2755, Fax: 805-482-3470, E-mail: rbensoncm@stjohnsem.edu. *Application contact:* Esme M. Takahashi, Registrar, 805-482-2755 Ext. 1014, Fax: 805-482-3470, E-mail: registrar-sjs@stjohnsem.edu.

St. John's University, St. John's College of Liberal Arts and Sciences, Department of Theology and Religious Studies, Queens, NY 11439. Offers pastoral ministry (Certificate); priestly studies (M Div); theology (MA, Certificate). *Accreditation:* ACIPE. Part-time and evening/weekend programs available. *Students:* 11 full-time (2 women), 29 part-time (22 women); includes 8 minority (3 African Americans, 2 Asian Americans or Pacific Islanders, 3 Hispanic Americans), 9 international. Average age 44. 27 applicants, 78% accepted, 9 enrolled. In 2009, 9 master's, 1 other advanced degree awarded. *Degree requirements:* For master's, thesis optional; for M Div, thesis/dissertation optional. *Entrance requirements:* For M Div and master's, minimum GPA of 3.0. Additional exam requirements/recommendations for international students: Required—TOEFL (minimum score 500 paper-based; 173 computer-based; 61 iBT), IELTS (minimum score 5.5). *Application deadline:* For fall admission, 5/1 priority date for domestic and international students; for spring admission, 11/1 priority date for domestic and international students. Applications are processed on a rolling basis. Application fee: $70. Electronic applications accepted. *Expenses:* Tuition: Full-time $16,290; part-time $905 per credit. Required fees: $300; $150 per semester. Tuition and fees vary according to program. *Financial support:* Research assistantships, scholarships/grants available. Support available to part-time students. Financial award application deadline: 3/1; financial award applicants required to submit FAFSA. *Faculty research:* Systematic theology, moral theory, Biblical studies, pastoral theology, church history. *Unit head:* Fr. Michael Whalen, Chair, 718-990-1556, E-mail: whalenm@stjohns.edu. *Application contact:* Kathleen Davis, Director of Graduate Admission, 718-990-2790, Fax: 718-990-5686, E-mail: gradhelp@stjohns.edu.

Saint John's University, Saint John's School of Theology and Seminary, Collegeville, MN 56321. Offers divinity (M Div); liturgical music (MA); liturgical studies (MA); pastoral ministry (MA); theology (MA), including church history, liturgy, monastic studies, scripture, spirituality, systematics; M Div/MA. *Accreditation:* ATS. Part-time programs available. Postbaccalaureate distance learning degree programs offered (no on-campus study). *Degree requirements:* For master's, one foreign language, comprehensive exam (for some programs), thesis (for some programs). *Entrance requirements:* For master's, GRE General Test or MAT. Electronic applications accepted. *Faculty research:* Religious education, biblical literature.

Saint Leo University, Graduate Studies in Theology, Saint Leo, FL 33574-6665. Offers theology (MA). Part-time and evening/weekend programs available. *Faculty:* 7 full-time (0 women), 1 part-time/adjunct (0 women). *Students:* 153 full-time (37 women); includes 15 minority (8 African Americans, 1 Asian American or Pacific Islander, 6 Hispanic Americans). Average age 52. In 2009, 3 master's awarded. *Degree requirements:* For master's, comprehensive project. *Entrance requirements:* For master's, bachelor's degree from regionally-accredited college or university with minimum GPA of 3.0, letter of recommendation. Additional exam requirements/recommendations for international students: Required—TOEFL (minimum score 550 paper-based; 213 computer-based; 80 iBT). *Application deadline:* For fall admission, 7/1 priority date for domestic and international students; for spring admission, 11/1 priority date for domestic and international students. Applications are processed on a rolling basis. Application fee: $75. Electronic applications accepted. *Expenses:* Tuition: Part-time $1767 per course. Required fees: $115 per course. *Financial support:* In 2009–10, 1 student received support. Federal Work-Study and health care benefits available. *Faculty research:* Ecclesiology and the Second Vatican Council, sacramental theology and the liturgical movement, Christian and Eastern religious traditions, Ecumenism, ministry and technology. *Unit head:* Dr. William Ditewig, Director, 352-588-7297, Fax: 352-588-8404, E-mail: william.ditewig@saintleo.edu. *Application contact:* Jared Welling, Director, Graduate/Weekend and Evening Admission, 800-707-8846, Fax: 352-588-7873, E-mail: grad.admissions@saintleo.edu.

Saint Mary-of-the-Woods College, Program in Pastoral Theology, Saint Mary-of-the-Woods, IN 47876. Offers pastoral theology (MA); youth ministry (Graduate Certificate). Part-time and evening/weekend programs available. Postbaccalaureate distance learning degree programs offered (minimal on-campus study). *Degree requirements:* For master's, thesis, qualifying exam.

St. Mary's University, Graduate School, Department of Theology, San Antonio, TX 78228-8507. Offers pastoral ministry (MA); theology (MA); JD/MA. Part-time and evening/weekend programs available. Postbaccalaureate distance learning degree programs offered (no on-campus study). *Degree requirements:* For master's, comprehensive exam, practicum (pastoral administration). *Entrance requirements:* For master's, GRE General Test, MAT, 12 credit hours in theology/philosophy. Additional exam requirements/recommendations for international students: Required—TOEFL (minimum score 550 paper-based; 213 computer-based; 80 iBT). Electronic applications accepted. *Expenses:* Tuition: Full-time $8004. Required fees: $536. One-time fee: $5 full-time. Full-time tuition and fees vary according to program. *Faculty research:* Bioethics; perceptions of ministry; Marian doctrines and the contemporary church; Jaspers, peace, and justice.

Saint Mary's University of Minnesota, Schools of Graduate and Professional Programs, Graduate School of Health and Human Services, Institute in Pastoral Ministries, Winona, MN 55987-1399. Offers Canon law (Certificate); pastoral administration (MA); pastoral ministries (MA). *Unit head:* Dr. Gregory Sobolewski, Director, 507-457-1767, Fax: 507-457-1752, E-mail: gsobolew@smumn.edu. *Application contact:* Jami Spitzer, Information Contact, 507-457-7500, E-mail: jspitzer@smumn.edu.

Saint Paul University, Faculty of Canon Law, Ottawa, ON K1S 1C4, Canada. Offers canon law (MCL, JCD, PhD, Graduate Certificate, JCL); canonical practice (Graduate Certificate); ecclesiastical administration (Graduate Certificate). Part-time programs available. *Faculty:* 9 full-time (1 woman), 8 part-time/adjunct (1 woman). *Students:* 54 full-time (10 women), 6 part-time (2 women); includes 31 minority (15 African Americans, 15 Asian Americans or Pacific Islanders, 1 Hispanic American). Average age 40. 45 applicants, 84% accepted, 38 enrolled. In 2009, 11 master's, 3 doctorates, 15 other advanced degrees awarded. *Degree requirements:* For master's, one foreign language; for doctorate, one foreign language, comprehensive exam, thesis/dissertation; for other advanced degree, one foreign language, comprehensive exam and seminar paper (JCL). *Entrance requirements:* For master's, appropriate bachelor's degree, 18 credits in theology; for doctorate, JCL or MCL; for other advanced degree, B Th or equivalent (JCL), appropriate bachelor's degree, 18 credits in theology. *Application deadline:* For fall admission, 8/15 priority date for domestic students, 3/15 priority date for international students. Applications are processed on a rolling basis. Application fee: $70 Canadian dollars. *Financial support:* Scholarships/grants and bursaries available. *Faculty research:* Questions related to Church law. *Unit head:* Dr. Anne Asselin, Dean, 613-751-4018, Fax: 613-751-4036, E-mail: canonlaw@ustpaul.ca. *Application contact:* Beverly Ruth Kavanaugh, Administrative Assistant, 613-751-4018, Fax: 613-751-4036, E-mail: bkavanaugh@ustpaul.ca.

Saint Paul University, Faculty of Human Sciences, Program in Counseling and Spirituality, Ottawa, ON K1S 1C4, Canada. Offers individual or marital/couple counseling (MA); spiritual care (MA). Part-time programs available. *Degree requirements:* For master's, research project or thesis. *Entrance requirements:* For master's, honors BA in human sciences, minimum B average, 12 theology credits.

St. Petersburg Theological Seminary, Graduate Programs, St. Petersburg, FL 33708. Offers Biblical studies (MA); counseling (MA); divinity (M Div); education (MA); Judaic studies (MA); ministry (MA, D Min); religious teacher (MA). Part-time and evening/weekend programs available. Postbaccalaureate distance learning degree programs offered (minimal on-campus study). *Degree requirements:* For master's, thesis; for doctorate, thesis/dissertation. *Entrance requirements:* For M Div, Bachelor degree; for doctorate, Master degree. Electronic applications accepted.

Saints Cyril and Methodius Seminary, Graduate and Professional Programs, Orchard Lake, MI 48324. Offers pastoral ministry (MAPM); religious education (MARE); theology (M Div, MA). *Accreditation:* ATS. Part-time programs available.

St. Stephen's College, Programs in Theology, Edmonton, AB T6G 2J6, Canada. Offers ministry (D Min); pastoral counseling (MA); social transformation ministry (MA); spirituality and liturgy (MA); theological studies (MTS); theology (M Th). Part-time and evening/weekend programs available. Postbaccalaureate distance learning degree programs offered (minimal on-campus study). Terminal master's awarded for partial completion of doctoral program. *Degree requirements:* For master's, thesis; for doctorate, thesis/dissertation. *Entrance requirements:* Additional exam requirements/recommendations for international students: Required—TOEFL. Electronic applications accepted. *Faculty research:* Methodology for theological education, practice and supervision for ministry.

St. Thomas University, School of Theology and Ministry, Institute for Pastoral Ministries, Miami Gardens, FL 33054-6459. Offers pastoral ministries (MA, Certificate); practical theology (PhD). Part-time and evening/weekend programs available. *Degree requirements:* For master's, comprehensive exam; for doctorate, comprehensive exam, thesis/dissertation. *Entrance requirements:* For master's, interview, minimum GPA of 3.0 or GRE; for doctorate, GRE, MA in

Pastoral Ministry and Counseling

St. Thomas University (continued)
theology. Additional exam requirements/recommendations for international students: Required—TOEFL (minimum score 550 paper-based; 213 computer-based; 79 iBT). Electronic applications accepted.

Santa Clara University, College of Arts and Sciences, Graduate Programs in Pastoral Ministries, Program in Pastoral Liturgy, Santa Clara, CA 95053. Offers MA. Part-time and evening/weekend programs available. *Students:* 4 part-time (0 women); includes 1 minority (Hispanic American), 1 international. Average age 48. *Degree requirements:* For master's, comprehensive exam, thesis (for some programs). *Entrance requirements:* For master's, 3 letters of recommendation, essay, resume. Additional exam requirements/recommendations for international students: Required—TOEFL. *Application deadline:* Applications are processed on a rolling basis. Application fee: $50. Electronic applications accepted. *Expenses:* Contact institution. *Financial support:* Fellowships, research assistantships, career-related internships or fieldwork, Federal Work-Study, and health care benefits available. Support available to part-time students. Financial award applicants required to submit FAFSA. *Unit head:* Fr. Paul Crowley, Department Chair of Religious Studies, 408-554-4542. *Application contact:* Fr. Paul Crowley, Department Chair of Religious Studies, 408-554-4542.

Seattle University, School of Theology and Ministry, Program in Pastoral Counseling, Seattle, WA 98122-1090. Offers MA.

Seattle University, School of Theology and Ministry, Program in Pastoral Studies, Seattle, WA 98122-1090. Offers MAPS. Part-time and evening/weekend programs available. *Degree requirements:* For master's, project. *Entrance requirements:* For master's, interview, minimum GPA of 2.75, 2 years of experience in field.

Seminary of the Immaculate Conception, School of Theology, Huntington, NY 11743-1696. Offers pastoral studies (MA); theology (M Div, MA, D Min, Certificate). *Accreditation:* ATS (one or more programs are accredited). Part-time and evening/weekend programs available. *Faculty:* 8 full-time (2 women), 12 part-time/adjunct (5 women). *Students:* 40 full-time (0 women), 105 part-time (47 women); includes 25 minority (8 African Americans, 7 Asian Americans or Pacific Islanders, 10 Hispanic Americans), 11 international. Average age 49. 35 applicants, 100% accepted, 34 enrolled. In 2009, 3 first professional degrees, 27 master's awarded. *Degree requirements:* For master's, comprehensive exam; for doctorate, thesis/dissertation; for M Div, one foreign language, thesis/dissertation. *Entrance requirements:* For M Div, college degree in philosophy-theology; for master's, undergraduate degree; for doctorate, MA plus 30 credits or M Div; for Certificate, MA in theology. *Application deadline:* For fall admission, 8/30 priority date for domestic students; for spring admission, 1/20 priority date for domestic students. Applications are processed on a rolling basis. Application fee: $75. *Expenses:* Tuition: Full-time $12,000; part-time $450 per credit. Required fees: $50 per semester. One-time fee: $200 part-time. *Financial support:* Scholarships/grants available. *Unit head:* Sr. Mary Louise Brink, Academic Dean, 631-423-0483 Ext. 130, Fax: 631-432-2346, E-mail: mlbrink@icseminary.edu. *Application contact:* Kathryn L. Zahner, Registrar, 631-423-0483 Ext. 147, Fax: 631-423-2346, E-mail: kzahner@icseminary.edu.

Seminary of the Southwest, Graduate and Professional Programs, Austin, TX 78768-2247. Offers Anglican studies (Advanced Diploma); chaplaincy (MCPC); counseling (MAC); divinity (M Div); religion (MAR); spiritual formation (MAPM); theological studies (Advanced Diploma). *Accreditation:* ACIPE; ATS (one or more programs are accredited). Part-time and evening/weekend programs available. *Faculty:* 10 full-time (3 women), 22 part-time/adjunct (4 women). *Students:* 56 full-time (37 women), 52 part-time (41 women); includes 10 minority (4 African Americans, 2 Asian Americans or Pacific Islanders, 4 Hispanic Americans). Average age 46. 47 applicants, 100% accepted, 46 enrolled. In 2009, 10 first professional degrees, 11 master's, 5 other advanced degrees awarded. *Degree requirements:* For master's, thesis (for some programs). *Entrance requirements:* For M Div and master's, GRE, MAT, interview; for Advanced Diploma, interview. *Application deadline:* For fall admission, 7/1 for domestic students; for spring admission, 11/1 for domestic students. Applications are processed on a rolling basis. Application fee: $50. *Expenses:* Tuition: Full-time $13,150; part-time $390 per credit hour. Required fees: $75. One-time fee: $20 part-time. *Financial support:* Career-related internships or fieldwork and scholarships/grants available. Support available to part-time students. Financial award application deadline: 6/17. *Unit head:* Very Rev. Douglas Travis, Dean and President, 512-472-4133 Ext. 307, Fax: 512-472-3098, E-mail: dtravis@ssw.edu. *Application contact:* Jennielle Strother, Director of Admissions, 512-472-4133 Ext. 375, Fax: 512-472-3098, E-mail: jstrother@ssw.edu.

Seton Hall University, Immaculate Conception Seminary School of Theology, South Orange, NJ 07079-2697. Offers great spiritual books (Certificate); pastoral ministry (M Div, MA, Certificate); scripture studies (Certificate); Seminary's Theological Education for Parish Services (STEPS) (Certificate); theology (MA); youth ministry (Certificate). *Accreditation:* ATS (one or more programs are accredited). Part-time and evening/weekend programs available. *Faculty:* 16 full-time (2 women), 13 part-time/adjunct (1 woman). *Students:* 132 full-time (3 women), 79 part-time (32 women); includes 38 minority (4 African Americans, 6 Asian Americans or Pacific Islanders, 28 Hispanic Americans), 81 international. Average age 38. 46 applicants, 100% accepted, 43 enrolled. In 2009, 12 first professional degrees, 24 master's, 3 other advanced degrees awarded. *Degree requirements:* For master's, one foreign language, comprehensive exam, thesis (for some programs), final project; for M Div, one foreign language, thesis/dissertation, final project and seminar, field education, spiritual formation. *Entrance requirements:* For M Div, GRE, MAT; for master's, GRE General Test or MAT. Additional exam requirements/recommendations for international students: Required—TOEFL (minimum score 600 paper-based; 250 computer-based; 100 iBT). *Application deadline:* For fall admission, 8/1 priority date for domestic and international students; for spring admission, 12/15 priority date for domestic and international students. Applications are processed on a rolling basis. Application fee: $50. Electronic applications accepted. *Expenses:* Contact institution. *Financial support:* In 2009–10, 211 students received support. Career-related internships or fieldwork, Federal Work-Study, scholarships/grants, tuition waivers (partial), and unspecified assistantships available. Support available to part-time students. Financial award application deadline: 8/1; financial award applicants required to submit FAFSA. *Unit head:* Rev. Msgr. Robert F. Coleman, Rector/Dean, 973-761-9016, Fax: 973-761-9577, E-mail: robert.coleman@shu.edu. *Application contact:* Rev. Msgr. Joseph R. Chapel, Associate Dean, 973-761-9633, Fax: 973-761-9577, E-mail: theology@shu.edu.

Shasta Bible College, Program in Biblical Counseling, Redding, CA 96002. Offers biblical counseling and Christian family life education (MA). Part-time programs available. *Degree requirements:* For master's, comprehensive exam (for some programs), thesis or alternative. *Entrance requirements:* For master's, minimum GPA of 2.5. Additional exam requirements/recommendations for international students: Required—TOEFL (minimum score 550 paper-based; 213 computer-based).

Shasta Bible College, Program in Christian Ministry, Redding, CA 96002. Offers MA. Part-time programs available. Postbaccalaureate distance learning degree programs offered (minimal on-campus study). *Entrance requirements:* Additional exam requirements/recommendations for international students: Required—TOEFL (minimum score 550 paper-based; 213 computer-based).

Simpson University, A.W. Tozer Theological Seminary, Redding, CA 96003-8606. Offers intellectual leadership (MA); ministry (M Div). Part-time and evening/weekend programs available. Postbaccalaureate distance learning degree programs offered (minimal on-campus study). *Faculty:* 17 part-time/adjunct (1 woman). *Students:* 35 full-time (10 women), 22 part-time (4 women); includes 1 minority (Asian American or Pacific Islander), 1 international. Average age 38. 22 applicants, 73% accepted, 16 enrolled. In 2009, 5 master's awarded. *Degree requirements:* For master's, student portfolio. *Entrance requirements:* For master's, GRE General Test (if undergraduate GPA less than 2.5), 2 letters of reference, Christian Experience statement. Additional exam requirements/recommendations for international students: Required—TOEFL. *Application deadline:* For fall admission, 9/4 priority date for domestic students, 9/4 for international students; for spring admission, 1/8 priority date for domestic students, 1/8 for international students. Applications are processed on a rolling basis. Application fee: $25. Electronic applications accepted. *Expenses:* Contact institution. *Financial support:* Scholarships/grants available. Support available to part-time students. Financial award application deadline: 3/20; financial award applicants required to submit FAFSA. *Unit head:* Dr. Sarah Sumner, Dean, 530-226-4144, Fax: 530-226-4871, E-mail: ssumner@simpsonu.edu. *Application contact:* Becky Durben, Enrollment Advisor, 530-226-4771, Fax: 530-226-4861, E-mail: rdurben@simpsonu.edu.

Sioux Falls Seminary, Graduate and Professional Programs, Professional Program in Pastoral Ministry, Sioux Falls, SD 57105-1599. Offers M Div. *Accreditation:* ACIPE. Part-time programs available. *Entrance requirements:* Minimum GPA of 2.5.

Sioux Falls Seminary, Graduate and Professional Programs, Program in Counseling, Sioux Falls, SD 57105-1599. Offers MA. Part-time programs available. *Entrance requirements:* For master's, minimum GPA of 2.5.

Southeastern University, College of Christian Ministries and Religion, Lakeland, FL 33801-6099. Offers ministerial leadership (MA). Evening/weekend programs available. Postbaccalaureate distance learning degree programs offered. *Degree requirements:* For master's, thesis/project.

Southern Baptist Theological Seminary, Billy Graham School of Missions, Evangelism and Church Growth, Louisville, KY 40280-0004. Offers Christian mission/world religion (PhD); evangelism/church growth (PhD); ministry (D Min); missiology (MA, D Miss); missions, evangelism and church growth (M Div); religion (Th M); theological studies (MA). *Accreditation:* ATS. Part-time and evening/weekend programs available. Postbaccalaureate distance learning degree programs offered (minimal on-campus study). *Faculty:* 12 full-time (0 women). *Students:* 608. In 2009, 27 first professional degrees, 4 master's, 3 doctorates awarded. *Degree requirements:* For master's and M Div, 2 foreign languages; for doctorate, 4 foreign languages, thesis/dissertation. *Entrance requirements:* For doctorate, GRE General Test, MAT, M Div. Additional exam requirements/recommendations for international students: Required—TOEFL, TWE. *Application deadline:* For fall admission, 8/1 priority date for domestic students; for spring admission, 1/2 for domestic students. Applications are processed on a rolling basis. Application fee: $35. *Faculty research:* Assimilation of church congregants, effective methodologies of evangelism, expectations of church members, spiritual warfare literature, formative church discipline. *Unit head:* Dr. Chuck Lawless, Dean, 800-626-5525, E-mail: clawless@sbts.edu. *Application contact:* Chuck Haddox, Director of Admissions, 800-626-5525 Ext. 4617, E-mail: chaddox@sbts.edu.

Southern Baptist Theological Seminary, School of Leadership and Church Ministry, Louisville, KY 40280-0004. Offers advanced youth ministry (M Div); Christian education (M Div, MACE); leadership (Ed D); leadership and church ministry (PhD); ministry (D Ed Min); women's leadership (M Div); youth ministry (M Div, MAYM). Part-time programs available. Postbaccalaureate distance learning degree programs offered (minimal on-campus study). *Degree requirements:* For doctorate, thesis/dissertation; for M Div, 2 foreign languages. *Entrance requirements:* For doctorate, GRE General Test, interview, M Div or MACE. Additional exam requirements/recommendations for international students: Required—TWE. *Faculty research:* Gerontology, creative teaching methods, faith development in children, faith development in youth, transformational learning.

Southern Baptist Theological Seminary, School of Theology, Louisville, KY 40280-0004. Offers biblical and theological studies (M Div); biblical counseling (M Div, MA, D Min); biblical spirituality (D Min); Christian ministry (M Div); expository preaching (D Min); pastoral studies (M Div); theological studies (MA); theology (Th M, PhD); theology and arts (MA); theology and law (MA); worldview and apologetics (M Div). *Accreditation:* ATS. Part-time and evening/weekend programs available. Postbaccalaureate distance learning degree programs offered (minimal on-campus study). *Degree requirements:* For master's, 2 foreign languages, thesis; for doctorate, 4 foreign languages, thesis/dissertation; for M Div, 2 foreign languages. *Entrance requirements:* For master's, GRE General Test, MAT, M Div; for doctorate, GRE General Test, MAT, interview, M Div, field essay. Additional exam requirements/recommendations for international students: Required—TOEFL, TWE. *Faculty research:* Biblical studies, contemporary theology, church history, pastoral care, ministry/missions studies.

Southern Evangelical Seminary, Graduate School of Ministry and Missions, Matthews, NC 28105. Offers apologetics (Certificate); Christian education (MA); church ministry (MA, Certificate); divinity (Certificate), including apologetics (M Div, Certificate); Islamic studies (Certificate); theology (M Div), including apologetics (M Div, Certificate), Biblical studies; youth ministry (MA). Part-time and evening/weekend programs available. Postbaccalaureate distance learning degree programs offered. *Degree requirements:* For master's, thesis (for some programs); for M Div, one foreign language. *Entrance requirements:* Additional exam requirements/recommendations for international students: Required—TOEFL (minimum score 600 paper-based; 250 computer-based).

Southern Wesleyan University, Program in Christian Ministries, Central, SC 29630-1020. Offers M Min. Evening/weekend programs available. *Degree requirements:* For master's, paper. *Entrance requirements:* For master's, GRE General Test or MAT.

Southwestern Assemblies of God University, Thomas F. Harrison School of Graduate Studies, Program in Theological Studies, Waxahachie, TX 75165-5735. Offers Bible and theology (MS); Biblical studies (M Div); counseling (M Div); cross cultural missions (M Div); practical theology (M Div); theological studies (M Div). Postbaccalaureate distance learning degree programs offered. *Degree requirements:* For master's, comprehensive written and oral exams. *Entrance requirements:* For master's, GRE General Test, minimum GPA of 2.5. Electronic applications accepted.

Southwestern Christian University, Program in Ministry, Bethany, OK 73008-0340. Offers church planting (M Min); church revitalization and renewal (M Min); intercultural studies (M Min); leadership (M Min); life coaching (M Min); pastoral ministries (M Min); work place ministries (M Min). Part-time programs available. *Degree requirements:* For master's, thesis. *Entrance requirements:* For master's, minimum GPA of 2.5. Additional exam requirements/recommendations for international students: Required—TOEFL (minimum score 500 paper-based). Electronic applications accepted.

Spring Arbor University, School of Arts and Sciences, Spring Arbor, MI 49283-9799. Offers communication (MA); spiritual formation and leadership (MA). Part-time programs available. Postbaccalaureate distance learning degree programs offered (no on-campus study). *Faculty:* 6 full-time (1 woman), 11 part-time/adjunct (5 women). *Students:* 107 full-time (73 women), 76 part-time (57 women); includes 8 minority (6 African Americans, 2 Hispanic Americans), 1 international. Average age 42. In 2009, 16 master's awarded. *Degree requirements:* For master's, thesis (for some programs). *Entrance requirements:* For master's, GRE (taken within the last 5 years), writing sample, 3 recommendations. Additional exam requirements/recommendations for international students: Required—TOEFL (minimum score 550 paper-based; 220 computer-based). Application fee: $40. *Expenses:* Contact institution. *Financial support:* Applicants required to submit FAFSA. *Unit head:* Dr. Wally Metts, Chair of the Department of Communication, 517-750-1200 Ext. 1491, E-mail: wmetts@arbor.edu. *Application contact:* Dale Glinz, Lead Recruitment Specialist/Trainer, Graduate and Professional Studies, 517-750-6703, E-mail: dglinz@arbor.edu.

Spring Hill College, Graduate Programs, Program in Theology, Mobile, AL 36608-1791. Offers pastoral studies (MPS); theological studies (MTS); theology (MA). Part-time and evening/weekend programs available. *Faculty:* 6 full-time (0 women), 5 part-time/adjunct (1 woman). *Students:* 2 full-time (0 women), 49 part-time (24 women); includes 8 minority (5 African

Americans, 1 Asian American or Pacific Islander, 2 Hispanic Americans). Average age 46. 35 applicants, 51% accepted, 1 enrolled. In 2009, 16 master's awarded. *Degree requirements:* For master's, variable foreign language requirement, comprehensive exam, thesis (for some programs), completion of program within 6 calendar years of initial enrollment (MTS, MPS), 4½ calendar years (MA). *Entrance requirements:* For master's, bachelor's degree with minimum undergraduate GPA of 3.0; six hours of undergraduate theology, religious studies, or unquestioned equivalency. Additional exam requirements/recommendations for international students: Required—TOEFL (minimum score 550 paper-based; 213 computer-based; 80 iBT), IELTS (minimum score 6.5). *Application deadline:* For fall admission, 8/1 priority date for domestic and international students; for spring admission, 12/1 priority date for domestic and international students. Applications are processed on a rolling basis. Application fee: $25 ($35 for international students). Electronic applications accepted. *Expenses:* Tuition: Full-time $5112; part-time $284 per credit hour. Tuition and fees vary according to program. *Financial support:* In 2009–10, 17 students received support. Career-related internships or fieldwork, institutionally sponsored loans, and scholarships/grants available. Support available to part-time students. Financial award applicants required to submit FAFSA. *Unit head:* Dr. John B. Switzer, Director, 251-380-4669, Fax: 251-460-2194, E-mail: jswitzer@shc.edu. *Application contact:* Donna B. Tarasavage, Director of Marketing and Recruiting, Graduate and Continuing Studies, 251-380-3067, Fax: 251-460-2190, E-mail: dtarasavage@shc.edu.

Trinity Baptist College, Graduate Programs, Jacksonville, FL 32221. Offers Bible (M Ed); Christian school administration (M Ed); classroom practices (M Ed); ministry (M Min); special education (M Ed). Postbaccalaureate distance learning degree programs offered. *Entrance requirements:* For master's, GRE (M Ed), 2 letters of recommendation; minimum GPA of 2.5 (M Min) or 3.0 (M Ed); computer proficiency.

Trinity International University, Trinity Evangelical Divinity School, Deerfield, IL 60015-1284. Offers Biblical and Near Eastern archaeology and languages (MA); Christian studies (MA, Certificate); Christian thought (MA); church history (MA, Th M); congregational ministry: pastor-teacher (M Div); congregational ministry: team ministry (M Div); counseling ministries (MA); counseling psychology (MA); cross-cultural ministry (M Div); educational studies (PhD); evangelism (MA); history of Christianity in America (MA); intercultural studies (MA, PhD); leadership and ministry management (D Min); military chaplaincy (D Min); ministry (MA); mission and evangelism (Th M); missions and evangelism (D Min); New Testament (MA, Th M); Old Testament (Th M); Old Testament and Semitic languages (MA); pastoral care (M Div); pastoral care and counseling (D Min); pastoral counseling and psychology (Th M); pastoral theology (Th M); philosophy of religion (MA); preaching (D Min); religion (MA); research ministry (M Div); systematic theology (Th M); theological studies (PhD); urban ministry (MA). *Accreditation:* ATS (one or more programs are accredited). Part-time programs available. Postbaccalaureate distance learning degree programs offered (minimal on-campus study). *Degree requirements:* For master's, comprehensive exam, thesis, fieldwork; for doctorate, comprehensive exam (for some programs), thesis/dissertation; for M Div, 2 foreign languages, fieldwork; for Certificate, comprehensive exam, integrative papers. *Entrance requirements:* For M Div, GRE, MAT; for master's, GRE, MAT, minimum cumulative undergraduate GPA of 3.0; for doctorate, GRE, minimum cumulative graduate GPA of 3.2; for Certificate, GRE, MAT, minimum undergraduate GPA of 2.5. Additional exam requirements/recommendations for international students: Required—TOEFL (minimum score 580 paper-based; 237 computer-based), TWE (minimum score 4). Electronic applications accepted.

Trinity Lutheran Seminary, Graduate and Professional Programs, Columbus, OH 43209-2334. Offers Christian education (MA); church music (MA); divinity (M Div); sacred theology (STM); theological studies (MTS); youth and family ministry (MA); MSN/MTS; MTS/JD. *Accreditation:* ACIPE; ATS. Part-time programs available. *Faculty:* 15 full-time (7 women), 10 part-time/adjunct (3 women). *Students:* 99 full-time (38 women), 44 part-time (18 women); includes 21 minority (15 African Americans, 4 Asian Americans or Pacific Islanders, 2 Hispanic Americans), 4 international. Average age 35. 71 applicants, 77% accepted, 49 enrolled. In 2009, 29 first professional degrees, 9 master's awarded. *Degree requirements:* For master's, comprehensive exam (for some programs), thesis (for some programs); for M Div, 2 foreign languages, internship. *Entrance requirements:* For master's, M Div or equivalent (STM). Additional exam requirements/recommendations for international students: Required—TOEFL (minimum score 500 paper-based; 173 computer-based; 61 iBT). *Application deadline:* For fall admission, 7/15 priority date for domestic and international students. Applications are processed on a rolling basis. Application fee: $25. *Expenses:* Tuition: Full-time $11,400; part-time $380 per semester hour. Required fees: $115 per semester. One-time fee: $150 full-time. *Financial support:* In 2009–10, 102 students received support. Career-related internships or fieldwork, Federal Work-Study, institutionally sponsored loans, and scholarships/grants available. Support available to part-time students. Financial award application deadline: 5/1; financial award applicants required to submit FAFSA. *Unit head:* Dr. James M. Childs, Interim Academic Dean, 614-235-4136, Fax: 614-384-4635, E-mail: jchilds@trinitylutheranseminary.edu. *Application contact:* Rev. Sheri L. Ayers, Director of Admissions, 614-235-4136 Ext. 4614, Fax: 866-610-8572, E-mail: sayers@trinitylutheranseminary.edu.

Trinity School for Ministry, Graduate Programs, Ambridge, PA 15003-2397. Offers Anglican studies (Diploma); basic Christian studies (Diploma); divinity (M Div); ministry (D Min); mission and evangelism (MAME, Diploma); religion (MAR); youth ministry (Diploma). *Accreditation:* ATS (one or more programs are accredited). Part-time programs available. *Degree requirements:* For master's, thesis optional; for doctorate, thesis/dissertation; for M Div, thesis/dissertation optional, Greek and Hebrew. *Entrance requirements:* Additional exam requirements/recommendations for international students: Required—TOEFL. *Faculty research:* Pauline Epistles, contemporary theology, history of Anglican liturgy, book of Ruth, biblical theology.

Trinity Western University, ACTS Seminaries, Langley, BC V2Y 1Y1, Canada. Offers Christian studies (MA); church ministries (MA); cross cultural ministries (MA); theology (M Div, M Th, MAMFT, MLE, MTS, D Min). *Accreditation:* ATS. Part-time programs available. *Degree requirements:* For master's, thesis (for some programs), internship. *Entrance requirements:* For doctorate, MDiv or equivalent. Additional exam requirements/recommendations for international students: Required—TOEFL. *Expenses:* Contact institution. *Faculty research:* Theology of leadership.

Tyndale University College & Seminary, Graduate Programs, Toronto, ON M2M 4B3, Canada. Offers Biblical studies (M Div); Christian foundations (MTS); Christian studies (Diploma); counseling (M Div); educational ministry (M Div); missions (M Div, Diploma); pastoral and Chinese ministry (M Div); pastoral ministry (M Div); Pentecostal studies (MTS); spiritual formation (M Div, Diploma); theological studies (M Div); theology (Th M); worship and liturgy (M Div, MTS); youth and family ministry (M Div). *Accreditation:* ATS. Part-time programs available. Postbaccalaureate distance learning degree programs offered (no on-campus study). *Degree requirements:* For M Div, one foreign language, thesis/dissertation optional. *Entrance requirements:* For M Div, master's, and Diploma, minimum C+ average in undergraduate course work. Additional exam requirements/recommendations for international students: Required—TOEFL (minimum score 570 paper-based; 230 computer-based), TWE (minimum score 5). Electronic applications accepted. *Faculty research:* Canadian church history, Chinese church history, Old Testament, counseling ministries (narrative therapy), world religions.

Union University, School of Christian Studies, Jackson, TN 38305-3697. Offers Christian studies (MCS); expository preaching (D Min).

United Theological Seminary of the Twin Cities, Professional Program, New Brighton, MN 55112-2598. Offers advanced theological studies (Diploma); justice and peace studies (M Div, MA); leadership toward racial justice (MA, Certificate); leadership towards racial justice (M Div); Methodist studies (M Div, MA, Certificate); ministry (D Min); ministry renewal and professional development (Certificate); pastoral care and counseling (M Div, MA, MARL); religion and theology (MA); theological and religious studies (Certificate); theology and the arts (M Div, MA); urban ministry (M Div, MA, MARL); women's studies: religions, theology and ministry (MA); women's studies: religions, theology and ministry (M Div). *Accreditation:* ACIPE; ATS. Part-time and evening/weekend programs available. *Faculty:* 9 full-time (6 women), 22 part-time/adjunct (10 women). *Students:* 49 full-time (34 women), 105 part-time (68 women). Average age 47. 41 applicants, 98% accepted, 34 enrolled. In 2009, 24 first professional degrees, 5 master's, 2 doctorates, 2 other advanced degrees awarded. *Degree requirements:* For master's, thesis; for doctorate, comprehensive exam, thesis/dissertation; for M Div, integrative notebook, spiritual chronicle. *Entrance requirements:* For M Div and master's, minimum GPA of 2.75; strong analytical, reflective thinking and writing skills; vocational and academic goals compatible with those of Seminary; for doctorate, M Div or equivalent, minimum GPA of 3.0, 3 years experience in professional ministry; for other advanced degree, BA or equivalent life experience; strong analytical, reflective thinking and writing skills (Certificate); proficiency in English language, previous study of theology at a theological school, recommendation of student's denomination (Diploma). Additional exam requirements/recommendations for international students: Required—TOEFL (minimum score 550 paper-based). *Application deadline:* For fall admission, 7/1 priority date for domestic students, 11/1 priority date for international students; for winter admission, 11/1 priority date for domestic students; for spring admission, 11/15 priority date for domestic students. Applications are processed on a rolling basis. Application fee: $50. *Expenses:* Tuition: Full-time $11,502; part-time $426 per credit hour. Required fees: $295; $155 per term. One-time fee: $25. Tuition and fees vary according to course load, degree level and program. *Financial support:* In 2009–10, 120 students received support. Career-related internships or fieldwork, institutionally sponsored loans, and scholarships/grants available. Support available to part-time students. Financial award application deadline: 5/1; financial award applicants required to submit FAFSA. *Unit head:* Dr. Richard D. Weis, Dean of the Seminary, 651-255-6108 Ext. 108, Fax: 651-633-4315, E-mail: rweis@unitedseminary.edu. *Application contact:* Rev. Glen Herrington-Hall, Director of Admissions, 651-255-6107 Ext. 107, Fax: 651-633-4315, E-mail: gherrington-hall@unitedseminary.edu.

University of Dallas, Institute for Religious and Pastoral Studies, Irving, TX 75062-4736. Offers MCSL, MPM, MRE, MTS. *Accreditation:* ACIPE. Part-time and evening/weekend programs available. Postbaccalaureate distance learning degree programs offered (no on-campus study). *Faculty:* 7 full-time (3 women), 1 part-time/adjunct (0 women). *Students:* 2 full-time (both women), 106 part-time (57 women); includes 14 minority (1 African American, 1 American Indian/Alaska Native, 3 Asian Americans or Pacific Islanders, 9 Hispanic Americans), 3 international. Average age 45. 38 applicants, 100% accepted, 27 enrolled. In 2009, 16 master's awarded. *Application deadline:* For fall admission, 7/15 for domestic students; for spring admission, 11/15 for domestic students. Application fee: $50. *Expenses:* Tuition: Full-time $10,080; part-time $560 per credit hour. Required fees: $50 per term. Tuition and fees vary according to program. *Financial support:* In 2009–10, 79 students received support. Scholarships/grants available. Financial award application deadline: 2/15. *Faculty research:* Scripture, pastoral theology, ecclesiology, systematic theology, theological anthropology. *Unit head:* Dr. Brian Schmisek, Director, 972-721-4068, Fax: 972-721-4076, E-mail: schmisek@acad.udallas.edu. *Application contact:* Program Coordinator, 972-721-5105, Fax: 972-721-4076, E-mail: irps@acad.udallas.edu.

University of Dayton, Graduate School, College of Arts and Sciences, Department of Religious Studies, Dayton, OH 45469-1300. Offers pastoral ministry (MA); theological studies (MA); theology (PhD). Part-time and evening/weekend programs available. *Faculty:* 19 full-time (5 women), 5 part-time/adjunct (1 woman). *Students:* 60 full-time (28 women), 21 part-time (12 women); includes 3 minority (1 Asian American or Pacific Islander, 2 Hispanic Americans), 1 international. Average age 33. 66 applicants, 65% accepted, 19 enrolled. In 2009, 14 master's, 1 doctorate awarded. Terminal master's awarded for partial completion of doctoral program. *Degree requirements:* For master's, thesis or alternative; for doctorate, 2 foreign languages, comprehensive exam, thesis/dissertation. *Entrance requirements:* For master's, minimum undergraduate GPA of 3.0, 3 letters of recommendation, personal statement, official transcript(s); for doctorate, GRE General Test (minimum score 600 verbal), minimum GPA of 3.5, academic writing sample, 3 letters of recommendation. Additional exam requirements/recommendations for international students: Required—TOEFL (minimum score 550 paper-based; 213 computer-based; 80 iBT). *Application deadline:* For fall admission, 3/1 priority date for domestic and international students; for winter admission, 7/1 priority date for international students; for spring admission, 1/1 priority date for international students. Applications are processed on a rolling basis. Application fee: $0 ($50 for international students). Electronic applications accepted. *Expenses:* Contact institution. *Financial support:* In 2009–10, 28 students received support, including 4 fellowships with full tuition reimbursements available (averaging $15,814 per year), 8 research assistantships with full tuition reimbursements available (averaging $9,457 per year), 16 teaching assistantships with full tuition reimbursements available (averaging $15,814 per year); career-related internships or fieldwork, institutionally sponsored loans, scholarships/grants, health care benefits, tuition waivers (full), and unspecified assistantships also available. Support available to part-time students. Financial award application deadline: 3/1; financial award applicants required to submit FAFSA. *Faculty research:* Practical/constructive theology, theological ethics, U. S. Catholic/Christian life and thought, methodologies in Biblical studies, religion and science. *Unit head:* Dr. Sandra Yocum, Chair, 937-229-4321, Fax: 937-229-4330, E-mail: sandra.yocum@notes.udayton.edu. *Application contact:* Graduate Admissions, 937-229-4411, Fax: 937-229-4729, E-mail: gradadmission@udayton.edu.

University of Portland, College of Arts and Sciences, Department of Theology, Portland, OR 97203-5798. Offers pastoral ministry (MA). *Students:* 26 part-time (15 women); includes 3 minority (2 Asian Americans or Pacific Islanders, 1 Hispanic American). Average age 50. In 2009, 5 master's awarded. *Entrance requirements:* For master's, GRE or MAT, 3 letters of recommendation, minimum GPA of 3.0. Additional exam requirements/recommendations for international students: Required—TOEFL (minimum score 550 paper-based; 80 iBT), IELTS (minimum score 7). *Application deadline:* For fall admission, 7/15 priority date for domestic and international students. Application fee: $45. *Expenses:* Tuition: Part-time $860 per semester hour. *Financial support:* Federal Work-Study and scholarships/grants available. Financial award application deadline: 3/1; financial award applicants required to submit FAFSA. *Unit head:* Dr. Matt Baasten, Head, 503-943-7160. *Application contact:* Dr. Mary Labarre, Director, 503-943-7365, E-mail: labarre@up.edu.

University of Puget Sound, Graduate Studies, School of Education, Program in Counseling, Tacoma, WA 98416. Offers mental health counseling (M Ed); pastoral counseling (M Ed); school counseling (M Ed). *Accreditation:* NCATE. Part-time programs available. *Faculty:* 2 full-time (both women). *Students:* 1 (woman) full-time, 26 part-time (20 women); includes 4 minority (1 African American, 3 Hispanic Americans). Average age 32. 25 applicants, 56% accepted, 11 enrolled. In 2009, 10 master's awarded. *Entrance requirements:* For master's, GRE General Test, minimum GPA of 3.0. Additional exam requirements/recommendations for international students: Required—TOEFL (minimum score 550 paper-based; 213 computer-based; 80 iBT). *Application deadline:* For fall admission, 3/1 priority date for domestic and international students. Applications are processed on a rolling basis. Application fee: $60. Electronic applications accepted. *Expenses:* Contact institution. *Financial support:* Teaching assistantships, career-related internships or fieldwork available. Financial award application deadline: 3/31; financial award applicants required to submit FAFSA. *Faculty research:* Cross-role professional preparation, suicide prevention. *Unit head:* Dr. John Woodward, Dean, 253-879-3375, E-mail: woodward@pugetsound.edu. *Application contact:* Dr. George H. Mills, Vice President for Enrollment, 253-879-3211, Fax: 253-879-3993, E-mail: admission@pugetsound.edu.

University of Saint Francis, Graduate School, Department of Psychology and Counseling, Fort Wayne, IN 46808-3994. Offers general psychology (MS); mental health counseling (MS); pastoral counseling (MS); school counseling (MS Ed). Part-time and evening/weekend programs available. *Entrance requirements:* For master's, interview, minimum undergraduate GPA of 3.0.

University of St. Michael's College, Faculty of Theology, Toronto, ON M5S 1J4, Canada. Offers Catholic leadership (MA); eastern Christian studies (Diploma); religious education (Diploma); theological studies (Diploma); theology (M Div, MA, MRE, MTS, D Min, PhD, Th D);

Pastoral Ministry and Counseling

University of St. Michael's College (continued)

theology and Jewish studies (MA). *Accreditation:* ATS (one or more programs are accredited). Part-time programs available. *Faculty:* 9 full-time (2 women), 23 part-time/adjunct (6 women). *Students:* 106 full-time (35 women), 98 part-time (59 women); includes 35 minority (13 African Americans, 21 Asian Americans or Pacific Islanders, 1 Hispanic American), 24 international. Average age 40. 72 applicants, 75% accepted, 44 enrolled. In 2009, 29 first professional degrees, 7 master's, 2 doctorates, 3 other advanced degrees awarded. *Degree requirements:* For master's, thesis (for some programs), 1 foreign language (MA), 2 foreign languages (Th M); for doctorate, 3 foreign languages, comprehensive exam, thesis/dissertation; for M Div, thesis/dissertation optional; for other advanced degree, thesis optional. *Entrance requirements:* For M Div and other advanced degree, minimum GPA of 2.7; for master's, M Div or BA, course work in an ancient or modern language, minimum GPA of 3.3; for doctorate, MA in theology, Th M, or M Div with thesis, minimum GPA of 3.7. Additional exam requirements/recommendations for international students: Required—TOEFL (minimum score 600 paper-based; 250 computer-based). *Application deadline:* For fall admission, 1/15 for domestic and international students. Applications are processed on a rolling basis. Application fee: $25 Canadian dollars. Electronic applications accepted. *Expenses:* Contact institution. *Financial support:* In 2009–10, 45 students received support, including fellowships with partial tuition reimbursements available (averaging $2,500 per year), research assistantships with partial tuition reimbursements available (averaging $2,400 per year), 4 teaching assistantships with partial tuition reimbursements available (averaging $2,400 per year); scholarships/grants, tuition waivers (partial), and bursaries also available. Financial award application deadline: 2/1. *Faculty research:* Patristics, eastern Christianity, ecology and theology, ecumenism, Jewish Christian studies. *Unit head:* Fr. Dr. Mario O. D'Souza, Dean, 416-926-7265, Fax: 416-926-7294, E-mail: mario.dsouza@utoronto.ca. *Application contact:* Allen Croxall, Student Recruitment and Advancement Officer, 416-926-1300 Ext. 3281, Fax: 416-926-7294, E-mail: allen.croxall@utoronto.ca.

University of St. Thomas, Graduate Studies, Saint Paul Seminary School of Divinity, Program in Theology/Pastoral Studies, St. Paul, MN 55105-1096. Offers religious education (MARE); theology (MA). *Accreditation:* ATS. Part-time and evening/weekend programs available. *Degree requirements:* For master's, one foreign language, comprehensive exam, thesis or alternative. *Entrance requirements:* For master's, GRE, interview, 3 letters of recommendation. Additional exam requirements/recommendations for international students: Required—TOEFL (minimum score 550 paper-based; 213 computer-based). Electronic applications accepted. *Expenses:* Contact institution. *Faculty research:* Theological education.

University of South Africa, College of Human Sciences, Pretoria, South Africa. Offers adult education (M Ed); African languages (MA, PhD); African politics (MA, PhD); Afrikaans (MA, PhD); ancient history (MA, PhD); ancient Near Eastern studies (MA, PhD); anthropology (MA, PhD); applied linguistics (MA); Arabic (MA, PhD); archaeology (MA); art history (MA); Biblical archaeology (MA); Biblical studies (M Th, D Th, PhD); Christian spirituality (M Th, D Th); church history (M Th, D Th); classical studies (MA, PhD); clinical psychology (MA); communication (MA, PhD); comparative education (M Ed, Ed D); consulting psychology (D Admin, D Com, PhD); curriculum studies (M Ed, Ed D); development studies (M Admin, MA, D Admin, PhD); didactics (M Ed, Ed D); education (M Tech); education management (M Ed, Ed D); educational psychology (M Ed); English (MA); environmental education (M Ed); French (MA, PhD); German (MA, PhD); Greek (MA); guidance and counseling (M Ed); health studies (MA, PhD), including health sciences education (MA), health services management (MA), medical and surgical nursing science (critical care general) (MA), midwifery and neonatal nursing science (MA), trauma and emergency care (MA); history (MA, PhD); history of education (Ed D); inclusive education (M Ed, Ed D); information and communications technology policy and regulation (MA); information science (MA, MIS, PhD); international politics (MA, PhD); Islamic studies (MA, PhD); Italian (MA, PhD); Judaica (MA, PhD); linguistics (MA, PhD); mathematical education (M Ed); mathematics education (MA); missiology (M Th, D Th); modern Hebrew (MA, PhD); musicology (MA, MMus, D Mus, PhD); natural science education (M Ed); New Testament (M Th, D Th); Old Testament (D Th); pastoral therapy (M Th, D Th); philosophy (MA); philosophy of education (M Ed, Ed D); politics (MA, PhD); Portuguese (MA, PhD); practical theology (M Th, D Th); psychology (MA, MS, PhD); psychology of education (M Ed, Ed D); public health (MA); religious studies (MA, D Th, PhD); Romance languages (MA); Russian (MA, PhD); Semitic languages (MA, PhD); social behavior studies in HIV/AIDS (MA); social science (mental health) (MA); social science in development studies (MA); social science in psychology (MA); social science in social work (MA); social science in sociology (MA); social work (MSW, DSW, PhD); socio-education (M Ed, Ed D); sociolinguistics (MA); sociology (MA, PhD); Spanish (MA, PhD); systematic theology (M Th, D Th); TESOL (teaching English to speakers of other languages) (MA); theological ethics (M Th, D Th); theory of literature (MA, PhD); urban ministries (D Th); urban ministry (M Th).

University of Trinity College, Faculty of Divinity, Toronto, ON M5S 1H8, Canada. Offers ministry (Diploma); ministry for church musicians (Diploma); theology (M Div, MTS, Th M, D Min, PhD, Th D, Diploma, L Th); M Div/MA. *Accreditation:* ATS. Part-time programs available. *Degree requirements:* For master's, 2 foreign languages, thesis (for some programs); for doctorate, 3 foreign languages, comprehensive exam, thesis/dissertation; for M Div, thesis/dissertation optional; for other advanced degree, thesis (for some programs). *Entrance requirements:* For M Div, interview; for master's, 1 language (modern or ancient), interview; for doctorate, 2 languages (modern and ancient). Additional exam requirements/recommendations for international students: Required—TOEFL, TWE. *Faculty research:* Interreligious dialogue, feminist theology, systematic theology, philosophy of religion, pastoral theology.

Warner Pacific College, Graduate Programs, Portland, OR 97215-4099. Offers biblical and theological studies (MA); biblical studies (M Rel); education (M Ed); management/organizational leadership (MS); pastoral ministries (M Rel); religion and ethics (M Rel); teaching (MA); theology (M Rel). Part-time programs available. *Degree requirements:* For master's, thesis or alternative, presentation of defense. *Entrance requirements:* For master's, interview, minimum GPA of 2.5, letters of recommendations. *Faculty research:* New Testament studies, nineteenth-century Wesleyan theology, preaching and church growth, Christian ethics.

Wayland Baptist University, Graduate Programs, Programs in Religion, Plainview, TX 79072-6998. Offers Christian ministry (MCM); religion (MA). Part-time and evening/weekend programs available. Postbaccalaureate distance learning degree programs offered (no on-campus study). *Faculty:* 6 full-time (1 woman). *Students:* 13 part-time (4 women); includes 3 minority (2 African Americans, 1 Hispanic American). Average age 38. 10 applicants, 90% accepted, 3 enrolled. In 2009, 2 master's awarded. *Degree requirements:* For master's, comprehensive exam. *Entrance requirements:* For master's, GRE or MAT. Additional exam requirements/recommendations for international students: Required—TOEFL (minimum score 500 paper-based; 173 computer-based; 61 iBT). *Application deadline:* Applications are processed on a rolling basis. Application fee: $50. Electronic applications accepted. *Expenses:* Tuition: Full-time $5796; part-time $322 per credit hour. Required fees: $782; $9 per credit hour. $60 per semester. Tuition and fees vary according to course load and campus/location. *Financial support:* Federal Work-Study, institutionally sponsored loans, and scholarships/grants available. Support available to part-time students. Financial award application deadline: 5/1; financial award applicants required to submit FAFSA. *Unit head:* Dr. Paul Sadler, Chairman, 806-291-1160, Fax: 806-291-1969, E-mail: sadlerp@wbu.edu. *Application contact:* Amanda Stanton, Graduate Studies, 806-291-3423, Fax: 806-291-1950, E-mail: stanton@wbu.edu.

Wesley Biblical Seminary, Graduate Programs, Jackson, MS 39206. Offers apologetics (MA); Biblical studies (MA); Christian studies (MA); evangelism (M Div); family life ministry (M Div); honors research (M Div); missions (M Div); pastoral ministry (M Div); teaching (M Div); theological studies (MA). *Accreditation:* ATS. Part-time programs available. *Faculty:* 11 full-time (2 women), 5 part-time/adjunct (0 women). *Students:* 43 full-time (5 women), 89 part-time (33 women). *Degree requirements:* For master's, thesis. *Entrance requirements:* Additional exam requirements/recommendations for international students: Required—TOEFL. *Application deadline:* For fall admission, 7/1 priority date for domestic students; for spring admission, 12/1 priority date for domestic students. Applications are processed on a rolling basis. Application fee: $40. Electronic applications accepted. *Expenses:* Tuition: Full-time $8000; part-time $320 per credit hour. Required fees: $310; $160 per semester. Tuition and fees vary according to course load, campus/location and program. *Financial support:* Scholarships/grants available. Support available to part-time students. *Faculty research:* Patristics, missiology, culture, hermeneutics. *Unit head:* Dr. Ray R. Easley, Vice President for Academic Affairs, 601-366-8880 Ext. 112, Fax: 601-366-8832. *Application contact:* Laura McMillan, Assistant to the Vice President for Business and Student Development, 601-366-8880 Ext. 110, Fax: 601-366-8832, E-mail: admissions@wbs.edu.

Western Seminary, Graduate Programs, Program in Counseling, Portland, OR 97215-3367. Offers counseling (MA, Certificate); pastoral counseling (M Div); M Div/MA. Part-time and evening/weekend programs available. *Faculty:* 93 full-time (38 women), 586 part-time/adjunct (198 women). *Students:* 85 full-time, 69 part-time; includes 20 minority (5 African Americans, 1 American Indian/Alaska Native, 11 Asian Americans or Pacific Islanders, 3 Hispanic Americans). Average age 29. 132 applicants, 92% accepted, 86 enrolled. *Degree requirements:* For master's, practicum; for M Div, 2 foreign languages, practicum. *Entrance requirements:* Additional exam requirements/recommendations for international students: Required—TOEFL. *Application deadline:* For fall admission, 7/19 priority date for domestic students; for winter admission, 11/8 priority date for domestic students; for spring admission, 3/14 priority date for domestic students. Applications are processed on a rolling basis. Application fee: $50. *Expenses:* Contact institution. *Financial support:* Career-related internships or fieldwork and institutionally sponsored loans available. Financial award application deadline: 7/19; financial award applicants required to submit FAFSA. *Unit head:* Dr. David Wenzel, Director, 503-517-1869, E-mail: dwenzel@westernseminary.edu. *Application contact:* Dr. Robert W. Wiggins, Registrar/Dean of Student Development, 503-517-1820, Fax: 503-517-1801, E-mail: rwiggins@westernseminary.edu.

Western Seminary, Graduate Programs, Program in Intercultural Studies, Portland, OR 97215-3367. Offers MA, D Miss, Certificate, G Dip. Part-time and evening/weekend programs available. *Faculty:* 2 full-time (1 woman), 5 part-time/adjunct (1 woman). *Students:* 93 full-time (38 women), 586 part-time (198 women); includes 20 minority (5 African Americans, 1 American Indian/Alaska Native, 11 Asian Americans or Pacific Islanders, 3 Hispanic Americans). Average age 39. 132 applicants, 92% accepted, 86 enrolled. *Degree requirements:* For master's, practicum; for doctorate, 2 foreign languages, thesis/dissertation. *Entrance requirements:* Additional exam requirements/recommendations for international students: Required—TOEFL. *Application deadline:* For fall admission, 7/9 priority date for domestic students; for winter admission, 10/8 priority date for domestic students; for spring admission, 3/4 priority date for domestic students. Applications are processed on a rolling basis. Application fee: $50. *Expenses:* Tuition: Full-time $3280; part-time $410 per credit hour. *Financial support:* Career-related internships or fieldwork available. Financial award applicants required to submit FAFSA. *Unit head:* Dr. Enoch Wan, Director, 503-233-1804, Fax: 503-517-1889, E-mail: ewan@westernseminary.edu. *Application contact:* Dr. Robert W. Wiggins, Registrar/Dean of Student Development, 503-517-1820, Fax: 503-517-1801, E-mail: rwiggins@westernseminary.edu.

Western Seminary, Graduate Programs, Program in Ministry and Leadership, Portland, OR 97215-3367. Offers chaplaincy (MA); coaching (MA); Jewish ministry (MA); pastoral care to women (MA); youth ministry (MA). *Students:* 93 full-time (38 women), 586 part-time (198 women); includes 20 minority (5 African Americans, 1 American Indian/Alaska Native, 11 Asian Americans or Pacific Islanders, 3 Hispanic Americans). Average age 29. 132 applicants, 92% accepted, 86 enrolled. *Degree requirements:* For master's, practicum. *Entrance requirements:* Additional exam requirements/recommendations for international students: Required—TOEFL. *Application deadline:* For fall admission, 7/19 priority date for domestic students; for winter admission, 11/8 priority date for domestic students; for spring admission, 3/14 priority date for domestic students. Applications are processed on a rolling basis. Application fee: $50. *Expenses:* Tuition: Full-time $3280; part-time $410 per credit hour. *Financial support:* Applicants required to submit FAFSA. *Unit head:* Beverly Hislop, Director, 503-517-1881, E-mail: bhislop@westernseminary.edu. *Application contact:* Dr. Robert W. Wiggins, Registrar/Dean of Student Development, 503-517-1820, Fax: 503-517-1801, E-mail: rwiggins@westernseminary.edu.

Western Seminary–Sacramento Campus, Graduate Programs, Sacramento, CA 95821. Offers exegetical theology (MA); marital and family therapy (MA); ministry (M Div); specialized ministry (MA). Postbaccalaureate distance learning degree programs offered. *Entrance requirements:* For M Div, minimum GPA of 2.5; for master's, minimum GPA of 3.0.

Western Seminary–San Jose Campus, Graduate Programs, Los Gatos, CA 95032-4520. Offers exegetical theology (MA); expositional ministry (M Div); marital and family therapy (MA); ministry (M Div); pastoral ministry (M Div); specialized ministry (MA). Postbaccalaureate distance learning degree programs offered. *Degree requirements:* For master's, 2 foreign languages; for M Div, 3 foreign languages. *Entrance requirements:* For M Div, minimum GPA of 2.5; for master's, minimum GPA of 3.0.

Westminster Theological Seminary, Graduate and Professional Programs, Philadelphia, PA 19118. Offers apologetics (Th M); Biblical and urban studies (Certificate); Biblical counseling (MA); biblical studies (MAR); Christian studies (Certificate); church history (Th M); counseling (M Div); general studies (M Div, MAR); hermeneutics and Bible interpretations (PhD); historical and theological studies (PhD); historical theology (Th M); New Testament (Th M); Old Testament (Th M); pastoral counseling (D Min); pastoral ministry (M Div, D Min); systematic theology (Th M); theological studies (MAR); urban missions (M Div, MA, MAR, D Min). *Accreditation:* ATS. Part-time programs available. Terminal master's awarded for partial completion of doctoral program. *Degree requirements:* For master's, thesis (for some programs); for doctorate, 4 foreign languages, comprehensive exam (for some programs), thesis/dissertation; for M Div, 2 foreign languages. *Entrance requirements:* For doctorate, GRE General Test. Additional exam requirements/recommendations for international students: Required—TOEFL, TWE.

Wheaton College, Graduate School, Department of Psychology, Wheaton, IL 60187-5593. Offers clinical psychology (MA, Psy D); counseling ministries (MA). *Accreditation:* APA (one or more programs are accredited). Terminal master's awarded for partial completion of doctoral program. *Degree requirements:* For master's, thesis or alternative; for doctorate, thesis/dissertation, internship. *Entrance requirements:* For master's, GRE General Test, 18 hours of course work in psychology; for doctorate, GRE General Test.

Wilfrid Laurier University, Waterloo Lutheran Seminary, Waterloo, ON N2L 3C5, Canada. Offers Christian ethics (M Th); divinity (M Div); homiletics (M Th); ministry (D Min); pastoral counseling (M Th); spirituality in a health care setting (Diploma); theological studies (MTS); theology (Diploma); M Div/MTS/MSW. *Accreditation:* ATS. Part-time programs available. *Degree requirements:* For master's, one foreign language, thesis (for some programs); for doctorate, thesis/dissertation; for M Div, one foreign language, thesis/dissertation. *Entrance requirements:* For M Div, denominational endorsement; for master's, M Div, 2 units of clinical pastoral education (M Th); for doctorate, M Div, 3 years of ministry experience, proficiency in a foreign language, basic training in clinical pastoral education. Additional exam requirements/recommendations for international students: Required—TOEFL (minimum score 573 paper-based; 230 computer-based; 89 iBT), IELTS (minimum score 7). Electronic applications accepted. *Expenses:* Contact institution. *Faculty research:* Biblical study, church history, systematic theology.

Xavier University, College of Arts and Sciences, Department of Theology, Cincinnati, OH 45207. Offers theology (MA), including religious education, social and pastoral ministry, theology. Part-time programs available. *Faculty:* 7 full-time (2 women). *Students:* 5 full-time (2 women), 23 part-time (10 women); includes 1 minority (Hispanic American). Average age 33. 11 applicants, 100% accepted, 11 enrolled. In 2009, 5 master's awarded. *Degree requirements:* For master's, thesis optional, final paper and defense. *Entrance requirements:* For master's, MAT or GRE, letters of recommendation. Additional exam requirements/recommendations for international students: Required—TOEFL (minimum score 550 paper-based; 213 computer-based). *Application deadline:* Applications are processed on a rolling basis. Application fee:

$35. Electronic applications accepted. *Expenses:* Tuition: Part-time $697 per credit hour. One-time fee: $35 part-time. *Financial support:* In 2009–10, 26 students received support. Scholarships/grants and unspecified assistantships available. Financial award applicants required to submit FAFSA. *Faculty research:* Scripture, ethics, constructive theology, historical theology. *Unit head:* Dr. Sarah Melcher, Chair, 513-745-2043, Fax: 513-745-3215, E-mail: melcher@xavier.edu. *Application contact:* Dr. Sarah Melcher, Chair, 513-745-2043, Fax: 513-745-3215, E-mail: melcher@xavier.edu.

Xavier University of Louisiana, Graduate School, Institute for Black Catholic Studies, New Orleans, LA 70125-1098. Offers pastoral theology (Th M). Part-time programs available. *Degree requirements:* For master's, comprehensive exam, practicum. *Entrance requirements:* For master's, GRE General Test, MAT, minimum GPA of 2.5. Additional exam requirements/recommendations for international students: Required—TOEFL.

Religion

Ambrose University College, Ambrose Seminary, Calgary, AB T2P 3T5, Canada. Offers biblical/theological studies (MA); Chinese ministries (Certificate); Christian studies (M Div, MA, Diploma); foundations for ministry (Certificate); intercultural ministries (M Div, MA, Certificate, Diploma); leadership and ministry (MA, Certificate, Diploma). *Accreditation:* ATS (one or more programs are accredited). Part-time programs available. *Faculty:* 7 full-time (0 women), 24 part-time/adjunct (2 women). *Students:* 44 full-time (15 women), 107 part-time (49 women). Average age 41. *Degree requirements:* For master's, 2 foreign languages, internship; for M Div, one foreign language, internship. *Entrance requirements:* For master's, bachelor's degree. Additional exam requirements/recommendations for international students: Required—TOEFL or IELTS. *Application deadline:* For fall admission, 7/31 priority date for domestic students, 3/1 priority date for international students; for winter admission, 11/30 priority date for domestic students, 6/1 priority date for international students. Applications are processed on a rolling basis. Application fee: $50. Electronic applications accepted. *Expenses:* Tuition: Full-time $6000; part-time $299 per credit hour. Required fees: $306; $17 per credit hour. *Financial support:* Career-related internships or fieldwork and scholarships/grants available. Support available to part-time students. Financial award application deadline: 3/30. *Faculty research:* Evangelicalism and sociology, missiological trends, chaplaincy, intertestamental studies, postmodernism. *Unit head:* Dr. Paul Spilsbury, Vice-President of Academic Affairs, 403-410-2000 Ext. 6905, Fax: 403-571-2556, E-mail: pspilsbury@ambrose.edu. *Application contact:* Dr. Paul Spilsbury, Vice-President of Academic Affairs, 403-410-2000 Ext. 6905, Fax: 403-571-2556, E-mail: pspilsbury@ambrose.edu.

Amridge University, Graduate and Professional Programs, Montgomery, AL 36117. Offers behavioral leadership and management (MA); biblical studies (MA, PhD); family therapy (D Min); leadership and management (MS); marriage and family therapy (M Div, MA, PhD); ministerial leadership (M Div, MS); pastoral counseling (M Div, MS); practical theology (MA); professional counseling (M Div, MA); theology (M Div, D Min). *Accreditation:* ATS. Part-time and evening/weekend programs available. Postbaccalaureate distance learning degree programs offered (no on-campus study). *Faculty:* 44 full-time (9 women), 18 part-time/adjunct (7 women). *Students:* 175 full-time (95 women), 192 part-time (93 women); includes 182 minority (172 African Americans, 1 American Indian/Alaska Native, 1 Asian American or Pacific Islander, 8 Hispanic Americans). Average age 35. *Degree requirements:* For master's, one foreign language, comprehensive exam (for some programs), thesis (for some programs); for doctorate, comprehensive exam (for some programs), thesis/dissertation; for M Div, comprehensive exam (for some programs). *Entrance requirements:* For M Div, master's, and doctorate, GRE General Test or MAT. Additional exam requirements/recommendations for international students: Required—TOEFL. *Application deadline:* For fall admission, 9/1 priority date for domestic students; for spring admission, 1/1 priority date for domestic students. Applications are processed on a rolling basis. Application fee: $75. Electronic applications accepted. *Expenses:* Tuition: Full-time $10,080; part-time $560 per semester hour. Required fees: $600 per term. *Financial support:* Federal Work-Study and scholarships/grants available. Support available to part-time students. Financial award applicants required to submit FAFSA. *Faculty research:* Homiletics, hermeneutics, ancient Near Eastern history. *Unit head:* Director of Enrollment Management, 800-351-4040 Ext. 7513, Fax: 334-387-3878. *Application contact:* Ora Davis, Admissions Officer, 334-387-3877 Ext. 7524, Fax: 334-387-3878, E-mail: admissions@amridgeuniversity.edu.

Arizona State University, Graduate College, College of Liberal Arts and Sciences, Division of Humanities, Department of Religious Studies, Tempe, AZ 85287. Offers MA, PhD. *Degree requirements:* For master's, thesis or alternative. *Entrance requirements:* For master's, GRE.

Azusa Pacific University, Haggard School of Theology, Program in Christian Education, Azusa, CA 91702-7000. Offers MAR.

Baptist Bible College of Pennsylvania, Baptist Bible Seminary, Clarks Summit, PA 18411-1297. Offers biblical studies (PhD); church planting (M Div); global missions (M Div); military chaplaincy (M Div); ministry (M Min, D Min); pastor of church education (M Div); pastor of outreach (M Div); pastoral counseling (M Div); pastoral leadership (M Div); theology (M Div, Th M); youth pastor (M Div). Part-time and evening/weekend programs available. Postbaccalaureate distance learning degree programs offered (minimal on-campus study). Terminal master's awarded for partial completion of doctoral program. *Degree requirements:* For master's, 2 foreign languages, thesis; for doctorate, 2 foreign languages, comprehensive exam (for some programs), thesis/dissertation, oral exam; for M Div, 2 foreign languages, thesis/dissertation, oral exam. *Entrance requirements:* For doctorate, Greek and Hebrew entrance exams (PhD). Electronic applications accepted.

Baptist Theological Seminary at Richmond, Graduate and Professional Programs, Richmond, VA 23227. Offers biblical interpretation (M Div); Christian education (M Div); theology (D Min); youth and student ministries (M Div); M Div/MS; M Div/MSW. *Accreditation:* ATS. Part-time programs available. Postbaccalaureate distance learning degree programs offered (minimal on-campus study). *Faculty:* 8 full-time (2 women), 9 part-time/adjunct (3 women). *Students:* 59 full-time (33 women), 30 part-time (17 women); includes 9 minority (all African Americans), 3 international. Average age 46. In 2009, 29 first professional degrees, 6 doctorates awarded. *Degree requirements:* For doctorate, one foreign language, comprehensive exam, thesis/dissertation, field study, independent study; for M Div, one foreign language, comprehensive exam (for some programs), thesis/dissertation optional, mission immersion experience, internship. *Entrance requirements:* For doctorate, MAT, M Div, 3 years of full-time ministry experience. Additional exam requirements/recommendations for international students: Required—TOEFL (minimum score 550 paper-based; 213 computer-based). *Application deadline:* For fall admission, 8/1 priority date for domestic students, 5/1 priority date for international students; for winter admission, 12/1 priority date for domestic students, 9/1 priority date for international students; for spring admission, 1/1 priority date for domestic students, 10/1 priority date for international students. Applications are processed on a rolling basis. Application fee: $35. *Financial support:* In 2009–10, 16 teaching assistantships (averaging $1,650 per year) were awarded; scholarships/grants and tuition waivers (partial) also available. Financial award application deadline: 2/1. *Faculty research:* New Testament studies, Old Testament studies, pastoral care, church history, theology. *Unit head:* Dr. Ronald W. Crawford, President, 804-204-1201, Fax: 804-355-8182, E-mail: rcrawford@btsr.edu. *Application contact:* Tiffany Kellogg Pittman, Director of Admissions, 804-204-1208, Fax: 804-355-8182, E-mail: admissions@btsr.edu.

Baylor University, Graduate School, College of Arts and Sciences, Department of Religion, Waco, TX 76798. Offers MA, PhD. *Students:* 57 full-time (9 women), 8 part-time (1 woman); includes 5 minority (1 American Indian/Alaska Native, 1 Asian American or Pacific Islander, 3 Hispanic Americans), 7 international. In 2009, 1 master's, 8 doctorates awarded. Terminal master's awarded for partial completion of doctoral program. *Degree requirements:* For master's, one foreign language, thesis; for doctorate, 2 foreign languages, thesis/dissertation. *Entrance requirements:* For master's and doctorate, GRE General Test. *Application deadline:* Applications are processed on a rolling basis. Application fee: $25. *Financial support:* Fellowships, research assistantships, teaching assistantships, Federal Work-Study, institutionally sponsored loans, and scholarships/grants available. *Unit head:* Dr. Bill Pitts, Graduate Program Director, 254-710-6321, Fax: 254-710-3740, E-mail: william_pitts@baylor.edu. *Application contact:* Lisa M. Long, Administrative Assistant, 254-710-3742, Fax: 254-710-3870, E-mail: lisa_m_long@baylor.edu.

Baylor University, Graduate School, College of Arts and Sciences, J. M. Dawson Institute of Church-State Studies, Waco, TX 76798. Offers MA, PhD. *Students:* 33 full-time (12 women), 6 part-time (2 women); includes 8 minority (1 American Indian/Alaska Native, 3 Asian Americans or Pacific Islanders, 4 Hispanic Americans), 7 international. In 2009, 5 master's, 3 doctorates awarded. *Degree requirements:* For master's, thesis, oral exam; for doctorate, one foreign language, thesis/dissertation, preliminary exams. *Entrance requirements:* For master's, GRE General Test; for doctorate, GRE General Test, MA or equivalent. *Application deadline:* For fall admission, 3/1 for domestic students. Applications are processed on a rolling basis. Application fee: $25. *Financial support:* Fellowships, research assistantships, teaching assistantships, Federal Work-Study and institutionally sponsored loans available. Financial award application deadline: 3/1. *Faculty research:* Religion and politics, religion and public education, religious freedom and international politics, First Amendment jurisprudence. *Unit head:* Dr. Christopher Marsh, Graduate Program Director, 254-710-4412, Fax: 254-710-1571, E-mail: chris_marsh@baylor.edu. *Application contact:* Suzanne Seller, Administrative Assistant, 254-710-1510, Fax: 254-710-1571, E-mail: suzanne_sellers@baylor.edu.

Bellarmine University, Bellarmine College of Arts and Sciences, Louisville, KY 40205-0671. Offers spirituality (MA). *Faculty:* 4 full-time (1 woman). *Students:* 9 part-time (7 women); includes 1 minority (African American). Average age 44. In 2009, 4 master's awarded. *Entrance requirements:* For master's, minimum GPA of 2.8, letter of recommendation, spirituality autobiography. Additional exam requirements/recommendations for international students: Required—TOEFL (minimum score 550 paper-based; 213 computer-based; 80 iBT). *Application deadline:* For spring admission, 3/15 for domestic students. Application fee: $25. *Expenses:* Contact institution. *Faculty research:* Early Christianity, catholic social teaching, Christian spirituality, social justice. *Unit head:* Dr. Gregory Hillis, Program Director, 502-473-3800, E-mail: ghillis@bellarmine.edu. *Application contact:* Sara Yount, Dean of Graduate Admission, 502-452-8401, E-mail: syount@bellarmine.edu.

Bethany Theological Seminary, Graduate and Professional Programs, Richmond, IN 47374-4019. Offers biblical studies (MA Th); ministry studies (M Div); peace studies (M Div, MA Th); theological studies (MA Th, CATS); youth ministry (M Div). *Accreditation:* ACIPE; ATS. Part-time programs available. Postbaccalaureate distance learning degree programs offered (minimal on-campus study). *Degree requirements:* For master's, thesis. *Entrance requirements:* For M Div, letters of reference, minimum GPA of 2.75; for master's, letters of reference, minimum GPA of 3.0. Additional exam requirements/recommendations for international students: Required—TOEFL (minimum score 550 paper-based; 218 computer-based).

Bethesda Christian University, Graduate and Professional Programs, Anaheim, CA 92801. Offers biblical studies (MA); music (MA); theology (M Div). *Entrance requirements:* For M Div and master's, interview.

Beulah Heights University, Graduate School, Atlanta, GA 30316. Offers biblical studies (MA); leadership studies (MA). *Entrance requirements:* Additional exam requirements/recommendations for international students: Required—TOEFL (minimum score 500 paper-based). Electronic applications accepted.

Biola University, Talbot School of Theology, La Mirada, CA 90639-0001. Offers Bible exposition (MA); biblical and theological studies (MA); Christian education (MACE); Christian ministry and leadership (MA); divinity (M Div); education (PhD); ministry (MA Min); New Testament (MA); Old Testament (MA); philosophy of religion and ethics (MA); spiritual formation (MA); spiritual formation and soul care (MA); theology (MA, Th M, D Min). *Accreditation:* ATS. Part-time and evening/weekend programs available. *Degree requirements:* For master's, variable foreign language requirement, thesis or alternative; for doctorate, variable foreign language requirement, thesis/dissertation; for M Div, thesis/dissertation or alternative. *Entrance requirements:* For M Div, minimum GPA of 2.6; for master's, minimum undergraduate GPA of 3.0; for doctorate, minimum GPA of 3.25. Additional exam requirements/recommendations for international students: Required—TOEFL (minimum score 550 paper-based; 213 computer-based). *Faculty research:* Moral development; biological, medical, and social ethics; ancient Near Eastern historical philosophy.

Bob Jones University, Graduate Programs, Greenville, SC 29614. Offers accountancy (MS); Bible (MA); Bible translation (MA); Biblical studies (Certificate); broadcast management (MS); business administration (MBA); church history (MA, PhD); church ministries (MA); church music (MM); cinema and video production (MA); counseling (MS); curriculum and instruction (Ed D); divinity (M Div); dramatic production (MA); educational leadership (MS, Ed D, Ed S); elementary education (M Ed, MAT); English (M Ed, MA, MAT); fine arts (MA); graphic design (MA); history (M Ed, MA); illustration (MA); interpretative speech (MA); mathematics (M Ed, MAT); medical missions (Certificate); ministry (MM, D Min); multi-categorical special education (M Ed, MAT); music (M Ed); New Testament interpretation (PhD); Old Testament interpretation (PhD); orchestral instrument performance (MM); organ performance (MM); pastoral studies (MA); personnel services (MS, Ed S); piano pedagogy (MM); piano performance (MM); platform arts (MA); radio and television broadcasting (MS); rhetoric and public address (MA); secondary education (M Ed); studio art (MA); teaching Bible (MA); theology (MA, PhD); voice performance (MM); youth ministries (MA); M Div/MM.

Boston University, Graduate School of Arts and Sciences, Division of Religious and Theological Studies, Boston, MA 02215. Offers MA, PhD. *Students:* 56 full-time (22 women), 11 part-time (7 women); includes 10 minority (2 African Americans, 8 Asian Americans or Pacific Islanders), 7 international. Average age 34. 149 applicants, 15% accepted, 5 enrolled. In 2009, 5 master's, 8 doctorates awarded. Terminal master's awarded for partial completion of doctoral program. *Degree requirements:* For master's, one foreign language, comprehensive exam, thesis; for doctorate, 2 foreign languages, comprehensive exam, thesis/dissertation. *Entrance requirements:* For master's and doctorate, GRE General Test, 3 letters of recommendation, academic writing sample. Additional exam requirements/recommendations for international students: Required—TOEFL (minimum score 550 paper-based; 213 computer-based). *Application deadline:* For fall admission, 1/1 for domestic and international students. Application fee: $70. Electronic applications accepted. *Expenses:* Tuition: Full-time $37,910; part-time $1184 per credit hour. Required

Religion

Boston University (continued)

fees: $386; $40 per semester. Part-time tuition and fees vary according to class time, course level, degree level and program. *Financial support:* In 2009–10, 46 students received support, including 2 fellowships with full tuition reimbursements available (averaging $18,900 per year), 1 research assistantship with full tuition reimbursement available (averaging $18,400 per year), 6 teaching assistantships with full tuition reimbursements available (averaging $18,400 per year); career-related internships or fieldwork, Federal Work-Study, tuition waivers (partial), and unspecified assistantships also available. Support available to part-time students. Financial award application deadline: 1/1; financial award applicants required to submit FAFSA. *Unit head:* Jonathan Klawans, Chairman, 617-353-4432, Fax: 617-353-5441, E-mail: jklawans@bu.edu. *Application contact:* Karen Nardella, Department Administrator, 617-353-2636, Fax: 617-353-5441, E-mail: kcn@bu.edu.

Briercrest Seminary, Graduate Programs, Program in Christian Ministries, Caronport, SK S0H 0S0, Canada. Offers leadership (MA); marriage and family counseling (MA); missions (MA); pastoral counseling (MA); worship (MA); youth and family ministry (MA). Part-time programs available. *Degree requirements:* For master's, comprehensive exam, thesis optional. *Entrance requirements:* Additional exam requirements/recommendations for international students: Required—TOEFL (minimum score 550 paper-based; 213 computer-based).

Briercrest Seminary, Graduate Programs, Program in Theology, Caronport, SK S0H 0S0, Canada. Offers Biblical studies (M Div); leadership and management (M Div); New Testament (MATS); Old Testament (MATS); pastoral counseling (M Div); pastoral ministry (M Div); theological studies (M Div); theology (MATS); worship (M Div); youth and family ministry (M Div). *Accreditation:* ATS. Part-time programs available. *Degree requirements:* For master's, comprehensive exam, thesis optional. *Entrance requirements:* Additional exam requirements/recommendations for international students: Required—TOEFL (minimum score 550 paper-based; 213 computer-based).

Brown University, Graduate School, Department of Religious Studies, Providence, RI 02912. Offers ancient Judaism (PhD); early Christianity (PhD); religion and critical thought (PhD); religion in the ancient Mediterranean (PhD); religion, culture, and comparison (PhD). *Degree requirements:* For doctorate, 2 foreign languages, thesis/dissertation. *Entrance requirements:* For doctorate, GRE General Test.

Bryn Athyn College of the New Church, Academy of the New Church Theological School, Bryn Athyn, PA 19009-0717. Offers divinity (M Div); religious studies (MA). Part-time programs available. Postbaccalaureate distance learning degree programs offered (minimal on-campus study). *Degree requirements:* For master's, thesis; for M Div, 3 foreign languages, thesis/dissertation. *Entrance requirements:* Additional exam requirements/recommendations for international students: Required—TOEFL.

California Institute of Integral Studies, School of Consciousness and Transformation, San Francisco, CA 94103. Offers creative inquiry (MFA); cultural anthropology and social transformation (MA); East-West psychology (MA, PhD); integrative health studies (MA); philosophy and religion (MA, PhD), including Asian and comparative studies, philosophy, cosmology, and consciousness, women's spirituality; social and cultural anthropology (PhD); transformative leadership (MA); transformative studies (PhD); writing and consciousness (MFA). Part-time and evening/weekend programs available. Postbaccalaureate distance learning degree programs offered (minimal on-campus study). *Students:* 334 full-time (218 women), 126 part-time (77 women); includes 116 minority (40 African Americans, 4 American Indian/Alaska Native, 42 Asian Americans or Pacific Islanders, 30 Hispanic Americans). Average age 38. 265 applicants, 90% accepted, 149 enrolled. In 2009, 64 master's, 22 doctorates awarded. Terminal master's awarded for partial completion of doctoral program. *Degree requirements:* For master's, comprehensive exam (for some programs), thesis optional; for doctorate, comprehensive exam, thesis/dissertation, 1 foreign language (Asian comparative studies). *Entrance requirements:* For master's, minimum GPA of 3.0, letters of recommendation, writing sample; for doctorate, master's degree, minimum GPA of 3.0, letters of recommendation, writing sample. Additional exam requirements/recommendations for international students: Required—TOEFL. *Application deadline:* For fall admission, 2/1 priority date for domestic and international students; for spring admission, 10/15 priority date for domestic and international students. Applications are processed on a rolling basis. Application fee: $65. Electronic applications accepted. *Expenses:* Tuition: Full-time $15,300; part-time $850 per credit hour. Required fees: $110 per semester. Tuition and fees vary according to degree level. *Financial support:* In 2009–10, 330 students received support; research assistantships, teaching assistantships, career-related internships or fieldwork, Federal Work-Study, scholarships/grants, and tuition waivers (partial) available. Support available to part-time students. Financial award application deadline: 4/15; financial award applicants required to submit FAFSA. *Faculty research:* Altered states of consciousness, dreams, cosmology, postcolonial studies, integrative health studies. *Application contact:* Allyson Werner, Associate Director of Admissions, 415-575-6155, Fax: 415-575-1268.

California State University, Long Beach, Graduate Studies, College of Liberal Arts, Department of Religious Studies, Long Beach, CA 90840. Offers MA. Part-time and evening/weekend programs available. *Faculty:* 4 full-time (1 woman). *Students:* 7 full-time (4 women), 18 part-time (8 women); includes 14 minority (1 African American, 3 Asian Americans or Pacific Islanders, 10 Hispanic Americans). Average age 33. 13 applicants, 54% accepted, 7 enrolled. *Entrance requirements:* Additional exam requirements/recommendations for international students: Required—TOEFL. *Application deadline:* For fall admission, 3/15 for domestic students, 7/1 for international students; for spring admission, 12/1 for international students. Applications are processed on a rolling basis. Application fee: $55. Electronic applications accepted. *Expenses:* Required fees: $1802 per semester. Part-time tuition and fees vary according to course load. *Financial support:* Application deadline: 3/2. *Unit head:* Dr. Peter Lowentrout, Chair, 562-985-4906, Fax: 562-985-5540. *Application contact:* Dr. Carlos R. Piar, Graduate Advisor, 562-985-8727, Fax: 562-985-5540, E-mail: crpiar@csulb.edu.

Calvin Theological Seminary, Graduate and Professional Programs, Grand Rapids, MI 49546-4387. Offers Bible and theology (MA); divinity (M Div), including ancient near eastern languages and literature, contextual ministry, evangelism and teaching, history of Christianity, new church development, New Testament, Old Testament, pastoral care and leadership, preaching and worship, theological studies, youth and family ministries; educational ministry (MA); historical theology (PhD); missions and evangelism (MA); pastoral care (MA); philosophical and moral theology (PhD); systematic theology (PhD); theological studies (MTS); theology (Th M); worship (MA); youth and family ministries (MA). *Accreditation:* ACIPE; ATS. Part-time programs available. *Faculty:* 28 full-time (2 women), 20 part-time/adjunct (7 women). *Students:* 203 full-time (39 women), 48 part-time (19 women); includes 28 minority (10 African Americans, 13 Asian Americans or Pacific Islanders, 5 Hispanic Americans), 69 international. Average age 31. 152 applicants, 89% accepted, 98 enrolled. In 2009, 45 first professional degrees, 42 master's, 6 doctorates awarded. *Degree requirements:* For master's, thesis (for some programs); for doctorate, 4 foreign languages, comprehensive exam, thesis/dissertation; for M Div, 2 foreign languages. *Entrance requirements:* For doctorate, GRE General Test, Hebrew, Greek, and a modern foreign language. Additional exam requirements/recommendations for international students: Required—TOEFL (minimum score 550 paper-based; 213 computer-based), TWE (minimum score 4). *Application deadline:* For fall admission, 3/1 priority date for domestic and international students. Applications are processed on a rolling basis. Application fee: $25. Electronic applications accepted. *Expenses:* Tuition: Full-time $11,814; part-time $358 per semester hour. Tuition and fees vary according to degree level. *Financial support:* In 2009–10, 187 students received support, including 4 fellowships with full tuition reimbursements available (averaging $8,405 per year), 4 teaching assistantships with full tuition reimbursements available (averaging $5,760 per year); career-related internships or fieldwork, institutionally sponsored loans, scholarships/grants, and tuition waivers (full) also available. Support available to part-time students. Financial award application deadline: 3/1; financial award applicants required to submit FAFSA. *Faculty research:* Recent Trinity theory, Christian anthropology, Proverbs, reformed confessions, Paul's view of law. *Unit head:* Dr. Cornelius Plantinga, Head, 616-957-6024, Fax: 616-957-6536, E-mail: sempres@calvinseminary.edu. *Application contact:* Rev. Gregory Janke, Director of Admissions, 616-957-7035, Fax: 616-957-6101, E-mail: gjanke@calvinseminary.edu.

Cardinal Stritch University, College of Arts and Sciences, Department of Religious Studies, Milwaukee, WI 53217-3985. Offers lay ministries (MA); ministry (MA); religious studies (MA). Part-time and evening/weekend programs available. *Degree requirements:* For master's, comprehensive exam, thesis, faculty recommendation, research project. *Entrance requirements:* For master's, interview, minimum GPA of 2.75.

The Catholic University of America, School of Arts and Sciences, Program in Early Christian Studies, Washington, DC 20064. Offers MA, PhD. Part-time programs available. *Faculty:* 1 full-time (0 women). *Students:* 1 (woman) full-time, 6 part-time (1 woman), 1 international. Average age 38. 4 applicants, 0% accepted, 0 enrolled. In 2009, 1 doctorate awarded. *Degree requirements:* For master's, one foreign language, comprehensive exam, thesis; for doctorate, 2 foreign languages, comprehensive exam, thesis/dissertation. *Entrance requirements:* For master's and doctorate, GRE General Test, statement of purpose, official copies of academic transcripts, three letters of recommendation. Additional exam requirements/recommendations for international students: Required—TOEFL (minimum score 580 paper-based; 237 computer-based). *Application deadline:* For fall admission, 8/1 priority date for domestic students, 7/15 for international students; for spring admission, 12/1 priority date for domestic students, 10/15 for international students. Applications are processed on a rolling basis. Application fee: $55. Electronic applications accepted. *Expenses:* Tuition: Full-time $31,740; part-time $1245 per credit hour. Required fees: $50; $25 per semester hour. One-time fee: $425. *Financial support:* Fellowships, research assistantships, teaching assistantships, Federal Work-Study, scholarships/grants, tuition waivers (full and partial), and unspecified assistantships available. Financial award application deadline: 2/1; financial award applicants required to submit FAFSA. *Faculty research:* Languages and literatures of the Christian Near East, systematic and fundamental theology, Greek and Latin patristics, early Christian poetry and hagiography, ancient and late antique philosophy. *Unit head:* Dr. Philip Rousseau, Director, 202-319-6217, Fax: 202-319-6609, E-mail: rousseau@cua.edu. *Application contact:* Julie Schwing, Director of Graduate Admissions, 202-319-5057, Fax: 202-319-6533, E-mail: cua-admissions@cua.edu.

The Catholic University of America, School of Theology and Religious Studies, Washington, DC 20064. Offers Biblical studies (STB, MA, PhD, STL); Catholic educational leadership (MA); church history (PhD); Hispanic pastoral leadership (Certificate); Hispanic/Latino ministry (M Div); historical theology (STB, STD); history of religions (Hinduism/Islam) (MA, PhD); liturgical studies/sacramental theology (MA, PhD, STD, STL); moral theology/ethics (STB, MA, PhD, STD, STL); pastoral studies (M Div, Certificate); religion and culture (PhD); religious education/catechetics (MA, MRE, PhD); spirituality (STB, PhD, STD, STL); systematic and historical theology (MA, PhD, STD, STL). *Accreditation:* ATS (one or more programs are accredited). Part-time programs available. *Faculty:* 40 full-time (6 women), 10 part-time/adjunct (2 women). *Students:* 169 full-time (26 women), 225 part-time (57 women); includes 33 minority (10 African Americans, 1 American Indian/Alaska Native, 9 Asian Americans or Pacific Islanders, 13 Hispanic Americans), 73 international. Average age 36. 226 applicants, 72% accepted, 75 enrolled. In 2009, 9 first professional degrees, 14 master's, 26 doctorates awarded. *Degree requirements:* For master's, variable foreign language requirement, comprehensive exam, thesis (for some programs); for doctorate, variable foreign language requirement, comprehensive exam, thesis/dissertation; for first professional degree, comprehensive exam. *Entrance requirements:* For first professional degree and master's, GRE General Test, statement of purpose, official copies of academic transcripts, three letters of recommendation; for doctorate, GRE General Test, 3 letters of recommendation. Additional exam requirements/recommendations for international students: Required—TOEFL (minimum score 580 paper-based; 237 computer-based). *Application deadline:* For fall admission, 8/1 priority date for domestic students, 7/15 for international students; for spring admission, 12/1 priority date for domestic students, 10/15 for international students. Applications are processed on a rolling basis. Application fee: $55. Electronic applications accepted. *Expenses:* Tuition: Full-time $31,740; part-time $1245 per credit hour. Required fees: $50; $25 per semester hour. One-time fee: $425. *Financial support:* Fellowships, research assistantships, teaching assistantships, Federal Work-Study, scholarships/grants, tuition waivers (full and partial), and unspecified assistantships available. Financial award application deadline: 2/1; financial award applicants required to submit FAFSA. *Faculty research:* Historical and systematic theology, religious education and catechetics, moral theology and ethics, Biblical studies, liturgical studies and sacramental theology. Total annual research expenditures: $66,740. *Unit head:* Msgr. Kevin W. Irwin, Dean, 202-319-5683, Fax: 202-319-4967, E-mail: irwin@cua.edu. *Application contact:* Julie Schwing, Director of Graduate Admissions, 202-319-5057, Fax: 202-319-6533, E-mail: cua-admissions@cua.edu.

Chestnut Hill College, School of Graduate Studies, Department of Religious Studies and Philosophy, Philadelphia, PA 19118-2693. Offers holistic spirituality (MA); holistic spirituality and healthcare (MA); holistic spirituality and spiritual direction (MA); holistic spirituality/health care (CAS); spiritual direction (CAS); spirituality (CAS); supervision of spiritual directors (CAS). Part-time and evening/weekend programs available. *Degree requirements:* For master's, thesis optional, practicum (spiritual direction and healthcare tracks). *Entrance requirements:* For master's, MAT or GRE, writing sample. Additional exam requirements/recommendations for international students: Required—TOEFL (minimum score 500 paper-based; 213 computer-based). *Faculty research:* Interfaith spiritual direction, supervisory issues for spiritual directors, ecclesial responsibility of reconciliation, globalization of the Magdalene laundry system, ethical issues at the end of life.

Chicago Theological Seminary, Graduate and Professional Programs, Chicago, IL 60637-1507. Offers preaching (D Min); religion and health (D Min); religious studies (MA); spirituality and spiritual direction (D Min); theology (M Div); theology, ethics and the human sciences (PhD); M Div/MSW. *Accreditation:* ACIPE; ATS. Part-time programs available. *Degree requirements:* For master's, thesis; for doctorate, 2 foreign languages, comprehensive exam, thesis/dissertation; for M Div, thesis/dissertation. *Entrance requirements:* For doctorate, GRE General Test. Additional exam requirements/recommendations for international students: Required—TOEFL (minimum score 217 computer-based). *Faculty research:* Bible, culture and hermeneutics, theology, gender and sexuality, black faith and life, spirituality and psychology, practical theology.

Christian Brothers University, School of Arts, Memphis, TN 38104-5581. Offers Catholic studies (MACS); curriculum and instruction (M Ed); educational leadership (MSEL); teacher-leadership (M Ed); teaching (MAT). Part-time and evening/weekend programs available. *Faculty:* 7 full-time (4 women), 10 part-time/adjunct (7 women). *Students:* 62 full-time (49 women), 175 part-time (125 women); includes 70 minority (60 African Americans, 5 Asian Americans or Pacific Islanders, 5 Hispanic Americans). Average age 32. In 2009, 92 master's awarded. *Entrance requirements:* For master's, GRE, GMAT, PRAXIS II. *Application deadline:* Applications are processed on a rolling basis. Application fee: $35. *Expenses:* Contact institution. *Financial support:* Institutionally sponsored loans available. Support available to part-time students. *Unit head:* Dr. Marius Carriere, Dean, 901-321-3366, Fax: 901-321-4340, E-mail: mcarrier@cbu.edu. *Application contact:* Dr. Talana L. Vogel, Director, 901-321-4101, Fax: 901-321-3408, E-mail: tvogel@cbu.edu.

Christian Theological Seminary, Graduate and Professional Programs, Indianapolis, IN 46208-3301. Offers educational and arts ministries (MA); marriage and family therapy (MA); pastoral care and counseling (D Min); psychotherapy and faith (MA); theological studies (MTS); theology (M Div). *Accreditation:* AAMFT/COAMFTE (one or more programs are accredited); ACIPE; ATS. Part-time programs available. *Faculty:* 18 full-time (8 women), 18 part-time/adjunct (4 women). *Students:* 152 full-time (98 women), 53 part-time (28 women); includes 73 minority (53 African Americans, 1 American Indian/Alaska Native, 4 Asian Americans or Pacific Islanders, 15 Hispanic Americans), 2 international. Average age 41. 120 applicants, 86% accepted, 71 enrolled. In 2009, 31 first professional degrees, 22 master's, 3 doctorates awarded. Terminal master's awarded for partial completion of doctoral program. *Degree* *requirements:* For master's, comprehensive exam (for some programs), thesis (for some programs); for doctorate, comprehensive exam, thesis/dissertation; for M Div, comprehensive exam, thesis/dissertation (for some programs), missionary and cross-cultural experience. *Entrance requirements:* For master's, GRE General Test, MAT; for doctorate, M Div or BD. *Application deadline:* For fall admission, 7/15 for domestic and international students; for spring admission, 11/15 for domestic and international students. Applications are processed on a rolling basis. Application fee: $30. Electronic applications accepted. *Expenses:* Tuition: Full-time $9310; part-time $490 per credit hour. Required fees: $180; $160 per semester. Tuition and fees vary according to course load. *Financial support:* In 2009–10, 187 students received support, including 12 teaching assistantships (averaging $350 per year); career-related internships or fieldwork, Federal Work-Study, scholarships/grants, and tuition waivers (full and partial) also available. Support available to part-time students. Financial award application deadline: 4/1; financial award applicants required to submit FAFSA. *Faculty research:* Faith formation, peer learning post graduation. *Unit head:* Dr. Edward L. Wheeler, President, 317-931-2304, Fax: 317-923-1961, E-mail: wheeler@cts.edu. *Application contact:* Rev. Mary Harris, Associate Dean for Student Services, 317-931-2300, Fax: 317-923-1961, E-mail: mharris@cts.edu.

Cincinnati Christian University, Graduate School, Cincinnati, OH 45204-3200. Offers biblical studies (MA); church history (MA); counseling (MAC); divinity (M Div); ministry (M Min); practical ministries (MA); theological studies (MA). *Accreditation:* ATS. Part-time programs available. *Degree requirements:* For master's, thesis (for some programs); for M Div, 2 foreign languages, oral exam. *Entrance requirements:* For master's, GRE General Test. Additional exam requirements/recommendations for international students: Required—TOEFL. Electronic applications accepted.

Claremont Graduate University, Graduate Programs, School of Religion, Claremont, CA 91711-6160. Offers Hebrew Bible (MA, PhD); history of Christianity and religions of North America (MA, PhD); New Testament (MA, PhD); philosophy of religion and theology (MA, PhD); theology, ethics and culture (MA, PhD); women's studies in religion (MA, PhD); MA/PhD; MBA/PhD. Part-time programs available. *Faculty:* 7 full-time (2 women), 2 part-time/adjunct (0 women). *Students:* 223 full-time (90 women), 7 part-time (4 women); includes 37 minority (14 African Americans, 11 Asian Americans or Pacific Islanders, 12 Hispanic Americans), 23 international. Average age 37. In 2009, 10 master's, 14 doctorates awarded. Terminal master's awarded for partial completion of doctoral program. *Entrance requirements:* For master's and doctorate, GRE General Test. Additional exam requirements/recommendations for international students: Required—TOEFL (minimum score 550 paper-based; 213 computer-based; 80 iBT). *Application deadline:* For fall admission, 2/1 priority date for domestic students. Applications are processed on a rolling basis. Application fee: $60. Electronic applications accepted. *Expenses:* Tuition: Full-time $35,046; part-time $1524 per credit. Required fees: $161 per semester. *Financial support:* Fellowships, research assistantships, teaching assistantships, Federal Work-Study, institutionally sponsored loans, and scholarships/grants available. Support available to part-time students. Financial award application deadline: 2/15; financial award applicants required to submit FAFSA. *Unit head:* Anselm Min, Dean, 909-607-3214, Fax: 909-621-9587, E-mail: anselm.min@cgu.edu. *Application contact:* Brent Smith, Recruiter, 909-607-2653, Fax: 909-607-9587, E-mail: brent.smith@cgu.edu.

Claremont School of Theology, Graduate and Professional Programs, Program in Religion, Claremont, CA 91711-3199. Offers practical theology (PhD), including religious education, spiritual care and counseling; religion (PhD), including Hebrew Bible, New Testament and Christian origins, process studies, religion, ethics, and society; religion and theology (MA); religious education (MARE). *Accreditation:* ACIPE; ATS. Terminal master's awarded for partial completion of doctoral program. *Degree requirements:* For master's, thesis; for doctorate, 2 foreign languages, thesis/dissertation. *Entrance requirements:* For doctorate, GRE General Test. Additional exam requirements/recommendations for international students: Required—TOEFL (minimum score 250 computer-based). Electronic applications accepted.

College of the Humanities and Sciences, Harrison Middleton University, Graduate Program, Tempe, AZ 85282. Offers education (MA, Ed D); humanities (MA); imaginative literature (MA); interdisciplinary studies (DA); jurisprudence (MA); natural science (MA); philosophy and religion (MA); social science (MA). Part-time and evening/weekend programs available. Postbaccalaureate distance learning degree programs offered (no on-campus study). *Faculty:* 17 full-time (7 women), 14 part-time/adjunct (6 women). *Students:* 49 full-time (18 women). In 2009, 4 master's awarded. *Application deadline:* Applications are processed on a rolling basis. Application fee: $50. Electronic applications accepted. *Application contact:* Deborah Deacon, Dean of Graduate Studies, 877-248-6724, Fax: 800-762-1622, E-mail: ddeacon@chumsci.edu.

Columbia University, Graduate School of Arts and Sciences, Division of Humanities, Department of Religion, New York, NY 10027. Offers M Phil, MA, PhD. *Degree requirements:* For master's, 2 foreign languages, thesis, oral and written exams; for doctorate, variable foreign language requirement, thesis/dissertation. *Entrance requirements:* For master's and doctorate, GRE General Test. Additional exam requirements/recommendations for international students: Required—TOEFL.

Concordia University, School of Graduate Studies, Faculty of Arts and Science, Department of Religion, Program in History and Philosophy of Religion, Montréal, QC H3G 1M8, Canada. Offers MA. *Degree requirements:* For master's, comprehensive exam, thesis optional. *Entrance requirements:* For master's, honors degree in religion or equivalent. *Faculty research:* Comparative ethics, social theory and political society, Judaic studies.

Concordia University, School of Graduate Studies, Faculty of Arts and Science, Department of Religion, Program in Religion, Montréal, QC H3G 1M8, Canada. Offers PhD. *Degree requirements:* For doctorate, one foreign language, comprehensive exam, thesis/dissertation.

Concordia University, School of Theology, Irvine, CA 92612-3299. Offers Christian leadership (MA); research in theology (MA); theology and culture (MA). Part-time and evening/weekend programs available. Postbaccalaureate distance learning degree programs offered (no on-campus study). *Faculty:* 9 full-time (2 women). *Students:* 32 full-time (4 women), 8 part-time (3 women); includes 5 minority (1 African American, 1 Asian American or Pacific Islander, 3 Hispanic Americans), 3 international. Average age 36. 7 applicants, 100% accepted, 5 enrolled. In 2009, 10 master's awarded. *Degree requirements:* For master's, project/thesis or vicarage. *Entrance requirements:* For master's, 2 references, interview. Additional exam requirements/recommendations for international students: Required—TOEFL. *Application deadline:* For fall admission, 7/1 priority date for domestic students, 6/1 for international students; for spring admission, 11/30 priority date for domestic students, 10/1 for international students. Applications are processed on a rolling basis. Application fee: $50 ($125 for international students). Electronic applications accepted. *Expenses:* Contact institution. *Financial support:* In 2009–10, 34 students received support. Scholarships/grants available. Financial award applicants required to submit FAFSA. *Unit head:* Rev. Dr. James Bachman, Dean, School of Theology Graduate Studies, 949-854-8002 Ext. 1751, E-mail: james.bachman@cui.edu. *Application contact:* Carrie Donohoe, Christ College Program Coordinator, 949-854-8002 Ext. 1407, E-mail: carrie.donohoe@cui.edu.

Concordia University Chicago, College of Graduate and Innovative Programs, Program in Religion, River Forest, IL 60305-1499. Offers MA. Part-time and evening/weekend programs available. *Degree requirements:* For master's, comprehensive exam, thesis. *Entrance requirements:* For master's, minimum GPA of 2.9. Additional exam requirements/recommendations for international students: Required—TOEFL (minimum score 550 paper-based; 195 computer-based). Electronic applications accepted. *Faculty research:* Dead Sea Scrolls, cultural construction of gender in early modern Europe, Luther, Luther's theology of the cross, gospels of Mark and John.

Cornell University, Graduate School, Graduate Fields of Arts and Sciences, Field of Asian Religions, Ithaca, NY 14853-0001. Offers PhD. *Faculty:* 9 full-time (3 women). *Students:* 6 full-time (1 woman), 1 international. Average age 30. 16 applicants, 19% accepted, 0 enrolled. In 2009, 2 doctorates awarded. *Degree requirements:* For doctorate, comprehensive exam, thesis/dissertation. *Entrance requirements:* For doctorate, GRE General Test, academic writing sample, 3 letters of recommendation. Additional exam requirements/recommendations for international students: Required—TOEFL (minimum score 600 paper-based; 250 computer-based; 77 iBT). *Application deadline:* For fall admission, 1/15 for domestic students. Application fee: $70. Electronic applications accepted. *Expenses:* Tuition: Full-time $29,500. Required fees: $70. Full-time tuition and fees vary according to degree level, program and student level. *Financial support:* In 2009–10, 5 students received support; fellowships with full tuition reimbursements available, research assistantships with full tuition reimbursements available, teaching assistantships with full tuition reimbursements available, institutionally sponsored loans, scholarships/grants, health care benefits, and unspecified assistantships available. *Unit head:* Director of Graduate Studies, 607-255-9099, Fax: 607-255-1345. *Application contact:* Graduate Field Assistant, 607-255-9099, Fax: 607-255-1345, E-mail: asian-religions@cornell.edu.

Denver Seminary, Graduate and Professional Programs, Littleton, CO 80120. Offers apologetics (Certificate); biblical studies (MA); Christian formation and soul care (MA, Certificate); Christian studies (MA, Certificate); church and parachurch leadership (D Min); counseling licensure (MA); counseling ministry (MA); intercultural ministry (Certificate); leadership (MA, Certificate); marriage and family counseling (D Min); pastoral ministry (D Min); philosophy of religion (MA); spiritual guidance (Certificate); theology (M Div, Certificate); worship (Certificate); youth and family ministry (MA). *Accreditation:* ACA; ACIPE; ATS (one or more programs are accredited). Part-time and evening/weekend programs available. Postbaccalaureate distance learning degree programs offered. *Degree requirements:* For master's, 2 foreign languages, thesis (for some programs); for doctorate, 2 foreign languages, thesis/dissertation; for M Div, 2 foreign languages. *Entrance requirements:* For M Div, minimum undergraduate GPA of 2.5; for master's, minimum undergraduate GPA of 3.0; for doctorate, M Div, 3 years of ministry experience. Additional exam requirements/recommendations for international students: Required—TOEFL (minimum score 575 paper-based; 233 computer-based; 90 iBT). Electronic applications accepted.

Duke University, Graduate School, Department of Religion, Durham, NC 27708. Offers MA, PhD. Part-time programs available. *Faculty:* 45 full-time. *Students:* 87 full-time (34 women); includes 12 minority (3 African Americans, 7 Asian Americans or Pacific Islanders, 2 Hispanic Americans), 13 international. 227 applicants, 17% accepted, 21 enrolled. In 2009, 7 master's, 15 doctorates awarded. Terminal master's awarded for partial completion of doctoral program. *Degree requirements:* For master's, one foreign language, thesis or alternative; for doctorate, 2 foreign languages, thesis/dissertation. *Entrance requirements:* For master's and doctorate, GRE General Test. Additional exam requirements/recommendations for international students: Required—TOEFL (minimum score 550 paper-based; 213 computer-based; 83 iBT), IELTS (minimum score 7). *Application deadline:* For fall admission, 12/8 priority date for domestic and international students. Application fee: $75. Electronic applications accepted. *Financial support:* Federal Work-Study available. Financial award application deadline: 12/31; financial award applicants required to submit FAFSA. *Unit head:* Grant Wacker, Director of Graduate Studies, 919-660-3512, Fax: 919-660-3530. *Application contact:* Gay C. Trotter, Staff Assistant, 919-660-3512, Fax: 919-660-3530, E-mail: gtrotter@duke.edu.

Earlham School of Religion, Graduate Programs, Richmond, IN 47374-5360. Offers religion (MA); theology (M Div, M Min). *Accreditation:* ACIPE; ATS. Part-time programs available. Postbaccalaureate distance learning degree programs offered (minimal on-campus study). *Degree requirements:* For master's, one foreign language, comprehensive exam, thesis; for M Div, project. *Entrance requirements:* For M Div and master's, 3 references. Additional exam requirements/recommendations for international students: Required—TOEFL (minimum score 550 paper-based; 218 computer-based; 82 iBT). Electronic applications accepted. *Faculty research:* Digitizing Quaker texts, vital Quaker ministry.

Eastern Mennonite University, Eastern Mennonite Seminary, Harrisonburg, VA 22802-2462. Offers church leadership (MA); divinity (M Div); ministry studies (Certificate); online theological studies (Certificate); religion (MA); theological studies (Certificate). *Accreditation:* ATS. Part-time programs available. *Faculty:* 11 full-time (2 women), 8 part-time/adjunct (3 women). *Students:* 45 full-time (20 women), 81 part-time (33 women); includes 9 minority (5 African Americans, 4 Hispanic Americans), 6 international. In 2009, 13 first professional degrees, 9 master's awarded. *Degree requirements:* For master's, thesis (for some programs); for M Div, thesis/dissertation (for some programs), supervised field education. *Entrance requirements:* For M Div and master's, minimum GPA of 2.5. Additional exam requirements/recommendations for international students: Required—TOEFL (minimum score 550 paper-based; 213 computer-based). *Application deadline:* For fall admission, 6/15 priority date for domestic and international students; for winter admission, 11/15 priority date for domestic and international students; for spring admission, 3/15 priority date for domestic and international students. Applications are processed on a rolling basis. Application fee: $25. *Expenses:* Contact institution. *Financial support:* Application deadline: 6/30. *Faculty research:* Spiritual direction and culture of call, leadership coaching: an approach to leadership in a culture of call, clarity of call in the probationary process for United Methodist clergy in Virginia, EMS women's experiences of culture of call efforts, practices of excellent and fruitful Mennonite pastoral ministry. *Unit head:* Dr. Ervin R. Stutzman, Dean, 540-432-4261, Fax: 540-432-4444, E-mail: stutzerv@emu.edu. *Application contact:* Don A. Yoder, Director of Seminary and Graduate Admissions, 540-432-4257, Fax: 540-432-4598, E-mail: yoderda@emu.edu.

Edgewood College, Program in Religious Studies, Madison, WI 53711-1997. Offers MA. Part-time and evening/weekend programs available. In 2009, 9 master's awarded. *Entrance requirements:* For master's, minimum GPA of 2.75, 2 letters of reference. Additional exam requirements/recommendations for international students: Required—TOEFL (minimum score 213 computer-based). *Application deadline:* For fall admission, 8/24 for domestic students, 8/1 for international students; for spring admission, 1/10 for domestic students, 10/1 for international students. Applications are processed on a rolling basis. Application fee: $25. Electronic applications accepted. *Expenses:* Tuition: Part-time $688 per credit hour. *Financial support:* Career-related internships or fieldwork, institutionally sponsored loans, scholarships/grants, and tuition waivers (partial) available. *Faculty research:* Interpretation theory and New Testament, women and religion, theology and literature, Hebrew poetry. *Unit head:* Dr. John Leonard, Chairperson, 608-663-2823, Fax: 608-663-3291, E-mail: jleonard@edgewood.edu. *Application contact:* Joann Eastman, Admissions Counselor, 608-663-3250, Fax: 608-663-2214, E-mail: gps@edgewood.edu.

Elms College, Religious Studies Department, Chicopee, MA 01013-2839. Offers MAAT. Part-time and evening/weekend programs available. *Faculty:* 3 full-time (1 woman), 1 part-time/adjunct (0 women). *Students:* 6 part-time (3 women). Average age 35. 2 applicants, 100% accepted, 2 enrolled. In 2009, 6 master's awarded. *Degree requirements:* For master's, thesis. *Entrance requirements:* For master's, minimum GPA of 3.0. Additional exam requirements/recommendations for international students: Required—TOEFL. *Application deadline:* For fall admission, 7/1 priority date for domestic students; for spring admission, 11/1 priority date for domestic students. Applications are processed on a rolling basis. Application fee: $30. *Financial support:* Tuition waivers (partial) available. Financial award applicants required to submit FAFSA. *Unit head:* Dr. Martin Pion, Director of MALA/MAAT Programs, 413-265-3581, Fax: 413-594-3951, E-mail: pionm@elms.edu. *Application contact:* Dr. Martin Pion, Director of MALA/MAAT Programs, 413-265-3581, Fax: 413-594-3951, E-mail: pionm@elms.edu.

Emmanuel School of Religion, Graduate and Professional Programs, Johnson City, TN 37601-9438. Offers Christian care and counseling (M Div); Christian doctrine (MAR); Christian education (M Div); church history (MAR); ministry (D Min); New Testament (MAR); Old Testament (MAR); urban ministry (M Div); world missions (M Div). *Accreditation:* ACIPE; ATS. Part-time programs available. *Faculty:* 10 full-time (2 women), 5 part-time/adjunct (0 women). *Students:* 108 full-time (27 women), 48 part-time (13 women). Average age 32. *Degree requirements:* For master's, 2 foreign languages, thesis; for M Div, 2 foreign languages, thesis/dissertation or alternative. *Entrance requirements:* For doctorate, GRE General Test, Minnesota Multiphasic

Religion

Emmanuel School of Religion (continued)

Personality Inventory, M Div or equivalent. *Application deadline:* For fall admission, 8/1 priority date for domestic students. Applications are processed on a rolling basis. Application fee: $25. *Expenses:* Tuition: Full-time $7800; part-time $325 per credit hour. Required fees: $137.50 per semester. One-time fee: $240. Tuition and fees vary according to course load. *Financial support:* Teaching assistantships with partial tuition reimbursements, career-related internships or fieldwork, institutionally sponsored loans, scholarships/grants, and tuition waivers (partial) available. Support available to part-time students. Financial award application deadline: 4/1; financial award applicants required to submit FAFSA. *Faculty research:* Theology of Old Testament prophets, spiritual formation for Christian leaders, history of African churches and religions, social world of early Christianity, lay pastoral counseling. Total annual research expenditures: $12,000. *Unit head:* Dr. Rollin A. Ramsaran, Dean and Professor of New Testament, 423-461-1524, Fax: 423-926-6198, E-mail: ramsaranr@esr.edu. *Application contact:* Shelley Gasser, Administrative Assistant for Admissions, 423-461-1535, Fax: 423-926-6198, E-mail: gassers@esr.edu.

Emory University, Graduate School of Arts and Sciences, Department of Comparative Literature, Atlanta, GA 30322-1100. Offers comparative literature (PhD); English (Certificate); French (Certificate); Middle Eastern studies (PhD); philosophy (Certificate); psychoanalytic studies (PhD); religion (PhD); Spanish (Certificate); women studies (Certificate). *Degree requirements:* For doctorate, 2 foreign languages, comprehensive exam, thesis/dissertation. *Entrance requirements:* For doctorate, GRE General Test, minimum GPA of 3.0. Additional exam requirements/recommendations for international students: Required—TOEFL. Electronic applications accepted. *Faculty research:* Literary theory, psychoanalysis trauma and testimony, literature and religion, literature and technology, literature and philosophy, politics and global culture, literature and aesthetics.

Emory University, Graduate School of Arts and Sciences, Division of Religion, Atlanta, GA 30322-1100. Offers PhD. *Degree requirements:* For doctorate, 2 foreign languages, comprehensive exam, thesis/dissertation. *Entrance requirements:* For doctorate, GRE General Test, minimum GPA of 3.0. Additional exam requirements/recommendations for international students: Required—TOEFL. Electronic applications accepted. *Faculty research:* Systematic and historical theology, biblical studies.

Faith Baptist Bible College and Theological Seminary, Graduate Program, Ankeny, IA 50023. Offers biblical studies (MA); pastoral studies (M Div); pastoral training (MA); religion (MA); theological studies (MA). Part-time programs available. *Faculty:* 4 full-time (0 women), 4 part-time/adjunct (0 women). *Students:* 31 full-time (6 women), 35 part-time (8 women); includes 2 minority (1 African American, 1 Asian American or Pacific Islander), 2 international. Average age 29. In 2009, 9 first professional degrees, 12 master's awarded. *Degree requirements:* For master's, thesis or alternative; for M Div, 2 foreign languages. *Entrance requirements:* Additional exam requirements/recommendations for international students: Required—TOEFL (minimum score 550 paper-based; 197 computer-based). *Application deadline:* For fall admission, 8/1 priority date for domestic students, 8/1 for international students; for spring admission, 12/15 for domestic and international students. Applications are processed on a rolling basis. Application fee: $25. *Financial support:* Career-related internships or fieldwork and scholarships/grants available. Support available to part-time students. Financial award application deadline: 3/1; financial award applicants required to submit FAFSA. *Faculty research:* Baptist theology, American church history. *Unit head:* Dr. Ernest Schmidt, Dean of Seminary, 515-964-0601, E-mail: schmidte@faith.edu. *Application contact:* Patrick Odle, Vice President of Enrollment, 888-FAITH4U, Fax: 515-964-1638, E-mail: odlep@faith.edu.

Florida International University, College of Arts and Sciences, Department of Religious Studies, Miami, FL 33199. Offers MA. Part-time and evening/weekend programs available. *Faculty:* 12 full-time (3 women). *Students:* 14 full-time (8 women), 12 part-time (4 women); includes 9 minority (1 African American, 8 Hispanic Americans), 3 international. Average age 28. 22 applicants, 45% accepted, 9 enrolled. In 2009, 12 master's awarded. *Degree requirements:* For master's, thesis or alternative. *Entrance requirements:* For master's, minimum GPA of 3.0, 2 letters of recommendation. Additional exam requirements/recommendations for international students: Required—TOEFL (minimum score 550 paper-based; 80 iBT). *Application deadline:* For fall admission, 2/15 for domestic and international students; for spring admission, 10/1 for domestic students, 9/1 for international students. Application fee: $30. Electronic applications accepted. *Expenses:* Tuition, state resident: full-time $8008; part-time $4004 per year. Tuition, nonresident: full-time $20,104; part-time $10,052 per year. Required fees: $298; $149 per term. *Financial support:* Institutionally sponsored loans and scholarships/grants available. Financial award application deadline: 3/1; financial award applicants required to submit FAFSA. *Unit head:* Dr. Christine Gudorf, Chair, 305-348-2186, Fax: 305-348-1879, E-mail: religion@fiu.edu. *Application contact:* Dr. Oren Stier, Graduate Program Director, 305-348-2186, Fax: 305-348-1879, E-mail: religion@fiu.edu.

Florida State University, The Graduate School, College of Arts and Sciences, Department of Religion, Tallahassee, FL 32306-1520. Offers humanities (PhD), including religion; religion (MA, PhD). *Faculty:* 18 full-time (6 women), 5 part-time/adjunct (2 women). *Students:* 45 full-time (19 women), 6 part-time (3 women); includes 5 minority (1 African American, 1 American Indian/Alaska Native, 3 Hispanic Americans). Average age 26. 75 applicants, 28% accepted, 15 enrolled. In 2009, 9 master's, 6 doctorates awarded. Terminal master's awarded for partial completion of doctoral program. *Degree requirements:* For master's, one foreign language, comprehensive exam (for some programs), thesis (for some programs); for doctorate, 2 foreign languages, thesis/dissertation. *Entrance requirements:* For master's, GRE General Test, minimum GPA of 3.0; for doctorate, GRE General Test, MA in religion. Additional exam requirements/recommendations for international students: Required—TOEFL. *Application deadline:* For fall admission, 1/15 for domestic students, 1/5 for international students. Application fee: $30. Electronic applications accepted. *Expenses:* Tuition, state resident: full-time $7413. Tuition, nonresident: full-time $22,567. *Financial support:* In 2009–10, 45 students received support, including 2 fellowships with partial tuition reimbursements available (averaging $6,300 per year), 14 research assistantships with partial tuition reimbursements available (averaging $6,935 per year), 31 teaching assistantships with partial tuition reimbursements available (averaging $9,074 per year); Federal Work-Study, institutionally sponsored loans, and unspecified assistantships also available. Financial award application deadline: 3/15; financial award applicants required to submit FAFSA. *Faculty research:* Wisdom literature, Hindu goddesses, feminist theology and medical ethics, Tibetan Buddhism, religion and emotion. *Unit head:* Dr. John Corrigan, Chair, 850-644-1020, Fax: 850-644-7225, E-mail: john.corrigan@fsu.edu. *Application contact:* Dr. Bryan Cuevas, Director of Graduate Studies, 850-644-1020, Fax: 850-644-7225, E-mail: bcuevas@fsu.edu.

Fordham University, Graduate School of Religion and Religious Education, New York, NY 10458. Offers pastoral counseling and spiritual care (MA); pastoral ministry/spirituality/pastoral counseling (D Min); religion and religious education (MA); religious education (MS, PhD, PD); spiritual direction (Certificate). Part-time programs available. Terminal master's awarded for partial completion of doctoral program. *Degree requirements:* For master's, research paper; for doctorate, comprehensive exam, thesis/dissertation. *Entrance requirements:* For doctorate, MAT. Electronic applications accepted. *Expenses:* Contact institution. *Faculty research:* Spirituality and spiritual direction, pastoral care and counseling, adult family and community, growth and young adult.

General Theological Seminary, Graduate and Professional Programs, New York, NY 10011-4977. Offers Anglican studies (STM, Th D, Certificate); ascetical theology (Certificate); biblical studies (Certificate); congregational development (Certificate); divinity (M Div); historical and theological studies (Certificate); spiritual direction (MASD, STM, Certificate); theology (MA). *Accreditation:* ACIPE; ATS. Part-time and evening/weekend programs available. Terminal master's awarded for partial completion of doctoral program. *Degree requirements:* For master's, thesis; for doctorate, 2 foreign languages, thesis/dissertation. *Entrance requirements:* For M Div, GRE General Test, bishop's endorsement; for master's, GRE General Test; for doctorate, GRE, M Div or MA. Additional exam requirements/recommendations for international students: Required—TOEFL. *Faculty research:* Liturgy, New Testament, ethics, history, ecumenical relations.

Georgetown University, Graduate School of Arts and Sciences, School of Continuing Studies, Washington, DC 20057. Offers American studies (MALS); Catholic studies (MALS); classical civilizations (MALS); ethics and the professions (MALS); human resources management (MPS); humanities (MALS); individualized study (MALS); international affairs (MALS); Islam and Muslim-Christian relations (MALS); journalism (MPS); liberal studies (DLS); literature and society (MALS); medieval and early modern European studies (MALS); public relations (MPS); real estate (MPS); religious studies (MALS); social and public policy (MALS); sports industry management (MPS); the theory and practice of American democracy (MALS); visual culture (MALS). *Entrance requirements:* Additional exam requirements/recommendations for international students: Required—TOEFL.

The George Washington University, Columbian College of Arts and Sciences, Department of Religion, Washington, DC 20052. Offers Hinduism and Islam (MA). Part-time and evening/weekend programs available. *Faculty:* 5 full-time (2 women), 14 part-time/adjunct (5 women). *Students:* 2 full-time (both women), 5 part-time (3 women); includes 2 minority (both Asian Americans or Pacific Islanders), 3 international. Average age 27. 7 applicants, 86% accepted, 3 enrolled. In 2009, 1 master's awarded. *Degree requirements:* For master's, one foreign language, comprehensive exam, thesis. *Entrance requirements:* For master's, GRE General Test, interview, minimum GPA of 3.0. Additional exam requirements/recommendations for international students: Required—TOEFL (minimum score 550 paper-based; 213 computer-based; 80 iBT). *Application deadline:* For fall admission, 4/1 priority date for domestic students, 1/15 priority date for international students; for spring admission, 10/1 priority date for domestic students, 9/1 priority date for international students. Applications are processed on a rolling basis. Application fee: $60. Electronic applications accepted. *Financial support:* In 2009–10, 1 student received support. Federal Work-Study and tuition waivers available. *Unit head:* Dr. Alfred Hiltebeitel, Chair, 202-994-1674, Fax: 202-994-9379, E-mail: religion@gwu.edu. *Application contact:* Information Contact, 202-994-6325, Fax: 202-994-9379, E-mail: religion@gwu.edu.

Georgia State University, College of Arts and Sciences, Department of Religious Studies, Atlanta, GA 30302-4089. Offers MA. Part-time programs available. *Degree requirements:* For master's, thesis optional. *Entrance requirements:* For master's, GRE, 3 letters of recommendation, writing sample. Electronic applications accepted. *Faculty research:* Comparative religions; history of religions; religious ethics; comparative religious ritual; Islam, Judaism, and the Middle East.

Gonzaga University, College of Arts and Sciences, Department of Religious Studies, Spokane, WA 99258. Offers pastoral ministry (MA); religious studies (MA); spirituality (MA). *Faculty:* 21 full-time (7 women), 1 part-time/adjunct (0 women). *Students:* 8 full-time (2 women), 33 part-time (20 women); includes 4 minority (1 Asian American or Pacific Islander, 3 Hispanic Americans), 1 international. Average age 43. 15 applicants, 87% accepted, 13 enrolled. In 2009, 7 master's awarded. *Degree requirements:* For master's, comprehensive exam. *Entrance requirements:* For master's, GRE General Test or MAT, minimum GPA of 3.0. Additional exam requirements/recommendations for international students: Required—TOEFL. *Application deadline:* For fall admission, 7/20 priority date for domestic students; for spring admission, 11/1 for domestic students. Applications are processed on a rolling basis. Application fee: $50. Tuition and fees vary according to course level, course load, degree level, campus/location and program. *Financial support:* Application deadline: 3/1. *Unit head:* Dr. Ron Large, Chairperson, 509-328-4220 Ext. 6782, E-mail: jennings@gonzaga.edu. *Application contact:* Dr. Ron Large, Chairperson, 509-328-4220 Ext. 6782, E-mail: jennings@gonzaga.edu.

Gordon-Conwell Theological Seminary, Graduate and Professional Programs, South Hamilton, MA 01982. Offers biblical languages (MABL); church history (MACH); counseling (MACO); ministry (D Min); missions/evangelism (MAME); New Testament (MANT); Old Testament (MAOT); religion (MAR); theology (M Div, MATH, Th M, Th D). *Accreditation:* ACIPE; ATS (one or more programs are accredited). Part-time and evening/weekend programs available. *Degree requirements:* For master's, one foreign language, thesis optional; for doctorate, 2 foreign languages, thesis/dissertation; for M Div, 2 foreign languages. *Entrance requirements:* For M Div and master's, minimum GPA of 2.5; for doctorate, minimum GPA of 3.0.

Graceland University, Community of Christ Seminary, Independence, MO 64050. Offers Christian ministry (MACM); religion (MAR). Part-time programs available. Postbaccalaureate distance learning degree programs offered (minimal on-campus study). *Faculty:* 3 full-time (2 women), 8 part-time/adjunct (4 women). *Students:* 6 full-time (3 women), 14 part-time (7 women), 1 international. Average age 39. 13 applicants, 85% accepted, 11 enrolled. In 2009, 7 master's awarded. *Degree requirements:* For master's, thesis optional, portfolio or thesis (MAR), practicum (MACM). *Entrance requirements:* For master's, minimum cumulative GPA of 3.0. Additional exam requirements/recommendations for international students: Required—TOEFL. *Application deadline:* For fall admission, 8/15 priority date for domestic students; for winter admission, 10/15 priority date for domestic students; for spring admission, 4/15 priority date for domestic students. Applications are processed on a rolling basis. Application fee: $50. *Expenses:* Contact institution. *Financial support:* Scholarships/grants available. Financial award application deadline: 12/15; financial award applicants required to submit FAFSA. *Faculty research:* Theology, scripture. *Unit head:* Dr. Don H. Compier, Dean, 800-833-0524 Ext. 4900, Fax: 816-833-2990, E-mail: dcompier@graceland.edu. *Application contact:* Judy K. Luffman, Executive Assistant, 816-833-0524 Ext. 4508, Fax: 816-833-2990, E-mail: luffman@graceland.edu.

Graduate Theological Union, Graduate Programs, Berkeley, CA 94709-1212. Offers art and religion (MA, PhD, Th D); biblical languages (MA); Biblical studies (PhD, Th D); biblical studies (MA); Buddhist studies (MA); Christian spirituality (MA, PhD, Th D); cultural and historical studies of religions (MA, PhD, Th D); ethics and social theory (PhD, Th D); history (MA, PhD, Th D); homiletics (MA, PhD, Th D); interdisciplinary studies (PhD, Th D); Jewish studies (MA, PhD, Th D, Certificate); liturgical studies (MA, PhD, Th D); Near Eastern religions (PhD, Th D); Orthodox Christian studies (MA); religion and psychology (MA, PhD, Th D); religion and society/ethics and social theory (MA); systematic and philosophical theology (MA, PhD, Th D). *Accreditation:* ATS. Terminal master's awarded for partial completion of doctoral program. *Degree requirements:* For master's, one foreign language, thesis; for doctorate, one foreign language, comprehensive exam, thesis/dissertation. *Entrance requirements:* For master's, GRE General Test; for doctorate, GRE General Test, MA or M Div. Additional exam requirements/recommendations for international students: Required—TOEFL. Electronic applications accepted.

Grand Rapids Theological Seminary of Cornerstone University, Graduate Programs, Grand Rapids, MI 49525-5897. Offers biblical counseling (MA); Biblical counseling (M Div); chaplaincy (M Div); Christian education (M Div, MA); intercultural studies (M Div, MA); New Testament (MA, Th M); Old Testament (MA, Th M); pastoral studies (M Div); systematic theology (MA); theology (Th M). *Accreditation:* ATS. Part-time programs available. Postbaccalaureate distance learning degree programs offered (minimal on-campus study). *Entrance requirements:* Additional exam requirements/recommendations for international students: Required—TOEFL (minimum score 577 paper-based; 233 computer-based; 90 iBT). Electronic applications accepted.

Harding University Graduate School of Religion, Graduate Programs, Memphis, TN 38117-5499. Offers Christian ministry (MA); counseling (MA); ministry (M Div, D Min); religion (MA). *Accreditation:* ATS. Part-time programs available. Postbaccalaureate distance learning degree programs offered (minimal on-campus study). *Degree requirements:* For master's, variable foreign language requirement, thesis (for some programs); for doctorate, one foreign language, thesis/dissertation; for M Div, 2 foreign languages, thesis/dissertation optional. *Entrance requirements:* For M Div, GRE General Test (for graduates of non-accredited schools), minimum

GPA of 2.5; for master's, minimum GPA of 2.7; for doctorate, minimum GPA of 3.0. Additional exam requirements/recommendations for international students: Required—TOEFL (minimum score 550 paper-based; 213 computer-based; 79 iBT). Electronic applications accepted.

Hardin-Simmons University, Graduate School, Logsdon School of Theology, Program in Religion, Abilene, TX 79698-0001. Offers MA. Part-time programs available. *Faculty:* 15 full-time (1 woman), 3 part-time/adjunct (2 women). *Students:* 7 full-time (2 women), 6 part-time (2 women). Average age 25. 9 applicants, 89% accepted, 4 enrolled. In 2009, 1 master's awarded. *Degree requirements:* For master's, one foreign language, comprehensive exam, thesis or alternative. *Entrance requirements:* For master's, minimum undergraduate GPA of 3.0 in major, 2.7 overall, 18 hours of course work in religious studies, interview. Additional exam requirements/recommendations for international students: Required—TOEFL (minimum score 550 paper-based; 213 computer-based; 75 iBT). *Application deadline:* For fall admission, 8/15 priority date for domestic students, 4/1 for international students; for spring admission, 1/5 priority date for domestic students, 9/1 for international students. Applications are processed on a rolling basis. Application fee: $50. *Expenses:* Tuition: Full-time $11,430; part-time $635 per credit hour. Required fees: $650; $110 per semester. Tuition and fees vary according to degree level. *Financial support:* In 2009–10, 13 students received support; fellowships, scholarships/grants available. Support available to part-time students. Financial award application deadline: 6/30; financial award applicants required to submit FAFSA. *Faculty research:* Archaeology research in Christian origins, Hebrew grammar, history of Christian education, training of ministers into the twenty-first century, role of women in the Old Testament, contemporary ethical issues. *Unit head:* Dr. Travis Frampton, Director, 325-670-1270, Fax: 325-670-1406, E-mail: frampton@hsutx.edu. *Application contact:* Dr. Gary Stanlake, Dean of Graduate Studies, 325-670-1298, Fax: 325-670-1564, E-mail: gradoff@hsutx.edu.

Hartford Seminary, Graduate Programs, Hartford, CT 06105-2279. Offers black ministry (Certificate); Islamic studies (MA); ministerios Hispanos (Certificate); ministry (D Min); religious studies (MA); women's leadership institute (Certificate). *Accreditation:* ATS (one or more programs are accredited). Part-time and evening/weekend programs available. Postbaccalaureate distance learning degree programs offered (no on-campus study). *Degree requirements:* For master's, thesis optional, oral exam; for doctorate, thesis/dissertation, oral exam. *Entrance requirements:* For doctorate, experience in ministry, M Div. Additional exam requirements/recommendations for international students: Required—TOEFL (minimum score 550 paper-based; 213 computer-based; 80 iBT). *Faculty research:* Liturgy and social justice, professional leadership in ministry, congregational studies, Christian-Muslim relations, American religion.

Harvard University, Graduate School of Arts and Sciences, Committee on the Study of Religion, Cambridge, MA 02138. Offers PhD. *Degree requirements:* For doctorate, 2 foreign languages, thesis/dissertation. *Entrance requirements:* For doctorate, GRE General Test. Additional exam requirements/recommendations for international students: Required—TOEFL. *Expenses:* Tuition: Full-time $33,696. Required fees: $1126. Full-time tuition and fees vary according to program.

Hebrew Union College–Jewish Institute of Religion, School of Graduate Studies, Cincinnati, OH 45220-2488. Offers Bible and the ancient Near East (M Phil, MA, PhD); Hebrew letters (DHL); history of biblical interpretation (M Phil, MA, PhD); Jewish and Christian studies in the Greco-Roman period (M Phil, PhD); Jewish and cognate studies (M Phil); Judaic and cognate studies (MA, PhD); modern Jewish history (M Phil, MA, PhD); philosophy and Jewish religious thought (M Phil, MA, PhD); rabbinics (M Phil, MA, PhD). Part-time programs available. Terminal master's awarded for partial completion of doctoral program. *Degree requirements:* For master's, one foreign language, thesis optional; for doctorate, 3 foreign languages, comprehensive exam, thesis/dissertation. *Entrance requirements:* For master's and doctorate, GRE General Test, knowledge of Hebrew. Additional exam requirements/recommendations for international students: Required—TOEFL. *Faculty research:* Aramaic lexicon translations, German-Jewish history, neo-Babylonian texts.

Heritage Christian University, Graduate Programs, Florence, AL 35630. Offers counseling (MM); Greek (MA); ministry (MM); New Testament (MA). *Degree requirements:* For master's, practicum (MM), major research paper (MA). *Entrance requirements:* For master's, MAT or GRE, bachelor's degree in Bible from an accredited college or university, minimum GPA of 2.75, 3 letters of recommendation.

Holy Names University, Graduate Division, Sophia Center in Culture and Spirituality, Oakland, CA 94619-1699. Offers MA, Certificate. *Degree requirements:* For master's, thesis or alternative. *Entrance requirements:* For master's, minimum undergraduate GPA of 2.6 overall, 3.0 in major. Additional exam requirements/recommendations for international students: Required—TOEFL. *Faculty research:* Medieval mystics, environmental justice, work and spirituality.

Hope International University, School of Graduate and Professional Studies, Programs in Ministry, Fullerton, CA 92831-3138. Offers Christian leadership (MCM); church music (MA); church music (Korean track) (MCM); church planting (MCM); intercultural studies (MCM); worship (MCM). Part-time and evening/weekend programs available. Postbaccalaureate distance learning degree programs offered (minimal on-campus study). *Degree requirements:* For master's, thesis (for some programs), project. *Entrance requirements:* For master's, minimum GPA of 3.0, MCM program requires an undergraduate degree in music, 2 references. Additional exam requirements/recommendations for international students: Required—TOEFL (minimum score 550 paper-based; 213 computer-based; 86 iBT); Recommended—IELTS (minimum score 6.5). Electronic applications accepted. *Expenses:* Contact institution. *Faculty research:* Church dynamics, growth methodologies.

Iliff School of Theology, Graduate and Professional Programs, Denver, CO 80210-4798. Offers biblical studies (MA); church history (MA); religion (MA); religion and social change (MA); specialized ministry (MASM), including justice and peace, pastoral theology and care, religions leadership; theology (M Div, MTS, D Min, PhD), including Biblical studies (PhD), religion and psychological studies (PhD), religion and social change (PhD), theology, philosophy and culture (PhD); theology/ethics (MA). *Accreditation:* ACIPE; ATS. Part-time and evening/weekend programs available. *Degree requirements:* For master's, one foreign language, thesis (for some programs); for doctorate, 2 foreign languages, comprehensive exam, thesis/dissertation; for M Div, thesis/dissertation optional. *Entrance requirements:* For M Div, minimum GPA of 2.75, references; for master's, minimum GPA of 3.0, writing sample, references; for doctorate, GRE General Test, minimum GPA of 3.0, writing sample, letters of recommendation. Additional exam requirements/recommendations for international students: Required—TOEFL (minimum score 550 paper-based). Electronic applications accepted. *Faculty research:* Pastoral care, history, church music, contemporary church, biblical studies.

Indiana University Bloomington, University Graduate School, College of Arts and Sciences, Department of Religious Studies, Bloomington, IN 47405-7005. Offers MA, PhD. Part-time programs available. *Faculty:* 7 full-time (2 women). *Students:* 32 full-time (18 women), 1 (woman) part-time; includes 2 minority (1 Asian American or Pacific Islander, 1 Hispanic American), 4 international. Average age 31. 121 applicants, 19% accepted, 14 enrolled. Terminal master's awarded for partial completion of doctoral program. *Degree requirements:* For master's, variable foreign language requirement, thesis or alternative; for doctorate, 2 foreign languages, thesis/dissertation. *Entrance requirements:* For master's, GRE General Test; for doctorate, GRE, MA, writing sample. Additional exam requirements/recommendations for international students: Required—TOEFL. *Application deadline:* For fall admission, 1/15 priority date for domestic students, 12/15 for international students; for spring admission, 9/1 for domestic and international students. Application fee: $55 ($65 for international students). *Financial support:* In 2009–10, 14 students received support, including 5 fellowships with full tuition reimbursements available (averaging $15,500 per year), 1 research assistantship with full tuition reimbursement available (averaging $15,000 per year), 14 teaching assistantships with full tuition reimbursements available (averaging $11,386 per year); Federal Work-Study and institutionally sponsored loans also available. Financial award application deadline: 2/1. *Unit head:* Prof. David Brakke, Chair, 812-855-3531, Fax: 812-855-4687, E-mail: dbrakke@indiana.edu. *Application contact:* Debra Melsheimer, Graduate Secretary, 812-855-3531, Fax: 812-855-4687, E-mail: dmelshei@indiana.edu.

The Jewish Theological Seminary, The Graduate School, New York, NY 10027-4649. Offers ancient Judaism (MA, DHL, PhD); Bible (MA, DHL, PhD); Jewish education (PhD); Jewish history (MA, DHL, PhD); Jewish literature (MA, DHL, PhD); Jewish philosophy (MA, DHL, PhD); liturgy (MA, DHL, PhD); medieval Jewish studies (MA, DHL, PhD); Midrash (MA, DHL, PhD); modern Jewish studies (MA, DHL, PhD); Talmud and rabbinics (MA, DHL, PhD); MA/MSW. *Accreditation:* ACIPE. Part-time programs available. Terminal master's awarded for partial completion of doctoral program. *Degree requirements:* For master's, one foreign language, comprehensive exam (for some programs), thesis (for some programs); for doctorate, 3 foreign languages, comprehensive exam (for some programs), thesis/dissertation. *Entrance requirements:* For master's, GRE or MAT, 3 letters of recommendation, writing sample; for doctorate, GRE or MAT, 3 letters of recommendation, writing research sample. Additional exam requirements/recommendations for international students: Required—TOEFL (minimum score 100 computer-based). *Expenses:* Tuition: Full-time $21,200; part-time $1000 per credit. Required fees: $400 per semester. Tuition and fees vary according to degree level.

See Close-Up on page 511.

John Carroll University, Graduate School, Department of Religious Studies, University Heights, OH 44118-4581. Offers MA. Part-time and evening/weekend programs available. *Degree requirements:* For master's, comprehensive exam, research essay or thesis, foreign language proficiency. *Entrance requirements:* For master's, GRE General Test or MAT, minimum GPA of 2.5. Additional exam requirements/recommendations for international students: Required—TOEFL. Electronic applications accepted. *Faculty research:* Ethics, women's studies, contemporary theology, Bible studies, Latin American theology.

Kentucky Christian University, Graduate School, Grayson, KY 41143-2205. Offers Christian leadership (MA); New Testament (MA). Part-time programs available. *Degree requirements:* For master's, comprehensive exam (for some programs), thesis optional. *Entrance requirements:* For master's, minimum cumulative GPA of 2.75 in major or 2.5 overall; 6 additional hours in Bible (for non-Biblical undergraduate majors). Additional exam requirements/recommendations for international students: Required—TOEFL (minimum score 550 paper-based; 213 computer-based). Electronic applications accepted.

Knox Theological Seminary, Graduate Programs, Program in Christianity and Culture, Fort Lauderdale, FL 33308. Offers MA. Part-time and evening/weekend programs available. *Entrance requirements:* Additional exam requirements/recommendations for international students: Required—TOEFL (minimum score 520 paper-based; 213 computer-based; 83 iBT), TWE (minimum score 5).

Lancaster Theological Seminary, Graduate and Professional Programs, Lancaster, PA 17603-2812. Offers biblical studies (MAR); Christian education (MAR); Christianity and the arts (MAR); church history (MAR); congregational life (MAR); lay leadership (Certificate); theological studies (M Div); theology (D Min); theology and ethics (MAR). *Accreditation:* ACIPE; ATS. *Faculty:* 11 full-time (4 women), 13 part-time/adjunct (9 women). *Students:* 91 full-time (48 women), 42 part-time (33 women). *Degree requirements:* For doctorate, thesis/dissertation; for M Div, one foreign language. *Application deadline:* For fall admission, 4/1 priority date for domestic students, 1/1 for international students; for spring admission, 11/15 priority date for domestic students. Applications are processed on a rolling basis. Application fee: $50. *Expenses:* Tuition: Full-time $12,600; part-time $490 per credit. Required fees: $125 per semester. One-time fee: $3000. Tuition and fees vary according to program and student level. *Financial support:* Career-related internships or fieldwork, scholarships/grants, and tuition waivers (partial) available. Financial award application deadline: 4/15; financial award applicants required to submit FAFSA. *Unit head:* Dr. Edwin D. Aponte, Vice President of Academic Affairs and Dean of the Seminary, 717-290-8754, Fax: 717-393-0423, E-mail: eaponte@lancasterseminary.edu. *Application contact:* Virginia Whitaker-Brooks, Assistant Director of Recruitment and Admissions, 717-290-8741, Fax: 717-393-0423.

La Salle University, School of Arts and Sciences, Program in Theological, Pastoral and Liturgical Studies, Philadelphia, PA 19141-1199. Offers pastoral studies (MA); religion (MA); theological studies (MA). Part-time and evening/weekend programs available. *Entrance requirements:* For master's, 26 credits in humanistic subjects, religion, theology, or ministry-related work.

La Sierra University, School of Religion, Riverside, CA 92515. Offers pastoral ministry (M Div); religion (MA); religious education (MA); religious studies (MA). *Accreditation:* ATS. Part-time programs available. *Degree requirements:* For master's, one foreign language, thesis or alternative. *Entrance requirements:* For master's, GRE General Test, minimum GPA of 3.0.

Lee University, Program in Religion, Cleveland, TN 37320-3450. Offers biblical studies (MA); theological studies (MA); youth and family ministry (MA). Part-time programs available. *Faculty:* 11 full-time (2 women), 1 part-time/adjunct (0 women). *Students:* 11 full-time (5 women), 16 part-time (7 women); includes 4 minority (2 African Americans, 1 American Indian/Alaska Native, 1 Asian American or Pacific Islander), 1 international. Average age 28. In 2009, 5 master's awarded. *Degree requirements:* For master's, comprehensive exam, thesis. *Entrance requirements:* For master's, GRE or MAT, minimum GPA of 3.0, 2 letters of recommendation, interview. Additional exam requirements/recommendations for international students: Required—TOEFL (minimum score 450 paper-based; 45 computer-based). *Application deadline:* For fall admission, 4/1 priority date for domestic students; for spring admission, 10/1 priority date for domestic students. Applications are processed on a rolling basis. Application fee: $25. *Expenses:* Tuition: Full-time $11,100; part-time $463 per credit. Required fees: $305. *Financial support:* Career-related internships or fieldwork, Federal Work-Study, institutionally sponsored loans, scholarships/grants, and unspecified assistantships available. Financial award application deadline: 3/1; financial award applicants required to submit FAFSA. *Faculty research:* Book of Isaiah, Gospel of Mark, school of St. Victor of 12th century, spirit Christology, people groups of New Testament and work. Total annual research expenditures: $3,000. *Unit head:* Dr. Bob Bayles, Director, 423-614-8338, E-mail: bbayles@leeuniversity.edu. *Application contact:* Vicki Glasscock, Graduate Admissions Director, 423-614-8059, E-mail: vglasscock@leeuniversity.edu.

Liberty University, Liberty Theological Seminary and Graduate School, Lynchburg, VA 24502. Offers religious studies (M Div, MA, MAR, MRE, D Min); theology (Th M). Part-time programs available. Postbaccalaureate distance learning degree programs offered (minimal on-campus study). *Degree requirements:* For master's, 2 foreign languages, thesis (for some programs); for doctorate, 2 foreign languages, thesis/dissertation. *Entrance requirements:* For M Div, minimum undergraduate GPA of 2.0; for master's, minimum undergraduate GPA of 2.0, 9 credit hours of course work in Greek, 9 credit hours of course work in Hebrew (Th M); for doctorate, GRE General Test or MAT. Additional exam requirements/recommendations for international students: Required—TOEFL (minimum score 550 paper-based; 213 computer-based). Electronic applications accepted. *Expenses:* Contact institution.

Lipscomb University, Hazelip School of Theology, Nashville, TN 37204-3951. Offers biblical studies (MA); Christian studies (MA); divinity (M Div); ministry (MA); New Testament (MA); Old Testament (MA); theological studies (MTS); theology (MA). Part-time and evening/weekend programs available. *Faculty:* 7 full-time (0 women), 3 part-time/adjunct (0 women). *Students:* 25 full-time (6 women), 72 part-time (10 women); includes 14 minority (all African Americans), 1 international. Average age 35. 46 applicants, 57% accepted, 23 enrolled. In 2009, 15 first professional degrees, 6 master's awarded. *Degree requirements:* For master's, 2 foreign languages, comprehensive exam (for some programs); for M Div, 2 foreign languages. *Entrance requirements:* For M Div and master's, 2 references. Additional exam requirements/recommendations for international students: Required—TOEFL (minimum score 570 paper-based; 230 computer-based). *Application deadline:* For fall admission, 8/14 priority date for

Religion

Lipscomb University (continued)
domestic students; for spring admission, 12/31 for domestic students. Applications are processed on a rolling basis. Application fee: $0 ($75 for international students). Electronic applications accepted. *Expenses:* Tuition: Full-time $16,002; part-time $889 per credit hour. Tuition and fees vary according to program. *Financial support:* Scholarships/grants available. Support available to part-time students. Financial award application deadline: 3/1; financial award applicants required to submit FAFSA. *Faculty research:* Status of Churches of Christ in foreign nations, Hebrew grammar, marriage and family. *Unit head:* Dr. Mark Black, Director, 615-966-1000 Ext. 5799, Fax: 615-966-1808, E-mail: mark.black@lipscomb.edu. *Application contact:* Kellye McCool, Information Contact, 615-966-6051, Fax: 615-966-6052, E-mail: kellye.mccool@lipscomb.edu.

Loma Linda University, Faculty of Religion, Program in Religion and Science, Loma Linda, CA 92350. Offers MA. *Degree requirements:* For master's, comprehensive exam, thesis optional. *Entrance requirements:* Additional exam requirements/recommendations for international students: Required—TOEFL. Electronic applications accepted.

Louisville Presbyterian Theological Seminary, Graduate and Professional Programs, Louisville, KY 40205-1798. Offers Bible (MAR); divinity (M Div); ministry (D Min); religious thought (MAR); theology (Th M); JD/M Div; M Div/MBA; M Div/MS; M Div/MSW. *Accreditation:* AAMFT/COAMFTE (one or more programs are accredited); ACIPE; ATS (one or more programs are accredited). Part-time and evening/weekend programs available. *Faculty:* 22 full-time (10 women), 30 part-time/adjunct (11 women). *Students:* 140 full-time (82 women), 72 part-time (45 women); includes 43 minority (37 African Americans, 2 Asian Americans or Pacific Islanders, 4 Hispanic Americans), 6 international. Average age 37. 139 applicants, 77% accepted, 79 enrolled. In 2009, 22 first professional degrees, 11 master's, 10 doctorates awarded. *Degree requirements:* For master's, one foreign language; for doctorate, thesis/dissertation; for M Div, 2 foreign languages. *Entrance requirements:* For master's, interview; for doctorate, M Div. Additional exam requirements/recommendations for international students: Required—TOEFL (minimum score 550 paper-based; 213 computer-based). *Application deadline:* For fall admission, 6/15 priority date for domestic students, 6/1 priority date for international students; for spring admission, 11/15 priority date for domestic and international students. Applications are processed on a rolling basis. Application fee: $62. Electronic applications accepted. *Expenses:* Tuition: Full-time $9660; part-time $322 per credit hour. Required fees: $286; $143 per semester. *Financial support:* In 2009–10, 132 students received support. Career-related internships or fieldwork, Federal Work-Study, institutionally sponsored loans, and scholarships/grants available. Financial award application deadline: 4/15; financial award applicants required to submit CSS PROFILE or FAFSA. *Unit head:* Dr. David C. Hester, Dean, 502-894-2282, Fax: 502-895-1096, E-mail: dhester@lpts.edu. *Application contact:* Cheri Harper, Director of Admission, 502-895-3411 Ext. 371, Fax: 502-895-1096, E-mail: charper@lpts.edu.

Lutheran Theological Seminary, Graduate and Professional Programs, Saskatoon, SK S7N 0X3, Canada. Offers Biblical studies (MTS); church history (MTS); ethics/church and society (MTS); history of Christianity (STM); New Testament (STM); Old Testament (STM); pastoral studies (STM); pastoral theology (MTS); systematic theology (MTS); systematic theology and philosophy of religion (STM); theology (M Div, D Div). *Accreditation:* ATS. Part-time programs available. *Degree requirements:* For master's, thesis; for M Div, Greek, Hebrew.

Lutheran Theological Seminary at Gettysburg, Graduate and Professional Programs, Gettysburg, PA 17325-1795. Offers divinity (M Div); ministerial studies (MAMS); outdoor ministry (MAR); parish ministry (D Min); theology (STM). *Accreditation:* ACIPE; ATS (one or more programs are accredited). Part-time programs available. Postbaccalaureate distance learning degree programs offered (no on-campus study). *Degree requirements:* For master's, thesis (for some programs); for M Div, one foreign language. Electronic applications accepted.

The Lutheran Theological Seminary at Philadelphia, Graduate School, Philadelphia, PA 19119-1794. Offers divinity (M Div); ministry (D Min); religion (MAR); social ministry (Certificate); theology (STM). *Accreditation:* ACIPE; ATS. Part-time and evening/weekend programs available. *Degree requirements:* For master's, one foreign language, comprehensive exam (for some programs), thesis (for some programs); for doctorate, thesis/dissertation; for M Div, 2 foreign languages. *Entrance requirements:* For M Div and master's, minimum undergraduate GPA of 2.8; for doctorate, minimum first professional GPA of 3.0. Additional exam requirements/recommendations for international students: Required—TOEFL (minimum score 550 paper-based; 213 computer-based), TWE. Electronic applications accepted.

Mars Hill Graduate School, Graduate Programs, Seattle, WA 98121. Offers Christian studies (MA); counseling psychology (MA); divinity (MS). Part-time programs available. *Entrance requirements:* For master's, MAT.

McGill University, Faculty of Graduate and Postdoctoral Studies, Faculty of Religious Studies, Montréal, QC H3A 2T5, Canada. Offers MA, STM, PhD. *Accreditation:* ATS.

McMaster University, School of Graduate Studies, Faculty of Social Sciences, Department of Religious Studies, Hamilton, ON L8S 4M2, Canada. Offers MA, PhD. Part-time programs available. *Degree requirements:* For master's, one foreign language, thesis; for doctorate, 2 foreign languages, comprehensive exam, thesis/dissertation. *Entrance requirements:* For master's, minimum B+ average. Additional exam requirements/recommendations for international students: Required—TOEFL (minimum score 580 paper-based; 237 computer-based). *Faculty research:* Hellenistic Judaism, religious biographies in Asia, medieval India, synoptic gospels, ritual and belief systems.

Memorial University of Newfoundland, School of Graduate Studies, Department of Religious Studies, St. John's, NL A1C 5S7, Canada. Offers MA. Part-time programs available. *Degree requirements:* For master's, one foreign language, thesis. *Entrance requirements:* For master's, honors degree in religious studies or equivalent. Electronic applications accepted. *Faculty research:* Biblical studies, Christian thought and history, world religions, ethics, contemporary spirituality.

Miami University, Graduate School, College of Arts and Sciences, Department of Comparative Religion, Oxford, OH 45056. Offers MA. Part-time programs available. *Students:* 5 full-time (2 women). *Entrance requirements:* For master's, minimum undergraduate GPA of 3.0 during previous 2 years or 2.75 overall. Additional exam requirements/recommendations for international students: Required—TOEFL. Application fee: $50. *Expenses:* Tuition, state resident: full-time $11,280. Tuition, nonresident: full-time $24,912. Required fees: $516. *Financial support:* Fellowships with full tuition reimbursements, research assistantships, teaching assistantships, Federal Work-Study, health care benefits, tuition waivers (full), and unspecified assistantships available. Financial award application deadline: 3/1; financial award applicants required to submit FAFSA. *Unit head:* Dr. Elizabeth Wilson, Chair, 513-529-4300, E-mail: wilsone@muohio.edu. *Application contact:* Dr. Lisa Poirier, Director of Graduate Studies, 513-529-4300, Fax: 513-529-1774, E-mail: poirelj@muohio.edu.

Michigan Theological Seminary, Graduate Programs, Plymouth, MI 48170. Offers Bible (Graduate Certificate); Christian education (MA); counseling psychology (MA); divinity (M Div); theological studies (MA). *Accreditation:* ATS. Part-time and evening/weekend programs available. *Degree requirements:* For master's, one foreign language, thesis; for M Div, 2 foreign languages. *Faculty research:* Judaism, cults, world religions.

Midwestern Baptist Theological Seminary, Graduate and Professional Programs, Kansas City, MO 64118-4697. Offers Biblical archaeology (MA); Biblical languages (MA); Christian education (M Div, MACE); Christian foundations—lay ministry (Graduate Certificate); collegiate ministries (M Div); counseling (MA); educational ministry (D Ed Min); international church planting (M Div); ministry (M Div, D Min); North American church planting (M Div); sacred music (MCM); urban ministry (M Div); worship leadership (M Div); youth ministry (M Div). *Accreditation:* ATS. Part-time programs available. Postbaccalaureate distance learning degree programs offered (minimal on-campus study). *Degree requirements:* For doctorate, thesis/dissertation; for M Div, 2 foreign languages. *Entrance requirements:* For doctorate, MAT. Electronic applications accepted. *Faculty research:* Ministerial studies, Biblical and theological studies, missions, counseling.

Missouri State University, Graduate College, College of Humanities and Public Affairs, Department of Religious Studies, Springfield, MO 65897. Offers MA. Part-time programs available. *Faculty:* 12 full-time (5 women). *Students:* 6 full-time (3 women), 22 part-time (9 women); includes 1 minority (Hispanic American). Average age 32. 7 applicants, 86% accepted, 4 enrolled. In 2009, 6 master's awarded. *Degree requirements:* For master's, one foreign language, comprehensive exam, thesis or alternative. *Entrance requirements:* For master's, GRE, minimum GPA of 3.2. Additional exam requirements/recommendations for international students: Required—TOEFL (minimum score 550 paper-based; 213 computer-based; 79 iBT). *Application deadline:* For fall admission, 7/20 priority date for domestic students, 5/1 for international students; for spring admission, 12/20 priority date for domestic students, 9/1 for international students. Applications are processed on a rolling basis. Application fee: $35 ($50 for international students). Electronic applications accepted. *Expenses:* Tuition, state resident: full-time $3852; part-time $214 per credit hour. Tuition, nonresident: full-time $7524; part-time $418 per credit hour. Required fees: $696; $172 per semester. Tuition and fees vary according to course level, course load, degree level and program. *Financial support:* Federal Work-Study, institutionally sponsored loans, scholarships/grants, and unspecified assistantships available. Financial award application deadline: 3/31; financial award applicants required to submit FAFSA. *Faculty research:* Apocalyptic literature, Protestantism in American society, contemporary Hinduism, Christian history. *Unit head:* Dr. J. E. Llewellyn, Head, 417-836-5514, Fax: 417-836-4757. *Application contact:* Eric Eckert, Coordinator of Admissions and Recruitment, 417-836-5331, Fax: 417-836-6888, E-mail: ericeckert@missouristate.edu.

Mount St. Mary's College, Graduate Division, Program in Religious Studies, Los Angeles, CA 90049-1599. Offers MA. Part-time and evening/weekend programs available. *Faculty:* 4 full-time (3 women). *Students:* 3 full-time (1 woman), 9 part-time (8 women); includes 4 minority (1 Asian American or Pacific Islander, 3 Hispanic Americans). Average age 39. In 2009, 4 master's awarded. *Degree requirements:* For master's, thesis. *Entrance requirements:* For master's, minimum GPA of 3.0. Additional exam requirements/recommendations for international students: Required—TOEFL (minimum score 550 iBT). *Application deadline:* For fall admission, 7/15 priority date for domestic students; for spring admission, 11/15 priority date for domestic students. *Expenses:* Tuition: Part-time $730 per unit. Part-time tuition and fees vary according to degree level and program. *Financial support:* Institutionally sponsored loans and tuition waivers (partial) available. Support available to part-time students. Financial award application deadline: 3/15; financial award applicants required to submit FAFSA. *Faculty research:* Scripture, systematics, ethics, religious education for Mexican-Americans. *Unit head:* Dr. Rosamund Rodman, Director, 213-477-2722, E-mail: ggarcia@msmc.la.edu. *Application contact:* Dr. Rosamund Rodman, Director, 213-477-2722, E-mail: ggarcia@msmc.la.edu.

Naropa University, Graduate Programs, Program in Indo-Tibetan Buddhism, Boulder, CO 80302-6697. Offers MA. *Degree requirements:* For master's, comprehensive exam, thesis. *Entrance requirements:* For master's, writing sample, interview (by phone or in-person), 3 letters of recommendation, letter of interest, resume. Additional exam requirements/recommendations for international students: Required—TOEFL (minimum score 600 paper-based; 250 computer-based). Electronic applications accepted.

Naropa University, Graduate Programs, Program in Indo-Tibetan Buddhism with Language, Boulder, CO 80302-6697. Offers MA. *Degree requirements:* For master's, comprehensive exam, thesis. *Entrance requirements:* For master's, writing sample, interview (by phone or in-person), resume, letter of interest, 3 letters of recommendation. Additional exam requirements/recommendations for international students: Required—TOEFL (minimum score 600 paper-based; 250 computer-based). Electronic applications accepted.

Naropa University, Graduate Programs, Program in Religious Studies, Boulder, CO 80302-6697. Offers MA. *Degree requirements:* For master's, thesis. *Entrance requirements:* For master's, interview (by phone or in-person), writing sample, letter of interest, resume, 3 letters of recommendation. Additional exam requirements/recommendations for international students: Required—TOEFL (minimum score 600 paper-based; 250 computer-based). Electronic applications accepted.

Naropa University, Graduate Programs, Program in Religious Studies with Language, Boulder, CO 80302-6697. Offers MA. *Degree requirements:* For master's, thesis. *Entrance requirements:* For master's, interview, writing sample, resume, 3 letters of recommendation, letter of interest. Additional exam requirements/recommendations for international students: Required—TOEFL (minimum score 600 paper-based; 250 computer-based). Electronic applications accepted.

New Life Theological Seminary, Graduate Program, Charlotte, NC 28206-7901. Offers urban Christian ministry (MA), including Biblical studies, church planting, divinity, youth/music. Part-time and evening/weekend programs available. *Degree requirements:* For master's, thesis. Electronic applications accepted.

New Saint Andrews College, Graduate Studies, Moscow, ID 83843. Offers classical Christian studies (Graduate Certificate); Trinitarian theology and culture (MA). Part-time programs available. *Degree requirements:* For master's, final oral exam. *Entrance requirements:* For master's, GRE, 2 letters of recommendation; for Graduate Certificate, GRE, bachelor's degree, essays, 2 letters of recommendation. Electronic applications accepted.

New York University, Graduate School of Arts and Science, Draper Interdisciplinary Program in Humanities and Social Thought, New York, NY 10012-1019. Offers humanities and social thought (MA); religion (Advanced Certificate); social theory (Advanced Certificate). Part-time programs available. *Faculty:* 6 full-time (3 women). *Students:* 104 full-time (62 women), 113 part-time (76 women); includes 35 minority (9 African Americans, 15 Asian Americans or Pacific Islanders, 11 Hispanic Americans), 11 international. Average age 27. 353 applicants, 57% accepted, 110 enrolled. In 2009, 76 master's awarded. *Degree requirements:* For master's, thesis, comprehensive exam or essay. *Entrance requirements:* For degree, master's degree. Additional exam requirements/recommendations for international students: Required—TOEFL. *Application deadline:* For fall admission, 7/1 for domestic students; for spring admission, 12/1 for domestic students. Applications are processed on a rolling basis. Application fee: $90. *Expenses:* Tuition: Full-time $30,528; part-time $1272 per credit. Required fees: $2177. *Financial support:* Teaching assistantships with tuition reimbursements, Federal Work-Study, institutionally sponsored loans, and tuition waivers (partial) available. Financial award application deadline: 7/1; financial award applicants required to submit FAFSA. *Faculty research:* Art world, gender politics, global histories, literary cultures, the city. *Unit head:* Robin Nagle, Director, 212-998-8070, Fax: 212-995-4691, E-mail: draper.program@nyu.edu. *Application contact:* Robert Dimit, Associate Director, 212-998-8070, Fax: 212-995-4691, E-mail: draper.program@nyu.edu.

New York University, Graduate School of Arts and Science, Program in Religious Studies, New York, NY 10012-1019. Offers MA. Part-time programs available. *Students:* 13 full-time (9 women), 5 part-time (4 women), 5 international. Average age 29. 35 applicants, 74% accepted, 11 enrolled. In 2009, 5 master's awarded. *Degree requirements:* For master's, one foreign language, thesis. *Entrance requirements:* For master's, GRE General Test. Additional exam requirements/recommendations for international students: Required—TOEFL. *Application deadline:* For fall admission, 1/4 priority date for domestic students. Application fee: $90. *Expenses:* Tuition: Full-time $30,528; part-time $1272 per credit. Required fees: $2177. *Financial support:* Teaching assistantships with tuition reimbursements, Federal Work-Study and institutionally sponsored loans available. Financial award application deadline: 4/15; financial award applicants required to submit FAFSA. *Faculty research:* Biblical and rabbinic Judaism, New Testament and early Christianity, comparative mysticism, gender and embodiment, East Asian religions. *Unit head:* Adam Becker, Director, 212-998-3756, Fax: 212-995-4827, E-mail:

religious.studies@nyu.edu. *Application contact:* J. Mercer Crenshaw, Department Administrator, 212-998-3756, Fax: 212-995-4827, E-mail: religious.studies@nyu.edu.

Northwestern University, School of Continuing Studies, Program in Liberal Studies, Evanston, IL 60208. Offers American studies (MA); history (MA); religious and ethical studies (MA).

Northwest Nazarene University, Graduate Studies, Program in Religion, Nampa, ID 83686-5897. Offers Christian education (MA); missional leadership (MA); pastoral ministry (MA); religion (M Div); spiritual formation (MA). Part-time and evening/weekend programs available. Postbaccalaureate distance learning degree programs offered (no on-campus study). Electronic applications accepted.

Oblate School of Theology, Graduate and Professional Programs, San Antonio, TX 78216-6693. Offers divinity (M Div); Hispanic ministry (D Min); pastoral ministry (MAP Min); pastoral studies (Certificate); spirituality (MA Sp); supervision (D Min), including clinical pastoral education, general supervision; theology (MA Th); M Div/MA Th. *Accreditation:* ACIPE; ATS (one or more programs are accredited). Part-time programs available. *Faculty:* 22 full-time (7 women), 7 part-time/adjunct (1 woman). *Students:* 91 full-time (5 women), 76 part-time (43 women); includes 69 minority (5 African Americans, 1 American Indian/Alaska Native, 15 Asian Americans or Pacific Islanders, 48 Hispanic Americans), 35 international. Average age 39. 29 applicants, 100% accepted, 29 enrolled. In 2009, 8 first professional degrees, 11 master's, 4 doctorates awarded. *Degree requirements:* For master's, thesis (for some programs), practicum; for doctorate, paper, practicum; for M Div, one foreign language, seminar. *Entrance requirements:* For M Div, MAT, interview, course work in philosophy and theology; for master's, MAT, interview, course work in theology or religious studies, minimum GPA of 2.5; for doctorate, M Div. Additional exam requirements/recommendations for international students: Required—TOEFL (minimum score 197 computer-based; 71 iBT). *Application deadline:* For fall admission, 6/15 priority date for domestic and international students; for spring admission, 12/30 for domestic and international students. Applications are processed on a rolling basis. Application fee: $45. *Expenses:* Tuition: Full-time $11,960; part-time $460 per credit. Required fees: $175 per semester. Tuition and fees vary according to course level, course load and degree level. *Financial support:* Scholarships/grants available. Support available to part-time students. Financial award application deadline: 8/1; financial award applicants required to submit FAFSA. *Unit head:* Sr. Elaine Brothers, Academic Dean, 210-341-1366, Fax: 214-341-4519, E-mail: ebrothers@ost.edu. *Application contact:* James Oberhausen, Director of Admission/Registrar, 210-341-1366 Ext. 212, Fax: 210-341-4519, E-mail: registrar@ost.edu.

Oklahoma City University, Petree College of Arts and Sciences, Wimberly School of Religion and Graduate Theological Center, Oklahoma City, OK 73106-1402. Offers M Rel. Part-time and evening/weekend programs available. *Faculty:* 5 full-time (2 women), 1 (woman) part-time/adjunct. *Students:* 5 full-time (4 women), 1 (woman) part-time; includes 3 minority (2 African Americans, 1 American Indian/Alaska Native), 1 international. Average age 33. 3 applicants, 100% accepted, 2 enrolled. *Degree requirements:* For master's, thesis optional. *Entrance requirements:* For master's, minimum GPA of 3.0. Additional exam requirements/recommendations for international students: Required—TOEFL (minimum score 550 paper-based). *Application deadline:* For fall admission, 8/20 for domestic students; for spring admission, 1/6 for domestic students. Applications are processed on a rolling basis. Application fee: $50 ($70 for international students). *Expenses:* Tuition: Full-time $15,930; part-time $885 per hour. *Financial support:* Fellowships with partial tuition reimbursements, career-related internships or fieldwork, Federal Work-Study, and tuition waivers (partial) available. Support available to part-time students. Financial award applicants required to submit FAFSA. *Faculty research:* Biblical studies, church history, social ethics, world religions. *Unit head:* Dr. Sharon Betsworth, Director, 405-208-5602, Fax: 405-208-6046, E-mail: sbetsworth@okcu.edu. *Application contact:* Michelle Lockhart, Director, Admissions, 800-633-7242, Fax: 405-208-5916, E-mail: gadmissions@okcu.edu.

Olivet Nazarene University, Graduate School, Division of Religion, Bourbonnais, IL 60914. Offers biblical literature (MA); religion (MA); theology (MA). Part-time programs available. *Degree requirements:* For master's, thesis or alternative.

Oxford Graduate School, Graduate Programs, Dayton, TN 37321-6736. Offers family life education (M Litt); organizational leadership in nonprofits (M Litt); religion and society (D Phil).

Pacific School of Religion, Graduate and Professional Programs, Berkeley, CA 94709-1323. Offers M Div, MA, MTS, D Min, PhD, Th D, CAPS, CMS, CSS, CTS. *Accreditation:* ACIPE; ATS (one or more programs are accredited). Part-time programs available. *Degree requirements:* For master's, one foreign language, thesis (for some programs); for doctorate, thesis/dissertation. *Entrance requirements:* For M Div and master's, minimum GPA of 3.0; for doctorate, M Div, minimum GPA of 3.0 (D Min); for other advanced degree, M Div, minimum GPA of 3.0 (CAPS). Additional exam requirements/recommendations for international students: Required—TOEFL (minimum score 550 paper-based; 213 computer-based). Electronic applications accepted. *Faculty research:* Medical ethics, gay/lesbian studies in religion, Asian-American religion, race, culture and theology, theology in context.

Pepperdine University, Seaver College, Division of Religion, Malibu, CA 90263. Offers ministry (MS); religion (M Div, MA). Part-time and evening/weekend programs available. *Degree requirements:* For master's, 2 foreign languages, thesis (for some programs). *Entrance requirements:* For master's, GRE General Test. Additional exam requirements/recommendations for international students: Required—TOEFL. *Expenses:* Tuition: Full-time $37,516; part-time $1310 per unit. Required fees: $80.

Point Loma Nazarene University, Program in Religion, San Diego, CA 92106-2899. Offers M Min, MA. Part-time programs available. *Students:* 8 full-time (2 women), 28 part-time (6 women); includes 9 minority (3 African Americans, 6 Hispanic Americans), 1 international. Average age 41. In 2009, 3 master's awarded. *Degree requirements:* For master's, thesis optional. *Entrance requirements:* For master's, GRE General Test, letters of recommendation, writing sample. *Application deadline:* For fall admission, 5/15 priority date for domestic students; for spring admission, 11/1 for domestic students. Applications are processed on a rolling basis. Application fee: $35. *Financial support:* Available to part-time students. Application deadline: 4/10. *Faculty research:* Theology, Christian education, church administration. *Unit head:* Dr. Bob Smith, Dean, 619-849-2594, E-mail: robertsmith@pointloma.edu. *Application contact:* Dejon Davis, Director of Graduate Admissions, 619-563-2856, E-mail: dejondavis@pointloma.edu.

Princeton Theological Seminary, Graduate and Professional Programs, Princeton, NJ 08542-0803. Offers M Div, MA, Th M, D Min, PhD. *Accreditation:* ACIPE; ATS. Part-time programs available. Terminal master's awarded for partial completion of doctoral program. *Degree requirements:* For doctorate, 2 foreign languages, thesis/dissertation, comprehensive exam (PhD), French and German. *Entrance requirements:* For doctorate, GRE General Test. Additional exam requirements/recommendations for international students: Required—TOEFL. Electronic applications accepted.

Princeton University, Graduate School, Department of Religion, Princeton, NJ 08544-1019. Offers PhD. *Degree requirements:* For doctorate, variable foreign language requirement, comprehensive exam, thesis/dissertation. *Entrance requirements:* For doctorate, GRE General Test. Additional exam requirements/recommendations for international students: Required—TOEFL (minimum score 600 paper-based; 250 computer-based). Electronic applications accepted.

Providence College, Graduate Studies, Department of Religious Studies, Providence, RI 02918. Offers Biblical studies (MA); theology (MA, MTS). Part-time and evening/weekend programs available. *Faculty:* 6 full-time (1 woman). *Students:* 4 full-time (2 women), 24 part-time (9 women), 1 international. Average age 40. 5 applicants, 100% accepted. In 2009, 11 master's awarded. *Degree requirements:* For master's, comprehensive exam, Greek and Hebrew (biblical studies). *Entrance requirements:* Additional exam requirements/recommendations for international students: Required—TOEFL (minimum score 550 paper-based; 213 computer-based; 80 iBT). *Application deadline:* For fall admission, 8/1 priority date for domestic and international students; for spring admission, 12/1 priority date for domestic and international students. Applications are processed on a rolling basis. Application fee: $55. *Expenses:* Tuition: Full-time $9909; part-time $367 per credit. One-time fee: $200. Tuition and fees vary according to course load and program. *Financial support:* In 2009–10, 4 research assistantships with full tuition reimbursements (averaging $8,400 per year) were awarded; career-related internships or fieldwork and unspecified assistantships also available. Support available to part-time students. Financial award application deadline: 8/1; financial award applicants required to submit FAFSA. *Unit head:* Rev. Thomas McCreesh, Director, 401-865-1150, Fax: 401-865-1830, E-mail: tmccrees@providence.edu. *Application contact:* Carol A. Daniels, Coordinator of Graduate Faculty and Administrative Services, 401-865-2247, Fax: 401-865-1147, E-mail: daniels@providence.edu.

Queen's University at Kingston, School of Graduate Studies and Research, Faculty of Arts and Sciences, Department of Religious Studies, Kingston, ON K7L 3N6, Canada. Offers MA. *Degree requirements:* For master's, one foreign language, essay. *Entrance requirements:* For master's, honors BA in religious studies or equivalent. Additional exam requirements/recommendations for international students: Required—TOEFL (minimum score 600 paper-based; 250 computer-based). *Faculty research:* Modernity, culture, feminism, world religions, traditions.

Reformed Theological Seminary–Charlotte Campus, Graduate and Professional Programs, Charlotte, NC 28226-6318. Offers biblical studies (MA); ministry (D Min); pastoral ministry (M Div); theological studies (MA). Part-time programs available. *Degree requirements:* For master's, comprehensive exam; for doctorate, thesis/dissertation; for M Div, 2 foreign languages, comprehensive exam. *Entrance requirements:* For master's, minimum GPA of 2.6; for doctorate, minimum GPA of 3.0. Additional exam requirements/recommendations for international students: Required—TOEFL (minimum score 550 paper-based; 213 computer-based). Electronic applications accepted.

Reformed Theological Seminary–Washington D.C., Graduate and Professional Programs, McLean, VA 22101. Offers Bible (M Div); practical theology (M Div); religion (MA); theology (M Div). Part-time and evening/weekend programs available. *Faculty:* 2 full-time (0 women), 5 part-time/adjunct (0 women). *Students:* 18 full-time (0 women), 89 part-time (14 women); includes 3 African Americans, 24 Asian Americans or Pacific Islanders, 3 Hispanic Americans. Average age 35. 50 applicants, 76% accepted, 35 enrolled. In 2009, 11 master's awarded. *Degree requirements:* For master's, integrative paper. *Entrance requirements:* For master's, minimum undergraduate GPA of 2.6. Additional exam requirements/recommendations for international students: Required—TOEFL (minimum score 550 paper-based; 213 computer-based), TWE. *Application deadline:* Applications are processed on a rolling basis. Application fee: $70. Electronic applications accepted. *Expenses:* Tuition: Full-time $6480; part-time $360 per credit. Tuition and fees vary according to campus/location. *Financial support:* In 2009–10, 89 students received support, including 7 fellowships (averaging $1,000 per year); institutionally sponsored loans, scholarships/grants, tuition waivers (partial), and unspecified assistantships also available. Support available to part-time students. Financial award application deadline: 6/1. *Faculty research:* Theology, biblical studies, cultural studies. *Unit head:* Hugh C. Whelchel, Executive Director, 703-448-3393, Fax: 703-738-7389, E-mail: hwhelchel@rts.edu. *Application contact:* Geoff M. Sackett, Director of Admissions, 800-639-0226, Fax: 703-738-7389, E-mail: gsackett@rts.edu.

Rice University, Graduate Programs, School of Humanities, Department of Religious Studies, Houston, TX 77251-1892. Offers African religions (PhD); African-American religions (PhD); contemplative studies (PhD); ghosticism, esotericism, mysticism (PhD); Islam (PhD); Jewish thought and philosophy (PhD); modern Christianity in thought and popular culture (PhD); psychology of religion (PhD); the Bible and beyond (PhD). *Faculty:* 11 full-time (3 women), 2 part-time/adjunct (both women). *Students:* 37 full-time (13 women); includes 10 minority (9 African Americans, 1 Asian American or Pacific Islander), 9 international. Average age 31. 42 applicants, 14% accepted, 6 enrolled. In 2009, 2 doctorates awarded. *Degree requirements:* For doctorate, 2 foreign languages, comprehensive exam, thesis/dissertation. *Entrance requirements:* For doctorate, GRE, letters of recommendation, writing sample. Additional exam requirements/recommendations for international students: Required—TOEFL (minimum score 600 paper-based; 90 iBT). *Application deadline:* For fall admission, 1/1 for domestic students, 1/15 for international students. Application fee: $70. Electronic applications accepted. *Financial support:* In 2009–10, 14 fellowships (averaging $15,900 per year) were awarded. Financial award application deadline: 5/15; financial award applicants required to submit FAFSA. *Faculty research:* Origins and historical development of Islam, history of Christianity, the study of comparative religion, African-American religion, religion and culture. Total annual research expenditures: $46,514. *Unit head:* Prof. William B. Parsons, Associate Professor, Religious Studies, 713-348-2712, Fax: 713-348-5486, E-mail: pars@rice.edu. *Application contact:* Sylvia Louie, Senior Department Coordinator, 713-348-5201, Fax: 713-348-5486, E-mail: reli@rice.edu.

Sacred Heart University, Graduate Programs, College of Arts and Sciences, Department of Philosophy and Religious Studies, Fairfield, CT 06825-1000. Offers religious studies (MA). Part-time programs available. *Faculty:* 6 full-time (2 women). *Students:* 2 full-time (1 woman), 16 part-time (8 women); includes 1 minority (Asian American or Pacific Islander). Average age 37. 7 applicants, 71% accepted, 4 enrolled. In 2009, 4 master's awarded. *Degree requirements:* For master's, comprehensive exam. *Entrance requirements:* Additional exam requirements/recommendations for international students: Required—TOEFL (minimum score 550 paper-based; 213 computer-based). *Application deadline:* Applications are processed on a rolling basis. Application fee: $50 ($100 for international students). Electronic applications accepted. *Expenses:* Contact institution. *Financial support:* Career-related internships or fieldwork, institutionally sponsored loans, and unspecified assistantships available. Support available to part-time students. Financial award applicants required to submit FAFSA. *Unit head:* Dr. June-Ann Greeley, Graduate Program Director, 203-371-7713, E-mail: greeleyj@sacredheart.edu. *Application contact:* Alexis Haakonsen, Dean of Graduate Admissions, 203-365-7619, Fax: 203-365-4732, E-mail: haakonsena@sacredheart.edu.

St. Charles Borromeo Seminary, Overbrook, Graduate and Professional Programs, Division of Religious Studies, Wynnewood, PA 19096. Offers MA. Part-time programs available. *Degree requirements:* For master's, comprehensive exam. *Entrance requirements:* For master's, 18 undergraduate credits in theology and/or philosophy or the equivalent.

Saint John's Seminary, Graduate Programs, Brighton, MA 02135. Offers M Div, MA Th, MAM. *Accreditation:* ATS.

Saint Mary's University, Faculty of Arts, Department of Religious Studies, Halifax, NS B3H 3C3, Canada. Offers theology and religious studies (MA). *Unit head:* Dr. Paul Bowlby, Chair, 902-420-5823, Fax: 902-491-6286, E-mail: paul.bowlby@smu.ca. *Application contact:* Dr. Anne-Marie Dalton, Graduate Coordinator, 902-420-5864, E-mail: adalton@smu.ca.

Santa Clara University, College of Arts and Sciences, Graduate Programs in Pastoral Ministries, Program in Catechetics, Santa Clara, CA 95053. Offers MA. Part-time and evening/weekend programs available. *Students:* 10 part-time (5 women); includes 1 minority (Asian American or Pacific Islander), 2 international. Average age 44. 3 applicants, 67% accepted, 2 enrolled. *Degree requirements:* For master's, comprehensive exam, thesis (for some programs). *Entrance requirements:* For master's, 3 letters of recommendation, resume. Additional exam requirements/recommendations for international students: Required—TOEFL. *Application deadline:* Applications are processed on a rolling basis. Application fee: $50. Electronic applications accepted. *Expenses:* Contact institution. *Financial support:* Fellowships, research assistantships, teaching assistantships, career-related internships or fieldwork, Federal Work-Study, and health care benefits available. Support available to part-time students. Financial award applicants required

Religion

Santa Clara University (continued)
to submit FAFSA. *Unit head:* Fr. Paul Crowley, Department Chair of Religious Studies, 408-554-4542. *Application contact:* Fr. Paul Crowley, Department Chair of Religious Studies, 408-554-4542.

Santa Clara University, College of Arts and Sciences, Graduate Programs in Pastoral Ministries, Program in Spirituality, Santa Clara, CA 95053. Offers MA. Part-time and evening/weekend programs available. *Students:* 3 full-time (all women), 12 part-time (8 women); includes 4 minority (2 Asian Americans or Pacific Islanders, 2 Hispanic Americans), 1 international. Average age 43. 4 applicants, 100% accepted, 4 enrolled. *Degree requirements:* For master's, comprehensive exam, thesis (for some programs). *Entrance requirements:* For master's, 3 letters of recommendation, resume. Additional exam requirements/recommendations for international students: Required—TOEFL. *Application deadline:* Applications are processed on a rolling basis. Application fee: $50. Electronic applications accepted. *Expenses:* Contact institution. *Financial support:* Fellowships, research assistantships, career-related internships or fieldwork, Federal Work-Study, and health care benefits available. Support available to part-time students. Financial award applicants required to submit FAFSA. *Unit head:* Fr. Paul Crowley, Department Chair of Religious Studies, 408-554-4542. *Application contact:* Fr. Paul Crowley, Department Chair of Religious Studies, 408-554-4542.

Seminary of the Southwest, Graduate and Professional Programs, Austin, TX 78768-2247. Offers Anglican studies (Advanced Diploma); chaplaincy (MCPC); counseling (MAC); divinity (M Div); religion (MAR); spiritual formation (MAPM); theological studies (Advanced Diploma). *Accreditation:* ACIPE; ATS (one or more programs are accredited). Part-time and evening/weekend programs available. *Faculty:* 10 full-time (3 women), 22 part-time/adjunct (4 women). *Students:* 56 full-time (37 women), 52 part-time (41 women); includes 10 minority (4 African Americans, 2 Asian Americans or Pacific Islanders, 4 Hispanic Americans). Average age 46. 47 applicants, 100% accepted, 46 enrolled. In 2009, 10 first professional degrees, 11 master's, 5 other advanced degrees awarded. *Degree requirements:* For master's, thesis (for some programs). *Entrance requirements:* For M Div and master's, GRE, MAT, interview; for Advanced Diploma, interview. *Application deadline:* For fall admission, 7/1 for domestic students; for spring admission, 11/1 for domestic students. Applications are processed on a rolling basis. Application fee: $50. *Expenses:* Tuition: Full-time $13,150; part-time $390 per credit hour. Required fees: $75. One-time fee: $20 part-time. *Financial support:* Career-related internships or fieldwork and scholarships/grants available. Support available to part-time students. Financial award application deadline: 6/17. *Unit head:* Very Rev. Douglas Travis, Dean and President, 512-472-4133 Ext. 307, Fax: 512-472-3098, E-mail: dtravis@ssw.edu. *Application contact:* Jennielle Strother, Director of Admissions, 512-472-4133 Ext. 375, Fax: 512-472-3098, E-mail: jstrother@ssw.edu.

Seton Hall University, College of Arts and Sciences, Department of Jewish-Christian Studies, South Orange, NJ 07079-2697. Offers Holocaust studies (MA); Jewish-Christian Studies (MA). Part-time and evening/weekend programs available. *Faculty:* 4 full-time (0 women). *Students:* 6 full-time (4 women), 5 part-time (4 women); includes 1 minority (Hispanic American), 1 international. Average age 45. 7 applicants, 100% accepted, 5 enrolled. In 2009, 6 master's awarded. *Degree requirements:* For master's, thesis optional. *Entrance requirements:* For master's, interview or suitable correspondence with department chair. Additional exam requirements/recommendations for international students: Required—TOEFL. *Application deadline:* For fall admission, 7/1 priority date for domestic and international students; for spring admission, 11/1 priority date for domestic and international students. Applications are processed on a rolling basis. Application fee: $50. Electronic applications accepted. *Financial support:* Fellowships, research assistantships, career-related internships or fieldwork, Federal Work-Study, scholarships/grants, tuition waivers (full and partial), and unspecified assistantships available. Support available to part-time students. Financial award application deadline: 8/31; financial award applicants required to submit FAFSA. *Faculty research:* Jewish-Christian issues, Biblical studies, Holocaust studies. *Unit head:* Fr. Lawrence Frizzell, Chair, 973-275-2177, Fax: 973-761-9596, E-mail: frizzela@shu.edu. *Application contact:* Sarah Caron, Director, Graduate Admissions, 973-275-2892, Fax: 973-275-2993, E-mail: shugrad@shu.edu.

Seton Hall University, Immaculate Conception Seminary School of Theology, South Orange, NJ 07079-2697. Offers great spiritual books (Certificate); pastoral ministry (M Div, MA, Certificate); scripture studies (Certificate); Seminary's Theological Education for Parish Services (STEPS) (Certificate); theology (MA); youth ministry (Certificate). *Accreditation:* ATS (one or more programs are accredited). Part-time and evening/weekend programs available. *Faculty:* 16 full-time (2 women), 13 part-time/adjunct (1 woman). *Students:* 132 full-time (3 women), 79 part-time (32 women); includes 38 minority (4 African Americans, 6 Asian Americans or Pacific Islanders, 28 Hispanic Americans), 81 international. Average age 38. 46 applicants, 100% accepted, 43 enrolled. In 2009, 12 first professional degrees, 24 master's, 3 other advanced degrees awarded. *Degree requirements:* For master's, one foreign language, comprehensive exam, thesis (for some programs), final project; for M Div, one foreign language, thesis/dissertation, final project and seminar, field education, spiritual formation. *Entrance requirements:* For M Div, GRE, MAT; for master's, GRE General Test or MAT. Additional exam requirements/recommendations for international students: Required—TOEFL (minimum score 600 paper-based; 250 computer-based; 100 iBT). *Application deadline:* For fall admission, 8/1 priority date for domestic and international students; for spring admission, 12/15 priority date for domestic and international students. Applications are processed on a rolling basis. Application fee: $50. Electronic applications accepted. *Expenses:* Contact institution. *Financial support:* In 2009–10, 211 students received support. Career-related internships or fieldwork, Federal Work-Study, scholarships/grants, tuition waivers (partial), and unspecified assistantships available. Support available to part-time students. Financial award application deadline: 8/1; financial award applicants required to submit FAFSA. *Unit head:* Rev. Msgr. Robert F. Coleman, Rector/Dean, 973-761-9016, Fax: 973-761-9577, E-mail: robert.coleman@shu.edu. *Application contact:* Rev. Msgr. Joseph R. Chapel, Associate Dean, 973-761-9633, Fax: 973-761-9577, E-mail: theology@shu.edu.

Sioux Falls Seminary, Graduate and Professional Programs, Program in Christian Leadership, Sioux Falls, SD 57105-1599. Offers MA.

Sioux Falls Seminary, Graduate and Professional Programs, Program in Religious Studies, Sioux Falls, SD 57105-1599. Offers MA. Part-time programs available. *Entrance requirements:* For master's, minimum GPA of 2.5.

Southern Adventist University, School of Religion, Collegedale, TN 37315-0370. Offers Biblical and theological studies (MA); church leadership and management (M Min); church ministry and homiletics (M Min); evangelism and world mission (M Min); religious studies (MA). Part-time programs available. *Faculty:* 5 full-time (0 women). *Students:* 1 (woman) full-time, 1 part-time (0 women); includes 1 minority (African American). Average age 36. 2 applicants, 100% accepted, 2 enrolled. In 2009, 6 master's awarded. *Degree requirements:* For master's, comprehensive exam, thesis (for some programs). *Entrance requirements:* For master's, GRE. Additional exam requirements/recommendations for international students: Required—TOEFL (minimum score 600 paper-based; 250 computer-based). *Application deadline:* For spring admission, 5/1 priority date for domestic students, 4/30 for international students. Applications are processed on a rolling basis. Application fee: $25. *Expenses:* Tuition: Full-time $13,149; part-time $487 per credit hour. *Financial support:* Tuition waivers (full) available. Support available to part-time students. Financial award application deadline: 4/1; financial award applicants required to submit FAFSA. *Faculty research:* Biblical archaeology. *Unit head:* Dr. Greg A. King, Dean, 423-236-2975, Fax: 423-236-1976, E-mail: gking@southern.edu. *Application contact:* Susan L. Brown, Administrative Assistant, 423-236-2977, Fax: 423-236-1977, E-mail: sbrown@southern.edu.

Southern Baptist Theological Seminary, Billy Graham School of Missions, Evangelism and Church Growth, Louisville, KY 40280-0004. Offers Christian mission/world religion (PhD); evangelism/church growth (PhD); ministry (D Min); missiology (MA, D Miss); missions, evangelism and church growth (M Div); religion (Th M); theological studies (MA). *Accreditation:* ATS. Part-time and evening/weekend programs available. Postbaccalaureate distance learning degree programs offered (minimal on-campus study). *Faculty:* 12 full-time (0 women). *Students:* 608. In 2009, 27 first professional degrees, 4 master's, 3 doctorates awarded. *Degree requirements:* For master's and M Div, 2 foreign languages; for doctorate, 4 foreign languages, thesis/dissertation. *Entrance requirements:* For doctorate, GRE General Test, MAT, M Div. Additional exam requirements/recommendations for international students: Required—TOEFL, TWE. *Application deadline:* For fall admission, 8/1 priority date for domestic students; for spring admission, 1/2 for domestic students. Applications are processed on a rolling basis. Application fee: $35. *Faculty research:* Assimilation of church congregants, effective methodologies of evangelism, expectations of church members, spiritual warfare literature, formative church discipline. *Unit head:* Dr. Chuck Lawless, Dean, 800-626-5525, E-mail: clawless@sbts.edu. *Application contact:* Chuck Haddox, Director of Admissions, 800-626-5525 Ext. 4617, E-mail: chaddox@sbts.edu.

Southern Baptist Theological Seminary, School of Church Music and Worship, Louisville, KY 40280-0004. Offers church music (M Div, MCM, MM); church music and worship (DMA, DMM); worship (M Div, MAW). *Accreditation:* NASM. *Degree requirements:* For master's, comprehensive exam; for doctorate, one foreign language, thesis/dissertation. *Entrance requirements:* For doctorate, GRE General Test, MAT, auditions. Additional exam requirements/recommendations for international students: Required—TOEFL, TWE. *Faculty research:* Baptist hymnody, church music drama, keyboard literature, impact of contemporary pop culture on church music.

Southern Baptist Theological Seminary, School of Theology, Louisville, KY 40280-0004. Offers biblical and theological studies (M Div); biblical counseling (M Div, MA, D Min); biblical spirituality (D Min); Christian ministry (M Div); expository preaching (D Min); pastoral studies (M Div); theological studies (MA); theology (Th M, PhD); theology and arts (MA); theology and law (MA); worldview and apologetics (M Div). *Accreditation:* ATS. Part-time and evening/weekend programs available. Postbaccalaureate distance learning degree programs offered (minimal on-campus study). *Degree requirements:* For master's, 2 foreign languages, thesis; for doctorate, 4 foreign languages, thesis/dissertation; for M Div, 2 foreign languages. *Entrance requirements:* For master's, GRE General Test, MAT, M Div; for doctorate, GRE General Test, MAT, interview, M Div, field essay. Additional exam requirements/recommendations for international students: Required—TOEFL, TWE. *Faculty research:* Biblical studies, contemporary theology, church history, pastoral care, ministry/missions studies.

Southern California Seminary, Graduate and Professional Programs, El Cajon, CA 92019. Offers biblical studies (MA); counseling psychology (MACP); psychology (Psy D); religious studies (MRS); theology (M Div). Part-time and evening/weekend programs available. Postbaccalaureate distance learning degree programs offered (minimal on-campus study). *Degree requirements:* For master's, thesis (for some programs); for doctorate, thesis/dissertation; for M Div, 2 foreign languages. *Entrance requirements:* For doctorate, master's degree in psychology. Additional exam requirements/recommendations for international students: Required—TOEFL (minimum score 550 paper-based). Electronic applications accepted.

Southern Evangelical Seminary, Graduate School of Ministry and Missions, Matthews, NC 28105. Offers apologetics (Certificate); Christian education (MA); church ministry (MA, Certificate); divinity (Certificate), including apologetics (M Div, Certificate); Islamic studies (Certificate); theology (M Div), including apologetics (M Div, Certificate), Biblical studies; youth ministry (MA). Part-time and evening/weekend programs available. Postbaccalaureate distance learning degree programs offered. *Degree requirements:* For master's, thesis (for some programs); for M Div, one foreign language. *Entrance requirements:* Additional exam requirements/recommendations for international students: Required—TOEFL (minimum score 600 paper-based; 250 computer-based).

Southern Evangelical Seminary, Veritas Graduate School of Apologetics and Counter-Cult Ministry, Matthews, NC 28105. Offers apologetics (MA, D Min, PhD, Certificate); Islamic studies (MA); Jewish studies (MA); philosophy (MA); religion (MA). Part-time and evening/weekend programs available. Postbaccalaureate distance learning degree programs offered (minimal on-campus study). *Degree requirements:* For master's, thesis optional; for doctorate, comprehensive exam (for some programs), thesis/dissertation. *Entrance requirements:* Additional exam requirements/recommendations for international students: Required—TOEFL (minimum score 600 paper-based; 250 computer-based).

Southern Methodist University, Dedman College, Graduate Program in Religious Studies, Dallas, TX 75275-0133. Offers MA, PhD. *Faculty:* 20 full-time (6 women), 4 part-time/adjunct (1 woman). *Students:* 31 full-time (12 women); includes 2 minority (1 African American, 1 American Indian/Alaska Native), 3 international. Average age 33. 60 applicants, 12% accepted, 5 enrolled. In 2009, 4 doctorates awarded. Terminal master's awarded for partial completion of doctoral program. *Degree requirements:* For master's, one foreign language, thesis, oral and written exams; for doctorate, variable foreign language requirement, thesis/dissertation, oral and written exams. *Entrance requirements:* For master's and doctorate, GRE General Test, minimum GPA of 3.0, course work in religion. Additional exam requirements/recommendations for international students: Required—TOEFL (minimum score 550 paper-based; 210 computer-based; 79 iBT). *Application deadline:* For fall admission, 1/15 for domestic and international students. Application fee: $75. Electronic applications accepted. *Financial support:* In 2009–10, 31 students received support, including 30 fellowships with full and partial tuition reimbursements available (averaging $10,966 per year), 11 research assistantships with full and partial tuition reimbursements available (averaging $650 per year), 2 teaching assistantships with full and partial tuition reimbursements available (averaging $2,000 per year); institutionally sponsored loans, scholarships/grants, and tuition waivers (full and partial) also available. Financial award application deadline: 2/1; financial award applicants required to submit FAFSA. *Faculty research:* Theology, religious ethics, Biblical studies, history of Christianity, religion and culture. *Unit head:* Prof. Bruce D. Marshall, Director, 214-768-2432, Fax: 214-768-2117. *Application contact:* Lucy Cobbe, Assistant to Director of Graduate Program, 214-768-2432, Fax: 214-768-2117, E-mail: gradreli@mail.smu.edu.

Southern Nazarene University, Graduate College, Department of Philosophy and Religion, Bethany, OK 73008. Offers theology (MA). Part-time programs available. *Degree requirements:* For master's, one foreign language, thesis optional. *Entrance requirements:* For master's, GMAT, English proficiency exam, minimum GPA of 3.0 in last 60 hours/major, 2.7 overall.

Southwestern Assemblies of God University, Thomas F. Harrison School of Graduate Studies, Program in Theological Studies, Waxahachie, TX 75165-5735. Offers Bible and theology (MS); Biblical studies (M Div); counseling (M Div); cross cultural missions (M Div); practical theology (M Div); theological studies (M Div). Postbaccalaureate distance learning degree programs offered. *Degree requirements:* For master's, comprehensive written and oral exams. *Entrance requirements:* For master's, GRE General Test, minimum GPA of 2.5. Electronic applications accepted.

Stanford University, School of Humanities and Sciences, Department of Religious Studies, Stanford, CA 94305-9991. Offers MA, PhD. Terminal master's awarded for partial completion of doctoral program. *Degree requirements:* For master's, one foreign language, thesis optional; for doctorate, 2 foreign languages, thesis/dissertation, qualifying exam. *Entrance requirements:* For master's and doctorate, GRE General Test. Additional exam requirements/recommendations for international students: Required—TOEFL. Electronic applications accepted. *Expenses:* Tuition: Full-time $37,380; part-time $2760 per quarter. Required fees: $501.

Syracuse University, College of Arts and Sciences, Program in Religion, Syracuse, NY 13244. Offers MA, PhD. Part-time programs available. *Students:* 37 full-time (19 women), 18 part-time (10 women); includes 3 minority (1 Asian American or Pacific Islander, 2 Hispanic Americans), 5 international. Average age 35. 79 applicants, 15% accepted, 6 enrolled. In 2009, 1 master's, 3 doctorates awarded. Terminal master's awarded for partial completion of doctoral program. *Degree requirements:* For master's, one foreign language, comprehensive exam, thesis optional; for doctorate, 2 foreign languages, comprehensive exam, thesis/dissertation. *Entrance requirements:* For master's and doctorate, GRE General Test. Additional exam requirements/recommendations for international students: Required—TOEFL (minimum score 100 iBT). *Application deadline:* For fall admission, 1/10 priority date for domestic and international students. Application fee: $75. Electronic applications accepted. *Expenses:* Tuition: Full-time $26,808; part-time $1117 per credit. Required fees: $1024. *Financial support:* Fellowships with full tuition reimbursements, teaching assistantships with full tuition reimbursements, tuition waivers (partial) available. Financial award application deadline: 1/1; financial award applicants required to submit FAFSA. *Unit head:* Dr. Joanne P. Waghorne, Director, 315-443-3861, Fax: 315-443-3958, E-mail: jpwaghor@syr.edu. *Application contact:* Jackie Borowre, Recruiting Contact, 315-443-3861, E-mail: jborowre@syr.edu.

Taylor University, Master of Arts in Religious Studies Program, Upland, IN 46989-1001. Offers biblical studies (MA); world religions (MA). Part-time programs available. *Faculty:* 2 part-time/adjunct (0 women). *Students:* 10 full-time (3 women); includes 1 minority (African American). Average age 31. 8 applicants, 75% accepted, 6 enrolled. *Degree requirements:* For master's, thesis. *Application deadline:* Applications are processed on a rolling basis. Application fee: $100. *Expenses:* Contact institution. *Financial support:* In 2009–10, 2 students received support, including 3 fellowships (averaging $2,000 per year). Financial award applicants required to submit FAFSA. *Unit head:* Dr. Sheri Klouda, Graduate Chair, 765-998-4786, Fax: 765-998-4930, E-mail: shklouda@taylor.edu. *Application contact:* Kari Manganello, Program Assistant, 765-998-5148, Fax: 765-998-4930, E-mail: krmangane@taylor.edu.

Temple Baptist Seminary, Program in Theology, Chattanooga, TN 37404-3530. Offers biblical languages (M Div); Biblical studies (MABS); Christian education (MACE); English Bible û language tools (M Div); theology (MM, D Min). Part-time and evening/weekend programs available. Postbaccalaureate distance learning degree programs offered (minimal on-campus study). *Degree requirements:* For doctorate, thesis/dissertation; for M Div, proficiency in Greek and Hebrew. *Entrance requirements:* For doctorate, minimum GPA of 3.0, M Div.

Temple University, Graduate School, College of Liberal Arts, Department of Religion, Philadelphia, PA 19122-6096. Offers MA, PhD. Part-time programs available. *Degree requirements:* For doctorate, variable foreign language requirement, thesis/dissertation. *Entrance requirements:* For doctorate, GRE General Test, minimum GPA of 3.0. Additional exam requirements/recommendations for international students: Required—TOEFL (minimum score 550 paper-based; 213 computer-based; 79 iBT). Electronic applications accepted. *Faculty research:* Textural and historical origins; philosophy of religion and religious thought; religion, culture, and society.

Trevecca Nazarene University, Graduate Division, Graduate Religion Programs, Nashville, TN 37210-2877. Offers biblical studies (MA); preaching and practical theology (MA); systematic theology/historical theology (MA). Part-time programs available. *Faculty:* 3 full-time (0 women). *Students:* 19 full-time (2 women), 22 part-time (5 women); includes 7 minority (6 African Americans, 1 Asian American or Pacific Islander), 1 international. Average age 34. In 2009, 17 master's awarded. *Degree requirements:* For master's, comprehensive exam, thesis optional. *Entrance requirements:* For master's, GRE General Test or MAT, minimum GPA of 2.7, 2 letters of recommendation. Additional exam requirements/recommendations for international students: Required—TOEFL (minimum score 550 paper-based; 213 computer-based). *Application deadline:* Applications are processed on a rolling basis. Application fee: $25. Electronic applications accepted. *Expenses:* Contact institution. *Financial support:* Applicants required to submit FAFSA. *Unit head:* Dr. Tim Green, Dean/Director, 615-248-1378, Fax: 615-248-7417, E-mail: admissions_rel@trevecca.edu. *Application contact:* Sherry Crutchfield, Secretary, 615-248-1378, Fax: 615-248-7417, E-mail: admissions_rel@trevecca.edu.

Trinity International University, South Florida Campus, Divinity School, Miami, FL 33132-1996. Offers MA, Certificate.

Trinity School for Ministry, Graduate Programs, Ambridge, PA 15003-2397. Offers Anglican studies (Diploma); basic Christian studies (Diploma); divinity (M Div); ministry (D Min); mission and evangelism (MAME, Diploma); religion (MAR); youth ministry (Diploma). *Accreditation:* ATS (one or more programs are accredited). Part-time programs available. *Degree requirements:* For master's, thesis optional; for doctorate, thesis/dissertation; for M Div, thesis/dissertation optional, Greek and Hebrew. *Entrance requirements:* Additional exam requirements/recommendations for international students: Required—TOEFL. *Faculty research:* Pauline Epistles, contemporary theology, history of Anglican liturgy, book of Ruth, biblical theology.

Union University, School of Christian Studies, Jackson, TN 38305-3697. Offers Christian studies (MCS); expository preaching (D Min).

United Theological Seminary of the Twin Cities, Professional Program, New Brighton, MN 55112-2598. Offers advanced theological studies (Diploma); justice and peace studies (M Div, MA); leadership toward racial justice (MA, Certificate); leadership towards racial justice (M Div); Methodist studies (M Div, MA, Certificate); ministry (D Min); ministry renewal and professional development (Certificate); pastoral care and counseling (M Div, MA, MARL); religion and theology (MA); theological and religious studies (Certificate); theology and the arts (M Div, MA); urban ministry (M Div, MA, MARL); women's studies: religion, theology and ministry (MA); women's studies: religions, theology and ministry (M Div). *Accreditation:* ACIPE; ATS. Part-time and evening/weekend programs available. *Faculty:* 9 full-time (6 women), 22 part-time/adjunct (10 women). *Students:* 49 full-time (34 women), 105 part-time (68 women). Average age 47. 41 applicants, 98% accepted, 34 enrolled. In 2009, 24 first professional degrees, 5 master's, 2 doctorates, 2 other advanced degrees awarded. *Degree requirements:* For master's, thesis; for doctorate, comprehensive exam, thesis/dissertation; for M Div, integrative notebook, spiritual chronicle. *Entrance requirements:* For M Div and master's, minimum GPA of 2.75; strong analytical, reflective thinking and writing skills; vocational and academic goals compatible with those of Seminary; for doctorate, M Div or equivalent, minimum GPA of 3.0, 3 years experience in professional ministry; for other advanced degree, BA or equivalent life experience; strong analytical, reflective thinking and writing skills (Certificate); proficiency in English language, previous study of theology at a theological school, recommendation of student's denomination (Diploma). Additional exam requirements/recommendations for international students: Required—TOEFL (minimum score 550 paper-based). *Application deadline:* For fall admission, 7/1 priority date for domestic students, 11/1 priority date for international students; for winter admission, 11/1 priority date for domestic students; for spring admission, 11/15 priority date for domestic students. Applications are processed on a rolling basis. Application fee: $50. *Expenses:* Tuition: Full-time $11,502; part-time $426 per credit hour. Required fees: $295; $155 per term. One-time fee: $25. Tuition and fees vary according to course load, degree level and program. *Financial support:* In 2009–10, 120 students received support. Career-related internships or fieldwork, institutionally sponsored loans, and scholarships/grants available. Support available to part-time students. Financial award application deadline: 5/1; financial award applicants required to submit FAFSA. *Unit head:* Dr. Richard D. Weis, Dean of the Seminary, 651-255-6108 Ext. 108, Fax: 651-633-4315, E-mail: rweis@unitedseminary.edu. *Application contact:* Rev. Glen Herrington-Hall, Director of Admissions, 651-255-6107 Ext. 107, Fax: 651-633-4315, E-mail: gherrington-hall@unitedseminary.edu.

Université de Sherbrooke, Faculty of Theology, Ethics and Philosophy, Sherbrooke, QC J1K 2R1, Canada. Offers applied ethics (Diploma); human science of religions (MA); intercultural training (Diploma); philosophy (MA, PhD); spiritual anthropology (Diploma); theology (MA, PhD, Diploma). Part-time and evening/weekend programs available. Postbaccalaureate distance learning degree programs offered. Terminal master's awarded for partial completion of doctoral program. *Entrance requirements:* For master's, bachelor's degree in related discipline; for doctorate, master's degree in related discipline. *Faculty research:* Faith and culture interrelation.

Université du Québec à Montréal, Graduate Programs, Program in Religious Sciences, Montréal, QC H3C 3P8, Canada. Offers MA, PhD. Part-time programs available. *Degree requirements:* For master's, thesis; for doctorate, thesis/dissertation. *Entrance requirements:* For master's, appropriate bachelor's degree or equivalent, proficiency in French; for doctorate, appropriate master's degree or equivalent, proficiency in French.

Université Laval, Faculty of Theology and Religious Sciences, Programs in Human Sciences of Religion, Québec, QC G1K 7P4, Canada. Offers MA, PhD. Terminal master's awarded for partial completion of doctoral program. *Degree requirements:* For master's, thesis (for some programs); for doctorate, comprehensive exam, thesis/dissertation. *Entrance requirements:* For master's, knowledge of French, comprehension of a second language; for doctorate, knowledge of French and English. Electronic applications accepted.

The University of British Columbia, Faculty of Arts and Faculty of Graduate Studies, Department of Classical, Near Eastern and Religious Studies, Program in Religious Studies, Vancouver, BC V6T 1Z1, Canada. Offers MA, PhD. Part-time programs available. *Degree requirements:* For master's, 2 foreign languages, comprehensive exam, thesis optional; for doctorate, 2 foreign languages, comprehensive exam, thesis/dissertation. *Entrance requirements:* For doctorate, MA. Additional exam requirements/recommendations for international students: Required—TOEFL (minimum score 600 paper-based; 250 computer-based), IELTS. Electronic applications accepted. *Faculty research:* Hebrew Bible in ancient Near Eastern context, Christian scriptures in Greco-Roman context, mystical aspects of religion, the feminine in western traditions, modern Jewish experience.

The University of British Columbia, Faculty of Arts and Faculty of Graduate Studies, Department of Classical, Near Eastern and Religious Studies, Programmes in Classics, Vancouver, BC V6T 1Z1, Canada. Offers ancient culture, religion, and ethnicity (MA); classical and near eastern archaeology (MA); classics (MA, PhD). Part-time programs available. *Degree requirements:* For master's, 2 foreign languages, thesis or comprehensive exam; for doctorate, 2 foreign languages, comprehensive exam, thesis/dissertation. *Entrance requirements:* For doctorate, MA. Additional exam requirements/recommendations for international students: Required—TOEFL (minimum score 600 paper-based; 250 computer-based), IELTS (minimum score 7.5). Electronic applications accepted. *Faculty research:* Classical archaeology, ancient historians, late antiquity, ancient prose fiction, epigraphy.

University of Calgary, Faculty of Graduate Studies, Faculty of Humanities, Department of Religious Studies, Calgary, AB T2N 1N4, Canada. Offers MA, PhD. Part-time programs available. *Degree requirements:* For master's, one foreign language, thesis; for doctorate, 2 foreign languages, thesis/dissertation, candidacy exam. *Entrance requirements:* For master's, minimum GPA of 3.3; for doctorate, minimum GPA of 3.5. Additional exam requirements/recommendations for international students: Required—TOEFL (minimum score 550 paper-based; 213 computer-based). *Faculty research:* Eastern religions, Western religions, nature of religion.

University of California, Berkeley, Graduate Division, College of Letters and Science, Department of Near Eastern Studies, Group in Near Eastern Religions, Berkeley, CA 94720-1500. Offers PhD. *Students:* 4 full-time (3 women). Average age 45. 8 applicants, 0 enrolled. *Degree requirements:* For doctorate, 2 foreign languages, thesis/dissertation, qualifying exam. *Entrance requirements:* For doctorate, GRE General Test, MA or equivalent in Near Eastern studies or related field; minimum GPA of 3.0, 3 letters of recommendation. *Application deadline:* For fall admission, 12/15 for domestic students. Application fee: $70 ($90 for international students). *Financial support:* Fellowships, research assistantships, teaching assistantships, unspecified assistantships available. *Unit head:* Prof. Niek Veldhuis, Chair, 510-642-3757, E-mail: nes@berkeley.edu. *Application contact:* Judy Shattuck, Graduate Assistant, 510-642-6162, Fax: 510-643-8430, E-mail: nes@berkeley.edu.

University of California, Berkeley, Graduate Division, College of Letters and Science, Group in Buddhist Studies, Berkeley, CA 94720-1500. Offers PhD. *Faculty:* 9 full-time. *Students:* 6 full-time (3 women). Average age 31. 14 applicants, 1 enrolled. *Degree requirements:* For doctorate, 4 foreign languages, thesis/dissertation, dissertation defense, qualifying exam. *Entrance requirements:* For doctorate, GRE General Test, MA in Japanese, Chinese, or Sanskrit; minimum GPA of 3.0, 3 letters of recommendation. *Application deadline:* For fall admission, 12/8 for domestic students. Application fee: $70 ($90 for international students). Electronic applications accepted. *Financial support:* Unspecified assistantships available. *Unit head:* Prof. Robert Sharf, Chair, 510-642-3480, E-mail: rsharf@berkeley.edu. *Application contact:* Information Contact, 510-642-3480, E-mail: gbs@berkeley.edu.

University of California, Santa Barbara, Graduate Division, College of Letters and Sciences, Division of Humanities and Fine Arts, Department of Religious Studies, Santa Barbara, CA 93106-3130. Offers European Medieval studies (PhD); feminist studies (PhD); global studies (PhD); religious studies (MA, PhD); MA/PhD. *Faculty:* 18 full-time (8 women), 11 part-time/adjunct (5 women). *Students:* 86 full-time (33 women). Average age 31. 151 applicants, 31% accepted, 17 enrolled. In 2009, 7 master's, 6 doctorates awarded. Terminal master's awarded for partial completion of doctoral program. *Degree requirements:* For master's, one foreign language, comprehensive exam (for some programs), thesis (for some programs); for doctorate, one foreign language, thesis/dissertation. *Entrance requirements:* For master's, GRE General Test; for doctorate, GRE General Test, MA in related field, 3 letters of recommendation, statement of purpose, personal achievements/contributions statement, resume/curriculum vitae, transcripts for post-secondary institutions attended. Additional exam requirements/recommendations for international students: Required—TOEFL (minimum score 550 paper-based; 213 computer-based; 80 iBT) or IELTS (minimum score 7). *Application deadline:* For fall admission, 12/1 for domestic and international students. Application fee: $70 ($90 for international students). Electronic applications accepted. *Financial support:* In 2009–10, 67 students received support, including 29 fellowships with full and partial tuition reimbursements available (averaging $12,600 per year), 5 research assistantships with full and partial tuition reimbursements available (averaging $7,900 per year), 46 teaching assistantships with partial tuition reimbursements available (averaging $8,400 per year); career-related internships or fieldwork, Federal Work-Study, institutionally sponsored loans, scholarships/grants, traineeships, health care benefits, tuition waivers (full and partial), and unspecified assistantships also available. Financial award application deadline: 12/1; financial award applicants required to submit FAFSA. *Faculty research:* Religion and politics, religion and violence, contemporary spirituality, religious traditions, theoretical approaches to the study of religion, area studies. *Unit head:* Prof. Catherine L. Albanese, Chair, 805-893-3564, Fax: 805-893-2059, E-mail: albanese@religion.ucsb.edu. *Application contact:* Sally J. Lombrozo, Graduate Program Assistant, 805-893-2744, Fax: 805-893-2059, E-mail: lombrozo@religion.ucsb.edu.

University of Chicago, Divinity School, Chicago, IL 60637-1513. Offers M Div, AM, AMRS, PhD, JD/M Div, JD/MA, JD/PhD, MPP/M Div, MSW/M Div. *Accreditation:* ATS (one or more programs are accredited). Part-time programs available. *Degree requirements:* For master's and M Div, one foreign language; for doctorate, 2 foreign languages, comprehensive exam, thesis/dissertation. *Entrance requirements:* For M Div, master's, and doctorate, GRE General Test. Additional exam requirements/recommendations for international students: Required—TOEFL (minimum score 600 paper-based; 250 computer-based). Electronic applications accepted. *Expenses:* Contact institution. *Faculty research:* Theology, history of religion, ethics, biblical studies, philosophy of religion.

University of Colorado at Boulder, Graduate School, College of Arts and Sciences, Department of Religious Studies, Boulder, CO 80309. Offers MA. *Faculty:* 8 full-time (4 women). *Students:* 25 full-time (11 women), 5 part-time (3 women); includes 3 minority (1 American Indian/Alaska Native, 2 Hispanic Americans), 2 international. Average age 29. 50 applicants, 42% accepted, 11 enrolled. In 2009, 5 master's awarded. *Degree requirements:* For master's, one foreign language, comprehensive exam, thesis. *Entrance requirements:* For master's, minimum undergraduate GPA of 2.75. *Application deadline:* For fall admission, 1/15 priority date for domestic students, 1/31 for international students; for spring admission, 10/15 for domestic students, 9/15 for international students. Applications are processed on a rolling basis. Application fee: $50 ($60 for international students). *Financial support:* In 2009–10, 6 fellowships (averaging

Religion

University of Colorado at Boulder (continued)
$6,063 per year), 5 research assistantships (averaging $6,388 per year) were awarded; tuition waivers (full) also available. Financial award application deadline: 1/15. *Faculty research:* Comparative studies in religion, methodologies in the study of religion, religion and dance, history of religions (including Hinduism, Buddhism, religions of China and Japan, Islam, and Christianity).

University of Denver, Division of Arts, Humanities and Social Sciences, Department of Religious Studies, Denver, CO 80208. Offers MA. *Faculty:* 6 full-time (2 women). *Students:* 1 (woman) full-time, 9 part-time (5 women); includes 1 minority (Hispanic American), 2 international. Average age 34. 12 applicants, 83% accepted, 7 enrolled. In 2009, 8 master's awarded. *Entrance requirements:* For master's, GRE. *Application deadline:* Applications are processed on a rolling basis. Application fee: $50. Electronic applications accepted. *Expenses:* Tuition: Full-time $34,596; part-time $961 per quarter hour. Required fees: $4 per quarter hour. Tuition and fees vary according to course load, campus/location and program. *Unit head:* Dr. Ginette Ishimatsu, Chairperson, 303-871-2755. *Application contact:* Dr. Carl Raschke, Information Contact, 303-371-2749, E-mail: rlgs@du.edu.

University of Denver, Joint Program in Religious and Theological Studies, Denver, CO 80208. Offers PhD. Part-time programs available. *Students:* 44 full-time (17 women), 49 part-time (21 women); includes 9 minority (3 African Americans, 1 American Indian/Alaska Native, 2 Asian Americans or Pacific Islanders, 3 Hispanic Americans), 6 international. Average age 39. 66 applicants, 56% accepted, 21 enrolled. In 2009, 11 doctorates awarded. *Entrance requirements:* For doctorate, GRE. *Application deadline:* For fall admission, 1/15 for domestic students. Application fee: $50. *Expenses:* Tuition: Full-time $34,596; part-time $961 per quarter hour. Required fees: $4 per quarter hour. Tuition and fees vary according to course load, campus/location and program. *Unit head:* Dr. Frank Seeburger, Head, 303-871-2766. *Application contact:* Dr. Frank Seeburger, Head, 303-871-2766.

University of Detroit Mercy, College of Liberal Arts and Education, Department of Religious Studies, Detroit, MI 48221. Offers MA. *Degree requirements:* For master's, thesis or alternative. *Entrance requirements:* For master's, minimum GPA of 3.0. *Faculty research:* History of religions, textual studies (Old and New Testaments), ethical and cultural studies.

University of Florida, Graduate School, College of Liberal Arts and Sciences, Department of Religion, Gainesville, FL 32611. Offers religion (MA, PhD), including religion and nature (PhD), religion in the Americas (PhD), religions of Asia (PhD). Part-time programs available. *Degree requirements:* For master's, one foreign language, thesis. *Entrance requirements:* For master's, GRE General Test, minimum GPA of 3.0. Additional exam requirements/recommendations for international students: Required—TOEFL (minimum score 550 paper-based; 213 computer-based). Electronic applications accepted. *Faculty research:* Religion in America, Christian thought, Islam, religions of India, comparative religion.

University of Georgia, Graduate School, College of Arts and Sciences, Department of Religion, Athens, GA 30602. Offers MA. *Faculty:* 11 full-time (1 woman). *Students:* 23 full-time (11 women), 3 part-time (0 women); includes 1 minority (Asian American or Pacific Islander), 3 international. 43 applicants, 51% accepted, 13 enrolled. In 2009, 11 master's awarded. *Degree requirements:* For master's, one foreign language, thesis. *Entrance requirements:* For master's, GRE General Test. *Application deadline:* For fall admission, 7/1 priority date for domestic students; for spring admission, 11/15 for domestic students. Application fee: $50. Electronic applications accepted. *Expenses:* Tuition, state resident: full-time $6000; part-time $250 per credit hour. Tuition, nonresident: full-time $20,904; part-time $871 per credit hour. Required fees: $730 per semester. *Financial support:* Fellowships, research assistantships, teaching assistantships, unspecified assistantships available. *Unit head:* Dr. Sandy D. Martin, Head, 706-542-5356, Fax: 706-542-6724, E-mail: martin@uga.edu. *Application contact:* Dr. Carolyn Medine, Graduate Coordinator, 706-543-0308, Fax: 706-542-6724, E-mail: medine@uga.edu.

University of Hawaii at Manoa, Graduate Division, College of Arts and Humanities, Department of Religion, Honolulu, HI 96822. Offers MA. Part-time programs available. *Faculty:* 6 full-time (1 woman), 4 part-time/adjunct (1 woman). *Students:* 11 full-time (7 women), 4 part-time (1 woman); includes 3 minority (all Asian Americans or Pacific Islanders), 1 international. Average age 28. 20 applicants, 35% accepted, 5 enrolled. In 2009, 5 master's awarded. *Degree requirements:* For master's, one foreign language, thesis optional. *Entrance requirements:* For master's, GRE General Test. Additional exam requirements/recommendations for international students: Required—TOEFL (minimum score 600 paper-based; 250 computer-based; 100 iBT), IELTS (minimum score 7). *Application deadline:* For fall admission, 3/1 for domestic students, 1/15 for international students; for spring admission, 9/1 for international students. Applications are processed on a rolling basis. Application fee: $60. *Expenses:* Tuition, state resident: full-time $8900; part-time $372 per credit. Tuition, nonresident: full-time $21,400; part-time $898 per credit. Required fees: $207 per semester. *Financial support:* In 2009–10, 1 student received support, including 3 fellowships (averaging $2,883 per year), 8 teaching assistantships (averaging $14,598 per year); career-related internships or fieldwork, scholarships/grants, and tuition waivers (full and partial) also available. Financial award application deadline: 3/1. *Faculty research:* Buddhism, East Asian religion, South Asian religion, Polynesian religion, Western religions. *Application contact:* Michel Mohr, Graduate Field Chairperson, 808-956-8299, Fax: 808-956-9894, E-mail: mmohr@hawaii.edu.

The University of Iowa, Graduate College, College of Liberal Arts and Sciences, Department of Religious Studies, Iowa City, IA 52242-1316. Offers MA, PhD, JD/MA. Terminal master's awarded for partial completion of doctoral program. *Degree requirements:* For master's, thesis optional, exam; for doctorate, comprehensive exam, thesis/dissertation. *Entrance requirements:* For master's and doctorate, GRE General Test, minimum GPA of 3.0. Additional exam requirements/recommendations for international students: Required—TOEFL (minimum score 550 paper-based; 213 computer-based; 81 iBT). Electronic applications accepted. *Faculty research:* Eastern and Western religion.

The University of Kansas, Graduate Studies, College of Liberal Arts and Sciences, Department of Religious Studies, Lawrence, KS 66045. Offers MA. Part-time programs available. *Faculty:* 8 full-time (0 women), 6 part-time/adjunct (4 women). *Students:* 9 full-time (4 women), 8 part-time (5 women); includes 1 minority (African American). Average age 29. 7 applicants, 86% accepted, 4 enrolled. In 2009, 4 master's awarded. *Degree requirements:* For master's, comprehensive exam, thesis optional. *Entrance requirements:* For master's, minimum GPA of 3.0. Additional exam requirements/recommendations for international students: Required—TOEFL. *Application deadline:* For fall admission, 2/1 for domestic and international students. Application fee: $45 ($55 for international students). Electronic applications accepted. *Expenses:* Tuition, state resident: full-time $6492; part-time $270.50 per credit hour. Tuition, nonresident: full-time $15,510; part-time $646.25 per credit hour. Required fees: $847; $70.56 per credit hour. Tuition and fees vary according to course load and program. *Financial support:* Fellowships, teaching assistantships with full and partial tuition reimbursements, unspecified assistantships available. Financial award application deadline: 1/1. *Faculty research:* Judaism and Christianity, Islam, religions in Asia, methods and theories, American and Native American religion. *Unit head:* Daniel B. Stevenson, Chair, 785-864-7258, Fax: 785-864-5205, E-mail: rstudies@ku.edu. *Application contact:* Paul Mirecki, Graduate Director, 785-864-7258, Fax: 785-864-5205, E-mail: pmirecki@ku.edu.

University of Lethbridge, School of Graduate Studies, Lethbridge, AB T1K 3M4, Canada. Offers accounting (MScM); addictions counseling (M Sc); agricultural biotechnology (M Sc); agricultural studies (M Sc, MA); anthropology (MA); archaeology (MA); art (MA, MFA); biochemistry (M Sc); biological sciences (M Sc); biomolecular science (PhD); biosystems and biodiversity (PhD); Canadian studies (MA); chemistry (M Sc); computer science (M Sc); computer science and geographical information science (M Sc); counseling psychology (M Ed); dramatic arts (MA); earth, space, and physical science (PhD); economics (MA); educational leadership (M Ed); English (MA); environmental science (M Sc); evolution and behavior (PhD); exercise science (M Sc); finance (MScM); French (MA); French/German (MA); French/Spanish (MA); general education (M Ed); general management (MScM); geography (M Sc, MA); German (MA); health science (M Sc); health sciences (MA); history (MA); human resource management and labour relations (MScM); individualized multidisciplinary (M Sc, MA); information systems (MScM); international management (MScM); kinesiology (M Sc, MA); management (M Sc, MA); marketing (MScM); mathematics (M Sc); music (M Mus, MA); Native American studies (MA); neuroscience (M Sc, PhD); new media (MA); nursing (M Sc); philosophy (MA); physics (M Sc); policy and strategy (MScM); political science (MA); psychology (M Sc, MA); religious studies (MA); social sciences (MA); sociology (MA); theatre and dramatic arts (MFA); theoretical and computational science (PhD); urban and regional studies (MA); women's studies (MA). Part-time and evening/weekend programs available. *Degree requirements:* For doctorate, comprehensive exam, thesis/dissertation. *Entrance requirements:* For master's, GMAT (M Sc in management), bachelor's degree in related field, minimum GPA of 3.0 during previous 20 graded semester courses, 2 years teaching or related experience (M Ed); for doctorate, master's degree, minimum graduate GPA of 3.5. Additional exam requirements/recommendations for international students: Required—TOEFL. *Faculty research:* Movement and brain plasticity, gibberellin physiology, photosynthesis, carbon cycling, molecular properties of main-group ring components.

University of Manitoba, Faculty of Graduate Studies, Faculty of Arts, Department of Religion, Winnipeg, MB R3T 2N2, Canada. Offers MA, PhD. *Degree requirements:* For master's, one foreign language, thesis or alternative.

University of Michigan, Horace H. Rackham School of Graduate Studies, College of Literature, Science, and the Arts, Department of Near Eastern Studies, Ann Arbor, MI 48109. Offers ancient Near Eastern studies (AM, PhD); Arabic for professional purposes (AM); Arabic language and literature (AM, PhD); Armenian studies (AM, PhD); Christianity in late antiquity (AM, PhD); Egyptology (AM, PhD); Hebrew Bible and ancient Israel (AM, PhD); Hebrew literature (AM, PhD); Islamic studies (AM, PhD); Jewish cultural studies (AM, PhD); Jewish mysticism (AM, PhD); Persian and Iranian studies (AM, PhD); Rabbinic literature (AM, PhD); Second Temple Judaism (AM, PhD); teaching of Arabic as a foreign language (AM); Turkish studies (AM, PhD). Part-time programs available. *Faculty:* 23 full-time (5 women), 15 part-time/adjunct (6 women). *Students:* 47 full-time (23 women), 1 part-time (0 women); includes 1 minority (Hispanic American), 8 international. Average age 31. 99 applicants, 15% accepted, 8 enrolled. In 2009, 4 master's, 4 doctorates awarded. Terminal master's awarded for partial completion of doctoral program. *Degree requirements:* For master's, 2 foreign languages; for doctorate, 4 foreign languages, comprehensive exam, thesis/dissertation. *Entrance requirements:* For master's, GRE General Test; for doctorate, GRE General Test, master's degree. Additional exam requirements/recommendations for international students: Required—TOEFL (minimum score 560 paper-based; 220 computer-based; 84 iBT). *Application deadline:* For fall admission, 12/15 for domestic and international students. Application fee: $60 ($75 for international students). Electronic applications accepted. *Expenses:* Tuition, state resident: full-time $17,286; part-time $1099 per credit hour. Tuition, nonresident: full-time $34,944; part-time $2080 per credit hour. Required fees: $95 per semester. Tuition and fees vary according to course load, degree level and program. *Financial support:* In 2009–10, 43 students received support, including 21 fellowships with full tuition reimbursements available (averaging $16,694 per year), research assistantships with tuition reimbursements available (averaging $16,694 per year), 22 teaching assistantships with full tuition reimbursements available (averaging $16,694 per year); scholarships/grants, health care benefits, unspecified assistantships, and spring/summer stipends also available. *Faculty research:* Middle and Near Eastern literatures, languages, cultures from ancient times to the present. *Unit head:* Prof. Michael Bonner, Chair, 734-764-0314, Fax: 734-936-2679, E-mail: mbonner@umich.edu. *Application contact:* Angela Beskow, Student Services Assistant, 734-763-4539, Fax: 734-936-2679, E-mail: aradjews@umich.edu.

University of Minnesota, Twin Cities Campus, Graduate School, College of Liberal Arts, Department of Classical and Near Eastern Studies, Minneapolis, MN 55455-0213. Offers ancient and medieval art and archaeology (MA, PhD); classics (MA, PhD); Greek (MA, PhD); Latin (MA, PhD); religions in antiquity (MA). Part-time programs available. *Faculty:* 22 full-time (6 women). *Students:* 24 full-time (10 women), 1 part-time (0 women), 1 international. Average age 29. 40 applicants, 20% accepted, 4 enrolled. In 2009, 5 master's awarded. Terminal master's awarded for partial completion of doctoral program. *Degree requirements:* For master's, 2 foreign languages, comprehensive exam, thesis or alternative; for doctorate, variable foreign language requirement, comprehensive exam, thesis/dissertation. *Entrance requirements:* For master's and doctorate, GRE, 3 letters of recommendation, department application, writing sample, copies of transcripts, personal statement. Additional exam requirements/recommendations for international students: Required—TOEFL. *Application deadline:* For fall admission, 1/4 priority date for domestic and international students. Application fee: $50 ($75 for international students). Electronic applications accepted. *Financial support:* In 2009–10, 24 students received support, including 2 fellowships with full tuition reimbursements available (averaging $22,500 per year), 2 research assistantships with partial tuition reimbursements available (averaging $7,000 per year), 20 teaching assistantships with full tuition reimbursements available (averaging $14,000 per year); career-related internships or fieldwork, Federal Work-Study, institutionally sponsored loans, health care benefits, and tuition waivers (full and partial) also available. Support available to part-time students. Financial award application deadline: 1/4. *Faculty research:* Greek and Latin literature, religions in antiquity, ancient Near East. *Unit head:* Christopher Nappa, Chair, 612-625-624-6339, Fax: 612-624-4894, E-mail: cnappa@umn.edu. *Application contact:* Victoria H. Keller, Administrative Specialist, 612-625-8371, Fax: 612-624-4894, E-mail: kell0801@umn.edu.

University of Missouri, Graduate School, College of Arts and Sciences, Department of Religious Studies, Columbia, MO 65211. Offers MA. *Faculty:* 9 full-time (2 women), 3 part-time/adjunct (1 woman). *Students:* 10 full-time (6 women), 2 part-time (both women); includes 2 minority (1 African American, 1 Hispanic American). Average age 30. 15 applicants, 80% accepted, 7 enrolled. In 2009, 3 master's awarded. *Entrance requirements:* For master's, GRE General Test, minimum GPA of 3.0. Additional exam requirements/recommendations for international students: Required—TOEFL (minimum score 550 paper-based; 213 computer-based; 79 iBT). *Application deadline:* For fall admission, 2/1 priority date for domestic students. Application fee: $45 ($60 for international students). Electronic applications accepted. *Financial support:* In 2009–10, 2 fellowships with full tuition reimbursements, 10 teaching assistantships with full tuition reimbursements were awarded; research assistantships, institutionally sponsored loans, health care benefits, and unspecified assistantships also available. *Faculty research:* American religious history; biblical studies; history of Christianity; religion and society; religions of East Asia; religions of Indigenous peoples; religions of South Asia; women and religion. *Unit head:* Dr. Robert Baum, Department Chair, E-mail: baumr@missouri.edu. *Application contact:* Dr. Signe Cohen, Director of Graduate Studies, 573-882-4769, E-mail: cohens@missouri.edu.

University of Mobile, Graduate Programs, Program in Religious Studies, Mobile, AL 36613. Offers biblical/theological studies (MA); marriage and family counseling (MA). Part-time and evening/weekend programs available. *Faculty:* 4 full-time (0 women), 1 (woman) part-time/adjunct. *Students:* 12 full-time (11 women), 34 part-time (22 women); includes 24 minority (23 African Americans, 1 American Indian/Alaska Native). Average age 32. 20 applicants, 100% accepted, 16 enrolled. In 2009, 12 master's awarded. *Degree requirements:* For master's, 2 foreign languages, comprehensive exam, thesis optional. *Entrance requirements:* For master's, GRE General Test. Additional exam requirements/recommendations for international students: Required—TOEFL (minimum score 550 paper-based; 213 computer-based; 80 iBT). *Application deadline:* For fall admission, 8/3 priority date for domestic students; for spring admission, 12/23 for domestic students. Applications are processed on a rolling basis. Application fee: $40 ($50 for international students). *Financial support:* Federal Work-Study available. Support available to part-time students. Financial award application deadline: 8/1. *Unit head:* Dr. Cecil Taylor, Dean, School of Christian Studies, 251-442-2255, Fax: 251-442-2523, E-mail: ctaylor@mail.umobile.edu. *Application contact:* Tammy C. Eubanks, Administrative Assistant to Dean of Graduate Programs, 251-442-2270, Fax: 251-442-2523, E-mail: teubanks@umobile.edu.

The University of North Carolina at Chapel Hill, Graduate School, College of Arts and Sciences, Department of Religious Studies, Chapel Hill, NC 27599. Offers MA, PhD. *Degree requirements:* For master's, one foreign language, comprehensive exam, thesis; for doctorate, 2 foreign languages, comprehensive exam, thesis/dissertation. *Entrance requirements:* For master's and doctorate, GRE General Test, minimum GPA of 3.0. Additional exam requirements/recommendations for international students: Required—TOEFL. *Faculty research:* Religion.

The University of North Carolina at Charlotte, Graduate School, College of Arts and Sciences, Department of Religious Studies, Charlotte, NC 28223-0001. Offers MA. *Faculty:* 16 full-time (4 women), 5 part-time/adjunct (4 women). *Students:* 5 full-time (1 woman), 19 part-time (8 women); includes 1 minority (African American). Average age 30. 18 applicants, 72% accepted, 9 enrolled. In 2009, 6 master's awarded. *Degree requirements:* For master's, comprehensive exam, thesis. *Entrance requirements:* For master's, GRE or MAT, 3 letters of reference. Additional exam requirements/recommendations for international students: Required—TOEFL (minimum score 557 paper-based; 220 computer-based; 83 iBT). *Application deadline:* For fall admission, 7/15 for domestic students, 5/1 for international students; for spring admission, 11/15 for domestic students, 10/1 for international students. Applications are processed on a rolling basis. Application fee: $55. Electronic applications accepted. *Financial support:* In 2009–10, 3 students received support, including 3 teaching assistantships (averaging $9,000 per year); career-related internships or fieldwork, Federal Work-Study, institutionally sponsored loans, scholarships/grants, and unspecified assistantships also available. Support available to part-time students. Financial award application deadline: 4/1; financial award applicants required to submit FAFSA. Total annual research expenditures: $18,803. *Unit head:* Dr. James D. Tabor, Chair, 704-687-2783, Fax: 704-687-3002, E-mail: jdtabor@uncc.edu. *Application contact:* Kathy B. Giddings, Director of Graduate Admissions, 704-687-5503, Fax: 704-687-3279, E-mail: gradadm@uncc.edu.

University of North Texas, Robert B. Toulouse School of Graduate Studies, College of Arts and Sciences, Department of Philosophy and Religion Studies, Denton, TX 76203. Offers philosophy (MA, PhD). *Degree requirements:* For master's, one foreign language, thesis or alternative; for doctorate, one foreign language, comprehensive exam, thesis/dissertation. *Entrance requirements:* For master's, GRE General Test. Additional exam requirements/recommendations for international students: Required—proof of English language proficiency required for non-native English speakers; Recommended—TOEFL (minimum score 550 paper-based; 213 computer-based; 79 iBT). Application fee: $50 ($75 for international students). *Expenses:* Tuition, state resident: full-time $4298; part-time $239 per contact hour. Tuition, nonresident: full-time $9878; part-time $549 per contact hour. Required fees: $265 per contact hour. *Financial support:* Application deadline: 4/1. *Application contact:* Associate Dean, 940-565-2383, Fax: 940-565-2141.

University of Notre Dame, Graduate School, College of Arts and Letters, Division of Humanities, Program in Early Christian Studies, Notre Dame, IN 46556. Offers MA. *Degree requirements:* For master's, 3 foreign languages, comprehensive exam. *Entrance requirements:* For master's, GRE General Test. Additional exam requirements/recommendations for international students: Required—TOEFL (minimum score 600 paper-based; 250 computer-based; 80 iBT). Electronic applications accepted. *Faculty research:* Early Christian theology, worship and scriptural interpretation; late antique and Byzantine history; art and culture; Greek and Latin literature.

University of Ottawa, Faculty of Graduate and Postdoctoral Studies, Faculty of Arts, Department of Classics and Religious Studies, Ottawa, ON K1N 6N5, Canada. Offers classical studies (MA); religious studies (PhD). *Degree requirements:* For master's, comprehensive exam, thesis or alternative; for doctorate, comprehensive exam, thesis/dissertation. *Entrance requirements:* For master's, honors degree or equivalent, minimum B average; for doctorate, master's degree, minimum B+ average. Electronic applications accepted. *Faculty research:* Religions in Canada, including Amerindian and Inuit religions; religion and culture; late antiquity.

University of Pennsylvania, School of Arts and Sciences, Graduate Group in Religious Studies, Philadelphia, PA 19104. Offers PhD. *Faculty:* 28 full-time (11 women), 6 part-time/adjunct (0 women). *Students:* 22 full-time (9 women), 4 part-time (2 women); includes 3 minority (2 American Indian/Alaska Native, 1 Asian American or Pacific Islander), 4 international. 55 applicants, 9% accepted, 5 enrolled. In 2009, 5 doctorates awarded. *Degree requirements:* For doctorate, thesis/dissertation, approved specialty languages, preliminary and final exams. *Entrance requirements:* For doctorate, GRE. Additional exam requirements/recommendations for international students: Required—TOEFL. *Application deadline:* For fall admission, 12/1 priority date for domestic students. Application fee: $70. Electronic applications accepted. *Expenses:* Tuition: Full-time $25,660; part-time $4758 per course. Required fees: $2152; $270 per course. Tuition and fees vary according to course load, degree level and program. *Financial support:* In 2009–10, 10 students received support, including 2 fellowships, 1 research assistantship, 3 teaching assistantships; institutionally sponsored loans, scholarships/grants, traineeships, health care benefits, and unspecified assistantships also available. Financial award application deadline: 12/15. *Faculty research:* Judaism and Christianity (ancient, medieval, modern), Islam, Hinduism, Buddhism, modern religious thought.

University of Pittsburgh, School of Arts and Sciences, Cooperative Doctoral Program in Religion, Pittsburgh, PA 15260. Offers PhD. *Faculty:* 6 full-time (2 women), 2 part-time/adjunct (both women). *Students:* 11 full-time (5 women); includes 1 minority (Hispanic American). Average age 39. 9 applicants, 11% accepted, 1 enrolled. In 2009, 1 doctorate awarded. *Degree requirements:* For doctorate, 2 foreign languages, comprehensive exam, thesis/dissertation, preliminary exam. *Entrance requirements:* For doctorate, GRE General Test, sample of research or written work, 3 letters of recommendation. Additional exam requirements/recommendations for international students: Required—TOEFL (minimum score 600 paper-based; 250 computer-based; 100 iBT). *Application deadline:* For fall admission, 1/15 for domestic and international students. Application fee: $50. Electronic applications accepted. *Expenses:* Tuition, state resident: full-time $16,402; part-time $665 per credit. Tuition, nonresident: full-time $28,694; part-time $1175 per credit. Required fees: $690; $175 per term. Tuition and fees vary according to program. *Financial support:* In 2009–10, 1 fellowship with full tuition reimbursement (averaging $16,000 per year), 2 teaching assistantships with full tuition reimbursements (averaging $15,000 per year) were awarded; research assistantships, health care benefits, tuition waivers (partial), and unspecified assistantships also available. Financial award application deadline: 1/15. *Faculty research:* Contemporary Catholicism and religion in America, Buddhism and East Asian religions, philosophy and religion and religious thought and language, medieval to modern Jewish history, theories and methods in the study of religion. *Unit head:* Dr. Adam Shear, Director of Graduate Studies, 412-624-2280, Fax: 412-624-5994, E-mail: ashear@pitt.edu. *Application contact:* Donna L. Walker, Department Administrator, 412-624-5990, Fax: 412-624-5994, E-mail: dlw5@pitt.edu.

University of Pittsburgh, School of Arts and Sciences, Department of Religious Studies, Pittsburgh, PA 15260. Offers MA. *Faculty:* 6 full-time (2 women), 3 part-time/adjunct (2 women). *Students:* 8 full-time (6 women). Average age 27. 12 applicants, 33% accepted, 3 enrolled. In 2009, 2 master's awarded. *Degree requirements:* For master's, comprehensive exam, thesis. *Entrance requirements:* For master's, GRE General Test, sample of written work, 3 letters of recommendation. Additional exam requirements/recommendations for international students: Required—TOEFL (minimum score 600 paper-based; 250 computer-based; 100 iBT). *Application deadline:* For fall admission, 1/15 for domestic and international students. Application fee: $50. Electronic applications accepted. *Expenses:* Tuition, state resident: full-time $16,402; part-time $665 per credit. Tuition, nonresident: full-time $28,694; part-time $1175 per credit. Required fees: $690; $175 per term. Tuition and fees vary according to program. *Financial support:* In 2009–10, 3 students received support, including 3 teaching assistantships with full tuition reimbursements available (averaging $15,000 per year); fellowships, research assistantships with full tuition reimbursements available, health care benefits and tuition waivers (partial) also available. Financial award application deadline: 1/15. *Faculty research:* Contemporary Catholicism and religion in America, Buddhism and East Asian religions, philosophy and religion and religious thought and language, Medieval to modern Jewish history, theories and methods in the study of religion. *Unit head:* Dr. Adam Shear, Director of Graduate Studies, 412-624-2280, Fax: 412-624-5994, E-mail: ashear@pitt.edu. *Application contact:* Donna L. Walker, Department Administrator, 412-624-5990, Fax: 412-624-5994, E-mail: dlw5@pitt.edu.

University of Regina, Faculty of Graduate Studies and Research, Faculty of Arts, Department of Religious Studies, Regina, SK S4S 0A2, Canada. Offers MA, PhD. Part-time programs available. *Faculty:* 10 full-time (3 women), 2 part-time/adjunct (0 women). *Students:* 3 full-time (2 women), 3 part-time (2 women). 4 applicants, 75% accepted. In 2009, 1 master's awarded. *Degree requirements:* For master's, thesis. *Entrance requirements:* Additional exam requirements/recommendations for international students: Required—TOEFL (minimum score 580 paper-based; 237 computer-based; 80 iBT). *Application deadline:* Applications are processed on a rolling basis. Application fee: $90 ($100 for international students). Electronic applications accepted. *Financial support:* In 2009–10, 1 fellowship (averaging $19,000 per year), 3 teaching assistantships (averaging $6,650 per year) were awarded; research assistantships, scholarships/grants also available. Financial award application deadline: 6/15. *Faculty research:* Christianity, Hinduism, Buddhism, Islam, Judaism. *Unit head:* Dr. Leona Anderson, Head, 306-585-4580, Fax: 306-585-4815, E-mail: leona.anderson@uregina.ca. *Application contact:* Dr. Leona Anderson, Head, 306-585-4580, Fax: 306-585-4815, E-mail: leona.anderson@uregina.ca.

University of St. Thomas, Graduate Studies, College of Arts and Sciences, Program in Catholic Studies, St. Paul, MN 55105-1096. Offers MA. Part-time and evening/weekend programs available. *Degree requirements:* For master's, thesis. *Entrance requirements:* For master's, bachelor's degree with minimum GPA of 3.0, writing sample, 3 letters of recommendation. Additional exam requirements/recommendations for international students: Required—TOEFL (minimum score 550 paper-based).

University of Saskatchewan, College of Graduate Studies and Research, College of Arts and Sciences, Department of Religious Studies and Anthropology, Saskatoon, SK S7N 5A2, Canada. Offers MA. *Faculty:* 20. *Students:* 1. *Degree requirements:* For master's, thesis. *Entrance requirements:* Additional exam requirements/recommendations for international students: Required—TOEFL (minimum score 80 iBT); Recommended—IELTS (minimum score 6.5). *Application deadline:* Applications are processed on a rolling basis. Application fee: $75. Electronic applications accepted. Tuition and fees charges are reported in Canadian dollars. *Expenses:* Tuition, area resident: Full-time $3000 Canadian dollars; part-time $500 Canadian dollars per term. Required fees: $700 Canadian dollars; $100 Canadian dollars per term. *Financial support:* Fellowships, research assistantships, teaching assistantships available. Financial award application deadline: 1/31. *Unit head:* Dr. Baj Sinha, Head, 306-966-4258, E-mail: baj.sinha@usask.ca. *Application contact:* Dr. Mary Beavis, Graduate Chair, 306-966-4258, E-mail: mary.beavis@usas.ca.

University of South Africa, College of Human Sciences, Pretoria, South Africa. Offers adult education (M Ed); African languages (MA, PhD); African politics (MA, PhD); Afrikaans (MA, PhD); ancient history (MA, PhD); ancient Near Eastern studies (MA, PhD); anthropology (MA, PhD); applied linguistics (MA); Arabic (MA, PhD); archaeology (MA); art history (MA); Biblical archaeology (MA); Biblical studies (M Th, D Th, PhD); Christian spirituality (M Th, D Th); church history (M Th, D Th); classical studies (MA, PhD); clinical psychology (MA); communication (MA, PhD); comparative education (M Ed, Ed D); consulting psychology (D Admin, D Com, PhD); curriculum studies (M Ed, Ed D); development studies (M Admin, MA, D Admin, PhD); didactics (M Ed, Ed D); education (M Tech); education management (M Ed, Ed D); educational psychology (M Ed); English (MA); environmental education (M Ed); French (MA, PhD); German (MA, PhD); Greek (MA); guidance and counseling (M Ed); health studies (MA, PhD), including health sciences education (MA), health services management (MA), medical and surgical nursing science (critical care general) (MA), midwifery and neonatal nursing science (MA), trauma and emergency care (MA); history (MA, PhD); history of education (Ed D); inclusive education (M Ed, Ed D); information and communications technology policy and regulation (MA); information science (MA, MIS, PhD); international politics (MA, PhD); Islamic studies (MA, PhD); Italian (MA, PhD); Judaica (MA, PhD); linguistics (MA, PhD); mathematical education (M Ed); mathematics education (MA); missiology (M Th, D Th); modern Hebrew (MA, PhD); musicology (MA, MMus, D Mus, PhD); natural science education (M Ed); New Testament (M Th, D Th); Old Testament (D Th); pastoral therapy (M Th, D Th); philosophy (MA); philosophy of education (M Ed, Ed D); politics (MA, PhD); Portuguese (MA, PhD); practical theology (M Th, D Th); psychology (MA, MS, PhD); psychology of education (M Ed, Ed D); public health (MA); religious studies (MA, D Th, PhD); Romance languages (MA); Russian (MA, PhD); Semitic languages (MA, PhD); social behavior studies in HIV/AIDS (MA); social science (mental health) (MA); social science in development studies (MA); social science in psychology (MA); social science in social work (MA); social science in sociology (MA); social work (MSW, DSW, PhD); socio-education (M Ed, Ed D); sociolinguistics (MA); sociology (MA, PhD); Spanish (MA, PhD); systematic theology (M Th, D Th); TESOL (teaching English to speakers of other languages) (MA); theological ethics (M Th, D Th); theory of literature (MA, PhD); urban ministries (D Th); urban ministry (M Th).

University of South Carolina, The Graduate School, College of Arts and Sciences, Department of Religious Studies, Columbia, SC 29208. Offers MA. Part-time programs available. *Degree requirements:* For master's, one foreign language, comprehensive exam, thesis. *Entrance requirements:* For master's, GRE General Test or MAT. Additional exam requirements/recommendations for international students: Required—TOEFL. Electronic applications accepted. *Faculty research:* Biblical and Near Eastern studies, theology and religious thought, religion and culture, South Asian religions, Islamic studies.

University of South Florida, Graduate School, College of Arts and Sciences, Department of Religious Studies, Tampa, FL 33620-9951. Offers MA. Part-time and evening/weekend programs available. *Faculty:* 11 full-time (3 women). *Students:* 15 full-time (9 women), 11 part-time (6 women); includes 6 minority (2 African Americans, 2 Asian Americans or Pacific Islanders, 2 Hispanic Americans). Average age 32. 29 applicants, 59% accepted, 12 enrolled. In 2009, 12 master's awarded. *Degree requirements:* For master's, comprehensive exam, thesis. *Entrance requirements:* For master's, GRE General Test, minimum GPA of 3.0 in last 60 hours. Additional exam requirements/recommendations for international students: Required—TOEFL (minimum score 550 paper-based; 213 computer-based). *Application deadline:* For fall admission, 2/15 priority date for domestic students, 1/2 priority date for international students; for spring admission, 10/15 priority date for domestic students, 6/1 priority date for international students. Applications are processed on a rolling basis. Application fee: $30. Electronic applications accepted. *Financial support:* In 2009–10, teaching assistantships with tuition reimbursements (averaging $9,000 per year); unspecified assistantships also available. Financial award applicants required to submit FAFSA. *Faculty research:* Scripture and history of Judaism, Christianity, and Islam; religion and society; new religions; comparative religious ethics; narrative and religion. Total annual research expenditures: $15,857. *Unit head:* Dr. Mozella G. Mitchell, Chairperson, 813-974-1852, Fax: 813-974-1853, E-mail: mitchellm@usf.edu. *Application contact:* Dr. Paul Schneider, Director, 813-974-2730, Fax: 813-974-1853, E-mail: pgschnei@cas.usf.edu.

The University of Tennessee, Graduate School, College of Arts and Sciences, Department of Philosophy, Knoxville, TN 37996. Offers medical ethics (MA, PhD); philosophy (MA, PhD); religious studies (MA). Part-time programs available. *Degree requirements:* For master's, thesis or alternative; for doctorate, one foreign language, thesis/dissertation. *Entrance requirements:* For master's and doctorate, GRE General Test, minimum GPA of 2.7. Additional exam requirements/recommendations for international students: Required—TOEFL. Electronic applications accepted. *Expenses:* Tuition, state resident: full-time $6826; part-time $380 per semester hour. Tuition, nonresident: full-time $21,844; part-time $1147 per semester hour. Tuition and fees vary according to program.

University of the Incarnate Word, School of Graduate Studies and Research, College of Humanities, Arts, and Social Sciences, Program in Religious Studies, San Antonio, TX 78209-6397. Offers MA. Part-time programs available. *Faculty:* 1 (woman) full-time, 1 part-time/adjunct (0 women). *Students:* 2 full-time (both women), 14 part-time (9 women); includes 7

Religion

University of the Incarnate Word (continued)
minority (1 African American, 6 Hispanic Americans), 1 international. Average age 42. In 2009, 3 master's awarded. *Degree requirements:* For master's, pastoral project. *Entrance requirements:* For master's, recommendation letters, 12 credit hours related undergraduate coursework. Additional exam requirements/recommendations for international students: Required—TOEFL (minimum score 560 paper-based; 220 computer-based; 83 iBT). *Application deadline:* Applications are processed on a rolling basis. Application fee: $20. Electronic applications accepted. *Expenses:* Tuition: Full-time $12,150; part-time $675 per credit hour. Required fees: $83 per credit hour. *Financial support:* Federal Work-Study, scholarships/grants, and tuition waivers (partial) available. Financial award applicants required to submit FAFSA. *Unit head:* Sr. Eilish Ryan, Chair, 210-829-3871, Fax: 210-829-3880, E-mail: eryan@uiwtx.edu. *Application contact:* Andrea Cyterski-Acosta, Dean of Enrollment, 210-829-6005, Fax: 210-829-3921, E-mail: admis@uiwtx.edu.

University of the West, Department of Religious Studies, Rosemead, CA 91770. Offers Buddhist studies (MA, DBS); comparative religions (MA); religious studies (PhD). Part-time and evening/weekend programs available. *Degree requirements:* For master's, thesis or comprehensive exam, competency in language associated with Buddhist Canon literature; for doctorate, one foreign language, comprehensive exam, thesis/dissertation.

University of Toronto, School of Graduate Studies, Humanities Division, Centre for the Study of Religion, Toronto, ON M5S 1A1, Canada. Offers MA, PhD. Part-time programs available. *Degree requirements:* For master's, one foreign language, research paper, language requirement examination; for doctorate, 2 foreign languages, thesis/dissertation, language examinations, general examinations, oral examination. *Entrance requirements:* For master's, BA in religion or a related field; minimum A- average in final year, 3 letters of recommendation, resume; for doctorate, MA in religion, minimum average of A- in MA courses with no individual grade below a B, 3 letters of recommendation, resumé, brief writing sample. Additional exam requirements/recommendations for international students: Required—TOEFL (minimum score 600 paper-based; 250 computer-based), TWE (minimum score 5).

University of Virginia, College and Graduate School of Arts and Sciences, Department of Religious Studies, Charlottesville, VA 22903. Offers MA, PhD. *Faculty:* 28 full-time (10 women), 6 part-time/adjunct (2 women). *Students:* 88 full-time (29 women), 4 part-time (2 women); includes 3 minority (1 African American, 2 Asian Americans or Pacific Islanders), 7 international. Average age 31. 146 applicants, 49% accepted, 30 enrolled. In 2009, 7 master's, 16 doctorates awarded. *Degree requirements:* For master's, one foreign language, thesis optional; for doctorate, 2 foreign languages, comprehensive exam, thesis/dissertation. *Entrance requirements:* For master's and doctorate, GRE General Test, 3 letters of recommendation. Additional exam requirements/recommendations for international students: Required—TOEFL (minimum score 600 paper-based; 250 computer-based; 90 iBT), IELTS (minimum score 7). *Application deadline:* For fall admission, 12/3 for domestic and international students. Applications are processed on a rolling basis. Application fee: $60. Electronic applications accepted. *Financial support:* Fellowships, teaching assistantships available. Financial award applicants required to submit FAFSA. *Unit head:* Kevin Hart, Chair, 434-924-6705, Fax: 434-924-1467. *Application contact:* Elizabeth Smith, Graduate and Fiscal Coordinator, 434-924-6706, Fax: 434-924-1467, E-mail: eas5x@virginia.edu.

University of Washington, Graduate School, College of Arts and Sciences, Department of Asian Languages and Literature, Seattle, WA 98195. Offers Buddhist studies (MA, PhD); Chinese language and literature (MA, PhD); Japanese language and literature (MA, PhD); Korean language and literature (MA, PhD); South Asian language and literature (MA, PhD). *Degree requirements:* For master's, 2 foreign languages, general exam, thesis or 2 research papers; for doctorate, 3 foreign languages, thesis/dissertation, general exam. *Entrance requirements:* For master's, GRE, minimum GPA of 3.0; for doctorate, GRE, master's degree in related field, minimum GPA of 3.0. Additional exam requirements/recommendations for international students: Required—TOEFL. Electronic applications accepted. *Faculty research:* Textual, linguistic, philological, and literary study of languages and literatures of Asia.

University of Washington, Graduate School, College of Arts and Sciences, Henry M. Jackson School of International Studies, Comparative Religion Program, Seattle, WA 98195. Offers MAIS. *Faculty:* 21 full-time (9 women). *Students:* 23 full-time (11 women); includes 2 minority (1 Asian American or Pacific Islander, 1 Hispanic American). 29 applicants, 59% accepted, 6 enrolled. In 2009, 14 master's awarded. *Degree requirements:* For master's, 2 foreign languages. *Entrance requirements:* For master's, GRE General Test, minimum GPA of 3.0. Additional exam requirements/recommendations for international students: Required—TOEFL (minimum score 500 paper-based; 213 computer-based; 92 iBT), or IELTS (minimum score 7). *Application deadline:* For fall admission, 12/30 for domestic students, 12/1 for international students. Application fee: $75. Electronic applications accepted. *Financial support:* In 2009–10, 1 fellowship, 2 teaching assistantships with full tuition reimbursements were awarded; research assistantships, career-related internships or fieldwork, Federal Work-Study, institutionally sponsored loans, scholarships/grants, and tuition waivers (partial) also available. Financial award application deadline: 12/30; financial award applicants required to submit FAFSA. *Unit head:* Prof. James K. Wellman, Chair, 206-543-0339, E-mail: jwellman@u.washington.edu. *Application contact:* 206-543-6001, Fax: 206-616-3170, E-mail: jsisinfo@u.washington.edu.

University of Waterloo, Graduate Studies, Faculty of Arts, Department of Religious Studies, Waterloo, ON N2L 3G1, Canada. Offers religious diversity in North America (PhD). *Degree requirements:* For doctorate, thesis/dissertation. *Entrance requirements:* Additional exam requirements/recommendations for international students: Required—TOEFL. Electronic applications accepted. *Faculty research:* Religious diversity in North America.

The University of Winnipeg, Graduate Studies, Department of Religious Studies, Winnipeg, MB R3B 2E9, Canada. Offers MA. Part-time programs available. *Faculty research:* Religion and culture, social ethics, religious liberalism, history of Canaanite and Israelite religion, literary criticism of the Hebrew Bible.

Vanderbilt University, Graduate School, Department of Religion, Nashville, TN 37240-1001. Offers MA, PhD. *Faculty:* 48 full-time (16 women). *Students:* 108 full-time (55 women), 1 part-time (0 women); includes 25 minority (18 African Americans, 1 American Indian/Alaska Native, 3 Asian Americans or Pacific Islanders, 3 Hispanic Americans), 12 international. Average age 35. 226 applicants, 9% accepted, 15 enrolled. In 2009, 25 master's, 10 doctorates awarded. *Degree requirements:* For master's, one foreign language, thesis; for doctorate, 2 foreign languages, thesis/dissertation, final and qualifying exams. *Entrance requirements:* For master's and doctorate, GRE General Test. Additional exam requirements/recommendations for international students: Required—TOEFL (minimum score 570 paper-based; 230 computer-based; 88 iBT). *Application deadline:* For fall admission, 1/15 for domestic and international students. Application fee: $0. Electronic applications accepted. *Financial support:* Fellowships with full and partial tuition reimbursements, teaching assistantships with full and partial tuition reimbursements, Federal Work-Study, institutionally sponsored loans, health care benefits, and tuition waivers (full and partial) available. Support available to part-time students. Financial award application deadline: 1/15; financial award applicants required to submit CSS PROFILE or FAFSA. *Faculty research:* Hebrew Bible, New Testament, church history, theology, ethics. *Unit head:* John S. McClure, Chair, 615-343-3977, Fax: 615-343-5449, E-mail: john.s.mcclure@vanderbilt.edu. *Application contact:* James P. Byrd, Director of Graduate Studies, 615-343-3977, Fax: 615-343-5449, E-mail: james.p.byrd@vanderbilt.edu.

Vanguard University of Southern California, Graduate Programs in Religion, Costa Mesa, CA 92626-9601. Offers leadership studies (MA); theological studies (MTS). Part-time and evening/weekend programs available. *Faculty:* 5 full-time (0 women), 1 part-time/adjunct (0 women). *Students:* 10 full-time (2 women), 60 part-time (17 women); includes 14 minority (1 African American, 4 Asian Americans or Pacific Islanders, 9 Hispanic Americans). Average age 38. 26 applicants, 73% accepted, 16 enrolled. *Degree requirements:* For master's, comprehensive exam (for some programs), thesis (for some programs). *Entrance requirements:* For master's, minimum GPA of 3.0 (MA), 2.5 (MTS). Additional exam requirements/recommendations for international students: Required—TOEFL (minimum score 550 paper-based; 213 computer-based; 79 iBT). *Application deadline:* For fall admission, 4/1 priority date for domestic and international students; for spring admission, 10/1 priority date for domestic and international students. Applications are processed on a rolling basis. Application fee: $45. Electronic applications accepted. *Expenses:* Contact institution. *Financial support:* Teaching assistantships, scholarships/grants and tuition waivers (partial) available. Support available to part-time students. Financial award application deadline: 3/2; financial award applicants required to submit FAFSA. *Faculty research:* Narrative theology, ecumenism and Pentecost, leadership studies. *Unit head:* Dr. Richard Israel, Associate Dean, 714-556-3610 Ext. 3223, Fax: 714-957-9317. *Application contact:* Angel McGee, Secretary, 714-556-3610 Ext. 3237, Fax: 714-957-9317, E-mail: angel.mcgee@vanguard.edu.

Virginia University of Lynchburg, Graduate Programs, Lynchburg, VA 24501-6417. Offers Christian ministry (M Div).

Wake Forest University, Graduate School of Arts and Sciences, Department of Religion, Winston-Salem, NC 27109. Offers MA. *Accreditation:* ACIPE. Part-time programs available. *Degree requirements:* For master's, one foreign language, thesis. *Entrance requirements:* For master's, GRE General Test. Additional exam requirements/recommendations for international students: Required—TOEFL (minimum score 213 computer-based; 79 iBT). Electronic applications accepted. *Faculty research:* Christian origins, biblical archaeology, psychology and religion, religion and literature.

Warner Pacific College, Graduate Programs, Portland, OR 97215-4099. Offers biblical and theological studies (MA); biblical studies (M Rel); education (M Ed); management/organizational leadership (MS); pastoral ministries (M Rel); religion and ethics (M Rel); teaching (MA); theology (M Rel). Part-time programs available. *Degree requirements:* For master's, thesis or alternative, presentation of defense. *Entrance requirements:* For master's, interview, minimum GPA of 2.5, letters of recommendations. *Faculty research:* New Testament studies, nineteenth-century Wesleyan theology, preaching and church growth, Christian ethics.

Washington Adventist University, Program in Religion, Takoma Park, MD 20912. Offers MAR. Part-time programs available. *Students:* 1 full-time (0 women), 13 part-time (8 women); includes 6 African Americans, 4 Asian Americans or Pacific Islanders, 1 Hispanic American. Average age 43. *Application deadline:* Applications are processed on a rolling basis. *Financial support:* Available to part-time students. Applicants required to submit FAFSA. *Unit head:* Dr. Davenia Lea, Dean, School of Graduate and Professional Studies, E-mail: dlea@wau.edu. *Application contact:* Dr. Davenia Lea, Dean, School of Graduate and Professional Studies, 301-891-4092, E-mail: dlea@wau.edu.

Wayland Baptist University, Graduate Programs, Programs in Religion, Plainview, TX 79072-6998. Offers Christian ministry (MCM); religion (MA). Part-time and evening/weekend programs available. Postbaccalaureate distance learning degree programs offered (no on-campus study). *Faculty:* 6 full-time (1 woman). *Students:* 13 part-time (4 women); includes 3 minority (2 African Americans, 1 Hispanic American). Average age 38. 10 applicants, 90% accepted, 3 enrolled. In 2009, 2 master's awarded. *Degree requirements:* For master's, comprehensive exam. *Entrance requirements:* For master's, GRE or MAT. Additional exam requirements/recommendations for international students: Required—TOEFL (minimum score 500 paper-based; 173 computer-based; 61 iBT). *Application deadline:* Applications are processed on a rolling basis. Application fee: $50. Electronic applications accepted. *Expenses:* Tuition: Full-time $5796; part-time $322 per credit hour. Required fees: $782; $9 per credit hour. $60 per semester. Tuition and fees vary according to course load and campus/location. *Financial support:* Federal Work-Study, institutionally sponsored loans, and scholarships/grants available. Support available to part-time students. Financial award application deadline: 5/1; financial award applicants required to submit FAFSA. *Unit head:* Dr. Paul Sadler, Chairman, 806-291-1160, Fax: 806-291-1969, E-mail: sadlerp@wbu.edu. *Application contact:* Amanda Stanton, Graduate Studies, 806-291-3423, Fax: 806-291-1950, E-mail: stanton@wbu.edu.

Wesley Biblical Seminary, Graduate Programs, Jackson, MS 39206. Offers apologetics (MA); Biblical studies (MA); Christian studies (MA); evangelism (M Div); family life ministry (M Div); honors research (M Div); missions (M Div); pastoral ministry (M Div); teaching (M Div); theological studies (MA). *Accreditation:* ATS. Part-time programs available. *Faculty:* 11 full-time (2 women), 5 part-time/adjunct (0 women). *Students:* 43 full-time (5 women), 89 part-time (33 women). *Degree requirements:* For master's, thesis. *Entrance requirements:* Additional exam requirements/recommendations for international students: Required—TOEFL. *Application deadline:* For fall admission, 7/1 priority date for domestic students; for spring admission, 12/1 priority date for domestic students. Applications are processed on a rolling basis. Application fee: $40. Electronic applications accepted. *Expenses:* Tuition: Full-time $8000; part-time $320 per credit hour. Required fees: $310; $160 per semester. Tuition and fees vary according to course load, campus/location and program. *Financial support:* Scholarships/grants available. Support available to part-time students. *Faculty research:* Patristics, missiology, culture, hermeneutics. *Unit head:* Dr. Ray R. Easley, Vice President for Academic Affairs, 601-366-8880 Ext. 112, Fax: 601-366-8832. *Application contact:* Laura McMillan, Assistant to the Vice President for Business and Student Development, 601-366-8880 Ext. 110, Fax: 601-366-8832, E-mail: admissions@wbs.edu.

Western Michigan University, Graduate College, College of Arts and Sciences, Department of Comparative Religion, Kalamazoo, MI 49008. Offers MA. *Degree requirements:* For master's, one foreign language, thesis optional, oral exam.

Western Seminary, Graduate Programs, Program in Biblical and Theological Studies, Portland, OR 97215-3367. Offers biblical and theological studies (MA, G Dip); biblical studies (Certificate); theology (Th M). *Accreditation:* ATS. Part-time and evening/weekend programs available. *Faculty:* 93 full-time (38 women), 586 part-time/adjunct (198 women). *Students:* 79 full-time, 123 part-time; includes 20 minority (5 African Americans, 1 American Indian/Alaska Native, 11 Asian Americans or Pacific Islanders, 3 Hispanic Americans). Average age 29. 132 applicants, 92% accepted, 86 enrolled. *Degree requirements:* For master's, thesis or alternative, practicum. *Entrance requirements:* Additional exam requirements/recommendations for international students: Required—TOEFL. *Application deadline:* For fall admission, 7/19 priority date for domestic students; for winter admission, 11/8 priority date for domestic students; for spring admission, 3/14 priority date for domestic students. Applications are processed on a rolling basis. Application fee: $50. *Expenses:* Tuition: Full-time $3280; part-time $410 per credit hour. *Financial support:* Fellowships, career-related internships or fieldwork available. Financial award applicants required to submit FAFSA. *Unit head:* Dr. Gerry Breshears, Director, 503-517-1870, E-mail: gbreshears@westernseminary.edu. *Application contact:* Dr. Robert W. Wiggins, Registrar/Dean of Student Development, 503-517-1820, Fax: 503-517-1820, E-mail: rwiggins@westernseminary.edu.

Westminster Seminary California, Programs in Theology, Escondido, CA 92027-4128. Offers Biblical studies (MA); historical theology (MA); theological studies (M Div, MA). *Accreditation:* ATS. Part-time and evening/weekend programs available. *Degree requirements:* For master's, 2 foreign languages, thesis (for some programs); for M Div, 2 foreign languages, internship. *Entrance requirements:* For M Div and master's, 2 letters of reference. Additional exam requirements/recommendations for international students: Required—TOEFL (minimum score 570 paper-based; 230 computer-based; 89 iBT), TWE (minimum score 4.5). *Faculty research:* Neo-paganism, New Testament background, eschatology, Protestant scholasticism, Ezekiel.

Westminster Theological Seminary, Graduate and Professional Programs, Philadelphia, PA 19118. Offers apologetics (Th M); Biblical and urban studies (Certificate); Biblical counseling (MA); biblical studies (MAR); Christian studies (Certificate); church history (Th M); counseling (M Div); general studies (M Div, MAR); hermeneutics and Bible interpretations (PhD); historical and theological studies (PhD); historical theology (Th M); New Testament (Th M); Old Testament

(Th M); pastoral counseling (D Min); pastoral ministry (M Div, D Min); systematic theology (Th M); theological studies (MAR); urban missions (M Div, MA, MAR, D Min). *Accreditation:* ATS. Part-time programs available. Terminal master's awarded for partial completion of doctoral program. *Degree requirements:* For master's, thesis (for some programs); for doctorate, 4 foreign languages, comprehensive exam (for some programs), thesis/dissertation; for M Div, 2 foreign languages. *Entrance requirements:* For doctorate, GRE General Test. Additional exam requirements/recommendations for international students: Required—TOEFL, TWE.

Wheaton College, Graduate School, Department of Biblical and Theological Studies, Program in Religion in American Life, Wheaton, IL 60187-5593. Offers MA. Part-time programs available. *Degree requirements:* For master's, thesis optional. *Entrance requirements:* For master's, GRE General Test, MAT. Electronic applications accepted.

Wilfrid Laurier University, Faculty of Graduate Studies, Faculty of Arts, Department of Religion and Culture, Waterloo, ON N2L 3C5, Canada. Offers MA, PhD. *Degree requirements:* For master's, thesis optional; for doctorate, thesis/dissertation. *Entrance requirements:* For master's, honors BA or the equivalent in religious studies or other interdisciplinary social science or humanities program, minimum B average in overall undergraduate course work, B+ average in the undergraduate major; for doctorate, MA in religious studies, minimum A- average. Additional exam requirements/recommendations for international students: Required—TOEFL (minimum score 230 computer-based; 89 iBT). Electronic applications accepted. *Faculty research:* Religious diversity in North America.

Wycliffe College, Division of Advanced Degree Studies, Toronto, ON M5S 1H7, Canada. Offers MA, Th M, D Min, PhD, Th D. *Accreditation:* ATS (one or more programs are accredited). Part-time programs available. Terminal master's awarded for partial completion of doctoral program. *Degree requirements:* For master's, 2 foreign languages, thesis (for some programs); for doctorate, 3 foreign languages, thesis/dissertation. *Entrance requirements:* Additional exam requirements/recommendations for international students: Required—TOEFL (minimum score 600 paper-based; 250 computer-based). *Expenses:* Contact institution. *Faculty research:* Old and New Testament, doctrine, ethics, philosophy, history.

Wycliffe College, Division of Basic Degree Studies, Toronto, ON M5S 1H7, Canada. Offers Christian Studies (Diploma); theology (M Div, M Rel, MTS). *Accreditation:* ATS. Part-time programs available. *Degree requirements:* For master's, one foreign language, thesis; for M Div, thesis/dissertation optional. *Entrance requirements:* Additional exam requirements/recommendations for international students: Required—TOEFL (minimum score 580 paper-based).

Yale University, Graduate School of Arts and Sciences, Department of Religious Studies, New Haven, CT 06520. Offers PhD. *Degree requirements:* For doctorate, 2 foreign languages, thesis/dissertation. *Entrance requirements:* For doctorate, GRE General Test.

Yeshiva Derech Chaim, Graduate Program, Brooklyn, NY 11218. Offers PhD. *Accreditation:* AARTS.

Theology

Abilene Christian University, Graduate School, College of Biblical Studies, Graduate School of Theology, Program in Divinity, Abilene, TX 79699-9100. Offers M Div. *Accreditation:* ATS. *Students:* 36 full-time (7 women), 26 part-time (2 women); includes 6 minority (3 African Americans, 3 Hispanic Americans). 29 applicants, 90% accepted, 26 enrolled. *Degree requirements:* For M Div, one foreign language, comprehensive exam. *Entrance requirements:* GMAT, GRE, or MAT. *Application deadline:* For fall admission, 4/1 priority date for domestic students; for spring admission, 11/1 for domestic students. Applications are processed on a rolling basis. Application fee: $40. Electronic applications accepted. *Expenses:* Tuition: Full-time $11,520; part-time $640 per hour. Required fees: $1090; $53.50 per hour. $10 per term. Tuition and fees vary according to program. *Financial support:* In 2009–10, 29 students received support. Applicants required to submit FAFSA. *Unit head:* Dr. Tim Sensing, Graduate Advisor, 325-674-3792, Fax: 325-674-6716, E-mail: sensingt@acu.edu. *Application contact:* William Horn, Graduate Admissions Counselor, 325-674-2656, Fax: 325-674-6717, E-mail: gradinfo@acu.edu.

Abilene Christian University, Graduate School, College of Biblical Studies, Graduate School of Theology, Program in History and Theology, Abilene, TX 79699-9100. Offers MA. *Students:* 4 full-time (0 women), 13 part-time (2 women); includes 1 minority (Hispanic American), 1 international. 4 applicants, 75% accepted, 3 enrolled. *Degree requirements:* For master's, comprehensive exam, thesis. *Application deadline:* For fall admission, 4/1 priority date for domestic students; for spring admission, 11/1 for domestic students. Applications are processed on a rolling basis. Application fee: $40. Electronic applications accepted. *Expenses:* Tuition: Full-time $11,520; part-time $640 per hour. Required fees: $1090; $53.50 per hour. $10 per term. Tuition and fees vary according to program. *Financial support:* In 2009–10, 9 students received support. Application deadline: 4/1. *Unit head:* Dr. Douglas Foster, Graduate Advisor, 325-674-3730, Fax: 325-674-6180, E-mail: foster@bible.acu.edu. *Application contact:* William Horn, Graduate Admissions Counselor, 325-674-2656, Fax: 325-674-6717, E-mail: gradinfo@acu.edu.

Abilene Christian University, Graduate School, College of Biblical Studies, Graduate School of Theology, Program in New Testament, Abilene, TX 79699-9100. Offers MA. *Accreditation:* ATS. *Students:* 1 full-time (0 women). 1 applicant. In 2009, 3 master's awarded. *Degree requirements:* For master's, comprehensive exam, thesis. *Entrance requirements:* For master's, GRE General Test or MAT. *Application deadline:* For fall admission, 4/1 priority date for domestic students; for spring admission, 11/1 for domestic students. Applications are processed on a rolling basis. Application fee: $40. Electronic applications accepted. *Expenses:* Tuition: Full-time $11,520; part-time $640 per hour. Required fees: $1090; $53.50 per hour. $10 per term. Tuition and fees vary according to program. *Financial support:* In 2009–10, 1 student received support. Application deadline: 4/1. *Unit head:* Dr. James Thompson, Graduate Advisor, 325-674-3781, Fax: 325-674-6180, E-mail: thompsonja@acu.edu. *Application contact:* William Horn, Graduate Admissions Counselor, 325-674-2656, Fax: 325-674-6717, E-mail: gradinfo@acu.edu.

Abilene Christian University, Graduate School, College of Biblical Studies, Graduate School of Theology, Program in Old Testament, Abilene, TX 79699-9100. Offers MA. *Students:* 1 full-time (0 women), 2 part-time (0 women). 1 applicant, 100% accepted, 1 enrolled. *Degree requirements:* For master's, comprehensive exam, thesis. *Application deadline:* For fall admission, 4/1 priority date for domestic students; for spring admission, 11/1 for domestic students. Applications are processed on a rolling basis. Application fee: $40. Electronic applications accepted. *Expenses:* Tuition: Full-time $11,520; part-time $640 per hour. Required fees: $1090; $53.50 per hour. $10 per term. Tuition and fees vary according to program. *Financial support:* In 2009–10, 2 students received support. Application deadline: 4/1. *Unit head:* Dr. Mark Hamilton, Graduate Advisor, 325-674-3765, Fax: 325-674-6180, E-mail: wmh00c@acu.edu. *Application contact:* William Horn, Graduate Admissions Counselor, 325-674-2656, Fax: 325-674-6717, E-mail: gradinfo@acu.edu.

Acadia University, Divinity College, Wolfville, NS B4P 2R6, Canada. Offers divinity (M Div); theology (MA, D Min), including biblical studies (MA), church history (MA), theology (MA). *Accreditation:* ATS. Part-time programs available. *Faculty:* 12 full-time (2 women), 12 part-time/adjunct (1 woman). *Students:* 59 full-time (25 women), 40 part-time (8 women). Average age 43. In 2009, 34 master's, 4 doctorates awarded. *Degree requirements:* For master's, one foreign language, thesis (for some programs); for doctorate, one foreign language, comprehensive exam, thesis/dissertation. *Entrance requirements:* For M Div, minimum GPA of 2.0; for master's, minimum GPA of 3.0; for doctorate, minimum GPA of 3.0, 3 years ministry experience. Additional exam requirements/recommendations for international students: Required—TOEFL. *Application deadline:* For fall admission, 6/30 priority date for domestic students, 4/1 priority date for international students; for spring admission, 4/30 priority date for domestic students. Applications are processed on a rolling basis. Application fee: $50. *Expenses:* Contact institution. *Financial support:* In 2009–10, 8 teaching assistantships (averaging $1,000 per year) were awarded; career-related internships or fieldwork, institutionally sponsored loans, and scholarships/grants also available. Support available to part-time students. Financial award application deadline: 8/12. *Faculty research:* Biblical canon, Jesus, Dead Sea Scrolls, Baptist studies, Old Testament–Septuagint. *Unit head:* Dr. Harry M. Gardner, President, 902-585-2212, Fax: 902-585-2233, E-mail: harry.gardner@acadiau.ca. *Application contact:* Shawna Peverill, Registrar, 902-585-2215, Fax: 902-585-2233, E-mail: shawna.peverill@acadiau.ca.

Alliance Theological Seminary, Graduate and Professional Programs, Nyack, NY 10960. Offers Christian ministry (MPS); counseling (MA); intercultural studies (MA); missions (MPS); New Testament (MA); Old Testament (MA); theology (M Div); urban ministry (MPS). *Accreditation:* ATS. Part-time programs available. *Degree requirements:* For master's, comprehensive exam (for some programs), thesis optional, internships; for M Div, 2 foreign languages, internship. *Entrance requirements:* Proficiency in New Testament Greek, minimum GPA of 2.5 (undergraduate). Additional exam requirements/recommendations for international students: Required—TOEFL (minimum score 550 paper-based; 213 computer-based).

Ambrose University College, Ambrose Seminary, Calgary, AB T2P 3T5, Canada. Offers biblical/theological studies (MA); Chinese ministries (Certificate); Christian studies (M Div, MA, Diploma); foundations for ministry (Certificate); intercultural ministries (M Div, MA, Certificate, Diploma); leadership and ministry (MA, Certificate, Diploma). *Accreditation:* ATS (one or more programs are accredited). Part-time programs available. *Faculty:* 7 full-time (0 women), 24 part-time/adjunct (2 women). *Students:* 44 full-time (15 women), 107 part-time (49 women). Average age 41. *Degree requirements:* For master's, 2 foreign languages, internship; for M Div, one foreign language, internship. *Entrance requirements:* For master's, bachelor's degree. Additional exam requirements/recommendations for international students: Required—TOEFL or IELTS. *Application deadline:* For fall admission, 7/31 priority date for domestic students, 3/1 priority date for international students; for winter admission, 11/30 priority date for domestic students, 6/1 priority date for international students. Applications are processed on a rolling basis. Application fee: $50. Electronic applications accepted. *Expenses:* Tuition: Full-time $6000; part-time $299 per credit hour. Required fees: $306; $17 per credit hour. *Financial support:* Career-related internships or fieldwork and scholarships/grants available. Support available to part-time students. Financial award application deadline: 3/30. *Faculty research:* Evangelicalism and sociology, missiological trends, chaplaincy, intertestamental studies, postmodernism. *Unit head:* Dr. Paul Spilsbury, Vice-President of Academic Affairs, 403-410-2000 Ext. 6905, Fax: 403-571-2556, E-mail: pspilsbury@ambrose.edu. *Application contact:* Dr. Paul Spilsbury, Vice-President of Academic Affairs, 403-410-2000 Ext. 6905, Fax: 403-571-2556, E-mail: pspilsbury@ambrose.edu.

American Baptist Seminary of the West, Graduate and Professional Programs, Berkeley, CA 94704-3029. Offers community leadership (MA); theology (M Div, MA). *Accreditation:* ACIPE; ATS (one or more programs are accredited). Part-time and evening/weekend programs available. *Faculty:* 6 full-time (4 women), 7 part-time/adjunct (2 women). *Students:* 25 full-time (9 women), 38 part-time (23 women); includes 50 minority (44 African Americans, 6 Asian Americans or Pacific Islanders), 13 international. *Entrance requirements:* For M Div, minimum GPA of 2.5; for master's, minimum GPA of 3.0. Additional exam requirements/recommendations for international students: Required—TOEFL (minimum score 550 paper-based; 250 computer-based). *Application deadline:* For fall admission, 4/15 priority date for domestic students, 4/15 for international students. Applications are processed on a rolling basis. Application fee: $25. Electronic applications accepted. *Expenses:* Tuition: Full-time $13,390; part-time $515 per credit. Required fees: $480; $515 per credit. $240 per semester. One-time fee: $250. *Financial support:* Career-related internships or fieldwork, institutionally sponsored loans, scholarships/grants, tuition waivers (partial), and tuition discount available. Support available to part-time students. Financial award application deadline: 4/15; financial award applicants required to submit FAFSA. *Unit head:* Dr. Paul M. Martin, President, 510-841-1905 Ext. 224, Fax: 510-841-2446, E-mail: pmartin@absw.edu. *Application contact:* Rev. Michelle M. Holmes, Vice President, 510-841-1905 Ext. 225, Fax: 510-841-2446, E-mail: mmholmes@absw.edu.

American Jewish University, Graduate School, Ziegler School of Rabbinic Studies, Bel Air, CA 90077-1599. Offers MARS. *Degree requirements:* For master's, one foreign language. *Entrance requirements:* For master's, GRE General Test, interview. Additional exam requirements/recommendations for international students: Required—TOEFL.

Amridge University, Graduate and Professional Programs, Montgomery, AL 36117. Offers behavioral leadership and management (MA); biblical studies (MA, PhD); family therapy (D Min); leadership and management (MS); marriage and family therapy (M Div, MA, PhD); ministerial leadership (M Div, MS); pastoral counseling (M Div, MS); practical theology (MA); professional counseling (M Div, MA); theology (M Div, D Min). *Accreditation:* ATS. Part-time and evening/weekend programs available. Postbaccalaureate distance learning degree programs offered (no on-campus study). *Faculty:* 44 full-time (9 women), 18 part-time/adjunct (7 women). *Students:* 175 full-time (95 women), 192 part-time (93 women); includes 182 minority (172 African Americans, 1 American Indian/Alaska Native, 1 Asian American or Pacific Islander, 8 Hispanic Americans). Average age 35. *Degree requirements:* For master's, one foreign language, comprehensive exam (for some programs), thesis (for some programs); for doctorate, comprehensive exam (for some programs), thesis/dissertation; for M Div, comprehensive exam (for some programs). *Entrance requirements:* For M Div, master's, and doctorate, GRE General Test or MAT. Additional exam requirements/recommendations for international students: Required—TOEFL. *Application deadline:* For fall admission, 9/1 priority date for domestic students; for spring admission, 1/1 priority date for domestic students. Applications are processed on a rolling basis. Application fee: $75. Electronic applications accepted. *Expenses:* Tuition: Full-time $10,080; part-time $560 per semester hour. Required fees: $600 per term. *Financial support:* Federal Work-Study and scholarships/grants available. Support available to part-time students. Financial award applicants required to submit FAFSA. *Faculty research:* Homiletics, hermeneutics, ancient Near Eastern history. *Unit head:* Director of Enrollment Management, 800-351-4040 Ext. 7513, Fax: 334-387-3878. *Application contact:* Ora Davis, Admissions Officer, 334-387-3877 Ext. 7524, Fax: 334-387-3878, E-mail: admissions@amridgeuniversity.edu.

Anderson University, School of Theology, Anderson, IN 46012-3495. Offers missions (MA); theology (M Div, MTS, D Min). *Accreditation:* ACIPE; ATS. Part-time programs available. *Degree requirements:* For master's, one foreign language, thesis, integrative senior seminar; for doctorate, thesis/dissertation; for M Div, thesis/dissertation (for some programs). *Faculty research:* Small-church/bivocational ministry, women in ministry.

Theology

Andover Newton Theological School, Graduate and Professional Programs, Newton Centre, MA 02459-2243. Offers divinity (M Div); general (MA); psychology and religion (MA); religious education (MA); research (MA); sacred theology (STM); theology (D Min); theology and the arts (MA). *Accreditation:* ACIPE; ATS. Part-time programs available. *Degree requirements:* For master's, comprehensive exam (for some programs), thesis (for some programs); for doctorate, comprehensive exam, thesis/dissertation. *Entrance requirements:* For doctorate, M Div or equivalent. Additional exam requirements/recommendations for international students: Required—TOEFL (minimum score 550 paper-based; 213 computer-based). Electronic applications accepted.

Andrews University, School of Graduate Studies, Seventh-day Adventist Theological Seminary, Berrien Springs, MI 49104. Offers ministry (M Div, D Min); pastoral ministry (MA); religious education (MA, Ed D, PhD, Ed S); theology (M Th, Th D); youth ministry (MA). *Accreditation:* ATS. *Faculty:* 35 full-time (3 women), 1 (woman) part-time/adjunct. *Students:* 390 full-time (63 women), 581 part-time (69 women); includes 381 minority (196 African Americans, 2 American Indian/Alaska Native, 50 Asian Americans or Pacific Islanders, 133 Hispanic Americans), 279 international. Average age 47. 468 applicants, 59% accepted, 77 enrolled. In 2009, 96 first professional degrees, 27 master's, 28 doctorates awarded. *Degree requirements:* For master's, thesis optional; for doctorate, variable foreign language requirement, thesis/dissertation; for M Div, one foreign language, thesis/dissertation optional. *Entrance requirements:* For master's, GRE Subject Test, minimum GPA of 2.0. Additional exam requirements/recommendations for international students: Required—TOEFL (minimum score 550 paper-based). *Application deadline:* Applications are processed on a rolling basis. Application fee: $40. *Financial support:* Fellowships, research assistantships, teaching assistantships, career-related internships or fieldwork, Federal Work-Study, and institutionally sponsored loans available. *Unit head:* Dr. Denis Fortin, Dean, 269-471-3537. *Application contact:* Carolyn Hurst, Director, 800-253-2874, Fax: 269-471-6321.

Apex School of Theology, Graduate Programs, Durham, NC 27703. Offers M Div, MACC, MCE, D Min. *Faculty:* 4 full-time (1 woman), 4 part-time/adjunct (1 woman). *Students:* 91 full-time (61 women), 16 part-time (11 women). Average age 45.Application fee: $50. *Expenses:* Tuition: Full-time $5600; part-time $300 per credit hour. Required fees: $800. One-time fee: $35 full-time. Tuition and fees vary according to class time, course level, course load, degree level, campus/location, program and student level. *Faculty research:* Sociology, educational sciences, economics. *Unit head:* Dr. LaFayette Maxwell, Academic Dean, 919-572-1625, Fax: 919-572-1762, E-mail: lmaxwell@apexsot.edu. *Application contact:* Dr. Henry O. Wells, Registrar, 919-572-1625, Fax: 919-572-1762, E-mail: registrar@apexsot.edu.

Aquinas Institute of Theology, Graduate and Professional Programs, St. Louis, MO 63108. Offers biblical studies (Certificate); health care mission (MAHCM); ministry (M Div); pastoral care (Certificate); pastoral ministry (MAPM); pastoral studies (MAPS); preaching (D Min); spiritual direction (Certificate); theology (M Div, MA); Thomistic studies (Certificate); M Div/MA; MAPS/MSW. *Accreditation:* ATS (one or more programs are accredited). Part-time and evening/weekend programs available. Postbaccalaureate distance learning degree programs offered (minimal on-campus study). *Faculty:* 17 full-time (10 women), 4 part-time/adjunct (2 women). *Students:* 65 full-time (21 women), 179 part-time (108 women); includes 37 minority (16 African Americans, 1 American Indian/Alaska Native, 8 Asian Americans or Pacific Islanders, 12 Hispanic Americans), 7 international. Average age 41. 39 applicants, 87% accepted, 27 enrolled. In 2009, 31 master's, 11 doctorates awarded. *Degree requirements:* For master's, one foreign language, comprehensive exam, thesis or major paper; for doctorate, thesis/dissertation. *Entrance requirements:* For M Div, master's, and Certificate, MAT; for doctorate, 3 years of ministerial experience, 6 hours of graduate course work in homiletics, M Div or the equivalent, minimum GPA of 3.0. Additional exam requirements/recommendations for international students: Required—TOEFL. *Application deadline:* For fall admission, 3/15 priority date for domestic and international students; for spring admission, 11/15 priority date for domestic and international students. Applications are processed on a rolling basis. Application fee: $50. *Expenses:* Tuition: Full-time $14,784; part-time $616 per credit hour. Required fees: $195 per semester. *Financial support:* Career-related internships or fieldwork, scholarships/grants, health care benefits, and tuition waivers (partial) available. Support available to part-time students. Financial award application deadline: 3/15; financial award applicants required to submit CSS PROFILE or FAFSA. *Faculty research:* Theology of preaching, hermeneutics, lay ecclesial ministry, pastoral and practical theology. *Unit head:* Fr. Gregory Heille, Academic Dean, 314-256-8800, Fax: 314-256-8888, E-mail: heille@ai.edu. *Application contact:* David Werthmann, Director of Admissions, 314-256-8806, Fax: 314-256-8888, E-mail: admissions@ai.edu.

Asbury Theological Seminary, Graduate and Professional Programs, Wilmore, KY 40390-1199. Offers MA, MAC, MACE, MACL, MAPC, MAYM, Th M, D Miss, PhD, Certificate. *Accreditation:* ATS. Part-time programs available. Postbaccalaureate distance learning degree programs offered (minimal on-campus study). *Faculty:* 64 full-time (11 women), 74 part-time/adjunct (14 women). *Students:* 760 full-time (226 women), 768 part-time (279 women); includes 155 minority (85 African Americans, 13 American Indian/Alaska Native, 25 Asian Americans or Pacific Islanders, 32 Hispanic Americans), 141 international. Average age 25. 765 applicants, 75% accepted, 364 enrolled. In 2009, 95 master's, 15 doctorates, 38 other advanced degrees awarded. Terminal master's awarded for partial completion of doctoral program. *Degree requirements:* For master's, thesis (for some programs); for doctorate, thesis/dissertation, qualifying exam. *Entrance requirements:* For master's, minimum GPA of 2.75; for doctorate, minimum GPA of 3.0. Additional exam requirements/recommendations for international students: Required—TOEFL, IELTS. *Application deadline:* Applications are processed on a rolling basis. Application fee: $50. Electronic applications accepted. *Financial support:* In 2009–10, 1,317 students received support. Career-related internships or fieldwork, Federal Work-Study, institutionally sponsored loans, and scholarships/grants available. Support available to part-time students. Financial award applicants required to submit FAFSA. *Unit head:* Dr. Leslie A. Andrews, Provost, 859-858-2206, Fax: 859-858-2025, E-mail: leslie.andrews@asburyseminary.edu. *Application contact:* Kevin Bush, Vice President of Enrollment Management, 859-858-2211, Fax: 859-858-2287, E-mail: admissions.office@asburyseminary.edu.

Ashland Theological Seminary, Graduate Programs, Ashland, OH 44805. Offers biblical and theological studies (MA, MAR), including New Testament (MA), Old Testament (MA); Christian ministry (MAPT); Christian studies (Diploma); clinical counseling (michigan) (MAC); clinical counseling (Ohio) (MACC), including anabaptism, pietism; historical studies (MA), including church history; ministry (D Min); pastoral ministry (M Div); theological studies (MA). *Accreditation:* ATS. Part-time programs available. *Faculty:* 23 full-time (7 women), 74 part-time/adjunct (28 women). *Students:* 663 full-time (343 women), 124 part-time (65 women); includes 312 minority (289 African Americans, 3 American Indian/Alaska Native, 8 Asian Americans or Pacific Islanders, 12 Hispanic Americans), 25 international. Average age 43. 173 applicants, 87% accepted, 142 enrolled. In 2009, 34 first professional degrees, 102 master's, 17 doctorates, 2 other advanced degrees awarded. *Degree requirements:* For master's, 2 foreign languages, comprehensive exam (for some programs), thesis (for some programs); for doctorate, thesis/dissertation; for M Div, 2 foreign languages, comprehensive exam (for some programs). *Entrance requirements:* For M Div, minimum GPA of 2.75; for master's, minimum undergraduate GPA of 2.75; for doctorate, M Div, minimum undergraduate GPA of 3.0. Additional exam requirements/recommendations for international students: Required—TOEFL (minimum score 500 paper-based; 65 computer-based; 173 iBT). *Application deadline:* For fall admission, 8/30 for domestic students. Applications are processed on a rolling basis. Application fee: $30. Electronic applications accepted. *Expenses:* Tuition: Full-time $10,476; part-time $345 per credit hour. Required fees: $180; $15 per course. Part-time tuition and fees vary according to course load. *Financial support:* In 2009–10, 311 students received support, including 17 teaching assistantships; research assistantships, career-related internships or fieldwork, institutionally sponsored loans, scholarships/grants, and unspecified assistantships also available. Support available to part-time students. Financial award application deadline: 5/15; financial award applicants required to submit FAFSA. *Faculty research:* Semitic languages and linguistics, rhetorical and social-scientific criticism, Anabaptist studies, inner spiritual healing, African-American clergy in film and literature. *Unit head:* Dr. John C. Shultz, President, 419-289-5160, Fax: 419-289-5969, E-mail: jshultz@ashland.edu. *Application contact:* Glenn Black, Director of Enrollment Management, 419-289-5151, Fax: 419-289-5969, E-mail: gblack@ashland.edu.

Assemblies of God Theological Seminary, Graduate and Professional Programs, Springfield, MO 65802. Offers Christian ministries (MA); counseling (MA); divinity (M Div); intercultural ministry (MA); intercultural studies (D Miss, PhD); relief and development (D Miss); theological studies (MA); women in leadership (D Min). *Accreditation:* ATS. Part-time and evening/weekend programs available. Postbaccalaureate distance learning degree programs offered (minimal on-campus study). *Faculty:* 12 full-time (3 women), 23 part-time/adjunct (5 women). *Students:* 195 full-time (70 women), 221 part-time (53 women); includes 48 minority (10 African Americans, 6 American Indian/Alaska Native, 16 Asian Americans or Pacific Islanders, 16 Hispanic Americans), 9 international. Average age 36. 109 applicants, 76% accepted, 62 enrolled. In 2009, 46 first professional degrees, 65 master's, 14 doctorates awarded. *Degree requirements:* For master's, analytical reflection paper, comprehensive exam or field education research project; for doctorate, thesis/dissertation; for M Div, one foreign language, analytical reflection paper or field education research project. *Entrance requirements:* For M Div, minimum GPA of 2.5; for master's, minimum GPA of 2.5; for doctorate, minimum GPA of 3.0. Additional exam requirements/recommendations for international students: Required—TOEFL (minimum score 550 paper-based; 213 computer-based; 80 iBT). *Application deadline:* For fall admission, 7/1 priority date for domestic students, 6/1 priority date for international students; for spring admission, 12/1 priority date for domestic students, 11/1 priority date for international students. Applications are processed on a rolling basis. Application fee: $75. Electronic applications accepted. *Financial support:* Career-related internships or fieldwork, Federal Work-Study, and scholarships/grants available. Support available to part-time students. Financial award application deadline: 7/15; financial award applicants required to submit FAFSA. *Unit head:* Stephen Lim, Academic Dean, 417-268-1000, Fax: 417-268-1001, E-mail: slim@agts.edu. *Application contact:* Stephen Lim, Academic Dean, 417-268-1000, Fax: 417-268-1001, E-mail: slim@agts.edu.

Associated Mennonite Biblical Seminary, Graduate and Professional Programs, Elkhart, IN 46517-1999. Offers Christian formation (MA); divinity (M Div); mission and evangelism (MA); peace studies (MA); theological studies (MA, Certificate). *Accreditation:* ACIPE; ATS. Part-time programs available. *Degree requirements:* For master's, comprehensive exam, thesis optional; for M Div, integration paper. *Entrance requirements:* For M Div, master's, and Certificate, 3 letters of reference. Additional exam requirements/recommendations for international students: Required—TOEFL (minimum score 550 paper-based; 213 computer-based). Electronic applications accepted. *Faculty research:* Biblical studies, theology, church history, church leadership.

The Athenaeum of Ohio, Graduate Programs, Cincinnati, OH 45230-5900. Offers biblical studies (MABS); divinity (M Div); lay ministry (Certificate); pastoral counseling (MAPC); pastoral ministry (MA); theology (MA Th); M Div/MA Th; M Div/MABS; M Div/MAPC. *Accreditation:* ATS (one or more programs are accredited). Part-time and evening/weekend programs available. *Degree requirements:* For master's, one foreign language, comprehensive exam (for some programs), thesis optional; for M Div, comprehensive exam.

Atlantic School of Theology, Graduate and Professional Programs, Halifax, NS B3H 3B5, Canada. Offers ministry (M Div); theological studies (Graduate Certificate). *Accreditation:* ATS. Part-time programs available. Postbaccalaureate distance learning degree programs offered (minimal on-campus study). *Faculty:* 6 full-time, 7 part-time/adjunct. *Students:* 50 full-time (31 women), 75 part-time (38 women). In 2009, 14 first professional degrees, 4 master's awarded. *Degree requirements:* For master's, thesis. *Entrance requirements:* For M Div, master's, and Graduate Certificate, minimum B average in undergraduate course work. *Application deadline:* For fall admission, 2/28 priority date for domestic students. Applications are processed on a rolling basis. Application fee: $40. Tuition charges are reported in Canadian dollars. *Expenses:* Tuition: Full-time $5210 Canadian dollars; part-time $521 Canadian dollars per credit. *Financial support:* Career-related internships or fieldwork available. Support available to part-time students. Financial award application deadline: 9/30. *Faculty research:* Ethics and biology; death, dying and pastoral care; theology and the economy; adult education; John and anti-Judaism. *Unit head:* Rev. Dr. David MacLachlan, Academic Dean, 902-496-7941, Fax: 902-492-4048. *Application contact:* Cynthia Thomson, Registrar, 902-425-3691, Fax: 902-492-4048, E-mail: registrar@astheology.ns.ca.

Austin Graduate School of Theology, Program in Theological Studies, Austin, TX 78752. Offers MATS. Part-time programs available. *Faculty:* 4 full-time (0 women), 4 part-time/adjunct (0 women). *Students:* 8 full-time (3 women), 24 part-time (6 women). Average age 42. *Degree requirements:* For master's, 2 foreign languages, comprehensive exam, faculty forums. *Entrance requirements:* For master's, 3 letters of reference. Additional exam requirements/recommendations for international students: Required—TOEFL (minimum score 530 paper-based). *Application deadline:* For fall admission, 7/1 priority date for domestic and international students; for spring admission, 10/1 priority date for domestic and international students. Applications are processed on a rolling basis. Application fee: $25. *Expenses:* Tuition: Part-time $275 per credit hour. Required fees: $50 per semester. One-time fee: $25 part-time. *Financial support:* Federal Work-Study and scholarships/grants available. Support available to part-time students. Financial award application deadline: 7/1. *Faculty research:* Revelation, synoptic problem, Acadian, Biblical archaeology, worship. *Unit head:* Dr. Jeffery Peterson, Graduate Student Advisor, 512-476-2772, Fax: 512-476-3919, E-mail: peterson@austingrad.edu. *Application contact:* Dr. Jeffery Peterson, Graduate Student Advisor, 512-476-2772, Fax: 512-476-3919, E-mail: peterson@austingrad.edu.

Austin Presbyterian Theological Seminary, Graduate and Professional Programs, Austin, TX 78705-5797. Offers divinity (M Div); ministry (D Min); theological studies (MA); M Div/MATS; M Div/MSSW. *Accreditation:* ACIPE; ATS. Part-time programs available. *Degree requirements:* For doctorate, thesis/dissertation; for M Div, Greek, Hebrew. *Entrance requirements:* References. Additional exam requirements/recommendations for international students: Required—TOEFL (minimum score 550 paper-based; 213 computer-based; 79 iBT). *Faculty research:* Mystical theology, religious pluralism, narrative preaching, social ethics, pastoral care and healing.

Ave Maria University, Graduate Programs, Ave Maria, FL 34142. Offers pastoral theology (MTS); theology (MA, PhD). Terminal master's awarded for partial completion of doctoral program. *Degree requirements:* For master's, one foreign language, thesis; for doctorate, 3 foreign languages, comprehensive exam, thesis/dissertation. *Entrance requirements:* For master's, GRE; for doctorate, GRE, M Div or equivalent; MA or MTS in religion, theology, or philosophy; bachelor's degree with strong background in religion, theology, and/or philosophy.

Ave Maria University, Institute for Pastoral Theology, Ave Maria, FL 34142. Offers MTS. Part-time and evening/weekend programs available.

Azusa Pacific University, Haggard School of Theology, Program in Ministry, Azusa, CA 91702-7000. Offers D Min.

Azusa Pacific University, Haggard School of Theology, Program in Non-Profit Leadership and Theology, Azusa, CA 91702-7000. Offers Christian non-profit leadership (MA).

Azusa Pacific University, Haggard School of Theology, Program in Religion: Biblical Studies, Azusa, CA 91702-7000. Offers MAR.

Azusa Pacific University, Haggard School of Theology, Program in Religion: Theology and Ethics, Azusa, CA 91702-7000. Offers MAR.

Bangor Theological Seminary, Professional Program, Bangor, ME 04401-4699. Offers M Div, MA, MTS, D Min. M Div not offered at Portland, ME campus. *Accreditation:* ACIPE; ATS. Part-time programs available. *Degree requirements:* For master's, thesis optional; for doctorate, project, report; for M Div, thesis/dissertation optional. *Entrance requirements:* For M Div and master's, Bachelor degree; for doctorate, M Div, 3 years in ministry. Additional exam requirements/recommendations for international students: Required—TOEFL (minimum score 550 paper-based; 213 computer-based; 80 iBT). *Faculty research:* Formation of the New Testament canon, critical pedagogy, history of theological education, human sexuality, the Isaiah Scroll.

Baptist Bible College, Graduate School of Theology, Springfield, MO 65803-3498. Offers biblical counseling (MA); biblical studies (MA); church ministry (MA); intercultural studies (MA); theology (M Div). Part-time programs available. *Degree requirements:* For master's, 2 foreign languages, thesis (for some programs); for M Div, 2 foreign languages, thesis/dissertation (for some programs). *Entrance requirements:* For master's, outcomes test. Electronic applications accepted.

Baptist Bible College of Pennsylvania, Baptist Bible Seminary, Clarks Summit, PA 18411-1297. Offers biblical studies (PhD); church planting (M Div); global missions (M Div); military chaplaincy (M Div); ministry (M Min, D Min); pastor of church education (M Div); pastor of outreach (M Div); pastoral counseling (M Div); pastoral leadership (M Div); theology (M Div, Th M); youth pastor (M Div). Part-time and evening/weekend programs available. Postbaccalaureate distance learning degree programs offered (minimal on-campus study). Terminal master's awarded for partial completion of doctoral program. *Degree requirements:* For master's, 2 foreign languages, thesis; for doctorate, 2 foreign languages, comprehensive exam (for some programs), thesis/dissertation, oral exam; for M Div, 2 foreign languages, thesis/dissertation, oral exam. *Entrance requirements:* For doctorate, Greek and Hebrew entrance exams (PhD). Electronic applications accepted.

Baptist Bible College of Pennsylvania, Graduate School, Clarks Summit, PA 18411-1297. Offers Bible (MA); biblical ministries (MS); Christian school education (MS); counseling (MS). Part-time and evening/weekend programs available. Postbaccalaureate distance learning degree programs offered (no on-campus study). *Faculty:* 2 full-time (0 women), 1 part-time/adjunct (0 women). *Students:* 12 full-time (7 women), 61 part-time (40 women); includes 3 minority (all African Americans), 1 international. Average age 31. In 2009, 13 master's awarded. *Entrance requirements:* Additional exam requirements/recommendations for international students: Required—TOEFL (minimum score 500 paper-based; 173 computer-based). *Application deadline:* Applications are processed on a rolling basis. Application fee: $30. *Financial support:* In 2009–10, 43 students received support. Institutionally sponsored loans and scholarships/grants available. Financial award application deadline: 8/20; financial award applicants required to submit FAFSA. *Unit head:* Dr. James Lytle, Provost, 570-586-2400 Ext. 9222, Fax: 570-586-1753. *Application contact:* Drew Whipple, Assitant Director of Enrollment, 570-585-9370, Fax: 570-585-9299, E-mail: gradadmissions@bbc.edu.

Baptist Missionary Association Theological Seminary, Graduate and Professional Programs, Jacksonville, TX 75766-5407. Offers M Div, MAR. *Accreditation:* ATS. Part-time programs available. *Degree requirements:* For master's, thesis optional; for M Div, 2 foreign languages, thesis/dissertation optional. *Entrance requirements:* Additional exam requirements/recommendations for international students: Required—TOEFL (minimum score 550 paper-based; 213 computer-based). Electronic applications accepted. *Faculty research:* Education, Biblical studies.

Baptist Theological Seminary at Richmond, Graduate and Professional Programs, Richmond, VA 23227. Offers biblical interpretation (M Div); Christian education (M Div); theology (D Min); youth and student ministries (M Div); M Div/MS; M Div/MSW. *Accreditation:* ATS. Part-time programs available. Postbaccalaureate distance learning degree programs offered (minimal on-campus study). *Faculty:* 8 full-time (2 women), 9 part-time/adjunct (3 women). *Students:* 59 full-time (33 women), 30 part-time (17 women); includes 9 minority (all African Americans), 3 international. Average age 46. In 2009, 29 first professional degrees, 6 doctorates awarded. *Degree requirements:* For doctorate, one foreign language, comprehensive exam, thesis/dissertation, field study, independent study; for M Div, one foreign language, comprehensive exam (for some programs), thesis/dissertation optional, mission immersion experience, internship. *Entrance requirements:* For doctorate, MAT, M Div, 3 years of full-time ministry experience. Additional exam requirements/recommendations for international students: Required—TOEFL (minimum score 550 paper-based; 213 computer-based). *Application deadline:* For fall admission, 8/1 priority date for domestic students, 5/1 priority date for international students; for winter admission, 12/1 priority date for domestic students, 9/1 priority date for international students; for spring admission, 1/1 priority date for domestic students, 10/1 priority date for international students. Applications are processed on a rolling basis. Application fee: $35. *Financial support:* In 2009–10, 16 teaching assistantships (averaging $1,650 per year) were awarded; scholarships/grants and tuition waivers (partial) also available. Financial award application deadline: 2/1. *Faculty research:* New Testament studies, Old Testament studies, pastoral care, church history, theology. *Unit head:* Dr. Ronald W. Crawford, President, 804-204-1201, Fax: 804-355-8182, E-mail: rcrawford@btsr.edu. *Application contact:* Tiffany Kellogg Pittman, Director of Admissions, 804-204-1208, Fax: 804-355-8182, E-mail: admissions@btsr.edu.

Barry University, School of Arts and Sciences, Department of Theology and Philosophy, Miami Shores, FL 33161-6695. Offers ministry (D Min); pastoral ministry for Hispanics (MA); pastoral theology (MA); practical theology (MA). *Accreditation:* ATS. Part-time and evening/weekend programs available. *Degree requirements:* For master's, comprehensive exam, thesis optional; for doctorate, thesis/dissertation. *Entrance requirements:* For master's, GRE General Test or MAT, minimum GPA of 3.0. Electronic applications accepted. *Faculty research:* Fundamental morals, bioethics, social ethics, liturgical and sacramental theology, biblical studies.

Baylor University, George W. Truett Theological Seminary, Waco, TX 76798. Offers M Div, MTS, D Min, M Div/MM, M Div/MSW, MTS/MSW. *Accreditation:* ATS. *Faculty:* 17 full-time (3 women), 7 part-time/adjunct (1 woman). *Students:* 306 full-time (110 women), 93 part-time (30 women); includes 75 minority (44 African Americans, 3 American Indian/Alaska Native, 6 Asian Americans or Pacific Islanders, 22 Hispanic Americans), 22 international. Average age 29. 144 applicants, 94% accepted, 102 enrolled. In 2009, 78 first professional degrees, 14 master's, 7 doctorates awarded. *Entrance requirements:* Additional exam requirements/recommendations for international students: Required—TOEFL (minimum score 82 computer-based). *Application deadline:* For fall admission, 5/1 for domestic and international students; for spring admission, 11/1 for domestic and international students. Applications are processed on a rolling basis. Application fee: $35. Electronic applications accepted. *Financial support:* In 2009–10, 207 students received support, including 1 research assistantship, 12 teaching assistantships; career-related internships or fieldwork, institutionally sponsored loans, scholarships/grants, tuition waivers (partial), and unspecified assistantships also available. Support available to part-time students. Financial award application deadline: 8/1; financial award applicants required to submit FAFSA. *Unit head:* Dr. David E. Garland, Dean, 254-710-3755, Fax: 254-710-3753, E-mail: david_e_garland@baylor.edu. *Application contact:* Dr. Edward Grear Howard, Director of Student Services, 254-710-6087, Fax: 254-710-7233, E-mail: grear_howard@baylor.edu.

Bethany Theological Seminary, Graduate and Professional Programs, Richmond, IN 47374-4019. Offers biblical studies (MA Th); ministry studies (M Div); peace studies (M Div, MA Th); theological studies (MA Th, CATS); youth ministry (M Div). *Accreditation:* ACIPE; ATS. Part-time programs available. Postbaccalaureate distance learning degree programs offered (minimal on-campus study). *Degree requirements:* For master's, thesis. *Entrance requirements:* For M Div, letters of reference, minimum GPA of 2.75; for master's, letters of reference, minimum GPA of 3.0. Additional exam requirements/recommendations for international students: Required—TOEFL (minimum score 550 paper-based; 218 computer-based).

Bethel College, Division of Graduate Studies, Program in Theological Studies, Mishawaka, IN 46545-5591. Offers MATS. Part-time and evening/weekend programs available. *Faculty:* 8 part-time/adjunct (0 women). *Students:* 4 full-time (1 woman), 13 part-time (2 women); includes 3 minority (all African Americans), 1 international. 2 applicants, 50% accepted, 1 enrolled. In 2009, 1 master's awarded. *Entrance requirements:* Additional exam requirements/recommendations for international students: Required—TOEFL (minimum score 540 paper-based; 207 computer-based). *Application deadline:* For fall admission, 5/1 for international students; for spring admission, 10/1 for international students. Applications are processed on a rolling basis. Application fee: $25. Electronic applications accepted. *Financial support:* Career-related internships or fieldwork available. Financial award applicants required to submit FAFSA. *Unit head:* Dr. Eugene Carpenter, Director, 574-257-3332, E-mail: carpeng@bethelcollege.edu. *Application contact:* Dr. John Dendiu, Advisor, 574-257-2675, Fax: 574-257-3385, E-mail: dendiuj@bethelcollege.edu.

Bethel Seminary, Graduate and Professional Programs, St. Paul, MN 55112-6998. Offers applied ministry (MA); biblical studies (MATS, Certificate); children's and family ministry (MACFM); Christian education (MACE); Christian thought (M Div, MACT); church leadership (D Min); community ministry leadership (MA, Certificate); congregation and family care (D Min); global and contextual studies (MA, MATS); historical studies (MATS); lay ministry (Certificate); marriage and family studies (M Div, MATS); marriage and family therapy (MAMFT, Certificate); ministry leadership (Certificate); pastoral care and counseling (MATS); pastoral ministries (M Div); spiritual formation (Certificate); theological studies (MATS, Certificate); transformational leadership (MATL, Certificate); youth ministries (MACE). *Accreditation:* ACIPE; ATS (one or more programs are accredited). Part-time and evening/weekend programs available. Postbaccalaureate distance learning degree programs offered (minimal on-campus study). *Faculty:* 26 full-time (3 women), 76 part-time/adjunct (30 women). *Students:* 725 full-time (269 women), 300 part-time (104 women); includes 204 minority (115 African Americans, 1 American Indian/Alaska Native, 65 Asian Americans or Pacific Islanders, 23 Hispanic Americans), 13 international. Average age 37. 516 applicants, 78% accepted, 261 enrolled. In 2009, 50 first professional degrees, 100 master's, 6 doctorates awarded. *Degree requirements:* For master's, variable foreign language requirement, thesis (for some programs); for doctorate, thesis/dissertation; for M Div, one foreign language. *Entrance requirements:* For M Div and master's, letters of reference, transcripts, personal statement; for doctorate, M Div, letters of reference, organizational support. Additional exam requirements/recommendations for international students: Required—TOEFL (minimum score 550 paper-based; 213 computer-based; 87 iBT). *Application deadline:* For fall admission, 8/1 priority date for domestic students, 3/1 for international students; for winter admission, 12/1 priority date for domestic students; for spring admission, 3/1 priority date for domestic students. Applications are processed on a rolling basis. Application fee: $20. Electronic applications accepted. *Financial support:* In 2009–10, 847 students received support, including 18 teaching assistantships; career-related internships or fieldwork, Federal Work-Study, scholarships/grants, and tuition waivers (full) also available. Financial award application deadline: 7/15; financial award applicants required to submit FAFSA. *Faculty research:* Nature of theology, ethics, Biblical commentaries, nature of God, science and theology. *Unit head:* Dr. David Ridder, Vice President and Dean, 651-638-6553. *Application contact:* Joseph V. Dworak, Director of Admissions, 651-638-6288, Fax: 651-638-6002, E-mail: j-dworak@bethel.edu.

Bethesda Christian University, Graduate and Professional Programs, Anaheim, CA 92801. Offers biblical studies (MA); music (MA); theology (M Div). *Entrance requirements:* For M Div and master's, interview.

Beth HaMedrash Shaarei Yosher Institute, Graduate Programs, Brooklyn, NY 11204. *Accreditation:* AARTS.

Beth Hatalmud Rabbinical College, Graduate Programs, Brooklyn, NY 11214. *Accreditation:* AARTS.

Beth Medrash Govoha, Graduate Programs, Lakewood, NJ 08701-2797. *Accreditation:* AARTS.

Bethune-Cookman University, School of Graduate and Professional Studies, Daytona Beach, FL 32114-3099. Offers transformative leadership (MS). Postbaccalaureate distance learning degree programs offered (minimal on-campus study). *Degree requirements:* For master's, thesis. *Entrance requirements:* For master's, GRE or MAT, minimum GPA of 2.75 in the last 60 semester hours; 3 letters of recommendation. Additional exam requirements/recommendations for international students: Required—TOEFL (minimum score 550 paper-based; 213 computer-based). Electronic applications accepted. *Faculty research:* Civic engagement, communication ethics, service learning in higher education women in leadership.

Bexley Hall Episcopal Seminary, Graduate Programs, Columbus, OH 43209-2325. Offers M Div, MA. *Accreditation:* ATS.

Biblical Theological Seminary, Graduate and Professional Programs, Hatfield, PA 19440-2499. Offers advanced missional leadership (D Min); advanced pastoral studies (Certificate); biblical counseling (Certificate); biblical studies (MA, Certificate); counseling (MA); ministry (MA); missional theology (MA); theology (M Div); youth ministry (Certificate). *Accreditation:* ATS. Part-time programs available. Postbaccalaureate distance learning degree programs offered. *Degree requirements:* For M Div, thesis/dissertation. *Entrance requirements:* Additional exam requirements/recommendations for international students: Required—TOEFL (minimum score 550 paper-based; 213 computer-based). *Application deadline:* Applications are processed on a rolling basis. Application fee: $30. *Expenses:* Tuition: Full-time $14,000; part-time $441 per credit hour. *Financial support:* Career-related internships or fieldwork, institutionally sponsored loans, and scholarships/grants available. Support available to part-time students. Financial award application deadline: 5/15. *Faculty research:* Old Testament narrative, Old Testament historiography, Hebrew syntax, parables, addictions. *Application contact:* Rev. Darryl John Lang, Director of Recruitment and Student Life, 215-368-5000 Ext. 147, Fax: 215-368-7002, E-mail: dlang@biblical.edu.

Biola University, School of Professional Studies, La Mirada, CA 90639-0001. Offers Christian apologetics (MA); organizational leadership (MA). Part-time and evening/weekend programs available. *Entrance requirements:* For master's, minimum undergraduate GPA of 3.0. Additional exam requirements/recommendations for international students: Required—TOEFL (minimum score 550 paper-based; 213 computer-based).

Biola University, Talbot School of Theology, La Mirada, CA 90639-0001. Offers Bible exposition (MA); biblical and theological studies (MA); Christian education (MACE); Christian ministry and leadership (MA); divinity (M Div); education (PhD); ministry (MA Min); New Testament (MA); Old Testament (MA); philosophy of religion and ethics (MA); spiritual formation (MA); spiritual formation and soul care (MA); theology (MA, Th M, D Min). *Accreditation:* ATS. Part-time and evening/weekend programs available. *Degree requirements:* For master's, variable foreign language requirement, thesis or alternative; for doctorate, variable foreign language requirement, thesis/dissertation; for M Div, thesis/dissertation or alternative. *Entrance requirements:* For M Div, minimum GPA of 2.6; for master's, minimum undergraduate GPA of 3.0; for doctorate, minimum GPA of 3.25. Additional exam requirements/recommendations for international students: Required—TOEFL (minimum score 550 paper-based; 213 computer-based). *Faculty research:* Moral development; biological, medical, and social ethics; ancient Near Eastern historical philosophy.

Blessed John XXIII National Seminary, School of Theology, Weston, MA 02493-2618. Offers M Div. *Accreditation:* ATS. *Entrance requirements:* Bachelor's degree or equivalent in life experience.

Bob Jones University, Graduate Programs, Greenville, SC 29614. Offers accountancy (MS); Bible (MA); Bible translation (MA); Biblical studies (Certificate); broadcast management (MS); business administration (MBA); church history (MA, PhD); church ministries (MA); church music (MM); cinema and video production (MA); counseling (MS); curriculum and instruction (Ed D); divinity (M Div); dramatic production (MA); educational leadership (MS, Ed D, Ed S); elementary education (M Ed, MAT); English (M Ed, MA, MAT); fine arts (MA); graphic design (MA); history (M Ed, MA); illustration (MA); interpretative speech (MA); mathematics (M Ed, MAT); medical missions (Certificate); ministry (MM, D Min); multi-categorical special education (M Ed, MAT); music (M Ed); New Testament interpretation (PhD); Old Testament interpretation

Theology

Bob Jones University (continued)
(PhD); orchestral instrument performance (MM); organ performance (MM); pastoral studies (MA); personnel services (MS, Ed S); piano pedagogy (MM); piano performance (MM); platform arts (MA); radio and television broadcasting (MS); rhetoric and public address (MA); secondary education (M Ed); studio art (MA); teaching Bible (MA); theology (MA, PhD); voice performance (MM); youth ministries (MA); M Div/MM.

Boston College, Graduate School of Arts and Sciences, Department of Theology, Chestnut Hill, MA 02467-3800. Offers PhD. *Accreditation:* ATS. Part-time programs available. *Students:* 138 full-time (60 women), 92 part-time (65 women); includes 22 minority (4 African Americans, 2 American Indian/Alaska Native, 4 Asian Americans or Pacific Islanders, 12 Hispanic Americans), 38 international. 223 applicants, 9% accepted, 14 enrolled. In 2009, 17 doctorates awarded. Terminal master's awarded for partial completion of doctoral program. *Degree requirements:* For doctorate, thesis/dissertation. *Entrance requirements:* For doctorate, GRE General Test. Additional exam requirements/recommendations for international students: Required—TOEFL (minimum score 590 paper-based; 250 computer-based; 91 iBT). *Application deadline:* For fall admission, 1/2 for domestic and international students. Application fee: $75. Electronic applications accepted. *Financial support:* Fellowships with full tuition reimbursements, research assistantships with full tuition reimbursements, teaching assistantships with full tuition reimbursements, Federal Work-Study and scholarships/grants available. Support available to part-time students. Financial award application deadline: 3/1; financial award applicants required to submit FAFSA. *Faculty research:* Roman Catholic theology, Christian social ethics, Bible, history of Christian life and thought. *Unit head:* Dr. Kenneth Himes, Chairperson, 617-552-8440, E-mail: kenneth.himes@bc.edu. *Application contact:* Dr. John Darr, Graduate Program Director, 617-552-4602, E-mail: john.darr@bc.edu.

Boston College, Graduate School of Arts and Sciences, School of Theology and Ministry, Chestnut Hill, MA 02467-3800. Offers church leadership (MA); divinity (M Div); pastoral ministry (MA), including Hispanic ministry, liturgy and worship, pastoral care and counseling, spirituality; religious education (MA, PhD); sacred theology (STD, STL); social justice/social ministry (MA); spiritual direction (MA); theological studies (MTS); theology (Th M, PhD); youth ministry (MA); MA/MA; MS/MA; MSW/MA. Part-time programs available. *Degree requirements:* For doctorate, one foreign language, thesis/dissertation. *Entrance requirements:* For doctorate, GRE. Additional exam requirements/recommendations for international students: Required—TOEFL (minimum score 550 paper-based; 213 computer-based). Electronic applications accepted. *Faculty research:* Philosophy and practice of religious education, pastoral psychology, liturgical and spiritual theology, spiritual formation for the practice of ministry.

Boston University, School of Theology, Boston, MA 02215. Offers M Div, MSM, MTS, STM, D Min, Th D, D Min/MSW, M Div/MSM, M Div/MSW, MTS/MSW. *Accreditation:* ACIPE; ATS. Part-time programs available. *Faculty:* 24 full-time (10 women), 18 part-time/adjunct (5 women). *Students:* 263 full-time (108 women), 19 part-time (8 women); includes 31 minority (17 African Americans, 6 Asian Americans or Pacific Islanders, 8 Hispanic Americans), 84 international. Average age 34. In 2009, 31 first professional degrees, 40 master's, 4 doctorates awarded. *Degree requirements:* For master's, comprehensive exam; for doctorate, 2 foreign languages, comprehensive exam, thesis/dissertation. *Entrance requirements:* For M Div and master's, GRE General Test or MAT, minimum GPA of 3.0; for doctorate, GRE General Test or MAT, minimum GPA of 3.3. *Application deadline:* For fall admission, 1/15 priority date for domestic students; for spring admission, 10/1 priority date for domestic students. Applications are processed on a rolling basis. Application fee: $70. Electronic applications accepted. *Expenses:* Contact institution. *Financial support:* Fellowships, research assistantships, teaching assistantships, Federal Work-Study, institutionally sponsored loans, and scholarships/grants available. Support available to part-time students. Financial award application deadline: 7/15; financial award applicants required to submit FAFSA. *Faculty research:* Israelite literature in its social and cultural context, New Testament literature in its social and cultural context, Reformation history, women in the church, social ethics. *Unit head:* Mary Elizabeth Moore, Interim Dean, 617-353-3050, Fax: 617-353-3061. *Application contact:* Anastasia Kidd, Director of Admissions, 617-353-3036, Fax: 617-358-0140, E-mail: sthadmis@bu.edu.

Briercrest Seminary, Graduate Programs, Program in Theology, Caronport, SK S0H 0S0, Canada. Offers Biblical studies (M Div); leadership and management (M Div); New Testament (MATS); Old Testament (MATS); pastoral counseling (M Div); pastoral ministry (M Div); theological studies (M Div); theology (MATS); worship (M Div); youth and family ministry (M Div). *Accreditation:* ATS. Part-time programs available. *Degree requirements:* For master's, comprehensive exam, thesis optional. *Entrance requirements:* Additional exam requirements/recommendations for international students: Required—TOEFL (minimum score 550 paper-based; 213 computer-based).

Bryn Athyn College of the New Church, Academy of the New Church Theological School, Bryn Athyn, PA 19009-0717. Offers divinity (M Div); religious studies (MA). Part-time programs available. Postbaccalaureate distance learning degree programs offered (minimal on-campus study). *Degree requirements:* For master's, thesis; for M Div, 3 foreign languages, thesis/dissertation. *Entrance requirements:* Additional exam requirements/recommendations for international students: Required—TOEFL.

California Institute of Integral Studies, School of Consciousness and Transformation, San Francisco, CA 94103. Offers creative inquiry (MFA); cultural anthropology and social transformation (MA); East-West psychology (MA, PhD); integrative health studies (MA); philosophy and religion (MA, PhD), including Asian and comparative studies, philosophy, cosmology, and consciousness, women's spirituality; social and cultural anthropology (PhD); transformative leadership (MA); transformative studies (PhD); writing and consciousness (MFA). Part-time and evening/weekend programs available. Postbaccalaureate distance learning degree programs offered (minimal on-campus study). *Students:* 334 full-time (218 women), 126 part-time (77 women); includes 116 minority (40 African Americans, 4 American Indian/Alaska Native, 42 Asian Americans or Pacific Islanders, 30 Hispanic Americans). Average age 38. 265 applicants, 90% accepted, 149 enrolled. In 2009, 64 master's, 22 doctorates awarded. Terminal master's awarded for partial completion of doctoral program. *Degree requirements:* For master's, comprehensive exam (for some programs), thesis optional; for doctorate, comprehensive exam, thesis/dissertation, 1 foreign language (Asian comparative studies). *Entrance requirements:* For master's, minimum GPA of 3.0, letters of recommendation, writing sample; for doctorate, master's degree, minimum GPA of 3.0, letters of recommendation, writing sample. Additional exam requirements/recommendations for international students: Required—TOEFL. *Application deadline:* For fall admission, 2/1 priority date for domestic and international students; for spring admission, 10/15 priority date for domestic and international students. Applications are processed on a rolling basis. Application fee: $65. Electronic applications accepted. *Expenses:* Tuition: Full-time $15,300; part-time $850 per credit hour. Required fees: $110 per semester. Tuition and fees vary according to degree level. *Financial support:* In 2009–10, 330 students received support; research assistantships, teaching assistantships, career-related internships or fieldwork, Federal Work-Study, scholarships/grants, and tuition waivers (partial) available. Support available to part-time students. Financial award application deadline: 4/15; financial award applicants required to submit FAFSA. *Faculty research:* Altered states of consciousness, dreams, cosmology, postcolonial studies, integrative health studies. *Application contact:* Allyson Werner, Associate Director of Admissions, 415-575-6155, Fax: 415-575-1268.

Calvary Bible College and Theological Seminary, Calvary Theological Seminary, Kansas City, MO 64147-1341. Offers Bible and theology (MS); Biblical counseling (MA); Biblical studies (MA); Christian ministry (MA); Christian studies (MS); Christian theology (MA); New Testament (MA); Old Testament (MA); pastoral studies (M Div). Part-time and evening/weekend programs available. *Faculty:* 4 full-time (0 women), 2 part-time/adjunct (0 women). *Students:* 20 full-time (7 women), 38 part-time (8 women); includes 4 African Americans, 4 Asian Americans or Pacific Islanders, 2 Hispanic Americans, 1 international. Average age 40. 27 applicants, 96% accepted, 20 enrolled. In 2009, 18 master's awarded. *Degree requirements:* For master's, one foreign language, comprehensive exam, thesis; for M Div, 2 foreign languages, comprehensive exam, thesis/dissertation. *Entrance requirements:* For M Div and master's, minimum GPA of 2.5, 50 semester hours of course work in liberal arts, BA or BS, doctrine agreement. Additional exam requirements/recommendations for international students: Required—TOEFL (minimum score 550 paper-based; 213 computer-based). *Application deadline:* For fall admission, 7/15 priority date for domestic and international students; for spring admission, 12/1 priority date for domestic and international students. Application fee: $25. *Expenses:* Tuition: Full-time $5400; part-time $300 per credit hour. Required fees: $267 per semester. *Financial support:* Scholarships/grants available. Financial award application deadline: 11/5. *Unit head:* Dr. Thomas Baurain, Academic Dean, 816-322-0110 Ext. 1502, Fax: 816-331-4474, E-mail: thomas.baurain@calvary.edu. *Application contact:* Bob Crank, Director of Admissions, 800-326-3960 Ext. 1326, Fax: 816-331-4474, E-mail: admissions@calvary.edu.

Calvin Theological Seminary, Graduate and Professional Programs, Grand Rapids, MI 49546-4387. Offers Bible and theology (MA); divinity (M Div), including ancient near eastern languages and literature, contextual ministry, evangelism and teaching, history of Christianity, new church development, New Testament, Old Testament, pastoral care and leadership, preaching and worship, theological studies, youth and family ministries; educational ministry (MA); historical theology (PhD); missions and evangelism (MA); pastoral care (MA); philosophical and moral theology (PhD); systematic theology (PhD); theological studies (MTS); theology (Th M); worship (MA); youth and family ministries (MA). *Accreditation:* ACIPE; ATS. Part-time programs available. *Faculty:* 28 full-time (2 women), 20 part-time/adjunct (7 women). *Students:* 203 full-time (39 women), 48 part-time (19 women); includes 28 minority (10 African Americans, 13 Asian Americans or Pacific Islanders, 5 Hispanic Americans), 69 international. Average age 31. 152 applicants, 89% accepted, 98 enrolled. In 2009, 45 first professional degrees, 42 master's, 6 doctorates awarded. *Degree requirements:* For master's, thesis (for some programs); for doctorate, 4 foreign languages, comprehensive exam, thesis/dissertation; for M Div, 2 foreign languages. *Entrance requirements:* For doctorate, GRE General Test, Hebrew, Greek, and a modern foreign language. Additional exam requirements/recommendations for international students: Required—TOEFL (minimum score 550 paper-based; 213 computer-based), TWE (minimum score 4). *Application deadline:* For fall admission, 3/1 priority date for domestic and international students. Applications are processed on a rolling basis. Application fee: $25. Electronic applications accepted. *Expenses:* Tuition: Full-time $11,814; part-time $358 per semester hour. Tuition and fees vary according to degree level. *Financial support:* In 2009–10, 187 students received support, including 4 fellowships with full tuition reimbursements available (averaging $8,405 per year), 4 teaching assistantships with full tuition reimbursements available (averaging $5,760 per year); career-related internships or fieldwork, institutionally sponsored loans, scholarships/grants, and tuition waivers (full) also available. Support available to part-time students. Financial award application deadline: 3/1; financial award applicants required to submit FAFSA. *Faculty research:* Recent Trinity theory, Christian anthropology, Proverbs, reformed confessions, Paul's view of law. *Unit head:* Dr. Cornelius Plantinga, Head, 616-957-6024, Fax: 616-957-6536, E-mail: sempres@calvinseminary.edu. *Application contact:* Rev. Gregory Janke, Director of Admissions, 616-957-7035, Fax: 616-957-6101, E-mail: gjanke@calvinseminary.edu.

Campbellsville University, School of Theology, Campbellsville, KY 42718-2799. Offers theology (M Th). Part-time programs available. *Degree requirements:* For master's, comprehensive exam, thesis optional. *Entrance requirements:* For master's, GRE General Test, minimum GPA of 3.0 in major, minimum GPA of 2.75 overall, 18 hours of undergraduate coursework in Christian studies. Electronic applications accepted. *Expenses:* Tuition: Full-time $6750; part-time $375 per credit hour. *Faculty research:* Clergy needing graduate theology education, trinity and Christian faith, Old Testament David narratives, leadership Principles on Christian University integration of Christian principles in counseling process.

Campbell University, Graduate and Professional Programs, Divinity School, Buies Creek, NC 27506. Offers Christian education (MA); divinity (M Div); ministry (D Min); M Div/MA; M Div/MBA. *Accreditation:* ATS. *Degree requirements:* For doctorate, final project. *Entrance requirements:* For master's, minimum GPA of 2.5; for doctorate, MAT, M Div, minimum graduate GPA of 3.0. Additional exam requirements/recommendations for international students: Required—TOEFL (minimum score 580 paper-based; 237 computer-based). *Expenses:* Contact institution. *Faculty research:* New Testament, theology, spiritual formation, Old Testament, Christian leadership.

Canadian Southern Baptist Seminary, Graduate Programs, Cochrane, AB T4C 2G1, Canada. Offers Christian education (MACE); ministry (M Div). *Accreditation:* ATS. Part-time programs available. *Faculty:* 8 full-time (0 women), 3 part-time/adjunct (1 woman). *Students:* 17 full-time (3 women), 25 part-time (4 women); includes 9 minority (1 African American, 5 Asian Americans or Pacific Islanders, 3 Hispanic Americans), 12 international. *Entrance requirements:* Additional exam requirements/recommendations for international students: Required—TOEFL (minimum score 560 paper-based; 220 computer-based), IELTS (minimum score 6.5). *Application deadline:* For fall admission, 7/1 priority date for domestic and international students; for winter admission, 11/15 priority date for domestic and international students. Applications are processed on a rolling basis. Application fee: $50. Tuition and fees charges are reported in Canadian dollars. *Expenses:* Tuition: Full-time $5280 Canadian dollars; part-time $220 Canadian dollars per credit hour. Required fees: $480 Canadian dollars; $20 Canadian dollars per credit hour. *Unit head:* Steve Booth, Academic Dean, 403-932-6622. *Application contact:* Kathleen McNaughton, Registrar, 403-932-6622 Ext. 221, E-mail: kathleen.mcnaughton@csbs.ca.

Capital Bible Seminary, Graduate and Professional Programs, Lanham, MD 20706-3599. Offers biblical studies (MA, Certificate); Christian counseling (MA); Christian counseling and discipleship (Certificate); ministry leadership (MA); theology (M Div, Th M). *Accreditation:* ATS (one or more programs are accredited). Part-time and evening/weekend programs available. *Degree requirements:* For master's, 2 foreign languages, comprehensive exam, thesis (for some programs); for M Div, 2 foreign languages, comprehensive exam. *Entrance requirements:* For M Div and master's, GRE General Test, Greek exam for those with 2 years of Greek, proficiency exam in theology, previous course work in Biblical studies. Additional exam requirements/recommendations for international students: Required—TOEFL (minimum score 550 paper-based; 213 computer-based). *Faculty research:* Dead Sea Scrolls, spiritual gifts, hermeneutics.

Carey Theological College, Graduate Programs, Vancouver, BC V6T 1J6, Canada. Offers M Div, MASF, D Min. *Accreditation:* ATS. Part-time programs available. *Faculty:* 8 full-time (2 women), 17 part-time/adjunct (2 women). *Students:* 2 full-time (0 women), 105 part-time (29 women); includes 38 minority (1 African American, 31 Asian Americans or Pacific Islanders, 6 Hispanic Americans). Average age 45. 27 applicants, 78% accepted, 21 enrolled. In 2009, 8 master's, 5 doctorates awarded. *Degree requirements:* For doctorate, thesis/dissertation. *Entrance requirements:* For master's, undergraduate degree with minimum GPA of 2.7; for doctorate, M Div with minimum GPA of 3.5. Additional exam requirements/recommendations for international students: Required—TOEFL (minimum score 577 paper-based; 233 computer-based; 90 iBT). *Application deadline:* Applications are processed on a rolling basis. Application fee: $60. Electronic applications accepted. *Expenses:* Tuition: Full-time $7500; part-time $250 per credit. One-time fee: $350. *Financial support:* In 2009–10, 4 students received support. Scholarships/grants available. *Faculty research:* Missional church, new monasticism, women in leadership, spiritual formation, applied theology. *Unit head:* Dr. Barbara Mutch, Academic Vice President, 604-224-4308, Fax: 604-224-5014, E-mail: barmutch@careytheologicalcollege.ca. *Application contact:* Rev. Myrna Sears, Registrar, 604-224-4308, Fax: 604-224-5014, E-mail: msears@careytheologicalcollege.ca.

Carolina Evangelical Divinity School, Divinity Program, High Point, NC 27265. Offers M Div.

Carolina Evangelical Divinity School, Program in Theological Studies, High Point, NC 27265. Offers MA.

The Catholic Distance University, Graduate Programs, Hamilton, VA 20158. Offers religious studies (MRS); theology (MA). Part-time and evening/weekend programs available. Postbaccalaureate distance learning degree programs offered (no on-campus study). *Degree requirements:* For master's, comprehensive exam, capstone paper or project.

Catholic Theological Union at Chicago, Graduate and Professional Programs, Chicago, IL 60615-5698. Offers biblical spirituality (Certificate); cross-cultural ministries (D Min); cross-cultural missions (Certificate); divinity (M Div); liturgical studies (Certificate); liturgy (D Min); pastoral studies (MAPS, Certificate); spiritual formation (Certificate); spirituality (D Min); theology (MA); M Div/MA; M Div/MSW; M Div/PhD. *Accreditation:* ACIPE; ATS (one or more programs are accredited). Part-time and evening/weekend programs available. *Degree requirements:* For master's, one foreign language, comprehensive exam (for some programs), thesis (for some programs); for doctorate, thesis/dissertation. *Entrance requirements:* For doctorate, master's degree, 5 years of active ministry. *Faculty research:* Doctrine, sacraments, ethics, Bible.

The Catholic University of America, School of Canon Law, Washington, DC 20064. Offers JCD, JCL, JD/JCL. Part-time programs available. *Faculty:* 7 full-time (1 woman), 1 part-time/adjunct (0 women). *Students:* 42 full-time (10 women), 48 part-time (5 women); includes 9 minority (1 African American, 3 Asian Americans or Pacific Islanders, 5 Hispanic Americans), 16 international. Average age 40. 42 applicants, 93% accepted, 30 enrolled. In 2009, 4 doctorates awarded. *Degree requirements:* For doctorate, 2 foreign languages, thesis/dissertation, fluency in canonical Latin; for JCL, one foreign language, comprehensive exam, thesis, fluency in canonical Latin. *Entrance requirements:* For doctorate, GRE General Test, 2 letters of recommendation; for JCL, GRE General Test, official copies of academic transcripts, two letters of recommendation. Additional exam requirements/recommendations for international students: Required—TOEFL (minimum score 580 paper-based; 237 computer-based). *Application deadline:* For fall admission, 8/1 priority date for domestic students, 7/15 for international students; for spring admission, 12/1 priority date for domestic students, 10/15 for international students. Applications are processed on a rolling basis. Application fee: $55. Electronic applications accepted. *Expenses:* Tuition: Full-time $31,740; part-time $1245 per credit hour. Required fees: $50; $25 per semester hour. One-time fee: $425. *Financial support:* Fellowships, research assistantships, teaching assistantships, Federal Work-Study, scholarships/grants, tuition waivers (full and partial), and unspecified assistantships available. Financial award application deadline: 2/1; financial award applicants required to submit FAFSA. *Faculty research:* Ecclesiology and the Sacrament of Orders, procedural law, temporal goods, matrimonial jurisprudence, sacramental and liturgical law. *Unit head:* Rev. Robert Kaslyn, Dean, 202-319-5492, Fax: 202-319-4187, E-mail: cua-canonlaw@cua.edu. *Application contact:* Julie Schwing, Director of Graduate Admissions, 202-319-5057, Fax: 202-319-6533, E-mail: cua-admissions@cua.edu.

The Catholic University of America, School of Theology and Religious Studies, Washington, DC 20064. Offers Biblical studies (STB, MA, PhD, STL); Catholic educational leadership (MA); church history (PhD); Hispanic pastoral leadership (Certificate); Hispanic/Latino ministry (M Div); historical theology (STB, STD); history of religions (Hinduism/Islam) (MA, PhD); liturgical studies/sacramental theology (MA, PhD, STD, STL); moral theology/ethics (STB, MA, PhD, STD, STL); pastoral studies (M Div, Certificate); religion and culture (PhD); religious education/catechetics (MA, MRE, PhD); spirituality (STB, PhD, STD, STL); systematic and historical theology (MA, PhD, STD, STL). *Accreditation:* ATS (one or more programs are accredited). Part-time programs available. *Faculty:* 40 full-time (6 women), 10 part-time/adjunct (2 women). *Students:* 169 full-time (26 women), 225 part-time (57 women); includes 33 minority (10 African Americans, 1 American Indian/Alaska Native, 9 Asian Americans or Pacific Islanders, 13 Hispanic Americans), 73 international. Average age 36. 226 applicants, 72% accepted, 75 enrolled. In 2009, 9 first professional degrees, 14 master's, 26 doctorates awarded. *Degree requirements:* For master's, variable foreign language requirement, comprehensive exam, thesis (for some programs); for doctorate, variable foreign language requirement, comprehensive exam, thesis/dissertation; for first professional degree, comprehensive exam. *Entrance requirements:* For first professional degree and master's, GRE General Test, statement of purpose, official copies of academic transcripts, three letters of recommendation; for doctorate, GRE General Test, 3 letters of recommendation. Additional exam requirements/recommendations for international students: Required—TOEFL (minimum score 580 paper-based; 237 computer-based). *Application deadline:* For fall admission, 8/1 priority date for domestic students, 7/15 for international students; for spring admission, 12/1 priority date for domestic students, 10/15 for international students. Applications are processed on a rolling basis. Application fee: $55. Electronic applications accepted. *Expenses:* Tuition: Full-time $31,740; part-time $1245 per credit hour. Required fees: $50; $25 per semester hour. One-time fee: $425. *Financial support:* Fellowships, research assistantships, teaching assistantships, Federal Work-Study, scholarships/grants, tuition waivers (full and partial), and unspecified assistantships available. Financial award application deadline: 2/1; financial award applicants required to submit FAFSA. *Faculty research:* Historical and systematic theology, religious education and catechetics, moral theology and ethics, Biblical studies, liturgical studies and sacramental theology. Total annual research expenditures: $66,740. *Unit head:* Msgr. Kevin W. Irwin, Dean, 202-319-5683, Fax: 202-319-4967, E-mail: irwin@cua.edu. *Application contact:* Julie Schwing, Director of Graduate Admissions, 202-319-5057, Fax: 202-319-6533, E-mail: cua-admissions@cua.edu.

Central Baptist Theological Seminary, Graduate and Professional Programs, Shawnee, KS 66226. Offers missional church studies (MA); theological studies (MA); theology (M Div, Diploma). *Accreditation:* ACIPE; ATS (one or more programs are accredited). Part-time programs available. *Degree requirements:* For master's, thesis optional, MMPI, Myers-Briggs, Enneagram; for M Div, thesis/dissertation optional. *Entrance requirements:* For master's, accredited bachelor's degree with minimum GPA of 2.3. Additional exam requirements/recommendations for international students: Required—TOEFL (minimum score 547 paper-based; 210 computer-based; 77 iBT). Electronic applications accepted.

Central Baptist Theological Seminary of Virginia Beach, Graduate Programs, Virginia Beach, VA 23464. Offers M Div, MBS, Th M. *Entrance requirements:* For M Div, GRE, interview, M Div or equivalent from an accredited seminary, minimum cumulative GPA of 2.7, church endorsement, 4 recommendations; for master's, GRE, interview, minimum cumulative GPA of 2.4, church endorsement, 4 recommendations. Electronic applications accepted.

Central Yeshiva Tomchei Tmimim-Lubavitch, Graduate Programs, Brooklyn, NY 11230. *Accreditation:* AARTS.

Chaminade University of Honolulu, Graduate Services, Program in Pastoral Theology, Honolulu, HI 96816-1578. Offers MPT. Part-time and evening/weekend programs available. Postbaccalaureate distance learning degree programs offered. *Degree requirements:* For master's, capstone course. *Entrance requirements:* For master's, 2 letters of recommendation. Additional exam requirements/recommendations for international students: Required—TOEFL (minimum score 550 paper-based). Electronic applications accepted.

Chicago Theological Seminary, Graduate and Professional Programs, Chicago, IL 60637-1507. Offers preaching (D Min); religion and health (D Min); religious studies (MA); spirituality and spiritual direction (D Min); theology (M Div); theology, ethics and the human sciences (PhD); M Div/MSW. *Accreditation:* ACIPE; ATS. Part-time programs available. *Degree requirements:* For master's, thesis; for doctorate, 2 foreign languages, comprehensive exam, thesis/dissertation; for M Div, thesis/dissertation. *Entrance requirements:* For doctorate, GRE General Test. Additional exam requirements/recommendations for international students: Required—TOEFL (minimum score 217 computer-based). *Faculty research:* Bible, culture and hermeneutics, theology, gender and sexuality, black faith and life, spirituality and psychology, practical theology.

Christendom College, Notre Dame Graduate School, Front Royal, VA 22630-5103. Offers theological studies (MA). Part-time and evening/weekend programs available. *Degree requirements:* For master's, one foreign language, thesis or alternative. Electronic applications accepted.

Christian Theological Seminary, Graduate and Professional Programs, Indianapolis, IN 46208-3301. Offers educational and arts ministries (MA); marriage and family therapy (MA); pastoral care and counseling (D Min); psychotherapy and faith (MA); theological studies (MTS); theology (M Div). *Accreditation:* AAMFT/COAMFTE (one or more programs are accredited); ACIPE; ATS. Part-time programs available. *Faculty:* 18 full-time (8 women), 18 part-time/adjunct (4 women). *Students:* 152 full-time (98 women), 53 part-time (28 women); includes 73 minority (53 African Americans, 1 American Indian/Alaska Native, 4 Asian Americans or Pacific Islanders, 15 Hispanic Americans), 2 international. Average age 41. 120 applicants, 86% accepted, 71 enrolled. In 2009, 31 first professional degrees, 22 master's, 3 doctorates awarded. Terminal master's awarded for partial completion of doctoral program. *Degree requirements:* For master's, comprehensive exam (for some programs), thesis (for some programs); for doctorate, comprehensive exam, thesis/dissertation; for M Div, comprehensive exam, thesis/dissertation (for some programs), missionary and cross-cultural experience. *Entrance requirements:* For master's, GRE General Test, MAT; for doctorate, M Div or BD. *Application deadline:* For fall admission, 7/15 for domestic and international students; for spring admission, 11/15 for domestic and international students. Applications are processed on a rolling basis. Application fee: $30. Electronic applications accepted. *Expenses:* Tuition: Full-time $9310; part-time $490 per credit hour. Required fees: $180; $160 per semester. Tuition and fees vary according to course load. *Financial support:* In 2009–10, 187 students received support, including 12 teaching assistantships (averaging $350 per year); career-related internships or fieldwork, Federal Work-Study, scholarships/grants, and tuition waivers (full and partial) also available. Support available to part-time students. Financial award application deadline: 4/1; financial award applicants required to submit FAFSA. *Faculty research:* Faith formation, peer learning post graduation. *Unit head:* Dr. Edward L. Wheeler, President, 317-931-2304, Fax: 317-923-1961, E-mail: wheeler@cts.edu. *Application contact:* Rev. Mary Harris, Associate Dean for Student Services, 317-931-2300, Fax: 317-923-1961, E-mail: mharris@cts.edu.

Christ the King Seminary, Graduate and Professional Programs, East Aurora, NY 14052. Offers divinity (M Div); pastoral ministry (MA); pastoral studies (Certificate); theology (MA). *Accreditation:* ATS. Part-time and evening/weekend programs available. *Degree requirements:* For master's, comprehensive exam, thesis; for M Div, comprehensive exam. *Entrance requirements:* For M Div and master's, previous course work in philosophy and religious studies.

Church Divinity School of the Pacific, Graduate and Professional Programs, Berkeley, CA 94709-1217. Offers M Div, MA, MTS, D Min, Certificate. *Accreditation:* ACIPE; ATS (one or more programs are accredited). Part-time programs available. *Degree requirements:* For master's, one foreign language, thesis; for doctorate, thesis/dissertation; for M Div, one foreign language. *Entrance requirements:* For M Div, master's, and Certificate, GRE General Test, letters of reference; for doctorate, letters of reference. Additional exam requirements/recommendations for international students: Required—TOEFL. Electronic applications accepted.

Church of God Theological Seminary, Graduate and Professional Programs, Cleveland, TN 37320-3330. Offers counseling (MA); discipleship and Christian formations (MA); ministry (D Min); theology (M Div). *Accreditation:* ACIPE. Part-time programs available. *Degree requirements:* For M Div, 2 foreign languages, thesis/dissertation, internship. *Faculty research:* Biblical exegesis.

Cincinnati Christian University, Graduate School, Cincinnati, OH 45204-3200. Offers biblical studies (MA); church history (MA); counseling (MAC); divinity (M Div); ministry (M Min); practical ministries (MA); theological studies (MA). *Accreditation:* ATS. Part-time programs available. *Degree requirements:* For master's, thesis (for some programs); for M Div, 2 foreign languages, oral exam. *Entrance requirements:* For master's, GRE General Test. Additional exam requirements/recommendations for international students: Required—TOEFL. Electronic applications accepted.

Claremont Graduate University, Graduate Programs, School of Religion, Claremont, CA 91711-6160. Offers Hebrew Bible (MA, PhD); history of Christianity and religions of North America (MA, PhD); New Testament (MA, PhD); philosophy of religion and theology (MA, PhD); theology, ethics and culture (MA, PhD); women's studies in religion (MA, PhD); MA/PhD; MBA/PhD. Part-time programs available. *Faculty:* 7 full-time (2 women), 2 part-time/adjunct (0 women). *Students:* 223 full-time (90 women), 7 part-time (4 women); includes 37 minority (14 African Americans, 11 Asian Americans or Pacific Islanders, 12 Hispanic Americans), 23 international. Average age 37. In 2009, 10 master's, 14 doctorates awarded. Terminal master's awarded for partial completion of doctoral program. *Entrance requirements:* For master's and doctorate, GRE General Test. Additional exam requirements/recommendations for international students: Required—TOEFL (minimum score 550 paper-based; 213 computer-based; 80 iBT). *Application deadline:* For fall admission, 2/1 priority date for domestic students. Applications are processed on a rolling basis. Application fee: $60. Electronic applications accepted. *Expenses:* Tuition: Full-time $35,046; part-time $1524 per credit. Required fees: $161 per semester. *Financial support:* Fellowships, research assistantships, teaching assistantships, Federal Work-Study, institutionally sponsored loans, and scholarships/grants available. Support available to part-time students. Financial award application deadline: 2/15; financial award applicants required to submit FAFSA. *Unit head:* Anselm Min, Dean, 909-607-3214, Fax: 909-621-9587, E-mail: anselm.min@cgu.edu. *Application contact:* Brent Smith, Recruiter, 909-607-2653, Fax: 909-607-9587, E-mail: brent.smith@cgu.edu.

Claremont School of Theology, Graduate and Professional Programs, Master of Divinity Program, Claremont, CA 91711-3199. Offers M Div. *Accreditation:* ACIPE; ATS. Part-time programs available. *Entrance requirements:* Additional exam requirements/recommendations for international students: Required—TOEFL (minimum score 230 computer-based). Electronic applications accepted.

Claremont School of Theology, Graduate and Professional Programs, Program in Religion, Claremont, CA 91711-3199. Offers practical theology (PhD), including religious education, spiritual care and counseling; religion (PhD), including Hebrew Bible, New Testament and Christian origins, process studies, religion, ethics, and society; religion and theology (MA); religious education (MARE). *Accreditation:* ACIPE; ATS. Terminal master's awarded for partial completion of doctoral program. *Degree requirements:* For master's, thesis; for doctorate, 2 foreign languages, thesis/dissertation. *Entrance requirements:* For doctorate, GRE General Test. Additional exam requirements/recommendations for international students: Required—TOEFL (minimum score 250 computer-based). Electronic applications accepted.

Colgate Rochester Crozer Divinity School, Graduate and Professional Programs, Rochester, NY 14620-2530. Offers M Div, MA, D Min, Certificate. *Accreditation:* ACIPE; ATS (one or more programs are accredited). Part-time programs available. Postbaccalaureate distance learning degree programs offered (minimal on-campus study). *Faculty:* 8 full-time (4 women), 15 part-time/adjunct (7 women). *Students:* 72 full-time, 45 part-time; includes 39 minority (33 African Americans, 1 Asian American or Pacific Islander, 5 Hispanic Americans), 5 international. Average age 43. 40 applicants, 90% accepted, 29 enrolled. In 2009, 13 first professional degrees, 5 master's, 3 doctorates awarded. *Degree requirements:* For master's, thesis; for doctorate, thesis/dissertation; for M Div, supervised ministry year. *Entrance requirements:* For M Div and master's, BA/BS, personal statement; for doctorate, M Div, 3 years professional experience. Additional exam requirements/recommendations for international students: Required—TOEFL (minimum score 600 paper-based; 237 computer-based; 93 iBT). *Application deadline:* For fall admission, 7/1 priority date for domestic students, 3/1 for international students; for spring admission, 12/1 priority date for domestic students. Applications are processed on a rolling basis. Application fee: $35. *Expenses:* Tuition: Full-time $12,160; part-time $1520 per course. Required fees: $165; $25 per course. Tuition and fees vary according to course level, course load, degree level and program. *Financial support:* In 2009–10, 55 students received support. Scholarships/grants available. Financial award application deadline: 9/1; financial award applicants required to submit FAFSA. *Faculty research:* Old Testament, New Testament, Christian ethics, black church studies, woman and gender

Theology

Colgate Rochester Crozer Divinity School (continued)
studies. *Unit head:* Dr. Eugene C. Bay, President, 585-271-1320 Ext. 680, Fax: 585-271-8013. *Application contact:* Melissa M. Morral, Vice President for Enrollment Services, 585-340-9500, Fax: 585-340-9644, E-mail: mmorral@crcds.edu.

Collège Dominicain de Philosophie et de Théologie, Graduate Programs, Faculty of Theology, Ottawa, ON K1R 7G3, Canada. Offers M Th, MA Th, PhD, Th D, L Th. Part-time and evening/weekend programs available. *Faculty:* 6 full-time (1 woman), 5 part-time/adjunct (2 women). *Students:* 28 full-time (5 women), 1 part-time (0 women); includes 7 minority (5 African Americans, 2 Asian Americans or Pacific Islanders), 11 international. Average age 44. 9 applicants, 78% accepted, 6 enrolled. In 2009, 2 master's awarded. *Degree requirements:* For master's, 2 foreign languages, research paper; for doctorate, 2 foreign languages, thesis/dissertation, candidacy exam. *Entrance requirements:* For master's, B Th or equivalent, minimum A- average in undergraduate course work; for doctorate, MA Th or equivalent, minimum A- average in graduate course work. *Application deadline:* For fall admission, 6/1 priority date for domestic students, 3/1 priority date for international students; for winter admission, 11/20 priority date for domestic students, 10/16 priority date for international students. Applications are processed on a rolling basis. Application fee: $40. Tuition and fees charges are reported in Canadian dollars. *Expenses:* Tuition: Full-time $3560 Canadian dollars; part-time $130 Canadian dollars per credit. Required fees: $125 Canadian dollars; $105 Canadian dollars per year. *Financial support:* In 2009–10, 13 fellowships (averaging $1,000 per year) were awarded. Financial award application deadline: 10/15. *Faculty research:* Exegese, bioethics, history of church, New Testament. *Unit head:* Sr. Marie-Therese Nadeau, Dean of the Faculty, 613-233-5696 Ext. 310, Fax: 613-233-6064, E-mail: marie-therese.nadeau@collegedominicain.ca. *Application contact:* Fr. Herve Tremblay, Registrar, 613-233-5696 Ext. 308, Fax: 613-233-6064, E-mail: registrar@collegedominicain.ca.

College of Emmanuel and St. Chad, Bachelor of Theology Program, Saskatoon, SK S7N 0W6, Canada. Offers B Th. Part-time programs available. Postbaccalaureate distance learning degree programs offered (minimal on-campus study). *Degree requirements:* For B Th, internship. *Entrance requirements:* 1 year of university-level work or equivalent. Additional exam requirements/recommendations for international students: Required—TOEFL. *Faculty research:* Pauline studies, New Testament, ethics, congregational development, trauma and spirituality.

College of Emmanuel and St. Chad, Graduate Programs, Saskatoon, SK S7N 0W6, Canada. Offers M Div, MTS, STM. Part-time programs available. *Degree requirements:* For master's, thesis optional. *Entrance requirements:* For master's, M Div or MTS (STM). Additional exam requirements/recommendations for international students: Required—TOEFL. *Faculty research:* New Testament, systematics, Christian education, theology, ethics.

College of Mount St. Joseph, Graduate Program in Religious Studies, Cincinnati, OH 45233-1670. Offers religious education (Certificate); spiritual and pastoral care (MA, Certificate); spiritual direction (Certificate). Part-time and evening/weekend programs available. *Faculty:* 4 full-time (2 women). *Students:* 25 part-time (20 women); includes 1 minority (African American). Average age 49. 5 applicants, 100% accepted, 3 enrolled. In 2009, 9 master's awarded. *Degree requirements:* For master's, comprehensive exam, integrating project. *Entrance requirements:* For master's, 3 letters of recommendation, interview, minimum GPA of 3.0. Additional exam requirements/recommendations for international students: Required—TOEFL (minimum score 560 paper-based; 220 computer-based; 83 iBT). *Application deadline:* Applications are processed on a rolling basis. Application fee: $50. Electronic applications accepted. *Expenses:* Tuition: Part-time $500 per hour. Required fees: $200 per year. Tuition and fees vary according to degree level and program. *Financial support:* In 2009–10, 20 students received support. Scholarships/grants available. Financial award applicants required to submit FAFSA. *Faculty research:* Contextual/cultural/systematic theology, historical/spiritual theology, business/economics ethics, social justice, Biblical/cultural/pastoral theology. *Unit head:* Dr. John Trokan, Chair of Religious/Pastoral Studies, 513-244-4272, Fax: 513-244-4222, E-mail: john_trokan@mail.msj.edu. *Application contact:* Marilyn Hoskins, Assistant Director of Graduate Recruitment, 513-244-4723, Fax: 513-244-4629, E-mail: marilyn_hoskins@mail.msj.edu.

College of Saint Elizabeth, Department of Theology, Morristown, NJ 07960-6989. Offers MA. Part-time and evening/weekend programs available. *Faculty:* 2 full-time (both women), 2 part-time/adjunct (0 women). *Students:* 16 part-time (12 women); includes 1 minority (Hispanic American), 1 international. Average age 54. 4 applicants, 100% accepted, 2 enrolled. In 2009, 4 master's awarded. *Degree requirements:* For master's, thesis or alternative, 3 essays, oral exam. *Entrance requirements:* For master's, interview, minimum GPA of 3.0. *Application deadline:* For fall admission, 3/1 priority date for domestic students; for spring admission, 9/1 for domestic students. Applications are processed on a rolling basis. Application fee: $35. Electronic applications accepted. *Expenses:* Tuition: Part-time $797 per credit hour. Required fees: $65 per credit hour. *Financial support:* Tuition waivers (partial) and unspecified assistantships available. Support available to part-time students. Financial award applicants required to submit FAFSA. *Unit head:* Sr. Kathleen Flanagan, Director of the Graduate Program, 973-290-4336, Fax: 973-290-4312, E-mail: kflanagan@cse.edu. *Application contact:* Donna Tatarka, Dean of Admission, 973-290-4705, Fax: 973-290-4710, E-mail: dtatarka@cse.edu.

Columbia International University, Columbia Biblical Seminary and School of Missions, Columbia, SC 29230-3122. Offers academic ministries (M Div); bible exposition (M Div, MABE); biblical studies (Certificate); counseling ministries (Certificate); divinity (M Div); educational ministries (M Div, MAEM, Certificate); intercultural studies (M Div, MAIS, Certificate); leadership (D Min); leadership for evangelism/mobilization (MALM); member care (D Min); ministry (Certificate); missions (D Min); pastoral counseling and spiritual formation (M Div, MAPS); preaching (D Min); theology (MA). *Accreditation:* ATS (one or more programs are accredited). Part-time and evening/weekend programs available. *Degree requirements:* For master's, integrative seminar; for doctorate, comprehensive exam, thesis/dissertation; for M Div, internship. *Entrance requirements:* For master's, minimum GPA of 2.7; for doctorate, 3 years of ministerial experience, M Div. Additional exam requirements/recommendations for international students: Required—TOEFL. Electronic applications accepted.

Columbia Theological Seminary, Graduate and Professional Programs, Decatur, GA 30031-0520. Offers M Div, MATS, Th M, D Min, Th D. *Accreditation:* ACIPE; ATS (one or more programs are accredited). Terminal master's awarded for partial completion of doctoral program. *Degree requirements:* For master's, thesis (for some programs); for doctorate, one foreign language, thesis/dissertation; for M Div, 2 foreign languages. *Entrance requirements:* For doctorate, M Div or equivalent, 3 years practice of ministry. Additional exam requirements/recommendations for international students: Required—TOEFL.

Concordia Lutheran Seminary, Graduate and Professional Programs, Edmonton, AB T5B 4E3, Canada. Offers M Div, Graduate Certificate. *Accreditation:* ATS (one or more programs are accredited). Part-time programs available. *Degree requirements:* For M Div, 2 foreign languages, thesis/dissertation. *Entrance requirements:* GRE General Test, 1 year of Greek, 1 year of Hebrew, minimum GPA of 2.0. Additional exam requirements/recommendations for international students: Required—TOEFL. *Faculty research:* Lutheran Pietism, Christianity and culture, missiology, Christian worship, homiletics.

Concordia Seminary, Graduate Programs, St. Louis, MO 63105-3199. Offers M Div, MA, STM, D Min, PhD, Certificate. *Accreditation:* ACIPE; ATS (one or more programs are accredited). Terminal master's awarded for partial completion of doctoral program. *Degree requirements:* For master's, 3 foreign languages, thesis optional; for doctorate, 4 foreign languages, thesis/dissertation; for M Div, 2 foreign languages, comprehensive exam (for some programs), thesis/dissertation (for some programs). *Entrance requirements:* For M Div, GRE General Test, previous course work in public speaking, Greek, Hebrew, Old Testament, New Testament, and Christian Doctrine; for master's, GRE General Test; for doctorate, GRE General Test, theological essay in English (foreign students only). Additional exam requirements/recommendations for international students: Required—TOEFL. *Faculty research:* Family counseling, educational administration, contemporary theology, pastoral office, humanism and education.

Concordia Theological Seminary, Graduate and Professional Programs, Fort Wayne, IN 46825-4996. Offers M Div, MA, STM, D Min, PhD. *Accreditation:* ATS. Part-time programs available. *Degree requirements:* For master's, 2 foreign languages, thesis, oral exam, language exam, comprehensive exam (STM); for doctorate, comprehensive exam, thesis/dissertation, oral exam; for M Div, one foreign language, 1 year of vicarage. *Entrance requirements:* GRE General Test, minimum GPA of 2.25.

Concordia University, School of Graduate Studies, Faculty of Arts and Science, Department of Theological Studies, Montréal, QC H3G 1M8, Canada. Offers MA. *Degree requirements:* For master's, one foreign language, research papers or thesis. *Entrance requirements:* For master's, minimum B average in theology. *Faculty research:* Interpretation theory, theological methodology.

Concordia University, School of Theology, Irvine, CA 92612-3299. Offers Christian leadership (MA); research in theology (MA); theology and culture (MA). Part-time and evening/weekend programs available. Postbaccalaureate distance learning degree programs offered (no on-campus study). *Faculty:* 9 full-time (2 women). *Students:* 32 full-time (4 women), 8 part-time (3 women); includes 5 minority (1 African American, 1 Asian American or Pacific Islander, 3 Hispanic Americans), 3 international. Average age 36. 7 applicants, 100% accepted, 5 enrolled. In 2009, 10 master's awarded. *Degree requirements:* For master's, project/thesis or vicarage. *Entrance requirements:* For master's, 2 references, interview. Additional exam requirements/recommendations for international students: Required—TOEFL. *Application deadline:* For fall admission, 7/1 priority date for domestic students, 6/1 for international students; for spring admission, 11/30 priority date for domestic students, 10/1 for international students. Applications are processed on a rolling basis. Application fee: $50 ($125 for international students). Electronic applications accepted. *Expenses:* Contact institution. *Financial support:* In 2009–10, 34 students received support. Scholarships/grants available. Financial award applicants required to submit FAFSA. *Unit head:* Rev. Dr. James Bachman, Dean, School of Theology Graduate Studies, 949-854-8002 Ext. 1751, E-mail: james.bachman@cui.edu. *Application contact:* Carrie Donohoe, Christ College Program Coordinator, 949-854-8002 Ext. 1407, E-mail: carrie.donohoe@cui.edu.

Concordia University, St. Paul, College of Vocation and Ministry, St. Paul, MN 55104-5494. Offers Christian education (Certificate); Christian outreach (MA); christian outreach (Certificate). Evening/weekend programs available. Postbaccalaureate distance learning degree programs offered (minimal on-campus study). *Faculty:* 4 full-time (0 women), 2 part-time/adjunct (1 woman). *Students:* 14 full-time (8 women), 4 part-time (2 women); includes 1 minority (Asian American or Pacific Islander). Average age 38. In 2009, 5 master's, 10 other advanced degrees awarded. *Application deadline:* Applications are processed on a rolling basis. Application fee: $50. Electronic applications accepted. *Financial support:* Applicants required to submit FAFSA. *Unit head:* Dr. David Lumpp, Dean, 651-641-8217, E-mail: lumpp@csp.edu. *Application contact:* Kimberly Craig, Director of Graduate and Cohort Admission, 651-603-6223, Fax: 651-603-6320, E-mail: craig@csp.edu.

Covenant Theological Seminary, Graduate and Professional Programs, St. Louis, MO 63141-8697. Offers M Div, MA, MAC, MAEM, Th M, D Min, Certificate. *Accreditation:* ATS (one or more programs are accredited). Part-time and evening/weekend programs available. Postbaccalaureate distance learning degree programs offered (minimal on-campus study). *Degree requirements:* For master's, 2 foreign languages, thesis (for some programs); for doctorate, 2 foreign languages, thesis/dissertation; for M Div and Certificate, 2 foreign languages. *Entrance requirements:* For doctorate and Certificate, M Div. Additional exam requirements/recommendations for international students: Required—TOEFL (minimum score 550 paper-based; 213 computer-based). Electronic applications accepted.

Creighton University, Graduate School, College of Arts and Sciences, Department of Theology, Omaha, NE 68178-0001. Offers Christian spirituality (MA); ministry (MA); theology (MA). Part-time and evening/weekend programs available. Postbaccalaureate distance learning degree programs offered (minimal on-campus study). *Faculty:* 18 full-time (7 women), 1 part-time/adjunct (0 women). *Students:* 20 part-time (10 women). Average age 44. 7 applicants, 71% accepted, 5 enrolled. In 2009, 32 master's awarded. *Entrance requirements:* For master's, GRE General Test, 9 hours of theology course work, 3 letters of recommendation. Additional exam requirements/recommendations for international students: Required—TOEFL (minimum score 550 paper-based; 213 computer-based; 80 iBT). *Application deadline:* For fall admission, 3/1 for domestic and international students. Applications are processed on a rolling basis. Application fee: $50. *Expenses:* Tuition: Full-time $11,700; part-time $650 per credit hour. Required fees: $126 per semester. *Financial support:* Scholarships/grants and tuition waivers (partial) available. Support available to part-time students. Financial award applicants required to submit FAFSA. *Unit head:* Dr. Richard Miller, Director, 402-280-3618, E-mail: richardmiller@creighton.edu. *Application contact:* Taunya Plater, Senior Program Coordinator, 402-280-2870, Fax: 402-280-2899, E-mail: taunyaplater@creighton.edu.

The Criswell College, Graduate School of the Bible, Dallas, TX 75246-1537. Offers biblical studies (M Div); Christian leadership (MA); counseling (MA); Jewish studies (MA); ministry (MA); theological and biblical studies (MA). Part-time programs available. *Degree requirements:* For master's, 2 foreign languages, thesis optional; for M Div, 2 foreign languages, thesis/dissertation optional. *Entrance requirements:* For M Div and master's, GRE General Test, minimum GPA of 2.5. Electronic applications accepted. *Faculty research:* Emphasis on biblical languages (Hebrew and Greek), expository preaching and evangelism in the local church.

Crown College, Graduate Studies, St. Bonifacius, MN 55375-9001. Offers Christian studies (MA); instructional leadership (MA); international leadership (MA); ministry leadership (MA); organizational leadership (MA). Part-time and evening/weekend programs available. Postbaccalaureate distance learning degree programs offered (no on-campus study). *Faculty:* 10 full-time (0 women), 75 part-time/adjunct (4 women). *Students:* 130 full-time (46 women), 30 part-time (11 women); includes 17 minority (9 African Americans, 5 Asian Americans or Pacific Islanders, 3 Hispanic Americans). Average age 37. 75 applicants, 77% accepted, 43 enrolled. In 2009, 30 master's awarded. *Degree requirements:* For master's, thesis optional. *Entrance requirements:* For master's, 12 credits in foundational studies, minimum GPA of 2.5. Additional exam requirements/recommendations for international students: Required—TOEFL (minimum score 500 paper-based). *Application deadline:* For fall admission, 8/1 priority date for domestic students; for winter admission, 1/1 priority date for domestic students; for spring admission, 6/1 priority date for domestic students. Applications are processed on a rolling basis. Application fee: $20. *Expenses:* Tuition: Full-time $7022; part-time $379 per credit. One-time fee: $20. Tuition and fees vary according to course load, degree level and student's religious affiliation. *Financial support:* Scholarships/grants available. *Unit head:* Matt Newby, Director of Adult and Graduate Studies, 952-446-4224, Fax: 952-416-4349, E-mail: grad@crown.edu. *Application contact:* Nate Erickson, Enrollment Coordinator, 952-446-4370, Fax: 952-446-4349, E-mail: grad@crown.edu.

Dallas Theological Seminary, Graduate Programs, Dallas, TX 75204-6499. Offers academic ministries (Th M); Bible translation (Th M); biblical and theological studies (CGS); biblical counseling (MA, Th M); biblical exegesis and linguistics (MA); biblical exposition (PhD); biblical studies (MA); Christian education (MA, D Min); cross-cultural ministries (MA, Th M); educational leadership (Th M); evangelism and discipleship (Th M); interdisciplinary studies (Th M); media and communication (MA); media arts in ministry (Th M); ministry (D Min); New Testament studies (Th M, PhD); Old Testament studies (PhD); parachurch ministries (Th M); pastoral ministries (Th M); sacred theology (STM); theological studies (PhD); women's ministry (Th M). *Accreditation:* ATS (one or more programs are accredited). Part-time and evening/weekend programs available. *Degree requirements:* For master's, variable foreign language requirement, thesis (for some programs); for doctorate, 2 foreign languages, thesis/dissertation. *Entrance* *requirements:* Additional exam requirements/recommendations for international students: Required—TOEFL, TWE. Electronic applications accepted.

Darkei Noam Rabbinical College, Graduate Programs, Brooklyn, NY 11210.

Denver Seminary, Graduate and Professional Programs, Littleton, CO 80120. Offers apologetics (Certificate); biblical studies (MA); Christian formation and soul care (MA, Certificate); Christian studies (MA, Certificate); church and parachurch leadership (D Min); counseling licensure (MA); counseling ministry (MA); intercultural ministry (Certificate); leadership (MA, Certificate); marriage and family counseling (D Min); pastoral ministry (D Min); philosophy of religion (MA); spiritual guidance (Certificate); theology (M Div, Certificate); worship (Certificate); youth and family ministry (MA). *Accreditation:* ACA; ACIPE; ATS (one or more programs are accredited). Part-time and evening/weekend programs available. Postbaccalaureate distance learning degree programs offered. *Degree requirements:* For master's, 2 foreign languages, thesis (for some programs); for doctorate, 2 foreign languages, thesis/dissertation; for M Div, 2 foreign languages. *Entrance requirements:* For M Div, minimum undergraduate GPA of 2.5; for master's, minimum undergraduate GPA of 3.0; for doctorate, M Div, 3 years of ministry experience. Additional exam requirements/recommendations for international students: Required—TOEFL (minimum score 575 paper-based; 233 computer-based; 90 iBT). Electronic applications accepted.

Dominican House of Studies, Pontifical Faculty of the Immaculate Conception, Graduate and Professional Programs in Theology, Washington, DC 20017-1585. Offers moral theology (STL); sacred scripture (STL); systematic theology (STL); theology (M Div, STB, MA); Thomistic studies (STL). *Accreditation:* ATS (one or more programs are accredited). Part-time programs available. *Faculty:* 17 full-time (1 woman), 6 part-time/adjunct (2 women). *Students:* 67 full-time (1 woman), 20 part-time (8 women). Average age 32. *Degree requirements:* For master's, one foreign language, thesis, thesis defense; for first professional degree, 2 foreign languages, comprehensive exam; for STL, 3 foreign languages, comprehensive exam (for some programs), thesis (for some programs), lecture. *Entrance requirements:* For first professional degree, 18 credits of philosophy (36 for STB); reading knowledge of Latin; BA with minimum GPA of 3.0 (3.25 for STB); for master's, 18 credits of philosophy, reading knowledge of Latin, BA with a minimum GPA of 3.0. Additional exam requirements/recommendations for international students: Required—TOEFL (minimum score 550 paper-based; 215 computer-based; 79 iBT). *Application deadline:* For fall admission, 7/1 priority date for domestic and international students; for spring admission, 12/1 priority date for domestic and international students. Applications are processed on a rolling basis. Application fee: $50. *Expenses:* Tuition: Full-time $15,120; part-time $630 per credit hour. Required fees: $50 per semester. One-time fee: $50. *Financial support:* Career-related internships or fieldwork and Federal Work-Study available. Financial award application deadline: 6/30; financial award applicants required to submit FAFSA. *Faculty research:* Sacred scripture, moral theology, systematic theology, philosophy, languages. *Unit head:* Rev. Gabriel O'Donnell, Vice-President/Academic Dean, 202-495-3832, Fax: 202-495-3873, E-mail: dean@dhs.edu. *Application contact:* Tobias John Nathe, Registrar, 202-495-3836, Fax: 202-495-3873, E-mail: registrar@dhs.edu.

Dominican School of Philosophy and Theology, Graduate Programs, Department of Theology, Berkeley, CA 94708. Offers M Div, Certificate, M Div/MA, MA/MA. *Accreditation:* ATS (one or more programs are accredited). Part-time programs available. *Entrance requirements:* Minimum GPA of 2.5. Additional exam requirements/recommendations for international students: Required—TOEFL (minimum score 550 paper-based; 68 computer-based). *Faculty research:* Literary and historical study of scripture, Christianity in late antiquity, homiletic theory, religion and art, Christology.

Drew University, The Theological School, Madison, NJ 07940-1493. Offers M Div, MTS, STM, D Min, Certificate. *Accreditation:* ACIPE; ATS. Part-time programs available. Postbaccalaureate distance learning degree programs offered (minimal on-campus study). *Degree requirements:* For doctorate, thesis/dissertation. *Entrance requirements:* For M Div, 3 years professional ministry experience; for master's, minimum GPA of 3.0. Additional exam requirements/recommendations for international students: Required—TOEFL (minimum score 516 paper-based; 230 computer-based; 88 iBT), TWE. Electronic applications accepted. *Expenses:* Contact institution. *Faculty research:* Biblical studies, constructive theology, ecology and religion, gender and religion, race/ethnicity and religion.

Duke University, Divinity School, Durham, NC 27708-0586. Offers M Div, MTS, Th M, Th D, JD/MTS, M Div/MSW. *Accreditation:* ACIPE; ATS. Part-time programs available. *Faculty:* 40 full-time (11 women), 19 part-time/adjunct (6 women). *Students:* 502 full-time (196 women), 35 part-time (15 women); includes 107 minority (65 African Americans, 4 American Indian/Alaska Native, 21 Asian Americans or Pacific Islanders, 17 Hispanic Americans). Average age 29. 636 applicants, 62% accepted, 201 enrolled. In 2009, 145 first professional degrees, 18 master's, 1 doctorate awarded. *Degree requirements:* For master's, thesis optional; for doctorate, 2 foreign languages, thesis/dissertation; for M Div, field experience, spiritual formation, faculty evaluation. *Entrance requirements:* For M Div, 5 letters of reference, 2 essays; for master's, 5 letters of reference; for doctorate, GRE, 4 letters of reference, 2-page statement of purpose, one sample of academic writing. Additional exam requirements/recommendations for international students: Required—TOEFL (minimum score 580 paper-based; 93 iBT). *Application deadline:* For fall admission, 4/1 for domestic students, 3/1 for international students. Application fee: $50. Electronic applications accepted. *Expenses:* Contact institution. *Financial support:* In 2009–10, 495 students received support. Career-related internships or fieldwork, Federal Work-Study, institutionally sponsored loans, scholarships/grants, and field education stipends available. Financial award application deadline: 5/1; financial award applicants required to submit FAFSA. *Faculty research:* Biblical studies, historical church studies, theological studies, church ministry studies. Total annual research expenditures: $4.1 million. *Unit head:* Dr. L. Gregory Jones, Dean, 919-660-3434, Fax: 919-660-3474, E-mail: gjones@div.duke.edu. *Application contact:* Rev. McKennon Shea, Director of Admissions, 919-660-3436, Fax: 919-660-3535, E-mail: admissions@div.duke.edu.

Duquesne University, Graduate School of Liberal Arts, Department of Theology, Pittsburgh, PA 15282-0001. Offers pastoral ministry (MA); religious education (MA); systematic theology (PhD); theology (MA). Part-time and evening/weekend programs available. *Faculty:* 13 full-time (4 women). *Students:* 59 full-time (20 women), 42 part-time (36 women); includes 3 minority (2 African Americans, 1 Asian American or Pacific Islander), 12 international. Average age 35. 28 applicants, 71% accepted, 15 enrolled. In 2009, 12 master's, 5 doctorates awarded. *Degree requirements:* For master's, comprehensive exam; for doctorate, 2 foreign languages, comprehensive exam, thesis/dissertation. *Entrance requirements:* For master's and doctorate, GRE General Test. Additional exam requirements/recommendations for international students: Required—TOEFL. *Application deadline:* For fall admission, 2/1 for domestic and international students. Electronic applications accepted. *Expenses:* Tuition: Part-time $851 per credit. Required fees: $81 per credit. *Financial support:* In 2009–10, 10 teaching assistantships with full tuition reimbursements (averaging $13,000 per year) were awarded; career-related internships or fieldwork, scholarships/grants, tuition waivers (partial), and unspecified assistantships also available. Support available to part-time students. Financial award application deadline: 5/1. *Unit head:* Dr. George Worgul, Chair, 412-396-6530. *Application contact:* Dr. Marie Baird, Director, 412-396-6530.

Earlham School of Religion, Graduate Programs, Richmond, IN 47374-5360. Offers religion (MA); theology (M Div, M Min). *Accreditation:* ACIPE; ATS. Part-time programs available. Postbaccalaureate distance learning degree programs offered (minimal on-campus study). *Degree requirements:* For master's, one foreign language, comprehensive exam, thesis; for M Div, project. *Entrance requirements:* For M Div and master's, 3 references. Additional exam requirements/recommendations for international students: Required—TOEFL (minimum score 550 paper-based; 218 computer-based; 82 iBT). Electronic applications accepted. *Faculty research:* Digitizing Quaker texts, vital Quaker ministry.

Eastern Mennonite University, Eastern Mennonite Seminary, Harrisonburg, VA 22802-2462. Offers church leadership (MA); divinity (M Div); ministry studies (Certificate); online theological studies (Certificate); religion (MA); theological studies (Certificate). *Accreditation:* ATS. Part-time programs available. *Faculty:* 11 full-time (2 women), 8 part-time/adjunct (3 women). *Students:* 45 full-time (20 women), 81 part-time (33 women); includes 9 minority (5 African Americans, 4 Hispanic Americans), 6 international. In 2009, 13 first professional degrees, 9 master's awarded. *Degree requirements:* For master's, thesis (for some programs); for M Div, thesis/dissertation (for some programs), supervised field education. *Entrance requirements:* For M Div and master's, minimum GPA of 2.5. Additional exam requirements/recommendations for international students: Required—TOEFL (minimum score 550 paper-based; 213 computer-based). *Application deadline:* For fall admission, 6/15 priority date for domestic and international students; for winter admission, 11/15 priority date for domestic and international students; for spring admission, 3/15 priority date for domestic and international students. Applications are processed on a rolling basis. Application fee: $25. *Expenses:* Contact institution. *Financial support:* Application deadline: 6/30. *Faculty research:* Spiritual direction and culture of call, leadership coaching: an approach to leadership in a culture of call, clarity of call in the probationary process for United Methodist clergy in Virginia, EMS women's experiences of culture of call efforts, practices of excellent and fruitful Mennonite pastoral ministry. *Unit head:* Dr. Ervin R. Stutzman, Dean, 540-432-4261, Fax: 540-432-4444, E-mail: stutzerv@emu.edu. *Application contact:* Don A. Yoder, Director of Seminary and Graduate Admissions, 540-432-4257, Fax: 540-432-4598, E-mail: yoderda@emu.edu.

Eastern University, Palmer Theological Seminary, Wynnewood, PA 19096-3430. Offers M Div, MTS, D Min, M Div/MBA, M Div/MSW. *Accreditation:* ACIPE; ATS; MSA/CIHE. Part-time and evening/weekend programs available. *Entrance requirements:* Additional exam requirements/recommendations for international students: Required—TOEFL.

Ecumenical Theological Seminary, Professional Program, Detroit, MI 48201. Offers M Div. *Accreditation:* ACIPE; ATS.

Eden Theological Seminary, Graduate and Professional Programs, St. Louis, MO 63119-3192. Offers M Div, MAPS, MTS, D Min. *Accreditation:* ACIPE; ATS. *Degree requirements:* For master's, comprehensive exam (for some programs), thesis (for some programs), 2 oral exams; for doctorate, professional essay, supervised in-service projects; for M Div, thesis/dissertation optional, 2 oral exams. *Entrance requirements:* For M Div and master's, interview, minimum GPA of 2.7; for doctorate, interview, minimum GPA of 3.0. Additional exam requirements/recommendations for international students: Required—TOEFL (minimum score 550 paper-based). Electronic applications accepted. *Faculty research:* Psalms, pastoral ethics, historical Jesus, leadership roles, congregational life.

Emmanuel School of Religion, Graduate and Professional Programs, Johnson City, TN 37601-9438. Offers Christian care and counseling (M Div); Christian doctrine (MAR); Christian education (M Div); church history (MAR); ministry (D Min); New Testament (MAR); Old Testament (MAR); urban ministry (M Div); world missions (M Div). *Accreditation:* ACIPE; ATS. Part-time programs available. *Faculty:* 10 full-time (2 women), 5 part-time/adjunct (0 women). *Students:* 108 full-time (27 women), 48 part-time (13 women). Average age 32. *Degree requirements:* For master's, 2 foreign languages, thesis; for M Div, 2 foreign languages, thesis/dissertation or alternative. *Entrance requirements:* For doctorate, GRE General Test, Minnesota Multiphasic Personality Inventory, M Div or equivalent. *Application deadline:* For fall admission, 8/1 priority date for domestic students. Applications are processed on a rolling basis. Application fee: $25. *Expenses:* Tuition: Full-time $7800; part-time $325 per credit hour. Required fees: $137.50 per semester. One-time fee: $240. Tuition and fees vary according to course load. *Financial support:* Teaching assistantships with partial tuition reimbursements, career-related internships or fieldwork, institutionally sponsored loans, scholarships/grants, and tuition waivers (partial) available. Support available to part-time students. Financial award application deadline: 4/1; financial award applicants required to submit FAFSA. *Faculty research:* Theology of Old Testament prophets, spiritual formation for Christian leaders, history of African churches and religions, social world of early Christianity, lay pastoral counseling. Total annual research expenditures: $12,000. *Unit head:* Dr. Rollin A. Ramsaran, Dean and Professor of New Testament, 423-461-1524, Fax: 423-926-6198, E-mail: ramsaranr@esr.edu. *Application contact:* Shelley Gasser, Administrative Assistant for Admissions, 423-461-1535, Fax: 423-926-6198, E-mail: gassers@esr.edu.

Emory University, Candler School of Theology, Atlanta, GA 30322. Offers formation and witness (M Div); leadership in church and community (M Div); religion and race (M Div); religion, health and science (M Div); scripture and interpretation (M Div); society and personality (M Div); theology (MTS, Th M, Th D); theology and ethics (M Div); theology and the arts (M Div); traditions of the church (M Div); women and religion (M Div); JD/M Div; JD/MTS; M Div/MBA; M Div/MPH; MBA/MTS; MTS/MPH. *Accreditation:* ACIPE; ATS. Part-time programs available. *Degree requirements:* For master's, thesis optional; for doctorate, thesis/dissertation; for M Div, thesis/dissertation optional. *Entrance requirements:* For M Div, minimum undergraduate GPA of 2.75; for master's, minimum undergraduate GPA of 3.0; for doctorate, GRE, M Div, 8 units of course work in clinical pastoral education. Additional exam requirements/recommendations for international students: Required—TOEFL (minimum score 600 paper-based; 250 computer-based; 95 iBT). Electronic applications accepted. *Expenses:* Contact institution. *Faculty research:* Biblical studies, church history, ministry practice, pastoral care and ethics.

Episcopal Divinity School, Graduate and Professional Programs, Cambridge, MA 02138-3494. Offers M Div, MATS, D Min, CTS. *Accreditation:* ACIPE; ATS (one or more programs are accredited). Part-time programs available. *Faculty:* 15 full-time (8 women), 9 part-time/adjunct (5 women). *Students:* 54 full-time (32 women), 37 part-time (27 women); includes 13 minority (8 African Americans, 1 American Indian/Alaska Native, 2 Asian Americans or Pacific Islanders, 2 Hispanic Americans), 10 international. Average age 43. 67 applicants, 79% accepted, 42 enrolled. In 2009, 16 M Divs, 5 master's, 3 doctorates, 8 other advanced degrees awarded. *Degree requirements:* For master's, thesis optional; for doctorate, thesis/dissertation, project; for M Div, thesis/dissertation optional, fieldwork. *Entrance requirements:* For M Div and master's, GRE General Test or MAT, 2 interviews, 4 letters of recommendation, 1500-word autobiographical statement; for doctorate, interview, M Div or equivalent, 3 letters of recommendation, 1500-word autobiographical statement; for CTS, GRE General Test, MAT, or advanced degree; interview; 2 letters of recommendation, 1000-word autobiographical statement. Additional exam requirements/recommendations for international students: Required—TOEFL. *Application deadline:* For fall admission, 3/5 for domestic students; for spring admission, 11/6 for domestic students. Applications are processed on a rolling basis. Application fee: $50. *Expenses:* Tuition: Full-time $12,500; part-time $6250 per year. Tuition and fees vary according to degree level, campus/location and program. *Financial support:* In 2009–10, 63 students received support. Career-related internships or fieldwork and scholarships/grants available. Support available to part-time students. Financial award application deadline: 5/1; financial award applicants required to submit FAFSA. *Faculty research:* Anglican, global, and ecumenical studies; congregational studies; feminist liberation theologies. *Unit head:* Katherine Ragsdale, President and Dean, 617-868-3450 Ext. 511, Fax: 617-864-5385, E-mail: kragsdale@eds.edu. *Application contact:* Christopher J. Medeiros, Director of Admissions, Recruitment, and Financial Aid, 617-682-1507, Fax: 617-864-5385, E-mail: admissions@eds.edu.

Erskine Theological Seminary, Graduate and Professional Programs, Due West, SC 29639-0668. Offers M Div, MACE, MACM, MAPM, MATS, MCM, D Min. *Accreditation:* ATS. Part-time and evening/weekend programs available. *Degree requirements:* For doctorate, thesis/dissertation; for M Div, 2 foreign languages. *Entrance requirements:* For master's, Myers-Briggs Type Indicator, Taylor Johnson Temperament Analysis, Ministry Specialties Test (MACM), minimum GPA of 3.0, interview with committee (MACM); for doctorate, minimum GPA of 3.0 during M Div. Additional exam requirements/recommendations for international students: Required—TOEFL (minimum score 550 paper-based). Electronic applications accepted. *Faculty research:* Church administration, biblical studies.

Evangelical Seminary of Puerto Rico, Graduate and Professional Programs, San Juan, PR 00925-2207. Offers M Div, MAR, D Min. *Accreditation:* ATS. Part-time programs available.

Theology

Evangelical Seminary of Puerto Rico (continued)

Degree requirements: For master's, comprehensive exam; for M Div, integration essay. *Entrance requirements:* For M Div, Admission Test for Graduate Studies, denominational endorsement; for doctorate, 3 years experience in ministry service. Additional exam requirements/recommendations for international students: Required—TOEFL, EXADEP. *Faculty research:* Protestantism in Puerto Rico.

Evangelical Theological Seminary, Graduate and Professional Programs, Myerstown, PA 17067-1212. Offers Biblical studies (MAR); congregational ministry (M Div); global and contextual studies (M Div, MAR); historical and theological studies (MAR); interdisciplinary studies (MAR); marriage and family counseling (M Div); marriage and family therapy (MA); New Testament (MAR); Old Testament (MAR); spiritual formation (MAR); teaching ministry (M Div); youth ministry (M Div). *Accreditation:* ATS (one or more programs are accredited). Part-time programs available. Postbaccalaureate distance learning degree programs offered (minimal on-campus study). *Degree requirements:* For master's, 2 foreign languages; for M Div, 2 foreign languages, ministry internship. *Entrance requirements:* For M Div and master's, minimum GPA of 2.5. Additional exam requirements/recommendations for international students: Required—TOEFL (minimum score 550 paper-based; 213 computer-based). *Faculty research:* Literary form and structure within the Hebrew and Greek scriptures, Wesley studies, esoteric biblical languages, the Mosaic law and the Christian, ethics.

Faith Baptist Bible College and Theological Seminary, Graduate Program, Ankeny, IA 50023. Offers biblical studies (MA); pastoral studies (M Div); pastoral training (MA); religion (MA); theological studies (MA). Part-time programs available. *Faculty:* 4 full-time (0 women), 4 part-time/adjunct (0 women). *Students:* 31 full-time (6 women), 35 part-time (8 women); includes 2 minority (1 African American, 1 Asian American or Pacific Islander), 2 international. Average age 29. In 2009, 9 first professional degrees, 12 master's awarded. *Degree requirements:* For master's, thesis or alternative; for M Div, 2 foreign languages. *Entrance requirements:* Additional exam requirements/recommendations for international students: Required—TOEFL (minimum score 550 paper-based; 197 computer-based). *Application deadline:* For fall admission, 8/1 priority date for domestic students, 8/1 for international students; for spring admission, 12/15 for domestic and international students. Applications are processed on a rolling basis. Application fee: $25. *Financial support:* Career-related internships or fieldwork and scholarships/grants available. Support available to part-time students. Financial award application deadline: 3/1; financial award applicants required to submit FAFSA. *Faculty research:* Baptist theology, American church history. *Unit head:* Dr. Ernest Schmidt, Dean of Seminary, 515-964-0601, E-mail: schmidte@faith.edu. *Application contact:* Patrick Odle, Vice President of Enrollment, 888-FAITH4U, Fax: 515-964-1638, E-mail: odlep@faith.edu.

Faith Evangelical Lutheran Seminary, Graduate and Professional Programs, Tacoma, WA 98407. Offers B Th, M Div, MCM, MTS, D Min. Part-time and evening/weekend programs available. Postbaccalaureate distance learning degree programs offered (minimal on-campus study). *Degree requirements:* For master's, thesis optional; for doctorate, thesis/dissertation; for first professional degree, thesis/dissertation (for some programs). *Entrance requirements:* For first professional degree and master's, minimum undergraduate GPA of 2.7; for doctorate, minimum graduate GPA of 3.0. Additional exam requirements/recommendations for international students: Required—TOEFL (minimum score 550 paper-based; 213 computer-based).

Fordham University, Graduate School of Arts and Sciences, Department of Theology, New York, NY 10458. Offers MA, PhD. Part-time and evening/weekend programs available. *Faculty:* 22 full-time (7 women). *Students:* 8 full-time (4 women), 58 part-time (21 women); includes 4 minority (1 American Indian/Alaska Native, 2 Asian Americans or Pacific Islanders, 1 Hispanic American), 1 international. Average age 36. 89 applicants, 42% accepted, 13 enrolled. In 2009, 3 master's, 5 doctorates awarded. Terminal master's awarded for partial completion of doctoral program. *Degree requirements:* For master's, one foreign language, comprehensive exam; for doctorate, 2 foreign languages, comprehensive exam, thesis/dissertation. *Entrance requirements:* For master's and doctorate, GRE General Test. Additional exam requirements/recommendations for international students: Required—TOEFL (minimum score 650 paper-based; 280 computer-based). *Application deadline:* For fall admission, 1/4 priority date for domestic students; for spring admission, 11/1 for domestic students. Application fee: $70. Electronic applications accepted. *Financial support:* In 2009–10, 28 students received support, including 2 fellowships with tuition reimbursements available (averaging $19,800 per year), 17 research assistantships with tuition reimbursements available (averaging $18,541 per year), 9 teaching assistantships with tuition reimbursements available (averaging $20,711 per year); institutionally sponsored loans, tuition waivers (full and partial), and unspecified assistantships also available. Support available to part-time students. Financial award application deadline: 1/4. *Faculty research:* History of Christian tradition, contemporary systematic theology, theological/feminist ethics, American Catholicism, Biblical exegesis and theology. Total annual research expenditures: $10,000. *Unit head:* Dr. Terrence Tilley, Chair, 718-817-3245, E-mail: ttilley@fordham.edu. *Application contact:* Charlene Dundie, Director of Graduate Admissions, 718-817-4420, Fax: 718-817-3566, E-mail: dundie@fordham.edu.

Franciscan School of Theology, Graduate and Professional Programs, Berkeley, CA 94709-1294. Offers M Div, MA, MAMC, MTS. *Accreditation:* ATS (one or more programs are accredited). Part-time programs available. *Degree requirements:* For master's, one foreign language, thesis. *Entrance requirements:* For master's, GRE General Test (MA). Additional exam requirements/recommendations for international students: Required—TOEFL (minimum score 550 paper-based; 213 computer-based). *Faculty research:* Church history, multicultural ministries, ethics and morality, catechesis, biblical studies.

Franciscan University of Steubenville, Graduate Programs, Department of Theology, Steubenville, OH 43952-1763. Offers theology and Christian ministry (MA). Part-time programs available. Postbaccalaureate distance learning degree programs offered (minimal on-campus study). *Degree requirements:* For master's, comprehensive exam. *Entrance requirements:* For master's, minimum undergraduate GPA of 3.0.

Freed-Hardeman University, School of Biblical Studies, Program in Divinity, Henderson, TN 38340-2399. Offers M Div. Part-time programs available. *Entrance requirements:* Additional exam requirements/recommendations for international students: Required—TOEFL (minimum score 500 paper-based; 173 computer-based).

Freed-Hardeman University, School of Biblical Studies, Program in New Testament, Henderson, TN 38340-2399. Offers MA. Part-time programs available. *Degree requirements:* For master's, one foreign language, comprehensive exam, thesis. *Entrance requirements:* For master's, GRE General Test or MAT. Additional exam requirements/recommendations for international students: Required—TOEFL (minimum score 500 paper-based; 173 computer-based).

Friends University, Graduate School, Division of Science, Arts, and Education, Program in Christian Ministry, Wichita, KS 67213. Offers MACM. Evening/weekend programs available. *Entrance requirements:* Additional exam requirements/recommendations for international students: Required—TOEFL (minimum score 560 paper-based; 220 computer-based). Electronic applications accepted.

Fuller Theological Seminary, Graduate School of Theology, Pasadena, CA 91182. Offers Christian leadership (MACL); evangelism (MA); family life education (MA); ministry (M Div, D Min); pastoral ministry (MA); recovery ministry (MA); theology (MAT, Th M, PhD); worship music ministry (MA); worship, theology, and the arts (MA); youth, family, and culture (MA). M Div offered jointly with Denver Conservative Baptist Seminary. *Accreditation:* ACIPE; ATS (one or more programs are accredited). Part-time and evening/weekend programs available. *Degree requirements:* For doctorate, variable foreign language requirement, thesis/dissertation; for M Div, 2 foreign languages. *Entrance requirements:* For doctorate, GRE General Test. *Faculty research:* New Testament, Old Testament, systematic theology, history, practical theology.

Gardner-Webb University, School of Divinity, Boiling Springs, NC 28017. Offers biblical studies (M Div); Christian education and formation (M Div); ministry (D Min); missiology (M Div); pastoral care and counseling (M Div); pastoral studies (M Div); M Div/MA; M Div/MBA. *Accreditation:* ACIPE; ATS. Part-time programs available. *Degree requirements:* For M Div, 2 foreign languages. *Entrance requirements:* For M Div, minimum GPA of 2.0; for doctorate, minimum GPA of 2.75. *Application deadline:* For fall admission, 8/1 priority date for domestic students; for spring admission, 12/15 priority date for domestic students. Applications are processed on a rolling basis. Application fee: $25. *Expenses:* Contact institution. *Financial support:* Fellowships, institutionally sponsored loans and unspecified assistantships available. Support available to part-time students. Financial award application deadline: 5/15. *Faculty research:* Jewish Christian dialogue, Islam. *Unit head:* Dr. Robert W. Canoy, Dean, 704-406-4400, Fax: 704-406-3935, E-mail: rcanoy@gardner-webb.edu. *Application contact:* Jeremy Fern, Director of Admissions, 704-406-3205, Fax: 704-406-3935, E-mail: jfern@gardner-webb.edu.

Garrett-Evangelical Theological Seminary, Graduate and Professional Programs, Evanston, IL 60201-3298. Offers Bible and culture (PhD); Christian education (MA); Christian education and congregational studies (PhD); contemporary theology and culture (PhD); divinity (M Div); ethics, church, and society (MA); liturgical studies (PhD); ministry (D Min); music ministry (MA); pastoral care and counseling (MA); pastoral theology, personality, and culture (PhD); spiritual formation and evangelism (MA); theological studies (MTS); M Div/MSW. *Accreditation:* ACIPE; ATS (one or more programs are accredited). Part-time programs available. *Degree requirements:* For master's, thesis (for some programs); for doctorate, thesis/dissertation. *Entrance requirements:* For doctorate, GRE (PhD). Additional exam requirements/recommendations for international students: Required—TOEFL (minimum score 560 paper-based; 230 computer-based). Electronic applications accepted.

General Theological Seminary, Graduate and Professional Programs, New York, NY 10011-4977. Offers Anglican studies (STM, Th D, Certificate); ascetical theology (Certificate); biblical studies (Certificate); congregational development (Certificate); divinity (M Div); historical and theological studies (Certificate); spiritual direction (MASD, STM, Certificate); theology (MA). *Accreditation:* ACIPE; ATS. Part-time and evening/weekend programs available. Terminal master's awarded for partial completion of doctoral program. *Degree requirements:* For master's, thesis; for doctorate, 2 foreign languages, thesis/dissertation. *Entrance requirements:* For M Div, GRE General Test, bishop's endorsement; for master's, GRE General Test; for doctorate, GRE, M Div or MA. Additional exam requirements/recommendations for international students: Required—TOEFL. *Faculty research:* Liturgy, New Testament, ethics, history, ecumenical relations.

George Fox University, George Fox Evangelical Seminary, Newberg, OR 97132-2697. Offers Biblical studies (M Div); chaplaincy (M Div); Christian earth keeping (M Div); ministry (D Min), including global missional leadership, leadership and spiritual formation, semiotics and future studies; ministry leadership (MA); pastoral studies (M Div); spiritual formation (M Div, MA); spiritual formation and discipleship (Certificate); theological studies (MA). *Accreditation:* ACIPE; ATS. Part-time programs available. Postbaccalaureate distance learning degree programs offered (minimal on-campus study). *Faculty:* 7 full-time (2 women), 16 part-time/adjunct (8 women). *Students:* 50 full-time (16 women), 292 part-time (88 women); includes 25 minority (6 African Americans, 2 American Indian/Alaska Native, 13 Asian Americans or Pacific Islanders, 4 Hispanic Americans), 5 international. Average age 41. 152 applicants, 88% accepted, 86 enrolled. In 2009, 14 first professional degrees, 8 master's, 12 doctorates, 4 other advanced degrees awarded. *Degree requirements:* For master's, variable foreign language requirement, thesis optional, internship; for doctorate, comprehensive exam (for some programs), thesis/dissertation, internship. *Entrance requirements:* For master's, resume, admission statement, three references (one pastoral, one academic or professional, one personal), one official transcript from each college or university attended; for doctorate, resume, 3 references (1 professional, 1 academic, 1 personal). Additional exam requirements/recommendations for international students: Required—TOEFL (minimum score 577 paper-based; 233 computer-based; 90 iBT). *Application deadline:* For fall admission, 7/1 for domestic and international students; for winter admission, 11/1 for domestic and international students; for spring admission, 4/1 for domestic and international students. Applications are processed on a rolling basis. Application fee: $40. Electronic applications accepted. *Expenses:* Contact institution. *Financial support:* Career-related internships or fieldwork and scholarships/grants available. Financial award application deadline: 5/1; financial award applicants required to submit FAFSA. *Unit head:* Dr. Chuck Conniry, Vice President/Dean, 503-554-6152, E-mail: cconniry@georgefox.edu. *Application contact:* Sheila Bartlett, Admissions Counselor, 800-631-0921, Fax: 503-554-6122, E-mail: seminary@georgefox.edu.

Georgetown University, Graduate School of Arts and Sciences, Department of Theology, Washington, DC 20057. Offers PhD.

Georgian Court University, School of Arts and Humanities, Lakewood, NJ 08701-2697. Offers Catholic school leadership (Certificate); parish business management (Certificate); pastoral administration (Certificate); pastoral ministry (Certificate); religious education (Certificate); theology (MA, Certificate). Part-time and evening/weekend programs available. *Faculty:* 3 full-time (2 women), 1 (woman) part-time/adjunct. *Students:* 57 part-time (39 women); includes 8 minority (3 African Americans, 1 Asian American or Pacific Islander, 4 Hispanic Americans). Average age 52. 20 applicants, 100% accepted, 14 enrolled. In 2009, 6 master's awarded. *Degree requirements:* For master's, thesis (for some programs). *Entrance requirements:* For master's, 3 letters of recommendation. Additional exam requirements/recommendations for international students: Required—TOEFL (minimum score 550 paper-based; 213 computer-based). *Application deadline:* For fall admission, 8/1 priority date for domestic students, 4/1 for international students; for spring admission, 1/1 priority date for domestic students, 7/1 for international students. Applications are processed on a rolling basis. Application fee: $40. Electronic applications accepted. *Expenses:* Tuition: Full-time $12,510; part-time $695 per credit. Required fees: $416 per year. Tuition and fees vary according to campus/location. *Financial support:* Scholarships/grants, health care benefits, and unspecified assistantships available. Financial award application deadline: 4/15; financial award applicants required to submit FAFSA. *Unit head:* Dr. Linda James, Dean, 732-987-2617, Fax: 732-987-2007. *Application contact:* Eugene Soltys, Director of Graduate Admissions, 732-987-2770, Fax: 732-987-2084, E-mail: graduateadmissions@georgian.edu.

Global University, Graduate School of Theology, Springfield, MO 65804. Offers biblical studies (MA); divinity (M Div); ministerial studies (MA), including education, leadership, missions, New Testament, Old Testament. Part-time and evening/weekend programs available. Postbaccalaureate distance learning degree programs offered (no on-campus study). *Degree requirements:* For master's, thesis (for some programs). *Entrance requirements:* For M Div, minimum undergraduate GPA of 3.0; for master's, minimum undergraduate GPA of 3.0, 15 undergraduate credit hours of course work in Bible or theology. Electronic applications accepted. *Faculty research:* Higher education, cross-cultural missions.

Golden Gate Baptist Theological Seminary, Graduate and Professional Programs, Mill Valley, CA 94941-3197. Offers divinity (M Div); early childhood education (Certificate); education leadership (MAEL, Diploma); ministry (D Min); theological studies (MTS); theology (Th M); youth ministry (Certificate). *Accreditation:* ACIPE; ATS (one or more programs are accredited). Part-time and evening/weekend programs available. *Degree requirements:* For master's, thesis (for some programs); for doctorate, 2 foreign languages, thesis/dissertation; for M Div, 2 foreign languages. *Entrance requirements:* For doctorate, MAT. Additional exam requirements/recommendations for international students: Required—TOEFL (minimum score 550 paper-based; 213 computer-based). Electronic applications accepted.

Gordon-Conwell Theological Seminary, Graduate and Professional Programs, South Hamilton, MA 01982. Offers Biblical languages (MABL); church history (MACH); counseling (MACO); ministry (D Min); missions/evangelism (MAME); New Testament (MANT); Old Testament (MAOT); religion (MAR); theology (M Div, MATH, Th M, Th D). *Accreditation:* ACIPE; ATS (one or more programs are accredited). Part-time and evening/weekend programs available. *Degree requirements:* For master's, one foreign language, thesis optional; for doctorate, 2 foreign languages, thesis/dissertation; for M Div, 2 foreign languages. *Entrance requirements:* For M Div and master's, minimum GPA of 2.5; for doctorate, minimum GPA of 3.0.

Grace Theological Seminary, Graduate and Professional Programs, Winona Lake, IN 46590-9907. Offers biblical studies (Certificate); camp administration (MA); counseling (M Div); exegetical studies (MA); intercultural studies (M Div, MA); local church studies (MA); pastoral studies (M Div); theological studies (MA); theology (D Min, Diploma). Part-time programs available. Postbaccalaureate distance learning degree programs offered (no on-campus study). *Degree requirements:* For master's, thesis optional; for doctorate, 2 foreign languages, thesis/dissertation; for M Div, 2 foreign languages, thesis/dissertation optional. *Entrance requirements:* For M Div and master's, MAT, minimum GPA of 2.5. Electronic applications accepted. *Faculty research:* Biblical theology, language, and church ministries.

Grace University, College of Graduate Studies, Bible Department, Omaha, NE 68108. Offers MA. *Degree requirements:* For master's, thesis optional. *Entrance requirements:* For master's, minimum undergraduate GPA of 3.0. Electronic applications accepted.

Graduate Theological Union, Graduate Programs, Berkeley, CA 94709-1212. Offers art and religion (MA, PhD, Th D); biblical languages (MA); Biblical studies (PhD, Th D); biblical studies (MA); Buddhist studies (MA); Christian spirituality (MA, PhD, Th D); cultural and historical studies of religions (MA, PhD, Th D); ethics and social theory (PhD, Th D); history (MA, PhD, Th D); homiletics (MA, PhD, Th D); interdisciplinary studies (PhD, Th D); Jewish studies (MA, PhD, Th D, Certificate); liturgical studies (MA, PhD, Th D); Near Eastern religions (PhD, Th D); Orthodox Christian studies (MA); religion and psychology (MA, PhD, Th D); religion and society/ethics and social theory (MA); systematic and philosophical theology (MA, PhD, Th D). *Accreditation:* ATS. Terminal master's awarded for partial completion of doctoral program. *Degree requirements:* For master's, one foreign language, thesis; for doctorate, one foreign language, comprehensive exam, thesis/dissertation. *Entrance requirements:* For master's, GRE General Test; for doctorate, GRE General Test, MA or M Div. Additional exam requirements/recommendations for international students: Required—TOEFL. Electronic applications accepted.

Grand Rapids Theological Seminary of Cornerstone University, Graduate Programs, Grand Rapids, MI 49525-5897. Offers biblical counseling (MA); Biblical counseling (M Div); chaplaincy (M Div); Christian education (M Div, MA); intercultural studies (M Div, MA); New Testament (MA, Th M); Old Testament (MA, Th M); pastoral studies (M Div); systematic theology (MA); theology (Th M). *Accreditation:* ATS. Part-time programs available. Postbaccalaureate distance learning degree programs offered (minimal on-campus study). *Entrance requirements:* Additional exam requirements/recommendations for international students: Required—TOEFL (minimum score 577 paper-based; 233 computer-based; 90 iBT). Electronic applications accepted.

Harding University Graduate School of Religion, Graduate Programs, Memphis, TN 38117-5499. Offers Christian ministry (MA); counseling (MA); ministry (M Div, D Min); religion (MA). *Accreditation:* ATS. Part-time programs available. Postbaccalaureate distance learning degree programs offered (minimal on-campus study). *Degree requirements:* For master's, variable foreign language requirement, thesis (for some programs); for doctorate, one foreign language, thesis/dissertation; for M Div, 2 foreign languages, thesis/dissertation optional. *Entrance requirements:* For M Div, GRE General Test (for graduates of non-accredited schools), minimum GPA of 2.5; for master's, minimum GPA of 2.7; for doctorate, minimum GPA of 3.0. Additional exam requirements/recommendations for international students: Required—TOEFL (minimum score 550 paper-based; 213 computer-based; 79 iBT). Electronic applications accepted.

Hardin-Simmons University, Graduate School, Logsdon School of Theology, Abilene, TX 79698-0001. Offers M Div, MA, D Min. Part-time and evening/weekend programs available. *Faculty:* 18 full-time (2 women), 3 part-time/adjunct (2 women). *Students:* 59 full-time (17 women), 64 part-time (14 women); includes 14 minority (3 African Americans, 2 American Indian/Alaska Native, 9 Hispanic Americans). Average age 32. 41 applicants, 98% accepted, 23 enrolled. In 2009, 15 first professional degrees, 3 master's awarded. *Entrance requirements:* Additional exam requirements/recommendations for international students: Required—TOEFL (minimum score 550 paper-based; 213 computer-based; 75 iBT). *Application deadline:* For fall admission, 8/15 priority date for domestic students, 4/1 for international students; for spring admission, 1/5 priority date for domestic students, 9/1 for international students. Applications are processed on a rolling basis. Application fee: $50. *Expenses:* Tuition: Full-time $11,430; part-time $635 per credit hour. Required fees: $650; $110 per semester. Tuition and fees vary according to degree level. *Financial support:* In 2009–10, 99 students received support; fellowships, scholarships/grants available. Support available to part-time students. Financial award application deadline: 6/30; financial award applicants required to submit FAFSA. *Unit head:* Dr. Thomas V. Brisco, Dean, 325-670-1266, Fax: 325-670-1406, E-mail: tbrisco@hsutx.edu. *Application contact:* Dr. Gary Stanlake, Dean of Graduate Studies, 325-670-1298, Fax: 325-670-1564, E-mail: gradoff@hsutx.edu.

Hardin-Simmons University, Graduate School, Logsdon School of Theology, Logsdon Seminary, Seminary Program in Theology, Abilene, TX 79698-0001. Offers M Div. *Accreditation:* ATS. Part-time programs available. *Faculty:* 15 full-time (1 woman), 3 part-time/adjunct (2 women). *Students:* 38 full-time (9 women), 41 part-time (8 women); includes 11 minority (2 African Americans, 2 American Indian/Alaska Native, 7 Hispanic Americans). Average age 32. 19 applicants, 95% accepted, 13 enrolled. In 2009, 15 M Divs awarded. *Degree requirements:* For M Div, 2 foreign languages, chapel/spiritual formations, colloquium, ministry retreat and formation conferences. *Entrance requirements:* Minimum GPA of 2.0, interview, 3 letters of recommendation. Additional exam requirements/recommendations for international students: Required—TOEFL (minimum score 550 paper-based; 213 computer-based; 75 iBT). *Application deadline:* For fall admission, 8/15 priority date for domestic students, 4/1 for international students; for spring admission, 1/5 priority date for domestic students, 9/1 for international students. Applications are processed on a rolling basis. Application fee: $50. *Expenses:* Tuition: Full-time $11,430; part-time $635 per credit hour. Required fees: $650; $110 per semester. Tuition and fees vary according to degree level. *Financial support:* In 2009–10, 59 students received support; fellowships, career-related internships or fieldwork and scholarships/grants available. Support available to part-time students. Financial award application deadline: 6/30; financial award applicants required to submit FAFSA. *Faculty research:* Hebrew grammar, history of Christian education, training of ministers into the twenty-first century, role of women in Old Testament, contemporary ethical issues, Ricouer in contemporary theology. *Unit head:* Dr. Robert Ellis, Director, 325-670-5841, E-mail: rellis@hsutx.edu. *Application contact:* Dr. Gary Stanlake, Dean of Graduate Studies, 325-670-1298, Fax: 325-670-1564, E-mail: gradoff@hsutx.edu.

Hartford Seminary, Graduate Programs, Hartford, CT 06105-2279. Offers black ministry (Certificate); Islamic studies (MA); ministerios Hispanos (Certificate); ministry (D Min); religious studies (MA); women's leadership institute (Certificate). *Accreditation:* ATS (one or more programs are accredited). Part-time and evening/weekend programs available. Postbaccalaureate distance learning degree programs offered (no on-campus study). *Degree requirements:* For master's, thesis optional, oral exam; for doctorate, thesis/dissertation, oral exam. *Entrance requirements:* For doctorate, experience in ministry, M Div. Additional exam requirements/recommendations for international students: Required—TOEFL (minimum score 550 paper-based; 213 computer-based; 80 iBT). *Faculty research:* Liturgy and social justice, professional leadership in ministry, congregational studies, Christian-Muslim relations, American religion.

Harvard University, Harvard Divinity School, Cambridge, MA 02138. Offers M Div, MTS, Th M, Th D. PhD offered by the Harvard Graduate School of Arts and Sciences. *Accreditation:* ACIPE; ATS. *Faculty:* 30 full-time (11 women), 51 part-time/adjunct (21 women). *Students:* 384 full-time (208 women); includes 88 minority (36 African Americans, 5 American Indian/Alaska Native, 20 Asian Americans or Pacific Islanders, 27 Hispanic Americans), 33 international. Average age 26. 514 applicants, 42% accepted, 140 enrolled. In 2009, 62 M Divs, 124 master's, 6 doctorates awarded. *Degree requirements:* For master's, one foreign language, thesis (for some programs); for doctorate, 3 foreign languages, comprehensive exam, thesis/dissertation; for M Div, one foreign language, thesis/dissertation, field education. *Entrance requirements:* For M Div, master's, and doctorate, GRE General Test. Additional exam requirements/recommendations for international students: Required—TOEFL (minimum score 600 paper-based; 250 computer-based; 100 iBT). *Application deadline:* For fall admission, 1/11 for domestic and international students. Application fee: $75. Electronic applications accepted. *Expenses:* Contact institution. *Financial support:* In 2009–10, 346 students received support, including 346 fellowships with tuition reimbursements available (averaging $25,262 per year); teaching assistantships, career-related internships or fieldwork, Federal Work-Study, and scholarships/grants also available. Support available to part-time students. Financial award application deadline: 2/1; financial award applicants required to submit FAFSA. *Faculty research:* Theology, women's studies, history, comparative religion. *Unit head:* William A. Graham, Dean of the Faculty of Divinity, 917-495-4513, Fax: 617-496-8026. *Application contact:* Loida Feliz, Director of Admissions, 617-495-5796, Fax: 617-495-0345, E-mail: admissions@hds.harvard.edu.

Hebrew College, Rabbinical School, Newton Centre, MA 02459. Offers MA. *Entrance requirements:* For master's, interview. Additional exam requirements/recommendations for international students: Required—TOEFL.

Hebrew Union College–Jewish Institute of Religion, Rabbinical School, New York, NY 10012-1186. Offers MAHL. *Degree requirements:* For MAHL, one foreign language, thesis/dissertation, fieldwork, sermons. *Entrance requirements:* GRE, language exam, minimum GPA of 3.0, minimum 2 years of college-level Hebrew. Additional exam requirements/recommendations for international students: Required—TOEFL. *Faculty research:* Philosophy and theology, Bible, Hebrew, pastoral care, history and Rabbinics.

Hebrew Union College–Jewish Institute of Religion, Rabbinic School, Cincinnati, OH 45220-2488. Offers MAHL. *Accreditation:* ACIPE. *Degree requirements:* For MAHL, one foreign language, thesis/dissertation. *Entrance requirements:* GRE General Test, Hebrew competency exam, interview, psychological test. *Faculty research:* Comprehensive Aramaic lexicon, four-volume history (German Jews and modern times).

Hebrew Union College–Jewish Institute of Religion, School of Graduate Studies, Program in Pastoral Counseling, New York, NY 10012-1186. Offers D Min. *Accreditation:* ACIPE. *Degree requirements:* For doctorate, thesis/dissertation. *Entrance requirements:* For doctorate, M Div (or higher), ordination/certification for ministry. Additional exam requirements/recommendations for international students: Required—TOEFL. *Expenses:* Contact institution. *Faculty research:* Philosophy and theology, Bible, Hebrew, pastoral care, history and Rabbinics.

Hebrew Union College–Jewish Institute of Religion, School of Rabbinical Studies, Los Angeles, CA 90007-3796. Offers MAHL. *Accreditation:* ACIPE. *Degree requirements:* For MAHL, one foreign language, thesis/dissertation, Hebrew. *Entrance requirements:* GRE General Test, interview, minimum undergraduate GPA of 3.0, 2 years of college-level Hebrew. Additional exam requirements/recommendations for international students: Required—TOEFL (minimum score 550 paper-based). Electronic applications accepted.

Heritage Baptist College and Heritage Theological Seminary, Program in Theological Studies, Cambridge, ON N3C 3T2, Canada. Offers chaplaincy (M Div); counselling (M Div); general (M Div); ministry (D Min); pastoral (M Div); research (M Div); theological studies (MA, Certificate). *Accreditation:* ATS.

Holy Apostles College and Seminary, Department of Theology, Cromwell, CT 06416-2005. Offers bioethics (MA, Certificate, Post Master's Certificate); church history (MA, Certificate, Post Master's Certificate); dogmatic theology (MA, Certificate, Post Master's Certificate); liturgical music (MA, Certificate, Post Master's Certificate); liturgy (MA, Certificate, Post Master's Certificate); moral theology (MA, Certificate, Post Master's Certificate); philosophical theology (MA, Certificate, Post Master's Certificate); religious education (MA, Certificate, Post Master's Certificate); sacred scripture (MA, Post Master's Certificate); sacred scriptures (Certificate); theology (M Div). Part-time and evening/weekend programs available. Postbaccalaureate distance learning degree programs offered (no on-campus study). *Degree requirements:* For master's, one foreign language, comprehensive exam, thesis optional; for other advanced degree, culminating paper. *Entrance requirements:* For M Div, interview; for master's, minimum undergraduate GPA of 3.0; for other advanced degree, minimum graduate GPA of 3.0. Electronic applications accepted. *Faculty research:* Roman Catholic theology, philosophy.

Holy Cross Greek Orthodox School of Theology, Theological Programs, Brookline, MA 02445-7496. Offers M Div, MTS, Th M. *Accreditation:* ATS. Part-time programs available. *Faculty:* 12 full-time (1 woman), 9 part-time/adjunct (2 women). *Students:* 116 full-time (15 women), 11 part-time (2 women); includes 1 minority (African American), 20 international. Average age 25. 74 applicants, 73% accepted, 48 enrolled. In 2009, 17 M Divs, 25 master's awarded. *Degree requirements:* For master's, 2 foreign languages, thesis (for some programs); for M Div, 2 foreign languages, thesis/dissertation (for some programs). *Entrance requirements:* For M Div and master's, GRE General Test, interview, written submission. Additional exam requirements/recommendations for international students: Required—TOEFL (minimum score 550 paper-based; 213 computer-based; 80 iBT). *Application deadline:* For fall admission, 8/15 for domestic students, 8/1 for international students; for spring admission, 1/3 for domestic students. Application fee: $50. *Expenses:* Tuition: Full-time $18,400; part-time $766 per credit hour. Required fees: $500. *Financial support:* In 2009–10, 26 students received support, including 20 teaching assistantships (averaging $525 per year); research assistantships, Federal Work-Study, scholarships/grants, and tuition waivers (partial) also available. Financial award application deadline: 4/1; financial award applicants required to submit FAFSA. *Faculty research:* Spirituality, liturgies, ecumenism, church history. *Unit head:* Rev. Dr. Thomas FitzGerald, Dean, 617-731-3500 Ext. 1213, Fax: 617-850-1460, E-mail: tfitzgerald@hchc.edu. *Application contact:* Gregory Floor, Director of Admissions, 617-731-3500 Ext. 1285, Fax: 617-850-1460, E-mail: gfloor@hchc.edu.

Hood Theological Seminary, Graduate and Professional Programs, Salisbury, NC 28144. Offers M Div, MTS, D Min. *Accreditation:* ATS. Evening/weekend programs available. *Degree requirements:* For master's, thesis optional; for doctorate, thesis/dissertation; for M Div, thesis/dissertation optional. *Faculty research:* Old Testament human sexuality, preaching and the vulnerable, socio-historical issues, Pauline studies, multiculturalism/African-American studies.

Houston Baptist University, College of Arts and Humanities, Program in Theological Studies, Houston, TX 77074-3298. Offers MATS. Part-time and evening/weekend programs available. *Degree requirements:* For master's, comprehensive exam. *Entrance requirements:* For master's, GRE General Test, 6 hours of course work in Greek or Hebrew (optional), interview, minimum GPA of 2.5. Additional exam requirements/recommendations for international students: Required—TOEFL (minimum score 550 paper-based; 213 computer-based). *Expenses:* Contact institution.

Houston Graduate School of Theology, Graduate School, Houston, TX 77092. Offers counseling (MA); pastoral ministry (M Div, D Min); theology (MA). *Accreditation:* ATS (one or more programs are accredited). Part-time and evening/weekend programs available. *Degree requirements:* For master's, thesis (for some programs); for doctorate, thesis/dissertation; for M Div, thesis/dissertation optional. *Entrance requirements:* For doctorate, GRE General Test or MAT, M Div or equivalent. Additional exam requirements/recommendations for international

Theology

Houston Graduate School of Theology (continued)
students: Required—TOEFL (minimum score 550 paper-based; 213 computer-based). *Faculty research:* Hermeneutics, spirituality, religion of Eastern Europe.

Howard University, School of Divinity, Washington, DC 20017. Offers M Div, MARS, D Min. *Accreditation:* ACIPE; ATS. Part-time and evening/weekend programs available. *Degree requirements:* For master's, thesis; for doctorate, thesis/dissertation; for M Div, thesis/dissertation optional. *Entrance requirements:* For M Div, minimum GPA of 2.0; for master's and doctorate, minimum GPA of 3.0. Electronic applications accepted. *Faculty research:* African-American religious experience, women in ministry, ecumenics, biblical studies.

Iliff School of Theology, Graduate and Professional Programs, Denver, CO 80210-4798. Offers biblical studies (MA); church history (MA); religion (MA); religion and social change (MA); specialized ministry (MASM), including justice and peace, pastoral theology and care, religions leadership; theology (M Div, MTS, D Min, PhD), including Biblical studies (PhD), religion and psychological studies (PhD), religion and social change (PhD), theology, philosophy and culture (PhD); theology/ethics (MA). *Accreditation:* ACIPE; ATS. Part-time and evening/weekend programs available. *Degree requirements:* For master's, one foreign language, thesis (for some programs); for doctorate, 2 foreign languages, comprehensive exam, thesis/dissertation; for M Div, thesis/dissertation optional. *Entrance requirements:* For M Div, minimum GPA of 2.75, references; for master's, minimum GPA of 3.0, writing sample, references; for doctorate, GRE General Test, minimum GPA of 3.0, writing sample, letters of recommendation. Additional exam requirements/recommendations for international students: Required—TOEFL (minimum score 550 paper-based). Electronic applications accepted. *Faculty research:* Pastoral care, history, church music, contemporary church, biblical studies.

Indiana Wesleyan University, College of Graduate Studies, Master of Divinity Program, Marion, IN 46953-4974. Offers M Div. Postbaccalaureate distance learning degree programs offered (minimal on-campus study). *Degree requirements:* For M Div, capstone. *Expenses:* Tuition: Full-time $7380; part-time $410 per credit. One-time fee: $85. Tuition and fees vary according to campus/location.

Indiana Wesleyan University, College of Graduate Studies, Wesley Seminary, Program in Ministry, Marion, IN 46953-4974. Offers ministerial leadership (MA); youth ministries (MA). Part-time programs available. Postbaccalaureate distance learning degree programs offered (minimal on-campus study). *Degree requirements:* For master's, one foreign language, capstone practicum and/or project. *Entrance requirements:* Additional exam requirements/recommendations for international students: Required—TOEFL. Electronic applications accepted. *Expenses:* Contact institution. *Faculty research:* History of worship innovation, history of New Testament afterlife traditions, second century mantanism, cross-cultural ministry, church health and growth, leadership in Christian organizations, managing change in the church, effective youth ministry, women in ministry, biblical hermeneutics.

Institute for Christian Studies, Graduate Programs, Toronto, ON M5T 1R4, Canada. Offers education (M Phil F, PhD); history of philosophy (M Phil F, PhD); philosophical aesthetics (M Phil F, PhD); philosophy of religion (M Phil F, PhD); political theory (M Phil F, PhD); systematic philosophy (M Phil F, PhD); theology (M Phil F, PhD); worldview studies (MWS). Part-time programs available. Postbaccalaureate distance learning degree programs offered (minimal on-campus study). *Degree requirements:* For master's, one foreign language, thesis; for doctorate, 2 foreign languages, thesis/dissertation. *Entrance requirements:* For master's and doctorate, philosophy background. Additional exam requirements/recommendations for international students: Required—TOEFL (minimum score 600 paper-based; 250 computer-based). *Faculty research:* Human rights, anthropology of self, medieval discourse, gender and body, post-modern thought; biblical hermeneutics, creational aesthetics, ecumenism, epistemology, political theory and public policy, relational psychotherapy.

Inter American University of Puerto Rico, Metropolitan Campus, Graduate Programs, Program in Theological Studies, San Juan, PR 00919-1293. Offers PhD.

Interdenominational Theological Center, Graduate and Professional Programs, Atlanta, GA 30314-4112. Offers M Div, MACE, MACM, D Min, Th D, M Div/MACE, M Div/MACM, MACM/MACE. *Accreditation:* ACIPE; ATS (one or more programs are accredited). Part-time and evening/weekend programs available. Postbaccalaureate distance learning degree programs offered (minimal on-campus study). *Faculty:* 21 full-time (8 women), 18 part-time/adjunct (7 women). *Students:* 241 full-time (111 women), 169 part-time (73 women); includes 383 minority (382 African Americans, 1 Hispanic American), 15 international. *Degree requirements:* For doctorate, thesis/dissertation. *Entrance requirements:* For M Div, bachelor's degree; for doctorate, master's degree. *Application deadline:* For fall admission, 7/1 for domestic and international students; for spring admission, 11/3 for domestic and international students. Applications are processed on a rolling basis. Application fee: $50. *Expenses:* Tuition: Part-time $632 per credit. Required fees: $424 per semester. *Financial support:* Research assistantships, career-related internships or fieldwork and Federal Work-Study available. Support available to part-time students. Financial award application deadline: 6/15; financial award applicants required to submit FAFSA. *Unit head:* Dr. Thomas W. Cole, President, 404-527-7702, Fax: 404-527-7770. *Application contact:* Walter Cabassa, Office of Admission and Recruitment, 404-527-7792, E-mail: wcabassa@itc.edu.

International Baptist College, Program in Biblical Studies, Chandler, AZ 85286. Offers MA.

Jesuit School of Theology at Berkeley, Programs in Theology, Berkeley, CA 94709-1193. Offers M Div, MA, MABL, MTS, Th M, STD, STL, MA/M Div. *Accreditation:* ATS (one or more programs are accredited). Part-time programs available. *Degree requirements:* For master's, one foreign language, thesis; for doctorate, 2 foreign languages, comprehensive exam, thesis/dissertation; for M Div, comprehensive exam. *Entrance requirements:* For M Div, GRE, undergraduate course work in philosophy; for master's, GRE. Additional exam requirements/recommendations for international students: Required—TOEFL, TWE.

The Jewish Theological Seminary, The Graduate School, New York, NY 10027-4649. Offers ancient Judaism (MA, DHL, PhD); Bible (MA, DHL, PhD); Jewish education (PhD); Jewish history (MA, DHL, PhD); Jewish literature (MA, DHL, PhD); Jewish philosophy (MA, DHL, PhD); liturgy (MA, DHL, PhD); medieval Jewish studies (MA, DHL, PhD); Midrash (MA, DHL, PhD); modern Jewish studies (MA, DHL, PhD); Talmud and rabbinics (MA, DHL, PhD); MA/MSW. *Accreditation:* ACIPE. Part-time programs available. Terminal master's awarded for partial completion of doctoral program. *Degree requirements:* For master's, one foreign language, comprehensive exam (for some programs), thesis (for some programs); for doctorate, 3 foreign languages, comprehensive exam (for some programs), thesis/dissertation. *Entrance requirements:* For master's, GRE or MAT, 3 letters of recommendation, writing sample; for doctorate, GRE or MAT, 3 letters of recommendation, writing research sample. Additional exam requirements/recommendations for international students: Required—TOEFL (minimum score 100 computer-based). *Expenses:* Tuition: Full-time $21,200; part-time $1000 per credit. Required fees: $400 per semester. Tuition and fees vary according to degree level.

See Close-Up on page 511.

The Jewish Theological Seminary, The Rabbinical School, New York, NY 10027-4649. Offers MA, Rabbi. *Accreditation:* ACIPE. *Degree requirements:* For master's and Rabbi, one foreign language, competency exams. *Entrance requirements:* For master's and Rabbi, GRE, interview, writing sample. Additional exam requirements/recommendations for international students: Required—TOEFL. *Expenses:* Contact institution.

See Close-Up on page 513.

Johnson Bible College, Program in New Testament, Knoxville, TN 37998-1001. Offers preaching (MA); research (MA). Part-time and evening/weekend programs available. Postbaccalaureate distance learning degree programs offered (no on-campus study). *Degree requirements:* For master's, one foreign language, comprehensive exam, thesis (for some programs). *Entrance requirements:* For master's, minimum GPA of 2.5. Additional exam requirements/recommendations for international students: Required—TOEFL.

Kehilath Yakov Rabbinical Seminary, Graduate Programs, Ossining, NY 10562. *Accreditation:* AARTS.

Kenrick-Glennon Seminary, Graduate and Professional Programs, St. Louis, MO 63119-4330. Offers M Div, MA. *Accreditation:* ATS. *Degree requirements:* For master's, thesis optional. *Entrance requirements:* MAT.

Kentucky Christian University, Graduate School, Grayson, KY 41143-2205. Offers Christian leadership (MA); New Testament (MA). Part-time programs available. *Degree requirements:* For master's, comprehensive exam (for some programs), thesis optional. *Entrance requirements:* For master's, minimum cumulative GPA of 2.75 in major or 2.5 overall; 6 additional hours in Bible (for non-Biblical undergraduate majors). Additional exam requirements/recommendations for international students: Required—TOEFL (minimum score 550 paper-based; 213 computer-based). Electronic applications accepted.

Knox College, College of Theology, Toronto, ON M5S 2E6, Canada. Offers M Div, MRE, MTS, Th M, D Min, Th D. Applicants for D Min, Th M, and Th D must apply to Toronto School of Theology. *Accreditation:* ATS. Part-time programs available. *Degree requirements:* For master's, one foreign language, thesis (for some programs); for doctorate, 2 foreign languages, thesis/dissertation. *Entrance requirements:* For doctorate, M Div. Additional exam requirements/recommendations for international students: Required—TOEFL (minimum score 580 paper-based; 237 computer-based), TWE (minimum score 5). *Faculty research:* Nineteenth century theologians.

Knox Theological Seminary, Graduate Programs, Program in Biblical Studies, Fort Lauderdale, FL 33308. Offers CBS. *Accreditation:* ATS. Part-time and evening/weekend programs available. *Entrance requirements:* Additional exam requirements/recommendations for international students: Required—TOEFL (minimum score 520 paper-based; 213 computer-based; 83 iBT), TWE (minimum score 5).

Knox Theological Seminary, Graduate Programs, Program in Divinity, Fort Lauderdale, FL 33308. Offers M Div. *Accreditation:* ATS. Part-time and evening/weekend programs available. *Entrance requirements:* Additional exam requirements/recommendations for international students: Required—TOEFL (minimum score 520 paper-based; 213 computer-based; 83 iBT), TWE (minimum score 5).

Knox Theological Seminary, Graduate Programs, Program in New and Old Testament, Fort Lauderdale, FL 33308. Offers MBT. *Accreditation:* ATS. Part-time and evening/weekend programs available. *Degree requirements:* For master's, one foreign language, thesis. *Entrance requirements:* Additional exam requirements/recommendations for international students: Required—TOEFL, TWE (minimum score 5).

Kol Yaakov Torah Center, Graduate Program, Monsey, NY 10952-2954. Offers Advanced Rabbinic Degree. *Accreditation:* AARTS. Part-time and evening/weekend programs available. *Faculty research:* Talmud, Jewish law.

Lakeland College, Graduate Studies Division, Program in Theology, Sheboygan, WI 53082-0359. Offers MAT.

Lancaster Bible College & Graduate School, Graduate School, Lancaster, PA 17601-5036. Offers Bible (MA); consulting resource teacher (M Ed); counseling (MA); ministry (MA); school counseling (M Ed). Part-time and evening/weekend programs available. *Degree requirements:* For master's, comprehensive exam (for some programs), thesis (for some programs). *Entrance requirements:* For master's, bachelor's degree with a minimum of 30 credits of course work in Bible, minimum undergraduate GPA of 3.0, interview. Additional exam requirements/recommendations for international students: Required—TOEFL.

Lancaster Theological Seminary, Graduate and Professional Programs, Lancaster, PA 17603-2812. Offers biblical studies (MAR); Christian education (MAR); Christianity and the arts (MAR); church history (MAR); congregational life (MAR); lay leadership (Certificate); theological studies (M Div); theology (D Min); theology and ethics (MAR). *Accreditation:* ACIPE; ATS. *Faculty:* 11 full-time (4 women), 13 part-time/adjunct (9 women). *Students:* 91 full-time (48 women), 42 part-time (33 women). *Degree requirements:* For doctorate, thesis/dissertation; for M Div, one foreign language. *Application deadline:* For fall admission, 4/1 priority date for domestic students, 1/1 for international students; for spring admission, 11/15 priority date for domestic students. Applications are processed on a rolling basis. Application fee: $50. *Expenses:* Tuition: Full-time $12,600; part-time $490 per credit. Required fees: $125 per semester. One-time fee: $3000. Tuition and fees vary according to program and student level. *Financial support:* Career-related internships or fieldwork, scholarships/grants, and tuition waivers (partial) available. Financial award application deadline: 4/15; financial award applicants required to submit FAFSA. *Unit head:* Dr. Edwin D. Aponte, Vice President of Academic Affairs and Dean of the Seminary, 717-290-8754, Fax: 717-393-0423, E-mail: eaponte@lancasterseminary.edu. *Application contact:* Virginia Whitaker-Brooks, Assistant Director of Recruitment and Admissions, 717-290-8741, Fax: 717-393-0423.

La Salle University, School of Arts and Sciences, Program in Theological, Pastoral and Liturgical Studies, Philadelphia, PA 19141-1199. Offers pastoral studies (MA); religion (MA); theological studies (MA). Part-time and evening/weekend programs available. *Entrance requirements:* For master's, 26 credits in humanistic subjects, religion, theology, or ministry-related work.

Lee University, Program in Religion, Cleveland, TN 37320-3450. Offers biblical studies (MA); theological studies (MA); youth and family ministry (MA). Part-time programs available. *Faculty:* 11 full-time (2 women), 1 part-time/adjunct (0 women). *Students:* 11 full-time (5 women), 16 part-time (7 women); includes 4 minority (2 African Americans, 1 American Indian/Alaska Native, 1 Asian American or Pacific Islander), 1 international. Average age 28. In 2009, 5 master's awarded. *Degree requirements:* For master's, comprehensive exam, thesis. *Entrance requirements:* For master's, GRE or MAT, minimum GPA of 3.0, 2 letters of recommendation, interview. Additional exam requirements/recommendations for international students: Required—TOEFL (minimum score 450 paper-based; 45 computer-based). *Application deadline:* For fall admission, 4/1 priority date for domestic students; for spring admission, 10/1 priority date for domestic students. Applications are processed on a rolling basis. Application fee: $25. *Expenses:* Tuition: Full-time $11,100; part-time $463 per credit. Required fees: $305. *Financial support:* Career-related internships or fieldwork, Federal Work-Study, institutionally sponsored loans, scholarships/grants, and unspecified assistantships available. Financial award application deadline: 3/1; financial award applicants required to submit FAFSA. *Faculty research:* Book of Isaiah, Gospel of Mark, school of St. Victor of 12th century, spirit Christology, people groups of New Testament and work. Total annual research expenditures: $3,000. *Unit head:* Dr. Bob Bayles, Director, 423-614-8338, E-mail: bbayles@leeuniversity.edu. *Application contact:* Vicki Glasscock, Graduate Admissions Director, 423-614-8059, E-mail: vglasscock@leeuniversity.edu.

Lexington Theological Seminary, Graduate and Professional Programs, Lexington, KY 40508-3218. Offers M Div, MA, MAPS, D Min, M Div/MSW. *Accreditation:* ACIPE; ATS. Part-time and evening/weekend programs available. *Degree requirements:* For master's, thesis; for doctorate, thesis/dissertation. *Entrance requirements:* Additional exam requirements/recommendations for international students: Required—TOEFL (minimum score 600 paper-based; 250 computer-based). *Faculty research:* History of biblical interpretation, biblical apocalyptic, psalms, history of Stone-Campbell traditions.

Liberty University, Liberty Theological Seminary and Graduate School, Lynchburg, VA 24502. Offers religious studies (M Div, MA, MAR, MRE, D Min); theology (Th M). Part-time programs available. Postbaccalaureate distance learning degree programs offered (minimal on-campus study). *Degree requirements:* For master's, 2 foreign languages, thesis (for some programs); for doctorate, 2 foreign languages, thesis/dissertation. *Entrance requirements:* For M Div, minimum undergraduate GPA of 2.0; for master's, minimum undergraduate GPA of 2.0, 9 credit hours of course work in Greek, 9 credit hours of course work in Hebrew (Th M); for doctorate, GRE General Test or MAT. Additional exam requirements/recommendations for international students: Required—TOEFL (minimum score 550 paper-based; 213 computer-based). Electronic applications accepted. *Expenses:* Contact institution.

Lincoln Christian Seminary, Graduate and Professional Programs, Lincoln, IL 62656-2167. Offers Bible and theology (MA); Christian ministries (MA); counseling (MA); divinity (M Div); leadership ministry (D Min); religious education (MRE). *Accreditation:* ACIPE; ATS. Part-time programs available. *Degree requirements:* For master's, 2 foreign languages, thesis; for doctorate, thesis/dissertation; for M Div, 2 foreign languages. *Entrance requirements:* For M Div and master's, minimum GPA of 2.5; for doctorate, M Div or equivalent. Additional exam requirements/recommendations for international students: Required—TOEFL (minimum score 550 paper-based; 213 computer-based). Electronic applications accepted.

Lipscomb University, Hazelip School of Theology, Nashville, TN 37204-3951. Offers biblical studies (MA); Christian studies (MA); divinity (M Div); ministry (MA); New Testament (MA); Old Testament (MA); theological studies (MTS); theology (MA). Part-time and evening/weekend programs available. *Faculty:* 7 full-time (0 women), 3 part-time/adjunct (0 women). *Students:* 25 full-time (6 women), 72 part-time (10 women); includes 14 minority (all African Americans), 1 international. Average age 35. 46 applicants, 57% accepted, 23 enrolled. In 2009, 15 first professional degrees, 6 master's awarded. *Degree requirements:* For master's, 2 foreign languages, comprehensive exam (for some programs); for M Div, 2 foreign languages. *Entrance requirements:* For M Div and master's, 2 references. Additional exam requirements/recommendations for international students: Required—TOEFL (minimum score 570 paper-based; 230 computer-based). *Application deadline:* For fall admission, 8/14 priority date for domestic students; for spring admission, 12/31 for domestic students. Applications are processed on a rolling basis. Application fee: $0 ($75 for international students). Electronic applications accepted. *Expenses:* Tuition: Full-time $16,002; part-time $889 per credit hour. Tuition and fees vary according to program. *Financial support:* Scholarships/grants available. Support available to part-time students. Financial award application deadline: 3/1; financial award applicants required to submit FAFSA. *Faculty research:* Status of Churches of Christ in foreign nations, Hebrew grammar, marriage and family. *Unit head:* Dr. Mark Black, Director, 615-966-1000 Ext. 5799, Fax: 615-966-1808, E-mail: mark.black@lipscomb.edu. *Application contact:* Kellye McCool, Information Contact, 615-966-6051, Fax: 615-966-6052, E-mail: kellye.mccool@lipscomb.edu.

Logos Evangelical Seminary, Graduate Programs, El Monte, CA 91731. Offers M Div, MA, Th M, D Min. *Accreditation:* ATS (one or more programs are accredited). Part-time programs available. *Faculty:* 11 full-time (2 women), 11 part-time/adjunct (3 women). *Students:* 58 full-time (31 women), 107 part-time (48 women); all minorities (all Asian Americans or Pacific Islanders). Average age 48. 53 applicants, 60% accepted, 30 enrolled. In 2009, 10 first professional degrees, 4 master's, 3 doctorates awarded. *Degree requirements:* For master's, 2 foreign languages, comprehensive exam, thesis; for doctorate, thesis/dissertation; for M Div, one foreign language, field education. *Entrance requirements:* For M Div, BA with a minimum GPA of 2.66, 2 recommendations, 3 years post-baptism; for master's, MA in Biblical studies with a minimum GPA of 3.33, 1.5 years of a Biblical language, 2 recommendations, 1 research paper; for doctorate, M Div with a minimum GPA of 3.0, 3 years ministry experience, 2 recommendations. Additional exam requirements/recommendations for international students: Required—TOEFL (minimum score 450 paper-based; 133 computer-based; 45 iBT). *Application deadline:* For fall admission, 7/15 for domestic students, 5/15 for international students; for spring admission, 12/15 for domestic students, 10/15 for international students. Applications are processed on a rolling basis. Application fee: $25 ($50 for international students). Electronic applications accepted. *Expenses:* Tuition: Full-time $8320; part-time $260 per credit hour. Tuition and fees vary according to course level and degree level. *Financial support:* Application deadline: 3/1. *Faculty research:* Asian-American hermaneutics, narrative theology, biblical studies, pastor's mental health. *Unit head:* Dr. Jeffrey Lu, Academic Dean, 626-571-5110 Ext. 126, Fax: 626-571-5119, E-mail: jefl@les.edu. *Application contact:* Becky Perng, Admission Officer, 626-571-5110 Ext. 112, Fax: 626-571-5119, E-mail: admission@les.edu.

Loras College, Graduate Division, Program in Theology and Ministry, Dubuque, IA 52004-0178. Offers ministry (MA); theology (MA). Part-time and evening/weekend programs available. *Degree requirements:* For master's, comprehensive exam (for some programs), thesis (for some programs). *Entrance requirements:* For master's, bachelor's degree or undergraduate minor in religious studies or equivalent, minimum undergraduate GPA of 2.75.

Louisville Presbyterian Theological Seminary, Graduate and Professional Programs, Louisville, KY 40205-1798. Offers Bible (MAR); divinity (M Div); ministry (D Min); religious thought (MAR); theology (Th M); JD/M Div; M Div/MBA; M Div/MS; M Div/MSW. *Accreditation:* AAMFT/COAMFTE (one or more programs are accredited); ACIPE; ATS (one or more programs are accredited). Part-time and evening/weekend programs available. *Faculty:* 22 full-time (10 women), 30 part-time/adjunct (11 women). *Students:* 140 full-time (82 women), 72 part-time (45 women); includes 43 minority (37 African Americans, 2 Asian Americans or Pacific Islanders, 4 Hispanic Americans), 6 international. Average age 37. 139 applicants, 77% accepted, 79 enrolled. In 2009, 22 first professional degrees, 11 master's, 10 doctorates awarded. *Degree requirements:* For master's, one foreign language; for doctorate, thesis/dissertation; for M Div, 2 foreign languages. *Entrance requirements:* For master's, interview; for doctorate, M Div. Additional exam requirements/recommendations for international students: Required—TOEFL (minimum score 550 paper-based; 213 computer-based). *Application deadline:* For fall admission, 6/15 priority date for domestic students, 6/1 priority date for international students; for spring admission, 11/15 priority date for domestic and international students. Applications are processed on a rolling basis. Application fee: $62. Electronic applications accepted. *Expenses:* Tuition: Full-time $9660; part-time $322 per credit hour. Required fees: $286; $143 per semester. *Financial support:* In 2009–10, 132 students received support. Career-related internships or fieldwork, Federal Work-Study, institutionally sponsored loans, and scholarships/grants available. Financial award application deadline: 4/15; financial award applicants required to submit CSS PROFILE or FAFSA. *Unit head:* Dr. David C. Hester, Dean, 502-894-2282, Fax: 502-895-1096, E-mail: dhester@lpts.edu. *Application contact:* Cheri Harper, Director of Admission, 502-895-3411 Ext. 371, Fax: 502-895-1096, E-mail: charper@lpts.edu.

Loyola Marymount University, College of Liberal Arts, Department of Theological Studies, Program in Theology, Los Angeles, CA 90045-8400. Offers MA. *Accreditation:* ATS. *Faculty:* 24 full-time (5 women). *Students:* 20 full-time (8 women), 25 part-time (9 women); includes 14 minority (3 African Americans, 4 Asian Americans or Pacific Islanders, 7 Hispanic Americans), 1 international. Average age 37. 35 applicants, 60% accepted, 17 enrolled. In 2009, 13 master's awarded. *Degree requirements:* For master's, comprehensive exam, thesis or alternative. *Entrance requirements:* For master's, GRE or MAT (recommended), 2 letters of recommendation. Additional exam requirements/recommendations for international students: Required—TOEFL (minimum score 600 paper-based; 250 computer-based; 100 iBT). *Application deadline:* For fall admission, 3/1 priority date for domestic students. Application fee: $50. Electronic applications accepted. *Financial support:* In 2009–10, 29 students received support, including 2 research assistantships (averaging $2,100 per year); Federal Work-Study, scholarships/grants, and unspecified assistantships also available. Support available to part-time students. Financial award application deadline: 6/1; financial award applicants required to submit FAFSA. Total annual research expenditures: $84,937. *Unit head:* Dr. Michael P. Horan, Graduate Director, 310-338-2755, E-mail: mhoran@lmu.edu. *Application contact:* Chake H. Kouyoumjian, Associate Dean of Graduate Studies, 310-338-2721, Fax: 310-338-6086, E-mail: ckouyoum@lmu.edu.

Loyola University Chicago, Graduate School, Department of Theology, Chicago, IL 60660. Offers MA, PhD. Part-time and evening/weekend programs available. *Faculty:* 16 full-time (5 women). *Students:* 80 full-time (27 women), 11 part-time (5 women); includes 5 minority (1 African American, 1 Asian American or Pacific Islander, 3 Hispanic Americans), 9 international. Average age 31. 82 applicants, 52% accepted, 15 enrolled. In 2009, 6 master's, 9 doctorates awarded. Terminal master's awarded for partial completion of doctoral program. *Degree requirements:* For master's, comprehensive exam; for doctorate, 2 foreign languages, comprehensive exam, thesis/dissertation. *Entrance requirements:* For master's, GRE General Test, minimum GPA of 3.0, 9 hours of course work in theology; for doctorate, GRE General Test, minimum GPA of 3.0, master's degree or equivalent. Additional exam requirements/recommendations for international students: Required—TOEFL. *Application deadline:* For fall admission, 1/15 for domestic and international students; for spring admission, 12/1 for domestic and international students. Application fee: $50. Electronic applications accepted. *Expenses:* Tuition: Full-time $14,220; part-time $790 per credit hour. Required fees: $60 per semester hour. Tuition and fees vary according to program. *Financial support:* In 2009–10, 12 students received support, including 12 research assistantships (averaging $16,500 per year); fellowships, teaching assistantships, institutionally sponsored loans also available. Financial award application deadline: 1/15; financial award applicants required to submit FAFSA. *Faculty research:* Systematics, historical theology, constructive theology, scripture, theological ethics. *Unit head:* Dr. Susan A. Ross, Department Chair, 773-508-2364, Fax: 773-508-2386, E-mail: sross@luc.edu. *Application contact:* Dr. Robert A. Divito, Graduate Program Director, 773-508-8453, Fax: 773-508-2386, E-mail: rdivito@luc.edu.

Loyola University Chicago, Institute of Pastoral Studies, Professional Program in Divinity, Chicago, IL 60660. Offers M Div, M Div/MA, M Div/MSN, M Div/MSW. *Accreditation:* ACIPE. *Faculty:* 8 full-time (2 women), 26 part-time/adjunct (12 women). *Students:* 19 full-time (11 women), 15 part-time (6 women); includes 5 minority (all African Americans), 1 international. Average age 40. 15 applicants, 87% accepted, 6 enrolled. In 2009, 4 first professional degrees awarded. *Degree requirements:* For M Div, project. *Entrance requirements:* Minimum GPA of 3.0, 1 year of ministry experience. Additional exam requirements/recommendations for international students: Required—TOEFL. *Application deadline:* For fall admission, 8/1 priority date for domestic students; for spring admission, 12/1 priority date for domestic students. Applications are processed on a rolling basis. Application fee: $50. Electronic applications accepted. *Expenses:* Contact institution. *Financial support:* In 2009–10, 9 students received support. Career-related internships or fieldwork, Federal Work-Study, institutionally sponsored loans, and scholarships/grants available. Support available to part-time students. Financial award application deadline: 2/1; financial award applicants required to submit FAFSA. *Faculty research:* Women leadership development for professionals in ministry, religious memoirs, passing on the values of Jesus, justice. *Unit head:* Dr. Robert T. O'Gorman, Professor, 312-915-7485, Fax: 312-915-7410, E-mail: rogorma@luc.edu. *Application contact:* Randy Gibbons, Administrative Assistant, 312-915-7450, Fax: 312-915-7410, E-mail: rgibbon@luc.edu.

Loyola University Chicago, Institute of Pastoral Studies, Program in Pastoral Counseling, Chicago, IL 60660. Offers pastoral care and counseling (MA); pastoral counseling (MA, Certificate). *Accreditation:* ACIPE. Part-time programs available. *Faculty:* 6 full-time (2 women), 12 part-time/adjunct (7 women). *Students:* 30 full-time (19 women), 20 part-time (14 women); includes 7 minority (2 African Americans, 3 Asian Americans or Pacific Islanders, 2 Hispanic Americans), 7 international. Average age 42. 31 applicants, 74% accepted, 18 enrolled. In 2009, 31 master's awarded. *Degree requirements:* For master's, thesis or alternative, integration project. *Application deadline:* For fall admission, 2/15 priority date for domestic students. Applications are processed on a rolling basis. Application fee: $50. Electronic applications accepted. *Expenses:* Tuition: Full-time $14,220; part-time $790 per credit hour. Required fees: $60 per semester hour. Tuition and fees vary according to program. *Financial support:* In 2009–10, 7 students received support. Career-related internships or fieldwork, Federal Work-Study, and institutionally sponsored loans available. Support available to part-time students. Financial award application deadline: 3/1; financial award applicants required to submit FAFSA. *Faculty research:* Pastoral psychotherapy, enrichment outcome, marriage and family therapy, marriage and family spirituality, gender and ethnicity issues, theological anthropology. *Unit head:* Dr. Paul R. Giblin, Associate Professor, 312-915-7483, Fax: 312-915-7410, E-mail: pgibli@luc.edu. *Application contact:* Dr. Paul R. Giblin, Associate Professor, 312-915-7483, Fax: 312-915-7410, E-mail: pgibli@luc.edu.

Loyola University Chicago, Institute of Pastoral Studies, Program in Spirituality/Spiritual Direction, Chicago, IL 60660. Offers spirituality (MA, Certificate); spirituality, contemporary (MA). *Students:* 10 full-time (7 women), 27 part-time (16 women); includes 4 minority (1 African American, 1 Asian American or Pacific Islander, 2 Hispanic Americans), 2 international. Average age 49. 8 applicants, 100% accepted, 7 enrolled. In 2009, 10 master's awarded. *Expenses:* Tuition: Full-time $14,220; part-time $790 per credit hour. Required fees: $60 per semester hour. Tuition and fees vary according to program. *Unit head:* Dr. Robert A. Ludwig. *Application contact:* Randy Gibbons, Administrative Assistant, 312-915-7450, Fax: 312-915-7410, E-mail: rgibbon@luc.edu.

Loyola University New Orleans, College of Social Sciences, Loyola Institute for Ministry, New Orleans, LA 70118-6195. Offers pastoral studies (MPS); religious education (MRE); theology and ministry (Certificate). Part-time and evening/weekend programs available. Post-baccalaureate distance learning degree programs offered (no on-campus study). *Students:* 5 full-time (2 women), 203 part-time (148 women); includes 31 minority (10 African Americans, 1 American Indian/Alaska Native, 4 Asian Americans or Pacific Islanders, 16 Hispanic Americans), 1 international. Average age 50. 74 applicants, 100% accepted, 61 enrolled. In 2009, 102 master's, 1 other advanced degree awarded. *Entrance requirements:* For master's, minimum GPA of 2.5, resume, 2 letters of recommendation, work experience. Additional exam requirements/recommendations for international students: Required—TOEFL (minimum score 550 paper-based; 213 computer-based). *Application deadline:* Applications are processed on a rolling basis. Application fee: $20. Electronic applications accepted. *Financial support:* Career-related internships or fieldwork, scholarships/grants, health care benefits, tuition waivers (partial), and room and board assistance available. Support available to part-time students. Financial award application deadline: 5/1; financial award applicants required to submit FAFSA. *Faculty research:* Practical theology, ministry education, small Christian communities, religion and ecology, Christian spirituality. *Unit head:* Tom Ryan, Director, 504-865-2069, Fax: 504-865-2066, E-mail: tfryan@loyno.edu. *Application contact:* Cecelia M. Bennett, Associate Director, 504-865-3398, Fax: 504-865-2066, E-mail: abennett@loyno.edu.

Lubbock Christian University, Graduate Biblical Studies, Lubbock, TX 79407-2099. Offers Bible and ministry (MS); biblical interpretation (MA). Part-time programs available. *Degree requirements:* For master's, one foreign language, thesis (for some programs). *Entrance requirements:* For master's, GRE General Test or MAT. *Faculty research:* Commentary on John, commentary on First and Second Thessalonians, mission teams, church leadership, family systems.

Lutheran School of Theology at Chicago, Graduate and Professional Programs, Chicago, IL 60615-5199. Offers ministry (MAM, D Min); theological studies (MATS, PhD); theology (M Div, Th M). *Accreditation:* ACIPE; ATS (one or more programs are accredited). Part-time programs available. *Faculty:* 20 full-time (6 women), 18 part-time/adjunct (5 women). *Students:* 214 full-time (103 women), 88 part-time (52 women). Terminal master's awarded for partial completion of doctoral program. *Degree requirements:* For master's, variable foreign language requirement; for doctorate, variable foreign language requirement, comprehensive exam, thesis/dissertation; for M Div, 2 foreign languages. *Entrance requirements:* For master's, GRE (Th M), M Div or equivalent (Th M); for doctorate, GRE, M Div or equivalent, 3 years of professional experience (D Min). Additional exam requirements/recommendations for international students: Required—TOEFL (Th M). *Application deadline:* Applications are processed on a rolling basis. Application fee: $50. *Expenses:* Tuition: Full-time $11,997; part-time $1333 per course. Required fees: $35 per semester. Tuition and fees vary according to degree level and program. *Financial support:* Career-related internships or fieldwork and scholarships/grants available. Support available to part-time students. *Unit head:* Michael Shelley, Dean, 773-256-0722, Fax: 773-256-0782, E-mail: mshelley@lstc.edu. *Application contact:* Dorothy

Theology

Lutheran School of Theology at Chicago (continued)

C. Dominiak, Director of Admissions and Financial Aid, 773-256-0726, Fax: 773-256-0782, E-mail: ddominia@lstc.edu.

Lutheran Theological Seminary, Graduate and Professional Programs, Saskatoon, SK S7N 0X3, Canada. Offers Biblical studies (MTS); church history (MTS); ethics/church and society (MTS); history of Christianity (STM); New Testament (STM); Old Testament (STM); pastoral studies (STM); pastoral theology (MTS); systematic theology (MTS); systematic theology and philosophy of religion (STM); theology (M Div, D Div). *Accreditation:* ATS. Part-time programs available. *Degree requirements:* For master's, thesis; for M Div, Greek, Hebrew.

Lutheran Theological Seminary at Gettysburg, Graduate and Professional Programs, Gettysburg, PA 17325-1795. Offers divinity (M Div); ministerial studies (MAMS); outdoor ministry (MAR); parish ministry (D Min); theology (STM). *Accreditation:* ACIPE; ATS (one or more programs are accredited). Part-time programs available. Postbaccalaureate distance learning degree programs offered (no on-campus study). *Degree requirements:* For master's, thesis (for some programs); for M Div, one foreign language. Electronic applications accepted.

The Lutheran Theological Seminary at Philadelphia, Graduate School, Philadelphia, PA 19119-1794. Offers divinity (M Div); ministry (D Min); religion (MAR); social ministry (Certificate); theology (STM). *Accreditation:* ACIPE; ATS. Part-time and evening/weekend programs available. *Degree requirements:* For master's, one foreign language, comprehensive exam (for some programs), thesis (for some programs); for doctorate, thesis/dissertation; for M Div, 2 foreign languages. *Entrance requirements:* For M Div and master's, minimum undergraduate GPA of 2.8; for doctorate, minimum first professional GPA of 3.0. Additional exam requirements/recommendations for international students: Required—TOEFL (minimum score 550 paper-based; 213 computer-based), TWE. Electronic applications accepted.

Lutheran Theological Southern Seminary, Graduate and Professional Programs, Columbia, SC 29203. Offers M Div, MAR, STM, D Min. *Accreditation:* ACIPE; ATS. Part-time programs available. *Degree requirements:* For master's, comprehensive exam (for some programs), thesis (for some programs); for M Div, 2 foreign languages. *Faculty research:* Theology in 21st century, Biblical interpretation.

Luther Rice University, Graduate Programs, Lithonia, GA 30038-2454. Offers Bible/theology (M Div); Christian education (M Div); Christian studies (MA); church ministry (D Min); counseling (M Div); discipleship counseling (MA); ministry (M Div, MA); missions/evangelism (M Div). Part-time programs available. Postbaccalaureate distance learning degree programs offered (no on-campus study). *Degree requirements:* For doctorate, thesis/dissertation. *Entrance requirements:* Additional exam requirements/recommendations for international students: Required—TOEFL (minimum score 500 paper-based; 173 computer-based).

Luther Seminary, Graduate and Professional Programs, St. Paul, MN 55108-1445. Offers M Div, M Th, MA, MSM, D Min, PhD. *Accreditation:* ACIPE; ATS. *Degree requirements:* For master's, thesis or alternative; for doctorate, 2 foreign languages, thesis/dissertation; for M Div, 2 foreign languages, 1 year internship. *Entrance requirements:* For M Div, minimum GPA of 3.0; for master's, minimum GPA of 2.8; for doctorate, GRE General Test. Electronic applications accepted. *Faculty research:* Theology, psychology (pastoral care), church history, Bible, Islamic studies.

Machzikei Hadath Rabbinical College, Graduate Programs, Brooklyn, NY 11204-1805. Offers First Talmudic Degree. *Accreditation:* AARTS.

Madonna University, Program in Religious Studies, Livonia, MI 48150-1173. Offers pastoral ministry (MA).

Malone University, Graduate Program in Theological Studies, Canton, OH 44709. Offers sports outreach ministries (MA); theological studies: general track (MA). Part-time and evening/weekend programs available. *Faculty:* 4 full-time (1 woman), 3 part-time/adjunct (0 women). *Students:* 1 full-time (0 women), 32 part-time (12 women); includes 6 minority (all African Americans). Average age 37. In 2009, 10 master's awarded. *Entrance requirements:* For master's, minimum GPA of 3.0. Additional exam requirements/recommendations for international students: Required—TOEFL (minimum score 550 paper-based; 213 computer-based; 79 iBT). *Application deadline:* Applications are processed on a rolling basis. Application fee: $25. *Expenses:* Contact institution. *Financial support:* Tuition waivers (partial) and unspecified assistantships available. Support available to part-time students. Financial award application deadline: 6/30. *Faculty research:* Pauline theology, history of Biblical interpretation, Johannine epistles, miracles in the New Testament, God's judgment and love. *Unit head:* Dr. Larry D. Reinhart, Interim Director, 330-471-8198, Fax: 330-471-8477, E-mail: lareinhart@malone.edu. *Application contact:* David L. Kleffman, Assistant Director of Enrollment, 330-471-8447, Fax: 330-471-8343, E-mail: dkleffman@malone.edu.

Maple Springs Baptist Bible College and Seminary, Graduate and Professional Programs, Capitol Heights, MD 20743. Offers biblical studies (MA, Certificate); Christian counseling (MA); church administration (MA); divinity (M Div); ministry (D Min); religious education (MRE).

Maranatha Baptist Bible College, Program in Biblical Studies, Watertown, WI 53094. Offers MA. Part-time programs available. *Degree requirements:* For master's, one foreign language, fieldwork. *Expenses:* Tuition: Full-time $4000; part-time $250 per credit. Required fees: $21 per credit. *Faculty research:* Bible structure, counseling techniques, church history.

Maranatha Baptist Bible College, Program in Theology, Watertown, WI 53094. Offers MA. Part-time programs available. *Expenses:* Tuition: Full-time $4000; part-time $250 per credit. Required fees: $21 per credit.

Marquette University, Graduate School, College of Arts and Sciences, Department of Theology, Milwaukee, WI 53201-1881. Offers ethics (PhD); historical theology (MA, PhD); religious studies (PhD), including scriptural theology (MA, PhD); systematic theology (MA, PhD); theology (MA), including scriptural theology (MA, PhD); theology and society (PhD). Part-time programs available. *Faculty:* 32 full-time (7 women), 22 part-time/adjunct (4 women). *Students:* 73 full-time (17 women), 44 part-time (14 women); includes 6 minority (2 African Americans, 2 Asian Americans or Pacific Islanders, 2 Hispanic Americans), 4 international. Average age 35. 154 applicants, 48% accepted, 20 enrolled. In 2009, 11 master's, 9 doctorates awarded. Terminal master's awarded for partial completion of doctoral program. *Degree requirements:* For master's, one foreign language, comprehensive exam, thesis or alternative; for doctorate, 2 foreign languages, thesis/dissertation, qualifying exam. *Entrance requirements:* For master's and doctorate, GRE General Test. Additional exam requirements/recommendations for international students: Required—TOEFL. Application fee: $40. *Financial support:* In 2009–10, 5 fellowships, 5 research assistantships, 14 teaching assistantships were awarded; Federal Work-Study, institutionally sponsored loans, scholarships/grants, and tuition waivers (full and partial) also available. Support available to part-time students. Financial award application deadline: 2/15. *Faculty research:* Old Testament theology, New Testament theology, church history, Christian ethics. *Unit head:* Rev. John Laurance, Acting Chair, 414-288-7170, Fax: 414-288-5548. *Application contact:* Dr. Christine Hinze, Director of Graduate Studies, 414-288-6802.

Mars Hill Graduate School, Graduate Programs, Seattle, WA 98121. Offers Christian studies (MA); counseling psychology (MA); divinity (MS). Part-time programs available. *Entrance requirements:* For master's, MAT.

Marylhurst University, Department of Religious Studies–Applied Theology Program, Marylhurst, OR 97036-0261. Offers applied theology (MA). Part-time and evening/weekend programs available. *Faculty:* 1 full-time (0 women), 9 part-time/adjunct (5 women). *Students:* 2 full-time (0 women), 17 part-time (14 women). Average age 48. 11 applicants, 91% accepted, 8 enrolled. In 2009, 3 master's awarded. *Degree requirements:* For master's, thesis. *Entrance requirements:* For master's, MAT, resume, 3 letters of recommendation, interview, autobiography. Additional exam requirements/recommendations for international students: Recommended—TOEFL (minimum score 550 paper-based; 213 computer-based; 80 iBT). *Application deadline:* For fall admission, 6/30 priority date for domestic students, 6/30 for international students; for winter admission, 11/30 priority date for domestic students, 11/30 for international students; for spring admission, 3/30 priority date for domestic students, 3/30 for international students. Applications are processed on a rolling basis. Application fee: $40 ($50 for international students). Electronic applications accepted. *Financial support:* Fellowships, research assistantships, teaching assistantships, scholarships/grants available. Support available to part-time students. Financial award applicants required to submit FAFSA. *Faculty research:* Pastoral care, scripture, world religions. *Unit head:* Dr. Jerry Roussell, Chair, 503-636-8141, Fax: 503-697-5597, E-mail: jroussell@marylhurst.edu. *Application contact:* Kathleen Schneff, Admissions Specialist, 800-634-9982 Ext. 3322, Fax: 503-635-6585, E-mail: admissions@marylhurst.edu.

Marylhurst University, Department of Religious Studies–Divinity Program, Marylhurst, OR 97036-0261. Offers M Div. Part-time and evening/weekend programs available. *Faculty:* 1 full-time (0 women), 9 part-time/adjunct (5 women). *Students:* 11 full-time (10 women), 22 part-time (18 women). Average age 48. 7 applicants, 100% accepted, 6 enrolled. *Degree requirements:* For M Div, thesis/dissertation. *Entrance requirements:* MAT, resume, 3 letters of recommendation, interview. Additional exam requirements/recommendations for international students: Required—TOEFL (minimum score 550 paper-based; 213 computer-based; 80 iBT). *Application deadline:* For fall admission, 6/30 for domestic students; for winter admission, 11/30 for domestic students; for spring admission, 3/30 for domestic students. Applications are processed on a rolling basis. Application fee: $40 ($50 for international students). Electronic applications accepted. *Financial support:* Fellowships, research assistantships, teaching assistantships, scholarships/grants available. Support available to part-time students. Financial award applicants required to submit FAFSA. *Faculty research:* Scripture-Biblical studies, theology, history, ministry, spirituality. *Unit head:* Dr. Jerry Roussell, Chair, 503-636-8141, Fax: 503-697-5597, E-mail: jroussell@marylhurst.edu. *Application contact:* Kathleen Schneff, Admissions Specialist, 800-634-9982 Ext. 3322, Fax: 503-635-6585, E-mail: admissions@marylhurst.edu.

The Master's College and Seminary, The Master's Seminary, Santa Clarita, CA 91321-1200. Offers biblical counseling (MABC); New Testament (Th D); Old Testament (Th D); preaching (D Min); theology (M Div, M Th, Th D). Part-time programs available. *Degree requirements:* For master's, 2 foreign languages, thesis; for doctorate, 4 foreign languages, thesis/dissertation; for M Div, 2 foreign languages, thesis/dissertation. *Entrance requirements:* For M Div, minimum 2 years of college; for master's, minimum GPA of 2.75; for doctorate, Th M, minimum GPA of 3.5. Additional exam requirements/recommendations for international students: Required—TOEFL (minimum score 550 paper-based).

McCormick Theological Seminary, Graduate and Professional Programs, Chicago, IL 60615. Offers ministry (D Min); theological studies (MATS, Certificate); theology (M Div); M Div/MSW. *Accreditation:* ACIPE; ATS (one or more programs are accredited). Part-time and evening/weekend programs available. *Degree requirements:* For master's, thesis (for some programs); for doctorate, thesis/dissertation. *Entrance requirements:* For M Div and master's, minimum GPA of 3.0; for doctorate, M Div, minimum 3 years in pastorate. *Faculty research:* Faith formation, families, biblical literature, Dead Sea scrolls, women in antiquity.

McGill University, Faculty of Graduate and Postdoctoral Studies, Faculty of Religious Studies, Montréal, QC H3A 2T5, Canada. Offers MA, STM, PhD. *Accreditation:* ATS.

McMaster University, McMaster Divinity College, Hamilton, ON L8S 4M2, Canada. Offers biblical studies (M Div); Biblical studies (MA, MTS, Diploma); Christian interpretation/history (M Div, MA, MTS, Diploma); Christian ministry (M Div, MA, MTS, Diploma); Christian Studies (Certificate); Christian theology (PhD). Affiliated with the Toronto School of Theology. *Accreditation:* ATS. Part-time programs available. *Degree requirements:* For master's, one foreign language, thesis optional; for doctorate, 3 foreign languages, comprehensive exam, thesis/dissertation; for other advanced degree, 2 foreign languages, thesis. *Entrance requirements:* For master's, minimum B average in undergraduate course work, 3 letters of reference; for doctorate, minimum B+ average in bachelor's and master's, appropriate modern/ancient language, interview; for other advanced degree, 6 units of related Biblical language, minimum B+ average in undergraduate course work, minimum 15 units of course work in related area of study, 3 letters of recommendation. Additional exam requirements/recommendations for international students: Required—TOEFL (minimum score 550 paper-based; 237 computer-based). *Faculty research:* Ethics, Biblical studies, language studies, church history, Christian ministry.

Meadville Lombard Theological School, Graduate and Professional Programs, Chicago, IL 60637-1602. Offers divinity (M Div); ministry (D Min); religion (MA); M Div/MSW. *Accreditation:* ACIPE; ATS. Part-time programs available. Postbaccalaureate distance learning degree programs offered (minimal on-campus study). *Entrance requirements:* For M Div and master's, bachelor's degree; for doctorate, bachelor's and masters degrees, 3 years of ministry.

Memphis Theological Seminary, Graduate and Professional Programs, Memphis, TN 38104-4395. Offers M Div, MAR, D Min. *Accreditation:* ATS. Part-time programs available. *Faculty:* 11 full-time (4 women), 7 part-time/adjunct (0 women). *Students:* 161 full-time (57 women), 92 part-time (46 women); includes 96 minority (94 African Americans, 1 American Indian/Alaska Native, 1 Asian American or Pacific Islander), 1 international. Average age 43. *Degree requirements:* For doctorate, thesis/dissertation. *Entrance requirements:* For doctorate, M Div, 3 years in ministry. *Application deadline:* For fall admission, 8/10 priority date for domestic students; for spring admission, 1/10 priority date for domestic students. Applications are processed on a rolling basis. Application fee: $35. *Expenses:* Tuition: Full-time $9120; part-time $380 per credit hour. Required fees: $40 per term. *Financial support:* Career-related internships or fieldwork and scholarships/grants available. Support available to part-time students. Financial award application deadline: 4/15. *Unit head:* Dr. Daniel J. Earheart-Brown, President, 901-458-8232, Fax: 901-452-4051, E-mail: jebrown@memphisseminary.edu. *Application contact:* Barry L. Anderson, Director of Admissions, 901-458-8232 Ext. 109, Fax: 901-452-4501, E-mail: banderson@mtscampus.edu.

Mennonite Brethren Biblical Seminary, School of Theology, Program in Divinity, Fresno, CA 93727-5097. Offers M Div. *Accreditation:* ATS. *Degree requirements:* For M Div, one foreign language.

Mennonite Brethren Biblical Seminary, School of Theology, Programs in New Testament, Old Testament, and Theology, Fresno, CA 93727-5097. Offers New Testament (MA); Old Testament (MA); theology (MA). Part-time programs available. *Entrance requirements:* Additional exam requirements/recommendations for international students: Required—TOEFL (minimum score 550 paper-based; 213 computer-based).

Mercer University, Graduate Studies, Cecil B. Day Campus, James and Carolyn McAfee School of Theology, Macon, GA 31207-0003. Offers M Div, MACM, D Min, M Div/MBA, M Div/MM, M Div/MS. *Accreditation:* ATS. Part-time programs available. *Faculty:* 14 full-time (3 women), 9 part-time/adjunct (3 women). *Students:* 159 full-time (78 women), 71 part-time (35 women); includes 80 minority (76 African Americans, 2 Asian Americans or Pacific Islanders, 2 Hispanic Americans), 2 international. Average age 32. 140 applicants, 70% accepted, 60 enrolled. In 2009, 38 master's, 5 doctorates awarded. *Degree requirements:* For doctorate, thesis/dissertation, fieldwork, seminars; for M Div, 2 foreign languages. *Entrance requirements:* For M Div, letters of recommendation, minimum B+ average in undergraduate course work; for master's, bachelor's degree with liberal arts core from regionally accredited college/university; for doctorate, MAT or GRE, minimum B+ average in undergraduate course work, letters of recommendation. Additional exam requirements/recommendations for international students: Required—TOEFL (minimum score 550 paper-based; 215 computer-based; 79 iBT). *Application* *deadline:* For fall admission, 7/1 for domestic students, 2/1 for international students; for spring admission, 1/4 for domestic students. Applications are processed on a rolling basis. Application fee: $35. *Expenses:* Contact institution. *Financial support:* In 2009–10, 30 students received support. Career-related internships or fieldwork, Federal Work-Study, institutionally sponsored loans, and merit-based scholarships available. Support available to part-time students. Financial award applicants required to submit FAFSA. *Faculty research:* Biblical studies, Baptist heritage, Christian heritage, theology, pastoral care, ethics, global missions, academic research. *Unit head:* Dr. R. Alan Culpepper, Dean, 678-547-6470, Fax: 678-547-6478, E-mail: culpepper_ra@mercer.edu. *Application contact:* Dr. Ryan A. Clark, Director of Admissions, 678-547-6451, Fax: 678-547-6478, E-mail: clark_ra@mercer.edu.

Mesivta of Eastern Parkway–Yeshiva Zichron Meilech, Graduate Programs, Brooklyn, NY 11218-5559. *Accreditation:* AARTS.

Mesivta Tifereth Jerusalem of America, Graduate Programs, New York, NY 10002-6301. *Accreditation:* AARTS.

Mesivta Torah Vodaath Rabbinical Seminary, Graduate Programs, Brooklyn, NY 11218-5299. *Accreditation:* AARTS.

Methodist Theological School in Ohio, Graduate and Professional Programs, Delaware, OH 43015-8004. Offers M Div, MACE, MACM, MTS, D Min. *Accreditation:* ACIPE; ATS. Part-time programs available. *Entrance requirements:* For master's, 3 letters of recommendation. Additional exam requirements/recommendations for international students: Required—TOEFL (minimum score 577 paper-based; 233 computer-based; 90 iBT).

Michigan Theological Seminary, Graduate Programs, Plymouth, MI 48170. Offers Bible (Graduate Certificate); Christian education (MA); counseling psychology (MA); divinity (M Div); theological studies (MA). *Accreditation:* ATS. Part-time and evening/weekend programs available. *Degree requirements:* For master's, one foreign language, thesis; for M Div, 2 foreign languages. *Faculty research:* Judaism, cults, world religions.

Mid-America Baptist Theological Seminary, Graduate and Professional Programs, Cordova, TN 38016. Offers M Div, MACE, MCE, MM, D Min, PhD. *Degree requirements:* For doctorate, 4 foreign languages, thesis/dissertation; for M Div, 2 foreign languages. *Entrance requirements:* For doctorate, MAT. Additional exam requirements/recommendations for international students: Required—TOEFL (minimum score 600 paper-based; 250 computer-based). Electronic applications accepted.

Mid-America Baptist Theological Seminary Northeast Branch, Program in Theology, Schenectady, NY 12303-3463. Offers M Div. Part-time and evening/weekend programs available. *Degree requirements:* For M Div, 2 foreign languages. *Entrance requirements:* Additional exam requirements/recommendations for international students: Required—TOEFL. Electronic applications accepted.

Mid-America Reformed Seminary, Graduate Programs, Dyer, IN 46311. Offers M Div, MTS. *Degree requirements:* For M Div, comprehensive exam. *Entrance requirements:* Additional exam requirements/recommendations for international students: Required—TOEFL (minimum score 550 paper-based).

Midwestern Baptist Theological Seminary, Graduate and Professional Programs, Kansas City, MO 64118-4697. Offers Biblical archaeology (MA); Biblical languages (MA); Christian education (M Div, MACE); Christian foundations—lay ministry (Graduate Certificate); collegiate ministries (M Div); counseling (MA); educational ministry (D Ed Min); international church planting (M Div); ministry (M Div, D Min); North American church planting (M Div); sacred music (MCM); urban ministry (M Div); worship leadership (M Div); youth ministry (M Div). *Accreditation:* ATS. Part-time programs available. Postbaccalaureate distance learning degree programs offered (minimal on-campus study). *Degree requirements:* For doctorate, thesis/dissertation; for M Div, 2 foreign languages. *Entrance requirements:* For doctorate, MAT. Electronic applications accepted. *Faculty research:* Ministerial studies, Biblical and theological studies, missions, counseling.

Midwest University, Graduate Programs, Wentzville, MO 63385. Offers social work (DSW); teaching English to speakers of other languages (MA); theology (M Div, MA, D Min). Part-time programs available. Postbaccalaureate distance learning degree programs offered (minimal on-campus study). *Degree requirements:* For master's, thesis (for some programs); for doctorate, thesis/dissertation; for M Div, thesis/dissertation (for some programs). *Entrance requirements:* Additional exam requirements/recommendations for international students: Recommended—TOEFL (minimum score 550 paper-based).

Mirrer Yeshiva, Graduate Programs, Brooklyn, NY 11223-2010. *Accreditation:* AARTS.

Moody Bible Institute, Graduate School, Chicago, IL 60610-3284. Offers biblical studies (MABS, Graduate Certificate); intercultural studies (MAIS, Graduate Certificate); ministry (M Div, M Min); spiritual formation and discipleship (MASF, Graduate Certificate); urban studies (MA, Graduate Certificate). Part-time programs available. *Degree requirements:* For master's, 2 foreign languages, fieldwork (MABS); colloquium, field research project (MA Min). *Entrance requirements:* For master's, 30 hours in Bible/theology, 2 years of ministry experience (MA Min).

Moravian Theological Seminary, Graduate and Professional Programs, Bethlehem, PA 18018-6614. Offers M Div, MAPC, MATS. *Accreditation:* ACIPE; ATS (one or more programs are accredited). Part-time programs available. *Degree requirements:* For master's, thesis. *Entrance requirements:* Additional exam requirements/recommendations for international students: Required—TOEFL.

Mount Angel Seminary, Program in Theology, Saint Benedict, OR 97373. Offers M Div, MA. *Accreditation:* ACIPE; ATS. Part-time programs available. *Degree requirements:* For master's, thesis optional.

Mount St. Mary's University, Graduate Seminary, Emmitsburg, MD 21727-7799. Offers M Div, MA. *Accreditation:* ATS. *Faculty:* 9 full-time (0 women), 4 part-time/adjunct (2 women). *Students:* 133 full-time (0 women), 3 part-time (1 woman); includes 8 minority (1 African American, 4 Asian Americans or Pacific Islanders, 3 Hispanic Americans), 12 international. Average age 30. 44 applicants, 95% accepted, 40 enrolled. In 2009, 25 first professional degrees, 9 master's awarded. *Degree requirements:* For master's, one foreign language, comprehensive exam, thesis, language proficiency exams. *Entrance requirements:* For M Div, 24 credits of course work in philosophy; for master's, 18 credits of course work in philosophy. Additional exam requirements/recommendations for international students: Required—TOEFL (minimum score 550 paper-based; 213 computer-based). *Application deadline:* For fall admission, 8/1 for domestic and international students. Application fee: $0. *Expenses:* Contact institution. *Financial support:* In 2009–10, 3 students received support. Career-related internships or fieldwork and scholarships/grants available. Financial award applicants required to submit FAFSA. *Faculty research:* Pope Benedict XVI and the Church's influence on modern society, Marian theology, eschatology, medical ethics, medieval catechesis. *Unit head:* Rev. Steven P. Rohlfs, Vice President/Rector, 301-447-5295, Fax: 301-447-5636, E-mail: rohlfs@msmary.edu. *Application contact:* Susan Nield, Seminary Admissions, 301-447-7423, Fax: 301-447-7402, E-mail: nield@msmary.edu.

Mount Vernon Nazarene University, Program in Ministry, Mount Vernon, OH 43050-9500. Offers M Min. Part-time and evening/weekend programs available. *Degree requirements:* For master's, project. *Faculty research:* Pastoral effectiveness and professional development.

Naropa University, Graduate Programs, Program in Divinity, Boulder, CO 80302-6697. Offers M Div. *Entrance requirements:* In-person interview, writing sample. Additional exam requirements/recommendations for international students: Required—TOEFL (minimum score 600 paper-based; 250 computer-based). Electronic applications accepted.

Nashotah House, School of Theology, Nashotah, WI 53058-9793. Offers M Div, MTS, STM, Certificate. *Accreditation:* ACIPE; ATS (one or more programs are accredited). Part-time programs available. *Degree requirements:* For master's, thesis optional; for M Div, 2 foreign languages, thesis/dissertation optional, clinical experience. *Entrance requirements:* For M Div, master's, and Certificate, GRE General Test or MAT, interview. Additional exam requirements/recommendations for international students: Required—TOEFL. *Faculty research:* Formation for parochial ministry, ancient Semitic epigraphy.

Nazarene Theological Seminary, Graduate and Professional Programs, Kansas City, MO 64131-1263. Offers Christian education (MA); intercultural studies (MA); theological studies (MA); theology (M Div, D Min). *Accreditation:* ACIPE; ATS. Part-time programs available. *Faculty:* 19 full-time (3 women), 12 part-time/adjunct (2 women). *Students:* 136 full-time (32 women), 118 part-time (32 women); includes 21 minority (5 African Americans, 1 American Indian/Alaska Native, 7 Asian Americans or Pacific Islanders, 8 Hispanic Americans), 14 international. Average age 31. 129 applicants, 77% accepted, 71 enrolled. In 2009, 40 first professional degrees, 22 master's, 2 doctorates awarded. *Degree requirements:* For master's, comprehensive exam (for some programs), thesis (for some programs); for doctorate, thesis/dissertation. *Entrance requirements:* Additional exam requirements/recommendations for international students: Required—TOEFL. *Application deadline:* For fall admission, 3/1 priority date for domestic and international students; for spring admission, 10/1 priority date for domestic and international students. Applications are processed on a rolling basis. Application fee: $25 ($200 for international students). Electronic applications accepted. *Financial support:* In 2009–10, 235 students received support, including 15 teaching assistantships (averaging $1,400 per year); institutionally sponsored loans and scholarships/grants also available. Support available to part-time students. Financial award application deadline: 3/1; financial award applicants required to submit FAFSA. *Unit head:* Dr. Roger L. Hahn, Dean of the Faculty, 816-268-5412, Fax: 816-268-5500, E-mail: rlhahn@nts.edu. *Application contact:* Jay A. Sandbloom, Director of Admissions, 816-268-5451, Fax: 816-268-5500, E-mail: jasandbloom@nts.edu.

Ner Israel Rabbinical College, Graduate Programs, Baltimore, MD 21208. Offers MTL, DTL, Professional Certificate. *Accreditation:* AARTS.

Ner Israel Yeshiva College of Toronto, Graduate Programs, Thornhill, ON L4J 8A7, Canada. *Accreditation:* AARTS.

New Brunswick Theological Seminary, Graduate and Professional Programs, New Brunswick, NJ 08901-1196. Offers metro-urban ministry (D Min), including theological studies; theological studies (M Div, MA); M Div/MA. *Accreditation:* ACIPE; ATS. Part-time and evening/weekend programs available. *Degree requirements:* For master's, thesis optional. *Entrance requirements:* For M Div, minimum GPA of 2.0; for master's, minimum GPA of 3.0; for doctorate, M Div. Additional exam requirements/recommendations for international students: Required—TOEFL. Electronic applications accepted.

Newman Theological College, Theology Program, Edmonton, AB T6V 1H3, Canada. Offers M Div, M Th, MTS. *Accreditation:* ATS. Part-time programs available. *Degree requirements:* For master's, comprehensive exam, thesis; for M Div, comprehensive exam, thesis/dissertation. *Entrance requirements:* For M Div, bachelor's degree including 12 credits in philosophy; for master's, M Div. Additional exam requirements/recommendations for international students: Required—TOEFL (minimum score 560 paper-based; 220 computer-based). Tuition and fees charges are reported in Canadian dollars. *Expenses:* Tuition: Full-time $5150 Canadian dollars; part-time $515 Canadian dollars per course. Required fees: $40 Canadian dollars per semester. Tuition and fees vary according to course level, course load, campus/location and program.

Newman University, School of Arts and Humanities, Wichita, KS 67213-2097. Offers theological studies (MTS); theology (MA). Part-time programs available. Postbaccalaureate distance learning degree programs offered (minimal on-campus study). *Faculty:* 1 full-time (0 women). *Students:* 43 part-time (22 women); includes 3 Hispanic Americans. Average age 48. 45 applicants, 98% accepted, 43 enrolled. *Degree requirements:* For master's, 2 foreign languages, comprehensive exam (for some programs). *Entrance requirements:* For master's, Master of Arts: bachelor's degree in theology or related field and letter of recommendation from pastor; Master in Theological Studies: bachelor's degree in any field and letter of recommendation from pastor. Additional exam requirements/recommendations for international students: Required—TOEFL (minimum score 600 paper-based; 250 computer-based; 100 iBT). *Application deadline:* For fall admission, 8/1 priority date for domestic students. Application fee: $25 ($40 for international students). *Expenses:* Contact institution. *Financial support:* Federal Work-Study available. Financial award application deadline: 8/15; financial award applicants required to submit FAFSA. *Unit head:* Fr. Gile Joseph, Assistant Professor of Theology and Graduate Theology Director, 316-942-4291 Ext. 2861, Fax: 316-942-4483, E-mail: gilej@newmanu.edu. *Application contact:* Linda Kay Sabala, Director of Graduate Admissions, 316-942-4291 Ext. 2230, Fax: 316-942-4483, E-mail: sabalal@newmanu.edu.

New Orleans Baptist Theological Seminary, Graduate and Professional Programs, Division of Biblical Studies, New Orleans, LA 70126-4858. Offers MA. *Accreditation:* ACIPE; ATS.

New Orleans Baptist Theological Seminary, Graduate and Professional Programs, Division of Theological and Historical Studies, New Orleans, LA 70126-4858. Offers M Div, D Min, PhD. *Accreditation:* ACIPE; ATS (one or more programs are accredited). *Degree requirements:* For doctorate, thesis/dissertation. *Entrance requirements:* For doctorate, GRE General Test.

New Saint Andrews College, Graduate Studies, Moscow, ID 83843. Offers classical Christian studies (Graduate Certificate); Trinitarian theology and culture (MA). Part-time programs available. *Degree requirements:* For master's, final oral exam. *Entrance requirements:* For master's, GRE, 2 letters of recommendation; for Graduate Certificate, GRE, bachelor's degree, essays, 2 letters of recommendation. Electronic applications accepted.

New York Theological Seminary, Graduate and Professional Programs, New York, NY 10115. Offers M Div, MPS, MSW, D Min. *Accreditation:* ACIPE; ATS (one or more programs are accredited). Part-time programs available. *Degree requirements:* For doctorate, thesis/dissertation; for M Div, thesis/dissertation, supervised ministry. *Entrance requirements:* For M Div, interview; for doctorate, M Div, 3 years of ministry experience, interview. Additional exam requirements/recommendations for international students: Required—TOEFL. *Faculty research:* Women in leadership; crime and punishment; church history; culture, politics and theology.

The Nigerian Baptist Theological Seminary, Graduate Studies, Ogbomoso, Nigeria. Offers church music (M Div, M Th, Diploma); divinity (M Div); ministry (D Min); religious education (M Div, M Th, PhD); theological studies (MATS); theology (M Th, PhD). Part-time programs available. *Degree requirements:* For master's, thesis, 2 Nigerian languages; for M Div, thesis/dissertation (for some programs), 2 biblical languages; for Diploma, thesis or alternative.

Northeastern Seminary at Roberts Wesleyan College, Graduate and Professional Programs, Rochester, NY 14624. Offers ministry (D Min); theological studies (MA); theology (M Div); M Div/MSW. *Accreditation:* ATS. Evening/weekend programs available. *Degree requirements:* For master's, thesis (for some programs); for doctorate, one foreign language, thesis/dissertation. *Entrance requirements:* For doctorate, M Div, 3 years of full-time ministry experience. Additional exam requirements/recommendations for international students: Required—TOEFL (minimum score 550 paper-based). Electronic applications accepted. *Faculty research:* Historical theology, spiritual formation, biblical theology, counseling education.

Northern Baptist Theological Seminary, Graduate and Professional Programs, Lombard, IL 60148-5698. Offers Biblical studies (MA); Christian ministries (MACM); divinity (M Div); ministry (D Min); New Testament (MA); Old Testament (MA); pastoral care and counseling (MA). *Accreditation:* ATS. Part-time programs available. *Faculty:* 5 full-time (0 women), 30 part-time/adjunct (5 women). *Students:* 42 full-time (6 women), 95 part-time (45 women); includes 67 minority (51 African Americans, 12 Asian Americans or Pacific Islanders, 4 Hispanic Americans),

Theology

Northern Baptist Theological Seminary (continued)

3 international. *Degree requirements:* For doctorate, thesis/dissertation; for M Div, field experience. *Entrance requirements:* For master's, official transcripts, letter of reference from pastor, autobiographical statement (400 words or more); for doctorate, 3 years in the ministry post-M Div, 3 letters of reference. Additional exam requirements/recommendations for international students: Required—TOEFL (minimum score 550 paper-based; 213 computer-based). *Application deadline:* Applications are processed on a rolling basis. Application fee: $35. Electronic applications accepted. *Expenses:* Tuition: Full-time $15,800; part-time $2640 per trimester. Required fees: $115 per trimester. One-time fee: $300. Tuition and fees vary according to course load. *Financial support:* Career-related internships or fieldwork and scholarships/grants available. Support available to part-time students. Financial award application deadline: 9/1. *Faculty research:* Theology, worship studies, church history, evangelism, Bible. *Unit head:* Alistair Brown, Chief Academic Officer, 630-620-2101, Fax: 630-620-2190. *Application contact:* Greg Henson, Executive Director of External Relations, 630-620-2180, Fax: 630-620-2190, E-mail: admissions@seminary.edu.

North Park Theological Seminary, Graduate and Professional Programs, Professional Program, Chicago, IL 60625-4895. Offers M Div, M Div/MBA, M Div/MM. *Accreditation:* ACIPE; ATS. Part-time programs available. *Faculty:* 17 full-time (4 women), 13 part-time/adjunct (3 women). *Students:* 59 full-time, 42 part-time; includes 13 minority (10 African Americans, 3 Asian Americans or Pacific Islanders), 15 international. Average age 33. 62 applicants, 79% accepted. In 2009, 12 first professional degrees awarded. *Degree requirements:* For M Div, 2 foreign languages. *Entrance requirements:* Minimum GPA of 2.5. Additional exam requirements/recommendations for international students: Required—TOEFL. *Application deadline:* For fall admission, 9/15 priority date for domestic students; for spring admission, 3/1 for domestic students. Applications are processed on a rolling basis. Application fee: $25. *Financial support:* Career-related internships or fieldwork available. Financial award application deadline: 9/7; financial award applicants required to submit FAFSA. *Application contact:* Mark Washington, Associate Director, 800-964-0101, Fax: 773-244-6244, E-mail: semadmissions@northpark.edu.

North Park Theological Seminary, Graduate and Professional Programs, Program in Christian Formation, Chicago, IL 60625-4895. Offers MA, MA/MM.

North Park Theological Seminary, Graduate and Professional Programs, Program in Preaching, Chicago, IL 60625-4895. Offers D Min. *Accreditation:* ACIPE; ATS. *Degree requirements:* For doctorate, thesis/dissertation. *Entrance requirements:* For doctorate, 3 years of preaching experience.

North Park Theological Seminary, Graduate and Professional Programs, Program in Theological Studies, Chicago, IL 60625-4895. Offers MATS, MATS/MBA, MATS/MM. *Accreditation:* ACIPE; ATS. Part-time programs available. *Degree requirements:* For master's, comprehensive exam or thesis. *Entrance requirements:* For master's, minimum GPA of 2.5. Additional exam requirements/recommendations for international students: Required—TOEFL.

Northwest Baptist Seminary, Programs in Theology, Tacoma, WA 98407. Offers M Div, M Min, MTS, STM, Th M, D Min, Certificate. Part-time and evening/weekend programs available. *Degree requirements:* For master's, thesis; for M Div, thesis/dissertation (for some programs). *Entrance requirements:* Greek placement exam. Additional exam requirements/recommendations for international students: Required—TOEFL (minimum score 550 paper-based; 213 computer-based), IELTS (minimum score 6).

Northwest University, College of Ministry, Kirkland, WA 98033. Offers ministry (MA); missional leadership (MA); theology and culture (MA). *Faculty:* 11 full-time (1 woman), 12 part-time/adjunct (2 women). *Students:* 16 full-time (3 women), 24 part-time (7 women); includes 3 minority (all African Americans). 39 applicants, 97% accepted, 22 enrolled. *Entrance requirements:* Additional exam requirements/recommendations for international students: Required—TOEFL (minimum score 550 paper-based). Application fee: $75. *Unit head:* Dr. Kent Ingle, Dean, 425-889-5253, E-mail: kent.ingle@northwestu.edu. *Application contact:* Roy Rowland, Director of Graduate and Professional Studies Enrollment, 425-889-7787, Fax: 425-803-3059, E-mail: gpse@northwestu.edu.

Notre Dame Seminary, Graduate School of Theology, New Orleans, LA 70118-4391. Offers M Div, MA. *Accreditation:* ACIPE; ATS. Part-time programs available. *Faculty:* 18 full-time (2 women), 11 part-time/adjunct (4 women). *Students:* 72 full-time (0 women), 33 part-time (17 women). *Degree requirements:* For master's, one foreign language, comprehensive exam, thesis. *Entrance requirements:* For M Div, GRE, previous course work in philosophy; for master's, GRE. Additional exam requirements/recommendations for international students: Required—TOEFL. *Application deadline:* For fall admission, 8/1 priority date for domestic students; for spring admission, 1/3 for domestic students. Applications are processed on a rolling basis. Application fee: $40. *Expenses:* Tuition: Part-time $625 per credit hour. Required fees: $50 per semester. One-time fee: $115 part-time. Tuition and fees vary according to course load and program. *Unit head:* Rev. Jose I. Lavastida, President/Rector, 504-866-7426 Ext. 3104, Fax: 504-861-1301, E-mail: rector@nds.edu. *Application contact:* Rev. David Liberto, Academic Dean, 504-866-7426 Ext. 3107, Fax: 504-866-3119, E-mail: dliberto@nds.edu.

Oakland City University, Chapman Seminary, Oakland City, IN 47660-1099. Offers M Div, D Min. *Accreditation:* ATS. Part-time programs available. *Degree requirements:* For doctorate, thesis/dissertation. *Entrance requirements:* For M Div, GRE General Test, minimum GPA of 2.75 in undergraduate major or 2.5 overall; for doctorate, GRE, MAT, letters of recommendation. Additional exam requirements/recommendations for international students: Required—TOEFL. *Expenses:* Contact institution. *Faculty research:* Pastoral ministry, Christian education, missions.

Oblate School of Theology, Graduate and Professional Programs, San Antonio, TX 78216-6693. Offers divinity (M Div); Hispanic ministry (D Min); pastoral ministry (MAP Min); pastoral studies (Certificate); spirituality (MA Sp); supervision (D Min), including clinical pastoral education, general supervision; theology (MA Th); M Div/MA Th. *Accreditation:* ACIPE; ATS (one or more programs are accredited). Part-time programs available. *Faculty:* 22 full-time (7 women), 7 part-time/adjunct (1 woman). *Students:* 91 full-time (5 women), 76 part-time (43 women); includes 69 minority (5 African Americans, 1 American Indian/Alaska Native, 15 Asian Americans or Pacific Islanders, 48 Hispanic Americans), 35 international. Average age 39. 29 applicants, 100% accepted, 29 enrolled. In 2009, 8 first professional degrees, 11 master's, 4 doctorates awarded. *Degree requirements:* For master's, thesis (for some programs), practicum; for doctorate, paper, practicum; for M Div, one foreign language, seminar. *Entrance requirements:* For M Div, MAT, interview, course work in philosophy and theology; for master's, MAT, interview, course work in theology or religious studies, minimum GPA of 2.5; for doctorate, M Div. Additional exam requirements/recommendations for international students: Required—TOEFL (minimum score 197 computer-based; 71 iBT). *Application deadline:* For fall admission, 6/15 priority date for domestic and international students; for spring admission, 12/30 for domestic and international students. Applications are processed on a rolling basis. Application fee: $45. *Expenses:* Tuition: Full-time $11,960; part-time $460 per credit. Required fees: $175 per semester. Tuition and fees vary according to course level, course load and degree level. *Financial support:* Scholarships/grants available. Support available to part-time students. Financial award application deadline: 8/1; financial award applicants required to submit FAFSA. *Unit head:* Sr. Elaine Brothers, Academic Dean, 210-341-1366, Fax: 214-341-4519, E-mail: ebrothers@ost.edu. *Application contact:* James Oberhausen, Director of Admission/Registrar, 210-341-1366 Ext. 212, Fax: 210-341-4519, E-mail: registrar@ost.edu.

Ohio Dominican University, Graduate Programs, Division of Theology, Arts and Ideas, Columbus, OH 43219-2099. Offers theology (MA). Part-time and evening/weekend programs available. *Students:* 4 full-time (all women), 15 part-time (all women). Average age 40. In 2009, 4 master's awarded. *Degree requirements:* For master's, thesis or alternative. *Entrance requirements:* For master's, 20 undergraduate semester hours of theology or the equivalent, 3 letters of recommendation, interview. Additional exam requirements/recommendations for international students: Required—TOEFL (minimum score 550 paper-based; 213 computer-based). *Application deadline:* For fall admission, 7/15 priority date for domestic and international students; for spring admission, 12/15 priority date for domestic and international students. Applications are processed on a rolling basis. Application fee: $25. *Financial support:* Applicants required to submit FAFSA. *Unit head:* Dr. Barbara Finan, Director, MA in Theology, 614-251-4721, E-mail: finanb@ohiodominican.edu. *Application contact:* Jill M. Westerfeld, Graduate Admissions Recruiter, 614-251-4725, Fax: 614-251-4634, E-mail: westerfj@ohiodominican.edu.

Ohr Hameir Theological Seminary, Graduate Programs, Cortlandt Manor, NY 10567. *Accreditation:* AARTS.

Oklahoma Christian University, Graduate School of Theology, Oklahoma City, OK 73136-1100. Offers family life ministry (MA); ministry (M Div, MA); youth ministry (MA). Part-time programs available. Postbaccalaureate distance learning degree programs offered (minimal on-campus study). *Degree requirements:* For master's, one foreign language, comprehensive exam, field experience; for M Div, 2 foreign languages, comprehensive exam, field experience. *Entrance requirements:* For M Div and master's, minimum undergraduate GPA of 3.0. Additional exam requirements/recommendations for international students: Required—TOEFL (minimum score 550 paper-based; 213 computer-based). Electronic applications accepted. *Faculty research:* Early marriage adjustment, new religions, Ethiopic language, church health, Hebrew rhetoric.

Olivet Nazarene University, Graduate School, Department of Practical Ministries, Bourbonnais, IL 60914. Offers MPM. Part-time programs available. *Degree requirements:* For master's, thesis or alternative.

Olivet Nazarene University, Graduate School, Division of Religion, Bourbonnais, IL 60914. Offers biblical literature (MA); religion (MA); theology (MA). Part-time programs available. *Degree requirements:* For master's, thesis or alternative.

Oral Roberts University, School of Theology and Missions, Tulsa, OK 74171. Offers biblical literature (MA), including advanced languages, Judaic-Christian studies; Christian counseling (MA), including marriage and family therapy; divinity (M Div); missions (MA); practical theology (MA); theological/historical studies (MA); theology (D Min). *Accreditation:* ATS; NASM. Part-time programs available. Postbaccalaureate distance learning degree programs offered (minimal on-campus study). *Degree requirements:* For master's, thesis (for some programs), practicum/internship; for doctorate, thesis/dissertation, applied research project; for M Div, one foreign language, field experience. *Entrance requirements:* For M Div and master's, GRE General Test or MAT, minimum GPA of 2.5; for doctorate, M Div, minimum GPA of 3.0, 3 years of full-time ministry experience. Additional exam requirements/recommendations for international students: Required—TOEFL (minimum score 550 paper-based; 213 computer-based; 79 iBT). Electronic applications accepted.

Pacific Lutheran Theological Seminary, Graduate and Professional Programs, Berkeley, CA 94708-1597. Offers M Div, MA, MCM, MTS, PhD, Th D, Certificate, M Div/MA. *Accreditation:* ACIPE; ATS (one or more programs are accredited). Part-time programs available. *Degree requirements:* For master's, variable foreign language requirement, thesis or alternative; for M Div, one foreign language. *Entrance requirements:* Minimum cumulative GPA of 2.5, two semesters of Greek. *Faculty research:* Theology and genetics, power and prayer, liturgy and ethics, Christianity and Confucianism, religion and abuse.

Pacific School of Religion, Graduate and Professional Programs, Berkeley, CA 94709-1323. Offers M Div, MA, MTS, D Min, PhD, Th D, CAPS, CMS, CSS, CTS. *Accreditation:* ACIPE; ATS (one or more programs are accredited). Part-time programs available. *Degree requirements:* For master's, one foreign language, thesis (for some programs); for doctorate, thesis/dissertation. *Entrance requirements:* For M Div and master's, minimum GPA of 3.0; for doctorate, M Div, minimum GPA of 3.0 (D Min); for other advanced degree, M Div, minimum GPA of 3.0 (CAPS). Additional exam requirements/recommendations for international students: Required—TOEFL (minimum score 550 paper-based; 213 computer-based). Electronic applications accepted. *Faculty research:* Medical ethics, gay/lesbian studies in religion, Asian-American religion, race, culture and theology, theology in context.

Payne Theological Seminary, Program in Theology, Wilberforce, OH 45384-3474. Offers M Div. *Accreditation:* ACIPE; ATS. Part-time and evening/weekend programs available. Postbaccalaureate distance learning degree programs offered (minimal on-campus study). *Degree requirements:* For M Div, 2 foreign languages, thesis/dissertation.

Philadelphia Biblical University, School of Biblical Studies, Langhorne, PA 19047-2990. Offers M Div, MSB. Part-time and evening/weekend programs available. *Faculty:* 6 full-time (0 women), 1 part-time/adjunct (0 women). *Students:* 23 full-time (2 women), 65 part-time (19 women); includes 36 minority (31 African Americans, 2 Asian Americans or Pacific Islanders, 3 Hispanic Americans), 3 international. Average age 38. 52 applicants, 67% accepted, 20 enrolled. In 2009, 5 M Divs, 4 master's awarded. *Entrance requirements:* Additional exam requirements/recommendations for international students: Required—TOEFL (minimum score 550 paper-based; 213 computer-based). *Application deadline:* Applications are processed on a rolling basis. Application fee: $25. Electronic applications accepted. *Expenses:* Tuition: Full-time $10,350; part-time $575 per credit. Required fees: $10; $10 per year. Tuition and fees vary according to program. *Financial support:* In 2009–10, 29 students received support. Scholarships/grants available. Support available to part-time students. Financial award applicants required to submit FAFSA. *Unit head:* Dr. O. Herbert Hirt, Dean, 215-702-4354, Fax: 215-702-4359, E-mail: bible@pbu.edu. *Application contact:* Timothy Nessler, Assistant Director, Graduate Admissions, 800-572-2472, Fax: 215-702-4248, E-mail: tnessler@pbu.edu.

Phillips Theological Seminary, Programs in Theology, Tulsa, OK 74116. Offers administration of church agencies (M Div); campus ministry (M Div); church-related social work (M Div); college and seminary teaching (M Div); global mission work (M Div); institutional chaplaincy (M Div); ministerial vocations in Christian education (M Div); ministry (D Min), including parish ministry, pastoral counseling, practices of ministry; ministry and culture (MAMC), including Christian education, congregational leadership, history and practice of Christian spirituality, theology, ethics, and culture; ministry of music (M Div); pastoral care and counseling (M Div); pastoral ministry (M Div); theological studies (MTS). *Accreditation:* ATS. Part-time programs available. Postbaccalaureate distance learning degree programs offered (minimal on-campus study). *Degree requirements:* For master's, thesis (for some programs); for doctorate, thesis/dissertation. *Entrance requirements:* For master's, minimum GPA of 2.5; for doctorate, M Div, minimum GPA of 3.0. *Faculty research:* Biblical studies, historical studies, theology and culture, practical theology, theology and film.

Phoenix Seminary, Graduate Programs, Scottsdale, AZ 85254. Offers biblical communication (M Div); biblical leadership (MA); biblical studies (Graduate Diploma); Christian counseling (Graduate Diploma); counseling and family (M Div); intercultural studies (Graduate Diploma); leadership development (M Div, Graduate Diploma); ministry (D Min); professional counseling (MA); women's studies (Graduate Diploma). *Accreditation:* ATS (one or more programs are accredited). Part-time and evening/weekend programs available. *Faculty:* 5 full-time (0 women), 5 part-time/adjunct (0 women). *Students:* 26 full-time (8 women), 151 part-time (39 women); includes 34 minority (18 African Americans, 2 American Indian/Alaska Native, 5 Asian Americans or Pacific Islanders, 9 Hispanic Americans), 1 international. 41 applicants, 90% accepted, 30 enrolled. In 2009, 21 master's, 2 doctorates, 12 other advanced degrees awarded. *Degree requirements:* For master's, 2 foreign languages, comprehensive exam; for doctorate, 2 foreign languages, thesis/dissertation. *Entrance requirements:* For master's, undergraduate degree with minimum GPA of 2.5; for doctorate, M Div (94 hours) with minimum GPA of 3.0. Additional exam requirements/recommendations for international students: Required—TOEFL (minimum score 587 paper-based; 240 computer-based; 92 iBT), TWE (minimum score 4.5). *Application deadline:* For fall admission, 7/1 for domestic students; for spring admission, 11/1 for domestic students. Applications are processed on a rolling basis. Application fee: $90. *Expenses:* Tuition: Full-time $9420; part-time $410 per credit hour. Required fees: $60 per semester. Tuition and fees vary according to course load and degree level. *Financial support:* Institutionally sponsored loans and scholarships/grants available. Support available to part-time students. Financial award application deadline: 6/1; financial award applicants required to submit FAFSA. *Application contact:* Roma Royer, Director of Admissions and Academic Services, 602-850-8000 Ext. 111, Fax: 602-850-8080, E-mail: rroyer@ps.edu.

Piedmont Baptist College and Graduate School, Piedmont Baptist Graduate School, Winston-Salem, NC 27101-5197. Offers chaplaincy track (MABS); non-language track (MABS); PhD preparation track (MABS); theology (M Min, PhD). Part-time programs available. Postbaccalaureate distance learning degree programs offered (no on-campus study). *Degree requirements:* For master's, 2 foreign languages, comprehensive exam, thesis or alternative; for doctorate, 2 foreign languages, comprehensive exam. *Entrance requirements:* For master's, GRE General Test; for doctorate, Hebrew and Greek proficiency, MA. Electronic applications accepted. *Faculty research:* Theological and biblical studies.

Pittsburgh Theological Seminary, Graduate and Professional Programs, Pittsburgh, PA 15206-2596. Offers divinity (M Div); ministry (D Min); theology (MA, STM); JD/M Div; M Div/MS; M Div/MSW. *Accreditation:* ATS (one or more programs are accredited). Part-time and evening/weekend programs available. *Faculty:* 17 full-time (3 women), 9 part-time/adjunct (3 women). *Students:* 272 full-time (91 women), 65 part-time (29 women); includes 47 minority (40 African Americans, 1 American Indian/Alaska Native, 5 Asian Americans or Pacific Islanders, 1 Hispanic American), 15 international. Average age 36. 126 applicants, 75% accepted, 88 enrolled. In 2009, 46 first professional degrees, 8 master's, 12 doctorates awarded. *Degree requirements:* For master's, comprehensive exam (for some programs), thesis (for some programs); for doctorate, thesis/dissertation; for M Div, one foreign language. *Entrance requirements:* For M Div and master's, bachelor's degree with minimum GPA of 2.7, interview, references; for doctorate, interview, references. Additional exam requirements/recommendations for international students: Required—TOEFL (minimum score 570 paper-based; 230 computer-based; 89 iBT). *Application deadline:* For fall admission, 6/30 priority date for domestic students, 12/1 for international students; for winter admission, 10/15 priority date for domestic students; for spring admission, 1/15 priority date for domestic students. Applications are processed on a rolling basis. Application fee: $40. *Expenses:* Tuition: Part-time $300 per credit. Required fees: $51 per term. Tuition and fees vary according to course load. *Financial support:* In 2009–10, 135 students received support. Career-related internships or fieldwork, scholarships/grants, and institutional work-study available. Financial award application deadline: 3/15; financial award applicants required to submit FAFSA. *Unit head:* Dr. Byron H. Jackson, Dean of Faculty and Vice President for Academic Affairs, 412-924-1374, Fax: 412-924-1774, E-mail: bjackson@pts.edu. *Application contact:* Sherry Sparks, Associate Dean of Admissions, 412-924-1382, Fax: 412-924-1782, E-mail: ssparks@pts.edu.

Pontifical Catholic University of Puerto Rico, College of Arts and Humanities, Department of Theology and Philosophy, Ponce, PR 00717-0777. Offers M Div.

Pontifical College Josephinum, School of Theology, Columbus, OH 43235. Offers M Div, MA. *Accreditation:* ATS. Part-time programs available. *Degree requirements:* For master's, 3 foreign languages, comprehensive exam, thesis; for M Div, 2 foreign languages, thesis/dissertation. *Entrance requirements:* For M Div, GRE General Test, 24 credit hours of course work in philosophy, 12 credit hours of course work in theology; for master's, GRE General Test, 15 credit hours of course work in philosophy, 6 credit hours of course work in scripture. Additional exam requirements/recommendations for international students: Required—TOEFL (minimum score 600 paper-based; 250 computer-based).

Princeton Theological Seminary, Graduate and Professional Programs, Princeton, NJ 08542-0803. Offers M Div, MA, Th M, D Min, PhD. *Accreditation:* ACIPE; ATS. Part-time programs available. Terminal master's awarded for partial completion of doctoral program. *Degree requirements:* For doctorate, 2 foreign languages, thesis/dissertation, comprehensive exam (PhD), French and German. *Entrance requirements:* For doctorate, GRE General Test. Additional exam requirements/recommendations for international students: Required—TOEFL. Electronic applications accepted.

Providence College, Graduate Studies, Department of Religious Studies, Providence, RI 02918. Offers Biblical studies (MA); theology (MA, MTS). Part-time and evening/weekend programs available. *Faculty:* 6 full-time (1 woman). *Students:* 4 full-time (2 women), 24 part-time (9 women), 1 international. Average age 40. 5 applicants, 100% accepted. In 2009, 11 master's awarded. *Degree requirements:* For master's, comprehensive exam, Greek and Hebrew (biblical studies). *Entrance requirements:* Additional exam requirements/recommendations for international students: Required—TOEFL (minimum score 550 paper-based; 213 computer-based; 80 iBT). *Application deadline:* For fall admission, 8/1 priority date for domestic and international students; for spring admission, 12/1 priority date for domestic and international students. Applications are processed on a rolling basis. Application fee: $55. *Expenses:* Tuition: Full-time $9909; part-time $367 per credit. One-time fee: $200. Tuition and fees vary according to course load and program. *Financial support:* In 2009–10, 4 research assistantships with full tuition reimbursements (averaging $8,400 per year) were awarded; career-related internships or fieldwork and unspecified assistantships also available. Support available to part-time students. Financial award application deadline: 8/1; financial award applicants required to submit FAFSA. *Unit head:* Rev. Thomas McCreesh, Director, 401-865-1150, Fax: 401-865-1830, E-mail: tmccrees@providence.edu. *Application contact:* Carol A. Daniels, Coordinator of Graduate Faculty and Administrative Services, 401-865-2247, Fax: 401-865-1147, E-mail: daniels@providence.edu.

Providence College and Theological Seminary, Theological Seminary, Otterburne, MB R0A 1G0, Canada. Offers children's ministry (Certificate); Christian studies (MA, Certificate); counseling (MA); cross-cultural discipleship (Certificate); divinity (M Div); educational studies (MA), including counseling psychology, educational ministries, student development, teaching English to speakers of other languages, training teachers of English to speakers of other languages; global studies (MA); lay counseling (Diploma); ministry (D Min); teaching English to speakers of other languages (Certificate); theological studies (MA); training teacher of English to speakers of other languages (Certificate); youth ministry (Certificate). *Accreditation:* ATS. Part-time programs available. *Degree requirements:* For master's, variable foreign language requirement, thesis (for some programs); for doctorate, thesis/dissertation; for M Div, 2 foreign languages, comprehensive exam, thesis/dissertation (for some programs). *Entrance requirements:* Additional exam requirements/recommendations for international students: Recommended—TOEFL (minimum score 550 paper-based; 213 computer-based). *Faculty research:* Studies in Isaiah, theology of sin.

Queen's University at Kingston, Queen's Theological College, Kingston, ON K7L 3N6, Canada. Offers M Div, MTS, Certificate. *Accreditation:* ATS. Part-time programs available. *Degree requirements:* For master's, thesis (for some programs); for M Div, 2 foreign languages. *Entrance requirements:* For master's, minimum undergraduate B average. Additional exam requirements/recommendations for international students: Required—TOEFL (minimum score 580 paper-based). *Faculty research:* Early Christian group formations, pastoral care and spiritual direction, feminist theology, public religion, interpretation of Biblical texts using psychologies of shame and trauma.

Quincy University, Program in Theological Studies, Quincy, IL 62301-2699. Offers MTS. Part-time and evening/weekend programs available. *Faculty:* 2 full-time (0 women). *Students:* 3 part-time (0 women). In 2009, 3 master's awarded. *Entrance requirements:* For master's, MAT or GRE. Additional exam requirements/recommendations for international students: Required—TOEFL. *Application deadline:* Applications are processed on a rolling basis. Application fee: $25. Electronic applications accepted. *Expenses:* Tuition: Full-time $8400; part-time $350 per credit hour. Required fees: $360; $15 per credit hour. Tuition and fees vary according to course load, campus/location and program. *Financial support:* Applicants required to submit FAFSA. *Unit head:* Dr. Ed Maniscalco, Director, 217-228-5432 Ext. 3201, E-mail: manised@quincy.edu. *Application contact:* Jennifer O'Donnell, Coordinator of Adult Studies, 217-228-5404, Fax: 217-228-5479, E-mail: admissions@quincy.edu.

Rabbi Isaac Elchanan Theological Seminary, Graduate Program, New York, NY 10033-1807. Offers Certificate of Advanced Ordination, Certificate of Ordination. *Degree requirements:* For other advanced degree, one foreign language, comprehensive exam. *Entrance requirements:* For degree, oral exam, 2 interview, undergraduate major in Jewish studies or equivalent. *Faculty research:* Talmud, rabbinics.

Rabbinical Academy Mesivta Rabbi Chaim Berlin, Graduate Program, Brooklyn, NY 11230-4715. Offers Advanced Talmudic Degree, Second Talmudic Degree. *Accreditation:* AARTS. *Degree requirements:* For other advanced degree, 2 foreign languages. *Entrance requirements:* For degree, must be a graduate of a rabbinical school.

Rabbinical College Beth Shraga, Graduate Programs, Monsey, NY 10952-3035. *Accreditation:* AARTS.

Rabbinical College Bobover Yeshiva B'nei Zion, Graduate Programs, Brooklyn, NY 11219. *Accreditation:* AARTS.

Rabbinical College Ch'san Sofer, Graduate Programs, Brooklyn, NY 11204. *Accreditation:* AARTS.

Rabbinical College of Long Island, Graduate Programs, Long Beach, NY 11561-3305. *Accreditation:* AARTS.

Rabbinical Seminary M'kor Chaim, Graduate Programs, Brooklyn, NY 11219. *Accreditation:* AARTS.

Rabbinical Seminary of America, Graduate Programs, Flushing, NY 11367. School offers a master's and first professional degree. *Accreditation:* AARTS.

Reconstructionist Rabbinical College, Graduate Program, Wyncote, PA 19095-1898. Offers MAHL, MAJS, DHL, Certificate. Part-time programs available. *Degree requirements:* For master's, one foreign language, thesis (MAJS), completion of rabbinical program (MAHL); for doctorate and MAHL, one foreign language. *Entrance requirements:* For MAHL and doctorate, GRE General Test, placement examinations in Hebrew and Judaism; for master's, GRE General Test. *Faculty research:* Bible, Hebrew Semitic texts, contemporary Judaism.

Reformed Presbyterian Theological Seminary, Graduate and Professional Programs, Pittsburgh, PA 15208-2594. Offers M Div, MTS, D Min. *Accreditation:* ATS. Part-time and evening/weekend programs available. Electronic applications accepted. *Faculty research:* Prayer.

Reformed Theological Seminary–Charlotte Campus, Graduate and Professional Programs, Charlotte, NC 28226-6318. Offers biblical studies (MA); ministry (D Min); pastoral ministry (M Div); theological studies (MA). Part-time programs available. *Degree requirements:* For master's, comprehensive exam; for doctorate, thesis/dissertation; for M Div, 2 foreign languages, comprehensive exam. *Entrance requirements:* For master's, minimum GPA of 2.6; for doctorate, minimum GPA of 3.0. Additional exam requirements/recommendations for international students: Required—TOEFL (minimum score 550 paper-based; 213 computer-based). Electronic applications accepted.

Reformed Theological Seminary–Jackson Campus, Graduate and Professional Programs, Jackson, MS 39209-3099. Offers Bible, theology, and missions (Certificate); biblical studies (MA); Christian education (M Div, MA); counseling (M Div); divinity (M Div, Diploma); marriage and family therapy (MA); ministry (D Min); missions (M Div, MA, D Min); New Testament (Th M); Old Testament (Th M); theological studies (MA); theology (Th M); M Div/MA. *Accreditation:* AAMFT/COAMFTE (one or more programs are accredited); ATS (one or more programs are accredited). *Degree requirements:* For master's, thesis (for some programs), fieldwork; for doctorate, 2 foreign languages, thesis/dissertation; for M Div, 2 foreign languages, thesis/dissertation (for some programs). *Entrance requirements:* For M Div and master's, minimum GPA of 2.6; for doctorate, minimum GPA of 3.0. Additional exam requirements/recommendations for international students: Required—TOEFL.

Reformed Theological Seminary–Orlando Campus, Graduate Program, Oviedo, FL 32765-7197. Offers biblical studies (MA); counseling (MA); ministry (D Min); reformation studies (Th M); theological studies (MA); theology (M Div); MA/Certificate. Part-time programs available. Postbaccalaureate distance learning degree programs offered (minimal on-campus study). *Entrance requirements:* For M Div and master's, minimum GPA of 2.6. Electronic applications accepted.

Reformed Theological Seminary–Washington D.C., Graduate and Professional Programs, McLean, VA 22101. Offers Bible (M Div); practical theology (M Div); religion (MA); theology (M Div). Part-time and evening/weekend programs available. *Faculty:* 2 full-time (0 women), 5 part-time/adjunct (0 women). *Students:* 18 full-time (0 women), 89 part-time (14 women); includes 3 African Americans, 24 Asian Americans or Pacific Islanders, 3 Hispanic Americans. Average age 35. 50 applicants, 76% accepted, 35 enrolled. In 2009, 11 master's awarded. *Degree requirements:* For master's, integrative paper. *Entrance requirements:* For master's, minimum undergraduate GPA of 2.6. Additional exam requirements/recommendations for international students: Required—TOEFL (minimum score 550 paper-based; 213 computer-based), TWE. *Application deadline:* Applications are processed on a rolling basis. Application fee: $70. Electronic applications accepted. *Expenses:* Tuition: Full-time $6480; part-time $360 per credit. Tuition and fees vary according to campus/location. *Financial support:* In 2009–10, 89 students received support, including 7 fellowships (averaging $1,000 per year); institutionally sponsored loans, scholarships/grants, tuition waivers (partial), and unspecified assistantships also available. Support available to part-time students. Financial award application deadline: 6/1. *Faculty research:* Theology, biblical studies, cultural studies. *Unit head:* Hugh C. Whelchel, Executive Director, 703-448-3393, Fax: 703-738-7389, E-mail: hwhelchel@rts.edu. *Application contact:* Geoff M. Sackett, Director of Admissions, 800-639-0226, Fax: 703-738-7389, E-mail: gsackett@rts.edu.

Regent College, Program in Theology, Vancouver, BC V6T 2E4, Canada. Offers M Div, MCS, Th M, Dip CS. *Accreditation:* ATS (one or more programs are accredited). Part-time and evening/weekend programs available. *Faculty:* 16 full-time (3 women), 19 part-time/adjunct (7 women). *Students:* 265 full-time (85 women), 248 part-time (104 women); includes 143 minority (2 African Americans, 131 Asian Americans or Pacific Islanders, 10 Hispanic Americans). Average age 33. 232 applicants, 89% accepted, 140 enrolled. In 2009, 53 M Divs, 97 master's, 87 other advanced degrees awarded. *Degree requirements:* For master's, thesis (for some programs). *Entrance requirements:* For M Div and Dip CS, minimum GPA of 2.8; for master's, minimum GPA of 2.8 (MCS), 3.5 (Th M). Additional exam requirements/recommendations for international students: Required—TOEFL (minimum score 575 paper-based; 230 computer-based; 90 iBT), TWE (minimum score 5). *Application deadline:* For fall admission, 2/1 priority date for domestic students, 1/1 priority date for international students; for winter admission, 7/1 priority date for domestic and international students; for spring admission, 2/1 priority date for domestic students, 1/1 priority date for international students. Applications are processed on a rolling basis. Application fee: $60 Canadian dollars. *Financial support:* In 2009–10, 84 students received support, including 150 teaching assistantships (averaging $2,500 per year); career-related internships or fieldwork, scholarships/grants, and health care benefits also available. Financial award application deadline: 3/1. *Faculty research:* Integration of theology with secular life, Biblical studies. *Unit head:* Dr. Rod Wilson, President, 604-221-3318, Fax: 604-224-3097, E-mail: presidentsoffice@regent-college.edu. *Application contact:* Cindy Y. Aalders, Director of Admissions, 604-224-3245 Ext. 335, Fax: 604-224-3097, E-mail: admissions@regent-college.edu.

Regent University, Graduate School, School of Divinity, Virginia Beach, VA 23464-9800. Offers Biblical studies (MA); leadership and renewal (D Min); missiology (M Div, MA); practical theology (M Div, MA); renewal studies (PhD); M Div/M Ed; M Div/MA; M Div/MBA; M Ed/MA; MBA/MA. *Accreditation:* ACIPE; ATS. Part-time programs available. Postbaccalaureate distance

Theology

Regent University (continued)
learning degree programs offered (minimal on-campus study). *Faculty:* 19 full-time (4 women), 28 part-time/adjunct (5 women). *Students:* 108 full-time (53 women), 436 part-time (171 women); includes 244 minority (214 African Americans, 2 American Indian/Alaska Native, 13 Asian Americans or Pacific Islanders, 15 Hispanic Americans), 19 international. Average age 40. 349 applicants, 63% accepted, 97 enrolled. In 2009, 31 first professional degrees, 39 master's, 5 doctorates awarded. *Degree requirements:* For master's, comprehensive exam, thesis or alternative, internship; for doctorate, thesis/dissertation or alternative; for M Div, internship. *Entrance requirements:* For M Div, GRE General Test or MAT, minimum undergraduate GPA of 3.0, minimum 3 years of ministry experience, transcripts, recommendations; for master's, GRE General Test or MAT, minimum undergraduate GPA of 2.75, writing sample, clergy recommendation; for doctorate, M Div or theological master's degree; minimum graduate GPA of 3.5 (PhD), 3.0 (D Min); recommendations; writing sample; transcripts. Additional exam requirements/recommendations for international students: Required—TOEFL (minimum score 577 paper-based; 233 computer-based). *Application deadline:* For fall admission, 5/1 priority date for domestic students. Applications are processed on a rolling basis. Application fee: $50. Electronic applications accepted. *Expenses:* Contact institution. *Financial support:* In 2009–10, 401 students received support; fellowships with full and partial tuition reimbursements available, career-related internships or fieldwork, scholarships/grants, tuition waivers (full and partial), and unspecified assistantships available. Support available to part-time students. Financial award application deadline: 9/1; financial award applicants required to submit FAFSA. *Faculty research:* Greek and Hebrew theology, spiritual formation, global missions and world Christianity, women's studies. *Unit head:* Dr. Michael Palmer, Dean, 757-352-4406, Fax: 757-352-4597, E-mail: mpalmer@regent.edu. *Application contact:* Matthew Chadwick, Director of Admissions, 800-373-5504, Fax: 757-352-4381, E-mail: admissions@regent.edu.

Regis College, Graduate and Professional Programs, Toronto, ON M4Y 2R5, Canada. Offers eastern Christian studies (Certificate); Ignatian studies (Diploma); Lonergan studies (Diploma); ministry (D Min); ministry and spirituality (MAMS); philosophical studies (Diploma); retreat direction (Certificate); sacred theology (STB, STM, STD, STL); spiritual direction (Diploma); spiritual theology (Diploma); theological studies (MTS, Diploma); theology (M Div, MA, Th M, PhD, Th D); M Div/MA. *Accreditation:* ATS (one or more programs are accredited). *Faculty:* 13 full-time (3 women), 6 part-time/adjunct (1 woman). *Students:* 86 full-time (28 women), 130 part-time (80 women); includes 39 minority (9 African Americans, 1 American Indian/Alaska Native, 27 Asian Americans or Pacific Islanders, 2 Hispanic Americans), 51 international. Average age 46. 116 applicants, 83% accepted, 67 enrolled. In 2009, 13 first professional degrees, 12 master's, 3 doctorates, 40 other advanced degrees awarded. Terminal master's awarded for partial completion of doctoral program. *Degree requirements:* For master's, 2 foreign languages, thesis; for doctorate, 3 foreign languages, comprehensive exam, thesis/dissertation; for first professional degree, comprehensive exam. *Entrance requirements:* For first professional degree and other advanced degree, minimum GPA of 3.0; for master's, minimum GPA of 3.3; for doctorate, minimum GPA of 3.7. Additional exam requirements/recommendations for international students: Required—TOEFL (minimum score 580 paper-based; 237 computer-based; 93 iBT), TWE (minimum score 5). *Application deadline:* For fall admission, 3/15 priority date for domestic and international students; for winter admission, 12/1 for domestic and international students; for spring admission, 3/15 for domestic and international students. Applications are processed on a rolling basis. Application fee: $25. *Financial support:* In 2009–10, 61 students received support. Career-related internships or fieldwork and scholarships/grants available. Support available to part-time students. Financial award application deadline: 3/15. *Unit head:* Dr. Gordon Rixon, Dean, 416-922-5474 Ext. 225, Fax: 416-922-2898, E-mail: gordon.rixon@utoronto.ca. *Application contact:* Elaine Chu, Registrar, 416-922-5474 Ext. 226, Fax: 416-922-2898, E-mail: regis.registrar@utoronto.ca.

Sacred Heart Major Seminary, School of Theology, Detroit, MI 48206-1799. Offers pastoral studies (MAPS); theology (M Div, MA). *Accreditation:* ACIPE; ATS. Part-time and evening/weekend programs available. *Degree requirements:* For master's, one foreign language, thesis optional, integrating project; for M Div, integrating seminar. *Entrance requirements:* For M Div and master's, GRE, previous course work in philosophy and theology. *Faculty research:* Local church history, patristics, spirituality, religious education.

Sacred Heart School of Theology, Graduate and Professional Programs, Hales Corners, WI 53130-0429. Offers theology (M Div, MA). *Accreditation:* ACIPE; ATS. Part-time programs available. *Faculty:* 29 full-time (6 women), 14 part-time/adjunct (6 women). *Students:* 79 full-time (0 women), 24 part-time (13 women); includes 4 minority (1 African American, 1 Asian American or Pacific Islander, 2 Hispanic Americans), 20 international. Average age 47. 20 applicants, 100% accepted, 20 enrolled. In 2009, 11 first professional degrees, 3 master's awarded. *Degree requirements:* For master's, essay or comprehensive exam; for M Div, integrating seminar. *Entrance requirements:* For master's, MAT, 6 hours of course work each in philosophy and theology, letter of recommendation. *Application deadline:* For fall admission, 8/1 for domestic students; for spring admission, 12/1 for domestic students. Application fee: $50. *Financial support:* In 2009–10, 10 students received support. Career-related internships or fieldwork and scholarships/grants available. Financial award application deadline: 9/30; financial award applicants required to submit FAFSA. *Unit head:* Very Rev. Jan de Jong, President-Rector, 414-425-8300, Fax: 414-529-6999, E-mail: jdejong@shst.edu. *Application contact:* Rev. Thomas L. Knoebel, Director of Admissions, 414-425-8300 Ext. 6984, Fax: 414-529-6999, E-mail: tknoebel@shst.edu.

St. Andrew's College in Winnipeg, Graduate Programs, Winnipeg, MB R3T 2M7, Canada. Offers M Div. *Degree requirements:* For M Div, one foreign language, thesis/dissertation. *Faculty research:* Church history, doctrine, liturgical theology.

St. Augustine's Seminary of Toronto, Graduate and Professional Programs, Scarborough, ON M1M 1M3, Canada. Offers divinity (M Div); lay ministry (Diploma); religious education (MRE); theological studies (MTS, Diploma). *Accreditation:* ATS. Part-time and evening/weekend programs available. *Degree requirements:* For M Div, comprehensive exam (for some programs), thesis/dissertation optional, field education. *Entrance requirements:* Course work in philosophy. Additional exam requirements/recommendations for international students: Required—TOEFL (minimum score 580 paper-based; 237 computer-based), TWE (minimum score 5).

Saint Bernard's School of Theology and Ministry, Graduate and Professional Programs, Rochester, NY 14618. Offers pastoral studies (MA, Certificate); theological studies (MA); theology (M Div). *Accreditation:* ATS (one or more programs are accredited). Part-time and evening/weekend programs available. *Faculty:* 3 full-time (2 women), 8 part-time/adjunct (3 women). *Students:* 2 full-time (1 woman), 125 part-time (58 women); includes 5 minority (2 African Americans, 1 Asian American or Pacific Islander, 2 Hispanic Americans). Average age 50. 42 applicants, 100% accepted, 42 enrolled. In 2009, 7 first professional degrees, 23 master's awarded. *Degree requirements:* For master's, variable foreign language requirement, thesis (for some programs). *Entrance requirements:* For M Div, minimum GPA of 2.0; for master's, minimum GPA of 2.5. *Application deadline:* Applications are processed on a rolling basis. Application fee: $75. *Expenses:* Tuition: Part-time $1464 per course. Required fees: $30 per semester. *Financial support:* In 2009–10, 33 students received support; fellowships, research assistantships, teaching assistantships, career-related internships or fieldwork, scholarships/grants, and tuition waivers (partial) available. Support available to part-time students. Financial award application deadline: 4/15; financial award applicants required to submit FAFSA. *Unit head:* Dr. Patricia Schoelles, President, 585-271-3657 Ext. 276, Fax: 585-271-2045, E-mail: pschoelles@stbernards.edu. *Application contact:* Laura Smith, Director of Admissions and Financial Aid, 585-271-3657 Ext. 289, Fax: 585-271-2045, E-mail: admissions@stbernards.edu.

St. Catherine University, Graduate Programs, Program in Theology, St. Paul, MN 55105. Offers MA. Part-time and evening/weekend programs available. *Faculty:* 7 full-time (2 women). *Students:* 10 full-time (8 women), 36 part-time (34 women); includes 3 minority (2 African Americans, 1 Asian American or Pacific Islander). Average age 44. 12 applicants, 92% accepted, 8 enrolled. In 2009, 8 master's awarded. *Degree requirements:* For master's, comprehensive exam, thesis (for some programs). *Entrance requirements:* For master's, MAT, minimum GPA of 3.0. Additional exam requirements/recommendations for international students: Required—Michigan English Language Assessment Battery or TOEFL (minimum score 600 paper-based; 250 computer-based; 100 iBT). *Application deadline:* For fall admission, 8/1 priority date for domestic students. Applications are processed on a rolling basis. Application fee: $35. *Expenses:* Contact institution. *Financial support:* In 2009–10, 9 students received support; research assistantships, career-related internships or fieldwork and institutionally sponsored loans available. Support available to part-time students. Financial award application deadline: 4/1; financial award applicants required to submit FAFSA. *Faculty research:* Feminist scholarship, historical theology, symbols, rites of purification, spirituality. *Unit head:* Dr. Catherine Michaud, Director, 651-690-6017, Fax: 651-690-6024. *Application contact:* 651-690-6933, Fax: 651-690-6064.

St. Charles Borromeo Seminary, Overbrook, Graduate and Professional Programs, Division of Theology, Wynnewood, PA 19096. Offers M Div, MA. *Accreditation:* ATS. Part-time programs available. *Degree requirements:* For master's, comprehensive exam, research papers; for M Div, comprehensive exam. *Entrance requirements:* For M Div, previous course work in philosophy and theology; for master's, M Div.

Saint Francis Seminary, Graduate and Professional Programs, St. Francis, WI 53235-3795. Offers M Div, MAPS. *Accreditation:* ACIPE; ATS. Part-time programs available. *Degree requirements:* For master's, comprehensive exam; for M Div, thesis/dissertation. *Entrance requirements:* For M Div and master's, Otis IQ Test, Terman Concept Mastery Test, interview. Additional exam requirements/recommendations for international students: Required—TOEFL (minimum score 550 paper-based).

St. John's Seminary, Graduate and Professional Programs, Camarillo, CA 93012-2598. Offers divinity (M Div); pastoral ministry (MAPM); theology (MA). *Accreditation:* ATS. Part-time programs available. *Faculty:* 21 full-time (4 women), 6 part-time/adjunct (1 woman). *Students:* 81 full-time (5 women), 10 part-time (4 women); includes 45 minority (18 Asian Americans or Pacific Islanders, 27 Hispanic Americans), 19 international. Average age 34. 37 applicants, 86% accepted, 32 enrolled. In 2009, 13 first professional degrees, 1 master's awarded. *Degree requirements:* For master's, comprehensive exam (for some programs), thesis optional, comprehensive integration paper (MAPM); for M Div, parish internship. *Entrance requirements:* For M Div, GRE General Test, bishop's approbation; for master's, GRE General Test, minimum GPA of 3.5 (MA), 2.5 (MAPM). Additional exam requirements/recommendations for international students: Required—TOEFL (minimum score 550 paper-based; 213 computer-based; 79 iBT). *Application deadline:* For fall admission, 7/15 priority date for domestic students. Applications are processed on a rolling basis. Application fee: $0. Electronic applications accepted. *Expenses:* Tuition: Full-time $13,250; part-time $442 per unit. One-time fee: $4446.52 full-time; $25 part-time. Full-time tuition and fees vary according to course load and program. *Faculty research:* Biblical studies, moral theology, historical studies, systematic theology, spiritual theology. *Unit head:* Rev. Richard Benson, Academic Dean, 805-482-2755, Fax: 805-482-3470, E-mail: rbensoncm@stjohnsem.edu. *Application contact:* Esme M. Takahashi, Registrar, 805-482-2755 Ext. 1014, Fax: 805-482-3470, E-mail: registrar-sjs@stjohnsem.edu.

Saint John's Seminary, Graduate Programs, Brighton, MA 02135. Offers M Div, MA Th, MAM. *Accreditation:* ATS.

St. John's University, St. John's College of Liberal Arts and Sciences, Department of Theology and Religious Studies, Queens, NY 11439. Offers pastoral ministry (Certificate); priestly studies (M Div); theology (MA, Certificate). *Accreditation:* ACIPE. Part-time and evening/weekend programs available. *Students:* 11 full-time (2 women), 29 part-time (22 women); includes 8 minority (3 African Americans, 2 Asian Americans or Pacific Islanders, 3 Hispanic Americans), 9 international. Average age 44. 27 applicants, 78% accepted, 9 enrolled. In 2009, 9 master's, 1 other advanced degree awarded. *Degree requirements:* For master's, thesis optional; for M Div, thesis/dissertation optional. *Entrance requirements:* For M Div and master's, minimum GPA of 3.0. Additional exam requirements/recommendations for international students: Required—TOEFL (minimum score 500 paper-based; 173 computer-based; 61 iBT), IELTS (minimum score 5.5). *Application deadline:* For fall admission, 5/1 priority date for domestic and international students; for spring admission, 11/1 priority date for domestic and international students. Applications are processed on a rolling basis. Application fee: $70. Electronic applications accepted. *Expenses:* Tuition: Full-time $16,290; part-time $905 per credit. Required fees: $300; $150 per semester. Tuition and fees vary according to program. *Financial support:* Research assistantships, scholarships/grants available. Support available to part-time students. Financial award application deadline: 3/1; financial award applicants required to submit FAFSA. *Faculty research:* Systematic theology, moral theory, Biblical studies, pastoral theology, church history. *Unit head:* Fr. Michael Whalen, Chair, 718-990-1556, E-mail: whalenm@stjohns.edu. *Application contact:* Kathleen Davis, Director of Graduate Admission, 718-990-2790, Fax: 718-990-5686, E-mail: gradhelp@stjohns.edu.

Saint John's University, Saint John's School of Theology and Seminary, Collegeville, MN 56321. Offers divinity (M Div); liturgical music (MA); liturgical studies (MA); pastoral ministry (MA); theology (MA), including church history, liturgy, monastic studies, scripture, spirituality, systematics; M Div/MA. *Accreditation:* ATS. Part-time programs available. Postbaccalaureate distance learning degree programs offered (no on-campus study). *Degree requirements:* For master's, one foreign language, comprehensive exam (for some programs), thesis (for some programs). *Entrance requirements:* For master's, GRE General Test or MAT. Electronic applications accepted. *Faculty research:* Religious education, biblical literature.

St. Joseph's Seminary, Institute of Religious Studies, Yonkers, NY 10704. Offers MA. *Accreditation:* ATS. Part-time and evening/weekend programs available. *Degree requirements:* For master's, comprehensive exam. *Entrance requirements:* For master's, 18 hours in theology and/or philosophy. Electronic applications accepted. *Expenses:* Contact institution. *Faculty research:* Medical ethics, mystical theology of Karl Rahner, medieval church history.

St. Joseph's Seminary, Professional Program, Yonkers, NY 10704. Offers divinity (M Div); theology (MA). *Accreditation:* ATS. *Degree requirements:* For master's, one foreign language, thesis; for M Div, comprehensive exam. *Entrance requirements:* For M Div and master's, 27 credits in philosophy and 9 in theology.

Saint Leo University, Graduate Studies in Theology, Saint Leo, FL 33574-6665. Offers theology (MA). Part-time and evening/weekend programs available. *Faculty:* 7 full-time (0 women), 1 part-time/adjunct (0 women). *Students:* 153 full-time (37 women); includes 15 minority (8 African Americans, 1 Asian American or Pacific Islander, 6 Hispanic Americans). Average age 52. In 2009, 3 master's awarded. *Degree requirements:* For master's, comprehensive project. *Entrance requirements:* For master's, bachelor's degree from regionally-accredited college or university with minimum GPA of 3.0, letter of recommendation. Additional exam requirements/recommendations for international students: Required—TOEFL (minimum score 550 paper-based; 213 computer-based; 80 iBT). *Application deadline:* For fall admission, 7/1 priority date for domestic and international students; for spring admission, 11/1 priority date for domestic and international students. Applications are processed on a rolling basis. Application fee: $75. Electronic applications accepted. *Expenses:* Tuition: Part-time $1767 per course. Required fees: $115 per course. *Financial support:* In 2009–10, 1 student received support. Federal Work-Study and health care benefits available. *Faculty research:* Ecclesiology and the Second Vatican Council, sacramental theology and the liturgical movement, Christian and Eastern religious traditions, Ecumenism, ministry and technology. *Unit head:* Dr. William Ditewig, Director, 352-588-7297, Fax: 352-588-8404, E-mail: william.ditewig@saintleo.edu. *Application contact:* Jared Welling, Director, Graduate/Weekend and Evening Admission, 800-707-8846, Fax: 352-588-7873, E-mail: grad.admissions@saintleo.edu.

Saint Louis University, Graduate School, College of Arts and Sciences and Graduate School, Department of Theological Studies, St. Louis, MO 63103-2097. Offers historical theology (MA,

PhD); theology (MA). Part-time programs available. *Degree requirements:* For master's, comprehensive exam; for doctorate, 4 foreign languages, comprehensive exam, thesis/dissertation, preliminary exams. *Entrance requirements:* For master's, GRE General Test, letters of recommendation, resume; for doctorate, GRE General Test, letters of recommendation, resumé, interview, transcripts, goal statement. Additional exam requirements/recommendations for international students: Required—TOEFL (minimum score 550 paper-based; 213 computer-based). Electronic applications accepted. *Faculty research:* Biblical and early church studies, medieval and renaissance studies, modern and American Christianity, comparative and interreligious studies, moral and ethical theology.

Saint Mary-of-the-Woods College, Program in Pastoral Theology, Saint Mary-of-the-Woods, IN 47876. Offers pastoral theology (MA); youth ministry (Graduate Certificate). Part-time and evening/weekend programs available. Postbaccalaureate distance learning degree programs offered (minimal on-campus study). *Degree requirements:* For master's, thesis, qualifying exam.

Saint Mary Seminary and Graduate School of Theology, School of Theology, Wickliffe, OH 44092-2527. Offers M Div, MA, D Min. *Accreditation:* ATS. Part-time programs available. *Degree requirements:* For master's, comprehensive exam, symposium; for doctorate, thesis/dissertation, final project, symposium; for M Div, one foreign language, evaluation by faculty for ordination. *Entrance requirements:* For M Div, GRE General Test, previous course work in religion and philosophy; for master's, GRE General Test, previous course work in religion; for doctorate, M Div or equivalent, 3 years in full-time ministry, interviews, ministry profile report. *Faculty research:* Pastoral ministry, theology of ministry, ecclesiology, American Catholics.

St. Mary's Seminary and University, Ecumenical Institute of Theology, Baltimore, MD 21210-1994. Offers church ministries (MA); theology (MA Th, Certificate). *Accreditation:* ATS. Part-time and evening/weekend programs available. *Degree requirements:* For master's, thesis or alternative, comprehensive exam or colloquium. *Expenses:* Contact institution. *Faculty research:* Scripture and ethics, theology and literature, early Christianity and Judaism, medical and social ethics.

See Display below.

St. Mary's Seminary and University, School of Theology, Baltimore, MD 21210-1994. Offers M Div, STB, MA Th, STD, STL. *Accreditation:* ATS (one or more programs are accredited). Part-time programs available. Terminal master's awarded for partial completion of doctoral program. *Degree requirements:* For master's and first professional degree, comprehensive exam. *Entrance requirements:* For master's, Computerized Adaptive Placement Assessment and Support System.

Saint Mary's University, Faculty of Arts, Department of Religious Studies, Halifax, NS B3H 3C3, Canada. Offers theology and religious studies (MA). *Unit head:* Dr. Paul Bowlby, Chair, 902-420-5823, Fax: 902-491-6286, E-mail: paul.bowlby@smu.ca. *Application contact:* Dr. Anne-Marie Dalton, Graduate Coordinator, 902-420-5864, E-mail: adalton@smu.ca.

St. Mary's University, Graduate School, Department of Theology, San Antonio, TX 78228-8507. Offers pastoral ministry (MA); theology (MA); JD/MA. Part-time and evening/weekend programs available. Postbaccalaureate distance learning degree programs offered (no on-campus study). *Degree requirements:* For master's, comprehensive exam, practicum (pastoral administration). *Entrance requirements:* For master's, GRE General Test, MAT, 12 credit hours in theology/philosophy. Additional exam requirements/recommendations for international students: Required—TOEFL (minimum score 550 paper-based; 213 computer-based; 80 iBT). Electronic applications accepted. *Expenses:* Tuition: Full-time $8004. Required fees: $536. One-time fee: $5 full-time. Full-time tuition and fees vary according to program. *Faculty research:* Bioethics; perceptions of ministry; Marian doctrines and the contemporary church; Jaspers, peace, and justice.

Saint Meinrad School of Theology, Professional Program, Saint Meinrad, IN 47577. Offers M Div. *Accreditation:* ATS. *Entrance requirements:* 30 credits in philosophy, 12 credits in theology. Additional exam requirements/recommendations for international students: Required—TOEFL (minimum score 550 paper-based). *Expenses:* Tuition: Full-time $16,865; part-time $340 per credit hour. Required fees: $275; $27 per course. One-time fee: $170 full-time.

Saint Meinrad School of Theology, Program in Catholic Thought and Life, Saint Meinrad, IN 47577. Offers MA. *Accreditation:* ATS. Part-time and evening/weekend programs available. *Degree requirements:* For master's, comprehensive exam. *Expenses:* Tuition: Full-time $16,865; part-time $340 per credit hour. Required fees: $275; $27 per course. One-time fee: $170 full-time.

Saint Meinrad School of Theology, Program in Theological Studies, Saint Meinrad, IN 47577. Offers MTS. *Accreditation:* ATS. Part-time and evening/weekend programs available. *Degree requirements:* For master's, thesis. *Expenses:* Tuition: Full-time $16,865; part-time $340 per credit hour. Required fees: $275; $27 per course. One-time fee: $170 full-time.

Saint Michael's College, Graduate Programs, Program in Theology and Pastoral Ministry, Colchester, VT 05439. Offers theology (MA, CAS, Certificate). Part-time and evening/weekend programs available. *Degree requirements:* For master's, thesis optional, 1 foreign language if thesis option selected. *Entrance requirements:* For master's, bachelor's degree in arts, science, philosophy, theology, or education; minimum GPA of 3.0; 24 hours of course work in theology and other humanistic disciplines. Additional exam requirements/recommendations for international students: Required—TOEFL (minimum score 550 paper-based; 213 computer-based; 80 iBT), IELTS (minimum score 6). Electronic applications accepted. *Expenses:* Contact institution.

St. Norbert College, Program in Theological Studies, De Pere, WI 54115-2099. Offers MTS. Part-time programs available. *Faculty:* 10 part-time/adjunct (4 women). *Students:* 59 part-time (42 women); includes 7 minority (1 Asian American or Pacific Islander, 6 Hispanic Americans). 6 applicants, 100% accepted, 6 enrolled. In 2009, 5 master's awarded. *Degree requirements:* For master's, comprehensive exam, thesis. *Entrance requirements:* For master's, minimum of 8 credits of course work in theology/religious studies, BA degree from an accredited institution. *Application deadline:* Applications are processed on a rolling basis. Application fee: $50. Electronic applications accepted. *Expenses:* Tuition: Part-time $390 per credit hour. *Financial support:* In 2009–10, 9 students received support. Scholarships/grants available. Support available to part-time students. *Faculty research:* Practical theology, Holocaust, Rahner, women in the Bible and Christian ethics. *Unit head:* Dr. Howard Ebert, Director, 920-403-3956, Fax: 920-403-4086, E-mail: howard.ebert@snc.edu. *Application contact:* Dinah Grassel, Program Coordinator, 920-403-3957, Fax: 920-403-4086, E-mail: dinah.grassel@snc.edu.

St. Patrick's Seminary & University, School of Theology, Menlo Park, CA 94025-3596. Offers M Div, STB, MA. *Accreditation:* ATS (one or more programs are accredited). Part-time programs available. *Degree requirements:* For master's, comprehensive exam, thesis or alternative. *Entrance requirements:* For first professional degree, GRE General Test or MAT, minimum GPA of 2.0, interview; for master's, GRE General Test, minimum GPA of 3.0, interview. Additional exam requirements/recommendations for international students: Required—TOEFL (minimum score 550 paper-based; 215 computer-based; 80 iBT), TWE. *Faculty research:* Systematic theology, sacred scripture, moral theology, liturgy.

Saint Paul School of Theology, Graduate and Professional Programs, Kansas City, MO 64127-2440. Offers M Div, MA, MTS, D Min. *Accreditation:* ACIPE; ATS. Part-time programs available. *Degree requirements:* For doctorate, thesis/dissertation. *Entrance requirements:* For

Theology

Saint Paul School of Theology (continued)
M Div and master's, minimum GPA of 2.75; for doctorate, minimum GPA of 3.0. Additional exam requirements/recommendations for international students: Required—TOEFL. *Faculty research:* Religion and aging; leadership development; feminist, African-American, and liberation theology; rural ministry; worship and the arts.

Saint Paul University, Faculty of Canon Law, Ottawa, ON K1S 1C4, Canada. Offers canon law (MCL, JCD, PhD, Graduate Certificate, JCL); canonical practice (Graduate Certificate); ecclesiastical administration (Graduate Certificate). Part-time programs available. *Faculty:* 9 full-time (1 woman), 8 part-time/adjunct (1 woman). *Students:* 54 full-time (10 women), 6 part-time (2 women); includes 31 minority (15 African Americans, 15 Asian Americans or Pacific Islanders, 1 Hispanic American). Average age 40. 45 applicants, 84% accepted, 38 enrolled. In 2009, 11 master's, 3 doctorates, 15 other advanced degrees awarded. *Degree requirements:* For master's, one foreign language; for doctorate, one foreign language, comprehensive exam, thesis/dissertation; for other advanced degree, one foreign language, comprehensive exam and seminar paper (JCL). *Entrance requirements:* For master's, appropriate bachelor's degree, 18 credits in theology; for doctorate, JCL or MCL; for other advanced degree, B Th or equivalent (JCL), appropriate bachelor's degree, 18 credits in theology. *Application deadline:* For fall admission, 8/15 priority date for domestic students, 3/15 priority date for international students. Applications are processed on a rolling basis. Application fee: $70 Canadian dollars. *Financial support:* Scholarships/grants and bursaries available. *Faculty research:* Questions related to Church law. *Unit head:* Dr. Anne Asselin, Dean, 613-751-4018, Fax: 613-751-4036, E-mail: canonlaw@ustpaul.ca. *Application contact:* Beverly Ruth Kavanaugh, Administrative Assistant, 613-751-4018, Fax: 613-751-4036, E-mail: bkavanaugh@ustpaul.ca.

Saint Paul University, Faculty of Human Sciences, Program in Counseling and Spirituality, Ottawa, ON K1S 1C4, Canada. Offers individual or marital/couple counseling (MA); spiritual care (MA). Part-time programs available. *Degree requirements:* For master's, research project or thesis. *Entrance requirements:* For master's, honors BA in human sciences, minimum B average, 12 theology credits.

Saint Paul University, Faculty of Theology, Ottawa, ON K1S 1C4, Canada. Offers MA Th, MP Th, MRE, D Min, D Th, PhD, L Th. *Degree requirements:* For master's and L Th, one foreign language; for doctorate, one foreign language, comprehensive exam, thesis/dissertation. *Entrance requirements:* For master's, B Th; for doctorate, MA Th, L Th, MP Th, M Div. *Faculty research:* Biblical studies, systematic and historical theology, ethics, spirituality, Eastern Christian studies, applied theology.

St. Petersburg Theological Seminary, Graduate Programs, St. Petersburg, FL 33708. Offers Biblical studies (MA); counseling (MA); divinity (M Div); education (MA); Judaic studies (MA); ministry (MA, D Min); religious teacher (MA). Part-time and evening/weekend programs available. Postbaccalaureate distance learning degree programs offered (minimal on-campus study). *Degree requirements:* For master's, thesis; for doctorate, thesis/dissertation. *Entrance requirements:* For M Div, Bachelor degree; for doctorate, Master degree. Electronic applications accepted.

St. Peter's Seminary, Department of Theology, London, ON N6A 3Y1, Canada. Offers M Div, MTS. *Accreditation:* ATS.

Saints Cyril and Methodius Seminary, Graduate and Professional Programs, Orchard Lake, MI 48324. Offers pastoral ministry (MAPM); religious education (MARE); theology (M Div, MA). *Accreditation:* ATS. Part-time programs available.

St. Stephen's College, Programs in Theology, Edmonton, AB T6G 2J6, Canada. Offers ministry (D Min); pastoral counseling (MA); social transformation ministry (MA); spirituality and liturgy (MA); theological studies (MTS); theology (M Th). Part-time and evening/weekend programs available. Postbaccalaureate distance learning degree programs offered (minimal on-campus study). Terminal master's awarded for partial completion of doctoral program. *Degree requirements:* For master's, thesis; for doctorate, thesis/dissertation. *Entrance requirements:* Additional exam requirements/recommendations for international students: Required—TOEFL. Electronic applications accepted. *Faculty research:* Methodology for theological education, practice and supervision for ministry.

St. Thomas University, School of Theology and Ministry, Institute for Pastoral Ministries, Miami Gardens, FL 33054-6459. Offers pastoral ministries (MA, Certificate); practical theology (PhD). Part-time and evening/weekend programs available. *Degree requirements:* For master's, comprehensive exam; for doctorate, comprehensive exam, thesis/dissertation. *Entrance requirements:* For master's, interview, minimum GPA of 3.0 or GRE; for doctorate, GRE, MA in theology. Additional exam requirements/recommendations for international students: Required—TOEFL (minimum score 550 paper-based; 213 computer-based; 79 iBT). Electronic applications accepted.

St. Tikhon's Orthodox Theological Seminary, Divinity Program, South Canaan, PA 18459. Offers M Div. *Accreditation:* ATS. *Degree requirements:* For M Div, one foreign language, thesis/dissertation optional. *Entrance requirements:* Letters of recommendation. *Faculty research:* Church history, patristics, scripture, spirituality.

Saint Vincent de Paul Regional Seminary, Graduate and Professional Programs, Boynton Beach, FL 33436-4899. Offers theology (M Div, MA Th). *Accreditation:* ATS. Part-time programs available. *Degree requirements:* For master's, comprehensive exam (for some programs), thesis optional; for M Div, one foreign language. *Entrance requirements:* For M Div and master's, GRE General Test, MAT. Additional exam requirements/recommendations for international students: Required—TOEFL.

Saint Vincent Seminary, School of Theology, Latrobe, PA 15650-2690. Offers M Div, MA. *Accreditation:* ATS. Part-time programs available. *Degree requirements:* For master's, one foreign language, comprehensive exam; for M Div, one foreign language. *Entrance requirements:* For M Div, minimum GPA of 2.5; for master's, minimum GPA of 3.0. Additional exam requirements/recommendations for international students: Required—TOEFL (minimum score 550 paper-based; 220 computer-based). Electronic applications accepted. *Faculty research:* Church history, preaching, psychology of religion, Biblical studies, moral theology.

St. Vladimir's Orthodox Theological Seminary, Graduate School of Theology, Crestwood, NY 10707-1699. Offers general theological studies (MA); liturgical music (MA); religious education (MA); theology (M Div, M Th, D Min); M Div/MA. MA in general theological studies, M Div offered jointly with St. Nersess Seminary. *Accreditation:* ATS. Part-time programs available. *Degree requirements:* For master's, one foreign language, thesis, fieldwork; for doctorate, thesis/dissertation, fieldwork; for M Div, one foreign language, thesis/dissertation, fieldwork. *Entrance requirements:* For doctorate, M Div, minimum GPA of 3.0. Additional exam requirements/recommendations for international students: Required—TOEFL (minimum score 250 computer-based).

Samford University, Beeson School of Divinity, Birmingham, AL 35229. Offers M Div, MTS, D Min, JD/M Div, JD/MTS, M Div/MBA, M Div/MM, M Div/MSE. *Accreditation:* ATS. *Faculty:* 14 full-time (3 women), 2 part-time/adjunct (0 women). *Students:* 193 full-time (31 women), 11 part-time (3 women); includes 30 minority (28 African Americans, 2 Hispanic Americans), 2 international. Average age 30. 70 applicants, 69% accepted, 37 enrolled. In 2009, 32 master's, 8 doctorates awarded. *Degree requirements:* For master's, one foreign language, thesis optional; for doctorate, thesis/dissertation; for M Div, 2 foreign languages, thesis/dissertation optional, 4 internships (including 1 cross-cultural experience). *Entrance requirements:* For M Div and master's, minimum GPA of 2.5; for doctorate, minimum GPA of 3.0. Additional exam requirements/recommendations for international students: Required—TOEFL (minimum score 550 paper-based; 213 computer-based). *Application deadline:* For fall admission, 3/1 for domestic and international students; for spring admission, 10/1 for domestic and international students. Application fee: $25. Electronic applications accepted. *Expenses:* Contact institution. *Financial support:* In 2009–10, 151 students received support. Scholarships/grants and tuition waivers (full and partial) available. Financial award applicants required to submit FAFSA. *Faculty research:* New Testament theology, exegesis of Psalms, doctrinal preaching, history of Anglicanism, racial reconciliation. *Unit head:* Dr. Timothy George, Dean, 205-726-2632, E-mail: tfgeorge@samford.edu. *Application contact:* Burch Rountree Barger, Director of Admission, Scholarship and Financial Aid, 205-726-2066, Fax: 205-726-4120, E-mail: brbarger@samford.edu.

San Francisco Theological Seminary, Graduate and Professional Programs, San Anselmo, CA 94960-2997. Offers M Div, MA, MATS, D Min, PhD, Th D, M Div/MA. *Accreditation:* ACIPE; ATS (one or more programs are accredited). Part-time programs available. *Degree requirements:* For master's, one foreign language, thesis (for some programs); for doctorate, thesis/dissertation; for M Div, one foreign language, internship. *Entrance requirements:* For master's, minimum GPA of 3.0; for doctorate, M Div. Additional exam requirements/recommendations for international students: Required—TOEFL.

Seabury-Western Theological Seminary, School of Theology, Evanston, IL 60201-2976. Offers advanced theological studies (Certificate); church music and liturgy (MTS); congregational development (D Min); preaching (D Min); theological studies (MA); theology (M Div, L Th). D Min in congregational development offered in summer only. *Accreditation:* ACIPE; ATS (one or more programs are accredited). Part-time programs available. *Degree requirements:* For master's, thesis; for doctorate, thesis/dissertation; for other advanced degree, thesis (for some programs). *Entrance requirements:* For M Div and master's, interview, sample of written work. *Faculty research:* Liturgical interpretations of baptism, trinitarian theology, congregational development, post modern biblical criticism-Matthew.

Seattle Pacific University, Master of Arts in Theology Program, Seattle, WA 98119-1997. Offers MA. *Faculty:* 7 full-time (1 woman). *Students:* 11 full-time (6 women), 2 part-time (1 woman); includes 1 minority (African American). Average age 33. 23 applicants, 57% accepted, 13 enrolled. *Degree requirements:* For master's, internship or thesis. *Entrance requirements:* For master's, minimum GPA of 3.0. Additional exam requirements/recommendations for international students: Required—TOEFL (minimum score 550 paper-based; 213 computer-based). *Application deadline:* For fall admission, 5/15 for domestic and international students. Applications are processed on a rolling basis. Application fee: $50. Electronic applications accepted. *Expenses:* Tuition: Part-time $485 per credit. Part-time tuition and fees vary according to course level, degree level and program. *Financial support:* In 2009–10, 8 students received support. Application deadline: 4/1. *Unit head:* Dr. Douglas Strong, Dean, 206-281-2473, E-mail: dstrong@spu.edu. *Application contact:* John Glancy, Director, Graduate Admissions/Marketing, 206-281-2325, Fax: 206-281-2877, E-mail: jglancy@spu.edu.

Seattle Pacific University, The Master of Divinity Program, Seattle, WA 98119-1997. Offers M Div. *Students:* 12 full-time (6 women), 2 part-time (0 women); includes 4 minority (1 African American, 2 Asian Americans or Pacific Islanders, 1 Hispanic American). Average age 33. 17 applicants, 82% accepted, 14 enrolled. *Entrance requirements:* Additional exam requirements/recommendations for international students: Required—TOEFL (minimum score 550 paper-based; 213 computer-based). *Application deadline:* For fall admission, 5/15 for domestic and international students. Application fee: $50. *Expenses:* Tuition: Part-time $485 per credit. Part-time tuition and fees vary according to course level, degree level and program. *Financial support:* In 2009–10, 11 students received support. Scholarships/grants available. Financial award applicants required to submit FAFSA. *Unit head:* Douglas Strong, Dean, 206-281-2473, E-mail: dstrong@spu.edu. *Application contact:* John Glancy, Director, Graduate Admissions/Marketing, 206-281-2325, Fax: 206-281-2877, E-mail: jglancy@spu.edu.

Seattle University, School of Theology and Ministry, Program in Divinity, Seattle, WA 98122-1090. Offers M Div. *Accreditation:* ATS. Part-time and evening/weekend programs available. *Degree requirements:* For M Div, project. *Entrance requirements:* Interview, minimum GPA of 2.75.

Seattle University, School of Theology and Ministry, Program in Transforming Spirituality, Seattle, WA 98122-1090. Offers MATS, Certificate. *Accreditation:* ATS. Part-time and evening/weekend programs available. *Degree requirements:* For master's, project. *Entrance requirements:* For master's, interview, minimum GPA of 2.75.

Seminary of the Immaculate Conception, School of Theology, Huntington, NY 11743-1696. Offers pastoral studies (MA); theology (M Div, MA, D Min, Certificate). *Accreditation:* ATS (one or more programs are accredited). Part-time and evening/weekend programs available. *Faculty:* 8 full-time (2 women), 12 part-time/adjunct (5 women). *Students:* 40 full-time (0 women), 105 part-time (47 women); includes 25 minority (8 African Americans, 7 Asian Americans or Pacific Islanders, 10 Hispanic Americans), 11 international. Average age 49. 35 applicants, 100% accepted, 34 enrolled. In 2009, 3 first professional degrees, 27 master's awarded. *Degree requirements:* For master's, comprehensive exam; for doctorate, thesis/dissertation; for M Div, one foreign language, thesis/dissertation. *Entrance requirements:* For M Div, college degree in philosophy-theology; for master's, undergraduate degree; for doctorate, MA plus 30 credits or M Div; for Certificate, MA in theology. *Application deadline:* For fall admission, 8/30 priority date for domestic students; for spring admission, 1/20 priority date for domestic students. Applications are processed on a rolling basis. Application fee: $75. *Expenses:* Tuition: Full-time $12,000; part-time $450 per credit. Required fees: $50 per semester. One-time fee: $200 part-time. *Financial support:* Scholarships/grants available. *Unit head:* Sr. Mary Louise Brink, Academic Dean, 631-423-0483 Ext. 130, Fax: 631-432-2346, E-mail: mlbrink@icseminary.edu. *Application contact:* Kathryn L. Zahner, Registrar, 631-423-0483 Ext. 147, Fax: 631-423-2346, E-mail: kzahner@icseminary.edu.

Seminary of the Southwest, Graduate and Professional Programs, Austin, TX 78768-2247. Offers Anglican studies (Advanced Diploma); chaplaincy (MCPC); counseling (MAC); divinity (M Div); religion (MAR); spiritual formation (MAPM); theological studies (Advanced Diploma). *Accreditation:* ACIPE; ATS (one or more programs are accredited). Part-time and evening/weekend programs available. *Faculty:* 10 full-time (3 women), 22 part-time/adjunct (4 women). *Students:* 56 full-time (37 women), 52 part-time (41 women); includes 10 minority (4 African Americans, 2 Asian Americans or Pacific Islanders, 4 Hispanic Americans). Average age 46. 47 applicants, 100% accepted, 46 enrolled. In 2009, 10 first professional degrees, 11 master's, 5 other advanced degrees awarded. *Degree requirements:* For master's, thesis (for some programs). *Entrance requirements:* For M Div and master's, GRE, MAT, interview; for Advanced Diploma, interview. *Application deadline:* For fall admission, 7/1 for domestic students; for spring admission, 11/1 for domestic students. Applications are processed on a rolling basis. Application fee: $50. *Expenses:* Tuition: Full-time $13,150; part-time $390 per credit hour. Required fees: $75. One-time fee: $20 part-time. *Financial support:* Career-related internships or fieldwork and scholarships/grants available. Support available to part-time students. Financial award application deadline: 6/17. *Unit head:* Very Rev. Douglas Travis, Dean and President, 512-472-4133 Ext. 307, Fax: 512-472-3098, E-mail: dtravis@ssw.edu. *Application contact:* Jennielle Strother, Director of Admissions, 512-472-4133 Ext. 375, Fax: 512-472-3098, E-mail: jstrother@ssw.edu.

Seton Hall University, Immaculate Conception Seminary School of Theology, South Orange, NJ 07079-2697. Offers great spiritual books (Certificate); pastoral ministry (M Div, MA, Certificate); scripture studies (Certificate); Seminary's Theological Education for Parish Services (STEPS) (Certificate); theology (MA); youth ministry (Certificate). *Accreditation:* ATS (one or more programs are accredited). Part-time and evening/weekend programs available. *Faculty:* 16 full-time (2 women), 13 part-time/adjunct (1 woman). *Students:* 132 full-time (3 women), 79 part-time (32 women); includes 38 minority (4 African Americans, 6 Asian Americans or Pacific Islanders, 28 Hispanic Americans), 81 international. Average age 38. 46 applicants, 100% accepted, 43 enrolled. In 2009, 12 first professional degrees, 24 master's, 3 other advanced degrees awarded. *Degree requirements:* For master's, one foreign language, comprehensive exam, thesis (for some programs), final project; for M Div, one foreign language, thesis/

dissertation, final project and seminar, field education, spiritual formation. *Entrance requirements:* For M Div, GRE, MAT; for master's, GRE General Test or MAT. Additional exam requirements/recommendations for international students: Required—TOEFL (minimum score 600 paper-based; 250 computer-based; 100 iBT). *Application deadline:* For fall admission, 8/1 priority date for domestic and international students; for spring admission, 12/15 priority date for domestic and international students. Applications are processed on a rolling basis. Application fee: $50. Electronic applications accepted. *Expenses:* Contact institution. *Financial support:* In 2009–10, 211 students received support. Career-related internships or fieldwork, Federal Work-Study, scholarships/grants, tuition waivers (partial), and unspecified assistantships available. Support available to part-time students. Financial award application deadline: 8/1; financial award applicants required to submit FAFSA. *Unit head:* Rev. Msgr. Robert F. Coleman, Rector/Dean, 973-761-9016, Fax: 973-761-9577, E-mail: robert.coleman@shu.edu. *Application contact:* Rev. Msgr. Joseph R. Chapel, Associate Dean, 973-761-9633, Fax: 973-761-9577, E-mail: theology@shu.edu.

Sewanee: The University of the South, School of Theology, Sewanee, TN 37383. Offers M Div, MA, STM, D Min. *Accreditation:* ACIPE; ATS. Part-time programs available. *Degree requirements:* For master's, thesis; for doctorate, thesis/dissertation. *Entrance requirements:* For M Div, GRE General Test, interview; for master's, GRE General Test, M Div (STM); for doctorate, M Div. Additional exam requirements/recommendations for international students: Required—TOEFL (minimum score 550 paper-based).

Shaw University, Divinity School, Raleigh, NC 27601-2399. Offers M Div, MRE. *Accreditation:* ATS. Part-time and evening/weekend programs available. *Degree requirements:* For master's, thesis; for M Div, thesis/dissertation. *Entrance requirements:* For M Div and master's, letters of reference. Electronic applications accepted. *Faculty research:* HIV/AIDS awareness through faith-based curriculum, domestic abuse and violence prevention, pedagogy for non-traditional theology education, health disparities in the African American community, technology and theological education.

Sh'or Yoshuv Rabbinical College, Graduate Programs, Far Rockaway, NY 11691-4002. *Accreditation:* AARTS.

Sioux Falls Seminary, Graduate and Professional Programs, Professional Program in Ministry, Sioux Falls, SD 57105-1599. Offers D Min. *Accreditation:* ACIPE. Part-time programs available. *Degree requirements:* For doctorate, thesis/dissertation. *Entrance requirements:* For doctorate, M Div, 3 years of ministry.

Sioux Falls Seminary, Graduate and Professional Programs, Program in Bible and Theology, Sioux Falls, SD 57105-1599. Offers MA. *Accreditation:* ACIPE; ATS. Part-time programs available. *Degree requirements:* For master's, 2 foreign languages, thesis or alternative. *Entrance requirements:* For master's, minimum GPA of 2.5.

Sioux Falls Seminary, Graduate and Professional Programs, Program in Theological Studies, Sioux Falls, SD 57105-1599. Offers Certificate.

Southeastern Baptist Theological Seminary, Graduate and Professional Programs, Wake Forest, NC 27588-1889. Offers advanced biblical studies (M Div); Christian education (M Div, MACE); Christian ethics (PhD); Christian ministry (M Div); Christian planting (M Div); church music (MACM); counseling (MACO); evangelism (PhD); language (M Div); ministry (D Min); New Testament (PhD); Old Testament (PhD); philosophy (PhD); theology (Th M, PhD); women's studies (M Div). *Accreditation:* ACIPE; ATS (one or more programs are accredited). *Degree requirements:* For master's, thesis (for some programs), oral exam; for doctorate, thesis/dissertation, fieldwork; for M Div, supervised ministry. *Entrance requirements:* For master's, Cooperative English Test, minimum GPA of 2.0, M Div or equivalent (Th M); for doctorate, GRE General Test or MAT, Cooperative English Test, M Div or equivalent, 3 years of professional experience.

Southern Adventist University, School of Religion, Collegedale, TN 37315-0370. Offers Biblical and theological studies (MA); church leadership and management (M Min); church ministry and homiletics (M Min); evangelism and world mission (M Min); religious studies (MA). Part-time programs available. *Faculty:* 5 full-time (0 women). *Students:* 1 (woman) full-time, 1 part-time (0 women); includes 1 minority (African American). Average age 36. 2 applicants, 100% accepted, 2 enrolled. In 2009, 6 master's awarded. *Degree requirements:* For master's, comprehensive exam, thesis (for some programs). *Entrance requirements:* For master's, GRE. Additional exam requirements/recommendations for international students: Required—TOEFL (minimum score 600 paper-based; 250 computer-based). *Application deadline:* For spring admission, 5/1 priority date for domestic students, 4/30 for international students. Applications are processed on a rolling basis. Application fee: $25. *Expenses:* Tuition: Full-time $13,149; part-time $487 per credit hour. *Financial support:* Tuition waivers (full) available. Support available to part-time students. Financial award application deadline: 4/1; financial award applicants required to submit FAFSA. *Faculty research:* Biblical archaeology. *Unit head:* Dr. Greg A. King, Dean, 423-236-2975, Fax: 423-236-1976, E-mail: gking@southern.edu. *Application contact:* Susan L. Brown, Administrative Assistant, 423-236-2977, Fax: 423-236-1977, E-mail: sbrown@southern.edu.

Southern Baptist Theological Seminary, Billy Graham School of Missions, Evangelism and Church Growth, Louisville, KY 40280-0004. Offers Christian mission/world religion (PhD); evangelism/church growth (PhD); ministry (D Min); missiology (MA, D Miss); missions, evangelism and church growth (M Div); religion (Th M); theological studies (MA). *Accreditation:* ATS. Part-time and evening/weekend programs available. Postbaccalaureate distance learning degree programs offered (minimal on-campus study). *Faculty:* 12 full-time (0 women). *Students:* 608. In 2009, 27 first professional degrees, 4 master's, 3 doctorates awarded. *Degree requirements:* For master's and M Div, 2 foreign languages; for doctorate, 4 foreign languages, thesis/dissertation. *Entrance requirements:* For doctorate, GRE General Test, MAT, M Div. Additional exam requirements/recommendations for international students: Required—TOEFL, TWE. *Application deadline:* For fall admission, 8/1 priority date for domestic students; for spring admission, 1/2 for domestic students. Applications are processed on a rolling basis. Application fee: $35. *Faculty research:* Assimilation of church congregants, effective methodologies of evangelism, expectations of church members, spiritual warfare literature, formative church discipline. *Unit head:* Dr. Chuck Lawless, Dean, 800-626-5525, E-mail: clawless@sbts.edu. *Application contact:* Chuck Haddox, Director of Admissions, 800-626-5525 Ext. 4617, E-mail: chaddox@sbts.edu.

Southern Baptist Theological Seminary, School of Theology, Louisville, KY 40280-0004. Offers biblical and theological studies (M Div); biblical counseling (M Div, MA, D Min); biblical spirituality (D Min); Christian ministry (M Div); expository preaching (D Min); pastoral studies (M Div); theological studies (MA); theology (Th M, PhD); theology and arts (MA); theology and law (MA); worldview and apologetics (M Div). *Accreditation:* ATS. Part-time and evening/weekend programs available. Postbaccalaureate distance learning degree programs offered (minimal on-campus study). *Degree requirements:* For master's, 2 foreign languages, thesis; for doctorate, 4 foreign languages, thesis/dissertation; for M Div, 2 foreign languages. *Entrance requirements:* For master's, GRE General Test, MAT, M Div; for doctorate, GRE General Test, MAT, interview, M Div, field essay. Additional exam requirements/recommendations for international students: Required—TOEFL, TWE. *Faculty research:* Biblical studies, contemporary theology, church history, pastoral care, ministry/missions studies.

Southern California Seminary, Graduate and Professional Programs, El Cajon, CA 92019. Offers biblical studies (MA); counseling psychology (MACP); psychology (Psy D); religious studies (MRS); theology (M Div). Part-time and evening/weekend programs available. Postbaccalaureate distance learning degree programs offered (minimal on-campus study). *Degree requirements:* For master's, thesis (for some programs); for doctorate, thesis/dissertation; for M Div, 2 foreign languages. *Entrance requirements:* For doctorate, master's degree in psychology. Additional exam requirements/recommendations for international students: Required—TOEFL (minimum score 550 paper-based). Electronic applications accepted.

Southern Evangelical Seminary, Graduate School of Ministry and Missions, Matthews, NC 28105. Offers apologetics (Certificate); Christian education (MA); church ministry (MA, Certificate); divinity (Certificate), including apologetics (M Div, Certificate); Islamic studies (Certificate); theology (M Div), including apologetics (M Div, Certificate), Biblical studies; youth ministry (MA). Part-time and evening/weekend programs available. Postbaccalaureate distance learning degree programs offered. *Degree requirements:* For master's, thesis (for some programs); for M Div, one foreign language. *Entrance requirements:* Additional exam requirements/recommendations for international students: Required—TOEFL (minimum score 600 paper-based; 250 computer-based).

Southern Evangelical Seminary, Veritas Graduate School of Apologetics and Counter-Cult Ministry, Matthews, NC 28105. Offers apologetics (MA, D Min, PhD, Certificate); Islamic studies (MA); Jewish studies (MA); philosophy (MA); religion (MA). Part-time and evening/weekend programs available. Postbaccalaureate distance learning degree programs offered (minimal on-campus study). *Degree requirements:* For master's, thesis optional; for doctorate, comprehensive exam (for some programs), thesis/dissertation. *Entrance requirements:* Additional exam requirements/recommendations for international students: Required—TOEFL (minimum score 600 paper-based; 250 computer-based).

Southern Methodist University, Perkins School of Theology, Dallas, TX 75275. Offers M Div, CMM, MSM, MTS, D Min. *Accreditation:* ACIPE; ATS. Part-time programs available. *Faculty:* 24 full-time (10 women), 11 part-time/adjunct (3 women). *Students:* 194 full-time (96 women), 137 part-time (72 women); includes 88 minority (62 African Americans, 1 American Indian/Alaska Native, 4 Asian Americans or Pacific Islanders, 21 Hispanic Americans), 8 international. Average age 40. 162 applicants, 80% accepted, 74 enrolled. In 2009, 59 M Divs, 26 master's, 6 doctorates awarded. *Degree requirements:* For master's, thesis (for some programs), internship; for doctorate, internship, oral exam, professional project; for M Div, internship. *Entrance requirements:* For M Div and master's, minimum GPA of 2.75; for doctorate, minimum graduate GPA of 3.0, M Div or equivalent, 3 years of ministry experience. Additional exam requirements/recommendations for international students: Required—TOEFL (minimum score 600 paper-based; 250 computer-based; 100 iBT), TWE. *Application deadline:* For fall admission, 5/1 for domestic students, 12/15 for international students; for spring admission, 11/1 for domestic students. Applications are processed on a rolling basis. Application fee: $50. *Expenses:* Contact institution. *Financial support:* In 2009–10, 188 students received support, including 3 fellowships with full tuition reimbursements available (averaging $5,000 per year); career-related internships or fieldwork, Federal Work-Study, scholarships/grants, and minister's family tuition awards also available. Support available to part-time students. Financial award application deadline: 3/1; financial award applicants required to submit FAFSA. Total annual research expenditures: $271,008. *Unit head:* Dr. William B. Lawrence, Dean, 214-768-2534, Fax: 214-768-2966. *Application contact:* Rev. Herbert S. Coleman, Director, Recruitment and Admissions, 214-768-2139, Fax: 214-768-4245, E-mail: theology@smu.edu.

Southern Nazarene University, Graduate College, Department of Philosophy and Religion, Bethany, OK 73008. Offers theology (MA). Part-time programs available. *Degree requirements:* For master's, one foreign language, thesis optional. *Entrance requirements:* For master's, GMAT, English proficiency exam, minimum GPA of 3.0 in last 60 hours/major, 2.7 overall.

Southwestern Assemblies of God University, Thomas F. Harrison School of Graduate Studies, Program in Theological Studies, Waxahachie, TX 75165-5735. Offers Bible and theology (MS); Biblical studies (M Div); counseling (M Div); cross cultural missions (M Div); practical theology (M Div); theological studies (M Div). Postbaccalaureate distance learning degree programs offered. *Degree requirements:* For master's, comprehensive written and oral exams. *Entrance requirements:* For master's, GRE General Test, minimum GPA of 2.5. Electronic applications accepted.

Southwestern Baptist Theological Seminary, School of Theology, Fort Worth, TX 76122-0000. Offers M Div, MA Islamic, MA Miss, MA Th, Th M, D Min, PhD, SPTH. *Accreditation:* ACIPE; ATS (one or more programs are accredited). Part-time and evening/weekend programs available. Terminal master's awarded for partial completion of doctoral program. *Degree requirements:* For master's, 2 foreign languages, thesis (for some programs); for doctorate, 2 foreign languages, comprehensive exam, thesis/dissertation, oral exams; for M Div, 2 foreign languages, thesis/dissertation (for some programs). *Entrance requirements:* For doctorate, GRE, M Div or equivalent. Additional exam requirements/recommendations for international students: Required—TOEFL. Electronic applications accepted.

Spring Arbor University, School of Arts and Sciences, Spring Arbor, MI 49283-9799. Offers communication (MA); spiritual formation and leadership (MA). Part-time programs available. Postbaccalaureate distance learning degree programs offered (no on-campus study). *Faculty:* 6 full-time (1 woman), 11 part-time/adjunct (5 women). *Students:* 107 full-time (73 women), 76 part-time (57 women); includes 8 minority (6 African Americans, 2 Hispanic Americans), 1 international. Average age 42. In 2009, 16 master's awarded. *Degree requirements:* For master's, thesis (for some programs). *Entrance requirements:* For master's, GRE (taken within the last 5 years), writing sample, 3 recommendations. Additional exam requirements/recommendations for international students: Required—TOEFL (minimum score 550 paper-based; 220 computer-based). Application fee: $40. *Expenses:* Contact institution. *Financial support:* Applicants required to submit FAFSA. *Unit head:* Dr. Wally Metts, Chair of the Department of Communication, 517-750-1200 Ext. 1491, E-mail: wmetts@arbor.edu. *Application contact:* Dale Glinz, Lead Recruitment Specialist/Trainer, Graduate and Professional Studies, 517-750-6703, E-mail: dglinz@arbor.edu.

Spring Hill College, Graduate Programs, Program in Theology, Mobile, AL 36608-1791. Offers pastoral studies (MPS); theological studies (MTS); theology (MA). Part-time and evening/weekend programs available. *Faculty:* 6 full-time (0 women), 5 part-time/adjunct (1 woman). *Students:* 2 full-time (0 women), 49 part-time (24 women); includes 8 minority (5 African Americans, 1 Asian American or Pacific Islander, 2 Hispanic Americans). Average age 46. 35 applicants, 51% accepted, 1 enrolled. In 2009, 16 master's awarded. *Degree requirements:* For master's, variable foreign language requirement, comprehensive exam, thesis (for some programs), completion of program within 6 calendar years of initial enrollment (MTS, MPS), 4½ calendar years (MA). *Entrance requirements:* For master's, bachelor's degree with minimum undergraduate GPA of 3.0; six hours of undergraduate theology, religious studies, or unquestioned equivalency. Additional exam requirements/recommendations for international students: Required—TOEFL (minimum score 550 paper-based; 213 computer-based; 80 iBT), IELTS (minimum score 6.5). *Application deadline:* For fall admission, 8/1 priority date for domestic and international students; for spring admission, 12/1 priority date for domestic and international students. Applications are processed on a rolling basis. Application fee: $25 ($35 for international students). Electronic applications accepted. *Expenses:* Tuition: Full-time $5112; part-time $284 per credit hour. Tuition and fees vary according to program. *Financial support:* In 2009–10, 17 students received support. Career-related internships or fieldwork, institutionally sponsored loans, and scholarships/grants available. Support available to part-time students. Financial award applicants required to submit FAFSA. *Unit head:* Dr. John B. Switzer, Director, 251-380-4669, Fax: 251-460-2194, E-mail: jswitzer@shc.edu. *Application contact:* Donna B. Tarasavage, Director of Marketing and Recruiting, Graduate and Continuing Studies, 251-380-3067, Fax: 251-460-2190, E-mail: dtarasavage@shc.edu.

Starr King School for the Ministry, Professional Program, Berkeley, CA 94709-1209. Offers M Div. *Accreditation:* ACIPE; ATS.

Talmudic College of Florida, Program in Talmudic Law, Miami Beach, FL 33139. Offers MRE, Master of Talmudic Law, Doctor of Talmudic Law. *Accreditation:* AARTS. Terminal master's awarded for partial completion of doctoral program. *Degree requirements:* For master's, 2 foreign languages; for doctorate, 2 foreign languages, thesis/dissertation. *Entrance requirements:* For master's, oral exam, undergraduate Judaic studies degree; for doctorate, oral exam, Judaic studies degree.

Theology

Taylor College and Seminary, Graduate and Professional Programs, Edmonton, AB T6J 4T3, Canada. Offers Christian studies (Diploma); intercultural studies (MA, Diploma), including intercultural studies (Diploma), TESOL; theology (M Div, MTS). *Accreditation:* ATS. Part-time programs available. Postbaccalaureate distance learning degree programs offered (minimal on-campus study). *Faculty:* 5 full-time (0 women), 5 part-time/adjunct (1 woman). *Students:* 13 full-time (4 women), 52 part-time (24 women); includes 18 minority (2 African Americans, 1 American Indian/Alaska Native, 15 Asian Americans or Pacific Islanders). Average age 38. 40 applicants, 73% accepted, 20 enrolled. In 2009, 11 first professional degrees awarded. *Degree requirements:* For master's, thesis optional. *Entrance requirements:* Additional exam requirements/recommendations for international students: Required—TOEFL (minimum score 550 paper-based; 80 iBT), IELTS (minimum score 6.5). *Application deadline:* For fall admission, 9/1 priority date for domestic and international students. Applications are processed on a rolling basis. Application fee: $35 ($70 for international students). *Financial support:* In 2009–10, 16 students received support. Career-related internships or fieldwork and scholarships/grants available. Financial award application deadline: 8/1. *Faculty research:* Biblical studies, administration and organization, world religions, ethics, missiology. *Unit head:* Dr. Joost Pikkert, Academic Dean, 780-431-5243, Fax: 780-436-9416, E-mail: joost.pikkert@taylor-edu.ca. *Application contact:* Craig Weston, Registrar and Director of Enrolment Services, 780-431-5208, Fax: 780-436-9416, E-mail: craig.weston@taylor-edu.ca.

Temple Baptist Seminary, Program in Theology, Chattanooga, TN 37404-3530. Offers biblical languages (M Div); Biblical studies (MABS); Christian education (MACE); English Bible û language tools (M Div); theology (MM, D Min). Part-time and evening/weekend programs available. Postbaccalaureate distance learning degree programs offered (minimal on-campus study). *Degree requirements:* For doctorate, thesis/dissertation; for M Div, proficiency in Greek and Hebrew. *Entrance requirements:* For doctorate, minimum GPA of 3.0, M Div.

Toronto School of Theology, Graduate Programs, Toronto, ON M5S 2C3, Canada. Offers M Div, M Mus, M Rel, MA, MAMS, MPS, MRE, MTS, Th M, D Min, PhD, Th D. Federation of seven Toronto-area theological colleges; basic degrees offered through the member colleges jointly with the University of Toronto. *Accreditation:* ATS. Postbaccalaureate distance learning degree programs offered (minimal on-campus study). Terminal master's awarded for partial completion of doctoral program. *Degree requirements:* For master's, 2 foreign languages, thesis; for doctorate, 3 foreign languages, comprehensive exam, thesis/dissertation. *Entrance requirements:* For master's, language exams, minimum B+ average in undergraduate course work; for doctorate, language exams, first-class standing in master's program. Additional exam requirements/recommendations for international students: Required—TOEFL. Electronic applications accepted.

Trevecca Nazarene University, Graduate Division, Graduate Religion Programs, Nashville, TN 37210-2877. Offers biblical studies (MA); preaching and practical theology (MA); systematic theology/historical theology (MA). Part-time programs available. *Faculty:* 3 full-time (0 women). *Students:* 19 full-time (2 women), 22 part-time (5 women); includes 7 minority (6 African Americans, 1 Asian American or Pacific Islander), 1 international. Average age 34. In 2009, 17 master's awarded. *Degree requirements:* For master's, comprehensive exam, thesis optional. *Entrance requirements:* For master's, GRE General Test or MAT, minimum GPA of 2.7, 2 letters of recommendation. Additional exam requirements/recommendations for international students: Required—TOEFL (minimum score 550 paper-based; 213 computer-based). *Application deadline:* Applications are processed on a rolling basis. Application fee: $25. Electronic applications accepted. *Expenses:* Contact institution. *Financial support:* Applicants required to submit FAFSA. *Unit head:* Dr. Tim Green, Dean/Director, 615-248-1378, Fax: 615-248-7417, E-mail: admissions_rel@trevecca.edu. *Application contact:* Sherry Crutchfield, Secretary, 615-248-1378, Fax: 615-248-7417, E-mail: admissions_rel@trevecca.edu.

Trinity International University, Trinity Evangelical Divinity School, Deerfield, IL 60015-1284. Offers Biblical and Near Eastern archaeology and languages (MA); Christian studies (MA, Certificate); Christian thought (MA); church history (MA, Th M); congregational ministry: pastor-teacher (M Div); congregational ministry: team ministry (M Div); counseling ministries (MA); counseling psychology (MA); cross-cultural ministry (M Div); educational studies (PhD); evangelism (MA); history of Christianity in America (MA); intercultural studies (MA, PhD); leadership and ministry management (D Min); military chaplaincy (D Min); ministry (MA); mission and evangelism (Th M); missions and evangelism (D Min); New Testament (MA, Th M); Old Testament (Th M); Old Testament and Semitic languages (MA); pastoral care (M Div); pastoral care and counseling (D Min); pastoral counseling and psychology (Th M); pastoral theology (Th M); philosophy of religion (MA); preaching (D Min); religion (MA); research ministry (M Div); systematic theology (Th M); theological studies (PhD); urban ministry (MA). *Accreditation:* ATS (one or more programs are accredited). Part-time programs available. Postbaccalaureate distance learning degree programs offered (minimal on-campus study). *Degree requirements:* For master's, comprehensive exam, thesis, fieldwork; for doctorate, comprehensive exam (for some programs), thesis/dissertation; for M Div, 2 foreign languages, fieldwork; for Certificate, comprehensive exam, integrative papers. *Entrance requirements:* For M Div, GRE, MAT; for master's, GRE, MAT, minimum cumulative undergraduate GPA of 3.0; for doctorate, GRE, minimum cumulative graduate GPA of 3.2; for Certificate, GRE, MAT, minimum undergraduate GPA of 2.5. Additional exam requirements/recommendations for international students: Required—TOEFL (minimum score 580 paper-based; 237 computer-based), TWE (minimum score 4). Electronic applications accepted.

Trinity Lutheran Seminary, Graduate and Professional Programs, Columbus, OH 43209-2334. Offers Christian education (MA); church music (MA); divinity (M Div); sacred theology (STM); theological studies (MTS); youth and family ministry (MA); MSN/MTS; MTS/JD. *Accreditation:* ACIPE; ATS. Part-time programs available. *Faculty:* 15 full-time (7 women), 10 part-time/adjunct (3 women). *Students:* 99 full-time (38 women), 44 part-time (18 women); includes 21 minority (15 African Americans, 4 Asian Americans or Pacific Islanders, 2 Hispanic Americans), 4 international. Average age 35. 71 applicants, 77% accepted, 49 enrolled. In 2009, 29 first professional degrees, 9 master's awarded. *Degree requirements:* For master's, comprehensive exam (for some programs), thesis (for some programs); for M Div, 2 foreign languages, internship. *Entrance requirements:* For master's, M Div or equivalent (STM). Additional exam requirements/recommendations for international students: Required—TOEFL (minimum score 500 paper-based; 173 computer-based; 61 iBT). *Application deadline:* For fall admission, 7/15 priority date for domestic and international students. Applications are processed on a rolling basis. Application fee: $25. *Expenses:* Tuition: Full-time $11,400; part-time $380 per semester hour. Required fees: $115 per semester. One-time fee: $150 full-time. *Financial support:* In 2009–10, 102 students received support. Career-related internships or fieldwork, Federal Work-Study, institutionally sponsored loans, and scholarships/grants available. Support available to part-time students. Financial award application deadline: 5/1; financial award applicants required to submit FAFSA. *Unit head:* Dr. James M. Childs, Interim Academic Dean, 614-235-4136, Fax: 614-384-4635, E-mail: jchilds@trinitylutheranseminary.edu. *Application contact:* Rev. Sheri L. Ayers, Director of Admissions, 614-235-4136 Ext. 4614, Fax: 866-610-8572, E-mail: sayers@trinitylutheranseminary.edu.

Trinity School for Ministry, Graduate Programs, Ambridge, PA 15003-2397. Offers Anglican studies (Diploma); basic Christian studies (Diploma); divinity (M Div); ministry (D Min); mission and evangelism (MAME, Diploma); religion (MAR); youth ministry (Diploma). *Accreditation:* ATS (one or more programs are accredited). Part-time programs available. *Degree requirements:* For master's, thesis optional; for doctorate, thesis/dissertation; for M Div, thesis/dissertation optional, Greek and Hebrew. *Entrance requirements:* Additional exam requirements/recommendations for international students: Required—TOEFL. *Faculty research:* Pauline Epistles, contemporary theology, history of Anglican liturgy, book of Ruth, biblical theology.

Trinity Western University, ACTS Seminaries, Langley, BC V2Y 1Y1, Canada. Offers Christian studies (MA); church ministries (MA); cross cultural ministries (MA); theology (M Div, M Th, MAMFT, MLE, MTS, D Min). *Accreditation:* ATS. Part-time programs available. *Degree requirements:* For master's, thesis (for some programs), internship. *Entrance requirements:* For doctorate, MDiv or equivalent. Additional exam requirements/recommendations for international students: Required—TOEFL. *Expenses:* Contact institution. *Faculty research:* Theology of leadership.

Trinity Western University, Faculty of Graduate Studies, Program in Biblical Studies, Langley, BC V2Y 1Y1, Canada. Offers MA. *Accreditation:* ATS. Part-time programs available. *Degree requirements:* For master's, 2 foreign languages, thesis, 2 years Greek, 2 years Hebrew. *Entrance requirements:* For master's, minimum GPA of 3.0, degree in biblical studies, master of divinity or 42 hours Biblical Study credit. Additional exam requirements/recommendations for international students: Required—TOEFL (minimum score 600 paper-based; 250 computer-based). Electronic applications accepted. *Faculty research:* Intertestamental literature, Dead Sea Scrolls, Biblical literature, history of Jesus, ancient languages.

Tyndale University College & Seminary, Graduate Programs, Toronto, ON M2M 4B3, Canada. Offers Biblical studies (M Div); Christian foundations (MTS); Christian studies (Diploma); counseling (M Div); educational ministry (M Div); missions (M Div, Diploma); pastoral and Chinese ministry (M Div); pastoral ministry (M Div); Pentecostal studies (MTS); spiritual formation (M Div, Diploma); theological studies (M Div); theology (Th M); worship and liturgy (M Div, MTS); youth and family ministry (M Div). *Accreditation:* ATS. Part-time programs available. Postbaccalaureate distance learning degree programs offered (no on-campus study). *Degree requirements:* For M Div, one foreign language, thesis/dissertation optional. *Entrance requirements:* For M Div, master's, and Diploma, minimum C+ average in undergraduate course work. Additional exam requirements/recommendations for international students: Required—TOEFL (minimum score 570 paper-based; 230 computer-based), TWE (minimum score 5). Electronic applications accepted. *Faculty research:* Canadian church history, Chinese church history, Old Testament, counseling ministries (narrative therapy), world religions.

Unification Theological Seminary, Graduate Program, Main Campus, Barrytown, NY 12507. Offers M Div, MRE, D Min. Part-time programs available. *Faculty:* 3 full-time (1 woman), 3 part-time/adjunct (0 women). *Students:* 33 full-time (8 women), 3 part-time (1 woman); includes 19 minority (9 African Americans, 2 American Indian/Alaska Native, 6 Asian Americans or Pacific Islanders, 2 Hispanic Americans), 6 international. Average age 45. In 2009, 3 first professional degrees, 32 master's, 1 doctorate awarded. *Degree requirements:* For master's, one foreign language, project; for doctorate, thesis/dissertation; for M Div, one foreign language, thesis/dissertation. *Entrance requirements:* For M Div and master's, bachelor's degree; for doctorate, M Div or equivalency. Additional exam requirements/recommendations for international students: Required—TOEFL (minimum score 450 paper-based; 133 computer-based; 45 iBT). *Application deadline:* For fall admission, 8/15 priority date for domestic students; for spring admission, 1/15 priority date for domestic students. Applications are processed on a rolling basis. Application fee: $30. *Expenses:* Tuition: Full-time $10,440; part-time $435 per credit. Required fees: $320; $435 per credit. $125 per semester. *Financial support:* Teaching assistantships, career-related internships or fieldwork, institutionally sponsored loans, scholarships/grants, and tuition waivers (partial) available. Financial award applicants required to submit FAFSA. *Faculty research:* Church leadership, church history, world religions, ecumenism, interfaith peace building, service-learning. *Unit head:* Dr. Kathy Winings, Academic Dean, 845-752-3000 Ext. 228, Fax: 845-752-3014, E-mail: academics@uts.edu. *Application contact:* Davetta Ogunlola, Director of Admissions, 212-563-6647 Ext. 105, Fax: 212-563-6431, E-mail: admissions@uts.edu.

Unification Theological Seminary, Graduate Program, New York Extension, New York, NY 10036. Offers M Div, MRE. Part-time and evening/weekend programs available. *Faculty:* 4 full-time (1 woman), 7 part-time/adjunct (2 women). *Students:* 44 full-time (14 women), 35 part-time (16 women); includes 39 minority (30 African Americans, 1 American Indian/Alaska Native, 5 Asian Americans or Pacific Islanders, 3 Hispanic Americans), 34 international. Average age 41. *Degree requirements:* For master's, thesis, project; for M Div, thesis/dissertation. *Entrance requirements:* For M Div and master's, bachelor's degree. Additional exam requirements/recommendations for international students: Required—TOEFL (minimum score 450 paper-based; 133 computer-based). *Application deadline:* For fall admission, 8/15 priority date for domestic students; for spring admission, 1/15 priority date for domestic students. Applications are processed on a rolling basis. Application fee: $30. *Expenses:* Tuition: Full-time $10,440; part-time $435 per credit. Required fees: $320; $435 per credit. $125 per semester. *Financial support:* Career-related internships or fieldwork, institutionally sponsored loans, scholarships/grants, and tuition waivers (partial) available. Financial award applicants required to submit FAFSA. *Faculty research:* Church history, world religions, ecumenism, interfaith peace building, service-learning. *Unit head:* Dr. Kathy Winings, Academic Dean, 212-563-6647 Ext. 101, Fax: 212-563-6431, E-mail: academics@uts.edu. *Application contact:* Davetta Ogunlola, Admissions Officer, 212-563-6647 Ext. 105, Fax: 212-563-6431, E-mail: admissions@uts.edu.

Union Theological Seminary and Presbyterian School of Christian Education, School of Theological Studies, Richmond, VA 23227-4597. Offers M Div, Th M, D Min, PhD, M Div/MA. *Accreditation:* ACIPE; ATS. Terminal master's awarded for partial completion of doctoral program. *Degree requirements:* For master's, oral and written exams; for doctorate, 2 foreign languages, comprehensive exam, thesis/dissertation; for M Div, 2 foreign languages. *Entrance requirements:* For doctorate, GRE General Test. Additional exam requirements/recommendations for international students: Required—TOEFL, TWE.

Union Theological Seminary in the City of New York, Graduate and Professional Programs, New York, NY 10027-5710. Offers M Div, MA, STM, Ed D, PhD, M Div/MSSW. *Accreditation:* ACIPE; ATS (one or more programs are accredited). Part-time programs available. *Degree requirements:* For master's, one foreign language, thesis; for doctorate, 2 foreign languages, thesis/dissertation; for M Div, one foreign language, thesis/dissertation. *Entrance requirements:* For doctorate, GRE General Test, sample of written work. *Faculty research:* American religious history, psychiatry and religion, Christian ethics, New Testament.

United Talmudical Seminary, Graduate Programs, Brooklyn, NY 11211. *Accreditation:* AARTS.

United Theological Seminary, Graduate and Professional Programs, Trotwood, OH 45426. Offers M Div, MA, MATS, D Min, M Div/MA. *Accreditation:* ATS. Part-time and evening/weekend programs available. *Faculty:* 14 full-time (5 women), 26 part-time/adjunct (6 women). *Students:* 212 full-time (83 women), 42 part-time (22 women). *Degree requirements:* For master's, thesis (for some programs), comprehensive evaluation; for doctorate, thesis/dissertation, final exam; for M Div, comprehensive evaluation. *Entrance requirements:* For M Div, minimum GPA of 2.5, 5 letters of recommendation, interview; for master's, minimum GPA of 2.5, interview, 5 letters of recommendation; for doctorate, minimum GPA of 3.0, 2 letters of recommendation, interview. Additional exam requirements/recommendations for international students: Required—TOEFL (minimum score 550 paper-based; 213 computer-based). *Application deadline:* For fall admission, 8/1 for domestic students, 1/15 for international students; for spring admission, 1/1 for domestic students. Applications are processed on a rolling basis. Application fee: $40. Electronic applications accepted. *Financial support:* Career-related internships or fieldwork, Federal Work-Study, and scholarships/grants available. Financial award application deadline: 4/1; financial award applicants required to submit CSS PROFILE or FAFSA. *Unit head:* M. Merritt Worthen, Director of Student Services, 937-529-2201 Ext. 3300, Fax: 937-529-2292, E-mail: meworthen@united.edu. *Application contact:* Thomas Miller, Admissions Officer, 937-529-2201 Ext. 3307, E-mail: utsadmis@united.edu.

United Theological Seminary of the Twin Cities, Professional Program, New Brighton, MN 55112-2598. Offers advanced theological studies (Diploma); justice and peace studies (M Div, MA); leadership toward racial justice (MA, Certificate); leadership towards racial justice (M Div); Methodist studies (M Div, MA, Certificate); ministry (D Min); ministry renewal and professional development (Certificate); pastoral care and counseling (M Div, MA, MARL); religion and theology (MA); theological and religious studies (Certificate); theology and the arts (M Div, MA); urban ministry (M Div, MA, MARL); women's studies: religion, theology and ministry (MA); women's studies: religions, theology and ministry (M Div). *Accreditation:* ACIPE; ATS.

Part-time and evening/weekend programs available. *Faculty:* 9 full-time (6 women), 22 part-time/adjunct (10 women). *Students:* 49 full-time (34 women), 105 part-time (68 women). Average age 47. 41 applicants, 98% accepted, 34 enrolled. In 2009, 24 first professional degrees, 5 master's, 2 doctorates, 2 other advanced degrees awarded. *Degree requirements:* For master's, thesis; for doctorate, comprehensive exam, thesis/dissertation; for M Div, integrative notebook, spiritual chronicle. *Entrance requirements:* For M Div and master's, minimum GPA of 2.75; strong analytical, reflective thinking and writing skills; vocational and academic goals compatible with those of Seminary; for doctorate, M Div or equivalent, minimum GPA of 3.0, 3 years experience in professional ministry; for other advanced degree, BA or equivalent life experience; strong analytical, reflective thinking and writing skills (Certificate); proficiency in English language, previous study of theology at a theological school, recommendation of student's denomination (Diploma). Additional exam requirements/recommendations for international students: Required—TOEFL (minimum score 550 paper-based). *Application deadline:* For fall admission, 7/1 priority date for domestic students, 11/1 priority date for international students; for winter admission, 11/1 priority date for domestic students; for spring admission, 11/15 priority date for domestic students. Applications are processed on a rolling basis. Application fee: $50. *Expenses:* Tuition: Full-time $11,502; part-time $426 per credit hour. Required fees: $295; $155 per term. One-time fee: $25. Tuition and fees vary according to course load, degree level and program. *Financial support:* In 2009–10, 120 students received support. Career-related internships or fieldwork, institutionally sponsored loans, and scholarships/grants available. Support available to part-time students. Financial award application deadline: 5/1; financial award applicants required to submit FAFSA. *Unit head:* Dr. Richard D. Weis, Dean of the Seminary, 651-255-6108 Ext. 108, Fax: 651-633-4315, E-mail: rweis@unitedseminary.edu. *Application contact:* Rev. Glen Herrington-Hall, Director of Admissions, 651-255-6107 Ext. 107, Fax: 651-633-4315, E-mail: gherrington-hall@unitedseminary.edu.

Universidad FLET, Department of Graduate Studies, Miami, FL 33186. Offers education (M Ed); theological studies (MTS). *Degree requirements:* For master's, thesis or project. *Entrance requirements:* For master's, letter of recommendation.

Université de Montréal, Faculty of Theology and Sciences of Religions, Montréal, QC H3C 3J7, Canada. Offers MA, D Th, PhD, Certificate, DESS, L Th. *Degree requirements:* For master's, one foreign language; for doctorate, 2 foreign languages, thesis/dissertation, general exam. Electronic applications accepted.

Université de Sherbrooke, Faculty of Theology, Ethics and Philosophy, Sherbrooke, QC J1K 2R1, Canada. Offers applied ethics (Diploma); human science of religions (MA); intercultural training (Diploma); philosophy (MA, PhD); spiritual anthropology (Diploma); theology (MA, PhD, Diploma). Part-time and evening/weekend programs available. Postbaccalaureate distance learning degree programs offered. Terminal master's awarded for partial completion of doctoral program. *Entrance requirements:* For master's, bachelor's degree in related discipline; for doctorate, master's degree in related discipline. *Faculty research:* Faith and culture interrelation.

Université du Québec à Chicoutimi, Graduate Programs, Program in Theology (Pastoral Studies), Chicoutimi, QC G7H 2B1, Canada. Offers MA, PhD. Part-time programs available. *Degree requirements:* For doctorate, thesis/dissertation. *Entrance requirements:* For master's, appropriate bachelor's degree, proficiency in French; for doctorate, appropriate master's degree, proficiency in French.

Université Laval, Faculty of Theology and Religious Sciences, Program in Practical Theology, Québec, QC G1K 7P4, Canada. Offers D Th P. Part-time programs available. *Degree requirements:* For doctorate, comprehensive exam, thesis/dissertation. *Entrance requirements:* For doctorate, knowledge of French and English. Electronic applications accepted.

Université Laval, Faculty of Theology and Religious Sciences, Programs in Theology, Québec, QC G1K 7P4, Canada. Offers MA, PhD. Terminal master's awarded for partial completion of doctoral program. *Degree requirements:* For master's, thesis (for some programs); for doctorate, comprehensive exam, thesis/dissertation. *Entrance requirements:* For master's and doctorate, knowledge of French, comprehension of written English. Electronic applications accepted.

University of Chicago, Divinity School, Chicago, IL 60637-1513. Offers M Div, AM, AMRS, PhD, JD/M Div, JD/MA, JD/PhD, MPP/M Div, MSW/M Div. *Accreditation:* ATS (one or more programs are accredited). Part-time programs available. *Degree requirements:* For master's and M Div, one foreign language; for doctorate, 2 foreign languages, comprehensive exam, thesis/dissertation. *Entrance requirements:* For M Div, master's, and doctorate, GRE General Test. Additional exam requirements/recommendations for international students: Required—TOEFL (minimum score 600 paper-based; 250 computer-based). Electronic applications accepted. *Expenses:* Contact institution. *Faculty research:* Theology, history of religion, ethics, biblical studies, philosophy of religion.

University of Dallas, Braniff Graduate School of Liberal Arts, Department of Theology, Irving, TX 75062-4736. Offers M Th, MA. Part-time programs available. *Faculty:* 5 full-time (0 women), 4 part-time/adjunct (0 women). *Students:* 17 full-time (8 women), 15 part-time (6 women); includes 2 minority (1 Asian American or Pacific Islander, 1 Hispanic American). Average age 28. 16 applicants, 81% accepted, 10 enrolled. In 2009, 5 master's awarded. *Degree requirements:* For master's, one foreign language, comprehensive exam, thesis (for some programs). *Entrance requirements:* For master's, GRE General Test. *Application deadline:* For fall admission, 2/15 priority date for domestic students; for spring admission, 11/15 for domestic students. Applications are processed on a rolling basis. Application fee: $50. *Expenses:* Tuition: Full-time $10,080; part-time $560 per credit hour. Required fees: $50 per term. Tuition and fees vary according to program. *Financial support:* In 2009–10, 30 students received support. Scholarships/grants available. Financial award application deadline: 2/15. *Faculty research:* Patristics, justice in the Old and New Testament, Pauline literature, Christology, theology of the Trinity. *Unit head:* Dr. Christopher J. Malloy, Chair, 972-721-4076, Fax: 972-721-4007, E-mail: cmalloy@udallas.edu. *Application contact:* Graduate Coordinator, 972-721-5106, Fax: 972-721-5280, E-mail: graduate@acad.udallas.edu.

University of Dayton, Graduate School, College of Arts and Sciences, Department of Religious Studies, Dayton, OH 45469-1300. Offers pastoral ministry (MA); theological studies (MA); theology (PhD). Part-time and evening/weekend programs available. *Faculty:* 19 full-time (5 women), 5 part-time/adjunct (1 woman). *Students:* 60 full-time (28 women), 21 part-time (12 women); includes 3 minority (1 Asian American or Pacific Islander, 2 Hispanic Americans), 1 international. Average age 33. 66 applicants, 65% accepted, 19 enrolled. In 2009, 14 master's, 1 doctorate awarded. Terminal master's awarded for partial completion of doctoral program. *Degree requirements:* For master's, thesis or alternative; for doctorate, 2 foreign languages, comprehensive exam, thesis/dissertation. *Entrance requirements:* For master's, minimum undergraduate GPA of 3.0, 3 letters of recommendation, personal statement, official transcript(s); for doctorate, GRE General Test (minimum score 600 verbal), minimum GPA of 3.5, academic writing sample, 3 letters of recommendation. Additional exam requirements/recommendations for international students: Required—TOEFL (minimum score 550 paper-based; 213 computer-based; 80 iBT). *Application deadline:* For fall admission, 3/1 priority date for domestic and international students; for winter admission, 7/1 priority date for international students; for spring admission, 1/1 priority date for international students. Applications are processed on a rolling basis. Application fee: $0 ($50 for international students). Electronic applications accepted. *Expenses:* Contact institution. *Financial support:* In 2009–10, 28 students received support, including 4 fellowships with full tuition reimbursements available (averaging $15,814 per year), 8 research assistantships with full tuition reimbursements available (averaging $9,457 per year), 16 teaching assistantships with full tuition reimbursements available (averaging $15,814 per year); career-related internships or fieldwork, institutionally sponsored loans, scholarships/grants, health care benefits, tuition waivers (full), and unspecified assistantships also available. Support available to part-time students. Financial award application deadline: 3/1; financial award applicants required to submit FAFSA. *Faculty research:* Practical/constructive theology, theological ethics, U. S. Catholic/Christian life and thought, methodologies in Biblical studies, religion and science. *Unit head:* Dr. Sandra Yocum, Chair, 937-229-4321, Fax: 937-229-4330, E-mail: sandra.yocum@notes.udayton.edu. *Application contact:* Graduate Admissions, 937-229-4411, Fax: 937-229-4729, E-mail: gradadmission@udayton.edu.

University of Denver, Joint Program in Religious and Theological Studies, Denver, CO 80208. Offers PhD. Part-time programs available. *Students:* 44 full-time (17 women), 49 part-time (21 women); includes 9 minority (3 African Americans, 1 American Indian/Alaska Native, 2 Asian Americans or Pacific Islanders, 3 Hispanic Americans), 6 international. Average age 39. 66 applicants, 56% accepted, 21 enrolled. In 2009, 11 doctorates awarded. *Entrance requirements:* For doctorate, GRE. *Application deadline:* For fall admission, 1/15 for domestic students. Application fee: $50. *Expenses:* Tuition: Full-time $34,596; part-time $961 per quarter hour. Required fees: $4 per quarter hour. Tuition and fees vary according to course load, campus/location and program. *Unit head:* Dr. Frank Seeburger, Head, 303-871-2766. *Application contact:* Dr. Frank Seeburger, Head, 303-871-2766.

University of Dubuque, Theological Seminary, Dubuque, IA 52001-5099. Offers M Div, MAR, D Min. *Accreditation:* ACIPE; ATS. Postbaccalaureate distance learning degree programs offered (minimal on-campus study). *Degree requirements:* For doctorate, thesis/dissertation. *Entrance requirements:* Additional exam requirements/recommendations for international students: Recommended—TOEFL (minimum score 550 paper-based; 220 computer-based; 80 iBT). *Faculty research:* Biblical archaeology, biblical theology, reformed history and theology, pastoral theology, homiletics.

University of Mobile, Graduate Programs, Program in Religious Studies, Mobile, AL 36613. Offers biblical/theological studies (MA); marriage and family counseling (MA). Part-time and evening/weekend programs available. *Faculty:* 4 full-time (0 women), 1 (woman) part-time/adjunct. *Students:* 12 full-time (11 women), 34 part-time (22 women); includes 24 minority (23 African Americans, 1 American Indian/Alaska Native). Average age 32. 20 applicants, 100% accepted, 16 enrolled. In 2009, 12 master's awarded. *Degree requirements:* For master's, 2 foreign languages, comprehensive exam, thesis optional. *Entrance requirements:* For master's, GRE General Test. Additional exam requirements/recommendations for international students: Required—TOEFL (minimum score 550 paper-based; 213 computer-based; 80 iBT). *Application deadline:* For fall admission, 8/3 priority date for domestic students; for spring admission, 12/23 for domestic students. Applications are processed on a rolling basis. Application fee: $40 ($50 for international students). *Financial support:* Federal Work-Study available. Support available to part-time students. Financial award application deadline: 8/1. *Unit head:* Dr. Cecil Taylor, Dean, School of Christian Studies, 251-442-2255, Fax: 251-442-2523, E-mail: ctaylor@mail.umobile.edu. *Application contact:* Tammy C. Eubanks, Administrative Assistant to Dean of Graduate Programs, 251-442-2270, Fax: 251-442-2523, E-mail: teubanks@umobile.edu.

University of Notre Dame, Graduate School, College of Arts and Letters, Division of Humanities, Department of Theology, Notre Dame, IN 46556. Offers M Div, MA, MSM, MTS, PhD. *Accreditation:* ACIPE; ATS. Terminal master's awarded for partial completion of doctoral program. *Degree requirements:* For master's, one foreign language, comprehensive exam, thesis or alternative; for doctorate, 3 foreign languages, comprehensive exam, thesis/dissertation, candidacy exam. *Entrance requirements:* For M Div, master's, and doctorate, GRE General Test. Additional exam requirements/recommendations for international students: Required—TOEFL (minimum score 600 paper-based; 250 computer-based; 80 iBT). Electronic applications accepted. *Faculty research:* Liturgy, ethics, historical studies, biblical studies, systematic theology.

University of Saint Mary of the Lake–Mundelein Seminary, Graduate School of Theology, Mundelein, IL 60060. Offers M Div, MA, D Min. *Accreditation:* ATS (one or more programs are accredited). *Faculty:* 42 full-time (6 women), 15 part-time/adjunct (3 women). *Students:* 223 full-time (7 women); includes 10 minority (2 African Americans, 3 Asian Americans or Pacific Islanders, 5 Hispanic Americans), 78 international. Average age 30. 95 applicants, 75% accepted, 71 enrolled. *Degree requirements:* For doctorate, thesis/dissertation; for M Div, thesis/dissertation (for some programs). *Entrance requirements:* For M Div, master's, and doctorate, bachelor's degree. Additional exam requirements/recommendations for international students: Required—TOEFL. *Application deadline:* Applications are processed on a rolling basis. Application fee: $0. Electronic applications accepted. *Expenses:* Tuition: Full-time $19,173. Required fees: $250. *Financial support:* Career-related internships or fieldwork available. *Unit head:* Rev. Raymond J. Webb, Academic Dean, 847-566-6401. *Application contact:* Rev. Raymond J. Webb, Academic Dean, 847-566-6401.

University of St. Michael's College, Faculty of Theology, Toronto, ON M5S 1J4, Canada. Offers Catholic leadership (MA); eastern Christian studies (Diploma); religious education (Diploma); theological studies (Diploma); theology (M Div, MA, MRE, MTS, D Min, PhD, Th D); theology and Jewish studies (MA). *Accreditation:* ATS (one or more programs are accredited). Part-time programs available. *Faculty:* 9 full-time (2 women), 23 part-time/adjunct (6 women). *Students:* 106 full-time (35 women), 98 part-time (59 women); includes 35 minority (13 African Americans, 21 Asian Americans or Pacific Islanders, 1 Hispanic American), 24 international. Average age 40. 72 applicants, 75% accepted, 44 enrolled. In 2009, 29 first professional degrees, 7 master's, 2 doctorates, 3 other advanced degrees awarded. *Degree requirements:* For master's, thesis (for some programs), 1 foreign language (MA), 2 foreign languages (Th M); for doctorate, 3 foreign languages, comprehensive exam, thesis/dissertation; for M Div, thesis/dissertation optional; for other advanced degree, thesis optional. *Entrance requirements:* For M Div and other advanced degree, minimum GPA of 2.7; for master's, M Div or BA, course work in an ancient or modern language, minimum GPA of 3.3; for doctorate, MA in theology, Th M, or M Div with thesis, minimum GPA of 3.7. Additional exam requirements/recommendations for international students: Required—TOEFL (minimum score 600 paper-based; 250 computer-based). *Application deadline:* For fall admission, 1/15 for domestic and international students. Applications are processed on a rolling basis. Application fee: $25 Canadian dollars. Electronic applications accepted. *Expenses:* Contact institution. *Financial support:* In 2009–10, 45 students received support, including fellowships with partial tuition reimbursements available (averaging $2,500 per year), research assistantships with partial tuition reimbursements available (averaging $2,400 per year), 4 teaching assistantships with partial tuition reimbursements available (averaging $2,400 per year); scholarships/grants, tuition waivers (partial), and bursaries also available. Financial award application deadline: 2/1. *Faculty research:* Patristics, eastern Christianity, ecology and theology, ecumenism, Jewish Christian studies. *Unit head:* Fr. Dr. Mario O. D'Souza, Dean, 416-926-7265, Fax: 416-926-7294, E-mail: mario.dsouza@utoronto.ca. *Application contact:* Allen Croxall, Student Recruitment and Advancement Officer, 416-926-1300 Ext. 3281, Fax: 416-926-7294, E-mail: allen.croxall@utoronto.ca.

University of St. Thomas, Graduate Studies, Saint Paul Seminary School of Divinity, Program in Divinity, St. Paul, MN 55105-1096. Offers M Div. *Accreditation:* ATS. Part-time programs available. *Entrance requirements:* MAT, interview, 3 letters of recommendation. Additional exam requirements/recommendations for international students: Required—TOEFL (minimum score 550 paper-based; 213 computer-based). *Faculty research:* Theological education.

University of St. Thomas, Graduate Studies, Saint Paul Seminary School of Divinity, Program in Theology/Pastoral Studies, St. Paul, MN 55105-1096. Offers religious education (MARE); theology (MA). *Accreditation:* ATS. Part-time and evening/weekend programs available. *Degree requirements:* For master's, one foreign language, comprehensive exam, thesis or alternative. *Entrance requirements:* For master's, GRE, interview, 3 letters of recommendation. Additional exam requirements/recommendations for international students: Required—TOEFL (minimum score 550 paper-based; 213 computer-based). Electronic applications accepted. *Expenses:* Contact institution. *Faculty research:* Theological education.

University of St. Thomas, School of Theology, Houston, TX 77006-4696. Offers M Div, MAPS, MAT. *Accreditation:* ATS. Part-time programs available. *Faculty:* 10 full-time (3 women), 6 part-time/adjunct (0 women). *Students:* 86 full-time (8 women), 115 part-time (40 women); includes 46 minority (5 African Americans, 14 Asian Americans or Pacific Islanders, 27 Hispanic Americans), 17 international. Average age 41. 45 applicants, 100% accepted, 40 enrolled. In 2009, 19 first professional degrees, 32 master's awarded. *Degree requirements:* For master's,

Theology

University of St. Thomas (continued)
comprehensive exam (MAT). *Entrance requirements:* For M Div, minimum GPA of 2.0 in philosophy and theology; for master's, minimum GPA of 2.3 (MAPS); 3.0 in theology, philosophy, or religious studies (MAT). Additional exam requirements/recommendations for international students: Required—TOEFL (minimum score 550 paper-based; 213 computer-based). *Application deadline:* Applications are processed on a rolling basis. Application fee: $35. Electronic applications accepted. *Expenses:* Contact institution. *Financial support:* In 2009–10, 9 students received support. Federal Work-Study and scholarships/grants available. Support available to part-time students. Financial award application deadline: 3/1; financial award applicants required to submit FAFSA. *Unit head:* Dr. Sandra C. Magie, Dean, 713-686-4345 Ext. 242, Fax: 713-683-8673, E-mail: smagie@stthom.edu. *Application contact:* Connie Henry, Office Manager, 713-686-4345 Ext. 231, Fax: 713-683-8673, E-mail: henryc@stthom.edu.

The University of Scranton, College of Graduate and Continuing Education, Program in Theology, Scranton, PA 18510. Offers MA. Part-time and evening/weekend programs available. *Faculty:* 14 full-time (5 women). *Students:* 10 full-time (3 women), 6 part-time (3 women); includes 1 minority (Hispanic American), 1 international. Average age 34. 4 applicants, 100% accepted. In 2009, 4 master's awarded. *Degree requirements:* For master's, thesis (for some programs), capstone experience. *Entrance requirements:* For master's, minimum GPA of 2.75. Additional exam requirements/recommendations for international students: Required—TOEFL (minimum score 500 paper-based; 173 computer-based), IELTS (minimum score 5.5). *Application deadline:* Applications are processed on a rolling basis. Application fee: $0. *Expenses:* Contact institution. *Financial support:* In 2009–10, 2 students received support, including 2 teaching assistantships with full tuition reimbursements available (averaging $3,300 per year); career-related internships or fieldwork, Federal Work-Study, and unspecified assistantships also available. Support available to part-time students. Financial award application deadline: 3/1. *Unit head:* Dr. Charles R. Pinches, Chair, 570-941-4302, Fax: 570-941-6369, E-mail: pinchesc1@scranton.edu. *Application contact:* Joseph M. Roback, Director of Admissions, 570-941-4385, Fax: 570-941-5928, E-mail: robackj2@scranton.edu.

University of South Africa, College of Human Sciences, Pretoria, South Africa. Offers adult education (M Ed); African languages (MA, PhD); African politics (MA, PhD); Afrikaans (MA, PhD); ancient history (MA, PhD); ancient Near Eastern studies (MA, PhD); anthropology (MA, PhD); applied linguistics (MA); Arabic (MA, PhD); archaeology (MA); art history (MA); Biblical archaeology (MA); Biblical studies (M Th, D Th, PhD); Christian spirituality (M Th, D Th); church history (M Th, D Th); classical studies (MA, PhD); clinical psychology (MA); communication (MA, PhD); comparative education (M Ed, Ed D); consulting psychology (D Admin, D Com, PhD); curriculum studies (M Ed, Ed D); development studies (M Admin, MA, D Admin, PhD); didactics (M Ed, Ed D); education (M Tech); education management (M Ed, Ed D); educational psychology (M Ed); English (MA); environmental education (M Ed); French (MA, PhD); German (MA, PhD); Greek (MA); guidance and counseling (M Ed); health studies (MA, PhD), including health sciences education (MA), health services management (MA), medical and surgical nursing science (critical care general) (MA), midwifery and neonatal nursing science (MA), trauma and emergency care (MA); history (MA, PhD); history of education (Ed D); inclusive education (M Ed, Ed D); information and communications technology policy and regulation (MA); information science (MA, MIS, PhD); international politics (MA, PhD); Islamic studies (MA, PhD); Italian (MA, PhD); Judaica (MA, PhD); linguistics (MA, PhD); mathematical education (M Ed); mathematics education (MA); missiology (M Th, D Th); modern Hebrew (MA, PhD); musicology (MA, MMus, D Mus, PhD); natural science education (M Ed); New Testament (M Th, D Th); Old Testament (D Th); pastoral therapy (M Th, D Th); philosophy (MA); philosophy of education (M Ed, Ed D); politics (MA, PhD); Portuguese (MA, PhD); practical theology (M Th, D Th); psychology (MA, MS, PhD); psychology of education (M Ed, Ed D); public health (MA); religious studies (MA, D Th, PhD); Romance languages (MA); Russian (MA, PhD); Semitic languages (MA, PhD); social behavior studies in HIV/AIDS (MA); social science (mental health) (MA); social science in development studies (MA); social science in psychology (MA); social science in social work (MA); social science in sociology (MA); social work (MSW, DSW, PhD); socio-education (M Ed, Ed D); sociolinguistics (MA); sociology (MA, PhD); Spanish (MA, PhD); systematic theology (M Th, D Th); TESOL (teaching English to speakers of other languages) (MA); theological ethics (M Th, D Th); theory of literature (MA, PhD); urban ministries (D Th); urban ministry (M Th).

University of Trinity College, Faculty of Divinity, Toronto, ON M5S 1H8, Canada. Offers ministry (Diploma); ministry for church musicians (Diploma); theology (M Div, MTS, Th M, D Min, PhD, Th D, Diploma, L Th); M Div/MA. *Accreditation:* ATS. Part-time programs available. *Degree requirements:* For master's, 2 foreign languages, thesis (for some programs); for doctorate, 3 foreign languages, comprehensive exam, thesis/dissertation; for M Div, thesis/dissertation optional; for other advanced degree, thesis (for some programs). *Entrance requirements:* For M Div, interview; for master's, 1 language (modern or ancient), interview; for doctorate, 2 languages (modern and ancient). Additional exam requirements/recommendations for international students: Required—TOEFL, TWE. *Faculty research:* Interreligious dialogue, feminist theology, systematic theology, philosophy of religion, pastoral theology.

The University of Winnipeg, Faculty of Theology, Winnipeg, MB R3B 2E9, Canada. Offers marriage and family therapy (MMFT, Certificate); sacred theology (STM); theology (M Div). *Accreditation:* AAMFT/COAMFTE; ATS. Part-time programs available. *Degree requirements:* For M Div, thesis/dissertation optional.

Ursuline College, School of Graduate Studies, Graduate Program in Ministry, Pepper Pike, OH 44124-4398. Offers MA. Part-time programs available. *Faculty:* 1 (woman) full-time, 1 (woman) part-time/adjunct. *Students:* 22 part-time (20 women); includes 4 minority (3 African Americans, 1 Hispanic American). Average age 48. 3 applicants, 100% accepted, 3 enrolled. In 2009, 8 master's awarded. *Degree requirements:* For master's, thesis. *Entrance requirements:* For master's, minimum undergraduate GPA of 3.0, interview. Additional exam requirements/recommendations for international students: Required—TOEFL (minimum score 500 paper-based; 173 computer-based). *Application deadline:* For fall admission, 8/1 priority date for domestic students. Applications are processed on a rolling basis. Application fee: $25. *Expenses:* Contact institution. *Financial support:* In 2009–10, 11 students received support. Federal Work-Study available. Financial award application deadline: 3/1; financial award applicants required to submit FAFSA. *Unit head:* Dr. Linda Martin, Co-Director, 440-646-8191, Fax: 440-684-6088, E-mail: lmartin@ursuline.edu. *Application contact:* Melanie Steele, Secretary, 440-646-8199, Fax: 440-684-6138, E-mail: gradsch@ursuline.edu.

Valparaiso University, Graduate School, Programs in Liberal Studies, Concentration in Theology, Valparaiso, IN 46383. Offers MALS, Post-Master's Certificate, JD/MALS. Part-time and evening/weekend programs available. *Students:* 1 (woman) part-time. Average age 36. In 2009, 1 master's awarded. *Entrance requirements:* For master's, minimum GPA of 3.0. Additional exam requirements/recommendations for international students: Required—TOEFL (minimum score 550 paper-based; 213 computer-based; 80 iBT). *Application deadline:* Applications are processed on a rolling basis. Application fee: $30 ($50 for international students). Electronic applications accepted. *Financial support:* Available to part-time students. Applicants required to submit FAFSA. *Unit head:* Dr. David L. Rowland, Dean, Graduate Studies and Continuing Education/Associate Provost, 219-464-5313, Fax: 219-464-5381, E-mail: david.rowland@valpo.edu. *Application contact:* Jamie Haney, Coordinator of Graduate Admission, 219-464-5313, Fax: 219-464-5381, E-mail: jamie.haney@valpo.edu.

Valparaiso University, Graduate School, Programs in Liberal Studies, Concentration in Theology and Ministry, Valparaiso, IN 46383. Offers MALS, Post-Master's Certificate. Part-time and evening/weekend programs available. *Entrance requirements:* For master's, minimum GPA of 3.0. Additional exam requirements/recommendations for international students: Required—TOEFL (minimum score 550 paper-based; 213 computer-based; 80 iBT). *Application deadline:* Applications are processed on a rolling basis. Application fee: $30 ($50 for international students). Electronic applications accepted. *Financial support:* Available to part-time students. Applicants required to submit FAFSA. *Unit head:* Dr. David L. Rowland, Dean, Graduate Studies and Continuing Education/Associate Provost, 219-464-5313, Fax: 219-464-5381, E-mail: david.rowland@valpo.edu. *Application contact:* Jamie Haney, Coordinator of Graduate Admission, 219-464-5313, Fax: 219-464-5381, E-mail: jamie.haney@valpo.edu.

Vancouver School of Theology, Graduate and Professional Programs, Vancouver, BC V6T 1L4, Canada. Offers spiritual direction (Graduate Diploma); theological studies (MATS); theology (M Div, Th M, Dip CS). *Accreditation:* ATS. Part-time programs available. *Degree requirements:* For master's, comprehensive exam (for some programs), thesis (for some programs); for M Div, thesis/dissertation (for some programs); for other advanced degree, one foreign language, thesis. *Entrance requirements:* Additional exam requirements/recommendations for international students: Required—TOEFL. Electronic applications accepted. *Faculty research:* Old Testament studies, pastoral theology, New Testament studies, field education, church history, systematic theology, spirituality.

Vanderbilt University, Divinity School, Nashville, TN 37240-1001. Offers M Div, MTS, JD/M Div, JD/MTS, MBA/M Div, MBA/MTS, MD/M Div, MD/MTS, MSN/M Div, MSN/MTS. *Accreditation:* ACIPE; ATS. Part-time programs available. *Faculty:* 30 full-time (11 women), 9 part-time/adjunct (3 women). *Students:* 222 full-time (104 women); includes 45 minority (38 African Americans, 1 American Indian/Alaska Native, 3 Asian Americans or Pacific Islanders, 3 Hispanic Americans). Average age 26. 177 applicants, 77% accepted, 72 enrolled. In 2009, 41 first professional degrees, 25 master's awarded. *Entrance requirements:* Additional exam requirements/recommendations for international students: Required—TOEFL (minimum score 630 paper-based; 250 computer-based; 100 iBT). *Application deadline:* For fall admission, 5/1 for domestic students, 4/1 for international students. Applications are processed on a rolling basis. Application fee: $50. Electronic applications accepted. *Expenses:* Contact institution. *Financial support:* In 2009–10, 200 students received support. Career-related internships or fieldwork, Federal Work-Study, institutionally sponsored loans, scholarships/grants, and tuition waivers (full and partial) available. Financial award application deadline: 5/1; financial award applicants required to submit CSS PROFILE or FAFSA. *Unit head:* Dr. James Hudnut-Beumler, Dean, 615-322-2776, Fax: 615-343-9957, E-mail: james.d.hudnut-beumler@vanderbilt.edu. *Application contact:* Dr. James Hudnut-Beumler, Dean, 615-322-2776, Fax: 615-343-9957, E-mail: james.d.hudnut-beumler@vanderbilt.edu.

Vanguard University of Southern California, Graduate Programs in Religion, Costa Mesa, CA 92626-9601. Offers leadership studies (MA); theological studies (MTS). Part-time and evening/weekend programs available. *Faculty:* 5 full-time (0 women), 1 part-time/adjunct (0 women). *Students:* 10 full-time (2 women), 60 part-time (17 women); includes 14 minority (1 African American, 4 Asian Americans or Pacific Islanders, 9 Hispanic Americans). Average age 38. 26 applicants, 73% accepted, 16 enrolled. *Degree requirements:* For master's, comprehensive exam (for some programs), thesis (for some programs). *Entrance requirements:* For master's, minimum GPA of 3.0 (MA), 2.5 (MTS). Additional exam requirements/recommendations for international students: Required—TOEFL (minimum score 550 paper-based; 213 computer-based; 79 iBT). *Application deadline:* For fall admission, 4/1 priority date for domestic and international students; for spring admission, 10/1 priority date for domestic and international students. Applications are processed on a rolling basis. Application fee: $45. Electronic applications accepted. *Expenses:* Contact institution. *Financial support:* Teaching assistantships, scholarships/grants and tuition waivers (partial) available. Support available to part-time students. Financial award application deadline: 3/2; financial award applicants required to submit FAFSA. *Unit head:* Dr. Richard Israel, Associate Dean, 714-556-3610 Ext. 3223, Fax: 714-957-9317. *Faculty research:* Narrative theology, ecumenism and Pentecost, leadership studies. *Unit head:* Dr. Richard Israel, Associate Dean, 714-556-3610 Ext. 3223, Fax: 714-957-9317. *Application contact:* Angel McGee, Secretary, 714-556-3610 Ext. 3237, Fax: 714-957-9317, E-mail: angel.mcgee@vanguard.edu.

Victoria University, Emmanuel College, Toronto, ON M5S 1K7, Canada. Offers M Div, MA, MPS, MRE, MSMus, MTS, Th M, D Min, PhD, Th D, Certificate, Diploma, L Th, M Div/MA, M Div/MPS, M Div/MRE. *Accreditation:* ATS. *Faculty:* 11 full-time (5 women), 5 part-time/adjunct (2 women). *Students:* 81 full-time (45 women), 74 part-time (51 women); includes 19 minority (1 African American, 1 American Indian/Alaska Native, 15 Asian Americans or Pacific Islanders, 2 Hispanic Americans), 9 international. Average age 43. 64 applicants, 94% accepted, 37 enrolled. In 2009, 18 first professional degrees, 5 master's, 2 doctorates, 2 other advanced degrees awarded. Terminal master's awarded for partial completion of doctoral program. *Degree requirements:* For master's, 2 foreign languages, thesis (for some programs); for doctorate, 2 foreign languages, thesis/dissertation; for M Div, thesis/dissertation optional. *Entrance requirements:* For M Div, BA, BSc, BMus; for master's and other advanced degree, BA, BSc; for doctorate, MDiv, MA, MTS, ThM. Additional exam requirements/recommendations for international students: Required—TOEFL (minimum score 600 paper-based; 250 computer-based; 100 iBT), IELTS (minimum score 7), TWE (minimum score 5). *Application deadline:* For fall admission, 6/30 for domestic students, 1/15 for international students; for winter admission, 11/30 for domestic students; for spring admission, 3/30 for domestic students. Applications are processed on a rolling basis. Application fee: $0. Electronic applications accepted. Tuition charges are reported in Canadian dollars. *Expenses:* Tuition: Full-time $5896 Canadian dollars. Full-time tuition and fees vary according to course load, degree level and program. *Financial support:* In 2009–10, 97 students received support, including 2 fellowships (averaging $11,000 per year), 12 teaching assistantships (averaging $11,000 per year); career-related internships or fieldwork, scholarships/grants, unspecified assistantships, and bursaries also available. Support available to part-time students. Financial award application deadline: 5/30. *Faculty research:* New Testament and Old Testament hermeneutics, religious symbolism, Reformation, liberation theology, Canadian church history. *Unit head:* Dr. Mark G. Toulouse, Principal, 416-585-4540, Fax: 416-585-4516, E-mail: m.toulouse@utoronto.ca. *Application contact:* Wanda Chin, Registrar, 416-585-4538, Fax: 416-585-4516, E-mail: wanda.chin@utoronto.ca.

Villanova University, Graduate School of Liberal Arts and Sciences, Department of Theology, Villanova, PA 19085-1699. Offers MA. Part-time and evening/weekend programs available. *Faculty:* 7 full-time (2 women). *Students:* 18 full-time (6 women), 16 part-time (10 women); includes 5 minority (2 African Americans, 2 Asian Americans or Pacific Islanders, 1 Hispanic American), 1 international. Average age 32. 28 applicants, 100% accepted, 12 enrolled. In 2009, 12 master's awarded. *Degree requirements:* For master's, one foreign language, comprehensive exam, thesis optional. *Entrance requirements:* For master's, GRE, minimum GPA of 3.0. Additional exam requirements/recommendations for international students: Required—TOEFL. *Application deadline:* For fall admission, 3/1 priority date for domestic and international students; for spring admission, 11/15 priority date for domestic students, 11/15 for international students. Applications are processed on a rolling basis. Application fee: $50. Electronic applications accepted. *Expenses:* Tuition: Part-time $630 per credit. Required fees: $60 per credit. Part-time tuition and fees vary according to degree level and program. *Financial support:* Research assistantships, Federal Work-Study and scholarships/grants available. Financial award applicants required to submit FAFSA. *Unit head:* Dr. Bernard Prusak, Chair, 610-519-7423. *Application contact:* Dr. Adele Lindenmeyr, Dean, Graduate School of Liberal Arts and Sciences, 610-519-7093, Fax: 610-519-7096.

See Close-Up on page 515.

Virginia Theological Seminary, Graduate and Professional Programs, Alexandria, VA 22304. Offers M Div, MACE, MTS, D Min. *Accreditation:* ATS. Part-time programs available. *Degree requirements:* For master's, 2 foreign languages, thesis; for doctorate, thesis/dissertation. *Entrance requirements:* For M Div, master's, and doctorate, GRE General Test.

Virginia Union University, School of Theology, Richmond, VA 23220-1170. Offers M Div, D Min. *Accreditation:* ACIPE; ATS. Part-time and evening/weekend programs available. *Entrance requirements:* Additional exam requirements/recommendations for international students: Required—TOEFL.

Walsh University, Graduate Studies, Program in Theology, North Canton, OH 44720-3396. Offers MA. Part-time and evening/weekend programs available. *Faculty:* 2 full-time (1 woman), 3 part-time/adjunct (2 women). *Students:* 17 part-time (11 women). Average age 48. 5 applicants,

80% accepted, 4 enrolled. In 2009, 1 master's awarded. *Degree requirements:* For master's, thesis (for some programs). *Entrance requirements:* For master's, MAT or GRE, minimum GPA of 3.0. *Application deadline:* For fall admission, 7/15 priority date for domestic students. Applications are processed on a rolling basis. Application fee: $25. Electronic applications accepted. *Expenses:* Tuition: Full-time $9630; part-time $535 per credit hour. Tuition and fees vary according to course load and program. *Financial support:* In 2009–10, 9 students received support; research assistantships available. Financial award application deadline: 12/31. *Faculty research:* Historical theology, patristics, twentieth century Catholic theologians, theological anthropology, peace studies. *Unit head:* Dr. Patrick Manning, Chair of Theology Division, 330-244-4922, Fax: 330-244-4955, E-mail: pmanning@walsh.edu. *Application contact:* Stephanie Wheeler, Director of Graduate and Transfer Admissions, 830-490-7174, Fax: 330-490-7165, E-mail: swheeler@walsh.edu.

Warner Pacific College, Graduate Programs, Portland, OR 97215-4099. Offers biblical and theological studies (MA); biblical studies (M Rel); education (M Ed); management/organizational leadership (MS); pastoral ministries (M Rel); religion and ethics (M Rel); teaching (MA); theology (M Rel). Part-time programs available. *Degree requirements:* For master's, thesis or alternative, presentation of defense. *Entrance requirements:* For master's, interview, minimum GPA of 2.5, letters of recommendations. *Faculty research:* New Testament studies, nineteenth-century Wesleyan theology, preaching and church growth, Christian ethics.

Wartburg Theological Seminary, Graduate and Professional Programs, Dubuque, IA 52004-5004. Offers diaconal ministry (MA); theology (M Div, MA, MATDE, STM). *Accreditation:* ACIPE; ATS. *Degree requirements:* For master's, thesis (for some programs); for M Div, thesis/dissertation optional. *Entrance requirements:* For M Div, minimum GPA of 2.5; for master's, minimum GPA of 3.0 (STM). Additional exam requirements/recommendations for international students: Required—TOEFL (minimum score 500 paper-based; 173 computer-based; 80 iBT). Electronic applications accepted.

Washington Theological Union, Graduate and Professional Programs, Washington, DC 20012. Offers M Div, MA, MAPS, MTS, D Min, M Div/MA. *Accreditation:* ACIPE; ATS. Part-time programs available. Postbaccalaureate distance learning degree programs offered. *Degree requirements:* For master's, one foreign language, comprehensive exam, thesis. *Entrance requirements:* For M Div, 18 hours of course work in philosophy; for master's, 18 hours of course work in philosophy and religious studies.

Wesley Biblical Seminary, Graduate Programs, Jackson, MS 39206. Offers apologetics (MA); Biblical studies (MA); Christian studies (MA); evangelism (M Div); family life ministry (M Div); honors research (M Div); missions (M Div); pastoral ministry (M Div); teaching (M Div); theological studies (MA). *Accreditation:* ATS. Part-time programs available. *Faculty:* 11 full-time (2 women), 5 part-time/adjunct (0 women). *Students:* 43 full-time (5 women), 89 part-time (33 women). *Degree requirements:* For master's, thesis. *Entrance requirements:* Additional exam requirements/recommendations for international students: Required—TOEFL. *Application deadline:* For fall admission, 7/1 priority date for domestic students; for spring admission, 12/1 priority date for domestic students. Applications are processed on a rolling basis. Application fee: $40. Electronic applications accepted. *Expenses:* Tuition: Full-time $8000; part-time $320 per credit hour. Required fees: $310; $160 per semester. Tuition and fees vary according to course load, campus/location and program. *Financial support:* Scholarships/grants available. Support available to part-time students. *Faculty research:* Patristics, missiology, culture, hermeneutics. *Unit head:* Dr. Ray R. Easley, Vice President for Academic Affairs, 601-366-8880 Ext. 112, Fax: 601-366-8832. *Application contact:* Laura McMillan, Assistant to the Vice President for Business and Student Development, 601-366-8880 Ext. 110, Fax: 601-366-8832, E-mail: admissions@wbs.edu.

Wesley Theological Seminary, Graduate and Professional Programs, Washington, DC 20016-5690. Offers M Div, MA, MTS, D Min, M Div/MA, M Div/MTS. *Accreditation:* ACIPE; ATS. Part-time programs available. *Degree requirements:* For master's, thesis; for doctorate, thesis/dissertation; for M Div, thesis/dissertation or alternative. *Entrance requirements:* For M Div and master's, minimum GPA of 2.7; for doctorate, minimum GPA of 3.0.

Western Seminary, Graduate Programs, Master of Divinity Program, Portland, OR 97215-3367. Offers D Min. *Faculty:* 3 full-time (1 woman), 3 part-time/adjunct (0 women). *Students:* 93 full-time (38 women), 586 part-time (198 women); includes 20 minority (5 African Americans, 1 American Indian/Alaska Native, 11 Asian Americans or Pacific Islanders, 3 Hispanic Americans). Average age 29. 186 applicants, 65% accepted, 86 enrolled. *Entrance requirements:* Additional exam requirements/recommendations for international students: Required—TOEFL. *Application deadline:* For fall admission, 7/9 priority date for domestic students; for winter admission, 10/8 priority date for domestic students; for spring admission, 3/4 priority date for domestic students. Applications are processed on a rolling basis. Application fee: $50. *Expenses:* Tuition: Full-time $3280; part-time $410 per credit hour. *Financial support:* Fellowships, career-related internships or fieldwork available. Support available to part-time students. Financial award applicants required to submit FAFSA. *Unit head:* Dr. Art Azurdia, Director, 503-517-1873, E-mail: aazurdia@westernseminary.edu. *Application contact:* Dr. Robert W. Wiggins, Registrar/Dean of Student Development, 503-517-1820, Fax: 503-517-1801, E-mail: rwiggins@westernseminary.edu.

Western Seminary, Graduate Programs, Program in Biblical and Theological Studies, Portland, OR 97215-3367. Offers biblical and theological studies (MA, G Dip); biblical studies (Certificate); theology (Th M). *Accreditation:* ATS. Part-time and evening/weekend programs available. *Faculty:* 93 full-time (38 women), 586 part-time/adjunct (198 women). *Students:* 79 full-time, 123 part-time; includes 20 minority (5 African Americans, 1 American Indian/Alaska Native, 11 Asian Americans or Pacific Islanders, 3 Hispanic Americans). Average age 29. 132 applicants, 92% accepted, 86 enrolled. *Degree requirements:* For master's, thesis or alternative, practicum. *Entrance requirements:* Additional exam requirements/recommendations for international students: Required—TOEFL. *Application deadline:* For fall admission, 7/19 priority date for domestic students; for winter admission, 11/8 priority date for domestic students; for spring admission, 3/14 priority date for domestic students. Applications are processed on a rolling basis. Application fee: $50. *Expenses:* Tuition: Full-time $3280; part-time $410 per credit hour. *Financial support:* Fellowships, career-related internships or fieldwork available. Financial award applicants required to submit FAFSA. *Unit head:* Dr. Gerry Breshears, Director, 503-517-1870, E-mail: gbreshears@westernseminary.edu. *Application contact:* Dr. Robert W. Wiggins, Registrar/Dean of Student Development, 503-517-1820, Fax: 503-517-1820, E-mail: rwiggins@westernseminary.edu.

Western Seminary–Sacramento Campus, Graduate Programs, Sacramento, CA 95821. Offers exegetical theology (MA); marital and family therapy (MA); ministry (M Div); specialized ministry (MA). Postbaccalaureate distance learning degree programs offered. *Entrance requirements:* For M Div, minimum GPA of 2.5; for master's, minimum GPA of 3.0.

Western Seminary–San Jose Campus, Graduate Programs, Los Gatos, CA 95032-4520. Offers exegetical theology (MA); expositional ministry (M Div); marital and family therapy (MA); ministry (M Div); pastoral ministry (M Div); specialized ministry (MA). Postbaccalaureate distance learning degree programs offered. *Degree requirements:* For master's, 2 foreign languages; for M Div, 3 foreign languages. *Entrance requirements:* For M Div, minimum GPA of 2.5; for master's, minimum GPA of 3.0.

Western Theological Seminary, Graduate and Professional Programs, Holland, MI 49423-3622. Offers M Div, M Th, D Min. *Accreditation:* ACIPE; ATS. Part-time programs available. Postbaccalaureate distance learning degree programs offered (minimal on-campus study). *Faculty:* 18 full-time (4 women), 9 part-time/adjunct (5 women). *Students:* 152 full-time (48 women), 96 part-time (35 women); includes 24 minority (19 African Americans, 1 Asian American or Pacific Islander, 4 Hispanic Americans), 1 international. Average age 29. 82 applicants, 98% accepted, 64 enrolled. In 2009, 35 first professional degrees, 5 master's, 1 doctorate awarded. *Degree requirements:* For doctorate, 2 foreign languages, thesis/dissertation; for M Div, 2 foreign languages. *Entrance requirements:* For doctorate, 5 years of experience in the ministry (must be ordained). Additional exam requirements/recommendations for international students: Required—TOEFL. *Application deadline:* For fall admission, 5/1 priority date for domestic students. Applications are processed on a rolling basis. Application fee: $50. *Expenses:* Tuition: Full-time $11,472; part-time $358.50 per credit. Required fees: $90. *Financial support:* In 2009–10, 125 students received support. Career-related internships or fieldwork, institutionally sponsored loans, and scholarships/grants available. Support available to part-time students. Financial award applicants required to submit FAFSA. *Unit head:* Dr. Timothy Brown, President, 616-392-8555, Fax: 616-392-7717, E-mail: dennis@westernsem.edu. *Application contact:* Rev. Mark Poppen, Director of Admissions, 616-392-8555, Fax: 616-392-7717, E-mail: mark@westernsem.edu.

Westminster Seminary California, Programs in Theology, Escondido, CA 92027-4128. Offers Biblical studies (MA); historical theology (MA); theological studies (M Div, MA). *Accreditation:* ATS. Part-time and evening/weekend programs available. *Degree requirements:* For master's, 2 foreign languages, thesis (for some programs); for M Div, 2 foreign languages, internship. *Entrance requirements:* For M Div and master's, 2 letters of reference. Additional exam requirements/recommendations for international students: Required—TOEFL (minimum score 570 paper-based; 230 computer-based; 89 iBT), TWE (minimum score 4.5). *Faculty research:* Neo-paganism, New Testament background, eschatology, Protestant scholasticism, Ezekiel.

Westminster Theological Seminary, Graduate and Professional Programs, Philadelphia, PA 19118. Offers apologetics (Th M); Biblical and urban studies (Certificate); Biblical counseling (MA); biblical studies (MAR); Christian studies (Certificate); church history (Th M); counseling (M Div); general studies (M Div, MAR); hermeneutics and Bible interpretations (PhD); historical and theological studies (PhD); historical theology (Th M); New Testament (Th M); Old Testament (Th M); pastoral counseling (D Min); pastoral ministry (M Div, D Min); systematic theology (Th M); theological studies (MAR); urban missions (M Div, MA, MAR, D Min). *Accreditation:* ATS. Part-time programs available. Terminal master's awarded for partial completion of doctoral program. *Degree requirements:* For master's, thesis (for some programs); for doctorate, 4 foreign languages, comprehensive exam (for some programs), thesis/dissertation; for M Div, 2 foreign languages. *Entrance requirements:* For doctorate, GRE General Test. Additional exam requirements/recommendations for international students: Required—TOEFL, TWE.

Wheaton College, Graduate School, Department of Biblical and Theological Studies, Program in Biblical and Theological Studies, Wheaton, IL 60187-5593. Offers PhD. *Degree requirements:* For doctorate, thesis/dissertation. *Entrance requirements:* For doctorate, GRE. Electronic applications accepted.

Wheaton College, Graduate School, Department of Biblical and Theological Studies, Program in Biblical Archaeology, Wheaton, IL 60187-5593. Offers MA. *Degree requirements:* For master's, thesis or alternative, semester of study in Israel. *Entrance requirements:* For master's, GRE General Test or MAT. Electronic applications accepted.

Wheaton College, Graduate School, Department of Biblical and Theological Studies, Program in Biblical Exegesis, Wheaton, IL 60187-5593. Offers MA. *Degree requirements:* For master's, 2 foreign languages, thesis or alternative. *Entrance requirements:* For master's, GRE General Test or MAT. Electronic applications accepted.

Wheaton College, Graduate School, Department of Biblical and Theological Studies, Program in Biblical Studies, Wheaton, IL 60187-5593. Offers MA. Part-time programs available. *Degree requirements:* For master's, one foreign language, thesis optional. *Entrance requirements:* For master's, GRE General Test, MAT. Electronic applications accepted.

Wheaton College, Graduate School, Department of Biblical and Theological Studies, Program in General History of Christianity, Wheaton, IL 60187-5593. Offers biblical and theological studies (MA). Part-time and evening/weekend programs available. *Degree requirements:* For master's, thesis optional. *Entrance requirements:* For master's, GRE General Test, MAT.

Wheaton College, Graduate School, Department of Biblical and Theological Studies, Program in Historical and Systematic Theology, Wheaton, IL 60187-5593. Offers biblical and theological studies (MA). Electronic applications accepted.

Whitworth University, Master of Arts in Theology Program, Spokane, WA 99251-0001. Offers MA. Part-time and evening/weekend programs available. Tuition and fees vary according to program.

Wilfrid Laurier University, Waterloo Lutheran Seminary, Waterloo, ON N2L 3C5, Canada. Offers Christian ethics (M Th); divinity (M Div); homiletics (M Th); ministry (D Min); pastoral counseling (M Th); spirituality in a health care setting (Diploma); theological studies (MTS); theology (Diploma); M Div/MTS/MSW. *Accreditation:* ATS. Part-time programs available. *Degree requirements:* For master's, one foreign language, thesis (for some programs); for doctorate, thesis/dissertation; for M Div, one foreign language, thesis/dissertation. *Entrance requirements:* For M Div, denominational endorsement; for master's, M Div, 2 units of clinical pastoral education (M Th); for doctorate, M Div, 3 years of ministry experience, proficiency in a foreign language, basic training in clinical pastoral education. Additional exam requirements/recommendations for international students: Required—TOEFL (minimum score 573 paper-based; 230 computer-based; 89 iBT), IELTS (minimum score 7). Electronic applications accepted. *Expenses:* Contact institution. *Faculty research:* Biblical study, church history, systematic theology.

Winebrenner Theological Seminary, Graduate Programs, Findlay, OH 45840. Offers church development (MA); family ministry (MA); theological study (MA); theological/ministerial studies (D Min); theology/ministerial studies (M Div). *Accreditation:* ATS (one or more programs are accredited). Part-time and evening/weekend programs available. *Faculty:* 6 full-time (1 woman), 5 part-time/adjunct (3 women). *Students:* 42 full-time (9 women), 42 part-time (15 women); includes 7 minority (all African Americans), 3 international. Average age 40. 13 applicants, 100% accepted, 9 enrolled. In 2009, 6 first professional degrees, 6 master's awarded. *Degree requirements:* For master's, supervised ministry, theological summit; for doctorate, thesis/dissertation, research project; for M Div, 2 foreign languages, supervised ministry, theological summit. *Entrance requirements:* For M Div and master's, background check; for doctorate, 3 years of post-M Div full-time ministry, background check. Additional exam requirements/recommendations for international students: Required—TOEFL (minimum score 550 paper-based; 213 computer-based). *Application deadline:* For fall admission, 8/15 priority date for domestic students, 7/15 priority date for international students; for winter admission, 12/15 priority date for domestic students, 11/15 priority date for international students; for spring admission, 4/15 priority date for domestic students, 3/15 priority date for international students. Applications are processed on a rolling basis. Application fee: $30. Electronic applications accepted. *Expenses:* Tuition: Full-time $10,920; part-time $426 per credit. Required fees: $115 per term. Tuition and fees vary according to program. *Financial support:* In 2009–10, 43 students received support, including 1 research assistantship with partial tuition reimbursement available, 2 teaching assistantships with partial tuition reimbursements available; institutionally sponsored loans, scholarships/grants, and tuition waivers (partial) also available. Support available to part-time students. Financial award application deadline: 7/1; financial award applicants required to submit FAFSA. *Faculty research:* Sound and silence, nineteenth century American Lutheranism, sexuality and spirituality/intimacy and marriage; eighteenth century feminism of Mary Asbell; late Colonial spirituality of Jonathan Edwards. *Unit head:* Dr. M. John Nissley, Vice President for Academic Advancement, 419-434-4247, Fax: 419-434-4267, E-mail: jnissley@winebrenner.edu. *Application contact:* Jim Wilder, Regional Coordinator, 419-434-4200, Fax: 419-434-4267, E-mail: admissions@winebrenner.edu.

Wycliffe College, Division of Advanced Degree Studies, Toronto, ON M5S 1H7, Canada. Offers MA, Th M, D Min, PhD, Th D. *Accreditation:* ATS (one or more programs are accredited). Part-time programs available. Terminal master's awarded for partial completion of doctoral program. *Degree requirements:* For master's, 2 foreign languages, thesis (for some programs); for doctorate, 3 foreign languages, thesis/dissertation. *Entrance requirements:* Additional exam requirements/recommendations for international students: Required—TOEFL (minimum score

Theology

Wycliffe College (continued)
600 paper-based; 250 computer-based). *Expenses:* Contact institution. *Faculty research:* Old and New Testament, doctrine, ethics, philosophy, history.

Wycliffe College, Division of Basic Degree Studies, Toronto, ON M5S 1H7, Canada. Offers Christian Studies (Diploma); theology (M Div, M Rel, MTS). *Accreditation:* ATS. Part-time programs available. *Degree requirements:* For master's, one foreign language, thesis; for M Div, thesis/dissertation optional. *Entrance requirements:* Additional exam requirements/recommendations for international students: Required—TOEFL (minimum score 580 paper-based).

Xavier University, College of Arts and Sciences, Department of Theology, Cincinnati, OH 45207. Offers theology (MA), including religious education, social and pastoral ministry, theology. Part-time programs available. *Faculty:* 7 full-time (2 women). *Students:* 5 full-time (2 women), 23 part-time (10 women); includes 1 minority (Hispanic American). Average age 33. 11 applicants, 100% accepted, 11 enrolled. In 2009, 5 master's awarded. *Degree requirements:* For master's, thesis optional, final paper and defense. *Entrance requirements:* For master's, MAT or GRE, letters of recommendation. Additional exam requirements/recommendations for international students: Required—TOEFL (minimum score 550 paper-based; 213 computer-based). *Application deadline:* Applications are processed on a rolling basis. Application fee: $35. Electronic applications accepted. *Expenses:* Tuition: Part-time $697 per credit hour. One-time fee: $35 part-time. *Financial support:* In 2009–10, 26 students received support. Scholarships/grants and unspecified assistantships available. Financial award applicants required to submit FAFSA. *Faculty research:* Scripture, ethics, constructive theology, historical theology. *Unit head:* Dr. Sarah Melcher, Chair, 513-745-2043, Fax: 513-745-3215, E-mail: melcher@xavier.edu. *Application contact:* Dr. Sarah Melcher, Chair, 513-745-2043, Fax: 513-745-3215, E-mail: melcher@xavier.edu.

Xavier University of Louisiana, Graduate School, Institute for Black Catholic Studies, New Orleans, LA 70125-1098. Offers pastoral theology (Th M). Part-time programs available. *Degree requirements:* For master's, comprehensive exam, practicum. *Entrance requirements:* For master's, GRE General Test, MAT, minimum GPA of 2.5. Additional exam requirements/recommendations for international students: Required—TOEFL.

Yale University, Divinity School, New Haven, CT 06511. Offers M Div, MAR, STM, JD/M Div, JD/MAR, M Div/MBA, M Div/MF, M Div/MSN, M Div/MSW, MAR/MSN, MAR/MSW, MD/M Div, MD/MAR. *Accreditation:* ACIPE; ATS. Part-time programs available. *Entrance requirements:* Additional exam requirements/recommendations for international students: Required—IELTS (minimum score 7). Electronic applications accepted. *Expenses:* Contact institution.

Yeshiva Beth Moshe, Graduate Programs, Scranton, PA 18505-2124. Offers Second Talmudical Degree, Talmudic Fellow Degree. *Accreditation:* AARTS.

Yeshiva Karlin Stolin Rabbinical Institute, Graduate Programs, Brooklyn, NY 11204. Offers Advanced Rabbinical Degree. *Accreditation:* AARTS.

Yeshiva of Nitra Rabbinical College, Graduate Programs, Mount Kisco, NY 10549. *Accreditation:* AARTS.

Yeshiva Shaar Hatorah Talmudic Research Institute, Graduate Programs, Kew Gardens, NY 11418-1469. *Accreditation:* AARTS.

Yeshivath Zichron Moshe, Graduate Programs, South Fallsburg, NY 12779. Offers Advanced Talmudic Degree, Talmudic Scholar Degree. *Accreditation:* AARTS. Part-time programs available.

Yeshiva Toras Chaim Talmudical Seminary, Graduate Programs, Denver, CO 80204-1415.

JTS
The Graduate School

THE JEWISH THEOLOGICAL SEMINARY

The Graduate School

Programs of Study

The Graduate School of The Jewish Theological Seminary (JTS) offers the most comprehensive program of advanced Jewish studies available in North America. Through specialized courses of study, students prepare to pursue careers in academia, Jewish art, or communal leadership. Programs leading to the M.A. and doctoral (D.H.L. and Ph.D.) degrees are offered in the following fields except as noted: ancient Judaism, Bible and ancient Semitic languages, interdepartmental studies (M.A. only), Jewish art and visual culture (M.A. only), Jewish history, Jewish literature, Jewish thought, Jewish gender and women's studies (M.A. only), liturgy, medieval Jewish studies, midrash and scriptural interpretation, modern Jewish studies, and Talmud and Rabbinics. In addition, The Graduate School offers dual-degree programs with the Columbia University School of Social Work leading to the M.A./M.S.S.W. degrees and with Columbia University's School of International and Public Affairs leading to the M.A./M.P.A. degrees to prepare students to enter the field of communal service.

Research Facilities

The Library of The Jewish Theological Seminary houses the most complete collection of Judaica in the Western Hemisphere. With more than 400,000 volumes on open shelves, it is ideally suited for the research needs of graduate students. The Library's special collection, with more than 78,000 items, affords many opportunities for original scholarship. Students also benefit from the library resources of neighboring Columbia University and Union Theological Seminary. M.A. and Ph.D. students also have access to the courses and facilities of several universities through a special consortial agreement.

Financial Aid

Financial aid based on need is available to U.S. and Canadian matriculated M.A. students in the form of scholarships, grants, and loans. There are also competitive merit awards available for outstanding M.A. candidates who apply by March 1. Moreover, some M.A. programs offer their own designated merit fellowships. Prospective Ph.D. students who complete their applications by January 2 are automatically considered for merit-based, five-year fellowships consisting of tuition, an annual stipend, pedagogic training, health insurance, and other benefits. Advanced doctoral students may be awarded teaching assistantships. Students may obtain information and applications for need-based aid from the Office of Financial Aid, Schiff 100, call 212-678-8007, or send an e-mail to financialaid@jtsa.edu.

Cost of Study

For the 2010–11 academic year, tuition is $27,900 for full-time Ph.D. study and $22,300 for full-time M.A. study. Part-time students are charged $1050 per credit. In addition to tuition, a fee of $520 is charged per semester.

Living and Housing Costs

Residence hall rooms are available to single students at a cost of approximately $10,490 per academic year. Apartments of various sizes and costs are also available to married students. The housing application deadline for all new students entering the following fall semester is May 15. For more information, prospective students should contact the Office of Residence Life at 212-678-8035 or or send an e-mail to reslife@jtsa.edu.

Student Group

The Graduate School enrolled 128 students in fall 2009. Forty-seven percent of the students are women, and approximately 65 percent of all students receive financial aid.

Location

JTS is located on the vibrant Upper West Side of New York City. Its proximity to Columbia University, Teachers College, Union Theological Seminary, and the Manhattan School of Music puts The Graduate School in the heart of a dynamic academic community. Students are encouraged to explore the wealth of cultural activities that New York City offers—from music and dance at Lincoln Center to theater on and off Broadway, from art at the Metropolitan and Whitney museums to the galleries in SoHo, Chelsea, and Williamsburg.

The Seminary

The Jewish Theological Seminary of America is a preeminent institution of Jewish higher education that integrates rigorous academic scholarship and teaching with a commitment to strengthening Jewish tradition, Jewish lives, and Jewish communities.

JTS articulates a vision of Judaism that is learned and passionate, pluralist and authentic, traditional and egalitarian; one that is thoroughly grounded in Jewish texts, history, and practices, and fully engaged with the societies and cultures of the present. The Seminary's vision joins faith with inquiry; the covenant of the ancestors with the creative insights of today; intense involvement in the society and State of Israel with devotion to the flowering of Judaism throughout the world; and service to the Jewish community, as well as to all of the communities of which Jews are a part: the society, the country, and the world.

JTS serves North American Jewry by educating intellectual and spiritual leaders for Conservative Judaism and the vital religious center; and training rabbis, cantors, scholars, educators, communal professionals, and lay activists who are inspired by the JTS vision of Torah and dedicated to assisting in its realization.

Applying

Application for admission to degree programs should be made as early as possible. Although applications are accepted and reviewed all year, The Graduate School sets deadlines for those who wish to receive fellowship consideration (January 2 for Ph.D. applicants and March 1 for M.A. applicants). Ph.D. applicants must submit a $65 application fee; official college transcripts; three letters of academic reference; GRE or MAT scores; and a sample of academic research in the field of study, written in English. M.A. applicants must submit a $65 application fee; official college transcripts; three letters of reference, at least two of which must be academic; GRE or MAT scores; and a sample of written English. Applicants whose native language is other than English and who have not been educated at a college where English is the language of instruction should submit official scores of the Test of English as a Foreign Language (TOEFL) in lieu of the GRE or MAT. A minimum TOEFL score of 100 (Internet-based) is required. The Graduate School may also require nonnative English speakers to demonstrate oral/aural English proficiency; for details, students should contact the Admissions Office. For M.A. and doctoral programs, an interview with a member of the admissions committee and/or the department chair is recommended and may be required. Ph.D. candidates may begin their studies in the fall only, whereas M.A. candidates enter The Graduate School in either the fall or the spring semester. Students who wish to attend The Graduate School on a nonmatriculated basis may do so by submitting a nonmatriculated status application form, accompanied by a $35 application fee and an official college transcript indicating receipt of a B.A. degree. The Graduate School accepts nonmatriculated applications until one month prior to either the fall or the spring semester. Two summer sessions are also available. The Graduate School is open to all men and women without regard to age, race, religion, sexual orientation, or national origin.

Correspondence and Information

The Graduate School
The Jewish Theological Seminary
3080 Broadway
Box 74
New York, New York 10027-4649
Phone: 212-678-8022
Fax: 212-280-6022
E-mail: gsadmissions@jtsa.edu
Web site: http://www.jtsa.edu/graduate

The Jewish Theological Seminary

THE FACULTY

Administration

Arnold M. Eisen, Chancellor.
Michael B. Greenbaum, Vice Chancellor and Chief Operating Officer.
Marc Wolf, Vice Chancellor and Chief Development Officer.
Alan M. Cooper, Provost.
Stephen Garfinkel, Associate Provost.
Shuly Rubin Schwartz, Dean of Graduate and Undergraduate Studies.

Ancient Judaism Program

Beth Berkowitz, Associate Professor and Program Adviser.
Richard Kalmin, Professor (on sabbatical).
Shani Tzoref, Adjunct Assistant Professor.

Department of Bible and Ancient Semitic Languages

Alan M. Cooper, Professor.
Stephen A. Geller, Professor.
David Marcus, Professor.
Benjamin Sommer, Professor.
Robert Alan Harris, Associate Professor (on sabbatical).
Stephen Garfinkel, Assistant Professor and Co-Chair.
Walter Herzberg, Assistant Professor.
Amy Kalmanofsky, Assistant Professor.
Leong Seow, Visiting Professor.

Department of Hebrew Language

Joel Roth, Chair.
Edna Nahshon, Professor.
Nitza Krohn, Assistant Professor and Director of Curriculum.
Shlomit Shraybom-Shivtiel, Adjunct Assistant Professor.
Tamar Ben Vered, Adjunct Instructor.
Cila Allon, Adjunct Lecturer.
Miriam Meir, Adjunct Lecturer.
Tsipi Rubin, Adjunct Lecturer.

Interdepartmental Studies Program

Neil Danzig, Professor.
Edna Nahshon, Professor.
Eitan Fishbane, Assistant Professor.
Shira Kohn, Program Adviser.

Jewish Art and Visual Culture Program

Vivian B. Mann, Adjunct Professor and Program Adviser.
Susan Chevlowe, Adjunct Assistant Professor.

Department of Jewish History

David Fishman, Professor.
Ismar Schorsch, Professor.
Jack Wertheimer, Professor and Chair.
Benjamin R. Gampel, Associate Professor.
Shuly Rubin Schwartz, Associate Professor.
Stefanie Siegmund, Associate Professor.
Shmuel Sandler, Visiting Professor.
Jenny Labendz, Adjunct Assistant Professor.
Robert Goldenberg, Adjunct Professor.

Department of Jewish Literature

Alan Mintz, Professor.
David G. Roskies, Professor.
Raymond P. Scheindlin, Professor.
Barbara Mann, Associate Professor and Chair.
Liati Myak-Hai, Adjunct Instructor.

Department of Jewish Thought

Arnold Eisen, Professor.
Alan Mittleman, Professor and Chair.
Eitan Fishbane, Assistant Professor.
Leonard Levin, Adjunct Assistant Professor.
Gordon Tucker, Adjunct Assistant Professor.
Leonard Sharzer, Adjunct Instructor.
Alvan Kaunfer, Adjunct Assistant.
Steven Kepnes, Adjunct Professor.

Jewish Professional Leadership: Jewish Studies and Social Work; Jewish Studies and Public Administration

Aryeh Davidson, Assistant Professor.
Rebecca Grabiner, Program Adviser.

Jewish Women's Studies Program

Judith Hauptman, Professor.
Stefanie Siegmund, Associate Professor and Program Adviser.
Barbara Mann, Associate Professor.
Daniel Belasco, Adjunct Assistant Professor.

Liturgy Program

Burton Visotzky, Chair.
Stephen Geller, Professor.
Reuven Kimelman, Adjunct Professor.
Tzvee Zahavy, Adjunct Professor.
Amy Wallk Katz, Adjunct Assistant Professor.

Medieval Jewish Studies Program

Raymond P. Scheindlin, Professor and Program Adviser.
Benjamin R. Gampel, Associate Professor.
Leonard Levin, Adjunct Assistant Professor.
Robert Harris, Associate Professor (on sabbatical).

Midrash and Scriptural Interpretation Program

Alan M. Cooper, Professor.
David C. Kraemer, Professor.
Burton L. Visotzky, Professor and Program Adviser.
Gila Vachman, Adjunct Assistant Professor.
Robert Harris, Associate Professor (on sabbatical).

Modern Jewish Studies Program

David Fishman, Professor and Program Adviser (fall 2010).
Alan Mintz, Professor and Program Adviser (spring 2011).
Aryeh Davidson, Assistant Professor.
Shmuel Sandler, Visiting Professor.
Shuly Rubin Schwartz, Associate Professor.

Department of Talmud and Rabbinics

Neil Danzig, Professor.
Judith Hauptman, Professor and Chair.
David C. Kraemer, Professor.
Eliezer Diamond, Associate Professor.
Beth Berkowitz, Associate Professor.
Marjorie Lehman, Assistant Professor.
Jonathan Milgram, Assistant Professor (on sabbatical).
Jay Rovner, Adjunct Assistant Professor.
David Hoffman, Adjunct Instructor.
Joshua Cahan, Adjunct Instructor.
Will Friedman, Adjunct Instructor.
Jenny Labendz, Adjunct Assistant Professor.
Michael Pitkowsky, Adjunct Instructor.
David M. Fishman, Adjunct Instructor.
Noah Bickart, Adjunct Instructor.

Students in the courtyard at The Jewish Theological Seminary.

The Library of The Jewish Theological Seminary.

THE JEWISH THEOLOGICAL SEMINARY

The Rabbinical School

Program of Study

The Rabbinical School of The Jewish Theological Seminary (JTS) offers a five-year program of study and field experience that leads to rabbinic ordination under the auspices of the Conservative Movement. The second year of learning is spent in Jerusalem at the Schechter Institute of Jewish Studies, JTS's Israeli affiliate. Through a consortium agreement, students can enroll in courses at Union Theological Seminary and Hebrew Union College. A Master of Arts (M.A.) degree is earned during the program from the Graduate School or the William Davidson School of Jewish Education at JTS. Concentrations include Bible, Talmud and rabbinics, Jewish history, Jewish gender and women's studies, Jewish literature, liturgy, Midrash, Jewish education, pastoral care, and sacred music.

Students entering without the requisite skills in Hebrew, and Bible and Talmud reading take skill level 1 courses and may require six years to graduate; advanced students begin at skill level 2 and may complete their studies in five years. Students with prior advanced degrees in Jewish studies may qualify for exemption from the M.A. requirement and pursue an accelerated path to ordination.

Research Facilities

Rabbinic students regularly study in *havruta* (in pairs) in the Eisenfeld/Duker Beit Midrash. In addition, the library of The Jewish Theological Seminary houses the most complete collection of Judaica in the Western Hemisphere. With more than 400,000 volumes on open shelves, it is ideally suited for the research needs of graduate students. The library's special collection, with more than 78,000 items, affords many opportunities for original scholarship. All students also benefit from the resources of neighboring Columbia University and Union Theological Seminary.

Financial Aid

The program at The Rabbinical School offers a significant number of merit-based fellowships. Applicants may obtain applications for merit-based fellowships directly from the office of The Rabbinical School. Candidates are encouraged to apply for the Wexner Graduate Fellowship from the Wexner Foundation.

Cost of Study

For the 2010–11 academic year, tuition is $11,850 per semester for full-time study. Part-time students are charged $1050 per credit.

Living and Housing Costs

Rooms and apartments (150 units) are available to single students at a cost of approximately $10,500 per academic year. Apartments of various costs are available to married students. The housing application deadline for incoming students is May 12. For more information, students should contact the Office of Residence Life by calling 212-678-8035 or by e-mailing reslife@jtsa.edu.

Student Group

In fall 2009, 117 students were enrolled in The Rabbinical School. Approximately 39 percent are women. A majority of students receive generous merit-based fellowships.

Location

JTS is located on the vibrant Upper West Side of New York City. Its proximity to Columbia University, Teachers College, Union Theological Seminary, and the Manhattan School of Music puts The Rabbinical School in the heart of a dynamic academic community. Students are encouraged to explore the wealth of cultural activities that New York City offers—from music and dance at Lincoln Center to theater on and off Broadway, from art at the Metropolitan and Whitney museums to the galleries in SoHo, Chelsea, and Williamsburg.

The Seminary

The Jewish Theological Seminary of America is a preeminent institution of Jewish higher education that integrates rigorous academic scholarship and teaching with a commitment to strengthening Jewish tradition, Jewish lives, and Jewish communities.

JTS articulates a vision of Judaism that is learned and passionate, pluralist and authentic, traditional and egalitarian; one that is thoroughly grounded in Jewish texts, history, and practices, and fully engaged with the societies and cultures of the present. The Seminary's vision joins faith with inquiry; the covenant of the ancestors with the creative insights of today; intense involvement in the society and State of Israel with devotion to the flowering of Judaism throughout the world; and service to the Jewish community, as well as to all of the communities of which Jews are a part: the society, the country, and the world.

JTS serves North American Jewry by educating intellectual and spiritual leaders for Conservative Judaism and the vital religious center, training rabbis, cantors, scholars, educators, communal professionals, and lay activists who are inspired by the JTS vision of Torah and dedicated to assisting in its realization.

Applying

Applications for regular admission should be submitted by February 15 for the following fall. There is also an early action deadline of November 15. Applicants from outside the U.S. should submit their materials by December 3. JTS does accept some late applications on a case-by-case basis. A $65 application fee, application, essays, official college transcripts, three letters of recommendation, and GRE or LSAT scores are required. All candidates are considered for merit-based fellowships.

Correspondence and Information

Rabbi David Levy
The Rabbinical School
The Jewish Theological Seminary
3080 Broadway
New York, New York 10027-4649
Phone: 212-678-8817
E-mail: rabschool@jtsa.edu
Web site: http://www.jtsa.edu/x731.xml

The Jewish Theological Seminary

THE FACULTY AND THEIR RESEARCH

Administration

Arnold M. Eisen, Chancellor.
Michael B. Greenbaum, Vice Chancellor and Chief Operating Officer.
Marc Wolf, Vice Chancellor and Chief Development Officer.
Alan M. Cooper, Provost.
Stephen Garfinkel, Associate Provost.
Daniel Nevins, Pearl Resnick Dean of The Rabbinical School and Dean of the Division of Religious Leadership.
Lisa Gelber, Associate Dean and Rabbi of the Women's League Seminary Synagogue.
Mychal Springer, Director, Clinical and Pastoral Education.
Matthew Berkowitz, Director of Israel Programs.
David Levy, Director of Admissions.
Jonathan Lipnick, Field Education Coordinator.

Faculty

Ancient Judaism Program
Beth Berkowitz, Associate Professor and Program Adviser.
Richard Kalmin, Professor (on sabbatical).
Shani Tzoref, Adjunct Assistant Professor.

Department of Bible and Ancient Semitic Languages
Alan M. Cooper, Professor.
Stephen A. Geller, Professor.
David Marcus, Professor.
Benjamin Sommer, Professor.
Robert Alan Harris, Associate Professor (on sabbatical).
Stephen Garfinkel, Assistant Professor and Co-Chair.
Walter Herzberg, Assistant Professor.
Amy Kalmanofsky, Assistant Professor.
Leong Seow, Visiting Professor.

Department of Hebrew Language
Joel Roth, Chair.
Edna Nahshon, Professor.
Nitza Krohn, Assistant Professor and Director of Curriculum.
Shlomit Shraybom-Shivtiel, Adjunct Assistant Professor.
Tamar Ben Vered, Adjunct Instructor.
Cila Allon, Adjunct Lecturer.
Miriam Meir, Adjunct Lecturer.
Tsipi Rubin, Adjunct Lecturer.

Interdepartmental Studies Program
Neil Danzig, Professor.
Edna Nahshon, Professor.
Eitan Fishbane, Assistant Professor.
Shira Kohn, Program Adviser.

Jewish Art and Visual Culture Program
Vivian B. Mann, Adjunct Professor and Program Adviser.
Susan Chevlowe, Adjunct Assistant Professor.

Department of Jewish History
David Fishman, Professor.
Ismar Schorsch, Professor.
Jack Wertheimer, Professor and Chair.
Benjamin R. Gampel, Associate Professor.
Shuly Rubin Schwartz, Associate Professor.
Stefanie Siegmund, Associate Professor.
Shmuel Sandler, Visiting Professor.
Jenny Labendz, Adjunct Assistant Professor.
Robert Goldenberg, Adjunct Professor.

Department of Jewish Literature
Alan Mintz, Professor.
David G. Roskies, Professor.
Raymond P. Scheindlin, Professor.
Barbara Mann, Associate Professor and Chair.
Liati Myak-Hai, Adjunct Instructor.

Department of Jewish Thought
Arnold Eisen, Professor.
Alan Mittleman, Professor and Chair.
Eitan Fishbane, Assistant Professor.
Leonard Levin, Adjunct Assistant Professor.
Gordon Tucker, Adjunct Assistant Professor.
Leonard Sharzer, Adjunct Instructor.
Alvan Kaunfer, Adjunct Assistant.
Steven Kepnes, Adjunct Professor.

Jewish Professional Leadership: Jewish Studies and Social Work; Jewish Studies and Public Administration
Aryeh Davidson, Assistant Professor.
Rebecca Grabiner, Program Adviser.

Jewish Women's Studies Program
Judith Hauptman, Professor.
Stefanie Siegmund, Associate Professor and Program Adviser.
Barbara Mann, Associate Professor.
Daniel Belasco, Adjunct Assistant Professor.

Liturgy Program
Burton Visotzky, Chair.
Stephen Geller, Professor.
Reuven Kimelman, Adjunct Professor.
Tzvee Zahavy, Adjunct Professor.
Amy Wallk Katz, Adjunct Assistant Professor.

Medieval Jewish Studies Program
Raymond P. Scheindlin, Professor and Program Adviser.
Benjamin R. Gampel, Associate Professor.
Leonard Levin, Adjunct Assistant Professor.
Robert Harris, Associate Professor (on sabbatical).

Midrash and Scriptural Interpretation Program
Alan M. Cooper, Professor.
David C. Kraemer, Professor.
Burton L. Visotzky, Professor and Program Adviser.
Gila Vachman, Adjunct Assistant Professor.
Robert Harris, Associate Professor (on sabbatical).

Modern Jewish Studies Program
David Fishman, Professor and Program Adviser (fall 2010).
Alan Mintz, Professor and Program Adviser (spring 2011).
Aryeh Davidson, Assistant Professor.
Shmuel Sandler, Visiting Professor.
Shuly Rubin Schwartz, Associate Professor.

Department of Talmud and Rabbinics
Neil Danzig, Professor.
Judith Hauptman, Professor and Chair.
David C. Kraemer, Professor.
Eliezer Diamond, Associate Professor.
Beth Berkowitz, Associate Professor.
Marjorie Lehman, Assistant Professor.
Jonathan Milgram, Assistant Professor (on sabbatical).
Jay Rovner, Adjunct Assistant Professor.
David Hoffman, Adjunct Instructor.
Joshua Cahan, Adjunct Instructor.
Will Friedman, Adjunct Instructor.
Jenny Labendz, Adjunct Assistant Professor.
Michael Pitkowsky, Adjunct Instructor.
David M. Fishman, Adjunct Instructor.
Noah Bickart, Adjunct Instructor.

VILLANOVA UNIVERSITY

Department of Theology and Religious Studies

Program of Study

In the Master of Arts in theology program, students and faculty together investigate the resources of the Christian tradition and of contemporary culture to serve the world and the Church. Academic study of theology is pursued in dialogue, with the questions raised by contemporary culture and the continuous experience of human life. Students must complete 36 credit hours (or twelve courses) of academic course work, including 6 credits each in Biblical literature, systematic theology, historical theology, and Christian ethics, as well as 12 credits in electives. Students are free to choose courses based on their academic and interdisciplinary interests. In addition, candidates are required to attend the Research Proseminar in the fall semester of their first year of studies, and they must pass a comprehensive exam and a language exam that demonstrates reading comprehension in a foreign language.

Four graduate certificate programs are open to national and regional applicants with diverse levels of academic and professional expertise interested in Catholic Christian theological studies. For students with a master's degree in theology or religion, programs are offered in advanced theological studies (18 credits) or advanced interdisciplinary theological inquiry; for those without an advanced theological or religious degree, certificates are available in theological studies (15 credits) and interdisciplinary theological inquiry (18 credits). It takes five or six courses to complete a certificate. Every program has a simple, transparent structure that invites students to design their own course of study, with courses in five areas: systematic theology, Biblical studies, historical studies and historical theology, Christian ethics, and spirituality. Students can also choose courses outside the department according to their professional and personal interests.

It is possible to combine programs, for example, the master's program with a certificate program or two certificate programs. Part-time students can enroll in as few as one course per semester. Most courses meet in the evening.

Research Facilities

The University library contains more than 780,000 volumes and 5,600 current periodicals. Special library holdings include the collection of the Augustinian Historical Institute and an extensive collection of works in contemporary Continental philosophy.

The Office of University Information Technologies provides data and voice communication, computing services, and access to remote computing and information services over the Internet; offers noncredit seminars and workshops on popular computer software and the use of the Villanova phone system; and maintains state-of-the-art computer labs for students on campus.

Financial Aid

The University supports all master's students in theology by offering the lowest tuition rate in the College of Liberal Arts and Sciences. Graduate assistantships are awarded on a competitive basis. The assistantship stipend began at approximately $13,100 in 2009–10 and carried with it a waiver of all tuition and academic fees. A few research fellowships are also awarded each year. A number of tuition scholarships are available; they provide a waiver of all tuition and academic fees. For priority consideration, candidates for an assistantship or a scholarship must submit their complete applications by March 1 for the following fall semester.

In addition, the office of the director of financial aid administers the Federal Stafford Student Loan, the unsubsidized Federal Stafford Student Loan, and the Federal Supplemental Loans for Students.

Cost of Study

Graduate tuition for theology courses was $470 per credit hour in 2009–10. The standard tuition rate was $630 per credit. In addition, there is a University fee of $30 each semester.

Living and Housing Costs

The University does not maintain accommodations for graduate students, but second-year students are eligible for positions as resident counselors in the dormitories. The area has a wide selection of living quarters that are convenient to the campus.

Student Group

Approximately 2,200 graduate students were enrolled for the fall 2008 term, of whom 985 were in liberal arts and sciences programs. Total University enrollment is approximately 12,000, including 7,577 full-time undergraduates, 1,000 part-time evening (undergraduate and continuing studies) students, and 1,000 students in the School of Law. There are about equal numbers of men and women graduate students.

Location

Located in the heart of the Delaware Valley's Main Line, the University occupies more than 200 handsomely landscaped acres in the town of Villanova, 12 miles west of Philadelphia. The location combines the advantages of a tranquil suburban setting with proximity to a large metropolitan city known for its outstanding historical, educational, and cultural resources.

The University

Villanova University is a private institution founded in 1842 by the Augustinian Fathers. Graduate programs were first administered separately in 1931. Currently, there are five academic units in addition to Graduate Studies: the Colleges of Arts and Sciences, Commerce and Finance, Engineering, Nursing, and the School of Law.

Applying

The theology program welcomes men and women, ordained and lay, from near and far, from all Christian traditions, of all ages, and with diverse educational and professional backgrounds and equally diverse professional goals. All applicants must submit to the Office of Graduate Studies the completed application and a nonrefundable $50 fee, official GRE scores, and official transcripts of all previous college work. To the graduate program director, students must provide a 500–700-word statement of their objectives; candidates for the master's and combined master's programs must send an academic writing sample (if available) and three letters of recommendation. Deadlines for the fall, spring, and summer semesters are August 1, December 1, and May 1, respectively.

Correspondence and Information

Peter Spitaler, Th.D.
Department of Theology and Religious Studies
Saint Augustine Center 124
Villanova University
800 Lancaster Avenue
Villanova, Pennsylvania 19085-1696

Phone: 610-519-4731
Fax: 610-519-6697
E-mail: peter.spitaler@villanova.edu
Web site: http://www.villanova.edu/artsci/theology/graduate/

Villanova University

THE FACULTY AND THEIR RESEARCH

Full-Time Faculty

Gustavo Benavides, Associate Professor; Ph.D., Temple. Far Eastern religions.
Timothy M. Brunk, Assistant Professor; Ph.D., Marquette. Systematic theology (sacraments).
Francis J. Caponi, OSA, Assistant Professor; Th.D., Harvard. Systematic theology.
Walter E. Conn, Professor; Ph.D., Columbia. Ethics.
Paul Danove, Professor; Ph.D., Graduate Theological Union. New Testament, narrative, rhetorical, and linguistic studies.
Edmund J. Dobbin, OSA, Professor; S.T.D., Louvain. Systematic theology.
Daniel Doyle, OSA, Assistant Professor; S.T.D., Institutum Patristicum Augustinianum. Patristics, St. Augustine, Augustinian theology.
Allan D. Fitzgerald, OSA, Professor and Director of the Augustinian Institute; Ph.D., Institut Catholique (Paris). Systematic theology, Augustinian studies.
Anthony J. Godzieba, Associate Professor and Editor of *Horizons: The Journal of the College Theology Society;* Ph.D., Catholic University. Fundamental theology, systematic theology, philosophy of religion, philosophical theology.
Mark Graham, Associate Professor; Ph.D., Boston College. Moral theology.
Judith M. Hadley, Associate Professor; Ph.D., Cambridge. Hebrew Bible, Near Eastern archaeology.
Kathleen A. Holscher, Assistant Professor; Ph.D., Princeton. U.S. Catholic history.
Kevin L. Hughes, Associate Professor and Chair of the Humanities Department and Classical Studies Program; Ph.D., Chicago. Medieval and early-modern theology and culture, historical theology.
Shams C. Inati, Professor; Ph.D., SUNY at Buffalo. Islamic philosophy and theology.
Martin Laird, OSA, Associate Professor; Ph.D., London. Early Christianity, patristics.
Joseph Loya, OSA, Associate Professor; Ph.D., Fordham. Eastern Christianity.
Jessica M. Murdoch, Assistant Professor; Ph.D., Fordham. Fundamental and systematic theology.
Bernard P. Prusak, STL, Professor; J.C.D., Lateran (Rome). Historical and systematic theology.
Michael J. Scanlon, OSA, Professor and Josephine C. Connelly Chair of Christian Theology; S.T.D., Catholic University. Foundational and systematic theology.
Peter Spitaler, Associate Professor and Graduate Program Director; Th.D., Ludwig Maximilian (Munich). New Testament, Pauline literature.
Suzanne C. Toton, Associate Professor; Ed.D., Columbia Teachers College. Social ethics, development ethics, justice education.
Rodger Van Allen, Professor; Ph.D., Temple. Catholicism in the United States, theology of Christian living.
Fayette B. Veverka, Associate Professor; Ed.D., Columbia Teachers College. Religious education, Catholicism in the United States.
Darlene Fozard Weaver, Associate Professor and Director of the Theology Institute; Ph.D., Chicago. Ethics.
William J. Werpehowski, Professor and Director of the Center for Peace and Justice Education; Ph.D., Princeton. Ethics, theology of Christian living.

Adjunct Faculty

Joseph C. Collins.
Joseph L. Farrell, OSA, Director of Programming and External Outreach, S.T.D.
Donald A. Giannella, Associate Director of Campus Ministry; M.A.
Gregory Grimes.
John Groch, M.A., M.S.
Beth Hassel, PBVM, Executive Director of Campus Ministry.
Alan Iser, Rabbi, M.A.
Margaret Kowalsky.
Charles P. Laferty, OSA, Ph.D.
Richard J. Lohkamp, Ph.D.
Michael A. McElwee, Ph.D.
Neil J. McGettigan, OSA, D.Min.
Gaile Pohlhaus, Ph.D.
Darren G. Poley, M.A., M.S.
Edward D. Ruscil, M.A.
Ernest J. Sherretta, D.Min.
Murray Silberman, Rabbi.
Joyce A. Zavarich, Associate Director of Campus Ministry, D.Min.

Section 13
Writing

This section contains a directory of institutions offering graduate work in writing. Additional information about programs listed in the directory but not augmented by an in-depth entry may be obtained by writing directly to the dean of a graduate school or chair of a department at the address given in the directory.

For programs offering related work, see also in this book *Communication and Media* and *Language and Literature.*

CONTENTS

Program Directories

Technical Writing 518
Writing 519

Close-Up

See:

Columbia University—Film, Theater Arts, Visual Arts, and Writing 261

Technical Writing

Carnegie Mellon University, College of Humanities and Social Sciences, Department of English, Program in Professional Writing, Pittsburgh, PA 15213-3891. Offers editing and publishing (MAPW); policy and non-profit communication (MAPW); public and media relations / corporate communications (MAPW); science or healthcare communication (MAPW); technical writing (MAPW); writing for new media (MAPW); writing for print media (MAPW). Part-time programs available. *Entrance requirements:* For master's, GRE General Test. Additional exam requirements/recommendations for international students: Required—TOEFL, TWE.

Colorado State University, Graduate School, College of Liberal Arts, Department of Journalism and Technical Communication, Fort Collins, CO 80523-1785. Offers public communication and technology (MS, PhD); technical communication (MS). Part-time programs available. *Faculty:* 19 full-time (8 women). *Students:* 26 full-time (21 women), 38 part-time (28 women); includes 5 minority (1 American Indian/Alaska Native, 1 Asian American or Pacific Islander, 3 Hispanic Americans), 3 international. Average age 33. 60 applicants, 48% accepted, 15 enrolled. In 2009, 13 master's awarded. *Degree requirements:* For master's, variable foreign language requirement, comprehensive exam (for some programs), thesis (for some programs); for doctorate, variable foreign language requirement, comprehensive exam (for some programs), thesis/dissertation (for some programs). *Entrance requirements:* For master's, GRE General Test, samples of written work, letters of recommendation, resume or curriculum vitae, 3 writing/communication projects; for doctorate, GRE General Test, master's degree, minimum GPA of 3.0, scholarly/professional work, letters of recommendation, statement of career plans, resume. Additional exam requirements/recommendations for international students: Required—TOEFL (minimum score 600 paper-based; 250 computer-based). *Application deadline:* For fall admission, 2/15 priority date for domestic students, 12/15 priority date for international students; for spring admission, 6/15 priority date for domestic students. Applications are processed on a rolling basis. Application fee: $50. Electronic applications accepted. *Expenses:* Tuition, state resident: full-time $6434; part-time $359.10 per credit. Tuition, nonresident: full-time $18,116; part-time $1006.45 per credit. Required fees: $1496; $83 per credit. *Financial support:* In 2009–10, 21 students received support, including 21 teaching assistantships with partial tuition reimbursements available (averaging $9,428 per year); fellowships with partial tuition reimbursements available, research assistantships with full and partial tuition reimbursements available, career-related internships or fieldwork, Federal Work-Study, institutionally sponsored loans, scholarships/grants, traineeships, and unspecified assistantships also available. Support available to part-time students. Financial award application deadline: 3/1; financial award applicants required to submit FAFSA. *Faculty research:* Technical/science communication, public relations, health/risk communication, web/new media technologies, environmental communication. Total annual research expenditures: $133,759. *Unit head:* Dr. Greg Luft, Chair, 970-491-1979, Fax: 970-491-2908, E-mail: greg.luft@colostate.edu. *Application contact:* Dr. Craig Trumbo, Graduate Program Coordinator, 970-491-2077, Fax: 970-491-2908, E-mail: craig.trumbo@colostate.edu.

DePaul University, College of Liberal Arts and Sciences, Department of English, Program in Writing, Rhetoric, and Discourse, Chicago, IL 60604-2287. Offers MA. *Students:* 24 full-time (16 women), 18 part-time (15 women); includes 8 minority (4 African Americans, 1 Asian American or Pacific Islander, 3 Hispanic Americans). *Expenses:* Tuition: Full-time $37,525; part-time $620 per credit hour. *Unit head:* Christine Tardy, Director, 773-325-4145. *Application contact:* Dr. Lesley Kordecki, Director, 773-325-1786, Fax: 773-325-8607, E-mail: lkordeck@depaul.edu.

Drexel University, College of Arts and Sciences, Department of Culture and Communication, Philadelphia, PA 19104-2875. Offers communication (MS), including public communication, science communication, technical communication; publication management (MS). Part-time and evening/weekend programs available. *Degree requirements:* For master's, internship, professional portfolio. *Entrance requirements:* Additional exam requirements/recommendations for international students: Required—TOEFL. Electronic applications accepted. *Faculty research:* Science information and attitudes, science influence on literature, process of technical writing, document design, software documentation.

Fitchburg State University, Division of Graduate and Continuing Education, Program in Applied Communications, Fitchburg, MA 01420-2697. Offers applied communications (MS, Certificate); library media (MS); technical and professional writing (MS). Part-time and evening/weekend programs available. *Students:* 3 full-time (2 women), 18 part-time (10 women), 2 international. Average age 33. 8 applicants, 88% accepted, 6 enrolled. In 2009, 10 master's awarded. *Entrance requirements:* For master's, GRE General Test or MAT, minimum 2 years of related experience, letters of recommendation, resume. Additional exam requirements/recommendations for international students: Required—TOEFL (minimum score 550 paper-based; 213 computer-based; 79 iBT). *Application deadline:* Applications are processed on a rolling basis. Application fee: $25 ($50 for international students). *Expenses:* Tuition, area resident: Part-time $150 per credit. Tuition, state resident: part-time $150 per credit. Tuition, nonresident: part-time $150 per credit. Required fees: $120 per credit. *Financial support:* In 2009–10, research assistantships with partial tuition reimbursements (averaging $5,500 per year); Federal Work-Study, scholarships/grants, and unspecified assistantships also available. Support available to part-time students. Financial award application deadline: 3/1; financial award applicants required to submit FAFSA. *Unit head:* Dr. John Chetro-Szivos, Chair, 978-665-3261, Fax: 978-665-3658, E-mail: gce@fsc.edu. *Application contact:* Director of Admissions, 978-665-3144, Fax: 978-665-4540, E-mail: admissions@fsc.edu.

Illinois Institute of Technology, Graduate College, College of Science and Letters, Lewis Department of Humanities, Chicago, IL 60616-3793. Offers information architecture (MS); technical communication (PhD); technical communication and information design (MS). Part-time and evening/weekend programs available. *Faculty:* 17 full-time (6 women), 11 part-time/adjunct (4 women). *Students:* 13 full-time (8 women), 34 part-time (24 women); includes 12 minority (11 African Americans, 1 Asian American or Pacific Islander), 6 international. Average age 34. 46 applicants, 52% accepted, 9 enrolled. In 2009, 9 master's, 2 doctorates awarded. *Degree requirements:* For master's, comprehensive exam, thesis or alternative, project; for doctorate, comprehensive exam, thesis/dissertation, qualifying exam. *Entrance requirements:* For master's, GRE General Test; for doctorate, GRE General Test, bachelor's degree in technical communication or other relevant field. Additional exam requirements/recommendations for international students: Required—TOEFL (minimum score 523 paper-based; 70 iBT). *Application deadline:* For fall admission, 5/1 for domestic and international students; for spring admission, 10/15 for domestic and international students. Applications are processed on a rolling basis. Application fee: $50. Electronic applications accepted. *Expenses:* Tuition: Full-time $17,550; part-time $888 per credit hour. Required fees: $850; $7.50 per credit hour. One-time fee: $50 full-time. Full-time tuition and fees vary according to program. *Financial support:* In 2009–10, 15 teaching assistantships with partial tuition reimbursements (averaging $9,000 per year) were awarded; career-related internships or fieldwork, Federal Work-Study, institutionally sponsored loans, scholarships/grants, health care benefits, tuition waivers (partial), and unspecified assistantships also available. Support available to part-time students. Financial award applicants required to submit FAFSA. *Faculty research:* Discourse analysis, linguistics, readability, ethics in professions, instructional and document design, knowledge management, usability testing and evaluation, history and philosophy of science. Total annual research expenditures: $34,161. *Unit head:* Dr. Kathryn Riley, Professor and Chair, 312-567-3566, Fax: 312-567-5187, E-mail: riley@iit.edu. *Application contact:* Dr. Kathryn Riley, Professor and Chair, 312-567-3566, Fax: 312-567-5187, E-mail: riley@iit.edu.

James Madison University, The Graduate School, College of Arts and Letters, School of Writing, Rhetoric, and Technical Communication, Harrisonburg, VA 22807. Offers MA, MS. Part-time programs available. *Faculty:* 5 full-time (2 women). *Students:* 14 full-time (10 women), 7 part-time (6 women); includes 2 minority (both Asian Americans or Pacific Islanders), 1 international. Average age 27. In 2009, 5 master's awarded. *Degree requirements:* For master's, one foreign language, thesis, internship, practicum. *Entrance requirements:* For master's, GRE General Test, GRE Subject Test, TSC application dossier, 3 letters of recommendation, 20-30 page writing samples. Additional exam requirements/recommendations for international students: Required—TOEFL (minimum score 550 paper-based). *Application deadline:* For fall admission, 5/31 priority date for domestic students; for spring admission, 8/31 priority date for domestic students. Applications are processed on a rolling basis. Application fee: $55. Electronic applications accepted. *Expenses:* Tuition, area resident: Part-time $305 per credit hour. Tuition, state resident: part-time $305 per credit hour. Tuition, nonresident: part-time $890 per credit hour. *Financial support:* In 2009–10, 9 students received support, including 1 teaching assistantship with full tuition reimbursement available (averaging $8,664 per year); Federal Work-Study and unspecified assistantships also available. Financial award application deadline: 3/1; financial award applicants required to submit FAFSA. *Unit head:* Dr. Shelley B. Aley, Interim Director, 540-568-2334. *Application contact:* Lynette M. Bible, Director of Graduate Admissions, 540-568-6395, Fax: 540-568-7860, E-mail: biblelm@jmu.edu.

The Johns Hopkins University, Zanvyl Krieger School of Arts and Sciences, The Writing Seminars, Baltimore, MD 21218-2699. Offers fiction writing (MFA); poetry (MFA); science writing (MA). *Faculty:* 11 full-time (3 women). *Students:* 28 full-time (19 women); includes 2 minority (both Asian Americans or Pacific Islanders), 1 international. Average age 29. 273 applicants, 9% accepted, 17 enrolled. In 2009, 13 master's awarded. *Degree requirements:* For master's, one foreign language, thesis, foreign language exam (MFA). *Entrance requirements:* For master's, GRE General Test, GRE Subject Test (recommended), foreign language exam, sample of written work, 3 letters of recommendation. Additional exam requirements/recommendations for international students: Required—TOEFL (minimum score 600 paper-based; 250 computer-based; 100 iBT). *Application deadline:* For fall admission, 1/15 for domestic and international students. Application fee: $75. Electronic applications accepted. *Financial support:* In 2009–10, 28 students received support, including 1 fellowship (averaging $5,000 per year), 1 research assistantship with full tuition reimbursement available (averaging $17,500 per year), 22 teaching assistantships with full tuition reimbursements available (averaging $17,500 per year); Federal Work-Study, institutionally sponsored loans, scholarships/grants, health care benefits, tuition waivers (partial), and two teaching assistantships with $5000 stipend and full tuition also available. Financial award application deadline: 3/1; financial award applicants required to submit FAFSA. *Faculty research:* Film theory, literary criticism, contemporary fiction. *Unit head:* Dave Smith, Chairman and Elliott Coleman Professor of Poetry, 410-516-3409, Fax: 410-516-6828, E-mail: davesmith@jhu.edu. *Application contact:* Gina Woloszyn, Application Contact, 410-516-6286, Fax: 410-516-6828, E-mail: regina@jhu.edu.

Laurentian University, School of Graduate Studies and Research, Programme in Science Communication, Sudbury, ON P3E 2C6, Canada. Offers G Dip.

Massachusetts Institute of Technology, School of Humanities, Arts, and Social Sciences, Program in Writing and Humanistic Studies, Cambridge, MA 02139-4307. Offers science writing (SM). *Faculty:* 9 full-time (2 women). *Students:* 7 full-time (4 women); includes 1 minority (Hispanic American), 1 international. Average age 25. 63 applicants, 29% accepted, 7 enrolled. In 2009, 7 master's awarded. *Degree requirements:* For master's, thesis, internship. *Entrance requirements:* For master's, GRE General Test. Additional exam requirements/recommendations for international students: Required—TOEFL (minimum score 600 paper-based; 250 computer-based), IELTS (minimum score 7.5). *Application deadline:* For fall admission, 1/15 for domestic and international students. Application fee: $75. Electronic applications accepted. *Expenses:* Tuition: Full-time $37,510; part-time $585 per unit. Required fees: $272. *Financial support:* In 2009–10, 7 students received support, including 7 fellowships with tuition reimbursements available; teaching assistantships with tuition reimbursements available, career-related internships or fieldwork, Federal Work-Study, institutionally sponsored loans, scholarships/grants, health care benefits, and unspecified assistantships also available. Total annual research expenditures: $74,000. *Unit head:* Prof. James Paradis, Head of Program, 617-253-7894, Fax: 617-253-6910. *Application contact:* Science Writing Graduate Admissions, 617-253-6668, Fax: 617-452-5100, E-mail: sciwrite-www@mit.edu.

Metropolitan State University, College of Arts and Sciences, St. Paul, MN 55106-5000. Offers computer science (MS); liberal studies (MA); technical communication (MS). Part-time and evening/weekend programs available. *Entrance requirements:* For master's, minimum GPA of 2.75, resumè. Additional exam requirements/recommendations for international students: Required—TOEFL (minimum score 550 paper-based; 213 computer-based). *Expenses:* Tuition, state resident: full-time $5520; part-time $276 per credit hour. Tuition, nonresident: full-time $11,040; part-time $552 per credit hour. Required fees: $209; $10 per credit hour. Tuition and fees vary according to degree level. *Faculty research:* Computer security, software engineering, distributed systems, document design, diffusing of innovations, social issues and communication technology.

Northern Arizona University, Graduate College, College of Arts and Letters, Department of English, Program in English, Flagstaff, AZ 86011. Offers creative writing (MA); English education (MA); general English studies (MA); literacy, technology and professional writing (MA); literature (MA). *Faculty:* 40 full-time (24 women). *Students:* 87 full-time (59 women), 94 part-time (70 women); includes 20 minority (6 African Americans, 6 American Indian/Alaska Native, 3 Asian Americans or Pacific Islanders, 5 Hispanic Americans), 1 international. Average age 31. 99 applicants, 66% accepted, 45 enrolled. In 2009, 77 master's awarded. *Degree requirements:* For master's, thesis (for some programs), departmental qualifying exam. *Entrance requirements:* For master's, minimum GPA of 3.0 or GRE. Additional exam requirements/recommendations for international students: Required—TOEFL (minimum score 550 paper-based; 213 computer-based; 80 iBT), IELTS (minimum score 7), or a bachelor's degree from an English-speaking university and demonstrated proficiency. *Application deadline:* For fall admission, 2/15 priority date for domestic students, 9/1 priority date for international students; for winter admission, 4/15 priority date for domestic students; for spring admission, 11/15 priority date for domestic students. Applications are processed on a rolling basis. Application fee: $65. Electronic applications accepted. *Financial support:* In 2009–10, 63 teaching assistantships with partial tuition reimbursements (averaging $11,623 per year) were awarded; Federal Work-Study, scholarships/grants, health care benefits, and unspecified assistantships also available. Support available to part-time students. Financial award application deadline: 3/30; financial award applicants required to submit FAFSA. *Unit head:* Dr. Allen Woodman, Chair, 928-523-5651, Fax: 928-523-7074, E-mail: allen.woodman@nau.edu. *Application contact:* Barbara Hanks, 928-523-4911, Fax: 928-523-7074, E-mail: barbara.hanks@nau.edu.

Polytechnic Institute of NYU, Department of Humanities and Social Sciences, Major in Technical Writing and Specialized Journalism, Brooklyn, NY 11201-2990. Offers MS. *Students:* 3 part-time (1 woman), 1 international. 2 applicants, 50% accepted, 0 enrolled.Application fee: $75. *Expenses:* Tuition: Full-time $21,492; part-time $1194 per credit hour. Required fees: $1160; $204 per course. *Unit head:* Teresa Feroli, Head, 718-260-3422, E-mail: tferoli@poly.edu. *Application contact:* Teresa Feroli, Head, 718-260-3422, E-mail: tferoli@poly.edu.

Regis University, College for Professional Studies, MA Program, Denver, CO 80221-1099. Offers criminology (MA); fine arts administration (Certificate); language and communication (MA); mediation (Certificate); psychology (MA); self-designed major (MA); social justice, peace, and reconciliation (Certificate); social science (MA); technical communication (Certificate). Program also offered in Henderson and Las Vegas (Summerlin), NV. Part-time and evening/weekend programs available. Postbaccalaureate distance learning degree programs offered (minimal on-campus study). *Degree requirements:* For master's, thesis, research project. *Entrance requirements:* For master's, resume, recommendations. Additional exam requirements/recommendations for international students: Required—TOEFL (minimum score 213 computer-based), TWE (minimum score 5). Electronic applications accepted. *Expenses:* Contact institution.

Faculty research: Independent/nonresidential graduate study: new methods and models, adult learning and the capstone experience, Goal Setting, behavior of Adult students, Innovative Studies for Community Colleges.

Texas Tech University, Graduate School, College of Arts and Sciences, Department of English, Lubbock, TX 79409. Offers English (MA, PhD); technical communication (MA); technical communication and rhetoric (PhD). Part-time programs available. *Faculty:* 38 full-time (15 women), 2 part-time/adjunct (both women). *Students:* 101 full-time (62 women), 94 part-time (58 women); includes 14 minority (4 African Americans, 2 American Indian/Alaska Native, 2 Asian Americans or Pacific Islanders, 6 Hispanic Americans), 15 international. Average age 35. 208 applicants, 31% accepted, 45 enrolled. In 2009, 30 master's, 10 doctorates awarded. *Degree requirements:* For master's, one foreign language, thesis (for some programs); for doctorate, thesis/dissertation. *Entrance requirements:* For master's and doctorate, GRE General Test. Additional exam requirements/recommendations for international students: Required—TOEFL (minimum score 550 paper-based; 213 computer-based). *Application deadline:* For fall admission, 3/1 priority date for international students; for spring admission, 11/1 priority date for international students. Applications are processed on a rolling basis. Application fee: $50 ($75 for international students). Electronic applications accepted. *Expenses:* Tuition, state resident: full-time $5100; part-time $213 per credit hour. Tuition, nonresident: full-time $11,748; part-time $490 per credit hour. Required fees: $2298; $50 per credit hour. $555 per semester. *Financial support:* In 2009–10, 8 research assistantships with partial tuition reimbursements (averaging $19,712 per year), 9 teaching assistantships with partial tuition reimbursements (averaging $14,010 per year) were awarded; Federal Work-Study and institutionally sponsored loans also available. Support available to part-time students. Financial award application deadline: 4/15; financial award applicants required to submit FAFSA. *Faculty research:* Computers and writing; technical communication and rhetoric; creative writing; nineteenth century studies; literature of social justice and the environment. *Unit head:* Dr. Sam Dragga, Chair, 806-742-2501, Fax: 806-742-0989, E-mail: sam.dragga@ttu.edu. *Application contact:* Dr. Brian McFadden, Director of Graduate Studies, 806-742-2501, Fax: 806-742-0989, E-mail: english.gradadvisor@ttu.edu.

The University of Alabama in Huntsville, School of Graduate Studies, College of Liberal Arts, Department of English, Huntsville, AL 35899. Offers English (MA); teaching of English to speakers of other languages (Certificate); technical communications (Certificate). Part-time and evening/weekend programs available. *Faculty:* 14 full-time (9 women). *Students:* 14 full-time (9 women), 39 part-time (31 women); includes 11 minority (8 African Americans, 1 American Indian/Alaska Native, 2 Hispanic Americans). Average age 33. 28 applicants, 86% accepted, 17 enrolled. In 2009, 23 master's, 1 other advanced degree awarded. *Degree requirements:* For master's, one foreign language, comprehensive exam, thesis or alternative, oral and written exams. *Entrance requirements:* For master's and Certificate, GRE General Test, minimum GPA of 3.0. Additional exam requirements/recommendations for international students: Required—TOEFL (minimum score 500 paper-based; 173 computer-based; 62 iBT). *Application deadline:* For fall admission, 7/15 for domestic students, 4/1 for international students; for spring admission, 11/30 for domestic students, 9/1 for international students. Applications are processed on a rolling basis. Application fee: $40 ($50 for international students). Electronic applications accepted. *Expenses:* Tuition, state resident: part-time $355.75 per credit hour. Tuition, nonresident: part-time $847.10 per credit hour. Required fees: $210.80 per semester. Tuition and fees vary according to course load and program. *Financial support:* In 2009–10, 9 students received support, including 4 teaching assistantships with full and partial tuition reimbursements available (averaging $8,460 per year); career-related internships or fieldwork, Federal Work-Study, institutionally sponsored loans, scholarships/grants, health care benefits, tuition waivers, and unspecified assistantships also available. Support available to part-time students. Financial award application deadline: 4/1; financial award applicants required to submit FAFSA. *Faculty research:* American and British literature, linguistics, technical writing, women's studies, rhetoric. *Unit head:* Dr. Rose Norman, Chair, 256-824-6320, Fax: 256-824-6949, E-mail: normanr@uah.edu. *Application contact:* Kathy Biggs, Graduate Studies Admissions Manager, 256-824-6199, Fax: 256-824-6405, E-mail: deangrad@uah.edu.

University of Arkansas at Little Rock, Graduate School, College of Arts, Humanities, and Social Science, Department of Rhetoric and Writing, Little Rock, AR 72204-1099. Offers professional and technical writing (MA). Part-time and evening/weekend programs available. *Degree requirements:* For master's, thesis or alternative, oral defense of final project. *Entrance requirements:* For master's, GRE, minimum GPA of 3.0, writing portfolio. *Faculty research:* Writing for industry, science, business, and government; composition and rhetorical theory; writing nonfiction; teaching of writing.

University of California, Santa Cruz, Division of Graduate Studies, Division of Physical and Biological Sciences, Program in Science Communication, Santa Cruz, CA 95064. Offers science illustration (Certificate); science writing (Certificate). *Entrance requirements:* For degree, GRE General Test, GRE Subject Test, bachelor's degree in science. Electronic applications accepted.

The University of North Carolina at Greensboro, Graduate School, College of Arts and Sciences, Department of English, Greensboro, NC 27412-5001. Offers creative writing (MFA); English (M Ed, MA, PhD, Certificate), including American literature (PhD), English (M Ed, MA), English literature (PhD), rhetoric and composition (PhD), technical writing (Certificate), women's studies (Certificate). *Degree requirements:* For master's, comprehensive exam; for doctorate, variable foreign language requirement, thesis/dissertation, preliminary exam. *Entrance requirements:* For master's, GRE General Test, minimum GPA of 3.0; for doctorate, GRE General Test, GRE Subject Test, critical writing sample, minimum GPA of 3.0. Additional exam requirements/recommendations for international students: Required—TOEFL. Electronic applications accepted.

University of the Sciences in Philadelphia, College of Graduate Studies, Program in Biomedical Writing, Philadelphia, PA 19104-4495. Offers biomedical writing (MS); medical marketing writing (Certificate); regulatory affairs writing (Certificate). Part-time and evening/weekend programs available. Postbaccalaureate distance learning degree programs offered (minimal on-campus study). *Entrance requirements:* For master's, GRE General Test. Additional exam requirements/recommendations for international students: Required—TOEFL, TWE. *Expenses:* Contact institution. *Faculty research:* History of medical writing and publishing, compliance, regulatory.

University of Waterloo, Graduate Studies, Faculty of Arts, Department of English, Language and Literature, Waterloo, ON N2L 3G1, Canada. Offers English language and literature (PhD); literary studies (MA); rhetoric and communication design (MA). Part-time programs available. *Degree requirements:* For master's, one foreign language, thesis optional; for doctorate, 2 foreign languages, thesis/dissertation. *Entrance requirements:* For master's, honors degree, minimum B+ average; for doctorate, master's degree, minimum A- average. Additional exam requirements/recommendations for international students: Required—TOEFL, TWE. Electronic applications accepted. *Faculty research:* Shakespeare, American literature, rhetoric, Romantics, moderns.

Writing

Abilene Christian University, Graduate School, College of Arts and Sciences, Department of English, Abilene, TX 79699-9100. Offers composition/rhetoric (MA); literature (MA); writing (MA). Part-time programs available. *Faculty:* 17 part-time/adjunct (7 women). *Students:* 15 full-time (7 women), 2 part-time (both women); includes 1 minority (Hispanic American), 1 international. 10 applicants, 100% accepted, 8 enrolled. In 2009, 6 master's awarded. *Degree requirements:* For master's, one foreign language, comprehensive exam, thesis optional. *Entrance requirements:* For master's, GRE General Test. *Application deadline:* For fall admission, 4/1 priority date for domestic students; for spring admission, 11/1 for domestic students. Applications are processed on a rolling basis. Application fee: $40. Electronic applications accepted. *Expenses:* Tuition: Full-time $11,520; part-time $640 per hour. Required fees: $1090; $53.50 per hour. $10 per term. Tuition and fees vary according to program. *Financial support:* Teaching assistantships, Federal Work-Study available. Support available to part-time students. Financial award application deadline: 4/1; financial award applicants required to submit FAFSA. *Faculty research:* Feminism, Shakespearean dimensions of new literature, poetic consciousness, deconstruction myths. *Unit head:* Dr. Dana McMichael, Graduate Adviser, 325-674-2083, Fax: 325-674-2408, E-mail: dana.mcmichael@acu.edu. *Application contact:* William Horn, Graduate Admissions Counselor, 325-674-2656, Fax: 325-674-6717, E-mail: gradinfo@acu.edu.

Adelphi University, Graduate School of Arts and Sciences, Program in Creative Writing, Garden City, NY 11530-0701. Offers MFA. Part-time and evening/weekend programs available. *Students:* 14 full-time (8 women), 17 part-time (9 women); includes 4 minority (1 African American, 1 Asian American or Pacific Islander, 2 Hispanic Americans). Average age 29. In 2009, 8 master's awarded. *Degree requirements:* For master's, thesis. *Entrance requirements:* For master's, 3 letters of reference, manuscript in chosen genre (poetry, fiction, playwriting). Additional exam requirements/recommendations for international students: Required—TOEFL (minimum score 550 paper-based; 213 computer-based; 80 iBT). *Application deadline:* For fall admission, 5/1 priority date for international students; for spring admission, 11/1 priority date for international students. Applications are processed on a rolling basis. Application fee: $50. Electronic applications accepted. *Expenses:* Tuition: Full-time $28,340; part-time $830 per credit. Required fees: $600; $250 per credit. Full-time tuition and fees vary according to course load and program. *Financial support:* Fellowships, Federal Work-Study available. *Unit head:* Judith Baumel, Director, 516-877-4031, E-mail: baumel@adelphi.edu. *Application contact:* Christine Murphy, Director of Admissions, 516-877-3050, Fax: 516-877-3039, E-mail: graduateadmissions@adelphi.edu.

American University, College of Arts and Sciences, Department of Literature, Program in Creative Writing, Washington, DC 20016-8047. Offers MFA. Part-time and evening/weekend programs available. *Students:* 36 full-time (23 women), 25 part-time (14 women); includes 6 minority (4 African Americans, 2 Hispanic Americans), 2 international. Average age 29. 156 applicants, 56% accepted, 22 enrolled. In 2009, 18 master's awarded. *Degree requirements:* For master's, comprehensive exam, thesis. *Entrance requirements:* For master's, GRE, sample of written work. Additional exam requirements/recommendations for international students: Required—TOEFL. *Application deadline:* For fall admission, 2/1 priority date for domestic students. Application fee: $80. *Expenses:* Tuition: Full-time $22,266; part-time $1237 per credit hour. Required fees: $430. Tuition and fees vary according to program. *Financial support:* Fellowships, research assistantships, teaching assistantships, career-related internships or fieldwork, institutionally sponsored loans, and tuition waivers (full and partial) available. Support available to part-time students. Financial award application deadline: 2/1. *Unit head:* Richard McCann, Co-Director, 202-885-2978, Fax: 202-885-2938. *Application contact:* Graduate Program Assistant.

Antioch University Los Angeles, Graduate Programs, Program in Creative Writing, Culver City, CA 90230. Offers creative writing (MFA); pedagogy of creative writing (Certificate). Postbaccalaureate distance learning degree programs offered (minimal on-campus study). *Degree requirements:* For master's, thesis. *Entrance requirements:* For master's, sample of written work. Additional exam requirements/recommendations for international students: Required—TOEFL. *Faculty research:* Creative nonfiction, fiction, poetry.

Antioch University Midwest, Graduate Programs, Individualized Liberal and Professional Studies Program, Yellow Springs, OH 45387-1609. Offers liberal and professional studies (MA), including counseling, creative writing, education, film studies, liberal studies, management, modern literature, psychology, theatre, visual arts. Part-time and evening/weekend programs available. Postbaccalaureate distance learning degree programs offered (minimal on-campus study). *Faculty:* 1 full-time (0 women), 2 part-time/adjunct (1 woman). *Students:* 23 full-time (13 women), 41 part-time (30 women); includes 13 minority (11 African Americans, 2 Hispanic Americans). Average age 40. 21 applicants, 76% accepted, 15 enrolled. In 2009, 24 master's awarded. *Degree requirements:* For master's, thesis or alternative. *Entrance requirements:* For master's, resume, 2 letters of reference. *Application deadline:* For fall admission, 8/1 for domestic students; for winter admission, 12/1 for domestic students; for spring admission, 3/10 for domestic students. Applications are processed on a rolling basis. Application fee: $50. Electronic applications accepted. *Expenses:* Contact institution. *Financial support:* Federal Work-Study available. Financial award applicants required to submit FAFSA. *Unit head:* Dr. Jon Saari, Chair, 937-769-1879, Fax: 937-769-1807, E-mail: jsaari@antioch.edu. *Application contact:* Seth Gordon, Assistant Director of Admissions, 937-769-1800 Ext. 1825, Fax: 937-769-1804, E-mail: sgordon@antioch.edu.

Arizona State University, Graduate College, College of Liberal Arts and Sciences, Division of Humanities, Department of English, Interdisciplinary Program in Creative Writing, Tempe, AZ 85287. Offers MFA. *Entrance requirements:* For master's, GRE.

Asbury University, School of Graduate and Professional Studies, Wilmore, KY 40390-1198. Offers biology: alternative certificate (MA Ed); chemistry: alternative certificate (MA Ed); English (MA Ed); English as a second language (MA Ed); ESL (MA Ed); French (MA Ed); Latin: alternative certificate (MA Ed); mathematics: alternative certificate (MA Ed); reading/writing endorsement (MA Ed); social studies (MA Ed); social work (MSW), including child and family services; Spanish (MA Ed); special education (MA Ed); special education: alternative certificate (MA Ed); teacher as leader endorsement (MA Ed). *Accreditation:* NCATE. Part-time programs available. *Faculty:* 8 full-time (7 women), 9 part-time/adjunct (4 women). *Students:* 108 part-time (87 women); includes 8 minority (4 African Americans, 2 Asian Americans or Pacific Islanders, 2 Hispanic Americans). Average age 36. 36 applicants, 86% accepted, 24 enrolled. In 2009, 20 master's awarded. *Degree requirements:* For master's, action research project, portfolio. *Entrance requirements:* For master's, PRAXIS/NTE, minimum GPA of 2.75, letters of recommendation. Additional exam requirements/recommendations for international students: Required—TOEFL (minimum score 550 paper-based). *Application deadline:* Applications are processed on a rolling basis. Application fee: $25. Electronic applications accepted. *Financial support:* Scholarships/grants and traineeships available. Financial award applicants required to submit FAFSA. *Unit head:* Dr. Bonnie J. Banker, Dean, School of Graduate and Professional Studies, 859-858-3511 Ext. 2221, Fax: 859-858-3921, E-mail: bonnie.banker@asbury.edu. *Application contact:* Lenore A. Sweigard, Graduate Program Assistant and Certification Specialist, 859-858-3511 Ext. 2502, Fax: 859-858-3921, E-mail: graded@asbury.edu.

Ashland University, College of Arts and Sciences, Program in Creative Writing, Ashland, OH 44805-3702. Offers MFA. Postbaccalaureate distance learning degree programs offered (minimal

Writing

Ashland University (continued)

on-campus study). *Faculty:* 8 part-time/adjunct (5 women). *Students:* 30 full-time (24 women); includes 3 minority (1 African American, 2 American Indian/Alaska Native). Average age 42. 34 applicants, 88% accepted, 20 enrolled. In 2009, 13 master's awarded. *Degree requirements:* For master's, thesis. *Entrance requirements:* For master's, writing sample, minimum GPA of 2.75. *Application deadline:* For fall admission, 2/1 priority date for domestic students; for winter admission, 10/1 priority date for domestic students. Application fee: $30. Electronic applications accepted. *Expenses:* Contact institution. *Financial support:* In 2009–10, 23 students received support. Career-related internships or fieldwork, Federal Work-Study, and institutionally sponsored loans available. Financial award application deadline: 4/15; financial award applicants required to submit FAFSA. *Unit head:* Dr. Stephen Haven, Director, MFA Program, 419-289-5979, Fax: 419-289-5255, E-mail: shaven@ashland.edu. *Application contact:* Sarah Marie Wells, Administrative Director, 419-289-5957, Fax: 419-289-5255, E-mail: swells@ashland.edu.

Ball State University, Graduate School, College of Sciences and Humanities, Department of English, Muncie, IN 47306-1099. Offers English (MA, PhD), including composition, creative writing (MA), general (MA), literature; linguistics (MA, PhD), including applied linguistics (PhD); linguistics and teaching English to speakers of other languages (MA); teaching English to speakers of other languages (MA). *Degree requirements:* For doctorate, variable foreign language requirement, thesis/dissertation. *Entrance requirements:* For master's, GRE General Test, writing sample; for doctorate, GRE General Test, GRE Subject Test, minimum graduate GPA of 3.2, writing sample. *Faculty research:* American literature; literary editing; Medieval, Renaissance, and eighteenth century British literature; rhetoric.

Belmont University, College of Arts and Sciences, Department of English, Nashville, TN 37212-3757. Offers literature (MA); writing (MA). Part-time and evening/weekend programs available. *Degree requirements:* For master's, one foreign language, comprehensive exam (for some programs), thesis optional. *Entrance requirements:* For master's, GRE, letters of recommendation, writing sample. Additional exam requirements/recommendations for international students: Required—TOEFL. Electronic applications accepted. *Expenses:* Contact institution. *Faculty research:* Gender, autobiography, folklore, Shakespeare, editing.

Bennington College, Graduate Programs, The Bennington Writing Seminars, Bennington, VT 05201. Offers creative writing (MFA). Postbaccalaureate distance learning degree programs offered (minimal on-campus study). *Faculty:* 16 full-time (7 women), 6 part-time/adjunct (2 women). *Students:* 106 full-time (80 women); includes 14 minority (4 African Americans, 1 American Indian/Alaska Native, 4 Asian Americans or Pacific Islanders, 5 Hispanic Americans), 1 international. Average age 38. 158 applicants, 37% accepted, 35 enrolled. In 2009, 50 master's awarded. *Degree requirements:* For master's, thesis, collection of essays or poems, or collection of short stories and/or a novel. *Entrance requirements:* For master's, manuscript. *Application deadline:* For fall admission, 3/1 for domestic students; for spring admission, 9/1 for domestic students. Application fee: $60. *Expenses:* Contact institution. *Financial support:* In 2009–10, 11 students received support. Scholarships/grants available. Financial award application deadline: 4/1; financial award applicants required to submit FAFSA. *Unit head:* Sven Birkerts, Director, 802-440-4452, Fax: 802-440-4453, E-mail: writing@bennington.edu. *Application contact:* Victoria Clausi, Associate Director, 802-440-4454, Fax: 802-440-4453, E-mail: writing@bennington.edu.

Boise State University, Graduate College, College of Arts and Sciences, Department of English, Program in Creative Writing, Boise, ID 83725-0399. Offers MFA. *Degree requirements:* For master's, thesis. *Entrance requirements:* For master's, GRE General Test, minimum GPA of 3.0. *Expenses:* Tuition, state resident: full-time $3106; part-time $209 per credit. Tuition, nonresident: part-time $284 per credit.

Boston University, Graduate School of Arts and Sciences, Creative Writing Program, Boston, MA 02215. Offers MFA. *Students:* 25 full-time (15 women), 7 part-time (5 women); includes 3 minority (1 African American, 2 Asian Americans or Pacific Islanders), 3 international. Average age 30. 318 applicants, 8% accepted, 26 enrolled. In 2009, 26 master's awarded. *Entrance requirements:* Additional exam requirements/recommendations for international students: Required—TOEFL. *Application deadline:* For fall admission, 3/1 for domestic students. Application fee: $70. Electronic applications accepted. *Expenses:* Tuition: Full-time $37,910; part-time $1184 per credit hour. Required fees: $386; $40 per semester. Part-time tuition and fees vary according to class time, course level, degree level and program. *Financial support:* In 2009–10, 22 students received support, including teaching assistantships with partial tuition reimbursements available (averaging $17,500 per year); Federal Work-Study and unspecified assistantships also available. Support available to part-time students. Financial award applicants required to submit FAFSA. *Unit head:* Leslie Epstein, Director, 617-353-2510, Fax: 617-353-3653, E-mail: leslieep@bu.edu. *Application contact:* Aaron Kerner, Administrative Coordinator, 617-353-2510, Fax: 617-353-3653, E-mail: crwr@bu.edu.

Boston University, Graduate School of Arts and Sciences, Department of English, Boston, MA 02215. Offers creative writing (MA); English (MA, PhD). *Students:* 53 full-time (35 women), 6 part-time (5 women); includes 1 minority (Asian American or Pacific Islander), 1 international. Average age 28. 278 applicants, 7% accepted, 15 enrolled. In 2009, 8 master's, 2 doctorates awarded. Terminal master's awarded for partial completion of doctoral program. *Degree requirements:* For master's, one foreign language, thesis; for doctorate, 2 foreign languages, comprehensive exam, thesis/dissertation, qualifying/oral exam. *Entrance requirements:* For master's and doctorate, GRE General Test, GRE Subject Test, sample of written work, 2 letters of recommendation. Additional exam requirements/recommendations for international students: Required—TOEFL (minimum score 550 paper-based; 213 computer-based). *Application deadline:* For fall admission, 1/1 for domestic and international students. Application fee: $70. Electronic applications accepted. *Expenses:* Tuition: Full-time $37,910; part-time $1184 per credit hour. Required fees: $386; $40 per semester. Part-time tuition and fees vary according to class time, course level, degree level and program. *Financial support:* In 2009–10, 39 students received support, including 2 fellowships with full tuition reimbursements available (averaging $18,900 per year), 25 teaching assistantships with partial tuition reimbursements available (averaging $18,400 per year); Federal Work-Study, scholarships/grants, and unspecified assistantships also available. Financial award application deadline: 1/15; financial award applicants required to submit FAFSA. *Unit head:* William Carroll, Interim Chairman, 617-353-2509, Fax: 617-353-3653, E-mail: wcarroll@bu.edu. *Application contact:* Amanda Trainor, Administrative Assistant, 617-353-2509, Fax: 617-353-3653, E-mail: hlane@bu.edu.

Boston University, Graduate School of Arts and Sciences, Editorial Institute, Boston, MA 02215. Offers MA, PhD. *Students:* 13 full-time (7 women), 1 part-time (0 women), 1 international. Average age 35. 13 applicants, 38% accepted, 5 enrolled. *Degree requirements:* For master's, one foreign language, thesis; for doctorate, one foreign language, comprehensive exam, thesis/dissertation. *Entrance requirements:* For master's and doctorate, GRE General Test, thesis proposal, 3 letters of recommendation. Additional exam requirements/recommendations for international students: Required—TOEFL (minimum score 550 paper-based; 213 computer-based). *Application deadline:* For fall admission, 3/30 for domestic and international students. Application fee: $70. Electronic applications accepted. *Expenses:* Tuition: Full-time $37,910; part-time $1184 per credit hour. Required fees: $386; $40 per semester. Part-time tuition and fees vary according to class time, course level, degree level and program. *Financial support:* In 2009–10, 13 students received support, including 3 teaching assistantships with full tuition reimbursements available (averaging $18,400 per year); Federal Work-Study, scholarships/grants, and unspecified assistantships also available. Support available to part-time students. Financial award application deadline: 1/15; financial award applicants required to submit FAFSA. *Unit head:* Archie Burnett, Co-Director, 617-353-6631, E-mail: burnetta@bu.edu. *Application contact:* Alex Effgen, Administrative Assistant, 617-353-6631, Fax: 617-353-6917, E-mail: editinst@bu.edu.

Bowling Green State University, Graduate College, College of Arts and Sciences, Department of English, Program in Creative Writing, Bowling Green, OH 43403. Offers fiction (MFA); poetry (MFA). Part-time programs available. *Degree requirements:* For master's, thesis or alternative. *Entrance requirements:* For master's, GRE General Test. Additional exam requirements/recommendations for international students: Required—TOEFL. Electronic applications accepted. *Faculty research:* Poetry, criticism, novels, translation, travel writing.

Bowling Green State University, Graduate College, College of Arts and Sciences, Department of English, Program in English, Bowling Green, OH 43403. Offers English (MA, PhD); literature (MA); rhetoric and writing (PhD); scientific and technical communication (MA). Part-time programs available. *Degree requirements:* For master's, thesis or alternative; for doctorate, comprehensive exam, thesis/dissertation, foreign language or proficiency in Old English. *Entrance requirements:* For master's and doctorate, GRE General Test. Additional exam requirements/recommendations for international students: Required—TOEFL. Electronic applications accepted. *Faculty research:* Postmodern literary theory, rhetorical theory, ethnic American literature, literature and culture, composition pedagogy.

Brigham Young University, Graduate Studies, College of Humanities, Department of English, Provo, UT 84602-1001. Offers creative writing (MFA); literature (MA); rhetoric/composition (MA). *Faculty:* 54 full-time (18 women). *Students:* 80 full-time (53 women), 5 part-time (3 women); includes 2 minority (both Asian Americans or Pacific Islanders). Average age 25. 98 applicants, 36% accepted, 29 enrolled. In 2009, 36 master's awarded. *Degree requirements:* For master's, thesis. *Entrance requirements:* For master's, GRE General Test. Additional exam requirements/recommendations for international students: Required—TOEFL. *Application deadline:* For fall admission, 1/15 for domestic students. Application fee: $50. Electronic applications accepted. *Expenses:* Tuition: Full-time $5580; part-time $301 per credit hour. Tuition and fees vary according to student's religious affiliation. *Financial support:* In 2009–10, 79 students received support, including 10 research assistantships (averaging $3,000 per year), 62 teaching assistantships (averaging $6,000 per year); career-related internships or fieldwork, institutionally sponsored loans, scholarships/grants, and tuition waivers (partial) also available. Support available to part-time students. Financial award application deadline: 3/15. *Faculty research:* English literature, American literature, rhetoric, creative writing. *Unit head:* Prof. Ed Cutler, Head, 801-422-3581, Fax: 801-422-0221, E-mail: ed_cutler@byu.edu. *Application contact:* Lou Ann C. Crisler, Graduate Secretary, 801-422-8673, Fax: 801-422-0221, E-mail: louann_crisler@byu.edu.

Brooklyn College of the City University of New York, Division of Graduate Studies, Department of English, Program in Creative Writing, Brooklyn, NY 11210-2889. Offers fiction (MFA); playwriting (MFA); poetry (MFA). Part-time and evening/weekend programs available. *Students:* 4 full-time (3 women), 65 part-time (38 women); includes 14 minority (4 African Americans, 6 Asian Americans or Pacific Islanders, 4 Hispanic Americans), 2 international. Average age 30. 437 applicants, 12% accepted, 28 enrolled. In 2009, 25 master's awarded. *Degree requirements:* For master's, comprehensive exam, thesis or alternative, 36 credits. *Entrance requirements:* For master's, 12 undergraduate advanced credits in English, writing sample, 2 letters of recommendation, manuscript. Additional exam requirements/recommendations for international students: Required—TOEFL (minimum score 650 paper-based; 280 computer-based; 114 iBT). *Application deadline:* For fall admission, 1/15 priority date for domestic students, 1/15 for international students. Applications are processed on a rolling basis. Application fee: $125. Electronic applications accepted. *Expenses:* Tuition, area resident: Full-time $7360; part-time $310 per credit hour. Tuition, state resident: full-time $7360; part-time $310 per credit hour. Tuition, nonresident: full-time $13,800; part-time $575 per credit hour. International tuition: $13,800 full-time. Required fees: $140.10 per semester. *Financial support:* Federal Work-Study, institutionally sponsored loans, and scholarships/grants available. Support available to part-time students. Financial award application deadline: 5/1; financial award applicants required to submit FAFSA. *Faculty research:* Postmodern fiction. *Unit head:* Dr. James Davis, Graduate Deputy Chairperson, 718-951-5195, E-mail: jcdavis@brooklyn.cuny.edu. *Application contact:* Herman Sierra, Graduate Admissions Coordinator, 718-951-4536, Fax: 718-951-4506, E-mail: grads@brooklyn.cuny.edu.

Brown University, Graduate School, Department of English, Program in Nonfiction Writing, Providence, RI 02912. Offers MFA. *Degree requirements:* For master's, thesis. *Entrance requirements:* For master's, GRE General Test, GRE Subject Test.

California College of the Arts, Graduate Programs, Program in Writing, San Francisco, CA 94107. Offers MFA. *Degree requirements:* For master's, thesis, exhibit. *Entrance requirements:* For master's, appropriate bachelor's degree, portfolio. Additional exam requirements/recommendations for international students: Required—TOEFL (minimum score 600 paper-based; 250 computer-based). Electronic applications accepted.

California Institute of Integral Studies, School of Consciousness and Transformation, San Francisco, CA 94103. Offers creative inquiry (MFA); cultural anthropology and social transformation (MA); East-West psychology (MA, PhD); integrative health studies (MA); philosophy and religion (MA, PhD), including Asian and comparative studies, philosophy, cosmology, and consciousness, women's spirituality; social and cultural anthropology (PhD); transformative leadership (MA); transformative studies (PhD); writing and consciousness (MFA). Part-time and evening/weekend programs available. Postbaccalaureate distance learning degree programs offered (minimal on-campus study). *Students:* 334 full-time (218 women), 126 part-time (77 women); includes 116 minority (40 African Americans, 4 American Indian/Alaska Native, 42 Asian Americans or Pacific Islanders, 30 Hispanic Americans). Average age 38. 265 applicants, 90% accepted, 149 enrolled. In 2009, 64 master's, 22 doctorates awarded. Terminal master's awarded for partial completion of doctoral program. *Degree requirements:* For master's, comprehensive exam (for some programs), thesis optional; for doctorate, comprehensive exam, thesis/dissertation, 1 foreign language (Asian comparative studies). *Entrance requirements:* For master's, minimum GPA of 3.0, letters of recommendation, writing sample; for doctorate, master's degree, minimum GPA of 3.0, letters of recommendation, writing sample. Additional exam requirements/recommendations for international students: Required—TOEFL. *Application deadline:* For fall admission, 2/1 priority date for domestic and international students; for spring admission, 10/15 priority date for domestic and international students. Applications are processed on a rolling basis. Application fee: $65. Electronic applications accepted. *Expenses:* Tuition: Full-time $15,300; part-time $850 per credit hour. Required fees: $110 per semester. Tuition and fees vary according to degree level. *Financial support:* In 2009–10, 330 students received support; research assistantships, teaching assistantships, career-related internships or fieldwork, Federal Work-Study, scholarships/grants, and tuition waivers (partial) available. Support available to part-time students. Financial award application deadline: 4/15; financial award applicants required to submit FAFSA. *Faculty research:* Altered states of consciousness, dreams, cosmology, postcolonial studies, integrative health studies. *Application contact:* Allyson Werner, Associate Director of Admissions, 415-575-6155, Fax: 415-575-1268.

California Institute of the Arts, School of Critical Studies, Valencia, CA 91355-2340. Offers writing (MFA, Adv C). *Entrance requirements:* For master's, portfolio. Additional exam requirements/recommendations for international students: Required—TOEFL.

California Institute of the Arts, School of Theatre, Valencia, CA 91355-2340. Offers acting (MFA, Adv C); design and technology (Adv C); directing (MFA); performing arts design and technology (MFA); theater management (MFA, Adv C); writing for performance (MFA). *Accreditation:* NAST. *Degree requirements:* For master's, thesis (for some programs), faculty review, performance or portfolio. *Entrance requirements:* For master's, audition or portfolio, interview. Additional exam requirements/recommendations for international students: Required—TOEFL. Electronic applications accepted.

California State University, Fresno, Division of Graduate Studies, College of Arts and Humanities, Department of English, Fresno, CA 93740-8027. Offers composition theory (MA); creative writing (MFA); literature (MA). Part-time and evening/weekend programs available. *Degree requirements:* For master's, one foreign language, thesis. *Entrance requirements:* For master's, GRE General Test, minimum GPA of 3.0, writing sample. Additional exam requirements/

recommendations for international students: Required—TOEFL. Electronic applications accepted. *Faculty research:* American literature, Renaissance literature, foreign literature.

California State University, Long Beach, Graduate Studies, College of Liberal Arts, Department of English, Long Beach, CA 90840. Offers creative writing (MFA); English (MA). Part-time programs available. *Faculty:* 28 full-time (12 women), 2 part-time/adjunct (1 woman). *Students:* 63 full-time (44 women), 106 part-time (76 women); includes 45 minority (4 African Americans, 19 Asian Americans or Pacific Islanders, 22 Hispanic Americans), 3 international. Average age 31. *Degree requirements:* For master's, one foreign language, comprehensive exam or thesis. *Entrance requirements:* For master's, GRE Subject Test, minimum GPA of 3.0 in English. *Application deadline:* For fall admission, 5/1 for domestic students. Applications are processed on a rolling basis. Application fee: $55. Electronic applications accepted. *Expenses:* Required fees: $1802 per semester. Part-time tuition and fees vary according to course load. *Financial support:* Federal Work-Study, institutionally sponsored loans, and scholarships/grants available. Financial award application deadline: 3/2. *Faculty research:* English and American literature, literary theory, linguistics, rhetoric and composition. *Unit head:* Dr. Eileen S. Klink, Chair, 562-985-4223, Fax: 562-985-2369, E-mail: eklink@csulb.edu. *Application contact:* Dr. Beth Lau, Graduate Adviser, 562-985-4252, Fax: 562-985-4223, E-mail: blau@csulb.edu.

California State University, Northridge, Graduate Studies, College of Humanities, Department of English, Northridge, CA 91330. Offers creative writing (MA); literature (MA); rhetoric and composition theory (MA). Part-time and evening/weekend programs available. *Faculty:* 31 full-time (13 women), 66 part-time/adjunct (58 women). *Students:* 36 full-time (22 women), 130 part-time (87 women); includes 1 American Indian/Alaska Native, 16 Asian Americans or Pacific Islanders, 22 Hispanic Americans, 1 international. Average age 33. 119 applicants, 65% accepted, 42 enrolled. In 2009, 36 master's awarded. *Degree requirements:* For master's, thesis or alternative. *Entrance requirements:* For master's, writing proficiency test, GRE General Test or minimum GPA of 3.0. Additional exam requirements/recommendations for international students: Required—TOEFL. *Application deadline:* For fall admission, 11/30 for domestic students. Application fee: $55. *Financial support:* Teaching assistantships available. Financial award application deadline: 3/1. *Faculty research:* Reading improvement, professional writing, Dickens, Shaw, English as a second language. *Unit head:* Dr. George Uba, Chair, 818-677-3434, E-mail: george.uba@csun.edu. *Application contact:* Dr. Marjie Seagoe, Graduate Studies Secretary, 818-677-3433.

California State University, Sacramento, Graduate Studies, College of Arts and Letters, Department of English, Sacramento, CA 95819. Offers creative writing (MA); teaching English to speakers of other languages (MA). Part-time programs available. *Degree requirements:* For master's, thesis, project, or comprehensive exam; writing proficiency exam. *Entrance requirements:* For master's, portfolio (creative writing); minimum GPA of 3.0 in English, 2.75 overall during previous 2 years. Additional exam requirements/recommendations for international students: Required—TOEFL. Electronic applications accepted. *Faculty research:* Teaching composition, remedial writing.

California State University, San Bernardino, Graduate Studies, College of Arts and Letters, Department of English, San Bernardino, CA 92407-2397. Offers creative writing (MFA); English composition (MA). Part-time and evening/weekend programs available. *Faculty:* 14 full-time (7 women). *Students:* 90 full-time (57 women), 46 part-time (34 women); includes 50 minority (12 African Americans, 6 Asian Americans or Pacific Islanders, 32 Hispanic Americans), 2 international. Average age 34. 105 applicants, 61% accepted, 44 enrolled. In 2009, 19 master's awarded. *Degree requirements:* For master's, one foreign language, thesis. *Entrance requirements:* For master's, BA in English or linguistics, minimum GPA of 3.0. Additional exam requirements/recommendations for international students: Required—TOEFL. *Application deadline:* For fall admission, 8/31 priority date for domestic students. Application fee: $55. *Financial support:* Research assistantships, teaching assistantships, career-related internships or fieldwork, Federal Work-Study, institutionally sponsored loans, and writing center tutorships available. Support available to part-time students. Financial award application deadline: 3/1. *Faculty research:* Composition and literary theory, theatrical theory, creative writing, relationship between evaluating writing and teaching composition. *Unit head:* Dr. Juan Delgado, Chair, 909-537-5834, Fax: 909-537-7086, E-mail: jdelgado@csusb.edu. *Application contact:* Olivia Rosas, Director of Admissions, 909-537-7577, Fax: 909-537-7034, E-mail: orosas@csusb.edu.

California State University, San Marcos, College of Arts and Sciences, Program in Literature and Writing Studies, San Marcos, CA 92096-0001. Offers MA. Part-time and evening/weekend programs available. *Degree requirements:* For master's, one foreign language, thesis. *Entrance requirements:* For master's, GRE General Test, minimum GPA of 3.0, writing sample. *Faculty research:* Postcolonialism, feminism rhetoric, cultural studies, creative writing, critical theory.

California State University, Stanislaus, College of Humanities and Social Sciences, Department of English, Turlock, CA 95382. Offers English (MA); literature (MA); rhetoric and teaching of writing (MA); TESOL (MA, Certificate). Part-time programs available. *Degree requirements:* For master's, one foreign language, comprehensive exam, thesis. *Entrance requirements:* For master's, GRE General Test, minimum GPA of 3.0, 2 letters of reference; for Certificate, minimum GPA of 3.0, 2 letters of reference. Additional exam requirements/recommendations for international students: Required—TOEFL (minimum score 550 paper-based; 213 computer-based), TWE (minimum score 4). Electronic applications accepted. *Faculty research:* Transnational literacies, Renaissance and Medieval literature, abolition writings and slave narratives, qualitative writing.

Carlow University, Humanities Division, Pittsburgh, PA 15213-3165. Offers creative writing (MFA), including fiction, nonfiction, poetry. Part-time and evening/weekend programs available. *Degree requirements:* For master's, thesis or alternative. *Entrance requirements:* For master's, minimum GPA of 3.0, resume, writing samples, 2 letters of recommendation. Additional exam requirements/recommendations for international students: Required—TOEFL (minimum score 550 paper-based; 213 computer-based). *Expenses:* Tuition: Full-time $11,250; part-time $625 per credit. Tuition and fees vary according to course load, degree level and program.

Carnegie Mellon University, College of Humanities and Social Sciences, Department of English, Program in Professional Writing, Pittsburgh, PA 15213-3891. Offers editing and publishing (MAPW); policy and non-profit communication (MAPW); public and media relations / corporate communications (MAPW); science or healthcare communication (MAPW); technical writing (MAPW); writing for new media (MAPW); writing for print media (MAPW). Part-time programs available. *Entrance requirements:* For master's, GRE General Test. Additional exam requirements/recommendations for international students: Required—TOEFL, TWE.

Central Michigan University, College of Graduate Studies, College of Humanities and Social and Behavioral Sciences, Department of English Language and Literature, Mount Pleasant, MI 48859. Offers English composition and communication (MA); English language and literature (MA), including children's and young adult literature, creative writing, general concentration; teaching English to speakers of other languages (TESOL) (MA). Part-time and evening/weekend programs available. *Degree requirements:* For master's, thesis or alternative. Electronic applications accepted. *Faculty research:* Composition theory, science fiction history and bibliography, children's and young adult literature, nineteenth century American literature, applied linguistics.

Chapman University, Graduate Studies, Wilkinson College of Humanities and Social Sciences, Department of English, Orange, CA 92866. Offers creative writing (MFA); English (MA). Part-time and evening/weekend programs available. *Faculty:* 20 full-time (8 women), 21 part-time/adjunct (8 women). *Students:* 35 full-time (18 women), 21 part-time (14 women); includes 8 minority (3 African Americans, 1 American Indian/Alaska Native, 1 Asian American or Pacific Islander, 3 Hispanic Americans). Average age 33. 55 applicants, 62% accepted, 17 enrolled. In 2009, 38 master's awarded. *Degree requirements:* For master's, comprehensive exam (for some programs), thesis (for some programs). *Entrance requirements:* For master's, GRE or MAT, minimum undergraduate GPA of 2.5. Additional exam requirements/recommendations for international students: Required—TOEFL (minimum score 550 paper-based; 213 computer-based; 80 iBT). *Application deadline:* For fall admission, 5/1 priority date for domestic students. Applications are processed on a rolling basis. Application fee: $50. Electronic applications accepted. *Expenses:* Contact institution. *Financial support:* Fellowships, Federal Work-Study and scholarships/grants available. Financial award application deadline: 3/2; financial award applicants required to submit FAFSA. *Unit head:* Dr. Patrick Fuery, Department Chair, 714-532-7789, E-mail: fuery@chapman.edu. *Application contact:* Priscilla Garcia Powers, Graduate Admission Counselor, 714-997-6711, E-mail: pgarcia@chapman.edu.

Chapman University, Graduate Studies, Wilkinson College of Humanities and Social Sciences, Program in Creative Writing, Orange, CA 92866. Offers MFA. Part-time and evening/weekend programs available. *Faculty:* 19 full-time (8 women), 19 part-time/adjunct (11 women). *Students:* 33 full-time (21 women), 25 part-time (13 women); includes 7 minority (1 African American, 2 Asian Americans or Pacific Islanders, 4 Hispanic Americans). Average age 29. 40 applicants, 80% accepted, 22 enrolled. In 2009, 19 master's awarded. *Degree requirements:* For master's, thesis, project. *Entrance requirements:* For master's, GRE General Test or MAT, minimum undergraduate GPA of 3.0, sample of creative writing. Additional exam requirements/recommendations for international students: Required—TOEFL (minimum score 550 paper-based). *Application deadline:* Applications are processed on a rolling basis. Application fee: $55. Electronic applications accepted. *Expenses:* Contact institution. *Financial support:* Fellowships, Federal Work-Study and scholarships/grants available. Financial award application deadline: 6/30; financial award applicants required to submit FAFSA. *Unit head:* Dr. Richard Ruppel, Chair, 714-997-6754, E-mail: ruppel@chapman.edu. *Application contact:* Jim Blaylock, Coordinator, 714-997-6750, E-mail: blaylock@chapman.edu.

Chatham University, Program in Writing, Pittsburgh, PA 15232-2826. Offers children's writing (MFA); fiction (MFA); non-fiction (MFA); poetry (MFA); professional writing (MPW); screenwriting (MFA). Part-time and evening/weekend programs available. Postbaccalaureate distance learning degree programs offered (minimal on-campus study). *Students:* 81 full-time (60 women), 85 part-time (69 women). Average age 32. 161 applicants, 79% accepted, 73 enrolled. In 2009, 43 master's awarded. *Entrance requirements:* For master's, minimum GPA of 3.0, writing sample, recommendation letters. Additional exam requirements/recommendations for international students: Required—TOEFL (minimum score 600 paper-based; 250 computer-based; 100 iBT), IELTS (minimum score 6.5), TWE. *Application deadline:* For fall admission, 3/15 priority date for domestic students, 5/1 priority date for international students; for spring admission, 10/15 priority date for domestic students, 10/1 priority date for international students. Applications are processed on a rolling basis. Application fee: $45. Electronic applications accepted. *Financial support:* Career-related internships or fieldwork available. Financial award applicants required to submit FAFSA. *Faculty research:* Ecopoetics; environment and culture; wilderness and literature; literature of exploration, exile, and home. *Unit head:* Dr. Sheryl St. Germain, Director, 412-365-1190, Fax: 412-365-1505, E-mail: sstgermain@chatham.edu. *Application contact:* Dory Perry, Associate Director of Graduate Admissions, 412-365-2758, Fax: 412-365-1609, E-mail: gradadmissions@chatham.edu.

Chicago State University, School of Graduate and Professional Studies, College of Arts and Sciences, Department of English, Chicago, IL 60628. Offers creative writing (MFA); English (MA). *Degree requirements:* For master's, comprehensive exam. *Entrance requirements:* For master's, minimum GPA of 2.75.

City College of the City University of New York, Graduate School, College of Liberal Arts and Science, Division of the Humanities and Arts, Department of English, Program in Creative Writing, New York, NY 10031-9198. Offers MA, MFA. *Degree requirements:* For master's, one foreign language, comprehensive exam, thesis. *Entrance requirements:* For master's, minimum GPA of 3.0, 10-15 poems or 30-50 pages of fiction (short stories or novel excerpt). Additional exam requirements/recommendations for international students: Required—TOEFL (minimum score 600 paper-based; 100 iBT). Electronic applications accepted.

Claremont Graduate University, Graduate Programs, School of Arts and Humanities, Department of English, Claremont, CA 91711-6160. Offers American studies (MA, PhD); critical theory (MA, PhD); early modern studies (MA, PhD); English (M Phil, MA, PhD); literary theory (PhD); literature (MA, PhD); literature and creative writing (MA); literature and film (MA); MBA/MA; MBA/PhD. Part-time programs available. *Faculty:* 2 full-time (1 woman), 2 part-time/adjunct (0 women). *Students:* 83 full-time (60 women), 19 part-time (11 women); includes 17 minority (1 African American, 1 American Indian/Alaska Native, 8 Asian Americans or Pacific Islanders, 7 Hispanic Americans), 4 international. Average age 35. In 2009, 6 master's, 4 doctorates awarded. *Entrance requirements:* For master's and doctorate, GRE General Test. Additional exam requirements/recommendations for international students: Required—TOEFL (minimum score 550 paper-based; 213 computer-based; 80 iBT). *Application deadline:* For fall admission, 2/1 priority date for domestic students. Applications are processed on a rolling basis. Application fee: $60. Electronic applications accepted. *Expenses:* Tuition: Full-time $35,046; part-time $1524 per credit. Required fees: $161 per semester. *Financial support:* Fellowships, Federal Work-Study, institutionally sponsored loans, and scholarships/grants available. Support available to part-time students. Financial award application deadline: 2/15; financial award applicants required to submit FAFSA. *Faculty research:* American, comparative, and English Renaissance literature; modernism; feminist literature and theory. *Unit head:* Wendy Martin, Chair, 909-621-8612, Fax: 909-607-1221, E-mail: wendy.martin@cgu.edu. *Application contact:* Susan Hampson, Admissions Coordinator, 909-607-1278, Fax: 909-607-1221, E-mail: humanities@cgu.edu.

Clemson University, Graduate School, College of Architecture, Arts, and Humanities, Department of English, Program in Professional Communication, Clemson, SC 29634. Offers MA. Part-time programs available. *Students:* 24 full-time (17 women), 8 part-time (6 women); includes 2 minority (1 Asian American or Pacific Islander, 1 Hispanic American), 3 international. Average age 27. 36 applicants, 44% accepted, 10 enrolled. In 2009, 17 master's awarded. *Degree requirements:* For master's, one foreign language, thesis optional, oral exam. *Entrance requirements:* For master's, GRE General Test, minimum GPA of 3.0. Additional exam requirements/recommendations for international students: Required—TOEFL, IELTS. *Application deadline:* For fall admission, 2/1 priority date for domestic students, 4/15 for international students; for spring admission, 11/1 priority date for domestic students, 9/15 for international students. Applications are processed on a rolling basis. Application fee: $70 ($80 for international students). Electronic applications accepted. *Expenses:* Tuition, state resident: full-time $8684; part-time $528 per credit hour. Tuition, nonresident: full-time $15,330; part-time $1078 per credit hour. Required fees: $736; $37 per semester. Part-time tuition and fees vary according to course load and program. *Financial support:* In 2009–10, 24 students received support, including 2 research assistantships with partial tuition reimbursements available (averaging $11,500 per year), 10 teaching assistantships with partial tuition reimbursements available (averaging $13,552 per year); fellowships with full and partial tuition reimbursements available, career-related internships or fieldwork, institutionally sponsored loans, scholarships/grants, health care benefits, and unspecified assistantships also available. Support available to part-time students. Financial award application deadline: 4/1; financial award applicants required to submit FAFSA. *Faculty research:* Usability testing, rhetoric, communication across the curriculum, intercultural communication. *Unit head:* Dr. Lee Morrissey, Coordinator, 864-656-3151, Fax: 864-656-1345, E-mail: lmorris@clemson.edu. *Application contact:* Dr. Summer Taylor, Graduate Coordinator, 864-656-6689, Fax: 864-656-1345, E-mail: slsmith@clemson.edu.

Cleveland State University, College of Graduate Studies, College of Liberal Arts and Social Sciences, Department of English, Cleveland, OH 44115. Offers creative writing (MFA); English (MA). Part-time and evening/weekend programs available. *Degree requirements:* For master's, comprehensive exam, thesis. *Entrance requirements:* For master's, minimum GPA of 2.75, undergraduate concentration in English, writing sample, portfolio. Additional exam requirements/recommendations for international students: Required—TOEFL (525 paper-based; 197

Writing

Cleveland State University (continued)
computer-based) or IELTS (6 paper-based). Electronic applications accepted. *Faculty research:* Literary history and criticism, linguistics, literature.

The College at Brockport, State University of New York, School of Arts, Humanities and Social Sciences, Department of English, Brockport, NY 14420-2997. Offers English (MA), including creative writing, literature. Part-time programs available. *Students:* 28 full-time (17 women), 30 part-time (18 women). 15 applicants, 87% accepted, 10 enrolled. In 2009, 8 master's awarded. *Degree requirements:* For master's, thesis. *Entrance requirements:* For master's, minimum GPA of 3.0, letters of recommendation, writing sample. Additional exam requirements/recommendations for international students: Required—TOEFL (minimum score 550 paper-based; 213 computer-based; 79 iBT). *Application deadline:* For fall admission, 4/15 priority date for domestic and international students; for spring admission, 11/15 priority date for domestic and international students. Application fee: $50. Electronic applications accepted. *Expenses:* Tuition, state resident: full-time $8370; part-time $349 per credit. Tuition, nonresident: full-time $13,250; part-time $522 per credit. *Financial support:* In 2009–10, 1 fellowship with full tuition reimbursement (averaging $7,500 per year), 3 teaching assistantships with full tuition reimbursements (averaging $6,000 per year) were awarded; Federal Work-Study, scholarships/grants, and unspecified assistantships also available. Support available to part-time students. Financial award application deadline: 3/15; financial award applicants required to submit FAFSA. *Faculty research:* British and American literature, creative writing, film studies, children's literature, ancient and modern world literature. *Unit head:* Dr. J. Roger Kurtz, Chairperson, 585-395-2503, Fax: 585-395-2391, E-mail: rkurtz@brockport.edu. *Application contact:* Dr. Stefan Jurasinski, Graduate Program Director, 585-395-5714, Fax: 585-395-2391, E-mail: sjurasin@brockport.edu.

Colorado State University, Graduate School, College of Liberal Arts, Department of English, Fort Collins, CO 80523-1773. Offers creative writing (MFA); English (MA). Part-time programs available. *Faculty:* 32 full-time (19 women). *Students:* 96 full-time (57 women), 46 part-time (32 women); includes 10 minority (1 American Indian/Alaska Native, 2 Asian Americans or Pacific Islanders, 7 Hispanic Americans), 15 international. Average age 30. 289 applicants, 34% accepted, 36 enrolled. In 2009, 53 master's awarded. *Degree requirements:* For master's, variable foreign language requirement, thesis (for some programs), exams. *Entrance requirements:* For master's, GRE, writing sample, BA/BS with minimum GPA of 3.0, letters of recommendation. Additional exam requirements/recommendations for international students: Required—TOEFL (minimum score 550 paper-based), TOEFL paper-based score of 575 required for creative writing. *Application deadline:* For fall admission, 4/1 priority date for domestic students; for spring admission, 9/1 priority date for domestic students. Applications are processed on a rolling basis. Application fee: $50. Electronic applications accepted. *Expenses:* Tuition, state resident: full-time $6434; part-time $359.10 per credit. Tuition, nonresident: full-time $18,116; part-time $1006.45 per credit. Required fees: $1496; $83 per credit. *Financial support:* In 2009–10, 36 students received support, including 36 teaching assistantships with full tuition reimbursements available (averaging $12,564 per year); fellowships, research assistantships, career-related internships or fieldwork, Federal Work-Study, institutionally sponsored loans, scholarships/grants, traineeships, and unspecified assistantships also available. Support available to part-time students. Financial award application deadline: 5/1; financial award applicants required to submit FAFSA. *Faculty research:* Computers and writing, environmental writing, cultural studies, new historicism, performance and identity. Total annual research expenditures: $43,684. *Unit head:* Dr. Bruce Ronda, Chair, 970-491-6428, Fax: 970-491-5601, E-mail: bruce.ronda@colostate.edu. *Application contact:* Marnie Leonard, Administrative Assistant, 970-491-2403, Fax: 970-491-7541, E-mail: marnie.leonard@colostate.edu.

Columbia College Chicago, Graduate School, Department of Fiction Writing, Chicago, IL 60605-1996. Offers creative writing (MFA); teaching of writing (MA); MFA/MA. Part-time programs available. *Degree requirements:* For master's, thesis. *Entrance requirements:* For master's, minimum GPA of 3.0, work sample, thirty pages of manuscript in roughly equal amounts of fiction and expository prose. Additional exam requirements/recommendations for international students: Required—TOEFL (minimum score 550 paper-based; 213 computer-based). Electronic applications accepted. *Expenses:* Tuition: Part-time $651 per credit hour. Required fees: $651 per credit hour. $205 per semester. One-time fee: $285 part-time. Tuition and fees vary according to program.

Columbia College Chicago, Graduate School, Program in Nonfiction Writing, Chicago, IL 60605-1996. Offers MFA. *Expenses:* Tuition: Part-time $651 per credit hour. Required fees: $651 per credit hour. $205 per semester. One-time fee: $285 part-time. Tuition and fees vary according to program.

Columbia College Chicago, Graduate School, Program in Poetry, Chicago, IL 60605-1996. Offers MFA. Part-time programs available. *Degree requirements:* For master's, thesis. *Entrance requirements:* For master's, interview, writing sample, minimum GPA of 3.0. Additional exam requirements/recommendations for international students: Required—TOEFL (minimum score 550 paper-based; 213 computer-based). Electronic applications accepted. *Expenses:* Tuition: Part-time $651 per credit hour. Required fees: $651 per credit hour. $205 per semester. One-time fee: $285 part-time. Tuition and fees vary according to program.

Columbia University, School of the Arts, Writing Division, New York, NY 10027. Offers fiction (MFA); nonfiction (MFA); poetry (MFA). *Degree requirements:* For master's, thesis. *Entrance requirements:* For master's, 3 letters of recommendation, writing sample. Additional exam requirements/recommendations for international students: Required—TOEFL (minimum score 600 paper-based; 250 computer-based). Electronic applications accepted.

See Close-Up on page 261.

Concordia University, School of Graduate Studies, Faculty of Arts and Science, Department of English, Program in Creative Writing, Montréal, QC H3G 1M8, Canada. Offers MA. *Degree requirements:* For master's, one foreign language, thesis. *Entrance requirements:* For master's, honors degree in English, minimum GPA of 3.3 in English literature, portfolio. *Faculty research:* Fiction, poetry, prose, drama.

Cornell University, Graduate School, Graduate Fields of Arts and Sciences, Field of English Language and Literature, Ithaca, NY 14853-0001. Offers African-American literature (PhD); American literature after 1865 (PhD); American literature to 1865 (PhD); American studies (PhD); colonial and postcolonial literature (PhD); creative writing (MFA); cultural studies (PhD); dramatic literature (PhD); English poetry (PhD); English Renaissance to 1660 (PhD); lesbian, bisexual, and gay literature studies (PhD); literary criticism and theory (PhD); nineteenth century (PhD); Old and Middle English (PhD); prose fiction (PhD); Restoration and eighteenth century (PhD); twentieth century (PhD); women's literature (PhD); MFA/PhD. *Faculty:* 74 full-time (35 women). *Students:* 100 full-time (55 women); includes 26 minority (9 African Americans, 3 American Indian/Alaska Native, 7 Asian Americans or Pacific Islanders, 7 Hispanic Americans), 11 international. Average age 28. 890 applicants, 4% accepted, 21 enrolled. In 2009, 21 master's, 12 doctorates awarded. Terminal master's awarded for partial completion of doctoral program. *Degree requirements:* For master's, one foreign language, thesis; for doctorate, one foreign language, comprehensive exam, thesis/dissertation, teaching experience. *Entrance requirements:* For master's, GRE General Test, 3 letters of recommendation, creative writing sample; for doctorate, GRE General Test, GRE Subject Test (English), 3 letters of recommendation, writing sample. Additional exam requirements/recommendations for international students: Required—TOEFL (minimum score 600 paper-based; 250 computer-based; 77 iBT). *Application deadline:* For fall admission, 1/10 for domestic students. Application fee: $70. Electronic applications accepted. *Expenses:* Tuition: Full-time $29,500. Required fees: $70. Full-time tuition and fees vary according to degree level, program and student level. *Financial support:* In 2009–10, 96 students received support, including 13 fellowships with full tuition reimbursements available, 8 teaching assistantships with full tuition reimbursements available; research assistantships with full tuition reimbursements available, institutionally sponsored loans, scholarships/grants, health care benefits, tuition waivers (full and partial), and unspecified assistantships also available. Financial award applicants required to submit FAFSA. *Faculty research:* English and American literature, women's writing, ethnic and post-colonial literature, critical theory, medievalism. *Unit head:* Director of Graduate Studies, 607-255-7989, Fax: 607-255-6661. *Application contact:* Graduate Field Assistant, 607-255-7989, Fax: 607-255-6661, E-mail: english_grad@cornell.edu.

Creighton University, Graduate School, College of Arts and Sciences, Department of English, Omaha, NE 68178-0001. Offers creative writing (MA). Part-time programs available. *Faculty:* 17 full-time (9 women). *Students:* 12 full-time (8 women), 4 part-time (2 women); includes 1 minority (Hispanic American), 3 international. 21 applicants, 95% accepted, 13 enrolled. In 2009, 6 master's awarded. *Degree requirements:* For master's, thesis optional. *Entrance requirements:* For master's, GRE, 10-15 page writing sample, 3 letters of recommendation. Additional exam requirements/recommendations for international students: Required—TOEFL (minimum score 550 paper-based; 213 computer-based; 80 iBT). *Application deadline:* For fall admission, 3/15 priority date for domestic and international students. Application fee: $50. Electronic applications accepted. *Expenses:* Tuition: Full-time $11,700; part-time $650 per credit hour. Required fees: $126 per semester. *Financial support:* In 2009–10, 5 fellowships with full and partial tuition reimbursements (averaging $10,437 per year) were awarded; tuition waivers (partial) also available. Financial award applicants required to submit FAFSA. *Unit head:* Dr. Greg Zacharias, Director, 402-280-2729, E-mail: gregzacharias@creighton.edu. *Application contact:* Taunya Plater, Senior Program Coordinator, 402-280-2870, Fax: 402-280-2899, E-mail: taunyaplater@creighton.edu.

DePaul University, College of Liberal Arts and Sciences, Department of English, Program in Writing, Rhetoric, and Discourse, Chicago, IL 60604-2287. Offers MA. *Students:* 24 full-time (16 women), 18 part-time (15 women); includes 8 minority (4 African Americans, 1 Asian American or Pacific Islander, 3 Hispanic Americans). *Expenses:* Tuition: Full-time $37,525; part-time $620 per credit hour. *Unit head:* Christine Tardy, Director, 773-325-4145. *Application contact:* Dr. Lesley Kordecki, Director, 773-325-1786, Fax: 773-325-8607, E-mail: lkordeck@depaul.edu.

Drew University, Caspersen School of Graduate Studies, Program in Poetry, Madison, NJ 07940-1493. Offers poetry (MFA); poetry in translation (MFA). *Students:* 24 full-time (19 women); includes 4 minority (1 African American, 3 Hispanic Americans). Average age 36. 12 applicants, 92% accepted, 8 enrolled. *Degree requirements:* For master's, thesis. *Entrance requirements:* For master's, transcripts, writing sample, recommendations. *Application deadline:* For fall admission, 5/1 priority date for domestic students; for spring admission, 12/1 priority date for domestic students. Applications are processed on a rolling basis. Application fee: $35. *Expenses:* Contact institution. *Financial support:* In 2009–10, 23 students received support. Federal Work-Study, scholarships/grants, and tuition waivers (partial) available. Financial award applicants required to submit FAFSA. *Unit head:* Anne Marie Macari, 973-408-3016, E-mail: amacari@drew.edu. *Application contact:* Carla J. Burns, Director of Graduate Admissions, 973-408-3110, Fax: 973-408-3242, E-mail: gradm@drew.edu.

Eastern Kentucky University, The Graduate School, College of Arts and Sciences, Department of English and Theatre, Richmond, KY 40475-3102. Offers creative writing (MFA); English (MA). Part-time and evening/weekend programs available. *Degree requirements:* For master's, thesis optional. *Entrance requirements:* For master's, GRE General Test, minimum GPA of 2.5, minor in English with 3.0 GPA. *Faculty research:* Old English, Victorian studies, women's studies, rhetoric, popular culture, novel studies.

Eastern Michigan University, Graduate School, College of Arts and Sciences, Department of English Language and Literature, Program in Creative Writing, Ypsilanti, MI 48197. Offers MA. Part-time and evening/weekend programs available. Postbaccalaureate distance learning degree programs offered (minimal on-campus study). *Students:* 3 full-time (1 woman), 4 part-time (1 woman); includes 1 minority (African American). Average age 27. In 2009, 7 master's awarded. *Entrance requirements:* Additional exam requirements/recommendations for international students: Required—TOEFL. *Application deadline:* Applications are processed on a rolling basis. Application fee: $35. Tuition and fees vary according to course level. *Financial support:* Fellowships, research assistantships with full tuition reimbursements, teaching assistantships with full tuition reimbursements, career-related internships or fieldwork, Federal Work-Study, institutionally sponsored loans, scholarships/grants, tuition waivers (partial), and unspecified assistantships available. Support available to part-time students. Financial award applicants required to submit FAFSA. *Unit head:* Dr. Rebecca Sipe, Department Head, 734-487-4220, Fax: 734-483-9744, E-mail: rebecca.sipe@emich.edu. *Application contact:* Christine Hume, Program Advisor, 734-487-1310, Fax: 734-483-9744, E-mail: chume@emich.edu.

Eastern Michigan University, Graduate School, College of Arts and Sciences, Department of English Language and Literature, Program in Teaching of Writing, Ypsilanti, MI 48197. Offers MA, Graduate Certificate. *Students:* 1 (woman) full-time. Average age 29. In 2009, 2 other advanced degrees awarded. Application fee: $35. Tuition and fees vary according to course level. *Unit head:* Dr. Rebecca Sipe, Department Head, 734-487-4220, Fax: 734-483-9744, E-mail: rebecca.sipe@emich.edu. *Application contact:* Dr. Cheryl Cassidy, Program Advisor, 734-487-0150, Fax: 734-483-9744, E-mail: cheryl.cassidy@emich.edu.

Eastern Michigan University, Graduate School, College of Arts and Sciences, Department of English Language and Literature, Program in Written Communication, Ypsilanti, MI 48197. Offers technical communications (MA, Graduate Certificate); written communications (MA). Part-time and evening/weekend programs available. Postbaccalaureate distance learning degree programs offered (minimal on-campus study). *Students:* 7 full-time (5 women), 35 part-time (27 women); includes 2 minority (both African Americans). Average age 35. In 2009, 21 master's awarded. *Entrance requirements:* Additional exam requirements/recommendations for international students: Required—TOEFL. *Application deadline:* Applications are processed on a rolling basis. Application fee: $35. Tuition and fees vary according to course level. *Financial support:* Fellowships, research assistantships with full tuition reimbursements, teaching assistantships with full tuition reimbursements, career-related internships or fieldwork, Federal Work-Study, institutionally sponsored loans, scholarships/grants, tuition waivers (partial), and unspecified assistantships available. Support available to part-time students. Financial award applicants required to submit FAFSA. *Unit head:* Dr. Rebecca Sipe, Department Head, 734-487-4220, Fax: 734-483-9744, E-mail: rebecca.sipe@emich.edu. *Application contact:* Dr. Cheryl Cassidy, Program Advisor, 734-487-0150, Fax: 734-483-9744, E-mail: cheryl.cassidy@emich.edu.

Eastern Washington University, Graduate Studies, College of Arts and Letters, Inland Northwest Center for Writers, Cheney, WA 99004-2431. Offers MFA. *Degree requirements:* For master's, comprehensive exam, thesis. *Entrance requirements:* For master's, GRE General Test, minimum GPA of 3.0, sample of written work. *Expenses:* Tuition, state resident: full-time $7476; part-time $249 per quarter hour. Tuition, nonresident: full-time $18,030; part-time $601 per quarter hour. Required fees: $3.50 per quarter hour. $142 per quarter.

Emerson College, Graduate Studies, School of the Arts, Department of Writing, Literature and Publishing, Program in Creative Writing, Boston, MA 02116-4624. Offers MFA. Part-time and evening/weekend programs available. *Faculty:* 43 full-time (19 women), 6 part-time/adjunct (1 woman). *Students:* 111 full-time (72 women), 29 part-time (15 women); includes 18 minority (3 African Americans, 1 American Indian/Alaska Native, 9 Asian Americans or Pacific Islanders, 5 Hispanic Americans), 1 international. Average age 24. 232 applicants, 54% accepted, 49 enrolled. In 2009, 46 master's awarded. *Entrance requirements:* For master's, GRE General Test, 15 page writing sample. Additional exam requirements/recommendations for international students: Required—TOEFL (minimum score 550 paper-based; 213 computer-based; 80 iBT), IELTS (minimum score 6.5). *Application deadline:* For fall admission, 1/5 for domestic and international students. Applications are processed on a rolling basis. Application fee: $60 ($75 for international students). Electronic applications accepted. *Expenses:* Tuition: Full-time $22,056; part-time $919 per credit. Required fees: $120; $120 per year. One-time fee: $170 full-time. *Financial support:* In 2009–10, 44 students received support, including 6 fellowships with partial tuition reimbursements available (averaging $14,000 per year), 16 research assistantships with partial tuition reimbursements available (averaging $10,000 per year); Federal Work-Study, scholarships/grants, and unspecified assistantships also available. Financial award application deadline: 1/5; financial award applicants required to submit FAFSA. *Unit head:* Prof. Frederick Reiken, Graduate Program Director, 617-824-8750, E-mail: frederick_reiken@emerson.edu. *Application contact:* Office of Graduate Admission, 617-824-8610, Fax: 617-824-8614, E-mail: gradapp@emerson.edu.

Emerson College, Graduate Studies, School of the Arts, Department of Writing, Literature and Publishing, Program in Publishing and Writing, Boston, MA 02116-4624. Offers MA. Part-time and evening/weekend programs available. *Faculty:* 43 full-time (19 women), 9 part-time/adjunct (6 women). *Students:* 92 full-time (75 women), 15 part-time (14 women); includes 8 minority (4 African Americans, 1 Asian American or Pacific Islander, 3 Hispanic Americans), 5 international. Average age 24. 130 applicants, 68% accepted, 49 enrolled. In 2009, 48 master's awarded. *Degree requirements:* For master's, thesis or alternative. *Entrance requirements:* For master's, GRE General Test, 15 page writing sample. Additional exam requirements/recommendations for international students: Required—TOEFL (minimum score 550 paper-based; 213 computer-based; 80 iBT), IELTS (minimum score 6.5). *Application deadline:* For fall admission, 1/5 for domestic and international students. Applications are processed on a rolling basis. Application fee: $60 ($75 for international students). Electronic applications accepted. *Expenses:* Tuition: Full-time $22,056; part-time $919 per credit. Required fees: $120; $120 per year. One-time fee: $170 full-time. *Financial support:* In 2009–10, 46 students received support, including 6 fellowships with partial tuition reimbursements available (averaging $14,000 per year), 24 research assistantships with partial tuition reimbursements available (averaging $10,000 per year); Federal Work-Study, scholarships/grants, and unspecified assistantships also available. Financial award application deadline: 1/5; financial award applicants required to submit FAFSA. *Faculty research:* Publishing. *Unit head:* Prof. Lisa Diercks, Graduate Program Director, 617-824-8750, E-mail: lisa_diercks@emerson.edu. *Application contact:* Office of Graduate Admission, 617-824-8610, Fax: 617-824-8614, E-mail: gradapp@emerson.edu.

Fairfield University, College of Arts and Sciences, Fairfield, CT 06824-5195. Offers American studies (MA); communication (MA); creative writing (MFA); mathematics (MS). Part-time and evening/weekend programs available. *Degree requirements:* For master's, capstone research course. *Entrance requirements:* For master's, minimum GPA of 3.0, 2 letters of recommendation, resume. Additional exam requirements/recommendations for international students: Required—TOEFL (minimum score 550 paper-based; 213 computer-based; 80 iBT). Electronic applications accepted. *Faculty research:* Non-commutative algebra, partial differential equations, writing (fiction, non-fiction and poetry), communication for social change, comparative media systems, negotiation and management.

Fairleigh Dickinson University, College at Florham, Maxwell Becton College of Arts and Sciences, Department of English, Communication and Philosophy, Program in Creative Writing, Madison, NJ 07940-1099. Offers MFA. *Students:* 35 full-time (19 women), 4 part-time (1 woman). Average age 33. 48 applicants, 38% accepted, 14 enrolled. In 2009, 11 master's awarded. *Application deadline:* Applications are processed on a rolling basis. Application fee: $40. *Unit head:* Dr. Martin Green, Chairperson, 973-443-8712. *Application contact:* Susan Brooman, University Director, Graduate Admissions, 973-443-8905, Fax: 973-443-8088, E-mail: grad@fdu.edu.

Florida Atlantic University, Dorothy F. Schmidt College of Arts and Letters, Department of English, Boca Raton, FL 33431-0991. Offers British and American literature (MA); creative nonfiction (MFA); creative writing (MA); fiction (MFA); multicultural literatures and literacies (MA); poetry (MFA); science fiction and fantasy (MA); teaching English (MAT). Part-time programs available. *Faculty:* 49 full-time (24 women), 17 part-time/adjunct (7 women). *Students:* 63 full-time (36 women), 28 part-time (21 women); includes 22 minority (6 African Americans, 2 American Indian/Alaska Native, 2 Asian Americans or Pacific Islanders, 12 Hispanic Americans), 1 international. Average age 31. 70 applicants, 54% accepted, 16 enrolled. In 2009, 21 master's awarded. *Degree requirements:* For master's, one foreign language, thesis. *Entrance requirements:* For master's, GRE General Test, minimum GPA of 3.0, writing samples, 2 letters of recommendation. *Application deadline:* For fall admission, 3/1 for domestic students, 2/15 for international students; for spring admission, 11/1 for domestic students, 7/15 for international students. Applications are processed on a rolling basis. Application fee: $30. Electronic applications accepted. *Expenses:* Tuition, state resident: full-time $7055; part-time $293.94 per credit hour. Tuition, nonresident: full-time $22,096; part-time $920.66 per credit hour. *Financial support:* Fellowships, teaching assistantships with partial tuition reimbursements, Federal Work-Study and tuition waivers available. Support available to part-time students. Financial award application deadline: 3/1. *Faculty research:* African-American writers, critical theory, British-American, Asian-American. *Unit head:* Dr. Wenying Xu, Chair, 561-297-2065, Fax: 561-297-3807, E-mail: wxu@fau.edu. *Application contact:* Dr. Andrew Furman, Director of Graduate Studies, 561-297-3835, Fax: 561-297-3807, E-mail: afurman@fau.edu.

Florida International University, College of Arts and Sciences, Department of English, Program in Creative Writing, Miami, FL 33199. Offers MFA. Part-time and evening/weekend programs available. *Students:* 20 full-time (10 women), 24 part-time (18 women); includes 11 minority (2 African Americans, 9 Hispanic Americans). Average age 39. 49 applicants, 24% accepted, 12 enrolled. In 2009, 6 master's awarded. *Degree requirements:* For master's, comprehensive exam. *Entrance requirements:* For master's, GRE General Test, minimum undergraduate GPA of 3.0, writing sample,2 letters of recommendation. Additional exam requirements/recommendations for international students: Required—TOEFL (minimum score 550 paper-based; 80 iBT). *Application deadline:* For fall admission, 1/15 for domestic and international students. Application fee: $30. Electronic applications accepted. *Expenses:* Tuition, state resident: full-time $8008; part-time $4004 per year. Tuition, nonresident: full-time $20,104; part-time $10,052 per year. Required fees: $298; $149 per term. *Financial support:* Institutionally sponsored loans and scholarships/grants available. Financial award application deadline: 3/1; financial award applicants required to submit FAFSA. *Unit head:* Dr. James Sutton, Chair, English Department, 305-348-2874, Fax: 305-348-3778, E-mail: james.sutton@fiu.edu. *Application contact:* Dr. Kimberly Harrision, Director, 305-348-2874, Fax: 305-348-3778, E-mail: kimberly.harrison@fiu.edu.

Florida State University, The Graduate School, College of Arts and Sciences, Department of English, Tallahassee, FL 32306. Offers creative writing (MFA); English (PhD), including creative writing, literature, rhetoric and composition; literature (MA); rhetoric and composition (MA). Part-time programs available. *Faculty:* 48 full-time (23 women), 6 part-time/adjunct (1 woman). *Students:* 150 full-time (90 women), 20 part-time (10 women); includes 31 minority (15 African Americans, 1 American Indian/Alaska Native, 5 Asian Americans or Pacific Islanders, 10 Hispanic Americans). Average age 30. 480 applicants, 21% accepted, 58 enrolled. In 2009, 22 master's, 14 doctorates awarded. *Degree requirements:* For master's, one foreign language, thesis or alternative; for doctorate, comprehensive exam, thesis/dissertation, 27 hours of coursework, 24 hours of dissertation work. *Entrance requirements:* For master's and doctorate, GRE General Test, GRE Subject Test (literature only), sample of written work, 3 letters of recommendation, resume. Additional exam requirements/recommendations for international students: Required—TOEFL. *Application deadline:* For fall admission, 1/1 priority date for domestic and international students. Application fee: $30. Electronic applications accepted. *Expenses:* Tuition, state resident: full-time $7413. Tuition, nonresident: full-time $22,567. *Financial support:* In 2009–10, 126 students received support, including 5 fellowships, teaching assistantships (averaging $11,375 per year); career-related internships or fieldwork, Federal Work-Study, and institutionally sponsored loans also available. Financial award application deadline: 1/1; financial award applicants required to submit FAFSA. *Faculty research:* British and Irish literature, American literature, creative writing, rhetoric and composition, multiethnic transnational literature. *Unit head:* Dr. Ralph Berry, Chairman, 850-644-4230, Fax: 850-644-0811, E-mail: rberry@fsu.edu. *Application contact:* Dr. Ralph Berry, Chairman, 850-644-4230, Fax: 850-644-0811, E-mail: rberry@fsu.edu.

George Mason University, College of Humanities and Social Sciences, Department of English, Program in Creative Writing, Fairfax, VA 22030. Offers MFA. *Faculty:* 82 full-time (47 women), 48 part-time/adjunct (29 women). *Students:* 41 full-time (30 women), 75 part-time (55 women); includes 15 minority (5 African Americans, 2 American Indian/Alaska Native, 8 Asian Americans or Pacific Islanders), 3 international. Average age 29. 191 applicants, 53% accepted, 40 enrolled. In 2009, 20 master's awarded. *Degree requirements:* For master's, one foreign language, thesis, exam or project. *Entrance requirements:* For master's, minimum GPA of 3.0 in last 60 hours, portfolio, 2 letters of recommendation. Additional exam requirements/recommendations for international students: Required—TOEFL. *Application deadline:* For fall admission, 1/2 priority date for domestic students. Application fee: $75. Electronic applications accepted. *Expenses:* Tuition, state resident: full-time $7568; part-time $315.33 per credit hour. Tuition, nonresident: full-time $21,704; part-time $904.33 per credit hour. Required fees: $2184; $91 per credit hour. *Financial support:* In 2009–10, 43 students received support, including 3 research assistantships with full and partial tuition reimbursements available (averaging $9,443 per year), 41 teaching assistantships with full and partial tuition reimbursements available (averaging $10,685 per year); Federal Work-Study, scholarships/grants, unspecified assistantships, and health care benefits (full-time research or teaching assistantship recipients) also available. Support available to part-time students. Financial award application deadline: 3/1; financial award applicants required to submit FAFSA. *Faculty research:* British Romantic poetry and literary celebrity, Arab feminist novelists in the West, masculinity and African American culture, public rhetoric and the South African Truth Commission, the origins of children's literature in eighteenth and nineteenth century Britain. *Unit head:* Denise Albanese, Director/Associate Professor, 703-993-1175, E-mail: dalbanes@gmu.edu. *Application contact:* Jennifer Stone, Graduate Programs Manager, 703-993-1180, E-mail: jstone22@gmu.edu.

Georgia College & State University, Graduate School, College of Arts and Sciences, Department of English and Rhetoric, Program in Creative Writing, Milledgeville, GA 31061. Offers MFA. Part-time and evening/weekend programs available. *Students:* 15 full-time (5 women), 15 part-time (8 women); includes 4 minority (3 African Americans, 1 Hispanic American). Average age 31. 36 applicants, 53% accepted, 10 enrolled. In 2009, 7 master's awarded. *Degree requirements:* For master's, one foreign language, thesis. *Entrance requirements:* For master's, GRE or MAT, writing portfolio, letters of recommendation. Additional exam requirements/recommendations for international students: Recommended—TOEFL (minimum score 550 paper-based; 213 computer-based; 79 iBT). *Application deadline:* For fall admission, 2/1 for domestic students. Application fee: $40. Electronic applications accepted. *Expenses:* Tuition, area resident: Part-time $241 per credit hour. Tuition, state resident: full-time $4338. Tuition, nonresident: full-time $17,352; part-time $964 per credit hour. Required fees: $609 per semester. Tuition and fees vary according to course load and campus/location. *Financial support:* In 2009–10, 22 teaching assistantships with full tuition reimbursements were awarded; unspecified assistantships also available. Financial award applicants required to submit FAFSA. *Unit head:* Dr. Martin Lammon, Graduate Coordinator, 478-445-3508, E-mail: mfa@gcsu.edu. *Application contact:* Dr. Martin Lammon, Graduate Coordinator, 478-445-3508, E-mail: mfa@gcsu.edu.

Georgia State University, College of Arts and Sciences, Department of English, Program in Creative Writing, Atlanta, GA 30302-3083. Offers fiction/poetry (MA, MFA). Part-time programs available. *Degree requirements:* For master's, variable foreign language requirement, comprehensive exam, thesis; for doctorate, one foreign language, comprehensive exam, thesis/dissertation. *Entrance requirements:* For master's and doctorate, GRE General Test, portfolio. Additional exam requirements/recommendations for international students: Required—TOEFL (minimum score 0 paper-based; 0 computer-based). Electronic applications accepted. *Faculty research:* Poetry and fiction.

Goddard College, Graduate Division, Master of Fine Arts in Creative Writing Program, Plainfield, VT 05667-9432. Offers MFA. Program residency available in Plainfield, VT or Port Townsend, WA. Postbaccalaureate distance learning degree programs offered (minimal on-campus study). *Faculty:* 29 part-time/adjunct (19 women). *Students:* 156 full-time. Average age 38. 129 applicants, 57% accepted, 57 enrolled. *Degree requirements:* For master's, thesis, completed manuscript, teaching practicum, 3 critical papers, reading of 45 to 60 literary works. *Entrance requirements:* For master's, 3 letters of recommendation, preliminary study plan and bibliography, creative writing sample or samples, current resume. *Application deadline:* Applications are processed on a rolling basis. Application fee: $40. Electronic applications accepted. *Expenses:* Contact institution. *Financial support:* In 2009–10, 145 students received support. Applicants required to submit FAFSA. *Unit head:* Paul Selig, Director, 802-454-8311, Fax: 802-454-7835, E-mail: paul.selig@goddard.edu. *Application contact:* David DeLucca, Senior Admissions Counselor, 800-906-8312 Ext. 248, Fax: 802-454-1029, E-mail: david.delucca@goddard.edu.

Goucher College, Program in Creative Nonfiction, Baltimore, MD 21204-2794. Offers MFA. Part-time and evening/weekend programs available. Postbaccalaureate distance learning degree programs offered (minimal on-campus study). *Degree requirements:* For master's, manuscript, portfolio. *Entrance requirements:* For master's, writing sample. *Expenses:* Contact institution.

Hofstra University, College of Liberal Arts and Sciences, Department of English, Hempstead, NY 11549. Offers English and creative writing (MA); English literature (MA). Part-time programs available. *Faculty:* 12 full-time (3 women), 1 part-time/adjunct (0 women). *Students:* 23 full-time (16 women), 12 part-time (9 women); includes 3 minority (1 African American, 1 Asian American or Pacific Islander, 1 Hispanic American). Average age 27. 28 applicants, 82% accepted, 14 enrolled. In 2009, 18 master's awarded. *Degree requirements:* For master's, thesis optional. *Entrance requirements:* For master's, writing sample, minimum GPA of 3.0 in literature courses. Additional exam requirements/recommendations for international students: Required—TOEFL (minimum score 550 paper-based; 213 computer-based; 80 iBT). *Application deadline:* Applications are processed on a rolling basis. Application fee: $60. Electronic applications accepted. *Expenses:* Tuition: Full-time $16,200; part-time $900 per credit hour. Required fees: $970; $145 per term. Tuition and fees vary according to program. *Financial support:* In 2009–10, 22 students received support, including 2 fellowships with full and partial tuition reimbursements available (averaging $3,250 per year), 1 research assistantship with full and partial tuition reimbursement available (averaging $21,930 per year); Federal Work-Study, institutionally sponsored loans, scholarships/grants, and tuition waivers (full and partial) also available. Support available to part-time students. Financial award applicants required to submit FAFSA. *Faculty research:* Herman Melville, disability studies, early American literature, Queer Theory, twentieth century popular culture. *Unit head:* Dr. Joseph A. Fichtelberg, Chairperson, 516-463-5455, Fax: 516-463-6395, E-mail: engjaf@hofstra.edu. *Application contact:* Carol Drummer, Dean of Graduate Admissions, 516-463-4876, Fax: 516-463-4664, E-mail: gradstudent@hofstra.edu.

Hollins University, Graduate Programs, Program in Creative Writing, Roanoke, VA 24020-1603. Offers MFA. *Faculty:* 7 full-time (2 women), 2 part-time/adjunct (1 woman). *Students:* 22 full-time (15 women); includes 2 minority (both African Americans). Average age 27. 233 applicants, 15% accepted, 10 enrolled. In 2009, 11 master's awarded. *Degree requirements:* For master's, comprehensive exam, thesis. *Entrance requirements:* For master's, manuscripts, 3 letters of recommendation. Additional exam requirements/recommendations for international students: Required—TOEFL (minimum score 550 paper-based; 213 computer-based; 79 iBT). *Application deadline:* For fall admission, 1/6 for domestic and international students. Application fee: $40. Electronic applications accepted. *Expenses:* Contact institution. *Financial support:* In 2009–10, 22 students received support, including 22 fellowships with full and partial tuition reimbursements available (averaging $9,460 per year), 4 teaching assistantships (averaging $6,000 per year); scholarships/grants and unspecified assistantships also available. Support available to part-time students. Financial award application deadline: 2/2; financial award applicants required to submit FAFSA. *Faculty research:* Poetry, fiction, creative nonfiction, literary criticism, literary theory. *Unit head:* Cathryn Hankla, Director, 540-362-6317, Fax: 540-362-6097, E-mail: creative.writing@hollins.edu. *Application contact:* Cathy S. Koon, Manager of Graduate Services, 540-362-6326, Fax: 540-362-6288, E-mail: ckoon@hollins.edu.

Writing

Hunter College of the City University of New York, Graduate School, School of Arts and Sciences, Department of English, Program in Creative Writing, New York, NY 10021-5085. Offers creative writing (MFA); fiction (MFA); nonfiction (MFA); poetry (MFA). Part-time and evening/weekend programs available. *Faculty:* 24 full-time (10 women), 3 part-time/adjunct (2 women). *Students:* 11 full-time (10 women), 30 part-time (all women); includes 3 minority (all African Americans). Average age 31. 503 applicants, 4% accepted, 19 enrolled. In 2009, 14 master's awarded. *Degree requirements:* For master's, thesis. *Entrance requirements:* For master's, creative writing manuscript (up to 10 pages of poetry or 25-30 pages of fiction or nonfiction), nonfiction proposal (for nonfiction applicants only). *Application deadline:* For fall admission, 2/1 for domestic and international students. Application fee: $125. *Expenses:* Tuition, state resident: full-time $7360; part-time $310 per credit. Required fees: $250 per semester. *Financial support:* In 2009–10, 18 students received support, including 12 fellowships (averaging $5,000 per year); Federal Work-Study and tuition waivers (partial) also available. Support available to part-time students. Financial award application deadline: 4/15. *Unit head:* Sue Nacey, Coordinator, 212-772-5164, Fax: 212-772-5076, E-mail: mfa@hunter.cuny.edu. *Application contact:* Elena Georgiou, Coordinator, 212-772-5164, Fax: 212-772-5076, E-mail: egeorgio@hunter.cuny.edu.

Illinois State University, Graduate School, College of Arts and Sciences, Department of English, Program in Writing, Normal, IL 61790-2200. Offers MA, MS. *Degree requirements:* For master's, comprehensive exam, internship or practicum. *Entrance requirements:* For master's, GRE General Test, minimum GPA of 3.0 in last 60 hours.

Indiana State University, School of Graduate Studies, College of Arts and Sciences, Department of English, Terre Haute, IN 47809. Offers English teaching (MA); history (MA); literature (MA). Part-time and evening/weekend programs available. *Degree requirements:* For master's, one foreign language, thesis optional. *Entrance requirements:* For master's, minimum GPA of 2.75 in all English courses above freshman level. Additional exam requirements/recommendations for international students: Required—TOEFL (minimum score 550 paper-based). Electronic applications accepted.

Indiana University Bloomington, University Graduate School, College of Arts and Sciences, Department of English, Bloomington, IN 47405-7000. Offers composition, literacy, and culture (PhD); creative writing (MA, MFA), including fiction, poetry; language (MA); literature (MA, PhD); writing (MA). Part-time programs available. *Faculty:* 51 full-time (23 women). *Students:* 221 full-time (139 women), 10 part-time (5 women); includes 27 minority (7 African Americans, 11 Asian Americans or Pacific Islanders, 9 Hispanic Americans), 9 international. Average age 30. 602 applicants, 15% accepted, 47 enrolled. In 2009, 21 master's, 9 doctorates awarded. Terminal master's awarded for partial completion of doctoral program. *Degree requirements:* For master's, one foreign language, thesis (for some programs); for doctorate, 2 foreign languages, thesis/dissertation, qualifying exam. *Entrance requirements:* For master's, GRE General Test, GRE Subject Test (for all but MFA and MA in creative writing), minimum GPA of 3.5; for doctorate, GRE General Test, GRE Subject Test, minimum GPA of 3.7. Additional exam requirements/recommendations for international students: Required—TOEFL. *Application deadline:* For fall admission, 1/15 priority date for domestic students, 12/15 for international students. Application fee: $55 ($65 for international students). Electronic applications accepted. *Financial support:* In 2009–10, 15 fellowships with full and partial tuition reimbursements (averaging $15,000 per year), 152 teaching assistantships with full tuition reimbursements (averaging $15,000 per year) were awarded; research assistantships with partial tuition reimbursements, career-related internships or fieldwork and health care benefits also available. Financial award application deadline: 2/1. *Unit head:* George Hutchinson, Chair, 812-855-8225, E-mail: gbhutchi@indiana.edu. *Application contact:* Patricia Ingham, Director of Admissions, 812-855-0521, Fax: 812-855-9535, E-mail: pingham@indiana.edu.

Indiana University of Pennsylvania, School of Graduate Studies and Research, College of Humanities and Social Sciences, Department of English, Program in Composition and Teaching English to Speakers of Other Languages, Indiana, PA 15705-1087. Offers composition and teaching English to speakers of other languages (PhD); teaching English (MAT); teaching English to speakers of other languages (MA). *Faculty:* 27 full-time (15 women). *Students:* 73 full-time (48 women), 142 part-time (95 women); includes 10 minority (2 African Americans, 6 Asian Americans or Pacific Islanders, 2 Hispanic Americans), 63 international. Average age 36. 203 applicants, 36% accepted, 45 enrolled. In 2009, 20 master's, 12 doctorates awarded. *Degree requirements:* For master's, thesis optional; for doctorate, one foreign language, comprehensive exam, thesis/dissertation. *Entrance requirements:* For master's and doctorate, 2 letters of recommendation. Additional exam requirements/recommendations for international students: Required—TOEFL. *Application deadline:* For fall admission, 7/1 priority date for domestic students; for spring admission, 11/1 for domestic students. Applications are processed on a rolling basis. Application fee: $40. *Expenses:* Tuition, state resident: full-time $6666; part-time $370 per credit hour. Tuition, nonresident: full-time $10,666; part-time $593 per credit hour. Required fees: $813 per semester. *Financial support:* In 2009–10, 4 fellowships (averaging $938 per year), 22 research assistantships with full and partial tuition reimbursements (averaging $5,922 per year), 8 teaching assistantships with partial tuition reimbursements (averaging $17,498 per year) were awarded. Financial award application deadline: 3/15; financial award applicants required to submit FAFSA. *Unit head:* Dr. Ben Rafoth, Graduate Coordinator, 724-357-2272. *Application contact:* Dr. Ben Rafoth, Graduate Coordinator, 724-357-2272.

Iowa State University of Science and Technology, Graduate College, College of Liberal Arts and Sciences, Department of English, Ames, IA 50011. Offers creative writing (MFA); English (MA); rhetoric and professional communication (PhD). *Faculty:* 53 full-time (26 women), 8 part-time/adjunct (6 women). *Students:* 105 full-time (68 women), 25 part-time (17 women); includes 3 minority (all Hispanic Americans), 28 international. 99 applicants, 62% accepted, 39 enrolled. In 2009, 30 master's, 3 doctorates awarded. *Degree requirements:* For master's, thesis or alternative; for doctorate, thesis/dissertation. *Entrance requirements:* For master's, GRE General Test, sample of written work, resume, portfolio in creative writing; for doctorate, GRE General Test, sample of written work, resume. Additional exam requirements/recommendations for international students: Required—TOEFL (minimum score 600 paper-based; 100 iBT) or IELTS (minimum score 7). *Application deadline:* For fall admission, 1/5 priority date for domestic and international students. Application fee: $40 ($90 for international students). Electronic applications accepted. *Expenses:* Tuition, state resident: full-time $6716. Tuition, nonresident: full-time $8908. Tuition and fees vary according to course level, course load, program and student level. *Financial support:* In 2009–10, 10 research assistantships with full and partial tuition reimbursements (averaging $18,120 per year), 84 teaching assistantships with full and partial tuition reimbursements (averaging $18,120 per year) were awarded; fellowships, scholarships/grants, health care benefits, and unspecified assistantships also available. *Faculty research:* Creative writing, literature, rhetoric, composition and professional communication, teaching English as a second language, applied linguistics. *Unit head:* Dr. Charles Kostelnick, Chair, 515-294-2477, Fax: 515-294-2125, E-mail: englgrad@iastate.edu. *Application contact:* Dr. Constance Post, Director of Graduate Education, 515-294-3175, E-mail: englgrad@iastate.edu.

The Johns Hopkins University, Zanvyl Krieger School of Arts and Sciences, Advanced Academic Programs, Program in Writing, Baltimore, MD 21218-2699. Offers MA. Part-time and evening/weekend programs available. *Faculty:* 1 full-time (0 women), 19 part-time/adjunct (9 women). *Students:* 6 full-time (4 women), 162 part-time (111 women); includes 20 minority (16 African Americans, 3 Asian Americans or Pacific Islanders, 1 Hispanic American), 4 international. Average age 38. 95 applicants, 54% accepted, 47 enrolled. In 2009, 44 master's awarded. *Degree requirements:* For master's, thesis. *Entrance requirements:* Additional exam requirements/recommendations for international students: Required—TOEFL (minimum score 600 paper-based; 250 computer-based; 100 iBT). *Application deadline:* For fall admission, 5/31 priority date for domestic students, 4/30 for international students; for spring admission, 10/31 priority date for domestic students, 10/31 for international students. Application fee: $75. *Financial support:* Applicants required to submit FAFSA. *Unit head:* Prof. David Everett, Associate Program Chair, 202-452-0758, Fax: 202-452-8713, E-mail: deverett@jhu.edu. *Application contact:* Valana M. McMickens, Admissions Manager, 202-452-1941, Fax: 202-452-1970, E-mail: aapadmissions@jhu.edu.

The Johns Hopkins University, Zanvyl Krieger School of Arts and Sciences, The Writing Seminars, Baltimore, MD 21218-2699. Offers fiction writing (MFA); poetry (MFA); science writing (MA). *Faculty:* 11 full-time (3 women). *Students:* 28 full-time (19 women); includes 2 minority (both Asian Americans or Pacific Islanders), 1 international. Average age 29. 273 applicants, 9% accepted, 17 enrolled. In 2009, 13 master's awarded. *Degree requirements:* For master's, one foreign language, thesis, foreign language exam (MFA). *Entrance requirements:* For master's, GRE General Test, GRE Subject Test (recommended), foreign language exam, sample of written work, 3 letters of recommendation. Additional exam requirements/recommendations for international students: Required—TOEFL (minimum score 600 paper-based; 250 computer-based; 100 iBT). *Application deadline:* For fall admission, 1/15 for domestic and international students. Application fee: $75. Electronic applications accepted. *Financial support:* In 2009–10, 28 students received support, including 1 fellowship (averaging $5,000 per year), 1 research assistantship with full tuition reimbursement available (averaging $17,500 per year), 22 teaching assistantships with full tuition reimbursements available (averaging $17,500 per year); Federal Work-Study, institutionally sponsored loans, scholarships/grants, health care benefits, tuition waivers (partial), and two teaching assistantships with $5000 stipend and full tuition also available. Financial award application deadline: 3/1; financial award applicants required to submit FAFSA. *Faculty research:* Film theory, literary criticism, contemporary fiction. *Unit head:* Dave Smith, Chairman and Elliott Coleman Professor of Poetry, 410-516-3409, Fax: 410-516-6828, E-mail: davesmith@jhu.edu. *Application contact:* Gina Woloszyn, Application Contact, 410-516-6286, Fax: 410-516-6828, E-mail: regina@jhu.edu.

Kean University, College of Humanities and Social Sciences, Program in English Writing, Union, NJ 07083. Offers MA. Part-time and evening/weekend programs available. *Faculty:* 25 full-time (14 women). *Students:* 1 full-time (0 women), 1 (woman) part-time; both minorities (1 African American, 1 Asian American or Pacific Islander). Average age 28. 2 applicants, 100% accepted, 2 enrolled. *Degree requirements:* For master's, thesis. *Entrance requirements:* For master's, GRE General Test, minimum GPA of 3.0, 12 credits in English or related area, 2 letters of recommendation. *Application deadline:* For fall admission, 5/1 for domestic students; for spring admission, 11/1 for domestic students. Application fee: $60 ($150 for international students). Electronic applications accepted. *Expenses:* Tuition, state resident: full-time $10,440; part-time $435 per credit. Tuition, nonresident: full-time $14,160; part-time $590 per credit. Required fees: $2642; $110 per credit. Part-time tuition and fees vary according to course load and degree level. *Financial support:* In 2009–10, 1 research assistantship with full tuition reimbursement (averaging $3,263 per year) was awarded; unspecified assistantships also available. *Unit head:* Dr. Sarah Chandler, Program Coordinator, 908-737-0380, E-mail: schandler@kean.edu. *Application contact:* Dorothy Rowe, Pre-Admissions Coordinator, 908-737-5928, Fax: 908-737-5965, E-mail: drowe@kean.edu.

Kennesaw State University, College of Humanities and Social Sciences, Program in Professional Writing, Kennesaw, GA 30144-5591. Offers MAPW. Part-time and evening/weekend programs available. *Faculty:* 18 full-time (9 women), 2 part-time/adjunct (1 woman). *Students:* 39 full-time (30 women), 79 part-time (59 women); includes 24 minority (20 African Americans, 1 American Indian/Alaska Native, 3 Hispanic Americans), 1 international. Average age 36. 57 applicants, 82% accepted, 34 enrolled. In 2009, 42 master's awarded. *Entrance requirements:* For master's, GRE General Test, minimum GPA of 2.5, writing sample. Additional exam requirements/recommendations for international students: Required—TOEFL (minimum score 550 paper-based; 213 computer-based; 80 iBT), IELTS (minimum score 6). *Application deadline:* For fall admission, 3/1 for domestic and international students. Application fee: $60. Electronic applications accepted. *Expenses:* Tuition, state resident: full-time $2341; part-time $196 per credit hour. Tuition, nonresident: full-time $9396; part-time $783 per credit hour. Required fees: $573 per semester. *Financial support:* In 2009–10, 2 research assistantships with full tuition reimbursements (averaging $15,000 per year) were awarded; Federal Work-Study also available. Support available to part-time students. Financial award application deadline: 6/15; financial award applicants required to submit FAFSA. *Unit head:* Dr. Jim Elledge, Director, 678-797-2039, E-mail: jellege1@kennesaw.edu. *Application contact:* Vilma Marquez, Admissions Counselor, 770-420-4377, Fax: 770-423-6885, E-mail: ksugrad@kennesaw.edu.

Kent State University, College of Arts and Sciences, Department of English, Kent, OH 44242-0001. Offers comparative literature (MA); creative writing (MFA); English (PhD); English for teachers (MA); literature and writing (MA); rhetoric and composition (PhD); teaching English as a second language (MA). Part-time programs available. Terminal master's awarded for partial completion of doctoral program. *Degree requirements:* For master's, one foreign language, thesis optional; for doctorate, one foreign language, thesis/dissertation, qualifying exams. *Entrance requirements:* For master's and doctorate, GRE General Test, writing sample, letters of recommendation. Additional exam requirements/recommendations for international students: Required—TOEFL (minimum score 600 paper-based). Electronic applications accepted. *Faculty research:* British and American literature, textual editing, rhetoric and composition, cultural studies, linguistic and critical theories.

La Sierra University, College of Arts and Sciences, Department of English and Communication, Riverside, CA 92515. Offers communication (MA), including public relations/advertising, theory emphasis; English (MA), including literary emphasis, writing emphasis. Part-time programs available. *Degree requirements:* For master's, one foreign language. *Entrance requirements:* For master's, GRE General Test.

Lesley University, Graduate School of Arts and Social Sciences, Program in Creative Writing, Cambridge, MA 02138-2790. Offers MFA. Part-time programs available. Postbaccalaureate distance learning degree programs offered (minimal on-campus study). *Degree requirements:* For master's, intensive residency. *Entrance requirements:* For master's, writing sample. Additional exam requirements/recommendations for international students: Required—TOEFL (minimum score 550 paper-based; 213 computer-based; 80 iBT). *Expenses:* Contact institution.

Lindenwood University, Graduate Programs, College of Individualized Education, St. Charles, MO 63301-1695. Offers administration (MSA); business administration (MBA); communications (MA); criminal justice and administration (MS); gerontology (MA); health management (MS); human resource management (MS); information technology (MBA, Certificate); management (MSA); managing information technology (MS); marketing (MSA); writing (MFA). Part-time and evening/weekend programs available. *Faculty:* 15 full-time (8 women), 128 part-time/adjunct (53 women). *Students:* 679 full-time (432 women), 90 part-time (57 women); includes 138 minority (121 African Americans, 2 American Indian/Alaska Native, 5 Asian Americans or Pacific Islanders, 10 Hispanic Americans), 18 international. Average age 34. 223 applicants, 44% accepted, 87 enrolled. In 2009, 478 master's awarded. *Degree requirements:* For master's, thesis (for some programs), 1 colloquium per term. *Entrance requirements:* For master's, interview, minimum GPA of 3.0. Additional exam requirements/recommendations for international students: Required—TOEFL (minimum score 550 paper-based; 213 computer-based; 80 iBT). *Application deadline:* For fall admission, 10/2 priority date for domestic and international students; for winter admission, 1/8 priority date for domestic and international students; for spring admission, 4/8 priority date for domestic and international students. Applications are processed on a rolling basis. Application fee: $30 ($100 for international students). *Expenses:* Tuition: Full-time $12,960; part-time $370 per credit hour. Required fees: $340. One-time fee: $30 full-time. Tuition and fees vary according to course level and course load. *Financial support:* In 2009–10, 631 students received support. Career-related internships or fieldwork, institutionally sponsored loans, tuition waivers (partial), and unspecified assistantships available. Financial award application deadline: 6/30; financial award applicants required to submit FAFSA. *Unit head:* Dan Kemper, Dean, 636-949-4501, Fax: 636-949-4505, E-mail: dkemper@lindenwood.edu. *Application contact:* Brett Barger, Dean of Evening Admissions and Extension Campuses, 636-949-4934, Fax: 636-949-4109, E-mail: adultadmissions@lindenwood.edu.

Writing

Long Island University, Brooklyn Campus, Richard L. Conolly College of Liberal Arts and Sciences, Department of English, Brooklyn, NY 11201-8423. Offers creative writing (MFA); literature (MA); professional writing (MA); writing and rhetoric (MA). Part-time and evening/weekend programs available. *Degree requirements:* For master's, thesis or alternative. *Entrance requirements:* For master's, 2 letters of recommendation (at least 1 from a former professor or teacher). Additional exam requirements/recommendations for international students: Required—TOEFL (minimum score 550 paper-based; 173 computer-based). Electronic applications accepted.

Longwood University, Office of Graduate Studies, Department of English and Modern Languages, Farmville, VA 23909. Offers 6-12 initial teaching/licensure (MA); creative writing (MA); English education and writing (MA); literature (MA). Part-time programs available. *Degree requirements:* For master's, comprehensive exam (for some programs), thesis (for some programs). *Entrance requirements:* For master's, minimum GPA of 2.75. Additional exam requirements/recommendations for international students: Required—TOEFL (minimum score 550 paper-based; 213 computer-based).

Louisiana State University and Agricultural and Mechanical College, Graduate School, College of Arts and Sciences, Department of English, Baton Rouge, LA 70803. Offers creative writing (MFA); English (MA, PhD). Part-time programs available. *Faculty:* 53 full-time (23 women). *Students:* 80 full-time (42 women), 9 part-time (6 women); includes 6 minority (2 African Americans, 1 American Indian/Alaska Native, 1 Asian American or Pacific Islander, 2 Hispanic Americans), 5 international. Average age 30. 218 applicants, 9% accepted, 18 enrolled. In 2009, 15 master's, 7 doctorates awarded. Terminal master's awarded for partial completion of doctoral program. *Degree requirements:* For master's, comprehensive exam; for doctorate, one foreign language, comprehensive exam, thesis/dissertation. *Entrance requirements:* For master's, GRE General Test, minimum GPA of 3.0; for doctorate, GRE General Test, GRE Subject Test, minimum GPA of 3.0. Additional exam requirements/recommendations for international students: Required—TOEFL (minimum score 550 paper-based; 213 computer-based; 79 iBT) or IELTS (minimum score 6.5). *Application deadline:* For fall admission, 5/15 priority date for domestic students, 5/15 for international students; for spring admission, 10/15 priority date for domestic students, 10/15 for international students. Applications are processed on a rolling basis. Application fee: $50 ($70 for international students). Electronic applications accepted. *Financial support:* In 2009–10, 82 students received support, including 1 fellowship with full tuition reimbursement available (averaging $19,109 per year), 3 research assistantships with partial tuition reimbursements available (averaging $16,333 per year), 74 teaching assistantships with partial tuition reimbursements available (averaging $16,547 per year); career-related internships or fieldwork, Federal Work-Study, traineeships, and health care benefits also available. Financial award application deadline: 2/1; financial award applicants required to submit FAFSA. *Faculty research:* American literature, British literature, cultural studies, rhetoric and composition, folklore. Total annual research expenditures: $152,193. *Unit head:* Dr. Richard Morland, Chair, 225-578-0812, Fax: 225-578-2214, E-mail: english@lsu.edu. *Application contact:* Dr. Sharon Weltman, Director of Graduate Studies, 225-578-0812, Fax: 225-578-4129, E-mail: egs@lsu.edu.

Loyola Marymount University, School of Film and Television, Department of Screenwriting, Program in Screen Writing, Los Angeles, CA 90045-8347. Offers MFA. *Faculty:* 4 full-time (3 women). *Students:* 27 full-time (10 women), 3 part-time (0 women); includes 8 minority (3 African Americans, 5 Hispanic Americans), 4 international. Average age 27. 50 applicants, 58% accepted, 12 enrolled. In 2009, 9 master's awarded. *Degree requirements:* For master's, thesis, project or script. *Entrance requirements:* For master's, GRE General Test, writing sample, 2 letters of recommendation. Additional exam requirements/recommendations for international students: Required—TOEFL (minimum score 600 paper-based; 250 computer-based; 100 iBT). *Application deadline:* For fall admission, 2/15 for domestic students. Application fee: $50. Electronic applications accepted. *Financial support:* In 2009–10, 28 students received support, including 1 research assistantship (averaging $480 per year); career-related internships or fieldwork and scholarships/grants also available. Support available to part-time students. Financial award application deadline: 6/1; financial award applicants required to submit FAFSA. *Unit head:* Jeffrey Davis, Acting Chair, 310-338-7834, E-mail: jdavis@lmu.edu. *Application contact:* Chake Kouyoumjian, Associate Dean of Graduate Admissions, 310-338-2721, Fax: 310-338-6086, E-mail: ckouyoum@lmu.edu.

Manhattanville College, Graduate Programs, Humanities and Social Sciences Programs, Program in Writing, Purchase, NY 10577-2132. Offers MA. Part-time and evening/weekend programs available. *Students:* 1 full-time (0 women), 41 part-time (26 women); includes 3 minority (1 Asian American or Pacific Islander, 2 Hispanic Americans). In 2009, 17 master's awarded. *Degree requirements:* For master's, thesis. *Entrance requirements:* For master's, interview, 2 letters of recommendation. Additional exam requirements/recommendations for international students: Required—TOEFL. *Application deadline:* Applications are processed on a rolling basis. Application fee: $70. *Financial support:* Career-related internships or fieldwork, Federal Work-Study, institutionally sponsored loans, and unspecified assistantships available. Financial award application deadline: 3/1; financial award applicants required to submit FAFSA. *Faculty research:* Published writers: fiction, poetry, essay. *Unit head:* Sr. Ruth M. Dowd, Dean Emeritus, 914-694-5483, Fax: 914-694-3488, E-mail: rdowd@mville.edu. *Application contact:* Office of Admissions for Graduate and Professional Studies, 914-323-5418, E-mail: gps@mville.edu.

Massachusetts Institute of Technology, School of Humanities, Arts, and Social Sciences, Program in Writing and Humanistic Studies, Cambridge, MA 02139-4307. Offers science writing (SM). *Faculty:* 9 full-time (2 women). *Students:* 7 full-time (4 women); includes 1 minority (Hispanic American), 1 international. Average age 25. 63 applicants, 29% accepted, 7 enrolled. In 2009, 7 master's awarded. *Degree requirements:* For master's, thesis, internship. *Entrance requirements:* For master's, GRE General Test. Additional exam requirements/recommendations for international students: Required—TOEFL (minimum score 600 paper-based; 250 computer-based), IELTS (minimum score 7.5). *Application deadline:* For fall admission, 1/15 for domestic and international students. Application fee: $75. Electronic applications accepted. *Expenses:* Tuition: Full-time $37,510; part-time $585 per unit. Required fees: $272. *Financial support:* In 2009–10, 7 students received support, including 7 fellowships with tuition reimbursements available; teaching assistantships with tuition reimbursements available, career-related internships or fieldwork, Federal Work-Study, institutionally sponsored loans, scholarships/grants, health care benefits, and unspecified assistantships also available. Total annual research expenditures: $74,000. *Unit head:* Prof. James Paradis, Head of Program, 617-253-7894, Fax: 617-253-6910. *Application contact:* Science Writing Graduate Admissions, 617-253-6668, Fax: 617-452-5100, E-mail: sciwrite-www@mit.edu.

McNeese State University, Doré School of Graduate Studies, College of Liberal Arts, Department of English and Foreign Languages, Program in Creative Writing, Lake Charles, LA 70609. Offers MFA. Evening/weekend programs available. *Faculty:* 15 full-time (9 women). *Students:* 20 full-time (9 women); includes 3 minority (2 African Americans, 1 Asian American or Pacific Islander). In 2009, 3 master's awarded. *Degree requirements:* For master's, thesis, public reading. *Entrance requirements:* For master's, GRE, writing sample. *Application deadline:* For fall admission, 5/15 priority date for domestic and international students; for spring admission, 10/15 priority date for domestic and international students. Applications are processed on a rolling basis. Application fee: $20 ($30 for international students). *Expenses:* Tuition, area resident: Full-time $2556. Tuition, state resident: full-time $2556. Required fees: $1031. Tuition and fees vary according to course load. *Financial support:* Teaching assistantships available. Financial award application deadline: 5/1. *Unit head:* Dr. Jacob D. Blevins, Head, 337-475-5325, Fax: 337-475-5327, E-mail: jblevins@mcneese.edu. *Application contact:* Dr. George F. Mead, Interim Dean of Dore' School of Graduate Studies, 337-475-5396, Fax: 337-475-5397, E-mail: admissions@mcneese.edu.

Michigan State University, The Graduate School, College of Arts and Letters, Program in Rhetoric and Writing, East Lansing, MI 48824. Offers critical studies in literacy and pedagogy (MA); digital rhetoric and professional writing (MA); rhetoric and writing (PhD). *Students:* 38 full-time (24 women), 15 part-time (8 women); includes 12 minority (5 African Americans, 1 Asian American or Pacific Islander, 6 Hispanic Americans), 3 international. Average age 31. 61 applicants, 16% accepted. In 2009, 6 master's, 7 doctorates awarded. *Entrance requirements:* Additional exam requirements/recommendations for international students: Required—TOEFL. Electronic applications accepted. *Expenses:* Tuition, state resident: part-time $478.25 per credit hour. Tuition, nonresident: part-time $966.50 per credit hour. Part-time tuition and fees vary according to program. *Financial support:* In 2009–10, 6 research assistantships with tuition reimbursements (averaging $6,452 per year), 30 teaching assistantships with tuition reimbursements (averaging $6,159 per year) were awarded. *Faculty research:* Rhetoric, writing and communication studies; media studies; technical communication, writing for digital environments. *Unit head:* Dr. Malea E. Powell, Director, Graduate Studies, 517-432-2583, Fax: 517-353-9162, E-mail: powell37@msu.edu. *Application contact:* Melissa Arthurton, Program Secretary, 517-353-9183, Fax: 517-353-9162, E-mail: arthurt1@msu.edu.

Mills College, Graduate Studies, Department of English, Oakland, CA 94613-1000. Offers book art and creative writing (MFA); creative writing, poetry (MFA); creative writing, prose (MFA); English and American literature (MA). Part-time programs available. *Faculty:* 10 full-time (8 women), 16 part-time/adjunct (13 women). *Students:* 92 full-time (71 women), 5 part-time (4 women); includes 26 minority (11 African Americans, 1 American Indian/Alaska Native, 8 Asian Americans or Pacific Islanders, 6 Hispanic Americans). Average age 31. 176 applicants, 85% accepted, 42 enrolled. In 2009, 63 master's awarded. *Degree requirements:* For master's, comprehensive exam, thesis. *Entrance requirements:* For master's, manuscript, writing sample. Additional exam requirements/recommendations for international students: Required—TOEFL. *Application deadline:* For fall admission, 2/1 priority date for domestic students; for spring admission, 11/1 for domestic students. Applications are processed on a rolling basis. Application fee: $50. Electronic applications accepted. *Expenses:* Tuition: Full-time $26,326; part-time $6584 per course. Required fees: $896. One-time fee: $896 part-time. Tuition and fees vary according to program. *Financial support:* In 2009–10, 85 students received support, including 85 fellowships (averaging $7,587 per year), 35 teaching assistantships with partial tuition reimbursements available (averaging $2,667 per year); scholarships/grants also available. Support available to part-time students. Financial award application deadline: 2/1; financial award applicants required to submit FAFSA. *Faculty research:* Creative writing, African-American literature, Victorian women writers, theories of sexuality, Shakespeare. *Unit head:* Dr. Cynthia Scheinberg, Chair, 510-430-2213, E-mail: cyns@mills.edu. *Application contact:* Jessica King, Graduate Admission Specialist, 510-430-3305, Fax: 510-430-2159, E-mail: grad-studies@mills.edu.

Minnesota State University Mankato, College of Graduate Studies, College of Arts and Humanities, Department of English, Mankato, MN 56001. Offers creative writing (MFA); English (MAT); English studies (MA); literature (MA); teaching English as a second language (MA, Certificate); technical communication (MA, Certificate). Part-time programs available. *Students:* 54 full-time (34 women), 114 part-time (78 women). *Degree requirements:* For master's, one foreign language, comprehensive exam, thesis or alternative. *Entrance requirements:* For master's, minimum GPA of 3.0 during previous 2 years, writing sample (MFA). Additional exam requirements/recommendations for international students: Required—TOEFL. *Application deadline:* Applications are processed on a rolling basis. Application fee: $40. Electronic applications accepted. *Expenses:* Tuition, state resident: full-time $5364. Tuition, nonresident: full-time $8314. *Financial support:* Research assistantships with full tuition reimbursements, teaching assistantships with full tuition reimbursements, career-related internships or fieldwork, Federal Work-Study, and unspecified assistantships available. Financial award application deadline: 3/15; financial award applicants required to submit FAFSA. *Faculty research:* Keats and Christianity. *Unit head:* Dr. John Banschbach, Chairperson, 507-389-2117. *Application contact:* 507-389-2321, E-mail: grad@mnsu.edu.

Minnesota State University Moorhead, Graduate Studies, College of Arts and Humanities, Program in Creative Writing, Moorhead, MN 56563-0002. Offers MFA. Part-time programs available. *Degree requirements:* For master's, thesis, final manuscript, final oral exam. *Entrance requirements:* For master's, manuscript, minimum GPA of 2.75, 3 letters of recommendation. Additional exam requirements/recommendations for international students: Required—TOEFL (minimum score 550 paper-based; 213 computer-based). Electronic applications accepted.

Monmouth University, Graduate School, Department of English, West Long Branch, NJ 07764-1898. Offers creative writing (MA); New Jersey studies (MA); rhetoric and writing (MA). Part-time and evening/weekend programs available. *Faculty:* 11 full-time (8 women). *Students:* 7 full-time (5 women), 26 part-time (20 women); includes 2 minority (1 African American, 1 Hispanic American). Average age 35. 22 applicants, 95% accepted, 10 enrolled. In 2009, 14 master's awarded. *Degree requirements:* For master's, comprehensive exam (for some programs), thesis (for some programs). *Entrance requirements:* For master's, minimum overall GPA of 2.75, at least 15 credits in literary studies. Additional exam requirements/recommendations for international students: Required—TOEFL (minimum score 550 paper-based; 213 computer-based; 79 iBT), IELTS (minimum score 5), Michigan English Language Assessment Battery (minimum score 77), Cambridge A, B, C. *Application deadline:* For fall admission, 7/15 for domestic students, 6/1 for international students; for spring admission, 11/15 for domestic students, 11/1 for international students. Application fee: $50. *Expenses:* Tuition: Part-time $773 per credit. Required fees: $157 per semester. *Financial support:* In 2009–10, 28 students received support, including 20 fellowships (averaging $1,891 per year), 4 research assistantships (averaging $3,334 per year); career-related internships or fieldwork, scholarships/grants, and unspecified assistantships also available. Support available to part-time students. Financial award applicants required to submit FAFSA. *Faculty research:* Renaissance and medieval literature, nineteenth century American literature, eighteenth century British literature and women's studies, Old English and Middle English, African diaspora and African post-colonial literature. *Unit head:* Dr. Hiede Estes, Program Director, 732-571-7547, E-mail: hestes@monmouth.edu. *Application contact:* Kevin Roane, Director, Office of Graduate Admission, 732-571-3452, Fax: 732-263-5123, E-mail: gradadm@monmouth.edu.

Murray State University, College of Humanities and Fine Arts, Department of English and Philosophy, Program in Creative Writing, Murray, KY 42071. Offers MFA.

Naropa University, Graduate Programs, Program in Creative Writing, Boulder, CO 80302-6697. Offers MFA. Program is offered online only. Part-time and evening/weekend programs available. Postbaccalaureate distance learning degree programs offered (minimal on-campus study). *Degree requirements:* For master's, manuscript. *Entrance requirements:* For master's, manuscript/writing sample; resume, 3 letters of recommendation, letter of interest, technology check list. Additional exam requirements/recommendations for international students: Required—TOEFL (minimum score 600 paper-based; 250 computer-based). Electronic applications accepted.

Naropa University, Graduate Programs, Program in Writing and Poetics, Boulder, CO 80302-6697. Offers MFA. *Degree requirements:* For master's, thesis. *Entrance requirements:* For master's, manuscript; resume, 3 letters of recommendation. Additional exam requirements/recommendations for international students: Required—TOEFL (minimum score 600 paper-based; 250 computer-based). Electronic applications accepted.

National-Louis University, College of Arts and Sciences, Program in Written Communication, Chicago, IL 60603. Offers corporate written communication (Certificate); written communication (MS). Part-time programs available. *Degree requirements:* For master's, thesis. *Entrance requirements:* For master's, GRE General Test, MAT, or Watson-Glaser Critical Thinking Appraisal, interview, minimum GPA of 3.0. *Expenses:* Tuition: Full-time $17,160; part-time $715 per semester hour. Tuition and fees vary according to course load, degree level, campus/location and program.

National University, Academic Affairs, College of Letters and Sciences, Department of Art and Humanities, La Jolla, CA 92037-1011. Offers creative writing (MFA); English (MA); history

Writing

National University (continued)

(MA). Part-time and evening/weekend programs available. Postbaccalaureate distance learning degree programs offered (no on-campus study). *Faculty:* 13 full-time (4 women), 24 part-time/adjunct (15 women). *Students:* 204 full-time (144 women), 499 part-time (340 women); includes 160 minority (77 African Americans, 6 American Indian/Alaska Native, 17 Asian Americans or Pacific Islanders, 60 Hispanic Americans). Average age 38. 440 applicants, 100% accepted, 280 enrolled. In 2009, 152 master's awarded. *Degree requirements:* For master's, thesis (for some programs). *Entrance requirements:* For master's, interview, minimum GPA of 2.5. Additional exam requirements/recommendations for international students: Required—TOEFL (minimum score 550 paper-based; 213 computer-based; 79 iBT), IELTS (minimum score 6). *Application deadline:* Applications are processed on a rolling basis. Application fee: $60 ($65 for international students). Electronic applications accepted. *Expenses:* Tuition: Part-time $338 per quarter hour. *Financial support:* Career-related internships or fieldwork, institutionally sponsored loans, scholarships/grants, and tuition waivers (partial) available. Support available to part-time students. Financial award application deadline: 6/30; financial award applicants required to submit FAFSA. *Unit head:* Dr. Janet Baker, Chair, 858-642-8472, Fax: 858-642-8715, E-mail: jbaker@nu.edu. *Application contact:* Dominick Giovanniello, Associate Regional Dean—San Diego, 800-NAT-UNIV, Fax: 858-541-7792, E-mail: dgiovann@nu.edu.

New England College, Programs in Writing, Henniker, NH 03242-3293. Offers poetry (MFA); professional writing (MA). Part-time and evening/weekend programs available. Electronic applications accepted. *Faculty research:* Poetry collections.

New Mexico Highlands University, Graduate Studies, College of Arts and Sciences, Department of Humanities, Las Vegas, NM 87701. Offers English (MA), including creative writing, language, rhetoric and composition, literature. *Degree requirements:* For master's, comprehensive exam, thesis. *Entrance requirements:* For master's, minimum undergraduate GPA of 3.0. Additional exam requirements/recommendations for international students: Required—TOEFL (minimum score 540 paper-based; 207 computer-based). *Faculty research:* 20th century literature, life path writing in homeless shelters, native American philosophy, medieval intellectual and cultural history, creating pedagogical tools for teaching law.

New Mexico State University, Graduate School, College of Arts and Sciences, Department of English, Las Cruces, NM 88003-8001. Offers creative writing (MFA); English (MA); rhetoric and professional communication (PhD). Part-time programs available. *Faculty:* 26 full-time (15 women). *Students:* 81 full-time (45 women), 35 part-time (19 women); includes 23 minority (4 African Americans, 3 Asian Americans or Pacific Islanders, 16 Hispanic Americans), 7 international. Average age 32. 89 applicants, 66% accepted, 26 enrolled. In 2009, 27 master's awarded. *Degree requirements:* For master's, one foreign language, thesis (for some programs); for doctorate, comprehensive exam, thesis/dissertation, internship. *Entrance requirements:* For master's and doctorate, sample of written work. *Application deadline:* For fall admission, 2/1 for domestic and international students. Application fee: $30 ($50 for international students). Electronic applications accepted. *Expenses:* Tuition, state resident: full-time $4080; part-time $223 per credit. Tuition, nonresident: full-time $14,256; part-time $647 per credit. Required fees: $1278; $639 per semester. *Financial support:* In 2009–10, 2 research assistantships (averaging $7,900 per year), 55 teaching assistantships (averaging $15,193 per year) were awarded; fellowships, career-related internships or fieldwork, Federal Work-Study, institutionally sponsored loans, scholarships/grants, health care benefits, and unspecified assistantships also available. Financial award application deadline: 2/1; financial award applicants required to submit FAFSA. *Faculty research:* Composition research, history and theory of rhetoric, technical/professional communication, creative writing, English and American literature. *Unit head:* Dr. Monica F. Torres, Head, 575-646-2319, Fax: 575-646-7725, E-mail: mftorres@nmsu.edu. *Application contact:* Dr. Elizabeth Schirmer, Director of Graduate Studies, 575-646-1733, E-mail: eschirme@nmsu.edu.

The New School: A University, The New School for General Studies, Program in Creative Writing, New York, NY 10011. Offers MFA. Evening/weekend programs available. *Faculty:* 6 full-time (2 women). *Students:* 205 full-time (132 women), 9 part-time (8 women); includes 39 minority (11 African Americans, 4 American Indian/Alaska Native, 8 Asian Americans or Pacific Islanders, 16 Hispanic Americans), 5 international. Average age 28. 658 applicants, 38% accepted, 106 enrolled. In 2009, 104 master's awarded. *Degree requirements:* For master's, thesis, literature project. *Entrance requirements:* For master's, portfolio. Additional exam requirements/recommendations for international students: Required—TOEFL (minimum score 600 paper-based; 250 computer-based; 100 iBT). *Application deadline:* For fall admission, 1/15 priority date for domestic and international students. Applications are processed on a rolling basis. Application fee: $50. Electronic applications accepted. *Expenses:* Contact institution. *Financial support:* Federal Work-Study, scholarships/grants, and tuition waivers (partial) available. Support available to part-time students. Financial award application deadline: 3/1; financial award applicants required to submit FAFSA. *Unit head:* Dr. Robert Polito, Director, 212-229-5611, Fax: 212-645-0661, E-mail: politor@newschool.edu. *Application contact:* Robert Macdonald, Director of Admissions, 212-229-5710 Ext. 3007, Fax: 212-989-3887, E-mail: macdonar@newschool.edu.

New York University, Graduate School of Arts and Science, Department of English, Program in Creative Writing, New York, NY 10012-1019. Offers MA, MFA. Part-time and evening/weekend programs available. *Students:* 88 full-time (53 women), 18 part-time (7 women); includes 9 minority (2 African Americans, 6 Asian Americans or Pacific Islanders, 1 Hispanic American), 9 international. Average age 28. 678 applicants, 13% accepted, 53 enrolled. In 2009, 38 master's awarded. *Degree requirements:* For master's, one foreign language, thesis or alternative. *Entrance requirements:* For master's, GRE General Test, sample of written work. Additional exam requirements/recommendations for international students: Required—TOEFL. *Application deadline:* For fall admission, 12/18 for domestic students. Application fee: $90. *Expenses:* Tuition: Full-time $30,528; part-time $1272 per credit. Required fees: $2177. *Financial support:* Fellowships with tuition reimbursements, teaching assistantships with tuition reimbursements, Federal Work-Study, institutionally sponsored loans, scholarships/grants, health care benefits, tuition waivers (full and partial), and unspecified assistantships available. Financial award application deadline: 12/18; financial award applicants required to submit FAFSA. *Faculty research:* Fiction, poetry. *Unit head:* Deborah Landau, Director, 212-998-9916, Fax: 212-995-4864, E-mail: creative.writing@nyu.edu. *Application contact:* Jessica Flynn, Program Coordinator, 212-998-8816, Fax: 212-995-4864, E-mail: creative.writing@nyu.edu.

New York University, NYU in Madrid, Madrid, NY 10012-1019, Spain. Offers creative writing in Spanish (MFA); Spanish (PhD); Spanish and Latin American literatures and cultures (MA); Spanish language and translation (MA). *Students:* 27 full-time (23 women), 1 part-time (0 women); includes 8 minority (2 African Americans, 1 Asian American or Pacific Islander, 5 Hispanic Americans), 1 international. Average age 26. 73 applicants, 90% accepted, 27 enrolled. In 2009, 22 master's awarded. Application fee: $90. *Expenses:* Tuition: Full-time $30,528; part-time $1272 per credit. Required fees: $2177. *Unit head:* Judith Nemethy, Director, 212-998-8770, Fax: 212-995-4149, E-mail: nyu-in-madrid@nyu.edu. *Application contact:* Judith Nemethy, Director, 212-998-8770, Fax: 212-995-4149, E-mail: nyu-in-madrid@nyu.edu.

New York University, Tisch School of the Arts Asia, Singapore, NY 248923, Singapore. Offers animation and digital arts (MFA); dramatic writing (MFA); film production (MFA). *Entrance requirements:* Additional exam requirements/recommendations for international students: Required—TOEFL (minimum score 610 paper-based; 250 computer-based; 105 iBT). Electronic applications accepted. *Expenses:* Tuition: Full-time $30,528; part-time $1272 per credit. Required fees: $2177.

New York University, Tisch School of the Arts, Rita and Burton Goldberg Department of Dramatic Writing, New York, NY 10012-1019. Offers MFA. *Faculty:* 15 full-time, 16 part-time/adjunct. *Students:* 41 full-time (17 women); includes 12 minority (6 African Americans, 4 Asian Americans or Pacific Islanders, 2 Hispanic Americans). Average age 30. 238 applicants, 15% accepted, 22 enrolled. In 2009, 20 master's awarded. *Degree requirements:* For master's, thesis, play or screenplay, internship. *Entrance requirements:* For master's, writing sample. Additional exam requirements/recommendations for international students: Required—TOEFL, IELTS or ALI. *Application deadline:* For fall admission, 12/1 for domestic and international students. Application fee: $60. Electronic applications accepted. *Expenses:* Tuition: Full-time $30,528; part-time $1272 per credit. Required fees: $2177. *Financial support:* In 2009–10, 19 students received support, including 5 fellowships with full and partial tuition reimbursements available; career-related internships or fieldwork, Federal Work-Study, institutionally sponsored loans, and scholarships/grants also available. Financial award application deadline: 2/15; financial award applicants required to submit FAFSA. *Faculty research:* Craft of screenwriting film story analysis, production elements in film and theatre. *Unit head:* Richard Wesley, Chair, 212-998-1940, Fax: 212-995-4069. *Application contact:* Dan Sandford, Director of Graduate Admissions, 212-998-1918, Fax: 212-995-4060, E-mail: tisch.gradadmissions@nyu.edu.

North Carolina State University, Graduate School, College of Humanities and Social Sciences, Department of English, Program in Creative Writing, Raleigh, NC 27695. Offers MFA. *Degree requirements:* For master's, thesis optional. *Entrance requirements:* For master's, GRE. Electronic applications accepted. *Faculty research:* Science fiction, Asian poetry, translation, Southern writers, satiric fiction.

Northeastern Illinois University, Graduate College, College of Arts and Sciences, Department of English, Programs in English, Chicago, IL 60625-4699. Offers composition/writing (MA); literature (MA). Part-time and evening/weekend programs available. *Degree requirements:* For master's, comprehensive exam, thesis optional. *Entrance requirements:* For master's, 30 hours of undergraduate course work in literature and composition (literature), BA in English or approval (composition/writing), minimum GPA of 2.75. Additional exam requirements/recommendations for international students: Required—TOEFL (minimum score 550 paper-based; 213 computer-based; 80 iBT). Electronic applications accepted. *Faculty research:* Arthurian literature, Southern American literature, rhetoric and theories of authorship.

Northern Arizona University, Graduate College, College of Arts and Letters, Department of English, Program in English, Flagstaff, AZ 86011. Offers creative writing (MA); English education (MA); general English studies (MA); literacy, technology and professional writing (MA); literature (MA). *Faculty:* 40 full-time (24 women). *Students:* 87 full-time (59 women), 94 part-time (70 women); includes 20 minority (6 African Americans, 6 American Indian/Alaska Native, 3 Asian Americans or Pacific Islanders, 5 Hispanic Americans), 1 international. Average age 31. 99 applicants, 66% accepted, 45 enrolled. In 2009, 77 master's awarded. *Degree requirements:* For master's, thesis (for some programs), departmental qualifying exam. *Entrance requirements:* For master's, minimum GPA of 3.0 or GRE. Additional exam requirements/recommendations for international students: Required—TOEFL (minimum score 550 paper-based; 213 computer-based; 80 iBT), IELTS (minimum score 7), or a bachelor's degree from an English-speaking university and demonstrated proficiency. *Application deadline:* For fall admission, 2/15 priority date for domestic students, 9/1 priority date for international students; for winter admission, 4/15 priority date for domestic students; for spring admission, 11/15 priority date for domestic students. Applications are processed on a rolling basis. Application fee: $65. Electronic applications accepted. *Financial support:* In 2009–10, 63 teaching assistantships with partial tuition reimbursements (averaging $11,623 per year) were awarded; Federal Work-Study, scholarships/grants, health care benefits, and unspecified assistantships also available. Support available to part-time students. Financial award application deadline: 3/30; financial award applicants required to submit FAFSA. *Unit head:* Dr. Allen Woodman, Chair, 928-523-5651, Fax: 928-523-7074, E-mail: allen.woodman@nau.edu. *Application contact:* Barbara Hanks, 928-523-4911, Fax: 928-523-7074, E-mail: barbara.hanks@nau.edu.

Northern Kentucky University, Office of Graduate Programs, College of Arts and Sciences, Program in English, Highland Heights, KY 41099. Offers composition and rhetoric (Certificate); English (MA); professional writing (Certificate). Part-time and evening/weekend programs available. *Students:* 7 full-time (4 women), 49 part-time (36 women); includes 3 minority (2 African Americans, 1 Hispanic American). Average age 33. 49 applicants, 76% accepted, 32 enrolled. *Degree requirements:* For master's, comprehensive exam or thesis. *Entrance requirements:* For master's, minimum GPA of 3.0, two letters of reference. Additional exam requirements/recommendations for international students: Required—TOEFL (minimum score 550 paper-based; 213 computer-based; 79 iBT); Recommended—IELTS (minimum score 6.5). *Application deadline:* For fall admission, 7/1 priority date for domestic students, 6/1 priority date for international students; for spring admission, 11/1 for domestic students, 10/1 for international students. Applications are processed on a rolling basis. Application fee: $40. Electronic applications accepted. *Expenses:* Tuition, state resident: full-time $6912; part-time $384 per credit hour. Tuition, nonresident: full-time $12,150; part-time $675 per credit hour. Tuition and fees vary according to course load, program and reciprocity agreements. *Financial support:* Unspecified assistantships available. Financial award applicants required to submit FAFSA. *Faculty research:* Professional writing and new media studies, composition and rhetoric, literary studies, creative writing, cinema studies. *Unit head:* Dr. Roxanne Kent-Drury, Coordinator, 859-572-6636, E-mail: rkdrury@nku.edu. *Application contact:* Dr. Peg Griffin, Director of Graduate Programs, 859-572-6934, Fax: 859-572-6670, E-mail: griffinp@nku.edu.

Northern Michigan University, College of Graduate Studies, College of Arts and Sciences, Department of English, Marquette, MI 49855-5301. Offers creative writing (MFA); literature (MA); pedagogy (MA); writing (MA). Part-time programs available. *Degree requirements:* For master's, thesis or alternative. *Entrance requirements:* For master's, minimum GPA of 2.75.

Northwestern University, Medill School of Journalism, Evanston, IL 60208. Offers broadcast journalism (MSJ); integrated marketing communications (MSIMC), including advertising/sales promotion, direct database and e-commerce marketing, general studies, public relations; magazine publishing (MSJ); new media (MSJ); reporting and writing (MSJ). *Accreditation:* ACEJMC (one or more programs are accredited). *Entrance requirements:* For master's, GRE General Test, GMAT or LSAT (MSJ). Additional exam requirements/recommendations for international students: Required—TOEFL. Electronic applications accepted. *Expenses:* Contact institution. *Faculty research:* Web business journalism, cultural stereotypes, voter apathy, digital television.

Northwestern University, School of Continuing Studies, Program in Creative Writing, Evanston, IL 60208. Offers MA, MFA.

Oklahoma City University, Petree College of Arts and Sciences, Program in Liberal Arts, Oklahoma City, OK 73106-1402. Offers art (MLA); general studies (MLA); leadership/management (MLA); literature (MLA); mass communications (MLA); philosophy (MLA); writing (MLA). Part-time and evening/weekend programs available. *Faculty:* 23 full-time (6 women), 5 part-time/adjunct (3 women). *Students:* 50 full-time (24 women), 23 part-time (14 women); includes 6 minority (4 African Americans, 1 Asian American or Pacific Islander, 1 Hispanic American), 50 international. Average age 31. 31 applicants, 94% accepted, 15 enrolled. In 2009, 21 master's awarded. *Degree requirements:* For master's, comprehensive exam, thesis optional. *Entrance requirements:* Additional exam requirements/recommendations for international students: Required—TOEFL (minimum score 550 paper-based). *Application deadline:* For fall admission, 8/20 for domestic students; for spring admission, 1/6 for domestic students. Applications are processed on a rolling basis. Application fee: $50 ($70 for international students). *Expenses:* Tuition: Full-time $15,930; part-time $885 per hour. *Financial support:* Fellowships with partial tuition reimbursements, career-related internships or fieldwork, Federal Work-Study, and tuition waivers (partial) available. Support available to part-time students. Financial award application deadline: 8/1; financial award applicants required to submit FAFSA. *Unit head:* Dr. Regina Bennett, Director, 405-208-5207, Fax: 405-208-5451, E-mail: rbennett@okcu.edu. *Application contact:* Michelle Lockhart, Director, Admissions, 800-633-7242, Fax: 405-208-5916, E-mail: gadmissions@okcu.edu.

Oklahoma State University, College of Arts and Sciences, Department of English, Stillwater, OK 74078. Offers creative writing (MFA); English (MA, PhD). *Faculty:* 50 full-time (31 women), 2 part-time/adjunct (both women). *Students:* 15 full-time (9 women), 134 part-time (72 women);

includes 15 minority (4 African Americans, 9 American Indian/Alaska Native, 1 Asian American or Pacific Islander, 1 Hispanic American), 21 international. Average age 32. 130 applicants, 49% accepted, 37 enrolled. In 2009, 15 master's, 7 doctorates awarded. *Degree requirements:* For master's, comprehensive exam, thesis; for doctorate, comprehensive exam, thesis/dissertation. *Entrance requirements:* For master's, GRE General Test, minimum GPA of 3.0, writing sample; for doctorate, GRE General Test, minimum GPA of 3.5, writing sample. Additional exam requirements/recommendations for international students: Required—TOEFL (minimum score 550 paper-based; 79 iBT). *Application deadline:* For fall admission, 3/1 priority date for international students; for spring admission, 8/1 priority date for international students. Applications are processed on a rolling basis. Application fee: $40 ($75 for international students). Electronic applications accepted. *Expenses:* Tuition, state resident: full-time $3716; part-time $154.85 per credit hour. Tuition, nonresident: full-time $14,448; part-time $602 per credit hour. Required fees: $1772; $73.85 per credit hour. One-time fee: $50. Tuition and fees vary according to course load and campus/location. *Financial support:* In 2009–10, 3 research assistantships (averaging $11,313 per year), 97 teaching assistantships (averaging $14,184 per year) were awarded; career-related internships or fieldwork, Federal Work-Study, scholarships/grants, health care benefits, tuition waivers (partial), and unspecified assistantships also available. Support available to part-time students. Financial award application deadline: 3/1; financial award applicants required to submit FAFSA. *Faculty research:* American and British novels, poetry, and autobiography; Native American languages and literature; institutional history of American film, history, and adaptations; rhetoric and theories of human communication; learning strategies of second language learners. *Unit head:* Dr. Carol Moder, Head, 405-744-9474, Fax: 405-744-6326. *Application contact:* Dr. Gordon Emslie, Dean, 405-744-6368, Fax: 405-744-0355, E-mail: grad-i@okstate.edu.

Old Dominion University, College of Arts and Letters, MFA Program in Creative Writing, Norfolk, VA 23529. Offers MFA. Part-time programs available. *Faculty:* 6 full-time (3 women), 1 part-time/adjunct (0 women). *Students:* 20 full-time (13 women), 10 part-time (7 women); includes 1 minority (African American). Average age 34. 56 applicants, 55% accepted, 12 enrolled. In 2009, 11 master's awarded. *Degree requirements:* For master's, comprehensive exam, thesis. *Entrance requirements:* For master's, GRE General Test, 24 hours previous course work in English, sample of written work. Additional exam requirements/recommendations for international students: Required—TOEFL. *Application deadline:* For fall admission, 2/15 for domestic students. Application fee: $40. Electronic applications accepted. *Expenses:* Tuition, state resident: full-time $8112; part-time $338 per credit. Tuition, nonresident: full-time $20,256; part-time $844 per credit. Required fees: $119 per semester. One-time fee: $50. *Financial support:* In 2009–10, 13 students received support, including 2 fellowships with tuition reimbursements available (averaging $13,000 per year), 3 research assistantships with tuition reimbursements available (averaging $10,000 per year), 8 teaching assistantships with tuition reimbursements available (averaging $10,000 per year); scholarships/grants and unspecified assistantships also available. Financial award application deadline: 2/15. *Faculty research:* Literary fiction, nonfiction, poetry. Total annual research expenditures: $35,000. *Unit head:* Dr. Luisa Igloria, Graduate Program Director, 757-683-3929, Fax: 757-683-3241, E-mail: cwgpd@odu.edu. *Application contact:* Dr. Robert Wojtowicz, Associate Dean, 757-683-6077, Fax: 757-683-5746, E-mail: rwojtowi@odu.edu.

Otis College of Art and Design, Program in Writing, Los Angeles, CA 90045-9785. Offers MFA. *Faculty:* 2 full-time (1 woman), 11 part-time/adjunct (3 women). *Students:* 17 full-time (14 women), 13 part-time (11 women); includes 11 minority (5 African Americans, 2 Asian Americans or Pacific Islanders, 4 Hispanic Americans), 1 international. Average age 34. 47 applicants, 38% accepted, 6 enrolled. In 2009, 6 master's awarded. *Degree requirements:* For master's, thesis. *Entrance requirements:* For master's, writing sample. *Application deadline:* For fall admission, 2/1 for domestic and international students; for spring admission, 11/1 for domestic and international students. Application fee: $50. Electronic applications accepted. *Expenses:* Tuition: Full-time $33,200. Required fees: $700. *Financial support:* Federal Work-Study, scholarships/grants, and tuition waivers (partial) available. Financial award applicants required to submit FAFSA. *Unit head:* Paul Vangelisti, Chair, 310-665-6891, Fax: 310-665-6890, E-mail: pvangel@otis.edu. *Application contact:* Information Contact, 310-665-6820, Fax: 310-665-6821, E-mail: admissions@otis.edu.

Our Lady of the Lake University of San Antonio, College of Arts and Sciences, Program in English, San Antonio, TX 78207-4689. Offers communication arts (MA); English and literature (MA); English education (MA); writing (MA). Part-time and evening/weekend programs available. *Students:* 9 full-time (5 women), 15 part-time (14 women); includes 16 minority (all Hispanic Americans). Average age 31. In 2009, 15 master's awarded. *Degree requirements:* For master's, comprehensive exam, thesis optional. *Entrance requirements:* For master's, GRE General Test or MAT, minimum GPA of 3.0 in last 60 hours, 2.5 overall. Additional exam requirements/recommendations for international students: Required—TOEFL. *Application deadline:* Applications are processed on a rolling basis. Application fee: $25 ($50 for international students). Electronic applications accepted. *Expenses:* Tuition: Full-time $12,330; part-time $685 per contact hour. Required fees: $139; $12 per contact hour. $57 per semester. Tuition and fees vary according to campus/location. *Financial support:* Research assistantships, teaching assistantships, career-related internships or fieldwork, Federal Work-Study, institutionally sponsored loans, and tuition waivers (partial) available. Financial award application deadline: 4/15. *Faculty research:* Writing theory and research, contemporary Southern literature, popular culture, poetry, literature of the Southwest. *Unit head:* Dr. Michael Lueker, Chair, 210-434-6711 Ext. 2242, E-mail: luekm@lake.ollusa.edu. *Application contact:* 210-434-6711, Fax: 210-431-4036, E-mail: gradadm@lake.ollusa.edu.

Pacific Lutheran University, Division of Graduate Studies, Division of Humanities, Tacoma, WA 98447. Offers creative writing (MFA). Offered during summer only. Part-time programs available. *Faculty:* 1 part-time/adjunct (0 women). *Students:* 53 part-time (40 women); includes 3 minority (2 American Indian/Alaska Native, 1 Asian American or Pacific Islander). Average age 42. In 2009, 13 master's awarded. *Degree requirements:* For master's, thesis, final residency including teaching class. *Entrance requirements:* For master's, portfolio, book review. Additional exam requirements/recommendations for international students: Required—TOEFL. *Application deadline:* For winter admission, 2/15 for domestic and international students. Application fee: $40. Electronic applications accepted. *Expenses:* Contact institution. *Financial support:* Fellowships, unspecified assistantships available. Financial award application deadline: 3/1; financial award applicants required to submit FAFSA. *Unit head:* Dr. Douglas E. Oakman, Dean, 253-535-7317, Fax: 253-536-7132, E-mail: oakmande@plu.edu. *Application contact:* Stan Sanvel Rubin, Director of MFA in Creative Writing Program, 253-535-7221, E-mail: mfa@plu.edu.

Pacific University, Program in Writing, Forest Grove, OR 97116-1797. Offers MFA. Part-time programs available.

Penn State University Park, Graduate School, College of the Liberal Arts, Department of English, State College, University Park, PA 16802-1503. Offers MA, MFA, PhD.

Purdue University, Graduate School, College of Liberal Arts, Department of English, West Lafayette, IN 47907. Offers creative writing (MFA); literature (MA, PhD), including linguistics, literature and philosophy (PhD), rhetoric and composition, theory and cultural studies (PhD). Part-time programs available. *Degree requirements:* For master's, one foreign language; for doctorate, one foreign language, thesis/dissertation. *Entrance requirements:* For master's and doctorate, GRE General Test, sample of written work. Additional exam requirements/recommendations for international students: Required—TOEFL. Electronic applications accepted. *Faculty research:* Cultural studies, postmodern narrative, contemporary women writers, composition theory, slave narratives.

Queens College of the City University of New York, Division of Graduate Studies, Arts and Humanities Division, Department of English, Flushing, NY 11367-1597. Offers creative writing (MA); English language and literature (MA). Part-time and evening/weekend programs available. *Faculty:* 53 full-time (25 women). *Students:* 2 full-time (1 woman), 118 part-time (81 women). 158 applicants, 38% accepted, 38 enrolled. In 2009, 47 master's awarded. *Degree requirements:* For master's, one foreign language, thesis (for some programs), oral exam (English language and literature). *Entrance requirements:* For master's, manuscript (creative writing), minimum GPA of 3.0. Additional exam requirements/recommendations for international students: Required—TOEFL. *Application deadline:* For fall admission, 4/1 for domestic students; for spring admission, 11/1 for domestic students. Applications are processed on a rolling basis. Application fee: $125. *Expenses:* Tuition, state resident: full-time $7360; part-time $310 per credit. Tuition, nonresident: part-time $575 per credit. One-time fee: $195.25 full-time; $145.25 part-time. *Financial support:* Career-related internships or fieldwork, Federal Work-Study, institutionally sponsored loans, and tuition waivers (partial) available. Support available to part-time students. Financial award application deadline: 4/1; financial award applicants required to submit FAFSA. *Unit head:* Dr. Nancy Comley, Chairperson, 718-997-4600, E-mail: nancy_comley@qc.edu. *Application contact:* Dr. Talia Schaffer, Graduate Adviser, 718-997-4600, E-mail: talia_schaffer@qc.edu.

Queens University of Charlotte, College of Arts and Sciences, Charlotte, NC 28274-0002. Offers creative writing (MFA). Part-time programs available. Postbaccalaureate distance learning degree programs offered (minimal on-campus study). Electronic applications accepted.

Rhode Island College, School of Graduate Studies, Faculty of Arts and Sciences, Department of English, Providence, RI 02908-1991. Offers creative writing (MA); English (MA). Part-time and evening/weekend programs available. *Faculty:* 9 full-time (7 women). *Students:* 3 full-time (all women), 17 part-time (11 women). Average age 35. In 2009, 6 master's awarded. *Degree requirements:* For master's, thesis (for some programs). *Entrance requirements:* For master's, GRE General Test, 3 letters of recommendation, interview. Additional exam requirements/recommendations for international students: Recommended—TOEFL (minimum score 550 paper-based; 213 computer-based; 79 iBT). *Application deadline:* For fall admission, 4/1 for domestic students; for spring admission, 11/1 for domestic students. Applications are processed on a rolling basis. Application fee: $50. *Expenses:* Tuition, state resident: full-time $7440; part-time $310 per credit hour. Tuition, nonresident: full-time $14,784; part-time $616 per credit hour. Required fees: $552; $20 per credit. $70 per term. *Financial support:* Teaching assistantships with full tuition reimbursements, career-related internships or fieldwork, Federal Work-Study, scholarships/grants, health care benefits, and unspecified assistantships available. Support available to part-time students. Financial award application deadline: 5/15; financial award applicants required to submit FAFSA. *Unit head:* Dr. Maureen Reddy, Chair, 401-456-8028. *Application contact:* Graduate Studies, 401-456-8700.

Rivier College, School of Graduate Studies, Department of English, Nashua, NH 03060. Offers English (MA, MAT); writing and literature (MA). Part-time and evening/weekend programs available. *Faculty:* 4 full-time (2 women), 2 part-time/adjunct (both women). *Students:* 1 (woman) full-time, 9 part-time (7 women). Average age 36. 4 applicants, 50% accepted, 1 enrolled. In 2009, 4 master's awarded. *Degree requirements:* For master's, comprehensive exam (for some programs). *Entrance requirements:* For master's, GRE Subject Test. *Application deadline:* Applications are processed on a rolling basis. Application fee: $25. *Expenses:* Tuition: Part-time $447 per credit. *Financial support:* Available to part-time students. Application deadline: 2/1. *Unit head:* Dr. Brad Stull, Chairman, 603-897-8238, E-mail: bstull@rivier.edu. *Application contact:* Mathew Kittredge, Director of Graduate Admissions, 603-897-8129, Fax: 603-897-8810, E-mail: mkittredge@rivier.edu.

Roosevelt University, Graduate Division, College of Arts and Sciences, Department of Literature and Languages, Program in Creative Writing, Chicago, IL 60605. Offers MFA. Part-time and evening/weekend programs available. *Faculty research:* Poetry, fiction, nonfiction, script writing.

Rosemont College, Schools of Graduate and Professional Studies, Program in Creative Writing, Rosemont, PA 19010-1699. Offers MFA.

Rowan University, Graduate School, College of Communication, Program in Writing, Glassboro, NJ 08028-1701. Offers MA. Part-time and evening/weekend programs available. *Students:* 7 full-time (6 women), 20 part-time (8 women); includes 5 minority (1 African American, 2 Asian Americans or Pacific Islanders, 2 Hispanic Americans). Average age 32. 11 applicants, 100% accepted, 8 enrolled. In 2009, 11 master's awarded. *Degree requirements:* For master's, thesis. *Entrance requirements:* For master's, GRE General Test. Additional exam requirements/recommendations for international students: Required—TOEFL. *Application deadline:* Applications are processed on a rolling basis. Application fee: $50. Electronic applications accepted. *Expenses:* Tuition, state resident: full-time $10,624; part-time $590 per semester hour. Tuition, nonresident: full-time $10,624; part-time $590 per semester hour. Required fees: $2320; $125 per semester hour. *Financial support:* Career-related internships or fieldwork, scholarships/grants, and health care benefits available. Support available to part-time students. *Unit head:* Dr. Mira Lalovic-Hand, Interim Associate Provost/Director of Graduate School, 856-256-5120, E-mail: lalovic-hand@rowan.edu. *Application contact:* Karen Haynes, Graduate Coordinator, 856-256-4052, E-mail: haynes@rowan.edu.

Rutgers, The State University of New Jersey, Camden, Graduate School of Arts and Sciences, Program in Creative Writing, Camden, NJ 08102-1401. Offers MFA. *Degree requirements:* For master's, thesis. *Entrance requirements:* For master's, GRE (for assistantships), 2 letters of recommendation, writing sample. Additional exam requirements/recommendations for international students: Required—TOEFL, IELTS. Electronic applications accepted. *Faculty research:* Poetry, fiction, nonfiction, short stories.

Rutgers, The State University of New Jersey, Newark, Graduate School, Program in Creative Writing, Newark, NJ 07102. Offers MFA. *Entrance requirements:* For master's, GRE, minimum undergraduate B average.

Rutgers, The State University of New Jersey, New Brunswick, Mason Gross School of the Arts, Department of Theater Arts, Piscataway, NJ 08854-8097. Offers acting (MFA); design (MFA); directing (MFA); playwriting (MFA); stage management (MFA). *Degree requirements:* For master's, thesis (for some programs), performance project. *Entrance requirements:* For master's, audition, interview, portfolio. Electronic applications accepted. *Faculty research:* Faculty of working professional.

Saint Joseph's University, College of Arts and Sciences, Program in Writing Studies, Philadelphia, PA 19131-1395. Offers MA. Part-time and evening/weekend programs available. *Students:* 1 full-time (0 women), 40 part-time (31 women); includes 8 minority (7 African Americans, 1 Asian American or Pacific Islander). Average age 30. In 2009, 13 master's awarded. *Entrance requirements:* For master's, 2 letters of recommendation, resume, 2 writing samples. Additional exam requirements/recommendations for international students: Required—TOEFL (minimum score 550 paper-based; 213 computer-based; 79 iBT). *Application deadline:* For fall admission, 7/15 priority date for domestic students, 4/15 priority date for international students; for winter admission, 1/15 priority date for international students; for spring admission, 11/15 priority date for domestic students, 10/15 priority date for international students. Applications are processed on a rolling basis. Application fee: $35. Electronic applications accepted. *Expenses:* Tuition: Part-time $729 per credit hour. Tuition and fees vary according to degree level and program. *Financial support:* Unspecified assistantships available. Financial award applicants required to submit FAFSA. *Unit head:* Dr. Ann Green, Director, 610-660-1889, E-mail: agreen@sju.edu. *Application contact:* Kate McConnell, Director, Graduate College of Arts and Sciences Admissions and Retention, 610-660-3184, Fax: 610-660-3230, E-mail: kate.mcconnell@sju.edu.

Saint Mary's College of California, School of Liberal Arts, MFA Program in Creative Writing, Moraga, CA 94556. Offers MFA. *Faculty:* 6 full-time (3 women), 4 part-time/adjunct (3 women). *Students:* 46 full-time (30 women); includes 3 minority (2 Asian Americans or Pacific Islanders, 1 Hispanic American). Average age 28. *Degree requirements:* For master's, thesis. *Entrance requirements:* For master's, sample of written work. *Application deadline:* For fall admission, 1/31 for domestic students, 10/31 for international students. Application fee: $50. Electronic applications accepted. *Expenses:* Tuition: Full-time $35,087; part-time $956 per credit hour.

Writing

Saint Mary's College of California (continued)

One-time fee: $50 full-time. Part-time tuition and fees vary according to course level, course load, degree level, campus/location and program. *Financial support:* In 2009–10, 22 students received support, including 3 fellowships (averaging $6,000 per year), 20 teaching assistantships (averaging $2,000 per year); career-related internships or fieldwork and Federal Work-Study also available. Support available to part-time students. Financial award application deadline: 1/31; financial award applicants required to submit FAFSA. *Faculty research:* Poetry, fiction, nonfiction. *Unit head:* Marilyn Abildskov, Director, 925-631-4457, Fax: 925-631-4471, E-mail: mabildsk@stmarys-ca.edu. *Application contact:* Thomas Cooney, MFA Program Coordinator, 925-631-4762, Fax: 925-631-4471, E-mail: writers@stmarys-ca.edu.

Saint Xavier University, Graduate Studies, School of Arts and Sciences, Department of English, Chicago, IL 60655-3105. Offers English (CAS); literary studies (MA); teaching of writing (MA); writing pedagogy (CAS). Part-time and evening/weekend programs available. *Entrance requirements:* For master's, MAT or GRE, minimum GPA of 3.0. *Expenses:* Tuition: Part-time $743 per credit hour. Required fees: $135 per semester.

Salisbury University, Graduate Division, Program in English, Salisbury, MD 21801-6837. Offers composition, language and rhetoric (MA); literature (MA); teaching English to speakers of other languages (MA). Part-time and evening/weekend programs available. *Faculty:* 11 full-time (6 women). *Students:* 17 full-time (14 women), 20 part-time (14 women); includes 2 minority (both Hispanic Americans), 1 international. Average age 28. 31 applicants, 52% accepted, 2 enrolled. In 2009, 16 master's awarded. *Degree requirements:* For master's, comprehensive exam (for some programs), thesis optional. *Entrance requirements:* For master's, GRE General Test, MAT or PRAXIS, minimum GPA of 3.0, 2 letters of recommendation. Additional exam requirements/recommendations for international students: Required—TOEFL (minimum score 550 paper-based; 213 computer-based). *Application deadline:* For fall admission, 8/1 for domestic students; for spring admission, 1/1 for domestic students. Applications are processed on a rolling basis. Application fee: $45. Electronic applications accepted. *Expenses:* Tuition, area resident: Part-time $278 per credit hour. Tuition, state resident: part-time $278 per credit hour. Tuition, nonresident: part-time $574 per credit hour. Required fees: $57 per credit hour. *Financial support:* In 2009–10, 9 students received support, including 14 teaching assistantships with full tuition reimbursements available; career-related internships or fieldwork and scholarships/grants also available. Support available to part-time students. Financial award applicants required to submit FAFSA. *Faculty research:* Shakespeare, Keats, J. D. Salinger, Samuel Johnson, post-colonial theory. *Unit head:* Dr. John D. Kalb, Director, 410-543-6049, Fax: 410-548-2142, E-mail: jdkalb@salisbury.edu. *Application contact:* Dr. John D. Kalb, Director, 410-543-6049, Fax: 410-548-2142, E-mail: jdkalb@salisbury.edu.

San Diego State University, Graduate and Research Affairs, College of Arts and Letters, Department of English and Comparative Literature, San Diego, CA 92182. Offers creative writing (MFA); English (MA). *Degree requirements:* For master's, one foreign language, comprehensive exam (for some programs), thesis (for some programs). *Entrance requirements:* For master's, GRE General Test, minimum GPA of 2.85, writing sample, 3 letters of recommendation. Additional exam requirements/recommendations for international students: Required—TOEFL. Electronic applications accepted.

San Diego State University, Graduate and Research Affairs, College of Arts and Letters, Department of Rhetoric and Writing, San Diego, CA 92182. Offers MA. Part-time programs available. *Degree requirements:* For master's, thesis. *Entrance requirements:* For master's, GRE General Test, writing sample, 3 letters of reference. Additional exam requirements/recommendations for international students: Required—TOEFL. Electronic applications accepted.

San Francisco State University, Division of Graduate Studies, College of Humanities, Department of Creative Writing, San Francisco, CA 94132-1722. Offers MA, MFA. Part-time programs available. *Degree requirements:* For master's, thesis.

Sarah Lawrence College, Graduate Studies, Program in Writing, Bronxville, NY 10708-5999. Offers creative non-fiction (MFA); fiction (MFA); poetry (MFA). Part-time programs available. *Faculty:* 43 part-time/adjunct (25 women). *Students:* 114 full-time (88 women), 32 part-time (26 women); includes 24 minority (6 African Americans, 8 Asian Americans or Pacific Islanders, 10 Hispanic Americans), 5 international. Average age 28. 368 applicants, 51% accepted, 61 enrolled. In 2009, 61 master's awarded. *Degree requirements:* For master's, thesis. *Entrance requirements:* For master's, sample of creative writing, minimum B average in undergraduate course work. Additional exam requirements/recommendations for international students: Required—TOEFL (minimum score 600 paper-based). *Application deadline:* For fall admission, 1/15 for domestic students. Application fee: $60. *Expenses:* Tuition: Part-time $1161 per credit. Required fees: $232 per semester. Part-time tuition and fees vary according to course load, program and student level. *Financial support:* In 2009–10, 85 fellowships (averaging $5,049 per year) were awarded; scholarships/grants and unspecified assistantships also available. Support available to part-time students. Financial award application deadline: 3/1; financial award applicants required to submit CSS PROFILE or FAFSA. *Unit head:* Kate Johnson, Co-Director, 914-395-2373. *Application contact:* Emanual Lomax, Dean of Graduate Studies, 914-395-2373, E-mail: elomax@sarahlawrence.edu.

Savannah College of Art and Design, Graduate School, Program in Professional Writing, Savannah, GA 31402-3146. Offers MFA. Part-time programs available. *Degree requirements:* For master's, thesis. *Entrance requirements:* Additional exam requirements/recommendations for international students: Required—TOEFL (minimum score 450 paper-based; 133 computer-based). Electronic applications accepted. *Expenses:* Tuition: Full-time $28,515; part-time $627 per credit hour. One-time fee: $500. Tuition and fees vary according to course load.

School of the Art Institute of Chicago, Graduate Division, Program in Writing, Chicago, IL 60603-3103. Offers MFA, Certificate. *Entrance requirements:* Additional exam requirements/recommendations for international students: Required—TOEFL.

Seattle Pacific University, Masters of Fine Arts in Creative Writing Program, Seattle, WA 98119-1997. Offers MFA. Part-time programs available. *Faculty:* 1 full-time (0 women), 6 part-time/adjunct (4 women). *Students:* 24 part-time (12 women); includes 6 minority (1 African American, 2 Asian Americans or Pacific Islanders, 3 Hispanic Americans). Average age 34. In 2009, 17 master's awarded. *Degree requirements:* For master's, thesis. *Entrance requirements:* For master's, 10 pages of poetry or 25 to 30 double-spaced pages of prose (fiction or creative nonfiction) in chosen genre. *Application deadline:* For fall admission, 2/15 for domestic students; for spring admission, 10/1 for domestic students. Application fee: $50. Electronic applications accepted. *Expenses:* Tuition: Part-time $485 per credit. Part-time tuition and fees vary according to course level, degree level and program. *Financial support:* In 2009–10, 14 students received support. Applicants required to submit FAFSA. *Unit head:* Dr. Gregory Wolfe, Director, 206-281-2109, E-mail: gwolfe@spu.edu. *Application contact:* The Grad Center, 206-281-2091.

Seton Hall University, College of Arts and Sciences, Department of English, South Orange, NJ 07079-2697. Offers English (MA), including literature, writing. Part-time and evening/weekend programs available. *Faculty:* 15 full-time (8 women). *Students:* 23 full-time (15 women), 20 part-time (15 women); includes 3 minority (2 African Americans, 1 Asian American or Pacific Islander), 1 international. Average age 28. 32 applicants, 91% accepted, 17 enrolled. In 2009, 11 master's awarded. *Degree requirements:* For master's, one foreign language, comprehensive exam, thesis. *Entrance requirements:* For master's, GRE, minimum of 21 undergraduate credits in English. Additional exam requirements/recommendations for international students: Required—TOEFL. *Application deadline:* For fall admission, 7/1 priority date for domestic and international students; for spring admission, 11/1 priority date for domestic and international students. Applications are processed on a rolling basis. Application fee: $50. Electronic applications accepted. *Financial support:* Teaching assistantships with full tuition reimbursements, Federal Work-Study and unspecified assistantships available. Financial award applicants required to submit FAFSA. *Faculty research:* The essay, modern poetry, the novel, medieval poetry, Renaissance drama. *Unit head:* Dr. Mary McAleer Balkun, Chair, 973-761-9387, Fax: 973-761-9596, E-mail: balkunma@shu.edu. *Application contact:* Dr. Angela Weisl, Director of Graduate Studies, 973-275-5889, Fax: 973-761-9596, E-mail: weislang@shu.edu.

Seton Hill University, Program in Writing Popular Fiction, Greensburg, PA 15601. Offers MA. Part-time programs available. Postbaccalaureate distance learning degree programs offered (minimal on-campus study). *Faculty:* 3 full-time (1 woman), 20 part-time/adjunct (11 women). *Students:* 31 full-time (25 women), 42 part-time (33 women); includes 5 minority (1 African American, 1 Asian American or Pacific Islander, 3 Hispanic Americans), 1 international. Average age 37. 44 applicants, 55% accepted, 12 enrolled. In 2009, 15 master's awarded. *Degree requirements:* For master's, thesis or alternative. *Entrance requirements:* For master's, writing sample. Additional exam requirements/recommendations for international students: Required—TOEFL (minimum score 650 paper-based; 280 computer-based), IELTS (minimum score 7). *Application deadline:* For fall admission, 6/1 for domestic students; for spring admission, 12/15 for domestic students. Applications are processed on a rolling basis. Application fee: $35. Electronic applications accepted. *Expenses:* Tuition: Full-time $12,780; part-time $710 per credit. Required fees: $300; $150 per semester. Tuition and fees vary according to course load and program. *Financial support:* Scholarships/grants, tuition waivers (partial), and unspecified assistantships available. Support available to part-time students. Financial award application deadline: 8/15; financial award applicants required to submit FAFSA. *Faculty research:* Romance novels, science fiction novels, children's fiction, mystery, horror. *Unit head:* Dr. Lee McClain, Director, 724-830-1040, Fax: 724-830-1294, E-mail: mcclain@setonhill.edu. *Application contact:* Laurel Pellis, Advisor, 724-838-4209, Fax: 724-830-1891, E-mail: lpellis@setonhill.edu.

Sewanee: The University of the South, Sewanee School of Letters, Sewanee, TN 37383-1000. Offers American literature and English literature (MA); creative writing (MFA). Programs offered only during the summer. Part-time programs available. *Degree requirements:* For master's, thesis (for some programs). *Entrance requirements:* For master's, writing sample, 2 letters of recommendation. Electronic applications accepted. *Expenses:* Contact institution.

Slippery Rock University of Pennsylvania, Graduate Studies (Recruitment), College of Humanities, Fine and Performing Arts, Department of English, Slippery Rock, PA 16057-1383. Offers literature and composition (MA); professional writing (MA). Part-time and evening/weekend programs available. *Degree requirements:* For master's, comprehensive exam (for some programs), thesis (for some programs). *Entrance requirements:* For master's, GRE General Test, MAT, minimum GPA of 2.75. *Application deadline:* For fall admission, 3/1 priority date for domestic students, 5/1 priority date for international students; for spring admission, 11/1 priority date for domestic students, 9/1 priority date for international students. Applications are processed on a rolling basis. Application fee: $25 ($30 for international students). Electronic applications accepted. *Expenses:* Tuition, state resident: full-time $6666; part-time $370 per credit. Tuition, nonresident: full-time $10,666; part-time $593 per credit. Required fees: $2184; $182 per credit. *Financial support:* Career-related internships or fieldwork, Federal Work-Study, scholarships/grants, and unspecified assistantships available. Support available to part-time students. Financial award application deadline: 5/1; financial award applicants required to submit FAFSA. *Unit head:* Dr. Joseph McCarren, Graduate Coordinator, 724-738-2868, Fax: 724-738-4829, E-mail: joseph.mccarren@sru.edu. *Application contact:* Angela Piverotto, Interim Director of Graduate Studies, 724-738-2051, Fax: 724-738-2146, E-mail: graduate.admissions@sru.edu.

Sonoma State University, School of Arts and Humanities, Department of English, Rohnert Park, CA 94928. Offers American literature (MA); creative writing (MA); English literature (MA); world literature (MA). Part-time and evening/weekend programs available. *Faculty:* 5 full-time (3 women), 2 part-time/adjunct (1 woman). *Students:* 22 full-time (14 women), 15 part-time (10 women); includes 1 minority (Asian American or Pacific Islander). Average age 34. 30 applicants, 90% accepted, 11 enrolled. In 2009, 11 master's awarded. *Degree requirements:* For master's, one foreign language, thesis or alternative. *Entrance requirements:* For master's, minimum GPA of 2.5. Additional exam requirements/recommendations for international students: Required—TOEFL (minimum score 500 paper-based; 173 computer-based). *Application deadline:* For fall admission, 11/30 priority date for domestic students. Application fee: $55. *Expenses:* Tuition, nonresident: full-time $11,160. Required fees: $6226. Full-time tuition and fees vary according to course load. *Financial support:* Teaching assistantships, career-related internships or fieldwork and Federal Work-Study available. Financial award application deadline: 3/2; financial award applicants required to submit FAFSA. *Unit head:* Dr. Thaine Stearns, Chair of Graduate Studies, 707-661-2882, E-mail: thaine.stearns@sonoma.edu. *Application contact:* Dr. Thaine Stearns, Chair of Graduate Studies, 707-661-2882, E-mail: thaine.stearns@sonoma.edu.

Southeastern Louisiana University, College of Arts, Humanities and Social Sciences, Department of English, Hammond, LA 70402. Offers creative writing (MA); language and literacy (MA); professional writing (MA). Part-time and evening/weekend programs available. *Faculty:* 15 full-time (7 women), 1 (woman) part-time/adjunct. *Students:* 27 full-time (15 women), 22 part-time (15 women); includes 4 minority (3 African Americans, 1 Asian American or Pacific Islander). Average age 29. 16 applicants, 94% accepted, 11 enrolled. In 2009, 12 master's awarded. *Degree requirements:* For master's, one foreign language, comprehensive exam, thesis optional. *Entrance requirements:* For master's, GRE General Test (850 or better), 24 undergraduate credit hours in English, minimum GPA of 2.5. Additional exam requirements/recommendations for international students: Required—TOEFL (minimum score 500 paper-based; 173 computer-based; 61 iBT). *Application deadline:* For fall admission, 7/15 priority date for domestic students, 6/1 priority date for international students; for spring admission, 12/1 priority date for domestic students, 10/1 priority date for international students. Applications are processed on a rolling basis. Application fee: $20 ($30 for international students). Electronic applications accepted. *Expenses:* Tuition, state resident: full-time $3086; part-time $225 per credit hour. Tuition, nonresident: part-time $529 per credit hour. Required fees: $1195. Tuition and fees vary according to course level and course load. *Financial support:* In 2009–10, 11 students received support, including 1 fellowship (averaging $13,050 per year), 9 research assistantships (averaging $8,078 per year), 1 teaching assistantship (averaging $6,700 per year); career-related internships or fieldwork, Federal Work-Study, institutionally sponsored loans, scholarships/grants, and administrative assistantships also available. Support available to part-time students. Financial award application deadline: 5/1; financial award applicants required to submit FAFSA. *Faculty research:* Composition/rhetoric, professional and technical writing, film and performance studies, literary criticism, creative writing. Total annual research expenditures: $34,307. *Unit head:* Dr. David Hanson, Department Head, 985-549-2100, Fax: 985-549-5021, E-mail: dhanson@selu.edu. *Application contact:* Sandra Meyers, Graduate Admissions Analyst, 985-549-5620, Fax: 985-549-5632, E-mail: admissions@selu.edu.

Southern Illinois University Carbondale, Graduate School, College of Liberal Arts, Department of English, Program in Creative Writing, Carbondale, IL 62901-4701. Offers MFA. *Degree requirements:* For master's, one foreign language, thesis. *Entrance requirements:* For master's, GRE General Test, GRE Subject Test, minimum GPA of 2.7. Additional exam requirements/recommendations for international students: Required—TOEFL.

Southern Illinois University Edwardsville, Graduate Studies and Research, College of Arts and Sciences, Department of English Language and Literature, Program in Creative Writing, Edwardsville, IL 62026-0001. Offers MA. Part-time programs available. *Students:* 4 full-time (all women), 12 part-time (all women); includes 2 minority (1 African American, 1 American Indian/Alaska Native). Average age 26. In 2009, 2 master's awarded. *Degree requirements:* For master's, one foreign language, thesis. *Entrance requirements:* Additional exam requirements/recommendations for international students: Required—TOEFL (minimum score 550 paper-based; 213 computer-based; 79 iBT), IELTS (minimum score 6.5). *Application deadline:* For fall admission, 7/23 for domestic students, 6/1 for international students; for spring admission, 12/11 for domestic students, 10/1 for international students. Applications are processed on a rolling basis. Application fee: $30. Electronic applications accepted. *Expenses:* Tuition, state resident: part-time $1252.50 per semester. Tuition, nonresident: part-time $3131.25

per semester. Required fees: $586.85 per semester. Tuition and fees vary according to course load. *Financial support:* Fellowships with full tuition reimbursements, research assistantships with full tuition reimbursements, teaching assistantships with full tuition reimbursements available. Financial award application deadline: 3/1; financial award applicants required to submit FAFSA. *Unit head:* Dr. Joel Hardman, Director, 618-650-5978, E-mail: jhardma@siue.edu. *Application contact:* Dr. Joel Hardman, Director, 618-650-5978, E-mail: jhardma@siue.edu.

Southern New Hampshire University, School of Liberal Arts, Manchester, NH 03106-1045. Offers clinical services for adults psychiatric disabilities (Certificate); clinical services for children and adolescents with psychiatric disabilities (Certificate); clinical services for persons with co-occurring substance abuse and psychiatric disabilities (Certificate); community mental health (MS); fiction writing (MFA); non-fiction writing (MFA); teaching English as a foreign language (MS). Part-time and evening/weekend programs available. *Degree requirements:* For master's, one foreign language, thesis. *Entrance requirements:* For master's, minimum GPA of 2.75: MS-TEFL, 3.0: MFA. Additional exam requirements/recommendations for international students: Required—TOEFL (minimum score 550 paper-based; 213 computer-based; 79 iBT), IELTS (minimum score 6.5), TWE (minimum score 5). Electronic applications accepted. *Expenses:* Contact institution. *Faculty research:* Action research, state of the art practice in behavioral health services, wraparound approaches to working with youth, learning styles.

Spalding University, Graduate Studies, College of Social Sciences and Humanities, Program in Writing, Louisville, KY 40203-2188. Offers MFA. Postbaccalaureate distance learning degree programs offered (minimal on-campus study). *Faculty:* 1 (woman) full-time, 1 (woman) part-time/adjunct. *Students:* 138 full-time (97 women), 1 (woman) part-time; includes 11 minority (8 African Americans, 1 American Indian/Alaska Native, 2 Hispanic Americans). Average age 42. 101 applicants, 62% accepted, 61 enrolled. In 2009, 46 master's awarded. *Degree requirements:* For master's, thesis. *Entrance requirements:* For master's, writing sample, letters of recommendation. Additional exam requirements/recommendations for international students: Required—TOEFL (minimum score 535 paper-based; 203 computer-based). *Application deadline:* For fall admission, 7/1 priority date for domestic and international students; for spring admission, 1/15 priority date for domestic and international students. Applications are processed on a rolling basis. Application fee: $29. Electronic applications accepted. *Expenses:* Tuition: Full-time $11,340; part-time $630 per credit hour. Tuition and fees vary according to program. *Financial support:* In 2009–10, 29 students received support. Scholarships/grants and unspecified assistantships available. Financial award application deadline: 3/15; financial award applicants required to submit FAFSA. *Faculty research:* Fiction, creative nonfiction, poetry, writing for children, playwriting/screenwriting. *Unit head:* Dr. Sena Jeter Naslund, Director, 502-585-9911 Ext. 2876, Fax: 502-585-7158, E-mail: mfa@spalding.edu. *Application contact:* Karen J. Mann, Administrative Director, 502-585-9911 Ext. 2786, Fax: 502-585-7158, E-mail: mfa@spalding.edu.

Stony Brook University, State University of New York, Graduate School, College of Arts and Sciences, Department of English, Program in Composition Studies, Stony Brook, NY 11794. Offers Certificate. *Expenses:* Tuition, state resident: full-time $8370; part-time $349 per credit. Tuition, nonresident: full-time $13,250; part-time $552 per credit. Required fees: $933.

Stony Brook University, State University of New York, Stony Brook Southampton, Program in Writing and Literature, Stony Brook, NY 11794. Offers fiction (MFA); poetry (MFA); scientific writing (MFA), including environmental, medical, technological; scriptwriting (MFA). *Faculty:* 1 (woman) full-time, 12 part-time/adjunct (6 women). *Students:* 6 full-time (4 women), 27 part-time (19 women); includes 2 minority (1 African American, 1 Asian American or Pacific Islander). 29 applicants, 66% accepted. In 2009, 5 master's awarded. *Expenses:* Tuition, state resident: full-time $8370; part-time $349 per credit. Tuition, nonresident: full-time $13,250; part-time $552 per credit. Required fees: $933. *Financial support:* In 2009–10, 6 teaching assistantships were awarded. *Unit head:* Dr. Robert Reeves, Director, 631-632-5030, Fax: 631-632-2576, E-mail: southamptonwriters@notes.cc.sunysb.edu. *Application contact:* Director of Graduate Admissions and Program Administration.

Syracuse University, College of Arts and Sciences, Program in Composition and Cultural Rhetoric, Syracuse, NY 13244. Offers PhD. *Students:* 31 full-time (21 women), 5 part-time (2 women); includes 5 minority (3 African Americans, 2 Hispanic Americans), 1 international. Average age 36. 31 applicants, 13% accepted, 3 enrolled. In 2009, 4 doctorates awarded. *Degree requirements:* For doctorate, comprehensive exam, thesis/dissertation. *Entrance requirements:* For doctorate, GRE. Additional exam requirements/recommendations for international students: Required—TOEFL (minimum score 100 iBT). *Application deadline:* For fall admission, 2/1 priority date for domestic and international students. Application fee: $75. Electronic applications accepted. *Expenses:* Tuition: Full-time $26,808; part-time $1117 per credit. Required fees: $1024. *Financial support:* Fellowships with full tuition reimbursements, teaching assistantships with full tuition reimbursements available. Financial award application deadline: 1/1; financial award applicants required to submit FAFSA. *Unit head:* Prof. Gwendolyn Pough, Graduate Director, 315-443-1067, E-mail: gdpough@syr.edu. *Application contact:* Velita Chapple, 315-443-5146, E-mail: vnchappl@syr.edu.

Syracuse University, College of Arts and Sciences, Program in Creative Writing, Syracuse, NY 13244. Offers MFA. *Students:* 33 full-time (20 women); includes 7 minority (1 African American, 4 Asian Americans or Pacific Islanders, 2 Hispanic Americans), 2 international. Average age 30. 330 applicants, 5% accepted, 11 enrolled. In 2009, 12 master's awarded. *Degree requirements:* For master's, thesis. *Entrance requirements:* For master's, GRE General Test, sample of written work. Additional exam requirements/recommendations for international students: Required—TOEFL (minimum score 100 iBT). *Application deadline:* For fall admission, 1/10 priority date for domestic and international students. Application fee: $75. Electronic applications accepted. *Expenses:* Tuition: Full-time $26,808; part-time $1117 per credit. Required fees: $1024. *Financial support:* Fellowships with full tuition reimbursements, teaching assistantships with full tuition reimbursements available. Financial award application deadline: 1/1; financial award applicants required to submit FAFSA. *Unit head:* Christopher Kennedy, Director, 315-443-3755, Fax: 315-443-3660, E-mail: ckennedy@syr.edu. *Application contact:* Terri Zollo, Information Contact, 315-443-2174, E-mail: tazollo@syr.edu.

Temple University, Graduate School, College of Liberal Arts, Department of English, Program in Creative Writing, Philadelphia, PA 19122-6096. Offers MA. Part-time programs available. *Degree requirements:* For master's, comprehensive exam, manuscript. *Entrance requirements:* For master's, GRE General Test, minimum GPA of 3.0. Additional exam requirements/recommendations for international students: Required—TOEFL (minimum score 550 paper-based; 213 computer-based; 79 iBT). Electronic applications accepted. *Faculty research:* Poetry, fiction, cultural studies.

Texas State University–San Marcos, Graduate School, College of Liberal Arts, Department of English, Program in Creative Writing, San Marcos, TX 78666. Offers MFA. Part-time and evening/weekend programs available. *Faculty:* 10 full-time (4 women). *Students:* 56 full-time (29 women), 12 part-time (6 women); includes 12 minority (1 African American, 3 Asian Americans or Pacific Islanders, 8 Hispanic Americans). Average age 29. 122 applicants, 43% accepted, 22 enrolled. In 2009, 20 master's awarded. *Degree requirements:* For master's, comprehensive exam, thesis. *Entrance requirements:* For master's, 24 hours of undergraduate course work in English (12 advanced) with minimum GPA of 3.25, 6 hours of course work in foreign language, minimum GPA of 2.75 in last 60 hours, writing portfolios (3 copies), 3 letters of recommendation. Additional exam requirements/recommendations for international students: Required—TOEFL (minimum score 550 paper-based; 213 computer-based). *Application deadline:* For fall admission, 1/15 priority date for domestic students, 1/15 for international students; for spring admission, 11/1 priority date for domestic students, 10/1 for international students. Applications are processed on a rolling basis. Application fee: $40 ($90 for international students). Electronic applications accepted. *Expenses:* Tuition, state resident: full-time $5784; part-time $241 per credit hour. Tuition, nonresident: part-time $551 per credit hour. Required fees: $1728; $48 per credit hour. $306. Tuition and fees vary according to course load. *Financial support:* In 2009–10, 58 students received support, including 1 research assistantship (averaging $6,478 per year), 38 teaching assistantships (averaging $6,102 per year); Federal Work-Study and institutionally sponsored loans also available. Support available to part-time students. Financial award application deadline: 4/1; financial award applicants required to submit FAFSA. *Unit head:* Tom Grimes, Graduate Adviser, 512-245-2163, Fax: 512-245-8546, E-mail: tg02@txstate.edu. *Application contact:* Dr. J. Michael Willoughby, Dean of Graduate School, 512-245-2581, Fax: 512-245-8365, E-mail: gradcollege@txstate.edu.

Towson University, College of Graduate Studies and Research, Program in Professional Writing, Towson, MD 21252-0001. Offers MS. Part-time and evening/weekend programs available. *Degree requirements:* For master's, thesis optional, exam. *Entrance requirements:* For master's, sample of written work, minimum GPA of 3.0, 2 letters of recommendation. Electronic applications accepted. *Faculty research:* Creative writing, essay writing, sociopsychological linguistics, interdisciplinary rhetoric, global communication.

Union Institute & University, Master of Arts Program–Online, Montpelier, VT 05602. Offers creativity studies (MA); education (MA); health and wellness (MA); history and culture (MA); leadership, public policy, and social issues (MA); literature and writing (MA); psychology (MA). Part-time programs available. Postbaccalaureate distance learning degree programs offered (no on-campus study). *Faculty:* 3 full-time (1 woman), 16 part-time/adjunct (11 women). *Students:* 27 full-time (23 women), 113 part-time (84 women); includes 30 minority (22 African Americans, 2 American Indian/Alaska Native, 1 Asian American or Pacific Islander, 5 Hispanic Americans). Average age 40. In 2009, 26 master's awarded. *Degree requirements:* For master's, thesis. *Application deadline:* Applications are processed on a rolling basis. Application fee: $50. Electronic applications accepted. *Expenses:* Contact institution. *Financial support:* Career-related internships or fieldwork and tuition waivers available. Financial award applicants required to submit FAFSA. *Unit head:* Dr. Brian Webb, Program Director, 802-828-8777, E-mail: brian.webb@tui.edu. *Application cohtact:* Kathleen Murphy, Interim Director of Admissions—Montpelier, 888-828-8575, E-mail: admissions@myunion.edu.

The University of Akron, Graduate School, Buchtel College of Arts and Sciences, Department of English, Akron, OH 44325. Offers composition (MA); creative writing (MFA); literature (MA). Part-time programs available. *Faculty:* 18 full-time (5 women). *Students:* 48 full-time (24 women), 45 part-time (31 women); includes 6 minority (4 African Americans, 1 Asian American or Pacific Islander, 1 Hispanic American), 1 international. Average age 32. 37 applicants, 89% accepted, 16 enrolled. In 2009, 20 master's awarded. *Degree requirements:* For master's, thesis optional. *Entrance requirements:* For master's, BA in English, minimum GPA of 2.75, writing portfolio, letters of recommendation. Additional exam requirements/recommendations for international students: Required—TOEFL (minimum score 580 paper-based; 237 computer-based; 92 iBT). *Application deadline:* Applications are processed on a rolling basis. Application fee: $30 ($40 for international students). Electronic applications accepted. *Expenses:* Tuition, state resident: full-time $6570; part-time $365 per credit hour. Tuition, nonresident: full-time $11,250; part-time $625 per credit hour. *Financial support:* In 2009–10, 5 research assistantships with full tuition reimbursements, 23 teaching assistantships with full tuition reimbursements were awarded. *Faculty research:* British and American literary studies, literary theory, creative writing, applied linguistics. Total annual research expenditures: $1,332. *Unit head:* Dr. Michael Schuldiner, Chair, 330-972-8556, E-mail: schuldi@uakron.edu. *Application contact:* Dr. Hillary Nunn, Director of Graduate Studies, 330-972-7601, E-mail: nunn@uakron.edu.

The University of Alabama, Graduate School, College of Arts and Sciences, Department of English, Tuscaloosa, AL 35487. Offers composition and rhetoric (PhD); creative writing (MFA), including fiction, poetry; literature (MA, PhD); rhetoric and composition (MA); teaching English as a second language (MATESOL). *Faculty:* 30 full-time (12 women). *Students:* 123 full-time (71 women), 12 part-time (9 women); includes 14 minority (9 African Americans, 2 American Indian/Alaska Native, 1 Asian American or Pacific Islander, 2 Hispanic Americans), 4 international. Average age 27. 339 applicants, 17% accepted, 39 enrolled. In 2009, 31 degrees awarded. *Degree requirements:* For master's, one foreign language, comprehensive exam, thesis (for some programs); for doctorate, 2 foreign languages, comprehensive exam, thesis/dissertation. *Entrance requirements:* For master's and doctorate, GRE, minimum GPA of 3.0, critical writing sample. Additional exam requirements/recommendations for international students: Required—TOEFL. *Application deadline:* For fall admission, 1/15 priority date for domestic students, 1/15 for international students. Application fee: $50 ($60 for international students). Electronic applications accepted. *Expenses:* Tuition, state resident: full-time $7000. Tuition, nonresident: full-time $19,200. *Financial support:* In 2009–10, 7 fellowships with full tuition reimbursements (averaging $15,000 per year), 1 research assistantship (averaging $11,708 per year), 106 teaching assistantships with full tuition reimbursements (averaging $11,708 per year) were awarded; career-related internships or fieldwork, scholarships/grants, health care benefits, and unspecified assistantships also available. Financial award application deadline: 1/15. *Faculty research:* Critical theory; modern, Renaissance, and African-American literature. *Unit head:* Dr. Catherine E. Davies, Director of Graduate Studies, 205-348-8499, E-mail: cdavies@bama.ua.edu. *Application contact:* Vernita W. James, Office Assistant II, 205-348-0766, Fax: 205-348-1388, E-mail: vwjames@bama.ua.edu.

University of Alaska Anchorage, College of Arts and Sciences, Program in Creative Writing and Literary Arts, Anchorage, AK 99508. Offers MFA. Part-time programs available. *Degree requirements:* For master's, comprehensive exam, thesis or alternative. *Entrance requirements:* For master's, portfolio, minimum GPA of 3.0. Additional exam requirements/recommendations for international students: Required—TOEFL (minimum score 550 paper-based; 213 computer-based). *Faculty research:* Alaska Quarterly Review publications, feminist studies, ecocriticism and native writing, poetry.

University of Alaska Fairbanks, College of Liberal Arts, Department of English, Fairbanks, AK 99775-5720. Offers creative writing (MFA); literature (MA); MA/MFA. Part-time programs available. *Faculty:* 15 full-time (6 women), 6 part-time/adjunct (5 women). *Students:* 33 full-time (14 women), 11 part-time (8 women); includes 5 minority (2 American Indian/Alaska Native, 2 Asian Americans or Pacific Islanders, 1 Hispanic American). Average age 42. 50 applicants, 30% accepted, 9 enrolled. In 2009, 6 master's awarded. *Degree requirements:* For master's, comprehensive exam, thesis or alternative, oral exams, oral defense. *Entrance requirements:* For master's, GRE General Test, academic writing sample. Additional exam requirements/recommendations for international students: Required—TOEFL (minimum score 550 paper-based; 213 computer-based; 80 iBT). *Application deadline:* For fall admission, 6/1 for domestic students, 3/1 for international students; for spring admission, 10/15 for domestic students, 9/1 for international students. Applications are processed on a rolling basis. Application fee: $60. Electronic applications accepted. *Expenses:* Tuition, state resident: full-time $7584; part-time $316 per credit. Tuition, nonresident: full-time $15,504; part-time $646 per credit. Required fees: $23 per credit. $135 per semester. Tuition and fees vary according to course level, course load and reciprocity agreements. *Financial support:* In 2009–10, 1 research assistantship (averaging $13,330 per year), 26 teaching assistantships (averaging $11,844 per year) were awarded; fellowships, Federal Work-Study, scholarships/grants, health care benefits, and unspecified assistantships also available. Support available to part-time students. Financial award application deadline: 7/1; financial award applicants required to submit FAFSA. *Faculty research:* Traditional Alaskan native literature, British literature, pedagogy, American literature, rhetoric/composition history. *Unit head:* Dr. Cooper Burns, Department Chair, 907-474-7193, Fax: 907-474-5247, E-mail: faengl@uaf.edu. *Application contact:* Dr. Cooper Burns, Department Chair, 907-474-7193, Fax: 907-474-5247, E-mail: faengl@uaf.edu.

The University of Arizona, Graduate College, College of Humanities, Department of English Program in Creative Writing, Tucson, AZ 85721. Offers MFA. *Students:* 43 full-time (26 women), 12 part-time (5 women); includes 3 minority (all Hispanic Americans), 2 international Average age 28. 306 applicants, 16% accepted, 24 enrolled. In 2009, 25 master's awardec *Entrance requirements:* Additional exam requirements/recommendations for internationa students: Required—TOEFL (minimum score 550 paper-based; 213 computer-based; 79 iBT *Application deadline:* For fall admission, 1/1 for domestic students, 12/1 for internatior students. Applications are processed on a rolling basis. Application fee: $75. Electronic applic tions accepted. *Expenses:* Tuition, state resident: full-time $9028. Tuition, nonresident: full-ti

Writing

The University of Arizona (continued)

$24,890. *Financial support:* Career-related internships or fieldwork, institutionally sponsored loans, and tuition waivers (partial) available. *Unit head:* Aurelie Sheehan, Director, 520-621-3880, E-mail: sheehan@email.arizona.edu. *Application contact:* Marlene Cooksey, Graduate Secretary, 520-621-3880, Fax: 520-621-7397, E-mail: mcooksey@email.arizona.edu.

University of Arkansas, Graduate School, J. William Fulbright College of Arts and Sciences, Department of English, Program in Creative Writing, Fayetteville, AR 72701-1201. Offers MFA. *Students:* 11 full-time (6 women), 26 part-time (13 women); includes 3 minority (2 Asian Americans or Pacific Islanders, 1 Hispanic American). In 2009, 10 master's awarded. *Degree requirements:* For master's, thesis. Application fee: $40 ($50 for international students). *Expenses:* Tuition, state resident: full-time $7355; part-time $356.58 per hour. Tuition, nonresident: full-time $17,401; part-time $775.17 per hour. Required fees: $1203. *Financial support:* In 2009–10, 30 teaching assistantships were awarded; fellowships with tuition reimbursements, research assistantships, career-related internships or fieldwork and Federal Work-Study also available. Support available to part-time students. Financial award application deadline: 4/1; financial award applicants required to submit FAFSA. *Unit head:* Dr. Geoffrey Brock, Interim Director, 479-575-4301, Fax: 479-575-5919, E-mail: mfa@uark.edu. *Application contact:* Dr. Geoffrey Brock, Interim Director, 479-575-4301, Fax: 479-575-5919, E-mail: mfa@uark.edu.

University of Arkansas at Little Rock, Graduate School, College of Arts, Humanities, and Social Science, Department of Rhetoric and Writing, Little Rock, AR 72204-1099. Offers professional and technical writing (MA). Part-time and evening/weekend programs available. *Degree requirements:* For master's, thesis or alternative, oral defense of final project. *Entrance requirements:* For master's, GRE, minimum GPA of 3.0, writing portfolio. *Faculty research:* Writing for industry, science, business, and government; composition and rhetorical theory; writing nonfiction; teaching of writing.

University of Baltimore, Graduate School, The Yale Gordon College of Liberal Arts, Program in Creative Writing and Publishing Arts, Baltimore, MD 21201-5779. Offers MFA. Part-time and evening/weekend programs available. *Entrance requirements:* Additional exam requirements/recommendations for international students: Required—TOEFL.

University of Baltimore, Graduate School, The Yale Gordon College of Liberal Arts, Program in Publications Design, Baltimore, MD 21201-5779. Offers MA. Part-time and evening/weekend programs available. *Degree requirements:* For master's, seminar project. *Entrance requirements:* For master's, minimum GPA of 3.0, portfolio, interview. Additional exam requirements/recommendations for international students: Required—TOEFL (minimum score 550 paper-based; 213 computer-based). Electronic applications accepted. *Faculty research:* Communication theory, graphic design, media technology.

The University of British Columbia, Faculty of Arts, Creative Writing Program, Vancouver, BC V6T 1Z1, Canada. Offers creative writing (MFA); creative writing and film (MFA); creative writing and theatre (MFA). Part-time programs available. Postbaccalaureate distance learning degree programs offered (minimal on-campus study). *Degree requirements:* For master's, thesis. *Entrance requirements:* For master's, sample of written work. Additional exam requirements/recommendations for international students: Required—TOEFL (minimum score 550 paper-based; 213 computer-based). Electronic applications accepted. *Expenses:* Contact institution. *Faculty research:* Writing of fiction; poetry, creative nonfiction, plays for stage, screen, television, radio, writing for children and translation, song lyrics and libretto, new media and graphic novel.

The University of British Columbia, Faculty of Arts and Faculty of Graduate Studies, Department of Theatre and Film, Film Program, Vancouver, BC V6T 1Z2, Canada. Offers creative writing and film production (MFA); film production (MFA, Diploma); film studies (MA). *Degree requirements:* For master's, variable foreign language requirement, comprehensive exam, thesis (MA), thesis or project (MFA). *Entrance requirements:* For master's, portfolio (MFA). Additional exam requirements/recommendations for international students: Required—TOEFL (minimum score 600 paper-based; 250 computer-based). Electronic applications accepted. *Faculty research:* Film theory and violence; American and European cinema; cult cinema; Irish cinema.

University of California, Berkeley, UC Berkeley Extension, Certificate Programs in Writing, Editing and Technical Communication, Berkeley, CA 94720-1500. Offers writing (Post-baccalaureate Certificate). Postbaccalaureate distance learning degree programs offered. *Unit head:* Diana Wu, Dean, 510-642-4181. *Application contact:* Writing, Editing, and Technical Communication, 510-642-6362, E-mail: letters@unex.berkeley.edu.

University of California, Davis, Graduate Studies, Program in English, Davis, CA 95616. Offers creative writing (MA); English (MA, PhD). Terminal master's awarded for partial completion of doctoral program. *Degree requirements:* For master's, one foreign language, thesis optional; for doctorate, 2 foreign languages, thesis/dissertation. *Entrance requirements:* For master's and doctorate, GRE General Test, GRE Subject Test, minimum GPA of 3.0, writing sample. Additional exam requirements/recommendations for international students: Required—TOEFL (minimum score 550 paper-based; 213 computer-based). Electronic applications accepted. *Faculty research:* Feminist theory, ethnic literature, literary theory, history of literature, literature of nature.

University of California, Irvine, Office of Graduate Studies, School of Humanities, Department of English and Comparative Literature, Program in Writing, Irvine, CA 92697. Offers creative writing (MFA), including fiction, poetry. *Faculty:* 4 full-time (1 woman), 2 part-time/adjunct (1 woman). *Students:* 32 full-time (16 women); includes 1 Asian American or Pacific Islander, 1 Hispanic American, 1 international. Average age 29. 416 applicants, 2% accepted, 10 enrolled. 'n 2009, 11 master's awarded. *Degree requirements:* For master's, thesis. *Entrance* *equirements:* For master's, minimum GPA of 3.0, sample of written work. *Application deadline:* r fall admission, 1/15 for domestic and international students. Application fee: $70 ($90 for rnational students). Electronic applications accepted. *Financial support:* In 2009–10, research istantships (averaging $15,000 per year), teaching assistantships with partial tuition bursements (averaging $14,145 per year) were awarded; fellowships with full and partial reimbursements, institutionally sponsored loans and tuition waivers (full and partial) vailable. Financial award application deadline: 3/2; financial award applicants required to FAFSA. *Unit head:* Director, 949-824-6718, Fax: 949-824-2916. *Application contact:* Read, Graduate Administrator, 949-824-6718, Fax: 949-824-2916, E-mail: eclgradapp@

ity of California, Riverside, Graduate Division, Department of Creative Writing, Palm CA 92211. Offers creative writing and writing for the performing arts (MFA). Program red at Palm Desert Graduate Center. *Faculty:* 15 part-time/adjunct (5 women). *Students:* time (42 women); includes 17 minority (8 African Americans, 4 Asian Americans or slanders, 5 Hispanic Americans). Average age 34. 57 applicants, 53% accepted, 27 In 2009, 11 master's awarded. *Degree requirements:* For master's, thesis, final *Entrance requirements:* For master's, writing sample. Additional exam requirements/ endations for international students: Required—TOEFL (minimum score 550 paper- 13 computer-based; 80 iBT). *Application deadline:* For fall admission, 8/1 for domestic , 6/1 for international students; for winter admission, 11/1 for domestic students, 8/1 ational students; for spring admission, 2/1 for domestic students, 12/1 for international . Applications are processed on a rolling basis. Application fee: $70 ($75 for inter- students). Electronic applications accepted. *Financial support:* In 2009–10, 1 fel- with partial tuition reimbursement (averaging $12,000 per year) was awarded; research ships, teaching assistantships with partial tuition reimbursements. *Faculty research:* on, playwriting, screenwriting, poetry, fiction. *Unit head:* Tod Goldberg, Administrative Director, 760-834-0928, Fax: 760-834-0800, E-mail: tod.goldberg@ucr.edu. *Application contact:* Michelle Harding, Program Representative, 760-834-0926, Fax: 760-834-0796, E-mail: michelle.harding@ucr.edu.

University of California, Santa Cruz, Division of Graduate Studies, Division of Social Sciences, Program in Social Documentation, Santa Cruz, CA 95064. Offers MA. *Entrance requirements:* For master's, resume or curriculum vitae, sample of documentary production work. Electronic applications accepted.

University of Central Florida, College of Arts and Humanities, Department of English, Program in English, Orlando, FL 32816. Offers creative writing (MFA); English (MA). *Students:* 44 full-time (30 women), 47 part-time (33 women); includes 14 minority (6 African Americans, 2 Asian Americans or Pacific Islanders, 6 Hispanic Americans). Average age 30. 87 applicants, 52% accepted, 35 enrolled. In 2009, 21 master's awarded. Application fee: $30. Electronic applications accepted. *Expenses:* Tuition, state resident: part-time $306.31 per credit hour. Tuition, nonresident: part-time $1099.01 per credit hour. Part-time tuition and fees vary according to degree level and program. *Financial support:* In 2009–10, 8 fellowships with partial tuition reimbursements (averaging $3,600 per year), 2 research assistantships with partial tuition reimbursements (averaging $10,200 per year), 20 teaching assistantships with partial tuition reimbursements (averaging $7,600 per year) were awarded.

University of Central Oklahoma, College of Graduate Studies and Research, College of Liberal Arts, Department of English, Edmond, OK 73034-5209. Offers composition skills (MA); contemporary literature (MA); creative writing (MA); teaching English as a second language (MA); traditional studies (MA). Part-time programs available. *Degree requirements:* For master's, one foreign language. *Entrance requirements:* For master's, 24 hours of course work in English language and literature. Additional exam requirements/recommendations for international students: Required—TOEFL (minimum score 550 paper-based; 213 computer-based). Electronic applications accepted. *Expenses:* Tuition, state resident: full-time $4128; part-time $172 per credit hour. Tuition, nonresident: full-time $10,373; part-time $432.20 per credit hour. Required fees: $433.20; $18.05 per credit hour. *Faculty research:* John Milton, Harriet Beecher Stowe.

University of Colorado at Boulder, Graduate School, College of Arts and Sciences, Department of English, Boulder, CO 80309. Offers literature (MA, PhD), including creative writing (MA). Part-time programs available. *Faculty:* 48 full-time (26 women). *Students:* 96 full-time (58 women), 22 part-time (14 women); includes 14 minority (6 African Americans, 1 American Indian/Alaska Native, 1 Asian American or Pacific Islander, 6 Hispanic Americans), 2 international. Average age 32. 334 applicants, 11% accepted, 32 enrolled. In 2009, 32 master's, 2 doctorates awarded. *Degree requirements:* For master's, one foreign language, comprehensive exam, thesis or alternative; for doctorate, 2 foreign languages, comprehensive exam, thesis/dissertation. *Entrance requirements:* For master's, GRE General Test, GRE Subject Test, minimum undergraduate GPA of 3.0; for doctorate, GRE General Test, GRE Subject Test. *Application deadline:* For fall admission, 1/1 for domestic students, 12/1 for international students. Application fee: $50 ($60 for international students). *Financial support:* In 2009–10, 22 fellowships (averaging $3,976 per year), 42 research assistantships (averaging $11,068 per year) were awarded; Federal Work-Study and tuition waivers (full) also available. Financial award application deadline: 1/1; financial award applicants required to submit FAFSA. *Faculty research:* Creative writing, literature, language, critical theory. Total annual research expenditures: $9,912.

University of Florida, Graduate School, College of Liberal Arts and Sciences, Department of English, Gainesville, FL 32611. Offers creative writing (MFA); English (MA, PhD). *Degree requirements:* For master's, variable foreign language requirement, thesis or alternative; for doctorate, thesis/dissertation. *Entrance requirements:* For master's and doctorate, GRE General Test, minimum GPA of 3.0. Additional exam requirements/recommendations for international students: Required—TOEFL (minimum score 550 paper-based; 213 computer-based). Electronic applications accepted.

University of Georgia, Graduate School, College of Arts and Sciences, Department of English, Athens, GA 30602. Offers creative writing (MFA, PhD); English (MA, MAT, PhD). *Faculty:* 35 full-time (13 women), 2 part-time/adjunct (0 women). *Students:* 77 full-time (45 women), 26 part-time (15 women); includes 7 minority (all African Americans), 1 international. 241 applicants, 33% accepted, 26 enrolled. In 2009, 17 master's, 14 doctorates awarded. *Degree requirements:* For master's, one foreign language, thesis (MA); for doctorate, 2 foreign languages, thesis/dissertation. *Entrance requirements:* For master's and doctorate, GRE General Test. Additional exam requirements/recommendations for international students: Required—TWE. *Application deadline:* For fall admission, 7/1 priority date for domestic students; for spring admission, 11/15 for domestic students. Application fee: $50. Electronic applications accepted. *Expenses:* Tuition, state resident: full-time $6000; part-time $250 per credit hour. Tuition, nonresident: full-time $20,904; part-time $871 per credit hour. Required fees: $730 per semester. *Financial support:* Fellowships, research assistantships, teaching assistantships, unspecified assistantships available. *Unit head:* Dr. Doug Anderson, Head, 706-543-2248, Fax: 706-542-2181, E-mail: anderson@uga.edu. *Application contact:* Dr. Kris Boudreau, Graduate Coordinator, 706-542-2197, E-mail: boudreau@uga.edu.

University of Houston, College of Liberal Arts and Social Sciences, Department of English, Houston, TX 77204. Offers applied English linguistics (MA); creative writing and literature (MA, PhD); English (MFA, PhD). *Faculty:* 25 full-time (10 women), 6 part-time/adjunct (2 women). *Students:* 93 full-time (45 women), 44 part-time (36 women); includes 25 minority (3 African Americans, 1 American Indian/Alaska Native, 13 Asian Americans or Pacific Islanders, 8 Hispanic Americans), 4 international. Average age 32. 357 applicants, 13% accepted, 34 enrolled. In 2009, 21 master's, 8 doctorates awarded. *Degree requirements:* For master's, one foreign language, comprehensive exam (for some programs), thesis (MFA); for doctorate, one foreign language, comprehensive exam, thesis/dissertation. *Entrance requirements:* For master's, GRE General Test, minimum GPA of 3.0 in last 60 hours of course work; for doctorate, GRE General Test, GRE Subject Test (literature), writing sample. Additional exam requirements/recommendations for international students: Required—TOEFL (minimum score 550 paper-based; 79 iBT). *Application deadline:* For fall admission, 1/15 for domestic and international students. Application fee: $50 ($75 for international students). Electronic applications accepted. *Expenses:* Tuition, state resident: full-time $7676; part-time $320 per credit hour. Tuition, nonresident: full-time $14,324; part-time $597 per credit hour. Required fees: $3034. *Financial support:* In 2009–10, 1 fellowship with full tuition reimbursement (averaging $7,100 per year), teaching assistantships with full tuition reimbursements (averaging $12,000 per year) were awarded; career-related internships or fieldwork, Federal Work-Study, institutionally sponsored loans, scholarships/grants, health care benefits, and unspecified assistantships also available. Support available to part-time students. Financial award application deadline: 2/1. *Unit head:* Wyman Henderson, Chairperson, 713-743-3004, Fax: 713-743-3215, E-mail: whh@uh.edu. *Application contact:* Julie Kofford, Academic Advisor, 713-743-3004, E-mail: jkofford@central.uh.edu.

University of Houston–Downtown, College of Humanities and Social Sciences, Department of English, Houston, TX 77002. Offers professional writing and technical communication (MS). Part-time and evening/weekend programs available. *Faculty:* 5 full-time (3 women). *Students:* 4 full-time (all women), 18 part-time (14 women); includes 9 minority (7 African Americans, 1 Asian American or Pacific Islander, 1 Hispanic American). Average age 37. 5 applicants, 80% accepted, 4 enrolled. In 2009, 4 master's awarded. *Degree requirements:* For master's, thesis optional, graduation portfolio with oral defense. *Entrance requirements:* For master's, GRE (including Analytical Writing section), personal application statement, resume, writing sample, 3 letters of recommendation. Additional exam requirements/recommendations for international students: Required—TOEFL (minimum score 600 paper-based; 250 computer-based; 86 iBT). *Application deadline:* For fall admission, 5/1 for domestic and international students; for spring admission, 11/1 for domestic and international students. Application fee: $35 ($60 for international students). Electronic applications accepted. *Expenses:* Tuition, state resident: full-time

$3150; part-time $175 per credit hour. Tuition, nonresident: full-time $7506; part-time $417 per credit hour. Required fees: $908; $322 per term. *Financial support:* Applicants required to submit FAFSA. *Faculty research:* Environmental rhetoric, instructional design, usability, assessment, presentation slides. *Unit head:* Dr. Robert Jarrett, Chair, 713-221-8013, Fax: 713-226-5205, E-mail: jarrettr@uhd.edu. *Application contact:* Dr. Michelle Moosally, Coordinator of MS in Professional Writing and Technical Communication and Professor, Department of English, 713-221-8013, Fax: 713-226-5205, E-mail: mspwtc@uhd.edu.

University of Idaho, College of Graduate Studies, College of Letters, Arts and Social Sciences, Department of English, Program in Creative Writing, Moscow, ID 83844-2282. Offers MFA. *Students:* 31 full-time, 2 part-time. In 2009, 17 master's awarded. *Entrance requirements:* For master's, minimum GPA of 2.8. *Application deadline:* For fall admission, 8/1 for domestic students; for spring admission, 12/15 for domestic students. Application fee: $55 ($60 for international students). *Expenses:* Tuition, state resident: full-time $6120. Tuition, nonresident: full-time $17,712. *Financial support:* Application deadline: 2/15. *Unit head:* Dr. Gary Williams, Chair, 208-883-6156. *Application contact:* Dr. Gary Williams, Chair, 208-883-6156.

University of Illinois at Chicago, Graduate College, College of Liberal Arts and Sciences, Department of English, Chicago, IL 60607-7128. Offers English (MA, PhD), including creative writing (PhD), English education (MA), English studies, writing (MA); linguistics (MA), including teaching English to speakers of other languages/applied linguistics. Part-time and evening/weekend programs available. *Degree requirements:* For doctorate, variable foreign language requirement, thesis/dissertation, written and oral exams. *Entrance requirements:* For master's, GRE General Test, GRE Subject Test; for doctorate, GRE General Test, GRE Subject Test, minimum GPA of 2.0. Additional exam requirements/recommendations for international students: Required—TOEFL. Electronic applications accepted. *Faculty research:* Literary history and theory.

University of Illinois at Urbana–Champaign, Graduate College, College of Liberal Arts and Sciences, Department of English, Champaign, IL 61820. Offers creative writing (MFA); English (MA, PhD). *Faculty:* 52 full-time (22 women), 2 part-time/adjunct (1 woman). *Students:* 101 full-time (63 women), 58 part-time (40 women); includes 22 minority (3 African Americans, 8 Asian Americans or Pacific Islanders, 11 Hispanic Americans), 12 international. 310 applicants, 18% accepted, 29 enrolled. In 2009, 19 master's, 14 doctorates awarded. *Entrance requirements:* For master's, GRE General Test, GRE Subject Test, minimum GPA of 3.0; writing sample. Additional exam requirements/recommendations for international students: Required—TOEFL (minimum score 550 paper-based; 213 computer-based). *Application deadline:* Applications are processed on a rolling basis. Application fee: $60 ($75 for international students). Electronic applications accepted. *Financial support:* In 2009–10, 64 fellowships, 22 research assistantships, 132 teaching assistantships were awarded; tuition waivers (full and partial) also available. *Faculty research:* English and American literature, cultural studies and critical theory. *Unit head:* Curtis Perry, Head, 217-333-2391, Fax: 217-333-4321, E-mail: cperry@illinois.edu. *Application contact:* Stephanie J. Shockey, Office Support Specialist, 217-333-3646, Fax: 217-333-4321, E-mail: shockey@illinois.edu.

The University of Iowa, Graduate College, College of Liberal Arts and Sciences, Department of English, Iowa City, IA 52242-1316. Offers English (PhD); literary criticism (PhD); literary history (PhD); literary studies (MA); nonfiction writing (MFA); rhetorical theory and stylistics (PhD); writer's workshop (MFA); JD/PhD. *Degree requirements:* For master's, thesis (for some programs), exam; for doctorate, comprehensive exam, thesis/dissertation. *Entrance requirements:* For master's and doctorate, GRE General Test, minimum GPA of 3.0. Additional exam requirements/recommendations for international students: Required—TOEFL (minimum score 640 paper-based; 273 computer-based; 111 iBT). Electronic applications accepted.

The University of Kansas, Graduate Studies, College of Liberal Arts and Sciences, Department of English, Lawrence, KS 66045. Offers creative writing (MFA); English (MA, PhD). Part-time programs available. *Faculty:* 39 full-time (18 women). *Students:* 72 full-time (49 women), 10 part-time (6 women); includes 9 minority (6 African Americans, 3 Hispanic Americans), 4 international. Average age 32. 173 applicants, 34% accepted, 27 enrolled. In 2009, 7 master's, 10 doctorates awarded. *Degree requirements:* For master's, one foreign language, comprehensive exam (for some programs), thesis or alternative; for doctorate, 2 foreign languages, comprehensive exam, thesis/dissertation. *Entrance requirements:* For master's and doctorate, GRE General Test, minimum GPA of 3.3. Additional exam requirements/recommendations for international students: Required—TOEFL. *Application deadline:* For fall admission, 12/31 for domestic and international students. Application fee: $45 ($55 for international students). Electronic applications accepted. *Expenses:* Tuition, state resident: full-time $6492; part-time $270.50 per credit hour. Tuition, nonresident: full-time $15,510; part-time $646.25 per credit hour. Required fees: $847; $70.56 per credit hour. Tuition and fees vary according to course load and program. *Financial support:* Fellowships with full tuition reimbursements, research assistantships, teaching assistantships with full and partial tuition reimbursements, unspecified assistantships available. Financial award application deadline: 12/31. *Faculty research:* African-American literature, twentieth century American literature, Renaissance literature, creative writing. *Unit head:* Marta Caminero-Santangelo, Chair, 785-864-4520, E-mail: camsan@ku.edu. *Application contact:* Joseph Harrington, Director of Graduate Studies, 785-864-4520, E-mail: jharring@ku.edu.

University of Louisiana at Lafayette, College of Liberal Arts, Department of English, Lafayette, LA 70504. Offers British and American literature (MA), including creative writing, folklore, rhetoric; creative writing (PhD); literature (PhD); rhetoric (PhD). Part-time programs available. Terminal master's awarded for partial completion of doctoral program. *Degree requirements:* For master's, one foreign language, thesis or alternative; for doctorate, 2 foreign languages, comprehensive exam, thesis/dissertation. *Entrance requirements:* For master's, GRE General Test, minimum GPA of 2.75; for doctorate, GRE General Test, minimum GPA of 3.0. Additional exam requirements/recommendations for international students: Required—TOEFL (minimum score 550 paper-based; 213 computer-based). Electronic applications accepted. *Faculty research:* Composition theory, Southern literature, medieval literature.

University of Louisville, Graduate School, College of Arts and Sciences, Department of English, Louisville, KY 40292. Offers English (MA), including creative writing, literature, rhetoric and composition (MA, PhD); English rhetoric and composition (PhD), including rhetoric and composition (MA, PhD). Part-time programs available. *Faculty:* 40 full-time (24 women). *Students:* 71 full-time (41 women), 29 part-time (20 women); includes 12 minority (7 African Americans, 1 American Indian/Alaska Native, 2 Asian Americans or Pacific Islanders, 2 Hispanic Americans), 5 international. Average age 30. 82 applicants, 65% accepted, 22 enrolled. In 2009, 22 master's, 7 doctorates awarded. *Degree requirements:* For master's, one foreign language, thesis or alternative, thesis or culminating project; for doctorate, 2 foreign languages, comprehensive exam, thesis/dissertation. *Entrance requirements:* For master's, GRE General Test, 2 academic letters of recommendation; for doctorate, GRE General Test, 15-20 page critical writing sample, 1000-word statement of professional goals, 3 academic letters of recommendation, application for graduate teaching assistantship (resume plus statement of teaching philosophy), transcripts of all college work. Additional exam requirements/recommendations for international students: Required—TOEFL (minimum score 600 paper-based; 210 computer-based; 100 iBT). *Application deadline:* For fall admission, 1/5 for domestic and international students. Applications are processed on a rolling basis. Application fee: $50. Electronic applications accepted. *Financial support:* Fellowships, teaching assistantships, health care benefits and unspecified assistantships available. Financial award application deadline: 1/5. *Faculty research:* American and English literatures and cultures, rhetoric and composition, critical theory and cultural studies, creative writing. Total annual research expenditures: $278,898. *Unit head:* Dr. Susan Griffin, Chair, 502-852-6801, Fax: 502-852-4182, E-mail: smgriff01@louisville.edu. *Application contact:* Libby Leggett, Director, Graduate Admissions, 502-852-3101, Fax: 502-852-6536, E-mail: gradadm@louisville.edu.

University of Maryland, College Park, Academic Affairs, College of Arts and Humanities, Department of English, Creative Writing Program, College Park, MD 20742. Offers MA, MFA, PhD. *Students:* 31 full-time (15 women), 9 part-time (6 women); includes 6 minority (2 African Americans, 3 Asian Americans or Pacific Islanders, 1 Hispanic American). 148 applicants, 36% accepted, 16 enrolled. In 2009, 10 master's awarded. *Degree requirements:* For master's, thesis optional, written exam; for doctorate, one foreign language, oral and written exams. *Entrance requirements:* For master's, GRE General Test, minimum GPA of 3.5, writing sample, 3 letters of recommendation. Additional exam requirements/recommendations for international students: Required—TOEFL. *Application deadline:* For fall admission, 1/15 for domestic and international students. Applications are processed on a rolling basis. Application fee: $60. Electronic applications accepted. *Expenses:* Tuition, area resident: Part-time $471 per credit hour. Tuition, state resident: part-time $471 per credit hour. Tuition, nonresident: part-time $1016 per credit hour. Required fees: $337.04 per term. *Financial support:* In 2009–10, 16 teaching assistantships (averaging $16,229 per year) were awarded; fellowships, research assistantships also available. Financial award applicants required to submit FAFSA. *Faculty research:* Early British literature, American literature. *Unit head:* Kent Cartwright, Chair, 301-405-3807, E-mail: kcartwri@umd.edu. *Application contact:* Dean of Graduate School, 301-405-0376, Fax: 301-314-9305.

University of Massachusetts Amherst, Graduate School, College of Humanities and Fine Arts, Department of English, Amherst, MA 01003. Offers creative writing (MFA); English and American literature (MA, PhD). Part-time programs available. *Faculty:* 47 full-time (23 women). *Students:* 115 full-time (65 women), 88 part-time (54 women); includes 27 minority (10 African Americans, 2 American Indian/Alaska Native, 7 Asian Americans or Pacific Islanders, 8 Hispanic Americans), 7 international. Average age 30. 864 applicants, 14% accepted, 49 enrolled. In 2009, 29 master's, 8 doctorates awarded. Terminal master's awarded for partial completion of doctoral program. *Degree requirements:* For master's, one foreign language, thesis optional; for doctorate, one foreign language, comprehensive exam, thesis/dissertation. *Entrance requirements:* For master's, GRE General Test, GRE Subject Test (MA), writing sample (MFA); for doctorate, GRE General Test, GRE Subject Test. Additional exam requirements/recommendations for international students: Required—TOEFL (minimum score 550 paper-based; 213 computer-based; 80 iBT), IELTS (minimum score 6.5). *Application deadline:* For fall admission, 12/1 for domestic and international students. Applications are processed on a rolling basis. Application fee: $50 ($65 for international students). Electronic applications accepted. *Expenses:* Tuition, state resident: full-time $2640; part-time $110 per credit. Tuition, nonresident: full-time $9936; part-time $414 per credit. Tuition and fees vary according to course load. *Financial support:* In 2009–10, 8 fellowships with full tuition reimbursements (averaging $4,868 per year), 5 research assistantships with full tuition reimbursements (averaging $8,729 per year), 48 teaching assistantships with full tuition reimbursements (averaging $8,846 per year) were awarded; career-related internships or fieldwork, Federal Work-Study, scholarships/grants, traineeships, health care benefits, tuition waivers (full), and unspecified assistantships also available. Support available to part-time students. Financial award application deadline: 12/1. *Unit head:* Dr. Joseph F. Bartolomeo, Department Head, 413-545-2575, Fax: 413-545-3880. *Application contact:* Jean M. Ames, Supervisor of Admissions, 413-545-0722, Fax: 413-577-0010, E-mail: gradadm@grad.umass.edu.

University of Massachusetts Dartmouth, Graduate School, College of Arts and Sciences, Program in Professional Writing, North Dartmouth, MA 02747-2300. Offers MA, Post-baccalaureate Certificate. Part-time programs available. *Faculty:* 23 full-time (11 women), 38 part-time/adjunct (23 women). *Students:* 9 full-time (7 women), 22 part-time (16 women). Average age 34. 16 applicants, 81% accepted, 10 enrolled. In 2009, 9 master's, 2 other advanced degrees awarded. *Degree requirements:* For master's, thesis. *Entrance requirements:* For master's, MAT or GRE; portfolio or writing sample (10-30 pages), 3 letters of recommendation. Additional exam requirements/recommendations for international students: Required—TOEFL (minimum score 500 paper-based). *Application deadline:* For fall admission, 4/1 for domestic students, 2/1 for international students; for spring admission, 11/1 for domestic students, 9/1 for international students. Application fee: $40 ($60 for international students). Electronic applications accepted. *Expenses:* Tuition, state resident: full-time $2071; part-time $86.29 per credit. Tuition, nonresident: full-time $8099; part-time $337.46 per credit. Required fees: $9446. Tuition and fees vary according to class time, course load and reciprocity agreements. *Financial support:* In 2009–10, 9 teaching assistantships with full tuition reimbursements (averaging $10,450 per year) were awarded; career-related internships or fieldwork, Federal Work-Study, and unspecified assistantships also available. Support available to part-time students. Financial award application deadline: 3/1; financial award applicants required to submit FAFSA. *Faculty research:* Rhetoric/communication studies, ethnic literatures, technology transfer, internet worked writing practices. *Unit head:* Dr. Christopher Eisenhart, Director, 508-910-6468, Fax: 508-999-9235, E-mail: ceisenhart@umassd.edu. *Application contact:* Elan Turcotte-Shamski, Graduate Admissions Officer, 508-999-8604, Fax: 508-999-8183, E-mail: graduate@umassd.edu.

University of Memphis, Graduate School, College of Arts and Sciences, Department of English, Memphis, TN 38152. Offers African-American literature (Graduate Certificate); applied linguistics (PhD); composition studies (PhD); creative writing (MFA); English as a second language (MA); linguistics (MA); literary and cultural studies (PhD), including African-American literature; literature (MA); professional writing (MA, PhD); teaching English as a second language (Graduate Certificate). Part-time and evening/weekend programs available. Post-baccalaureate distance learning degree programs offered (no on-campus study). *Faculty:* 31 full-time (15 women), 2 part-time/adjunct (both women). *Students:* 98 full-time (59 women), 99 part-time (66 women); includes 36 minority (28 African Americans, 5 Asian Americans or Pacific Islanders, 3 Hispanic Americans), 7 international. Average age 34. 128 applicants, 71% accepted, 29 enrolled. In 2009, 38 master's, 4 doctorates, 21 other advanced degrees awarded. Terminal master's awarded for partial completion of doctoral program. *Degree requirements:* For master's, one foreign language, comprehensive exam, thesis optional; for doctorate, 2 foreign languages, comprehensive exam, thesis/dissertation. *Entrance requirements:* For master's, GRE; for doctorate, GRE. Additional exam requirements/recommendations for international students: Required—TOEFL. *Application deadline:* For fall admission, 7/1 for domestic students; for spring admission, 10/15 for domestic students. Applications are processed on a rolling basis. Application fee: $35 ($60 for international students). Electronic applications accepted. *Expenses:* Tuition, state resident: full-time $6246; part-time $347 per credit hour. Tuition, nonresident: full-time $15,894; part-time $883 per credit hour. Required fees: $1160. Full-time tuition and fees vary according to course load, degree level and program. *Financial support:* In 2009–10, 123 students received support; research assistantships with full tuition reimbursements available, teaching assistantships with full tuition reimbursements available, Federal Work-Study, scholarships/grants, and unspecified assistantships available. Financial award application deadline: 2/15; financial award applicants required to submit FAFSA. *Faculty research:* Applied linguistis, British and American literature, professional writing, composition studies. *Unit head:* Dr. Eric C. Link, Chair, 901-678-2651, Fax: 901-678-2226, E-mail: eclink@memphis.edu. *Application contact:* Dr. Verner D. Mitchell, Director, Graduate Studies, 901-678-3099, Fax: 901-678-2226, E-mail: vdmtchll@memphis.edu.

University of Miami, Graduate School, College of Arts and Sciences, Department of English, Coral Gables, FL 33124. Offers creative writing (MFA); English (MA, PhD). Part-time programs available. Terminal master's awarded for partial completion of doctoral program. *Degree requirements:* For master's, one foreign language, thesis optional; for doctorate, one foreign language, thesis/dissertation. *Entrance requirements:* For master's and doctorate, GRE General Test. Electronic applications accepted. *Faculty research:* Anglo-Irish literature, feminist criticism and theory, Caribbean literature, early modern literature and culture, postcolonial and ethnic studies.

University of Michigan, Horace H. Rackham School of Graduate Studies, College of Literature, Science, and the Arts, Department of English Language and Literature, Creative Writing Program, Ann Arbor, MI 48109. Offers MFA. *Faculty:* 9 full-time (4 women). *Students:* 48 full-time (32 women); includes 13 minority (3 African Americans, 5 Asian Americans or Pacific Islanders, 5 Hispanic Americans), 2 international. 780 applicants, 4% accepted, 24 enrolled. In 2009, 24 master's awarded. *Degree requirements:* For master's, comprehensive exam, thesis.

Writing

University of Michigan (continued)

Entrance requirements: For master's, writing sample. Additional exam requirements/recommendations for international students: Required—TOEFL (minimum score 620 paper-based; 260 computer-based; 106 iBT). *Application deadline:* For fall admission, 1/1 for domestic and international students. Application fee: $60 ($75 for international students). Electronic applications accepted. *Expenses:* Tuition, state resident: full-time $17,286; part-time $1099 per credit hour. Tuition, nonresident: full-time $34,944; part-time $2080 per credit hour. Required fees: $95 per semester. Tuition and fees vary according to course load, degree level and program. *Financial support:* In 2009–10, 48 students received support; fellowships with tuition reimbursements available, teaching assistantships with tuition reimbursements available, health care benefits and summer funding available. *Faculty research:* Prose, poetry. *Unit head:* Prof. Eileen Pollack, Director, 734-936-2274. *Application contact:* Graduate Admissions Office, 734-936-2274, Fax: 734-763-3128, E-mail: grad.eng.admis@um.cc.umich.edu.

University of Missouri–Kansas City, College of Arts and Sciences, Department of English, Kansas City, MO 64110-2499. Offers creative writing and media arts (MFA); English (MA, PhD). PhD (interdisciplinary) offered through the School of Graduate Studies. Part-time and evening/weekend programs available. *Faculty:* 22 full-time (15 women), 18 part-time/adjunct (11 women). *Students:* 10 full-time (6 women), 39 part-time (22 women); includes 5 minority (4 African Americans, 1 Asian American or Pacific Islander). Average age 31. 38 applicants, 63% accepted, 12 enrolled. In 2009, 13 master's awarded. *Degree requirements:* For master's, one foreign language; for doctorate, 2 foreign languages, comprehensive exam, thesis/dissertation. *Entrance requirements:* For master's, GRE General Test, 3 letters of recommendation. Additional exam requirements/recommendations for international students: Required—TOEFL (minimum score 550 paper-based; 213 computer-based; 80 iBT). *Application deadline:* For fall admission, 1/15 for domestic students, 1/15 priority date for international students. Applications are processed on a rolling basis. Application fee: $45 ($50 for international students). Electronic applications accepted. *Expenses:* Tuition, state resident: full-time $5378; part-time $299 per credit hour. Tuition, nonresident: full-time $13,881; part-time $771 per credit hour. Required fees: $641; $71 per credit hour. Tuition and fees vary according to course load and program. *Financial support:* In 2009–10, 15 teaching assistantships (averaging $12,180 per year) were awarded; career-related internships or fieldwork, Federal Work-Study, and institutionally sponsored loans also available. Support available to part-time students. Financial award application deadline: 3/1; financial award applicants required to submit FAFSA. *Faculty research:* Creative writing: poetry and prose, computational linguistics, rhetoric and composition, African-American and British literature, print culture. Total annual research expenditures: $105,946. *Unit head:* Dr. Jeff Rydberg-Cox, Co-Chair, 816-235-2560, Fax: 816-235-1308, E-mail: rydbergcoxj@umkc.edu. *Application contact:* Dr. Joan Dean, Director of Graduate Studies, 816-235-2555, E-mail: deanj@umkc.edu.

University of Missouri–St. Louis, College of Arts and Sciences, Department of English, St. Louis, MO 63121. Offers American literature (MA); creative writing (MFA); English (MA); English literature (MA); linguistics (MA); teaching of writing (Graduate Certificate). Part-time and evening/weekend programs available. *Faculty:* 21 full-time (11 women), 2 part-time/adjunct (1 woman). *Students:* 32 full-time (15 women), 97 part-time (62 women); includes 10 minority (5 African Americans, 2 American Indian/Alaska Native, 2 Asian Americans or Pacific Islanders, 1 Hispanic American), 1 international. Average age 31. 114 applicants, 46% accepted, 36 enrolled. In 2009, 28 master's, 1 other advanced degree awarded. *Degree requirements:* For master's, thesis optional. *Entrance requirements:* For master's, writing sample. Additional exam requirements/recommendations for international students: Required—TOEFL (minimum score 550 paper-based; 213 computer-based). *Application deadline:* For fall admission, 7/1 priority date for domestic and international students; for spring admission, 12/1 priority date for domestic and international students. Applications are processed on a rolling basis. Application fee: $35 ($40 for international students). Electronic applications accepted. *Expenses:* Tuition, state resident: full-time $5377; part-time $297.70 per credit hour. Tuition, nonresident: full-time $13,882; part-time $771.20 per credit hour. Required fees: $220; $12.20 per credit hour. One-time fee: $12. Tuition and fees vary according to course level, campus/location and program. *Financial support:* In 2009–10, 4 research assistantships (averaging $5,500 per year), 7 teaching assistantships with full and partial tuition reimbursements (averaging $9,000 per year) were awarded. Financial award applicants required to submit FAFSA. *Faculty research:* Victorian literature, Shakespeare and Renaissance literature, eighteenth century literature, composition theory. *Unit head:* Dr. Frank Grady, Director of Graduate Studies, 314-516-5541, Fax: 314-516-5781, E-mail: fgrady@umsl.edu. *Application contact:* 314-516-5458, Fax: 314-516-5310, E-mail: gradadm@umsl.edu.

The University of Montana, Graduate School, College of Arts and Sciences, Department of English, Program in Creative Writing, Missoula, MT 59812-0002. Offers fiction (MFA); non-fiction (MFA); poetry (MFA). *Degree requirements:* For master's, final creative paper. *Entrance requirements:* For master's, GRE General Test, sample of written work. Additional exam requirements/recommendations for international students: Required—TOEFL. *Faculty research:* Fiction, poetry, nonfiction.

University of Nebraska at Kearney, College of Graduate Study, College of Fine Arts and Humanities, Department of English, Kearney, NE 68849-0001. Offers creative writing (MA); literature (MA). Part-time and evening/weekend programs available. *Degree requirements:* For master's, thesis optional. *Entrance requirements:* For master's, GRE General Test. Additional exam requirements/recommendations for international students: Required—TOEFL (minimum score 550 paper-based; 213 computer-based). Electronic applications accepted. *Faculty research:* Narrative theory, popular culture, western and plains literature, women's studies, media studies.

University of Nebraska at Omaha, Graduate Studies, College of Arts and Sciences, Department of English, Omaha, NE 68182. Offers advanced writing (Certificate); English (MA); teaching of English to speakers of other languages (Certificate); technical communication (Certificate). Part-time and evening/weekend programs available. *Faculty:* 20 full-time (10 women). *Students:* 11 full-time (4 women), 59 part-time (43 women); includes 2 minority (1 African American, 1 Asian American or Pacific Islander), 3 international. Average age 32. 40 applicants, 68% accepted, 17 enrolled. In 2009, 13 master's, 8 other advanced degrees awarded. *Degree requirements:* For master's, comprehensive exam, thesis (for some programs). *Entrance requirements:* For master's, minimum GPA of 3.0, 3 letters of recommendation, writing sample. Additional exam requirements/recommendations for international students: Required—TOEFL (minimum score 600 paper-based; 250 computer-based; 100 iBT). *Application deadline:* For fall admission, 8/1 priority date for domestic students; for spring admission, 12/1 priority date for domestic students. Applications are processed on a rolling basis. Application fee: $45. Electronic applications accepted. *Financial support:* In 2009–10, 34 students received support; fellowships, teaching assistantships with tuition reimbursements available, Federal Work-Study, institutionally sponsored loans, scholarships/grants, tuition waivers (partial), and unspecified assistantships available. Support available to part-time students. Financial award application deadline: 3/1; financial award applicants required to submit FAFSA. *Unit head:* Dr. Susan Maher, Chairperson, 402-554-3636. *Application contact:* Dr. Joan Latchaw, Student Contact, 402-554-3636.

University of Nebraska at Omaha, Graduate Studies, Program in Writing, Omaha, NE 68182. Offers MFA. Postbaccalaureate distance learning degree programs offered (no on-campus study). *Students:* 35 full-time (20 women); includes 3 minority (1 African American, 2 Hispanic Americans). Average age 38. 28 applicants, 75% accepted, 11 enrolled. In 2009, 16 master's awarded. *Degree requirements:* For master's, comprehensive exam. *Entrance requirements:* For master's, portfolio, letters of recommendation. Additional exam requirements/recommendations for international students: Required—TOEFL (minimum score 550 paper-based; 213 computer-based; 80 iBT). *Application deadline:* For fall admission, 2/15 priority date for domestic students; for spring admission, 7/15 priority date for domestic students. Applications are processed on a rolling basis. Application fee: $45. Electronic applications accepted. *Financial support:* In 2009–10, 15 students received support. Scholarships/grants and tuition waivers (partial) available. Financial award application deadline: 3/1; financial award applicants required to submit FAFSA. *Unit head:* Dr. Richard Duggin, Director, 402-554-4801. *Application contact:* Penny Harmoney, Director, Graduate Studies, 402-554-2341, Fax: 402-554-3143, E-mail: graduate@unomaha.edu.

University of Nebraska–Lincoln, Graduate College, College of Arts and Sciences, Department of English, Lincoln, NE 68588-0333. Offers composition and rhetoric (MA, PhD); creative writing (MA, PhD); literature studies (MA, PhD). *Degree requirements:* For master's, thesis optional; for doctorate, one foreign language, comprehensive exam, thesis/dissertation. *Entrance requirements:* For master's, writing sample; for doctorate, GRE General Test, writing sample. Additional exam requirements/recommendations for international students: Required—TOEFL (minimum score 600 paper-based; 250 computer-based). Electronic applications accepted. *Faculty research:* Creative writing, composition and rhetoric, women's studies, North American literature, medieval/Renaissance studies.

University of Nevada, Las Vegas, Graduate College, College of Liberal Arts, Department of English, Las Vegas, NV 89154-5011. Offers creative writing (MFA); English (MA, PhD). Part-time programs available. *Faculty:* 32 full-time (12 women), 5 part-time/adjunct (0 women). *Students:* 66 full-time (31 women), 21 part-time (14 women); includes 7 minority (1 Asian American or Pacific Islander, 6 Hispanic Americans), 4 international. Average age 36. 170 applicants, 19% accepted, 23 enrolled. In 2009, 21 master's, 5 doctorates awarded. *Degree requirements:* For master's, one foreign language, comprehensive exam, thesis (for some programs); for doctorate, 2 foreign languages, comprehensive exam, thesis/dissertation. *Entrance requirements:* For master's, GRE General Test (verbal); for doctorate, GRE General Test (Verbal and Subject). Additional exam requirements/recommendations for international students: Required—TOEFL (minimum score 550 paper-based; 213 computer-based; 80 iBT), IELTS (minimum score 7). *Application deadline:* For fall admission, 2/15 priority date for domestic and international students. Applications are processed on a rolling basis. Application fee: $60 ($95 for international students). Electronic applications accepted. *Financial support:* In 2009–10, 68 students received support, including 1 fellowship with full tuition reimbursement available (averaging $20,000 per year), 12 research assistantships with partial tuition reimbursements available (averaging $13,782 per year), 55 teaching assistantships with partial tuition reimbursements available (averaging $11,127 per year); institutionally sponsored loans, scholarships/grants, health care benefits, and unspecified assistantships also available. Financial award application deadline: 3/1. *Faculty research:* Contemporary poetry and fiction, Renaissance literature and Renaissance studies, Post-Structuralist literary theory and criticism, business and professional writing, nineteenth and twentieth century British and American literature. *Unit head:* Dr. Richard Harp, Chair/ Professor, 702-895-0919, Fax: 702-895-4801, E-mail: richard.harp@unlv.edu. *Application contact:* Graduate College Admissions Evaluator, 702-895-3320, Fax: 702-895-4180, E-mail: gradcollege@unlv.edu.

University of New Hampshire, Graduate School, College of Liberal Arts, Department of English, Durham, NH 03824. Offers English (MFA, PhD); English education (MST); language and linguistics (MA); literature (MA); writing (MA). Part-time programs available. *Faculty:* 35 full-time (18 women). *Students:* 54 full-time (33 women), 64 part-time (40 women); includes 5 minority (1 African American, 2 American Indian/Alaska Native, 2 Hispanic Americans), 5 international. Average age 34. 279 applicants, 43% accepted, 38 enrolled. In 2009, 32 master's, 5 doctorates awarded. *Degree requirements:* For master's, one foreign language; for doctorate, 2 foreign languages, thesis/dissertation. *Entrance requirements:* For master's, GRE General Test, sample of written work; for doctorate, GRE General Test, GRE Subject Test, sample of written work. Additional exam requirements/recommendations for international students: Required—TOEFL (minimum score 550 paper-based; 213 computer-based; 80 iBT). *Application deadline:* For fall admission, 6/1 priority date for domestic students, 2/15 for international students; for spring admission, 12/1 for domestic students. Applications are processed on a rolling basis. Application fee: $65. Electronic applications accepted. *Expenses:* Tuition, state resident: full-time $10,380; part-time $577 per credit hour. Tuition, nonresident: full-time $24,350; part-time $1002 per credit hour. Required fees: $1550; $387.50 per semester. Tuition and fees vary according to course load and program. *Financial support:* In 2009–10, 57 students received support, including 4 fellowships, 46 teaching assistantships; research assistantships, career-related internships or fieldwork, Federal Work-Study, scholarships/grants, and tuition waivers (full and partial) also available. Support available to part-time students. Financial award application deadline: 2/15. *Unit head:* Dr. Andrew Merton, Chairperson, 603-862-3963. *Application contact:* Jamie Auger, Administrative Assistant, 603-862-3963, E-mail: engl.grad@unh.edu.

University of New Mexico, Graduate School, College of Arts and Sciences, Department of English, Albuquerque, NM 87131-2039. Offers creative writing (MFA); English (MA, PhD). Part-time programs available. *Faculty:* 38 full-time (22 women), 31 part-time/adjunct (20 women). *Students:* 75 full-time (56 women), 29 part-time (22 women); includes 20 minority (1 African American, 5 American Indian/Alaska Native, 2 Asian Americans or Pacific Islanders, 12 Hispanic Americans), 2 international. Average age 35. 133 applicants, 35% accepted, 24 enrolled. In 2009, 17 master's, 10 doctorates awarded. *Degree requirements:* For master's, one foreign language, comprehensive exam (for some programs), portfolio; thesis (MFA); for doctorate, 2 foreign languages, comprehensive exam, thesis/dissertation. *Entrance requirements:* For master's, GRE General Test, writing sample; for doctorate, GRE General Test, GRE Subject Test (literature), writing sample. *Application deadline:* For fall admission, 1/15 for domestic students. Application fee: $50. Electronic applications accepted. *Expenses:* Tuition, state resident: full-time $2099; part-time $233.20 per credit hour. Tuition, nonresident: full-time $6650. Required fees: $25 per semester. Tuition and fees vary according to course load, program and reciprocity agreements. *Financial support:* In 2009–10, 44 students received support, including 3 fellowships (averaging $11,283 per year), 75 teaching assistantships with full tuition reimbursements available (averaging $13,184 per year); career-related internships or fieldwork, scholarships/grants, health care benefits, and unspecified assistantships also available. Financial award application deadline: 1/15; financial award applicants required to submit FAFSA. *Faculty research:* American literature, Native American literature, Chicana/o literature, British and Irish literature, creative writing, rhetoric and writing. Total annual research expenditures: $3,000. *Unit head:* Dr. Gail Turley Houston, Chair, 505-277-6347, Fax: 505-277-0021, E-mail: ghouston@unm.edu. *Application contact:* N. Ezra Meier, Graduate Advisor, 505-277-4437, Fax: 505-277-0021, E-mail: nezra@unm.edu.

University of New Mexico, Graduate School, College of Arts and Sciences, Program in Creative Writing, Albuquerque, NM 87131-2039. Offers MFA. Part-time programs available. *Students:* 25 full-time (19 women), 10 part-time (8 women); includes 13 minority (3 American Indian/Alaska Native, 2 Asian Americans or Pacific Islanders, 8 Hispanic Americans), 1 international. Average age 37. 68 applicants, 19% accepted, 6 enrolled. In 2009, 9 master's awarded. *Degree requirements:* For master's, comprehensive exam, thesis. *Entrance requirements:* For master's, writing sample. *Application deadline:* For fall admission, 1/15 for domestic and international students. Application fee: $50. Electronic applications accepted. *Expenses:* Tuition, state resident: full-time $2099; part-time $233.20 per credit hour. Tuition, nonresident: full-time $6650. Required fees: $25 per semester. Tuition and fees vary according to course load, program and reciprocity agreements. *Financial support:* Health care benefits and unspecified assistantships available. Financial award application deadline: 1/15. *Faculty research:* Creative writing, fiction, creative non-fiction, poetry. *Unit head:* Dr. Gail Turley Houston, Chair, 505-277-6347, Fax: 505-277-0021, E-mail: ghouston@unm.edu. *Application contact:* Ezra Meir, Graduate Advisor, 505-277-4437, Fax: 505-277-0021, E-mail: nezra@unm.edu.

University of New Mexico, Graduate School, College of Fine Arts, Department of Theatre and Dance, Albuquerque, NM 87131-2039. Offers dramatic writing (MFA); theater and dance (MA). *Accreditation:* NASD; NAST. *Faculty:* 21 full-time (12 women), 16 part-time/adjunct (6 women). *Students:* 23 full-time (19 women), 5 part-time (4 women); includes 7 minority (1 Asian American or Pacific Islander, 6 Hispanic Americans), 2 international. Average age 31. 34

applicants, 53% accepted, 12 enrolled. In 2009, 10 master's awarded. *Degree requirements:* For master's, comprehensive exam (for some programs), thesis (for some programs). *Entrance requirements:* For master's, minimum GPA of 3.0, undergraduate major in theatre, dance or closely related field, 3 letters of recommendation, letter of intent. *Application deadline:* For fall admission, 4/15 for domestic students; for spring admission, 11/10 for domestic students. Application fee: $50. Electronic applications accepted. *Expenses:* Tuition, state resident: full-time $2099; part-time $233.20 per credit hour. Tuition, nonresident: full-time $6650. Required fees: $25 per semester. Tuition and fees vary according to course load, program and reciprocity agreements. *Financial support:* In 2009–10, 14 students received support, including 5 research assistantships with partial tuition reimbursements available (averaging $8,000 per year), 6 teaching assistantships with partial tuition reimbursements available (averaging $8,000 per year); Federal Work-Study, health care benefits, tuition waivers (partial), and unspecified assistantships also available. Financial award application deadline: 3/1; financial award applicants required to submit FAFSA. *Faculty research:* Theater education and outreach, choreography, dramatic writing, dance history/criticism. *Unit head:* Bill Liotta, Chair, 505-277-4332, Fax: 505-277-8921, E-mail: wliotta@unm.edu. *Application contact:* Christina Squire, Administrator II, 505-277-7362, Fax: 505-277-8921, E-mail: csquire@unm.edu.

The University of North Carolina at Greensboro, Graduate School, College of Arts and Sciences, Department of English, Program in Creative Writing, Greensboro, NC 27412-5001. Offers MFA. *Degree requirements:* For master's, comprehensive exam, thesis. *Entrance requirements:* For master's, GRE General Test, minimum GPA of 3.0, writing sample. Additional exam requirements/recommendations for international students: Required—TOEFL. Electronic applications accepted. *Faculty research:* Fiction, poetry, science fiction, film studies.

The University of North Carolina Wilmington, College of Arts and Sciences, Department of Creative Writing, Wilmington, NC 28403-3297. Offers MFA. Part-time programs available. *Degree requirements:* For master's, comprehensive exam, thesis. *Entrance requirements:* For master's, writing sample. Additional exam requirements/recommendations for international students: Required—TOEFL (minimum score 550 paper-based; 217 computer-based; 79 iBT), IELTS (minimum score 6.5).

University of North Florida, College of Arts and Sciences, Department of English, Jacksonville, FL 32224. Offers MA. Part-time and evening/weekend programs available. *Faculty:* 15 full-time (7 women). *Students:* 17 full-time (11 women), 45 part-time (35 women); includes 4 minority (1 African American, 2 Asian Americans or Pacific Islanders, 1 Hispanic American), 1 international. Average age 30. 27 applicants, 26% accepted, 4 enrolled. In 2009, 33 master's awarded. *Degree requirements:* For master's, comprehensive exam, thesis optional. *Entrance requirements:* For master's, GRE General Test, minimum GPA of 3.0 in last 60 hours, writing sample. Additional exam requirements/recommendations for international students: Required—TOEFL (minimum score 500 paper-based; 173 computer-based). *Application deadline:* For fall admission, 7/1 priority date for domestic students, 5/1 for international students; for spring admission, 11/1 priority date for domestic students, 10/1 for international students. Applications are processed on a rolling basis. Application fee: $30. Electronic applications accepted. *Expenses:* Tuition, state resident: full-time $6649.20; part-time $277.05 per credit hour. Tuition, nonresident: full-time $22,970; part-time $957.08 per credit hour. Required fees: $985; $41.03 per credit hour. *Financial support:* In 2009–10, 39 students received support, including 1 teaching assistantship (averaging $2,000 per year); research assistantships, Federal Work-Study and tuition waivers (partial) also available. Support available to part-time students. Financial award application deadline: 4/1; financial award applicants required to submit FAFSA. *Faculty research:* Genre, period, and individual author studies in British, American, and world literature; literary criticism and theory—psychological, new historical and cultural, deconstructive, feminist, narrative, mythic; film and popular culture; online poetry publishing. *Unit head:* Dr. Samuel A. Kimball, Chair, 904-620-2273, Fax: 904-620-3940, E-mail: skimball@unf.edu. *Application contact:* Dr. Jason Mauro, Graduate Coordinator, 904-620-2273, Fax: 904-620-3940, E-mail: jmauro@unf.edu.

University of North Texas, Robert B. Toulouse School of Graduate Studies, College of Arts and Sciences, Department of English, Denton, TX 76203. Offers creative writing (MA); English (MA, PhD). Terminal master's awarded for partial completion of doctoral program. *Degree requirements:* For master's, one foreign language, comprehensive exam, thesis optional; for doctorate, one foreign language, comprehensive exam, thesis/dissertation. *Entrance requirements:* For master's, GRE General Test, minimum GPA of 3.0, personal statement, current curriculum vitae/resume, writing sample (for creative writing program); for doctorate, GRE General Test, minimum GPA of 3.5, 3 letters of recommendation, personal statement, writing sample. Additional exam requirements/recommendations for international students: Required—proof of English language proficiency required for non-native English speakers; Recommended—TOEFL (minimum score 550 paper-based; 213 computer-based; 79 iBT). Application fee: $50 ($75 for international students). *Expenses:* Tuition, state resident: full-time $4298; part-time $239 per contact hour. Tuition, nonresident: full-time $9878; part-time $549 per contact hour. Required fees: $265 per contact hour. *Financial support:* Fellowships with full tuition reimbursements, teaching assistantships with partial tuition reimbursements, career-related internships or fieldwork, Federal Work-Study, institutionally sponsored loans, scholarships/grants, health care benefits, and unspecified assistantships available. Financial award application deadline: 4/1; financial award applicants required to submit FAFSA. *Faculty research:* Creative writing, British and American literature, composition and rhetoric. *Application contact:* Chair of Graduate Studies, 940-565-2114, Fax: 940-565-4355.

University of Notre Dame, Graduate School, College of Arts and Letters, Division of Humanities, Department of English, Creative Writing Program, Notre Dame, IN 46556. Offers MFA. *Degree requirements:* For master's, thesis. *Entrance requirements:* For master's, GRE General Test, minimum GPA of 3.0. Additional exam requirements/recommendations for international students: Required—TOEFL (minimum score 600 paper-based; 250 computer-based; 80 iBT). Electronic applications accepted. *Faculty research:* Novels, stories, poetry.

University of Oklahoma, Graduate College, Gaylord College of Journalism and Mass Communication, Program in Journalism and Mass Communication, Norman, OK 73019-0390. Offers advertising and public relations (MA); information gathering and distribution (MA); mass communication management and policy (MA); professional writing (MA); telecommunication and new technology (MA). Part-time programs available. *Students:* 34 full-time (18 women), 43 part-time (23 women); includes 13 minority (4 African Americans, 5 American Indian/Alaska Native, 4 Hispanic Americans), 9 international. 45 applicants, 42% accepted, 9 enrolled. *Degree requirements:* For master's, thesis optional. *Entrance requirements:* For master's, GRE General Test, minimum GPA of 3.2, 9 hours of course work in journalism, course work in statistics. Additional exam requirements/recommendations for international students: Required—TOEFL (minimum score 600 paper-based; 250 computer-based), TWE (minimum score 5). *Application deadline:* For fall admission, 2/1 for domestic students, 4/1 for international students; for spring admission, 11/1 for domestic students, 9/1 for international students. Application fee: $40 ($90 for international students). Electronic applications accepted. *Expenses:* Tuition, state resident: full-time $3744; part-time $156 per credit hour. Tuition, nonresident: full-time $13,577; part-time $565.70 per credit hour. Required fees: $2415; $90.10 per credit hour. *Financial support:* In 2009–10, 43 students received support, including 4 fellowships (averaging $5,000 per year); career-related internships or fieldwork, scholarships/grants, health care benefits, and unspecified assistantships also available. *Faculty research:* Organizational management, rhetorical analysis, international public relations, digital production, normative theory. *Unit head:* Dr. Joe Foote, Dean, 405-325-2721, Fax: 405-325-7565, E-mail: jfoote@ou.edu. *Application contact:* Kelly Storm, Graduate Advisor, 405-325-2722, Fax: 405-325-7565, E-mail: kstorm@ou.edu.

University of Oklahoma, Graduate College, Gaylord College of Journalism and Mass Communication, Program in Professional Writing, Norman, OK 73019-0390. Offers MPW. Part-time programs available. *Students:* 12 full-time (8 women), 11 part-time (6 women); includes 3 minority (all American Indian/Alaska Native). 11 applicants, 100% accepted, 11 enrolled. In 2009, 23 master's awarded. *Degree requirements:* For master's, project. *Entrance requirements:* For master's, GRE General Test, 2 letters of recommendation, resume, writing sample. Additional exam requirements/recommendations for international students: Required—TOEFL (minimum score 600 paper-based; 250 computer-based), TWE (minimum score 5). *Application deadline:* For fall admission, 7/1 for domestic students, 4/1 for international students; for spring admission, 11/1 for domestic students, 9/1 for international students. Application fee: $40 ($90 for international students). Electronic applications accepted. *Expenses:* Tuition, state resident: full-time $3744; part-time $156 per credit hour. Tuition, nonresident: full-time $13,577; part-time $565.70 per credit hour. Required fees: $2415; $90.10 per credit hour. *Financial support:* In 2009–10, 16 students received support. Career-related internships or fieldwork, scholarships/grants, health care benefits, and unspecified assistantships available. Financial award applicants required to submit FAFSA. *Faculty research:* Creative writing, script writing, nonfiction. *Unit head:* Dr. Joe Foote, Dean, 405-325-2721, Fax: 405-325-7565, E-mail: jfoote@ou.edu. *Application contact:* Kelly Storm, Graduate Advisor, 405-325-2722, Fax: 405-325-7565, E-mail: kstorm@ou.edu.

University of Oregon, Graduate School, College of Arts and Sciences, Department of Creative Writing, Eugene, OR 97403. Offers MFA. *Degree requirements:* For master's, thesis, exam. *Entrance requirements:* For master's, minimum GPA of 3.0. Additional exam requirements/recommendations for international students: Required—TOEFL. *Faculty research:* Poetry, fiction, literary nonfiction.

University of Pennsylvania, Graduate School of Education, Division of Language in Education, Program in Reading, Writing, and Literacy, Philadelphia, PA 19104. Offers MS Ed, Ed D, PhD. Part-time programs available. *Students:* 87 full-time (77 women), 43 part-time (41 women); includes 31 minority (14 African Americans, 14 Asian Americans or Pacific Islanders, 3 Hispanic Americans), 4 international. 104 applicants, 71% accepted, 46 enrolled. In 2009, 33 master's, 3 doctorates awarded. *Degree requirements:* For master's, comprehensive exam; for doctorate, one foreign language, thesis/dissertation, preliminary exam. *Entrance requirements:* For master's and doctorate, GRE General Test or MAT. Additional exam requirements/recommendations for international students: Required—TOEFL. *Application deadline:* For fall admission, 12/15 priority date for domestic students. Applications are processed on a rolling basis. Application fee: $70. Electronic applications accepted. *Expenses:* Contact institution. *Financial support:* Fellowships, institutionally sponsored loans, scholarships/grants, traineeships, health care benefits, and unspecified assistantships available. *Faculty research:* Reading and writing relationships, classroom teachers as researchers, comprehension processes.

University of Pittsburgh, School of Arts and Sciences, Department of English, Pittsburgh, PA 15260. Offers cultural and critical studies (PhD); English (MA); writing (MFA). Part-time programs available. *Faculty:* 53 full-time (25 women). *Students:* 170 full-time (106 women), 37 part-time (33 women); includes 21 minority (8 African Americans, 1 American Indian/Alaska Native, 6 Asian Americans or Pacific Islanders, 6 Hispanic Americans), 5 international. Average age 23. 410 applicants, 12% accepted, 19 enrolled. In 2009, 22 master's, 10 doctorates awarded. *Degree requirements:* For master's, one foreign language; for doctorate, 2 foreign languages, comprehensive exam, thesis/dissertation. *Entrance requirements:* For master's and doctorate, GRE General Test, writing sample. Additional exam requirements/recommendations for international students: Required—TOEFL (minimum score 550 paper-based; 213 computer-based; 80 iBT). *Application deadline:* For fall admission, 12/10 for domestic and international students. Application fee: $50. *Expenses:* Tuition, state resident: full-time $16,402; part-time $665 per credit. Tuition, nonresident: full-time $28,694; part-time $1175 per credit. Required fees: $690; $175 per term. Tuition and fees vary according to program. *Financial support:* In 2009–10, 100 students received support, including 19 fellowships with full tuition reimbursements available (averaging $17,822 per year), 5 research assistantships with full and partial tuition reimbursements available (averaging $12,300 per year), 64 teaching assistantships with full tuition reimbursements available (averaging $15,065 per year); Federal Work-Study, tuition waivers (full and partial), and unspecified assistantships also available. Financial award application deadline: 12/12. *Faculty research:* Cultural studies, literary history and theory, film, composition. *Unit head:* Dr. John Twyning, Chairman, 412-624-6509, Fax: 412-624-6639, E-mail: twyning@pitt.edu. *Application contact:* Michelle Delie, Graduate Administrator, 412-624-6549, Fax: 412-624-6639, E-mail: mid29@pitt.edu.

University of San Francisco, College of Arts and Sciences, Program in Writing, San Francisco, CA 94117-1080. Offers MFA. Part-time and evening/weekend programs available. *Faculty:* 2 full-time (1 woman), 13 part-time/adjunct (5 women). *Students:* 63 full-time (44 women), 11 part-time (8 women); includes 14 minority (4 African Americans, 7 Asian Americans or Pacific Islanders, 3 Hispanic Americans), 2 international. Average age 36. 242 applicants, 36% accepted, 31 enrolled. In 2009, 24 master's awarded. *Degree requirements:* For master's, thesis. *Entrance requirements:* For master's, minimum overall GPA of 2.7, writing sample, 2 letters of recommendation, resume, interview. Additional exam requirements/recommendations for international students: Required—TOEFL (minimum score 550 paper-based; 79 iBT). *Application deadline:* For fall admission, 2/1 for domestic students. Applications are processed on a rolling basis. Application fee: $55 ($65 for international students). *Expenses:* Tuition: Full-time $19,710; part-time $1095 per unit. Part-time tuition and fees vary according to degree level, campus/location and program. *Financial support:* In 2009–10, 49 students received support; fellowships, institutionally sponsored loans available. Support available to part-time students. Financial award application deadline: 3/2; financial award applicants required to submit FAFSA. *Faculty research:* Techniques of teaching the novel to writers, oral history. *Unit head:* Dr. Aaron Shurin, Director, 415-422-5357, Fax: 415-422-6996, E-mail: mfaw@usfca.edu. *Application contact:* Dr. Aaron Shurin, Director, 415-422-5357, Fax: 415-422-6996, E-mail: mfaw@usfca.edu.

University of South Carolina, The Graduate School, College of Arts and Sciences, Department of English Language and Literature, Columbia, SC 29208. Offers creative writing (MFA); English (MA, PhD); English education (MAT); MLIS/MA. MAT offered in cooperation with the College of Education. Part-time programs available. *Degree requirements:* For master's, one foreign language, comprehensive exam, thesis; for doctorate, 2 foreign languages, comprehensive exam, thesis/dissertation. *Entrance requirements:* For master's, GRE General Test (MFA), GRE Subject Test (MA; MAT), sample of written work; for doctorate, GRE General Test, GRE Subject Test, sample of written work. Additional exam requirements/recommendations for international students: Required—TOEFL. Electronic applications accepted. *Faculty research:* American literature, British literature, composition and rhetoric, linguistics, speech communication.

University of Southern California, Graduate School, College of Letters, Arts and Sciences, Department of English, Los Angeles, CA 90089. Offers English (MA, PhD); literature and creative writing (PhD). *Faculty:* 37 full-time (18 women), 12 part-time/adjunct (5 women). *Students:* 110 full-time (68 women), 3 part-time (1 woman); includes 20 minority (1 African American, 1 American Indian/Alaska Native, 6 Asian Americans or Pacific Islanders, 12 Hispanic Americans), 9 international. 90 applicants, 16% accepted, 12 enrolled. In 2009, 5 master's, 21 doctorates awarded. Terminal master's awarded for partial completion of doctoral program. *Degree requirements:* For doctorate, one foreign language, comprehensive exam, thesis/dissertation. *Entrance requirements:* For doctorate, GRE General Test, GRE Subject Test (English literature). Additional exam requirements/recommendations for international students: Required—TOEFL. *Application deadline:* For fall admission, 12/1 for domestic and international students. Application fee: $85. Electronic applications accepted. *Expenses:* Tuition: Full-time $25,980; part-time $1315 per unit. Required fees: $554. One-time fee: $35 full-time. Full-time tuition and fees vary according to degree level and program. *Financial support:* In 2009–10, 11 students received support, including 14 fellowships with full tuition reimbursements available (averaging $21,000 per year), 2 research assistantships with full tuition reimbursements available (averaging $19,500 per year), 30 teaching assistantships with full tuition reimbursements available (averaging $21,000 per year); scholarships/grants, health care benefits, tuition waivers, and unspecified assistantships also available. *Faculty research:* Creative writing and literature; early modern studies; gender and sexuality; narrative studies; poetry and poetics; media, film, and popular culture; studies in race and minority literature. *Unit*

Writing

University of Southern California (continued)
head: Dr. Margaret Russett, Chair, 213-740-3737, Fax: 213-741-0377, E-mail: russett@usc.edu. *Application contact:* Flora Ruiz, Graduate Coordinator of Student Affairs, 213-740-3725, Fax: 213-741-0377, E-mail: fruiz@usc.edu.

University of Southern California, Graduate School, College of Letters, Arts and Sciences, Master of Professional Writing Program, Los Angeles, CA 90089. Offers Internet (MPW). Part-time and evening/weekend programs available. *Faculty:* 4 full-time (3 women), 13 part-time/adjunct (9 women). *Students:* 54 full-time (32 women), 35 part-time (21 women); includes 25 minority (8 African Americans, 1 American Indian/Alaska Native, 8 Asian Americans or Pacific Islanders, 8 Hispanic Americans), 4 international. 52 applicants, 87% accepted, 33 enrolled. In 2009, 54 master's awarded. *Degree requirements:* For master's, thesis. *Entrance requirements:* For master's, GRE, minimum GPA of 3.0. Additional exam requirements/recommendations for international students: Required—TOEFL. *Application deadline:* For fall admission, 6/1 priority date for domestic and international students; for spring admission, 11/1 priority date for domestic and international students. Applications are processed on a rolling basis. Application fee: $85. Electronic applications accepted. *Expenses:* Tuition: Full-time $25,980; part-time $1315 per unit. Required fees: $554. One-time fee: $35 full-time. Full-time tuition and fees vary according to degree level and program. *Financial support:* In 2009–10, 10 students received support, including 10 fellowships with full tuition reimbursements available (averaging $19,600 per year). Financial award application deadline: 12/1. *Faculty research:* Creative writing including fiction, creative nonfiction, screenwriting, television writing, playwriting, poetry, internet writing; publishing in electronic media; book and film reviewing; teaching. *Unit head:* Brighde Mullins, Director, 213-740-4718, Fax: 213-740-5002, E-mail: bmullins@college.usc.edu. *Application contact:* Natalie Inouye, Student Service Advisor, 213-740-1384, Fax: 213-740-5002, E-mail: natalie.inouye@college.usc.edu.

University of Southern Maine, College of Arts and Sciences, Program in Creative Writing, Portland, ME 04104. Offers MFA.

The University of Tennessee at Chattanooga, Graduate School, College of Arts and Sciences, Department of English, Chattanooga, TN 37403. Offers creative writing (MA); literary study (MA); rhetoric and writing (MA, Graduate Certificate). Part-time and evening/weekend programs available. *Faculty:* 12 full-time (7 women). *Students:* 11 full-time (10 women), 28 part-time (13 women); includes 2 minority (both African Americans). Average age 32. 27 applicants, 81% accepted, 11 enrolled. In 2009, 15 master's awarded. *Degree requirements:* For master's, one foreign language, comprehensive exam, thesis. *Entrance requirements:* For master's, GRE General Test or GRE Subject Test in literature, minimum GPA of 3.0 in English. Additional exam requirements/recommendations for international students: Required—TOEFL (minimum score 550 paper-based; 213 computer-based; 79 iBT), IELTS (minimum score 6). *Application deadline:* For fall admission, 8/1 priority date for domestic students, 6/1 for international students; for spring admission, 12/1 priority date for domestic students, 10/1 for international students. Applications are processed on a rolling basis. Application fee: $35. Electronic applications accepted. *Expenses:* Tuition, state resident: full-time $5404; part-time $300 per credit hour. Tuition, nonresident: full-time $16,702; part-time $928 per credit hour. Required fees: $1150; $130 per credit hour. *Financial support:* In 2009–10, 6 research assistantships with full and partial tuition reimbursements (averaging $5,500 per year) were awarded; career-related internships or fieldwork, scholarships/grants, and unspecified assistantships also available. Support available to part-time students. *Faculty research:* Technical writing, African-American literature, Milton, creative writing and poetry, American modernism and gender theory. Total annual research expenditures: $74,953. *Unit head:* Dr. Verbie Prevost, Head, 423-425-4238, Fax: 423-785-2282, E-mail: verbie-prevost@utc.edu. *Application contact:* Dr. Stephanie Bellar, Dean of Graduate Studies, 423-425-4666, Fax: 423-425-5223, E-mail: stephanie-bellar@utc.edu.

The University of Texas at Austin, Graduate School, College of Liberal Arts, Department of English, Austin, TX 78712-1111. Offers creative writing (MA); English (MA, PhD). Part-time programs available. Terminal master's awarded for partial completion of doctoral program. *Degree requirements:* For master's, 2 foreign languages; for doctorate, variable foreign language requirement. *Entrance requirements:* For master's and doctorate, GRE General Test. Electronic applications accepted.

The University of Texas at Austin, Graduate School, Program in Writing, Austin, TX 78712-1111. Offers MFA. Electronic applications accepted.

The University of Texas at El Paso, Graduate School, College of Liberal Arts, Department of Creative Writing, El Paso, TX 79968-0001. Offers creative writing (on-line) (MFA); creative writing in English (MFA); creative writing in Spanish (MFA). Part-time and evening/weekend programs available. Postbaccalaureate distance learning degree programs offered (no on-campus study). *Students:* 47 (25 women); includes 21 minority (1 African American, 20 Hispanic Americans), 13 international. Average age 34. In 2009, 7 master's awarded. *Degree requirements:* For master's, thesis. *Entrance requirements:* For master's, Minimum GPA of 3.0, Letters of Recommendation, Writing Sample. Additional exam requirements/recommendations for international students: Required—TOEFL; Recommended—IELTS. *Application deadline:* For fall admission, 8/1 priority date for domestic students, 3/1 for international students; for spring admission, 11/1 for domestic students, 9/1 for international students. Applications are processed on a rolling basis. Application fee: $45 ($80 for international students). Electronic applications accepted. *Financial support:* In 2009–10, research assistantships (averaging $18,625 per year), teaching assistantships with partial tuition reimbursements (averaging $14,900 per year) were awarded; fellowships with partial tuition reimbursements, institutionally sponsored loans, scholarships/grants, health care benefits, tuition waivers (partial), and unspecified assistantships also available. Support available to part-time students. Financial award application deadline: 3/15; financial award applicants required to submit FAFSA. *Unit head:* Dr. Johnny Payne, Chair, 915-747-5713, Fax: 915-747-5523, E-mail: jpayne@utep.edu. *Application contact:* Dr. Patricia D. Witherspoon, Dean of the Graduate School, 915-747-5491, Fax: 915-747-5788, E-mail: withersp@utep.edu.

The University of Texas at El Paso, Graduate School, College of Liberal Arts, Department of English, El Paso, TX 79968-0001. Offers bilingual professional writing (Certificate); English and American literature (MA); rhetoric and composition (PhD); rhetoric and writing studies (MA); teaching English (MAT). Part-time and evening/weekend programs available. *Degree requirements:* For master's, thesis optional. *Entrance requirements:* For master's, GRE General Test, minimum GPA of 3.0. Additional exam requirements/recommendations for international students: Required—TOEFL. Electronic applications accepted. *Faculty research:* Literature, creative writing, literary theory.

University of the Sacred Heart, Graduate Programs, Department of Communication, San Juan, PR 00914-0383. Offers contemporary culture and media (MA); digital journalism (Certificate); editing for media (MA, Certificate); public relations (MA, Certificate); publicity (MA, Certificate); scriptwriting (MA, Certificate). Part-time and evening/weekend programs available. *Degree requirements:* For master's, thesis.

University of the Sacred Heart, Graduate Programs, Program in Creative Writing, San Juan, PR 00914-0383. Offers MA, Certificate.

The University of Toledo, College of Graduate Studies, College of Arts and Sciences, Department of English Language and Literature, Toledo, OH 43606-3390. Offers English as a second language (MA); literature (MA); teaching of writing (Certificate). Part-time programs available. *Degree requirements:* For master's, one foreign language. *Entrance requirements:* For master's, minimum GPA of 2.7. Electronic applications accepted. *Faculty research:* Literary criticism, linguistics, creative writing, folklore and cultural studies.

University of Utah, The Graduate School, College of Humanities, Department of English, Program in Creative Writing, Salt Lake City, UT 84112. Offers rhetoric/composition (MA, PhD). *Students:* 8 full-time (5 women), 6 part-time (4 women); includes 2 minority (1 African American, 1 American Indian/Alaska Native). Average age 27. 30 applicants, 20% accepted, 6 enrolled. In 2009, 5 master's awarded. *Degree requirements:* For master's, variable foreign language requirement, comprehensive exam, thesis optional; for doctorate, variable foreign language requirement, comprehensive exam, thesis/dissertation. *Entrance requirements:* For master's and doctorate, GRE. *Application deadline:* For fall admission, 1/15 for domestic students. Application fee: $55 ($65 for international students). *Expenses:* Tuition, state resident: full-time $4004; part-time $1674 per semester. Tuition, nonresident: full-time $14,134; part-time $5915 per semester. Required fees: $324 per semester. Tuition and fees vary according to course load, degree level and program. *Financial support:* In 2009–10, 9 teaching assistantships with full tuition reimbursements (averaging $12,430 per year) were awarded; institutionally sponsored loans, scholarships/grants, health care benefits, and unspecified assistantships also available. *Unit head:* Dr. Maureen Ann Mathison, Director, 801-581-7090, E-mail: maureen.mathison@hum.utah.edu. *Application contact:* Pauline Frances Light, Office Support Coordinator, 801-581-7098, E-mail: plight@utah.edu.

University of Victoria, Faculty of Graduate Studies, Faculty of Fine Arts, Department of Writing, Victoria, BC V8W 2Y2, Canada. Offers MFA. *Entrance requirements:* For master's, portfolio, 2 letters of reference.

University of Virginia, College and Graduate School of Arts and Sciences, Department of English Language and Literature, Program in Creative Writing, Charlottesville, VA 22903. Offers MFA. *Students:* 30 full-time (18 women), 1 part-time (0 women); includes 4 minority (1 African American, 2 Asian Americans or Pacific Islanders, 1 Hispanic American), 1 international. Average age 28. 646 applicants, 2% accepted, 12 enrolled. In 2009, 9 master's awarded. *Degree requirements:* For master's, comprehensive exam, thesis. *Entrance requirements:* For master's, GRE General Test, writing sample. Additional exam requirements/recommendations for international students: Required—TOEFL (minimum score 600 paper-based; 250 computer-based; 90 iBT), IELTS (minimum score 7). *Application deadline:* For fall admission, 1/4 for domestic and international students. Application fee: $60. Electronic applications accepted. *Financial support:* Fellowships, teaching assistantships available. Financial award application deadline: 1/4; financial award applicants required to submit FAFSA. *Unit head:* Christopher Tilghman, Director, 434-924-6675, Fax: 434-924-1478, E-mail: ct2a@virginia.edu. *Application contact:* Barbara Moriarty, Administrative Assistant, 434-924-6074, Fax: 434-924-1478, E-mail: bam9s@virginia.edu.

University of Washington, Graduate School, College of Arts and Sciences, Department of English, Program in Creative Writing, Seattle, WA 98195. Offers MFA. *Entrance requirements:* For master's, GRE, GMAT. Additional exam requirements/recommendations for international students: Required—TOEFL (minimum score 550 paper-based; 213 computer-based). Electronic applications accepted.

University of West Florida, College of Arts and Sciences: Arts, Department of English and Foreign Languages, Pensacola, FL 32514-5750. Offers creative writing (MA); literature (MA). Part-time and evening/weekend programs available. *Faculty:* 5 full-time (2 women). *Students:* 12 full-time (8 women), 31 part-time (19 women); includes 4 minority (2 African Americans, 2 American Indian/Alaska Native). Average age 32. 24 applicants, 79% accepted, 10 enrolled. In 2009, 1 master's awarded. *Degree requirements:* For master's, thesis. *Entrance requirements:* For master's, GRE General Test, minimum GPA of 3.0. Additional exam requirements/recommendations for international students: Required—TOEFL (minimum score 550 paper-based; 213 computer-based). *Application deadline:* For fall admission, 6/1 for domestic students, 5/15 for international students; for spring admission, 11/1 for domestic students, 10/1 for international students. Applications are processed on a rolling basis. Application fee: $30. *Expenses:* Tuition, state resident: full-time $4982; part-time $260 per credit hour. Tuition, nonresident: full-time $20,059; part-time $919 per credit hour. Required fees: $1247; $52 per credit hour. *Financial support:* In 2009–10, 4 research assistantships with partial tuition reimbursements (averaging $3,280 per year), 12 teaching assistantships with partial tuition reimbursements (averaging $5,884 per year) were awarded; unspecified assistantships also available. Financial award application deadline: 4/15; financial award applicants required to submit FAFSA. *Faculty research:* Faulkner, Shakespeare, American humor, women's studies, poetry. *Unit head:* Dr. Bob Yeager, Chairperson, 850-474-2923. *Application contact:* Terry McCray, Assistant Director of Graduate Admissions, 850-473-7718, Fax: 850-473-7714, E-mail: gradadmissions@uwf.edu.

University of Windsor, Faculty of Graduate Studies, Faculty of Arts and Social Sciences, Department of English Language, Literature and Creative Writing, Windsor, ON N9B 3P4, Canada. Offers English: creative writing and language and literature (MA); English: language and literature (MA). Part-time programs available. *Degree requirements:* For master's, thesis. *Entrance requirements:* For master's, minimum B average, portfolio. Additional exam requirements/recommendations for international students: Required—TOEFL (minimum score 600 paper-based; 250 computer-based). Electronic applications accepted. *Faculty research:* Use of gender-related terms in popular culture; international and Aboriginal literatures: expression of cultural identity; critical analysis of authors: Pope, Munroe, Lady Morgan, Orwell, Thomas; the 'feminine" voice in literature and contemporary culture.

University of Wisconsin–Madison, Graduate School, College of Letters and Science, Department of English, Madison, WI 53706-1380. Offers applied English linguistics (MA); composition and rhetoric (PhD); creative writing (MFA); English language and linguistics (PhD); literary studies (MA, PhD). *Degree requirements:* For doctorate, thesis/dissertation. *Expenses:* Tuition, state resident: part-time $594 per credit. Tuition, nonresident: part-time $1504 per credit. Required fees: $65 per credit. Tuition and fees vary according to course load, program and reciprocity agreements.

University of Wisconsin–Milwaukee, Graduate School, College of Letters and Sciences, Department of English, Milwaukee, WI 53201-0413. Offers creative writing (PhD); English (MA); international technical communication (Certificate); linguistics (PhD); professional writing (PhD); professional writing and communication (Certificate); rhetoric and composition (PhD); MLIS/MA. *Faculty:* 38 full-time (19 women). *Students:* 107 full-time (64 women), 82 part-time (54 women); includes 13 minority (8 African Americans, 1 American Indian/Alaska Native, 2 Asian Americans or Pacific Islanders, 2 Hispanic Americans), 23 international. Average age 34. 193 applicants, 51% accepted, 31 enrolled. In 2009, 26 master's, 16 doctorates awarded. *Degree requirements:* For master's, thesis or alternative; for doctorate, one foreign language, thesis/dissertation. *Entrance requirements:* For master's, GRE General Test, GRE Subject Test; for doctorate, GRE. Additional exam requirements/recommendations for international students: Required—TOEFL (minimum score 550 paper-based; 79 iBT), IELTS (minimum score 6.5). *Application deadline:* For fall admission, 1/1 priority date for domestic students; for spring admission, 9/1 for domestic students. Applications are processed on a rolling basis. Application fee: $45 ($75 for international students). *Expenses:* Tuition, state resident: full-time $8800. Tuition, nonresident: full-time $20,760. Tuition and fees vary according to program and reciprocity agreements. *Financial support:* In 2009–10, 75 teaching assistantships were awarded; career-related internships or fieldwork and unspecified assistantships also available. Support available to part-time students. Financial award application deadline: 4/15. Total annual research expenditures: $41,495. *Unit head:* Tasha Oren, Representative, 414-229-4637, Fax: 414-229-2643, E-mail: tgoren@uwm.edu. *Application contact:* General Information Contact, 414-229-4982, Fax: 414-229-6967, E-mail: gradschool@uwm.edu.

University of Wyoming, College of Arts and Sciences, Department of English, Laramie, WY 82070. Offers creative writing (MFA); English (MA). Part-time programs available. *Degree requirements:* For master's, thesis or alternative, internship. *Entrance requirements:* For master's, GRE General Test, minimum GPA of 3.0. Electronic applications accepted. *Faculty research:* Literature and theory, creative writing, English as a second language, ethnic and women's studies, composition.

Utah State University, School of Graduate Studies, College of Humanities, Arts and Social Sciences, Department of English, Logan, UT 84322. Offers American studies (MA, MS), including folklore, western American literature and culture; English (MA, MS), including literature and writing, technical writing. Part-time and evening/weekend programs available. *Degree requirements:* For master's, thesis or alternative. *Entrance requirements:* For master's, GRE General Test or MAT, minimum GPA of 3.0, recommendation letters, writing samples. Additional exam requirements/recommendations for international students: Required—TOEFL. *Faculty research:* Scottish enlightenment, material culture, composition theory, creative nonfiction, literary criticism.

Vanderbilt University, Graduate School, Program in Creative Writing, Nashville, TN 37240-1001. Offers MFA. *Faculty:* 10 full-time (6 women). *Students:* 10 full-time (6 women), 1 (woman) part-time; includes 2 minority (1 African American, 1 Asian American or Pacific Islander). Average age 28. 307 applicants, 3% accepted, 6 enrolled. In 2009, 6 master's awarded. *Degree requirements:* For master's, comprehensive exam, thesis. *Entrance requirements:* For master's, GRE General Test, sample of written work. Additional exam requirements/recommendations for international students: Required—TOEFL (minimum score 570 paper-based; 230 computer-based; 88 iBT). *Application deadline:* For fall admission, 1/15 for domestic and international students. Application fee: $0. Electronic applications accepted. *Financial support:* Fellowships with full and partial tuition reimbursements, teaching assistantships with full and partial tuition reimbursements, Federal Work-Study, institutionally sponsored loans, and health care benefits available. Financial award application deadline: 1/15; financial award applicants required to submit CSS PROFILE or FAFSA. *Unit head:* Mark Jarman, Director, 615-322-2618, E-mail: mark.jarman@vanderbilt.edu. *Application contact:* Margaret Quigley, MFA Graduate Assistant, 615-322-2765, E-mail: creativewriting@vanderbilt.edu.

Virginia Commonwealth University, Graduate School, College of Humanities and Sciences, Department of English, Program in Creative Writing, Richmond, VA 23284-9005. Offers fiction (MFA); fictional poetry (MFA); poetry (MFA). *Entrance requirements:* For master's, portfolio.

Virginia Commonwealth University, Graduate School, College of Humanities and Sciences, Department of English, Program in English, Richmond, VA 23284-9005. Offers literature (MA); writing and rhetoric (MA).

Warren Wilson College, MFA Program for Writers, Swannanoa, Asheville, NC 28815-9000. Offers MFA. Postbaccalaureate distance learning degree programs offered (minimal on-campus study). *Degree requirements:* For master's, thesis, public reading, teaching experience. *Entrance requirements:* For master's, manuscript of creative work. *Faculty research:* Analytic writing, creative and analytic study of literature.

Washington University in St. Louis, Graduate School of Arts and Sciences, Department of English and American Literature, Writing Program, St. Louis, MO 63130-4899. Offers MFAW. *Degree requirements:* For master's, thesis or written exam. *Entrance requirements:* For master's, GRE General Test, sample of written work. Electronic applications accepted.

Wayne State University, College of Liberal Arts and Sciences, Department of English, Detroit, MI 48202. Offers comparative literature (MA); English (MA, PhD). *Degree requirements:* For master's, one foreign language, essay or thesis; for doctorate, one foreign language, thesis/dissertation. *Entrance requirements:* For master's, GRE General Test, minimum GPA of 3.25 in English, 3.0 overall; references; for doctorate, GRE General Test, GRE Subject Test, statement of purpose, references, sample essay. Additional exam requirements/recommendations for international students: Required—TOEFL (minimum score 550 paper-based; 213 computer-based); Recommended—TWE (minimum score 6). Electronic applications accepted. *Faculty research:* English and American literature, cultural studies, composition, linguistics, film.

Western Connecticut State University, Division of Graduate Studies, School of Arts and Sciences, Department of English, Danbury, CT 06810-6885. Offers English (MA); literature option (MA); TESOL option (MA); writing option (MA). Part-time programs available. *Faculty:* 4 full-time (3 women), 1 part-time/adjunct (0 women). *Students:* 3 full-time (2 women), 33 part-time (24 women); includes 5 minority (2 African Americans, 3 Hispanic Americans). Average age 40. 15 applicants, 73% accepted, 7 enrolled. In 2009, 6 master's awarded. *Degree requirements:* For master's, thesis (writing option), completion of program in 6 years. *Entrance requirements:* For master's, minimum GPA of 2.5, writing sample. Additional exam requirements/recommendations for international students: Recommended—TOEFL (minimum score 550 paper-based; 213 computer-based; 79 iBT), IELTS (minimum score 6). *Application deadline:* For fall admission, 8/5 priority date for domestic students; for spring admission, 1/5 priority date for domestic students. Applications are processed on a rolling basis. Application fee: $50. *Expenses:* Tuition, state resident: full-time $5012; part-time $278 per credit hour. Tuition, nonresident: full-time $13,962; part-time $284 per credit hour. Required fees: $3886; $139 per credit hour. Full-time tuition and fees vary according to course load and program. Part-time tuition and fees vary according to course level, degree level and program. *Financial support:* Application deadline: 5/1. *Unit head:* Dr. Shouhua Qi, Co-Coordinator, 203-837-9048, Fax: 203-837-8525, E-mail: qis@wcsu.edu. *Application contact:* Chris Shankle, Associate Director of Graduate Studies, 203-837-9005, Fax: 203-837-8326, E-mail: shanklec@wcsu.edu.

Western Connecticut State University, Division of Graduate Studies, School of Arts and Sciences, Department of Writing, Linguistics, and Creative Process, Danbury, CT 06810-6885. Offers professional writing (MFA). Part-time programs available. *Faculty:* 5 full-time (1 woman), 32 part-time/adjunct (13 women). *Students:* 21 full-time (11 women), 12 part-time (9 women); includes 6 minority (3 African Americans, 1 American Indian/Alaska Native, 1 Asian American or Pacific Islander, 1 Hispanic American). Average age 36. 27 applicants, 70% accepted, 14 enrolled. In 2009, 19 master's awarded. *Degree requirements:* For master's, thesis, completion of program within 4 years, enrichment project that compliments course of study. *Entrance requirements:* For master's, 2 writing samples: a 20-50 page portfolio of previous writing and a brief essay. Additional exam requirements/recommendations for international students: Recommended—TOEFL (minimum score 550 paper-based; 213 computer-based; 79 iBT), IELTS (minimum score 6). *Application deadline:* For fall admission, 8/5 priority date for domestic students; for spring admission, 1/5 priority date for domestic students. Application fee: $50. *Expenses:* Contact institution. *Financial support:* In 2009–10, 1 student received support. Scholarships/grants available. *Unit head:* Dr. Brian Clements, Associate Professor/MFA Coordinator, 203-837-8876, Fax: 636-246-7589, E-mail: clementsb@wcsu.edu. *Application contact:* Chris Shankle, Associate Director of Graduate Admissions, 203-837-9005, Fax: 203-837-8326, E-mail: shanklec@wcsu.edu.

Western Kentucky University, Graduate Studies, Potter College of Arts and Letters, Department of English, Bowling Green, KY 42101. Offers education (MA); English (MA Ed); literature (MA), including American literature, British literature, literary theory, women writers, world literature; teaching English as a second language (MA); writing (MA). Part-time and evening/weekend programs available. *Degree requirements:* For master's, comprehensive exam, thesis optional, final exam. *Entrance requirements:* For master's, GRE General Test, minimum GPA of 2.75. Additional exam requirements/recommendations for international students: Required—TOEFL (minimum score 555 paper-based; 213 computer-based; 79 iBT). *Expenses:* Tuition, state resident: full-time $4160; part-time $416 per credit hour. Tuition, nonresident: full-time $9550; part-time $506 per credit hour. Tuition and fees vary according to campus/location and reciprocity agreements. *Faculty research:* Improving writing, linking teacher knowledge and performance, Victorian women writers, Kentucky women writers, Kentucky poets.

Western Michigan University, Graduate College, College of Arts and Sciences, Department of English, Kalamazoo, MI 49008. Offers creative writing (MFA, PhD); English (MA, PhD); English education (MA, PhD). *Degree requirements:* For master's, oral exams; for doctorate, one foreign language, thesis/dissertation, oral exam, written exams. *Entrance requirements:* For master's and doctorate, GRE General Test, GRE Subject Test.

Westminster College, Program in Professional Communication, Salt Lake City, UT 84105-3697. Offers MPC. Part-time and evening/weekend programs available. *Faculty:* 7 full-time (3 women), 6 part-time/adjunct (4 women). *Students:* 22 full-time (17 women), 53 part-time (31 women); includes 6 minority (2 American Indian/Alaska Native, 3 Asian Americans or Pacific Islanders, 1 Hispanic American), 2 international. Average age 34. 40 applicants, 55% accepted, 18 enrolled. In 2009, 13 master's awarded. *Degree requirements:* For master's, field project. *Entrance requirements:* For master's, resume, professional writing sample, 2 letters of recommendation. Additional exam requirements/recommendations for international students: Required—TOEFL (minimum score 600 paper-based; 250 computer-based; 100 iBT). *Application deadline:* For fall admission, 7/9 for domestic and international students. Applications are processed on a rolling basis. Application fee: $40. Electronic applications accepted. *Expenses:* Tuition: Part-time $555 per credit hour. Part-time tuition and fees vary according to program. *Financial support:* In 2009–10, 31 students received support. Career-related internships or fieldwork and tuition reimbursement, tuition remission available. Support available to part-time students. Financial award applicants required to submit FAFSA. *Faculty research:* Critical communication pedagogy, sexuality and gender, autoethnography, regulation of broadcast indecency, hypertext theory. *Unit head:* Dr. Helen Hodgson, Director, 801-832-2821, Fax: 801-832-3102, E-mail: hhodgson@westminstercollege.edu. *Application contact:* Joel Bauman, Vice President of Enrollment Services, 801-832-2200, Fax: 801-832-3101, E-mail: admission@westminstercollege.edu.

West Virginia University, Eberly College of Arts and Sciences, Department of English, Program in Creative Writing, Morgantown, WV 26506. Offers MFA. Part-time and evening/weekend programs available.

Wichita State University, Graduate School, Fairmount College of Liberal Arts and Sciences, Department of English, Wichita, KS 67260. Offers creative writing (MFA); English (MA). Part-time and evening/weekend programs available. *Entrance requirements:* For master's, writing sample (MFA). *Expenses:* Tuition, state resident: full-time $4247; part-time $235.95 per credit hour. Tuition, nonresident: full-time $11,171; part-time $620.60 per credit hour. Required fees: $34; $3.60 per credit hour. $17 per term. Tuition and fees vary according to campus/location and program. *Unit head:* Dr. Donald Wineke, Chair, 316-978-3130, Fax: 316-978-3548, E-mail: donald.wineke@wichita.edu. *Application contact:* Dr. Donald Wineke, Chair, 316-978-3130, Fax: 316-978-3548, E-mail: donald.wineke@wichita.edu.

Wilkes University, College of Graduate and Professional Studies, College of Arts, Humanities and Social Sciences, Program in Creative Writing, Wilkes-Barre, PA 18766-0002. Offers MA, MFA. Part-time programs available. Postbaccalaureate distance learning degree programs offered (minimal on-campus study). *Students:* 94 full-time (60 women), 29 part-time (14 women); includes 14 minority (10 African Americans, 4 Hispanic Americans). Average age 37. In 2009, 27 master's awarded. *Entrance requirements:* Additional exam requirements/recommendations for international students: Required—TOEFL (minimum score 500 paper-based; 173 computer-based; 79 iBT). Application fee: $35. *Expenses:* Contact institution. *Financial support:* Application deadline: 3/1. *Unit head:* Dr. Bonnie Culver, Director, 570-408-4527, Fax: 570-408-7846, E-mail: bonnie.culver@wilkes.edu. *Application contact:* Kathleen Houlihan, Director of Graduate Studies, 570-408-3235, Fax: 570-408-7846, E-mail: kathleen.houlihan@wilkes.edu.

Wright State University, School of Graduate Studies, College of Liberal Arts, Department of English Language and Literatures, Dayton, OH 45435. Offers composition and rhetoric (MA); English (MA); literature (MA); teaching English to speakers of other languages (MA). *Degree requirements:* For master's, thesis optional, portfolio. *Entrance requirements:* For master's, 20 hours in upper-level English. Additional exam requirements/recommendations for international students: Required—TOEFL. *Faculty research:* American literature, world literature in English, applied linguistics, writing theory and pedagogy.

ACADEMIC AND PROFESSIONAL PROGRAMS IN INTERDISCIPLINARY STUDIES

Section 14
Interdisciplinary Studies

This section contains a directory of institutions offering graduate work in interdisciplinary studies, followed by an in-depth entry submitted by an institution that chose to prepare a detailed program description. Additional information about programs listed in the directory but not augmented by an in-depth entry may be obtained by writing directly to the dean of a graduate school or chair of a department at the address given in the directory.

For programs offering related work, see also in this book *Comparative and Interdisciplinary Arts, Humanities,* and *Social Sciences.*

CONTENTS

Program Directory

Interdisciplinary Studies 540

Close-Up

New York University 551

Interdisciplinary Studies

Alaska Pacific University, Graduate Programs, Liberal Studies Department, Self-Designed Programs, Anchorage, AK 99508-4672. Offers MA. Part-time and evening/weekend programs available. *Degree requirements:* For master's, thesis or project. *Entrance requirements:* For master's, MAT (preferred), GRE General Test or GMAT. *Expenses:* Contact institution.

Amberton University, Graduate School, Program in Professional Development, Garland, TX 75041-5595. Offers MA. *Entrance requirements:* For master's, minimum GPA of 3.0.

American University, College of Arts and Sciences, Interdisciplinary Programs, Washington, DC 20016-8001. Offers MA. Application fee: $80. *Expenses:* Tuition: Full-time $22,266; part-time $1237 per credit hour. Required fees: $430. Tuition and fees vary according to program.

Angelo State University, College of Graduate Studies, Program in Interdisciplinary Studies, San Angelo, TX 76909. Offers MA, MS. Part-time and evening/weekend programs available. *Students:* 1 full-time (0 women); minority (Hispanic American). Average age 23. In 2009, 2 master's awarded. *Degree requirements:* For master's, comprehensive exam. *Entrance requirements:* For master's, GRE General Test. Additional exam requirements/recommendations for international students: Required—TOEFL or IELTS. *Application deadline:* For fall admission, 7/15 priority date for domestic students, 6/10 for international students; for spring admission, 12/1 priority date for domestic students, 11/1 for international students. Applications are processed on a rolling basis. Application fee: $25 ($50 for international students). Electronic applications accepted. *Expenses:* Tuition, state resident: full-time $3396; part-time $142 per credit hour. Tuition, nonresident: full-time $10,152; part-time $423 per credit hour. Required fees: $1786; $36.25 per credit hour. $494 per semester. Full-time tuition and fees vary according to course load, degree level and program. *Financial support:* Federal Work-Study and scholarships/grants available. Support available to part-time students. Financial award application deadline: 3/1; financial award applicants required to submit FAFSA. *Unit head:* Dr. Brian J. May, Interim Dean of Graduate Studies, 325-942-2169, Fax: 325-942-2194, E-mail: brian.may@angelo.edu. *Application contact:* Theresa Fortin, Graduate Admissions Assistant, 325-942-2169, Fax: 325-942-2194, E-mail: theresa.fortin@angelo.edu.

Antioch University New England, Graduate School, Department of Environmental Studies, Individualized Program, Keene, NH 03431-3552. Offers MS. *Degree requirements:* For master's, practicum, seminar, thesis or project. *Entrance requirements:* For master's, detailed proposal.

Arizona State University, Graduate College, New College of Interdisciplinary Arts and Sciences, Tempe, AZ 85287. Offers communication studies (MA); interdisciplinary studies (MA); social justice and human rights (MA). Part-time and evening/weekend programs available. *Degree requirements:* For master's, applied project. *Entrance requirements:* For master's, GRE, letter of recommendation, writing sample. Additional exam requirements/recommendations for international students: Required—TOEFL (minimum score 550 paper-based; 213 computer-based; 83 iBT), IELTS (minimum score 6.5). Electronic applications accepted.

Athabasca University, Centre for Integrated Studies, Athabasca, AB T9S 3A3, Canada. Offers adult education (MA); community studies (MA); cultural studies (MA); educational studies (MA); global change (MA); work, organization, and leadership (MA). Part-time and evening/weekend programs available. Postbaccalaureate distance learning degree programs offered (no on-campus study). *Faculty:* 10 full-time (4 women), 12 part-time/adjunct (9 women). *Students:* 705 part-time. Average age 35. 195 applicants, 38 enrolled. In 2009, 52 master's awarded. *Degree requirements:* For master's, project. *Entrance requirements:* Additional exam requirements/recommendations for international students: Required—TOEFL (minimum score 560 paper-based; 220 computer-based). *Application deadline:* For fall admission, 3/1 for domestic and international students; for winter admission, 9/1 for domestic and international students. Application fee: $80. Electronic applications accepted. *Expenses:* Tuition: Part-time $16,500 per degree program. Required fees: $200 per year. One-time fee: $80 part-time. *Faculty research:* Women's history, literature and culture studies, sustainable development, labor and education. *Unit head:* Dr. Michael Gismondi, Program Director, 780-675-6218, Fax: 780-675-6921, E-mail: mikeg@athabascau.ca. *Application contact:* Derek Stovin, Program Administrator, 780-675-6236, Fax: 780-675-6921, E-mail: dereks@athabascau.ca.

Baylor University, Graduate School, College of Arts and Sciences, J. M. Dawson Institute of Church-State Studies, Waco, TX 76798. Offers MA, PhD. *Students:* 33 full-time (12 women), 6 part-time (2 women); includes 8 minority (1 American Indian/Alaska Native, 3 Asian Americans or Pacific Islanders, 4 Hispanic Americans), 7 international. In 2009, 5 master's, 3 doctorates awarded. *Degree requirements:* For master's, thesis, oral exam; for doctorate, one foreign language, thesis/dissertation, preliminary exams. *Entrance requirements:* For master's, GRE General Test; for doctorate, GRE General Test, MA or equivalent. *Application deadline:* For fall admission, 3/1 for domestic students. Applications are processed on a rolling basis. Application fee: $25. *Financial support:* Fellowships, research assistantships, teaching assistantships, Federal Work-Study and institutionally sponsored loans available. Financial award application deadline: 3/1. *Faculty research:* Religion and politics, religion and public education, religious freedom and international politics, First Amendment jurisprudence. *Unit head:* Dr. Christopher Marsh, Graduate Program Director, 254-710-4412, Fax: 254-710-1571, E-mail: chris_marsh@baylor.edu. *Application contact:* Suzanne Seller, Administrative Assistant, 254-710-1510, Fax: 254-710-1571, E-mail: suzanne_sellers@baylor.edu.

Boise State University, Graduate College, College of Arts and Sciences, Program in Interdisciplinary Studies, Boise, ID 83725-0399. Offers MA, MS. Part-time programs available. *Degree requirements:* For master's, thesis. *Entrance requirements:* For master's, minimum GPA of 3.0. Electronic applications accepted. *Expenses:* Tuition, state resident: full-time $3106; part-time $209 per credit. Tuition, nonresident: part-time $284 per credit.

Boston University, Metropolitan College, Interdisciplinary Studies, Boston, MA 02215. Offers interdisciplinary studies (MLA). Part-time and evening/weekend programs available. *Students:* 1 (woman) full-time, 17 part-time (12 women). Average age 29. 2 applicants, 100% accepted, 1 enrolled. *Degree requirements:* For master's, thesis. *Entrance requirements:* For master's, interview. Additional exam requirements/recommendations for international students: Required—TOEFL (minimum score 560 paper-based). *Application deadline:* For fall admission, 3/31 priority date for domestic and international students; for winter admission, 11/30 priority date for domestic students; for spring admission, 11/15 priority date for international students. Applications are processed on a rolling basis. Application fee: $70. Electronic applications accepted. *Expenses:* Tuition: Full-time $37,910; part-time $1184 per credit hour. Required fees: $386; $40 per semester. Part-time tuition and fees vary according to class time, course level, degree level and program. *Financial support:* Research assistantships with partial tuition reimbursements, scholarships/grants available. Support available to part-time students. *Unit head:* Prof. Daniel Ranall, Interim Chair, 617-358-0005, Fax: 617-358-1230, E-mail: dranalli@bu.edu. *Application contact:* Prof. Daniel Ranall, Interim Chair, 617-358-0005, Fax: 617-358-1230, E-mail: dranalli@bu.edu.

Bowling Green State University, Graduate College, Interdisciplinary Studies, Bowling Green, OH 43403. Offers M Ed, MA, MS, PhD. Part-time programs available. *Degree requirements:* For master's, thesis or alternative; for doctorate, comprehensive exam, thesis/dissertation. *Entrance requirements:* For master's and doctorate, GRE General Test. Additional exam requirements/recommendations for international students: Required—TOEFL. Electronic applications accepted.

Buffalo State College, State University of New York, The Graduate School, Program in Multidisciplinary Studies, Buffalo, NY 14222-1095. Offers MA, MS. Part-time and evening/weekend programs available. *Degree requirements:* For master's, thesis or project. *Entrance requirements:* For master's, minimum GPA of 2.5. Additional exam requirements/recommendations for international students: Required—TOEFL (minimum score 550 paper-based; 213 computer-based).

California State University, Bakersfield, Division of Graduate Studies, Program in Interdisciplinary Studies, Bakersfield, CA 93311. Offers MA. *Degree requirements:* For master's, thesis or project. *Entrance requirements:* For master's, minimum GPA of 3.0 in last 90 quarter units. Additional exam requirements/recommendations for international students: Required—TOEFL (minimum score 550 paper-based; 213 computer-based). *Faculty research:* Ethics, physical education and health.

California State University, Chico, Graduate School, Interdisciplinary Programs, Chico, CA 95929-0722. Offers interdisciplinary studies (MA, MS); science teaching (MS); simulation science (MS). Part-time programs available. *Students:* 21 full-time (18 women), 10 part-time (9 women); includes 7 minority (1 African American, 1 Asian American or Pacific Islander, 5 Hispanic Americans), 7 international. Average age 35. 23 applicants, 91% accepted, 11 enrolled. In 2009, 8 master's awarded. *Degree requirements:* For master's, thesis or alternative, oral exam. *Entrance requirements:* For master's, GRE General Test or MAT, 3 letters of recommendation. Additional exam requirements/recommendations for international students: Required—TOEFL (minimum score 550 paper-based; 213 computer-based; 80 iBT), IELTS (minimum score 6.5). *Application deadline:* For fall admission, 3/1 priority date for domestic students, 3/1 for international students; for spring admission, 9/15 priority date for domestic students, 9/15 for international students. Applications are processed on a rolling basis. Application fee: $55. *Financial support:* Fellowships, Federal Work-Study available. Support available to part-time students. *Unit head:* Dr. Sara Trechter, Graduate Coordinator, 530-898-5447. *Application contact:* School of Graduate, International, and Interdisciplinary Studies, 530-898-6880, Fax: 530-898-6889, E-mail: grin@csuchico.edu.

California State University, East Bay, Academic Programs and Graduate Studies, Interdisciplinary Programs, Hayward, CA 94542-3000. Offers MA, MS, Certificate. Part-time programs available. *Students:* 1 (woman) full-time, 6 part-time (4 women); includes 1 minority (African American), 1 international. Average age 40. 5 applicants, 80% accepted, 0 enrolled. In 2009, 8 master's awarded. *Degree requirements:* For master's, comprehensive exam, project or thesis. *Entrance requirements:* Additional exam requirements/recommendations for international students: Required—TOEFL (minimum score 550 paper-based; 213 computer-based). *Application deadline:* For fall admission, 6/30 for domestic and international students; for winter admission, 10/31 for domestic students; for spring admission, 11/30 for domestic students. Applications are processed on a rolling basis. Application fee: $55. Electronic applications accepted. *Financial support:* Fellowships, teaching assistantships, Federal Work-Study, institutionally sponsored loans, and scholarships/grants available. Support available to part-time students. Financial award application deadline: 3/1; financial award applicants required to submit FAFSA. *Unit head:* Dr. Susan Opp, Associate Vice President, 510-885-3716, Fax: 510-885-4777, E-mail: susan.opp@csueastbay.edu. *Application contact:* Donna Wiley, Interim Associate Director, 510-885-2928, Fax: 510-885-4777, E-mail: donna.wiley@csueastbay.edu.

California State University, Long Beach, Graduate Studies, Interdisciplinary Studies Program, Long Beach, CA 90840. Offers MA, MS. Part-time programs available. *Students:* 1 (woman) full-time, 6 part-time (4 women); includes 2 minority (1 American Indian/Alaska Native, 1 Hispanic American). Average age 36. *Degree requirements:* For master's, thesis. *Entrance requirements:* For master's, minimum undergraduate GPA of 3.0. *Application deadline:* For fall admission, 3/30 for domestic students. Applications are processed on a rolling basis. Application fee: $55. Electronic applications accepted. *Expenses:* Required fees: $1802 per semester. Part-time tuition and fees vary according to course load. *Financial support:* Federal Work-Study, institutionally sponsored loans, and scholarships/grants available. Financial award application deadline: 3/2. *Unit head:* Dr. Cecile Lindsay, Director, 562-985-8225, Fax: 562-985-1680, E-mail: clindsay@csulb.edu. *Application contact:* Dr. Cecile Lindsay, Director, 562-985-8225, Fax: 562-985-1680, E-mail: clindsay@csulb.edu.

California State University, Monterey Bay, College of Science, Media Arts and Technology, School of Information Technology and Communication Design, Seaside, CA 93955-8001. Offers interdisciplinary studies (MA), including instructional science and technology; management and information technology (MA). *Degree requirements:* For master's, capstone or thesis. *Entrance requirements:* For master's, GRE, 2 letters of recommendation, minimum GPA of 3.0, technology screening assessment. Additional exam requirements/recommendations for international students: Required—TOEFL (minimum score 550 paper-based; 213 computer-based; 71 iBT). Electronic applications accepted. *Faculty research:* Electronic commerce, e-learning, knowledge management, international business, business and public policy.

California State University, Northridge, Graduate Studies, Interdisciplinary Studies, Northridge, CA 91330. Offers MA, MS. *Faculty:* 13 part-time/adjunct (7 women). *Students:* 12 full-time (9 women), 17 part-time (11 women); includes 14 African Americans, 1 Asian American or Pacific Islander, 2 Hispanic Americans. Average age 41. 1,071 applicants, 71% accepted. In 2009, 6 master's awarded. *Entrance requirements:* For master's, GRE (if cumulative undergraduate GPA less than 3.0). Additional exam requirements/recommendations for international students: Required—TOEFL. *Application deadline:* For fall admission, 11/30 for domestic students. Application fee: $55. *Financial support:* Federal Work-Study available. Financial award application deadline: 3/1. *Unit head:* Hedy Carpenter, Associate Director of Graduate Programs, 818-677-2138. *Application contact:* Hedy Carpenter, Associate Director of Graduate Programs, 818-677-2138.

California State University, San Bernardino, Graduate Studies, Interdisciplinary Programs, San Bernardino, CA 92407-2397. Offers MA. Part-time and evening/weekend programs available. *Students:* 1 full-time (0 women), 2 part-time (1 woman). Average age 34. 7 applicants, 43% accepted, 1 enrolled. In 2009, 3 master's awarded. *Degree requirements:* For master's, thesis or alternative, advancement to candidacy. *Entrance requirements:* For master's, writing exam, minimum overall undergraduate GPA of 2.5; 3.0 in major. *Application deadline:* For fall admission, 8/31 priority date for domestic students. Application fee: $55. *Financial support:* Career-related internships or fieldwork, Federal Work-Study, and institutionally sponsored loans available. Support available to part-time students. Financial award application deadline: 3/1. *Unit head:* Dr. Sandra Kamusikiri, Dean of Graduate Studies, 909-537-5058, Fax: 909-537-7034, E-mail: skamusik@csusb.edu. *Application contact:* Olivia Rosas, Director of Admissions, 909-537-7577, Fax: 909-537-7034, E-mail: orosas@csusb.edu.

California State University, Stanislaus, Programs in Interdisciplinary Studies, Turlock, CA 95382. Offers MA, MS. Part-time and evening/weekend programs available. *Degree requirements:* For master's, thesis. *Entrance requirements:* For master's, GRE, minimum GPA of 3.0. Electronic applications accepted.

Cambridge College, School of Education, Cambridge, MA 02138-5304. Offers autism specialist (M Ed); autism/behavior analyst (Post-Master's Certificate); behavioral management (M Ed); early childhood teacher (M Ed); education specialist in curriculum and instruction (CAGS); educational leadership (Ed D); elementary teacher (M Ed); English as a second language (M Ed, Certificate); general science (M Ed); health education, health promotion (Post-Master's Certificate); health/family and consumer sciences (M Ed); history (M Ed); individualized degree (M Ed); information technology literacy (M Ed); instructional technology (M Ed); interdisciplinary studies (M Ed); library teacher (M Ed); literacy education (M Ed); mathematics (M Ed); mathematics specialist (Certificate); middle school mathematics and science (M Ed); school administration (M Ed, CAGS); school guidance counselor (M Ed); school nurse education (M Ed); school social worker/school adjustment counselor (M Ed); special education administrator (CAGS); special education/moderate disabilities (M Ed); teaching skills and methodologies (M Ed). Part-time and evening/weekend programs available. Postbaccalaureate distance learning degree programs offered (minimal on-campus study). *Faculty:* 10 full-time (3 women), 283 part-time/adjunct (187 women). *Students:* 974 full-time (755 women), 1,071 part-time (835 women); includes 940 minority (762 African Americans, 4 American Indian/Alaska Native, 22 Asian Americans or Pacific Islanders, 152 Hispanic

Americans), 28 international. Average age 39. In 2009, 866 master's, 4 doctorates, 209 other advanced degrees awarded. *Degree requirements:* For master's, thesis, internship/practicum (licensure program only); for doctorate, thesis/dissertation; for other advanced degree, thesis. *Entrance requirements:* For master's, interview, resume, documentation of licensure, 2 professional references; for doctorate, official transcripts, interview, resume, documentation of licensure (if any), written personal statement/essay, portfolio of scholarly and professional work, qualifying assessment, 2 professional references, health insurance, immunizations form; for other advanced degree, official transcripts, interview, resume, documentation of licensure (if any), written personal statement/essay, 2 professional references, health insurance, immunizations form. Additional exam requirements/recommendations for international students: Required—TOEFL (minimum score 550 paper-based; 213 computer-based; 79 iBT); Recommended—IELTS (minimum score 6). *Application deadline:* Applications are processed on a rolling basis. Application fee: $30. Electronic applications accepted. *Expenses:* Contact institution. *Financial support:* In 2009–10, 1,373 students received support. Career-related internships or fieldwork, Federal Work-Study, and scholarships/grants available. Financial award applicants required to submit FAFSA. *Faculty research:* Adult education, accelerated learning, mathematics education, brain compatible learning, special education and law. *Unit head:* Dr. N. Alan Sheppard, Interim Associate Dean, 617-873-0619, E-mail: alan.sheppard@cambridgecollege.edu. *Application contact:* Stephen Lyons, Director of Enrollment, Graduate and N.I.T.E. Programs, 617-868-1000, Fax: 617-349-3561, E-mail: stephen.lyons@cambridgecollege.edu.

Campbell University, Graduate and Professional Programs, School of Education, Buies Creek, NC 27506. Offers administration (MSA); community counseling (MA); elementary education (M Ed); English education (M Ed); interdisciplinary studies (M Ed); mathematics education (M Ed); middle grades education (M Ed); physical education (M Ed); school counseling (M Ed); secondary education (M Ed); social science education (M Ed). *Accreditation:* NCATE. Part-time and evening/weekend programs available. *Degree requirements:* For master's, comprehensive exam. *Entrance requirements:* For master's, GRE General Test, minimum GPA of 2.7. *Faculty research:* Spiritual values and wellness issues in counseling, stress and professional burnout among counselors, thinking strategies, leadership, adaptive technology.

Central Washington University, Graduate Studies and Research, Individual Studies Program, Ellensburg, WA 98926. Offers M Ed, MA, MS. Part-time programs available. *Faculty:* 354 full-time (133 women). *Students:* 1 (woman) full-time, 3 part-time (1 woman). 2 applicants, 50% accepted, 0 enrolled. In 2009, 2 master's awarded. *Degree requirements:* For master's, thesis. *Entrance requirements:* For master's, GRE General Test, minimum GPA of 3.0. Additional exam requirements/recommendations for international students: Required—TOEFL (minimum score 550 paper-based; 213 computer-based; 79 iBT). *Application deadline:* For fall admission, 2/1 priority date for domestic students; for winter admission, 10/1 for domestic students; for spring admission, 1/1 for domestic students. Applications are processed on a rolling basis. Application fee: $50. *Expenses:* Tuition, state resident: full-time $7353; part-time $245 per credit. Tuition, nonresident: full-time $16,383; part-time $546 per credit. Required fees: $882. Tuition and fees vary according to degree level. *Financial support:* Application deadline: 3/1. *Unit head:* Dr. Roger S. Fouts, Associate Vice President for Graduate Studies, Research and Continuing Education, 509-963-3101, Fax: 509-963-1799, E-mail: masters@cwu.edu. *Application contact:* Justine Eason, Admissions Program Coordinator, 509-963-3103, Fax: 509-963-1799, E-mail: masters@cwu.edu.

College of the Humanities and Sciences, Harrison Middleton University, Graduate Program, Tempe, AZ 85282. Offers education (MA, Ed D); humanities (MA); imaginative literature (MA); interdisciplinary studies (DA); jurisprudence (MA); natural science (MA); philosophy and religion (MA); social science (MA). Part-time and evening/weekend programs available. Postbaccalaureate distance learning degree programs offered (no on-campus study). *Faculty:* 17 full-time (7 women), 14 part-time/adjunct (6 women). *Students:* 49 full-time (18 women). In 2009, 4 master's awarded. *Application deadline:* Applications are processed on a rolling basis. Application fee: $50. Electronic applications accepted. *Application contact:* Deborah Deacon, Dean of Graduate Studies, 877-248-6724, Fax: 800-762-1622, E-mail: ddeacon@chumsci.edu.

Columbia University, Graduate School of Arts and Sciences, Program in Liberal Studies, New York, NY 10027. Offers American studies (MA); East Asian studies (MA); human rights studies (MA); Islamic culture studies (MA); Jewish studies (MA); medieval studies (MA); modern European studies (MA); South Asian studies (MA). Part-time and evening/weekend programs available. *Degree requirements:* For master's, thesis.

Concordia University, School of Graduate Studies, Special Individualized Programs, Montréal, QC H3G 1M8, Canada. Offers M Sc, MA, PhD. *Degree requirements:* For master's, comprehensive exam, thesis; for doctorate, one foreign language, comprehensive exam, thesis/dissertation.

Dalhousie University, Faculty of Graduate Studies, Interdisciplinary PhD Program, Halifax, NS B3H 4H6, Canada. Offers PhD. *Students:* 11 full-time (7 women). In 2009, 1 doctorate awarded. *Degree requirements:* For doctorate, thesis/dissertation. *Entrance requirements:* Additional exam requirements/recommendations for international students: Required—TOEFL, IELTS, CANTEST, CAEL, or Michigan English Language Assessment Battery. *Application deadline:* For fall admission, 6/1 for domestic students, 4/1 for international students; for winter admission, 10/31 for domestic students, 8/31 for international students; for spring admission, 2/28 for domestic students, 12/31 for international students. Applications are processed on a rolling basis. Application fee: $70. Electronic applications accepted. *Expenses:* Contact institution. *Financial support:* Fellowships available. *Unit head:* Dr. Marina Pluzhenskaya, Graduate Coordinator, E-mail: marina.pluzhenskaya@dal.ca. *Application contact:* Elizabeth Clark, Administrative Secretary, 902-494-8078, Fax: 902-494-8797, E-mail: elizabethclark@dal.ca.

Dallas Baptist University, College of Adult Education, Professional Development Program, Dallas, TX 75211-9299. Offers accounting (MA); church leadership (MA); counseling (MA); criminal justice (MA); English as a second language (MA); finance (MA); higher education (MA); leadership studies (MA); management (MA); management information systems (MA); marketing (MA); missions (MA). Part-time and evening/weekend programs available. *Entrance requirements:* For master's, minimum GPA of 3.0. Additional exam requirements/recommendations for international students: Required—TOEFL, IELTS. *Expenses:* Tuition: Full-time $10,674; part-time $593 per credit hour.

DePaul University, College of Liberal Arts and Sciences, Department of Interdisciplinary Studies, Chicago, IL 60614. Offers MA, MS. Part-time and evening/weekend programs available. *Students:* 84 full-time (54 women), 118 part-time (84 women); includes 42 minority (13 African Americans, 2 Asian Americans or Pacific Islanders, 27 Hispanic Americans), 6 international. Average age 31. 10 applicants, 90% accepted. In 2009, 10 master's awarded. *Degree requirements:* For master's, thesis optional. *Application deadline:* Applications are processed on a rolling basis. Application fee: $25. *Expenses:* Tuition: Full-time $37,525; part-time $620 per credit hour. *Unit head:* Dr. Fassil Demissie, Director, 773-325-7356, E-mail: fdemissie@depaul.edu. *Application contact:* Ann Spittle, Director of Graduate Admissions, 312-362-8300, Fax: 312-362-5749, E-mail: admitdpu@depaul.edu.

Drew University, Caspersen School of Graduate Studies, Program in Arts and Letters, Madison, NJ 07940-1493. Offers holocaust and genocide studies (Certificate); interdisciplinary studies (M Litt, D Litt). Part-time and evening/weekend programs available. *Students:* 19 full-time (13 women), 162 part-time (94 women); includes 12 minority (7 African Americans, 2 Asian Americans or Pacific Islanders, 3 Hispanic Americans), 2 international. Average age 46. 33 applicants, 91% accepted, 23 enrolled. In 2009, 17 master's, 17 doctorates awarded. Terminal master's awarded for partial completion of doctoral program. *Degree requirements:* For master's, thesis optional; for doctorate, thesis/dissertation. *Entrance requirements:* For master's and doctorate, transcripts, writing sample, personal statement, recommendations. Additional exam requirements/recommendations for international students: Required—TOEFL (minimum score 585 paper-based; 240 computer-based; 95 iBT), TWE. *Application deadline:* Applications are processed on a rolling basis. Application fee: $35. *Expenses:* Contact institution. *Financial support:* In 2009–10, 102 students received support. Federal Work-Study, scholarships/grants, and tuition waivers (partial) available. Support available to part-time students. Financial award application deadline: 2/15; financial award applicants required to submit FAFSA. *Faculty research:* Interdisciplinary studies across art, literature, music, philosophy, religion, and history. *Unit head:* Dr. Robert Ready, Director, 973-408-3302, E-mail: rready@drew.edu. *Application contact:* Carla J. Burns, Director of Graduate Admissions, 973-408-3110, Fax: 973-408-3040, E-mail: gradm@drew.edu.

Eastern Washington University, Graduate Studies, Interdisciplinary Studies, Cheney, WA 99004-2431. Offers MA, MS. *Degree requirements:* For master's, comprehensive exam, thesis or alternative. *Entrance requirements:* For master's, minimum GPA of 3.0. *Expenses:* Tuition, state resident: full-time $7476; part-time $249 per quarter hour. Tuition, nonresident: full-time $18,030; part-time $601 per quarter hour. Required fees: $3.50 per quarter hour. $142 per quarter.

Emory University, Graduate School of Arts and Sciences, Graduate Institute of Liberal Arts, Atlanta, GA 30322-1100. Offers PhD. *Degree requirements:* For doctorate, one foreign language, comprehensive exam, thesis/dissertation. *Entrance requirements:* For doctorate, GRE General Test. Electronic applications accepted. *Faculty research:* American cultural criticism, intellectual history, psychoanalysis, history of science, popular culture.

Fitchburg State University, Division of Graduate and Continuing Education, Program in Interdisciplinary Studies, Fitchburg, MA 01420-2697. Offers CAGS. Part-time and evening/weekend programs available. *Students:* 1 (woman) full-time, 39 part-time (31 women). Average age 43. 11 applicants, 100% accepted, 5 enrolled. In 2009, 10 CAGSs awarded. *Entrance requirements:* For degree, master's degree, letters of recommendation, resume. Additional exam requirements/recommendations for international students: Required—TOEFL (minimum score 550 paper-based; 213 computer-based; 79 iBT). *Application deadline:* Applications are processed on a rolling basis. Application fee: $25 ($50 for international students). *Expenses:* Tuition, area resident: Part-time $150 per credit. Tuition, state resident: part-time $150 per credit. Tuition, nonresident: part-time $150 per credit. Required fees: $120 per credit. *Financial support:* In 2009–10, research assistantships with partial tuition reimbursements (averaging $5,500 per year); Federal Work-Study, scholarships/grants, and unspecified assistantships also available. Support available to part-time students. Financial award application deadline: 3/1; financial award applicants required to submit FAFSA. *Unit head:* Dr. Harry Semerjian, Chair, 978-665-3279, Fax: 978-665-3658, E-mail: gce@fsc.edu. *Application contact:* Director of Admissions, 978-665-3144, Fax: 978-665-4540, E-mail: admissions@fsc.edu.

Florida Gulf Coast University, College of Health Professions, Department of Health Sciences, Fort Myers, FL 33965-6565. Offers MS. Part-time and evening/weekend programs available. Postbaccalaureate distance learning degree programs offered (no on-campus study). *Faculty:* 42 full-time (33 women), 30 part-time/adjunct (20 women). *Students:* 25 full-time (20 women), 23 part-time (15 women); includes 12 minority (7 African Americans, 1 American Indian/Alaska Native, 4 Hispanic Americans). Average age 32. 13 applicants, 100% accepted, 12 enrolled. In 2009, 9 master's awarded. *Degree requirements:* For master's, final project or thesis. *Entrance requirements:* For master's, GRE General Test or MAT, minimum GPA of 3.0. Additional exam requirements/recommendations for international students: Required—TOEFL (minimum score 550 paper-based; 213 computer-based). *Application deadline:* For fall admission, 7/1 priority date for domestic students; for spring admission, 11/15 for domestic students. Applications are processed on a rolling basis. Application fee: $30. Electronic applications accepted. *Financial support:* Career-related internships or fieldwork available. *Faculty research:* Health services administration, gerontology, therapeutic recreation, health professions education, exercise physiology. *Unit head:* Dr. Joan Glacken, Chair, 239-590-7498, Fax: 239-590-7474, E-mail: jglacken@fgcu.edu. *Application contact:* Dr. Joan Glacken, Chair, 239-590-7498, Fax: 239-590-7474, E-mail: jglacken@fgcu.edu.

Franklin Pierce University, Graduate Studies, Rindge, NH 03461-0060. Offers emerging network technology (Graduate Certificate); health practice management (MBA, Graduate Certificate); human resource management (MBA); human resources management (Graduate Certificate); information technology management (MS); leadership (MBA, DA), including transformational leadership (DA); nursing (MS); physical therapy (DPT); physician assistant (MPAS); sports facilities management (MS); teacher education (M Ed). *Accreditation:* APTA. Part-time programs available. Postbaccalaureate distance learning degree programs offered (no on-campus study). *Faculty:* 27 full-time (16 women), 18 part-time/adjunct (4 women). *Students:* 296 full-time (172 women), 249 part-time (165 women); includes 18 minority (5 African Americans, 7 Asian Americans or Pacific Islanders, 6 Hispanic Americans), 31 international. Average age 38. 227 applicants, 97% accepted, 185 enrolled. In 2009, 76 master's, 46 doctorates awarded. *Degree requirements:* For master's, Program specific. Concentrated original research projects; student teaching, fieldwork and/or internship; leadership project.; for doctorate, concentrated original research projects, clinical fieldwork and/or internship, leadership project. *Entrance requirements:* For master's, minimum GPA of 2.5 GPA, 3 letters of recommendation; for doctorate, Demonstrated success at previous academic institutions (GPA of 2.5 or higher), cover letter, 3 letters of recommendation, personal mission statement. Interview. Writing sample required for Doctor of Arts program. Additional exam requirements/recommendations for international students: Required—TOEFL (minimum score 550 paper-based; 195 computer-based). *Application deadline:* Applications are processed on a rolling basis. Application fee: $0. Electronic applications accepted. *Expenses:* Tuition: Part-time $1560 per course. Part-time tuition and fees vary according to degree level, campus/location and program. *Financial support:* In 2009–10, 36 students received support, including 22 teaching assistantships with full and partial tuition reimbursements available; career-related internships or fieldwork and unspecified assistantships also available. Support available to part-time students. Financial award applicants required to submit FAFSA. *Faculty research:* Evidence based practice in sports physical therapy, human resource management in economic crisis, leadership in nursing, innovation in sports facility management, differentiated learning and understanding by design. *Unit head:* Dr. Robert G. Goddard, Assistant Dean, 603-899-4361, Fax: 603-229-4580, E-mail: goddardr@franklinpierce.edu. *Application contact:* 800-325-1090, Fax: 603-898-0827, E-mail: gpsadmin@franklinpierce.edu.

Fresno Pacific University, Graduate Programs, Individualized Study Program, Fresno, CA 93702-4709. Offers MA. Part-time and evening/weekend programs available. *Degree requirements:* For master's, thesis. *Entrance requirements:* For master's, GMAT, GRE General Test, or MAT, 2 writing samples, interview. Additional exam requirements/recommendations for international students: Required—TOEFL (minimum score 550 paper-based; 213 computer-based). Electronic applications accepted.

Frostburg State University, Graduate School, College of Education, Department of Educational Professions, Program in Interdisciplinary Education, Frostburg, MD 21532-1099. Offers M Ed. Part-time and evening/weekend programs available. *Students:* 17 full-time (5 women), 16 part-time (13 women); includes 3 minority (all African Americans), 2 international. Average age 31. 22 applicants, 73% accepted, 13 enrolled. In 2009, 12 master's awarded. *Degree requirements:* For master's, thesis or alternative. *Entrance requirements:* Additional exam requirements/recommendations for international students: Required—TOEFL. *Application deadline:* For fall admission, 7/15 priority date for domestic students. Applications are processed on a rolling basis. Application fee: $30. Electronic applications accepted. *Expenses:* Tuition, state resident: full-time $5706; part-time $317 per credit hour. Tuition, nonresident: full-time $6948; part-time $386 per credit hour. Required fees: $1476; $82 per credit hour. $11 per term. One-time fee: $30 full-time. *Financial support:* In 2009–10, 1 research assistantship with full tuition reimbursement (averaging $5,000 per year) was awarded; career-related internships or fieldwork also available. Financial award application deadline: 4/1; financial award applicants required to submit FAFSA. *Unit head:* Dr. Thomas Palardy, Coordinator, 301-687-3095, E-mail: tpalardy@frostburg.edu. *Application contact:* Vickie Mazer, Director, Graduate Services, 301-687-7053, Fax: 301-687-4597, E-mail: vmmazer@frostburg.edu.

Interdisciplinary Studies

George Mason University, College of Humanities and Social Sciences, Interdisciplinary Studies Program, Fairfax, VA 22030. Offers interdisciplinary studies (MAIS). Part-time and evening/weekend programs available. *Faculty:* 5 full-time (2 women), 5 part-time/adjunct (4 women). *Students:* 18 full-time (16 women), 96 part-time (70 women); includes 25 minority (6 African Americans, 1 American Indian/Alaska Native, 4 Asian Americans or Pacific Islanders, 14 Hispanic Americans), 3 international. Average age 34. 94 applicants, 47% accepted, 31 enrolled. In 2009, 25 master's awarded. *Degree requirements:* For master's, project or thesis. *Entrance requirements:* For master's, minimum GPA of 3.0 in last 60 hours of course work, resume, 3 letters of recommendation, writing sample. Additional exam requirements/recommendations for international students: Required—TOEFL. *Application deadline:* For fall admission, 3/1 priority date for domestic students; for spring admission, 10/15 for domestic students. Application fee: $75. Electronic applications accepted. *Expenses:* Tuition, state resident: full-time $7568; part-time $315.33 per credit hour. Tuition, nonresident: full-time $21,704; part-time $904.33 per credit hour. Required fees: $2184; $91 per credit hour. *Financial support:* In 2009–10, 3 students received support, including 1 research assistantship (averaging $5,542 per year), 2 teaching assistantships (averaging $7,931 per year); Federal Work-Study, scholarships/grants, unspecified assistantships, and health care benefits (full-time research or teaching assistantship recipients) also available. Support available to part-time students. Financial award application deadline: 3/1. *Faculty research:* Combined English and folklore, religious and cultural studies (Christianity and Muslim society). *Unit head:* Clare Snyder-Hall, Chair, 703-993-2308, E-mail: rcsnyder@gmu.edu. *Application contact:* Charles Milling, Administrative Coordinator, 703-993-8762, E-mail: cmilling@gmu.edu.

Georgetown University, Graduate School of Arts and Sciences, School of Continuing Studies, Washington, DC 20057. Offers American studies (MALS); Catholic studies (MALS); classical civilizations (MALS); ethics and the professions (MALS); human resources management (MPS); humanities (MALS); individualized study (MALS); international affairs (MALS); Islam and Muslim-Christian relations (MALS); journalism (MPS); liberal studies (DLS); literature and society (MALS); medieval and early modern European studies (MALS); public relations (MPS); real estate (MPS); religious studies (MALS); social and public policy (MALS); sports industry management (MPS); the theory and practice of American democracy (MALS); visual culture (MALS). *Entrance requirements:* Additional exam requirements/recommendations for international students: Required—TOEFL.

Goddard College, Graduate Division, Master of Arts in Individualized Studies Program, Plainfield, VT 05667-9432. Offers consciousness studies (MA); environmental studies (MA); transformative language arts (MA). Postbaccalaureate distance learning degree programs offered (minimal on-campus study). *Faculty:* 10 part-time/adjunct (7 women). *Students:* 42. Average age 37. 31 applicants, 81% accepted, 17 enrolled. *Degree requirements:* For master's, thesis. *Entrance requirements:* For master's, 3 letters of recommendation, study plan, bibliography/ resource list, interview. *Application deadline:* Applications are processed on a rolling basis. Application fee: $40. Electronic applications accepted. *Expenses:* Contact institution. *Financial support:* In 2009–10, 36 students received support. Applicants required to submit FAFSA. *Unit head:* Prof. Ruth Farmer, Director, 802-454-8311, Fax: 802-454-7835, E-mail: ruth.farmer@goddard.edu. *Application contact:* Jamie Kline, Admissions Counselor, 800-468-4888 Ext. 311, Fax: 802-454-1029, E-mail: jamie.kline@goddard.edu.

Graduate School and University Center of the City University of New York, Graduate Studies, Interdisciplinary Studies, New York, NY 10016-4039. Offers language in social context (PhD); medieval studies (PhD); public policy (MA, PhD); urban studies (MA, PhD); women's studies (MA, PhD). Terminal master's awarded for partial completion of doctoral program. *Degree requirements:* For master's, thesis; for doctorate, comprehensive exam, thesis/dissertation. *Entrance requirements:* For master's and doctorate, GRE General Test.

Hiram College, Graduate Studies, Hiram, OH 44234-0067. Offers MAIS. Part-time and evening/weekend programs available. *Degree requirements:* For master's, two seminars, capstone research project. *Entrance requirements:* For master's, bachelor's degree from an accredited institution, 2 letters of recommendation, writing sample, interview.

Hodges University, Graduate Programs, Naples, FL 34119. Offers business administration (MBA); computer information technology (MS); criminal justice (MCJ); education (MPS); information systems management (MIS); interdisciplinary (MPS); law (MPS); management (MSM); professional studies (MPS); psychology (MPS); public administration (MPA). Part-time and evening/weekend programs available. Postbaccalaureate distance learning degree programs offered (no on-campus study). *Faculty:* 14 full-time (4 women), 4 part-time/adjunct (3 women). *Students:* 37 full-time (28 women), 217 part-time (142 women); includes 76 minority (35 African Americans, 5 Asian Americans or Pacific Islanders, 36 Hispanic Americans). Average age 36. 92 applicants, 91% accepted, 81 enrolled. In 2009, 92 master's awarded. *Degree requirements:* For master's, comprehensive exam (for some programs), thesis (for some programs). *Entrance requirements:* For master's, in-house entrance exam. *Application deadline:* Applications are processed on a rolling basis. Application fee: $50. Electronic applications accepted. *Expenses:* Tuition: Full-time $16,605; part-time $615 per credit hour. Required fees: $570. *Financial support:* In 2009–10, 200 students received support. Federal Work-Study and scholarships/grants available. Financial award application deadline: 7/9; financial award applicants required to submit FAFSA. *Unit head:* Terry McMahan, President, 239-513-1122, Fax: 239-598-6253, E-mail: tmcmahan@hodges.edu. *Application contact:* Rita Lampus, Vice President of Student Enrollment Management, 239-513-1122, Fax: 239-598-6253, E-mail: rlampus@hodges.edu.

Hollins University, Graduate Programs, Program in Liberal Studies, Roanoke, VA 24020-1603. Offers humanities (MALS); interdisciplinary studies (MALS); justice and legal studies (MALS); liberal studies (CAS); social science (MALS); visual and performing arts (MALS). Part-time and evening/weekend programs available. *Faculty:* 7 full-time (1 woman), 4 part-time/adjunct (2 women). *Students:* 23 full-time (22 women), 73 part-time (57 women); includes 15 minority (13 African Americans, 2 Asian Americans or Pacific Islanders), 4 international. Average age 39. 31 applicants, 94% accepted, 25 enrolled. In 2009, 30 master's awarded. *Degree requirements:* For master's, thesis. *Entrance requirements:* For master's, letters of recommendation, interview. Additional exam requirements/recommendations for international students: Required—TOEFL (minimum score 550 paper-based; 213 computer-based; 79 iBT). *Application deadline:* For fall admission, 7/1 priority date for domestic and international students; for spring admission, 12/10 priority date for domestic and international students. Applications are processed on a rolling basis. Application fee: $40. Electronic applications accepted. *Expenses:* Tuition: Full-time $27,780; part-time $295 per contact hour. Required fees: $280; $70 per unit. Part-time tuition and fees vary according to course load and program. *Financial support:* In 2009–10, 31 students received support, including 2 fellowships (averaging $902 per year); Federal Work-Study and scholarships/grants also available. Support available to part-time students. Financial award application deadline: 7/15; financial award applicants required to submit FAFSA. *Faculty research:* Elderly blacks, film, feminist economics, US voting patterns, Wagner, diversity. *Unit head:* Dr. Edward A. Lynch, Director, 540-362-6475, Fax: 540-362-6288, E-mail: elynch@hollins.edu. *Application contact:* Cathy S. Koon, Manager of Graduate Services, 540-362-6326, Fax: 540-362-6288, E-mail: ckoon@hollins.edu.

Idaho State University, Office of Graduate Studies, Department of Interdisciplinary Studies, Pocatello, ID 83209. Offers general interdisciplinary (M Ed, MA, MNS); waste management and environmental science (MS). Part-time programs available. *Faculty:* 2 full-time (1 woman). In 2009, 2 master's awarded. *Degree requirements:* For master's, comprehensive exam, thesis optional. *Entrance requirements:* For master's, GRE General Test or MAT, minimum GPA of 3.0. Additional exam requirements/recommendations for international students: Required—TOEFL (minimum score 550 paper-based; 213 computer-based; 80 iBT). *Application deadline:* For fall admission, 7/1 for domestic students, 6/1 for international students; for spring admission, 12/1 for domestic students, 11/1 for international students. Applications are processed on a rolling basis. Application fee: $55. *Expenses:* Tuition, state resident: full-time $3318; part-time $297 per credit hour. Tuition, nonresident: full-time $13,120; part-time $437 per credit hour. Required fees: $2530. Tuition and fees vary according to program. *Financial support:* Career-related internships or fieldwork, Federal Work-Study, scholarships/grants, and unspecified assistantships available. Support available to part-time students. Financial award application deadline: 1/1; financial award applicants required to submit FAFSA. *Unit head:* Dr. Pamela Crowell, Vice President for Research, 208-282-2714, Fax: 208-282-4529. *Application contact:* Ellen Combs, Graduate School Technical Records Specialist, 208-282-2150, Fax: 208-282-4847.

Iowa State University of Science and Technology, Graduate College, Interdisciplinary Programs, Program in Interdisciplinary Graduate Studies, Ames, IA 50011. Offers MA, MS. *Students:* 27 full-time (18 women), 48 part-time (32 women); includes 15 minority (10 African Americans, 2 American Indian/Alaska Native, 3 Hispanic Americans), 12 international. 38 applicants, 71% accepted, 22 enrolled. In 2009, 13 master's awarded. *Degree requirements:* For master's, thesis or alternative. *Entrance requirements:* Additional exam requirements/recommendations for international students: Required—TOEFL (minimum score 550 paper-based; 79 iBT) or IELTS (minimum score 6.5). *Application deadline:* Applications are processed on a rolling basis. Application fee: $40 ($90 for international students). Electronic applications accepted. *Expenses:* Tuition, state resident: full-time $6716. Tuition, nonresident: full-time $8908. Tuition and fees vary according to course level, course load, program and student level. *Financial support:* In 2009–10, 11 research assistantships with full and partial tuition reimbursements (averaging $13,770 per year), 3 teaching assistantships with full and partial tuition reimbursements (averaging $14,000 per year) were awarded; fellowships, scholarships/grants, health care benefits, and unspecified assistantships also available. *Unit head:* Chair, Supervisory Committee, 515-294-1170. *Application contact:* Linda Thorson, Information Contact, 515-294-1170, Fax: 515-294-3003, E-mail: grad_admissions@iastate.edu.

John F. Kennedy University, Graduate School of Holistic Studies, Department of Integral Studies, Program in Consciousness Studies, Pleasant Hill, CA 94523-4817. Offers MA. Part-time and evening/weekend programs available. *Degree requirements:* For master's, thesis or alternative. *Entrance requirements:* For master's, interview. Additional exam requirements/recommendations for international students: Required—TOEFL.

Lehigh University, P.C. Rossin College of Engineering and Applied Science and College of Arts and Sciences, Center for Polymer Science and Engineering, Bethlehem, PA 18015. Offers M Eng, MS, PhD. Part-time and evening/weekend programs available. Postbaccalaureate distance learning degree programs offered (no on-campus study). *Faculty:* 1 part-time/adjunct (0 women). *Students:* 4 full-time (1 woman), 9 part-time (2 women); includes 1 minority (Asian American or Pacific Islander), 2 international. Average age 34. 45 applicants, 0% accepted, 0 enrolled. In 2009, 2 master's, 1 doctorate awarded. Terminal master's awarded for partial completion of doctoral program. *Degree requirements:* For master's, thesis (for some programs); for doctorate, thesis/dissertation. *Entrance requirements:* For master's and doctorate, GRE General Test. Additional exam requirements/recommendations for international students: Required—TOEFL (minimum score 550 paper-based; 213 computer-based; 82 iBT). *Application deadline:* For fall admission, 7/15 for domestic students, 1/15 for international students; for spring admission, 12/1 for domestic and international students. Applications are processed on a rolling basis. Application fee: $65. Electronic applications accepted. *Financial support:* In 2009–10, 5 students received support, including fellowships (averaging $17,667 per year), 5 research assistantships (averaging $26,670 per year), teaching assistantships (averaging $17,667 per year); Royal Thai scholarship also available. Financial award application deadline: 1/15. *Faculty research:* Polymer colloids, polymer coatings, blends and composites, polymer interfaces, emulsion polymer. *Unit head:* Dr. Raymond A. Pearson, Director, 610-758-3857, Fax: 610-758-3526, E-mail: rp02@lehigh.edu. *Application contact:* James E. Roberts, Chair, Polymer Education Committee, 610-758-4841, Fax: 610-758-6536, E-mail: jer1@lehigh.edu.

Lesley University, Graduate School of Arts and Social Sciences, Self-Designed Master's Program in Interdisciplinary Studies, Cambridge, MA 02138-2790. Offers individualized studies (MA); integrative holistic health (MA); women's studies (MA). Part-time and evening/weekend programs available. Postbaccalaureate distance learning degree programs offered (no on-campus study). *Entrance requirements:* For master's, 3 letters of recommendation. Additional exam requirements/recommendations for international students: Required—TOEFL (minimum score 550 paper-based; 213 computer-based; 80 iBT).

Long Island University, C.W. Post Campus, College of Liberal Arts and Sciences, Program in Interdisciplinary Studies, Brookville, NY 11548-1300. Offers MA, MS. Part-time and evening/weekend programs available. *Degree requirements:* For master's, thesis. *Entrance requirements:* For master's, minimum GPA of 3.0. Electronic applications accepted.

Marquette University, Graduate School, Interdisciplinary PhD and Transfusion Medicine Programs, Milwaukee, WI 53201-1881. Offers interdisciplinary studies (PhD); transfusion medicine (MS). *Students:* 2 full-time (1 woman), 10 part-time (9 women); includes 1 minority (African American), 2 international. Average age 40. 5 applicants, 60% accepted, 1 enrolled. In 2009, 4 master's, 2 doctorates awarded. *Degree requirements:* For doctorate, thesis/dissertation. *Entrance requirements:* For doctorate, GRE General Test. Additional exam requirements/recommendations for international students: Required—TOEFL. Application fee: $40. *Financial support:* Fellowships, research assistantships, teaching assistantships, career-related internships or fieldwork, Federal Work-Study, institutionally sponsored loans, scholarships/grants, and tuition waivers (full and partial) available. Support available to part-time students. Financial award application deadline: 2/15. *Unit head:* Dr. William Wiener, Vice Provost for Research/Dean, 414-288-1532, Fax: 414-288-1578. *Application contact:* Craig Pierce, Director of Admissions, Graduate School, 414-288-7137, Fax: 414-288-1902, E-mail: craig.pierce@marquette.edu.

Marylhurst University, Department of Interdisciplinary Studies, Marylhurst, OR 97036-0261. Offers MA. Part-time and evening/weekend programs available. *Faculty:* 2 full-time (both women), 2 part-time/adjunct (1 woman). *Students:* 1 full-time (0 women), 28 part-time (19 women); includes 1 minority (Hispanic American). Average age 47. 5 applicants, 80% accepted, 4 enrolled. In 2009, 8 master's awarded. *Degree requirements:* For master's, thesis. *Entrance requirements:* For master's, 2 letters of recommendation, writing sample, interview. Additional exam requirements/recommendations for international students: Recommended—TOEFL (minimum score 550 paper-based; 213 computer-based; 80 iBT). *Application deadline:* Applications are processed on a rolling basis. Application fee: $40 ($50 for international students). Electronic applications accepted. *Financial support:* Federal Work-Study and scholarships/grants available. Support available to part-time students. Financial award applicants required to submit FAFSA. *Faculty research:* World religions, spirituality and literature, philosophy, humanities. *Unit head:* Dr. Debrah B. Bokowski, Chair, 503-636-8141, Fax: 503-697-5597, E-mail: dbokowski@marylhurst.edu. *Application contact:* Kathleen Schneff, Admissions Specialist, 800-634-9982 Ext. 3322, Fax: 503-635-6585, E-mail: admissions@marylhurst.edu.

Marywood University, Academic Affairs, Insalaco College of Creative and Performing Arts, Department of Communication Arts, Program in Communication Arts, Scranton, PA 18509-1598. Offers interdisciplinary (MA); media management (MA); production (MA). *Students:* 12 full-time (7 women), 25 part-time (13 women); includes 5 minority (2 African Americans, 1 Asian American or Pacific Islander, 2 Hispanic Americans). Average age 33. In 2009, 11 master's awarded. *Entrance requirements:* Additional exam requirements/recommendations for international students: Required—TOEFL (minimum score 550 paper-based; 213 computer-based; 79 iBT). *Application deadline:* For fall admission, 4/1 for domestic students, 3/31 for international students; for spring admission, 11/1 for domestic students, 8/31 for international students. Applications are processed on a rolling basis. Application fee: $35. Electronic applications accepted. *Expenses:* Tuition: Part-time $715 per credit. Required fees: $270 per semester. Tuition and fees vary according to degree level, campus/location and program. *Financial support:* Career-related internships or fieldwork, scholarships/grants, and unspecified assistantships available. Support available to part-time students. Financial award application deadline: 6/30; financial award applicants required to submit FAFSA. *Application contact:* Tammy Manka, Assistant Director of Admissions, 866-279-9663, E-mail: tmanka@marywood.edu.

Mills College, Graduate Studies, Program in Computer Science, Oakland, CA 94613-1000. Offers computer science (Certificate); interdisciplinary computer science (MA). Part-time programs available. *Faculty:* 7 full-time (6 women), 2 part-time/adjunct (1 woman). *Students:* 5 full-time (4 women), 2 part-time (1 woman); includes 2 minority (1 African American, 1 Asian American or Pacific Islander). Average age 28. 11 applicants, 100% accepted, 6 enrolled. In 2009, 2 master's awarded. *Degree requirements:* For master's, thesis. *Entrance requirements:* Additional exam requirements/recommendations for international students: Required—TOEFL. *Application deadline:* For fall admission, 2/1 priority date for domestic students; for spring admission, 11/1 for domestic students. Applications are processed on a rolling basis. Application fee: $50. Electronic applications accepted. *Expenses:* Tuition: Full-time $26,326; part-time $6584 per course. Required fees: $896. One-time fee: $896 part-time. Tuition and fees vary according to program. *Financial support:* In 2009–10, 3 students received support. Career-related internships or fieldwork and residence awards available. Financial award application deadline: 2/1; financial award applicants required to submit FAFSA. *Faculty research:* Dynamical systems, linear programming, theory of computer viruses, interface design, intelligent tutoring systems. *Unit head:* Susan S. Wang, Department Head, 510-430-2138, E-mail: wang@mills.edu. *Application contact:* Jessica King, Graduate Admission Specialist, 510-430-3305, Fax: 510-430-2159, E-mail: rmcglaut@mills.edu.

Minnesota State University Mankato, College of Graduate Studies, Program in Cross-disciplinary Studies, Mankato, MN 56001. Offers MS. Part-time and evening/weekend programs available. *Students:* 5 part-time (4 women). *Degree requirements:* For master's, comprehensive exam, thesis or alternative. *Entrance requirements:* For master's, GRE General Test, minimum GPA of 3.0 during previous 2 years. Additional exam requirements/recommendations for international students: Required—TOEFL. *Application deadline:* For fall admission, 7/1 priority date for domestic students; for spring admission, 11/1 for domestic students. Applications are processed on a rolling basis. Application fee: $40. Electronic applications accepted. *Expenses:* Tuition, state resident: full-time $5364. Tuition, nonresident: full-time $8314. *Financial support:* Research assistantships with full tuition reimbursements, teaching assistantships with full tuition reimbursements, career-related internships or fieldwork, Federal Work-Study, and unspecified assistantships available. Support available to part-time students. Financial award application deadline: 3/15; financial award applicants required to submit FAFSA. *Unit head:* Chris Mickle, Graduate Coordinator, 507-389-2321. *Application contact:* 507-389-2321, E-mail: grad@mnsu.edu.

Mississippi State University, College of Arts and Sciences, Department of Chemistry, Mississippi State, MS 39762. Offers chemistry (MS, PhD); interdisciplinary sciences (MA), including biological sciences, chemistry. *Faculty:* 11 full-time (0 women), 1 part-time/adjunct (0 women). *Students:* 46 full-time (13 women), 4 part-time (2 women); includes 5 minority (4 African Americans, 1 Asian American or Pacific Islander), 37 international. Average age 30. 121 applicants, 13% accepted, 15 enrolled. In 2009, 3 doctorates awarded. Terminal master's awarded for partial completion of doctoral program. *Degree requirements:* For master's, thesis, comprehensive oral or written exam; for doctorate, thesis/dissertation, comprehensive oral or written exam. *Entrance requirements:* For master's, minimum GPA of 2.75 on last two years of undergraduate courses; for doctorate, minimum GPA of 2.75. Additional exam requirements/recommendations for international students: Required—TOEFL (minimum score 475 paper-based; 153 computer-based). *Application deadline:* For fall admission, 7/1 for domestic students, 5/1 for international students; for spring admission, 11/1 for domestic students, 9/1 for international students. Applications are processed on a rolling basis. Application fee: $40. Electronic applications accepted. *Expenses:* Tuition, state resident: full-time $2575.50; part-time $286.25 per credit hour. Tuition, nonresident: full-time $6510; part-time $723.50 per credit hour. Tuition and fees vary according to course load. *Financial support:* In 2009–10, 9 research assistantships with full tuition reimbursements (averaging $12,610 per year), 37 teaching assistantships with full tuition reimbursements (averaging $13,900 per year) were awarded; Federal Work-Study, institutionally sponsored loans, scholarships/grants, and unspecified assistantships also available. Financial award applicants required to submit FAFSA. *Faculty research:* Spectroscopy, fluorometry, organic and inorganic synthesis, electrochemistry. Total annual research expenditures: $4.5 million. *Unit head:* Dr. Edwin A. Lewis, Department Head, 662-325-3584, Fax: 662-325-1618, E-mail: elewis@chemistry.msstate.edu. *Application contact:* Dr. Stephen Foster, Graduate Coordinator, 662-325-8854, E-mail: grad@chemistry.msstate.edu.

Montana State University Billings, College of Education, Department of Educational Theory and Practice, Option in Interdisciplinary Studies, Billings, MT 59101-0298. Offers M Ed. *Degree requirements:* For master's, thesis or alternative. *Entrance requirements:* For master's, GRE General Test or MAT, minimum GPA of 3.0 (undergraduate), 3.25 (graduate).

Montana Tech of The University of Montana, Graduate School, Interdisciplinary Program, Butte, MT 59701-8997. Offers MS. Part-time programs available. *Students:* 4 full-time (2 women), 1 (woman) part-time, 1 international. 4 applicants, 75% accepted, 1 enrolled. In 2009, 1 master's awarded. *Degree requirements:* For master's, comprehensive exam (for some programs), thesis optional. *Entrance requirements:* For master's, GRE General Test, minimum GPA of 3.0. Additional exam requirements/recommendations for international students: Required—TOEFL (minimum score 525 paper-based; 195 computer-based; 71 iBT). *Application deadline:* For fall admission, 4/1 for domestic students, 3/1 priority date for international students; for spring admission, 10/1 for domestic students, 7/1 priority date for international students. Application fee: $30. *Expenses:* Tuition, state resident: full-time $5068; part-time $319 per credit. Tuition, nonresident: full-time $14,815; part-time $875 per credit. Tuition and fees vary according to course load and campus/location. *Financial support:* In 2009–10, 5 students received support, including 4 teaching assistantships (averaging $8,000 per year); research assistantships, career-related internships or fieldwork, tuition waivers (full and partial), and unspecified assistantships also available. *Unit head:* Dr. Joseph Figueira, Associate Vice Chancellor of Academic Affairs and Research/Dean of the Graduate School, 406-496-4456. *Application contact:* Cindy Dunstan, Administrator, Graduate School, 406-496-4304, Fax: 406-496-4710, E-mail: cdunstan@mtech.edu.

Mountain State University, Graduate Studies, Program in Interdisciplinary Studies, Beckley, WV 25802-9003. Offers MA, MS. Part-time and evening/weekend programs available. Postbaccalaureate distance learning degree programs offered (no on-campus study). *Faculty:* 7 full-time (2 women), 15 part-time/adjunct (6 women). *Students:* 56 full-time (40 women); includes 13 minority (12 African Americans, 1 Asian American or Pacific Islander), 1 international. Average age 38. 52 applicants, 77% accepted, 29 enrolled. In 2009, 6 master's awarded. *Degree requirements:* For master's, thesis or alternative. *Entrance requirements:* Additional exam requirements/recommendations for international students: Required—TOEFL (minimum score 550 paper-based; 213 computer-based); Recommended—IELTS (minimum score 6.5). *Application deadline:* For fall admission, 5/31 priority date for domestic and international students. Applications are processed on a rolling basis. Application fee: $25 ($50 for international students). Electronic applications accepted. *Expenses:* Tuition: Full-time $6450. Tuition and fees vary according to program. *Financial support:* Federal Work-Study, scholarships/grants, and unspecified assistantships available. Support available to part-time students. Financial award applicants required to submit FAFSA. *Unit head:* Dr. William White, Interim Dean, School of Graduate Studies/Dean, School of Leadership and Professional Development, 304-929-1658, Fax: 304-929-1637, E-mail: wwhite@mountainstate.edu. *Application contact:* Anita Diaz, Enrollment Coordinator for Graduate Studies, 304-461-3213, Fax: 304-929-1637, E-mail: adiaz@mountainstate.edu.

New Mexico State University, Graduate School, Interdisciplinary Program, Las Cruces, NM 88003-8001. Offers MA, MS, PhD. Part-time programs available. Postbaccalaureate distance learning degree programs offered (minimal on-campus study). *Faculty:* 1 (woman) full-time. *Students:* 68 full-time (38 women), 189 part-time (122 women); includes 122 minority (8 African Americans, 9 American Indian/Alaska Native, 3 Asian Americans or Pacific Islanders, 102 Hispanic Americans), 3 international. Average age 36. 335 applicants, 92% accepted. In 2009, 1 master's awarded. *Degree requirements:* For master's, comprehensive exam, thesis; for doctorate, comprehensive exam, thesis/dissertation. *Entrance requirements:* For master's, GRE General Test, minimum GPA of 2.5; for doctorate, GRE General Test, minimum GPA of 3.0. Additional exam requirements/recommendations for international students: Required—TOEFL (minimum score 550 paper-based; 213 computer-based; 79 iBT), IELTS. *Application deadline:* Applications are processed on a rolling basis. Application fee: $30 ($50 for international students). *Expenses:* Tuition, state resident: full-time $4080; part-time $223 per credit. Tuition, nonresident: full-time $14,256; part-time $647 per credit. Required fees: $1278; $639 per semester. *Financial support:* In 2009–10, 2 research assistantships with full tuition reimbursements (averaging $9,140 per year), 2 teaching assistantships with full tuition reimbursements (averaging $16,000 per year) were awarded; fellowships, career-related internships or fieldwork, Federal Work-Study, and health care benefits also available. Financial award application deadline: 3/1. *Faculty research:* Bioinformatics, molecular genetics, plant pathology. *Unit head:* Dr. Linda Lacey, Dean, 575-646-5746, Fax: 575-646-7721, E-mail: lacey@nmsu.edu. *Application contact:* Dr. Linda Lacey, Dean, 575-646-5746, Fax: 575-646-7721, E-mail: lacey@nmsu.edu.

New York University, Gallatin School of Individualized Study, New York, NY 10003. Offers MA. Part-time and evening/weekend programs available. *Faculty:* 39 full-time (21 women), 47 part-time/adjunct (31 women). *Students:* 57 full-time (41 women), 152 part-time (114 women); includes 54 minority (25 African Americans, 1 American Indian/Alaska Native, 14 Asian Americans or Pacific Islanders, 14 Hispanic Americans), 12 international. Average age 34. 290 applicants, 47% accepted, 56 enrolled. In 2009, 44 master's awarded. *Degree requirements:* For master's, thesis. *Entrance requirements:* Additional exam requirements/recommendations for international students: Required—TOEFL. *Application deadline:* For fall admission, 1/15 priority date for domestic and international students; for spring admission, 10/15 for domestic and international students. Applications are processed on a rolling basis. Application fee: $50. Electronic applications accepted. *Expenses:* Contact institution. *Financial support:* In 2009–10, 97 students received support, including 5 fellowships (averaging $25,000 per year), 4 research assistantships with full tuition reimbursements available (averaging $17,280 per year); Federal Work-Study, scholarships/grants, and unspecified assistantships also available. Support available to part-time students. Financial award application deadline: 2/1; financial award applicants required to submit FAFSA. *Faculty research:* Arts and culture, gender studies, political and social thought, literature, classical studies. *Unit head:* Dr. Susanne L. Wofford, Dean, 212-998-7370. *Application contact:* Frances R. Levin, Director of Enrollment, 212-998-7370, Fax: 212-995-4150, E-mail: gallatin.gradadmissions@nyu.edu.

See Close-Up on page 551.

Niagara University, Graduate Division of Arts and Sciences, Program in Interdisciplinary Studies, Niagara Falls, Niagara University, NY 14109. Offers MA.

Northeastern University, College of Engineering, Program in Interdisciplinary Engineering, Boston, MA 02115-5096. Offers PhD. *Students:* 7 full-time (3 women). Average age 25. *Entrance requirements:* Additional exam requirements/recommendations for international students: Required—TOEFL (minimum score 550 paper-based; 213 computer-based). *Application deadline:* For fall admission, 1/15 priority date for domestic and international students. Applications are processed on a rolling basis. Application fee: $50. Electronic applications accepted. *Financial support:* In 2009–10, 3 students received support, including 3 research assistantships with full tuition reimbursements available (averaging $18,320 per year), 2 teaching assistantships with full tuition reimbursements available (averaging $18,320 per year); fellowships, career-related internships or fieldwork, Federal Work-Study, scholarships/grants, tuition waivers, and unspecified assistantships also available. Support available to part-time students. Financial award application deadline: 1/15. *Unit head:* Dr. Yaman Yener, Associate Dean of Engineering for Research and Graduate Studies, 617-373-2711, Fax: 617-373-2501. *Application contact:* Stephen L. Gibson, Associate Director, 617-373-2711, Fax: 617-373-2501, E-mail: grad-eng@coe.neu.edu.

Nova Southeastern University, Graduate School of Humanities and Social Sciences, Department of Multi-Disciplinary Studies, Program in Cross-Disciplinary Studies, Fort Lauderdale, FL 33314-7796. Offers MA. *Unit head:* Dr. Judith McKay, Chair, 954-262-3060. *Application contact:* Marcia Arango, Student Recruitment Coordinator, 954-262-3006, Fax: 954-262-3968, E-mail: marango@nsu.nova.edu.

The Ohio State University, Graduate School, College of Humanities, Department of Comparative Studies, Columbus, OH 43210. Offers MA, PhD. *Faculty:* 71. *Students:* 19 full-time (10 women), 11 part-time (8 women); includes 4 minority (all African Americans), 4 international. Average age 35. In 2009, 5 master's, 2 doctorates awarded. *Entrance requirements:* For master's and doctorate, GRE General Test. Additional exam requirements/recommendations for international students: Required—TOEFL (minimum score 600 paper-based; 250 computer-based). *Application deadline:* For fall admission, 8/15 priority date for domestic students, 7/1 priority date for international students; for winter admission, 12/1 priority date for domestic students, 11/1 priority date for international students; for spring admission, 3/1 priority date for domestic students, 2/1 priority date for international students. Applications are processed on a rolling basis. Application fee: $40 ($50 for international students). Electronic applications accepted. *Expenses:* Tuition, state resident: full-time $10,683. Tuition, nonresident: full-time $25,923. Tuition and fees vary according to course load and program. *Financial support:* Fellowships, research assistantships, teaching assistantships, Federal Work-Study, institutionally sponsored loans, and unspecified assistantships available. Support available to part-time students. *Unit head:* Ruby Tapia, Graduate Studies Committee Chair, E-mail: tapia.14@osu.edu. *Application contact:* 614-292-9444, Fax: 614-292-3895, E-mail: domestic.grad@osu.edu.

Oregon State University, Graduate School, Program in Interdisciplinary Studies, Corvallis, OR 97331. Offers MAIS. Program focuses on three areas of study and must include at least one area of study in liberal arts. Part-time programs available. *Students:* 39 full-time (28 women), 16 part-time (9 women); includes 11 minority (1 American Indian/Alaska Native, 2 Asian Americans or Pacific Islanders, 8 Hispanic Americans), 4 international. Average age 31. In 2009, 22 master's awarded. *Degree requirements:* For master's, thesis optional. *Entrance requirements:* For master's, minimum GPA of 3.0 in last 90 hours of course work. Additional exam requirements/recommendations for international students: Required—TOEFL. *Application deadline:* For fall admission, 3/1 for domestic students. Applications are processed on a rolling basis. Application fee: $50. *Expenses:* Tuition, state resident: full-time $9774; part-time $362 per credit. Tuition, nonresident: full-time $15,849; part-time $587 per credit. Required fees: $1639. Full-time tuition and fees vary according to course load and program. *Financial support:* Fellowships, research assistantships, teaching assistantships, career-related internships or fieldwork, Federal Work-Study, and institutionally sponsored loans available. Support available to part-time students. Financial award application deadline: 2/1. *Unit head:* Dr. Mary Ann Matzke, Head Advisor, 541-737-3880, Fax: 541-737-1009, E-mail: maryann.matzke@oregonstate.edu. *Application contact:* Rosemary Garagnani, Assistant Dean, 541-737-1465, Fax: 541-737-3313.

Polytechnic Institute of NYU, Department of Interdisciplinary Studies, Brooklyn, NY 11201-2990. Offers bioinformatics (MS); industrial engineering (MS); manufacturing engineering (MS). Part-time programs available. *Students:* 61 full-time (19 women), 51 part-time (22 women); includes 15 minority (3 African Americans, 5 Asian Americans or Pacific Islanders, 7 Hispanic Americans), 54 international. Average age 30. 176 applicants, 60% accepted, 45 enrolled. In 2009, 37 master's awarded. *Degree requirements:* For master's, comprehensive exam (for some programs), thesis (for some programs). *Entrance requirements:* Additional exam requirements/recommendations for international students: Required—TOEFL (minimum score 550 paper-based; 213 computer-based; 80 iBT); Recommended—IELTS (minimum score 6.5). *Application deadline:* For fall admission, 7/31 priority date for domestic students, 4/30 priority date for international students; for spring admission, 12/31 priority date for domestic students, 11/30 priority date for international students. Applications are processed on a rolling basis. Application fee: $75. Electronic applications accepted. *Expenses:* Tuition: Full-time $21,492; part-time $1194 per credit hour. Required fees: $1160; $204 per course.

Interdisciplinary Studies

Polytechnic Institute of NYU (continued)
Financial support: Institutionally sponsored loans, scholarships/grants, and unspecified assistantships available. Support available to part-time students. *Application contact:* JeanCarlo Bonilla, Dir. Graduate Enrollment Management, 718-260-3182, Fax: 718-260-3624, E-mail: gradinfo@poly.edu.

Polytechnic Institute of NYU, Long Island Graduate Center, Graduate Programs, Department of Interdisciplinary Studies, Melville, NY 11747. Offers bioinformatics (MS); industrial engineering (MS); manufacturing engineering (MS). Part-time and evening/weekend programs available. *Students:* 2 full-time (0 women), 4 part-time (all women); includes 1 minority (African American), 1 international. Average age 36. *Entrance requirements:* Additional exam requirements/recommendations for international students: Required—TOEFL (minimum score 550 paper-based; 213 computer-based; 80 iBT); Recommended—IELTS (minimum score 6.5). *Application deadline:* For fall admission, 7/31 priority date for domestic students, 4/30 priority date for international students; for spring admission, 12/31 priority date for domestic students, 11/30 priority date for international students. Applications are processed on a rolling basis. Application fee: $75. Electronic applications accepted. *Financial support:* Institutionally sponsored loans, scholarships/grants, and unspecified assistantships available. Support available to part-time students. *Application contact:* JeanCarlo Bonilla, Director of Graduate Enrollment Management, 718-260-3182, Fax: 718-260-3624, E-mail: gradinfo@poly.edu.

Polytechnic Institute of NYU, Westchester Graduate Center, Graduate Programs, Department of Interdisciplinary Studies, Hawthorne, NY 10532-1507. Offers bioinformatics (MS); industrial engineering (MS); manufacturing engineering (MS); wireless innovation (ME). *Students:* 1 full-time (0 women), 1 part-time (0 women), both international. Average age 24. *Entrance requirements:* Additional exam requirements/recommendations for international students: Required—TOEFL (minimum score 550 paper-based; 213 computer-based; 80 iBT); Recommended—IELTS (minimum score 6.5). *Application deadline:* For fall admission, 7/31 priority date for domestic students, 4/30 priority date for international students; for spring admission, 12/31 priority date for domestic students, 11/30 priority date for international students. Applications are processed on a rolling basis. Application fee: $75. Electronic applications accepted. *Financial support:* Institutionally sponsored loans, scholarships/grants, and unspecified assistantships available. Support available to part-time students. *Application contact:* JeanCarlo Bonilla, Director of Graduate Enrollment Management, 718-260-3182, Fax: 718-260-3624, E-mail: gradinfo@poly.edu.

Regis University, College for Professional Studies, MA Program, Denver, CO 80221-1099. Offers criminology (MA); fine arts administration (Certificate); language and communication (MA); mediation (Certificate); psychology (MA); self-designed major (MA); social justice, peace, and reconciliation (Certificate); social science (MA); technical communication (Certificate). Program also offered in Henderson and Las Vegas (Summerlin), NV. Part-time and evening/weekend programs available. Postbaccalaureate distance learning degree programs offered (minimal on-campus study). *Degree requirements:* For master's, thesis, research project. *Entrance requirements:* For master's, resume, recommendations. Additional exam requirements/recommendations for international students: Required—TOEFL (minimum score 213 computer-based), TWE (minimum score 5). Electronic applications accepted. *Expenses:* Contact institution. *Faculty research:* Independent/nonresidential graduate study: new methods and models, adult learning and the capstone experience, Goal Setting, behavior of Adult students, Innovative Studies for Community Colleges.

Rensselaer Polytechnic Institute, Graduate School, School of Science, Program in Multidisciplinary Science, Troy, NY 12180-3590. Offers MS, PhD. Part-time programs available. *Students:* 5 full-time (1 woman); includes 1 minority (Asian American or Pacific Islander). 7 applicants, 14% accepted, 0 enrolled. Terminal master's awarded for partial completion of doctoral program. *Degree requirements:* For master's, comprehensive exam (for some programs), thesis optional; for doctorate, comprehensive exam, thesis/dissertation. *Entrance requirements:* For doctorate, GRE General Test. Additional exam requirements/recommendations for international students: Required—TOEFL. *Application deadline:* For fall admission, 1/15 priority date for domestic and international students. Applications are processed on a rolling basis. Application fee: $75. Electronic applications accepted. *Expenses:* Tuition: Full-time $38,100. *Financial support:* In 2009–10, 5 students received support, including 1 fellowship with full tuition reimbursement available (averaging $18,000 per year), 3 research assistantships with full tuition reimbursements available (averaging $16,500 per year), 1 teaching assistantship with full tuition reimbursement available (averaging $16,500 per year); career-related internships or fieldwork and institutionally sponsored loans also available. Financial award application deadline: 2/1. *Faculty research:* Bioinformatics, astrobiology, nanotechnology, biotechnology, scientific computation. *Unit head:* Dr. William L. Siegmann, Associate Dean for Graduate Education and Research, 518-276-6905, Fax: 518-276-2825, E-mail: siegmw@rpi.edu. *Application contact:* Dr. William L. Siegmann, Associate Dean for Graduate Education and Research, 518-276-6905, Fax: 518-276-2825, E-mail: siegmw@rpi.edu.

Rochester Institute of Technology, Graduate Enrollment Services, College of Applied Science and Technology, Center for Multidisciplinary Studies, Program in Professional Studies, Rochester, NY 14623-5603. Offers MS. Part-time and evening/weekend programs available. Postbaccalaureate distance learning degree programs offered (no on-campus study). *Students:* 28 full-time (12 women), 137 part-time (67 women); includes 7 African Americans, 6 Asian Americans or Pacific Islanders, 3 Hispanic Americans, 17 international. Average age 36. 65 applicants, 62% accepted, 35 enrolled. In 2009, 49 master's awarded. *Degree requirements:* For master's, thesis or alternative. *Entrance requirements:* For master's, minimum GPA of 3.0. Additional exam requirements/recommendations for international students: Required—TOEFL (minimum score 550 paper-based; 213 computer-based; 79 iBT), or IELTS (minimum score 6.5). *Application deadline:* For fall admission, 2/15 priority date for domestic and international students; for winter admission, 11/1 for domestic and international students; for spring admission, 2/1 for domestic and international students. Applications are processed on a rolling basis. Application fee: $50. *Expenses:* Tuition: Full-time $31,533; part-time $876 per credit hour. Required fees: $210. *Financial support:* In 2009–10, 42 students received support. Career-related internships or fieldwork available. Support available to part-time students. Financial award application deadline: 2/15; financial award applicants required to submit FAFSA. *Unit head:* Dr. Samuel McQuade, Graduate Program Coordinator, 585-475-5230, Fax: 585-475-6292, E-mail: scmcms@rit.edu. *Application contact:* Diane Ellison, Assistant Vice President, Graduate Enrollment Services, 585-475-2229, Fax: 585-475-7164, E-mail: gradinfo@rit.edu.

Rosalind Franklin University of Medicine and Science, College of Health Professions, Department of Interprofessional Healthcare Studies, Interprofessional Healthcare Studies Program, North Chicago, IL 60064-3095. Offers interprofessional studies (D Sc). Part-time programs available. Postbaccalaureate distance learning degree programs offered (minimal on-campus study). *Faculty:* 1 (woman) full-time, 6 part-time/adjunct (4 women). *Students:* 13; includes 2 minority (both Hispanic Americans), 1 international. Average age 35. *Degree requirements:* For doctorate, comprehensive exam, thesis/dissertation. *Entrance requirements:* For doctorate, GRE. Additional exam requirements/recommendations for international students: Required—TOEFL. *Application deadline:* For fall admission, 6/1 for domestic students. Application fee: $50. *Financial support:* Tuition waivers available. *Faculty research:* Interprofessional education. *Unit head:* Dr. Judith Stoecker, Vice Dean and Program Director, 847-578-8694, Fax: 847-578-8623, E-mail: judith.stoecker@rosalindfranklin.edu. *Application contact:* Melissa Knox, Admissions Officer, 847-578-8772, Fax: 847-775-6559, E-mail: melissa.knox@rosalindfranklin.edu.

Rutgers, The State University of New Jersey, New Brunswick, Graduate School-New Brunswick, BioMaPS Institute for Quantitative Biology, Piscataway, NJ 08854-8097. Offers computational biology and molecular biophysics (PhD). *Degree requirements:* For doctorate, comprehensive exam, thesis/dissertation. *Entrance requirements:* For doctorate, GRE. Additional exam requirements/recommendations for international students: Required—TOEFL. Electronic applications accepted. *Faculty research:* Structural biology, systems biology, bioinformatics, translational medicine, genomics.

San Diego State University, Graduate and Research Affairs, Interdisciplinary Studies, San Diego, CA 92182. Offers MA, MS. Part-time programs available. *Degree requirements:* For master's, thesis. *Entrance requirements:* For master's, GRE General Test. Additional exam requirements/recommendations for international students: Required—TOEFL. Electronic applications accepted.

San Jose State University, Graduate Studies and Research, Program in Interdisciplinary Studies, San Jose, CA 95192-0001. Offers MA, MS. *Students:* 1 (woman) full-time, 7 part-time (4 women); includes 3 minority (1 Asian American or Pacific Islander, 2 Hispanic Americans). Average age 37. 1 applicant, 0% accepted. In 2009, 1 master's awarded. *Application deadline:* For fall admission, 6/29 for domestic students; for spring admission, 11/30 for domestic students. Applications are processed on a rolling basis. Electronic applications accepted. *Financial support:* Applicants required to submit FAFSA. *Unit head:* David Bruck, Interim Associate Dean, 408-924-2427, Fax: 408-924-2477. *Application contact:* David Bruck, Interim Associate Dean, 408-924-2427, Fax: 408-924-2477.

Sarah Lawrence College, Graduate Studies, Individualized Study Program, Bronxville, NY 10708-5999. Offers MA. Part-time programs available. *Degree requirements:* For master's, thesis. Application fee: $60. *Expenses:* Tuition: Part-time $1161 per credit. Required fees: $232 per semester. Part-time tuition and fees vary according to course load, program and student level. *Financial support:* Career-related internships or fieldwork, scholarships/grants, and unspecified assistantships available. Support available to part-time students. Financial award application deadline: 3/1; financial award applicants required to submit FAFSA. *Unit head:* Susan Guma, Dean of Graduate Studies, 914-395-2373, E-mail: sguma@mail.slc.edu. *Application contact:* Susan Guma, Dean of Graduate Studies, 914-395-2373, E-mail: sguma@mail.slc.edu.

Sonoma State University, Institute of Interdisciplinary Studies/Special Major, Rohnert Park, CA 94928. Offers special major (MA, MS). Part-time programs available. *Faculty:* 1 (woman) full-time. *Students:* 5 full-time (4 women), 23 part-time (20 women); includes 1 minority (Hispanic American). Average age 43. 26 applicants, 62% accepted, 3 enrolled. In 2009, 8 master's awarded. *Degree requirements:* For master's, thesis or alternative. *Entrance requirements:* For master's, written English proficiency test, minimum GPA of 3.0 in last 60 hours. Additional exam requirements/recommendations for international students: Required—TOEFL (minimum score 500 paper-based; 173 computer-based). *Application deadline:* For fall admission, 1/31 for domestic students; for spring admission, 10/31 for domestic students. Application fee: $55. *Expenses:* Tuition, nonresident: full-time $11,160. Required fees: $6226. Full-time tuition and fees vary according to course load. *Financial support:* Career-related internships or fieldwork, Federal Work-Study, and institutionally sponsored loans available. Support available to part-time students. Financial award applicants required to submit FAFSA. *Unit head:* Dr. Ellen Carlton, Coordinator, 707-664-3918, E-mail: ellen.carlton@sonoma.edu. *Application contact:* Elaine Sundberg, Associate Vice Provost, Academic Programs/Graduate Studies, 707-664-2215, Fax: 707-664-4060, E-mail: elaine.sundberg@sonoma.edu.

Southern Oregon University, Graduate Studies, College of Arts and Sciences, Program in Interdisciplinary Studies, Ashland, OR 97520. Offers MIS.

Stanford University, School of Education, Program in Social Sciences, Policy, and Educational Practice, Stanford, CA 94305-9991. Offers administration and policy analysis (Ed D, PhD); anthropology of education (PhD); economics of education (PhD); educational linguistics (PhD); evaluation (MA), including interdisciplinary studies; higher education (PhD); history of education (PhD); interdisciplinary studies (PhD); international comparative education (MA, PhD); international education administration and policy analysis (MA); philosophy of education (PhD); policy analysis (MA); prospective principal's program (MA); sociology of education (PhD). *Degree requirements:* For master's, thesis (for some programs); for doctorate, thesis/dissertation. *Entrance requirements:* For master's and doctorate, GRE General Test. Electronic applications accepted. *Expenses:* Tuition: Full-time $37,380; part-time $2760 per quarter. Required fees: $501.

State University of New York at Fredonia, Graduate Studies, Graduate Programs in Interdisciplinary Studies, Fredonia, NY 14063-1136. Offers MA, MS. Part-time and evening/weekend programs available. *Degree requirements:* For master's, thesis optional. *Expenses:* Tuition, state resident: full-time $8370; part-time $349 per credit. Tuition, nonresident: full-time $13,250; part-time $552 per credit. Required fees: $1289; $53.55 per credit.

Stephen F. Austin State University, Graduate School, College of Applied Arts and Science, Program in Interdisciplinary Studies, Nacogdoches, TX 75962. Offers MIS. Part-time programs available. *Degree requirements:* For master's, comprehensive exam, thesis optional. *Entrance requirements:* For master's, GRE General Test. Additional exam requirements/recommendations for international students: Required—TOEFL (minimum score 550 paper-based; 213 computer-based).

Teachers College, Columbia University, Graduate Faculty of Education, Interdisciplinary Programs, New York, NY 10027-6696. Offers Ed M, MA, Ed D. Part-time programs available. *Students:* 7 full-time (5 women), 24 part-time (12 women); includes 9 minority (3 African Americans, 3 Asian Americans or Pacific Islanders, 3 Hispanic Americans), 2 international. Average age 41. 5 applicants, 80% accepted, 3 enrolled. In 2009, 4 master's, 1 doctorate awarded. Terminal master's awarded for partial completion of doctoral program. *Degree requirements:* For doctorate, thesis/dissertation. *Application deadline:* For fall admission, 5/15 for domestic students. Application fee: $65. *Financial support:* Fellowships, career-related internships or fieldwork, Federal Work-Study, institutionally sponsored loans, and tuition waivers (full and partial) available. Support available to part-time students. Financial award application deadline: 2/1. *Unit head:* Susan Furhman, President, 212-678-3050. *Application contact:* Director of Admissions, 212-678-3083, Fax: 212-678-4171.

Texas A&M University–Texarkana, Graduate Studies and Research, College of Education and Liberal Arts, Texarkana, TX 75505-5518. Offers adult education (MS); curriculum and instruction (M Ed); education (MS); educational administration (M Ed); English (MA); instructional technology (MS); interdisciplinary studies (MA, MS); special education (MS). Part-time and evening/weekend programs available. *Degree requirements:* For master's, comprehensive exam (for some programs), thesis optional. *Entrance requirements:* For master's, minimum GPA of 2.5 on last 60 hours of bachelor's degree. Additional exam requirements/recommendations for international students: Required—TOEFL. Electronic applications accepted.

Texas State University–San Marcos, Graduate School, Interdisciplinary Studies in Political Science, San Marcos, TX 78666. Offers MAIS. *Students:* 1 part-time (0 women). Average age 35. 1 applicant, 100% accepted, 1 enrolled. *Degree requirements:* For master's, comprehensive exam, thesis optional. *Entrance requirements:* For master's, minimum GPA of 2.9 or GRE (minimum combined score of 900 Verbal and Quantitative preferred). Additional exam requirements/recommendations for international students: Required—TOEFL (minimum score 550 paper-based; 213 computer-based). *Application deadline:* For fall admission, 6/15 priority date for domestic students, 6/1 for international students; for spring admission, 10/15 priority date for domestic students, 10/1 for international students. Applications are processed on a rolling basis. Application fee: $40 ($90 for international students). *Expenses:* Tuition, state resident: full-time $5784; part-time $241 per credit hour. Tuition, nonresident: part-time $551 per credit hour. Required fees: $1728; $48 per credit hour. $306. Tuition and fees vary according to course load. *Financial support:* Application deadline: 4/1. *Unit head:* Dr. Cecilia Castillio, Graduate Advisor, 512-245-3255, Fax: 512-345-7815, E-mail: cr09@txstate.edu. *Application contact:* Dr. J. Michael Willoughby, Dean of Graduate School, 512-245-2581, Fax: 512-245-8365, E-mail: gradcollege@txstate.edu.

Texas State University–San Marcos, Graduate School, Interdisciplinary Studies Program in Applied Sociology, San Marcos, TX 78666. Offers MAIS. Part-time and evening/weekend programs available. *Students:* 1 applicant, 100% accepted, 0 enrolled. *Degree requirements:* For master's, comprehensive exam. *Entrance requirements:* For master's, minimum GPA of 3.0 on last 60 hours of undergraduate work, 3 letters of reference, letter of intent. Additional exam requirements/recommendations for international students: Required—TOEFL (minimum score 550 paper-based; 213 computer-based). *Application deadline:* For fall admission, 6/15 priority date for domestic students; for spring admission, 10/15 priority date for domestic students. Applications are processed on a rolling basis. Application fee: $40 ($90 for international students). Electronic applications accepted. *Expenses:* Tuition, state resident: full-time $5784; part-time $241 per credit hour. Tuition, nonresident: part-time $551 per credit hour. Required fees: $1728; $48 per credit hour. $306. Tuition and fees vary according to course load. *Financial support:* Teaching assistantships available. Financial award application deadline: 4/1; financial award applicants required to submit FAFSA. *Unit head:* Dr. Audwin Anderson, Head, 512-245-2113, E-mail: aa04@txstate.edu. *Application contact:* Dr. J. Michael Willoughby, Dean of Graduate School, 512-245-2581, Fax: 512-245-8365, E-mail: gradcollege@txstate.edu.

Texas State University–San Marcos, Graduate School, Interdisciplinary Studies Program in Biology, San Marcos, TX 78666. Offers MSIS. *Students:* 1 applicant, 0% accepted, 0 enrolled. *Degree requirements:* For master's, comprehensive exam, thesis optional. *Entrance requirements:* For master's, GRE (minimum score 1000 verbal and quantitative preferred), bachelor's degree in biology or related field, minimum GPA of 3.0 in last 60 hours of undergraduate work. Additional exam requirements/recommendations for international students: Required—TOEFL (minimum score 550 paper-based; 213 computer-based). *Application deadline:* For fall admission, 6/15 priority date for domestic students, 6/1 for international students; for spring admission, 10/15 priority date for domestic students, 10/1 for international students. Applications are processed on a rolling basis. Application fee: $40 ($90 for international students). *Expenses:* Tuition, state resident: full-time $5784; part-time $241 per credit hour. Tuition, nonresident: part-time $551 per credit hour. Required fees: $1728; $48 per credit hour. $306. Tuition and fees vary according to course load. *Financial support:* Application deadline: 4/1. *Unit head:* Dr. David Lemker, Graduate Advisor, 512-245-2178, E-mail: dl10@txstate.edu. *Application contact:* Dr. J. Michael Willoughby, Dean of Graduate School, 512-245-2581, Fax: 512-245-8365, E-mail: gradcollege@txstate.edu.

Texas State University–San Marcos, Graduate School, Interdisciplinary Studies Program in Criminal Justice, San Marcos, TX 78666. Offers MSIS. Part-time and evening/weekend programs available. *Degree requirements:* For master's, comprehensive exam, thesis optional. *Entrance requirements:* For master's, minimum GPA of 2.75 in last 60 hours of undergraduate work. Additional exam requirements/recommendations for international students: Required—TOEFL (minimum score 550 paper-based; 213 computer-based). *Application deadline:* For fall admission, 6/15 priority date for domestic students, 6/1 for international students; for spring admission, 10/15 priority date for domestic students, 10/1 for international students. Applications are processed on a rolling basis. Application fee: $40 ($90 for international students). *Expenses:* Tuition, state resident: full-time $5784; part-time $241 per credit hour. Tuition, nonresident: part-time $551 per credit hour. Required fees: $1728; $48 per credit hour. $306. Tuition and fees vary according to course load. *Financial support:* Application deadline: 4/1 *Unit head:* Dr. Donna Vandiver, Advisor, 512-245-2174, Fax: 512-245-2174, E-mail: dv14@txstate.edu. *Application contact:* Dr. J. Michael Willoughby, Dean of Graduate School, 512-245-2581, Fax: 512-245-8365, E-mail: gradcollege@txstate.edu.

Texas State University–San Marcos, Graduate School, Interdisciplinary Studies Program in Educational Administration and Psychological Services, San Marcos, TX 78666. Offers MAIS. *Degree requirements:* For master's, comprehensive exam. *Application deadline:* For fall admission, 6/15 priority date for domestic students; for spring admission, 10/15 priority date for domestic students. Applications are processed on a rolling basis. Application fee: $40 ($90 for international students). *Expenses:* Tuition, state resident: full-time $5784; part-time $241 per credit hour. Tuition, nonresident: part-time $551 per credit hour. Required fees: $1728; $48 per credit hour. $306. Tuition and fees vary according to course load. *Financial support:* Application deadline: 4/1. *Unit head:* Dr. Stan Carpenter, Dean, 512-245-2575, Fax: 512-245-8345, E-mail: sc33@txstate.edu. *Application contact:* Dr. J. Michael Willoughby, Dean of Graduate School, 512-245-2581, Fax: 512-245-8365, E-mail: gradcollege@txstate.edu.

Texas State University–San Marcos, Graduate School, Interdisciplinary Studies Program in Elementary Mathematics, Science, and Technology, San Marcos, TX 78666. Offers MSIS. *Students:* 1 full-time (0 women), 4 part-time (3 women). Average age 32. 1 applicant, 100% accepted, 0 enrolled. In 2009, 1 master's awarded. *Degree requirements:* For master's, comprehensive exam, thesis optional. *Entrance requirements:* For master's, minimum GPA of 2.75 in the last 60 hours of undergraduate work. Additional exam requirements/recommendations for international students: Required—TOEFL (minimum score 550 paper-based; 213 computer-based). *Application deadline:* For fall admission, 6/15 priority date for domestic students, 6/1 priority date for international students; for spring admission, 10/15 priority date for domestic students, 10/1 priority date for international students. Applications are processed on a rolling basis. Application fee: $40 ($90 for international students). Electronic applications accepted. *Expenses:* Tuition, state resident: full-time $5784; part-time $241 per credit hour. Tuition, nonresident: part-time $551 per credit hour. Required fees: $1728; $48 per credit hour. $306. Tuition and fees vary according to course load. *Financial support:* In 2009–10, 3 students received support; research assistantships, teaching assistantships available. Financial award application deadline: 4/1; financial award applicants required to submit FAFSA. *Unit head:* Dr. Sandra Mody, Acting Dean, 512-245-3360, Fax: 512-245-8095, E-mail: sw04@txstate.edu. *Application contact:* Dr. J. Michael Willoughby, Dean of Graduate School, 512-245-2581, Fax: 512-245-8365, E-mail: gradcollege@txstate.edu.

Texas State University–San Marcos, Graduate School, Interdisciplinary Studies Program in Health, Physical Education, and Recreation, San Marcos, TX 78666. Offers MAIS. Part-time and evening/weekend programs available. *Students:* 7 full-time (5 women), 4 part-time (0 women); includes 1 minority (Hispanic American). Average age 28. 5 applicants, 100% accepted, 5 enrolled. In 2009, 1 master's awarded. *Degree requirements:* For master's, comprehensive exam, thesis optional. *Entrance requirements:* For master's, GRE General Test, minimum GPA of 2.75 in last 60 hours of course work. Additional exam requirements/recommendations for international students: Required—TOEFL (minimum score 550 paper-based; 213 computer-based). *Application deadline:* For fall admission, 6/15 priority date for domestic students, 6/1 for international students; for spring admission, 10/15 priority date for domestic students, 10/1 for international students. Applications are processed on a rolling basis. Application fee: $40 ($90 for international students). *Expenses:* Tuition, state resident: full-time $5784; part-time $241 per credit hour. Tuition, nonresident: part-time $551 per credit hour. Required fees: $1728; $48 per credit hour. $306. Tuition and fees vary according to course load. *Financial support:* In 2009–10, 8 students received support, including 2 teaching assistantships (averaging $5,751 per year); career-related internships or fieldwork, Federal Work-Study, and institutionally sponsored loans also available. Support available to part-time students. Financial award application deadline: 4/1; financial award applicants required to submit FAFSA. *Unit head:* Dr. Tinker Murray, Head, 512-245-2561, Fax: 512-245-8678, E-mail: tm05@txstate.edu. *Application contact:* Dr. J. Michael Willoughby, Dean of Graduate School, 512-245-2581, Fax: 512-245-8365, E-mail: gradcollege@txstate.edu.

Texas State University–San Marcos, Graduate School, Interdisciplinary Studies Program in Modern Languages, San Marcos, TX 78666. Offers MAIS. *Degree requirements:* For master's, comprehensive exam, thesis optional. *Entrance requirements:* For master's, minimum GPA of 2.75 in last 60 hours of course work. Additional exam requirements/recommendations for international students: Required—TOEFL (minimum score 550 paper-based; 213 computer-based). *Application deadline:* For fall admission, 6/15 priority date for domestic students, 6/1 for international students; for spring admission, 10/15 priority date for domestic students, 10/1 for international students. Applications are processed on a rolling basis. Application fee: $40 ($90 for international students). *Expenses:* Tuition, state resident: full-time $5784; part-time $241 per credit hour. Tuition, nonresident: part-time $551 per credit hour. Required fees: $1728; $48 per credit hour. $306. Tuition and fees vary according to course load. *Financial support:* Application deadline: 4/1. *Unit head:* Dr. Catherine Jaffe, Advisor, 512-245-2360, Fax: 512-245-8298, E-mail: cj10@txstate.edu. *Application contact:* Dr. Catherine Jaffe, Advisor, 512-245-2360, Fax: 512-245-8298, E-mail: cj10@txstate.edu.

Texas State University–San Marcos, Graduate School, Interdisciplinary Studies Program in Occupational Education, San Marcos, TX 78666. Offers MAIS, MSIS. *Faculty:* 4 full-time (0 women), 1 (woman) part-time/adjunct. *Students:* 8 full-time (4 women), 51 part-time (26 women); includes 28 minority (9 African Americans, 19 Hispanic Americans), 1 international. Average age 41. 23 applicants, 100% accepted, 12 enrolled. In 2009, 8 master's awarded. *Degree requirements:* For master's, comprehensive exam, thesis optional. *Entrance requirements:* For master's, minimum GPA of 2.75 for undergraduate work, statement of personal goals. Additional exam requirements/recommendations for international students: Required—TOEFL (minimum score 550 paper-based; 213 computer-based). *Application deadline:* For fall admission, 6/15 priority date for domestic students, 6/1 priority date for international students; for spring admission, 10/15 priority date for domestic students, 10/1 priority date for international students. Applications are processed on a rolling basis. Application fee: $40 ($90 for international students). *Expenses:* Tuition, state resident: full-time $5784; part-time $241 per credit hour. Tuition, nonresident: part-time $551 per credit hour. Required fees: $1728; $48 per credit hour. $306. Tuition and fees vary according to course load. *Financial support:* In 2009–10, 37 students received support, including 2 teaching assistantships (averaging $5,076 per year). Financial award application deadline: 4/1; financial award applicants required to submit FAFSA. *Unit head:* Dr. Stephen Springer, Director, 512-245-2115, E-mail: ss01@txstate.edu. *Application contact:* Dr. J. Michael Willoughby, Dean of Graduate School, 512-245-2581, Fax: 512-245-8365, E-mail: gradcollege@txstate.edu.

Texas State University–San Marcos, Graduate School, Interdisciplinary Studies Program in Psychology, San Marcos, TX 78666. Offers MAIS. *Degree requirements:* For master's, comprehensive exam. *Application deadline:* For fall admission, 6/15 priority date for domestic students; for spring admission, 10/15 priority date for domestic students. Applications are processed on a rolling basis. Application fee: $40 ($90 for international students). *Expenses:* Tuition, state resident: full-time $5784; part-time $241 per credit hour. Tuition, nonresident: part-time $551 per credit hour. Required fees: $1728; $48 per credit hour. $306. Tuition and fees vary according to course load. *Financial support:* Application deadline: 4/1. *Unit head:* Dr. Francisco Barrios, Advisor, 512-245-3159, E-mail: fb12@txstate.edu. *Application contact:* Dr. J. Michael Willoughby, Dean of Graduate School, 512-245-2581, Fax: 512-245-8365, E-mail: gradcollege@txstate.edu.

Texas Tech University, Graduate School, Program in Interdisciplinary Studies, Lubbock, TX 79409. Offers MA, MS. Part-time and evening/weekend programs available. *Faculty:* 3 full-time (1 woman). *Students:* 69 full-time (42 women), 59 part-time (41 women); includes 41 minority (7 African Americans, 1 American Indian/Alaska Native, 4 Asian Americans or Pacific Islanders, 29 Hispanic Americans), 12 international. Average age 32. 171 applicants, 86% accepted, 55 enrolled. In 2009, 17 master's awarded. *Degree requirements:* For master's, comprehensive exam, thesis or alternative. *Entrance requirements:* For master's, GRE General Test. Additional exam requirements/recommendations for international students: Required—TOEFL (minimum score 550 paper-based; 213 computer-based). *Application deadline:* For fall admission, 3/1 priority date for international students; for spring admission, 11/1 priority date for international students. Applications are processed on a rolling basis. Application fee: $50 ($75 for international students). Electronic applications accepted. *Expenses:* Tuition, state resident: full-time $5100; part-time $213 per credit hour. Tuition, nonresident: full-time $11,748; part-time $490 per credit hour. Required fees: $2298; $50 per credit hour. $555 per semester. *Financial support:* Teaching assistantships with partial tuition reimbursements, career-related internships or fieldwork, Federal Work-Study, and institutionally sponsored loans available. Support available to part-time students. Financial award application deadline: 4/15; financial award applicants required to submit FAFSA. *Faculty research:* Literature-short story, comparative literature. *Unit head:* Dr. Wendell Aycock, Associate Dean, 806-742-2781 Ext. 228, E-mail: wendell.aycock@ttu.edu. *Application contact:* Graduate Adviser, 806-742-2781 Ext. 228.

Trinity Western University, Faculty of Graduate Studies, Program in Interdisciplinary Humanities, Langley, BC V2Y 1Y1, Canada. Offers general humanities (MAIH); specialized (MAIH), including English, history, philosophy. Part-time and evening/weekend programs available. Postbaccalaureate distance learning degree programs offered (minimal on-campus study). *Entrance requirements:* For master's, strong undergraduate degree in Humanities or English, History or Philosophy. *Faculty research:* Literary theory, gender, medieval and early modern literature, philosophy of religion, Thomas Merton's poetics.

Tulane University, School of Science and Engineering, Interdisciplinary PhD Program, New Orleans, LA 70118-5669. Offers PhD.

Union Institute & University, Master of Arts Program–Online, Montpelier, VT 05602. Offers creativity studies (MA); education (MA); health and wellness (MA); history and culture (MA); leadership, public policy, and social issues (MA); literature and writing (MA); psychology (MA). Part-time programs available. Postbaccalaureate distance learning degree programs offered (no on-campus study). *Faculty:* 3 full-time (1 woman), 16 part-time/adjunct (11 women). *Students:* 27 full-time (23 women), 113 part-time (84 women); includes 30 minority (22 African Americans, 2 American Indian/Alaska Native, 1 Asian American or Pacific Islander, 5 Hispanic Americans). Average age 40. In 2009, 26 master's awarded. *Degree requirements:* For master's, thesis. *Application deadline:* Applications are processed on a rolling basis. Application fee: $50. Electronic applications accepted. *Expenses:* Contact institution. *Financial support:* Career-related internships or fieldwork and tuition waivers available. Financial award applicants required to submit FAFSA. *Unit head:* Dr. Brian Webb, Program Director, 802-828-8777, E-mail: brian.webb@tui.edu. *Application contact:* Kathleen Murphy, Interim Director of Admissions—Montpelier, 888-828-8575, E-mail: admissions@myunion.edu.

Union Institute & University, PhD Program in Interdisciplinary Studies, Cincinnati, OH 45206-1925. Offers public policy and social change (PhD), including Martin Luther King studies. Postbaccalaureate distance learning degree programs offered (minimal on-campus study). *Faculty:* 4 full-time (1 woman), 15 part-time/adjunct (9 women). *Students:* 77 full-time (45 women), 7 part-time (4 women); includes 34 minority (31 African Americans, 3 Hispanic Americans). Average age 45. In 2009, 3 doctorates awarded. *Degree requirements:* For doctorate, comprehensive exam, thesis/dissertation. *Entrance requirements:* For doctorate, master's degree, letters of recommendation, interview. *Application deadline:* Applications are processed on a rolling basis. Application fee: $50. Tuition and fees vary according to course load, degree level, campus/location and program. *Financial support:* Federal Work-Study, scholarships/grants, and tuition waivers (partial) available. Financial award application deadline: 5/1; financial award applicants required to submit FAFSA. *Unit head:* Dr. Larry Preston, Dean, 513-861-6400 Ext. 1151, E-mail: larry.preston@tui.edu. *Application contact:* Dr. Larry Preston, Dean, 513-861-6400 Ext. 1151, E-mail: larry.preston@tui.edu.

The University of Alabama in Huntsville, School of Graduate Studies, Interdisciplinary Studies, Huntsville, AL 35899. Offers MS, PhD, Certificate. Part-time and evening/weekend programs available. *Faculty:* 78 full-time (9 women), 2 part-time/adjunct (0 women). *Students:* 35 full-time (16 women), 25 part-time (2 women); includes 9 minority (7 African Americans, 2 American Indian/Alaska Native), 23 international. Average age 32. 40 applicants, 50% accepted, 11 enrolled. In 2009, 2 master's, 2 doctorates, 14 other advanced degrees awarded. *Degree requirements:* For master's, comprehensive exam, thesis or alternative, oral and written exams; for doctorate, comprehensive exam, thesis/dissertation, oral and written exams. *Entrance requirements:* For master's and doctorate, GRE General Test, minimum GPA of 3.0; for Certificate, GMAT (score of at least 500), minimum AACSB index of 1080. Additional exam requirements/recommendations for international students: Required—TOEFL (minimum score 500 paper-based; 173 computer-based; 62 iBT). *Application deadline:* For fall admission, 7/15 for domestic students, 4/1 for international students; for spring admission, 11/30 for domestic

Interdisciplinary Studies

The University of Alabama in Huntsville (continued)

students, 9/1 for international students. Applications are processed on a rolling basis. Application fee: $40 ($50 for international students). Electronic applications accepted. *Expenses:* Tuition, state resident: part-time $355.75 per credit hour. Tuition, nonresident: part-time $847.10 per credit hour. Required fees: $210.80 per semester. Tuition and fees vary according to course load and program. *Financial support:* In 2009–10, 35 students received support, including 13 research assistantships with full and partial tuition reimbursements available (averaging $1,221 per year), 19 teaching assistantships with full and partial tuition reimbursements available (averaging $11,347 per year); career-related internships or fieldwork, Federal Work-Study, institutionally sponsored loans, scholarships/grants, health care benefits, tuition waivers, and unspecified assistantships also available. Support available to part-time students. Financial award application deadline: 4/1; financial award applicants required to submit FAFSA. Total annual research expenditures: $1.3 million. *Unit head:* Dr. Debra Moriarity, Dean of Graduate Studies, 256-824-6002, Fax: 256-824-6405, E-mail: deangrad@uah.edu. *Application contact:* Kathy Biggs, Graduate Studies Admissions Manager, 256-824-6199, Fax: 256-824-6405, E-mail: deangrad@uah.edu.

University of Alaska Anchorage, College of Arts and Sciences, Program in Interdisciplinary Studies, Anchorage, AK 99508. Offers MA, MS. Part-time programs available. *Entrance requirements:* For master's, GRE General Test, GRE Subject Test, minimum GPA of 3.0. Additional exam requirements/recommendations for international students: Required—TOEFL (minimum score 550 paper-based; 213 computer-based).

University of Alaska Fairbanks, Graduate School for Interdisciplinary Studies, Fairbanks, AK 99775-7560. Offers indigenous studies (PhD); interdisciplinary studies (MA, MS, PhD). Part-time programs available. *Students:* 2 full-time (both women), 5 part-time (3 women); includes 3 minority (all American Indian/Alaska Native). Average age 49. 33 applicants, 36% accepted, 5 enrolled. In 2009, 1 doctorate awarded. Terminal master's awarded for partial completion of doctoral program. *Degree requirements:* For master's, comprehensive exam (for some programs), thesis (for some programs); for doctorate, one foreign language, comprehensive exam, thesis/dissertation, oral defense, oral exam. *Entrance requirements:* For master's and doctorate, GRE General Test. Additional exam requirements/recommendations for international students: Required—TOEFL (minimum score 550 paper-based; 213 computer-based; 80 iBT). *Application deadline:* For fall admission, 6/1 for domestic students, 3/1 for international students; for spring admission, 10/15 for domestic students, 9/1 for international students. Applications are processed on a rolling basis. Application fee: $60. Electronic applications accepted. *Expenses:* Tuition, state resident: full-time $7584; part-time $316 per credit. Tuition, nonresident: full-time $15,504; part-time $646 per credit. Required fees: $23 per credit. $135 per semester. Tuition and fees vary according to course level, course load and reciprocity agreements. *Financial support:* In 2009–10, 1 research assistantship (averaging $7,081 per year) was awarded; fellowships, teaching assistantships, career-related internships or fieldwork, Federal Work-Study, scholarships/grants, health care benefits, and unspecified assistantships also available. Support available to part-time students. Financial award application deadline: 2/15; financial award applicants required to submit FAFSA. *Unit head:* Lawrence Duffy, Interim Dean, 907-474-7716, Fax: 907-474-1984, E-mail: fyinds@uaf.edu. *Application contact:* Lawrence Duffy, Interim Dean, 907-474-7716, Fax: 907-474-1984, E-mail: fyinds@uaf.edu.

The University of Arizona, Graduate College, Graduate Interdisciplinary Programs, Tucson, AZ 85721. Offers American Indian studies (MA, PhD); applied mathematics (MS, PMS, PhD), including applied mathematics (MS, PhD), mathematical sciences (PMS); biomedical engineering (MS, PhD); cancer biology (PhD); entomology (MA, MS); genetics (MS, PhD); insect science (PhD); neuroscience (PhD); physiological sciences (MS, PhD); second language acquisition and teaching (PhD); statistics (MS, PhD); JD/MA. Part-time programs available. *Faculty:* 40 full-time (14 women). *Students:* 197 full-time (93 women), 146 part-time (89 women); includes 60 minority (3 African Americans, 22 American Indian/Alaska Native, 18 Asian Americans or Pacific Islanders, 17 Hispanic Americans), 86 international. Average age 30. 540 applicants, 40% accepted, 143 enrolled. In 2009, 42 master's, 47 doctorates awarded. *Entrance requirements:* Additional exam requirements/recommendations for international students: Required—TOEFL (minimum score 550 paper-based; 213 computer-based; 79 iBT). *Application deadline:* For fall admission, 2/1 for domestic students, 1/15 for international students. Application fee: $65. *Expenses:* Tuition, state resident: full-time $9028. Tuition, nonresident: full-time $24,890. *Financial support:* In 2009–10, 115 research assistantships with full tuition reimbursements (averaging $18,401 per year), 38 teaching assistantships with full tuition reimbursements (averaging $16,320 per year) were awarded; career-related internships or fieldwork, Federal Work-Study, institutionally sponsored loans, scholarships/grants, health care benefits, tuition waivers (full and partial), and unspecified assistantships also available. Support available to part-time students. Total annual research expenditures: $9.9 million. *Unit head:* Dr. Andrew Comrie, Dean, 520-621-3512, Fax: 520-621-4101, E-mail: gradadm@grad.arizona.edu. *Application contact:* Jolene M. Gruener, Associate Director, 520-621-8368, E-mail: gidp@email.arizona.edu.

University of Arkansas, Graduate School, Interdisciplinary Program in Comparative Literature and Cultural Studies, Fayetteville, AR 72701-1201. Offers classical studies (MA); comparative literature (PhD). *Degree requirements:* For master's, one foreign language, comprehensive exam, thesis optional; for doctorate, 2 foreign languages, comprehensive exam, thesis/dissertation. *Entrance requirements:* For master's and doctorate, GRE General Test. *Expenses:* Tuition, state resident: full-time $7355; part-time $356.58 per hour. Tuition, nonresident: full-time $17,401; part-time $775.17 per hour. Required fees: $1203. *Faculty research:* Literary and cultural theory, cultural studies, postcolonial theory, gender studies, world literature.

University of Arkansas, Graduate School, Interdisciplinary Program in Environmental Dynamics, Fayetteville, AR 72701-1201. Offers PhD. *Students:* 1 full-time (0 women), 26 part-time (14 women); includes 2 minority (1 African American, 1 Hispanic American), 5 international. In 2009, 3 doctorates awarded. *Degree requirements:* For doctorate, thesis/dissertation. Application fee: $40 ($50 for international students). *Expenses:* Tuition, state resident: full-time $7355; part-time $356.58 per hour. Tuition, nonresident: full-time $17,401; part-time $775.17 per hour. Required fees: $1203. *Financial support:* In 2009–10, 12 fellowships with tuition reimbursements, 2 research assistantships, 10 teaching assistantships were awarded. Financial award application deadline: 4/1. *Unit head:* Dr. Stephen Boss, Head, 479-575-6603, Fax: 479-575-3469, E-mail: sboss@uark.edu. *Application contact:* Graduate Admissions, 479-575-6246, Fax: 479-575-5908, E-mail: gradinfo@uark.edu.

University of Central Florida, College of Graduate Studies, Program in Interdisciplinary Studies, Orlando, FL 32816. Offers MA, MS. *Students:* 6 full-time (4 women), 15 part-time (11 women); includes 5 minority (1 African American, 1 Asian American or Pacific Islander, 3 Hispanic Americans). Average age 35. 5 applicants, 60% accepted, 2 enrolled. In 2009, 12 master's awarded. *Degree requirements:* For master's, thesis or alternative. *Entrance requirements:* For master's, GRE General Test, minimum GPA of 3.0 in last 60 hours. Additional exam requirements/recommendations for international students: Required—TOEFL. Application fee: $30. Electronic applications accepted. *Expenses:* Tuition, state resident: part-time $306.31 per credit hour. Tuition, nonresident: part-time $1099.01 per credit hour. Part-time tuition and fees vary according to degree level and program. *Financial support:* In 2009–10, 4 students received support, including 2 fellowships (averaging $5,700 per year), 2 teaching assistantships (averaging $7,700 per year). *Unit head:* Dr. Michael Hampton, Director, 407-823-2136, E-mail: mhampton@mail.ucf.edu. *Application contact:* Dr. Michael Hampton, Director, 407-823-2136, E-mail: mhampton@mail.ucf.edu.

University of Chicago, Division of the Biological Sciences, The Interdisciplinary Scientist Training Program, Chicago, IL 60637-1513. Offers PhD. *Students:* 2 full-time (0 women). Average age 27. 3 applicants, 0% accepted, 0 enrolled. *Degree requirements:* For doctorate, thesis/dissertation, ethics class, 2 teaching assistantships. *Entrance requirements:* Additional exam requirements/recommendations for international students: Required—TOEFL (minimum score 600 paper-based; 250 computer-based; 104 iBT), IELTS (minimum score 7). *Application deadline:* For fall admission, 12/1 for domestic and international students. Application fee: $55. Electronic applications accepted. *Financial support:* In 2009–10, 2 students received support, including fellowships (averaging $29,781 per year), research assistantships (averaging $29,781 per year). Financial award applicants required to submit FAFSA. *Unit head:* Dr. Daniel Margoliash, Program Director, 773-702-3224, Fax: 773-702-0037. *Application contact:* Diane Hall, Student Contact, E-mail: djh8@uchicago.edu.

University of Cincinnati, Graduate School, McMicken College of Arts and Sciences, Interdisciplinary Studies Program, Cincinnati, OH 45221. Offers PhD. *Entrance requirements:* For doctorate, GRE General Test. Electronic applications accepted.

University of Houston–Victoria, School of Arts and Sciences, Program in Interdisciplinary Studies, Victoria, TX 77901-4450. Offers MAIS. Part-time and evening/weekend programs available. Postbaccalaureate distance learning degree programs offered (no on-campus study). *Degree requirements:* For master's, comprehensive exam or thesis. *Entrance requirements:* For master's, GRE General Test. Additional exam requirements/recommendations for international students: Required—TOEFL (minimum score 550 paper-based; 213 computer-based).

University of Idaho, College of Graduate Studies, Program in Interdisciplinary Studies, Moscow, ID 83844-2282. Offers MA, MS. *Students:* 3 full-time, 3 part-time. In 2009, 1 master's awarded. *Entrance requirements:* For master's, minimum GPA of 2.8. *Application deadline:* For fall admission, 8/1 for domestic students; for spring admission, 12/15 for domestic students. Application fee: $55 ($60 for international students). *Expenses:* Tuition, state resident: full-time $6120. Tuition, nonresident: full-time $17,712. *Financial support:* Application deadline: 2/15. *Unit head:* Dr. Margrit von Braun, Dean of Graduate Studies, 208-885-6243. *Application contact:* Dr. Margrit von Braun, Dean of Graduate Studies, 208-885-6243.

University of Illinois at Springfield, Graduate Programs, College of Liberal Arts and Sciences, Individual Option Program, Springfield, IL 62703-5407. Offers MA. Part-time and evening/weekend programs available. *Faculty:* 5 full-time (3 women). *Students:* 9 full-time (4 women), 25 part-time (14 women); includes 5 minority (4 African Americans, 1 Asian American or Pacific Islander), 2 international. Average age 41. 34 applicants. In 2009, 10 master's awarded. *Degree requirements:* For master's, project or thesis. *Entrance requirements:* For master's, 2 letters of reference, interview. Additional exam requirements/recommendations for international students: Required—TOEFL (minimum score 500 paper-based; 176 computer-based; 61 iBT). *Application deadline:* Applications are processed on a rolling basis. Application fee: $50 ($60 for international students). *Expenses:* Tuition, state resident: full-time $6390; part-time $266.25 per credit hour. Tuition, nonresident: full-time $14,226; part-time $592.75 per credit hour. Required fees: $2044; $14.36 per credit hour. $722.50 per term. *Financial support:* In 2009–10, research assistantships with full tuition reimbursements (averaging $8,109 per year), teaching assistantships with full tuition reimbursements (averaging $8,109 per year) were awarded; career-related internships or fieldwork, Federal Work-Study, scholarships/grants, health care benefits, and unspecified assistantships also available. Support available to part-time students. Financial award application deadline: 11/15; financial award applicants required to submit FAFSA. *Unit head:* Dr. Annette Van Dyke, Program Administrator, 217-206-7420, Fax: 217-206-6217, E-mail: vandyke.annette@uis.edu. *Application contact:* Dr. Lynn Pardie, Office of Graduate Studies, 800-252-8533, Fax: 217-206-7623, E-mail: pardie.lynn@uis.edu.

The University of Kansas, University of Kansas Medical Center, School of Medicine, Interdisciplinary Graduate Program in Biomedical Sciences (IGPBS), Kansas City, KS 66160. Offers MA, MPH, MS, PhD, MD/MPH, MD/MS, MD/PhD. Part-time and evening/weekend programs available. *Students:* 20 full-time (13 women); includes 1 minority (Asian American or Pacific Islander), 6 international. Average age 25. 160 applicants, 25% accepted, 20 enrolled. Terminal master's awarded for partial completion of doctoral program. *Degree requirements:* For master's, thesis; for doctorate, comprehensive exam, thesis/dissertation. *Entrance requirements:* For master's and doctorate, GRE. Additional exam requirements/recommendations for international students: Required—TOEFL. *Application deadline:* For fall admission, 1/15 priority date for domestic and international students. Applications are processed on a rolling basis. Application fee: $0. Electronic applications accepted. *Expenses:* Tuition, state resident: full-time $6492; part-time $270.50 per credit hour. Tuition, nonresident: full-time $15,510; part-time $646.25 per credit hour. Required fees: $847; $70.56 per credit hour. Tuition and fees vary according to course load and program. *Financial support:* In 2009–10, 20 students received support, including fellowships with full tuition reimbursements available (averaging $24,000 per year), research assistantships with full tuition reimbursements available (averaging $24,000 per year), teaching assistantships with full tuition reimbursements available (averaging $24,000 per year); Federal Work-Study also available. Support available to part-time students. Financial award application deadline: 3/30; financial award applicants required to submit FAFSA. *Faculty research:* Cardiovascular biology, neurosciences, signal transduction and cancer biology, molecular biology and genetics, developmental biology. *Unit head:* Dr. Michael J. Werle, Graduate Advisor, 913-588-7491, Fax: 913-588-2710, E-mail: mwerle@kumc.edu. *Application contact:* Miranda Olenhouse, Coordinator, 913-588-2719, Fax: 913-588-2711, E-mail: molenhouse@kumc.edu.

University of Louisville, School of Interdisciplinary and Graduate Studies, Louisville, KY 40292. Offers MA, MS, PhD. Part-time and evening/weekend programs available. *Students:* 7 full-time (6 women), 10 part-time (7 women); includes 2 minority (1 Asian American or Pacific Islander, 1 Hispanic American). Average age 33. 15 applicants, 47% accepted, 5 enrolled. In 2009, 4 master's awarded. Terminal master's awarded for partial completion of doctoral program. *Degree requirements:* For master's, thesis (for some programs); for doctorate, thesis/dissertation. *Entrance requirements:* For master's, GRE General Test, baccalaureate degree, minimum GPA of 3.0; for doctorate, GRE General Test, minimum GPA of 3.0. Additional exam requirements/recommendations for international students: Required—TOEFL (minimum score 550 paper-based; 213 computer-based; 79 iBT). *Application deadline:* For fall admission, 5/1 for international students; for spring admission, 11/1 for international students. Applications are processed on a rolling basis. Application fee: $50. Electronic applications accepted. *Financial support:* In 2009–10, 110 fellowships (averaging $12,662 per year) were awarded; career-related internships or fieldwork, Federal Work-Study, institutionally sponsored loans, scholarships/grants, and tuition waivers (full and partial) also available. Financial award application deadline: 2/1; financial award applicants required to submit FAFSA. *Unit head:* Dr. Beth A. Boehm, Interim Dean/Associate Provost for Faculty Personnel/Professor of English, 502-852-6590, Fax: 502-852-6616, E-mail: beth.boehm@louisville.edu. *Application contact:* Libby Leggett, Executive Director of Graduate Admissions and Recruitment, 502-852-3108, Fax: 502-852-3111, E-mail: melegg02@louisville.edu.

University of Maine, Graduate School, Interdisciplinary Doctoral Program, Orono, ME 04469. Offers PhD. Part-time and evening/weekend programs available. *Students:* 19 full-time (9 women), 26 part-time (15 women), 4 international. Average age 38. 21 applicants, 48% accepted, 7 enrolled. In 2009, 5 doctorates awarded. *Degree requirements:* For doctorate, comprehensive exam, thesis/dissertation. *Entrance requirements:* For doctorate, GRE General Test. Additional exam requirements/recommendations for international students: Required—TOEFL. *Application deadline:* For fall admission, 4/1 for domestic students; for spring admission, 11/1 for domestic students. Applications are processed on a rolling basis. Application fee: $65. Electronic applications accepted. *Unit head:* Scott G. Delcourt, Associate Dean of the Graduate School, 207-581-3291, Fax: 207-581-3232, E-mail: graduate@maine.edu. *Application contact:* Scott G. Delcourt, Associate Dean of the Graduate School, 207-581-3291, Fax: 207-581-3232, E-mail: graduate@maine.edu.

University of Manitoba, Faculty of Graduate Studies, Interdisciplinary Programs, Individual Interdisciplinary Programs, Winnipeg, MB R3T 2N2, Canada. Offers M Sc, MA, PhD.

University of Medicine and Dentistry of New Jersey, School of Health Related Professions, Department of Interdisciplinary Studies, Program in Health Sciences, Newark, NJ 07107-1709.

Offers cardiopulmonary sciences (PhD); clinical laboratory sciences (PhD); health sciences (MS); interdisciplinary studies (PhD); nutrition (PhD); physical therapy/movement science (PhD). *Degree requirements:* For doctorate, thesis/dissertation. *Entrance requirements:* For doctorate, interview, writing sample. Additional exam requirements/recommendations for international students: Required—TOEFL. Electronic applications accepted.

University of Minnesota, Twin Cities Campus, Graduate School, College of Liberal Arts, Department of Cultural Studies and Comparative Literature, Program in Comparative Studies in Discourse and Society, Minneapolis, MN 55455-0213. Offers PhD. *Faculty:* 14 full-time (2 women), 9 part-time/adjunct (7 women). *Students:* 22 full-time (10 women); includes 3 minority (2 Asian Americans or Pacific Islanders, 1 Hispanic American), 2 international. Average age 26. 56 applicants, 5% accepted, 3 enrolled. In 2009, 1 doctorate awarded. *Degree requirements:* For doctorate, 2 foreign languages, thesis/dissertation. *Entrance requirements:* For doctorate, GRE General Test, sample of written work. Additional exam requirements/recommendations for international students: Required—TOEFL. *Application deadline:* For fall admission, 12/10 for domestic students. Application fee: $55 ($75 for international students). *Financial support:* In 2009–10, 1 fellowship with full tuition reimbursement (averaging $22,500 per year), 1 research assistantship with full tuition reimbursement (averaging $6,232 per year), 25 teaching assistantships with full tuition reimbursements (averaging $13,800 per year) were awarded; Federal Work-Study, institutionally sponsored loans, and tuition waivers (full and partial) also available. Financial award application deadline: 12/10. *Faculty research:* Cultural theory; music; architecture, space, and urbanism; body and gender; film and popular culture. *Unit head:* Robert I. Brown, Director of Graduate Studies, 612-624-8878, Fax: 612-626-0228, E-mail: brown004@umn.edu. *Application contact:* Robert L. Brown, Director of Graduate Studies, 612-624-8878, Fax: 612-626-0228, E-mail: brown004@umn.edu.

University of Missouri–Kansas City, School of Graduate Studies, Kansas City, MO 64110-2499. Offers interdisciplinary studies (PhD), including art history, cell biology and biophysics, chemistry, computer and electrical engineering, computer science and informatics, economics, education, engineering, English, entrepreneurship and innovation, geosciences, history, mathematics and statistics, molecular biology and biochemistry, music education, oral biology, pharmaceutical sciences, pharmacology, physics, political science, psychology, public affairs and administration, religious studies, social science consortium, sociology, telecommunications and computer networking, urban leadership and policy studies in education. Students select two or more subjects. *Students:* 91 full-time (43 women), 295 part-time (115 women); includes 26 minority (13 African Americans, 9 Asian Americans or Pacific Islanders, 4 Hispanic Americans), 172 international. Average age 35. 352 applicants, 22% accepted, 42 enrolled. In 2009, 24 doctorates awarded. *Degree requirements:* For doctorate, comprehensive exam, thesis/dissertation, residency. *Entrance requirements:* For doctorate, GRE General Test, minimum GPA of 2.75 (undergraduate), 3.0 (graduate). Additional exam requirements/recommendations for international students: Required—TOEFL (minimum score 550 paper-based; 213 computer-based; 80 iBT), TWE (minimum score 4). *Application deadline:* For fall admission, 1/15 priority date for domestic and international students. Applications are processed on a rolling basis. Application fee: $45 ($50 for international students). Electronic applications accepted. *Expenses:* Tuition, state resident: full-time $5378; part-time $299 per credit hour. Tuition, nonresident: full-time $13,881; part-time $771 per credit hour. Required fees: $641; $71 per credit hour. Tuition and fees vary according to course load and program. *Financial support:* Career-related internships or fieldwork, Federal Work-Study, tuition waivers (partial), and unspecified assistantships available. Support available to part-time students. Financial award application deadline: 3/1; financial award applicants required to submit FAFSA. *Unit head:* Dr. Ronald MacQuarrie, Dean, 816-235-1301, Fax: 816-235-1310, E-mail: macquarrier@umkc.edu. *Application contact:* Qunicy Bennett Johnson, Administrative Assistant, 816-235-1559, Fax: 816-235-1310, E-mail: bennettq@umkc.edu.

The University of Montana, Graduate School, Program in Interdisciplinary Studies, Missoula, MT 59812-0002. Offers individual interdisciplinary programs (IIP) (PhD); interdisciplinary studies (MIS). *Degree requirements:* For doctorate, thesis/dissertation. *Entrance requirements:* For master's, GRE General Test. Additional exam requirements/recommendations for international students: Required—TOEFL.

University of New Brunswick Fredericton, School of Graduate Studies, Interdisciplinary Studies Program, Fredericton, NB E3B 5A3, Canada. Offers M IDST, PhD. *Faculty:* 27 full-time (17 women), 5 part-time/adjunct (2 women). *Students:* 35 full-time (26 women), 9 part-time (4 women). In 2009, 1 master's, 1 doctorate awarded. *Degree requirements:* For master's, thesis; for doctorate, comprehensive exam, thesis/dissertation. *Entrance requirements:* For master's, BA honours degree with A- average, minimum GPA of 3.3; for doctorate, master's degree with thesis; A- average. Additional exam requirements/recommendations for international students: Required—TOEFL (minimum score 600 paper-based; 250 computer-based; 100 iBT), TWE (minimum score 4), or IELTS (minimum score 7). Application fee: $50 Canadian dollars. Tuition and fees charges are reported in Canadian dollars. *Expenses:* Tuition, area resident: Full-time $5562 Canadian dollars; part-time $2781 Canadian dollars per year. Required fees: $49.75 Canadian dollars per term. *Financial support:* In 2009–10, 5 research assistantships (averaging $7,000 per year), 1 teaching assistantship (averaging $4,400 per year) were awarded. *Faculty research:* Support needs of young adults with cancer; risk analysis, cervical cancer; treatment of persons with disabilities; tourism strategy; farm-related injuries. *Unit head:* Dr. Linda Eyre, Assistant Dean of Graduate Studies, 506-447-3044, Fax: 506-453-4817, E-mail: gradidst@unb.ca. *Application contact:* Janet Amirault, Graduate Secretary, 506-458-7558, Fax: 506-453-4817, E-mail: jamiraul@unb.ca.

University of Northern British Columbia, Office of Graduate Studies, Prince George, BC V2N 4Z9, Canada. Offers business administration (Diploma); community health science (M Sc); disability management (MA); education (M Ed); first nations studies (MA); gender studies (MA); history (MA); interdisciplinary studies (MA); international studies (MA); mathematical, computer and physical sciences (M Sc); natural resources and environmental studies (M Sc, MA, MNRES, PhD); political science (MA); psychology (M Sc, PhD); social work (MSW). Part-time and evening/weekend programs available. Postbaccalaureate distance learning degree programs offered (no on-campus study). *Degree requirements:* For master's, thesis; for doctorate, thesis/dissertation. *Entrance requirements:* For master's, GRE, minimum B average in undergraduate course work; for doctorate, candidacy exam, minimum A average in graduate course work.

University of North Texas, Robert B. Toulouse School of Graduate Studies, Interdisciplinary Studies, Denton, TX 76203. Offers MA, MS. Part-time programs available. *Degree requirements:* For master's, comprehensive exam, thesis optional. *Entrance requirements:* For master's, GRE General Test, minimum GPA of 2.8, 3 letters of reference. Additional exam requirements/recommendations for international students: Required—proof of English language proficiency required for non-native English speakers; Recommended—TOEFL (minimum score 550 paper-based; 213 computer-based; 79 iBT). *Application deadline:* Applications are processed on a rolling basis. Application fee: $50 ($75 for international students). Electronic applications accepted. *Expenses:* Tuition, state resident: full-time $4298; part-time $239 per contact hour. Tuition, nonresident: full-time $9878; part-time $549 per contact hour. Required fees: $265 per contact hour. *Financial support:* In 2009–10, 1 fellowship was awarded; career-related internships or fieldwork, Federal Work-Study, and institutionally sponsored loans also available. Financial award application deadline: 4/1; financial award applicants required to submit FAFSA.

University of Oklahoma, Graduate College, Program in Interdisciplinary Studies, Norman, OK 73019-0390. Offers MA, MS, PhD. Part-time and evening/weekend programs available. *Students:* 118 full-time (55 women), 465 part-time (172 women); includes 118 minority (54 African Americans, 6 American Indian/Alaska Native, 21 Asian Americans or Pacific Islanders, 37 Hispanic Americans), 11 international. 143 applicants, 94% accepted, 134 enrolled. In 2009, 132 master's, 4 doctorates awarded. *Entrance requirements:* Additional exam requirements/recommendations for international students: Recommended—TOEFL (minimum score 550 paper-based; 213 computer-based). *Application deadline:* For fall admission, 6/1 for domestic students, 4/1 for international students; for spring admission, 11/1 for domestic students, 9/1 for international students. Applications are processed on a rolling basis. Application fee: $40 ($90 for international students). Electronic applications accepted. *Expenses:* Tuition, state resident: full-time $3744; part-time $156 per credit hour. Tuition, nonresident: full-time $13,577; part-time $565.70 per credit hour. Required fees: $2415; $90.10 per credit hour. *Financial support:* In 2009–10, 25 students received support. Tuition waivers (full and partial) and unspecified assistantships available. Financial award applicants required to submit FAFSA. Total annual research expenditures: $1,240. *Unit head:* Lee Williams, Dean/Vice President of Research, 405-325-3811, Fax: 405-325-5346, E-mail: lwilliams@ou.edu. *Application contact:* Angela Castillo, Academic Counselor II, 405-325-3841, Fax: 405-325-5346, E-mail: acastillo@ou.edu.

University of Oregon, Graduate School, Interdisciplinary Program in Applied Information Management, Eugene, OR 97403. Offers MS. Part-time and evening/weekend programs available. *Degree requirements:* For master's, project. *Entrance requirements:* For master's, GMAT, GRE, or MAT. Additional exam requirements/recommendations for international students: Required—TOEFL. Electronic applications accepted. *Expenses:* Contact institution. *Faculty research:* Business management, information design.

University of Ottawa, Faculty of Graduate and Postdoctoral Studies, Interdisciplinary Programs, Ottawa, ON K1N 6N5, Canada. Offers e-business (Certificate); e-commerce (Certificate); finance (Certificate); health services and policies research (Diploma); population health (PhD); population health risk assessment and management (Certificate); public management and governance (Certificate); systems science (Certificate).

University of Pittsburgh, School of Medicine, Graduate Programs in Medicine, Interdisciplinary Biomedical Sciences Program, Pittsburgh, PA 15260. Offers PhD. *Faculty:* 257 full-time (58 women). *Students:* 15 full-time (5 women); includes 3 minority (1 Asian American or Pacific Islander, 2 Hispanic Americans), 5 international. Average age 27. 655 applicants, 10% accepted. In 2009, 37 doctorates awarded. *Degree requirements:* For doctorate, comprehensive exam, thesis/dissertation. *Entrance requirements:* For doctorate, GRE General Test, GRE Subject Test, minimum QPA of 3.0. Additional exam requirements/recommendations for international students: Required—TOEFL (minimum score 600 paper-based; 250 computer-based; 100 iBT), IELTS (minimum score 7). *Application deadline:* For fall admission, 12/15 priority date for domestic and international students. Application fee: $40. Electronic applications accepted. *Expenses:* Tuition, state resident: full-time $16,402; part-time $665 per credit. Tuition, nonresident: full-time $28,694; part-time $1175 per credit. Required fees: $690; $175 per term. Tuition and fees vary according to program. *Financial support:* In 2009–10, 15 research assistantships with full tuition reimbursements (averaging $24,650 per year) were awarded; teaching assistantships, institutionally sponsored loans, scholarships/grants, traineeships, and unspecified assistantships also available. *Faculty research:* Biochemistry and molecular genetics, cell biology and molecular physiology, cellular and molecular pathology, immunology, molecular pharmacology. *Unit head:* Dr. John P. Horn, Associate Dean for Graduate Studies, 412-648-8957, Fax: 412-648-1077, E-mail: gradstudies@medschool.pitt.edu. *Application contact:* Graduate Studies Administrator, 412-648-8957, Fax: 412-648-1077, E-mail: gradstudies@medschool.pitt.edu.

The University of South Dakota, Graduate School, Interdisciplinary Studies Program, Vermillion, SD 57069-2390. Offers interdisciplinary studies (MA). Part-time programs available. Postbaccalaureate distance learning degree programs offered. *Degree requirements:* For master's, thesis or alternative. *Entrance requirements:* For master's, minimum GPA of 2.7; supplemental packet. Additional exam requirements/recommendations for international students: Required—TOEFL (minimum score 550 paper-based; 213 computer-based; 79 iBT). Electronic applications accepted.

University of South Florida, Graduate School, College of Marine Science, St. Petersburg, FL 33701. Offers biological oceanography (MS, PhD); chemical oceanography (MS, PhD); geological oceanography (MS, PhD); interdisciplinary (MS, PhD); marine resource assessment (MS, PhD); physical oceanography (MS, PhD). Part-time programs available. *Faculty:* 24 full-time (4 women). *Students:* 73 full-time (44 women), 26 part-time (18 women); includes 16 minority (7 African Americans, 9 Hispanic Americans), 10 international. Average age 32. 80 applicants, 34% accepted, 19 enrolled. In 2009, 14 master's, 10 doctorates awarded. Terminal master's awarded for partial completion of doctoral program. *Degree requirements:* For master's, thesis, successful oral defense; for doctorate, comprehensive exam, thesis/dissertation, successful oral defense. *Entrance requirements:* For master's, GRE General Test; for doctorate, GRE General Test, bachelor's degree or equivalent from regionally-accredited university, minimum B average or GPA of 3.0 in all upper-division work attempted. Additional exam requirements/recommendations for international students: Required—TOEFL (minimum score 550 paper-based; 213 computer-based; 79 iBT). *Application deadline:* For fall admission, 1/15 for domestic students, 1/2 for international students; for spring admission, 10/1 for domestic students, 7/1 for international students. Applications are processed on a rolling basis. Application fee: $30. *Financial support:* In 2009–10, 73 students received support, including 19 fellowships with partial tuition reimbursements available (averaging $13,972 per year), 36 research assistantships with partial tuition reimbursements available (averaging $13,972 per year), 7 teaching assistantships with partial tuition reimbursements available (averaging $13,972 per year); health care benefits and unspecified assistantships also available. Financial award application deadline: 1/15. *Faculty research:* Trace metal chemistry, water quality, organic and isotopic geochemistry, physical chemistry, nutrient chemistry. Total annual research expenditures: $11.9 million. *Unit head:* Dr. Edward S. Van Vleet, Professor and Director of Academic Programs and Student Affairs, 727-553-1165, Fax: 727-553-1189, E-mail: vanvleet@marine.usf.edu. *Application contact:* Dawna L. Ishler, Academic Services Administrator, 727-553-3944, Fax: 727-553-1189, E-mail: dishler@usf.edu.

The University of Texas at Arlington, Graduate School, School of Urban and Public Affairs, Department of Interdisciplinary Science, Arlington, TX 76019. Offers MA. Part-time and evening/weekend programs available. *Students:* 1 (woman) part-time. *Entrance requirements:* For master's, GRE. Additional exam requirements/recommendations for international students: Required—TOEFL (minimum score 550 paper-based; 213 computer-based). *Application deadline:* For fall admission, 6/15 for domestic students. Application fee: $35 ($50 for international students). *Unit head:* Dr. Allen Repko, Director, 817-272-2338, E-mail: repko@uta.edu. *Application contact:* Dr. Allen Repko, Director, 817-272-2338, E-mail: repko@uta.edu.

The University of Texas at Brownsville, Graduate Studies, College of Liberal Arts, Department of English, Brownsville, TX 78520-4991. Offers English (MA); interdisciplinary studies (MAIS). Part-time and evening/weekend programs available. *Degree requirements:* For master's, comprehensive exam or thesis. *Entrance requirements:* For master's, GRE General Test. Additional exam requirements/recommendations for international students: Required—TOEFL. *Faculty research:* Sandra Cisneros, Nathaniel Hawthorne, Rodolfo Araya, Isabel Allende, linguistics.

The University of Texas at Brownsville, Graduate Studies, College of Liberal Arts, Department of Modern Languages, Brownsville, TX 78520-4991. Offers interdisciplinary studies (MAIS); Spanish (MA). Part-time and evening/weekend programs available. *Degree requirements:* For master's, comprehensive exam, thesis optional. *Entrance requirements:* For master's, GRE General Test, letters of recommendation, interview. Additional exam requirements/recommendations for international students: Required—TOEFL. *Faculty research:* Children's literature, Hispanic folklore, translation.

The University of Texas at Dallas, School of Interdisciplinary Studies, Richardson, TX 75080. Offers interdisciplinary studies (MA). Part-time and evening/weekend programs available. *Faculty:* 3 full-time (2 women). *Students:* 9 full-time (8 women), 24 part-time (16 women); includes 13 minority (6 African Americans, 4 Asian Americans or Pacific Islanders, 3 Hispanic Americans). Average age 40. 13 applicants, 62% accepted, 7 enrolled. In 2009, 16 master's awarded. *Degree requirements:* For master's, research project, seminar. *Entrance requirements:*

Interdisciplinary Studies

The University of Texas at Dallas (continued)

For master's, GRE General Test, minimum GPA of 3.0. Additional exam requirements/recommendations for international students: Required—TOEFL (minimum score 550 paper-based; 213 computer-based). *Application deadline:* For fall admission, 7/15 for domestic students, 5/1 priority date for international students; for spring admission, 11/15 for domestic students, 9/1 priority date for international students. Applications are processed on a rolling basis. Application fee: $50 ($100 for international students). Electronic applications accepted. *Expenses:* Tuition, state resident: full-time $11,068; part-time $461 per credit hour. Tuition, nonresident: full-time $21,178; part-time $882 per credit hour. Tuition and fees vary according to course load. *Financial support:* Fellowships, research assistantships, teaching assistantships, career-related internships or fieldwork, Federal Work-Study, institutionally sponsored loans, and scholarships/grants available. Support available to part-time students. Financial award application deadline: 4/30; financial award applicants required to submit FAFSA. *Faculty research:* Biomedical ethics, history and philosophy of science, social control and regulation, national security, education policy. *Unit head:* Dr. George Fair, Dean, 972-883-2350, Fax: 972-883-2440, E-mail: gwfair@utdallas.edu. *Application contact:* Dr. Elizabeth Salter, Associate Dean, 972-883-2323, Fax: 972-883-2440, E-mail: emsalter@utdallas.edu.

The University of Texas at El Paso, Graduate School, College of Liberal Arts, Interdisciplinary Program in Liberal Arts, El Paso, TX 79968-0001. Offers MAIS. Part-time and evening/weekend programs available. *Students:* 12 (5 women); includes 5 minority (all Hispanic Americans), 4 international. Average age 34. In 2009, 5 master's awarded. *Entrance requirements:* For master's, GRE, minimum GPA of 3.0, letters of recommendation. Additional exam requirements/recommendations for international students: Required—TOEFL; Recommended—IELTS. *Application deadline:* For fall admission, 8/1 priority date for domestic students, 3/1 for international students; for spring admission, 11/1 priority date for domestic students, 9/1 for international students. Applications are processed on a rolling basis. Application fee: $45 ($80 for international students). Electronic applications accepted. *Financial support:* In 2009–10, research assistantships with tuition reimbursements (averaging $18,625 per year), teaching assistantships with partial tuition reimbursements (averaging $14,900 per year) were awarded; fellowships with partial tuition reimbursements, institutionally sponsored loans, scholarships/grants, health care benefits, tuition waivers (partial), and unspecified assistantships also available. Support available to part-time students. Financial award application deadline: 3/15; financial award applicants required to submit FAFSA. *Unit head:* Dr. Ronald Weber, Director, 915-747-7073, E-mail: rweber@utep.edu. *Application contact:* Dr. Patricia D. Witherspoon, Dean of the Graduate School, 915-747-5491, Fax: 915-747-5788, E-mail: withersp@utep.edu.

The University of Texas at El Paso, Graduate School, College of Science, Interdisciplinary Studies Program, El Paso, TX 79968-0001. Offers MSIS. Part-time and evening/weekend programs available. *Students:* 6 (3 women); includes 4 minority (all Hispanic Americans), 2 international. Average age 34. In 2009, 4 master's awarded. *Degree requirements:* For master's, thesis optional. *Entrance requirements:* For master's, GRE. Additional exam requirements/recommendations for international students: Required—TOEFL; Recommended—IELTS. *Application deadline:* For fall admission, 8/1 priority date for domestic students, 3/1 for international students; for spring admission, 11/1 priority date for domestic students, 9/1 for international students. Applications are processed on a rolling basis. Application fee: $45 ($80 for international students). Electronic applications accepted. *Financial support:* In 2009–10, research assistantships (averaging $21,812 per year), teaching assistantships (averaging $17,450 per year) were awarded; fellowships with partial tuition reimbursements, institutionally sponsored loans, scholarships/grants, health care benefits, tuition waivers (partial), and unspecified assistantships also available. Support available to part-time students. Financial award application deadline: 3/15; financial award applicants required to submit FAFSA. *Unit head:* Joel Gilbert, Program Coordinator, 915-747-5554, E-mail: esci@utep.edu. *Application contact:* Dr. Patricia D. Witherspoon, Dean of the Graduate School, 915-747-5491, Fax: 915-747-5788, E-mail: withersp@utep.edu.

The University of Texas at San Antonio, College of Education and Human Development, Department of Interdisciplinary Learning and Teaching, San Antonio, TX 78249-0617. Offers curriculum and instruction (MA); early childhood education (MA); instructional technology (MA); reading (MA); special education (MA). Part-time and evening/weekend programs available. *Faculty:* 28 full-time (24 women), 1 part-time/adjunct (0 women). *Students:* 103 full-time (83 women), 317 part-time (253 women); includes 227 minority (36 African Americans, 11 Asian Americans or Pacific Islanders, 180 Hispanic Americans), 17 international. Average age 33. 212 applicants, 90% accepted, 140 enrolled. In 2009, 74 master's awarded. *Degree requirements:* For master's, comprehensive exam (for some programs), thesis (for some programs). *Entrance requirements:* For master's, GRE General Test, minimum GPA of 3.0. Additional exam requirements/recommendations for international students: Required—TOEFL (minimum score 500 paper-based; 173 computer-based; 61 iBT), IELTS (minimum score 5). *Application deadline:* For fall admission, 7/1 for domestic students, 4/1 for international students; for spring admission, 11/1 for domestic students, 9/1 for international students. Applications are processed on a rolling basis. Application fee: $45 ($80 for international students). Electronic applications accepted. *Expenses:* Tuition, state resident: full-time $3975; part-time $221 per contact hour. Tuition, nonresident: full-time $13,947; part-time $775 per contact hour. Required fees: $1853. *Financial support:* In 2009–10, 76 students received support, including 25 research assistantships (averaging $11,599 per year), 4 teaching assistantships (averaging $8,800 per year); scholarships/grants, tuition waivers, and unspecified assistantships also available. Support available to part-time students. *Faculty research:* Adult education; early childhood education; literacy; special education; science, technology, engineering and math fields. Total annual research expenditures: $57,097. *Unit head:* Dr. Belinda B. Flores, Chair, 210-458-5969, Fax: 210-458-7281, E-mail: belinda.flores@utsa.edu. *Application contact:* Mari Cortez, Graduate Advisor, 210-458-4414, E-mail: mari.cortez@utsa.edu.

The University of Texas at Tyler, College of Arts and Sciences, Department of Art and Art History, Tyler, TX 75799-0001. Offers art history (MA); interdisciplinary (MAIS); studio art (MFA). *Faculty:* 7 full-time (4 women). *Students:* 9 full-time (6 women), 2 part-time (both women); includes 1 minority (Hispanic American). Average age 31. 2 applicants, 100% accepted, 1 enrolled. In 2009, 3 master's awarded. *Degree requirements:* For master's, thesis, graduate committee review. *Entrance requirements:* For master's, minimum GPA of 3.0. Additional exam requirements/recommendations for international students: Required—TOEFL (minimum score 79 computer-based). *Application deadline:* For fall admission, 8/17 priority date for domestic students, 7/1 priority date for international students; for spring admission, 12/21 priority date for domestic students, 11/1 priority date for international students. Applications are processed on a rolling basis. Application fee: $25 ($50 for international students). *Expenses:* Tuition, state resident: part-time $665 per semester hour. Tuition, nonresident: part-time $942 per semester hour. Part-time tuition and fees vary according to degree level and program. *Financial support:* Application deadline: 7/1. *Faculty research:* Classical myths in contemporary art, social issues in contemporary art, casting methods, Renaissance art. *Unit head:* Gary Hatcher, Chair, 903-566-7486, Fax: 903-566-7062, E-mail: ghatcher@mail.uttyl.edu. *Application contact:* Dr. Rachel Sailor, Program Chair, Art History, 903-566-7398, E-mail: rasailor@uttyler.edu.

The University of Texas at Tyler, College of Arts and Sciences, Department of Biology, Tyler, TX 75799-0001. Offers biology (MS); interdisciplinary studies (MSIS). *Faculty:* 10 full-time (1 woman). *Students:* 11 full-time (5 women), 6 part-time (3 women); includes 1 minority (Asian American or Pacific Islander), 1 international. Average age 26. 14 applicants, 57% accepted, 7 enrolled. In 2009, 5 master's awarded. *Degree requirements:* For master's, comprehensive exam, thesis, oral qualifying exam, thesis defense. *Entrance requirements:* For master's, GRE General Test, GRE Subject Test, bachelor's degree in biology or equivalent. Additional exam requirements/recommendations for international students: Required—TOEFL (minimum score 79 computer-based). *Application deadline:* For fall admission, 8/17 priority date for domestic students, 7/1 priority date for international students; for spring admission, 12/21 priority date for domestic students, 11/1 priority date for international students. Applications are processed on a rolling basis. Application fee: $25 ($50 for international students). Electronic applications accepted. *Expenses:* Tuition, state resident: part-time $665 per semester hour. Tuition, nonresident: part-time $942 per semester hour. Part-time tuition and fees vary according to degree level and program. *Financial support:* In 2009–10, 2 research assistantships (averaging $10,000 per year), 10 teaching assistantships (averaging $10,000 per year) were awarded; scholarships/grants also available. Financial award application deadline: 7/1; financial award applicants required to submit FAFSA. *Faculty research:* Phenotypic plasticity and heritability of life history traits, invertebrate ecology and genetics, systematics and phylogenetics of reptiles, hibernation physiology in turtles, landscape ecology, host-microbe interaction, outer membrane proteins in bacteria. Total annual research expenditures: $200,000. *Unit head:* Dr. Don Killebrew, Chair, 903-566-7252, E-mail: dkillebrew@uttyler.edu. *Application contact:* Dr. Neil Ford, Program Chair, 903-566-7249, E-mail: nford@uttyler.edu.

The University of Texas at Tyler, College of Arts and Sciences, Department of Literature and Languages, Tyler, TX 75799-0001. Offers English (MA); interdisciplinary studies (MAIS). Part-time and evening/weekend programs available. *Faculty:* 12 full-time (7 women). *Students:* 6 full-time (3 women), 19 part-time (16 women); includes 1 minority (Hispanic American). Average age 34. 9 applicants, 100% accepted, 5 enrolled. In 2009, 2 master's awarded. *Degree requirements:* For master's, one foreign language, comprehensive exam, thesis optional. *Entrance requirements:* For master's, GRE General Test, minimum GPA of 3.0; four semesters or the equivalent of one foreign language. Additional exam requirements/recommendations for international students: Required—TOEFL (minimum score 79 computer-based). *Application deadline:* For fall admission, 8/17 priority date for domestic students, 7/1 priority date for international students; for spring admission, 12/21 priority date for domestic students, 11/1 priority date for international students. Applications are processed on a rolling basis. Application fee: $25 ($50 for international students). Electronic applications accepted. *Expenses:* Tuition, state resident: part-time $665 per semester hour. Tuition, nonresident: part-time $942 per semester hour. Part-time tuition and fees vary according to degree level and program. *Financial support:* In 2009–10, fellowships with full and partial tuition reimbursements (averaging $1,000 per year), 1 research assistantship with full and partial tuition reimbursement (averaging $6,000 per year) were awarded; teaching assistantships with full and partial tuition reimbursements, Federal Work-Study, institutionally sponsored loans, scholarships/grants, tuition waivers, and unspecified assistantships also available. Financial award application deadline: 7/1; financial award applicants required to submit FAFSA. *Faculty research:* Medieval and Tudor drama, Shakespeare, British Romanticism, British and Irish modernism, American realism, Greek drama, nineteenth century American literature. *Unit head:* Dr. Hui Wu, Chair, 903-566-7289, Fax: 903-565-5700, E-mail: hui_wu@uttyler.edu. *Application contact:* Dr. Hui Wu, Chair, 903-566-7289, Fax: 903-565-5700, E-mail: hui_wu@uttyler.edu.

The University of Texas at Tyler, College of Education and Psychology, Department of Psychology and Counseling, Tyler, TX 75799-0001. Offers clinical psychology (MS), including neuropsychology, school psychology; counseling psychology (MA), including general, marriage and family; interdisciplinary studies (MSIS); school counseling (MA). Part-time and evening/weekend programs available. *Faculty:* 11 full-time (3 women). *Students:* 80 full-time (63 women), 46 part-time (38 women); includes 5 minority (3 African Americans, 1 American Indian/Alaska Native, 1 Hispanic American). Average age 29. 64 applicants, 77% accepted, 28 enrolled. In 2009, 36 master's awarded. *Degree requirements:* For master's, comprehensive exam, thesis optional. *Entrance requirements:* For master's, GRE General Test, minimum GPA of 3.0. Additional exam requirements/recommendations for international students: Required—TOEFL (minimum score 79 computer-based). *Application deadline:* For fall admission, 8/17 priority date for domestic students, 7/1 priority date for international students; for spring admission, 12/21 priority date for domestic students, 11/1 priority date for international students. Application fee: $25 ($50 for international students). Electronic applications accepted. *Expenses:* Tuition, state resident: part-time $665 per semester hour. Tuition, nonresident: part-time $942 per semester hour. Part-time tuition and fees vary according to degree level and program. *Financial support:* In 2009–10, fellowships with partial tuition reimbursements (averaging $3,000 per year), research assistantships (averaging $5,000 per year), teaching assistantships (averaging $1,500 per year) were awarded; career-related internships or fieldwork, Federal Work-Study, and institutionally sponsored loans also available. Support available to part-time students. Financial award application deadline: 7/1. *Faculty research:* Neuropsychology, child abuse, psychometric properties of psychological instruments, maternal behavior, clinical practice issues, victimization of women, post-traumatic stress disorder. *Unit head:* Dr. Charles B. Barke, Chair/Professor, 903-565-5875, Fax: 903-565-5560, E-mail: cbarke@uttyler.edu. *Application contact:* Dr. Charles Barke.

The University of Texas at Tyler, College of Engineering and Computer Science, Department of Computer Science, Tyler, TX 75799-0001. Offers computer science (MS); interdisciplinary studies (MSIS). *Faculty:* 7 full-time (0 women). *Students:* 15 full-time (4 women), 15 part-time (5 women), 23 international. Average age 25. 28 applicants, 68% accepted, 5 enrolled. In 2009, 10 master's awarded. *Degree requirements:* For master's, comprehensive exam, thesis optional. *Entrance requirements:* For master's, GRE General Test, previous course work in data structures and computer organization, 6 hours of course work in calculus and statistics. Additional exam requirements/recommendations for international students: Required—TOEFL (minimum score 79 computer-based). *Application deadline:* For fall admission, 6/15 priority date for domestic students, 7/1 priority date for international students; for spring admission, 10/15 priority date for domestic students, 11/1 priority date for international students. Applications are processed on a rolling basis. Application fee: $25 ($50 for international students). Electronic applications accepted. *Expenses:* Tuition, state resident: part-time $665 per semester hour. Tuition, nonresident: part-time $942 per semester hour. Part-time tuition and fees vary according to degree level and program. *Financial support:* In 2009–10, 5 research assistantships (averaging $2,590 per year), 5 teaching assistantships (averaging $3,090 per year) were awarded; scholarships/grants also available. Financial award application deadline: 7/1; financial award applicants required to submit FAFSA. *Faculty research:* Database design, software engineering, client-server architecture, visual programming, data mining, computer security, digital image processing, simulation and modeling, computer science education. Total annual research expenditures: $20,000. *Unit head:* Dr. Stephen Rainwater, Acting Chair, 903-566-7235, Fax: 903-565-5607, E-mail: srainwater@uttyler.edu. *Application contact:* Dr. Stephen Rainwater.

The University of Texas–Pan American, College of Arts and Humanities, Program in Interdisciplinary Studies, Edinburg, TX 78539. Offers MAIS, MSIS. Part-time and evening/weekend programs available. *Degree requirements:* For master's, comprehensive exam, thesis or alternative. *Entrance requirements:* For master's, GRE General Test, minimum GPA of 3.0. *Expenses:* Tuition, state resident: full-time $3630.60; part-time $201.70 per credit hour. Tuition, nonresident: full-time $8617; part-time $478.70 per credit hour. Required fees: $806.50.

University of the Incarnate Word, School of Graduate Studies and Research, College of Humanities, Arts, and Social Sciences, Program in Multidisciplinary Studies, San Antonio, TX 78209-6397. Offers MA. Part-time and evening/weekend programs available. *Students:* 8 part-time (5 women); includes 3 minority (all Hispanic Americans). Average age 36. *Degree requirements:* For master's, thesis or capstone experience in one area of focus which incorporates the integration of all disciplines from which work is taken. *Entrance requirements:* For master's, GRE (minimum score 800 verbal and quantitative, 3.5 analytical), MAT (minimum score 40), GMAT (minimum score 450). Additional exam requirements/recommendations for international students: Required—TOEFL (minimum score 560 paper-based; 220 computer-based; 83 iBT). *Application deadline:* Applications are processed on a rolling basis. Application fee: $20. Electronic applications accepted. *Expenses:* Tuition: Full-time $12,150; part-time $675 per credit hour. Required fees: $83 per credit hour. *Financial support:* Federal Work-Study and scholarships/grants available. Financial award applicants required to submit FAFSA. *Unit head:* Dr. Kevin Vichcales, Dean, School of Graduate Studies and Research, 210-829-3157. *Application contact:* Andrea Cyterski-Acosta, Dean of Enrollment, 210-829-6005, Fax: 210-829-3921, E-mail: admis@uiwtx.edu.

University of the Incarnate Word, School of Graduate Studies and Research, School of Mathematics, Science, and Engineering, Program in Multidisciplinary Sciences, San Antonio, TX 78209-6397. Offers MA. Part-time and evening/weekend programs available. *Students:* 17 part-time (11 women); includes 12 minority (1 Asian American or Pacific Islander, 11 Hispanic Americans). Average age 36. In 2009, 3 master's awarded. *Degree requirements:* For master's, capstone. *Entrance requirements:* For master's, GRE (minimum score 800 verbal and quantitative, 3.5 analytical), elementary certification with science endorsement (18 hours of science) or secondary certification, or equivalent professional experience teaching service. Additional exam requirements/recommendations for international students: Required—TOEFL (minimum score 560 paper-based; 220 computer-based; 83 iBT). *Application deadline:* Applications are processed on a rolling basis. Application fee: $20. Electronic applications accepted. *Expenses:* Tuition: Full-time $12,150; part-time $675 per credit hour. Required fees: $83 per credit hour. *Financial support:* Federal Work-Study and scholarships/grants available. Financial award applicants required to submit FAFSA. *Unit head:* Dr. Alakananda Chaudhuri, 210-829-3145, Fax: 210-829-3153, E-mail: alakanan@uiwtx.edu. *Application contact:* Andrea Cyterski-Acosta, Dean of Enrollment, 210-829-6005, Fax: 210-829-3921, E-mail: admis@uiwtx.edu.

University of Vermont, Graduate College, College of Education and Social Services, Department of Integrated Professional Studies, Interdisciplinary Major, Burlington, VT 05405. Offers M Ed. *Students:* 31 (25 women); includes 9 minority (4 African Americans, 3 Asian Americans or Pacific Islanders, 2 Hispanic Americans), 2 international. 24 applicants, 88% accepted, 11 enrolled. In 2009, 10 master's awarded. *Degree requirements:* For master's, thesis or alternative. *Entrance requirements:* Additional exam requirements/recommendations for international students: Required—TOEFL (minimum score 550 paper-based; 213 computer-based; 80 iBT). *Application deadline:* For fall admission, 8/1 priority date for domestic students. Applications are processed on a rolling basis. Application fee: $40. Electronic applications accepted. *Expenses:* Tuition, state resident: part-time $508 per credit hour. Tuition, nonresident: part-time $1281 per credit hour. *Financial support:* Research assistantships, teaching assistantships available. Financial award application deadline: 3/1. *Unit head:* Dr. R. Nash, Coordinator, 802-656-2030. *Application contact:* Dr. R. Nash, Coordinator, 802-656-2030.

University of Virginia, College and Graduate School of Arts and Sciences, Program in Art and Architectural History, Charlottesville, VA 22903. Offers MA, PhD. *Faculty:* 25 full-time (9 women), 5 part-time/adjunct (3 women). *Students:* 48 full-time (37 women), 1 (woman) part-time; includes 1 minority (African American), 1 international. Average age 31. 81 applicants, 33% accepted, 9 enrolled. In 2009, 7 master's, 7 doctorates awarded. *Degree requirements:* For master's, one foreign language, comprehensive exam, thesis; for doctorate, 2 foreign languages, thesis/dissertation, oral exam. *Entrance requirements:* For master's and doctorate, GRE, 2 letters of recommendation. *Application deadline:* For fall admission, 12/7 for domestic and international students. Applications are processed on a rolling basis. Electronic applications accepted. *Financial support:* Application deadline: 12/7. *Unit head:* Lawrence O. Goedde, Chair, 434-924-6123, Fax: 434-924-3647, E-mail: artdept@virginia.edu. *Application contact:* Daniel Ehnbom, Director of Graduate Studies, 434-924-6130, Fax: 434-924-3647, E-mail: dje6r@virginia.edu.

University of Washington, Tacoma, Graduate Programs, Interdisciplinary Studies Program, Tacoma, WA 98402-3100. Offers MA. *Faculty:* 60 full-time (34 women), 22 part-time/adjunct (11 women). *Students:* 22 full-time (13 women), 25 part-time (21 women); includes 10 minority (1 American Indian/Alaska Native, 3 Asian Americans or Pacific Islanders, 6 Hispanic Americans). Average age 36. 25 applicants, 76% accepted, 17 enrolled. In 2009, 15 master's awarded. *Degree requirements:* For master's, thesis or masters project. *Entrance requirements:* For master's, GRE, Statement of intended area of focus GRE scores Two official transcripts from every college attended Copy of current resume Three recommendations. *Application deadline:* For fall admission, 5/1 priority date for domestic students; for winter admission, 11/1 for domestic students. Applications are processed on a rolling basis. Application fee: $65. Electronic applications accepted. *Expenses:* Tuition, state resident: full-time $10,660; part-time $484 per credit. Tuition, nonresident: full-time $24,000; part-time $1119 per credit. Required fees: $150 per term. Tuition and fees vary according to course load and program. *Faculty research:* Interdisciplinary arts, interdisciplinary physical sciences, interdisciplinary social and behavioral sciences, environmental science, liberal studies. *Unit head:* Dr. Larry Knopp, Director, 253-692-4450, Fax: 253-692-5718, E-mail: ias@u.washington.edu. *Application contact:* Dr. Linda Kachinsky, M.A. Adviser, 253-692-4450, Fax: 253-692-5718, E-mail: ias@u.washington.edu.

The University of Western Ontario, Faculty of Graduate Studies, Center for the Study of Theory and Criticism, London, ON N6A 5B8, Canada. Offers MA, PhD. *Degree requirements:* For master's, one foreign language, thesis; for doctorate, one foreign language, comprehensive exam, thesis/dissertation. *Entrance requirements:* For master's, honors degree or equivalent, minimum B+ average, 2 samples of written work; for doctorate, MA in humanitites or social sciences.

University of Wisconsin–Milwaukee, Graduate School, Program in Multidisciplinary Studies, Milwaukee, WI 53201-0413. Offers PhD. *Students:* 2 full-time (both women). Average age 43. *Degree requirements:* For doctorate, thesis/dissertation. *Application deadline:* For fall admission, 1/1 priority date for domestic students; for spring admission, 9/1 for domestic students. Applications are processed on a rolling basis. Application fee: $45 ($75 for international students). *Expenses:* Tuition, state resident: full-time $8800. Tuition, nonresident: full-time $20,760. Tuition and fees vary according to program and reciprocity agreements. *Financial support:* Career-related internships or fieldwork and unspecified assistantships available. Support available to part-time students. Financial award application deadline: 4/15. *Application contact:* Patricia J. Hayes, Senior Student Services Specialist, 414-229-6263, Fax: 414-229-6967, E-mail: hayes@uwm.edu.

Virginia Commonwealth University, Graduate School, Program in Interdisciplinary Studies, Richmond, VA 23284-9005. Offers MIS. Part-time programs available. *Degree requirements:* For master's, thesis optional. *Entrance requirements:* For master's, GRE General Test, minimum GPA of 2.8.

Virginia Polytechnic Institute and State University, Graduate School, College of Liberal Arts and Human Sciences, Program in Social, Political, Ethical and Cultural Thought, Blacksburg, VA 24061. Offers PhD. *Expenses:* Tuition, area resident: Full-time $10,228; part-time $459 per credit hour. Tuition, nonresident: full-time $17,892; part-time $865 per credit hour. Required fees: $1966; $451 per semester. *Unit head:* Dr. Sue Ott Rowlands, Dean, 540-231-6779, Fax: 540-231-7157, E-mail: sottrowlands@vt.edu. *Application contact:* Dr. Sue Ott Rowlands, Dean, 540-231-6779, Fax: 540-231-7157, E-mail: sottrowlands@vt.edu.

Virginia Polytechnic Institute and State University, Graduate School, College of Natural Resources, Program in Geospatial and Environmental Analysis, Blacksburg, VA 24061. Offers PhD.

Virginia Polytechnic Institute and State University, Graduate School, Intercollege, Blacksburg, VA 24061. Offers MIT, MS, PhD. *Students:* 197 full-time (73 women), 292 part-time (72 women); includes 92 minority (28 African Americans, 1 American Indian/Alaska Native, 47 Asian Americans or Pacific Islanders, 16 Hispanic Americans), 127 international. Average age 32. 931 applicants, 69% accepted, 426 enrolled. In 2009, 94 master's, 20 doctorates awarded. *Entrance requirements:* For master's and doctorate, GRE, GMAT. Additional exam requirements/recommendations for international students: Required—TOEFL (minimum score 550 paper-based; 213 computer-based). *Application deadline:* For fall admission, 5/15 for international students; for spring admission, 10/15 for international students. Applications are processed on a rolling basis. Application fee: $65. Electronic applications accepted. *Expenses:* Tuition, area resident: Full-time $10,228; part-time $459 per credit hour. Tuition, nonresident: full-time $17,892; part-time $865 per credit hour. Required fees: $1966; $451 per semester. *Financial support:* In 2009–10, 44 research assistantships with full tuition reimbursements (averaging $22,224 per year), 3 teaching assistantships with full tuition reimbursements (averaging $11,902 per year) were awarded; career-related internships or fieldwork, Federal Work-Study, scholarships/grants, and unspecified assistantships also available. Financial award application deadline: 1/15. *Unit head:* Dr. Karen P. DePauw, Vice President and Dean for Graduate Education, 540-231-7581, Fax: 540-231-1670, E-mail: kpdepauw@vt.edu. *Application contact:* Dr. Karen P. DePauw, Vice President and Dean for Graduate Education, 540-231-7581, Fax: 540-231-1670, E-mail: kpdepauw@vt.edu.

Virginia State University, School of Graduate Studies, Research, and Outreach, Program in Interdisciplinary Studies, Petersburg, VA 23806-0001. Offers MIS. *Degree requirements:* For master's, thesis optional.

Washington State University, Graduate School, Individual Interdisciplinary Doctoral Program, Pullman, WA 99164. Offers PhD. *Degree requirements:* For doctorate, comprehensive exam, thesis/dissertation. *Entrance requirements:* For doctorate, minimum GPA of 3.5, master's degree from an accredited institution. Additional exam requirements/recommendations for international students: Required—TOEFL.

Wayland Baptist University, Graduate Programs, Program in Multidisciplinary Science, Plainview, TX 79072-6998. Offers MS. Part-time and evening/weekend programs available. *Faculty:* 9 full-time (2 women), 1 part-time/adjunct (0 women). *Students:* 10 part-time (all women); includes 1 minority (Hispanic American). Average age 34. 2 applicants, 100% accepted, 2 enrolled. In 2009, 4 master's awarded. *Degree requirements:* For master's, comprehensive exam. *Entrance requirements:* For master's, GRE or MAT. Additional exam requirements/recommendations for international students: Required—TOEFL (minimum score 500 paper-based; 173 computer-based; 61 iBT). *Application deadline:* Applications are processed on a rolling basis. Application fee: $50. Electronic applications accepted. *Expenses:* Tuition: Full-time $5796; part-time $322 per credit hour. Required fees: $782; $9 per credit hour. $60 per semester. Tuition and fees vary according to course load and campus/location. *Financial support:* Federal Work-Study, institutionally sponsored loans, and scholarships/grants available. Support available to part-time students. Financial award application deadline: 5/1; financial award applicants required to submit FAFSA. *Unit head:* Dr. Herbert Grover, Chairman, Division of Mathematics and Science, 806-291-1115, Fax: 806-291-1968, E-mail: groverh@wbu.edu. *Application contact:* Amanda Stanton, Graduate Studies, 806-291-3423, Fax: 806-291-1950, E-mail: stanton@wbu.edu.

Western Kentucky University, Graduate Studies, College of Education and Behavioral Sciences, Department of Special Instructional Programs, Bowling Green, KY 42101. Offers exceptional child education (MAE); interdisciplinary early child education (MAE); library media education (MS); literacy (MAE). Part-time and evening/weekend programs available. Postbaccalaureate distance learning degree programs offered (minimal on-campus study). *Degree requirements:* For master's, comprehensive exam. *Entrance requirements:* For master's, GRE General Test. Additional exam requirements/recommendations for international students: Required—TOEFL (minimum score 555 paper-based; 213 computer-based; 79 iBT). *Expenses:* Tuition, state resident: full-time $4160; part-time $416 per credit hour. Tuition, nonresident: full-time $9550; part-time $506 per credit hour. Tuition and fees vary according to campus/location and reciprocity agreements. *Faculty research:* Teacher preparation in moderate/severe disabilities.

Western New Mexico University, Graduate Division, Interdisciplinary Studies, Silver City, NM 88062-0680. Offers MA. Part-time programs available. *Degree requirements:* For master's, comprehensive exam (for some programs), thesis optional. *Entrance requirements:* For master's, GRE General Test, GRE Subject Test, minimum GPA of 3.2 in last 64 hours of undergraduate study. Additional exam requirements/recommendations for international students: Required—TOEFL (minimum score 550 paper-based; 213 computer-based).

West Texas A&M University, Program in Interdisciplinary Studies, Canyon, TX 79016-0001. Offers MA, MS. Part-time and evening/weekend programs available. Postbaccalaureate distance learning degree programs offered (minimal on-campus study). *Degree requirements:* For master's, comprehensive exam, thesis or alternative. *Entrance requirements:* For master's, GRE General Test, interview with graduate Dean. Additional exam requirements/recommendations for international students: Required—TOEFL (minimum score 550 paper-based). Electronic applications accepted.

Worcester Polytechnic Institute, Graduate Studies and Research, Department of Social Science and Policy Studies, Worcester, MA 01609-2280. Offers interdisciplinary social science (PhD); system dynamics (MS, Graduate Certificate). Part-time and evening/weekend programs available. Postbaccalaureate distance learning degree programs offered (no on-campus study). *Faculty:* 3 full-time (0 women), 2 part-time/adjunct (0 women). *Students:* 12 part-time (11 women). 13 applicants, 85% accepted, 5 enrolled. In 2009, 2 master's awarded. *Entrance requirements:* For master's, GRE General Test, 3 letters of recommendation. Additional exam requirements/recommendations for international students: Required—TOEFL (minimum score 550 paper-based; 213 computer-based; 79 iBT), IELTS (minimum score 6.5). *Application deadline:* For fall admission, 1/15 priority date for domestic students, 1/15 for international students; for spring admission, 10/15 priority date for domestic students, 10/15 for international students. Applications are processed on a rolling basis. Application fee: $70. Electronic applications accepted. *Financial support:* Career-related internships or fieldwork, institutionally sponsored loans, scholarships/grants, and unspecified assistantships available. Financial award application deadline: 1/15. *Faculty research:* Sustainable development, information economics, judgment and decision making, learning science, system dynamics, social simulation, political economies. *Unit head:* Dr. James K. Doyle, Head, 508-831-5296, Fax: 508-831-5896, E-mail: doyle@wpi.edu. *Application contact:* Dr. Oleg Pavlov, Graduate Coordinator, 508-831-5296, Fax: 508-831-5896, E-mail: opavlov@wpi.edu.

Worcester Polytechnic Institute, Graduate Studies and Research, Programs in Interdisciplinary Studies, Worcester, MA 01609-2280. Offers bioscience administration (MS); impact engineering (MS); manufacturing engineering management (MS); power systems management (MS); social science (PhD); systems modeling (MS). Part-time and evening/weekend programs available. *Faculty:* 1 part-time/adjunct (0 women). *Students:* 3 full-time (1 woman), 126 part-time (24 women). 184 applicants, 68% accepted, 100 enrolled. In 2009, 19 master's awarded. *Degree requirements:* For master's, thesis; for doctorate, comprehensive exam, thesis/dissertation. *Entrance requirements:* For master's and doctorate, 3 letters of recommendation. Additional exam requirements/recommendations for international students: Required—TOEFL (minimum score 550 paper-based; 213 computer-based; 79 iBT), IELTS (minimum score 6.5). *Application deadline:* For fall admission, 1/15 priority date for domestic students; for spring admission, 10/15 priority date for domestic students. Application fee: $70. *Financial support:* Institutionally sponsored loans, scholarships/grants, and unspecified assistantships available. Financial award application deadline: 1/15. *Unit head:* Dr. Fred J. Looft, Head, 508-831-5231, Fax: 508-831-5491, E-mail: fjlooft@wpi.edu. *Application contact:* Lynne Dougherty, Administrative Assistant, 508-831-5301, Fax: 508-831-5717, E-mail: grad@wpi.edu.

Wright State University, School of Graduate Studies, Interdisciplinary Programs, Program in Interdisciplinary Studies, Dayton, OH 45435. Offers MA, MS. *Degree requirements:* For master's, thesis optional. *Entrance requirements:* Additional exam requirements/recommendations for international students: Required—TOEFL.

York University, Faculty of Graduate Studies, Program in Interdisciplinary Studies, Toronto, ON M3J 1P3, Canada. Offers MA. Part-time programs available. *Degree requirements:* For master's, thesis or alternative. Electronic applications accepted.

NEW YORK UNIVERSITY

NEW YORK UNIVERSITY

Gallatin School of Individualized Study

Program of Study

The Gallatin School offers an M.A. degree in individualized study. Working closely with a faculty adviser, self-motivated students have the opportunity to develop an individually tailored, interdisciplinary educational program. Students master an area of concentration that integrates study in several disciplines. For example, a student who is interested in the arts and community could combine courses in educational theater, arts administration, and sociology; a student with an interest in the cultural history of the United States might combine English with history and museum studies; a student with an interest in communications might develop a program to include course work in cinema studies, gender studies, and media ecology; and a student wishing to study the European Union might combine course work in politics, history, and social policy. A student's course of study is not limited to these examples. Students are encouraged to design a program according to their individual needs and interests. With the adviser, the student designs a 40-credit M.A. program consisting of course work and other options that may include independent study, tutorials, internships, and private lessons in the arts.

The course work is taken in the various graduate schools of New York University (NYU), such as the Graduate School of Arts and Science; the Stern School of Business; the Wagner Graduate School of Public Service; the Steinhardt School of Culture, Education, and Human Development; the School of Continuing and Professional Studies; the Silver School of Social Work; and the Tisch School of the Arts (selected courses). In addition to course work, independent study and tutorials allow students to pursue in-depth research, while internships and private lessons enable students to take advantage of the resources of New York City. The program requires 40 credits; students may apply for a maximum of 12 transfer credits and/or course-equivalency credits, which are based on previous work experience or training. A thesis is required and can be a traditional research paper, an applied project, or an artistic endeavor, such as a performance, a novel, or a work of visual art.

During the first year and a half, the curriculum for full-time students consists primarily of course work from the various schools of NYU along with independent study, tutorials, and internships (if desired). Students may attend on a full-time or part-time basis. Full-time students usually complete the program in 2 or 2½ years; part-time students generally complete the program in three to four years but are given up to six years.

Research Facilities

NYU's Holmes Bobst Library is the flagship of a five-library system that provides access to the world's scholarship and serves as a center for the NYU community's intellectual life. The collections include 4 million print volumes, 68,000 serial subscriptions, 50,000 electronic journals, 500,000 e-books, 105,000 audio and video recordings, and 25,000 linear feet of archival materials.

Bobst Library offers 45 miles of open stacks and approximately 2,500 seats for student study. The Avery Fisher Center for Music and Media has 134 carrels for audio listening and video viewing and three multimedia classrooms. The Digital Studio offers a leading-edge resource for faculty and student projects and promotes and supports access to digital resources for teaching, learning, research, and arts events. The Data Service Studio provides expert staff and access to software, statistical computing, geographical information systems analysis, data collection resources, and data management services in support of quantitative research at NYU.

The Fales Library, a special collection within Bobst Library, is home to the Fales Collection of English and American Literature; the Food Studies Collection, comprised of cookbooks, food writing, pamphlets, paper, and archives dating from the 1790s; and the Downtown Collection, a multimedia archive documenting the avant-garde New York art world since 1975. Bobst Library also houses the Tamiment Library, with research materials in the history of left politics and labor organizations. Two fellowship programs explore the impact of the Cold War on American institutions and the history and role in our society of academic freedom. Tamiment also houses the Wagner Labor Archives.

The Barbara Goldsmith Preservation and Conservation Department in Bobst Library comprises laboratories for book, paper, film, media, and audio/video conservation and preservation. Library research funded by the Mellon Foundation has developed groundbreaking strategies in preservation for moving image and audio, with the best practices identified and tested and the results disseminated throughout the archival community.

Beyond the Bobst facility, the Courant Institute of Mathematical Sciences library focuses on research-level material in mathematics and computer science. The Stephen Chan Library of Fine Arts at the Institute of Fine Arts (IFA) houses collections that support the research needs of graduate programs in art history and archaeology. The Jack Brause Real Estate Library at the Real Estate Institute serves the information needs of the real estate community. The library of the Institute for the Study of the Ancient World (ISAW) is a resource for advanced research and graduate education in ancient civilizations from the western Mediterranean to China. Complementing these collections are those of the Ehrman Medical Library of NYU's School of Medicine, the Dental Center's Waldmann Library, and the School of Law's library.

The Grey Art Gallery, the University's fine arts museum, presents three to four innovative exhibitions each year that encompass all aspects of the visual arts. The gallery also sponsors lectures, seminars, symposia, and film series in conjunction with its exhibitions.

In addition to dozens of other research centers are the following international cultural centers that are available for student use: Casa Italiana Zerilli-Marimò, Glucksman Ireland House, Bronfman Center for Jewish Student Life, King Juan Carlos I of Spain Center, La Maison Française, Deutsches Haus, and Hagop Kevorkian Center.

NYU's Information Technology Services (ITS) provides computer, network, telephone, and Internet services to students and the entire University. It connects people to their work and studies and to the information, training, and technical resources they need to achieve their goals. ITS supports the broad spectrum of University activities and technology services for students, in support of research, scholarship, and instruction.

Financial Aid

Scholarships, work-study opportunities, loans, and a deferred-payment plan are available. Financial aid is awarded on the basis of merit and demonstrated financial need to both full-time and part-time students. In 2009–10, 60 percent of graduate students received some form of aid; of those receiving aid, 77 percent received scholarships/grants, 82 percent received loans, and 10 percent received work-study. The range of scholarship/grant packages was $419–$54,998. The range of loan packages was $3200–$61,567.

To be considered for a Gallatin Scholarship, students must submit the Free Application for Federal Student Aid (FAFSA). Resident assistantships and student employment are also available.

In addition to the Gallatin Scholarship, other sources of financial support include the following:

The Catherine B. Reynolds Program in Social Entrepreneurship at New York University: A comprehensive initiative designed to train the next generation of leaders in public service, offering up to 20 graduate fellowships each year to students across the University. The graduate fellowship provides up to $50,000 over two years and dedicated curricular and cocurricular activities. For more information, visit the Web site at http://www.nyu.edu/reynolds.

Foreign Language and Area Studies (FLAS) Fellowships: To apply or for further information, visit the Web site of either the Center for European and Mediterranean Studies (http://cems.as.nyu.edu/object/cems.grad.fellowships.html), the Hagop Kevorkian Center (http://www.nyu.edu/gsas/program/neareast/4_FLAS.html), or the Center for Latin American and Caribbean Studies (http://www.nyu.edu/gsas/program/latin/FLAS_PAGE.htm).

Residential Education Assistantship Opportunities: These are available for Resident Assistants (RAs) and Community Education Assistants (CEAs). For additional information and to apply, visit the department's student staff selection Web site at http://www.nyu.edu/residential.education/staff/studentselection/index.html.

NYU America Reads/America Counts: For more information, visit http://www.steinhardt.nyu.edu/americareads.

New York State Tuition Assistance Program (TAP): Visit http://www.nyu.edu/financial.aid/tap.html.

Part-Time Students and International Students: Visit http://www.nyu.edu/financial.aid.

Cost of Study

Tuition for the 2009–10 academic year at Gallatin was $1214 per credit per term, plus additional nonrefundable registration and services fees. Tuition is paid per credit, per term. The University offers a basic health insurance benefit plan at $1261 per year for full-time students and a comprehensive health insurance benefit plan at $1963 per year for international students. Students are automatically enrolled in these plans unless they already have comparable coverage.

Living and Housing Costs

Graduate student housing at NYU provides the advantages of apartment-style living with the convenience and security of residence hall life. Generally, accommodations are in shared studios for two students. Off-campus housing is also available at market rates. Meal plans are available but not required. For further information, students may visit http://www.nyu.edu/housing.

Student Group

There are approximately 200 graduate students in the Gallatin School. Half of the students are from the New York metropolitan area, while the other half comes from across the country as well as from international locations. Because of the diversity offered in the Gallatin School, students come from a wide range of undergraduate disciplines.

Student Outcomes

Because of the individualized nature of Gallatin, graduates embark on a wide variety of professions. In the arts, graduates include choreographers, artistic directors of dance and theater companies, performers, writers, arts administrators, curators, and museum directors. Graduates in the arts often remain in academia, teaching the arts at all levels, from elementary to university. In the field of finance, Gallatin graduates hold positions in such firms as Oppenheimer & Company, the Bank of America, and Citigroup. Others enter the fields of nutrition, psychotherapy, journalism, education, and communications, while many have obtained positions in government, social, and environmental agencies. Graduates have also entered Ph.D. programs in such areas as literature, sociology, cinema, performance studies, cultural studies, educational theater, history, music composition, and political science.

Location

NYU's Gallatin School is located in historic Greenwich Village, which is known for its small-scale, European style of living. NYU's campus is within minutes of Broadway and off-Broadway drama and dance, art galleries, coffeehouses, restaurants, clubs, bookstores, and world-renowned museums and libraries. The Jerome S. Coles Sports and Recreation Center and the Palladium Athletic Facility serve the recreational needs of all students.

The University

NYU is a private university, comprising eighteen schools, colleges, and institutes at major centers in Manhattan, Brooklyn, and Abu Dhabi (UAE). The University was founded in 1831 by Albert Gallatin, treasury secretary under Thomas Jefferson, and other prominent New Yorkers who believed that the place for a university was not in "the seclusion of cloistered halls but in the throbbing heart of a great city." In this spirit, the Gallatin School was founded in 1972.

Applying

Students may be admitted for the fall or spring semesters. In addition to official transcripts, two letters of recommendation and a statement of purpose are required.

Correspondence and Information

Director of Graduate Admissions
Gallatin School of Individualized Study
New York University
715 Broadway, 6th Floor
New York, New York 10003-6806
Phone: 212-998-7370
Web site: http://www.nyu.edu/info/gallatin09

New York University

THE FACULTY

Students in the Gallatin School take courses in the various graduate schools of New York University. Essentially, the entire graduate faculty of the University instructs Gallatin students. The following is a list of Gallatin faculty members.

Susanne Wofford, Ph.D., Yale. Dean, Gallatin School of Individualized Study. Shakespeare, Spenser, Renaissance and classical epic, comparative European drama, and narrative and literary theory.

Peder Anker, Ph.D., Harvard. History of science, ecology, environmentalism, design, and environmental philosophy.

Sinan Antoon, Ph.D., Harvard. Premodern Arabo-Islamic culture and contemporary Arab culture and politics.

Gene Cittadino, Ph.D., Wisconsin. Understanding and interpreting the historical and present role of scientific knowledge in our culture, the interaction of science and cultural values in the shaping of environmental policy.

Nina Cornyetz, Ph.D., Columbia. Critical, literary, and filmic theory; intellectual history; gender and sexuality; cultural studies with a specialization in Japan.

Kimberly McClain DaCosta, Ph.D., Berkeley. Intersection of cultural ideas about race, family, and consumption; contemporary production of racial boundaries.

Michael D. Dinwiddie, M.F.A., NYU. Cultural studies, African American theater history, dramatic writing, filmmaking, ragtime music.

Stephen Duncombe, Ph.D., CUNY Graduate Center. Media and cultural studies, history of the mass and alternative media, intersection of culture and politics.

Hallie Franks, Ph.D., Harvard. Art and archaeology of Greece, Rome, and the ancient Near East.

Sharon Friedman, Ph.D., NYU. Literary interpretation, feminist criticism, women dramatists, critical writing across the curriculum.

Lisa Goldfarb, Ph.D., CUNY Graduate Center. Comparative literature and writing, nineteenth- and twentieth-century European and American poetry and fiction, music and literature, philosophic questions in literature, literature and history of New York City.

Jean Graybeal, Ph.D., Syracuse. Philosophy and psychology of religion, phenomenology, feminist theory, the question of embodiment.

Karen Hornick, Ph.D., Columbia. Literature, media, philosophy, cultural history, writing.

Kristin Horton, M.F.A., Iowa. Directing, Shakespeare, new play development, theater and cross-cultural dialogue, reinventing the classics for the contemporary stage.

Steven Hutkins, Ph.D., NYU. Theme of place and literature: the places where we live and travel, the places that have been imagined by writers and philosophers.

Bradley Lewis, Ph.D., George Washington; M.D., Tennessee. Interface of medicine, humanities, cultural studies of science, disability studies.

Ritty Lukose, Ph.D., Chicago. Gender, globalization, and colonial, postcolonial, and diasporic modernities as they impact South Asia—particularly youth development, consumption, citizenship, politics, and gender and feminist issues.

Julie Malnig, Ph.D., NYU. Social and popular dance, the history of popular entertainments, performance art, feminist performance and criticism, performance writing.

Eve Meltzer, Ph.D., Berkeley. Contemporary art history; photography; material culture; and a range of philosophical and theoretical discourses including psychoanalysis, structuralism, and phenomenology.

M. Bella Mirabella, Ph.D., Rutgers. Literature and culture of the Renaissance, including the ancient and medieval periods, with a focus on drama, theater, performance, and gender.

Ali Mirsepassi, Ph.D., American. Middle Eastern studies, social theory, sociology of religion, Islam and modernity, intellectual history, Iranian studies.

David Thornton Moore, Ed.D., Harvard. History of social thought and contemporary social issues, work reform and experiential learning, innovations in higher education.

Sara Murphy, Ph.D. NYU. Literature and philosophy, critical theory, feminist and gender studies, nineteenth-century literary cultures.

Kimberly Phillips-Fein, Ph.D., Columbia. American political, business, and labor history; history of economic thought; the role of business in the development of the modern conservative movement in the second half of the twentieth century; the role of economic ideas in the rise of conservatism.

Stacy Pies, Ph.D., CUNY, Graduate Center. Poetry, world literature—narrative across the disciplines and narrative theology, literary criticism, literature and philosophy, writing on cities and urbanism.

René Francisco Poitevin, Ph.D., California, Davis. Local labor markets, gentrification, race and ethnicity in the United States, geographic information systems.

Millery Polyné, Ph.D., Michigan. History of African American and Afro-Caribbean/Afro-Latino cultural, political, and economic initiatives in the nineteenth and twentieth centuries; cultural studies; dance; race and sports; jazz.

Myisha Priest, Ph.D., Berkeley. African American literature and material culture.

Laurin Raiken, M.A., Adelphi. Sociology and political economy of the arts; arts management and cultural policy; arts, community, and social change; Native American studies; the relationship between Kabbalah and art.

George Shulman, Ph.D., Berkeley. Political thought and American studies, political thought in Europe and the United States, tragic and biblical traditions.

Laura M. Slatkin, Ph.D., Harvard. Ancient Greek and Roman poetry—especially epic and drama, wisdom traditions in classical and Near Eastern antiquity, gender studies, anthropological approaches to the literature of the ancient Mediterranean world, cultural poetics.

Matthew Stanley, Ph.D., Harvard. History and philosophy of science.

Clyde R. Taylor, Ph.D., Wayne State. Politics of representation, vernacular modernisms, cinema and society, African American and African literature, cultural symbolism.

Jack (John Kuo Wei) Tchen, Ph.D., NYU. Cross-cultural and community studies; New York City history; Asians in the Americas; race, colonialism, and museums; dialogic theory; radical pedagogy.

Alejandro Velasco, Ph.D., Duke. History of modern Latin America, social movements, urban culture, democratization.

E. Frances White, Ph.D., Boston University. History of Africa and its diaspora; history of gender and sexuality; critical race theory.

A Gallatin professor talks with students.

Gallatin students use Washington Square Park as an outdoor classroom.

ACADEMIC AND PROFESSIONAL PROGRAMS IN THE SOCIAL SCIENCES

Section 15
Area and Cultural Studies

This section contains a directory of institutions offering graduate work in area and cultural studies, followed by an in-depth entry submitted by an institution that chose to prepare a detailed program description. Additional information about programs listed in the directory but not augmented by an in-depth entry may be obtained by writing directly to the dean of a graduate school or chair of a department at the address given in the directory.

For programs offering related work, see also in this book *Geography, History, Language and Literature, Political Science and International Affairs,* and *Sociology, Anthropology, and Archaeology.*

CONTENTS

Program Directories

African-American Studies 556
African Studies 558
American Indian/Native American Studies 560
American Studies 561
Asian-American Studies 567
Asian Studies 567
Canadian Studies 573
Cultural Studies 574
East European and Russian Studies 578
Ethnic Studies 579
Folklore 580
Gender Studies 581
Hispanic Studies 583
Holocaust and Genocide Studies 585
Jewish Studies 586
Latin American Studies 589
Near and Middle Eastern Studies 592
Northern Studies 596
Pacific Area/Pacific Rim Studies 596
Western European Studies 597
Women's Studies 599

Close-Up

Villanova University 607

See also:

American University—International Service 849
The Jewish Theological Seminary—Graduate Studies 511

African-American Studies

Boston University, Graduate School of Arts and Sciences, Program in African American Studies, Boston, MA 02215. Offers MA. *Students:* 4 full-time (3 women); includes 1 minority (African American), 2 international. Average age 25. 7 applicants, 57% accepted, 4 enrolled. *Degree requirements:* For master's, one foreign language, comprehensive exam. *Entrance requirements:* For master's, GRE General Test, 2 letters of recommendation. Additional exam requirements/recommendations for international students: Required—TOEFL (minimum score 550 paper-based; 213 computer-based). *Application deadline:* For fall admission, 7/1 for domestic and international students. Application fee: $70. Electronic applications accepted. *Expenses:* Tuition: Full-time $37,910; part-time $1184 per credit hour. Required fees: $386; $40 per semester. Part-time tuition and fees vary according to class time, course level, degree level and program. *Financial support:* Career-related internships or fieldwork, Federal Work-Study, scholarships/grants, and unspecified assistantships available. Support available to part-time students. Financial award application deadline: 1/15; financial award applicants required to submit FAFSA. *Unit head:* Allison Blakely, Director, 617-358-1420, Fax: 617-353-0455, E-mail: ablakely@bu.edu. *Application contact:* Katy Evans, Program Administrator, 617-358-1421, Fax: 617-353-0455, E-mail: kaevans@bu.edu.

Carnegie Mellon University, College of Humanities and Social Sciences, Department of History, Pittsburgh, PA 15213-3891. Offers African and African-American diaspora (PhD); culture and power (PhD); gender and the family (PhD); history (MA, MS); history and policy (MA); labor and politics (PhD); science, technology, medicine and environment (PhD). Part-time programs available. *Degree requirements:* For doctorate, oral and written comprehensive exams, dissertation defense. *Entrance requirements:* For doctorate, GRE General Test. Additional exam requirements/recommendations for international students: Required—TOEFL. Electronic applications accepted. *Faculty research:* Anthropology and history, African American history, technology/environment, cultural history analysis.

Clark Atlanta University, School of Arts and Sciences, Department of African-American Studies, Atlanta, GA 30314. Offers MA, DAH. Part-time programs available. *Faculty:* 1 full-time (0 women), 1 (woman) part-time/adjunct. *Students:* 12 full-time (5 women), 24 part-time (15 women); includes 30 minority (all African Americans), 4 international. Average age 37. 15 applicants, 93% accepted, 10 enrolled. In 2009, 2 master's, 1 doctorate awarded. *Degree requirements:* For master's, one foreign language, comprehensive exam, thesis optional; for doctorate, one foreign language, comprehensive exam, thesis/dissertation. *Entrance requirements:* For master's, GRE General Test, minimum GPA of 2.5. Additional exam requirements/recommendations for international students: Required—TOEFL (minimum score 500 paper-based; 173 computer-based). *Application deadline:* For fall admission, 4/1 for domestic and international students; for spring admission, 11/1 for domestic and international students. Applications are processed on a rolling basis. Application fee: $40 ($55 for international students). Electronic applications accepted. *Expenses:* Tuition: Full-time $12,240; part-time $680 per credit hour. Required fees: $710; $355 per semester. *Financial support:* In 2009–10, 10 fellowships were awarded; scholarships/grants also available. Financial award application deadline: 4/30; financial award applicants required to submit FAFSA. *Unit head:* Dr. Josephine Bradley, Chairperson, 404-880-6810, E-mail: jbradley@cau.edu. *Application contact:* Michelle Clark-Davis, Graduate Program Admissions, 404-880-6605, E-mail: cauadmissions@cau.edu.

Clark Atlanta University, School of Arts and Sciences, Department of Africana Women's Studies, Atlanta, GA 30314. Offers MA, DAH. Part-time programs available. *Faculty:* 1 (woman) full-time, 1 (woman) part-time/adjunct. *Students:* 5 full-time (all women), 6 part-time (5 women); includes 10 minority (all African Americans), 1 international. Average age 39. 10 applicants, 90% accepted, 1 enrolled. In 2009, 1 doctorate awarded. *Degree requirements:* For master's, one foreign language, comprehensive exam, thesis optional; for doctorate, one foreign language, comprehensive exam, thesis/dissertation. *Entrance requirements:* For master's, GRE General Test, minimum GPA of 2.5; for doctorate, GRE General Test, minimum graduate GPA of 3.0. Additional exam requirements/recommendations for international students: Required—TOEFL (minimum score 500 paper-based; 173 computer-based). *Application deadline:* For fall admission, 4/1 for domestic and international students; for spring admission, 11/1 for domestic and international students. Applications are processed on a rolling basis. Application fee: $40 ($55 for international students). Electronic applications accepted. *Expenses:* Tuition: Full-time $12,240; part-time $680 per credit hour. Required fees: $710; $355 per semester. *Financial support:* In 2009–10, 4 fellowships were awarded; scholarships/grants also available. Financial award application deadline: 4/30; financial award applicants required to submit FAFSA. *Faculty research:* Concerns of women of African descent globally. *Unit head:* Dr. Josephine Bradley, Chairperson, 404-880-6810, E-mail: jbradley@cau.edu. *Application contact:* Michelle Clark-Davis, Graduate Program Admissions, 404-880-6605, E-mail: cauadmissions@cau.edu.

Columbia University, Graduate School of Arts and Sciences, Program in African-American Studies, New York, NY 10027. Offers MA. Part-time programs available.

Cornell University, Graduate School, Graduate Fields of Arts and Sciences, Field of African and African-American Studies, Ithaca, NY 14853-0001. Offers African studies (MPS); African-American studies (MPS). *Faculty:* 27 full-time (10 women). *Students:* 12 full-time (9 women); includes 9 minority (7 African Americans, 2 Hispanic Americans), 1 international. Average age 28. 26 applicants, 27% accepted, 5 enrolled. In 2009, 13 master's awarded. *Degree requirements:* For master's, thesis. *Entrance requirements:* For master's, GRE General Test (recommended), 3 letters of recommendation. Additional exam requirements/recommendations for international students: Required—TOEFL (minimum score 550 paper-based; 213 computer-based; 77 iBT). *Application deadline:* For fall admission, 1/30 for domestic students. Application fee: $70. Electronic applications accepted. *Expenses:* Tuition: Full-time $29,500. Required fees: $70. Full-time tuition and fees vary according to degree level, program and student level. *Financial support:* In 2009–10, 5 fellowships with full tuition reimbursements were awarded; research assistantships, teaching assistantships with full tuition reimbursements, institutionally sponsored loans, scholarships/grants, health care benefits, tuition waivers (full and partial), and unspecified assistantships also available. Financial award applicants required to submit FAFSA. *Faculty research:* African-American literature, art, cinema and theater; African-American politics and public policy; African history, politics and art; Caribbean politics and Africana Diaspora. *Unit head:* Director of Graduate Studies, 607-255-4625, Fax: 607-255-0784. *Application contact:* Graduate Field Assistant, 607-255-4625, Fax: 607-255-0784, E-mail: spt1@cornell.edu.

Cornell University, Graduate School, Graduate Fields of Arts and Sciences, Field of English Language and Literature, Ithaca, NY 14853-0001. Offers African-American literature (PhD); American literature after 1865 (PhD); American literature to 1865 (PhD); American studies (PhD); colonial and postcolonial literature (PhD); creative writing (MFA); cultural studies (PhD); dramatic literature (PhD); English poetry (PhD); English Renaissance to 1660 (PhD); lesbian, bisexual, and gay literature studies (PhD); literary criticism and theory (PhD); nineteenth century (PhD); Old and Middle English (PhD); prose fiction (PhD); Restoration and eighteenth century (PhD); twentieth century (PhD); women's literature (PhD); MFA/PhD. *Faculty:* 74 full-time (35 women). *Students:* 100 full-time (55 women); includes 26 minority (9 African Americans, 3 American Indian/Alaska Native, 7 Asian Americans or Pacific Islanders, 7 Hispanic Americans), 11 international. Average age 28. 890 applicants, 4% accepted, 21 enrolled. In 2009, 21 master's, 12 doctorates awarded. Terminal master's awarded for partial completion of doctoral program. *Degree requirements:* For master's, one foreign language, thesis; for doctorate, one foreign language, comprehensive exam, thesis/dissertation, teaching experience. *Entrance requirements:* For master's, GRE General Test, 3 letters of recommendation, creative writing sample; for doctorate, GRE General Test, GRE Subject Test (English), 3 letters of recommendation, writing sample. Additional exam requirements/recommendations for international students: Required—TOEFL (minimum score 600 paper-based; 250 computer-based; 77 iBT). *Application deadline:* For fall admission, 1/10 for domestic students. Application fee: $70. Electronic applications accepted. *Expenses:* Tuition: Full-time $29,500. Required fees: $70. Full-time tuition and fees vary according to degree level, program and student level. *Financial support:* In 2009–10, 96 students received support, including 13 fellowships with full tuition reimbursements available, 8 teaching assistantships with full tuition reimbursements available; research assistantships with full tuition reimbursements available, institutionally sponsored loans, scholarships/grants, health care benefits, tuition waivers (full and partial), and unspecified assistantships also available. Financial award applicants required to submit FAFSA. *Faculty research:* English and American literature, women's writing, ethnic and post-colonial literature, critical theory, medievalism. *Unit head:* Director of Graduate Studies, 607-255-7989, Fax: 607-255-6661. *Application contact:* Graduate Field Assistant, 607-255-7989, Fax: 607-255-6661, E-mail: english_grad@cornell.edu.

Eastern Michigan University, Graduate School, College of Arts and Sciences, Department of African-American Studies, Ypsilanti, MI 48197. Offers Graduate Certificate. *Faculty:* 3 full-time (0 women). *Students:* 2 full-time (1 woman), 6 part-time (4 women); includes 6 minority (all African Americans). Average age 27. 8 applicants, 88% accepted, 5 enrolled. In 2009, 1 Graduate Certificate awarded. *Entrance requirements:* For degree, bachelor's degree with minimum GPA of 2.7, two letters of reference. *Application deadline:* Applications are processed on a rolling basis. Application fee: $35. Tuition and fees vary according to course level. *Unit head:* Dr. Victor Okafor, Head, 734-487-3460, Fax: 734-487-6891, E-mail: victor.okafor@emich.edu. *Application contact:* Dr. Robert Perry, Graduate Advisor, 734-487-3460, Fax: 734-487-6891, E-mail: robert.perry@emich.edu.

Florida Agricultural and Mechanical University, Division of Graduate Studies, Research, and Continuing Education, College of Arts and Sciences, Division of History and Political Sciences, Program in Applied Social Science, Tallahassee, FL 32307-3200. Offers African American history (MASS); criminal justice (MASS); economics (MASS); history (MASS); political science (MASS); public administration (MASS); public management (MASS); social work (MASS); sociology (MASS). Part-time programs available. *Faculty:* 17 full-time (2 women). *Students:* 54 full-time (42 women), 4 part-time (2 women); includes 57 minority (all African Americans). In 2009, 14 master's awarded. *Degree requirements:* For master's, thesis optional. *Entrance requirements:* For master's, GRE General Test, minimum GPA of 3.0. *Application deadline:* For fall admission, 5/18 for domestic students, 12/18 for international students; for spring admission, 11/12 for domestic students, 5/12 for international students. Application fee: $20. *Financial support:* Fellowships, research assistantships, career-related internships or fieldwork, Federal Work-Study, and tuition waivers (full) available. Financial award application deadline: 4/1. *Faculty research:* Southern history, black history, election trends, presidential history. *Unit head:* Dr. Gary Paul, Director, 850-599-3447. *Application contact:* Dr. Chanta M. Haywood, Dean of Graduate Studies, Research, and Continuing Education, 850-599-3315, Fax: 850-599-3727.

Harvard University, Graduate School of Arts and Sciences, Department of African and African American Studies, Cambridge, MA 02138. Offers PhD. *Expenses:* Tuition: Full-time $33,696. Required fees: $1126. Full-time tuition and fees vary according to program.

Indiana University Bloomington, University Graduate School, College of Arts and Sciences, Department of African American and African Diaspora Studies, Bloomington, IN 47405-7000. Offers MA. Part-time programs available. *Faculty:* 3 full-time (1 woman). *Students:* 18 full-time (12 women), 4 part-time (2 women); includes 18 minority (all African Americans), 4 international. Average age 28. 42 applicants, 43% accepted, 8 enrolled. In 2009, 7 master's awarded. *Entrance requirements:* For master's, GRE, minimum GPA of 3.0. Additional exam requirements/recommendations for international students: Required—TOEFL. *Application deadline:* For fall admission, 1/15 priority date for domestic students, 12/15 for international students; for spring admission, 9/1 for domestic and international students. Applications are processed on a rolling basis. Application fee: $55 ($65 for international students). Electronic applications accepted. *Financial support:* In 2009–10, 17 students received support, including 5 fellowships with tuition reimbursements available (averaging $15,000 per year), 6 teaching assistantships with tuition reimbursements available (averaging $11,300 per year). *Unit head:* Dr. Valerie Grim, Chair, 812-855-3875. *Application contact:* Yunika Jackson, Department Secretary, 812-855-3875, E-mail: ytjackso@indiana.edu.

Michigan State University, The Graduate School, College of Arts and Letters, Program in African American and African Studies, East Lansing, MI 48824. Offers MA, PhD. *Students:* 23 full-time (14 women), 2 part-time (both women); includes 24 minority (22 African Americans, 1 American Indian/Alaska Native, 1 Hispanic American), 1 international. Average age 29. 13 applicants, 23% accepted. In 2009, 1 master's, 3 doctorates awarded. *Entrance requirements:* Additional exam requirements/recommendations for international students: Required—TOEFL. Electronic applications accepted. *Expenses:* Tuition, state resident: part-time $478.25 per credit hour. Tuition, nonresident: part-time $966.50 per credit hour. Part-time tuition and fees vary according to program. *Financial support:* In 2009–10, 6 research assistantships with tuition reimbursements (averaging $5,967 per year), 3 teaching assistantships with tuition reimbursements (averaging $5,874 per year) were awarded. *Faculty research:* Black American and diasporic studies, comparative communities of color. *Unit head:* Dr. Geneva Smitherman, III, Acting Director, 517-432-0869, Fax: 517-432-6246, E-mail: smither4@msu.edu. *Application contact:* Linda Cornish, Office Manager, 517-432-0869, Fax: 517-432-6246, E-mail: aaas@msu.edu.

Morgan State University, School of Graduate Studies, College of Liberal Arts, Department of History and Geography, Baltimore, MD 21251. Offers African-American studies (MA); history (MA, PhD). Part-time and evening/weekend programs available. *Degree requirements:* For master's, comprehensive exam, thesis; for doctorate, comprehensive exam, thesis/dissertation. *Entrance requirements:* For master's, minimum GPA of 2.5; for doctorate, GRE or MAT. Additional exam requirements/recommendations for international students: Required—TOEFL (minimum score 550 paper-based; 213 computer-based). *Faculty research:* Women's history, African diaspora history, urban history.

North Carolina Agricultural and Technical State University, Graduate School, College of Arts and Sciences, Department of English, Program in English and Afro-American Literature, Greensboro, NC 27411. Offers MA. Part-time and evening/weekend programs available. *Degree requirements:* For master's, comprehensive exam, qualifying exam. *Entrance requirements:* For master's, GRE General Test, minimum GPA of 3.0.

Northwestern University, The Graduate School, Judd A. and Marjorie Weinberg College of Arts and Sciences, Department of African American Studies, Evanston, IL 60208. Offers PhD.

The Ohio State University, Graduate School, College of Humanities, Department of African-American and African Studies, Columbus, OH 43210. Offers MA. *Faculty:* 18. *Students:* 11 full-time (6 women); includes 7 minority (all African Americans). Average age 26. In 2009, 4 master's awarded. *Degree requirements:* For master's, comprehensive exam, internship or thesis. *Entrance requirements:* For master's, GRE General Test. Additional exam requirements/recommendations for international students: Required—TOEFL (minimum score 600 paper-based; 250 computer-based). *Application deadline:* For fall admission, 8/15 priority date for domestic students, 7/1 priority date for international students; for winter admission, 12/1 priority date for domestic students, 11/1 priority date for international students; for spring admission, 3/1 priority date for domestic students, 2/1 priority date for international students. Applications are processed on a rolling basis. Application fee: $40 ($50 for international students). Electronic applications accepted. *Expenses:* Tuition, state resident: full-time $10,683. Tuition, nonresident: full-time $25,923. Tuition and fees vary according to course load and program. *Financial support:* In 2009–10, 9 teaching assistantships were awarded; fellowships, research assistantships, Federal Work-Study, institutionally sponsored loans, and unspecified assistantships also available. Support available to part-time students. *Unit head:* James Upton,

Graduate Studies Committee Chair, E-mail: upton.2@osu.edu. *Application contact:* 614-292-9444, Fax: 614-292-3895, E-mail: domestic.grad@osu.edu.

Rutgers, The State University of New Jersey, New Brunswick, Graduate School-New Brunswick, Program in History, Piscataway, NJ 08854-8097. Offers African-American history (PhD); early American history (PhD); early modern European history (PhD); east Asian history (PhD); global and comparative history (PhD); history (PhD); history of diplomacy and foreign relations (PhD); history of technology, environment and health (PhD); history of the Atlantic cultures and African diaspora (PhD); Latin American history (PhD); medieval history (PhD); modern European history (PhD); nineteenth and twentieth century American history (PhD); women's and gender history (PhD). *Degree requirements:* For doctorate, thesis/dissertation. *Entrance requirements:* For doctorate, GRE General Test, sample of written work. Electronic applications accepted. *Faculty research:* American history, European history, Afro-American history, women's history, Latin American history.

Syracuse University, College of Arts and Sciences, Program in Pan-African Studies, Syracuse, NY 13244. Offers MA. *Students:* 15 full-time (11 women); includes 10 minority (all African Americans), 2 international. Average age 26. 21 applicants, 52% accepted, 9 enrolled. In 2009, 9 master's awarded. *Degree requirements:* For master's, thesis. *Entrance requirements:* For master's, GRE General Test. Additional exam requirements/recommendations for international students: Required—TOEFL (minimum score 100 iBT). *Application deadline:* For fall admission, 1/10 priority date for domestic and international students. Application fee: $75. Electronic applications accepted. *Expenses:* Tuition: Full-time $26,808; part-time $1117 per credit. Required fees: $1024. *Financial support:* Fellowships with tuition reimbursements available. Financial award application deadline: 1/1; financial award applicants required to submit FAFSA. *Unit head:* Dr. Linda Carter, Graduate Studies Director, 315-443-5599, E-mail: lcarty@syr.edu. *Application contact:* Aja Brown, Information Contact, 315-443-5599, E-mail: aabrow02@syr.edu.

Temple University, Graduate School, College of Liberal Arts, Department of African American Studies, Philadelphia, PA 19122-6096. Offers MA, PhD. Terminal master's awarded for partial completion of doctoral program. *Degree requirements:* For master's, comprehensive exam; for doctorate, one foreign language, thesis/dissertation, oral and written qualifying exams. *Entrance requirements:* For doctorate, MA in African American studies. Additional exam requirements/recommendations for international students: Required—TOEFL (minimum score 550 paper-based; 213 computer-based; 79 iBT). Electronic applications accepted. *Faculty research:* Afrocentric theory; African-American youth; centered drama, literature, and history; comparative analysis; South and West Africa; Nile Valley.

University at Albany, State University of New York, College of Arts and Sciences, Department of Africana Studies, Albany, NY 12222-0001. Offers African studies (MA); Afro-American studies (MA). Part-time and evening/weekend programs available. *Entrance requirements:* Additional exam requirements/recommendations for international students: Required—TOEFL (minimum score 550 paper-based; 213 computer-based). Electronic applications accepted. *Faculty research:* The black family, Afro-centricity in poetry, black women in U.S. literature, African economic development, African American history.

University of California, Berkeley, Graduate Division, College of Letters and Science, Department of African American Studies, Berkeley, CA 94720-1500. Offers PhD. *Faculty:* 4 full-time. *Students:* 27 full-time (16 women). Average age 30. 67 applicants, 4 enrolled. In 2009, 3 doctorates awarded. *Degree requirements:* For doctorate, one foreign language, thesis/dissertation. *Entrance requirements:* For doctorate, minimum GPA of 3.0, 3 letters of recommendation. Additional exam requirements/recommendations for international students: Required—TOEFL (minimum score 570 paper-based; 230 computer-based) or IELTS (minimum score 7). *Application deadline:* For fall admission, 12/15 for domestic students. Application fee: $70 ($90 for international students). *Financial support:* Fellowships with full tuition reimbursements, research assistantships with partial tuition reimbursements, teaching assistantships with partial tuition reimbursements, unspecified assistantships available. Financial award applicants required to submit FAFSA. *Faculty research:* Black influence on U. S. foreign policy, black intellectuals, ethnic space in urban society, representation in museums of African-Americans and British Americans during slavery. *Unit head:* Prof. Charles P. Henry, Chair, 510-643-7972, Fax: 510-642-7089, E-mail: ch_africanamerican@ls.berkeley.edu. *Application contact:* Margaret B. Wilkerson, Professor, 510-642-7084, E-mail: africam@berkeley.edu.

University of California, Los Angeles, Graduate Division, College of Letters and Science, Program in Afro-American Studies, Los Angeles, CA 90095. Offers MA, MA/JD. *Students:* 25 full-time (17 women); includes 24 minority (22 African Americans, 2 Hispanic Americans). Average age 29. 29 applicants, 48% accepted, 8 enrolled. In 2009, 14 master's awarded. *Degree requirements:* For master's, one foreign language, comprehensive exam or thesis. *Entrance requirements:* For master's, GRE General Test, minimum GPA of 3.0, sample of written work. *Application deadline:* For fall admission, 12/15 for domestic and international students. Application fee: $70 ($90 for international students). Electronic applications accepted. *Financial support:* In 2009–10, 24 fellowships with full and partial tuition reimbursements, 5 research assistantships with full and partial tuition reimbursements, 5 teaching assistantships with full and partial tuition reimbursements were awarded; Federal Work-Study, institutionally sponsored loans, scholarships/grants, health care benefits, tuition waivers (full and partial), and unspecified assistantships also available. Financial award application deadline: 3/1; financial award applicants required to submit FAFSA. *Unit head:* Brenda Stevenson, Chair, 310-825-9420. *Application contact:* Department Office, 310-825-9821, E-mail: idpstaff@bunche.ucla.edu.

The University of Iowa, Graduate College, College of Liberal Arts and Sciences, Program in African American World Studies, Iowa City, IA 52242-1316. Offers MA. *Degree requirements:* For master's, thesis optional, exam. *Entrance requirements:* For master's, GRE General Test, minimum GPA of 3.0. Additional exam requirements/recommendations for international students: Required—TOEFL (minimum score 550 paper-based; 213 computer-based; 81 iBT). Electronic applications accepted.

The University of Kansas, Graduate Studies, College of Liberal Arts and Sciences, Department of African and African-American Studies, Lawrence, KS 66045. Offers African and African-American studies (MA); African Studies (Graduate Certificate). Part-time programs available. *Faculty:* 11 full-time (5 women), 35 part-time/adjunct (18 women). *Students:* 3 full-time (2 women), 1 part-time (0 women); includes 3 minority (all African Americans). Average age 27. 8 applicants, 63% accepted, 4 enrolled. *Degree requirements:* For master's, variable foreign language requirement, thesis or alternative. *Entrance requirements:* For master's, GRE, all academic transcripts, 3 letters of recommendation, personal statement of purpose, writing sample. Additional exam requirements/recommendations for international students: Required—TOEFL. *Application deadline:* For fall admission, 5/1 for domestic students. Applications are processed on a rolling basis. Application fee: $45 ($55 for international students). Electronic applications accepted. *Expenses:* Tuition, state resident: full-time $6492; part-time $270.50 per credit hour. Tuition, nonresident: full-time $15,510; part-time $646.25 per credit hour. Required fees: $847; $70.56 per credit hour. Tuition and fees vary according to course load and program. *Faculty research:* African theatre, YaKuur culture, interracial communication, African development and urban planning, African literature, Muslim women in West Africa, identity formation in African and Disaporan settings, African American history, North African and Arab societies, civil rights. *Unit head:* Dr. Peter Ukpokodu, Chair, 785-864-3054, Fax: 785-864-5330, E-mail: afs@ku.edu. *Application contact:* Lisa Brown, Administrative Associate Sr, 785-864-3054, Fax: 785-864-5330, E-mail: lisabrown@ku.edu.

University of Louisville, Graduate School, College of Arts and Sciences, Department of Pan-African Studies, Louisville, KY 40292. Offers African and Diaspora studies (MA); African-American studies (MA); MA/MSW; MSSW/MA. Part-time programs available. *Faculty:* 12 full-time (6 women). *Students:* 14 full-time (10 women), 6 part-time (4 women); includes 15 minority (all African Americans), 2 international. Average age 29. 14 applicants, 57% accepted, 6 enrolled. In 2009, 3 master's awarded. *Degree requirements:* For master's, comprehensive exam, thesis optional. *Entrance requirements:* For master's, GRE General Test. Additional exam requirements/recommendations for international students: Recommended—TOEFL (minimum score 550 paper-based; 213 computer-based; 79 iBT). *Application deadline:* For fall admission, 10/15 for domestic and international students; for spring admission, 3/15 for domestic and international students. Application fee: $50. Electronic applications accepted. *Financial support:* In 2009–10, 10 students received support; teaching assistantships available. Financial award applicants required to submit FAFSA. *Faculty research:* African popular culture, black male identity development, education and retention, contemporary politics in Nigeria, poverty in the Caribbean. *Unit head:* Dr. Theresa Rajack-Talley, Chair, 502-852-4192, Fax: 502-852-5954, E-mail: tatall01@gwise.louisville.edu. *Application contact:* Dr. Theresa Rajack-Talley, Acting Graduate Studies Director, 502-852-4192, Fax: 502-852-5954, E-mail: tatall01@louisville.edu.

University of Massachusetts Amherst, Graduate School, College of Humanities and Fine Arts, Department of Afro-American Studies, Amherst, MA 01003. Offers MA, PhD. Part-time programs available. *Faculty:* 13 full-time (5 women). *Students:* 28 full-time (16 women), 1 part-time (0 women); includes 18 minority (17 African Americans, 1 Hispanic American), 3 international. Average age 32. 43 applicants, 21% accepted, 4 enrolled. In 2009, 3 doctorates awarded. Terminal master's awarded for partial completion of doctoral program. *Degree requirements:* For master's, thesis or alternative; for doctorate, comprehensive exam, thesis/dissertation. *Entrance requirements:* For doctorate, writing sample. Additional exam requirements/recommendations for international students: Required—TOEFL (minimum score 550 paper-based; 213 computer-based; 80 iBT), IELTS (minimum score 6.5). *Application deadline:* For fall admission, 1/15 for domestic and international students. Applications are processed on a rolling basis. Application fee: $50 ($65 for international students). Electronic applications accepted. *Expenses:* Tuition, state resident: full-time $2640; part-time $110 per credit. Tuition, nonresident: full-time $9936; part-time $414 per credit. Tuition and fees vary according to course load. *Financial support:* In 2009–10, 5 fellowships with full tuition reimbursements (averaging $6,000 per year), 6 research assistantships with full tuition reimbursements (averaging $4,950 per year), 5 teaching assistantships with full tuition reimbursements (averaging $14,516 per year) were awarded; career-related internships or fieldwork, Federal Work-Study, scholarships/grants, traineeships, health care benefits, tuition waivers (full), and unspecified assistantships also available. Support available to part-time students. Financial award application deadline: 1/15. *Unit head:* Dr. A. Yemisi Jimoh, Graduate Program Director, 413-545-2751, Fax: 413-545-0628. *Application contact:* Jean M. Ames, Supervisor of Admissions, 413-545-0722, Fax: 413-577-0100, E-mail: gradadm@grad.umass.edu.

University of Memphis, Graduate School, College of Arts and Sciences, Department of English, Memphis, TN 38152. Offers African-American literature (Graduate Certificate); applied linguistics (PhD); composition studies (PhD); creative writing (MFA); English as a second language (MA); linguistics (MA); literary and cultural studies (PhD), including African-American literature; literature (MA); professional writing (MA, PhD); teaching English as a second language (Graduate Certificate). Part-time and evening/weekend programs available. Post-baccalaureate distance learning degree programs offered (no on-campus study). *Faculty:* 31 full-time (15 women), 2 part-time/adjunct (both women). *Students:* 98 full-time (59 women), 99 part-time (66 women); includes 36 minority (28 African Americans, 5 Asian Americans or Pacific Islanders, 3 Hispanic Americans), 7 international. Average age 34. 128 applicants, 71% accepted, 29 enrolled. In 2009, 38 master's, 4 doctorates, 21 other advanced degrees awarded. Terminal master's awarded for partial completion of doctoral program. *Degree requirements:* For master's, one foreign language, comprehensive exam, thesis optional; for doctorate, 2 foreign languages, comprehensive exam, thesis/dissertation. *Entrance requirements:* For master's, GRE; for doctorate, GRE. Additional exam requirements/recommendations for international students: Required—TOEFL. *Application deadline:* For fall admission, 7/1 for domestic students; for spring admission, 10/15 for domestic students. Applications are processed on a rolling basis. Application fee: $35 ($60 for international students). Electronic applications accepted. *Expenses:* Tuition, state resident: full-time $6246; part-time $347 per credit hour. Tuition, nonresident: full-time $15,894; part-time $883 per credit hour. Required fees: $1160. Full-time tuition and fees vary according to course load, degree level and program. *Financial support:* In 2009–10, 123 students received support; research assistantships with full tuition reimbursements available, teaching assistantships with full tuition reimbursements available, Federal Work-Study, scholarships/grants, and unspecified assistantships available. Financial award application deadline: 2/15; financial award applicants required to submit FAFSA. *Faculty research:* Applied linguistis, British and American literature, professional writing, composition studies. *Unit head:* Dr. Eric C. Link, Chair, 901-678-2651, Fax: 901-678-2226, E-mail: eclink@memphis.edu. *Application contact:* Dr. Verner D. Mitchell, Director, Graduate Studies, 901-678-3099, Fax: 901-678-2226, E-mail: vdmtchll@memphis.edu.

University of Wisconsin–Madison, Graduate School, College of Letters and Science, Department of Afro-American Studies, Madison, WI 53706-1380. Offers MA. *Degree requirements:* For master's, thesis or alternative. *Entrance requirements:* For master's, bachelor's degree in related field, minimum GPA of 3.0. Additional exam requirements/recommendations for international students: Required—TOEFL. Electronic applications accepted. *Expenses:* Tuition, state resident: part-time $594 per credit. Tuition, nonresident: part-time $1504 per credit. Required fees: $65 per credit. Tuition and fees vary according to course load, program and reciprocity agreements. *Faculty research:* Afro American art, history, music, literature, and culture.

West Virginia University, Eberly College of Arts and Sciences, Department of History, Morgantown, WV 26506. Offers African history (MA, PhD); African-American history (MA, PhD); American history (MA, PhD); Appalachian/regional history (MA, PhD); East Asian history (MA, PhD); European history (MA, PhD); history of science and technology (MA, PhD); Latin American history (MA). Part-time programs available. *Degree requirements:* For master's, one foreign language, thesis (for some programs), oral exam, thesis defense; for doctorate, one foreign language, comprehensive exam, thesis/dissertation, dissertation defense. *Entrance requirements:* For master's, GRE General Test, minimum GPA of 3.0; for doctorate, GRE General Test. Additional exam requirements/recommendations for international students: Required—TOEFL (minimum score 550 paper-based), IELTS (minimum score 6.5). Electronic applications accepted. *Faculty research:* U.S., Appalachia, modern Europe, Africa, colonial and post-colonial societies.

Yale University, Graduate School of Arts and Sciences, Interdisciplinary Program in African-American Studies, New Haven, CT 06520. Offers PhD. *Entrance requirements:* For doctorate, GRE General Test.

African Studies

Boston University, Graduate School of Arts and Sciences, Department of International Relations, Boston, MA 02215. Offers African studies (Certificate); international relations (MA); international relations and environmental policy management (MA); international relations and international communication (MA); JD/MA; MBA/MA. *Students:* 66 full-time (41 women), 16 part-time (10 women); includes 7 minority (3 African Americans, 3 Asian Americans or Pacific Islanders, 1 Hispanic American), 16 international. Average age 27. 417 applicants, 59% accepted, 50 enrolled. In 2009, 43 master's awarded. *Degree requirements:* For master's, one foreign language, comprehensive exam, thesis. *Entrance requirements:* For master's, GRE General Test, 3 letters of recommendation; for Certificate, GRE General Test. Additional exam requirements/recommendations for international students: Required—TOEFL (minimum score 600 paper-based; 250 computer-based). *Application deadline:* For fall admission, 4/15 for domestic and international students; for spring admission, 10/15 for domestic and international students. Application fee: $70. Electronic applications accepted. *Expenses:* Tuition: Full-time $37,910; part-time $1184 per credit hour. Required fees: $386; $40 per semester. Part-time tuition and fees vary according to class time, course level, degree level and program. *Financial support:* In 2009–10, 17 students received support. Federal Work-Study, scholarships/grants, and unspecified assistantships available. Support available to part-time students. Financial award application deadline: 1/15; financial award applicants required to submit FAFSA. *Unit head:* Dr. Erik Goldstein, Chairman, 617-353-9280, Fax: 617-353-9290, E-mail: goldstee@bu.edu. *Application contact:* Michael Williams, Graduate Program Administrator, 617-353-9349, Fax: 617-353-9290, E-mail: mawillia@bu.edu.

California State University, Long Beach, Graduate Studies, College of Liberal Arts, Department of History, Long Beach, CA 90840. Offers Africa and the Middle East (MA); ancient/Medieval Europe (MA); Asia (MA); Latin America (MA); modern Europe (MA); United States (MA); world (MA). Part-time and evening/weekend programs available. *Faculty:* 9 full-time (6 women), 1 (woman) part-time/adjunct. *Students:* 10 full-time (3 women), 56 part-time (21 women); includes 19 minority (2 African Americans, 1 American Indian/Alaska Native, 4 Asian Americans or Pacific Islanders, 12 Hispanic Americans), 1 international. Average age 31. 40 applicants, 50% accepted, 11 enrolled. *Degree requirements:* For master's, one foreign language, comprehensive exam or thesis. *Application deadline:* For fall admission, 3/1 for domestic students. Applications are processed on a rolling basis. Application fee: $55. Electronic applications accepted. *Expenses:* Required fees: $1802 per semester. Part-time tuition and fees vary according to course load. *Financial support:* Research assistantships, Federal Work-Study, institutionally sponsored loans, and scholarships/grants available. Financial award application deadline: 3/2. *Faculty research:* All periods of European and American history, recent Asian and African history. *Unit head:* Dr. Nancy Quam-Wickham, Department Chair, 562-985-4431, Fax: 562-985-5431, E-mail: quamwick@csulb.edu. *Application contact:* Dr. Houri Berberian, Graduate Advisor, 562-985-4524, Fax: 562-985-4431, E-mail: hberber@csulb.edu.

Carnegie Mellon University, College of Humanities and Social Sciences, Department of History, Pittsburgh, PA 15213-3891. Offers African and African-American diaspora (PhD); culture and power (PhD); gender and the family (PhD); history (MA, MS); history and policy (MA); labor and politics (PhD); science, technology, medicine and environment (PhD). Part-time programs available. *Degree requirements:* For doctorate, oral and written comprehensive exams, dissertation defense. *Entrance requirements:* For doctorate, GRE General Test. Additional exam requirements/recommendations for international students: Required—TOEFL. Electronic applications accepted. *Faculty research:* Anthropology and history, African American history, technology/environment, cultural history analysis.

Claremont Graduate University, Graduate Programs, School of Arts and Humanities, Department of History, Claremont, CA 91711-6160. Offers Africana history (Certificate); American studies and U.S. history (MA, PhD); archival studies (MA); early modern studies (MA, PhD); European studies (MA, PhD); oral history (MA, PhD); MBA/MA; MBA/PhD. *Faculty:* 4 full-time (2 women). *Students:* 69 full-time (31 women), 5 part-time (3 women); includes 13 minority (1 African American, 4 Asian Americans or Pacific Islanders, 8 Hispanic Americans), 2 international. Average age 36. In 2009, 10 master's, 3 doctorates awarded. Terminal master's awarded for partial completion of doctoral program. *Entrance requirements:* For master's and doctorate, GRE General Test. Additional exam requirements/recommendations for international students: Required—TOEFL (minimum score 550 paper-based; 213 computer-based; 80 iBT). *Application deadline:* For fall admission, 2/1 priority date for domestic students. Applications are processed on a rolling basis. Application fee: $60. Electronic applications accepted. *Expenses:* Tuition: Full-time $35,046; part-time $1524 per credit. Required fees: $161 per semester. *Financial support:* Fellowships, research assistantships, Federal Work-Study, institutionally sponsored loans, and scholarships/grants available. Support available to part-time students. Financial award application deadline: 2/15; financial award applicants required to submit FAFSA. *Faculty research:* Intellectual and social history, cultural studies, gender studies, Western history, Chicano history. *Unit head:* Janet Farrell Brodie, Chair, 909-621-8880, Fax: 909-621-8609, E-mail: janet.brodie@cgu.edu. *Application contact:* Susan Hampson, Admissions Coordinator, 909-607-1278, E-mail: humanities@cgu.edu.

Claremont Graduate University, Graduate Programs, School of Educational Studies, Claremont, CA 91711-6160. Offers Africana education (Certificate); education and policy (MA, PhD); higher education/student affairs (MA, PhD); human development (MA, PhD); public school administration (MA, PhD); quantitative evaluation (MA, PhD); special education (MA, PhD); teacher education (MA); teaching and learning (MA, PhD); urban leadership (PhD); MBA/PhD. Part-time programs available. *Faculty:* 18 full-time (12 women), 1 part-time/adjunct (0 women). *Students:* 279 full-time (190 women), 174 part-time (122 women); includes 196 minority (50 African Americans, 1 American Indian/Alaska Native, 37 Asian Americans or Pacific Islanders, 108 Hispanic Americans), 10 international. Average age 37. In 2009, 84 master's, 23 doctorates awarded. Terminal master's awarded for partial completion of doctoral program. *Entrance requirements:* For master's and doctorate, GRE General Test. Additional exam requirements/recommendations for international students: Required—TOEFL (minimum score 550 paper-based; 213 computer-based; 80 iBT). *Application deadline:* For fall admission, 2/1 priority date for domestic students. Applications are processed on a rolling basis. Application fee: $60. Electronic applications accepted. *Expenses:* Tuition: Full-time $35,046; part-time $1524 per credit. Required fees: $161 per semester. *Financial support:* Fellowships, research assistantships, Federal Work-Study, institutionally sponsored loans, and scholarships/grants available. Support available to part-time students. Financial award application deadline: 2/15; financial award applicants required to submit FAFSA. *Faculty research:* Education administration, K-12 and higher education, multicultural education, education policy, diversity in higher education, faculty issues. *Unit head:* Margaret Grogan, Dean, 909-621-8075, Fax: 909-621-8734, E-mail: margaret.grogan@cgu.edu. *Application contact:* Nicole Kouyoumdjian, Director of External Affairs, 909-607-8493, Fax: 909-621-8734, E-mail: nicole.kouyoumdjian@cgu.edu.

Columbia University, School of International and Public Affairs, Institute of African Studies, New York, NY 10027. Offers Certificate. Students must be enrolled in a separate graduate degree program at Columbia University. Electronic applications accepted.

Cornell University, Graduate School, Graduate Fields of Arts and Sciences, Field of African and African-American Studies, Ithaca, NY 14853-0001. Offers African studies (MPS); African-American studies (MPS). *Faculty:* 27 full-time (10 women). *Students:* 12 full-time (9 women); includes 9 minority (7 African Americans, 2 Hispanic Americans), 1 international. Average age 28. 26 applicants, 27% accepted, 5 enrolled. In 2009, 13 master's awarded. *Degree requirements:* For master's, thesis. *Entrance requirements:* For master's, GRE General Test (recommended), 3 letters of recommendation. Additional exam requirements/recommendations for international students: Required—TOEFL (minimum score 550 paper-based; 213 computer-based; 77 iBT). *Application deadline:* For fall admission, 1/30 for domestic students. Application fee: $70. Electronic applications accepted. *Expenses:* Tuition: Full-time $29,500. Required fees: $70. Full-time tuition and fees vary according to degree level, program and student level. *Financial support:* In 2009–10, 5 fellowships with full tuition reimbursements were awarded; research assistantships, teaching assistantships with full tuition reimbursements, institutionally sponsored loans, scholarships/grants, health care benefits, tuition waivers (full and partial), and unspecified assistantships also available. Financial award applicants required to submit FAFSA. *Faculty research:* African-American literature, art, cinema and theater; African-American politics and public policy; African history, politics and art; Caribbean politics and Africana Diaspora. *Unit head:* Director of Graduate Studies, 607-255-4625, Fax: 607-255-0784. *Application contact:* Graduate Field Assistant, 607-255-4625, Fax: 607-255-0784, E-mail: spt1@cornell.edu.

Cornell University, Graduate School, Graduate Fields of Arts and Sciences, Field of History, Ithaca, NY 14853-0001. Offers African history (MA, PhD); American history (MA, PhD); ancient history (MA, PhD); early modern European history (MA, PhD); English history (MA, PhD); French history (MA, PhD); German history (MA, PhD); history of science (MA, PhD); Latin American history (MA, PhD); medieval Chinese history (MA, PhD); medieval history (MA, PhD); modern Chinese history (MA, PhD); modern European history (MA, PhD); modern Japanese history (MA, PhD); premodern Islamic history (MA, PhD); premodern Japanese history (MA, PhD); Renaissance history (MA, PhD); Russian history (MA, PhD); Southeast Asian history (MA, PhD). *Faculty:* 62 full-time (19 women). *Students:* 67 full-time (33 women); includes 10 minority (4 African Americans, 3 Asian Americans or Pacific Islanders, 3 Hispanic Americans), 24 international. Average age 31. 195 applicants, 7% accepted, 10 enrolled. In 2009, 11 master's, 3 doctorates awarded. Terminal master's awarded for partial completion of doctoral program. *Degree requirements:* For master's, thesis; for doctorate, 2 foreign languages, comprehensive exam, thesis/dissertation, 1 year of teaching experience. *Entrance requirements:* For master's and doctorate, GRE General Test, writing sample, 3 letters of recommendation. Additional exam requirements/recommendations for international students: Required—TOEFL (minimum score 550 paper-based; 213 computer-based; 77 iBT). *Application deadline:* For fall admission, 1/15 for domestic students. Application fee: $70. Electronic applications accepted. *Expenses:* Tuition: Full-time $29,500. Required fees: $70. Full-time tuition and fees vary according to degree level, program and student level. *Financial support:* In 2009–10, 54 students received support, including 8 fellowships with full tuition reimbursements available; research assistantships with full tuition reimbursements available, teaching assistantships with full tuition reimbursements available, institutionally sponsored loans, scholarships/grants, health care benefits, tuition waivers (full and partial), and unspecified assistantships also available. Financial award applicants required to submit FAFSA. *Unit head:* Director of Graduate Studies, 607-255-6738, Fax: 607-255-0469. *Application contact:* Graduate Field Assistant, 607-255-6738, Fax: 607-255-0469, E-mail: history_grad_info@cornell.edu.

Florida International University, College of Arts and Sciences, Program in African-New World Studies, Miami, FL 33199. Offers MA. Part-time and evening/weekend programs available. *Faculty:* 1 full-time (0 women). *Students:* 4 full-time (3 women), 3 part-time (1 woman); includes 3 minority (2 African Americans, 1 Hispanic American). Average age 30. 7 applicants, 14% accepted, 1 enrolled. In 2009, 3 master's awarded. Terminal master's awarded for partial completion of doctoral program. *Degree requirements:* For master's, one foreign language, thesis optional, minimum GPA of 3.0. *Entrance requirements:* For master's, GRE General Test, BA with minimum GPA of 3.0, 2 letters of recommendation, examples of written work. Additional exam requirements/recommendations for international students: Required—TOEFL (minimum score 80 iBT). *Application deadline:* For fall admission, 2/1 for domestic and international students; for spring admission, 10/1 for domestic students, 9/1 for international students. Application fee: $30. Electronic applications accepted. *Expenses:* Tuition, state resident: full-time $8008; part-time $4004 per year. Tuition, nonresident: full-time $20,104; part-time $10,052 per year. Required fees: $298; $149 per term. *Financial support:* In 2009–10, 1 student received support, including 3 teaching assistantships with full tuition reimbursements available (averaging $8,000 per year); institutionally sponsored loans, scholarships/grants and unspecified assistantships also available. Financial award application deadline: 3/1; financial award applicants required to submit FAFSA. *Faculty research:* African Diaspora in Latin America; Haitian creole phonology and culture; racial/ethnic minority sexual health; African American labor and southern history; gendered perspective of the development of racial science. *Unit head:* Dr. Jean Muteba Rahier, Director, African—African Diaspora Studies, 305-348-6860, Fax: 305-348-3270, E-mail: africana@fiu.edu. *Application contact:* Dr. Alex Lichtenstein, Director of Graduate Studies, 305-348-1535, Fax: 305-348-3270, E-mail: africana@fiu.edu.

Harvard University, Graduate School of Arts and Sciences, Department of African and African American Studies, Cambridge, MA 02138. Offers PhD. *Expenses:* Tuition: Full-time $33,696. Required fees: $1126. Full-time tuition and fees vary according to program.

Howard University, Graduate School, Department of African Studies, Washington, DC 20059-0002. Offers MA, PhD. Part-time programs available. *Degree requirements:* For master's, one foreign language, comprehensive exam, thesis, internship; for doctorate, 2 foreign languages, comprehensive exam, thesis/dissertation, field research for some. *Entrance requirements:* For master's, GRE General Test, minimum GPA of 3.0; for doctorate, GRE General Test, minimum GPA of 3.5. Electronic applications accepted. *Faculty research:* African literature and film, economics of Africa, international relations, public policy analysis, gender.

Indiana University Bloomington, University Graduate School, College of Arts and Sciences, African Studies Program, Bloomington, IN 47405-7000. Offers MA. *Students:* 5 full-time (4 women), 1 part-time (0 women); includes 2 minority (both African Americans), 1 international. Average age 30. 20 applicants, 70% accepted.Application fee: $55 ($65 for international students). *Financial support:* In 2009–10, 4 students received support, including 3 fellowships with tuition reimbursements available (averaging $15,000 per year). *Unit head:* Dr. Samuel Obeng, Director, 812-855-8284, E-mail: sobeng@indiana.edu. *Application contact:* Sue Hanson, Graduate Secretary, 812-855-8284, E-mail: shanson@indiana.edu.

Michigan State University, The Graduate School, College of Arts and Letters, Program in African American and African Studies, East Lansing, MI 48824. Offers MA, PhD. *Students:* 23 full-time (14 women), 2 part-time (both women); includes 24 minority (22 African Americans, 1 American Indian/Alaska Native, 1 Hispanic American), 1 international. Average age 29. 13 applicants, 23% accepted. In 2009, 1 master's, 3 doctorates awarded. *Entrance requirements:* Additional exam requirements/recommendations for international students: Required—TOEFL. Electronic applications accepted. *Expenses:* Tuition, state resident: part-time $478.25 per credit hour. Tuition, nonresident: part-time $966.50 per credit hour. Part-time tuition and fees vary according to program. *Financial support:* In 2009–10, 6 research assistantships with tuition reimbursements (averaging $5,967 per year), 3 teaching assistantships with tuition reimbursements (averaging $5,874 per year) were awarded. *Faculty research:* Black American and diasporic studies, comparative communities of color. *Unit head:* Dr. Geneva Smitherman, III, Acting Director, 517-432-0869, Fax: 517-432-6246, E-mail: smither4@msu.edu. *Application contact:* Linda Cornish, Office Manager, 517-432-0869, Fax: 517-432-6246, E-mail: aaas@msu.edu.

New York University, Graduate School of Arts and Science, Department of History, New York, NY 10012-1019. Offers African diaspora (PhD); African history (PhD); archival management and historical editing (Advanced Certificate); Atlantic history (PhD); French studies/history (PhD); Hebrew and Judaic studies/history (PhD); history (MA, PhD), including Europe (PhD), Latin American and the Caribbean (PhD), United States (PhD), women's history (MA); Middle Eastern history (MA); Middle Eastern studies/history (PhD); public history (Advanced Certificate); world history (MA); JD/MA; MA/Advanced Certificate. Part-time programs available. *Faculty:* 43 full-time (19 women). *Students:* 141 full-time (87 women), 43 part-time (35 women); includes 33 minority (20 African Americans, 5 Asian Americans or Pacific Islanders, 8 Hispanic Americans), 32 international. Average age 30. 406 applicants, 30% accepted, 51 enrolled. In

2009, 21 master's, 10 doctorates, 4 other advanced degrees awarded. Terminal master's awarded for partial completion of doctoral program. *Degree requirements:* For master's, seminar paper; for doctorate, one foreign language, thesis/dissertation, oral and written exams; for Advanced Certificate, internship. *Entrance requirements:* For master's, GRE General Test, minimum GPA of 3.0, writing sample; for doctorate, GRE. Additional exam requirements/recommendations for international students: Required—TOEFL. *Application deadline:* For fall admission, 12/12 for domestic students. Application fee: $90. *Expenses:* Tuition: Full-time $30,528; part-time $1272 per credit. Required fees: $2177. *Financial support:* Fellowships with tuition reimbursements, research assistantships, teaching assistantships with tuition reimbursements, career-related internships or fieldwork, Federal Work-Study, institutionally sponsored loans, scholarships/grants, health care benefits, and unspecified assistantships available. Financial award application deadline: 12/12; financial award applicants required to submit FAFSA. *Faculty research:* African, East Asian, Medieval, early modern, and modern European history; U.S. history; African and African Diaspora; Latin American history; Atlantic World. *Unit head:* Joanna Waley-Cohen, Chair, 212-998-8600, Fax: 212-995-4017, E-mail: history.dept@nyu.edu. *Application contact:* Barbara Weinstein, Director of Graduate Studies, 212-998-8600, Fax: 212-995-4017, E-mail: history.dept@nyu.edu.

New York University, Graduate School of Arts and Science, Program in Africana Studies, New York, NY 10012-1019. Offers MA. *Students:* 8 full-time (all women), 6 part-time (4 women); includes 9 minority (all African Americans), 3 international. Average age 25. 36 applicants, 47% accepted, 8 enrolled. In 2009, 2 master's awarded. *Degree requirements:* For master's, thesis or alternative. *Entrance requirements:* For master's, GRE, sample of written work. Additional exam requirements/recommendations for international students: Required—TOEFL. *Application deadline:* For fall admission, 1/4 priority date for domestic students. Application fee: $90. *Expenses:* Tuition: Full-time $30,528; part-time $1272 per credit. Required fees: $2177. *Financial support:* Fellowships with tuition reimbursements, Federal Work-Study and institutionally sponsored loans available. Financial award application deadline: 1/4; financial award applicants required to submit FAFSA. *Faculty research:* Pan-Africanism, black urban studies, film and literature of black Diaspora, cultural politics and theory, politics of identity. *Unit head:* Awam Amkpa, Director, 212-992-9650, Fax: 212-995-4665, E-mail: africana@nyu.edu. *Application contact:* Jennifer Morgan, Director of Graduate Studies, 212-998-9650, Fax: 212-995-4665, E-mail: africana@nyu.edu.

New York University, Graduate School of Arts and Science, Program in Museum Studies, New York, NY 10012-1019. Offers museum studies (MA, Advanced Certificate), including Africana studies (MA), Hebrew and Judaic studies (MA), Latin American and Caribbean studies (MA), Near Eastern studies (MA). Part-time and evening/weekend programs available. *Students:* 62 full-time (57 women), 23 part-time (21 women); includes 13 minority (1 African American, 2 American Indian/Alaska Native, 3 Asian Americans or Pacific Islanders, 7 Hispanic Americans), 15 international. Average age 27. 220 applicants, 52% accepted, 37 enrolled. In 2009, 37 master's awarded. *Entrance requirements:* For degree, master's degree or PhD. Additional exam requirements/recommendations for international students: Required—TOEFL. *Application deadline:* For fall admission, 2/1 for domestic students; for spring admission, 11/1 for domestic students. Application fee: $90. *Expenses:* Tuition: Full-time $30,528; part-time $1272 per credit. Required fees: $2177. *Financial support:* Application deadline: 2/1. *Faculty research:* Modern and contemporary art, history of museums and exhibitions, conservation of cultural materials, museum anthropology, ethnography. *Unit head:* Haidy Geismar, Director, 212-998-8080, Fax: 212-995-4185, E-mail: museum.studies@nyu.edu. *Application contact:* Tatiana Kamorina, Department Administrator, 212-998-8080, Fax: 212-995-4185, E-mail: museum.studies@nyu.edu.

Northwestern University, The Graduate School, Program of African Studies, Evanston, IL 60208. Offers Certificate. *Degree requirements:* For Certificate, one foreign language. *Faculty research:* Collapsing states in Africa, HIV/AIDS in Africa, Islam in Africa, African philosophy.

The Ohio State University, Graduate School, College of Humanities, Department of African-American and African Studies, Columbus, OH 43210. Offers MA. *Faculty:* 18. *Students:* 11 full-time (6 women); includes 7 minority (all African Americans). Average age 26. In 2009, 4 master's awarded. *Degree requirements:* For master's, comprehensive exam, internship or thesis. *Entrance requirements:* For master's, GRE General Test. Additional exam requirements/recommendations for international students: Required—TOEFL (minimum score 600 paper-based; 250 computer-based). *Application deadline:* For fall admission, 8/15 priority date for domestic students, 7/1 priority date for international students; for winter admission, 12/1 priority date for domestic students, 11/1 priority date for international students; for spring admission, 3/1 priority date for domestic students, 2/1 priority date for international students. Applications are processed on a rolling basis. Application fee: $40 ($50 for international students). Electronic applications accepted. *Expenses:* Tuition, state resident: full-time $10,683. Tuition, nonresident: full-time $25,923. Tuition and fees vary according to course load and program. *Financial support:* In 2009–10, 9 teaching assistantships were awarded; fellowships, research assistantships, Federal Work-Study, institutionally sponsored loans, and unspecified assistantships also available. Support available to part-time students. *Unit head:* James Upton, Graduate Studies Committee Chair, E-mail: upton.2@osu.edu. *Application contact:* 614-292-9444, Fax: 614-292-3895, E-mail: domestic.grad@osu.edu.

Ohio University, Graduate College, Center for International Studies, Program in African Studies, Athens, OH 45701. Offers MA. Part-time programs available. *Faculty:* 21 full-time (7 women). *Students:* 31 full-time (20 women), 1 (woman) part-time; includes 6 minority (all African Americans), 18 international. Average age 30. 56 applicants, 68% accepted, 14 enrolled. In 2009, 25 master's awarded. *Degree requirements:* For master's, one foreign language, thesis optional. *Entrance requirements:* For master's, minimum GPA of 3.0. Additional exam requirements/recommendations for international students: Required—TOEFL (minimum score 550 paper-based; 213 computer-based; 80 iBT), IELTS (minimum score 6.5). *Application deadline:* For fall admission, 1/1 for domestic and international students. Application fee: $50 ($55 for international students). *Expenses:* Tuition, state resident: full-time $7839; part-time $323 per quarter hour. Tuition, nonresident: full-time $15,831; part-time $654 per quarter hour. Required fees: $2931. *Financial support:* In 2009–10, fellowships with full tuition reimbursements (averaging $15,000 per year), research assistantships with full tuition reimbursements (averaging $11,499 per year), teaching assistantships with full tuition reimbursements (averaging $11,499 per year) were awarded; Federal Work-Study, institutionally sponsored loans, scholarships/grants, tuition waivers (partial), and unspecified assistantships also available. Financial award application deadline: 1/1. *Faculty research:* African social sciences and the humanities. Total annual research expenditures: $110,000. *Unit head:* Dr. William Stephen Howard, Director, E-mail: showard1@ohio.edu. *Application contact:* Joan Kraynanski, Administrative Assistant, 740-593-1840, Fax: 740-593-1837, E-mail: kraynans@ohio.edu.

Rice University, Graduate Programs, School of Humanities, Department of Religious Studies, Houston, TX 77251-1892. Offers African religions (PhD); African-American religions (PhD); contemplative studies (PhD); ghosticism, esotericism, mysticism (PhD); Islam (PhD); Jewish thought and philosophy (PhD); modern Christianity in thought and popular culture (PhD); psychology of religion (PhD); the Bible and beyond (PhD). *Faculty:* 11 full-time (3 women), 2 part-time/adjunct (both women). *Students:* 37 full-time (13 women); includes 10 minority (9 African Americans, 1 Asian American or Pacific Islander), 9 international. Average age 31. 42 applicants, 14% accepted, 6 enrolled. In 2009, 2 doctorates awarded. *Degree requirements:* For doctorate, 2 foreign languages, comprehensive exam, thesis/dissertation. *Entrance requirements:* For doctorate, GRE, letters of recommendation, writing sample. Additional exam requirements/recommendations for international students: Required—TOEFL (minimum score 600 paper-based; 90 iBT). *Application deadline:* For fall admission, 1/1 for domestic students, 1/15 for international students. Application fee: $70. Electronic applications accepted. *Financial support:* In 2009–10, 14 fellowships (averaging $15,900 per year) were awarded. Financial award application deadline: 5/15; financial award applicants required to submit FAFSA. *Faculty research:* Origins and historical development of Islam, history of Christianity, the study of comparative religion, African-American religion, religion and culture. Total annual research expenditures: $46,514. *Unit head:* Prof. William B. Parsons, Associate Professor, Religious Studies, 713-348-2712, Fax: 713-348-5486, E-mail: pars@rice.edu. *Application contact:* Sylvia Louie, Senior Department Coordinator, 713-348-5201, Fax: 713-348-5486, E-mail: reli@rice.edu.

Rutgers, The State University of New Jersey, New Brunswick, Graduate School-New Brunswick, Program in History, Piscataway, NJ 08854-8097. Offers African-American history (PhD); early American history (PhD); early modern European history (PhD); east Asian history (PhD); global and comparative history (PhD); history (PhD); history of diplomacy and foreign relations (PhD); history of technology, environment and health (PhD); history of the Atlantic cultures and African diaspora (PhD); Latin American history (PhD); medieval history (PhD); modern European history (PhD); nineteenth and twentieth century American history (PhD); women's and gender history (PhD). *Degree requirements:* For doctorate, thesis/dissertation. *Entrance requirements:* For doctorate, GRE General Test, sample of written work. Electronic applications accepted. *Faculty research:* American history, European history, Afro-American history, women's history, Latin American history.

St. John's University, St. John's College of Liberal Arts and Sciences, Institute of Asian Studies, Queens, NY 11439. Offers Asian and African cultural studies (Adv C); Asian studies (Adv C); Chinese studies (MA, Adv C); East Asian culture studies (Adv C); East Asian studies (MA). Part-time and evening/weekend programs available. *Students:* 8 full-time (6 women), 6 part-time (5 women); includes 5 minority (3 Asian Americans or Pacific Islanders, 2 Hispanic Americans), 8 international. Average age 30. 22 applicants, 68% accepted, 6 enrolled. In 2009, 6 master's awarded. *Degree requirements:* For master's, one foreign language, comprehensive exam, thesis optional. *Entrance requirements:* For master's, 18 hours of course work in the field, minimum GPA of 3.0. Additional exam requirements/recommendations for international students: Required—TOEFL (minimum score 500 paper-based; 173 computer-based; 61 iBT), IELTS (minimum score 5.5). *Application deadline:* For fall admission, 5/1 priority date for domestic and international students; for spring admission, 11/1 priority date for domestic and international students. Applications are processed on a rolling basis. Application fee: $70. Electronic applications accepted. *Expenses:* Tuition: Full-time $16,290; part-time $905 per credit. Required fees: $300; $150 per semester. Tuition and fees vary according to program. *Financial support:* Research assistantships, scholarships/grants available. Support available to part-time students. Financial award application deadline: 3/1; financial award applicants required to submit FAFSA. *Faculty research:* East Asian philosophy and religion, Chinese language and literature, Japanese language, modern Japan, Chinese art and history. *Unit head:* Dr. Bernadette Li, Chair, 718-990-1657, E-mail: lib@stjohns.edu. *Application contact:* Kathleen Davis, Director of Graduate Admission, 718-990-2790, Fax: 718-990-5686, E-mail: gradhelp@stjohns.edu.

Stony Brook University, State University of New York, Graduate School, College of Arts and Sciences, Department of Africana Studies, Stony Brook, NY 11794. Offers MA. *Degree requirements:* For master's, research thesis project, research seminar. *Entrance requirements:* For master's, GRE General Test, minimum GPA of 3.0, 3 letters of recommendation. *Expenses:* Tuition, state resident: full-time $8370; part-time $349 per credit. Tuition, nonresident: full-time $13,250; part-time $552 per credit. Required fees: $933. *Unit head:* Floris Cash, Chairperson, 631-632-7472. *Application contact:* Anthony Hurley, Graduate Program Director, 631-632-1366.

Syracuse University, College of Arts and Sciences, Program in Pan-African Studies, Syracuse, NY 13244. Offers MA. *Students:* 15 full-time (11 women); includes 10 minority (all African Americans), 2 international. Average age 26. 21 applicants, 52% accepted, 9 enrolled. In 2009, 9 master's awarded. *Degree requirements:* For master's, thesis. *Entrance requirements:* For master's, GRE General Test. Additional exam requirements/recommendations for international students: Required—TOEFL (minimum score 100 iBT). *Application deadline:* For fall admission, 1/10 priority date for domestic and international students. Application fee: $75. Electronic applications accepted. *Expenses:* Tuition: Full-time $26,808; part-time $1117 per credit. Required fees: $1024. *Financial support:* Fellowships with tuition reimbursements available. Financial award application deadline: 1/1; financial award applicants required to submit FAFSA. *Unit head:* Dr. Linda Carter, Graduate Studies Director, 315-443-5599, E-mail: lcarty@syr.edu. *Application contact:* Aja Brown, Information Contact, 315-443-5599, E-mail: aabrow02@syr.edu.

University at Albany, State University of New York, College of Arts and Sciences, Department of Africana Studies, Albany, NY 12222-0001. Offers African studies (MA); Afro-American studies (MA). Part-time and evening/weekend programs available. *Entrance requirements:* Additional exam requirements/recommendations for international students: Required—TOEFL (minimum score 550 paper-based; 213 computer-based). Electronic applications accepted. *Faculty research:* The black family, Afro-centricity in poetry, black women in U.S. literature, African economic development, African American history.

University of California, Los Angeles, Graduate Division, International Institute, Program in African Studies, Los Angeles, CA 90095. Offers MA, MPH/MA. *Students:* 15 full-time (8 women); includes 5 minority (all African Americans). Average age 29. 19 applicants, 47% accepted, 6 enrolled. In 2009, 6 master's awarded. *Degree requirements:* For master's, one foreign language, comprehensive exam or thesis. *Entrance requirements:* For master's, GRE General Test, minimum GPA of 3.0, sample of research writing. *Application deadline:* For fall admission, 12/15 for domestic and international students. Application fee: $70 ($90 for international students). Electronic applications accepted. *Financial support:* In 2009–10, 11 fellowships with full and partial tuition reimbursements, 5 research assistantships with full and partial tuition reimbursements, 6 teaching assistantships with full and partial tuition reimbursements were awarded; Federal Work-Study, institutionally sponsored loans, scholarships/grants, health care benefits, tuition waivers (full and partial), and unspecified assistantships also available. Financial award application deadline: 3/1; financial award applicants required to submit FAFSA. *Unit head:* Ghislaine Lydon, Chair, 310-825-4214. *Application contact:* Department Office, 310-825-4214, E-mail: idpgrads@international.ucla.edu.

University of Connecticut, Graduate School, College of Liberal Arts and Sciences, Field of International Studies, Program in African Studies, Storrs, CT 06269. Offers MA. *Faculty:* 38 full-time (23 women). *Students:* 1 full-time (0 women). Average age 23. 1 applicant, 100% accepted, 1 enrolled. *Degree requirements:* For master's, comprehensive exam. *Entrance requirements:* For master's, GRE General Test. Additional exam requirements/recommendations for international students: Required—TOEFL (minimum score 550 paper-based; 213 computer-based). *Application deadline:* For fall admission, 2/1 priority date for domestic and international students; for spring admission, 11/1 for domestic students, 10/1 for international students. Applications are processed on a rolling basis. Application fee: $55. Electronic applications accepted. *Expenses:* Tuition, state resident: full-time $4725; part-time $525 per credit. Tuition, nonresident: full-time $12,267; part-time $1363 per credit. Required fees: $346 per semester. Tuition and fees vary according to course load. *Financial support:* In 2009–10, 1 teaching assistantship with full tuition reimbursement was awarded; research assistantships with full tuition reimbursements, Federal Work-Study, scholarships/grants, health care benefits, and unspecified assistantships also available. Financial award application deadline: 2/1; financial award applicants required to submit FAFSA.

University of Florida, Graduate School, College of Liberal Arts and Sciences, Center for African Studies, Gainesville, FL 32611. Offers Certificate. Part-time programs available. *Faculty research:* Governance, human rights, African archaeology, southern African history, wildlife conservation and natural resources.

University of Illinois at Urbana–Champaign, Graduate College, College of Liberal Arts and Sciences, Center for African Studies, Champaign, IL 61820. Offers MA. *Students:* 7 full-time (5 women), 1 part-time (0 women); includes 3 minority (2 African Americans, 1 Hispanic American), 1 international. 12 applicants, 50% accepted, 4 enrolled. In 2009, 9 master's awarded. *Entrance requirements:* For master's, minimum GPA of 3.0. Additional exam requirements/

African Studies

University of Illinois at Urbana–Champaign (continued)
recommendations for international students: Required—TOEFL (minimum score 550 paper-based; 213 computer-based; 79 iBT). *Application deadline:* Applications are processed on a rolling basis. Application fee: $60 ($75 for international students). Electronic applications accepted. *Financial support:* In 2009–10, 6 fellowships, 2 teaching assistantships were awarded; research assistantships, tuition waivers (full and partial) also available. *Unit head:* Merle L. Bowen, Director, 217-333-6335, Fax: 217-244-2429, E-mail: bowen@illinois.edu. *Application contact:* Maimouna Barro, Associate Director, 217-333-6335, Fax: 217-244-2429, E-mail: barro@illinois.edu.

The University of Kansas, Graduate Studies, College of Liberal Arts and Sciences, Department of African and African-American Studies, Lawrence, KS 66045. Offers African and African-American studies (MA); African Studies (Graduate Certificate). Part-time programs available. *Faculty:* 11 full-time (5 women), 35 part-time/adjunct (18 women). *Students:* 3 full-time (2 women), 1 part-time (0 women); includes 3 minority (all African Americans). Average age 27. 8 applicants, 63% accepted, 4 enrolled. *Degree requirements:* For master's, variable foreign language requirement, thesis or alternative. *Entrance requirements:* For master's, GRE, all academic transcripts, 3 letters of recommendation, personal statement of purpose, writing sample. Additional exam requirements/recommendations for international students: Required—TOEFL. *Application deadline:* For fall admission, 5/1 for domestic students. Applications are processed on a rolling basis. Application fee: $45 ($55 for international students). Electronic applications accepted. *Expenses:* Tuition, state resident: full-time $6492; part-time $270.50 per credit hour. Tuition, nonresident: full-time $15,510; part-time $646.25 per credit hour. Required fees: $847; $70.56 per credit hour. Tuition and fees vary according to course load and program. *Faculty research:* African theatre, YaKuur culture, interracial communication, African development and urban planning, African literature, Muslim women in West Africa, identity formation in African and Disaporan settings, African American history, North African and Arab societies, civil rights. *Unit head:* Dr. Peter Ukpokodu, Chair, 785-864-3054, Fax: 785-864-5330, E-mail: afs@ku.edu. *Application contact:* Lisa Brown, Administrative Associate Sr, 785-864-3054, Fax: 785-864-5330, E-mail: lisabrown@ku.edu.

University of Louisville, Graduate School, College of Arts and Sciences, Department of Pan-African Studies, Louisville, KY 40292. Offers African and Diaspora studies (MA); African-American studies (MA); MA/MSW; MSSW/MA. Part-time programs available. *Faculty:* 12 full-time (6 women). *Students:* 14 full-time (10 women), 6 part-time (4 women); includes 15 minority (all African Americans), 2 international. Average age 29. 14 applicants, 57% accepted, 6 enrolled. In 2009, 3 master's awarded. *Degree requirements:* For master's, comprehensive exam, thesis optional. *Entrance requirements:* For master's, GRE General Test. Additional exam requirements/recommendations for international students: Recommended—TOEFL (minimum score 550 paper-based; 213 computer-based; 79 iBT). *Application deadline:* For fall admission, 10/15 for domestic and international students; for spring admission, 3/15 for domestic and international students. Application fee: $50. Electronic applications accepted. *Financial support:* In 2009–10, 10 students received support; teaching assistantships available. Financial award applicants required to submit FAFSA. *Faculty research:* African popular culture, black male identity development, education and retention, contemporary politics in Nigeria, poverty in the Caribbean. *Unit head:* Dr. Theresa Rajack-Talley, Chair, 502-852-4192, Fax: 502-852-5954, E-mail: tatall01@gwise.louisville.edu. *Application contact:* Dr. Theresa Rajack-Talley, Acting Graduate Studies Director, 502-852-4192, Fax: 502-852-5954, E-mail: tatall01@louisville.edu.

University of Pennsylvania, School of Arts and Sciences, Program in Africana Studies, Philadelphia, PA 19104. Offers MA, PhD. *Faculty:* 27 full-time (14 women), 1 part-time/adjunct (0 women). *Students:* 4 full-time (1 woman); includes 1 African American, 1 Hispanic American. Application fee: $70. *Expenses:* Tuition: Full-time $25,660; part-time $4758 per course. Required fees: $2152; $270 per course. Tuition and fees vary according to course load, degree level and program. *Unit head:* Dr. Barbara Savage, Program Chair, 215-898-4965, Fax: 215-573-2052, E-mail: africana-grad@sas.upenn.edu. *Application contact:* Patricia Rea, Associate Director for Admissions, 215-573-5816, Fax: 215-573-8068, E-mail: gdasadmis@sas.upenn.edu.

University of Pittsburgh, University Center for International Studies, Pittsburgh, PA 15260. Offers African studies (Certificate); Asian studies (Certificate); European Union studies (Certificate); global studies (Certificate); Latin American studies (Certificate); Russian and East European studies (Certificate); West European studies (Certificate). *Students:* 332 (129 women); includes 31 minority (7 African Americans, 10 Asian Americans or Pacific Islanders, 14 Hispanic Americans), 136 international. In 2009, 59 Certificates awarded. *Degree requirements:* For Certificate, one foreign language, study abroad. *Application deadline:* Applications are processed on a rolling basis. *Expenses:* Tuition, state resident: full-time $16,402; part-time $665 per credit. Tuition, nonresident: full-time $28,694; part-time $1175 per credit. Required fees: $690; $175 per term. Tuition and fees vary according to program. *Unit head:* Lawrence F. Feick, Director, 412-648-7374, Fax: 412-624-4672, E-mail: feick@pitt.edu. *Application contact:* Information Contact, 412-624-4141, E-mail: graduate@pitt.edu.

University of South Florida, Graduate School, College of Arts and Sciences, Department of Africana Studies, Tampa, FL 33620-9951. Offers MLA. *Faculty:* 5 full-time (2 women). *Degree requirements:* For master's, comprehensive exam, thesis. *Entrance requirements:* For master's, GRE, 3 letters of recommendation. Additional exam requirements/recommendations for international students: Required—TOEFL (minimum score 550 paper-based; 213 computer-based). *Application deadline:* For fall admission, 2/15 for domestic students, 1/2 for international students; for spring admission, 10/15 for domestic students, 6/1 for international students. Application fee: $30. *Financial support:* In 2009–10, teaching assistantships with tuition reimbursements (averaging $9,000 per year); tuition waivers (full) also available. Financial award applicants required to submit FAFSA. *Unit head:* Eric D. Duke, Director, 813-974-4442, Fax: 813-974-2668, E-mail: eduke@cas.usf.edu. *Application contact:* Eric D. Duke, Director, 813-974-4442, Fax: 813-974-2668, E-mail: eduke@cas.usf.edu.

The University of Texas at Austin, Graduate School, College of Liberal Arts, John L. Warfield Center for African and African American Studies, Austin, TX 78712-1111. Offers African Diaspora studies (MA, PhD). Part-time programs available. *Degree requirements:* For master's, one foreign language, thesis. *Entrance requirements:* For master's, GRE General Test. Electronic applications accepted.

University of Wisconsin–Madison, Graduate School, College of Letters and Science, Department of African Languages and Literature, Madison, WI 53706-1380. Offers MA, PhD. Part-time programs available. *Degree requirements:* For master's, one foreign language, thesis; for doctorate, 2 foreign languages, comprehensive exam, thesis/dissertation. *Entrance requirements:* For master's, BA in African language and literature; for doctorate, MA in African language and literature. Electronic applications accepted. *Expenses:* Tuition, state resident: part-time $594 per credit. Tuition, nonresident: part-time $1504 per credit. Required fees: $65 per credit. Tuition and fees vary according to course load, program and reciprocity agreements. *Faculty research:* Oral traditions, language pedagogy, stylistics, sociolinguistics, literary criticism.

University of Wisconsin–Madison, Graduate School, College of Letters and Science, Department of History, Madison, WI 53706-1380. Offers African history (MA, PhD); Central Asian history (MA, PhD); comparative world history (MA, PhD); East Asian history (MA, PhD); European history (MA, PhD); gender and women's history (MA, PhD); Latin American and Caribbean history (MA, PhD); Middle Eastern history (MA, PhD); South Asian history (MA, PhD); Southeast Asian history (MA, PhD); United States history (MA, PhD). Terminal master's awarded for partial completion of doctoral program. *Degree requirements:* For master's, thesis (for some programs); for doctorate, variable foreign language requirement, thesis/dissertation. *Entrance requirements:* For master's and doctorate, GRE General Test. Additional exam requirements/recommendations for international students: Required—Michigan English Language Assessment Battery or TOEFL. Electronic applications accepted. *Expenses:* Tuition, state resident: part-time $594 per credit. Tuition, nonresident: part-time $1504 per credit. Required fees: $65 per credit. Tuition and fees vary according to course load, program and reciprocity agreements. *Faculty research:* American, African, European, Asian, Latin American, and Middle Eastern history.

University of Wisconsin–Milwaukee, Graduate School, College of Letters and Sciences, Department of Africology, Milwaukee, WI 53201-0413. Offers PhD. *Faculty:* 9 full-time (5 women). *Degree requirements:* For doctorate, comprehensive exam. *Entrance requirements:* For doctorate, GRE General Test. Additional exam requirements/recommendations for international students: Required—TOEFL (minimum score 550 paper-based; 79 iBT), IELTS (minimum score 6.5). *Expenses:* Tuition, state resident: full-time $8800. Tuition, nonresident: full-time $20,760. Tuition and fees vary according to program and reciprocity agreements. *Financial support:* In 2009–10, 1 teaching assistantship was awarded. *Unit head:* Abera Gelan, Representative, 414-229-4155, E-mail: agelan@uwm.edu. *Application contact:* General Information Contact, 414-229-4982, Fax: 414-229-6967, E-mail: gradschool@uwm.edu.

West Virginia University, Eberly College of Arts and Sciences, Department of History, Morgantown, WV 26506. Offers African history (MA, PhD); African-American history (MA, PhD); American history (MA, PhD); Appalachian/regional history (MA, PhD); East Asian history (MA, PhD); European history (MA, PhD); history of science and technology (MA, PhD); Latin American history (MA). Part-time programs available. *Degree requirements:* For master's, one foreign language, thesis (for some programs), oral exam, thesis defense; for doctorate, one foreign language, comprehensive exam, thesis/dissertation, dissertation defense. *Entrance requirements:* For master's, GRE General Test, minimum GPA of 3.0; for doctorate, GRE General Test. Additional exam requirements/recommendations for international students: Required—TOEFL (minimum score 550 paper-based), IELTS (minimum score 6.5). Electronic applications accepted. *Faculty research:* U.S., Appalachia, modern Europe, Africa, colonial and post-colonial societies.

Yale University, Graduate School of Arts and Sciences, Interdisciplinary Program in African Studies, New Haven, CT 06520. Offers MA. *Degree requirements:* For master's, one foreign language, thesis. *Entrance requirements:* For master's, GRE General Test.

American Indian/Native American Studies

Central Michigan University, College of Graduate Studies, College of Humanities and Social and Behavioral Sciences, Program in Humanities, Mount Pleasant, MI 48859. Offers humanities (MA), including contemporary issues in the humanities: race, class, and gender, images and ideas of self, Native American issues in modern culture, popular culture studies, the rise of industrial society. Part-time and evening/weekend programs available. *Degree requirements:* For master's, thesis or alternative. Electronic applications accepted. *Faculty research:* Rise of industrial society; images and ideas of self; contemporary issues of race, class, and gender; popular culture; Native American issues in modern culture.

Montana State University, College of Graduate Studies, College of Letters and Science, Department of Native American Studies, Bozeman, MT 59717. Offers MA. Part-time programs available. Postbaccalaureate distance learning degree programs offered (no on-campus study). *Faculty:* 5 full-time (1 woman). *Students:* 3 full-time (all women), 10 part-time (6 women); includes 7 minority (all American Indian/Alaska Native). Average age 42. 11 applicants, 64% accepted, 7 enrolled. In 2009, 3 master's awarded. *Degree requirements:* For master's, comprehensive exam. *Entrance requirements:* For master's, minimum GPA of 3.0. Additional exam requirements/recommendations for international students: Required—TOEFL (minimum score 550 paper-based; 213 computer-based). *Application deadline:* For fall admission, 7/15 priority date for domestic students, 5/15 priority date for international students; for spring admission, 12/1 priority date for domestic students, 10/1 priority date for international students. Applications are processed on a rolling basis. Application fee: $30. Electronic applications accepted. *Expenses:* Tuition, state resident: full-time $5635; part-time $3492 per year. Tuition, nonresident: full-time $17,212; part-time $7865.10 per year. Required fees: $1441; $153.15 per credit. Tuition and fees vary according to course load and program. *Financial support:* In 2009–10, 8 students received support, including 4 teaching assistantships with partial tuition reimbursements available (averaging $10,243 per year); career-related internships or fieldwork, institutionally sponsored loans, scholarships/grants, and unspecified assistantships also available. Financial award application deadline: 3/1; financial award applicants required to submit FAFSA. *Faculty research:* Federal Indian law and policy, American Indian literature and film, Native American higher education, indigenous political theory, ethnoecology and effects of colonization. Total annual research expenditures: $25,984. *Unit head:* Dr. Walter Fleming, Head, 406-994-3881, Fax: 406-994-6879, E-mail: wfleming@montana.edu. *Application contact:* Dr. Carl A. Fox, Vice Provost for Graduate Education, 406-994-4145, Fax: 406-994-7433, E-mail: gradstudy@montana.edu.

Trent University, Graduate Studies, The Frost Centre for Canadian Studies and Indigenous Studies, Peterborough, ON K9J 7B8, Canada. Offers Canadian studies (PhD); Canadian studies and indigenous studies (MA). Part-time programs available. *Degree requirements:* For master's, thesis. *Entrance requirements:* For master's, honors degree. *Faculty research:* Native community-based socioeconomic development, environmental and social impact inventory, regional studies.

Trent University, Graduate Studies, Program in Indigenous Studies, Peterborough, ON K9J 7B8, Canada. Offers PhD. Part-time programs available. *Degree requirements:* For doctorate, thesis/dissertation. *Entrance requirements:* For doctorate, master's degree.

The University of Arizona, Graduate College, Graduate Interdisciplinary Programs, Graduate Interdisciplinary Program in American Indian Studies, Tucson, AZ 85721. Offers MA, PhD, JD/MA. Part-time programs available. *Faculty:* 7 full-time (6 women). *Students:* 24 full-time (17 women), 24 part-time (14 women); includes 19 minority (all American Indian/Alaska Native), 6 international. Average age 37. 24 applicants, 58% accepted, 9 enrolled. In 2009, 7 master's, 2 doctorates awarded. *Degree requirements:* For master's, thesis; for doctorate, one foreign language, comprehensive exam, thesis/dissertation. *Entrance requirements:* For master's, 3 letters of recommendation, 2 writing samples, resume; for doctorate, statement of purpose, 3 letters of recommendation, 2 writing samples, resume. Additional exam requirements/recommendations for international students: Required—TOEFL (minimum score 550 paper-based; 213 computer-based; 79 iBT). *Application deadline:* For fall admission, 1/15 for domestic and international students; for spring admission, 8/1 for domestic and international students. Application fee: $65. Electronic applications accepted. *Expenses:* Tuition, state resident: full-time $9028. Tuition, nonresident: full-time $24,890. *Financial support:* In 2009–10, 13 teaching assistantships with full tuition reimbursements (averaging $16,835 per year) were awarded; institutionally sponsored loans, scholarships/grants, health care benefits, tuition waivers (partial), and unspecified assistantships also available. Support available to part-time students. Financial award application deadline: 1/15. *Faculty research:* Indian law and policy, Indian societies, Indian language and literature, Indian education. *Unit head:* Dr. Jospeh Hiller, Head, 520-626-9772, Fax: 520-621-7952, E-mail: jghiller@cals.arizona.edu. *Application contact:* Beverly Larson, Administrative Secretary, 520-621-7108, Fax: 520-621-7952, E-mail: aisp@email.arizona.edu.

University of California, Davis, Graduate Studies, Program in Native American Studies, Davis, CA 95616. Offers MA, PhD. Terminal master's awarded for partial completion of doctoral program. *Degree requirements:* For master's, comprehensive exam (for some programs), thesis (for some programs); for doctorate, thesis/dissertation. *Entrance requirements:* For doctorate, GRE. Additional exam requirements/recommendations for international students: Required—TOEFL (minimum score 550 paper-based; 213 computer-based).

University of California, Los Angeles, Graduate Division, College of Letters and Science, Program in American Indian Studies, Los Angeles, CA 90095. Offers MA, JD/MA. *Students:* 25 full-time (17 women); includes 12 minority (11 American Indian/Alaska Native, 1 Hispanic American). Average age 27. 12 applicants, 67% accepted, 6 enrolled. In 2009, 6 master's awarded. *Degree requirements:* For master's, comprehensive exam or thesis. *Entrance requirements:* For master's, GRE General Test (recommended), minimum GPA of 3.0, sample of written work. *Application deadline:* For fall admission, 12/15 for domestic and international students. Application fee: $70 ($90 for international students). Electronic applications accepted. *Financial support:* In 2009–10, 12 fellowships with full and partial tuition reimbursements, 2 teaching assistantships with full and partial tuition reimbursements were awarded; research assistantships with full and partial tuition reimbursements, Federal Work-Study, institutionally sponsored loans, scholarships/grants, health care benefits, tuition waivers (full and partial), and unspecified assistantships also available. Financial award application deadline: 3/1; financial award applicants required to submit FAFSA. *Unit head:* Dr. Felicia Hodge, Chair, 310-794-9997. *Application contact:* Department Office, 310-794-9997, E-mail: aisc@ucla.edu.

The University of Kansas, Graduate Studies, College of Liberal Arts and Sciences, Global Indigenous Nations Studies Program, Lawrence, KS 66045-7515. Offers MA, JD/MA. Part-time programs available. *Faculty:* 6 full-time (3 women). *Students:* 14 full-time (8 women), 3 part-time (2 women); includes 13 minority (all American Indian/Alaska Native). Average age 35. 5 applicants, 80% accepted, 1 enrolled. In 2009, 7 master's awarded. *Degree requirements:* For master's, thesis or alternative. *Entrance requirements:* For master's, GRE, resume, writing sample, minimum GPA of 3.0 (preferred), 3 recommendations. Additional exam requirements/recommendations for international students: Required—TOEFL. *Application deadline:* For fall admission, 3/15 priority date for domestic and international students. Applications are processed on a rolling basis. Application fee: $45 ($50 for international students). Electronic applications accepted. *Expenses:* Tuition, state resident: full-time $6492; part-time $270.50 per credit hour. Tuition, nonresident: full-time $15,510; part-time $646.25 per credit hour. Required fees: $847; $70.56 per credit hour. Tuition and fees vary according to course load and program. *Financial support:* Fellowships, teaching assistantships, Federal Work-Study, institutionally sponsored loans, and scholarships/grants available. Support available to part-time students. Financial award application deadline: 3/15; financial award applicants required to submit FAFSA. *Faculty research:* American Indian history, religion, literature, law, languages, decolonization, sovereignty, pre-Columbian cultures of Latin America. *Unit head:* Dr. John Hoopes, Director, 785-864-2660, Fax: 785-864-0370, E-mail: indigenous@ku.edu. *Application contact:* Prof. Sharon O'Brien, Graduate Coordinator, 785-864-2660, Fax: 785-864-0370, E-mail: indigenous@ku.edu.

University of Lethbridge, School of Graduate Studies, Lethbridge, AB T1K 3M4, Canada. Offers accounting (MScM); addictions counseling (M Sc); agricultural biotechnology (M Sc); agricultural studies (M Sc, MA); anthropology (MA); archaeology (MA); art (MA, MFA); biochemistry (M Sc); biological sciences (M Sc); biomolecular science (PhD); biosystems and biodiversity (PhD); Canadian studies (MA); chemistry (M Sc); computer science (M Sc); computer science and geographical information science (M Sc); counseling psychology (M Ed); dramatic arts (MA); earth, space, and physical science (PhD); economics (MA); educational leadership (M Ed); English (MA); environmental science (M Sc); evolution and behavior (PhD); exercise science (M Sc); finance (MScM); French (MA); French/German (MA); French/Spanish (MA); general education (M Ed); general management (MScM); geography (M Sc, MA); German (MA); health science (M Sc); health sciences (MA); history (MA); human resource management and labour relations (MScM); individualized multidisciplinary (M Sc, MA); information systems (MScM); international management (MScM); kinesiology (M Sc, MA); management (M Sc, MA); marketing (MScM); mathematics (M Sc); music (M Mus, MA); Native American studies (MA); neuroscience (M Sc, PhD); new media (MA); nursing (M Sc); philosophy (MA); physics (M Sc); policy and strategy (MScM); political science (MA); psychology (M Sc, MA); religious studies (MA); social sciences (MA); sociology (MA); theatre and dramatic arts (MFA); theoretical and computational science (PhD); urban and regional studies (MA); women's studies (MA). Part-time and evening/weekend programs available. *Degree requirements:* For doctorate, comprehensive exam, thesis/dissertation. *Entrance requirements:* For master's, GMAT (M Sc in management), bachelor's degree in related field, minimum GPA of 3.0 during previous 20 graded semester courses, 2 years teaching or related experience (M Ed); for doctorate, master's degree, minimum graduate GPA of 3.5. Additional exam requirements/recommendations for international students: Required—TOEFL. *Faculty research:* Movement and brain plasticity, gibberellin physiology, photosynthesis, carbon cycling, molecular properties of main-group ring components.

University of Manitoba, Faculty of Graduate Studies, Faculty of Arts, Department of Native Studies, Winnipeg, MB R3T 2N2, Canada. Offers MA.

University of Oklahoma, Graduate College, College of Arts and Sciences, Department of Native American Studies, Norman, OK 73019. Offers MA. Part-time programs available. *Faculty:* 6 full-time (2 women), 1 (woman) part-time/adjunct. *Students:* 26 full-time (18 women), 6 part-time (4 women); includes 23 minority (22 American Indian/Alaska Native, 1 Hispanic American), 1 international. 15 applicants, 100% accepted, 15 enrolled. In 2009, 3 master's awarded. *Degree requirements:* For master's, thesis. *Entrance requirements:* For master's, minimum undergraduate GPA of 3.0, 3 letters of recommendation. *Application deadline:* For fall admission, 2/1 for domestic students, 4/1 for international students; for spring admission, 11/1 for domestic students, 9/1 for international students. Applications are processed on a rolling basis. Application fee: $40 ($90 for international students). Electronic applications accepted. *Expenses:* Tuition, state resident: full-time $3744; part-time $156 per credit hour. Tuition, nonresident: full-time $13,577; part-time $565.70 per credit hour. Required fees: $2415; $90.10 per credit hour. *Financial support:* In 2009–10, 31 students received support, including 11 teaching assistantships with partial tuition reimbursements available (averaging $10,000 per year); career-related internships or fieldwork, Federal Work-Study, and unspecified assistantships also available. Financial award application deadline: 2/1; financial award applicants required to submit FAFSA. *Faculty research:* Higher education and retention among American Indian students, contemporary Native American artists, indigenous archaeology, tribal economic development. *Unit head:* Joe Watkins, Director, 405-325-2312, Fax: 405-325-0842, E-mail: jwatkins@ou.edu. *Application contact:* Barbara T. Hobson, Assistant Director, 405-325-2324, Fax: 405-325-0842, E-mail: bhobson@ou.edu.

University of Regina, Faculty of Graduate Studies and Research, Faculty of Arts, Program in Indigenous Studies, Regina, SK S4S 0A2, Canada. Offers MA. Offered as special case program. Part-time programs available. *Faculty:* 10 full-time (3 women). In 2009, 1 master's awarded. *Degree requirements:* For master's, thesis. *Entrance requirements:* For master's, honors degree in Indian studies or related field. Additional exam requirements/recommendations for international students: Required—TOEFL (minimum score 580 paper-based; 237 computer-based; 80 iBT). *Application deadline:* For fall admission, 3/15 for domestic students. Application fee: $90 ($100 for international students). Electronic applications accepted. *Financial support:* Fellowships, research assistantships, teaching assistantships, scholarships/grants available. Financial award application deadline: 6/15. *Unit head:* Dr. David Miller, Professor, 306-790-5950 Ext. 3209, E-mail: dmiller@firstnationsuniversity.ca. *Application contact:* Dr. David Miller, Professor, 306-790-5950 Ext. 3209, E-mail: dmiller@firstnationsuniversity.ca.

American Studies

American University, School of International Service, Washington, DC 20016-8071. Offers comparative and regional studies (Certificate); cross-cultural communication (Certificate); development management (MS); ethics, peace, and global affairs (MA); European studies (Certificate); global environmental policy (MA, Certificate); international affairs (MA), including comparative and regional studies, environmental policy, international economic policy, international politics, natural resources and sustainable development, U.S. foreign policy; international communication (MA, Certificate); international development (MA, Certificate); international development management (Certificate); international economic policy (Certificate); international economic relations (Certificate); international media (MA); international peace and conflict resolution (MA, Certificate); international relations (PhD); international service (MIS); peace building (Certificate); the Americas (Certificate); United States foreign policy (Certificate); JD/MA. Part-time and evening/weekend programs available. *Faculty:* 98 full-time (42 women), 48 part-time/adjunct (13 women). *Students:* 565 full-time (349 women), 329 part-time (189 women); includes 128 minority (44 African Americans, 2 American Indian/Alaska Native, 37 Asian Americans or Pacific Islanders, 45 Hispanic Americans), 102 international. Average age 27. 2,034 applicants, 63% accepted, 344 enrolled. In 2009, 326 master's, 6 doctorates, 9 other advanced degrees awarded. Terminal master's awarded for partial completion of doctoral program. *Degree requirements:* For master's, one foreign language, comprehensive exam, thesis or alternative; for doctorate, one foreign language, comprehensive exam, thesis/dissertation, research practicum; for Certificate, minimum 15 credit hours related course work. *Entrance requirements:* For master's, GRE, 24 credits of course work in related social sciences, minimum GPA of 3.5, 2 letters of recommendation, bachelor's degree, resume; for doctorate, GRE, 2 letters of recommendation, 24 credits in related social sciences; for Certificate, bachelor's degree. Additional exam requirements/recommendations for international students: Required—TOEFL (minimum score 600 paper-based; 250 computer-based; 100 iBT). *Application deadline:* For fall admission, 1/15 priority date for domestic students; for spring admission, 10/1 priority date for domestic students. Applications are processed on a rolling basis. Application fee: $50. *Expenses:* Tuition: Full-time $22,266; part-time $1237 per credit hour. Required fees: $430. Tuition and fees vary according to program. *Financial support:* Career-related internships or fieldwork, Federal Work-Study, and institutionally sponsored loans available. Financial award application deadline: 1/15. *Faculty research:* International intellectual property, international environmental issues, international law and legal order, international telecommunications/technology, international sustainable development. *Unit head:* Dr. Louis W. Goodman, Dean, 202-885-1600, Fax: 202-885-2494. *Application contact:* Yasmin Quianzon, Director of Graduate Admissions and Financial Aid, 202-885-2496, Fax: 202-885-1109.

See Close-Up on page 849.

Appalachian State University, Cratis D. Williams Graduate School, Center for Appalachian Studies, Boone, NC 28608. Offers culture (MA); music (MA); sustainable development (MA). Part-time programs available. *Faculty:* 14 full-time (5 women). *Students:* 24 full-time (18 women), 4 part-time (3 women). 20 applicants, 75% accepted, 10 enrolled. In 2009, 12 master's awarded. *Degree requirements:* For master's, one foreign language, comprehensive exam, thesis optional. *Entrance requirements:* For master's, GRE General Test, 3 letters of recommendation. Additional exam requirements/recommendations for international students: Required—TOEFL (minimum score 570 paper-based; 230 computer-based; 79 iBT), IELTS (minimum score 6.5). *Application deadline:* For fall admission, 7/1 for domestic students, 2/1 for international students; for spring admission, 11/1 for domestic students, 7/1 for international students. Applications are processed on a rolling basis. Application fee: $50. Electronic applications accepted. *Expenses:* Tuition, state resident: full-time $2960. Tuition, nonresident: full-time $14,051. Required fees: $2320. *Financial support:* In 2009–10, 8 research assistantships (averaging $8,000 per year) were awarded; fellowships, teaching assistantships, career-related internships or fieldwork, Federal Work-Study, scholarships/grants, and unspecified assistantships also available. Financial award application deadline: 4/1; financial award applicants required to submit FAFSA. *Faculty research:* Appalachian culture, sustainable development, Appalachian music. Total annual research expenditures: $11,250. *Unit head:* Dr. Pat Beaver, Center Director, 828-262-2550, E-mail: beaverpd@appstate.edu. *Application contact:* Dr. Katherine Ledford, Graduate Program Director, 828-262-4089, E-mail: ledfordke@appstate.edu.

Baylor University, Graduate School, College of Arts and Sciences, Program in American Studies, Waco, TX 76798. Offers MA. *Students:* 4 full-time (2 women), 1 part-time (0 women), 2 international. In 2009, 1 master's awarded. *Degree requirements:* For master's, thesis, final oral exam. *Entrance requirements:* For master's, GRE General Test, 24 semester hours of course work in subjects with American content. *Application deadline:* For fall admission, 8/1 for domestic students. Applications are processed on a rolling basis. Application fee: $25. *Financial support:* Fellowships, Federal Work-Study and institutionally sponsored loans available. Financial award application deadline: 4/15. *Unit head:* Dr. Doug Ferdon, Graduate Program Director, 254-710-6350, Fax: 254-710-3600, E-mail: doug_ferdon@baylor.edu. *Application contact:* Margaret Kramer, Administrative Assistant, 254-710-4350, Fax: 254-710-3870, E-mail: margaret_kramer@baylor.edu.

Boston University, Graduate School of Arts and Sciences, Program in American and New England Studies, Boston, MA 02215. Offers PhD. *Students:* 42 full-time (26 women), 11 part-time (4 women); includes 5 minority (4 African Americans, 1 American Indian/Alaska Native), 1 international. Average age 35. 80 applicants, 18% accepted, 8 enrolled. In 2009, 3 doctorates awarded. *Degree requirements:* For doctorate, one foreign language, comprehensive exam, thesis/dissertation. *Entrance requirements:* For doctorate, GRE General Test, scholarly writing sample, 3 letters of recommendation. Additional exam requirements/recommendations for international students: Required—TOEFL (minimum score 550 paper-based; 213 computer-based). *Application deadline:* For fall admission, 1/15 for domestic and international students. Application fee: $70. Electronic applications accepted. *Expenses:* Tuition: Full-time $37,910; part-time $1184 per credit hour. Required fees: $386; $40 per semester. Part-time tuition and fees vary according to class time, course level, degree level and program. *Financial support:* In 2009–10, 15 students received support, including 1 fellowship with full tuition reimbursement available (averaging $1,800 per year), 1 research assistantship with full tuition reimbursement available (averaging $18,400 per year), 4 teaching assistantships with full tuition reimbursements available (averaging $18,400 per year); career-related internships or fieldwork, Federal

American Studies

Boston University (continued)
Work-Study, scholarships/grants, and unspecified assistantships also available. Support available to part-time students. Financial award application deadline: 1/15; financial award applicants required to submit FAFSA. *Unit head:* Kim Sichel, Director, 617-353-9912, Fax: 617-353-2556, E-mail: ksichel@bu.edu. *Application contact:* Jessica Hill, Senior Program Coordinator, 617-353-2948, Fax: 617-353-2556, E-mail: jesshill@bu.edu.

Bowling Green State University, Graduate College, College of Arts and Sciences, American Culture Studies Program, Bowling Green, OH 43403. Offers MA, PhD. Part-time programs available. *Degree requirements:* For master's, thesis or alternative; for doctorate, comprehensive exam, thesis/dissertation. *Entrance requirements:* For master's and doctorate, GRE General Test. Additional exam requirements/recommendations for international students: Required—TOEFL. Electronic applications accepted. *Faculty research:* Race and ethnicity, gender, popular culture.

Bowling Green State University, Graduate College, College of Arts and Sciences, Department of Popular Culture, Bowling Green, OH 43403. Offers MA. Part-time programs available. *Degree requirements:* For master's, thesis or alternative. *Entrance requirements:* For master's, GRE General Test. Additional exam requirements/recommendations for international students: Required—TOEFL. Electronic applications accepted. *Faculty research:* Mass media (popular film, TV, and music); folklore/folklife; ritual, festival, celebration, and holidays; global, international, and popular culture; nineteenth century everyday life.

Brown University, Graduate School, Department of American Civilization, Providence, RI 02912. Offers American civilization (MA, PhD); public humanities (MA). *Degree requirements:* For doctorate, thesis/dissertation, preliminary exam.

California State University, Fullerton, Graduate Studies, College of Humanities and Social Sciences, Department of American Studies, Fullerton, CA 92834-9480. Offers MA. Part-time programs available. *Students:* 11 full-time (9 women), 41 part-time (24 women); includes 19 minority (1 American Indian/Alaska Native, 7 Asian Americans or Pacific Islanders, 11 Hispanic Americans), 1 international. Average age 28. 36 applicants, 72% accepted, 21 enrolled. In 2009, 17 master's awarded. *Degree requirements:* For master's, comprehensive exam or thesis. *Entrance requirements:* For master's, minimum GPA of 3.0 in major, 2.5 in last 60 hours. Application fee: $55. *Expenses:* Tuition, nonresident: full-time $11,160; part-time $373 per credit. Required fees: $1440 per term. Tuition and fees vary according to course load, degree level and program. *Financial support:* Federal Work-Study, institutionally sponsored loans, and scholarships/grants available. Support available to part-time students. Financial award application deadline: 3/1; financial award applicants required to submit FAFSA. *Unit head:* Dr. Jesse Battan, Chair, 657-278-2441. *Application contact:* Admissions/Applications, 657-278-2371.

California State University, Long Beach, Graduate Studies, College of Liberal Arts, Department of History, Long Beach, CA 90840. Offers Africa and the Middle East (MA); ancient/Medieval Europe (MA); Asia (MA); Latin America (MA); modern Europe (MA); United States (MA); world (MA). Part-time and evening/weekend programs available. *Faculty:* 9 full-time (6 women), 1 (woman) part-time/adjunct. *Students:* 10 full-time (3 women), 56 part-time (21 women); includes 19 minority (2 African Americans, 1 American Indian/Alaska Native, 4 Asian Americans or Pacific Islanders, 12 Hispanic Americans), 1 international. Average age 31. 40 applicants, 50% accepted, 11 enrolled. *Degree requirements:* For master's, one foreign language, comprehensive exam or thesis. *Application deadline:* For fall admission, 3/1 for domestic students. Applications are processed on a rolling basis. Application fee: $55. Electronic applications accepted. *Expenses:* Required fees: $1802 per semester. Part-time tuition and fees vary according to course load. *Financial support:* Research assistantships, Federal Work-Study, institutionally sponsored loans, and scholarships/grants available. Financial award application deadline: 3/2. *Faculty research:* All periods of European and American history, recent Asian and African history. *Unit head:* Dr. Nancy Quam-Wickham, Department Chair, 562-985-4431, Fax: 562-985-5431, E-mail: quamwick@csulb.edu. *Application contact:* Dr. Houri Berberian, Graduate Advisor, 562-985-4524, Fax: 562-985-4431, E-mail: hberber@csulb.edu.

The Catholic University of America, School of Arts and Sciences, Department of History, Washington, DC 20064. Offers Medieval Europe (MA, PhD); modern Europe (PhD); religion and society in the late Medieval and early modern world (MA); United States (MA); MA/JD; MSLS/MA. Part-time programs available. *Faculty:* 13 full-time (6 women), 3 part-time/adjunct (1 woman). *Students:* 14 full-time (9 women), 28 part-time (11 women); includes 1 minority (American Indian/Alaska Native), 3 international. Average age 33. 38 applicants, 50% accepted, 7 enrolled. In 2009, 8 master's, 2 doctorates awarded. *Degree requirements:* For master's, one foreign language, comprehensive exam, thesis optional; for doctorate, 2 foreign languages, comprehensive exam, thesis/dissertation, oral exams. *Entrance requirements:* For master's, GRE General Test, statement of purpose, official copies of academic transcripts, three letters of recommendation, writing sample; for doctorate, GRE General Test, MA in history, statement of purpose, official copies of academic transcripts, three letters of recommendation, writing sample. Additional exam requirements/recommendations for international students: Required—TOEFL (minimum score 580 paper-based; 237 computer-based). *Application deadline:* For fall admission, 8/1 priority date for domestic students, 7/15 for international students; for spring admission, 12/1 priority date for domestic students, 10/15 for international students. Applications are processed on a rolling basis. Application fee: $55. Electronic applications accepted. *Expenses:* Tuition: Full-time $31,740; part-time $1245 per credit hour. Required fees: $50; $25 per semester hour. One-time fee: $425. *Financial support:* Fellowships, research assistantships, teaching assistantships, Federal Work-Study, scholarships/grants, tuition waivers (full and partial), and unspecified assistantships available. Financial award application deadline: 2/1; financial award applicants required to submit FAFSA. *Faculty research:* Modern European intellectual history, history of mathematics and sciences, Renaissance, Catholic reformation, medieval women and gender. *Unit head:* Dr. Jerry Muller, Chair, 202-319-5484, Fax: 202-319-5569, E-mail: mullerj@cua.edu. *Application contact:* Julie Schwing, Director of Graduate Admissions, 202-319-5057, Fax: 202-319-6533, E-mail: cua-admissions@cua.edu.

Central Michigan University, College of Graduate Studies, College of Humanities and Social and Behavioral Sciences, Department of History, Mount Pleasant, MI 48859. Offers European history (Graduate Certificate); history (MA, PhD); modern history (Graduate Certificate); United States history (Graduate Certificate). Offered jointly with the University of Stratclyde, Scotland. Part-time programs available. *Degree requirements:* For master's, thesis or alternative; for doctorate, comprehensive exam, thesis/dissertation. Electronic applications accepted. *Faculty research:* Colonial and revolutionary United States history, modern European history, Latin American and transatlantic history, transnational and comparative history, United States social history.

Claremont Graduate University, Graduate Programs, School of Arts and Humanities, Department of English, Claremont, CA 91711-6160. Offers American studies (MA, PhD); critical theory (MA, PhD); early modern studies (MA, PhD); English (M Phil, MA, PhD); literary theory (PhD); literature (MA, PhD); literature and creative writing (MA); literature and film (MA); MBA/MA; MBA/PhD. Part-time programs available. *Faculty:* 2 full-time (1 woman), 2 part-time/adjunct (0 women). *Students:* 83 full-time (60 women), 19 part-time (11 women); includes 17 minority (1 African American, 1 American Indian/Alaska Native, 8 Asian Americans or Pacific Islanders, 7 Hispanic Americans), 4 international. Average age 35. In 2009, 6 master's, 4 doctorates awarded. *Entrance requirements:* For master's and doctorate, GRE General Test. Additional exam requirements/recommendations for international students: Required—TOEFL (minimum score 550 paper-based; 213 computer-based; 80 iBT). *Application deadline:* For fall admission, 2/1 priority date for domestic students. Applications are processed on a rolling basis. Application fee: $60. Electronic applications accepted. *Expenses:* Tuition: Full-time $35,046; part-time $1524 per credit. Required fees: $161 per semester. *Financial support:* Fellowships, Federal Work-Study, institutionally sponsored loans, and scholarships/grants available. Support available to part-time students. Financial award application deadline: 2/15; financial award applicants required to submit FAFSA. *Faculty research:* American, comparative, and English Renaissance literature; modernism; feminist literature and theory. *Unit head:* Wendy Martin, Chair, 909-621-8612, Fax: 909-607-1221, E-mail: wendy.martin@cgu.edu. *Application contact:* Susan Hampson, Admissions Coordinator, 909-607-1278, Fax: 909-607-1221, E-mail: humanities@cgu.edu.

Claremont Graduate University, Graduate Programs, School of Arts and Humanities, Department of History, Claremont, CA 91711-6160. Offers Africana history (Certificate); American studies and U.S. history (MA, PhD); archival studies (MA); early modern studies (MA, PhD); European studies (MA, PhD); oral history (MA, PhD); MBA/MA; MBA/PhD. *Faculty:* 4 full-time (2 women). *Students:* 69 full-time (31 women), 5 part-time (3 women); includes 13 minority (1 African American, 4 Asian Americans or Pacific Islanders, 8 Hispanic Americans), 2 international. Average age 36. In 2009, 10 master's, 3 doctorates awarded. Terminal master's awarded for partial completion of doctoral program. *Entrance requirements:* For master's and doctorate, GRE General Test. Additional exam requirements/recommendations for international students: Required—TOEFL (minimum score 550 paper-based; 213 computer-based; 80 iBT). *Application deadline:* For fall admission, 2/1 priority date for domestic students. Applications are processed on a rolling basis. Application fee: $60. Electronic applications accepted. *Expenses:* Tuition: Full-time $35,046; part-time $1524 per credit. Required fees: $161 per semester. *Financial support:* Fellowships, research assistantships, Federal Work-Study, institutionally sponsored loans, and scholarships/grants available. Support available to part-time students. Financial award application deadline: 2/15; financial award applicants required to submit FAFSA. *Faculty research:* Intellectual and social history, cultural studies, gender studies, Western history, Chicano history. *Unit head:* Janet Farrell Brodie, Chair, 909-621-8880, Fax: 909-621-8609, E-mail: janet.brodie@cgu.edu. *Application contact:* Susan Hampson, Admissions Coordinator, 909-607-1278, E-mail: humanities@cgu.edu.

Clark University, Graduate School, Department of History, Program in American History, Worcester, MA 01610-1477. Offers MA, PhD. *Faculty:* 9 full-time (4 women). *Students:* 14 full-time (6 women). Average age 28. 16 applicants, 63% accepted, 10 enrolled. In 2009, 4 master's awarded. *Application deadline:* For fall admission, 1/15 for domestic students. Application fee: $50. *Expenses:* Tuition: Full-time $34,900; part-time $4362.50 per course. *Financial support:* In 2009–10, fellowships with full and partial tuition reimbursements (averaging $11,850 per year), research assistantships with full and partial tuition reimbursements (averaging $11,850 per year), teaching assistantships with full and partial tuition reimbursements (averaging $11,850 per year) were awarded. *Faculty research:* American political history, comparative history, American family history. Total annual research expenditures: $15,000. *Unit head:* Dr. Amy Richter, Chair, 508-793-7288. *Application contact:* Diane Fenner, Academic Secretary, 508-793-7288, Fax: 508-793-8816, E-mail: history@clarku.edu.

The College at Brockport, State University of New York, School of Arts, Humanities and Social Sciences, Department of History, Brockport, NY 14420-2997. Offers history (MA), including American history, American/world history, world history. Part-time and evening/weekend programs available. *Students:* 17 full-time (8 women), 31 part-time (11 women); includes 2 minority (both Hispanic Americans). 21 applicants, 76% accepted, 15 enrolled. In 2009, 16 master's awarded. *Degree requirements:* For master's, thesis or alternative. *Entrance requirements:* For master's, GRE General Test (recommended), minimum GPA of 3.0, writing sample, letters of recommendation, statement of objectives. Additional exam requirements/recommendations for international students: Required—TOEFL (minimum score 550 paper-based; 213 computer-based; 79 iBT). *Application deadline:* For fall admission, 6/1 priority date for domestic and international students; for spring admission, 11/15 priority date for domestic and international students. Application fee: $50. Electronic applications accepted. *Expenses:* Tuition, state resident: full-time $8370; part-time $349 per credit. Tuition, nonresident: full-time $13,250; part-time $522 per credit. *Financial support:* In 2009–10, 1 fellowship with tuition reimbursement (averaging $1,600 per year), 1 teaching assistantship with full tuition reimbursement (averaging $6,000 per year) were awarded; Federal Work-Study, scholarships/grants, and unspecified assistantships also available. Support available to part-time students. Financial award application deadline: 3/15; financial award applicants required to submit FAFSA. *Faculty research:* American history, women's history, European history, world history, cultural history. *Unit head:* Dr. Alison Parker, Chairperson, 585-395-5694, Fax: 585-395-2620, E-mail: jlloyd@brockport.edu. *Application contact:* Dr. Morag Martin, Graduate Director, 585-395-5690, Fax: 585-395-2620, E-mail: mmartin@brockport.edu.

The College of William and Mary, Faculty of Arts and Sciences, Program in American Studies, Williamsburg, VA 23187-8795. Offers MA, PhD, JD/MA. Part-time programs available. *Students:* 43 full-time (26 women), 2 part-time (both women); includes 8 minority (7 African Americans, 1 Asian American or Pacific Islander), 3 international. Average age 32. 85 applicants, 0% accepted, 0 enrolled. In 2009, 7 master's, 4 doctorates awarded. Terminal master's awarded for partial completion of doctoral program. *Degree requirements:* For master's, thesis; for doctorate, one foreign language, comprehensive exam, thesis/dissertation. *Entrance requirements:* For master's, GRE; for doctorate, GRE, MA. Additional exam requirements/recommendations for international students: Required—TOEFL. *Application deadline:* For fall admission, 1/15 for domestic and international students. Application fee: $45. Electronic applications accepted. *Expenses:* Tuition, state resident: full-time $6400; part-time $315 per credit hour. Tuition, nonresident: full-time $19,720; part-time $840 per credit hour. Required fees: $4114. *Financial support:* Fellowships with full tuition reimbursements, career-related internships or fieldwork, tuition waivers (full and partial), and unspecified assistantships available. Financial award application deadline: 3/15; financial award applicants required to submit FAFSA. *Faculty research:* Native American literature and environment, Guada canal and memory, twentieth century African-American celebrity, African-American's relation to war, American religious nationalism. *Unit head:* Dr. Maureen F. Fitzgerald, Director/Dean, 757-221-1281, Fax: 757-221-1287, E-mail: mafitz@wm.edu. *Application contact:* Jean Brown, Program Administrator, 757-221-1275, Fax: 757-221-1287, E-mail: jxbrow@wm.edu.

The Colorado College, Department of Education, Experienced Teacher Program, Colorado Springs, CO 80903-3294. Offers arts and humanities (MAT); liberal arts (MAT); Southwest studies (MAT). Programs offered during summer only. Part-time programs available. *Degree requirements:* For master's, thesis, oral exam, 50-page paper. *Application deadline:* Applications are processed on a rolling basis. Application fee: $50. *Expenses:* Contact institution. *Financial support:* Institutionally sponsored loans and half-tuition scholarships to teachers with a contract available.

Columbia University, Graduate School of Arts and Sciences, Program in Liberal Studies, New York, NY 10027. Offers American studies (MA); East Asian studies (MA); human rights studies (MA); Islamic culture studies (MA); Jewish studies (MA); medieval studies (MA); modern European studies (MA); South Asian studies (MA). Part-time and evening/weekend programs available. *Degree requirements:* For master's, thesis.

Cornell University, Graduate School, Graduate Fields of Arts and Sciences, Field of English Language and Literature, Ithaca, NY 14853-0001. Offers African-American literature (PhD); American literature after 1865 (PhD); American literature to 1865 (PhD); American studies (PhD); colonial and postcolonial literature (PhD); creative writing (MFA); cultural studies (PhD); dramatic literature (PhD); English poetry (PhD); English Renaissance to 1660 (PhD); lesbian, bisexual, and gay literature studies (PhD); literary criticism and theory (PhD); nineteenth century (PhD); Old and Middle English (PhD); prose fiction (PhD); Restoration and eighteenth century (PhD); twentieth century (PhD); women's literature (PhD); MFA/PhD. *Faculty:* 74 full-time (35 women). *Students:* 100 full-time (55 women); includes 26 minority (9 African Americans, 3 American Indian/Alaska Native, 7 Asian Americans or Pacific Islanders, 7 Hispanic Americans), 11 international. Average age 28. 890 applicants, 4% accepted, 21 enrolled. In 2009, 21 master's, 12 doctorates awarded. Terminal master's awarded for partial completion of doctoral program. *Degree requirements:* For master's, one foreign language, thesis; for doctorate, one foreign language, comprehensive exam, thesis/dissertation, teaching experience. *Entrance requirements:* For master's, GRE General Test, 3 letters of recommendation, creative writing sample; for doctorate, GRE General Test, GRE Subject Test (English), 3 letters of recommendation, writing sample. Additional exam requirements/recommendations for international students: Required—TOEFL (minimum score 600 paper-based; 250 computer-based; 77 iBT). *Application deadline:* For fall admission, 1/10 for domestic students. Application fee: $70. Electronic applications accepted. *Expenses:* Tuition: Full-time $29,500. Required fees: $70. Full-time tuition and fees vary according to degree level, program and student level. *Financial support:* In 2009–10, 96 students received support, including 13 fellowships with full tuition reimbursements available, 8 teaching assistantships with full tuition reimbursements available; research assistantships with full tuition reimbursements available, institutionally sponsored loans, scholarships/grants, health care benefits, tuition waivers (full and partial), and unspecified assistantships also available. Financial award applicants required to submit FAFSA. *Faculty research:* English and American literature, women's writing, ethnic and post-colonial literature, critical theory, medievalism. *Unit head:* Director of Graduate Studies, 607-255-7989, Fax: 607-255-6661. *Application contact:* Graduate Field Assistant, 607-255-7989, Fax: 607-255-6661, E-mail: english_grad@cornell.edu.

Cornell University, Graduate School, Graduate Fields of Arts and Sciences, Field of History, Ithaca, NY 14853-0001. Offers African history (MA, PhD); American history (MA, PhD); ancient history (MA, PhD); early modern European history (MA, PhD); English history (MA, PhD); French history (MA, PhD); German history (MA, PhD); history of science (MA, PhD); Latin American history (MA, PhD); medieval Chinese history (MA, PhD); medieval history (MA, PhD); modern Chinese history (MA, PhD); modern European history (MA, PhD); modern Japanese history (MA, PhD); premodern Islamic history (MA, PhD); premodern Japanese history (MA, PhD); Renaissance history (MA, PhD); Russian history (MA, PhD); Southeast Asian history (MA, PhD). *Faculty:* 62 full-time (19 women). *Students:* 67 full-time (33 women); includes 10 minority (4 African Americans, 3 Asian Americans or Pacific Islanders, 3 Hispanic Americans), 24 international. Average age 31. 195 applicants, 7% accepted, 10 enrolled. In 2009, 11 master's, 3 doctorates awarded. Terminal master's awarded for partial completion of doctoral program. *Degree requirements:* For master's, thesis; for doctorate, 2 foreign languages, comprehensive exam, thesis/dissertation, 1 year of teaching experience. *Entrance requirements:* For master's and doctorate, GRE General Test, writing sample, 3 letters of recommendation. Additional exam requirements/recommendations for international students: Required—TOEFL (minimum score 550 paper-based; 213 computer-based; 77 iBT). *Application deadline:* For fall admission, 1/15 for domestic students. Application fee: $70. Electronic applications accepted. *Expenses:* Tuition: Full-time $29,500. Required fees: $70. Full-time tuition and fees vary according to degree level, program and student level. *Financial support:* In 2009–10, 54 students received support, including 8 fellowships with full tuition reimbursements available; research assistantships with full tuition reimbursements available, teaching assistantships with full tuition reimbursements available, institutionally sponsored loans, scholarships/grants, health care benefits, tuition waivers (full and partial), and unspecified assistantships also available. Financial award applicants required to submit FAFSA. *Unit head:* Director of Graduate Studies, 607-255-6738, Fax: 607-255-0469. *Application contact:* Graduate Field Assistant, 607-255-6738, Fax: 607-255-0469, E-mail: history_grad_info@cornell.edu.

Cornell University, Graduate School, Graduate Fields of Arts and Sciences, Field of History of Art, Archaeology and Visual Studies, Ithaca, NY 14853. Offers American art (PhD); ancient art and archaeology (PhD); Asian art (PhD); baroque art (PhD); medieval art (PhD); modern art (PhD); Renaissance art (PhD); Southeast Asian art (PhD); theory and criticism (PhD). *Faculty:* 23 full-time (14 women). *Students:* 20 full-time (18 women); includes 4 minority (1 African American, 1 American Indian/Alaska Native, 1 Asian American or Pacific Islander, 1 Hispanic American), 5 international. Average age 35. 73 applicants. In 2009, 3 doctorates awarded. *Degree requirements:* For doctorate, one foreign language, comprehensive exam, thesis/dissertation, general exams in 3 areas. *Entrance requirements:* For doctorate, GRE General Test, sample of written work, 3 letters of recommendation. Additional exam requirements/recommendations for international students: Required—TOEFL (minimum score 550 paper-based; 213 computer-based; 77 iBT). *Application deadline:* For fall admission, 1/15 for domestic students. Application fee: $70. Electronic applications accepted. *Expenses:* Tuition: Full-time $29,500. Required fees: $70. Full-time tuition and fees vary according to degree level, program and student level. *Financial support:* In 2009–10, 17 students received support, including 3 fellowships with full tuition reimbursements available; research assistantships with full tuition reimbursements available, teaching assistantships with full tuition reimbursements available, institutionally sponsored loans, scholarships/grants, health care benefits, tuition waivers (full and partial), and unspecified assistantships also available. Financial award applicants required to submit FAFSA. *Unit head:* Director of Graduate Studies, 607-255-4905, Fax: 607-255-0566, E-mail: art_history@cornell.edu. *Application contact:* Graduate Field Assistant, 607-255-4905, Fax: 607-255-0566, E-mail: art_history@cornell.edu.

East Carolina University, Graduate School, Thomas Harriot College of Arts and Sciences, Department of History, Greenville, NC 27858-4353. Offers American history (MA); European history (MA); maritime history (MA). Part-time and evening/weekend programs available. *Degree requirements:* For master's, one foreign language, comprehensive exam, thesis. *Entrance requirements:* For master's, GRE General Test, GRE Subject Test. Additional exam requirements/recommendations for international students: Required—TOEFL.

Eastern Michigan University, Graduate School, College of Arts and Sciences, Department of History and Philosophy, Programs in Social Sciences, Ypsilanti, MI 48197. Offers social science (MA, Graduate Certificate); social science and American culture (MLS). Part-time and evening/weekend programs available. Postbaccalaureate distance learning degree programs offered (minimal on-campus study). *Students:* 7 full-time (3 women), 23 part-time (14 women); includes 2 minority (1 African American, 1 Asian American or Pacific Islander), 2 international. Average age 32. In 2009, 10 master's awarded. *Degree requirements:* For master's, thesis optional. *Entrance requirements:* Additional exam requirements/recommendations for international students: Required—TOEFL. *Application deadline:* Applications are processed on a rolling basis. Application fee: $35. Tuition and fees vary according to course level. *Financial support:* Fellowships, research assistantships with full tuition reimbursements, teaching assistantships with full tuition reimbursements, career-related internships or fieldwork, Federal Work-Study, institutionally sponsored loans, scholarships/grants, tuition waivers (partial), and unspecified assistantships available. Support available to part-time students. Financial award applicants required to submit FAFSA. *Application contact:* Dr. Ronald Delph, Coordinator, 734-487-0053, Fax: 734-487-6835, E-mail: rdelph@emich.edu.

Emory & Henry College, Graduate Programs, Emory, VA 24327-0947. Offers American history (MA Ed); organizational leadership (MOL); professional studies (M Ed); reading specialist (MA Ed). Part-time and evening/weekend programs available. *Entrance requirements:* For master's, GRE or PRAXIS I, recommendations, writing sample.

Fairfield University, College of Arts and Sciences, Fairfield, CT 06824-5195. Offers American studies (MA); communication (MA); creative writing (MFA); mathematics (MS). Part-time and evening/weekend programs available. *Degree requirements:* For master's, capstone research course. *Entrance requirements:* For master's, minimum GPA of 3.0, 2 letters of recommendation, resume. Additional exam requirements/recommendations for international students: Required—TOEFL (minimum score 550 paper-based; 213 computer-based; 80 iBT). Electronic applications accepted. *Faculty research:* Non-commutative algebra, partial differential equations, writing (fiction, non-fiction and poetry), communication for social change, comparative media systems, negotiation and management.

Georgetown University, Graduate School of Arts and Sciences, School of Continuing Studies, Washington, DC 20057. Offers American studies (MALS); Catholic studies (MALS); classical civilizations (MALS); ethics and the professions (MALS); human resources management (MPS); humanities (MALS); individualized study (MALS); international affairs (MALS); Islam and Muslim-Christian relations (MALS); journalism (MPS); liberal studies (DLS); literature and society (MALS); medieval and early modern European studies (MALS); public relations (MPS); real estate (MPS); religious studies (MALS); social and public policy (MALS); sports industry management (MPS); the theory and practice of American democracy (MALS); visual culture (MALS). *Entrance requirements:* Additional exam requirements/recommendations for international students: Required—TOEFL.

The George Washington University, Columbian College of Arts and Sciences, Department of American Studies, Washington, DC 20052. Offers American studies (PhD); folklife (MA); historic preservation (MA); material culture (MA). Part-time and evening/weekend programs available. *Faculty:* 10 full-time (4 women), 5 part-time/adjunct (4 women). *Students:* 24 full-time (16 women), 26 part-time (14 women); includes 7 minority (5 African Americans, 1 Asian American or Pacific Islander, 1 Hispanic American), 3 international. Average age 31. 116 applicants, 43% accepted, 17 enrolled. In 2009, 10 master's, 4 doctorates awarded. Terminal master's awarded for partial completion of doctoral program. *Degree requirements:* For master's, comprehensive exam; for doctorate, one foreign language, thesis/dissertation, general exam. *Entrance requirements:* For master's and doctorate, GRE General Test, minimum GPA of 3.0. Additional exam requirements/recommendations for international students: Required—TOEFL (minimum score 550 paper-based; 213 computer-based; 80 iBT). *Application deadline:* For fall admission, 1/15 priority date for domestic and international students; for spring admission, 10/1 for domestic students. Application fee: $60. *Financial support:* In 2009–10, 22 students received support; fellowships, research assistantships, teaching assistantships, career-related internships or fieldwork, Federal Work-Study, institutionally sponsored loans, and tuition waivers available. Financial award application deadline: 1/15. *Unit head:* James A. Miller, Chair, 202-994-6743, E-mail: jam@gwu.edu. *Application contact:* Information Contact, 202-994-6070, Fax: 202-994-8651, E-mail: amst@gwu.edu.

Harvard University, Graduate School of Arts and Sciences, Committee on History of American Civilization, Cambridge, MA 02138. Offers PhD. *Degree requirements:* For doctorate, 2 foreign languages, thesis/dissertation. *Entrance requirements:* For doctorate, GRE General Test, GRE Subject Test (recommended). Additional exam requirements/recommendations for international students: Required—TOEFL. *Expenses:* Tuition: Full-time $33,696. Required fees: $1126. Full-time tuition and fees vary according to program. *Faculty research:* American history, literature, and religion in the Colonial era; twentieth century American history, literature, and law; Southern literature, history, and sociology.

Inter American University of Puerto Rico, Metropolitan Campus, Graduate Programs, Program in History, San Juan, PR 00919-1293. Offers American history (PhD); history (MA, PhD).

Kennesaw State University, College of Humanities and Social Sciences, Master of Arts in American Studies Program, Kennesaw, GA 30144-5591. Offers MA. Part-time programs available. *Students:* 10 full-time (7 women), 8 part-time (6 women); includes 1 minority (African American). Average age 33. 26 applicants, 77% accepted, 16 enrolled. *Degree requirements:* For master's, one foreign language. *Entrance requirements:* For master's, GRE. Additional exam requirements/recommendations for international students: Required—TOEFL (minimum score 550 paper-based; 213 computer-based; 80 iBT), IELTS (minimum score 6). *Application deadline:* For fall admission, 5/1 for domestic and international students; for winter admission, 11/1 for domestic and international students. Applications are processed on a rolling basis. Application fee: $60. Electronic applications accepted. *Expenses:* Tuition, state resident: full-time $2341; part-time $196 per credit hour. Tuition, nonresident: full-time $9396; part-time $783 per credit hour. Required fees: $573 per semester. *Unit head:* LeeAnn Lands. *Application contact:* Vilma Marquez, Admissions Counselor, 770-420-4377, Fax: 770-423-6885, E-mail: ksugrad@kennesaw.edu.

Lehigh University, College of Arts and Sciences, Department of History, Bethlehem, PA 18015. Offers American history (PhD); British history (PhD); history (MA). Part-time programs available. *Faculty:* 14 full-time (4 women), 2 part-time/adjunct (1 woman). *Students:* 17 full-time (7 women), 17 part-time (4 women); includes 1 minority (Asian American or Pacific Islander), 1 international. Average age 32. 19 applicants, 68% accepted, 3 enrolled. In 2009, 2 master's, 3 doctorates awarded. Terminal master's awarded for partial completion of doctoral program. *Degree requirements:* For master's, thesis optional, comprehensive exam or thesis; for doctorate, comprehensive exam, thesis/dissertation. *Entrance requirements:* For master's, GRE General Test, recommendations; for doctorate, GRE General Test, recommendations, writing samples. Additional exam requirements/recommendations for international students: Required—TOEFL. *Application deadline:* For fall admission, 7/15 for domestic students; for winter admission, 1/15 priority date for domestic and international students. Applications are processed on a rolling basis. Application fee: $65. Electronic applications accepted. *Financial support:* In 2009–10, 27 students received support, including research assistantships with full tuition reimbursements available (averaging $15,600 per year), 10 teaching assistantships with full tuition reimbursements available (averaging $18,400 per year); fellowships with full tuition reimbursements available, career-related internships or fieldwork, Federal Work-Study, institutionally sponsored loans, scholarships/grants, tuition waivers (full and partial), and unspecified assistantships also available. Support available to part-time students. Financial award application deadline: 1/15. *Faculty research:* Colonial America, modern America, history of technology. *Unit head:* Dr. Stephen H. Cutcliffe, Chairman, 610-758-3360, Fax: 610-758-6554, E-mail: shc0@lehigh.edu. *Application contact:* Dr. Roger D. Simon, Graduate Coordinator, 610-758-3368, Fax: 610-758-6554, E-mail: rds2@lehigh.edu.

Lehigh University, College of Arts and Sciences, Program in American Studies, Bethlehem, PA 18015. Offers MA. Part-time programs available. *Students:* 9 full-time (all women), 3 part-time (2 women), 2 international. Average age 25. 13 applicants, 77% accepted, 8 enrolled. In 2009, 4 master's awarded. *Degree requirements:* For master's, thesis. *Entrance requirements:* For master's, GRE, writing sample. Additional exam requirements/recommendations for international students: Required—TOEFL. *Application deadline:* For fall admission, 7/15 for domestic and international students; for spring admission, 12/1 for domestic and international students. Application fee: $65. Electronic applications accepted. *Financial support:* In 2009–10, 4 students received support, including 1 fellowship with full tuition reimbursement available; institutionally sponsored loans, scholarships/grants, tuition waivers (full), and unspecified assistantships also available. Support available to part-time students. Financial award application deadline: 1/15; financial award applicants required to submit FAFSA. *Unit head:* Prof. Edward Whitley, Director, 610-758-4745, Fax: 610-758-6554, E-mail: amstdgrad@lehigh.edu. *Application contact:* Mary T. Harnett, Coordinator, 610-758-4745, Fax: 610-758-6554, E-mail: amstdgrad@lehigh.edu.

Lindenwood University, Graduate Programs, School of Humanities, St. Charles, MO 63301-1695. Offers American studies (MA); international studies (MA). Part-time programs available. *Faculty:* 4 full-time (2 women), 5 part-time/adjunct (1 woman). *Students:* 11 full-time (4 women), 8 part-time (6 women); includes 1 minority (African American), 9 international. Average age 30. 8 applicants, 6 enrolled. In 2009, 2 master's awarded. *Entrance requirements:* For master's, minimum GPA of 2.5, 2 letters of recommendation. Additional exam requirements/recommendations for international students: Required—TOEFL (minimum score 550 paper-based; 213 computer-based; 80 iBT). *Application deadline:* For fall admission, 8/27 priority date for domestic and international students; for spring admission, 1/28 for domestic students, 1/28 priority date for international students. Applications are processed on a rolling basis. Application fee: $30 ($100 for international students). Electronic applications accepted. *Expenses:* Tuition: Full-time $12,960; part-time $370 per credit hour. Required fees: $340. One-time fee: $30 full-time. Tuition and fees vary according to course level and course load. *Financial support:* In 2009–10, 19 students received support. Career-related internships or fieldwork, institutionally sponsored loans, tuition waivers (partial), and unspecified assistantships available. Financial award application deadline: 6/30; financial award applicants required to submit FAFSA. *Unit head:* Dr. Ana Schnellmann, Dean, 636-949-4873, E-mail: aschnellmann@lindenwood.edu. *Application contact:* Brett Barger, Dean of Evening Admissions and Extension Campuses, 636-949-4934, Fax: 636-949-4109, E-mail: adultadmissions@lindenwood.edu.

Michigan State University, The Graduate School, College of Arts and Letters, Program in American Studies, East Lansing, MI 48824. Offers MA, PhD. *Students:* 35 full-time (15

American Studies

Michigan State University (continued)

women), 4 part-time (2 women); includes 12 minority (4 African Americans, 4 American Indian/Alaska Native, 2 Asian Americans or Pacific Islanders, 2 Hispanic Americans), 4 international. Average age 34. 39 applicants, 26% accepted. In 2009, 2 master's, 4 doctorates awarded. *Entrance requirements:* Additional exam requirements/recommendations for international students: Required—TOEFL. Electronic applications accepted. *Expenses:* Tuition, state resident: part-time $478.25 per credit hour. Tuition, nonresident: part-time $966.50 per credit hour. Part-time tuition and fees vary according to program. *Financial support:* In 2009–10, 2 research assistantships with tuition reimbursements (averaging $6,197 per year), 15 teaching assistantships with tuition reimbursements (averaging $6,170 per year) were awarded. *Unit head:* Dr. Ann Larabee, Director, 517-432-2565, Fax: 517-353-5250, E-mail: larabee@msu.edu. *Application contact:* Patience Adibe, Office Manager, 517-432-3791, Fax: 517-353-5250, E-mail: amstudys@msu.edu.

Mississippi State University, College of Arts and Sciences, Department of History, Mississippi State, MS 39762. Offers history (PhD); U. S. and European history (MA). Part-time programs available. *Faculty:* 17 full-time (6 women). *Students:* 34 full-time (13 women), 13 part-time (4 women); includes 2 minority (1 African American, 1 Asian American or Pacific Islander). Average age 32. 30 applicants, 80% accepted, 12 enrolled. In 2009, 7 master's, 2 doctorates awarded. *Degree requirements:* For master's, one foreign language, comprehensive exam, thesis optional; for doctorate, 2 foreign languages, thesis/dissertation, comprehensive oral and written exam. *Entrance requirements:* For master's, GRE (except for those with MA in history from MSU), minimum GPA of 3.0 on last two years of undergraduate courses; for doctorate, GRE, writing sample, minimum graduate GPA of 3.0. Additional exam requirements/recommendations for international students: Required—TOEFL (minimum score 475 paper-based; 153 computer-based; 53 iBT); Recommended—IELTS (minimum score 4.5). *Application deadline:* For fall admission, 4/1 for domestic students, 5/1 for international students; for spring admission, 11/1 for domestic students, 9/1 for international students. Applications are processed on a rolling basis. Application fee: $40. Electronic applications accepted. *Expenses:* Tuition, state resident: full-time $2575.50; part-time $286.25 per credit hour. Tuition, nonresident: full-time $6510; part-time $723.50 per credit hour. Tuition and fees vary according to course load. *Financial support:* In 2009–10, 2 research assistantships (averaging $9,333 per year), 26 teaching assistantships with full tuition reimbursements (averaging $11,005 per year) were awarded; Federal Work-Study, institutionally sponsored loans, scholarships/grants, and unspecified assistantships also available. Financial award application deadline: 4/1; financial award applicants required to submit FAFSA. *Faculty research:* U. S. political, diplomatic, military, social, and cultural history; modern Europe; Latin America; Asian history; African history. *Unit head:* Dr. Alan I. Marcus, Head, 662-325-3604, Fax: 662-325-1139, E-mail: aim10@msstate.edu. *Application contact:* Dr. Richard Damms, Associate Professor/Graduate Coordinator, 662-325-8821, E-mail: correspondence@history.msstate.edu.

Monmouth University, Graduate School, Department of History, West Long Branch, NJ 07764-1898. Offers European specialization (MA); U.S. specialization (MA); world specialization (MA). Part-time and evening/weekend programs available. *Faculty:* 13 full-time (3 women), 1 part-time/adjunct (0 women). *Students:* 3 full-time (1 woman), 59 part-time (27 women); includes 5 minority (1 Asian American or Pacific Islander, 4 Hispanic Americans). Average age 38. 31 applicants, 100% accepted, 15 enrolled. In 2009, 16 master's awarded. *Degree requirements:* For master's, comprehensive exam, thesis or alternative. *Entrance requirements:* For master's, minimum GPA of 3.0 in major, 2.5 overall. Additional exam requirements/recommendations for international students: Required—TOEFL (minimum score 550 paper-based; 213 computer-based; 79 iBT), IELTS (minimum score 5), Michigan English Language Assessment Battery (minimum score 77), Cambridge A, B, C. *Application deadline:* For fall admission, 7/15 priority date for domestic students, 6/1 for international students; for spring admission, 11/15 priority date for domestic students, 11/1 for international students. Applications are processed on a rolling basis. Application fee: $50. Electronic applications accepted. *Expenses:* Tuition: Part-time $773 per credit. Required fees: $157 per semester. *Financial support:* In 2009–10, 47 students received support, including 39 fellowships (averaging $1,270 per year), 22 research assistantships (averaging $6,668 per year); career-related internships or fieldwork, scholarships/grants, and unspecified assistantships also available. Support available to part-time students. Financial award applicants required to submit FAFSA. *Faculty research:* U.S. business; labor; British, German, and French Revolutions; Soviet Union; Africa. *Unit head:* Dr. Aaron Ansell, Director, 732-571-4495, Fax: 732-263-5112, E-mail: aansell@monmouth.edu. *Application contact:* Kevin Roane, Director, Office of Graduate Admission, 732-571-3452, Fax: 732-263-5123, E-mail: gradadm@monmouth.edu.

New Mexico Highlands University, Graduate Studies, College of Arts and Sciences, Program in Southwest Studies, Las Vegas, NM 87701. Offers anthropology (MA). Program is interdisciplinary. Part-time programs available. *Degree requirements:* For master's, comprehensive exam, thesis or alternative. *Entrance requirements:* For master's, minimum undergraduate GPA of 3.0. Additional exam requirements/recommendations for international students: Required—TOEFL (minimum score 540 paper-based; 207 computer-based).

New York University, Graduate School of Arts and Science, Program in American Studies, New York, NY 10012-1019. Offers MA, PhD. Part-time programs available. *Faculty:* 4 full-time (1 woman), 2 part-time/adjunct (0 women). *Students:* 41 full-time (26 women), 8 part-time (3 women); includes 26 minority (12 African Americans, 1 American Indian/Alaska Native, 5 Asian Americans or Pacific Islanders, 8 Hispanic Americans), 4 international. Average age 32. 222 applicants, 9% accepted, 11 enrolled. In 2009, 2 master's, 7 doctorates awarded. *Degree requirements:* For master's, one foreign language, thesis; for doctorate, 2 foreign languages, thesis/dissertation. *Entrance requirements:* For master's and doctorate, GRE General Test, writing sample. Additional exam requirements/recommendations for international students: Required—TOEFL. *Application deadline:* For fall admission, 12/18 for domestic students. Application fee: $90. *Expenses:* Tuition: Full-time $30,528; part-time $1272 per credit. Required fees: $2177. *Financial support:* Fellowships with tuition reimbursements, teaching assistantships with tuition reimbursements, Federal Work-Study, institutionally sponsored loans, and unspecified assistantships available. Financial award application deadline: 12/18; financial award applicants required to submit FAFSA. *Faculty research:* Cultural politics; race, gender, and sexuality studies; nationalism and transnationalism; science and technology; urban and suburban studies. *Unit head:* Nikhil Singh, Director of American Studies, 212-998-9650, Fax: 212-995-4665, E-mail: amstudies@nyu.edu. *Application contact:* Jennifer Morgan, Director of Graduate Studies, 212-998-9650, Fax: 212-995-4665, E-mail: amstudies@nyu.edu.

New York University, Graduate School of Arts and Science, Program in Irish and Irish American Studies, New York, NY 10012-1019. Offers MA. Part-time programs available. *Students:* 7 full-time (6 women), 16 part-time (10 women), 1 international. Average age 33. 23 applicants, 87% accepted, 9 enrolled. In 2009, 10 master's awarded. *Degree requirements:* For master's, one foreign language. *Entrance requirements:* For master's, GRE General Test. Additional exam requirements/recommendations for international students: Required—TOEFL. *Application deadline:* For fall admission, 4/15 priority date for domestic students. Application fee: $90. *Expenses:* Tuition: Full-time $30,528; part-time $1272 per credit. Required fees: $2177. *Financial support:* Federal Work-Study, scholarships/grants, health care benefits, and unspecified assistantships available. Financial award application deadline: 4/15. *Unit head:* John Waters, Director of Graduate Studies, 212-998-3950, Fax: 212-995-4373, E-mail: gsas.irishstudies.ma@nyu.edu. *Application contact:* Anne Solari, Program Coordinator, 212-998-3950, Fax: 212-995-4373, E-mail: gsas.irishstudies.ma@nyu.edu.

Northeastern State University, Graduate College, College of Liberal Arts, Program in American Studies, Tahlequah, OK 74464-2399. Offers MA. Part-time and evening/weekend programs available. *Degree requirements:* For master's, thesis, written and oral examinations. *Entrance requirements:* For master's, GRE, minimum GPA of 2.5. Additional exam requirements/recommendations for international students: Required—TOEFL (minimum score 213 computer-based). Electronic applications accepted.

Northwestern University, School of Continuing Studies, Program in Liberal Studies, Evanston, IL 60208. Offers American studies (MA); history (MA); religious and ethical studies (MA).

Norwich University, School of Graduate and Continuing Studies, Program in Military History, Northfield, VT 05663. Offers race and gender in military history (MA); U. S. military history (MA). Evening/weekend programs available. *Faculty:* 33 part-time/adjunct (2 women). *Students:* 531 full-time (85 women); includes 30 minority (3 African Americans, 6 American Indian/Alaska Native, 6 Asian Americans or Pacific Islanders, 15 Hispanic Americans). Average age 42. 736 applicants, 80% accepted, 531 enrolled. In 2009, 503 master's awarded. *Entrance requirements:* For master's, minimum undergraduate GPA of 2.75. Additional exam requirements/recommendations for international students: Required—TOEFL (minimum score 550 paper-based; 212 computer-based; 83 iBT). *Application deadline:* For fall admission, 8/10 for domestic and international students; for winter admission, 11/7 for domestic and international students; for spring admission, 2/6 for domestic and international students. Application fee: $50. Electronic applications accepted. Full-time tuition and fees vary according to course level and course load. *Financial support:* Scholarships/grants available. Financial award applicants required to submit FAFSA. *Unit head:* Dr. James Erhman, Program Director, 802-485-2567, Fax: 802-485-2533. *Application contact:* Lars Nielsen, Administrative Director, 802-485-2853, Fax: 802-485-2533, E-mail: lnielsen@norwich.edu.

Penn State Harrisburg, Graduate School, School of Humanities, Middletown, PA 17057-4898. Offers American studies (MA). Evening/weekend programs available. *Unit head:* Dr. Kathryn Robinson, Director, 717-948-6470, E-mail: kdr12@psu.edu. *Application contact:* Robert Coffman, Director of Admissions, 717-948-6250, Fax: 717-948-6325, E-mail: ric1@psu.edu.

Pepperdine University, Seaver College, Humanities Division, Malibu, CA 90263. Offers American studies (MA); history (MA). *Degree requirements:* For master's, oral and written exams. *Entrance requirements:* For master's, GRE General Test, undergraduate major or 15 upper-division units in history. Additional exam requirements/recommendations for international students: Required—TOEFL. *Expenses:* Tuition: Full-time $37,516; part-time $1310 per unit. Required fees: $80.

Providence College, Graduate Studies, Department of History, Providence, RI 02918. Offers American history (MA); European history (MA). Part-time and evening/weekend programs available. *Faculty:* 6 full-time (1 woman), 4 part-time/adjunct (1 woman). *Students:* 25 full-time (10 women), 31 part-time (16 women), 1 international. Average age 29. 19 applicants, 100% accepted. In 2009, 28 master's awarded. *Degree requirements:* For master's, comprehensive exam, thesis optional. *Entrance requirements:* Additional exam requirements/recommendations for international students: Required—TOEFL (minimum score 550 paper-based; 213 computer-based; 80 iBT). *Application deadline:* For fall admission, 8/1 priority date for domestic and international students; for spring admission, 12/31 priority date for domestic students, 12/1 priority date for international students. Applications are processed on a rolling basis. Application fee: $55. *Expenses:* Tuition: Full-time $9909; part-time $367 per credit. One-time fee: $200. Tuition and fees vary according to course load and program. *Financial support:* In 2009–10, 8 research assistantships with full tuition reimbursements (averaging $8,400 per year) were awarded; career-related internships or fieldwork, institutionally sponsored loans, and unspecified assistantships also available. Support available to part-time students. Financial award application deadline: 8/1; financial award applicants required to submit FAFSA. *Faculty research:* Modern Europe, American social and political history, modern Ireland, Rhode Island, eastern European history. *Unit head:* Dr. Paul O'Malley, Director of Graduate Program in History, 401-865-2193, Fax: 401-865-1193, E-mail: pomalley@providence.edu. *Application contact:* Phyllis S. Cardullo, Senior Administrative Coordinator, 401-865-2193, Fax: 401-865-1193, E-mail: pcardull@providence.edu.

Purdue University, Graduate School, College of Liberal Arts, Program in American Studies, West Lafayette, IN 47907. Offers MA, PhD. *Degree requirements:* For master's, essay; for doctorate, one foreign language, thesis/dissertation. *Entrance requirements:* For master's and doctorate, GRE General Test, sample of written work. Additional exam requirements/recommendations for international students: Required—TOEFL, TWE. Electronic applications accepted. *Faculty research:* American history, literature, politics, sociology, women's studies, African-American studies, mass culture.

Regent University, Graduate School, Robertson School of Government, Virginia Beach, VA 23464. Offers american government (MA); global politics (MA); health care policy and administration (MA); international politics (MA); law and public policy (MA); Mid-East Politics (MA); political leadership and management (MA); political management (MA); political theory (MA); public administration (MA); public policy (MA); terrorism and homeland defense (MA); world economies and political development (MA); JD/MA; M Div/MA; M Ed/MA; MBA/MA. Part-time and evening/weekend programs available. Postbaccalaureate distance learning degree programs offered (minimal on-campus study). *Faculty:* 6 full-time (2 women), 11 part-time/adjunct (1 woman). *Students:* 77 full-time (55 women), 65 part-time (36 women); includes 47 minority (38 African Americans, 2 Asian Americans or Pacific Islanders, 7 Hispanic Americans), 4 international. Average age 30. 131 applicants, 65% accepted, 54 enrolled. In 2009, 51 master's awarded. *Degree requirements:* For master's, thesis optional, internship. *Entrance requirements:* For master's, GRE General Test or LSAT, minimum undergraduate GPA of 3.0, writing sample, resume, interview, references. Additional exam requirements/recommendations for international students: Required—TOEFL (minimum score 577 paper-based; 233 computer-based). *Application deadline:* For fall admission, 5/1 priority date for domestic students; for spring admission, 11/1 priority date for domestic students. Applications are processed on a rolling basis. Application fee: $50. Electronic applications accepted. *Expenses:* Contact institution. *Financial support:* In 2009–10, 130 students received support. Career-related internships or fieldwork, scholarships/grants, tuition waivers (full and partial), and unspecified assistantships available. Support available to part-time students. Financial award application deadline: 9/1; financial award applicants required to submit FAFSA. *Faculty research:* Education reform, political character issues, social capital concerns, administrative ethics, Biblical law and public policy. *Unit head:* Dr. Charles W. Dunn, Dean, 757-352-4322, Fax: 757-352-4643, E-mail: cwdunn@regent.edu. *Application contact:* Matthew Chadwick, Director of Admissions, 800-373-5504, Fax: 757-352-4381, E-mail: admissions@regent.edu.

Rice University, Graduate Programs, School of Humanities, Department of Religious Studies, Houston, TX 77251-1892. Offers African religions (PhD); African-American religions (PhD); contemplative studies (PhD); gnosticism, esotericism, mysticism (PhD); Islam (PhD); Jewish thought and philosophy (PhD); modern Christianity in thought and popular culture (PhD); psychology of religion (PhD); the Bible and beyond (PhD). *Faculty:* 11 full-time (3 women), 2 part-time/adjunct (both women). *Students:* 37 full-time (13 women); includes 10 minority (9 African Americans, 1 Asian American or Pacific Islander), 9 international. Average age 31. 42 applicants, 14% accepted, 6 enrolled. In 2009, 2 doctorates awarded. *Degree requirements:* For doctorate, 2 foreign languages, comprehensive exam, thesis/dissertation. *Entrance requirements:* For doctorate, GRE, letters of recommendation, writing sample. Additional exam requirements/recommendations for international students: Required—TOEFL (minimum score 600 paper-based; 90 iBT). *Application deadline:* For fall admission, 1/1 for domestic students, 1/15 for international students. Application fee: $70. Electronic applications accepted. *Financial support:* In 2009–10, 14 fellowships (averaging $15,900 per year) were awarded. Financial award application deadline: 5/15; financial award applicants required to submit FAFSA. *Faculty research:* Origins and historical development of Islam, history of Christianity, the study of comparative religion, African-American religion, religion and culture. Total annual research expenditures: $46,514. *Unit head:* Prof. William B. Parsons, Associate Professor, Religious Studies, 713-348-2712, Fax: 713-348-5486, E-mail: pars@rice.edu. *Application contact:* Sylvia Louie, Senior Department Coordinator, 713-348-5201, Fax: 713-348-5486, E-mail: reli@rice.edu.

Rutgers, The State University of New Jersey, Newark, Graduate School, Program in American Studies, Newark, NJ 07102. Offers MA, PhD. *Entrance requirements:* For master's and doctorate, GRE, minimum undergraduate B average.

Saint Louis University, Graduate School, College of Arts and Sciences and Graduate School, Department of American Studies, St. Louis, MO 63103-2097. Offers MA, MA-R, PhD. Part-time programs available. *Degree requirements:* For master's, thesis optional, comprehensive written and oral exams; for doctorate, one foreign language, comprehensive exam, thesis/dissertation, preliminary exams. *Entrance requirements:* For master's, GRE General Test, letters of recommendation, resume; for doctorate, GRE General Test, letters of recommendation, resumé, goal statement, transcripts. Additional exam requirements/recommendations for international students: Required—TOEFL (minimum score 525 paper-based; 194 computer-based). Electronic applications accepted. *Faculty research:* Urban studies, American religion, intellectual history, southern culture, African-American literature.

State University of New York College at Cortland, Graduate Studies, School of Arts and Sciences, Program in American Civilization and Culture, Cortland, NY 13045. Offers CAS. Part-time and evening/weekend programs available. *Entrance requirements:* Additional exam requirements/recommendations for international students: Required—TOEFL.

Trinity College, Graduate Programs, Program in American Studies, Hartford, CT 06106-3100. Offers MA. Part-time and evening/weekend programs available. *Faculty:* 2 part-time/adjunct (1 woman). *Students:* 34 part-time (21 women); includes 2 African Americans, 1 Hispanic American. Average age 38. In 2009, 10 master's awarded. *Degree requirements:* For master's, thesis or alternative. *Entrance requirements:* For master's, minimum GPA of 3.0. *Application deadline:* For fall admission, 4/15 for domestic students; for spring admission, 11/15 for domestic students. Application fee: $50. *Expenses:* Tuition: Part-time $1700 per course. One-time fee: $75 full-time. *Financial support:* In 2009–10, 4 students received support, including 4 fellowships; tuition waivers (full) also available. Support available to part-time students. Financial award application deadline: 4/1. *Unit head:* Dr. Paul Lauter, Graduate Director, 860-297-2303. *Application contact:* Nicola Dawkins, Program Manager for Graduate Studies, 860-297-2151, Fax: 860-297 5179, E-mail: nicola.dawkins@trincoll.edu.

Universidad de las Américas–Puebla, Division of Graduate Studies, School of Social Sciences, Program in American Studies, Puebla, Mexico. Offers MA. Part-time and evening/weekend programs available. *Degree requirements:* For master's, one foreign language, thesis. *Faculty research:* NAFTA, technology, culture, politics and economics in NAFTA region.

University at Buffalo, the State University of New York, Graduate School, College of Arts and Sciences, Department of American Studies, Buffalo, NY 14260. Offers MA, PhD. Post-baccalaureate distance learning degree programs offered (minimal on-campus study). Terminal master's awarded for partial completion of doctoral program. *Degree requirements:* For master's, comprehensive exam, thesis (for some programs); for doctorate, comprehensive exam, thesis/dissertation. *Entrance requirements:* For master's, minimum GPA of 3.0; for doctorate, GRE, minimum GPA of 3.0. Additional exam requirements/recommendations for international students: Required—TOEFL (minimum score 550 paper-based; 213 computer-based; 79 iBT). Electronic applications accepted. *Faculty research:* Native American studies, intercultural studies, indigenous people's studies, multiculturalism, border theory, cultural studies, American popular culture.

The University of Alabama, Graduate School, College of Arts and Sciences, Department of American Studies, Tuscaloosa, AL 35487. Offers MA. Part-time programs available. *Faculty:* 7 full-time (2 women). *Students:* 17 full-time (9 women), 2 part-time (1 woman); includes 1 minority (Asian American or Pacific Islander). Average age 27. 21 applicants, 62% accepted, 11 enrolled. In 2009, 5 degrees awarded. *Degree requirements:* For master's, comprehensive exam, thesis optional. *Entrance requirements:* For master's, GRE or MAT. Additional exam requirements/recommendations for international students: Required—TOEFL. *Application deadline:* For fall admission, 1/15 priority date for domestic and international students; for spring admission, 11/30 priority date for domestic and international students. Applications are processed on a rolling basis. Application fee: $50 ($60 for international students). Electronic applications accepted. *Expenses:* Tuition, state resident: full-time $7000. Tuition, nonresident: full-time $19,200. *Financial support:* In 2009–10, 12 students received support; teaching assistantships, career-related internships or fieldwork, tuition waivers (full), and unspecified assistantships available. *Faculty research:* Social and cultural history, popular music, African-American arts, the South, women's history, Asian-American studies, sports, Latino Studies. *Unit head:* Dr. Lynne M. Adrian, Associate Professor, 205-348-5940, Fax: 205-348-9766, E-mail: ladrian@tenhoor.as.ua.edu. *Application contact:* Dr. Lynne M. Adrian, Associate Professor, 205-348-5940, Fax: 205-348-9766, E-mail: ladrian@tenhoor.as.ua.edu.

University of Central Oklahoma, College of Graduate Studies and Research, College of Liberal Arts, Department of History, Edmond, OK 73034-5209. Offers history (MA); museum studies (MA); social studies teaching (MA); Southwestern studies (MA). Part-time programs available. *Degree requirements:* For master's, thesis optional. *Entrance requirements:* Additional exam requirements/recommendations for international students: Required—TOEFL (minimum score 550 paper-based; 213 computer-based). Electronic applications accepted. *Expenses:* Tuition, state resident: full-time $4128; part-time $172 per credit hour. Tuition, nonresident: full-time $10,373; part-time $432.20 per credit hour. Required fees: $433.20; $18.05 per credit hour. *Faculty research:* China, Russia, civil war, American naval logistics.

University of Dallas, Braniff Graduate School of Liberal Arts, Program in American Studies, Irving, TX 75062-4736. Offers MAS. Part-time programs available. *Faculty:* 1 full-time (0 women). *Students:* 2 full-time (1 woman), 5 part-time (2 women); includes 1 minority (Hispanic American). Average age 35. 4 applicants, 100% accepted, 2 enrolled. In 2009, 1 master's awarded. *Degree requirements:* For master's, comprehensive exam. *Entrance requirements:* For master's, GRE General Test. *Application deadline:* For fall admission, 2/15 priority date for domestic students; for spring admission, 11/15 for domestic students. Applications are processed on a rolling basis. Application fee: $50. *Expenses:* Tuition: Full-time $10,080; part-time $560 per credit hour. Required fees: $50 per term. Tuition and fees vary according to program. *Financial support:* In 2009–10, 7 students received support. Scholarships/grants available. Financial award application deadline: 2/15. *Faculty research:* Shakespeare, Milton, Melville, Hawthorne, liberty and American literature. *Unit head:* Dr. John Alvis, Director, 972-721-5365, Fax: 972-721-4007, E-mail: alvis@udallas.edu. *Application contact:* Graduate Coordinator, 972-721-5106, Fax: 972-721-5280, E-mail: graduate@acad.udallas.edu.

University of Delaware, College of Arts and Sciences, Winterthur Program in Early American Culture, Newark, DE 19716. Offers MA. *Degree requirements:* For master's, thesis. *Entrance requirements:* For master's, GRE General Test, minimum GPA of 3.0. Electronic applications accepted. *Faculty research:* American material culture, American studies, decorative arts.

University of Hawaii at Manoa, Graduate Division, College of Arts and Humanities, Department of American Studies, Honolulu, HI 96822. Offers American studies (MA, PhD); historic preservation (Graduate Certificate); museum studies (Graduate Certificate). Part-time programs available. *Faculty:* 15 full-time (4 women), 3 part-time/adjunct (all women). *Students:* 45 full-time (32 women), 27 part-time (19 women); includes 25 minority (2 American Indian/Alaska Native, 21 Asian Americans or Pacific Islanders, 2 Hispanic Americans), 12 international. Average age 32. 36 applicants, 69% accepted, 19 enrolled. In 2009, 6 master's awarded. *Degree requirements:* For master's, comprehensive exam (for some programs), thesis (for some programs); for doctorate, comprehensive exam, thesis/dissertation. *Entrance requirements:* For master's and doctorate, GRE General Test. Additional exam requirements/recommendations for international students: Required—TOEFL (minimum score 600 paper-based; 250 computer-based; 100 iBT), IELTS (minimum score 7). *Application deadline:* For fall admission, 2/1 for domestic students, 1/15 for international students; for spring admission, 9/1 for domestic students, 8/1 for international students. Application fee: $60. *Expenses:* Tuition, state resident: full-time $8900; part-time $372 per credit. Tuition, nonresident: full-time $21,400; part-time $898 per credit. Required fees: $207 per semester. *Financial support:* In 2009–10, 5 students received support, including 14 fellowships (averaging $1,127 per year), 2 research assistantships (averaging $17,496 per year), 6 teaching assistantships (averaging $15,362 per year); institutionally sponsored loans and tuition waivers (full and partial) also available. Support available to part-time students. Financial award application deadline: 3/31. *Faculty research:* Ethnicity and race, popular culture, historic preservation, arts and culture, international relations. Total annual research expenditures: $7,500. *Application contact:* Robert Perkinson, Graduate Chairperson, 808-956-8570, Fax: 808-956-4733, E-mail: perk@hawaii.edu.

The University of Iowa, Graduate College, College of Liberal Arts and Sciences, Department of American Studies, Iowa City, IA 52242-1316. Offers MA, PhD. *Degree requirements:* For master's, thesis optional, exam; for doctorate, comprehensive exam, thesis/dissertation. *Entrance requirements:* For master's and doctorate, GRE General Test, minimum GPA of 3.0. Additional exam requirements/recommendations for international students: Required—TOEFL (minimum score 550 paper-based; 213 computer-based; 81 iBT). Electronic applications accepted.

The University of Kansas, Graduate Studies, College of Liberal Arts and Sciences, Program in American Studies, Lawrence, KS 66045. Offers MA, PhD, MUP/MA. Part-time programs available. *Faculty:* 10 full-time (5 women). *Students:* 34 full-time (19 women), 8 part-time (5 women); includes 6 minority (3 African Americans, 1 American Indian/Alaska Native, 2 Hispanic Americans), 6 international. Average age 35. 34 applicants, 56% accepted, 5 enrolled. In 2009, 7 master's, 3 doctorates awarded. Terminal master's awarded for partial completion of doctoral program. *Degree requirements:* For master's, thesis or alternative; for doctorate, comprehensive exam, thesis/dissertation. *Entrance requirements:* For master's and doctorate, GRE General Test. Additional exam requirements/recommendations for international students: Required—TOEFL. *Application deadline:* For fall admission, 12/1 for domestic and international students; for spring admission, 5/1 for domestic and international students. Applications are processed on a rolling basis. Application fee: $45 ($55 for international students). Electronic applications accepted. *Expenses:* Tuition, state resident: full-time $6492; part-time $270.50 per credit hour. Tuition, nonresident: full-time $15,510; part-time $646.25 per credit hour. Required fees: $847; $70.56 per credit hour. Tuition and fees vary according to course load and program. *Financial support:* Fellowships with full tuition reimbursements, research assistantships with partial tuition reimbursements, teaching assistantships with full and partial tuition reimbursements, Federal Work-Study, scholarships/grants, health care benefits, and unspecified assistantships available. Financial award application deadline: 12/21. *Faculty research:* Transnational and global American studies of race, gender, class, religion, ethnicity, sexuality, jazz studies, public health and medicine; migration and immigration; Latino/a studies; African-American studies; Jewish studies; women's studies; oral history; ethnography; environmental studies. *Unit head:* Cheryl Lester, Director, 785-864-2309, Fax: 785-864-5772, E-mail: chlester@ku.edu. *Application contact:* Kay Isbell, Information Contact, 785-864-2306, Fax: 785-864-5772, E-mail: kisbell@ku.edu.

University of Louisiana at Lafayette, College of Liberal Arts, Department of Modern Languages, Program in Francophone Studies, Lafayette, LA 70504. Offers PhD. *Degree requirements:* For doctorate, 2 foreign languages, comprehensive exam, thesis/dissertation. *Entrance requirements:* For doctorate, GRE General Test, minimum GPA of 2.75. Additional exam requirements/recommendations for international students: Required—TOEFL (minimum score 550 paper-based; 213 computer-based). Electronic applications accepted. *Faculty research:* Louisiana folklore, eighteenth century French literature, contemporary criticism.

University of Maryland, College Park, Academic Affairs, College of Arts and Humanities, Department of American Studies, College Park, MD 20742. Offers MA, PhD. *Faculty:* 44 full-time (20 women), 8 part-time/adjunct (5 women). *Students:* 51 full-time (34 women), 11 part-time (8 women); includes 28 minority (19 African Americans, 3 Asian Americans or Pacific Islanders, 6 Hispanic Americans), 5 international. 115 applicants, 16% accepted, 9 enrolled. In 2009, 3 master's, 8 doctorates awarded. *Degree requirements:* For master's, thesis or scholarly paper and exam; for doctorate, thesis/dissertation, 3 comprehensive exams. *Entrance requirements:* For master's, GRE General Test, minimum GPA of 3.0, writing sample, 3 letters of recommendation; for doctorate, GRE General Test. Additional exam requirements/recommendations for international students: Required—TOEFL. *Application deadline:* For fall admission, 12/1 for domestic students, 2/1 for international students. Applications are processed on a rolling basis. Application fee: $60. Electronic applications accepted. *Expenses:* Tuition, area resident: Part-time $471 per credit hour. Tuition, state resident: part-time $471 per credit hour. Tuition, nonresident: part-time $1016 per credit hour. Required fees: $337.04 per term. *Financial support:* In 2009–10, 6 fellowships with full and partial tuition reimbursements (averaging $16,618 per year), 24 teaching assistantships with tuition reimbursements (averaging $17,472 per year) were awarded; research assistantships, career-related internships or fieldwork, Federal Work-Study, and scholarships/grants also available. Support available to part-time students. Financial award applicants required to submit FAFSA. *Faculty research:* Material culture, modes of culture, cultural movements, popular culture, ethnography. *Unit head:* Nancy L. Struna, Chair, 301-405-1354, Fax: 301-314-9453, E-mail: nlstruna@umd.edu. *Application contact:* Dean of Graduate School, 301-405-0376, Fax: 301-314-9305.

University of Massachusetts Boston, Office of Graduate Studies, College of Liberal Arts, Program in American Studies, Boston, MA 02125-3393. Offers MA. Part-time and evening/weekend programs available. *Degree requirements:* For master's, thesis or capstone project. *Entrance requirements:* For master's, minimum GPA of 2.75. *Faculty research:* War in American culture, immigration history, Latin Americans, history of race and popular music, education and Asian Americans.

University of Michigan, Horace H. Rackham School of Graduate Studies, College of Literature, Science, and the Arts, Interdepartmental Program in American Culture, Ann Arbor, MI 48109-1045. Offers AM, PhD. *Faculty:* 40 full-time (20 women). *Students:* 51 full-time (30 women); includes 32 minority (10 African Americans, 4 American Indian/Alaska Native, 11 Asian Americans or Pacific Islanders, 7 Hispanic Americans), 2 international. 102 applicants, 10% accepted, 8 enrolled. In 2009, 2 master's, 6 doctorates awarded. Terminal master's awarded for partial completion of doctoral program. *Degree requirements:* For doctorate, field and preliminary exams, oral defense of dissertation. *Entrance requirements:* For master's, GRE General Test; for doctorate, GRE General Test, sample of written work. Additional exam requirements/recommendations for international students: Required—TOEFL. *Application deadline:* For fall admission, 12/1 for domestic and international students. Application fee: $60 ($75 for international students). Electronic applications accepted. *Expenses:* Tuition, state resident: full-time $17,286; part-time $1099 per credit hour. Tuition, nonresident: full-time $34,944; part-time $2080 per credit hour. Required fees: $95 per semester. Tuition and fees vary according to course load, degree level and program. *Financial support:* In 2009–10, 19 students received support, including 8 fellowships with full tuition reimbursements available (averaging $46,000 per year), 12 teaching assistantships with full tuition reimbursements available (averaging $28,000 per year); research assistantships, Federal Work-Study, health care benefits, and tuition waivers (full) also available. *Faculty research:* Cultural studies; ethnic studies, American culture methodology, literature, history. *Unit head:* Gregory Dowd, Director, 734-763-1460, Fax: 734-936-1967, E-mail: ac.inq@umich.edu. *Application contact:* Marlene Moore, Graduate Student Coordinator, 734-647-9533, Fax: 734-936-1967, E-mail: ac.inq@umich.edu.

University of Michigan–Flint, Graduate Programs, Program in American Culture, Flint, MI 48502-1950. Offers MLS. Part-time programs available. *Faculty:* 6 full-time (3 women). *Students:* 5 full-time (2 women), 25 part-time (15 women); includes 6 minority (4 African Americans, 2 Hispanic Americans). Average age 39. 8 applicants, 75% accepted, 5 enrolled. In 2009, 14 master's awarded. *Degree requirements:* For master's, thesis or alternative. *Entrance requirements:* For master's, minimum GPA of 3.0, 24 undergraduate credits in humanities and social sciences. Additional exam requirements/recommendations for international students: Required—TOEFL (minimum score 560 paper-based; 220 computer-based; 84 iBT), IELTS (minimum score 6.5). *Application deadline:* For fall admission, 8/1 for domestic students, 5/1 for international students; for winter admission, 11/15 for domestic students, 9/1 for international students; for spring admission, 3/15 for domestic students, 1/1 for international students. Application fee: $55. Electronic applications accepted. *Expenses:* Tuition, state resident: full-time $10,469.50; part-time $436.25 per credit hour. Tuition, nonresident: full-time $15,704; part-time $654.40 per credit hour. Required fees: $380; $144.50 per term. Tuition and

American Studies

University of Michigan–Flint (continued)
fees vary according to course level, course load, degree level and student level. *Financial support:* Federal Work-Study, scholarships/grants, and unspecified assistantships available. Support available to part-time students. Financial award application deadline: 6/1; financial award applicants required to submit FAFSA. *Unit head:* Dr. M. Jan Furman, Director, 810-762-3285, E-mail: jfurman@umflint.edu. *Application contact:* Bradley T. Maki, Director of Graduate Admissions, 810-762-3171, Fax: 810-766-6789, E-mail: bmaki@umflint.edu.

University of Minnesota, Twin Cities Campus, Graduate School, College of Liberal Arts, Department of American Studies, Minneapolis, MN 55455-0213. Offers PhD. *Degree requirements:* For doctorate, one foreign language, comprehensive exam, thesis/dissertation. *Entrance requirements:* For doctorate, GRE General Test, sample of written work, 3 letters of recommendation. Additional exam requirements/recommendations for international students: Required—TOEFL (minimum score 550 paper-based; 213 computer-based). *Faculty research:* American Indian history, nationalism/transnationalism, gender and sexuality, race and ethnicity.

University of Mississippi, Graduate School, College of Liberal Arts, Interdisciplinary Program in Southern Studies, Oxford, University, MS 38677. Offers MA. *Faculty:* 1 full-time (0 women). *Students:* 26 full-time (15 women), 4 part-time (3 women); includes 8 minority (7 African Americans, 1 Hispanic American), 1 international. In 2009, 6 master's awarded. *Entrance requirements:* For master's, GRE General Test, minimum GPA of 3.0. Additional exam requirements/recommendations for international students: Required—TOEFL. *Application deadline:* For fall admission, 2/1 for domestic students; for spring admission, 10/1 for domestic students. Applications are processed on a rolling basis. Application fee: $25. Electronic applications accepted. *Financial support:* Scholarships/grants available. Financial award application deadline: 3/1; financial award applicants required to submit FAFSA. *Unit head:* Dr. Ted Ownby, Interim Director, 662-915-5993, Fax: 662-915-5814, E-mail: cssc@olemiss.edu. *Application contact:* Dr. Christy M. Wyandt, Associate Dean, 662-915-7474, Fax: 662-915-7577, E-mail: cwyandt@olemiss.edu.

University of New Mexico, Graduate School, College of Arts and Sciences, Department of American Studies, Albuquerque, NM 87131-2039. Offers MA, PhD. Part-time programs available. *Faculty:* 9 full-time (4 women), 3 part-time/adjunct (1 woman). *Students:* 43 full-time (30 women), 12 part-time (9 women); includes 18 minority (1 African American, 4 American Indian/Alaska Native, 13 Hispanic Americans), 3 international. Average age 37. 71 applicants, 23% accepted, 9 enrolled. In 2009, 63 master's, 1 doctorate awarded. Terminal master's awarded for partial completion of doctoral program. *Degree requirements:* For master's, comprehensive exam (for some programs), thesis (for some programs); for doctorate, one foreign language, comprehensive exam, thesis/dissertation. *Entrance requirements:* For master's, BA in related field; for doctorate, MA in related field, complete dossier. Additional exam requirements/recommendations for international students: Required—TOEFL. *Application deadline:* For fall admission, 1/15 for domestic students. Application fee: $50. Electronic applications accepted. *Expenses:* Tuition, state resident: full-time $2099; part-time $233.20 per credit hour. Tuition, nonresident: full-time $6650. Required fees: $25 per semester. Tuition and fees vary according to course load, program and reciprocity agreements. *Financial support:* In 2009–10, 29 students received support, including 24 teaching assistantships with tuition reimbursements available (averaging $6,024 per year); research assistantships, career-related internships or fieldwork, Federal Work-Study, health care benefits, tuition waivers (full), and unspecified assistantships also available. Support available to part-time students. Financial award application deadline: 2/20; financial award applicants required to submit FAFSA. *Faculty research:* Culture studies environment/science/technology, gender, race/class/ethnicity, popular culture, Southwest studies. *Unit head:* Dr. Alex Lubin, Chair, 505-277-3929, Fax: 505-277-1208, E-mail: alubin@unm.edu. *Application contact:* Dr. Sandy Rodrigue, Department Administrator, 505-277-3929, Fax: 505-277-1208, E-mail: amstudy@unm.edu.

University of Southern California, Graduate School, College of Letters, Arts and Sciences, Department of American Studies and Ethnicity, Los Angeles, CA 90089. Offers PhD. *Faculty:* 30 full-time (16 women). *Students:* 54 full-time (36 women); includes 47 minority (14 African Americans, 1 American Indian/Alaska Native, 16 Asian Americans or Pacific Islanders, 16 Hispanic Americans), 2 international. 149 applicants, 7% accepted. In 2009, 6 doctorates awarded. Terminal master's awarded for partial completion of doctoral program. *Degree requirements:* For doctorate, one foreign language, thesis/dissertation, qualifying exam. *Entrance requirements:* For doctorate, GRE. *Application deadline:* For fall admission, 12/1 for domestic students. Application fee: $85. Electronic applications accepted. *Expenses:* Tuition: Full-time $25,980; part-time $1315 per unit. Required fees: $554. One-time fee: $35 full-time. Full-time tuition and fees vary according to degree level and program. *Financial support:* In 2009–10, 38 students received support, including 13 fellowships with full tuition reimbursements available (averaging $22,000 per year), 6 research assistantships with full tuition reimbursements available (averaging $19,000 per year), 19 teaching assistantships with full tuition reimbursements available (averaging $19,000 per year); tuition waivers (full) also available. Financial award application deadline: 2/1. *Faculty research:* Interdisciplinary study of race and ethnicity, regional focus on Los Angeles and the American West, multidisciplinary exploration of culture, interdisciplinary study of gender and sexuality. *Unit head:* Prof. John Carlos Rowe, Chair, 213-740-2426, Fax: 213-821-0409, E-mail: johnrowe@usc.edu. *Application contact:* Kitty Lai, Graduate Staff Advisor, 213-740-2426, Fax: 213-821-0409, E-mail: kittylai@usc.edu.

University of Southern Maine, College of Arts and Sciences, Program in American and New England Studies, Portland, ME 04104-9300. Offers MA. Part-time and evening/weekend programs available. *Degree requirements:* For master's, thesis optional. *Entrance requirements:* For master's, GRE General Test or MAT. Additional exam requirements/recommendations for international students: Required—TOEFL. *Faculty research:* Social history, regional culture, landscape of literature, material culture, art and architecture.

University of South Florida, Graduate School, College of Arts and Sciences, Department of Humanities and Cultural Studies, Tampa, FL 33617. Offers American studies (MA); film studies (MLA); humanities (MLA). Part-time and evening/weekend programs available. *Faculty:* 8 full-time (4 women). *Students:* 26 full-time (18 women), 14 part-time (9 women); includes 10 minority (7 African Americans, 3 Hispanic Americans). Average age 32. 24 applicants, 58% accepted, 11 enrolled. In 2009, 15 master's awarded. *Degree requirements:* For master's, comprehensive exam, thesis. *Entrance requirements:* For master's, GRE General Test, minimum GPA of 3.0 in last 60 hours, academic writing sample. Additional exam requirements/recommendations for international students: Required—TOEFL (minimum score 550 paper-based; 213 computer-based). *Application deadline:* For fall admission, 2/15 priority date for domestic students, 1/2 for international students; for spring admission, 10/15 priority date for domestic students, 6/1 for international students. Application fee: $30. *Financial support:* In 2009–10, 4 teaching assistantships with tuition reimbursements were awarded; scholarships/grants also available. Financial award application deadline: 4/4. *Faculty research:* American South, American autobiography, material culture, critical theory, cultural studies. *Unit head:* Daniel Belgrad, Chairperson, 813-974-9388, Fax: 813-974-9409, E-mail: dbelgrad@cas.usf.edu. *Application contact:* Maria Cizmic, Program Director, 813-974-9383, Fax: 813-974-9409, E-mail: mcizmic@cas.usf.edu.

The University of Texas at Austin, Graduate School, College of Liberal Arts, Department of American Studies, Austin, TX 78712-1111. Offers MA, PhD. Part-time programs available. *Degree requirements:* For master's, thesis; for doctorate, one foreign language, thesis/dissertation, qualifying oral exam. *Entrance requirements:* For master's and doctorate, GRE General Test, minimum GPA of 3.5. Electronic applications accepted. *Faculty research:* Race, gender, and ethnicity; history of the American West; American design and archaeology; literary cultural history; religion and psychology in American culture.

University of Utah, The Graduate School, College of Humanities, Department of English, Salt Lake City, UT 84112. Offers American studies (MA, PhD), including rhetoric/composition; British American literature (MA, PhD); creative writing (MA, MFA, PhD), including rhetoric/composition (MA, PhD); literature (PhD); rhetoric and composition (PhD). *Faculty:* 36 full-time (16 women). *Students:* 57 full-time (36 women), 17 part-time (13 women); includes 5 minority (3 African Americans, 1 American Indian/Alaska Native, 1 Asian American or Pacific Islander), 2 international. Average age 33. 270 applicants, 10% accepted, 24 enrolled. In 2009, 20 master's, 8 doctorates awarded. Terminal master's awarded for partial completion of doctoral program. *Degree requirements:* For master's, one foreign language, comprehensive exam, thesis (for some programs), written exam; for doctorate, 2 foreign languages, comprehensive exam, thesis/dissertation. *Entrance requirements:* For master's and doctorate, GRE General Test, minimum GPA of 3.2. Additional exam requirements/recommendations for international students: Required—TOEFL (minimum score 650 paper-based; 280 computer-based; 115 iBT). *Application deadline:* For fall admission, 12/15 for domestic and international students. Application fee: $55 ($65 for international students). Electronic applications accepted. *Expenses:* Tuition, state resident: full-time $4004; part-time $1674 per semester. Tuition, nonresident: full-time $14,134; part-time $5915 per semester. Required fees: $324 per semester. Tuition and fees vary according to course load, degree level and program. *Financial support:* In 2009–10, 52 students received support, including 9 fellowships with full tuition reimbursements available (averaging $12,400 per year), 43 teaching assistantships with full tuition reimbursements available (averaging $12,400 per year); research assistantships, health care benefits also available. Financial award application deadline: 12/15; financial award applicants required to submit FAFSA. *Faculty research:* Poetics and modern poetry, nineteenth and twentieth century British and American literature, the American west, environmental studies, critical theory and race and gender studies. Total annual research expenditures: $45,462. *Unit head:* Prof. Vincent P. Pecora, Chair, 801-581-6168, E-mail: v.pecora@utah.edu. *Application contact:* Prof. Scott Black, Director of Graduate Studies, 801-581-5137, E-mail: scott.black@utah.edu.

University of Wisconsin–Madison, Graduate School, College of Letters and Science, Department of History, Madison, WI 53706-1380. Offers African history (MA, PhD); Central Asian history (MA, PhD); comparative world history (MA, PhD); East Asian history (MA, PhD); European history (MA, PhD); gender and women's history (MA, PhD); Latin American and Caribbean history (MA, PhD); Middle Eastern history (MA, PhD); South Asian history (MA, PhD); Southeast Asian history (MA, PhD); United States history (MA, PhD). Terminal master's awarded for partial completion of doctoral program. *Degree requirements:* For master's, thesis (for some programs); for doctorate, variable foreign language requirement, thesis/dissertation. *Entrance requirements:* For master's and doctorate, GRE General Test. Additional exam requirements/recommendations for international students: Required—Michigan English Language Assessment Battery or TOEFL. Electronic applications accepted. *Expenses:* Tuition, state resident: part-time $594 per credit. Tuition, nonresident: part-time $1504 per credit. Required fees: $65 per credit. Tuition and fees vary according to course load, program and reciprocity agreements. *Faculty research:* American, African, European, Asian, Latin American, and Middle Eastern history.

University of Wyoming, College of Arts and Sciences, American Studies Program, Laramie, WY 82070. Offers MA. Part-time programs available. *Degree requirements:* For master's, thesis optional. *Entrance requirements:* For master's, GRE General Test, minimum GPA of 3.0. *Faculty research:* Material culture, American culture, ethnicity, cultural environments, public culture.

Utah State University, School of Graduate Studies, College of Humanities, Arts and Social Sciences, Department of English and Department of History, Program in American Studies, Logan, UT 84322. Offers folklore (MA, MS); western American literature and culture (MA, MS). Part-time and evening/weekend programs available. *Degree requirements:* For master's, thesis or alternative. *Entrance requirements:* For master's, GRE General Test or MAT, minimum GPA of 3.0, 3 letters of recommendation, writing sample. Additional exam requirements/recommendations for international students: Required—TOEFL. *Faculty research:* Folklore and folklife, American culture, regional studies, material culture, Jewish folklore, Native American folklore.

Washington State University, Graduate School, College of Liberal Arts, Department of History, Pullman, WA 99164. Offers early and modern European history (MA, PhD); environmental history (MA, PhD); Latin American history (MA, PhD); modern East Asia history (MA, PhD); public history (MA, PhD); US history (MA, PhD); women's history (MA, PhD); world history (MA, PhD). Part-time programs available. *Faculty:* 25. *Students:* 38 full-time (22 women), 10 part-time (4 women); includes 3 minority (1 American Indian/Alaska Native, 2 Hispanic Americans), 2 international. Average age 33. 57 applicants, 47% accepted, 10 enrolled. In 2009, 10 master's, 2 doctorates awarded. *Degree requirements:* For master's, comprehensive exam (for some programs), thesis, oral exam; for doctorate, one foreign language, comprehensive exam, thesis/dissertation, oral and written exam. *Entrance requirements:* For master's and doctorate, GRE General Test, Graduate School Application form; official transcripts from all universities attended; GRE scores; TOEFL or IELTS scores (international students only); three letters of recommendation; a statement of purpose; a writing sample, Preferred Fields of Study form; and the Language Background form. Additional exam requirements/recommendations for international students: Required—TOEFL (minimum score 550 paper-based), IELTS. *Application deadline:* For fall admission, 1/10 for domestic and international students; for spring admission, 7/1 for domestic and international students. Applications are processed on a rolling basis. Application fee: $50. Electronic applications accepted. *Financial support:* In 2009–10, 1 fellowship with partial tuition reimbursement (averaging $3,000 per year), research assistantships with full and partial tuition reimbursements (averaging $13,917 per year), 28 teaching assistantships with full and partial tuition reimbursements (averaging $13,056 per year) were awarded; career-related internships or fieldwork, Federal Work-Study, institutionally sponsored loans, scholarships/grants, and health care benefits also available. Financial award application deadline: 2/15; financial award applicants required to submit FAFSA. *Faculty research:* Public, world, environmental, women's and U. S. history. *Unit head:* Dr. Raymond Sun, Chair, 509-335-5139, Fax: 509-335-4171, E-mail: pietz@wsu.edu. *Application contact:* Graduate Studies Director, 509-335-4030, Fax: 509-335-4171, E-mail: kale@wsu.edu.

Washington State University, Graduate School, College of Liberal Arts, Program in American Studies, Pullman, WA 99164. Offers ethnic studies (MA, PhD); feminist studies (MA, PhD); history (MA, PhD); literature (MA, PhD). Part-time programs available. *Faculty:* 35. *Students:* 23 full-time (14 women), 4 part-time (2 women); includes 17 minority (5 African Americans, 4 American Indian/Alaska Native, 4 Asian Americans or Pacific Islanders, 4 Hispanic Americans), 2 international. Average age 35. 55 applicants, 7% accepted, 3 enrolled. In 2009, 1 master's, 3 doctorates awarded. *Degree requirements:* For master's, one foreign language, comprehensive exam (for some programs), thesis optional, oral exam; for doctorate, one foreign language, comprehensive exam (for some programs), thesis/dissertation, oral exam. *Entrance requirements:* For master's, GRE General Test, * Send to the Graduate School an official application form and official college transcripts sent directly from each institution attended. * Send to the American Studies program: A 3 to 5 page statement of purpose describing your areas of interest and why the program minimum GPA of 3.0, writing sample, 3 letters of recommendation; for doctorate, GRE General Test, * Send to the Graduate School an official application form and official college transcripts sent directly from each institution attended. * Send to the American Studies program: A 3 to 5 page statement of purpose describing your areas of interest and why the program minimum GPA of 3.0, writing sample, 3 letters of recommendation. Additional exam requirements/recommendations for international students: Required—TOEFL, IELTS. *Application deadline:* For fall admission, 1/10 priority date for domestic and international students; for spring admission, 7/1 priority date for domestic and international students. Applications are processed on a rolling basis. Application fee: $50. *Financial support:* In 2009–10, 1 fellowship (averaging $6,950 per year), 3 research assistantships with full and partial tuition reimbursements (averaging $14,634 per year), 17 teaching assistantships with full and partial tuition reimbursements (averaging $13,383 per year) were awarded; career-related internships or fieldwork, Federal Work-Study, institutionally sponsored loans, health care benefits, tuition waivers (partial), and teaching associateships also available. Financial award application deadline: 2/15; financial award applicants required to submit

FAFSA. *Faculty research:* The American West in multicultural perspective; nineteenth century historical, literary, and cultural studies; comparative American ethnic literatures and cultures; American cultures and the environment; American rhetoric. *Unit head:* Dr. Rory J. Ong, Director, 509-335-1560, E-mail: rjong@mail.wsu.edu. *Application contact:* Graduate School Admissions, 800-GRADWSU, Fax: 509-335-1949, E-mail: gradsch@wsu.edu.

West Virginia University, Eberly College of Arts and Sciences, Department of History, Morgantown, WV 26506. Offers African history (MA, PhD); African-American history (MA, PhD); American history (MA, PhD); Appalachian/regional history (MA, PhD); East Asian history (MA, PhD); European history (MA, PhD); history of science and technology (MA, PhD); Latin American history (MA). Part-time programs available. *Degree requirements:* For master's, one foreign language, thesis (for some programs), oral exam, thesis defense; for doctorate, one foreign language, comprehensive exam, thesis/dissertation, dissertation defense. *Entrance requirements:* For master's, GRE General Test, minimum GPA of 3.0; for doctorate, GRE General Test. Additional exam requirements/recommendations for international students: Required—TOEFL (minimum score 550 paper-based), IELTS (minimum score 6.5). Electronic applications accepted. *Faculty research:* U.S., Appalachia, modern Europe, Africa, colonial and post-colonial societies.

Wheaton College, Graduate School, Department of Biblical and Theological Studies, Program in Religion in American Life, Wheaton, IL 60187-5593. Offers MA. Part-time programs available. *Degree requirements:* For master's, thesis optional. *Entrance requirements:* For master's, GRE General Test, MAT. Electronic applications accepted.

Yale University, Graduate School of Arts and Sciences, Interdisciplinary Program in American Studies, New Haven, CT 06520. Offers PhD. *Degree requirements:* For doctorate, one foreign language, thesis/dissertation. *Entrance requirements:* For doctorate, GRE General Test.

Asian-American Studies

California State University, Long Beach, Graduate Studies, College of Liberal Arts, Department of Asian and Asian American Studies, Long Beach, CA 90840. Offers Asian studies (MA). Part-time programs available. *Faculty:* 4 full-time (all women). *Students:* 11 full-time (7 women), 10 part-time (6 women); includes 11 minority (all Asian Americans or Pacific Islanders), 3 international. Average age 34. 12 applicants, 75% accepted, 5 enrolled. *Degree requirements:* For master's, one foreign language, comprehensive exam or thesis. *Application deadline:* For fall admission, 5/1 for domestic students. Applications are processed on a rolling basis. Application fee: $55. Electronic applications accepted. *Expenses:* Required fees: $1802 per semester. Part-time tuition and fees vary according to course load. *Financial support:* Federal Work-Study, institutionally sponsored loans, and scholarships/grants available. Financial award application deadline: 3/2. *Faculty research:* South Asia, China, Japan, Southeast Asia, Asian-Americans in the U. S. *Unit head:* Dr. John N. Tsuchida, Chair, 562-985-8085, Fax: 562-985-1535, E-mail: jtsuchid@csulb.edu. *Application contact:* Dr. Linda Espana-Maram, Graduate Advisor, 562-985-4822, Fax: 562-985-1535, E-mail: lnemaram@csulb.edu.

San Francisco State University, Division of Graduate Studies, College of Ethnic Studies, Program in Asian American Studies, San Francisco, CA 94132-1722. Offers MA.

University of California, Los Angeles, Graduate Division, College of Letters and Science, Program in Asian-American Studies, Los Angeles, CA 90095. Offers MA, MA/MPH, MA/MSW. *Students:* 16 full-time (10 women); includes 10 minority (all Asian Americans or Pacific Islanders), 2 international. Average age 26. 21 applicants, 48% accepted, 9 enrolled. In 2009, 13 master's awarded. *Degree requirements:* For master's, one foreign language, comprehensive exam or thesis, research tool. *Entrance requirements:* For master's, minimum GPA of 3.0, sample of written work. *Application deadline:* For fall admission, 12/15 for domestic and international students. Application fee: $70 ($90 for international students). Electronic applications accepted. *Financial support:* In 2009–10, 12 fellowships with full and partial tuition reimbursements, 2 research assistantships with full and partial tuition reimbursements, 8 teaching assistantships with full and partial tuition reimbursements were awarded; Federal Work-Study, institutionally sponsored loans, scholarships/grants, health care benefits, tuition waivers (full and partial), and unspecified assistantships also available. Financial award application deadline: 3/1; financial award applicants required to submit FAFSA. *Unit head:* Dr. Lane Hirabayashi, Chair, 310-206-8020. *Application contact:* Department Office, 310-267-5592, E-mail: maprogram@asianam.ucla.edu.

Asian Studies

California Institute of Integral Studies, School of Consciousness and Transformation, San Francisco, CA 94103. Offers creative inquiry (MFA); cultural anthropology and social transformation (MA); East-West psychology (MA, PhD); integrative health studies (MA); philosophy and religion (MA, PhD), including Asian and comparative studies, philosophy, cosmology, and consciousness, women's spirituality; social and cultural anthropology (PhD); transformative leadership (MA); transformative studies (PhD); writing and consciousness (MFA). Part-time and evening/weekend programs available. Postbaccalaureate distance learning degree programs offered (minimal on-campus study). *Students:* 334 full-time (218 women), 126 part-time (77 women); includes 116 minority (40 African Americans, 4 American Indian/Alaska Native, 42 Asian Americans or Pacific Islanders, 30 Hispanic Americans). Average age 38. 265 applicants, 90% accepted, 149 enrolled. In 2009, 64 master's, 22 doctorates awarded. Terminal master's awarded for partial completion of doctoral program. *Degree requirements:* For master's, comprehensive exam (for some programs), thesis optional; for doctorate, comprehensive exam, thesis/dissertation, 1 foreign language (Asian comparative studies). *Entrance requirements:* For master's, minimum GPA of 3.0, letters of recommendation, writing sample; for doctorate, master's degree, minimum GPA of 3.0, letters of recommendation, writing sample. Additional exam requirements/recommendations for international students: Required—TOEFL. *Application deadline:* For fall admission, 2/1 priority date for domestic and international students; for spring admission, 10/15 priority date for domestic and international students. Applications are processed on a rolling basis. Application fee: $65. Electronic applications accepted. *Expenses:* Tuition: Full-time $15,300; part-time $850 per credit hour. Required fees: $110 per semester. Tuition and fees vary according to degree level. *Financial support:* In 2009–10, 330 students received support; research assistantships, teaching assistantships, career-related internships or fieldwork, Federal Work-Study, scholarships/grants, and tuition waivers (partial) available. Support available to part-time students. Financial award application deadline: 4/15; financial award applicants required to submit FAFSA. *Faculty research:* Altered states of consciousness, dreams, cosmology, postcolonial studies, integrative health studies. *Application contact:* Allyson Werner, Associate Director of Admissions, 415-575-6155, Fax: 415-575-1268.

California State University, Long Beach, Graduate Studies, College of Liberal Arts, Department of Asian and Asian American Studies, Long Beach, CA 90840. Offers Asian studies (MA). Part-time programs available. *Faculty:* 4 full-time (all women). *Students:* 11 full-time (7 women), 10 part-time (6 women); includes 11 minority (all Asian Americans or Pacific Islanders), 3 international. Average age 34. 12 applicants, 75% accepted, 5 enrolled. *Degree requirements:* For master's, one foreign language, comprehensive exam or thesis. *Application deadline:* For fall admission, 5/1 for domestic students. Applications are processed on a rolling basis. Application fee: $55. Electronic applications accepted. *Expenses:* Required fees: $1802 per semester. Part-time tuition and fees vary according to course load. *Financial support:* Federal Work-Study, institutionally sponsored loans, and scholarships/grants available. Financial award application deadline: 3/2. *Faculty research:* South Asia, China, Japan, Southeast Asia, Asian-Americans in the U. S. *Unit head:* Dr. John N. Tsuchida, Chair, 562-985-8085, Fax: 562-985-1535, E-mail: jtsuchid@csulb.edu. *Application contact:* Dr. Linda Espana-Maram, Graduate Advisor, 562-985-4822, Fax: 562-985-1535, E-mail: lnemaram@csulb.edu.

California State University, Long Beach, Graduate Studies, College of Liberal Arts, Department of History, Long Beach, CA 90840. Offers Africa and the Middle East (MA); ancient/Medieval Europe (MA); Asia (MA); Latin America (MA); modern Europe (MA); United States (MA); world (MA). Part-time and evening/weekend programs available. *Faculty:* 9 full-time (6 women), 1 (woman) part-time/adjunct. *Students:* 10 full-time (3 women), 56 part-time (21 women); includes 19 minority (2 African Americans, 1 American Indian/Alaska Native, 4 Asian Americans or Pacific Islanders, 12 Hispanic Americans), 1 international. Average age 31. 40 applicants, 50% accepted, 11 enrolled. *Degree requirements:* For master's, one foreign language, comprehensive exam or thesis. *Application deadline:* For fall admission, 3/1 for domestic students. Applications are processed on a rolling basis. Application fee: $55. Electronic applications accepted. *Expenses:* Required fees: $1802 per semester. Part-time tuition and fees vary according to course load. *Financial support:* Research assistantships, Federal Work-Study, institutionally sponsored loans, and scholarships/grants available. Financial award application deadline: 3/2. *Faculty research:* All periods of European and American history, recent Asian and African history. *Unit head:* Dr. Nancy Quam-Wickham, Department Chair, 562-985-4431, Fax: 562-985-5431, E-mail: quamwick@csulb.edu. *Application contact:* Dr. Houri Berberian, Graduate Advisor, 562-985-4524, Fax: 562-985-4431, E-mail: hberber@csulb.edu.

Columbia University, Graduate School of Arts and Sciences, Division of Humanities, Department of East Asian Languages and Cultures, New York, NY 10027. Offers East Asian languages and cultures (M Phil, MA, PhD); Oriental studies (M Phil, MA, PhD). *Degree requirements:* For master's, one foreign language, comprehensive exam, thesis; for doctorate, 2 foreign languages, thesis/dissertation. *Entrance requirements:* For master's and doctorate, GRE General Test. Additional exam requirements/recommendations for international students: Required—TOEFL.

Columbia University, Graduate School of Arts and Sciences, Division of Humanities, Department of Middle East Languages and Cultures, New York, NY 10027. Offers Hebrew language and literature (M Phil, MA, PhD); Middle Eastern languages and cultures (M Phil, MA, PhD); South Asian languages and cultures (M Phil, MA, PhD). Part-time programs available. *Degree requirements:* For master's, thesis, oral and written exams; for doctorate, 3 foreign languages, thesis/dissertation. *Entrance requirements:* For master's and doctorate, GRE General Test. Additional exam requirements/recommendations for international students: Required—TOEFL. *Faculty research:* Indo-Iranian, Turkish, central Asian, and Armenian studies; Arabic and ancient Semitics.

Columbia University, Graduate School of Arts and Sciences, Program in East Asian Regional Studies, New York, NY 10027. Offers MA. *Degree requirements:* For master's, 2 foreign languages. *Entrance requirements:* For master's, GRE General Test.

Columbia University, Graduate School of Arts and Sciences, Program in Liberal Studies, New York, NY 10027. Offers American studies (MA); East Asian studies (MA); human rights studies (MA); Islamic culture studies (MA); Jewish studies (MA); medieval studies (MA); modern European studies (MA); South Asian studies (MA). Part-time and evening/weekend programs available. *Degree requirements:* For master's, thesis.

Columbia University, School of International and Public Affairs, Weatherhead East Asian Institute, New York, NY 10027. Offers Asian studies (Certificate). Students must be enrolled in a separate graduate degree program at Columbia University. *Entrance requirements:* For degree, proficiency in East Asian language. Electronic applications accepted.

Columbia University, South Asia Institute, New York, NY 10027. Offers Certificate. Students must be enrolled in a separate graduate degree program at Columbia University. Electronic applications accepted.

Cornell University, Graduate School, Graduate Fields of Arts and Sciences, Field of Asian Religions, Ithaca, NY 14853-0001. Offers PhD. *Faculty:* 9 full-time (3 women). *Students:* 6 full-time (1 woman), 1 international. Average age 30. 16 applicants, 19% accepted, 0 enrolled. In 2009, 2 doctorates awarded. *Degree requirements:* For doctorate, comprehensive exam, thesis/dissertation. *Entrance requirements:* For doctorate, GRE General Test, academic writing sample, 3 letters of recommendation. Additional exam requirements/recommendations for international students: Required—TOEFL (minimum score 600 paper-based; 250 computer-based; 77 iBT). *Application deadline:* For fall admission, 1/15 for domestic students. Application fee: $70. Electronic applications accepted. *Expenses:* Tuition: Full-time $29,500. Required fees: $70. Full-time tuition and fees vary according to degree level, program and student level. *Financial support:* In 2009–10, 5 students received support; fellowships with full tuition reimbursements available, research assistantships with full tuition reimbursements available, teaching assistantships with full tuition reimbursements available, institutionally sponsored loans, scholarships/grants, health care benefits, and unspecified assistantships available. *Unit head:* Director of Graduate Studies, 607-255-9099, Fax: 607-255-1345. *Application contact:* Graduate Field Assistant, 607-255-9099, Fax: 607-255-1345, E-mail: asian-religions@cornell.edu.

Cornell University, Graduate School, Graduate Fields of Arts and Sciences, Field of Asian Studies, Ithaca, NY 14853-0001. Offers East Asian linguistics (MA); East Asian studies (MA); South Asian linguistics (MA); South Asian studies (MA); Southeast Asian linguistics (MA); Southeast Asian studies (MA). *Faculty:* 59 full-time (21 women). *Students:* 7 full-time (1 woman); includes 3 minority (all Asian Americans or Pacific Islanders), 1 international. Average

Asian Studies

Cornell University (continued)
age 31. 51 applicants, 24% accepted. In 2009, 5 master's awarded. *Degree requirements:* For master's, one foreign language, thesis. *Entrance requirements:* For master's, GRE General Test, 3 letters of recommendation. Additional exam requirements/recommendations for international students: Required—TOEFL (minimum score 550 paper-based; 213 computer-based; 77 iBT). *Application deadline:* Applications are processed on a rolling basis. Application fee: $70. Electronic applications accepted. *Expenses:* Tuition: Full-time $29,500. Required fees: $70. Full-time tuition and fees vary according to degree level, program and student level. *Financial support:* In 2009–10, 5 students received support, including 1 fellowship with full tuition reimbursement available, 2 research assistantships with full tuition reimbursements available; teaching assistantships with full tuition reimbursements available, institutionally sponsored loans, scholarships/grants, health care benefits, tuition waivers (full and partial), and unspecified assistantships also available. Financial award applicants required to submit FAFSA. *Faculty research:* East Asian studies, South Asian studies, Southeast Asian studies. *Unit head:* Director of Graduate Studies, 607-255-9099, Fax: 607-255-1345. *Application contact:* Graduate Field Assistant, 607-255-9099, Fax: 607-255-1345, E-mail: asian@cornell.edu.

Cornell University, Graduate School, Graduate Fields of Arts and Sciences, Field of East Asian Literature, Ithaca, NY 14853-0001. Offers Asian religions (MA, PhD); Chinese linguistics (MA, PhD); Chinese philology (MA, PhD); classical Chinese literature (MA, PhD); classical Japanese literature (MA, PhD); Japanese linguistics (MA, PhD); Korean literature (MA, PhD); modern Chinese literature (MA, PhD); modern Japanese literature (MA, PhD). *Faculty:* 17 full-time (7 women). *Students:* 16 full-time (7 women); includes 4 minority (all Asian Americans or Pacific Islanders), 8 international. Average age 32. 49 applicants, 6% accepted, 2 enrolled. In 2009, 3 doctorates awarded. *Degree requirements:* For master's, 2 foreign languages, thesis, teaching experience; for doctorate, 2 foreign languages, comprehensive exam, thesis/dissertation, teaching experience. *Entrance requirements:* For master's, GRE General Test, 3 years of study in Chinese, Japanese, Korean, or Vietnamese; 3 letters of recommendation; academic writing sample; for doctorate, GRE General Test, 3 years of study in Chinese, Japanese, Korean, or Vietnamese, 3 letters of recommendation, academic writing sample. Additional exam requirements/recommendations for international students: Required—TOEFL (minimum score 600 paper-based; 250 computer-based; 77 iBT). *Application deadline:* For fall admission, 1/10 priority date for domestic students. Application fee: $70. Electronic applications accepted. *Expenses:* Tuition: Full-time $29,500. Required fees: $70. Full-time tuition and fees vary according to degree level, program and student level. *Financial support:* In 2009–10, 2 fellowships with full tuition reimbursements were awarded; research assistantships with full tuition reimbursements, teaching assistantships with full tuition reimbursements, institutionally sponsored loans, scholarships/grants, health care benefits, tuition waivers (full and partial), and unspecified assistantships also available. Financial award applicants required to submit FAFSA. *Faculty research:* Vietnamese literature; Chinese literature, drama, and film; Japanese theater and literature; popular culture in East Asia; Korean literature; Asian linguistics. *Unit head:* Director of Graduate Studies, 607-255-9099. *Application contact:* Graduate Field Assistant, 607-255-9099, E-mail: east_asian_lit@cornell.edu.

Cornell University, Graduate School, Graduate Fields of Arts and Sciences, Field of History, Ithaca, NY 14853-0001. Offers African history (MA, PhD); American history (MA, PhD); ancient history (MA, PhD); early modern European history (MA, PhD); English history (MA, PhD); French history (MA, PhD); German history (MA, PhD); history of science (MA, PhD); Latin American history (MA, PhD); medieval Chinese history (MA, PhD); medieval history (MA, PhD); modern Chinese history (MA, PhD); modern European history (MA, PhD); modern Japanese history (MA, PhD); premodern Islamic history (MA, PhD); premodern Japanese history (MA, PhD); Renaissance history (MA, PhD); Russian history (MA, PhD); Southeast Asian history (MA, PhD). *Faculty:* 62 full-time (19 women). *Students:* 67 full-time (33 women); includes 10 minority (4 African Americans, 3 Asian Americans or Pacific Islanders, 3 Hispanic Americans), 24 international. Average age 31. 195 applicants, 7% accepted, 10 enrolled. In 2009, 11 master's, 3 doctorates awarded. Terminal master's awarded for partial completion of doctoral program. *Degree requirements:* For master's, thesis; for doctorate, 2 foreign languages, comprehensive exam, thesis/dissertation, 1 year of teaching experience. *Entrance requirements:* For master's and doctorate, GRE General Test, writing sample, 3 letters of recommendation. Additional exam requirements/recommendations for international students: Required—TOEFL (minimum score 550 paper-based; 213 computer-based; 77 iBT). *Application deadline:* For fall admission, 1/15 for domestic students. Application fee: $70. Electronic applications accepted. *Expenses:* Tuition: Full-time $29,500. Required fees: $70. Full-time tuition and fees vary according to degree level, program and student level. *Financial support:* In 2009–10, 54 students received support, including 8 fellowships with full tuition reimbursements available; research assistantships with full tuition reimbursements available, teaching assistantships with full tuition reimbursements available, institutionally sponsored loans, scholarships/grants, health care benefits, tuition waivers (full and partial), and unspecified assistantships also available. Financial award applicants required to submit FAFSA. *Unit head:* Director of Graduate Studies, 607-255-6738, Fax: 607-255-0469. *Application contact:* Graduate Field Assistant, 607-255-6738, Fax: 607-255-0469, E-mail: history_grad_info@cornell.edu.

Cornell University, Graduate School, Graduate Fields of Arts and Sciences, Field of History of Art, Archaeology and Visual Studies, Ithaca, NY 14853. Offers American art (PhD); ancient art and archaeology (PhD); Asian art (PhD); baroque art (PhD); medieval art (PhD); modern art (PhD); Renaissance art (PhD); Southeast Asian art (PhD); theory and criticism (PhD). *Faculty:* 23 full-time (14 women). *Students:* 20 full-time (18 women); includes 4 minority (1 African American, 1 American Indian/Alaska Native, 1 Asian American or Pacific Islander, 1 Hispanic American), 5 international. Average age 35. 73 applicants. In 2009, 3 doctorates awarded. *Degree requirements:* For doctorate, one foreign language, comprehensive exam, thesis/dissertation, general exams in 3 areas. *Entrance requirements:* For doctorate, GRE General Test, sample of written work, 3 letters of recommendation. Additional exam requirements/recommendations for international students: Required—TOEFL (minimum score 550 paper-based; 213 computer-based; 77 iBT). *Application deadline:* For fall admission, 1/15 for domestic students. Application fee: $70. Electronic applications accepted. *Expenses:* Tuition: Full-time $29,500. Required fees: $70. Full-time tuition and fees vary according to degree level, program and student level. *Financial support:* In 2009–10, 17 students received support, including 3 fellowships with full tuition reimbursements available; research assistantships with full tuition reimbursements available, teaching assistantships with full tuition reimbursements available, institutionally sponsored loans, scholarships/grants, health care benefits, tuition waivers (full and partial), and unspecified assistantships also available. Financial award applicants required to submit FAFSA. *Unit head:* Director of Graduate Studies, 607-255-4905, Fax: 607-255-0566, E-mail: art_history@cornell.edu. *Application contact:* Graduate Field Assistant, 607-255-4905, Fax: 607-255-0566, E-mail: art_history@cornell.edu.

Cornell University, Graduate School, Graduate Fields of Arts and Sciences, Field of Linguistics, Ithaca, NY 14853-0001. Offers applied linguistics (MA, PhD); East Asian linguistics (MA, PhD); English linguistics (MA, PhD); general linguistics (MA, PhD); Germanic linguistics (MA, PhD); Indo-European linguistics (MA, PhD); phonetics (MA, PhD); phonological theory (MA, PhD); Romance linguistics (MA, PhD); second language acquisition (MA, PhD); semantics (MA, PhD); Slavic linguistics (MA, PhD); sociolinguistics (MA, PhD); South Asian linguistics (MA, PhD); Southeast Asian linguistics (MA, PhD); syntactic theory (MA, PhD). *Faculty:* 21 full-time (10 women). *Students:* 31 full-time (17 women), 14 international. Average age 30. 95 applicants, 12% accepted, 5 enrolled. In 2009, 5 master's, 6 doctorates awarded. Terminal master's awarded for partial completion of doctoral program. *Degree requirements:* For master's, one foreign language, thesis; for doctorate, one foreign language, comprehensive exam, thesis/dissertation. *Entrance requirements:* For master's and doctorate, GRE General Test, 2 letters of recommendation. Additional exam requirements/recommendations for international students: Required—TOEFL (minimum score 600 paper-based; 250 computer-based; 77 iBT). *Application deadline:* For fall admission, 1/15 for domestic students. Application fee: $70. Electronic applications accepted. *Expenses:* Tuition: Full-time $29,500. Required fees: $70. Full-time tuition and fees vary according to degree level, program and student level. *Financial support:* In 2009–10, 3 fellowships with full tuition reimbursements, 1 teaching assistantship with full tuition reimbursement were awarded; research assistantships with full tuition reimbursements, institutionally sponsored loans, scholarships/grants, health care benefits, tuition waivers (full and partial), and unspecified assistantships also available. Financial award applicants required to submit FAFSA. *Faculty research:* Phonology and phonetics; syntax and semantics; historical linguistics; philosophy of language; language acquisition. *Unit head:* Director of Graduate Studies, 607-255-1105. *Application contact:* Graduate Field Assistant, 607-255-1105, E-mail: lingfield@cornell.edu.

Duke University, Graduate School, Department of East Asian Studies, Durham, NC 27708. Offers AM, Certificate. Part-time programs available. *Faculty:* 41 full-time. *Students:* 14 full-time (10 women); includes 6 minority (1 African American, 4 Asian Americans or Pacific Islanders, 1 Hispanic American), 4 international. 42 applicants, 55% accepted, 8 enrolled. In 2009, 6 master's awarded. *Entrance requirements:* For master's, GRE General Test. Additional exam requirements/recommendations for international students: Required—TOEFL (minimum score 550 paper-based; 213 computer-based; 83 iBT), IELTS (minimum score 7). *Application deadline:* For fall admission, 12/8 priority date for domestic and international students; for spring admission, 11/1 for domestic students. Application fee: $75. Electronic applications accepted. *Financial support:* Application deadline: 12/31. *Unit head:* Kristina Troost, Director, Fax: 919-684-2604, E-mail: dana.watson@duke.edu. *Application contact:* Cynthia Robertson, Associate Dean for Academic Services, 919-684-3913, E-mail: grad-admissions@duke.edu.

Florida International University, College of Arts and Sciences, Program in Asian Studies, Miami, FL 33199. Offers MA. Part-time and evening/weekend programs available. *Students:* 7 full-time (5 women), 13 part-time (5 women); includes 8 minority (1 African American, 2 Asian Americans or Pacific Islanders, 5 Hispanic Americans), 2 international. Average age 28. 12 applicants, 58% accepted, 7 enrolled. In 2009, 4 master's awarded. *Degree requirements:* For master's, thesis. *Entrance requirements:* For master's, minimum GPA of 3.0, letter of intent, letter of recommendation. Additional exam requirements/recommendations for international students: Required—TOEFL (minimum score 550 paper-based; 80 iBT). *Application deadline:* For fall admission, 6/1 for domestic students, 4/1 for international students; for spring admission, 10/1 for domestic students, 9/1 for international students. Applications are processed on a rolling basis. Application fee: $30. Electronic applications accepted. *Expenses:* Tuition, state resident: full-time $8008; part-time $4004 per year. Tuition, nonresident: full-time $20,104; part-time $10,052 per year. Required fees: $298; $149 per term. *Financial support:* Institutionally sponsored loans, scholarships/grants, and tuition waivers available. Financial award application deadline: 3/1; financial award applicants required to submit FAFSA. *Unit head:* Dr. Steven Heine, Director, 305-348-1914, Fax: 305-348-6586, E-mail: asian@fiu.edu. *Application contact:* Nanett Rojas, Assistant Director of Graduate Admissions, 305-348-7442, Fax: 305-348-7441, E-mail: gradadm@fiu.edu.

Florida State University, The Graduate School, College of Social Sciences and Public Policy, Program in Asian Studies, Tallahassee, FL 32306. Offers MA. Part-time programs available. *Students:* 3 full-time (1 woman), 10 part-time (6 women); includes 4 minority (all Asian Americans or Pacific Islanders), 3 international. Average age 24. 16 applicants, 100% accepted, 4 enrolled. In 2009, 1 master's awarded. *Degree requirements:* For master's, one foreign language, comprehensive exam, thesis optional. *Entrance requirements:* For master's, GRE General Test, minimum GPA of 3.0. Additional exam requirements/recommendations for international students: Required—TOEFL (minimum score 550 paper-based; 213 computer-based; 80 iBT). *Application deadline:* For fall admission, 7/1 for domestic and international students; for spring admission, 11/1 for domestic and international students. Applications are processed on a rolling basis. Application fee: $30. Electronic applications accepted. *Expenses:* Tuition, state resident: full-time $7413. Tuition, nonresident: full-time $22,567. *Financial support:* In 2009–10, 1 student received support, including 1 research assistantship with full tuition reimbursement available (averaging $5,000 per year); Federal Work-Study, institutionally sponsored loans, and unspecified assistantships also available. Financial award application deadline: 2/15; financial award applicants required to submit FAFSA. *Faculty research:* Art history of the Orient, Asian history and politics. *Unit head:* Dr. Lee K. Metcalf, Director, 850-644-7327, Fax: 850-645-4981, E-mail: lmetcalf@fsu.edu. *Application contact:* Patty Lollis, Program Assistant, 850-644-4418, Fax: 850-645-4981, E-mail: plollis@.fsu.edu.

The George Washington University, Elliott School of International Affairs, Program in Asian Studies, Washington, DC 20052. Offers MA, JD/MA, MBA/MA, MPH/MA. Part-time and evening/weekend programs available. *Students:* 25 full-time (10 women), 8 part-time (4 women); includes 5 minority (all Asian Americans or Pacific Islanders), 5 international. Average age 27. 60 applicants, 55% accepted, 11 enrolled. In 2009, 10 master's awarded. *Degree requirements:* For master's, one foreign language, capstone project. *Entrance requirements:* For master's, GRE General Test, 2 years (or the equivalent) of an approved Asian language. Additional exam requirements/recommendations for international students: Required—TOEFL. *Application deadline:* For fall admission, 2/1 for domestic students; for spring admission, 10/1 for domestic students. Application fee: $60. Electronic applications accepted. *Financial support:* In 2009–10, 7 students received support; fellowships with tuition reimbursements available, research assistantships with tuition reimbursements available, career-related internships or fieldwork, Federal Work-Study, institutionally sponsored loans, and tuition waivers (full) available. Financial award application deadline: 1/15; financial award applicants required to submit FAFSA. *Faculty research:* Sino-Soviet studies, Japanese-U. S. relations, Chinese foreign policy, economic development in China. *Unit head:* Elizabeth Chacko, Director, 202-994-5328, Fax: 202-994-2484, E-mail: echacko@gwu.edu. *Application contact:* Jeff V. Miles, Director of Graduate Admissions, 202-994-7050, Fax: 202-994-9537, E-mail: esiagrad@gwu.edu.

Harvard University, Graduate School of Arts and Sciences, Committee on Inner Asian and Altaic Studies, Cambridge, MA 02138. Offers PhD. *Degree requirements:* For doctorate, 2 foreign languages, thesis/dissertation, oral general exam. *Entrance requirements:* For doctorate, GRE General Test, proficiency in a related foreign language. Additional exam requirements/recommendations for international students: Required—TOEFL. *Expenses:* Tuition: Full-time $33,696. Required fees: $1126. Full-time tuition and fees vary according to program.

Harvard University, Graduate School of Arts and Sciences, Committee on Regional Studies–East Asia, Cambridge, MA 02138. Offers Chinese studies (AM); Japanese studies (AM); Korean studies (AM); Mongolian studies (AM); Vietnamese studies (AM). *Degree requirements:* For master's, one foreign language, seminar paper. *Entrance requirements:* For master's, GRE General Test. Additional exam requirements/recommendations for international students: Required—TOEFL. *Expenses:* Tuition: Full-time $33,696. Required fees: $1126. Full-time tuition and fees vary according to program.

Harvard University, Graduate School of Arts and Sciences, Department of Sanskrit and Indian Studies, Cambridge, MA 02138. Offers Indian philosophy (AM, PhD); Pali (AM, PhD); Sanskrit (AM, PhD); Tibetan (AM, PhD); Urdu (AM, PhD). Terminal master's awarded for partial completion of doctoral program. *Degree requirements:* For master's, 3 foreign languages; for doctorate, 3 foreign languages, thesis/dissertation. *Entrance requirements:* For master's, GRE General Test; for doctorate, GRE General Test, proficiency in French and German. Additional exam requirements/recommendations for international students: Required—TOEFL. *Expenses:* Tuition: Full-time $33,696. Required fees: $1126. Full-time tuition and fees vary according to program.

Indiana University Bloomington, University Graduate School, College of Arts and Sciences, Department of Central Eurasian Studies, Bloomington, IN 47405-7000. Offers MA, PhD. *Faculty:* 11 full-time (0 women). *Students:* 42 full-time (16 women), 4 part-time (1 woman); includes 2 minority (1 American Indian/Alaska Native, 1 Asian American or Pacific Islander), 13 international. Average age 32. 34 applicants, 79% accepted, 14 enrolled. In 2009, 25 master's, 1 doctorate awarded. Terminal master's awarded for partial completion of doctoral program. *Degree requirements:* For master's, one foreign language, thesis; for doctorate, 2 foreign languages, thesis/dissertation, qualifying exams. *Entrance requirements:* For master's, minimum GPA of 3.0, 2 years of a foreign language; for doctorate, minimum GPA of 3.5, 1 research language. Additional exam requirements/recommendations for international students: Required—TOEFL. *Application deadline:* For fall admission, 1/15 priority date for domestic students, 12/15 for international students; for spring admission, 9/1 priority date for domestic students, 9/1 for international students. Applications are processed on a rolling basis. Application fee: $55 ($65 for international students). Electronic applications accepted. *Financial support:* Fellowships with full tuition reimbursements, research assistantships with full tuition reimbursements, teaching assistantships with full tuition reimbursements, Federal Work-Study available. Financial award application deadline: 2/16. *Faculty research:* Central Asia, Hungarian civilization, Tibetan civilization, Turkish studies, Mongolian philology. *Unit head:* Christopher Atwood, Chair, 812-855-2233, E-mail: catwood@indiana.edu. *Application contact:* April Younger, Graduate Secretary, 812-855-2233, E-mail: ayounger@indiana.edu.

Indiana University Bloomington, University Graduate School, College of Arts and Sciences, Department of East Asian Languages and Cultures, Bloomington, IN 47405-7000. Offers Chinese (MA, PhD); East Asian languages and cultures (PhD); East Asian studies (MA); Japanese (MA, PhD); language pedagogy (MA). Part-time programs available. *Faculty:* 7 full-time (2 women). *Students:* 21 full-time (12 women), 11 part-time (8 women); includes 1 minority (Asian American or Pacific Islander), 11 international. Average age 30. 85 applicants, 38% accepted, 12 enrolled. In 2009, 6 master's, 1 doctorate awarded. *Degree requirements:* For master's, 2 foreign languages, thesis; for doctorate, 2 foreign languages, thesis/dissertation. *Entrance requirements:* Additional exam requirements/recommendations for international students: Required—TOEFL. *Application deadline:* For fall admission, 1/15 for domestic students, 12/15 for international students; for spring admission, 9/1 for domestic and international students. Applications are processed on a rolling basis. Application fee: $55 ($65 for international students). Electronic applications accepted. *Financial support:* In 2009–10, 6 fellowships with full tuition reimbursements (averaging $15,500 per year), 11 teaching assistantships with full tuition reimbursements (averaging $13,000 per year) were awarded; Federal Work-Study and tuition waivers (full) also available. Financial award application deadline: 3/1. *Faculty research:* Postwar/postmodern Japanese fiction, modern Chinese film and literature, classical Chinese literature and philosophy, Chinese and Japanese linguistics and pedagogy, East Asian politics. *Unit head:* Robert Eno, Chair, 812-855-0856, E-mail: eno@indiana.edu. *Application contact:* Edith Sarra, Director of Graduate Studies, 812-855-4031, Fax: 812-855-6402, E-mail: eserra@indiana.edu.

The Johns Hopkins University, Paul H. Nitze School of Advanced International Studies, Washington, DC 20036. Offers international development (MA, Certificate), including international economics (MA); international public policy (MIPP); international relations (PhD); international studies (Certificate); Japan studies (MA), including international economics; Korea Studies (MA), including international economics; South Asia studies (MA), including international economics; Southeast Asia studies (MA), including international economics; JD/MA; MBA/MA; MHS/MA. *Faculty:* 57 full-time (18 women), 125 part-time/adjunct (40 women). *Students:* 623 full-time (291 women), 38 part-time (17 women); includes 94 minority (11 African Americans, 55 Asian Americans or Pacific Islanders, 28 Hispanic Americans), 173 international. Average age 29. 1,444 applicants, 38% accepted, 212 enrolled. In 2009, 395 master's, 7 doctorates awarded. Terminal master's awarded for partial completion of doctoral program. *Degree requirements:* For master's, 2 core examinations, oral exam, proficiency in language other than native language (MA); for doctorate, 2 foreign languages, thesis/dissertation, 3 comprehensive exams, economics, quantitative and qualitative course, dissertation prospectus and defense. *Entrance requirements:* For master's, GMAT or GRE General Test, previous course work in economics, foreign language, undergraduate degree; for doctorate, GRE General Test, master's degree. Additional exam requirements/recommendations for international students: Required—TOEFL (minimum score 600 paper-based; 250 computer-based; 100 iBT), IELTS (minimum score 7), TOEFL (minimum score 600 paper-based; 250 computer-based; 100 iBT) or IELTS (minimum score 7). *Application deadline:* For fall admission, 1/7 for domestic and international students. Application fee: $85. Electronic applications accepted. *Expenses:* Contact institution. *Financial support:* In 2009–10, 450 students received support, including 450 fellowships (averaging $7,500 per year); teaching assistantships, career-related internships or fieldwork, Federal Work-Study, and scholarships/grants also available. Financial award application deadline: 2/15; financial award applicants required to submit FAFSA. *Faculty research:* Regional studies, international relations, international economics, energy and environment, international development. Total annual research expenditures: $7 million. *Unit head:* Sidney Jackson, Director of Admissions, 202-663-5700, Fax: 202-663-7788. *Application contact:* Admissions, 202-663-5700, Fax: 202-663-7788, E-mail: admissions.sais@jhu.edu.

Maharishi University of Management, Graduate Studies, Program in Maharishi Vedic Science, Fairfield, IA 52557. Offers MA, PhD. Evening/weekend programs available. *Degree requirements:* For master's, thesis; for doctorate, thesis/dissertation. *Entrance requirements:* For master's, minimum GPA of 3.0; for doctorate, GRE, minimum GPA of 3.0. Additional exam requirements/recommendations for international students: Required—TOEFL. *Faculty research:* Modern science and Vedic science, unification of knowledge, philosophy of science, Sanskrit.

McGill University, Faculty of Graduate and Postdoctoral Studies, Faculty of Arts, Department of East Asian Studies, Montréal, QC H3A 2T5, Canada. Offers MA, PhD.

New York University, Graduate School of Arts and Science, Department of East Asian Studies, New York, NY 10012-1019. Offers MA, PhD. Part-time programs available. *Students:* 14 full-time (8 women), 4 part-time (all women); includes 2 minority (both Asian Americans or Pacific Islanders), 10 international. Average age 29. 86 applicants, 19% accepted, 5 enrolled. In 2009, 1 master's awarded. *Degree requirements:* For master's and doctorate, one foreign language. *Entrance requirements:* For master's and doctorate, GRE General Test. Additional exam requirements/recommendations for international students: Required—TOEFL. Application fee: $90. Electronic applications accepted. *Expenses:* Tuition: Full-time $30,528; part-time $1272 per credit. Required fees: $2177. *Financial support:* Fellowships with tuition reimbursements, teaching assistantships with tuition reimbursements, Federal Work-Study, institutionally sponsored loans, scholarships/grants, health care benefits, and unspecified assistantships available. Financial award application deadline: 1/4. *Unit head:* Xudong Zhang, Chair, 212-998-7620, Fax: 212-995-4682, E-mail: gsas.eas.graduate@nyu.edu. *Application contact:* Mitsuhiro Yoshimoto, Associate Dean of Enrollment, 212-998-7620, Fax: 212-995-4682, E-mail: gsas.eas.graduate@nyu.edu.

Ohio University, Graduate College, Center for International Studies, Program in Southeast Asian Studies, Athens, OH 45701-2979. Offers MA. Part-time programs available. *Faculty:* 37 full-time (10 women), 9 part-time/adjunct (4 women). *Students:* 17 full-time (11 women), 3 part-time (2 women), 14 international. Average age 31. 16 applicants, 94% accepted, 5 enrolled. In 2009, 6 master's awarded. *Degree requirements:* For master's, one foreign language, thesis optional. *Entrance requirements:* For master's, minimum GPA of 3.0. Additional exam requirements/recommendations for international students: Required—TOEFL (minimum score 550 paper-based; 213 computer-based). *Application deadline:* For fall admission, 1/1 for domestic and international students. Application fee: $50 ($55 for international students). Electronic applications accepted. *Expenses:* Tuition, state resident: full-time $7839; part-time $323 per quarter hour. Tuition, nonresident: full-time $15,831; part-time $654 per quarter hour. Required fees: $2931. *Financial support:* In 2009–10, research assistantships with full tuition reimbursements (averaging $11,499 per year), teaching assistantships with full tuition reimbursements (averaging $11,499 per year) were awarded; career-related internships or fieldwork, Federal Work-Study, institutionally sponsored loans, scholarships/grants, tuition waivers (partial), and unspecified assistantships also available. Financial award application deadline: 1/1. *Faculty research:* Indonesian and Malaysian: political, history, literature, media, Islam, and environmental problems. Total annual research expenditures: $36,000. *Unit head:* Dr. Gene Amarelle, Program Director, E-mail: ammarell@ohio.edu. *Application contact:* Joan Kraynanski, Administrative Assistant, 740-593-1840, Fax: 740-593-1837, E-mail: kraynans@ohio.edu.

Princeton University, Graduate School, Department of East Asian Studies, Princeton, NJ 08544-1019. Offers PhD. *Degree requirements:* For doctorate, 2 foreign languages, thesis/dissertation. *Entrance requirements:* For doctorate, GRE General Test, fluency in Japanese and/or Chinese. Additional exam requirements/recommendations for international students: Required—TOEFL (minimum score 600 paper-based; 250 computer-based). Electronic applications accepted. *Faculty research:* Modern and classical Japanese literature, premodern Chinese and Japanese history, Chinese narrative and poetry.

Rutgers, The State University of New Jersey, New Brunswick, Graduate School-New Brunswick, Program in History, Piscataway, NJ 08854-8097. Offers African-American history (PhD); early American history (PhD); early modern European history (PhD); east Asian history (PhD); global and comparative history (PhD); history (PhD); history of diplomacy and foreign relations (PhD); history of technology, environment and health (PhD); history of the Atlantic cultures and African diaspora (PhD); Latin American history (PhD); medieval history (PhD); modern European history (PhD); nineteenth and twentieth century American history (PhD); women's and gender history (PhD). *Degree requirements:* For doctorate, thesis/dissertation. *Entrance requirements:* For doctorate, GRE General Test, sample of written work. Electronic applications accepted. *Faculty research:* American history, European history, Afro-American history, women's history, Latin American history.

St. John's College, Graduate Institute in Liberal Education, Program in Eastern Classics, Santa Fe, NM 87505. Offers MA. Part-time and evening/weekend programs available. *Entrance requirements:* For master's, 2 letters of recommendation. Additional exam requirements/recommendations for international students: Required—TOEFL, TWE. *Expenses:* Contact institution.

St. John's University, St. John's College of Liberal Arts and Sciences, Institute of Asian Studies, Queens, NY 11439. Offers Asian and African cultural studies (Adv C); Asian studies (Adv C); Chinese studies (MA, Adv C); East Asian culture studies (Adv C); East Asian studies (MA). Part-time and evening/weekend programs available. *Students:* 8 full-time (6 women), 6 part-time (5 women); includes 5 minority (3 Asian Americans or Pacific Islanders, 2 Hispanic Americans), 8 international. Average age 30. 22 applicants, 68% accepted, 6 enrolled. In 2009, 6 master's awarded. *Degree requirements:* For master's, one foreign language, comprehensive exam, thesis optional. *Entrance requirements:* For master's, 18 hours of course work in the field, minimum GPA of 3.0. Additional exam requirements/recommendations for international students: Required—TOEFL (minimum score 500 paper-based; 173 computer-based; 61 iBT), IELTS (minimum score 5.5). *Application deadline:* For fall admission, 5/1 priority date for domestic and international students; for spring admission, 11/1 priority date for domestic and international students. Applications are processed on a rolling basis. Application fee: $70. Electronic applications accepted. *Expenses:* Tuition: Full-time $16,290; part-time $905 per credit. Required fees: $300; $150 per semester. Tuition and fees vary according to program. *Financial support:* Research assistantships, scholarships/grants available. Support available to part-time students. Financial award application deadline: 3/1; financial award applicants required to submit FAFSA. *Faculty research:* East Asian philosophy and religion, Chinese language and literature, Japanese language, modern Japan, Chinese art and history. *Unit head:* Dr. Bernadette Li, Chair, 718-990-1657, E-mail: lib@stjohns.edu. *Application contact:* Kathleen Davis, Director of Graduate Admission, 718-990-2790, Fax: 718-990-5686, E-mail: gradhelp@stjohns.edu.

San Diego State University, Graduate and Research Affairs, College of Arts and Letters, Center for Asian Studies, San Diego, CA 92182. Offers MA. *Degree requirements:* For master's, one foreign language, thesis. *Entrance requirements:* For master's, GRE General Test, 3 letters of reference, writing sample. Additional exam requirements/recommendations for international students: Required—TOEFL. Electronic applications accepted. *Faculty research:* Language acquisition process, social organization of Asia, economic development.

Seton Hall University, College of Arts and Sciences, Department of Asian Studies, South Orange, NJ 07079-2697. Offers Asian languages (MA); Asian studies (MA); teaching Chinese language and culture (MA). Part-time and evening/weekend programs available. *Faculty:* 5 full-time (2 women), 3 part-time/adjunct (2 women). *Students:* 21 full-time (9 women), 7 part-time (6 women). Average age 30. 26 applicants, 92% accepted, 10 enrolled. In 2009, 14 master's awarded. *Degree requirements:* For master's, thesis optional. *Entrance requirements:* For master's, strong background in Asian studies or related discipline. Additional exam requirements/recommendations for international students: Required—TOEFL. *Application deadline:* For fall admission, 7/1 priority date for domestic and international students; for spring admission, 11/1 priority date for domestic and international students. Applications are processed on a rolling basis. Application fee: $50. Electronic applications accepted. *Financial support:* Teaching assistantships with full tuition reimbursements, career-related internships or fieldwork, Federal Work-Study, institutionally sponsored loans, and unspecified assistantships available. Financial award applicants required to submit FAFSA. *Faculty research:* Modern Chinese history, contemporary Chinese politics, ancient Chinese history, Hinduism, Asian business, Japanese history. *Unit head:* Dr. Edwin Pak-Wah Leung, Chair, 973-761-9464, Fax: 973-761-9596, E-mail: leungedw@shu.edu. *Application contact:* Dr. Shigeru Osuka, Director of Graduate Studies, 973-275-2712, Fax: 973-761-9596, E-mail: osukashi@shu.edu.

Stanford University, School of Humanities and Sciences, Center for East Asian Studies, Stanford, CA 94305-9991. Offers MA. *Degree requirements:* For master's, one foreign language, thesis. *Entrance requirements:* For master's, GRE General Test. Additional exam requirements/recommendations for international students: Required—TOEFL. Electronic applications accepted. *Expenses:* Tuition: Full-time $37,380; part-time $2760 per quarter. Required fees: $501.

United Theological Seminary of the Twin Cities, Professional Program, New Brighton, MN 55112-2598. Offers advanced theological studies (Diploma); justice and peace studies (M Div, MA); leadership toward racial justice (MA, Certificate); leadership towards racial justice (M Div); Methodist studies (M Div, MA, Certificate); ministry (D Min); ministry renewal and professional development (Certificate); pastoral care and counseling (M Div, MA, MARL); religion and theology (MA); theological and religious studies (Certificate); theology and the arts (M Div, MA); urban ministry (M Div, MA, MARL); women's studies: religion, theology and ministry (MA); women's studies: religions, theology and ministry (M Div). *Accreditation:* ACIPE; ATS. Part-time and evening/weekend programs available. *Faculty:* 9 full-time (6 women), 22 part-time/adjunct (10 women). *Students:* 49 full-time (34 women), 105 part-time (68 women). Average age 47. 41 applicants, 98% accepted, 34 enrolled. In 2009, 24 first professional degrees, 5 master's, 2 doctorates, 2 other advanced degrees awarded. *Degree requirements:* For master's, thesis; for doctorate, comprehensive exam, thesis/dissertation; for M Div, integrative notebook, spiritual chronicle. *Entrance requirements:* For M Div and master's, minimum GPA of 2.75; strong analytical, reflective thinking and writing skills; vocational and academic goals compatible with those of Seminary; for doctorate, M Div or equivalent, minimum GPA of 3.0, 3 years experience in professional ministry; for other advanced degree, BA or equivalent life experience; strong analytical, reflective thinking and writing skills (Certificate); proficiency in English language, previous study of theology at a theological school, recommendation of student's denomination (Diploma). Additional exam requirements/recommendations for international students: Required—TOEFL (minimum score 550 paper-based). *Application deadline:* For fall admission, 7/1 priority date for domestic students, 11/1 priority date for international students; for winter admission, 11/1 priority date for domestic students; for spring admission, 11/15 priority date for domestic students. Applications are processed on a rolling basis. Application fee: $50. *Expenses:* Tuition: Full-time $11,502; part-time $426 per credit hour. Required fees: $295; $155 per term. One-time fee: $25. Tuition and fees vary according to course load, degree level and program. *Financial support:* In 2009–10, 120 students received support. Career-related internships or fieldwork, institutionally sponsored loans, and scholarships/grants available. Support available to part-time students. Financial award application deadline: 5/1; financial award applicants required to submit FAFSA. *Unit head:* Dr. Richard D. Weis, Dean of the Seminary, 651-255-6108 Ext. 108, Fax: 651-633-4315, E-mail: rweis@unitedseminary.edu. *Application contact:* Rev. Glen Herrington-Hall, Director of Admissions, 651-255-6107 Ext. 107, Fax: 651-633-4315, E-mail: gherrington-hall@unitedseminary.edu.

Asian Studies

University of Alberta, Faculty of Graduate Studies and Research, Department of East Asian Studies, Edmonton, AB T6G 2E1, Canada. Offers Chinese literature (MA); East Asian interdisciplinary studies (MA); Japanese literature (MA). Part-time programs available. *Faculty:* 7 full-time (4 women). *Students:* 4 full-time. Average age 23. 8 applicants, 50% accepted, 4 enrolled. In 2009, 3 master's awarded. *Degree requirements:* For master's, one foreign language, thesis. *Entrance requirements:* Additional exam requirements/recommendations for international students: Required—TOEFL. *Application deadline:* Applications are processed on a rolling basis. Application fee: $0. Electronic applications accepted. Tuition and fees charges are reported in Canadian dollars. *Expenses:* Tuition, area resident: Full-time $4626 Canadian dollars; part-time $99.72 Canadian dollars per unit. International tuition: $8216 Canadian dollars full-time. Required fees: $3590 Canadian dollars; $99.72 Canadian dollars per unit. $215 Canadian dollars per term. *Financial support:* In 2009–10, 4 students received support, including 3 teaching assistantships with tuition reimbursements available (averaging $10,500 per year); scholarships/grants also available. Financial award application deadline: 12/1. *Faculty research:* Classical Chinese poetry and poetics, Chinese philosophy, modern/contemporary Chinese literature, modern Japanese literature and culture, Japanese women's writing. Total annual research expenditures: $15,000. *Unit head:* Dr. Janice Brown, Chair, 780-492-3038, Fax: 780-492-7440, E-mail: janice.brown@gpu.srv.ualberta.ca. *Application contact:* Heather McDonald, Administrative Assistant, 780-492-2836, Fax: 780-492-7440, E-mail: eastasia.grad@ualberta.ca.

The University of Arizona, Graduate College, College of Humanities, Department of East Asian Studies, Tucson, AZ 85721. Offers MA, PhD. Part-time programs available. *Faculty:* 11. *Students:* 13 full-time (9 women), 16 part-time (8 women); includes 2 minority (1 Asian American or Pacific Islander, 1 Hispanic American), 17 international. Average age 33. 64 applicants, 19% accepted, 8 enrolled. In 2009, 6 master's, 4 doctorates awarded. Terminal master's awarded for partial completion of doctoral program. *Degree requirements:* For master's, one foreign language; for doctorate, 2 foreign languages. *Entrance requirements:* For master's, GRE General Test, 2 letters of recommendation; for doctorate, GRE General Test, 2 letters of recommendation, statement of purpose, writing sample. Additional exam requirements/recommendations for international students: Required—TOEFL (minimum score 550 paper-based; 213 computer-based; 79 iBT). *Application deadline:* For fall admission, 2/1 for domestic and international students. Applications are processed on a rolling basis. Application fee: $75. Electronic applications accepted. *Expenses:* Tuition, state resident: full-time $9028. Tuition, nonresident: full-time $24,890. *Financial support:* In 2009–10, 20 teaching assistantships with full tuition reimbursements (averaging $14,454 per year) were awarded; health care benefits, tuition waivers (partial), and unspecified assistantships also available. Financial award application deadline: 2/1. *Faculty research:* Chinese history, Chinese/Japanese linguistics, Chinese/Japanese literature, Chinese/Japanese religion. Total annual research expenditures: $30,001. *Unit head:* Dr. J. Philip Gabriel, Head, 520-621-7505, Fax: 520-621-1149, E-mail: jgabriel@u.arizona.edu. *Application contact:* Janet Kania, Administrative Associate, 520-621-5452, Fax: 520-621-1149, E-mail: kaniaj@u.arizona.edu.

The University of British Columbia, Faculty of Arts, Department of Asian Studies, Vancouver, CA V6T 1Z2, Canada. Offers MA, PhD. *Degree requirements:* For master's, one foreign language, thesis; for doctorate, 2 foreign languages, thesis/dissertation. *Entrance requirements:* For master's, BA; for doctorate, master's degree in Asian studies or equivalent. Additional exam requirements/recommendations for international students: Required—TOEFL (minimum score 570 paper-based; 230 computer-based; 85 iBT). Electronic applications accepted. *Faculty research:* Language; linguistics; literature; religion and philosophy; premodern history of China, Japan, Korea, South and South East Asia.

The University of British Columbia, Institute of Asian Research, Vancouver, BC V6T 1Z2, Canada. Offers MAPPS. *Degree requirements:* For master's, thesis optional. *Entrance requirements:* Additional exam requirements/recommendations for international students: Required—TOEFL (minimum score 600 paper-based; 250 computer-based; 100 iBT), GRE (recommended). Electronic applications accepted. *Faculty research:* Social cohesion, globalization, social safety nets, policy research, research and development alliances, knowledge-based workshops on Asia-Pacific studies.

University of California, Berkeley, Graduate Division, College of Letters and Science, Department of South and Southeast Asian Studies, Berkeley, CA 94720-1500. Offers Hindi (MA, PhD); Indonesian (MA, PhD); Sanskrit (MA, PhD); Tamil (MA, PhD). *Faculty:* 6 full-time, 14 part-time/adjunct. *Students:* 31 full-time (14 women). Average age 34. 362 applicants, 16 enrolled. In 2009, 18 master's, 13 doctorates awarded. Terminal master's awarded for partial completion of doctoral program. *Degree requirements:* For master's, 2 foreign languages, thesis; for doctorate, 2 foreign languages, thesis/dissertation, oral qualifying exam. *Entrance requirements:* For master's and doctorate, GRE General Test, minimum GPA of 3.0, 3 letters of recommendation. *Application deadline:* For fall admission, 12/3 for domestic students. Application fee: $70 ($90 for international students). Electronic applications accepted. *Financial support:* Fellowships, research assistantships, teaching assistantships, unspecified assistantships available. *Unit head:* Prof. Alexander von Rospatt, Chair, 510-642-4564, E-mail: ch_sseas@ls.berkeley.edu. *Application contact:* Lee Amazonas, Student Affairs Officer, 510-642-4219, E-mail: casmauga@berkeley.edu.

University of California, Berkeley, Graduate Division, College of Letters and Science, Group in Buddhist Studies, Berkeley, CA 94720-1500. Offers PhD. *Faculty:* 9 full-time. *Students:* 6 full-time (3 women). Average age 31. 14 applicants, 1 enrolled. *Degree requirements:* For doctorate, 4 foreign languages, thesis/dissertation, dissertation defense, qualifying exam. *Entrance requirements:* For doctorate, GRE General Test, MA in Japanese, Chinese, or Sanskrit; minimum GPA of 3.0, 3 letters of recommendation. *Application deadline:* For fall admission, 12/8 for domestic students. Application fee: $70 ($90 for international students). Electronic applications accepted. *Financial support:* Unspecified assistantships available. *Unit head:* Prof. Robert Sharf, Chair, 510-642-3480, E-mail: rsharf@berkeley.edu. *Application contact:* Information Contact, 510-642-3480, E-mail: gbs@berkeley.edu.

University of California, Berkeley, Graduate Division, Group in International and Area Studies, Group in Asian Studies, Berkeley, CA 94720-1500. Offers Asian studies (PhD); East Asian studies (MA); Northeast Asian studies (MA); South Asian studies (MA); Southeast Asian studies (MA); JD/MA; MBA/MA; MJ/MA. *Students:* 20 full-time (13 women). Average age 30. 68 applicants, 6 enrolled. In 2009, 4 master's awarded. *Degree requirements:* For master's, one foreign language, comprehensive exam or thesis; for doctorate, 2 foreign languages, thesis/dissertation, qualifying exam. *Entrance requirements:* For master's and doctorate, GRE General Test, minimum GPA of 3.0, 3 letters of recommendation. *Application deadline:* For fall admission, 12/1 for domestic students. Application fee: $70 ($90 for international students). *Financial support:* Fellowships, research assistantships, teaching assistantships, Federal Work-Study and unspecified assistantships available. Financial award applicants required to submit FAFSA. *Unit head:* Prof. Bonnie Wade, Chair, 510-642-0333, E-mail: asianst@berkeley.edu. *Application contact:* Hilary Vanessa Finchum-Sung, Student Affairs Officer, 510-642-0333, Fax: 510-643-7062, E-mail: hfinchum_sung@berkeley.edu.

University of California, Los Angeles, Graduate Division, College of Letters and Science, Department of Asian Languages and Cultures, Los Angeles, CA 90095. Offers MA, PhD. *Students:* 52 full-time (30 women); includes 14 minority (all Asian Americans or Pacific Islanders), 17 international. Average age 34. 49 applicants, 16% accepted, 4 enrolled. In 2009, 3 master's, 4 doctorates awarded. Terminal master's awarded for partial completion of doctoral program. *Degree requirements:* For master's, one foreign language, comprehensive exam or thesis; for doctorate, 2 foreign languages, thesis/dissertation, oral and written qualifying exams. *Entrance requirements:* For master's, GRE General Test, minimum GPA of 3.0, sample of written work; for doctorate, GRE General Test, minimum undergraduate GPA of 3.0, sample of research writing or thesis in English. Additional exam requirements/recommendations for international students: Required—TOEFL. *Application deadline:* For fall admission, 12/1 for domestic and international students. Application fee: $70 ($90 for international students). Electronic applications accepted. *Financial support:* In 2009–10, 36 fellowships with full and partial tuition reimbursements, 22 research assistantships with full and partial tuition reimbursements, 25 teaching assistantships with full and partial tuition reimbursements were awarded; Federal Work-Study, institutionally sponsored loans, scholarships/grants, health care benefits, tuition waivers (full and partial), and unspecified assistantships also available. Financial award application deadline: 3/1; financial award applicants required to submit FAFSA. *Unit head:* Dr. David Schaberg, Chair, 310-206-8235. *Application contact:* Department Office, 310-206-8235, E-mail: alcgen@humnet.ucla.edu.

University of California, Los Angeles, Graduate Division, International Institute, Interdepartmental Program in East Asian Studies, Los Angeles, CA 90095. Offers MA. *Students:* 16 full-time (7 women); includes 9 minority (1 African American, 8 Asian Americans or Pacific Islanders), 2 international. Average age 28. 59 applicants, 42% accepted, 9 enrolled. In 2009, 6 master's awarded. *Degree requirements:* For master's, one foreign language, comprehensive exam. *Entrance requirements:* For master's, GRE General Test, minimum undergraduate GPA of 3.0. *Application deadline:* For fall admission, 12/15 for domestic and international students. Application fee: $70 ($90 for international students). Electronic applications accepted. *Financial support:* In 2009–10, 3 fellowships with full and partial tuition reimbursements, 2 research assistantships with full and partial tuition reimbursements, 3 teaching assistantships with full and partial tuition reimbursements were awarded; Federal Work-Study, institutionally sponsored loans, scholarships/grants, health care benefits, tuition waivers (full and partial), and unspecified assistantships also available. Financial award application deadline: 3/1; financial award applicants required to submit FAFSA. *Unit head:* Cindy Fan, Director, 310-825-3821. *Application contact:* Program Office, 310-825-3821, E-mail: idgrads@international.ucla.edu.

University of California, Riverside, Graduate Division, Program in Southeast Asian Studies, Riverside, CA 92521-0102. Offers MA. *Faculty:* 11 full-time (6 women). *Students:* 2 full-time (1 woman); both minorities (both Asian Americans or Pacific Islanders). Average age 28. 4 applicants, 50% accepted, 2 enrolled. *Degree requirements:* For master's, one foreign language, thesis. *Entrance requirements:* For master's, GRE, statement of purpose to indicate serious interest in Southeast Asian Studies (or specific country or area in this region), writing sample. Additional exam requirements/recommendations for international students: Required—TOEFL. *Application deadline:* For fall admission, 5/1 for domestic students, 2/1 for international students; for winter admission, 9/1 for domestic students, 7/1 for international students; for spring admission, 12/1 for domestic students, 10/1 for international students. Application fee: $60 ($75 for international students). Electronic applications accepted. *Financial support:* In 2009–10, 2 students received support, including teaching assistantships with tuition reimbursements available (averaging $16,500 per year); tuition waivers (full and partial) and unspecified assistantships also available. *Faculty research:* Southeast Asian texts, rituals and performance, music and technoculture, dance ethnography, ethnomusicology. *Unit head:* Dr. Rene Lysloff, Director, 951-827-3606, Fax: 951-827-2237, E-mail: rene.lysloff@ucr.edu. *Application contact:* Sharon L. Payne, Graduate Admissions, 951-827-2742, Fax: 951-827-2237, E-mail: sharon.payne@ucr.edu.

University of California, Santa Barbara, Graduate Division, College of Letters and Sciences, Division of Humanities and Fine Arts, Department of East Asian Languages and Cultural Studies, Santa Barbara, CA 93106-7075. Offers Asian Studies (MA), including Asian Studies, East Asian language and cultural studies; Asian studies (MA), including Asian Studies, East Asian language and cultural studies; East Asian language and cultural studies (PhD); MA/PhD. *Students:* 13 full-time (8 women). Average age 27. 76 applicants, 28% accepted, 6 enrolled. In 2009, 2 master's awarded. *Degree requirements:* For master's, one foreign language, thesis or alternative; for doctorate, 2 foreign languages, thesis/dissertation. *Entrance requirements:* For master's and doctorate, GRE, 3 letters of recommendation, statement of purpose, personal achievements/contributions statement, resume/curriculum vitae, transcripts for post-secondary institutions attended. Additional exam requirements/recommendations for international students: Required—TOEFL (minimum score 550 paper-based; 213 computer-based; 80 iBT) or IELTS (minimum score 7). *Application deadline:* For fall admission, 4/1 for domestic and international students. Application fee: $70 ($90 for international students). Electronic applications accepted. *Financial support:* In 2009–10, 10 students received support, including 5 fellowships with full and partial tuition reimbursements available (averaging $11,000 per year), 10 teaching assistantships with partial tuition reimbursements available (averaging $8,200 per year); Federal Work-Study, institutionally sponsored loans, scholarships/grants, health care benefits, and unspecified assistantships also available. Financial award application deadline: 12/15; financial award applicants required to submit FAFSA. *Faculty research:* Chinese literature, Chinese film, Japanese society, Japanese literature, East Asian cultural studies. *Unit head:* Dr. William Powell, Chair, 805-893-4455, Fax: 805-893-3011, E-mail: bpowell@religion.ucsb.edu. *Application contact:* Dr. Ronald Egan, Faculty Graduate Advisor, 805-893-3770, Fax: 805-893-3011, E-mail: ronegan@eastasian.ucsb.edu.

University of Chicago, Division of the Humanities, Department of East Asian Languages and Civilizations, Chicago, IL 60637-1513. Offers AM, PhD. Terminal master's awarded for partial completion of doctoral program. *Degree requirements:* For master's, one foreign language, thesis; for doctorate, 2 foreign languages, thesis/dissertation. *Entrance requirements:* For master's and doctorate, GRE General Test. Additional exam requirements/recommendations for international students: Required—TOEFL.

University of Chicago, Division of the Humanities, Department of South Asian Languages and Civilizations, Chicago, IL 60637-1513. Offers South Asian languages and civilizations (AM, PhD), including Bengali (PhD), Hindi (PhD), Sanskrit (PhD), Tamil (PhD), Urdu (PhD). Terminal master's awarded for partial completion of doctoral program. *Degree requirements:* For master's, one foreign language, thesis; for doctorate, 2 foreign languages, thesis/dissertation. *Entrance requirements:* For master's and doctorate, GRE General Test. Additional exam requirements/recommendations for international students: Required—TOEFL.

University of Colorado at Boulder, Graduate School, College of Arts and Sciences, Department of Asian Languages and Civilizations, Boulder, CO 80309. Offers Chinese (MA, PhD); Japanese (MA, PhD). Part-time programs available. *Faculty:* 10 full-time (6 women). *Students:* 30 full-time (19 women), 4 part-time (3 women); includes 9 minority (1 American Indian/Alaska Native, 6 Asian Americans or Pacific Islanders, 2 Hispanic Americans), 7 international. Average age 27. 30 applicants, 30% accepted, 9 enrolled. In 2009, 16 master's awarded. *Degree requirements:* For master's, comprehensive exam. *Entrance requirements:* For master's, BA in Chinese or Japanese, minimum undergraduate GPA of 3.0. Additional exam requirements/recommendations for international students: Required—TOEFL. *Application deadline:* For fall admission, 1/1 priority date for domestic students, 12/1 for international students; for spring admission, 10/1 for domestic students, 9/1 for international students. Applications are processed on a rolling basis. Application fee: $50 ($60 for international students). *Financial support:* In 2009–10, 7 fellowships (averaging $13,865 per year), 10 research assistantships (averaging $6,596 per year) were awarded; career-related internships or fieldwork and Federal Work-Study also available. Financial award application deadline: 2/1. *Faculty research:* Chinese and Japanese modern and classical literature, religions, linguistics, language pedagogy, pre-modern and contemporary fiction, sociolinguistics. Total annual research expenditures: $819,946.

University of Hawaii at Hilo, Program in China-US Relations, Hilo, HI 96720-4091. Offers MA.

University of Hawaii at Manoa, Graduate Division, School of Pacific and Asian Studies, Program in Asian Studies, Concentration in Korean Studies, Honolulu, HI 96822. Offers Graduate Certificate. Part-time programs available. In 2009, 3 Graduate Certificates awarded. *Degree requirements:* For Graduate Certificate, one foreign language. *Entrance requirements:* For degree, GRE. Additional exam requirements/recommendations for international students: Required—TOEFL (minimum score 560 paper-based; 220 computer-based; 83 iBT), IELTS (minimum score 5). Application fee: $60. *Expenses:* Tuition, state resident: full-time $8900; part-time $372 per credit. Tuition, nonresident: full-time $21,400; part-time $898 per credit.

Required fees: $207 per semester. Total annual research expenditures: $40,000. *Application contact:* Ho-Min Sohn, Director, 808-956-7041, Fax: 808-956-2213, E-mail: homin@hawaii.edu.

University of Hawaii at Manoa, Graduate Division, School of Pacific and Asian Studies, Program in Asian Studies, Concentration in Southeast Asian Studies, Honolulu, HI 96822. Offers Graduate Certificate. Part-time programs available. *Students:* 1 full-time (0 women). In 2009, 7 Graduate Certificates awarded. *Degree requirements:* For Graduate Certificate, one foreign language. *Entrance requirements:* For degree, GRE. Additional exam requirements/recommendations for international students: Required—TOEFL (minimum score 560 paper-based; 220 computer-based; 83 iBT), IELTS (minimum score 5). Application fee: $60. *Expenses:* Tuition, state resident: full-time $8900; part-time $372 per credit. Tuition, nonresident: full-time $21,400; part-time $898 per credit. Required fees: $207 per semester. *Financial support:* In 2009–10, 1 fellowship (averaging $2,000 per year) was awarded. *Application contact:* Barbara Andaya, Director, 808-956-2688, Fax: 808-956-6345, E-mail: dirseas@hawaii.edu.

University of Illinois at Urbana–Champaign, Graduate College, College of Liberal Arts and Sciences, School of Literatures, Cultures and Linguistics, Department of East Asian Languages and Cultures, Champaign, IL 61820. Offers Asian studies (MA); East Asian languages and cultures (PhD). *Faculty:* 16 full-time (6 women). *Students:* 37 full-time (32 women), 3 part-time (1 woman); includes 5 minority (1 American Indian/Alaska Native, 3 Asian Americans or Pacific Islanders, 1 Hispanic American), 28 international. 67 applicants, 16% accepted, 7 enrolled. In 2009, 7 master's, 1 doctorate awarded. *Entrance requirements:* For master's, GRE General Test, minimum GPA of 3.0; writing sample; for doctorate, GRE, minimum GPA of 3.0; writing sample. Additional exam requirements/recommendations for international students: Required—TOEFL (minimum score 103 iBT). *Application deadline:* Applications are processed on a rolling basis. Application fee: $60 ($75 for international students). Electronic applications accepted. *Financial support:* In 2009–10, 7 fellowships, 2 research assistantships, 26 teaching assistantships were awarded; tuition waivers (full and partial) also available. *Unit head:* Brian D. Ruppert, Head, 217-244-4012, Fax: 217-244-2223, E-mail: ruppert@illinois.edu. *Application contact:* Lynn Stanke, Office Support Specialist, 217-333-6269, Fax: 217-244-3050, E-mail: stanke@illinois.edu.

The University of Iowa, Graduate College, College of Liberal Arts and Sciences, Program in Asian Languages and Literature, Iowa City, IA 52242-1316. Offers MA. *Degree requirements:* For master's, thesis optional, exam. *Entrance requirements:* For master's, GRE General Test, minimum GPA of 3.0. Additional exam requirements/recommendations for international students: Required—TOEFL (minimum score 590 paper-based; 243 computer-based; 96 iBT). Electronic applications accepted.

The University of Kansas, Graduate Studies, College of Liberal Arts and Sciences, Department of East Asian Languages and Cultures, Lawrence, KS 66045. Offers MA, MBA/MA. Part-time programs available. *Faculty:* 7. *Students:* 16 full-time (11 women), 4 part-time (1 woman); includes 2 minority (1 African American, 1 American Indian/Alaska Native), 7 international. Average age 29. 23 applicants, 52% accepted, 7 enrolled. In 2009, 3 master's awarded. *Degree requirements:* For master's, one foreign language, thesis. *Entrance requirements:* For master's, GRE, 3 letters of recommendation, writing sample. Additional exam requirements/recommendations for international students: Required—TOEFL. *Application deadline:* For fall admission, 5/1 priority date for domestic students, 5/1 for international students; for spring admission, 12/1 priority date for domestic students, 12/1 for international students. Applications are processed on a rolling basis. Application fee: $45 ($55 for international students). Electronic applications accepted. *Expenses:* Tuition, state resident: full-time $6492; part-time $270.50 per credit hour. Tuition, nonresident: full-time $15,510; part-time $646.25 per credit hour. Required fees: $847; $70.56 per credit hour. Tuition and fees vary according to course load and program. *Financial support:* Fellowships, teaching assistantships with full and partial tuition reimbursements, unspecified assistantships available. Financial award application deadline: 2/1. *Faculty research:* Gender relations in literature, ancient Chinese law, visual culture of modern Japan, Japanese language pedagogy, Chinese paleography, Korean shamanism, folklore, traditional Chinese and Japanese literature, Chinese linguistics and language pedagogy. *Unit head:* Margaret Childs, Chair and Graduate Director, 785-864-3100, E-mail: mgchilds@ku.edu. *Application contact:* Georgia Damis, Administrative Specialist, 785-864-3100, Fax: 785-864-4298, E-mail: ealc@ku.edu.

University of Michigan, Horace H. Rackham School of Graduate Studies, College of Literature, Science, and the Arts, Center for Chinese Studies, Ann Arbor, MI 48109. Offers Asian studies: China (AM, Graduate Certificate); JD/AM; MBA/AM; MPP/AM. Part-time programs available. *Faculty:* 30 full-time. *Students:* 9 full-time; includes 4 Asian Americans or Pacific Islanders. Average age 21. 33 applicants, 42% accepted, 5 enrolled. In 2009, 2 master's awarded. *Degree requirements:* For master's, one foreign language, thesis. *Entrance requirements:* For master's, GRE General Test. Additional exam requirements/recommendations for international students: Required—TOEFL. *Application deadline:* For winter admission, 1/15 for domestic and international students. Application fee: $60 ($75 for international students). Electronic applications accepted. *Expenses:* Tuition, state resident: full-time $17,286; part-time $1099 per credit hour. Tuition, nonresident: full-time $34,944; part-time $2080 per credit hour. Required fees: $95 per semester. Tuition and fees vary according to course load, degree level and program. *Financial support:* Fellowships, Federal Work-Study available. *Faculty research:* Economic reform in China, Chinese religion, history of late Imperial China, Chinese foreign policy, Chinese music and music history. *Unit head:* Mary Gallagher, Director, 734-764-6308, Fax: 734-764-5540. *Application contact:* Carol Stepanchuk, Student Services Coordinator, 734-936-3961, Fax: 734-764-5540, E-mail: cstep@umich.edu.

University of Michigan, Horace H. Rackham School of Graduate Studies, College of Literature, Science, and the Arts, Center for Japanese Studies, Ann Arbor, MI 48109-1106. Offers AM, JD/AM, MBA/AM. Part-time programs available. *Faculty:* 40 full-time (16 women), 12 part-time/adjunct (3 women). *Students:* 15 full-time (8 women), 1 (woman) part-time; includes 3 minority (all Asian Americans or Pacific Islanders). Average age 26. 28 applicants, 68% accepted, 8 enrolled. In 2009, 12 master's awarded. *Degree requirements:* For master's, thesis optional, 3rd year proficiency in Japanese language, distribution requirement (3 disciplines). *Entrance requirements:* For master's, GRE General Test, previous study of Japanese language (highly recommended). Additional exam requirements/recommendations for international students: Required—TOEFL (minimum score 560 paper-based; 84 iBT); Recommended—IELTS (minimum score 6.5). *Application deadline:* For fall admission, 1/10 for domestic and international students. Application fee: $60 ($75 for international students). Electronic applications accepted. *Expenses:* Tuition, state resident: full-time $17,286; part-time $1099 per credit hour. Tuition, nonresident: full-time $34,944; part-time $2080 per credit hour. Required fees: $95 per semester. Tuition and fees vary according to course load, degree level and program. *Financial support:* In 2009–10, 6 students received support, including 1 fellowship with full tuition reimbursement available (averaging $15,000 per year), teaching assistantships with full tuition reimbursements available (averaging $16,135 per year); research assistantships with full tuition reimbursements available, career-related internships or fieldwork, Federal Work-Study, scholarships/grants, health care benefits, unspecified assistantships, and 5 partial tuition fellowships also available. Support available to part-time students. Financial award application deadline: 1/15; financial award applicants required to submit FAFSA. *Faculty research:* Japanese literature; Japanese history (premodern and modern); Japanese linguistics and language pedagogy; modern Japanese society and culture; Japanese elections and politics; gender and sexuality in Japan; Japanese art, art history and visual culture; Japanese film; Buddhism and religion in Japan; Japanese law. *Unit head:* Prof. Ken K. Ito, Director, 734-764-6307, Fax: 734-936-2948, E-mail: umcjs@umich.edu. *Application contact:* Azumi Ann Takata, Student Services Coordinator, 734-764-6307, Fax: 734-936-2948, E-mail: cjsadmissions@umich.edu.

University of Michigan, Horace H. Rackham School of Graduate Studies, College of Literature, Science, and the Arts, Center for South Asian Studies, Ann Arbor, MI 48109. Offers MA, Certificate, MBA/MA. Part-time programs available. *Faculty:* 40 full-time (13 women), 2 part-time/adjunct (both women). *Students:* 6 full-time (3 women); includes 5 minority (all Asian Americans or Pacific Islanders). Average age 30. 11 applicants, 64% accepted, 3 enrolled. In 2009, 1 master's awarded. *Degree requirements:* For master's, one foreign language, thesis, 24 credits; for Certificate, one foreign language. *Entrance requirements:* For master's, GRE General Test, 3 letters of recommendation; for Certificate, GRE General Test, GMAT (MA/MBA), 2 letters of recommendation, transcripts. Additional exam requirements/recommendations for international students: Required—TOEFL (minimum score 560 paper-based; 220 computer-based; 84 iBT). *Application deadline:* For fall admission, 1/15 for domestic and international students; for winter admission, 1/15 priority date for domestic and international students. Application fee: $60 ($75 for international students). Electronic applications accepted. *Expenses:* Tuition, state resident: full-time $17,286; part-time $1099 per credit hour. Tuition, nonresident: full-time $34,944; part-time $2080 per credit hour. Required fees: $95 per semester. Tuition and fees vary according to course load, degree level and program. *Financial support:* In 2009–10, 2 fellowships with full tuition reimbursements (averaging $15,000 per year) were awarded; career-related internships or fieldwork, Federal Work-Study, institutionally sponsored loans, scholarships/grants, and health care benefits also available. Financial award application deadline: 2/1; financial award applicants required to submit FAFSA. *Faculty research:* History of Islam and South Asia; ethnicity and nationalism; global and transnational feminism; South Asian architecture and urbanism; mysticism and politics in Indian religions. *Unit head:* Dr. Juan R. Cole, Director, 734-764-0352, Fax: 734-936-0996, E-mail: jrcole@umich.edu. *Application contact:* Nancy A. Becker, Student Services Coordinator, 734-764-0448, Fax: 734-936-0996, E-mail: nbecker@umich.edu.

University of Michigan, Horace H. Rackham School of Graduate Studies, College of Literature, Science, and the Arts, Center for Southeast Asian Studies, Ann Arbor, MI 48109-1106. Offers MA, Graduate Certificate, MBA/MA, MPP/MA. Part-time programs available. *Faculty:* 31 full-time (17 women). *Students:* 7 full-time (2 women), 3 part-time (2 women); includes 2 minority (both Asian Americans or Pacific Islanders), 1 international. Average age 30. 12 applicants, 75% accepted, 3 enrolled. In 2009, 6 master's, 1 other advanced degree awarded. *Degree requirements:* For master's, one foreign language, thesis, 25 credits, with specific requirements; for Graduate Certificate, one foreign language. *Entrance requirements:* For master's, GRE General Test, 3 recommendations, curriculum vitae; for Graduate Certificate, GRE General Test, 2 recommendations, transcripts, statement of purpose. Additional exam requirements/recommendations for international students: Required—TOEFL (minimum score 560 paper-based; 220 computer-based; 84 iBT), or IELTS. *Application deadline:* For fall admission, 1/15 for domestic and international students; for winter admission, 1/15 priority date for domestic and international students. Application fee: $60 ($75 for international students). Electronic applications accepted. *Expenses:* Tuition, state resident: full-time $17,286; part-time $1099 per credit hour. Tuition, nonresident: full-time $34,944; part-time $2080 per credit hour. Required fees: $95 per semester. Tuition and fees vary according to course load, degree level and program. *Financial support:* In 2009–10, 3 students received support, including 3 fellowships with full tuition reimbursements available (averaging $15,000 per year); career-related internships or fieldwork, Federal Work-Study, institutionally sponsored loans, scholarships/grants, health care benefits, and Foreign Language and Area Studies (FLAS) fellowships also available. Financial award application deadline: 2/1. *Faculty research:* Politics, political parties, civil society, the law and human rights in Southeast Asia; Nationalism and modernity in late colonial Southeast Asia; Islam, religion, language and media; urbanization, globalization and business; pre-modern Southeast Asia in a global/Eurasian context. *Unit head:* Dr. Allen Hicken, Director, 734-764-0352, Fax: 734-936-0996, E-mail: ahicken@umich.edu. *Application contact:* Nancy Becker, Student Services Coordinator, 734-764-0352, Fax: 734-936-0996, E-mail: nbecker@umich.edu.

University of Michigan, Horace H. Rackham School of Graduate Studies, College of Literature, Science, and the Arts, Department of Asian Languages and Cultures, Ann Arbor, MI 48104. Offers MA, PhD. Students cannot apply directly to a terminal masters degree in this program. Masters are only awarded to PhD program students for partial completion of the degree. *Faculty:* 20 full-time (8 women). *Students:* 26 full-time (11 women); includes 4 minority (3 Asian Americans or Pacific Islanders, 1 Hispanic American). Average age 32. 58 applicants, 9% accepted, 2 enrolled. In 2009, 2 master's, 3 doctorates awarded. Terminal master's awarded for partial completion of doctoral program. *Degree requirements:* For master's, variable foreign language requirement, thesis; for doctorate, 2 foreign languages, thesis/dissertation, oral defense of dissertation, preliminary exam. *Entrance requirements:* For master's and doctorate, GRE General Test. Additional exam requirements/recommendations for international students: Required—TOEFL (minimum score 600 paper-based; 250 computer-based; 106 iBT). *Application deadline:* For fall admission, 12/15 for domestic and international students. Application fee: $75. Electronic applications accepted. *Expenses:* Tuition, state resident: full-time $17,286; part-time $1099 per credit hour. Tuition, nonresident: full-time $34,944; part-time $2080 per credit hour. Required fees: $95 per semester. Tuition and fees vary according to course load, degree level and program. *Financial support:* In 2009–10, 20 students received support, including 10 fellowships with full tuition reimbursements available (averaging $16,500 per year), 1 research assistantship with full tuition reimbursement available (averaging $16,500 per year), 9 teaching assistantships with full tuition reimbursements available (averaging $16,500 per year); Federal Work-Study and health care benefits also available. Support available to part-time students. Financial award application deadline: 12/15; financial award applicants required to submit FAFSA. *Faculty research:* Literature, linguistics, religion, music, cinema. *Unit head:* Prof. Donald Lopez, Chair, 734-764-8286, Fax: 734-647-0157, E-mail: alcgradinfo@umich.edu. *Application contact:* Nicole Baker, Graduate Program Coordinator, 734-936-3915, Fax: 734-647-0157, E-mail: nicolmba@umich.edu.

University of Minnesota, Twin Cities Campus, Graduate School, College of Liberal Arts, Department of Asian Languages and Literatures, Minneapolis, MN 55455-0213. Offers Asian literatures, cultures, and media (PhD). *Degree requirements:* For doctorate, comprehensive exam, thesis/dissertation. *Entrance requirements:* For doctorate, GRE, 3 letters of recommendation. Additional exam requirements/recommendations for international students: Required—TOEFL (minimum score 550 paper-based; 213 computer-based), IELTS (minimum score 6.5). Electronic applications accepted. *Faculty research:* Gender studies, post-colonial theory, poetics and poetic theory, film studies, post modernist thought.

University of Oregon, Graduate School, College of Arts and Sciences, Program in Asian Studies, Eugene, OR 97403. Offers MA. Part-time programs available. *Degree requirements:* For master's, one foreign language, thesis or alternative. *Entrance requirements:* For master's, GRE General Test. Additional exam requirements/recommendations for international students: Required—TOEFL. *Faculty research:* East and Southeast Asia, Pacific Islands.

University of Pennsylvania, School of Arts and Sciences, Graduate Group in East Asian Languages and Civilization, Philadelphia, PA 19104. Offers AM, PhD. *Faculty:* 15 full-time (6 women), 2 part-time/adjunct (1 woman). *Students:* 48 full-time (28 women), 2 part-time (both women); includes 2 minority (both Asian Americans or Pacific Islanders), 21 international. 80 applicants, 13% accepted, 10 enrolled. In 2009, 11 master's, 2 doctorates awarded. Application fee: $70. *Expenses:* Tuition: Full-time $25,660; part-time $4758 per course. Required fees: $2152; $270 per course. Tuition and fees vary according to course load, degree level and program. *Financial support:* Institutionally sponsored loans, scholarships/grants, traineeships, health care benefits, and unspecified assistantships available.

University of Pennsylvania, School of Arts and Sciences, Graduate Group in South Asian Regional Studies, Philadelphia, PA 19104. Offers AM, PhD. *Faculty:* 16 full-time (7 women), 9 part-time/adjunct (1 woman). *Students:* 19 full-time (10 women), 2 part-time (1 woman); includes 2 minority (1 American Indian/Alaska Native, 1 Asian American or Pacific Islander), 4 international. 32 applicants, 31% accepted, 5 enrolled. In 2009, 2 master's, 1 doctorate awarded. Terminal master's awarded for partial completion of doctoral program. *Degree requirements:* For master's, one foreign language, thesis, written exam; for doctorate, 3 foreign languages, thesis/dissertation, written exam. *Entrance requirements:* For master's, GRE General Test. Additional exam requirements/recommendations for international students: Required—TOEFL. *Application deadline:* For fall admission, 12/1 priority date for domestic

Asian Studies

University of Pennsylvania (continued)
students. Application fee: $70. Electronic applications accepted. *Expenses:* Tuition: Full-time $25,660; part-time $4758 per course. Required fees: $2152; $270 per course. Tuition and fees vary according to course load, degree level and program. *Financial support:* Fellowships, research assistantships, teaching assistantships, institutionally sponsored loans, scholarships/grants, traineeships, health care benefits, and unspecified assistantships available. Financial award application deadline: 12/15. *Faculty research:* South Asian linguistics, literature, and history; economic history.

University of Pittsburgh, School of Arts and Sciences, Department of East Asian Languages and Literatures, Pittsburgh, PA 15260. Offers East Asian studies (MA). Part-time programs available. *Faculty:* 7 full-time (3 women), 6 part-time/adjunct (4 women). *Students:* 7 full-time (4 women), 3 international. Average age 26. 31 applicants, 35% accepted, 3 enrolled. *Degree requirements:* For master's, one foreign language, thesis, oral comprehensive exam. *Entrance requirements:* For master's, GRE General Test, 2 years of Chinese or Japanese, minimum QPA of 3.0. Additional exam requirements/recommendations for international students: Required—TOEFL (minimum score 600 paper-based). *Application deadline:* For fall admission, 1/15 for domestic and international students. Application fee: $50. Electronic applications accepted. *Expenses:* Tuition, state resident: full-time $16,402; part-time $665 per credit. Tuition, nonresident: full-time $28,694; part-time $1175 per credit. Required fees: $690; $175 per term. Tuition and fees vary according to program. *Financial support:* In 2009–10, 6 students received support, including 2 fellowships with full and partial tuition reimbursements available (averaging $15,070 per year); Federal Work-Study, scholarships/grants, health care benefits, and unspecified assistantships also available. Financial award application deadline: 1/30. *Faculty research:* Chinese literature, film, and poetry; Japanese literature, film, and theater; Chinese society and culture; east Asian foreign policy, security studies, and economic history; Japanese performing arts and fine arts. *Unit head:* Dr. Hiroshi Nara, Chairman, 412-624-5568, Fax: 412-624-3458, E-mail: hnara@pitt.edu. *Application contact:* Paula Locante, Administrator, 412-624-5568, Fax: 412-624-3458, E-mail: plocante@pitt.edu.

University of Pittsburgh, University Center for International Studies, Pittsburgh, PA 15260. Offers African studies (Certificate); Asian studies (Certificate); European Union studies (Certificate); global studies (Certificate); Latin American studies (Certificate); Russian and East European studies (Certificate); West European studies (Certificate). *Students:* 332 (129 women); includes 31 minority (7 African Americans, 10 Asian Americans or Pacific Islanders, 14 Hispanic Americans), 136 international. In 2009, 59 Certificates awarded. *Degree requirements:* For Certificate, one foreign language, study abroad. *Application deadline:* Applications are processed on a rolling basis. *Expenses:* Tuition, state resident: full-time $16,402; part-time $665 per credit. Tuition, nonresident: full-time $28,694; part-time $1175 per credit. Required fees: $690; $175 per term. Tuition and fees vary according to program. *Unit head:* Lawrence F. Feick, Director, 412-648-7374, Fax: 412-624-4672, E-mail: feick@pitt.edu. *Application contact:* Information Contact, 412-624-4141, E-mail: graduate@pitt.edu.

University of San Francisco, College of Arts and Sciences, Program in Asia Pacific Studies, San Francisco, CA 94117-1080. Offers MA, MA/MBA. Part-time and evening/weekend programs available. *Faculty:* 1 full-time (0 women), 5 part-time/adjunct (4 women). *Students:* 36 full-time (22 women), 4 part-time (3 women); includes 14 minority (4 African Americans, 9 Asian Americans or Pacific Islanders, 1 Hispanic American), 15 international. Average age 28. 44 applicants, 86% accepted, 20 enrolled. In 2009, 19 master's awarded. *Degree requirements:* For master's, one foreign language, thesis. *Entrance requirements:* For master's, minimum GPA of 3.0. *Application deadline:* Applications are processed on a rolling basis. Application fee: $55 ($65 for international students). *Expenses:* Tuition: Full-time $19,710; part-time $1095 per unit. Part-time tuition and fees vary according to degree level, campus/location and program. *Financial support:* In 2009–10, 22 students received support. Career-related internships or fieldwork, Federal Work-Study, and institutionally sponsored loans available. Financial award application deadline: 3/2; financial award applicants required to submit FAFSA. *Faculty research:* History of Christianity in China, U. S.-China policy, East Asian economies and political systems, sociolinguistic aspects of Japanese. *Unit head:* Dr. Ken Kopp, Director, 415-422-6357, Fax: 415-422-5933. *Application contact:* Information Contact, 415-422-5135, Fax: 415-422-2217, E-mail: asgraduate@usfca.edu.

University of Southern California, Graduate School, College of Letters, Arts and Sciences, Department of East Asian Languages and Cultures, Los Angeles, CA 90089. Offers classical Chinese literature (MA, PhD); classical Japanese literature (MA, PhD); linguistics (MA, PhD); modern Chinese literature (MA, PhD); modern Japanese literature (MA, PhD); modern Korean literature (MA, PhD). *Faculty:* 15 full-time (8 women). *Students:* 22 full-time (14 women); includes 6 minority (1 African American, 5 Asian Americans or Pacific Islanders), 10 international. 53 applicants, 21% accepted, 7 enrolled. In 2009, 5 master's, 1 doctorate awarded. *Degree requirements:* For master's, one foreign language, thesis; for doctorate, 2 foreign languages, comprehensive exam, thesis/dissertation. *Entrance requirements:* For master's and doctorate, GRE, BA in relevant field. Additional exam requirements/recommendations for international students: Required—TOEFL. *Application deadline:* For fall admission, 12/1 priority date for domestic and international students. Application fee: $85. Electronic applications accepted. *Expenses:* Tuition: Full-time $25,980; part-time $1315 per unit. Required fees: $554. One-time fee: $35 full-time. Full-time tuition and fees vary according to degree level and program. *Financial support:* In 2009–10, 18 students received support, including 4 fellowships with full tuition reimbursements available (averaging $23,650 per year), 10 teaching assistantships with partial tuition reimbursements available (averaging $18,800 per year); scholarships/grants, health care benefits, and unspecified assistantships also available. Financial award application deadline: 12/1. *Faculty research:* East Asian (Chinese, Japanese and Korean) language, literature, and culture; visual cultures and media studies with focus in East Asian visual arts; films; pre-modern Japanese, Korean and Chinese literature and cultures; modern and contemporary Chinese, Korean and Japanese literature. *Unit head:* Dominic Cheung, Chair, 213-740-3707, Fax: 213-740-9295, E-mail: dcheung@usc.edu. *Application contact:* Sherall R. Preyer, Administrative Coordinator, 213-740-3709, Fax: 213-740-9295, E-mail: preyer@college.usc.edu.

University of Southern California, Graduate School, College of Letters, Arts and Sciences, East Asian Studies Center, Los Angeles, CA 90089. Offers MA, MA/MBA. Part-time programs available. *Faculty:* 13 full-time (4 women). *Students:* 8 full-time (6 women); includes 2 minority (both Asian Americans or Pacific Islanders), 4 international. 32 applicants, 41% accepted, 2 enrolled. In 2009, 3 master's awarded. *Degree requirements:* For master's, one foreign language, thesis, language proficiency in an East Asian language (equivalent to 3 years of study). *Entrance requirements:* For master's, GRE (minimum score 1000). Additional exam requirements/recommendations for international students: Required—TOEFL (minimum score 600 paper-based; 250 computer-based; 100 iBT). *Application deadline:* For fall admission, 1/7 for domestic and international students. Application fee: $85. Electronic applications accepted. *Expenses:* Tuition: Full-time $25,980; part-time $1315 per unit. Required fees: $554. One-time fee: $35 full-time. Full-time tuition and fees vary according to degree level and program. *Financial support:* In 2009–10, 14 fellowships with full tuition reimbursements (averaging $15,000 per year), 5 teaching assistantships with full tuition reimbursements (averaging $19,000 per year) were awarded; scholarships/grants and unspecified assistantships also available. Financial award application deadline: 5/3; financial award applicants required to submit FAFSA. *Faculty research:* East Asian visual cultures (Chinese, Japanese, and Korean film, culture and art); East Asian politics, society and history; East Asian literature and culture. Total annual research expenditures: $283,607. *Unit head:* Prof. Stanley Rosen, Director/Professor of Political Science, 213-740-6661, Fax: 213-740-8409, E-mail: rosen@usc.edu. *Application contact:* Lily Glenn, Program Specialist, 213-740-2992, Fax: 213-740-8409, E-mail: lglenn@usc.edu.

The University of Texas at Austin, Graduate School, College of Liberal Arts, Department of Asian Studies, Austin, TX 78712-1111. Offers Asian cultures and languages (MA, PhD); Asian studies (MA). Part-time programs available. *Degree requirements:* For master's, thesis; for doctorate, 3 foreign languages, thesis/dissertation. *Entrance requirements:* For master's and doctorate, GRE General Test. Electronic applications accepted. *Faculty research:* Modern Taiwanese fiction, modern Japanese literature, religious studies in South Asia during classical period.

University of Toronto, School of Graduate Studies, Humanities Division, Centre for South Asian Studies, Toronto, ON M5S 1A1, Canada. Offers MA, PhD. Students who wish to be admitted into the Collaborative Program in South Asian Studies must apply to one of the following units: anthropology, English, history, geography, political science (PhD only), religious studies, social work. Part-time programs available. *Degree requirements:* For master's, thesis optional; for doctorate, one foreign language, thesis/dissertation.

University of Toronto, School of Graduate Studies, Humanities Division, Department of East Asian Studies, Toronto, ON M5S 1A1, Canada. Offers MA, PhD. Part-time programs available. *Degree requirements:* For master's, thesis optional; for doctorate, 2 foreign languages, comprehensive exam, thesis/dissertation. *Entrance requirements:* For master's, writing sample, 2 letters of recommendation, BA in a specialist or East Asian studies program, minimum B+ average in final year; for doctorate, writing sample, 3 letters of recommendation, MA in East Asian studies. Additional exam requirements/recommendations for international students: Required—TOEFL (minimum score 600 paper-based), TWE (minimum score 5). Electronic applications accepted.

University of Utah, The Graduate School, College of Humanities, Asian Studies Program, Salt Lake City, UT 84112. Offers MA. Part-time and evening/weekend programs available. *Faculty:* 47 full-time (20 women), 4 part-time/adjunct (0 women). *Students:* 6 full-time (3 women), 1 part-time (0 women); includes 1 minority (Asian American or Pacific Islander), 2 international. Average age 27. 9 applicants, 44% accepted, 3 enrolled. In 2009, 2 master's awarded. *Degree requirements:* For master's, one foreign language, thesis. *Entrance requirements:* For master's, GRE. Additional exam requirements/recommendations for international students: Required—TOEFL (minimum score 580 paper-based; 237 computer-based). *Application deadline:* For fall admission, 1/15 for domestic and international students; for spring admission, 9/15 for domestic and international students. Application fee: $55 ($65 for international students). Electronic applications accepted. *Expenses:* Tuition, state resident: full-time $4004; part-time $1674 per semester. Tuition, nonresident: full-time $14,134; part-time $5915 per semester. Required fees: $324 per semester. Tuition and fees vary according to course load, degree level and program. *Financial support:* In 2009–10, 2 students received support. Tuition waivers (partial) and unspecified assistantships available. Financial award application deadline: 1/15; financial award applicants required to submit FAFSA. *Faculty research:* Asian health studies; Asian history, literature, culture, politics, economics. *Unit head:* Dr. Janet Theiss, Director, 801-585-6477, Fax: 801-581-6105, E-mail: janet.theiss@utah.edu. *Application contact:* Caitlin G. McDonald, Administrative Program Coordinator, 801-581-6101, Fax: 801-581-6105, E-mail: caitlin.g.mcdonald@utah.edu.

University of Victoria, Faculty of Graduate Studies, Faculty of Humanities, Department of Pacific and Asian Studies, Victoria, BC V8W 2Y2, Canada. Offers MA. *Degree requirements:* For master's, thesis. *Entrance requirements:* For master's, minimum B+ average, writing sample. Additional exam requirements/recommendations for international students: Required—TOEFL (minimum score 575 paper-based; 233 computer-based), IELTS (minimum score 7). Electronic applications accepted. *Faculty research:* Culture, ethnicity and identity; economy and society; gender studies; languages and linguistics; literature.

University of Virginia, College and Graduate School of Arts and Sciences, Department of East Asian Languages, Literatures, and Cultures, Charlottesville, VA 22903. Offers East Asian studies (MA); MBA/MA. *Faculty:* 14 full-time (12 women), 3 part-time/adjunct (2 women). *Students:* 3 full-time (2 women); includes 1 minority (American Indian/Alaska Native). Average age 27. 12 applicants, 33% accepted, 2 enrolled. In 2009, 1 master's awarded. *Degree requirements:* For master's, one foreign language, comprehensive exam, thesis. *Entrance requirements:* For master's, GRE General Test, 2 letters of recommendation. Additional exam requirements/recommendations for international students: Required—TOEFL, IELTS. *Application deadline:* For fall admission, 1/15 for domestic and international students; for winter admission, 9/15 for domestic and international students. Applications are processed on a rolling basis. Application fee: $60. Electronic applications accepted. *Financial support:* Applicants required to submit FAFSA. *Unit head:* Anne Kinney, Chair, 434-982-2304, Fax: 434-924-6977, E-mail: deal-lc@virginia.edu. *Application contact:* Anne Kinney, Chair, 434-982-2304, Fax: 434-924-6977, E-mail: deal-lc@virginia.edu.

University of Washington, Graduate School, College of Arts and Sciences, Department of Asian Languages and Literature, Seattle, WA 98195. Offers Buddhist studies (MA, PhD); Chinese language and literature (MA, PhD); Japanese language and literature (MA, PhD); Korean language and literature (MA, PhD); South Asian language and literature (MA, PhD). *Degree requirements:* For master's, 2 foreign languages, general exam, thesis or 2 research papers; for doctorate, 3 foreign languages, thesis/dissertation, general exam. *Entrance requirements:* For master's, GRE, minimum GPA of 3.0; for doctorate, GRE, master's degree in related field, minimum GPA of 3.0. Additional exam requirements/recommendations for international students: Required—TOEFL. Electronic applications accepted. *Faculty research:* Textual, linguistic, philological, and literary study of languages and literatures of Asia.

University of Washington, Graduate School, College of Arts and Sciences, Henry M. Jackson School of International Studies, China Studies Program, Seattle, WA 98195. Offers MAIS. *Faculty:* 25 full-time (8 women). *Students:* 22 full-time (9 women); includes 4 minority (1 African American, 3 Asian Americans or Pacific Islanders), 1 international. 38 applicants, 74% accepted, 8 enrolled. In 2009, 8 master's awarded. *Degree requirements:* For master's, one foreign language, thesis optional. *Entrance requirements:* For master's, GRE General Test, minimum GPA of 3.0. Additional exam requirements/recommendations for international students: Required—TOEFL (minimum score 500 paper-based; 213 computer-based; 92 iBT), or IELTS (minimum score 7). *Application deadline:* For fall admission, 12/30 for domestic students, 12/1 for international students. Application fee: $75. Electronic applications accepted. *Financial support:* In 2009–10, 3 fellowships were awarded; research assistantships with tuition reimbursements, teaching assistantships with tuition reimbursements, career-related internships or fieldwork, Federal Work-Study, institutionally sponsored loans, and scholarships/grants also available. Financial award application deadline: 12/30; financial award applicants required to submit FAFSA. *Unit head:* Prof. Yue Dong, Chair, 206-543-4999. *Application contact:* 206-543-6001, Fax: 206-616-3170, E-mail: jsisinfo@u.washington.edu.

University of Washington, Graduate School, College of Arts and Sciences, Henry M. Jackson School of International Studies, Japan Studies Program, Seattle, WA 98195. Offers MAIS. *Faculty:* 15 full-time (6 women). *Students:* 24 full-time (8 women); includes 4 minority (all Asian Americans or Pacific Islanders), 2 international. 21 applicants, 90% accepted, 12 enrolled. In 2009, 5 master's awarded. *Degree requirements:* For master's, one foreign language. *Entrance requirements:* For master's, GRE General Test, minimum GPA of 3.0. Additional exam requirements/recommendations for international students: Required—TOEFL (minimum score 500 paper-based; 213 computer-based; 92 iBT), or IELTS (minimum score 7). *Application deadline:* For fall admission, 12/30 for domestic students, 12/1 for international students. Application fee: $75. Electronic applications accepted. *Financial support:* In 2009–10, 4 fellowships with full tuition reimbursements, 3 research assistantships with full and partial tuition reimbursements, 2 teaching assistantships with full and partial tuition reimbursements were awarded; career-related internships or fieldwork, Federal Work-Study, institutionally sponsored loans, scholarships/grants, and tuition waivers (partial) also available. Financial award application deadline: 12/30; financial award applicants required to submit FAFSA. *Unit head:* Prof. Marie Anchordoguy, Chair, 206-543-4994. *Application contact:* 206-543-6001, Fax: 206-616-3170, E-mail: jsisinfo@u.washington.edu.

University of Washington, Graduate School, College of Arts and Sciences, Henry M. Jackson School of International Studies, Korea Studies Program, Seattle, WA 98195. Offers MAIS.

Faculty: 4 full-time (1 woman). *Students:* 13 full-time (4 women); includes 5 minority (all Asian Americans or Pacific Islanders), 1 international. 12 applicants, 100% accepted, 5 enrolled. In 2009, 1 master's awarded. *Degree requirements:* For master's, one foreign language. *Entrance requirements:* For master's, GRE General Test, minimum GPA of 3.0. Additional exam requirements/recommendations for international students: Required—TOEFL (minimum score 500 paper-based; 213 computer-based; 92 iBT), or IELTS (minimum score 7). *Application deadline:* For fall admission, 12/30 for domestic students, 12/1 for international students. Application fee: $75. Electronic applications accepted. *Financial support:* In 2009–10, 1 fellowship with full tuition reimbursement was awarded; research assistantships, career-related internships or fieldwork, Federal Work-Study, institutionally sponsored loans, scholarships/grants, and summer language study awards also available. Financial award application deadline: 12/30; financial award applicants required to submit FAFSA. *Unit head:* Prof. Clark Sorensen. *Application contact:* 206-543-6001, Fax: 206-616-3170, E-mail: jsisinfo@u.washington.edu.

University of Washington, Graduate School, College of Arts and Sciences, Henry M. Jackson School of International Studies, Program in Southeast Asian Studies, Seattle, WA 98195. Offers MAIS. *Faculty:* 15 full-time (5 women). *Degree requirements:* For master's, one foreign language, thesis optional. *Entrance requirements:* For master's, GRE General Test, minimum GPA of 3.00. Additional exam requirements/recommendations for international students: Required—TOEFL (minimum score 500 paper-based; 213 computer-based; 92 iBT) or IELTS (minimum score 7). *Application deadline:* For fall admission, 12/30 for domestic students, 12/1 for international students. Application fee: $75. Electronic applications accepted. *Financial support:* Career-related internships or fieldwork, Federal Work-Study, institutionally sponsored loans, and summer language study awards available. Financial award application deadline: 12/30; financial award applicants required to submit FAFSA. *Unit head:* Prof. Laurie J. Sears, Chair, 206-543-4370. *Application contact:* Prof. Laurie J. Sears, Chair, 206-543-4370.

University of Washington, Graduate School, College of Arts and Sciences, Henry M. Jackson School of International Studies, Russian, East European and Central Asian Studies Program, Seattle, WA 98195. Offers Central Asian studies (MAIS); East European studies (MAIS); Russian studies (MAIS). *Faculty:* 59 full-time (24 women). *Students:* 23 full-time (12 women); includes 3 minority (1 African American, 1 Asian American or Pacific Islander, 1 Hispanic American), 1 international. 32 applicants, 91% accepted, 9 enrolled. In 2009, 7 master's awarded. *Degree requirements:* For master's, one foreign language, thesis. *Entrance requirements:* For master's, GRE General Test, 2 years of relevant language, minimum GPA of 3.0. Additional exam requirements/recommendations for international students: Required—TOEFL (minimum score 500 paper-based; 213 computer-based; 92 iBT), or IELTS. *Application deadline:* For fall admission, 12/30 for domestic students, 12/1 for international students. Application fee: $75. Electronic applications accepted. *Financial support:* In 2009–10, 8 fellowships with full tuition reimbursements were awarded; research assistantships, teaching assistantships, career-related internships or fieldwork, Federal Work-Study, institutionally sponsored loans, and summer language study awards also available. Financial award application deadline: 12/30. *Unit head:* Prof. James Augerot, Chair, 206-543-6848, E-mail: bigjim@u.washington.edu. *Application contact:* 206-543-6001, Fax: 206-616-3170, E-mail: jsisinfo@u.washington.edu.

University of Washington, Graduate School, College of Arts and Sciences, Henry M. Jackson School of International Studies, South Asian Studies Program, Seattle, WA 98195. Offers MAIS. *Faculty:* 25 full-time (12 women). *Students:* 8 full-time (6 women). 16 applicants, 81% accepted, 4 enrolled. In 2009, 2 master's awarded. *Degree requirements:* For master's, one foreign language, thesis optional. *Entrance requirements:* For master's, GRE General Test, minimum GPA of 3.0. Additional exam requirements/recommendations for international students: Required—TOEFL (minimum score 500 paper-based; 213 computer-based; 92 iBT), or IELTS (minimum score 7). *Application deadline:* For fall admission, 12/30 for domestic students, 12/1 for international students. Application fee: $75. Electronic applications accepted. *Financial support:* In 2009–10, 4 fellowships with full tuition reimbursements were awarded; research assistantships, career-related internships or fieldwork, Federal Work-Study, institutionally sponsored loans, scholarships/grants, tuition waivers (partial), and summer language study awards also available. Financial award application deadline: 12/30; financial award applicants required to submit FAFSA. *Unit head:* Prof. Priti Ramamurthy, Chair, 206-543-6984, E-mail: priti@u.washington.edu. *Application contact:* 206-543-6001, Fax: 206-616-3170, E-mail: jsisinfo@u.washington.edu.

University of Wisconsin–Madison, Graduate School, College of Letters and Science, Center for Southeast Asian Studies, Madison, WI 53706. Offers MA. Part-time programs available. *Degree requirements:* For master's, one foreign language, oral defense of seminar paper. Electronic applications accepted. *Expenses:* Tuition, state resident: part-time $594 per credit. Tuition, nonresident: part-time $1504 per credit. Required fees: $65 per credit. Tuition and fees vary according to course load, program and reciprocity agreements. *Faculty research:* Economic development, censorship, political change, pedagogical developments in Indonesia, Philippine historical demography, environment photography.

University of Wisconsin–Madison, Graduate School, College of Letters and Science, Department of East Asian Languages and Literature, Madison, WI 53706-1380. Offers Chinese literature (MA, PhD); Chinese thought (MA, PhD); Japanese linguistics (MA, PhD); Japanese literature (MA, PhD). Part-time programs available. Terminal master's awarded for partial completion of doctoral program. *Degree requirements:* For master's, one foreign language, seminars, written exam; for doctorate, 3 foreign languages, thesis/dissertation, seminars, preliminary exams, oral exams. *Entrance requirements:* For master's, GRE General Test, BA or equivalent in major field; for doctorate, GRE General Test, MA or equivalent in major field. Electronic applications accepted. *Expenses:* Tuition, state resident: part-time $594 per credit. Tuition, nonresident: part-time $1504 per credit. Required fees: $65 per credit. Tuition and fees vary according to course load, program and reciprocity agreements. *Faculty research:* Modern and historical linguistics, literature, literary and cultural history.

University of Wisconsin–Madison, Graduate School, College of Letters and Science, Department of History, Madison, WI 53706-1380. Offers African history (MA, PhD); Central Asian history (MA, PhD); comparative world history (MA, PhD); East Asian history (MA, PhD); European history (MA, PhD); gender and women's history (MA, PhD); Latin American and Caribbean history (MA, PhD); Middle Eastern history (MA, PhD); South Asian history (MA, PhD); Southeast Asian history (MA, PhD); United States history (MA, PhD). Terminal master's awarded for partial completion of doctoral program. *Degree requirements:* For master's, thesis (for some programs); for doctorate, variable foreign language requirement, thesis/dissertation. *Entrance requirements:* For master's and doctorate, GRE General Test. Additional exam requirements/recommendations for international students: Required—Michigan English Language Assessment Battery or TOEFL. Electronic applications accepted. *Expenses:* Tuition, state resident: part-time $594 per credit. Tuition, nonresident: part-time $1504 per credit. Required fees: $65 per credit. Tuition and fees vary according to course load, program and reciprocity agreements. *Faculty research:* American, African, European, Asian, Latin American, and Middle Eastern history.

University of Wisconsin–Madison, Graduate School, College of Letters and Science, Department of Languages and Cultures of Asia, Madison, WI 53706-1380. Offers civilizations and cultures (PhD); languages and cultures of Asia (MA); languages and literatures (PhD); religions of Asia (PhD). Part-time programs available. Terminal master's awarded for partial completion of doctoral program. *Degree requirements:* For master's, one foreign language, thesis or alternative; for doctorate, 2 foreign languages, thesis/dissertation. *Entrance requirements:* For master's, minimum GPA of 3.0; for doctorate, minimum GPA of 3.25, master's degree. Electronic applications accepted. *Expenses:* Tuition, state resident: part-time $594 per credit. Tuition, nonresident: part-time $1504 per credit. Required fees: $65 per credit. Tuition and fees vary according to course load, program and reciprocity agreements. *Faculty research:* Literature, folklore, religion.

Valparaiso University, Graduate School, Program in Chinese Studies, Valparaiso, IN 46383. Offers MA, JD/MA. Part-time and evening/weekend programs available. *Faculty:* 3 part-time/adjunct (0 women). *Students:* 8 full-time (3 women), 6 part-time (3 women); includes 7 minority (3 African Americans, 1 American Indian/Alaska Native, 2 Asian Americans or Pacific Islanders, 1 Hispanic American). Average age 30. In 2009, 12 master's awarded. *Entrance requirements:* For master's, minimum GPA of 3.0, Chinese language proficiency. Additional exam requirements/recommendations for international students: Required—TOEFL (minimum score 550 paper-based; 213 computer-based; 80 iBT). *Application deadline:* Applications are processed on a rolling basis. Application fee: $30 ($50 for international students). Electronic applications accepted. *Financial support:* Scholarships/grants and unspecified assistantships available. Support available to part-time students. Financial award applicants required to submit FAFSA. *Unit head:* Dr. David L. Rowland, Dean, Graduate Studies and Continuing Education/Associate Provost, 219-464-5313, Fax: 219-464-5381, E-mail: david.rowland@valpo.edu. *Application contact:* Jamie Haney, Coordinator of Graduate Admission, 219-464-5313, Fax: 219-464-5381, E-mail: jamie.haney@valpo.edu.

Washington State University, Graduate School, College of Liberal Arts, Department of History, Pullman, WA 99164. Offers early and modern European history (MA, PhD); environmental history (MA, PhD); Latin American history (MA, PhD); modern East Asia history (MA, PhD); public history (MA, PhD); US history (MA, PhD); women's history (MA, PhD); world history (MA, PhD). Part-time programs available. *Faculty:* 25. *Students:* 38 full-time (22 women), 10 part-time (4 women); includes 3 minority (1 American Indian/Alaska Native, 2 Hispanic Americans), 2 international. Average age 33. 57 applicants, 47% accepted, 10 enrolled. In 2009, 10 master's, 2 doctorates awarded. *Degree requirements:* For master's, comprehensive exam (for some programs), thesis, oral exam; for doctorate, one foreign language, comprehensive exam, thesis/dissertation, oral and written exam. *Entrance requirements:* For master's and doctorate, GRE General Test, Graduate School Application form; official transcripts from all universities attended; GRE scores; TOEFL or IELTS scores (international students only); three letters of recommendation; a statement of purpose; a writing sample, Preferred Fields of Study form; and the Language Background form. Additional exam requirements/recommendations for international students: Required—TOEFL (minimum score 550 paper-based), IELTS. *Application deadline:* For fall admission, 1/10 for domestic and international students; for spring admission, 7/1 for domestic and international students. Applications are processed on a rolling basis. Application fee: $50. Electronic applications accepted. *Financial support:* In 2009–10, 1 fellowship with partial tuition reimbursement (averaging $3,000 per year), research assistantships with full and partial tuition reimbursements (averaging $13,917 per year), 28 teaching assistantships with full and partial tuition reimbursements (averaging $13,056 per year) were awarded; career-related internships or fieldwork, Federal Work-Study, institutionally sponsored loans, scholarships/grants, and health care benefits also available. Financial award application deadline: 2/15; financial award applicants required to submit FAFSA. *Faculty research:* Public, world, environmental, women's and U. S. history. *Unit head:* Dr. Raymond Sun, Chair, 509-335-5139, Fax: 509-335-4171, E-mail: pietz@wsu.edu. *Application contact:* Graduate Studies Director, 509-335-4030, Fax: 509-335-4171, E-mail: kale@wsu.edu.

Washington University in St. Louis, Graduate School of Arts and Sciences, Program in East Asian Studies, St. Louis, MO 63130-4899. Offers East Asian studies (MA); JD/MA. PhD offered through specific departments. *Entrance requirements:* For master's, GRE General Test. Electronic applications accepted.

West Virginia University, Eberly College of Arts and Sciences, Department of History, Morgantown, WV 26506. Offers African history (MA, PhD); African-American history (MA, PhD); American history (MA, PhD); Appalachian/regional history (MA, PhD); East Asian history (MA, PhD); European history (MA, PhD); history of science and technology (MA, PhD); Latin American history (MA). Part-time programs available. *Degree requirements:* For master's, one foreign language, thesis (for some programs), oral exam, thesis defense; for doctorate, one foreign language, comprehensive exam, thesis/dissertation, dissertation defense. *Entrance requirements:* For master's, GRE General Test, minimum GPA of 3.0; for doctorate, GRE General Test. Additional exam requirements/recommendations for international students: Required—TOEFL (minimum score 550 paper-based), IELTS (minimum score 6.5). Electronic applications accepted. *Faculty research:* U.S., Appalachia, modern Europe, Africa, colonial and post-colonial societies.

Yale University, Graduate School of Arts and Sciences, Program in East Asian Studies, New Haven, CT 06520. Offers MA. *Degree requirements:* For master's, one foreign language. *Entrance requirements:* For master's, GRE General Test.

Canadian Studies

Carleton University, Faculty of Graduate Studies, Faculty of Arts and Social Sciences, School of Canadian Studies, Ottawa, ON K1S 5B6, Canada. Offers MA, PhD. *Degree requirements:* For master's, one foreign language, thesis optional; for doctorate, one foreign language, thesis/dissertation. *Entrance requirements:* For master's, honors degree. Additional exam requirements/recommendations for international students: Required—TOEFL. Electronic applications accepted. *Faculty research:* Modern Canada, cultural studies, women's studies, aboriginal studies and the north, heritage conservation.

Collège universitaire de Saint-Boniface, Program in Canadian Studies, Saint-Boniface, MB R2H 0H7, Canada. Offers MA.

Queen's University at Kingston, School of Graduate Studies and Research, Faculty of Arts and Sciences, Department of Political Studies, Kingston, ON K7L 3N6, Canada. Offers Canadian politics (PhD); comparative politics (PhD); gender and politics (PhD); international relations (PhD); political theory (PhD). *Degree requirements:* For master's, thesis or alternative; for doctorate, one foreign language, thesis/dissertation, qualifying exams. *Entrance requirements:* Additional exam requirements/recommendations for international students: Required—TOEFL (minimum score 600 paper-based; 250 computer-based). *Faculty research:* Canadian politics, comparative politics, political thought, international politics, women and politics.

Saint Mary's University, Faculty of Arts, Program in Atlantic Canada Studies, Halifax, NS B3H 3C3, Canada. Offers MA, Certificate. Part-time and evening/weekend programs available. *Degree requirements:* For master's, thesis. *Entrance requirements:* For master's, honors degree. *Application deadline:* For fall admission, 5/31 for domestic students. Application fee: $35. Electronic applications accepted. *Expenses:* Contact institution. *Financial support:* Fellowships, research assistantships available. *Unit head:* Dr. Peter L. Twohig, Chair, 902-420-5447, E-mail: peter.twohig@smu.ca. *Application contact:* Dr. Peter L. Twohig, Chair, 902-420-5447, E-mail: peter.twohig@smu.ca.

Canadian Studies

Trent University, Graduate Studies, The Frost Centre for Canadian Studies and Indigenous Studies, Peterborough, ON K9J 7B8, Canada. Offers Canadian studies (PhD); Canadian studies and indigenous studies (MA). Part-time programs available. *Degree requirements:* For master's, thesis. *Entrance requirements:* For master's, honors degree. *Faculty research:* Native community-based socioeconomic development, environmental and social impact inventory, regional studies.

Université de Sherbrooke, Faculty of Letters and Human Sciences, Department of Letters and Communications, Sherbrooke, QC J1K 2R1, Canada. Offers comparative Canadian literature (MA, PhD); French literature (MA, PhD); linguistics (MA); theatre (MA). *Degree requirements:* For master's, thesis or alternative; for doctorate, thesis/dissertation. *Entrance requirements:* For master's, minimum GPA of 2.8; for doctorate, minimum GPA of 3.0.

Université du Québec à Chicoutimi, Graduate Programs, Program in Regional Studies, Chicoutimi, QC G7H 2B1, Canada. Offers MA. Part-time programs available. *Degree requirements:* For master's, thesis. *Entrance requirements:* For master's, appropriate bachelor's degree, proficiency in French.

University of Lethbridge, School of Graduate Studies, Lethbridge, AB T1K 3M4, Canada. Offers accounting (MScM); addictions counseling (M Sc); agricultural biotechnology (M Sc); agricultural studies (M Sc, MA); anthropology (MA); archaeology (MA); art (MA, MFA); biochemistry (M Sc); biological sciences (M Sc); biomolecular science (PhD); biosystems and biodiversity (PhD); Canadian studies (MA); chemistry (M Sc); computer science (M Sc); computer science and geographical information science (M Sc); counseling psychology (M Ed); dramatic arts (MA); earth, space, and physical science (PhD); economics (MA); educational leadership (M Ed); English (MA); environmental science (M Sc); evolution and behavior (PhD); exercise science (M Sc); finance (MScM); French (MA); French/German (MA); French/Spanish (MA); general education (M Ed); general management (MScM); geography (M Sc, MA); German (MA); health science (M Sc); health sciences (MA); history (MA); human resource management and labour relations (MScM); individualized multidisciplinary (M Sc, MA); information systems (MScM); international management (MScM); kinesiology (M Sc, MA); management (M Sc, MA); marketing (MScM); mathematics (M Sc); music (M Mus, MA); Native American studies (MA); neuroscience (M Sc, PhD); new media (MA); nursing (M Sc); philosophy (MA); physics (M Sc); policy and strategy (MScM); political science (MA); psychology (M Sc, MA); religious studies (MA); social sciences (MA); sociology (MA); theatre and dramatic arts (MFA); theoretical and computational science (PhD); urban and regional studies (MA); women's studies (MA). Part-time and evening/weekend programs available. *Degree requirements:* For doctorate, comprehensive exam, thesis/dissertation. *Entrance requirements:* For master's, GMAT (M Sc in management), bachelor's degree in related field, minimum GPA of 3.0 during previous 20 graded semester courses, 2 years teaching or related experience (M Ed); for doctorate, master's degree, minimum graduate GPA of 3.5. Additional exam requirements/recommendations for international students: Required—TOEFL. *Faculty research:* Movement and brain plasticity, gibberellin physiology, photosynthesis, carbon cycling, molecular properties of main-group ring components.

University of Manitoba, Faculty of Graduate Studies, College Universitaire de Saint Boniface, Program in Canadian Studies, Winnipeg, MB R3T 2N2, Canada. Offers MA.

University of Ottawa, Faculty of Graduate and Postdoctoral Studies, Faculty of Arts, Institute of Canadian Studies, Ottawa, ON K1N 6N5, Canada. Offers economics (PhD); English (PhD); geography (PhD); history (PhD); lettres Françaises (PhD); linguistics (PhD); philosophy (PhD); political science (PhD); psychology (PhD); religious studies (PhD); translation studies (PhD). *Degree requirements:* For doctorate, comprehensive exam, thesis/dissertation.

University of Regina, Faculty of Graduate Studies and Research, Faculty of Arts, Canadian Plains Studies Program, Regina, SK S4S 0A2, Canada. Offers MA, PhD. Offered as special case program. Part-time programs available. *Faculty:* 1 full-time (0 women). *Students:* 6 full-time (3 women), 1 (woman) part-time. 2 applicants, 100% accepted. In 2009, 1 doctorate awarded. *Degree requirements:* For master's, thesis; for doctorate, thesis/dissertation. *Entrance requirements:* Additional exam requirements/recommendations for international students: Required—TOEFL (minimum score 580 paper-based; 237 computer-based; 80 iBT). *Application deadline:* Applications are processed on a rolling basis. Application fee: $90 ($100 for international students). Electronic applications accepted. *Financial support:* Fellowships, research assistantships, teaching assistantships, scholarships/grants available. Financial award application deadline: 6/15. *Faculty research:* Prairie region. *Unit head:* Dr. Harry Diaz, Graduate Program Coordinator, 306-585-4758, Fax: 306-585-4699, E-mail: canadian.plains@uregina.ca. *Application contact:* Dr. Dongyan Blachford, Associate Dean, 306-585-5186, Fax: 306-337-2444, E-mail: dongyan.blachford@uregina.ca.

University of Saskatchewan, College of Graduate Studies and Research, College of Arts and Sciences, Department of Native Studies, Saskatoon, SK S7N 5A2, Canada. Offers MA, PhD. *Faculty:* 6. *Students:* 8. In 2009, 1 master's awarded. *Degree requirements:* For master's, thesis; for doctorate, comprehensive exam (for some programs), thesis/dissertation. *Entrance requirements:* Additional exam requirements/recommendations for international students: Required—TOEFL (minimum score 80 iBT); Recommended—IELTS (minimum score 6.5). *Application deadline:* For fall admission, 7/1 priority date for domestic students. Applications are processed on a rolling basis. Application fee: $75. Electronic applications accepted. Tuition and fees charges are reported in Canadian dollars. *Expenses:* Tuition, area resident: Full-time $3000 Canadian dollars; part-time $500 Canadian dollars per term. Required fees: $700 Canadian dollars; $100 Canadian dollars per term. *Financial support:* Fellowships, research assistantships, teaching assistantships available. Financial award application deadline: 1/31. *Unit head:* Dr. Benda Mcdougall, Head, 306-966-6210, Fax: 306-966-6242, E-mail: b.macdougall@usask.ca. *Application contact:* Dr. Caroline Tait, Graduate Chair, 306-966-6210, Fax: 306-966-6242, E-mail: caroline.tait@usask.ca.

Cultural Studies

Ambrose University College, Ambrose Seminary, Calgary, AB T2P 3T5, Canada. Offers biblical/theological studies (MA); Chinese ministries (Certificate); Christian studies (M Div, MA, Diploma); foundations for ministry (Certificate); intercultural ministries (M Div, MA, Certificate, Diploma); leadership and ministry (MA, Certificate, Diploma). *Accreditation:* ATS (one or more programs are accredited). Part-time programs available. *Faculty:* 7 full-time (0 women), 24 part-time/adjunct (2 women). *Students:* 44 full-time (15 women), 107 part-time (49 women). Average age 41. *Degree requirements:* For master's, 2 foreign languages, internship; for M Div, one foreign language, internship. *Entrance requirements:* For master's, bachelor's degree. Additional exam requirements/recommendations for international students: Required—TOEFL or IELTS. *Application deadline:* For fall admission, 7/31 priority date for domestic students, 3/1 priority date for international students; for winter admission, 11/30 priority date for domestic students, 6/1 priority date for international students. Applications are processed on a rolling basis. Application fee: $50. Electronic applications accepted. *Expenses:* Tuition: Full-time $6000; part-time $299 per credit hour. Required fees: $306; $17 per credit hour. *Financial support:* Career-related internships or fieldwork and scholarships/grants available. Support available to part-time students. Financial award application deadline: 3/30. *Faculty research:* Evangelicalism and sociology, missiological trends, chaplaincy, intertestamental studies, postmodernism. *Unit head:* Dr. Paul Spilsbury, Vice-President of Academic Affairs, 403-410-2000 Ext. 6905, Fax: 403-571-2556, E-mail: pspilsbury@ambrose.edu. *Application contact:* Dr. Paul Spilsbury, Vice-President of Academic Affairs, 403-410-2000 Ext. 6905, Fax: 403-571-2556, E-mail: pspilsbury@ambrose.edu.

American University, School of International Service, Washington, DC 20016-8071. Offers comparative and regional studies (Certificate); cross-cultural communication (Certificate); development management (MS); ethics, peace, and global affairs (MA); European studies (Certificate); global environmental policy (MA, Certificate); international affairs (MA), including comparative and regional studies, environmental policy, international economic policy, international politics, natural resources and sustainable development, U.S. foreign policy; international communication (MA, Certificate); international development (MA, Certificate); international development management (Certificate); international economic policy (Certificate); international economic relations (Certificate); international media (MA); international peace and conflict resolution (MA, Certificate); international relations (PhD); international service (MIS); peace building (Certificate); the Americas (Certificate); United States foreign policy (Certificate); JD/MA. Part-time and evening/weekend programs available. *Faculty:* 98 full-time (42 women), 48 part-time/adjunct (13 women). *Students:* 565 full-time (349 women), 329 part-time (189 women); includes 128 minority (44 African Americans, 2 American Indian/Alaska Native, 37 Asian Americans or Pacific Islanders, 45 Hispanic Americans), 102 international. Average age 27. 2,034 applicants, 63% accepted, 344 enrolled. In 2009, 326 master's, 6 doctorates, 9 other advanced degrees awarded. Terminal master's awarded for partial completion of doctoral program. *Degree requirements:* For master's, one foreign language, comprehensive exam, thesis or alternative; for doctorate, one foreign language, comprehensive exam, thesis/dissertation, research practicum; for Certificate, minimum 15 credit hours related course work. *Entrance requirements:* For master's, GRE, 24 credits of course work in related social sciences, minimum GPA of 3.5, 2 letters of recommendation, bachelor's degree, resume; for doctorate, GRE, 2 letters of recommendation, 24 credits in related social sciences; for Certificate, bachelor's degree. Additional exam requirements/recommendations for international students: Required—TOEFL (minimum score 600 paper-based; 250 computer-based; 100 iBT). *Application deadline:* For fall admission, 1/15 priority date for domestic students; for spring admission, 10/1 priority date for domestic students. Applications are processed on a rolling basis. Application fee: $50. *Expenses:* Tuition: Full-time $22,266; part-time $1237 per credit hour. Required fees: $430. Tuition and fees vary according to program. *Financial support:* Career-related internships or fieldwork, Federal Work-Study, and institutionally sponsored loans available. Financial award application deadline: 1/15. *Faculty research:* International intellectual property, international environmental issues, international law and legal order, international telecommunications/technology, international sustainable development. *Unit head:* Dr. Louis W. Goodman, Dean, 202-885-1600, Fax: 202-885-2494. *Application contact:* Yasmin Quianzon, Director of Graduate Admissions and Financial Aid, 202-885-2496, Fax: 202-885-1109.

See Close-Up on page 849.

The American University of Paris, Graduate Programs, Paris, France. Offers cross-cultural and sustainable business management (MA); cultural translation (MA); global communications (MA); global communications and civil society (MA); international affairs, conflict resolution and civil society development (MA); Middle East and Islamic studies (MA); Middle East and Islamic studies and international affairs (MA); public policy and international affairs (MA); public policy and international law (MA). *Faculty:* 14 full-time (3 women). *Students:* 143 full-time (109 women). 71 applicants, 92% accepted, 34 enrolled. *Degree requirements:* For master's, thesis. *Entrance requirements:* For master's, minimum undergraduate GPA of 3.0. *Application deadline:* For fall admission, 4/15 priority date for international students; for spring admission, 11/15 priority date for international students. Applications are processed on a rolling basis. Application fee: $75. Tuition charges are reported in euros. *Expenses:* Tuition: Full-time 23,460 euros. *Financial support:* Scholarships/grants available. Financial award applicants required to submit FAFSA. *Unit head:* Celeste Schenk, President, 33 1-40620659, E-mail: president@aup.fr. *Application contact:* International Admissions Counselor, 33 1-40620720, Fax: 33 1-47053432, E-mail: admissions@aup.edu.

Appalachian State University, Cratis D. Williams Graduate School, Center for Appalachian Studies, Boone, NC 28608. Offers culture (MA); music (MA); sustainable development (MA). Part-time programs available. *Faculty:* 14 full-time (5 women). *Students:* 24 full-time (18 women), 4 part-time (3 women). 20 applicants, 75% accepted, 10 enrolled. In 2009, 12 master's awarded. *Degree requirements:* For master's, one foreign language, comprehensive exam, thesis optional. *Entrance requirements:* For master's, GRE General Test, 3 letters of recommendation. Additional exam requirements/recommendations for international students: Required—TOEFL (minimum score 570 paper-based; 230 computer-based; 79 iBT), IELTS (minimum score 6.5). *Application deadline:* For fall admission, 7/1 for domestic students, 2/1 for international students; for spring admission, 11/1 for domestic students, 7/1 for international students. Applications are processed on a rolling basis. Application fee: $50. Electronic applications accepted. *Expenses:* Tuition, state resident: full-time $2960. Tuition, nonresident: full-time $14,051. Required fees: $2320. *Financial support:* In 2009–10, 8 research assistantships (averaging $8,000 per year) were awarded; fellowships, teaching assistantships, career-related internships or fieldwork, Federal Work-Study, scholarships/grants, and unspecified assistantships also available. Financial award application deadline: 4/1; financial award applicants required to submit FAFSA. *Faculty research:* Appalachian culture, sustainable development, Appalachian music. Total annual research expenditures: $11,250. *Unit head:* Dr. Pat Beaver, Center Director, 828-262-2550, E-mail: beaverpd@appstate.edu. *Application contact:* Dr. Katherine Ledford, Graduate Program Director, 828-262-4089, E-mail: ledfordke@appstate.edu.

Arizona State University, Graduate College, College of Liberal Arts and Sciences, Division of Humanities, Program in Film and Media Studies, Tempe, AZ 85287. Offers American media and popular culture (MAS); film analysis (MLS); screenwriting (MAS).

Assemblies of God Theological Seminary, Graduate and Professional Programs, Springfield, MO 65802. Offers Christian ministries (MA); counseling (MA); divinity (M Div); intercultural ministry (MA); intercultural studies (D Miss, PhD); relief and development (D Miss); theological studies (MA); women in leadership (D Min). *Accreditation:* ATS. Part-time and evening/weekend programs available. Postbaccalaureate distance learning degree programs offered (minimal on-campus study). *Faculty:* 12 full-time (3 women), 23 part-time/adjunct (5 women). *Students:* 195 full-time (70 women), 221 part-time (53 women); includes 48 minority (10 African Americans, 6 American Indian/Alaska Native, 16 Asian Americans or Pacific Islanders, 16 Hispanic Americans), 9 international. Average age 36. 109 applicants, 76% accepted, 62 enrolled. In 2009, 46 first professional degrees, 65 master's, 14 doctorates awarded. *Degree requirements:* For master's, analytical reflection paper, comprehensive exam or field education research project; for doctorate, thesis/dissertation; for M Div, one foreign language, analytical reflection paper or field education research project. *Entrance requirements:* For M Div, minimum GPA of 2.5; for master's, minimum GPA of 2.5; for doctorate, minimum GPA of 3.0. Additional exam requirements/recommendations for international students: Required—TOEFL (minimum score 550 paper-based; 213 computer-based; 80 iBT). *Application deadline:* For fall admission, 7/1 priority date for domestic students, 6/1 priority date for international students; for spring admission, 12/1 priority date for domestic students, 11/1 priority date for international students. Applications are processed on a rolling basis. Application fee: $75. Electronic applications accepted. *Financial support:* Career-related internships or fieldwork, Federal Work-Study, and scholarships/grants available. Support available to part-time students. Financial award application deadline: 7/15; financial award applicants required to submit FAFSA. *Unit head:* Stephen Lim, Academic Dean, 417-268-1000, Fax: 417-268-1001, E-mail: slim@agts.edu. *Application contact:* Stephen Lim, Academic Dean, 417-268-1000, Fax: 417-268-1001, E-mail: slim@agts.edu.

Athabasca University, Centre for Integrated Studies, Athabasca, AB T9S 3A3, Canada. Offers adult education (MA); community studies (MA); cultural studies (MA); educational studies (MA); global change (MA); work, organization, and leadership (MA). Part-time and evening/weekend programs available. Postbaccalaureate distance learning degree programs offered (no on-campus study). *Faculty:* 10 full-time (4 women), 12 part-time/adjunct (9 women). *Students:* 705 part-time. Average age 35. 195 applicants, 38 enrolled. In 2009, 52 master's awarded. *Degree requirements:* For master's, project. *Entrance requirements:* Additional exam requirements/recommendations for international students: Required—TOEFL (minimum score 560 paper-based; 220 computer-based). *Application deadline:* For fall admission, 3/1 for domestic and international students; for winter admission, 9/1 for domestic and international students. Application fee: $80. Electronic applications accepted. *Expenses:* Tuition: Part-time $16,500 per degree program. Required fees: $200 per year. One-time fee: $80 part-time. *Faculty research:* Women's history, literature and culture studies, sustainable development, labor and education. *Unit head:* Dr. Michael Gismondi, Program Director, 780-675-6218, Fax: 780-675-6921, E-mail: mikeg@athabascau.ca. *Application contact:* Derek Stovin, Program Administrator, 780-675-6236, Fax: 780-675-6921, E-mail: dereks@athabascau.ca.

Baptist Bible College, Graduate School of Theology, Springfield, MO 65803-3498. Offers biblical counseling (MA); biblical studies (MA); church ministry (MA); intercultural studies (MA); theology (M Div). Part-time programs available. *Degree requirements:* For master's, 2 foreign languages, thesis (for some programs); for M Div, 2 foreign languages, thesis/dissertation (for some programs). *Entrance requirements:* For master's, outcomes test. Electronic applications accepted.

Biola University, School of Intercultural Studies, La Mirada, CA 90639-0001. Offers applied linguistics (MA); intercultural education (PhD); intercultural studies (MAICS); missiology (D Miss); missions (MA); teaching English to speakers of other languages (MA, Certificate). Part-time and evening/weekend programs available. Terminal master's awarded for partial completion of doctoral program. *Degree requirements:* For master's, one foreign language, comprehensive exam; for doctorate, one foreign language, comprehensive exam, thesis/dissertation. *Entrance requirements:* For master's, minimum undergraduate GPA of 3.0; for doctorate, MA, 3 years of ministry experience, minimum graduate GPA of 3.3. Additional exam requirements/recommendations for international students: Required—TOEFL (minimum score 550 paper-based; 213 computer-based). Electronic applications accepted.

Brandeis University, Graduate School of Arts and Sciences, Program in Cultural Production, Waltham, MA 02454-9110. Offers MA. Part-time programs available. *Faculty:* 20 full-time (10 women), 1 (woman) part-time/adjunct. *Students:* 23 full-time (20 women), 2 part-time (both women); includes 5 minority (3 African Americans, 1 Asian American or Pacific Islander, 1 Hispanic American), 4 international. 26 applicants, 92% accepted, 13 enrolled. In 2009, 6 master's awarded. *Degree requirements:* For master's, thesis. *Entrance requirements:* For master's, GRE (recommended), 2 letters of recommendation, resume, portfolio/writing sample. Additional exam requirements/recommendations for international students: Required—TOEFL (minimum score 650 paper-based; 250 computer-based; 100 iBT), IELTS (minimum score 7). *Application deadline:* For fall admission, 1/15 priority date for domestic students. Applications are processed on a rolling basis. Application fee: $75. Electronic applications accepted. *Financial support:* In 2009–10, fellowships with full tuition reimbursements (averaging $17,500 per year), teaching assistantships with partial tuition reimbursements (averaging $3,200 per year) were awarded; scholarships/grants and tuition waivers (partial) also available. Support available to part-time students. Financial award application deadline: 4/15; financial award applicants required to submit FAFSA. *Unit head:* Dr. Mark Auslander, Program Chair, 781-736-2214, E-mail: mausland@brandeis.edu. *Application contact:* David F. Cotter, Graduate School of Arts and Sciences, 781-736-3410, Fax: 781-736-3412, E-mail: gradschool@brandeis.edu.

Brock University, Faculty of Graduate Studies, Faculty of Social Sciences, Program in Popular Culture, St. Catharines, ON L2S 3A1, Canada. Offers MA. Part-time programs available. *Degree requirements:* For master's, thesis optional. *Entrance requirements:* For master's, honors BA. Additional exam requirements/recommendations for international students: Required—TOEFL (minimum score 550 paper-based; 213 computer-based; 80 iBT), IELTS (minimum score 6.5), TWE (minimum score 4). Electronic applications accepted. *Faculty research:* Film and television studies, popular music, historical aspects of popular culture, popular literature.

Carnegie Mellon University, College of Humanities and Social Sciences, Department of History, Pittsburgh, PA 15213-3891. Offers African and African-American diaspora (PhD); culture and power (PhD); gender and the family (PhD); history (MA, MS); history and policy (MA); labor and politics (PhD); science, technology, medicine and environment (PhD). Part-time programs available. *Degree requirements:* For doctorate, oral and written comprehensive exams, dissertation defense. *Entrance requirements:* For doctorate, GRE General Test. Additional exam requirements/recommendations for international students: Required—TOEFL. Electronic applications accepted. *Faculty research:* Anthropology and history, African American history, technology/environment, cultural history analysis.

The Catholic University of America, School of Architecture and Planning, Washington, DC 20064. Offers cultural studies/sacred space (M Arch); design technologies (M Arch); digital media (M Arch); urban design (M Arch). Part-time programs available. *Faculty:* 20 full-time (7 women), 34 part-time/adjunct (4 women). *Students:* 110 full-time (46 women), 37 part-time (16 women); includes 40 minority (12 African Americans, 11 Asian Americans or Pacific Islanders, 17 Hispanic Americans), 9 international. Average age 27. 154 applicants, 80% accepted, 55 enrolled. In 2009, 39 master's awarded. *Degree requirements:* For master's, thesis. *Entrance requirements:* For master's, GRE (minimum score: 1000), minimum GPA of 2.8, portfolio, statement of purpose, official copies of academic transcripts, three letters of recommendation. Additional exam requirements/recommendations for international students: Required—TOEFL (minimum score 580 paper-based; 237 computer-based). *Application deadline:* For fall admission, 1/15 priority date for domestic students, 1/15 for international students; for spring admission, 10/15 priority date for domestic students, 10/15 for international students. Applications are processed on a rolling basis. Application fee: $55. Electronic applications accepted. *Expenses:* Contact institution. *Financial support:* Fellowships, research assistantships, teaching assistantships, Federal Work-Study, scholarships/grants, tuition waivers (full and partial), and unspecified assistantships available. Financial award application deadline: 2/1; financial award applicants required to submit FAFSA. *Faculty research:* Architectural history, cultural studies/scared space, design technologies, digital media, real estate development, urban design. *Unit head:* Randall Ott, Dean, 202-319-5784, Fax: 202-319-2023, E-mail: ott@cua.edu. *Application contact:* Julie Schwing, Director of Graduate Admissions, 202-319-5057, Fax: 202-319-6533, E-mail: cua-admissions@cua.edu.

Central Michigan University, College of Graduate Studies, College of Humanities and Social and Behavioral Sciences, Program in Humanities, Mount Pleasant, MI 48859. Offers humanities (MA), including contemporary issues in the humanities: race, class, and gender, images and ideas of self, Native American issues in modern culture, popular culture studies, the rise of industrial society. Part-time and evening/weekend programs available. *Degree requirements:* For master's, thesis or alternative. Electronic applications accepted. *Faculty research:* Rise of industrial society; images and ideas of self; contemporary issues of race, class, and gender; popular culture; Native American issues in modern culture.

Chapman University, Graduate Studies, College of Educational Studies, Program in Education: Cultural and Curricular Studies, Orange, CA 92866. Offers PhD. Part-time and evening/weekend programs available. *Faculty:* 24 full-time (15 women), 25 part-time/adjunct (16 women). *Students:* 23 part-time (18 women); includes 9 minority (2 African Americans, 1 Asian American or Pacific Islander, 6 Hispanic Americans). Average age 37. 23 applicants, 70% accepted, 10 enrolled. *Degree requirements:* For doctorate, thesis/dissertation. Tuition and fees vary according to course load, degree level and program. *Financial support:* Fellowships, Federal Work-Study and scholarships/grants available. *Unit head:* Dr. Joel Colbert, Director, 714-744-7076. *Application contact:* Rika Judd, Graduate Admission Counselor, 714-997-6786, Fax: 714-997-6713, E-mail: rjudd@chapman.edu.

Claremont Graduate University, Graduate Programs, School of Arts and Humanities, Department of Cultural Studies, Claremont, CA 91711-6160. Offers Africana studies (Certificate); cultural studies (MA, PhD); media studies (MA, PhD); museum studies (MA). Part-time programs available. *Faculty:* 3 full-time (2 women). *Students:* 67 full-time (43 women), 8 part-time (6 women); includes 28 minority (14 African Americans, 1 American Indian/Alaska Native, 5 Asian Americans or Pacific Islanders, 8 Hispanic Americans), 7 international. Average age 36. In 2009, 7 master's, 3 doctorates awarded. *Entrance requirements:* For master's and doctorate, GRE General Test. Additional exam requirements/recommendations for international students: Required—TOEFL (minimum score 550 paper-based; 213 computer-based; 80 iBT). *Application deadline:* For fall admission, 2/1 priority date for domestic students. Applications are processed on a rolling basis. Application fee: $60. Electronic applications accepted. *Expenses:* Tuition: Full-time $35,046; part-time $1524 per credit. Required fees: $161 per semester. *Financial support:* Fellowships, research assistantships, Federal Work-Study, institutionally sponsored loans, and scholarships/grants available. Support available to part-time students. Financial award application deadline: 2/15; financial award applicants required to submit FAFSA. *Unit head:* Eve Oishi, Chair, 909-607-7587, E-mail: eve.oishi@cgu.edu. *Application contact:* Susan Hampson, Admissions Coordinator, 909-607-1278, Fax: 909-607-1221, E-mail: humanities@cgu.edu.

Columbia International University, Columbia Biblical Seminary and School of Missions, Columbia, SC 29230-3122. Offers academic ministries (M Div); bible exposition (M Div, MABE); biblical studies (Certificate); counseling ministries (Certificate); divinity (M Div); educational ministries (M Div, MAEM, Certificate); intercultural studies (M Div, MAIS, Certificate); leadership (D Min); leadership for evangelism/mobilization (MALM); member care (D Min); ministry (Certificate); missions (D Min); pastoral counseling and spiritual formation (M Div, MAPS); preaching (D Min); theology (MA). *Accreditation:* ATS (one or more programs are accredited). Part-time and evening/weekend programs available. *Degree requirements:* For master's, integrative seminar; for doctorate, comprehensive exam, thesis/dissertation; for M Div, internship. *Entrance requirements:* For master's, minimum GPA of 2.7; for doctorate, 3 years of ministerial experience, M Div. Additional exam requirements/recommendations for international students: Required—TOEFL. Electronic applications accepted.

Concordia University, School of Theology, Irvine, CA 92612-3299. Offers Christian leadership (MA); research in theology (MA); theology and culture (MA). Part-time and evening/weekend programs available. Postbaccalaureate distance learning degree programs offered (no on-campus study). *Faculty:* 9 full-time (2 women). *Students:* 32 full-time (4 women), 8 part-time (3 women); includes 5 minority (1 African American, 1 Asian American or Pacific Islander, 3 Hispanic Americans), 3 international. Average age 36. 7 applicants, 100% accepted, 5 enrolled. In 2009, 10 master's awarded. *Degree requirements:* For master's, project/thesis or vicarage. *Entrance requirements:* For master's, 2 references, interview. Additional exam requirements/recommendations for international students: Required—TOEFL. *Application deadline:* For fall admission, 7/1 priority date for domestic students, 6/1 for international students; for spring admission, 11/30 priority date for domestic students, 10/1 for international students. Applications are processed on a rolling basis. Application fee: $50 ($125 for international students). Electronic applications accepted. *Expenses:* Contact institution. *Financial support:* In 2009–10, 34 students received support. Scholarships/grants available. Financial award applicants required to submit FAFSA. *Unit head:* Rev. Dr. James Bachman, Dean, School of Theology Graduate Studies, 949-854-8002 Ext. 1751, E-mail: james.bachman@cui.edu. *Application contact:* Carrie Donohoe, Christ College Program Coordinator, 949-854-8002 Ext. 1407, E-mail: carrie.donohoe@cui.edu.

Cornell University, Graduate School, Graduate Fields of Arts and Sciences, Field of English Language and Literature, Ithaca, NY 14853-0001. Offers African-American literature (PhD); American literature after 1865 (PhD); American literature to 1865 (PhD); American studies (PhD); colonial and postcolonial literature (PhD); creative writing (MFA); cultural studies (PhD); dramatic literature (PhD); English poetry (PhD); English Renaissance to 1660 (PhD); lesbian, bisexual, and gay literature studies (PhD); literary criticism and theory (PhD); nineteenth century (PhD); Old and Middle English (PhD); prose fiction (PhD); Restoration and eighteenth century (PhD); twentieth century (PhD); women's literature (PhD); MFA/PhD. *Faculty:* 74 full-time (35 women). *Students:* 100 full-time (55 women); includes 26 minority (9 African Americans, 3 American Indian/Alaska Native, 7 Asian Americans or Pacific Islanders, 7 Hispanic Americans), 11 international. Average age 28. 890 applicants, 4% accepted, 21 enrolled. In 2009, 21 master's, 12 doctorates awarded. Terminal master's awarded for partial completion of doctoral program. *Degree requirements:* For master's, one foreign language, thesis; for doctorate, one foreign language, comprehensive exam, thesis/dissertation, teaching experience. *Entrance requirements:* For master's, GRE General Test, 3 letters of recommendation, creative writing sample; for doctorate, GRE General Test, GRE Subject Test (English), 3 letters of recommendation, writing sample. Additional exam requirements/recommendations for international students: Required—TOEFL (minimum score 600 paper-based; 250 computer-based; 77 iBT). *Application deadline:* For fall admission, 1/10 for domestic students. Application fee: $70. Electronic applications accepted. *Expenses:* Tuition: Full-time $29,500. Required fees: $70. Full-time tuition and fees vary according to degree level, program and student level. *Financial support:* In 2009–10, 96 students received support, including 13 fellowships with full tuition reimbursements available, 8 teaching assistantships with full tuition reimbursements available; research assistantships with full tuition reimbursements available, institutionally sponsored loans, scholarships/grants, health care benefits, tuition waivers (full and partial), and unspecified assistantships also available. Financial award applicants required to submit FAFSA. *Faculty research:* English and American literature, women's writing, ethnic and post-colonial literature, critical theory, medievalism. *Unit head:* Director of Graduate Studies, 607-255-7989, Fax: 607-255-6661. *Application contact:* Graduate Field Assistant, 607-255-7989, Fax: 607-255-6661, E-mail: english_grad@cornell.edu.

Eastern Michigan University, Graduate School, College of Education, Department of Teacher Education, Program in Culture and Diversity, Ypsilanti, MI 48197. Offers MA. *Students:* 3 full-time (2 women), 15 part-time (12 women); includes 14 minority (all African Americans). Average age 39. In 2009, 9 master's awarded. Tuition and fees vary according to course level. *Unit head:* Dr. Wendy Burke, Coordinator, 734-487-3260, Fax: 734-487-2101, E-mail: wendy.burke@emich.edu. *Application contact:* Dr. Wendy Burke, Coordinator, 734-487-3260, Fax: 734-487-2101, E-mail: wendy.burke@emich.edu.

George Mason University, College of Humanities and Social Sciences, Program in Cultural Studies, Fairfax, VA 22030. Offers PhD. Part-time and evening/weekend programs available. *Faculty:* 22 full-time (11 women). *Students:* 7 full-time (2 women), 60 part-time (38 women); includes 6 minority (3 African Americans, 3 Asian Americans or Pacific Islanders), 15 international. Average age 36. 51 applicants, 55% accepted, 11 enrolled. In 2009, 2 doctorates awarded. *Degree requirements:* For doctorate, one foreign language, comprehensive exam, thesis/dissertation, foreign language exams. *Entrance requirements:* For doctorate, GRE General Test, sample of written work, MA or simultaneous application to related MA program at George Mason University. Additional exam requirements/recommendations for international students: Required—TOEFL. *Application deadline:* For fall admission, 1/15 for domestic students. Application fee: $75. Electronic applications accepted. *Expenses:* Tuition, state resident: full-time $7568; part-time $315.33 per credit hour. Tuition, nonresident: full-time $21,704; part-time $904.33 per credit hour. Required fees: $2184; $91 per credit hour. *Financial support:* In 2009–10, 24 students received support, including 3 fellowships with full tuition reimbursements available (averaging $18,000 per year), 1 research assistantship with full and

Cultural Studies

George Mason University (continued)
partial tuition reimbursement available (averaging $15,800 per year), 20 teaching assistantships with full and partial tuition reimbursements available (averaging $9,529 per year); Federal Work-Study, unspecified assistantships, and health care benefits (full-time research or teaching assistantship recipients) also available. Support available to part-time students. Financial award application deadline: 1/15; financial award applicants required to submit FAFSA. *Faculty research:* Early Modern cultural studies, Shakespeare and film, feminism, Foucault, science and technology studies. *Unit head:* Roger N. Lancaster, Director, 703-993-2851, Fax: 703-993-2852, E-mail: rlancast@gmu.edu. *Application contact:* Dr. Matt Zingraff, Associate Dean, Research and Graduate Programs, 703-993-4769, E-mail: zingraff@gmu.edu.

Goucher College, Program in Cultural Sustainability, Baltimore, MD 21204-2794. Offers MA. Postbaccalaureate distance learning degree programs offered (minimal on-campus study). *Degree requirements:* For master's, capstone project.

Grace Theological Seminary, Graduate and Professional Programs, Winona Lake, IN 46590-9907. Offers biblical studies (Certificate); camp administration (MA); counseling (M Div); exegetical studies (MA); intercultural studies (M Div, MA); local church studies (MA); pastoral studies (M Div); theological studies (MA); theology (D Min, Diploma). Part-time programs available. Postbaccalaureate distance learning degree programs offered (no on-campus study). *Degree requirements:* For master's, thesis optional; for doctorate, 2 foreign languages, thesis/dissertation; for M Div, 2 foreign languages, thesis/dissertation optional. *Entrance requirements:* For M Div and master's, MAT, minimum GPA of 2.5. Electronic applications accepted. *Faculty research:* Biblical theology, language, and church ministries.

Graduate Theological Union, Graduate Programs, Berkeley, CA 94709-1212. Offers art and religion (MA, PhD, Th D); biblical languages (MA); Biblical studies (PhD, Th D); biblical studies (MA); Buddhist studies (MA); Christian spirituality (MA, PhD, Th D); cultural and historical studies of religions (MA, PhD, Th D); ethics and social theory (PhD, Th D); history (MA, PhD, Th D); homiletics (MA, PhD, Th D); interdisciplinary studies (PhD, Th D); Jewish studies (MA, PhD, Th D, Certificate); liturgical studies (MA, PhD, Th D); Near Eastern religions (PhD, Th D); Orthodox Christian studies (MA); religion and psychology (MA, PhD, Th D); religion and society/ethics and social theory (MA); systematic and philosophical theology (MA, PhD, Th D). *Accreditation:* ATS. Terminal master's awarded for partial completion of doctoral program. *Degree requirements:* For master's, one foreign language, thesis; for doctorate, one foreign language, comprehensive exam, thesis/dissertation. *Entrance requirements:* For master's, GRE General Test; for doctorate, GRE General Test, MA or M Div. Additional exam requirements/recommendations for international students: Required—TOEFL. Electronic applications accepted.

Lewis & Clark College, Graduate School of Education and Counseling, Department of Counseling Psychology, Portland, OR 97219-7899. Offers addictions treatment (MA, MS); community counseling (MA, MS); marriage, couple and family therapy (MA, MS); psychological and cultural studies (MA, MS); school psychology (Ed S). Part-time and evening/weekend programs available. *Faculty:* 11 full-time (7 women), 22 part-time/adjunct (15 women). *Students:* 103 full-time (87 women), 146 part-time (115 women); includes 22 minority (3 African Americans, 9 Asian Americans or Pacific Islanders, 10 Hispanic Americans), 3 international. Average age 31. 157 applicants, 78% accepted, 75 enrolled. In 2009, 69 master's, 13 other advanced degrees awarded. *Degree requirements:* For master's, thesis proposal (MS). *Entrance requirements:* For master's, GRE General Test, minimum undergraduate GPA of 2.75. Additional exam requirements/recommendations for international students: Required—TOEFL (minimum score 575 paper-based; 233 computer-based). *Application deadline:* For fall admission, 2/1 priority date for domestic and international students; for spring admission, 10/1 priority date for domestic and international students. Application fee: $50. Electronic applications accepted. *Expenses:* Tuition: Part-time $713 per semester hour. Tuition and fees vary according to course level and campus/location. *Financial support:* In 2009–10, 230 students received support. Career-related internships or fieldwork, Federal Work-Study, institutionally sponsored loans, scholarships/grants, health care benefits, and tuition waivers (partial) available. Support available to part-time students. Financial award application deadline: 3/1; financial award applicants required to submit FAFSA. *Unit head:* Dr. Tod Sloan, Chair, 503-768-6060, Fax: 503-768-6065, E-mail: cpsy@lclark.edu. *Application contact:* Becky Haas, Director of Admissions, 503-768-6200, Fax: 503-768-6205, E-mail: gseadmit@lclark.edu.

Maranatha Baptist Bible College, Program in Cross-Cultural Studies, Watertown, WI 53094. Offers MA. Part-time programs available. *Expenses:* Tuition: Full-time $4000; part-time $250 per credit. Required fees: $21 per credit.

McMaster University, School of Graduate Studies, Faculty of Humanities, Department of English and Cultural Studies, Hamilton, ON L8S 4M2, Canada. Offers cultural studies and critical theory (MA); English (MA, PhD). Part-time programs available. *Degree requirements:* For master's, one foreign language, thesis; for doctorate, one foreign language, comprehensive exam, thesis/dissertation. *Entrance requirements:* For master's, honors degree, minimum B+ average in at least 6 full courses of English beyond year 1; for doctorate, MA; minimum A-average in two of three courses. Additional exam requirements/recommendations for international students: Required—TOEFL (minimum score 580 paper-based; 237 computer-based). *Faculty research:* Literary theory, feminist theory, literature of migration, Bakhting globalization.

New York University, NYU in Madrid, Madrid, NY 10012-1019, Spain. Offers creative writing in Spanish (MFA); Spanish (PhD); Spanish and Latin American literatures and cultures (MA); Spanish language and translation (MA). *Students:* 27 full-time (23 women), 1 part-time (0 women); includes 8 minority (2 African Americans, 1 Asian American or Pacific Islander, 5 Hispanic Americans), 1 international. Average age 26. 73 applicants, 90% accepted, 27 enrolled. In 2009, 22 master's awarded. Application fee: $90. *Expenses:* Tuition: Full-time $30,528; part-time $1272 per credit. Required fees: $2177. *Unit head:* Judith Nemethy, Director, 212-998-8770, Fax: 212-995-4149, E-mail: nyu-in-madrid@nyu.edu. *Application contact:* Judith Nemethy, Director, 212-998-8770, Fax: 212-995-4149, E-mail: nyu-in-madrid@nyu.edu.

New York University, Steinhardt School of Culture, Education, and Human Development, New York, NY 10003. Offers MA, MFA, MM, MPH, MS, DPS, DPT, Ed D, PhD, Advanced Certificate, MM/Advanced Certificate, MPA/MA. *Accreditation:* Teacher Education Accreditation Council. Part-time programs available. *Faculty:* 259 full-time (151 women), 898 part-time/adjunct (488 women). *Students:* 2,357 full-time (1,841 women), 1,414 part-time (1,098 women); includes 820 minority (242 African Americans, 7 American Indian/Alaska Native, 289 Asian Americans or Pacific Islanders, 282 Hispanic Americans), 552 international. Average age 30. 6,436 applicants, 47% accepted, 1308 enrolled. In 2009, 1,286 master's, 122 doctorates, 18 other advanced degrees awarded. *Degree requirements:* For master's, thesis (for some programs); for doctorate, comprehensive exam (for some programs), thesis/dissertation. *Entrance requirements:* For doctorate, GRE General Test, interview. Additional exam requirements/recommendations for international students: Required—TOEFL. *Application deadline:* For fall admission, 12/15 priority date for domestic students, 12/15 for international students; for spring admission, 1/1 for domestic and international students. Applications are processed on a rolling basis. Application fee: $75. Electronic applications accepted. *Expenses:* Contact institution. *Financial support:* Fellowships with full and partial tuition reimbursements, research assistantships with full and partial tuition reimbursements, teaching assistantships with full and partial tuition reimbursements, career-related internships or fieldwork, Federal Work-Study, institutionally sponsored loans, scholarships/grants, traineeships, tuition waivers (partial), and unspecified assistantships available. Support available to part-time students. Financial award application deadline: 2/1; financial award applicants required to submit FAFSA. *Faculty research:* Equity, urban adolescents, arts in education, globalization, community and public health. Total annual research expenditures: $22.8 million. *Unit head:* Dr. Mary Brabeck, Dean, 212-998-5000. *Application contact:* John Myers, Director of Enrollment Management, 212-998-5030, Fax: 212-995-4328, E-mail: steinhardt.gradadmissions@nyu.edu.

Northeastern University, College of Arts, Media and Design, Department of Communication Studies, Boston, MA 02115-5096. Offers communication, media, and cultural studies (MA). *Faculty:* 25 full-time (10 women), 6 part-time/adjunct (3 women). *Students:* 5 full-time (all women); includes 1 minority (African American), 1 international. 59 applicants, 42% accepted, 4 enrolled. In 2009, 3 master's awarded. *Degree requirements:* For master's, thesis (for some programs). *Entrance requirements:* For master's, GRE. Additional exam requirements/recommendations for international students: Required—TOEFL or IELTS. *Application deadline:* For fall admission, 2/1 priority date for domestic and international students. Applications are processed on a rolling basis. Application fee: $50. Electronic applications accepted. *Financial support:* Federal Work-Study and scholarships/grants available. *Unit head:* Dr. Joanne Morreale, Graduate Coordinator, 617-373-2506, E-mail: j.morreale@neu.edu. *Application contact:* Jo-Anne Dickinson, Admissions Contact, 617-373-5990, Fax: 617-373-7281, E-mail: gsas@neu.edu.

Northwest University, College of Ministry, Kirkland, WA 98033. Offers ministry (MA); missional leadership (MA); theology and culture (MA). *Faculty:* 11 full-time (1 woman), 12 part-time/adjunct (2 women). *Students:* 16 full-time (3 women), 24 part-time (7 women); includes 3 minority (all African Americans). 39 applicants, 97% accepted, 22 enrolled. *Entrance requirements:* Additional exam requirements/recommendations for international students: Required—TOEFL (minimum score 550 paper-based). Application fee: $75. *Unit head:* Dr. Kent Ingle, Dean, 425-889-5253, E-mail: kent.ingle@northwestu.edu. *Application contact:* Roy Rowland, Director of Graduate and Professional Studies Enrollment, 425-889-7787, Fax: 425-803-3059, E-mail: gpse@northwestu.edu.

Phoenix Seminary, Graduate Programs, Scottsdale, AZ 85254. Offers biblical communication (M Div); biblical leadership (MA); biblical studies (Graduate Diploma); Christian counseling (Graduate Diploma); counseling and family (M Div); intercultural studies (Graduate Diploma); leadership development (M Div, Graduate Diploma); ministry (D Min); professional counseling (MA); women's studies (Graduate Diploma). *Accreditation:* ATS (one or more programs are accredited). Part-time and evening/weekend programs available. *Faculty:* 5 full-time (0 women), 5 part-time/adjunct (0 women). *Students:* 26 full-time (8 women), 151 part-time (39 women); includes 34 minority (18 African Americans, 2 American Indian/Alaska Native, 5 Asian Americans or Pacific Islanders, 9 Hispanic Americans), 1 international. 41 applicants, 90% accepted, 30 enrolled. In 2009, 21 master's, 2 doctorates, 12 other advanced degrees awarded. *Degree requirements:* For master's, 2 foreign languages, comprehensive exam; for doctorate, 2 foreign languages, thesis/dissertation. *Entrance requirements:* For master's, undergraduate degree with minimum GPA of 2.5; for doctorate, M Div (94 hours) with minimum GPA of 3.0. Additional exam requirements/recommendations for international students: Required—TOEFL (minimum score 587 paper-based; 240 computer-based; 92 iBT), TWE (minimum score 4.5). *Application deadline:* For fall admission, 7/1 for domestic students; for spring admission, 11/1 for domestic students. Applications are processed on a rolling basis. Application fee: $90. *Expenses:* Tuition: Full-time $9420; part-time $410 per credit hour. Required fees: $60 per semester. Tuition and fees vary according to course load and degree level. *Financial support:* Institutionally sponsored loans and scholarships/grants available. Support available to part-time students. Financial award application deadline: 6/1; financial award applicants required to submit FAFSA. *Application contact:* Roma Royer, Director of Admissions and Academic Services, 602-850-8000 Ext. 111, Fax: 602-850-8080, E-mail: rroyer@ps.edu.

St. Francis Xavier University, Graduate Studies, Department of Celtic Studies, Antigonish, NS B2G 2W5, Canada. Offers MA. *Degree requirements:* For master's, thesis. *Entrance requirements:* Additional exam requirements/recommendations for international students: Required—TOEFL (minimum score 580 paper-based; 236 computer-based). *Faculty research:* Scottish Gaelic in Nova Scotia.

San Francisco State University, Division of Graduate Studies, College of Behavioral and Social Sciences, Human Sexuality Studies Program, San Francisco, CA 94132-1722. Offers MA.

Simmons College, College of Arts and Sciences Graduate Studies, Program in Gender/Cultural Studies, Boston, MA 02115. Offers MA, MA/MAT, MA/MS. Part-time programs available. *Students:* 1 (woman) full-time, 24 part-time (all women); includes 5 minority (1 African American, 1 American Indian/Alaska Native, 3 Hispanic Americans), 2 international. Average age 26. 42 applicants, 62% accepted, 12 enrolled. In 2009, 16 master's awarded. *Degree requirements:* For master's, thesis. *Entrance requirements:* For master's, academic writing sample. Additional exam requirements/recommendations for international students: Required—TOEFL (minimum score 600 paper-based; 250 computer-based; 100 iBT). *Application deadline:* For fall admission, 8/1 priority date for domestic and international students; for winter admission, 12/15 priority date for domestic and international students; for spring admission, 5/1 priority date for domestic and international students. Applications are processed on a rolling basis. Application fee: $35. Electronic applications accepted. *Expenses:* Tuition: Part-time $925 per credit hour. Part-time tuition and fees vary according to program. *Financial support:* Application deadline: 3/1. *Faculty research:* Gender and sexuality, queer theory, gender and the media, race, feminist film theory. *Unit head:* Dr. Sarah Leonard, Director, 617-521-2254, Fax: 617-521-3090. *Application contact:* Kristen Haack, Director, Graduate Studies Admission, 617-521-2917, Fax: 617-521-3058, E-mail: gsa@simmons.edu.

Southern Illinois University Carbondale, Graduate School, College of Liberal Arts, Department of Foreign Languages and Literatures, Carbondale, IL 62901-4701. Offers MA. Part-time programs available. *Degree requirements:* For master's, one foreign language, thesis. *Entrance requirements:* For master's, minimum GPA of 2.7. Additional exam requirements/recommendations for international students: Required—TOEFL. *Faculty research:* Bibliography, historical linguistics, language pedagogy, philology, commercial facets.

State University of New York at Binghamton, Graduate School, School of Arts and Sciences, Philosophy, Interpretation and Culture Program, Binghamton, NY 13902-6000. Offers MA, PhD. *Students:* 12 full-time (4 women), 37 part-time (19 women); includes 15 minority (6 African Americans, 2 Asian Americans or Pacific Islanders, 7 Hispanic Americans), 17 international. Average age 35. 34 applicants, 35% accepted, 4 enrolled. In 2009, 2 master's, 1 doctorate awarded. Application fee: $60. *Financial support:* In 2009–10, 21 students received support, including 5 fellowships with full tuition reimbursements available (averaging $14,500 per year), 1 research assistantship with full tuition reimbursement available (averaging $14,500 per year), 11 teaching assistantships with full tuition reimbursements available (averaging $14,500 per year); career-related internships or fieldwork, Federal Work-Study, institutionally sponsored loans, scholarships/grants, health care benefits, and unspecified assistantships also available. Financial award application deadline: 2/15; financial award applicants required to submit FAFSA. *Unit head:* Dr. Joshua Price, Director, 607-777-2348, E-mail: jmprice@binghamton.edu. *Application contact:* Victoria Williams, Recruiting and Admissions Coordinator, 607-777-2151, Fax: 607-777-2501, E-mail: vwilliam@binghamton.edu.

Stony Brook University, State University of New York, Graduate School, College of Arts and Sciences, Department of Comparative Literary and Cultural Studies, Stony Brook, NY 11794. Offers comparative literature (MA, PhD); cultural studies (PhD). Evening/weekend programs available. *Faculty:* 7 full-time (1 woman). *Students:* 35 full-time (21 women), 4 part-time (3 women); includes 6 minority (5 Asian Americans or Pacific Islanders, 1 Hispanic American), 17 international. Average age 30. 101 applicants, 19% accepted. In 2009, 1 master's, 1 doctorate awarded. Terminal master's awarded for partial completion of doctoral program. *Degree requirements:* For master's, 2 foreign languages, exam; for doctorate, 3 foreign languages, comprehensive exam, thesis/dissertation. *Entrance requirements:* For master's and doctorate, GRE General Test, minimum GPA of 3.5 in major, 3.0 overall. Additional exam requirements/recommendations for international students: Required—TOEFL. *Application deadline:* For fall admission, 1/15 for domestic students. Application fee: $60. *Expenses:* Tuition, state resident: full-time $8370; part-time $349 per credit. Tuition, nonresident: full-time $13,250; part-time $552 per credit. Required fees: $933. *Financial support:* In 2009–10, 24 teaching assistantships were awarded; fellowships, research assistantships also available. *Faculty research:* Literary theory, interdisciplinary studies, literary history. *Unit head:* Prof. Krin

Gabbard, Chairman, 631-632-7456. *Application contact:* Dr. Kent Marks, Assistant Dean, Admissions and Records, 631-632-4723, Fax: 631-632-7243, E-mail: kmarks@notes.cc.sunysb.edu.

Taylor College and Seminary, Graduate and Professional Programs, Edmonton, AB T6J 4T3, Canada. Offers Christian studies (Diploma); intercultural studies (MA, Diploma), including intercultural studies (Diploma), TESOL; theology (M Div, MTS). *Accreditation:* ATS. Part-time programs available. Postbaccalaureate distance learning degree programs offered (minimal on-campus study). *Faculty:* 5 full-time (0 women), 5 part-time/adjunct (1 woman). *Students:* 13 full-time (4 women), 52 part-time (24 women); includes 18 minority (2 African Americans, 1 American Indian/Alaska Native, 15 Asian Americans or Pacific Islanders). Average age 38. 40 applicants, 73% accepted, 20 enrolled. In 2009, 11 first professional degrees awarded. *Degree requirements:* For master's, thesis optional. *Entrance requirements:* Additional exam requirements/recommendations for international students: Required—TOEFL (minimum score 550 paper-based; 80 iBT), IELTS (minimum score 6.5). *Application deadline:* For fall admission, 9/1 priority date for domestic and international students. Applications are processed on a rolling basis. Application fee: $35 ($70 for international students). *Financial support:* In 2009–10, 16 students received support. Career-related internships or fieldwork and scholarships/grants available. Financial award application deadline: 8/1. *Faculty research:* Biblical studies, administration and organization, world religions, ethics, missiology. *Unit head:* Dr. Joost Pikkert, Academic Dean, 780-431-5243, Fax: 780-436-9416, E-mail: joost.pikkert@taylor-edu.ca. *Application contact:* Craig Weston, Registrar and Director of Enrolment Services, 780-431-5208, Fax: 780-436-9416, E-mail: craig.weston@taylor-edu.ca.

Trent University, Graduate Studies, Program in Cultural Studies, Peterborough, ON K9J 7B8, Canada. Offers PhD.

Union Institute & University, Master of Arts Program–Online, Montpelier, VT 05602. Offers creativity studies (MA); education (MA); health and wellness (MA); history and culture (MA); leadership, public policy, and social issues (MA); literature and writing (MA); psychology (MA). Part-time programs available. Postbaccalaureate distance learning degree programs offered (no on-campus study). *Faculty:* 3 full-time (1 woman), 16 part-time/adjunct (11 women). *Students:* 27 full-time (23 women), 113 part-time (84 women); includes 30 minority (22 African Americans, 2 American Indian/Alaska Native, 1 Asian American or Pacific Islander, 5 Hispanic Americans). Average age 40. In 2009, 26 master's awarded. *Degree requirements:* For master's, thesis. *Application deadline:* Applications are processed on a rolling basis. Application fee: $50. Electronic applications accepted. *Expenses:* Contact institution. *Financial support:* Career-related internships or fieldwork and tuition waivers available. Financial award applicants required to submit FAFSA. *Unit head:* Dr. Brian Webb, Program Director, 802-828-8777, E-mail: brian.webb@tui.edu. *Application contact:* Kathleen Murphy, Interim Director of Admissions—Montpelier, 888-828-8575, E-mail: admissions@myunion.edu.

Union University, Institute for International and Intercultural Studies, Jackson, TN 38305-3697. Offers MAIS. Part-time and evening/weekend programs available. *Degree requirements:* For master's, capstone course. *Entrance requirements:* For master's, GRE, minimum undergraduate GPA of 3.0, 3 letters of reference. Additional exam requirements/recommendations for international students: Required—TOEFL (minimum score 560 paper-based; 220 computer-based). Electronic applications accepted. *Faculty research:* International education, ethnographic field research, intercultural training for professionals and students, language and culture.

University of Alaska Fairbanks, College of Liberal Arts, Department of Alaska Native Studies, Fairbanks, AK 99775-6300. Offers cross cultural studies (MA). *Faculty:* 4 full-time (1 woman), 1 part-time/adjunct (0 women). *Students:* 2 full-time (1 woman), 7 part-time (5 women); includes 4 minority (all American Indian/Alaska Native). Average age 42. 5 applicants, 20% accepted, 0 enrolled. In 2009, 3 master's awarded. *Degree requirements:* For master's, comprehensive exam. *Entrance requirements:* Additional exam requirements/recommendations for international students: Required—TOEFL (minimum score 550 paper-based; 213 computer-based; 80 iBT). *Application deadline:* For fall admission, 6/1 for domestic students, 3/1 for international students; for spring admission, 10/15 for domestic students, 9/1 for international students. Applications are processed on a rolling basis. Application fee: $60. Electronic applications accepted. *Expenses:* Tuition, state resident: full-time $7584; part-time $316 per credit. Tuition, nonresident: full-time $15,504; part-time $646 per credit. Required fees: $23 per credit. $135 per semester. Tuition and fees vary according to course level, course load and reciprocity agreements. *Financial support:* In 2009–10, 1 fellowship (averaging $13,500 per year) was awarded; research assistantships, teaching assistantships, Federal Work-Study, scholarships/grants, health care benefits, and unspecified assistantships also available. Support available to part-time students. Financial award application deadline: 7/1; financial award applicants required to submit FAFSA. *Faculty research:* Alaska native literature, oral traditions, history, law and policy; Alaska native cultures, art, native American religion and philosophy. *Unit head:* Dr. James K. Ruppert, Chair, 907-474-7181, Fax: 907-474-5666, E-mail: jkruppert@alaska.edu. *Application contact:* Dr. James K. Ruppert, Chair, 907-474-7181, Fax: 907-474-5666, E-mail: jkruppert@alaska.edu.

University of California, Davis, Graduate Studies, Graduate Group in Cultural Studies, Davis, CA 95616. Offers MA, PhD. *Degree requirements:* For master's, thesis; for doctorate, thesis/dissertation. *Entrance requirements:* For doctorate, GRE. Additional exam requirements/recommendations for international students: Required—TOEFL (minimum score 550 paper-based; 213 computer-based). Electronic applications accepted.

University of Hawaii at Hilo, Program in Hawaiian and Indigenous Language and Cultural Revitalization, Hilo, HI 96720-4091. Offers PhD.

University of Hawaii at Hilo, Program in Indigenous Language and Culture Education, Hilo, HI 96720-4091. Offers MA.

University of Houston–Clear Lake, School of Human Sciences and Humanities, Programs in Human Sciences, Houston, TX 77058-1098. Offers behavioral sciences (MA), including criminology, cross cultural studies, general psychology, sociology; clinical psychology (MA); criminology (MA); cross cultural studies (MA); family therapy (MA); fitness and human performance (MA); school psychology (MA). *Accreditation:* AAMFT/COAMFTE. Part-time and evening/weekend programs available. Postbaccalaureate distance learning degree programs offered (minimal on-campus study). *Degree requirements:* For master's, thesis or alternative. *Entrance requirements:* For master's, GRE General Test. Additional exam requirements/recommendations for international students: Required—TOEFL (minimum score 550 paper-based; 213 computer-based). Electronic applications accepted. *Faculty research:* Smoking cessation, adolescent sexuality, white collar crime, serial murder, human factors/human computer interaction.

University of Minnesota, Twin Cities Campus, Graduate School, College of Liberal Arts, Department of Cultural Studies and Comparative Literature, Program in Comparative Studies in Discourse and Society, Minneapolis, MN 55455-0213. Offers PhD. *Faculty:* 14 full-time (2 women), 9 part-time/adjunct (7 women). *Students:* 22 full-time (10 women); includes 3 minority (2 Asian Americans or Pacific Islanders, 1 Hispanic American), 2 international. Average age 26. 56 applicants, 5% accepted, 3 enrolled. In 2009, 1 doctorate awarded. *Degree requirements:* For doctorate, 2 foreign languages, thesis/dissertation. *Entrance requirements:* For doctorate, GRE General Test, sample of written work. Additional exam requirements/recommendations for international students: Required—TOEFL. *Application deadline:* For fall admission, 12/10 for domestic students. Application fee: $55 ($75 for international students). *Financial support:* In 2009–10, 1 fellowship with full tuition reimbursement (averaging $22,500 per year), 1 research assistantship with full tuition reimbursement (averaging $6,232 per year), 25 teaching assistantships with full tuition reimbursements (averaging $13,800 per year) were awarded; Federal Work-Study, institutionally sponsored loans, and tuition waivers (full and partial) also available. Financial award application deadline: 12/10. *Faculty research:* Cultural theory; music; architecture, space, and urbanism; body and gender; film and popular culture. *Unit head:* Robert I. Brown, Director of Graduate Studies, 612-624-8878, Fax: 612-626-0228, E-mail: brown004@umn.edu. *Application contact:* Robert L. Brown, Director of Graduate Studies, 612-624-8878, Fax: 612-626-0228, E-mail: brown004@umn.edu.

University of Pittsburgh, School of Arts and Sciences, Department of English, Pittsburgh, PA 15260. Offers cultural and critical studies (PhD); English (MA); writing (MFA). Part-time programs available. *Faculty:* 53 full-time (25 women). *Students:* 170 full-time (106 women), 37 part-time (33 women); includes 21 minority (8 African Americans, 1 American Indian/Alaska Native, 6 Asian Americans or Pacific Islanders, 6 Hispanic Americans), 5 international. Average age 23. 410 applicants, 12% accepted, 19 enrolled. In 2009, 22 master's, 10 doctorates awarded. *Degree requirements:* For master's, one foreign language; for doctorate, 2 foreign languages, comprehensive exam, thesis/dissertation. *Entrance requirements:* For master's and doctorate, GRE General Test, writing sample. Additional exam requirements/recommendations for international students: Required—TOEFL (minimum score 550 paper-based; 213 computer-based; 80 iBT). *Application deadline:* For fall admission, 12/10 for domestic and international students. Application fee: $50. *Expenses:* Tuition, state resident: full-time $16,402; part-time $665 per credit. Tuition, nonresident: full-time $28,694; part-time $1175 per credit. Required fees: $690; $175 per term. Tuition and fees vary according to program. *Financial support:* In 2009–10, 100 students received support, including 19 fellowships with full tuition reimbursements available (averaging $17,822 per year), 5 research assistantships with full and partial tuition reimbursements available (averaging $12,300 per year), 64 teaching assistantships with full tuition reimbursements available (averaging $15,065 per year); Federal Work-Study, tuition waivers (full and partial), and unspecified assistantships also available. Financial award application deadline: 12/12. *Faculty research:* Cultural studies, literary history and theory, film, composition. *Unit head:* Dr. John Twyning, Chairman, 412-624-6509, Fax: 412-624-6639, E-mail: twyning@pitt.edu. *Application contact:* Michelle Delie, Graduate Administrator, 412-624-6549, Fax: 412-624-6639, E-mail: mid29@pitt.edu.

The University of Texas at San Antonio, College of Education and Human Development, Division of Bicultural-Bilingual Studies, San Antonio, TX 78249-0617. Offers bicultural-bilingual studies (MA); culture, literacy, and language (PhD); teaching English as a second language (MA). Part-time and evening/weekend programs available. *Faculty:* 13 full-time (7 women). *Students:* 48 full-time (36 women), 94 part-time (75 women); includes 108 minority (5 African Americans, 8 Asian Americans or Pacific Islanders, 95 Hispanic Americans), 10 international. Average age 35. 76 applicants, 89% accepted, 36 enrolled. In 2009, 27 master's, 3 doctorates awarded. *Degree requirements:* For master's, comprehensive exam (for some programs), thesis (for some programs); for doctorate, comprehensive exam, thesis/dissertation. *Entrance requirements:* For master's and doctorate, GRE General Test. Additional exam requirements/recommendations for international students: Required—TOEFL (minimum score 500 paper-based; 173 computer-based; 61 iBT), IELTS (minimum score 5). *Application deadline:* For fall admission, 7/1 for domestic students, 4/1 for international students; for spring admission, 11/1 for domestic students, 9/1 for international students. Applications are processed on a rolling basis. Application fee: $45 ($80 for international students). Electronic applications accepted. *Expenses:* Tuition, state resident: full-time $3975; part-time $221 per contact hour. Tuition, nonresident: full-time $13,947; part-time $775 per contact hour. Required fees: $1853. *Financial support:* In 2009–10, 24 students received support, including 2 research assistantships (averaging $11,660 per year), 9 teaching assistantships (averaging $8,439 per year); fellowships, career-related internships or fieldwork and tuition waivers also available. Support available to part-time students. *Faculty research:* Globalization, migration and immigrant education, integrating language and content in PK-12 instruction, language and cultural policies in multilingual societies, multiple literacies. *Unit head:* Dr. Robert D. Milk, Director, 210-458-4426, Fax: 210-458-5962, E-mail: rmilk@utsa.edu. *Application contact:* Dr. Dorothy A. Flannagan, Dean of the Graduate School, 210-458-4330, Fax: 210-458-4332, E-mail: dorothy.flannagan@utsa.edu.

University of the Sacred Heart, Graduate Programs, Department of Communication, Program in Contemporary Culture and Media, San Juan, PR 00914-0383. Offers MA. *Degree requirements:* For master's, thesis.

University of Washington, Bothell, Program in Cultural Studies, Bothell, WA 98011-8246. Offers MA. Evening/weekend programs available. *Faculty:* 9 full-time (5 women), 5 part-time/adjunct (1 woman). *Students:* 36 full-time (25 women), 1 (woman) part-time; includes 8 minority (2 African Americans, 1 American Indian/Alaska Native, 3 Asian Americans or Pacific Islanders, 2 Hispanic Americans), 2 international. Average age 33. 60 applicants, 40% accepted, 20 enrolled. *Degree requirements:* For master's, thesis. *Entrance requirements:* Additional exam requirements/recommendations for international students: Required—TOEFL. *Application deadline:* For fall admission, 2/1 for domestic and international students. Application fee: $65. Electronic applications accepted. *Expenses:* Tuition, state resident: full-time $10,160; part-time $484 per credit hour. Tuition, nonresident: full-time $23,500; part-time $1120 per credit hour. Required fees: $567; $21.50 per credit hour. Tuition and fees vary according to course load and program. *Financial support:* In 2009–10, 9 students received support, including 5 fellowships (averaging $1,000 per year), 1 research assistantship (averaging $1,000 per year); Federal Work-Study and unspecified assistantships also available. *Unit head:* Prof. Bruce Burgett, Director, 425-352-5452, Fax: 425-352-3462, E-mail: bburgett@uwb.edu. *Application contact:* Andrew Brusletten, Program Manager, 425-352-5427, Fax: 425-352-3462, E-mail: abrusletten@uwb.edu.

Washington State University, Graduate School, College of Liberal Arts, Edward R. Murrow College of Communication, Pullman, WA 99164. Offers health communications (MA, PhD); intercultural and international communications (MA, PhD); media and society (MA, PhD); media process and effects (MA, PhD); organizational communications (MA, PhD). *Degree requirements:* For master's, comprehensive exam (for some programs), thesis optional, oral exam; for doctorate, comprehensive exam, thesis/dissertation. *Entrance requirements:* For master's, GRE General Test, minimum GPA of 3.25, 3 letters of recommendation; for doctorate, GRE General Test, minimum undergraduate GPA of 3.25, graduate 3.5; MA in communication; 3 letters of recommendation. Additional exam requirements/recommendations for international students: Required—TOEFL (minimum score 580 paper-based; 237 computer-based). Electronic applications accepted. *Faculty research:* Advocacy communication, mediated communication in decision making, communication technology policy and effects, multicultural and international psychology and physiology of communication.

Wheaton College, Graduate School, Department of Intercultural Studies, Wheaton, IL 60187-5593. Offers evangelism (MA); intercultural studies (MA); intercultural studies/teaching English as a second language (MA); missions (MA); teaching English as a second language (Certificate). Part-time programs available. *Degree requirements:* For master's, thesis or alternative. *Entrance requirements:* For master's, GRE General Test, MAT. Electronic applications accepted.

Wilfrid Laurier University, Faculty of Graduate Studies, Faculty of Arts, Cultural Analysis and Social Theory Program, Waterloo, ON N2L 3C5, Canada. Offers MA. *Entrance requirements:* For master's, honours BA in humanities, social science or interdisciplinary program with social theory, minimum B+ in final year of full-time study. Additional exam requirements/recommendations for international students: Required—TOEFL (minimum score 230 computer-based; 89 iBT). Electronic applications accepted. *Faculty research:* Globalization, identify and social movements, body politics: gender, sexuality and embodiment, cultural representation and social theory.

East European and Russian Studies

Boston College, Graduate School of Arts and Sciences, Department of Slavic and Eastern Languages, Program in Slavic Studies, Chestnut Hill, MA 02467-3800. Offers MA, MA/JD, MBA/MA. Part-time programs available. *Degree requirements:* For master's, 3 foreign languages, comprehensive exam, thesis or alternative. *Entrance requirements:* Additional exam requirements/recommendations for international students: Required—TOEFL (minimum score 600 paper-based; 250 computer-based; 100 iBT). *Application deadline:* For fall admission, 1/15 for domestic students. Application fee: $75. Electronic applications accepted. *Financial support:* Application deadline: 3/1. *Unit head:* Dr. Maxin Shrayer, Chairperson, 617-552-3910. *Application contact:* Dr. Maxin Shrayer, Chairperson, 617-552-3910.

Brown University, Graduate School, Department of Slavic Languages, Providence, RI 02912. Offers Russian language and literature (AM); Slavic languages (AM); Slavic studies (PhD). *Degree requirements:* For master's, one foreign language; for doctorate, 2 foreign languages, thesis/dissertation, preliminary exam.

Carleton University, Faculty of Graduate Studies, Faculty of Public Affairs and Management, Institute of European and Russian Studies, Ottawa, ON K1S 5B6, Canada. Offers European and European Union studies (MA); European integration studies (Diploma); Russian, Eurasian and transition studies (MA). *Degree requirements:* For master's, one foreign language, thesis optional. *Entrance requirements:* For master's, honors degree or equivalent; 2 years of Russian, German or other central east European language. Additional exam requirements/recommendations for international students: Required—TOEFL. *Faculty research:* East-West relations, minority rights in Russia and Eastern Europe.

Columbia University, Graduate School of Arts and Sciences, Program in Russian, Eurasian and East European Regional Studies, New York, NY 10027. Offers MA. Part-time programs available.

Columbia University, School of International and Public Affairs, The East Central Europe Center, New York, NY 10027. Offers Certificate. Students must be enrolled in a separate graduate degree program at Columbia University. Electronic applications accepted. *Faculty research:* Ethnic politics, modern East Central European history, post-Communist economic and political transitions, East Central European language and literature.

Columbia University, School of International and Public Affairs, The Harriman Institute, New York, NY 10027. Offers Certificate. Students must be enrolled in a separate graduate degree program at Columbia University. Part-time programs available. *Degree requirements:* For Certificate, one foreign language, thesis. *Entrance requirements:* For degree, minimum 2 years of Russian. Electronic applications accepted.

Cornell University, Graduate School, Graduate Fields of Arts and Sciences, Field of History, Ithaca, NY 14853-0001. Offers African history (MA, PhD); American history (MA, PhD); ancient history (MA, PhD); early modern European history (MA, PhD); English history (MA, PhD); French history (MA, PhD); German history (MA, PhD); history of science (MA, PhD); Latin American history (MA, PhD); medieval Chinese history (MA, PhD); medieval history (MA, PhD); modern Chinese history (MA, PhD); modern European history (MA, PhD); modern Japanese history (MA, PhD); premodern Islamic history (MA, PhD); premodern Japanese history (MA, PhD); Renaissance history (MA, PhD); Russian history (MA, PhD); Southeast Asian history (MA, PhD). *Faculty:* 62 full-time (19 women). *Students:* 67 full-time (33 women); includes 10 minority (4 African Americans, 3 Asian Americans or Pacific Islanders, 3 Hispanic Americans), 24 international. Average age 31. 195 applicants, 7% accepted, 10 enrolled. In 2009, 11 master's, 3 doctorates awarded. Terminal master's awarded for partial completion of doctoral program. *Degree requirements:* For master's, thesis; for doctorate, 2 foreign languages, comprehensive exam, thesis/dissertation, 1 year of teaching experience. *Entrance requirements:* For master's and doctorate, GRE General Test, writing sample, 3 letters of recommendation. Additional exam requirements/recommendations for international students: Required—TOEFL (minimum score 550 paper-based; 213 computer-based; 77 iBT). *Application deadline:* For fall admission, 1/15 for domestic students. Application fee: $70. Electronic applications accepted. *Expenses:* Tuition: Full-time $29,500. Required fees: $70. Full-time tuition and fees vary according to degree level, program and student level. *Financial support:* In 2009–10, 54 students received support, including 8 fellowships with full tuition reimbursements available; research assistantships with full tuition reimbursements available, teaching assistantships with full tuition reimbursements available, institutionally sponsored loans, scholarships/grants, health care benefits, tuition waivers (full and partial), and unspecified assistantships also available. Financial award applicants required to submit FAFSA. *Unit head:* Director of Graduate Studies, 607-255-6738, Fax: 607-255-0469. *Application contact:* Graduate Field Assistant, 607-255-6738, Fax: 607-255-0469, E-mail: history_grad_info@cornell.edu.

Florida State University, The Graduate School, College of Social Sciences and Public Policy, Program in Russian and East European Studies, Tallahassee, FL 32306. Offers MA. Part-time programs available. *Students:* 4 full-time (3 women), 2 part-time (1 woman), 1 international. Average age 26. 9 applicants, 100% accepted, 1 enrolled. In 2009, 2 master's awarded. *Degree requirements:* For master's, one foreign language, comprehensive exam, thesis optional. *Entrance requirements:* For master's, GRE General Test, minimum GPA of 3.0. Additional exam requirements/recommendations for international students: Required—TOEFL (minimum score 550 paper-based; 213 computer-based; 80 iBT). *Application deadline:* For fall admission, 7/1 for domestic and international students; for spring admission, 11/1 for domestic and international students. Applications are processed on a rolling basis. Application fee: $30. Electronic applications accepted. *Expenses:* Tuition, state resident: full-time $7413. Tuition, nonresident: full-time $22,567. *Financial support:* In 2009–10, research assistantships with full tuition reimbursements (averaging $5,000 per year); fellowships, career-related internships or fieldwork, Federal Work-Study, institutionally sponsored loans, and unspecified assistantships also available. Financial award application deadline: 2/15; financial award applicants required to submit FAFSA. *Unit head:* Dr. Lee K. Metcalf, Director, 850-644-7327, Fax: 850-645-4981, E-mail: lmetcalf@fsu.edu. *Application contact:* Patty Lollis, Academic Program Specialist, 850-644-4418, Fax: 850-645-4981, E-mail: plollis@fsu.edu.

Georgetown University, Graduate School of Arts and Sciences, Program in Russian and East European Studies, Washington, DC 20057. Offers MA, MA/JD, MA/PhD. *Degree requirements:* For master's, one foreign language, comprehensive exam, thesis optional. *Entrance requirements:* For master's, GRE General Test. Additional exam requirements/recommendations for international students: Required—TOEFL. *Faculty research:* East-West trade.

The George Washington University, Elliott School of International Affairs, Program in European and Eurasian Studies, Washington, DC 20052. Offers MA, JD/MA, MBA/MA. Part-time and evening/weekend programs available. *Students:* 16 full-time (5 women), 9 part-time (5 women), 3 international. Average age 26. 45 applicants, 80% accepted, 9 enrolled. In 2009, 2 master's awarded. *Degree requirements:* For master's, one foreign language, capstone project. *Entrance requirements:* For master's, GRE General Test, 2 years (or the equivalent) of a modern European language or Russian, 2 semesters of introductory economics (macro or micro). Additional exam requirements/recommendations for international students: Required—TOEFL. *Application deadline:* For fall admission, 2/1 for domestic students; for spring admission, 10/1 for domestic students. Application fee: $60. Electronic applications accepted. *Financial support:* In 2009–10, 3 students received support; fellowships with tuition reimbursements available, research assistantships with tuition reimbursements available, career-related internships or fieldwork, Federal Work-Study, institutionally sponsored loans, and tuition waivers available. Financial award application deadline: 1/15; financial award applicants required to submit FAFSA. *Faculty research:* NATO, European economics, European history, European Union. *Unit head:* Hope Harrison, Director, 202-994-5439, Fax: 202-994-5436, E-mail: hopeharr@gwu.edu. *Application contact:* Jeff V. Miles, Director of Graduate Admissions, 202-994-7050, Fax: 202-994-9537, E-mail: esiagrad@gwu.edu.

Harvard University, Graduate School of Arts and Sciences, Committee on Regional Studies-Russia, Eastern Europe, and Central Asia, Cambridge, MA 02138. Offers AM. *Degree requirements:* For master's, one foreign language. *Entrance requirements:* For master's, GRE General Test. Additional exam requirements/recommendations for international students: Required—TOEFL. *Expenses:* Tuition: Full-time $33,696. Required fees: $1126. Full-time tuition and fees vary according to program. *Faculty research:* Strategic policy, ethnography and demography of U.S.S.R., non-Russian nationality language training.

Indiana University Bloomington, University Graduate School, College of Arts and Sciences, Russian and East European Institute, Bloomington, IN 47405-7000. Offers MA, Certificate, MBA/MA, MIS/MA, MLS/MA, MPA/MA. Part-time programs available. *Students:* 19 full-time (12 women), 2 part-time (both women); includes 1 minority (Asian American or Pacific Islander). Average age 27. 46 applicants, 54% accepted, 9 enrolled. In 2009, 11 master's awarded. *Degree requirements:* For master's, one foreign language, essay, proficiency and written exams; for Certificate, one foreign language, oral and proficiency exams. *Entrance requirements:* For master's, GRE General Test, minimum 2 years of college Russian (Russian area studies); for Certificate, GRE General Test. Additional exam requirements/recommendations for international students: Required—TOEFL. *Application deadline:* For fall admission, 1/15 priority date for domestic students, 12/15 for international students; for spring admission, 9/1 priority date for domestic students, 9/1 for international students. Applications are processed on a rolling basis. Application fee: $55 ($65 for international students). *Financial support:* Fellowships, research assistantships with full tuition reimbursements, teaching assistantships, career-related internships or fieldwork, Federal Work-Study, and institutionally sponsored loans available. Financial award application deadline: 2/15; financial award applicants required to submit FAFSA. *Faculty research:* Political and economic transition of former Soviet Union and eastern Europe, Russian and Soviet history, Slavic literature and linguistics, education and mass media of former Soviet Union and Eastern Europe. *Unit head:* David Ransel, Director, 812-855-7309, Fax: 812-855-6411, E-mail: ransel@indiana.edu. *Application contact:* Marianne Davis, Administrative Secretary, 812-855-3869, Fax: 812-855-6411, E-mail: marwdavi@indiana.edu.

La Salle University, School of Arts and Sciences, Central and Eastern European Studies Program, Philadelphia, PA 19141-1199. Offers MA. Part-time and evening/weekend programs available. *Degree requirements:* For master's, one foreign language, thesis or alternative. *Entrance requirements:* For master's, MAT. Additional exam requirements/recommendations for international students: Required—TOEFL. *Expenses:* Contact institution. *Faculty research:* Ukrainian culture, Russian studies, business in Central and Eastern European countries.

The Ohio State University, Graduate School, College of Humanities, Department of Slavic and East European Languages and Literatures, Program in Slavic and East European Studies, Columbus, OH 43210. Offers MA. *Degree requirements:* For master's, thesis optional. *Entrance requirements:* For master's, GRE General Test. Additional exam requirements/recommendations for international students: Required—TOEFL (paper-based 550; computer-based 213) or IELTS (7) or Michigan English Language Assessment Battery (82). Electronic applications accepted. *Expenses:* Tuition, state resident: full-time $10,683. Tuition, nonresident: full-time $25,923. Tuition and fees vary according to course load and program.

Stanford University, School of Humanities and Sciences, Center for Russian and East European Studies, Stanford, CA 94305-9991. Offers MA. *Degree requirements:* For master's, one foreign language. *Entrance requirements:* For master's, GRE General Test. Additional exam requirements/recommendations for international students: Required—TOEFL. Electronic applications accepted. *Expenses:* Tuition: Full-time $37,380; part-time $2760 per quarter. Required fees: $501.

University of Alberta, Faculty of Graduate Studies and Research, Department of Modern Languages and Cultural Studies, Edmonton, AB T6G 2E1, Canada. Offers applied linguistics (Germanic, Romance, Slavic) (MA); French language, literatures and linguistics (PhD); French language, literatures, and linguistics (MA); Germanic languages, literatures and linguistics (PhD); Germanic languages, literatures, and linguistics (MA); Italian studies (MA); Slavic languages and literatures (Russian, Ukrainian) (MA, PhD); Slavic linguistics (Russian, Ukrainian) (MA, PhD); Spanish and Latin American studies (MA, PhD); Ukrainian folklore (MA, PhD). Part-time programs available. *Faculty:* 33 full-time (15 women), 2 part-time/adjunct (1 woman). *Students:* 39 full-time (29 women), 13 part-time (12 women). 300 applicants, 10% accepted. In 2009, 12 master's, 2 doctorates awarded. *Degree requirements:* For master's, one foreign language, thesis; for doctorate, 2 foreign languages, comprehensive exam, thesis/dissertation. *Entrance requirements:* For master's and doctorate, 1 language other than English. Additional exam requirements/recommendations for international students: Required—Michigan English Language Assessment Battery or TOEFL (minimum score 550 paper-based; 213 computer-based). *Application deadline:* For fall admission, 7/1 for domestic and international students; for winter admission, 11/1 for domestic and international students; for spring admission, 3/1 for domestic students. Applications are processed on a rolling basis. Electronic applications accepted. Tuition and fees charges are reported in Canadian dollars. *Expenses:* Tuition, area resident: Full-time $4626 Canadian dollars; part-time $99.72 Canadian dollars per unit. International tuition: $8216 Canadian dollars full-time. Required fees: $3590 Canadian dollars; $99.72 Canadian dollars per unit. $215 Canadian dollars per term. *Financial support:* In 2009–10, 2 fellowships with full and partial tuition reimbursements (averaging $18,000 per year), 23 research assistantships with full and partial tuition reimbursements (averaging $10,450 per year), 21 teaching assistantships with full and partial tuition reimbursements (averaging $12,572 per year) were awarded; scholarships/grants also available. Support available to part-time students. Financial award application deadline: 3/31. *Faculty research:* Russian/Ukrainian studies; German studies; contemporary Latin American, French and Francophone studies; Italian studies. *Unit head:* Dr. Don Bruce, Chair, 780-492-3273, Fax: 780-492-9106. *Application contact:* Jane Wilson, Graduate Programs Secretary, 780-492-3273, Fax: 780-492-9106, E-mail: mlcsgrad@ualberta.ca.

The University of British Columbia, Faculty of Arts and Faculty of Graduate Studies, Department of Central, Eastern and Northern European Studies, Vancouver, BC V6T2Z1, Canada. Offers Germanic studies (MA, PhD). Part-time programs available. *Degree requirements:* For master's, one foreign language, thesis optional, exam; for doctorate, comprehensive exam, thesis/dissertation. *Entrance requirements:* For master's, BA in German; for doctorate, MA in German. Additional exam requirements/recommendations for international students: Required—TOEFL (minimum score 550 paper-based; 213 computer-based). Electronic applications accepted. *Faculty research:* Second language acquisition, media theory, performance theory, gender studies, cultural studies.

University of Illinois at Urbana–Champaign, Graduate College, College of Liberal Arts and Sciences, Russian, East European and Eurasian Center, Champaign, IL 61820. Offers MA. *Students:* 13 full-time (4 women). 16 applicants, 50% accepted, 6 enrolled. In 2009, 3 master's awarded. *Entrance requirements:* For master's, GRE, writing sample. Additional exam requirements/recommendations for international students: Required—TOEFL (minimum score 550 paper-based; 213 computer-based). *Application deadline:* Applications are processed on a rolling basis. Application fee: $60 ($75 for international students). Electronic applications accepted. *Financial support:* In 2009–10, 10 fellowships, 1 teaching assistantship were awarded; research assistantships, tuition waivers (full and partial) also available. *Unit head:* Richard Tempest, Director, 217-244-4720, Fax: 217-333-7310, E-mail: rtempest@illinois.edu. *Application contact:* Theresa Jo Schafroth, Office Manager, 217-333-3278, Fax: 217-333-1582, E-mail: schafrot@illinois.edu.

The University of Kansas, Graduate Studies, College of Liberal Arts and Sciences, Center for Russian, East European and Eurasian Studies, Lawrence, KS 66045. Offers MA. Part-time programs available. *Faculty:* 38 full-time (17 women), 4 part-time/adjunct (1 woman). *Students:* 9 full-time (2 women), 1 part-time (0 women), 1 international. Average age 28. 18 applicants, 83% accepted, 4 enrolled. In 2009, 1 master's awarded. *Degree requirements:* For master's, one foreign language, comprehensive exam, interdisciplinary capstone research seminar. *Entrance requirements:* For master's, GRE General Test, 3 letters of recommendation. Additional exam requirements/recommendations for international students: Required—TOEFL. *Application deadline:* For fall admission, 1/1 priority date for domestic and international students. Application fee: $45 ($55 for international students). Electronic applications accepted. *Expenses:* Tuition, state resident: full-time $6492; part-time $270.50 per credit hour. Tuition, nonresident: full-time $15,510; part-time $646.25 per credit hour. Required fees: $847; $70.56 per credit hour. Tuition and fees vary according to course load and program. *Financial support:* Fellowships with full tuition reimbursements, research assistantships with partial tuition reimbursements, scholarships/grants available. Financial award application deadline: 1/31; financial award applicants required to submit FAFSA. *Faculty research:* Russian and East Central European history and culture; Ukrainian, Russian, and Central Asian domestic politics and international security; Slavic languages, linguistics, and literatures. *Unit head:* Dr. Edith Clowes, Director, 785-864-4236, Fax: 785-864-3800, E-mail: crees@ku.edu. *Application contact:* Dr. Eve Levin, Associate Director, 785-864-4236, Fax: 785-864-4236, E-mail: evelevin@ku.edu.

University of Michigan, Horace H. Rackham School of Graduate Studies, College of Literature, Science, and the Arts, Center for Russian and East European Studies, Ann Arbor, MI 48109-1106. Offers AM, Certificate, JD/AM, MBA/AM, MPP/AM. Part-time programs available. *Faculty:* 67 full-time (24 women), 8 part-time/adjunct (6 women). *Students:* 14 full-time (8 women). Average age 27. 37 applicants, 59% accepted, 6 enrolled. In 2009, 4 master's, 1 other advanced degree awarded. *Degree requirements:* For master's and Certificate, one foreign language, thesis. *Entrance requirements:* For master's, GRE General Test. Additional exam requirements/recommendations for international students: Required—TOEFL. *Application deadline:* For fall admission, 1/15 for domestic and international students. Application fee: $60 ($75 for international students). Electronic applications accepted. *Expenses:* Tuition, state resident: full-time $17,286; part-time $1099 per credit hour. Tuition, nonresident: full-time $34,944; part-time $2080 per credit hour. Required fees: $95 per semester. Tuition and fees vary according to course load, degree level and program. *Financial support:* In 2009–10, 6 students received support, including 3 fellowships with full and partial tuition reimbursements available (averaging $15,000 per year), 3 teaching assistantships with full tuition reimbursements available (averaging $8,000 per year); scholarships/grants also available. Financial award application deadline: 2/1. *Faculty research:* Russia; East Europe; Eurasia; Central Asia; Caucasus. *Unit head:* Dr. Douglas Taylor Northrop, Director, 734-764-0351, Fax: 734-763-4765, E-mail: crees@umich.edu. *Application contact:* Julie E. Claus, Student Services Associate, 734-764-0351, Fax: 734-763-4765, E-mail: crees.admissions@umich.edu.

The University of North Carolina at Chapel Hill, Graduate School, Curriculum in Russian and East European Studies, Chapel Hill, NC 27599. Offers MA. Part-time programs available. *Degree requirements:* For master's, one foreign language, thesis. *Entrance requirements:* For master's, GRE General Test. Additional exam requirements/recommendations for international students: Required—TOEFL. Electronic applications accepted. *Faculty research:* Language, area studies, social sciences, sciences, professional schools.

University of Pittsburgh, University Center for International Studies, Pittsburgh, PA 15260. Offers African studies (Certificate); Asian studies (Certificate); European Union studies (Certificate); global studies (Certificate); Latin American studies (Certificate); Russian and East European studies (Certificate); West European studies (Certificate). *Students:* 332 (129 women); includes 31 minority (7 African Americans, 10 Asian Americans or Pacific Islanders, 14 Hispanic Americans), 136 international. In 2009, 59 Certificates awarded. *Degree requirements:* For Certificate, one foreign language, study abroad. *Application deadline:* Applications are processed on a rolling basis. *Expenses:* Tuition, state resident: full-time $16,402; part-time $665 per credit. Tuition, nonresident: full-time $28,694; part-time $1175 per credit. Required fees: $690; $175 per term. Tuition and fees vary according to program. *Unit head:* Lawrence F. Feick, Director, 412-648-7374, Fax: 412-624-4672, E-mail: feick@pitt.edu. *Application contact:* Information Contact, 412-624-4141, E-mail: graduate@pitt.edu.

University of Saskatchewan, College of Graduate Studies and Research, College of Arts and Sciences, Department of Languages and Linguistics, Saskatoon, SK S7N 5A2, Canada. Offers MA. *Faculty:* 10. *Degree requirements:* For master's, 2 foreign languages, thesis. *Entrance requirements:* Additional exam requirements/recommendations for international students: Required—TOEFL (minimum score 80 iBT); Recommended—IELTS (minimum score 6.5). *Application deadline:* For fall admission, 7/1 priority date for domestic students. Applications are processed on a rolling basis. Application fee: $75. Electronic applications accepted. Tuition and fees charges are reported in Canadian dollars. *Expenses:* Tuition, area resident: Full-time $3000 Canadian dollars; part-time $500 Canadian dollars per term. Required fees: $700 Canadian dollars; $100 Canadian dollars per term. *Financial support:* Fellowships, research assistantships, teaching assistantships available. Financial award application deadline: 1/31. *Unit head:* Dr. Richard Julien, Head, 306-966-6920, Fax: 306-966-5782, E-mail: richard.julien@usask.ca. *Application contact:* Dr. Alex Sokalski, Graduate Chair, 306-966-5648, Fax: 306-966-5782.

The University of Texas at Austin, Graduate School, College of Liberal Arts, Center for Russian, East European, and Eurasian Studies, Austin, TX 78712-1111. Offers MA, JD/MA, MBA/MA, MP Aff/MA. Part-time programs available. *Degree requirements:* For master's, one foreign language, report or thesis. *Entrance requirements:* For master's, GRE General Test, 3 years of formal language training or equivalent, minimum GPA of 3.0. Electronic applications accepted. *Faculty research:* East European gypsies, elite transformation and democracy in Eastern Europe, elite partisanship as an intervening variable in Russian politics, post-Soviet youth in Russia.

University of Toronto, School of Graduate Studies, Social Sciences Division, Centre for European, Russian and Eurasian Studies, Toronto, ON M5S 1A1, Canada. Offers MA. *Degree requirements:* For master's, one foreign language, language proficiency test. *Entrance requirements:* For master's, minimum B+ average in final year, coursework in Russian/East European subjects, 2 years of study in a relevant language.

University of Washington, Graduate School, College of Arts and Sciences, Henry M. Jackson School of International Studies, Russian, East European and Central Asian Studies Program, Seattle, WA 98195. Offers Central Asian studies (MAIS); East European studies (MAIS); Russian studies (MAIS). *Faculty:* 59 full-time (24 women). *Students:* 23 full-time (12 women); includes 3 minority (1 African American, 1 Asian American or Pacific Islander, 1 Hispanic American), 1 international. 32 applicants, 91% accepted, 9 enrolled. In 2009, 7 master's awarded. *Degree requirements:* For master's, one foreign language, thesis. *Entrance requirements:* For master's, GRE General Test, 2 years of relevant language, minimum GPA of 3.0. Additional exam requirements/recommendations for international students: Required—TOEFL (minimum score 500 paper-based; 213 computer-based; 92 iBT), or IELTS. *Application deadline:* For fall admission, 12/30 for domestic students, 12/1 for international students. Application fee: $75. Electronic applications accepted. *Financial support:* In 2009–10, 8 fellowships with full tuition reimbursements were awarded; research assistantships, teaching assistantships, career-related internships or fieldwork, Federal Work-Study, institutionally sponsored loans, and summer language study awards also available. Financial award application deadline: 12/30. *Unit head:* Prof. James Augerot, Chair, 206-543-6848, E-mail: bigjim@u.washington.edu. *Application contact:* 206-543-6001, Fax: 206-616-3170, E-mail: jsisinfo@u.washington.edu.

Yale University, Graduate School of Arts and Sciences, Department of Slavic Languages and Literatures, New Haven, CT 06520. Offers medieval Slavic literature and philology (PhD); Polish literature (PhD); Russian literature (PhD); Slavic languages and literatures and film studies (PhD). *Degree requirements:* For doctorate, 3 foreign languages, thesis/dissertation. *Entrance requirements:* For doctorate, GRE General Test.

Yale University, Graduate School of Arts and Sciences, Program in Russian and East European Studies, New Haven, CT 06520. Offers MA. *Degree requirements:* For master's, 2 foreign languages. *Entrance requirements:* For master's, GRE General Test.

Ethnic Studies

Cornell University, Graduate School, Graduate Fields of Arts and Sciences, Field of Sociology, Ithaca, NY 14853-0001. Offers economy and society (MA, PhD); gender and life course (MA, PhD); methodology (MA, PhD); organizations (MA, PhD); policy analysis (MA, PhD); political sociology/social movements (MA, PhD); racial and ethnic relations (MA, PhD); social networks (MA, PhD); social psychology (MA, PhD); social stratification (MA, PhD). *Faculty:* 41 full-time (17 women). *Students:* 39 full-time (19 women); includes 4 minority (all Asian Americans or Pacific Islanders), 10 international. Average age 31. 153 applicants, 8% accepted, 7 enrolled. In 2009, 2 master's, 2 doctorates awarded. Terminal master's awarded for partial completion of doctoral program. *Degree requirements:* For master's, thesis; for doctorate, thesis/dissertation, 1 year of teaching experience. *Entrance requirements:* For master's and doctorate, GRE General Test, 2 letters of recommendation, writing sample. Additional exam requirements/recommendations for international students: Required—TOEFL (minimum score 550 paper-based; 213 computer-based; 77 iBT). *Application deadline:* For fall admission, 1/15 for domestic students. Application fee: $70. Electronic applications accepted. *Expenses:* Tuition: Full-time $29,500. Required fees: $70. Full-time tuition and fees vary according to degree level, program and student level. *Financial support:* In 2009–10, 32 students received support, including 6 fellowships with full tuition reimbursements available; research assistantships with full tuition reimbursements available, teaching assistantships with full tuition reimbursements available, institutionally sponsored loans, scholarships/grants, health care benefits, tuition waivers (full and partial), and unspecified assistantships also available. Financial award applicants required to submit FAFSA. *Faculty research:* Comparative societal analysis, work and family, simulations, social class and mobility, racial segregation and inequality. *Unit head:* Director of Graduate Studies, 607-255-4266. *Application contact:* Graduate Field Assistant, 607-255-4266, E-mail: sociology@cornell.edu.

Minnesota State University Mankato, College of Graduate Studies, College of Social and Behavioral Sciences, Department of Ethnic Studies, Mankato, MN 56001. Offers MS, Certificate. *Students:* 4 full-time (3 women), 9 part-time (3 women). *Application deadline:* For fall admission, 7/1 for domestic students, 5/1 for international students; for winter admission, 11/1 for domestic students; for spring admission, 10/1 for international students. Applications are processed on a rolling basis. Electronic applications accepted. *Expenses:* Tuition, state resident: full-time $5364. Tuition, nonresident: full-time $8314. *Unit head:* Dr. Wayne Allen, Graduate Coordinator, 507-389-1185. *Application contact:* Dr. Wayne Allen, Graduate Coordinator, 507-389-1185.

Northern Arizona University, Graduate College, College of Social and Behavioral Sciences, Ethnic Studies Program, Flagstaff, AZ 86011. Offers Graduate Certificate. *Faculty:* 1 (woman) full-time. *Students:* 1 (woman) part-time. Average age 25. 1 applicant, 100% accepted, 1 enrolled. *Entrance requirements:* For degree, bachelor's degree with minimum GPA of 2.5. Additional exam requirements/recommendations for international students: Required—TOEFL (minimum score 550 paper-based; 213 computer-based; 80 iBT), IELTS (minimum score 7), or a bachelor's degree from an English-speaking university and demonstrated proficiency. *Application deadline:* Applications are processed on a rolling basis. Application fee: $65. Electronic applications accepted. *Unit head:* Dr. Sara Aleman, Director, 928-523-3886, Fax: 928-522-6777, E-mail: sara.aleman@nau.edu. *Application contact:* Dr. Sara Aleman, Director, 928-523-3886, Fax: 928-522-6777, E-mail: sara.aleman@nau.edu.

Norwich University, School of Graduate and Continuing Studies, Program in Military History, Northfield, VT 05663. Offers race and gender in military history (MA); U. S. military history (MA). Evening/weekend programs available. *Faculty:* 33 part-time/adjunct (2 women). *Students:* 531 full-time (85 women); includes 30 minority (3 African Americans, 6 American Indian/Alaska Native, 6 Asian Americans or Pacific Islanders, 15 Hispanic Americans). Average age 42. 736 applicants, 80% accepted, 531 enrolled. In 2009, 503 master's awarded. *Entrance requirements:* For master's, minimum undergraduate GPA of 2.75. Additional exam requirements/recommendations for international students: Required—TOEFL (minimum score 550 paper-based; 212 computer-based; 83 iBT). *Application deadline:* For fall admission, 8/10 for domestic and international students; for winter admission, 11/7 for domestic and international students; for spring admission, 2/6 for domestic and international students. Application fee: $50. Electronic applications accepted. Full-time tuition and fees vary according to course level and course load. *Financial support:* Scholarships/grants available. Financial award applicants required to submit FAFSA. *Unit head:* Dr. James Ehrman, Program Director, 802-485-2567, Fax: 802-485-2533. *Application contact:* Lars Nielsen, Administrative Director, 802-485-2853, Fax: 802-485-2533, E-mail: lnielsen@norwich.edu.

San Francisco State University, Division of Graduate Studies, College of Ethnic Studies, Program in Ethnic Studies, San Francisco, CA 94132-1722. Offers MA.

United Theological Seminary of the Twin Cities, Professional Program, New Brighton, MN 55112-2598. Offers advanced theological studies (Diploma); justice and peace studies (M Div, MA); leadership toward racial justice (MA, Certificate); leadership towards racial justice (M Div); Methodist studies (M Div, MA, Certificate); ministry (D Min); ministry renewal and professional development (Certificate); pastoral care and counseling (M Div, MA, MARL); religion and theology (MA); theological and religious studies (Certificate); theology and the arts (M Div, MA); urban ministry (M Div, MA, MARL); women's studies: religion, theology and ministry (MA); women's studies: religions, theology and ministry (M Div). *Accreditation:* ACIPE; ATS. Part-time and evening/weekend programs available. *Faculty:* 9 full-time (6 women), 22 part-time/adjunct (10 women). *Students:* 49 full-time (34 women), 105 part-time (68 women). Average age 47. 41 applicants, 98% accepted, 34 enrolled. In 2009, 24 first professional degrees, 5 master's, 2 doctorates, 2 other advanced degrees awarded. *Degree requirements:* For master's, thesis; for doctorate, comprehensive exam, thesis/dissertation; for M Div, integrative notebook, spiritual chronicle. *Entrance requirements:* For M Div and master's, minimum GPA of 2.75; strong analytical, reflective thinking and writing skills; vocational and academic goals compatible with those of Seminary; for doctorate, M Div or equivalent, minimum GPA of 3.0, 3 years experience in professional ministry; for other advanced degree, BA or equivalent life experience; strong analytical, reflective thinking and writing skills (Certificate); proficiency in English language, previous study of theology at a theological school, recommendation of student's denomination (Diploma). Additional exam requirements/recommendations for inter-

Ethnic Studies

United Theological Seminary of the Twin Cities (continued)
national students: Required—TOEFL (minimum score 550 paper-based). *Application deadline:* For fall admission, 7/1 priority date for domestic students, 11/1 priority date for international students; for winter admission, 11/1 priority date for domestic students; for spring admission, 11/15 priority date for domestic students. Applications are processed on a rolling basis. Application fee: $50. *Expenses:* Tuition: Full-time $11,502; part-time $426 per credit hour. Required fees: $295; $155 per term. One-time fee: $25. Tuition and fees vary according to course load, degree level and program. *Financial support:* In 2009–10, 120 students received support. Career-related internships or fieldwork, institutionally sponsored loans, and scholarships/grants available. Support available to part-time students. Financial award application deadline: 5/1; financial award applicants required to submit FAFSA. *Unit head:* Dr. Richard D. Weis, Dean of the Seminary, 651-255-6108 Ext. 108, Fax: 651-633-4315, E-mail: rweis@unitedseminary.edu. *Application contact:* Rev. Glen Herrington-Hall, Director of Admissions, 651-255-6107 Ext. 107, Fax: 651-633-4315, E-mail: gherrington-hall@unitedseminary.edu.

Université Laval, Faculty of Letters, Department of History, Programs in Ethnology of French-Speaking People in North America, Québec, QC G1K 7P4, Canada. Offers MA, PhD. Terminal master's awarded for partial completion of doctoral program. *Degree requirements:* For master's, thesis; for doctorate, comprehensive exam, thesis/dissertation. *Entrance requirements:* For master's and doctorate, English exam (comprehension of written English), knowledge of French. Electronic applications accepted.

University of California, Berkeley, Graduate Division, College of Letters and Science, Group in Ethnic Studies, Berkeley, CA 94720-1500. Offers PhD. *Faculty:* 17 full-time. *Students:* 52 full-time (31 women). Average age 34. 101 applicants, 8 enrolled. In 2009, 3 doctorates awarded. *Degree requirements:* For doctorate, one foreign language, thesis/dissertation, qualifying exam. *Entrance requirements:* For doctorate, minimum GPA of 3.0, 3 letters of recommendation. *Application deadline:* For fall admission, 12/15 for domestic students. Application fee: $70 ($90 for international students). *Financial support:* Fellowships with full tuition reimbursements, research assistantships with partial tuition reimbursements, teaching assistantships with partial tuition reimbursements, unspecified assistantships available. *Faculty research:* Gender and race, Asian American visual art, racial theory and politics, Chicana/o literature and visual arts, history of Native North Americans. *Unit head:* Prof. Thomas Biolsi, Chair, 510-643-0796, E-mail: ethnicst@berkeley.edu. *Application contact:* Information Contact, 510-642-6643, Fax: 510-642-6456, E-mail: ethnicst@berkeley.edu.

University of California, Riverside, Graduate Division, Department of Ethnic Studies, Riverside, CA 92521. Offers PhD. *Faculty:* 12 full-time (4 women). *Students:* 4 full-time (3 women); includes 2 African Americans, 1 Hispanic American. Average age 29. 46 applicants, 28% accepted, 4 enrolled. *Degree requirements:* For doctorate, variable foreign language requirement, comprehensive exam, thesis/dissertation. *Entrance requirements:* For doctorate, GRE, writing sample. Additional exam requirements/recommendations for international students: Required—TOEFL (minimum score 550 paper-based; 213 computer-based; 80 iBT). *Application deadline:* For fall admission, 5/1 for domestic students, 2/1 for international students. Applications are processed on a rolling basis. Application fee: $70 ($85 for international students). Electronic applications accepted. *Expenses:* Contact institution. *Financial support:* In 2009–10, 4 students received support, including 4 fellowships with full tuition reimbursements available (averaging $10,000 per year), 4 teaching assistantships (averaging $16,500 per year). Financial award application deadline: 1/5; financial award applicants required to submit FAFSA. *Faculty research:* The political economy of race, class, gender, sexuality, cultural production, the state, law, criminal justice and grass roots responses. *Unit head:* Dr. Dylan Rodriguez, Chair, 951-827-4707, E-mail: dylan.rodriguez@ucr.edu. *Application contact:* Andrea Gonzales, Graduate Program Coordinator, 951-827-1821, E-mail: andrea.gonzales@ucr.edu.

University of California, San Diego, Office of Graduate Studies, Department of Ethnic Studies, La Jolla, CA 92093. Offers MA, PhD. Electronic applications accepted.

Washington State University, Graduate School, College of Liberal Arts, Program in American Studies, Pullman, WA 99164. Offers ethnic studies (MA, PhD); feminist studies (MA, PhD); history (MA, PhD); literature (MA, PhD). Part-time programs available. *Faculty:* 35. *Students:* 23 full-time (14 women), 4 part-time (2 women); includes 17 minority (5 African Americans, 4 American Indian/Alaska Native, 4 Asian Americans or Pacific Islanders, 4 Hispanic Americans), 2 international. Average age 35. 55 applicants, 7% accepted, 3 enrolled. In 2009, 1 master's, 3 doctorates awarded. *Degree requirements:* For master's, one foreign language, comprehensive exam (for some programs), thesis optional, oral exam; for doctorate, one foreign language, comprehensive exam (for some programs), thesis/dissertation, oral exam. *Entrance requirements:* For master's, GRE General Test, * Send to the Graduate School an official application form and official college transcripts sent directly from each institution attended. * Send to the American Studies program: A 3 to 5 page statement of purpose describing your areas of interest and why the program minimum GPA of 3.0, writing sample, 3 letters of recommendation; for doctorate, GRE General Test, * Send to the Graduate School an official application form and official college transcripts sent directly from each institution attended. * Send to the American Studies program: A 3 to 5 page statement of purpose describing your areas of interest and why the program minimum GPA of 3.0, writing sample, 3 letters of recommendation. Additional exam requirements/recommendations for international students: Required—TOEFL, IELTS. *Application deadline:* For fall admission, 1/10 priority date for domestic and international students; for spring admission, 7/1 priority date for domestic and international students. Applications are processed on a rolling basis. Application fee: $50. *Financial support:* In 2009–10, 1 fellowship (averaging $6,950 per year), 3 research assistantships with full and partial tuition reimbursements (averaging $14,634 per year), 17 teaching assistantships with full and partial tuition reimbursements (averaging $13,383 per year) were awarded; career-related internships or fieldwork, Federal Work-Study, institutionally sponsored loans, health care benefits, tuition waivers (partial), and teaching associateships also available. Financial award application deadline: 2/15; financial award applicants required to submit FAFSA. *Faculty research:* The American West in multicultural perspective; nineteenth century historical, literary, and cultural studies; comparative American ethnic literatures and cultures; American cultures and the environment; American rhetoric. *Unit head:* Dr. Rory J. Ong, Director, 509-335-1560, E-mail: rjong@mail.wsu.edu. *Application contact:* Graduate School Admissions, 800-GRADWSU, Fax: 509-335-1949, E-mail: gradsch@wsu.edu.

Folklore

George Mason University, College of Humanities and Social Sciences, Department of English, Fairfax, VA 22030. Offers creative writing (MFA); English (MA); folklore studies (Certificate); linguistics (PhD); professional writing and rhetoric (Certificate); teaching English as a second language (Certificate). *Faculty:* 82 full-time (47 women), 48 part-time/adjunct (29 women). *Students:* 72 full-time (51 women), 228 part-time (172 women); includes 39 minority (12 African Americans, 3 American Indian/Alaska Native, 20 Asian Americans or Pacific Islanders, 4 Hispanic Americans), 10 international. Average age 31. 314 applicants, 57% accepted, 86 enrolled. In 2009, 63 master's, 12 other advanced degrees awarded. *Degree requirements:* For master's, thesis (for some programs), proficiency in a foreign language by course work or translation test. *Entrance requirements:* For master's, 30 credits in graduate English courses, minimum undergraduate GPA of 3.0, 2 letters of recommendation. Additional exam requirements/recommendations for international students: Required—TOEFL. *Application deadline:* For fall admission, 3/15 priority date for domestic students; for spring admission, 10/15 for domestic students. Application fee: $75. Electronic applications accepted. *Expenses:* Tuition, state resident: full-time $7568; part-time $315.33 per credit hour. Tuition, nonresident: full-time $21,704; part-time $904.33 per credit hour. Required fees: $2184; $91 per credit hour. *Financial support:* In 2009–10, 49 students received support, including 1 fellowship with full tuition reimbursement available (averaging $18,000 per year), 3 research assistantships with full and partial tuition reimbursements available (averaging $9,443 per year), 46 teaching assistantships with full and partial tuition reimbursements available (averaging $10,509 per year); Federal Work-Study, scholarships/grants, unspecified assistantships, and health care benefits (full-time research or teaching assistantship recipients) also available. Support available to part-time students. Financial award application deadline: 3/1; financial award applicants required to submit FAFSA. *Faculty research:* Literature, professional writing and editing, writing of fiction or poetry. Total annual research expenditures: $1.2 million. *Unit head:* Robert Matz, Chair, 703-993-1170, E-mail: rmatz@gmu.edu. *Application contact:* Denise Albanese, Graduate Director, 703-993-1175, E-mail: dalbanes@gmu.edu.

The George Washington University, Columbian College of Arts and Sciences, Department of American Studies, Washington, DC 20052. Offers American studies (PhD); folklife (MA); historic preservation (MA); material culture (MA). Part-time and evening/weekend programs available. *Faculty:* 10 full-time (4 women), 5 part-time/adjunct (4 women). *Students:* 24 full-time (16 women), 26 part-time (14 women); includes 7 minority (5 African Americans, 1 Asian American or Pacific Islander, 1 Hispanic American), 3 international. Average age 31. 116 applicants, 43% accepted, 17 enrolled. In 2009, 10 master's, 4 doctorates awarded. Terminal master's awarded for partial completion of doctoral program. *Degree requirements:* For master's, comprehensive exam; for doctorate, one foreign language, thesis/dissertation, general exam. *Entrance requirements:* For master's and doctorate, GRE General Test, minimum GPA of 3.0. Additional exam requirements/recommendations for international students: Required—TOEFL (minimum score 550 paper-based; 213 computer-based; 80 iBT). *Application deadline:* For fall admission, 1/15 priority date for domestic and international students; for spring admission, 10/1 for domestic students. Application fee: $60. *Financial support:* In 2009–10, 22 students received support; fellowships, research assistantships, teaching assistantships, career-related internships or fieldwork, Federal Work-Study, institutionally sponsored loans, and tuition waivers available. Financial award application deadline: 1/15. *Unit head:* James A. Miller, Chair, 202-994-6743, E-mail: jam@gwu.edu. *Application contact:* Information Contact, 202-994-6070, Fax: 202-994-8651, E-mail: amst@gwu.edu.

The George Washington University, Columbian College of Arts and Sciences, Department of Anthropology, Concentration in Folklife, Washington, DC 20052. Offers MA. *Degree requirements:* For master's, comprehensive exam, thesis or alternative. *Entrance requirements:* For master's, GRE General Test, minimum GPA of 3.0.

Indiana University Bloomington, University Graduate School, College of Arts and Sciences, Department of Folklore and Ethnomusicology, Bloomington, IN 47408-3890. Offers folklore (MA, PhD), including ethnomusicology. Part-time programs available. *Faculty:* 12 full-time (5 women), 11 part-time/adjunct (6 women). *Students:* 110 full-time (69 women), 5 part-time (all women); includes 24 minority (13 African Americans, 1 American Indian/Alaska Native, 5 Asian Americans or Pacific Islanders, 5 Hispanic Americans), 21 international. Average age 34. 74 applicants, 61% accepted, 17 enrolled. In 2009, 14 master's, 9 doctorates awarded. *Degree requirements:* For master's, one foreign language, comprehensive exam, thesis or alternative, project or thesis; for doctorate, 2 foreign languages, comprehensive exam, thesis/dissertation. *Entrance requirements:* For master's and doctorate, GRE General Test, minimum GPA of 3.0. Additional exam requirements/recommendations for international students: Required—TOEFL (minimum score 550 paper-based; 213 computer-based; 79 iBT). *Application deadline:* For fall admission, 1/15 for domestic students, 12/1 for international students. Application fee: $55 ($65 for international students). Electronic applications accepted. *Financial support:* In 2009–10, 38 students received support, including 9 fellowships with full tuition reimbursements available (averaging $18,000 per year), 23 research assistantships with full tuition reimbursements available (averaging $11,500 per year), 22 teaching assistantships with full tuition reimbursements available (averaging $12,500 per year); Federal Work-Study and unspecified assistantships also available. Financial award application deadline: 3/1; financial award applicants required to submit FAFSA. *Faculty research:* Narrative, performance studies, material culture, popular culture, music. *Unit head:* Dr. Portia Maultsby, Chair, 812-855-0395, Fax: 812-855-4008, E-mail: maultsby@indiana.edu. *Application contact:* Christopher Roush, Graduate Secretary, 812-855-0389, Fax: 812-855-4008, E-mail: croush@indiana.edu.

Memorial University of Newfoundland, School of Graduate Studies, Department of Folklore, St. John's, NL A1C 5S7, Canada. Offers MA, PhD. Part-time programs available. *Degree requirements:* For master's, thesis optional; for doctorate, one foreign language, comprehensive exam, thesis/dissertation, oral thesis defense. *Entrance requirements:* For master's, 36 credit hours of course work in folklore, humanities, or social studies; honors degree; for doctorate, MA in folklore or related field. Electronic applications accepted. *Faculty research:* Narrative, folklife, belief theory, methodology, popular culture.

University of Alberta, Faculty of Graduate Studies and Research, Department of Modern Languages and Cultural Studies, Edmonton, AB T6G 2E1, Canada. Offers applied linguistics (Germanic, Romance, Slavic) (MA); French language, literatures and linguistics (PhD); French language, literatures, and linguistics (MA); Germanic languages, literatures and linguistics (PhD); Germanic languages, literatures, and linguistics (MA); Italian studies (MA); Slavic languages and literatures (Russian, Ukrainian) (MA, PhD); Slavic linguistics (Russian, Ukrainian) (MA, PhD); Spanish and Latin American studies (MA, PhD); Ukrainian folklore (MA, PhD). Part-time programs available. *Faculty:* 33 full-time (15 women), 2 part-time/adjunct (1 woman). *Students:* 39 full-time (29 women), 13 part-time (12 women). 300 applicants, 10% accepted. In 2009, 12 master's, 2 doctorates awarded. *Degree requirements:* For master's, one foreign language, thesis; for doctorate, 2 foreign languages, comprehensive exam, thesis/dissertation. *Entrance requirements:* For master's and doctorate, 1 language other than English. Additional exam requirements/recommendations for international students: Required—Michigan English Language Assessment Battery or TOEFL (minimum score 550 paper-based; 213 computer-based). *Application deadline:* For fall admission, 7/1 for domestic and international students; for winter admission, 11/1 for domestic and international students; for spring admission, 3/1 for domestic students. Applications are processed on a rolling basis. Electronic applications accepted. Tuition and fees charges are reported in Canadian dollars. *Expenses:* Tuition, area resident: Full-time $4626 Canadian dollars; part-time $99.72 Canadian dollars per unit. International tuition: $8216 Canadian dollars full-time. Required fees: $3590 Canadian dollars; $99.72 Canadian dollars per unit. $215 Canadian dollars per term. *Financial support:* In 2009–10, 2 fellowships with full and partial tuition reimbursements (averaging $18,000 per year), 23 research assistantships with full and partial tuition reimbursements (averaging $10,450 per year), 21 teaching assistantships with full and partial tuition reimbursements (averaging $12,572 per year) were awarded; scholarships/grants also available. Support available to part-time students. Financial award application deadline: 3/31. *Faculty research:* Russian/Ukrainian studies; German studies; contemporary Latin American, French and Francophone studies; Italian studies. *Unit head:* Dr. Don Bruce, Chair, 780-492-3273, Fax: 780-492-9106.

Application contact: Jane Wilson, Graduate Programs Secretary, 780-492-3273, Fax: 780-492-9106, E-mail: mlcsgrad@ualberta.ca.

University of California, Berkeley, Graduate Division, College of Letters and Science, Department of Anthropology, Group in Folklore, Berkeley, CA 94720-1500. Offers MA. *Students:* 9 full-time (7 women). Average age 29. 18 applicants, 4 enrolled. In 2009, 5 master's awarded. *Entrance requirements:* For master's, GRE General Test, minimum GPA of 3.0, 3 letters of recommendation. *Application deadline:* For fall admission, 12/15 for domestic students. Application fee: $70 ($90 for international students). *Unit head:* Prof. Charles Briggs, Chair, 510-643-7934, E-mail: ucbfolklore@berkeley.edu. *Application contact:* Information Contact, 510-643-7934, E-mail: ucbfolklore@berkeley.edu.

University of Louisiana at Lafayette, College of Liberal Arts, Department of English, Lafayette, LA 70504. Offers British and American literature (MA), including creative writing, folklore, rhetoric; creative writing (PhD); literature (PhD); rhetoric (PhD). Part-time programs available. Terminal master's awarded for partial completion of doctoral program. *Degree requirements:* For master's, one foreign language, thesis or alternative; for doctorate, 2 foreign languages, comprehensive exam, thesis/dissertation. *Entrance requirements:* For master's, GRE General Test, minimum GPA of 2.75; for doctorate, GRE General Test, minimum GPA of 3.0. Additional exam requirements/recommendations for international students: Required—TOEFL (minimum score 550 paper-based; 213 computer-based). Electronic applications accepted. *Faculty research:* Composition theory, Southern literature, medieval literature.

The University of North Carolina at Chapel Hill, Graduate School, College of Arts and Sciences, Curriculum in Folklore, Chapel Hill, NC 27599. Offers MA. *Degree requirements:* For master's, one foreign language, comprehensive exam, thesis. *Entrance requirements:* For master's, GRE General Test, minimum GPA of 3.0, writing sample. Electronic applications accepted. *Faculty research:* Public folklore, politics of culture, folklore and feminist theory, belief and health systems, Southern culture.

University of Oregon, Graduate School, College of Arts and Sciences, Folklore Program, Eugene, OR 97403. Offers independent study: folklore (MA, MS). Part-time programs available. *Degree requirements:* For master's, one foreign language, project or thesis. *Entrance requirements:* For master's, GRE General Test, minimum GPA of 3.0. Additional exam requirements/recommendations for international students: Required—TOEFL. *Faculty research:* American folklore, East European folklore, film and folklore, folk religion and belief, ballad.

The University of Texas at Austin, Graduate School, College of Liberal Arts, Department of Anthropology, Program in Folklore and Public Culture, Austin, TX 78712-1111. Offers MA, PhD. Part-time programs available. Terminal master's awarded for partial completion of doctoral program. *Degree requirements:* For master's, one foreign language, thesis, report; for doctorate, one foreign language, thesis/dissertation. *Entrance requirements:* For master's and doctorate, GRE General Test. Electronic applications accepted. *Faculty research:* Expressive culture, gender, genre, folklore and culture of British Isles, ethnography of speaking.

University of Wisconsin–Madison, Graduate School, College of Letters and Science, Department of Scandinavian Studies, Madison, WI 53706-1380. Offers area studies (MA); folklore (PhD); literature (MA, PhD); philology (PhD). Part-time programs available. *Degree requirements:* For master's, 2 foreign languages, exam; for doctorate, thesis/dissertation, exam. *Entrance requirements:* For master's, minimum GPA of 3.25; for doctorate, minimum GPA of 3.5. Electronic applications accepted. *Expenses:* Tuition, state resident: part-time $594 per credit. Tuition, nonresident: part-time $1504 per credit. Required fees: $65 per credit. Tuition and fees vary according to course load, program and reciprocity agreements. *Faculty research:* Historical fiction, Icelandic poetry, nineteenth-century literature, theater, gender studies, folklore.

Utah State University, School of Graduate Studies, College of Humanities, Arts and Social Sciences, Department of English and Department of History, Program in American Studies, Logan, UT 84322. Offers folklore (MA, MS); western American literature and culture (MA, MS). Part-time and evening/weekend programs available. *Degree requirements:* For master's, thesis or alternative. *Entrance requirements:* For master's, GRE General Test or MAT, minimum GPA of 3.0, 3 letters of recommendation, writing sample. Additional exam requirements/recommendations for international students: Required—TOEFL. *Faculty research:* Folklore and folklife, American culture, regional studies, material culture, Jewish folklore, Native American folklore.

Gender Studies

The American University in Cairo, Graduate Studies and Research, School of Humanities and Social Sciences, Program in Gender and Women's Studies, Cairo, Egypt. Offers gender and development (MA, Diploma); gender and justice (MA, Diploma); gender and women's studies in the Middle East and North Africa (MA, Diploma).

Arizona State University, Graduate College, College of Liberal Arts and Sciences, Division of Social Sciences, Women and Gender Studies Program, Tempe, AZ 85287. Offers gender studies (PhD).

Brandeis University, Graduate School of Arts and Sciences, Department of Anthropology, Waltham, MA 02454. Offers anthropology (MA, PhD); anthropology and women's and gender studies (MA). Part-time programs available. *Faculty:* 9 full-time (4 women), 1 part-time/adjunct (0 women). *Students:* 39 full-time (25 women), 2 part-time (1 woman); includes 5 minority (1 Asian American or Pacific Islander, 4 Hispanic Americans), 13 international. Average age 34. 68 applicants, 44% accepted, 12 enrolled. In 2009, 12 master's awarded. Terminal master's awarded for partial completion of doctoral program. *Degree requirements:* For master's, thesis; for doctorate, one foreign language, comprehensive exam, thesis/dissertation. *Entrance requirements:* For master's, GRE General Test (recommended), sample of written work, resume, letters of recommendation; for doctorate, GRE General Test, sample of written work, resume, letters of recommendation. Additional exam requirements/recommendations for international students: Required—TOEFL (minimum score 600 paper-based; 250 computer-based; 100 iBT); Recommended—IELTS (minimum score 7). *Application deadline:* For fall admission, 1/15 for domestic students. Applications are processed on a rolling basis. Application fee: $75. Electronic applications accepted. *Financial support:* In 2009–10, 23 students received support, including 12 fellowships with full tuition reimbursements available (averaging $20,000 per year), 11 teaching assistantships with partial tuition reimbursements available (averaging $3,200 per year); research assistantships with partial tuition reimbursements available, career-related internships or fieldwork, scholarships/grants, health care benefits, tuition waivers (full and partial), and unspecified assistantships also available. Support available to part-time students. Financial award application deadline: 4/15; financial award applicants required to submit FAFSA. *Faculty research:* Technology and culture, comparative methods, economic anthropology, gender studies, semiotic anthropology. *Unit head:* Dr. Elizabeth Ferry, Associate Professor/Director of Graduate Studies, 781-736-2210, Fax: 781-736-2232, E-mail: ferry@brandeis.edu. *Application contact:* Laurel Carpenter, Academic Administrator, 781-736-2210, Fax: 781-736-2232, E-mail: lcarpenter@brandeis.edu.

Brandeis University, Graduate School of Arts and Sciences, Department of English and American Literature, Waltham, MA 02454-9110. Offers English (MA, PhD); English and women's and gender studies (MA). Part-time programs available. *Faculty:* 15 full-time (8 women), 7 part-time/adjunct (4 women). *Students:* 50 full-time (24 women), 2 part-time (1 woman); includes 3 minority (1 Asian American or Pacific Islander, 2 Hispanic Americans), 4 international. 154 applicants, 20% accepted, 10 enrolled. In 2009, 10 master's, 3 doctorates awarded. *Degree requirements:* For master's, one foreign language, thesis, symposium; for doctorate, 2 foreign languages, thesis/dissertation, field exam, symposium presentation, prospectus defense. *Entrance requirements:* For master's, GRE General Test, resume, sample of work, letters of recommendation; for doctorate, GRE General Test, GRE Subject Test, resume, sample of work, letters of recommendation. Additional exam requirements/recommendations for international students: Required—TOEFL (minimum score 600 paper-based; 250 computer-based; 100 iBT); Recommended—IELTS (minimum score 7). *Application deadline:* For fall admission, 1/5 for domestic students. Application fee: $75. Electronic applications accepted. *Financial support:* In 2009–10, 27 fellowships with full tuition reimbursements (averaging $20,000 per year), 4 teaching assistantships with partial tuition reimbursements (averaging $3,200 per year) were awarded; research assistantships with full tuition reimbursements, scholarships/grants, health care benefits, and tuition waivers (full and partial) also available. Financial award application deadline: 4/15; financial award applicants required to submit FAFSA. *Faculty research:* Feminist and gender theory, American literature, Anglophone literature, early modern literature, modernism. *Unit head:* Dr. John Burt, Director of Graduate Studies, 781-736-2130, Fax: 781-736-2179, E-mail: chaucer@brandeis.edu. *Application contact:* Shannon Hunt, Department Administrator, 781-736-2130, Fax: 781-736-2179, E-mail: shuntl@brandeis.edu.

Brandeis University, Graduate School of Arts and Sciences, Department of Music, Waltham, MA 02454-9110. Offers composition and theory (MA, MFA, PhD); music and women's and gender studies (MA); musicology (MA, MFA, PhD). Part-time programs available. *Faculty:* 7 full-time (1 woman), 8 part-time/adjunct (3 women). *Students:* 46 full-time (18 women), 1 (woman) part-time; includes 2 minority (1 Asian American or Pacific Islander, 1 Hispanic American), 9 international. Average age 28. 73 applicants, 33% accepted, 15 enrolled. In 2009, 6 master's, 4 doctorates awarded. Terminal master's awarded for partial completion of doctoral program. *Degree requirements:* For master's, one foreign language, thesis or alternative; for doctorate, 2 foreign languages, comprehensive exam, thesis/dissertation. *Entrance requirements:* For master's, GRE General Test (musicology), resume, sample of work (music composition), letters of recommendation; for doctorate, GRE General Test (musicology), resume, writing sample (musicology), letters of recommendation, sample of work—recording (composition). Additional exam requirements/recommendations for international students: Required—TOEFL (minimum score 600 paper-based; 250 computer-based; 100 iBT); Recommended—IELTS (minimum score 7). *Application deadline:* For fall admission, 1/31 for domestic and international students. Application fee: $75. Electronic applications accepted. *Financial support:* In 2009–10, 23 students received support, including 24 fellowships with full tuition reimbursements available (averaging $20,000 per year), 4 teaching assistantships with partial tuition reimbursements available (averaging $3,200 per year); research assistantships, scholarships/grants, health care benefits, and tuition waivers (full and partial) also available. Support available to part-time students. Financial award application deadline: 4/15; financial award applicants required to submit FAFSA. *Faculty research:* History of theory; music of Monteverdi, Bach, Mozart, Lizst, and Wagner; compositional process; computer music. *Unit head:* Prof. Mary Ruth Ray, Chair, 781-736-3310, E-mail: ray@brandeis.edu. *Application contact:* Mark Kagan, Senior Academic Administrator, 781-736-3311, E-mail: kagan@brandeis.edu.

Brandeis University, Graduate School of Arts and Sciences, Department of Near Eastern and Judaic Studies, Waltham, MA 02454-9110. Offers Near Eastern and Judaic studies (MA, PhD); Near Eastern and Judaic studies and sociology (PhD); Near Eastern and Judaic studies and women's and gender studies (MA); teaching of Hebrew (MAT). Part-time programs available. *Faculty:* 26 full-time (11 women), 4 part-time/adjunct (1 woman). *Students:* 62 full-time (30 women), 1 part-time (0 women); includes 2 minority (1 African American, 1 Hispanic American), 7 international. Average age 33. 88 applicants, 67% accepted, 28 enrolled. In 2009, 10 master's, 6 doctorates awarded. Terminal master's awarded for partial completion of doctoral program. *Degree requirements:* For master's, one foreign language, comprehensive exam, thesis or alternative; for doctorate, 3 foreign languages, comprehensive exam, thesis/dissertation. *Entrance requirements:* For master's, GRE General Test (recommended), letters of recommendation; for doctorate, GRE General Test (recommended), letters of recommendation, transcripts, statement of purpose. Additional exam requirements/recommendations for international students: Required—TOEFL (minimum score 600 paper-based; 250 computer-based; 100 iBT); Recommended—IELTS (minimum score 7). *Application deadline:* For fall admission, 1/15 priority date for domestic and international students. Applications are processed on a rolling basis. Application fee: $75. Electronic applications accepted. *Financial support:* In 2009–10, 17 students received support, including 14 fellowships with full tuition reimbursements available (averaging $20,000 per year), 3 teaching assistantships with partial tuition reimbursements available (averaging $3,200 per year); research assistantships with full and partial tuition reimbursements available, scholarships/grants, health care benefits, and tuition waivers (full and partial) also available. Support available to part-time students. Financial award application deadline: 4/15; financial award applicants required to submit FAFSA. *Faculty research:* Ancient Near East and Bible, philosophy, history, modern Middle East, Islamic studies. *Unit head:* Dr. David Wright, Chair, 781-736-2954, Fax: 781-736-2070, E-mail: wright@brandeis.edu. *Application contact:* Joanne Arnish, Department Administrator, 781-736-2950, Fax: 781-736-2070, E-mail: arnish@brandeis.edu.

Brandeis University, Graduate School of Arts and Sciences, Joint Master's Programs in Women's and Gender Studies, Waltham, MA 02454-9110. Offers anthropology and women's and gender studies (MA); English and women's and gender studies (MA); music and women's and gender studies (MA); Near Eastern and Judaic studies and women's and gender studies (MA); public policy and women's and gender studies (MA); sociology and women's and gender studies (MA); sustainable international development and women's/gender studies (MA). Part-time programs available. *Faculty:* 18 full-time (17 women), 2 part-time/adjunct (both women). *Students:* 17 full-time (15 women), 4 international. Average age 25. 35 applicants, 49% accepted, 6 enrolled. In 2009, 8 master's awarded. *Degree requirements:* For master's, thesis. *Entrance requirements:* For master's, GRE, sample of written work, resume. Additional exam requirements/recommendations for international students: Required—TOEFL (minimum score 600 paper-based; 250 computer-based; 100 iBT); Recommended—IELTS (minimum score 7). *Application deadline:* For fall admission, 1/15 for domestic students. Application fee: $75. Electronic applications accepted. *Financial support:* In 2009–10, 6 students received support, including 2 fellowships with partial tuition reimbursements available (averaging $4,450 per year), 1 teaching assistantship with partial tuition reimbursement available (averaging $3,200 per year); research assistantships, scholarships/grants and tuition waivers (full and partial) also available. Support available to part-time students. Financial award application deadline: 4/15; financial award applicants required to submit FAFSA. *Unit head:* Prof. James Mandrell, Chair, 781-736-3042, Fax: 781-736-3044, E-mail: mandrell@brandeis.edu. *Application contact:* Kathryn Dalton, Program Administrator, 781-736-3045, Fax: 781-736-3044, E-mail: daltonka@brandeis.edu.

Brandeis University, Graduate School of Arts and Sciences, MA Program in Women's and Gender Studies, Waltham, MA 02454-9110. Offers MA. *Degree requirements:* For master's,

Gender Studies

Brandeis University (continued)
thesis. *Entrance requirements:* For master's, GRE, three letters of recommendation, curriculum vitae or resume, statement of purpose, critical writing sample. Additional exam requirements/recommendations for international students: Required—TOEFL (minimum score 600 paper-based; 250 computer-based; 100 iBT); Recommended—IELTS (minimum score 7). *Application deadline:* For fall admission, 1/15 for domestic students. Application fee: $75. Electronic applications accepted. *Financial support:* Scholarships/grants available. Financial award application deadline: 4/15; financial award applicants required to submit FAFSA. *Faculty research:* Gender and legal studies, sexuality studies, social and public policy, comparative literature and culture, anthropology, English, music, Near Eastern and Judaic Studies, public policy, sociology, sustainable international development. *Unit head:* Prof. James Mandrell, Chair, 781-736-3045, Fax: 781-736-3044, E-mail: wgstudies@brandeis.edu. *Application contact:* Katie Dalton, Department Administrator, 781-736-3045, Fax: 781-736-3044, E-mail: daltonka@brandeis.edu.

Carnegie Mellon University, College of Humanities and Social Sciences, Department of History, Pittsburgh, PA 15213-3891. Offers African and African-American diaspora (PhD); culture and power (PhD); gender and the family (PhD); history (MA, MS); history and policy (MA); labor and politics (PhD); science, technology, medicine and environment (PhD). Part-time programs available. *Degree requirements:* For doctorate, oral and written comprehensive exams, dissertation defense. *Entrance requirements:* For doctorate, GRE General Test. Additional exam requirements/recommendations for international students: Required—TOEFL. Electronic applications accepted. *Faculty research:* Anthropology and history, African American history, technology/environment, cultural history analysis.

Central European University, Graduate Studies, School of Social Sciences and Humanities, Budapest, Hungary. Offers economics (MA, PhD); gender studies (MA, PhD); international relations and European studies (MA, PhD); mathematics and its applications (MS, PhD); medieval studies (MA, PhD); nationalism studies (MA, PhD); philosophy (MA, PhD); political science (MA, PhD); public policy (MA, PhD); sociology and social anthropology (MA, PhD). Terminal master's awarded for partial completion of doctoral program. *Degree requirements:* For master's, one foreign language, thesis; for doctorate, one foreign language, comprehensive exam, thesis/dissertation. *Entrance requirements:* For master's, interview; for doctorate, GRE, CEU subject test, interview. Additional exam requirements/recommendations for international students: Required—TOEFL (minimum score 570 paper-based; 230 computer-based). Electronic applications accepted. *Faculty research:* Civil society, fiscal decentralization, party politics, political philosophy (especially Liberalism, theory of Democracy).

Central Michigan University, College of Graduate Studies, College of Humanities and Social and Behavioral Sciences, Program in Humanities, Mount Pleasant, MI 48859. Offers humanities (MA), including contemporary issues in the humanities: race, class, and gender, images and ideas of self, Native American issues in modern culture, popular culture studies, the rise of industrial society. Part-time and evening/weekend programs available. *Degree requirements:* For master's, thesis or alternative. Electronic applications accepted. *Faculty research:* Rise of industrial society; images and ideas of self; contemporary issues of race, class, and gender; popular culture; Native American issues in modern culture.

Cornell University, Graduate School, Graduate Fields of Arts and Sciences, Field of Sociology, Ithaca, NY 14853-0001. Offers economy and society (MA, PhD); gender and life course (MA, PhD); methodology (MA, PhD); organizations (MA, PhD); policy analysis (MA, PhD); political sociology/social movements (MA, PhD); racial and ethnic relations (MA, PhD); social networks (MA, PhD); social psychology (MA, PhD); social stratification (MA, PhD). *Faculty:* 41 full-time (17 women). *Students:* 39 full-time (19 women); includes 4 minority (all Asian Americans or Pacific Islanders), 10 international. Average age 31. 153 applicants, 8% accepted, 7 enrolled. In 2009, 2 master's, 2 doctorates awarded. Terminal master's awarded for partial completion of doctoral program. *Degree requirements:* For master's, thesis; for doctorate, thesis/dissertation, 1 year of teaching experience. *Entrance requirements:* For master's and doctorate, GRE General Test, 2 letters of recommendation, writing sample. Additional exam requirements/recommendations for international students: Required—TOEFL (minimum score 550 paper-based; 213 computer-based; 77 iBT). *Application deadline:* For fall admission, 1/15 for domestic students. Application fee: $70. Electronic applications accepted. *Expenses:* Tuition: Full-time $29,500. Required fees: $70. Full-time tuition and fees vary according to degree level, program and student level. *Financial support:* In 2009–10, 32 students received support, including 6 fellowships with full tuition reimbursements available; research assistantships with full tuition reimbursements available, teaching assistantships with full tuition reimbursements available, institutionally sponsored loans, scholarships/grants, health care benefits, tuition waivers (full and partial), and unspecified assistantships also available. Financial award applicants required to submit FAFSA. *Faculty research:* Comparative societal analysis, work and family, simulations, social class and mobility, racial segregation and inequality. *Unit head:* Director of Graduate Studies, 607-255-4266. *Application contact:* Graduate Field Assistant, 607-255-4266, E-mail: sociology@cornell.edu.

Eastern Michigan University, Graduate School, College of Arts and Sciences, Department of Women's and Gender Studies, Ypsilanti, MI 48197. Offers MA, Graduate Certificate. Part-time and evening/weekend programs available. *Students:* 3 full-time (all women), 6 part-time (all women); includes 4 minority (3 African Americans, 1 Hispanic American), 1 international. Average age 38. 17 applicants, 76% accepted, 4 enrolled. In 2009, 6 master's awarded. *Degree requirements:* For master's, thesis, research project, or practicum. *Entrance requirements:* Additional exam requirements/recommendations for international students: Required—TOEFL. *Application deadline:* For fall admission, 6/15 for domestic and international students; for winter admission, 9/15 for domestic and international students; for spring admission, 3/1 for domestic and international students. Applications are processed on a rolling basis. Application fee: $35. Tuition and fees vary according to course level. *Financial support:* Fellowships, research assistantships with full tuition reimbursements, teaching assistantships with full tuition reimbursements, career-related internships or fieldwork, Federal Work-Study, institutionally sponsored loans, scholarships/grants, tuition waivers (partial), and unspecified assistantships available. Support available to part-time students. Financial award applicants required to submit FAFSA. *Unit head:* Dr. Linda Pritchard, Department Head, 734-487-1177, Fax: 734-487-5029, E-mail: linda.pritchard@emich.edu. *Application contact:* Dr. Deanna Mihaly, Program Advisor, 734-487-1177, Fax: 734-487-5029, E-mail: dmihaly@emich.edu.

Indiana University Bloomington, University Graduate School, College of Arts and Sciences, Gender Studies Program, Bloomington, IN 47405-7000. Offers PhD. *Faculty:* 4 full-time (all women). *Students:* 23 full-time (19 women); includes 5 minority (1 African American, 2 American Indian/Alaska Native, 2 Hispanic Americans), 3 international. Average age 29. 79 applicants, 20% accepted, 5 enrolled. *Application deadline:* For fall admission, 1/12 priority date for domestic students, 12/1 priority date for international students. Application fee: $55 ($65 for international students). *Financial support:* Fellowships with tuition reimbursements, research assistantships with tuition reimbursements, teaching assistantships with tuition reimbursements available. *Unit head:* Helen Gremillion, Director of Graduate Studies, 812-855-0101, E-mail: hgremill@indiana.edu. *Application contact:* Nina Taylor, Graduate Secretary, 812-855-4848, E-mail: nitaylor@indiana.edu.

Indiana University–Purdue University Indianapolis, School of Liberal Arts, Department of Sociology, Indianapolis, IN 46202-2896. Offers family/gender studies (MA); medical sociology (MA); work/occupations (MA). *Faculty:* 17 full-time (8 women). *Students:* 13 full-time (8 women), 10 part-time (8 women), 3 international. Average age 29. 26 applicants, 73% accepted, 12 enrolled. In 2009, 5 master's awarded. Application fee: $55 ($65 for international students). *Financial support:* In 2009–10, 2 fellowships (averaging $9,500 per year), 2 teaching assistantships (averaging $6,309 per year) were awarded. *Unit head:* Carrie Foote, Director of Graduate Studies, 317-274-8981, E-mail: sociology@iupui.edu. *Application contact:* Director of Research and Graduate Programs, 317-274-8305.

Memorial University of Newfoundland, School of Graduate Studies, Department of Sociology, St. John's, NL A1C 5S7, Canada. Offers gender (PhD); maritime sociology (PhD); sociology (M Phil, MA); work and development (PhD). Part-time programs available. *Degree requirements:* For master's, comprehensive exam, thesis optional, program journal (M Phil); for doctorate, one foreign language, comprehensive exam, thesis/dissertation, oral defense of thesis. *Entrance requirements:* For master's, 2nd class degree from university of recognized standing in area of study; for doctorate, MA, M Phil, or equivalent. Electronic applications accepted. *Faculty research:* Work and development, gender, maritime sociology.

Minnesota State University Mankato, College of Graduate Studies, College of Social and Behavioral Sciences, Department of Gender and Women's Studies, Mankato, MN 56001. Offers MS, Certificate. Part-time programs available. *Students:* 8 full-time (7 women), 6 part-time (5 women). *Degree requirements:* For master's, comprehensive exam, thesis or alternative. *Entrance requirements:* For master's, minimum GPA of 3.0 during previous 2 years of course work. Additional exam requirements/recommendations for international students: Required—TOEFL. *Application deadline:* For fall admission, 7/1 priority date for domestic students; for spring admission, 11/1 for domestic students. Applications are processed on a rolling basis. Application fee: $40. *Expenses:* Tuition, state resident: full-time $5364. Tuition, nonresident: full-time $8314. *Financial support:* Research assistantships, teaching assistantships with full tuition reimbursements, career-related internships or fieldwork, Federal Work-Study, institutionally sponsored loans, and unspecified assistantships available. Support available to part-time students. Financial award application deadline: 3/15; financial award applicants required to submit FAFSA. *Unit head:* Dr. Maria Bevacqua, Chairperson, 507-389-2077. *Application contact:* 507-389-2321, E-mail: grad@mnsu.edu.

Northern Arizona University, Graduate College, College of Social and Behavioral Sciences, Women's and Gender Studies Program, Flagstaff, AZ 86011. Offers Graduate Certificate. *Faculty:* 2 full-time (both women). *Students:* 1 (woman) part-time. Average age 25. 8 applicants, 50% accepted, 1 enrolled. *Application deadline:* Applications are processed on a rolling basis. Application fee: $65. Electronic applications accepted. *Unit head:* Dr. Sanjam Ahluwalia, Chair, 928-523-8709, E-mail: sanjam.ahluwalia@nau.edu. *Application contact:* Dr. Sanjam Ahluwalia, Chair, 928-523-8709, E-mail: sanjam.ahluwalia@nau.edu.

Northwestern University, The Graduate School, Program in Gender Studies, Evanston, IL 60208. Offers PhD/Certificate. *Faculty research:* Anthropology, gender in Victorian period, autobiography, performance ethnographies, Slavic literature, women in the law.

Norwich University, School of Graduate and Continuing Studies, Program in Military History, Northfield, VT 05663. Offers race and gender in military history (MA); U. S. military history (MA). Evening/weekend programs available. *Faculty:* 33 part-time/adjunct (2 women). *Students:* 531 full-time (85 women); includes 30 minority (3 African Americans, 6 American Indian/Alaska Native, 6 Asian Americans or Pacific Islanders, 15 Hispanic Americans). Average age 42. 736 applicants, 80% accepted, 531 enrolled. In 2009, 503 master's awarded. *Entrance requirements:* For master's, minimum undergraduate GPA of 2.75. Additional exam requirements/recommendations for international students: Required—TOEFL (minimum score 550 paper-based; 212 computer-based; 83 iBT). *Application deadline:* For fall admission, 8/10 for domestic and international students; for winter admission, 11/7 for domestic and international students; for spring admission, 2/6 for domestic and international students. Application fee: $50. Electronic applications accepted. Full-time tuition and fees vary according to course level and course load. *Financial support:* Scholarships/grants available. Financial award applicants required to submit FAFSA. *Unit head:* Dr. James Erhman, Program Director, 802-485-2567, Fax: 802-485-2533. *Application contact:* Lars Nielsen, Administrative Director, 802-485-2853, Fax: 802-485-2533, E-mail: lnielsen@norwich.edu.

Queen's University at Kingston, School of Graduate Studies and Research, Faculty of Arts and Sciences, Department of Political Studies, Kingston, ON K7L 3N6, Canada. Offers Canadian politics (PhD); comparative politics (PhD); gender and politics (PhD); international relations (PhD); political theory (PhD). *Degree requirements:* For master's, thesis or alternative; for doctorate, one foreign language, thesis/dissertation, qualifying exams. *Entrance requirements:* Additional exam requirements/recommendations for international students: Required—TOEFL (minimum score 600 paper-based; 250 computer-based). *Faculty research:* Canadian politics, comparative politics, political thought, international politics, women and politics.

Roosevelt University, Graduate Division, College of Arts and Sciences, Department of Literature and Languages, Program in Women's and Gender Studies, Chicago, IL 60605. Offers MA, Certificate. Part-time and evening/weekend programs available. *Degree requirements:* For master's, thesis. *Entrance requirements:* For master's, minimum GPA of 2.7. *Faculty research:* Feminist economics; philosophy of feminism; race, class, and gender; women and art; women's history.

Rutgers, The State University of New Jersey, New Brunswick, Graduate School-New Brunswick, Program in Women's and Gender Studies, Piscataway, NJ 08854-8097. Offers MA, PhD. Part-time programs available. *Degree requirements:* For master's, thesis or alternative; for doctorate, comprehensive exam, thesis/dissertation. *Entrance requirements:* For master's and doctorate, GRE General Test, writing sample, 3 letters of recommendation. Additional exam requirements/recommendations for international students: Required—TOEFL. *Faculty research:* Feminist theory, gender and sexuality, global and cultural studies, women in history, literature, and politics, feminist politics.

Saint Mary's University, Faculty of Arts, Program in Women and Gender Studies, Halifax, NS B3H 3C3, Canada. Offers MA. Part-time programs available. *Faculty:* 50. *Students:* 40. *Degree requirements:* For master's, thesis. *Entrance requirements:* For master's, honors degree. *Application deadline:* For fall admission, 5/31 for domestic students. Application fee: $35. *Unit head:* Dr. Michele Byers, Director, 902-420-5869, E-mail: michele.byers@smu.ca. *Application contact:* Dr. Michele Byers, Director, 902-420-5869, E-mail: michele.byers@smu.ca.

Simmons College, College of Arts and Sciences Graduate Studies, Program in Gender/Cultural Studies, Boston, MA 02115. Offers MA, MA/MAT, MA/MS. Part-time programs available. *Students:* 1 (woman) full-time, 24 part-time (all women); includes 5 minority (1 African American, 1 American Indian/Alaska Native, 3 Hispanic Americans), 2 international. Average age 26. 42 applicants, 62% accepted, 12 enrolled. In 2009, 16 master's awarded. *Degree requirements:* For master's, thesis. *Entrance requirements:* For master's, academic writing sample. Additional exam requirements/recommendations for international students: Required—TOEFL (minimum score 600 paper-based; 250 computer-based; 100 iBT). *Application deadline:* For fall admission, 8/1 priority date for domestic and international students; for winter admission, 12/15 priority date for domestic and international students; for spring admission, 5/1 priority date for domestic and international students. Applications are processed on a rolling basis. Application fee: $35. Electronic applications accepted. *Expenses:* Tuition: Part-time $925 per credit hour. Part-time tuition and fees vary according to program. *Financial support:* Application deadline: 3/1. *Faculty research:* Gender and sexuality, queer theory, gender and the media, race, feminist film theory. *Unit head:* Dr. Sarah Leonard, Director, 617-521-2254, Fax: 617-521-3090. *Application contact:* Kristen Haack, Director, Graduate Studies Admission, 617-521-2917, Fax: 617-521-3058, E-mail: gsa@simmons.edu.

Syracuse University, College of Arts and Sciences, Program in Women's and Gender Studies, Syracuse, NY 13244. Offers CAS. *Students:* 3 applicants, 100% accepted, 0 enrolled. In 2009, 3 CASs awarded. *Entrance requirements:* For degree, Must be matriculated in an SU graduate Program. Additional exam requirements/recommendations for international students: Required—TOEFL (minimum score 100 iBT). *Application deadline:* For fall admission, 2/1 priority date for domestic and international students. Application fee: $75. Electronic applications accepted. *Expenses:* Tuition: Full-time $26,808; part-time $1117 per credit. Required fees: $1024. *Unit head:* Dr. Chandra Talpade Mohanty, Chair, 315-443-3707, E-mail: ctmohant@syr.edu.

Application contact: Susann Democker-Shedd, Program Contact, 315-443-3560, E-mail: sademock@syr.edu.

University of Florida, Graduate School, College of Liberal Arts and Sciences, Center for Women's Studies and Gender Research, Gainesville, FL 32611. Offers gender and development (Graduate Certificate); women's studies (MA, MWS, Graduate Certificate); MA/JD; MA/MA.

The University of North Carolina at Greensboro, Graduate School, College of Arts and Sciences, Program in Women's and Gender Studies, Greensboro, NC 27412-5001. Offers MA, Certificate. Electronic applications accepted.

University of Northern British Columbia, Office of Graduate Studies, Prince George, BC V2N 4Z9, Canada. Offers business administration (Diploma); community health science (M Sc); disability management (MA); education (M Ed); first nations studies (MA); gender studies (MA); history (MA); interdisciplinary studies (MA); international studies (MA); mathematical, computer and physical sciences (M Sc); natural resources and environmental studies (M Sc, MA, MNRES, PhD); political science (MA); psychology (M Sc, PhD); social work (MSW). Part-time and evening/weekend programs available. Postbaccalaureate distance learning degree programs offered (no on-campus study). *Degree requirements:* For master's, thesis; for doctorate, thesis/dissertation. *Entrance requirements:* For master's, GRE, minimum B average in undergraduate course work; for doctorate, candidacy exam, minimum A average in graduate course work.

University of Northern Iowa, Graduate College, Program in Women's and Gender Studies, Cedar Falls, IA 50614. Offers MA. *Students:* 4 full-time (3 women), 1 (woman) part-time; includes 1 minority (African American), 1 international. 4 applicants, 75% accepted, 3 enrolled. In 2009, 3 master's awarded. *Degree requirements:* For master's, comprehensive exam (for some programs), thesis or alternative. *Entrance requirements:* For master's, minimum GPA of 3.0. Additional exam requirements/recommendations for international students: Required—TOEFL (minimum score 500 paper-based; 180 computer-based; 61 iBT). *Application deadline:* Applications are processed on a rolling basis. Application fee: $30 ($50 for international students). Electronic applications accepted. *Financial support:* Application deadline: 2/1. *Unit head:* Dr. Phyllis L. Baker, Director/Professor, 319-273-7102, Fax: 319-273-3053, E-mail: phyllis.baker@uni.edu. *Application contact:* Laurie S. Russell, Record Analyst, 319-273-2623, Fax: 319-273-6792, E-mail: laurie.russell@uni.edu.

University of Saskatchewan, College of Graduate Studies and Research, College of Arts and Sciences, Department of Women's and Gender Studies, Saskatoon, SK S7N 5A2, Canada. Offers MA, PhD. *Faculty:* 5. *Degree requirements:* For master's, thesis; for doctorate, comprehensive exam (for some programs), thesis/dissertation. *Entrance requirements:* Additional exam requirements/recommendations for international students: Required—TOEFL (minimum score 80 iBT); Recommended—IELTS (minimum score 6.5). *Application deadline:* For fall admission, 7/1 priority date for domestic students. Applications are processed on a rolling basis. Application fee: $75. Electronic applications accepted. Tuition and fees charges are reported in Canadian dollars. *Expenses:* Tuition, area resident: Full-time $3000 Canadian dollars; part-time $500 Canadian dollars per term. Required fees: $700 Canadian dollars; $100 Canadian dollars per term. *Financial support:* Fellowships, research assistantships, teaching assistantships available. *Unit head:* Dr. Joan Brsa, Acting Head, 306-966-4256, Fax: 306-966-4559, E-mail: jan.borsa@usask.ca. *Application contact:* Dr. Pamela Downe, Graduate Chair, 306-966-1974, E-mail: pamela.downe@usask.ca.

The University of Texas at El Paso, Graduate School, College of Liberal Arts, Women's Studies Program, El Paso, TX 79968-0001. Offers women's and gender studies (Certificate).

Virginia Commonwealth University, Graduate School, College of Humanities and Sciences, Wilder School of Government and Public Affairs, Department of Sociology, Program in Gender Violence Intervention, Richmond, VA 23284-9005. Offers Certificate, MSW/Certificate.

Hispanic Studies

Brown University, Graduate School, Department of Hispanic Studies, Providence, RI 02912. Offers MA, PhD. *Degree requirements:* For master's, one foreign language, thesis; for doctorate, 2 foreign languages, thesis/dissertation, preliminary exam.

California State University, Los Angeles, Graduate Studies, College of Natural and Social Sciences, Department of Chicano Studies, Los Angeles, CA 90032-8530. Offers Mexican-American studies (MA). Part-time and evening/weekend programs available. *Faculty:* 2 full-time (both women), 3 part-time/adjunct (1 woman). *Students:* 7 full-time (5 women), 13 part-time (10 women); includes 18 minority (2 African Americans, 16 Hispanic Americans). Average age 30. 10 applicants, 100% accepted, 6 enrolled. In 2009, 6 master's awarded. *Degree requirements:* For master's, one foreign language, comprehensive exam or thesis. *Entrance requirements:* For master's, undergraduate major in Mexican-American studies or related area, 12 units in Chicano studies. Additional exam requirements/recommendations for international students: Required—TOEFL (minimum score 500 paper-based; 173 computer-based). *Application deadline:* For fall admission, 5/1 for domestic and international students. Applications are processed on a rolling basis. Application fee: $55. Electronic applications accepted. *Financial support:* Career-related internships or fieldwork and Federal Work-Study available. Support available to part-time students. Financial award application deadline: 3/1. *Faculty research:* U.S.-Mexican relations, Chicano literature, community organization among Chicanos and Hispanics, Spanish language in the American Southwest. *Unit head:* Dr. Michael Soldatenko, Chair, 323-343-2400, Fax: 323-343-5609, E-mail: msoldat@calstatela.edu. *Application contact:* Dr. Cheryl L. Ney, Associate Vice President for Academic Affairs and Dean of Graduate Studies, 323-343-3820, Fax: 323-343-5653, E-mail: cney@cslanet.calstatela.edu.

California State University, Northridge, Graduate Studies, College of Humanities, Department of Chicana and Chicano Studies, Northridge, CA 91330. Offers MA. *Faculty:* 18 full-time (12 women), 40 part-time/adjunct (15 women). *Students:* 14 full-time (7 women), 24 part-time (15 women); includes 35 minority (all Hispanic Americans). Average age 30. 29 applicants, 52% accepted, 12 enrolled. In 2009, 9 master's awarded. *Degree requirements:* For master's, thesis, project. *Entrance requirements:* Additional exam requirements/recommendations for international students: Required—TOEFL. *Application deadline:* For fall admission, 11/30 for domestic students. Application fee: $55. *Financial support:* Application deadline: 3/1. *Unit head:* Dr. David Rodriguez, Chair, 818-677-2734. *Application contact:* Dr. David Rodriguez, Chair, 818-677-2734.

Eastern Michigan University, Graduate School, College of Arts and Sciences, Department of World Languages, Programs in Foreign Languages, Ypsilanti, MI 48197. Offers French (MA); German (MA); German for business (Graduate Certificate); Hispanic language and cultures (Graduate Certificate); Japanese business practices (Graduate Certificate); Spanish (MA). Part-time and evening/weekend programs available. Postbaccalaureate distance learning degree programs offered (minimal on-campus study). *Students:* 1 full-time (0 women), 15 part-time (14 women); includes 4 minority (1 African American, 3 Hispanic Americans), 1 international. Average age 39. In 2009, 6 master's awarded. *Degree requirements:* For master's, one foreign language, thesis optional. *Entrance requirements:* Additional exam requirements/recommendations for international students: Required—TOEFL. *Application deadline:* Applications are processed on a rolling basis. Application fee: $35. Tuition and fees vary according to course level. *Financial support:* Fellowships, research assistantships with full tuition reimbursements, teaching assistantships with full tuition reimbursements, career-related internships or fieldwork, Federal Work-Study, institutionally sponsored loans, scholarships/grants, tuition waivers (partial), and unspecified assistantships available. Support available to part-time students. Financial award applicants required to submit FAFSA. *Application contact:* Dr. Genevieve Peden, Program Advisor, 734-487-2283, Fax: 734-487-3411, E-mail: gpeden@emich.edu.

La Salle University, School of Arts and Sciences, Program in Bilingual/Bicultural Studies (Spanish), Philadelphia, PA 19141-1199. Offers MA. Part-time and evening/weekend programs available. *Degree requirements:* For master's, one foreign language, thesis or alternative, project. *Entrance requirements:* For master's, GRE or MAT. *Expenses:* Contact institution. *Faculty research:* Puerto Rican literature, cross-cultural communication, English as a second language methodology, Spanish language.

Louisiana State University and Agricultural and Mechanical College, Graduate School, College of Arts and Sciences, Department of Foreign Languages and Literatures, Baton Rouge, LA 70803. Offers Hispanic studies (MA). Part-time programs available. *Faculty:* 23 full-time (8 women). *Students:* 8 full-time (6 women), 5 part-time (all women); includes 2 minority (1 American Indian/Alaska Native, 1 Hispanic American), 1 international. Average age 26. 5 applicants, 80% accepted, 4 enrolled. In 2009, 4 master's awarded. *Degree requirements:* For master's, 2 foreign languages, thesis optional. *Entrance requirements:* For master's, GRE General Test, minimum GPA of 3.0. Additional exam requirements/recommendations for international students: Required—TOEFL (minimum score 550 paper-based; 213 computer-based; 79 iBT) or IELTS (minimum score 6.5). *Application deadline:* For fall admission, 1/25 priority date for domestic students, 5/15 for international students; for spring admission, 10/15 for international students. Applications are processed on a rolling basis. Application fee: $50 ($70 for international students). Electronic applications accepted. *Financial support:* In 2009–10, 10 students received support, including 8 teaching assistantships with partial tuition reimbursements available (averaging $10,500 per year); fellowships with full tuition reimbursements available, research assistantships with partial tuition reimbursements available, Federal Work-Study, scholarships/grants, health care benefits, and tuition waivers (full and partial) also available. Financial award application deadline: 4/1; financial award applicants required to submit FAFSA. *Faculty research:* Hispanic cultural studies, linguistics, literary and cultural theory, peninsular and Latin American literature. Total annual research expenditures: $67,651. *Unit head:* Dr. Emily E. Batinski, Chair, 225-578-6616, Fax: 225-578-5074, E-mail: slbati@lsu.edu. *Application contact:* Dr. Alejandro Cortazar, Graduate Adviser, 225-578-5169, Fax: 225-578-5074, E-mail: acorta1@lsu.edu.

McGill University, Faculty of Graduate and Postdoctoral Studies, Faculty of Arts, Department of Hispanic Studies, Montréal, QC H3A 2T5, Canada. Offers MA, PhD.

Michigan State University, The Graduate School, College of Arts and Letters, Department of Spanish and Portuguese, East Lansing, MI 48824. Offers applied Spanish linguistics (MA); Hispanic cultural studies (PhD); Hispanic literatures (MA). *Faculty:* 14 full-time (7 women). *Students:* 26 full-time (17 women), 3 part-time (2 women); includes 10 minority (1 African American, 1 Asian American or Pacific Islander, 8 Hispanic Americans), 6 international. Average age 31. 23 applicants, 39% accepted. In 2009, 4 master's, 6 doctorates awarded. *Entrance requirements:* Additional exam requirements/recommendations for international students: Required—TOEFL. Electronic applications accepted. *Expenses:* Tuition, state resident: part-time $478.25 per credit hour. Tuition, nonresident: part-time $966.50 per credit hour. Part-time tuition and fees vary according to program. *Financial support:* In 2009–10, 20 teaching assistantships with tuition reimbursements (averaging $6,017 per year) were awarded. *Unit head:* Dr. Douglas Noverr, Acting Chairperson, 517-353-4939, Fax: 517-432-3844, E-mail: noverr@msu.edu. *Application contact:* Victoria Reynaga, Graduate Secretary, 517-355-8350, Fax: 517-432-3844, E-mail: reynagav@cal.msu.edu.

New York University, NYU in Madrid, Madrid, NY 10012-1019, Spain. Offers creative writing in Spanish (MFA); Spanish (PhD); Spanish and Latin American literatures and cultures (MA); Spanish language and translation (MA). *Students:* 27 full-time (23 women), 1 part-time (0 women); includes 8 minority (2 African Americans, 1 Asian American or Pacific Islander, 5 Hispanic Americans), 1 international. Average age 26. 73 applicants, 90% accepted, 27 enrolled. In 2009, 22 master's awarded. Application fee: $90. *Expenses:* Tuition: Full-time $30,528; part-time $1272 per credit. Required fees: $2177. *Unit head:* Judith Nemethy, Director, 212-998-8770, Fax: 212-995-4149, E-mail: nyu-in-madrid@nyu.edu. *Application contact:* Judith Nemethy, Director, 212-998-8770, Fax: 212-995-4149, E-mail: nyu-in-madrid@nyu.edu.

Pontifical Catholic University of Puerto Rico, College of Arts and Humanities, Department of Hispanic Studies, Ponce, PR 00717-0777. Offers grammar and writing (Professional Certificate); Hispanic studies (MA). Part-time and evening/weekend programs available. *Degree requirements:* For master's, variable foreign language requirement, comprehensive exam, thesis or alternative. *Entrance requirements:* For master's, GRE General Test, 2 letters of recommendation, interview, minimum GPA of 2.75. Electronic applications accepted.

Queen's University at Kingston, School of Graduate Studies and Research, Faculty of Arts and Sciences, Department of Spanish and Italian, Kingston, ON K7L 3N6, Canada. Offers Spanish language and literature (MA). Part-time programs available. *Degree requirements:* For master's, one foreign language, thesis. *Entrance requirements:* Additional exam requirements/recommendations for international students: Required—TOEFL. Electronic applications accepted. *Faculty research:* Golden Age, nineteenth- and twentieth-century Peninsular novel, literary theory, colonial Latin America, nineteenth-and-twentieth century Latin America.

St. Thomas University, School of Leadership Studies, Program in Hispanic Media, Miami Gardens, FL 33054-6459. Offers MA, Certificate. Part-time and evening/weekend programs available. *Degree requirements:* For master's, comprehensive exam. *Entrance requirements:* Additional exam requirements/recommendations for international students: Required—TOEFL (minimum score 550 paper-based; 213 computer-based; 79 iBT). Electronic applications accepted.

San Jose State University, Graduate Studies and Research, College of Social Sciences, Department of Mexican American Studies, San Jose, CA 95192-0001. Offers MA. *Students:* 8 full-time (6 women), 16 part-time (10 women); includes 23 minority (all Hispanic Americans). Average age 28. 24 applicants, 50% accepted, 8 enrolled. In 2009, 4 master's awarded. *Application deadline:* For fall admission, 6/29 for domestic students; for spring admission, 11/30 for domestic students. Applications are processed on a rolling basis. Application fee: $59. Electronic applications accepted. *Financial support:* Application deadline: 5/31. *Unit head:* Marcos Pizarro, Chair, 408-924-5760, Fax: 408-924-5700. *Application contact:* Marcos Pizarro, Chair, 408-924-5760, Fax: 408-924-5700.

Stony Brook University, State University of New York, Graduate School, College of Arts and Sciences, Department of Hispanic Languages and Literature, Stony Brook, NY 11794. Offers MA, PhD. Evening/weekend programs available. *Faculty:* 12 full-time (6 women). *Students:* 39 full-time (26 women), 15 part-time (11 women); includes 23 minority (1 African

Hispanic Studies

Stony Brook University, State University of New York (continued)
American, 22 Hispanic Americans), 16 international. Average age 33. 30 applicants, 53% accepted. In 2009, 6 master's, 4 doctorates awarded. *Degree requirements:* For master's, one foreign language, thesis or alternative; for doctorate, 2 foreign languages, thesis/dissertation. *Entrance requirements:* For master's, GRE General Test, BA in Spanish; for doctorate, GRE General Test, MA in Spanish. Additional exam requirements/recommendations for international students: Required—TOEFL. *Application deadline:* For fall admission, 1/15 for domestic students. Application fee: $60. *Expenses:* Contact institution. *Financial support:* In 2009–10, 22 teaching assistantships were awarded; fellowships, research assistantships, tuition waivers and unspecified assistantships also available. *Faculty research:* Spanish language and literature. *Unit head:* Dr. Victoriano Roncero-Lopez, Chair, 631-632-9669, E-mail: roncero@oponline.net. *Application contact:* Dr. Kathleen Vernon, Director of Graduate Studies, 631-632-9668, Fax: 631-632-9724, E-mail: kvernon@notes.cc.sunysb.edu.

Texas A&M International University, Office of Graduate Studies and Research, College of Arts and Sciences, Department of Language and Literature, Laredo, TX 78041-1900. Offers English (MA); Hispanic studies (PhD); Spanish (MA). *Faculty:* 6 full-time (3 women). *Students:* 4 full-time (3 women), 49 part-time (33 women); includes 46 minority (all Hispanic Americans), 1 international. Average age 34. 26 applicants. In 2009, 3 master's awarded. *Entrance requirements:* For master's, GRE General Test. Additional exam requirements/recommendations for international students: Required—TOEFL (minimum score 550 paper-based; 213 computer-based). *Application deadline:* For fall admission, 4/30 priority date for domestic students; for spring admission, 11/30 for domestic students. Applications are processed on a rolling basis. Application fee: $25. *Financial support:* In 2009–10, 12 students received support, including 1 fellowship, 1 research assistantship, 6 teaching assistantships. Financial award application deadline: 11/1. *Unit head:* Dr. Manuel Broncano, Chair, 956-326-2470, E-mail: manuel.broncano@tamiu.edu. *Application contact:* Rosie Espinoza-Dickinson, Director of Admissions, 956-326-2200, Fax: 956-326-2199, E-mail: enroll@tamiu.edu.

Universidad Metropolitana, School of Social Sciences, Humanities and Communications, Program in Interdisciplinary Puerto Rican Studies, San Juan, PR 00928-1150. Offers MA.

Université de Montréal, Faculty of Arts and Sciences, Department of Literatures and Modern Languages, Montréal, QC H3C 3J7, Canada. Offers German literature (PhD); German studies (MA); Hispanic literature (PhD); Hispanic studies (MA); literature and cinema (PhD). Terminal master's awarded for partial completion of doctoral program. *Degree requirements:* For master's, 2 foreign languages, thesis; for doctorate, 2 foreign languages, thesis/dissertation, general exam. Electronic applications accepted.

University of Alberta, Faculty of Graduate Studies and Research, Department of Modern Languages and Cultural Studies, Edmonton, AB T6G 2E1, Canada. Offers applied linguistics (Germanic, Romance, Slavic) (MA); French language, literatures and linguistics (PhD); French language, literatures, and linguistics (MA); Germanic languages, literatures and linguistics (PhD); Germanic languages, literatures, and linguistics (MA); Italian studies (MA); Slavic languages and literatures (Russian, Ukrainian) (MA, PhD); Slavic linguistics (Russian, Ukrainian) (MA, PhD); Spanish and Latin American studies (MA, PhD); Ukrainian folklore (MA, PhD). Part-time programs available. *Faculty:* 33 full-time (15 women), 2 part-time/adjunct (1 woman). *Students:* 39 full-time (29 women), 13 part-time (12 women). 300 applicants, 10% accepted. In 2009, 12 master's, 2 doctorates awarded. *Degree requirements:* For master's, one foreign language, thesis; for doctorate, 2 foreign languages, comprehensive exam, thesis/dissertation. *Entrance requirements:* For master's and doctorate, 1 language other than English. Additional exam requirements/recommendations for international students: Required—Michigan English Language Assessment Battery or TOEFL (minimum score 550 paper-based; 213 computer-based). *Application deadline:* For fall admission, 7/1 for domestic and international students; for winter admission, 11/1 for domestic and international students; for spring admission, 3/1 for domestic students. Applications are processed on a rolling basis. Electronic applications accepted. Tuition and fees charges are reported in Canadian dollars. *Expenses:* Tuition, area resident: Full-time $4626 Canadian dollars; part-time $99.72 Canadian dollars per unit. International tuition: $8216 Canadian dollars full-time. Required fees: $3590 Canadian dollars; $99.72 Canadian dollars per unit. $215 Canadian dollars per term. *Financial support:* In 2009–10, 2 fellowships with full and partial tuition reimbursements (averaging $18,000 per year), 23 research assistantships with full and partial tuition reimbursements (averaging $10,450 per year), 21 teaching assistantships with full and partial tuition reimbursements (averaging $12,572 per year) were awarded; scholarships/grants also available. Support available to part-time students. Financial award application deadline: 3/31. *Faculty research:* Russian/Ukrainian studies; German studies; contemporary Latin American, French and Francophone studies; Italian studies. *Unit head:* Dr. Don Bruce, Chair, 780-492-3273, Fax: 780-492-9106. *Application contact:* Jane Wilson, Graduate Programs Secretary, 780-492-3273, Fax: 780-492-9106, E-mail: mlcsgrad@ualberta.ca.

The University of British Columbia, Faculty of Arts and Faculty of Graduate Studies, Department of French, Hispanic and Italian Studies, Vancouver, BC V6T 1Z1, Canada. Offers French (MA, PhD); Hispanic studies (MA, PhD). Part-time programs available. *Degree requirements:* For master's, thesis optional; for doctorate, 2 foreign languages, comprehensive exam, thesis/dissertation. *Entrance requirements:* For doctorate, MA. Additional exam requirements/recommendations for international students: Required—TOEFL (minimum score 550 paper-based; 213 computer-based; 80 iBT). Electronic applications accepted. *Faculty research:* Medieval and Renaissance literature, modern literature, romance philology and linguistics, cultural studies, women's literature.

University of California, Berkeley, Graduate Division, College of Letters and Science, Department of Hispanic Languages and Literature, Berkeley, CA 94720-1500. Offers PhD. *Faculty:* 16 full-time (6 women). *Students:* 42 full-time (23 women). Average age 33. 56 applicants, 4 enrolled. In 2009, 8 doctorates awarded. *Degree requirements:* For doctorate, thesis/dissertation, qualifying exam. *Entrance requirements:* For doctorate, GRE General Test, minimum GPA of 3.0, 3 letters of recommendation. Additional exam requirements/recommendations for international students: Required—TOEFL (minimum score 570 paper-based; 230 computer-based). *Application deadline:* For fall admission, 12/15 for domestic students. Application fee: $70 ($90 for international students). *Financial support:* Fellowships with full tuition reimbursements, research assistantships, teaching assistantships with partial tuition reimbursements, unspecified assistantships available. Financial award applicants required to submit FAFSA. *Unit head:* Prof. Michael Mascuch, Chair, 510-642-0471, E-mail: ch_spanport@ls.berkeley.edu. *Application contact:* Veronica Lopez, Student Affairs Officer, 510-642-8037, E-mail: spanga@berkeley.edu.

University of California, Los Angeles, Graduate Division, College of Letters and Science, Department of Spanish and Portuguese, Program in Hispanic Languages and Literature, Los Angeles, CA 90095. Offers PhD. *Students:* 47 full-time (35 women); includes 22 minority (2 African Americans, 2 Asian Americans or Pacific Islanders, 18 Hispanic Americans), 6 international. Average age 32. 29 applicants, 31% accepted, 7 enrolled. In 2009, 5 doctorates awarded. *Degree requirements:* For doctorate, 2 foreign languages, thesis/dissertation, oral and written exams. *Entrance requirements:* For doctorate, GRE General Test, minimum undergraduate GPA of 3.0, sample of written work (recommended), master's degree. *Application deadline:* For fall admission, 12/31 for domestic and international students. Application fee: $70 ($90 for international students). Electronic applications accepted. *Financial support:* In 2009–10, 42 fellowships with full and partial tuition reimbursements, 16 research assistantships with full and partial tuition reimbursements, 39 teaching assistantships with full and partial tuition reimbursements were awarded; Federal Work-Study, scholarships/grants, health care benefits, tuition waivers (full and partial), and unspecified assistantships also available. Financial award applicants required to submit FAFSA. *Unit head:* Dr. Maarten Van Delden, Chair, 310-825-1220. *Application contact:* Department Office, 310-825-1036, E-mail: peinado@humnet.ucla.edu.

University of California, Riverside, Graduate Division, Department of Hispanic Studies, Riverside, CA 92521-0102. Offers Spanish (MA, PhD). Terminal master's awarded for partial completion of doctoral program. *Degree requirements:* For master's, one foreign language, comprehensive exam; for doctorate, one foreign language, thesis/dissertation, qualifying exams, 1 quarter of teaching experience. *Entrance requirements:* For master's and doctorate, GRE General Test, minimum GPA of 3.2. Additional exam requirements/recommendations for international students: Required—TOEFL (minimum score 550 paper-based; 213 computer-based; 80 iBT). Electronic applications accepted. *Faculty research:* Spanish literature of sixteenth, seventeenth and twentieth century; pre-Columbian and colonial Latin American literature; nineteenth and twentieth century Latin American literature.

University of California, Santa Barbara, Graduate Division, College of Letters and Sciences, Division of Humanities and Fine Arts, Department of Spanish and Portuguese, Santa Barbara, CA 93106-4150. Offers Hispanic languages and literature (PhD), including applied linguistics, European Medieval studies, feminist studies, Hispanic languages and literature; Portuguese (MA); Spanish (MA); Spanish and Portuguese (MA); MA/PhD. Spanish Language Institute available during summer session. *Faculty:* 16 full-time (6 women). *Students:* 29 full-time (16 women). Average age 30. 46 applicants, 39% accepted, 9 enrolled. In 2009, 4 master's, 2 doctorates awarded. *Degree requirements:* For master's, 2 foreign languages, comprehensive exam (for some programs), thesis optional; for doctorate, 2 foreign languages, comprehensive exam, thesis/dissertation. *Entrance requirements:* For master's, GRE, 2 writing samples, undergraduate major in Spanish or equivalent, 3 letters of recommendation, resume/curriculum vitae; for doctorate, GRE, 2 writing samples, master's degree, 3 letters of recommendation, statement of purpose, personal achievements/contributions statement, resume/curriculum vitae, transcripts for post-secondary institutions attended. Additional exam requirements/recommendations for international students: Required—TOEFL (minimum score 550 paper-based; 213 computer-based; 80 iBT), or IELTS (minimum score 7). *Application deadline:* For fall admission, 3/1 for domestic and international students; for winter admission, 11/1 for domestic and international students; for spring admission, 2/1 for domestic and international students. Application fee: $70 ($90 for international students). Electronic applications accepted. *Financial support:* In 2009–10, 9 fellowships with full and partial tuition reimbursements (averaging $7,000 per year), 29 teaching assistantships with partial tuition reimbursements (averaging $11,500 per year) were awarded; career-related internships or fieldwork, Federal Work-Study, institutionally sponsored loans, scholarships/grants, health care benefits, tuition waivers (full and partial), and unspecified assistantships also available. Financial award application deadline: 1/7; financial award applicants required to submit FAFSA. *Faculty research:* Nineteenth century Spanish and Portuguese literature, Spanish and Spanish American literature, nineteenth and twentieth century Portuguese and Brazilian literatures, Hispanic linguistics, Catalan language and culture. *Unit head:* Prof. Francisco A. Lomeli, Chair, 805-893-5715, Fax: 805-893-8341, E-mail: lomeli@spanport.ucsb.edu. *Application contact:* Carol Conley, Graduate Program Assistant, 805-893-3162, Fax: 805-893-8341, E-mail: cconley@spanport.ucsb.edu.

University of California, Santa Barbara, Graduate Division, College of Letters and Sciences, Division of Social Sciences, Department of Chicana and Chicano Studies, Santa Barbara, CA 93106-4120. Offers PhD, MA/PhD. *Faculty:* 9 full-time (5 women), 1 part-time/adjunct (0 women). *Students:* 20 full-time (10 women). Average age 30. 19 applicants, 32% accepted, 3 enrolled. *Degree requirements:* For doctorate, one foreign language, comprehensive exam, thesis/dissertation. *Entrance requirements:* For doctorate, GRE, writing sample, 3 letters of recommendation, resume/curriculum vitae. Additional exam requirements/recommendations for international students: Required—TOEFL (minimum score 550 paper-based; 213 computer-based; 80 iBT) or IELTS. *Application deadline:* For fall admission, 12/15 for domestic and international students. Application fee: $70 ($90 for international students). Electronic applications accepted. *Financial support:* In 2009–10, 19 students received support, including 12 fellowships with full and partial tuition reimbursements available (averaging $9,150 per year), 17 teaching assistantships with partial tuition reimbursements available (averaging $9,700 per year); career-related internships or fieldwork, Federal Work-Study, institutionally sponsored loans, scholarships/grants, health care benefits, tuition waivers (full and partial), and unspecified assistantships also available. Financial award application deadline: 12/15; financial award applicants required to submit FAFSA. *Faculty research:* Global, postcolonial and border studies; literature, culture and representation; political history and community; critical and cultural theory; gender and sexuality studies. *Unit head:* Dr. Juan Vincente Palerm, Chair, 805-893-3601, Fax: 805-893-4076, E-mail: palerm@anth.ucsb.edu. *Application contact:* Katherine G. Morales, Staff Graduate Advisor, 805-893-5269, Fax: 805-893-4076, E-mail: kmorales@chicst.ucsb.edu.

University of Houston, College of Liberal Arts and Social Sciences, Department of Hispanic Studies, Houston, TX 77204. Offers MA, PhD. Part-time and evening/weekend programs available. *Faculty:* 12 full-time (6 women), 2 part-time/adjunct (both women). *Students:* 34 full-time (26 women), 40 part-time (30 women); includes 50 minority (2 African Americans, 2 Asian Americans or Pacific Islanders, 46 Hispanic Americans), 11 international. Average age 36. 17 applicants, 94% accepted, 9 enrolled. In 2009, 14 master's, 7 doctorates awarded. *Degree requirements:* For master's, comprehensive exam, thesis optional; for doctorate, 2 foreign languages, comprehensive exam, thesis/dissertation. *Entrance requirements:* For master's, GRE. Additional exam requirements/recommendations for international students: Required—TOEFL (minimum score 550 paper-based; 79 iBT); Recommended—IELTS (minimum score 6.5). *Application deadline:* For fall admission, 2/1 for domestic and international students; for spring admission, 10/1 for domestic and international students. Applications are processed on a rolling basis. Application fee: $40. Electronic applications accepted. *Expenses:* Tuition, state resident: full-time $7676; part-time $320 per credit hour. Tuition, nonresident: full-time $14,324; part-time $597 per credit hour. Required fees: $3034. *Financial support:* In 2009–10, 8 research assistantships with full tuition reimbursements (averaging $10,400 per year), 18 teaching assistantships with full tuition reimbursements (averaging $10,400 per year) were awarded. *Unit head:* Dr. Manuel J. Gutierrez, Interim Chair, 713-743-3067, E-mail: mjgutierrez@uh.edu. *Application contact:* Debra Frazier, Academic Advisor, 713-743-3059, E-mail: dfrazier@uh.edu.

University of Illinois at Chicago, Graduate College, College of Liberal Arts and Sciences, Department of Spanish, French, Italian and Portuguese, Program in Hispanic Studies, Chicago, IL 60607-7128. Offers Hispanic linguistics (MA, PhD); Hispanic literary and cultural studies (MA, PhD). Part-time programs available. Terminal master's awarded for partial completion of doctoral program. *Degree requirements:* For master's, one foreign language, departmental qualifying exam. *Entrance requirements:* For master's, GRE General Test, minimum GPA of 2.75, undergraduate major in Spanish. Additional exam requirements/recommendations for international students: Required—TOEFL. Electronic applications accepted.

University of Kentucky, Graduate School, College of Arts and Sciences, Program in Hispanic Studies, Lexington, KY 40506-0032. Offers MA, PhD. *Degree requirements:* For master's, one foreign language, comprehensive exam, thesis optional; for doctorate, 2 foreign languages, comprehensive exam, thesis/dissertation. *Entrance requirements:* For master's, GRE General Test, minimum undergraduate GPA of 2.75; for doctorate, GRE General Test, minimum graduate GPA of 3.0. Additional exam requirements/recommendations for international students: Required—TOEFL (minimum score 550 paper-based; 213 computer-based). Electronic applications accepted. *Faculty research:* Hispanic linguistics, medieval Spanish literature and civilization, Renaissance and Golden Age literature and civilization, Spanish American literature and civilization.

University of Nevada, Las Vegas, Graduate College, College of Liberal Arts, Department of Foreign Languages, Las Vegas, NV 89154-5047. Offers Hispanic studies (MA); Spanish translation (Certificate). Part-time programs available. *Faculty:* 5 full-time (4 women). *Students:* 2 full-time (both women), 10 part-time (6 women); includes 8 minority (1 Asian American or Pacific Islander, 7 Hispanic Americans). Average age 41. 8 applicants, 63% accepted, 3 enrolled. In 2009, 5 master's, 1 other advanced degree awarded. *Degree requirements:* For master's and Certificate, one foreign language, comprehensive exam. *Entrance requirements:*

Additional exam requirements/recommendations for international students: Required—TOEFL (minimum score 550 paper-based; 213 computer-based; 80 iBT), IELTS (minimum score 7). *Application deadline:* For fall admission, 8/1 priority date for domestic students, 5/1 for international students; for spring admission, 12/1 priority date for domestic students, 10/1 for international students. Applications are processed on a rolling basis. Application fee: $60 ($95 for international students). Electronic applications accepted. *Financial support:* In 2009–10, 2 students received support, including 2 teaching assistantships with partial tuition reimbursements available (averaging $10,000 per year); institutionally sponsored loans, scholarships/grants, health care benefits, and unspecified assistantships also available. Financial award application deadline: 3/1. *Faculty research:* Second language acquisition/Romance languages, Old French, sociolinguistics/Romance languages, Spanish poetry of the twenties and thirties, post-Spanish Civil War women's fiction. *Unit head:* Dr. Ralph Buechler, Chair/Associate Professor, 702-895-3546, Fax: 702-895-3431, E-mail: ralph.buechler@unlv.edu. *Application contact:* Graduate College Admissions Evaluator, 702-895-3320, Fax: 702-895-4180, E-mail: gradcollege@unlv.edu.

The University of North Carolina at Greensboro, Graduate School, College of Arts and Sciences, Department of Romance Languages, Program in Spanish, Greensboro, NC 27412-5001. Offers advanced Spanish language and Hispanic cultural studies (Certificate); Spanish (MA). *Degree requirements:* For master's, one foreign language, comprehensive exam, thesis or alternative. *Entrance requirements:* For master's, GRE General Test, 3-5 minute tape demonstrating foreign language proficiency, composition in Spanish, sample paper in English. Additional exam requirements/recommendations for international students: Required—TOEFL. Electronic applications accepted.

The University of North Carolina Wilmington, College of Arts and Sciences, Department of Foreign Languages and Literature, Wilmington, NC 28403-3297. Offers Hispanic studies (Graduate Certificate). Part-time programs available. Postbaccalaureate distance learning degree programs offered. *Degree requirements:* For master's, one foreign language, comprehensive exam, thesis or alternative. *Entrance requirements:* For master's, GRE. Additional exam requirements/recommendations for international students: Required—TOEFL (minimum score 550 paper-based; 217 computer-based; 79 iBT), IELTS (minimum score 6.5).

University of Pittsburgh, School of Arts and Sciences, Department of Hispanic Languages and Literatures, Pittsburgh, PA 15260. Offers MA, PhD. Part-time programs available. *Faculty:* 9 full-time (1 woman). *Students:* 39 full-time (22 women); includes 13 minority (2 African Americans, 2 Asian Americans or Pacific Islanders, 9 Hispanic Americans), 20 international. Average age 33. 82 applicants, 34% accepted, 8 enrolled. In 2009, 6 master's, 3 doctorates awarded. Terminal master's awarded for partial completion of doctoral program. *Degree requirements:* For master's, one foreign language, comprehensive exam (for some programs), thesis or alternative, research paper; for doctorate, 2 foreign languages, comprehensive exam, thesis/dissertation. *Entrance requirements:* Additional exam requirements/recommendations for international students: Required—TOEFL (minimum score 550 paper-based; 213 computer-based; 80 iBT). *Application deadline:* For fall admission, 1/15 priority date for domestic and international students. Application fee: $50. Electronic applications accepted. *Expenses:* Tuition, state resident: full-time $16,402; part-time $665 per credit. Tuition, nonresident: full-time $28,694; part-time $1175 per credit. Required fees: $690; $175 per term. Tuition and fees vary according to program. *Financial support:* In 2009–10, 35 students received support, including 7 fellowships with full tuition reimbursements available (averaging $17,927 per year), 26 teaching assistantships with full tuition reimbursements available (averaging $15,065 per year); scholarships/grants, health care benefits, and tuition waivers (partial) also available. Financial award application deadline: 1/15. *Faculty research:* Latin American, Luso-Brazilian, and peninsular literature; cultural theory; cultural studies; race, ethnicity, and post-colonial studies; gender and sexuality studies. *Unit head:* Dr. Elizabeth Monasterios, Chair, 412-624-5226, Fax: 412-624-8505, E-mail: elm15@pitt.edu. *Application contact:* Dr. Daniel Balderston, Director of Graduate Studies, 412-628-0279, Fax: 412-624-8505, E-mail: dbalder@pitt.edu.

University of Puerto Rico, Mayagüez Campus, Graduate Studies, College of Arts and Sciences, Department of Hispanic Studies, Mayagüez, PR 00681-9000. Offers MA. Part-time programs available. *Degree requirements:* For master's, comprehensive exam, thesis. *Entrance requirements:* For master's, minimum GPA of 2.75, BA degree in Hispanic studies or its equivalent. *Faculty research:* Spanish literature, Hispanic-American literature, Puerto Rican literature, stylistics, linguistics.

University of Puerto Rico, Río Piedras, College of Humanities, Department of Hispanic Studies, San Juan, PR 00931-3300. Offers Hispanic studies (MA); Latin American literature (PhD); Puerto Rican literature (PhD); Spanish linguistics (PhD); Spanish literature (PhD). Part-time programs available. *Degree requirements:* For master's, one foreign language, comprehensive exam, thesis; for doctorate, one foreign language, comprehensive exam, thesis/dissertation. *Entrance requirements:* For master's, PAEG or GRE, interview, minimum GPA of 3.0, letter of recommendation (2); for doctorate, PAEG or GRE, interview, master's degree, minimum GPA of 3.0, letter of recommendation (2). *Faculty research:* Poetry of Luis Palés Matos, short stories in Puerto Rico, language in the social process, 'Decima Popular", Anglicism.

The University of Texas at Austin, Graduate School, College of Liberal Arts, Center for Mexican American Studies, Austin, TX 78712-1111. Offers MA.

University of Victoria, Faculty of Graduate Studies, Faculty of Humanities, Department of Hispanic and Italian Studies, Victoria, BC V8W 2Y2, Canada. Offers Hispanic and Italian studies (MA); Hispanic studies (MA). *Degree requirements:* For master's, one foreign language, comprehensive exam, thesis (for some programs). *Entrance requirements:* For master's, undergraduate major in Hispanic studies, minimum B+ average. Additional exam requirements/recommendations for international students: Required—TOEFL (minimum score 575 paper-based; 233 computer-based), IELTS (minimum score 7). Electronic applications accepted. *Faculty research:* Medieval/Renaissance Spanish and Italian literature, Golden Age literature, Latin American literature.

University of Washington, Graduate School, College of Arts and Sciences, Department of Romance Languages and Literature, Division of Spanish and Portuguese Studies, Seattle, WA 98195. Offers Hispanic literary and cultural studies (MA). *Degree requirements:* For master's, 2 foreign languages, thesis optional, exam. *Entrance requirements:* For master's, GRE General Test, minimum GPA of 3.0. Additional exam requirements/recommendations for international students: Required—TOEFL. Electronic applications accepted. *Faculty research:* Medieval through modern Spanish literature and film, Latin American literature, poetry and essay, pan-Hispanic ballad, Hispanic cultural studies, second language acquisition and applied linguistics.

Villanova University, Graduate School of Liberal Arts and Sciences, Department of Modern Languages and Literature, Villanova, PA 19085-1699. Offers Hispanic studies (MA). Part-time and evening/weekend programs available. *Faculty:* 4 full-time (3 women). *Students:* 5 full-time (1 woman), 12 part-time (8 women); includes 5 minority (all Hispanic Americans), 5 international. Average age 34. 8 applicants, 88% accepted, 3 enrolled. In 2009, 10 master's awarded. *Degree requirements:* For master's, one foreign language, comprehensive exam. *Entrance requirements:* For master's, minimum GPA of 3.0, writing sample in Spanish. Additional exam requirements/recommendations for international students: Required—TOEFL. *Application deadline:* For fall admission, 2/1 priority date for domestic and international students; for spring admission, 11/15 priority date for domestic and international students. Applications are processed on a rolling basis. Application fee: $50. Electronic applications accepted. *Expenses:* Tuition: Part-time $630 per credit. Required fees: $60 per credit. Part-time tuition and fees vary according to degree level and program. *Financial support:* Teaching assistantships with tuition reimbursements, Federal Work-Study and scholarships/grants available. Financial award applicants required to submit FAFSA. *Unit head:* Silvia Nagy-Zekmi, Chair, 610-519-7478. *Application contact:* Dr. Adele Lindenmeyr, Dean, Graduate School of Liberal Arts and Sciences, 610-519-7093, Fax: 610-519-7096.

See Close-Up on page 607.

Holocaust and Genocide Studies

Clark University, Graduate School, Department of History, Program in Holocaust History, Worcester, MA 01610-1477. Offers PhD. *Faculty:* 3 full-time (1 woman), 1 part-time/adjunct (0 women). *Students:* 10 full-time (6 women), 4 international. Average age 30. 25 applicants, 12% accepted, 3 enrolled. *Degree requirements:* For doctorate, thesis/dissertation. *Entrance requirements:* Additional exam requirements/recommendations for international students: Required—TOEFL. *Application deadline:* For fall admission, 1/15 for domestic students. Application fee: $50. *Expenses:* Tuition: Full-time $34,900; part-time $4362.50 per course. *Financial support:* In 2009–10, fellowships with full and partial tuition reimbursements (averaging $11,850 per year), research assistantships with full and partial tuition reimbursements (averaging $11,850 per year), teaching assistantships with full and partial tuition reimbursements (averaging $11,850 per year) were awarded; tuition waivers (partial) also available. *Faculty research:* Jewish persecution, children and survivors, Germany's role in the Holocaust. *Unit head:* Deborah Dwork, Professor, 508-421-3745. *Application contact:* Tatyana Macaulay, Program Officer, 508-793-7764, Fax: 508-793-8827, E-mail: chgs@clarku.edu.

Drew University, Caspersen School of Graduate Studies, Program in Arts and Letters, Madison, NJ 07940-1493. Offers holocaust and genocide studies (Certificate); interdisciplinary studies (M Litt, D Litt). Part-time and evening/weekend programs available. *Students:* 19 full-time (13 women), 162 part-time (94 women); includes 12 minority (7 African Americans, 2 Asian Americans or Pacific Islanders, 3 Hispanic Americans), 2 international. Average age 46. 33 applicants, 91% accepted, 23 enrolled. In 2009, 17 master's, 17 doctorates awarded. Terminal master's awarded for partial completion of doctoral program. *Degree requirements:* For master's, thesis optional; for doctorate, thesis/dissertation. *Entrance requirements:* For master's and doctorate, transcripts, writing sample, personal statement, recommendations. Additional exam requirements/recommendations for international students: Required—TOEFL (minimum score 585 paper-based; 240 computer-based; 95 iBT), TWE. *Application deadline:* Applications are processed on a rolling basis. Application fee: $35. *Expenses:* Contact institution. *Financial support:* In 2009–10, 102 students received support. Federal Work-Study, scholarships/grants, and tuition waivers (partial) available. Support available to part-time students. Financial award application deadline: 2/15; financial award applicants required to submit FAFSA. *Faculty research:* Interdisciplinary studies across art, literature, music, philosophy, religion, and history. *Unit head:* Dr. Robert Ready, Director, 973-408-3302, E-mail: rready@drew.edu. *Application contact:* Carla J. Burns, Director of Graduate Admissions, 973-408-3110, Fax: 973-408-3040, E-mail: gradm@drew.edu.

Gratz College, Graduate Programs, Program in Jewish Studies, Melrose Park, PA 19027. Offers classical studies (MA); Holocaust studies (Certificate); Jewish studies (MA, Certificate); modern studies (MA). Part-time programs available. Postbaccalaureate distance learning degree programs offered. *Degree requirements:* For master's, one foreign language, comprehensive exam, thesis optional.

Kean University, Nathan Weiss Graduate College, Program in Holocaust and Genocide Studies, Union, NJ 07083. Offers MA. Part-time and evening/weekend programs available. *Students:* 5 full-time (3 women), 15 part-time (9 women); includes 2 minority (both Hispanic Americans). Average age 33. 5 applicants, 100% accepted, 3 enrolled. In 2009, 4 master's awarded. *Degree requirements:* For master's, comprehensive exam, thesis. *Entrance requirements:* For master's, GRE General Test or MAT, minimum GPA of 3.0 or experience, 2 letters of recommendation, interview, official transcripts from all institutions attended. *Application deadline:* For fall admission, 5/1 for domestic students; for spring admission, 11/1 for domestic students. Application fee: $60 ($150 for international students). Electronic applications accepted. *Expenses:* Tuition, state resident: full-time $10,440; part-time $435 per credit. Tuition, nonresident: full-time $14,160; part-time $590 per credit. Required fees: $2642; $110 per credit. Part-time tuition and fees vary according to course load and degree level. *Financial support:* In 2009–10, 2 research assistantships with full tuition reimbursements (averaging $3,263 per year) were awarded; unspecified assistantships also available. *Unit head:* Dr. Keith Nunes, Program Coordinator, 908-737-5987, E-mail: knunes@kean.edu. *Application contact:* Dororthy Rowe, Pre-Admissions Coordinator, 908-737-5928, Fax: 908-737-5965, E-mail: drowe@kean.edu.

Laura and Alvin Siegal College of Judaic Studies, Graduate Programs, Beachwood, OH 44122-7116. Offers humanities (MA), including Holocaust studies; religious education (MAJS), including Jewish education, Judaic studies. Part-time and evening/weekend programs available. Postbaccalaureate distance learning degree programs offered (no on-campus study). *Degree requirements:* For master's, one foreign language, thesis. *Entrance requirements:* For master's, interview.

The Richard Stockton College of New Jersey, School of Graduate and Continuing Education, Program in Holocaust and Genocide Studies, Pomona, NJ 08240-0195. Offers MA. Part-time programs available. *Degree requirements:* For master's, thesis optional. *Entrance requirements:* Additional exam requirements/recommendations for international students: Required—TOEFL. *Expenses:* Tuition, state resident: part-time $497.36 per credit hour. Tuition, nonresident: part-time $765.61 per credit hour. Required fees: $129.12 per credit hour. Tuition and fees vary according to degree level. *Faculty research:* Women and the Holocaust, survivor perspectives, liberty and persecution.

Seton Hall University, College of Arts and Sciences, Department of Jewish-Christian Studies, South Orange, NJ 07079-2697. Offers Holocaust studies (MA); Jewish-Christian Studies (MA). Part-time and evening/weekend programs available. *Faculty:* 4 full-time (0 women). *Students:* 6 full-time (4 women), 5 part-time (4 women); includes 1 minority (Hispanic American), 1 international. Average age 45. 7 applicants, 100% accepted, 5 enrolled. In 2009, 6 master's awarded. *Degree requirements:* For master's, thesis optional. *Entrance requirements:* For master's, interview or suitable correspondence with department chair. Additional exam requirements/recommendations for international students: Required—TOEFL. *Application deadline:* For fall admission, 7/1 priority date for domestic and international students; for spring admission, 11/1 priority date for domestic and international students. Applications are processed on a rolling basis. Application fee: $50. Electronic applications accepted. *Financial support:* Fellowships, research assistantships, career-related internships or fieldwork, Federal Work-Study, scholarships/grants, tuition waivers (full and partial), and unspecified assistantships

Holocaust and Genocide Studies

Seton Hall University (continued)
available. Support available to part-time students. Financial award application deadline: 8/31; financial award applicants required to submit FAFSA. *Faculty research:* Jewish-Christian issues, Biblical studies, Holocaust studies. *Unit head:* Fr. Lawrence Frizzell, Chair, 973-275-2177, Fax: 973-761-9596, E-mail: frizzela@shu.edu. *Application contact:* Sarah Caron, Director, Graduate Admissions, 973-275-2892, Fax: 973-275-2993, E-mail: shugrad@shu.edu.

Seton Hill University, Program in Genocide and Holocaust Studies, Greensburg, PA 15601. Offers Certificate. Part-time programs available. Postbaccalaureate distance learning degree programs offered (no on-campus study). *Faculty:* 2 full-time (1 woman), 3 part-time/adjunct (1 woman). *Students:* 8 part-time (4 women). 14 applicants, 100% accepted, 5 enrolled. *Entrance requirements:* Additional exam requirements/recommendations for international students: Required—TOEFL (minimum score 600 paper-based; 250 computer-based), IELTS (minimum score 6.5). *Expenses:* Tuition: Full-time $12,780; part-time $710 per credit. Required fees: $300; $150 per semester. Tuition and fees vary according to course load and program. *Unit head:* Dr. Terrance DePasquale, Dean of Graduate and International Programs, 724-838-4256, E-mail: depasquale@setonhill.edu. *Application contact:* Tracey Bartos, Director of Graduate and Adult Studies, 724-838-4283, Fax: 724-830-1891, E-mail: bartos@setonhill.edu.

West Chester University of Pennsylvania, Office of Graduate Studies, College of Arts and Sciences, Department of History, West Chester, PA 19383. Offers history (M Ed, MA); holocaust and genocide studies (MA, Certificate); social studies/history (Teaching Certificate). Part-time and evening/weekend programs available. *Students:* 58 part-time (30 women); includes 3 minority (1 African American, 2 Asian Americans or Pacific Islanders). Average age 28. 38 applicants, 95% accepted, 24 enrolled. In 2009, 14 master's awarded. *Degree requirements:* For master's, thesis optional. *Entrance requirements:* For master's, GMAT, statement of professional goals, writing sample, minimum GPA of 3.0 in history, three letters of recommendation . Additional exam requirements/recommendations for international students: Required—TOEFL (minimum score 550 paper-based; 213 computer-based; 80 iBT). *Application deadline:* For fall admission, 4/15 priority date for domestic students, 3/15 for international students; for spring admission, 10/15 for domestic students, 9/1 for international students. Applications are processed on a rolling basis. Application fee: $35. Electronic applications accepted. *Expenses:* Tuition, state resident: full-time $6666; part-time $370 per credit. Tuition, nonresident: full-time $10,666; part-time $593 per credit. Required fees: $122.56 per credit. *Financial support:* In 2009–10, 5 research assistantships with full and partial tuition reimbursements (averaging $5,000 per year) were awarded; unspecified assistantships also available. Support available to part-time students. Financial award application deadline: 2/15; financial award applicants required to submit FAFSA. *Faculty research:* Oral histories, siege of Leningrad. *Unit head:* Dr. Wayne Hanley, Chair, 610-436-2201, E-mail: whanley@wcupa.edu. *Application contact:* Dr. Jonathan Friedman, Director of the Holocaust/Genocide Education Center and Graduate Coordinator of Holocaust and Genocide Studies, 610-436-2972, E-mail: jfriedmans@wcupa.edu.

Jewish Studies

American Jewish University, Graduate School, Bel Air, CA 90077-1599. Offers MA Ed, MAJCS, MARS, MBA. Part-time and evening/weekend programs available. *Entrance requirements:* For master's, interview, minimum undergraduate GPA of 3.0. Additional exam requirements/recommendations for international students: Required—TOEFL.

American Jewish University, Graduate School, David Lieber School of Graduate Studies, Program in Jewish Communal Studies, Bel Air, CA 90077-1599. Offers MAJCS. *Degree requirements:* For master's, thesis. *Entrance requirements:* For master's, GMAT or GRE General Test, interview.

Brandeis University, Graduate School of Arts and Sciences, Department of Near Eastern and Judaic Studies, Waltham, MA 02454-9110. Offers Near Eastern and Judaic studies (MA, PhD); Near Eastern and Judaic studies and sociology (PhD); Near Eastern and Judaic studies and women's and gender studies (MA); teaching of Hebrew (MAT). Part-time programs available. *Faculty:* 26 full-time (11 women), 4 part-time/adjunct (1 woman). *Students:* 62 full-time (30 women), 1 part-time (0 women); includes 2 minority (1 African American, 1 Hispanic American), 7 international. Average age 33. 88 applicants, 67% accepted, 28 enrolled. In 2009, 10 master's, 6 doctorates awarded. Terminal master's awarded for partial completion of doctoral program. *Degree requirements:* For master's, one foreign language, comprehensive exam, thesis or alternative; for doctorate, 3 foreign languages, comprehensive exam, thesis/dissertation. *Entrance requirements:* For master's, GRE General Test (recommended), letters of recommendation; for doctorate, GRE General Test (recommended), letters of recommendation, transcripts, statement of purpose. Additional exam requirements/recommendations for international students: Required—TOEFL (minimum score 600 paper-based; 250 computer-based; 100 iBT); Recommended—IELTS (minimum score 7). *Application deadline:* For fall admission, 1/15 priority date for domestic and international students. Applications are processed on a rolling basis. Application fee: $75. Electronic applications accepted. *Financial support:* In 2009–10, 17 students received support, including 14 fellowships with full tuition reimbursements available (averaging $20,000 per year), 3 teaching assistantships with partial tuition reimbursements available (averaging $3,200 per year); research assistantships with full and partial tuition reimbursements available, scholarships/grants, health care benefits, and tuition waivers (full and partial) also available. Support available to part-time students. Financial award application deadline: 4/15; financial award applicants required to submit FAFSA. *Faculty research:* Ancient Near East and Bible, philosophy, history, modern Middle East, Islamic studies. *Unit head:* Dr. David Wright, Chair, 781-736-2954, Fax: 781-736-2070, E-mail: wright@brandeis.edu. *Application contact:* Joanne Arnish, Department Administrator, 781-736-2950, Fax: 781-736-2070, E-mail: arnish@brandeis.edu.

Brandeis University, Graduate School of Arts and Sciences, Hornstein Jewish Professional Leadership Program, Waltham, MA 02454-9110. Offers MA/MA, MBA/MA, MPP/MA. Part-time programs available. *Faculty:* 4 full-time (1 woman). *Students:* 5 full-time (3 women), 1 (woman) part-time; includes 1 minority (Hispanic American), 3 international. Average age 25. 30 applicants, 60% accepted. *Entrance requirements:* Additional exam requirements/recommendations for international students: Required—TOEFL (minimum score 600 paper-based; 250 computer-based; 100 iBT); Recommended—IELTS (minimum score 7). *Application deadline:* For fall admission, 2/15 priority date for domestic and international students. Applications are processed on a rolling basis. Application fee: $75. Electronic applications accepted. *Financial support:* In 2009–10, 2 fellowships with full tuition reimbursements were awarded; research assistantships, career-related internships or fieldwork, institutionally sponsored loans, scholarships/grants, tuition waivers (full), and living expense stipends also available. Support available to part-time students. Financial award application deadline: 3/30; financial award applicants required to submit FAFSA. *Faculty research:* Leadership, informal education, demography, Jewish identity, Israel-Diaspora relations. *Unit head:* Dr. Jonathan D. Sarna, Director, 781-736-2990, Fax: 781-736-2070, E-mail: hornstein@brandeis.edu. *Application contact:* Carol Hengerle, Program Administrator, 781-736-2990, Fax: 781-736-2070, E-mail: hornstein@brandeis.edu.

Brooklyn College of the City University of New York, Division of Graduate Studies, Department of Judaic Studies, Brooklyn, NY 11210-2889. Offers MA. Part-time and evening/weekend programs available. *Students:* 1 (woman) part-time. 1 applicant, 0% accepted, 0 enrolled. *Degree requirements:* For master's, 2 foreign languages, thesis or alternative, comprehensive exam or thesis. *Entrance requirements:* For master's, 18 upper-level credits in Judaic studies, interview, 2 letters of recommendation. Additional exam requirements/recommendations for international students: Required—TOEFL (minimum score 525 paper-based; 195 computer-based; 70 iBT). *Application deadline:* For fall admission, 3/1 priority date for domestic students, 2/1 priority date for international students; for spring admission, 11/1 priority date for domestic students, 10/1 priority date for international students. Applications are processed on a rolling basis. Application fee: $125. Electronic applications accepted. *Expenses:* Tuition, area resident: Full-time $7360; part-time $310 per credit hour. Tuition, state resident: full-time $7360; part-time $310 per credit hour. Tuition, nonresident: full-time $13,800; part-time $575 per credit hour. International tuition: $13,800 full-time. Required fees: $140.10 per semester. *Financial support:* Federal Work-Study, institutionally sponsored loans, and scholarships/grants available. Support available to part-time students. Financial award application deadline: 5/1; financial award applicants required to submit FAFSA. *Faculty research:* Biblical studies, Talmud and Midrash, modern Jewish history and thought. *Unit head:* Dr. Sara Reguer, Chairperson, 718-951-5229, Fax: 718-951-4703, E-mail: sreguer@brooklyn.cuny.edu. *Application contact:* Hernan Sierra, Graduate Admissions Coordinator, 718-951-4536, Fax: 718-951-4506, E-mail: grads@brooklyn.cuny.edu.

Brown University, Graduate School, Department of Religious Studies, Providence, RI 02912. Offers ancient Judaism (PhD); early Christianity (PhD); religion and critical thought (PhD); religion in the ancient Mediterranean (PhD); religion, culture, and comparison (PhD). *Degree requirements:* For doctorate, 2 foreign languages, thesis/dissertation. *Entrance requirements:* For doctorate, GRE General Test.

Columbia University, Graduate School of Arts and Sciences, Division of Humanities, Program in Jewish Studies, New York, NY 10027. Offers M Phil, MA, PhD. *Degree requirements:* For master's, variable foreign language requirement; for doctorate, variable foreign language requirement, thesis/dissertation. *Entrance requirements:* For master's and doctorate, GRE General Test. Additional exam requirements/recommendations for international students: Required—TOEFL. *Faculty research:* Jewish history, culture, and institutions; Hebrew, Yiddish, and Jewish languages and literatures; history of Jewish philosophy and religion.

Columbia University, Graduate School of Arts and Sciences, Interdepartmental Committee on Yiddish Studies, New York, NY 10027. Offers MA. Applicants must apply for admission to one of the participating departments: Germanic Languages, History, Middle East Languages and Cultures, Religion. *Entrance requirements:* For master's, high degree of proficiency in Yiddish.

Columbia University, Graduate School of Arts and Sciences, Program in Liberal Studies, New York, NY 10027. Offers American studies (MA); East Asian studies (MA); human rights studies (MA); Islamic culture studies (MA); Jewish studies (MA); medieval studies (MA); modern European studies (MA); South Asian studies (MA). Part-time and evening/weekend programs available. *Degree requirements:* For master's, thesis.

Concordia University, School of Graduate Studies, Faculty of Arts and Science, Department of Religion, Program in Judaic Studies, Montréal, QC H3G 1M8, Canada. Offers MA. *Degree requirements:* For master's, one foreign language, comprehensive exam, thesis optional. *Entrance requirements:* For master's, Hebrew exam, honors degree in Judaic studies or equivalent. Additional exam requirements/recommendations for international students: Required—TOEFL. *Faculty research:* Jewish religious reflections and modern philosophy of religion, Judaism and modernity, Judaism in late antiquity.

Cornell University, Graduate School, Graduate Fields of Arts and Sciences, Field of Near Eastern Studies, Ithaca, NY 14853-0001. Offers ancient Near Eastern studies (MA, PhD); Arabic and Islamic studies (MA, PhD); biblical studies (MA, PhD); Hebrew and Judaic studies (MA, PhD). *Faculty:* 18 full-time (6 women). *Students:* 5 full-time (2 women), 1 international. Average age 26. 26 applicants. In 2009, 1 master's, 1 doctorate awarded. Terminal master's awarded for partial completion of doctoral program. *Degree requirements:* For master's, one foreign language, thesis; for doctorate, 2 foreign languages, comprehensive exam, thesis/dissertation. *Entrance requirements:* For master's and doctorate, GRE General Test, 2 years of 1 Near Eastern language, 3 letters of recommendation, writing sample. Additional exam requirements/recommendations for international students: Required—TOEFL (minimum score 550 paper-based; 213 computer-based; 77 iBT). *Application deadline:* For fall admission, 2/1 for domestic students. Application fee: $70. Electronic applications accepted. *Expenses:* Tuition: Full-time $29,500. Required fees: $70. Full-time tuition and fees vary according to degree level, program and student level. *Financial support:* In 2009–10, 5 students received support; fellowships with full tuition reimbursements available, research assistantships with full tuition reimbursements available, teaching assistantships with full tuition reimbursements available, institutionally sponsored loans, scholarships/grants, health care benefits, tuition waivers (full and partial), and unspecified assistantships available. Financial award applicants required to submit FAFSA. *Faculty research:* Ancient Near East (including archeology), Hebrew and Judaic studies (including Bible), early Christianity, Arabic and Islamic studies, modern Middle East. *Unit head:* Director of Graduate Studies, 607-255-1329, Fax: 607-255-6450. *Application contact:* Graduate Field Assistant, 607-255-1329, Fax: 607-255-6450, E-mail: neareastern@cornell.edu.

The Criswell College, Graduate School of the Bible, Dallas, TX 75246-1537. Offers biblical studies (M Div); Christian leadership (MA); counseling (MA); Jewish studies (MA); ministry (MA); theological and biblical studies (MA). Part-time programs available. *Degree requirements:* For master's, 2 foreign languages, thesis optional; for M Div, 2 foreign languages, thesis/dissertation optional. *Entrance requirements:* For M Div and master's, GRE General Test, minimum GPA of 2.5. Electronic applications accepted. *Faculty research:* Emphasis on biblical languages (Hebrew and Greek), expository preaching and evangelism in the local church.

Emory University, Graduate School of Arts and Sciences, Program in Jewish Studies, Atlanta, GA 30322-1100. Offers MA. *Degree requirements:* For master's, one foreign language, thesis optional. *Entrance requirements:* For master's, GRE General Test, 2 years of course work in Hebrew or equivalent, writing sample. Additional exam requirements/recommendations for international students: Required—TOEFL. Electronic applications accepted. *Faculty research:* Medieval Jewish history and culture, Hebrew language and linguistics, Jewish law, Jewish ethics, Holocaust studies.

Graduate Theological Union, Graduate Programs, Berkeley, CA 94709-1212. Offers art and religion (MA, PhD, Th D); biblical languages (MA); Biblical studies (PhD, Th D); biblical studies (MA); Buddhist studies (MA); Christian spirituality (MA, PhD, Th D); cultural and historical studies of religions (MA, PhD, Th D); ethics and social theory (PhD, Th D); history (MA, PhD, Th D); homiletics (MA, PhD, Th D); interdisciplinary studies (PhD, Th D); Jewish studies (MA, PhD, Th D, Certificate); liturgical studies (MA, PhD, Th D); Near Eastern religions (PhD, Th D); Orthodox Christian studies (MA); religion and psychology (MA, PhD, Th D); religion and society/ethics and social theory (MA); systematic and philosophical theology (MA, PhD, Th D). *Accreditation:* ATS. Terminal master's awarded for partial completion of doctoral program. *Degree requirements:* For master's, one foreign language, thesis; for doctorate, one foreign language, comprehensive exam, thesis/dissertation. *Entrance requirements:* For master's,

GRE General Test; for doctorate, GRE General Test, MA or M Div. Additional exam requirements/recommendations for international students: Required—TOEFL. Electronic applications accepted.

Gratz College, Graduate Programs, Program in Jewish Studies, Melrose Park, PA 19027. Offers classical studies (MA); Holocaust studies (Certificate); Jewish studies (MA, Certificate); modern studies (MA). Part-time programs available. Postbaccalaureate distance learning degree programs offered. *Degree requirements:* For master's, one foreign language, comprehensive exam, thesis optional.

Harvard University, Graduate School of Arts and Sciences, Department of Near Eastern Languages and Civilizations, Cambridge, MA 02138. Offers Akkadian and Sumerian (AM, PhD); Arabic (AM, PhD); Armenian (AM, PhD); biblical history (AM, PhD); Hebrew (AM, PhD); Indo-Muslim culture (AM, PhD); Iranian (AM, PhD); Jewish history and literature (AM, PhD); Persian (AM, PhD); Semitic philology (AM, PhD); Syro-Palestinian archaeology (AM, PhD); Turkish (AM, PhD). *Degree requirements:* For doctorate, variable foreign language requirement, thesis/dissertation, general exams. *Entrance requirements:* For master's, GRE General Test; for doctorate, GRE General Test, proficiency in a Near Eastern language. Additional exam requirements/recommendations for international students: Required—TOEFL. *Expenses:* Tuition: Full-time $33,696. Required fees: $1126. Full-time tuition and fees vary according to program.

Hebrew College, Cantor Educator Program, Newton Centre, MA 02459. Offers MJ Ed. *Entrance requirements:* For master's, GRE, interview. Additional exam requirements/recommendations for international students: Required—TOEFL.

Hebrew College, Program in Jewish Studies, Newton Centre, MA 02459. Offers Jewish liturgical music (Certificate); Jewish music education (Certificate); Jewish studies (MA). Part-time and evening/weekend programs available. Postbaccalaureate distance learning degree programs offered (minimal on-campus study). *Degree requirements:* For master's, one foreign language. *Entrance requirements:* For master's, GRE, interview. Additional exam requirements/recommendations for international students: Required—TOEFL.

Hebrew Union College–Jewish Institute of Religion, Edgar F. Magnin School of Graduate Studies, Los Angeles, CA 90007-3796. Offers MAJS, DHL, DHS. Part-time programs available. Terminal master's awarded for partial completion of doctoral program. *Degree requirements:* For master's, one foreign language, thesis, Hebrew; for doctorate, one foreign language, thesis/dissertation, Hebrew. *Entrance requirements:* For master's, GRE General Test, Hebrew Language Test, interview, minimum undergraduate GPA of 3.0; for doctorate, GRE General Test, Hebrew Language Test, interview, minimum graduate GPA of 3.0. Additional exam requirements/recommendations for international students: Required—TOEFL (minimum score 550 paper-based). Electronic applications accepted.

Hebrew Union College–Jewish Institute of Religion, Rabbinic School, Cincinnati, OH 45220-2488. Offers MAHL. *Accreditation:* ACIPE. *Degree requirements:* For MAHL, one foreign language, thesis/dissertation. *Entrance requirements:* GRE General Test, Hebrew competency exam, interview, psychological test. *Faculty research:* Comprehensive Aramaic lexicon, four-volume history (German Jews and modern times).

Hebrew Union College–Jewish Institute of Religion, School of Graduate Studies, Cincinnati, OH 45220-2488. Offers Bible and the ancient Near East (M Phil, MA, PhD); Hebrew letters (DHL); history of biblical interpretation (M Phil, MA, PhD); Jewish and Christian studies in the Greco-Roman period (M Phil, PhD); Jewish and cognate studies (M Phil); Judaic and cognate studies (MA, PhD); modern Jewish history (M Phil, MA, PhD); philosophy and Jewish religious thought (M Phil, MA, PhD); rabbinics (M Phil, MA, PhD). Part-time programs available. Terminal master's awarded for partial completion of doctoral program. *Degree requirements:* For master's, one foreign language, thesis optional; for doctorate, 3 foreign languages, comprehensive exam, thesis/dissertation. *Entrance requirements:* For master's and doctorate, GRE General Test, knowledge of Hebrew. Additional exam requirements/recommendations for international students: Required—TOEFL. *Faculty research:* Aramaic lexicon translations, German-Jewish history, neo-Babylonian texts.

Hebrew Union College–Jewish Institute of Religion, School of Graduate Studies, Program in Judaic Studies, New York, NY 10012-1186. Offers MAJS. Part-time programs available. *Degree requirements:* For master's, one foreign language, thesis. *Entrance requirements:* For master's, GRE, minimum 2 years of college-level Hebrew. *Faculty research:* Philosophy and theology, Bible, Hebrew, history and Rabbinics.

The Jewish Theological Seminary, The Graduate School, New York, NY 10027-4649. Offers ancient Judaism (MA, DHL, PhD); Bible (MA, DHL, PhD); Jewish education (PhD); Jewish history (MA, DHL, PhD); Jewish literature (MA, DHL, PhD); Jewish philosophy (MA, DHL, PhD); liturgy (MA, DHL, PhD); medieval Jewish studies (MA, DHL, PhD); Midrash (MA, DHL, PhD); modern Jewish studies (MA, DHL, PhD); Talmud and rabbinics (MA, DHL, PhD); MA/MSW. *Accreditation:* ACIPE. Part-time programs available. Terminal master's awarded for partial completion of doctoral program. *Degree requirements:* For master's, one foreign language, comprehensive exam (for some programs), thesis (for some programs); for doctorate, 3 foreign languages, comprehensive exam (for some programs), thesis/dissertation. *Entrance requirements:* For master's, GRE or MAT, 3 letters of recommendation, writing sample; for doctorate, GRE or MAT, 3 letters of recommendation, writing research sample. Additional exam requirements/recommendations for international students: Required—TOEFL (minimum score 100 computer-based). *Expenses:* Tuition: Full-time $21,200; part-time $1000 per credit. Required fees: $400 per semester. Tuition and fees vary according to degree level.

See Close-Up on page 511.

The Jewish Theological Seminary, William Davidson Graduate School of Jewish Education, New York, NY 10027-4649. Offers MA, Ed D. Offered in conjunction with Rabbinical School; H. L. Miller Cantorial School and College of Jewish Music; Teacher's College, Columbia University; and Union Theological Seminary. Part-time programs available. Postbaccalaureate distance learning degree programs offered (minimal on-campus study). *Degree requirements:* For master's, one foreign language, thesis optional; for doctorate, one foreign language, comprehensive exam, thesis/dissertation. *Entrance requirements:* For master's, GRE or MAT, 3 letters of recommendation; for doctorate, GRE or MAT, writing sample, 3 letters of recommendation. *Expenses:* Tuition: Full-time $21,200; part-time $1000 per credit. Required fees: $400 per semester. Tuition and fees vary according to degree level.

Jewish University of America, Graduate School, Graduate Research Division, Skokie, IL 60077-3248. Offers Bible (MHL, DHL); Hebrew (MHL, DHL); history (MHL, DHL); Jewish studies (MHL, DHL); philosophy (MHL, DHL); rabbinics (MHL, DHL). Part-time programs available. *Degree requirements:* For doctorate, one foreign language, thesis/dissertation; for MHL, thesis/dissertation optional. *Entrance requirements:* For MHL and doctorate, interview.

Laura and Alvin Siegal College of Judaic Studies, Graduate Programs, Program in Religious Education, Beachwood, OH 44122-7116. Offers Jewish education (MAJS); Judaic studies (MAJS). Part-time and evening/weekend programs available. Postbaccalaureate distance learning degree programs offered (minimal on-campus study). *Degree requirements:* For master's, one foreign language, thesis. *Entrance requirements:* For master's, interview.

McGill University, Faculty of Graduate and Postdoctoral Studies, Faculty of Arts, Department of Jewish Studies, Montréal, QC H3A 2T5, Canada. Offers MA.

New York University, Graduate School of Arts and Science, Program in Museum Studies, New York, NY 10012-1019. Offers museum studies (MA, Advanced Certificate), including Africana studies (MA), Hebrew and Judaic studies (MA), Latin American and Caribbean studies (MA), Near Eastern studies (MA). Part-time and evening/weekend programs available. *Students:* 62 full-time (57 women), 23 part-time (21 women); includes 13 minority (1 African American, 2 American Indian/Alaska Native, 3 Asian Americans or Pacific Islanders, 7 Hispanic Americans), 15 international. Average age 27. 220 applicants, 52% accepted, 37 enrolled. In 2009, 37 master's awarded. *Entrance requirements:* For degree, master's degree or PhD. Additional exam requirements/recommendations for international students: Required—TOEFL. *Application deadline:* For fall admission, 2/1 for domestic students; for spring admission, 11/1 for domestic students. Application fee: $90. *Expenses:* Tuition: Full-time $30,528; part-time $1272 per credit. Required fees: $2177. *Financial support:* Application deadline: 2/1. *Faculty research:* Modern and contemporary art, history of museums and exhibitions, conservation of cultural materials, museum anthropology, ethnography. *Unit head:* Haidy Geismar, Director, 212-998-8080, Fax: 212-995-4185, E-mail: museum.studies@nyu.edu. *Application contact:* Tatiana Kamorina, Department Administrator, 212-998-8080, Fax: 212-995-4185, E-mail: museum.studies@nyu.edu.

New York University, Graduate School of Arts and Science, Skirball Department of Hebrew and Judaic Studies, New York, NY 10012-1019. Offers Hebrew and Judaic studies (MA, PhD); Hebrew and Judaic studies/museum studies (MA). Part-time programs available. *Students:* 52 full-time (30 women), 34 part-time (25 women); includes 3 minority (1 African American, 1 Asian American or Pacific Islander, 1 Hispanic American), 23 international. Average age 32. 103 applicants, 45% accepted, 11 enrolled. In 2009, 8 master's, 3 doctorates awarded. Terminal master's awarded for partial completion of doctoral program. *Degree requirements:* For master's, 2 foreign languages, comprehensive exam, thesis optional; for doctorate, 4 foreign languages, comprehensive exam, thesis/dissertation. *Entrance requirements:* For master's, GRE General Test, minimum 2 years of undergraduate course work in Hebrew; for doctorate, GRE General Test. Additional exam requirements/recommendations for international students: Required—TOEFL. *Application deadline:* For fall admission, 12/18 priority date for domestic students. Application fee: $90. *Expenses:* Tuition: Full-time $30,528; part-time $1272 per credit. Required fees: $2177. *Financial support:* Fellowships with tuition reimbursements, teaching assistantships with tuition reimbursements, Federal Work-Study and institutionally sponsored loans available. Financial award application deadline: 1/4; financial award applicants required to submit FAFSA. *Faculty research:* Post-biblical and Talmudic literature and history, mysticism, Bible and ancient Near East, medieval and modern Jewish history, medieval and modern Jewish philosophy. *Unit head:* Lawrence Schiffman, Chair, 212-98-8980, Fax: 212-995-4178, E-mail: gsas.hebrewjudaic@nyu.edu. *Application contact:* Mark Smith, Director of Graduate Studies, 212-998-8980, Fax: 212-995-4178, E-mail: gsas.hebrewjudaic@nyu.edu.

New York University, Steinhardt School of Culture, Education, and Human Development, Department of Humanities and Social Sciences in the Professions, Program in Education and Jewish Studies, New York, NY 10012-1019. Offers MA, PhD, MPA/MA. Part-time programs available. *Students:* 18 full-time (10 women), 5 part-time (3 women); includes 2 minority (both Hispanic Americans), 2 international. Average age 33. 21 applicants, 71% accepted, 10 enrolled. In 2009, 3 doctorates awarded. *Degree requirements:* For doctorate, thesis/dissertation. *Entrance requirements:* For doctorate, GRE General Test, interview. Additional exam requirements/recommendations for international students: Required—TOEFL. *Application deadline:* For fall admission, 12/15 priority date for domestic and international students; for spring admission, 11/1 for domestic and international students. Applications are processed on a rolling basis. Application fee: $75. Electronic applications accepted. *Expenses:* Tuition: Full-time $30,528; part-time $1272 per credit. Required fees: $2177. *Financial support:* Fellowships with full and partial tuition reimbursements, teaching assistantships with partial tuition reimbursements, career-related internships or fieldwork, Federal Work-Study, institutionally sponsored loans, scholarships/grants, tuition waivers (partial), and unspecified assistantships available. Support available to part-time students. Financial award application deadline: 2/1; financial award applicants required to submit FAFSA. *Faculty research:* Jewish education, educational history, Judaic studies. *Unit head:* Dr. Harold Wechsler, Director, 212-992-9475, Fax: 212-995-4178. *Application contact:* 212-998-5030, Fax: 212-995-4328, E-mail: steinhardt.gradadmissions@nyu.edu.

Rice University, Graduate Programs, School of Humanities, Department of Religious Studies, Houston, TX 77251-1892. Offers African religions (PhD); African-American religions (PhD); contemplative studies (PhD); ghosticism, esotericism, mysticism (PhD); Islam (PhD); Jewish thought and philosophy (PhD); modern Christianity in thought and popular culture (PhD); psychology of religion (PhD); the Bible and beyond (PhD). *Faculty:* 11 full-time (3 women), 2 part-time/adjunct (both women). *Students:* 37 full-time (13 women); includes 10 minority (9 African Americans, 1 Asian American or Pacific Islander), 9 international. Average age 31. 42 applicants, 14% accepted, 6 enrolled. In 2009, 2 doctorates awarded. *Degree requirements:* For doctorate, 2 foreign languages, comprehensive exam, thesis/dissertation. *Entrance requirements:* For doctorate, GRE, letters of recommendation, writing sample. Additional exam requirements/recommendations for international students: Required—TOEFL (minimum score 600 paper-based; 90 iBT). *Application deadline:* For fall admission, 1/1 for domestic students, 1/15 for international students. Application fee: $70. Electronic applications accepted. *Financial support:* In 2009–10, 14 fellowships (averaging $15,900 per year) were awarded. Financial award application deadline: 5/15; financial award applicants required to submit FAFSA. *Faculty research:* Origins and historical development of Islam, history of Christianity, the study of comparative religion, African-American religion, religion and culture. Total annual research expenditures: $46,514. *Unit head:* Prof. William B. Parsons, Associate Professor, Religious Studies, 713-348-2712, Fax: 713-348-5486, E-mail: pars@rice.edu. *Application contact:* Sylvia Louie, Senior Department Coordinator, 713-348-5201, Fax: 713-348-5486, E-mail: reli@rice.edu.

St. Petersburg Theological Seminary, Graduate Programs, St. Petersburg, FL 33708. Offers Biblical studies (MA); counseling (MA); divinity (M Div); education (MA); Judaic studies (MA); ministry (MA, D Min); religious teacher (MA). Part-time and evening/weekend programs available. Postbaccalaureate distance learning degree programs offered (minimal on-campus study). *Degree requirements:* For master's, thesis; for doctorate, thesis/dissertation. *Entrance requirements:* For M Div, Bachelor degree; for doctorate, Master degree. Electronic applications accepted.

Seton Hall University, College of Arts and Sciences, Department of Jewish-Christian Studies, South Orange, NJ 07079-2697. Offers Holocaust studies (MA); Jewish-Christian Studies (MA). Part-time and evening/weekend programs available. *Faculty:* 4 full-time (0 women). *Students:* 6 full-time (4 women), 5 part-time (4 women); includes 1 minority (Hispanic American), 1 international. Average age 45. 7 applicants, 100% accepted, 5 enrolled. In 2009, 6 master's awarded. *Degree requirements:* For master's, thesis optional. *Entrance requirements:* For master's, interview or suitable correspondence with department chair. Additional exam requirements/recommendations for international students: Required—TOEFL. *Application deadline:* For fall admission, 7/1 priority date for domestic and international students; for spring admission, 11/1 priority date for domestic and international students. Applications are processed on a rolling basis. Application fee: $50. Electronic applications accepted. *Financial support:* Fellowships, research assistantships, career-related internships or fieldwork, Federal Work-Study, scholarships/grants, tuition waivers (full and partial), and unspecified assistantships available. Support available to part-time students. Financial award application deadline: 8/31; financial award applicants required to submit FAFSA. *Faculty research:* Jewish-Christian issues, Biblical studies, Holocaust studies. *Unit head:* Fr. Lawrence Frizzell, Chair, 973-275-2177, Fax: 973-761-9596, E-mail: frizzela@shu.edu. *Application contact:* Sarah Caron, Director, Graduate Admissions, 973-275-2892, Fax: 973-275-2993, E-mail: shugrad@shu.edu.

Southern Evangelical Seminary, Veritas Graduate School of Apologetics and Counter-Cult Ministry, Matthews, NC 28105. Offers apologetics (MA, D Min, PhD, Certificate); Islamic studies (MA); Jewish studies (MA); philosophy (MA); religion (MA). Part-time and evening/weekend programs available. Postbaccalaureate distance learning degree programs offered (minimal on-campus study). *Degree requirements:* For master's, thesis optional; for doctorate, comprehensive exam (for some programs), thesis/dissertation. *Entrance requirements:* Additional exam requirements/recommendations for international students: Required—TOEFL (minimum score 600 paper-based; 250 computer-based).

Jewish Studies

Spertus Institute of Jewish Studies, Graduate Programs, Program in Jewish Studies, Chicago, IL 60605-1901. Offers MAJS, MSJE, MSJS, DJS, DSJS. Part-time and evening/weekend programs available. Postbaccalaureate distance learning degree programs offered (minimal on-campus study). *Degree requirements:* For master's, one foreign language, thesis (for some programs); for doctorate, one foreign language, thesis/dissertation. *Entrance requirements:* For master's, interview, BAJS (MAJS); for doctorate, MAJS.

Telshe Yeshiva–Chicago, Graduate Program, Chicago, IL 60625-5598. Offers Second Talmudic Degree. *Accreditation:* AARTS.

Touro College, Graduate School of Jewish Studies, New York, NY 10010. Offers MA. Part-time programs available. *Degree requirements:* For master's, one foreign language, thesis. *Entrance requirements:* For master's, previous course work in Jewish studies, proficiency in Hebrew. *Faculty research:* Medieval and modern Jewish history, Jewish philosophy, holocaust studies, Jewish education.

Towson University, College of Graduate Studies and Research, Baltimore Hebrew Institute, Towson, MD 21252. Offers Jewish communal service (MAJCS); Jewish education (MAJE); Jewish studies (MAJS).

University of California, Berkeley, Graduate Division, College of Letters and Science, Program in Jewish Studies, Berkeley, CA 94720-1500. Offers PhD. *Students:* 9 full-time (6 women). Average age 39. 31 applicants, 6 enrolled. *Entrance requirements:* For doctorate, GRE General Test, 3 letters of recommendation. *Application deadline:* For fall admission, 12/15 for domestic students. Application fee: $70 ($90 for international students). *Unit head:* Robert Alter, Chair, 510-643-2995, E-mail: altcos@berkeley.edu. *Application contact:* Sandra J. B. Richmond, Program Analyst, 510-643-2995, Fax: 510-643-3927, E-mail: info@jewishstudies.berkeley.edu.

University of California, San Diego, Office of Graduate Studies, Department of History, La Jolla, CA 92093. Offers history (MA, PhD); Judaic studies (MA); science studies (PhD). *Degree requirements:* For doctorate, thesis/dissertation. *Entrance requirements:* For master's and doctorate, GRE General Test. Electronic applications accepted.

University of Connecticut, Graduate School, College of Liberal Arts and Sciences, Field of International Studies, Program in Judaic Studies, Storrs, CT 06269. Offers MA. *Faculty:* 51 full-time (29 women). *Students:* 5 full-time (3 women), 4 part-time (all women); includes 6 minority (all Hispanic Americans), 1 international. Average age 32. 12 applicants, 33% accepted, 1 enrolled. In 2009, 2 master's awarded. *Entrance requirements:* Additional exam requirements/recommendations for international students: Required—TOEFL (minimum score 550 paper-based; 213 computer-based). *Application deadline:* For fall admission, 2/1 priority date for domestic and international students; for spring admission, 11/1 for domestic students, 10/1 for international students. Applications are processed on a rolling basis. Electronic applications accepted. *Expenses:* Tuition, state resident: full-time $4725; part-time $525 per credit. Tuition, nonresident: full-time $12,267; part-time $1363 per credit. Required fees: $346 per semester. Tuition and fees vary according to course load. *Financial support:* In 2009–10, 4 research assistantships with full tuition reimbursements, 1 teaching assistantship with full tuition reimbursement were awarded; Federal Work-Study, scholarships/grants, health care benefits, and unspecified assistantships also available. Financial award application deadline: 2/1. *Unit head:* Arnold Dashefsky, Director, 860-486-4289, Fax: 860-486-6332, E-mail: arnold.dashefsky@uconn.edu. *Application contact:* Arnold Dashefsky, Director, 860-486-4289, Fax: 860-486-6332, E-mail: arnold.dashefsky@uconn.edu.

University of Maryland, College Park, Academic Affairs, College of Arts and Humanities, Program in Jewish Studies, College Park, MD 20742. Offers MA. *Faculty:* 3 full-time (all women), 1 part-time/adjunct (0 women). *Students:* 5 full-time (all women), 1 (woman) part-time, 2 international. 5 applicants, 60% accepted, 2 enrolled. In 2009, 2 master's awarded. *Degree requirements:* For master's, thesis or 2 major research papers. *Entrance requirements:* For master's, GRE General Test, 3 letters of recommendation, writing sample. Additional exam requirements/recommendations for international students: Required—TOEFL. *Application deadline:* For fall admission, 12/15 for domestic and international students. Application fee: $60. *Expenses:* Tuition, area resident: Part-time $471 per credit hour. Tuition, state resident: part-time $471 per credit hour. Tuition, nonresident: part-time $1016 per credit hour. Required fees: $337.04 per term. *Financial support:* In 2009–10, 2 teaching assistantships (averaging $19,000 per year) were awarded; fellowships also available. *Unit head:* Hayim Lapin, Director, Meyerhoff Program and Center for Jewish Studies, 301-405-4734, E-mail: hlapin@umd.edu. *Application contact:* Dean of Graduate Studies, 301-405-0376, Fax: 301-314-9305.

University of Michigan, Horace H. Rackham School of Graduate Studies, College of Literature, Science, and the Arts, Department of Near Eastern Studies, Ann Arbor, MI 48109. Offers ancient Near Eastern studies (AM, PhD); Arabic for professional purposes (AM); Arabic language and literature (AM, PhD); Armenian studies (AM, PhD); Christianity in late antiquity (AM, PhD); Egyptology (AM, PhD); Hebrew Bible and ancient Israel (AM, PhD); Hebrew literature (AM, PhD); Islamic studies (AM, PhD); Jewish cultural studies (AM, PhD); Jewish mysticism (AM, PhD); Persian and Iranian studies (AM, PhD); Rabbinic literature (AM, PhD); Second Temple Judaism (AM, PhD); teaching of Arabic as a foreign language (AM); Turkish studies (AM, PhD). Part-time programs available. *Faculty:* 23 full-time (5 women), 15 part-time/adjunct (6 women). *Students:* 47 full-time (23 women), 1 part-time (0 women); includes 1 minority (Hispanic American), 8 international. Average age 31. 99 applicants, 15% accepted, 8 enrolled. In 2009, 4 master's, 4 doctorates awarded. Terminal master's awarded for partial completion of doctoral program. *Degree requirements:* For master's, 2 foreign languages; for doctorate, 4 foreign languages, comprehensive exam, thesis/dissertation. *Entrance requirements:* For master's, GRE General Test; for doctorate, GRE General Test, master's degree. Additional exam requirements/recommendations for international students: Required—TOEFL (minimum score 560 paper-based; 220 computer-based; 84 iBT). *Application deadline:* For fall admission, 12/15 for domestic and international students. Application fee: $60 ($75 for international students). Electronic applications accepted. *Expenses:* Tuition, state resident: full-time $17,286; part-time $1099 per credit hour. Tuition, nonresident: full-time $34,944; part-time $2080 per credit hour. Required fees: $95 per semester. Tuition and fees vary according to course load, degree level and program. *Financial support:* In 2009–10, 43 students received support, including 21 fellowships with full tuition reimbursements available (averaging $16,694 per year), research assistantships with tuition reimbursements available (averaging $16,694 per year), 22 teaching assistantships with full tuition reimbursements available (averaging $16,694 per year); scholarships/grants, health care benefits, unspecified assistantships, and spring/summer stipends also available. *Faculty research:* Middle and Near Eastern literatures, languages, cultures from ancient times to the present. *Unit head:* Prof. Michael Bonner, Chair, 734-764-0314, Fax: 734-936-2679, E-mail: mbonner@umich.edu. *Application contact:* Angela Beskow, Student Services Assistant, 734-763-4539, Fax: 734-936-2679, E-mail: aradjews@umich.edu.

University of Michigan, Jean and Samuel Frankel Center for Judaic Studies, Ann Arbor, MI 48178. Offers MA, Graduate Certificate. Part-time programs available. *Faculty:* 32 full-time (14 women). *Students:* 10 full-time (5 women), 1 (woman) part-time. Average age 26. 10 applicants, 80% accepted, 5 enrolled. In 2009, 2 master's awarded. *Degree requirements:* For master's, thesis, Fourth-term proficiency in either Hebrew or Yiddish; for Graduate Certificate, capstone course (including public lecture), reading knowledge of 1 Jewish language. *Entrance requirements:* For master's, GRE General Test; for Graduate Certificate, Admission to a U-M doctoral program. Additional exam requirements/recommendations for international students: Required—TOEFL (minimum score 540 paper-based; 220 computer-based). *Application deadline:* For fall admission, 1/10 for domestic and international students; for winter admission, 9/1 for domestic and international students. Application fee: $60 ($75 for international students). Electronic applications accepted. *Expenses:* Tuition, state resident: full-time $17,286; part-time $1099 per credit hour. Tuition, nonresident: full-time $34,944; part-time $2080 per credit hour. Required fees: $95 per semester. Tuition and fees vary according to course load, degree level and program. *Financial support:* In 2009–10, 2 students received support, including 12 fellowships (averaging $3,000 per year); summer research fellowships also available. *Faculty research:* Jewish history (antique to modern); Jewish literature; Yiddish language and literature; Jewish cultural studies; Jewish political and social studies. *Unit head:* Prof. Deborah Dash Moore, Director, 734-763-9047, Fax: 734-936-2186, E-mail: ddmoore@umich.edu. *Application contact:* Tracy Ann Darnell, Student/Fellow Coordinator, 734-615-6097, Fax: 734-936-2186, E-mail: tdarnell@umich.edu.

The University of Montana, Graduate School, School of Fine Arts, Department of Art, Missoula, MT 59812-0002. Offers fine arts (MA, MFA), including art (MA), art history (MA), ceramics (MFA), integrated arts and education (MA), media arts (MFA), painting and drawing (MFA), photography (MFA), printmaking (MFA), sculpture (MFA). *Accreditation:* NASAD (one or more programs are accredited). *Degree requirements:* For master's, thesis exhibit. *Entrance requirements:* For master's, GRE General Test, portfolio.

University of St. Michael's College, Faculty of Theology, Toronto, ON M5S 1J4, Canada. Offers Catholic leadership (MA); eastern Christian studies (Diploma); religious education (Diploma); theological studies (Diploma); theology (M Div, MA, MRE, MTS, D Min, PhD, Th D); theology and Jewish studies (MA). *Accreditation:* ATS (one or more programs are accredited). Part-time programs available. *Faculty:* 9 full-time (2 women), 23 part-time/adjunct (6 women). *Students:* 106 full-time (35 women), 98 part-time (59 women); includes 35 minority (13 African Americans, 21 Asian Americans or Pacific Islanders, 1 Hispanic American), 24 international. Average age 40. 72 applicants, 75% accepted, 44 enrolled. In 2009, 29 first professional degrees, 7 master's, 2 doctorates, 3 other advanced degrees awarded. *Degree requirements:* For master's, thesis (for some programs), 1 foreign language (MA), 2 foreign languages (Th M); for doctorate, 3 foreign languages, comprehensive exam, thesis/dissertation; for M Div, thesis/dissertation optional; for other advanced degree, thesis optional. *Entrance requirements:* For M Div and other advanced degree, minimum GPA of 2.7; for master's, M Div or BA, course work in an ancient or modern language, minimum GPA of 3.3; for doctorate, MA in theology, Th M, or M Div with thesis, minimum GPA of 3.7. Additional exam requirements/recommendations for international students: Required—TOEFL (minimum score 600 paper-based; 250 computer-based). *Application deadline:* For fall admission, 1/15 for domestic and international students. Applications are processed on a rolling basis. Application fee: $25 Canadian dollars. Electronic applications accepted. *Expenses:* Contact institution. *Financial support:* In 2009–10, 45 students received support, including fellowships with partial tuition reimbursements available (averaging $2,500 per year), research assistantships with partial tuition reimbursements available (averaging $2,400 per year), 4 teaching assistantships with partial tuition reimbursements available (averaging $2,400 per year); scholarships/grants, tuition waivers (partial), and bursaries also available. Financial award application deadline: 2/1. *Faculty research:* Patristics, eastern Christianity, ecology and theology, ecumenism, Jewish Christian studies. *Unit head:* Fr. Dr. Mario O. D'Souza, Dean, 416-926-7265, Fax: 416-926-7294, E-mail: mario.dsouza@utoronto.ca. *Application contact:* Allen Croxall, Student Recruitment and Advancement Officer, 416-926-1300 Ext. 3281, Fax: 416-926-7294, E-mail: allen.croxall@utoronto.ca.

University of Wisconsin–Madison, Graduate School, College of Letters and Science, Department of Hebrew and Semitic Studies, Madison, WI 53706-1380. Offers MA, PhD. Terminal master's awarded for partial completion of doctoral program. *Degree requirements:* For master's, 2 foreign languages; for doctorate, thesis/dissertation. *Entrance requirements:* For master's and doctorate, GRE. Electronic applications accepted. *Expenses:* Tuition, state resident: part-time $594 per credit. Tuition, nonresident: part-time $1504 per credit. Required fees: $65 per credit. Tuition and fees vary according to course load, program and reciprocity agreements. *Faculty research:* Biblical language and literature, Northwest Semitic languages.

University of Wisconsin–Milwaukee, Graduate School, College of Letters and Sciences, Interdepartmental Program in Foreign Language and Literature, Milwaukee, WI 53201-0413. Offers classics and Hebrew studies (MAFLL); comparative literature (MAFLL); French and Italian (MAFLL); German (MAFLL); Slavic studies (MAFLL); translation (Certificate). Part-time programs available. *Faculty:* 37 full-time (18 women). *Students:* 32 full-time (25 women), 28 part-time (19 women); includes 5 minority (1 Asian American or Pacific Islander, 4 Hispanic Americans), 22 international. Average age 33. 54 applicants, 69% accepted, 20 enrolled. In 2009, 24 master's awarded. *Degree requirements:* For master's, 2 foreign languages, thesis or alternative. *Entrance requirements:* Additional exam requirements/recommendations for international students: Required—TOEFL (minimum score 550 paper-based; 79 iBT), IELTS (minimum score 6.5). *Application deadline:* For fall admission, 1/1 priority date for domestic students; for spring admission, 9/1 for domestic students. Applications are processed on a rolling basis. Application fee: $45 ($75 for international students). *Expenses:* Tuition, state resident: full-time $8800. Tuition, nonresident: full-time $20,760. Tuition and fees vary according to program and reciprocity agreements. *Financial support:* In 2009–10, 2 research assistantships, 21 teaching assistantships were awarded; career-related internships or fieldwork and unspecified assistantships also available. Support available to part-time students. Financial award application deadline: 4/15. Total annual research expenditures: $285,237. *Unit head:* Gabrielle Verdier, Representative, 414-229-3346, Fax: 414-229-2741, E-mail: verdier@uwm.edu. *Application contact:* General Information Contact, 414-229-4982, Fax: 414-229-6967, E-mail: gradschool@uwm.edu.

Yeshiva University, Bernard Revel Graduate School of Jewish Studies, New York, NY 10033-3201. Offers MA, PhD. Part-time programs available. *Faculty:* 9 full-time (0 women), 5 part-time/adjunct (1 woman). *Students:* 46 full-time (24 women), 92 part-time (34 women); includes 1 minority (Hispanic American). Average age 25. In 2009, 42 master's, 2 doctorates awarded. Terminal master's awarded for partial completion of doctoral program. *Degree requirements:* For master's, comprehensive exam; for doctorate, 2 foreign languages, comprehensive exam, thesis/dissertation. *Entrance requirements:* For master's and doctorate, GRE General Test (recommended), reading knowledge of Hebrew, minimum GPA of 3.0. *Application deadline:* Applications are processed on a rolling basis. Application fee: $25. *Expenses:* Tuition: Full-time $24,918; part-time $1022 per credit. Required fees: $175. *Financial support:* In 2009–10, 49 fellowships with full and partial tuition reimbursements (averaging $5,322 per year) were awarded; institutionally sponsored loans, scholarships/grants, and tuition waivers (full and partial) also available. Support available to part-time students. Financial award application deadline: 3/1. *Faculty research:* Bible, Jewish history, Jewish philosophy and mysticism, Talmud, Semitic languages. *Unit head:* Dr. David Berger, Dean, 212-960-5253, Fax: 212-960-5245, E-mail: dberger@yu.edu. *Application contact:* Sheniagia Alise Warren, Executive Secretary, 212-960-5254, Fax: 212-960-5245, E-mail: swarren@yu.edu.

Latin American Studies

American University, College of Arts and Sciences, Department of Language and Foreign Studies, Program in Spanish: Latin American Studies, Washington, DC 20016-8045. Offers Spanish: Latin American studies (MA); translation (Certificate). Part-time and evening/weekend programs available. *Students:* 11 full-time (9 women), 8 part-time (4 women); includes 8 minority (3 African Americans, 5 Hispanic Americans). Average age 26. 23 applicants, 87% accepted, 7 enrolled. In 2009, 11 master's, 7 other advanced degrees awarded. *Degree requirements:* For master's, one foreign language, comprehensive exam, thesis or alternative, research. *Entrance requirements:* For master's, GRE, bachelor's degree in language or equivalent, essay in Spanish, minimum GPA of 3.2; for Certificate, bachelor's degree in Spanish or BA in any field plus Spanish proficiency. Additional exam requirements/recommendations for international students: Required—TOEFL. *Application deadline:* For fall admission, 2/1 for domestic students; for spring admission, 10/1 for domestic students. Application fee: $80. *Expenses:* Tuition: Full-time $22,266; part-time $1237 per credit hour. Required fees: $430. Tuition and fees vary according to program. *Financial support:* Fellowships, career-related internships or fieldwork, Federal Work-Study, and institutionally sponsored loans available. Financial award application deadline: 2/1. *Faculty research:* Latin American culture, literature, and history; computer-aided instruction.

Arizona State University, Graduate College, College of Liberal Arts and Sciences, Division of Humanities, Department of History, Tempe, AZ 85287. Offers East/Southeast Asian history (MA, PhD); European history (MA, PhD); Latin American studies (MA, PhD); North American history (MA, PhD); public history (MA). *Degree requirements:* For master's, thesis or alternative; for doctorate, 2 foreign languages, thesis/dissertation. *Entrance requirements:* For master's and doctorate, GRE.

Boricua College, Program in Latin American and Caribbean Studies (Brooklyn Campus), New York, NY 10032-1560. Offers MA. Evening/weekend programs available. *Degree requirements:* For master's, thesis. *Entrance requirements:* For master's, interview by the faculty. Additional exam requirements/recommendations for international students: Required—Boricua College's exam.

Boricua College, Program in Latin American and Caribbean Studies (Manhattan Campus), New York, NY 10032-1560. Offers MA. Evening/weekend programs available. *Degree requirements:* For master's, thesis. *Entrance requirements:* For master's, interview by the faculty. Additional exam requirements/recommendations for international students: Required—Boricua College's exam.

Brown University, Graduate School, Center for Portuguese and Brazilian Studies, Providence, RI 02912. Offers Brazilian studies (AM); Portuguese and Brazilian studies (AM, PhD); Portuguese Bilingual Education and Cross-Cultural Studies (AM); MA/PhD. *Degree requirements:* For doctorate, thesis/dissertation.

California State University, Long Beach, Graduate Studies, College of Liberal Arts, Department of History, Long Beach, CA 90840. Offers Africa and the Middle East (MA); ancient/Medieval Europe (MA); Asia (MA); Latin America (MA); modern Europe (MA); United States (MA); world (MA). Part-time and evening/weekend programs available. *Faculty:* 9 full-time (6 women), 1 (woman) part-time/adjunct. *Students:* 10 full-time (3 women), 56 part-time (21 women); includes 19 minority (2 African Americans, 1 American Indian/Alaska Native, 4 Asian Americans or Pacific Islanders, 12 Hispanic Americans), 1 international. Average age 31. 40 applicants, 50% accepted, 11 enrolled. *Degree requirements:* For master's, one foreign language, comprehensive exam or thesis. *Application deadline:* For fall admission, 3/1 for domestic students. Applications are processed on a rolling basis. Application fee: $55. Electronic applications accepted. *Expenses:* Required fees: $1802 per semester. Part-time tuition and fees vary according to course load. *Financial support:* Research assistantships, Federal Work-Study, institutionally sponsored loans, and scholarships/grants available. Financial award application deadline: 3/2. *Faculty research:* All periods of European and American history, recent Asian and African history. *Unit head:* Dr. Nancy Quam-Wickham, Department Chair, 562-985-4431, Fax: 562-985-5431, E-mail: quamwick@csulb.edu. *Application contact:* Dr. Houri Berberian, Graduate Advisor, 562-985-4524, Fax: 562-985-4431, E-mail: hberber@csulb.edu.

California State University, Los Angeles, Graduate Studies, College of Natural and Social Sciences, Department of Latin American Studies, Los Angeles, CA 90032-8530. Offers MA. Part-time and evening/weekend programs available. *Students:* 13 full-time (8 women), 36 part-time (18 women); includes 36 minority (all Hispanic Americans), 1 international. Average age 33. 12 applicants, 100% accepted, 10 enrolled. In 2009, 11 master's awarded. *Degree requirements:* For master's, one foreign language, comprehensive exam, thesis. *Entrance requirements:* For master's, minimum GPA of 2.5. Additional exam requirements/recommendations for international students: Required—TOEFL (minimum score 500 paper-based; 173 computer-based). *Application deadline:* For fall admission, 5/1 for domestic and international students. Applications are processed on a rolling basis. Application fee: $55. Electronic applications accepted. *Financial support:* Federal Work-Study available. Support available to part-time students. Financial award application deadline: 3/1. *Faculty research:* Central America, Cuba, Third World development, labor history, redemocratization. *Unit head:* Dr. Marjorie W. Bray, Director, 323-343-2180, Fax: 323-343-5485, E-mail: mbray@calstatela.edu. *Application contact:* Dr. Cheryl L. Ney, Associate Vice President for Academic Affairs and Dean of Graduate Studies, 323-343-3820, Fax: 323-343-5653, E-mail: cney@cslanet.calstatela.edu.

Centro de Estudios Avanzados de Puerto Rico y el Caribe, Graduate Program in Puerto Rican and Caribbean Studies, Old San Juan, PR 00902-3970. Offers Puerto Rican and Caribbean history (MA, PhD); Puerto Rican and Caribbean literature (MA, PhD); Puerto Rican studies (MA). Part-time and evening/weekend programs available. *Degree requirements:* For master's, comprehensive exam, thesis; for doctorate, 2 foreign languages, comprehensive exam, thesis/dissertation. *Entrance requirements:* For master's and doctorate, interview. *Faculty research:* Literature, history, art, folklore, and culture of Puerto Rico and Caribbean countries.

Cleveland State University, College of Graduate Studies, College of Liberal Arts and Social Sciences, Department of Modern Languages, Cleveland, OH 44115. Offers French (M Ed); Spanish (M Ed, MA), including language and linguistics (MA), Latin American studies (MA), peninsular studies (MA), Spanish (MA). Part-time and evening/weekend programs available. *Degree requirements:* For master's, one foreign language, comprehensive exam, thesis optional, study abroad. *Entrance requirements:* For master's, undergraduate major in Spanish or equivalent, essay in Spanish, writing sample. Additional exam requirements/recommendations for international students: Required—TOEFL (minimum score 525 paper-based; 197 computer-based). Electronic applications accepted. *Faculty research:* Second language acquisition, sociolinguistics, contemporary Spanish novel, Arabic diaspora in Latin America, border literature.

Columbia University, School of International and Public Affairs, Institute of Latin American Studies, New York, NY 10027. Offers Latin American and Caribbean studies (MA); Latin American studies (Certificate). Students must also be enrolled in a separate graduate degree program at Columbia University. *Degree requirements:* For master's, 2 foreign languages, thesis. Electronic applications accepted. *Faculty research:* Rights vs. efficiency in a globalized era, citizenship and governance in Latin America and Western Europe.

Cornell University, Graduate School, Graduate Fields of Arts and Sciences, Field of Archaeology, Ithaca, NY 14853-0001. Offers environmental archaeology (MA); historical archaeology (MA); Latin American archaeology (MA); medieval archaeology (MA); Mediterranean and Near Eastern archaeology (MA); Stone Age archaeology (MA). *Faculty:* 13 full-time (3 women). *Students:* 7 full-time (5 women). Average age 25. 20 applicants, 35% accepted, 4 enrolled. *Degree requirements:* For master's, one foreign language, thesis. *Entrance requirements:* For master's, GRE General Test, 3 letters of recommendation, sample of written work. Additional exam requirements/recommendations for international students: Required—TOEFL (minimum score 550 paper-based; 213 computer-based; 77 iBT). *Application deadline:* For fall admission, 1/15 for domestic students. Application fee: $70. Electronic applications accepted. *Expenses:* Tuition: Full-time $29,500. Required fees: $70. Full-time tuition and fees vary according to degree level, program and student level. *Financial support:* In 2009–10, 4 students received support; fellowships with full tuition reimbursements available, research assistantships with full tuition reimbursements available, teaching assistantships with full tuition reimbursements available, institutionally sponsored loans, scholarships/grants, health care benefits, tuition waivers (full and partial), and unspecified assistantships available. Financial award applicants required to submit FAFSA. *Faculty research:* Anatolia, Lydia, Sardis, classical and Hellenistic Greece; science in archaeology; North American Indians; Stone Age Africa; Maya trade. *Unit head:* Director of Graduate Studies, 607-255-6768, E-mail: blj7@cornell.edu. *Application contact:* Graduate Field Assistant, 607-255-6768, E-mail: dsd6@cornell.edu.

Cornell University, Graduate School, Graduate Fields of Arts and Sciences, Field of History, Ithaca, NY 14853-0001. Offers African history (MA, PhD); American history (MA, PhD); ancient history (MA, PhD); early modern European history (MA, PhD); English history (MA, PhD); French history (MA, PhD); German history (MA, PhD); history of science (MA, PhD); Latin American history (MA, PhD); medieval Chinese history (MA, PhD); medieval history (MA, PhD); modern Chinese history (MA, PhD); modern European history (MA, PhD); modern Japanese history (MA, PhD); premodern Islamic history (MA, PhD); premodern Japanese history (MA, PhD); Renaissance history (MA, PhD); Russian history (MA, PhD); Southeast Asian history (MA, PhD). *Faculty:* 62 full-time (19 women). *Students:* 67 full-time (33 women); includes 10 minority (4 African Americans, 3 Asian Americans or Pacific Islanders, 3 Hispanic Americans), 24 international. Average age 31. 195 applicants, 7% accepted, 10 enrolled. In 2009, 11 master's, 3 doctorates awarded. Terminal master's awarded for partial completion of doctoral program. *Degree requirements:* For master's, thesis; for doctorate, 2 foreign languages, comprehensive exam, thesis/dissertation, 1 year of teaching experience. *Entrance requirements:* For master's and doctorate, GRE General Test, writing sample, 3 letters of recommendation. Additional exam requirements/recommendations for international students: Required—TOEFL (minimum score 550 paper-based; 213 computer-based; 77 iBT). *Application deadline:* For fall admission, 1/15 for domestic students. Application fee: $70. Electronic applications accepted. *Expenses:* Tuition: Full-time $29,500. Required fees: $70. Full-time tuition and fees vary according to degree level, program and student level. *Financial support:* In 2009–10, 54 students received support, including 8 fellowships with full tuition reimbursements available; research assistantships with full tuition reimbursements available, teaching assistantships with full tuition reimbursements available, institutionally sponsored loans, scholarships/grants, health care benefits, tuition waivers (full and partial), and unspecified assistantships also available. Financial award applicants required to submit FAFSA. *Unit head:* Director of Graduate Studies, 607-255-6738, Fax: 607-255-0469. *Application contact:* Graduate Field Assistant, 607-255-6738, Fax: 607-255-0469, E-mail: history_grad_info@cornell.edu.

Duke University, Graduate School, Department of History, Durham, NC 27708. Offers history (AM, PhD); Latin American studies (PhD); JD/AM; MD/PhD. *Faculty:* 37 full-time. *Students:* 56 full-time (32 women); includes 7 minority (all African Americans), 10 international. 199 applicants, 10% accepted, 5 enrolled. In 2009, 4 master's, 7 doctorates awarded. *Degree requirements:* For doctorate, 2 foreign languages, thesis/dissertation. *Entrance requirements:* For doctorate, GRE General Test. Additional exam requirements/recommendations for international students: Required—TOEFL (minimum score 550 paper-based; 213 computer-based; 83 iBT), IELTS (minimum score 7). *Application deadline:* For fall admission, 12/8 priority date for domestic and international students. Application fee: $75. Electronic applications accepted. *Financial support:* Fellowships, research assistantships, teaching assistantships, Federal Work-Study available. Financial award application deadline: 12/31. *Unit head:* Anna Krylova, Director of Graduate Studies, Fax: 919-681-5746, E-mail: rmennis@duke.edu. *Application contact:* Cynthia Robertson, Associate Dean for Enrollment Services, 919-684-3913, E-mail: grad-admissions@duke.edu.

Florida International University, College of Arts and Sciences, Program in Latin American and Caribbean Studies, Miami, FL 33199. Offers MA. Part-time and evening/weekend programs available. *Faculty:* 1 (woman) full-time. *Students:* 13 full-time (8 women), 9 part-time (4 women); includes 10 minority (1 African American, 9 Hispanic Americans), 4 international. Average age 30. 18 applicants, 44% accepted, 8 enrolled. In 2009, 11 master's awarded. *Degree requirements:* For master's, one foreign language, thesis or alternative. *Entrance requirements:* For master's, GRE General Test (minimum score 1000); GMAT, LSAT, or EXADEP (minimum 62nd percentile), minimum GPA of 3.0, 3 letters of recommendation, letter of intent. Additional exam requirements/recommendations for international students: Required—TOEFL (minimum score 550 paper-based; 80 iBT). *Application deadline:* For fall admission, 2/1 for domestic and international students; for spring admission, 10/1 for domestic students, 9/1 for international students. Applications are processed on a rolling basis. Application fee: $30. Electronic applications accepted. *Expenses:* Tuition, state resident: full-time $8008; part-time $4004 per year. Tuition, nonresident: full-time $20,104; part-time $10,052 per year. Required fees: $298; $149 per term. *Financial support:* Institutionally sponsored loans and scholarships/grants available. Financial award application deadline: 3/1; financial award applicants required to submit FAFSA. *Unit head:* Dr. Cristina Eguizabal, Director, 305-348-2894, Fax: 305-348-3593, E-mail: lacc@fiu.edu. *Application contact:* Dr. Astrid Arraras, Director of Graduate Programs, 305-348-2894, Fax: 305-348-3593, E-mail: astrid.arraras@fiu.edu.

Fordham University, Graduate School of Arts and Sciences, Program in Latin American and Latino Studies, New York, NY 10458. Offers MA, Certificate. *Students:* 1 (woman) full-time, 5 part-time (4 women); includes 1 minority (Hispanic American), 2 international. 12 applicants, 58% accepted, 3 enrolled. In 2009, 2 other advanced degrees awarded. *Entrance requirements:* Additional exam requirements/recommendations for international students: Required—TOEFL (minimum score 650 paper-based; 280 computer-based). *Application deadline:* For fall admission, 1/4 priority date for domestic students; for spring admission, 11/1 for domestic students. Application fee: $65. Electronic applications accepted. *Financial support:* Application deadline: 1/4. *Faculty research:* Latinos and Hollywood, Puerto Rican women and labor history, education and the state in El Salvador, Avant-garde literature in twentieth century Latin America. *Unit head:* Dr. Arnaldo Cruz-Malave, Director, 718-817-6571, E-mail: lalsi@fordham.edu. *Application contact:* Charlene Dundie, Director of Graduate Admissions, 718-817-4420, Fax: 718-817-3566, E-mail: dundie@fordham.edu.

Georgetown University, Graduate School of Arts and Sciences, Center for Latin American Studies, Washington, DC 20057-1026. Offers MA, MA/JD, MA/PhD. *Degree requirements:* For master's, one foreign language, comprehensive exam, thesis optional. *Entrance requirements:* For master's, GRE General Test, minimum B average. Additional exam requirements/recommendations for international students: Required—TOEFL.

The George Washington University, Elliott School of International Affairs, Program in Latin American and Hemispheric Studies, Washington, DC 20052. Offers MA, JD/MA, MBA/MA. Part-time and evening/weekend programs available. *Students:* 18 full-time (16 women), 4 part-time (2 women); includes 6 minority (2 African Americans, 4 Hispanic Americans). Average age 25. 45 applicants, 87% accepted, 11 enrolled. In 2009, 8 master's awarded. *Degree requirements:* For master's, one foreign language, capstone project. *Entrance requirements:* For master's, GRE General Test, 2 years (or the equivalent) of Spanish or Portuguese. Additional exam requirements/recommendations for international students: Required—TOEFL. *Application deadline:* For fall admission, 2/1 for domestic students; for spring admission, 10/1 for domestic students. Application fee: $60. Electronic applications accepted. *Financial support:* In 2009–10, 4 students received support; fellowships with tuition reimbursements available, research assistantships with tuition reimbursements available, career-related internships or fieldwork, Federal Work-Study, institutionally sponsored loans, and tuition waivers (full) available. Financial award application deadline: 1/15; financial award applicants required to submit

Latin American Studies

The George Washington University (continued)
FAFSA. *Faculty research:* Democracy and change in Andean nations, rural economic development, peasant cooperatives and political change. *Unit head:* Cynthia McClintock, Director, 202-994-6589, Fax: 202-994-7743, E-mail: mcclin@gwu.edu. *Application contact:* Jeff V. Miles, Director of Graduate Admissions, 202-994-7050, Fax: 202-994-9537, E-mail: esiagrad@gwu.edu.

Georgia State University, College of Arts and Sciences, Department of History, Atlanta, GA 30302-3083. Offers heritage preservation (MHP, Certificate); history (MA, PhD); Latin American studies (Certificate). Part-time and evening/weekend programs available. *Degree requirements:* For master's, one foreign language, comprehensive exam, thesis; for doctorate, 2 foreign languages, comprehensive exam, thesis/dissertation, exam. *Entrance requirements:* For master's, GRE General Test; for doctorate, GRE General Test, sample of written work. Additional exam requirements/recommendations for international students: Required—TOEFL. Electronic applications accepted. *Faculty research:* Historic preservation, labor history, twentieth-century U.S. history, American South, world history.

Indiana University Bloomington, University Graduate School, College of Arts and Sciences, Center for Latin American and Caribbean Studies, Bloomington, IN 47405-7000. Offers MA, MBA/MA, MLS/MA, MPA/MA. Part-time programs available. *Students:* 8 full-time (5 women), 1 (woman) part-time; includes 4 minority (1 African American, 3 Hispanic Americans), 1 international. Average age 28. 22 applicants, 77% accepted, 8 enrolled. In 2009, 4 master's awarded. *Degree requirements:* For master's, one foreign language, oral and written exam. *Entrance requirements:* For master's, GRE General Test. Additional exam requirements/recommendations for international students: Required—TOEFL. *Application deadline:* For fall admission, 1/15 priority date for domestic students, 12/15 for international students; for spring admission, 9/1 priority date for domestic students, 9/1 for international students. Applications are processed on a rolling basis. Application fee: $55 ($65 for international students). *Financial support:* In 2009–10, 9 students received support, including 5 fellowships with tuition reimbursements available (averaging $9,200 per year), 2 teaching assistantships with tuition reimbursements available (averaging $15,300 per year); research assistantships with tuition reimbursements available, career-related internships or fieldwork, Federal Work-Study, institutionally sponsored loans, scholarships/grants, and unspecified assistantships also available. Financial award application deadline: 7/15; financial award applicants required to submit FAFSA. *Unit head:* Dr. Jeffrey Gould, Director, 812-855-9098, Fax: 812-855-5345, E-mail: gouldj@indiana.edu. *Application contact:* Amy Belcher, Information Contact, 812-855-9097, Fax: 812-855-5345, E-mail: clacs@indiana.edu.

La Salle University, School of Arts and Sciences, Program in Bilingual/Bicultural Studies (Spanish), Philadelphia, PA 19141-1199. Offers MA. Part-time and evening/weekend programs available. *Degree requirements:* For master's, one foreign language, thesis or alternative, project. *Entrance requirements:* For master's, GRE or MAT. *Expenses:* Contact institution. *Faculty research:* Puerto Rican literature, cross-cultural communication, English as a second language methodology, Spanish language.

Michigan State University, The Graduate School, College of Social Science, Program in Chicano/Latino Studies, East Lansing, MI 48824. Offers PhD. *Students:* 7 full-time (0 women), 1 (woman) part-time; includes 7 minority (all Hispanic Americans). Average age 42. 6 applicants, 33% accepted. *Entrance requirements:* Additional exam requirements/recommendations for international students: Required—TOEFL. *Application deadline:* For fall admission, 12/27 for domestic students. Electronic applications accepted. *Expenses:* Tuition, state resident: part-time $478.25 per credit hour. Tuition, nonresident: part-time $966.50 per credit hour. Part-time tuition and fees vary according to program. *Financial support:* In 2009–10, 1 research assistantship with tuition reimbursement (averaging $6,193 per year), 4 teaching assistantships with tuition reimbursements (averaging $6,061 per year) were awarded; scholarships/grants and unspecified assistantships also available. *Unit head:* Dr. Sheila M. Contreras, Director, 517-353-8685, Fax: 517-432-8662, E-mail: sheilac@msu.edu. *Application contact:* Information Contact, 517-432-7187, Fax: 517-432-8662, E-mail: cls@msu.edu.

New York University, Graduate School of Arts and Science, Center for Latin American and Caribbean Studies, New York, NY 10012-1019. Offers MA, JD/MA. Part-time programs available. *Students:* 24 full-time (17 women), 12 part-time (9 women); includes 10 minority (1 African American, 9 Hispanic Americans), 6 international. Average age 27. 46 applicants, 67% accepted, 12 enrolled. In 2009, 16 master's awarded. *Degree requirements:* For master's, one foreign language, thesis or alternative, major project. *Entrance requirements:* For master's, GRE General Test, knowledge of Portuguese or Spanish. Additional exam requirements/recommendations for international students: Required—TOEFL. *Application deadline:* For fall admission, 1/4 priority date for domestic students. Application fee: $90. *Expenses:* Tuition: Full-time $30,528; part-time $1272 per credit. Required fees: $2177. *Financial support:* Fellowships with tuition reimbursements, teaching assistantships with tuition reimbursements, Federal Work-Study, institutionally sponsored loans, scholarships/grants, health care benefits, and unspecified assistantships available. Financial award application deadline: 1/4; financial award applicants required to submit FAFSA. *Faculty research:* Latin American politics, Caribbean societies, Andean history, political economy of cultural policies. *Unit head:* Ada Ferrer, Director, 212-998-8686, Fax: 212-995-4163, E-mail: clacs.info@nyu.edu. *Application contact:* Jennifer Lewis, Assistant Director, 212-998-8686, Fax: 212-995-4163, E-mail: clacs.info@nyu.edu.

New York University, Graduate School of Arts and Science, Program in Museum Studies, New York, NY 10012-1019. Offers museum studies (MA, Advanced Certificate), including Africana studies (MA), Hebrew and Judaic studies (MA), Latin American and Caribbean studies (MA), Near Eastern studies (MA). Part-time and evening/weekend programs available. *Students:* 62 full-time (57 women), 23 part-time (21 women); includes 13 minority (1 African American, 2 American Indian/Alaska Native, 3 Asian Americans or Pacific Islanders, 7 Hispanic Americans), 15 international. Average age 27. 220 applicants, 52% accepted, 37 enrolled. In 2009, 37 master's awarded. *Entrance requirements:* For degree, master's degree or PhD. Additional exam requirements/recommendations for international students: Required—TOEFL. *Application deadline:* For fall admission, 2/1 for domestic students; for spring admission, 11/1 for domestic students. Application fee: $90. *Expenses:* Tuition: Full-time $30,528; part-time $1272 per credit. Required fees: $2177. *Financial support:* Application deadline: 2/1. *Faculty research:* Modern and contemporary art, history of museums and exhibitions, conservation of cultural materials, museum anthropology, ethnography. *Unit head:* Haidy Geismar, Director, 212-998-8080, Fax: 212-995-4185, E-mail: museum.studies@nyu.edu. *Application contact:* Tatiana Kamorina, Department Administrator, 212-998-8080, Fax: 212-995-4185, E-mail: museum.studies@nyu.edu.

New York University, NYU in Madrid, Madrid, NY 10012-1019, Spain. Offers creative writing in Spanish (MFA); Spanish (PhD); Spanish and Latin American literatures and cultures (MA); Spanish language and translation (MA). *Students:* 27 full-time (23 women), 1 part-time (0 women); includes 8 minority (2 African Americans, 1 Asian American or Pacific Islander, 5 Hispanic Americans), 1 international. Average age 26. 73 applicants, 90% accepted, 27 enrolled. In 2009, 22 master's awarded. Application fee: $90. *Expenses:* Tuition: Full-time $30,528; part-time $1272 per credit. Required fees: $2177. *Unit head:* Judith Nemethy, Director, 212-998-8770, Fax: 212-995-4149, E-mail: nyu-in-madrid@nyu.edu. *Application contact:* Judith Nemethy, Director, 212-998-8770, Fax: 212-995-4149, E-mail: nyu-in-madrid@nyu.edu.

Ohio University, Graduate College, Center for International Studies, Program in Latin American Studies, Athens, OH 45701-2979. Offers MA. Part-time programs available. *Faculty:* 24 full-time (5 women). *Students:* 18 full-time (11 women), 1 (woman) part-time; includes 4 minority (1 African American, 3 Hispanic Americans), 5 international. Average age 25. 17 applicants, 71% accepted, 6 enrolled. In 2009, 14 master's awarded. *Degree requirements:* For master's, one foreign language, thesis optional. *Entrance requirements:* For master's, minimum GPA of 3.0. Additional exam requirements/recommendations for international students: Required—TOEFL (minimum score 550 paper-based; 213 computer-based; 80 iBT), IELTS (minimum score 6.5). *Application deadline:* For fall admission, 1/1 priority date for domestic and international students. Applications are processed on a rolling basis. Application fee: $50 ($55 for international students). Electronic applications accepted. *Expenses:* Tuition, state resident: full-time $7839; part-time $323 per quarter hour. Tuition, nonresident: full-time $15,831; part-time $654 per quarter hour. Required fees: $2931. *Financial support:* In 2009–10, 4 research assistantships with full tuition reimbursements (averaging $11,499 per year) were awarded; career-related internships or fieldwork, Federal Work-Study, institutionally sponsored loans, scholarships/grants, tuition waivers (partial), and unspecified assistantships also available. Financial award application deadline: 1/1. *Faculty research:* Central America, Ecuador, Brazil, transnational migration, microfinance. *Unit head:* Dr. Jose Delgado, Director, E-mail: delgadoj@ohio.edu. *Application contact:* Joan Kraynanski, Administrative Assistant, 740-593-1840, Fax: 740-593-1837, E-mail: kraynans@ohio.edu.

San Diego State University, Graduate and Research Affairs, College of Arts and Letters, Center for Latin American Studies, San Diego, CA 92182. Offers MA, MBA/MA. *Degree requirements:* For master's, 2 foreign languages, thesis or alternative. *Entrance requirements:* For master's, GRE General Test, 3 letters of reference. Additional exam requirements/recommendations for international students: Required—TOEFL. Electronic applications accepted. *Faculty research:* Latin American politics and economics.

Simon Fraser University, Graduate Studies, Faculty of Arts and Social Sciences, Latin American Studies Program, Burnaby, BC V5A 1S6, Canada. Offers MA. *Degree requirements:* For master's, thesis. *Entrance requirements:* For master's, minimum GPA of 3.0. Additional exam requirements/recommendations for international students: Required—TOEFL or IELTS. *Faculty research:* Sociology theory, social and cultural anthropology, political sociology, religion and society, Canadian native people.

Syracuse University, Maxwell School of Citizenship and Public Affairs, Program in Latin American Studies, Syracuse, NY 13244. Offers CAS. *Entrance requirements:* For degree, Must be matriculated in a degree program. Additional exam requirements/recommendations for international students: Required—TOEFL (minimum score 100 iBT). *Application deadline:* For fall admission, 2/1 priority date for domestic and international students. Application fee: $75. Electronic applications accepted. *Expenses:* Tuition: Full-time $26,808; part-time $1117 per credit. Required fees: $1024. *Financial support:* Application deadline: 1/1. *Unit head:* Tom Perreault, Associate Professor, 315-443-9467, Fax: 315-443-3385, E-mail: taperrea@maxwell.syr.edu. *Application contact:* Tom Perreault, Associate Professor, 315-443-9467, Fax: 315-443-3385, E-mail: taperrea@maxwell.syr.edu.

Tulane University, School of Liberal Arts, Roger Thayer Stone Center for Latin American Studies, New Orleans, LA 70118-5669. Offers MA, PhD, MBA/MA, MCL/MA. Terminal master's awarded for partial completion of doctoral program. *Degree requirements:* For master's, one foreign language, thesis optional; for doctorate, 2 foreign languages, thesis/dissertation. *Entrance requirements:* For master's, GRE General Test, minimum B average in undergraduate course work; for doctorate, GRE General Test. Additional exam requirements/recommendations for international students: Required—TOEFL. Electronic applications accepted.

University at Albany, State University of New York, College of Arts and Sciences, Latin American, Caribbean, and US Latino Studies, Albany, NY 12222-0001. Offers MA, Certificate. Part-time programs available. *Degree requirements:* For master's, thesis. *Entrance requirements:* For master's, ability to read and write Spanish. Additional exam requirements/recommendations for international students: Required—TOEFL (minimum score 550 paper-based; 213 computer-based). Electronic applications accepted. *Faculty research:* Meso-American anthropology, Latin American women's studies, Latinos in the U.S.

The University of Arizona, Graduate College, College of Social and Behavioral Sciences, Center for Latin American Studies, Tucson, AZ 85721. Offers MA. Part-time programs available. *Faculty:* 2. *Students:* 26 full-time (14 women), 9 part-time (4 women); includes 2 minority (both Hispanic Americans), 3 international. Average age 28. 69 applicants, 52% accepted, 15 enrolled. In 2009, 10 master's awarded. *Degree requirements:* For master's, 2 foreign languages, comprehensive exam, thesis optional. *Entrance requirements:* For master's, GRE, 2 letters of recommendation, resume. Additional exam requirements/recommendations for international students: Required—TOEFL (minimum score 550 paper-based; 213 computer-based; 79 iBT). *Application deadline:* For fall admission, 2/1 for domestic students, 12/1 for international students. Application fee: $65. Electronic applications accepted. *Expenses:* Tuition, state resident: full-time $9028. Tuition, nonresident: full-time $24,890. *Financial support:* In 2009–10, 1 research assistantship with full tuition reimbursement (averaging $14,451 per year), 5 teaching assistantships with full tuition reimbursements (averaging $13,443 per year) were awarded; career-related internships or fieldwork, Federal Work-Study, institutionally sponsored loans, scholarships/grants, health care benefits, tuition waivers (full and partial), and unspecified assistantships also available. *Faculty research:* Comparative analyses of national identities and of democratization across Latin America, environmental problems and management along the U. S.-Mexican border, integration efforts along the Peru/Ecuador border, social justice issues in Guatemala. Total annual research expenditures: $78,887. *Unit head:* Dr. Scott Whiteford, Director, 520-626-7207, Fax: 520-626-7248, E-mail: eljete@email.arizona.edu. *Application contact:* Brittany Kaza, Information Contact, 520-626-3317, Fax: 520-626-7248, E-mail: bkaza@email.arizona.edu.

University of California, Berkeley, Graduate Division, Group in International and Area Studies, Group in Latin American Studies, Berkeley, CA 94720-1500. Offers MA, MJ/MA. *Students:* 14 full-time (7 women). Average age 29. 34 applicants, 5 enrolled. In 2009, 5 master's awarded. *Degree requirements:* For master's, 2 foreign languages. *Entrance requirements:* For master's, GRE General Test, minimum GPA of 3.0, reading knowledge of Spanish or Portuguese, 3 letters of recommendation. Additional exam requirements/recommendations for international students: Required—TOEFL. *Application deadline:* For fall admission, 12/15 for domestic students. Application fee: $70 ($90 for international students). Electronic applications accepted. *Financial support:* Fellowships, teaching assistantships with tuition reimbursements, unspecified assistantships available. *Faculty research:* Rural development, border communities, political economy, geography, history. *Unit head:* Prof. John Lie, Chair, 510-642-4466, E-mail: iasone@berkeley.edu. *Application contact:* Information Contact, 510-642-4466, E-mail: lasgrad@berkeley.edu.

University of California, Los Angeles, Graduate Division, International Institute, Program in Latin American Studies, Los Angeles, CA 90095. Offers MA, M Ed/MA, MA/MA, MBA/MA, MLIS/MA, MPH/MA. *Students:* 26 full-time (20 women); includes 18 minority (1 African American, 17 Hispanic Americans). Average age 27. 30 applicants, 63% accepted, 11 enrolled. In 2009, 14 master's awarded. *Degree requirements:* For master's, 2 foreign languages, comprehensive exam or thesis. *Entrance requirements:* For master's, GRE General Test, minimum GPA of 3.0. *Application deadline:* For fall admission, 12/15 for domestic and international students. Application fee: $70 ($90 for international students). Electronic applications accepted. *Financial support:* In 2009–10, 10 fellowships with full and partial tuition reimbursements, 3 research assistantships with full and partial tuition reimbursements, 8 teaching assistantships with full and partial tuition reimbursements were awarded; Federal Work-Study, institutionally sponsored loans, scholarships/grants, health care benefits, tuition waivers (full and partial), and unspecified assistantships also available. Financial award application deadline: 3/1; financial award applicants required to submit FAFSA. *Unit head:* Dr. Kevin Terraciano, Chair, 310-825-8410. *Application contact:* Department Office, 310-825-8410, E-mail: idpgrads@international.ucla.edu.

University of California, San Diego, Office of Graduate Studies, Department of Political Science, Latin American Studies Program, La Jolla, CA 92093. Offers MA. *Entrance requirements:* For master's, GRE General Test, GRE Subject Test. Electronic applications accepted.

University of California, Santa Barbara, Graduate Division, College of Letters and Sciences, Division of Humanities and Fine Arts, Department of Spanish and Portuguese, Santa Barbara,

CA 93106-4150. Offers Hispanic languages and literature (PhD), including applied linguistics, European Medieval studies, feminist studies, Hispanic languages and literature; Portuguese (MA); Spanish (MA); Spanish and Portuguese (MA); MA/PhD. Spanish Language Institute available during summer session. *Faculty:* 16 full-time (6 women). *Students:* 29 full-time (16 women). Average age 30. 46 applicants, 39% accepted, 9 enrolled. In 2009, 4 master's, 2 doctorates awarded. *Degree requirements:* For master's, 2 foreign languages, comprehensive exam (for some programs), thesis optional; for doctorate, 2 foreign languages, comprehensive exam, thesis/dissertation. *Entrance requirements:* For master's, GRE, 2 writing samples, undergraduate major in Spanish or equivalent, 3 letters of recommendation, resume/curriculum vitae; for doctorate, GRE, 2 writing samples, master's degree, 3 letters of recommendation, statement of purpose, personal achievements/contributions statement, resume/curriculum vitae, transcripts for post-secondary institutions attended. Additional exam requirements/recommendations for international students: Required—TOEFL (minimum score 550 paper-based; 213 computer-based; 80 iBT), or IELTS (minimum score 7). *Application deadline:* For fall admission, 3/1 for domestic and international students; for winter admission, 11/1 for domestic and international students; for spring admission, 2/1 for domestic and international students. Application fee: $70 ($90 for international students). Electronic applications accepted. *Financial support:* In 2009–10, 9 fellowships with full and partial tuition reimbursements (averaging $7,000 per year), 29 teaching assistantships with partial tuition reimbursements (averaging $11,500 per year) were awarded; career-related internships or fieldwork, Federal Work-Study, institutionally sponsored loans, scholarships/grants, health care benefits, tuition waivers (full and partial), and unspecified assistantships also available. Financial award application deadline: 1/7; financial award applicants required to submit FAFSA. *Faculty research:* Nineteenth century Spanish and Portuguese literature, Spanish and Spanish American literature, nineteenth and twentieth century Portuguese and Brazilian literatures, Hispanic linguistics, Catalan language and culture. *Unit head:* Prof. Francisco A. Lomeli, Chair, 805-893-5715, Fax: 805-893-8341, E-mail: lomeli@spanport.ucsb.edu. *Application contact:* Carol Conley, Graduate Program Assistant, 805-893-3162, Fax: 805-893-8341, E-mail: cconley@spanport.ucsb.edu.

University of California, Santa Barbara, Graduate Division, College of Letters and Sciences, Division of Humanities and Fine Arts, Program in Latin American and Iberian Studies, Santa Barbara, CA 93106-4150. Offers MA. *Faculty:* 56 part-time/adjunct (26 women). *Students:* 10 full-time (4 women). Average age 33. 23 applicants, 65% accepted, 4 enrolled. In 2009, 8 master's awarded. *Degree requirements:* For master's, one foreign language, comprehensive exam (for some programs), thesis. *Entrance requirements:* For master's, GRE, 2 writing samples, 3 letters of recommendation, resume/curriculum vitae. Additional exam requirements/recommendations for international students: Required—TOEFL (minimum score 550 paper-based; 213 computer-based; 80 iBT), or IELTS (minimum score 7). *Application deadline:* For fall admission, 5/1 for domestic and international students. Applications are processed on a rolling basis. Application fee: $70 ($90 for international students). Electronic applications accepted. *Financial support:* In 2009–10, 6 students received support, including 5 fellowships with full and partial tuition reimbursements available (averaging $9,900 per year), 3 teaching assistantships with partial tuition reimbursements available (averaging $10,000 per year); Federal Work-Study, institutionally sponsored loans, scholarships/grants, and health care benefits also available. Financial award application deadline: 1/15; financial award applicants required to submit FAFSA. *Faculty research:* Political science, anthropology, history, sociology, Portuguese. *Unit head:* Prof. Kathleen Bruhn, Director, 805-893-2999, Fax: 805-893-8341, E-mail: laisdirector@spanport.ucsb.edu. *Application contact:* Carol Conley, Graduate Program Assistant, 805-893-3162, Fax: 805-893-8341, E-mail: cconley@spanport.ucsb.edu.

University of Central Florida, College of Sciences, Department of Sociology, Orlando, FL 32816. Offers applied sociology (MA); Maya studies (Certificate); sociology (PhD). Part-time and evening/weekend programs available. *Faculty:* 18 full-time (10 women), 2 part-time/adjunct (1 woman). *Students:* 47 full-time (37 women), 16 part-time (9 women); includes 15 minority (6 African Americans, 1 Asian American or Pacific Islander, 8 Hispanic Americans), 1 international. Average age 30. 49 applicants, 73% accepted, 20 enrolled. In 2009, 16 master's, 4 doctorates, 4 other advanced degrees awarded. *Degree requirements:* For master's, comprehensive written exam or thesis. *Entrance requirements:* For master's, GRE General Test, minimum GPA of 3.0 in last 60 hours of course work. Additional exam requirements/recommendations for international students: Required—TOEFL. *Application deadline:* For fall admission, 7/15 for domestic students; for spring admission, 12/1 for domestic students. Application fee: $30. Electronic applications accepted. *Expenses:* Tuition, state resident: part-time $306.31 per credit hour. Tuition, nonresident: part-time $1099.01 per credit hour. Part-time tuition and fees vary according to degree level and program. *Financial support:* In 2009–10, 31 students received support, including 13 fellowships with partial tuition reimbursements available (averaging $5,800 per year), 2 research assistantships with partial tuition reimbursements available (averaging $4,900 per year), 26 teaching assistantships with partial tuition reimbursements available (averaging $9,700 per year); career-related internships or fieldwork, Federal Work-Study, institutionally sponsored loans, tuition waivers (partial), and unspecified assistantships also available. Financial award application deadline: 3/1; financial award applicants required to submit FAFSA. *Faculty research:* Religious subcultures, attitudes toward abortion, population, sport research, stratification. *Unit head:* Dr. Jay Corzine, Chair, 407-823-2227, Fax: 407-823-5156, E-mail: hcorzine@mail.ucf.edu. *Application contact:* Dr. Jay Corzine, Chair, 407-823-2227, Fax: 407-823-5156, E-mail: hcorzine@mail.ucf.edu.

University of Chicago, Division of Social Sciences and Division of the Humanities, Latin American and Caribbean Studies Program, Chicago, IL 60637-1513. Offers AM, MBA/AM. *Students:* 6. In 2009, 5 master's awarded. *Degree requirements:* For master's, one foreign language, thesis. *Entrance requirements:* For master's, GRE General Test. Additional exam requirements/recommendations for international students: Required—TOEFL. *Application deadline:* For fall admission, 1/4 for domestic and international students. Application fee: $55. Electronic applications accepted. *Financial support:* Federal Work-Study, institutionally sponsored loans, and scholarships/grants available. Financial award application deadline: 1/4. *Unit head:* Prof. Mauricio Tenorio, Director, 773-702-9741. *Application contact:* Office of the Dean of Students, 773-702-8415, E-mail: admissions@ssd.uchicago.edu.

University of Connecticut, Graduate School, College of Liberal Arts and Sciences, Field of International Studies, Program in Latin American Studies, Storrs, CT 06269. Offers MA. *Faculty:* 51 full-time (29 women). *Students:* 5 full-time (3 women), 4 part-time (all women); includes 6 minority (all Hispanic Americans), 1 international. Average age 32. 12 applicants, 33% accepted, 1 enrolled. In 2009, 2 master's awarded. *Degree requirements:* For master's, comprehensive exam. *Entrance requirements:* For master's, GRE General Test. Additional exam requirements/recommendations for international students: Required—TOEFL (minimum score 550 paper-based; 213 computer-based). *Application deadline:* For fall admission, 2/1 priority date for domestic students, 2/1 for international students; for spring admission, 11/1 for domestic students, 10/1 for international students. Applications are processed on a rolling basis. Application fee: $55. Electronic applications accepted. *Expenses:* Tuition, state resident: full-time $4725; part-time $525 per credit. Tuition, nonresident: full-time $12,267; part-time $1363 per credit. Required fees: $346 per semester. Tuition and fees vary according to course load. *Financial support:* In 2009–10, 4 research assistantships with full tuition reimbursements, 1 teaching assistantship with full tuition reimbursement were awarded; fellowships, Federal Work-Study, scholarships/grants, health care benefits, and unspecified assistantships also available. Financial award application deadline: 2/1; financial award applicants required to submit FAFSA. *Unit head:* Tricia Gabany-Guerrero, Chairperson, 860-486-2814, Fax: 860-486-2963, E-mail: t.gabany_guerrero@uconn.edu. *Application contact:* Ludmilla Burns, Administrative Assistant, 860-486-5888, Fax: 860-486-0641, E-mail: ludmilla.burns@uconn.edu.

University of Florida, Graduate School, College of Liberal Arts and Sciences, Center for Latin American Studies, Gainesville, FL 32611. Offers MA, Certificate, JD/MA. Part-time programs available. *Degree requirements:* For master's, thesis. *Entrance requirements:* For master's, GRE General Test, minimum GPA of 3.0. Additional exam requirements/recommendations for international students: Required—TOEFL (minimum score 550 paper-based; 213 computer-based). Electronic applications accepted. *Faculty research:* Tropical conservation and development; ethnicity in the Americas, Brazil, and Cuba; North American Free Trade Agreement.

University of Illinois at Urbana–Champaign, Graduate College, College of Liberal Arts and Sciences, Center for Latin American and Caribbean Studies, Champaign, IL 61820. Offers Latin American studies (MA). *Students:* 9 full-time (4 women), 1 (woman) part-time; includes 6 minority (1 African American, 1 Asian American or Pacific Islander, 4 Hispanic Americans), 2 international. 12 applicants, 42% accepted, 4 enrolled. In 2009, 2 master's awarded. *Entrance requirements:* For master's, GRE, minimum GPA of 3.0; writing sample. Additional exam requirements/recommendations for international students: Required—TOEFL (minimum score 550 paper-based; 213 computer-based). *Application deadline:* Applications are processed on a rolling basis. Application fee: $60 ($75 for international students). Electronic applications accepted. *Financial support:* In 2009–10, 5 fellowships, 2 teaching assistantships were awarded; research assistantships, tuition waivers (full and partial) also available. *Unit head:* Andrew Orta, Director, 217-244-7108, Fax: 217-244-7333, E-mail: njacobse@illinois.edu. *Application contact:* Angelina Cotler, Associate Director, 217-333-8419, Fax: 217-244-7333, E-mail: cotler@illinois.edu.

The University of Kansas, Graduate Studies, College of Liberal Arts and Sciences, Center of Latin American Studies, Lawrence, KS 66045. Offers Brazilian studies (Graduate Certificate); Central American and Mexican studies (Graduate Certificate); Latin American studies (MA). Part-time programs available. *Students:* 5 full-time (2 women), 7 part-time (3 women); includes 2 minority (both Hispanic Americans), 2 international. Average age 30. 13 applicants, 92% accepted, 6 enrolled. In 2009, 5 master's awarded. *Degree requirements:* For master's, 2 foreign languages, comprehensive exam, thesis optional. *Entrance requirements:* For master's, GRE, minimum GPA of 3.0, references, writing sample. Additional exam requirements/recommendations for international students: Required—TOEFL. *Application deadline:* For fall admission, 2/1 priority date for domestic and international students; for spring admission, 11/15 priority date for domestic and international students. Applications are processed on a rolling basis. Application fee: $45 ($55 for international students). Electronic applications accepted. *Expenses:* Tuition, state resident: full-time $6492; part-time $270.50 per credit hour. Tuition, nonresident: full-time $15,510; part-time $646.25 per credit hour. Required fees: $847; $70.56 per credit hour. Tuition and fees vary according to course load and program. *Financial support:* Fellowships with full tuition reimbursements, research assistantships with full and partial tuition reimbursements, teaching assistantships with full and partial tuition reimbursements, scholarships/grants and unspecified assistantships available. Financial award application deadline: 2/1. *Faculty research:* Democracy, ethnicity, literature, environment, gender. *Unit head:* Peter Herlihy, Graduate Advisor, 785-864-4213, Fax: 785-864-3800, E-mail: herlihy@ku.edu. *Application contact:* Judy Farmer, Office Manager, 785-864-4213, Fax: 785-864-3800, E-mail: jfarmer@ku.edu.

University of Massachusetts Dartmouth, Graduate School, College of Arts and Sciences, Department of Portuguese, North Dartmouth, MA 02747-2300. Offers Luso-Afro-Brazilian studies (PhD); Portuguese (MA). Part-time programs available. *Faculty:* 6 full-time (2 women), 2 part-time/adjunct (0 women). *Students:* 9 full-time (7 women), 11 part-time (7 women); includes 4 minority (1 African American, 3 Hispanic Americans), 4 international. Average age 36. 12 applicants, 83% accepted, 5 enrolled. In 2009, 2 master's awarded. *Degree requirements:* For master's, comprehensive exam (for some programs). *Entrance requirements:* For master's, GRE (recommended), 10 page writing sample; for doctorate, GRE. Additional exam requirements/recommendations for international students: Required—TOEFL (minimum score 500 paper-based). *Application deadline:* For fall admission, 4/20 priority date for domestic students, 2/20 priority date for international students; for spring admission, 11/15 priority date for domestic students, 9/15 priority date for international students. Applications are processed on a rolling basis. Application fee: $40 ($60 for international students). Electronic applications accepted. *Expenses:* Tuition, state resident: full-time $2071; part-time $86.29 per credit. Tuition, nonresident: full-time $8099; part-time $337.46 per credit. Required fees: $9446. Tuition and fees vary according to class time, course load and reciprocity agreements. *Financial support:* In 2009–10, 2 research assistantships with full tuition reimbursements (averaging $18,558 per year), 8 teaching assistantships with full tuition reimbursements (averaging $15,000 per year) were awarded. Financial award application deadline: 3/1; financial award applicants required to submit FAFSA. *Faculty research:* Translation studies, ethnicity and migration, literature in Luso-Afro-Brazilian studies, anaphoric direct objects in Portuguese. *Unit head:* Victor J. Mendes, Director, Graduate Studies, 508-999-8338, Fax: 508-999-9272, E-mail: vmendes@umassd.edu. *Application contact:* Elan Turcotte-Shamski, Graduate Admissions Officer, 508-999-8604, Fax: 508-999-8183, E-mail: graduate@umassd.edu.

University of Miami, Graduate School, College of Arts and Sciences, Department of Latin American and Caribbean Studies, Coral Gables, FL 33124. Offers Latin American studies (MA). Part-time programs available. *Degree requirements:* For master's, comprehensive exam (for some programs), thesis, linguistic competency in Spanish or Portuguese, reading competency in a second Latin American language. *Entrance requirements:* For master's, GRE, 3 letters of recommendation. Additional exam requirements/recommendations for international students: Required—TOEFL. Electronic applications accepted. *Faculty research:* Literary, media, religious, visual and cultural studies; environment and tourism studies; US-Latin American Relations and drug trafficking; migration, globalization, and social movements; democratization, regime transitions, and citizenship.

University of New Mexico, Graduate School, College of Arts and Sciences, Committee on Latin American Studies, Albuquerque, NM 87131-2039. Offers MA, PhD, JD/MA, MA/MA, MBA/MA, MCRP/MA, MSN/MA. Part-time programs available. *Faculty:* 1 part-time/adjunct (0 women). *Students:* 18 full-time (9 women), 12 part-time (8 women); includes 11 minority (1 African American, 1 American Indian/Alaska Native, 2 Asian Americans or Pacific Islanders, 7 Hispanic Americans), 2 international. Average age 29. 51 applicants, 78% accepted, 13 enrolled. In 2009, 14 master's awarded. *Degree requirements:* For master's, one foreign language, comprehensive exam (for some programs), thesis (for some programs); for doctorate, 2 foreign languages, comprehensive exam, thesis/dissertation. *Entrance requirements:* For master's, GRE General Test, Intermediate competence in Spanish, Portuguese or indigenous Latin American Language, background in LAS-related coursework; for doctorate, GRE General Test, master's degree in related field, one Latin American language. Additional exam requirements/recommendations for international students: Required—TOEFL. *Application deadline:* For fall admission, 2/1 priority date for domestic and international students; for spring admission, 11/1 for domestic and international students. Application fee: $50. Electronic applications accepted. *Expenses:* Tuition, state resident: full-time $2099; part-time $233.20 per credit hour. Tuition, nonresident: full-time $6650. Required fees: $25 per semester. Tuition and fees vary according to course load, program and reciprocity agreements. *Financial support:* In 2009–10, 27 students received support, including 8 research assistantships with full tuition reimbursements available (averaging $12,223 per year), 2 teaching assistantships with full tuition reimbursements available (averaging $12,223 per year); fellowships, Federal Work-Study, scholarships/grants, health care benefits, tuition waivers (full), and unspecified assistantships also available. Financial award application deadline: 2/1; financial award applicants required to submit FAFSA. *Unit head:* Dr. Kathryn McKnight, Associate Director for Academic Programs, 505-277-7042, Fax: 505-277-5989, E-mail: mcknight@unm.edu. *Application contact:* Kathryn McKnight, Associate Director for Academic Programs, 505-277-7042, Fax: 505-277-5989, E-mail: mcknight@unm.edu.

The University of North Carolina at Chapel Hill, Graduate School, College of Arts and Sciences, Department of Political Science, Chapel Hill, NC 27599. Offers Latin American studies (Certificate); political science (MA, PhD); trans-Atlantic studies (MA). *Degree requirements:* For master's, comprehensive exam; for doctorate, one foreign language, comprehensive exam, thesis/dissertation. *Entrance requirements:* For master's and doctorate, GRE General Test, minimum GPA of 3.0 recommended. Electronic applications accepted.

The University of North Carolina at Charlotte, Graduate School, College of Arts and Sciences, Department of Languages and Culture Studies, Charlotte, NC 28223-0001. Offers

Latin American Studies

The University of North Carolina at Charlotte (continued)
Latin American studies (MA); Spanish (MA). Part-time and evening/weekend programs available. *Faculty:* 21 full-time (11 women). *Students:* 10 full-time (8 women), 12 part-time (10 women); includes 5 minority (2 African Americans, 3 Hispanic Americans). Average age 27. 15 applicants, 87% accepted, 9 enrolled. In 2009, 7 master's awarded. *Degree requirements:* For master's, thesis optional. *Entrance requirements:* For master's, GRE, 3 letters of reference, minimum GPA of 2.75. Additional exam requirements/recommendations for international students: Required—TOEFL (minimum score 557 paper-based; 220 computer-based; 83 iBT). *Application deadline:* For fall admission, 7/15 for domestic students, 5/1 for international students; for spring admission, 11/15 for domestic students, 10/1 for international students. Applications are processed on a rolling basis. Application fee: $55. Electronic applications accepted. *Financial support:* In 2009–10, 9 students received support, including 8 teaching assistantships (averaging $3,750 per year); career-related internships or fieldwork, Federal Work-Study, institutionally sponsored loans, scholarships/grants, and administrative assistantship also available. Support available to part-time students. Financial award application deadline: 4/1; financial award applicants required to submit FAFSA. *Faculty research:* Twentieth and twenty-first century Spanish literature, Central American literature, Caribbean literature, Mexican literature, literature of the Southern Cone. Total annual research expenditures: $53,920. *Unit head:* Robert L. Reimer, Chair, 704-687-8767, Fax: 704-687-3496, E-mail: rcreimer@uncc.edu. *Application contact:* Kathy B. Giddings, Director of Graduate Admissions, 704-687-5503, Fax: 704-687-3279, E-mail: gradadm@uncc.edu.

University of Notre Dame, Graduate School, College of Arts and Letters, Division of Humanities, Department of Romance Languages and Literatures, Notre Dame, IN 46556. Offers French and Francophone studies (MA); Iberian and Latin American studies (MA); Italian studies (MA); Romance literatures (MA). *Degree requirements:* For master's, 2 foreign languages, comprehensive exam, thesis optional. *Entrance requirements:* For master's, GRE General Test, BA in target language. Additional exam requirements/recommendations for international students: Required—TOEFL (minimum score 600 paper-based; 250 computer-based; 80 iBT). Electronic applications accepted. *Faculty research:* Literature of discovery and exploration, modern literature, literary criticism, medieval literature, feminist critical theory.

University of Pittsburgh, University Center for International Studies, Pittsburgh, PA 15260. Offers African studies (Certificate); Asian studies (Certificate); European Union studies (Certificate); global studies (Certificate); Latin American studies (Certificate); Russian and East European studies (Certificate); West European studies (Certificate). *Students:* 332 (129 women); includes 31 minority (7 African Americans, 10 Asian Americans or Pacific Islanders, 14 Hispanic Americans), 136 international. In 2009, 59 Certificates awarded. *Degree requirements:* For Certificate, one foreign language, study abroad. *Application deadline:* Applications are processed on a rolling basis. *Expenses:* Tuition, state resident: full-time $16,402; part-time $665 per credit. Tuition, nonresident: full-time $28,694; part-time $1175 per credit. Required fees: $690; $175 per term. Tuition and fees vary according to program. *Unit head:* Lawrence F. Feick, Director, 412-648-7374, Fax: 412-624-4672, E-mail: feick@pitt.edu. *Application contact:* Information Contact, 412-624-4141, E-mail: graduate@pitt.edu.

University of South Florida, Graduate School, College of Arts and Sciences, Department of Government and International Affairs, Tampa, FL 33620-9951. Offers Latin American Caribbean and Latino Studies (MA); government (PhD); political science (MA); public administration (MPA). Part-time and evening/weekend programs available. *Faculty:* 19 full-time (4 women), 1 (woman) part-time/adjunct. *Students:* 31 full-time (16 women), 76 part-time (37 women); includes 28 minority (16 African Americans, 1 American Indian/Alaska Native, 4 Asian Americans or Pacific Islanders, 7 Hispanic Americans), 3 international. Average age 32. 126 applicants, 38% accepted, 24 enrolled. In 2009, 28 master's awarded. *Degree requirements:* For master's, comprehensive exam, thesis; for doctorate, comprehensive exam, thesis/dissertation. *Entrance requirements:* For master's, GRE (minimum score 470 verbal, 470 quantitative), minimum GPA of 3.0 in last 60 hours of course work. Additional exam requirements/recommendations for international students: Required—TOEFL (minimum score 550 paper-based; 213 computer-based). *Application deadline:* For fall admission, 2/15 for domestic students, 1/2 for international students; for spring admission, 10/15 for domestic students, 6/1 for international students. Applications are processed on a rolling basis. Application fee: $30. Electronic applications accepted. *Financial support:* In 2009–10, teaching assistantships with tuition reimbursements (averaging $24,000 per year); unspecified assistantships also available. Financial award application deadline: 4/1. *Unit head:* Dr. Mohsen Milani, Chairperson, 813-974-2384, Fax: 813-974-0832, E-mail: milani@chuma1.cas.usf.edu. *Application contact:* Dr. Stephen Tauber, Graduate Coordinator, 813-974-0781, Fax: 813-974-0832, E-mail: stauber@chuma1.cas.usf.edu.

The University of Texas at Austin, Graduate School, College of Liberal Arts, Teresa Lozano Long Institute of Latin American Studies, Austin, TX 78712-1111. Offers MA, PhD, JD/MA, MBA/MA, MP Aff/MA, MSCRP/MA. *Entrance requirements:* For master's and doctorate, GRE General Test.

The University of Texas at Dallas, School of Arts and Humanities, Richardson, TX 75080. Offers arts and technology (MFA); emerging media and communications (MA); humanities (MA, MAT, PhD), including aesthetic studies, history of ideas, humanities, studies in literature; Latin American studies (MA). Part-time and evening/weekend programs available. *Faculty:* 57 full-time (19 women), 3 part-time/adjunct (1 woman). *Students:* 240 full-time (127 women), 221 part-time (115 women); includes 90 minority (30 African Americans, 5 American Indian/Alaska Native, 21 Asian Americans or Pacific Islanders, 34 Hispanic Americans), 36 international. Average age 37. 186 applicants, 70% accepted, 106 enrolled. In 2009, 57 master's, 13 doctorates awarded. *Degree requirements:* For master's, one foreign language, portfolio; for doctorate, one foreign language, thesis/dissertation. *Entrance requirements:* For master's and doctorate, minimum GPA of 3.0 in undergraduate course work in field. Additional exam requirements/recommendations for international students: Required—TOEFL (minimum score 550 paper-based; 213 computer-based). *Application deadline:* For fall admission, 7/15 for domestic students, 5/1 priority date for international students; for spring admission, 11/15 for domestic students, 9/1 priority date for international students. Applications are processed on a rolling basis. Application fee: $50 ($100 for international students). Electronic applications accepted. *Expenses:* Tuition, state resident: full-time $11,068; part-time $461 per credit hour. Tuition, nonresident: full-time $21,178; part-time $882 per credit hour. Tuition and fees vary according to course load. *Financial support:* In 2009–10, 23 research assistantships with full tuition reimbursements (averaging $10,108 per year), 92 teaching assistantships with full tuition reimbursements (averaging $10,115 per year) were awarded; fellowships, Federal Work-Study, institutionally sponsored loans, scholarships/grants, and unspecified assistantships also available. Support available to part-time students. Financial award application deadline: 4/30; financial award applicants required to submit FAFSA. *Faculty research:* Translation, science and the arts and humanities, intellectual and philosophical history, cultural studies. Total annual research expenditures: $726,917. *Unit head:* Dr. Dennis M. Kratz, Dean, 972-883-2984, Fax: 972-883-2989, E-mail: dkratz@utdallas.edu. *Application contact:* Dr. Michael Wilson, Associate Dean of Graduate Studies, 972-883-2756, Fax: 972-883-2989, E-mail: mwilson@utdallas.edu.

The University of Texas at El Paso, Graduate School, College of Liberal Arts, Department of Sociology and Anthropology, El Paso, TX 79968-0001. Offers Latin American and border studies (MA, Certificate); sociology (MA). Part-time and evening/weekend programs available. *Degree requirements:* For master's, thesis optional. *Entrance requirements:* For master's, GRE General Test, minimum GPA of 3.0. Additional exam requirements/recommendations for international students: Required—TOEFL. Electronic applications accepted.

University of Wisconsin–Madison, Graduate School, College of Letters and Science, Department of History, Madison, WI 53706-1380. Offers African history (MA, PhD); Central Asian history (MA, PhD); comparative world history (MA, PhD); East Asian history (MA, PhD); European history (MA, PhD); gender and women's history (MA, PhD); Latin American and Caribbean history (MA, PhD); Middle Eastern history (MA, PhD); South Asian history (MA, PhD); Southeast Asian history (MA, PhD); United States history (MA, PhD). Terminal master's awarded for partial completion of doctoral program. *Degree requirements:* For master's, thesis (for some programs); for doctorate, variable foreign language requirement, thesis/dissertation. *Entrance requirements:* For master's and doctorate, GRE General Test. Additional exam requirements/recommendations for international students: Required—Michigan English Language Assessment Battery or TOEFL. Electronic applications accepted. *Expenses:* Tuition, state resident: part-time $594 per credit. Tuition, nonresident: part-time $1504 per credit. Required fees: $65 per credit. Tuition and fees vary according to course load, program and reciprocity agreements. *Faculty research:* American, African, European, Asian, Latin American, and Middle Eastern history.

University of Wisconsin–Madison, Graduate School, College of Letters and Science, Latin American, Caribbean and Iberian Studies Program, Madison, WI 53706-1380. Offers MA, MA/JD. *Degree requirements:* For master's, 2 foreign languages, thesis. *Entrance requirements:* For master's, minimum GPA of 3.0. Electronic applications accepted. *Expenses:* Tuition, state resident: part-time $594 per credit. Tuition, nonresident: part-time $1504 per credit. Required fees: $65 per credit. Tuition and fees vary according to course load, program and reciprocity agreements. *Faculty research:* Development, gender, social movements, cultural studies, history.

Vanderbilt University, Graduate School, Program in Latin American Studies, Nashville, TN 37240-1001. Offers MA, LL M/MA, MBA/MA. *Students:* 10 full-time (6 women); includes 3 minority (1 African American, 2 Hispanic Americans), 1 international. Average age 26. 31 applicants, 26% accepted, 6 enrolled. In 2009, 7 master's awarded. *Degree requirements:* For master's, 2 foreign languages, thesis or alternative. *Entrance requirements:* For master's, GRE General Test. Additional exam requirements/recommendations for international students: Required—TOEFL (minimum score 570 paper-based; 230 computer-based; 88 iBT). *Application deadline:* For fall admission, 1/15 for domestic and international students. Application fee: $0. Electronic applications accepted. *Financial support:* Teaching assistantships with full tuition reimbursements, Federal Work-Study, institutionally sponsored loans, and health care benefits available. Financial award application deadline: 1/15; financial award applicants required to submit CSS PROFILE or FAFSA. *Faculty research:* Latin American and Iberian studies, anthropology, history, Spanish and Portuguese, social and political science. *Unit head:* Edward Fischer, Director, 615-322-2527, Fax: 615-322-2305, E-mail: edward.f.fischer@vanderbilt.edu. *Application contact:* Frank Robinson, Associate Director, 615-322-2527, Fax: 615-322-2305, E-mail: william.f.robinson@vanderbilt.edu.

West Virginia University, Eberly College of Arts and Sciences, Department of History, Morgantown, WV 26506. Offers African history (MA, PhD); African-American history (MA, PhD); American history (MA, PhD); Appalachian/regional history (MA, PhD); East Asian history (MA, PhD); European history (MA, PhD); history of science and technology (MA, PhD); Latin American history (MA). Part-time programs available. *Degree requirements:* For master's, one foreign language, thesis (for some programs), oral exam, thesis defense; for doctorate, one foreign language, comprehensive exam, thesis/dissertation, dissertation defense. *Entrance requirements:* For master's, GRE General Test, minimum GPA of 3.0; for doctorate, GRE General Test. Additional exam requirements/recommendations for international students: Required—TOEFL (minimum score 550 paper-based), IELTS (minimum score 6.5). Electronic applications accepted. *Faculty research:* U.S., Appalachia, modern Europe, Africa, colonial and post-colonial societies.

Yale University, Graduate School of Arts and Sciences, Department of Spanish and Portuguese, New Haven, CT 06520. Offers Latin American literature (PhD); Luso-Brazilian and Spanish/Spanish American literatures (PhD); Spanish peninsular literature (PhD). Terminal master's awarded for partial completion of doctoral program. *Degree requirements:* For doctorate, 3 foreign languages, thesis/dissertation. *Entrance requirements:* For doctorate, GRE General Test.

Near and Middle Eastern Studies

The American University in Cairo, Graduate Studies and Research, School of Humanities and Social Sciences, Department of Arabic Studies, Cairo, Egypt. Offers Arab language and literature (MA); Islamic art and architecture (MA); Islamic studies (Diploma); Middle East studies (MA, Diploma); Middle Eastern history (MA). Part-time programs available. *Degree requirements:* For master's, thesis optional, proficiency in French or German. *Entrance requirements:* Additional exam requirements/recommendations for international students: Required—English entrance exam and/or TOEFL. Electronic applications accepted. *Faculty research:* History of early Islam, Ayubbid, and Mamluk periods; nineteenth- and twentieth-century Middle East Islamic jurisprudence; contemporary Arabic literary criticism.

The American University in Cairo, Graduate Studies and Research, School of Humanities and Social Sciences, Department of Sociology, Anthropology, Psychology, and Egyptology, Cairo, Egypt. Offers sociology and anthropology (MA). *Degree requirements:* For master's, one foreign language, thesis. *Entrance requirements:* Additional exam requirements/recommendations for international students: Required—English entrance exam and/or TOEFL. Electronic applications accepted. *Faculty research:* Development, gender, sociopolitical economic formulations, social science indigenization, Arab world.

American University of Beirut, Graduate Programs, Faculty of Arts and Sciences, Beirut, Lebanon. Offers anthropology (MA); Arabic language and literature (MA); archaeology (MA); biology (MS); chemistry (MS); computer science (MS); economics (MA); education (MA); English language (MA); English literature (MA); environmental policy planning (MSES); financial economics (MAFE); geology (MS); history (MA); mathematics (MA, MS); Middle Eastern studies (MA); philosophy (MA); physics (MS); political studies (MA); psychology (MA); public administration (MA); sociology (MA); statistics (MA, MS). Part-time programs available. *Degree requirements:* For master's, one foreign language, comprehensive exam, thesis (for some programs). *Entrance requirements:* For master's, GRE, letter of recommendation. Additional exam requirements/recommendations for international students: Required—TOEFL (minimum score 600 paper-based; 250 computer-based; 100 iBT), IELTS (minimum score 7.5). *Faculty research:* String theory and supergravity; computer graphics; algebra and number theory; popular Arabic literature; marine and freshwater biology; integrating science, math and technology.

The American University of Paris, Graduate Programs, Paris, France. Offers cross-cultural and sustainable business management (MA); cultural translation (MA); global communications

(MA); global communications and civil society (MA); international affairs, conflict resolution and civil society development (MA); Middle East and Islamic studies (MA); Middle East and Islamic studies and international affairs (MA); public policy and international affairs (MA); public policy and international law (MA). *Faculty:* 14 full-time (3 women). *Students:* 143 full-time (109 women). 71 applicants, 92% accepted, 34 enrolled. *Degree requirements:* For master's, thesis. *Entrance requirements:* For master's, minimum undergraduate GPA of 3.0. *Application deadline:* For fall admission, 4/15 priority date for international students; for spring admission, 11/15 priority date for international students. Applications are processed on a rolling basis. Application fee: $75. Tuition charges are reported in euros. *Expenses:* Tuition: Full-time 23,460 euros. *Financial support:* Scholarships/grants available. Financial award applicants required to submit FAFSA. *Unit head:* Celeste Schenk, President, 33 1-40620659, E-mail: president@aup.fr. *Application contact:* International Admissions Counselor, 33 1-40620720, Fax: 33 1-47053432, E-mail: admissions@aup.edu.

Brandeis University, Graduate School of Arts and Sciences, Department of Near Eastern and Judaic Studies, Waltham, MA 02454-9110. Offers Near Eastern and Judaic studies (MA, PhD); Near Eastern and Judaic studies and sociology (PhD); Near Eastern and Judaic studies and women's and gender studies (MA); teaching of Hebrew (MAT). Part-time programs available. *Faculty:* 26 full-time (11 women), 4 part-time/adjunct (1 woman). *Students:* 62 full-time (30 women), 1 part-time (0 women); includes 2 minority (1 African American, 1 Hispanic American), 7 international. Average age 33. 88 applicants, 67% accepted, 28 enrolled. In 2009, 10 master's, 6 doctorates awarded. Terminal master's awarded for partial completion of doctoral program. *Degree requirements:* For master's, one foreign language, comprehensive exam, thesis or alternative; for doctorate, 3 foreign languages, comprehensive exam, thesis/dissertation. *Entrance requirements:* For master's, GRE General Test (recommended), letters of recommendation; for doctorate, GRE General Test (recommended), letters of recommendation, transcripts, statement of purpose. Additional exam requirements/recommendations for international students: Required—TOEFL (minimum score 600 paper-based; 250 computer-based; 100 IBT); Recommended—IELTS (minimum score 7). *Application deadline:* For fall admission, 1/15 priority date for domestic and international students. Applications are processed on a rolling basis. Application fee: $75. Electronic applications accepted. *Financial support:* In 2009–10, 17 students received support, including 14 fellowships with full tuition reimbursements available (averaging $20,000 per year), 3 teaching assistantships with partial tuition reimbursements available (averaging $3,200 per year); research assistantships with full and partial tuition reimbursements available, scholarships/grants, health care benefits, and tuition waivers (full and partial) also available. Support available to part-time students. Financial award application deadline: 4/15; financial award applicants required to submit FAFSA. *Faculty research:* Ancient Near East and Bible, philosophy, history, modern Middle East, Islamic studies. *Unit head:* Dr. David Wright, Chair, 781-736-2954, Fax: 781-736-2070, E-mail: wright@brandeis.edu. *Application contact:* Joanne Arnish, Department Administrator, 781-736-2950, Fax: 781-736-2070, E-mail: arnish@brandeis.edu.

California State University, Long Beach, Graduate Studies, College of Liberal Arts, Department of History, Long Beach, CA 90840. Offers Africa and the Middle East (MA); ancient/Medieval Europe (MA); Asia (MA); Latin America (MA); modern Europe (MA); United States (MA); world (MA). Part-time and evening/weekend programs available. *Faculty:* 9 full-time (6 women), 1 (woman) part-time/adjunct. *Students:* 10 full-time (3 women), 56 part-time (21 women); includes 19 minority (2 African Americans, 1 American Indian/Alaska Native, 4 Asian Americans or Pacific Islanders, 12 Hispanic Americans), 1 international. Average age 31. 40 applicants, 50% accepted, 11 enrolled. *Degree requirements:* For master's, one foreign language, comprehensive exam or thesis. *Application deadline:* For fall admission, 3/1 for domestic students. Applications are processed on a rolling basis. Application fee: $55. Electronic applications accepted. *Expenses:* Required fees: $1802 per semester. Part-time tuition and fees vary according to course load. *Financial support:* Research assistantships, Federal Work-Study, institutionally sponsored loans, and scholarships/grants available. Financial award application deadline: 3/2. *Faculty research:* All periods of European and American history, recent Asian and African history. *Unit head:* Dr. Nancy Quam-Wickham, Department Chair, 562-985-4431, Fax: 562-985-5431, E-mail: quamwick@csulb.edu. *Application contact:* Dr. Houri Berberian, Graduate Advisor, 562-985-4524, Fax: 562-985-4431, E-mail: hberber@csulb.edu.

The Catholic University of America, School of Arts and Sciences, Department of Semitic and Egyptian Languages and Literature, Washington, DC 20064. Offers Ancient Near East (Biblical Hebrew/Aramaic) (MA); ancient Near East (Biblical Hebrew/Aramaic) (PhD); Arabic (PhD); Christian Near East (Biblical Hebrew/Aramaic) (MA); Coptic (MA, PhD); Syriac (MA). Part-time programs available. *Faculty:* 3 full-time (0 women), 2 part-time/adjunct (1 woman). *Students:* 14 full-time (5 women), 17 part-time (3 women); includes 4 minority (2 African Americans, 2 Asian Americans or Pacific Islanders), 4 international. Average age 36. 17 applicants, 88% accepted, 9 enrolled. In 2009, 2 master's, 1 doctorate awarded. *Degree requirements:* For master's, one foreign language, comprehensive exam; for doctorate, 2 foreign languages, comprehensive exam, thesis/dissertation. *Entrance requirements:* For master's, GRE General Test, 3 letters of recommendation; for doctorate, GRE General Test, statement of purpose, official copies of academic transcripts, three letters of recommendation. Additional exam requirements/recommendations for international students: Required—TOEFL (minimum score 580 paper-based; 237 computer-based). *Application deadline:* For fall admission, 8/1 priority date for domestic students, 7/15 for international students; for spring admission, 12/1 priority date for domestic students, 10/15 for international students. Applications are processed on a rolling basis. Application fee: $55. Electronic applications accepted. *Expenses:* Tuition: Full-time $31,740; part-time $1245 per credit hour. Required fees: $50; $25 per semester hour. One-time fee: $425. *Financial support:* Fellowships, research assistantships, teaching assistantships, Federal Work-Study, scholarships/grants, tuition waivers (full and partial), and unspecified assistantships available. Financial award application deadline: 2/1; financial award applicants required to submit FAFSA. *Faculty research:* Christian history and literature of the Near East, Biblical Hebrew, Arabic Christianity, Coptic, and Syriac. *Unit head:* Rev. Sidney H. Griffith, Chair, 202-319-5084, Fax: 202-319-4735, E-mail: griffith@cua.edu. *Application contact:* Julie Schwing, Director of Graduate Admissions, 202-319-5057, Fax: 202-319-6533, E-mail: cua-admissions@cua.edu.

Columbia University, Graduate School of Arts and Sciences, Division of Humanities, Department of Middle East Languages and Cultures, New York, NY 10027. Offers Hebrew language and literature (M Phil, MA, PhD); Middle Eastern languages and cultures (M Phil, MA, PhD); South Asian languages and cultures (M Phil, MA, PhD). Part-time programs available. *Degree requirements:* For master's, thesis, oral and written exams; for doctorate, 3 foreign languages, thesis/dissertation. *Entrance requirements:* For master's and doctorate, GRE General Test. Additional exam requirements/recommendations for international students: Required—TOEFL. *Faculty research:* Indo-Iranian, Turkish, central Asian, and Armenian studies; Arabic and ancient Semitics.

Columbia University, Graduate School of Arts and Sciences, Program in Liberal Studies, New York, NY 10027. Offers American studies (MA); East Asian studies (MA); human rights studies (MA); Islamic culture studies (MA); Jewish studies (MA); medieval studies (MA); modern European studies (MA); South Asian studies (MA). Part-time and evening/weekend programs available. *Degree requirements:* For master's, thesis.

Columbia University, School of International and Public Affairs, Middle East Institute, New York, NY 10027. Offers Certificate. Students must also be enrolled in a separate graduate degree program at Columbia University. Electronic applications accepted.

Cornell University, Graduate School, Graduate Fields of Arts and Sciences, Field of Archaeology, Ithaca, NY 14853-0001. Offers environmental archaeology (MA); historical archaeology (MA); Latin American archaeology (MA); medieval archaeology (MA); Mediterranean and Near Eastern archaeology (MA); Stone Age archaeology (MA). *Faculty:* 13 full-time (3 women). *Students:* 7 full-time (5 women). Average age 25. 20 applicants, 35% accepted, 4 enrolled. *Degree requirements:* For master's, one foreign language, thesis. *Entrance requirements:* For master's, GRE General Test, 3 letters of recommendation, sample of written work. Additional exam requirements/recommendations for international students: Required—TOEFL (minimum score 550 paper-based; 213 computer-based; 77 iBT). *Application deadline:* For fall admission, 1/15 for domestic students. Application fee: $70. Electronic applications accepted. *Expenses:* Tuition: Full-time $29,500. Required fees: $70. Full-time tuition and fees vary according to degree level, program and student level. *Financial support:* In 2009–10, 4 students received support; fellowships with full tuition reimbursements available, research assistantships with full tuition reimbursements available, teaching assistantships with full tuition reimbursements available, institutionally sponsored loans, scholarships/grants, health care benefits, tuition waivers (full and partial), and unspecified assistantships available. Financial award applicants required to submit FAFSA. *Faculty research:* Anatolia, Lydia, Sardis, classical and Hellenistic Greece; science in archaeology; North American Indians; Stone Age Africa; Maya trade. *Unit head:* Director of Graduate Studies, 607-255-6768, E-mail: blj7@cornell.edu. *Application contact:* Graduate Field Assistant, 607-255-6768, E-mail: dsd6@cornell.edu.

Cornell University, Graduate School, Graduate Fields of Arts and Sciences, Field of History, Ithaca, NY 14853-0001. Offers African history (MA, PhD); American history (MA, PhD); ancient history (MA, PhD); early modern European history (MA, PhD); English history (MA, PhD); French history (MA, PhD); German history (MA, PhD); history of science (MA, PhD); Latin American history (MA, PhD); medieval Chinese history (MA, PhD); medieval history (MA, PhD); modern Chinese history (MA, PhD); modern European history (MA, PhD); modern Japanese history (MA, PhD); premodern Islamic history (MA, PhD); premodern Japanese history (MA, PhD); Renaissance history (MA, PhD); Russian history (MA, PhD); Southeast Asian history (MA, PhD). *Faculty:* 62 full-time (19 women). *Students:* 67 full-time (33 women); includes 10 minority (4 African Americans, 3 Asian Americans or Pacific Islanders, 3 Hispanic Americans), 24 international. Average age 31. 195 applicants, 7% accepted, 10 enrolled. In 2009, 11 master's, 3 doctorates awarded. Terminal master's awarded for partial completion of doctoral program. *Degree requirements:* For master's, thesis; for doctorate, 2 foreign languages, comprehensive exam, thesis/dissertation, 1 year of teaching experience. *Entrance requirements:* For master's and doctorate, GRE General Test, writing sample, 3 letters of recommendation. Additional exam requirements/recommendations for international students: Required—TOEFL (minimum score 550 paper-based; 213 computer-based; 77 iBT). *Application deadline:* For fall admission, 1/15 for domestic students. Application fee: $70. Electronic applications accepted. *Expenses:* Tuition: Full-time $29,500. Required fees: $70. Full-time tuition and fees vary according to degree level, program and student level. *Financial support:* In 2009–10, 54 students received support, including 8 fellowships with full tuition reimbursements available; research assistantships with full tuition reimbursements available, teaching assistantships with full tuition reimbursements available, institutionally sponsored loans, scholarships/grants, health care benefits, tuition waivers (full and partial), and unspecified assistantships also available. Financial award applicants required to submit FAFSA. *Unit head:* Director of Graduate Studies, 607-255-6738, Fax: 607-255-0469. *Application contact:* Graduate Field Assistant, 607-255-6738, Fax: 607-255-0469, E-mail: history_grad_info@cornell.edu.

Cornell University, Graduate School, Graduate Fields of Arts and Sciences, Field of Near Eastern Studies, Ithaca, NY 14853-0001. Offers ancient Near Eastern studies (MA, PhD); Arabic and Islamic studies (MA, PhD); biblical studies (MA, PhD); Hebrew and Judaic studies (MA, PhD). *Faculty:* 18 full-time (6 women). *Students:* 5 full-time (2 women), 1 international. Average age 26. 26 applicants. In 2009, 1 master's, 1 doctorate awarded. Terminal master's awarded for partial completion of doctoral program. *Degree requirements:* For master's, one foreign language, thesis; for doctorate, 2 foreign languages, comprehensive exam, thesis/dissertation. *Entrance requirements:* For master's and doctorate, GRE General Test, 2 years of 1 Near Eastern language, 3 letters of recommendation, writing sample. Additional exam requirements/recommendations for international students: Required—TOEFL (minimum score 550 paper-based; 213 computer-based; 77 iBT). *Application deadline:* For fall admission, 2/1 for domestic students. Application fee: $70. Electronic applications accepted. *Expenses:* Tuition: Full-time $29,500. Required fees: $70. Full-time tuition and fees vary according to degree level, program and student level. *Financial support:* In 2009–10, 5 students received support; fellowships with full tuition reimbursements available, research assistantships with full tuition reimbursements available, teaching assistantships with full tuition reimbursements available, institutionally sponsored loans, scholarships/grants, health care benefits, tuition waivers (full and partial), and unspecified assistantships available. Financial award applicants required to submit FAFSA. *Faculty research:* Ancient Near East (including archeology), Hebrew and Judaic studies (including Bible), early Christianity, Arabic and Islamic studies, modern Middle East. *Unit head:* Director of Graduate Studies, 607-255-1329, Fax: 607-255-6450. *Application contact:* Graduate Field Assistant, 607-255-1329, Fax: 607-255-6450, E-mail: neareastern@cornell.edu.

Emory University, Graduate School of Arts and Sciences, Department of Comparative Literature, Atlanta, GA 30322-1100. Offers comparative literature (PhD); English (Certificate); French (Certificate); Middle Eastern studies (PhD); philosophy (Certificate); psychoanalytic studies (PhD); religion (PhD); Spanish (Certificate); women studies (Certificate). *Degree requirements:* For doctorate, 2 foreign languages, comprehensive exam, thesis/dissertation. *Entrance requirements:* For doctorate, GRE General Test, minimum GPA of 3.0. Additional exam requirements/recommendations for international students: Required—TOEFL. Electronic applications accepted. *Faculty research:* Literary theory, psychoanalysis trauma and testimony, literature and religion, literature and technology, literature and philosophy, politics and global culture, literature and aesthetics.

Georgetown University, Graduate School of Arts and Sciences, The Center for Contemporary Arab Studies, Washington, DC 20057. Offers MA, Certificate, MA/JD, MA/PhD. *Degree requirements:* For master's, comprehensive exam, proficiency in Arabic. *Entrance requirements:* For master's, GRE, minimum GPA of 3.0. Additional exam requirements/recommendations for international students: Required—TOEFL. *Faculty research:* Contemporary Arab world.

Georgetown University, Graduate School of Arts and Sciences, Department of Arabic and Islamic Studies, Washington, DC 20057. Offers Arabic area studies (PhD); Islamic studies (MA, PhD); linguistics (MA, PhD). *Degree requirements:* For master's, comprehensive exam, research project; for doctorate, one foreign language, comprehensive exam, thesis/dissertation. *Entrance requirements:* Additional exam requirements/recommendations for international students: Required—TOEFL.

The George Washington University, Elliott School of International Affairs, Program in Middle East Studies, Washington, DC 20052. Offers MA. *Students:* 36 full-time (22 women), 15 part-time (7 women); includes 3 minority (2 African Americans, 1 Asian American or Pacific Islander), 2 international. Average age 24. 99 applicants, 68% accepted, 27 enrolled. In 2009, 2 master's awarded. *Application deadline:* For fall admission, 2/1 for domestic students; for spring admission, 10/1 for domestic students. *Financial support:* In 2009–10, 7 students received support. Tuition waivers available. Financial award application deadline: 1/15. *Unit head:* Nathan J. Brown, Director, 202-994-2123, Fax: 202-994-5477, E-mail: nbrown@gwu.edu. *Application contact:* Jeff V. Miles, Director of Graduate Admissions, 202-994-7050, Fax: 202-994-9537, E-mail: esiagrad@gwu.edu.

Harvard University, Graduate School of Arts and Sciences, Committee on Middle Eastern Studies, Cambridge, MA 02138. Offers anthropology and Middle Eastern studies (PhD); economics and Middle Eastern studies (PhD); fine arts and Middle Eastern studies (PhD); history and Middle Eastern studies (PhD); regional studies–Middle East (AM). Terminal master's awarded for partial completion of doctoral program. *Degree requirements:* For master's, one foreign language; for doctorate, 2 foreign languages, thesis/dissertation. *Entrance requirements:* For master's, GRE General Test; for doctorate, GRE General Test, 1 year of course work in Middle Eastern regional studies, proficiency in a related language. Additional exam requirements/recommendations for international students: Required—TOEFL. *Expenses:* Tuition: Full-time $33,696. Required fees: $1126. Full-time tuition and fees vary according to program.

Near and Middle Eastern Studies

Harvard University, Graduate School of Arts and Sciences, Department of Near Eastern Languages and Civilizations, Cambridge, MA 02138. Offers Akkadian and Sumerian (AM, PhD); Arabic (AM, PhD); Armenian (AM, PhD); biblical history (AM, PhD); Hebrew (AM, PhD); Indo-Muslim culture (AM, PhD); Iranian (AM, PhD); Jewish history and literature (AM, PhD); Persian (AM, PhD); Semitic philology (AM, PhD); Syro-Palestinian archaeology (AM, PhD); Turkish (AM, PhD). *Degree requirements:* For doctorate, variable foreign language requirement, thesis/dissertation, general exams. *Entrance requirements:* For master's, GRE General Test; for doctorate, GRE General Test, proficiency in a Near Eastern language. Additional exam requirements/recommendations for international students: Required—TOEFL. *Expenses:* Tuition: Full-time $33,696. Required fees: $1126. Full-time tuition and fees vary according to program.

Hebrew Union College–Jewish Institute of Religion, School of Graduate Studies, Cincinnati, OH 45220-2488. Offers Bible and the ancient Near East (M Phil, MA, PhD); Hebrew letters (DHL); history of biblical interpretation (M Phil, MA, PhD); Jewish and Christian studies in the Greco-Roman period (M Phil, PhD); Jewish and cognate studies (M Phil); Judaic and cognate studies (MA, PhD); modern Jewish history (M Phil, MA, PhD); philosophy and Jewish religious thought (M Phil, MA, PhD); rabbinics (M Phil, MA, PhD). Part-time programs available. Terminal master's awarded for partial completion of doctoral program. *Degree requirements:* For master's, one foreign language, thesis optional; for doctorate, 3 foreign languages, comprehensive exam, thesis/dissertation. *Entrance requirements:* For master's and doctorate, GRE General Test, knowledge of Hebrew. Additional exam requirements/recommendations for international students: Required—TOEFL. *Faculty research:* Aramaic lexicon translations, German-Jewish history, neo-Babylonian texts.

The Johns Hopkins University, Zanvyl Krieger School of Arts and Sciences, Department of Near Eastern Studies, Baltimore, MD 21218-2699. Offers PhD. Part-time programs available. *Faculty:* 6 full-time (1 woman), 11 part-time/adjunct (7 women). *Students:* 23 full-time (13 women); includes 2 minority (1 African American, 1 Hispanic American), 2 international. Average age 30. 64 applicants, 16% accepted, 7 enrolled. In 2009, 4 doctorates awarded. *Degree requirements:* For doctorate, 2 foreign languages, comprehensive exam, thesis/dissertation. *Entrance requirements:* Additional exam requirements/recommendations for international students: Required—TOEFL (minimum score 600 paper-based; 250 computer-based; 100 iBT), IELTS. *Application deadline:* For fall admission, 1/15 for domestic and international students. Application fee: $75. Electronic applications accepted. *Financial support:* In 2009–10, 22 students received support, including 20 fellowships with full tuition reimbursements available (averaging $17,000 per year), 2 teaching assistantships with full tuition reimbursements available (averaging $17,000 per year); career-related internships or fieldwork, Federal Work-Study, scholarships/grants, and health care benefits also available. Financial award application deadline: 4/15; financial award applicants required to submit FAFSA. *Faculty research:* Egyptology, Assyriology, religions of ancient Israel and Syria, ancient and biblical law, demotic Egyptian. Total annual research expenditures: $64,479. *Unit head:* Dr. Theodore Lewis, Chair, 410-516-6791, Fax: 410-516-5218, E-mail: tjl@jhu.edu. *Application contact:* Glenda Hogan, Academic Program Coordinator, 410-516-7394, Fax: 410-516-5218, E-mail: ghogan@jhu.edu.

McGill University, Faculty of Graduate and Postdoctoral Studies, Faculty of Arts, Institute of Islamic Studies, Montréal, QC H3A 2T5, Canada. Offers MA, PhD, Diploma.

New York University, Graduate School of Arts and Science, Hagop Kevorkian Center for Near Eastern Studies, Department of Middle Eastern and Islamic Studies, New York, NY 10012-1019. Offers Middle Eastern and Islamic studies (MA, PhD); Middle Eastern and Islamic studies/history (PhD). Part-time programs available. *Faculty:* 17 full-time (6 women). *Students:* 40 full-time (22 women), 2 part-time (0 women); includes 5 minority (4 Asian Americans or Pacific Islanders, 1 Hispanic American), 11 international. Average age 31. 109 applicants, 11% accepted, 5 enrolled. In 2009, 9 doctorates awarded. Terminal master's awarded for partial completion of doctoral program. *Degree requirements:* For master's, 2 foreign languages, thesis; for doctorate, 4 foreign languages, comprehensive exam, thesis/dissertation. *Entrance requirements:* For master's and doctorate, GRE General Test. Additional exam requirements/recommendations for international students: Required—TOEFL. *Application deadline:* For fall admission, 12/18 for domestic students. Application fee: $90. *Expenses:* Tuition: Full-time $30,528; part-time $1272 per credit. Required fees: $2177. *Financial support:* Fellowships with tuition reimbursements, teaching assistantships with tuition reimbursements, Federal Work-Study and institutionally sponsored loans available. Financial award application deadline: 12/18; financial award applicants required to submit FAFSA. *Faculty research:* Middle Eastern history, Arabic/Persian/Turkish language and literature, cultures and societies of Middle East, Islamic studies. *Unit head:* Marion Katz, Chair, 212-998-8880, Fax: 212-995-4689, E-mail: mideast.studies@nyu.edu. *Application contact:* Khaled Fahmy, Director of Graduate Studies, 212-998-8880, Fax: 212-995-4689, E-mail: mideast.studies@nyu.edu.

New York University, Graduate School of Arts and Science, Hagop Kevorkian Center for Near Eastern Studies, Program in Near Eastern Studies, New York, NY 10012-1019. Offers Near Eastern studies (MA); Near Eastern studies (museum studies) (MA); Near Eastern studies/journalism (MA). Part-time programs available. *Faculty:* 2 full-time (0 women). *Students:* 32 full-time (24 women), 5 part-time (1 woman); includes 4 minority (all Asian Americans or Pacific Islanders), 11 international. Average age 26. 126 applicants, 44% accepted, 19 enrolled. In 2009, 14 master's awarded. *Degree requirements:* For master's, one foreign language, thesis. *Entrance requirements:* For master's, GRE General Test. Additional exam requirements/recommendations for international students: Required—TOEFL. *Application deadline:* For fall admission, 1/4 for domestic students. Application fee: $90. *Expenses:* Tuition: Full-time $30,528; part-time $1272 per credit. Required fees: $2177. *Financial support:* Fellowships with tuition reimbursements, teaching assistantships with tuition reimbursements, Federal Work-Study and institutionally sponsored loans available. Financial award application deadline: 1/4; financial award applicants required to submit FAFSA. *Faculty research:* Politics, political economy, anthropology, history and culture of the Middle East. *Unit head:* Michael Gilsenan, Director, 212-998-8877, Fax: 212-995-4144, E-mail: kevorkian.center@nyu.edu. *Application contact:* Greta Scharnweber, Associate Director, 212-998-8877, Fax: 212-995-4144, E-mail: kevorkian.center@nyu.edu.

New York University, Graduate School of Arts and Science, Program in Museum Studies, New York, NY 10012-1019. Offers museum studies (MA, Advanced Certificate), including Africana studies (MA), Hebrew and Judaic studies (MA), Latin American and Caribbean studies (MA), Near Eastern studies (MA). Part-time and evening/weekend programs available. *Students:* 62 full-time (57 women), 23 part-time (21 women); includes 13 minority (1 African American, 2 American Indian/Alaska Native, 3 Asian Americans or Pacific Islanders, 7 Hispanic Americans), 15 international. Average age 27. 220 applicants, 52% accepted, 37 enrolled. In 2009, 37 master's awarded. *Entrance requirements:* For degree, master's degree or PhD. Additional exam requirements/recommendations for international students: Required—TOEFL. *Application deadline:* For fall admission, 2/1 for domestic students; for spring admission, 11/1 for domestic students. Application fee: $90. *Expenses:* Tuition: Full-time $30,528; part-time $1272 per credit. Required fees: $2177. *Financial support:* Application deadline: 2/1. *Faculty research:* Modern and contemporary art, history of museums and exhibitions, conservation of cultural materials, museum anthropology, ethnography. *Unit head:* Haidy Geismar, Director, 212-998-8080, Fax: 212-995-4185, E-mail: museum.studies@nyu.edu. *Application contact:* Tatiana Kamorina, Department Administrator, 212-998-8080, Fax: 212-995-4185, E-mail: museum.studies@nyu.edu.

Princeton University, Graduate School, Department of Near Eastern Studies, Princeton, NJ 08544-1019. Offers MA, PhD. *Degree requirements:* For master's, one foreign language, thesis; for doctorate, 2 foreign languages, thesis/dissertation. *Entrance requirements:* For master's and doctorate, GRE General Test. Additional exam requirements/recommendations for international students: Required—TOEFL. Electronic applications accepted.

Regent University, Graduate School, Robertson School of Government, Virginia Beach, VA 23464. Offers american government (MA); global politics (MA); health care policy and administration (MA); international politics (MA); law and public policy (MA); Mid-East Politics (MA); political leadership and management (MA); political management (MA); political theory (MA); public administration (MA); public policy (MA); terrorism and homeland defense (MA); world economies and political development (MA); JD/MA; M Div/MA; M Ed/MA; MBA/MA. Part-time and evening/weekend programs available. Postbaccalaureate distance learning degree programs offered (minimal on-campus study). *Faculty:* 6 full-time (2 women), 11 part-time/adjunct (1 woman). *Students:* 77 full-time (55 women), 65 part-time (36 women); includes 47 minority (38 African Americans, 2 Asian Americans or Pacific Islanders, 7 Hispanic Americans), 4 international. Average age 30. 131 applicants, 65% accepted, 54 enrolled. In 2009, 51 master's awarded. *Degree requirements:* For master's, thesis optional, internship. *Entrance requirements:* For master's, GRE General Test or LSAT, minimum undergraduate GPA of 3.0, writing sample, resume, interview, references. Additional exam requirements/recommendations for international students: Required—TOEFL (minimum score 577 paper-based; 233 computer-based). *Application deadline:* For fall admission, 5/1 priority date for domestic students; for spring admission, 11/1 priority date for domestic students. Applications are processed on a rolling basis. Application fee: $50. Electronic applications accepted. *Expenses:* Contact institution. *Financial support:* In 2009–10, 130 students received support. Career-related internships or fieldwork, scholarships/grants, tuition waivers (full and partial), and unspecified assistantships available. Support available to part-time students. Financial award application deadline: 9/1; financial award applicants required to submit FAFSA. *Faculty research:* Education reform, political character issues, social capital concerns, administrative ethics, Biblical law and public policy. *Unit head:* Dr. Charles W. Dunn, Dean, 757-352-4322, Fax: 757-352-4643, E-mail: cwdunn@regent.edu. *Application contact:* Matthew Chadwick, Director of Admissions, 800-373-5504, Fax: 757-352-4381, E-mail: admissions@regent.edu.

Rice University, Graduate Programs, School of Humanities, Department of Religious Studies, Houston, TX 77251-1892. Offers African religions (PhD); African-American religions (PhD); contemplative studies (PhD); ghosticism, esotericism, mysticism (PhD); Islam (PhD); Jewish thought and philosophy (PhD); modern Christianity in thought and popular culture (PhD); psychology of religion (PhD); the Bible and beyond (PhD). *Faculty:* 11 full-time (3 women), 2 part-time/adjunct (both women). *Students:* 37 full-time (13 women); includes 10 minority (9 African Americans, 1 Asian American or Pacific Islander), 9 international. Average age 31. 42 applicants, 14% accepted, 6 enrolled. In 2009, 2 doctorates awarded. *Degree requirements:* For doctorate, 2 foreign languages, comprehensive exam, thesis/dissertation. *Entrance requirements:* For doctorate, GRE, letters of recommendation, writing sample. Additional exam requirements/recommendations for international students: Required—TOEFL (minimum score 600 paper-based; 90 iBT). *Application deadline:* For fall admission, 1/1 for domestic students, 1/15 for international students. Application fee: $70. Electronic applications accepted. *Financial support:* In 2009–10, 14 fellowships (averaging $15,900 per year) were awarded. Financial award application deadline: 5/15; financial award applicants required to submit FAFSA. *Faculty research:* Origins and historical development of Islam, history of Christianity, the study of comparative religion, African-American religion, religion and culture. Total annual research expenditures: $46,514. *Unit head:* Prof. William B. Parsons, Associate Professor, Religious Studies, 713-348-2712, Fax: 713-348-5486, E-mail: pars@rice.edu. *Application contact:* Sylvia Louie, Senior Department Coordinator, 713-348-5201, Fax: 713-348-5486, E-mail: reli@rice.edu.

SIT Graduate Institute, Graduate Programs, Program in Global Management (Oman), Brattleboro, VT 05302-0676. Offers MGM. Program offered in the Sultanate of Oman. Part-time programs available. *Degree requirements:* For master's, capstone project. *Entrance requirements:* Additional exam requirements/recommendations for international students: Required—TOEFL (minimum score of 550 paper-based, 213 computer-based, 79 iBT) or IELTS (minimum score of 6.0).

Southern Evangelical Seminary, Veritas Graduate School of Apologetics and Counter-Cult Ministry, Matthews, NC 28105. Offers apologetics (MA, D Min, PhD, Certificate); Islamic studies (MA); Jewish studies (MA); philosophy (MA); religion (MA). Part-time and evening/weekend programs available. Postbaccalaureate distance learning degree programs offered (minimal on-campus study). *Degree requirements:* For master's, thesis optional; for doctorate, comprehensive exam (for some programs), thesis/dissertation. *Entrance requirements:* Additional exam requirements/recommendations for international students: Required—TOEFL (minimum score 600 paper-based; 250 computer-based).

Syracuse University, College of Arts and Sciences, Program in Middle Eastern Studies, Syracuse, NY 13244. Offers CAS. Part-time programs available. *Students:* 3 applicants, 100% accepted, 0 enrolled. In 2009, 2 CASs awarded. *Entrance requirements:* For degree, Must be matriculated in a graduate SU program. *Application deadline:* For fall admission, 2/1 priority date for domestic students, 1/1 priority date for international students. Application fee: $75. Electronic applications accepted. *Expenses:* Tuition: Full-time $26,808; part-time $1117 per credit. Required fees: $1024. *Unit head:* Mehrzad Boroujerdi, Program Contact, 315-443-9082, E-mail: mborouje@maxwell.syr.edu. *Application contact:* Mehrzad Boroujerdi, Program Contact, 315-443-9082, E-mail: mborouje@maxwell.syr.edu.

The University of Arizona, Graduate College, College of Social and Behavioral Sciences, Department of Near Eastern Studies, Tucson, AZ 85721. Offers MA, PhD. Part-time and evening/weekend programs available. *Faculty:* 11. *Students:* 33 full-time (11 women), 26 part-time (20 women); includes 3 minority (1 African American, 2 Hispanic Americans), 13 international. Average age 31. 91 applicants, 49% accepted, 24 enrolled. In 2009, 14 master's awarded. Terminal master's awarded for partial completion of doctoral program. *Degree requirements:* For master's, one foreign language; for doctorate, 3 foreign languages, thesis/dissertation. *Entrance requirements:* For master's, GRE General Test, 3 letters of recommendation, statement of purpose, curriculum vitae, writing sample; for doctorate, GRE General Test, 3 letters of recommendation, curriculum vitae, writing sample. Additional exam requirements/recommendations for international students: Required—TOEFL (minimum score 550 paper-based; 213 computer-based; 79 iBT). *Application deadline:* For fall admission, 1/15 for domestic students, 12/1 for international students; for spring admission, 10/1 for domestic students, 6/1 for international students. Applications are processed on a rolling basis. Application fee: $65. Electronic applications accepted. *Expenses:* Tuition, state resident: full-time $9028. Tuition, nonresident: full-time $24,890. *Financial support:* In 2009–10, 1 research assistantship with full tuition reimbursement (averaging $11,538 per year), 21 teaching assistantships with full tuition reimbursements (averaging $12,508 per year) were awarded; Federal Work-Study, institutionally sponsored loans, health care benefits, tuition waivers (full), and unspecified assistantships also available. Support available to part-time students. Total annual research expenditures: $8,946. *Unit head:* Dr. Michael E. Bonine, Head, 520-626-9140, Fax: 520-621-2333, E-mail: bonine@u.arizona.edu. *Application contact:* Kathleen A. Landeen, Graduate Coordinator, 520-626-8731, Fax: 520-621-2333, E-mail: klandeen@email.arizona.edu.

University of California, Berkeley, Graduate Division, College of Letters and Science, Department of Near Eastern Studies, Group in Near Eastern Religions, Berkeley, CA 94720-1500. Offers PhD. *Students:* 4 full-time (3 women). Average age 45. 8 applicants, 0 enrolled. *Degree requirements:* For doctorate, 2 foreign languages, thesis/dissertation, qualifying exam. *Entrance requirements:* For doctorate, GRE General Test, MA or equivalent in Near Eastern studies or related field; minimum GPA of 3.0, 3 letters of recommendation. *Application deadline:* For fall admission, 12/15 for domestic students. Application fee: $70 ($90 for international students). *Financial support:* Fellowships, research assistantships, teaching assistantships, unspecified assistantships available. *Unit head:* Prof. Niek Veldhuis, Chair, 510-642-3757, E-mail: nes@berkeley.edu. *Application contact:* Judy Shattuck, Graduate Assistant, 510-642-6162, Fax: 510-643-8430, E-mail: nes@berkeley.edu.

University of California, Berkeley, Graduate Division, College of Letters and Science, Department of Near Eastern Studies, Program in Near Eastern Studies, Berkeley, CA 94720-1500. Offers MA, PhD. *Students:* 28 full-time (20 women). Average age 32. 66 applicants, 2 enrolled. In 2009, 6 master's, 6 doctorates awarded. *Degree requirements:* For doctorate, 2 foreign languages, thesis/dissertation, qualifying exam. *Entrance requirements:* For master's and doctorate, GRE General Test, minimum GPA of 3.0, 3 letters of recommendation. *Application deadline:* For fall admission, 12/15 for domestic students. Application fee: $70 ($90 for international students). *Financial support:* Unspecified assistantships available. *Unit head:* Prof. Carol Redmount, Chair, 510-642-3757, E-mail: nes@berkeley.edu. *Application contact:* Judy Shattuck, Graduate Assistant, 510-642-6162, Fax: 510-643-8430, E-mail: nes@berkeley.edu.

University of California, Los Angeles, Graduate Division, College of Letters and Science, Department of Near Eastern Languages and Cultures, Los Angeles, CA 90034. Offers MA, PhD. *Students:* 43 full-time (21 women); includes 2 minority (both Hispanic Americans), 2 international. Average age 29. 60 applicants, 23% accepted, 6 enrolled. In 2009, 9 master's, 2 doctorates awarded. *Degree requirements:* For master's, one foreign language, comprehensive exam; for doctorate, 2 foreign languages, thesis/dissertation, oral and written qualifying exams. *Entrance requirements:* For master's and doctorate, GRE General Test, minimum GPA of 3.25, sample of written work (recommended). Additional exam requirements/recommendations for international students: Required—TOEFL. *Application deadline:* For fall admission, 12/1 for domestic and international students. Application fee: $70 ($90 for international students). Electronic applications accepted. *Financial support:* In 2009–10, 30 fellowships with full and partial tuition reimbursements, 24 research assistantships with full and partial tuition reimbursements, 22 teaching assistantships with full and partial tuition reimbursements were awarded; Federal Work-Study, institutionally sponsored loans, scholarships/grants, health care benefits, tuition waivers (full and partial), and unspecified assistantships also available. Financial award application deadline: 3/1; financial award applicants required to submit FAFSA. *Unit head:* Dr. Elizabeth Carter, Chair, 310-206-5474. *Application contact:* Department Office, 310-825-4165, E-mail: nreast@humnet.ucla.edu.

University of California, Los Angeles, Graduate Division, College of Letters and Science, Program in Indo-European Studies, Los Angeles, CA 90095. Offers PhD. *Students:* 15 full-time (6 women), 4 international. Average age 28. 20 applicants, 30% accepted, 4 enrolled. *Degree requirements:* For doctorate, 2 foreign languages, thesis/dissertation, oral and written qualifying exams. *Entrance requirements:* For doctorate, minimum undergraduate GPA of 3.0, writing sample, competency in Classical Latin. *Application deadline:* For fall admission, 1/15 for domestic and international students. Application fee: $70 ($90 for international students). Electronic applications accepted. *Financial support:* In 2009–10, 9 fellowships with full and partial tuition reimbursements, 7 research assistantships with full and partial tuition reimbursements, 5 teaching assistantships with full and partial tuition reimbursements were awarded; Federal Work-Study, institutionally sponsored loans, scholarships/grants, health care benefits, tuition waivers (full and partial), and unspecified assistantships also available. Financial award application deadline: 3/1; financial award applicants required to submit FAFSA. *Unit head:* Dr. Stephanie Jamison, Chair, 310-206-7736. *Application contact:* Department Office, 310-206-1590, E-mail: dabugheida@humnet.ucla.edu.

University of California, Los Angeles, Graduate Division, International Institute, Program in Islamic Studies, Los Angeles, CA 90095. Offers MA, PhD, MPH/MA. *Students:* 21 full-time (7 women); includes 1 minority (Hispanic American), 4 international. Average age 32. In 2009, 1 master's, 1 doctorate awarded. *Degree requirements:* For master's, one foreign language, comprehensive exam; for doctorate, 2 foreign languages, thesis/dissertation, oral and written qualifying exams. *Entrance requirements:* For master's, GRE General Test, minimum GPA of 3.0; for doctorate, GRE General Test, minimum undergraduate GPA of 3.0, master's degree, advanced level proficiency in Arabic. *Application deadline:* For fall admission, 12/15 for domestic students. Application fee: $70 ($90 for international students). Electronic applications accepted. *Financial support:* In 2009–10, 6 fellowships with full and partial tuition reimbursements, 4 research assistantships with full and partial tuition reimbursements, 8 teaching assistantships with full and partial tuition reimbursements were awarded; Federal Work-Study, institutionally sponsored loans, scholarships/grants, health care benefits, tuition waivers (full and partial), and unspecified assistantships also available. Financial award application deadline: 3/1; financial award applicants required to submit FAFSA. *Unit head:* Dr. Khaled Abou El Fadl, Chair, 310-206-5401. *Application contact:* Department Office, 310-206-5401, E-mail: idpgrads@international.ucla.edu.

University of Chicago, Division of Social Sciences and Division of the Humanities, Middle Eastern Studies Program, Chicago, IL 60637-1513. Offers AM, MBA/AM, MPP/AM. *Students:* 20. In 2009, 11 master's awarded. *Degree requirements:* For master's, one foreign language, thesis. *Entrance requirements:* For master's, GRE General Test. Additional exam requirements/recommendations for international students: Required—TOEFL. *Application deadline:* For fall admission, 1/4 for domestic and international students. Application fee: $55. Electronic applications accepted. *Financial support:* Federal Work-Study, institutionally sponsored loans, and scholarships/grants available. Financial award application deadline: 1/4. *Unit head:* Prof. Fred Donner, Director, 773-702-8297. *Application contact:* Office of the Dean of Students, 773-702-8415, E-mail: admissions@ssd.uchicago.edu.

University of Chicago, Division of the Humanities, Department of Near Eastern Languages and Civilizations, Chicago, IL 60637-1513. Offers AM, PhD. Terminal master's awarded for partial completion of doctoral program. *Degree requirements:* For master's, one foreign language, comprehensive exam, thesis; for doctorate, 2 foreign languages, comprehensive exam, thesis/dissertation. *Entrance requirements:* For master's and doctorate, GRE General Test. Additional exam requirements/recommendations for international students: Required—TOEFL.

The University of Kansas, Graduate Studies, College of Liberal Arts and Sciences, Center for Russian, East European and Eurasian Studies, Lawrence, KS 66045. Offers MA. Part-time programs available. *Faculty:* 38 full-time (17 women), 4 part-time/adjunct (1 woman). *Students:* 9 full-time (2 women), 1 part-time (0 women), 1 international. Average age 28. 18 applicants, 83% accepted, 4 enrolled. In 2009, 1 master's awarded. *Degree requirements:* For master's, one foreign language, comprehensive exam, interdisciplinary capstone research seminar. *Entrance requirements:* For master's, GRE General Test, 3 letters of recommendation. Additional exam requirements/recommendations for international students: Required—TOEFL. *Application deadline:* For fall admission, 1/1 priority date for domestic and international students. Application fee: $45 ($55 for international students). Electronic applications accepted. *Expenses:* Tuition, state resident: full-time $6492; part-time $270.50 per credit hour. Tuition, nonresident: full-time $15,510; part-time $646.25 per credit hour. Required fees: $847; $70.56 per credit hour. Tuition and fees vary according to course load and program. *Financial support:* Fellowships with full tuition reimbursements, research assistantships with partial tuition reimbursements, scholarships/grants available. Financial award application deadline: 1/31; financial award applicants required to submit FAFSA. *Faculty research:* Russian and East Central European history and culture; Ukrainian, Russian, and Central Asian domestic politics and international security; Slavic languages, linguistics, and literatures. *Unit head:* Dr. Edith Clowes, Director, 785-864-4236, Fax: 785-864-3800, E-mail: crees@ku.edu. *Application contact:* Dr. Eve Levin, Associate Director, 785-864-4236, Fax: 785-864-4236, E-mail: evelevin@ku.edu.

University of Michigan, Horace H. Rackham School of Graduate Studies, College of Literature, Science, and the Arts, Department of Near Eastern Studies, Ann Arbor, MI 48109. Offers ancient Near Eastern studies (AM, PhD); Arabic for professional purposes (AM); Arabic language and literature (AM, PhD); Armenian studies (AM, PhD); Christianity in late antiquity (AM, PhD); Egyptology (AM, PhD); Hebrew Bible and ancient Israel (AM, PhD); Hebrew literature (AM, PhD); Islamic studies (AM, PhD); Jewish cultural studies (AM, PhD); Jewish mysticism (AM, PhD); Persian and Iranian studies (AM, PhD); Rabbinic literature (AM, PhD); Second Temple Judaism (AM, PhD); teaching of Arabic as a foreign language (AM); Turkish studies (AM, PhD). Part-time programs available. *Faculty:* 23 full-time (5 women), 15 part-time/adjunct (6 women). *Students:* 47 full-time (23 women), 1 part-time (0 women); includes 1 minority (Hispanic American), 8 international. Average age 31. 99 applicants, 15% accepted, 8 enrolled. In 2009, 4 master's, 4 doctorates awarded. Terminal master's awarded for partial completion of doctoral program. *Degree requirements:* For master's, 2 foreign languages; for doctorate, 4 foreign languages, comprehensive exam, thesis/dissertation. *Entrance requirements:* For master's, GRE General Test; for doctorate, GRE General Test, master's degree. Additional exam requirements/recommendations for international students: Required—TOEFL (minimum score 560 paper-based; 220 computer-based; 84 iBT). *Application deadline:* For fall admission, 12/15 for domestic and international students. Application fee: $60 ($75 for international students). Electronic applications accepted. *Expenses:* Tuition, state resident: full-time $17,286; part-time $1099 per credit hour. Tuition, nonresident: full-time $34,944; part-time $2080 per credit hour. Required fees: $95 per semester. Tuition and fees vary according to course load, degree level and program. *Financial support:* In 2009–10, 43 students received support, including 21 fellowships with full tuition reimbursements available (averaging $16,694 per year), research assistantships with tuition reimbursements available (averaging $16,694 per year), 22 teaching assistantships with full tuition reimbursements available (averaging $16,694 per year); scholarships/grants, health care benefits, unspecified assistantships, and spring/summer stipends also available. *Faculty research:* Middle and Near Eastern literatures, languages, cultures from ancient times to the present. *Unit head:* Prof. Michael Bonner, Chair, 734-764-0314, Fax: 734-936-2679, E-mail: mbonner@umich.edu. *Application contact:* Angela Beskow, Student Services Assistant, 734-763-4539, Fax: 734-936-2679, E-mail: aradjews@umich.edu.

University of Michigan, Horace H. Rackham School of Graduate Studies, Interdepartmental Program in Modern Middle Eastern and North African Studies, Ann Arbor, MI 48109. Offers AM, JD/AM, MBA/AM. *Faculty:* 46 full-time (12 women). *Students:* 20 full-time (12 women), 2 international. Average age 26. 58 applicants, 52% accepted, 8 enrolled. In 2009, 3 master's awarded. *Degree requirements:* For master's, one foreign language, thesis or alternative. *Entrance requirements:* For master's, GRE General Test. Additional exam requirements/recommendations for international students: Required—TOEFL (minimum score 560 paper-based; 84 iBT). *Application deadline:* For fall admission, 1/15 for domestic and international students. Application fee: $65 ($75 for international students). Electronic applications accepted. *Expenses:* Tuition, state resident: full-time $17,286; part-time $1099 per credit hour. Tuition, nonresident: full-time $34,944; part-time $2080 per credit hour. Required fees: $95 per semester. Tuition and fees vary according to course load, degree level and program. *Financial support:* In 2009–10, 1 student received support, including 3 fellowships with full and partial tuition reimbursements available (averaging $45,000 per year); Federal Work-Study also available. Financial award application deadline: 3/15; financial award applicants required to submit FAFSA. *Faculty research:* Middle east and north Africa. Total annual research expenditures: $300,000. *Unit head:* Dr. Gottfried Hagen, Director, 734-764-0350, Fax: 734-764-8523, E-mail: cmenas@umich.edu. *Application contact:* Susan Barrera, Administrative Assistant, 734-764-0350, Fax: 734-764-8523, E-mail: cmenas@umich.edu.

University of Pennsylvania, School of Arts and Sciences, Graduate Group in Near Eastern Languages and Civilization, Philadelphia, PA 19104. Offers AM, PhD. *Faculty:* 21 full-time (6 women), 2 part-time/adjunct (0 women). *Students:* 33 full-time (17 women), 20 part-time (13 women); includes 1 minority (Asian American or Pacific Islander), 6 international. 77 applicants, 10% accepted, 5 enrolled. In 2009, 7 master's, 5 doctorates awarded. Application fee: $70. *Expenses:* Tuition: Full-time $25,660; part-time $4758 per course. Required fees: $2152; $270 per course. Tuition and fees vary according to course load, degree level and program. *Financial support:* Institutionally sponsored loans, scholarships/grants, traineeships, health care benefits, and unspecified assistantships available.

University of South Africa, College of Human Sciences, Pretoria, South Africa. Offers adult education (M Ed); African languages (MA, PhD); African politics (MA, PhD); Afrikaans (MA, PhD); ancient history (MA, PhD); ancient Near Eastern studies (MA, PhD); anthropology (MA, PhD); applied linguistics (MA); Arabic (MA, PhD); archaeology (MA); art history (MA); Biblical archaeology (MA); Biblical studies (M Th, D Th, PhD); Christian spirituality (M Th, D Th); church history (M Th, D Th); classical studies (MA, PhD); clinical psychology (MA); communication (MA, PhD); comparative education (M Ed, Ed D); consulting psychology (D Admin, D Com, PhD); curriculum studies (M Ed, Ed D); development studies (M Admin, MA, D Admin, PhD); didactics (M Ed, Ed D); education (M Tech); education management (M Ed, Ed D); educational psychology (M Ed); English (MA); environmental education (M Ed); French (MA, PhD); German (MA, PhD); Greek (MA); guidance and counseling (M Ed); health studies (MA, PhD), including health sciences education (MA), health services management (MA), medical and surgical nursing science (critical care general) (MA), midwifery and neonatal nursing science (MA), trauma and emergency care (MA); history (MA, PhD); history of education (Ed D); inclusive education (M Ed, Ed D); information and communications technology policy and regulation (MA); information science (MA, MIS, PhD); international politics (MA, PhD); Islamic studies (MA, PhD); Italian (MA, PhD); Judaica (MA, PhD); linguistics (MA, PhD); mathematical education (M Ed); mathematics education (MA); missiology (M Th, D Th); modern Hebrew (MA, PhD); musicology (MA, MMus, D Mus, PhD); natural science education (M Ed); New Testament (M Th, D Th); Old Testament (D Th); pastoral therapy (M Th, D Th); philosophy (MA); philosophy of education (M Ed, Ed D); politics (MA, PhD); Portuguese (MA, PhD); practical theology (M Th, D Th); psychology (MA, MS, PhD); psychology of education (M Ed, Ed D); public health (MA); religious studies (MA, D Th, PhD); Romance languages (MA); Russian (MA, PhD); Semitic languages (MA, PhD); social behavior studies in HIV/AIDS (MA); social science (mental health) (MA); social science in development studies (MA); social science in psychology (MA); social science in social work (MA); social science in sociology (MA); social work (MSW, DSW, PhD); socio-education (M Ed, Ed D); sociolinguistics (MA); sociology (MA, PhD); Spanish (MA, PhD); systematic theology (M Th, D Th); TESOL (teaching English to speakers of other languages) (MA); theological ethics (M Th, D Th); theory of literature (MA, PhD); urban ministries (D Th); urban ministry (M Th).

The University of Texas at Austin, Graduate School, College of Liberal Arts, Center for Middle Eastern Studies, Austin, TX 78712-1111. Offers MA, JD/MA, MBA/MA, MLIS/MA, MP Aff/MA. *Degree requirements:* For master's, one foreign language, thesis optional. *Entrance requirements:* For master's, GRE General Test. Electronic applications accepted.

The University of Texas at Austin, Graduate School, College of Liberal Arts, Department of Middle Eastern Studies, Austin, TX 78712-1111. Offers Arabic (MA, PhD); Hebrew (MA). *Degree requirements:* For master's, one foreign language, comprehensive exam, thesis; for doctorate, 2 foreign languages, comprehensive exam, thesis/dissertation. *Entrance requirements:* For master's and doctorate, GRE General Test. Additional exam requirements/recommendations for international students: Required—TOEFL. Electronic applications accepted. *Faculty research:* Islamic studies, Persian language and literature, Hebrew language, Jewish studies, Arabic literature and language.

University of Toronto, School of Graduate Studies, Humanities Division, Department of Near and Middle Eastern Civilizations, Toronto, ON M5S 1A1, Canada. Offers MA, PhD. Part-time programs available. *Degree requirements:* For master's, thesis optional; for doctorate, 2 foreign languages, thesis/dissertation, language proficiency exams. *Entrance requirements:* For master's, BA in relevant area, minimum B+ average in final year, prior coursework in ancient Near Eastern or Islamic civilizations, 2 letters of reference; for doctorate, MA in relevant area with a minimum A– average, 2 letters of reference. Additional exam requirements/recommendations for international students: Required—TOEFL (minimum score 580 paper-based; 237 computer-based), TWE (minimum score 5).

University of Utah, The Graduate School, College of Humanities, Program in Middle East Studies, Salt Lake City, UT 84112. Offers anthropology (MA); Arabic (MA, PhD); Arabic and linguistics (MA, PhD); Hebrew (MA); history (MA, PhD); Persian (MA, PhD); political science (MA, PhD); Turkish (MA). *Students:* 24 full-time (8 women), 19 part-time (9 women), 13 international. Average age 33. 33 applicants, 48% accepted, 10 enrolled. In 2009, 8 master's, 2 doctorates awarded. Terminal master's awarded for partial completion of doctoral program. *Degree requirements:* For master's, 2 foreign languages, comprehensive exam, thesis optional; for doctorate, 3 foreign languages, comprehensive exam, thesis/dissertation. *Entrance requirements:* For master's, GRE General Test, minimum GPA of 3.2; for doctorate, GRE General Test, MA in Middle East studies or equivalent, minimum GPA of 3.2. Additional exam requirements/recommendations for international students: Required—TOEFL (minimum score

Near and Middle Eastern Studies

University of Utah (continued)
580 paper-based; 237 computer-based; 92 iBT). *Application deadline:* For fall admission, 1/15 priority date for domestic and international students; for spring admission, 9/15 priority date for domestic and international students. Application fee: $55 ($65 for international students). Electronic applications accepted. *Expenses:* Tuition, state resident: full-time $4004; part-time $1674 per semester. Tuition, nonresident: full-time $14,134; part-time $5915 per semester. Required fees: $324 per semester. Tuition and fees vary according to course load, degree level and program. *Financial support:* In 2009–10, 19 students received support, including 15 fellowships with full tuition reimbursements available (averaging $14,000 per year), 3 teaching assistantships with full tuition reimbursements available (averaging $12,000 per year); unspecified assistantships also available. Financial award application deadline: 1/15. *Faculty research:* Arabic linguistics; Islamic studies; Middle Eastern history; political science; Judaic studies; anthropology; Arabic, Persian, Hebrew, and Turkish language and literature. *Unit head:* Dr. Bahman Baktiari, Director, 801-581-6181, Fax: 801-581-6183, E-mail: b.baktiari@utah.edu. *Application contact:* Peter von Sivers, Director of Graduate Studies, 801-581-9028, Fax: 801-581-6183, E-mail: peter.vonsivers@utah.edu.

University of Washington, Graduate School, College of Arts and Sciences, Department of Near Eastern Languages and Civilization, Seattle, WA 98195. Offers MA. *Degree requirements:* For master's, 2 foreign languages, exams. *Entrance requirements:* For master's, GRE, minimum GPA of 3.0. Additional exam requirements/recommendations for international students: Required—TOEFL. Electronic applications accepted. *Faculty research:* Arabic, Hebrew, Persian, and Turkish literature; Islamic civilization and religion; Central Asian Turkic language and literature; Hebrew Bible and ancient Near East; ancient Christianity.

University of Washington, Graduate School, College of Arts and Sciences, Henry M. Jackson School of International Studies, Middle East Studies Program, Seattle, WA 98195. Offers MAIS. *Faculty:* 36 full-time (13 women). *Students:* 14 full-time (10 women), 1 international. 60 applicants, 33% accepted, 4 enrolled. In 2009, 5 master's awarded. *Degree requirements:* For master's, one foreign language, thesis optional. *Entrance requirements:* For master's, GRE General Test, minimum GPA of 3.0. Additional exam requirements/recommendations for international students: Required—TOEFL (minimum score 500 paper-based; 213 computer-based; 92 iBT), or IELTS (minimum score 7). *Application deadline:* For fall admission, 12/30 for domestic students, 12/1 for international students. Application fee: $75. Electronic applications accepted. *Financial support:* In 2009–10, 3 fellowships with full tuition reimbursements were awarded; research assistantships, teaching assistantships, career-related internships or fieldwork, Federal Work-Study, institutionally sponsored loans, scholarships/grants, and summer language study awards also available. Financial award application deadline: 12/30; financial award applicants required to submit FAFSA. *Unit head:* Prof. Philip D. Schuyler, Chair, 206-543-9878. *Application contact:* 206-543-6001, Fax: 206-616-3170, E-mail: jsisinfo@u.washington.edu.

University of Washington, Graduate School, Interdisciplinary Program in Near and Middle Eastern Studies, Seattle, WA 98195. Offers PhD. *Degree requirements:* For doctorate, 3 foreign languages, thesis/dissertation. *Entrance requirements:* For doctorate, GRE General Test, minimum GPA of 3.0. Additional exam requirements/recommendations for international students: Required—TOEFL. Electronic applications accepted.

University of Waterloo, Graduate Studies, Faculty of Arts, Department of Classical Studies, Waterloo, ON N2L 3G1, Canada. Offers ancient Mediterranean cultures (MA). *Degree requirements:* For master's, one foreign language. *Faculty research:* Ancient history, philosophy, anthropology, religion, culture.

University of Wisconsin–Madison, Graduate School, College of Letters and Science, Department of History, Madison, WI 53706-1380. Offers African history (MA, PhD); Central Asian history (MA, PhD); comparative world history (MA, PhD); East Asian history (MA, PhD); European history (MA, PhD); gender and women's history (MA, PhD); Latin American and Caribbean history (MA, PhD); Middle Eastern history (MA, PhD); South Asian history (MA, PhD); Southeast Asian history (MA, PhD); United States history (MA, PhD). Terminal master's awarded for partial completion of doctoral program. *Degree requirements:* For master's, thesis (for some programs); for doctorate, variable foreign language requirement, thesis/dissertation. *Entrance requirements:* For master's and doctorate, GRE General Test. Additional exam requirements/recommendations for international students: Required—Michigan English Language Assessment Battery or TOEFL. Electronic applications accepted. *Expenses:* Tuition, state resident: part-time $594 per credit. Tuition, nonresident: part-time $1504 per credit. Required fees: $65 per credit. Tuition and fees vary according to course load, program and reciprocity agreements. *Faculty research:* American, African, European, Asian, Latin American, and Middle Eastern history.

Wayne State University, College of Liberal Arts and Sciences, Department of Classical and Modern Languages, Literatures, and Cultures, Program in Near Eastern and Asian Studies, Detroit, MI 48202. Offers language learning (MA); Near Eastern studies (MA). *Degree requirements:* For master's, one foreign language. *Entrance requirements:* For master's, GRE General Test. Additional exam requirements/recommendations for international students: Required—TOEFL (minimum score 550 paper-based; 213 computer-based); Recommended—TWE (minimum score 6). Electronic applications accepted. *Faculty research:* Modern Middle East history, Arabic language and culture studies, Chinese linguistics, Islamic studies, Judaic studies.

Yale University, Graduate School of Arts and Sciences, Department of Near Eastern Languages and Civilizations, New Haven, CT 06520. Offers Arabic and Islamic studies (MA, PhD); archaeology of the ancient Near East (MA, PhD); Assyriology (MA, PhD); Egyptology (MA, PhD); Graeco-Arabic studies (MA, PhD); Northwest Semitic, Bible, comparative Semitics (MA, PhD). *Degree requirements:* For doctorate, 2 foreign languages, thesis/dissertation. *Entrance requirements:* For doctorate, GRE General Test.

Northern Studies

University of Alaska Fairbanks, College of Liberal Arts, Department of Northern Studies, Fairbanks, AK 99775-6460. Offers environmental politics and policy (MA); Northern history (MA). Part-time programs available. *Faculty:* 9 full-time (5 women), 1 part-time/adjunct (0 women). *Students:* 14 full-time (6 women), 21 part-time (15 women); includes 2 minority (1 African American, 1 American Indian/Alaska Native), 5 international. Average age 39. 19 applicants, 63% accepted, 9 enrolled. In 2009, 11 master's awarded. *Degree requirements:* For master's, comprehensive exam, thesis or alternative. *Entrance requirements:* Additional exam requirements/recommendations for international students: Required—TOEFL (minimum score 550 paper-based; 213 computer-based; 80 iBT). *Application deadline:* For fall admission, 6/1 for domestic students, 3/1 for international students; for spring admission, 10/15 for domestic students, 9/1 for international students. Applications are processed on a rolling basis. Application fee: $60. Electronic applications accepted. *Expenses:* Tuition, state resident: full-time $7584; part-time $316 per credit. Tuition, nonresident: full-time $15,504; part-time $646 per credit. Required fees: $23 per credit. $135 per semester. Tuition and fees vary according to course level, course load and reciprocity agreements. *Financial support:* In 2009–10, 3 research assistantships (averaging $7,517 per year), 11 teaching assistantships (averaging $7,671 per year) were awarded; fellowships, career-related internships or fieldwork, Federal Work-Study, scholarships/grants, health care benefits, and unspecified assistantships also available. Support available to part-time students. Financial award application deadline: 1/1; financial award applicants required to submit FAFSA. *Faculty research:* Canadian history, environmental history, Native Alaskan history and art, fetal alcohol syndrome. *Unit head:* Dr. Judith S. Kleinfeld, Co-Director, 907-474-7126, Fax: 907-474-5817, E-mail: fynors@uaf.edu. *Application contact:* Dr. Judith S. Kleinfeld, Co-Director, 907-474-7126, Fax: 907-474-5817, E-mail: fynors@uaf.edu.

University of Manitoba, Faculty of Graduate Studies, Faculty of Arts, Department of Icelandic Language and Literature, Winnipeg, MB R3T 2N2, Canada. Offers MA.

Pacific Area/Pacific Rim Studies

University of California, San Diego, Office of Graduate Studies, Graduate School of International Relations and Pacific Studies, La Jolla, CA 92093. Offers economics and international affairs (PhD); Pacific international affairs (MPIA); political science and international affairs (PhD). *Degree requirements:* For master's, one foreign language; for doctorate, thesis/dissertation. *Entrance requirements:* For master's, GMAT or GRE General Test; for doctorate, GRE General Test. Additional exam requirements/recommendations for international students: Required—TOEFL (minimum score 550 paper-based; 213 computer-based). Electronic applications accepted. *Faculty research:* Pacific Rim as system and placement in global relations; studies in international economics, management and finance; analysis of patterns of policymaking in countries of the Pacific.

University of Guam, Office of Graduate Studies, College of Liberal Arts and Social Sciences, Micronesian Studies Program, Mangilao, GU 96923. Offers MA. *Degree requirements:* For master's, thesis. *Entrance requirements:* For master's, GRE General Test. Additional exam requirements/recommendations for international students: Required—TOEFL. *Faculty research:* Adolescent suicide in Micronesia, history of Micronesia, traditional agriculture in the Pacific, Micronesian languages, health and cultural practices.

University of Hawaii at Manoa, Graduate Division, School of Pacific and Asian Studies, Program in Pacific Island Studies, Honolulu, HI 96822. Offers MA, Graduate Certificate. Part-time programs available. *Faculty:* 27 full-time (8 women), 3 part-time/adjunct (2 women). *Students:* 17 full-time (11 women), 8 part-time (6 women); includes 11 minority (10 Asian Americans or Pacific Islanders, 1 Hispanic American), 5 international. Average age 31. 19 applicants, 53% accepted, 9 enrolled. In 2009, 7 master's awarded. *Degree requirements:* For master's, thesis optional. *Entrance requirements:* Additional exam requirements/recommendations for international students: Required—TOEFL (minimum score 580 paper-based; 237 computer-based; 92 iBT), IELTS (minimum score 5). *Application deadline:* For fall admission, 3/1 for domestic and international students; for spring admission, 9/1 for domestic and international students. Application fee: $60. *Expenses:* Tuition, state resident: full-time $8900; part-time $372 per credit. Tuition, nonresident: full-time $21,400; part-time $898 per credit. Required fees: $207 per semester. *Financial support:* In 2009–10, 9 fellowships (averaging $8,613 per year), 1 research assistantship (averaging $17,496 per year), 1 teaching assistantship (averaging $14,382 per year) were awarded. Total annual research expenditures: $271,000. *Application contact:* Terence Wesley-Smith, Associate Professor/Graduate Chair, 808-956-7700, Fax: 808-956-7053, E-mail: twsmith@hawaii.edu.

University of San Francisco, College of Arts and Sciences, Program in Asia Pacific Studies, San Francisco, CA 94117-1080. Offers MA, MA/MBA. Part-time and evening/weekend programs available. *Faculty:* 1 full-time (0 women), 5 part-time/adjunct (4 women). *Students:* 36 full-time (22 women), 4 part-time (3 women); includes 14 minority (4 African Americans, 9 Asian Americans or Pacific Islanders, 1 Hispanic American), 15 international. Average age 28. 44 applicants, 86% accepted, 20 enrolled. In 2009, 19 master's awarded. *Degree requirements:* For master's, one foreign language, thesis. *Entrance requirements:* For master's, minimum GPA of 3.0. *Application deadline:* Applications are processed on a rolling basis. Application fee: $55 ($65 for international students). *Expenses:* Tuition: Full-time $19,710; part-time $1095 per unit. Part-time tuition and fees vary according to degree level, campus/location and program. *Financial support:* In 2009–10, 22 students received support. Career-related internships or fieldwork, Federal Work-Study, and institutionally sponsored loans available. Financial award application deadline: 3/2; financial award applicants required to submit FAFSA. *Faculty research:* History of Christianity in China, U. S.-China policy, East Asian economies and political systems, sociolinguistic aspects of Japanese. *Unit head:* Dr. Ken Kopp, Director, 415-422-6357, Fax: 415-422-5933. *Application contact:* Information Contact, 415-422-5135, Fax: 415-422-2217, E-mail: asgraduate@usfca.edu.

University of Victoria, Faculty of Graduate Studies, Faculty of Humanities, Department of Pacific and Asian Studies, Victoria, BC V8W 2Y2, Canada. Offers MA. *Degree requirements:* For master's, thesis. *Entrance requirements:* For master's, minimum B+ average, writing sample. Additional exam requirements/recommendations for international students: Required—TOEFL (minimum score 575 paper-based; 233 computer-based), IELTS (minimum score 7). Electronic applications accepted. *Faculty research:* Culture, ethnicity and identity; economy and society; gender studies; languages and linguistics; literature.

Western European Studies

American University, School of International Service, Washington, DC 20016-8071. Offers comparative and regional studies (Certificate); cross-cultural communication (Certificate); development management (MS); ethics, peace, and global affairs (MA); European studies (Certificate); global environmental policy (MA, Certificate); international affairs (MA), including comparative and regional studies, environmental policy, international economic policy, international politics, natural resources and sustainable development, U.S. foreign policy; international communication (MA, Certificate); international development (MA, Certificate); international development management (Certificate); international economic policy (Certificate); international economic relations (Certificate); international media (MA); international peace and conflict resolution (MA, Certificate); international relations (PhD); international service (MIS); peace building (Certificate); the Americas (Certificate); United States foreign policy (Certificate); JD/MA. Part-time and evening/weekend programs available. *Faculty:* 98 full-time (42 women), 48 part-time/adjunct (13 women). *Students:* 565 full-time (349 women), 329 part-time (189 women); includes 128 minority (44 African Americans, 2 American Indian/Alaska Native, 37 Asian Americans or Pacific Islanders, 45 Hispanic Americans), 102 international. Average age 27. 2,034 applicants, 63% accepted, 344 enrolled. In 2009, 326 master's, 6 doctorates, 9 other advanced degrees awarded. Terminal master's awarded for partial completion of doctoral program. *Degree requirements:* For master's, one foreign language, comprehensive exam, thesis or alternative; for doctorate, one foreign language, comprehensive exam, thesis/dissertation, research practicum; for Certificate, minimum 15 credit hours related course work. *Entrance requirements:* For master's, GRE, 24 credits of course work in related social sciences, minimum GPA of 3.5, 2 letters of recommendation, bachelor's degree, resume; for doctorate, GRE, 2 letters of recommendation, 24 credits in related social sciences; for Certificate, bachelor's degree. Additional exam requirements/recommendations for international students: Required—TOEFL (minimum score 600 paper-based; 250 computer-based; 100 iBT). *Application deadline:* For fall admission, 1/15 priority date for domestic students; for spring admission, 10/1 priority date for domestic students. Applications are processed on a rolling basis. Application fee: $50. *Expenses:* Tuition: Full-time $22,266; part-time $1237 per credit hour. Required fees: $430. Tuition and fees vary according to program. *Financial support:* Career-related internships or fieldwork, Federal Work-Study, and institutionally sponsored loans available. Financial award application deadline: 1/15. *Faculty research:* International intellectual property, international environmental issues, international law and legal order, international telecommunications/technology, international sustainable development. *Unit head:* Dr. Louis W. Goodman, Dean, 202-885-1600, Fax: 202-885-2494. *Application contact:* Yasmin Quianzon, Director of Graduate Admissions and Financial Aid, 202-885-2496, Fax: 202-885-1109.

See Close-Up on page 849.

Boston College, Graduate School of Arts and Sciences, Department of History, Chestnut Hill, MA 02467-3800. Offers European national studies (MA); history (MA, PhD); medieval studies (MA). *Students:* 70 full-time (38 women), 9 part-time (6 women); includes 4 minority (2 African Americans, 2 Asian Americans or Pacific Islanders), 7 international. 229 applicants, 21% accepted, 11 enrolled. In 2009, 20 master's, 7 doctorates awarded. Terminal master's awarded for partial completion of doctoral program. *Degree requirements:* For master's, one foreign language, comprehensive exam, thesis optional; for doctorate, 2 foreign languages, comprehensive exam, thesis/dissertation. *Entrance requirements:* For master's and doctorate, GRE General Test, writing sample. Additional exam requirements/recommendations for international students: Required—TOEFL (minimum score 600 paper-based; 250 computer-based; 100 iBT). *Application deadline:* For fall admission, 1/2 for domestic and international students. Application fee: $70. Electronic applications accepted. *Financial support:* In 2009–10, fellowships with full tuition reimbursements (averaging $17,000 per year), teaching assistantships with full tuition reimbursements (averaging $17,400 per year) were awarded; Federal Work-Study and scholarships/grants also available. Support available to part-time students. Financial award application deadline: 3/1; financial award applicants required to submit FAFSA. *Faculty research:* Modern and early modern European, U. S., Russian, and Soviet history; European and U. S. intellectual history. *Unit head:* Dr. Marilynn Johnson, Chairperson, 617-552-3781. *Application contact:* Dr. David Quigley, Director of Graduate Studies, 617-552-2267, E-mail: david.quigley@bc.edu.

Brown University, Graduate School, Center for Portuguese and Brazilian Studies, Providence, RI 02912. Offers Brazilian studies (AM); Portuguese and Brazilian studies (AM, PhD); Portuguese Bilingual Education and Cross-Cultural Studies (AM); MA/PhD. *Degree requirements:* For doctorate, thesis/dissertation.

California State University, Long Beach, Graduate Studies, College of Liberal Arts, Department of History, Long Beach, CA 90840. Offers Africa and the Middle East (MA); ancient/Medieval Europe (MA); Asia (MA); Latin America (MA); modern Europe (MA); United States (MA); world (MA). Part-time and evening/weekend programs available. *Faculty:* 9 full-time (6 women), 1 (woman) part-time/adjunct. *Students:* 10 full-time (3 women), 56 part-time (21 women); includes 19 minority (2 African Americans, 1 American Indian/Alaska Native, 4 Asian Americans or Pacific Islanders, 12 Hispanic Americans), 1 international. Average age 31. 40 applicants, 50% accepted, 11 enrolled. *Degree requirements:* For master's, one foreign language, comprehensive exam or thesis. *Application deadline:* For fall admission, 3/1 for domestic students. Applications are processed on a rolling basis. Application fee: $55. Electronic applications accepted. *Expenses:* Required fees: $1802 per semester. Part-time tuition and fees vary according to course load. *Financial support:* Research assistantships, Federal Work-Study, institutionally sponsored loans, and scholarships/grants available. Financial award application deadline: 3/2. *Faculty research:* All periods of European and American history, recent Asian and African history. *Unit head:* Dr. Nancy Quam-Wickham, Department Chair, 562-985-4431, Fax: 562-985-5431, E-mail: quamwick@csulb.edu. *Application contact:* Dr. Houri Berberian, Graduate Advisor, 562-985-4524, Fax: 562-985-4431, E-mail: hberber@csulb.edu.

Carleton University, Faculty of Graduate Studies, Faculty of Public Affairs and Management, Institute of European and Russian Studies, Ottawa, ON K1S 5B6, Canada. Offers European and European Union studies (MA); European integration studies (Diploma); Russian, Eurasian and transition studies (MA). *Degree requirements:* For master's, one foreign language, thesis optional. *Entrance requirements:* For master's, honors degree or equivalent; 2 years of Russian, German or other central east European language. Additional exam requirements/recommendations for international students: Required—TOEFL. *Faculty research:* East-West relations, minority rights in Russia and Eastern Europe.

The Catholic University of America, School of Arts and Sciences, Department of History, Washington, DC 20064. Offers Medieval Europe (MA, PhD); modern Europe (PhD); religion and society in the late Medieval and early modern world (MA); United States (MA); MA/JD; MSLS/MA. Part-time programs available. *Faculty:* 13 full-time (6 women), 3 part-time/adjunct (1 woman). *Students:* 14 full-time (9 women), 28 part-time (11 women); includes 1 minority (American Indian/Alaska Native), 3 international. Average age 33. 38 applicants, 50% accepted, 7 enrolled. In 2009, 8 master's, 2 doctorates awarded. *Degree requirements:* For master's, one foreign language, comprehensive exam, thesis optional; for doctorate, 2 foreign languages, comprehensive exam, thesis/dissertation, oral exams. *Entrance requirements:* For master's, GRE General Test, statement of purpose, official copies of academic transcripts, three letters of recommendation, writing sample; for doctorate, GRE General Test, MA in history, statement of purpose, official copies of academic transcripts, three letters of recommendation, writing sample. Additional exam requirements/recommendations for international students: Required—TOEFL (minimum score 580 paper-based; 237 computer-based). *Application deadline:* For fall admission, 8/1 priority date for domestic students, 7/15 for international students; for spring admission, 12/1 priority date for domestic students, 10/15 for international students. Applications are processed on a rolling basis. Application fee: $55. Electronic applications accepted. *Expenses:* Tuition: Full-time $31,740; part-time $1245 per credit hour. Required fees: $50; $25 per semester hour. One-time fee: $425. *Financial support:* Fellowships, research assistantships, teaching assistantships, Federal Work-Study, scholarships/grants, tuition waivers (full and partial), and unspecified assistantships available. Financial award application deadline: 2/1; financial award applicants required to submit FAFSA. *Faculty research:* Modern European intellectual history, history of mathematics and sciences, Renaissance, Catholic reformation, medieval women and gender. *Unit head:* Dr. Jerry Muller, Chair, 202-319-5484, Fax: 202-319-5569, E-mail: mullerj@cua.edu. *Application contact:* Julie Schwing, Director of Graduate Admissions, 202-319-5057, Fax: 202-319-6533, E-mail: cua-admissions@cua.edu.

Central Michigan University, College of Graduate Studies, College of Humanities and Social and Behavioral Sciences, Department of History, Mount Pleasant, MI 48859. Offers European history (Graduate Certificate); history (MA, PhD); modern history (Graduate Certificate); United States history (Graduate Certificate). Offered jointly with the University of Stratclyde, Scotland. Part-time programs available. *Degree requirements:* For master's, thesis or alternative; for doctorate, comprehensive exam, thesis/dissertation. Electronic applications accepted. *Faculty research:* Colonial and revolutionary United States history, modern European history, Latin American and transatlantic history, transnational and comparative history, United States social history.

Claremont Graduate University, Graduate Programs, School of Arts and Humanities, Department of History, Claremont, CA 91711-6160. Offers Africana history (Certificate); American studies and U.S. history (MA, PhD); archival studies (MA); early modern studies (MA, PhD); European studies (MA, PhD); oral history (MA, PhD); MBA/MA; MBA/PhD. *Faculty:* 4 full-time (2 women). *Students:* 69 full-time (31 women), 5 part-time (3 women); includes 13 minority (1 African American, 4 Asian Americans or Pacific Islanders, 8 Hispanic Americans), 2 international. Average age 36. In 2009, 10 master's, 3 doctorates awarded. Terminal master's awarded for partial completion of doctoral program. *Entrance requirements:* For master's and doctorate, GRE General Test. Additional exam requirements/recommendations for international students: Required—TOEFL (minimum score 550 paper-based; 213 computer-based; 80 iBT). *Application deadline:* For fall admission, 2/1 priority date for domestic students. Applications are processed on a rolling basis. Application fee: $60. Electronic applications accepted. *Expenses:* Tuition: Full-time $35,046; part-time $1524 per credit. Required fees: $161 per semester. *Financial support:* Fellowships, research assistantships, Federal Work-Study, institutionally sponsored loans, and scholarships/grants available. Support available to part-time students. Financial award application deadline: 2/15; financial award applicants required to submit FAFSA. *Faculty research:* Intellectual and social history, cultural studies, gender studies, Western history, Chicano history. *Unit head:* Janet Farrell Brodie, Chair, 909-621-8880, Fax: 909-621-8609, E-mail: janet.brodie@cgu.edu. *Application contact:* Susan Hampson, Admissions Coordinator, 909-607-1278, E-mail: humanities@cgu.edu.

Columbia University, Graduate School of Arts and Sciences, Program in Liberal Studies, New York, NY 10027. Offers American studies (MA); East Asian studies (MA); human rights studies (MA); Islamic culture studies (MA); Jewish studies (MA); medieval studies (MA); modern European studies (MA); South Asian studies (MA). Part-time and evening/weekend programs available. *Degree requirements:* For master's, thesis.

Columbia University, School of International and Public Affairs, Institute for the Study of Europe, New York, NY 10027. Offers Certificate. Students must be enrolled in a separate graduate degree program at Columbia University. Electronic applications accepted.

Cornell University, Graduate School, Graduate Fields of Arts and Sciences, Field of History, Ithaca, NY 14853-0001. Offers African history (MA, PhD); American history (MA, PhD); ancient history (MA, PhD); early modern European history (MA, PhD); English history (MA, PhD); French history (MA, PhD); German history (MA, PhD); history of science (MA, PhD); Latin American history (MA, PhD); medieval Chinese history (MA, PhD); medieval history (MA, PhD); modern Chinese history (MA, PhD); modern European history (MA, PhD); modern Japanese history (MA, PhD); premodern Islamic history (MA, PhD); premodern Japanese history (MA, PhD); Renaissance history (MA, PhD); Russian history (MA, PhD); Southeast Asian history (MA, PhD). *Faculty:* 62 full-time (19 women). *Students:* 67 full-time (33 women); includes 10 minority (4 African Americans, 3 Asian Americans or Pacific Islanders, 3 Hispanic Americans), 24 international. Average age 31. 195 applicants, 7% accepted, 10 enrolled. In 2009, 11 master's, 3 doctorates awarded. Terminal master's awarded for partial completion of doctoral program. *Degree requirements:* For master's, thesis; for doctorate, 2 foreign languages, comprehensive exam, thesis/dissertation, 1 year of teaching experience. *Entrance requirements:* For master's and doctorate, GRE General Test, writing sample, 3 letters of recommendation. Additional exam requirements/recommendations for international students: Required—TOEFL (minimum score 550 paper-based; 213 computer-based; 77 iBT). *Application deadline:* For fall admission, 1/15 for domestic students. Application fee: $70. Electronic applications accepted. *Expenses:* Tuition: Full-time $29,500. Required fees: $70. Full-time tuition and fees vary according to degree level, program and student level. *Financial support:* In 2009–10, 54 students received support, including 8 fellowships with full tuition reimbursements available; research assistantships with full tuition reimbursements available, teaching assistantships with full tuition reimbursements available, institutionally sponsored loans, scholarships/grants, health care benefits, tuition waivers (full and partial), and unspecified assistantships also available. Financial award applicants required to submit FAFSA. *Unit head:* Director of Graduate Studies, 607-255-6738, Fax: 607-255-0469. *Application contact:* Graduate Field Assistant, 607-255-6738, Fax: 607-255-0469, E-mail: history_grad_info@cornell.edu.

East Carolina University, Graduate School, Thomas Harriot College of Arts and Sciences, Department of History, Greenville, NC 27858-4353. Offers American history (MA); European history (MA); maritime history (MA). Part-time and evening/weekend programs available. *Degree requirements:* For master's, one foreign language, comprehensive exam, thesis. *Entrance requirements:* For master's, GRE General Test, GRE Subject Test. Additional exam requirements/recommendations for international students: Required—TOEFL.

Georgetown University, Graduate School of Arts and Sciences, BMW Center for German and European Studies, Washington, DC 20057. Offers MA, MA/JD, MA/PhD. *Degree requirements:* For master's, 2 foreign languages, comprehensive exam. *Entrance requirements:* For master's, GRE General Test. Additional exam requirements/recommendations for international students: Required—TOEFL. *Faculty research:* Trans-Atlantic relations, European Union, German and European Studies.

The George Washington University, Elliott School of International Affairs, Program in European and Eurasian Studies, Washington, DC 20052. Offers MA, JD/MA, MBA/MA. Part-time and evening/weekend programs available. *Students:* 16 full-time (5 women), 9 part-time (5 women), 3 international. Average age 26. 45 applicants, 80% accepted, 9 enrolled. In 2009, 2 master's awarded. *Degree requirements:* For master's, one foreign language, capstone project. *Entrance requirements:* For master's, GRE General Test, 2 years (or the equivalent) of a modern European language or Russian, 2 semesters of introductory economics (macro or micro). Additional exam requirements/recommendations for international students: Required—TOEFL. *Application deadline:* For fall admission, 2/1 for domestic students; for spring admission, 10/1 for domestic students. Application fee: $60. Electronic applications accepted. *Financial support:* In 2009–10, 3 students received support; fellowships with tuition reimbursements available, research assistantships with tuition reimbursements available, career-related internships or fieldwork, Federal Work-Study, institutionally sponsored loans, and tuition waivers available. Financial award application deadline: 1/15; financial award applicants required to submit FAFSA. *Faculty research:* NATO, European economics, European history, European Union. *Unit head:* Hope Harrison, Director, 202-994-5439, Fax: 202-994-5436, E-mail: hopeharr@

Western European Studies

The George Washington University (continued)

gwu.edu. *Application contact:* Jeff V. Miles, Director of Graduate Admissions, 202-994-7050, Fax: 202-994-9537, E-mail: esiagrad@gwu.edu.

Indiana University Bloomington, University Graduate School, College of Arts and Sciences, Department of West European Studies, Bloomington, IN 47405-7000. Offers MA. *Faculty:* 1 full-time (0 women). *Students:* 6 full-time (2 women), 2 part-time (both women); includes 1 minority (Hispanic American). Average age 28. 7 applicants, 100% accepted, 5 enrolled. In 2009, 1 master's awarded. *Degree requirements:* For master's, 2 foreign languages, thesis. *Entrance requirements:* For master's, GRE General Test. Additional exam requirements/recommendations for international students: Required—TOEFL. *Application deadline:* For fall admission, 1/15 priority date for domestic students, 12/15 for international students; for spring admission, 9/1 priority date for domestic students, 9/1 for international students. Applications are processed on a rolling basis. Application fee: $55 ($65 for international students). *Financial support:* Fellowships with full tuition reimbursements, research assistantships with full tuition reimbursements, teaching assistantships with partial tuition reimbursements available. *Faculty research:* European integration, economics of Europe, European union, European culture and identity, expansion of European union. *Unit head:* Dr. Patricia McManus, Director, 812-855-3280, E-mail: pmcmanus@indiana.edu. *Application contact:* Deborah Piston-Hatlen, Associate Director, 812-855-3280, Fax: 812-855-7695, E-mail: weur@indiana.edu.

Mississippi State University, College of Arts and Sciences, Department of History, Mississippi State, MS 39762. Offers history (PhD); U. S. and European history (MA). Part-time programs available. *Faculty:* 17 full-time (6 women). *Students:* 34 full-time (13 women), 13 part-time (4 women); includes 2 minority (1 African American, 1 Asian American or Pacific Islander). Average age 32. 30 applicants, 80% accepted, 12 enrolled. In 2009, 7 master's, 2 doctorates awarded. *Degree requirements:* For master's, one foreign language, comprehensive exam, thesis optional; for doctorate, 2 foreign languages, thesis/dissertation, comprehensive oral and written exam. *Entrance requirements:* For master's, GRE (except for those with MA in history from MSU), minimum GPA of 3.0 on last two years of undergraduate courses; for doctorate, GRE, writing sample, minimum graduate GPA of 3.0. Additional exam requirements/recommendations for international students: Required—TOEFL (minimum score 475 paper-based; 153 computer-based; 53 iBT); Recommended—IELTS (minimum score 4.5). *Application deadline:* For fall admission, 4/1 for domestic students, 5/1 for international students; for spring admission, 11/1 for domestic students, 9/1 for international students. Applications are processed on a rolling basis. Application fee: $40. Electronic applications accepted. *Expenses:* Tuition, state resident: full-time $2575.50; part-time $286.25 per credit hour. Tuition, nonresident: full-time $6510; part-time $723.50 per credit hour. Tuition and fees vary according to course load. *Financial support:* In 2009–10, 2 research assistantships (averaging $9,333 per year), 26 teaching assistantships with full tuition reimbursements (averaging $11,005 per year) were awarded; Federal Work-Study, institutionally sponsored loans, scholarships/grants, and unspecified assistantships also available. Financial award application deadline: 4/1; financial award applicants required to submit FAFSA. *Faculty research:* U. S. political, diplomatic, military, social, and cultural history; modern Europe; Latin America; Asian history; African history. *Unit head:* Dr. Alan I. Marcus, Head, 662-325-3604, Fax: 662-325-1139, E-mail: aim10@msstate.edu. *Application contact:* Dr. Richard Damms, Associate Professor/Graduate Coordinator, 662-325-8821, E-mail: correspondence@history.msstate.edu.

Monmouth University, Graduate School, Department of History, West Long Branch, NJ 07764-1898. Offers European specialization (MA); U.S. specialization (MA); world specialization (MA). Part-time and evening/weekend programs available. *Faculty:* 13 full-time (3 women), 1 part-time/adjunct (0 women). *Students:* 3 full-time (1 woman), 59 part-time (27 women); includes 5 minority (1 Asian American or Pacific Islander, 4 Hispanic Americans). Average age 38. 31 applicants, 100% accepted, 15 enrolled. In 2009, 16 master's awarded. *Degree requirements:* For master's, comprehensive exam, thesis or alternative. *Entrance requirements:* For master's, minimum GPA of 3.0 in major, 2.5 overall. Additional exam requirements/recommendations for international students: Required—TOEFL (minimum score 550 paper-based; 213 computer-based; 79 iBT), IELTS (minimum score 5), Michigan English Language Assessment Battery (minimum score 77), Cambridge A, B, C. *Application deadline:* For fall admission, 7/15 priority date for domestic students, 6/1 for international students; for spring admission, 11/15 priority date for domestic students, 11/1 for international students. Applications are processed on a rolling basis. Application fee: $50. Electronic applications accepted. *Expenses:* Tuition: Part-time $773 per credit. Required fees: $157 per semester. *Financial support:* In 2009–10, 47 students received support, including 39 fellowships (averaging $1,270 per year), 22 research assistantships (averaging $6,668 per year); career-related internships or fieldwork, scholarships/grants, and unspecified assistantships also available. Support available to part-time students. Financial award applicants required to submit FAFSA. *Faculty research:* U.S. business; labor; British, German, and French Revolutions; Soviet Union; Africa. *Unit head:* Dr. Aaron Ansell, Director, 732-571-4495, Fax: 732-263-5112, E-mail: aansell@monmouth.edu. *Application contact:* Kevin Roane, Director, Office of Graduate Admission, 732-571-3452, Fax: 732-263-5123, E-mail: gradadm@monmouth.edu.

New York University, Graduate School of Arts and Science, Center for European Studies, New York, NY 10012-1019. Offers MA. *Faculty:* 4 full-time (0 women). *Students:* 18 full-time (12 women), 2 part-time (1 woman), 4 international. Average age 26. 29 applicants, 86% accepted, 13 enrolled. In 2009, 10 master's awarded. *Entrance requirements:* For master's, GRE General Test. Additional exam requirements/recommendations for international students: Required—TOEFL. *Application deadline:* For fall admission, 1/4 priority date for domestic students. Application fee: $90. Electronic applications accepted. *Expenses:* Tuition: Full-time $30,528; part-time $1272 per credit. Required fees: $2177. *Financial support:* Fellowships with tuition reimbursements, teaching assistantships with tuition reimbursements, career-related internships or fieldwork, Federal Work-Study, institutionally sponsored loans, and scholarships/grants available. Financial award application deadline: 1/4; financial award applicants required to submit FAFSA. *Faculty research:* Xenophobia, migration, and identity politics in Europe; European Union and political economy; Central Eastern Europe. *Unit head:* Larry Wolff, Director, 212-998-3838, Fax: 212-995-4188, E-mail: european.studies@nyu.edu. *Application contact:* Jennifer Denbo, Department Graduate Administrator, 212-998-3838, Fax: 212-995-4188, E-mail: european.studies@nyu.edu.

San Diego State University, Graduate and Research Affairs, College of Arts and Letters, Department of European Studies, San Diego, CA 92182. Offers MA. *Degree requirements:* For master's, one foreign language. *Entrance requirements:* For master's, GRE General Test. Additional exam requirements/recommendations for international students: Required—TOEFL. Electronic applications accepted.

Syracuse University, Maxwell School of Citizenship and Public Affairs, Program in European Union and Contemporary Europe, Syracuse, NY 13244. Offers CAS. *Entrance requirements:* Additional exam requirements/recommendations for international students: Required—TOEFL (minimum score 100 iBT). *Application deadline:* For fall admission, 2/1 priority date for domestic and international students. Application fee: $75. Electronic applications accepted. *Expenses:* Tuition: Full-time $26,808; part-time $1117 per credit. Required fees: $1024. *Financial support:* Application deadline: 1/1. *Unit head:* Margaret Lane, Director of Executive Education, 315-443-8708, E-mail: melane@syr.edu. *Application contact:* Margaret Lane, Director of Executive Education, 315-443-8708, E-mail: melane@syr.edu.

The University of British Columbia, College for Interdisciplinary Studies, Institute for European Studies, Vancouver, BC V6T 1Z2, Canada. Offers MA. *Faculty research:* Canada and the EU as global players, China and the transatlantic relation, European environmental policy, nationalism, global currency competition.

University of Connecticut, Graduate School, College of Liberal Arts and Sciences, Field of International Studies, Program in European Studies, Storrs, CT 06269. Offers MA. *Faculty:* 31 full-time (19 women). *Students:* 1 full-time (0 women), 1 (woman) part-time, 1 international. Average age 25. 5 applicants, 20% accepted, 1 enrolled. In 2009, 1 master's awarded. *Degree requirements:* For master's, comprehensive exam. *Entrance requirements:* For master's, GRE General Test. Additional exam requirements/recommendations for international students: Required—TOEFL (minimum score 550 paper-based; 213 computer-based). *Application deadline:* For fall admission, 2/1 priority date for domestic and international students; for spring admission, 11/1 for domestic students, 10/1 for international students. Applications are processed on a rolling basis. Application fee: $40 ($45 for international students). Electronic applications accepted. *Expenses:* Tuition, state resident: full-time $4725; part-time $525 per credit. Tuition, nonresident: full-time $12,267; part-time $1363 per credit. Required fees: $346 per semester. Tuition and fees vary according to course load. *Financial support:* In 2009–10, 1 research assistantship with full tuition reimbursement was awarded; teaching assistantships with full tuition reimbursements, Federal Work-Study, scholarships/grants, health care benefits, and unspecified assistantships also available. Financial award application deadline: 2/1; financial award applicants required to submit FAFSA. *Unit head:* John Davis, Chairperson, 860-486-2752, Fax: 860-486-0641, E-mail: john.davis@uconn.edu. *Application contact:* Ludmilla Burns, Administrative Assistant, 860-486-5888, Fax: 860-486-0641, E-mail: ludmilla.burns@uconn.edu.

University of Connecticut, Graduate School, College of Liberal Arts and Sciences, Field of International Studies, Program in Italian History and Culture, Storrs, CT 06269. Offers MA. *Faculty:* 31 full-time (19 women). *Students:* 1 (woman) full-time. Average age 23. 2 applicants, 0% accepted, 0 enrolled. *Entrance requirements:* Additional exam requirements/recommendations for international students: Required—TOEFL (minimum score 550 paper-based; 213 computer-based). *Application deadline:* For fall admission, 2/1 priority date for domestic and international students; for spring admission, 11/1 for domestic students, 10/1 for international students. Applications are processed on a rolling basis. Electronic applications accepted. *Expenses:* Tuition, state resident: full-time $4725; part-time $525 per credit. Tuition, nonresident: full-time $12,267; part-time $1363 per credit. Required fees: $346 per semester. Tuition and fees vary according to course load. *Financial support:* In 2009–10, 1 research assistantship with full tuition reimbursement was awarded; teaching assistantships, Federal Work-Study, scholarships/grants, health care benefits, and unspecified assistantships also available. Financial award application deadline: 2/1. *Unit head:* John Davis, Chairperson, 860-486-2752, Fax: 860-486-0641, E-mail: john.davis@uconn.edu. *Application contact:* John Davis, Chairperson, 860-486-2752, Fax: 860-486-0641, E-mail: john.davis@uconn.edu.

University of Guelph, Graduate Program Services, College of Arts, School of Languages and Literatures, Program in European Studies, Guelph, ON N1G 2W1, Canada. Offers MA. *Degree requirements:* For master's, research paper. *Entrance requirements:* For master's, curriculum vitae, writing sample, 2 letters of recommendation.

University of Illinois at Urbana–Champaign, Graduate College, College of Liberal Arts and Sciences, European Union Center, Champaign, IL 61820. Offers MA.

University of Nevada, Reno, Graduate School, Interdisciplinary Program in Basque Studies, Reno, NV 89557. Offers PhD. *Degree requirements:* For doctorate, thesis/dissertation. *Entrance requirements:* For doctorate, GRE General Test, master's degree in related field, minimum GPA of 3.0. Additional exam requirements/recommendations for international students: Required—TOEFL (minimum score 500 paper-based; 173 computer-based; 61 iBT), IELTS (minimum score 6). Electronic applications accepted. *Faculty research:* Ethnic groups, Basque society, migration studies, symbolic anthropology, terrorism.

University of Pittsburgh, University Center for International Studies, Pittsburgh, PA 15260. Offers African studies (Certificate); Asian studies (Certificate); European Union studies (Certificate); global studies (Certificate); Latin American studies (Certificate); Russian and East European studies (Certificate); West European studies (Certificate). *Students:* 332 (129 women); includes 31 minority (7 African Americans, 10 Asian Americans or Pacific Islanders, 14 Hispanic Americans), 136 international. In 2009, 59 Certificates awarded. *Degree requirements:* For Certificate, one foreign language, study abroad. *Application deadline:* Applications are processed on a rolling basis. *Expenses:* Tuition, state resident: full-time $16,402; part-time $665 per credit. Tuition, nonresident: full-time $28,694; part-time $1175 per credit. Required fees: $690; $175 per term. Tuition and fees vary according to program. *Unit head:* Lawrence F. Feick, Director, 412-648-7374, Fax: 412-624-4672, E-mail: feick@pitt.edu. *Application contact:* Information Contact, 412-624-4141, E-mail: graduate@pitt.edu.

Washington State University, Graduate School, College of Liberal Arts, Department of History, Pullman, WA 99164. Offers early and modern European history (MA, PhD); environmental history (MA, PhD); Latin American history (MA, PhD); modern East Asia history (MA, PhD); public history (MA, PhD); US history (MA, PhD); women's history (MA, PhD); world history (MA, PhD). Part-time programs available. *Faculty:* 25. *Students:* 38 full-time (22 women), 10 part-time (4 women); includes 3 minority (1 American Indian/Alaska Native, 2 Hispanic Americans), 2 international. Average age 33. 57 applicants, 47% accepted, 10 enrolled. In 2009, 10 master's, 2 doctorates awarded. *Degree requirements:* For master's, comprehensive exam (for some programs), thesis, oral exam; for doctorate, one foreign language, comprehensive exam, thesis/dissertation, oral and written exam. *Entrance requirements:* For master's and doctorate, GRE General Test, Graduate School Application form; official transcripts from all universities attended; GRE scores; TOEFL or IELTS scores (international students only); three letters of recommendation; a statement of purpose; a writing sample, Preferred Fields of Study form; and the Language Background form. Additional exam requirements/recommendations for international students: Required—TOEFL (minimum score 550 paper-based), IELTS. *Application deadline:* For fall admission, 1/10 for domestic and international students; for spring admission, 7/1 for domestic and international students. Applications are processed on a rolling basis. Application fee: $50. Electronic applications accepted. *Financial support:* In 2009–10, 1 fellowship with partial tuition reimbursement (averaging $3,000 per year), research assistantships with full and partial tuition reimbursements (averaging $13,917 per year), 28 teaching assistantships with full and partial tuition reimbursements (averaging $13,056 per year) were awarded; career-related internships or fieldwork, Federal Work-Study, institutionally sponsored loans, scholarships/grants, and health care benefits also available. Financial award application deadline: 2/15; financial award applicants required to submit FAFSA. *Faculty research:* Public, world, environmental, women's and U. S. history. *Unit head:* Dr. Raymond Sun, Chair, 509-335-5139, Fax: 509-335-4171, E-mail: pietz@wsu.edu. *Application contact:* Graduate Studies Director, 509-335-4030, Fax: 509-335-4171, E-mail: kale@wsu.edu.

Women's Studies

The American University in Cairo, Graduate Studies and Research, School of Humanities and Social Sciences, Program in Gender and Women's Studies, Cairo, Egypt. Offers gender and development (MA, Diploma); gender and justice (MA, Diploma); gender and women's studies in the Middle East and North Africa (MA, Diploma).

Assemblies of God Theological Seminary, Graduate and Professional Programs, Springfield, MO 65802. Offers Christian ministries (MA); counseling (MA); divinity (M Div); intercultural ministry (MA); intercultural studies (D Miss, PhD); relief and development (D Miss); theological studies (MA); women in leadership (D Min). *Accreditation:* ATS. Part-time and evening/weekend programs available. Postbaccalaureate distance learning degree programs offered (minimal on-campus study). *Faculty:* 12 full-time (3 women), 23 part-time/adjunct (5 women). *Students:* 195 full-time (70 women), 221 part-time (53 women); includes 48 minority (10 African Americans, 6 American Indian/Alaska Native, 16 Asian Americans or Pacific Islanders, 16 Hispanic Americans), 9 international. Average age 36. 109 applicants, 76% accepted, 62 enrolled. In 2009, 46 first professional degrees, 65 master's, 14 doctorates awarded. *Degree requirements:* For master's, analytical reflection paper, comprehensive exam or field education research project; for doctorate, thesis/dissertation; for M Div, one foreign language, analytical reflection paper or field education research project. *Entrance requirements:* For M Div, minimum GPA of 2.5; for master's, minimum GPA of 2.5; for doctorate, minimum GPA of 3.0. Additional exam requirements/recommendations for international students: Required—TOEFL (minimum score 550 paper-based; 213 computer-based; 80 iBT). *Application deadline:* For fall admission, 7/1 priority date for domestic students, 6/1 priority date for international students; for spring admission, 12/1 priority date for domestic students, 11/1 priority date for international students. Applications are processed on a rolling basis. Application fee: $75. Electronic applications accepted. *Financial support:* Career-related internships or fieldwork, Federal Work-Study, and scholarships/grants available. Support available to part-time students. Financial award application deadline: 7/15; financial award applicants required to submit FAFSA. *Unit head:* Stephen Lim, Academic Dean, 417-268-1000, Fax: 417-268-1001, E-mail: slim@agts.edu. *Application contact:* Stephen Lim, Academic Dean, 417-268-1000, Fax: 417-268-1001, E-mail: slim@agts.edu.

Brandeis University, Graduate School of Arts and Sciences, Department of Anthropology, Waltham, MA 02454. Offers anthropology (MA, PhD); anthropology and women's and gender studies (MA). Part-time programs available. *Faculty:* 9 full-time (4 women), 1 part-time/adjunct (0 women). *Students:* 39 full-time (25 women), 2 part-time (1 woman); includes 5 minority (1 Asian American or Pacific Islander, 4 Hispanic Americans), 13 international. Average age 34. 68 applicants, 44% accepted, 12 enrolled. In 2009, 12 master's awarded. Terminal master's awarded for partial completion of doctoral program. *Degree requirements:* For master's, thesis; for doctorate, one foreign language, comprehensive exam, thesis/dissertation. *Entrance requirements:* For master's, GRE General Test (recommended), sample of written work, resume, letters of recommendation; for doctorate, GRE General Test, sample of written work, resume, letters of recommendation. Additional exam requirements/recommendations for international students: Required—TOEFL (minimum score 600 paper-based; 250 computer-based; 100 iBT); Recommended—IELTS (minimum score 7). *Application deadline:* For fall admission, 1/15 for domestic students. Applications are processed on a rolling basis. Application fee: $75. Electronic applications accepted. *Financial support:* In 2009–10, 23 students received support, including 12 fellowships with full tuition reimbursements available (averaging $20,000 per year), 11 teaching assistantships with partial tuition reimbursements available (averaging $3,200 per year); research assistantships with partial tuition reimbursements available, career-related internships or fieldwork, scholarships/grants, health care benefits, tuition waivers (full and partial), and unspecified assistantships also available. Support available to part-time students. Financial award application deadline: 4/15; financial award applicants required to submit FAFSA. *Faculty research:* Technology and culture, comparative methods, economic anthropology, gender studies, semiotic anthropology. *Unit head:* Dr. Elizabeth Ferry, Associate Professor/Director of Graduate Studies, 781-736-2210, Fax: 781-736-2232, E-mail: ferry@brandeis.edu. *Application contact:* Laurel Carpenter, Academic Administrator, 781-736-2210, Fax: 781-736-2232, E-mail: lcarpenter@brandeis.edu.

Brandeis University, Graduate School of Arts and Sciences, Department of English and American Literature, Waltham, MA 02454-9110. Offers English (MA, PhD); English and women's and gender studies (MA). Part-time programs available. *Faculty:* 15 full-time (8 women), 7 part-time/adjunct (4 women). *Students:* 50 full-time (24 women), 2 part-time (1 woman); includes 3 minority (1 Asian American or Pacific Islander, 2 Hispanic Americans), 4 international. 154 applicants, 20% accepted, 10 enrolled. In 2009, 10 master's, 3 doctorates awarded. *Degree requirements:* For master's, one foreign language, thesis, symposium; for doctorate, 2 foreign languages, thesis/dissertation, field exam, symposium presentation, prospectus defense. *Entrance requirements:* For master's, GRE General Test, resume, sample of work, letters of recommendation; for doctorate, GRE General Test, GRE Subject Test, resume, sample of work, letters of recommendation. Additional exam requirements/recommendations for international students: Required—TOEFL (minimum score 600 paper-based; 250 computer-based; 100 iBT); Recommended—IELTS (minimum score 7). *Application deadline:* For fall admission, 1/5 for domestic students. Application fee: $75. Electronic applications accepted. *Financial support:* In 2009–10, 27 fellowships with full tuition reimbursements (averaging $20,000 per year), 4 teaching assistantships with partial tuition reimbursements (averaging $3,200 per year) were awarded; research assistantships with full tuition reimbursements, scholarships/grants, health care benefits, and tuition waivers (full and partial) also available. Financial award application deadline: 4/15; financial award applicants required to submit FAFSA. *Faculty research:* Feminist and gender theory, American literature, Anglophone literature, early modern literature, modernism. *Unit head:* Dr. John Burt, Director of Graduate Studies, 781-736-2130, Fax: 781-736-2179, E-mail: chaucer@brandeis.edu. *Application contact:* Shannon Hunt, Department Administrator, 781-736-2130, Fax: 781-736-2179, E-mail: shuntl@brandeis.edu.

Brandeis University, Graduate School of Arts and Sciences, Department of Music, Waltham, MA 02454-9110. Offers composition and theory (MA, MFA, PhD); music and women's and gender studies (MA); musicology (MA, MFA, PhD). Part-time programs available. *Faculty:* 7 full-time (1 woman), 8 part-time/adjunct (3 women). *Students:* 46 full-time (18 women), 1 (woman) part-time; includes 2 minority (1 Asian American or Pacific Islander, 1 Hispanic American), 9 international. Average age 28. 73 applicants, 33% accepted, 15 enrolled. In 2009, 6 master's, 4 doctorates awarded. Terminal master's awarded for partial completion of doctoral program. *Degree requirements:* For master's, one foreign language, thesis or alternative; for doctorate, 2 foreign languages, comprehensive exam, thesis/dissertation. *Entrance requirements:* For master's, GRE General Test (musicology), resume, sample of work (music composition), letters of recommendation; for doctorate, GRE General Test (musicology), resume, writing sample (musicology), letters of recommendation, sample of work—recording (composition). Additional exam requirements/recommendations for international students: Required—TOEFL (minimum score 600 paper-based; 250 computer-based; 100 iBT); Recommended—IELTS (minimum score 7). *Application deadline:* For fall admission, 1/31 for domestic and international students. Application fee: $75. Electronic applications accepted. *Financial support:* In 2009–10, 23 students received support, including 24 fellowships with full tuition reimbursements available (averaging $20,000 per year), 4 teaching assistantships with partial tuition reimbursements available (averaging $3,200 per year); research assistantships, scholarships/grants, health care benefits, and tuition waivers (full and partial) also available. Support available to part-time students. Financial award application deadline: 4/15; financial award applicants required to submit FAFSA. *Faculty research:* History of theory; music of Monteverdi, Bach, Mozart, Lizst, and Wagner; compositional process; computer music. *Unit head:* Prof. Mary Ruth Ray, Chair, 781-736-3310, E-mail: ray@brandeis.edu. *Application contact:* Mark Kagan, Senior Academic Administrator, 781-736-3311, E-mail: kagan@brandeis.edu.

Brandeis University, Graduate School of Arts and Sciences, Department of Near Eastern and Judaic Studies, Waltham, MA 02454-9110. Offers Near Eastern and Judaic studies (MA, PhD); Near Eastern and Judaic studies and sociology (PhD); Near Eastern and Judaic studies and women's and gender studies (MA); teaching of Hebrew (MAT). Part-time programs available. *Faculty:* 26 full-time (11 women), 4 part-time/adjunct (1 woman). *Students:* 62 full-time (30 women), 1 part-time (0 women); includes 2 minority (1 African American, 1 Hispanic American), 7 international. Average age 33. 88 applicants, 67% accepted, 28 enrolled. In 2009, 10 master's, 6 doctorates awarded. Terminal master's awarded for partial completion of doctoral program. *Degree requirements:* For master's, one foreign language, comprehensive exam, thesis or alternative; for doctorate, 3 foreign languages, comprehensive exam, thesis/dissertation. *Entrance requirements:* For master's, GRE General Test (recommended), letters of recommendation; for doctorate, GRE General Test (recommended), letters of recommendation, transcripts, statement of purpose. Additional exam requirements/recommendations for international students: Required—TOEFL (minimum score 600 paper-based; 250 computer-based; 100 iBT); Recommended—IELTS (minimum score 7). *Application deadline:* For fall admission, 1/15 priority date for domestic and international students. Applications are processed on a rolling basis. Application fee: $75. Electronic applications accepted. *Financial support:* In 2009–10, 17 students received support, including 14 fellowships with full tuition reimbursements available (averaging $20,000 per year), 3 teaching assistantships with partial tuition reimbursements available (averaging $3,200 per year); research assistantships with full and partial tuition reimbursements available, scholarships/grants, health care benefits, and tuition waivers (full and partial) also available. Support available to part-time students. Financial award application deadline: 4/15; financial award applicants required to submit FAFSA. *Faculty research:* Ancient Near East and Bible, philosophy, history, modern Middle East, Islamic studies. *Unit head:* Dr. David Wright, Chair, 781-736-2954, Fax: 781-736-2070, E-mail: wright@brandeis.edu. *Application contact:* Joanne Arnish, Department Administrator, 781-736-2950, Fax: 781-736-2070, E-mail: arnish@brandeis.edu.

Brandeis University, Graduate School of Arts and Sciences, Joint Master's Programs in Women's and Gender Studies, Waltham, MA 02454-9110. Offers anthropology and women's and gender studies (MA); English and women's and gender studies (MA); music and women's and gender studies (MA); Near Eastern and Judaic studies and women's and gender studies (MA); public policy and women's and gender studies (MA); sociology and women's and gender studies (MA); sustainable international development and women's/gender studies (MA). Part-time programs available. *Faculty:* 18 full-time (17 women), 2 part-time/adjunct (both women). *Students:* 17 full-time (15 women), 4 international. Average age 25. 35 applicants, 49% accepted, 6 enrolled. In 2009, 8 master's awarded. *Degree requirements:* For master's, thesis. *Entrance requirements:* For master's, GRE, sample of written work, resume. Additional exam requirements/recommendations for international students: Required—TOEFL (minimum score 600 paper-based; 250 computer-based; 100 iBT); Recommended—IELTS (minimum score 7). *Application deadline:* For fall admission, 1/15 for domestic students. Application fee: $75. Electronic applications accepted. *Financial support:* In 2009–10, 6 students received support, including 2 fellowships with partial tuition reimbursements available (averaging $4,450 per year), 1 teaching assistantship with partial tuition reimbursement available (averaging $3,200 per year); research assistantships, scholarships/grants and tuition waivers (full and partial) also available. Support available to part-time students. Financial award application deadline: 4/15; financial award applicants required to submit FAFSA. *Unit head:* Prof. James Mandrell, Chair, 781-736-3042, Fax: 781-736-3044, E-mail: mandrell@brandeis.edu. *Application contact:* Kathryn Dalton, Program Administrator, 781-736-3045, Fax: 781-736-3044, E-mail: daltonka@brandeis.edu.

Brandeis University, Graduate School of Arts and Sciences, MA Program in Women's and Gender Studies, Waltham, MA 02454-9110. Offers MA. *Degree requirements:* For master's, thesis. *Entrance requirements:* For master's, GRE, three letters of recommendation, curriculum vitae or resume, statement of purpose, critical writing sample. Additional exam requirements/recommendations for international students: Required—TOEFL (minimum score 600 paper-based; 250 computer-based; 100 iBT); Recommended—IELTS (minimum score 7). *Application deadline:* For fall admission, 1/15 for domestic students. Application fee: $75. Electronic applications accepted. *Financial support:* Scholarships/grants available. Financial award application deadline: 4/15; financial award applicants required to submit FAFSA. *Faculty research:* Gender and legal studies, sexuality studies, social and public policy, comparative literature and culture, anthropology, English, music, Near Eastern and Judaic Studies, public policy, sociology, sustainable international development. *Unit head:* Prof. James Mandrell, Chair, 781-736-3045, Fax: 781-736-3044, E-mail: wgstudies@brandeis.edu. *Application contact:* Katie Dalton, Department Administrator, 781-736-3045, Fax: 781-736-3044, E-mail: daltonka@brandeis.edu.

California Institute of Integral Studies, School of Consciousness and Transformation, San Francisco, CA 94103. Offers creative inquiry (MFA); cultural anthropology and social transformation (MA); East-West psychology (MA, PhD); integrative health studies (MA); philosophy and religion (MA, PhD), including Asian and comparative studies, philosophy, cosmology, and consciousness, women's spirituality; social and cultural anthropology (PhD); transformative leadership (MA); transformative studies (PhD); writing and consciousness (MFA). Part-time and evening/weekend programs available. Postbaccalaureate distance learning degree programs offered (minimal on-campus study). *Students:* 334 full-time (218 women), 126 part-time (77 women); includes 116 minority (40 African Americans, 4 American Indian/Alaska Native, 42 Asian Americans or Pacific Islanders, 30 Hispanic Americans). Average age 38. 265 applicants, 90% accepted, 149 enrolled. In 2009, 64 master's, 22 doctorates awarded. Terminal master's awarded for partial completion of doctoral program. *Degree requirements:* For master's, comprehensive exam (for some programs), thesis optional; for doctorate, comprehensive exam, thesis/dissertation, 1 foreign language (Asian comparative studies). *Entrance requirements:* For master's, minimum GPA of 3.0, letters of recommendation, writing sample; for doctorate, master's degree, minimum GPA of 3.0, letters of recommendation, writing sample. Additional exam requirements/recommendations for international students: Required—TOEFL. *Application deadline:* For fall admission, 2/1 priority date for domestic and international students; for spring admission, 10/15 priority date for domestic and international students. Applications are processed on a rolling basis. Application fee: $65. Electronic applications accepted. *Expenses:* Tuition: Full-time $15,300; part-time $850 per credit hour. Required fees: $110 per semester. Tuition and fees vary according to degree level. *Financial support:* In 2009–10, 330 students received support; research assistantships, teaching assistantships, career-related internships or fieldwork, Federal Work-Study, scholarships/grants, and tuition waivers (partial) available. Support available to part-time students. Financial award application deadline: 4/15; financial award applicants required to submit FAFSA. *Faculty research:* Altered states of consciousness, dreams, cosmology, postcolonial studies, integrative health studies. *Application contact:* Allyson Werner, Associate Director of Admissions, 415-575-6155, Fax: 415-575-1268.

Claremont Graduate University, Graduate Programs, School of Arts and Humanities, Program in Applied Women's Studies, Claremont, CA 91711-6160. Offers MA. *Faculty:* 1 (woman) full-time. *Students:* 13 full-time (12 women); includes 4 minority (2 African Americans, 1 Asian American or Pacific Islander, 1 Hispanic American). Average age 27. In 2009, 11 master's awarded. *Entrance requirements:* For master's, GRE General Test. Additional exam requirements/recommendations for international students: Required—TOEFL (minimum score 550 paper-based; 213 computer-based; 80 iBT). *Application deadline:* For fall admission, 2/1 priority date for domestic students. Applications are processed on a rolling basis. Application fee: $60. Electronic applications accepted. *Expenses:* Tuition: Full-time $35,046; part-time $1524 per credit. Required fees: $161 per semester. *Financial support:* Fellowships, research assistantships, teaching assistantships, Federal Work-Study, institutionally sponsored loans, and scholarships/grants available. Support available to part-time students. Financial award application deadline: 2/15; financial award applicants required to submit FAFSA. *Unit head:* Linda Perkins, Director, 909-621-8696, E-mail: linda.perkins@cgu.edu. *Application contact:*

Women's Studies

Claremont Graduate University (continued)
Susan Hampson, Admissions Coordinator, 909-607-1278, Fax: 909-607-1221, E-mail: susan.hampson@cgu.edu.

Claremont Graduate University, Graduate Programs, School of Religion, Claremont, CA 91711-6160. Offers Hebrew Bible (MA, PhD); history of Christianity and religions of North America (MA, PhD); New Testament (MA, PhD); philosophy of religion and theology (MA, PhD); theology, ethics and culture (MA, PhD); women's studies in religion (MA, PhD); MA/PhD; MBA/PhD. Part-time programs available. *Faculty:* 7 full-time (2 women), 2 part-time/adjunct (0 women). *Students:* 223 full-time (90 women), 7 part-time (4 women); includes 37 minority (14 African Americans, 11 Asian Americans or Pacific Islanders, 12 Hispanic Americans), 23 international. Average age 37. In 2009, 10 master's, 14 doctorates awarded. Terminal master's awarded for partial completion of doctoral program. *Entrance requirements:* For master's and doctorate, GRE General Test. Additional exam requirements/recommendations for international students: Required—TOEFL (minimum score 550 paper-based; 213 computer-based; 80 iBT). *Application deadline:* For fall admission, 2/1 priority date for domestic students. Applications are processed on a rolling basis. Application fee: $60. Electronic applications accepted. *Expenses:* Tuition: Full-time $35,046; part-time $1524 per credit. Required fees: $161 per semester. *Financial support:* Fellowships, research assistantships, teaching assistantships, Federal Work-Study, institutionally sponsored loans, and scholarships/grants available. Support available to part-time students. Financial award application deadline: 2/15; financial award applicants required to submit FAFSA. *Unit head:* Anselm Min, Dean, 909-607-3214, Fax: 909-621-9587, E-mail: anselm.min@cgu.edu. *Application contact:* Brent Smith, Recruiter, 909-607-2653, Fax: 909-607-9587, E-mail: brent.smith@cgu.edu.

Clark Atlanta University, School of Arts and Sciences, Department of Africana Women's Studies, Atlanta, GA 30314. Offers MA, DAH. Part-time programs available. *Faculty:* 1 (woman) full-time, 1 (woman) part-time/adjunct. *Students:* 5 full-time (all women), 6 part-time (5 women); includes 10 minority (all African Americans), 1 international. Average age 39. 10 applicants, 90% accepted, 1 enrolled. In 2009, 1 doctorate awarded. *Degree requirements:* For master's, one foreign language, comprehensive exam, thesis optional; for doctorate, one foreign language, comprehensive exam, thesis/dissertation. *Entrance requirements:* For master's, GRE General Test, minimum GPA of 2.5; for doctorate, GRE General Test, minimum graduate GPA of 3.0. Additional exam requirements/recommendations for international students: Required—TOEFL (minimum score 500 paper-based; 173 computer-based). *Application deadline:* For fall admission, 4/1 for domestic and international students; for spring admission, 11/1 for domestic and international students. Applications are processed on a rolling basis. Application fee: $40 ($55 for international students). Electronic applications accepted. *Expenses:* Tuition: Full-time $12,240; part-time $680 per credit hour. Required fees: $710; $355 per semester. *Financial support:* In 2009–10, 4 fellowships were awarded; scholarships/grants also available. Financial award application deadline: 4/30; financial award applicants required to submit FAFSA. *Faculty research:* Concerns of women of African descent globally. *Unit head:* Dr. Josephine Bradley, Chairperson, 404-880-6810, E-mail: jbradley@cau.edu. *Application contact:* Michelle Clark-Davis, Graduate Program Admissions, 404-880-6605, E-mail: cauadmissions@cau.edu.

Cornell University, Graduate School, Graduate Fields of Arts and Sciences, Field of English Language and Literature, Ithaca, NY 14853-0001. Offers African-American literature (PhD); American literature after 1865 (PhD); American literature to 1865 (PhD); American studies (PhD); colonial and postcolonial literature (PhD); creative writing (MFA); cultural studies (PhD); dramatic literature (PhD); English poetry (PhD); English Renaissance to 1660 (PhD); lesbian, bisexual, and gay literature studies (PhD); literary criticism and theory (PhD); nineteenth century (PhD); Old and Middle English (PhD); prose fiction (PhD); Restoration and eighteenth century (PhD); twentieth century (PhD); women's literature (PhD); MFA/PhD. *Faculty:* 74 full-time (35 women). *Students:* 100 full-time (55 women); includes 26 minority (9 African Americans, 3 American Indian/Alaska Native, 7 Asian Americans or Pacific Islanders, 7 Hispanic Americans), 11 international. Average age 28. 890 applicants, 4% accepted, 21 enrolled. In 2009, 21 master's, 12 doctorates awarded. Terminal master's awarded for partial completion of doctoral program. *Degree requirements:* For master's, one foreign language, thesis; for doctorate, one foreign language, comprehensive exam, thesis/dissertation, teaching experience. *Entrance requirements:* For master's, GRE General Test, 3 letters of recommendation, creative writing sample; for doctorate, GRE General Test, GRE Subject Test (English), 3 letters of recommendation, writing sample. Additional exam requirements/recommendations for international students: Required—TOEFL (minimum score 600 paper-based; 250 computer-based; 77 iBT). *Application deadline:* For fall admission, 1/10 for domestic students. Application fee: $70. Electronic applications accepted. *Expenses:* Tuition: Full-time $29,500. Required fees: $70. Full-time tuition and fees vary according to degree level, program and student level. *Financial support:* In 2009–10, 96 students received support, including 13 fellowships with full tuition reimbursements available, 8 teaching assistantships with full tuition reimbursements available; research assistantships with full tuition reimbursements available, institutionally sponsored loans, scholarships/grants, health care benefits, tuition waivers (full and partial), and unspecified assistantships also available. Financial award applicants required to submit FAFSA. *Faculty research:* English and American literature, women's writing, ethnic and post-colonial literature, critical theory, medievalism. *Unit head:* Director of Graduate Studies, 607-255-7989, Fax: 607-255-6661. *Application contact:* Graduate Field Assistant, 607-255-7989, Fax: 607-255-6661, E-mail: english_grad@cornell.edu.

Eastern Michigan University, Graduate School, College of Arts and Sciences, Department of Women's and Gender Studies, Ypsilanti, MI 48197. Offers MA, Graduate Certificate. Part-time and evening/weekend programs available. *Students:* 3 full-time (all women), 6 part-time (all women); includes 4 minority (3 African Americans, 1 Hispanic American), 1 international. Average age 38. 17 applicants, 76% accepted, 4 enrolled. In 2009, 6 master's awarded. *Degree requirements:* For master's, thesis, research project, or practicum. *Entrance requirements:* Additional exam requirements/recommendations for international students: Required—TOEFL. *Application deadline:* For fall admission, 6/15 for domestic and international students; for winter admission, 9/15 for domestic and international students; for spring admission, 3/1 for domestic and international students. Applications are processed on a rolling basis. Application fee: $35. Tuition and fees vary according to course level. *Financial support:* Fellowships, research assistantships with full tuition reimbursements, teaching assistantships with full tuition reimbursements, career-related internships or fieldwork, Federal Work-Study, institutionally sponsored loans, scholarships/grants, tuition waivers (partial), and unspecified assistantships available. Support available to part-time students. Financial award applicants required to submit FAFSA. *Unit head:* Dr. Linda Pritchard, Department Head, 734-487-1177, Fax: 734-487-5029, E-mail: linda.pritchard@emich.edu. *Application contact:* Dr. Deanna Mihaly, Program Advisor, 734-487-1177, Fax: 734-487-5029, E-mail: dmihaly@emich.edu.

Emory University, Graduate School of Arts and Sciences, Department of Comparative Literature, Atlanta, GA 30322-1100. Offers comparative literature (PhD); English (Certificate); French (Certificate); Middle Eastern studies (PhD); philosophy (Certificate); psychoanalytic studies (PhD); religion (PhD); Spanish (Certificate); women studies (Certificate). *Degree requirements:* For doctorate, 2 foreign languages, comprehensive exam, thesis/dissertation. *Entrance requirements:* For doctorate, GRE General Test, minimum GPA of 3.0. Additional exam requirements/recommendations for international students: Required—TOEFL. Electronic applications accepted. *Faculty research:* Literary theory, psychoanalysis trauma and testimony, literature and religion, literature and technology, literature and philosophy, politics and global culture, literature and aesthetics.

Emory University, Graduate School of Arts and Sciences, Department of Spanish and Portuguese, Atlanta, GA 30322-1100. Offers comparative literature (Certificate); film studies (Certificate); Spanish (PhD); women's studies (Certificate). *Degree requirements:* For doctorate, 2 foreign languages, comprehensive exam, thesis/dissertation. *Entrance requirements:* For doctorate, GRE General Test. Additional exam requirements/recommendations for international students: Required—TOEFL. Electronic applications accepted. *Faculty research:* Spanish literature, Spanish-American literature, literary theory, criticism, cultural studies.

Emory University, Graduate School of Arts and Sciences, Department of Women's Studies, Atlanta, GA 30322-1100. Offers PhD. *Degree requirements:* For doctorate, comprehensive exam, thesis/dissertation. *Entrance requirements:* For doctorate, GRE General Test, writing sample. Additional exam requirements/recommendations for international students: Required—TOEFL. Electronic applications accepted. *Faculty research:* Feminist theory, women's literature, African-American literature, gender in cross-cultural perspective, public policy and globalization.

Florida Atlantic University, Dorothy F. Schmidt College of Arts and Letters, Women's Studies Center, Boca Raton, FL 33431-0991. Offers MA, Certificate. *Faculty:* 2 full-time (both women), 1 (woman) part-time/adjunct. *Students:* 3 full-time (all women), 1 (woman) part-time. Average age 36. 6 applicants, 50% accepted, 0 enrolled. In 2009, 7 master's awarded. *Degree requirements:* For master's, comprehensive exam, thesis or alternative. *Entrance requirements:* For master's, GRE General Test, minimum GPA of 3.0. *Application deadline:* For fall admission, 7/1 for domestic students, 2/15 for international students; for spring admission, 11/1 for domestic students, 7/15 for international students. Applications are processed on a rolling basis. Application fee: $30. *Expenses:* Tuition, state resident: full-time $7055; part-time $293.94 per credit hour. Tuition, nonresident: full-time $22,096; part-time $920.66 per credit hour. *Financial support:* Fellowships with full and partial tuition reimbursements, teaching assistantships with full and partial tuition reimbursements, career-related internships or fieldwork, Federal Work-Study, institutionally sponsored loans, scholarships/grants, and unspecified assistantships available. Support available to part-time students. *Faculty research:* Women and science/technology, feminist theory, violence against women, women and international development, feminist medical anthropology. *Unit head:* Dr. Josephine Beoku-Betts, Director, 561-297-3865, Fax: 561-297-2127. *Application contact:* Dr. Jane Caputi, Professor, 561-297-2056, Fax: 561-297-2127, E-mail: jcaputi@fau.edu.

The George Washington University, Columbian College of Arts and Sciences, Department of Women's Studies, Washington, DC 20052. Offers MA, Certificate. Part-time and evening/weekend programs available. *Faculty:* 1 (woman) full-time, 4 part-time/adjunct (all women). *Students:* 19 full-time (all women), 14 part-time (13 women); includes 4 minority (2 African Americans, 2 Hispanic Americans), 2 international. Average age 25. 41 applicants, 95% accepted, 17 enrolled. In 2009, 15 master's awarded. *Degree requirements:* For master's, comprehensive exam, thesis or alternative. *Entrance requirements:* For master's, GRE General Test, minimum GPA of 3.0. Additional exam requirements/recommendations for international students: Required—TOEFL (minimum score 550 paper-based; 213 computer-based; 80 iBT). *Application deadline:* For fall admission, 4/1 priority date for domestic students, 1/15 priority date for international students; for spring admission, 10/1 priority date for domestic students, 9/1 priority date for international students. Applications are processed on a rolling basis. Application fee: $60. Electronic applications accepted. *Financial support:* In 2009–10, 2 students received support; fellowships with tuition reimbursements available, teaching assistantships with tuition reimbursements available, Federal Work-Study, institutionally sponsored loans, and tuition waivers available. Financial award application deadline: 1/15. *Unit head:* Dr. Daniel Moshenberg, Director, 202-994-9086, Fax: 202-994-7249. *Application contact:* Information Contact, 202-994-6942, Fax: 202-994-2249, E-mail: wstu@gwu.edu.

The George Washington University, Columbian College of Arts and Sciences, Trachtenberg School of Public Policy and Public Administration, Washington, DC 20052. Offers public administration (MPA), including budget and public finance, federal policy, politics, and management, international development management, managing public organizations, managing state and local governments, nonprofit management, policy analysis and evaluation, public administration, public-private policy and management; public policy (MA, MPP), including environmental and resource policy (MA), philosophy and social policy (MA), women's studies (MA); public policy and administration (PhD); JD/MPP; MPA/JD; PhD/MPP. Part-time and evening/weekend programs available. *Faculty:* 35 full-time (12 women), 19 part-time/adjunct (10 women). *Students:* 187 full-time (114 women), 232 part-time (151 women); includes 62 minority (15 African Americans, 3 American Indian/Alaska Native, 29 Asian Americans or Pacific Islanders, 15 Hispanic Americans), 23 international. Average age 26. 913 applicants, 56% accepted, 186 enrolled. In 2009, 106 master's, 9 doctorates awarded. *Degree requirements:* For doctorate, thesis/dissertation, general exam. *Entrance requirements:* For master's, GRE General Test, minimum GPA of 3.0; for doctorate, GRE General Test, interview, minimum GPA of 3.0. Additional exam requirements/recommendations for international students: Required—TOEFL (minimum score 600 paper-based; 250 computer-based; 100 iBT). *Application deadline:* For fall admission, 1/15 priority date for domestic and international students; for spring admission, 10/1 priority date for domestic students, 9/1 priority date for international students. Applications are processed on a rolling basis. Application fee: $60. Electronic applications accepted. *Financial support:* In 2009–10, 87 students received support; fellowships, research assistantships, teaching assistantships, institutionally sponsored loans available. Financial award application deadline: 1/15. *Unit head:* Dr. Kathyrn E. Newcomer, Director, 202-994-3959, Fax: 202-994-3959, E-mail: newcomer@gwu.edu. *Application contact:* Information Contact, 202-994-6295, Fax: 202-994-6295, E-mail: tspppa@gwu.edu.

The George Washington University, Columbian College of Arts and Sciences, Trachtenberg School of Public Policy and Public Administration, Interdisciplinary Programs in Public Policy, Program in Women's Studies, Washington, DC 20052. Offers MA. Part-time and evening/weekend programs available. *Students:* 2 full-time (both women), 9 part-time (8 women). Average age 26. 12 applicants, 67% accepted, 5 enrolled. In 2009, 9 master's awarded. *Degree requirements:* For master's, comprehensive exam. *Entrance requirements:* For master's, GRE General Test, minimum GPA of 3.0. Additional exam requirements/recommendations for international students: Required—TOEFL (minimum score 600 paper-based; 250 computer-based; 100 iBT). *Application deadline:* For fall admission, 4/1 priority date for domestic and international students; for spring admission, 10/1 priority date for domestic students, 9/1 priority date for international students. Applications are processed on a rolling basis. Application fee: $60. Electronic applications accepted. *Financial support:* In 2009–10, 4 students received support; fellowships with tuition reimbursements available, teaching assistantships with tuition reimbursements available, tuition waivers available. Financial award application deadline: 1/15. *Unit head:* Prof. Daniel Moshenberg, Director, 202-994-9086, E-mail: dym@gwu.edu. *Application contact:* Information Contact, 202-994-6942, Fax: 202-994-7249, E-mail: wstu@gwu.edu.

Georgia State University, College of Arts and Sciences, Women's Studies Institute, Atlanta, GA 30302-3083. Offers MA, Graduate Certificate. Part-time programs available. *Degree requirements:* For master's, comprehensive exam, thesis. *Entrance requirements:* For master's, GRE General Test. Additional exam requirements/recommendations for international students: Required—TOEFL. *Faculty research:* Globalization and gender, womanism, sexuality studies, activism, feminist theories.

Graduate School and University Center of the City University of New York, Graduate Studies, Interdisciplinary Studies, New York, NY 10016-4039. Offers language in social context (PhD); medieval studies (PhD); public policy (MA, PhD); urban studies (MA, PhD); women's studies (MA, PhD). Terminal master's awarded for partial completion of doctoral program. *Degree requirements:* For master's, thesis; for doctorate, comprehensive exam, thesis/dissertation. *Entrance requirements:* For master's and doctorate, GRE General Test.

Institute of Transpersonal Psychology, Low-Residency Programs, Palo Alto, CA 94303. Offers counseling psychology (online) (MA); spiritual guidance (MA); women's spirituality (MA). Postbaccalaureate distance learning degree programs offered (minimal on-campus study).

Inter American University of Puerto Rico, Metropolitan Campus, Graduate Programs, Program in Women's Studies, San Juan, PR 00919-1293. Offers MA.

Lakehead University, Graduate Studies, Department of History, Thunder Bay, ON P7B 5E1, Canada. Offers gerontology (MA); history (MA); women's studies (MA). Part-time programs available. *Degree requirements:* For master's, one foreign language, thesis. *Entrance requirements:* For master's, minimum B average. Additional exam requirements/recommendations for international students: Required—TOEFL. *Faculty research:* Canadian history, British history, Russian/German history, women's studies.

Lakehead University, Graduate Studies, Faculty of Education, Thunder Bay, ON P7B 5E1, Canada. Offers educational studies (PhD); gerontology (M Ed); women's studies (M Ed). Part-time and evening/weekend programs available. *Degree requirements:* For master's, project or thesis. *Entrance requirements:* For master's, minimum B average. Additional exam requirements/recommendations for international students: Required—TOEFL. *Faculty research:* Art education, AIDS education, language arts education, gerontology, women's studies.

Lakehead University, Graduate Studies, Faculty of Social Sciences and Humanities, Department of English, Thunder Bay, ON P7B 5E1, Canada. Offers English (MA); women's studies (MA). Part-time and evening/weekend programs available. *Degree requirements:* For master's, one foreign language, thesis optional. *Entrance requirements:* For master's, minimum B average. Additional exam requirements/recommendations for international students: Required—TOEFL. *Faculty research:* Rhetoric and literary studies, children's literature, nineteenth- and twentieth-century American literature, modern literature, women's studies.

Lakehead University, Graduate Studies, Faculty of Social Sciences and Humanities, Department of Sociology, Thunder Bay, ON P7B 5E1, Canada. Offers gerontology (MA); health services and policy research (MA); sociology (MA); women's studies (MA). Part-time and evening/weekend programs available. *Degree requirements:* For master's, research project or thesis. *Entrance requirements:* For master's, minimum B average. Additional exam requirements/recommendations for international students: Required—TOEFL. *Faculty research:* Sociology of medicine, cultural and social change, health human resources, gerontology, women's studies.

Lakehead University, Graduate Studies, School of Social Work, Thunder Bay, ON P7B 5E1, Canada. Offers gerontology (MSW); social work (MSW); women's studies (MSW). Part-time programs available. *Degree requirements:* For master's, thesis or project. *Entrance requirements:* For master's, minimum B average. Additional exam requirements/recommendations for international students: Required—TOEFL. *Faculty research:* Clinical psychology, social work and practice theory, long-term care, health care for frail elderly, women's studies.

Lakehead University, Graduate Studies, Women's Studies Collaborative Program, Thunder Bay, ON P7B 5E1, Canada. Offers M Ed, MA, MSW. Part-time programs available. *Degree requirements:* For master's, thesis (for some programs). *Entrance requirements:* Additional exam requirements/recommendations for international students: Required—TOEFL. *Faculty research:* Feminist thought, feminist pedagogy, women of literature, Canadian women's history, well-being of women.

Lesley University, Graduate School of Arts and Social Sciences, Self-Designed Master's Program in Interdisciplinary Studies, Cambridge, MA 02138-2790. Offers individualized studies (MA); integrative holistic health (MA); women's studies (MA). Part-time and evening/weekend programs available. Postbaccalaureate distance learning degree programs offered (no on-campus study). *Entrance requirements:* For master's, 3 letters of recommendation. Additional exam requirements/recommendations for international students: Required—TOEFL (minimum score 550 paper-based; 213 computer-based; 80 iBT).

Memorial University of Newfoundland, School of Graduate Studies, Interdisciplinary Program in Women's Studies, St. John's, NL A1C 5S7, Canada. Offers MWS.

Minnesota State University Mankato, College of Graduate Studies, College of Social and Behavioral Sciences, Department of Gender and Women's Studies, Mankato, MN 56001. Offers MS, Certificate. Part-time programs available. *Students:* 8 full-time (7 women), 6 part-time (5 women). *Degree requirements:* For master's, comprehensive exam, thesis or alternative. *Entrance requirements:* For master's, minimum GPA of 3.0 during previous 2 years of course work. Additional exam requirements/recommendations for international students: Required—TOEFL. *Application deadline:* For fall admission, 7/1 priority date for domestic students; for spring admission, 11/1 for domestic students. Applications are processed on a rolling basis. Application fee: $40. *Expenses:* Tuition, state resident: full-time $5364. Tuition, nonresident: full-time $8314. *Financial support:* Research assistantships, teaching assistantships with full tuition reimbursements, career-related internships or fieldwork, Federal Work-Study, institutionally sponsored loans, and unspecified assistantships available. Support available to part-time students. Financial award application deadline: 3/15; financial award applicants required to submit FAFSA. *Unit head:* Dr. Maria Bevacqua, Chairperson, 507-389-2077. *Application contact:* 507-389-2321, E-mail: grad@mnsu.edu.

Mount Saint Vincent University, Graduate Programs, Department of Women's Studies, Halifax, NS B3M 2J6, Canada. Offers MA. Part-time programs available. *Degree requirements:* For master's, thesis. Electronic applications accepted.

Northern Arizona University, Graduate College, College of Social and Behavioral Sciences, Women's and Gender Studies Program, Flagstaff, AZ 86011. Offers Graduate Certificate. *Faculty:* 2 full-time (both women). *Students:* 1 (woman) part-time. Average age 25. 8 applicants, 50% accepted, 1 enrolled. *Application deadline:* Applications are processed on a rolling basis. Application fee: $65. Electronic applications accepted. *Unit head:* Dr. Sanjam Ahluwalia, Chair, 928-523-8709, E-mail: sanjam.ahluwalia@nau.edu. *Application contact:* Dr. Sanjam Ahluwalia, Chair, 928-523-8709, E-mail: sanjam.ahluwalia@nau.edu.

The Ohio State University, Graduate School, College of Humanities, Department of Women's Studies, Columbus, OH 43210. Offers MA, PhD. *Faculty:* 63. *Students:* 16 full-time (14 women); includes 1 minority (African American), 1 international. Average age 27. In 2009, 4 master's, 1 doctorate awarded. *Degree requirements:* For master's, thesis optional. *Entrance requirements:* Additional exam requirements/recommendations for international students: Required—TOEFL (minimum score 600 paper-based; 250 computer-based). *Application deadline:* For fall admission, 8/15 priority date for domestic students, 7/1 priority date for international students; for winter admission, 12/1 priority date for domestic students, 11/1 priority date for international students; for spring admission, 3/1 priority date for domestic students, 2/1 priority date for international students. Applications are processed on a rolling basis. Application fee: $40 ($50 for international students). Electronic applications accepted. *Expenses:* Tuition, state resident: full-time $10,683. Tuition, nonresident: full-time $25,923. Tuition and fees vary according to course load and program. *Financial support:* Fellowships, research assistantships, teaching assistantships, career-related internships or fieldwork, Federal Work-Study, institutionally sponsored loans, and unspecified assistantships available. Support available to part-time students. *Unit head:* Linda Mizejewski, Graduate Studies Committee Chair, E-mail: mizejewski.1@osu.edu. *Application contact:* 614-292-9444, Fax: 614-292-3895, E-mail: domestic.grad@osu.edu.

Old Dominion University, College of Arts and Letters, Graduate Programs in International Studies, Norfolk, VA 23529. Offers conflict and cooperation (PhD), including women's studies certificate; U.S. foreign policy (MA), including modeling and simulation certificate. Part-time programs available. *Faculty:* 14 full-time (3 women). *Students:* 53 full-time (26 women), 44 part-time (17 women); includes 6 minority (3 African Americans, 3 Hispanic Americans), 29 international. Average age 32. 99 applicants, 54% accepted, 30 enrolled. In 2009, 18 master's, 5 doctorates awarded. Terminal master's awarded for partial completion of doctoral program. *Degree requirements:* For master's, one foreign language, comprehensive exam, thesis optional; for doctorate, one foreign language, comprehensive exam, thesis/dissertation. *Entrance requirements:* For master's, GRE General Test, sample of written work, 2 letters of recommendation; for doctorate, GRE General Test, sample of written work, 3 letters of recommendation. Additional exam requirements/recommendations for international students: Required—TOEFL (minimum score 570 paper-based; 230 computer-based). *Application deadline:* For fall admission, 3/15 for domestic students, 2/15 for international students; for spring admission, 10/15 for domestic and international students. Application fee: $40. Electronic applications accepted. *Expenses:* Tuition, state resident: full-time $8112; part-time $338 per credit. Tuition, nonresident: full-time $20,256; part-time $844 per credit. Required fees: $119 per semester. One-time fee: $50. *Financial support:* In 2009–10, 20 students received support, including 2 fellowships (averaging $13,000 per year), 9 research assistantships with tuition reimbursements available (averaging $11,000 per year), 9 teaching assistantships with tuition reimbursements available (averaging $11,000 per year); career-related internships or fieldwork, institutionally sponsored loans, scholarships/grants, and unspecified assistantships also available. Support available to part-time students. Financial award application deadline: 2/15; financial award applicants required to submit FAFSA. *Faculty research:* U. S. foreign policy, international security, transatlantic and transpacific relations, transnational issues, IPE and development. Total annual research expenditures: $330,391. *Unit head:* Dr. Regina Karp, Graduate Program Director, 757-683-5700, Fax: 757-683-5701, E-mail: rkarp@odu.edu. *Application contact:* Dr. Angelica Huizar, 757-683-3988, Fax: 757-683-5701, E-mail: ahuizar@odu.edu.

Phoenix Seminary, Graduate Programs, Scottsdale, AZ 85254. Offers biblical communication (M Div); biblical leadership (MA); biblical studies (Graduate Diploma); Christian counseling (Graduate Diploma); counseling and family (M Div); intercultural studies (Graduate Diploma); leadership development (M Div, Graduate Diploma); ministry (D Min); professional counseling (MA); women's studies (Graduate Diploma). *Accreditation:* ATS (one or more programs are accredited). Part-time and evening/weekend programs available. *Faculty:* 5 full-time (0 women), 5 part-time/adjunct (0 women). *Students:* 26 full-time (8 women), 151 part-time (39 women); includes 34 minority (18 African Americans, 2 American Indian/Alaska Native, 5 Asian Americans or Pacific Islanders, 9 Hispanic Americans), 1 international. 41 applicants, 90% accepted, 30 enrolled. In 2009, 21 master's, 2 doctorates, 12 other advanced degrees awarded. *Degree requirements:* For master's, 2 foreign languages, comprehensive exam; for doctorate, 2 foreign languages, thesis/dissertation. *Entrance requirements:* For master's, undergraduate degree with minimum GPA of 2.5; for doctorate, M Div (94 hours) with minimum GPA of 3.0. Additional exam requirements/recommendations for international students: Required—TOEFL (minimum score 587 paper-based; 240 computer-based; 92 iBT), TWE (minimum score 4.5). *Application deadline:* For fall admission, 7/1 for domestic students; for spring admission, 11/1 for domestic students. Applications are processed on a rolling basis. Application fee: $90. *Expenses:* Tuition: Full-time $9420; part-time $410 per credit hour. Required fees: $60 per semester. Tuition and fees vary according to course load and degree level. *Financial support:* Institutionally sponsored loans and scholarships/grants available. Support available to part-time students. Financial award application deadline: 6/1; financial award applicants required to submit FAFSA. *Application contact:* Roma Royer, Director of Admissions and Academic Services, 602-850-8000 Ext. 111, Fax: 602-850-8080, E-mail: rroyer@ps.edu.

Queen's University at Kingston, School of Graduate Studies and Research, Faculty of Arts and Sciences, Department of Sociology, Kingston, ON K7L 3N6, Canada. Offers communication and Information technology (MA, PhD); feminist sociology (MA, PhD); socio-legal studies (MA, PhD); sociological theory (MA, PhD). Part-time programs available. *Degree requirements:* For master's, thesis; for doctorate, comprehensive exam, thesis/dissertation. *Entrance requirements:* For master's, honors bachelors degree in sociology; for doctorate, honors bachelors degree, masters degree in sociology. Additional exam requirements/recommendations for international students: Required—TOEFL. *Faculty research:* Social change and modernization, social control, deviance and criminology, surveillance.

Roosevelt University, Graduate Division, College of Arts and Sciences, Department of Literature and Languages, Program in Women's and Gender Studies, Chicago, IL 60605. Offers MA, Certificate. Part-time and evening/weekend programs available. *Degree requirements:* For master's, thesis. *Entrance requirements:* For master's, minimum GPA of 2.7. *Faculty research:* Feminist economics; philosophy of feminism; race, class, and gender; women and art; women's history.

Rutgers, The State University of New Jersey, New Brunswick, Graduate School-New Brunswick, Department of Political Science, Piscataway, NJ 08854-8097. Offers American politics (PhD); comparative politics (PhD); international relations (PhD); political theory (PhD); public law (PhD); women and politics (PhD). *Degree requirements:* For doctorate, one foreign language, comprehensive exam, thesis/dissertation. *Entrance requirements:* For doctorate, GRE General Test. Additional exam requirements/recommendations for international students: Required—TOEFL.

Rutgers, The State University of New Jersey, New Brunswick, Graduate School-New Brunswick, Program in Women's and Gender Studies, Piscataway, NJ 08854-8097. Offers MA, PhD. Part-time programs available. *Degree requirements:* For master's, thesis or alternative; for doctorate, comprehensive exam, thesis/dissertation. *Entrance requirements:* For master's and doctorate, GRE General Test, writing sample, 3 letters of recommendation. Additional exam requirements/recommendations for international students: Required—TOEFL. *Faculty research:* Feminist theory, gender and sexuality, global and cultural studies, women in history, literature, and politics, feminist politics.

Saint Mary's University, Faculty of Arts, Program in Women and Gender Studies, Halifax, NS B3H 3C3, Canada. Offers MA. Part-time programs available. *Faculty:* 50. *Students:* 40. *Degree requirements:* For master's, thesis. *Entrance requirements:* For master's, honors degree. *Application deadline:* For fall admission, 5/31 for domestic students. Application fee: $35. *Unit head:* Dr. Michele Byers, Director, 902-420-5869, E-mail: michele.byers@smu.ca. *Application contact:* Dr. Michele Byers, Director, 902-420-5869, E-mail: michele.byers@smu.ca.

San Diego State University, Graduate and Research Affairs, College of Arts and Letters, Department of Women's Studies, San Diego, CA 92182. Offers MA. *Entrance requirements:* For master's, GRE General Test, 2 letters of reference. Additional exam requirements/recommendations for international students: Required—TOEFL. Electronic applications accepted.

San Francisco State University, Division of Graduate Studies, College of Humanities, Department of Women Studies, San Francisco, CA 94132-1722. Offers MA. Part-time and evening/weekend programs available.

Sarah Lawrence College, Graduate Studies, Program in Women's History, Bronxville, NY 10708-5999. Offers MA. Part-time programs available. *Faculty:* 9 part-time/adjunct (8 women). *Students:* 28 full-time (26 women), 5 part-time (all women); includes 7 minority (6 African Americans, 1 Asian American or Pacific Islander), 2 international. Average age 27. 54 applicants, 63% accepted, 17 enrolled. In 2009, 12 master's awarded. *Degree requirements:* For master's, thesis. *Entrance requirements:* For master's, previous course work in history, minimum B average in undergraduate course work. Additional exam requirements/recommendations for international students: Required—TOEFL (minimum score 600 paper-based). *Application deadline:* For fall admission, 2/1 priority date for domestic students. Applications are processed on a rolling basis. Application fee: $60. *Expenses:* Tuition: Part-time $1161 per credit. Required fees: $232 per semester. Part-time tuition and fees vary according to course load, program and student level. *Financial support:* In 2009–10, 25 fellowships (averaging $5,563 per year)

Women's Studies

Sarah Lawrence College (continued)
were awarded; career-related internships or fieldwork also available. Support available to part-time students. Financial award application deadline: 3/1; financial award applicants required to submit CSS PROFILE or FAFSA. *Unit head:* Priscilla Murolo, Director, 914-395-2405. *Application contact:* Emanual Lomax, Dean of Graduate Studies, 914-395-2371, E-mail: elomax@sarahlawrence.edu.

Simon Fraser University, Graduate Studies, Faculty of Arts and Social Sciences, Department of Women's Studies, Burnaby, BC V5A 1S6, Canada. Offers MA, PhD. *Degree requirements:* For master's, thesis or alternative. *Entrance requirements:* For master's, minimum GPA of 3.8. Additional exam requirements/recommendations for international students: Required—TOEFL or IELTS. *Faculty research:* Theory development, disability, economics, globalization.

Southeastern Baptist Theological Seminary, Graduate and Professional Programs, Wake Forest, NC 27588-1889. Offers advanced biblical studies (M Div); Christian education (M Div, MACE); Christian ethics (PhD); Christian ministry (M Div); Christian planting (M Div); church music (MACM); counseling (MACO); evangelism (PhD); language (M Div); ministry (D Min); New Testament (PhD); Old Testament (PhD); philosophy (PhD); theology (Th M, PhD); women's studies (M Div). *Accreditation:* ACIPE; ATS (one or more programs are accredited). *Degree requirements:* For master's, thesis (for some programs), oral exam; for doctorate, thesis/dissertation, fieldwork; for M Div, supervised ministry. *Entrance requirements:* For master's, Cooperative English Test, minimum GPA of 2.0, M Div or equivalent (Th M); for doctorate, GRE General Test or MAT, Cooperative English Test, M Div or equivalent, 3 years of professional experience.

Southern Connecticut State University, School of Graduate Studies, School of Arts and Sciences, Program in Women's Studies, New Haven, CT 06515-1355. Offers MA. Part-time and evening/weekend programs available. *Students:* 6 full-time (all women), 13 part-time (all women); includes 2 minority (both Hispanic Americans). 12 applicants, 67% accepted, 7 enrolled. In 2009, 5 master's awarded. *Degree requirements:* For master's, thesis or alternative. *Entrance requirements:* For master's, interview. *Application deadline:* Applications are processed on a rolling basis. Application fee: $50. Electronic applications accepted. Tuition and fees vary according to program. *Financial support:* Application deadline: 4/15. *Unit head:* Dr. Tricia Lin, Director, 203-392-6832, Fax: 203-392-5670, E-mail: liny4@southernct.edu. *Application contact:* Dr. Tricia Lin, Director, 203-392-6832, Fax: 203-392-5670, E-mail: liny4@southernct.edu.

Stony Brook University, State University of New York, Graduate School, College of Arts and Sciences, Program in Women's Studies, Stony Brook, NY 11794. Offers Certificate. *Degree requirements:* For Certificate, interdisciplinary research colloquium. *Entrance requirements:* For degree, GRE, minimum GPA of 2.75, 3 letters of recommendation. *Expenses:* Tuition, state resident: full-time $8370; part-time $349 per credit. Tuition, nonresident: full-time $13,250; part-time $552 per credit. Required fees: $933.

Suffolk University, College of Arts and Sciences, Program in Women's Health, Boston, MA 02108-2770. Offers MA. *Faculty:* 15 full-time (10 women). *Students:* 25 full-time (all women), 14 part-time (all women); includes 24 minority (14 African Americans, 10 Hispanic Americans). Average age 27. 128 applicants, 50% accepted, 24 enrolled. In 2009, 3 master's awarded. *Entrance requirements:* For master's, statement of professional goals, official transcripts, 2 letters of recommendation, resume. Additional exam requirements/recommendations for international students: Required—TOEFL (minimum score 550 paper-based; 213 computer-based; 80 iBT). *Application deadline:* For fall admission, 6/15 priority date for domestic students, 6/15 for international students; for spring admission, 11/1 priority date for domestic students, 11/1 for international students. Applications are processed on a rolling basis. Application fee: $50. Electronic applications accepted. *Expenses:* Contact institution. *Financial support:* In 2009–10, 38 students received support, including 36 fellowships (averaging $6,929 per year). Financial award applicants required to submit FAFSA. *Unit head:* Dr. Amy Agigian, Co-Director, 617-573-8487, Fax: 617-994-4278, E-mail: aagigian@suffolk.edu. *Application contact:* Judith Reynolds, Director of Graduate Admissions, 617-573-8302, Fax: 617-305-1733, E-mail: grad.admission@suffolk.edu.

Syracuse University, College of Arts and Sciences, Program in Women's and Gender Studies, Syracuse, NY 13244. Offers CAS. *Students:* 3 applicants, 100% accepted, 0 enrolled. In 2009, 3 CASs awarded. *Entrance requirements:* For degree, Must be matriculated in an SU graduate Program. Additional exam requirements/recommendations for international students: Required—TOEFL (minimum score 100 iBT). *Application deadline:* For fall admission, 2/1 priority date for domestic and international students. Application fee: $75. Electronic applications accepted. *Expenses:* Tuition: Full-time $26,808; part-time $1117 per credit. Required fees: $1024. *Unit head:* Dr. Chandra Talpade Mohanty, Chair, 315-443-3707, E-mail: ctmohant@syr.edu. *Application contact:* Susann Democker-Shedd, Program Contact, 315-443-3560, E-mail: sademock@syr.edu.

Texas Woman's University, Graduate School, College of Arts and Sciences, Program in Women's Studies, Denton, TX 76201. Offers MA, PhD. Part-time and evening/weekend programs available. *Faculty:* 4 full-time (all women), 2 part-time/adjunct (both women). *Students:* 16 full-time (15 women), 23 part-time (all women); includes 12 minority (6 African Americans, 1 American Indian/Alaska Native, 1 Asian American or Pacific Islander, 4 Hispanic Americans), 2 international. Average age 34. 34 applicants, 68% accepted, 14 enrolled. In 2009, 5 master's awarded. *Degree requirements:* For master's, thesis. *Entrance requirements:* For master's, 2 letters of reference. Additional exam requirements/recommendations for international students: Required—TOEFL (minimum score 550 paper-based; 213 computer-based; 79 iBT). *Application deadline:* For fall admission, 7/1 priority date for domestic students, 3/1 for international students; for spring admission, 12/1 priority date for domestic students, 7/1 for international students. Applications are processed on a rolling basis. Application fee: $50. Electronic applications accepted. *Expenses:* Tuition, state resident: full-time $3564; part-time $198 per credit hour. Tuition, nonresident: full-time $8550; part-time $475 per credit hour. Required fees: $69.26 per credit hour. Tuition and fees vary according to course load. *Financial support:* In 2009–10, 14 students received support, including 12 research assistantships (averaging $10,440 per year), 8 teaching assistantships (averaging $10,440 per year); career-related internships or fieldwork, Federal Work-Study, institutionally sponsored loans, scholarships/grants, traineeships, health care benefits, and unspecified assistantships also available. Support available to part-time students. Financial award application deadline: 3/1; financial award applicants required to submit FAFSA. *Faculty research:* Feminism and religion, family violence, feminist theory, women of color, feminist ethics. *Unit head:* Dr. Claire L. Sahlin, Director, 940-898-2119, Fax: 940-898-2101, E-mail: womenstudies@twu.edu. *Application contact:* Samuel Wheeler, Assistant Director of Admissions, 940-898-3188, Fax: 940-898-3081, E-mail: wheelersr@twu.edu.

Towson University, College of Graduate Studies and Research, Program in Women's Studies, Towson, MD 21252-0001. Offers MS, Certificate. *Degree requirements:* For master's, thesis optional. *Entrance requirements:* For master's, minimum GPA of 3.0, 9 credits of course work in women's studies and/or the social sciences. Electronic applications accepted. *Faculty research:* Gender and international relations, health, economics, violence against women, public policy.

United Theological Seminary of the Twin Cities, Professional Program, New Brighton, MN 55112-2598. Offers advanced theological studies (Diploma); justice and peace studies (M Div, MA); leadership toward racial justice (MA, Certificate); leadership towards racial justice (M Div); Methodist studies (M Div, MA, Certificate); ministry (D Min); ministry renewal and professional development (Certificate); pastoral care and counseling (M Div, MA, MARL); religion and theology (MA); theological and religious studies (Certificate); theology and the arts (M Div, MA); urban ministry (M Div, MA, MARL); women's studies: religion, theology and ministry (MA); women's studies: religions, theology and ministry (M Div). *Accreditation:* ACIPE; ATS. Part-time and evening/weekend programs available. *Faculty:* 9 full-time (6 women), 22 part-time/adjunct (10 women). *Students:* 49 full-time (34 women), 105 part-time (68 women). Average age 47. 41 applicants, 98% accepted, 34 enrolled. In 2009, 24 first professional degrees, 5 master's, 2 doctorates, 2 other advanced degrees awarded. *Degree requirements:* For master's, thesis; for doctorate, comprehensive exam, thesis/dissertation; for M Div, integrative notebook, spiritual chronicle. *Entrance requirements:* For M Div and master's, minimum GPA of 2.75; strong analytical, reflective thinking and writing skills; vocational and academic goals compatible with those of Seminary; for doctorate, M Div or equivalent, minimum GPA of 3.0, 3 years experience in professional ministry; for other advanced degree, BA or equivalent life experience; strong analytical, reflective thinking and writing skills (Certificate); proficiency in English language, previous study of theology at a theological school, recommendation of student's denomination (Diploma). Additional exam requirements/recommendations for international students: Required—TOEFL (minimum score 550 paper-based). *Application deadline:* For fall admission, 7/1 priority date for domestic students, 11/1 priority date for international students; for winter admission, 11/1 priority date for domestic students; for spring admission, 11/15 priority date for domestic students. Applications are processed on a rolling basis. Application fee: $50. *Expenses:* Tuition: Full-time $11,502; part-time $426 per credit hour. Required fees: $295; $155 per term. One-time fee: $25. Tuition and fees vary according to course load, degree level and program. *Financial support:* In 2009–10, 120 students received support. Career-related internships or fieldwork, institutionally sponsored loans, and scholarships/grants available. Support available to part-time students. Financial award application deadline: 5/1; financial award applicants required to submit FAFSA. *Unit head:* Dr. Richard D. Weis, Dean of the Seminary, 651-255-6108 Ext. 108, Fax: 651-633-4315, E-mail: rweis@unitedseminary.edu. *Application contact:* Rev. Glen Herrington-Hall, Director of Admissions, 651-255-6107 Ext. 107, Fax: 651-633-4315, E-mail: gherrington-hall@unitedseminary.edu.

Université Laval, Faculty of Social Sciences, Program in Feminist Studies, Québec, QC G1K 7P4, Canada. Offers Diploma. Part-time programs available. *Entrance requirements:* For degree, knowledge of French, comprehension of written English. Electronic applications accepted.

University at Albany, State University of New York, College of Arts and Sciences, Department of Women's Studies, Albany, NY 12222-0001. Offers MA, DA. *Entrance requirements:* Additional exam requirements/recommendations for international students: Required—TOEFL (minimum score 550 paper-based; 213 computer-based). Electronic applications accepted. *Faculty research:* Feminist pedagogy, lesbian and gay studies, women in the African diaspora, women's health policy, literature of feminism.

The University of Alabama, Graduate School, College of Arts and Sciences, Department of Gender and Race Studies, Program in Women's Studies, Tuscaloosa, AL 35487. Offers MA. *Faculty:* 4 full-time (all women). *Students:* 9 full-time (all women); includes 2 minority (both African Americans). Average age 25. 9 applicants, 56% accepted, 1 enrolled. In 2009, 4 degrees awarded. *Degree requirements:* For master's, comprehensive exam, thesis optional, teaching women's studies course. *Entrance requirements:* For master's, GRE or MAT, minimum GPA of 3.0. Additional exam requirements/recommendations for international students: Required—TOEFL. *Application deadline:* For winter admission, 2/1 for domestic students. Applications are processed on a rolling basis. Electronic applications accepted. *Expenses:* Tuition, state resident: full-time $7000. Tuition, nonresident: full-time $19,200. *Financial support:* Unspecified assistantships available. Financial award application deadline: 2/15. *Faculty research:* Black feminist criticism, black women's written and oral discourse, black women's leadership, hip-hop and feminism, queer theory, feminist theory, women and spirituality, nineteenth century African-American literature, black popular culture, African Diaspora religion. Total annual research expenditures: $7,488. *Unit head:* Dr. DoVeanna S. Minor, Chair, 205-348-8462, Fax: 205-348-3584, E-mail: dfulton@as.ua.edu. *Application contact:* Dr. DoVeanna S. Minor, Chair and Director of Graduate Studies, 205-348-8462, Fax: 205-348-3584, E-mail: dfulton@as.ua.edu.

The University of Arizona, Graduate College, College of Social and Behavioral Sciences, Department of Women's Studies, Tucson, AZ 85721. Offers MA, PhD. Part-time programs available. *Faculty:* 9 full-time (8 women). *Students:* 7 full-time (6 women), 2 part-time (both women); includes 1 minority (Hispanic American), 1 international. Average age 28. 18 applicants, 44% accepted, 1 enrolled. In 2009, 4 master's awarded. *Degree requirements:* For master's, thesis/project. *Entrance requirements:* For master's and doctorate, GRE (minimum score: 500 verbal, 500 quantitative, 4.5 analytical), 3 letters of recommendation. Additional exam requirements/recommendations for international students: Required—TOEFL (minimum score 600 paper-based; 250 computer-based; 100 iBT). *Application deadline:* For fall admission, 12/1 for domestic and international students. Applications are processed on a rolling basis. Application fee: $65. Electronic applications accepted. *Expenses:* Tuition, state resident: full-time $9028. Tuition, nonresident: full-time $24,890. *Financial support:* In 2009–10, 8 teaching assistantships with full tuition reimbursements (averaging $14,009 per year) were awarded; career-related internships or fieldwork, scholarships/grants, health care benefits, tuition waivers (full and partial), and unspecified assistantships also available. Financial award application deadline: 1/15. *Faculty research:* Gender race and border studies, sexuality and the body, gender health and science, cultural representation and theory, public policy and social movements. Total annual research expenditures: $106,592. *Unit head:* Dr. Laura Briggs, Department Head, 520-626-9149, Fax: 520-621-1533, E-mail: lbriggs@email.arizona.edu. *Application contact:* Susan D. Whitworth, Information Contact, 520-626-5657, Fax: 520-621-1533, E-mail: whitwort@email.arizona.edu.

University of California, Los Angeles, Graduate Division, College of Letters and Science, Program in Women's Studies, Los Angeles, CA 90095. Offers MA, PhD. *Students:* 26 full-time (25 women); includes 10 minority (4 African Americans, 1 American Indian/Alaska Native, 1 Asian American or Pacific Islander, 4 Hispanic Americans), 2 international. Average age 30. 53 applicants, 21% accepted, 6 enrolled. In 2009, 2 master's, 1 doctorate awarded. Terminal master's awarded for partial completion of doctoral program. *Degree requirements:* For master's, comprehensive exam or thesis; for doctorate, one foreign language, thesis/dissertation, written and oral exams. *Entrance requirements:* For master's, GRE General Test; for doctorate, GRE General Test, minimum undergraduate GPA of 3.0. *Application deadline:* For fall admission, 12/15 for domestic and international students. Application fee: $70 ($90 for international students). Electronic applications accepted. *Financial support:* In 2009–10, 23 fellowships with full and partial tuition reimbursements, 13 research assistantships with full and partial tuition reimbursements, 13 teaching assistantships with full and partial tuition reimbursements were awarded; Federal Work-Study, institutionally sponsored loans, scholarships/grants, health care benefits, tuition waivers (full and partial), and unspecified assistantships also available. Financial award applicants required to submit FAFSA. *Unit head:* Dr. Christine Littleton, Chair, 310-206-8101. *Application contact:* Department Office, 310-206-8101, E-mail: women@women.ucla.edu.

University of California, Santa Barbara, Graduate Division, College of Letters and Sciences, Division of Humanities and Fine Arts, Department of English, Santa Barbara, CA 93106-3170. Offers English (PhD); feminist studies (PhD); global studies (PhD); MA/PhD. *Faculty:* 26 full-time (13 women), 17 part-time/adjunct (12 women). *Students:* 81 full-time (43 women). Average age 30. 151 applicants, 19% accepted, 13 enrolled. In 2009, 12 doctorates awarded. Terminal master's awarded for partial completion of doctoral program. *Degree requirements:* For doctorate, one foreign language, comprehensive exam, thesis/dissertation. *Entrance requirements:* For doctorate, GRE General Test, GRE Subject Test (literature), sample of written work, 3 letters of recommendation, resume/curriculum vitae. Additional exam requirements/recommendations for international students: Required—TOEFL (minimum score 550 paper-based; 213 computer-based; 80 iBT) or IELTS (minimum score 7). *Application deadline:* For fall admission, 12/15 for domestic and international students. Application fee:

$70 ($90 for international students). Electronic applications accepted. *Financial support:* In 2009–10, 70 students received support, including 32 fellowships with full and partial tuition reimbursements available (averaging $10,800 per year), 6 research assistantships with full and partial tuition reimbursements available (averaging $4,200 per year), 54 teaching assistantships with partial tuition reimbursements available (averaging $10,800 per year); Federal Work-Study, institutionally sponsored loans, scholarships/grants, health care benefits, tuition waivers (full and partial), and unspecified assistantships also available. Financial award application deadline: 12/15; financial award applicants required to submit FAFSA. *Faculty research:* Renaissance literature, eighteenth century literature, American literature, race and ethnic studies, literature and theory of technology/media/information. *Unit head:* Prof. Alan Liu, Chair, 805-893-3478, Fax: 805-893-4622, E-mail: ayliu@english.ucsb.edu. *Application contact:* Chelsea Houdyshell, Staff Graduate Advisor, 805-893-2639, Fax: 805-893-4622, E-mail: chelsea@english.ucsb.edu.

University of California, Santa Barbara, Graduate Division, College of Letters and Sciences, Division of Humanities and Fine Arts, Department of French and Italian, Santa Barbara, CA 93106-4140. Offers French (MA, MABL, PhD), including applied linguistics (PhD), European Medieval studies (PhD), feminist studies (PhD), French (MABL, PhD); MA/PhD. French Language Institute available during summer sessions. *Faculty:* 21 full-time (12 women). *Students:* 11 full-time (7 women). Average age 31. 16 applicants, 63% accepted, 3 enrolled. In 2009, 1 master's, 5 doctorates awarded. Terminal master's awarded for partial completion of doctoral program. *Degree requirements:* For master's, 2 foreign languages, comprehensive exam; for doctorate, 2 foreign languages, comprehensive exam, thesis/dissertation. *Entrance requirements:* For master's, GRE, sample of written work, tape of spoken French, BA or the equivalent, 3 letters of recommendation, resume/curriculum vitae; for doctorate, GRE, sample of written work, tape of spoken French, MA or the equivalent, 3 letters of recommendation, statement of purpose, personal achievements/contributions statement, resume/curriculum vitae, transcripts for post-secondary institutions attended. Additional exam requirements/recommendations for international students: Required—TOEFL (minimum score 550 paper-based; 213 computer-based; 80 iBT) or IELTS (minimum score 7). *Application deadline:* For fall admission, 5/1 for domestic and international students; for winter admission, 10/1 for domestic and international students; for spring admission, 1/15 for domestic and international students. Application fee: $70 ($90 for international students). Electronic applications accepted. *Financial support:* In 2009–10, 11 students received support, including 5 fellowships with full and partial tuition reimbursements available (averaging $8,100 per year), 11 teaching assistantships with partial tuition reimbursements available (averaging $11,400 per year); career-related internships or fieldwork, Federal Work-Study, institutionally sponsored loans, scholarships/grants, traineeships, health care benefits, tuition waivers (full and partial), and unspecified assistantships also available. Financial award applicants required to submit FAFSA. *Faculty research:* French and Francophone studies, comparative literature, second language acquisition, applied linguistics, performance studies, feminist and gender studies. Total annual research expenditures: $2,500. *Unit head:* Prof. Jon Snyder, Chair, 805-893-2220, Fax: 805-893-8826, E-mail: snyder@frit.ucsb.edu. *Application contact:* Rosa Pinter, Graduate Staff Advisor, 805-893-3398, Fax: 805-893-8826, E-mail: pinter@frit.ucsb.edu.

University of California, Santa Barbara, Graduate Division, College of Letters and Sciences, Division of Humanities and Fine Arts, Department of Germanic, Slavic, and Semitic Studies, Santa Barbara, CA 93106-4130. Offers Germanic languages and literature (MA, PhD), including applied linguistics (PhD), feminist studies (PhD); MA/PhD. *Faculty:* 7 full-time (4 women). *Students:* 2 full-time (0 women). Average age 31. 6 applicants, 50% accepted, 1 enrolled. In 2009, 1 master's awarded. Terminal master's awarded for partial completion of doctoral program. *Degree requirements:* For master's, 2 foreign languages, comprehensive exam, thesis; for doctorate, 3 foreign languages, comprehensive exam, thesis/dissertation. *Entrance requirements:* For master's and doctorate, GRE. Additional exam requirements/recommendations for international students: Required—TOEFL (minimum score 550 paper-based; 213 computer-based; 80 iBT), or IELTS (minimum score 7). *Application deadline:* For fall admission, 12/31 priority date for domestic students, 5/1 priority date for international students; for winter admission, 11/1 priority date for domestic and international students; for spring admission, 2/1 priority date for domestic and international students. Applications are processed on a rolling basis. Application fee: $70 ($90 for international students). Electronic applications accepted. *Financial support:* In 2009–10, 2 students received support, including 2 fellowships with full and partial tuition reimbursements available (averaging $10,100 per year), 1 teaching assistantship with partial tuition reimbursement available (averaging $11,600 per year); Federal Work-Study, institutionally sponsored loans, scholarships/grants, health care benefits, and tuition waivers (full and partial) also available. Financial award application deadline: 12/31; financial award applicants required to submit FAFSA. *Faculty research:* Critical theory, media technology, psychoanalysis, German romanticism, Goethe. *Unit head:* Prof. Elisabeth Weber, Chair, 805-893-3527, Fax: 805-893-2374, E-mail: weber@gss.ucsb.edu. *Application contact:* Sierra Gray, Graduate Program Assistant, 805-893-2131, Fax: 805-893-2374, E-mail: sierra@gss.ucsb.edu.

University of California, Santa Barbara, Graduate Division, College of Letters and Sciences, Division of Humanities and Fine Arts, Department of History, Santa Barbara, CA 93106-9410. Offers feminist studies (PhD); global studies (PhD); public history (PhD); MA/PhD. *Faculty:* 40 full-time (17 women), 11 part-time/adjunct (6 women). *Students:* 120 full-time (62 women). Average age 34. 130 applicants, 38% accepted, 22 enrolled. In 2009, 9 doctorates awarded. Terminal master's awarded for partial completion of doctoral program. *Degree requirements:* For doctorate, variable foreign language requirement, comprehensive exam, thesis/dissertation. *Entrance requirements:* For doctorate, GRE, 3 letters of recommendation, resume/curriculum vitae. Additional exam requirements/recommendations for international students: Required—TOEFL (minimum score 550 paper-based; 213 computer-based; 80 iBT) or IELTS (minimum score 7). *Application deadline:* For fall admission, 12/5 for domestic and international students. Application fee: $70 ($90 for international students). Electronic applications accepted. *Financial support:* In 2009–10, 94 students received support, including 53 fellowships with full and partial tuition reimbursements available (averaging $8,600 per year), 2 research assistantships with full and partial tuition reimbursements available (averaging $7,400 per year), 70 teaching assistantships with partial tuition reimbursements available (averaging $9,400 per year); Federal Work-Study, institutionally sponsored loans, scholarships/grants, traineeships, health care benefits, tuition waivers (full and partial), and unspecified assistantships also available. Financial award application deadline: 12/5; financial award applicants required to submit FAFSA. *Faculty research:* Europe, U. S., Latin America, Africa, Middle East, East Asia. *Unit head:* Kenneth J. Moure, Chair, 805-893-2993, Fax: 805-893-8795, E-mail: moure@history.ucrb.edu. *Application contact:* Prof. Sharon Farmer, Director of Graduate Studies, 805-893-2543, Fax: 805-893-8795, E-mail: farmer@history.ucsb.edu.

University of California, Santa Barbara, Graduate Division, College of Letters and Sciences, Division of Humanities and Fine Arts, Department of Music, Santa Barbara, CA 93106-6070. Offers brass (MM); composition (MA, PhD); conducting (MM, DMA); ethnomusicology (MA, PhD); feminist studies (PhD); keyboard (MM, DMA); musicology (MA, PhD); piano accompanying (MM); strings (MM, DMA); theory (MA, PhD); voice (MM, DMA); woodwinds (MM); MA/PhD; MM/DMA. *Faculty:* 28 full-time (6 women), 17 part-time/adjunct (6 women). *Students:* 71 full-time (34 women). Average age 30. 103 applicants, 31% accepted, 24 enrolled. In 2009, 13 master's, 11 doctorates awarded. Terminal master's awarded for partial completion of doctoral program. *Degree requirements:* For master's, variable foreign language requirement, comprehensive exam (for some programs), thesis (for some programs); for doctorate, variable foreign language requirement, comprehensive exam, thesis/dissertation. *Entrance requirements:* For master's, GRE, tape/audition, media (performance), portfolio (composition), writing sample, 3 letters of recommendation, resume/curriculum vitae; for doctorate, tape/audition (DMA), media (performance), portfolio (composition), writing sample, 3 letters of recommendation, statement of purpose, personal achievements/contributions statement, resume/curriculum vitae, transcripts for post-secondary institutions attended. Additional exam requirements/recommendations for international students: Required—TOEFL (minimum score 550 paper-based; 213 computer-based; 80 iBT) or IELTS (minimum score 7). Application fee: $70 ($90 for international students). Electronic applications accepted. *Financial support:* In 2009–10, 62 students received support, including 31 fellowships with full and partial tuition reimbursements available (averaging $7,700 per year), 2 research assistantships with full and partial tuition reimbursements available (averaging $6,200 per year), 42 teaching assistantships with partial tuition reimbursements available (averaging $8,500 per year); Federal Work-Study, institutionally sponsored loans, scholarships/grants, health care benefits, tuition waivers (full and partial), and unspecified assistantships also available. Financial award applicants required to submit FAFSA. *Faculty research:* Music theory, ethnomusicology, musicology, music performance, music composition. *Unit head:* Dr. Paul Berkowitz, Chair, Fax: 805-893-7194, E-mail: berkowit@music.ucsb.edu. *Application contact:* David L. Holmes, Student Affairs Officer, 805-893-4603, Fax: 805-893-7194, E-mail: dholmes@music.ucsb.edu.

University of California, Santa Barbara, Graduate Division, College of Letters and Sciences, Division of Humanities and Fine Arts, Department of Religious Studies, Santa Barbara, CA 93106-3130. Offers European Medieval studies (PhD); feminist studies (PhD); global studies (PhD); religious studies (MA, PhD); MA/PhD. *Faculty:* 18 full-time (8 women), 11 part-time/adjunct (5 women). *Students:* 86 full-time (33 women). Average age 31. 151 applicants, 31% accepted, 17 enrolled. In 2009, 7 master's, 6 doctorates awarded. Terminal master's awarded for partial completion of doctoral program. *Degree requirements:* For master's, one foreign language, comprehensive exam (for some programs), thesis (for some programs); for doctorate, one foreign language, thesis/dissertation. *Entrance requirements:* For master's, GRE General Test; for doctorate, GRE General Test, MA in related field, 3 letters of recommendation, statement of purpose, personal achievements/contributions statement, resume/curriculum vitae, transcripts for post-secondary institutions attended. Additional exam requirements/recommendations for international students: Required—TOEFL (minimum score 550 paper-based; 213 computer-based; 80 iBT) or IELTS (minimum score 7). *Application deadline:* For fall admission, 12/1 for domestic and international students. Application fee: $70 ($90 for international students). Electronic applications accepted. *Financial support:* In 2009–10, 67 students received support, including 29 fellowships with full and partial tuition reimbursements available (averaging $12,600 per year), 5 research assistantships with full and partial tuition reimbursements available (averaging $7,900 per year), 46 teaching assistantships with partial tuition reimbursements available (averaging $8,400 per year); career-related internships or fieldwork, Federal Work-Study, institutionally sponsored loans, scholarships/grants, traineeships, health care benefits, tuition waivers (full and partial), and unspecified assistantships also available. Financial award application deadline: 12/1; financial award applicants required to submit FAFSA. *Faculty research:* Religion and politics, religion and violence, contemporary spirituality, religious traditions, theoretical approaches to the study of religion, area studies. *Unit head:* Prof. Catherine L. Albanese, Chair, 805-893-3564, Fax: 805-893-2059, E-mail: albanese@religion.ucsb.edu. *Application contact:* Sally J. Lombrozo, Graduate Program Assistant, 805-893-2744, Fax: 805-893-2059, E-mail: lombrozo@religion.ucsb.edu.

University of California, Santa Barbara, Graduate Division, College of Letters and Sciences, Division of Humanities and Fine Arts, Department of Spanish and Portuguese, Santa Barbara, CA 93106-4150. Offers Hispanic languages and literature (PhD), including applied linguistics, European Medieval studies, feminist studies, Hispanic languages and literature; Portuguese (MA); Spanish (MA); Spanish and Portuguese (MA); MA/PhD. Spanish Language Institute available during summer session. *Faculty:* 16 full-time (6 women). *Students:* 29 full-time (16 women). Average age 30. 46 applicants, 39% accepted, 9 enrolled. In 2009, 4 master's, 2 doctorates awarded. *Degree requirements:* For master's, 2 foreign languages, comprehensive exam (for some programs), thesis optional; for doctorate, 2 foreign languages, comprehensive exam, thesis/dissertation. *Entrance requirements:* For master's, GRE, 2 writing samples, undergraduate major in Spanish or equivalent, 3 letters of recommendation, resume/curriculum vitae; for doctorate, GRE, 2 writing samples, master's degree, 3 letters of recommendation, statement of purpose, personal achievements/contributions statement, resume/curriculum vitae, transcripts for post-secondary institutions attended. Additional exam requirements/recommendations for international students: Required—TOEFL (minimum score 550 paper-based; 213 computer-based; 80 iBT), or IELTS (minimum score 7). *Application deadline:* For fall admission, 3/1 for domestic and international students; for winter admission, 11/1 for domestic and international students; for spring admission, 2/1 for domestic and international students. Application fee: $70 ($90 for international students). Electronic applications accepted. *Financial support:* In 2009–10, 9 fellowships with full and partial tuition reimbursements (averaging $7,000 per year), 29 teaching assistantships with partial tuition reimbursements (averaging $11,500 per year) were awarded; career-related internships or fieldwork, Federal Work-Study, institutionally sponsored loans, scholarships/grants, health care benefits, tuition waivers (full and partial), and unspecified assistantships also available. Financial award application deadline: 1/7; financial award applicants required to submit FAFSA. *Faculty research:* Nineteenth century Spanish and Portuguese literature, Spanish and Spanish American literature, nineteenth and twentieth century Portuguese and Brazilian literatures, Hispanic linguistics, Catalan language and culture. *Unit head:* Prof. Francisco A. Lomeli, Chair, 805-893-5715, Fax: 805-893-8341, E-mail: lomeli@spanport.ucsb.edu. *Application contact:* Carol Conley, Graduate Program Assistant, 805-893-3162, Fax: 805-893-8341, E-mail: cconley@spanport.ucsb.edu.

University of California, Santa Barbara, Graduate Division, College of Letters and Sciences, Division of Humanities and Fine Arts, Department of Theatre and Dance, Santa Barbara, CA 93106-7060. Offers theater studies (MA, PhD), including European Medieval studies (PhD), feminist studies (PhD), theater studies (PhD); MA/PhD. *Faculty:* 7 full-time (3 women), 1 (woman) part-time/adjunct. *Students:* 22 full-time (15 women). Average age 33. 22 applicants, 36% accepted, 5 enrolled. In 2009, 3 master's, 5 doctorates awarded. Terminal master's awarded for partial completion of doctoral program. *Degree requirements:* For master's, variable foreign language requirement, comprehensive exam, thesis; for doctorate, one foreign language, comprehensive exam, thesis/dissertation. *Entrance requirements:* For master's, GRE, sample of written work, 3 letters of recommendation, resume/curriculum vitae; for doctorate, GRE, sample of written work, 3 letters of recommendation, statement of purpose, personal achievements/contributions statement, resume/curriculum vitae, transcripts for post-secondary institutions attended. Additional exam requirements/recommendations for international students: Required—TOEFL (minimum score 550 paper-based; 213 computer-based; 80 iBT) or IELTS (minimum score 7). *Application deadline:* For fall admission, 1/5 for domestic and international students. Application fee: $70 ($90 for international students). Electronic applications accepted. *Financial support:* In 2009–10, 13 fellowships with full and partial tuition reimbursements (averaging $11,600 per year), 29 teaching assistantships with partial tuition reimbursements (averaging $11,500 per year) were awarded; Federal Work-Study, scholarships/grants, traineeships, health care benefits, and unspecified assistantships also available. Support available to part-time students. Financial award application deadline: 1/5; financial award applicants required to submit FAFSA. *Faculty research:* Spanish/Latin American drama, performance studies and European theatre history, East Asian and Russian studies, playwriting, Medieval theatre. *Unit head:* Prof. Simon Williams, Chair, 805-893-5515, Fax: 805-893-7029, E-mail: williams@theaterdance.ucsb.edu. *Application contact:* Mary Tench, Graduate Program Assistant, 805-893-3147, Fax: 805-893-7029, E-mail: mtench@theaterdance.ucsb.edu.

University of California, Santa Barbara, Graduate Division, College of Letters and Sciences, Division of Humanities and Fine Arts, Program in Comparative Literature, Santa Barbara, CA 93106-4130. Offers comparative literature (PhD); East Asian literatures (PhD); feminist studies (PhD); MA/PhD. *Faculty:* 56 full-time (24 women). *Students:* 24 full-time (18 women). Average age 29. 43 applicants, 40% accepted, 5 enrolled. In 2009, 5 doctorates awarded. Terminal master's awarded for partial completion of doctoral program. *Degree requirements:* For doctorate, 2 foreign languages, comprehensive exam, thesis/dissertation. *Entrance requirements:* For doctorate, GRE. Additional exam requirements/recommendations for international students: Required—TOEFL (minimum score 550 paper-based; 213 computer-based; 80 iBT) or IELTS (minimum score 7). *Application deadline:* For fall admission, 12/15 for domestic and inter-

Women's Studies

University of California, Santa Barbara (continued)
national students. Application fee: $70 ($90 for international students). Electronic applications accepted. *Financial support:* In 2009–10, 24 students received support, including 15 fellowships with full and partial tuition reimbursements available (averaging $6,900 per year), 1 research assistantship (averaging $10,600 per year), 18 teaching assistantships with partial tuition reimbursements available (averaging $10,400 per year); Federal Work-Study, institutionally sponsored loans, scholarships/grants, health care benefits, and tuition waivers (full and partial) also available. Financial award application deadline: 12/15; financial award applicants required to submit FAFSA. *Faculty research:* Media studies, literary theory, cultural studies, early modern and modern literature, critical theory. *Unit head:* Prof. Elisabeth Weber, Chair, 805-893-3527, Fax: 805-893-2374, E-mail: weber@gss.ucsb.edu. *Application contact:* Sierra Gray, Graduate Program Assistant, 805-893-2131, Fax: 805-893-2374, E-mail: sierra@gss.ucsb.edu.

University of California, Santa Barbara, Graduate Division, College of Letters and Sciences, Division of Social Sciences, Department of Feminist Studies, Santa Barbara, CA 93106-7110. Offers MA, PhD, MA/PhD. *Entrance requirements:* For master's, GRE, writing sample, 3 letters of recommendation, statement of purpose, personal achievements/contributions statement, resume/curriculum vitae, transcripts for post-secondary institutions attended; for doctorate, GRE, writing sample, 3 letters of recommendation, resume/curriculum vitae. Additional exam requirements/recommendations for international students: Required—TOEFL (minimum score 550 paper-based; 213 computer-based; 80 iBT) or IELTS. *Application deadline:* For fall admission, 12/15 for domestic and international students. Application fee: $70 ($90 for international students). Electronic applications accepted. *Unit head:* Eileen Boris, Chair, 805-893-8444, E-mail: boris@femst.ucsb.edu. *Application contact:* Christina Toy, Graduate Admissions Officer, 805-893-4330, Fax: 805-893-8676, E-mail: christina@femst.ucsb.edu.

University of California, Santa Barbara, Graduate Division, College of Letters and Sciences, Division of Social Sciences, Department of Political Science, Santa Barbara, CA 93106-9420. Offers political science (MA); women's studies (PhD); MA/PhD. Part-time programs available. *Faculty:* 22 full-time (10 women), 5 part-time/adjunct (2 women). *Students:* 51 full-time (22 women). Average age 30. 94 applicants, 32% accepted, 7 enrolled. In 2009, 9 master's, 4 doctorates awarded. Terminal master's awarded for partial completion of doctoral program. *Degree requirements:* For master's, comprehensive exam (for some programs), thesis optional; for doctorate, one foreign language, comprehensive exam, thesis/dissertation. *Entrance requirements:* For master's, GRE General Test, minimum undergraduate GPA of 3.0, 3 letters of recommendation, resume/curriculum vitae; for doctorate, GRE General Test, master's degree with minimum GPA of 3.0, 3 letters of recommendation, statement of purpose, personal achievements/contributions statement, resume/curriculum vitae, transcripts for post-secondary institutions attended. Additional exam requirements/recommendations for international students: Required—TOEFL (minimum score 600 paper-based; 250 computer-based; 100 iBT), or IELTS. *Application deadline:* For fall admission, 1/1 priority date for domestic and international students. Application fee: $70 ($90 for international students). Electronic applications accepted. *Financial support:* In 2009–10, 43 students received support, including 25 fellowships with full tuition reimbursements available (averaging $8,200 per year), 42 teaching assistantships with partial tuition reimbursements available (averaging $8,900 per year); Federal Work-Study, institutionally sponsored loans, scholarships/grants, and health care benefits also available. Financial award applicants required to submit FAFSA. *Faculty research:* American politics, comparative politics, international relations, political theory, methodology. *Unit head:* Dr. John Woolley, Chair, 805-893-3432, Fax: 805-893-3309, E-mail: woolley@polsci.ucsb.edu. *Application contact:* Linda James, Staff Graduate Advisor, 805-893-3626, Fax: 805-893-3309, E-mail: james@polsci.ucsb.edu.

University of California, Santa Barbara, Graduate Division, College of Letters and Sciences, Division of Social Sciences, Department of Sociology, Santa Barbara, CA 93106-9430. Offers global studies (PhD); human development (PhD); language, interaction and social organization (PhD); technology and society (PhD); women's studies (PhD); MA/PhD. *Faculty:* 35 full-time (14 women). *Students:* 77 full-time (50 women). Average age 30. 155 applicants, 9% accepted, 8 enrolled. In 2009, 10 doctorates awarded. Terminal master's awarded for partial completion of doctoral program. *Degree requirements:* For doctorate, comprehensive exam, thesis/dissertation. *Entrance requirements:* For doctorate, GRE General Test, sample of written work, 3 letters of recommendation, resume/curriculum vitae. Additional exam requirements/recommendations for international students: Required—TOEFL (minimum score 550 paper-based; 213 computer-based; 80 iBT), or IELTS. *Application deadline:* For fall admission, 12/10 for domestic students. Application fee: $70 ($90 for international students). Electronic applications accepted. *Financial support:* In 2009–10, 69 students received support, including 50 fellowships with full tuition reimbursements available (averaging $7,900 per year), 6 research assistantships with full and partial tuition reimbursements available (averaging $2,600 per year), 53 teaching assistantships with partial tuition reimbursements available (averaging $9,200 per year); career-related internships or fieldwork, Federal Work-Study, institutionally sponsored loans, scholarships/grants, health care benefits, and unspecified assistantships also available. Financial award applicants required to submit FAFSA. *Faculty research:* Conversation analysis, social movements, human sexuality, urban sociology, race and ethnic relations. *Unit head:* Prof. Verta Taylor, Chair, 805-893-3118, Fax: 805-893-3324, E-mail: grad-soc@soc.ucsb.edu. *Application contact:* Ra Thea, Graduate Staff Advisor, 805-893-3328, Fax: 805-893-3324, E-mail: grad-soc@soc.ucsb.edu.

University of Cincinnati, Graduate School, McMicken College of Arts and Sciences, Department of Women's, Gender, and Sexuality Studies, Cincinnati, OH 45221-0164. Offers MA, Certificate, MA/JD. Part-time programs available. *Degree requirements:* For master's, comprehensive exam, final paper/project. *Entrance requirements:* For master's, GRE General Test, 3 letters of recommendation. Additional exam requirements/recommendations for international students: Required—TOEFL (minimum score 600 paper-based), IELTS (minimum score 6.5). Electronic applications accepted. *Faculty research:* Feminist legal issues, sexuality, international political economy, Latin America, cultural/literary and environmental studies.

University of Florida, Graduate School, College of Liberal Arts and Sciences, Center for Women's Studies and Gender Research, Gainesville, FL 32611. Offers gender and development (Graduate Certificate); women's studies (MA, MWS, Graduate Certificate); MA/JD; MA/MA.

University of Georgia, Graduate School, College of Arts and Sciences, Institute for Women's Studies, Athens, GA 30602. Offers Certificate. *Students:* 1 (woman) part-time; minority (African American). 1 applicant, 100% accepted, 1 enrolled. *Expenses:* Tuition, state resident: full-time $6000; part-time $250 per credit hour. Tuition, nonresident: full-time $20,904; part-time $871 per credit hour. Required fees: $730 per semester. *Unit head:* Dr. Chris Cuomo, Director, 706-542-2846, E-mail: cuomo@uga.edu. *Application contact:* Dr. Blaise Parker, Assistant Director, 706-542-2846, Fax: 706-542-0049, E-mail: blaze@uga.edu.

University of Hawaii at Manoa, Graduate Division, College of Social Sciences, Advanced Women's Studies Program, Honolulu, HI 96822. Offers Graduate Certificate. Part-time programs available. *Students:* 7 full-time (6 women), 4 part-time (all women); includes 5 minority (all Asian Americans or Pacific Islanders), 1 international. Average age 36. 4 applicants, 50% accepted, 2 enrolled. *Entrance requirements:* Additional exam requirements/recommendations for international students: Required—TOEFL (minimum score 500 paper-based; 173 computer-based; 61 iBT), IELTS (minimum score 5). *Application deadline:* For fall admission, 3/1 for domestic and international students. Application fee: $60. *Expenses:* Tuition, state resident: full-time $8900; part-time $372 per credit. Tuition, nonresident: full-time $21,400; part-time $898 per credit. Required fees: $207 per semester. *Financial support:* In 2009–10, 1 student received support, including 7 fellowships (averaging $2,408 per year), 1 research assistantship (averaging $17,496 per year), 3 teaching assistantships (averaging $15,558 per year). *Application contact:* Susan Hippensteele, Director, 808-956-6313, Fax: 808-956-9616, E-mail: hippenst@hawaii.edu.

The University of Iowa, Graduate College, College of Liberal Arts and Sciences, Department of Women's Studies, Iowa City, IA 52242-1316. Offers PhD. *Degree requirements:* For doctorate, comprehensive exam, thesis/dissertation. *Entrance requirements:* For doctorate, GRE General Test, minimum GPA of 3.0. Additional exam requirements/recommendations for international students: Required—TOEFL (minimum score 550 paper-based; 213 computer-based; 81 iBT).

University of Lethbridge, School of Graduate Studies, Lethbridge, AB T1K 3M4, Canada. Offers accounting (MScM); addictions counseling (M Sc); agricultural biotechnology (M Sc); agricultural studies (M Sc, MA); anthropology (MA); archaeology (MA); art (MA, MFA); biochemistry (M Sc); biological sciences (M Sc); biomolecular science (PhD); biosystems and biodiversity (PhD); Canadian studies (MA); chemistry (M Sc); computer science (M Sc); computer science and geographical information science (M Sc); counseling psychology (M Ed); dramatic arts (MA); earth, space, and physical science (PhD); economics (MA); educational leadership (M Ed); English (MA); environmental science (M Sc); evolution and behavior (PhD); exercise science (M Sc); finance (MScM); French (MA); French/German (MA); French/Spanish (MA); general education (M Ed); general management (MScM); geography (M Sc, MA); German (MA); health science (M Sc); health sciences (MA); history (MA); human resource management and labour relations (MScM); individualized multidisciplinary (M Sc, MA); information systems (MScM); international management (MScM); kinesiology (M Sc, MA); management (M Sc, MA); marketing (MScM); mathematics (M Sc); music (M Mus, MA); Native American studies (MA); neuroscience (M Sc, PhD); new media (MA); nursing (M Sc); philosophy (MA); physics (M Sc); policy and strategy (MScM); political science (MA); psychology (M Sc, MA); religious studies (MA); social sciences (MA); sociology (MA); theatre and dramatic arts (MFA); theoretical and computational science (PhD); urban and regional studies (MA); women's studies (MA). Part-time and evening/weekend programs available. *Degree requirements:* For doctorate, comprehensive exam, thesis/dissertation. *Entrance requirements:* For master's, GMAT (M Sc in management), bachelor's degree in related field, minimum GPA of 3.0 during previous 20 graded semester courses, 2 years teaching or related experience (M Ed); for doctorate, master's degree, minimum graduate GPA of 3.5. Additional exam requirements/recommendations for international students: Required—TOEFL. *Faculty research:* Movement and brain plasticity, gibberellin physiology, photosynthesis, carbon cycling, molecular properties of main-group ring components.

University of Louisville, Graduate School, College of Arts and Sciences, Department of Women's and Gender Studies, Louisville, KY 40292. Offers MA, Certificate, MSSW/MA. Part-time and evening/weekend programs available. *Faculty:* 6 full-time (all women), 7 part-time/adjunct (6 women). *Students:* 17 full-time (15 women), 8 part-time (7 women); includes 3 minority (all African Americans). Average age 28. 22 applicants, 82% accepted, 12 enrolled. In 2009, 5 master's, 2 other advanced degrees awarded. *Degree requirements:* For master's, thesis or alternative. *Entrance requirements:* For master's, GRE. *Application deadline:* For fall admission, 8/1 for domestic students, 7/15 for international students; for spring admission, 12/20 for domestic students, 12/1 for international students. Application fee: $50. Electronic applications accepted. *Financial support:* In 2009–10, 9 students received support, including 1 teaching assistantship with full tuition reimbursement available (averaging $12,000 per year); scholarships/grants also available. Financial award application deadline: 5/1; financial award applicants required to submit FAFSA. *Faculty research:* Gender representation in popular media; intersections of race, class, gender and sexuality in U.S. popular culture and popular music; interconnectedness between the performance of identity and racialized body politics for African diasporan women and men; nineteenth century women/gender in the U.S.; medicine as a gendered practice; gender, race, and class dynamics in parenting and the workplace. *Unit head:* Nancy M. Theriot, Chairperson, 502-852-8160, Fax: 502-852-4421, E-mail: nancyt@louisville.edu. *Application contact:* Libby Leggett, Director, Graduate Admissions, 502-852-3101, Fax: 502-852-6536, E-mail: gradadm@louisville.edu.

University of Maryland, Baltimore County, Graduate School, College of Arts, Humanities and Social Sciences, Program in Gender and Women's Studies, Baltimore, MD 21250. Offers Postbaccalaureate Certificate. Part-time and evening/weekend programs available. *Students:* 2 applicants, 50% accepted, 0 enrolled. In 2009, 1 Postbaccalaureate Certificate awarded. *Application deadline:* Applications are processed on a rolling basis. Application fee: $50. Electronic applications accepted. *Financial support:* In 2009–10, 1 teaching assistantship with partial tuition reimbursement (averaging $7,500 per year) was awarded; health care benefits also available. *Faculty research:* Feminist theory, reproductive and sexual politics, U.S. women's history. *Unit head:* Dr. Carole McCann, Director/Associate Professor, 410-455-2161, E-mail: gwst@umbc.edu. *Application contact:* Dr. Carole McCann, Director/Associate Professor, 410-455-2161, E-mail: gwst@umbc.edu.

University of Maryland, College Park, Academic Affairs, College of Arts and Humanities, Department of Women's Studies, College Park, MD 20742. Offers MA, PhD. *Faculty:* 69 full-time (66 women), 1 (woman) part-time/adjunct. *Students:* 26 full-time (all women), 1 (woman) part-time; includes 7 minority (5 African Americans, 1 Asian American or Pacific Islander, 1 Hispanic American), 4 international. 59 applicants, 14% accepted, 4 enrolled. In 2009, 5 master's, 2 doctorates awarded. *Degree requirements:* For master's, thesis or alternative; for doctorate, one foreign language, thesis/dissertation or alternative. *Entrance requirements:* For master's, GRE General Test, writing sample, 3 letters of recommendation. Additional exam requirements/recommendations for international students: Required—TOEFL. *Application deadline:* For fall admission, 12/15 for domestic and international students. Application fee: $60. *Expenses:* Tuition, area resident: Part-time $471 per credit hour. Tuition, state resident: part-time $471 per credit hour. Tuition, nonresident: part-time $1016 per credit hour. Required fees: $337.04 per term. *Financial support:* In 2009–10, 7 fellowships with full and partial tuition reimbursements (averaging $12,809 per year), 17 teaching assistantships with tuition reimbursements (averaging $16,860 per year) were awarded; research assistantships, career-related internships or fieldwork, Federal Work-Study, and scholarships/grants also available. Support available to part-time students. *Faculty research:* Gender roles, national and global diversity, sexuality. *Unit head:* Seung-kyung Kim, Acting Chair, 301-450-7293, E-mail: skim2@umd.edu. *Application contact:* Dean of Graduate School, 301-405-0376, Fax: 301-314-9305.

University of Massachusetts Boston, Office of Graduate Studies, Division of Continuing Education and John W. McCormack Graduate School of Policy Studies, Program in Women in Politics and Government, Boston, MA 02125-3393. Offers Certificate. Part-time and evening/weekend programs available. *Degree requirements:* For Certificate, practicum, final project. *Entrance requirements:* For degree, interview, minimum GPA of 2.75.

University of Massachusetts Boston, Office of Graduate Studies, John W. McCormack Graduate School of Policy Studies, Boston, MA 02125-3393. Offers gerontology (MA, MS, PhD, Certificate), including gerontology (MS, PhD, Certificate), gerontology research (MA), management in aging services (MA); public affairs (MS); public policy (PhD); women in politics and government (Certificate). Certificate program in women in politics and government offered jointly with Division of Continuing Education. Part-time and evening/weekend programs available. *Degree requirements:* For doctorate, thesis/dissertation; for Certificate, practicum, final project. *Entrance requirements:* For doctorate, GRE General Test; for Certificate, interview, minimum GPA of 2.5.

University of Michigan, Horace H. Rackham School of Graduate Studies, College of Literature, Science, and the Arts, Department of Women's Studies, Ann Arbor, MI 48109. Offers English and women's studies (PhD); history and women's studies (PhD); lesbian, gay, bisexual, transgender, queer (LGBTQ) studies (Certificate); psychology and women's studies (PhD); sociology and women's studies (PhD); women's studies (Certificate). *Faculty:* 74 full-time (68 women). *Students:* 68 full-time (63 women); includes 21 minority (7 African Americans, 1 American Indian/Alaska Native, 8 Asian Americans or Pacific Islanders, 5 Hispanic Americans), 12 international. Average age 31. 119 applicants, 9% accepted, 7 enrolled. In 2009, 5 doctorates, 8 other advanced degrees awarded. *Degree requirements:* For doctorate, variable foreign language requirement, comprehensive exam (for some programs), thesis/dissertation. *Entrance requirements:* For doctorate, GRE General Test, previous undergraduate course work in women's studies. *Application deadline:* For fall admission, 12/1 for domestic and international students. Application fee: $60 ($75 for international students). Electronic applications accepted. *Expenses:* Tuition, state resident: full-time $17,286; part-time $1099 per credit hour. Tuition, nonresident: full-time $34,944; part-time $2080 per credit hour. Required fees: $95 per semester. Tuition and fees vary according to course load, degree level and program. *Financial support:* In 2009–10, 34 students received support, including 19 fellowships with full tuition reimbursements available (averaging $16,000 per year), 15 teaching assistantships with full and partial tuition reimbursements available (averaging $16,135 per year); career-related internships or fieldwork, institutionally sponsored loans, scholarships/grants, traineeships, health care benefits, and unspecified assistantships also available. *Faculty research:* Gender issues; LGBTQ studies; sexuality; women and science; global feminism. *Unit head:* Anne Herrmann, Chair, 734-763-2047, Fax: 734-647-4943, E-mail: anneh@umich.edu. *Application contact:* Aimee Germain, Graduate Program Coordinator, 734-763-2047, Fax: 734-647-4943, E-mail: wsdgradlnquiry@umich.edu.

University of Minnesota, Twin Cities Campus, Graduate School, College of Liberal Arts, Department of Gender, Women, and Sexuality Studies, Minneapolis, MN 55455-0213. Offers feminist studies (PhD). *Degree requirements:* For doctorate, comprehensive exam, thesis/dissertation. *Entrance requirements:* For doctorate, GRE. Additional exam requirements/recommendations for international students: Required—TOEFL (minimum score 550 paper-based). Electronic applications accepted. *Faculty research:* Transnational feminist theories, critical development theory, feminist postcolonialisms, feminist science studies and studying of health, literature, Asian diasporas, sexuality and queer theory.

University of Nevada, Las Vegas, Graduate College, College of Liberal Arts, Women's Studies Department, Las Vegas, NV 89154-5055. Offers Certificate. *Faculty:* 4 full-time (all women). *Students:* 3 part-time (all women). Average age 33. 4 applicants, 75% accepted, 3 enrolled. In 2009, 2 Certificates awarded. *Entrance requirements:* Additional exam requirements/recommendations for international students: Required—TOEFL (minimum score 550 paper-based; 213 computer-based; 80 iBT), IELTS (minimum score 7). *Application deadline:* For fall admission, 6/15 priority date for domestic students, 5/1 for international students; for spring admission, 11/15 priority date for domestic students, 10/1 for international students. Applications are processed on a rolling basis. Application fee: $60 ($95 for international students). Electronic applications accepted. *Financial support:* In 2009–10, 2 students received support, including 2 research assistantships with partial tuition reimbursements available (averaging $11,000 per year); institutionally sponsored loans, scholarships/grants, health care benefits, and unspecified assistantships also available. Financial award application deadline: 3/1. *Faculty research:* Transnational feminism; intersection of gender, race, class and sexuality; sexuality studies; Chicana/Latina feminism; gender and development. *Unit head:* Dr. S. Charusheela, Chair/ Associate Professor, 702-895-0467, Fax: 702-895-0850, E-mail: s.charusheela@unlv.edu. *Application contact:* Graduate College Admissions Evaluator, 702-895-3320, Fax: 702-895-4180, E-mail: gradcollege@unlv.edu.

University of New Mexico, Graduate School, College of Arts and Sciences, Program in Women Studies, Albuquerque, NM 87131-2039. Offers Graduate Certificate. *Faculty:* 1 (woman) full-time, 1 (woman) part-time/adjunct. *Entrance requirements:* For degree, must be enrolled in degree-granting program before acceptance for Graduate Certification in Women Studies. *Application deadline:* Applications are processed on a rolling basis. Application fee: $50. *Expenses:* Tuition, state resident: full-time $2099; part-time $233.20 per credit hour. Tuition, nonresident: full-time $6650. Required fees: $25 per semester. Tuition and fees vary according to course load, program and reciprocity agreements. *Unit head:* Dr. Rajeshwar Vallury, Director, 505-277-3854, Fax: 505-277-0267, E-mail: rvallury@unm.edu. *Application contact:* Dr. Rajeshwar Vallury, Director, 505-277-3854, Fax: 505-277-0267, E-mail: rvallury@unm.edu.

The University of North Carolina at Greensboro, Graduate School, College of Arts and Sciences, Department of English, Greensboro, NC 27412-5001. Offers creative writing (MFA); English (M Ed, MA, PhD, Certificate), including American literature (PhD), English (M Ed, MA), English literature (PhD), rhetoric and composition (PhD), technical writing (Certificate), women's studies (Certificate). *Degree requirements:* For master's, comprehensive exam; for doctorate, variable foreign language requirement, thesis/dissertation, preliminary exam. *Entrance requirements:* For master's, GRE General Test, minimum GPA of 3.0; for doctorate, GRE General Test, GRE Subject Test, critical writing sample, minimum GPA of 3.0. Additional exam requirements/recommendations for international students: Required—TOEFL. Electronic applications accepted.

The University of North Carolina at Greensboro, Graduate School, College of Arts and Sciences, Program in Women's and Gender Studies, Greensboro, NC 27412-5001. Offers MA, Certificate. Electronic applications accepted.

University of Northern Iowa, Graduate College, Program in Women's and Gender Studies, Cedar Falls, IA 50614. Offers MA. *Students:* 4 full-time (3 women), 1 (woman) part-time; includes 1 minority (African American), 1 international. 4 applicants, 75% accepted, 3 enrolled. In 2009, 3 master's awarded. *Degree requirements:* For master's, comprehensive exam (for some programs), thesis or alternative. *Entrance requirements:* For master's, minimum GPA of 3.0. Additional exam requirements/recommendations for international students: Required—TOEFL (minimum score 500 paper-based; 180 computer-based; 61 iBT). *Application deadline:* Applications are processed on a rolling basis. Application fee: $30 ($50 for international students). Electronic applications accepted. *Financial support:* Application deadline: 2/1. *Unit head:* Dr. Phyllis L. Baker, Director/Professor, 319-273-7102, Fax: 319-273-3053, E-mail: phyllis.baker@uni.edu. *Application contact:* Laurie S. Russell, Record Analyst, 319-273-2623, Fax: 319-273-6792, E-mail: laurie.russell@uni.edu.

University of Ottawa, Faculty of Graduate and Postdoctoral Studies, Faculty of Social Sciences, Institute of Women's Studies, Ottawa, ON K1N 6N5, Canada. Offers criminology (MA, MCA); education (MA); English (MA); history (MA); human kinetics (MA); law (LL M); lettres Françaises (MA); nursing (M Sc); pastoral studies (MA); political science (MA); religious studies (MA); sociology (MA). *Degree requirements:* For master's, thesis or alternative.

University of Pittsburgh, School of Arts and Sciences, Program in Women's Studies, Pittsburgh, PA 15260. Offers Doctoral Certificate, Master's Certificate. Part-time programs available. *Faculty:* 64 full-time (52 women). *Students:* 26 full-time (24 women); includes 1 minority (African American). Average age 30. 2 applicants, 100% accepted, 2 enrolled. *Degree requirements:* For other advanced degree, scholarly essay. *Entrance requirements:* Additional exam requirements/recommendations for international students: Required—TOEFL. *Application deadline:* Applications are processed on a rolling basis. Application fee: $50. Electronic applications accepted. *Expenses:* Tuition, state resident: full-time $16,402; part-time $665 per credit. Tuition, nonresident: full-time $28,694; part-time $1175 per credit. Required fees: $690; $175 per term. Tuition and fees vary according to program. *Financial support:* In 2009–10, 2 students received support, including 2 teaching assistantships with full tuition reimbursements available (averaging $15,675 per year); unspecified assistantships also available. Financial award application deadline: 2/20. *Faculty research:* Global feminisms; gender and interpersonal violence; race and gender studies; representation and gender in media, arts, and literature; concepts of the body. *Unit head:* Jean Ferguson Carr, Director, 412-624-6486, Fax: 412-624-6492, E-mail: wstudies@pitt.edu. *Application contact:* Jean Ferguson Carr, Director, 412-624-6486, Fax: 412-624-6492, E-mail: wstudies@pitt.edu.

University of Regina, Faculty of Graduate Studies and Research, Faculty of Arts, Department of Women's Studies, Regina, SK S4S 0A2, Canada. Offers MA. Offered as a special case program. Part-time programs available. *Faculty:* 2 full-time (both women). *Students:* 1 (woman) full-time, 1 (woman) part-time. 2 applicants, 50% accepted. *Degree requirements:* For master's, thesis. *Entrance requirements:* Additional exam requirements/recommendations for international students: Required—TOEFL (minimum score 580 paper-based; 237 computer-based; 80 iBT). *Application deadline:* Applications are processed on a rolling basis. Application fee: $90 ($100 for international students). Electronic applications accepted. *Financial support:* Fellowships, research assistantships, teaching assistantships, scholarships/grants available. Financial award application deadline: 6/15. *Unit head:* Dr. Wendee Kubik, Graduate Program Coordinator, 306-585-4668, E-mail: wendee.kubik@uregina.ca. *Application contact:* Dr. Dongyan Blachford, Associate Dean, 306-585-5186, Fax: 306-337-2444, E-mail: dongyan.blachford@uregina.ca.

University of Saskatchewan, College of Graduate Studies and Research, College of Arts and Sciences, Department of Women's and Gender Studies, Saskatoon, SK S7N 5A2, Canada. Offers MA, PhD. *Faculty:* 5. *Degree requirements:* For master's, thesis; for doctorate, comprehensive exam (for some programs), thesis/dissertation. *Entrance requirements:* Additional exam requirements/recommendations for international students: Required—TOEFL (minimum score 80 iBT); Recommended—IELTS (minimum score 6.5). *Application deadline:* For fall admission, 7/1 priority date for domestic students. Applications are processed on a rolling basis. Application fee: $75. Electronic applications accepted. Tuition and fees charges are reported in Canadian dollars. *Expenses:* Tuition, area resident: Full-time $3000 Canadian dollars; part-time $500 Canadian dollars per term. Required fees: $700 Canadian dollars; $100 Canadian dollars per term. *Financial support:* Fellowships, research assistantships, teaching assistantships available. *Unit head:* Dr. Joan Brsa, Acting Head, 306-966-4256, Fax: 306-966-4559, E-mail: jan.borsa@usask.ca. *Application contact:* Dr. Pamela Downe, Graduate Chair, 306-966-1974, E-mail: pamela.downe@usask.ca.

University of South Carolina, The Graduate School, College of Arts and Sciences, Program in Women's Studies, Columbia, SC 29208. Offers Certificate. Part-time programs available. *Entrance requirements:* For degree, GRE General Test or MAT. Additional exam requirements/recommendations for international students: Required—TOEFL. Electronic applications accepted. *Faculty research:* Health; pedagogy; intersection of race, class, gender; public policy; politics of culture and representations, feminist political economics.

University of South Florida, Graduate School, College of Arts and Sciences, Department of Women's Studies, Tampa, FL 33620-9951. Offers MA. Part-time programs available. *Students:* 8 full-time (all women); includes 1 minority (American Indian/Alaska Native), 1 international. Average age 32. 6 applicants, 83% accepted, 4 enrolled. In 2009, 5 master's awarded. *Degree requirements:* For master's, comprehensive exam, thesis or internship. *Entrance requirements:* For master's, GRE General Test, 3 letters of reference, writing sample, minimum GPA of 3.0 in last 60 hours. Additional exam requirements/recommendations for international students: Required—TOEFL (minimum score 550 paper-based; 213 computer-based). *Application deadline:* For fall admission, 2/15 for domestic students, 1/2 for international students; for spring admission, 10/15 for domestic students, 6/1 for international students. Applications are processed on a rolling basis. Application fee: $30. *Financial support:* In 2009–10, 7 students received support, including teaching assistantships with tuition reimbursements available (averaging $9,000 per year). Financial award application deadline: 3/1. *Unit head:* Dr. Kim Vaz, Chairperson, 813-974-0985, Fax: 813-974-0336, E-mail: vaz@cas.usf.edu. *Application contact:* Marilyn Myerson, Director, 813-974-0979, Fax: 813-974-0336, E-mail: myerson@cas.l.usf.edu.

The University of Texas at El Paso, Graduate School, College of Liberal Arts, Women's Studies Program, El Paso, TX 79968-0001. Offers women's and gender studies (Certificate).

University of Washington, Graduate School, College of Arts and Sciences, Department of Women Studies, Seattle, WA 98195. Offers PhD. Terminal master's awarded for partial completion of doctoral program. *Degree requirements:* For doctorate, one foreign language, thesis/dissertation, exam. *Entrance requirements:* For doctorate, GRE General Test. Additional exam requirements/recommendations for international students: Required—TOEFL. Electronic applications accepted. *Faculty research:* Women's history in U.S. and China; Native American ethnography and identity; women, science, and technology; political economy of development, feminism and nationalism.

University of Wisconsin–Madison, Graduate School, College of Letters and Science, Department of History, Madison, WI 53706-1380. Offers African history (MA, PhD); Central Asian history (MA, PhD); comparative world history (MA, PhD); East Asian history (MA, PhD); European history (MA, PhD); gender and women's history (MA, PhD); Latin American and Caribbean history (MA, PhD); Middle Eastern history (MA, PhD); South Asian history (MA, PhD); Southeast Asian history (MA, PhD); United States history (MA, PhD). Terminal master's awarded for partial completion of doctoral program. *Degree requirements:* For master's, thesis (for some programs); for doctorate, variable foreign language requirement, thesis/dissertation. *Entrance requirements:* For master's and doctorate, GRE General Test. Additional exam requirements/recommendations for international students: Required—Michigan English Language Assessment Battery or TOEFL. Electronic applications accepted. *Expenses:* Tuition, state resident: part-time $594 per credit. Tuition, nonresident: part-time $1504 per credit. Required fees: $65 per credit. Tuition and fees vary according to course load, program and reciprocity agreements. *Faculty research:* American, African, European, Asian, Latin American, and Middle Eastern history.

Washington State University, Graduate School, College of Liberal Arts, Program in American Studies, Pullman, WA 99164. Offers ethnic studies (MA, PhD); feminist studies (MA, PhD); history (MA, PhD); literature (MA, PhD). Part-time programs available. *Faculty:* 35. *Students:* 23 full-time (14 women), 4 part-time (2 women); includes 17 minority (5 African Americans, 4 American Indian/Alaska Native, 4 Asian Americans or Pacific Islanders, 4 Hispanic Americans), 2 international. Average age 35. 55 applicants, 7% accepted, 3 enrolled. In 2009, 1 master's, 3 doctorates awarded. *Degree requirements:* For master's, one foreign language, comprehensive exam (for some programs), thesis optional, oral exam; for doctorate, one foreign language, comprehensive exam (for some programs), thesis/dissertation, oral exam. *Entrance requirements:* For master's, GRE General Test, * Send to the Graduate School an official application form and official college transcripts sent directly from each institution attended. * Send to the American Studies program: A 3 to 5 page statement of purpose describing your areas of interest and why the program minimum GPA of 3.0, writing sample, 3 letters of recommendation; for doctorate, GRE General Test, * Send to the Graduate School an official application form and official college transcripts sent directly from each institution attended. * Send to the American Studies program: A 3 to 5 page statement of purpose describing your areas of interest and why the program minimum GPA of 3.0, writing sample, 3 letters of recommendation. Additional exam requirements/recommendations for international students: Required—TOEFL, IELTS. *Application deadline:* For fall admission, 1/10 priority date for domestic and international students; for spring admission, 7/1 priority date for domestic and international students. Applications are processed on a rolling basis. Application fee: $50. *Financial support:* In 2009–10, 1 fellowship (averaging $6,950 per year), 3 research assistantships with full and partial tuition reimbursements (averaging $14,634 per year), 17 teaching assistantships with full and partial tuition reimbursements (averaging $13,383 per year) were awarded; career-related internships or fieldwork, Federal Work-Study, institutionally sponsored loans, health care benefits, tuition waivers (partial), and teaching associateships also available. Financial award application deadline: 2/15; financial award applicants required to submit FAFSA. *Faculty research:* The American West in multicultural perspective; nineteenth century historical, literary, and cultural studies; comparative American ethnic literatures and cultures; American cultures and the environment; American rhetoric. *Unit head:* Dr. Rory J. Ong, Director, 509-335-1560, E-mail: rjong@mail.wsu.edu. *Application contact:* Graduate School Admissions, 800-GRADWSU, Fax: 509-335-1949, E-mail: gradsch@wsu.edu.

Women's Studies

West Chester University of Pennsylvania, Office of Graduate Studies, College of Arts and Sciences, Department of Women's Studies, West Chester, PA 19383. Offers leadership for women (MSA, Certificate). Part-time and evening/weekend programs available. *Students:* 1 applicant, 100% accepted, 0 enrolled. *Degree requirements:* For master's, comprehensive exam. *Entrance requirements:* For master's, GMAT, GRE General Test, or MAT, resume, 2 letters of reference, interview. Additional exam requirements/recommendations for international students: Required—TOEFL (minimum score 550 paper-based; 213 computer-based; 80 iBT). *Application deadline:* For fall admission, 4/15 priority date for domestic students, 3/15 for international students; for spring admission, 10/15 for domestic students, 9/1 for international students. Applications are processed on a rolling basis. Application fee: $35. Electronic applications accepted. *Expenses:* Tuition, state resident: full-time $6666; part-time $370 per credit. Tuition, nonresident: full-time $10,666; part-time $593 per credit. Required fees: $122.56 per credit. *Financial support:* In 2009–10, research assistantships with full and partial tuition reimbursements (averaging $5,000 per year); unspecified assistantships also available. Support available to part-time students. Financial award application deadline: 2/15; financial award applicants required to submit FAFSA. *Unit head:* Dr. Jen Bacon, Director, 610-436-2464, E-mail: jbacon@wcupa.edu. *Application contact:* Dr. Lorraine Bernotsky, Graduate Coordinator, 610-738-0576, E-mail: lbernotsky@wcupa.edu.

Western Seminary, Graduate Programs, Program in Ministry and Leadership, Portland, OR 97215-3367. Offers chaplaincy (MA); coaching (MA); Jewish ministry (MA); pastoral care to women (MA); youth ministry (MA). *Students:* 93 full-time (38 women), 586 part-time (198 women); includes 20 minority (5 African Americans, 1 American Indian/Alaska Native, 11 Asian Americans or Pacific Islanders, 3 Hispanic Americans). Average age 29. 132 applicants, 92% accepted, 86 enrolled. *Degree requirements:* For master's, practicum. *Entrance requirements:* Additional exam requirements/recommendations for international students: Required—TOEFL. *Application deadline:* For fall admission, 7/19 priority date for domestic students; for winter admission, 11/8 priority date for domestic students; for spring admission, 3/14 priority date for domestic students. Applications are processed on a rolling basis. Application fee: $50. *Expenses:* Tuition: Full-time $3280; part-time $410 per credit hour. *Financial support:* Applicants required to submit FAFSA. *Unit head:* Beverly Hislop, Director, 503-517-1881, E-mail: bhislop@westernseminary.edu. *Application contact:* Dr. Robert W. Wiggins, Registrar/Dean of Student Development, 503-517-1820, Fax: 503-517-1801, E-mail: rwiggins@westernseminary.edu.

York University, Faculty of Graduate Studies, Faculty of Arts, Program in Women's Studies, Toronto, ON M3J 1P3, Canada. Offers MA, PhD. *Degree requirements:* For master's, thesis or alternative; for doctorate, comprehensive exam, thesis/dissertation. Electronic applications accepted.

VILLANOVA UNIVERSITY

Department of Modern Languages and Literature
Program in Hispanic Studies

Program of Study

The Graduate Program in Hispanic Studies of the Department of Modern Languages and Literature at Villanova University provides students with a critical and theoretical foundation in literary studies as well as ample opportunities for interdisciplinary work in specialized areas of the literatures and cultures of Spain and Latin America. The Department prides itself on its small classes and warm and friendly atmosphere in which regular and informal interaction between faculty and students is encouraged. In and out of class, students enjoy an open and supportive environment.

The 30-credit-hour Master of Arts (M.A.) can be completed by full-time students within one year, although many students obtain their degree in two years. The program is geared to prepare students to pursue a Ph.D. in Spanish or Latin American literature, European studies, cultural studies, and/or comparative literature. Students may also enroll in the program to pursue a career in teaching in higher education or at the secondary level. High school teachers can enhance their knowledge and skills as a means of career advancement. Upon successful completion of course work, with a minimum GPA of 3.0 (3.5 for teaching assistants), each candidate must pass a written comprehensive exam. It is strongly recommended that each student meet with the faculty members of his or her chosen area to discuss readings, literary criticism, possible questions, and strategies for successful completion of the exam.

Certificates of advanced study at the pre-master's and post-master's level are also offered. The program emphasizes the contextualization of literary production and changing relations between the literatures and cultures of Spain and Latin America. The aim of the program is to prepare students to become first-rate scholars and teachers. To this end, the faculty places emphasis on providing students with a solid knowledge of literature and critical theory, without neglecting a professional pedagogical training. Eighteen (18) semester graduate credit hours of study are required of pre-master's certificate candidates. Those who already hold an M.A. in Spanish may pursue specialized studies toward a post-master's certificate. Upon completion of 15 credits in the M.A. program, and with a minimum GPA of 3.0, the student is awarded a post-master's certificate.

Research Facilities

The University library contains more than 780,000 volumes and 5,600 current periodicals. Special library holdings include the collection of the Augustinian Historical Institute and an extensive collection of works in contemporary Continental philosophy.

The Office of University Information Technologies provides data and voice communication, computing services, and access to remote computing and information services over the Internet; offers noncredit seminars and workshops on popular computer software and the use of the Villanova phone system; and maintains state-of-the-art computer labs for students on campus.

Financial Aid

Graduate assistantships are awarded on a competitive basis. The assistantship stipend began at approximately $13,100 in 2009–10 and carried with it a waiver of all tuition and academic fees. A few research fellowships are also awarded each year. A number of tuition scholarships are available; they provide a waiver of all tuition and academic fees. In addition, teachers who enroll in a program in the College of Liberal Arts and Sciences may be entitled to a tuition reduction. Application materials must be received by March 1 for consideration to receive an assistantship or scholarship.

In addition, the office of the director of financial aid administers the Federal Stafford Student Loan, the unsubsidized Federal Stafford Student Loan, and the Federal Supplemental Loans for Students.

Cost of Study

Graduate tuition ranged from approximately $630 to $700 per credit hour in 2009–10. In addition, there is a University fee of $30 each semester.

Living and Housing Costs

The University does not maintain accommodations for graduate students, but second-year students are eligible for positions as resident counselors in the dormitories. The area has a wide selection of living quarters that are convenient to the campus.

Student Group

Approximately 2,200 graduate students were enrolled for the fall 2008 term, of whom 985 were in liberal arts and sciences programs. Total University enrollment is approximately 12,000, including 7,577 full-time undergraduates, 1,000 part-time evening (undergraduate and continuing studies) students, and 1,000 students in the School of Law. There are about equal numbers of men and women graduate students.

Location

Located in the heart of the Delaware Valley's Main Line, the University occupies more than 200 handsomely landscaped acres in the town of Villanova, 12 miles west of Philadelphia. The location combines the advantages of a tranquil suburban setting with proximity to a large metropolitan city known for its outstanding historical, educational, and cultural resources.

The University

Villanova University is a private institution founded in 1842 by the Augustinian Fathers. Graduate programs were first administered separately in 1931. Currently, there are five academic units in addition to graduate studies: the Colleges of Arts and Sciences, Commerce and Finance, Engineering, Nursing, and the School of Law.

Applying

Applicants should have at least 18 undergraduate credits and a 3.0 average in history. The Graduate Record Examinations General Test is required for admission to the program. International applicants must take the TOEFL examination. Application deadlines are March 1 for fall admission, November 15 for spring admission, and May 1 for summer admission. The deadline is March 1 for those applying for a graduate assistantship.

Applicants should have a minimum of 30 undergraduate credits in one of three curriculum tracks, with at least a 3.0 GPA, or an undergraduate degree from an accredited institution. Students must submit to the Office of Graduate Studies the completed application and nonrefundable $50 fee (online), official GRE scores, and two official undergraduate transcripts, as well as TOEFL scores (if applicable). In addition, applicants must submit three letters of recommendation and a writing sample in Spanish (no more than ten pages) to the graduate program director. Those applying to the pre- or post-M.A. certificate program need only to submit the application, fee, and official undergraduate and graduate transcripts. Deadlines for the fall, spring, and summer semesters are May 1, November 15, and May 1, respectively.

Correspondence and Information

Carlos Trujillo, Director
Graduate Program in Hispanic Studies
Department of Modern Languages and Literatures
Villanova University, SAC303
Villanova, Pennsylvania 19085-1696
Phone: 610-519-6956
E-mail: carlos.trujillo@villanova.edu
Web site: http://www.villanova.edu/artsci/modernlanglit/graduate/

Villanova University

THE FACULTY AND THEIR RESEARCH

Lee B. Abraham, Assistant Professor of Spanish; Ph.D., New Mexico. Language variation in Spanish, sociolinguistic approaches to second-language acquisition, new technologies in language learning and teaching.

Jose Luis Gastanaga Ponce de Leon, Assistant Professor; Ph.D., Princeton. Colonial Latin American historiography and literature, early-modern Spanish literature, autobiography and subject formation.

Mercedes Juliá, Professor and Chair of the Department; Ph.D., Chicago. Nineteenth-, twentieth-, and twenty-first-century Hispanic literature; cultural studies; translation skills.

Silvia Nagy-Zekmi, Professor of Hispanic and Cultural Studies and Director of the Center for Arab and Islamic Studies; Ph.D., Eötvös Loránd (Budapest). Cultural and postcolonial theories, gender studies, contemporary Latin American literature and culture, literary and cultural practices of the Arab world and North Africa.

Estrella Ogden, Professor; Ph.D., Temple. Latin American poetry, narrative, theater, literature through the arts.

Carmen Peraita, Professor and Coordinator of Spanish Studies; Ph.D., California, Santa Barbara. Early-modern Peninsular literature, historiographical discourse, cultural studies.

Salvatore Poeta, Associate Professor and Director of the Spanish Internship Program; Ph.D., Pennsylvania. Early-modern Spanish poetry, Spanish poetry (modern to present day), Spanish theater (modern to present day), Spanish short narrative, literary theory and genre studies.

Carlos Trujillo, Associate Professor and Director of the Graduate Program in Hispanic Studies; Ph.D., Pennsylvania. Latin American narrative and poetry, Chilean literature from the twentieth century, creative writing.

Section 16
Communication and Media

This section contains a directory of institutions offering graduate work in communication and media, followed by in-depth entries submitted by institutions that chose to prepare detailed program descriptions. Additional information about programs listed in the directory but not augmented by an in-depth entry may be obtained by writing directly to the dean of a graduate school or chair of a department at the address given in the directory.

For programs offering related work, see also in this book *Film, Television, and Video; Language and Literature;* and *Psychology and Counseling.* In the other guides in this series:

Graduate Programs in Engineering & Applied Sciences

See *Computer Science and Information Technology* and *Telecommunications*

Graduate Programs in Business, Education, Health, Information Studies, Law & Social Work

See *Advertising and Public Relations*

CONTENTS

Program Directories

Communication—General 610
Arts Journalism 632
Broadcast Journalism 632
Corporate and Organizational Communication 633
Health Communication 638
Internet and Interactive Multimedia 639
Journalism 642
Mass Communication 648
Media Studies 654
Publishing 661
Rhetoric 662
Speech and Interpersonal Communication 666
Technical Communication 671

Close-Ups

American University 673
Boston University 675
CUNY Graduate School of Journalism 677
Hawai'i Pacific University 679
Point Park University 681
Syracuse University 683
Communications (Display) 622
University of Southern California 685
Communications (Display) 629

See also:

American University—International Service 849
Pratt Institute—Art and Design 119

Communication—General

Abilene Christian University, Graduate School, College of Arts and Sciences, Department of Communication, Program in Communication, Abilene, TX 79699-9100. Offers MA. Part-time programs available. *Faculty:* 8 part-time/adjunct (2 women). *Students:* 16 full-time (5 women), 9 part-time (8 women); includes 5 minority (4 African Americans, 1 Hispanic American), 7 international. 20 applicants, 80% accepted, 8 enrolled. In 2009, 11 master's awarded. *Degree requirements:* For master's, one foreign language, comprehensive exam, thesis optional. *Entrance requirements:* For master's, GRE General Test. Additional exam requirements/recommendations for international students: Required—TOEFL (minimum score 213 computer-based). *Application deadline:* For fall admission, 4/1 priority date for domestic students; for spring admission, 11/1 for domestic students. Applications are processed on a rolling basis. Application fee: $40. Electronic applications accepted. *Expenses:* Tuition: Full-time $11,520; part-time $640 per hour. Required fees: $1090; $53.50 per hour. $10 per term. Tuition and fees vary according to program. *Financial support:* In 2009–10, 22 students received support; teaching assistantships, Federal Work-Study available. Support available to part-time students. Financial award application deadline: 4/1; financial award applicants required to submit FAFSA. *Faculty research:* Intercultural communication, family communication, forensics, organizational communication. *Unit head:* Dr. Paul Lakey, Graduate Adviser, 325-674-2292, Fax: 325-674-6966, E-mail: lakeyp@acu.edu. *Application contact:* William Horn, Graduate Admissions Counselor, 325-674-2656, Fax: 325-674-6717, E-mail: gradinfo@acu.edu.

American University, School of Communication, Washington, DC 20016-8001. Offers MA, MFA. *Accreditation:* ACEJMC (one or more programs are accredited). Part-time and evening/weekend programs available. *Faculty:* 44 full-time (23 women), 15 part-time/adjunct. *Students:* 171 full-time (109 women), 199 part-time (125 women); includes 91 minority (65 African Americans, 17 Asian Americans or Pacific Islanders, 9 Hispanic Americans), 26 international. Average age 27. 685 applicants, 64% accepted, 200 enrolled. In 2009, 185 degrees awarded. *Degree requirements:* For master's, comprehensive exam, thesis or alternative. *Entrance requirements:* For master's, GRE General Test. Additional exam requirements/recommendations for international students: Required—TOEFL (minimum score 600 paper-based; 260 computer-based; 100 iBT), IELTS (minimum score 7). *Application deadline:* For fall admission, 2/1 priority date for domestic students, 4/1 priority date for international students; for spring admission, 11/15 for domestic students. Applications are processed on a rolling basis. Application fee: $50. Electronic applications accepted. *Expenses:* Tuition: Full-time $22,266; part-time $1237 per credit hour. Required fees: $430. Tuition and fees vary according to program. *Financial support:* In 2009–10, 64 students received support, including 6 fellowships with partial tuition reimbursements available (averaging $23,000 per year), 15 research assistantships with partial tuition reimbursements available (averaging $18,000 per year), 15 teaching assistantships with partial tuition reimbursements available (averaging $18,000 per year); career-related internships or fieldwork, Federal Work-Study, institutionally sponsored loans, scholarships/grants, and tuition waivers (partial) also available. Financial award application deadline: 2/1; financial award applicants required to submit FAFSA. *Faculty research:* New communication technology, documentaries and public broadcasting, litigation and public relations, dissident media, race and gender and the media, international journalism and human rights, social media. *Unit head:* Larry Kirkman, Dean, 202-885-2058, Fax: 202-885-2099, E-mail: larry@american.edu. *Application contact:* Sharmeen Ahsan-Bracciale, Director of Graduate Services, 202-885-2040, Fax: 202-885-2019, E-mail: sharmeen@american.edu.

See Close-Up on page 673.

The American University in Cairo, Graduate Studies and Research, School of Business, Economics and Communication, Department of Journalism and Mass Communication, Cairo, Egypt. Offers journalism and mass communication (MA); television and digital journalism (MA). Part-time programs available. *Degree requirements:* For master's, thesis (for some programs). *Entrance requirements:* For master's, English entrance exam, GMAT. Electronic applications accepted. *Faculty research:* Mass media and national development/censorship, intercultural photo communication, comparative journalism/television.

The American University of Paris, Graduate Programs, Paris, France. Offers cross-cultural and sustainable business management (MA); cultural translation (MA); global communications (MA); global communications and civil society (MA); international affairs, conflict resolution and civil society development (MA); Middle East and Islamic studies (MA); Middle East and Islamic studies and international affairs (MA); public policy and international affairs (MA); public policy and international law (MA). *Faculty:* 14 full-time (3 women). *Students:* 143 full-time (109 women). 71 applicants, 92% accepted, 34 enrolled. *Degree requirements:* For master's, thesis. *Entrance requirements:* For master's, minimum undergraduate GPA of 3.0. *Application deadline:* For fall admission, 4/15 priority date for international students; for spring admission, 11/15 priority date for international students. Applications are processed on a rolling basis. Application fee: $75. Tuition charges are reported in euros. *Expenses:* Tuition: Full-time 23,460 euros. *Financial support:* Scholarships/grants available. Financial award applicants required to submit FAFSA. *Unit head:* Celeste Schenk, President, 33 1-40620659, E-mail: president@aup.fr. *Application contact:* International Admissions Counselor, 33 1-40620720, Fax: 33 1-47053432, E-mail: admissions@aup.edu.

Andrews University, School of Graduate Studies, College of Arts and Sciences, Interdisciplinary Studies in Communication Program, Berrien Springs, MI 49104. Offers MA. *Students:* 8 full-time (all women), 6 part-time (5 women); includes 11 minority (10 African Americans, 1 Asian American or Pacific Islander), 1 international. Average age 29. 7 applicants, 57% accepted, 1 enrolled. In 2009, 6 master's awarded. *Application deadline:* Applications are processed on a rolling basis. Application fee: $43. *Unit head:* Dr. Janice Y. Watson, Area Coordinator, 269-471-3126. *Application contact:* Carolyn Hurst, Supervisor of Graduate Admission, 800-253-2874, Fax: 269-471-3228, E-mail: graduate@andrews.edu.

Angelo State University, College of Graduate Studies, College of Liberal and Fine Arts, Department of Communication, Mass Media and Theatre, San Angelo, TX 76909. Offers communication systems management (MA). Part-time and evening/weekend programs available. *Faculty:* 2 full-time (0 women). *Students:* 8 full-time (5 women), 4 part-time (2 women); includes 2 minority (both Hispanic Americans). Average age 30. 7 applicants, 100% accepted, 6 enrolled. *Degree requirements:* For master's, comprehensive exam, thesis optional. *Entrance requirements:* For master's, GRE General Test. Additional exam requirements/recommendations for international students: Required—TOEFL or IELTS. *Application deadline:* For fall admission, 7/15 priority date for domestic students, 6/10 for international students; for spring admission, 12/1 priority date for domestic students, 11/1 for international students. Applications are processed on a rolling basis. Application fee: $40 ($50 for international students). Electronic applications accepted. *Expenses:* Tuition, state resident: full-time $3396; part-time $142 per credit hour. Tuition, nonresident: full-time $10,152; part-time $423 per credit hour. Required fees: $1786; $36.25 per credit hour. $494 per semester. Full-time tuition and fees vary according to course load, degree level and program. *Financial support:* In 2009–10, 5 students received support, including 3 teaching assistantships (averaging $10,251 per year); career-related internships or fieldwork, Federal Work-Study, scholarships/grants, and unspecified assistantships also available. Support available to part-time students. Financial award application deadline: 3/1; financial award applicants required to submit FAFSA. *Unit head:* Dr. Shawn T. Wahl, Department Head, 325-942-2031 Ext. 228, Fax: 325-942-2551, E-mail: swahl1@angelo.edu. *Application contact:* Dr. Lana Marlow, Graduate Advisor, 325-942-2032 Ext. 356, Fax: 325-942-2551, E-mail: lana.marlow@angelo.edu.

Arizona State University, Graduate College, College of Liberal Arts and Sciences, Division of Social Sciences, Hugh Downs School of Human Communication, Tempe, AZ 85287. Offers communication (MA, PhD). *Degree requirements:* For master's, thesis or alternative; for doctorate, thesis/dissertation.

Arizona State University, Graduate College, New College of Interdisciplinary Arts and Sciences, Department of Communication Studies, Tempe, AZ 85287. Offers MA. Part-time and evening/weekend programs available. *Degree requirements:* For master's, comprehensive exams or thesis. *Entrance requirements:* For master's, GRE (if GPA less than 3.0 in last 60 hours of undergraduate study), 2 letters of recommendation, minimum GPA of 3.0 in last 2 years of undergraduate study, writing sample of scholarly work. Additional exam requirements/recommendations for international students: Required—TOEFL (minimum score 550 paper-based; 213 computer-based; 83 iBT), IELTS (minimum score 6.5). Electronic applications accepted. *Faculty research:* Research regarding various ways in which communication shapes social contexts, constructs people's realities, and constitutes human relationships.

Arkansas State University—Jonesboro, Graduate School, College of Communications, Jonesboro, State University, AR 72467. Offers MA, MSMC, SCCT. Part-time programs available. *Faculty:* 13 full-time (5 women), 1 part-time/adjunct (0 women). *Students:* 28 full-time (14 women), 28 part-time (17 women); includes 16 minority (15 African Americans, 1 Asian American or Pacific Islander), 24 international. Average age 27. 57 applicants, 89% accepted, 32 enrolled. In 2009, 14 master's awarded. *Degree requirements:* For master's, one foreign language, comprehensive exam, thesis or alternative. *Entrance requirements:* For master's, GRE General Test, appropriate bachelor's degree, letters of reference; for SCCT, GRE, interview, master's degree, official transcript, immunization records. Additional exam requirements/recommendations for international students: Required—TOEFL (minimum score 550 paper-based; 213 computer-based; 79 iBT), IELTS (minimum score 6). *Application deadline:* For fall admission, 7/15 for domestic students, 7/1 for international students; for spring admission, 12/1 for domestic students, 11/13 for international students. Applications are processed on a rolling basis. Application fee: $30 ($40 for international students). Electronic applications accepted. *Expenses:* Tuition, state resident: full-time $3744; part-time $208 per credit hour. Tuition, nonresident: full-time $9540; part-time $530 per credit hour. Required fees: $896; $47 per credit hour. $25 per term. One-time fee: $50. Tuition and fees vary according to course load and program. *Financial support:* In 2009–10, 20 students received support. Career-related internships or fieldwork, scholarships/grants, and unspecified assistantships available. Financial award application deadline: 7/1; financial award applicants required to submit FAFSA. *Unit head:* Dr. Osabuohien Amienyi, Interim Dean, 870-972-2468, Fax: 870-972-3856, E-mail: osami@astate.edu. *Application contact:* Dr. Andrew Sustich, Dean of the Graduate School, 870-972-3029, Fax: 870-972-3857, E-mail: sustich@astate.edu.

Arkansas Tech University, Graduate College, College of Arts and Humanities, Russellville, AR 72801. Offers communication (MLA); English (M Ed, MA); fine arts (MLA); history (MA); multi-media journalism (MA); psychology (MS); social science (MLA); Spanish (MA, MLA); teaching English as a second language (MA, MLA). Part-time programs available. *Students:* 39 full-time (30 women), 80 part-time (63 women); includes 11 minority (3 African Americans, 1 American Indian/Alaska Native, 1 Asian American or Pacific Islander, 6 Hispanic Americans), 23 international. Average age 33. In 2009, 70 master's awarded. *Degree requirements:* For master's, comprehensive exam (for some programs), thesis (for some programs), project. *Entrance requirements:* For master's, GRE General Test or MAT. Additional exam requirements/recommendations for international students: Required—TOEFL (minimum score 550 paper-based; 213 computer-based; 79 iBT), IELTS (minimum score 6). *Application deadline:* For fall admission, 3/1 priority date for domestic students, 5/1 priority date for international students; for spring admission, 10/1 priority date for domestic and international students. Applications are processed on a rolling basis. Application fee: $0 ($50 for international students). Electronic applications accepted. *Expenses:* Tuition, state resident: full-time $3438; part-time $191 per hour. Tuition, nonresident: full-time $6876; part-time $382 per hour. Required fees: $482; $9 per credit hour. $140 per semester. Tuition and fees vary according to course load. *Financial support:* In 2009–10, teaching assistantships with full tuition reimbursements (averaging $4,000 per year); research assistantships, career-related internships or fieldwork, Federal Work-Study, scholarships/grants, health care benefits, and unspecified assistantships also available. Support available to part-time students. Financial award application deadline: 4/15; financial award applicants required to submit FAFSA. *Unit head:* Dr. Micheal Tarver, Dean, 479-968-0274, Fax: 479-964-0812, E-mail: mtarver@atu.edu. *Application contact:* Dr. Mary B. Gunter, Dean of Graduate College, 479-968-0398, Fax: 479-964-0542, E-mail: graduate.school@atu.edu.

Auburn University, Graduate School, College of Liberal Arts, Department of Communication and Journalism, Auburn University, AL 36849. Offers communication (MA); mass communications (MA). Part-time programs available. *Faculty:* 24 full-time (13 women), 10 part-time/adjunct (5 women). *Students:* 21 full-time (15 women), 6 part-time (4 women); includes 4 minority (3 African Americans, 1 Hispanic American), 1 international. Average age 26. 26 applicants, 65% accepted, 13 enrolled. In 2009, 14 master's awarded. *Degree requirements:* For master's, thesis (for some programs). *Entrance requirements:* For master's, GRE General Test. *Application deadline:* For fall admission, 7/7 for domestic students; for spring admission, 11/24 for domestic students. Applications are processed on a rolling basis. Application fee: $50 ($60 for international students). Electronic applications accepted. *Expenses:* Tuition, state resident: full-time $6240. Tuition, nonresident: full-time $18,720. International tuition: $18,938 full-time. Required fees: $492. Tuition and fees vary according to course load, program and reciprocity agreements. *Financial support:* Teaching assistantships, Federal Work-Study available. Support available to part-time students. Financial award application deadline: 3/15; financial award applicants required to submit FAFSA. *Unit head:* Dr. Mary Helen Brown, Acting Chair, 334-844-2727. *Application contact:* Dr. George Flowers, Dean of the Graduate School, 334-844-2125.

Austin Peay State University, College of Graduate Studies, College of Arts and Letters, Department of Communication, Clarksville, TN 37044. Offers communication arts (MA). Part-time and evening/weekend programs available. Postbaccalaureate distance learning degree programs offered (no on-campus study). *Faculty:* 9 full-time (4 women), 3 part-time/adjunct (2 women). *Students:* 3 full-time (2 women), 75 part-time (47 women); includes 20 minority (15 African Americans, 2 Asian Americans or Pacific Islanders, 3 Hispanic Americans). Average age 31. 35 applicants, 100% accepted, 24 enrolled. In 2009, 18 master's awarded. *Degree requirements:* For master's, comprehensive exam, thesis (for some programs). *Entrance requirements:* For master's, GRE General Test, 3 letters of recommendation. Additional exam requirements/recommendations for international students: Required—TOEFL (minimum score 500 paper-based; 173 computer-based). *Application deadline:* For fall admission, 7/27 priority date for domestic students; for spring admission, 12/17 priority date for domestic students. Applications are processed on a rolling basis. Application fee: $25. Electronic applications accepted. *Expenses:* Tuition, state resident: full-time $6160; part-time $608 per credit hour. Tuition, nonresident: full-time $17,080; part-time $854 per credit hour. Required fees: $1224; $61.20 per credit hour. *Financial support:* In 2009–10, 7 students received support, including 7 research assistantships with full tuition reimbursements available (averaging $5,184 per year); career-related internships or fieldwork, Federal Work-Study, institutionally sponsored loans, scholarships/grants, and unspecified assistantships also available. Support available to part-time students. Financial award application deadline: 3/1; financial award applicants required to submit FAFSA. *Unit head:* Dr. Mike Gotcher, Chair, 931-221-7378, Fax: 931-221-7265, E-mail: comm@apsu.edu. *Application contact:* Dr. Dixie Dennis, Dean, College of Graduate Studies, 931-221-7662, Fax: 931-221-7641, E-mail: dennisdi@apsu.edu.

Ball State University, Graduate School, College of Communication, Information, and Media, Muncie, IN 47306-1099. Offers MA, MS. Part-time programs available. Postbaccalaureate distance learning degree programs offered (no on-campus study). *Degree requirements:* For master's, comprehensive exam (for some programs), thesis (for some programs). *Entrance requirements:* For master's, GRE (for some programs). Additional exam requirements/recommendations for international students: Required—TOEFL (minimum score 550 paper-based; 213 computer-based), IELTS (minimum score 6.5). Electronic applications accepted.

Barry University, School of Arts and Sciences, Department of Communication, Miami Shores, FL 33161-6695. Offers broadcasting (Certificate); communication (MA), including broadcast communication, public relations and corporate communications; organizational communication (MS). Part-time and evening/weekend programs available. *Degree requirements:* For master's, thesis (for some programs). *Entrance requirements:* For master's, GRE General Test, MAT, minimum GPA of 3.0. Electronic applications accepted. *Faculty research:* Organizational communication, broadcast communication, intercultural communication, advertising, leadership.

Baylor University, Graduate School, College of Arts and Sciences, Department of Communication Studies, Waco, TX 76798. Offers MA. Part-time programs available. *Students:* 16 full-time (7 women), 5 part-time (2 women); includes 1 minority (Asian American or Pacific Islander), 1 international. Average age 22. In 2009, 13 master's awarded. *Degree requirements:* For master's, thesis or alternative. *Entrance requirements:* For master's, GRE General Test. *Application deadline:* For fall admission, 8/1 for domestic students. Applications are processed on a rolling basis. Application fee: $25. *Financial support:* In 2009–10, 12 teaching assistantships were awarded; career-related internships or fieldwork, Federal Work-Study, institutionally sponsored loans, and scholarships/grants also available. Financial award application deadline: 4/1. *Faculty research:* Rhetoric and debate, organizational communication, media studies, new technology. *Unit head:* Dr. Mark Morman, Graduate Program Director, 254-710-1621, E-mail: mark_morman@baylor.edu. *Application contact:* Marilyn Spivey, Administrative Assistant, 254-710-1621, Fax: 254-710-3870, E-mail: marilyn_spivey@baylor.edu.

Bellarmine University, School of Communication, Louisville, KY 40205-0671. Offers MA. Part-time and evening/weekend programs available. *Faculty:* 7 full-time (5 women), 5 part-time/adjunct (2 women). *Students:* 2 full-time (1 woman), 41 part-time (31 women); includes 2 minority (both African Americans), 1 international. Average age 32. *Entrance requirements:* For master's, GRE, GMAT or LSAT. Additional exam requirements/recommendations for international students: Required—TOEFL (minimum score 550 paper-based; 213 computer-based; 80 iBT). *Application deadline:* Applications are processed on a rolling basis. Application fee: $30. *Unit head:* Edward Manasssah, Executive Director, 502-452-8324, E-mail: emahassah@bellarmine.edu. *Application contact:* Dr. Sara Yount, Dean of Graduate Admission, 502-452-8401, Fax: 502-452-8002, E-mail: syount@bellarmine.edu.

Bethel University, Graduate School, Program in Communication, St. Paul, MN 55112-6999. Offers communication (MA); post-secondary teaching (Certificate). Part-time and evening/weekend programs available. *Faculty:* 3 full-time (1 woman), 3 part-time/adjunct (1 woman). *Students:* 47 full-time (30 women), 16 part-time (10 women); includes 3 minority (2 African Americans, 1 Asian American or Pacific Islander), 1 international. Average age 38. 28 applicants, 89% accepted, 18 enrolled. In 2009, 19 master's awarded. *Degree requirements:* For master's, comprehensive exam, thesis. *Entrance requirements:* For master's, MAT, baccalaureate degree, interview, minimum GPA of 3.0, course work in communication and statistics, references, sample of written work, interview. Additional exam requirements/recommendations for international students: Required—TOEFL (minimum score 550 paper-based; 213 computer-based; 80 iBT). *Application deadline:* For fall admission, 5/15 priority date for domestic students. Applications are processed on a rolling basis. Application fee: $25. Electronic applications accepted. *Expenses:* Tuition: Full-time $7920; part-time $440 per credit. One-time fee: $25. Tuition and fees vary according to course load, degree level and program. *Financial support:* Applicants required to submit FAFSA. *Unit head:* Dr. Lori J. Jass, Assistant Dean, 651-635-8000, Fax: 651-635-8039, E-mail: l-jass@bethel.edu. *Application contact:* Michael Price, Director of Admissions, 651-635-8000, Fax: 651-635-8004, E-mail: m-price@bethel.edu.

Boise State University, Graduate College, College of Social Sciences and Public Affairs, Department of Communication, Boise, ID 83725-0399. Offers MA. Part-time programs available. *Degree requirements:* For master's, thesis. *Entrance requirements:* For master's, minimum GPA of 3.0, writing sample. Electronic applications accepted. *Expenses:* Tuition, state resident: full-time $3106; part-time $209 per credit. Tuition, nonresident: part-time $284 per credit.

Boston University, College of Communication, Boston, MA 02215. Offers MFA, MS, JD/MS, MBA/MS. Part-time programs available. *Faculty:* 57 full-time, 81 part-time/adjunct. *Students:* 286 full-time (184 women), 25 part-time (15 women); includes 31 minority (9 African Americans, 2 American Indian/Alaska Native, 14 Asian Americans or Pacific Islanders, 6 Hispanic Americans), 65 international. Average age 26. 875 applicants, 48% accepted. In 2009, 146 master's awarded. *Degree requirements:* For master's, comprehensive exam (for some programs), thesis (for some programs). *Entrance requirements:* For master's, GRE General Test. Additional exam requirements/recommendations for international students: Required—TOEFL (minimum score 600 paper-based; 250 computer-based; 100 iBT). *Application deadline:* For fall admission, 2/1 for domestic and international students. Application fee: $70. Electronic applications accepted. *Expenses:* Tuition: Full-time $37,910; part-time $1184 per credit hour. Required fees: $386; $40 per semester. Part-time tuition and fees vary according to class time, course level, degree level and program. *Financial support:* In 2009–10, 290 students received support, including 18 teaching assistantships with partial tuition reimbursements available; career-related internships or fieldwork, Federal Work-Study, institutionally sponsored loans, scholarships/grants, and unspecified assistantships also available. Support available to part-time students. Financial award application deadline: 2/1; financial award applicants required to submit FAFSA. *Unit head:* Thomas Fiedler, Dean, 617-353-3450, Fax: 617-358-0399, E-mail: com@bu.edu. *Application contact:* Kate Iserman, Administrator of Graduate Services, 617-353-3481, Fax: 617-358-0399, E-mail: comgrad@bu.edu.

See Close-Up on page 675.

Bowling Green State University, Graduate College, College of Arts and Sciences, School of Communication Studies, Bowling Green, OH 43403. Offers MA, PhD. Part-time programs available. Terminal master's awarded for partial completion of doctoral program. *Degree requirements:* For master's, thesis or alternative; for doctorate, comprehensive exam, thesis/dissertation. *Entrance requirements:* For master's and doctorate, GRE General Test. Additional exam requirements/recommendations for international students: Required—TOEFL. Electronic applications accepted.

Brandeis University, Rabb School of Continuing Studies, Division of Graduate Professional Studies, Virtual Team Management and Communication Program, Waltham, MA 02454-9110. Offers MS, Graduate Certificate. Part-time and evening/weekend programs available. Post-baccalaureate distance learning degree programs offered (no on-campus study). *Faculty:* 2 full-time (both women), 32 part-time/adjunct (8 women). *Students:* 1 part-time (0 women). Average age 35. *Entrance requirements:* For master's, statement of goals, resume, official transcripts, recommendations; for Graduate Certificate, resume, recommendations. Additional exam requirements/recommendations for international students: Recommended—TOEFL (minimum score 600 paper-based; 250 computer-based; 100 iBT). *Application deadline:* For fall admission, 6/15 priority date for domestic students; for winter admission, 10/15 priority date for domestic students; for spring admission, 2/15 priority date for domestic students. Applications are processed on a rolling basis. Application fee: $50. Electronic applications accepted. *Unit head:* Dr. Aline Yurik, Program Chair, 781-736-8787, Fax: 781-736-3420, E-mail: ayurik@brandeis.edu. *Application contact:* Frances Stearns, Associate Director of Admissions and Student Services, 781-736-8785, Fax: 781-736-3420, E-mail: fstearns@brandeis.edu.

Brigham Young University, Graduate Studies, College of Fine Arts and Communications, Department of Communications, Provo, UT 84602. Offers mass communications (MA). *Faculty:* 19 full-time (3 women). *Students:* 22 full-time (15 women), 16 part-time (8 women); includes 3 minority (1 African American, 1 American Indian/Alaska Native, 1 Hispanic American). Average age 29. 32 applicants, 44% accepted, 14 enrolled. In 2009, 14 master's awarded. *Degree requirements:* For master's, comprehensive exam, thesis. *Entrance requirements:* For master's, GRE, minimum GPA of 3.0 in last 60 hours of course work. Additional exam requirements/recommendations for international students: Required—TOEFL (minimum score 580 paper-based; 237 computer-based; 85 iBT). *Application deadline:* For fall admission, 2/28 for domestic and international students. Application fee: $50. Electronic applications accepted. *Expenses:* Tuition: Full-time $5580; part-time $301 per credit hour. Tuition and fees vary according to student's religious affiliation. *Financial support:* In 2009–10, 24 students received support, including 20 research assistantships with full and partial tuition reimbursements available (averaging $4,563 per year), 9 teaching assistantships with full and partial tuition reimbursements available (averaging $5,676 per year); career-related internships or fieldwork, institutionally sponsored loans, scholarships/grants, unspecified assistantships, and supplementary awards also available. Financial award application deadline: 4/15; financial award applicants required to submit FAFSA. *Faculty research:* Ethics, international, magazine, newspaper, media effects. *Unit head:* Dr. Bradley L. Rawlins, Chair, 801-422-2997, Fax: 801-422-0160, E-mail: comms_secretary@byu.edu. *Application contact:* Dr. Steven R. Thomsen, Graduate Coordinator, 801-422-2078, Fax: 801-422-0160, E-mail: steven_thomsen@byu.edu.

California State University, Chico, Graduate School, College of Communication and Education, Department of Communication Arts and Sciences, Program in Communication Studies, Chico, CA 95929-0722. Offers MA. *Students:* 4 full-time (3 women), 17 part-time (10 women); includes 4 minority (1 American Indian/Alaska Native, 3 Hispanic Americans), 4 international. Average age 27. 30 applicants, 67% accepted, 13 enrolled. In 2009, 3 master's awarded. *Degree requirements:* For master's, thesis. *Entrance requirements:* Additional exam requirements/recommendations for international students: Required—TOEFL (minimum score 550 paper-based; 213 computer-based; 80 iBT), IELTS (minimum score 6.5). *Application deadline:* For fall admission, 3/1 priority date for domestic students, 3/1 for international students; for spring admission, 9/15 priority date for domestic students, 9/15 for international students. Applications are processed on a rolling basis. Application fee: $55. Electronic applications accepted. *Application contact:* Dr. Ruth Guzley, Graduate Coordinator, 530-898-5751.

California State University, East Bay, Academic Programs and Graduate Studies, College of Letters, Arts, and Social Sciences, Department of Communication, Hayward, CA 94542-3000. Offers MA. Part-time programs available. *Faculty:* 7 full-time (3 women). *Students:* 9 full-time (7 women), 14 part-time (10 women); includes 9 minority (4 African Americans, 4 Asian Americans or Pacific Islanders, 1 Hispanic American), 3 international. Average age 29. 16 applicants, 56% accepted, 8 enrolled. In 2009, 6 master's awarded. *Degree requirements:* For master's, comprehensive exam, project or thesis. *Entrance requirements:* For master's, GRE, minimum GPA of 3.0 in field. Additional exam requirements/recommendations for international students: Required—TOEFL (minimum score 550 paper-based; 213 computer-based). *Application deadline:* For fall admission, 2/25 for domestic and international students. Applications are processed on a rolling basis. Application fee: $55. Electronic applications accepted. *Financial support:* Fellowships, teaching assistantships, career-related internships or fieldwork, Federal Work-Study, institutionally sponsored loans, scholarships/grants, and unspecified assistantships available. Support available to part-time students. Financial award application deadline: 3/1; financial award applicants required to submit FAFSA. *Unit head:* Dr. Gale Young, Interim Chair, 510-885-3292, Fax: 510-885-4099, E-mail: gale.young@csueastbay.edu. *Application contact:* Donna Wiley, Interim Associate Director, 510-885-2928, Fax: 510-885-4777, E-mail: donna.wiley@csueastbay.edu.

California State University, Fresno, Division of Graduate Studies, College of Arts and Humanities, Department of Communication, Fresno, CA 93740-8027. Offers MA. Part-time and evening/weekend programs available. *Degree requirements:* For master's, thesis or alternative. *Entrance requirements:* For master's, GRE General Test, minimum GPA of 3.1. Additional exam requirements/recommendations for international students: Required—TOEFL. Electronic applications accepted. *Faculty research:* Learning styles, education, critical thinking.

California State University, Fullerton, Graduate Studies, College of Communications, Department of Communications, Fullerton, CA 92834-9480. Offers communications—advertising (MA); communications—entertainment and tourism (MA); communications—journalism (MA); communications—public relations (MA). Part-time programs available. *Students:* 18 full-time (14 women), 38 part-time (30 women); includes 21 minority (2 African Americans, 8 Asian Americans or Pacific Islanders, 11 Hispanic Americans), 4 international. Average age 28. 121 applicants, 23% accepted, 17 enrolled. In 2009, 33 master's awarded. *Degree requirements:* For master's, project or thesis. *Entrance requirements:* For master's, GRE General Test. Application fee: $55. *Expenses:* Tuition, nonresident: full-time $11,160; part-time $373 per credit. Required fees: $1440 per term. Tuition and fees vary according to course load, degree level and program. *Financial support:* Teaching assistantships, career-related internships or fieldwork, Federal Work-Study, institutionally sponsored loans, and scholarships/grants available. Support available to part-time students. Financial award application deadline: 3/1; financial award applicants required to submit FAFSA. *Unit head:* Dr. Tony Fellow, Chair, 657-278-3517. *Application contact:* Coordinator, 657-278-3832.

California State University, Long Beach, Graduate Studies, College of Liberal Arts, Department of Communication Studies, Long Beach, CA 90840. Offers MA. Part-time programs available. *Faculty:* 6 full-time (3 women). *Students:* 12 full-time (8 women), 21 part-time (15 women); includes 10 minority (1 American Indian/Alaska Native, 3 Asian Americans or Pacific Islanders, 6 Hispanic Americans). Average age 30. 64 applicants, 20% accepted, 11 enrolled. *Degree requirements:* For master's, comprehensive exam or thesis. *Entrance requirements:* For master's, GRE. *Application deadline:* For fall admission, 2/27 for domestic students. Applications are processed on a rolling basis. Application fee: $55. Electronic applications accepted. *Expenses:* Required fees: $1802 per semester. Part-time tuition and fees vary according to course load. *Financial support:* Federal Work-Study, institutionally sponsored loans, and scholarships/grants available. Financial award application deadline: 3/2. *Faculty research:* Rhetoric, public address, communication theory, interpersonal communication, intercultural communication. *Unit head:* Dr. Sharon Downey, Chair, 562-985-4301, Fax: 562-985-4259. *Application contact:* Dr. Ann Johnson, Graduate Adviser, 562-985-9190, Fax: 562-985-4259, E-mail: ajohnso7@csulb.edu.

California State University, Los Angeles, Graduate Studies, College of Arts and Letters, Department of Communication Studies, Los Angeles, CA 90032-8530. Offers speech communication (MA); television, film and theatre (MFA). Part-time and evening/weekend programs available. *Faculty:* 6 full-time (3 women), 8 part-time/adjunct (4 women). *Students:* 69 full-time (40 women), 52 part-time (38 women); includes 48 minority (18 African Americans, 9 Asian Americans or Pacific Islanders, 21 Hispanic Americans), 18 international. Average age 31. 92 applicants, 99% accepted, 34 enrolled. In 2009, 17 master's awarded. *Degree requirements:* For master's, comprehensive exam or thesis. *Entrance requirements:* For master's, minimum GPA of 2.75 in last 90 units of course work. Additional exam requirements/recommendations for international students: Required—TOEFL (minimum score 500 paper-based; 173 computer-based). *Application deadline:* For fall admission, 5/1 for domestic and international students. Applications are processed on a rolling basis. Application fee: $55. Electronic applications accepted. *Financial support:* Career-related internships or fieldwork and Federal Work-Study available. Support available to part-time students. Financial award application deadline: 3/1. *Faculty research:* Organizational, interpersonal, intercultural, and instructional communication; rhetorical theories. *Unit head:* Dr. Suzanne Regan, Chair, 323-343-4200, Fax: 323-343-6467, E-mail: sregan@calstatela.edu. *Application contact:* Dr. Cheryl L. Ney, Associate Vice President for Academic Affairs and Dean of Graduate Studies, 323-343-3820, Fax: 323-343-5653, E-mail: cney@cslanet.calstatela.edu.

California State University, Northridge, Graduate Studies, College of Arts, Media, and Communication, Northridge, CA 91330. Offers MA, MFA, MM. Part-time and evening/weekend programs available. *Faculty:* 86 full-time (37 women), 149 part-time/adjunct (59 women). *Students:* 108 full-time (79 women), 154 part-time (104 women); includes 63 minority (15 African Americans, 2 American Indian/Alaska Native, 15 Asian Americans or Pacific Islanders, 31 Hispanic Americans), 28 international. Average age 32. 389 applicants, 38% accepted, 88 enrolled. In 2009, 79 master's awarded. *Entrance requirements:* Additional exam requirements/recommendations for international students: Required—TOEFL. *Application deadline:* For fall admission, 11/30 for domestic students. Application fee: $55. *Financial support:* Teaching assistantships, career-related internships or fieldwork, Federal Work-Study, and unspecified

Communication—General

California State University, Northridge (continued)
assistantships available. Support available to part-time students. Financial award application deadline: 3/1. *Unit head:* Robert Bucker, Dean, 818-677-2246, E-mail: robert.bucker@csun.edu. *Application contact:* Robert Bucker, Dean, 818-677-2246, E-mail: robert.bucker@csun.edu.

California State University, Sacramento, Graduate Studies, College of Arts and Letters, Department of Communication Studies, Sacramento, CA 95819. Offers MA. Part-time programs available. *Degree requirements:* For master's, thesis or alternative, writing proficiency exam. *Entrance requirements:* For master's, minimum GPA of 3.25 during previous 2 years. Additional exam requirements/recommendations for international students: Required—TOEFL. Electronic applications accepted.

California State University, San Bernardino, Graduate Studies, College of Arts and Letters, Department of Communication Studies, San Bernardino, CA 92407-2397. Offers communication studies (MA); integrated marketing communication (MA). *Faculty:* 5 full-time (3 women), 3 part-time/adjunct (1 woman). *Students:* 30 full-time (20 women), 14 part-time (12 women); includes 18 minority (6 African Americans, 12 Hispanic Americans), 15 international. Average age 30. 92 applicants, 66% accepted. In 2009, 18 master's awarded. *Degree requirements:* For master's, comprehensive exam, advancement to candidacy. *Entrance requirements:* Additional exam requirements/recommendations for international students: Required—TOEFL. *Application deadline:* For fall admission, 8/31 priority date for domestic students. Application fee: $55. *Unit head:* Dr. Mo Bahk, Chair, 909-537-5820, Fax: 909-537-7009, E-mail: mbahk@csusb.edu. *Application contact:* Olivia Rosas, Director of Admissions, 909-537-7577, Fax: 909-537-7034, E-mail: orosas@csusb.edu.

Carleton University, Faculty of Graduate Studies, Faculty of Public Affairs and Management, School of Journalism and Communication, Program in Communication, Ottawa, ON K1S 5B6, Canada. Offers MA, PhD. *Degree requirements:* For master's, thesis optional; for doctorate, comprehensive exam, thesis/dissertation. *Entrance requirements:* For master's, honors degree. Additional exam requirements/recommendations for international students: Required—TOEFL. *Faculty research:* History of communication and media systems, communication/information technologies and society, communication and social relations, communication policy and political economy.

Carnegie Mellon University, College of Fine Arts, School of Design, Program in Communication Planning and Information Design, Pittsburgh, PA 15213-3891. Offers M Des. Part-time programs available. *Degree requirements:* For master's, thesis. *Entrance requirements:* For master's, GRE, portfolio of relevant work. Additional exam requirements/recommendations for international students: Required—TOEFL (minimum score 600 paper-based). *Faculty research:* Dynamic information design, communication design, systems design, strategic planning, kinetic typography and emotion.

Carnegie Mellon University, College of Humanities and Social Sciences, Department of English, Pittsburgh, PA 15213-3891. Offers communication planning and design (M Des); literary and cultural studies (MA, PhD); professional writing (MAPW), including editing and publishing, policy and non-profit communication, public and media relations / corporate communications, science or healthcare communication, technical writing, writing for new media, writing for print media; rhetoric (MA, PhD). Part-time programs available. Terminal master's awarded for partial completion of doctoral program. *Degree requirements:* For doctorate, 2 foreign languages, comprehensive exam, thesis/dissertation. *Entrance requirements:* For master's and doctorate, GRE General Test. Additional exam requirements/recommendations for international students: Required—TOEFL, TWE. *Faculty research:* Cognitive processes in discourse with emphasis on writing, testing, and evaluation.

Central Connecticut State University, School of Graduate Studies, School of Arts and Sciences, Department of Communication, New Britain, CT 06050-4010. Offers organizational communication (MS); public relations/promotions (Certificate). Part-time and evening/weekend programs available. *Faculty:* 12 full-time (4 women), 8 part-time/adjunct (2 women). *Students:* 10 full-time (5 women), 23 part-time (13 women); includes 7 minority (4 African Americans, 1 Asian American or Pacific Islander, 2 Hispanic Americans), 1 international. Average age 29. 30 applicants, 50% accepted, 15 enrolled. In 2009, 9 master's awarded. *Degree requirements:* For master's, comprehensive exam, thesis or alternative; for Certificate, qualifying exam. *Entrance requirements:* For master's, minimum undergraduate GPA of 3.0. Additional exam requirements/recommendations for international students: Required—TOEFL. *Application deadline:* For fall admission, 7/1 for domestic students; for spring admission, 12/1 for domestic students. Applications are processed on a rolling basis. Application fee: $50. Electronic applications accepted. *Expenses:* Tuition, area resident: Full-time $4662; part-time $440 per credit. Tuition, state resident: full-time $6994; part-time $440 per credit. Tuition, nonresident: full-time $12,988; part-time $440 per credit. Required fees: $3606. One-time fee: $62 part-time. *Financial support:* In 2009–10, 5 students received support, including 1 research assistantship; career-related internships or fieldwork, Federal Work-Study, scholarships/grants, and unspecified assistantships also available. Support available to part-time students. Financial award application deadline: 3/1; financial award applicants required to submit FAFSA. *Faculty research:* Organizational communication, mass communication, intercultural communication, political communication, information management. *Unit head:* Dr. Serafin Mendez-Mendez, Chair, 860-832-2690. *Application contact:* Dr. Serafin Mendez-Mendez, Chair, 860-832-2690.

Central Michigan University, College of Graduate Studies, College of Communication and Fine Arts, Department of Communication and Dramatic Arts, Mount Pleasant, MI 48859. Offers interpersonal and public communication (MA), including communication and dramatic arts. Part-time programs available. *Degree requirements:* For master's, thesis. Electronic applications accepted. *Faculty research:* Communication theory, interpersonal/nonverbal communication, organizational communication, family and interpersonal communication, political communication.

Clarion University of Pennsylvania, Office of Research and Graduate Studies, College of Arts and Sciences, Department of Mass Media Arts, Journalism, and Communication Studies, Clarion, PA 16214. Offers MS. Part-time programs available. *Degree requirements:* For master's, comprehensive exam, thesis or alternative. *Entrance requirements:* For master's, minimum QPA of 3.0. Additional exam requirements/recommendations for international students: Required—TOEFL (minimum score 600 paper-based; 250 computer-based; 100 iBT). Electronic applications accepted.

Clark University, Graduate School, College of Professional and Continuing Education, Program in Professional Communication, Worcester, MA 01610-1477. Offers MSPC. *Students:* 24 full-time (17 women), 20 part-time (12 women); includes 2 minority (1 American Indian/Alaska Native, 1 Hispanic American), 7 international. Average age 29. 29 applicants, 97% accepted, 22 enrolled. In 2009, 23 master's awarded. *Degree requirements:* For master's, thesis optional. *Application deadline:* Applications are processed on a rolling basis. Application fee: $50. Electronic applications accepted. *Expenses:* Tuition: Full-time $34,900; part-time $4362.50 per course. *Unit head:* Max E. Hess, Director of Graduate Studies, 508-793-7217, Fax: 508-793-7232. *Application contact:* Julia Parent, Director of Marketing, Communications, and Admissions, 508-793-7217, Fax: 508-793-7232, E-mail: jparent@clarku.edu.

Clemson University, Graduate School, College of Architecture, Arts, and Humanities, Department of English, Program in Professional Communication, Clemson, SC 29634. Offers MA. Part-time programs available. *Students:* 24 full-time (17 women), 8 part-time (6 women); includes 2 minority (1 Asian American or Pacific Islander, 1 Hispanic American), 3 international. Average age 27. 36 applicants, 44% accepted, 10 enrolled. In 2009, 17 master's awarded. *Degree requirements:* For master's, one foreign language, thesis optional, oral exam. *Entrance requirements:* For master's, GRE General Test, minimum GPA of 3.0. Additional exam requirements/recommendations for international students: Required—TOEFL, IELTS. *Application deadline:* For fall admission, 2/1 priority date for domestic students, 4/15 for international students; for spring admission, 11/1 priority date for domestic students, 9/15 for international students. Applications are processed on a rolling basis. Application fee: $70 ($80 for international students). Electronic applications accepted. *Expenses:* Tuition, state resident: full-time $8684; part-time $528 per credit hour. Tuition, nonresident: full-time $15,330; part-time $1078 per credit hour. Required fees: $736; $37 per semester. Part-time tuition and fees vary according to course load and program. *Financial support:* In 2009–10, 24 students received support, including 2 research assistantships with partial tuition reimbursements available (averaging $11,500 per year), 10 teaching assistantships with partial tuition reimbursements available (averaging $13,552 per year); fellowships with full and partial tuition reimbursements available, career-related internships or fieldwork, institutionally sponsored loans, scholarships/grants, health care benefits, and unspecified assistantships also available. Support available to part-time students. Financial award application deadline: 4/1; financial award applicants required to submit FAFSA. *Faculty research:* Usability testing, rhetoric, communication across the curriculum, intercultural communication. *Unit head:* Dr. Lee Morrissey, Coordinator, 864-656-3151, Fax: 864-656-1345, E-mail: lmorris@clemson.edu. *Application contact:* Dr. Summer Taylor, Graduate Coordinator, 864-656-6689, Fax: 864-656-1345, E-mail: slsmith@clemson.edu.

Clemson University, Graduate School, College of Architecture, Arts, and Humanities, Program in Rhetorics, Communication and Information Design, Clemson, SC 29634. Offers PhD. *Faculty:* 25 full-time (10 women). *Students:* 23 full-time (9 women), 6 part-time (2 women); includes 6 minority (4 African Americans, 1 Asian American or Pacific Islander, 1 Hispanic American), 5 international. Average age 36. 17 applicants, 59% accepted, 8 enrolled. In 2009, 1 doctorate awarded. *Degree requirements:* For doctorate, thesis/dissertation (for some programs). *Entrance requirements:* For doctorate, GRE, master's degree in English, communications studies, art, professional communication or related field; portfolio; 3 letters of reference; minimum graduate GPA of 3.5. Additional exam requirements/recommendations for international students: Required—TOEFL (minimum score 550 paper-based; 213 computer-based). *Application deadline:* For fall admission, 1/1 priority date for domestic students, 4/15 for international students. Applications are processed on a rolling basis. Application fee: $70 ($80 for international students). Electronic applications accepted. *Expenses:* Tuition, state resident: full-time $8684; part-time $528 per credit hour. Tuition, nonresident: full-time $15,330; part-time $1078 per credit hour. Required fees: $736; $37 per semester. Part-time tuition and fees vary according to course load and program. *Financial support:* In 2009–10, 22 students received support, including 22 teaching assistantships with partial tuition reimbursements available (averaging $19,709 per year); career-related internships or fieldwork, institutionally sponsored loans, scholarships/grants, health care benefits, and unspecified assistantships also available. Support available to part-time students. *Unit head:* Dr. Victor Vitanza, Director, 864-656-6411, Fax: 864-656-0599, E-mail: sophist@clemson.edu. *Application contact:* Dr. Victor Vitanza, Director, 864-656-6411, Fax: 864-656-0599, E-mail: sophist@clemson.edu.

Clemson University, Graduate School, College of Business and Behavioral Science, Department of Graphic Communications, Clemson, SC 29634. Offers MS. *Faculty:* 11 full-time (2 women), 1 (woman) part-time/adjunct. *Students:* 10 full-time (6 women), 2 part-time (1 woman), 2 international. Average age 25. 8 applicants, 63% accepted, 5 enrolled. In 2009, 4 master's awarded. *Entrance requirements:* For master's, GRE General Test. Additional exam requirements/recommendations for international students: Required—TOEFL. *Application deadline:* For fall admission, 4/15 for international students; for spring admission, 9/15 for international students. Application fee: $70 ($80 for international students). Electronic applications accepted. *Expenses:* Tuition, state resident: full-time $8684; part-time $528 per credit hour. Tuition, nonresident: full-time $15,330; part-time $1078 per credit hour. Required fees: $736; $37 per semester. Part-time tuition and fees vary according to course load and program. *Financial support:* In 2009–10, 8 students received support; research assistantships with partial tuition reimbursements available, teaching assistantships with partial tuition reimbursements available, career-related internships or fieldwork, institutionally sponsored loans, scholarships/grants, health care benefits, and unspecified assistantships available. Support available to part-time students. Financial award applicants required to submit FAFSA. *Unit head:* Dr. Samuel T. Ingram, Chair, 864-656-3447, E-mail: sting@clemson.edu. *Application contact:* Nancy Leininger, 864-656-3447, Fax: 864-656-5344, E-mail: lnancy@clemson.edu.

Cleveland State University, College of Graduate Studies, College of Liberal Arts and Social Sciences, School of Communication, Cleveland, OH 44115. Offers applied communication theory and methodology (MA); culture, communication and health care (Certificate). Part-time and evening/weekend programs available. *Degree requirements:* For master's, variable foreign language requirement, thesis, project, comprehensive exam, or collaborative project. *Entrance requirements:* For master's, GRE or MAT, minimum undergraduate GPA of 2.75, 2 letters of recommendation. Additional exam requirements/recommendations for international students: Required—TOEFL (minimum score 525 paper-based; 197 computer-based). Electronic applications accepted. *Faculty research:* Interpersonal, organizational, and mass communication; health communication.

The College at Brockport, State University of New York, School of Arts, Humanities and Social Sciences, Department of Communication, Brockport, NY 14420-2997. Offers MA. Part-time and evening/weekend programs available. *Students:* 17 full-time (12 women), 20 part-time (17 women); includes 6 minority (4 African Americans, 1 Asian American or Pacific Islander, 1 Hispanic American). 35 applicants, 100% accepted, 31 enrolled. In 2009, 7 master's awarded. *Degree requirements:* For master's, thesis or alternative, research project. *Entrance requirements:* For master's, minimum GPA of 3.0, letters of recommendation. Additional exam requirements/recommendations for international students: Required—TOEFL (minimum score 550 paper-based; 213 computer-based; 79 iBT). *Application deadline:* For fall admission, 7/15 priority date for domestic and international students; for spring admission, 11/15 priority date for domestic and international students. Application fee: $50. Electronic applications accepted. *Expenses:* Tuition, state resident: full-time $8370; part-time $349 per credit. Tuition, nonresident: full-time $13,250; part-time $522 per credit. *Financial support:* In 2009–10, 3 teaching assistantships with full tuition reimbursements (averaging $6,000 per year) were awarded; Federal Work-Study, scholarships/grants, and unspecified assistantships also available. Support available to part-time students. Financial award application deadline: 3/15; financial award applicants required to submit FAFSA. *Faculty research:* Organizational communication, rhetorical theory and criticism, media theory and criticism, interpersonal communication, communication theory. *Unit head:* Dr. Monica Brasted, Chairperson, 585-395-2511, Fax: 585-395-5771, E-mail: mbrasted@brockport.edu. *Application contact:* Dr. Alex Lyon, Graduate Director, 585-395-5772, Fax: 585-395-5771, E-mail: alyon@brockport.edu.

College of Charleston, Graduate School, School of Humanities and Social Sciences, Program in Communication, Charleston, SC 29424-0001. Offers MA. Part-time and evening/weekend programs available. *Faculty:* 21 full-time (10 women). *Students:* 15 full-time (13 women), 15 part-time (12 women); includes 2 minority (1 American Indian/Alaska Native, 1 Hispanic American), 1 international. Average age 27. 22 applicants, 41% accepted, 8 enrolled. In 2009, 7 master's awarded. *Degree requirements:* For master's, comprehensive exam or thesis. *Entrance requirements:* For master's, GRE, writing sample; 2 letters of recommendation; minimum GPA of 2.75 overall, 3.0 in major. Additional exam requirements/recommendations for international students: Required—TOEFL. *Application deadline:* For fall admission, 4/1 for domestic students; for spring admission, 11/1 for domestic students. Applications are processed on a rolling basis. Application fee: $45. Electronic applications accepted. *Financial support:* Research assistantships, teaching assistantships, career-related internships or fieldwork, scholarships/grants, and unspecified assistantships available. Financial award applicants required to submit FAFSA. *Unit head:* Dr. Vincent Benigni, Director, 844-983-7854, E-mail: fergusond@cofc.edu. *Application contact:* Susan Hallatt, Director of Graduate Admissions, 843-953-5614, Fax: 843-953-1434, E-mail: hallatts@cofc.edu.

The College of New Rochelle, Graduate School, Division of Art and Communication Studies, Program in Communication Studies, New Rochelle, NY 10805-2308. Offers MS, Certificate. Part-time and evening/weekend programs available. *Degree requirements:* For master's, thesis or alternative. *Entrance requirements:* For master's, GRE General Test, interview, minimum

GPA of 3.0. Additional exam requirements/recommendations for international students: Required—TOEFL.

College of Notre Dame of Maryland, Graduate Studies, Program in Contemporary Communication, Baltimore, MD 21210-2476. Offers MA. Part-time and evening/weekend programs available. *Degree requirements:* For master's, thesis optional. *Entrance requirements:* For master's, minimum GPA of 3.0. Additional exam requirements/recommendations for international students: Required—TOEFL (minimum score 500 paper-based; 173 computer-based; 61 iBT). Electronic applications accepted.

Columbia University, Graduate School of Business, Doctoral Program in Business, New York, NY 10027. Offers business (PhD), including accounting, decision, risk, and operations, finance and economics, management, marketing. *Accreditation:* AACSB. *Faculty:* 149 full-time (23 women), 134 part-time/adjunct (16 women). *Students:* 91 full-time (37 women); includes 10 minority (8 Asian Americans or Pacific Islanders, 2 Hispanic Americans), 64 international. Average age 27. 758 applicants, 6% accepted, 20 enrolled. In 2009, 15 doctorates awarded. *Degree requirements:* For doctorate, comprehensive exam, thesis/dissertation, major field exam, research paper, thesis proposal. *Entrance requirements:* For doctorate, GMAT or GRE (finance), 2 letters of reference, resume. Additional exam requirements/recommendations for international students: Required—TOEFL. *Application deadline:* For fall admission, 1/1 for domestic and international students. Application fee: $75. Electronic applications accepted. *Expenses:* Contact institution. *Financial support:* In 2009–10, 91 students received support, including fellowships with full tuition reimbursements available (averaging $22,000 per year), research assistantships (averaging $4,000 per year); teaching assistantships, career-related internships or fieldwork, health care benefits, and tuition waivers (full) also available. *Faculty research:* Human decision making and behavioral research; real estate market and mortgage defaults; financial crisis and corporate governance; international business; security analysis and accounting. *Unit head:* Elizabeth Elam Chang, Administrative Director, 212-854-2836, Fax: 212-932-2359, E-mail: phdinfo@gsb.columbia.edu. *Application contact:* Elizabeth Elam Chang, Administrative Director, 212-854-2836, Fax: 212-932-2359, E-mail: phdinfo@gsb.columbia.edu.

Columbia University, Graduate School of Business, MBA Program, New York, NY 10027. Offers accounting (MBA); decision, risk, and operations (MBA); entrepreneurship (MBA); finance and economics (MBA); healthcare and pharmaceutical management (MBA); human resource management (MBA); international business (MBA); leadership and ethics (MBA); management (MBA); marketing (MBA); media (MBA); private equity (MBA); real estate (MBA); social enterprise (MBA); value investing (MBA); DDS/MBA; JD/MBA; MBA/MIA; MBA/MPH; MBA/MS; MD/MBA. *Faculty:* 149 full-time (23 women), 134 part-time/adjunct (16 women). *Students:* 1,293 full-time (435 women); includes 235 minority (65 African Americans, 4 American Indian/Alaska Native, 135 Asian Americans or Pacific Islanders, 31 Hispanic Americans), 417 international. Average age 28. 6,885 applicants, 15% accepted, 737 enrolled. In 2009, 696 master's awarded. *Entrance requirements:* For master's, GMAT, 2 letters of recommendation. Additional exam requirements/recommendations for international students: Required—TOEFL. *Application deadline:* For fall admission, 4/14 for domestic students, 3/3 for international students; for spring admission, 10/7 for domestic and international students. Applications are processed on a rolling basis. Application fee: $250. Electronic applications accepted. *Expenses:* Contact institution. *Financial support:* In 2009–10, 358 students received support, including 101 fellowships (averaging $23,250 per year); research assistantships, teaching assistantships, career-related internships or fieldwork, institutionally sponsored loans, and scholarships/grants also available. Financial award application deadline: 3/1; financial award applicants required to submit CSS PROFILE or FAFSA. *Faculty research:* Human decision making and behavioral research; real estate market and mortgage defaults; financial crisis and corporate governance; international business; security analysis and accounting. *Unit head:* Prof. Amir Ziv, Vice Dean of Students and the MBA Program, 212-854-3485, Fax: 212-932-0545, E-mail: az50@columbia.edu. *Application contact:* Mary J. Miller, Assistant Dean of Admissions, 212-854-1961, Fax: 212-662-6754, E-mail: apply@gsb.columbia.edu.

Columbia University, School of Continuing Education, Program in Communications Practice, New York, NY 10027. Offers MS. *Faculty:* 11. Application fee: $65. Electronic applications accepted. *Unit head:* Trudi Baldwin, Director, 212-854-9666, E-mail: ce-info@columbia.edu. *Application contact:* Trudi Baldwin, Director, 212-854-9666, E-mail: ce-info@columbia.edu.

Concordia University, School of Graduate Studies, Faculty of Arts and Science, Department of Communication Studies, Montréal, QC H3G 1M8, Canada. Offers communication (PhD); communication studies (Diploma); media studies (MA). *Degree requirements:* For master's, thesis optional; for doctorate, one foreign language, comprehensive exam, thesis/dissertation, research practicum, seminar. *Entrance requirements:* For master's, bachelor's degree in communications, 2 years of media-related experience; for doctorate, MA in communications. *Faculty research:* Communication and development, organizational communication, cultural studies, rhetoric, future studies.

Cornell University, Graduate School, Graduate Fields of Agriculture and Life Sciences, Field of Communication, Ithaca, NY 14853-0001. Offers communication (MPS, MS, PhD); communication research methods (MS, PhD); international communication (MS, PhD); science and environmental communication (MS, PhD); social psychology of communication (MS, PhD); uses and effects of communication (MS, PhD). *Faculty:* 24 full-time (8 women). *Students:* 31 full-time (18 women); includes 2 minority (1 Asian American or Pacific Islander, 1 Hispanic American), 11 international. Average age 30. 144 applicants, 10% accepted, 9 enrolled. In 2009, 6 master's, 3 doctorates awarded. *Degree requirements:* For master's, thesis (MS); for doctorate, comprehensive exam, thesis/dissertation. *Entrance requirements:* For master's and doctorate, GRE General Test, 3 letters of recommendation. Additional exam requirements/recommendations for international students: Required—TOEFL (minimum score 600 paper-based; 250 computer-based; 100 iBT). *Application deadline:* For fall admission, 1/15 for domestic students. Application fee: $70. Electronic applications accepted. *Expenses:* Tuition: Full-time $29,500. Required fees: $70. Full-time tuition and fees vary according to degree level, program and student level. *Financial support:* In 2009–10, 28 students received support, including 1 fellowship with full tuition reimbursement available, 2 research assistantships with full tuition reimbursements available, 6 teaching assistantships with full tuition reimbursements available; institutionally sponsored loans, scholarships/grants, health care benefits, tuition waivers (full and partial), and unspecified assistantships also available. Financial award applicants required to submit FAFSA. *Faculty research:* Mass communication, communication technologies, science and environmental communication. *Unit head:* Director of Graduate Studies, 607-255-2112. *Application contact:* Graduate Field Assistant, 607-255-2112, E-mail: commgrad@cornell.edu.

DePaul University, College of Communication, Chicago, IL 60614. Offers journalism (MA); media, culture and society (MA); organizational and multicultural communication (MA); public relations and advertising (MA). Part-time and evening/weekend programs available. *Faculty:* 31 full-time (17 women), 15 part-time/adjunct (7 women). *Students:* 159 full-time (127 women), 50 part-time (40 women); includes 56 minority (29 African Americans, 9 Asian Americans or Pacific Islanders, 18 Hispanic Americans), 11 international. Average age 29. 354 applicants, 44% accepted, 79 enrolled. In 2009, 64 master's awarded. *Degree requirements:* For master's, comprehensive exam (for some programs), final exam or thesis/project. *Entrance requirements:* For master's, GRE General Test (public relations and advertising), minimum GPA of 3.0, writing sample, letters of recommendation, resume. Additional exam requirements/recommendations for international students: Required—TOEFL (minimum score 590 paper-based; 243 computer-based; 96 iBT). Application fee: $40. Electronic applications accepted. *Expenses:* Tuition: Full-time $37,525; part-time $620 per credit hour. *Financial support:* In 2009–10, 8 students received support, including 4 research assistantships with partial tuition reimbursements available, 2 teaching assistantships with full tuition reimbursements available (averaging $12,000 per year); fellowships with full tuition reimbursements available, career-related internships or fieldwork, scholarships/grants, and tuition waivers (partial) also available. Support available to part-time students. Financial award applicants required to submit FAFSA. *Faculty research:* Intercultural communication, corporate culture, diversity in the working place, organizational socialization, critical cultural studies. *Unit head:* Dr. Jacqueline Taylor, Dean, 773-325-7216, Fax: 773-325-7584, E-mail: jtaylor@depaul.edu. *Application contact:* Ann Spittle, Director of Graduate Admission, 773-325-7315, Fax: 773-325-2395, E-mail: gradcom@depaul.edu.

DeVry University, Keller Graduate School of Management, Downers Grove, IL 60515. Offers accounting and financial management (MAFM); business administration (MBA); human resources management (MHRM); information systems management (MISM); network and communications management (MNCM); project management (MPM); public administration (MPA).

Drake University, School of Journalism and Mass Communication, Des Moines, IA 50311-4516. Offers MCL. *Faculty:* 1 (woman) part-time/adjunct. *Students:* 15 part-time (13 women). Average age 35. 8 applicants, 0% accepted, 0 enrolled. *Expenses:* Tuition: Part-time $475 per credit hour. *Unit head:* Dr. Charles Edwards, Dean, 515-271-2871, Fax: 515-271-4518, E-mail: charles.edwards@drake.edu. *Application contact:* Ann J. Martin, Graduate Coordinator, 515-271-2034, Fax: 515-271-2831, E-mail: ann.martin@drake.edu.

Drexel University, College of Arts and Sciences, Department of Culture and Communication, Philadelphia, PA 19104-2875. Offers communication (MS), including public communication, science communication, technical communication; publication management (MS). Part-time and evening/weekend programs available. *Degree requirements:* For master's, internship, professional portfolio. *Entrance requirements:* Additional exam requirements/recommendations for international students: Required—TOEFL. Electronic applications accepted. *Faculty research:* Science information and attitudes, science influence on literature, process of technical writing, document design, software documentation.

Drury University, Program in Communication, Springfield, MO 65802. Offers MA. Part-time and evening/weekend programs available. *Entrance requirements:* For master's, GMAT or MAT. Additional exam requirements/recommendations for international students: Required—TOEFL. Electronic applications accepted. *Expenses:* Contact institution.

Duquesne University, Graduate School of Liberal Arts, Department of Communication and Rhetorical Studies, Pittsburgh, PA 15282-0001. Offers communication (MA); rhetoric (PhD). Part-time and evening/weekend programs available. *Faculty:* 6 full-time (3 women), 5 part-time/adjunct (3 women). *Students:* 100 full-time (52 women), 34 part-time (31 women); includes 5 minority (4 African Americans, 1 Hispanic American), 12 international. Average age 27. 50 applicants, 86% accepted, 28 enrolled. In 2009, 19 master's, 9 doctorates awarded. *Degree requirements:* For master's, thesis optional, practicum; for doctorate, 2 foreign languages, comprehensive exam, thesis/dissertation. *Entrance requirements:* For master's, GRE General Test, MAT or GMAT; for doctorate, GRE General Test. Additional exam requirements/recommendations for international students: Required—TOEFL. *Application deadline:* For fall admission, 2/1 priority date for domestic and international students; for spring admission, 11/1 priority date for domestic and international students. Applications are processed on a rolling basis. Electronic applications accepted. *Expenses:* Tuition: Part-time $851 per credit. Required fees: $81 per credit. *Financial support:* In 2009–10, 9 research assistantships with full tuition reimbursements (averaging $9,000 per year), 10 teaching assistantships with full tuition reimbursements (averaging $13,000 per year) were awarded; career-related internships or fieldwork, Federal Work-Study, institutionally sponsored loans, scholarships/grants, tuition waivers (full and partial), and unspecified assistantships also available. Financial award application deadline: 5/1. *Unit head:* Dr. Ronald Arnett, Chair, 412-396-5076. *Application contact:* Dr. Janie Fritz, Director, 412-396-6460.

Eastern Michigan University, Graduate School, College of Arts and Sciences, Department of Communication, Media and Theatre Arts, Program in Communication, Ypsilanti, MI 48197. Offers MA. Part-time and evening/weekend programs available. Postbaccalaureate distance learning degree programs offered (minimal on-campus study). *Students:* 9 full-time (5 women), 25 part-time (19 women); includes 8 minority (6 African Americans, 2 Asian Americans or Pacific Islanders). Average age 31. In 2009, 11 master's awarded. *Degree requirements:* For master's, thesis or alternative. *Entrance requirements:* Additional exam requirements/recommendations for international students: Required—TOEFL. *Application deadline:* Applications are processed on a rolling basis. Application fee: $35. Tuition and fees vary according to course level. *Financial support:* Fellowships, research assistantships with full tuition reimbursements, teaching assistantships with full tuition reimbursements, career-related internships or fieldwork, Federal Work-Study, institutionally sponsored loans, scholarships/grants, tuition waivers (partial), and unspecified assistantships available. Support available to part-time students. Financial award applicants required to submit FAFSA. *Unit head:* Dr. Kathleen Stacey, Coordinator, 734-487-3198, Fax: 734-487-3443, E-mail: kathleen.stacey@emich.edu. *Application contact:* Graduate Coordinator.

Eastern New Mexico University, Graduate School, College of Liberal Arts and Sciences, Department of Communicative Arts and Sciences, Portales, NM 88130. Offers MA. Part-time programs available. Postbaccalaureate distance learning degree programs offered (minimal on-campus study). *Faculty:* 6 full-time (3 women). *Students:* 2 full-time (both women), 21 part-time (9 women); includes 5 minority (all Hispanic Americans), 3 international. Average age 30. 13 applicants, 31% accepted, 4 enrolled. In 2009, 4 master's awarded. *Degree requirements:* For master's, comprehensive exam, thesis optional. *Entrance requirements:* For master's, minimum GPA of 3.0. Additional exam requirements/recommendations for international students: Required—TOEFL (minimum score 550 paper-based; 213 computer-based; 79 iBT), IELTS (minimum score 6). *Application deadline:* For fall admission, 7/20 priority date for domestic students, 6/20 priority date for international students. Applications are processed on a rolling basis. Application fee: $10. Electronic applications accepted. *Expenses:* Tuition, state resident: full-time $2922; part-time $121.75 per credit hour. Tuition, nonresident: full-time $8454; part-time $352.25 per credit hour. Required fees: $1038; $43.25 per credit hour. *Financial support:* In 2009–10, research assistantships (averaging $4,250 per year), 2 teaching assistantships with tuition reimbursements (averaging $4,250 per year) were awarded; fellowships, unspecified assistantships also available. Support available to part-time students. Financial award applicants required to submit FAFSA. *Faculty research:* Radio and television production. *Unit head:* Graduate Coordinator, 575-562-2272. *Application contact:* Dr. Linda Weems, Dean, Graduate School, 575-562-2148, E-mail: linda.weems@enmu.edu.

Eastern Washington University, Graduate Studies, College of Social and Behavioral Sciences, Department of Communication Studies, Cheney, WA 99004-2431. Offers MSC. Part-time and evening/weekend programs available. *Degree requirements:* For master's, comprehensive exam, thesis or alternative. *Entrance requirements:* For master's, GRE General Test, minimum GPA of 3.0. *Expenses:* Tuition, state resident: full-time $7476; part-time $249 per quarter hour. Tuition, nonresident: full-time $18,030; part-time $601 per quarter hour. Required fees: $3.50 per quarter hour. $142 per quarter.

East Tennessee State University, School of Graduate Studies, College of Arts and Sciences, Department of Communication, Johnson City, TN 37614. Offers MA. *Entrance requirements:* For master's, GRE. Additional exam requirements/recommendations for international students: Required—TOEFL (minimum score 550 paper-based; 213 computer-based). *Faculty research:* Political communications, visual communication, depictions of gender and ethnicity in print and online media and online corporate media, presidential rhetoric and newspaper coverage of presidential speeches.

Edinboro University of Pennsylvania, School of Graduate Studies and Research, School of Liberal Arts, Department of Communications and Media Studies, Edinboro, PA 16444. Offers MA, Certificate. Part-time and evening/weekend programs available. *Faculty:* 5 full-time (2 women). *Students:* 29 full-time (18 women), 14 part-time (10 women); includes 6 minority (4 African Americans, 1 Asian American or Pacific Islander, 1 Hispanic American). Average age

Communication—General

Edinboro University of Pennsylvania (continued)

29. In 2009, 18 master's, 10 other advanced degrees awarded. *Degree requirements:* For master's, thesis or alternative, competency exam. *Entrance requirements:* For master's, GRE or MAT, minimum QPA of 2.5. *Application deadline:* Applications are processed on a rolling basis. Application fee: $30. Electronic applications accepted. *Expenses:* Tuition, state resident: full-time $6666; part-time $370 per credit. Tuition, nonresident: full-time $10,666; part-time $593 per credit. Required fees: $2206.28. One-time fee: $204 part-time. *Financial support:* In 2009–10, 13 research assistantships with full and partial tuition reimbursements (averaging $4,050 per year) were awarded; career-related internships or fieldwork, Federal Work-Study, scholarships/grants, and unspecified assistantships also available. Support available to part-time students. Financial award application deadline: 2/15; financial award applicants required to submit FAFSA. *Unit head:* Dr. Andrew Smith, Program Head, 814-732-2165, E-mail: arsmith@edinboro.edu. *Application contact:* Dr. Andrew Smith, Program Head, 814-732-2165, E-mail: arsmith@edinboro.edu.

Emerson College, Graduate Studies, School of Communication, Department of Communication Studies, Boston, MA 02116-4624. Offers communication management (MA). Part-time and evening/weekend programs available. *Faculty:* 19 full-time (9 women). *Students:* 42 full-time (30 women), 11 part-time (7 women); includes 3 minority (1 African American, 2 Asian Americans or Pacific Islanders), 18 international. Average age 23. 64 applicants, 86% accepted, 25 enrolled. In 2009, 18 master's awarded. *Entrance requirements:* For master's, GMAT or GRE General Test. Additional exam requirements/recommendations for international students: Required—TOEFL (minimum score 550 paper-based; 213 computer-based; 80 iBT), IELTS (minimum score 6.5). *Application deadline:* For fall admission, 6/1 priority date for domestic students, 5/1 priority date for international students; for spring admission, 11/1 priority date for domestic and international students. Applications are processed on a rolling basis. Application fee: $60 ($75 for international students). Electronic applications accepted. *Expenses:* Tuition: Full-time $22,056; part-time $919 per credit. Required fees: $120; $120 per year. One-time fee: $170 full-time. *Financial support:* In 2009–10, 17 students received support, including 2 fellowships (averaging $14,000 per year), 9 research assistantships (averaging $10,000 per year); Federal Work-Study, scholarships/grants, and unspecified assistantships also available. Financial award application deadline: 3/1; financial award applicants required to submit FAFSA. *Unit head:* Prof. Richard West, Chair, 617-824-8491, E-mail: richard_west@emerson.edu. *Application contact:* Office of Graduate Admission, 617-824-8610, Fax: 617-824-8614, E-mail: gradapp@emerson.edu.

Fairfield University, College of Arts and Sciences, Fairfield, CT 06824-5195. Offers American studies (MA); communication (MA); creative writing (MFA); mathematics (MS). Part-time and evening/weekend programs available. *Degree requirements:* For master's, capstone research course. *Entrance requirements:* For master's, minimum GPA of 3.0, 2 letters of recommendation, resume. Additional exam requirements/recommendations for international students: Required—TOEFL (minimum score 550 paper-based; 213 computer-based; 80 iBT). Electronic applications accepted. *Faculty research:* Non-commutative algebra, partial differential equations, writing (fiction, non-fiction and poetry), communication for social change, comparative media systems, negotiation and management.

Fairleigh Dickinson University, Metropolitan Campus, University College: Arts, Sciences, and Professional Studies, School of Art and Media Studies, Program in Media and Communications, Teaneck, NJ 07666-1914. Offers MA. *Students:* 15 full-time (12 women), 11 part-time (7 women), 5 international. Average age 28. 16 applicants, 81% accepted, 8 enrolled. In 2009, 7 master's awarded. Application fee: $40. *Application contact:* Susan Brooman, University Director of Graduate Admissions, 201-692-2554, Fax: 201-692-2560, E-mail: globaleducation@fdu.edu.

Fitchburg State University, Division of Graduate and Continuing Education, Program in Applied Communications, Fitchburg, MA 01420-2697. Offers applied communications (MS, Certificate); library media (MS); technical and professional writing (MS). Part-time and evening/weekend programs available. *Students:* 3 full-time (2 women), 18 part-time (10 women), 2 international. Average age 33. 8 applicants, 88% accepted, 6 enrolled. In 2009, 10 master's awarded. *Entrance requirements:* For master's, GRE General Test or MAT, minimum 2 years of related experience, letters of recommendation, resume. Additional exam requirements/recommendations for international students: Required—TOEFL (minimum score 550 paper-based; 213 computer-based; 79 iBT). *Application deadline:* Applications are processed on a rolling basis. Application fee: $25 ($50 for international students). *Expenses:* Tuition, area resident: Part-time $150 per credit. Tuition, state resident: part-time $150 per credit. Tuition, nonresident: part-time $150 per credit. Required fees: $120 per credit. *Financial support:* In 2009–10, research assistantships with partial tuition reimbursements (averaging $5,500 per year); Federal Work-Study, scholarships/grants, and unspecified assistantships also available. Support available to part-time students. Financial award application deadline: 3/1; financial award applicants required to submit FAFSA. *Unit head:* Dr. John Chetro-Szivos, Chair, 978-665-3261, Fax: 978-665-3658, E-mail: gce@fsc.edu. *Application contact:* Director of Admissions, 978-665-3144, Fax: 978-665-4540, E-mail: admissions@fsc.edu.

Florida Atlantic University, Dorothy F. Schmidt College of Arts and Letters, School of Communication and Multimedia Studies, Boca Raton, FL 33431-0991. Offers communication studies (MA); film and video (Certificate); film studies (MA); multimedia journalism studies (MA). Part-time programs available. *Faculty:* 21 full-time (10 women), 14 part-time/adjunct (3 women). *Students:* 14 full-time (11 women), 13 part-time (8 women); includes 3 minority (1 African American, 1 Asian American or Pacific Islander, 1 Hispanic American), 3 international. Average age 28. 39 applicants, 26% accepted, 6 enrolled. In 2009, 7 master's awarded. *Degree requirements:* For master's, one foreign language, comprehensive exam (for some programs), thesis (for some programs). *Entrance requirements:* For master's, GRE General Test, minimum GPA of 3.0. *Application deadline:* For fall admission, 7/1 priority date for domestic students, 4/1 for international students; for spring admission, 11/1 for domestic students, 10/1 for international students. Applications are processed on a rolling basis. Application fee: $30. Electronic applications accepted. *Expenses:* Tuition, state resident: full-time $7055; part-time $293.94 per credit hour. Tuition, nonresident: full-time $22,096; part-time $920.66 per credit hour. *Financial support:* Teaching assistantships with partial tuition reimbursements, Federal Work-Study and institutionally sponsored loans available. Support available to part-time students. Financial award application deadline: 3/1. *Faculty research:* Cultural studies, gender studies, film, communication theory, journalism, new media. *Unit head:* Dr. Susan S. Reilly, Director, 561-297-1095, Fax: 561-297-2615, E-mail: sreilly@fau.edu. *Application contact:* Dr. Eric M. Freedman, Graduate Coordinator, 561-297-2534, Fax: 561-297-2615, E-mail: efreedma@fau.edu.

Florida Institute of Technology, Graduate Programs, College of Psychology and Liberal Arts, Department of Humanities and Communication, Melbourne, FL 32901-6975. Offers technical and professional communication (MS). Part-time and evening/weekend programs available. *Faculty:* 4 full-time (all women). *Students:* 6 full-time (2 women), 11 part-time (9 women); includes 5 minority (2 African Americans, 1 American Indian/Alaska Native, 1 Asian American or Pacific Islander, 1 Hispanic American), 2 international. Average age 38. 4 applicants, 100% accepted, 2 enrolled. In 2009, 2 master's awarded. *Degree requirements:* For master's, comprehensive exam (for some programs), thesis optional. *Entrance requirements:* For master's, GRE (minimum score 1000 verbal and analytical), minimum GPA of 3.0, 2 letters of recommendation, discursive writing sample. Additional exam requirements/recommendations for international students: Required—TOEFL (minimum score 550 paper-based; 213 computer-based; 79 iBT). *Application deadline:* For fall admission, 4/1 for international students; for spring admission, 9/30 for international students. Applications are processed on a rolling basis. Application fee: $50. Electronic applications accepted. *Expenses:* Tuition: Part-time $1015 per credit. Tuition and fees vary according to campus/location and program. *Financial support:* Career-related internships or fieldwork and tuition remissions available. Support available to part-time students. Financial award application deadline: 3/1; financial award applicants required to submit FAFSA. *Faculty research:* Communication of astronomy in the seventeenth century, persuasion and patronage in seventeenth century work, technical and cross-cultural communication. *Unit head:* Dr. Robert A. Taylor, Department Head, 321-674-7384, Fax: 321-674-8109, E-mail: rotaylor@fit.edu. *Application contact:* Thomas M. Shea, Director of Graduate Admissions, 321-674-7577, Fax: 321-723-9468, E-mail: tshea@fit.edu.

Florida State University, The Graduate School, College of Communication and Information, School of Communication, Tallahassee, FL 32306. Offers corporate and public communication (MA, MS); integrated marketing communication (MA, MS); mass communication (PhD); media and communication studies (MA, MS); speech communication (PhD). Part-time programs available. *Faculty:* 24 full-time (9 women), 6 part-time/adjunct (1 woman). *Students:* 153 full-time (110 women), 65 part-time (34 women); includes 62 minority (37 African Americans, 1 American Indian/Alaska Native, 24 Hispanic Americans). Average age 24. 230 applicants, 76% accepted, 85 enrolled. In 2009, 84 master's, 6 doctorates awarded. *Degree requirements:* For master's, thesis (for some programs); for doctorate, comprehensive exam, thesis/dissertation. *Entrance requirements:* For master's, GRE General Test, minimum GPA of 3.0; for doctorate, GRE General Test, minimum GPA of 3.3 in graduate course work. Additional exam requirements/recommendations for international students: Required—TOEFL (minimum score 600 paper-based; 250 computer-based; 100 iBT). *Application deadline:* For fall admission, 7/1 priority date for domestic students, 5/1 priority date for international students; for spring admission, 11/1 priority date for domestic and international students. Applications are processed on a rolling basis. Application fee: $30. Electronic applications accepted. *Expenses:* Tuition, state resident: full-time $7413. Tuition, nonresident: full-time $22,567. *Financial support:* In 2009–10, 52 students received support, including 1 fellowship with full tuition reimbursement available, 8 research assistantships with full tuition reimbursements available (averaging $14,000 per year), 40 teaching assistantships with full tuition reimbursements available (averaging $5,000 per year); career-related internships or fieldwork, Federal Work-Study, institutionally sponsored loans, scholarships/grants, tuition waivers (partial), and unspecified assistantships also available. Support available to part-time students. Financial award application deadline: 2/1; financial award applicants required to submit FAFSA. *Faculty research:* Communication technology and policy, marketing communication, communication content and effect, new communication/information technologies. Total annual research expenditures: $600,000. *Unit head:* Dr. Stephen D. McDowell, Director, 850-644-2276, Fax: 850-644-8642, E-mail: steve.mcdowell@cci.fsu.edu. *Application contact:* Natashia Hinson-Turner, Graduate Coordinator, 850-644-8746, Fax: 850-644-8642, E-mail: natashia.turner@cci.fsu.edu.

Fordham University, Graduate School of Arts and Sciences, Department of Communication and Media Studies, New York, NY 10458. Offers public communications (MA). Part-time and evening/weekend programs available. *Faculty:* 11 full-time (3 women). *Students:* 12 full-time (9 women), 35 part-time (23 women); includes 3 minority (all African Americans), 12 international. Average age 26. 77 applicants, 44% accepted, 14 enrolled. In 2009, 24 master's awarded. *Degree requirements:* For master's, thesis, internship. *Entrance requirements:* For master's, GRE General Test. Additional exam requirements/recommendations for international students: Required—TOEFL (minimum score 600 paper-based; 250 computer-based). *Application deadline:* For fall admission, 1/4 priority date for domestic students; for spring admission, 11/1 for domestic students. Application fee: $70. Electronic applications accepted. *Financial support:* In 2009–10, 3 students received support, including 3 research assistantships with tuition reimbursements available (averaging $19,000 per year); fellowships, career-related internships or fieldwork, Federal Work-Study, institutionally sponsored loans, scholarships/grants, tuition waivers (full and partial), and unspecified assistantships also available. Financial award application deadline: 1/4. Total annual research expenditures: $80,000. *Unit head:* Dr. Paul Levinson, Chair, 718-817-4860, Fax: 718-817-4868, E-mail: levinson@fordham.edu. *Application contact:* Charlene Dundie, Director of Graduate Admissions, 718-817-4420, Fax: 718-817-3566, E-mail: dundie@fordham.edu.

Fort Hays State University, Graduate School, College of Arts and Sciences, Department of Communication, Hays, KS 67601-4099. Offers MS. Part-time programs available. *Degree requirements:* For master's, comprehensive exam, thesis optional. *Entrance requirements:* Additional exam requirements/recommendations for international students: Required—TOEFL (minimum score 550 paper-based; 213 computer-based). Electronic applications accepted. *Faculty research:* Listening skills development, oral sensory motor skills, speech, reading, articulation in preschool children.

George Mason University, College of Humanities and Social Sciences, Program in Communications, Fairfax, VA 22030. Offers MA, PhD. *Faculty:* 33 full-time (14 women), 41 part-time/adjunct (16 women). *Students:* 24 full-time (18 women), 31 part-time (18 women); includes 3 minority (1 African American, 2 Asian Americans or Pacific Islanders), 3 international. Average age 33. 96 applicants, 51% accepted, 29 enrolled. In 2009, 18 master's awarded. *Degree requirements:* For master's, comprehensive exam, thesis or project; for doctorate, comprehensive exam, thesis/dissertation. *Entrance requirements:* For master's, GRE, 3 letters of recommendation, resume; for doctorate, GRE, 3 letters of recommendation, essay addressing communication area, resume, expanded goals statement. Additional exam requirements/recommendations for international students: Required—TOEFL. *Application deadline:* For fall admission, 3/1 for domestic students. Applications are processed on a rolling basis. Application fee: $75. Electronic applications accepted. *Expenses:* Tuition, state resident: full-time $7568; part-time $315.33 per credit hour. Tuition, nonresident: full-time $21,704; part-time $904.33 per credit hour. Required fees: $2184; $91 per credit hour. *Financial support:* In 2009–10, 21 students received support, including 2 fellowships with full tuition reimbursements available (averaging $18,000 per year), 6 research assistantships with full and partial tuition reimbursements available (averaging $10,409 per year), 14 teaching assistantships with full and partial tuition reimbursements available (averaging $9,239 per year); Federal Work-Study, scholarships/grants, unspecified assistantships, and health care benefits (full-time research or teaching assistantship recipients) also available. Support available to part-time students. *Faculty research:* Theoretical and multi-methodological promotion, disease prevention, quality of care, risk assessment, crisis management, consumer/provider relationships, health campaigns, communication policy. Total annual research expenditures: $378,090. *Unit head:* Gary Kreps, Chair, 703-993-1094, Fax: 703-993-1096, E-mail: gkreps@gmu.edu. *Application contact:* Maria Carabelli, Graduate Coordinator, 703-993-3552, E-mail: mverdino@gmu.edu.

Georgetown University, Graduate School of Arts and Sciences, Program in Communication, Culture, and Technology, Washington, DC 20057. Offers MA. Part-time and evening/weekend programs available. *Degree requirements:* For master's, thesis (for some programs). *Entrance requirements:* For master's, GRE General Test, 3 letters of recommendation, writing sample. Additional exam requirements/recommendations for international students: Required—TOEFL (minimum score 600 paper-based; 250 computer-based). Electronic applications accepted.

The George Washington University, Elliott School of International Affairs, Program in Global Communication, Washington, DC 20052. Offers MA. *Students:* 19 full-time (15 women), 9 part-time (8 women); includes 6 minority (2 African Americans, 2 Asian Americans or Pacific Islanders, 2 Hispanic Americans), 3 international. Average age 26. 93 applicants, 62% accepted, 21 enrolled. *Application deadline:* For fall admission, 2/1 for domestic students; for spring admission, 10/1 for domestic students. *Financial support:* Application deadline: 1/15. *Unit head:* Sean Aday, Director, 202-994-4220, Fax: 202-994-5806, E-mail: seanaday@gwu.edu. *Application contact:* Jeff V. Miles, Director of Graduate Admissions, 202-994-7050, Fax: 202-994-9537, E-mail: esiagrad@gwu.edu.

Georgia State University, College of Arts and Sciences, Department of Communication, Atlanta, GA 30302-3083. Offers film/video/digital imaging (MA); human communication and social influence (MA); mass communication (MA); moving image studies (PhD); public communication (PhD). Part-time programs available. *Degree requirements:* For master's, one foreign language, thesis or alternative; for doctorate, comprehensive exam, thesis/dissertation. *Entrance requirements:* For master's and doctorate, GRE General Test. Additional exam requirements/recommendations for international students: Required—TOEFL (minimum score

80 computer-based). Electronic applications accepted. *Faculty research:* Critical/cultural studies, rhetoric studies, film/media studies, mass communications/journalism, audience studies.

Gonzaga University, School of Professional Studies, Program in Communication and Leadership Studies, Spokane, WA 99258. Offers MA. Postbaccalaureate distance learning degree programs offered. *Faculty:* 4 full-time (2 women), 10 part-time/adjunct (4 women). *Students:* 41 full-time (25 women), 373 part-time (264 women); includes 75 minority (38 African Americans, 6 American Indian/Alaska Native, 12 Asian Americans or Pacific Islanders, 19 Hispanic Americans). Average age 33. In 2009, 61 master's awarded. Tuition and fees vary according to course level, course load, degree level, campus/location and program. *Unit head:* Dr. Mary McFarland, Dean, 509-328-4220 Ext. 3542. *Application contact:* Dr. Mary McFarland, Dean, 509-328-4220 Ext. 3542.

Governors State University, College of Arts and Sciences, Program in Communication and Training, University Park, IL 60466-0975. Offers communication studies (MA); instructional and training technology (MA); media communication (MA). Part-time and evening/weekend programs available. *Degree requirements:* For master's, thesis or alternative.

Grand Valley State University, College of Liberal Arts and Sciences, School of Communications, Allendale, MI 49401-9403. Offers MS. Part-time and evening/weekend programs available. *Faculty:* 3 full-time (0 women), 1 part-time/adjunct (0 women). *Students:* 21 full-time (12 women), 37 part-time (25 women); includes 15 minority (11 African Americans, 1 American Indian/Alaska Native, 1 Asian American or Pacific Islander, 2 Hispanic Americans), 5 international. Average age 31. 29 applicants, 83% accepted, 19 enrolled. In 2009, 25 master's awarded. *Degree requirements:* For master's, thesis or alternative. *Entrance requirements:* For master's, minimum GPA of 3.0 in last 60 hours, 2 letters of recommendation. Additional exam requirements/recommendations for international students: Required—TOEFL (minimum score 550 paper-based; 213 computer-based). *Application deadline:* For fall admission, 8/15 priority date for domestic students; for winter admission, 12/15 priority date for domestic students; for spring admission, 4/15 priority date for domestic students. Applications are processed on a rolling basis. Application fee: $30. Electronic applications accepted. *Expenses:* Tuition, state resident: part-time $471 per credit hour. Tuition, nonresident: part-time $646 per credit hour. Tuition and fees vary according to course level. *Financial support:* In 2009–10, 7 students received support, including 4 fellowships (averaging $7,372 per year), 3 research assistantships with tuition reimbursements available (averaging $12,091 per year); career-related internships or fieldwork, Federal Work-Study, and institutionally sponsored loans also available. Support available to part-time students. Financial award application deadline: 4/15. *Faculty research:* Communication technology, databases, organizational communication, systems theory, public relations and advertising. *Unit head:* Dr. Anthony Thompson, Director, 616-331-3606, Fax: 616-895-2700, E-mail: thompsoa@gvsu.edu. *Application contact:* Dr. Alex Nesterenko, Coordinator, 616-331-3668, Fax: 616-331-2700, E-mail: nesterea@gvsu.edu.

Harvard University, Extension School, Cambridge, MA 02138-3722. Offers applied sciences (CAS); biotechnology (ALM); educational technologies (ALM); educational technology (CET); English for graduate and professional studies (DGP); environmental management (ALM, CEM); information technology (ALM); journalism (ALM); liberal arts (ALM); management (ALM, CM); mathematics for teaching (ALM); museum studies (ALM); premedical studies (Diploma); publication and communication (CPC). Part-time and evening/weekend programs available. *Degree requirements:* For master's, thesis. *Entrance requirements:* For master's, 3 completed graduate courses with grade of B or higher. Additional exam requirements/recommendations for international students: Required—TOEFL (minimum score 600 paper-based; 250 computer-based), TWE (minimum score 5). *Expenses:* Contact institution.

Hawai'i Pacific University, College of Humanities and Social Sciences, Program in Communication, Honolulu, HI 96813. Offers MA. Part-time and evening/weekend programs available. *Faculty:* 7 full-time (2 women), 4 part-time/adjunct (3 women). *Students:* 58 full-time (36 women), 49 part-time (33 women); includes 37 minority (4 African Americans, 3 American Indian/Alaska Native, 24 Asian Americans or Pacific Islanders, 6 Hispanic Americans), 39 international. Average age 29. 61 applicants, 93% accepted, 26 enrolled. In 2009, 40 master's awarded. *Degree requirements:* For master's, thesis. *Entrance requirements:* Additional exam requirements/recommendations for international students: Recommended—TOEFL (minimum score 550 paper-based; 213 computer-based; 80 iBT), TWE (minimum score 5). *Application deadline:* For fall admission, 2/15 priority date for domestic students; for spring admission, 10/15 priority date for domestic students. Applications are processed on a rolling basis. Application fee: $50. Electronic applications accepted. *Expenses:* Tuition: Full-time $12,600; part-time $700 per credit hour. Tuition and fees vary according to program. *Financial support:* In 2009–10, 65 students received support. Career-related internships or fieldwork, Federal Work-Study, scholarships/grants, and unspecified assistantships available. Support available to part-time students. Financial award application deadline: 3/1; financial award applicants required to submit FAFSA. *Unit head:* Dr. Steven Combs, Dean, 808-544-0828, Fax: 808-544-0835, E-mail: scombs@hpu.edu. *Application contact:* Danny Lam, Assistant Director of Graduate Admissions, 808-544-1135, Fax: 808-544-0280, E-mail: graduate@hpu.edu.

See Close-Up on page 679.

Hofstra University, School of Communication, Hempstead, NY 11549. Offers MA, MFA. Part-time and evening/weekend programs available. *Faculty:* 14 full-time (4 women), 3 part-time/adjunct (1 woman). *Students:* 43 full-time (24 women), 30 part-time (19 women); includes 17 minority (9 African Americans, 1 American Indian/Alaska Native, 3 Asian Americans or Pacific Islanders, 4 Hispanic Americans), 7 international. Average age 28. 77 applicants, 87% accepted, 32 enrolled. In 2009, 8 master's awarded. *Degree requirements:* For master's, thesis, thesis project. *Entrance requirements:* For master's, letters of recommendation, interview. Additional exam requirements/recommendations for international students: Required—TOEFL (minimum score 550 paper-based; 213 computer-based; 80 iBT). *Application deadline:* Applications are processed on a rolling basis. Application fee: $60. Electronic applications accepted. *Expenses:* Tuition: Full-time $16,200; part-time $900 per credit hour. Required fees: $970; $145 per term. Tuition and fees vary according to program. *Financial support:* In 2009–10, 24 students received support, including 8 fellowships with full and partial tuition reimbursements available (averaging $3,188 per year), 7 research assistantships with full and partial tuition reimbursements available (averaging $15,650 per year); Federal Work-Study, institutionally sponsored loans, scholarships/grants, tuition waivers (full and partial), and unspecified assistantships also available. Support available to part-time students. Financial award applicants required to submit FAFSA. *Faculty research:* Public deliberation; community and citizen's media; public deliberations; media ethics/law; performance of race and gender; environmental and health journalism, communication, development, and globalization. *Unit head:* Dr. Cliff Jernigan, Acting Dean, 516-463-5214, Fax: 516-463-4866, E-mail: avfczj@hofstra.edu. *Application contact:* Carol Drummer, Dean of Graduate Admissions, 516-463-4876, Fax: 516-463-4664, E-mail: gradstudent@hofstra.edu.

Howard University, School of Communications, Washington, DC 20059-0002. Offers MA, MFA, MS, PhD. Part-time and evening/weekend programs available. Terminal master's awarded for partial completion of doctoral program. *Degree requirements:* For master's, comprehensive exam (for some programs), thesis optional; for doctorate, one foreign language, comprehensive exam, thesis/dissertation. *Entrance requirements:* For master's, GRE General Test, minimum GPA of 3.0; for doctorate, GRE General Test, minimum GPA of 3.2. Additional exam requirements/recommendations for international students: Required—TOEFL. Electronic applications accepted. *Expenses:* Contact institution. *Faculty research:* Communication disorders, intercultural communication, communication skills, race and media.

Illinois Institute of Technology, Graduate College, College of Science and Letters, Lewis Department of Humanities, Chicago, IL 60616-3793. Offers information architecture (MS); technical communication (PhD); technical communication and information design (MS). Part-time and evening/weekend programs available. *Faculty:* 17 full-time (6 women), 11 part-time/adjunct (4 women). *Students:* 13 full-time (8 women), 34 part-time (24 women); includes 12 minority (11 African Americans, 1 Asian American or Pacific Islander), 6 international. Average age 34. 46 applicants, 52% accepted, 9 enrolled. In 2009, 9 master's, 2 doctorates awarded. *Degree requirements:* For master's, comprehensive exam, thesis or alternative, project; for doctorate, comprehensive exam, thesis/dissertation, qualifying exam. *Entrance requirements:* For master's, GRE General Test; for doctorate, GRE General Test, bachelor's degree in technical communication or other relevant field. Additional exam requirements/recommendations for international students: Required—TOEFL (minimum score 523 paper-based; 70 iBT). *Application deadline:* For fall admission, 5/1 for domestic and international students; for spring admission, 10/15 for domestic and international students. Applications are processed on a rolling basis. Application fee: $50. Electronic applications accepted. *Expenses:* Tuition: Full-time $17,550; part-time $888 per credit hour. Required fees: $850; $7.50 per credit hour. One-time fee: $50 full-time. Full-time tuition and fees vary according to program. *Financial support:* In 2009–10, 15 teaching assistantships with partial tuition reimbursements (averaging $9,000 per year) were awarded; career-related internships or fieldwork, Federal Work-Study, institutionally sponsored loans, scholarships/grants, health care benefits, tuition waivers (partial), and unspecified assistantships also available. Support available to part-time students. Financial award applicants required to submit FAFSA. *Faculty research:* Discourse analysis, linguistics, readability, ethics in professions, instructional and document design, knowledge management, usability testing and evaluation, history and philosophy of science. Total annual research expenditures: $34,161. *Unit head:* Dr. Kathryn Riley, Professor and Chair, 312-567-3566, Fax: 312-567-5187, E-mail: riley@iit.edu. *Application contact:* Dr. Kathryn Riley, Professor and Chair, 312-567-3566, Fax: 312-567-5187, E-mail: riley@iit.edu.

Illinois State University, Graduate School, College of Arts and Sciences, School of Communication, Normal, IL 61790-2200. Offers MA, MS. *Degree requirements:* For master's, thesis or alternative. *Entrance requirements:* For master's, GRE General Test, minimum GPA of 2.8 in last 60 hours of course work. Additional exam requirements/recommendations for international students: Required—TOEFL. *Faculty research:* Corporation for public broadcasting, FY2007, community service grant for WGLT-FM, Illinois public broadcasting grant FY2007 for WGLT-FM; WGLT digital conversion fund.

Immaculata University, College of Graduate Studies, Program in Applied Communication, Immaculata, PA 19345. Offers MA.

Indiana State University, School of Graduate Studies, College of Arts and Sciences, Department of Communication, Terre Haute, IN 47809. Offers communication studies (MA, MS); radio, television and film (MA, MS). Part-time programs available. *Degree requirements:* For master's, thesis (for some programs), oral and written exam. *Entrance requirements:* For master's, GRE General Test. Additional exam requirements/recommendations for international students: Required—TOEFL. *Faculty research:* Women in media, communication apprehension, media history.

Indiana University Bloomington, University Graduate School, College of Arts and Sciences, Department of Telecommunications, Bloomington, IN 47405-7000. Offers mass communications (PhD); telecommunications (MA, MS). *Faculty:* 11 full-time (4 women). *Students:* 55 full-time (28 women), 8 part-time (3 women); includes 4 minority (3 African Americans, 1 Asian American or Pacific Islander), 26 international. Average age 30. 61 applicants, 43% accepted, 17 enrolled. In 2009, 17 master's, 8 doctorates awarded. Terminal master's awarded for partial completion of doctoral program. *Degree requirements:* For master's, thesis (for some programs); for doctorate, thesis/dissertation. *Entrance requirements:* For master's and doctorate, GRE General Test. Additional exam requirements/recommendations for international students: Required—TOEFL. *Application deadline:* For fall admission, 1/15 priority date for domestic students, 12/15 for international students. Applications are processed on a rolling basis. Application fee: $55 ($65 for international students). *Financial support:* Fellowships, research assistantships, teaching assistantships, tuition waivers (full) available. *Faculty research:* Media processes and effects, media law and policy, media management, media design and production. *Unit head:* Tamera Theodore, Graduate Secretary, 812-855-2017, E-mail: ttheodor@indiana.edu. *Application contact:* Tamera Theodore, Graduate Secretary, 812-855-2017, E-mail: ttheodor@indiana.edu.

Indiana University of Pennsylvania, School of Graduate Studies and Research, College of Education and Educational Technology, Department of Communications Media, Indiana, PA 15705-1087. Offers adult education and communications technology (MA); communications media and instructional technology (PhD). *Faculty:* 8 full-time (1 woman). *Students:* 16 full-time (7 women), 24 part-time (13 women); includes 3 minority (2 African Americans, 1 Asian American or Pacific Islander), 2 international. Average age 35. 40 applicants, 53% accepted, 20 enrolled.Application fee: $40. *Expenses:* Tuition, state resident: full-time $6666; part-time $370 per credit hour. Tuition, nonresident: full-time $10,666; part-time $593 per credit hour. Required fees: $813 per semester. *Financial support:* In 2009–10, 4 fellowships (averaging $1,000 per year), 8 research assistantships (averaging $5,936 per year), 3 teaching assistantships (averaging $21,536 per year) were awarded. *Unit head:* Dr. Mark Piwinsky, Chairperson, 724-357-3954, Fax: 724-357-5503, E-mail: mark.piwinsky@iup.edu. *Application contact:* Dr. Edward Nardi, Associate Dean, 724-357-2480, Fax: 724-357-5595, E-mail: ewnardi@iup.edu.

Indiana University–Purdue University Fort Wayne, College of Arts and Sciences, Department of Communication, Fort Wayne, IN 46805-1499. Offers professional communication (MA, MS). Part-time programs available. *Faculty:* 3 full-time (all women). *Students:* 8 full-time (4 women), 22 part-time (11 women); includes 3 minority (all African Americans), 2 international. Average age 32. 15 applicants, 100% accepted, 11 enrolled. In 2009, 10 master's awarded. *Entrance requirements:* For master's, minimum GPA of 3.0. Additional exam requirements/recommendations for international students: Required—TOEFL (minimum score 550 paper-based; 213 computer-based; 77 iBT); Recommended—TWE. *Application deadline:* For fall admission, 4/15 priority date for domestic students, 2/15 priority date for international students; for spring admission, 11/30 priority date for domestic students, 9/15 priority date for international students. Applications are processed on a rolling basis. Application fee: $55 ($60 for international students). Electronic applications accepted. *Expenses:* Tuition, state resident: full-time $4595; part-time $255 per credit. Tuition, nonresident: full-time $10,963; part-time $609 per credit. Required fees: $528; $29.35 per credit. Tuition and fees vary according to course load. *Financial support:* In 2009–10, 9 teaching assistantships with partial tuition reimbursements (averaging $12,740 per year) were awarded; scholarships/grants also available. Support available to part-time students. Financial award application deadline: 3/1; financial award applicants required to submit FAFSA. *Faculty research:* National Woman Suffrage Association, Clinton's Presidential Campaign. *Unit head:* Dr. Marcia Dixson, Chair and Associate Professor, 260-481-6558, Fax: 260-481-6183, E-mail: dixson@ipfw.edu. *Application contact:* Dr. Steven Carr, Graduate Program Director, 260-481-6545, Fax: 260-481-6183, E-mail: carr@ipfw.edu.

Instituto Tecnológico y de Estudios Superiores de Monterrey, Campus Ciudad Obregón, Programs in Education, Program in Communications, Ciudad Obregón, Mexico. Offers ME.

Instituto Tecnológico y de Estudios Superiores de Monterrey, Campus Monterrey, Graduate and Research Division, Program in Natural and Social Sciences, Monterrey, Mexico. Offers biotechnology (MS); chemistry (MS, PhD); communications (MS); education (MA). Part-time programs available. *Degree requirements:* For master's, one foreign language, thesis; for doctorate, one foreign language, thesis/dissertation. *Entrance requirements:* For master's, EXADEP; for doctorate, EXADEP, master's degree in related field. Additional exam requirements/recommendations for international students: Required—TOEFL. *Faculty research:* Cultural industries, mineral substances, bioremediation, food processing, CQ in industrial chemical processing.

International University in Geneva, Master of Arts in Media and Communication Program, Geneva, Switzerland. Offers luxury management (MA); marketing (MA). *Degree requirements:* For master's, comprehensive exam. *Entrance requirements:* Additional exam requirements/recommendations for international students: Required—TOEFL. Electronic applications accepted.

Communication—General

Ithaca College, Division of Graduate and Professional Studies, Roy H. Park School of Communications, Program in Communications, Ithaca, NY 14850. Offers MS. Part-time programs available. *Faculty:* 6 full-time (1 woman). *Students:* 27 full-time (19 women), 8 part-time (all women); includes 2 minority (1 American Indian/Alaska Native, 1 Hispanic American), 8 international. Average age 29. 45 applicants, 76% accepted, 17 enrolled. In 2009, 14 master's awarded. *Degree requirements:* For master's, comprehensive exam (for some programs), thesis optional. *Entrance requirements:* For master's, minimum GPA of 3.0. Additional exam requirements/recommendations for international students: Required—TOEFL (minimum score 550 paper-based; 213 computer-based; 80 iBT). *Application deadline:* For fall admission, 7/1 for domestic and international students; for spring admission, 12/1 for domestic and international students. Applications are processed on a rolling basis. Application fee: $40. Electronic applications accepted. *Expenses:* Tuition: Full-time $18,960; part-time $632 per credit hour. *Financial support:* In 2009–10, 30 students received support, including 16 teaching assistantships (averaging $7,538 per year); career-related internships or fieldwork, Federal Work-Study, scholarships/grants, and unspecified assistantships also available. Support available to part-time students. Financial award application deadline: 3/1; financial award applicants required to submit CSS PROFILE or FAFSA. *Faculty research:* Managing corporate communication and learning, social systems design, crisis communication and diversity, social marketing, instructional design and interactive technologies. *Unit head:* Dr. Howard Kalman, Chairperson, 607-274-3527, Fax: 607-274-1263, E-mail: gps@ithaca.edu. *Application contact:* Rob Gearhart, Dean, Graduate and Professional Studies, 607-274-3527, Fax: 607-274-1263, E-mail: gps@ithaca.edu.

The Johns Hopkins University, Zanvyl Krieger School of Arts and Sciences, Advanced Academic Programs, Program in Communication, Baltimore, MD 21218-2699. Offers MA, MA/MBA. Part-time and evening/weekend programs available. *Faculty:* 4 full-time (all women), 18 part-time/adjunct (10 women). *Students:* 22 full-time (18 women), 229 part-time (184 women); includes 42 minority (22 African Americans, 1 American Indian/Alaska Native, 9 Asian Americans or Pacific Islanders, 10 Hispanic Americans), 9 international. Average age 30. 211 applicants, 38% accepted, 42 enrolled. In 2009, 40 master's awarded. *Degree requirements:* For master's, thesis. *Entrance requirements:* For master's, minimum GPA of 3.0, strong writing skills. Additional exam requirements/recommendations for international students: Required—TOEFL (minimum score 250 computer-based; 100 iBT). *Application deadline:* For fall admission, 5/31 priority date for domestic students, 4/30 priority date for international students; for spring admission, 10/31 priority date for domestic and international students. Applications are processed on a rolling basis. Application fee: $75. Electronic applications accepted. *Financial support:* Applicants required to submit FAFSA. *Unit head:* Dr. Erika Falk, Associate Program Chair, 202-452-8711, E-mail: erikafalk@jhu.edu. *Application contact:* Valana M. McMickens, Admissions Manager, 202-452-1941, Fax: 202-452-1970, E-mail: aapadmissions@jhu.edu.

Kansas State University, Graduate School, College of Arts and Sciences, Department of Communication Studies, Theatre and Dance, Manhattan, KS 66505. Offers rhetoric/communication (MA); theatre (MA). *Faculty:* 17 full-time (8 women), 1 (woman) part-time/adjunct. *Students:* 10 applicants, 100% accepted, 10 enrolled. In 2009, 15 master's awarded. *Degree requirements:* For master's, thesis or alternative. *Entrance requirements:* For master's, GRE General Test (recommended), minimum GPA of 3.0. Additional exam requirements/recommendations for international students: Required—TOEFL. *Application deadline:* For fall admission, 2/1 priority date for domestic and international students; for spring admission, 8/1 priority date for domestic and international students. Applications are processed on a rolling basis. Application fee: $40 ($55 for international students). Electronic applications accepted. *Financial support:* In 2009–10, 23 teaching assistantships with full tuition reimbursements (averaging $9,391 per year) were awarded; career-related internships or fieldwork, institutionally sponsored loans, and scholarships/grants also available. Support available to part-time students. Financial award application deadline: 3/1; financial award applicants required to submit FAFSA. *Faculty research:* Drama therapy, directing, costume design, scenic design, technical theatre mechanics and safety. Total annual research expenditures: $10,294. *Unit head:* Charles Griffin, Head, 785-532-6860, Fax: 785-532-3714, E-mail: charlieg@ksu.edu. *Application contact:* William Schenck-Hamlin, Director, 785-532-6861, Fax: 785-532-3714, E-mail: billsh@ksu.edu.

Kean University, College of Humanities and Social Sciences, Program in Communication Studies, Union, NJ 07083. Offers MA. Part-time and evening/weekend programs available. *Faculty:* 12 full-time (5 women). *Students:* 4 full-time (3 women), 10 part-time (7 women); includes 5 minority (3 African Americans, 1 Asian American or Pacific Islander, 1 Hispanic American), 2 international. Average age 31. 9 applicants, 89% accepted, 4 enrolled. In 2009, 10 master's awarded. *Degree requirements:* For master's, comprehensive exam, thesis optional. *Entrance requirements:* For master's, GRE General Test, minimum GPA of 3.0, 3 letters of recommendation, interview. *Application deadline:* For fall admission, 5/1 for domestic students; for spring admission, 11/1 for domestic students. Application fee: $60 ($150 for international students). Electronic applications accepted. *Expenses:* Tuition, state resident: full-time $10,440; part-time $435 per credit. Tuition, nonresident: full-time $14,160; part-time $590 per credit. Required fees: $2642; $110 per credit. Part-time tuition and fees vary according to course load and degree level. *Financial support:* In 2009–10, 3 research assistantships with full tuition reimbursements (averaging $3,263 per year) were awarded; unspecified assistantships also available. *Unit head:* Dr. Wenli Yuan, Program Coordinator, 908-737-0471, E-mail: wyuan@kean.edu. *Application contact:* Steven Koch, Pre-Admissions Coordinator, 908-737-5924, Fax: 908-737-5965, E-mail: skoch@kean.edu.

Kent State University, College of Communication and Information, School of Communication Studies, Kent, OH 44242-0001. Offers MA, PhD. *Degree requirements:* For master's, thesis optional; for doctorate, variable foreign language requirement, thesis/dissertation. *Entrance requirements:* For master's and doctorate, GRE General Test, minimum GPA of 3.0. Additional exam requirements/recommendations for international students: Required—TOEFL (minimum score 600 paper-based), TWE (minimum score 5). Electronic applications accepted. *Faculty research:* Interpersonal communication, organizational communication, mass communication, new technologies and communication.

Lasell College, Graduate and Professional Studies in Communication, Newton, MA 02466-2709. Offers integrated marketing communication (MSC, Graduate Certificate); public relations (MSC, Graduate Certificate). Part-time and evening/weekend programs available. Postbaccalaureate distance learning degree programs offered (minimal on-campus study). *Faculty:* 3 full-time (all women), 1 part-time/adjunct (0 women). *Students:* 5 full-time (all women), 13 part-time (12 women); includes 3 minority (all African Americans). Average age 29. 19 applicants, 89% accepted, 11 enrolled. *Entrance requirements:* For master's and Graduate Certificate, bachelor's degree from an accredited institution. Additional exam requirements/recommendations for international students: Required—TOEFL (minimum score 550 paper-based; 213 computer-based; 75 iBT) or IELTS. *Application deadline:* For fall admission, 8/31 priority date for domestic students, 6/30 priority date for international students; for spring admission, 12/31 priority date for domestic students, 10/31 priority date for international students. Applications are processed on a rolling basis. Application fee: $40. Electronic applications accepted. *Expenses:* Tuition: Full-time $4890; part-time $525 per credit hour. Required fees: $55 per term. *Financial support:* Available to part-time students. Application deadline: 8/30. *Unit head:* Dr. Joan Dolamore, Dean of Graduate and Professional Studies, 617-243-2485, Fax: 617-243-2450, E-mail: gradinfo@lasell.edu. *Application contact:* Adrienne Franciosi, Director of Graduate Admission, 617-243-2214, Fax: 617-243-2450, E-mail: gradinfo@lasell.edu.

La Sierra University, College of Arts and Sciences, Department of English and Communication, Riverside, CA 92515. Offers communication (MA), including public relations/advertising, theory emphasis; English (MA), including literary emphasis, writing emphasis. Part-time programs available. *Degree requirements:* For master's, one foreign language. *Entrance requirements:* For master's, GRE General Test.

Liberty University, School of Communications, Lynchburg, VA 24502. Offers MA. Part-time programs available. *Degree requirements:* For master's, thesis. *Entrance requirements:* For master's, minimum undergraduate GPA of 3.0, 2 faculty recommendations, 1 pastoral recommendation. Additional exam requirements/recommendations for international students: Required—TOEFL (minimum score 600 paper-based; 250 computer-based). Electronic applications accepted. *Expenses:* Tuition: Full-time $7110; part-time $415 per credit hour. Required fees: $150 per semester. Tuition and fees vary according to course load, degree level, campus/location and program.

Lindenwood University, Graduate Programs, College of Individualized Education, St. Charles, MO 63301-1695. Offers administration (MSA); business administration (MBA); communications (MA); criminal justice and administration (MS); gerontology (MA); health management (MS); human resource management (MS); information technology (MBA, Certificate); management (MSA); managing information technology (MS); marketing (MSA); writing (MFA). Part-time and evening/weekend programs available. *Faculty:* 15 full-time (8 women), 128 part-time/adjunct (53 women). *Students:* 679 full-time (432 women), 90 part-time (57 women); includes 138 minority (121 African Americans, 2 American Indian/Alaska Native, 5 Asian Americans or Pacific Islanders, 10 Hispanic Americans), 18 international. Average age 34. 223 applicants, 44% accepted, 87 enrolled. In 2009, 478 master's awarded. *Degree requirements:* For master's, thesis (for some programs), 1 colloquium per term. *Entrance requirements:* For master's, interview, minimum GPA of 3.0. Additional exam requirements/recommendations for international students: Required—TOEFL (minimum score 550 paper-based; 213 computer-based; 80 iBT). *Application deadline:* For fall admission, 10/2 priority date for domestic and international students; for winter admission, 1/8 priority date for domestic and international students; for spring admission, 4/8 priority date for domestic and international students. Applications are processed on a rolling basis. Application fee: $30 ($100 for international students). *Expenses:* Tuition: Full-time $12,960; part-time $370 per credit hour. Required fees: $340. One-time fee: $30 full-time. Tuition and fees vary according to course level and course load. *Financial support:* In 2009–10, 631 students received support. Career-related internships or fieldwork, institutionally sponsored loans, tuition waivers (partial), and unspecified assistantships available. Financial award application deadline: 6/30; financial award applicants required to submit FAFSA. *Unit head:* Dan Kemper, Dean, 636-949-4501, Fax: 636-949-4505, E-mail: dkemper@lindenwood.edu. *Application contact:* Brett Barger, Dean of Evening Admissions and Extension Campuses, 636-949-4934, Fax: 636-949-4109, E-mail: adultadmissions@lindenwood.edu.

Lindenwood University, Graduate Programs, School of Communications, St. Charles, MO 63301-1695. Offers MA. Part-time and evening/weekend programs available. *Faculty:* 5 full-time (0 women), 6 part-time/adjunct (2 women). *Students:* 4 full-time (3 women), 2 part-time (1 woman); includes 1 minority (African American), 3 international. Average age 34. 12 applicants, 5 enrolled. In 2009, 3 master's awarded. *Degree requirements:* For master's, thesis (for some programs). *Entrance requirements:* For master's, minimum GPA of 3.0, resume. Additional exam requirements/recommendations for international students: Required—TOEFL (minimum score 550 paper-based; 213 computer-based; 80 iBT). *Application deadline:* For fall admission, 8/27 priority date for domestic and international students; for spring admission, 1/28 priority date for domestic and international students. Application fee: $30 ($100 for international students). *Expenses:* Tuition: Full-time $12,960; part-time $370 per credit hour. Required fees: $340. One-time fee: $30 full-time. Tuition and fees vary according to course level and course load. *Financial support:* In 2009–10, 6 students received support. Career-related internships or fieldwork, institutionally sponsored loans, tuition waivers (partial), and unspecified assistantships available. Financial award application deadline: 6/30; financial award applicants required to submit FAFSA. *Unit head:* Mike Wall, Dean, 636-949-4880. *Application contact:* Brett Barger, Dean of Evening Admissions and Extension Campuses, 636-949-4934, Fax: 636-949-4109, E-mail: adultadmissions@lindenwood.edu.

Louisiana State University and Agricultural and Mechanical College, Graduate School, College of Arts and Sciences, Department of Communication Studies, Baton Rouge, LA 70803. Offers MA, PhD. *Faculty:* 12 full-time (7 women). *Students:* 35 full-time (14 women), 7 part-time (5 women); includes 4 African Americans, 1 international. Average age 31. 31 applicants, 61% accepted, 8 enrolled. In 2009, 5 master's, 4 doctorates awarded. *Degree requirements:* For master's, thesis; for doctorate, one foreign language, thesis/dissertation. *Entrance requirements:* For master's and doctorate, GRE General Test, minimum GPA of 3.0. Additional exam requirements/recommendations for international students: Required—TOEFL (minimum score 550 paper-based; 213 computer-based; 79 iBT) or IELTS (minimum score 6.5). *Application deadline:* For fall admission, 1/25 priority date for domestic students, 5/15 for international students; for spring admission, 10/15 for international students. Applications are processed on a rolling basis. Application fee: $50 ($70 for international students). Electronic applications accepted. *Financial support:* In 2009–10, 39 students received support, including 2 fellowships with full and partial tuition reimbursements available (averaging $31,005 per year), 2 research assistantships with full and partial tuition reimbursements available (averaging $18,650 per year), 26 teaching assistantships with full and partial tuition reimbursements available (averaging $11,403 per year); career-related internships or fieldwork, Federal Work-Study, institutionally sponsored loans, scholarships/grants, health care benefits, tuition waivers (full and partial), and unspecified assistantships also available. Support available to part-time students. Financial award applicants required to submit FAFSA. *Faculty research:* Rhetorical theory and criticism, performance studies, interpersonal communication. Total annual research expenditures: $5,302. *Unit head:* Dr. Renee Edwards, Chair, 225-578-4172, Fax: 225-578-4828, E-mail: edwards@lsu.edu. *Application contact:* Dr. Ruth Bowman, Graduate Adviser, 225-578-6812, Fax: 225-578-4828, E-mail: spbowm@lsu.edu.

Marquette University, Graduate School, College of Communication, Milwaukee, WI 53201-1881. Offers advertising and public relations (MA); broadcasting and electronic communications (MA); communications studies (MA); journalism (MA); mass communications (MA); religious communications (MA); science, health and environmental communications (MA). *Accreditation:* ACEJMC. Part-time and evening/weekend programs available. *Faculty:* 31 full-time (17 women), 35 part-time/adjunct (16 women). *Students:* 28 full-time (21 women), 30 part-time (24 women); includes 3 minority (1 African American, 2 American Indian/Alaska Native), 7 international. Average age 26. 81 applicants, 47% accepted, 22 enrolled. In 2009, 17 master's awarded. *Degree requirements:* For master's, comprehensive exam. *Entrance requirements:* For master's, GRE. Additional exam requirements/recommendations for international students: Required—TOEFL. Application fee: $40. *Financial support:* In 2009–10, 6 research assistantships, 12 teaching assistantships were awarded; career-related internships or fieldwork, Federal Work-Study, institutionally sponsored loans, scholarships/grants, and tuition waivers (full and partial) also available. Support available to part-time students. Financial award application deadline: 2/15. *Faculty research:* Urban journalism, gender and communication, intercultural communication, religious communication. *Unit head:* Dr. Ana Garner, Dean, 414-288-3588, Fax: 414-288-1578. *Application contact:* Erin Fox, Assistant Director for Recruitment, 414-288-5319, Fax: 414-288-1902, E-mail: erin.fox@marquette.edu.

Marshall University, Academic Affairs Division, College of Liberal Arts, Department of Communication Studies, Huntington, WV 25755. Offers MA. *Faculty:* 9 full-time (3 women), 19 part-time/adjunct (14 women). *Students:* 19 full-time (14 women), 7 part-time (4 women); includes 1 minority (African American), 3 international. Average age 29. In 2009, 10 master's awarded. *Degree requirements:* For master's, thesis optional. Application fee: $40. *Financial support:* Fellowships available. *Unit head:* Dr. Robert Bookwalter, Interim Chair, 304-696-2815, E-mail: bookwalt@marshall.edu. *Application contact:* Dr. Edward Woods, Information Contact, 304-7696-3104, Fax: 304-746-1902, E-mail: services@marshall.edu.

Marywood University, Academic Affairs, Insalaco College of Creative and Performing Arts, Department of Communication Arts, Program in Communication Arts, Scranton, PA 18509-1598. Offers interdisciplinary (MA); media management (MA); production (MA). *Students:* 12 full-time (7 women), 25 part-time (13 women); includes 5 minority (2 African Americans, 1 Asian American or Pacific Islander, 2 Hispanic Americans). Average age 33. In 2009, 11 master's awarded. *Entrance requirements:* Additional exam requirements/recommendations for international students: Required—TOEFL (minimum score 550 paper-based; 213 computer-based; 79 iBT). *Application deadline:* For fall admission, 4/1 for domestic students, 3/31 for international students; for spring admission, 11/1 for domestic students, 8/31 for international students. Applications are processed on a rolling basis. Application fee: $35. Electronic applications accepted. *Expenses:* Tuition: Part-time $715 per credit. Required fees: $270 per semester. Tuition and fees vary according to degree level, campus/location and program. *Financial support:* Career-related internships or fieldwork, scholarships/grants, and unspecified assistantships available. Support available to part-time students. Financial award application deadline: 6/30; financial award applicants required to submit FAFSA. *Application contact:* Tammy Manka, Assistant Director of Admissions, 866-279-9663, E-mail: tmanka@marywood.edu.

McGill University, Faculty of Graduate and Postdoctoral Studies, Faculty of Arts, Department of Art History and Communication Studies, Montréal, QC H3A 2T5, Canada. Offers MA, PhD.

Michigan State University, The Graduate School, College of Communication Arts and Sciences, Department of Communication, East Lansing, MI 48824. Offers MA, PhD. *Faculty:* 17 full-time (8 women). *Students:* 40 full-time (29 women), 9 part-time (7 women); includes 4 minority (1 African American, 1 American Indian/Alaska Native, 2 Asian Americans or Pacific Islanders), 12 international. Average age 29. 141 applicants, 28% accepted. In 2009, 12 master's, 4 doctorates awarded. *Entrance requirements:* Additional exam requirements/recommendations for international students: Required—TOEFL (minimum score 580 paper-based; 237 computer-based). Electronic applications accepted. *Expenses:* Tuition, state resident: part-time $478.25 per credit hour. Tuition, nonresident: part-time $966.50 per credit hour. Part-time tuition and fees vary according to program. *Financial support:* In 2009–10, 14 research assistantships with tuition reimbursements (averaging $6,754 per year), 24 teaching assistantships with tuition reimbursements (averaging $6,760 per year) were awarded. Total annual research expenditures: $181,084. *Unit head:* Dr. Charles Atkin, Chairperson, 517-353-3259, Fax: 517-432-1192, E-mail: atkin@msu.edu. *Application contact:* Marge Barkman, Academic Programs Coordinator, 517-355-3471, Fax: 517-432-1192, E-mail: barkman@msu.edu.

Minnesota State University Mankato, College of Graduate Studies, College of Arts and Humanities, Department of Communication Studies, Mankato, MN 56001. Offers communication studies (MA, MS, Certificate); forensics (MFA). *Students:* 18 full-time (15 women), 16 part-time (6 women). *Degree requirements:* For master's, one foreign language, comprehensive exam, thesis. *Entrance requirements:* For master's, minimum GPA of 3.0 during previous 2 years, writing sample. *Application deadline:* For fall admission, 7/1 priority date for domestic students, 5/1 for international students; for spring admission, 11/1 for domestic students, 10/1 for international students. Applications are processed on a rolling basis. Application fee: $40. Electronic applications accepted. *Expenses:* Tuition, state resident: full-time $5364. Tuition, nonresident: full-time $8314. *Financial support:* Research assistantships, teaching assistantships with full tuition reimbursements, career-related internships or fieldwork, Federal Work-Study, and institutionally sponsored loans available. Support available to part-time students. Financial award application deadline: 3/15; financial award applicants required to submit FAFSA. *Unit head:* Dr. Daniel Cronn-Mills, Chairperson, 507-389-2213. *Application contact:* 507-389-2321, E-mail: grad@mnsu.edu.

Mississippi College, Graduate School, College of Arts and Sciences, School of Christian Studies and the Arts, Department of Communication, Clinton, MS 39058. Offers applied communication (MSC); public relations and corporate communication (MSC). Part-time programs available. *Faculty:* 6 full-time (2 women), 1 part-time/adjunct (0 women). *Students:* 14 full-time (7 women), 18 part-time (13 women); includes 5 minority (all African Americans), 10 international. Average age 28. In 2009, 6 master's awarded. *Degree requirements:* For master's, comprehensive exam, thesis optional. *Entrance requirements:* For master's, GRE or NTE, minimum GPA of 2.5. Additional exam requirements/recommendations for international students: Recommended—IELTS. *Application deadline:* For fall admission, 8/15 priority date for domestic and international students. Applications are processed on a rolling basis. Application fee: $30. Electronic applications accepted. *Expenses:* Tuition: Part-time $452 per credit hour. Required fees: $101 per semester. Tuition and fees vary according to degree level, campus/location, program and student level. *Financial support:* Career-related internships or fieldwork, Federal Work-Study, and unspecified assistantships available. Support available to part-time students. Financial award application deadline: 4/1; financial award applicants required to submit FAFSA. *Unit head:* Dr. Cliff Fortenberry, Chair, 601-925-3457, E-mail: fortenbe@mc.edu. *Application contact:* Elnora Lewis, Secretary, 601-925-3225, Fax: 601-925-3889, E-mail: lewis09@mc.edu.

Missouri State University, Graduate College, College of Arts and Letters, Department of Communication and Mass Media, Springfield, MO 65897. Offers MA. Part-time programs available. *Faculty:* 13 full-time (8 women). *Students:* 29 full-time (18 women), 26 part-time (14 women); includes 2 minority (1 African American, 1 Hispanic American), 1 international. Average age 29. 29 applicants, 93% accepted, 19 enrolled. In 2009, 13 master's awarded. *Degree requirements:* For master's, comprehensive exam, thesis or alternative. *Entrance requirements:* For master's, GRE General Test, minimum GPA of 3.0. Additional exam requirements/recommendations for international students: Required—TOEFL (minimum score 550 paper-based; 213 computer-based; 79 iBT). *Application deadline:* For fall admission, 7/20 for domestic students, 5/1 for international students; for spring admission, 12/20 for domestic students, 9/1 for international students. Applications are processed on a rolling basis. Application fee: $35 ($50 for international students). Electronic applications accepted. *Expenses:* Tuition, state resident: full-time $3852; part-time $214 per credit hour. Tuition, nonresident: full-time $7524; part-time $418 per credit hour. Required fees: $696; $172 per semester. Tuition and fees vary according to course level, course load, degree level and program. *Financial support:* In 2009–10, 6 teaching assistantships with full tuition reimbursements (averaging $7,340 per year) were awarded; career-related internships or fieldwork, Federal Work-Study, institutionally sponsored loans, scholarships/grants, and unspecified assistantships also available. Support available to part-time students. Financial award application deadline: 3/31; financial award applicants required to submit FAFSA. *Faculty research:* Conflict resolution, media analysis, intercultural communication, rhetorical criticism. *Unit head:* Dr. Kelly Wood, Head, 417-836-4423, Fax: 417-836-4774, E-mail: communication@missouristate.edu. *Application contact:* Eric Eckert, Coordinator of Graduate Admissions and Recruitment, 417-836-5331, Fax: 417-836-6888, E-mail: ericeckert@missouristate.edu.

Missouri State University, Graduate College, Interdisciplinary Program in Administrative Studies, Springfield, MO 65897. Offers applied communication (MS); criminal justice (MS); environmental management (MS); project management (MS); sports management (MS). Part-time and evening/weekend programs available. Postbaccalaureate distance learning degree programs offered (no on-campus study). *Students:* 17 full-time (11 women), 60 part-time (26 women); includes 6 minority (4 African Americans, 1 Asian American or Pacific Islander, 1 Hispanic American), 2 international. Average age 35. 24 applicants, 100% accepted, 19 enrolled. In 2009, 16 master's awarded. *Degree requirements:* For master's, comprehensive exam, thesis or alternative. *Entrance requirements:* For master's, GRE, GMAT, 3 years of work experience. Additional exam requirements/recommendations for international students: Required—TOEFL (minimum score 550 paper-based; 213 computer-based; 79 iBT). *Application deadline:* For fall admission, 7/20 priority date for domestic students; for spring admission, 12/20 priority date for domestic students. Applications are processed on a rolling basis. Application fee: $35 ($50 for international students). Electronic applications accepted. *Expenses:* Tuition, state resident: full-time $3852; part-time $214 per credit hour. Tuition, nonresident: full-time $7524; part-time $418 per credit hour. Required fees: $696; $172 per semester. Tuition and fees vary according to course level, course load, degree level and program. *Financial support:* In 2009–10, 1 teaching assistantship with full tuition reimbursement (averaging $7,340 per year) was awarded; career-related internships or fieldwork, Federal Work-Study, institutionally sponsored loans, scholarships/grants, and unspecified assistantships also available. Support available to part-time students. Financial award application deadline: 3/31; financial award applicants required to submit FAFSA. *Unit head:* John Bourhis, Director, 417-836-6390, E-mail: johnbourhis@missouristate.edu. *Application contact:* Eric Eckert, Coordinator of Graduate Admissions and Recruitment, 417-836-5331, Fax: 417-836-6200, E-mail: ericeckert@missouristate.edu.

Monmouth University, Graduate School, Department of Corporate and Public Communication, West Long Branch, NJ 07764-1898. Offers corporate and public communication (MA); human resources communication (Certificate); public relations (Certificate); public service communication specialist (Certificate). Part-time and evening/weekend programs available. *Faculty:* 8 full-time (4 women), 2 part-time/adjunct (1 woman). *Students:* 6 full-time (3 women), 45 part-time (31 women); includes 8 minority (3 African Americans, 1 Asian American or Pacific Islander, 4 Hispanic Americans), 3 international. Average age 31. 39 applicants, 95% accepted, 20 enrolled. In 2009, 19 master's awarded. *Degree requirements:* For master's, comprehensive exam, project. *Entrance requirements:* For master's, GRE, minimum GPA of 3.0 in major, 2.75 overall. Additional exam requirements/recommendations for international students: Required—TOEFL (minimum score 550 paper-based; 213 computer-based; 79 iBT), IELTS (minimum score 5), Michigan English Language Assessment Battery (minimum score 77), Cambridge A, B, C. *Application deadline:* For fall admission, 7/15 priority date for domestic students, 6/1 for international students; for spring admission, 11/15 priority date for domestic students, 11/1 for international students. Applications are processed on a rolling basis. Application fee: $50. Electronic applications accepted. *Expenses:* Tuition: Part-time $773 per credit. Required fees: $157 per semester. *Financial support:* In 2009–10, 37 students received support, including 24 fellowships (averaging $1,242 per year), 7 research assistantships (averaging $5,715 per year); scholarships/grants and unspecified assistantships also available. Support available to part-time students. Financial award applicants required to submit FAFSA. *Faculty research:* Service-learning, history of television, feminism and the media, executive communication, public relations pedagogy. *Unit head:* Dr. Sherry Wien, Program Director, 732-263-5354, Fax: 732-571-3609, E-mail: swien@monmouth.edu. *Application contact:* Kevin Roane, Director, Office of Graduate Admission, 732-571-3452, Fax: 732-263-5123, E-mail: gradadm@monmouth.edu.

Montana State University Billings, College of Arts and Sciences, Department of Communication and Theater, Billings, MT 59101-0298. Offers public relations (MS). Part-time programs available. Postbaccalaureate distance learning degree programs offered. *Degree requirements:* For master's, thesis optional. *Entrance requirements:* For master's, GRE General Test, minimum undergraduate GPA of 3.0, 3 letters of recommendation.

Montclair State University, The Graduate School, School of the Arts, Department of Communication Studies, Montclair, NJ 07043-1624. Offers organizational communication (MA); public relations (MA); speech communication (MA). Part-time and evening/weekend programs available. *Faculty:* 5 full-time (2 women), 41 part-time/adjunct (24 women). *Students:* 16 full-time (15 women), 20 part-time (17 women). Average age 30. 23 applicants, 65% accepted, 12 enrolled. In 2009, 12 master's awarded. *Degree requirements:* For master's, comprehensive exam. *Entrance requirements:* For master's, GRE General Test, 2 letters of recommendation. Additional exam requirements/recommendations for international students: Required—TOEFL (minimum score 83 computer-based), or IELTS. *Application deadline:* For fall admission, 6/1 for international students; for spring admission, 10/1 for international students. Applications are processed on a rolling basis. Application fee: $60. Electronic applications accepted. *Expenses:* Tuition, area resident: Part-time $486.74 per credit. Tuition, state resident: part-time $486.74 per credit. Tuition, nonresident: part-time $751.34 per credit. Tuition and fees vary according to degree level and program. *Financial support:* In 2009–10, 3 research assistantships with full tuition reimbursements (averaging $7,000 per year) were awarded; Federal Work-Study, scholarships/grants, and unspecified assistantships also available. Support available to part-time students. Financial award application deadline: 3/1; financial award applicants required to submit FAFSA. *Unit head:* Dr. Harry Haines, Chair, 973-655-4200. *Application contact:* Amy Aiello, Director of Graduate Admissions and Operations, 973-655-5147, Fax: 973-655-7869, E-mail: graduate.school@montclair.edu.

Morehead State University, Graduate Programs, Caudill College of Arts, Humanities and Social Sciences, Department of Communication, Media and Leadership Studies, Morehead, KY 40351. Offers communication (MA). Part-time and evening/weekend programs available. *Faculty:* 6 full-time (3 women). *Students:* 13 full-time (7 women), 7 part-time (4 women); includes 1 minority (African American), 3 international. Average age 27. 9 applicants, 100% accepted, 6 enrolled. In 2009, 16 master's awarded. *Degree requirements:* For master's, comprehensive exam, exit assessment, written examination, oral interview. *Entrance requirements:* For master's, GRE General Test, bachelor's degree in communications or closely related field. Additional exam requirements/recommendations for international students: Required—TOEFL (minimum score 500 paper-based; 173 computer-based). *Application deadline:* For fall admission, 8/1 priority date for domestic and international students; for spring admission, 12/1 priority date for domestic and international students. Applications are processed on a rolling basis. Application fee: $30. Electronic applications accepted. *Expenses:* Tuition, state resident: full-time $6318; part-time $351 per credit hour. Tuition, nonresident: full-time $15,804; part-time $878 per credit hour. *Financial support:* In 2009–10, 2 research assistantships (averaging $10,000 per year), 1 teaching assistantship (averaging $10,000 per year) were awarded; career-related internships or fieldwork, Federal Work-Study, and unspecified assistantships also available. Financial award application deadline: 3/15; financial award applicants required to submit FAFSA. *Faculty research:* Mass media effects, organizational communications, advertising/public relations. *Unit head:* Dr. Calvin Lindell, Chair, 606-783-2693, Fax: 606-783-2457, E-mail: c.lindell@moreheadstate.edu. *Application contact:* Michelle Barber, Graduate Recruitment and Retention Assistant Director, 606-783-5127, Fax: 606-783-5061, E-mail: m.barber@moreheadstate.edu.

National University, Academic Affairs, School of Media and Communication, La Jolla, CA 92037-1011. Offers MA, MFA, MS. Part-time and evening/weekend programs available. Postbaccalaureate distance learning degree programs offered (no on-campus study). *Faculty:* 12 full-time (6 women), 14 part-time/adjunct (5 women). *Students:* 85 full-time (36 women), 142 part-time (60 women); includes 75 minority (34 African Americans, 12 Asian Americans or Pacific Islanders, 29 Hispanic Americans), 1 international. Average age 39. 164 applicants, 100% accepted, 102 enrolled. In 2009, 62 master's awarded. *Degree requirements:* For master's, thesis (for some programs). *Entrance requirements:* For master's, interview, minimum GPA of 2.5. Additional exam requirements/recommendations for international students: Required—TOEFL (minimum score 550 paper-based; 213 computer-based; 79 iBT), IELTS (minimum score 6). *Application deadline:* Applications are processed on a rolling basis. Application fee: $60 ($65 for international students). Electronic applications accepted. *Expenses:* Tuition: Part-time $338 per quarter hour. *Financial support:* Career-related internships or fieldwork, institutionally sponsored loans, scholarships/grants, and tuition waivers (partial) available. Support available to part-time students. Financial award application deadline: 6/30; financial award applicants required to submit FAFSA. *Faculty research:* Digital media, film, journalism. *Unit head:* Karla Berry, Dean, 858-309-3442, Fax: 858-309-3450, E-mail: kberry@nu.edu. *Application contact:* Dominick Giovanniello, Associate Regional Dean—San Diego, 800-NAT-UNIV, Fax: 858-541-7792, E-mail: dgiovann@nu.edu.

New Mexico State University, Graduate School, College of Arts and Sciences, Department of Communication Studies, Las Cruces, NM 88003-8001. Offers MA. Part-time programs available. *Faculty:* 6 full-time (4 women), 1 (woman) part-time/adjunct. *Students:* 27 full-time (20 women), 4 part-time (2 women); includes 12 minority (3 African Americans, 9 Hispanic Americans), 4 international. Average age 28. 26 applicants, 88% accepted, 14 enrolled. In 2009, 10 master's awarded. *Degree requirements:* For master's, comprehensive exam (for some programs), thesis (for some programs). *Entrance requirements:* For master's, minimum GPA of 3.0. *Application deadline:* For fall admission, 7/1 priority date for domestic students; for spring admission, 4/1 priority date for domestic students. Applications are processed on a rolling basis. Application fee: $30 ($50 for international students). Electronic applications accepted. *Expenses:* Tuition, state resident: full-time $4080; part-time $223 per credit. Tuition, nonresident: full-time $14,256; part-time $647 per credit. Required fees: $1278; $639 per semester. *Financial*

Communication—General

New Mexico State University (continued)
support: In 2009–10, 1 research assistantship with tuition reimbursement (averaging $3,950 per year), 20 teaching assistantships with partial tuition reimbursements (averaging $14,725 per year) were awarded; fellowships, Federal Work-Study and health care benefits also available. Financial award application deadline: 3/1. *Faculty research:* Interpersonal, organizational, intercultural, political, and health communication. *Unit head:* Dr. Anne P. Hubbell, Head, 575-646-2801, Fax: 575-646-1603, E-mail: ahubbell@nmsu.edu. *Application contact:* Dr. Anne P. Hubbell, Head, 575-646-2801, Fax: 575-646-1603, E-mail: ahubbell@nmsu.edu.

New York Institute of Technology, Graduate Division, School of Arts and Sciences, Program in Communication Arts, Old Westbury, NY 11568-8000. Offers MA. Part-time and evening/weekend programs available. *Students:* 112 full-time (82 women), 83 part-time (48 women); includes 44 minority (26 African Americans, 4 Asian Americans or Pacific Islanders, 14 Hispanic Americans), 59 international. Average age 28. In 2009, 66 master's awarded. *Degree requirements:* For master's, thesis or alternative. *Entrance requirements:* For master's, minimum QPA of 2.85. Additional exam requirements/recommendations for international students: Required—TOEFL (minimum score 550 paper-based; 213 computer-based). *Application deadline:* For fall admission, 7/1 priority date for domestic students; for spring admission, 12/1 priority date for domestic students. Applications are processed on a rolling basis. Application fee: $50. Electronic applications accepted. *Expenses:* Tuition: Part-time $825 per credit. *Financial support:* Research assistantships with partial tuition reimbursements, career-related internships or fieldwork, Federal Work-Study, institutionally sponsored loans, tuition waivers (partial), and unspecified assistantships available. Support available to part-time students. Financial award applicants required to submit FAFSA. *Faculty research:* Distance learning technology, computer animation, intercultural communication, multimedia technology. *Unit head:* Dr. Dena Winokur, Director, 212-261-1636, Fax: 516-686-7736, E-mail: dwinokur@nyit.edu. *Application contact:* Dr. Jacquelyn Nealon, Vice President for Enrollment Services, 516-686-7925, Fax: 516-686-7597, E-mail: jnealon@nyit.edu.

New York University, Steinhardt School of Culture, Education, and Human Development, Department of Media, Culture and Communication, New York, NY 10012-1019. Offers media, culture, and communication (MA, PhD). Part-time programs available. *Faculty:* 22 full-time (9 women), 43 part-time/adjunct (22 women). *Students:* 84 full-time (62 women), 42 part-time (24 women); includes 13 minority (7 African Americans, 5 Asian Americans or Pacific Islanders, 1 Hispanic American), 46 international. Average age 33. 289 applicants, 44% accepted, 52 enrolled. In 2009, 45 master's, 5 doctorates awarded. Terminal master's awarded for partial completion of doctoral program. *Degree requirements:* For master's, thesis (for some programs); for doctorate, thesis/dissertation. *Entrance requirements:* For doctorate, GRE General Test, interview. Additional exam requirements/recommendations for international students: Required—TOEFL. *Application deadline:* For fall admission, 12/15 priority date for domestic and international students; for spring admission, 11/1 for domestic and international students. Applications are processed on a rolling basis. Application fee: $75. Electronic applications accepted. *Expenses:* Tuition: Full-time $30,528; part-time $1272 per credit. Required fees: $2177. *Financial support:* Fellowships with full and partial tuition reimbursements, teaching assistantships with full and partial tuition reimbursements, career-related internships or fieldwork, Federal Work-Study, institutionally sponsored loans, scholarships/grants, tuition waivers (partial), and unspecified assistantships available. Support available to part-time students. Financial award application deadline: 2/1; financial award applicants required to submit FAFSA. *Faculty research:* Digital media and new technologies, media criticism, flow of media and culture transnationally and transculturally. *Unit head:* Dr. Marita Sturken, Chairperson, 212-992-9424, Fax: 212-995-4046, E-mail: marita.sturken@nyu.edu. *Application contact:* 212-998-5030, Fax: 212-995-4328, E-mail: steinhardt.gradadmissions@nyu.edu.

Norfolk State University, School of Graduate Studies, School of Liberal Arts, Department of Media and Communication, Norfolk, VA 23504. Offers MA. Part-time programs available. *Degree requirements:* For master's, thesis. *Entrance requirements:* For master's, GRE, minimum GPA of 2.5, letters of recommendation. Additional exam requirements/recommendations for international students: Required—TOEFL.

North Carolina State University, Graduate School, College of Humanities and Social Sciences, Department of Communication, Raleigh, NC 27695. Offers MS. Part-time programs available. *Degree requirements:* For master's, thesis optional. *Entrance requirements:* For master's, GRE, minimum undergraduate GPA of 3.0 during last 60 hours. Electronic applications accepted. *Faculty research:* Instructional communication, political communication, organizational conflict management, intercultural communication, communication technology.

North Dakota State University, College of Graduate and Interdisciplinary Studies, College of Arts, Humanities and Social Sciences, Department of Communication, Fargo, ND 58108. Offers communication (PhD); mass communication (MA, MS); speech communication (MA, MS). Part-time programs available. Postbaccalaureate distance learning degree programs offered (no on-campus study). *Faculty:* 11 full-time (5 women), 3 part-time/adjunct (1 woman). *Students:* 38 full-time (25 women), 23 part-time (17 women); includes 4 minority (1 African American, 2 Asian Americans or Pacific Islanders, 1 Hispanic American), 3 international. Average age 27. 62 applicants, 40% accepted, 19 enrolled. In 2009, 15 master's, 8 doctorates awarded. Terminal master's awarded for partial completion of doctoral program. *Degree requirements:* For master's, thesis (for some programs); for doctorate, comprehensive exam, thesis/dissertation, 2-3 publications referred before comps. *Entrance requirements:* For master's, GRE, minimum undergraduate GPA of 3.25; for doctorate, GRE, minimum undergraduate GPA of 3.5. Additional exam requirements/recommendations for international students: Required—TOEFL (minimum score 600 paper-based; 250 computer-based; 100 iBT), IELTS (minimum score 7). *Application deadline:* For fall admission, 2/15 priority date for domestic students; for winter admission, 10/15 priority date for domestic students. Applications are processed on a rolling basis. Application fee: $45 ($60 for international students). Electronic applications accepted. *Financial support:* In 2009–10, 38 students received support, including 1 fellowship with full tuition reimbursement available (averaging $16,000 per year), 10 research assistantships with full tuition reimbursements available (averaging $12,000 per year), 10 teaching assistantships with full tuition reimbursements available (averaging $8,100 per year); career-related internships or fieldwork, Federal Work-Study, institutionally sponsored loans, tuition waivers (full), and unspecified assistantships also available. Financial award application deadline: 2/1. *Faculty research:* Communication and rhetorical theory, organizational communication, broadcast and print journalism, international communication, public relations and advertising. Total annual research expenditures: $148,496. *Unit head:* Dr. Paul E. Nelson, Chair, 701-231-7705, Fax: 701-231-7784, E-mail: paul.nelson.1@ndsu.edu. *Application contact:* Dr. Judy C. Pearson, Director of Graduate Studies, 701-231-6551, Fax: 701-231-1074, E-mail: judy.pearson@ndsu.edu.

Northeastern State University, Graduate College, College of Liberal Arts, Department of Communication, Tahlequah, OK 74464-2399. Offers MA. Part-time and evening/weekend programs available. *Degree requirements:* For master's, comprehensive exam. *Entrance requirements:* For master's, GRE, MAT, minimum GPA of 2.5. Additional exam requirements/recommendations for international students: Required—TOEFL (minimum score 213 computer-based). Electronic applications accepted.

Northeastern University, College of Arts, Media and Design, Department of Communication Studies, Boston, MA 02115-5096. Offers communication, media, and cultural studies (MA). *Faculty:* 25 full-time (10 women), 6 part-time/adjunct (3 women). *Students:* 5 full-time (all women); includes 1 minority (African American), 1 international. 59 applicants, 42% accepted, 4 enrolled. In 2009, 3 master's awarded. *Degree requirements:* For master's, thesis (for some programs). *Entrance requirements:* For master's, GRE. Additional exam requirements/recommendations for international students: Required—TOEFL or IELTS. *Application deadline:* For fall admission, 2/1 priority date for domestic and international students. Applications are processed on a rolling basis. Application fee: $50. Electronic applications accepted. *Financial support:* Federal Work-Study and scholarships/grants available. *Unit head:* Dr. Joanne Morreale, Graduate Coordinator, 617-373-2506, E-mail: j.morreale@neu.edu. *Application contact:* Jo-Anne Dickinson, Admissions Contact, 617-373-5990, Fax: 617-373-7281, E-mail: gsas@neu.edu.

Northern Arizona University, Graduate College, College of Social and Behavioral Sciences, School of Communication, Flagstaff, AZ 86011. Offers applied communication (MA). *Faculty:* 39 full-time (17 women). *Students:* 10 full-time (3 women), 25 part-time (19 women); includes 8 minority (1 African American, 2 American Indian/Alaska Native, 1 Asian American or Pacific Islander, 4 Hispanic Americans), 2 international. Average age 28. 18 applicants, 83% accepted, 12 enrolled. *Degree requirements:* For master's, thesis or two projects. *Entrance requirements:* For master's, GRE General Test. Additional exam requirements/recommendations for international students: Required—TOEFL (minimum score 550 paper-based; 213 computer-based; 80 iBT), IELTS (minimum score 7), or a bachelor's degree from an English-speaking university and demonstrated proficiency. *Application deadline:* For fall admission, 3/1 priority date for domestic students, 9/1 priority date for international students. Applications are processed on a rolling basis. Application fee: $65. Electronic applications accepted. *Financial support:* In 2009–10, 6 teaching assistantships with partial tuition reimbursements (averaging $10,439 per year) were awarded; unspecified assistantships also available. Financial award application deadline: 3/1. *Unit head:* Dr. Mark Neumann, Chair, 928-523-8887, Fax: 928-523-8056, E-mail: mark.neumann@nau.edu. *Application contact:* Dr. Richard Rogers, Coordinator, 928-523-2330, Fax: 928-523-8056, E-mail: richard.rogers@nau.edu.

Northern Illinois University, Graduate School, College of Liberal Arts and Sciences, Department of Communication, De Kalb, IL 60115-2854. Offers communication studies (MA). Part-time programs available. *Faculty:* 24 full-time (11 women), 1 part-time/adjunct (0 women). *Students:* 39 full-time (22 women), 16 part-time (9 women); includes 10 minority (6 African Americans, 1 American Indian/Alaska Native, 3 Hispanic Americans), 1 international. Average age 26. 42 applicants, 67% accepted, 18 enrolled. In 2009, 21 master's awarded. *Degree requirements:* For master's, comprehensive exam, thesis optional. *Entrance requirements:* For master's, GRE General Test, minimum GPA of 2.75. Additional exam requirements/recommendations for international students: Required—TOEFL (minimum score 550 paper-based; 213 computer-based). *Application deadline:* For fall admission, 6/1 for domestic students, 5/1 for international students; for spring admission, 11/1 for domestic students, 10/1 for international students. Applications are processed on a rolling basis. Application fee: $30. Electronic applications accepted. *Expenses:* Tuition, state resident: full-time $6576; part-time $274 per credit hour. Tuition, nonresident: full-time $13,152; part-time $548 per credit hour. Required fees: $1813; $75.53 per credit hour. Part-time tuition and fees vary according to course load. *Financial support:* In 2009–10, 34 teaching assistantships with full tuition reimbursements were awarded; fellowships with full tuition reimbursements, research assistantships with full tuition reimbursements, career-related internships or fieldwork, Federal Work-Study, scholarships/grants, tuition waivers (full), and unspecified assistantships also available. Support available to part-time students. Financial award applicants required to submit FAFSA. *Faculty research:* Journalism, history film studies, rhetoric or criticism, globalization, mass media law. *Unit head:* Dr. Jeffrey Chown, Chair, 815-753-7028, Fax: 815-753-7109, E-mail: jchown@niu.edu. *Application contact:* Dr. Jeffrey Chown, Director, Graduate Studies, 815-753-1711, E-mail: schown@niu.edu.

Northern Kentucky University, Office of Graduate Programs, College of Informatics, Program in Communication, Highland Heights, KY 41099. Offers communication (MA); communication teaching (Certificate); documentary studies (Certificate); public relations (Certificate); relationships (Certificate). Part-time and evening/weekend programs available. *Students:* 9 full-time (8 women), 42 part-time (32 women); includes 5 minority (4 African Americans, 1 Asian American or Pacific Islander), 1 international. Average age 31. 48 applicants, 63% accepted, 23 enrolled. In 2009, 20 master's awarded. *Degree requirements:* For master's, thesis (for some programs), capstone experience, internship. *Entrance requirements:* For master's, GRE, minimum GPA of 3.0, 3 letters of recommendation. Additional exam requirements/recommendations for international students: Required—TOEFL (minimum score 550 paper-based; 213 computer-based; 79 iBT); Recommended—IELTS (minimum score 6.5). *Application deadline:* For fall admission, 2/1 priority date for domestic students, 6/1 for international students; for spring admission, 7/1 priority date for domestic students, 10/1 for international students. Applications are processed on a rolling basis. Application fee: $40. Electronic applications accepted. *Expenses:* Tuition, state resident: full-time $6912; part-time $384 per credit hour. Tuition, nonresident: full-time $12,150; part-time $675 per credit hour. Tuition and fees vary according to course load, program and reciprocity agreements. *Financial support:* Unspecified assistantships available. Financial award applicants required to submit FAFSA. *Faculty research:* Business/organizational communication, interpersonal/relational communication, public relations, communication teaching/pedagogy, media (production, criticism, popular culture). Total annual research expenditures: $29,000. *Unit head:* Dr. Jimmy Manning, Graduate Program Director, 859-572-1329, E-mail: manningj1@nku.edu. *Application contact:* Dr. Peg Griffin, Director of Graduate Programs, 859-572-6934, Fax: 859-572-6670, E-mail: griffinp@nku.edu.

Northwestern University, The Graduate School, School of Communication, Department of Communication Studies, Evanston, IL 60208. Offers communication studies (MA, PhD); communication systems strategy and management (MSC); managerial communication (MSC). MA and PhD admissions and degrees offered through The Graduate School. Terminal master's awarded for partial completion of doctoral program. *Degree requirements:* For doctorate, thesis/dissertation. *Entrance requirements:* For master's and doctorate, GRE General Test. Additional exam requirements/recommendations for international students: Required—TOEFL. Electronic applications accepted.

The Ohio State University, Graduate School, College of Social and Behavioral Sciences, School of Communication, Program in Communication, Columbus, OH 43210. Offers MA, PhD. *Degree requirements:* For doctorate, thesis/dissertation. *Entrance requirements:* For master's and doctorate, GRE General Test. Additional exam requirements/recommendations for international students: Required—TOEFL (minimum score 620 paper-based; 250 computer-based). Electronic applications accepted. *Expenses:* Tuition, state resident: full-time $10,683. Tuition, nonresident: full-time $25,923. Tuition and fees vary according to course load and program.

The Ohio State University, Graduate School, College of Social and Behavioral Sciences, School of Communication, Program in Journalism and Communication, Columbus, OH 43210. Offers MA. *Entrance requirements:* For master's, GRE General Test. Electronic applications accepted. *Expenses:* Tuition, state resident: full-time $10,683. Tuition, nonresident: full-time $25,923. Tuition and fees vary according to course load and program.

Ohio University, Graduate College, Scripps College of Communication, Athens, OH 45701-2979. Offers MA, MCTP, MS, PhD. Part-time programs available. *Faculty:* 93 full-time (33 women). *Students:* 153 full-time (95 women), 62 part-time (39 women); includes 21 minority (12 African Americans, 2 American Indian/Alaska Native, 3 Asian Americans or Pacific Islanders, 4 Hispanic Americans), 48 international. 235 applicants, 57% accepted, 76 enrolled. In 2009, 67 master's, 24 doctorates awarded. *Degree requirements:* For master's, comprehensive exam (for some programs), thesis or alternative; for doctorate, comprehensive exam, thesis/dissertation. *Entrance requirements:* For master's and doctorate, GRE General Test. Additional exam requirements/recommendations for international students: Required—TOEFL or IELTS Academic. Application fee: $50 ($55 for international students). Electronic applications accepted. *Expenses:* Contact institution. *Financial support:* Fellowships with tuition reimbursements, research assistantships with full and partial tuition reimbursements, teaching assistantships with full tuition reimbursements, career-related internships or fieldwork, Federal Work-Study, institutionally sponsored loans, tuition waivers (full and partial), and unspecified assistantships available. Financial award applicants required to submit FAFSA. *Unit head:* Dr. Gregory J. Shepherd, Dean, 740-593-4883, Fax: 740-593-0459, E-mail: shepherg@ohio.edu. *Application contact:* Dr. Eric Rothenbuhler, Associate Dean, 740-593-4885, Fax: 740-593-0459.

Our Lady of the Lake University of San Antonio, College of Arts and Sciences, Program in English, San Antonio, TX 78207-4689. Offers communication arts (MA); English and literature

(MA); English education (MA); writing (MA). Part-time and evening/weekend programs available. *Students:* 9 full-time (5 women), 15 part-time (14 women); includes 16 minority (all Hispanic Americans). Average age 31. In 2009, 15 master's awarded. *Degree requirements:* For master's, comprehensive exam, thesis optional. *Entrance requirements:* For master's, GRE General Test or MAT, minimum GPA of 3.0 in last 60 hours, 2.5 overall. Additional exam requirements/recommendations for international students: Required—TOEFL. *Application deadline:* Applications are processed on a rolling basis. Application fee: $25 ($50 for international students). Electronic applications accepted. *Expenses:* Tuition: Full-time $12,330; part-time $685 per contact hour. Required fees: $139; $12 per contact hour. $57 per semester. Tuition and fees vary according to campus/location. *Financial support:* Research assistantships, teaching assistantships, career-related internships or fieldwork, Federal Work-Study, institutionally sponsored loans, and tuition waivers (partial) available. Financial award application deadline: 4/15. *Faculty research:* Writing theory and research, contemporary Southern literature, popular culture, poetry, literature of the Southwest. *Unit head:* Dr. Michael Lueker, Chair, 210-434-6711 Ext. 2242, E-mail: luekm@lake.ollusa.edu. *Application contact:* 210-434-6711, Fax: 210-431-4036, E-mail: gradadm@lake.ollusa.edu.

Penn State University Park, Graduate School, College of Communications, State College, University Park, PA 16802-1503. Offers MA, PhD. *Accreditation:* ACEJMC (one or more programs are accredited). *Students:* 71 full-time (46 women), 15 part-time (9 women). Average age 31. 195 applicants, 35% accepted, 32 enrolled. In 2009, 5 master's, 14 doctorates awarded. *Entrance requirements:* For master's and doctorate, GRE General Test. Additional exam requirements/recommendations for international students: Required—TOEFL (minimum score 550 paper-based; 213 computer-based; 80 iBT). *Application deadline:* Applications are processed on a rolling basis. Application fee: $65. Electronic applications accepted. *Financial support:* Fellowships, research assistantships, teaching assistantships available. Financial award applicants required to submit FAFSA. *Unit head:* Dr. Douglas A. Anderson, Dean, 814-863-1484, Fax: 814-863-8044, E-mail: doug-anderson@psu.edu. *Application contact:* Cynthia E. Nicosia, Director, Graduate Enrollment Services, 814-865-1834, E-mail: cey1@psu.edu.

Penn State University Park, Graduate School, College of the Liberal Arts, Department of Communication Arts and Sciences, State College, University Park, PA 16802-1503. Offers MA, PhD.

Pepperdine University, Seaver College, Division of Communication, Malibu, CA 90263. Offers MA. Part-time programs available. *Degree requirements:* For master's, thesis or alternative. *Entrance requirements:* For master's, GRE General Test, bachelor's degree in communication or related field. Additional exam requirements/recommendations for international students: Required—TOEFL. *Expenses:* Tuition: Full-time $37,516; part-time $1310 per unit. Required fees: $80.

Pittsburg State University, Graduate School, College of Arts and Sciences, Department of Communication, Pittsburg, KS 66762. Offers applied communication (MA); communication education (MA); theatre (MA). *Degree requirements:* For master's, thesis or alternative. *Expenses:* Tuition, state resident: full-time $4212; part-time $176 per credit. Tuition, nonresident: full-time $11,530; part-time $480 per credit. Required fees: $940; $43 per credit. Tuition and fees vary according to course level, course load, degree level, campus/location, reciprocity agreements and student level.

Point Park University, School of Communication, Pittsburgh, PA 15222-1984. Offers MA. Part-time and evening/weekend programs available. *Faculty:* 10 full-time, 7 part-time/adjunct. *Students:* 28 full-time (18 women), 33 part-time (22 women); includes 14 minority (12 African Americans, 2 Asian Americans or Pacific Islanders), 3 international. Average age 27. 114 applicants, 45% accepted, 20 enrolled. In 2009, 19 master's awarded. *Degree requirements:* For master's, comprehensive exam (for some programs), thesis or alternative. *Entrance requirements:* For master's, GRE (if GPA less than 2.75), minimum GPA of 2.75, 2 letters of recommendation. Additional exam requirements/recommendations for international students: Required—TOEFL (minimum score 570 paper-based; 88 iBT). *Application deadline:* Applications are processed on a rolling basis. Application fee: $30. Electronic applications accepted. *Expenses:* Tuition: Full-time $11,880; part-time $660 per credit. Required fees: $486; $27 per credit. *Financial support:* In 2009–10, 43 students received support, including 7 research assistantships with full tuition reimbursements available (averaging $6,400 per year); scholarships/grants and unspecified assistantships also available. Financial award application deadline: 4/15; financial award applicants required to submit FAFSA. *Unit head:* Dr. Tim Hudson, Chair, 412-392-4748, E-mail: thudson@pointpark.edu. *Application contact:* Emily R. Quidetto, Recruiter/Counselor, 412-392-4794, Fax: 412-392-6164, E-mail: equidetto@pointpark.edu.

See Close-Up on page 681.

Polytechnic Institute of NYU, Department of Electrical and Computer Engineering, Major in Wireless Communications, Brooklyn, NY 11201-2990. Offers Certificate. *Entrance requirements:* Additional exam requirements/recommendations for international students: Required—TOEFL (minimum score 550 paper-based; 213 computer-based; 80 iBT); Recommended—IELTS (minimum score 6.5). *Application deadline:* For fall admission, 7/31 priority date for domestic students, 4/30 priority date for international students; for spring admission, 12/31 priority date for domestic students, 11/30 priority date for international students. Applications are processed on a rolling basis. Application fee: $75. Electronic applications accepted. *Expenses:* Tuition: Full-time $21,492; part-time $1194 per credit hour. Required fees: $1160; $204 per course. *Unit head:* Dr. Jonathan Chao, Head, 718-860-3478, Fax: 718-260-3302, E-mail: chao@poly.edu. *Application contact:* JeanCarlo Bonilla, Director of Graduate Enrollment Management, 718-260-3182, Fax: 718-260-3624, E-mail: gradinfo@poly.edu.

Purdue University, Graduate School, College of Liberal Arts, Department of Communication, West Lafayette, IN 47907. Offers MA, MS, PhD. *Degree requirements:* For master's, comprehensive exams or thesis; for doctorate, thesis/dissertation. *Entrance requirements:* For master's, GRE General Test, writing sample; for doctorate, GRE General Test, master's degree, writing sample. Additional exam requirements/recommendations for international students: Required—TOEFL, TWE. Electronic applications accepted. *Faculty research:* Interpersonal communication, mass communication, organizational communication, public affairs and issue management, rhetorical studies.

Purdue University Calumet, Graduate School, School of Liberal Arts and Social Sciences, Department of Communication and Creative Arts, Hammond, IN 46323-2094. Offers communication (MA). Part-time and evening/weekend programs available. *Degree requirements:* For master's, comprehensive exam, thesis or extended course work. *Entrance requirements:* For master's, minimum GPA of 3.0. Additional exam requirements/recommendations for international students: Required—TOEFL. Electronic applications accepted. *Faculty research:* International communication, gender studies, political rhetoric, media effects, media accountability.

Queen's University at Kingston, School of Graduate Studies and Research, Faculty of Arts and Sciences, Department of Sociology, Kingston, ON K7L 3N6, Canada. Offers communication and information technology (MA, PhD); feminist sociology (MA, PhD); socio-legal studies (MA, PhD); sociological theory (MA, PhD). Part-time programs available. *Degree requirements:* For master's, thesis; for doctorate, comprehensive exam, thesis/dissertation. *Entrance requirements:* For master's, honors bachelors degree in sociology; for doctorate, honors bachelors degree, masters degree in sociology. Additional exam requirements/recommendations for international students: Required—TOEFL. *Faculty research:* Social change and modernization, social control, deviance and criminology, surveillance.

Quinnipiac University, School of Communications, Hamden, CT 06518-1940. Offers MS. Part-time and evening/weekend programs available. *Faculty:* 15 full-time (6 women), 16 part-time/adjunct (4 women). *Students:* 34 full-time (17 women), 82 part-time (49 women); includes 9 minority (4 African Americans, 1 Asian American or Pacific Islander, 4 Hispanic Americans), 4 international. 64 applicants, 97% accepted, 36 enrolled. In 2009, 46 master's awarded. *Entrance requirements:* For master's, GRE (public relations), minimum GPA of 2.8, portfolio or writing sample. Additional exam requirements/recommendations for international students: Required—TOEFL (minimum score 575 paper-based; 233 computer-based; 90 iBT), IELTS (minimum score 6.5). *Application deadline:* For fall admission, 7/30 priority date for domestic students, 4/30 priority date for international students; for spring admission, 12/15 priority date for domestic students, 9/15 priority date for international students. Applications are processed on a rolling basis. Application fee: $45. Electronic applications accepted. *Expenses:* Tuition: Full-time $16,030; part-time $770 per credit. Required fees: $630; $35 per credit. *Financial support:* In 2009–10, 1 fellowship with full tuition reimbursement was awarded; career-related internships or fieldwork, tuition waivers (partial), and unspecified assistantships also available. Support available to part-time students. Financial award application deadline: 4/30; financial award applicants required to submit FAFSA. *Unit head:* Graduate Admissions Office, 800-462-1944, Fax: 203-582-3443, E-mail: graduate@quinnipiac.edu. *Application contact:* Scott Farber, Information Contact, 203-582-8672, Fax: 203-582-3443, E-mail: graduate@quinnipiac.edu.

Regent University, Graduate School, School of Communication and the Arts, Virginia Beach, VA 23464-9800. Offers acting (MFA); acting and directing (MFA); cinema arts/television arts (MA); communication (MA, PhD); digital media (MA); directing for cinema/TV (MA); journalism (MA); producing for cinema/TV (MA); script and screenwriting (MFA); theatre (MA). Part-time programs available. Postbaccalaureate distance learning degree programs offered (minimal on-campus study). *Faculty:* 27 full-time (3 women), 24 part-time/adjunct (8 women). *Students:* 120 full-time (65 women), 160 part-time (82 women); includes 70 minority (53 African Americans, 2 American Indian/Alaska Native, 4 Asian Americans or Pacific Islanders, 11 Hispanic Americans), 10 international. Average age 31. 221 applicants, 58% accepted, 62 enrolled. In 2009, 61 master's, 13 doctorates awarded. *Degree requirements:* For master's, thesis or alternative; for doctorate, thesis/dissertation. *Entrance requirements:* For master's, GRE General Test or MAT, minimum undergraduate GPA of 3.0, writing sample, computer literacy survey, recommendation, resume, interview, audition (MFA programs); for doctorate, GRE General Test, minimum graduate GPA of 3.0, writing sample, computer literacy survey, recommendation, interview, transcripts. Additional exam requirements/recommendations for international students: Required—TOEFL (minimum score 577 paper-based; 233 computer-based). *Application deadline:* For fall admission, 3/1 priority date for domestic students; for spring admission, 10/1 priority date for domestic students. Applications are processed on a rolling basis. Application fee: $50. Electronic applications accepted. *Expenses:* Contact institution. *Financial support:* In 2009–10, 229 students received support; fellowships with full and partial tuition reimbursements available, career-related internships or fieldwork, scholarships/grants, tuition waivers (full and partial), and unspecified assistantships available. Support available to part-time students. Financial award application deadline: 9/1; financial award applicants required to submit FAFSA. *Faculty research:* Southern gospel music, education and entertainment, celebrities and the media, journalism and ethics, C. S. Lewis. *Unit head:* Michael Patrick, Dean, 757-352-4970, Fax: 757-352-4279, E-mail: michpat@regent.edu. *Application contact:* Matthew Chadwick, Director of Admissions, 800-373-5504, Fax: 757-352-4381, E-mail: admissions@regent.edu.

Regis University, College for Professional Studies, MA Program, Denver, CO 80221-1099. Offers criminology (MA); fine arts administration (Certificate); language and communication (MA); mediation (Certificate); psychology (MA); self-designed major (MA); social justice, peace, and reconciliation (Certificate); social science (MA); technical communication (Certificate). Program also offered in Henderson and Las Vegas (Summerlin), NV. Part-time and evening/weekend programs available. Postbaccalaureate distance learning degree programs offered (minimal on-campus study). *Degree requirements:* For master's, thesis, research project. *Entrance requirements:* For master's, resume, recommendations. Additional exam requirements/recommendations for international students: Required—TOEFL (minimum score 213 computer-based), TWE (minimum score 5). Electronic applications accepted. *Expenses:* Contact institution. *Faculty research:* Independent/nonresidential graduate study: new methods and models, adult learning and the capstone experience, Goal Setting, behavior of Adult students, Innovative Studies for Community Colleges.

Rensselaer Polytechnic Institute, Graduate School, School of Humanities and Social Sciences, Department of Language, Literature, and Communication, Troy, NY 12180-3590. Offers communication and rhetoric (MS, PhD); human-computer interaction (MS); technical communication (MS). Part-time programs available. *Faculty:* 14 full-time (8 women). *Students:* 27 full-time (12 women), 24 part-time (16 women); includes 5 minority (3 African Americans, 1 Asian American or Pacific Islander, 1 Hispanic American), 2 international. 60 applicants, 53% accepted, 21 enrolled. In 2009, 14 master's, 4 doctorates awarded. Terminal master's awarded for partial completion of doctoral program. *Degree requirements:* For master's, thesis optional; for doctorate, comprehensive exam, thesis/dissertation. *Entrance requirements:* For master's, GRE General Test, resume; for doctorate, GRE General Test, writing sample, resume or curriculum vitae. Additional exam requirements/recommendations for international students: Required—TOEFL (minimum score 570 paper-based; 230 computer-based). *Application deadline:* For fall admission, 1/15 priority date for domestic students; for spring admission, 10/15 priority date for domestic students. Applications are processed on a rolling basis. Application fee: $75. Electronic applications accepted. *Expenses:* Tuition: Full-time $38,100. *Financial support:* In 2009–10, 19 students received support, including 10 fellowships with full tuition reimbursements available (averaging $16,500 per year), 1 research assistantship with full tuition reimbursement available (averaging $16,500 per year), 9 teaching assistantships with full tuition reimbursements available (averaging $16,500 per year); career-related internships or fieldwork, institutionally sponsored loans, and unspecified assistantships also available. Financial award application deadline: 1/15. *Faculty research:* Human-computer interaction, virtual institutions/communities, media design, theory and culture, usability, digital and visual rhetoric. *Unit head:* Prof. James P. Zappen, Acting Department Head, 518-276-6468, Fax: 518-276-4092, E-mail: zappenj@rpi.edu. *Application contact:* Kathy A. Colman, Recruitment Coordinator, 518-276-6469, Fax: 518-276-4092, E-mail: colmak@rpi.edu.

Rochester Institute of Technology, Graduate Enrollment Services, College of Imaging Arts and Sciences, School of Print Media, Rochester, NY 14623-5603. Offers print media (MS). Part-time programs available. *Students:* 26 full-time (11 women), 8 part-time (3 women); includes 4 minority (3 Asian Americans or Pacific Islanders, 1 Hispanic American), 23 international. Average age 27. 15 applicants, 67% accepted, 9 enrolled. In 2009, 19 master's awarded. *Entrance requirements:* For master's, minimum GPA of 3.0. Additional exam requirements/recommendations for international students: Required—TOEFL (minimum score 550 paper-based; 213 computer-based; 79 iBT), or IELTS (minimum score 6.5). *Application deadline:* For fall admission, 2/15 priority date for domestic and international students. Applications are processed on a rolling basis. Application fee: $50. Electronic applications accepted. *Expenses:* Tuition: Full-time $31,533; part-time $876 per credit hour. Required fees: $210. *Financial support:* In 2009–10, 14 students received support; research assistantships with partial tuition reimbursements available, teaching assistantships with partial tuition reimbursements available, career-related internships or fieldwork, institutionally sponsored loans, scholarships/grants, and unspecified assistantships available. Support available to part-time students. Financial award application deadline: 8/30; financial award applicants required to submit FAFSA. *Faculty research:* Printing Industry Center. *Unit head:* Dr. Patricia Sorce, Administrative Chair, 585-475-2728, Fax: 585-475-5336, E-mail: spminfo@rit.edu. *Application contact:* Diane Ellison, Assistant Vice President, Graduate Enrollment Services, 585-475-2229, Fax: 585-475-7164, E-mail: gradinfo@rit.edu.

Rochester Institute of Technology, Graduate Enrollment Services, College of Liberal Arts, Department of Communications, Program in Communication and Media Technologies, Rochester, NY 14623-5603. Offers MS. Part-time programs available. *Students:* 29 full-time (19 women), 13 part-time (12 women); includes 5 African Americans, 1 Asian American or Pacific Islander, 6 international. Average age 29. 41 applicants, 63% accepted, 21 enrolled. In 2009, 10 master's awarded. *Degree requirements:* For master's, thesis or project. *Entrance*

Communication—General

Rochester Institute of Technology (continued)
requirements: For master's, minimum GPA of 3.0, writing sample. Additional exam requirements/recommendations for international students: Required—TOEFL (minimum score 600 paper-based; 250 computer-based; 100 iBT), or IELTS (minimum score 7). *Application deadline:* For fall admission, 2/15 priority date for domestic and international students; for winter admission, 11/1 for domestic and international students; for spring admission, 2/1 for domestic and international students. Applications are processed on a rolling basis. Application fee: $50. Electronic applications accepted. *Expenses:* Tuition: Full-time $31,533; part-time $876 per credit hour. Required fees: $210. *Financial support:* In 2009–10, 17 students received support; research assistantships with partial tuition reimbursements available, teaching assistantships with partial tuition reimbursements available, career-related internships or fieldwork, scholarships/grants, and unspecified assistantships available. Support available to part-time students. Financial award applicants required to submit FAFSA. *Unit head:* Dr. Rudy Pugliese, Coordinator for Graduate Programs, 585-475-5925, Fax: 585-475-7732, E-mail: rrpgsl@rit.edu. *Application contact:* Diane Ellison, Assistant Vice President, Graduate Enrollment Services, 585-475-2229, Fax: 585-475-7164, E-mail: gradinfo@rit.edu.

Roosevelt University, Graduate Division, College of Arts and Sciences, Department of Communication, Chicago, IL 60605. Offers integrated marketing communications (MSIMC); journalism (MSJ). Part-time and evening/weekend programs available.

Rutgers, The State University of New Jersey, New Brunswick, School of Communication, Information and Library Studies, Program in Communication, Library and Information Science and Media Studies, Piscataway, NJ 08854-8097. Offers PhD. Part-time programs available. *Degree requirements:* For doctorate, comprehensive exam, thesis/dissertation, qualifying exams. *Entrance requirements:* For doctorate, GRE General Test, proficiency in statistics. Additional exam requirements/recommendations for international students: Required—TOEFL (minimum score 600 paper-based; 250 computer-based). Electronic applications accepted. *Faculty research:* Information science, media studies.

Saginaw Valley State University, College of Arts and Behavioral Sciences, Program in Communication and Digital Media Design, University Center, MI 48710. Offers MA. Part-time and evening/weekend programs available. *Students:* 21 full-time (14 women), 14 part-time (5 women); includes 5 minority (3 African Americans, 1 Asian American or Pacific Islander, 1 Hispanic American), 14 international. Average age 30. 20 applicants, 90% accepted, 12 enrolled. In 2009, 17 master's awarded. *Degree requirements:* For master's, thesis. *Entrance requirements:* For master's, minimum GPA of 2.75. Additional exam requirements/recommendations for international students: Required—TOEFL. *Application deadline:* Applications are processed on a rolling basis. Application fee: $25. Electronic applications accepted. *Financial support:* Federal Work-Study and scholarships/grants available. Support available to part-time students. Financial award application deadline: 4/1; financial award applicants required to submit FAFSA. *Unit head:* Dr. David Schneider, Professor of Communication, 989-964-4398, E-mail: erickson@svsu.edu. *Application contact:* Dr. David Schneider, Professor of Communication, 989-964-4398, E-mail: erickson@svsu.edu.

Saint Louis University, Graduate School, College of Arts and Sciences and Graduate School, Department of Communication, St. Louis, MO 63103-2097. Offers MA, MA-R. Part-time programs available. *Degree requirements:* For master's, thesis (for some programs), comprehensive oral and written exams. *Entrance requirements:* For master's, GRE General Test, letters of recommendation, resume, interview. Additional exam requirements/recommendations for international students: Required—TOEFL (minimum score 525 paper-based; 194 computer-based). Electronic applications accepted. *Faculty research:* Media studies, organizational communication, dialogue, intercultural communication, qualitative research methods.

St. Mary's University, Graduate School, Department of English and Communication Studies, Program in Communication Studies, San Antonio, TX 78228-8507. Offers MA. Part-time programs available. Postbaccalaureate distance learning degree programs offered (minimal on-campus study). *Degree requirements:* For master's, comprehensive exam. *Entrance requirements:* For master's, GRE General Test, MAT. Additional exam requirements/recommendations for international students: Required—TOEFL (minimum score 550 paper-based; 213 computer-based; 80 iBT). Electronic applications accepted. *Expenses:* Tuition: Full-time $8004. Required fees: $536. One-time fee: $5 full-time. Full-time tuition and fees vary according to program. *Faculty research:* Persuasion and negotiation, group dynamics, language and communication, business communication, organizational communication.

St. Thomas University, School of Leadership Studies, Miami Gardens, FL 33054-6459. Offers MA, MPS, MS, Ed D, Certificate. Part-time and evening/weekend programs available. *Entrance requirements:* Additional exam requirements/recommendations for international students: Required—TOEFL (minimum score 550 paper-based; 213 computer-based; 79 iBT).

San Diego State University, Graduate and Research Affairs, College of Professional Studies and Fine Arts, School of Communication, San Diego, CA 92182. Offers advertising and public relations (MA); critical-cultural studies (MA); interaction studies (MA); intercultural and international studies (MA); new media studies (MA); news and information studies (MA); telecommunications and media management (MA). *Degree requirements:* For master's, thesis. *Entrance requirements:* For master's, GRE General Test, 3 letters of recommendation. Additional exam requirements/recommendations for international students: Required—TOEFL. Electronic applications accepted.

San Jose State University, Graduate Studies and Research, College of Social Sciences, Department of Communication Studies, San Jose, CA 95192-0001. Offers MA. *Students:* 20 full-time (16 women), 27 part-time (20 women); includes 16 minority (2 African Americans, 6 Asian Americans or Pacific Islanders, 8 Hispanic Americans), 2 international. Average age 30. 38 applicants, 42% accepted, 15 enrolled. In 2009, 11 master's awarded. *Degree requirements:* For master's, comprehensive exam, thesis or alternative, project. *Entrance requirements:* For master's, minimum GPA of 3.0. *Application deadline:* For fall admission, 6/29 for domestic students; for spring admission, 11/30 for domestic students. Applications are processed on a rolling basis. Application fee: $59. Electronic applications accepted. *Financial support:* Applicants required to submit FAFSA. *Unit head:* Prof. Stephanie J. Coopman, Chair, 408-924-5360, Fax: 408-924-5396, E-mail: stephanie.coopman@sjsu.edu. *Application contact:* Prof. Stephanie J. Coopman, Chair, 408-924-5360, Fax: 408-924-5396, E-mail: stephanie.coopman@sjsu.edu.

Seton Hall University, College of Arts and Sciences, Department of Communication, South Orange, NJ 07079-2697. Offers corporate and professional communication (MA); intercultural communication (MA); organizational communication (MA); public relations (MA); strategic communication and leadership (MA); strategic communication planning (MA). Part-time and evening/weekend programs available. Postbaccalaureate distance learning degree programs offered (minimal on-campus study). *Faculty:* 3 full-time (1 woman), 15 part-time/adjunct (6 women). *Students:* 30 full-time (19 women), 92 part-time (56 women); includes 42 minority (33 African Americans, 1 Asian American or Pacific Islander, 8 Hispanic Americans), 3 international. Average age 33. 66 applicants, 97% accepted, 39 enrolled. In 2009, 64 master's awarded. *Degree requirements:* For master's, thesis. *Entrance requirements:* Additional exam requirements/recommendations for international students: Required—TOEFL. *Application deadline:* For fall admission, 7/1 priority date for domestic and international students; for spring admission, 11/1 priority date for domestic and international students. Applications are processed on a rolling basis. Application fee: $50. Electronic applications accepted. *Financial support:* Research assistantships, career-related internships or fieldwork, Federal Work-Study, and unspecified assistantships available. Financial award applicants required to submit FAFSA. *Faculty research:* Managerial communication, communication consulting, communication and development. *Unit head:* Prof. Peter Reader, Chair, 973-761-9474, Fax: 973-761-9234, E-mail: readerpe@shu.edu. *Application contact:* Dr. Richard Dool, Director of Graduate Studies, 973-275-2794, Fax: 973-761-9234, E-mail: doolrich@shu.edu.

Shippensburg University of Pennsylvania, School of Graduate Studies, College of Arts and Sciences, Department of Communication/Journalism, Shippensburg, PA 17257-2299. Offers communication studies (MS). Part-time and evening/weekend programs available. *Degree requirements:* For master's, 6 credit thesis option or 3 credit professional project, candidacy. *Entrance requirements:* For master's, GRE or MAT (if GPA less than 2.75), 3 professional references, resume. Additional exam requirements/recommendations for international students: Required—TOEFL (minimum score 580 paper-based; 237 computer-based); Recommended—IELTS (minimum score 6). Electronic applications accepted. *Expenses:* Contact institution.

Shippensburg University of Pennsylvania, School of Graduate Studies, College of Arts and Sciences, Department of Sociology and Anthropology, Shippensburg, PA 17257-2299. Offers organizational development and leadership (MS), including business, communications, education, environmental management, higher education, historical administration, individual and organizational development, public organizations, social structures and organizations. Part-time and evening/weekend programs available. *Degree requirements:* For master's, capstone experience. *Entrance requirements:* For master's, interview (if GPA less than 2.75), resume. Additional exam requirements/recommendations for international students: Required—TOEFL (minimum score 560 paper-based; 220 computer-based); Recommended—IELTS (minimum score 6). Electronic applications accepted.

Simon Fraser University, Graduate Studies, Faculty of Applied Sciences, School of Communication, Burnaby, BC V5A 1S6, Canada. Offers MA, PhD. *Degree requirements:* For master's, thesis optional; for doctorate, thesis/dissertation. *Entrance requirements:* For master's, minimum GPA of 3.0; for doctorate, minimum GPA of 3.5. Additional exam requirements/recommendations for international students: Required—TOEFL or IELTS. Electronic applications accepted. *Faculty research:* Theory and methodology, policy studies in communication media and telecommunication, international development, journalism studies, telelearning and telework.

South Dakota State University, Graduate School, College of Arts and Science, Department of Journalism and Mass Communication, Brookings, SD 57007. Offers communication studies and journalism (MS). *Accreditation:* ACEJMC. Part-time and evening/weekend programs available. *Degree requirements:* For master's, thesis, oral exam. *Entrance requirements:* Additional exam requirements/recommendations for international students: Required—TOEFL (minimum score 550 paper-based; 213 computer-based; 79 iBT). *Faculty research:* Mass communication applications.

Southeastern Louisiana University, College of Arts, Humanities and Social Sciences, Department of Communication, Hammond, LA 70402. Offers organizational communication (MA). Part-time and evening/weekend programs available. *Faculty:* 6 full-time (4 women). *Students:* 10 full-time (8 women), 26 part-time (23 women); includes 4 minority (all African Americans), 1 international. Average age 29. 19 applicants, 100% accepted, 14 enrolled. In 2009, 8 master's awarded. *Degree requirements:* For master's, comprehensive exam. *Entrance requirements:* For master's, GRE General Test (800 or better), bachelor's degree in communication or related field, minimum GPA of 3.0. Additional exam requirements/recommendations for international students: Required—TOEFL (minimum score 500 paper-based; 173 computer-based; 61 iBT). *Application deadline:* For fall admission, 7/15 priority date for domestic students, 6/1 priority date for international students; for spring admission, 12/1 priority date for domestic students, 10/1 priority date for international students. Applications are processed on a rolling basis. Application fee: $20 ($30 for international students). Electronic applications accepted. *Expenses:* Tuition, state resident: full-time $3086; part-time $225 per credit hour. Tuition, nonresident: part-time $529 per credit hour. Required fees: $1195. Tuition and fees vary according to course level and course load. *Financial support:* In 2009–10, 5 students received support, including 5 research assistantships (averaging $9,500 per year); career-related internships or fieldwork, Federal Work-Study, institutionally sponsored loans, and administrative assistantships also available. Support available to part-time students. Financial award application deadline: 5/1; financial award applicants required to submit FAFSA. *Faculty research:* Cross cultural communication in multi-national organizations, health communication among women, leadership communication, new media in organizations, crisis communication in organizations. Total annual research expenditures: $11,554. *Unit head:* Dr. Suzette Bryan, Interim Department Head, 985-549-2105, Fax: 985-549-5014, E-mail: suzette.bryan@selu.edu. *Application contact:* Sandra Meyers, Graduate Admissions Analyst, 985-549-5620, Fax: 985-549-5632, E-mail: admissions@selu.edu.

Southern Illinois University Carbondale, Graduate School, College of Mass Communication and Media Arts, Carbondale, IL 62901-4701. Offers MA, MFA, PhD, MBA/MA. Part-time programs available. *Degree requirements:* For doctorate, thesis/dissertation. *Entrance requirements:* For doctorate, GRE General Test, minimum GPA of 3.25. Additional exam requirements/recommendations for international students: Required—TOEFL.

Southern Methodist University, Meadows School of the Arts, Division of Communication Arts, Dallas, TX 75275. Offers MA. Part-time and evening/weekend programs available. *Faculty:* 9 full-time (4 women), 2 part-time/adjunct (both women). *Students:* 27 full-time (19 women), 1 (woman) part-time; includes 6 minority (1 American Indian/Alaska Native, 5 Hispanic Americans), 5 international. Average age 27. 9 applicants, 78% accepted, 4 enrolled. In 2009, 6 master's awarded. *Degree requirements:* For master's, thesis or alternative. *Entrance requirements:* For master's, GRE General Test, minimum undergraduate GPA of 3.0 in major field during last 2 years. Additional exam requirements/recommendations for international students: Required—TOEFL (minimum score 550 paper-based; 213 computer-based; 80 iBT). *Application deadline:* For fall admission, 3/1 priority date for domestic and international students. Application fee: $75. *Financial support:* In 2009–10, 7 students received support, including 7 teaching assistantships (averaging $6,500 per year); research assistantships, scholarships/grants, tuition waivers (full), and unspecified assistantships also available. Financial award application deadline: 3/15. *Faculty research:* Digital sound, new technology, film and gender study, popular film and TV genres, Asian cinema. Total annual research expenditures: $10,000. *Unit head:* Rick Worland, Chair, 214-768-3708, Fax: 214-768-2784, E-mail: rworland@smu.edu. *Application contact:* Jean Cherry, Director of Graduate Admissions and Records, 214-768-3765, Fax: 214-768-3272, E-mail: jcherry@smu.edu.

Southern Polytechnic State University, School of Arts and Sciences, Department of English, Technical Communication, and Media Arts, Marietta, GA 30060-2896. Offers communications management (Graduate Certificate); content development (Graduate Certificate); information and instructional design (MSIID); information design and communication (MS); instructional design (Graduate Certificate); technical and professional communication (Graduate Certificate); visual communication and graphics (Graduate Certificate). Part-time and evening/weekend programs available. Postbaccalaureate distance learning degree programs offered (no on-campus study). *Faculty:* 4 full-time (3 women), 1 part-time/adjunct (0 women). *Students:* 5 full-time (all women), 50 part-time (32 women); includes 18 African Americans, 2 international. Average age 38. 32 applicants, 94% accepted, 26 enrolled. In 2009, 8 master's awarded. *Degree requirements:* For master's, thesis or internship; for Graduate Certificate, thesis optional, 18 hours completed through thesis option (6 hours), internship option (6 hours) or advanced coursework option (6 hours). *Entrance requirements:* For master's, GRE, statement of purpose, writing sample, professional recommendations, timed essay; for Graduate Certificate, writing sample, professional recommendations. Additional exam requirements/recommendations for international students: Required—TOEFL (minimum score 550 paper-based; 213 computer-based; 79 iBT), IELTS (minimum score 6.5). *Application deadline:* For fall admission, 5/1 priority date for domestic students, 7/1 priority date for international students; for spring admission, 9/1 priority date for domestic students, 11/1 priority date for international students. Applications are processed on a rolling basis. Application fee: $20. Electronic applications accepted. *Expenses:* Tuition, state resident: full-time $2896; part-time $181 per credit hour. Tuition, nonresident: full-time $11,552; part-time $722 per credit hour. Required fees: $1096; $1096 per year. *Financial support:* In 2009–10, 1 research assistantship with full tuition reimbursement (averaging $4,000 per year), 1 teaching assistantship with partial tuition reimbursement (averaging $4,000 per year) were awarded; career-related internships or fieldwork, Federal Work-Study, scholarships/grants, and unspecified assistantships also available. Support available to part-time students. Financial award application deadline: 5/1; financial award applicants required to submit FAFSA. *Faculty research:* Usability, user-centered design, instructional design, information architecture, information design. *Unit head:* Dr. Mark Nunes, Chair, 678-915-7202, Fax: 678-915-7425, E-mail: mnunes@spsu.edu. *Application contact:* Nikki Palamiotis, Director of Graduate Studies, 678-915-4276, Fax: 678-915-7292, E-mail: npalamio@spsu.edu.

Southern Utah University, College of Humanities and Social Sciences, Program in Communication, Cedar City, UT 84720-2498. Offers MA. *Faculty:* 9 full-time (1 woman). *Students:* 3 full-time (2 women), 37 part-time (19 women); includes 1 African American, 1 Hispanic American. 5 applicants, 100% accepted, 4 enrolled. In 2009, 12 master's awarded. *Application deadline:* Applications are processed on a rolling basis. Application fee: $50 ($65 for international students). Electronic applications accepted. *Financial support:* In 2009–10, 6 research assistantships (averaging $800 per year), 6 teaching assistantships (averaging $4,200 per year) were awarded. *Unit head:* Dr. James McDonald, Dean, 435-586-7898, Fax: 435-865-8193, E-mail: mcdonaldj@suu.edu. *Application contact:* Pam Halgren, Administrative Assistant, 435-586-7861, Fax: 435-865-8352, E-mail: halgren@suu.edu.

Spalding University, Graduate Studies, College of Business and Communication, Louisville, KY 40203-2188. Offers business communication (MS). Part-time and evening/weekend programs available. *Faculty:* 6 full-time (2 women), 3 part-time/adjunct (2 women). *Students:* 39 full-time (30 women), 29 part-time (22 women); includes 19 minority (17 African Americans, 1 Asian American or Pacific Islander, 1 Hispanic American). Average age 37. 33 applicants, 73% accepted, 24 enrolled. In 2009, 20 master's awarded. *Degree requirements:* For master's, project. *Entrance requirements:* For master's, GRE or GMAT, writing sample, interview, letters of recommendation. Additional exam requirements/recommendations for international students: Required—TOEFL (minimum score 535 paper-based; 203 computer-based). *Application deadline:* Applications are processed on a rolling basis. Application fee: $30. Electronic applications accepted. *Expenses:* Tuition: Full-time $11,340; part-time $630 per credit hour. Tuition and fees vary according to program. *Financial support:* In 2009–10, 17 students received support, including 1 research assistantship (averaging $4,815 per year). Financial award application deadline: 3/15; financial award applicants required to submit FAFSA. *Faculty research:* Curriculum development, consumer behavior, interdisciplinary pedagogy. *Unit head:* Dr. Diane Tobin, Dean, 502-585-9911 Ext. 2747, E-mail: dtobin@spalding.edu. *Application contact:* Claire Rayburn, Administrative Assistant, 502-585-9911 Ext. 2120, E-mail: cbc@spalding.edu.

Spring Arbor University, School of Arts and Sciences, Spring Arbor, MI 49283-9799. Offers communication (MA); spiritual formation and leadership (MA). Part-time programs available. Postbaccalaureate distance learning degree programs offered (no on-campus study). *Faculty:* 6 full-time (1 woman), 11 part-time/adjunct (5 women). *Students:* 107 full-time (73 women), 76 part-time (57 women); includes 8 minority (6 African Americans, 2 Hispanic Americans), 1 international. Average age 42. In 2009, 16 master's awarded. *Degree requirements:* For master's, thesis (for some programs). *Entrance requirements:* For master's, GRE (taken within the last 5 years), writing sample, 3 recommendations. Additional exam requirements/recommendations for international students: Required—TOEFL (minimum score 550 paper-based; 220 computer-based). Application fee: $40. *Expenses:* Contact institution. *Financial support:* Applicants required to submit FAFSA. *Unit head:* Dr. Wally Metts, Chair of the Department of Communication, 517-750-1200 Ext. 1491, E-mail: wmetts@arbor.edu. *Application contact:* Dale Glinz, Lead Recruitment Specialist/Trainer, Graduate and Professional Studies, 517-750-6703, E-mail: dglinz@arbor.edu.

Stanford University, School of Humanities and Sciences, Department of Communication, Stanford, CA 94305-9991. Offers communication (journalism specialization) (MA); communication theory and research (PhD). *Faculty:* 11 full-time (1 woman). *Students:* 62 full-time (38 women). Average age 27. 164 applicants, 27% accepted, 34 enrolled. In 2009, 26 master's, 4 doctorates awarded. Terminal master's awarded for partial completion of doctoral program. *Degree requirements:* For master's, thesis, project; for doctorate, thesis/dissertation, qualifying examination, area examination, 2 projects. *Entrance requirements:* For master's and doctorate, GRE General Test. Additional exam requirements/recommendations for international students: Required—TOEFL (minimum score 650 paper-based; 280 computer-based; 115 iBT). *Application deadline:* For fall admission, 12/1 for domestic and international students. Application fee: $125. Electronic applications accepted. *Expenses:* Tuition: Full-time $37,380; part-time $2760 per quarter. Required fees: $501. *Financial support:* Fellowships, research assistantships, teaching assistantships available. *Unit head:* James S. Fishkin, Chair, 650-723-4611. *Application contact:* Student Services Manager, 650-723-2075, Fax: 650-725-2472, E-mail: comm-studentservices@stanford.edu.

State University of New York College at Potsdam, School of Arts and Sciences, Department of English and Communication, Potsdam, NY 13676. Offers English and communication (MA). Part-time and evening/weekend programs available. *Faculty:* 5 full-time (3 women). *Students:* 4 full-time (all women), 9 part-time (7 women); includes 1 minority (African American), 1 international. 4 applicants, 75% accepted, 3 enrolled. In 2009, 5 master's awarded. *Degree requirements:* For master's, one foreign language, thesis or alternative. *Entrance requirements:* For master's, minimum GPA of 3.0 in last 60 hours of undergraduate course work. Additional exam requirements/recommendations for international students: Required—TOEFL (minimum score 550 paper-based; 213 computer-based; 80 iBT), IELTS (minimum score 6). *Application deadline:* For fall admission, 4/1 priority date for domestic and international students; for spring admission, 10/15 priority date for domestic and international students. Applications are processed on a rolling basis. Application fee: $50. *Expenses:* Tuition, state resident: full-time $8370; part-time $349 per credit hour. Tuition, nonresident: full-time $13,250; part-time $552 per credit hour. Required fees: $942; $38.70 per credit hour. *Financial support:* In 2009–10, 1 student received support; teaching assistantships with full tuition reimbursements available, Federal Work-Study and unspecified assistantships available. Support available to part-time students. Financial award application deadline: 3/1; financial award applicants required to submit FAFSA. *Unit head:* Dr. Sharmain van Blommestein, Director of Graduate Studies, 315-267-3158, Fax: 315-267-3256, E-mail: vanblos@potsdam.edu. *Application contact:* Peter Cutler, Graduate Admissions Counselor, 315-267-3154, Fax: 315-267-4802, E-mail: cutlerpj@potsdam.edu.

State University of New York College of Environmental Science and Forestry, Program in Environmental Science, Syracuse, NY 13210-2779. Offers environmental and community land planning (MPS, MS, PhD); environmental and natural resources policy (PhD); environmental communication and participatory processes (MPS, MS, PhD); environmental policy and democratic processes (MPS, MS, PhD); environmental systems and risk management (MPS, MS, PhD); water and wetland resource studies (MPS, MS, PhD). Part-time programs available. *Degree requirements:* For master's, thesis (for some programs); for doctorate, comprehensive exam, thesis/dissertation. *Entrance requirements:* For master's and doctorate, GRE General Test, minimum GPA of 3.0. Additional exam requirements/recommendations for international students: Required—TOEFL (minimum score 550 paper-based; 213 computer-based; 80 iBT), IELTS (minimum score 6). *Faculty research:* Environmental education/communications, water resources, land resources, waste management.

Stephen F. Austin State University, Graduate School, College of Applied Arts and Science, Department of Communication, Nacogdoches, TX 75962. Offers communication (MA); mass communication (MA). Part-time programs available. *Degree requirements:* For master's, comprehensive exam, thesis optional. *Entrance requirements:* For master's, GRE General Test. Additional exam requirements/recommendations for international students: Required—TOEFL (minimum score 550 paper-based; 213 computer-based).

Stevens Institute of Technology, Graduate School, Charles V. Schaefer Jr. School of Engineering, Department of Electrical and Computer Engineering, Program in Electrical Engineering, Hoboken, NJ 07030. Offers computer architecture and digital system design (M Eng); electrical engineering (PhD); microelectronics and photonics science and technology (M Eng); signal processing for communications (M Eng); telecommunications systems engineering (M Eng); wireless communications (M Eng, Certificate). *Degree requirements:* For master's, thesis optional; for doctorate, variable foreign language requirement, thesis/dissertation. *Entrance requirements:* For master's, doctorate, and Certificate, GRE. Additional exam requirements/recommendations for international students: Required—TOEFL. Electronic applications accepted. *Expenses:* Tuition: Full-time $9900; part-time $1100 per credit. Required fees: $286 per semester.

Suffolk University, College of Arts and Sciences, Department of Communication, Boston, MA 02108-2770. Offers communication studies (MAC); integrated marketing communication (MAC); organizational communication (MAC); public relations and advertising (MAC). Part-time and evening/weekend programs available. *Faculty:* 20 full-time (10 women). *Students:* 14 full-time (12 women), 28 part-time (22 women), 2 international. Average age 27. 85 applicants, 58% accepted, 8 enrolled. In 2009, 21 master's awarded. *Degree requirements:* For master's, thesis optional. *Entrance requirements:* For master's, GRE General Test, MAT, or GMAT, 2 letters of recommendation, resume. Additional exam requirements/recommendations for international students: Required—TOEFL (minimum score 550 paper-based; 213 computer-based; 80 iBT). *Application deadline:* For fall admission, 6/15 priority date for domestic students, 6/15 for international students; for spring admission, 11/1 priority date for domestic students, 11/1 for international students. Applications are processed on a rolling basis. Application fee: $50. Electronic applications accepted. *Expenses:* Contact institution. *Financial support:* In 2009–10, 30 students received support, including 20 fellowships with partial tuition reimbursements available (averaging $3,413 per year); career-related internships or fieldwork, Federal Work-Study, and institutionally sponsored loans also available. Support available to part-time students. Financial award application deadline: 4/1; financial award applicants required to submit FAFSA. *Faculty research:* New media and new markets for advertising, First Amendment issues with the Internet, gender and intercultural communication, organizational development. *Unit head:* Dr. Robert Rosenthal, Chair, 617-573-8502, Fax: 617-742-6982, E-mail: rrosenth@suffolk.edu. *Application contact:* Judith Reynolds, Director of Graduate Admissions, 617-573-8302, Fax: 617-305-1733, E-mail: grad.admission@suffolk.edu.

Syracuse University, College of Visual and Performing Arts, Program in Communication and Rhetorical Studies, Syracuse, NY 13244. Offers MA. Part-time programs available. *Students:* 14 full-time (6 women), 2 part-time (both women); includes 1 minority (African American), 2 international. Average age 25. 23 applicants, 74% accepted, 9 enrolled. In 2009, 8 master's awarded. *Degree requirements:* For master's, thesis or alternative. *Entrance requirements:* For master's, GRE General Test, writing sample. Additional exam requirements/recommendations for international students: Required—TOEFL (minimum score 100 iBT). *Application deadline:* For fall admission, 2/1 priority date for domestic and international students. Application fee: $75. Electronic applications accepted. *Expenses:* Tuition: Full-time $26,808; part-time $1117 per credit. Required fees: $1024. *Financial support:* In 2009–10, 9 students received support; fellowships with full tuition reimbursements available, teaching assistantships with full and partial tuition reimbursements available, tuition waivers (partial) available. Financial award application deadline: 1/1; financial award applicants required to submit FAFSA. *Unit head:* Dr. Kendall Phillips, Chair, 315-443-2883, E-mail: kphillip@syr.edu. *Application contact:* Harriett Conti, Assistant Dean for Recruitment and Admissions, 315-443-5755, E-mail: hmconti@syr.edu.

Syracuse University, S. I. Newhouse School of Public Communications, Syracuse, NY 13244. Offers MA, MS, PhD, JD/MA, JD/MS, MS/MA. *Accreditation:* ACEJMC (one or more programs are accredited). Postbaccalaureate distance learning degree programs offered (minimal on-campus study). *Faculty:* 60 full-time (23 women), 45 part-time/adjunct (16 women). *Students:* 266 full-time (163 women), 88 part-time (62 women); includes 67 minority (37 African Americans, 16 Asian Americans or Pacific Islanders, 14 Hispanic Americans), 55 international. Average age 28. 839 applicants, 57% accepted, 241 enrolled. In 2009, 225 master's, 4 doctorates awarded. *Degree requirements:* For master's, comprehensive exam (for some programs); for doctorate, thesis/dissertation, qualifying exams. *Entrance requirements:* For master's and doctorate, GRE General Test. Additional exam requirements/recommendations for international students: Required—TOEFL (minimum score 600 paper-based; 250 computer-based; 100 iBT), IELTS (minimum score 7). *Application deadline:* For fall admission, 2/1 priority date for domestic and international students. Application fee: $45. Electronic applications accepted. *Expenses:* Tuition: Full-time $26,808; part-time $1117 per credit. Required fees: $1024. *Financial support:* In 2009–10, fellowships with tuition reimbursements (averaging $11,000 per year), teaching assistantships with tuition reimbursements (averaging $7,500 per year) were awarded; research assistantships with tuition reimbursements, career-related internships or fieldwork, Federal Work-Study, scholarships/grants, and tuition waivers (partial) also available. Support available to part-time students. Financial award application deadline: 2/1; financial award applicants required to submit FAFSA. *Faculty research:* Media convergence, political reporting, interactive multimedia, popular television, advertising effectiveness. *Unit head:* Dr. Lorraine Branham, Dean, 315-443-3627, Fax: 315-443-3946. *Application contact:* Martha Coria, Graduate Records Office, 315-443-5749, Fax: 315-443-1834, E-mail: pcgrad@syr.edu.

See Display on page 622 and Close-Up on page 683.

Teachers College, Columbia University, Graduate Faculty of Education, Department of Math, Science and Technology, Program in Communications, New York, NY 10027-6696. Offers Ed M, MA, Ed D. Part-time and evening/weekend programs available. *Faculty:* 24 part-time/adjunct. *Students:* 9 full-time (7 women), 29 part-time (18 women); includes 9 minority (4 African Americans, 3 Asian Americans or Pacific Islanders, 2 Hispanic Americans), 6 international. Average age 33. 19 applicants, 89% accepted, 8 enrolled. In 2009, 10 master's, 5 doctorates awarded. Terminal master's awarded for partial completion of doctoral program. *Degree requirements:* For doctorate, thesis/dissertation. *Entrance requirements:* For doctorate, GRE General Test or MAT. *Application deadline:* For fall admission, 5/15 for domestic students; for spring admission, 12/1 for domestic students. Application fee: $65. *Financial support:* Career-related internships or fieldwork, Federal Work-Study, institutionally sponsored loans, and tuition waivers (full and partial) available. Support available to part-time students. Financial award application deadline: 2/1. *Faculty research:* Television and youth, application of digital technology to education reform. *Unit head:* Dr. O. Roger Anderson, Chair, 212-678-3405. *Application contact:* Deanna Ghozati, Assistant Director of Admission, 212-678-4018, Fax: 212-678-4171, E-mail: ghozati@tc.edu.

Temple University, Graduate School, School of Communications and Theater, Philadelphia, PA 19122-6096. Offers MA, MFA, MJ, MS, PhD. Part-time and evening/weekend programs available. *Degree requirements:* For doctorate, one foreign language, thesis/dissertation. *Entrance requirements:* For master's, minimum GPA of 3.0; for doctorate, GRE General Test, minimum GPA of 3.0. Additional exam requirements/recommendations for international students: Required—TOEFL (minimum score 550 paper-based; 213 computer-based; 79 iBT). Electronic applications accepted.

Temple University, Health Sciences Center and Graduate School, College of Health Professions, Department of Communication Sciences, Philadelphia, PA 19122-6096. Offers communication sciences (PhD); linguistics (MA); speech-language-hearing (MA). *Accreditation:* ASHA. Part-time and evening/weekend programs available. *Degree requirements:* For doctorate, thesis/dissertation. *Entrance requirements:* For master's and doctorate, GRE General Test, minimum GPA of 3.0. Additional exam requirements/recommendations for international students: Required—TOEFL (minimum score 550 paper-based; 213 computer-based; 79 iBT). Electronic applications accepted. *Faculty research:* Fluency, infants and families, multilingual/multicultural communication, geriatrics, conflict process, language, health communication.

Texas A&M University, College of Liberal Arts, Department of Communication, College Station, TX 77843. Offers MA, PhD. *Faculty:* 16. *Students:* 38 full-time (23 women), 25 part-time (14 women); includes 13 minority (6 African Americans, 7 Hispanic Americans), 10 international. Average age 27. In 2009, 11 master's, 10 doctorates awarded. *Degree*

Communication—General

Texas A&M University (continued)

requirements: For master's, thesis or alternative; for doctorate, thesis/dissertation. *Entrance requirements:* For master's, GRE General Test. Additional exam requirements/recommendations for international students: Required—TOEFL. *Application deadline:* For fall admission, 2/15 priority date for domestic students; for spring admission, 10/15 for domestic students. Applications are processed on a rolling basis. Application fee: $50 ($75 for international students). Electronic applications accepted. *Expenses:* Tuition, state resident: full-time $3991; part-time $221.74 per credit hour. Tuition, nonresident: full-time $9049; part-time $502.74 per credit hour. *Financial support:* In 2009–10, fellowships with partial tuition reimbursements (averaging $12,000 per year), research assistantships with partial tuition reimbursements (averaging $11,000 per year), teaching assistantships with partial tuition reimbursements (averaging $11,000 per year) were awarded; institutionally sponsored loans also available. Financial award application deadline: 2/1; financial award applicants required to submit FAFSA. *Faculty research:* Rhetoric and public affairs, communication and health, communication and organizations. *Unit head:* Dr. Richard L. Street, Head, 979-845-0209, E-mail: r-street@tamu.edu. *Application contact:* Barbara F. Sharf, Director of Graduate Studies, 979-845-0625, Fax: 979-845-6594, E-mail: bsharf@tamu.edu.

Texas Southern University, Tavis Smiley School of Communication, Houston, TX 77004-4584. Offers MA. Part-time programs available. *Faculty:* 3 full-time (2 women), 1 part-time/adjunct (0 women). *Students:* 22 full-time (15 women), 37 part-time (25 women); includes 53 African Americans, 1 Hispanic American, 1 international. Average age 31. 38 applicants, 97% accepted, 28 enrolled. In 2009, 9 master's awarded. *Degree requirements:* For master's, comprehensive exam, thesis. *Entrance requirements:* For master's, GRE General Test, minimum GPA of 2.5. Additional exam requirements/recommendations for international students: Required—TOEFL. *Application deadline:* For fall admission, 7/1 for domestic and international students; for spring admission, 11/1 for domestic and international students. Applications are processed on a rolling basis. Application fee: $50 ($75 for international students). Electronic applications accepted. *Expenses:* Tuition, state resident: full-time $1805; part-time $100 per credit hour. Tuition, nonresident: full-time $6470; part-time $343 per credit hour. Tuition and fees vary according to course level, course load and degree level. *Financial support:* In 2009–10, 2 teaching assistantships (averaging $5,800 per year) were awarded; unspecified assistantships also available. Financial award application deadline: 5/1. *Unit head:* Dr. James Ward, Dean, 713-313-7740, E-mail: ward_jw@tsu.edu. *Application contact:* Dr. Louis Browne, Graduate Adviser, 713-313-7024.

Texas State University–San Marcos, Graduate School, College of Fine Arts and Communication, San Marcos, TX 78666. Offers MA, MFA, MM. Part-time and evening/weekend programs available. *Faculty:* 50 full-time (21 women), 6 part-time/adjunct (4 women). *Students:* 134 full-time (83 women), 76 part-time (44 women); includes 67 minority (7 African Americans, 1 American Indian/Alaska Native, 12 Asian Americans or Pacific Islanders, 47 Hispanic Americans), 12 international. Average age 29. 133 applicants, 74% accepted, 71 enrolled. In 2009, 77 master's awarded. *Degree requirements:* For master's, comprehensive exam, thesis (for some programs). *Entrance requirements:* For master's, GRE General Test (for some programs), minimum GPA of 2.75 in last 60 hours of course work. Additional exam requirements/recommendations for international students: Required—TOEFL (minimum score 550 paper-based; 213 computer-based). *Application deadline:* For fall admission, 6/15 priority date for domestic students; for spring admission, 10/15 priority date for domestic students. Applications are processed on a rolling basis. Application fee: $40 ($90 for international students). Electronic applications accepted. *Expenses:* Tuition, state resident: full-time $5784; part-time $241 per credit hour. Tuition, nonresident: part-time $551 per credit hour. Required fees: $1728; $48 per credit hour. $306. Tuition and fees vary according to course load. *Financial support:* In 2009–10, 194 students received support, including 4 research assistantships (averaging $5,160 per year), 65 teaching assistantships (averaging $4,246 per year); career-related internships or fieldwork, Federal Work-Study, institutionally sponsored loans, scholarships/grants, and unspecified assistantships also available. Support available to part-time students. Financial award application deadline: 4/1; financial award applicants required to submit FAFSA. *Faculty research:* Latino news media, emergency communication, Afred Survey-propane. Total annual research expenditures: $44,034. *Unit head:* Dr. T. Richard Cheatham, Dean, 512-245-2308, Fax: 512-245-8334, E-mail: tc02@txstate.edu. *Application contact:* Dr. J. Michael Willoughby, Dean of Graduate School, 512-245-2581, Fax: 512-245-8365, E-mail: gradcollege@txstate.edu.

Texas State University–San Marcos, Graduate School, College of Fine Arts and Communication, Department of Communication Studies, Program in Communication Studies, San Marcos, TX 78666. Offers MA. Part-time and evening/weekend programs available. *Faculty:* 4 full-time (2 women). *Students:* 25 full-time (21 women), 18 part-time (13 women); includes 13 minority (3 African Americans, 1 American Indian/Alaska Native, 1 Asian American or Pacific Islander, 8 Hispanic Americans), 1 international. Average age 26. 32 applicants, 69% accepted, 14 enrolled. In 2009, 22 master's awarded. *Degree requirements:* For master's, comprehensive exam, thesis optional. *Entrance requirements:* For master's, minimum GPA of 3.0 in last 60 hours. Additional exam requirements/recommendations for international students: Required—TOEFL (minimum score 550 paper-based; 213 computer-based). *Application deadline:* For fall admission, 6/15 priority date for domestic students; for spring admission, 10/15 priority date for domestic students. Applications are processed on a rolling basis. Application fee: $40 ($90 for international students). Electronic applications accepted. *Expenses:* Tuition, state resident: full-time $5784; part-time $241 per credit hour. Tuition, nonresident: part-time $551 per credit hour. Required fees: $1728; $48 per credit hour. $306. Tuition and fees vary according to course load. *Financial support:* In 2009–10, 36 students received support, including 1 research assistantship (averaging $5,859 per year), 19 teaching assistantships (averaging $6,232 per year); career-related internships or fieldwork, Federal Work-Study, and institutionally sponsored loans also available. Support available to part-time students. Financial award application deadline: 4/1; financial award applicants required to submit FAFSA. *Faculty research:* Speech education, rhetoric and criticism, interpersonal and group communication, communication theory, rhetoric of Sojourner Truth. *Unit head:* Dr. Phillip Salem, Graduate Adviser, 512-245-2165, Fax: 512-245-3138, E-mail: ps05@txstate.edu. *Application contact:* Dr. J. Michael Willoughby, Dean of Graduate School, 512-245-2581, Fax: 512-245-8365, E-mail: gradcollege@txstate.edu.

Texas Tech University, Graduate School, College of Arts and Sciences, Department of Communication Studies, Lubbock, TX 79409. Offers MA. Part-time programs available. *Faculty:* 7 full-time (3 women). *Students:* 21 full-time (10 women), 4 part-time (3 women); includes 6 minority (1 African American, 5 Hispanic Americans), 1 international. Average age 26. 35 applicants, 40% accepted, 11 enrolled. In 2009, 4 master's awarded. *Degree requirements:* For master's, thesis. *Entrance requirements:* For master's, GRE General Test. Additional exam requirements/recommendations for international students: Required—TOEFL (minimum score 550 paper-based; 213 computer-based). *Application deadline:* For fall admission, 3/1 priority date for international students; for spring admission, 11/1 priority date for international students. Applications are processed on a rolling basis. Application fee: $50 ($75 for international students). Electronic applications accepted. *Expenses:* Tuition, state resident: full-time $5100; part-time $213 per credit hour. Tuition, nonresident: full-time $11,748; part-time $490 per credit hour. Required fees: $2298; $50 per credit hour. $555 per semester. *Financial support:* In 2009–10, 9 teaching assistantships with partial tuition reimbursements (averaging $10,273 per year) were awarded; research assistantships with partial tuition reimbursements, Federal Work-Study and institutionally sponsored loans also available. Support available to part-time students. Financial award application deadline: 4/15; financial award applicants required to submit FAFSA. *Faculty research:* Computer mediated communication, intercultural communication, health communication, interpersonal communication, family communication. *Unit head:* Dr. Bolanle A. Olaniran, Chair, 806-742-3911, Fax: 806-742-1025, E-mail: b.olaniran@ttu.edu. *Application contact:* Dr. Juliann Scholl, Graduate Director, 806-742-1675, Fax: 806-742-1025, E-mail: juliann.scholl@ttu.edu.

Towson University, College of Graduate Studies and Research, Program in Communications Management, Towson, MD 21252-0001. Offers MS. *Degree requirements:* For master's, thesis. *Entrance requirements:* For master's, 24 credits in mass communications, public relations and/or advertising, writing and statistics; professional experience; minimum GPA of 3.0. Electronic applications accepted.

Towson University, College of Graduate Studies and Research, Program in Strategic Public Relations and Integrated Communications, Towson, MD 21252-0001. Offers Certificate. Evening/weekend programs available. Postbaccalaureate distance learning degree programs offered (no on-campus study). *Entrance requirements:* For degree, 24 credits in related course work, minimum GPA of 3.0. Electronic applications accepted.

Trinity International University, Trinity Graduate School, Deerfield, IL 60015-1284. Offers bioethics (MA); communication and culture (MA); counseling psychology (MA); instructional leadership (M Ed); teaching (MA). Part-time and evening/weekend programs available. Postbaccalaureate distance learning degree programs offered (minimal on-campus study). *Degree requirements:* For master's, comprehensive exam. *Entrance requirements:* For master's, GRE General Test or MAT, minimum undergraduate GPA of 3.0. Additional exam requirements/recommendations for international students: Required—TOEFL (minimum score 580 paper-based; 237 computer-based), TWE (minimum score 4). Electronic applications accepted.

Trinity (Washington) University, School of Professional Studies, Washington, DC 20017-1094. Offers business administration (MBA); communication (MA); international security studies (MA); organizational management (MSA), including federal program management, human resource management, nonprofit management, organizational development, public and community health. Part-time and evening/weekend programs available. *Degree requirements:* For master's, thesis (for some programs), capstone project (MSA). *Entrance requirements:* For master's, minimum GPA of 2.5. Additional exam requirements/recommendations for international students: Required—TOEFL (minimum score 550 paper-based; 213 computer-based).

Universidad Metropolitana, School of Social Sciences, Humanities and Communications, Program in Communications, San Juan, PR 00928-1150. Offers MA.

Université de Montréal, Faculty of Arts and Sciences, Department of Communication, Montréal, QC H3C 3J7, Canada. Offers communication (PhD); communication in changing organizations (Certificate); communication sciences (M Sc). *Degree requirements:* For master's, thesis; for doctorate, one foreign language, thesis/dissertation, general exam. *Entrance requirements:* For doctorate, proficiency in French. Electronic applications accepted. *Faculty research:* Mass media/new communication technologies, organizational communication.

Université du Québec à Montréal, Graduate Programs, Program in Communications, Montréal, QC H3C 3P8, Canada. Offers MA, PhD. Part-time programs available. *Degree requirements:* For master's, thesis; for doctorate, thesis/dissertation. *Entrance requirements:* For master's, appropriate bachelor's degree or equivalent, proficiency in French; for doctorate, appropriate master's degree or equivalent, proficiency in French.

Université du Québec à Trois-Rivières, Graduate Programs, Program in Social Communication, Trois-Rivières, QC G9A 5H7, Canada. Offers MA, DESS.

University at Albany, State University of New York, College of Arts and Sciences, Department of Communication, Albany, NY 12222-0001. Offers communication (MA); sociology and communication (PhD). Part-time programs available. *Degree requirements:* For master's, comprehensive exam, thesis or alternative; for doctorate, comprehensive exam, thesis/dissertation. *Entrance requirements:* For master's, minimum GPA of 3.0; for doctorate, GRE, minimum GPA of 3.0. Additional exam requirements/recommendations for international students: Required—TOEFL (minimum score 550 paper-based; 213 computer-based). Electronic applications accepted. *Faculty research:* Language and social interaction, campaign communication, media agenda-setting, high-speed management, organizational boundary-spanning.

University at Buffalo, the State University of New York, Graduate School, College of Arts and Sciences, Department of Communication, Buffalo, NY 14260. Offers MA, PhD. Part-time programs available. *Faculty:* 12 full-time (2 women), 16 part-time/adjunct (4 women). *Students:* 19 full-time (13 women), 34 part-time (17 women); includes 10 minority (1 African American, 9 Asian Americans or Pacific Islanders), 17 international. Average age 33. 121 applicants, 28% accepted. In 2009, 3 master's, 3 doctorates awarded. Terminal master's awarded for partial completion of doctoral program. *Degree requirements:* For master's, thesis; for doctorate, comprehensive exam, thesis/dissertation. *Entrance requirements:* For master's and doctorate, GRE General Test, minimum GPA of 3.0. Additional exam requirements/recommendations for international students: Required—TOEFL (minimum score 600 paper-based; 250 computer-based; 100 iBT); Recommended—TWE. *Application deadline:* For fall admission, 1/1 priority date for domestic and international students. Applications are processed on a rolling basis. Application fee: $75. Electronic applications accepted. *Financial support:* In 2009–10, 18 students received support, including 2 fellowships, 5 research assistantships with full tuition reimbursements available (averaging $12,500 per year), 13 teaching assistantships with full tuition reimbursements available (averaging $13,605 per year); career-related internships or fieldwork, institutionally sponsored loans, health care benefits, and unspecified assistantships also available. Financial award application deadline: 1/1; financial award applicants required to submit FAFSA. *Faculty research:* Technology, health, international, interpersonal. Total annual research expenditures: $231,588. *Unit head:* Dr. Thomas H. Feeley, Chairman, 716-645-1160, Fax: 716-645-2086, E-mail: thfeeley@buffalo.edu. *Application contact:* Rose Gryckiewicz, Graduate Secretary, 716-645-1505, E-mail: rfg@buffalo.edu.

The University of Akron, Graduate School, College of Creative and Professional Arts, School of Communication, Akron, OH 44325. Offers MA. Part-time and evening/weekend programs available. *Faculty:* 15 full-time (8 women), 2 part-time/adjunct (1 woman). *Students:* 22 full-time (13 women), 12 part-time (9 women); includes 5 minority (4 African Americans, 1 Hispanic American), 4 international. Average age 26. 21 applicants, 81% accepted, 12 enrolled. In 2009, 8 master's awarded. *Degree requirements:* For master's, thesis, project or written comprehensive exam. *Entrance requirements:* For master's, undergraduate major in communication or related area, minimum GPA of 2.75. Additional exam requirements/recommendations for international students: Required—TOEFL (minimum score 550 paper-based; 213 computer-based; 79 iBT). *Application deadline:* For fall admission, 5/31 for domestic students; for spring admission, 12/31 for domestic students. Application fee: $30 ($40 for international students). Electronic applications accepted. *Expenses:* Tuition, state resident: full-time $6570; part-time $365 per credit hour. Tuition, nonresident: full-time $11,250; part-time $625 per credit hour. *Financial support:* In 2009–10, 13 teaching assistantships with full tuition reimbursements were awarded; research assistantships, institutionally sponsored loans also available. *Faculty research:* Communications theory, business and organization communications, criticism of communications, film and video studies, interpersonal and intercultural communications. Total annual research expenditures: $22,535. *Unit head:* Dr. Carolyn Anderson, Director, 330-972-7600, E-mail: canderson@uakron.edu. *Application contact:* Dr. Richard Caplan, Graduate Coordinator, 330-972-5565, E-mail: caplan@uakron.edu.

The University of Alabama, Graduate School, College of Communication and Information Sciences, Tuscaloosa, AL 35487-0172. Offers MA, MFA, MLIS, PhD. *Accreditation:* ACEJMC (one or more programs are accredited at the [master's] level). *Faculty:* 53 full-time (25 women), 4 part-time/adjunct (3 women). *Students:* 200 full-time (134 women), 214 part-time (158 women); includes 48 minority (32 African Americans, 3 American Indian/Alaska Native, 8 Asian Americans or Pacific Islanders, 5 Hispanic Americans), 20 international. Average age 31. 526 applicants, 37% accepted, 144 enrolled. In 2009, 145 master's, 17 doctorates awarded. *Degree requirements:* For master's, comprehensive exam, thesis or alternative; for doctorate, comprehensive exam, thesis/dissertation. *Entrance requirements:* For master's, GRE; for doctorate, GRE, minimum graduate GPA of 3.0, master's degree. Additional exam requirements/recommendations for international students: Required—TOEFL (minimum score 600 paper-based; 250 computer-based; 100 iBT). *Application deadline:* For fall admission, 2/15 priority date for domestic and international students; for winter admission, 11/1 priority date for international students; for spring admission, 11/1 priority date for domestic students. Applications are processed on a rolling basis. Application fee: $50 ($60 for international students). Electronic applications accepted. *Expenses:* Tuition, state resident: full-time $7000. Tuition, nonresident: full-time $19,200. *Financial support:* In 2009–10, 78 students received support, including 3 fellowships with tuition reimbursements available (averaging $15,000 per year), 34 research assistantships with tuition reimbursements available (averaging $13,045 per year), 38 teaching assistantships with tuition reimbursements available (averaging $13,045 per year); institutionally sponsored loans, health care benefits, and unspecified assistantships also available. Financial award application deadline: 2/15. *Faculty research:* Mass media research; media effects; information studies; cultural, critical, and rhetorical studies; electronic media; law and policy. *Unit head:* Dr. Jennings Bryant, Associate Dean for Graduate Studies, 205-348-8593, Fax: 205-348-6774. *Application contact:* Diane Shaddix, Information Contact, 205-348-8593, Fax: 205-348-6774, E-mail: dshaddix@bama.ua.edu.

The University of Alabama at Birmingham, College of Arts and Sciences, Program in Communication Management, Birmingham, AL 35294. Offers MA.

University of Alaska Fairbanks, College of Liberal Arts, Department of Communications, Fairbanks, AK 99775-5680. Offers professional communications (MA). Part-time programs available. *Faculty:* 4 full-time (3 women), 1 (woman) part-time/adjunct. *Students:* 13 full-time (10 women), 7 part-time (5 women); includes 3 minority (1 African American, 1 Asian American or Pacific Islander, 1 Hispanic American), 2 international. Average age 31. 9 applicants, 67% accepted, 6 enrolled. In 2009, 3 master's awarded. *Degree requirements:* For master's, comprehensive exam, thesis, oral defense. *Entrance requirements:* Additional exam requirements/recommendations for international students: Required—TOEFL (minimum score 550 paper-based; 213 computer-based; 80 iBT). *Application deadline:* For fall admission, 6/1 for domestic students, 3/1 for international students; for spring admission, 10/15 for domestic students, 9/1 for international students. Applications are processed on a rolling basis. Application fee: $60. Electronic applications accepted. *Expenses:* Tuition, state resident: full-time $7584; part-time $316 per credit. Tuition, nonresident: full-time $15,504; part-time $646 per credit. Required fees: $23 per credit. $135 per semester. Tuition and fees vary according to course level, course load and reciprocity agreements. *Financial support:* In 2009–10, 10 teaching assistantships (averaging $12,006 per year) were awarded; fellowships, Federal Work-Study, scholarships/grants, tuition waivers, and unspecified assistantships also available. Support available to part-time students. Financial award application deadline: 7/1; financial award applicants required to submit FAFSA. *Faculty research:* Interpersonal communications, health communications, intercultural communications, politeness and face management in conversation, gender communication. *Unit head:* Dr. Robert Arundale, Department Chair, 907-474-6591, Fax: 907-474-5858, E-mail: fycomm@uaf.edu. *Application contact:* Dr. Robert Arundale, Department Chair, 907-474-6591, Fax: 907-474-5858, E-mail: fycomm@uaf.edu.

University of Alberta, Faculty of Extension, Edmonton, AB T6G 2E1, Canada. Offers communications and technology (MA). Tuition and fees charges are reported in Canadian dollars. *Expenses:* Tuition, area resident: Full-time $4626 Canadian dollars; part-time $99.72 Canadian dollars per unit. International tuition: $8216 Canadian dollars full-time. Required fees: $3590 Canadian dollars; $99.72 Canadian dollars per unit. $215 Canadian dollars per term. *Unit head:* Katy Campbell, Dean. *Application contact:* Eileen Crookes, Information Contact, 780-492-1501, Fax: 780-492-0627.

University of Alberta, Faculty of Graduate Studies and Research, Program in Communications and Technology, Edmonton, AB T6G 2E1, Canada. Offers MACT. Tuition and fees charges are reported in Canadian dollars. *Expenses:* Tuition, area resident: Full-time $4626 Canadian dollars; part-time $99.72 Canadian dollars per unit. International tuition: $8216 Canadian dollars full-time. Required fees: $3590 Canadian dollars; $99.72 Canadian dollars per unit. $215 Canadian dollars per term. *Unit head:* K. Campbell, Unit Head, 780-492-1501, E-mail: mact@ualberta.ca. *Application contact:* Information Contact, 780-492-3499, E-mail: grad.mail@ualberta.ca.

The University of Arizona, Graduate College, College of Social and Behavioral Sciences, Department of Communication, Tucson, AZ 85721. Offers MA, PhD. Part-time programs available. *Faculty:* 8 full-time (2 women). *Students:* 12 full-time (8 women), 15 part-time (12 women); includes 2 minority (both Hispanic Americans), 4 international. Average age 28. 45 applicants, 18% accepted, 8 enrolled. In 2009, 3 master's, 2 doctorates awarded. Terminal master's awarded for partial completion of doctoral program. *Degree requirements:* For master's, thesis optional; for doctorate, comprehensive exam, thesis/dissertation. *Entrance requirements:* For master's, GRE General Test, minimum GPA of 3.25, writing sample, 3 letters of recommendation; for doctorate, GRE General Test, minimum GPA of 3.5, writing sample, 3 letters of recommendation, statement of purpose. Additional exam requirements/recommendations for international students: Required—TOEFL (minimum score 600 paper-based; 250 computer-based; 90 iBT). *Application deadline:* For fall admission, 2/1 for domestic and international students. Applications are processed on a rolling basis. Application fee: $65. Electronic applications accepted. *Expenses:* Tuition, state resident: full-time $9028. Tuition, nonresident: full-time $24,890. *Financial support:* In 2009–10, 21 teaching assistantships with full tuition reimbursements (averaging $15,017 per year) were awarded; career-related internships or fieldwork, Federal Work-Study, scholarships/grants, health care benefits, tuition waivers (full), and unspecified assistantships also available. *Faculty research:* Health communication, new communication technologies. Total annual research expenditures: $202,495. *Unit head:* Dr. Chris Segrin, Department Head, 520-621-1366, Fax: 520-621-5504, E-mail: segrin@email.arizona.edu. *Application contact:* Dr. Peggy Flyntz, Graduate Coordinator, 520-307-0695, Fax: 520-621-5504, E-mail: commgrad@email.arizona.edu.

University of Arkansas, Graduate School, J. William Fulbright College of Arts and Sciences, Department of Communication, Fayetteville, AR 72701-1201. Offers MA. Part-time programs available. *Students:* 14 full-time (9 women), 22 part-time (15 women); includes 5 minority (3 African Americans, 2 Hispanic Americans), 4 international. In 2009, 14 master's awarded. *Degree requirements:* For master's, thesis. *Entrance requirements:* For master's, GRE General Test. Application fee: $40 ($50 for international students). *Expenses:* Tuition, state resident: full-time $7355; part-time $356.58 per hour. Tuition, nonresident: full-time $17,401; part-time $775.17 per hour. Required fees: $1203. *Financial support:* In 2009–10, 22 teaching assistantships were awarded; fellowships, research assistantships, career-related internships or fieldwork and Federal Work-Study also available. Support available to part-time students. Financial award application deadline: 4/1; financial award applicants required to submit FAFSA. *Unit head:* Dr. Robert Brady, Department Chairperson, 479-575-3046, Fax: 479-575-6734, E-mail: rbrady@uark.edu. *Application contact:* Dr. Ron Warren, Graduate Coordinator, 479-575-3046, Fax: 479-575-6734, E-mail: rwarren@uark.edu.

University of Calgary, Faculty of Graduate Studies, Faculty of Communication and Culture, Calgary, AB T2N 1N4, Canada. Offers MA, MCS, PhD. Part-time and evening/weekend programs available. *Degree requirements:* For master's, project (MCS), thesis (MA); for doctorate, thesis/dissertation. *Entrance requirements:* For master's, minimum GPA of 3.0; for doctorate, master's degree, minimum GPA of 3.0, BA degree, min GPA of 3.0. Additional exam requirements/recommendations for international students: Required—TOEFL (minimum score 600 paper-based; 250 computer-based); Recommended—IELTS (minimum score 8). Electronic applications accepted. *Faculty research:* Science communications, structuration theory, organizational communication, communication theory, media law.

Communication—General

University of California, Davis, Graduate Studies, Program in Communication, Davis, CA 95616. Offers MA. *Degree requirements:* For master's, comprehensive exam (for some programs), thesis (for some programs). *Entrance requirements:* For master's, GRE. Additional exam requirements/recommendations for international students: Required—TOEFL (minimum score 550 paper-based; 213 computer-based).

University of California, San Diego, Office of Graduate Studies, Department of Communication, La Jolla, CA 92093. Offers MA, PhD. *Entrance requirements:* For doctorate, GRE General Test. Electronic applications accepted.

University of California, San Diego, Office of Graduate Studies, Interdisciplinary Program in Cognitive Science, La Jolla, CA 92093. Offers cognitive science/anthropology (PhD); cognitive science/communication (PhD); cognitive science/computer science and engineering (PhD); cognitive science/linguistics (PhD); cognitive science/neuroscience (PhD); cognitive science/philosophy (PhD); cognitive science/psychology (PhD); cognitive science/sociology (PhD). Admissions offered through affiliated departments. *Degree requirements:* For doctorate, thesis/dissertation. *Entrance requirements:* For doctorate, GRE General Test, acceptance into one of the eight participating departments. *Faculty research:* Language and cognition, philosophy of mind, visual perception, biological anthropology, sociolinguistics.

University of California, Santa Barbara, Graduate Division, College of Letters and Sciences, Division of Social Sciences, Department of Communication, Santa Barbara, CA 93106-4020. Offers human development (PhD); MA/PhD. *Faculty:* 20 full-time (8 women), 1 part-time/adjunct (0 women). *Students:* 38 full-time (26 women). Average age 28. 155 applicants, 12% accepted, 10 enrolled. In 2009, 2 doctorates awarded. *Degree requirements:* For doctorate, comprehensive exam, thesis/dissertation. *Entrance requirements:* For doctorate, GRE General Test, 3 letters of recommendation, resume/curriculum vitae. Additional exam requirements/recommendations for international students: Required—TOEFL (minimum score 550 paper-based; 213 computer-based; 80 iBT), or IELTS. *Application deadline:* For fall admission, 1/1 for domestic and international students. Application fee: $70 ($90 for international students). Electronic applications accepted. *Financial support:* In 2009–10, 38 students received support, including 38 fellowships with full and partial tuition reimbursements available (averaging $5,500 per year), 5 research assistantships with full and partial tuition reimbursements available (averaging $7,800 per year), 34 teaching assistantships with partial tuition reimbursements available (averaging $11,000 per year); Federal Work-Study, institutionally sponsored loans, scholarships/grants, health care benefits, tuition waivers (full and partial), and unspecified assistantships also available. Financial award application deadline: 1/1; financial award applicants required to submit FAFSA. *Faculty research:* Interpersonal communication, organizational communication, media communication, political communication, intrapersonal communication. Total annual research expenditures: $100,000. *Unit head:* Prof. Michael Stohl, Chair, 805-893-7935, Fax: 805-893-7102, E-mail: mstohl@comm.ucsb.edu. *Application contact:* Nancy Siris-Rawls, Graduate Program Assistant, 805-893-3046, Fax: 805-893-7102, E-mail: nsiris@comm.ucsb.edu.

University of California, Santa Cruz, Division of Graduate Studies, Division of Physical and Biological Sciences, Program in Science Communication, Santa Cruz, CA 95064. Offers science illustration (Certificate); science writing (Certificate). *Entrance requirements:* For degree, GRE General Test, GRE Subject Test, bachelor's degree in science. Electronic applications accepted.

University of Central Florida, College of Sciences, Nicholson School of Communication, Orlando, FL 32816. Offers MA. Part-time and evening/weekend programs available. *Faculty:* 40 full-time (18 women), 24 part-time/adjunct (10 women). *Students:* 43 full-time (37 women), 36 part-time (27 women); includes 13 minority (6 African Americans, 1 Asian American or Pacific Islander, 6 Hispanic Americans), 8 international. Average age 27. 61 applicants, 74% accepted, 29 enrolled. In 2009, 34 master's awarded. *Degree requirements:* For master's, thesis or comprehensive exam. *Entrance requirements:* For master's, GRE General Test, minimum GPA of 3.0 in last 60 hours of course work. Additional exam requirements/recommendations for international students: Required—TOEFL. *Application deadline:* For fall admission, 7/15 for domestic students; for spring admission, 12/7 for domestic students. Application fee: $30. Electronic applications accepted. *Expenses:* Tuition, state resident: part-time $306.31 per credit hour. Tuition, nonresident: part-time $1099.01 per credit hour. Part-time tuition and fees vary according to degree level and program. *Financial support:* In 2009–10, 19 students received support, including 5 fellowships with partial tuition reimbursements available (averaging $4,200 per year), 1 research assistantship with partial tuition reimbursement available (averaging $6,600 per year), 14 teaching assistantships with partial tuition reimbursements available (averaging $600 per year); career-related internships or fieldwork, Federal Work-Study, institutionally sponsored loans, tuition waivers (partial), and unspecified assistantships also available. Financial award application deadline: 3/1; financial award applicants required to submit FAFSA. *Faculty research:* Persuasion, communication apprehension, nonverbal communication, conflict resolution. *Unit head:* Dr. Robert Chandler, Director, 407-823-2683, Fax: 407-823-5216, E-mail: rcchandl@mail.ucf.edu. *Application contact:* Dr. Robert Chandler, Director, 407-823-2683, Fax: 407-823-5216, E-mail: rcchandl@mail.ucf.edu.

University of Cincinnati, Graduate School, McMicken College of Arts and Sciences, Department of Communication, Cincinnati, OH 45221. Offers MA. Part-time programs available. *Degree requirements:* For master's, comprehensive exam, thesis or alternative. *Entrance requirements:* For master's, GRE General Test, undergraduate course work in communication. Additional exam requirements/recommendations for international students: Required—TOEFL. Electronic applications accepted. *Faculty research:* Political communication, health communication, organizational communication, interpersonal communication.

University of Colorado at Boulder, Graduate School, College of Arts and Sciences, Department of Communication, Boulder, CO 80309. Offers MA, PhD. *Faculty:* 18 full-time (7 women). *Students:* 48 full-time (33 women), 5 part-time (all women); includes 9 minority (1 African American, 2 Asian Americans or Pacific Islanders, 6 Hispanic Americans), 3 international. Average age 33. 79 applicants, 14% accepted, 11 enrolled. In 2009, 7 master's, 5 doctorates awarded. *Degree requirements:* For master's, comprehensive exam, thesis optional; for doctorate, comprehensive exam, thesis/dissertation. *Entrance requirements:* For master's and doctorate, GRE General Test, minimum undergraduate GPA of 3.2. *Application deadline:* For fall admission, 12/31 priority date for domestic students, 12/15 for international students; for spring admission, 9/15 for domestic students, 8/15 for international students. Applications are processed on a rolling basis. Application fee: $50 ($60 for international students). *Financial support:* In 2009–10, 15 fellowships (averaging $860 per year), 29 research assistantships (averaging $12,099 per year) were awarded; tuition waivers (full) also available. Financial award application deadline: 12/15. *Faculty research:* Organizational communication, computer-mediated communication and new technology, critical cultural studies, rhetoric and civil discourse, interpersonal communication, language and social interaction. Total annual research expenditures: $12,690.

University of Colorado at Boulder, Graduate School, School of Journalism and Mass Communication, Boulder, CO 80309. Offers communication (PhD), including media studies; mass communication research (MA); newsgathering (MA). *Accreditation:* ACEJMC (one or more programs are accredited). Part-time programs available. *Faculty:* 22 full-time (11 women). *Students:* 77 full-time (50 women), 16 part-time (12 women); includes 6 minority (1 African American, 5 Hispanic Americans), 14 international. Average age 32. 181 applicants, 26% accepted, 30 enrolled. In 2009, 22 master's, 3 doctorates awarded. *Degree requirements:* For master's, comprehensive exam, thesis or alternative; for doctorate, comprehensive exam, thesis/dissertation. *Entrance requirements:* For master's, GRE General Test, minimum undergraduate GPA of 2.75; for doctorate, GRE General Test, minimum undergraduate GPA of 3.2, 3.5 graduate. *Application deadline:* For fall admission, 2/15 for domestic students, 12/1 for international students. Applications are processed on a rolling basis. Application fee: $50 ($60 for international students). *Financial support:* In 2009–10, 14 fellowships (averaging $1,807 per year), 21 research assistantships with tuition reimbursements (averaging $11,554 per year) were awarded; institutionally sponsored loans and unspecified assistantships also available. Financial award application deadline: 3/1. *Faculty research:* Writing on science and the environment, mass communication and public opinion, minority representation in the media, media and culture. Total annual research expenditures: $141,446.

University of Colorado at Colorado Springs, Graduate School, College of Letters, Arts and Sciences, Department of Communication, Colorado Springs, CO 80933-7150. Offers MA. Part-time programs available. *Faculty:* 16 full-time (12 women). *Students:* 36 full-time (23 women), 11 part-time (7 women); includes 7 minority (4 African Americans, 3 Hispanic Americans), 3 international. Average age 33. 25 applicants, 92% accepted, 17 enrolled. In 2009, 12 master's awarded. *Degree requirements:* For master's, thesis optional. *Entrance requirements:* For master's, GRE General Test. *Application deadline:* Applications are processed on a rolling basis. Application fee: $60. *Expenses:* Tuition, state resident: full-time $8922; part-time $639 per credit hour. Tuition, nonresident: full-time $19,372; part-time $1154 per credit hour. Tuition and fees vary according to course level, course load, degree level, program, reciprocity agreements and student level. *Financial support:* Teaching assistantships, career-related internships or fieldwork, Federal Work-Study, and scholarships/grants available. Support available to part-time students. Financial award application deadline: 3/1; financial award applicants required to submit FAFSA. *Faculty research:* Organizational communication, interpersonal communication, communication education, oral communication, cultural diversity. *Unit head:* Dr. David Nelson, Chair, 719-255-4129, Fax: 719-255-4030, E-mail: drnelson@uccs.edu. *Application contact:* Debbie MacDonald, Program Assistant, 719-255-4114, Fax: 719-255-4030, E-mail: knorris@uccs.edu.

University of Colorado Denver, College of Liberal Arts and Sciences, Department of Communication, Denver, CO 80217-3364. Offers communication (MA); technical communication (MS). Part-time and evening/weekend programs available. *Students:* 5 full-time (4 women), 11 part-time (7 women), 1 international. 14 applicants, 57% accepted, 3 enrolled. In 2009, 6 master's awarded. *Degree requirements:* For master's, comprehensive exam, thesis or alternative. *Entrance requirements:* For master's, GRE General Test. Additional exam requirements/recommendations for international students: Required—TOEFL (minimum score 525 paper-based; 197 computer-based). *Application deadline:* For fall admission, 6/1 for domestic students. Applications are processed on a rolling basis. Application fee: $50 ($75 for international students). Electronic applications accepted. *Financial support:* Fellowships with partial tuition reimbursements, research assistantships with partial tuition reimbursements, teaching assistantships, Federal Work-Study and institutionally sponsored loans available. Financial award application deadline: 4/1; financial award applicants required to submit FAFSA. *Unit head:* Dr. Stephen J. Hartnett, Chair, 303-556-2778, E-mail: stephen.hartnett@ucdenver.edu. *Application contact:* Dr. Stephen J. Hartnett, Chair, 303-556-2778, E-mail: stephen.hartnett@ucdenver.edu.

University of Connecticut, Graduate School, College of Liberal Arts and Sciences, Department of Communication Sciences, Program in Communication Processes, Storrs, CT 06269. Offers MA. *Faculty:* 13 full-time (7 women). *Students:* 8 full-time (6 women); includes 1 minority (Hispanic American). Average age 25. 48 applicants, 8% accepted, 2 enrolled. In 2009, 3 master's awarded. *Degree requirements:* For master's, comprehensive exam. *Entrance requirements:* For master's, GRE General Test. Additional exam requirements/recommendations for international students: Required—TOEFL (minimum score 550 paper-based; 213 computer-based). *Application deadline:* For fall admission, 2/1 priority date for domestic and international students; for spring admission, 11/1 for domestic students, 10/1 for international students. Applications are processed on a rolling basis. Application fee: $55. Electronic applications accepted. *Expenses:* Tuition, state resident: full-time $4725; part-time $525 per credit. Tuition, nonresident: full-time $12,267; part-time $1363 per credit. Required fees: $346 per semester. Tuition and fees vary according to course load. *Financial support:* In 2009–10, 6 teaching assistantships with full tuition reimbursements were awarded; research assistantships with full tuition reimbursements, Federal Work-Study, scholarships/grants, health care benefits, and unspecified assistantships also available. Financial award application deadline: 2/1; financial award applicants required to submit FAFSA. *Unit head:* Carl A. Coelho, Chair, 860-486-2628. *Application contact:* Sue Kiss, Administrative Assistant, 860-486-2628, Fax: 860-486-5422, E-mail: susan.kiss@uconn.edu.

University of Dayton, Graduate School, College of Arts and Sciences, Department of Communication, Dayton, OH 45469-1300. Offers MA. Part-time and evening/weekend programs available. *Faculty:* 8 full-time (5 women), 1 part-time/adjunct (0 women). *Students:* 18 full-time (15 women), 2 part-time (both women); includes 1 minority (African American), 3 international. Average age 28. 26 applicants, 46% accepted, 6 enrolled. In 2009, 8 master's awarded. *Degree requirements:* For master's, comprehensive exam, thesis optional. *Entrance requirements:* For master's, GRE General Test, minimum undergraduate GPA of 3.0. Additional exam requirements/recommendations for international students: Required—TOEFL (minimum score 550 paper-based; 213 computer-based; 80 iBT). *Application deadline:* For fall admission, 3/1 priority date for domestic and international students; for winter admission, 7/1 priority date for international students; for spring admission, 1/1 priority date for international students. Applications are processed on a rolling basis. Application fee: $0 ($50 for international students). Electronic applications accepted. *Expenses:* Tuition: Full-time $8412; part-time $701 per credit hour. Required fees: $325; $65 per course. $25 per semester. Tuition and fees vary according to course load, degree level and program. *Financial support:* In 2009–10, 8 teaching assistantships with full tuition reimbursements (averaging $9,517 per year) were awarded; career-related internships or fieldwork, institutionally sponsored loans, health care benefits, and unspecified assistantships also available. Support available to part-time students. Financial award applicants required to submit FAFSA. *Faculty research:* Health communication, organizational communication, mass communication. *Unit head:* Dr. Jon Hess, Chair, 937-229-2028, E-mail: jonathan.hess@notes.udayton.edu. *Application contact:* Graduate Admissions, 937-229-4411, Fax: 937-229-4729, E-mail: gradadmission@udayton.edu.

University of Delaware, College of Arts and Sciences, Department of Communication, Newark, DE 19716. Offers MA. Part-time and evening/weekend programs available. *Degree requirements:* For master's, comprehensive exam (for some programs), thesis (for some programs). *Entrance requirements:* For master's, GRE General Test, minimum GPA of 3.0. Additional exam requirements/recommendations for international students: Required—TOEFL (minimum score 600 paper-based; 270 computer-based). Electronic applications accepted. *Faculty research:* Politics and the media, online social interaction technologies, mass communication law, media and the perceptions of reality, the role of communication in public opinion processes, small group research, communication during resource dilemmas.

University of Denver, University College, Denver, CO 80208. Offers applied communication (MAS, MPS, Certificate); computer information systems (MAS, Certificate); environmental policy and management (MAS, Certificate); geographic information systems (MAS, Certificate); human resource administration (MPS, Certificate); knowledge and information technologies (MAS); liberal studies (MLS, Certificate); modern languages (MLS, Certificate); organizational leadership (MPS, Certificate); security management (Certificate); technology management (MAS, Certificate), including 21st century strategic management (MAS), international markets (MAS), project management (MAS), research and development management (MAS); telecommunications (MAS, Certificate), including broadband (MAS), telecommunications management and policy (MAS), telecommunications technology (MAS), wireless networks (MAS). Part-time and evening/weekend programs available. Postbaccalaureate distance learning degree programs offered (no on-campus study). *Faculty:* 160 part-time/adjunct (64 women). *Students:* 53 full-time (25 women), 984 part-time (551 women); includes 171 minority (72 African Americans, 10 American Indian/Alaska Native, 33 Asian Americans or Pacific Islanders, 56 Hispanic Americans), 75 international. Average age 36. 537 applicants, 96% accepted, 494 enrolled. In 2009, 229 master's, 109 Certificates awarded. *Entrance requirements:* Additional exam requirements/recommendations for international students: Required—TOEFL (minimum score 550 paper-based; 213 computer-based). *Application deadline:* Applications are processed on a rolling basis

basis. Application fee: $75. Electronic applications accepted. *Expenses:* Contact institution. *Financial support:* Applicants required to submit FAFSA. *Unit head:* Dr. James Davis, Dean, 303-871-2291, Fax: 303-871-4047, E-mail: jdavis@du.edu. *Application contact:* Information Contact, 303-871-3155.

University of Dubuque, Program in Communication, Dubuque, IA 52001-5099. Offers information technologies communication (MAC); leadership and management (MAC); strategic and corporate communication (MAC). Part-time and evening/weekend programs available. *Degree requirements:* For master's, thesis optional. *Entrance requirements:* For master's, GRE, minimum GPA of 2.5, 3 recommendations. Additional exam requirements/ recommendations for international students: Required—TOEFL (minimum score 550 paper-based; 213 computer-based). Electronic applications accepted. *Faculty research:* Intercultural communication, management communication.

University of Florida, Graduate School, College of Journalism and Communications, Gainesville, FL 32611. Offers advertising (M Adv); journalism (MAMC); mass communication (MAMC, PhD); public relations (MAMC); telecommunication (MAMC); JD/MAMC; JD/PhD. *Accreditation:* ACEJMC (one or more programs are accredited). Part-time programs available. Terminal master's awarded for partial completion of doctoral program. *Degree requirements:* For master's, thesis optional; for doctorate, thesis/dissertation. *Entrance requirements:* For master's and doctorate, GRE General Test, minimum GPA of 3.0. Additional exam requirements/ recommendations for international students: Required—TOEFL (minimum score 550 paper-based; 213 computer-based). Electronic applications accepted. *Faculty research:* Public opinion, law and policy, regulation, environmental communication, international communication.

University of Georgia, Grady School of Journalism and Mass Communication, Athens, GA 30602. Offers journalism and mass communication (MA); mass communication (PhD). *Accreditation:* ACEJMC (one or more programs are accredited). *Faculty:* 39 full-time (16 women). *Students:* 75 full-time (48 women), 45 part-time (32 women); includes 17 minority (14 African Americans, 3 Hispanic Americans), 16 international. 263 applicants, 34% accepted, 38 enrolled. In 2009, 27 master's, 4 doctorates awarded. *Degree requirements:* For master's, comprehensive exam, thesis (MA); for doctorate, comprehensive exam, thesis/dissertation. *Entrance requirements:* For master's and doctorate, GRE General Test. Additional exam requirements/recommendations for international students: Required—TOEFL, TWE (PhD). *Application deadline:* For spring admission, 2/15 for domestic students. Application fee: $50. Electronic applications accepted. *Expenses:* Tuition, state resident: full-time $6000; part-time $250 per credit hour. Tuition, nonresident: full-time $20,904; part-time $871 per credit hour. Required fees: $730 per semester. *Financial support:* Research assistantships, teaching assistantships, tuition waivers (full) and unspecified assistantships available. *Unit head:* Dr. E. Culpepper Clark, Dean, 706-542-1704, Fax: 706-542-2183, E-mail: cully@uga.edu. *Application contact:* Dr. Jeffrey K. Springston, Graduate Coordinator, 706-542-7833, Fax: 706-542-2183, E-mail: jspring@grady.uga.edu.

University of Hartford, College of Arts and Sciences, Program in Communication, West Hartford, CT 06117-1599. Offers MA. Part-time and evening/weekend programs available. *Degree requirements:* For master's, comprehensive exam, thesis optional. *Entrance requirements:* For master's, GRE, 3 letters of recommendation. Additional exam requirements/ recommendations for international students: Required—TOEFL (minimum score 550 paper-based; 213 computer-based). Electronic applications accepted. *Expenses:* Contact institution. *Faculty research:* Communication reticence, relational communication, media literacy, journalism history, media audience attitude and behavior.

University of Hawaii at Manoa, Graduate Division, College of Social Sciences, School of Communications, Honolulu, HI 96822. Offers communication (MA); telecommunication and information resource management (Graduate Certificate). Part-time programs available. *Faculty:* 13 full-time (2 women), 8 part-time/adjunct (2 women). *Students:* 16 full-time (11 women), 16 part-time (9 women); includes 15 minority (12 Asian Americans or Pacific Islanders, 3 Hispanic Americans), 6 international. Average age 29. 63 applicants, 44% accepted, 15 enrolled. In 2009, 11 master's awarded. *Degree requirements:* For master's, thesis optional. *Entrance requirements:* Additional exam requirements/recommendations for international students: Required—TOEFL (minimum score 600 paper-based; 250 computer-based; 100 iBT), IELTS (minimum score 7). *Application deadline:* For fall admission, 2/1 for domestic students, 1/15 for international students. Application fee: $60. *Expenses:* Tuition, state resident: full-time $8900; part-time $372 per credit. Tuition, nonresident: full-time $21,400; part-time $898 per credit. Required fees: $207 per semester. *Financial support:* In 2009–10, 2 students received support, including 9 fellowships (averaging $2,910 per year), 1 teaching assistantship (averaging $14,382 per year); career-related internships or fieldwork, institutionally sponsored loans, and tuition waivers (full) also available. Financial award application deadline: 2/1. *Faculty research:* Communication technology policy and development, intercultural communication, organizational communication. *Application contact:* Gary Fotaine, Chair, 808-956-8715, Fax: 808-956-5396, E-mail: fontaine@hawaii.edu.

University of Houston, College of Liberal Arts and Social Sciences, School of Communication, Houston, TX 77204. Offers health communication (MA); mass communication studies (MA); public relations studies (MA); speech communication (MA). Part-time and evening/weekend programs available. *Faculty:* 9 full-time (5 women), 2 part-time/adjunct (0 women). *Students:* 42 full-time (38 women), 49 part-time (44 women); includes 31 minority (17 African Americans, 2 American Indian/Alaska Native, 2 Asian Americans or Pacific Islanders, 10 Hispanic Americans), 24 international. Average age 28. 92 applicants, 47% accepted, 28 enrolled. In 2009, 19 master's awarded. *Degree requirements:* For master's, comprehensive exam, thesis. *Entrance requirements:* For master's, GRE. Additional exam requirements/ recommendations for international students: Required—TOEFL. *Application deadline:* For fall admission, 6/1 for domestic students, 4/1 for international students; for spring admission, 11/1 for domestic students, 10/1 for international students. Application fee: $25 ($75 for international students). Electronic applications accepted. *Expenses:* Tuition, state resident: full-time $7676; part-time $320 per credit hour. Tuition, nonresident: full-time $14,324; part-time $597 per credit hour. Required fees: $3034. *Financial support:* In 2009–10, 2 fellowships with full tuition reimbursements (averaging $9,750 per year), 5 teaching assistantships with full tuition reimbursements (averaging $9,750 per year) were awarded; career-related internships or fieldwork, Federal Work-Study, institutionally sponsored loans, scholarships/grants, health care benefits, and unspecified assistantships also available. Support available to part-time students. Financial award application deadline: 2/1. *Unit head:* Dr. Beth Olson, Chairperson, 713-743-2873, Fax: 713-743-2876, E-mail: bolson@uh.edu. *Application contact:* Salima B. Haji, Academic Advisor, 713-743-2575, Fax: 713-743-2876, E-mail: sbhaji@central.uh.edu.

University of Illinois at Chicago, Graduate College, College of Liberal Arts and Sciences, Department of Communication, Chicago, IL 60607-7128. Offers MA, PhD. Evening/weekend programs available. *Degree requirements:* For master's, thesis. *Entrance requirements:* For master's, GRE General Test, minimum GPA of 3.0 in last 90 hours. Additional exam requirements/ recommendations for international students: Required—TOEFL. Electronic applications accepted. *Faculty research:* Organizational, political, and interpersonal communication; public relations.

University of Illinois at Springfield, Graduate Programs, College of Liberal Arts and Sciences, Program in Communication, Springfield, IL 62703-5407. Offers MA. Part-time and evening/weekend programs available. *Faculty:* 11 full-time (6 women), 3 part-time/adjunct (1 woman). *Students:* 17 full-time (11 women), 24 part-time (15 women); includes 4 minority (all African Americans), 2 international. Average age 32. 39 applicants, 62% accepted, 20 enrolled. In 2009, 15 master's awarded. *Degree requirements:* For master's, comprehensive exam, thesis, or project. *Entrance requirements:* For master's, in-house Graduate Admission Writing Exam, departmental writing proficiency exam, minimum undergraduate GPA of 3.0. Additional exam requirements/recommendations for international students: Required—TOEFL (minimum score 580 paper-based). *Application deadline:* Applications are processed on a rolling basis. Application fee: $50 ($60 for international students). Electronic applications accepted. *Expenses:* Tuition, state resident: full-time $6390; part-time $266.25 per credit hour. Tuition, nonresident: full-time $14,226; part-time $592.75 per credit hour. Required fees: $2044; $14.36 per credit hour. $722.50 per term. *Financial support:* In 2009–10, research assistantships with full tuition reimbursements (averaging $8,109 per year), teaching assistantships with full tuition reimbursements (averaging $8,109 per year) were awarded; career-related internships or fieldwork, Federal Work-Study, scholarships/grants, health care benefits, and unspecified assistantships also available. Support available to part-time students. Financial award application deadline: 11/15; financial award applicants required to submit FAFSA. *Unit head:* Dr. Mary Bohlen, Program Administrator, 217-206-7362, Fax: 217-206-6217. *Application contact:* Dr. Lynn Pardie, Office of Graduate Studies, 800-252-8533, Fax: 217-206-7623, E-mail: pardie.lynn@uis.edu.

University of Illinois at Urbana–Champaign, Graduate College, College of Liberal Arts and Sciences, Department of Communication, Champaign, IL 61820. Offers communication (MA). Postbaccalaureate distance learning degree programs offered (no on-campus study). *Faculty:* 24 full-time (11 women). *Students:* 40 full-time (25 women), 15 part-time (8 women); includes 9 minority (3 African Americans, 4 Asian Americans or Pacific Islanders, 2 Hispanic Americans), 2 international. 162 applicants, 18% accepted, 12 enrolled. In 2009, 14 master's, 7 doctorates awarded. *Entrance requirements:* For master's and doctorate, GRE, minimum GPA of 3.0; writing sample. Additional exam requirements/recommendations for international students: Required—TOEFL (minimum score 611 paper-based; 245 computer-based; 103 iBT). *Application deadline:* Applications are processed on a rolling basis. Application fee: $60 ($75 for international students). Electronic applications accepted. *Financial support:* In 2009–10, 2 fellowships, 21 research assistantships, 52 teaching assistantships were awarded; tuition waivers (full and partial) also available. *Unit head:* Dale E. Brashers, Head, 217-333-2683, Fax: 217-244-1598, E-mail: dbrasher@illinois.edu. *Application contact:* Mary Strum, Office Support Specialist, 217-244-1595, Fax: 217-244-1598, E-mail: strum@illinois.edu.

University of Illinois at Urbana–Champaign, Graduate College, College of Media, Institute of Communications Research, Champaign, IL 61820. Offers communications and media (PhD). *Faculty:* 10 full-time (5 women). *Students:* 38 full-time (21 women), 13 part-time (6 women); includes 16 minority (5 African Americans, 4 Asian Americans or Pacific Islanders, 7 Hispanic Americans), 22 international. 111 applicants, 8% accepted, 6 enrolled. In 2009, 7 doctorates awarded. *Entrance requirements:* For doctorate, GRE General Test, minimum GPA of 3.0. Additional exam requirements/recommendations for international students: Required—TOEFL (minimum score 550 paper-based). *Application deadline:* Applications are processed on a rolling basis. Application fee: $60 ($75 for international students). Electronic applications accepted. *Financial support:* In 2009–10, 14 fellowships, 12 research assistantships, 28 teaching assistantships were awarded; tuition waivers (full and partial) also available. *Faculty research:* Feminist cultural studies, media technology, international communications, Latino studies, economics of media. *Unit head:* Angharad N. Valdivia, Interim Director, 217-244-1422, Fax: 217-244-7695, E-mail: valdivia@illinois.edu. *Application contact:* Andrea Ray, Office Manager, 217-333-1549, Fax: 217-333-7695, E-mail: aray@illinois.edu.

The University of Iowa, Graduate College, College of Liberal Arts and Sciences, Department of Communication Studies, Iowa City, IA 52242-1316. Offers communication research (MA, PhD); rhetorical studies (MA, PhD). *Degree requirements:* For master's, thesis optional, exam; for doctorate, comprehensive exam, thesis/dissertation. *Entrance requirements:* For master's and doctorate, GRE General Test, minimum GPA of 3.0. Additional exam requirements/ recommendations for international students: Required—TOEFL (minimum score 550 paper-based; 213 computer-based; 81 iBT). Electronic applications accepted.

The University of Kansas, Graduate Studies, College of Liberal Arts and Sciences, Department of Communication Studies, Lawrence, KS 66045-7574. Offers MA, PhD. Evening/weekend programs available. *Faculty:* 19 full-time (12 women). *Students:* 61 full-time (40 women), 20 part-time (12 women); includes 1 minority (Asian American or Pacific Islander), 8 international. Average age 32. 77 applicants, 32% accepted, 13 enrolled. In 2009, 8 master's, 7 doctorates awarded. *Degree requirements:* For master's, comprehensive exam (for some programs), thesis or alternative; for doctorate, comprehensive exam, thesis/dissertation. *Entrance requirements:* For master's, GRE General Test, minimum GPA of 3.1; for doctorate, GRE General Test, minimum GPA of 3.2 (undergraduate), 3.6 (graduate). Additional exam requirements/recommendations for international students: Required—TOEFL. *Application deadline:* For fall admission, 1/15 priority date for domestic and international students; for spring admission, 11/15 for domestic and international students. Applications are processed on a rolling basis. Application fee: $45 ($55 for international students). Electronic applications accepted. *Expenses:* Tuition, state resident: full-time $6492; part-time $270.50 per credit hour. Tuition, nonresident: full-time $15,510; part-time $646.25 per credit hour. Required fees: $847; $70.56 per credit hour. Tuition and fees vary according to course load and program. *Financial support:* Fellowships with tuition reimbursements, research assistantships, teaching assistantships with full and partial tuition reimbursements, unspecified assistantships available. Financial award application deadline: 1/15. *Faculty research:* Rhetoric, organizational communication, political communication, interpersonal communication, new technology. *Unit head:* Dr. Beth Innocenti, Associate Professor and Chair, 785-864-9018, Fax: 785-864-5203, E-mail: bimanole@ku.edu. *Application contact:* Dr. Robert C. Rowland, Professor and Director of Graduate Studies, 785-864-9868, Fax: 785-864-5203, E-mail: rrowland@ku.edu.

University of Kentucky, Graduate School, College of Communications and Information Studies, Program in Communication, Lexington, KY 40506-0032. Offers MA, PhD. *Degree requirements:* For master's, comprehensive exam, thesis optional; for doctorate, comprehensive exam, thesis/dissertation. *Entrance requirements:* For master's, GRE General Test, minimum undergraduate GPA of 2.75; for doctorate, GRE General Test, minimum graduate GPA of 3.0, undergraduate 2.75. Additional exam requirements/recommendations for international students: Required—TOEFL (minimum score 550 paper-based; 213 computer-based). Electronic applications accepted. *Faculty research:* Public service campaigns, health communication, mass media law and public policy, political communication, international and intercultural communication.

University of Louisiana at Lafayette, College of Liberal Arts, Department of Communication, Lafayette, LA 70504. Offers mass communications (MS). Part-time programs available. *Degree requirements:* For master's, thesis optional. *Entrance requirements:* For master's, GRE General Test, minimum GPA of 2.75. Additional exam requirements/recommendations for international students: Required—TOEFL (minimum score 550 paper-based; 213 computer-based). Electronic applications accepted. *Faculty research:* Mass media problems, issues and ethics, mass communication, historical studies, conflict of interest and law and ethics in journalism, contemporary issues and trends in publications.

University of Louisiana at Monroe, Graduate School, College of Arts and Sciences, Department of Communication, Monroe, LA 71209-0001. Offers MA. *Faculty:* 4 full-time (2 women). *Students:* 10 full-time (5 women), 2 part-time (1 woman); includes 2 African Americans, 1 international. Average age 28. In 2009, 4 master's awarded. *Degree requirements:* For master's, thesis. *Entrance requirements:* For master's, GRE (minimum verbal and quantitative score: 900), minimum GPA of 2.5. Additional exam requirements/recommendations for international students: Required—TOEFL (minimum score 500 paper-based; 173 computer-based; 61 iBT). *Application deadline:* For fall admission, 8/24 priority date for domestic students, 7/1 for international students; for winter admission, 12/14 priority date for domestic students; for spring admission, 1/19 priority date for domestic students, 11/1 for international students. Applications are processed on a rolling basis. Application fee: $20 ($30 for international students). Electronic applications accepted. *Expenses:* Tuition, state resident: part-time $159 per credit hour. Tuition, nonresident: part-time $159 per credit hour. Required fees: $1300 per year. Tuition and fees vary according to course load. *Financial support:* In 2009–10, 2 research assistantships (averaging $2,500 per year), 1 teaching assistantship with full and partial tuition reimbursement (averaging $2,500 per year) were awarded; career-related internships or fieldwork, Federal Work-Study, and unspecified assistantships also available. Financial award application deadline: 4/1; financial award applicants required to submit FAFSA. *Faculty research:* Interactive media, rhetoric progress, interpersonal, journalism history, gender/multicultural issues, forensics. *Unit head:* Dr. Carl L. Thameling, Interim Head, 318-342-1406, Fax: 318-

Communication—General

University of Louisiana at Monroe (continued)
342-1422, E-mail: thameling@ulm.edu. *Application contact:* Dr. Lesli K. Pace, Graduate Coordinator, 318-342-1165, Fax: 318-342-1422, E-mail: pace@ulm.edu.

University of Louisville, Graduate School, College of Arts and Sciences, Department of Communication, Louisville, KY 40292-0001. Offers MA. *Students:* 11 full-time (8 women), 19 part-time (16 women); includes 3 minority (2 African Americans, 1 Hispanic American), 1 international. Average age 29. 35 applicants, 49% accepted, 9 enrolled. In 2009, 14 master's awarded. *Unit head:* Dr. J. Blaine Hudson, Dean, 502-852-2234, Fax: 502-852-6888, E-mail: jbhuds01@louisville.edu. *Application contact:* Libby Leggett, Director, Graduate Admissions, 502-852-3101, Fax: 502-852-6536, E-mail: gradadm@louisville.edu.

University of Maine, Graduate School, College of Liberal Arts and Sciences, Department of Communication and Journalism, Orono, ME 04469. Offers communication (MA). Part-time programs available. *Faculty:* 8 full-time (3 women), 5 part-time/adjunct (2 women). *Students:* 16 full-time (9 women), 5 part-time (2 women); includes 1 minority (American Indian/Alaska Native), 1 international. Average age 27. 22 applicants, 50% accepted, 9 enrolled. In 2009, 6 master's awarded. *Degree requirements:* For master's, thesis or alternative. *Entrance requirements:* For master's, GRE General Test. Additional exam requirements/recommendations for international students: Required—TOEFL. *Application deadline:* For fall admission, 2/1 priority date for domestic students. Applications are processed on a rolling basis. Application fee: $65. Electronic applications accepted. *Financial support:* In 2009–10, 15 teaching assistantships with tuition reimbursements (averaging $12,790 per year) were awarded; career-related internships or fieldwork, Federal Work-Study, institutionally sponsored loans, and tuition waivers (full and partial) also available. Support available to part-time students. Financial award application deadline: 3/1. *Faculty research:* Rhetorical theory, semiotics, discourse analysis, gender and communication, children's talk/communication disorders. *Unit head:* Dr. Paul Grosswiler, Chair, 207-581-1287, Fax: 207-581-1286. *Application contact:* Scott G. Delcourt, Associate Dean of the Graduate School, 207-581-3291, Fax: 207-581-3232, E-mail: graduate@maine.edu.

University of Maryland, Baltimore County, Graduate School, College of Arts, Humanities and Social Sciences, Department of Modern Languages and Linguistics, Program in Intercultural Communication, Baltimore, MD 21250. Offers MA. Part-time and evening/weekend programs available. *Faculty:* 18 full-time (6 women), 3 part-time/adjunct (2 women). *Students:* 14 full-time (10 women), 29 part-time (20 women); includes 4 minority (1 African American, 3 Hispanic Americans), 14 international. 30 applicants, 57% accepted, 13 enrolled. In 2009, 7 master's awarded. *Degree requirements:* For master's, one foreign language, comprehensive exam (for some programs), thesis (for some programs). *Entrance requirements:* For master's, GRE General Test, minimum GPA of 3.0, 3 letters of recommendation, self-evaluation and statement of support, resume. Additional exam requirements/recommendations for international students: Required—TOEFL (minimum score 213 computer-based). *Application deadline:* For fall admission, 1/31 for domestic and international students. Application fee: $45. Electronic applications accepted. *Financial support:* In 2009–10, 8 students received support, including 5 teaching assistantships with full tuition reimbursements available (averaging $11,324 per year); tuition waivers also available. Financial award applicants required to submit FAFSA. *Faculty research:* Comparative television research–cross-cultural; cultural studies; social developments in Latin America; intercultural communication; French civilization and cultural studies; language, gender and sexuality; sociolinguistics; African linguistics; immigrants in U.S. and Latin American societies. *Unit head:* Dr. Edward Larkey, Director, 410-455-2104, Fax: 410-455-1025, E-mail: larkey@umbc.edu. *Application contact:* Dr. Edward Larkey, Director, 410-455-2104, Fax: 410-455-1025, E-mail: larkey@umbc.edu.

University of Maryland, College Park, Academic Affairs, College of Arts and Humanities, Department of Communication, College Park, MD 20742. Offers MA, PhD. *Faculty:* 24 full-time (14 women), 5 part-time/adjunct (3 women). *Students:* 68 full-time (50 women), 3 part-time (all women); includes 6 minority (1 African American, 4 Asian Americans or Pacific Islanders, 1 Hispanic American), 18 international. 194 applicants, 10% accepted, 17 enrolled. In 2009, 3 master's, 7 doctorates awarded. *Degree requirements:* For master's, thesis optional; for doctorate, comprehensive exam, thesis/dissertation. *Entrance requirements:* For master's, GRE General Test, minimum GPA of 3.0, sample of scholarly writing, 3 letters of recommendation; for doctorate, GRE General Test. Additional exam requirements/recommendations for international students: Required—TOEFL. *Application deadline:* For fall admission, 2/1 for domestic and international students. Applications are processed on a rolling basis. Application fee: $60. Electronic applications accepted. *Expenses:* Tuition, area resident: Part-time $471 per credit hour. Tuition, state resident: part-time $471 per credit hour. Tuition, nonresident: part-time $1016 per credit hour. Required fees: $337.04 per term. *Financial support:* In 2009–10, 6 fellowships with partial tuition reimbursements (averaging $7,917 per year), 56 teaching assistantships with tuition reimbursements (averaging $16,047 per year) were awarded; Federal Work-Study, scholarships/grants, and unspecified assistantships also available. Support available to part-time students. Financial award applicants required to submit FAFSA. *Faculty research:* Health communication, interpersonal communication, persuasion, intercultural communication, contemporary rhetoric theory. Total annual research expenditures: $50,458. *Unit head:* Dr. Elizabeth L. Toth, Chair, 301-405-0870, Fax: 301-314-9471, E-mail: eltoth@umd.edu. *Application contact:* Dean of Graduate School, 301-405-0376, Fax: 301-314-9305.

University of Massachusetts Amherst, Graduate School, College of Social and Behavioral Sciences, Department of Communication, Amherst, MA 01003. Offers MA, PhD. Part-time programs available. *Faculty:* 23 full-time (11 women). *Students:* 65 full-time (38 women), 13 part-time (10 women); includes 14 minority (3 African Americans, 5 Asian Americans or Pacific Islanders, 6 Hispanic Americans), 30 international. Average age 35. 171 applicants, 11% accepted, 10 enrolled. In 2009, 2 master's, 6 doctorates awarded. Terminal master's awarded for partial completion of doctoral program. *Degree requirements:* For master's, thesis or alternative; for doctorate, comprehensive exam, thesis/dissertation. *Entrance requirements:* For master's and doctorate, GRE General Test, 3 letters of recommendation. Additional exam requirements/recommendations for international students: Required—TOEFL (minimum score 550 paper-based; 213 computer-based; 80 iBT), IELTS (minimum score 6.5). *Application deadline:* For fall admission, 1/2 for domestic and international students. Applications are processed on a rolling basis. Application fee: $50 ($65 for international students). Electronic applications accepted. *Expenses:* Tuition, state resident: full-time $2640; part-time $110 per credit. Tuition, nonresident: full-time $9936; part-time $414 per credit. Tuition and fees vary according to course load. *Financial support:* In 2009–10, 1 fellowship with full tuition reimbursement (averaging $14,516 per year), 15 research assistantships with full tuition reimbursements (averaging $4,292 per year), 53 teaching assistantships with full tuition reimbursements (averaging $10,354 per year) were awarded; career-related internships or fieldwork, Federal Work-Study, scholarships/grants, traineeships, health care benefits, tuition waivers (full), and unspecified assistantships also available. Support available to part-time students. Financial award application deadline: 1/2. *Unit head:* Dr. Donal A. Hanson, Graduate Program Director, 413-545-2795, Fax: 413-545-6399. *Application contact:* Jean M. Ames, Supervisor of Admissions, 413-545-0722, Fax: 413-577-0010, E-mail: gradadm@grad.umass.edu.

University of Memphis, Graduate School, College of Communication and Fine Arts, Department of Communication, Memphis, TN 38152. Offers communication (MA); communication arts (PhD); film and video production (MA). Part-time programs available. *Faculty:* 12 full-time (6 women). *Students:* 35 full-time (21 women), 15 part-time (9 women); includes 8 minority (6 African Americans, 1 American Indian/Alaska Native, 1 Asian American or Pacific Islander), 1 international. Average age 35. 47 applicants, 66% accepted, 13 enrolled. In 2009, 6 master's, 4 doctorates awarded. *Degree requirements:* For master's, comprehensive exam, thesis or alternative; for doctorate, comprehensive exam, thesis/dissertation. *Entrance requirements:* For master's and doctorate, GRE General Test. Additional exam requirements/recommendations for international students: Required—TOEFL (minimum score 550 paper-based; 210 computer-based). *Application deadline:* For fall admission, 8/1 for domestic students. Application fee: $35 ($60 for international students). *Expenses:* Tuition, state resident: full-time $6246; part-time $347 per credit hour. Tuition, nonresident: full-time $15,894; part-time $883 per credit hour. Required fees: $1160. Full-time tuition and fees vary according to course load, degree level and program. *Financial support:* In 2009–10, 27 students received support; research assistantships with full tuition reimbursements available, teaching assistantships with full tuition reimbursements available, Federal Work-Study, scholarships/grants, and unspecified assistantships available. Financial award application deadline: 2/15; financial award applicants required to submit FAFSA. *Faculty research:* Rhetoric, media studies, applied communication (health communication). *Unit head:* Dr. Mike Leff, Chair, 901-678-2565, Fax: 901-678-4331, E-mail: m_leff@bellsouth.net. *Application contact:* Dr. Sandra Sarkela, Coordinator of Graduate Studies, 901-678-3173, Fax: 901-678-4331, E-mail: ssarkela@memphis.edu.

University of Miami, Graduate School, School of Communication, Coral Gables, FL 33124. Offers communication (PhD); communication studies (MA); film studies (MA, PhD); motion pictures (MFA), including production, producing, and screenwriting; print journalism (MA); public relations (MA); Spanish language journalism (MA); television broadcast journalism (MA). *Accreditation:* ACEJMC. Part-time programs available. *Degree requirements:* For master's, comprehensive exam (for some programs), thesis (for some programs); for doctorate, comprehensive exam, thesis/dissertation. *Entrance requirements:* For master's, GRE General Test; for doctorate, GRE General Test, master's thesis or scholarly research. Additional exam requirements/recommendations for international students: Required—TOEFL (minimum score 600 paper-based; 250 computer-based; 100 iBT). Electronic applications accepted. *Faculty research:* Communication studies, mass communication, international/interpersonal communication, film studies, journalism.

University of Michigan, Horace H. Rackham School of Graduate Studies, College of Literature, Science, and the Arts, Department of Communication Studies, Ann Arbor, MI 48104-2523. Offers PhD. *Faculty:* 15 full-time (5 women), 1 part-time/adjunct (0 women). *Students:* 31 full-time (23 women); includes 4 minority (1 African American, 2 Asian Americans or Pacific Islanders, 1 Hispanic American), 10 international. Average age 28. 95 applicants, 8% accepted, 5 enrolled. In 2009, 4 doctorates awarded. *Degree requirements:* For doctorate, comprehensive exam, thesis/dissertation, first-year research project, 2 terms as in graduate student instructor position. *Entrance requirements:* For doctorate, GRE. Additional exam requirements/recommendations for international students: Required—TOEFL (minimum score 560 paper-based; 220 computer-based; 84 iBT). *Application deadline:* For fall admission, 12/1 for domestic and international students. Application fee: $60 ($75 for international students). Electronic applications accepted. *Expenses:* Tuition, state resident: full-time $17,286; part-time $1099 per credit hour. Tuition, nonresident: full-time $34,944; part-time $2080 per credit hour. Required fees: $95 per semester. Tuition and fees vary according to course load, degree level and program. *Financial support:* In 2009–10, 31 students received support, including 4 fellowships with full tuition reimbursements available (averaging $16,400 per year), 1 research assistantship with full tuition reimbursement available (averaging $16,400 per year), 22 teaching assistantships with full tuition reimbursements available (averaging $16,135 per year); scholarships/grants, health care benefits, tuition waivers (full and partial), and unspecified assistantships also available. Financial award application deadline: 2/15; financial award applicants required to submit FAFSA. *Faculty research:* Political communication; media, culture and society; media effects; race, gender, and the media; new media, media law and policy. *Unit head:* Prof. Susan J. Douglas, Professor and Chair, 734-764-0420, Fax: 734-764-3288, E-mail: sdoug@umich.edu. *Application contact:* Amy B. Eaton, Graduate Program Coordinator, 734-615-8974, Fax: 734-764-3288, E-mail: lsa-commphd@umich.edu.

University of Minnesota, Twin Cities Campus, Graduate School, College of Design, Department of Design, Housing, and Apparel, Minneapolis, MN 55455-0213. Offers apparel (MA, MS, PhD); design communication (MA, MS, PhD); housing studies (MA, MS, PhD, Postbaccalaureate Certificate); interactive design (MFA); interior design (MA, MS, PhD). Part-time programs available. *Degree requirements:* For master's and Postbaccalaureate Certificate, comprehensive exam, thesis (for some programs); for doctorate, comprehensive exam, thesis/dissertation. *Entrance requirements:* For master's, GRE General Test, minimum GPA of 3.0 (preferred), portfolio, 3 letters of recommendation; for doctorate, GRE General Test, minimum GPA of 3.0 (preferred), portfolio, 3 letters of recommendation, writing sample; for Post-baccalaureate Certificate, GRE General Test, minimum GPA of 3.0 (preferred). Additional exam requirements/recommendations for international students: Required—TOEFL (minimum score 550 paper-based; 213 computer-based; 79 iBT). Electronic applications accepted. *Faculty research:* Housing policy and community development; consumer behavior; interactive design; design history; social, cultural, and behavioral issues related to designed environments.

University of Minnesota, Twin Cities Campus, Graduate School, College of Liberal Arts, Department of Communication Studies, Minneapolis, MN 55455-0213. Offers MA, PhD. *Degree requirements:* For master's, thesis or alternative; for doctorate, thesis/dissertation. *Entrance requirements:* For master's, GRE General Test, minimum GPA of 3.0; for doctorate, GRE General Test, minimum graduate GPA of 3.5. Additional exam requirements/recommendations for international students: Required—TOEFL. Electronic applications accepted. *Faculty research:* Rhetorical studies, communication theory, media studies, gender and communication, public address.

University of Missouri, Graduate School, College of Arts and Sciences, Department of Communication, Columbia, MO 65211. Offers MA, PhD. *Faculty:* 12 full-time (6 women), 1 (woman) part-time/adjunct. *Students:* 23 full-time (13 women), 20 part-time (17 women); includes 5 minority (3 African Americans, 2 Asian Americans or Pacific Islanders), 5 international. Average age 30. 82 applicants, 15% accepted, 9 enrolled. In 2009, 1 master's awarded. Terminal master's awarded for partial completion of doctoral program. *Degree requirements:* For doctorate, comprehensive exam, thesis/dissertation. *Entrance requirements:* For master's, GRE General Test (minimum 500 verbal, 500 quantitative, 4.0 analytical preferred), minimum GPA of 3.0; for doctorate, GRE General Test; preferred is V and Q at least 500 each; A = 4.0, minimum GPA of 3.0. Additional exam requirements/recommendations for international students: Required—TOEFL (minimum score 600 paper-based; 250 computer-based; 100 iBT). *Application deadline:* For fall admission, 2/15 priority date for domestic students. Applications are processed on a rolling basis. Application fee: $45 ($60 for international students). Electronic applications accepted. *Financial support:* In 2009–10, 2 fellowships with full tuition reimbursements, 29 teaching assistantships with full tuition reimbursements were awarded; research assistantships with full tuition reimbursements, institutionally sponsored loans, health care benefits, and unspecified assistantships also available. *Unit head:* Dr. Mike Kramer, Department Chair, 573-882-6980, E-mail: kramerm@missouri.edu. *Application contact:* Martha Crump, Administrative Assistant, 573-882-4432, E-mail: crumpm@missouri.edu.

University of Missouri–St. Louis, College of Fine Arts and Communication, Department of Communication, St. Louis, MO 63121. Offers MA. Part-time and evening/weekend programs available. *Faculty:* 7 full-time (6 women). *Students:* 5 full-time (all women), 20 part-time (14 women); includes 4 minority (3 African Americans, 1 Hispanic American), 2 international. Average age 31. In 2009, 12 master's awarded. *Degree requirements:* For master's, thesis optional. *Entrance requirements:* For master's, 3 letters of recommendation, minimum GPA of 3.25. Additional exam requirements/recommendations for international students: Required—TOEFL (minimum score 600 paper-based; 233 computer-based). *Application deadline:* For fall admission, 7/1 for domestic and international students; for spring admission, 12/1 for domestic and international students. Application fee: $35 ($40 for international students). Electronic applications accepted. *Expenses:* Tuition, state resident: full-time $5377; part-time $297.70 per credit hour. Tuition, nonresident: full-time $13,882; part-time $771.20 per credit hour. Required fees: $220; $12.20 per credit hour. One-time fee: $12. Tuition and fees vary according to course level, campus/location and program. *Financial support:* In 2009–10, 5 teaching assistantships (averaging $12,000 per year) were awarded. Financial award application deadline: 4/1; financial award applicants required to submit FAFSA. *Faculty research:* Theory and methodology: intercultural, interpersonal, and mass organizational. *Unit head:* Dr. Alice Hall,

Director of Graduate Studies, 314-516-5485, Fax: 314-516-5816, E-mail: halla@umsl.edu. *Application contact:* 314-516-5458, Fax: 314-516-6996, E-mail: gradadm@umsl.edu.

The University of Montana, Graduate School, College of Arts and Sciences, Department of Communication Studies, Missoula, MT 59812-0002. Offers MA. *Degree requirements:* For master's, thesis (for some programs). *Entrance requirements:* For master's, GRE General Test. Additional exam requirements/recommendations for international students: Required—TOEFL (minimum score 525 paper-based; 197 computer-based). *Faculty research:* Conflict management, organizational communication, language, personal relationships, rhetoric.

University of Nebraska at Omaha, Graduate Studies, College of Communication, Fine Arts and Media, School of Communication, Omaha, NE 68182. Offers MA. Part-time and evening/weekend programs available. *Faculty:* 22 full-time (12 women). *Students:* 13 full-time (9 women), 56 part-time (39 women); includes 7 minority (5 African Americans, 1 American Indian/Alaska Native, 1 Asian American or Pacific Islander), 3 international. Average age 33. 26 applicants, 58% accepted, 8 enrolled. In 2009, 11 master's awarded. *Degree requirements:* For master's, comprehensive exam, thesis (for some programs). *Entrance requirements:* For master's, minimum GPA of 3.25, 15 undergraduate communication courses. Additional exam requirements/recommendations for international students: Required—TOEFL (minimum score 550 paper-based; 213 computer-based; 80 iBT). *Application deadline:* For fall admission, 6/1 priority date for domestic students; for spring admission, 11/1 priority date for domestic students. Applications are processed on a rolling basis. Application fee: $45. Electronic applications accepted. *Financial support:* In 2009–10, 26 students received support; fellowships, research assistantships with tuition reimbursements available, teaching assistantships with tuition reimbursements available, Federal Work-Study, institutionally sponsored loans, scholarships/grants, tuition waivers (partial), and unspecified assistantships available. Support available to part-time students. Financial award application deadline: 3/1; financial award applicants required to submit FAFSA. *Unit head:* Dr. Jeremy Lipschultz, Director, 402-554-2600. *Application contact:* Dr. Barbara Pickering, Student Contact, 402-554-2600.

University of Nebraska–Lincoln, Graduate College, College of Arts and Sciences, Department of Communication Studies, Lincoln, NE 68588. Offers instructional communication (MA, PhD); interpersonal communication (MA, PhD); marketing, communication studies, and advertising (MA, PhD); organizational communication (MA, PhD); rhetoric and culture (MA, PhD). *Degree requirements:* For master's, thesis optional; for doctorate, comprehensive exam, thesis/dissertation. *Entrance requirements:* For master's and doctorate, GRE General Test, writing sample. Additional exam requirements/recommendations for international students: Required—TOEFL (minimum score 600 paper-based; 250 computer-based). Electronic applications accepted. *Faculty research:* Message strategies, gender communication, political communication, organizational communication, instructional communication.

University of Nevada, Las Vegas, Graduate College, Greenspun College of Urban Affairs, Department of Communication Studies, Las Vegas, NV 89154-4052. Offers MA. Part-time programs available. *Faculty:* 9 full-time (4 women). *Students:* 15 full-time (9 women), 4 part-time (3 women); includes 5 minority (1 African American, 4 Hispanic Americans). Average age 31. 14 applicants, 57% accepted, 5 enrolled. In 2009, 3 master's awarded. *Degree requirements:* For master's, comprehensive exam (for some programs), thesis (for some programs). *Entrance requirements:* For master's, GRE General Test. Additional exam requirements/recommendations for international students: Required—TOEFL (minimum score 550 paper-based; 213 computer-based; 80 iBT), IELTS (minimum score 7). *Application deadline:* For fall admission, 1/15 priority date for domestic and international students. Applications are processed on a rolling basis. Application fee: $60 ($95 for international students). Electronic applications accepted. *Financial support:* In 2009–10, 12 students received support, including 12 teaching assistantships with partial tuition reimbursements available (averaging $10,000 per year); institutionally sponsored loans, scholarships/grants, health care benefits, and unspecified assistantships also available. Financial award application deadline: 3/1. *Faculty research:* Rhetoric (public influence), interpersonal communication. *Unit head:* Dr. Tom Burkholder, Chair/Associate Professor, 702-895-5125, Fax: 702-895-4805, E-mail: tom.burkholder@unlv.edu. *Application contact:* Graduate College Admissions Evaluator, 702-895-3320, Fax: 702-895-4180, E-mail: gradcollege@unlv.edu.

University of New Mexico, Graduate School, College of Arts and Sciences, Department of Communication and Journalism, Albuquerque, NM 87131-2039. Offers communication (MA, PhD). Part-time programs available. *Faculty:* 22 full-time (15 women), 10 part-time/adjunct (6 women). *Students:* 50 full-time (41 women), 20 part-time (13 women); includes 17 minority (3 African Americans, 2 American Indian/Alaska Native, 2 Asian Americans or Pacific Islanders, 10 Hispanic Americans), 19 international. Average age 33. 61 applicants, 38% accepted, 15 enrolled. In 2009, 10 master's, 9 doctorates awarded. *Degree requirements:* For master's, 30 hours class work and 6 hour thesis or project or 36 hours class work and comprehensive exam; for doctorate, 2 foreign languages, comprehensive exam, thesis/dissertation. *Entrance requirements:* For master's, GRE General Test, letters of recommendation, letter of intent, curriculum vitae, transcripts; for doctorate, GRE General Test, letters of recommendation, writing sample, letter of intent, curriculum vitae, transcripts. Additional exam requirements/recommendations for international students: Required—TOEFL (minimum score 550 paper-based; 213 computer-based). *Application deadline:* For fall admission, 1/15 for domestic students. Application fee: $50. Electronic applications accepted. *Expenses:* Tuition, state resident: full-time $2099; part-time $233.20 per credit hour. Tuition, nonresident: full-time $6650. Required fees: $25 per semester. Tuition and fees vary according to course load, program and reciprocity agreements. *Financial support:* In 2009–10, 19 students received support, including 45 teaching assistantships with tuition reimbursements available (averaging $14,250 per year); fellowships with tuition reimbursements available, research assistantships, career-related internships or fieldwork, scholarships/grants, health care benefits, and unspecified assistantships also available. Financial award application deadline: 3/1; financial award applicants required to submit FAFSA. *Faculty research:* Health communication, intercultural communication, interpersonal/organizational communication, mass communication. *Unit head:* Dr. Glenda Balas, Chair, 505-277-5305, Fax: 505-277-4206, E-mail: gbalas@unm.edu. *Application contact:* Nancy Montoya, Department Administrator, 505-277-5305, Fax: 505-277-4206, E-mail: cjadvise@unm.edu.

The University of North Carolina at Chapel Hill, Graduate School, College of Arts and Sciences, Department of Communication Studies, Chapel Hill, NC 27599. Offers MA, PhD. *Degree requirements:* For master's, comprehensive exam, thesis; for doctorate, thesis/dissertation. *Entrance requirements:* For master's and doctorate, GRE General Test, minimum GPA of 3.0. Electronic applications accepted.

The University of North Carolina at Charlotte, Graduate School, College of Arts and Sciences, Department of Communication Studies, Charlotte, NC 28223-0001. Offers MA. Part-time and evening/weekend programs available. *Faculty:* 10 full-time (3 women). *Students:* 10 full-time (5 women), 18 part-time (15 women); includes 4 minority (all African Americans), 2 international. Average age 28. 55 applicants, 36% accepted, 9 enrolled. In 2009, 7 master's awarded. Terminal master's awarded for partial completion of doctoral program. *Degree requirements:* For master's, project, thesis, or comprehensive exam. *Entrance requirements:* For master's, GRE General Test, minimum GPA of 2.75 overall. Additional exam requirements/recommendations for international students: Required—TOEFL (minimum score 557 paper-based; 220 computer-based; 83 iBT). *Application deadline:* For fall admission, 3/15 for domestic students, 5/1 for international students; for spring admission, 11/15 for domestic students, 10/1 for international students. Applications are processed on a rolling basis. Application fee: $55. Electronic applications accepted. *Financial support:* In 2009–10, 10 students received support, including 1 research assistantship (averaging $18,000 per year), 9 teaching assistantships (averaging $11,889 per year); career-related internships or fieldwork, institutionally sponsored loans, scholarships/grants, and unspecified assistantships also available. Support available to part-time students. Financial award application deadline: 4/1; financial award applicants required to submit FAFSA. *Faculty research:* Health literacy, systems of care and mental illness, the communication of emotions in gendered workplaces, international constructs of public relations managerial responsibilities, sports culture and the construction of social contracts, African American oratory. Total annual research expenditures: $34,835. *Unit head:* Dr. Richard W. Leeman, Chair, 704-687-2086, Fax: 704-687-6900, E-mail: rwleeman@uncc.edu. *Application contact:* Kathy B. Giddings, Director of Graduate Admissions, 704-687-5503, Fax: 704-687-3279, E-mail: gradadm@uncc.edu.

The University of North Carolina at Greensboro, Graduate School, College of Arts and Sciences, Department of Communication, Greensboro, NC 27412-5001. Offers communication studies (MA). Part-time programs available. *Degree requirements:* For master's, thesis or alternative. *Entrance requirements:* For master's, GRE General Test, MAT, or PRAXIS. Additional exam requirements/recommendations for international students: Required—TOEFL. Electronic applications accepted.

University of North Dakota, Graduate School, College of Arts and Sciences, School of Communication, Grand Forks, ND 58202. Offers MA, PhD. Part-time programs available. *Degree requirements:* For master's, comprehensive exam, thesis or alternative; for doctorate, thesis/dissertation. *Entrance requirements:* For master's and doctorate, GRE General Test, minimum GPA of 3.0. Additional exam requirements/recommendations for international students: Required—TOEFL (minimum score 550 paper-based; 213 computer-based; 79 iBT), IELTS (minimum score 6.5). Electronic applications accepted. *Faculty research:* Communication technologies, mass communication in diverse society, acculturation and socialization functions.

University of Northern Colorado, Graduate School, College of Humanities and Social Sciences, School of Communication, Program in Communication Studies, Greeley, CO 80639. Offers MA. Part-time programs available. *Faculty:* 4 full-time (1 woman). *Students:* 13 full-time (9 women), 8 part-time (7 women); includes 2 minority (1 African American, 1 Asian American or Pacific Islander), 2 international. Average age 28. 24 applicants, 83% accepted, 13 enrolled. In 2009, 7 master's awarded. *Degree requirements:* For master's, comprehensive exam, thesis or alternative. *Entrance requirements:* For master's, GRE General Test, 3 letters of recommendation. *Application deadline:* Applications are processed on a rolling basis. Application fee: $50 ($60 for international students). Electronic applications accepted. *Expenses:* Tuition, state resident: full-time $5770; part-time $320.55 per credit hour. Tuition, nonresident: full-time $13,847; part-time $769.27 per credit hour. Required fees: $948.78; $52.72 per credit. *Financial support:* In 2009–10, 6 teaching assistantships (averaging $7,884 per year) were awarded; research assistantships. Financial award application deadline: 3/1; financial award applicants required to submit FAFSA. *Unit head:* Dr. James Keaton, Program Coordinator, 970-351-2045, Fax: 970-351-2336. *Application contact:* Linda Sisson, Graduate Student Admission Coordinator, 970-351-1807, Fax: 970-351-2371, E-mail: linda.sisson@unco.edu.

University of Northern Iowa, Graduate College, College of Humanities and Fine Arts, Department of Communication Studies, Cedar Falls, IA 50614. Offers MA. Part-time and evening/weekend programs available. *Students:* 31 full-time (22 women), 15 part-time (12 women); includes 5 minority (3 African Americans, 2 Hispanic Americans), 8 international. 33 applicants, 45% accepted, 12 enrolled. In 2009, 19 master's awarded. *Degree requirements:* For master's, comprehensive exam, thesis or alternative. *Entrance requirements:* For master's, minimum GPA of 3.0. Additional exam requirements/recommendations for international students: Required—TOEFL (minimum score 500 paper-based; 180 computer-based; 61 iBT). *Application deadline:* For fall admission, 8/1 priority date for domestic students. Applications are processed on a rolling basis. Application fee: $30 ($50 for international students). Electronic applications accepted. *Financial support:* Career-related internships or fieldwork, Federal Work-Study, scholarships/grants, and tuition waivers (full and partial) available. Support available to part-time students. Financial award application deadline: 2/1. *Unit head:* Dr. John Fritch, Department Head/Associate Professor, 319-273-6118, Fax: 319-273-7356, E-mail: john.fritch@uni.edu. *Application contact:* Laurie S. Russell, Record Analyst, 319-273-2623, Fax: 319-273-6792, E-mail: laurie.russell@uni.edu.

University of North Texas, Robert B. Toulouse School of Graduate Studies, College of Arts and Sciences, Department of Communication Studies, Denton, TX 76203. Offers MA, MS. Part-time programs available. In 2009, 13 master's awarded. *Degree requirements:* For master's, one foreign language, comprehensive exam, internship or problem or thesis. *Entrance requirements:* For master's, GRE General Test, statement of purpose, curriculum vitae/resume, transcripts. Additional exam requirements/recommendations for international students: Required—proof of English language proficiency required for non-native English speakers; Recommended—TOEFL (minimum score 550 paper-based; 213 computer-based; 79 iBT). Application fee: $50 ($75 for international students). *Expenses:* Tuition, state resident: full-time $4298; part-time $239 per contact hour. Tuition, nonresident: full-time $9878; part-time $549 per contact hour. Required fees: $265 per contact hour. *Financial support:* Teaching assistantships, career-related internships or fieldwork, Federal Work-Study, and institutionally sponsored loans available. Financial award application deadline: 4/15; financial award applicants required to submit FAFSA. *Faculty research:* Rhetoric, performance studies, interpersonal communication, organizational communication, health communication. *Unit head:* Jay Allison, Chair, 940-565-2588, E-mail: allison@unt.edu. *Application contact:* Jay Allison, Chair, 940-565-2588, E-mail: allison@unt.edu.

University of Oklahoma, Graduate College, College of Arts and Sciences, Department of Communication, Norman, OK 73019. Offers MA, PhD. Postbaccalaureate distance learning degree programs offered (no on-campus study). *Faculty:* 17 full-time (8 women), 2 part-time/adjunct (1 woman). *Students:* 43 full-time (26 women), 49 part-time (24 women); includes 19 minority (8 African Americans, 2 American Indian/Alaska Native, 4 Asian Americans or Pacific Islanders, 5 Hispanic Americans), 12 international. 46 applicants, 78% accepted, 12 enrolled. In 2009, 15 master's, 5 doctorates awarded. Terminal master's awarded for partial completion of doctoral program. *Degree requirements:* For master's, comprehensive exam, thesis or alternative; for doctorate, thesis/dissertation, general exam. *Entrance requirements:* For master's, GRE General Test, minimum undergraduate GPA of 3.0; for doctorate, GRE General Test, minimum graduate GPA of 3.5. Additional exam requirements/recommendations for international students: Required—TOEFL (minimum score 550 paper-based; 213 computer-based). *Application deadline:* For fall admission, 4/1 priority date for domestic students, 4/1 for international students; for spring admission, 11/1 for domestic students, 9/1 for international students. Applications are processed on a rolling basis. Application fee: $40 ($90 for international students). Electronic applications accepted. *Expenses:* Tuition, state resident: full-time $3744; part-time $156 per credit hour. Tuition, nonresident: full-time $13,577; part-time $565.70 per credit hour. Required fees: $2415; $90.10 per credit hour. *Financial support:* In 2009–10, 47 students received support, including 28 teaching assistantships with partial tuition reimbursements available (averaging $11,985 per year); Federal Work-Study, scholarships/grants, tuition waivers (partial), and unspecified assistantships also available. Support available to part-time students. Financial award applicants required to submit FAFSA. *Faculty research:* Health communication; political, social influence; intercultural communication; interpersonal communication. Total annual research expenditures: $247,495. *Unit head:* Dr. Kevin Wright, Interim Chair, 405-325-3111, Fax: 405-325-7625, E-mail: kbwright@ou.edu. *Application contact:* Amy Johnson, Graduate Liaison, 405-325-2561, Fax: 405-325-7625, E-mail: amyjj@ou.edu.

University of Oregon, Graduate School, School of Journalism and Communication, Eugene, OR 97403. Offers MA, MS, PhD. *Accreditation:* ACEJMC (one or more programs are accredited); ASHA. Part-time programs available. *Degree requirements:* For master's, thesis or alternative. *Entrance requirements:* For master's, GRE General Test; for doctorate, master's degree. *Faculty research:* Impact of mass communication, media technology, media accountability, craft attitudes, media economics.

University of Ottawa, Faculty of Graduate and Postdoctoral Studies, Faculty of Arts, Department of Communication, Ottawa, ON K1N 6N5, Canada. Offers MA. Electronic applications accepted. *Faculty research:* Media studies, organizational communications.

Communication—General

University of Pennsylvania, Annenberg School for Communication, Philadelphia, PA 19104. Offers PhD. *Faculty:* 20 full-time (8 women), 4 part-time/adjunct (0 women). *Students:* 89 full-time (56 women), 1 part-time (0 women); includes 12 minority (10 African Americans, 2 Hispanic Americans), 25 international. 371 applicants, 6% accepted, 14 enrolled. In 2009, 13 doctorates awarded. *Degree requirements:* For doctorate, thesis/dissertation. *Entrance requirements:* For doctorate, GRE General Test. *Application deadline:* For fall admission, 1/2 for domestic students. Application fee: $70. Electronic applications accepted. *Expenses:* Tuition: Full-time $25,660; part-time $4758 per course. Required fees: $2152; $270 per course. Tuition and fees vary according to course load, degree level and program. *Financial support:* In 2009–10, 86 students received support; fellowships, research assistantships, teaching assistantships, institutionally sponsored loans, scholarships/grants, traineeships, health care benefits, and unspecified assistantships available. Financial award application deadline: 12/15. *Unit head:* Dr. Michael X. Delli Carpini, Dean. *Application contact:* Beverly Henry, Graduate Studies Coordinator, 215-573-1091, Fax: 215-898-2024, E-mail: bhenry@asc.upenn.edu.

University of Pittsburgh, School of Arts and Sciences, Department of Communication, Pittsburgh, PA 15260. Offers MA, PhD. *Faculty:* 11 full-time (3 women), 1 (woman) part-time/adjunct. *Students:* 42 full-time (22 women); includes 10 minority (3 African Americans, 2 Asian Americans or Pacific Islanders, 5 Hispanic Americans), 2 international. Average age 30. 103 applicants, 6% accepted, 0 enrolled. In 2009, 3 master's, 1 doctorate awarded. *Degree requirements:* For master's, comprehensive exam, thesis optional; for doctorate, comprehensive exam, thesis/dissertation. *Entrance requirements:* For master's and doctorate, GRE General Test, sample of written work. Additional exam requirements/recommendations for international students: Required—TOEFL (minimum score 550 paper-based; 213 computer-based; 80 iBT). *Application deadline:* For fall admission, 1/2 priority date for domestic and international students. Application fee: $50. Electronic applications accepted. *Expenses:* Tuition, state resident: full-time $16,402; part-time $665 per credit. Tuition, nonresident: full-time $28,694; part-time $1175 per credit. Required fees: $690; $175 per term. Tuition and fees vary according to program. *Financial support:* In 2009–10, 24 students received support, including 18 fellowships with full tuition reimbursements available (averaging $15,675 per year), 6 teaching assistantships with full tuition reimbursements available (averaging $15,065 per year); Federal Work-Study, scholarships/grants, health care benefits, tuition waivers (full), and unspecified assistantships also available. Financial award application deadline: 1/2; financial award applicants required to submit FAFSA. *Faculty research:* Media and cultural studies, public argument and discourse, rhetoric of science, history, criticism and theory of rhetoric. *Unit head:* Dr. Barbara Warnick, Department Chair, 412-624-1564, Fax: 412-624-1878, E-mail: bwarnick@pitt.edu. *Application contact:* Dr. Gordon R. Mitchell, Director of Graduate Studies, 412-624-8531, Fax: 412-624-1878, E-mail: gordonm@pitt.edu.

University of Portland, College of Arts and Sciences, Department of Communication Studies, Portland, OR 97203-5798. Offers communication (MA); management communication (MS). Part-time and evening/weekend programs available. *Faculty:* 7 full-time (2 women), 1 part-time/adjunct (0 women). *Students:* 2 full-time (both women), 11 part-time (10 women); includes 2 minority (1 African American, 1 Asian American or Pacific Islander), 2 international. Average age 27. In 2009, 4 master's awarded. *Degree requirements:* For master's, thesis optional. *Entrance requirements:* For master's, GRE General Test, minimum GPA of 3.25, 3 letters of recommendation, resume, statement of goals, official transcripts. Additional exam requirements/recommendations for international students: Required—TOEFL (minimum score 600 paper-based; 100 iBT), IELTS (minimum score 7.5). *Application deadline:* For fall admission, 7/15 priority date for domestic and international students; for spring admission, 12/15 priority date for domestic and international students. Applications are processed on a rolling basis. Application fee: $50. *Expenses:* Tuition: Part-time $860 per semester hour. *Financial support:* Career-related internships or fieldwork, Federal Work-Study, scholarships/grants, and tuition waivers (partial) available. Financial award application deadline: 3/1; financial award applicants required to submit FAFSA. *Unit head:* Dr. Jeffrey Kerssen-Griep, Director, 503-943-7167, E-mail: kerssen@up.edu. *Application contact:* Chris James Olinger, Administrative Assistant, 503-943-7107, Fax: 503-943-7315, E-mail: olingerc@up.edu.

University of Puerto Rico, Río Piedras, School of Communication, Program in Communication Theory and Research, San Juan, PR 00931-3300. Offers MA.

University of Rhode Island, Graduate School, College of Arts and Sciences, Department of Communication Studies, Kingston, RI 02881. Offers MA. Part-time programs available. *Faculty:* 29 full-time (16 women). *Students:* 18 full-time (9 women), 11 part-time (8 women); includes 2 minority (both African Americans), 3 international. In 2009, 4 master's awarded. *Degree requirements:* For master's, comprehensive exam (for some programs), thesis optional. *Entrance requirements:* For master's, GRE, 2 letters of recommendation. Additional exam requirements/recommendations for international students: Required—TOEFL (minimum score 550 paper-based; 230 computer-based; 88 iBT). *Application deadline:* For fall admission, 7/15 for domestic students, 2/1 for international students. Application fee: $65. Electronic applications accepted. *Expenses:* Tuition, state resident: full-time $8828; part-time $490 per credit hour. Tuition, nonresident: full-time $22,100; part-time $1228 per credit hour. Required fees: $1118; $57 per semester. Tuition and fees vary according to program. *Financial support:* In 2009–10, 1 research assistantship with partial tuition reimbursement (averaging $6,947 per year), 4 teaching assistantships with full tuition reimbursements (averaging $13,894 per year) were awarded. Financial award application deadline: 2/1; financial award applicants required to submit FAFSA. Total annual research expenditures: $43,689. *Unit head:* Dr. Lynne Derbyshire, Chair, 401-874-4732, Fax: 401-874-4722, E-mail: derbyshire@uri.edu. *Application contact:* Dr. Norbert Mundorf, Director of Graduate Studies, 401-874-4725, Fax: 401-874-4722, E-mail: mundorf@uri.edu.

University of South Africa, College of Human Sciences, Pretoria, South Africa. Offers adult education (M Ed); African languages (MA, PhD); African politics (MA, PhD); Afrikaans (MA, PhD); ancient history (MA, PhD); ancient Near Eastern studies (MA, PhD); anthropology (MA, PhD); applied linguistics (MA); Arabic (MA, PhD); archaeology (MA); art history (MA); Biblical archaeology (MA); Biblical studies (M Th, D Th, PhD); Christian spirituality (M Th, D Th); church history (M Th, D Th); classical studies (MA, PhD); clinical psychology (MA); communication (MA, PhD); comparative education (M Ed, Ed D); consulting psychology (D Admin, D Com, PhD); curriculum studies (M Ed, Ed D); development studies (M Admin, MA, D Admin, PhD); didactics (M Ed, Ed D); education (M Tech); education management (M Ed, Ed D); educational psychology (M Ed); English (MA); environmental education (M Ed); French (MA, PhD); German (MA, PhD); Greek (MA); guidance and counseling (M Ed); health studies (MA, PhD), including health sciences education (MA), health services management (MA), medical and surgical nursing science (critical care general) (MA), midwifery and neonatal nursing science (MA), trauma and emergency care (MA); history (MA, PhD); history of education (Ed D); inclusive education (M Ed, Ed D); information and communications technology policy and regulation (MA); information science (MA, MIS, PhD); international politics (MA, PhD); Islamic studies (MA, PhD); Italian (MA, PhD); Judaica (MA, PhD); linguistics (MA, PhD); mathematical education (M Ed); mathematics education (MA); missiology (M Th, D Th); modern Hebrew (MA, PhD); musicology (MA, MMus, D Mus, PhD); natural science education (M Ed); New Testament (M Th, D Th); Old Testament (D Th); pastoral therapy (M Th, D Th); philosophy (MA); philosophy of education (M Ed, Ed D); politics (MA, PhD); Portuguese (MA, PhD); practical theology (M Th, D Th); psychology (MA, MS, PhD); psychology of education (M Ed, Ed D); public health (MA); religious studies (MA, D Th, PhD); Romance languages (MA); Russian (MA, PhD); Semitic languages (MA, PhD); social behavior studies in HIV/AIDS (MA); social science (mental health) (MA); social science in development studies (MA); social science in psychology (MA); social science in social work (MA); social science in sociology (MA); social work (MSW, DSW, PhD); socio-education (M Ed, Ed D); sociolinguistics (MA); sociology (MA, PhD); Spanish (MA, PhD); systematic theology (M Th, D Th); TESOL (teaching English to speakers of other languages) (MA); theological ethics (M Th, D Th); theory of literature (MA, PhD); urban ministries (D Th); urban ministry (M Th).

University of South Alabama, Graduate School, College of Arts and Sciences, Department of Communication, Mobile, AL 36688-0002. Offers MA. *Degree requirements:* For master's, comprehensive exam, thesis optional. *Entrance requirements:* For master's, GRE, GMAT, minimum GPA of 3.0, BA in communication or 36 semester hours. *Expenses:* Tuition, state resident: part-time $218 per contact hour. Required fees: $1102 per year.

The University of South Dakota, Graduate School, College of Arts and Sciences, Department of Communication Studies, Vermillion, SD 57069-2390. Offers MA. Part-time programs available. *Degree requirements:* For master's, comprehensive exam (for some programs), thesis (for some programs). *Entrance requirements:* For master's, minimum GPA of 2.7. Additional exam requirements/recommendations for international students: Required—TOEFL (minimum score 575 paper-based; 213 computer-based; 79 iBT). Electronic applications accepted. *Faculty research:* Male/female communication, interpersonal communication, relational communication, rhetoric and public address, organizational communication.

University of Southern California, Graduate School, Annenberg School for Communication and Journalism, Los Angeles, CA 90089. Offers MA, MCM, MPD, PhD, JD/MCM, MA/M Sc, MCM/MAJCS. Part-time and evening/weekend programs available. Terminal master's awarded for partial completion of doctoral program. *Degree requirements:* For master's, comprehensive exam (for some programs), thesis (for some programs); for doctorate, thesis/dissertation. *Entrance requirements:* For master's, GRE General Test (or GMAT for Communication Management degree program only), resume, writing samples, letters of recommendation, statement of purpose; for doctorate, GRE General Test, resume, writing samples, letters of recommendation, statement of purpose, interest survey. Additional exam requirements/recommendations for international students: Required—TOEFL (minimum score 280 computer-based; 114 iBT). Electronic applications accepted. *Expenses:* Tuition: Full-time $25,980; part-time $1315 per unit. Required fees: $554. One-time fee: $35 full-time. Full-time tuition and fees vary according to degree level and program.

See Display on page 629 and Close-Up on page 685.

University of Southern California, Graduate School, Annenberg School for Communication and Journalism, School of Communication, Program in Communication, Los Angeles, CA 90089. Offers communication (MA, PhD), including interpersonal and social dynamics (PhD), mass communication, technology, and public policy (PhD), organizational communication (PhD), rhetorical and cultural studies (PhD). *Degree requirements:* For doctorate, thesis/dissertation. *Entrance requirements:* For master's and doctorate, GRE General Test, resume, writing samples, 3 letters of recommendation, interest survey questionnaire, statement of purpose. Additional exam requirements/recommendations for international students: Required—TOEFL (minimum score 280 computer-based; 114 iBT); Recommended—TWE. Electronic applications accepted. *Expenses:* Tuition: Full-time $25,980; part-time $1315 per unit. Required fees: $554. One-time fee: $35 full-time. Full-time tuition and fees vary according to degree level and program. *Faculty research:* Computer-mediated communication, public health campaigns, communication democracy and the public sphere, new communication technologies in organizations, communication and community.

See Display on page 629 and Close-Up on page 685.

University of Southern California, Graduate School, Annenberg School for Communication and Journalism, School of Communication, Program in Global Communication, Los Angeles, CA 90089. Offers MA/M Sc. Program offered jointly with London School of Economics. *Entrance requirements:* Additional exam requirements/recommendations for international students: Required—TOEFL (minimum score 280 computer-based; 114 iBT), IELTS. Electronic applications accepted. *Expenses:* Tuition: Full-time $25,980; part-time $1315 per unit. Required fees: $554. One-time fee: $35 full-time. Full-time tuition and fees vary according to degree level and program. *Faculty research:* New technology, audience analysis, globalization, entertainment industry, integrated communication.

See Display on page 629 and Close-Up on page 685.

University of South Florida, Graduate School, College of Arts and Sciences, Department of Communication, Tampa, FL 33620-9951. Offers MA, PhD. Part-time programs available. *Faculty:* 18 full-time (9 women). *Students:* 42 full-time (27 women), 19 part-time (10 women); includes 9 minority (4 African Americans, 1 Asian American or Pacific Islander, 4 Hispanic Americans), 1 international. Average age 32. 83 applicants, 30% accepted, 14 enrolled. In 2009, 2 master's, 4 doctorates awarded. *Degree requirements:* For master's, comprehensive exam (for some programs), thesis (for some programs); for doctorate, comprehensive exam, thesis/dissertation. *Entrance requirements:* For master's, GRE General Test, minimum GPA of 3.0. Additional exam requirements/recommendations for international students: Required—TOEFL (minimum score 550 paper-based; 213 computer-based). *Application deadline:* For fall admission, 1/15 for domestic students, 1/2 for international students; for spring admission, 11/1 for domestic students, 6/1 for international students. Applications are processed on a rolling basis. Application fee: $30. Electronic applications accepted. *Financial support:* In 2009–10, 3 students received support, including teaching assistantships with full tuition reimbursements available (averaging $12,500 per year); unspecified assistantships also available. Financial award application deadline: 1/15; financial award applicants required to submit FAFSA. *Faculty research:* Organizational, interpersonal, and health communication; media and cultural studies; rhetoric; performance studies; qualitative research methods. *Unit head:* Dr. Kenneth Cissna, Chairperson, 813-974-6820, Fax: 813-974-6817, E-mail: kcissna@usf.edu. *Application contact:* Stacy Holman Jones, Program Director, 813-974-6827, Fax: 813-974-6817, E-mail: holmanjo@usf.edu.

The University of Tennessee, Graduate School, College of Communication and Information, Knoxville, TN 37996. Offers advertising (MS, PhD); broadcasting (MS, PhD); communications (MS, PhD); information sciences (MS, PhD); journalism (MS, PhD); public relations (MS, PhD); speech communication (MS, PhD). *Accreditation:* ACEJMC (one or more programs are accredited at the [master's] level). Part-time and evening/weekend programs available. Postbaccalaureate distance learning degree programs offered (no on-campus study). *Degree requirements:* For master's, thesis or alternative; for doctorate, thesis/dissertation. *Entrance requirements:* For master's and doctorate, GRE General Test, minimum GPA of 2.7. Additional exam requirements/recommendations for international students: Required—TOEFL. Electronic applications accepted. *Expenses:* Tuition, state resident: full-time $6826; part-time $380 per semester hour. Tuition, nonresident: full-time $21,844; part-time $1147 per semester hour. Tuition and fees vary according to program.

The University of Texas at Arlington, Graduate School, College of Liberal Arts, Department of Communication, Arlington, TX 76019. Offers MA. Part-time and evening/weekend programs available. *Faculty:* 15 full-time (5 women). *Students:* 6 full-time (2 women), 14 part-time (10 women); includes 6 minority (2 African Americans, 4 Hispanic Americans), 3 international. 31 applicants, 100% accepted, 9 enrolled. In 2009, 10 master's awarded. *Degree requirements:* For master's, comprehensive exam (for some programs), thesis or alternative. *Entrance requirements:* For master's, GRE General Test. Additional exam requirements/recommendations for international students: Required—TOEFL (minimum score 550 paper-based; 213 computer-based). Application fee: $35 ($50 for international students). *Financial support:* In 2009–10, 2 research assistantships (averaging $7,200 per year), 1 teaching assistantship (averaging $2,500 per year) were awarded. *Unit head:* Dr. Charla Markham-Shaw, Chair, 817-272-2163, E-mail: markham@uta.edu. *Application contact:* Dr. Tom Christie, Graduate Advisor, 817-272-2163, E-mail: christie@uta.edu.

The University of Texas at Austin, Graduate School, College of Communication, Austin, TX 78712-1111. Offers MA, MFA, Au D, PhD, MBA/MA, MP Aff/MA. Part-time programs available. *Entrance requirements:* For master's and doctorate, GRE General Test. Electronic applications accepted.

The University of Texas at Dallas, School of Behavioral and Brain Sciences, Program in Communication Sciences and Disorders, Richardson, TX 75080. Offers communication disorders (MS); communication sciences (PhD). Part-time and evening/weekend programs available.

Faculty: 19 full-time (10 women), 2 part-time/adjunct (both women). *Students:* 221 full-time (216 women), 15 part-time (13 women); includes 35 minority (7 African Americans, 1 American Indian/Alaska Native, 15 Asian Americans or Pacific Islanders, 12 Hispanic Americans), 7 international. Average age 25. 295 applicants, 28% accepted, 65 enrolled. In 2009, 96 master's, 4 doctorates awarded. *Degree requirements:* For doctorate, thesis/dissertation. *Entrance requirements:* For master's and doctorate, GRE General Test, minimum GPA of 3.0 in upper-level course work in field. Additional exam requirements/recommendations for international students: Required—TOEFL (minimum score 550 paper-based; 213 computer-based). *Application deadline:* For fall admission, 7/15 for domestic students, 5/1 priority date for international students; for spring admission, 11/15 for domestic students, 9/1 priority date for international students. Applications are processed on a rolling basis. Application fee: $50 ($100 for international students). Electronic applications accepted. *Expenses:* Tuition, state resident: full-time $11,068; part-time $461 per credit hour. Tuition, nonresident: full-time $21,178; part-time $882 per credit hour. Tuition and fees vary according to course load. *Financial support:* In 2009–10, 6 research assistantships with full tuition reimbursements (averaging $18,317 per year), 11 teaching assistantships with full tuition reimbursements (averaging $10,681 per year) were awarded; fellowships, Federal Work-Study, institutionally sponsored loans, scholarships/grants, and unspecified assistantships also available. Support available to part-time students. Financial award application deadline: 4/30; financial award applicants required to submit FAFSA. *Faculty research:* Speech perception, auditory processing, language acquisition by young children, language development. *Unit head:* Dr. Robert D. Stillman, Program Head, 972-883-3106, Fax: 972-883-3022, E-mail: stillman@utdallas.edu. *Application contact:* Dr. Robert D. Stillman, Program Head, 972-883-3106, Fax: 972-883-3022, E-mail: stillman@utdallas.edu.

The University of Texas at El Paso, Graduate School, College of Liberal Arts, Department of Communication, El Paso, TX 79968-0001. Offers MA. Part-time and evening/weekend programs available. *Degree requirements:* For master's, thesis optional. *Entrance requirements:* For master's, GRE General Test, minimum GPA of 3.0. Additional exam requirements/recommendations for international students: Required—TOEFL. Electronic applications accepted. *Faculty research:* Cross-cultural communication, information media, telecommunication technology, trans-border communication, human communication.

The University of Texas at San Antonio, College of Liberal and Fine Arts, Department of Communication, San Antonio, TX 78249-0617. Offers MA. Part-time and evening/weekend programs available. *Faculty:* 6 full-time (3 women). *Students:* 6 full-time (5 women), 24 part-time (15 women); includes 13 minority (3 African Americans, 10 Hispanic Americans), 1 international. Average age 29. 27 applicants, 70% accepted, 12 enrolled. In 2009, 8 master's awarded. *Degree requirements:* For master's, comprehensive exam (for some programs), thesis (for some programs). *Entrance requirements:* For master's, GRE. Additional exam requirements/recommendations for international students: Required—TOEFL (minimum score 500 paper-based; 173 computer-based; 61 iBT), IELTS (minimum score 5). *Application deadline:* For fall admission, 7/1 for domestic students, 4/1 for international students; for spring admission, 11/1 for domestic students, 9/1 for international students. Applications are processed on a rolling basis. Application fee: $45 ($80 for international students). Electronic applications accepted. *Expenses:* Tuition, state resident: full-time $3975; part-time $221 per contact hour. Tuition, nonresident: full-time $13,947; part-time $775 per contact hour. Required fees: $1853. *Financial support:* In 2009–10, 4 students received support, including 1 research assistantship (averaging $10,660 per year), 3 teaching assistantships (averaging $5,320 per year); career-related internships or fieldwork, scholarships/grants, tuition waivers, and unspecified assistantships also available. Support available to part-time students. *Unit head:* Dr. Steven Levitt, Chair, 210-458-5990, E-mail: steven.levitt@utsa.edu. *Application contact:* H. Paul LeBlanc, Graduate Advisor, 210-458-7724, E-mail: paul.leblanc@utsa.edu.

The University of Texas at Tyler, College of Arts and Sciences, Department of Communication, Tyler, TX 75799-0001. Offers communication (MA); interdisciplinary studies (MAIS, MSIS). Part-time programs available. *Faculty:* 5 full-time (2 women). *Students:* 4 full-time (all women), 14 part-time (9 women); includes 4 minority (all African Americans). Average age 31. 10 applicants, 100% accepted, 7 enrolled. *Degree requirements:* For master's, comprehensive exam. *Entrance requirements:* For master's, GRE General Test, minimum GPA of 2.5. Additional exam requirements/recommendations for international students: Required—TOEFL (minimum score 79 computer-based). *Application deadline:* For fall admission, 8/17 priority date for domestic students, 5/31 priority date for international students; for spring admission, 12/21 priority date for domestic students, 11/1 priority date for international students. Applications are processed on a rolling basis. Application fee: $25 ($50 for international students). Electronic applications accepted. *Expenses:* Tuition, state resident: part-time $665 per semester hour. Tuition, nonresident: part-time $942 per semester hour. Part-time tuition and fees vary according to degree level and program. *Financial support:* Fellowships, research assistantships, teaching assistantships available. Financial award application deadline: 7/1; financial award applicants required to submit FAFSA. *Faculty research:* Organizational communication, feminist criticism, religions communication, mass media. *Unit head:* Dr. Dennis D. Cali, Chair, 903-566-7253, E-mail: dcali@uttyler.edu. *Application contact:* Dr. Dennis D. Cali, Chair, 903-566-7253, E-mail: dcali@uttyler.edu.

The University of Texas–Pan American, College of Arts and Humanities, Department of Communications, Edinburg, TX 78539. Offers communication (MA); theatre (MA). *Accreditation:* NAST. Part-time and evening/weekend programs available. *Degree requirements:* For master's, comprehensive exam, thesis or alternative. *Entrance requirements:* For master's, minimum GPA of 3.0. Additional exam requirements/recommendations for international students: Required—TOEFL. *Expenses:* Tuition, state resident: full-time $3630.60; part-time $201.70 per credit hour. Tuition, nonresident: full-time $8617; part-time $478.70 per credit hour. Required fees: $806.50. *Faculty research:* Rhetorical theory, intercultural and mass communication, American theatre, multicultural theatre and drama, television and film.

University of the Incarnate Word, School of Graduate Studies and Research, H-E-B School of Business and Administration, Programs in Administration, San Antonio, TX 78209-6397. Offers adult education (MAA); applied administration (MAA); communication arts (MAA); healthcare administration (MAA); instructional technology (MAA); international business (Certificate); nutrition (MAA); organizational development (MAA, Certificate); project management (Certificate); sports management (MAA). Part-time and evening/weekend programs available. Postbaccalaureate distance learning degree programs offered (no on-campus study). *Students:* 30 full-time (17 women), 163 part-time (114 women); includes 128 minority (18 African Americans, 3 Asian Americans or Pacific Islanders, 107 Hispanic Americans), 8 international. Average age 35. In 2009, 68 master's awarded. *Degree requirements:* For master's, capstone. *Entrance requirements:* For master's, GRE, GMAT, undergraduate degree, minimum GPA of 2.5. Additional exam requirements/recommendations for international students: Required—TOEFL (minimum score 560 paper-based; 220 computer-based; 83 iBT). *Application deadline:* Applications are processed on a rolling basis. Application fee: $20. Electronic applications accepted. *Expenses:* Tuition: Full-time $12,150; part-time $675 per credit hour. Required fees: $83 per credit hour. *Financial support:* Federal Work-Study and scholarships/grants available. Financial award applicants required to submit FAFSA. *Unit head:* Dr. Daniel Dominguez, MAA Director, 210-829-3180, Fax: 210-805-3564, E-mail: domingue@uiwtx.edu. *Application contact:* Andrea Cyterski-Acosta, Dean of Enrollment, 210-829-6005, Fax: 210-829-3921, E-mail: admis@uiwtx.edu.

University of the Incarnate Word, School of Graduate Studies and Research, School of Interactive Media and Design, Program in Communication Arts, San Antonio, TX 78209-6397. Offers communication arts (MA). Part-time and evening/weekend programs available. *Faculty:* 3 full-time (1 woman), 2 part-time/adjunct (0 women). *Students:* 9 full-time (5 women), 25 part-time (16 women); includes 23 minority (2 African Americans, 21 Hispanic Americans), 2 international. Average age 31. In 2009, 9 master's awarded. *Degree requirements:* For master's, thesis or alternative. *Entrance requirements:* For master's, GMAT, GRE General Test, interview, writing sample. Additional exam requirements/recommendations for international students: Required—TOEFL (minimum score 560 paper-based; 220 computer-based; 83 iBT). *Application*

Communication—General

University of the Incarnate Word (continued)
deadline: Applications are processed on a rolling basis. Application fee: $20. Electronic applications accepted. *Expenses:* Tuition: Full-time $12,150; part-time $675 per credit hour. Required fees: $83 per credit hour. *Financial support:* Federal Work-Study and scholarships/grants available. Financial award applicants required to submit FAFSA. *Unit head:* Dr. Valerie Greenberg, 210-829-3891, Fax: 210-829-3196, E-mail: greenber@uiwtx.edu. *Application contact:* Andrea Cyterski-Acosta, Dean of Enrollment, 210-829-6005, Fax: 210-829-3921, E-mail: admis@uiwtx.edu.

University of the Pacific, College of the Pacific, Department of Communication, Stockton, CA 95211-0197. Offers MA. *Faculty:* 9 full-time (2 women), 3 part-time/adjunct (2 women). *Students:* 7 full-time (4 women), 14 part-time (8 women); includes 3 minority (1 African American, 1 Asian American or Pacific Islander, 1 Hispanic American), 2 international. Average age 28. 37 applicants, 51% accepted, 13 enrolled. In 2009, 10 master's awarded. *Degree requirements:* For master's, thesis. *Entrance requirements:* For master's, GRE General Test. Additional exam requirements/recommendations for international students: Required—TOEFL (minimum score 475 paper-based; 150 computer-based). *Application deadline:* For fall admission, 3/1 priority date for domestic students; for spring admission, 10/1 for domestic students. Applications are processed on a rolling basis. Application fee: $75. *Financial support:* In 2009–10, 8 teaching assistantships were awarded. Support available to part-time students. Financial award application deadline: 3/1; financial award applicants required to submit FAFSA. *Unit head:* Dr. Qingwen Dong, Chairman, 209-946-2505, E-mail: qdong@pacific.edu. *Application contact:* Information Contact, 209-946-2261.

University of the Sacred Heart, Graduate Programs, Department of Communication, San Juan, PR 00914-0383. Offers contemporary culture and media (MA); digital journalism (Certificate); editing for media (MA, Certificate); public relations (MA, Certificate); publicity (MA, Certificate); scriptwriting (MA, Certificate). Part-time and evening/weekend programs available. *Degree requirements:* For master's, thesis.

The University of Toledo, College of Graduate Studies, College of Arts and Sciences, Department of Communications, Toledo, OH 43606-3390. Offers communication studies (Certificate).

University of Utah, The Graduate School, College of Humanities, Department of Communication, Salt Lake City, UT 84112. Offers MA, MS, PhD. *Faculty:* 28 full-time (14 women). *Students:* 42 full-time (28 women), 33 part-time (18 women); includes 8 minority (4 Asian Americans or Pacific Islanders, 4 Hispanic Americans), 2 international. Average age 35. 125 applicants, 30% accepted, 20 enrolled. In 2009, 9 master's, 14 doctorates awarded. *Degree requirements:* For master's, thesis or alternative; for doctorate, comprehensive exam, thesis/dissertation. *Entrance requirements:* For master's and doctorate, GRE General Test, minimum GPA of 3.0. Additional exam requirements/recommendations for international students: Required—TOEFL (minimum score 500 paper-based; 173 computer-based). *Application deadline:* For fall admission, 1/15 for domestic and international students. Application fee: $55 ($65 for international students). Electronic applications accepted. *Expenses:* Tuition, state resident: full-time $4004; part-time $1674 per semester. Tuition, nonresident: full-time $14,134; part-time $5915 per semester. Required fees: $324 per semester. Tuition and fees vary according to course load, degree level and program. *Financial support:* In 2009–10, 3 students received support, including 14 teaching assistantships with full tuition reimbursements available (averaging $13,000 per year); fellowships with full tuition reimbursements available, health care benefits also available. Financial award application deadline: 1/15; financial award applicants required to submit FAFSA. *Faculty research:* Communication theory and history, rhetoric, mass communications, journalism, public address and forensics. Total annual research expenditures: $36,247. *Unit head:* Dr. Ann L. Darling, Chair, 801-581-3912, Fax: 801-585-6255, E-mail: ann.darling@utah.edu. *Application contact:* Dr. Connie Bullis, Director of Graduate Studies, 801-581-6664, Fax: 801-585-6255, E-mail: connie.bullis@utah.edu.

University of Vermont, Graduate College, College of Arts and Sciences, Department of Communication Sciences, Burlington, VT 05405. Offers MS. *Accreditation:* ASHA. *Students:* 45 (44 women); includes 2 minority (both Asian Americans or Pacific Islanders), 2 international. 95 applicants, 47% accepted, 20 enrolled. In 2009, 14 master's awarded. *Entrance requirements:* For master's, GRE General Test. Additional exam requirements/recommendations for international students: Required—TOEFL (minimum score 550 paper-based; 213 computer-based; 80 iBT). *Application deadline:* For fall admission, 2/1 for domestic students. Application fee: $40. Electronic applications accepted. *Expenses:* Tuition, state resident: part-time $508 per credit hour. Tuition, nonresident: part-time $1281 per credit hour. *Financial support:* Fellowships available. Financial award application deadline: 3/1. *Unit head:* Prof. P. Prelock, Chair, 802-656-3861. *Application contact:* Prof. Barry Guitar, Coordinator, 802-656-3861.

University of Washington, Graduate School, College of Arts and Sciences, Department of Communication, Seattle, WA 98195. Offers MA, MC, PhD. Part-time programs available. Terminal master's awarded for partial completion of doctoral program. *Degree requirements:* For master's, thesis, project (MC); for doctorate, thesis/dissertation. *Entrance requirements:* For master's and doctorate, GRE, minimum GPA of 3.0, writing sample. Additional exam requirements/recommendations for international students: Required—TOEFL. Electronic applications accepted. *Faculty research:* Communication and culture, communication technology and society, international communication, political communication, rhetoric and critical studies.

University of Washington, Graduate School, College of Arts and Sciences, School of Art, Division of Design, Seattle, WA 98195. Offers industrial design (MFA); visual communication design (MFA).

University of West Florida, College of Arts and Sciences: Arts, Department of Communication Arts, Pensacola, FL 32514-5750. Offers MA. Part-time and evening/weekend programs available. *Faculty:* 2 full-time (both women). *Students:* 12 full-time (10 women), 10 part-time (all women); includes 2 minority (both African Americans), 2 international. Average age 28. 17 applicants, 76% accepted, 9 enrolled. In 2009, 11 master's awarded. *Degree requirements:* For master's, thesis or alternative. *Entrance requirements:* For master's, GRE General Test, minimum GPA of 3.0. Additional exam requirements/recommendations for international students: Required—TOEFL (minimum score 550 paper-based; 213 computer-based). *Application deadline:* For fall admission, 6/1 for domestic students, 5/15 for international students; for spring admission, 11/1 for domestic students, 10/1 for international students. Applications are processed on a rolling basis. Application fee: $30. *Expenses:* Tuition, state resident: full-time $4982; part-time $260 per credit hour. Tuition, nonresident: full-time $20,059; part-time $919 per credit hour. Required fees: $1247; $52 per credit hour. *Financial support:* In 2009–10, 3 teaching assistantships with partial tuition reimbursements (averaging $4,588 per year) were awarded; unspecified assistantships also available. Financial award application deadline: 4/15; financial award applicants required to submit FAFSA. *Faculty research:* Equity studies. *Unit head:* Dr. Bruce M. Swain, Chairperson, 850-474-3278. *Application contact:* Terry McCray, Assistant Director of Graduate Admissions, 850-473-7718, Fax: 850-473-7714, E-mail: gradadmissions@uwf.edu.

University of Windsor, Faculty of Graduate Studies, Faculty of Arts and Social Sciences, Department of Communication Studies, Windsor, ON N9B 3P4, Canada. Offers communication and social justice (MA). *Degree requirements:* For master's, thesis. *Entrance requirements:* For master's, writing sample/media production or multimedia portfolio. Additional exam requirements/recommendations for international students: Required—TOEFL (minimum score 600 paper-based; 250 computer-based). Electronic applications accepted. *Faculty research:* Sociology of news, media ownership and control, communication networks and social movements, issues of media representation.

University of Wisconsin–Madison, Graduate School, College of Letters and Science, Department of Communication Arts, Madison, WI 53706-1380. Offers communication science (MA, PhD); film (MA, PhD); media and cultural studies (MA, PhD); rhetoric (MA, PhD). Terminal master's awarded for partial completion of doctoral program. *Degree requirements:* For master's, one foreign language, thesis (for some programs); for doctorate, one foreign language, thesis/dissertation. *Entrance requirements:* For master's and doctorate, GRE General Test, minimum GPA of 3.5. Electronic applications accepted. *Expenses:* Tuition, state resident: part-time $594 per credit. Tuition, nonresident: part-time $1504 per credit. Required fees: $65 per credit. Tuition and fees vary according to course load, program and reciprocity agreements.

University of Wisconsin–Madison, Graduate School, College of Letters and Science, School of Journalism and Mass Communication, Madison, WI 53706-1380. Offers family and consumer journalism (PhD); journalism and mass communication (MA); mass communication (PhD). Part-time programs available. *Degree requirements:* For master's, thesis (for some programs); for doctorate, thesis/dissertation. *Entrance requirements:* For master's, GRE General Test, minimum GPA of 3.0; for doctorate, GRE General Test, minimum GPA of 3.5. Additional exam requirements/recommendations for international students: Required—TOEFL. Electronic applications accepted. *Expenses:* Tuition, state resident: part-time $594 per credit. Tuition, nonresident: part-time $1504 per credit. Required fees: $65 per credit. Tuition and fees vary according to course load, program and reciprocity agreements. *Faculty research:* International/development communication; strategic mass communication; mass communication and the individual; science, technology, and environment communication; mass communication and societal institutions.

University of Wisconsin–Milwaukee, Graduate School, College of Letters and Sciences, Department of Communication, Milwaukee, WI 53201-0413. Offers communication (MA, PhD); mediation and negotiation (Certificate); rhetorical leadership (Certificate). Part-time programs available. *Faculty:* 19 full-time (11 women). *Students:* 17 full-time (14 women), 34 part-time (26 women); includes 4 minority (2 American Indian/Alaska Native, 2 Hispanic Americans), 7 international. Average age 30. 59 applicants, 68% accepted, 8 enrolled. In 2009, 13 master's awarded. *Degree requirements:* For master's, thesis or alternative; for doctorate, comprehensive exam. *Entrance requirements:* For master's, GRE General Test, minimum GPA of 3.0. Additional exam requirements/recommendations for international students: Required—TOEFL (minimum score 550 paper-based; 79 iBT), IELTS (minimum score 6). *Application deadline:* For fall admission, 1/1 priority date for domestic students; for spring admission, 9/1 for domestic students. Applications are processed on a rolling basis. Application fee: $45 ($75 for international students). *Expenses:* Tuition, state resident: full-time $8800. Tuition, nonresident: full-time $20,760. Tuition and fees vary according to program and reciprocity agreements. *Financial support:* In 2009–10, 30 teaching assistantships were awarded; career-related internships or fieldwork and unspecified assistantships also available. Support available to part-time students. Financial award application deadline: 4/15. *Unit head:* Mike R. Allen, Representative, 414-229-4261, Fax: 414-229-3859, E-mail: mikealle@uwm.edu. *Application contact:* General Information Contact, 414-229-4982, Fax: 414-229-6967, E-mail: gradschool@uwm.edu.

University of Wisconsin–Stevens Point, College of Fine Arts and Communication, Division of Communication, Stevens Point, WI 54481-3897. Offers interpersonal communication (MA); mass communication (MA); organizational communication (MA); public relations (MA). Part-time programs available. *Students:* 7 full-time (3 women), 19 part-time (11 women). *Degree requirements:* For master's, thesis or alternative. *Entrance requirements:* For master's, GRE. Additional exam requirements/recommendations for international students: Required—TOEFL (minimum score 575 paper-based). *Application deadline:* For fall admission, 3/1 priority date for domestic students. Applications are processed on a rolling basis. Application fee: $45. *Expenses:* Tuition, state resident: full-time $7740; part-time $430 per credit hour. Tuition, nonresident: full-time $17,804; part-time $989 per credit hour. Tuition and fees vary according to course load and reciprocity agreements. *Financial support:* In 2009–10, 9 teaching assistantships were awarded; career-related internships or fieldwork, Federal Work-Study, institutionally sponsored loans, and unspecified assistantships also available. Support available to part-time students. Financial award application deadline: 5/1; financial award applicants required to submit FAFSA. *Faculty research:* Communication theory and research, film history. *Unit head:* Dr. James Haney, Chair, 715-346-3409, E-mail: jhaney@uwsp.edu. *Application contact:* Dr. Chris Sadler, Graduate Coordinator, 715-346-3898, E-mail: csadler@uwsp.edu.

University of Wisconsin–Superior, Graduate Division, Department of Communicating Arts, Superior, WI 54880-4500. Offers mass communication (MA); speech communication (MA); theater (MA). Part-time programs available. *Faculty:* 9 full-time (3 women), 1 (woman) part-time/adjunct. *Students:* 14 full-time (9 women), 5 part-time (3 women). Average age 30. 9 applicants, 100% accepted. In 2009, 7 master's awarded. *Degree requirements:* For master's, comprehensive exam, thesis or alternative, position paper or project. *Entrance requirements:* For master's, minimum GPA of 2.75. *Application deadline:* For fall admission, 4/1 priority date for domestic students; for spring admission, 10/15 priority date for domestic students. Applications are processed on a rolling basis. Application fee: $45. *Financial support:* Career-related internships or fieldwork, Federal Work-Study, institutionally sponsored loans, scholarships/grants, and tuition waivers (partial) available. Support available to part-time students. Financial award application deadline: 4/15; financial award applicants required to submit FAFSA. *Faculty research:* Multimedia technology, ethics in journalism, diversity, electronic portfolio assessment. *Unit head:* Dr. Martha Einerson, Program Coordinator, 715-394-8477, E-mail: meinerso@uwsuper.edu. *Application contact:* Sandy Wallgren, Program Assistant/Status Examiner, 715-394-8295, Fax: 715-394-8146, E-mail: swallgr1@uwsuper.edu.

University of Wisconsin–Whitewater, School of Graduate Studies, College of Arts and Communications, Department of Communication, Whitewater, WI 53190-1790. Offers corporate communication (MS); mass communication (MS). Part-time and evening/weekend programs available. Postbaccalaureate distance learning degree programs offered (no on-campus study). *Degree requirements:* For master's, thesis or alternative. *Entrance requirements:* For master's, 2 letters of recommendation. Additional exam requirements/recommendations for international students: Required—TOEFL (minimum score 550 paper-based; 213 computer-based). Electronic applications accepted.

University of Wyoming, College of Arts and Sciences, Department of Communication and Journalism, Laramie, WY 82070. Offers communication (MA). Part-time programs available. *Degree requirements:* For master's, thesis. *Entrance requirements:* For master's, GRE General Test, minimum GPA of 3.0. *Faculty research:* Personal relations, nonverbal behavior, media management, communication technology, conversation analysis.

Utah State University, School of Graduate Studies, College of Humanities, Arts and Social Sciences, Department of Journalism and Communication, Logan, UT 84322. Offers MA, MS. Part-time programs available. *Degree requirements:* For master's, comprehensive exam, thesis. *Entrance requirements:* For master's, GRE General Test or MAT, minimum GPA of 3.0. Additional exam requirements/recommendations for international students: Required—TOEFL. Electronic applications accepted. *Faculty research:* Race and gender and media, history of censorship, internet design and advertising, technology gap.

Valparaiso University, Graduate School, Program in Media and Communication, Valparaiso, IN 46383. Offers digital media (MS); sports media (MS). Part-time and evening/weekend programs available. *Students:* 10 full-time (6 women), 8 part-time (6 women); includes 1 minority (Asian American or Pacific Islander), 8 international. Average age 25. *Entrance requirements:* For master's, minimum GPA of 3.0, undergraduate minor in communication. Additional exam requirements/recommendations for international students: Required—TOEFL (minimum score 550 paper-based; 213 computer-based; 80 iBT). *Application deadline:* Applications are processed on a rolling basis. Application fee: $30 ($50 for international students). Electronic applications accepted. *Financial support:* Available to part-time students. Applicants required to submit FAFSA. *Unit head:* Dr. David L. Rowland, Dean, Graduate Studies and Continuing Education/Associate Provost, 219-464-5313, Fax: 219-464-5381, E-mail: david.rowland@valpo.edu. *Application contact:* Jamie Haney, Coordinator of Graduate Admission, 219-464-5313, Fax: 219-464-5381, E-mail: jamie.haney@valpo.edu.

Villanova University, Graduate School of Liberal Arts and Sciences, Department of Communication, Villanova, PA 19085-1699. Offers MA. Part-time and evening/weekend programs available. *Faculty:* 6 full-time (3 women). *Students:* 18 full-time (11 women), 31 part-time (22 women); includes 9 minority (6 African Americans, 2 Asian Americans or Pacific Islanders, 1 Hispanic American), 1 international. Average age 28. 15 applicants, 33% accepted, 0 enrolled. In 2009, 15 master's awarded. *Degree requirements:* For master's, comprehensive exam (for some programs), thesis optional. *Entrance requirements:* For master's, GRE or GMAT, minimum GPA of 3.0, writing sample, personal essay. Additional exam requirements/recommendations for international students: Required—TOEFL. *Application deadline:* For fall admission, 2/1 priority date for domestic and international students; for spring admission, 11/15 priority date for domestic and international students. Applications are processed on a rolling basis. Application fee: $50. Electronic applications accepted. *Expenses:* Tuition: Part-time $630 per credit. Required fees: $60 per credit. Part-time tuition and fees vary according to degree level and program. *Financial support:* Research assistantships, Federal Work-Study available. Financial award applicants required to submit FAFSA. *Unit head:* Dr. Emory Woodard, Director of Graduate Studies in Communication, 610-519-4780. *Application contact:* Dr. Emory Woodard, Director of Graduate Studies in Communication, 610-519-4780.

Virginia Commonwealth University, Graduate School, College of Humanities and Sciences, School of Mass Communications, Program in Media, Art, and Text, Richmond, VA 23284-9005. Offers PhD. *Entrance requirements:* For doctorate, GRE, MA, MAE, or MFA in appropriate field of study (English, art history, studio art, poetry, mass communications); 3 letters of recommendation.

Virginia Polytechnic Institute and State University, Graduate School, College of Liberal Arts and Human Sciences, Department of Communication, Blacksburg, VA 24061. Offers MA. *Faculty:* 24 full-time (9 women). *Students:* 16 full-time (12 women), 5 part-time (all women); includes 2 minority (1 American Indian/Alaska Native, 1 Asian American or Pacific Islander). Average age 26. 32 applicants, 44% accepted, 10 enrolled. In 2009, 10 master's awarded. *Entrance requirements:* For master's, GRE, GMAT. Additional exam requirements/recommendations for international students: Required—TOEFL (minimum score 550 paper-based; 213 computer-based). *Application deadline:* For fall admission, 5/15 for international students; for spring admission, 10/15 for international students. Applications are processed on a rolling basis. Application fee: $65. Electronic applications accepted. *Expenses:* Tuition, area resident: Full-time $10,228; part-time $459 per credit hour. Tuition, nonresident: full-time $17,892; part-time $865 per credit hour. Required fees: $1966; $451 per semester. *Financial support:* In 2009–10, 12 teaching assistantships with full tuition reimbursements (averaging $11,917 per year) were awarded; career-related internships or fieldwork, Federal Work-Study, scholarships/grants, and unspecified assistantships also available. Financial award application deadline: 1/15. *Unit head:* Dr. Robert E. Denton, Head, 540-231-7166, Fax: 540-231-9817, E-mail: rdenton@vt.edu. *Application contact:* Beth Waggenspack, Information Contact, 540-231-7625, Fax: 540-231-9817, E-mail: bwaggens@vt.edu.

Wake Forest University, Graduate School of Arts and Sciences, Department of Communication, Winston-Salem, NC 27109. Offers speech communication (MA). Part-time programs available. *Degree requirements:* For master's, one foreign language, thesis. *Entrance requirements:* For master's, GRE General Test, writing sample. Additional exam requirements/recommendations for international students: Required—TOEFL (minimum score 213 computer-based; 79 iBT). Electronic applications accepted.

Washington State University, Graduate School, College of Liberal Arts, Edward R. Murrow College of Communication, Pullman, WA 99164. Offers health communications (MA, PhD); intercultural and international communications (MA, PhD); media and society (MA, PhD); media process and effects (MA, PhD); organizational communications (MA, PhD). *Degree requirements:* For master's, comprehensive exam (for some programs), thesis optional, oral exam; for doctorate, comprehensive exam, thesis/dissertation. *Entrance requirements:* For master's, GRE General Test, minimum GPA of 3.25, 3 letters of recommendation; for doctorate, GRE General Test, minimum undergraduate GPA of 3.25, graduate 3.5; MA in communication; 3 letters of recommendation. Additional exam requirements/recommendations for international students: Required—TOEFL (minimum score 580 paper-based; 237 computer-based). Electronic applications accepted. *Faculty research:* Advocacy communication, mediated communication in decision making, communication technology policy and effects, multicultural and international psychology and physiology of communication.

Wayne State College, School of Education and Counseling, Department of Educational Foundations and Leadership, Program in Curriculum and Instruction, Wayne, NE 68787. Offers alternative education (MSE); business and information technology education (MSE); communication arts education (MSE); early childhood education (MSE); elementary education (MSE); English as a second language (MSE); English education (MSE); family and consumer sciences education (MSE); industrial technology and vocational education (MSE); learning communities (MSE); mathematics education (MSE); music education (MSE); science education (MSE); social science education (MSE). *Accreditation:* NCATE. Part-time and evening/weekend programs available. *Degree requirements:* For master's, comprehensive exam, thesis optional. *Entrance requirements:* For master's, GRE General Test. Additional exam requirements/recommendations for international students: Required—TOEFL (minimum score 550 paper-based; 213 computer-based).

Wayne State University, College of Fine, Performing and Communication Arts, Department of Communication, Detroit, MI 48202. Offers communication studies (MA, PhD); public relations and organizational communication (MA); radio-TV-film (MA, PhD); speech communication (MA, PhD). *Degree requirements:* For master's, thesis, essay, or comprehensive exam; for doctorate, thesis/dissertation. *Entrance requirements:* For master's, minimum GPA of 3.0, sample of academic writing; for doctorate, GRE, minimum GPA of 3.3, MA; letters of recommendation; personal statement; sample of written scholarship. Additional exam requirements/recommendations for international students: Required—TOEFL (minimum score 550 paper-based; 213 computer-based); Recommended—TWE (minimum score 6). Electronic applications accepted. *Faculty research:* Rhetorical theory and criticism; mass media theory and research; argumentation; organizational communication; risk and crisis communication; interpersonal, family, and health communication.

Webster University, School of Communications, St. Louis, MO 63119-3194. Offers MA. Part-time and evening/weekend programs available. Postbaccalaureate distance learning degree programs offered. *Faculty:* 8 full-time, 29 part-time/adjunct. *Students:* 55 full-time (35 women), 291 part-time (209 women); includes 128 minority (118 African Americans, 1 American Indian/Alaska Native, 3 Asian Americans or Pacific Islanders, 6 Hispanic Americans), 2 international. Average age 32. 100 applicants, 98% accepted, 71 enrolled. In 2009, 83 master's awarded. *Degree requirements:* For master's, thesis (for some programs). *Entrance requirements:* For master's, 36 hours of graduate course work. Additional exam requirements/recommendations for international students: Required—TOEFL. *Application deadline:* Applications are processed on a rolling basis. Application fee: $35 ($50 for international students). *Expenses:* Tuition: Part-time $565 per credit hour. Tuition and fees vary according to degree level, campus/location and program. *Financial support:* Career-related internships or fieldwork and Federal Work-Study available. Support available to part-time students. Financial award application deadline: 4/1; financial award applicants required to submit FAFSA. *Unit head:* Debra Carpenter, Dean, 314-968-7154, Fax: 314-963-6106, E-mail: carpenda@webster.edu. *Application contact:* Matt Nolan, Assoc. V.P.—Enrollment Management / Dean of Admissions, Fax: 314-968-7116, E-mail: gadmit@webster.edu.

West Chester University of Pennsylvania, Office of Graduate Studies, College of Arts and Sciences, Department of Communication Studies, West Chester, PA 19383. Offers communication studies (MA). Part-time and evening/weekend programs available. *Students:* 1 (woman) full-time, 30 part-time (24 women); includes 5 minority (2 African Americans, 2 Asian Americans or Pacific Islanders, 1 Hispanic American). Average age 26. 28 applicants, 100% accepted, 16 enrolled. In 2009, 8 master's awarded. *Degree requirements:* For master's, comprehensive exam, thesis optional. *Entrance requirements:* For master's, GRE or MAT, minimum overall GPA of 2.75, 3.0 in major; writing sample; 3 letters of reference. Additional exam requirements/recommendations for international students: Required—TOEFL (minimum score 550 paper-based; 213 computer-based; 80 iBT). *Application deadline:* For fall admission, 4/15 priority date for domestic students, 3/15 for international students; for spring admission, 10/15 for domestic students, 9/1 for international students. Applications are processed on a rolling basis. Application fee: $35. Electronic applications accepted. *Expenses:* Tuition, state resident: full-time $6666; part-time $370 per credit. Tuition, nonresident: full-time $10,666; part-time $593 per credit. Required fees: $122.56 per credit. *Financial support:* In 2009–10, 4 research assistantships with partial tuition reimbursements (averaging $5,000 per year) were awarded; unspecified assistantships also available. Support available to part-time students. Financial award application deadline: 2/15; financial award applicants required to submit FAFSA. *Faculty research:* Documentary of the Dalai Lama. *Unit head:* Dr. Timothy Brown, Chair, 610-436-2500, E-mail: tbrown@wcupa.edu. *Application contact:* Dr. Jack Orr, Graduate Coordinator, 610-436-2870, E-mail: jorr@wcupa.edu.

Western Illinois University, School of Graduate Studies, College of Fine Arts and Communication, Department of Communication, Macomb, IL 61455-1390. Offers MA. Part-time programs available. *Students:* 13 full-time (10 women), 10 part-time (6 women); includes 3 minority (1 African American, 1 Asian American or Pacific Islander, 1 Hispanic American), 3 international. Average age 30. 16 applicants, 56% accepted. In 2009, 11 master's awarded. *Degree requirements:* For master's, comprehensive exam (for some programs), thesis or alternative. *Entrance requirements:* Additional exam requirements/recommendations for international students: Required—TOEFL (minimum score 580 paper-based; 237 computer-based; 92 iBT). *Application deadline:* Applications are processed on a rolling basis. Application fee: $30. Electronic applications accepted. *Expenses:* Tuition, state resident: full-time $4486; part-time $249.21 per credit hour. Tuition, nonresident: full-time $8972; part-time $498.42 per credit hour. Required fees: $72.62 per credit hour. *Financial support:* In 2009–10, 11 students received support, including 5 research assistantships with full tuition reimbursements available (averaging $7,280 per year), 6 teaching assistantships with full tuition reimbursements available (averaging $8,400 per year). Financial award applicants required to submit FAFSA. *Unit head:* Dr. Lisa Miczo, Interim Chairperson, 309-298-1507. *Application contact:* Evelyn Hoing, Assistant Director of Graduate Studies, 309-298-1806, Fax: 309-298-2345, E-mail: grad-office@wiu.edu.

Western Kentucky University, Graduate Studies, Potter College of Arts and Letters, Department of Communication, Bowling Green, KY 42101. Offers communication (MA). Part-time and evening/weekend programs available. *Degree requirements:* For master's, comprehensive exam, thesis optional, final exam. *Entrance requirements:* For master's, GRE General Test, minimum GPA of 2.75. Additional exam requirements/recommendations for international students: Required—TOEFL (minimum score 555 paper-based; 213 computer-based; 79 iBT). *Expenses:* Tuition, state resident: full-time $4160; part-time $416 per credit hour. Tuition, nonresident: full-time $9550; part-time $506 per credit hour. Tuition and fees vary according to campus/location and reciprocity agreements. *Faculty research:* Public rhetoric and public address organization communication, teamwork in communication, intercultural crisis communication.

Western Michigan University, Graduate College, College of Arts and Sciences, Department of Communication, Kalamazoo, MI 49008. Offers MA.

Westminster College, Program in Professional Communication, Salt Lake City, UT 84105-3697. Offers MPC. Part-time and evening/weekend programs available. *Faculty:* 7 full-time (3 women), 6 part-time/adjunct (4 women). *Students:* 22 full-time (17 women), 53 part-time (31 women); includes 6 minority (2 American Indian/Alaska Native, 3 Asian Americans or Pacific Islanders, 1 Hispanic American), 2 international. Average age 34. 40 applicants, 55% accepted, 18 enrolled. In 2009, 13 master's awarded. *Degree requirements:* For master's, field project. *Entrance requirements:* For master's, resume, professional writing sample, 2 letters of recommendation. Additional exam requirements/recommendations for international students: Required—TOEFL (minimum score 600 paper-based; 250 computer-based; 100 iBT). *Application deadline:* For fall admission, 7/9 for domestic and international students. Applications are processed on a rolling basis. Application fee: $40. Electronic applications accepted. *Expenses:* Tuition: Part-time $555 per credit hour. Part-time tuition and fees vary according to program. *Financial support:* In 2009–10, 31 students received support. Career-related internships or fieldwork and tuition reimbursement, tuition remission available. Support available to part-time students. Financial award applicants required to submit FAFSA. *Faculty research:* Critical communication pedagogy, sexuality and gender, autoethnography, regulation of broadcast indecency, hypertext theory. *Unit head:* Dr. Helen Hodgson, Director, 801-832-2821, Fax: 801-832-3102, E-mail: hhodgson@westminstercollege.edu. *Application contact:* Joel Bauman, Vice President of Enrollment Services, 801-832-2200, Fax: 801-832-3101, E-mail: admission@westminstercollege.edu.

West Texas A&M University, College of Fine Arts and Humanities, Department of Art, Communication, and Theater, Program in Communication, Canyon, TX 79016-0001. Offers MA. Part-time programs available. *Degree requirements:* For master's, comprehensive exam, thesis optional. *Entrance requirements:* For master's, GRE General Test, 24 hours of undergraduate communications courses, 1 letter of recommendation, interview with communication advisor. Additional exam requirements/recommendations for international students: Required—TOEFL (minimum score 550 paper-based). Electronic applications accepted. *Faculty research:* Comparison student learning in basic public speaking in traditional versus online format, impact of supervisor immediacy and power on organizational outcomes, storytelling, gender, nonverbal.

West Virginia University, Eberly College of Arts and Sciences, Department of Communication Studies, Morgantown, WV 26506. Offers communication in instruction (MA); communication studies (PhD); communication theory and research (MA); corporate and organizational communication (MA). Part-time programs available. *Degree requirements:* For master's, comprehensive exam (for some programs), thesis (for some programs); for doctorate, comprehensive exam, thesis/dissertation. *Entrance requirements:* For master's and doctorate, minimum GPA of 3.0. Additional exam requirements/recommendations for international students: Required—TOEFL. Electronic applications accepted. *Faculty research:* Instructional communication, interpersonal communication, health communication, influence, instructional communication, social influence.

West Virginia University, Perley Isaac Reed School of Journalism, Program in Integrated Marketing Communications, Morgantown, WV 26506. Offers MS. Part-time programs available. Postbaccalaureate distance learning degree programs offered (no on-campus study). *Entrance requirements:* For master's, GRE or GMAT. Additional exam requirements/recommendations for international students: Required—TOEFL.

Wichita State University, Graduate School, Fairmount College of Liberal Arts and Sciences, Elliot School of Communication, Wichita, KS 67260. Offers MA. Part-time programs available. *Expenses:* Tuition, state resident: full-time $4247; part-time $235.95 per credit hour. Tuition, nonresident: full-time $11,171; part-time $620.60 per credit hour. Required fees: $34; $3.60 per credit hour. $17 per term. Tuition and fees vary according to campus/location and program. *Unit head:* Dr. Susan Huxman, Director, 316-978-3185, Fax: 316-978-3006, E-mail: susan.huxman@wichita.edu. *Application contact:* Dr. Susan Huxman, Director, 316-978-3185, Fax: 316-978-3006, E-mail: susan.huxman@wichita.edu.

Wilfrid Laurier University, Faculty of Graduate Studies, Faculty of Arts, Department of Communication Studies, Waterloo, ON N2L 3C5, Canada. Offers MA. *Degree requirements:* For master's, thesis optional. *Entrance requirements:* For master's, honours BA in communication studies or a cognate discipline from an approved university with a minimum B+ overall in last two years of study and in undergraduate major. Additional exam requirements/recommendations for international students: Required—TOEFL (minimum score 230 computer-based; 89 iBT). Electronic applications accepted. *Faculty research:* Visual communication and culture, media, technology and culture.

Communication—General

William Paterson University of New Jersey, College of the Arts and Communication, Wayne, NJ 07470-8420. Offers art (MFA); music (MM); professional communication (MA). Part-time and evening/weekend programs available. *Students:* 27 full-time (11 women), 28 part-time (11 women); includes 3 minority (1 African American, 1 Asian American or Pacific Islander, 1 Hispanic American), 4 international. *Entrance requirements:* For master's, minimum GPA of 2.75. *Application deadline:* Applications are processed on a rolling basis. Application fee: $50. Electronic applications accepted. *Financial support:* In 2009–10, 3 students received support; research assistantships with full tuition reimbursements available, career-related internships or fieldwork, Federal Work-Study, and unspecified assistantships available. Support available to part-time students. Financial award application deadline: 4/1; financial award applicants required to submit FAFSA. *Unit head:* Dr. Raymond Torres-Santos, Dean, College of Arts and Communication, 973-720-2232, E-mail: torressantosr@wpunj.edu. *Application contact:* Christina Aiello, Assistant Director, Graduate Admissions, 973-720-2506, Fax: 973-720-2035, E-mail: aielloc@wpunj.edu.

York University, Faculty of Graduate Studies, Program in Communication and Culture, Toronto, ON M3J 1P3, Canada. Offers MA, PhD. *Degree requirements:* For master's, thesis or alternative; for doctorate, comprehensive exam, thesis/dissertation. Electronic applications accepted.

Arts Journalism

School of the Art Institute of Chicago, Graduate Division, Program in New Arts Journalism, Chicago, IL 60603-3103. Offers MA. *Entrance requirements:* Additional exam requirements/recommendations for international students: Required—TOEFL, IELTS.

Syracuse University, S. I. Newhouse School of Public Communications, Program in Arts Journalism, Syracuse, NY 13244. Offers MA. *Students:* 20 full-time (13 women); includes 2 minority (1 African American, 1 Hispanic American), 2 international. Average age 24. 45 applicants, 64% accepted, 20 enrolled. In 2009, 1 master's awarded. *Degree requirements:* For master's, capstone project. *Entrance requirements:* For master's, GRE General Test. Additional exam requirements/recommendations for international students: Required—TOEFL (minimum score 600 paper-based; 250 computer-based; 100 iBT). *Application deadline:* For fall admission, 2/1 priority date for domestic and international students. Application fee: $45. Electronic applications accepted. *Expenses:* Tuition: Full-time $26,808; part-time $1117 per credit. Required fees: $1024. *Financial support:* Fellowships with tuition reimbursements, research assistantships with tuition reimbursements, teaching assistantships with tuition reimbursements, tuition waivers (partial) available. Financial award application deadline: 2/1; financial award applicants required to submit FAFSA. *Unit head:* Johanna Keller, Director, 315-443-9251, Fax: 315-443-3946, E-mail: pcgrad@syr.edu. *Application contact:* Martha Coria, Graduate Records Office, 315-443-5749, Fax: 315-443-1834, E-mail: pcgrad@syr.edu.

Broadcast Journalism

American University, School of Communication, Program in Journalism and Public Affairs, Washington, DC 20016-8001. Offers broadcast journalism (MA), including economic communication, international journalism, public policy journalism; interactive journalism (MA); news media studies (MA); print journalism (MA), including economic communication, international journalism, public policy journalism. *Accreditation:* ACEJMC. Part-time and evening/weekend programs available. *Faculty:* 13 full-time (5 women), 4 part-time/adjunct (all women). *Students:* 24 full-time (16 women). 190 applicants, 63% accepted. In 2009, 40 master's awarded. *Degree requirements:* For master's, comprehensive exam, thesis or alternative. *Entrance requirements:* For master's, GRE General Test. Additional exam requirements/recommendations for international students: Required—TOEFL (minimum score 600 paper-based; 250 computer-based). *Application deadline:* For fall admission, 2/1 priority date for domestic students, 4/1 priority date for international students. Applications are processed on a rolling basis. Application fee: $50. Electronic applications accepted. *Expenses:* Tuition: Full-time $22,266; part-time $1237 per credit hour. Required fees: $430. Tuition and fees vary according to program. *Financial support:* In 2009–10, 3 fellowships with partial tuition reimbursements (averaging $27,000 per year), 14 research assistantships with tuition reimbursements (averaging $7,000 per year), 3 teaching assistantships with tuition reimbursements (averaging $7,000 per year) were awarded; career-related internships or fieldwork, Federal Work-Study, institutionally sponsored loans, scholarships/grants, tuition waivers (partial), and unspecified assistantships also available. Financial award application deadline: 2/1. *Faculty research:* Government and media effects of journalistic practices and policies, race and gender and the media, investigative reporting, computer assisted reporting. *Unit head:* Wendell Cochran, Division Director, 202-885-2075. *Application contact:* Sharmeen Ahsan-Bracciale, Graduate Admissions Office, 202-885-2040, Fax: 202-885-2019, E-mail: sharmeen@american.edu.

See Close-Up on page 673.

The American University in Cairo, Graduate Studies and Research, School of Business, Economics and Communication, Department of Journalism and Mass Communication, Cairo, Egypt. Offers journalism and mass communication (MA); television and digital journalism (MA). Part-time programs available. *Degree requirements:* For master's, thesis (for some programs). *Entrance requirements:* For master's, English entrance exam, GMAT. Electronic applications accepted. *Faculty research:* Mass media and national development/censorship, intercultural photo communication, comparative journalism/television.

Boston University, College of Communication, Department of Journalism, Boston, MA 02215. Offers broadcast journalism (MS); business and economics journalism (MS); photojournalism (MS); print journalism (MS); science journalism (MS). Part-time programs available. *Faculty:* 23 full-time, 26 part-time/adjunct. *Students:* 94 full-time (67 women), 9 part-time (6 women); includes 14 minority (3 African Americans, 1 American Indian/Alaska Native, 9 Asian Americans or Pacific Islanders, 1 Hispanic American), 20 international. Average age 26. In 2009, 72 master's awarded. *Degree requirements:* For master's, thesis. *Entrance requirements:* For master's, GRE General Test, sample of written work. Additional exam requirements/recommendations for international students: Required—TOEFL (minimum score 600 paper-based; 250 computer-based; 100 iBT). *Application deadline:* For fall admission, 2/1 for domestic and international students. Application fee: $70. Electronic applications accepted. *Expenses:* Tuition: Full-time $37,910; part-time $1184 per credit hour. Required fees: $386; $40 per semester. Part-time tuition and fees vary according to class time, course level, degree level and program. *Financial support:* Teaching assistantships with partial tuition reimbursements, career-related internships or fieldwork, Federal Work-Study, institutionally sponsored loans, scholarships/grants, and unspecified assistantships available. Support available to part-time students. Financial award application deadline: 2/1; financial award applicants required to submit FAFSA. *Unit head:* Lou Ureneck, Chairman, 617-353-3484, Fax: 617-353-1086, E-mail: lureneck@bu.edu. *Application contact:* Kate Iserman, Administrator of Graduate Services, 617-353-3481, Fax: 617-358-0399, E-mail: comgrad@bu.edu.

See Close-Up on page 675.

Emerson College, Graduate Studies, School of Communication, Department of Journalism, Boston, MA 02116-4624. Offers journalism (MA), including broadcast journalism, print/multimedia journalism. *Faculty:* 15 full-time (5 women), 5 part-time/adjunct (1 woman). *Students:* 66 full-time (47 women), 3 part-time (all women); includes 7 minority (3 African Americans, 2 Asian Americans or Pacific Islanders, 2 Hispanic Americans), 8 international. Average age 24. 101 applicants, 86% accepted, 35 enrolled. In 2009, 32 master's awarded. *Entrance requirements:* For master's, GRE General Test. Additional exam requirements/recommendations for international students: Required—TOEFL (minimum score 550 paper-based; 213 computer-based; 80 iBT), IELTS (minimum score 6.5). *Application deadline:* For fall admission, 6/1 priority date for domestic students, 5/1 priority date for international students. Applications are processed on a rolling basis. Application fee: $60 ($75 for international students). Electronic applications accepted. *Expenses:* Tuition: Full-time $22,056; part-time $919 per credit. Required fees: $120; $120 per year. One-time fee: $170 full-time. *Financial support:* In 2009–10, 18 students received support, including 5 fellowships with partial tuition reimbursements available (averaging $14,000 per year), 9 research assistantships with partial tuition reimbursements available (averaging $10,000 per year); Federal Work-Study, scholarships/grants, and unspecified assistantships also available. Financial award application deadline: 3/1; financial award applicants required to submit FAFSA. *Faculty research:* Journalism. *Unit head:* Prof. Ted Gup, Chair, 617-824-8805, E-mail: ted_gup@emerson.edu. *Application contact:* Office of Graduate Admission, 617-824-8610, Fax: 617-824-8614, E-mail: gradapp@emerson.edu.

Northwestern University, Medill School of Journalism, Evanston, IL 60208. Offers broadcast journalism (MSJ); integrated marketing communications (MSIMC), including advertising/sales promotion, direct database and e-commerce marketing, general studies, public relations; magazine publishing (MSJ); new media (MSJ); reporting and writing (MSJ). *Accreditation:* ACEJMC (one or more programs are accredited). *Entrance requirements:* For master's, GRE General Test, GMAT or LSAT (MSJ). Additional exam requirements/recommendations for international students: Required—TOEFL. Electronic applications accepted. *Expenses:* Contact institution. *Faculty research:* Web business journalism, cultural stereotypes, voter apathy, digital television.

Syracuse University, S. I. Newhouse School of Public Communications, Program in Broadcast Journalism, Syracuse, NY 13244. Offers MS. *Students:* 31 full-time (18 women), 1 (woman) part-time; includes 13 minority (8 African Americans, 4 Asian Americans or Pacific Islanders, 1 Hispanic American), 2 international. Average age 23. 105 applicants, 70% accepted, 31 enrolled. In 2009, 33 master's awarded. *Degree requirements:* For master's, capstone course. *Entrance requirements:* For master's, GRE General Test. Additional exam requirements/recommendations for international students: Required—TOEFL (minimum score 100 iBT). *Application deadline:* For fall admission, 2/1 priority date for domestic and international students. Application fee: $45. Electronic applications accepted. *Expenses:* Tuition: Full-time $26,808; part-time $1117 per credit. Required fees: $1024. *Financial support:* Fellowships with tuition reimbursements, research assistantships with tuition reimbursements, teaching assistantships with tuition reimbursements, tuition waivers (partial) available. Financial award application deadline: 2/1. *Unit head:* Dona Hayes, Chair, 315-443-1944, Fax: 315-443-3946, E-mail: pcgrad@syr.edu. *Application contact:* Martha Coria, Graduate Records Office, 315-443-5749, Fax: 315-443-1834, E-mail: pcgrad@syr.edu.

See Display on page 622 and Close-Up on page 683.

University of Maryland, College Park, Academic Affairs, Phillip Merrill College of Journalism, College Park, MD 20742. Offers broadcast journalism (MA); journalism (MA); journalism and media studies (PhD); online news (MA); public affairs reporting (MA). *Accreditation:* ACEJMC (one or more programs are accredited). Part-time and evening/weekend programs available. *Faculty:* 22 full-time (11 women), 40 part-time/adjunct (15 women). *Students:* 75 full-time (46 women), 10 part-time (5 women); includes 19 minority (13 African Americans, 5 Asian Americans or Pacific Islanders, 1 Hispanic American), 12 international. 250 applicants, 36% accepted, 27 enrolled. In 2009, 25 master's, 5 doctorates awarded. *Degree requirements:* For doctorate, thesis/dissertation, preliminary written and oral comprehensive exams. *Entrance requirements:* For master's and doctorate, GRE General Test, minimum GPA of 3.0, 3 letters of recommendation. Additional exam requirements/recommendations for international students: Required—TOEFL. *Application deadline:* For fall admission, 2/1 for domestic and international students. Applications are processed on a rolling basis. Application fee: $60. Electronic applications accepted. *Expenses:* Tuition, area resident: Part-time $471 per credit hour. Tuition, state resident: part-time $471 per credit hour. Tuition, nonresident: part-time $1016 per credit hour. Required fees: $337.04 per term. *Financial support:* In 2009–10, 6 fellowships with full and partial tuition reimbursements (averaging $15,296 per year), 1 research assistantship with tuition reimbursement (averaging $15,266 per year), 19 teaching assistantships with tuition reimbursements (averaging $16,778 per year) were awarded; career-related internships or fieldwork, Federal Work-Study, and scholarships/grants also available. Support available to part-time students. Financial award applicants required to submit FAFSA. *Faculty research:* Mass communication theory, specialized journalism, new telecommunication technologies, press integration. Total annual research expenditures: $642,886. *Unit head:* Kevin Klose, Dean, 301-405-2393, E-mail: kklose@umd.edu. *Application contact:* Dean of Graduate School, 301-405-0376, Fax: 301-314-9305.

University of Miami, Graduate School, School of Communication, Coral Gables, FL 33124. Offers communication (PhD); communication studies (MA); film studies (MA, PhD); motion pictures (MFA), including production, producing, and screenwriting; print journalism (MA); public relations (MA); Spanish language journalism (MA); television broadcast journalism (MA). *Accreditation:* ACEJMC. Part-time programs available. *Degree requirements:* For master's, comprehensive exam (for some programs), thesis (for some programs); for doctorate, comprehensive exam, thesis/dissertation. *Entrance requirements:* For master's, GRE General Test; for doctorate, GRE General Test, master's thesis or scholarly research. Additional exam requirements/recommendations for international students: Required—TOEFL (minimum score 600 paper-based; 250 computer-based; 100 iBT). Electronic applications accepted. *Faculty research:* Communication studies, mass communication, international/interpersonal communication, film studies, journalism.

University of Southern California, Graduate School, Annenberg School for Communication and Journalism, School of Journalism, Program in Broadcast Journalism, Los Angeles, CA 90089. Offers MA. *Degree requirements:* For master's, comprehensive exam. *Entrance requirements:* For master's, GRE General Test, resume, writing samples, letters of recommendation, statement of purpose. Additional exam requirements/recommendations for international students: Required—TOEFL (minimum score 280 computer-based; 114 iBT). Electronic applications accepted. *Expenses:* Tuition: Full-time $25,980; part-time $1315 per unit. Required fees: $554. One-time fee: $35 full-time. Full-time tuition and fees vary according to degree level and program.

See Display on page 629 and Close-Up on page 685.

University of the Sacred Heart, Graduate Programs, Department of Communication, San Juan, PR 00914-0383. Offers contemporary culture and media (MA); digital journalism (Certificate); editing for media (MA, Certificate); public relations (MA, Certificate); publicity (MA, Certificate); scriptwriting (MA, Certificate). Part-time and evening/weekend programs available. *Degree requirements:* For master's, thesis.

Corporate and Organizational Communication

American International College, School of Business Administration, MBA Program, Springfield, MA 01109-3189. Offers accounting (MBA); corporate/public communication (MBA); finance (MBA); general business (MBA); hospitality, hotel and service management (MBA); international business (MBA); international business practice (MBA); management (MBA); management information systems (MBA); marketing (MBA). International business practice program developed in cooperation with the Mountbatten Institute. *Expenses:* Tuition: Full-time $12,510; part-time $695 per credit hour. Required fees: $35 per term.

The American University of Athens, The School of Graduate Studies, Athens, Greece. Offers biomedical sciences (MS); business (MBA); business communication (MA); computer sciences (MS); engineering and applied sciences (MS); politics and policy making (MA); systems engineering (MS); telecommunications (MS). *Entrance requirements:* For master's, resum&e, 2 recommendation letters. Additional exam requirements/recommendations for international students: Required—TOEFL (minimum score 550 paper-based; 213 computer-based). *Faculty research:* Nanotechnology, environmental sciences, rock mechanics, human skin studies, Monte Carlo algorithms and software.

Antioch University Seattle, Graduate Programs, Center for Creative Change, Seattle, WA 98121-1814. Offers environment and community (MA); management (MS); organizational psychology (MA); strategic communications (MA); whole system design (MA). Evening/weekend programs available. Electronic applications accepted. *Expenses:* Contact institution.

Argosy University, Schaumburg, College of Business, Schaumburg, IL 60173-5403. Offers accounting (DBA, Adv C); customized professional concentration (MBA, DBA); finance (MBA, Certificate); fraud examination (MBA); global business sustainability (DBA); healthcare administration (MBA, Certificate); information systems (DBA, Adv C, Certificate); information systems management (MBA); international business (MBA, DBA, Adv C, Certificate); management (MBA, MSM, DBA, Adv C, Certificate); marketing (MBA, DBA, Adv C, Certificate); organizational leadership (Ed D); public administration (MBA); sustainable management (MBA).

Barry University, School of Arts and Sciences, Department of Communication, Miami Shores, FL 33161-6695. Offers broadcasting (Certificate); communication (MA), including broadcast communication, public relations and corporate communications; organizational communication (MS). Part-time and evening/weekend programs available. *Degree requirements:* For master's, thesis (for some programs). *Entrance requirements:* For master's, GRE General Test, MAT, minimum GPA of 3.0. Electronic applications accepted. *Faculty research:* Organizational communication, broadcast communication, intercultural communication, advertising, leadership.

Bernard M. Baruch College of the City University of New York, Weissman School of Arts and Sciences, Program in Corporate Communication, New York, NY 10010-5585. Offers MA.

Bowie State University, Graduate Programs, Program in Organizational Communication, Bowie, MD 20715-9465. Offers MA, Certificate. Part-time and evening/weekend programs available. *Degree requirements:* For master's, comprehensive exam, thesis optional, research paper. *Entrance requirements:* For master's, minimum GPA of 2.5. Electronic applications accepted. *Faculty research:* International telecommunications, developmental communications.

California State University, San Bernardino, Graduate Studies, College of Arts and Letters, Department of Communication Studies, San Bernardino, CA 92407-2397. Offers communication studies (MA); integrated marketing communication (MA). *Faculty:* 5 full-time (3 women), 3 part-time/adjunct (1 woman). *Students:* 30 full-time (20 women), 14 part-time (12 women); includes 18 minority (6 African Americans, 12 Hispanic Americans), 15 international. Average age 30. 92 applicants, 66% accepted. In 2009, 18 master's awarded. *Degree requirements:* For master's, comprehensive exam, advancement to candidacy. *Entrance requirements:* Additional exam requirements/recommendations for international students: Required—TOEFL. *Application deadline:* For fall admission, 8/31 priority date for domestic students. Application fee: $55. *Unit head:* Dr. Mo Bahk, Chair, 909-537-5820, Fax: 909-537-7009, E-mail: mbahk@csusb.edu. *Application contact:* Olivia Rosas, Director of Admissions, 909-537-7577, Fax: 909-537-7034, E-mail: orosas@csusb.edu.

Canisius College, Graduate Division, College of Arts and Sciences, Department of Communication and Leadership, Buffalo, NY 14208-1098. Offers MS. Part-time and evening/weekend programs available. *Faculty:* 10 full-time (4 women), 2 part-time/adjunct (1 woman). *Students:* 11 full-time (6 women), 34 part-time (25 women); includes 8 minority (4 African Americans, 1 Asian American or Pacific Islander, 3 Hispanic Americans), 1 international. Average age 30. 24 applicants, 71% accepted, 13 enrolled. In 2009, 13 master's awarded. *Degree requirements:* For master's, thesis. *Entrance requirements:* For master's, GRE General Test or GMAT. *Application deadline:* For fall admission, 7/15 priority date for domestic students; for spring admission, 4/15 priority date for domestic students. Applications are processed on a rolling basis. Application fee: $25. Electronic applications accepted. *Financial support:* In 2009–10, 1 research assistantship with tuition reimbursement was awarded. *Unit head:* Dr. Rosanne L. Hartman, Director, 716-888-2589, Fax: 716-888-3118, E-mail: hartmanr@canisius.edu. *Application contact:* Dr. Rosanne L. Hartman, Director, Communication and Leadership, 716-888-2589, Fax: 716-888-3118, E-mail: hartmanr@canisius.edu.

Carnegie Mellon University, College of Humanities and Social Sciences, Department of English, Program in Professional Writing, Pittsburgh, PA 15213-3891. Offers editing and publishing (MAPW); policy and non-profit communication (MAPW); public and media relations / corporate communications (MAPW); science or healthcare communication (MAPW); technical writing (MAPW); writing for new media (MAPW); writing for print media (MAPW). Part-time programs available. *Entrance requirements:* For master's, GRE General Test. Additional exam requirements/recommendations for international students: Required—TOEFL, TWE.

Central Connecticut State University, School of Graduate Studies, School of Arts and Sciences, Department of Communication, New Britain, CT 06050-4010. Offers organizational communication (MS); public relations/promotions (Certificate). Part-time and evening/weekend programs available. *Faculty:* 12 full-time (4 women), 8 part-time/adjunct (2 women). *Students:* 10 full-time (5 women), 23 part-time (13 women); includes 7 minority (4 African Americans, 1 Asian American or Pacific Islander, 2 Hispanic Americans), 1 international. Average age 29. 30 applicants, 50% accepted, 15 enrolled. In 2009, 9 master's awarded. *Degree requirements:* For master's, comprehensive exam, thesis or alternative; for Certificate, qualifying exam. *Entrance requirements:* For master's, minimum undergraduate GPA of 3.0. Additional exam requirements/recommendations for international students: Required—TOEFL. *Application deadline:* For fall admission, 7/1 for domestic students; for spring admission, 12/1 for domestic students. Applications are processed on a rolling basis. Application fee: $50. Electronic applications accepted. *Expenses:* Tuition, area resident: Full-time $4662; part-time $440 per credit. Tuition, state resident: full-time $6994; part-time $440 per credit. Tuition, nonresident: full-time $12,988; part-time $440 per credit. Required fees: $3606. One-time fee: $62 part-time. *Financial support:* In 2009–10, 5 students received support, including 1 research assistantship; career-related internships or fieldwork, Federal Work-Study, scholarships/grants, and unspecified assistantships also available. Support available to part-time students. Financial award application deadline: 3/1; financial award applicants required to submit FAFSA. *Faculty research:* Organizational communication, mass communication, intercultural communication, political communication, information management. *Unit head:* Dr. Serafin Mendez-Mendez, Chair, 860-832-2690. *Application contact:* Dr. Serafin Mendez-Mendez, Chair, 860-832-2690.

Central Michigan University, College of Graduate Studies, Interdisciplinary Administration Programs, Mount Pleasant, MI 48859. Offers acquisitions administration (MSA, Graduate Certificate); general administration (MSA, Graduate Certificate); health services administration (MSA, Graduate Certificate); human resource administration (Graduate Certificate); human resources administration (MSA); information resource management (MSA, Graduate Certificate); international administration (MSA, Graduate Certificate); leadership (MSA); organizational communication (MSA, Graduate Certificate); public administration (MSA, Graduate Certificate); recreation and park administration (MSA); sport administration (MSA). *Accreditation:* AACSB. Part-time and evening/weekend programs available. Postbaccalaureate distance learning degree programs offered (no on-campus study). *Degree requirements:* For master's, thesis or alternative. *Entrance requirements:* For master's, bachelor's degree with minimum GPA of 2.7. Electronic applications accepted. *Faculty research:* Interdisciplinary studies in acquisitions administration, health services administration, sport administration, recreation and park administration, and international administration.

College of Charleston, Graduate School, School of Humanities and Social Sciences, Program in Organizational and Corporate Communication, Charleston, SC 29424-0001. Offers Certificate. *Faculty:* 21 full-time (10 women). *Students:* 8 part-time (5 women); includes 1 minority (African American). Average age 29. 4 applicants, 100% accepted, 0 enrolled. In 2009, 4 Certificates awarded. *Entrance requirements:* For degree, minimum GPA of 2.5. Additional exam requirements/recommendations for international students: Required—TOEFL. *Application deadline:* For fall admission, 4/1 for domestic students; for spring admission, 11/1 for domestic students. Application fee: $45. Electronic applications accepted. *Unit head:* Dr. Vincent Benigni, Director, 844-983-7017, E-mail: benigniv@cofc.edu. *Application contact:* Susan Hallatt, Director of Graduate Admissions, 843-953-5614, Fax: 843-953-1434, E-mail: hallatts@cofc.edu.

Columbia University, Graduate School of Business, MBA Program, New York, NY 10027. Offers accounting (MBA); decision, risk, and operations (MBA); entrepreneurship (MBA); finance and economics (MBA); healthcare and pharmaceutical management (MBA); human resource management (MBA); international business (MBA); leadership and ethics (MBA); management (MBA); marketing (MBA); media (MBA); private equity (MBA); real estate (MBA); social enterprise (MBA); value investing (MBA); DDS/MBA; JD/MBA; MBA/MIA; MBA/MPH; MBA/MS; MD/MBA. *Faculty:* 149 full-time (23 women), 134 part-time/adjunct (16 women). *Students:* 1,293 full-time (435 women); includes 235 minority (65 African Americans, 4 American Indian/Alaska Native, 135 Asian Americans or Pacific Islanders, 31 Hispanic Americans), 417 international. Average age 28. 6,885 applicants, 15% accepted, 737 enrolled. In 2009, 696 master's awarded. *Entrance requirements:* For master's, GMAT, 2 letters of recommendation. Additional exam requirements/recommendations for international students: Required—TOEFL. *Application deadline:* For fall admission, 4/14 for domestic students, 3/3 for international students; for spring admission, 10/7 for domestic and international students. Applications are processed on a rolling basis. Application fee: $250. Electronic applications accepted. *Expenses:* Contact institution. *Financial support:* In 2009–10, 358 students received support, including 101 fellowships (averaging $23,250 per year); research assistantships, teaching assistantships, career-related internships or fieldwork, institutionally sponsored loans, and scholarships/grants also available. Financial award application deadline: 3/1; financial award applicants required to submit CSS PROFILE or FAFSA. *Faculty research:* Human decision making and behavioral research; real estate market and mortgage defaults; financial crisis and corporate governance; international business; security analysis and accounting. *Unit head:* Prof. Amir Ziv, Vice Dean of Students and the MBA Program, 212-854-3485, Fax: 212-932-0545, E-mail: az50@columbia.edu. *Application contact:* Mary J. Miller, Assistant Dean of Admissions, 212-854-1961, Fax: 212-662-6754, E-mail: apply@gsb.columbia.edu.

Columbia University, School of Continuing Education, Program in Strategic Communications, New York, NY 10027. Offers MS. Part-time and evening/weekend programs available. *Faculty:* 1 (woman) full-time, 39 part-time/adjunct (19 women). *Students:* 1 (woman) full-time, 108 part-time (79 women); includes 29 minority (9 African Americans, 14 Asian Americans or Pacific Islanders, 6 Hispanic Americans), 8 international. Average age 33. 69 applicants, 54% accepted, 25 enrolled. In 2009, 14 master's awarded. *Entrance requirements:* For master's, minumum undergraduate GPA of 3.0. Additional exam requirements/recommendations for international students: Required—American Language Program placement test. *Application deadline:* For fall admission, 4/15 priority date for domestic students. Applications are processed on a rolling basis. Application fee: $50. Electronic applications accepted. *Financial support:* Institutionally sponsored loans available. Financial award applicants required to submit FAFSA. *Faculty research:* Marketing communications, public relations, crisis management. *Unit head:* Trudi Baldwin, Director, 212-854-0541, Fax: 212-854-5861, E-mail: tb293@columbia.edu. *Application contact:* Bryce Weinert, Admissions Adviser, 212-854-9666, E-mail: sce-apply@columbia.edu.

Concordia University Wisconsin, Graduate Programs, School of Business and Legal Studies, MBA Program, Mequon, WI 53097-2402. Offers finance (MBA); health care administration (MBA); human resource management (MBA); international business (MBA); international business-bilingual English/Chinese (MBA); management (MBA); management information systems (MBA); managerial communications (MBA); marketing (MBA); public administration (MBA); risk management (MBA). Postbaccalaureate distance learning degree programs offered (minimal on-campus study). *Degree requirements:* For master's, comprehensive exam, thesis or alternative. *Entrance requirements:* Additional exam requirements/recommendations for international students: Required—TOEFL. *Expenses:* Contact institution.

Corporate and Organizational Communication

Dallas Baptist University, College of Business, Business Administration Program, Dallas, TX 75211-9299. Offers accounting (MBA); business communication (MBA); conflict resolution management (MBA); e-business (MBA); entrepreneurship (MBA); finance (MBA); health care management (MBA); international business (MBA); leading the non-profit organization (MBA); management (MBA); management information systems (MBA); marketing (MBA); project management (MBA); technology and engineering management (MBA). *Accreditation:* ACBSP. Part-time and evening/weekend programs available. *Entrance requirements:* For master's, GMAT, minimum GPA of 3.0. Additional exam requirements/recommendations for international students: Required—TOEFL, IELTS. Electronic applications accepted. *Expenses:* Tuition: Full-time $10,674; part-time $593 per credit hour. *Faculty research:* Sports management, services marketing, retailing, strategic management, financial planning/investments.

Dallas Baptist University, College of Business, Management Program, Dallas, TX 75211-9299. Offers business communication (MA); conflict resolution management (MA); general management (MA); health care management (MA); human resource management (MA); performance management (MA). Part-time and evening/weekend programs available. *Entrance requirements:* For master's, GRE General Test, minimum GPA of 3.0. Additional exam requirements/recommendations for international students: Required—TOEFL, IELTS. Electronic applications accepted. *Expenses:* Tuition: Full-time $10,674; part-time $593 per credit hour. *Faculty research:* Organizational behavior, conflict personalities.

Dallas Baptist University, Gary Cook School of Leadership, Program in Global Leadership, Dallas, TX 75211-9299. Offers business communication (MA); Christian education/missions (MA); ESL (MA); general studies (MA); global studies (MA); international business (MA); missions (MA); worship/missions (MA). Part-time and evening/weekend programs available. *Entrance requirements:* For master's, minimum GPA of 3.0. Additional exam requirements/recommendations for international students: Required—TOEFL, IELTS. *Expenses:* Tuition: Full-time $10,674; part-time $593 per credit hour.

DePaul University, College of Communication, Chicago, IL 60614. Offers journalism (MA); media, culture and society (MA); organizational and multicultural communication (MA); public relations and advertising (MA). Part-time and evening/weekend programs available. *Faculty:* 31 full-time (17 women), 15 part-time/adjunct (7 women). *Students:* 159 full-time (127 women), 50 part-time (40 women); includes 56 minority (29 African Americans, 9 Asian Americans or Pacific Islanders, 18 Hispanic Americans), 11 international. Average age 29. 354 applicants, 44% accepted, 79 enrolled. In 2009, 64 master's awarded. *Degree requirements:* For master's, comprehensive exam (for some programs), final exam or thesis/project. *Entrance requirements:* For master's, GRE General Test (public relations and advertising), minimum GPA of 3.0, writing sample, letters of recommendation, resume. Additional exam requirements/recommendations for international students: Required—TOEFL (minimum score 590 paper-based; 243 computer-based; 96 iBT). Application fee: $40. Electronic applications accepted. *Expenses:* Tuition: Full-time $37,525; part-time $620 per credit hour. *Financial support:* In 2009–10, 8 students received support, including 4 research assistantships with partial tuition reimbursements available, 2 teaching assistantships with full tuition reimbursements available (averaging $12,000 per year); fellowships with full tuition reimbursements available, career-related internships or fieldwork, scholarships/grants, and tuition waivers (partial) also available. Support available to part-time students. Financial award applicants required to submit FAFSA. *Faculty research:* Intercultural communication, corporate culture, diversity in the working place, organizational socialization, critical cultural studies. *Unit head:* Dr. Jacqueline Taylor, Dean, 773-325-7216, Fax: 773-325-7584, E-mail: jtaylor@depaul.edu. *Application contact:* Ann Spittle, Director of Graduate Admission, 773-325-7315, Fax: 773-325-2395, E-mail: gradcom@depaul.edu.

Drexel University, College of Arts and Sciences, Department of Culture and Communication, Program in Communication, Philadelphia, PA 19104-2875. Offers public communication (MS); science communication (MS); technical communication (MS). Part-time and evening/weekend programs available. *Degree requirements:* For master's, internship, professional portfolio. *Entrance requirements:* For master's, GRE or minimum GPA of 3.0. Additional exam requirements/recommendations for international students: Required—TOEFL. Electronic applications accepted.

Emerson College, Graduate Studies, School of Communication, Department of Communication Studies, Program in Communication Management, Boston, MA 02116-4624. Offers MA. Part-time and evening/weekend programs available. *Faculty:* 19 full-time (9 women). *Students:* 42 full-time (30 women), 11 part-time (7 women); includes 3 minority (1 African American, 2 Asian Americans or Pacific Islanders), 18 international. Average age 23. 64 applicants, 86% accepted, 25 enrolled. In 2009, 18 master's awarded. *Entrance requirements:* For master's, GMAT or GRE General Test. Additional exam requirements/recommendations for international students: Required—TOEFL (minimum score 550 paper-based; 213 computer-based; 80 iBT), IELTS (minimum score 6.5). *Application deadline:* For fall admission, 6/1 priority date for domestic students, 5/1 priority date for international students; for spring admission, 11/1 priority date for domestic and international students. Applications are processed on a rolling basis. Application fee: $60 ($75 for international students). Electronic applications accepted. *Expenses:* Tuition: Full-time $22,056; part-time $919 per credit. Required fees: $120; $120 per year. One-time fee: $170 full-time. *Financial support:* In 2009–10, 17 students received support, including 2 fellowships with partial tuition reimbursements available (averaging $14,000 per year), 9 research assistantships with partial tuition reimbursements available (averaging $10,000 per year); Federal Work-Study, scholarships/grants, and unspecified assistantships also available. Financial award application deadline: 3/1; financial award applicants required to submit FAFSA. *Faculty research:* Organizational management, corporate and organizational communication. *Unit head:* Prof. Linda Gallant, Graduate Program Director, 617-824-8491, E-mail: linda_gallant@emerson.edu. *Application contact:* Office of Graduate Admission, 617-824-8610, Fax: 617-824-8614, E-mail: gradapp@emerson.edu.

Fairleigh Dickinson University, College at Florham, Maxwell Becton College of Arts and Sciences, Department of English, Communication and Philosophy, Program in Corporate and Organizational Communication, Madison, NJ 07940-1099. Offers MA, MA/MBA. *Students:* 12 full-time (9 women), 28 part-time (21 women), 4 international. Average age 32. 30 applicants, 77% accepted, 16 enrolled. In 2009, 17 master's awarded. *Entrance requirements:* For master's, GRE General Test. *Application deadline:* Applications are processed on a rolling basis. Application fee: $40. *Application contact:* Susan Brooman, University Director, Graduate Admissions, 973-443-8905, Fax: 973-443-8088, E-mail: grad@fdu.edu.

Florida Institute of Technology, Graduate Programs, College of Psychology and Liberal Arts, Department of Humanities and Communication, Melbourne, FL 32901-6975. Offers technical and professional communication (MS). Part-time and evening/weekend programs available. *Faculty:* 4 full-time (all women). *Students:* 6 full-time (2 women), 11 part-time (9 women); includes 5 minority (2 African Americans, 1 American Indian/Alaska Native, 1 Asian American or Pacific Islander, 1 Hispanic American), 2 international. Average age 38. 4 applicants, 100% accepted, 2 enrolled. In 2009, 2 master's awarded. *Degree requirements:* For master's, comprehensive exam (for some programs), thesis optional. *Entrance requirements:* For master's, GRE (minimum score 1000 verbal and analytical), minimum GPA of 3.0, 2 letters of recommendation, discursive writing sample. Additional exam requirements/recommendations for international students: Required—TOEFL (minimum score 550 paper-based; 213 computer-based; 79 iBT). *Application deadline:* For fall admission, 4/1 for international students; for spring admission, 9/30 for international students. Applications are processed on a rolling basis. Application fee: $50. Electronic applications accepted. *Expenses:* Tuition: Part-time $1015 per credit. Tuition and fees vary according to campus/location and program. *Financial support:* Career-related internships or fieldwork and tuition remissions available. Support available to part-time students. Financial award application deadline: 3/1; financial award applicants required to submit FAFSA. *Faculty research:* Communication of astronomy in the seventeenth century, persuasion and patronage in seventeenth century work, technical and cross-cultural communication. *Unit head:* Dr. Robert A. Taylor, Department Head, 321-674-7384, Fax: 321-674-8109, E-mail: rotaylor@fit.edu. *Application contact:* Thomas M. Shea, Director of Graduate Admissions, 321-674-7577, Fax: 321-723-9468, E-mail: tshea@fit.edu.

Florida State University, The Graduate School, College of Communication and Information, School of Communication, Tallahassee, FL 32306. Offers corporate and public communication (MA, MS); integrated marketing communication (MA, MS); mass communication (PhD); media and communication studies (MA, MS); speech communication (PhD). Part-time programs available. *Faculty:* 24 full-time (9 women), 6 part-time/adjunct (1 woman). *Students:* 153 full-time (110 women), 65 part-time (34 women); includes 62 minority (37 African Americans, 1 American Indian/Alaska Native, 24 Hispanic Americans). Average age 24. 230 applicants, 76% accepted, 85 enrolled. In 2009, 84 master's, 6 doctorates awarded. *Degree requirements:* For master's, thesis (for some programs); for doctorate, comprehensive exam, thesis/dissertation. *Entrance requirements:* For master's, GRE General Test, minimum GPA of 3.0; for doctorate, GRE General Test, minimum GPA of 3.3 in graduate course work. Additional exam requirements/recommendations for international students: Required—TOEFL (minimum score 600 paper-based; 250 computer-based; 100 iBT). *Application deadline:* For fall admission, 7/1 priority date for domestic students, 5/1 priority date for international students; for spring admission, 11/1 priority date for domestic and international students. Applications are processed on a rolling basis. Application fee: $30. Electronic applications accepted. *Expenses:* Tuition, state resident: full-time $7413. Tuition, nonresident: full-time $22,567. *Financial support:* In 2009–10, 52 students received support, including 1 fellowship with full tuition reimbursement available, 8 research assistantships with full tuition reimbursements available (averaging $14,000 per year), 40 teaching assistantships with full tuition reimbursements available (averaging $5,000 per year); career-related internships or fieldwork, Federal Work-Study, institutionally sponsored loans, scholarships/grants, tuition waivers (partial), and unspecified assistantships also available. Support available to part-time students. Financial award application deadline: 2/1; financial award applicants required to submit FAFSA. *Faculty research:* Communication technology and policy, marketing communication, communication content and effect, new communication/information technologies. Total annual research expenditures: $600,000. *Unit head:* Dr. Stephen D. McDowell, Director, 850-644-2276, Fax: 850-644-8642, E-mail: steve.mcdowell@cci.fsu.edu. *Application contact:* Natashia Hinson-Turner, Graduate Coordinator, 850-644-8746, Fax: 850-644-8642, E-mail: natashia.turner@cci.fsu.edu.

Fordham University, Graduate School of Business Administration, New York, NY 10023. Offers accounting (MBA); communications and media management (MBA); executive business administration (EMBA); finance (MBA, MS); information systems (MBA, MS); management systems (MBA); marketing (MBA); media management (MS); taxation (MS); taxation and accounting (MTA);); JD/MBA; MBA/MIM; MS/MBA. *Accreditation:* AACSB. Part-time and evening/weekend programs available. *Entrance requirements:* For master's, GMAT, 2 letters of recommendation, resume. Additional exam requirements/recommendations for international students: Required—TOEFL (minimum score 600 paper-based; 250 computer-based; 100 iBT). Electronic applications accepted. *Expenses:* Contact institution.

Franklin University, Marketing and Communications Program, Columbus, OH 43215-5399. Offers MS. Part-time and evening/weekend programs available. *Faculty:* 2 full-time (1 woman), 9 part-time/adjunct (7 women). *Students:* 74 full-time (50 women), 12 part-time (8 women); includes 18 minority (12 African Americans, 4 Asian Americans or Pacific Islanders, 2 Hispanic Americans), 3 international. Average age 34. 98 applicants. In 2009, 59 master's awarded. *Degree requirements:* For master's, thesis or alternative. *Entrance requirements:* For master's, minimum undergraduate GPA of 2.75, undergraduate course work in marketing and statistics. Additional exam requirements/recommendations for international students: Required—TOEFL (minimum score 600 paper-based; 232 computer-based). *Application deadline:* For fall admission, 8/15 priority date for domestic students; for winter admission, 12/20 priority date for domestic students; for spring admission, 4/4 priority date for domestic students. Applications are processed on a rolling basis. Application fee: $30. Electronic applications accepted. *Expenses:* Tuition: Full-time $5880; part-time $490 per credit hour. *Financial support:* Application deadline: 6/30. *Unit head:* Dr. Doug Ross, Program Chair, 614-947-6149. *Application contact:* Graduate Services Office, 614-797-4700, Fax: 614-224-7723, E-mail: gradschl@franklin.edu.

HEC Montreal, School of Business Administration, Diploma Programs in Administration, Program in Marketing Communication, Montréal, QC H3T 2A7, Canada. Offers Diploma. All courses are given in French. Program offered on part-time basis only. Part-time programs available. *Students:* 90 part-time (73 women). 91 applicants, 40% accepted, 33 enrolled. In 2009, 28 Diplomas awarded. *Degree requirements:* For Diploma, one foreign language. *Entrance requirements:* For degree, relevant work experience, letters of recommendation. *Application deadline:* For fall admission, 4/15 for domestic and international students. Application fee: $77 Canadian dollars. Electronic applications accepted. Tuition and fees charges are reported in Canadian dollars. *Expenses:* Tuition, area resident: Part-time $65.60 Canadian dollars per credit. Tuition, state resident: full-time $2361.60 Canadian dollars; part-time $183.36 Canadian dollars per credit. Tuition, nonresident: full-time $6601 Canadian dollars; part-time $448.13 Canadian dollars per credit. International tuition: $16,132.68 Canadian dollars full-time. Required fees: $1254.15 Canadian dollars; $28.99 Canadian dollars per course. $91.68 Canadian dollars per term. Tuition and fees vary according to degree level and program. *Financial support:* Research assistantships, teaching assistantships, scholarships/grants available. Financial award application deadline: 10/2. *Unit head:* Louise Cote, Director, 514-340-6205, Fax: 514-340-5640, E-mail: louise.cote@hec.ca. *Application contact:* Marie Deshaies, Senior Student Advisor, 514-340-6135, Fax: 514-340-6411, E-mail: marie.deshaies@hec.ca.

Howard University, School of Communications, Department of Communication and Culture, Washington, DC 20059-0002. Offers intercultural communication (MA, PhD); organizational communication (MA, PhD). Offered through the Graduate School of Arts and Sciences. Part-time programs available. Terminal master's awarded for partial completion of doctoral program. *Degree requirements:* For master's, comprehensive exam or thesis; for doctorate, one foreign language, comprehensive exam, thesis/dissertation. *Entrance requirements:* For master's, English proficiency exam, GRE General Test, minimum GPA of 3.0; for doctorate, English proficiency exam, GRE General Test, master's degree in related field, minimum GPA of 3.5. Additional exam requirements/recommendations for international students: Required—TOEFL. *Faculty research:* Media effects, black discourse, development communication, African-American organizations.

Illinois Institute of Technology, Stuart School of Business, Program in Marketing Communication, Chicago, IL 60616-3793. Offers MS, MBA/MS. Part-time and evening/weekend programs available. *Faculty:* 2 full-time (0 women), 5 part-time/adjunct (2 women). *Students:* 40 full-time (28 women), 9 part-time (6 women); includes 3 minority (1 Asian American or Pacific Islander, 2 Hispanic Americans), 42 international. Average age 24. 157 applicants, 69% accepted, 28 enrolled. In 2009, 17 master's awarded. *Entrance requirements:* For master's, GMAT or GRE General Test. Additional exam requirements/recommendations for international students: Required—TOEFL (minimum score 575 paper-based; 90 iBT). *Application deadline:* For fall admission, 8/1 for domestic students, 5/1 for international students; for spring admission, 12/15 for domestic students, 10/15 for international students. Applications are processed on a rolling basis. Application fee: $75. Electronic applications accepted. *Expenses:* Contact institution. *Financial support:* Career-related internships or fieldwork, Federal Work-Study, institutionally sponsored loans, scholarships/grants, traineeships, health care benefits, and tuition waivers (partial) available. Support available to part-time students. Financial award applicants required to submit FAFSA. *Unit head:* Thomas Anderson, Associate Dean, 312-906-6525, Fax: 312-906-6549, E-mail: anderson@stuart.iit.edu. *Application contact:* Thomas Anderson, Associate Dean, 312-906-6525, Fax: 312-906-6549, E-mail: anderson@stuart.iit.edu.

Iowa State University of Science and Technology, Graduate College, College of Liberal Arts and Sciences, Department of English, Ames, IA 50011. Offers creative writing (MFA); English (MA); rhetoric and professional communication (PhD). *Faculty:* 53 full-time (26 women), 8 part-time/adjunct (6 women). *Students:* 105 full-time (68 women), 25 part-time (17 women); includes 3 minority (all Hispanic Americans), 28 international. 99 applicants, 62% accepted, 39 enrolled. In 2009, 30 master's, 3 doctorates awarded. *Degree requirements:* For master's, thesis or alternative; for doctorate, thesis/dissertation. *Entrance requirements:* For master's, GRE General Test, sample of written work, resume, portfolio in creative writing; for doctorate, GRE General Test, sample of written work, resume. Additional exam requirements/recommendations for international students: Required—TOEFL (minimum score 600 paper-based; 100 iBT) or IELTS (minimum score 7). *Application deadline:* For fall admission, 1/5 priority date for domestic and international students. Application fee: $40 ($90 for international students). Electronic applications accepted. *Expenses:* Tuition, state resident: full-time $6716. Tuition, nonresident: full-time $8908. Tuition and fees vary according to course level, course load, program and student level. *Financial support:* In 2009–10, 10 research assistantships with full and partial tuition reimbursements (averaging $18,120 per year), 84 teaching assistantships with full and partial tuition reimbursements (averaging $18,120 per year) were awarded; fellowships, scholarships/grants, health care benefits, and unspecified assistantships also available. *Faculty research:* Creative writing, literature, rhetoric, composition and professional communication, teaching English as a second language, applied linguistics. *Unit head:* Dr. Charles Kostelnick, Chair, 515-294-2477, Fax: 515-294-2125, E-mail: englgrad@iastate.edu. *Application contact:* Dr. Constance Post, Director of Graduate Education, 515-294-3175, E-mail: englgrad@iastate.edu.

John Carroll University, Graduate School, Department of Communications Management, University Heights, OH 44118-4581. Offers MA. Part-time and evening/weekend programs available. *Degree requirements:* For master's, comprehensive exam, thesis or project. *Entrance requirements:* For master's, GRE General Test, minimum GPA of 3.0. Additional exam requirements/recommendations for international students: Required—TOEFL. Electronic applications accepted. *Faculty research:* Communication law, media ethics, international studies, international broadcasting, media history.

Jones International University, School of Business, Centennial, CO 80112. Offers accounting (MBA); business communication (MABC); entrepreneurship (MABC, MBA); finance (MBA); global enterprise management (MBA); health care management (MBA); information security management (MBA); information technology management (MBA); leadership and influence (MABC); leading the customer-driven organization (MABC); negotiation and conflict management (MBA); project management (MABC, MBA). Program only offered online. Part-time and evening/weekend programs available. Postbaccalaureate distance learning degree programs offered (no on-campus study). *Degree requirements:* For master's, capstone project. *Entrance requirements:* For master's, minimum cumulative GPA of 2.5. Additional exam requirements/recommendations for international students: Recommended—TOEFL (minimum score 550 paper-based; 213 computer-based). Electronic applications accepted.

La Salle University, School of Arts and Sciences, Program in Professional Communication, Philadelphia, PA 19141-1199. Offers MA. Part-time and evening/weekend programs available. *Degree requirements:* For master's, exam or project. *Entrance requirements:* For master's, GRE or MAT. *Expenses:* Contact institution.

Lasell College, Graduate and Professional Studies in Communication, Newton, MA 02466-2709. Offers integrated marketing communication (MSC, Graduate Certificate); public relations (MSC, Graduate Certificate). Part-time and evening/weekend programs available. Postbaccalaureate distance learning degree programs offered (minimal on-campus study). *Faculty:* 3 full-time (all women), 1 part-time/adjunct (0 women). *Students:* 5 full-time (all women), 13 part-time (12 women); includes 3 minority (all African Americans). Average age 29. 19 applicants, 89% accepted, 11 enrolled. *Entrance requirements:* For master's and Graduate Certificate, bachelor's degree from an accredited institution. Additional exam requirements/recommendations for international students: Required—TOEFL (minimum score 550 paper-based; 213 computer-based; 75 iBT) or IELTS. *Application deadline:* For fall admission, 8/31 priority date for domestic students, 6/30 priority date for international students; for spring admission, 12/31 priority date for domestic students, 10/31 priority date for international students. Applications are processed on a rolling basis. Application fee: $40. Electronic applications accepted. *Expenses:* Tuition: Full-time $4890; part-time $525 per credit hour. Required fees: $55 per term. *Financial support:* Available to part-time students. Application deadline: 8/30. *Unit head:* Dr. Joan Dolamore, Dean of Graduate and Professional Studies, 617-243-2485, Fax: 617-243-2450, E-mail: gradinfo@lasell.edu. *Application contact:* Adrienne Franciosi, Director of Graduate Admission, 617-243-2214, Fax: 617-243-2450, E-mail: gradinfo@lasell.edu.

Loyola University Chicago, Graduate School of Business, Marketing Department, Chicago, IL 60660. Offers integrated marketing communications (MS); marketing (MSIMC). Part-time and evening/weekend programs available. *Entrance requirements:* For master's, GMAT, v. Additional exam requirements/recommendations for international students: Required—TOEFL (minimum score 550 paper-based; 213 computer-based; 80 iBT). Electronic applications accepted. *Expenses:* Contact institution. *Faculty research:* Web performance metrics, new venture marketing strategies over consumption, benefit segmentation strategies.

Marietta College, Program in Corporate Media, Marietta, OH 45750-4000. Offers MCM.

Marist College, Graduate Programs, School of Communication and the Arts, Poughkeepsie, NY 12601-1387. Offers organizational communication and leadership (MA). Part-time programs available. Postbaccalaureate distance learning degree programs offered (no on-campus study). *Degree requirements:* For master's, thesis or comprehensive exam. *Entrance requirements:* For master's, GRE, minimum undergraduate GPA of 3.0, resume, 3 letters of recommendation. Additional exam requirements/recommendations for international students: Required—TOEFL (minimum score 550 paper-based; 213 computer-based; 80 iBT); Recommended—IELTS (minimum score 6.5). Electronic applications accepted. *Expenses:* Tuition: Full-time $12,510; part-time $695 per credit hour.

Marywood University, Academic Affairs, Insalaco College of Creative and Performing Arts, Department of Communication Arts, Program in Information Sciences, Scranton, PA 18509-1598. Offers corporate communication (Certificate); e-business (Certificate); health communication (Certificate); information sciences (MS), including library science/information specialist; instructional technology (Certificate). *Students:* 1 full-time (0 women), 4 part-time (3 women). Average age 32. In 2009, 3 master's awarded. *Entrance requirements:* Additional exam requirements/recommendations for international students: Required—TOEFL (minimum score 550 paper-based; 213 computer-based; 79 iBT). *Application deadline:* For fall admission, 4/1 priority date for domestic students, 3/31 priority date for international students; for spring admission, 11/1 priority date for domestic students, 8/31 priority date for international students. Applications are processed on a rolling basis. Application fee: $35. Electronic applications accepted. *Expenses:* Tuition: Part-time $715 per credit. Required fees: $270 per semester. Tuition and fees vary according to degree level, campus/location and program. *Financial support:* Career-related internships or fieldwork, scholarships/grants, and unspecified assistantships available. Support available to part-time students. Financial award application deadline: 6/30; financial award applicants required to submit FAFSA. *Application contact:* Tammy Manka, Assistant Director of Graduate Admissions, 866-279-9663, E-mail: tmanka@marywood.edu.

Metropolitan College of New York, Program in Media Management, New York, NY 10013. Offers MBA. Evening/weekend programs available. *Degree requirements:* For master's, thesis, 10 day study abroad. *Entrance requirements:* For master's, GMAT or GRE General Test, appropriate work experience, interview, minimum GPA of 2.7. Additional exam requirements/recommendations for international students: Required—TOEFL (minimum score 600 paper-based; 220 computer-based). Electronic applications accepted. *Expenses:* Contact institution.

Mississippi College, Graduate School, College of Arts and Sciences, School of Christian Studies and the Arts, Department of Communication, Clinton, MS 39058. Offers applied communication (MSC); public relations and corporate communication (MSC). Part-time programs available. *Faculty:* 6 full-time (2 women), 1 part-time/adjunct (0 women). *Students:* 14 full-time (7 women), 18 part-time (13 women); includes 5 minority (all African Americans), 10 international. Average age 28. In 2009, 6 master's awarded. *Degree requirements:* For master's, comprehensive exam, thesis optional. *Entrance requirements:* For master's, GRE or NTE, minimum GPA of 2.5. Additional exam requirements/recommendations for international students: Recommended—IELTS. *Application deadline:* For fall admission, 8/15 priority date for domestic and international students. Applications are processed on a rolling basis. Application fee: $30. Electronic applications accepted. *Expenses:* Tuition: Part-time $452 per credit hour. Required fees: $101 per semester. Tuition and fees vary according to degree level, campus/location, program and student level. *Financial support:* Career-related internships or fieldwork, Federal Work-Study, and unspecified assistantships available. Support available to part-time students. Financial award application deadline: 4/1; financial award applicants required to submit FAFSA. *Unit head:* Dr. Cliff Fortenberry, Chair, 601-925-3457, E-mail: fortenbe@mc.edu. *Application contact:* Elnora Lewis, Secretary, 601-925-3225, Fax: 601-925-3889, E-mail: lewis09@mc.edu.

Monmouth University, Graduate School, Department of Corporate and Public Communication, West Long Branch, NJ 07764-1898. Offers corporate and public communication (MA); human resources communication (Certificate); public relations (Certificate); public service communication specialist (Certificate). Part-time and evening/weekend programs available. *Faculty:* 8 full-time (4 women), 2 part-time/adjunct (1 woman). *Students:* 6 full-time (3 women), 45 part-time (31 women); includes 8 minority (3 African Americans, 1 Asian American or Pacific Islander, 4 Hispanic Americans), 3 international. Average age 31. 39 applicants, 95% accepted, 20 enrolled. In 2009, 19 master's awarded. *Degree requirements:* For master's, comprehensive exam, project. *Entrance requirements:* For master's, GRE, minimum GPA of 3.0 in major, 2.75 overall. Additional exam requirements/recommendations for international students: Required—TOEFL (minimum score 550 paper-based; 213 computer-based; 79 iBT), IELTS (minimum score 5), Michigan English Language Assessment Battery (minimum score 77), Cambridge A, B, C. *Application deadline:* For fall admission, 7/15 priority date for domestic students, 6/1 for international students; for spring admission, 11/15 priority date for domestic students, 11/1 for international students. Applications are processed on a rolling basis. Application fee: $50. Electronic applications accepted. *Expenses:* Tuition: Part-time $773 per credit. Required fees: $157 per semester. *Financial support:* In 2009–10, 37 students received support, including 24 fellowships (averaging $1,242 per year), 7 research assistantships (averaging $5,715 per year); scholarships/grants and unspecified assistantships also available. Support available to part-time students. Financial award applicants required to submit FAFSA. *Faculty research:* Service-learning, history of television, feminism and the media, executive communication, public relations pedagogy. *Unit head:* Dr. Sherry Wien, Program Director, 732-263-5354, Fax: 732-571-3609, E-mail: swien@monmouth.edu. *Application contact:* Kevin Roane, Director, Office of Graduate Admission, 732-571-3452, Fax: 732-263-5123, E-mail: gradadm@monmouth.edu.

Montclair State University, The Graduate School, School of the Arts, Department of Communication Studies, Montclair, NJ 07043-1624. Offers organizational communication (MA); public relations (MA); speech communication (MA). Part-time and evening/weekend programs available. *Faculty:* 5 full-time (2 women), 41 part-time/adjunct (24 women). *Students:* 16 full-time (15 women), 20 part-time (17 women). Average age 30. 23 applicants, 65% accepted, 12 enrolled. In 2009, 12 master's awarded. *Degree requirements:* For master's, comprehensive exam. *Entrance requirements:* For master's, GRE General Test, 2 letters of recommendation. Additional exam requirements/recommendations for international students: Required—TOEFL (minimum score 83 computer-based), or IELTS. *Application deadline:* For fall admission, 6/1 for international students; for spring admission, 10/1 for international students. Applications are processed on a rolling basis. Application fee: $60. Electronic applications accepted. *Expenses:* Tuition, area resident: Part-time $486.74 per credit. Tuition, state resident: part-time $486.74 per credit. Tuition, nonresident: part-time $751.34 per credit. Tuition and fees vary according to degree level and program. *Financial support:* In 2009–10, 3 research assistantships with full tuition reimbursements (averaging $7,000 per year) were awarded; Federal Work-Study, scholarships/grants, and unspecified assistantships also available. Support available to part-time students. Financial award application deadline: 3/1; financial award applicants required to submit FAFSA. *Unit head:* Dr. Harry Haines, Chair, 973-655-4200. *Application contact:* Amy Aiello, Director of Graduate Admissions and Operations, 973-655-5147, Fax: 973-655-7869, E-mail: graduate.school@montclair.edu.

Murray State University, College of Business and Public Affairs, Program in Organizational Communication, Murray, KY 42071. Offers MA, MS. Part-time programs available. *Degree requirements:* For master's, thesis (for some programs). *Entrance requirements:* For master's, minimum GPA of 2.5 for conditional admittance, 3.0 for unconditional admittance. Additional exam requirements/recommendations for international students: Required—TOEFL (minimum score 550 paper-based; 213 computer-based). *Faculty research:* Organizational learning, organizational culture, leadership, health communication, personality.

National-Louis University, College of Arts and Sciences, Program in Written Communication, Chicago, IL 60603. Offers corporate written communication (Certificate); written communication (MS). Part-time programs available. *Degree requirements:* For master's, thesis. *Entrance requirements:* For master's, GRE General Test, MAT, or Watson-Glaser Critical Thinking Appraisal, interview, minimum GPA of 3.0. *Expenses:* Tuition: Full-time $17,160; part-time $715 per semester hour. Tuition and fees vary according to course load, degree level, campus/location and program.

National University, Academic Affairs, School of Media and Communication, Department of Communication, La Jolla, CA 92037-1011. Offers strategic communication (MA). Part-time and evening/weekend programs available. Postbaccalaureate distance learning degree programs offered (no on-campus study). *Faculty:* 3 full-time (2 women), 1 (woman) part-time/adjunct. *Students:* 17 full-time (10 women), 24 part-time (15 women); includes 11 minority (5 African Americans, 2 Asian Americans or Pacific Islanders, 4 Hispanic Americans). 46 applicants, 100% accepted, 32 enrolled. In 2009, 3 master's awarded. *Degree requirements:* For master's, thesis. *Entrance requirements:* Additional exam requirements/recommendations for international students: Required—TOEFL (minimum score 550 paper-based; 213 computer-based; 79 iBT), IELTS (minimum score 6). *Application deadline:* For fall admission, 6/30 for international students. Applications are processed on a rolling basis. Application fee: $60 ($65 for international students). Electronic applications accepted. *Expenses:* Tuition: Part-time $338 per quarter hour. *Financial support:* Application deadline: 6/30. *Unit head:* Dr. Joan Vas Tassel, Dean, 858-309-3446, Fax: 858-309-3450, E-mail: jvantassel@nu.edu. *Application contact:* Dominick Giovanniello, Associate Regional Dean—San Diego, 800-NAT-UNIV, Fax: 858-541-7792, E-mail: dgiovann@nu.edu.

New Mexico State University, Graduate School, College of Arts and Sciences, Department of English, Las Cruces, NM 88003-8001. Offers creative writing (MFA); English (MA); rhetoric and professional communication (PhD). Part-time programs available. *Faculty:* 26 full-time (15 women). *Students:* 81 full-time (45 women), 35 part-time (19 women); includes 23 minority (4 African Americans, 3 Asian Americans or Pacific Islanders, 16 Hispanic Americans), 7 international. Average age 32. 89 applicants, 66% accepted, 26 enrolled. In 2009, 27 master's awarded. *Degree requirements:* For master's, one foreign language, thesis (for some programs); for doctorate, comprehensive exam, thesis/dissertation, internship. *Entrance requirements:* For master's and doctorate, sample of written work. *Application deadline:* For fall admission, 2/1 for domestic and international students. Application fee: $30 ($50 for international students). Electronic applications accepted. *Expenses:* Tuition, state resident: full-time $4080; part-time $223 per credit. Tuition, nonresident: full-time $14,256; part-time $647 per credit. Required fees: $1278; $639 per semester. *Financial support:* In 2009–10, 2 research assistantships (averaging $7,900 per year), 55 teaching assistantships (averaging $15,193 per year) were awarded; fellowships, career-related internships or fieldwork, Federal Work-Study, institutionally sponsored loans, scholarships/grants, health care benefits, and unspecified assistantships also available. Financial award application deadline: 2/1; financial award applicants required to submit FAFSA. *Faculty research:* Composition research, history and theory of rhetoric, technical/professional communication, creative writing, English and American literature. *Unit head:* Dr.

Corporate and Organizational Communication

New Mexico State University (continued)
Monica F. Torres, Head, 575-646-2319, Fax: 575-646-7725, E-mail: mftorres@nmsu.edu. *Application contact:* Dr. Elizabeth Schirmer, Director of Graduate Studies, 575-646-1733, E-mail: eschirme@nmsu.edu.

New York University, School of Continuing and Professional Studies, Division of Programs in Business, Program in Public Relations and Corporate Communications, New York, NY 10012-1019. Offers corporate and organizational communications (MS); public relations management (MS). Part-time and evening/weekend programs available. *Faculty:* 2 full-time (0 women), 28 part-time/adjunct (13 women). *Students:* 46 full-time (39 women), 93 part-time (67 women). Average age 28. 169 applicants, 52% accepted, 47 enrolled. In 2009, 81 master's awarded. *Degree requirements:* For master's, capstone project. *Entrance requirements:* For master's, GRE General Test or GMAT (for recent graduates), 2 letters of recommendation, resume. Additional exam requirements/recommendations for international students: Required—TOEFL (minimum score 600 paper-based; 250 computer-based; 100 iBT), TWE. *Application deadline:* For fall admission, 2/1 priority date for domestic and international students; for spring admission, 10/15 priority date for domestic students, 8/15 priority date for international students. Applications are processed on a rolling basis. Application fee: $75. Electronic applications accepted. *Expenses:* Tuition: Full-time $30,528; part-time $1272 per credit. Required fees: $2177. *Financial support:* In 2009–10, 67 students received support, including 67 fellowships (averaging $2,735 per year); institutionally sponsored loans and scholarships/grants also available. Financial award application deadline: 3/1; financial award applicants required to submit FAFSA. *Unit head:* John Doorley, Director, 212-992-3600, Fax: 212-992-3650. *Application contact:* Angrand Fadia, Assistant Director, 212-992-3600, Fax: 212-992-3650, E-mail: fs20@nyu.edu.

Northwestern University, The Graduate School, School of Communication, Department of Communication Studies, Managerial Communication Program, Evanston, IL 60208. Offers MSC. *Entrance requirements:* For master's, GRE General Test.

Northwestern University, Medill School of Journalism, Integrated Marketing Communications Program, Evanston, IL 60208. Offers advertising/sales promotion (MSIMC); direct database and e-commerce marketing (MSIMC); general studies (MSIMC); public relations (MSIMC). Part-time programs available. *Entrance requirements:* For master's, GRE General Test or GMAT, full-time work experience (preferred). Additional exam requirements/recommendations for international students: Required—TOEFL. Electronic applications accepted. *Faculty research:* Data mining, business to business marketing, values in advertising, political advertising.

Ohio University, Graduate College, Scripps College of Communication, School of Communication Studies, Athens, OH 45701-2979. Offers health communication (PhD); organizational communication (MA); relating and organizing (PhD); rhetoric and public culture (PhD). Part-time programs available. Postbaccalaureate distance learning degree programs offered (minimal on-campus study). *Faculty:* 24 full-time (9 women), 4 part-time/adjunct (1 woman). *Students:* 48 full-time (33 women), 31 part-time (25 women); includes 5 minority (4 African Americans, 1 Hispanic American), 12 international. 98 applicants, 46% accepted, 36 enrolled. In 2009, 7 master's, 12 doctorates awarded. Terminal master's awarded for partial completion of doctoral program. *Degree requirements:* For master's, capstone; for doctorate, comprehensive exam, thesis/dissertation. *Entrance requirements:* For master's, GRE; for doctorate, GRE General Test, minimum GPA of 3.0. Additional exam requirements/recommendations for international students: Required—TOEFL (minimum score 550 paper-based; 80 iBT) or IELTS Academic (minimum score 6.5). *Application deadline:* For fall admission, 1/15 priority date for domestic and international students. Application fee: $50 ($55 for international students). Electronic applications accepted. *Expenses:* Tuition, state resident: full-time $7839; part-time $323 per quarter hour. Tuition, nonresident: full-time $15,831; part-time $654 per quarter hour. Required fees: $2931. *Financial support:* In 2009–10, 12 students received support, including fellowships with full tuition reimbursements available (averaging $13,600 per year), research assistantships with full tuition reimbursements available (averaging $13,600 per year), teaching assistantships with full tuition reimbursements available (averaging $13,600 per year); career-related internships or fieldwork, Federal Work-Study, and institutionally sponsored loans also available. Financial award application deadline: 1/15. *Faculty research:* Rhetoric and public culture, relating and organizing, health communication. Total annual research expenditures: $200,000. *Unit head:* Dr. Claudia Hale, Director, 740-593-4832, Fax: 740-593-4810, E-mail: hale@ohio.edu. *Application contact:* Dr. Scott Titsworth, Graduate Chairman, 740-593-9160, Fax: 740-593-4810, E-mail: titswort@ohio.edu.

Oklahoma City University, Meinders School of Business, Program in Business Administration, Oklahoma City, OK 73106-1402. Offers finance (MBA); health administration (MBA); information technology (MBA); integrated marketing communications (MBA); international business (MBA); marketing (MBA); JD/MBA. *Accreditation:* ACBSP. Part-time and evening/weekend programs available. *Faculty:* 24 full-time (7 women), 11 part-time/adjunct (1 woman). *Students:* 268 full-time (91 women), 180 part-time (62 women); includes 51 minority (20 African Americans, 7 American Indian/Alaska Native, 11 Asian Americans or Pacific Islanders, 13 Hispanic Americans), 257 international. Average age 30. 158 applicants, 90% accepted, 35 enrolled. In 2009, 236 master's awarded. *Degree requirements:* For master's, comprehensive exam. *Entrance requirements:* Additional exam requirements/recommendations for international students: Required—TOEFL (minimum score 560 paper-based; 220 computer-based; 83 iBT). *Application deadline:* For fall admission, 8/20 for domestic students; for spring admission, 1/6 for domestic students. Applications are processed on a rolling basis. Application fee: $50 ($70 for international students). *Expenses:* Tuition: Full-time $15,930; part-time $885 per hour. *Financial support:* Fellowships with partial tuition reimbursements, career-related internships or fieldwork, Federal Work-Study, institutionally sponsored loans, and tuition waivers (partial) available. Support available to part-time students. Financial award application deadline: 8/1. *Faculty research:* Management information systems, international business strategies. *Unit head:* Dr. Mahmood Shandiz, Senior Associate Dean, 405-208-5130, Fax: 405-208-5098, E-mail: mshandiz@okcu.edu. *Application contact:* Michelle Lockhart, Director, Graduate Admissions, 800-633-7242, Fax: 405-208-5916, E-mail: gadmissions@okcu.edu.

Queens University of Charlotte, School of Communication, Charlotte, NC 28274-0002. Offers organizational and strategic communication (MA). Part-time and evening/weekend programs available. *Degree requirements:* For master's, capstone course. *Entrance requirements:* Additional exam requirements/recommendations for international students: Required—TOEFL. *Expenses:* Contact institution.

Radford University, College of Graduate and Professional Studies, College of Humanities and Behavioral Sciences, School of Communication, Radford, VA 24142. Offers corporate and professional communication (MS). Part-time and evening/weekend programs available. *Faculty:* 11 full-time (6 women). *Students:* 27 full-time (16 women), 5 part-time (4 women); includes 5 minority (3 African Americans, 2 Hispanic Americans), 4 international. Average age 26. 25 applicants, 72% accepted, 15 enrolled. In 2009, 10 master's awarded. *Degree requirements:* For master's, comprehensive exam, thesis optional. *Entrance requirements:* For master's, GRE, minimum GPA of 2.75; short essay; 3 letters of reference. Additional exam requirements/recommendations for international students: Required—TOEFL (minimum score 550 paper-based; 213 computer-based; 79 iBT). *Application deadline:* For fall admission, 12/1 for international students; for spring admission, 7/1 for international students. Applications are processed on a rolling basis. Application fee: $50. Electronic applications accepted. *Expenses:* Tuition, state resident: full-time $5086; part-time $211 per credit hour. Tuition, nonresident: full-time $12,608; part-time $525 per credit hour. Required fees: $2508; $105 per credit hour. *Financial support:* In 2009–10, 15 students received support, including 2 research assistantships with partial tuition reimbursements available (averaging $8,000 per year), 10 teaching assistantships with partial tuition reimbursements available (averaging $8,700 per year); career-related internships or fieldwork, Federal Work-Study, institutionally sponsored loans, and scholarships/grants also available. Financial award application deadline: 3/1; financial award applicants required to submit FAFSA. *Unit head:* Dr. Lynn M. Zoch, Director, 540-831-6553, Fax: 540-831-5883, E-mail: lzoch@radford.edu. *Application contact:* Graduate Admissions, 540-831-5431, Fax: 540-831-6061, E-mail: gradcollege@radford.edu.

Regis College, Department of Organizational and Professional Communication, Weston, MA 02493. Offers MS. Part-time and evening/weekend programs available. *Faculty:* 1 (woman) full-time, 3 part-time/adjunct (1 woman). *Students:* 15 part-time (all women); includes 2 minority (1 Asian American or Pacific Islander, 1 Hispanic American). Average age 34. 8 applicants, 100% accepted, 6 enrolled. In 2009, 13 master's awarded. *Degree requirements:* For master's, thesis. *Entrance requirements:* For master's, GRE or MAT. Additional exam requirements/recommendations for international students: Required—TOEFL (minimum score 550 paper-based; 213 computer-based). *Application deadline:* Applications are processed on a rolling basis. Application fee: $50. *Expenses:* Tuition: Full-time $29,000; part-time $800 per credit. Tuition and fees vary according to course load, degree level and program. *Financial support:* In 2009–10, 9 students received support. Scholarships/grants available. Financial award applicants required to submit FAFSA. *Unit head:* Dr. Joan Murray, Director, 781-768-7416, Fax: 781-768-7159, E-mail: joan.murray@regiscollege.edu. *Application contact:* Christine Petherick, Administrative Coordinator, Graduate Admission, 866-438-7344, Fax: 781-768-7071, E-mail: christine.petherick@regiscollege.edu.

Roosevelt University, Graduate Division, College of Arts and Sciences, Department of Communication, Program in Integrated Marketing Communications, Chicago, IL 60605. Offers MSIMC. Part-time and evening/weekend programs available. *Faculty research:* Print journalism, urban high school journalism.

St. Bonaventure University, School of Graduate Studies, Russell J. Jandoli School of Journalism and Mass Communication, St. Bonaventure, NY 14778-2284. Offers integrated marketing communications (MA). Evening/weekend programs available. *Faculty:* 3 full-time (2 women), 2 part-time/adjunct (1 woman). *Students:* 40 full-time (24 women), 9 part-time (3 women); includes 2 American Indian/Alaska Native, 1 international. Average age 26. 37 applicants, 78% accepted, 23 enrolled. In 2009, 12 master's awarded. *Entrance requirements:* For master's, GRE (waived if undergraduate GPA is 3.25 or higher), interview, writing sample. Additional exam requirements/recommendations for international students: Required—TOEFL. *Application deadline:* For fall admission, 2/15 priority date for domestic students, 12/15 for international students. Applications are processed on a rolling basis. Application fee: $30. *Expenses:* Tuition: Full-time $11,700; part-time $650 per credit. *Financial support:* In 2009–10, 8 research assistantships with full and partial tuition reimbursements were awarded; scholarships/grants also available. Financial award application deadline: 4/15; financial award applicants required to submit FAFSA. *Faculty research:* Public relations, branding, new media. *Unit head:* Lee Coppola, Dean, 716-375-2520, E-mail: lcoppola@sbu.edu. *Application contact:* Prof. Kathleen J. Mason, Program Director, 716-375-2578, E-mail: kmason@sbu.edu.

Schiller International University, Graduate Programs, London, Program in Communications, London, United Kingdom. Offers business communication (MA).

Seton Hall University, College of Arts and Sciences, Department of Communication, South Orange, NJ 07079-2697. Offers corporate and professional communication (MA); intercultural communication (MA); organizational communication (MA); public relations (MA); strategic communication and leadership (MA); strategic communication planning (MA). Part-time and evening/weekend programs available. Postbaccalaureate distance learning degree programs offered (minimal on-campus study). *Faculty:* 3 full-time (1 woman), 15 part-time/adjunct (6 women). *Students:* 30 full-time (19 women), 92 part-time (56 women); includes 42 minority (33 African Americans, 1 Asian American or Pacific Islander, 8 Hispanic Americans), 3 international. Average age 33. 66 applicants, 97% accepted, 39 enrolled. In 2009, 64 master's awarded. *Degree requirements:* For master's, thesis. *Entrance requirements:* Additional exam requirements/recommendations for international students: Required—TOEFL. *Application deadline:* For fall admission, 7/1 priority date for domestic and international students; for spring admission, 11/1 priority date for domestic and international students. Applications are processed on a rolling basis. Application fee: $50. Electronic applications accepted. *Financial support:* Research assistantships, career-related internships or fieldwork, Federal Work-Study, and unspecified assistantships available. Financial award applicants required to submit FAFSA. *Faculty research:* Managerial communication, communication consulting, communication and development. *Unit head:* Prof. Peter Reader, Chair, 973-761-9474, Fax: 973-761-9234, E-mail: readerpe@shu.edu. *Application contact:* Dr. Richard Dool, Director of Graduate Studies, 973-275-2794, Fax: 973-761-9234, E-mail: doolrich@shu.edu.

Simmons College, College of Arts and Sciences Graduate Studies, Program in Communications Management, Boston, MA 02115. Offers MS, MS/MA. Part-time programs available. *Students:* 7 full-time (6 women), 64 part-time (58 women); includes 11 minority (5 African Americans, 2 Asian Americans or Pacific Islanders, 4 Hispanic Americans), 3 international. 47 applicants, 74% accepted, 26 enrolled. In 2009, 32 master's awarded. *Degree requirements:* For master's, thesis. *Entrance requirements:* For master's, GRE General Test, MAT, or GMAT, 2 years of professional experience. Additional exam requirements/recommendations for international students: Required—TOEFL (minimum score 600 paper-based; 250 computer-based; 100 iBT). *Application deadline:* For fall admission, 8/1 priority date for domestic and international students; for winter admission, 12/15 priority date for domestic and international students; for spring admission, 5/1 priority date for domestic and international students. Applications are processed on a rolling basis. Application fee: $35. Electronic applications accepted. *Expenses:* Tuition: Part-time $925 per credit hour. Part-time tuition and fees vary according to program. *Financial support:* In 2009–10, 11 students received support. Career-related internships or fieldwork, scholarships/grants, and unspecified assistantships available. Financial award application deadline: 3/1; financial award applicants required to submit FAFSA. *Faculty research:* Communications in non-profit management, online communications, communication across cultures. *Unit head:* Joan C. Abrams, Director/Assistant Professor, 617-521-2845, Fax: 617-521-3149, E-mail: abrams@simmons.edu. *Application contact:* Kristen Haack, Director, Graduate Studies Admission, 617-521-2917, Fax: 617-521-3058, E-mail: gsa@simmons.edu.

Southern Illinois University Edwardsville, Graduate Studies and Research, College of Arts and Sciences, Department of Speech Communication, Program in Corporate and Organizational Communication, Edwardsville, IL 62026-0001. Offers Postbaccalaureate Certificate. Part-time programs available. *Students:* 1 (woman) part-time. Average age 26. 8 applicants, 0% accepted. *Entrance requirements:* Additional exam requirements/recommendations for international students: Required—TOEFL (minimum score 550 paper-based; 213 computer-based; 79 iBT), IELTS (minimum score 6.5). *Application deadline:* For fall admission, 7/20 for domestic students, 6/1 for international students; for spring admission, 12/14 for domestic students, 10/1 for international students. Applications are processed on a rolling basis. Application fee: $30. Electronic applications accepted. *Expenses:* Tuition, state resident: part-time $1252.50 per semester. Tuition, nonresident: part-time $3131.25 per semester. Required fees: $586.85 per semester. Tuition and fees vary according to course load. *Financial support:* Fellowships with full tuition reimbursements, research assistantships with full tuition reimbursements, teaching assistantships with full tuition reimbursements available. Financial award application deadline: 3/1; financial award applicants required to submit FAFSA. *Unit head:* Dr. Wai Hsien Cheah, Director, 618 650-5016, E-mail: wcheah@siue.edu. *Application contact:* Dr. Wai Hsien Cheah, Director, 618-650-5016, E-mail: wcheah@siue.edu.

Southern Polytechnic State University, School of Arts and Sciences, Department of English, Technical Communication, and Media Arts, Marietta, GA 30060-2896. Offers communications management (Graduate Certificate); content development (Graduate Certificate); information and instructional design (MSIID); information design and communication (MS); instructional design (Graduate Certificate); technical and professional communication (Graduate Certificate); visual communication and graphics (Graduate Certificate). Part-time and evening/weekend programs available. Postbaccalaureate distance learning degree programs offered (no on-campus study). *Faculty:* 4 full-time (3 women), 1 part-time/adjunct (0 women). *Students:* 5 full-time (all women), 50 part-time (32 women); includes 18 African Americans, 2 international.

Average age 38. 32 applicants, 94% accepted, 26 enrolled. In 2009, 8 master's awarded. *Degree requirements:* For master's, thesis or internship; for Graduate Certificate, thesis optional, 18 hours completed through thesis option (6 hours), internship option (6 hours) or advanced coursework option (6 hours). *Entrance requirements:* For master's, GRE, statement of purpose, writing sample, professional recommendations, timed essay; for Graduate Certificate, writing sample, professional recommendations. Additional exam requirements/recommendations for international students: Required—TOEFL (minimum score 550 paper-based; 213 computer-based; 79 iBT), IELTS (minimum score 6.5). *Application deadline:* For fall admission, 5/1 priority date for domestic students, 7/1 priority date for international students; for spring admission, 9/1 priority date for domestic students, 11/1 priority date for international students. Applications are processed on a rolling basis. Application fee: $20. Electronic applications accepted. *Expenses:* Tuition, state resident: full-time $2896; part-time $181 per credit hour. Tuition, nonresident: full-time $11,552; part-time $722 per credit hour. Required fees: $1096; $1096 per year. *Financial support:* In 2009–10, 1 research assistantship with full tuition reimbursement (averaging $4,000 per year), 1 teaching assistantship with partial tuition reimbursement (averaging $4,000 per year) were awarded; career-related internships or fieldwork, Federal Work-Study, scholarships/grants, and unspecified assistantships also available. Support available to part-time students. Financial award application deadline: 5/1; financial award applicants required to submit FAFSA. *Faculty research:* Usability, user-centered design, instructional design, information architecture, information design. *Unit head:* Dr. Mark Nunes, Chair, 678-915-7202, Fax: 678-915-7425, E-mail: mnunes@spsu.edu. *Application contact:* Nikki Palamiotis, Director of Graduate Studies, 678-915-4276, Fax: 678-915-7292, E-mail: npalamio@spsu.edu.

Spalding University, Graduate Studies, College of Business and Communication, Louisville, KY 40203-2188. Offers business communication (MS). Part-time and evening/weekend programs available. *Faculty:* 6 full-time (2 women), 3 part-time/adjunct (2 women). *Students:* 39 full-time (30 women), 29 part-time (22 women); includes 19 minority (17 African Americans, 1 Asian American or Pacific Islander, 1 Hispanic American). Average age 37. 33 applicants, 73% accepted, 24 enrolled. In 2009, 20 master's awarded. *Degree requirements:* For master's, project. *Entrance requirements:* For master's, GRE or GMAT, writing sample, interview, letters of recommendation. Additional exam requirements/recommendations for international students: Required—TOEFL (minimum score 535 paper-based; 203 computer-based). *Application deadline:* Applications are processed on a rolling basis. Application fee: $30. Electronic applications accepted. *Expenses:* Tuition: Full-time $11,340; part-time $630 per credit hour. Tuition and fees vary according to program. *Financial support:* In 2009–10, 17 students received support, including 1 research assistantship (averaging $4,815 per year). Financial award application deadline: 3/15; financial award applicants required to submit FAFSA. *Faculty research:* Curriculum development, consumer behavior, interdisciplinary pedagogy. *Unit head:* Dr. Diane Tobin, Dean, 502-585-9911 Ext. 2747, E-mail: dtobin@spalding.edu. *Application contact:* Claire Rayburn, Administrative Assistant, 502-585-9911 Ext. 2120, E-mail: cbc@spalding.edu.

Stevens Institute of Technology, Graduate School, Wesley J. Howe School of Technology Management, Program in Professional Communications, Hoboken, NJ 07030. Offers Certificate. *Expenses:* Tuition: Full-time $9900; part-time $1100 per credit. Required fees: $286 per semester.

Suffolk University, College of Arts and Sciences, Department of Communication, Boston, MA 02108-2770. Offers communication studies (MAC); integrated marketing communication (MAC); organizational communication (MAC); public relations and advertising (MAC). Part-time and evening/weekend programs available. *Faculty:* 20 full-time (10 women). *Students:* 14 full-time (12 women), 28 part-time (22 women), 2 international. Average age 27. 85 applicants, 58% accepted, 8 enrolled. In 2009, 21 master's awarded. *Degree requirements:* For master's, thesis optional. *Entrance requirements:* For master's, GRE General Test, MAT, or GMAT, 2 letters of recommendation, resume. Additional exam requirements/recommendations for international students: Required—TOEFL (minimum score 550 paper-based; 213 computer-based; 80 iBT). *Application deadline:* For fall admission, 6/15 priority date for domestic students, 6/15 for international students; for spring admission, 11/1 priority date for domestic students, 11/1 for international students. Applications are processed on a rolling basis. Application fee: $50. Electronic applications accepted. *Expenses:* Contact institution. *Financial support:* In 2009–10, 30 students received support, including 20 fellowships with partial tuition reimbursements available (averaging $3,413 per year); career-related internships or fieldwork, Federal Work-Study, and institutionally sponsored loans also available. Support available to part-time students. Financial award application deadline: 4/1; financial award applicants required to submit FAFSA. *Faculty research:* New media and new markets for advertising, First Amendment issues with the Internet, gender and intercultural communication, organizational development. *Unit head:* Dr. Robert Rosenthal, Chair, 617-573-8502, Fax: 617-742-6982, E-mail: rrosenth@suffolk.edu. *Application contact:* Judith Reynolds, Director of Graduate Admissions, 617-573-8302, Fax: 617-305-1733, E-mail: grad.admission@suffolk.edu.

Temple University, Graduate School, School of Communications and Theater, Department of Strategic and Organizational Communication, Philadelphia, PA 19122-6096. Offers communication management (MS); mass media and communication (PhD). *Entrance requirements:* Additional exam requirements/recommendations for international students: Required—TOEFL (minimum score 550 paper-based; 213 computer-based; 79 iBT).

Towson University, College of Graduate Studies and Research, Program in Communications Management, Towson, MD 21252-0001. Offers MS. *Degree requirements:* For master's, thesis. *Entrance requirements:* For master's, 24 credits in mass communications, public relations and/or advertising, writing and statistics; professional experience; minimum GPA of 3.0. Electronic applications accepted.

Universidad Autonoma de Guadalajara, Graduate Programs, Guadalajara, Mexico. Offers administrative law and justice (LL M); advertising and corporate communications (MA); architecture (M Arch); business (MBA); computational science (MCC); education (Ed M, Ed D); English-Spanish translation (MA); fiscal law (MA); integrated management of digital animation (MA); international business (MIB); international corporate law (LL M); internet technologies (MS); labor health (MS); manufacturing systems (MMS); philosophy (MA, PhD); power electronics (MS); quality systems (MQS); renewable energy (MS); social evaluation of projects (MBA); strategic market research (MBA); teaching mathematics (MA).

University of Alaska Fairbanks, College of Liberal Arts, Department of Communications, Fairbanks, AK 99775-5680. Offers professional communications (MA). Part-time programs available. *Faculty:* 4 full-time (3 women), 1 (woman) part-time/adjunct. *Students:* 13 full-time (10 women), 7 part-time (5 women); includes 3 minority (1 African American, 1 Asian American or Pacific Islander, 1 Hispanic American), 2 international. Average age 31. 9 applicants, 67% accepted, 6 enrolled. In 2009, 3 master's awarded. *Degree requirements:* For master's, comprehensive exam, thesis, oral defense. *Entrance requirements:* Additional exam requirements/recommendations for international students: Required—TOEFL (minimum score 550 paper-based; 213 computer-based; 80 iBT). *Application deadline:* For fall admission, 6/1 for domestic students, 3/1 for international students; for spring admission, 10/15 for domestic students, 9/1 for international students. Applications are processed on a rolling basis. Application fee: $60. Electronic applications accepted. *Expenses:* Tuition, state resident: full-time $7584; part-time $316 per credit. Tuition, nonresident: full-time $15,504; part-time $646 per credit. Required fees: $23 per credit. $135 per semester. Tuition and fees vary according to course level, course load and reciprocity agreements. *Financial support:* In 2009–10, 10 teaching assistantships (averaging $12,006 per year) were awarded; fellowships, Federal Work-Study, scholarships/grants, tuition waivers, and unspecified assistantships also available. Support available to part-time students. Financial award application deadline: 7/1; financial award applicants required to submit FAFSA. *Faculty research:* Interpersonal communications, health communications, intercultural communications, politeness and face management in conversation, gender communication. *Unit head:* Dr. Robert Arundale, Department Chair, 907-474-6591, Fax: 907-474-5858, E-mail: fycomm@uaf.edu. *Application contact:* Dr. Robert Arundale, Department Chair, 907-474-6591, Fax: 907-474-5858, E-mail: fycomm@uaf.edu.

University of Connecticut, Graduate School, College of Liberal Arts and Sciences, Department of Communication Sciences, Program in Communication Processes and Marketing Communication, Storrs, CT 06269. Offers PhD. *Faculty:* 16 full-time (6 women). *Students:* 20 full-time (7 women), 6 part-time (4 women); includes 1 minority (African American), 4 international. Average age 31. 32 applicants, 16% accepted, 2 enrolled. In 2009, 3 doctorates awarded. *Degree requirements:* For doctorate, thesis/dissertation. *Entrance requirements:* For doctorate, GMAT or GRE General Test. Additional exam requirements/recommendations for international students: Required—TOEFL (minimum score 550 paper-based; 213 computer-based). *Application deadline:* For fall admission, 2/1 priority date for domestic and international students; for spring admission, 11/1 for domestic students, 10/1 for international students. Applications are processed on a rolling basis. Application fee: $55. Electronic applications accepted. *Expenses:* Tuition, state resident: full-time $4725; part-time $525 per credit. Tuition, nonresident: full-time $12,267; part-time $1363 per credit. Required fees: $346 per semester. Tuition and fees vary according to course load. *Financial support:* In 2009–10, 2 research assistantships with full tuition reimbursements, 17 teaching assistantships with full tuition reimbursements were awarded; fellowships, Federal Work-Study, scholarships/grants, health care benefits, and unspecified assistantships also available. Financial award application deadline: 2/1; financial award applicants required to submit FAFSA. *Unit head:* Carl A. Coelho, Chair, 860-486-2628. *Application contact:* Sue Kiss, Administrative Assistant, 860-486-2628, Fax: 860-486-5422, E-mail: susan.kiss@uconn.edu.

University of Nebraska–Lincoln, Graduate College, College of Arts and Sciences, Department of Communication Studies, Lincoln, NE 68588. Offers instructional communication (MA, PhD); interpersonal communication (MA, PhD); marketing, communication studies, and advertising (MA, PhD); organizational communication (MA, PhD); rhetoric and culture (MA, PhD). *Degree requirements:* For master's, thesis optional; for doctorate, comprehensive exam, thesis/dissertation. *Entrance requirements:* For master's and doctorate, GRE General Test, writing sample. Additional exam requirements/recommendations for international students: Required—TOEFL (minimum score 600 paper-based; 250 computer-based). Electronic applications accepted. *Faculty research:* Message strategies, gender communication, political communication, organizational communication, instructional communication.

University of Portland, College of Arts and Sciences, Department of Communication Studies, Portland, OR 97203-5798. Offers communication (MA); management communication (MS). Part-time and evening/weekend programs available. *Faculty:* 7 full-time (2 women), 1 part-time/adjunct (0 women). *Students:* 2 full-time (both women), 11 part-time (10 women); includes 2 minority (1 African American, 1 Asian American or Pacific Islander), 2 international. Average age 27. In 2009, 4 master's awarded. *Degree requirements:* For master's, thesis optional. *Entrance requirements:* For master's, GRE General Test, minimum GPA of 3.25, 3 letters of recommendation, resume, statement of goals, official transcripts. Additional exam requirements/recommendations for international students: Required—TOEFL (minimum score 600 paper-based; 100 iBT), IELTS (minimum score 7.5). *Application deadline:* For fall admission, 7/15 priority date for domestic and international students; for spring admission, 12/15 priority date for domestic and international students. Applications are processed on a rolling basis. Application fee: $50. *Expenses:* Tuition: Part-time $860 per semester hour. *Financial support:* Career-related internships or fieldwork, Federal Work-Study, scholarships/grants, and tuition waivers (partial) available. Financial award application deadline: 3/1; financial award applicants required to submit FAFSA. *Unit head:* Dr. Jeffrey Kerssen-Griep, Director, 503-943-7167, E-mail: kerssen@up.edu. *Application contact:* Chris James Olinger, Administrative Assistant, 503-943-7107, Fax: 503-943-7315, E-mail: olingerc@up.edu.

University of St. Thomas, Graduate Studies, Opus College of Business, Master of Business Communication Program, Minneapolis, MN 55403. Offers MBC. Part-time and evening/weekend programs available. *Students:* 82 part-time (65 women); includes 5 minority (1 American Indian/Alaska Native, 3 Asian Americans or Pacific Islanders, 1 Hispanic American), 2 international. Average age 34. In 2009, 80 master's awarded. *Entrance requirements:* For master's, GMAT or GRE. Additional exam requirements/recommendations for international students: Required—TOEFL, IELTS or Michigan English Language Assessment Battery. *Application deadline:* For fall admission, 8/2 priority date for domestic students; for spring admission, 1/4 priority date for domestic students. Application fee: $40. Electronic applications accepted. *Financial support:* Institutionally sponsored loans and scholarships/grants available. Financial award application deadline: 7/1; financial award applicants required to submit FAFSA. *Unit head:* Dr. Michael Porter, Director, 651-962-4380, Fax: 651-962-4710, E-mail: businesscom@stthomas.edu. *Application contact:* Leslie Krona, Program Manager/Advisor, 612-962-4380, Fax: 612-962-4710, E-mail: businesscom@stthomas.edu.

University of Southern California, Graduate School, Annenberg School for Communication and Journalism, School of Communication, Program in Communication, Los Angeles, CA 90089. Offers communication (MA, PhD), including interpersonal and social dynamics (PhD), mass communication, technology, and public policy (PhD), organizational communication (PhD), rhetorical and cultural studies (PhD). *Degree requirements:* For doctorate, thesis/dissertation. *Entrance requirements:* For master's and doctorate, GRE General Test, resume, writing samples, 3 letters of recommendation, interest survey questionnaire, statement of purpose. Additional exam requirements/recommendations for international students: Required—TOEFL (minimum score 280 computer-based; 114 iBT); Recommended—TWE. Electronic applications accepted. *Expenses:* Tuition: Full-time $25,980; part-time $1315 per unit. Required fees: $554. One-time fee: $35 full-time. Full-time tuition and fees vary according to degree level and program. *Faculty research:* Computer-mediated communication, public health campaigns, communication democracy and the public sphere, new communication technologies in organizations, communication and community.

See Display on page 629 and Close-Up on page 685.

University of Southern California, Graduate School, Annenberg School for Communication and Journalism, School of Communication, Program in Communication Management, Los Angeles, CA 90089. Offers MCM, JD/MCM, MCM/MAJCS. Part-time and evening/weekend programs available. *Degree requirements:* For master's, professional project. *Entrance requirements:* For master's, GRE General Test or GMAT, resume, writing samples, recommendation letters, statement of purpose. Additional exam requirements/recommendations for international students: Required—TOEFL (minimum score 280 computer-based; 114 iBT). Electronic applications accepted. *Expenses:* Tuition: Full-time $25,980; part-time $1315 per unit. Required fees: $554. One-time fee: $35 full-time. Full-time tuition and fees vary according to degree level and program. *Faculty research:* Global communication, communication law and policy, entertainment management, marketing communication, strategic and corporate communication management.

See Display on page 629 and Close-Up on page 685.

University of Wisconsin–Stevens Point, College of Fine Arts and Communication, Division of Communication, Stevens Point, WI 54481-3897. Offers interpersonal communication (MA); mass communication (MA); organizational communication (MA); public relations (MA). Part-time programs available. *Students:* 7 full-time (3 women), 19 part-time (11 women). *Degree requirements:* For master's, thesis or alternative. *Entrance requirements:* For master's, GRE. Additional exam requirements/recommendations for international students: Required—TOEFL (minimum score 575 paper-based). *Application deadline:* For fall admission, 3/1 priority date for domestic students. Applications are processed on a rolling basis. Application fee: $45. *Expenses:* Tuition, state resident: full-time $7740; part-time $430 per credit hour. Tuition, nonresident: full-time $17,804; part-time $989 per credit hour. Tuition and fees vary according to course load and reciprocity agreements. *Financial support:* In 2009–10, 9 teaching assistantships were awarded; career-related internships or fieldwork, Federal Work-Study, institutionally sponsored loans, and unspecified assistantships also available. Support available to part-time

Corporate and Organizational Communication

University of Wisconsin–Stevens Point (continued)
students. Financial award application deadline: 5/1; financial award applicants required to submit FAFSA. *Faculty research:* Communication theory and research, film history. *Unit head:* Dr. James Haney, Chair, 715-346-3409, E-mail: jhaney@uwsp.edu. *Application contact:* Dr. Chris Sadler, Graduate Coordinator, 715-346-3898, E-mail: csadler@uwsp.edu.

University of Wisconsin–Whitewater, School of Graduate Studies, College of Arts and Communications, Department of Communication, Whitewater, WI 53190-1790. Offers corporate communication (MS); mass communication (MS). Part-time and evening/weekend programs available. Postbaccalaureate distance learning degree programs offered (no on-campus study). *Degree requirements:* For master's, thesis or alternative. *Entrance requirements:* For master's, 2 letters of recommendation. Additional exam requirements/recommendations for international students: Required—TOEFL (minimum score 550 paper-based; 213 computer-based). Electronic applications accepted.

Washington State University, Graduate School, College of Liberal Arts, Edward R. Murrow College of Communication, Pullman, WA 99164. Offers health communications (MA, PhD); intercultural and international communications (MA, PhD); media and society (MA, PhD); media process and effects (MA, PhD); organizational communications (MA, PhD). *Degree requirements:* For master's, comprehensive exam (for some programs), thesis optional, oral exam; for doctorate, comprehensive exam, thesis/dissertation. *Entrance requirements:* For master's, GRE General Test, minimum GPA of 3.25, 3 letters of recommendation; for doctorate, GRE General Test, minimum undergraduate GPA of 3.25, graduate 3.5; MA in communication; 3 letters of recommendation. Additional exam requirements/recommendations for international students: Required—TOEFL (minimum score 580 paper-based; 237 computer-based). Electronic applications accepted. *Faculty research:* Advocacy communication, mediated communication in decision making, communication technology policy and effects, multicultural and international psychology and physiology of communication.

Wayne State University, College of Fine, Performing and Communication Arts, Department of Communication, Detroit, MI 48202. Offers communication studies (MA, PhD); public relations and organizational communication (MA); radio-TV-film (MA, PhD); speech communication (MA, PhD). *Degree requirements:* For master's, thesis, essay, or comprehensive exam; for doctorate, thesis/dissertation. *Entrance requirements:* For master's, minimum GPA of 3.0, sample of academic writing; for doctorate, GRE, minimum GPA of 3.3, MA; letters of recommendation; personal statement; sample of written scholarship. Additional exam requirements/recommendations for international students: Required—TOEFL (minimum score 550 paper-based; 213 computer-based); Recommended—TWE (minimum score 6). Electronic applications accepted. *Faculty research:* Rhetorical theory and criticism; mass media theory and research; argumentation; organizational communication; risk and crisis communication; interpersonal, family, and health communication.

Webster University, School of Communications, Program in Communications Management, St. Louis, MO 63119-3194. Offers MA. *Expenses:* Tuition: Part-time $565 per credit hour. Tuition and fees vary according to degree level, campus/location and program.

Western Michigan University, Graduate College, College of Arts and Sciences, Department of Communication, Kalamazoo, MI 49008. Offers MA.

West Virginia University, Eberly College of Arts and Sciences, Department of Communication Studies, Morgantown, WV 26506. Offers communication in instruction (MA); communication studies (PhD); communication theory and research (MA); corporate and organizational communication (MA). Part-time programs available. *Degree requirements:* For master's, comprehensive exam (for some programs), thesis (for some programs); for doctorate, comprehensive exam, thesis/dissertation. *Entrance requirements:* For master's and doctorate, minimum GPA of 3.0. Additional exam requirements/recommendations for international students: Required—TOEFL. Electronic applications accepted. *Faculty research:* Instructional communication, interpersonal communication, health communication, influence, instructional communication, social influence.

West Virginia University, Perley Isaac Reed School of Journalism, Program in Digital Marketing Communications, Morgantown, WV 26506. Offers Graduate Certificate. Postbaccalaureate distance learning degree programs offered (no on-campus study). *Entrance requirements:* For degree, resume. Electronic applications accepted.

Health Communication

Chapman University, Graduate Studies, Schmid College of Science, Health Communication Program, Orange, CA 92866. Offers MS. Part-time and evening/weekend programs available. *Faculty:* 1 (woman) full-time, 1 part-time/adjunct (0 women). *Students:* 6 full-time (5 women), 3 part-time (all women); includes 1 minority (Asian American or Pacific Islander). Average age 28. 17 applicants, 59% accepted, 7 enrolled. *Entrance requirements:* For master's, GRE, minimum undergraduate GPA of 3.0. Additional exam requirements/recommendations for international students: Required—TOEFL (minimum score 550 paper-based; 213 computer-based; 80 iBT). *Application deadline:* Applications are processed on a rolling basis. Application fee: $50. Electronic applications accepted. Tuition and fees vary according to course load, degree level and program. *Financial support:* Fellowships, Federal Work-Study and scholarships/grants available. Financial award application deadline: 6/30; financial award applicants required to submit FAFSA. *Unit head:* Dr. Lisa Sparks, Interim Dean, 714-997-6703, E-mail: sparks@chapman.edu. *Application contact:* Saundra Hoover, Director of Graduate Admissions, 714-997-6786, Fax: 714-997-6713, E-mail: shoover@chapman.edu.

Cleveland State University, College of Graduate Studies, College of Liberal Arts and Social Sciences, School of Communication, Cleveland, OH 44115. Offers applied communication theory and methodology (MA); culture, communication and health care (Certificate). Part-time and evening/weekend programs available. *Degree requirements:* For master's, variable foreign language requirement, thesis, project, comprehensive exam, or collaborative project. *Entrance requirements:* For master's, GRE or MAT, minimum undergraduate GPA of 2.75, 2 letters of recommendation. Additional exam requirements/recommendations for international students: Required—TOEFL (minimum score 525 paper-based; 197 computer-based). Electronic applications accepted. *Faculty research:* Interpersonal, organizational, and mass communication; health communication.

East Carolina University, Graduate School, College of Fine Arts and Communication, School of Communication, Greenville, NC 27858-4353. Offers health communication (MA). *Entrance requirements:* For master's, GRE.

Emerson College, Graduate Studies, School of Communication, Department of Communication Sciences and Disorders, Program in Health Communication, Boston, MA 02116-4624. Offers MA. Part-time programs available. *Faculty:* 2 full-time (1 woman). *Students:* 37 full-time (33 women), 2 part-time (both women); includes 2 minority (1 African American, 1 Asian American or Pacific Islander), 2 international. Average age 24. 66 applicants, 58% accepted, 20 enrolled. In 2009, 15 master's awarded. *Entrance requirements:* For master's, GMAT or GRE General Test. Additional exam requirements/recommendations for international students: Required—TOEFL (minimum score 550 paper-based; 213 computer-based; 80 iBT), IELTS (minimum score 6.5). *Application deadline:* For fall admission, 6/1 priority date for domestic students, 5/1 for international students. Applications are processed on a rolling basis. Application fee: $60 ($75 for international students). Electronic applications accepted. *Expenses:* Tuition: Full-time $22,056; part-time $919 per credit. Required fees: $120; $120 per year. One-time fee: $170 full-time. *Financial support:* In 2009–10, 14 students received support, including 1 fellowship with partial tuition reimbursement available (averaging $14,000 per year), 11 research assistantships with partial tuition reimbursements available (averaging $10,000 per year); Federal Work-Study, scholarships/grants, and unspecified assistantships also available. Financial award application deadline: 3/1; financial award applicants required to submit FAFSA. *Faculty research:* Health promotion, health communications. *Unit head:* Dr. Timothy Edgar, Graduate Program Director, 617-824-8492, E-mail: timothy_edgar@emerson.edu. *Application contact:* Office of Graduate Admission, 617-824-8610, Fax: 617-824-8614, E-mail: gradapp@emerson.edu.

The Johns Hopkins University, Bloomberg School of Public Health, Department of Health, Behavior and Society, Baltimore, MD 21218-2699. Offers genetic counseling (Sc M); health education and health communication (MHS); social and behavioral sciences (Dr PH, PhD, Sc D); social factors in health (MHS). *Faculty:* 43 full-time (30 women), 59 part-time/adjunct (40 women). *Students:* 100 full-time (89 women), 4 part-time (3 women); includes 28 minority (13 African Americans, 12 Asian Americans or Pacific Islanders, 3 Hispanic Americans), 13 international. Average age 29. 227 applicants, 31% accepted, 26 enrolled. In 2009, 25 master's, 8 doctorates awarded. *Degree requirements:* For master's, comprehensive exam (for some programs), thesis (for some programs); for doctorate, comprehensive exam, thesis/dissertation. *Entrance requirements:* For master's, GRE, curriculum vitae, 3 letters of recommendation; for doctorate, GRE, transcripts, curriculum vitae, statement, 3 recommendation letters. Additional exam requirements/recommendations for international students: Required—TOEFL (minimum score 600 paper-based; 250 computer-based; 100 iBT). *Application deadline:* For fall admission, 12/1 for domestic and international students. Applications are processed on a rolling basis. Application fee: $45. Electronic applications accepted. *Financial support:* In 2009–10, 96 students received support, including 17 fellowships with tuition reimbursements available (averaging $23,634 per year), 30 research assistantships (averaging $7,800 per year), 25 teaching assistantships (averaging $2,759 per year); career-related internships or fieldwork, Federal Work-Study, scholarships/grants, traineeships, health care benefits, unspecified assistantships, and stipends also available. Financial award application deadline: 3/15. *Faculty research:* Social determinants of health, and structural- and community-level inventions to improve health; communication and health education; behavioral and social aspects of genetic counseling. Total annual research expenditures: $6.3 million. *Unit head:* Georgean Smith, Administrator, 410-502-3715, Fax: 410-502-4333, E-mail: gcsmith@jhsph.edu. *Application contact:* Barbara W. Diehl, Senior Academic Program Coordinator, 410-502-4415, Fax: 410-502-4333, E-mail: bdiehl@jhsph.edu.

Marquette University, Graduate School, College of Communication, Milwaukee, WI 53201-1881. Offers advertising and public relations (MA); broadcasting and electronic communications (MA); communications studies (MA); journalism (MA); mass communications (MA); religious communications (MA); science, health and environmental communications (MA). *Accreditation:* ACEJMC. Part-time and evening/weekend programs available. *Faculty:* 31 full-time (17 women), 35 part-time/adjunct (16 women). *Students:* 28 full-time (21 women), 30 part-time (24 women); includes 3 minority (1 African American, 2 American Indian/Alaska Native), 7 international. Average age 26. 81 applicants, 47% accepted, 22 enrolled. In 2009, 17 master's awarded. *Degree requirements:* For master's, comprehensive exam. *Entrance requirements:* For master's, GRE. Additional exam requirements/recommendations for international students: Required—TOEFL. Application fee: $40. *Financial support:* In 2009–10, 6 research assistantships, 12 teaching assistantships were awarded; career-related internships or fieldwork, Federal Work-Study, institutionally sponsored loans, scholarships/grants, and tuition waivers (full and partial) also available. Support available to part-time students. Financial award application deadline: 2/15. *Faculty research:* Urban journalism, gender and communication, intercultural communication, religious communication. *Unit head:* Dr. Ana Garner, Dean, 414-288-3588, Fax: 414-288-1578. *Application contact:* Erin Fox, Assistant Director for Recruitment, 414-288-5319, Fax: 414-288-1902, E-mail: erin.fox@marquette.edu.

Marywood University, Academic Affairs; Insalaco College of Creative and Performing Arts, Department of Communication Arts, Program in Information Sciences, Scranton, PA 18509-1598. Offers corporate communication (Certificate); e-business (Certificate); health communication (Certificate); information sciences (MS), including library science/information specialist; instructional technology (Certificate). *Students:* 1 full-time (0 women), 4 part-time (3 women). Average age 32. In 2009, 3 master's awarded. *Entrance requirements:* Additional exam requirements/recommendations for international students: Required—TOEFL (minimum score 550 paper-based; 213 computer-based; 79 iBT). *Application deadline:* For fall admission, 4/1 priority date for domestic students, 3/31 priority date for international students; for spring admission, 11/1 priority date for domestic students, 8/31 priority date for international students. Applications are processed on a rolling basis. Application fee: $35. Electronic applications accepted. *Expenses:* Tuition: Part-time $715 per credit. Required fees: $270 per semester. Tuition and fees vary according to degree level, campus/location and program. *Financial support:* Career-related internships or fieldwork, scholarships/grants, and unspecified assistantships available. Support available to part-time students. Financial award application deadline: 6/30; financial award applicants required to submit FAFSA. *Application contact:* Tammy Manka, Assistant Director of Graduate Admissions, 866-279-9663, E-mail: tmanka@marywood.edu.

Michigan State University, The Graduate School, College of Communication Arts and Sciences, Program in Health Communication, East Lansing, MI 48824. Offers MA. *Students:* 9 full-time (8 women), 6 part-time (4 women); includes 1 minority (Asian American or Pacific Islander), 3 international. Average age 27. 31 applicants, 74% accepted. In 2009, 7 master's awarded. *Entrance requirements:* Additional exam requirements/recommendations for international students: Required—TOEFL. Electronic applications accepted. *Expenses:* Tuition, state resident: part-time $478.25 per credit hour. Tuition, nonresident: part-time $966.50 per credit hour. Part-time tuition and fees vary according to program. *Financial support:* In 2009–10, 2 research assistantships with tuition reimbursements (averaging $6,746 per year), 2 teaching assistantships with tuition reimbursements (averaging $6,662 per year) were awarded. *Faculty research:* Mass communication and public health, health communication for diverse populations, descriptive and analytical epidemiology. *Unit head:* Dr. Sandi Smith, Director, Health and Risk Communication Center, 517-353-3715, Fax: 517-432-1192, E-mail: smiths@msu.edu. *Application contact:* Marge Barkman, Coordinator for Academic Programs, 517-355-3471, Fax: 517-432-1192, E-mail: hrcc@msu.edu.

Ohio University, Graduate College, Scripps College of Communication, School of Communication Studies, Athens, OH 45701-2979. Offers health communication (PhD); organizational communication (MA); relating and organizing (PhD); rhetoric and public culture (PhD). Part-time programs available. Postbaccalaureate distance learning degree programs offered (minimal on-campus study). *Faculty:* 24 full-time (9 women), 4 part-time/adjunct (1 woman). *Students:* 48 full-time (33 women), 31 part-time (25 women); includes 5 minority (4 African Americans, 1 Hispanic American), 12 international. 98 applicants, 46% accepted, 36 enrolled. In 2009, 7 master's, 12 doctorates awarded. Terminal master's awarded for partial completion of doctoral program. *Degree requirements:* For master's, capstone; for doctorate, comprehensive exam, thesis/dissertation. *Entrance requirements:* For master's, GRE; for doctorate, GRE General Test, minimum GPA of 3.0. Additional exam requirements/recommendations for international students: Required—TOEFL (minimum score 550 paper-based; 80 iBT) or IELTS Academic (minimum score 6.5). *Application deadline:* For fall admission, 1/15 priority date for domestic and international students. Application fee: $50 ($55 for international students). Electronic applications accepted. *Expenses:* Tuition, state resident: full-time $7839; part-time $323 per quarter hour. Tuition, nonresident: full-time $15,831; part-time $654 per quarter hour. Required fees: $2931. *Financial support:* In 2009–10, 12 students received support, including fellowships with full tuition reimbursements available (averaging $13,600 per year), research assistantships with full tuition reimbursements available (averaging $13,600 per year), teaching assistantships with full tuition reimbursements available (averaging $13,600 per year); career-related internships or fieldwork, Federal Work-Study, and institutionally sponsored loans also available. Financial award application deadline: 1/15. *Faculty research:* Rhetoric and public culture, relating and organizing, health communication. Total annual research expenditures: $200,000. *Unit head:* Dr. Claudia Hale, Director, 740-593-4832, Fax: 740-593-4810, E-mail: hale@ohio.edu. *Application contact:* Dr. Scott Titsworth, Graduate Chairman, 740-593-9160, Fax: 740-593-4810, E-mail: titswort@ohio.edu.

Tufts University, School of Medicine, Public Health and Professional Degree Programs, Boston, MA 02111. Offers biomedical sciences (MS); health communication (MS); pain research, education and policy (MS); public health (MPH). *Accreditation:* CEPH (one or more programs are accredited). Part-time and evening/weekend programs available. *Faculty:* 57 full-time (25 women), 44 part-time/adjunct (17 women). *Students:* 210 full-time (123 women), 68 part-time (54 women); includes 94 minority (19 African Americans, 1 American Indian/Alaska Native, 58 Asian Americans or Pacific Islanders, 16 Hispanic Americans), 13 international. Average age 27. 857 applicants, 55% accepted, 173 enrolled. In 2009, 97 master's awarded. *Degree requirements:* For master's, thesis (for some programs). *Entrance requirements:* For master's, GRE General Test. Additional exam requirements/recommendations for international students: Required—TOEFL. *Application deadline:* For fall admission, 3/15 priority date for domestic students, 3/15 for international students; for spring admission, 10/25 priority date for domestic students, 10/25 for international students. Applications are processed on a rolling basis. Application fee: $70. Electronic applications accepted. *Expenses:* Contact institution. *Financial support:* Federal Work-Study and scholarships/grants available. Support available to part-time students. Financial award application deadline: 2/27; financial award applicants required to submit FAFSA. *Faculty research:* Environmental and occupational health, nutrition, epidemiology, health communication, health services management and policy, biostatics, protein interaction, mRNA processing, vascular pathology. *Unit head:* Dr. Aviva Must, Dean, Public Health and Professional Degree Programs, 617-636-0935, Fax: 617-636-0898, E-mail: aviva.must@tufts.edu. *Application contact:* Emily Keily, Director of Admissions, 617-636-6645, Fax: 617-636-0898, E-mail: med-phpd@tufts.edu.

Tulane University, School of Public Health and Tropical Medicine, Department of Community Health Sciences, Program in Health Education and Communication, New Orleans, LA 70118-5669. Offers MPH. *Accreditation:* CEPH. *Degree requirements:* For master's, comprehensive exam. *Entrance requirements:* For master's, GRE General Test. Additional exam requirements/recommendations for international students: Required—TOEFL.

University of Florida, Graduate School, College of Health and Human Performance, Department of Health Education and Behavior, Gainesville, FL 32611. Offers health behavior (PhD); health communication (Graduate Certificate); health education and behavior (MS). *Accreditation:* NCATE (one or more programs are accredited). Part-time programs available. Terminal master's awarded for partial completion of doctoral program. *Degree requirements:* For master's, thesis (for some programs); for doctorate, thesis/dissertation. *Entrance requirements:* For master's and doctorate, GRE General Test, minimum GPA of 3.0. Additional exam requirements/recommendations for international students: Required—TOEFL (minimum score 550 paper-based; 213 computer-based). Electronic applications accepted. *Faculty research:* Adolescent health, human sexuality and HIV/AIDS, substance use, nutrition.

University of Houston, College of Liberal Arts and Social Sciences, School of Communication, Houston, TX 77204. Offers health communication (MA); mass communication studies (MA); public relations studies (MA); speech communication (MA). Part-time and evening/weekend programs available. *Faculty:* 9 full-time (5 women), 2 part-time/adjunct (0 women). *Students:* 42 full-time (38 women), 49 part-time (44 women); includes 31 minority (17 African Americans, 2 American Indian/Alaska Native, 2 Asian Americans or Pacific Islanders, 10 Hispanic Americans), 24 international. Average age 28. 92 applicants, 47% accepted, 28 enrolled. In 2009, 19 master's awarded. *Degree requirements:* For master's, comprehensive exam, thesis. *Entrance requirements:* For master's, GRE. Additional exam requirements/recommendations for international students: Required—TOEFL. *Application deadline:* For fall admission, 6/1 for domestic students, 4/1 for international students; for spring admission, 11/1 for domestic students, 10/1 for international students. Application fee: $25 ($75 for international students). Electronic applications accepted. *Expenses:* Tuition, state resident: full-time $7676; part-time $320 per credit hour. Tuition, nonresident: full-time $14,324; part-time $597 per credit hour. Required fees: $3034. *Financial support:* In 2009–10, 2 fellowships with full tuition reimbursements (averaging $9,750 per year), 5 teaching assistantships with full tuition reimbursements (averaging $9,750 per year) were awarded; career-related internships or fieldwork, Federal Work-Study, institutionally sponsored loans, scholarships/grants, health care benefits, and unspecified assistantships also available. Support available to part-time students. Financial award application deadline: 2/1. *Unit head:* Dr. Beth Olson, Chairperson, 713-743-2873, Fax: 713-743-2876, E-mail: bolson@uh.edu. *Application contact:* Salima B. Haji, Academic Advisor, 713-743-2575, Fax: 713-743-2876, E-mail: sbhaji@central.uh.edu.

University of Southern California, Keck School of Medicine and Graduate School, Graduate Programs in Medicine, Department of Preventive Medicine, Master of Public Health Program, Alhambra, CA 91803. Offers biostatistics/epidemiology (MPH); child and family health (MPH); global health leadership (MPH); health communication (MPH); health promotion (MPH). *Accreditation:* CEPH. Part-time programs available. *Faculty:* 22 full-time (12 women), 3 part-time/adjunct (0 women). *Students:* 215 full-time (158 women), 3 part-time (2 women); includes 148 minority (13 African Americans, 3 American Indian/Alaska Native, 114 Asian Americans or Pacific Islanders, 18 Hispanic Americans), 25 international. Average age 26. 208 applicants, 74% accepted, 76 enrolled. In 2009, 60 master's awarded. *Degree requirements:* For master's, practicum, final report, oral presentation. *Entrance requirements:* For master's, GRE General Test, MCAT, GMAT, minimum GPA of 3.0. Additional exam requirements/recommendations for international students: Required—TOEFL (minimum score 600 paper-based; 250 computer-based; 100 iBT). *Application deadline:* For fall admission, 6/1 priority date for domestic and international students; for spring admission, 11/1 priority date for domestic students, 10/1 priority date for international students. Applications are processed on a rolling basis. Application fee: $85. Electronic applications accepted. *Expenses:* Tuition: Full-time $25,980; part-time $1315 per unit. Required fees: $554. One-time fee: $35 full-time. Full-time tuition and fees vary according to degree level and program. *Financial support:* In 2009–10, 175 students received support, including 20 fellowships (averaging $3,200 per year); career-related internships or fieldwork, Federal Work-Study, institutionally sponsored loans, and scholarships/grants also available. Support available to part-time students. Financial award application deadline: 5/1; financial award applicants required to submit CSS PROFILE or FAFSA. *Faculty research:* Substance abuse prevention, cancer and heart disease prevention, mass media and health communication research, health promotion, treatment compliance. *Unit head:* Dr. Thomas W. Valente, Director, 626-457-4139, Fax: 626-457-6699, E-mail: tvalente@usc.edu. *Application contact:* Chrystal Romero, Admissions Counselor, 626-457-6676, Fax: 626-457-6699, E-mail: ccromero@usc.edu.

Washington State University, Graduate School, College of Liberal Arts, Edward R. Murrow College of Communication, Pullman, WA 99164. Offers health communications (MA, PhD); intercultural and international communications (MA, PhD); media and society (MA, PhD); media process and effects (MA, PhD); organizational communications (MA, PhD). *Degree requirements:* For master's, comprehensive exam (for some programs), thesis optional, oral exam; for doctorate, comprehensive exam, thesis/dissertation. *Entrance requirements:* For master's, GRE General Test, minimum GPA of 3.25, 3 letters of recommendation; for doctorate, GRE General Test, minimum undergraduate GPA of 3.25, graduate 3.5; MA in communication; 3 letters of recommendation. Additional exam requirements/recommendations for international students: Required—TOEFL (minimum score 580 paper-based; 237 computer-based). Electronic applications accepted. *Faculty research:* Advocacy communication, mediated communication in decision making, communication technology policy and effects, multicultural and international psychology and physiology of communication.

Internet and Interactive Multimedia

Academy of Art University, Graduate Program, School of Multimedia Communications, San Francisco, CA 94105-3410. Offers MA. Part-time and evening/weekend programs available. *Degree requirements:* For master's, final review. Electronic applications accepted.

Alfred University, Graduate School, New York State College of Ceramics, School of Art and Design, Alfred, NY 14802-1205. Offers ceramic art (MFA); electronic integrated arts (MFA); glass art (MFA); sculpture (MFA). *Accreditation:* NASAD. *Degree requirements:* For master's, exhibit. *Entrance requirements:* For master's, portfolio. Additional exam requirements/recommendations for international students: Required—TOEFL (minimum score 550 paper-based; 213 computer-based; 80 iBT), IELTS (minimum score 6). Electronic applications accepted. *Expenses:* Tuition: Full-time $33,296; part-time $708 per credit hour. Required fees: $880; $144 per year. Full-time tuition and fees vary according to program. *Faculty research:* Ceramic sculpture, functional ceramics, wood, mixed media, hot and cold glass.

Brooklyn College of the City University of New York, Division of Graduate Studies, Program in Performance and Interactive Media Arts, Brooklyn, NY 11210-2889. Offers MFA, CAS. *Students:* 11 full-time (7 women), 14 part-time (9 women); includes 6 minority (2 African Americans, 4 Hispanic Americans), 3 international. Average age 31. In 2009, 3 master's, 1 other advanced degree awarded. *Entrance requirements:* For master's, 2 letters of recommendation, resume, portfolio, interview; for CAS, 2 letters of recommendation. Additional exam requirements/recommendations for international students: Required—TOEFL (minimum score 500 paper-based; 173 computer-based; 61 iBT). *Application deadline:* For fall admission, 2/15 priority date for domestic students, 2/1 priority date for international students. Applications are processed on a rolling basis. Application fee: $125. Electronic applications accepted. *Expenses:* Tuition, area resident: Full-time $7360; part-time $310 per credit hour. Tuition, state resident: full-time $7360; part-time $310 per credit hour. Tuition, nonresident: full-time $13,800; part-time $575 per credit hour. International tuition: $13,800 full-time. Required fees: $140.10 per semester. *Financial support:* Application deadline: 5/1. *Unit head:* Dr. David Grubbs, Director, 718-951-4203, E-mail: dgrubbs@brooklyn.cuny.edu. *Application contact:* Hernan Sierra, Graduate Admissions Coordinator, 718-951-4536, Fax: 718-951-4506, E-mail: grads@brooklyn.cuny.edu.

California State University, East Bay, Academic Programs and Graduate Studies, College of Letters, Arts, and Social Sciences, Multimedia Program, Hayward, CA 94542-3000. Offers MA. Part-time programs available. *Faculty:* 4 full-time (2 women). *Students:* 21 full-time (10 women), 12 part-time (4 women); includes 15 minority (4 African Americans, 6 Asian Americans or Pacific Islanders, 5 Hispanic Americans), 2 international. Average age 32. 37 applicants, 57% accepted, 17 enrolled. In 2009, 14 master's awarded. *Degree requirements:* For master's, multimedia project. *Entrance requirements:* For master's, minimum GPA of 2.5. Additional exam requirements/recommendations for international students: Required—TOEFL (minimum score 550 paper-based; 213 computer-based). *Application deadline:* For fall admission, 3/1 for domestic and international students. Application fee: $55. Electronic applications accepted. *Financial support:* Fellowships, teaching assistantships, Federal Work-Study, institutionally sponsored loans, and scholarships/grants available. Support available to part-time students. Financial award application deadline: 3/1; financial award applicants required to submit FAFSA. *Unit head:* Dr. Rafael Hernandez, Program Director, 510-885-3204, Fax: 510-885-4301, E-mail: rafael.hernandez@csueastbay.edu. *Application contact:* Donna Wiley, Interim Associate Director, 510-885-2928, Fax: 510-885-4777, E-mail: donna.wiley@csueastbay.edu.

Concordia University, School of Graduate Studies, Faculty of Engineering and Computer Science, Concordia Institute for Information Systems Engineering (CIISE), Montréal, QC H3G 1M8, Canada. Offers 3D graphics and game development (Certificate); information systems security (M Eng, MA Sc); quality systems engineering (M Eng, MA Sc); service engineering and network management (Certificate).

DePaul University, College of Computing and Digital Media, Chicago, IL 60604. Offers business information technology (MS); computational finance (MS); computer and information sciences (PhD); computer game development (MS); computer graphics and motion technology (MS); computer science (MS); computer, information and network security (MS), including applied technology; digital cinema (MFA, MS), including information technology project management (MS); e-commerce technology (MS); human-computer interaction (MS); information systems (MS); information technology (MA); information technology project management (MS); software engineering (MS); telecommunications systems (MS); JD/MS. Part-time and evening/weekend programs available. Postbaccalaureate distance learning degree programs offered (no on-campus study). *Faculty:* 78 full-time (16 women), 191 part-time/adjunct (51 women). *Students:* 922 full-time (239 women), 887 part-time (209 women); includes 466 minority (193 African Americans, 3 American Indian/Alaska Native, 162 Asian Americans or Pacific Islanders, 108 Hispanic Americans), 276 international. Average age 31. 853 applicants, 67% accepted, 294 enrolled. In 2009, 444 master's, 4 doctorates awarded. *Degree requirements:* For master's, thesis (for some programs); for doctorate, comprehensive exam, thesis/dissertation. *Entrance requirements:* For master's, GRE or GMAT (MS in computational finance only), bachelor's degree; for doctorate, GRE, master's degree in computer science. Additional exam requirements/recommendations for international students: Required—TOEFL (minimum score 550 paper-based; 213 computer-based), IELTS (minimum score 6.5), Pearson Test of English (minimum score 53). *Application deadline:* For fall admission, 8/15 priority date for domestic students, 6/1 priority date for international students; for winter admission, 12/15 priority date for domestic students, 9/15 priority date for international students; for spring admission, 3/1 priority date for domestic students, 12/15 priority date for international students. Applications are processed on a rolling basis. Application fee: $25. Electronic applications accepted. *Expenses:* Contact institution. *Financial support:* In 2009–10, 69 students received support, including 6 fellow-

Internet and Interactive Multimedia

DePaul University (continued)
ships with full tuition reimbursements available (averaging $25,858 per year), 75 teaching assistantships with full and partial tuition reimbursements available (averaging $5,780 per year); research assistantships, Federal Work-Study, scholarships/grants, tuition waivers (full and partial), and unspecified assistantships also available. Support available to part-time students. Financial award application deadline: 4/30; financial award applicants required to submit FAFSA. *Faculty research:* Bioinformatics, visual computing, graphics and animation, high performance and scientific computing, databases. Total annual research expenditures: $790,000. *Unit head:* Dr. David Miller, Dean, 312-362-8381, Fax: 312-362-5185. *Application contact:* Dr. Liz Friedman, Assistant Dean of Student Services, 312-362-5384, Fax: 312-362-5327, E-mail: efriedm2@cdm.depaul.edu.

Duquesne University, Graduate School of Liberal Arts, Program in Multimedia Technology, Pittsburgh, PA 15282-0001. Offers MS, Certificate. Part-time and evening/weekend programs available. *Faculty:* 10 full-time (1 woman), 3 part-time/adjunct (0 women). *Students:* 36 full-time (17 women), 15 part-time (5 women); includes 1 minority (Hispanic American), 2 international. Average age 22. 21 applicants, 100% accepted, 19 enrolled. In 2009, 43 master's awarded. *Entrance requirements:* For master's, MAT or GRE General Test, portfolio. Additional exam requirements/recommendations for international students: Required—TOEFL. *Application deadline:* For fall admission, 8/1 for domestic students, 5/1 for international students; for spring admission, 11/1 for domestic students. Applications are processed on a rolling basis. Electronic applications accepted. *Expenses:* Tuition: Part-time $851 per credit. Required fees: $81 per credit. *Financial support:* In 2009–10, 5 research assistantships with full tuition reimbursements (averaging $8,400 per year) were awarded; Federal Work-Study also available. Support available to part-time students. Financial award application deadline: 5/1. *Unit head:* Dr. John Shepherd, Director, 412-396-5772. *Application contact:* Dr. John Shepherd, Assistant to the Dean, 412-396-5772, E-mail: shepherd@duq.edu.

Elon University, Program in Interactive Media, Elon, NC 27244-2010. Offers MA. *Faculty:* 16 full-time (6 women). *Students:* 37 full-time (16 women); includes 3 African Americans, 2 Asian Americans or Pacific Islanders, 1 Hispanic American. Average age 27. 76 applicants, 78% accepted, 37 enrolled. *Degree requirements:* For master's, 6-hour capstone. *Entrance requirements:* For master's, GRE. Additional exam requirements/recommendations for international students: Required—TOEFL (minimum score 550 paper-based; 213 computer-based; 79 iBT). *Application deadline:* For fall admission, 5/1 priority date for domestic students. Applications are processed on a rolling basis. Application fee: $50. Electronic applications accepted. *Expenses:* Contact institution. *Financial support:* In 2009–10, 22 students received support. Federal Work-Study and scholarships/grants available. Financial award application deadline: 3/15; financial award applicants required to submit FAFSA. *Unit head:* Dr. David Alan Copeland, Director, 336-278-5662, Fax: 336-278-5734, E-mail: dcopeland@elon.edu. *Application contact:* Art Fadde, Director of Graduate Admissions, 800-334-8448 Ext. 3, Fax: 336-278-7699, E-mail: afadde@elon.edu.

Full Sail University, Education Media Design and Technology Master of Science Program—Online, Winter Park, FL 32792-7437. Offers MS. Postbaccalaureate distance learning degree programs offered (no on-campus study). *Entrance requirements:* Additional exam requirements/recommendations for international students: Required—TOEFL (minimum score 550 paper-based; 213 computer-based; 79 iBT).

Full Sail University, Game Design Master of Science Program—Campus, Winter Park, FL 32792-7437. Offers MS.

Full Sail University, Internet Marketing Master of Science Program—Online, Winter Park, FL 32792-7437. Offers MS. Postbaccalaureate distance learning degree programs offered.

George Mason University, Volgenau School of Information Technology and Engineering, Department of Computer Science, Fairfax, VA 22030. Offers biometrics (Certificate); computer games technology (Certificate); computer networking (Certificate); computer science (MS, PhD); data mining (Certificate); database management (Certificate); electronic commerce (Certificate); foundations of information systems (Certificate); information engineering (Certificate); information security and assurance (MS, Certificate); information systems (MS); intelligent agents (Certificate); software architecture (Certificate); software engineering (MS, Certificate); systems engineering (MS); Web-based software engineering (Certificate). Part-time and evening/weekend programs available. Postbaccalaureate distance learning degree programs offered. *Faculty:* 42 full-time (9 women), 18 part-time/adjunct (0 women). *Students:* 121 full-time (36 women), 489 part-time (118 women); includes 90 minority (11 African Americans, 70 Asian Americans or Pacific Islanders, 9 Hispanic Americans), 222 international. Average age 29. 882 applicants, 58% accepted, 147 enrolled. In 2009, 202 master's, 6 doctorates, 21 other advanced degrees awarded. *Degree requirements:* For master's, thesis optional; for doctorate, comprehensive exam, thesis/dissertation. *Entrance requirements:* For master's, GRE General Test, minimum GPA of 3.0 in last 60 hours, 3 letters of recommendation; for doctorate, GRE, 4-year BA degree, academic work in computer science, 3 letters of recommendation, statement of career goals and aspirations. Additional exam requirements/recommendations for international students: Required—TOEFL. *Application deadline:* For fall admission, 4/15 priority date for domestic students, 1/15 for international students; for spring admission, 11/15 for domestic students. Application fee: $75. Electronic applications accepted. *Expenses:* Tuition, state resident: full-time $7568; part-time $315.33 per credit hour. Tuition, nonresident: full-time $21,704; part-time $904.33 per credit hour. Required fees: $2184; $91 per credit hour. *Financial support:* In 2009–10, 106 students received support, including 3 fellowships (averaging $18,000 per year), 53 research assistantships (averaging $11,119 per year), 53 teaching assistantships (averaging $7,881 per year); unspecified assistantships and health care benefits (full-time research or teaching assistantship recipients) also available. Financial award application deadline: 3/1; financial award applicants required to submit FAFSA. *Faculty research:* Artificial intelligence, image processing/graphics, parallel/distributed systems, software engineering systems. Total annual research expenditures: $1.3 million. *Unit head:* Dr. Arun Sood, Director, 703-993-1524, Fax: 703-993-1710, E-mail: asood@gmu.edu. *Application contact:* Jay Shapiro, Professor, 703-993-1485, E-mail: jshapiro@gmu.edu.

Georgetown University, Graduate School of Arts and Sciences, Program in Communication, Culture, and Technology, Washington, DC 20057. Offers MA. Part-time and evening/weekend programs available. *Degree requirements:* For master's, thesis (for some programs). *Entrance requirements:* For master's, GRE General Test, 3 letters of recommendation, writing sample. Additional exam requirements/recommendations for international students: Required—TOEFL (minimum score 600 paper-based; 250 computer-based). Electronic applications accepted.

Georgia Institute of Technology, Graduate Studies and Research, Ivan Allen College of Policy and International Affairs, School of Literature, Communication and Culture, Atlanta, GA 30332-0001. Offers digital media (MS, PhD); human computer interaction (MSHCI). *Degree requirements:* For master's, thesis or alternative. *Entrance requirements:* Additional exam requirements/recommendations for international students: Required—TOEFL. Electronic applications accepted. *Faculty research:* New media studies.

Indiana University–Purdue University Indianapolis, School of Informatics, Indianapolis, IN 46202-2896. Offers informatics (PhD); media arts and science (MS). Part-time and evening/weekend programs available. *Faculty:* 3 full-time (0 women). *Students:* 36 full-time (11 women), 76 part-time (29 women); includes 19 minority (12 African Americans, 5 Asian Americans or Pacific Islanders, 2 Hispanic Americans), 29 international. Average age 34. 70 applicants, 71% accepted, 33 enrolled. In 2009, 39 master's awarded. *Degree requirements:* For master's, multimedia project. *Entrance requirements:* For master's, minimum undergraduate GPA of 3.0, graduate 3.2; interview; portfolio; BA with demonstrated media arts skills. Additional exam requirements/recommendations for international students: Required—TOEFL. *Application deadline:* For fall admission, 3/15 for domestic students; for spring admission, 11/15 for domestic students. Application fee: $55 ($65 for international students). *Financial support:* In 2009–10, 6 fellowships (averaging $17,447 per year), 13 teaching assistantships (averaging $9,392 per year) were awarded; career-related internships or fieldwork, Federal Work-Study, institutionally sponsored loans, and scholarships/grants also available. Support available to part-time students. *Unit head:* Darrell L. Bailey, Executive Associate Dean, 317-278-4636, Fax: 317-278-7769. *Application contact:* Dr. Sherry Queener, Director, Graduate Studies and Associate Dean, 317-274-1577, Fax: 317-278-2380.

Long Island University, C.W. Post Campus, School of Visual and Performing Arts, Department of Theatre, Film, Dance and Arts Management, Brookville, NY 11548-1300. Offers interactive multimedia (MA); theatre (MA). Part-time and evening/weekend programs available. *Degree requirements:* For master's, thesis. *Entrance requirements:* For master's, placement exam. Electronic applications accepted. *Faculty research:* Playwriting, intercultural dance and theatre, translation, Suzuki, set and costume design.

Marlboro College, Graduate School, Program in Teaching with Technology, Marlboro, VT 05344. Offers MAT. Part-time and evening/weekend programs available. Postbaccalaureate distance learning degree programs offered (minimal on-campus study). *Faculty:* 7 part-time/adjunct (5 women). *Students:* 6 full-time (3 women), 4 part-time (2 women). Average age 38. 5 applicants, 100% accepted, 5 enrolled. In 2009, 4 master's awarded. *Degree requirements:* For master's, capstone project. *Entrance requirements:* For master's, 2 letters of recommendation. *Application deadline:* Applications are processed on a rolling basis. Application fee: $0. Electronic applications accepted. *Expenses:* Tuition: Full-time $9520; part-time $680 per credit. Tuition and fees vary according to course load and program. *Financial support:* Available to part-time students. Applicants required to submit FAFSA. *Application contact:* Joe Heslin, Associate Director of Admissions, 802-258-9209, Fax: 802-258-9201, E-mail: jheslin@gradcenter.marlboro.edu.

National University, Academic Affairs, School of Media and Communication, Department of Media, La Jolla, CA 92037-1011. Offers digital cinema (MFA); educational and instructional technology (MS); video game production and design (MFA). Part-time and evening/weekend programs available. Postbaccalaureate distance learning degree programs offered (no on-campus study). *Faculty:* 9 full-time (4 women), 13 part-time/adjunct (4 women). *Students:* 68 full-time (26 women), 118 part-time (45 women); includes 64 minority (29 African Americans, 10 Asian Americans or Pacific Islanders, 25 Hispanic Americans), 1 international. Average age 39. 118 applicants, 100% accepted, 70 enrolled. In 2009, 58 master's awarded. *Degree requirements:* For master's, thesis. *Entrance requirements:* For master's, interview, minimum GPA of 2.5. Additional exam requirements/recommendations for international students: Required—TOEFL (minimum score 550 paper-based; 213 computer-based; 79 iBT), IELTS (minimum score 6). *Application deadline:* Applications are processed on a rolling basis. Application fee: $60 ($65 for international students). Electronic applications accepted. *Expenses:* Tuition: Part-time $338 per quarter hour. *Financial support:* Career-related internships or fieldwork, institutionally sponsored loans, scholarships/grants, and tuition waivers (partial) available. Support available to part-time students. Financial award application deadline: 6/30; financial award applicants required to submit FAFSA. *Unit head:* Dr. Timothy Langdell, Department Chair, 310-662-2149, Fax: 858-309-3450, E-mail: tlangdell@nu.edu. *Application contact:* Dominick Giovanniello, Associate Regional Dean—San Diego, 800-NAT-UNIV, Fax: 858-541-7792, E-mail: dgiovann@nu.edu.

New Mexico Highlands University, Graduate Studies, College of Arts and Sciences, Program in Media Arts and Computer Science, Las Vegas, NM 87701. Offers media arts and computer science (MS). *Degree requirements:* For master's, comprehensive exam, thesis. *Entrance requirements:* For master's, minimum undergraduate GPA of 3.0. Additional exam requirements/recommendations for international students: Required—TOEFL (minimum score 540 paper-based; 270 computer-based). *Faculty research:* Advanced digital compositing, photographic installations and exhibition design, pattern recognition, parallel and distributed computing, computer security education.

New York University, Tisch School of the Arts, Interactive Telecommunications Program, New York, NY 10012-1019. Offers MPS. *Faculty:* 9 full-time, 40 part-time/adjunct. *Students:* 197 full-time (80 women), 18 part-time (8 women); includes 42 minority (7 African Americans, 23 Asian Americans or Pacific Islanders, 12 Hispanic Americans). Average age 29. 271 applicants, 74% accepted, 109 enrolled. In 2009, 102 master's awarded. *Degree requirements:* For master's, thesis. *Entrance requirements:* Additional exam requirements/recommendations for international students: Required—TOEFL (minimum score 600 paper-based; 250 computer-based; 100 iBT) or IELTS (minimum score 6). *Application deadline:* For fall admission, 12/1 priority date for domestic and international students. Application fee: $60. Electronic applications accepted. *Expenses:* Tuition: Full-time $30,528; part-time $1272 per credit. Required fees: $2177. *Financial support:* In 2009–10, 90 students received support, including 24 fellowships with full and partial tuition reimbursements available; career-related internships or fieldwork, Federal Work-Study, institutionally sponsored loans, scholarships/grants, and tuition waivers (partial) also available. Financial award application deadline: 2/15; financial award applicants required to submit FAFSA. *Faculty research:* Interactive narrative/storytelling, interactive media, web technology, physical computing, ubiquitous computing. *Unit head:* Red Burns, Chair, 212-998-1880, Fax: 212-998-1898, E-mail: itp.inquiries@nyu.edu. *Application contact:* Dan Sandford, Director of Graduate Admissions, 212-998-1918, Fax: 212-995-4060, E-mail: tisch.gradadmissions@nyu.edu.

Northwestern University, School of Continuing Studies, Program in Information Systems, Evanston, IL 60208. Offers database and Internet technologies (MS); information systems management (MS); information systems security (MS); software project management and development (MS).

Pace University, Seidenberg School of Computer Science and Information Systems, New York, NY 10038. Offers computer communications and networks (Certificate); computer science (MS); computing studies (DPS); information systems (MS); Internet technologies for e-commerce (MS); Internet technology (MS); object-oriented programming (Certificate); security and information assurance (Certificate); software development and engineering (MS); telecommunications (MS, Certificate). Part-time and evening/weekend programs available. *Students:* 122 full-time (37 women), 424 part-time (131 women); includes 188 minority (76 African Americans, 1 American Indian/Alaska Native, 65 Asian Americans or Pacific Islanders, 46 Hispanic Americans), 110 international. Average age 35. 352 applicants, 89% accepted, 128 enrolled. In 2009, 137 master's, 11 doctorates, 3 other advanced degrees awarded. *Entrance requirements:* For master's, GRE General Test. Additional exam requirements/recommendations for international students: Required—TOEFL. *Application deadline:* For fall admission, 7/31 priority date for domestic students; for spring admission, 11/30 for domestic students. Applications are processed on a rolling basis. Application fee: $70. Electronic applications accepted. *Expenses:* Contact institution. *Financial support:* Research assistantships, career-related internships or fieldwork available. Support available to part-time students. Financial award applicants required to submit FAFSA. *Unit head:* Dr. Constance Knapp, Interim Dean, 914-773-3750, Fax: 914-773-3533, E-mail: cknapp@pace.edu. *Application contact:* Joanna Broda, Director of Graduate Admissions, 914-422-4283, Fax: 914-422-4287, E-mail: gradwp@pace.edu.

Polytechnic Institute of NYU, Department of Humanities and Social Sciences, Major in Integrated Digital Media, Brooklyn, NY 11201-2990. Offers MS, Graduate Certificate. *Students:* 25 full-time (12 women), 5 part-time (2 women); includes 3 minority (2 African Americans, 1 Hispanic American), 15 international. 35 applicants, 74% accepted, 19 enrolled. In 2009, 18 master's awarded. *Entrance requirements:* Additional exam requirements/recommendations for international students: Required—TOEFL (minimum score 550 paper-based; 213 computer-based; 80 iBT); Recommended—IELTS (minimum score 6.5). *Application deadline:* For fall admission, 7/31 priority date for domestic students, 4/30 priority date for international students; for spring admission, 12/31 priority date for domestic students, 11/30 priority date for international students. Applications are processed on a rolling basis. Application fee: $75. Electronic applications accepted. *Expenses:* Tuition: Full-time $21,492; part-time $1194 per credit hour. Required fees: $1160; $204 per course. *Financial support:* Institutionally sponsored loans, scholarships/grants, and unspecified assistantships available. Support available to part-time students. *Unit head:* Teresa Feroli, Head, 718-260-3422, E-mail: tferoli@poly.edu. *Application contact:* Jearcarlo Bonilla, Director of Graduate Enrollment Management, 718-260-3182, Fax: 718-260-3624, E-mail: gradinfo@poly.edu.

Pratt Institute, School of Art and Design, Program in Digital Arts, Brooklyn, NY 11205-3899. Offers MFA, MS/MFA. *Accreditation:* NASAD. *Faculty:* 6 full-time (1 woman), 17 part-time/adjunct (8 women). *Students:* 55 full-time (30 women), 1 (woman) part-time; includes 6 minority (2 African Americans, 2 Asian Americans or Pacific Islanders, 2 Hispanic Americans), 30 international. Average age 29. 140 applicants, 29% accepted, 10 enrolled. In 2009, 19 master's awarded. *Degree requirements:* For master's, thesis, exhibit. *Entrance requirements:* For master's, portfolio or video tape, letters of recommendation. Additional exam requirements/recommendations for international students: Required—TOEFL (minimum score 550 paper-based; 213 computer-based; 79 iBT). *Application deadline:* For fall admission, 1/5 for domestic and international students; for spring admission, 10/1 for domestic and international students. Applications are processed on a rolling basis. Application fee: $50 ($90 for international students). Electronic applications accepted. *Expenses:* Tuition: Full-time $22,734. Required fees: $1280. *Financial support:* Career-related internships or fieldwork, Federal Work-Study, institutionally sponsored loans, scholarships/grants, health care benefits, and unspecified assistantships available. Support available to part-time students. Financial award application deadline: 2/1; financial award applicants required to submit FAFSA. *Unit head:* Peter Patchen, Chair, 718-636-3693, E-mail: ppatchen@pratt.edu. *Application contact:* Young Hah, Director of Graduate Admissions, 718-636-3683, Fax: 718-399-4242, E-mail: yhah@pratt.edu.

See Close-Up on page 119.

Quinnipiac University, School of Communications, Program in Interactive Communications, Hamden, CT 06518-1940. Offers MS. Part-time and evening/weekend programs available. *Faculty:* 5 full-time (2 women), 5 part-time/adjunct (1 woman). *Students:* 17 full-time (8 women), 61 part-time (36 women); includes 2 African Americans, 1 Asian American or Pacific Islander, 3 Hispanic Americans, 1 international. Average age 26. 28 applicants, 100% accepted, 20 enrolled. In 2009, 21 master's awarded. *Entrance requirements:* For master's, minimum GPA of 2.8, portfolio or writing sample. Additional exam requirements/recommendations for international students: Required—TOEFL (minimum score 575 paper-based; 233 computer-based; 90 iBT), IELTS (minimum score 6.5). *Application deadline:* For fall admission, 7/30 priority date for domestic students, 4/30 priority date for international students; for spring admission, 12/15 priority date for domestic students, 9/15 priority date for international students. Applications are processed on a rolling basis. Application fee: $45. Electronic applications accepted. *Expenses:* Tuition: Full-time $16,030; part-time $770 per credit. Required fees: $630; $35 per credit. *Financial support:* Federal Work-Study, tuition waivers (partial), and unspecified assistantships available. Support available to part-time students. Financial award application deadline: 4/30; financial award applicants required to submit FAFSA. *Faculty research:* Technology and democracy, the role of computing in social change. *Unit head:* Phillip Simon, Director, 203-582-8274, Fax: 203-582-5310, E-mail: phillip.simon@quinnipiac.edu. *Application contact:* Scott Farber, Director of Graduate Admissions, 800-462-1944, Fax: 203-582-3443, E-mail: scott.farber@quinnipiac.edu.

Robert Morris University, Graduate Studies, School of Communications and Information Systems, Moon Township, PA 15108-1189. Offers communication and information systems (MS); competitive intelligence systems (MS); information security and assurance (MS); information systems and communications (D Sc); information systems management (MS); information technology project management (MS); Internet information systems (MS); organizational studies (MS). Part-time and evening/weekend programs available. *Faculty:* 28 full-time (9 women), 9 part-time/adjunct (3 women). *Students:* 257 part-time (76 women); includes 41 minority (31 African Americans, 8 Asian Americans or Pacific Islanders, 2 Hispanic Americans), 16 international. Average age 33. 106 applicants, 100% accepted, 106 enrolled. In 2009, 84 master's, 8 doctorates awarded. *Degree requirements:* For doctorate, thesis/dissertation. *Entrance requirements:* For doctorate, employer letter of endorsement, interview. Additional exam requirements/recommendations for international students: Required—TOEFL (minimum score 550 paper-based; 213 computer-based; 79 iBT). *Application deadline:* For fall admission, 7/1 priority date for domestic and international students; for spring admission, 11/1 priority date for domestic and international students. Applications are processed on a rolling basis. Application fee: $35. Electronic applications accepted. *Expenses:* Contact institution. *Financial support:* Research assistantships with partial tuition reimbursements, institutionally sponsored loans and unspecified assistantships available. Support available to part-time students. Financial award application deadline: 5/1. *Unit head:* Dr. Barbara J. Levine, Dean, 412-397-2591, Fax: 412-397-2481, E-mail: levine@rmu.edu. *Application contact:* Deborah Roach, Assistant Dean, Graduate Admissions, 412-397-5200, Fax: 412-397-2425, E-mail: graduateadmissions@rmu.edu.

Rochester Institute of Technology, Graduate Enrollment Services, B. Thomas Golisano College of Computing and Information Sciences, Department of Information Technology, Program in Interactive Multimedia Development, Rochester, NY 14623-5603. Offers AC. Part-time and evening/weekend programs available. *Students:* 3 full-time (2 women), 3 part-time (2 women); includes 1 African American, 1 Hispanic American. Average age 44. 4 applicants, 100% accepted, 4 enrolled. In 2009, 5 ACs awarded. *Entrance requirements:* For degree, GRE, minimum GPA of 3.0. Additional exam requirements/recommendations for international students: Required—TOEFL (minimum score 570 paper-based; 230 computer-based; 88 iBT), or IELTS (minimum score 6.5). *Application deadline:* For fall admission, 8/1 for domestic students, 7/1 for international students; for spring admission, 2/1 for domestic students. Applications are processed on a rolling basis. Application fee: $50. Electronic applications accepted. *Expenses:* Tuition: Full-time $31,533; part-time $876 per credit hour. Required fees: $210. *Financial support:* In 2009–10, 5 students received support. Career-related internships or fieldwork, scholarships/grants, and unspecified assistantships available. Support available to part-time students. Financial award applicants required to submit FAFSA. *Unit head:* Prof. Dianne Bills, Graduate Program Coordinator, 585-475-2700, Fax: 585-475-6584, E-mail: informaticsgrad@rit.edu. *Application contact:* Diane Ellison, Assistant Vice President, Graduate Enrollment Services, 585-475-2229, Fax: 585-475-7164, E-mail: gradinfo@rit.edu.

Rochester Institute of Technology, Graduate Enrollment Services, B. Thomas Golisano College of Computing and Information Sciences, Department of Interactive Games and Media, Rochester, NY 14623-5603. Offers game design and development (MS). Part-time programs available. *Students:* 19 full-time (3 women), 2 part-time (0 women); includes 1 minority (Hispanic American), 2 international. Average age 26. 24 applicants, 54% accepted, 8 enrolled. In 2009, 3 master's awarded. *Degree requirements:* For master's, thesis. *Entrance requirements:* For master's, GRE, minimum GPA of 3.25. Additional exam requirements/recommendations for international students: Required—TOEFL (minimum score 570 paper-based; 230 computer-based; 88 iBT), or IELTS (minimum score 6.5). *Application deadline:* For fall admission, 1/15 priority date for domestic students, 1/1 priority date for international students. Applications are processed on a rolling basis. Application fee: $50. Electronic applications accepted. *Expenses:* Tuition: Full-time $31,533; part-time $876 per credit hour. Required fees: $210. *Financial support:* In 2009–10, 19 students received support; research assistantships with partial tuition reimbursements available, teaching assistantships with partial tuition reimbursements available, career-related internships or fieldwork, scholarships/grants, and unspecified assistantships available. Support available to part-time students. Financial award applicants required to submit FAFSA. *Faculty research:* Experimental game design and development, exploratory research in visualization environments and integrated media frameworks, outreach efforts that surround games and underlying technologies, support of STEM learning through games and interactive entertainment, the application of games and game technology to non-entertainment domains (Serious Games), small, discrete play experiences (Casual Games). *Unit head:* Andrew Phelps, Chair, 585-475-6464, Fax: 585-475-2181, E-mail: informaticsgrad@rit.edu. *Application contact:* Diane Ellison, Assistant Vice President, Graduate Enrollment Services, 585-475-2229, Fax: 585-475-7164, E-mail: gradinfo@rit.edu.

Sacred Heart University, Graduate Programs, College of Arts and Sciences, Department of Computer Science and Information Technology, Fairfield, CT 06825-1000. Offers computer science (MS); database (CPS); information technology (MS, CPS); information technology and network security (CPS); interactive multimedia (CPS); Web development (CPS). Part-time and evening/weekend programs available. *Faculty:* 7 full-time (4 women). *Students:* 20 full-time (6 women), 79 part-time (25 women); includes 10 minority (2 African Americans, 1 American Indian/Alaska Native, 5 Asian Americans or Pacific Islanders, 2 Hispanic Americans), 30 international. Average age 33. 66 applicants, 97% accepted, 26 enrolled. In 2009, 17 master's awarded. *Degree requirements:* For master's, thesis optional. *Entrance requirements:* Additional exam requirements/recommendations for international students: Required—TOEFL (minimum score 550 paper-based; 213 computer-based). *Application deadline:* Applications are processed on a rolling basis. Application fee: $50 ($100 for international students). Electronic applications accepted. *Expenses:* Tuition: Full-time $24,000; part-time $650 per credit. Required fees: $248. *Financial support:* Career-related internships or fieldwork, institutionally sponsored loans, and unspecified assistantships available. Support available to part-time students. Financial award applicants required to submit FAFSA. *Faculty research:* Contemporary market software. *Unit head:* Domenick Pinto, Academic Director and Chairperson, 203-371-7789, Fax: 203-371-0506, E-mail: pintod@sacredheart.edu. *Application contact:* Dean Alexis Haakonsen, Office of Graduate Admissions, 203-365-7619, Fax: 203-365-4732, E-mail: gradstudies@sacredheart.edu.

San Diego State University, Graduate and Research Affairs, College of Professional Studies and Fine Arts, School of Communication, San Diego, CA 92182. Offers advertising and public relations (MA); critical-cultural studies (MA); interaction studies (MA); intercultural and international studies (MA); new media studies (MA); news and information studies (MA); telecommunications and media management (MA). *Degree requirements:* For master's, thesis. *Entrance requirements:* For master's, GRE General Test, 3 letters of recommendation. Additional exam requirements/recommendations for international students: Required—TOEFL. Electronic applications accepted.

Savannah College of Art and Design, Graduate School, Program in Interactive Design and Game Development, Savannah, GA 31402-3146. Offers MA, MFA. Part-time programs available. *Degree requirements:* For master's, thesis, internships. *Entrance requirements:* For master's, interview, portfolio. Additional exam requirements/recommendations for international students: Required—TOEFL (minimum score 450 paper-based; 133 computer-based). Electronic applications accepted. *Expenses:* Tuition: Full-time $28,515; part-time $627 per credit hour. One-time fee: $500. Tuition and fees vary according to course load.

School of Visual Arts, Graduate Programs, Program in Photography, Video and Related Media, New York, NY 10010-3994. Offers MFA. *Accreditation:* NASAD. *Degree requirements:* For master's, final review, project or thesis. *Entrance requirements:* For master's, portfolio. Additional exam requirements/recommendations for international students: Required—TOEFL (minimum score 550 paper-based; 213 computer-based; 79 iBT). Electronic applications accepted.

Simon Fraser University, Graduate Studies, Faculty of Applied Sciences, School of Interactive Arts and Technology, Surrey, BC V3T 2W1, Canada. Offers information technology (M Sc, PhD); interactive arts (M Sc, PhD). *Degree requirements:* For master's, thesis; for doctorate, comprehensive exam, thesis/dissertation. *Entrance requirements:* For master's, 2 references, curriculum vitae; for doctorate, 3 references, curriculum vitae, minimum GPA of 3.0. Additional exam requirements/recommendations for international students: Required—TOEFL (minimum score 570 paper-based; 230 computer-based), TWE (minimum score 5). Electronic applications accepted.

Southern Polytechnic State University, School of Arts and Sciences, Department of English, Technical Communication, and Media Arts, Marietta, GA 30060-2896. Offers communications management (Graduate Certificate); content development (Graduate Certificate); information and instructional design (MSIID); information design and communication (MS); instructional design (Graduate Certificate); technical and professional communication (Graduate Certificate); visual communication and graphics (Graduate Certificate). Part-time and evening/weekend programs available. Postbaccalaureate distance learning degree programs offered (no on-campus study). *Faculty:* 4 full-time (3 women), 1 part-time/adjunct (0 women). *Students:* 5 full-time (all women), 50 part-time (32 women); includes 18 African Americans, 2 international. Average age 38. 32 applicants, 94% accepted, 26 enrolled. In 2009, 8 master's awarded. *Degree requirements:* For master's, thesis or internship; for Graduate Certificate, thesis optional, 18 hours completed through thesis option (6 hours), internship option (6 hours) or advanced coursework option (6 hours). *Entrance requirements:* For master's, GRE, statement of purpose, writing sample, professional recommendations, timed essay; for Graduate Certificate, writing sample, professional recommendations. Additional exam requirements/recommendations for international students: Required—TOEFL (minimum score 550 paper-based; 213 computer-based; 79 iBT), IELTS (minimum score 6.5). *Application deadline:* For fall admission, 5/1 priority date for domestic students, 7/1 priority date for international students; for spring admission, 9/1 priority date for domestic students, 11/1 priority date for international students. Applications are processed on a rolling basis. Application fee: $20. Electronic applications accepted. *Expenses:* Tuition, state resident: full-time $2896; part-time $181 per credit hour. Tuition, nonresident: full-time $11,552; part-time $722 per credit hour. Required fees: $1096; $1096 per year. *Financial support:* In 2009–10, 1 research assistantship with full tuition reimbursement (averaging $4,000 per year), 1 teaching assistantship with partial tuition reimbursement (averaging $4,000 per year) were awarded; career-related internships or fieldwork, Federal Work-Study, scholarships/grants, and unspecified assistantships also available. Support available to part-time students. Financial award application deadline: 5/1; financial award applicants required to submit FAFSA. *Faculty research:* Usability, user-centered design, instructional design, information architecture, information design. *Unit head:* Dr. Mark Nunes, Chair, 678-915-7202, Fax: 678-915-7425, E-mail: mnunes@spsu.edu. *Application contact:* Nikki Palamiotis, Director of Graduate Studies, 678-915-4276, Fax: 678-915-7292, E-mail: npalamio@spsu.edu.

Stevens Institute of Technology, Graduate School, Charles V. Schaefer Jr. School of Engineering, Department of Computer Science, Hoboken, NJ 07030. Offers computer graphics (Certificate); computer science (MS, PhD); computer systems (Certificate); database management systems (Certificate); distributed systems (Certificate); elements of computer science (Certificate); enterprise computing (Certificate); enterprise security and information assurance (Certificate); health informatics (Certificate); multimedia experience and management (Certificate); networks and systems administration (Certificate); security and privacy (Certificate); service oriented computing (Certificate); software design (Certificate); theoretical computer science (Certificate). Part-time and evening/weekend programs available. Terminal master's awarded for partial completion of doctoral program. *Degree requirements:* For master's, thesis optional; for doctorate, variable foreign language requirement, comprehensive exam, thesis/dissertation. *Entrance requirements:* For master's and doctorate, GRE, minimum GPA of 3.0. Additional exam requirements/recommendations for international students: Required—TOEFL. Electronic applications accepted. *Expenses:* Tuition: Full-time $9900; part-time $1100 per credit. Required fees: $286 per semester. *Faculty research:* Semantics, reliability theory, programming language, cyber security.

Towson University, College of Graduate Studies and Research, Program in Applied Information Technology, Towson, MD 21252-0001. Offers applied information technology (D Sc); database management (Certificate); information security and assurance (Certificate); information systems management (Certificate); Internet application development (Certificate); networking technologies (Certificate); software engineering (Certificate). *Entrance requirements:* For doctorate, minimum GPA 3.0, letter of intent, resumé, 2 letters of recommendation, personal assessment forms, official transcripts. Additional exam requirements/recommendations for international students: Required—TOEFL (minimum score 550 paper-based). Electronic applications accepted.

Towson University, College of Graduate Studies and Research, Program in Interactive Media Design, Towson, MD 21252-0001. Offers Certificate. Postbaccalaureate distance learning

Internet and Interactive Multimedia

Towson University (continued)
degree programs offered (no on-campus study). *Entrance requirements:* For degree, minimum GPA of 3.0, resume, letter of intent, BA in art education or coursework, professional experience in graphic design or art education. Additional exam requirements/recommendations for international students: Required—TOEFL (minimum score 550 paper-based).

Towson University, College of Graduate Studies and Research, Program in Internet Application Development, Towson, MD 21252-0001. Offers Certificate. Part-time and evening/weekend programs available. Electronic applications accepted.

Universidad Autonoma de Guadalajara, Graduate Programs, Guadalajara, Mexico. Offers administrative law and justice (LL M); advertising and corporate communications (MA); architecture (M Arch); business (MBA); computational science (MCC); education (Ed M, Ed D); English-Spanish translation (MA); fiscal law (MA); integrated management of digital animation (MA); international business (MIB); international corporate law (LL M); internet technologies (MS); labor health (MS); manufacturing systems (MMS); philosophy (MA, PhD); power electronics (MS); quality systems (MQS); renewable energy (MS); social evaluation of projects (MBA); strategic market research (MBA); teaching mathematics (MA).

University of Advancing Technology, Master of Science Program in Technology, Tempe, AZ 85283-1042. Offers advancing computer science (MS); emerging technologies (MS); game production and management (MS); information assurance (MS); technology leadership (MS). *Degree requirements:* For master's, project or thesis. *Entrance requirements:* Additional exam requirements/recommendations for international students: Required—TOEFL (minimum score 550 paper-based). Electronic applications accepted. *Faculty research:* Artificial intelligence, fractals, organizational management.

University of Central Florida, College of Arts and Humanities, Division of Film and Digital Media, Orlando, FL 32816. Offers interactive entertainment (MS). *Students:* 50 full-time (5 women), 49 part-time (5 women); includes 31 minority (5 African Americans, 5 Asian Americans or Pacific Islanders, 21 Hispanic Americans), 6 international. Average age 25. 92 applicants, 64% accepted, 49 enrolled. In 2009, 31 master's awarded. Application fee: $30. *Expenses:* Tuition, state resident: part-time $306.31 per credit hour. Tuition, nonresident: part-time $1099.01 per credit hour. Part-time tuition and fees vary according to degree level and program. *Financial support:* In 2009–10, 1 student received support, including 1 fellowship with partial tuition reimbursement available (averaging $10,000 per year), 3 research assistantships (averaging $3,200 per year), 2 teaching assistantships (averaging $6,400 per year). *Unit head:* Dr. Jose Maunez-Cuadra, Interim Chair, 407-823-2121, Fax: 407-317-7094, E-mail: info@fiea.ucf.edu. *Application contact:* Dr. Jose Maunez-Cuadra, Interim Chair, 407-823-2121, Fax: 407-317-7094, E-mail: info@fiea.ucf.edu.

University of Florida, Graduate School, College of Fine Arts, School of Art and Art History, Gainesville, FL 32611. Offers art (MFA), including ceramics, creative photography, drawing, electronic intermedia, graphic design, painting, printmaking, sculpture; art education (MA); art history (MA, PhD); digital arts and sciences (MA); museology (museum studies) (MA). *Accreditation:* NASAD. *Degree requirements:* For master's, variable foreign language requirement, project or thesis (MFA). *Entrance requirements:* For master's, portfolio (MFA), writing sample (MA), GRE General Test or minimum GPA of 3.0. Additional exam requirements/recommendations for international students: Required—TOEFL (minimum score 550 paper-based; 213 computer-based). Electronic applications accepted. *Faculty research:* Studio production, art historical studies of style context.

University of Georgia, Graduate School, Terry College of Business, Program in Internet Technology, Athens, GA 30602. Offers MIT. *Students:* 51 applicants, 61% accepted. *Application deadline:* For fall admission, 7/1 priority date for domestic students; for spring admission, 11/15 for domestic students. Application fee: $50. *Expenses:* Tuition, state resident: full-time $6000; part-time $250 per credit hour. Tuition, nonresident: full-time $20,904; part-time $871 per credit hour. Required fees: $730 per semester. *Unit head:* Dr. Craig A. Piercy, Director, 706-542-3589, Fax: 706-583-0037, E-mail: cpiercy@terry.uga.edu. *Application contact:* Dr. Craig A. Piercy, Director, 706-542-3589, Fax: 706-583-0037, E-mail: cpiercy@terry.uga.edu.

University of Miami, Graduate School, College of Arts and Sciences, Department of Art and Art History, Coral Gables, FL 33124. Offers art history (MA); ceramics/glass (MFA); graphic design/multimedia (MFA); painting (MFA); photography/digital imaging (MFA); printmaking (MFA); sculpture (MFA). Part-time programs available. *Degree requirements:* For master's, variable foreign language requirement, thesis, exhibit (MFA), comprehensive exam (MA). *Entrance requirements:* For master's, GRE General Test (MA), research paper (MA), slide portfolio (MFA). Additional exam requirements/recommendations for international students: Required—TOEFL. Electronic applications accepted. *Faculty research:* Installation art, public art.

University of Phoenix–Madison Campus, College of Graduate Business and Management, Madison, WI 53718-2416. Offers accounting (MBA); business and management (MBA); e-business (MBA); global management (MBA); human resources management (MBA, MM); management (MM); marketing (MBA); public administration (MBA).

University of San Francisco, College of Arts and Sciences, Department of Computer Science, Program in Web Science, San Francisco, CA 94117-1080. Offers MS. *Faculty:* 5 full-time (1 woman). *Students:* 18 full-time (2 women), 3 part-time (0 women), 13 international. Average age 29. 28 applicants, 71% accepted, 8 enrolled. In 2009, 4 master's awarded. *Expenses:* Tuition: Full-time $19,710; part-time $1095 per unit. Part-time tuition and fees vary according to degree level, campus/location and program. *Financial support:* In 2009–10, 12 students received support. *Unit head:* Terence Parr, Graduate Director, 415-422-6530, Fax: 415-422-5800. *Application contact:* Mark Landerghini, Graduate Adviser, 415-422-5135, E-mail: asgraduate@usfca.edu.

University of Southern California, Graduate School, Annenberg School for Communication and Journalism, School of Journalism, Program in Online Journalism, Los Angeles, CA 90089. Offers MA. Part-time programs available. *Degree requirements:* For master's, comprehensive exam, thesis. *Entrance requirements:* For master's, GRE General Test, resume, writing samples, letters of recommendation, statement of purpose. Additional exam requirements/recommendations for international students: Required—TOEFL (minimum score 280 computer-based; 114 iBT). Electronic applications accepted. *Expenses:* Tuition: Full-time $25,980; part-time $1315 per unit. Required fees: $554. One-time fee: $35 full-time. Full-time tuition and fees vary according to degree level and program.

See Display on page 629 and Close-Up on page 685.

University of Southern California, Graduate School, School of Cinematic Arts, Interactive Media Division, Los Angeles, CA 90089. Offers interactive media (MFA); media arts and practice (PhD). *Faculty:* 9 full-time (2 women), 13 part-time/adjunct (4 women). *Students:* 34 full-time (12 women); includes 3 minority (2 Asian Americans or Pacific Islanders, 1 Hispanic American), 6 international. In 2009, 10 master's awarded. *Degree requirements:* For master's, thesis, thesis project. *Entrance requirements:* Additional exam requirements/recommendations for international students: Required—TOEFL (minimum score 600 paper-based; 250 computer-based; 100 iBT). *Application deadline:* For fall admission, 12/1 for domestic and international students. Application fee: $85. *Expenses:* Contact institution. *Financial support:* In 2009–10, 25 students received support, including 6 fellowships with full tuition reimbursements available (averaging $20,000 per year), 6 research assistantships with full tuition reimbursements available (averaging $9,750 per year); career-related internships or fieldwork, Federal Work-Study, institutionally sponsored loans, scholarships/grants, health care benefits, and research assistantships through grant funded projects also available. Financial award application deadline: 5/3; financial award applicants required to submit CSS PROFILE or FAFSA. *Faculty research:* Game design and development, mobile media, stereoscopic/immersive media, game for health, serious games, experiments in gameplay, games for learning. Total annual research expenditures: $989,031. *Unit head:* Dr. Scott S. Fisher, Professor and Department Chair, 213-821-4472, Fax: 213-821-2665, E-mail: sfisher@cinema.usc.edu. *Application contact:* Adrienne Capirchio, Program Manager, 213-821-2515, Fax: 213-821-2665, E-mail: acapirchio@cinema.usc.edu.

University of Southern California, Graduate School, Viterbi School of Engineering, Department of Computer Science, Los Angeles, CA 90089. Offers computer networks (MS); computer science (MS, PhD); computer security (MS); game development (MS); high performance computing and simulations (MS); human language technology (MS); intelligent robotics (MS); multimedia and creative technologies (MS); software engineering (MS). Part-time programs available. Postbaccalaureate distance learning degree programs offered (no on-campus study). *Faculty:* 26 full-time (2 women), 56 part-time/adjunct (7 women). *Students:* 711 full-time (148 women), 304 part-time (55 women); includes 76 minority (5 African Americans, 59 Asian Americans or Pacific Islanders, 12 Hispanic Americans), 816 international. 2,017 applicants, 39% accepted, 382 enrolled. In 2009, 332 master's, 32 doctorates awarded. Terminal master's awarded for partial completion of doctoral program. *Degree requirements:* For doctorate, comprehensive exam, thesis/dissertation. *Entrance requirements:* For master's, GRE General Test; for doctorate, General GRE. *Application deadline:* For fall admission, 3/1 priority date for domestic and international students; for spring admission, 10/1 priority date for domestic and international students. Applications are processed on a rolling basis. Application fee: $85. Electronic applications accepted. *Expenses:* Tuition: Full-time $25,980; part-time $1315 per unit. Required fees: $554. One-time fee: $35 full-time. Full-time tuition and fees vary according to degree level and program. *Financial support:* In 2009–10, fellowships with full tuition reimbursements (averaging $30,000 per year), research assistantships with full tuition reimbursements (averaging $19,250 per year), teaching assistantships with full tuition reimbursements (averaging $19,250 per year) were awarded; career-related internships or fieldwork, scholarships/grants, health care benefits, and unspecified assistantships also available. Financial award application deadline: 12/1; financial award applicants required to submit CSS PROFILE or FAFSA. *Faculty research:* Databases, computer graphics and computer vision, software engineering, networks and security, robotics, multimedia and virtual reality. Total annual research expenditures: $10 million. *Unit head:* Dr. Shanghua Teng, Seeley G. Mudd Professor of Engineering and Department Chair, 213-740-4498, E-mail: shanghua@ usc.edu. *Application contact:* Steve Schrader, Director of Student Affairs, 213-740-4779, E-mail: steve.schrader@usc.edu.

University of the Sacred Heart, Graduate Programs, Department of Education, San Juan, PR 00914-0383. Offers early childhood education (M Ed); information technology and multimedia (Certificate); instruction systems and education technology (M Ed), including English, information technology and multimedia, instructional design, mathematics, Spanish. Part-time and evening/weekend programs available. *Degree requirements:* For master's, thesis. *Entrance requirements:* For master's, EXADEP, minimum undergraduate GPA of 2.75, interview.

Virginia Commonwealth University, Graduate School, School of the Arts, Department of Graphic Design, Richmond, VA 23284-9005. Offers design/visual communications (MFA); interior environment (MFA); photography and film (MFA). *Accreditation:* NASAD. *Degree requirements:* For master's, thesis, exhibition. *Entrance requirements:* For master's, portfolio. *Faculty research:* Film, photography, interior environments, visual communication.

Western Illinois University, School of Graduate Studies, College of Education and Human Services, Department of Instructional Design and Technology, Macomb, IL 61455-1390. Offers distance learning (Certificate); graphic applications (Certificate); instructional design and technology (MS); multimedia (Certificate); technology integration in education (Certificate); training development (Certificate). Part-time programs available. Postbaccalaureate distance learning degree programs offered (no on-campus study). *Students:* 23 full-time (13 women), 56 part-time (37 women); includes 18 minority (12 African Americans, 2 American Indian/Alaska Native, 3 Asian Americans or Pacific Islanders, 1 Hispanic American), 8 international. Average age 36. 18 applicants, 72% accepted. In 2009, 25 master's, 2 other advanced degrees awarded. *Degree requirements:* For master's, thesis or alternative. *Entrance requirements:* Additional exam requirements/recommendations for international students: Required—TOEFL (minimum score 550 paper-based; 213 computer-based; 80 iBT). *Application deadline:* Applications are processed on a rolling basis. Application fee: $30. Electronic applications accepted. *Expenses:* Tuition, state resident: full-time $4486; part-time $249.21 per credit hour. Tuition, nonresident: full-time $8972; part-time $498.42 per credit hour. Required fees: $72.62 per credit hour. *Financial support:* In 2009–10, 16 students received support, including 11 research assistantships with full tuition reimbursements available (averaging $7,280 per year), 5 teaching assistantships with full tuition reimbursements available (averaging $8,400 per year). Financial award applicants required to submit FAFSA. *Unit head:* Dr. Hoyet Hemphill, Chairperson, 309-298-1952. *Application contact:* Evelyn Hoing, Assistant Director of Graduate Studies, 309-298-1806, Fax: 309-298-2345, E-mail: grad-office@wiu.edu.

Wilmington University, College of Technology, New Castle, DE 19720-6491. Offers corporate training (MS); information assurance (MS); information systems technologies (MS); Internet web design (MS); management information systems (MS). Part-time and evening/weekend programs available. *Entrance requirements:* Additional exam requirements/recommendations for international students: Required—TOEFL (minimum score 500 paper-based; 173 computer-based). Electronic applications accepted.

Journalism

American University, School of Communication, Program in Journalism and Public Affairs, Washington, DC 20016-8001. Offers broadcast journalism (MA), including economic communication, international journalism, public policy journalism; interactive journalism (MA); news media studies (MA); print journalism (MA), including economic communication, international journalism, public policy journalism. *Accreditation:* ACEJMC. Part-time and evening/weekend programs available. *Faculty:* 13 full-time (5 women), 4 part-time/adjunct (all women). *Students:* 24 full-time (16 women). 190 applicants, 63% accepted. In 2009, 40 master's awarded. *Degree requirements:* For master's, comprehensive exam, thesis or alternative. *Entrance requirements:* For master's, GRE General Test. Additional exam requirements/recommendations for international students: Required—TOEFL (minimum score 600 paper-based; 250 computer-based). *Application deadline:* For fall admission, 2/1 priority date for domestic students, 4/1 priority date for international students. Applications are processed on a rolling basis. Application fee: $50. Electronic applications accepted. *Expenses:* Tuition: Full-time $22,266; part-time $1237 per credit hour. Required fees: $430. Tuition and fees vary according to program. *Financial support:* In 2009–10, 3 fellowships with partial tuition reimbursements (averaging $27,000 per year), 14 research assistantships with tuition reimbursements (averaging $7,000 per year), 3 teaching assistantships with tuition reimbursements (averaging $7,000 per year) were awarded; career-related internships or fieldwork, Federal Work-Study, institutionally sponsored loans, scholarships/grants, tuition waivers (partial), and unspecified assistantships also available. Financial award application deadline: 2/1. *Faculty research:* Government and media effects of journalistic practices and policies, race and gender and the media, investigative reporting, computer assisted reporting. *Unit head:* Wendell Cochran, Division Director, 202-885-2075. *Application contact:* Sharmeen Ahsan-Bracciale, Graduate Admissions Office, 202-885-2040, Fax: 202-885-2019, E-mail: sharmeen@american.edu.

See Close-Up on page 673.

American University, School of Communication, Weekend Programs in Communication, Washington, DC 20016-8001. Offers interactive journalism (MA); news media studies (MA); producing for film and video (MA); public communication (MA). *Accreditation:* ACEJMC. Part-time and evening/weekend programs available. *Faculty:* 5 part-time/adjunct (2 women). *Students:* 112 part-time (75 women). 137 applicants, 61% accepted, 61 enrolled. In 2009, 15 master's awarded. *Degree requirements:* For master's, comprehensive exam, thesis or alternative. *Entrance requirements:* Additional exam requirements/recommendations for international students: Required—TOEFL (minimum score 600 paper-based; 250 computer-based). *Application deadline:* For fall admission, 8/1 for domestic students. Applications are processed on a rolling basis. Application fee: $50. Electronic applications accepted. *Expenses:* Tuition: Full-time $22,266; part-time $1237 per credit hour. Required fees: $430. Tuition and fees vary according to program. *Financial support:* In 2009–10, 3 fellowships (averaging $3,500 per year) were awarded; institutionally sponsored loans also available. *Unit head:* Wendell Cochran, Journalism Weekend Program Director, 202-885-2075, E-mail: cochran@american.edu. *Application contact:* Sharmeen Ahsan-Bracciale, Graduate Admissions Office, 202-885-2040, Fax: 202-885-2019, E-mail: sharmeen@american.edu.

See Close-Up on page 673.

The American University in Cairo, Graduate Studies and Research, School of Business, Economics and Communication, Department of Journalism and Mass Communication, Cairo, Egypt. Offers journalism and mass communication (MA); television and digital journalism (MA). Part-time programs available. *Degree requirements:* For master's, thesis (for some programs). *Entrance requirements:* For master's, English entrance exam, GMAT. Electronic applications accepted. *Faculty research:* Mass media and national development/censorship, intercultural photo communication, comparative journalism/television.

Angelo State University, College of Graduate Studies, College of Liberal and Fine Arts, Department of Communication, Mass Media and Theatre, San Angelo, TX 76909. Offers communication systems management (MA). Part-time and evening/weekend programs available. *Faculty:* 2 full-time (0 women). *Students:* 8 full-time (5 women), 4 part-time (2 women); includes 2 minority (both Hispanic Americans). Average age 30. 7 applicants, 100% accepted, 6 enrolled. *Degree requirements:* For master's, comprehensive exam, thesis optional. *Entrance requirements:* For master's, GRE General Test. Additional exam requirements/recommendations for international students: Required—TOEFL or IELTS. *Application deadline:* For fall admission, 7/15 priority date for domestic students, 6/10 for international students; for spring admission, 12/1 priority date for domestic students, 11/1 for international students. Applications are processed on a rolling basis. Application fee: $40 ($50 for international students). Electronic applications accepted. *Expenses:* Tuition, state resident: full-time $3396; part-time $142 per credit hour. Tuition, nonresident: full-time $10,152; part-time $423 per credit hour. Required fees: $1786; $36.25 per credit hour. $494 per semester. Full-time tuition and fees vary according to course load, degree level and program. *Financial support:* In 2009–10, 5 students received support, including 3 teaching assistantships (averaging $10,251 per year); career-related internships or fieldwork, Federal Work-Study, scholarships/grants, and unspecified assistantships also available. Support available to part-time students. Financial award application deadline: 3/1; financial award applicants required to submit FAFSA. *Unit head:* Dr. Shawn T. Wahl, Department Head, 325-942-2031 Ext. 228, Fax: 325-942-2551, E-mail: swahl1@angelo.edu. *Application contact:* Dr. Lana Marlow, Graduate Advisor, 325-942-2032 Ext. 356, Fax: 325-942-2551, E-mail: lana.marlow@angelo.edu.

Arizona State University, Graduate College, Walter Cronkite School of Journalism and Mass Communication, Tempe, AZ 85287. Offers MMC. *Accreditation:* ACEJMC. *Entrance requirements:* For master's, GRE, minimum GPA of 3.0 in the last 60 semester hours or 90 quarter hours of undergraduate coursework; resume and/or biographical sketch; 3 letters of recommendation. Additional exam requirements/recommendations for international students: Required—TOEFL. Electronic applications accepted.

Arkansas State University—Jonesboro, Graduate School, College of Communications, Department of Journalism, Jonesboro, State University, AR 72467. Offers MSMC. *Accreditation:* ACEJMC. Part-time programs available. *Faculty:* 4 full-time (2 women), 1 part-time/adjunct (0 women). *Students:* 11 full-time (5 women), 10 part-time (6 women); includes 2 minority (1 African American, 1 Asian American or Pacific Islander), 12 international. Average age 26. 16 applicants, 94% accepted, 9 enrolled. In 2009, 5 master's awarded. *Degree requirements:* For master's, comprehensive exam, thesis or alternative. *Entrance requirements:* For master's, GRE General Test, appropriate bachelor's degree, letters of reference, educational experience, professional experience. Additional exam requirements/recommendations for international students: Required—TOEFL (minimum score 550 paper-based; 213 computer-based; 79 iBT), IELTS (minimum score 6). *Application deadline:* For fall admission, 7/15 for domestic students, 7/1 for international students; for spring admission, 12/1 for domestic students, 11/13 for international students. Applications are processed on a rolling basis. Application fee: $30 ($40 for international students). Electronic applications accepted. *Expenses:* Tuition, state resident: full-time $3744; part-time $208 per credit hour. Tuition, nonresident: full-time $9540; part-time $530 per credit hour. Required fees: $896; $47 per credit hour. $25 per term. One-time fee: $50. Tuition and fees vary according to course load and program. *Financial support:* In 2009–10, 5 students received support. Career-related internships or fieldwork, scholarships/grants, and unspecified assistantships available. Financial award application deadline: 7/1; financial award applicants required to submit FAFSA. *Unit head:* Dr. Gil Fowler, Chair, 870-972-3075, Fax: 870-972-3321, E-mail: gfowler@astate.edu. *Application contact:* Dr. Andrew Sustich, Dean of the Graduate School, 870-972-3029, Fax: 870-972-3857, E-mail: sustich@astate.edu.

Arkansas Tech University, Graduate College, College of Arts and Humanities, Russellville, AR 72801. Offers communication (MLA); English (M Ed, MA); fine arts (MLA); history (MA); multi-media journalism (MA); psychology (MS); social science (MLA); Spanish (MA, MLA); teaching English as a second language (MA, MLA). Part-time programs available. *Students:* 39 full-time (30 women), 80 part-time (63 women); includes 11 minority (3 African Americans, 1 American Indian/Alaska Native, 1 Asian American or Pacific Islander, 6 Hispanic Americans), 23 international. Average age 33. In 2009, 70 master's awarded. *Degree requirements:* For master's, comprehensive exam (for some programs), thesis (for some programs), project. *Entrance requirements:* For master's, GRE General Test or MAT. Additional exam requirements/recommendations for international students: Required—TOEFL (minimum score 550 paper-based; 213 computer-based; 79 iBT), IELTS (minimum score 6). *Application deadline:* For fall admission, 3/1 priority date for domestic students, 5/1 priority date for international students; for spring admission, 10/1 priority date for domestic and international students. Applications are processed on a rolling basis. Application fee: $0 ($50 for international students). Electronic applications accepted. *Expenses:* Tuition, state resident: full-time $3438; part-time $191 per hour. Tuition, nonresident: full-time $6876; part-time $382 per hour. Required fees: $482; $9 per credit hour. $140 per semester. Tuition and fees vary according to course load. *Financial support:* In 2009–10, teaching assistantships with full tuition reimbursements (averaging $4,000 per year); research assistantships, career-related internships or fieldwork, Federal Work-Study, scholarships/grants, health care benefits, and unspecified assistantships also available. Support available to part-time students. Financial award application deadline: 4/15; financial award applicants required to submit FAFSA. *Unit head:* Dr. Micheal Tarver, Dean, 479-968-0274, Fax: 479-964-0812, E-mail: mtarver@atu.edu. *Application contact:* Dr. Mary B. Gunter, Dean of Graduate College, 479-968-0398, Fax: 479-964-0542, E-mail: graduate.school@atu.edu.

Ball State University, Graduate School, College of Communication, Information, and Media, Department of Journalism, Muncie, IN 47306-1099. Offers journalism (MA); public relations (MA). *Accreditation:* ACEJMC. *Entrance requirements:* For master's, resume. *Faculty research:* Image studies, readership surveys, audience perception studies.

Baylor University, Graduate School, College of Arts and Sciences, Department of Journalism, Waco, TX 76798. Offers international journalism (MIJ); journalism (MA). *Accreditation:* ACEJMC. *Students:* 10 full-time (7 women), 7 part-time (3 women); includes 3 minority (2 Asian Americans or Pacific Islanders, 1 Hispanic American), 4 international. Average age 24. In 2009, 6 master's awarded. *Degree requirements:* For master's, proficiency in 1 foreign language (MIJ). *Entrance requirements:* For master's, GRE General Test. *Application deadline:* Applications are processed on a rolling basis. Application fee: $25. *Financial support:* Research assistantships, teaching assistantships, career-related internships or fieldwork, Federal Work-Study, and institutionally sponsored loans available. Support available to part-time students. *Faculty research:* International politics, mass media and society, journalism history, editing practices. *Unit head:* Dr. Amanda Sturgill, Graduate Program Director, 254-710-6322, Fax: 254-710-3363, E-mail: amanda_sturgill@baylor.edu. *Application contact:* Jan Loosier, Administrative Assistant, 254-710-3261, Fax: 254-710-3870, E-mail: jan_loosier@baylor.edu.

Bob Jones University, Graduate Programs, Greenville, SC 29614. Offers accountancy (MS); Bible (MA); Bible translation (MA); Biblical studies (Certificate); broadcast management (MS); business administration (MBA); church history (MA, PhD); church ministries (MA); church music (MM); cinema and video production (MA); counseling (MS); curriculum and instruction (Ed D); divinity (M Div); dramatic production (MA); educational leadership (MS, Ed D, Ed S); elementary education (M Ed, MAT); English (M Ed, MA, MAT); fine arts (MA); graphic design (MA); history (M Ed, MA); illustration (MA); interpretative speech (MA); mathematics (M Ed, MAT); medical missions (Certificate); ministry (MM, D Min); multi-categorical special education (M Ed, MAT); music (M Ed); New Testament interpretation (PhD); Old Testament interpretation (PhD); orchestral instrument performance (MM); organ performance (MM); pastoral studies (MA); personnel services (MS, Ed S); piano pedagogy (MM); piano performance (MM); platform arts (MA); radio and television broadcasting (MS); rhetoric and public address (MA); secondary education (M Ed); studio art (MA); teaching Bible (MA); theology (MA, PhD); voice performance (MM); youth ministries (MA); M Div/MM.

Boston University, College of Communication, Department of Journalism, Boston, MA 02215. Offers broadcast journalism (MS); business and economics journalism (MS); photojournalism (MS); print journalism (MS); science journalism (MS). Part-time programs available. *Faculty:* 23 full-time, 26 part-time/adjunct. *Students:* 94 full-time (67 women), 9 part-time (6 women); includes 14 minority (3 African Americans, 1 American Indian/Alaska Native, 9 Asian Americans or Pacific Islanders, 1 Hispanic American), 20 international. Average age 26. In 2009, 72 master's awarded. *Degree requirements:* For master's, thesis. *Entrance requirements:* For master's, GRE General Test, sample of written work. Additional exam requirements/recommendations for international students: Required—TOEFL (minimum score 600 paper-based; 250 computer-based; 100 iBT). *Application deadline:* For fall admission, 2/1 for domestic and international students. Application fee: $70. Electronic applications accepted. *Expenses:* Tuition: Full-time $37,910; part-time $1184 per credit hour. Required fees: $386; $40 per semester. Part-time tuition and fees vary according to class time, course level, degree level and program. *Financial support:* Teaching assistantships with partial tuition reimbursements, career-related internships or fieldwork, Federal Work-Study, institutionally sponsored loans, scholarships/grants, and unspecified assistantships available. Support available to part-time students. Financial award application deadline: 2/1; financial award applicants required to submit FAFSA. *Unit head:* Lou Ureneck, Chairman, 617-353-3484, Fax: 617-353-1086, E-mail: lureneck@bu.edu. *Application contact:* Kate Iserman, Administrator of Graduate Services, 617-353-3481, Fax: 617-358-0399, E-mail: comgrad@bu.edu.

See Close-Up on page 675.

California State University, Fresno, Division of Graduate Studies, College of Arts and Humanities, Department of Mass Communication and Journalism, Fresno, CA 93740-8027. Offers MA. Part-time and evening/weekend programs available. *Degree requirements:* For master's, thesis. *Entrance requirements:* For master's, GRE General Test, minimum GPA of 3.0. Additional exam requirements/recommendations for international students: Required—TOEFL. Electronic applications accepted.

California State University, Fullerton, Graduate Studies, College of Communications, Department of Communications, Fullerton, CA 92834-9480. Offers communications—advertising (MA); communications—entertainment and tourism (MA); communications—journalism (MA); communications—public relations (MA). Part-time programs available. *Students:* 18 full-time (14 women), 38 part-time (30 women); includes 21 minority (2 African Americans, 8 Asian Americans or Pacific Islanders, 11 Hispanic Americans), 4 international. Average age 28. 121 applicants, 23% accepted, 17 enrolled. In 2009, 33 master's awarded. *Degree requirements:* For master's, project or thesis. *Entrance requirements:* For master's, GRE General Test. Application fee: $55. *Expenses:* Tuition, nonresident: full-time $11,160; part-time $373 per credit. Required fees: $1440 per term. Tuition and fees vary according to course load, degree level and program. *Financial support:* Teaching assistantships, career-related internships or fieldwork, Federal Work-Study, institutionally sponsored loans, and scholarships/grants available. Support available to part-time students. Financial award application deadline: 3/1; financial award applicants required to submit FAFSA. *Unit head:* Dr. Tony Fellow, Chair, 657-278-3517. *Application contact:* Coordinator, 657-278-3832.

California State University, Northridge, Graduate Studies, College of Arts, Media, and Communication, Department of Journalism, Northridge, CA 91330. Offers mass communication (MA). *Accreditation:* ACEJMC. Part-time and evening/weekend programs available. *Faculty:* 9 full-time (4 women), 12 part-time/adjunct (4 women). *Students:* 8 full-time (7 women), 30 part-time (24 women); includes 14 minority (2 African Americans, 2 Asian Americans or Pacific Islanders, 10 Hispanic Americans), 4 international. Average age 28. 62 applicants, 45% accepted, 15 enrolled. In 2009, 10 master's awarded. *Degree requirements:* For master's, thesis. *Entrance requirements:* For master's, GRE General Test. Additional exam requirements/recommendations for international students: Required—TOEFL. *Application deadline:* For fall admission, 11/30 for domestic students. Application fee: $55. *Financial support:* Career-related internships or fieldwork and Federal Work-Study available. Financial award application deadline: 3/1. *Unit head:* Dr. José Luis Benavides, Chair, 818-677-3135, E-mail: jose.benavides@csun.edu. *Application contact:* Dr. José Luis Benavides, Chair, 818-677-3135, E-mail: jose.benavides@csun.edu.

Carleton University, Faculty of Graduate Studies, Faculty of Public Affairs and Management, School of Journalism and Communication, Ottawa, ON K1S 5B6, Canada. Offers communication (MA, PhD); journalism (MJ). *Degree requirements:* For master's, thesis optional; for doctorate, comprehensive exam, thesis/dissertation. *Entrance requirements:* For master's, honors degree. Additional exam requirements/recommendations for international students: Required—TOEFL. *Faculty research:* Specialized print reporting, broadcast journalism, journalism studies.

Columbia College Chicago, Graduate School, Department of Journalism, Chicago, IL 60605-1996. Offers public affairs journalism (MA). *Degree requirements:* For master's, thesis. *Entrance requirements:* For master's, interview, minimum GPA of 3.0, writing sample. Additional exam

Journalism

Columbia College Chicago (continued)
requirements/recommendations for international students: Required—TOEFL (minimum score 550 paper-based; 213 computer-based). Electronic applications accepted. *Expenses:* Tuition: Part-time $651 per credit hour. Required fees: $651 per credit hour. $205 per semester. One-time fee: $285 part-time. Tuition and fees vary according to program.

Columbia University, Graduate School of Journalism, New York, NY 10027. Offers MA, MS, PhD, JD/MS, MIA/MS, MS/MBA. *Accreditation:* ACEJMC. Part-time programs available. *Degree requirements:* For master's, thesis; for doctorate, thesis/dissertation. *Entrance requirements:* For master's, writing test, 2-3 samples of journalistic work, minimum typing speed of 50 words per minute; for doctorate, GRE. Additional exam requirements/recommendations for international students: Required—TOEFL. *Expenses:* Contact institution. *Faculty research:* International communication, communication technologies, ethics in journalism, journalism history.

Concordia University, School of Graduate Studies, Faculty of Arts and Science, Department of Journalism, Montréal, QC H3G 1M8, Canada. Offers Diploma. *Degree requirements:* For Diploma, one foreign language. *Entrance requirements:* Additional exam requirements/recommendations for international students: Required—departmental English test or TOEFL.

CUNY Graduate School of Journalism, Graduate Program, New York, NY 10018. Offers MA. *Faculty:* 10 full-time (3 women), 64 part-time/adjunct. *Students:* 137 full-time (88 women); includes 46 minority (15 African Americans, 15 Asian Americans or Pacific Islanders, 16 Hispanic Americans). Average age 27. 329 applicants, 50% accepted, 84 enrolled. In 2009, 58 master's awarded. *Degree requirements:* For master's, internship, final or capstone project. *Entrance requirements:* For master's, GRE, admissions exam, 3 letters of recommendation, resume, interview, 3 writing samples. Additional exam requirements/recommendations for international students: Required—TOEFL (minimum score 260 computer-based; 105 iBT). *Application deadline:* For fall admission, 1/2 for domestic students. Application fee: $65. Electronic applications accepted. *Expenses:* Tuition, state resident: full-time $11,040; part-time $3680 per semester. Tuition, nonresident: full-time $20,930; part-time $8625 per semester. International tuition: $25,875 full-time. Required fees: $1795. *Financial support:* Career-related internships or fieldwork, Federal Work-Study, and scholarships/grants available. Financial award application deadline: 2/1; financial award applicants required to submit FAFSA. *Unit head:* Stephen B. Shepard, Dean, 646-758-7800. *Application contact:* Colleen Marshall, Admissions/Outreach Counselor, 646-758-7852, Fax: 646-758-7709, E-mail: colleen.marshall@journalism.cuny.edu.

See Close-Up on page 677.

DePaul University, College of Communication, Chicago, IL 60614. Offers journalism (MA); media, culture and society (MA); organizational and multicultural communication (MA); public relations and advertising (MA). Part-time and evening/weekend programs available. *Faculty:* 31 full-time (17 women), 15 part-time/adjunct (7 women). *Students:* 159 full-time (127 women), 50 part-time (40 women); includes 56 minority (29 African Americans, 9 Asian Americans or Pacific Islanders, 18 Hispanic Americans), 11 international. Average age 29. 354 applicants, 44% accepted, 79 enrolled. In 2009, 64 master's awarded. *Degree requirements:* For master's, comprehensive exam (for some programs), final exam or thesis/project. *Entrance requirements:* For master's, GRE General Test (public relations and advertising), minimum GPA of 3.0, writing sample, letters of recommendation, resume. Additional exam requirements/recommendations for international students: Required—TOEFL (minimum score 590 paper-based; 243 computer-based; 96 iBT). Application fee: $40. Electronic applications accepted. *Expenses:* Tuition: Full-time $37,525; part-time $620 per credit hour. *Financial support:* In 2009–10, 8 students received support, including 4 research assistantships with partial tuition reimbursements available, 2 teaching assistantships with full tuition reimbursements available (averaging $12,000 per year); fellowships with full tuition reimbursements available, career-related internships or fieldwork, scholarships/grants, and tuition waivers (partial) also available. Support available to part-time students. Financial award applicants required to submit FAFSA. *Faculty research:* Intercultural communication, corporate culture, diversity in the working place, organizational socialization, critical cultural studies. *Unit head:* Dr. Jacqueline Taylor, Dean, 773-325-7216, Fax: 773-325-7584, E-mail: jtaylor@depaul.edu. *Application contact:* Ann Spittle, Director of Graduate Admission, 773-325-7315, Fax: 773-325-2395, E-mail: gradcom@depaul.edu.

Drexel University, School of Journalism, Philadelphia, PA 19104-2875. Offers MA. *Entrance requirements:* Additional exam requirements/recommendations for international students: Required—TOEFL.

Emerson College, Graduate Studies, School of Communication, Department of Journalism, Boston, MA 02116-4624. Offers journalism (MA), including broadcast journalism, print/multimedia journalism. *Faculty:* 15 full-time (5 women), 5 part-time/adjunct (1 woman). *Students:* 66 full-time (47 women), 3 part-time (all women); includes 7 minority (3 African Americans, 2 Asian Americans or Pacific Islanders, 2 Hispanic Americans), 8 international. Average age 24. 101 applicants, 86% accepted, 35 enrolled. In 2009, 32 master's awarded. *Entrance requirements:* For master's, GRE General Test. Additional exam requirements/recommendations for international students: Required—TOEFL (minimum score 550 paper-based; 213 computer-based; 80 iBT), IELTS (minimum score 6.5). *Application deadline:* For fall admission, 6/1 priority date for domestic students, 5/1 priority date for international students. Applications are processed on a rolling basis. Application fee: $60 ($75 for international students). Electronic applications accepted. *Expenses:* Tuition: Full-time $22,056; part-time $919 per credit. Required fees: $120; $120 per year. One-time fee: $170 full-time. *Financial support:* In 2009–10, 18 students received support, including 5 fellowships with partial tuition reimbursements available (averaging $14,000 per year), 9 research assistantships with partial tuition reimbursements available (averaging $10,000 per year); Federal Work-Study, scholarships/grants, and unspecified assistantships also available. Financial award application deadline: 3/1; financial award applicants required to submit FAFSA. *Faculty research:* Journalism. *Unit head:* Prof. Ted Gup, Chair, 617-824-8805, E-mail: ted_gup@emerson.edu. *Application contact:* Office of Graduate Admission, 617-824-8610, Fax: 617-824-8614, E-mail: gradapp@emerson.edu.

Florida Agricultural and Mechanical University, Division of Graduate Studies, Research, and Continuing Education, School of Journalism and Graphic Communication, Tallahassee, FL 32307-3200. Offers journalism (MS). *Accreditation:* ACEJMC. *Faculty:* 20 full-time (10 women). *Students:* 8 full-time (all women), 4 part-time (2 women); includes 11 minority (all African Americans). In 2009, 3 master's awarded. *Degree requirements:* For master's, comprehensive exam, thesis (for some programs). *Entrance requirements:* For master's, GRE General Test, minimum GPA of 3.0. Additional exam requirements/recommendations for international students: Required—TOEFL. *Application deadline:* For fall admission, 5/18 for domestic students, 12/18 for international students; for spring admission, 11/12 for domestic students, 5/12 for international students. Application fee: $30. *Unit head:* Dr. James E. Hawkins, Interim Dean, 850-599-3379, Fax: 850-561-2399. *Application contact:* Dr. Michael Abrams, Graduate Program Director, 850-561-2766.

Florida Atlantic University, Dorothy F. Schmidt College of Arts and Letters, School of Communication and Multimedia Studies, Boca Raton, FL 33431-0991. Offers communication studies (MA); film and video (Certificate); film studies (MA); multimedia journalism studies (MA). Part-time programs available. *Faculty:* 21 full-time (10 women), 14 part-time/adjunct (3 women). *Students:* 14 full-time (11 women), 13 part-time (8 women); includes 3 minority (1 African American, 1 Asian American or Pacific Islander, 1 Hispanic American), 3 international. Average age 28. 39 applicants, 26% accepted, 6 enrolled. In 2009, 7 master's awarded. *Degree requirements:* For master's, one foreign language, comprehensive exam (for some programs), thesis (for some programs). *Entrance requirements:* For master's, GRE General Test, minimum GPA of 3.0. *Application deadline:* For fall admission, 7/1 priority date for domestic students, 4/1 for international students; for spring admission, 11/1 for domestic students, 10/1 for international students. Applications are processed on a rolling basis. Application fee: $30. Electronic applications accepted. *Expenses:* Tuition, state resident: full-time $7055; part-time $293.94 per credit hour. Tuition, nonresident: full-time $22,096; part-time $920.66 per credit hour. *Financial support:* Teaching assistantships with partial tuition reimbursements, Federal Work-Study and institutionally sponsored loans available. Support available to part-time students. Financial award application deadline: 3/1. *Faculty research:* Cultural studies, gender studies, film, communication theory, journalism, new media. *Unit head:* Dr. Susan S. Reilly, Director, 561-297-1095, Fax: 561-297-2615, E-mail: sreilly@fau.edu. *Application contact:* Dr. Eric M. Freedman, Graduate Coordinator, 561-297-2534, Fax: 561-297-2615, E-mail: efreedma@fau.edu.

Georgetown University, Graduate School of Arts and Sciences, School of Continuing Studies, Washington, DC 20057. Offers American studies (MALS); Catholic studies (MALS); classical civilizations (MALS); ethics and the professions (MALS); human resources management (MPS); humanities (MALS); individualized study (MALS); international affairs (MALS); Islam and Muslim-Christian relations (MALS); journalism (MPS); liberal studies (DLS); literature and society (MALS); medieval and early modern European studies (MALS); public relations (MPS); real estate (MPS); religious studies (MALS); social and public policy (MALS); sports industry management (MPS); the theory and practice of American democracy (MALS); visual culture (MALS). *Entrance requirements:* Additional exam requirements/recommendations for international students: Required—TOEFL.

Harvard University, Extension School, Cambridge, MA 02138-3722. Offers applied sciences (CAS); biotechnology (ALM); educational technologies (ALM); educational technology (CET); English for graduate and professional studies (DGP); environmental management (ALM, CEM); information technology (ALM); journalism (ALM); liberal arts (ALM); management (ALM, CM); mathematics for teaching (ALM); museum studies (ALM); premedical studies (Diploma); publication and communication (CPC). Part-time and evening/weekend programs available. *Degree requirements:* For master's, thesis. *Entrance requirements:* For master's, 3 completed graduate courses with grade of B or higher. Additional exam requirements/recommendations for international students: Required—TOEFL (minimum score 600 paper-based; 250 computer-based), TWE (minimum score 5). *Expenses:* Contact institution.

Hofstra University, School of Communication, Department of Journalism, Media Studies, and Public Relations, Hempstead, NY 11549. Offers journalism (MA). *Accreditation:* ACEJMC. Part-time and evening/weekend programs available. *Faculty:* 6 full-time (3 women), 3 part-time/adjunct (1 woman). *Students:* 20 full-time (12 women), 12 part-time (8 women); includes 4 minority (1 African American, 1 American Indian/Alaska Native, 2 Hispanic Americans), 2 international. Average age 26. 40 applicants, 78% accepted, 13 enrolled. In 2009, 5 master's awarded. *Degree requirements:* For master's, thesis. *Entrance requirements:* For master's, minimum GPA of 2.75; bachelor's degree. Additional exam requirements/recommendations for international students: Required—TOEFL (minimum score 550 paper-based; 213 computer-based; 80 iBT). *Application deadline:* Applications are processed on a rolling basis. Application fee: $60. Electronic applications accepted. *Expenses:* Tuition: Full-time $16,200; part-time $900 per credit hour. Required fees: $970; $145 per term. Tuition and fees vary according to program. *Financial support:* In 2009–10, 15 students received support, including 4 fellowships with full and partial tuition reimbursements available (averaging $2,625 per year), 3 research assistantships with full and partial tuition reimbursements available (averaging $20,514 per year); Federal Work-Study, institutionally sponsored loans, scholarships/grants, tuition waivers (full and partial), and unspecified assistantships also available. Support available to part-time students. Financial award applicants required to submit FAFSA. *Faculty research:* Media ethics/law; environmental, science, and health journalism; multimedia/future of news; race, gender, cultural issues, social justice; RTNDA/Hofstra University Annual Survey. *Unit head:* Dr. Kristal Zook, Program Director, 516-463-4304, E-mail: jrnkzb@hofstra.edu. *Application contact:* Carol Drummer, Dean of Graduate Admissions, 516-463-4876, Fax: 516-463-4664, E-mail: gradstudent@hofstra.edu.

Indiana University Bloomington, School of Journalism, Bloomington, IN 47405-7000. Offers journalism (MA, MAT); mass communication (PhD); MA/JD; MA/MA. *Accreditation:* ACEJMC. *Faculty:* 11 full-time (5 women). *Students:* 63 full-time (35 women), 14 part-time (8 women); includes 7 minority (4 African Americans, 3 Asian Americans or Pacific Islanders), 26 international. Average age 32. 109 applicants, 62% accepted, 22 enrolled. In 2009, 26 master's, 2 doctorates awarded. Terminal master's awarded for partial completion of doctoral program. *Degree requirements:* For master's, thesis (for some programs); for doctorate, thesis/dissertation. *Entrance requirements:* For master's and doctorate, GRE General Test. Additional exam requirements/recommendations for international students: Required—TOEFL. *Application deadline:* For fall admission, 1/15 priority date for domestic students; for spring admission, 9/1 priority date for domestic students. Applications are processed on a rolling basis. Application fee: $55 ($65 for international students). *Financial support:* Fellowships, research assistantships with full tuition reimbursements, teaching assistantships with partial tuition reimbursements, career-related internships or fieldwork, Federal Work-Study, institutionally sponsored loans, and tuition waivers (full) available. Financial award application deadline: 1/15. *Faculty research:* Political communication, international communication, communication history, communication law, visual communication. Total annual research expenditures: $165,185. *Unit head:* Bradley Hamm, Dean, 812-855-9247. *Application contact:* Amy Reynolds, Associate Dean of Graduate Studies, 812-855-8111.

Iona College, School of Arts and Science, Department of Mass Communication, New Rochelle, NY 10801-1890. Offers journalism (MS); public relations (MA). *Accreditation:* ACEJMC (one or more programs are accredited). Part-time and evening/weekend programs available. *Faculty:* 6 full-time (1 woman), 6 part-time/adjunct (3 women). *Students:* 14 full-time (all women), 40 part-time (33 women); includes 15 minority (5 African Americans, 2 Asian Americans or Pacific Islanders, 8 Hispanic Americans), 4 international. Average age 27. 46 applicants, 50% accepted, 15 enrolled. In 2009, 23 master's awarded. *Degree requirements:* For master's, comprehensive exam or thesis. *Entrance requirements:* For master's, GRE General Test, minimum GPA of 3.0. Additional exam requirements/recommendations for international students: Required—TOEFL (minimum score 550 paper-based; 213 computer-based). *Application deadline:* Applications are processed on a rolling basis. Application fee: $50. Electronic applications accepted. *Expenses:* Contact institution. *Financial support:* Career-related internships or fieldwork, tuition waivers (partial), and unspecified assistantships available. Support available to part-time students. Financial award application deadline: 4/15; financial award applicants required to submit FAFSA. *Faculty research:* Media ecology, new media, corporate communication, media images, organizational learning in public relations. *Unit head:* Br. Raymond Smith, Chair, 914-633-2354, E-mail: rrsmith@iona.edu. *Application contact:* Veronica Jarek-Prinz, Director of Graduate Admissions, 914-633-2420, Fax: 914-633-2277, E-mail: vjarekprinz@iona.edu.

Iowa State University of Science and Technology, Graduate College, College of Liberal Arts and Sciences, Greenlee School of Journalism and Mass Communication, Ames, IA 50011. Offers MS. *Accreditation:* ACEJMC. *Faculty:* 70 full-time (56 women). *Students:* 25 full-time (19 women), 15 part-time (8 women); includes 6 minority (1 African American, 1 Asian American or Pacific Islander, 4 Hispanic Americans), 22 international. 42 applicants, 60% accepted, 13 enrolled. In 2009, 12 master's awarded. *Degree requirements:* For master's, thesis or alternative. *Entrance requirements:* For master's, GRE General Test. Additional exam requirements/recommendations for international students: Required—TOEFL (minimum score 570 paper-based; 88 iBT) or IELTS (minimum score 6.5). *Application deadline:* For fall admission, 4/1 priority date for international students; for spring admission, 11/1 priority date for international students. Applications are processed on a rolling basis. Application fee: $40 ($90 for international students). Electronic applications accepted. *Expenses:* Tuition, state resident: full-time $6716. Tuition, nonresident: full-time $8908. Tuition and fees vary according to course level, course load, program and student level. *Financial support:* In 2009–10, 15 research assistantships with full and partial tuition reimbursements (averaging $13,500 per year) were awarded; fellowships, teaching assistantships with partial tuition reimbursements, scholarships/grants, health care benefits, and unspecified assistantships also available. *Unit head:* Dr. Michael Bugeja, Chair, 515-294-0481, Fax: 515-294-5108, E-mail: greenlee@iastate.edu.

Application contact: Dr. Eric Abbott, Director of Graduate Education, 515-294-0492, E-mail: masscomm@iastate.edu.

Kent State University, College of Communication and Information, School of Journalism and Mass Communication, Kent, OH 44242-0001. Offers MA. *Accreditation:* ACEJMC. Part-time programs available. *Degree requirements:* For master's, thesis optional. *Entrance requirements:* For master's, GRE General Test, minimum GPA of 3.0. Additional exam requirements/recommendations for international students: Recommended—TOEFL (minimum score 600 paper-based; 250 computer-based). Electronic applications accepted. *Faculty research:* Electronic tablet newspapers, accuracy and ethics in broadcast news, internet credibility, First Amendment, HDTV.

Marquette University, Graduate School, College of Communication, Milwaukee, WI 53201-1881. Offers advertising and public relations (MA); broadcasting and electronic communications (MA); communications studies (MA); journalism (MA); mass communications (MA); religious communications (MA); science, health and environmental communications (MA). *Accreditation:* ACEJMC. Part-time and evening/weekend programs available. *Faculty:* 31 full-time (17 women), 35 part-time/adjunct (16 women). *Students:* 28 full-time (21 women), 30 part-time (24 women); includes 3 minority (1 African American, 2 American Indian/Alaska Native), 7 international. Average age 26. 81 applicants, 47% accepted, 22 enrolled. In 2009, 17 master's awarded. *Degree requirements:* For master's, comprehensive exam. *Entrance requirements:* For master's, GRE. Additional exam requirements/recommendations for international students: Required—TOEFL. Application fee: $40. *Financial support:* In 2009–10, 6 research assistantships, 12 teaching assistantships were awarded; career-related internships or fieldwork, Federal Work-Study, institutionally sponsored loans, scholarships/grants, and tuition waivers (full and partial) also available. Support available to part-time students. Financial award application deadline: 2/15. *Faculty research:* Urban journalism, gender and communication, intercultural communication, religious communication. *Unit head:* Dr. Ana Garner, Dean, 414-288-3588, Fax: 414-288-1578. *Application contact:* Erin Fox, Assistant Director for Recruitment, 414-288-5319, Fax: 414-288-1902, E-mail: erin.fox@marquette.edu.

Marshall University, Academic Affairs Division, School of Journalism and Mass Communications, Huntington, WV 25755. Offers MAJ. *Accreditation:* ACEJMC. *Faculty:* 3 full-time (0 women), 4 part-time/adjunct (1 woman). *Students:* 26 full-time (14 women), 3 part-time (all women); includes 2 minority (both African Americans), 8 international. Average age 27. In 2009, 8 master's awarded. *Degree requirements:* For master's, thesis optional. *Entrance requirements:* For master's, GRE General Test. Application fee: $40. *Unit head:* Dr. Corley F. Dennison, Dean, 304-696-2809, E-mail: dennisoc@marshall.edu. *Application contact:* Janet Dooley, Assistant Dean, 304-696-2734, Fax: 304-746-1902, E-mail: dooley@marshall.edu.

Michigan State University, The Graduate School, College of Communication Arts and Sciences, School of Journalism, East Lansing, MI 48824. Offers MA. *Accreditation:* ACEJMC. *Faculty:* 11 full-time (5 women). *Students:* 24 full-time (17 women), 15 part-time (10 women); includes 2 minority (both African Americans), 7 international. Average age 29. 58 applicants, 59% accepted. In 2009, 15 master's awarded. *Entrance requirements:* Additional exam requirements/recommendations for international students: Required—TOEFL. Electronic applications accepted. *Expenses:* Tuition, state resident: part-time $478.25 per credit hour. Tuition, nonresident: part-time $966.50 per credit hour. Part-time tuition and fees vary according to program. *Financial support:* In 2009–10, 5 research assistantships with tuition reimbursements (averaging $5,747 per year) were awarded. Total annual research expenditures: $100,323. *Unit head:* Dr. Lucinda Davenport, Director, 517-355-6574, Fax: 517-355-7710, E-mail: ludavenp@msu.edu. *Application contact:* Estrella Starn, Graduate Programs Coordinator, 517-353-6431, Fax: 517-355-7710, E-mail: jrnma@msu.edu.

New York University, Graduate School of Arts and Science, Department of Biology, New York, NY 10012-1019. Offers biology (PhD); biomedical journalism (MS); cancer and molecular biology (PhD); computational biology (PhD); computers in biological research (MS); developmental genetics (PhD); general biology (MS); immunology and microbiology (PhD); molecular genetics (PhD); neurobiology (PhD); oral biology (MS); plant biology (PhD); recombinant DNA technology (MS); MS/MBA. Part-time programs available. *Faculty:* 24 full-time (5 women). *Students:* 142 full-time (79 women), 44 part-time (28 women); includes 34 minority (1 African American, 25 Asian Americans or Pacific Islanders, 8 Hispanic Americans), 82 international. Average age 27. 362 applicants, 71% accepted, 72 enrolled. In 2009, 43 master's, 9 doctorates awarded. Terminal master's awarded for partial completion of doctoral program. *Degree requirements:* For master's, thesis or alternative, qualifying paper; for doctorate, comprehensive exam, thesis/dissertation. *Entrance requirements:* For master's, GRE General Test; for doctorate, GRE General Test, GRE Subject Test. Additional exam requirements/recommendations for international students: Required—TOEFL. *Application deadline:* For fall admission, 12/12 priority date for domestic students. Application fee: $90. *Expenses:* Tuition: Full-time $30,528; part-time $1272 per credit. Required fees: $2177. *Financial support:* Fellowships with tuition reimbursements, research assistantships with tuition reimbursements, teaching assistantships with tuition reimbursements, career-related internships or fieldwork, Federal Work-Study, institutionally sponsored loans, scholarships/grants, health care benefits, and unspecified assistantships available. Financial award application deadline: 12/12; financial award applicants required to submit FAFSA. *Faculty research:* Genomics, molecular and cell biology, development and molecular genetics, molecular evolution of plants and animals. *Unit head:* Gloria Coruzzi, Chair, 212-998-8200, Fax: 212-995-4015, E-mail: biology@nyu.edu. *Application contact:* Stephen Small, Director of Graduate Studies, 212-998-8200, Fax: 212-995-4015, E-mail: biology@nyu.edu.

New York University, Graduate School of Arts and Science, Department of Journalism, New York, NY 10012-1019. Offers biomedical journalism (MS); cultural reporting and criticism (MA); French studies/journalism (MA); journalism (MA); Latin American and Caribbean studies/journalism (MA); Near Eastern studies/journalism (MA); science and environmental reporting (Advanced Certificate); MA/Advanced Certificate. *Accreditation:* ACEJMC. Part-time programs available. *Students:* 186 full-time (132 women), 39 part-time (22 women); includes 25 minority (9 African Americans, 13 Asian Americans or Pacific Islanders, 3 Hispanic Americans), 47 international. Average age 27. 537 applicants, 50% accepted, 130 enrolled. In 2009, 88 master's, 22 other advanced degrees awarded. *Degree requirements:* For master's, written projects. *Entrance requirements:* For master's, GRE General Test, sample of written work. Additional exam requirements/recommendations for international students: Required—TOEFL. *Application deadline:* For fall admission, 1/4 priority date for domestic students. Application fee: $90. *Expenses:* Tuition: Full-time $30,528; part-time $1272 per credit. Required fees: $2177. *Financial support:* Fellowships with tuition reimbursements, teaching assistantships with tuition reimbursements, Federal Work-Study, institutionally sponsored loans, scholarships/grants, and tuition waivers (partial) available. Financial award application deadline: 1/4; financial award applicants required to submit FAFSA. *Faculty research:* Newspaper, magazine, and broadcast journalism; business and financial reporting; media studies. *Unit head:* Brooke Kroeger, Chair, 212-998-7980, Fax: 212-995-4148, E-mail: graduate.journalism@nyu.edu. *Application contact:* Perri Klass, Director of Graduate Studies, 212-998-7980, Fax: 212-995-4148, E-mail: graduate.journalism@nyu.edu.

Northeastern University, College of Arts, Media and Design, School of Journalism, Boston, MA 02115-5096. Offers MA. Part-time and evening/weekend programs available. *Faculty:* 12 full-time (4 women), 6 part-time/adjunct (4 women). *Students:* 17 full-time (11 women), 4 part-time (3 women); includes 2 African Americans, 1 Asian American or Pacific Islander, 1 Hispanic American, 1 international. 62 applicants, 71% accepted, 11 enrolled. In 2009, 17 master's awarded. *Degree requirements:* For master's, thesis (for some programs). *Entrance requirements:* For master's, GRE General Test, minimum GPA of 3.0. *Application deadline:* For fall admission, 2/1 priority date for domestic students, 2/1 for international students. Applications are processed on a rolling basis. Application fee: $50. Electronic applications accepted. *Financial support:* Career-related internships or fieldwork, Federal Work-Study, institutionally sponsored loans, scholarships/grants, tuition waivers (partial), and unspecified assistantships available. Financial award application deadline: 3/1; financial award applicants required to submit FAFSA. *Faculty research:* Online journalism, broadcast news, foreign reporting, presidential debates, sporting society. *Unit head:* Prof. Belle Adler, Graduate Coordinator, 617-373-3238, Fax: 617-373-8773, E-mail: b.adler@neu.edu. *Application contact:* Jo-Anne Dickinson, Graduate Assistant, 617-373-5990, Fax: 617-373-7281, E-mail: gsas@neu.edu.

Northwestern University, Medill School of Journalism, Evanston, IL 60208. Offers broadcast journalism (MSJ); integrated marketing communications (MSIMC), including advertising/sales promotion, direct database and e-commerce marketing, general studies, public relations; magazine publishing (MSJ); new media (MSJ); reporting and writing (MSJ). *Accreditation:* ACEJMC (one or more programs are accredited). *Entrance requirements:* For master's, GRE General Test, GMAT or LSAT (MSJ). Additional exam requirements/recommendations for international students: Required—TOEFL. Electronic applications accepted. *Expenses:* Contact institution. *Faculty research:* Web business journalism, cultural stereotypes, voter apathy, digital television.

The Ohio State University, Graduate School, College of Social and Behavioral Sciences, School of Communication, Program in Journalism and Communication, Columbus, OH 43210. Offers MA. *Entrance requirements:* For master's, GRE General Test. Electronic applications accepted. *Expenses:* Tuition, state resident: full-time $10,683. Tuition, nonresident: full-time $25,923. Tuition and fees vary according to course load and program.

Ohio University, Graduate College, Scripps College of Communication, E.W. Scripps School of Journalism, Athens, OH 45701-2979. Offers MS, PhD. *Accreditation:* ACEJMC (one or more programs are accredited). Part-time programs available. *Faculty:* 26 full-time (12 women), 4 part-time/adjunct (1 woman). *Students:* 34 full-time (22 women), 12 part-time (8 women); includes 3 minority (2 African Americans, 1 Asian American or Pacific Islander), 10 international. 94 applicants, 51% accepted, 25 enrolled. In 2009, 16 master's, 7 doctorates awarded. *Degree requirements:* For master's, thesis or alternative; for doctorate, comprehensive exam, thesis/dissertation. *Entrance requirements:* For master's and doctorate, GRE General Test, minimum GPA of 3.0. Additional exam requirements/recommendations for international students: Required—TOEFL (minimum score 550 paper-based; 80 iBT) or IELTS Academic (minimum score 6.5). *Application deadline:* For fall admission, 2/1 for domestic and international students. Application fee: $50 ($55 for international students). Electronic applications accepted. *Expenses:* Tuition, state resident: full-time $7839; part-time $323 per quarter hour. Tuition, nonresident: full-time $15,831; part-time $654 per quarter hour. Required fees: $2931. *Financial support:* In 2009–10, 30 students received support, including fellowships (averaging $7,000 per year), research assistantships with full tuition reimbursements available (averaging $9,300 per year), teaching assistantships with full tuition reimbursements available (averaging $15,500 per year); career-related internships or fieldwork, Federal Work-Study, institutionally sponsored loans, and unspecified assistantships also available. Financial award application deadline: 2/1. *Faculty research:* Newspaper, magazine, broadcasting, public relations, advertising. Total annual research expenditures: $120,000. *Unit head:* Thomas Hodson, Director, 740-593-2550, Fax: 740-593-2592, E-mail: hodson@ohio.edu. *Application contact:* Dr. Michael Sweeney, Associate Director, 740-593-2589 Ext. 740, Fax: 740-593-2592, E-mail: sweenem3@ohio.edu.

Point Park University, School of Communication, Pittsburgh, PA 15222-1984. Offers MA. Part-time and evening/weekend programs available. *Faculty:* 10 full-time, 7 part-time/adjunct. *Students:* 28 full-time (18 women), 33 part-time (22 women); includes 14 minority (12 African Americans, 2 Asian Americans or Pacific Islanders), 3 international. Average age 27. 114 applicants, 45% accepted, 20 enrolled. In 2009, 19 master's awarded. *Degree requirements:* For master's, comprehensive exam (for some programs), thesis or alternative. *Entrance requirements:* For master's, GRE (if GPA less than 2.75), minimum GPA of 2.75, 2 letters of recommendation. Additional exam requirements/recommendations for international students: Required—TOEFL (minimum score 570 paper-based; 88 iBT). *Application deadline:* Applications are processed on a rolling basis. Application fee: $30. Electronic applications accepted. *Expenses:* Tuition: Full-time $11,880; part-time $660 per credit. Required fees: $486; $27 per credit. *Financial support:* In 2009–10, 43 students received support, including 7 research assistantships with full tuition reimbursements available (averaging $6,400 per year); scholarships/grants and unspecified assistantships also available. Financial award application deadline: 4/15; financial award applicants required to submit FAFSA. *Unit head:* Dr. Tim Hudson, Chair, 412-392-4748, E-mail: thudson@pointpark.edu. *Application contact:* Emily R. Quidetto, Recruiter/Counselor, 412-392-4794, Fax: 412-392-6164, E-mail: equidetto@pointpark.edu.

See Close-Up on page 681.

Polytechnic Institute of NYU, Department of Humanities and Social Sciences, Major in Technical Writing and Specialized Journalism, Brooklyn, NY 11201-2990. Offers MS. *Students:* 3 part-time (1 woman), 1 international. 2 applicants, 50% accepted, 0 enrolled. Application fee: $75. *Expenses:* Tuition: Full-time $21,492; part-time $1194 per credit hour. Required fees: $1160; $204 per course. *Unit head:* Teresa Feroli, Head, 718-260-3422, E-mail: tferoli@poly.edu. *Application contact:* Teresa Feroli, Head, 718-260-3422, E-mail: tferoli@poly.edu.

Quinnipiac University, School of Communications, Program in Journalism, Hamden, CT 06518-1940. Offers MS. Part-time and evening/weekend programs available. *Faculty:* 4 full-time (1 woman), 9 part-time/adjunct (3 women). *Students:* 14 full-time (8 women), 19 part-time (11 women); includes 2 minority (1 African American, 1 Hispanic American), 3 international. 28 applicants, 93% accepted, 10 enrolled. In 2009, 25 master's awarded. *Degree requirements:* For master's, project. *Entrance requirements:* For master's, minimum GPA of 2.8, portfolio or writing sample. Additional exam requirements/recommendations for international students: Required—TOEFL (minimum score 575 paper-based; 233 computer-based; 90 iBT), IELTS (minimum score 6.5). *Application deadline:* For fall admission, 7/30 priority date for domestic students, 4/30 priority date for international students; for spring admission, 12/15 priority date for domestic students, 9/15 priority date for international students. Applications are processed on a rolling basis. Application fee: $45. Electronic applications accepted. *Expenses:* Tuition: Full-time $16,030; part-time $770 per credit. Required fees: $630; $35 per credit. *Financial support:* In 2009–10, 1 fellowship with full tuition reimbursement was awarded; career-related internships or fieldwork and unspecified assistantships also available. Support available to part-time students. Financial award application deadline: 4/15; financial award applicants required to submit FAFSA. *Faculty research:* Journalism history, media representation, media and politics, media influence. *Unit head:* Richard Hanley, Director, 203-582-8439, Fax: 203-582-5310, E-mail: rich.hanley@quinnipiac.edu. *Application contact:* Scott Farber, Director of Graduate Admissions, 800-462-1944, Fax: 203-582-3443, E-mail: scott.farber@quinnipiac.edu.

Regent University, Graduate School, School of Communication and the Arts, Virginia Beach, VA 23464-9800. Offers acting (MFA); acting and directing (MFA); cinema arts/television arts (MA); communication (MA, PhD); digital media (MA); directing for cinema/TV (MA); journalism (MA); producing for cinema/TV (MA); script and screenwriting (MFA); theatre (MA). Part-time programs available. Postbaccalaureate distance learning degree programs offered (minimal on-campus study). *Faculty:* 27 full-time (3 women), 24 part-time/adjunct (8 women). *Students:* 120 full-time (65 women), 160 part-time (82 women); includes 70 minority (53 African Americans, 2 American Indian/Alaska Native, 4 Asian Americans or Pacific Islanders, 11 Hispanic Americans), 10 international. Average age 31. 221 applicants, 58% accepted, 62 enrolled. In 2009, 61 master's, 13 doctorates awarded. *Degree requirements:* For master's, thesis or alternative; for doctorate, thesis/dissertation. *Entrance requirements:* For master's, GRE General Test or MAT, minimum undergraduate GPA of 3.0, writing sample, computer literacy survey, recommendation, resume, interview, audition (MFA programs); for doctorate, GRE General Test, minimum graduate GPA of 3.0, writing sample, computer literacy survey, recommendation, interview, transcripts. Additional exam requirements/recommendations for international students: Required—TOEFL (minimum score 577 paper-based; 233 computer-based). *Application deadline:* For fall admission, 3/1 priority date for domestic students; for spring admission, 10/1 priority date for domestic students. Applications are processed on a rolling basis. Application fee: $50. Electronic applications accepted. *Expenses:* Contact institution. *Financial support:* In

Journalism

Regent University (continued)
2009–10, 229 students received support; fellowships with full and partial tuition reimbursements available, career-related internships or fieldwork, scholarships/grants, tuition waivers (full and partial), and unspecified assistantships available. Support available to part-time students. Financial award application deadline: 9/1; financial award applicants required to submit FAFSA. *Faculty research:* Southern gospel music, education and entertainment, celebrities and the media, journalism and ethics, C. S. Lewis. *Unit head:* Michael Patrick, Dean, 757-352-4970, Fax: 757-352-4279, E-mail: michpat@regent.edu. *Application contact:* Matthew Chadwick, Director of Admissions, 800-373-5504, Fax: 757-352-4381, E-mail: admissions@regent.edu.

Roosevelt University, Graduate Division, College of Arts and Sciences, Department of Communication, Program in Journalism, Chicago, IL 60605. Offers MSJ. Part-time and evening/weekend programs available.

School of the Art Institute of Chicago, Graduate Division, Program in New Arts Journalism, Chicago, IL 60603-3103. Offers MA. *Entrance requirements:* Additional exam requirements/recommendations for international students: Required—TOEFL, IELTS.

South Dakota State University, Graduate School, College of Arts and Science, Department of Journalism and Mass Communication, Brookings, SD 57007. Offers communication studies and journalism (MS). *Accreditation:* ACEJMC. Part-time and evening/weekend programs available. *Degree requirements:* For master's, thesis, oral exam. *Entrance requirements:* Additional exam requirements/recommendations for international students: Required—TOEFL (minimum score 550 paper-based; 213 computer-based; 79 iBT). *Faculty research:* Mass communication applications.

Southern Illinois University Carbondale, Graduate School, College of Mass Communication and Media Arts, Department of Journalism, Carbondale, IL 62901-4701. Offers PhD. *Accreditation:* ACEJMC.

Stanford University, School of Humanities and Sciences, Department of Communication, Stanford, CA 94305-9991. Offers communication (journalism specialization) (MA); communication theory and research (PhD). *Faculty:* 11 full-time (1 woman). *Students:* 62 full-time (38 women). Average age 27. 164 applicants, 27% accepted, 34 enrolled. In 2009, 26 master's, 4 doctorates awarded. Terminal master's awarded for partial completion of doctoral program. *Degree requirements:* For master's, thesis, project; for doctorate, thesis/dissertation, qualifying examination, area examination, 2 projects. *Entrance requirements:* For master's and doctorate, GRE General Test. Additional exam requirements/recommendations for international students: Required—TOEFL (minimum score 650 paper-based; 280 computer-based; 115 iBT). *Application deadline:* For fall admission, 12/1 for domestic and international students. Application fee: $125. Electronic applications accepted. *Expenses:* Tuition: Full-time $37,380; part-time $2760 per quarter. Required fees: $501. *Financial support:* Fellowships, research assistantships, teaching assistantships available. *Unit head:* James S. Fishkin, Chair, 650-723-4611. *Application contact:* Student Services Manager, 650-723-2075, Fax: 650-725-2472, E-mail: comm-studentservices@stanford.edu.

Syracuse University, S. I. Newhouse School of Public Communications, Program in Arts Journalism, Syracuse, NY 13244. Offers MA. *Students:* 20 full-time (13 women); includes 2 minority (1 African American, 1 Hispanic American), 2 international. Average age 24. 45 applicants, 64% accepted, 20 enrolled. In 2009, 1 master's awarded. *Degree requirements:* For master's, capstone project. *Entrance requirements:* For master's, GRE General Test. Additional exam requirements/recommendations for international students: Required—TOEFL (minimum score 600 paper-based; 250 computer-based; 100 iBT). *Application deadline:* For fall admission, 2/1 priority date for domestic and international students. Application fee: $45. Electronic applications accepted. *Expenses:* Tuition: Full-time $26,808; part-time $1117 per credit. Required fees: $1024. *Financial support:* Fellowships with tuition reimbursements, research assistantships with tuition reimbursements, teaching assistantships with tuition reimbursements, tuition waivers (partial) available. Financial award application deadline: 2/1; financial award applicants required to submit FAFSA. *Unit head:* Johanna Keller, Director, 315-443-9251, Fax: 315-443-3946, E-mail: pcgrad@syr.edu. *Application contact:* Martha Coria, Graduate Records Office, 315-443-5749, Fax: 315-443-1834, E-mail: pcgrad@syr.edu.

Syracuse University, S. I. Newhouse School of Public Communications, Program in Broadcast Journalism, Syracuse, NY 13244. Offers MS. *Students:* 31 full-time (18 women), 1 (woman) part-time; includes 13 minority (8 African Americans, 4 Asian Americans or Pacific Islanders, 1 Hispanic American), 2 international. Average age 23. 105 applicants, 70% accepted, 31 enrolled. In 2009, 33 master's awarded. *Degree requirements:* For master's, capstone course. *Entrance requirements:* For master's, GRE General Test. Additional exam requirements/recommendations for international students: Required—TOEFL (minimum score 100 iBT). *Application deadline:* For fall admission, 2/1 priority date for domestic and international students. Application fee: $45. Electronic applications accepted. *Expenses:* Tuition: Full-time $26,808; part-time $1117 per credit. Required fees: $1024. *Financial support:* Fellowships with tuition reimbursements, research assistantships with tuition reimbursements, teaching assistantships with tuition reimbursements, tuition waivers (partial) available. Financial award application deadline: 2/1. *Unit head:* Dona Hayes, Chair, 315-443-1944, Fax: 315-443-3946, E-mail: pcgrad@syr.edu. *Application contact:* Martha Coria, Graduate Records Office, 315-443-5749, Fax: 315-443-1834, E-mail: pcgrad@syr.edu.

See Display on page 622 and Close-Up on page 683.

Syracuse University, S. I. Newhouse School of Public Communications, Program in Magazine, Newspaper and Online Journalism, Syracuse, NY 13244. Offers MA. *Students:* 45 full-time (22 women), 8 part-time (7 women); includes 14 minority (8 African Americans, 2 Asian Americans or Pacific Islanders, 4 Hispanic Americans), 5 international. Average age 24. 147 applicants, 78% accepted, 47 enrolled. In 2009, 46 master's awarded. *Degree requirements:* For master's, capstone course. *Entrance requirements:* For master's, GRE General Test. Additional exam requirements/recommendations for international students: Required—TOEFL (minimum score 600 paper-based; 250 computer-based; 100 iBT). *Application deadline:* For fall admission, 2/1 priority date for domestic and international students. Application fee: $45. Electronic applications accepted. *Expenses:* Tuition: Full-time $26,808; part-time $1117 per credit. Required fees: $1024. *Financial support:* Fellowships with tuition reimbursements, research assistantships with tuition reimbursements, teaching assistantships with tuition reimbursements, tuition waivers (full and partial) available. Financial award application deadline: 2/1; financial award applicants required to submit FAFSA. *Unit head:* Melissa Chessher, Director, 315-443-4004, Fax: 315-443-3946, E-mail: pcgrad@syr.edu. *Application contact:* Martha Coria, Graduate Records Office, 315-443-5749, Fax: 315-443-1834, E-mail: pcgrad@syr.edu.

See Display on page 622 and Close-Up on page 683.

Temple University, Graduate School, School of Communications and Theater, Department of Journalism, Philadelphia, PA 19122-6096. Offers MJ. *Accreditation:* ACEJMC. Part-time programs available. *Degree requirements:* For master's, written exam. *Entrance requirements:* For master's, GRE General Test, minimum GPA of 3.0. Additional exam requirements/recommendations for international students: Required—TOEFL (minimum score 550 paper-based; 213 computer-based; 79 iBT). Electronic applications accepted. *Faculty research:* Journalism history, advertising research, media law, media institutions.

Texas Christian University, College of Communication, Schieffer School of Journalism, Fort Worth, TX 76129-0002. Offers advertising/public relations (MS); news-editorial (MS). *Accreditation:* ACEJMC. Part-time and evening/weekend programs available. *Degree requirements:* For master's, thesis, written exam. *Entrance requirements:* For master's, GRE General Test. Additional exam requirements/recommendations for international students: Required—TOEFL. *Application deadline:* For fall admission, 3/1 for domestic students; for spring admission, 12/1 for domestic students. Applications are processed on a rolling basis. Application fee: $0. *Expenses:* Tuition: Full-time $17,640; part-time $980 per credit hour. Tuition and fees vary according to program. *Financial support:* Tuition waivers (full and partial) and unspecified assistantships available. Financial award application deadline: 3/1. *Unit head:* Dr. John Lumpkin, Director, 817-257-4908, E-mail: j.lumpkin@tcu.edu. *Application contact:* Dr. John Tisdale, Associate Director, 817-257-7425, E-mail: j.tisdale@tcu.edu.

Université Laval, Faculty of Letters, Department of Information and Communication, Program in International Journalism, Québec, QC G1K 7P4, Canada. Offers Diploma. Offered jointly with École Supérieure De Journalisme De Lille (France). *Entrance requirements:* For degree, English exam, French exam, test on international current events, interview, knowledge of French, knowledge of English. Electronic applications accepted.

The University of Alabama, Graduate School, College of Communication and Information Sciences, Department of Journalism, Tuscaloosa, AL 35487-0172. Offers MA. *Faculty:* 10 full-time (3 women). *Students:* 13 full-time (11 women), 4 part-time (3 women); includes 3 minority (2 African Americans, 1 Hispanic American). Average age 24. 30 applicants, 40% accepted, 10 enrolled. In 2009, 14 degrees awarded. Terminal master's awarded for partial completion of doctoral program. *Degree requirements:* For master's, comprehensive exam (for some programs), thesis or alternative. *Entrance requirements:* For master's, GRE or MAT, minimum GPA of 3.0. Additional exam requirements/recommendations for international students: Required—TOEFL (minimum score 550 paper-based; 213 computer-based; 79 iBT). *Application deadline:* For fall admission, 3/31 priority date for domestic students, 1/15 priority date for international students; for spring admission, 11/1 priority date for domestic students, 9/15 priority date for international students. Applications are processed on a rolling basis. Application fee: $50 ($60 for international students). Electronic applications accepted. *Expenses:* Tuition, state resident: full-time $7000. Tuition, nonresident: full-time $19,200. *Financial support:* In 2009–10, 7 students received support, including 8 fellowships with partial tuition reimbursements available, 3 research assistantships with full tuition reimbursements available (averaging $11,000 per year), 3 teaching assistantships with full tuition reimbursements available (averaging $11,000 per year); career-related internships or fieldwork, Federal Work-Study, institutionally sponsored loans, scholarships/grants, health care benefits, and unspecified assistantships also available. Financial award application deadline: 2/15; financial award applicants required to submit FAFSA. *Faculty research:* Journalistic processes, practices and ethics, media effects, media sociology, history, law. *Unit head:* Dr. Jennifer Greer, Chair, 205-348-6304, Fax: 205-348-2780, E-mail: jdgreer@ua.edu. *Application contact:* Dr. Wilson Lowrey, Graduate Coordinator, 205-348-8608, Fax: 205-348-2780, E-mail: wlowrey@ua.edu.

University of Arkansas, Graduate School, J. William Fulbright College of Arts and Sciences, Department of Journalism, Fayetteville, AR 72701-1201. Offers MA. *Accreditation:* ACEJMC. *Students:* 5 full-time (2 women), 10 part-time (8 women); includes 1 minority (African American), 2 international. In 2009, 2 master's awarded. Application fee: $40 ($50 for international students). *Expenses:* Tuition, state resident: full-time $7355; part-time $356.58 per hour. Tuition, nonresident: full-time $17,401; part-time $775.17 per hour. Required fees: $1203. *Financial support:* In 2009–10, 1 research assistantship, 2 teaching assistantships were awarded; fellowships with tuition reimbursements, career-related internships or fieldwork and Federal Work-Study also available. Support available to part-time students. Financial award application deadline: 4/1; financial award applicants required to submit FAFSA. *Unit head:* Dr. Patsy Watkins, Department Chairperson, 479-575-3601, Fax: 479-575-4314, E-mail: pwatkins@uark.edu. *Application contact:* Dr. Jan Wicks, Graduate Coordinator, 479-575-2006, Fax: 479-575-4314, E-mail: jwicks@uark.edu.

University of Arkansas at Little Rock, Graduate School, College of Professional Studies, School of Mass Communication, Little Rock, AR 72204-1099. Offers journalism (MA). Part-time and evening/weekend programs available. *Degree requirements:* For master's, comprehensive exam, thesis optional. *Entrance requirements:* For master's, GRE General Test, minimum GPA of 2.7. *Faculty research:* Theory and practice of mass communication, social role of the mass media.

The University of British Columbia, Faculty of Arts and Faculty of Graduate Studies, The School of Journalism, Vancouver, BC V6T 1Z2, Canada. Offers MJ. *Degree requirements:* For master's, thesis, 3 month internship. *Entrance requirements:* For master's, portfolio, resume with cover letter, letters of reference. Additional exam requirements/recommendations for international students: Required—TOEFL (minimum score 615 paper-based; 260 computer-based), IELTS (minimum score 7.5). Electronic applications accepted. *Expenses:* Contact institution. *Faculty research:* New media, media coverage, journalistic ethics, international journalism, multimedia.

University of California, Berkeley, Graduate Division, Graduate School of Journalism, Berkeley, CA 94720-1500. Offers MJ, JD/MJ, MJ/MA. *Accreditation:* ACEJMC. *Students:* 108 full-time (71 women); includes 41 minority (11 African Americans, 5 American Indian/Alaska Native, 9 Asian Americans or Pacific Islanders, 16 Hispanic Americans), 8 international. Average age 29. 261 applicants, 48 enrolled. In 2009, 54 master's awarded. *Degree requirements:* For master's, project. *Entrance requirements:* For master's, GRE General Test, 3 work samples, minimum GPA of 3.0, 3 letters of recommendation. Additional exam requirements/recommendations for international students: Required—TOEFL (minimum score 600 paper-based; 250 computer-based). *Application deadline:* For fall admission, 12/1 for domestic students. Application fee: $70 ($90 for international students). *Financial support:* Fellowships, research assistantships, career-related internships or fieldwork, Federal Work-Study, institutionally sponsored loans, scholarships/grants, tuition waivers (full and partial), and unspecified assistantships available. Financial award applicants required to submit FAFSA. *Faculty research:* Documentary, new media, print (newspaper and magazine), broadcast (television and radio), photography. *Unit head:* Prof. Neil Henry, Dean, 510-642-3383. *Application contact:* Information Contact, 510-642-7928, E-mail: applysoj@journalism. berkeley.edu.

University of Colorado at Boulder, Graduate School, School of Journalism and Mass Communication, Boulder, CO 80309. Offers communication (PhD), including media studies; mass communication research (MA); newsgathering (MA). *Accreditation:* ACEJMC (one or more programs are accredited). Part-time programs available. *Faculty:* 22 full-time (11 women). *Students:* 77 full-time (50 women), 16 part-time (12 women); includes 6 minority (1 African American, 5 Hispanic Americans), 14 international. Average age 32. 181 applicants, 26% accepted, 30 enrolled. In 2009, 22 master's, 3 doctorates awarded. *Degree requirements:* For master's, comprehensive exam, thesis or alternative; for doctorate, comprehensive exam, thesis/dissertation. *Entrance requirements:* For master's, GRE General Test, minimum undergraduate GPA of 2.75; for doctorate, GRE General Test, minimum undergraduate GPA of 3.2, 3.5 graduate. *Application deadline:* For fall admission, 2/15 for domestic students, 12/1 for international students. Applications are processed on a rolling basis. Application fee: $50 ($60 for international students). *Financial support:* In 2009–10, 14 fellowships (averaging $1,807 per year), 21 research assistantships with tuition reimbursements (averaging $11,554 per year) were awarded; institutionally sponsored loans and unspecified assistantships also available. Financial award application deadline: 3/1. *Faculty research:* Writing on science and the environment, mass communication and public opinion, minority representation in the media, media and culture. Total annual research expenditures: $141,446.

University of Florida, Graduate School, College of Journalism and Communications, Department of Journalism, Gainesville, FL 32611. Offers MAMC. *Degree requirements:* For master's, thesis optional. *Entrance requirements:* For master's, GRE General Test, minimum GPA of 3.0. Additional exam requirements/recommendations for international students: Required—TOEFL (minimum score 550 paper-based; 213 computer-based).

University of Georgia, Grady School of Journalism and Mass Communication, Athens, GA 30602. Offers journalism and mass communication (MA); mass communication (PhD). *Accreditation:* ACEJMC (one or more programs are accredited). *Faculty:* 39 full-time (16 women). *Students:* 75 full-time (48 women), 45 part-time (32 women); includes 17 minority (14 African Americans, 3 Hispanic Americans), 16 international. 263 applicants, 34% accepted, 38 enrolled. In 2009, 27 master's, 4 doctorates awarded. *Degree requirements:* For master's, comprehensive exam, thesis (MA); for doctorate, comprehensive exam, thesis/dissertation. *Entrance requirements:* For master's and doctorate, GRE General Test. Additional exam requirements/recommendations for international students: Required—TOEFL, TWE (PhD). *Application deadline:* For spring admission, 2/15 for domestic students. Application fee: $50. Electronic applications accepted. *Expenses:* Tuition, state resident: full-time $6000; part-time $250 per credit hour. Tuition, nonresident: full-time $20,904; part-time $871 per credit hour. Required fees: $730 per semester. *Financial support:* Research assistantships, teaching assistantships, tuition waivers (full) and unspecified assistantships available. *Unit head:* Dr. E. Culpepper Clark, Dean, 706-542-1704, Fax: 706-542-2183, E-mail: cully@uga.edu. *Application contact:* Dr. Jeffrey K. Springston, Graduate Coordinator, 706-542-7833, Fax: 706-542-2183, E-mail: jspring@grady.uga.edu.

University of Illinois at Springfield, Graduate Programs, College of Public Affairs and Administration, Public Affairs Reporting Program, Springfield, IL 62703-5407. Offers MA. Part-time and evening/weekend programs available. *Faculty:* 1 full-time (0 women). *Students:* 19 full-time (9 women); includes 1 minority (African American). Average age 23. 33 applicants, 64% accepted, 19 enrolled. In 2009, 17 master's awarded. *Degree requirements:* For master's, internship, professional portfolio. *Entrance requirements:* For master's, literacy/competency writing test, interview, written work sample, 3 letters of reference. Additional exam requirements/recommendations for international students: Required—TOEFL (minimum score 500 paper-based; 176 computer-based; 61 iBT). Application fee: $50 ($60 for international students). Electronic applications accepted. *Expenses:* Tuition, state resident: full-time $6390; part-time $266.25 per credit hour. Tuition, nonresident: full-time $14,226; part-time $592.75 per credit hour. Required fees: $2044; $14.36 per credit hour. $722.50 per term. *Financial support:* Career-related internships or fieldwork, Federal Work-Study, scholarships/grants, and health care benefits available. Support available to part-time students. Financial award application deadline: 11/15; financial award applicants required to submit FAFSA. *Unit head:* Dr. Charles Wheeler, Director, 217-206-6535, Fax: 217-206-7807, E-mail: wheeler.charles@uis.edu. *Application contact:* Dr. Lynn Pardie, Office of Graduate Studies, 800-252-8533, Fax: 217-206-7623, E-mail: pardie.lynn@uis.edu.

University of Illinois at Urbana–Champaign, Graduate College, College of Media, Department of Journalism, Champaign, IL 61820. Offers MS, MS/JD, MS/MBA. *Accreditation:* ACEJMC. *Faculty:* 14 full-time (3 women). *Students:* 19 full-time (13 women), 6 part-time (4 women); includes 7 minority (4 African Americans, 2 Asian Americans or Pacific Islanders, 1 Hispanic American), 4 international. 79 applicants, 19% accepted, 13 enrolled. In 2009, 18 master's awarded. *Entrance requirements:* For master's, GRE, minimum GPA of 3.0. Additional exam requirements/recommendations for international students: Required—TOEFL (minimum score 600 paper-based; 250 computer-based). *Application deadline:* Applications are processed on a rolling basis. Application fee: $60 ($75 for international students). Electronic applications accepted. *Financial support:* In 2009–10, 2 fellowships, 6 research assistantships, 13 teaching assistantships were awarded; tuition waivers (full and partial) also available. *Unit head:* Brian K. Johnson, Interim Head, 217-333-0709, Fax: 217-333-7931, E-mail: bkj@illinois.edu. *Application contact:* Diana King Schwanke, Office Administrator, 217-333-0709, Fax: 217-333-7931, E-mail: dking6@illinois.edu.

The University of Iowa, Graduate College, College of Liberal Arts and Sciences, School of Journalism and Mass Communication, Program in Professional Journalism, Iowa City, IA 52242-1316. Offers MA, JD/MA. *Accreditation:* ACEJMC. *Degree requirements:* For master's, thesis optional, exam. *Entrance requirements:* For master's, GRE General Test, minimum GPA of 3.0. Additional exam requirements/recommendations for international students: Required—TOEFL (minimum score 637 paper-based; 270 computer-based; 110 iBT). Electronic applications accepted. *Faculty research:* Verbal and visual aspects of historical, legal, social, and cross-cultural communication.

The University of Kansas, Graduate Studies, School of Journalism and Mass Communications, Lawrence, KS 66045. Offers journalism (MS). *Accreditation:* ACEJMC. Part-time programs available. *Faculty:* 23 full-time (8 women), 7 part-time/adjunct (4 women). *Students:* 26 full-time (16 women), 56 part-time (43 women); includes 7 minority (3 African Americans, 1 American Indian/Alaska Native, 1 Asian American or Pacific Islander, 2 Hispanic Americans), 6 international. Average age 30. 67 applicants, 58% accepted, 19 enrolled. In 2009, 25 master's awarded. *Degree requirements:* For master's, comprehensive exam, thesis. *Entrance requirements:* For master's, GRE General Test, minimum GPA of 3.0. Additional exam requirements/recommendations for international students: Required—TOEFL or IELTS. *Application deadline:* For fall admission, 2/1 for domestic and international students; for spring admission, 11/1 for domestic and international students. Application fee: $45 ($55 for international students). Electronic applications accepted. *Expenses:* Tuition, state resident: full-time $6492; part-time $270.50 per credit hour. Tuition, nonresident: full-time $15,510; part-time $646.25 per credit hour. Required fees: $847; $70.56 per credit hour. Tuition and fees vary according to course load and program. *Financial support:* Fellowships, research assistantships, teaching assistantships with full and partial tuition reimbursements, career-related internships or fieldwork, scholarships/grants, and unspecified assistantships available. Support available to part-time students. Financial award application deadline: 2/1; financial award applicants required to submit FAFSA. *Faculty research:* Advertising, creativity, media economics, public relations, press law, online journalism, political journalism, marketing communication, new media, visual communication. *Unit head:* Ann Brill, Dean, 785-864-4755, Fax: 785-864-4396, E-mail: abrill@ku.edu. *Application contact:* Cindy Nesvarba, Graduate Records Coordinator, 785-864-7649, Fax: 785-864-5318, E-mail: cnesvarb@ku.edu.

University of Maryland, College Park, Academic Affairs, Phillip Merrill College of Journalism, College Park, MD 20742. Offers broadcast journalism (MA); journalism (MA); journalism and media studies (PhD); online news (MA); public affairs reporting (MA). *Accreditation:* ACEJMC (one or more programs are accredited). Part-time and evening/weekend programs available. *Faculty:* 22 full-time (11 women), 40 part-time/adjunct (15 women). *Students:* 75 full-time (46 women), 10 part-time (5 women); includes 19 minority (13 African Americans, 5 Asian Americans or Pacific Islanders, 1 Hispanic American), 12 international. 250 applicants, 36% accepted, 27 enrolled. In 2009, 25 master's, 5 doctorates awarded. *Degree requirements:* For doctorate, thesis/dissertation, preliminary written and oral comprehensive exams. *Entrance requirements:* For master's and doctorate, GRE General Test, minimum GPA of 3.0, 3 letters of recommendation. Additional exam requirements/recommendations for international students: Required—TOEFL. *Application deadline:* For fall admission, 2/1 for domestic and international students. Applications are processed on a rolling basis. Application fee: $60. Electronic applications accepted. *Expenses:* Tuition, area resident: Part-time $471 per credit hour. Tuition, state resident: part-time $471 per credit hour. Tuition, nonresident: part-time $1016 per credit hour. Required fees: $337.04 per term. *Financial support:* In 2009–10, 6 fellowships with full and partial tuition reimbursements (averaging $15,296 per year), 1 research assistantship with tuition reimbursement (averaging $15,266 per year), 19 teaching assistantships with tuition reimbursements (averaging $16,778 per year) were awarded; career-related internships or fieldwork, Federal Work-Study, and scholarships/grants also available. Support available to part-time students. Financial award applicants required to submit FAFSA. *Faculty research:* Mass communication theory, specialized journalism, new telecommunication technologies, press integration. Total annual research expenditures: $642,886. *Unit head:* Kevin Klose, Dean, 301-405-2393, E-mail: kklose@umd.edu. *Application contact:* Dean of Graduate School, 301-405-0376, Fax: 301-314-9305.

University of Memphis, Graduate School, College of Communication and Fine Arts, Department of Journalism, Memphis, TN 38152. Offers general journalism (MA); journalism administration (MA). *Accreditation:* ACEJMC. Postbaccalaureate distance learning degree programs offered (no on-campus study). *Faculty:* 6 full-time (3 women), 2 part-time/adjunct (1 woman). *Students:* 16 full-time (13 women), 29 part-time (17 women); includes 8 minority (7 African Americans, 1 Hispanic American). Average age 34. 34 applicants, 79% accepted, 11 enrolled. In 2009, 9 master's awarded. *Degree requirements:* For master's, comprehensive exam. *Entrance requirements:* For master's, GRE General Test, MAT. *Application deadline:* For fall admission, 8/1 for domestic students; for spring admission, 12/1 for domestic students. Applications are processed on a rolling basis. Application fee: $35 ($60 for international students). *Expenses:* Tuition, state resident: full-time $6246; part-time $347 per credit hour. Tuition, nonresident: full-time $15,894; part-time $883 per credit hour. Required fees: $1160. Full-time tuition and fees vary according to course load, degree level and program. *Financial support:* In 2009–10, 25 students received support; research assistantships with full tuition reimbursements available, teaching assistantships with full tuition reimbursements available, Federal Work-Study, scholarships/grants, and unspecified assistantships available. Support available to part-time students. Financial award application deadline: 2/15; financial award applicants required to submit FAFSA. *Faculty research:* Spirit of libel law, statistical software packages, college yearbooks, computer-assisted grammar project, newspaper in education. *Unit head:* Dr. David Arant, Chair, 901-678-2401, Fax: 901-678-4287, E-mail: darant@memphis.edu. *Application contact:* Dr. Rick Fischer, Coordinator of Graduate Studies, 901-678-2853, Fax: 901-678-4287, E-mail: rfischer@memphis.edu.

University of Miami, Graduate School, School of Communication, Coral Gables, FL 33124. Offers communication (PhD); communication studies (MA); film studies (MA, PhD); motion pictures (MFA), including production, producing, and screenwriting; print journalism (MA); public relations (MA); Spanish language journalism (MA); television broadcast journalism (MA). *Accreditation:* ACEJMC. Part-time programs available. *Degree requirements:* For master's, comprehensive exam (for some programs), thesis (for some programs); for doctorate, comprehensive exam, thesis/dissertation. *Entrance requirements:* For master's, GRE General Test; for doctorate, GRE General Test, master's thesis or scholarly research. Additional exam requirements/recommendations for international students: Required—TOEFL (minimum score 600 paper-based; 250 computer-based; 100 iBT). Electronic applications accepted. *Faculty research:* Communication studies, mass communication, international/interpersonal communication, film studies, journalism.

University of Mississippi, Graduate School, College of Liberal Arts, Department of Journalism, Oxford, University, MS 38677. Offers MA. *Accreditation:* ACEJMC. *Faculty:* 18 full-time (9 women), 5 part-time/adjunct (2 women). *Students:* 18 full-time (10 women), 4 part-time (1 woman); includes 2 minority (both African Americans), 2 international. In 2009, 6 master's awarded. *Degree requirements:* For master's, thesis. *Entrance requirements:* For master's, GRE General Test, minimum GPA of 3.0. Additional exam requirements/recommendations for international students: Required—TOEFL. *Application deadline:* For fall admission, 8/1 for domestic students. Applications are processed on a rolling basis. Application fee: $25. Electronic applications accepted. *Financial support:* Career-related internships or fieldwork and scholarships/grants available. Financial award application deadline: 3/1; financial award applicants required to submit FAFSA. *Unit head:* Dr. Samir Husni, Chairman, 662-915-7146, Fax: 662-915-7765, E-mail: jour@olemiss.edu. *Application contact:* Dr. Christy M. Wyandt, Associate Dean, 662-915-7474, Fax: 662-915-7577, E-mail: cwyandt@olemiss.edu.

University of Missouri, Graduate School, School of Journalism, Columbia, MO 65211. Offers MA, PhD. *Accreditation:* ACEJMC (one or more programs are accredited). Part-time programs available. Terminal master's awarded for partial completion of doctoral program. *Degree requirements:* For master's, thesis (for some programs); for doctorate, 2 foreign languages, thesis/dissertation. *Entrance requirements:* For master's and doctorate, GRE General Test, minimum GPA of 3.0. Additional exam requirements/recommendations for international students: Required—TOEFL (minimum score 600 paper-based; 250 computer-based; 100 iBT).

The University of Montana, Graduate School, School of Journalism, Missoula, MT 59812-0002. Offers MA. *Accreditation:* ACEJMC. *Degree requirements:* For master's, thesis or alternative, professional project. *Entrance requirements:* For master's, GRE. Additional exam requirements/recommendations for international students: Required—TOEFL (minimum score 580 paper-based). Electronic applications accepted. *Faculty research:* Native American issues, natural resources, public affairs, economy, photojournalism, multimedia, media law.

University of Nebraska–Lincoln, Graduate College, College of Journalism and Mass Communications, Lincoln, NE 68588. Offers marketing, communication and advertising (MA); professional journalism (MA). *Accreditation:* ACEJMC. Postbaccalaureate distance learning degree programs offered (no on-campus study). *Degree requirements:* For master's, thesis. *Entrance requirements:* For master's, samples of work. Additional exam requirements/recommendations for international students: Required—TOEFL (minimum score 600 paper-based; 250 computer-based). Electronic applications accepted. *Faculty research:* Interactive media and the Internet, community newspapers, children's radio, advertising involvement, telecommunications policy.

University of Nevada, Las Vegas, Graduate College, Greenspun College of Urban Affairs, School of Journalism and Media Studies, Las Vegas, NV 89154-5007. Offers MA. *Faculty:* 10 full-time (2 women). *Students:* 13 full-time (7 women), 11 part-time (8 women); includes 6 minority (3 African Americans, 1 Asian American or Pacific Islander, 2 Hispanic Americans), 2 international. Average age 30. 26 applicants, 69% accepted, 12 enrolled. In 2009, 10 master's awarded. *Entrance requirements:* For master's, GRE General Test. Additional exam requirements/recommendations for international students: Required—TOEFL (minimum score 550 paper-based; 213 computer-based; 80 iBT), IELTS (minimum score 7). *Application deadline:* For fall admission, 3/15 priority date for domestic and international students. Applications are processed on a rolling basis. Application fee: $60 ($95 for international students). Electronic applications accepted. *Financial support:* In 2009–10, 8 students received support, including 4 research assistantships with partial tuition reimbursements available (averaging $10,000 per year), 4 teaching assistantships with partial tuition reimbursements available (averaging $10,000 per year); institutionally sponsored loans, scholarships/grants, health care benefits, and unspecified assistantships also available. Financial award application deadline: 3/1. *Faculty research:* Media and religion, science and communications, ethnic communities and journalism, journalism history, emerging technologies. *Unit head:* Dr. Ardyth Sohn, Director/ Professor, 702-895-3270, Fax: 702-895-5189, E-mail: ardyth.sohn@unlv.edu. *Application contact:* Graduate College Admissions Evaluator, 702-895-3320, Fax: 702-895-4180, E-mail: gradcollege@unlv.edu.

University of Nevada, Reno, Graduate School, Donald W. Reynolds School of Journalism, Reno, NV 89557. Offers MA. *Accreditation:* ACEJMC. *Degree requirements:* For master's, thesis. *Entrance requirements:* For master's, GRE General Test, minimum GPA of 2.75. Additional exam requirements/recommendations for international students: Required—TOEFL (minimum score 500 paper-based; 173 computer-based; 61 iBT), IELTS (minimum score 6). Electronic applications accepted. *Faculty research:* Interactive environmental journalism.

University of North Texas, Robert B. Toulouse School of Graduate Studies, College of Arts and Sciences, Mayborn School of Journalism, Denton, TX 76203. Offers journalism (MA, MJ); narrative journalism (Graduate Certificate). *Accreditation:* ACEJMC (one or more programs are accredited). Part-time programs available. *Degree requirements:* For master's, variable foreign language requirement, comprehensive exam, thesis or alternative. *Entrance requirements:* For master's, GRE General Test, portfolio. Additional exam requirements/recommendations for international students: Recommended—TOEFL (minimum score 550 paper-based; 213 computer-based; 79 iBT). Application fee: $50 ($75 for international students). *Expenses:* Tuition, state resident: full-time $4298; part-time $239 per contact hour. Tuition, nonresident: full-time $9878; part-time $549 per contact hour. Required fees: $265 per contact hour. *Financial support:* Research assistantships, teaching assistantships, career-related internships or fieldwork, Federal Work-Study, and institutionally sponsored loans available. Financial award application deadline: 4/1; financial award applicants required to submit FAFSA. *Faculty research:* Mass communication theory, public relations, advertising, mass communication technology, journalism ethics. *Application contact:* Graduate Adviser, 940-565-4564, Fax: 940-369-8959, E-mail: mland@unt.edu.

Journalism

University of Oklahoma, Graduate College, Gaylord College of Journalism and Mass Communication, Program in Journalism and Mass Communication, Norman, OK 73019-0390. Offers advertising and public relations (MA); information gathering and distribution (MA); mass communication management and policy (MA); professional writing (MA); telecommunication and new technology (MA). Part-time programs available. *Students:* 34 full-time (18 women), 43 part-time (23 women); includes 13 minority (4 African Americans, 5 American Indian/Alaska Native, 4 Hispanic Americans), 9 international. 45 applicants, 42% accepted, 9 enrolled. *Degree requirements:* For master's, thesis optional. *Entrance requirements:* For master's, GRE General Test, minimum GPA of 3.2, 9 hours of course work in journalism, course work in statistics. Additional exam requirements/recommendations for international students: Required—TOEFL (minimum score 600 paper-based; 250 computer-based), TWE (minimum score 5). *Application deadline:* For fall admission, 2/1 for domestic students, 4/1 for international students; for spring admission, 11/1 for domestic students, 9/1 for international students. Application fee: $40 ($90 for international students). Electronic applications accepted. *Expenses:* Tuition, state resident: full-time $3744; part-time $156 per credit hour. Tuition, nonresident: full-time $13,577; part-time $565.70 per credit hour. Required fees: $2415; $90.10 per credit hour. *Financial support:* In 2009–10, 43 students received support, including 4 fellowships (averaging $5,000 per year); career-related internships or fieldwork, scholarships/grants, health care benefits, and unspecified assistantships also available. *Faculty research:* Organizational management, rhetorical analysis, international public relations, digital production, normative theory. *Unit head:* Dr. Joe Foote, Dean, 405-325-2721, Fax: 405-325-7565, E-mail: jfoote@ou.edu. *Application contact:* Kelly Storm, Graduate Advisor, 405-325-2722, Fax: 405-325-7565, E-mail: kstorm@ou.edu.

University of Oregon, Graduate School, School of Journalism and Communication, Eugene, OR 97403. Offers MA, MS, PhD. *Accreditation:* ACEJMC (one or more programs are accredited); ASHA. Part-time programs available. *Degree requirements:* For master's, thesis or alternative. *Entrance requirements:* For master's, GRE General Test; for doctorate, master's degree. *Faculty research:* Impact of mass communication, media technology, media accountability, craft attitudes, media economics.

University of Puerto Rico, Río Piedras, School of Communication, Program in Journalism, San Juan, PR 00931-3300. Offers MA.

University of South Carolina, The Graduate School, College of Mass Communications and Information Studies, School of Journalism and Mass Communications, Columbia, SC 29208. Offers MA, MMC, PhD. *Accreditation:* ACEJMC (one or more programs are accredited). Part-time programs available. *Degree requirements:* For master's, comprehensive exam, thesis (for some programs); for doctorate, one foreign language, comprehensive exam, thesis/dissertation. *Entrance requirements:* For master's and doctorate, GRE General Test, minimum GPA of 3.0. Additional exam requirements/recommendations for international students: Required—TOEFL (minimum score 600 paper-based; 250 computer-based; 75 iBT). Electronic applications accepted. *Faculty research:* Ethics, communications law, international communications, science/health/environmental/risk communications, convergent media.

University of Southern California, Graduate School, Annenberg School for Communication and Journalism, School of Journalism, Program in Broadcast Journalism, Los Angeles, CA 90089. Offers MA. *Degree requirements:* For master's, comprehensive exam. *Entrance requirements:* For master's, GRE General Test, resume, writing samples, letters of recommendation, statement of purpose. Additional exam requirements/recommendations for international students: Required—TOEFL (minimum score 280 computer-based; 114 iBT). Electronic applications accepted. *Expenses:* Tuition: Full-time $25,980; part-time $1315 per unit. Required fees: $554. One-time fee: $35 full-time. Full-time tuition and fees vary according to degree level and program.

See Display on page 629 and Close-Up on page 685.

University of Southern California, Graduate School, Annenberg School for Communication and Journalism, School of Journalism, Program in Print Journalism, Los Angeles, CA 90089. Offers MA. *Degree requirements:* For master's, comprehensive exam. *Entrance requirements:* For master's, GRE General Test, resume, writing samples, letters of recommendation. Additional exam requirements/recommendations for international students: Required—TOEFL (minimum score 280 computer-based; 114 iBT). Electronic applications accepted. *Expenses:* Tuition: Full-time $25,980; part-time $1315 per unit. Required fees: $554. One-time fee: $35 full-time. Full-time tuition and fees vary according to degree level and program.

See Display on page 629 and Close-Up on page 685.

University of Southern California, Graduate School, Annenberg School for Communication and Journalism, School of Journalism, Program in Specialized Journalism, Los Angeles, CA 90089. Offers specialized journalism (MA); specialized journalism (the arts) (MA). Available in summer term only. *Degree requirements:* For master's, thesis. *Entrance requirements:* For master's, GRE General Test, resume, professional work samples, letters of recommendation, statement of purpose. Additional exam requirements/recommendations for international students: Required—TOEFL (minimum score 280 computer-based; 114 iBT). Electronic applications accepted. *Expenses:* Tuition: Full-time $25,980; part-time $1315 per unit. Required fees: $554. One-time fee: $35 full-time. Full-time tuition and fees vary according to degree level and program.

See Display on page 629 and Close-Up on page 685.

The University of Tennessee, Graduate School, College of Communication and Information, Knoxville, TN 37996. Offers advertising (MS, PhD); broadcasting (MS, PhD); communications (MS, PhD); information sciences (MS, PhD); journalism (MS, PhD); public relations (MS, PhD); speech communication (MS, PhD). *Accreditation:* ACEJMC (one or more programs are accredited at the [master's] level). Part-time and evening/weekend programs available. Postbaccalaureate distance learning degree programs offered (no on-campus study). *Degree requirements:* For master's, thesis or alternative; for doctorate, thesis/dissertation. *Entrance requirements:* For master's and doctorate, GRE General Test, minimum GPA of 2.7. Additional exam requirements/recommendations for international students: Required—TOEFL. Electronic applications accepted. *Expenses:* Tuition, state resident: full-time $6826; part-time $380 per semester hour. Tuition, nonresident: full-time $21,844; part-time $1147 per semester hour. Tuition and fees vary according to program.

The University of Texas at Austin, Graduate School, College of Communication, School of Journalism, Austin, TX 78712-1111. Offers MA, PhD. *Accreditation:* ACEJMC. Part-time programs available. *Degree requirements:* For master's, thesis; for doctorate, one foreign language, thesis/dissertation. *Entrance requirements:* For master's and doctorate, GRE General Test. Electronic applications accepted. *Faculty research:* Politics of race, gender, and sexuality; visual ethics; media law and ethics; national television violence study; agenda setting and public opinion.

The University of Western Ontario, Faculty of Graduate Studies, Faculty of Information and Media Studies, Program in Journalism, London, ON N6A 5B8, Canada. Offers MA. *Degree requirements:* For master's, internship. *Entrance requirements:* For master's, honors degree, minimum B average during previous 2 years of course work. Additional exam requirements/recommendations for international students: Required—TOEFL (minimum score 640 paper-based; 273 computer-based), TWE (minimum score 5). Electronic applications accepted.

University of Wisconsin–Madison, Graduate School, College of Agricultural and Life Sciences, Department of Life Sciences Communication, Madison, WI 53706-1380. Offers life sciences communication (MPS, MS); mass communication (PhD). *Degree requirements:* For doctorate, thesis/dissertation. *Expenses:* Tuition, state resident: part-time $594 per credit. Tuition, nonresident: part-time $1504 per credit. Required fees: $65 per credit. Tuition and fees vary according to course load, program and reciprocity agreements.

University of Wisconsin–Madison, Graduate School, College of Letters and Science, School of Journalism and Mass Communication, Program in Journalism and Mass Communication, Madison, WI 53706-1380. Offers MA. *Expenses:* Tuition, state resident: part-time $594 per credit. Tuition, nonresident: part-time $1504 per credit. Required fees: $65 per credit. Tuition and fees vary according to course load, program and reciprocity agreements.

Virginia Commonwealth University, Graduate School, College of Humanities and Sciences, School of Mass Communications, Program in Mass Communications, Richmond, VA 23284-9005. Offers scholastic journalism (MS); strategic public relations (MS). *Accreditation:* ACEJMC. *Degree requirements:* For master's, comprehensive exam, thesis optional. *Entrance requirements:* For master's, GRE General Test.

West Virginia University, Perley Isaac Reed School of Journalism, Morgantown, WV 26506. Offers digital marketing communications (Graduate Certificate); integrated marketing communications (MS); journalism (MSJ). MS program taught exclusively online. *Accreditation:* ACEJMC. Part-time programs available. Postbaccalaureate distance learning degree programs offered (no on-campus study). *Degree requirements:* For master's, thesis or alternative. *Entrance requirements:* For master's, GRE General Test, minimum GPA of 3.0, writing samples. Additional exam requirements/recommendations for international students: Required—TOEFL. Electronic applications accepted. *Faculty research:* History, law, and women in media; press management; public opinion; advertising effectiveness; international advertising.

Mass Communication

American University, School of Communication, Program in International Media, Washington, DC 20016-8001. Offers MA. *Students:* 4 full-time (all women), 1 (woman) part-time. *Degree requirements:* For master's, one foreign language, comprehensive exam. *Entrance requirements:* For master's, GRE, bachelor's degree with minimum cumulative GPA of 3.3, 2 letters of reference. Additional exam requirements/recommendations for international students: Required—TOEFL. *Application deadline:* For fall admission, 6/1 for domestic students. Applications are processed on a rolling basis. *Expenses:* Tuition: Full-time $22,266; part-time $1237 per credit hour. Required fees: $430. Tuition and fees vary according to program. *Unit head:* Prof. Larry Kirkman, Dean, 202-885-2058, Fax: 202-885-2099, E-mail: larry@american.edu. *Application contact:* Sharmeen Ahsan-Bracciale, Graduate Admissions Office, 202-885-2040, Fax: 202-885-2019, E-mail: sharmeen@american.edu.

American University, School of Communication, Program in Public Communication, Washington, DC 20016-8001. Offers MA. *Accreditation:* ACEJMC. Part-time and evening/weekend programs available. *Faculty:* 11 full-time (6 women), 6 part-time/adjunct (2 women). *Students:* 45 full-time (32 women), 13 part-time (12 women); includes 6 African Americans, 3 Asian Americans or Pacific Islanders, 2 Hispanic Americans, 5 international. 153 applicants, 68% accepted, 43 enrolled. In 2009, 61 master's awarded. *Degree requirements:* For master's, comprehensive exam, thesis or alternative. *Entrance requirements:* For master's, GRE General Test. Additional exam requirements/recommendations for international students: Required—TOEFL (minimum score 600 paper-based; 250 computer-based). *Application deadline:* For fall admission, 2/1 priority date for domestic students, 4/1 priority date for international students. Applications are processed on a rolling basis. Application fee: $50. Electronic applications accepted. *Expenses:* Tuition: Full-time $22,266; part-time $1237 per credit hour. Required fees: $430. Tuition and fees vary according to program. *Financial support:* In 2009–10, 10 research assistantships with partial tuition reimbursements (averaging $11,000 per year), 2 teaching assistantships with partial tuition reimbursements (averaging $11,000 per year) were awarded; career-related internships or fieldwork, Federal Work-Study, institutionally sponsored loans, scholarships/grants, and tuition waivers (partial) also available. Financial award application deadline: 2/1. *Faculty research:* Litigation and public relations, cross-cultural and intercultural communication, statistical public relations, African-Americans and women in public communication, international public relations. *Unit head:* Leonard Steinhorn, Director, Public Communication Division, 202-885-2031, E-mail: lsteinh@american.edu. *Application contact:* Sharmeen Ahsan-Bracciale, Graduate Admissions Office, 202-885-2040, Fax: 202-885-2019, E-mail: sharmeen@american.edu.

See Close-Up on page 673.

American University, School of Communication, Weekend Programs in Communication, Washington, DC 20016-8001. Offers interactive journalism (MA); news media studies (MA); producing for film and video (MA); public communication (MA). *Accreditation:* ACEJMC. Part-time and evening/weekend programs available. *Faculty:* 5 part-time/adjunct (2 women). *Students:* 112 part-time (75 women). 137 applicants, 61% accepted, 61 enrolled. In 2009, 15 master's awarded. *Degree requirements:* For master's, comprehensive exam, thesis or alternative. *Entrance requirements:* Additional exam requirements/recommendations for international students: Required—TOEFL (minimum score 600 paper-based; 250 computer-based). *Application deadline:* For fall admission, 8/1 for domestic students. Applications are processed on a rolling basis. Application fee: $50. Electronic applications accepted. *Expenses:* Tuition: Full-time $22,266; part-time $1237 per credit hour. Required fees: $430. Tuition and fees vary according to program. *Financial support:* In 2009–10, 3 fellowships (averaging $3,500 per year) were awarded; institutionally sponsored loans also available. *Unit head:* Wendell Cochran, Journalism Weekend Program Director, 202-885-2075, E-mail: cochran@american.edu. *Application contact:* Sharmeen Ahsan-Bracciale, Graduate Admissions Office, 202-885-2040, Fax: 202-885-2019, E-mail: sharmeen@american.edu.

See Close-Up on page 673.

American University, School of International Service, Washington, DC 20016-8071. Offers comparative and regional studies (Certificate); cross-cultural communication (Certificate); development management (MS); ethics, peace, and global affairs (MA); European studies (Certificate); global environmental policy (MA, Certificate); international affairs (MA), including comparative and regional studies, environmental policy, international economic policy, international politics, natural resources and sustainable development, U.S. foreign policy; international communication (MA, Certificate); international development (MA, Certificate); international development management (Certificate); international economic policy (Certificate); international economic relations (Certificate); international media (MA); international peace and conflict resolution (MA, Certificate); international relations (PhD); international service (MIS); peace building (Certificate); the Americas (Certificate); United States foreign policy (Certificate); JD/MA. Part-time and evening/weekend programs available. *Faculty:* 98 full-time (42 women), 48 part-time/adjunct (13 women). *Students:* 565 full-time (349 women), 329 part-time (189 women); includes 128 minority (44 African Americans, 2 American Indian/Alaska Native, 37 Asian Americans or Pacific Islanders, 45 Hispanic Americans), 102 international. Average age 27. 2,034 applicants, 63% accepted, 344 enrolled. In 2009, 326 master's, 6 doctorates, 9 other advanced degrees awarded. Terminal master's awarded for partial completion of doctoral program. *Degree requirements:* For master's, one foreign language, comprehensive exam, thesis or alternative; for doctorate, one foreign language, comprehensive exam, thesis/dissertation, research practicum; for Certificate, minimum 15 credit hours related course work. *Entrance requirements:* For master's, GRE, 24 credits of course work in related social sciences, minimum GPA of 3.5, 2 letters of recommendation, bachelor's degree, resume; for doctorate, GRE, 2 letters of recommendation, 24 credits in related social sciences; for Certificate, bachelor's degree. Additional exam requirements/recommendations for international students: Required—TOEFL (minimum score 600 paper-based; 250 computer-based; 100 iBT). *Application deadline:* For fall admission, 1/15 priority date for domestic students; for spring admission, 10/1 priority date for domestic students. Applications are processed on a rolling basis. Application fee: $50. *Expenses:* Tuition: Full-time $22,266; part-time $1237 per credit hour. Required fees: $430. Tuition and fees vary according to program. *Financial support:* Career-related internships or fieldwork, Federal Work-Study, and institutionally sponsored loans available. Financial award application deadline: 1/15. *Faculty research:* International intellectual property, international environmental issues, international law and legal order, international telecommunications/technology, international sustainable development. *Unit head:* Dr. Louis W. Goodman, Dean, 202-885-1600, Fax: 202-885-2494. *Application contact:* Yasmin Quianzon, Director of Graduate Admissions and Financial Aid, 202-885-2496, Fax: 202-885-1109.

See Close-Up on page 849.

The American University in Cairo, Graduate Studies and Research, School of Business, Economics and Communication, Department of Journalism and Mass Communication, Cairo, Egypt. Offers journalism and mass communication (MA); television and digital journalism (MA). Part-time programs available. *Degree requirements:* For master's, thesis (for some programs). *Entrance requirements:* For master's, English entrance exam, GMAT. Electronic applications accepted. *Faculty research:* Mass media and national development/censorship, intercultural photo communication, comparative journalism/television.

Arizona State University, Graduate College, Walter Cronkite School of Journalism and Mass Communication, Tempe, AZ 85287. Offers MMC. *Accreditation:* ACEJMC. *Entrance requirements:* For master's, GRE, minimum GPA of 3.0 in the last 60 semester hours or 90 quarter hours of undergraduate coursework; resume and/or biographical sketch; 3 letters of recommendation. Additional exam requirements/recommendations for international students: Required—TOEFL. Electronic applications accepted.

Auburn University, Graduate School, College of Liberal Arts, Department of Communication and Journalism, Auburn University, AL 36849. Offers communication (MA); mass communications (MA). Part-time programs available. *Faculty:* 24 full-time (13 women), 10 part-time/adjunct (5 women). *Students:* 21 full-time (15 women), 6 part-time (4 women); includes 4 minority (3 African Americans, 1 Hispanic American), 1 international. Average age 26. 26 applicants, 65% accepted, 13 enrolled. In 2009, 14 master's awarded. *Degree requirements:* For master's, thesis (for some programs). *Entrance requirements:* For master's, GRE General Test. *Application deadline:* For fall admission, 7/7 for domestic students; for spring admission, 11/24 for domestic students. Applications are processed on a rolling basis. Application fee: $50 ($60 for international students). Electronic applications accepted. *Expenses:* Tuition, state resident: full-time $6240. Tuition, nonresident: full-time $18,720. International tuition: $18,938 full-time. Required fees: $492. Tuition and fees vary according to course load, program and reciprocity agreements. *Financial support:* Teaching assistantships, Federal Work-Study available. Support available to part-time students. Financial award application deadline: 3/15; financial award applicants required to submit FAFSA. *Unit head:* Dr. Mary Helen Brown, Acting Chair, 334-844-2727. *Application contact:* Dr. George Flowers, Dean of the Graduate School, 334-844-2125.

Boston University, College of Communication, Department of Mass Communication, Advertising, and Public Relations, Boston, MA 02215. Offers advertising (MS); communication research (MS); communication studies (MS); public relations (MS); JD/MS. Part-time programs available. *Faculty:* 21 full-time, 28 part-time/adjunct. *Students:* 84 full-time (68 women), 72 part-time (57 women); includes 12 minority (5 African Americans, 3 Asian Americans or Pacific Islanders, 4 Hispanic Americans), 26 international. Average age 30. In 2009, 58 master's awarded. *Degree requirements:* For master's, comprehensive exam (for some programs), thesis (for some programs). *Entrance requirements:* For master's, GRE General Test, samples of written work. Additional exam requirements/recommendations for international students: Required—TOEFL (minimum score 600 paper-based; 250 computer-based; 100 iBT). *Application deadline:* For fall admission, 2/1 for domestic and international students. Application fee: $70. Electronic applications accepted. *Expenses:* Tuition: Full-time $37,910; part-time $1184 per credit hour. Required fees: $386; $40 per semester. Part-time tuition and fees vary according to class time, course level, degree level and program. *Financial support:* Research assistantships, teaching assistantships with partial tuition reimbursements, career-related internships or fieldwork, Federal Work-Study, institutionally sponsored loans, scholarships/grants, and unspecified assistantships available. Support available to part-time students. Financial award application deadline: 2/1; financial award applicants required to submit FAFSA. *Unit head:* T. Barton Carter, Chairman, 617-353-3482, E-mail: comlaw@bu.edu. *Application contact:* Kate Iserman, Administrator of Graduate Services, 617-353-3481, Fax: 617-358-0399, E-mail: comgrad@bu.edu.

See Close-Up on page 675.

Brigham Young University, Graduate Studies, College of Fine Arts and Communications, Department of Communications, Provo, UT 84602. Offers mass communications (MA). *Faculty:* 19 full-time (3 women). *Students:* 22 full-time (15 women), 16 part-time (8 women); includes 3 minority (1 African American, 1 American Indian/Alaska Native, 1 Hispanic American). Average age 29. 32 applicants, 44% accepted, 14 enrolled. In 2009, 14 master's awarded. *Degree requirements:* For master's, comprehensive exam, thesis. *Entrance requirements:* For master's, GRE, minimum GPA of 3.0 in last 60 hours of course work. Additional exam requirements/recommendations for international students: Required—TOEFL (minimum score 580 paper-based; 237 computer-based; 85 iBT). *Application deadline:* For fall admission, 2/28 for domestic and international students. Application fee: $50. Electronic applications accepted. *Expenses:* Tuition: Full-time $5580; part-time $301 per credit hour. Tuition and fees vary according to student's religious affiliation. *Financial support:* In 2009–10, 24 students received support, including 20 research assistantships with full and partial tuition reimbursements available (averaging $4,563 per year), 9 teaching assistantships with full and partial tuition reimbursements available (averaging $5,676 per year); career-related internships or fieldwork, institutionally sponsored loans, scholarships/grants, unspecified assistantships, and supplementary awards also available. Financial award application deadline: 4/15; financial award applicants required to submit FAFSA. *Faculty research:* Ethics, international, magazine, newspaper, media effects. *Unit head:* Dr. Bradley L. Rawlins, Chair, 801-422-2997, Fax: 801-422-0160, E-mail: comms_secretary@byu.edu. *Application contact:* Dr. Steven R. Thomsen, Graduate Coordinator, 801-422-2078, Fax: 801-422-0160, E-mail: steven_thomsen@byu.edu.

California State University, Fresno, Division of Graduate Studies, College of Arts and Humanities, Department of Mass Communication and Journalism, Fresno, CA 93740-8027. Offers MA. Part-time and evening/weekend programs available. *Degree requirements:* For master's, thesis. *Entrance requirements:* For master's, GRE General Test, minimum GPA of 3.0. Additional exam requirements/recommendations for international students: Required—TOEFL. Electronic applications accepted.

California State University, Northridge, Graduate Studies, College of Arts, Media, and Communication, Department of Journalism, Northridge, CA 91330. Offers mass communication (MA). *Accreditation:* ACEJMC. Part-time and evening/weekend programs available. *Faculty:* 9 full-time (4 women), 12 part-time/adjunct (4 women). *Students:* 8 full-time (7 women), 30 part-time (24 women); includes 14 minority (2 African Americans, 2 Asian Americans or Pacific Islanders, 10 Hispanic Americans), 4 international. Average age 28. 62 applicants, 45% accepted, 15 enrolled. In 2009, 10 master's awarded. *Degree requirements:* For master's, thesis. *Entrance requirements:* For master's, GRE General Test. Additional exam requirements/recommendations for international students: Required—TOEFL. *Application deadline:* For fall admission, 11/30 for domestic students. Application fee: $55. *Financial support:* Career-related internships or fieldwork and Federal Work-Study available. Financial award application deadline: 3/1. *Unit head:* Dr. José Luis Benavides, Chair, 818-677-3135, E-mail: jose.benavides@csun.edu. *Application contact:* Dr. José Luis Benavides, Chair, 818-677-3135, E-mail: jose.benavides@csun.edu.

Central Michigan University, College of Graduate Studies, College of Communication and Fine Arts, Department of Communication and Dramatic Arts, Concentration in Interpersonal and Public Communication, Mount Pleasant, MI 48859. Offers MA. *Accreditation:* ACEJMC. Part-time programs available. *Degree requirements:* For master's, thesis. *Entrance requirements:* For master's, minimum GPA of 3.0 in last 60 hours of undergraduate study and in last 15 hours of communication courses or other courses approved by department. Electronic applications accepted. *Faculty research:* Communication theory, interpersonal/nonverbal communication, organizational communication, family and interpersonal communication, political communication.

The College of Saint Rose, Graduate Studies, School of Arts and Humanities, Department of Public Communications, Albany, NY 12203-1419. Offers MA. Part-time and evening/weekend programs available. *Degree requirements:* For master's, final project or thesis. *Entrance requirements:* For master's, minimum undergraduate GPA of 3.0, 2 writing samples. Additional exam requirements/recommendations for international students: Required—TOEFL (minimum score 550 paper-based; 213 computer-based). Electronic applications accepted.

Colorado State University, Graduate School, College of Liberal Arts, Department of Journalism and Technical Communication, Fort Collins, CO 80523-1785. Offers public communication and technology (MS, PhD); technical communication (MS). Part-time programs available. *Faculty:* 19 full-time (8 women). *Students:* 26 full-time (21 women), 38 part-time (28 women); includes 5 minority (1 American Indian/Alaska Native, 1 Asian American or Pacific Islander, 3 Hispanic Americans), 3 international. Average age 33. 60 applicants, 48% accepted, 15 enrolled. In 2009, 13 master's awarded. *Degree requirements:* For master's, variable foreign language requirement, comprehensive exam (for some programs), thesis (for some programs); for doctorate, variable foreign language requirement, comprehensive exam (for some programs), thesis/dissertation (for some programs). *Entrance requirements:* For master's, GRE General Test, samples of written work, letters of recommendation, resume or curriculum vitae, 3 writing/communication projects; for doctorate, GRE General Test, master's degree, minimum GPA of 3.0, scholarly/professional work, letters of recommendation, statement of career plans, resume. Additional exam requirements/recommendations for international students: Required—TOEFL (minimum score 600 paper-based; 250 computer-based). *Application deadline:* For fall admission, 2/15 priority date for domestic students, 12/15 priority date for international students; for spring admission, 6/15 priority date for domestic students. Applications are processed on a rolling basis. Application fee: $50. Electronic applications accepted. *Expenses:* Tuition, state resident: full-time $6434; part-time $359.10 per credit. Tuition, nonresident: full-time $18,116; part-time $1006.45 per credit. Required fees: $1496; $83 per credit. *Financial support:* In 2009–10, 21 students received support, including 21 teaching assistantships with partial tuition reimbursements available (averaging $9,428 per year); fellowships with partial tuition reimbursements available, research assistantships with full and partial tuition reimbursements available, career-related internships or fieldwork, Federal Work-Study, institutionally sponsored loans, scholarships/grants, traineeships, and unspecified assistantships also available. Support available to part-time students. Financial award application deadline: 3/1; financial award applicants required to submit FAFSA. *Faculty research:* Technical/science communication, public relations, health/risk communication, web/new media technologies, environmental communication. Total annual research expenditures: $133,759. *Unit head:* Dr. Greg Luft, Chair, 970-491-1979, Fax: 970-491-2908, E-mail: greg.luft@colostate.edu. *Application contact:* Dr. Craig Trumbo, Graduate Program Coordinator, 970-491-2077, Fax: 970-491-2908, E-mail: craig.trumbo@colostate.edu.

Drexel University, College of Arts and Sciences, Department of Culture and Communication, Program in Communication, Philadelphia, PA 19104-2875. Offers public communication (MS); science communication (MS); technical communication (MS). Part-time and evening/weekend programs available. *Degree requirements:* For master's, internship, professional portfolio. *Entrance requirements:* For master's, GRE or minimum GPA of 3.0. Additional exam requirements/recommendations for international students: Required—TOEFL. Electronic applications accepted.

Florida International University, School of Journalism and Mass Communication, Miami, FL 33199. Offers mass communication (MS). *Accreditation:* ACEJMC. Part-time and evening/weekend programs available. *Faculty:* 19 full-time (12 women). *Students:* 99 full-time (76 women), 95 part-time (76 women); includes 138 minority (26 African Americans, 9 Asian Americans or Pacific Islanders, 103 Hispanic Americans), 23 international. Average age 28. 151 applicants, 50% accepted, 73 enrolled. In 2009, 38 master's awarded. *Degree requirements:* For master's, thesis optional. *Entrance requirements:* For master's, 2 letters of recommendation; minimum GPA of 3.0 during last 60 hours of upper-level work; resume. Additional exam requirements/recommendations for international students: Required—TOEFL (minimum score 550 paper-based; 80 iBT). *Application deadline:* For fall admission, 6/1 for domestic students, 4/1 for international students; for spring admission, 10/1 for domestic students, 9/1 for international students. Applications are processed on a rolling basis. Application fee: $30. Electronic applications accepted. *Expenses:* Tuition, state resident: full-time $8008; part-time $4004 per year. Tuition, nonresident: full-time $20,104; part-time $10,052 per year. Required fees: $298; $149 per term. *Financial support:* Institutionally sponsored loans and scholarships/grants available. Financial award application deadline: 3/1; financial award applicants required to submit FAFSA. *Faculty research:* Post-Hurricane Andrew population studies, Central American journalism, employment discrimination. *Unit head:* Dr. Lillian Kopenhaver, Dean, 305-919-5674, Fax: 305-919-5203, E-mail: kopenha@fiu.edu. *Application contact:* Nanett Rojas, Assistant Director of Graduate Admissions, 305-348-7442, Fax: 305-348-7441, E-mail: gradadm@fiu.edu.

Florida State University, The Graduate School, College of Communication and Information, School of Communication, Tallahassee, FL 32306. Offers corporate and public communication (MA, MS); integrated marketing communication (MA, MS); mass communication (PhD); media and communication studies (MA, MS); speech communication (PhD). Part-time programs available. *Faculty:* 24 full-time (9 women), 6 part-time/adjunct (1 woman). *Students:* 153 full-time (110 women), 65 part-time (34 women); includes 62 minority (37 African Americans, 1 American Indian/Alaska Native, 24 Hispanic Americans). Average age 24. 230 applicants, 76% accepted, 85 enrolled. In 2009, 84 master's, 6 doctorates awarded. *Degree requirements:* For master's, thesis (for some programs); for doctorate, comprehensive exam, thesis/dissertation. *Entrance requirements:* For master's, GRE General Test, minimum GPA of 3.0; for doctorate, GRE General Test, minimum GPA of 3.3 in graduate course work. Additional exam requirements/recommendations for international students: Required—TOEFL (minimum score 600 paper-based; 250 computer-based; 100 iBT). *Application deadline:* For fall admission, 7/1 priority date for domestic students, 5/1 priority date for international students; for spring admission, 11/1 priority date for domestic and international students. Applications are processed on a rolling basis. Application fee: $30. Electronic applications accepted. *Expenses:* Tuition, state resident: full-time $7413. Tuition, nonresident: full-time $22,567. *Financial support:* In 2009–10, 52 students received support, including 1 fellowship with full tuition reimbursement available, 8 research assistantships with full tuition reimbursements available (averaging $14,000 per year), 40 teaching assistantships with full tuition reimbursements available (averaging $5,000 per year); career-related internships or fieldwork, Federal Work-Study,

Mass Communication

Florida State University (continued)
institutionally sponsored loans, scholarships/grants, tuition waivers (partial), and unspecified assistantships also available. Support available to part-time students. Financial award application deadline: 2/1; financial award applicants required to submit FAFSA. *Faculty research:* Communication technology and policy, marketing communication, communication content and effect, new communication/information technologies. Total annual research expenditures: $600,000. *Unit head:* Dr. Stephen D. McDowell, Director, 850-644-2276, Fax: 850-644-8642, E-mail: steve.mcdowell@cci.fsu.edu. *Application contact:* Natashia Hinson-Turner, Graduate Coordinator, 850-644-8746, Fax: 850-644-8642, E-mail: natashia.turner@cci.fsu.edu.

Fordham University, Graduate School of Arts and Sciences, Department of Communication and Media Studies, New York, NY 10458. Offers public communications (MA). Part-time and evening/weekend programs available. *Faculty:* 11 full-time (3 women). *Students:* 12 full-time (9 women), 35 part-time (23 women); includes 3 minority (all African Americans), 12 international. Average age 26. 77 applicants, 44% accepted, 14 enrolled. In 2009, 24 master's awarded. *Degree requirements:* For master's, thesis, internship. *Entrance requirements:* For master's, GRE General Test. Additional exam requirements/recommendations for international students: Required—TOEFL (minimum score 600 paper-based; 250 computer-based). *Application deadline:* For fall admission, 1/4 priority date for domestic students; for spring admission, 11/1 for domestic students. Application fee: $70. Electronic applications accepted. *Financial support:* In 2009–10, 3 students received support, including 3 research assistantships with tuition reimbursements available (averaging $19,000 per year); fellowships, career-related internships or fieldwork, Federal Work-Study, institutionally sponsored loans, scholarships/grants, tuition waivers (full and partial), and unspecified assistantships also available. Financial award application deadline: 1/4. Total annual research expenditures: $80,000. *Unit head:* Dr. Paul Levinson, Chair, 718-817-4860, Fax: 718-817-4868, E-mail: levinson@fordham.edu. *Application contact:* Charlene Dundie, Director of Graduate Admissions, 718-817-4420, Fax: 718-817-3566, E-mail: dundie@fordham.edu.

The George Washington University, Columbian College of Arts and Sciences, School of Media and Public Affairs, Washington, DC 20052. Offers MA. *Faculty:* 22 full-time (6 women), 20 part-time/adjunct (4 women). *Students:* 17 full-time (11 women), 10 part-time (8 women); includes 3 minority (1 American Indian/Alaska Native, 1 Asian American or Pacific Islander, 1 Hispanic American), 5 international. Average age 26. 106 applicants, 56% accepted, 14 enrolled. In 2009, 22 master's awarded. *Degree requirements:* For master's, thesis optional. *Entrance requirements:* For master's, GRE General Test. Additional exam requirements/recommendations for international students: Required—TOEFL (minimum score 550 paper-based; 213 computer-based; 80 iBT). *Application deadline:* For fall admission, 4/1 priority date for domestic students, 1/15 priority date for international students; for spring admission, 10/1 priority date for domestic students, 9/1 priority date for international students. Applications are processed on a rolling basis. Application fee: $60. Electronic applications accepted. *Financial support:* In 2009–10, fellowships with tuition reimbursements (averaging $10,000 per year), teaching assistantships with tuition reimbursements (averaging $5,000 per year) were awarded. Financial award application deadline: 1/15. *Unit head:* Lee W. Huebner, Director, 202-994-6227, E-mail: huebner@gwu.edu. *Application contact:* Information Contact, 202-994-6227, Fax: 202-994-5806, E-mail: smpa@gwu.edu.

Georgia State University, College of Arts and Sciences, Department of Communication, Atlanta, GA 30302-3083. Offers film/video/digital imaging (MA); human communication and social influence (MA); mass communication (MA); moving image studies (PhD); public communication (PhD). Part-time programs available. *Degree requirements:* For master's, one foreign language, thesis or alternative; for doctorate, comprehensive exam, thesis/dissertation. *Entrance requirements:* For master's and doctorate, GRE General Test. Additional exam requirements/recommendations for international students: Required—TOEFL (minimum score 80 computer-based). Electronic applications accepted. *Faculty research:* Critical/cultural studies, rhetoric studies, film/media studies, mass communications/journalism, audience studies.

Grambling State University, School of Graduate Studies and Research, College of Professional Studies, Program in Mass Communication, Grambling, LA 71245. Offers MA. *Accreditation:* ACEJMC. Part-time programs available. *Faculty:* 6 full-time (2 women). *Students:* 5 full-time (4 women), 1 (woman) part-time; includes 4 minority (3 African Americans, 1 Hispanic American), 2 international. Average age 26. In 2009, 8 master's awarded. *Degree requirements:* For master's, comprehensive exam, thesis optional. *Entrance requirements:* For master's, GRE, minimum GPA of 2.5 on last degree. Additional exam requirements/recommendations for international students: Required—TOEFL (minimum score 500 paper-based; 173 computer-based; 61 iBT). *Application deadline:* For fall admission, 7/1 for domestic and international students; for spring admission, 12/1 for domestic and international students. Applications are processed on a rolling basis. Application fee: $20 ($30 for international students). Electronic applications accepted. *Expenses:* Tuition, state resident: full-time $2610. Tuition, nonresident: full-time $2610. *Financial support:* In 2009–10, 1 research assistantship (averaging $6,500 per year) was awarded; career-related internships or fieldwork, health care benefits, tuition waivers (full and partial), and unspecified assistantships also available. Financial award application deadline: 5/31; financial award applicants required to submit FAFSA. *Unit head:* Dr. Martin Adu, Acting Department Head, 318-274-2189, Fax: 318-274-3194, E-mail: edum@gram.edu. *Application contact:* Katina Crowe, Special Assistant to Associate Vice President/Dean, 318-274-2158, Fax: 318-274-7373, E-mail: croweks@gram.edu.

Howard University, School of Communications, Division of Mass Communication and Media Studies, Washington, DC 20059-0002. Offers mass communication (MA, PhD); media studies (MA, PhD). *Accreditation:* ACEJMC. Part-time and evening/weekend programs available. *Degree requirements:* For master's, comprehensive exam (for some programs), thesis optional; for doctorate, one foreign language, comprehensive exam, thesis/dissertation. *Entrance requirements:* For master's, GRE, minimum GPA of 3.0; for doctorate, GRE, minimum graduate GPA of 3.5. Additional exam requirements/recommendations for international students: Required—TOEFL. Electronic applications accepted. *Faculty research:* Advertising, public relations, journalism new media.

Indiana University Bloomington, School of Journalism, Bloomington, IN 47405-7000. Offers journalism (MA, MAT); mass communication (PhD); MA/JD; MA/MA. *Accreditation:* ACEJMC. *Faculty:* 11 full-time (5 women). *Students:* 63 full-time (35 women), 14 part-time (8 women); includes 7 minority (4 African Americans, 3 Asian Americans or Pacific Islanders), 26 international. Average age 32. 109 applicants, 62% accepted, 22 enrolled. In 2009, 26 master's, 2 doctorates awarded. Terminal master's awarded for partial completion of doctoral program. *Degree requirements:* For master's, thesis (for some programs); for doctorate, thesis/dissertation. *Entrance requirements:* For master's and doctorate, GRE General Test. Additional exam requirements/recommendations for international students: Required—TOEFL. *Application deadline:* For fall admission, 1/15 priority date for domestic students; for spring admission, 9/1 priority date for domestic students. Applications are processed on a rolling basis. Application fee: $55 ($65 for international students). *Financial support:* Fellowships, research assistantships with full tuition reimbursements, teaching assistantships with partial tuition reimbursements, career-related internships or fieldwork, Federal Work-Study, institutionally sponsored loans, and tuition waivers (full) available. Financial award application deadline: 1/15. *Faculty research:* Political communication, international communication, communication history, communication law, visual communication. Total annual research expenditures: $165,185. *Unit head:* Bradley Hamm, Dean, 812-855-9247. *Application contact:* Amy Reynolds, Associate Dean of Graduate Studies, 812-855-8111.

Indiana University Bloomington, University Graduate School, College of Arts and Sciences, Department of Telecommunications, Program in Mass Communications, Bloomington, IN 47405-7000. Offers PhD. *Faculty:* 18 full-time (5 women). *Students:* 35 full-time (17 women); includes 1 minority (African American), 26 international. Average age 35. 23 applicants, 26% accepted, 4 enrolled. In 2009, 8 doctorates awarded. *Degree requirements:* For doctorate, comprehensive exam, thesis/dissertation. *Entrance requirements:* For doctorate, GRE General Test, minimum graduate GPA of 3.5, 3 letters of recommendation. Additional exam requirements/recommendations for international students: Required—TOEFL (minimum score 600 paper-based; 250 computer-based; 100 iBT). *Application deadline:* For fall admission, 1/15 priority date for domestic students, 12/15 priority date for international students. Applications are processed on a rolling basis. Application fee: $50 ($60 for international students). Electronic applications accepted. *Financial support:* In 2009–10, 14 students received support, including 5 research assistantships with full tuition reimbursements available (averaging $11,869 per year), 9 teaching assistantships with full tuition reimbursements available (averaging $11,869 per year); scholarships/grants and health care benefits also available. Financial award application deadline: 1/15. *Faculty research:* Media management, media psychology, telecommunications law and policy, media processes and effects, media design and production (e.g., video games, virtual worlds, documentary, multi-media art). Total annual research expenditures: $152,000. *Unit head:* Tamera Theodore, Graduate Program Administrator, 812-855-2017, Fax: 812-855-7955, E-mail: ttheodor@indiana.edu. *Application contact:* Tamera Theodore, Graduate Program Administrator, 812-855-2017, Fax: 812-855-7955, E-mail: ttheodor@indiana.edu.

Iona College, School of Arts and Science, Department of Mass Communication, New Rochelle, NY 10801-1890. Offers journalism (MS); public relations (MA). *Accreditation:* ACEJMC (one or more programs are accredited). Part-time and evening/weekend programs available. *Faculty:* 6 full-time (1 woman), 6 part-time/adjunct (3 women). *Students:* 14 full-time (all women), 40 part-time (33 women); includes 15 minority (5 African Americans, 2 Asian Americans or Pacific Islanders, 8 Hispanic Americans), 4 international. Average age 27. 46 applicants, 50% accepted, 15 enrolled. In 2009, 23 master's awarded. *Degree requirements:* For master's, comprehensive exam or thesis. *Entrance requirements:* For master's, GRE General Test, minimum GPA of 3.0. Additional exam requirements/recommendations for international students: Required—TOEFL (minimum score 550 paper-based; 213 computer-based). *Application deadline:* Applications are processed on a rolling basis. Application fee: $50. Electronic applications accepted. *Expenses:* Contact institution. *Financial support:* Career-related internships or fieldwork, tuition waivers (partial), and unspecified assistantships available. Support available to part-time students. Financial award application deadline: 4/15; financial award applicants required to submit FAFSA. *Faculty research:* Media ecology, new media, corporate communication, media images, organizational learning in public relations. *Unit head:* Br. Raymond Smith, Chair, 914-633-2354, E-mail: rrsmith@iona.edu. *Application contact:* Veronica Jarek-Prinz, Director of Graduate Admissions, 914-633-2420, Fax: 914-633-2277, E-mail: vjarekprinz@iona.edu.

Iowa State University of Science and Technology, Graduate College, College of Liberal Arts and Sciences, Greenlee School of Journalism and Mass Communication, Ames, IA 50011. Offers MS. *Accreditation:* ACEJMC. *Faculty:* 70 full-time (56 women). *Students:* 25 full-time (19 women), 15 part-time (8 women); includes 6 minority (1 African American, 1 Asian American or Pacific Islander, 4 Hispanic Americans), 22 international. 42 applicants, 60% accepted, 13 enrolled. In 2009, 12 master's awarded. *Degree requirements:* For master's, thesis or alternative. *Entrance requirements:* For master's, GRE General Test. Additional exam requirements/recommendations for international students: Required—TOEFL (minimum score 570 paper-based; 88 iBT) or IELTS (minimum score 6.5). *Application deadline:* For fall admission, 4/1 priority date for international students; for spring admission, 11/1 priority date for international students. Applications are processed on a rolling basis. Application fee: $40 ($90 for international students). Electronic applications accepted. *Expenses:* Tuition, state resident: full-time $6716. Tuition, nonresident: full-time $8908. Tuition and fees vary according to course level, course load, program and student level. *Financial support:* In 2009–10, 15 research assistantships with full and partial tuition reimbursements (averaging $13,500 per year) were awarded; fellowships, teaching assistantships with partial tuition reimbursements, scholarships/grants, health care benefits, and unspecified assistantships also available. *Unit head:* Dr. Michael Bugeja, Chair, 515-294-0481, Fax: 515-294-5108, E-mail: greenlee@iastate.edu. *Application contact:* Dr. Eric Abbott, Director of Graduate Education, 515-294-0492, E-mail: masscomm@iastate.edu.

Jackson State University, Graduate School, School of Liberal Arts, Department of Mass Communications, Jackson, MS 39217. Offers MS. *Accreditation:* ACEJMC. Part-time and evening/weekend programs available. *Degree requirements:* For master's, comprehensive exam, thesis optional. *Entrance requirements:* For master's, GRE General Test. Additional exam requirements/recommendations for international students: Required—TOEFL.

Kansas State University, Graduate School, College of Arts and Sciences, A. Q. Miller School of Journalism and Mass Communications, Manhattan, KS 66506. Offers mass communications (MS). *Accreditation:* ACEJMC. Part-time programs available. *Faculty:* 14 full-time (7 women). *Students:* 13 full-time (10 women), 2 part-time (0 women), 9 international. Average age 28. 22 applicants, 77% accepted, 6 enrolled. In 2009, 15 master's awarded. *Degree requirements:* For master's, thesis or alternative. *Entrance requirements:* For master's, GRE General Test, minimum GPA of 3.0. Additional exam requirements/recommendations for international students: Required—TOEFL (minimum score 600 paper-based). *Application deadline:* For fall admission, 2/1 priority date for domestic and international students; for spring admission, 8/1 priority date for domestic and international students. Applications are processed on a rolling basis. Application fee: $40 ($55 for international students). Electronic applications accepted. *Financial support:* In 2009–10, 1 research assistantship (averaging $12,538 per year), 6 teaching assistantships with full tuition reimbursements (averaging $7,434 per year) were awarded; career-related internships or fieldwork, institutionally sponsored loans, and scholarships/grants also available. Support available to part-time students. Financial award application deadline: 3/1; financial award applicants required to submit FAFSA. *Faculty research:* Synergistic effects of integrated marketing communications, risk and hazard communication, leadership in media coverage, political communication, advertising psycholinguistic effects. Total annual research expenditures: $119,736. *Unit head:* Angela Powers, Head, 785-532-3955, Fax: 785-532-5484, E-mail: apowers@ksu.edu. *Application contact:* Hyun-Seung Jin, Director, 785-532-3959, Fax: 785-532-5484, E-mail: hsjin@ksu.edu.

Kent State University, College of Communication and Information, School of Journalism and Mass Communication, Kent, OH 44242-0001. Offers MA. *Accreditation:* ACEJMC. Part-time programs available. *Degree requirements:* For master's, thesis optional. *Entrance requirements:* For master's, GRE General Test, minimum GPA of 3.0. Additional exam requirements/recommendations for international students: Recommended—TOEFL (minimum score 600 paper-based; 250 computer-based). Electronic applications accepted. *Faculty research:* Electronic tablet newspapers, accuracy and ethics in broadcast news, internet credibility, First Amendment, HDTV.

Louisiana State University and Agricultural and Mechanical College, Graduate School, Manship School of Mass Communication, Baton Rouge, LA 70803. Offers MMC, PhD. *Accreditation:* ACEJMC. Part-time programs available. Postbaccalaureate distance learning degree programs offered (minimal on-campus study). *Faculty:* 25 full-time (11 women). *Students:* 54 full-time (36 women), 19 part-time (15 women); includes 16 minority (12 African Americans, 2 American Indian/Alaska Native, 2 Hispanic Americans), 8 international. Average age 31. 107 applicants, 40% accepted, 26 enrolled. In 2009, 11 master's, 4 doctorates awarded. *Degree requirements:* For master's, thesis; for doctorate, thesis/dissertation. *Entrance requirements:* For master's, GRE General Test, minimum GPA of 3.0. Additional exam requirements/recommendations for international students: Required—TOEFL (minimum score 550 paper-based; 213 computer-based; 79 iBT) or IELTS (minimum score 6.5). *Application deadline:* For fall admission, 1/25 priority date for domestic students, 5/15 for international students; for spring admission, 10/15 for international students. Applications are processed on a rolling basis. Application fee: $50 ($70 for international students). Electronic applications accepted. *Financial support:* In 2009–10, 55 students received support, including 2 fellowships (averaging $29,476 per year), 32 research assistantships with full and partial tuition reimbursements available (averaging $15,234 per year), 7 teaching assistantships with full and partial tuition reimbursements available (averaging $16,671 per year); career-related internships or fieldwork, Federal Work-Study, institutionally sponsored loans, scholarships/grants, health care benefits, tuition waivers (full and partial), and unspecified assistantships also available. Support available to part-time students. Financial award application deadline: 3/1; financial award applicants required to submit FAFSA. *Faculty research:* Media effects, political communication, new media technologies, persuasive communication, journalism processes and practice. Total annual research expenditures: $38,772. *Unit head:* Dr. John Maxwell Hamilton, Dean, 225-578-2002, Fax: 225-578-2125, E-mail: jhamilt@lsu.edu. *Application contact:* Dr. Amy L. Reynolds, Associate Dean of Graduate Studies and Research, 225-578-9294, Fax: 225-578-2125, E-mail: defleur@lsu.edu.

Lynn University, College of Business and Management, Boca Raton, FL 33431-5598. Offers aviation management (MBA); financial valuation and investment management (MBA); hospitality management (MBA); international business (MBA); marketing (MBA); mass communication and media management (MBA); sports and athletics administration (MBA). Part-time and evening/weekend programs available. Postbaccalaureate distance learning degree programs offered. *Degree requirements:* For master's, project. *Entrance requirements:* For master's, GMAT or GRE, minimum undergraduate GPA of 3.0, resume, 2 letters of recommendation. Additional exam requirements/recommendations for international students: Required—TOEFL (minimum score 550 paper-based; 213 computer-based). *Application deadline:* Applications are processed on a rolling basis. Application fee: $50. Electronic applications accepted. *Expenses:* Tuition: Part-time $580 per credit. One-time fee: $200 part-time. Part-time tuition and fees vary according to degree level. *Financial support:* Career-related internships or fieldwork, Federal Work-Study, institutionally sponsored loans, scholarships/grants, tuition waivers (full and partial), and unspecified assistantships available. Support available to part-time students. Financial award application deadline: 8/1; financial award applicants required to submit FAFSA. *Faculty research:* Labor relations, dynamic balance in leisure-time skills, ethics in athletics, hotel development. *Unit head:* Dr. Ralph Norcio, Associate Dean, 561-237-7010, Fax: 561-237-7014, E-mail: rnorcio@lynn.edu. *Application contact:* Dr. Larissa Baia, Assistant Director of Graduate Admissions, 561-237-7916, Fax: 561-237-7100, E-mail: admissionpm@lynn.edu.

Lynn University, Eugene M. and Christine E. Lynn College of International Communication, Boca Raton, FL 33431-5598. Offers communication and media (MS). Part-time and evening/weekend programs available. *Entrance requirements:* For master's, GRE, resume, 2 letters of recommendation, minimum GPA of 3.0. Additional exam requirements/recommendations for international students: Required—TOEFL (minimum score 550 paper-based; 213 computer-based). Application fee: $50. *Expenses:* Tuition: Part-time $580 per credit. One-time fee: $200 part-time. Part-time tuition and fees vary according to degree level. *Financial support:* Career-related internships or fieldwork, Federal Work-Study, institutionally sponsored loans, scholarships/grants, tuition waivers (partial), and unspecified assistantships available. Support available to part-time students. Financial award application deadline: 8/1; financial award applicants required to submit FAFSA. *Unit head:* Dr. David L. Jaffe, Dean, 561-237-7099, Fax: 561-237-7097, E-mail: djaffe@lynn.edu. *Application contact:* Dr. Larissa Baia, Assistant Director of Graduate Admissions, 561-237-7916, Fax: 561-237-7100, E-mail: admissionspm@lynn.edu.

Marquette University, Graduate School, College of Communication, Milwaukee, WI 53201-1881. Offers advertising and public relations (MA); broadcasting and electronic communications (MA); communications studies (MA); journalism (MA); mass communications (MA); religious communications (MA); science, health and environmental communications (MA). *Accreditation:* ACEJMC. Part-time and evening/weekend programs available. *Faculty:* 31 full-time (17 women), 35 part-time/adjunct (16 women). *Students:* 28 full-time (21 women), 30 part-time (24 women); includes 3 minority (1 African American, 2 American Indian/Alaska Native), 7 international. Average age 26. 81 applicants, 47% accepted, 22 enrolled. In 2009, 17 master's awarded. *Degree requirements:* For master's, comprehensive exam. *Entrance requirements:* For master's, GRE. Additional exam requirements/recommendations for international students: Required—TOEFL. Application fee: $40. *Financial support:* In 2009–10, 6 research assistantships, 12 teaching assistantships were awarded; career-related internships or fieldwork, Federal Work-Study, institutionally sponsored loans, scholarships/grants, and tuition waivers (full and partial) also available. Support available to part-time students. Financial award application deadline: 2/15. *Faculty research:* Urban journalism, gender and communication, intercultural communication, religious communication. *Unit head:* Dr. Ana Garner, Dean, 414-288-3588, Fax: 414-288-1578. *Application contact:* Erin Fox, Assistant Director for Recruitment, 414-288-5319, Fax: 414-288-1902, E-mail: erin.fox@marquette.edu.

Marshall University, Academic Affairs Division, School of Journalism and Mass Communications, Huntington, WV 25755. Offers MAJ. *Accreditation:* ACEJMC. *Faculty:* 3 full-time (0 women), 4 part-time/adjunct (1 woman). *Students:* 26 full-time (14 women), 3 part-time (all women); includes 2 minority (both African Americans), 8 international. Average age 27. In 2009, 8 master's awarded. *Degree requirements:* For master's, thesis optional. *Entrance requirements:* For master's, GRE General Test. Application fee: $40. *Unit head:* Dr. Corley F. Dennison, Dean, 304-696-2809, E-mail: dennisoc@marshall.edu. *Application contact:* Janet Dooley, Assistant Dean, 304-696-2734, Fax: 304-746-1902, E-mail: dooley@marshall.edu.

Middle Tennessee State University, College of Graduate Studies, College of Mass Communication, Program in Mass Communication, Murfreesboro, TN 37132. Offers MS. Part-time and evening/weekend programs available. Postbaccalaureate distance learning degree programs offered. *Faculty:* 17 full-time (2 women). *Students:* 1 full-time (0 women), 34 part-time (24 women); includes 12 minority (7 African Americans, 3 Asian Americans or Pacific Islanders, 2 Hispanic Americans). Average age 27. 40 applicants, 78% accepted, 31 enrolled. In 2009, 18 master's awarded. *Degree requirements:* For master's, comprehensive exam, thesis optional. *Entrance requirements:* For master's, GRE. Additional exam requirements/recommendations for international students: Required—TOEFL (minimum score 525 paper-based; 195 computer-based; 71 iBT) or IELTS (minimum score 6). *Application deadline:* For fall admission, 6/1 for domestic and international students. Applications are processed on a rolling basis. Application fee: $25 ($30 for international students). *Expenses:* Tuition, state resident: full-time $4404. Tuition, nonresident: full-time $10,956. *Financial support:* In 2009–10, 8 students received support. Institutionally sponsored loans available. Support available to part-time students. Financial award application deadline: 5/1. *Faculty research:* Ethics of digital media, communication administration, international media issues. *Unit head:* Dr. Clare Bratten, Director, 615-898-2795. *Application contact:* Dr. Michael Allen, Dean and Vice Provost for Research, 615-898-2840, Fax: 615-904-8020, E-mail: mallen@mtsu.edu.

Murray State University, College of Business and Public Affairs, Program in Mass Communications, Murray, KY 42071. Offers MA, MS. *Accreditation:* ACEJMC. Part-time programs available. *Entrance requirements:* Additional exam requirements/recommendations for international students: Required—TOEFL (minimum score 550 paper-based; 213 computer-based). *Faculty research:* AH media on the Internet, visual communication and learning, persuasion, media framing, history of radio and wireless technology.

North Dakota State University, College of Graduate and Interdisciplinary Studies, College of Arts, Humanities and Social Sciences, Department of Communication, Fargo, ND 58108. Offers communication (PhD); mass communication (MA, MS); speech communication (MA, MS). Part-time programs available. Postbaccalaureate distance learning degree programs offered (no on-campus study). *Faculty:* 11 full-time (5 women), 3 part-time/adjunct (1 woman). *Students:* 38 full-time (25 women), 23 part-time (17 women); includes 4 minority (1 African American, 2 Asian Americans or Pacific Islanders, 1 Hispanic American), 3 international. Average age 27. 62 applicants, 40% accepted, 19 enrolled. In 2009, 15 master's, 8 doctorates awarded. Terminal master's awarded for partial completion of doctoral program. *Degree requirements:* For master's, thesis (for some programs); for doctorate, comprehensive exam, thesis/dissertation, 2-3 publications referred before comps. *Entrance requirements:* For master's, GRE, minimum undergraduate GPA of 3.25; for doctorate, GRE, minimum undergraduate GPA of 3.5. Additional exam requirements/recommendations for international students: Required—TOEFL (minimum score 600 paper-based; 250 computer-based; 100 iBT), IELTS (minimum score 7). *Application deadline:* For fall admission, 2/15 priority date for domestic students; for winter admission, 10/15 priority date for domestic students. Applications are processed on a rolling basis. Application fee: $45 ($60 for international students). Electronic applications accepted. *Financial support:* In 2009–10, 38 students received support, including 1 fellowship with full tuition reimbursement available (averaging $16,000 per year), 10 research assistantships with full tuition reimbursements available (averaging $12,000 per year), 10 teaching assistantships with full tuition reimbursements available (averaging $8,100 per year); career-related internships or fieldwork, Federal Work-Study, institutionally sponsored loans, tuition waivers (full), and unspecified assistantships also available. Financial award application deadline: 2/1. *Faculty research:* Communication and rhetorical theory, organizational communication, broadcast and print journalism, international communication, public relations and advertising. Total annual research expenditures: $148,496. *Unit head:* Dr. Paul E. Nelson, Chair, 701-231-7705, Fax: 701-231-7784, E-mail: paul.nelson.1@ndsu.edu. *Application contact:* Dr. Judy C. Pearson, Director of Graduate Studies, 701-231-6551, Fax: 701-231-1074, E-mail: judy.pearson@ndsu.edu.

Oklahoma City University, Petree College of Arts and Sciences, Program in Liberal Arts, Oklahoma City, OK 73106-1402. Offers art (MLA); general studies (MLA); leadership/management (MLA); literature (MLA); mass communications (MLA); philosophy (MLA); writing (MLA). Part-time and evening/weekend programs available. *Faculty:* 23 full-time (6 women), 5 part-time/adjunct (3 women). *Students:* 50 full-time (24 women), 23 part-time (14 women); includes 6 minority (4 African Americans, 1 Asian American or Pacific Islander, 1 Hispanic American), 50 international. Average age 31. 31 applicants, 94% accepted, 15 enrolled. In 2009, 21 master's awarded. *Degree requirements:* For master's, comprehensive exam, thesis optional. *Entrance requirements:* Additional exam requirements/recommendations for international students: Required—TOEFL (minimum score 550 paper-based). *Application deadline:* For fall admission, 8/20 for domestic students; for spring admission, 1/6 for domestic students. Applications are processed on a rolling basis. Application fee: $50 ($70 for international students). *Expenses:* Tuition: Full-time $15,930; part-time $885 per hour. *Financial support:* Fellowships with partial tuition reimbursements, career-related internships or fieldwork, Federal Work-Study, and tuition waivers (partial) available. Support available to part-time students. Financial award application deadline: 8/1; financial award applicants required to submit FAFSA. *Unit head:* Dr. Regina Bennett, Director, 405-208-5207, Fax: 405-208-5451, E-mail: rbennett@okcu.edu. *Application contact:* Michelle Lockhart, Director, Admissions, 800-633-7242, Fax: 405-208-5916, E-mail: gadmissions@okcu.edu.

Oklahoma State University, College of Arts and Sciences, School of Journalism and Broadcasting, Stillwater, OK 74078. Offers mass communication (MS). *Accreditation:* ACEJMC. *Faculty:* 18 full-time (5 women), 4 part-time/adjunct (1 woman). *Students:* 9 full-time (5 women), 19 part-time (8 women); includes 5 minority (2 African Americans, 3 American Indian/Alaska Native), 4 international. Average age 30. 33 applicants, 42% accepted, 10 enrolled. In 2009, 6 master's awarded. *Degree requirements:* For master's, thesis, project/creative component. *Entrance requirements:* For master's, GRE, minimum GPA of 3.0. Additional exam requirements/recommendations for international students: Required—TOEFL (minimum score 550 paper-based; 79 iBT). *Application deadline:* For fall admission, 3/1 priority date for international students; for spring admission, 8/1 priority date for international students. Applications are processed on a rolling basis. Application fee: $40 ($75 for international students). Electronic applications accepted. *Expenses:* Tuition, state resident: full-time $3716; part-time $154.85 per credit hour. Tuition, nonresident: full-time $14,448; part-time $602 per credit hour. Required fees: $1772; $73.85 per credit hour. One-time fee: $50. Tuition and fees vary according to course load and campus/location. *Financial support:* In 2009–10, 1 research assistantship (averaging $5,550 per year), 5 teaching assistantships (averaging $9,324 per year) were awarded; career-related internships or fieldwork, Federal Work-Study, scholarships/grants, health care benefits, tuition waivers (partial), and unspecified assistantships also available. Support available to part-time students. Financial award application deadline: 3/1; financial award applicants required to submit FAFSA. *Unit head:* Dr. Derina Holtzhausen, Director, 405-744-6354, Fax: 405-744-7104. *Application contact:* Dr. Gordon Emslie, Dean, 405-744-6368, Fax: 405-744-0355, E-mail: grad-i@okstate.edu.

Point Park University, School of Communication, Pittsburgh, PA 15222-1984. Offers MA. Part-time and evening/weekend programs available. *Faculty:* 10 full-time, 7 part-time/adjunct. *Students:* 28 full-time (18 women), 33 part-time (22 women); includes 14 minority (12 African Americans, 2 Asian Americans or Pacific Islanders), 3 international. Average age 27. 114 applicants, 45% accepted, 20 enrolled. In 2009, 19 master's awarded. *Degree requirements:* For master's, comprehensive exam (for some programs), thesis or alternative. *Entrance requirements:* For master's, GRE (if GPA less than 2.75), minimum GPA of 2.75, 2 letters of recommendation. Additional exam requirements/recommendations for international students: Required—TOEFL (minimum score 570 paper-based; 88 iBT). *Application deadline:* Applications are processed on a rolling basis. Application fee: $30. Electronic applications accepted. *Expenses:* Tuition: Full-time $11,880; part-time $660 per credit. Required fees: $486; $27 per credit. *Financial support:* In 2009–10, 43 students received support, including 7 research assistantships with full tuition reimbursements available (averaging $6,400 per year); scholarships/grants and unspecified assistantships also available. Financial award application deadline: 4/15; financial award applicants required to submit FAFSA. *Unit head:* Dr. Tim Hudson, Chair, 412-392-4748, E-mail: thudson@pointpark.edu. *Application contact:* Emily R. Quidetto, Recruiter/Counselor, 412-392-4794, Fax: 412-392-6164, E-mail: equidetto@pointpark.edu.

See Close-Up on page 681.

St. Cloud State University, School of Graduate Studies, College of Fine Arts and Humanities, Department of Mass Communication, St. Cloud, MN 56301-4498. Offers MS. *Accreditation:* ACEJMC. *Faculty:* 11 full-time (5 women). *Students:* 26 full-time (15 women), 19 part-time (12 women); includes 5 minority (3 African Americans, 2 Asian Americans or Pacific Islanders), 12 international. 11 applicants, 100% accepted, 0 enrolled. In 2009, 12 master's awarded. *Degree requirements:* For master's, thesis or alternative. *Entrance requirements:* For master's, GRE General Test, minimum GPA of 2.75. Additional exam requirements/recommendations for international students: Required—Michigan English Language Assessment Battery; Recommended—TOEFL (minimum score 550 paper-based; 213 computer-based), IELTS (minimum score 6.5). *Application deadline:* For fall admission, 6/1 priority date for domestic students, 4/1 for international students; for spring admission, 10/1 priority date for domestic students, 8/1 for international students. Applications are processed on a rolling basis. Application fee: $35. Electronic applications accepted. *Financial support:* Federal Work-Study, scholarships/grants, and unspecified assistantships available. Financial award application deadline: 3/1. *Unit head:* Dr. Roya Akhavan-Majid, Chairperson, 320-308-3293, E-mail: comm@stcloudstate.edu. *Application contact:* Linda Lou Krueger, School of Graduate Studies, 320-308-2113, Fax: 320-308-5371, E-mail: lekrueger@stcloudstate.edu.

San Jose State University, Graduate Studies and Research, College of Applied Sciences and Arts, School of Journalism and Mass Communications, San Jose, CA 95192-0001. Offers mass communications (MS). *Accreditation:* ACEJMC. Part-time programs available. *Students:* 18 full-time (11 women), 38 part-time (27 women); includes 22 minority (4 African Americans, 7 Asian Americans or Pacific Islanders, 11 Hispanic Americans), 8 international. Average age 31. 37 applicants, 51% accepted, 17 enrolled. In 2009, 21 master's awarded. *Degree requirements:* For master's, thesis or alternative. *Entrance requirements:* For master's, GRE, minimum GPA of 3.0. *Application deadline:* For fall admission, 6/29 for domestic students; for spring admission, 11/30 for domestic students. Applications are processed on a rolling basis. Application fee: $59. Electronic applications accepted. *Financial support:* Applicants required to submit FAFSA. *Faculty research:* Communications theory, mass media effects, public relations, international communications. *Unit head:* William Briggs, Director, 408-924-3249, Fax: 408-924-3299, E-mail: william.briggs@sjsu.edu. *Application contact:* William Briggs, Director, 408-924-3249, Fax: 408-924-3299, E-mail: william.briggs@sjsu.edu.

Southern Illinois University Carbondale, Graduate School, College of Mass Communication and Media Arts, Department of Mass Communication and Media Arts, Carbondale, IL 62901-4701. Offers MA, MFA. *Accreditation:* ACEJMC.

Mass Communication

Southern Illinois University Edwardsville, Graduate Studies and Research, College of Arts and Sciences, Department of Mass Communications, Program in Mass Communications, Edwardsville, IL 62026-0001. Offers MS. *Accreditation:* ACEJMC. Part-time programs available. *Faculty:* 8 full-time (2 women). *Students:* 13 full-time (11 women), 19 part-time (15 women); includes 6 minority (4 African Americans, 1 American Indian/Alaska Native, 1 Hispanic American), 7 international. Average age 26. 34 applicants, 50% accepted. In 2009, 3 master's awarded. *Degree requirements:* For master's, comprehensive exam (for some programs), thesis (for some programs). *Entrance requirements:* Additional exam requirements/recommendations for international students: Required—TOEFL (minimum score 550 paper-based; 213 computer-based; 79 iBT), IELTS (minimum score 6.5). *Application deadline:* For fall admission, 7/23 for domestic students, 6/1 for international students; for spring admission, 12/11 for domestic students, 10/1 for international students. Applications are processed on a rolling basis. Application fee: $30. Electronic applications accepted. *Expenses:* Tuition, state resident: part-time $1252.50 per semester. Tuition, nonresident: part-time $3131.25 per semester. Required fees: $586.85 per semester. Tuition and fees vary according to course load. *Financial support:* In 2009–10, 1 research assistantship with full tuition reimbursement (averaging $8,064 per year), 10 teaching assistantships with full tuition reimbursements (averaging $8,064 per year) were awarded; fellowships with full tuition reimbursements, career-related internships or fieldwork, Federal Work-Study, institutionally sponsored loans, scholarships/grants, traineeships, and unspecified assistantships also available. Support available to part-time students. Financial award application deadline: 3/1; financial award applicants required to submit FAFSA. *Unit head:* Dr. Elza Ibroscheva, Director, 618-650-2242, E-mail: eibrosc@siue.edu. *Application contact:* Dr. Elza Ibroscheva, Director, 618-650-2242, E-mail: eibrosc@siue.edu.

Southern University and Agricultural and Mechanical College, Graduate School, College of Arts and Humanities, Department of Mass Communications, Baton Rouge, LA 70813. Offers MA. *Accreditation:* ACEJMC. *Degree requirements:* For master's, comprehensive exam, thesis. *Entrance requirements:* For master's, GRE General Test. Additional exam requirements/recommendations for international students: Required—TOEFL (minimum score 525 paper-based; 193 computer-based). *Faculty research:* Photojournalism, textbook on broadcast.

Stephen F. Austin State University, Graduate School, College of Applied Arts and Science, Department of Communication, Nacogdoches, TX 75962. Offers communication (MA); mass communication (MA). Part-time programs available. *Degree requirements:* For master's, comprehensive exam, thesis optional. *Entrance requirements:* For master's, GRE General Test. Additional exam requirements/recommendations for international students: Required—TOEFL (minimum score 550 paper-based; 213 computer-based).

Syracuse University, S. I. Newhouse School of Public Communications, Program in Communications Management, Syracuse, NY 13244. Offers MS. Part-time programs available. Postbaccalaureate distance learning degree programs offered (minimal on-campus study). *Students:* 57 part-time (38 women); includes 5 minority (2 African Americans, 1 Asian American or Pacific Islander, 2 Hispanic Americans), 6 international. Average age 43. 17 applicants, 100% accepted, 14 enrolled. In 2009, 13 master's awarded. *Degree requirements:* For master's, comprehensive exam, internship. *Entrance requirements:* For master's, GRE General Test, 5 years minimum experience in public relations or related field; portfolio; 3 letters of recommendation including 1 from current employer, client, or business partner. Additional exam requirements/recommendations for international students: Required—TOEFL (minimum score 100 iBT). *Application deadline:* For fall admission, 5/15 priority date for domestic and international students. Application fee: $45. Electronic applications accepted. *Expenses:* Tuition: Full-time $26,808; part-time $1117 per credit. Required fees: $1024. *Financial support:* Fellowships with tuition reimbursements, teaching assistantships with tuition reimbursements available. Financial award application deadline: 1/1; financial award applicants required to submit FAFSA. *Unit head:* Maria Russell, Academic Director, 315-443-3368. *Application contact:* Maria Russell, Academic Director, 315-443-3368.

See Display on page 622 and Close-Up on page 683.

Syracuse University, S. I. Newhouse School of Public Communications, Program in Mass Communications, Syracuse, NY 13244. Offers PhD. *Students:* 20 full-time (13 women), 5 part-time (4 women); includes 3 minority (2 African Americans, 1 Hispanic American), 8 international. Average age 33. 53 applicants, 11% accepted, 6 enrolled. In 2009, 4 doctorates awarded. *Degree requirements:* For doctorate, thesis/dissertation, qualifying exams. *Entrance requirements:* For doctorate, GRE General Test. Additional exam requirements/recommendations for international students: Required—TOEFL (minimum score 100 iBT). *Application deadline:* For fall admission, 12/10 priority date for domestic and international students. Application fee: $45. Electronic applications accepted. *Expenses:* Tuition: Full-time $26,808; part-time $1117 per credit. Required fees: $1024. *Financial support:* Fellowships with tuition reimbursements, research assistantships with tuition reimbursements, teaching assistantships with tuition reimbursements, career-related internships or fieldwork and tuition waivers (partial) available. Financial award application deadline: 12/10. *Unit head:* Carol M. Liebler, Director, 315-443-3372, Fax: 315-443-3946, E-mail: masscomm@syr.edu. *Application contact:* Amy Arends, Doctoral Office, 315-443-3372, E-mail: masscomm@syr.edu.

See Display on page 622 and Close-Up on page 683.

Temple University, Graduate School, School of Communications and Theater, Department of Strategic and Organizational Communication, Program in Mass Media and Communication, Philadelphia, PA 19122-6096. Offers PhD. Part-time programs available. *Degree requirements:* For doctorate, one foreign language, thesis/dissertation. *Entrance requirements:* For doctorate, GRE General Test, minimum GPA of 3.0, sample of written work. Additional exam requirements/recommendations for international students: Required—TOEFL (minimum score 550 paper-based; 213 computer-based; 79 iBT). Electronic applications accepted. *Faculty research:* Aesthetics and criticism, media institutions, social theory and processes.

Texas State University–San Marcos, Graduate School, College of Fine Arts and Communication, School of Journalism and Mass Communication, San Marcos, TX 78666. Offers MA. *Accreditation:* ACEJMC. *Faculty:* 8 full-time (5 women), 1 (woman) part-time/adjunct. *Students:* 33 full-time (20 women), 15 part-time (10 women); includes 17 minority (1 African American, 1 Asian American or Pacific Islander, 15 Hispanic Americans), 1 international. Average age 29. 23 applicants, 91% accepted, 14 enrolled. In 2009, 18 master's awarded. *Degree requirements:* For master's, comprehensive exam, thesis optional. *Entrance requirements:* For master's, GRE General Test, departmental grammar test, minimum GPA of 3.0 in last 60 hours of course work. Additional exam requirements/recommendations for international students: Required—TOEFL (minimum score 550 paper-based; 213 computer-based). *Application deadline:* For fall admission, 2/1 priority date for domestic students, 2/1 for international students; for spring admission, 10/15 priority date for domestic students, 10/1 for international students. Applications are processed on a rolling basis. Application fee: $40 ($90 for international students). Electronic applications accepted. *Expenses:* Tuition, state resident: full-time $5784; part-time $241 per credit hour. Tuition, nonresident: part-time $551 per credit hour. Required fees: $1728; $48 per credit hour. $306. Tuition and fees vary according to course load. *Financial support:* In 2009–10, 40 students received support, including 3 research assistantships (averaging $4,927 per year), 14 teaching assistantships (averaging $4,551 per year); career-related internships or fieldwork, Federal Work-Study, and institutionally sponsored loans also available. Support available to part-time students. Financial award application deadline: 4/1; financial award applicants required to submit FAFSA. *Faculty research:* Latino news media, emergency communication. Total annual research expenditures: $44,034. *Unit head:* Dr. Bruce Smith, Director, 512-245-2656, Fax: 512-245-7649, E-mail: bs20@txstate.edu. *Application contact:* Dr. Sandyha Rao, Graduate Adviser, 512-245-3790, Fax: 512-245-7649, E-mail: sr02@txstate.edu.

Texas Tech University, Graduate School, College of Mass Communications, Lubbock, TX 79409. Offers MA, PhD. *Accreditation:* ACEJMC. Part-time programs available. *Faculty:* 13 full-time (4 women). *Students:* 30 full-time (16 women), 15 part-time (8 women); includes 6 minority (1 American Indian/Alaska Native, 5 Hispanic Americans), 10 international. Average age 31. 62 applicants, 50% accepted, 13 enrolled. In 2009, 11 master's, 3 doctorates awarded. *Degree requirements:* For master's, thesis or alternative; for doctorate, thesis/dissertation. *Entrance requirements:* For master's, GRE General Test. Additional exam requirements/recommendations for international students: Required—TOEFL (minimum score 550 paper-based; 213 computer-based). *Application deadline:* For fall admission, 3/1 priority date for international students; for spring admission, 11/1 priority date for international students. Applications are processed on a rolling basis. Application fee: $50 ($75 for international students). Electronic applications accepted. *Expenses:* Tuition, state resident: full-time $5100; part-time $213 per credit hour. Tuition, nonresident: full-time $11,748; part-time $490 per credit hour. Required fees: $2298; $50 per credit hour. $555 per semester. *Financial support:* In 2009–10, 19 teaching assistantships with partial tuition reimbursements (averaging $17,443 per year) were awarded; research assistantships with partial tuition reimbursements, Federal Work-Study and institutionally sponsored loans also available. Support available to part-time students. Financial award application deadline: 4/15; financial award applicants required to submit FAFSA. *Faculty research:* Contemporary media use and structure; Hispanic media; characteristics of public relations spokesperson credibility; psychological measures of advertising effectiveness; media law. Total annual research expenditures: $149,348. *Unit head:* Dr. Jerry C. Hudson, Dean, 806-742-3385 Ext. 224, Fax: 806-742-1085, E-mail: jerry.hudson@ttu.edu. *Application contact:* Dr. Coy Callison, Associate Dean of Graduate Studies, 806-742-3385 Ext. 235, Fax: 806-742-1085, E-mail: coy.callison@ttu.edu.

Université Laval, Faculty of Letters, Department of Information and Communication, Program in Public Communication, Québec, QC G1K 7P4, Canada. Offers MA, PhD. Part-time programs available. *Degree requirements:* For master's, thesis (for some programs). *Entrance requirements:* For master's, knowledge of French, knowledge of English. Electronic applications accepted.

The University of Alabama, Graduate School, College of Communication and Information Sciences, Communication and Information Sciences Program, Tuscaloosa, AL 35487-0172. Offers PhD. *Faculty:* 9 full-time (7 women). *Students:* 44 full-time (19 women), 14 part-time (7 women); includes 7 minority (6 African Americans, 1 American Indian/Alaska Native), 10 international. Average age 35. 53 applicants, 43% accepted, 16 enrolled. In 2009, 17 degrees awarded. *Degree requirements:* For doctorate, comprehensive exam, thesis/dissertation. *Entrance requirements:* For doctorate, GRE, master's degree, minimum undergraduate and graduate GPA of 3.0. Additional exam requirements/recommendations for international students: Required—TOEFL. *Application deadline:* For fall admission, 2/15 for domestic and international students; for winter admission, 11/1 for domestic and international students. Application fee: $50 ($60 for international students). *Expenses:* Tuition, state resident: full-time $7000. Tuition, nonresident: full-time $19,200. *Financial support:* In 2009–10, 4 fellowships with full tuition reimbursements (averaging $15,000 per year), 14 research assistantships with full tuition reimbursements (averaging $13,045 per year), 10 teaching assistantships with full tuition reimbursements (averaging $13,045 per year) were awarded; institutionally sponsored loans, health care benefits, and unspecified assistantships also available. Financial award application deadline: 2/15. *Faculty research:* Mass media; mass media effects; information studies; cultural, critical and rhetorical studies; policy and law; electronic media. Total annual research expenditures: $5,591. *Unit head:* Dr. Jennings Bryant, Associate Dean for Graduate Studies, 205-348-8593, Fax: 205-348-6774. *Application contact:* Diane Shaddix, Information Contact, 205-348-8593, Fax: 205-348-6774, E-mail: dshaddix@bama.ua.edu.

University of Arkansas at Little Rock, Graduate School, College of Professional Studies, School of Mass Communication, Little Rock, AR 72204-1099. Offers journalism (MA). Part-time and evening/weekend programs available. *Degree requirements:* For master's, comprehensive exam, thesis optional. *Entrance requirements:* For master's, GRE General Test, minimum GPA of 2.7. *Faculty research:* Theory and practice of mass communication, social role of the mass media.

University of Central Missouri, The Graduate School, College of Arts, Humanities and Social Sciences, Warrensburg, MO 64093. Offers English (MA); history (MA); mass communication (MA); music (MA); psychology (MS); speech communication (MA); teaching english as a second language (MA); theatre (MA). Part-time programs available. *Faculty:* 82. *Students:* 60 full-time (35 women), 101 part-time (61 women); includes 11 minority (5 African Americans, 3 Asian Americans or Pacific Islanders, 3 Hispanic Americans), 17 international. Average age 30. 80 applicants, 80% accepted, 58 enrolled. In 2009, 51 master's awarded. *Entrance requirements:* Additional exam requirements/recommendations for international students: Required—TOEFL (minimum score 550 paper-based; 79 computer-based). *Application deadline:* For fall admission, 6/1 priority date for domestic students, 5/1 for international students; for spring admission, 10/1 priority date for domestic students, 10/1 for international students. Applications are processed on a rolling basis. Application fee: $30 ($75 for international students). Electronic applications accepted. *Expenses:* Tuition, area resident: Part-time $245.80 per credit hour. Tuition, nonresident: part-time $491.60 per credit hour. Required fees: $24.20 per credit hour. Full-time tuition and fees vary according to course load, degree level, campus/location and reciprocity agreements. *Financial support:* Research assistantships with full and partial tuition reimbursements, teaching assistantships with full and partial tuition reimbursements, career-related internships or fieldwork, Federal Work-Study, scholarships/grants, and administrative and laboratory assistantships available. Support available to part-time students. Financial award application deadline: 3/1; financial award applicants required to submit FAFSA. *Unit head:* Dr. Gersham Nelson, Dean, 660-543-4750, Fax: 660-543-8271, E-mail: nelson@ucmo.edu. *Application contact:* Laurie Delap, Admissions Coordinator, 660-543-4621, Fax: 660-543-4778, E-mail: gradinfo@ucmo.edu.

University of Colorado at Boulder, Graduate School, School of Journalism and Mass Communication, Boulder, CO 80309. Offers communication (PhD), including media studies; mass communication research (MA); newsgathering (MA). *Accreditation:* ACEJMC (one or more programs are accredited). Part-time programs available. *Faculty:* 22 full-time (11 women). *Students:* 77 full-time (50 women), 16 part-time (12 women); includes 6 minority (1 African American, 5 Hispanic Americans), 14 international. Average age 32. 181 applicants, 26% accepted, 30 enrolled. In 2009, 22 master's, 3 doctorates awarded. *Degree requirements:* For master's, comprehensive exam, thesis or alternative; for doctorate, comprehensive exam, thesis/dissertation. *Entrance requirements:* For master's, GRE General Test, minimum undergraduate GPA of 2.75; for doctorate, GRE General Test, minimum undergraduate GPA of 3.2, 3.5 graduate. *Application deadline:* For fall admission, 2/15 for domestic students, 12/1 for international students. Applications are processed on a rolling basis. Application fee: $50 ($60 for international students). *Financial support:* In 2009–10, 14 fellowships (averaging $1,807 per year), 21 research assistantships with tuition reimbursements (averaging $11,554 per year) were awarded; institutionally sponsored loans and unspecified assistantships also available. Financial award application deadline: 3/1. *Faculty research:* Writing on science and the environment, mass communication and public opinion, minority representation in the media, media and culture. Total annual research expenditures: $141,446.

University of Denver, Division of Arts, Humanities and Social Sciences, Department of Mass Communications, Denver, CO 80208. Offers advertising management (MS); digital media studies (MA); mass communications (MA); public relations (MS); video production (MA). Part-time programs available. *Faculty:* 14 full-time (8 women), 4 part-time/adjunct (3 women). *Students:* 37 full-time (28 women), 32 part-time (27 women); includes 8 minority (1 African American, 2 Asian Americans or Pacific Islanders, 5 Hispanic Americans), 3 international. Average age 26. 163 applicants, 64% accepted, 45 enrolled. In 2009, 24 master's awarded. *Degree requirements:* For master's, thesis (for some programs). *Entrance requirements:* For master's, GRE General Test. Additional exam requirements/recommendations for international students: Required—TOEFL, TWE. *Application deadline:* Applications are processed on a rolling basis. Application fee: $50. Electronic applications accepted. *Expenses:* Tuition: Full-time $34,596; part-time $961 per quarter hour. Required fees: $4 per quarter hour. Tuition and fees vary according to course load, campus/location and program. *Financial support:* In 2009–10,

10 research assistantships with full and partial tuition reimbursements (averaging $14,000 per year), 5 teaching assistantships with full and partial tuition reimbursements (averaging $11,500 per year) were awarded; career-related internships or fieldwork, Federal Work-Study, institutionally sponsored loans, and scholarships/grants also available. Support available to part-time students. Financial award application deadline: 3/1; financial award applicants required to submit FAFSA. *Faculty research:* Youth and civic engagement. Total annual research expenditures: $162,000. *Unit head:* Dr. Diane Waldman, Chair, 303-871-2008. *Application contact:* Information Contact, 303-871-2008, E-mail: mcom@du.edu.

University of Florida, Graduate School, College of Journalism and Communications, Gainesville, FL 32611. Offers advertising (M Adv); journalism (MAMC); mass communication (MAMC, PhD); public relations (MAMC); telecommunication (MAMC); JD/MAMC; JD/PhD. *Accreditation:* ACEJMC (one or more programs are accredited). Part-time programs available. Terminal master's awarded for partial completion of doctoral program. *Degree requirements:* For master's, thesis optional; for doctorate, thesis/dissertation. *Entrance requirements:* For master's and doctorate, GRE General Test, minimum GPA of 3.0. Additional exam requirements/recommendations for international students: Required—TOEFL (minimum score 550 paper-based; 213 computer-based). Electronic applications accepted. *Faculty research:* Public opinion, law and policy, regulation, environmental communication, international communication.

University of Georgia, Grady School of Journalism and Mass Communication, Athens, GA 30602. Offers journalism and mass communication (MA); mass communication (PhD). *Accreditation:* ACEJMC (one or more programs are accredited). *Faculty:* 39 full-time (16 women). *Students:* 75 full-time (48 women), 45 part-time (32 women); includes 17 minority (14 African Americans, 3 Hispanic Americans), 16 international. 263 applicants, 34% accepted, 38 enrolled. In 2009, 27 master's, 4 doctorates awarded. *Degree requirements:* For master's, comprehensive exam, thesis (MA); for doctorate, comprehensive exam, thesis/dissertation. *Entrance requirements:* For master's and doctorate, GRE General Test. Additional exam requirements/recommendations for international students: Required—TOEFL, TWE (PhD). *Application deadline:* For spring admission, 2/15 for domestic students. Application fee: $50. Electronic applications accepted. *Expenses:* Tuition, state resident: full-time $6000; part-time $250 per credit hour. Tuition, nonresident: full-time $20,904; part-time $871 per credit hour. Required fees: $730 per semester. *Financial support:* Research assistantships, teaching assistantships, tuition waivers (full) and unspecified assistantships available. *Unit head:* Dr. E. Culpepper Clark, Dean, 706-542-1704, Fax: 706-542-2183, E-mail: cully@uga.edu. *Application contact:* Dr. Jeffrey K. Springston, Graduate Coordinator, 706-542-7833, Fax: 706-542-2183, E-mail: jspring@grady.uga.edu.

University of Houston, College of Liberal Arts and Social Sciences, School of Communication, Houston, TX 77204. Offers health communication (MA); mass communication studies (MA); public relations studies (MA); speech communication (MA). Part-time and evening/weekend programs available. *Faculty:* 9 full-time (5 women), 2 part-time/adjunct (0 women). *Students:* 42 full-time (38 women), 49 part-time (44 women); includes 31 minority (17 African Americans, 2 American Indian/Alaska Native, 2 Asian Americans or Pacific Islanders, 10 Hispanic Americans), 24 international. Average age 28. 92 applicants, 47% accepted, 28 enrolled. In 2009, 19 master's awarded. *Degree requirements:* For master's, comprehensive exam, thesis. *Entrance requirements:* For master's, GRE. Additional exam requirements/recommendations for international students: Required—TOEFL. *Application deadline:* For fall admission, 6/1 for domestic students, 4/1 for international students; for spring admission, 11/1 for domestic students, 10/1 for international students. Application fee: $25 ($75 for international students). Electronic applications accepted. *Expenses:* Tuition, state resident: full-time $7676; part-time $320 per credit hour. Tuition, nonresident: full-time $14,324; part-time $597 per credit hour. Required fees: $3034. *Financial support:* In 2009–10, 2 fellowships with full tuition reimbursements (averaging $9,750 per year), 5 teaching assistantships with full tuition reimbursements (averaging $9,750 per year) were awarded; career-related internships or fieldwork, Federal Work-Study, institutionally sponsored loans, scholarships/grants, health care benefits, and unspecified assistantships also available. Support available to part-time students. Financial award application deadline: 2/1. *Unit head:* Dr. Beth Olson, Chairperson, 713-743-2873, Fax: 713-743-2876, E-mail: bolson@uh.edu. *Application contact:* Salima B. Haji, Academic Advisor, 713-743-2575, Fax: 713-743-2876, E-mail: sbhaji@central.uh.edu.

The University of Iowa, Graduate College, College of Liberal Arts and Sciences, School of Journalism and Mass Communication, Iowa City, IA 52242-1316. Offers mass communication (PhD); media communication (MA); professional journalism (MA); JD/MA. *Accreditation:* ACEJMC (one or more programs are accredited). *Degree requirements:* For master's, thesis optional, exam; for doctorate, comprehensive exam, thesis/dissertation. *Entrance requirements:* For master's and doctorate, GRE General Test, minimum GPA of 3.0. Additional exam requirements/recommendations for international students: Required—TOEFL (minimum score 637 paper-based; 270 computer-based; 110 iBT). Electronic applications accepted. *Faculty research:* Verbal and visual aspects of historical, legal, social, and cross-cultural communication.

University of Louisiana at Lafayette, College of Liberal Arts, Department of Communication, Lafayette, LA 70504. Offers mass communications (MS). Part-time programs available. *Degree requirements:* For master's, thesis optional. *Entrance requirements:* For master's, GRE General Test, minimum GPA of 2.75. Additional exam requirements/recommendations for international students: Required—TOEFL (minimum score 550 paper-based; 213 computer-based). Electronic applications accepted. *Faculty research:* Mass media problems, issues and ethics, mass communication, historical studies, conflict of interest and law and ethics in journalism, contemporary issues and trends in publications.

University of Michigan, Horace H. Rackham School of Graduate Studies, College of Literature, Science, and the Arts, Department of Communication Studies, Ann Arbor, MI 48104-2523. Offers PhD. *Faculty:* 15 full-time (5 women), 1 part-time/adjunct (0 women). *Students:* 31 full-time (23 women); includes 4 minority (1 African American, 2 Asian Americans or Pacific Islanders, 1 Hispanic American), 10 international. Average age 28. 95 applicants, 8% accepted, 5 enrolled. In 2009, 4 doctorates awarded. *Degree requirements:* For doctorate, comprehensive exam, thesis/dissertation, first-year research project, 2 terms as in graduate student instructor position. *Entrance requirements:* For doctorate, GRE. Additional exam requirements/recommendations for international students: Required—TOEFL (minimum score 560 paper-based; 220 computer-based; 84 iBT). *Application deadline:* For fall admission, 12/1 for domestic and international students. Application fee: $60 ($75 for international students). Electronic applications accepted. *Expenses:* Tuition, state resident: full-time $17,286; part-time $1099 per credit hour. Tuition, nonresident: full-time $34,944; part-time $2080 per credit hour. Required fees: $95 per semester. Tuition and fees vary according to course load, degree level and program. *Financial support:* In 2009–10, 31 students received support, including 4 fellowships with full tuition reimbursements available (averaging $16,400 per year), 1 research assistantship with full tuition reimbursement available (averaging $16,400 per year), 22 teaching assistantships with full tuition reimbursements available (averaging $16,135 per year); scholarships/grants, health care benefits, tuition waivers (full and partial), and unspecified assistantships also available. Financial award application deadline: 2/15; financial award applicants required to submit FAFSA. *Faculty research:* Political communication; media, culture and society; media effects; race, gender, and the media; new media, media law and policy. *Unit head:* Prof. Susan J. Douglas, Professor and Chair, 734-764-0420, Fax: 734-764-3288, E-mail: sdoug@umich.edu. *Application contact:* Amy B. Eaton, Graduate Program Coordinator, 734-615-8974, Fax: 734-764-3288, E-mail: lsa-commphd@umich.edu.

University of Minnesota, Twin Cities Campus, Graduate School, College of Liberal Arts, School of Journalism and Mass Communication, Minneapolis, MN 55455-0213. Offers mass communication (MA, PhD); strategic communication (professional program) (MA). *Faculty:* 23 full-time (12 women), 4 part-time/adjunct (1 woman). *Students:* 89 full-time (68 women), 33 part-time (27 women); includes 13 minority (7 African Americans, 3 Asian Americans or Pacific Islanders, 3 Hispanic Americans), 21 international. 109 applicants, 41% accepted, 36 enrolled. In 2009, 29 master's, 8 doctorates awarded. *Degree requirements:* For master's, thesis; for doctorate, comprehensive exam, thesis/dissertation. *Entrance requirements:* For master's, GRE (OR GMAT for Strat Comm Program), letters of recommendation, minimum undergraduate GPA of 3.0, writing sample (Plus two years professional experience for Strat Comm program); for doctorate, GRE, letters of recommendation, minimum undergraduate GPA of 3.0, writing sample. Additional exam requirements/recommendations for international students: Required—TOEFL (minimum score 79 iBT). *Application deadline:* For fall admission, 12/15 for domestic and international students. Application fee: $75 ($95 for international students). Electronic applications accepted. *Financial support:* In 2009–10, 60 students received support, including 2 fellowships with full and partial tuition reimbursements available (averaging $26,500 per year), 58 teaching assistantships with full and partial tuition reimbursements available (averaging $26,500 per year); career-related internships or fieldwork, Federal Work-Study, institutionally sponsored loans, tuition waivers (partial), and unspecified assistantships also available. Support available to part-time students. Financial award application deadline: 12/15; financial award applicants required to submit FAFSA. *Faculty research:* Communication law, regulation, and ethics; history; mass media effects; new media, health communication. Total annual research expenditures: $150,000. *Unit head:* Dr. Albert R. Tims, Director, 612-625-1338, Fax: 612-626-8251. *Application contact:* Heather Myers Larson, Coordinator of Graduate Student Services, 612-625-4054, Fax: 612-626-8251, E-mail: sjmcgrad@umn.edu.

University of Nebraska–Lincoln, Graduate College, College of Journalism and Mass Communications, Lincoln, NE 68588. Offers marketing, communication and advertising (MA); professional journalism (MA). *Accreditation:* ACEJMC. Postbaccalaureate distance learning degree programs offered (no on-campus study). *Degree requirements:* For master's, thesis. *Entrance requirements:* For master's, samples of work. Additional exam requirements/recommendations for international students: Required—TOEFL (minimum score 600 paper-based; 250 computer-based). Electronic applications accepted. *Faculty research:* Interactive media and the Internet, community newspapers, children's radio, advertising involvement, telecommunications policy.

The University of North Carolina at Chapel Hill, Graduate School, School of Journalism and Mass Communication, Chapel Hill, NC 27599. Offers mass communication (MA, PhD). *Accreditation:* ACEJMC (one or more programs are accredited). Part-time programs available. *Degree requirements:* For master's, comprehensive exam, thesis; for doctorate, comprehensive exam, thesis/dissertation. *Entrance requirements:* For master's and doctorate, GRE General Test, minimum GPA of 3.0. Additional exam requirements/recommendations for international students: Required—TOEFL (minimum score 620 paper-based; 260 computer-based; 105 iBT). Electronic applications accepted. *Expenses:* Contact institution. *Faculty research:* Media processes and production, legal and regulatory issues, media effects, media history.

University of Oklahoma, Graduate College, Gaylord College of Journalism and Mass Communication, Program in Journalism and Mass Communication, Norman, OK 73019-0390. Offers advertising and public relations (MA); information gathering and distribution (MA); mass communication management and policy (MA); professional writing (MA); telecommunication and new technology (MA). Part-time programs available. *Students:* 34 full-time (18 women), 43 part-time (23 women); includes 13 minority (4 African Americans, 5 American Indian/Alaska Native, 4 Hispanic Americans), 9 international. 45 applicants, 42% accepted, 9 enrolled. *Degree requirements:* For master's, thesis optional. *Entrance requirements:* For master's, GRE General Test, minimum GPA of 3.2, 9 hours of course work in journalism, course work in statistics. Additional exam requirements/recommendations for international students: Required—TOEFL (minimum score 600 paper-based; 250 computer-based), TWE (minimum score 5). *Application deadline:* For fall admission, 2/1 for domestic students, 4/1 for international students; for spring admission, 11/1 for domestic students, 9/1 for international students. Application fee: $40 ($90 for international students). Electronic applications accepted. *Expenses:* Tuition, state resident: full-time $3744; part-time $156 per credit hour. Tuition, nonresident: full-time $13,577; part-time $565.70 per credit hour. Required fees: $2415; $90.10 per credit hour. *Financial support:* In 2009–10, 43 students received support, including 4 fellowships (averaging $5,000 per year); career-related internships or fieldwork, scholarships/grants, health care benefits, and unspecified assistantships also available. *Faculty research:* Organizational management, rhetorical analysis, international public relations, digital production, normative theory. *Unit head:* Dr. Joe Foote, Dean, 405-325-2721, Fax: 405-325-7565, E-mail: jfoote@ou.edu. *Application contact:* Kelly Storm, Graduate Advisor, 405-325-2722, Fax: 405-325-7565, E-mail: kstorm@ou.edu.

University of Puerto Rico, Río Piedras, School of Communication, San Juan, PR 00931-3300. Offers MA. Part-time programs available. *Degree requirements:* For master's, comprehensive exam, thesis. *Entrance requirements:* For master's, GRE, PAEG, minimum GPA of 3.0, 2 letters of recommendation, interview.

University of Southern California, Graduate School, Annenberg School for Communication and Journalism, School of Communication, Program in Communication, Los Angeles, CA 90089. Offers communication (MA, PhD), including interpersonal and social dynamics (PhD), mass communication, technology, and public policy (PhD), organizational communication (PhD), rhetorical and cultural studies (PhD). *Degree requirements:* For doctorate, thesis/dissertation. *Entrance requirements:* For master's and doctorate, GRE General Test, resume, writing samples, 3 letters of recommendation, interest survey questionnaire, statement of purpose. Additional exam requirements/recommendations for international students: Required—TOEFL (minimum score 280 computer-based; 114 iBT); Recommended—TWE. Electronic applications accepted. *Expenses:* Tuition: Full-time $25,980; part-time $1315 per unit. Required fees: $554. One-time fee: $35 full-time. Full-time tuition and fees vary according to degree level and program. *Faculty research:* Computer-mediated communication, public health campaigns, communication democracy and the public sphere, new communication technologies in organizations, communication and community.

See Display on page 629 and Close-Up on page 685.

University of Southern Mississippi, Graduate School, College of Arts and Letters, School of Mass Communication and Journalism, Hattiesburg, MS 39406-0001. Offers mass communication (MA, MS, PhD); public relations (MS). *Accreditation:* ACEJMC. *Faculty:* 10 full-time (3 women), 1 part-time/adjunct (0 women). *Students:* 28 full-time (18 women), 57 part-time (43 women); includes 13 minority (12 African Americans, 1 Hispanic American), 5 international. Average age 34. 44 applicants, 66% accepted, 18 enrolled. In 2009, 24 master's, 4 doctorates awarded. *Degree requirements:* For master's, comprehensive exam, thesis optional; for doctorate, comprehensive exam, thesis/dissertation. *Entrance requirements:* For master's, GRE General Test, minimum GPA of 3.0 in field of study, 2.75 in last 2 years; for doctorate, GRE General Test, minimum GPA of 3.5. Additional exam requirements/recommendations for international students: Required—TOEFL. *Application deadline:* For fall admission, 3/1 priority date for domestic students, 3/1 for international students. Applications are processed on a rolling basis. Application fee: $35. *Expenses:* Tuition, state resident: full-time $5096; part-time $284 per hour. Tuition, nonresident: full-time $13,052; part-time $726 per hour. Required fees: $402. Tuition and fees vary according to course level and course load. *Financial support:* In 2009–10, 18 students received support, including 12 teaching assistantships with full tuition reimbursements available (averaging $8,000 per year); fellowships with full tuition reimbursements available, research assistantships with full tuition reimbursements available, career-related internships or fieldwork, Federal Work-Study, and unspecified assistantships also available. Financial award application deadline: 3/15; financial award applicants required to submit FAFSA. *Unit head:* Dr. Christopher Campbell, Director, 601-266-5650, Fax: 601-266-4263. *Application contact:* Dr. Fei Xue, Graduate Coordinator, 601-266-5652, Fax: 601-266-6473, E-mail: fei.xue@usm.edu.

University of South Florida, Graduate School, College of Arts and Sciences, School of Mass Communications, Tampa, FL 33620-9951. Offers MA. *Accreditation:* ACEJMC. Part-time and evening/weekend programs available. *Faculty:* 6 full-time (3 women), 1 (woman) part-time/adjunct. *Students:* 17 full-time (13 women), 26 part-time (19 women); includes 8 minority (6 African Americans, 2 Hispanic Americans), 4 international. Average age 32. 51 applicants,

Mass Communication

University of South Florida (continued)
31% accepted, 7 enrolled. In 2009, 7 master's awarded. *Degree requirements:* For master's, comprehensive exam, thesis. *Entrance requirements:* For master's, GRE General Test, minimum GPA of 3.0 in last 60 hours of course work. Additional exam requirements/recommendations for international students: Required—TOEFL (minimum score 550 paper-based; 213 computer-based). *Application deadline:* For fall admission, 2/15 for domestic students, 1/2 for international students; for spring admission, 10/15 for domestic students, 6/1 for international students. Application fee: $30. Electronic applications accepted. *Financial support:* In 2009–10, teaching assistantships with tuition reimbursements (averaging $10,152 per year); unspecified assistantships also available. Financial award application deadline: 2/28. *Faculty research:* First Amendment analysis, civic journalism, public opinion, media ethics, public relation management. Total annual research expenditures: $72,008. *Unit head:* Dr. Edward Jay Friedlander, Chairperson, 813-974-6461, Fax: 813-974-2592, E-mail: efriedla@luna.cas.usf.edu. *Application contact:* Kelly Page Werder, Director, 813-974-6790, Fax: 813-974-2592, E-mail: kgpage@.cas.usf.edu.

University of Wisconsin–Madison, Graduate School, College of Letters and Science, School of Journalism and Mass Communication, Program in Journalism and Mass Communication, Madison, WI 53706-1380. Offers MA. *Expenses:* Tuition, state resident: part-time $594 per credit. Tuition, nonresident: part-time $1504 per credit. Required fees: $65 per credit. Tuition and fees vary according to course load, program and reciprocity agreements.

University of Wisconsin–Madison, Graduate School, College of Letters and Science, School of Journalism and Mass Communication, Program in Mass Communication, Madison, WI 53706-1380. Offers PhD. *Degree requirements:* For doctorate, thesis/dissertation. *Expenses:* Tuition, state resident: part-time $594 per credit. Tuition, nonresident: part-time $1504 per credit. Required fees: $65 per credit. Tuition and fees vary according to course load, program and reciprocity agreements.

University of Wisconsin–Stevens Point, College of Fine Arts and Communication, Division of Communication, Stevens Point, WI 54481-3897. Offers interpersonal communication (MA); mass communication (MA); organizational communication (MA); public relations (MA). Part-time programs available. *Students:* 7 full-time (3 women), 19 part-time (11 women). *Degree requirements:* For master's, thesis or alternative. *Entrance requirements:* For master's, GRE. Additional exam requirements/recommendations for international students: Required—TOEFL (minimum score 575 paper-based). *Application deadline:* For fall admission, 3/1 priority date for domestic students. Applications are processed on a rolling basis. Application fee: $45. *Expenses:* Tuition, state resident: full-time $7740; part-time $430 per credit hour. Tuition, nonresident: full-time $17,804; part-time $989 per credit hour. Tuition and fees vary according to course load and reciprocity agreements. *Financial support:* In 2009–10, 9 teaching assistantships were awarded; career-related internships or fieldwork, Federal Work-Study, institutionally sponsored loans, and unspecified assistantships also available. Support available to part-time students. Financial award application deadline: 5/1; financial award applicants required to submit FAFSA. *Faculty research:* Communication theory and research, film history. *Unit head:* Dr. James Haney, Chair, 715-346-3409, E-mail: jhaney@uwsp.edu. *Application contact:* Dr. Chris Sadler, Graduate Coordinator, 715-346-3898, E-mail: csadler@uwsp.edu.

University of Wisconsin–Superior, Graduate Division, Department of Communicating Arts, Superior, WI 54880-4500. Offers mass communication (MA); speech communication (MA); theater (MA). Part-time programs available. *Faculty:* 9 full-time (3 women), 1 (woman) part-time/adjunct. *Students:* 14 full-time (9 women), 5 part-time (3 women). Average age 30. 9 applicants, 100% accepted. In 2009, 7 master's awarded. *Degree requirements:* For master's, comprehensive exam, thesis or alternative, position paper or project. *Entrance requirements:* For master's, minimum GPA of 2.75. *Application deadline:* For fall admission, 4/1 priority date for domestic students; for spring admission, 10/15 priority date for domestic students. Applications are processed on a rolling basis. Application fee: $45. *Financial support:* Career-related internships or fieldwork, Federal Work-Study, institutionally sponsored loans, scholarships/grants, and tuition waivers (partial) available. Support available to part-time students. Financial award application deadline: 4/15; financial award applicants required to submit FAFSA. *Faculty research:* Multimedia technology, ethics in journalism, diversity, electronic portfolio assessment. *Unit head:* Dr. Martha Einerson, Program Coordinator, 715-394-8477, E-mail: meinerso@uwsuper.edu. *Application contact:* Sandy Wallgren, Program Assistant/Status Examiner, 715-394-8295, Fax: 715-394-8146, E-mail: swallgr1@uwsuper.edu.

University of Wisconsin–Whitewater, School of Graduate Studies, College of Arts and Communications, Department of Communication, Whitewater, WI 53190-1790. Offers corporate communication (MS); mass communication (MS). Part-time and evening/weekend programs available. Postbaccalaureate distance learning degree programs offered (no on-campus study). *Degree requirements:* For master's, thesis or alternative. *Entrance requirements:* For master's, 2 letters of recommendation. Additional exam requirements/recommendations for international students: Required—TOEFL (minimum score 550 paper-based; 213 computer-based). Electronic applications accepted.

Virginia Commonwealth University, Graduate School, College of Humanities and Sciences, School of Mass Communications, Program in Mass Communications, Richmond, VA 23284-9005. Offers scholastic journalism (MS); strategic public relations (MS). *Accreditation:* ACEJMC. *Degree requirements:* For master's, comprehensive exam, thesis optional. *Entrance requirements:* For master's, GRE General Test.

Media Studies

American University, School of Communication, Film and Electronic Media Program, Washington, DC 20016-8001. Offers MFA. *Faculty:* 14 full-time (6 women). *Students:* 34 full-time (16 women), 39 part-time (19 women). 51 applicants, 73% accepted, 22 enrolled. In 2009, 141 master's awarded. *Degree requirements:* For master's, comprehensive exam, thesis or alternative. *Entrance requirements:* For master's, GRE General Test. Additional exam requirements/recommendations for international students: Required—TOEFL (minimum score 600 paper-based; 250 computer-based). *Application deadline:* For fall admission, 2/1 priority date for domestic and international students; for spring admission, 11/15 for domestic and international students. Applications are processed on a rolling basis. Application fee: $50. Electronic applications accepted. *Expenses:* Tuition: Full-time $22,266; part-time $1237 per credit hour. Required fees: $430. Tuition and fees vary according to program. *Financial support:* In 2009–10, 10 students received support, including 2 fellowships with partial tuition reimbursements available (averaging $13,000 per year), 2 research assistantships with partial tuition reimbursements available (averaging $11,000 per year), 4 teaching assistantships with partial tuition reimbursements available (averaging $11,000 per year); career-related internships or fieldwork, Federal Work-Study, institutionally sponsored loans, scholarships/grants, tuition waivers (partial), and unspecified assistantships also available. Financial award application deadline: 2/1. *Faculty research:* Documentary film production, social media, media and public policy, visual literacy, new technology. *Unit head:* Prof. John Douglass, Director, Film and Media Arts Division, 202-885-2045, Fax: 202-885-2019, E-mail: jdougla@american.edu. *Application contact:* Sharmeen Ahsan-Bracciale, Graduate Admissions Office, 202-885-2040, Fax: 202-885-2019, E-mail: sharmeen@american.edu.

Arizona State University, Graduate College, College of Liberal Arts and Sciences, Division of Humanities, Program in Film and Media Studies, Tempe, AZ 85287. Offers American media and popular culture (MAS); film analysis (MLS); screenwriting (MAS).

Arkansas State University—Jonesboro, Graduate School, College of Communications, Department of Radio-Television, Jonesboro, State University, AR 72467. Offers MSMC. Part-time programs available. *Faculty:* 4 full-time (1 woman). *Students:* 11 full-time (6 women), 14 part-time (9 women); includes 12 minority (all African Americans), 10 international. Average age 27. 30 applicants, 93% accepted, 18 enrolled. In 2009, 5 master's awarded. *Degree requirements:* For master's, comprehensive exam, thesis or alternative. *Entrance requirements:* For master's, GRE General Test or MAT, appropriate bachelor's degree, letters of reference, educational experience, professional experience. Additional exam requirements/recommendations for international students: Required—TOEFL (minimum score 550 paper-based; 213 computer-based; 79 iBT), IELTS (minimum score 6). *Application deadline:* For fall admission, 7/15 for domestic students, 7/1 for international students; for spring admission, 12/1 for domestic students, 11/13 for international students. Applications are processed on a rolling basis. Application fee: $30 ($40 for international students). Electronic applications accepted. *Expenses:* Tuition, state resident: full-time $3744; part-time $208 per credit hour. Tuition, nonresident: full-time $9540; part-time $530 per credit hour. Required fees: $896; $47 per credit hour. $25 per term. One-time fee: $50. Tuition and fees vary according to course load and program. *Financial support:* In 2009–10, 9 students received support. Career-related internships or fieldwork, scholarships/grants, and unspecified assistantships available. Financial award application deadline: 7/1; financial award applicants required to submit FAFSA. *Unit head:* Dr. Mary Jackson-Pitts, Interim Chair, 870-972-3070, Fax: 870-972-2997, E-mail: mpitts@astate.edu. *Application contact:* Dr. Andrew Sustich, Dean of the Graduate School, 870-972-3029, Fax: 870-972-3857, E-mail: sustich@astate.edu.

Bob Jones University, Graduate Programs, Greenville, SC 29614. Offers accountancy (MS); Bible (MA); Bible translation (MA); Biblical studies (Certificate); broadcast management (MS); business administration (MBA); church history (MA, PhD); church ministries (MA); church music (MM); cinema and video production (MA); counseling (MS); curriculum and instruction (Ed D); divinity (M Div); dramatic production (MA); educational leadership (MS, Ed D, Ed S); elementary education (M Ed, MAT); English (M Ed, MA, MAT); fine arts (MA); graphic design (MA); history (M Ed, MA); illustration (MA); interpretative speech (MA); mathematics (M Ed, MAT); medical missions (Certificate); ministry (MM, D Min); multi-categorical special education (M Ed, MAT); music (M Ed); New Testament interpretation (PhD); Old Testament interpretation (PhD); orchestral instrument performance (MM); organ performance (MM); pastoral studies (MA); personnel services (MS, Ed S); piano pedagogy (MM); piano performance (MM); platform arts (MA); radio and television broadcasting (MS); rhetoric and public address (MA); secondary education (M Ed); studio art (MA); teaching Bible (MA); theology (MA, PhD); voice performance (MM); youth ministries (MA); M Div/MM.

Boston University, College of Communication, Department of Film and Television, Boston, MA 02215. Offers film production (MFA); film studies (MFA); media ventures (MS); screenwriting (MFA); television production (MS); MBA/MS. Part-time programs available. *Faculty:* 13 full-time, 27 part-time/adjunct. *Students:* 108 full-time (49 women), 5 part-time (2 women); includes 11 minority (4 African Americans, 1 American Indian/Alaska Native, 3 Asian Americans or Pacific Islanders, 3 Hispanic Americans), 19 international. Average age 27. In 2009, 16 master's awarded. *Degree requirements:* For master's, thesis. *Entrance requirements:* For master's, GRE General Test, sample of written or creative work. Additional exam requirements/recommendations for international students: Required—TOEFL (minimum score 600 paper-based; 250 computer-based; 100 iBT). *Application deadline:* For fall admission, 2/1 for domestic and international students. Application fee: $70. Electronic applications accepted. *Expenses:* Tuition: Full-time $37,910; part-time $1184 per credit hour. Required fees: $386; $40 per semester. Part-time tuition and fees vary according to class time, course level, degree level and program. *Financial support:* Teaching assistantships with partial tuition reimbursements, career-related internships or fieldwork, Federal Work-Study, institutionally sponsored loans, scholarships/grants, and unspecified assistantships available. Support available to part-time students. Financial award application deadline: 2/1; financial award applicants required to submit FAFSA. *Unit head:* Paul Schneider, Chairman, 617-353-3483, Fax: 617-353-1084, E-mail: ftvchair@bu.edu. *Application contact:* Kate Iserman, Administrator of Graduate Services, 617-353-3481, Fax: 617-358-0399, E-mail: comgrad@bu.edu.

See Close-Up on page 675.

Brooklyn College of the City University of New York, Division of Graduate Studies, Department of Television and Radio, Brooklyn, NY 11210-2889. Offers media studies (MS); television production (MFA). Part-time and evening/weekend programs available. *Students:* 11 full-time (6 women), 40 part-time (11 women); includes 17 minority (10 African Americans, 2 Asian Americans or Pacific Islanders, 5 Hispanic Americans), 17 international. Average age 31. 36 applicants, 86% accepted, 16 enrolled. In 2009, 14 master's awarded. *Degree requirements:* For master's, comprehensive exam. *Entrance requirements:* For master's, GRE General Test or MAT, 12 credits in television/radio with a minimum B average, 2 letters of recommendation. Additional exam requirements/recommendations for international students: Required—TOEFL (minimum score 580 paper-based; 237 computer-based; 92 iBT). *Application deadline:* For fall admission, 3/1 priority date for domestic students, 2/1 priority date for international students; for spring admission, 11/1 priority date for domestic students, 10/1 priority date for international students. Applications are processed on a rolling basis. Application fee: $125. Electronic applications accepted. *Expenses:* Tuition, area resident: Full-time $7360; part-time $310 per credit hour. Tuition, state resident: full-time $7360; part-time $310 per credit hour. Tuition, nonresident: full-time $13,800; part-time $575 per credit hour. International tuition: $13,800 full-time. Required fees: $140.10 per semester. *Financial support:* Career-related internships or fieldwork, Federal Work-Study, and institutionally sponsored loans available. Support available to part-time students. Financial award application deadline: 5/1; financial award applicants required to submit FAFSA. *Faculty research:* Criticism, research methods, audience behavior, policy and regulation, program history, international television and radio. *Unit head:* Dr. Fred Wasser, Chairperson, 718-951-5555, E-mail: fwasser@brooklyn.cuny.edu. *Application contact:* Hernan Sierra, Graduate Admissions Coordinator, 718-951-4536, Fax: 718-951-4506, E-mail: grads@brooklyn.cuny.edu.

California State University, Fullerton, Graduate Studies, College of Communications, Department of Communications, Fullerton, CA 92834-9480. Offers communications—advertising (MA); communications—entertainment and tourism (MA); communications—journalism (MA); communications—public relations (MA). Part-time programs available. *Students:* 18 full-time (14 women), 38 part-time (30 women); includes 21 minority (2 African Americans, 8 Asian Americans or Pacific Islanders, 11 Hispanic Americans), 4 international. Average age 28. 121 applicants, 23% accepted, 17 enrolled. In 2009, 33 master's awarded. *Degree requirements:* For master's, project or thesis. *Entrance requirements:* For master's, GRE General Test. Application fee: $55. *Expenses:* Tuition, nonresident: full-time $11,160; part-time $373 per credit. Required fees: $1440 per term. Tuition and fees vary according to course load, degree level and program. *Financial support:* Teaching assistantships, career-related internships or fieldwork, Federal Work-Study, institutionally sponsored loans, and scholarships/grants available.

Support available to part-time students. Financial award application deadline: 3/1; financial award applicants required to submit FAFSA. *Unit head:* Dr. Tony Fellow, Chair, 657-278-3517. *Application contact:* Coordinator, 657-278-3832.

Carnegie Mellon University, School of Computer Science and College of Fine Arts, Program in Entertainment Technology, Pittsburgh, PA 15213-3891. Offers MET.

Central Michigan University, College of Graduate Studies, College of Communication and Fine Arts, School of Broadcasting and Cinematic Arts, Mount Pleasant, MI 48859. Offers electronic media management (MA); electronic media studies (MA); film theory and criticism (MA); media production (MA). Part-time programs available. *Degree requirements:* For master's, thesis or alternative. *Entrance requirements:* For master's, undergraduate degree in broadcasting, film studies, or an associated discipline with minimum GPA of 2.7. Electronic applications accepted. *Faculty research:* Multimedia production, film history and criticism, writing and promotions, international broadcasting and media systems, history of American broadcasting.

City College of the City University of New York, Graduate School, College of Liberal Arts and Science, Division of the Humanities and Arts, Department of Media Arts Production, New York, NY 10031-9198. Offers MFA. *Entrance requirements:* For master's, videotape portfolio. Additional exam requirements/recommendations for international students: Required—TOEFL (minimum score 575 paper-based; 90 iBT). Electronic applications accepted.

Claremont Graduate University, Graduate Programs, School of Arts and Humanities, Department of Cultural Studies, Claremont, CA 91711-6160. Offers Africana studies (Certificate); cultural studies (MA, PhD); media studies (MA, PhD); museum studies (MA). Part-time programs available. *Faculty:* 3 full-time (2 women). *Students:* 67 full-time (43 women), 8 part-time (6 women); includes 28 minority (14 African Americans, 1 American Indian/Alaska Native, 5 Asian Americans or Pacific Islanders, 8 Hispanic Americans), 7 international. Average age 36. In 2009, 7 master's, 3 doctorates awarded. *Entrance requirements:* For master's and doctorate, GRE General Test. Additional exam requirements/recommendations for international students: Required—TOEFL (minimum score 550 paper-based; 213 computer-based; 80 iBT). *Application deadline:* For fall admission, 2/1 priority date for domestic students. Applications are processed on a rolling basis. Application fee: $60. Electronic applications accepted. *Expenses:* Tuition: Full-time $35,046; part-time $1524 per credit. Required fees: $161 per semester. *Financial support:* Fellowships, research assistantships, Federal Work-Study, institutionally sponsored loans, and scholarships/grants available. Support available to part-time students. Financial award application deadline: 2/15; financial award applicants required to submit FAFSA. *Unit head:* Eve Oishi, Chair, 909-607-7587, E-mail: eve.oishi@cgu.edu. *Application contact:* Susan Hampson, Admissions Coordinator, 909-607-1278, Fax: 909-607-1221, E-mail: humanities@cgu.edu.

College of Staten Island of the City University of New York, Graduate Programs, Program in Cinema and Media Studies, Staten Island, NY 10314-6600. Offers MA. Part-time and evening/weekend programs available. *Faculty:* 3 full-time (2 women). *Students:* 1 full-time (0 women), 18 part-time (7 women); includes 1 minority (African American), 4 international. Average age 28. 31 applicants, 65% accepted, 10 enrolled. In 2009, 7 master's awarded. *Degree requirements:* For master's, comprehensive exam, original film, media or production thesis or written examination. *Entrance requirements:* For master's, 10-12 page critical writing sample on film or media topic, 3 letters of recommendation. Additional exam requirements/recommendations for international students: Required—TOEFL (minimum score 550 paper-based; 213 computer-based; 79 iBT). *Application deadline:* For fall admission, 4/15 priority date for domestic and international students; for spring admission, 11/15 for domestic and international students. Applications are processed on a rolling basis. Application fee: $125. Electronic applications accepted. *Expenses:* Tuition, state resident: full-time $7360; part-time $310 per credit. Tuition, nonresident: part-time $575 per credit. Required fees: $378; $113 per semester. *Financial support:* In 2009–10, 4 teaching assistantships (averaging $1,250 per year) were awarded; career-related internships or fieldwork, Federal Work-Study, and scholarships/grants also available. Support available to part-time students. Financial award applicants required to submit FAFSA. *Unit head:* Dr. Matthew Solomon, Coordinator/Associate Professor, 718-982-2548, E-mail: cinemamasters@mail.csi.cuny.edu. *Application contact:* Sasha Spence, Assistant Director of Graduate Recruitment and Admissions, 718-982-2699, Fax: 718-982-2500, E-mail: sasha.spence@csi.cuny.edu.

Columbia College Chicago, Graduate School, Department of Arts, Entertainment and Media Management, Chicago, IL 60605-1996. Offers arts, entertainment and media management (MA), including media management, music business management, performing arts management, visual arts management. Evening/weekend programs available. *Degree requirements:* For master's, thesis, internship. *Entrance requirements:* For master's, self-assessment essay. Additional exam requirements/recommendations for international students: Required—TOEFL (minimum score 550 paper-based; 213 computer-based). Electronic applications accepted. *Expenses:* Tuition: Part-time $651 per credit hour. Required fees: $651 per credit hour. $205 per semester. One-time fee: $285 part-time. Tuition and fees vary according to program.

Concordia University, School of Graduate Studies, Faculty of Arts and Science, Department of Communication Studies, Montréal, QC H3G 1M8, Canada. Offers communication (PhD); communication studies (Diploma); media studies (MA). *Degree requirements:* For master's, thesis optional; for doctorate, one foreign language, comprehensive exam, thesis/dissertation, research practicum, seminar. *Entrance requirements:* For master's, bachelor's degree in communications, 2 years of media-related experience; for doctorate, MA in communications. *Faculty research:* Communication and development, organizational communication, cultural studies, rhetoric, future studies.

Concordia University, School of Graduate Studies, Faculty of Fine Arts, Department of Studio Arts, Montréal, QC H3G 1M8, Canada. Offers studio arts (MFA), including film production, open media, painting, photography, print media, sculpture, ceramics and fibers. *Degree requirements:* For master's, thesis or alternative. *Entrance requirements:* For master's, portfolio.

Dallas Theological Seminary, Graduate Programs, Dallas, TX 75204-6499. Offers academic ministries (Th M); Bible translation (Th M); biblical and theological studies (CGS); biblical counseling (MA, Th M); biblical exegesis and linguistics (MA); biblical exposition (PhD); biblical studies (MA); Christian education (MA, D Min); cross-cultural ministries (MA, Th M); educational leadership (Th M); evangelism and discipleship (Th M); interdisciplinary studies (Th M); media and communication (MA); media arts in ministry (Th M); ministry (D Min); New Testament studies (Th M, PhD); Old Testament studies (PhD); parachurch ministries (Th M); pastoral ministries (Th M); sacred theology (STM); theological studies (PhD); women's ministry (Th M). *Accreditation:* ATS (one or more programs are accredited). Part-time and evening/weekend programs available. *Degree requirements:* For master's, variable foreign language requirement, thesis (for some programs); for doctorate, 2 foreign languages, thesis/dissertation. *Entrance requirements:* Additional exam requirements/recommendations for international students: Required—TOEFL, TWE. Electronic applications accepted.

DePaul University, College of Communication, Chicago, IL 60614. Offers journalism (MA); media, culture and society (MA); organizational and multicultural communication (MA); public relations and advertising (MA). Part-time and evening/weekend programs available. *Faculty:* 31 full-time (17 women), 15 part-time/adjunct (7 women). *Students:* 159 full-time (127 women), 50 part-time (40 women); includes 56 minority (29 African Americans, 9 Asian Americans or Pacific Islanders, 18 Hispanic Americans), 11 international. Average age 29. 354 applicants, 44% accepted, 79 enrolled. In 2009, 64 master's awarded. *Degree requirements:* For master's, comprehensive exam (for some programs), final exam or thesis/project. *Entrance requirements:* For master's, GRE General Test (public relations and advertising), minimum GPA of 3.0, writing sample, letters of recommendation, resume. Additional exam requirements/recommendations for international students: Required—TOEFL (minimum score 590 paper-based; 243 computer-based; 96 iBT). Application fee: $40. Electronic applications accepted. *Expenses:* Tuition: Full-time $37,525; part-time $620 per credit hour. *Financial support:* In 2009–10, 8 students received support, including 4 research assistantships with partial tuition reimbursements available, 2 teaching assistantships with full tuition reimbursements available (averaging $12,000 per year); fellowships with full tuition reimbursements available, career-related internships or fieldwork, scholarships/grants, and tuition waivers (partial) also available. Support available to part-time students. Financial award applicants required to submit FAFSA. *Faculty research:* Intercultural communication, corporate culture, diversity in the working place, organizational socialization, critical cultural studies. *Unit head:* Dr. Jacqueline Taylor, Dean, 773-325-7216, Fax: 773-325-7584, E-mail: jtaylor@depaul.edu. *Application contact:* Ann Spittle, Director of Graduate Admission, 773-325-7315, Fax: 773-325-2395, E-mail: gradcom@depaul.edu.

Digital Media Arts College, Graduate Programs, Boca Raton, FL 33431. Offers graphic design (MFA); special FX animation (MFA).

Edinboro University of Pennsylvania, School of Graduate Studies and Research, School of Liberal Arts, Department of Communications and Media Studies, Edinboro, PA 16444. Offers MA, Certificate. Part-time and evening/weekend programs available. *Faculty:* 5 full-time (2 women). *Students:* 29 full-time (18 women), 14 part-time (10 women); includes 6 minority (4 African Americans, 1 Asian American or Pacific Islander, 1 Hispanic American). Average age 29. In 2009, 18 master's, 10 other advanced degrees awarded. *Degree requirements:* For master's, thesis or alternative, competency exam. *Entrance requirements:* For master's, GRE or MAT, minimum QPA of 2.5. *Application deadline:* Applications are processed on a rolling basis. Application fee: $30. Electronic applications accepted. *Expenses:* Tuition, state resident: full-time $6666; part-time $370 per credit. Tuition, nonresident: full-time $10,666; part-time $593 per credit. Required fees: $2206.28. One-time fee: $204 part-time. *Financial support:* In 2009–10, 13 research assistantships with full and partial tuition reimbursements (averaging $4,050 per year) were awarded; career-related internships or fieldwork, Federal Work-Study, scholarships/grants, and unspecified assistantships also available. Support available to part-time students. Financial award application deadline: 2/15; financial award applicants required to submit FAFSA. *Unit head:* Dr. Andrew Smith, Program Head, 814-732-2165, E-mail: arsmith@edinboro.edu. *Application contact:* Dr. Andrew Smith, Program Head, 814-732-2165, E-mail: arsmith@edinboro.edu.

Emerson College, Graduate Studies, School of the Arts, Department of Visual and Media Arts, Program in Media Art, Boston, MA 02116-4624. Offers MFA. *Faculty:* 42 full-time (15 women), 18 part-time/adjunct (8 women). *Students:* 67 full-time (33 women), 33 part-time (15 women); includes 12 minority (5 African Americans, 3 Asian Americans or Pacific Islanders, 4 Hispanic Americans), 13 international. Average age 25. 109 applicants, 59% accepted, 36 enrolled. In 2009, 50 master's awarded. *Entrance requirements:* For master's, creative portfolio. Additional exam requirements/recommendations for international students: Required—TOEFL (minimum score 550 paper-based; 213 computer-based; 80 iBT), IELTS (minimum score 6.5). *Application deadline:* For fall admission, 3/1 for domestic and international students. Applications are processed on a rolling basis. Application fee: $60 ($75 for international students). Electronic applications accepted. *Expenses:* Tuition: Full-time $22,056; part-time $919 per credit. Required fees: $120; $120 per year. One-time fee: $170 full-time. *Financial support:* In 2009–10, 19 students received support, including 9 fellowships with partial tuition reimbursements available (averaging $22,056 per year), 8 research assistantships with partial tuition reimbursements available (averaging $10,000 per year); Federal Work-Study, scholarships/grants, and unspecified assistantships also available. Financial award application deadline: 1/5; financial award applicants required to submit FAFSA. *Faculty research:* Media studies. *Unit head:* Prof. Jan Roberts-Breslin, Graduate Program Director, 617-824-8800, E-mail: jan_roberts_breslin@emerson.edu. *Application contact:* Office of Graduate Admission, 617-824-8610, Fax: 617-824-8614, E-mail: gradapp@emerson.edu.

Fairleigh Dickinson University, Metropolitan Campus, University College: Arts, Sciences, and Professional Studies, School of Art and Media Studies, Program in Media and Communications, Teaneck, NJ 07666-1914. Offers MA. *Students:* 15 full-time (12 women), 11 part-time (7 women), 5 international. Average age 28. 16 applicants, 81% accepted, 8 enrolled. In 2009, 7 master's awarded. Application fee: $40. *Application contact:* Susan Brooman, University Director of Graduate Admissions, 201-692-2554, Fax: 201-692-2560, E-mail: globaleducation@fdu.edu.

Florida State University, The Graduate School, College of Communication and Information, School of Communication, Tallahassee, FL 32306. Offers corporate and public communication (MA, MS); integrated marketing communication (MA, MS); mass communication (PhD); media and communication studies (MA, MS); speech communication (PhD). Part-time programs available. *Faculty:* 24 full-time (9 women), 6 part-time/adjunct (1 woman). *Students:* 153 full-time (110 women), 65 part-time (34 women); includes 62 minority (37 African Americans, 1 American Indian/Alaska Native, 24 Hispanic Americans). Average age 24. 230 applicants, 76% accepted, 85 enrolled. In 2009, 84 master's, 6 doctorates awarded. *Degree requirements:* For master's, thesis (for some programs); for doctorate, comprehensive exam, thesis/dissertation. *Entrance requirements:* For master's, GRE General Test, minimum GPA of 3.0; for doctorate, GRE General Test, minimum GPA of 3.3 in graduate course work. Additional exam requirements/recommendations for international students: Required—TOEFL (minimum score 600 paper-based; 250 computer-based; 100 iBT). *Application deadline:* For fall admission, 7/1 priority date for domestic students, 5/1 priority date for international students; for spring admission, 11/1 priority date for domestic and international students. Applications are processed on a rolling basis. Application fee: $30. Electronic applications accepted. *Expenses:* Tuition, state resident: full-time $7413. Tuition, nonresident: full-time $22,567. *Financial support:* In 2009–10, 52 students received support, including 1 fellowship with full tuition reimbursement available, 8 research assistantships with full tuition reimbursements available (averaging $14,000 per year), 40 teaching assistantships with full tuition reimbursements available (averaging $5,000 per year); career-related internships or fieldwork, Federal Work-Study, institutionally sponsored loans, scholarships/grants, tuition waivers (partial), and unspecified assistantships also available. Support available to part-time students. Financial award application deadline: 2/1; financial award applicants required to submit FAFSA. *Faculty research:* Communication technology and policy, marketing communication, communication content and effect, new communication/information technologies. Total annual research expenditures: $600,000. *Unit head:* Dr. Stephen D. McDowell, Director, 850-644-2276, Fax: 850-644-8642, E-mail: steve.mcdowell@cci.fsu.edu. *Application contact:* Natashia Hinson-Turner, Graduate Coordinator, 850-644-8746, Fax: 850-644-8642, E-mail: natashia.turner@cci.fsu.edu.

Fordham University, Graduate School of Business Administration, New York, NY 10023. Offers accounting (MBA); communications and media management (MBA); executive business administration (EMBA); finance (MBA, MS); information systems (MBA, MS); management systems (MBA); marketing (MBA); media management (MS); taxation (MS); taxation and accounting (MTA);); JD/MBA; MBA/MIM; MS/MBA. *Accreditation:* AACSB. Part-time and evening/weekend programs available. *Entrance requirements:* For master's, GMAT, 2 letters of recommendation, resume. Additional exam requirements/recommendations for international students: Required—TOEFL (minimum score 600 paper-based; 250 computer-based; 100 iBT). Electronic applications accepted. *Expenses:* Contact institution.

Full Sail University, Media Design Master of Fine Arts Program—Online, Winter Park, FL 32792-7437. Offers MFA. Postbaccalaureate distance learning degree programs offered.

Georgetown University, Graduate School of Arts and Sciences, School of Continuing Studies, Washington, DC 20057. Offers American studies (MALS); Catholic studies (MALS); classical civilizations (MALS); ethics and the professions (MALS); human resources management (MPS); humanities (MALS); individualized study (MALS); international affairs (MALS); Islam and Muslim-Christian relations (MALS); journalism (MPS); liberal studies (DLS); literature and society (MALS); medieval and early modern European studies (MALS); public relations (MPS); real estate (MPS); religious studies (MALS); social and public policy (MALS); sports industry management (MPS); the theory and practice of American democracy (MALS); visual culture

Media Studies

Georgetown University (continued)
(MALS). *Entrance requirements:* Additional exam requirements/recommendations for international students: Required—TOEFL.

Governors State University, College of Arts and Sciences, Program in Communication and Training, University Park, IL 60466-0975. Offers communication studies (MA); instructional and training technology (MA); media communication (MA). Part-time and evening/weekend programs available. *Degree requirements:* For master's, thesis or alternative.

Howard University, School of Communications, Division of Mass Communication and Media Studies, Washington, DC 20059-0002. Offers mass communication (MA, PhD); media studies (MA, PhD). *Accreditation:* ACEJMC. Part-time and evening/weekend programs available. *Degree requirements:* For master's, comprehensive exam (for some programs), thesis optional; for doctorate, one foreign language, comprehensive exam, thesis/dissertation. *Entrance requirements:* For master's, GRE, minimum GPA of 3.0; for doctorate, GRE, minimum graduate GPA of 3.5. Additional exam requirements/recommendations for international students: Required—TOEFL. Electronic applications accepted. *Faculty research:* Advertising, public relations, journalism new media.

Hunter College of the City University of New York, Graduate School, School of Arts and Sciences, Department of Film and Media Studies, Program in Integrated Media Arts, New York, NY 10021-5085. Offers MA, MFA. Part-time and evening/weekend programs available. *Faculty:* 7 full-time (1 woman), 3 part-time/adjunct (2 women). *Students:* 13 full-time (11 women), 56 part-time (36 women); includes 8 minority (2 African Americans, 3 Asian Americans or Pacific Islanders, 3 Hispanic Americans). Average age 33. 88 applicants, 35% accepted, 22 enrolled. In 2009, 16 master's awarded. *Entrance requirements:* For master's, GRE General Test, 3 letters of recommendation, portfolio of media works, minimum GPA of 3.0. Additional exam requirements/recommendations for international students: Required—TOEFL, TWE. *Application deadline:* For fall admission, 2/1 for domestic students. Application fee: $125. *Expenses:* Tuition, state resident: full-time $7360; part-time $310 per credit. Required fees: $250 per semester. *Financial support:* Federal Work-Study and tuition waivers (partial) available. Support available to part-time students. *Faculty research:* Nonfiction production, Internet as medium, public interest journalism, social and historical roots of media arts. *Unit head:* Kelly Anderson, Deputy Chair, 212-772-6008. *Application contact:* Mary Flanagan, New Media Advisor, 212-650-3219, E-mail: maryflanagan@hunter.cuny.edu.

Indiana State University, School of Graduate Studies, College of Arts and Sciences, Department of Communication, Terre Haute, IN 47809. Offers communication studies (MA, MS); radio, television and film (MA, MS). Part-time programs available. *Degree requirements:* For master's, thesis (for some programs), oral and written exam. *Entrance requirements:* For master's, GRE General Test. Additional exam requirements/recommendations for international students: Required—TOEFL. *Faculty research:* Women in media, communication apprehension, media history.

Indiana University Bloomington, University Graduate School, College of Arts and Sciences, Department of Communication and Culture, Bloomington, IN 47405-7000. Offers film and media studies (PhD); performance and ethnography (PhD); rhetoric and public culture (PhD). *Faculty:* 24 full-time (12 women). *Students:* 85 full-time (43 women), 1 (woman) part-time; includes 9 minority (1 African American, 1 Asian American or Pacific Islander, 7 Hispanic Americans), 9 international. Average age 32. 179 applicants, 15% accepted, 15 enrolled. In 2009, 5 master's, 11 doctorates awarded. *Degree requirements:* For master's, comprehensive exam; for doctorate, one foreign language, comprehensive exam, thesis/dissertation, student teaching. *Entrance requirements:* For master's and doctorate, GRE General Test (recommended), minimum GPA of 3.0, 3 letters of recommendation, writing sample. Additional exam requirements/recommendations for international students: Required—TOEFL (minimum score 550 paper-based; 213 computer-based). *Application deadline:* For winter admission, 1/1 for domestic students, 12/1 for international students. Application fee: $55 ($65 for international students). Electronic applications accepted. *Financial support:* In 2009–10, 65 students received support, including 4 fellowships with full tuition reimbursements available (averaging $18,000 per year), 61 teaching assistantships with full tuition reimbursements available (averaging $12,961 per year). Financial award application deadline: 4/15. *Faculty research:* Rhetoric and public culture, film and media studies, performance ethnography. *Unit head:* Prof. Gregory A. Waller, Chair, 812-855-2367, Fax: 812-855-6014, E-mail: cmcl@indiana.edu. *Application contact:* Kathy P. Teige, Graduate Secretary, 812-855-6389, Fax: 812-855-6014, E-mail: kteige@indiana.edu.

Indiana University of Pennsylvania, School of Graduate Studies and Research, College of Education and Educational Technology, Department of Communications Media, Indiana, PA 15705-1087. Offers adult education and communications technology (MA); communications media and instructional technology (PhD). *Faculty:* 8 full-time (1 woman). *Students:* 16 full-time (7 women), 24 part-time (13 women); includes 3 minority (2 African Americans, 1 Asian American or Pacific Islander), 2 international. Average age 35. 40 applicants, 53% accepted, 20 enrolled.Application fee: $40. *Expenses:* Tuition, state resident: full-time $6666; part-time $370 per credit hour. Tuition, nonresident: full-time $10,666; part-time $593 per credit hour. Required fees: $813 per semester. *Financial support:* In 2009–10, 4 fellowships (averaging $1,000 per year), 8 research assistantships (averaging $5,936 per year), 3 teaching assistantships (averaging $21,536 per year) were awarded. *Unit head:* Dr. Mark Piwinsky, Chairperson, 724-357-3954, Fax: 724-357-5503, E-mail: mark.piwinsky@iup.edu. *Application contact:* Dr. Edward Nardi, Associate Dean, 724-357-2480, Fax: 724-357-5595, E-mail: ewnardi@iup.edu.

International University in Geneva, Master of Arts in Media and Communication Program, Geneva, Switzerland. Offers luxury management (MA); marketing (MA). *Degree requirements:* For master's, comprehensive exam. *Entrance requirements:* Additional exam requirements/recommendations for international students: Required—TOEFL. Electronic applications accepted.

Kutztown University of Pennsylvania, College of Liberal Arts and Sciences, Program in Electronic Media, Kutztown, PA 19530-0730. Offers MS. Part-time and evening/weekend programs available. *Faculty:* 4 full-time (2 women). *Students:* 8 full-time (4 women), 5 part-time (1 woman), 1 international. Average age 25. 14 applicants, 71% accepted, 6 enrolled. In 2009, 3 master's awarded. *Degree requirements:* For master's, thesis. *Entrance requirements:* For master's, GRE General Test. Additional exam requirements/recommendations for international students: Required—TOEFL. *Application deadline:* For fall admission, 8/15 priority date for domestic and international students; for spring admission, 12/15 priority date for domestic and international students. Applications are processed on a rolling basis. Application fee: $35. Electronic applications accepted. *Expenses:* Tuition, state resident: full-time $6666; part-time $370 per credit. Tuition, nonresident: full-time $10,666; part-time $593 per credit. Required fees: $62 per credit. $60 per semester. *Financial support:* Career-related internships or fieldwork, Federal Work-Study, scholarships/grants, and unspecified assistantships available. Financial award application deadline: 3/1; financial award applicants required to submit FAFSA. *Unit head:* Dr. Joseph Chuk, Chairperson, 610-683-4492, Fax: 610-683-4659, E-mail: chuk@kutztown.edu. *Application contact:* Kelly D. Burr, Associate Director, Graduate Admissions, 610-683-4200, Fax: 610-683-1393, E-mail: graduate@kutztown.edu.

Louisiana State University and Agricultural and Mechanical College, Graduate School, Manship School of Mass Communication, Baton Rouge, LA 70803. Offers MMC, PhD. *Accreditation:* ACEJMC. Part-time programs available. Postbaccalaureate distance learning degree programs offered (minimal on-campus study). *Faculty:* 25 full-time (11 women). *Students:* 54 full-time (36 women), 19 part-time (15 women); includes 16 minority (12 African Americans, 2 American Indian/Alaska Native, 2 Hispanic Americans), 8 international. Average age 31. 107 applicants, 40% accepted, 26 enrolled. In 2009, 11 master's, 4 doctorates awarded. *Degree requirements:* For master's, thesis; for doctorate, thesis/dissertation. *Entrance requirements:* For master's, GRE General Test, minimum GPA of 3.0. Additional exam requirements/recommendations for international students: Required—TOEFL (minimum score 550 paper-based; 213 computer-based; 79 iBT) or IELTS (minimum score 6.5). *Application deadline:* For fall admission, 1/25 priority date for domestic students, 5/15 for international students; for spring admission, 10/15 for international students. Applications are processed on a rolling basis. Application fee: $50 ($70 for international students). Electronic applications accepted. *Financial support:* In 2009–10, 55 students received support, including 2 fellowships (averaging $29,476 per year), 32 research assistantships with full and partial tuition reimbursements available (averaging $15,234 per year), 7 teaching assistantships with full and partial tuition reimbursements available (averaging $16,671 per year); career-related internships or fieldwork, Federal Work-Study, institutionally sponsored loans, scholarships/grants, health care benefits, tuition waivers (full and partial), and unspecified assistantships also available. Support available to part-time students. Financial award application deadline: 3/1; financial award applicants required to submit FAFSA. *Faculty research:* Media effects, political communication, new media technologies, persuasive communication, journalism processes and practice. Total annual research expenditures: $38,772. *Unit head:* Dr. John Maxwell Hamilton, Dean, 225-578-2002, Fax: 225-578-2125, E-mail: jhamilt@lsu.edu. *Application contact:* Dr. Amy L. Reynolds, Associate Dean of Graduate Studies and Research, 225-578-9294, Fax: 225-578-2125, E-mail: defleur@lsu.edu.

Lynn University, College of Business and Management, Boca Raton, FL 33431-5598. Offers aviation management (MBA); financial valuation and investment management (MBA); hospitality management (MBA); international business (MBA); marketing (MBA); mass communication and media management (MBA); sports and athletics administration (MBA). Part-time and evening/weekend programs available. Postbaccalaureate distance learning degree programs offered. *Degree requirements:* For master's, project. *Entrance requirements:* For master's, GMAT or GRE, minimum undergraduate GPA of 3.0, resume, 2 letters of recommendation. Additional exam requirements/recommendations for international students: Required—TOEFL (minimum score 550 paper-based; 213 computer-based). *Application deadline:* Applications are processed on a rolling basis. Application fee: $50. Electronic applications accepted. *Expenses:* Tuition: Part-time $580 per credit. One-time fee: $200 part-time. Part-time tuition and fees vary according to degree level. *Financial support:* Career-related internships or fieldwork, Federal Work-Study, institutionally sponsored loans, scholarships/grants, tuition waivers (full and partial), and unspecified assistantships available. Support available to part-time students. Financial award application deadline: 8/1; financial award applicants required to submit FAFSA. *Faculty research:* Labor relations, dynamic balance in leisure-time skills, ethics in athletics, hotel development. *Unit head:* Dr. Ralph Norcio, Associate Dean, 561-237-7010, Fax: 561-237-7014, E-mail: rnorcio@lynn.edu. *Application contact:* Dr. Larissa Baia, Assistant Director of Graduate Admissions, 561-237-7916, Fax: 561-237-7100, E-mail: admissionpm@lynn.edu.

Lynn University, Eugene M. and Christine E. Lynn College of International Communication, Boca Raton, FL 33431-5598. Offers communication and media (MS). Part-time and evening/weekend programs available. *Entrance requirements:* For master's, GRE, resume, 2 letters of recommendation, minimum GPA of 3.0. Additional exam requirements/recommendations for international students: Required—TOEFL (minimum score 550 paper-based; 213 computer-based). Application fee: $50. *Expenses:* Tuition: Part-time $580 per credit. One-time fee: $200 part-time. Part-time tuition and fees vary according to degree level. *Financial support:* Career-related internships or fieldwork, Federal Work-Study, institutionally sponsored loans, scholarships/grants, tuition waivers (partial), and unspecified assistantships available. Support available to part-time students. Financial award application deadline: 8/1; financial award applicants required to submit FAFSA. *Unit head:* Dr. David L. Jaffe, Dean, 561-237-7099, Fax: 561-237-7097, E-mail: djaffe@lynn.edu. *Application contact:* Dr. Larissa Baia, Assistant Director of Graduate Admissions, 561-237-7916, Fax: 561-237-7100, E-mail: admissionpm@lynn.edu.

Marquette University, Graduate School, College of Communication, Milwaukee, WI 53201-1881. Offers advertising and public relations (MA); broadcasting and electronic communications (MA); communications studies (MA); journalism (MA); mass communications (MA); religious communications (MA); science, health and environmental communications (MA). *Accreditation:* ACEJMC. Part-time and evening/weekend programs available. *Faculty:* 31 full-time (17 women), 35 part-time/adjunct (16 women). *Students:* 28 full-time (21 women), 30 part-time (24 women); includes 3 minority (1 African American, 2 American Indian/Alaska Native), 7 international. Average age 26. 81 applicants, 47% accepted, 22 enrolled. In 2009, 17 master's awarded. *Degree requirements:* For master's, comprehensive exam. *Entrance requirements:* For master's, GRE. Additional exam requirements/recommendations for international students: Required—TOEFL. Application fee: $40. *Financial support:* In 2009–10, 6 research assistantships, 12 teaching assistantships were awarded; career-related internships or fieldwork, Federal Work-Study, institutionally sponsored loans, scholarships/grants, and tuition waivers (full and partial) also available. Support available to part-time students. Financial award application deadline: 2/15. *Faculty research:* Urban journalism, gender and communication, intercultural communication, religious communication. *Unit head:* Dr. Ana Garner, Dean, 414-288-3588, Fax: 414-288-1578. *Application contact:* Erin Fox, Assistant Director for Recruitment, 414-288-5319, Fax: 414-288-1902, E-mail: erin.fox@marquette.edu.

Marywood University, Academic Affairs, Insalaco College of Creative and Performing Arts, Department of Communication Arts, Program in Communication Arts, Scranton, PA 18509-1598. Offers interdisciplinary (MA); media management (MA); production (MA). *Students:* 12 full-time (7 women), 25 part-time (13 women); includes 5 minority (2 African Americans, 1 Asian American or Pacific Islander, 2 Hispanic Americans). Average age 33. In 2009, 11 master's awarded. *Entrance requirements:* Additional exam requirements/recommendations for international students: Required—TOEFL (minimum score 550 paper-based; 213 computer-based; 79 iBT). *Application deadline:* For fall admission, 4/1 for domestic students, 3/31 for international students; for spring admission, 11/1 for domestic students, 8/31 for international students. Applications are processed on a rolling basis. Application fee: $35. Electronic applications accepted. *Expenses:* Tuition: Part-time $715 per credit. Required fees: $270 per semester. Tuition and fees vary according to degree level, campus/location and program. *Financial support:* Career-related internships or fieldwork, scholarships/grants, and unspecified assistantships available. Support available to part-time students. Financial award application deadline: 6/30; financial award applicants required to submit FAFSA. *Application contact:* Tammy Manka, Assistant Director of Admissions, 866-279-9663, E-mail: tmanka@marywood.edu.

Massachusetts Institute of Technology, School of Architecture and Planning, Program in Media Arts and Sciences, Cambridge, MA 02139-4307. Offers media arts and sciences (SM, PhD); media technology (SM). *Faculty:* 20 full-time (4 women). *Students:* 138 full-time (26 women), 1 part-time (0 women); includes 17 minority (3 African Americans, 2 American Indian/Alaska Native, 11 Asian Americans or Pacific Islanders, 1 Hispanic American), 42 international. Average age 29. 595 applicants, 9% accepted, 44 enrolled. In 2009, 27 master's, 5 doctorates awarded. Terminal master's awarded for partial completion of doctoral program. *Degree requirements:* For master's, thesis; for doctorate, comprehensive exam, thesis/dissertation. *Entrance requirements:* Additional exam requirements/recommendations for international students: Required—TOEFL (minimum score 600 paper-based; 250 computer-based; 100 iBT), or IELTS (minimum score 7). *Application deadline:* For fall admission, 12/15 for domestic and international students. Application fee: $75. Electronic applications accepted. *Expenses:* Tuition: Full-time $37,510; part-time $585 per unit. Required fees: $272. *Financial support:* In 2009–10, 138 students received support, including 4 fellowships with tuition reimbursements available (averaging $24,071 per year), 132 research assistantships with tuition reimbursements available (averaging $29,098 per year); Federal Work-Study, institutionally sponsored loans, scholarships/grants, health care benefits, and unspecified assistantships also available. *Faculty research:* Human machine interaction, communications technologies, new media technologies, physical computing, learning and creativity. Total annual research expenditures: $16.6 million. *Unit head:* Prof. Mitchel J. Resnick, Department Head, 617-253-5114, Fax: 617-253-8542, E-mail: mas-info@media.mit.edu. *Application contact:* Graduate Admissions, 617-253-5114, Fax: 617-253-8542.

Massachusetts Institute of Technology, School of Humanities, Arts, and Social Sciences, Program in Comparative Media Studies, Cambridge, MA 02139-4307. Offers SM. *Faculty:* 15

full-time (5 women). *Students:* 12 full-time (9 women); includes 1 minority (Asian American or Pacific Islander), 1 international. Average age 28. In 2009, 9 master's awarded. *Degree requirements:* For master's, thesis. Application fee: $75. Electronic applications accepted. *Expenses:* Tuition: Full-time $37,510; part-time $585 per unit. Required fees: $272. *Financial support:* In 2009–10, 11 students received support, including 10 research assistantships with tuition reimbursements available (averaging $27,000 per year); fellowships with tuition reimbursements available, Federal Work-Study, institutionally sponsored loans, scholarships/grants, health care benefits, and unspecified assistantships also available. *Faculty research:* Game design and games and education, new media literacies, civic media, media history, digital humanities. Total annual research expenditures: $3.7 million. *Unit head:* Prof. William Uricchio, Director, 617-253-3599, Fax: 617-258-5133, E-mail: cms@mit.edu. *Application contact:* Graduate Admissions, 617-253-3599, Fax: 617-258-5133, E-mail: cms-admissions@mit.edu.

Metropolitan College of New York, Program in Media Management, New York, NY 10013. Offers MBA. Evening/weekend programs available. *Degree requirements:* For master's, thesis, 10 day study abroad. *Entrance requirements:* For master's, GMAT or GRE General Test, appropriate work experience, interview, minimum GPA of 2.7. Additional exam requirements/recommendations for international students: Required—TOEFL (minimum score 600 paper-based; 220 computer-based). Electronic applications accepted. *Expenses:* Contact institution.

Michigan State University, The Graduate School, College of Communication Arts and Sciences, Department of Telecommunication, Information Studies, and Media, East Lansing, MI 48824. Offers digital media arts and technology (MA); information and telecommunication management (MA); information, policy and society (MA); serious game design (MA). *Faculty:* 15 full-time (3 women). *Students:* 35 full-time (10 women), 28 part-time (6 women); includes 8 minority (4 African Americans, 3 Asian Americans or Pacific Islanders, 1 Hispanic American), 18 international. Average age 29. 57 applicants, 56% accepted. In 2009, 13 degrees awarded. *Entrance requirements:* Additional exam requirements/recommendations for international students: Required—TOEFL. Electronic applications accepted. *Financial support:* In 2009–10, 1 research assistantship with tuition reimbursement (averaging $13,239 per year), 5 teaching assistantships with tuition reimbursements (averaging $11,902 per year) were awarded. Total annual research expenditures: $741,489. *Unit head:* Dr. Charles Steinfield, Chairperson, 517-355-8372, Fax: 517-355-1292, E-mail: steinfie@msu.edu. *Application contact:* Rachel Iseler, Academic Programs Coordinator, 517-432-3676, Fax: 517-355-1292, E-mail: tism@msu.edu.

Michigan State University, The Graduate School, College of Communication Arts and Sciences, Program in Communication Arts and Sciences–Media and Information Studies, East Lansing, MI 48824. Offers PhD. *Students:* 53 full-time (33 women), 7 part-time (2 women); includes 5 minority (2 African Americans, 1 Asian American or Pacific Islander, 2 Hispanic Americans), 35 international. Average age 34. 64 applicants, 27% accepted. In 2009, 11 doctorates awarded. *Entrance requirements:* Additional exam requirements/recommendations for international students: Required—TOEFL. Electronic applications accepted. *Expenses:* Tuition, state resident: part-time $478.25 per credit hour. Tuition, nonresident: part-time $966.50 per credit hour. Part-time tuition and fees vary according to program. *Financial support:* In 2009–10, 23 research assistantships with tuition reimbursements (averaging $6,545 per year), 15 teaching assistantships with tuition reimbursements (averaging $6,977 per year) were awarded. *Faculty research:* Mass media, comparative media. *Unit head:* Dr. Stephen Lacy, Graduate Director, 517-432-1332, Fax: 517-432-1244, E-mail: slacy@msu.edu. *Application contact:* Nancy Ashley, Academic Program Coordinator, 517-432-1526, Fax: 517-432-1244, E-mail: ashleyn@msu.edu.

National University, Academic Affairs, School of Media and Communication, Department of Media, La Jolla, CA 92037-1011. Offers digital cinema (MFA); educational and instructional technology (MS); video game production and design (MFA). Part-time and evening/weekend programs available. Postbaccalaureate distance learning degree programs offered (no on-campus study). *Faculty:* 9 full-time (4 women), 13 part-time/adjunct (4 women). *Students:* 68 full-time (26 women), 118 part-time (45 women); includes 64 minority (29 African Americans, 10 Asian Americans or Pacific Islanders, 25 Hispanic Americans), 1 international. Average age 39. 118 applicants, 100% accepted, 70 enrolled. In 2009, 58 master's awarded. *Degree requirements:* For master's, thesis. *Entrance requirements:* For master's, interview, minimum GPA of 2.5. Additional exam requirements/recommendations for international students: Required—TOEFL (minimum score 550 paper-based; 213 computer-based; 79 iBT), IELTS (minimum score 6). *Application deadline:* Applications are processed on a rolling basis. Application fee: $60 ($65 for international students). Electronic applications accepted. *Expenses:* Tuition: Part-time $338 per quarter hour. *Financial support:* Career-related internships or fieldwork, institutionally sponsored loans, scholarships/grants, and tuition waivers (partial) available. Support available to part-time students. Financial award application deadline: 6/30; financial award applicants required to submit FAFSA. *Unit head:* Dr. Timothy Langdell, Department Chair, 310-662-2149, Fax: 858-309-3450, E-mail: tlangdell@nu.edu. *Application contact:* Dominick Giovanniello, Associate Regional Dean—San Diego, 800-NAT-UNIV, Fax: 858-541-7792, E-mail: dgiovann@nu.edu.

New Mexico Highlands University, Graduate Studies, College of Arts and Sciences, Program in Media Arts and Computer Science, Las Vegas, NM 87701. Offers media arts and computer science (MS). *Degree requirements:* For master's, comprehensive exam, thesis. *Entrance requirements:* For master's, minimum undergraduate GPA of 3.0. Additional exam requirements/recommendations for international students: Required—TOEFL (minimum score 540 paper-based; 270 computer-based). *Faculty research:* Advanced digital compositing, photographic installations and exhibition design, pattern recognition, parallel and distributed computing, computer security education.

The New School: A University, The New School for General Studies, Program in Media Studies, New York, NY 10011. Offers documentary media studies (Graduate Certificate); media management (Graduate Certificate); media studies (MA). Part-time and evening/weekend programs available. Postbaccalaureate distance learning degree programs offered (no on-campus study). *Faculty:* 22 full-time (10 women). *Students:* 244 full-time (158 women), 270 part-time (180 women); includes 115 minority (41 African Americans, 2 American Indian/Alaska Native, 26 Asian Americans or Pacific Islanders, 46 Hispanic Americans), 71 international. Average age 30. 451 applicants, 74% accepted, 153 enrolled. In 2009, 137 master's, 64 other advanced degrees awarded. *Degree requirements:* For master's, thesis optional. *Entrance requirements:* For master's, interview. Additional exam requirements/recommendations for international students: Required—TOEFL (minimum score 600 paper-based; 250 computer-based; 100 iBT). *Application deadline:* For fall admission, 2/15 priority date for domestic students, 2/15 for international students; for spring admission, 10/15 for domestic and international students. Applications are processed on a rolling basis. Application fee: $50. Electronic applications accepted. *Financial support:* Research assistantships, teaching assistantships, Federal Work-Study, scholarships/grants, tuition waivers (partial), and unspecified assistantships available. Support available to part-time students. Financial award application deadline: 3/1; financial award applicants required to submit FAFSA. *Faculty research:* Effect of technology on society, effect of U. S. media on international affairs, effect of media on corporate affairs. *Unit head:* Dr. Peter L. Haratonik, Interim Chair, Media Studies and Film, 212-229-8903, Fax: 212-465-0661, E-mail: haraton@newschool.edu. *Application contact:* Robert MacDonald, Director of Admissions, 212-229-5630, Fax: 212-989-3887, E-mail: macdonar@newschool.edu.

New York University, Graduate School of Arts and Science, Department of Anthropology, Program in Culture and Media, New York, NY 10012-1019. Offers MA/Advanced Certificate, PhD/Advanced Certificate. Awarded with MA or PhD in anthropology. *Faculty:* 1 (woman) full-time. *Students:* 7 full-time (6 women), 1 international. Average age 31. 43 applicants, 2% accepted, 1 enrolled. *Entrance requirements:* Additional exam requirements/recommendations for international students: Required—TOEFL. *Application deadline:* For fall admission, 1/4 priority date for domestic students. Application fee: $90. *Expenses:* Tuition: Full-time $30,528; part-time $1272 per credit. Required fees: $2177. *Financial support:* Fellowships, research assistantships, teaching assistantships, career-related internships or fieldwork, institutionally sponsored loans, scholarships/grants, health care benefits, and unspecified assistantships available. Financial award application deadline: 1/4. *Faculty research:* Critical history of ethnographic film, ethnography of media, indigenous media, politics of reproduction and disability, social movements. *Unit head:* Faye Ginsburg, Director, 212-998-8558, Fax: 212-995-4014, E-mail: anthropology@nyu.edu. *Application contact:* Susan Carol-Rogers, Director of Graduate Studies, 212-998-8550, Fax: 212-995-4014, E-mail: anthropology@nyu.edu.

New York University, Steinhardt School of Culture, Education, and Human Development, Department of Media, Culture and Communication, New York, NY 10012-1019. Offers media, culture, and communication (MA, PhD). Part-time programs available. *Faculty:* 22 full-time (9 women), 43 part-time/adjunct (22 women). *Students:* 84 full-time (62 women), 42 part-time (24 women); includes 13 minority (7 African Americans, 5 Asian Americans or Pacific Islanders, 1 Hispanic American), 46 international. Average age 33. 289 applicants, 44% accepted, 52 enrolled. In 2009, 45 master's, 5 doctorates awarded. Terminal master's awarded for partial completion of doctoral program. *Degree requirements:* For master's, thesis (for some programs); for doctorate, thesis/dissertation. *Entrance requirements:* For doctorate, GRE General Test, interview. Additional exam requirements/recommendations for international students: Required—TOEFL. *Application deadline:* For fall admission, 12/15 priority date for domestic and international students; for spring admission, 11/1 for domestic and international students. Applications are processed on a rolling basis. Application fee: $75. Electronic applications accepted. *Expenses:* Tuition: Full-time $30,528; part-time $1272 per credit. Required fees: $2177. *Financial support:* Fellowships with full and partial tuition reimbursements, teaching assistantships with full and partial tuition reimbursements, career-related internships or fieldwork, Federal Work-Study, institutionally sponsored loans, scholarships/grants, tuition waivers (partial), and unspecified assistantships available. Support available to part-time students. Financial award application deadline: 2/1; financial award applicants required to submit FAFSA. *Faculty research:* Digital media and new technologies, media criticism, flow of media and culture transnationally and transculturally. *Unit head:* Dr. Marita Sturken, Chairperson, 212-992-9424, Fax: 212-995-4046, E-mail: marita.sturken@nyu.edu. *Application contact:* 212-998-5030, Fax: 212-995-4328, E-mail: steinhardt.gradadmissions@nyu.edu.

Norfolk State University, School of Graduate Studies, School of Liberal Arts, Department of Media and Communication, Norfolk, VA 23504. Offers MA. Part-time programs available. *Degree requirements:* For master's, thesis. *Entrance requirements:* For master's, GRE, minimum GPA of 2.5, letters of recommendation. Additional exam requirements/recommendations for international students: Required—TOEFL.

Northeastern University, College of Arts, Media and Design, Department of Communication Studies, Boston, MA 02115-5096. Offers communication, media, and cultural studies (MA). *Faculty:* 25 full-time (10 women), 6 part-time/adjunct (3 women). *Students:* 5 full-time (all women); includes 1 minority (African American), 1 international. 59 applicants, 42% accepted, 4 enrolled. In 2009, 3 master's awarded. *Degree requirements:* For master's, thesis (for some programs). *Entrance requirements:* For master's, GRE. Additional exam requirements/recommendations for international students: Required—TOEFL or IELTS. *Application deadline:* For fall admission, 2/1 priority date for domestic and international students. Applications are processed on a rolling basis. Application fee: $50. Electronic applications accepted. *Financial support:* Federal Work-Study and scholarships/grants available. *Unit head:* Dr. Joanne Morreale, Graduate Coordinator, 617-373-2506, E-mail: j.morreale@neu.edu. *Application contact:* Jo-Anne Dickinson, Admissions Contact, 617-373-5990, Fax: 617-373-7281, E-mail: gsas@neu.edu.

Northern Kentucky University, Office of Graduate Programs, College of Informatics, Program in Communication, Highland Heights, KY 41099. Offers communication (MA); communication teaching (Certificate); documentary studies (Certificate); public relations (Certificate); relationships (Certificate). Part-time and evening/weekend programs available. *Students:* 9 full-time (8 women), 42 part-time (32 women); includes 5 minority (4 African Americans, 1 Asian American or Pacific Islander), 1 international. Average age 31. 48 applicants, 63% accepted, 23 enrolled. In 2009, 20 master's awarded. *Degree requirements:* For master's, thesis (for some programs), capstone experience, internship. *Entrance requirements:* For master's, GRE, minimum GPA of 3.0, 3 letters of recommendation. Additional exam requirements/recommendations for international students: Required—TOEFL (minimum score 550 paper-based; 213 computer-based; 79 iBT); Recommended—IELTS (minimum score 6.5). *Application deadline:* For fall admission, 2/1 priority date for domestic students, 6/1 for international students; for spring admission, 7/1 priority date for domestic students, 10/1 for international students. Applications are processed on a rolling basis. Application fee: $40. Electronic applications accepted. *Expenses:* Tuition, state resident: full-time $6912; part-time $384 per credit hour. Tuition, nonresident: full-time $12,150; part-time $675 per credit hour. Tuition and fees vary according to course load, program and reciprocity agreements. *Financial support:* Unspecified assistantships available. Financial award applicants required to submit FAFSA. *Faculty research:* Business/organizational communication, interpersonal/relational communication, public relations, communication teaching/pedagogy, media (production, criticism, popular culture). Total annual research expenditures: $29,000. *Unit head:* Dr. Jimmy Manning, Graduate Program Director, 859-572-1329, E-mail: manningj1@nku.edu. *Application contact:* Dr. Peg Griffin, Director of Graduate Programs, 859-572-6934, Fax: 859-572-6670, E-mail: griffinp@nku.edu.

Northwestern University, The Graduate School, School of Communication, Department of Radio/Television/Film, Evanston, IL 60208. Offers MA, MFA, PhD. Admissions and degrees offered through The Graduate School. Part-time programs available. Terminal master's awarded for partial completion of doctoral program. *Degree requirements:* For master's, comprehensive exam or thesis; for doctorate, thesis/dissertation, qualifying exam. *Entrance requirements:* For master's and doctorate, GRE General Test. Additional exam requirements/recommendations for international students: Required—TOEFL. Electronic applications accepted. *Faculty research:* Art and new media, media theory and criticism, gender, media history, documentary.

Northwestern University, Medill School of Journalism, Evanston, IL 60208. Offers broadcast journalism (MSJ); integrated marketing communications (MSIMC), including advertising/sales promotion, direct database and e-commerce marketing, general studies, public relations; magazine publishing (MSJ); new media (MSJ); reporting and writing (MSJ). *Accreditation:* ACEJMC (one or more programs are accredited). *Entrance requirements:* For master's, GRE General Test, GMAT or LSAT (MSJ). Additional exam requirements/recommendations for international students: Required—TOEFL. Electronic applications accepted. *Expenses:* Contact institution. *Faculty research:* Web business journalism, cultural stereotypes, voter apathy, digital television.

Ohio University, Graduate College, Scripps College of Communication, School of Media Arts and Studies, Athens, OH 45701-2979. Offers mass communication (PhD); media arts and studies (MA). *Faculty:* 20 full-time (5 women), 2 part-time/adjunct (1 woman). *Students:* 31 full-time (22 women), 10 part-time (3 women); includes 6 minority (4 African Americans, 1 American Indian/Alaska Native, 1 Hispanic American), 10 international. 53 applicants, 43% accepted, 13 enrolled. In 2009, 9 master's, 5 doctorates awarded. *Degree requirements:* For master's, comprehensive exam (for some programs), thesis or alternative; for doctorate, comprehensive exam, thesis/dissertation. *Entrance requirements:* For master's, GRE General Test or MAT, minimum GPA of 3.0; for doctorate, GRE General Test or MAT. Additional exam requirements/recommendations for international students: Required—TOEFL (minimum score 600 paper-based; 100 iBT) or IELTS Academic (minimum score 7). *Application deadline:* For fall admission, 1/31 priority date for domestic students, 12/31 priority date for international students. Application fee: $50 ($55 for international students). Electronic applications accepted. *Expenses:* Tuition, state resident: full-time $7839; part-time $323 per quarter hour. Tuition, nonresident: full-time $15,831; part-time $654 per quarter hour. Required fees: $2931. *Financial support:* Research assistantships with full tuition reimbursements, teaching assistantships with full tuition reimbursements, career-related internships or fieldwork, Federal Work-Study, institutionally sponsored loans, and unspecified assistantships available. Financial award application deadline: 1/31; financial award applicants required to submit FAFSA. *Faculty*

Media Studies

Ohio University (continued)

research: Media and development communication, new media and society, and industry studies. *Unit head:* Dr. Roger Cooper, Director, Fax: 740-593-9184, E-mail: cooperr@ohio.edu. *Application contact:* Dr. Gregory Newton, Interim Director for Graduate Studies, 740-593-4870, Fax: 740-593-9184, E-mail: newtong@ohio.edu.

Ohio University, Graduate College, Scripps College of Communication, School of Visual Communication, Athens, OH 45701-2979. Offers MA. *Accreditation:* NASAD. *Faculty:* 11 full-time (2 women). *Students:* 29 full-time (14 women), 5 part-time (3 women); includes 5 minority (2 African Americans, 1 American Indian/Alaska Native, 2 Hispanic Americans), 5 international. 46 applicants, 50% accepted, 16 enrolled. In 2009, 18 master's awarded. *Entrance requirements:* For master's, minimum GPA of 2.5, portfolio. Additional exam requirements/recommendations for international students: Required—TOEFL (minimum score 600 paper-based; 100 iBT) or IELTS (minimum score 7). *Application deadline:* For fall admission, 2/1 for domestic students, 12/14 for international students. Application fee: $50 ($55 for international students). Electronic applications accepted. *Expenses:* Tuition, state resident: full-time $7839; part-time $323 per quarter hour. Tuition, nonresident: full-time $15,831; part-time $654 per quarter hour. Required fees: $2931. *Financial support:* Federal Work-Study, institutionally sponsored loans, and tuition waivers (partial) available. Financial award applicants required to submit FAFSA. *Faculty research:* Photojournalism (including documentary photography), commercial photography (including illustrative photography), picture editing, informational graphics/publication design, interactive multimedia, and visual media management. *Unit head:* Terry Eiler, Director, 740-595-4895, E-mail: eiler@ohio.edu. *Application contact:* Stan Alost, Assistant Director, 740-597-1778, Fax: 740-593-0190, E-mail: alost@ohio.edu.

Rochester Institute of Technology, Graduate Enrollment Services, College of Liberal Arts, Department of Communications, Program in Communication and Media Technologies, Rochester, NY 14623-5603. Offers MS. Part-time programs available. *Students:* 29 full-time (19 women), 13 part-time (12 women); includes 5 African Americans, 1 Asian American or Pacific Islander, 6 international. Average age 29. 41 applicants, 63% accepted, 21 enrolled. In 2009, 10 master's awarded. *Degree requirements:* For master's, thesis or project. *Entrance requirements:* For master's, minimum GPA of 3.0, writing sample. Additional exam requirements/recommendations for international students: Required—TOEFL (minimum score 600 paper-based; 250 computer-based; 100 iBT), or IELTS (minimum score 7). *Application deadline:* For fall admission, 2/15 priority date for domestic and international students; for winter admission, 11/1 for domestic and international students; for spring admission, 2/1 for domestic and international students. Applications are processed on a rolling basis. Application fee: $50. Electronic applications accepted. *Expenses:* Tuition: Full-time $31,533; part-time $876 per credit hour. Required fees: $210. *Financial support:* In 2009–10, 17 students received support; research assistantships with partial tuition reimbursements available, teaching assistantships with partial tuition reimbursements available, career-related internships or fieldwork, scholarships/grants, and unspecified assistantships available. Support available to part-time students. Financial award applicants required to submit FAFSA. *Unit head:* Dr. Rudy Pugliese, Coordinator for Graduate Programs, 585-475-5925, Fax: 585-475-7732, E-mail: rrpgsl@rit.edu. *Application contact:* Diane Ellison, Assistant Vice President, Graduate Enrollment Services, 585-475-2229, Fax: 585-475-7164, E-mail: gradinfo@rit.edu.

Saginaw Valley State University, College of Arts and Behavioral Sciences, Program in Communication and Digital Media Design, University Center, MI 48710. Offers MA. Part-time and evening/weekend programs available. *Students:* 21 full-time (14 women), 14 part-time (5 women); includes 5 minority (3 African Americans, 1 Asian American or Pacific Islander, 1 Hispanic American), 14 international. Average age 30. 20 applicants, 90% accepted, 12 enrolled. In 2009, 17 master's awarded. *Degree requirements:* For master's, thesis. *Entrance requirements:* For master's, minimum GPA of 2.75. Additional exam requirements/recommendations for international students: Required—TOEFL. *Application deadline:* Applications are processed on a rolling basis. Application fee: $25. Electronic applications accepted. *Financial support:* Federal Work-Study and scholarships/grants available. Support available to part-time students. Financial award application deadline: 4/1; financial award applicants required to submit FAFSA. *Unit head:* Dr. David Schneider, Professor of Communication, 989-964-4398, E-mail: erickson@svsu.edu. *Application contact:* Dr. David Schneider, Professor of Communication, 989-964-4398, E-mail: erickson@svsu.edu.

San Diego State University, Graduate and Research Affairs, College of Professional Studies and Fine Arts, School of Communication, San Diego, CA 92182. Offers advertising and public relations (MA); critical-cultural studies (MA); interaction studies (MA); intercultural and international studies (MA); new media studies (MA); news and information studies (MA); telecommunications and media management (MA). *Degree requirements:* For master's, thesis. *Entrance requirements:* For master's, GRE General Test, 3 letters of recommendation. Additional exam requirements/recommendations for international students: Required—TOEFL. Electronic applications accepted.

San Diego State University, Graduate and Research Affairs, College of Professional Studies and Fine Arts, School of Theater, Television and Film, Program in Television, Film, and New Media Production, San Diego, CA 92182. Offers MA. *Entrance requirements:* For master's, GRE General Test, 3 letters of recommendation, resume, sample reel, influential book list, influential films list, hobby list. Additional exam requirements/recommendations for international students: Required—TOEFL. Electronic applications accepted. *Faculty research:* Experimental film and television programs, documentary film, television research and production.

San Francisco State University, Division of Graduate Studies, College of Creative Arts, Department of Broadcast and Electronic Communication Arts, San Francisco, CA 94132-1722. Offers radio and television (MA).

Savannah College of Art and Design, Graduate School, Program in Broadcast Design, Savannah, GA 31402-3146. Offers MA, MFA. Part-time programs available. *Degree requirements:* For master's, thesis, internships. *Entrance requirements:* For master's, interview, portfolio. Additional exam requirements/recommendations for international students: Required—TOEFL (minimum score 450 paper-based; 133 computer-based). Electronic applications accepted. *Expenses:* Tuition: Full-time $28,515; part-time $627 per credit hour. One-time fee: $500. Tuition and fees vary according to course load.

Savannah College of Art and Design, Graduate School, Program in Performing Arts, Savannah, GA 31402-3146. Offers MA, MFA. *Degree requirements:* For master's, thesis, internship. *Entrance requirements:* For master's, audition, interview. Additional exam requirements/recommendations for international students: Required—TOEFL (minimum score 450 paper-based; 133 computer-based). Electronic applications accepted. *Expenses:* Tuition: Full-time $28,515; part-time $627 per credit hour. One-time fee: $500. Tuition and fees vary according to course load.

Southern Illinois University Carbondale, Graduate School, College of Mass Communication and Media Arts, Department of Mass Communication and Media Arts, Carbondale, IL 62901-4701. Offers MA, MFA. *Accreditation:* ACEJMC.

Southern Illinois University Carbondale, Graduate School, College of Mass Communication and Media Arts, Department of Professional Media and Media Management Studies, Carbondale, IL 62901-4701. Offers MA.

Southern Illinois University Carbondale, Graduate School, College of Mass Communication and Media Arts, Program in Media Theory and Research, Carbondale, IL 62901-4701. Offers MA.

Southern Illinois University Edwardsville, Graduate Studies and Research, College of Arts and Sciences, Department of Mass Communications, Program in Media Literacy, Edwardsville, IL 62026-0001. Offers Postbaccalaureate Certificate. Part-time programs available. *Students:* 1 (woman) full-time. Average age 26. 2 applicants, 50% accepted. *Entrance requirements:* Additional exam requirements/recommendations for international students: Required—TOEFL (minimum score 550 paper-based; 213 computer-based; 79 iBT), IELTS (minimum score 6.5). *Application deadline:* For fall admission, 7/23 for domestic students, 6/1 for international students; for spring admission, 12/11 for domestic students, 10/1 for international students. Applications are processed on a rolling basis. Application fee: $30. Electronic applications accepted. *Expenses:* Tuition, state resident: part-time $1252.50 per semester. Tuition, nonresident: part-time $3131.25 per semester. Required fees: $586.85 per semester. Tuition and fees vary according to course load. *Financial support:* Fellowships with full tuition reimbursements, research assistantships with full tuition reimbursements, teaching assistantships with full tuition reimbursements, career-related internships or fieldwork, Federal Work-Study, institutionally sponsored loans, scholarships/grants, traineeships, and unspecified assistantships available. Support available to part-time students. Financial award application deadline: 3/1; financial award applicants required to submit FAFSA. *Unit head:* Dr. Elza Ibroscheva, Director, 618-650-2242, E-mail: eibrosc@siue.edu. *Application contact:* Dr. Elza Ibroscheva, Director, 618-650-2242, E-mail: eibrosc@siue.edu.

Syracuse University, S. I. Newhouse School of Public Communications, Program in Media Management, Syracuse, NY 13244. Offers MS. *Students:* 13 full-time (8 women), 1 (woman) part-time; includes 2 minority (1 African American, 1 Asian American or Pacific Islander), 3 international. Average age 24. 70 applicants, 37% accepted, 14 enrolled. In 2009, 6 master's awarded. *Degree requirements:* For master's, thesis optional, capstone course. *Entrance requirements:* For master's, GRE General Test or GMAT. Additional exam requirements/recommendations for international students: Required—TOEFL (minimum score 600 paper-based; 250 computer-based; 100 iBT). *Application deadline:* For fall admission, 2/1 priority date for domestic and international students. Application fee: $45. Electronic applications accepted. *Expenses:* Tuition: Full-time $26,808; part-time $1117 per credit. Required fees: $1024. *Financial support:* Fellowships with tuition reimbursements, research assistantships with tuition reimbursements, teaching assistantships with tuition reimbursements, tuition waivers (partial) available. Financial award application deadline: 2/1. *Unit head:* Stephen Masiclat, Director, 315-443-9243, Fax: 315-443-3946, E-mail: pcgrad@syr.edu. *Application contact:* Martha Coria, Graduate Records Office, 315-443-5749, Fax: 315-334-1834, E-mail: pcgrad@syr.edu.

See Display on page 622 and Close-Up on page 683.

Syracuse University, S. I. Newhouse School of Public Communications, Program in Media Studies, Syracuse, NY 13244. Offers MA. *Students:* 21 full-time (17 women), 5 part-time (3 women); includes 2 minority (1 African American, 1 Asian American or Pacific Islander), 5 international. Average age 26. 56 applicants, 52% accepted, 11 enrolled. In 2009, 6 master's awarded. *Degree requirements:* For master's, thesis. *Entrance requirements:* For master's, GRE General Test. Additional exam requirements/recommendations for international students: Required—TOEFL (minimum score 600 paper-based; 250 computer-based; 100 iBT). *Application deadline:* For fall admission, 2/1 priority date for domestic and international students. Application fee: $45. Electronic applications accepted. *Expenses:* Tuition: Full-time $26,808; part-time $1117 per credit. Required fees: $1024. *Financial support:* Fellowships with tuition reimbursements, research assistantships with tuition reimbursements, teaching assistantships with tuition reimbursements, tuition waivers (partial) available. Financial award application deadline: 2/1. *Unit head:* Carol M. Liebler, Director, 315-443-3372, Fax: 315-443-3946, E-mail: pcgrad@syr.edu. *Application contact:* Martha Coria, 315-443-5749, E-mail: pcgrad@syr.edu.

Syracuse University, S. I. Newhouse School of Public Communications, Program in Television, Radio, and Film, Syracuse, NY 13244. Offers MA. *Students:* 43 full-time (25 women), 2 part-time (1 woman); includes 10 minority (6 African Americans, 1 Asian American or Pacific Islander, 3 Hispanic Americans), 7 international. Average age 26. 72 applicants, 81% accepted, 42 enrolled. In 2009, 40 master's awarded. *Degree requirements:* For master's, comprehensive exam. *Entrance requirements:* For master's, GRE General Test. Additional exam requirements/recommendations for international students: Required—TOEFL (minimum score 600 paper-based; 250 computer-based; 100 iBT). *Application deadline:* For fall admission, 2/1 priority date for domestic and international students. Application fee: $45. Electronic applications accepted. *Expenses:* Tuition: Full-time $26,808; part-time $1117 per credit. Required fees: $1024. *Financial support:* Fellowships with tuition reimbursements, research assistantships with tuition reimbursements, teaching assistantships with tuition reimbursements, tuition waivers (partial) available. Financial award application deadline: 2/1. *Unit head:* Michael Schoonmaker, Chair, 315-443-4004, Fax: 315-443-3946, E-mail: pcgrad@syr.edu. *Application contact:* Martha Coria, Graduate Records Office, 315-443-5749, Fax: 315-443-1834, E-mail: pcgrad@syr.edu.

See Display on page 622 and Close-Up on page 683.

Temple University, Graduate School, School of Communications and Theater, Department of Broadcasting, Telecommunications and Mass Media, Philadelphia, PA 19122-6096. Offers MA. Part-time programs available. *Degree requirements:* For master's, thesis optional, written exam. *Entrance requirements:* For master's, GRE General Test, minimum GPA of 3.0. Additional exam requirements/recommendations for international students: Required—TOEFL (minimum score 550 paper-based; 213 computer-based; 79 iBT). Electronic applications accepted. *Faculty research:* Media institutions, international communications, communication policy, media theory.

Temple University, Graduate School, School of Communications and Theater, Department of Strategic and Organizational Communication, Program in Mass Media and Communication, Philadelphia, PA 19122-6096. Offers PhD. Part-time programs available. *Degree requirements:* For doctorate, one foreign language, thesis/dissertation. *Entrance requirements:* For doctorate, GRE General Test, minimum GPA of 3.0, sample of written work. Additional exam requirements/recommendations for international students: Required—TOEFL (minimum score 550 paper-based; 213 computer-based; 79 iBT). Electronic applications accepted. *Faculty research:* Aesthetics and criticism, media institutions, social theory and processes.

University at Buffalo, the State University of New York, Graduate School, College of Arts and Sciences, Department of Media Study, Buffalo, NY 14260. Offers humanities (film studies concentration) (MA); media arts production (MFA); new media design (Certificate); M Arch/MFA. *Faculty:* 12 full-time (4 women), 10 part-time/adjunct (5 women). *Students:* 60 (25 women); includes 14 minority (3 African Americans, 7 Asian Americans or Pacific Islanders, 4 Hispanic Americans), 6 international. 71 applicants, 59% accepted, 21 enrolled. In 2009, 12 master's awarded. *Degree requirements:* For master's, thesis. *Entrance requirements:* For master's, portfolio. Additional exam requirements/recommendations for international students: Required—TOEFL (minimum score 550 paper-based; 213 computer-based; 79 iBT), SPEAK (for those awarded assistantships). *Application deadline:* For fall admission, 1/15 priority date for domestic and international students. Applications are processed on a rolling basis. Application fee: $50. Electronic applications accepted. *Financial support:* In 2009–10, 16 students received support, including 1 fellowship (averaging $4,000 per year), 12 teaching assistantships with full tuition reimbursements available (averaging $13,387 per year); career-related internships or fieldwork, Federal Work-Study, scholarships/grants, and unspecified assistantships also available. Support available to part-time students. Financial award application deadline: 1/15; financial award applicants required to submit FAFSA. *Faculty research:* Digital arts, video, documentary, film, virtual reality, digital poetics, locative media. Total annual research expenditures: $63,000. *Unit head:* Dr. Roy Roussel, Chair, 716-645-6902, Fax: 716-645-6979, E-mail: roussel@buffalo.edu. *Application contact:* LuAnn Zak, Graduate Secretary, 716-645-0924, Fax: 716-645-6979, E-mail: luannzak@buffalo.edu.

The University of Alabama, Graduate School, College of Communication and Information Sciences, Department of Telecommunication and Film, Tuscaloosa, AL 35487-0152. Offers MA. *Faculty:* 8 full-time (2 women). *Students:* 7 full-time (3 women), 1 part-time (0 women), 3 international. Average age 27. 12 applicants, 25% accepted, 3 enrolled. In 2009, 5 degrees awarded. Terminal master's awarded for partial completion of doctoral program. *Degree requirements:* For master's, comprehensive exam, thesis or alternative. *Entrance requirements:*

For master's, GRE, minimum GPA of 3.0. Additional exam requirements/recommendations for international students: Required—TOEFL (minimum score 600 paper-based; 79 iBT). *Application deadline:* For fall admission, 4/15 priority date for domestic students, 1/15 priority date for international students; for spring admission, 11/1 for domestic students, 10/1 priority date for international students. Applications are processed on a rolling basis. Application fee: $50 ($60 for international students). Electronic applications accepted. *Expenses:* Tuition, state resident: full-time $7000. Tuition, nonresident: full-time $19,200. *Financial support:* In 2009–10, 6 students received support, including 2 research assistantships with tuition reimbursements available (averaging $9,825 per year), 2 teaching assistantships with tuition reimbursements available (averaging $9,825 per year); institutionally sponsored loans also available. Financial award application deadline: 2/15. *Faculty research:* Entertainment theory, news and public affairs, effects of telecommunications, management, media law and policy. *Unit head:* Dr. Gary A. Copeland, Chair, 205-348-6350, Fax: 205-348-5162, E-mail: copeland@ua.edu. *Application contact:* Dr. Shuhua Zhou, Graduate Coordinator, 205-348-8653, Fax: 205-348-5162, E-mail: szhou@bama.ua.edu.

The University of Arizona, Graduate College, College of Fine Arts, School of Media Arts, Tucson, AZ 85721. Offers MA. Part-time programs available. *Faculty:* 8. *Students:* 14 full-time (9 women), 4 part-time (1 woman); includes 2 minority (1 African American, 1 Hispanic American), 2 international. Average age 29. 34 applicants, 47% accepted, 10 enrolled. In 2009, 5 master's awarded. *Degree requirements:* For master's, comprehensive exam. *Entrance requirements:* For master's, GRE. Additional exam requirements/recommendations for international students: Required—TOEFL (minimum score 550 paper-based; 213 computer-based; 79 iBT). *Application deadline:* For fall admission, 2/15 for domestic students, 1/31 for international students. Applications are processed on a rolling basis. Application fee: $75. Electronic applications accepted. *Expenses:* Tuition, state resident: full-time $9028. Tuition, nonresident: full-time $24,890. *Financial support:* In 2009–10, 9 teaching assistantships with full tuition reimbursements (averaging $12,119 per year) were awarded; career-related internships or fieldwork, scholarships/grants, health care benefits, tuition waivers (full and partial), and unspecified assistantships also available. Financial award applicants required to submit FAFSA. *Unit head:* Beverly Seckinger, Interim Director, 520-621-1239, Fax: 520-621-9662, E-mail: bsecking@email.arizona.edu. *Application contact:* Sylvia Jo Miles, Administrative Secretary, 520-626-2847, Fax: 520-621-9662, E-mail: sjmiles@u.arizona.edu.

University of California, Santa Barbara, Graduate Division, College of Letters and Sciences, Division of Humanities and Fine Arts, Department of Media Arts and Technology, Santa Barbara, CA 93106-6065. Offers electronic music and sound design (MA); media arts and technology (PhD); multimedia engineering (MS); visual and spatial arts (MA). *Faculty:* 33 full-time (3 women). *Students:* 29 full-time (3 women). Average age 30. 55 applicants, 33% accepted, 8 enrolled. In 2009, 5 master's awarded. Terminal master's awarded for partial completion of doctoral program. *Degree requirements:* For master's, comprehensive exam, thesis; for doctorate, comprehensive exam, thesis/dissertation. *Entrance requirements:* For master's, GRE, portfolios; programming language and calculus-based math (expertise in 1 discipline and experience in another); 3 letters of recommendation; resume/curriculum vitae; for doctorate, GRE, portfolios; programming language and calculus-based math (expertise in 1 discipline and experience in another); 3 letters of recommendation; statement of purpose; personal achievements/contributions statement; resume/curriculum vitae; transcripts for post-secondary institutions attended. Additional exam requirements/recommendations for international students: Required—TOEFL (minimum score 550 paper-based; 213 computer-based; 80 iBT), or IELTS (minimum score 7). *Application deadline:* For fall admission, 1/15 for domestic and international students. Application fee: $70 ($90 for international students). Electronic applications accepted. *Financial support:* In 2009–10, 23 students received support, including 10 fellowships with full and partial tuition reimbursements available (averaging $4,800 per year), 6 research assistantships with full and partial tuition reimbursements available (averaging $8,300 per year), 18 teaching assistantships with partial tuition reimbursements available (averaging $7,300 per year); career-related internships or fieldwork, Federal Work-Study, institutionally sponsored loans, scholarships/grants, health care benefits, tuition waivers (full and partial), and unspecified assistantships also available. Financial award application deadline: 1/15; financial award applicants required to submit FAFSA. *Faculty research:* Electronic music and sound design: computer music and algorithmic composition, computer generated music, human-computer cooperation in music, design and synthesis of new sounds, sonic diffusion, 3D spatial sound; interactive art: installations, generative and algorithmic art, immersive art environments, computational photography; visualization; transarchitecture, multimedia signal processing, human-computer interaction, multimedia systems. *Unit head:* Prof. Matthew A. Turk, Chair, 805-893-4236, Fax: 805-893-2930, E-mail: mturk@cs.ucsb.edu. *Application contact:* Diane E. Harden, Graduate Program Assistant, 805-893-2887, Fax: 805-893-2930, E-mail: diane@mat.ucsb.edu.

University of Chicago, Division of the Humanities, Committee on Cinema and Media Studies, Chicago, IL 60637-1513. Offers AM, PhD. *Degree requirements:* For master's, one foreign language, thesis; for doctorate, 2 foreign languages, thesis/dissertation.

University of Colorado at Boulder, Graduate School, ATLAS Institute (Alliance for Technology, Learning, and Society), Boulder, CO 80309. Offers technology, media, and society (PhD). *Students:* 6 full-time (4 women), 1 (woman) part-time; includes 3 minority (1 African American, 1 American Indian/Alaska Native, 1 Asian American or Pacific Islander). Average age 37. 20 applicants, 5% accepted, 1 enrolled. *Application deadline:* For fall admission, 1/28 for domestic students, 12/1 for international students. *Financial support:* In 2009–10, 2 fellowships (averaging $33,692 per year), 5 research assistantships (averaging $13,970 per year) were awarded. Financial award application deadline: 1/15. *Faculty research:* Evaluation of the Dissector Tool based on the Visible Human Data Project, assessing student outcomes for SENCER (an NSF-sponsored program using civic engagement to increase the interest and learning in undergraduate science at over 300 U. S. universities). Total annual research expenditures: $1.8 million.

University of Colorado at Boulder, Graduate School, School of Journalism and Mass Communication, Program in Communication, Boulder, CO 80309. Offers media studies (PhD). *Students:* 21 full-time (13 women), 7 part-time (4 women); includes 3 minority (1 African American, 2 Hispanic Americans), 7 international. Average age 35. 38 applicants, 16% accepted, 6 enrolled. In 2009, 3 doctorates awarded. *Entrance requirements:* For doctorate, GRE General Test, minimum undergraduate GPA of 3.25. Additional exam requirements/recommendations for international students: Required—TOEFL. *Application deadline:* For fall admission, 2/15 for domestic and international students. Application fee: $50 ($60 for international students). *Financial support:* In 2009–10, 5 fellowships (averaging $1,400 per year), 15 research assistantships (averaging $12,251 per year) were awarded; unspecified assistantships also available. Financial award application deadline: 3/1.

University of Denver, Division of Arts, Humanities and Social Sciences, Department of Mass Communications, Denver, CO 80208. Offers advertising management (MS); digital media studies (MA); mass communications (MA); public relations (MS); video production (MA). Part-time programs available. *Faculty:* 14 full-time (8 women), 4 part-time/adjunct (3 women). *Students:* 37 full-time (28 women), 32 part-time (27 women); includes 8 minority (1 African American, 2 Asian Americans or Pacific Islanders, 5 Hispanic Americans), 3 international. Average age 26. 163 applicants, 64% accepted, 45 enrolled. In 2009, 24 master's awarded. *Degree requirements:* For master's, thesis (for some programs). *Entrance requirements:* For master's, GRE General Test. Additional exam requirements/recommendations for international students: Required—TOEFL, TWE. *Application deadline:* Applications are processed on a rolling basis. Application fee: $50. Electronic applications accepted. *Expenses:* Tuition: Full-time $34,596; part-time $961 per quarter hour. Required fees: $4 per quarter hour. Tuition and fees vary according to course load, campus/location and program. *Financial support:* In 2009–10, 10 research assistantships with full and partial tuition reimbursements (averaging $14,000 per year), 5 teaching assistantships with full and partial tuition reimbursements (averaging $11,500 per year) were awarded; career-related internships or fieldwork, Federal Work-Study, institutionally sponsored loans, and scholarships/grants also available. Support available to part-time students. Financial award application deadline: 3/1; financial award applicants required to submit FAFSA. *Faculty research:* Youth and civic engagement. Total annual research expenditures: $162,000. *Unit head:* Dr. Diane Waldman, Chair, 303-871-2008. *Application contact:* Information Contact, 303-871-2008, E-mail: mcom@du.edu.

University of Florida, Graduate School, College of Journalism and Communications, Department of Telecommunication, Gainesville, FL 32611. Offers MAMC. *Degree requirements:* For master's, thesis optional. *Entrance requirements:* For master's, GRE General Test, minimum GPA of 3.0.

University of Illinois at Urbana–Champaign, Graduate College, College of Fine and Applied Arts, School of Art and Design, Program in Design and Media, Champaign, IL 61820. Offers art and design (MFA), including new media; graphic design (MFA); industrial design (MFA). *Accreditation:* NASAD. *Students:* 18 full-time (9 women), 2 part-time (1 woman); includes 2 minority (both Asian Americans or Pacific Islanders), 10 international. 109 applicants, 7% accepted, 8 enrolled. In 2009, 4 master's awarded. *Entrance requirements:* For master's, minimum GPA of 3.0. Additional exam requirements/recommendations for international students: Required—TOEFL (minimum score 550 paper-based; 213 computer-based; 79 iBT). *Application deadline:* Applications are processed on a rolling basis. Application fee: $60 ($75 for international students). Electronic applications accepted. *Financial support:* Fellowships, research assistantships, teaching assistantships, tuition waivers (full and partial) available. *Unit head:* Ernest Scott, Chair, 217-333-1579, E-mail: ernscott@illinois.edu. *Application contact:* Marsha Biddle, Coordinator of Graduate Academic Affairs, 217-333-0642, Fax: 217-244-7688, E-mail: mbiddle@illinois.edu.

University of Illinois at Urbana–Champaign, Graduate College, College of Media, Institute of Communications Research, Champaign, IL 61820. Offers communications and media (PhD). *Faculty:* 10 full-time (5 women). *Students:* 38 full-time (21 women), 13 part-time (6 women); includes 16 minority (5 African Americans, 4 Asian Americans or Pacific Islanders, 7 Hispanic Americans), 22 international. 111 applicants, 8% accepted, 6 enrolled. In 2009, 7 doctorates awarded. *Entrance requirements:* For doctorate, GRE General Test, minimum GPA of 3.0. Additional exam requirements/recommendations for international students: Required—TOEFL (minimum score 550 paper-based). *Application deadline:* Applications are processed on a rolling basis. Application fee: $60 ($75 for international students). Electronic applications accepted. *Financial support:* In 2009–10, 14 fellowships, 12 research assistantships, 28 teaching assistantships were awarded; tuition waivers (full and partial) also available. *Faculty research:* Feminist cultural studies, media technology, international communications, Latino studies, economics of media. *Unit head:* Angharad N. Valdivia, Interim Director, 217-244-1422, Fax: 217-244-7695, E-mail: valdivia@illinois.edu. *Application contact:* Andrea Ray, Office Manager, 217-333-1549, Fax: 217-333-7695, E-mail: aray@illinois.edu.

The University of Iowa, Graduate College, College of Liberal Arts and Sciences, School of Journalism and Mass Communication, Iowa City, IA 52242-1316. Offers mass communication (PhD); media communication (MA); professional journalism (MA); JD/MA. *Accreditation:* ACEJMC (one or more programs are accredited). *Degree requirements:* For master's, thesis optional, exam; for doctorate, comprehensive exam, thesis/dissertation. *Entrance requirements:* For master's and doctorate, GRE General Test, minimum GPA of 3.0. Additional exam requirements/recommendations for international students: Required—TOEFL (minimum score 637 paper-based; 270 computer-based; 110 iBT). Electronic applications accepted. *Faculty research:* Verbal and visual aspects of historical, legal, social, and cross-cultural communication.

The University of Kansas, Graduate Studies, College of Liberal Arts and Sciences, Department of Film and Media Studies, Lawrence, KS 66045. Offers MA, PhD. *Faculty:* 10 full-time (2 women). *Students:* 24 full-time (7 women), 2 part-time (0 women); includes 1 minority (Asian American or Pacific Islander), 5 international. Average age 34. 8 applicants, 100% accepted, 7 enrolled. *Degree requirements:* For master's, thesis; for doctorate, one foreign language, comprehensive exam, thesis/dissertation. *Entrance requirements:* For master's, GRE General Test, minimum GPA of 3.2; for doctorate, GRE General Test, minimum GPA of 3.5; MA in film, or related field. Additional exam requirements/recommendations for international students: Required—TOEFL. *Application deadline:* For fall admission, 2/15 for domestic and international students. *Expenses:* Tuition, state resident: full-time $6492; part-time $270.50 per credit hour. Tuition, nonresident: full-time $15,510; part-time $646.25 per credit hour. Required fees: $847; $70.56 per credit hour. Tuition and fees vary according to course load and program. *Financial support:* Teaching assistantships with full and partial tuition reimbursements available. Financial award application deadline: 1/1; financial award applicants required to submit FAFSA. *Faculty research:* Film and media theory, film and media history, East Asian cinema, Latin American cinema, film and video production. *Unit head:* Dr. Tamara L. Falicov, Chair, 785-864-1353, Fax: 785-331-2671, E-mail: tfalicov@ku.edu. *Application contact:* Dr. Michael Baskett, Associate Professor, 785-864-1384, Fax: 785-331-2671, E-mail: eiga@ku.edu.

University of Lethbridge, School of Graduate Studies, Lethbridge, AB T1K 3M4, Canada. Offers accounting (MScM); addictions counseling (M Sc); agricultural biotechnology (M Sc); agricultural studies (M Sc, MA); anthropology (MA); archaeology (MA); art (MA, MFA); biochemistry (M Sc); biological sciences (M Sc); biomolecular science (PhD); biosystems and biodiversity (PhD); Canadian studies (MA); chemistry (M Sc); computer science (M Sc); computer science and geographical information science (M Sc); counseling psychology (M Ed); dramatic arts (MA); earth, space, and physical science (PhD); economics (MA); educational leadership (M Ed); English (MA); environmental science (M Sc); evolution and behavior (PhD); exercise science (M Sc); finance (MScM); French (MA); French/German (MA); French/Spanish (MA); general education (M Ed); general management (MScM); geography (M Sc, MA); German (MA); health science (M Sc); health sciences (MA); history (MA); human resource management and labour relations (MScM); individualized multidisciplinary (M Sc, MA); information systems (MScM); international management (MScM); kinesiology (M Sc, MA); management (M Sc, MA); marketing (MScM); mathematics (M Sc); music (M Mus, MA); Native American studies (MA); neuroscience (M Sc, PhD); new media (MA); nursing (M Sc); philosophy (MA); physics (M Sc); policy and strategy (MScM); political science (MA); psychology (M Sc, MA); religious studies (MA); social sciences (MA); sociology (MA); theatre and dramatic arts (MFA); theoretical and computational science (PhD); urban and regional studies (MA); women's studies (MA). Part-time and evening/weekend programs available. *Degree requirements:* For doctorate, comprehensive exam, thesis/dissertation. *Entrance requirements:* For master's, GMAT (M Sc in management), bachelor's degree in related field, minimum GPA of 3.0 during previous 20 graded semester courses, 2 years teaching or related experience (M Ed); for doctorate, master's degree, minimum graduate GPA of 3.5. Additional exam requirements/recommendations for international students: Required—TOEFL. *Faculty research:* Movement and brain plasticity, gibberellin physiology, photosynthesis, carbon cycling, molecular properties of main-group ring components.

University of Maryland, College Park, Academic Affairs, Phillip Merrill College of Journalism, College Park, MD 20742. Offers broadcast journalism (MA); journalism (MA); journalism and media studies (PhD); online news (MA); public affairs reporting (MA). *Accreditation:* ACEJMC (one or more programs are accredited). Part-time and evening/weekend programs available. *Faculty:* 22 full-time (11 women), 40 part-time/adjunct (15 women). *Students:* 75 full-time (46 women), 10 part-time (5 women); includes 19 minority (13 African Americans, 5 Asian Americans or Pacific Islanders, 1 Hispanic American), 12 international. 250 applicants, 36% accepted, 27 enrolled. In 2009, 25 master's, 5 doctorates awarded. *Degree requirements:* For doctorate, thesis/dissertation, preliminary written and oral comprehensive exams. *Entrance requirements:* For master's and doctorate, GRE General Test, minimum GPA of 3.0, 3 letters of recommendation. Additional exam requirements/recommendations for international students: Required—TOEFL. *Application deadline:* For fall admission, 2/1 for domestic and international students. Applications are processed on a rolling basis. Application fee: $60. Electronic applications accepted. *Expenses:* Tuition, area resident: Part-time $471 per credit hour. Tuition, state

Media Studies

University of Maryland, College Park (continued)
resident: part-time $471 per credit hour. Tuition, nonresident: part-time $1016 per credit hour. Required fees: $337.04 per term. *Financial support:* In 2009–10, 6 fellowships with full and partial tuition reimbursements (averaging $15,296 per year), 1 research assistantship with tuition reimbursement (averaging $15,266 per year), 19 teaching assistantships with tuition reimbursements (averaging $16,778 per year) were awarded; career-related internships or fieldwork, Federal Work-Study, and scholarships/grants also available. Support available to part-time students. Financial award applicants required to submit FAFSA. *Faculty research:* Mass communication theory, specialized journalism, new telecommunication technologies, press integration. Total annual research expenditures: $642,886. *Unit head:* Kevin Klose, Dean, 301-405-2393, E-mail: kklose@umd.edu. *Application contact:* Dean of Graduate School, 301-405-0376, Fax: 301-314-9305.

University of Michigan, Horace H. Rackham School of Graduate Studies, The School of Music, Theatre, and Dance, Program in Media Arts, Ann Arbor, MI 48109-2085. Offers MA. *Students:* 3 full-time (1 woman). Average age 22. *Entrance requirements:* For master's, GRE, portfolio. Additional exam requirements/recommendations for international students: Required—TOEFL (minimum score 600 paper-based; 250 computer-based; 100 iBT). *Application deadline:* For fall admission, 12/1 for domestic and international students. *Expenses:* Tuition, state resident: full-time $17,286; part-time $1099 per credit hour. Tuition, nonresident: full-time $34,944; part-time $2080 per credit hour. Required fees: $95 per semester. Tuition and fees vary according to course load, degree level and program. *Financial support:* In 2009–10, 2 research assistantships with full and partial tuition reimbursements (averaging $38,208 per year) were awarded. *Unit head:* Steven M. Whiting, Associate Dean for Graduate Studies, 734-764-0590, Fax: 734-763-5097, E-mail: stevenmw@umich.edu. *Application contact:* Karen A. Frye, Admin. Asst., 734-764-0590, Fax: 734-763-5097, E-mail: hoshi@umich.edu.

University of Missouri–Kansas City, College of Arts and Sciences, Department of English, Kansas City, MO 64110-2499. Offers creative writing and media arts (MFA); English (MA, PhD). PhD (interdisciplinary) offered through the School of Graduate Studies. Part-time and evening/weekend programs available. *Faculty:* 22 full-time (15 women), 18 part-time/adjunct (11 women). *Students:* 10 full-time (6 women), 39 part-time (22 women); includes 5 minority (4 African Americans, 1 Asian American or Pacific Islander). Average age 31. 38 applicants, 63% accepted, 12 enrolled. In 2009, 13 master's awarded. *Degree requirements:* For master's, one foreign language; for doctorate, 2 foreign languages, comprehensive exam, thesis/dissertation. Additional *Entrance requirements:* For master's, GRE General Test, 3 letters of recommendation. Additional exam requirements/recommendations for international students: Required—TOEFL (minimum score 550 paper-based; 213 computer-based; 80 iBT). *Application deadline:* For fall admission, 1/15 for domestic students, 1/15 priority date for international students. Applications are processed on a rolling basis. Application fee: $45 ($50 for international students). Electronic applications accepted. *Expenses:* Tuition, state resident: full-time $5378; part-time $299 per credit hour. Tuition, nonresident: full-time $13,881; part-time $771 per credit hour. Required fees: $641; $71 per credit hour. Tuition and fees vary according to course load and program. *Financial support:* In 2009–10, 15 teaching assistantships (averaging $12,180 per year) were awarded; career-related internships or fieldwork, Federal Work-Study, and institutionally sponsored loans also available. Support available to part-time students. Financial award application deadline: 3/1; financial award applicants required to submit FAFSA. *Faculty research:* Creative writing: poetry and prose, computational linguistics, rhetoric and composition, African-American and British literature, print culture. Total annual research expenditures: $105,946. *Unit head:* Dr. Jeff Rydberg-Cox, Co-Chair, 816-235-2560, Fax: 816-235-1308, E-mail: rydbergcoxj@umkc.edu. *Application contact:* Dr. Joan Dean, Director of Graduate Studies, 816-235-2555, E-mail: deanj@umkc.edu.

University of Nevada, Las Vegas, Graduate College, Greenspun College of Urban Affairs, School of Journalism and Media Studies, Las Vegas, NV 89154-5007. Offers MA. *Faculty:* 10 full-time (2 women). *Students:* 13 full-time (7 women), 11 part-time (8 women); includes 6 minority (3 African Americans, 1 Asian American or Pacific Islander, 2 Hispanic Americans), 2 international. Average age 30. 26 applicants, 69% accepted, 12 enrolled. In 2009, 10 master's awarded. *Entrance requirements:* For master's, GRE General Test. Additional exam requirements/recommendations for international students: Required—TOEFL (minimum score 550 paper-based; 213 computer-based; 80 iBT), IELTS (minimum score 7). *Application deadline:* For fall admission, 3/15 priority date for domestic and international students. Applications are processed on a rolling basis. Application fee: $60 ($95 for international students). Electronic applications accepted. *Financial support:* In 2009–10, 8 students received support, including 4 research assistantships with partial tuition reimbursements available (averaging $10,000 per year), 4 teaching assistantships with partial tuition reimbursements available (averaging $10,000 per year); institutionally sponsored loans, scholarships/grants, health care benefits, and unspecified assistantships also available. Financial award application deadline: 3/1. *Faculty research:* Media and religion, science and communications, ethnic communities and journalism, journalism history, emerging technologies. *Unit head:* Dr. Ardyth Sohn, Director/ Professor, 702-895-3270, Fax: 702-895-5189, E-mail: ardyth.sohn@unlv.edu. *Application contact:* Graduate College Admissions Evaluator, 702-895-3320, Fax: 702-895-4180, E-mail: gradcollege@unlv.edu.

The University of North Carolina at Greensboro, Graduate School, College of Arts and Sciences, Department of Broadcasting and Cinema, Greensboro, NC 27412-5001. Offers film and video production (MFA).

University of Oregon, Graduate School, School of Architecture and Allied Arts, Program in Arts and Administration, Eugene, OR 97403. Offers arts management (MA, MS); media management (MA, MS). *Degree requirements:* For master's, summer internship, thesis/project. *Entrance requirements:* For master's, minimum GPA of 3.0; bachelor's degree in history, practice of visual, performing arts or other related degree. Additional exam requirements/recommendations for international students: Required—TOEFL. *Faculty research:* Museum education, arts program evaluation, community arts, information management, arts marketing.

University of South Carolina, The Graduate School, College of Arts and Sciences, Department of Art, Division of Media Arts, Columbia, SC 29208. Offers MMA. *Degree requirements:* For master's, thesis. *Entrance requirements:* For master's, GRE General Test, interview, portfolio. Additional exam requirements/recommendations for international students: Required—TOEFL. Electronic applications accepted. *Faculty research:* Three dimensional imaging, script writing.

University of Southern California, Graduate School, Annenberg School for Communication and Journalism, School of Communication, Program in Communication Management, Los Angeles, CA 90089. Offers MCM, JD/MCM, MCM/MAJCS. Part-time and evening/weekend programs available. *Degree requirements:* For master's, professional project. *Entrance requirements:* For master's, GRE General Test or GMAT, resume, writing samples, recommendation letters, statement of purpose. Additional exam requirements/recommendations for international students: Required—TOEFL (minimum score 280 computer-based; 114 iBT). Electronic applications accepted. *Expenses:* Tuition: Full-time $25,980; part-time $1315 per unit. Required fees: $554. One-time fee: $35 full-time. Full-time tuition and fees vary according to degree level and program. *Faculty research:* Global communication, communication law and policy, entertainment management, marketing communication, strategic and corporate communication management.

See Display on page 629 and Close-Up on page 685.

University of Southern California, Graduate School, Annenberg School for Communication and Journalism, School of Journalism, Program in Broadcast Journalism, Los Angeles, CA 90089. Offers MA. *Degree requirements:* For master's, comprehensive exam. *Entrance requirements:* For master's, GRE General Test, resume, writing samples, letters of recommendation, statement of purpose. Additional exam requirements/recommendations for international students: Required—TOEFL (minimum score 280 computer-based; 114 iBT). Electronic applications accepted. *Expenses:* Tuition: Full-time $25,980; part-time $1315 per unit. Required fees: $554. One-time fee: $35 full-time. Full-time tuition and fees vary according to degree level and program.

See Display on page 629 and Close-Up on page 685.

University of Southern California, Graduate School, School of Cinematic Arts, Interactive Media Division, Los Angeles, CA 90089. Offers interactive media (MFA); media arts and practice (PhD). *Faculty:* 9 full-time (2 women), 13 part-time/adjunct (4 women). *Students:* 34 full-time (12 women); includes 3 minority (2 Asian Americans or Pacific Islanders, 1 Hispanic American), 6 international. In 2009, 10 master's awarded. *Degree requirements:* For master's, thesis, thesis project. *Entrance requirements:* Additional exam requirements/recommendations for international students: Required—TOEFL (minimum score 600 paper-based; 250 computer-based; 100 iBT). *Application deadline:* For fall admission, 12/1 for domestic and international students. Application fee: $85. *Expenses:* Contact institution. *Financial support:* In 2009–10, 25 students received support, including 6 fellowships with full tuition reimbursements available (averaging $20,000 per year), 6 research assistantships with full tuition reimbursements available (averaging $9,750 per year); career-related internships or fieldwork, Federal Work-Study, institutionally sponsored loans, scholarships/grants, health care benefits, and research assistantships through grant funded projects also available. Financial award application deadline: 5/3; financial award applicants required to submit CSS PROFILE or FAFSA. *Faculty research:* Game design and development, mobile media, stereoscopic/immersive media, game for health, serious games, experiments in gameplay, games for learning. Total annual research expenditures: $989,031. *Unit head:* Dr. Scott S. Fisher, Professor and Department Chair, 213-821-4472, Fax: 213-821-2665, E-mail: sfisher@cinema.usc.edu. *Application contact:* Adrienne Capirchio, Program Manager, 213-821-2515, Fax: 213-821-2665, E-mail: acapirchio@cinema.usc.edu.

University of Southern California, Graduate School, School of Cinematic Arts, Interdivisional Program in Media Arts and Practice, Los Angeles, CA 90089. Offers PhD. *Faculty:* 1 full-time (0 women), 8 part-time/adjunct (4 women). *Students:* 9 full-time (6 women); includes 3 minority (1 Asian American or Pacific Islander, 2 Hispanic Americans), 2 international. *Degree requirements:* For doctorate, comprehensive exam, thesis/dissertation, fluency in 1 programming language. *Entrance requirements:* For doctorate, GRE. Additional exam requirements/recommendations for international students: Required—TOEFL. *Application deadline:* For fall admission, 12/1 for domestic and international students. Application fee: $85. Electronic applications accepted. *Expenses:* Tuition: Full-time $25,980; part-time $1315 per unit. Required fees: $554. One-time fee: $35 full-time. Full-time tuition and fees vary according to degree level and program. *Financial support:* In 2009–10, 3 students received support, including 3 fellowships with full tuition reimbursements available (averaging $30,000 per year), 2 teaching assistantships (averaging $20,000 per year); research assistantships, Federal Work-Study and scholarships/grants also available. Support available to part-time students. Financial award application deadline: 12/1; financial award applicants required to submit FAFSA. *Faculty research:* Interactive, mobile, and immersive media design and theory; digital arts and animation. *Unit head:* Dr. Steve F. Anderson, Director, 213-743-4421, Fax: 213-746-1226, E-mail: sfanders@usc.edu. *Application contact:* Cecilia Fletcher, Program Coordinator, 213-743-4421, Fax: 213-746-1226, E-mail: imap@cinema.usc.edu.

The University of Tennessee, Graduate School, College of Communication and Information, Knoxville, TN 37996. Offers advertising (MS, PhD); broadcasting (MS, PhD); communications (MS, PhD); information sciences (MS, PhD); journalism (MS, PhD); public relations (MS, PhD); speech communication (MS, PhD). *Accreditation:* ACEJMC (one or more programs are accredited at the [master's] level). Part-time and evening/weekend programs available. Post-baccalaureate distance learning degree programs offered (no on-campus study). *Degree requirements:* For master's, thesis or alternative; for doctorate, thesis/dissertation. *Entrance requirements:* For master's and doctorate, GRE General Test, minimum GPA of 2.7. Additional exam requirements/recommendations for international students: Required—TOEFL. Electronic applications accepted. *Expenses:* Tuition, state resident: full-time $6826; part-time $380 per semester hour. Tuition, nonresident: full-time $21,844; part-time $1147 per semester hour. Tuition and fees vary according to program.

The University of Texas at Austin, Graduate School, College of Communication, Department of Radio-Television-Film, Austin, TX 78712-1111. Offers film and video production (MFA); radio-television-film (MA, PhD); screenwriting (MFA). *Degree requirements:* For master's, thesis (for some programs); for doctorate, thesis/dissertation. *Entrance requirements:* For master's and doctorate, GRE General Test. Electronic applications accepted. *Faculty research:* International communication, film studies, media and culture, telecommunication and new media, gender and sexuality.

The University of Western Ontario, Faculty of Graduate Studies, Faculty of Information and Media Studies, Programs in Media Studies, London, ON N6A 5B8, Canada. Offers MA, PhD. Part-time programs available. *Degree requirements:* For master's, thesis; for doctorate, comprehensive exam, thesis/dissertation. *Entrance requirements:* For master's, 2 letters of reference; for doctorate, MA in media studies, communications or related field. Additional exam requirements/recommendations for international students: Required—TOEFL (minimum score 625 paper-based), TWE (minimum score 5). Electronic applications accepted. *Faculty research:* Media cultures, media industries, media technologies.

University of Wisconsin–Madison, Graduate School, College of Letters and Science, Department of Communication Arts, Madison, WI 53706-1380. Offers communication science (MA, PhD); film (MA, PhD); media and cultural studies (MA, PhD); rhetoric (MA, PhD). Terminal master's awarded for partial completion of doctoral program. *Degree requirements:* For master's, one foreign language, thesis (for some programs); for doctorate, one foreign language, thesis/dissertation. *Entrance requirements:* For master's and doctorate, GRE General Test, minimum GPA of 3.5. Electronic applications accepted. *Expenses:* Tuition, state resident: part-time $594 per credit. Tuition, nonresident: part-time $1504 per credit. Required fees: $65 per credit. Tuition and fees vary according to course load, program and reciprocity agreements.

University of Wisconsin–Milwaukee, Graduate School, College of Letters and Sciences, Department of Media Studies, Milwaukee, WI 53201-0413. Offers media studies (MA); rhetorical leadership (Certificate). Part-time programs available. *Faculty:* 9 full-time (3 women). *Students:* 11 full-time (10 women), 16 part-time (8 women); includes 2 minority (both African Americans), 5 international. Average age 27. 28 applicants, 50% accepted, 6 enrolled. In 2009, 10 master's awarded. *Degree requirements:* For master's, thesis or alternative. *Entrance requirements:* For master's, GRE General Test, minimum GPA of 3.0. Additional exam requirements/recommendations for international students: Required—TOEFL (minimum score 550 paper-based; 79 iBT), IELTS (minimum score 6.5). *Application deadline:* For fall admission, 1/1 priority date for domestic students; for spring admission, 9/1 for domestic students. Applications are processed on a rolling basis. Application fee: $45 ($75 for international students). *Expenses:* Tuition, state resident: full-time $8800. Tuition, nonresident: full-time $20,760. Tuition and fees vary according to program and reciprocity agreements. *Financial support:* In 2009–10, 20 teaching assistantships were awarded; career-related internships or fieldwork and unspecified assistantships also available. Support available to part-time students. Financial award application deadline: 4/15. *Unit head:* Barbara Ley, Representative, 414-229-6273, Fax: 414-229-2411, E-mail: barbley@uwm.edu. *Application contact:* General Information Contact, 414-229-4982, Fax: 414-229-6967, E-mail: gradschool@uwm.edu.

Valparaiso University, Graduate School, Program in Media and Communication, Valparaiso, IN 46383. Offers digital media (MS); sports media (MS). Part-time and evening/weekend programs available. *Students:* 10 full-time (6 women), 8 part-time (6 women); includes 1 minority (Asian American or Pacific Islander), 8 international. Average age 25. *Entrance requirements:* For master's, minimum GPA of 3.0, undergraduate minor in communication. Additional exam requirements/recommendations for international students: Required—TOEFL (minimum score 550 paper-based; 213 computer-based; 80 iBT). *Application deadline:* Applications are processed on a rolling basis. Application fee: $30 ($50 for international students).

Electronic applications accepted. *Financial support:* Available to part-time students. Applicants required to submit FAFSA. *Unit head:* Dr. David L. Rowland, Dean, Graduate Studies and Continuing Education/Associate Provost, 219-464-5313, Fax: 219-464-5381, E-mail: david.rowland@valpo.edu. *Application contact:* Jamie Haney, Coordinator of Graduate Admission, 219-464-5313, Fax: 219-464-5381, E-mail: jamie.haney@valpo.edu.

Virginia Commonwealth University, Graduate School, College of Humanities and Sciences, School of Mass Communications, Program in Media, Art, and Text, Richmond, VA 23284-9005. Offers PhD. *Entrance requirements:* For doctorate, GRE, MA, MAE, or MFA in appropriate field of study (English, art history, studio art, poetry, mass communications); 3 letters of recommendation.

Washington State University, Graduate School, College of Liberal Arts, Edward R. Murrow College of Communication, Pullman, WA 99164. Offers health communications (MA, PhD); intercultural and international communications (MA, PhD); media and society (MA, PhD); media process and effects (MA, PhD); organizational communications (MA, PhD). *Degree requirements:* For master's, comprehensive exam (for some programs), thesis optional, oral exam; for doctorate, comprehensive exam, thesis/dissertation. *Entrance requirements:* For master's, GRE General Test, minimum GPA of 3.25, 3 letters of recommendation; for doctorate, GRE General Test, minimum undergraduate GPA of 3.25, graduate 3.5; MA in communication; 3 letters of recommendation. Additional exam requirements/recommendations for international students: Required—TOEFL (minimum score 580 paper-based; 237 computer-based). Electronic applications accepted. *Faculty research:* Advocacy communication, mediated communication in decision making, communication technology policy and effects, multicultural and international psychology and physiology of communication.

Wayne State University, College of Fine, Performing and Communication Arts, Department of Communication, Detroit, MI 48202. Offers communication studies (MA, PhD); public relations and organizational communication (MA); radio-TV-film (MA, PhD); speech communication (MA, PhD). *Degree requirements:* For master's, thesis, essay, or comprehensive exam; for doctorate, thesis/dissertation. *Entrance requirements:* For master's, minimum GPA of 3.0, sample of academic writing; for doctorate, GRE, minimum GPA of 3.3, MA; letters of recommendation; personal statement; sample of written scholarship. Additional exam requirements/recommendations for international students: Required—TOEFL (minimum score 550 paper-based; 213 computer-based); Recommended—TWE (minimum score 6). Electronic applications accepted. *Faculty research:* Rhetorical theory and criticism; mass media theory and research; argumentation; organizational communication; risk and crisis communication; interpersonal, family, and health communication.

Webster University, School of Communications, Program in Media Communications, St. Louis, MO 63119-3194. Offers MA. *Expenses:* Tuition: Part-time $565 per credit hour. Tuition and fees vary according to degree level, campus/location and program.

Webster University, School of Communications, Program in Media Literacy, St. Louis, MO 63119-3194. Offers MA. *Expenses:* Tuition: Part-time $565 per credit hour. Tuition and fees vary according to degree level, campus/location and program.

West Virginia State University, Graduate Programs, Institute, WV 25112-1000. Offers biotechnology (MA, MS); media studies (MA). *Students:* 41 full-time (19 women), 8 part-time (6 women); includes 7 minority (5 African Americans, 1 Asian American or Pacific Islander, 1 Hispanic American), 8 international. *Entrance requirements:* For master's, GRE General Test, minimum GPA of 3.0, 3 letters of recommendation. Additional exam requirements/recommendations for international students: Required—TOEFL (minimum score 550 paper-based). *Financial support:* Research assistantships with tuition reimbursements, teaching assistantships with tuition reimbursements available. *Application contact:* Dr. John Teeuwissen, Assistant Vice President, Academic Affairs, 304-766-3147, E-mail: johntee@wvstateu.edu.

Publishing

Carnegie Mellon University, College of Humanities and Social Sciences, Department of English, Program in Professional Writing, Pittsburgh, PA 15213-3891. Offers editing and publishing (MAPW); policy and non-profit communication (MAPW); public and media relations / corporate communications (MAPW); science or healthcare communication (MAPW); technical writing (MAPW); writing for new media (MAPW); writing for print media (MAPW). Part-time programs available. *Entrance requirements:* For master's, GRE General Test. Additional exam requirements/recommendations for international students: Required—TOEFL, TWE.

DePaul University, College of Liberal Arts and Sciences, Department of English, Chicago, IL 60614. Offers English (MA); writing and publishing (MA); writing, rhetoric, and discourse (MA). Part-time and evening/weekend programs available. *Faculty:* 29 full-time (12 women). *Students:* 112 full-time (74 women), 77 part-time (67 women); includes 19 minority (7 African Americans, 4 Asian Americans or Pacific Islanders, 8 Hispanic Americans), 1 international. Average age 27. 95 applicants, 56% accepted. In 2009, 100 master's awarded. *Degree requirements:* For master's, written exam. *Entrance requirements:* Additional exam requirements/recommendations for international students: Required—TOEFL. *Application deadline:* For fall admission, 7/1 priority date for domestic students; for winter admission, 10/1 priority date for domestic students; for spring admission, 2/1 priority date for domestic students. Applications are processed on a rolling basis. Application fee: $40. Electronic applications accepted. *Expenses:* Tuition: Full-time $37,525; part-time $620 per credit hour. *Financial support:* In 2009–10, 2 research assistantships with full tuition reimbursements, 7 teaching assistantships with full tuition reimbursements (averaging $7,500 per year) were awarded; fellowships with partial tuition reimbursements, career-related internships or fieldwork, institutionally sponsored loans, scholarships/grants, tuition waivers (partial), and unspecified assistantships also available. Support available to part-time students. Financial award application deadline: 4/1. *Faculty research:* Rhetoric and composition, technical writing, creative writing, linguistics, literacy theory. *Unit head:* Dr. Janet Hickey, Chairperson, 773-325-4635, E-mail: jhicke11@depaul.edu. *Application contact:* Dr. Lesley Kordecki, Director, 773-325-1786, Fax: 773-325-8607, E-mail: lkordeck@depaul.edu.

Drexel University, College of Arts and Sciences, Department of Culture and Communication, Program in Publication Management, Philadelphia, PA 19104-2875. Offers MS. Part-time and evening/weekend programs available. *Degree requirements:* For master's, research project. *Entrance requirements:* Additional exam requirements/recommendations for international students: Required—TOEFL. Electronic applications accepted.

Emerson College, Graduate Studies, School of the Arts, Department of Writing, Literature and Publishing, Program in Publishing and Writing, Boston, MA 02116-4624. Offers MA. Part-time and evening/weekend programs available. *Faculty:* 43 full-time (19 women), 9 part-time/adjunct (6 women). *Students:* 92 full-time (75 women), 15 part-time (14 women); includes 8 minority (4 African Americans, 1 Asian American or Pacific Islander, 3 Hispanic Americans), 5 international. Average age 24. 130 applicants, 68% accepted, 49 enrolled. In 2009, 48 master's awarded. *Degree requirements:* For master's, thesis or alternative. *Entrance requirements:* For master's, GRE General Test, 15 page writing sample. Additional exam requirements/recommendations for international students: Required—TOEFL (minimum score 550 paper-based; 213 computer-based; 80 iBT), IELTS (minimum score 6.5). *Application deadline:* For fall admission, 1/5 for domestic and international students. Applications are processed on a rolling basis. Application fee: $60 ($75 for international students). Electronic applications accepted. *Expenses:* Tuition: Full-time $22,056; part-time $919 per credit. Required fees: $120; $120 per year. One-time fee: $170 full-time. *Financial support:* In 2009–10, 46 students received support, including 6 fellowships with partial tuition reimbursements available (averaging $14,000 per year), 24 research assistantships with partial tuition reimbursements available (averaging $10,000 per year); Federal Work-Study, scholarships/grants, and unspecified assistantships also available. Financial award application deadline: 1/5; financial award applicants required to submit FAFSA. *Faculty research:* Publishing. *Unit head:* Prof. Lisa Diercks, Graduate Program Director, 617-824-8750, E-mail: lisa_diercks@emerson.edu. *Application contact:* Office of Graduate Admission, 617-824-8610, Fax: 617-824-8614, E-mail: gradapp@emerson.edu.

The George Washington University, College of Professional Studies, Program in Publishing, Washington, DC 20052. Offers MPS. Program offered at Alexandria, VA education center. *Students:* 55 part-time (45 women); includes 15 minority (9 African Americans, 2 American Indian/Alaska Native, 2 Asian Americans or Pacific Islanders, 2 Hispanic Americans), 1 international. Average age 32. 62 applicants, 90% accepted, 31 enrolled. In 2009, 24 master's awarded. *Entrance requirements:* For master's, minimum cumulative GPA of 3.0. *Application deadline:* For fall admission, 4/1 for domestic and international students. Electronic applications accepted. *Unit head:* Dr. Arnold Grossblatt, Director, 202-994-7220, E-mail: arnieg@gwu.edu. *Application contact:* Kristin Williams, Assistant Vice President for Graduate and Special Enrollment Management, 202-994-0467, Fax: 202-994-0371, E-mail: ksw@gwu.edu.

New York University, School of Continuing and Professional Studies, Division for Media Industry Studies and Design, Center for Publishing, New York, NY 10012-1019. Offers publishing (MS), including book publishing, electronic publishing, magazine publishing. Part-time and evening/weekend programs available. *Faculty:* 41 part-time/adjunct (23 women). *Students:* 41 full-time (35 women), 56 part-time (48 women); includes 3 minority (all Asian Americans or Pacific Islanders), 3 international. Average age 26. 91 applicants, 64% accepted, 27 enrolled. In 2009, 52 master's awarded. *Degree requirements:* For master's, thesis. *Entrance requirements:* For master's, GMAT or GRE General Test (for recent graduates), 2 letters of recommendation, resume, essay. Additional exam requirements/recommendations for international students: Required—TOEFL (minimum score 600 paper-based; 250 computer-based; 100 iBT), TWE. *Application deadline:* For fall admission, 2/1 priority date for domestic and international students; for spring admission, 10/15 priority date for domestic students, 8/15 priority date for international students. Applications are processed on a rolling basis. Application fee: $75. Electronic applications accepted. *Expenses:* Tuition: Full-time $30,528; part-time $1272 per credit. Required fees: $2177. *Financial support:* In 2009–10, 70 students received support, including 70 fellowships (averaging $2,853 per year); career-related internships or fieldwork, Federal Work-Study, institutionally sponsored loans, and scholarships/grants also available. Support available to part-time students. Financial award application deadline: 3/1; financial award applicants required to submit FAFSA. *Faculty research:* Digital publishing and marketing. *Unit head:* Andrea Chambers, Director, 212-992-3226, Fax: 212-790-3233, E-mail: andrea.chambers@nyu.edu. *Application contact:* Sarah Cobb, Associate Director, 212-792-3236, Fax: 212-790-3233, E-mail: alyssa.leal@nyu.edu.

Northwestern University, Medill School of Journalism, Evanston, IL 60208. Offers broadcast journalism (MSJ); integrated marketing communications (MSIMC), including advertising/sales promotion, direct database and e-commerce marketing, general studies, public relations; magazine publishing (MSJ); new media (MSJ); reporting and writing (MSJ). *Accreditation:* ACEJMC (one or more programs are accredited). *Entrance requirements:* For master's, GRE General Test, GMAT or LSAT (MSJ). Additional exam requirements/recommendations for international students: Required—TOEFL. Electronic applications accepted. *Expenses:* Contact institution. *Faculty research:* Web business journalism, cultural stereotypes, voter apathy, digital television.

Pace University, Dyson College of Arts and Sciences, Program in Publishing, New York, NY 10038. Offers book publishing (Certificate); business side of publishing (Certificate); magazine publishing (Certificate); publishing (MS). Part-time and evening/weekend programs available. Postbaccalaureate distance learning degree programs offered. *Faculty:* 2 full-time (1 woman), 12 part-time/adjunct (8 women). *Students:* 72 full-time (65 women), 76 part-time (65 women); includes 32 minority (15 African Americans, 8 Asian Americans or Pacific Islanders, 9 Hispanic Americans), 13 international. Average age 27. 93 applicants, 95% accepted, 53 enrolled. In 2009, 40 master's awarded. *Degree requirements:* For master's, internship or thesis. *Entrance requirements:* For master's, GRE General Test. Additional exam requirements/recommendations for international students: Required—TOEFL. *Application deadline:* For fall admission, 7/31 priority date for domestic students; for spring admission, 11/30 priority date for domestic students. Applications are processed on a rolling basis. Application fee: $70. Electronic applications accepted. *Expenses:* Tuition: Part-time $954 per credit. Tuition and fees vary according to course load, degree level and program. *Financial support:* Research assistantships, career-related internships or fieldwork available. Support available to part-time students. Financial award applicants required to submit FAFSA. *Unit head:* Prof. Sherman Raskin, Chairperson and Director, 212-346-1417. *Application contact:* Susan Ford-Goldschein, Director of Graduate Admissions, 212-346-1652, Fax: 212-346-1585, E-mail: gradnyc@pace.edu.

Rosemont College, Schools of Graduate and Professional Studies, Program in English and Publishing and English Literature, Rosemont, PA 19010-1699. Offers English and publishing (MA); English literature (MA). Part-time programs available. *Degree requirements:* For master's, comprehensive exam (for some programs), thesis. *Entrance requirements:* For master's, 3 letters of recommendation. Additional exam requirements/recommendations for international students: Required—TOEFL. Electronic applications accepted.

Simon Fraser University, Graduate Studies, Faculty of Arts and Social Sciences, Canadian Centre for Studies in Publishing, Burnaby, BC V5A 1S6, Canada. Offers M Pub. *Degree requirements:* For master's, internship, project report. *Entrance requirements:* For master's, minimum GPA of 3.0. Additional exam requirements/recommendations for international students: Required—TWE, TOEFL or IELTS. *Expenses:* Contact institution. *Faculty research:* History of publishing, electronic publishing, editing, multimedia, publication design.

University of Baltimore, Graduate School, The Yale Gordon College of Liberal Arts, Program in Creative Writing and Publishing Arts, Baltimore, MD 21201-5779. Offers MFA. Part-time and evening/weekend programs available. *Entrance requirements:* Additional exam requirements/recommendations for international students: Required—TOEFL.

University of Baltimore, Graduate School, The Yale Gordon College of Liberal Arts, Program in Publications Design, Baltimore, MD 21201-5779. Offers MA. Part-time and evening/weekend programs available. *Degree requirements:* For master's, seminar project. *Entrance requirements:* For master's, minimum GPA of 3.0, portfolio, interview. Additional exam

Publishing

University of Baltimore (continued)
requirements/recommendations for international students: Required—TOEFL (minimum score 550 paper-based; 213 computer-based). Electronic applications accepted. *Faculty research:* Communication theory, graphic design, media technology.

University of Houston–Victoria, School of Arts and Sciences, Program in Publishing, Victoria, TX 77901-4450. Offers MS. *Degree requirements:* For master's, internship. *Entrance requirements:* For master's, GMAT or GRE, 2 letters of recommendation, writing sample.

Rhetoric

Abilene Christian University, Graduate School, College of Arts and Sciences, Department of English, Abilene, TX 79699-9100. Offers composition/rhetoric (MA); literature (MA); writing (MA). Part-time programs available. *Faculty:* 17 part-time/adjunct (7 women). *Students:* 15 full-time (7 women), 2 part-time (both women); includes 1 minority (Hispanic American), 1 international. 10 applicants, 100% accepted, 8 enrolled. In 2009, 6 master's awarded. *Degree requirements:* For master's, one foreign language, comprehensive exam, thesis optional. *Entrance requirements:* For master's, GRE General Test. *Application deadline:* For fall admission, 4/1 priority date for domestic students; for spring admission, 11/1 for domestic students. Applications are processed on a rolling basis. Application fee: $40. Electronic applications accepted. *Expenses:* Tuition: Full-time $11,520; part-time $640 per hour. Required fees: $1090; $53.50 per hour. $10 per term. Tuition and fees vary according to program. *Financial support:* Teaching assistantships, Federal Work-Study available. Support available to part-time students. Financial award application deadline: 4/1; financial award applicants required to submit FAFSA. *Faculty research:* Feminism, Shakespearean dimensions of new literature, poetic consciousness, deconstruction myths. *Unit head:* Dr. Dana McMichael, Graduate Adviser, 325-674-2083, Fax: 325-674-2408, E-mail: dana.mcmichael@acu.edu. *Application contact:* William Horn, Graduate Admissions Counselor, 325-674-2656, Fax: 325-674-6717, E-mail: gradinfo@acu.edu.

Ball State University, Graduate School, College of Communication, Information, and Media, Department of Communication Studies, Muncie, IN 47306-1099. Offers speech, public address, forensics, and rhetoric (MA). *Entrance requirements:* For master's, GRE General Test.

Bob Jones University, Graduate Programs, Greenville, SC 29614. Offers accountancy (MS); Bible (MA); Bible translation (MA); Biblical studies (Certificate); broadcast management (MS); business administration (MBA); church history (MA, PhD); church ministries (MA); church music (MM); cinema and video production (MA); counseling (MS); curriculum and instruction (Ed D); divinity (M Div); dramatic production (MA); educational leadership (MS, Ed D, Ed S); elementary education (M Ed, MAT); English (M Ed, MA, MAT); fine arts (MA); graphic design (MA); history (M Ed, MA); illustration (MA); interpretative speech (MA); mathematics (M Ed, MAT); medical missions (Certificate); ministry (MM, D Min); multi-categorical special education (M Ed, MAT); music (M Ed); New Testament interpretation (PhD); Old Testament interpretation (PhD); orchestral instrument performance (MM); organ performance (MM); pastoral studies (MA); personnel services (MS, Ed S); piano pedagogy (MM); piano performance (MM); platform arts (MA); radio and television broadcasting (MS); rhetoric and public address (MA); secondary education (M Ed); studio art (MA); teaching Bible (MA); theology (MA, PhD); voice performance (MM); youth ministries (MA); M Div/MM.

Bowling Green State University, Graduate College, College of Arts and Sciences, Department of English, Program in English, Bowling Green, OH 43403. Offers English (MA, PhD); literature (MA); rhetoric and writing (PhD); scientific and technical communication (MA). Part-time programs available. *Degree requirements:* For master's, thesis or alternative; for doctorate, comprehensive exam, thesis/dissertation, foreign language or proficiency in Old English. *Entrance requirements:* For master's and doctorate, GRE General Test. Additional exam requirements/recommendations for international students: Required—TOEFL. Electronic applications accepted. *Faculty research:* Postmodern literary theory, rhetorical theory, ethnic American literature, literature and culture, composition pedagogy.

Brigham Young University, Graduate Studies, College of Humanities, Department of English, Provo, UT 84602-1001. Offers creative writing (MFA); literature (MA); rhetoric/composition (MA). *Faculty:* 54 full-time (18 women). *Students:* 80 full-time (53 women), 5 part-time (3 women); includes 2 minority (both Asian Americans or Pacific Islanders). Average age 25. 98 applicants, 36% accepted, 29 enrolled. In 2009, 36 master's awarded. *Degree requirements:* For master's, thesis. *Entrance requirements:* For master's, GRE General Test. Additional exam requirements/recommendations for international students: Required—TOEFL. *Application deadline:* For fall admission, 1/15 for domestic students. Application fee: $50. Electronic applications accepted. *Expenses:* Tuition: Full-time $5580; part-time $301 per credit hour. Tuition and fees vary according to student's religious affiliation. *Financial support:* In 2009–10, 79 students received support, including 10 research assistantships (averaging $3,000 per year), 62 teaching assistantships (averaging $6,000 per year); career-related internships or fieldwork, institutionally sponsored loans, scholarships/grants, and tuition waivers (partial) also available. Support available to part-time students. Financial award application deadline: 3/15. *Faculty research:* English literature, American literature, rhetoric, creative writing. *Unit head:* Prof. Ed Cutler, Head, 801-422-3581, Fax: 801-422-0221, E-mail: ed_cutler@byu.edu. *Application contact:* Lou Ann C. Crisler, Graduate Secretary, 801-422-8673, Fax: 801-422-0221, E-mail: louann_crisler@byu.edu.

California State University, Dominguez Hills, College of Arts and Humanities, Department of English, Carson, CA 90747-0001. Offers English (MA); rhetoric and composition (Certificate); teaching English as a second language (Certificate). Part-time and evening/weekend programs available. *Faculty:* 13 full-time (5 women). *Students:* 23 full-time (14 women), 52 part-time (33 women); includes 34 minority (9 African Americans, 5 Asian Americans or Pacific Islanders, 20 Hispanic Americans), 3 international. Average age 39. 39 applicants, 79% accepted, 19 enrolled. In 2009, 20 master's awarded. *Degree requirements:* For master's, comprehensive exam (for some programs), thesis or alternative. *Entrance requirements:* For master's, minimum GPA of 3.0 in last 60 units. Additional exam requirements/recommendations for international students: Required—TOEFL (minimum score 550 paper-based; 213 computer-based). *Application deadline:* Applications are processed on a rolling basis. Application fee: $55. Electronic applications accepted. *Expenses:* Tuition, nonresident: full-time $6696; part-time $372 per unit. Required fees: $5946; $1752 per semester. *Faculty research:* Gender studies, transnationalism, discourse analysis, visual culture, Shakespeare. *Unit head:* Dr. Helen Oesterheld, Chair, 310-243-3322, E-mail: hoesterheld@csudh.edu. *Application contact:* 310-243-3600.

California State University, Northridge, Graduate Studies, College of Humanities, Department of English, Northridge, CA 91330. Offers creative writing (MA); literature (MA); rhetoric and composition theory (MA). Part-time and evening/weekend programs available. *Faculty:* 31 full-time (13 women), 66 part-time/adjunct (58 women). *Students:* 36 full-time (22 women), 130 part-time (87 women); includes 1 American Indian/Alaska Native, 16 Asian Americans or Pacific Islanders, 22 Hispanic Americans, 1 international. Average age 33. 119 applicants, 65% accepted, 42 enrolled. In 2009, 36 master's awarded. *Degree requirements:* For master's, thesis or alternative. *Entrance requirements:* For master's, writing proficiency test, GRE General Test or minimum GPA of 3.0. Additional exam requirements/recommendations for international students: Required—TOEFL. *Application deadline:* For fall admission, 11/30 for domestic students. Application fee: $55. *Financial support:* Teaching assistantships available. Financial award application deadline: 3/1. *Faculty research:* Reading improvement, professional writing, Dickens, Shaw, English as a second language. *Unit head:* Dr. George Uba, Chair, 818-677-3434, E-mail: george.uba@csun.edu. *Application contact:* Dr. Marjie Seagoe, Graduate Studies Secretary, 818-677-3433.

California State University, Stanislaus, College of Humanities and Social Sciences, Department of English, Turlock, CA 95382. Offers English (MA); literature (MA); rhetoric and teaching of writing (MA); TESOL (MA, Certificate). Part-time programs available. *Degree requirements:* For master's, one foreign language, comprehensive exam, thesis. *Entrance requirements:* For master's, GRE General Test, minimum GPA of 3.0, 2 letters of reference; for Certificate, minimum GPA of 3.0, 2 letters of reference. Additional exam requirements/recommendations for international students: Required—TOEFL (minimum score 550 paper-based; 213 computer-based), TWE (minimum score 4). Electronic applications accepted. *Faculty research:* Transnational literacies, Renaissance and Medieval literature, abolition writings and slave narratives, qualitative writing.

Carnegie Mellon University, College of Humanities and Social Sciences, Department of English, Pittsburgh, PA 15213-3891. Offers communication planning and design (M Des); literary and cultural studies (MA, PhD); professional writing (MAPW), including editing and publishing, policy and non-profit communication, public and media relations / corporate communications, science or healthcare communication, technical writing, writing for new media, writing for print media; rhetoric (MA, PhD). Part-time programs available. Terminal master's awarded for partial completion of doctoral program. *Degree requirements:* For doctorate, 2 foreign languages, comprehensive exam, thesis/dissertation. *Entrance requirements:* For master's and doctorate, GRE General Test. Additional exam requirements/recommendations for international students: Required—TOEFL, TWE. *Faculty research:* Cognitive processes in discourse with emphasis on writing, testing, and evaluation.

The Catholic University of America, School of Arts and Sciences, Department of English Language and Literature, Washington, DC 20064. Offers English language and literature (MA, PhD); rhetoric (MA, PhD); MSLS/MA. Part-time programs available. *Faculty:* 13 full-time (5 women), 3 part-time/adjunct (0 women). *Students:* 20 full-time (15 women), 36 part-time (26 women), 1 international. Average age 28. 85 applicants, 52% accepted, 14 enrolled. In 2009, 10 master's, 3 doctorates awarded. *Degree requirements:* For master's, one foreign language, comprehensive exam, thesis or alternative; for doctorate, 2 foreign languages, comprehensive exam, thesis/dissertation. *Entrance requirements:* For master's, GRE General Test, 3 letters of recommendation; for doctorate, GRE General Test, statement of purpose, official copies of academic transcripts, three letters of recommendation. Additional exam requirements/recommendations for international students: Required—TOEFL (minimum score 580 paper-based; 237 computer-based). *Application deadline:* For fall admission, 8/1 priority date for domestic students, 7/15 for international students; for spring admission, 12/1 priority date for domestic students, 10/15 for international students. Applications are processed on a rolling basis. Application fee: $55. Electronic applications accepted. *Expenses:* Tuition: Full-time $31,740; part-time $1245 per credit hour. Required fees: $50; $25 per semester hour. One-time fee: $425. *Financial support:* Fellowships, research assistantships, teaching assistantships, Federal Work-Study, scholarships/grants, tuition waivers (full and partial), and unspecified assistantships available. Financial award application deadline: 2/1; financial award applicants required to submit FAFSA. *Faculty research:* Medieval literature, theory and history of rhetoric, Renaissance literature, religion and literature, English and American drama. *Unit head:* Dr. Ernest Suarez, Chair, 202-319-5488, Fax: 202-319-4188, E-mail: suarez@cua.edu. *Application contact:* Julie Schwing, Director of Graduate Admissions, 202-319-5057, Fax: 202-319-6533, E-mail: cua-admissions@cua.edu.

Clemson University, Graduate School, College of Architecture, Arts, and Humanities, Program in Rhetorics, Communication and Information Design, Clemson, SC 29634. Offers PhD. *Faculty:* 25 full-time (10 women). *Students:* 23 full-time (9 women), 6 part-time (2 women); includes 6 minority (4 African Americans, 1 Asian American or Pacific Islander, 1 Hispanic American), 5 international. Average age 36. 17 applicants, 59% accepted, 8 enrolled. In 2009, 1 doctorate awarded. *Degree requirements:* For doctorate, thesis/dissertation (for some programs). *Entrance requirements:* For doctorate, GRE, master's degree in English, communications studies, art, professional communication or related field; portfolio; 3 letters of reference; minimum graduate GPA of 3.5. Additional exam requirements/recommendations for international students: Required—TOEFL (minimum score 550 paper-based; 213 computer-based). *Application deadline:* For fall admission, 1/1 priority date for domestic students, 4/15 for international students. Applications are processed on a rolling basis. Application fee: $70 ($80 for international students). Electronic applications accepted. *Expenses:* Tuition, state resident: full-time $8684; part-time $528 per credit hour. Tuition, nonresident: full-time $15,330; part-time $1078 per credit hour. Required fees: $736; $37 per semester. Part-time tuition and fees vary according to course load and program. *Financial support:* In 2009–10, 22 students received support, including 22 teaching assistantships with partial tuition reimbursements available (averaging $19,709 per year); career-related internships or fieldwork, institutionally sponsored loans, scholarships/grants, health care benefits, and unspecified assistantships also available. Support available to part-time students. *Unit head:* Dr. Victor Vitanza, Director, 864-656-6411, Fax: 864-656-0599, E-mail: sophist@clemson.edu. *Application contact:* Dr. Victor Vitanza, Director, 864-656-6411, Fax: 864-656-0599, E-mail: sophist@clemson.edu.

DePaul University, College of Liberal Arts and Sciences, Department of English, Program in Writing, Rhetoric, and Discourse, Chicago, IL 60604-2287. Offers MA. *Students:* 24 full-time (16 women), 18 part-time (15 women); includes 8 minority (4 African Americans, 1 Asian American or Pacific Islander, 3 Hispanic Americans). *Expenses:* Tuition: Full-time $37,525; part-time $620 per credit hour. *Unit head:* Christine Tardy, Director, 773-325-4145. *Application contact:* Dr. Lesley Kordecki, Director, 773-325-1786, Fax: 773-325-8607, E-mail: lkordeck@depaul.edu.

Duquesne University, Graduate School of Liberal Arts, Department of Communication and Rhetorical Studies, Pittsburgh, PA 15282-0001. Offers communication (MA); rhetoric (PhD). Part-time and evening/weekend programs available. *Faculty:* 6 full-time (3 women), 5 part-time/adjunct (3 women). *Students:* 100 full-time (52 women), 34 part-time (31 women); includes 5 minority (4 African Americans, 1 Hispanic American), 12 international. Average age 27. 50 applicants, 86% accepted, 28 enrolled. In 2009, 19 master's, 9 doctorates awarded. *Degree requirements:* For master's, thesis optional, practicum; for doctorate, 2 foreign languages, comprehensive exam, thesis/dissertation. *Entrance requirements:* For master's, GRE General Test, MAT or GMAT; for doctorate, GRE General Test. Additional exam requirements/recommendations for international students: Required—TOEFL. *Application deadline:* For fall admission, 2/1 priority date for domestic and international students; for spring admission, 11/1 priority date for domestic and international students. Applications are processed on a rolling basis. Electronic applications accepted. *Expenses:* Tuition: Part-time $851 per credit. Required fees: $81 per credit. *Financial support:* In 2009–10, 9 research assistantships with full tuition reimbursements (averaging $9,000 per year), 10 teaching assistantships with full tuition reimbursements (averaging $13,000 per year) were awarded; career-related internships or fieldwork, Federal Work-Study, institutionally sponsored loans, scholarships/grants, tuition waivers (full and partial), and unspecified assistantships also available. Financial award application deadline: 5/1. *Unit head:* Dr. Ronald Arnett, Chair, 412-396-5076. *Application contact:* Dr. Janie Fritz, Director, 412-396-6460.

Eastern Washington University, Graduate Studies, College of Arts and Letters, Department of English, Cheney, WA 99004-2431. Offers literature (MA); rhetoric, composition, and technical communication (MA); teaching English as a second language (MA). *Degree requirements:* For master's, comprehensive exam, thesis or alternative. *Entrance requirements:* For master's, GRE General Test, minimum GPA of 3.0. *Expenses:* Tuition, state resident: full-time $7476; part-time $249 per quarter hour. Tuition, nonresident: full-time $18,030; part-time $601 per quarter hour. Required fees: $3.50 per quarter hour. $142 per quarter.

Florida State University, The Graduate School, College of Arts and Sciences, Department of English, Tallahassee, FL 32306. Offers creative writing (MFA); English (PhD), including creative writing, literature, rhetoric and composition; literature (MA); rhetoric and composition (MA). Part-time programs available. *Faculty:* 48 full-time (23 women), 6 part-time/adjunct (1 woman). *Students:* 150 full-time (90 women), 20 part-time (10 women); includes 31 minority (15 African Americans, 1 American Indian/Alaska Native, 5 Asian Americans or Pacific Islanders, 10 Hispanic Americans). Average age 30. 480 applicants, 21% accepted, 58 enrolled. In 2009, 22 master's, 14 doctorates awarded. *Degree requirements:* For master's, one foreign language, thesis or alternative; for doctorate, comprehensive exam, thesis/dissertation, 27 hours of coursework, 24 hours of dissertation work. *Entrance requirements:* For master's and doctorate, GRE General Test, GRE Subject Test (literature only), sample of written work, 3 letters of recommendation, resume. Additional exam requirements/recommendations for international students: Required—TOEFL. *Application deadline:* For fall admission, 1/1 priority date for domestic and international students. Application fee: $30. Electronic applications accepted. *Expenses:* Tuition, state resident: full-time $7413. Tuition, nonresident: full-time $22,567. *Financial support:* In 2009–10, 126 students received support, including 5 fellowships, teaching assistantships (averaging $11,375 per year); career-related internships or fieldwork, Federal Work-Study, and institutionally sponsored loans also available. Financial award application deadline: 1/1; financial award applicants required to submit FAFSA. *Faculty research:* British and Irish literature, American literature, creative writing, rhetoric and composition, multiethnic transnational literature. *Unit head:* Dr. Ralph Berry, Chairman, 850-644-4230, Fax: 850-644-0811, E-mail: rberry@fsu.edu. *Application contact:* Dr. Ralph Berry, Chairman, 850-644-4230, Fax: 850-644-0811, E-mail: rberry@fsu.edu.

Georgia State University, College of Arts and Sciences, Department of English, Atlanta, GA 30302-3083. Offers creative writing (MA, MFA, PhD), including fiction/poetry; English (MA, PhD); fiction (MFA); literary studies (MA, PhD); poetry (MFA); rhetoric and composition (MA, PhD). Part-time and evening/weekend programs available. *Degree requirements:* For master's, variable foreign language requirement, thesis; for doctorate, one foreign language, comprehensive exam, thesis/dissertation, second exam. *Entrance requirements:* For master's and doctorate, GRE General Test. Additional exam requirements/recommendations for international students: Required—TOEFL (minimum score 0 paper-based; 0 computer-based). Electronic applications accepted. *Faculty research:* Literature, theory, culture, rhetoric/composition, professional/technical writing.

Hofstra University, School of Communication, Department of Speech Communication, Rhetoric, and Performance Studies, Hempstead, NY 11549. Offers speech communication and rhetorical studies (MA). Part-time and evening/weekend programs available. *Faculty:* 4 full-time (1 woman). *Students:* 10 full-time (6 women), 13 part-time (7 women); includes 9 minority (8 African Americans, 1 Hispanic American), 2 international. Average age 29. 18 applicants, 100% accepted, 10 enrolled. In 2009, 3 master's awarded. *Degree requirements:* For master's, thesis. *Entrance requirements:* For master's, 2 letters of recommendation, interview. Additional exam requirements/recommendations for international students: Required—TOEFL (minimum score 550 paper-based; 213 computer-based; 80 iBT). *Application deadline:* Applications are processed on a rolling basis. Application fee: $60. Electronic applications accepted. *Expenses:* Tuition: Full-time $16,200; part-time $900 per credit hour. Required fees: $970; $145 per term. Tuition and fees vary according to program. *Financial support:* In 2009–10, 6 students received support, including 3 fellowships with full and partial tuition reimbursements available (averaging $4,000 per year), 3 research assistantships with full and partial tuition reimbursements available (averaging $12,494 per year); Federal Work-Study, institutionally sponsored loans, scholarships/grants, tuition waivers (full and partial), and unspecified assistantships also available. Support available to part-time students. Financial award applicants required to submit FAFSA. *Faculty research:* Performance of race and gender, public deliberation, public memory, civic engagement and political participation, popular culture. *Unit head:* Dr. Maryanne Trasciatti, Chairperson, 516-463-5427, Fax: 516-463-7012, E-mail: sphmat@hofstra.edu. *Application contact:* Carol Drummer, Dean of Graduate Admissions, 516-463-4876, Fax: 516-463-4664, E-mail: gradstudent@hofstra.edu.

Idaho State University, Office of Graduate Studies, College of Arts and Sciences, Department of Communication and Rhetorical Studies, Pocatello, ID 83209-8115. Offers communication and rhetorical studies (MA). Part-time programs available. *Faculty:* 4 full-time (1 woman). *Students:* 8 full-time (3 women), 7 part-time (4 women); includes 1 minority (Hispanic American), 1 international. Average age 36. In 2009, 3 master's awarded. *Degree requirements:* For master's, comprehensive exam, paper or thesis. *Entrance requirements:* For master's, GRE General Test, minimum GPA of 3.0 in all upper-level courses. Additional exam requirements/recommendations for international students: Required—TOEFL (minimum score 550 paper-based; 213 computer-based; 80 iBT). *Application deadline:* For fall admission, 7/1 for domestic students, 6/1 for international students; for spring admission, 12/1 for domestic students, 11/1 for international students. Applications are processed on a rolling basis. Application fee: $55. Electronic applications accepted. *Expenses:* Tuition, state resident: full-time $3318; part-time $297 per credit hour. Tuition, nonresident: full-time $13,120; part-time $437 per credit hour. Required fees: $2530. Tuition and fees vary according to program. *Financial support:* In 2009–10, 2 teaching assistantships with full and partial tuition reimbursements (averaging $10,841 per year) were awarded; Federal Work-Study, institutionally sponsored loans, scholarships/grants, health care benefits, and unspecified assistantships also available. Support available to part-time students. Financial award application deadline: 1/1; financial award applicants required to submit FAFSA. *Faculty research:* Metaphor and cognition in organizational groups and teams; rhetorical criticism of contemporary culture, including music, film, television, and advertising; communication pedagogy; the effect of language on organizational identification and commitment; risk communication and crisis communication. *Unit head:* Dr. James DiSanza, Chairman, 208-282-3395, Fax: 208-282-4598, E-mail: disajame@isu.edu. *Application contact:* Tami Carson, Graduate School Technical Records Specialist, 208-282-2150, Fax: 208-282-4847, E-mail: carstami@isu.edu.

Indiana University Bloomington, University Graduate School, College of Arts and Sciences, Department of Communication and Culture, Bloomington, IN 47405-7000. Offers film and media studies (PhD); performance and ethnography (PhD); rhetoric and public culture (PhD). *Faculty:* 24 full-time (12 women). *Students:* 85 full-time (43 women), 1 (woman) part-time; includes 9 minority (1 African American, 1 Asian American or Pacific Islander, 7 Hispanic Americans), 9 international. Average age 32. 179 applicants, 15% accepted, 15 enrolled. In 2009, 5 master's, 11 doctorates awarded. *Degree requirements:* For master's, comprehensive exam; for doctorate, one foreign language, comprehensive exam, thesis/dissertation, student teaching. *Entrance requirements:* For master's and doctorate, GRE General Test (recommended), minimum GPA of 3.0, 3 letters of recommendation, writing sample. Additional exam requirements/recommendations for international students: Required—TOEFL (minimum score 550 paper-based; 213 computer-based). *Application deadline:* For winter admission, 1/1 for domestic students, 12/1 for international students. Application fee: $55 ($65 for international students). Electronic applications accepted. *Financial support:* In 2009–10, 65 students received support, including 4 fellowships with full tuition reimbursements available (averaging $18,000 per year), 61 teaching assistantships with full tuition reimbursements available (averaging $12,961 per year). Financial award application deadline: 4/15. *Faculty research:* Rhetoric and public culture, film and media studies, performance ethnography. *Unit head:* Prof. Gregory A. Waller, Chair, 812-855-2367, Fax: 812-855-6014, E-mail: cmcl@indiana.edu. *Application contact:* Kathy P. Teige, Graduate Secretary, 812-855-6389, Fax: 812-855-6014, E-mail: kteige@indiana.edu.

Indiana University of Pennsylvania, School of Graduate Studies and Research, College of Humanities and Social Sciences, Department of English, Indiana, PA 15705-1087. Offers composition and teaching English to speakers of other languages (MA, MAT, PhD), including composition and teaching English to speakers of other languages (PhD), teaching English (MAT), teaching English to speakers of other languages (MA); literature and criticism (MA, PhD), including generalist (MA), literature (MA), literature and criticism (PhD); rhetoric and linguistics (PhD). Part-time programs available. *Faculty:* 31 full-time (17 women). *Students:* 133 full-time (80 women), 235 part-time (141 women); includes 15 minority (5 African Americans, 7 Asian Americans or Pacific Islanders, 3 Hispanic Americans), 98 international. Average age 35. 326 applicants, 41% accepted, 82 enrolled. In 2009, 40 master's, 28 doctorates awarded. *Degree requirements:* For master's, thesis optional; for doctorate, one foreign language, comprehensive exam, thesis/dissertation. *Entrance requirements:* For master's and doctorate, 2 letters of recommendation. Additional exam requirements/recommendations for international students: Required—TOEFL. *Application deadline:* For fall admission, 7/1 priority date for domestic students; for spring admission, 11/1 for domestic students. Applications are processed on a rolling basis. Application fee: $40. *Expenses:* Tuition, state resident: full-time $6666; part-time $370 per credit hour. Tuition, nonresident: full-time $10,666; part-time $593 per credit hour. Required fees: $813 per semester. *Financial support:* In 2009–10, 11 fellowships (averaging $1,455 per year), 40 research assistantships with full and partial tuition reimbursements (averaging $5,973 per year), 17 teaching assistantships with partial tuition reimbursements (averaging $15,308 per year) were awarded. Financial award application deadline: 3/15; financial award applicants required to submit FAFSA. *Unit head:* Dr. Gail I. Berlin, Chairperson, 724-357-2261, E-mail: ivy@iup.edu. *Application contact:* Dr. Gail I. Berlin, Chairperson, 724-357-2261, E-mail: ivy@iup.edu.

Iowa State University of Science and Technology, Graduate College, College of Liberal Arts and Sciences, Department of English, Ames, IA 50011. Offers creative writing (MFA); English (MA); rhetoric and professional communication (PhD). *Faculty:* 53 full-time (26 women), 8 part-time/adjunct (6 women). *Students:* 105 full-time (68 women), 25 part-time (17 women); includes 3 minority (all Hispanic Americans), 28 international. 99 applicants, 62% accepted, 39 enrolled. In 2009, 30 master's, 3 doctorates awarded. *Degree requirements:* For master's, thesis or alternative; for doctorate, thesis/dissertation. *Entrance requirements:* For master's, GRE General Test, sample of written work, resume, portfolio in creative writing; for doctorate, GRE General Test, sample of written work, resume. Additional exam requirements/recommendations for international students: Required—TOEFL (minimum score 600 paper-based; 100 iBT) or IELTS (minimum score 7). *Application deadline:* For fall admission, 1/5 priority date for domestic and international students. Application fee: $40 ($90 for international students). Electronic applications accepted. *Expenses:* Tuition, state resident: full-time $6716. Tuition, nonresident: full-time $8908. Tuition and fees vary according to course level, course load, program and student level. *Financial support:* In 2009–10, 10 research assistantships with full and partial tuition reimbursements (averaging $18,120 per year), 84 teaching assistantships with full and partial tuition reimbursements (averaging $18,120 per year) were awarded; fellowships, scholarships/grants, health care benefits, and unspecified assistantships also available. *Faculty research:* Creative writing, literature, rhetoric, composition and professional communication, teaching English as a second language, applied linguistics. *Unit head:* Dr. Charles Kostelnick, Chair, 515-294-2477, Fax: 515-294-2125, E-mail: englgrad@iastate.edu. *Application contact:* Dr. Constance Post, Director of Graduate Education, 515-294-3175, E-mail: englgrad@iastate.edu.

Kansas State University, Graduate School, College of Arts and Sciences, Department of Communication Studies, Theatre and Dance, Manhattan, KS 66505. Offers rhetoric/communication (MA); theatre (MA). *Faculty:* 17 full-time (8 women), 1 (woman) part-time/adjunct. *Students:* 10 applicants, 100% accepted, 10 enrolled. In 2009, 15 master's awarded. *Degree requirements:* For master's, thesis or alternative. *Entrance requirements:* For master's, GRE General Test (recommended), minimum GPA of 3.0. Additional exam requirements/recommendations for international students: Required—TOEFL. *Application deadline:* For fall admission, 2/1 priority date for domestic and international students; for spring admission, 8/1 priority date for domestic and international students. Applications are processed on a rolling basis. Application fee: $40 ($55 for international students). Electronic applications accepted. *Financial support:* In 2009–10, 23 teaching assistantships with full tuition reimbursements (averaging $9,391 per year) were awarded; career-related internships or fieldwork, institutionally sponsored loans, and scholarships/grants also available. Support available to part-time students. Financial award application deadline: 3/1; financial award applicants required to submit FAFSA. *Faculty research:* Drama therapy, directing, costume design, scenic design, technical theatre mechanics and safety. Total annual research expenditures: $10,294. *Unit head:* Charles Griffin, Head, 785-532-6860, Fax: 785-532-3714, E-mail: charlieg@ksu.edu. *Application contact:* William Schenck-Hamlin, Director, 785-532-6861, Fax: 785-532-3714, E-mail: billsh@ksu.edu.

Kent State University, College of Arts and Sciences, Department of English, Kent, OH 44242-0001. Offers comparative literature (MA); creative writing (MFA); English (PhD); English for teachers (MA); literature and writing (MA); rhetoric and composition (PhD); teaching English as a second language (MA). Part-time programs available. Terminal master's awarded for partial completion of doctoral program. *Degree requirements:* For master's, one foreign language, thesis optional; for doctorate, one foreign language, thesis/dissertation, qualifying exams. *Entrance requirements:* For master's and doctorate, GRE General Test, writing sample, letters of recommendation. Additional exam requirements/recommendations for international students: Required—TOEFL (minimum score 600 paper-based). Electronic applications accepted. *Faculty research:* British and American literature, textual editing, rhetoric and composition, cultural studies, linguistic and critical theories.

Michigan State University, The Graduate School, College of Arts and Letters, Program in Rhetoric and Writing, East Lansing, MI 48824. Offers critical studies in literacy and pedagogy (MA); digital rhetoric and professional writing (MA); rhetoric and writing (PhD). *Students:* 38 full-time (24 women), 15 part-time (8 women); includes 12 minority (5 African Americans, 1 Asian American or Pacific Islander, 6 Hispanic Americans), 3 international. Average age 31. 61 applicants, 16% accepted. In 2009, 6 master's, 7 doctorates awarded. *Entrance requirements:* Additional exam requirements/recommendations for international students: Required—TOEFL. Electronic applications accepted. *Expenses:* Tuition, state resident: part-time $478.25 per credit hour. Tuition, nonresident: part-time $966.50 per credit hour. Part-time tuition and fees vary according to program. *Financial support:* In 2009–10, 6 research assistantships with tuition reimbursements (averaging $6,452 per year), 30 teaching assistantships with tuition reimbursements (averaging $6,159 per year) were awarded. *Faculty research:* Rhetoric, writing and communication studies; media studies; technical communication, writing for digital environments. *Unit head:* Dr. Malea E. Powell, Director, Graduate Studies, 517-432-2583, Fax: 517-353-9162, E-mail: powell37@msu.edu. *Application contact:* Melissa Arthurton, Program Secretary, 517-353-9183, Fax: 517-353-9162, E-mail: arthurt1@msu.edu.

Michigan Technological University, Graduate School, College of Sciences and Arts, Department of Humanities, Program in Rhetoric and Technical Communication, Houghton, MI 49931. Offers MS, PhD. Part-time programs available. Terminal master's awarded for partial completion of doctoral program. *Degree requirements:* For master's, comprehensive exam; for doctorate, one foreign language, comprehensive exam, thesis/dissertation. *Entrance requirements:* Additional exam requirements/recommendations for international students: Required—TOEFL (minimum score 600 paper-based; 250 computer-based). Electronic applications accepted.

Monmouth University, Graduate School, Department of English, West Long Branch, NJ 07764-1898. Offers creative writing (MA); New Jersey studies (MA); rhetoric and writing (MA).

Rhetoric

Monmouth University (continued)

Part-time and evening/weekend programs available. *Faculty:* 11 full-time (8 women). *Students:* 7 full-time (5 women), 26 part-time (20 women); includes 2 minority (1 African American, 1 Hispanic American). Average age 35. 22 applicants, 95% accepted, 10 enrolled. In 2009, 14 master's awarded. *Degree requirements:* For master's, comprehensive exam (for some programs), thesis (for some programs). *Entrance requirements:* For master's, minimum overall GPA of 2.75, at least 15 credits in literary studies. Additional exam requirements/recommendations for international students: Required—TOEFL (minimum score 550 paper-based; 213 computer-based; 79 iBT), IELTS (minimum score 5), Michigan English Language Assessment Battery (minimum score 77), Cambridge A, B, C. *Application deadline:* For fall admission, 7/15 for domestic students, 6/1 for international students; for spring admission, 11/15 for domestic students, 11/1 for international students. Application fee: $50. *Expenses:* Tuition: Part-time $773 per credit. Required fees: $157 per semester. *Financial support:* In 2009–10, 28 students received support, including 20 fellowships (averaging $1,891 per year), 4 research assistantships (averaging $3,334 per year); career-related internships or fieldwork, scholarships/grants, and unspecified assistantships also available. Support available to part-time students. Financial award applicants required to submit FAFSA. *Faculty research:* Renaissance and medieval literature, nineteenth century American literature, eighteenth century British literature and women's studies, Old English and Middle English, African diaspora and African post-colonial literature. *Unit head:* Dr. Hiede Estes, Program Director, 732-571-7547, E-mail: hestes@monmouth.edu. *Application contact:* Kevin Roane, Director, Office of Graduate Admission, 732-571-3452, Fax: 732-263-5123, E-mail: gradadm@monmouth.edu.

New Mexico Highlands University, Graduate Studies, College of Arts and Sciences, Department of Humanities, Las Vegas, NM 87701. Offers English (MA), including creative writing, language, rhetoric and composition, literature. *Degree requirements:* For master's, comprehensive exam, thesis. *Entrance requirements:* For master's, minimum undergraduate GPA of 3.0. Additional exam requirements/recommendations for international students: Required—TOEFL (minimum score 540 paper-based; 207 computer-based). *Faculty research:* 20th century literature, life path writing in homeless shelters, native American philosophy, medieval intellectual and cultural history, creating pedagogical tools for teaching law.

New Mexico State University, Graduate School, College of Arts and Sciences, Department of English, Las Cruces, NM 88003-8001. Offers creative writing (MFA); English (MA); rhetoric and professional communication (PhD). Part-time programs available. *Faculty:* 26 full-time (15 women). *Students:* 81 full-time (45 women), 35 part-time (19 women); includes 23 minority (4 African Americans, 3 Asian Americans or Pacific Islanders, 16 Hispanic Americans), 7 international. Average age 32. 89 applicants, 66% accepted, 26 enrolled. In 2009, 27 master's awarded. *Degree requirements:* For master's, one foreign language, thesis (for some programs); for doctorate, comprehensive exam, thesis/dissertation, internship. *Entrance requirements:* For master's and doctorate, sample of written work. *Application deadline:* For fall admission, 2/1 for domestic and international students. Application fee: $30 ($50 for international students). Electronic applications accepted. *Expenses:* Tuition, state resident: full-time $4080; part-time $223 per credit. Tuition, nonresident: full-time $14,256; part-time $647 per credit. Required fees: $1278; $639 per semester. *Financial support:* In 2009–10, 2 research assistantships (averaging $7,900 per year), 55 teaching assistantships (averaging $15,193 per year) were awarded; fellowships, career-related internships or fieldwork, Federal Work-Study, institutionally sponsored loans, scholarships/grants, health care benefits, and unspecified assistantships also available. Financial award application deadline: 2/1; financial award applicants required to submit FAFSA. *Faculty research:* Composition research, history and theory of rhetoric, technical/professional communication, creative writing, English and American literature. *Unit head:* Dr. Monica F. Torres, Head, 575-646-2319, Fax: 575-646-7725, E-mail: mftorres@nmsu.edu. *Application contact:* Dr. Elizabeth Schirmer, Director of Graduate Studies, 575-646-1733, E-mail: eschirme@nmsu.edu.

North Carolina State University, Graduate School, College of Humanities and Social Sciences, Program in Communication, Rhetoric, and Digital Media, Raleigh, NC 27695. Offers PhD.

Northern Kentucky University, Office of Graduate Programs, College of Arts and Sciences, Program in English, Highland Heights, KY 41099. Offers composition and rhetoric (Certificate); English (MA); professional writing (Certificate). Part-time and evening/weekend programs available. *Students:* 7 full-time (4 women), 49 part-time (36 women); includes 3 minority (2 African Americans, 1 Hispanic American). Average age 33. 49 applicants, 76% accepted, 32 enrolled. *Degree requirements:* For master's, comprehensive exam or thesis. *Entrance requirements:* For master's, minimum GPA of 3.0, two letters of reference. Additional exam requirements/recommendations for international students: Required—TOEFL (minimum score 550 paper-based; 213 computer-based; 79 iBT); Recommended—IELTS (minimum score 6.5). *Application deadline:* For fall admission, 7/1 priority date for domestic students, 6/1 priority date for international students; for spring admission, 11/1 for domestic students, 10/1 for international students. Applications are processed on a rolling basis. Application fee: $40. Electronic applications accepted. *Expenses:* Tuition, state resident: full-time $6912; part-time $384 per credit hour. Tuition, nonresident: full-time $12,150; part-time $675 per credit hour. Tuition and fees vary according to course load, program and reciprocity agreements. *Financial support:* Unspecified assistantships available. Financial award applicants required to submit FAFSA. *Faculty research:* Professional writing and new media studies, composition and rhetoric, literary studies, creative writing, cinema studies. *Unit head:* Dr. Roxanne Kent-Drury, Coordinator, 859-572-6636, E-mail: rkdrury@nku.edu. *Application contact:* Dr. Peg Griffin, Director of Graduate Programs, 859-572-6934, Fax: 859-572-6670, E-mail: griffinp@nku.edu.

Ohio University, Graduate College, Scripps College of Communication, School of Communication Studies, Athens, OH 45701-2979. Offers health communication (PhD); organizational communication (MA); relating and organizing (PhD); rhetoric and public culture (PhD). Part-time programs available. Postbaccalaureate distance learning degree programs offered (minimal on-campus study). *Faculty:* 24 full-time (9 women), 4 part-time/adjunct (1 woman). *Students:* 48 full-time (33 women), 31 part-time (25 women); includes 5 minority (4 African Americans, 1 Hispanic American), 12 international. 98 applicants, 46% accepted, 36 enrolled. In 2009, 7 master's, 12 doctorates awarded. Terminal master's awarded for partial completion of doctoral program. *Degree requirements:* For master's, capstone; for doctorate, comprehensive exam, thesis/dissertation. *Entrance requirements:* For master's, GRE; for doctorate, GRE General Test, minimum GPA of 3.0. Additional exam requirements/recommendations for international students: Required—TOEFL (minimum score 550 paper-based; 80 iBT) or IELTS Academic (minimum score 6.5). *Application deadline:* For fall admission, 1/15 priority date for domestic and international students. Application fee: $50 ($55 for international students). Electronic applications accepted. *Expenses:* Tuition, state resident: full-time $7839; part-time $323 per quarter hour. Tuition, nonresident: full-time $15,831; part-time $654 per quarter hour. Required fees: $2931. *Financial support:* In 2009–10, 12 students received support, including fellowships with full tuition reimbursements available (averaging $13,600 per year), research assistantships with full tuition reimbursements available (averaging $13,600 per year), teaching assistantships with full tuition reimbursements available (averaging $13,600 per year); career-related internships or fieldwork, Federal Work-Study, and institutionally sponsored loans also available. Financial award application deadline: 1/15. *Faculty research:* Rhetoric and public culture, relating and organizing, health communication. Total annual research expenditures: $200,000. *Unit head:* Dr. Claudia Hale, Director, 740-593-4832, Fax: 740-593-4810, E-mail: hale@ohio.edu. *Application contact:* Dr. Scott Titsworth, Graduate Chairman, 740-593-9160, Fax: 740-593-4810, E-mail: titswort@ohio.edu.

Rensselaer Polytechnic Institute, Graduate School, School of Humanities and Social Sciences, Department of Language, Literature, and Communication, Programs in Communication and Rhetoric, Troy, NY 12180-3590. Offers MS, PhD. *Faculty:* 14 full-time (8 women). *Students:* 20 full-time (11 women); includes 2 minority (1 African American, 1 Hispanic American), 1 international. 21 applicants, 48% accepted, 5 enrolled. In 2009, 1 master's, 4 doctorates awarded. Terminal master's awarded for partial completion of doctoral program. *Degree requirements:* For master's, thesis optional; for doctorate, comprehensive exam, thesis/dissertation. *Entrance requirements:* For master's, GRE General Test, resume; for doctorate, GRE General Test, writing sample, resume or curriculum vitae. Additional exam requirements/recommendations for international students: Required—TOEFL (minimum score 570 paper-based; 230 computer-based). *Application deadline:* For fall admission, 1/15 priority date for domestic students; for spring admission, 10/15 priority date for domestic students. Applications are processed on a rolling basis. Application fee: $75. Electronic applications accepted. *Expenses:* Tuition: Full-time $38,100. *Financial support:* In 2009–10, 18 students received support, including 10 fellowships with full tuition reimbursements available (averaging $16,500 per year), 1 research assistantship with full tuition reimbursement available (averaging $16,500 per year), 8 teaching assistantships with full tuition reimbursements available (averaging $16,500 per year); career-related internships or fieldwork, institutionally sponsored loans, and unspecified assistantships also available. Financial award application deadline: 1/15. *Faculty research:* Human-computer interaction; media design and theory; rhetoric and culture; virtual institutions/communities; usability, digital and visual rhetoric. *Unit head:* Prof. James P. Zappen, Head, 518-276-6468, Fax: 518-276-4092, E-mail: zappenj@rpi.edu. *Application contact:* Kathy A. Colman, Recruitment Coordinator, 518-276-6469, Fax: 518-276-4092, E-mail: colmak@rpi.edu.

San Diego State University, Graduate and Research Affairs, College of Arts and Letters, Department of Rhetoric and Writing, San Diego, CA 92182. Offers MA. Part-time programs available. *Degree requirements:* For master's, thesis. *Entrance requirements:* For master's, GRE General Test, writing sample, 3 letters of reference. Additional exam requirements/recommendations for international students: Required—TOEFL. Electronic applications accepted.

Southern Illinois University Carbondale, Graduate School, College of Liberal Arts, Department of English, Carbondale, IL 62901-4701. Offers composition (MA, PhD), including composition, literature, rhetoric; creative writing (MFA). *Degree requirements:* For master's, one foreign language, thesis; for doctorate, 2 foreign languages, thesis/dissertation. *Entrance requirements:* For master's, GRE General Test, GRE Subject Test, minimum GPA of 2.7; for doctorate, GRE General Test, GRE Subject Test, minimum GPA of 3.25. Additional exam requirements/recommendations for international students: Required—TOEFL. *Faculty research:* British literature, English literature, modern Continental literature, literary criticism and theory, film studies, Irish studies.

Syracuse University, College of Arts and Sciences, Program in Composition and Cultural Rhetoric, Syracuse, NY 13244. Offers PhD. *Students:* 31 full-time (21 women), 5 part-time (2 women); includes 5 minority (3 African Americans, 2 Hispanic Americans), 1 international. Average age 36. 31 applicants, 13% accepted, 3 enrolled. In 2009, 4 doctorates awarded. *Degree requirements:* For doctorate, comprehensive exam, thesis/dissertation. *Entrance requirements:* For doctorate, GRE. Additional exam requirements/recommendations for international students: Required—TOEFL (minimum score 100 iBT). *Application deadline:* For fall admission, 2/1 priority date for domestic and international students. Application fee: $75. Electronic applications accepted. *Expenses:* Tuition: Full-time $26,808; part-time $1117 per credit. Required fees: $1024. *Financial support:* Fellowships with full tuition reimbursements, teaching assistantships with full tuition reimbursements available. Financial award application deadline: 1/1; financial award applicants required to submit FAFSA. *Unit head:* Prof. Gwendolyn Pough, Graduate Director, 315-443-1067, E-mail: gdpough@syr.edu. *Application contact:* Velita Chapple, 315-443-5146, E-mail: vnchappl@syr.edu.

Syracuse University, College of Visual and Performing Arts, Program in Communication and Rhetorical Studies, Syracuse, NY 13244. Offers MA. Part-time programs available. *Students:* 14 full-time (6 women), 2 part-time (both women); includes 1 minority (African American), 2 international. Average age 25. 23 applicants, 74% accepted, 9 enrolled. In 2009, 8 master's awarded. *Degree requirements:* For master's, thesis or alternative. *Entrance requirements:* For master's, GRE General Test, writing sample. Additional exam requirements/recommendations for international students: Required—TOEFL (minimum score 100 iBT). *Application deadline:* For fall admission, 2/1 priority date for domestic and international students. Application fee: $75. Electronic applications accepted. *Expenses:* Tuition: Full-time $26,808; part-time $1117 per credit. Required fees: $1024. *Financial support:* In 2009–10, 9 students received support; fellowships with full tuition reimbursements available, teaching assistantships with full and partial tuition reimbursements available, tuition waivers (partial) available. Financial award application deadline: 1/1; financial award applicants required to submit FAFSA. *Unit head:* Dr. Kendall Phillips, Chair, 315-443-2883, E-mail: kphillip@syr.edu. *Application contact:* Harriett Conti, Assistant Dean for Recruitment and Admissions, 315-443-5755, E-mail: hmconti@syr.edu.

Texas Christian University, AddRan College of Liberal Arts, Department of English, Fort Worth, TX 76129-0002. Offers composition (MA); English (PhD), including rhetoric and/or literature; literature (MA); rhetoric (MA); rhetoric/composition (PhD). Part-time and evening/weekend programs available. *Degree requirements:* For master's, one foreign language, thesis, candidacy exam; for doctorate, one foreign language, comprehensive exam, thesis/dissertation, 66 hours, diagnostic exam, qualifying exam. *Entrance requirements:* For master's and doctorate, GRE General Test, 30 hours of English; 12 hours of foreign language study. Additional exam requirements/recommendations for international students: Required—TOEFL. *Application deadline:* For fall admission, 1/31 for domestic and international students; for spring admission, 10/15 for domestic and international students. Application fee: $0. *Expenses:* Tuition: Full-time $17,640; part-time $980 per credit hour. Tuition and fees vary according to program. *Financial support:* In 2009–10, 28 students received support; fellowships with full tuition reimbursements available, research assistantships with full tuition reimbursements available, teaching assistantships with full tuition reimbursements available, tuition waivers (full) and unspecified assistantships available. Financial award application deadline: 3/1; financial award applicants required to submit FAFSA. *Unit head:* Dr. Brad Lucas, Chairperson, 817-257-7240. *Application contact:* Dr. Bonnie Carol Blackwell, Associate Professor/Director of Graduate Studies, 817-257-6263, E-mail: b.blackwell@tcu.edu.

Texas State University–San Marcos, Graduate School, College of Liberal Arts, Department of English, Program in Rhetoric and Composition, San Marcos, TX 78666. Offers MA. Part-time programs available. *Faculty:* 5 full-time (3 women). *Students:* 4 full-time (3 women), 10 part-time (7 women); includes 5 minority (1 American Indian/Alaska Native, 1 Asian American or Pacific Islander, 3 Hispanic Americans). Average age 33. 9 applicants, 100% accepted, 5 enrolled. In 2009, 4 master's awarded. *Degree requirements:* For master's, comprehensive exam, thesis optional. *Entrance requirements:* For master's, minimum GPA of 3.25 in minimum of 24 hours of undergraduate English, 6 hours of a foreign language. Additional exam requirements/recommendations for international students: Required—TOEFL (minimum score 550 paper-based; 213 computer-based). *Application deadline:* For fall admission, 6/15 for domestic students, 6/1 for international students; for spring admission, 10/15 for domestic students, 10/1 for international students. Applications are processed on a rolling basis. Application fee: $40 ($90 for international students). Electronic applications accepted. *Expenses:* Tuition, state resident: full-time $5784; part-time $241 per credit hour. Tuition, nonresident: part-time $551 per credit hour. Required fees: $1728; $48 per credit hour. $306. Tuition and fees vary according to course load. *Financial support:* In 2009–10, 9 students received support, including 1 research assistantship (averaging $6,290 per year); teaching assistantships, Federal Work-Study and institutionally sponsored loans also available. Support available to part-time students. Financial award application deadline: 4/1; financial award applicants required to submit FAFSA. *Unit head:* Dr. Rebecca Jackson, Graduate Advisor, 512-245-2163, E-mail: rj10@txstate.edu. *Application contact:* Dr. J. Michael Willoughby, Dean of Graduate School, 512-245-2581, Fax: 512-245-8365, E-mail: gradcollege@txstate.edu.

Texas Tech University, Graduate School, College of Arts and Sciences, Department of English, Lubbock, TX 79409. Offers English (MA, PhD); technical communication (MA); technical communication and rhetoric (PhD). Part-time programs available. *Faculty:* 38 full-time (15 women), 2 part-time/adjunct (both women). *Students:* 101 full-time (62 women), 94 part-time (58 women); includes 14 minority (4 African Americans, 2 American Indian/Alaska Native, 2 Asian Americans or Pacific Islanders, 6 Hispanic Americans), 15 international. Average age 35. 208 applicants, 31% accepted, 45 enrolled. In 2009, 30 master's, 10 doctorates awarded. *Degree requirements:* For master's, one foreign language, thesis (for some programs); for doctorate, thesis/dissertation. *Entrance requirements:* For master's and doctorate, GRE General Test. Additional exam requirements/recommendations for international students: Required—TOEFL (minimum score 550 paper-based; 213 computer-based). *Application deadline:* For fall admission, 3/1 priority date for international students; for spring admission, 11/1 priority date for international students. Applications are processed on a rolling basis. Application fee: $50 ($75 for international students). Electronic applications accepted. *Expenses:* Tuition, state resident: full-time $5100; part-time $213 per credit hour. Tuition, nonresident: full-time $11,748; part-time $490 per credit hour. Required fees: $2298; $50 per credit hour. $555 per semester. *Financial support:* In 2009–10, 8 research assistantships with partial tuition reimbursements (averaging $19,712 per year), 9 teaching assistantships with partial tuition reimbursements (averaging $14,010 per year) were awarded; Federal Work-Study and institutionally sponsored loans also available. Support available to part-time students. Financial award application deadline: 4/15; financial award applicants required to submit FAFSA. *Faculty research:* Computers and writing; technical communication and rhetoric; creative writing; nineteenth century studies; literature of social justice and the environment. *Unit head:* Dr. Sam Dragga, Chair, 806-742-2501, Fax: 806-742-0989, E-mail: sam.dragga@ttu.edu. *Application contact:* Dr. Brian McFadden, Director of Graduate Studies, 806-742-2501, Fax: 806-742-0989, E-mail: english.gradadvisor@ttu.edu.

Texas Woman's University, Graduate School, College of Arts and Sciences, Department of English, Speech, and Foreign Languages, Denton, TX 76201. Offers English (MA); rhetoric (PhD). Part-time programs available. *Faculty:* 16 full-time (10 women). *Students:* 9 full-time (8 women), 50 part-time (43 women); includes 11 minority (4 African Americans, 1 American Indian/Alaska Native, 2 Asian Americans or Pacific Islanders, 4 Hispanic Americans). Average age 38. 12 applicants, 75% accepted, 5 enrolled. In 2009, 4 master's, 5 doctorates awarded. *Degree requirements:* For master's, comprehensive exam, thesis; for doctorate, comprehensive exam, thesis/dissertation. *Entrance requirements:* For master's, GRE General Test (minimum score 500 verbal, 350 quantitative), 3 letters of reference, interview, minimum GPA of 3.0; for doctorate, GRE General Test, writing sample, 3 letters of reference, interview, minimum GPA of 3.0 on previous upper-division and graduate work. Additional exam requirements/recommendations for international students: Recommended—TOEFL (minimum score 600 paper-based; 213 computer-based; 79 iBT). *Application deadline:* For fall admission, 7/1 priority date for domestic students, 3/1 for international students; for spring admission, 12/1 priority date for domestic students, 7/1 for international students. Applications are processed on a rolling basis. Application fee: $50. Electronic applications accepted. *Expenses:* Tuition, state resident: full-time $3564; part-time $198 per credit hour. Tuition, nonresident: full-time $8550; part-time $475 per credit hour. Required fees: $69.26 per credit hour. Tuition and fees vary according to course load. *Financial support:* In 2009–10, 24 students received support, including 6 research assistantships (averaging $10,746 per year), 15 teaching assistantships (averaging $10,746 per year); career-related internships or fieldwork, Federal Work-Study, institutionally sponsored loans, scholarships/grants, traineeships, health care benefits, and unspecified assistantships also available. Support available to part-time students. Financial award application deadline: 3/1; financial award applicants required to submit FAFSA. *Faculty research:* British and American literature, rhetoric: historical and applied, composition studies and technology, literary theory and criticism, women's literature and feminist rhetoric. *Unit head:* Dr. Genevieve West, Chair, 940-898-2324, Fax: 940-898-2297, E-mail: engspfl@twu.edu. *Application contact:* Samuel Wheeler, Assistant Director of Admissions, 940-898-3188, Fax: 940-898-3081, E-mail: wheelersr@twu.edu.

The University of Alabama, Graduate School, College of Arts and Sciences, Department of English, Tuscaloosa, AL 35487. Offers composition and rhetoric (PhD); creative writing (MFA), including fiction, poetry; literature (MA, PhD); rhetoric and composition (MA); teaching English as a second language (MATESOL). *Faculty:* 30 full-time (12 women). *Students:* 123 full-time (71 women), 12 part-time (9 women); includes 14 minority (9 African Americans, 2 American Indian/Alaska Native, 1 Asian American or Pacific Islander, 2 Hispanic Americans), 4 international. Average age 27. 339 applicants, 17% accepted, 39 enrolled. In 2009, 31 degrees awarded. *Degree requirements:* For master's, one foreign language, comprehensive exam, thesis (for some programs); for doctorate, 2 foreign languages, comprehensive exam, thesis/dissertation. *Entrance requirements:* For master's and doctorate, GRE, minimum GPA of 3.0, critical writing sample. Additional exam requirements/recommendations for international students: Required—TOEFL. *Application deadline:* For fall admission, 1/15 priority date for domestic students, 1/15 for international students. Application fee: $50 ($60 for international students). Electronic applications accepted. *Expenses:* Tuition, state resident: full-time $7000. Tuition, nonresident: full-time $19,200. *Financial support:* In 2009–10, 7 fellowships with full tuition reimbursements (averaging $15,000 per year), 1 research assistantship (averaging $11,708 per year), 106 teaching assistantships with full tuition reimbursements (averaging $11,708 per year) were awarded; career-related internships or fieldwork, scholarships/grants, health care benefits, and unspecified assistantships also available. Financial award application deadline: 1/15. *Faculty research:* Critical theory; modern, Renaissance, and African-American literature. *Unit head:* Dr. Catherine E. Davies, Director of Graduate Studies, 205-348-8499, E-mail: cdavies@bama.ua.edu. *Application contact:* Vernita W. James, Office Assistant II, 205-348-0766, Fax: 205-348-1388, E-mail: vwjames@bama.ua.edu.

The University of Arizona, Graduate College, College of Humanities, Department of English, Rhetoric, Composition and the Teaching of English Program, Tucson, AZ 85721. Offers PhD. *Students:* 8 full-time (7 women), 45 part-time (37 women); includes 3 minority (1 American Indian/Alaska Native, 2 Hispanic Americans), 2 international. Average age 34. 41 applicants, 15% accepted, 6 enrolled. In 2009, 17 doctorates awarded. *Degree requirements:* For doctorate, one foreign language, comprehensive exam, thesis/dissertation. *Entrance requirements:* For doctorate, GRE General Test, 3 letters of recommendation, writing sample. Additional exam requirements/recommendations for international students: Required—TOEFL (minimum score 550 paper-based; 213 computer-based; 79 iBT). *Application deadline:* Applications are processed on a rolling basis. Application fee: $75. Electronic applications accepted. *Expenses:* Tuition, state resident: full-time $9028. Tuition, nonresident: full-time $24,890. *Unit head:* Theresa Enos, Director, 520-621-3255, Fax: 520-621-7397, E-mail: enos@u.arizona.edu. *Application contact:* Alison Miller, Program Assistant, 520-621-7213, Fax: 520-621-7397, E-mail: admiller@u.arizona.edu.

University of Arkansas at Little Rock, Graduate School, College of Arts, Humanities, and Social Science, Department of Rhetoric and Writing, Little Rock, AR 72204-1099. Offers professional and technical writing (MA). Part-time and evening/weekend programs available. *Degree requirements:* For master's, thesis or alternative, oral defense of final project. *Entrance requirements:* For master's, GRE, minimum GPA of 3.0, writing portfolio. *Faculty research:* Writing for industry, science, business, and government; composition and rhetorical theory; writing nonfiction; teaching of writing.

University of California, Berkeley, Graduate Division, College of Letters and Science, Department of Rhetoric, Berkeley, CA 94720-1500. Offers PhD. *Students:* 74 full-time (39 women). Average age 31. 358 applicants, 11 enrolled. In 2009, 11 doctorates awarded. *Degree requirements:* For doctorate, 2 foreign languages, thesis/dissertation, qualifying exam. *Entrance requirements:* For doctorate, GRE General Test, minimum GPA of 3.0, 3 letters of recommendation. *Application deadline:* For fall admission, 12/8 for domestic students. Application fee: $70 ($90 for international students). *Financial support:* Fellowships, research assistantships, teaching assistantships, unspecified assistantships available. *Faculty research:* History and theory of rhetoric, public discourse (law, politics, and science), literature and philosophy, film. *Unit head:* Prof. Marianne Constable, Chair, 510-642-1415, E-mail: rfa@berkeley.edu. *Application contact:* Maxine Fredericksen, Student Assistant, 510-642-3522, E-mail: trout@berkeley.edu.

The University of Iowa, Graduate College, College of Liberal Arts and Sciences, Department of Communication Studies, Iowa City, IA 52242-1316. Offers communication research (MA, PhD); rhetorical studies (MA, PhD). *Degree requirements:* For master's, thesis optional, exam; for doctorate, comprehensive exam, thesis/dissertation. *Entrance requirements:* For master's and doctorate, GRE General Test, minimum GPA of 3.0. Additional exam requirements/recommendations for international students: Required—TOEFL (minimum score 550 paper-based; 213 computer-based; 81 iBT). Electronic applications accepted.

The University of Iowa, Graduate College, College of Liberal Arts and Sciences, Department of English, Iowa City, IA 52242-1316. Offers English (PhD); literary criticism (PhD); literary history (PhD); literary studies (MA); nonfiction writing (MFA); rhetorical theory and stylistics (PhD); writer's workshop (MFA); JD/PhD. *Degree requirements:* For master's, thesis (for some programs), exam; for doctorate, comprehensive exam, thesis/dissertation. *Entrance requirements:* For master's and doctorate, GRE General Test, minimum GPA of 3.0. Additional exam requirements/recommendations for international students: Required—TOEFL (minimum score 640 paper-based; 273 computer-based; 111 iBT). Electronic applications accepted.

University of Louisiana at Lafayette, College of Liberal Arts, Department of English, Lafayette, LA 70504. Offers British and American literature (MA), including creative writing, folklore, rhetoric; creative writing (PhD); literature (PhD); rhetoric (PhD). Part-time programs available. Terminal master's awarded for partial completion of doctoral program. *Degree requirements:* For master's, one foreign language, thesis or alternative; for doctorate, 2 foreign languages, comprehensive exam, thesis/dissertation. *Entrance requirements:* For master's, GRE General Test, minimum GPA of 2.75; for doctorate, GRE General Test, minimum GPA of 3.0. Additional exam requirements/recommendations for international students: Required—TOEFL (minimum score 550 paper-based; 213 computer-based). Electronic applications accepted. *Faculty research:* Composition theory, Southern literature, medieval literature.

University of Louisville, Graduate School, College of Arts and Sciences, Department of English, Louisville, KY 40292. Offers English (MA), including creative writing, literature, rhetoric and composition (MA, PhD); English rhetoric and composition (PhD), including rhetoric and composition (MA, PhD). Part-time programs available. *Faculty:* 40 full-time (24 women). *Students:* 71 full-time (41 women), 29 part-time (20 women); includes 12 minority (7 African Americans, 1 American Indian/Alaska Native, 2 Asian Americans or Pacific Islanders, 2 Hispanic Americans), 5 international. Average age 30. 82 applicants, 65% accepted, 22 enrolled. In 2009, 22 master's, 7 doctorates awarded. *Degree requirements:* For master's, one foreign language, thesis or alternative, thesis or culminating project; for doctorate, 2 foreign languages, comprehensive exam, thesis/dissertation. *Entrance requirements:* For master's, GRE General Test, 2 academic letters of recommendation; for doctorate, GRE General Test, 15-20 page critical writing sample, 1000-word statement of professional goals, 3 academic letters of recommendation, application for graduate teaching assistantship (resume plus statement of teaching philosophy), transcripts of all college work. Additional exam requirements/recommendations for international students: Required—TOEFL (minimum score 600 paper-based; 210 computer-based; 100 iBT). *Application deadline:* For fall admission, 1/5 for domestic and international students. Applications are processed on a rolling basis. Application fee: $50. Electronic applications accepted. *Financial support:* Fellowships, teaching assistantships, health care benefits and unspecified assistantships available. Financial award application deadline: 1/5. *Faculty research:* American and English literatures and cultures, rhetoric and composition, critical theory and cultural studies, creative writing. Total annual research expenditures: $278,898. *Unit head:* Dr. Susan Griffin, Chair, 502-852-6801, Fax: 502-852-4182, E-mail: smgriff01@louisville.edu. *Application contact:* Libby Leggett, Director, Graduate Admissions, 502-852-3101, Fax: 502-852-6536, E-mail: gradadm@louisville.edu.

University of Nebraska–Lincoln, Graduate College, College of Arts and Sciences, Department of Communication Studies, Lincoln, NE 68588. Offers instructional communication (MA, PhD); interpersonal communication (MA, PhD); marketing, communication studies, and advertising (MA, PhD); organizational communication (MA, PhD); rhetoric and culture (MA, PhD). *Degree requirements:* For master's, thesis optional; for doctorate, comprehensive exam, thesis/dissertation. *Entrance requirements:* For master's and doctorate, GRE General Test, writing sample. Additional exam requirements/recommendations for international students: Required—TOEFL (minimum score 600 paper-based; 250 computer-based). Electronic applications accepted. *Faculty research:* Message strategies, gender communication, political communication, organizational communication, instructional communication.

University of Nebraska–Lincoln, Graduate College, College of Arts and Sciences, Department of English, Lincoln, NE 68588-0333. Offers composition and rhetoric (MA, PhD); creative writing (MA, PhD); literature studies (MA, PhD). *Degree requirements:* For master's, thesis optional; for doctorate, one foreign language, comprehensive exam, thesis/dissertation. *Entrance requirements:* For master's, writing sample; for doctorate, GRE General Test, writing sample. Additional exam requirements/recommendations for international students: Required—TOEFL (minimum score 600 paper-based; 250 computer-based). Electronic applications accepted. *Faculty research:* Creative writing, composition and rhetoric, women's studies, North American literature, medieval/Renaissance studies.

The University of North Carolina at Greensboro, Graduate School, College of Arts and Sciences, Department of English, Program in English, Greensboro, NC 27412-5001. Offers American literature (PhD); English (M Ed, MA); English literature (PhD); rhetoric and composition (PhD). *Degree requirements:* For master's, comprehensive exam, thesis or alternative; for doctorate, variable foreign language requirement, thesis/dissertation, preliminary exam. *Entrance requirements:* For master's, GRE General Test, GRE Subject Test, minimum GPA of 3.0; for doctorate, GRE General Test, GRE Subject Test, critical writing sample, minimum GPA of 3.0. Additional exam requirements/recommendations for international students: Required—TOEFL. Electronic applications accepted.

The University of Tennessee at Chattanooga, Graduate School, College of Arts and Sciences, Department of English, Chattanooga, TN 37403. Offers creative writing (MA); literary study (MA); rhetoric and writing (MA, Graduate Certificate). Part-time and evening/weekend programs available. *Faculty:* 12 full-time (7 women). *Students:* 11 full-time (10 women), 28 part-time (13 women); includes 2 minority (both African Americans). Average age 32. 27 applicants, 81% accepted, 11 enrolled. In 2009, 15 master's awarded. *Degree requirements:* For master's, one foreign language, comprehensive exam, thesis. *Entrance requirements:* For master's, GRE General Test or GRE Subject Test in literature, minimum GPA of 3.0 in English. Additional exam requirements/recommendations for international students: Required—TOEFL (minimum score 550 paper-based; 213 computer-based; 79 iBT), IELTS (minimum score 6). *Application deadline:* For fall admission, 8/1 priority date for domestic students, 6/1 for international students; for spring admission, 12/1 priority date for domestic students, 10/1 for international students. Applications are processed on a rolling basis. Application fee: $35. Electronic applications accepted. *Expenses:* Tuition, state resident: full-time $5404; part-time $300 per credit hour. Tuition, nonresident: full-time $16,702; part-time $928 per credit hour. Required fees: $1150; $130 per credit hour. *Financial support:* In 2009–10, 6 research assistantships with full and partial tuition reimbursements (averaging $5,500 per year) were awarded; career-related internships or fieldwork, scholarships/grants, and unspecified assistantships also available. Support available to part-time students. *Faculty research:* Technical writing, African-American literature, Milton, creative writing and poetry, American modernism and gender theory. Total annual research expenditures: $74,953. *Unit head:* Dr. Verbie Prevost, Head, 423-425-4238, Fax: 423-785-2282, E-mail: verbie-prevost@utc.edu. *Application contact:* Dr. Stephanie Bellar, Dean of Graduate Studies, 423-425-4666, Fax: 423-425-5223, E-mail: stephanie-bellar@utc.edu.

The University of Texas at El Paso, Graduate School, College of Liberal Arts, Department of English, El Paso, TX 79968-0001. Offers bilingual professional writing (Certificate); English and American literature (MA); rhetoric and composition (PhD); rhetoric and writing studies (MA); teaching English (MAT). Part-time and evening/weekend programs available. *Degree requirements:* For master's, thesis optional. *Entrance requirements:* For master's, GRE General

Rhetoric

The University of Texas at El Paso (continued)
Test, minimum GPA of 3.0. Additional exam requirements/recommendations for international students: Required—TOEFL. Electronic applications accepted. *Faculty research:* Literature, creative writing, literary theory.

University of Utah, The Graduate School, College of Humanities, Department of English, Program in Creative Writing, Salt Lake City, UT 84112. Offers rhetoric/composition (MA, PhD). *Students:* 8 full-time (5 women), 6 part-time (4 women); includes 2 minority (1 African American, 1 American Indian/Alaska Native). Average age 27. 30 applicants, 20% accepted, 6 enrolled. In 2009, 5 master's awarded. *Degree requirements:* For master's, variable foreign language requirement, comprehensive exam, thesis optional; for doctorate, variable foreign language requirement, comprehensive exam, thesis/dissertation. *Entrance requirements:* For master's and doctorate, GRE. *Application deadline:* For fall admission, 1/15 for domestic students. Application fee: $55 ($65 for international students). *Expenses:* Tuition, state resident: full-time $4004; part-time $1674 per semester. Tuition, nonresident: full-time $14,134; part-time $5915 per semester. Required fees: $324 per semester. Tuition and fees vary according to course load, degree level and program. *Financial support:* In 2009–10, 9 teaching assistantships with full tuition reimbursements (averaging $12,430 per year) were awarded; institutionally sponsored loans, scholarships/grants, health care benefits, and unspecified assistantships also available. *Unit head:* Dr. Maureen Ann Mathison, Director, 801-581-7090, E-mail: maureen.mathison@hum.utah.edu. *Application contact:* Pauline Frances Light, Office Support Coordinator, 801-581-7098, E-mail: plight@utah.edu.

University of Wisconsin–Madison, Graduate School, College of Letters and Science, Department of Communication Arts, Madison, WI 53706-1380. Offers communication science (MA, PhD); film (MA, PhD); media and cultural studies (MA, PhD); rhetoric (MA, PhD). Terminal master's awarded for partial completion of doctoral program. *Degree requirements:* For master's, one foreign language, thesis (for some programs); for doctorate, one foreign language, thesis/dissertation. *Entrance requirements:* For master's and doctorate, GRE General Test, minimum GPA of 3.5. Electronic applications accepted. *Expenses:* Tuition, state resident: part-time $594 per credit. Tuition, nonresident: part-time $1504 per credit. Required fees: $65 per credit. Tuition and fees vary according to course load, program and reciprocity agreements.

University of Wisconsin–Milwaukee, Graduate School, College of Letters and Sciences, Department of Communication, Milwaukee, WI 53201-0413. Offers communication (MA, PhD); mediation and negotiation (Certificate); rhetorical leadership (Certificate). Part-time programs available. *Faculty:* 19 full-time (11 women). *Students:* 17 full-time (14 women), 34 part-time (26 women); includes 4 minority (2 American Indian/Alaska Native, 2 Hispanic Americans), 7 international. Average age 30. 59 applicants, 68% accepted, 8 enrolled. In 2009, 13 master's awarded. *Degree requirements:* For master's, thesis or alternative; for doctorate, comprehensive exam. *Entrance requirements:* For master's, GRE General Test, minimum GPA of 3.0. Additional exam requirements/recommendations for international students: Required—TOEFL (minimum score 550 paper-based; 79 iBT), IELTS (minimum score 6). *Application deadline:* For fall admission, 1/1 priority date for domestic students; for spring admission, 9/1 for domestic students. Applications are processed on a rolling basis. Application fee: $45 ($75 for international students). *Expenses:* Tuition, state resident: full-time $8800. Tuition, nonresident: full-time $20,760. Tuition and fees vary according to program and reciprocity agreements. *Financial support:* In 2009–10, 30 teaching assistantships were awarded; career-related internships or fieldwork and unspecified assistantships also available. Support available to part-time students. Financial award application deadline: 4/15. *Unit head:* Mike R. Allen, Representative, 414-229-4261, Fax: 414-229-3859, E-mail: mikealle@uwm.edu. *Application contact:* General Information Contact, 414-229-4982, Fax: 414-229-6967, E-mail: gradschool@uwm.edu.

University of Wisconsin–Milwaukee, Graduate School, College of Letters and Sciences, Department of English, Milwaukee, WI 53201-0413. Offers creative writing (PhD); English (MA); international technical communication (Certificate); linguistics (PhD); professional writing (PhD); professional writing and communication (Certificate); rhetoric and composition (PhD); MLIS/MA. *Faculty:* 38 full-time (19 women). *Students:* 107 full-time (64 women), 82 part-time (54 women); includes 13 minority (8 African Americans, 1 American Indian/Alaska Native, 2 Asian Americans or Pacific Islanders, 2 Hispanic Americans), 23 international. Average age 34. 193 applicants, 51% accepted, 31 enrolled. In 2009, 26 master's, 16 doctorates awarded. *Degree requirements:* For master's, thesis or alternative; for doctorate, one foreign language, thesis/dissertation. *Entrance requirements:* For master's, GRE General Test, GRE Subject Test; for doctorate, GRE. Additional exam requirements/recommendations for international students: Required—TOEFL (minimum score 550 paper-based; 79 iBT), IELTS (minimum score 6.5). *Application deadline:* For fall admission, 1/1 priority date for domestic students; for spring admission, 9/1 for domestic students. Applications are processed on a rolling basis. Application fee: $45 ($75 for international students). *Expenses:* Tuition, state resident: full-time $8800. Tuition, nonresident: full-time $20,760. Tuition and fees vary according to program and reciprocity agreements. *Financial support:* In 2009–10, 75 teaching assistantships were awarded; career-related internships or fieldwork and unspecified assistantships also available. Support available to part-time students. Financial award application deadline: 4/15. Total annual research expenditures: $41,495. *Unit head:* Tasha Oren, Representative, 414-229-4637, Fax: 414-229-2643, E-mail: tgoren@uwm.edu. *Application contact:* General Information Contact, 414-229-4982, Fax: 414-229-6967, E-mail: gradschool@uwm.edu.

Virginia Commonwealth University, Graduate School, College of Humanities and Sciences, Department of English, Program in English, Richmond, VA 23284-9005. Offers literature (MA); writing and rhetoric (MA).

Wright State University, School of Graduate Studies, College of Liberal Arts, Department of English Language and Literatures, Dayton, OH 45435. Offers composition and rhetoric (MA); English (MA); literature (MA); teaching English to speakers of other languages (MA). *Degree requirements:* For master's, thesis optional, portfolio. *Entrance requirements:* For master's, 20 hours in upper-level English. Additional exam requirements/recommendations for international students: Required—TOEFL. *Faculty research:* American literature, world literature in English, applied linguistics, writing theory and pedagogy.

Speech and Interpersonal Communication

Arizona State University, Graduate College, College of Liberal Arts and Sciences, Division of Social Sciences, Hugh Downs School of Human Communication, Tempe, AZ 85287. Offers communication (MA, PhD). *Degree requirements:* For master's, thesis or alternative; for doctorate, thesis/dissertation.

Arkansas State University—Jonesboro, Graduate School, College of Communications, Department of Communication Studies, Jonesboro, State University, AR 72467. Offers communication studies and theatre arts (MA); communication studies and theatre arts education (SCCT). Part-time programs available. *Faculty:* 5 full-time (2 women). *Students:* 6 full-time (3 women), 4 part-time (2 women); includes 2 minority (both African Americans), 2 international. Average age 28. 11 applicants, 73% accepted, 5 enrolled. In 2009, 4 master's awarded. *Degree requirements:* For master's, one foreign language, comprehensive exam, thesis or alternative; for SCCT, comprehensive exam. *Entrance requirements:* For master's, GRE General Test or MAT, appropriate bachelor's degree, writing sample, letter of recommendation; for SCCT, GRE or MAT, appropriate master's degree, interview, official transcript, immunization records. Additional exam requirements/recommendations for international students: Required—TOEFL (minimum score 550 paper-based; 213 computer-based; 79 iBT), IELTS (minimum score 6). *Application deadline:* For fall admission, 7/15 for domestic students, 7/1 for international students; for spring admission, 12/1 for domestic students, 11/13 for international students. Applications are processed on a rolling basis. Application fee: $30 ($40 for international students). Electronic applications accepted. *Expenses:* Tuition, state resident: full-time $3744; part-time $208 per credit hour. Tuition, nonresident: full-time $9540; part-time $530 per credit hour. Required fees: $896; $47 per credit hour. $25 per term. One-time fee: $50. Tuition and fees vary according to course load and program. *Financial support:* In 2009–10, 6 students received support; teaching assistantships, career-related internships or fieldwork, scholarships/grants, and unspecified assistantships available. Financial award application deadline: 7/1; financial award applicants required to submit FAFSA. *Unit head:* Dr. Thomas Bagland, Chair, 870-972-3091, Fax: 870-972-3856, E-mail: tbaglan@astate.edu. *Application contact:* Dr. Andrew Sustich, Dean of the Graduate School, 870-972-3029, Fax: 870-972-3857, E-mail: sustich@astate.edu.

Ball State University, Graduate School, College of Communication, Information, and Media, Department of Communication Studies, Muncie, IN 47306-1099. Offers speech, public address, forensics, and rhetoric (MA). *Entrance requirements:* For master's, GRE General Test.

Bob Jones University, Graduate Programs, Greenville, SC 29614. Offers accountancy (MS); Bible (MA); Bible translation (MA); Biblical studies (Certificate); broadcast management (MS); business administration (MBA); church history (MA, PhD); church ministries (MA); church music (MM); cinema and video production (MA); counseling (MS); curriculum and instruction (Ed D); divinity (M Div); dramatic production (MA); educational leadership (MS, Ed D, Ed S); elementary education (M Ed, MAT); English (M Ed, MA, MAT); fine arts (MA); graphic design (MA); history (M Ed, MA); illustration (MA); interpretative speech (MA); mathematics (M Ed, MAT); medical missions (Certificate); ministry (MM, D Min); multi-categorical special education (M Ed, MAT); music (M Ed); New Testament interpretation (PhD); Old Testament interpretation (PhD); orchestral instrument performance (MM); organ performance (MM); pastoral studies (MA); personnel services (MS, Ed S); piano pedagogy (MM); piano performance (MM); platform arts (MA); radio and television broadcasting (MS); rhetoric and public address (MA); secondary education (M Ed); studio art (MA); teaching Bible (MA); theology (MA, PhD); voice performance (MM); youth ministries (MA); M Div/MM.

Bowling Green State University, Graduate College, College of Arts and Sciences, School of Communication Studies, Program of Communication Studies, Bowling Green, OH 43403. Offers MA, PhD. Terminal master's awarded for partial completion of doctoral program. *Degree requirements:* For master's, thesis or alternative; for doctorate, comprehensive exam, thesis/dissertation. *Entrance requirements:* For master's and doctorate, GRE General Test. Additional exam requirements/recommendations for international students: Required—TOEFL. Electronic applications accepted. *Faculty research:* Rhetorical theory and criticism, culture and communication, interpersonal/organizational communication.

Brooklyn College of the City University of New York, Division of Graduate Studies, Department of Speech Communication Arts and Sciences, Brooklyn, NY 11210-2889. Offers audiology (Au D); speech (MA), including public communication; speech and hearing sciences (PhD); speech pathology (MS). *Accreditation:* ASHA (one or more programs are accredited). Part-time programs available. *Students:* 31 full-time (all women), 51 part-time (50 women); includes 14 minority (6 African Americans, 2 Asian Americans or Pacific Islanders, 6 Hispanic Americans), 1 international. Average age 26. 313 applicants, 23% accepted, 31 enrolled. In 2009, 42 master's awarded. Terminal master's awarded for partial completion of doctoral program. *Degree requirements:* For master's, comprehensive exam, NTE. *Entrance requirements:* For master's, GRE, minimum GPA of 3.0, interview, essay. Additional exam requirements/recommendations for international students: Required—TOEFL (minimum score 500 paper-based; 173 computer-based; 61 iBT). *Application deadline:* For fall admission, 2/1 priority date for domestic and international students. Applications are processed on a rolling basis. Electronic applications accepted. *Expenses:* Tuition, area resident: Full-time $7360; part-time $310 per credit hour. Tuition, state resident: full-time $7360; part-time $310 per credit hour. Tuition, nonresident: full-time $13,800; part-time $575 per credit hour. International tuition: $13,800 full-time. Required fees: $140.10 per semester. *Financial support:* Career-related internships or fieldwork, Federal Work-Study, institutionally sponsored loans, scholarships/grants, and traineeships available. Support available to part-time students. Financial award application deadline: 5/1; financial award applicants required to submit FAFSA. *Faculty research:* Language and learning disorders, aphasia, auditory disorders, public and business communication, voice and fluency disorders. *Unit head:* Dr. Michele Emmer, Chairperson, 718-951-5225, Fax: 718-951-4167, E-mail: memmer@brooklyn.cuny.edu. *Application contact:* Hernan Sierra, Graduate Admissions Coordinator, 718-951-4536, Fax: 718-951-4506, E-mail: grads@brooklyn.cuny.edu.

California State University, Fullerton, Graduate Studies, College of Communications, Department of Human Communications, Fullerton, CA 92834-9480. Offers communicative disorders (MA); speech communication (MA). *Accreditation:* ASHA. Part-time programs available. *Students:* 79 full-time (69 women), 42 part-time (31 women); includes 44 minority (8 African Americans, 14 Asian Americans or Pacific Islanders, 22 Hispanic Americans), 6 international. Average age 31. 266 applicants, 14% accepted, 29 enrolled. In 2009, 47 master's awarded. *Degree requirements:* For master's, comprehensive exam, thesis or alternative. *Entrance requirements:* For master's, minimum GPA of 3.0 in major. Application fee: $55. *Expenses:* Tuition, nonresident: full-time $11,160; part-time $373 per credit. Required fees: $1440 per term. Tuition and fees vary according to course load, degree level and program. *Financial support:* Teaching assistantships, career-related internships or fieldwork, Federal Work-Study, institutionally sponsored loans, and scholarships/grants available. Support available to part-time students. Financial award application deadline: 3/1; financial award applicants required to submit FAFSA. *Faculty research:* Speech therapy. *Unit head:* Dr. John Reinard, Chair, 657-278-3617. *Application contact:* Dr. John Reinard, Chair, 657-278-3617.

California State University, Fullerton, Graduate Studies, College of Humanities and Social Sciences, Program in Linguistics, Fullerton, CA 92834-9480. Offers analysis of specific language structures (MA); anthropological linguistics (MA); applied linguistics (MA); communication and semantics (MA); disorders of communication (MA); experimental phonetics (MA). Part-time programs available. *Students:* 20 full-time (10 women), 8 part-time (5 women); includes 5 minority (1 Asian American or Pacific Islander, 4 Hispanic Americans), 11 international. Average age 31. 21 applicants, 71% accepted, 8 enrolled. In 2009, 3 master's awarded. *Degree requirements:* For master's, one foreign language, thesis or alternative, project. *Entrance requirements:* For master's, minimum GPA of 3.0, undergraduate major in linguistics or related field. Application fee: $55. *Expenses:* Tuition, nonresident: full-time $11,160; part-time $373 per credit. Required fees: $1440 per term. Tuition and fees vary according to course load, degree level and program. *Financial support:* Career-related internships or fieldwork, Federal Work-Study, institutionally sponsored loans, and scholarships/grants available. Support available to part-time students. Financial award application deadline: 3/1; financial award applicants required to submit FAFSA. *Unit head:* Dr. Franz Muller-Gotama, Adviser, 657-278-2441. *Application contact:* Admissions/Applications, 657-278-2371.

California State University, Los Angeles, Graduate Studies, College of Arts and Letters, Department of Communication Studies, Los Angeles, CA 90032-8530. Offers speech communication (MA); television, film and theatre (MFA). Part-time and evening/weekend programs available. *Faculty:* 6 full-time (3 women), 8 part-time/adjunct (4 women). *Students:* 69 full-time (40 women), 52 part-time (38 women); includes 48 minority (18 African Americans, 9 Asian Americans or Pacific Islanders, 21 Hispanic Americans), 18 international. Average age 31. 92 applicants, 99% accepted, 34 enrolled. In 2009, 17 master's awarded. *Degree requirements:* For master's, comprehensive exam or thesis. *Entrance requirements:* For master's, minimum GPA of 2.75 in last 90 units of course work. Additional exam requirements/recommendations for international students: Required—TOEFL (minimum score 500 paper-based; 173 computer-based). *Application deadline:* For fall admission, 5/1 for domestic and international students. Applications are processed on a rolling basis. Application fee: $55. Electronic applications accepted. *Financial support:* Career-related internships or fieldwork and Federal Work-Study available. Support available to part-time students. Financial award application deadline: 3/1. *Faculty research:* Organizational, interpersonal, intercultural, and instructional communication; rhetorical theories. *Unit head:* Dr. Suzanne Regan, Chair, 323-343-4200, Fax: 323-343-6467, E-mail: sregan@calstatela.edu. *Application contact:* Dr. Cheryl L. Ney, Associate Vice President for Academic Affairs and Dean of Graduate Studies, 323-343-3820, Fax: 323-343-5653, E-mail: cney@cslanet.calstatela.edu.

California State University, Northridge, Graduate Studies, College of Arts, Media, and Communication, Department of Communication Studies, Northridge, CA 91330. Offers MA. *Faculty:* 13 full-time (4 women), 24 part-time/adjunct (9 women). *Students:* 26 full-time (21 women), 23 part-time (16 women); includes 6 African Americans, 3 Asian Americans or Pacific Islanders, 3 Hispanic Americans, 10 international. Average age 29. 74 applicants, 46% accepted, 19 enrolled. In 2009, 6 master's awarded. *Entrance requirements:* For master's, GRE General Test. Additional exam requirements/recommendations for international students: Required—TOEFL. *Application deadline:* For fall admission, 11/30 for domestic students. Application fee: $55. *Financial support:* Teaching assistantships available. Financial award application deadline: 3/1. *Unit head:* Dr. Bernardo Attias, Chair, 818-677-2853. *Application contact:* Dr. Bernardo Attias, Chair, 818-677-2853.

Central Michigan University, College of Graduate Studies, College of Communication and Fine Arts, Department of Communication and Dramatic Arts, Concentration in Interpersonal and Public Communication, Mount Pleasant, MI 48859. Offers MA. *Accreditation:* ACEJMC. Part-time programs available. *Degree requirements:* For master's, thesis. *Entrance requirements:* For master's, minimum GPA of 3.0 in last 60 hours of undergraduate study and in last 15 hours of communication courses or other courses approved by department. Electronic applications accepted. *Faculty research:* Communication theory, interpersonal/nonverbal communication, organizational communication, family and interpersonal communication, political communication.

Colorado State University, Graduate School, College of Liberal Arts, Department of Communication Studies, Fort Collins, CO 80523-1783. Offers MA. *Faculty:* 14 full-time (6 women), 1 part-time/adjunct (0 women). *Students:* 23 full-time (14 women), 4 part-time (3 women); includes 3 minority (all Hispanic Americans). Average age 25. 44 applicants, 32% accepted, 10 enrolled. In 2009, 10 master's awarded. *Entrance requirements:* For master's, GRE General Test, minimum GPA of 3.0; writing sample, letters of recommendation. Additional exam requirements/recommendations for international students: Required—TOEFL (minimum score 550 paper-based; 230 computer-based). *Application deadline:* For fall admission, 1/31 priority date for domestic and international students. Applications are processed on a rolling basis. Application fee: $50. Electronic applications accepted. *Expenses:* Tuition, state resident: full-time $6434; part-time $359.10 per credit. Tuition, nonresident: full-time $18,116; part-time $1006.45 per credit. Required fees: $1496; $83 per credit. *Financial support:* In 2009–10, 20 students received support, including 20 teaching assistantships with full and partial tuition reimbursements available (averaging $12,176 per year); scholarships/grants and unspecified assistantships also available. Financial award application deadline: 3/1; financial award applicants required to submit FAFSA. *Faculty research:* Rhetorical theory and criticism, media and popular culture, intercultural communication, freedom of speech, communication theory. Total annual research expenditures: $23,076. *Unit head:* Dr. Sue Pendell, Head, 970-491-6140, Fax: 970-491-2160, E-mail: sue.pendell@colostate.edu. *Application contact:* Dr. Greg Dickinson, Director of Graduate Studies, 970-491-6893, Fax: 970-491-2160, E-mail: greg.dickinson@colostate.edu.

Eastern Illinois University, Graduate School, College of Arts and Humanities, Department of Communication Studies, Charleston, IL 61920-3099. Offers MA. Part-time programs available. *Faculty:* 11 full-time (2 women). In 2009, 21 master's awarded. *Degree requirements:* For master's, major paper. *Application deadline:* For fall admission, 3/31 priority date for domestic students. Applications are processed on a rolling basis. Application fee: $30. *Expenses:* Tuition, state resident: full-time $9434; part-time $239 per credit hour. Tuition, nonresident: full-time $23,774; part-time $717 per credit hour. Required fees: $802.63. *Financial support:* In 2009–10, 1 research assistantship with tuition reimbursement (averaging $8,100 per year), 6 teaching assistantships with tuition reimbursements (averaging $8,100 per year) were awarded. *Unit head:* Dr. Mark Borzi, Chairperson, 217-581-2016, E-mail: cfmgb@eiu.edu. *Application contact:* Dr. Olaf Hoerschelmann, Coordinator, 217-581-6984, E-mail: ohoerschelmann@eiu.edu.

Florida State University, The Graduate School, College of Communication and Information, School of Communication, Tallahassee, FL 32306. Offers corporate and public communication (MA, MS); integrated marketing communication (MA, MS); mass communication (PhD); media and communication studies (MA, MS); speech communication (PhD). Part-time programs available. *Faculty:* 24 full-time (9 women), 6 part-time/adjunct (1 woman). *Students:* 153 full-time (110 women), 65 part-time (34 women); includes 62 minority (37 African Americans, 1 American Indian/Alaska Native, 24 Hispanic Americans). Average age 24. 230 applicants, 76% accepted, 85 enrolled. In 2009, 84 master's, 6 doctorates awarded. *Degree requirements:* For master's, thesis (for some programs); for doctorate, comprehensive exam, thesis/dissertation. *Entrance requirements:* For master's, GRE General Test, minimum GPA of 3.0; for doctorate, GRE General Test, minimum GPA of 3.3 in graduate course work. Additional exam requirements/recommendations for international students: Required—TOEFL (minimum score 600 paper-based; 250 computer-based; 100 iBT). *Application deadline:* For fall admission, 7/1 priority date for domestic students, 5/1 priority date for international students; for spring admission, 11/1 priority date for domestic and international students. Applications are processed on a rolling basis. Application fee: $30. Electronic applications accepted. *Expenses:* Tuition, state resident: full-time $7413. Tuition, nonresident: full-time $22,567. *Financial support:* In 2009–10, 52 students received support, including 1 fellowship with full tuition reimbursement available, 8 research assistantships with full tuition reimbursements available (averaging $14,000 per year), 40 teaching assistantships with full tuition reimbursements available (averaging $5,000 per year); career-related internships or fieldwork, Federal Work-Study, institutionally sponsored loans, scholarships/grants, tuition waivers (partial), and unspecified assistantships also available. Support available to part-time students. Financial award application deadline: 2/1; financial award applicants required to submit FAFSA. *Faculty research:* Communication technology and policy, marketing communication, communication content and effect, new communication/information technologies. Total annual research expenditures: $600,000. *Unit head:* Dr. Stephen D. McDowell, Director, 850-644-2276, Fax: 850-644-8642, E-mail: steve.mcdowell@cci.fsu.edu. *Application contact:* Natashia Hinson-Turner, Graduate Coordinator, 850-644-8746, Fax: 850-644-8642, E-mail: natashia.turner@cci.fsu.edu.

Georgia State University, College of Arts and Sciences, Department of Communication, Atlanta, GA 30302-3083. Offers film/video/digital imaging (MA); human communication and social influence (MA); mass communication (MA); moving image studies (PhD); public communication (PhD). Part-time programs available. *Degree requirements:* For master's, one foreign language, thesis or alternative; for doctorate, comprehensive exam, thesis/dissertation. *Entrance requirements:* For master's and doctorate, GRE General Test. Additional exam requirements/recommendations for international students: Required—TOEFL (minimum score 80 computer-based). Electronic applications accepted. *Faculty research:* Critical/cultural studies, rhetoric studies, film/media studies, mass communications/journalism, audience studies.

Hofstra University, School of Communication, Department of Speech Communication, Rhetoric, and Performance Studies, Hempstead, NY 11549. Offers speech communication and rhetorical studies (MA). Part-time and evening/weekend programs available. *Faculty:* 4 full-time (1 woman). *Students:* 10 full-time (6 women), 13 part-time (7 women); includes 9 minority (8 African Americans, 1 Hispanic American), 2 international. Average age 29. 18 applicants, 100% accepted, 10 enrolled. In 2009, 3 master's awarded. *Degree requirements:* For master's, thesis. *Entrance requirements:* For master's, 2 letters of recommendation, interview. Additional exam requirements/recommendations for international students: Required—TOEFL (minimum score 550 paper-based; 213 computer-based; 80 iBT). *Application deadline:* Applications are processed on a rolling basis. Application fee: $60. Electronic applications accepted. *Expenses:* Tuition: Full-time $16,200; part-time $900 per credit hour. Required fees: $970; $145 per term. Tuition and fees vary according to program. *Financial support:* In 2009–10, 6 students received support, including 3 fellowships with full and partial tuition reimbursements available (averaging $4,000 per year), 3 research assistantships with full and partial tuition reimbursements available (averaging $12,494 per year); Federal Work-Study, institutionally sponsored loans, scholarships/grants, tuition waivers (full and partial), and unspecified assistantships also available. Support available to part-time students. Financial award applicants required to submit FAFSA. *Faculty research:* Performance of race and gender, public deliberation, public memory, civic engagement and political participation, popular culture. *Unit head:* Dr. Maryanne Trasciatti, Chairperson, 516-463-5427, Fax: 516-463-7012, E-mail: sphmat@hofstra.edu. *Application contact:* Carol Drummer, Dean of Graduate Admissions, 516-463-4876, Fax: 516-463-4664, E-mail: gradstudent@hofstra.edu.

Idaho State University, Office of Graduate Studies, College of Arts and Sciences, Department of Communication and Rhetorical Studies, Pocatello, ID 83209-8115. Offers communication and rhetorical studies (MA). Part-time programs available. *Faculty:* 4 full-time (1 woman). *Students:* 8 full-time (3 women), 7 part-time (4 women); includes 1 minority (Hispanic American), 1 international. Average age 36. In 2009, 3 master's awarded. *Degree requirements:* For master's, comprehensive exam, paper or thesis. *Entrance requirements:* For master's, GRE General Test, minimum GPA of 3.0 in all upper-level courses. Additional exam requirements/recommendations for international students: Required—TOEFL (minimum score 550 paper-based; 213 computer-based; 80 iBT). *Application deadline:* For fall admission, 7/1 for domestic students, 6/1 for international students; for spring admission, 12/1 for domestic students, 11/1 for international students. Applications are processed on a rolling basis. Application fee: $55. Electronic applications accepted. *Expenses:* Tuition, state resident: full-time $3318; part-time $297 per credit hour. Tuition, nonresident: full-time $13,120; part-time $437 per credit hour. Required fees: $2530. Tuition and fees vary according to program. *Financial support:* In 2009–10, 2 teaching assistantships with full and partial tuition reimbursements (averaging $10,841 per year) were awarded; Federal Work-Study, institutionally sponsored loans, scholarships/grants, health care benefits, and unspecified assistantships also available. Support available to part-time students. Financial award application deadline: 1/1; financial award applicants required to submit FAFSA. *Faculty research:* Metaphor and cognition in organizational groups and teams; rhetorical criticism of contemporary culture, including music, film, television, and advertising; communication pedagogy; the effect of language on organizational identification and commitment; risk communication and crisis communication. *Unit head:* Dr. James DiSanza, Chairman, 208-282-3395, Fax: 208-282-4598, E-mail: disajame@isu.edu. *Application contact:* Tami Carson, Graduate School Technical Records Specialist, 208-282-2150, Fax: 208-282-4847, E-mail: carstami@isu.edu.

Indiana University Bloomington, University Graduate School, College of Arts and Sciences, Department of Communication and Culture, Bloomington, IN 47405-7000. Offers film and media studies (PhD); performance and ethnography (PhD); rhetoric and public culture (PhD). *Faculty:* 24 full-time (12 women). *Students:* 85 full-time (43 women), 1 (woman) part-time; includes 9 minority (1 African American, 1 Asian American or Pacific Islander, 7 Hispanic Americans), 9 international. Average age 32. 179 applicants, 15% accepted, 15 enrolled. In 2009, 5 master's, 11 doctorates awarded. *Degree requirements:* For master's, comprehensive exam; for doctorate, one foreign language, comprehensive exam, thesis/dissertation, student teaching. *Entrance requirements:* For master's and doctorate, GRE General Test (recommended), minimum GPA of 3.0, 3 letters of recommendation, writing sample. Additional exam requirements/recommendations for international students: Required—TOEFL (minimum score 550 paper-based; 213 computer-based). *Application deadline:* For winter admission, 1/1 for domestic students, 12/1 for international students. Application fee: $55 ($65 for international students). Electronic applications accepted. *Financial support:* In 2009–10, 65 students received support, including 4 fellowships with full tuition reimbursements available (averaging $18,000 per year), 61 teaching assistantships with full tuition reimbursements available (averaging $12,961 per year). Financial award application deadline: 4/15. *Faculty research:* Rhetoric and public culture, film and media studies, performance ethnography. *Unit head:* Prof. Gregory A. Waller, Chair, 812-855-2367, Fax: 812-855-6014, E-mail: cmcl@indiana.edu. *Application contact:* Kathy P. Teige, Graduate Secretary, 812-855-6389, Fax: 812-855-6014, E-mail: kteige@indiana.edu.

Kansas State University, Graduate School, College of Arts and Sciences, Department of Communication Studies, Theatre and Dance, Manhattan, KS 66505. Offers rhetoric/communication (MA); theatre (MA). *Faculty:* 17 full-time (8 women), 1 (woman) part-time/adjunct. *Students:* 10 applicants, 100% accepted, 10 enrolled. In 2009, 15 master's awarded. *Degree requirements:* For master's, thesis or alternative. *Entrance requirements:* For master's, GRE General Test (recommended), minimum GPA of 3.0. Additional exam requirements/recommendations for international students: Required—TOEFL. *Application deadline:* For fall admission, 2/1 priority date for domestic and international students; for spring admission, 8/1 priority date for domestic and international students. Applications are processed on a rolling basis. Application fee: $40 ($55 for international students). Electronic applications accepted. *Financial support:* In 2009–10, 23 teaching assistantships with full tuition reimbursements (averaging $9,391 per year) were awarded; career-related internships or fieldwork, institutionally sponsored loans, and scholarships/grants also available. Support available to part-time students. Financial award application deadline: 3/1; financial award applicants required to submit FAFSA. *Faculty research:* Drama therapy, directing, costume design, scenic design, technical theatre mechanics and safety. Total annual research expenditures: $10,294. *Unit head:* Charles Griffin, Head, 785-532-6860, Fax: 785-532-3714, E-mail: charlieg@ksu.edu. *Application contact:* William Schenck-Hamlin, Director, 785-532-6861, Fax: 785-532-3714, E-mail: billsh@ksu.edu.

Louisiana Tech University, Graduate School, College of Liberal Arts, Department of Speech, Ruston, LA 71272. Offers speech (MA); speech pathology and audiology (MA). *Accreditation:* ASHA. *Degree requirements:* For master's, thesis or alternative. *Entrance requirements:* For master's, GRE General Test.

Marquette University, Graduate School, College of Communication, Milwaukee, WI 53201-1881. Offers advertising and public relations (MA); broadcasting and electronic communications (MA); communications studies (MA); journalism (MA); mass communications (MA); religious communications (MA); science, health and environmental communications (MA). *Accreditation:* ACEJMC. Part-time and evening/weekend programs available. *Faculty:* 31 full-time (17 women), 35 part-time/adjunct (16 women). *Students:* 28 full-time (21 women), 30 part-time (24 women); includes 3 minority (1 African American, 2 American Indian/Alaska Native), 7 international. Average age 26. 81 applicants, 47% accepted, 22 enrolled. In 2009, 17 master's awarded. *Degree requirements:* For master's, comprehensive exam. *Entrance requirements:* For master's, GRE. Additional exam requirements/recommendations for international students: Required—TOEFL. Application fee: $40. *Financial support:* In 2009–10, 6 research assistantships, 12 teaching assistantships were awarded; career-related internships or fieldwork, Federal Work-Study, institutionally sponsored loans, scholarships/grants, and tuition waivers (full and partial) also available. Support available to part-time students. Financial award application deadline: 2/15. *Faculty research:* Urban journalism, gender and com-

Speech and Interpersonal Communication

Marquette University (continued)
munication, intercultural communication, religious communication. *Unit head:* Dr. Ana Garner, Dean, 414-288-3588, Fax: 414-288-1578. *Application contact:* Erin Fox, Assistant Director for Recruitment, 414-288-5319, Fax: 414-288-1902, E-mail: erin.fox@marquette.edu.

Montclair State University, The Graduate School, School of the Arts, Department of Communication Studies, Montclair, NJ 07043-1624. Offers organizational communication (MA); public relations (MA); speech communication (MA). Part-time and evening/weekend programs available. *Faculty:* 5 full-time (2 women), 41 part-time/adjunct (24 women). *Students:* 16 full-time (15 women), 20 part-time (17 women). Average age 30. 23 applicants, 65% accepted, 12 enrolled. In 2009, 12 master's awarded. *Degree requirements:* For master's, comprehensive exam. *Entrance requirements:* For master's, GRE General Test, 2 letters of recommendation. Additional exam requirements/recommendations for international students: Required—TOEFL (minimum score 83 computer-based), or IELTS. *Application deadline:* For fall admission, 6/1 for international students; for spring admission, 10/1 for international students. Applications are processed on a rolling basis. Application fee: $60. Electronic applications accepted. *Expenses:* Tuition, area resident: Part-time $486.74 per credit. Tuition, state resident: part-time $486.74 per credit. Tuition, nonresident: part-time $751.34 per credit. Tuition and fees vary according to degree level and program. *Financial support:* In 2009–10, 3 research assistantships with full tuition reimbursements (averaging $7,000 per year) were awarded; Federal Work-Study, scholarships/grants, and unspecified assistantships also available. Support available to part-time students. Financial award application deadline: 3/1; financial award applicants required to submit FAFSA. *Unit head:* Dr. Harry Haines, Chair, 973-655-4200. *Application contact:* Amy Aiello, Director of Graduate Admissions and Operations, 973-655-5147, Fax: 973-655-7869, E-mail: graduate.school@montclair.edu.

New York University, Steinhardt School of Culture, Education, and Human Development, Department of Media, Culture and Communication, New York, NY 10012-1019. Offers media, culture, and communication (MA, PhD). Part-time programs available. *Faculty:* 22 full-time (9 women), 43 part-time/adjunct (22 women). *Students:* 84 full-time (62 women), 42 part-time (24 women); includes 13 minority (7 African Americans, 5 Asian Americans or Pacific Islanders, 1 Hispanic American), 46 international. Average age 33. 289 applicants, 44% accepted, 52 enrolled. In 2009, 45 master's, 5 doctorates awarded. Terminal master's awarded for partial completion of doctoral program. *Degree requirements:* For master's, thesis (for some programs); for doctorate, thesis/dissertation. *Entrance requirements:* For doctorate, GRE General Test, interview. Additional exam requirements/recommendations for international students: Required—TOEFL. *Application deadline:* For fall admission, 12/15 priority date for domestic and international students; for spring admission, 11/1 for domestic and international students. Applications are processed on a rolling basis. Application fee: $75. Electronic applications accepted. *Expenses:* Tuition: Full-time $30,528; part-time $1272 per credit. Required fees: $2177. *Financial support:* Fellowships with full and partial tuition reimbursements, teaching assistantships with full and partial tuition reimbursements, career-related internships or fieldwork, Federal Work-Study, institutionally sponsored loans, scholarships/grants, tuition waivers (partial), and unspecified assistantships available. Support available to part-time students. Financial award application deadline: 2/1; financial award applicants required to submit FAFSA. *Faculty research:* Digital media and new technologies, media criticism, flow of media and culture transnationally and transculturally. *Unit head:* Dr. Marita Sturken, Chairperson, 212-992-9424, Fax: 212-995-4046, E-mail: marita.sturken@nyu.edu. *Application contact:* 212-998-5030, Fax: 212-995-4328, E-mail: steinhardt.gradadmissions@nyu.edu.

North Dakota State University, College of Graduate and Interdisciplinary Studies, College of Arts, Humanities and Social Sciences, Department of Communication, Fargo, ND 58108. Offers communication (PhD); mass communication (MA, MS); speech communication (MA, MS). Part-time programs available. Postbaccalaureate distance learning degree programs offered (no on-campus study). *Faculty:* 11 full-time (5 women), 3 part-time/adjunct (1 woman). *Students:* 38 full-time (25 women), 23 part-time (17 women); includes 4 minority (1 African American, 2 Asian Americans or Pacific Islanders, 1 Hispanic American), 3 international. Average age 27. 62 applicants, 40% accepted, 19 enrolled. In 2009, 15 master's, 8 doctorates awarded. Terminal master's awarded for partial completion of doctoral program. *Degree requirements:* For master's, thesis (for some programs); for doctorate, comprehensive exam, thesis/dissertation, 2-3 publications referred before comps. *Entrance requirements:* For master's, GRE, minimum undergraduate GPA of 3.25; for doctorate, GRE, minimum undergraduate GPA of 3.5. Additional exam requirements/recommendations for international students: Required—TOEFL (minimum score 600 paper-based; 250 computer-based; 100 iBT), IELTS (minimum score 7). *Application deadline:* For fall admission, 2/15 priority date for domestic students; for winter admission, 10/15 priority date for domestic students. Applications are processed on a rolling basis. Application fee: $45 ($60 for international students). Electronic applications accepted. *Financial support:* In 2009–10, 38 students received support, including 1 fellowship with full tuition reimbursement available (averaging $16,000 per year), 10 research assistantships with full tuition reimbursements available (averaging $12,000 per year), 10 teaching assistantships with full tuition reimbursements available (averaging $8,100 per year); career-related internships or fieldwork, Federal Work-Study, institutionally sponsored loans, tuition waivers (full), and unspecified assistantships also available. Financial award application deadline: 2/1. *Faculty research:* Communication and rhetorical theory, organizational communication, broadcast and print journalism, international communication, public relations and advertising. Total annual research expenditures: $148,496. *Unit head:* Dr. Paul E. Nelson, Chair, 701-231-7705, Fax: 701-231-7784, E-mail: paul.nelson.1@ndsu.edu. *Application contact:* Dr. Judy C. Pearson, Director of Graduate Studies, 701-231-6551, Fax: 701-231-1074, E-mail: judy.pearson@ndsu.edu.

Northeastern Illinois University, Graduate College, College of Arts and Sciences, Department of Communication, Media and Theatre, Program in Communication, Media and Theatre, Chicago, IL 60625-4699. Offers MA. Part-time and evening/weekend programs available. *Degree requirements:* For master's, comprehensive exam, oral exams, thesis or 3 term papers. *Entrance requirements:* For master's, 15 undergraduate hours in speech and performing arts, minimum GPA of 2.75. Additional exam requirements/recommendations for international students: Required—TOEFL (minimum score 550 paper-based; 213 computer-based; 80 iBT). Electronic applications accepted. *Faculty research:* Creative drama, family communication, fine arts and general education, playwriting techniques, interpersonal communications.

Northeastern University, Bouvé College of Health Sciences Graduate School, Department of Speech-Language Pathology, Program in Audiology, Boston, MA 02115-5096. Offers Au D. *Faculty:* 12 full-time (8 women), 6 part-time/adjunct (5 women). *Students:* 14 full-time (all women); includes 1 Asian American or Pacific Islander, 1 Hispanic American, 1 international. 53 applicants, 40% accepted, 9 enrolled. In 2009, 6 doctorates awarded. *Entrance requirements:* For doctorate, GRE, minimum GPA of 3.2. Additional exam requirements/recommendations for international students: Required—TOEFL (minimum score 100 iBT). *Application deadline:* For fall admission, 2/15 for domestic students. Application fee: $50. Electronic applications accepted. *Financial support:* Research assistantships, teaching assistantships, scholarships/grants, traineeships, and unspecified assistantships available. *Unit head:* Dr. Sandra Cleveland, Director, 617-373-2496, Fax: 617-373-8756, E-mail: sa.cleveland@neu.edu. *Application contact:* Margaret Schnabel, Director of Graduate Admissions, 617-373-2708, E-mail: bouvegrad@neu.edu.

Northwestern University, The Graduate School, School of Communication, Department of Performance Studies, Evanston, IL 60208. Offers MA, PhD. Admissions and degrees offered through The Graduate School. Part-time programs available. Terminal master's awarded for partial completion of doctoral program. *Degree requirements:* For master's, recital; for doctorate, one foreign language, thesis/dissertation, recital. *Entrance requirements:* For master's and doctorate, GRE General Test. Additional exam requirements/recommendations for international students: Required—TOEFL. *Faculty research:* Adaptation/performance of literature, ethnography of performance, critical cultural studies, performance theory, intercultural performance, gender studies.

Ohio University, Graduate College, Scripps College of Communication, School of Communication Studies, Athens, OH 45701-2979. Offers health communication (PhD); organizational communication (MA); relating and organizing (PhD); rhetoric and public culture (PhD). Part-time programs available. Postbaccalaureate distance learning degree programs offered (minimal on-campus study). *Faculty:* 24 full-time (9 women), 4 part-time/adjunct (1 woman). *Students:* 48 full-time (33 women), 31 part-time (25 women); includes 5 minority (4 African Americans, 1 Hispanic American), 12 international. 98 applicants, 46% accepted, 36 enrolled. In 2009, 7 master's, 12 doctorates awarded. Terminal master's awarded for partial completion of doctoral program. *Degree requirements:* For master's, capstone; for doctorate, comprehensive exam, thesis/dissertation. *Entrance requirements:* For master's, GRE; for doctorate, GRE General Test, minimum GPA of 3.0. Additional exam requirements/recommendations for international students: Required—TOEFL (minimum score 550 paper-based; 80 iBT) or IELTS Academic (minimum score 6.5). *Application deadline:* For fall admission, 1/15 priority date for domestic and international students. Application fee: $50 ($55 for international students). Electronic applications accepted. *Expenses:* Tuition, state resident: full-time $7839; part-time $323 per quarter hour. Tuition, nonresident: full-time $15,831; part-time $654 per quarter hour. Required fees: $2931. *Financial support:* In 2009–10, 12 students received support, including fellowships with full tuition reimbursements available (averaging $13,600 per year), research assistantships with full tuition reimbursements available (averaging $13,600 per year), teaching assistantships with full tuition reimbursements available (averaging $13,600 per year); career-related internships or fieldwork, Federal Work-Study, and institutionally sponsored loans also available. Financial award application deadline: 1/15. *Faculty research:* Rhetoric and public culture, relating and organizing, health communication. Total annual research expenditures: $200,000. *Unit head:* Dr. Claudia Hale, Director, 740-593-4832, Fax: 740-593-4810, E-mail: hale@ohio.edu. *Application contact:* Dr. Scott Titsworth, Graduate Chairman, 740-593-9160, Fax: 740-593-4810, E-mail: titswort@ohio.edu.

Portland State University, Graduate Studies, College of Liberal Arts and Sciences, Department of Communication, Portland, OR 97207-0751. Offers general speech communication (MA, MS, Certificate). Part-time programs available. *Degree requirements:* For master's, thesis. *Entrance requirements:* For master's, GRE General Test, minimum GPA of 3.0 in upper-division course work or 2.75 overall, 3 letters of recommendation. Additional exam requirements/recommendations for international students: Required—TOEFL (minimum score 550 paper-based; 213 computer-based).

Rensselaer Polytechnic Institute, Graduate School, School of Humanities and Social Sciences, Department of Language, Literature, and Communication, Programs in Communication and Rhetoric, Troy, NY 12180-3590. Offers MS, PhD. *Faculty:* 14 full-time (8 women). *Students:* 20 full-time (11 women); includes 2 minority (1 African American, 1 Hispanic American), 1 international. 21 applicants, 48% accepted, 5 enrolled. In 2009, 1 master's, 4 doctorates awarded. Terminal master's awarded for partial completion of doctoral program. *Degree requirements:* For master's, thesis optional; for doctorate, comprehensive exam, thesis/dissertation. *Entrance requirements:* For master's, GRE General Test, resume; for doctorate, GRE General Test, writing sample, resume or curriculum vitae. Additional exam requirements/recommendations for international students: Required—TOEFL (minimum score 570 paper-based; 230 computer-based). *Application deadline:* For fall admission, 1/15 priority date for domestic students; for spring admission, 10/15 priority date for domestic students. Applications are processed on a rolling basis. Application fee: $75. Electronic applications accepted. *Expenses:* Tuition: Full-time $38,100. *Financial support:* In 2009–10, 18 students received support, including 10 fellowships with full tuition reimbursements available (averaging $16,500 per year), 1 research assistantship with full tuition reimbursement available (averaging $16,500 per year), 8 teaching assistantships with full tuition reimbursements available (averaging $16,500 per year); career-related internships or fieldwork, institutionally sponsored loans, and unspecified assistantships also available. Financial award application deadline: 1/15. *Faculty research:* Human-computer interaction; media design and theory; rhetoric and culture; virtual institutions/communities; usability, digital and visual rhetoric. *Unit head:* Prof. James P. Zappen, Head, 518-276-6468, Fax: 518-276-4092, E-mail: zappenj@rpi.edu. *Application contact:* Kathy A. Colman, Recruitment Coordinator, 518-276-6469, Fax: 518-276-4092, E-mail: colmak@rpi.edu.

Sam Houston State University, College of Humanities and Social Sciences, Huntsville, TX 77341. Offers English and foreign languages (MA), including English; family and consumer sciences (MS), including dietetics, family and consumer sciences; history (MA); political science (MA, MPA), including political science (MA), public administration (MPA); psychology and philosophy (MA, PhD), including clinical psychology (PhD), psychology (MA); sociology (MA); speech communication (MA). *Faculty:* 60 full-time (30 women), 1 part-time/adjunct (0 women). *Students:* 115 full-time (85 women), 167 part-time (90 women); includes 39 minority (11 African Americans, 1 American Indian/Alaska Native, 5 Asian Americans or Pacific Islanders, 22 Hispanic Americans), 9 international. Average age 30. 216 applicants, 56% accepted, 96 enrolled. In 2009, 67 master's, 4 doctorates awarded. *Entrance requirements:* For master's, GRE General Test. Additional exam requirements/recommendations for international students: Required—TOEFL (minimum score 550 paper-based; 213 computer-based; 79 iBT). *Application deadline:* For fall admission, 8/1 for domestic students; for spring admission, 12/1 for domestic students. Application fee: $20. *Expenses:* Tuition, state resident: full-time $3690; part-time $205 per credit hour. Tuition, nonresident: full-time $8676; part-time $482 per credit hour. Required fees: $1474. Tuition and fees vary according to course load and campus/location. *Unit head:* Dr. John deCastro, Dean, 936-294-2200, Fax: 936-294-2207, E-mail: jmd018@shsu.edu. *Application contact:* Dr. Kandi Tayebi, Dean of Graduate Studies and Associate Vice President for Academic Affairs, 936-294-1971, Fax: 936-294-1271, E-mail: graduate@shsu.edu.

San Francisco State University, Division of Graduate Studies, College of Humanities, Department of Communication Studies, San Francisco, CA 94132-1722. Offers MA. Part-time programs available.

San Jose State University, Graduate Studies and Research, College of Social Sciences, Department of History, San Jose, CA 95192-0001. Offers history (MA); history education (MA). *Students:* 11 full-time (5 women), 53 part-time (34 women); includes 15 minority (1 African American, 7 Asian Americans or Pacific Islanders, 7 Hispanic Americans). Average age 35. 59 applicants, 34% accepted, 16 enrolled. In 2009, 10 master's awarded. *Degree requirements:* For master's, comprehensive exam, thesis or alternative. *Entrance requirements:* For master's, bachelor's degree or 15 units of course work in history, minimum GPA of 3.0. *Application deadline:* For fall admission, 2/15 for domestic students. Applications are processed on a rolling basis. Application fee: $59. Electronic applications accepted. *Financial support:* Fellowships available. Financial award applicants required to submit FAFSA. *Unit head:* Patricia Evridge Hill, Chair, 408-924-5755, Fax: 408-924-5531. *Application contact:* Libra Hilde, Graduate Advisor, 408-924-5500.

Seton Hall University, School of Health and Medical Sciences, Program in Speech-Language Pathology, South Orange, NJ 07079-2697. Offers MS. *Accreditation:* ASHA. *Entrance requirements:* For master's, GRE, bachelor's degree, clinical experience; minimum GPA of 3.0, undergraduate preprofessional coursework in communication sciences and disorders. Electronic applications accepted. *Faculty research:* Child language disorders, motor speech control, voice disorders, dysphagia, early intervention/teaming.

Southern Illinois University Carbondale, Graduate School, College of Liberal Arts, Department of Speech Communication, Carbondale, IL 62901-4701. Offers speech communication (MA, MS, PhD); speech/theater (PhD). *Degree requirements:* For master's, one foreign language, thesis or alternative; for doctorate, one foreign language, thesis/dissertation. *Entrance requirements:* For master's, GRE General Test or MAT, minimum GPA of 2.7; for doctorate, GRE General Test or MAT, minimum GPA of 3.25. Additional exam requirements/recommendations for international students: Required—TOEFL.

Southern Illinois University Edwardsville, Graduate Studies and Research, College of Arts and Sciences, Department of Speech Communication, Program in Speech Communication, Edwardsville, IL 62026-0001. Offers MA. Part-time and evening/weekend programs available. *Faculty:* 9 full-time (6 women). *Students:* 11 full-time (9 women), 10 part-time (9 women); includes 4 minority (3 African Americans, 1 Asian American or Pacific Islander). Average age 26. 25 applicants, 52% accepted. In 2009, 11 master's awarded. *Degree requirements:* For master's, thesis (for some programs), final exam. *Entrance requirements:* Additional exam requirements/recommendations for international students: Required—TOEFL (minimum score 550 paper-based; 213 computer-based; 79 iBT), IELTS (minimum score 6.5). *Application deadline:* For fall admission, 7/23 for domestic students, 6/1 for international students; for spring admission, 12/11 for domestic students, 10/1 for international students. Applications are processed on a rolling basis. Application fee: $30. Electronic applications accepted. *Expenses:* Tuition, state resident: part-time $1252.50 per semester. Tuition, nonresident: part-time $3131.25 per semester. Required fees: $586.85 per semester. Tuition and fees vary according to course load. *Financial support:* In 2009–10, 12 teaching assistantships with full tuition reimbursements (averaging $8,064 per year) were awarded; fellowships with full tuition reimbursements, research assistantships with full tuition reimbursements, career-related internships or fieldwork, Federal Work-Study, institutionally sponsored loans, scholarships/grants, traineeships, and unspecified assistantships also available. Support available to part-time students. Financial award application deadline: 3/1; financial award applicants required to submit FAFSA. *Unit head:* Dr. Wai Hsien Cheah, Director, 618-650-5016, E-mail: wcheah@siue.edu. *Application contact:* Dr. Wai Hsien Cheah, Director, 618-650-5016, E-mail: wcheah@siue.edu.

Texas A&M University–Commerce, Graduate School, College of Arts and Sciences, Department of Communication and Theatre, Commerce, TX 75429-3011. Offers theatre (MA, MS). Part-time programs available. *Degree requirements:* For master's, comprehensive exam, thesis (for some programs). *Entrance requirements:* For master's, GRE General Test. Electronic applications accepted. *Faculty research:* Theater history.

Texas Christian University, College of Communication, Department of Communication Studies, Fort Worth, TX 76129. Offers c (MS). Part-time programs available. *Degree requirements:* For master's, comprehensive exam, thesis optional. *Entrance requirements:* For master's, GRE General Test. Additional exam requirements/recommendations for international students: Required—TOEFL. *Application deadline:* For spring admission, 3/1 for domestic and international students. Applications are processed on a rolling basis. Application fee: $50. *Expenses:* Tuition: Full-time $17,640; part-time $980 per credit hour. Tuition and fees vary according to program. *Financial support:* In 2009–10, 12 students received support, including 9 teaching assistantships with full tuition reimbursements available (averaging $7,000 per year); tuition waivers (full) and unspecified assistantships also available. Financial award application deadline: 3/1. *Faculty research:* Interpersonal communication, family communication, instructional communication, public speaking anxiety, social cognition, conflict. *Unit head:* Dr. Paul King, Chairperson, 817-257-7610, E-mail: p.king@tcu.edu. *Application contact:* Dr. Paul Schrodt, Director of Graduate Studies, 817-257-5674, Fax: 817-257-6580, E-mail: p.schrodt@tcu.edu.

The University of Alabama, Graduate School, College of Communication and Information Sciences, Department of Communication Studies, Tuscaloosa, AL 35487. Offers MA. *Faculty:* 9 full-time (7 women). *Students:* 28 full-time (18 women), 2 part-time (both women); includes 7 minority (6 African Americans, 1 Hispanic American), 3 international. Average age 24. 32 applicants, 44% accepted, 11 enrolled. In 2009, 8 degrees awarded. *Degree requirements:* For master's, comprehensive exam (for some programs), thesis optional, research colloquium presentation, final practicum report. *Entrance requirements:* For master's, GRE, MAT. Additional exam requirements/recommendations for international students: Required—TOEFL (minimum score 550 paper-based; 213 computer-based). *Application deadline:* For fall admission, 5/1 for domestic and international students; for spring admission, 11/1 for domestic and international students. Applications are processed on a rolling basis. Application fee: $50 ($60 for international students). Electronic applications accepted. *Expenses:* Tuition, state resident: full-time $7000. Tuition, nonresident: full-time $19,200. *Financial support:* In 2009–10, 7 students received support, including 12 teaching assistantships with full tuition reimbursements available (averaging $10,908 per year); health care benefits and unspecified assistantships also available. Financial award application deadline: 5/1. *Faculty research:* Rhetorical theory, organizational communication, interpersonal communication, rhetorical criticism, gender and communication, health communication. *Unit head:* Dr. Beth S. Bennett, Chair and Professor, 205-348-8073, Fax: 205-348-8080, E-mail: bbennett@ua.edu. *Application contact:* Dr. Mary M. Meares, Graduate Program Director and Assistant Professor, 205-348-8072, Fax: 205-348-8080, E-mail: mmmeares@ua.edu.

University of Arkansas at Little Rock, Graduate School, College of Professional Studies, Department of Speech Communication, Little Rock, AR 72204-1099. Offers applied communication studies (MA). Part-time and evening/weekend programs available. *Degree requirements:* For master's, comprehensive exam, internship, paper, or thesis. *Entrance requirements:* For master's, GRE General Test, MAT, minimum GPA of 2.7. *Faculty research:* Communication theory and applications, managerial communication, human resource training and development, relational communication.

University of California, Santa Barbara, Graduate Division, College of Letters and Sciences, Division of Humanities and Fine Arts, Department of Linguistics, Santa Barbara, CA 93106-3100. Offers applied linguistics (PhD); cognitive science (PhD); human development (PhD); language, interaction, and social organizations (PhD); MA/PhD. *Faculty:* 23 full-time (12 women). *Students:* 25 full-time (14 women). Average age 32. 63 applicants, 17% accepted, 5 enrolled. In 2009, 5 doctorates awarded. *Degree requirements:* For doctorate, one foreign language, comprehensive exam, thesis/dissertation. *Entrance requirements:* For doctorate, GRE, 3 letters of recommendation, resume/curriculum vitae. Additional exam requirements/recommendations for international students: Required—TOEFL (minimum score 550 paper-based; 213 computer-based; 80 iBT), or IELTS (minimum score 7). *Application deadline:* For fall admission, 12/1 priority date for domestic and international students. Application fee: $70 ($90 for international students). Electronic applications accepted. *Financial support:* In 2009–10, 24 students received support, including 19 fellowships with full and partial tuition reimbursements available (averaging $12,400 per year), 1 research assistantship with full and partial tuition reimbursement available (averaging $3,000 per year), 13 teaching assistantships with partial tuition reimbursements available (averaging $5,600 per year); Federal Work-Study, institutionally sponsored loans, scholarships/grants, health care benefits, and unspecified assistantships also available. Financial award application deadline: 12/1; financial award applicants required to submit FAFSA. *Faculty research:* Language, race and subcultural identities among California teenagers; language acquisition, psycholinguistics; language documentation, fieldwork; syntax of nominalization in 5 Tibeto-Burman languages; perceptual correlates of syllable weight. *Unit head:* Prof. Patricia M. Clancy, Chair, 805-893-8658, Fax: 805-893-7769, E-mail: pclancy@linguistics.ucsb.edu. *Application contact:* Mary Rae Staton, Graduate Program Assistant, 805-893-3776, Fax: 805-893-7769, E-mail: staton@linguistics.ucsb.edu.

University of California, Santa Barbara, Graduate Division, College of Letters and Sciences, Division of Social Sciences, Department of Sociology, Santa Barbara, CA 93106-9430. Offers global studies (PhD); human development (PhD); language, interaction and social organization (PhD); technology and society (PhD); women's studies (PhD); MA/PhD. *Faculty:* 35 full-time (14 women). *Students:* 77 full-time (50 women). Average age 30. 155 applicants, 9% accepted, 8 enrolled. In 2009, 10 doctorates awarded. Terminal master's awarded for partial completion of doctoral program. *Degree requirements:* For doctorate, comprehensive exam, thesis/dissertation. *Entrance requirements:* For doctorate, GRE General Test, sample of written work, 3 letters of recommendation, resume/curriculum vitae. Additional exam requirements/recommendations for international students: Required—TOEFL (minimum score 550 paper-based; 213 computer-based; 80 iBT), or IELTS. *Application deadline:* For fall admission, 12/10 for domestic students. Application fee: $70 ($90 for international students). Electronic applications accepted. *Financial support:* In 2009–10, 69 students received support, including 50 fellowships with full tuition reimbursements available (averaging $7,900 per year), 6 research assistantships with full and partial tuition reimbursements available (averaging $2,600 per year), 53 teaching assistantships with partial tuition reimbursements available (averaging $9,200 per year); career-related internships or fieldwork, Federal Work-Study, institutionally sponsored loans, scholarships/grants, health care benefits, and unspecified assistantships also available. Financial award applicants required to submit FAFSA. *Faculty research:* Conversation analysis, social movements, human sexuality, urban sociology, race and ethnic relations. *Unit head:* Prof. Verta Taylor, Chair, 805-893-3118, Fax: 805-893-3324, E-mail: grad-soc@soc.ucsb.edu. *Application contact:* Ra Thea, Graduate Staff Advisor, 805-893-3328, Fax: 805-893-3324, E-mail: grad-soc@soc.ucsb.edu.

University of Central Missouri, The Graduate School, College of Arts, Humanities and Social Sciences, Warrensburg, MO 64093. Offers English (MA); history (MA); mass communication (MA); music (MA); psychology (MS); speech communication (MA); teaching english as a second language (MA); theatre (MA). Part-time programs available. *Faculty:* 82. *Students:* 60 full-time (35 women), 101 part-time (61 women); includes 11 minority (5 African Americans, 3 Asian Americans or Pacific Islanders, 3 Hispanic Americans), 17 international. Average age 30. 80 applicants, 80% accepted, 58 enrolled. In 2009, 51 master's awarded. *Entrance requirements:* Additional exam requirements/recommendations for international students: Required—TOEFL (minimum score 550 paper-based; 79 computer-based). *Application deadline:* For fall admission, 6/1 priority date for domestic students, 5/1 for international students; for spring admission, 10/1 priority date for domestic students, 10/1 for international students. Applications are processed on a rolling basis. Application fee: $30 ($75 for international students). Electronic applications accepted. *Expenses:* Tuition, area resident: Part-time $245.80 per credit hour. Tuition, nonresident: part-time $491.60 per credit hour. Required fees: $24.20 per credit hour. Full-time tuition and fees vary according to course load, degree level, campus/location and reciprocity agreements. *Financial support:* Research assistantships with full and partial tuition reimbursements, teaching assistantships with full and partial tuition reimbursements, career-related internships or fieldwork, Federal Work-Study, scholarships/grants, and administrative and laboratory assistantships available. Support available to part-time students. Financial award application deadline: 3/1; financial award applicants required to submit FAFSA. *Unit head:* Dr. Gersham Nelson, Dean, 660-543-4750, Fax: 660-543-8271, E-mail: nelson@ucmo.edu. *Application contact:* Laurie Delap, Admissions Coordinator, 660-543-4621, Fax: 660-543-4778, E-mail: gradinfo@ucmo.edu.

University of Denver, Division of Arts, Humanities and Social Sciences, Department of Human Communication Studies, Denver, CO 80208. Offers MA, PhD. Part-time programs available. *Faculty:* 11 full-time (7 women), 7 part-time/adjunct (1 woman). *Students:* 26 full-time (19 women), 6 part-time (4 women); includes 5 minority (2 African Americans, 1 Asian American or Pacific Islander, 2 Hispanic Americans), 5 international. Average age 32. 61 applicants, 57% accepted, 13 enrolled. In 2009, 2 master's, 6 doctorates awarded. *Degree requirements:* For master's, comprehensive exam or thesis; for doctorate, one foreign language, thesis/dissertation. *Entrance requirements:* For master's and doctorate, GRE General Test. Additional exam requirements/recommendations for international students: Required—TOEFL, TWE. *Application deadline:* Applications are processed on a rolling basis. Application fee: $50. *Expenses:* Tuition: Full-time $34,596; part-time $961 per quarter hour. Required fees: $4 per quarter hour. Tuition and fees vary according to course load, campus/location and program. *Financial support:* In 2009–10, 30 students received support, including 15 teaching assistantships with full and partial tuition reimbursements available (averaging $14,200 per year); career-related internships or fieldwork, Federal Work-Study, institutionally sponsored loans, and scholarships/grants also available. Support available to part-time students. Financial award application deadline: 2/10; financial award applicants required to submit FAFSA. *Faculty research:* Successful community collaborative efforts, long-term marriages, cross-ethnic friendships, public dialogue about environmental risk, women's international cooperation. *Unit head:* Dr. Roy Wood, Chair, 303-871-2385. *Application contact:* Information Contact, 303-871-2385, E-mail: hcom@du.edu.

University of Georgia, Graduate School, College of Arts and Sciences, Department of Speech Communication, Athens, GA 30602. Offers MA, PhD. *Faculty:* 13 full-time (8 women). *Students:* 26 full-time (16 women), 6 part-time (3 women); includes 2 minority (both African Americans). 66 applicants, 27% accepted, 9 enrolled. In 2009, 5 master's, 5 doctorates awarded. *Degree requirements:* For master's, thesis; for doctorate, one foreign language, thesis/dissertation. *Entrance requirements:* For master's and doctorate, GRE General Test. *Application deadline:* For fall admission, 7/1 priority date for domestic students; for spring admission, 11/15 for domestic students. Application fee: $50. Electronic applications accepted. *Expenses:* Tuition, state resident: full-time $6000; part-time $250 per credit hour. Tuition, nonresident: full-time $20,904; part-time $871 per credit hour. Required fees: $730 per semester. *Financial support:* Fellowships, research assistantships, teaching assistantships, unspecified assistantships available. *Unit head:* Dr. Jerold L. Hale, Head, 706-542-4893, Fax: 706-542-3245, E-mail: jhale@uga.edu. *Application contact:* Dr. Jennifer A. Samp, Graduate Coordinator, 706-542-3246, E-mail: jasamp@uga.edu.

University of Hawaii at Manoa, Graduate Division, College of Arts and Humanities, Department of Speech, Honolulu, HI 96822. Offers MA. Part-time programs available. *Faculty:* 7 full-time (4 women), 6 part-time/adjunct (1 woman). *Students:* 10 full-time (all women), 2 part-time (both women); includes 4 minority (all Asian Americans or Pacific Islanders), 2 international. Average age 26. 12 applicants, 67% accepted, 7 enrolled. In 2009, 4 master's awarded. *Degree requirements:* For master's, thesis optional. *Entrance requirements:* For master's, GRE General Test. Additional exam requirements/recommendations for international students: Required—TOEFL (minimum score 600 paper-based; 250 computer-based; 100 iBT), IELTS (minimum score 7). *Application deadline:* For fall admission, 3/1 for domestic students, 1/15 for international students; for spring admission, 9/1 for domestic students, 8/1 for international students. Application fee: $60. *Expenses:* Tuition, state resident: full-time $8900; part-time $372 per credit. Tuition, nonresident: full-time $21,400; part-time $898 per credit. Required fees: $207 per semester. *Financial support:* In 2009–10, 2 fellowships (averaging $2,600 per year), 7 teaching assistantships (averaging $14,547 per year) were awarded; tuition waivers (full) also available. *Faculty research:* Social influence, relational management, message processing, intercultural communication. *Application contact:* Amy Hubbard, Graduate Chairperson, 808-956-3316, Fax: 808-956-3947, E-mail: aebesu@hawaii.edu.

University of Houston, College of Liberal Arts and Social Sciences, School of Communication, Houston, TX 77204. Offers health communication (MA); mass communication studies (MA); public relations studies (MA); speech communication (MA). Part-time and evening/weekend programs available. *Faculty:* 9 full-time (5 women), 2 part-time/adjunct (0 women). *Students:* 42 full-time (38 women), 49 part-time (44 women); includes 31 minority (17 African Americans, 2 American Indian/Alaska Native, 2 Asian Americans or Pacific Islanders, 10 Hispanic Americans), 24 international. Average age 28. 92 applicants, 47% accepted, 28 enrolled. In 2009, 19 master's awarded. *Degree requirements:* For master's, comprehensive exam, thesis. *Entrance requirements:* For master's, GRE. Additional exam requirements/recommendations for international students: Required—TOEFL. *Application deadline:* For fall admission, 6/1 for domestic students, 4/1 for international students; for spring admission, 11/1 for domestic students, 10/1 for international students. Application fee: $25 ($75 for international students). Electronic applications accepted. *Expenses:* Tuition, state resident: full-time $7676; part-time $320 per credit hour. Tuition, nonresident: full-time $14,324; part-time $597 per credit hour. Required fees: $3034. *Financial support:* In 2009–10, 2 fellowships with full tuition reimbursements (averaging $9,750 per year), 5 teaching assistantships with full tuition reimbursements (averaging $9,750 per year) were awarded; career-related internships or fieldwork, Federal Work-Study, institutionally sponsored loans, scholarships/grants, health care benefits, and unspecified assistantships also available. Support available to part-time students. Financial award application deadline: 2/1. *Unit head:* Dr. Beth Olson, Chairperson, 713-743-2873, Fax: 713-743-2876, E-mail: bolson@uh.edu. *Application contact:* Salima B. Haji, Academic Advisor, 713-743-2575, Fax: 713-743-2876, E-mail: sbhaji@central.uh.edu.

Speech and Interpersonal Communication

University of Maryland, College Park, Academic Affairs, College of Behavioral and Social Sciences, Department of Hearing and Speech Sciences, College Park, MD 20742. Offers audiology (MA, PhD); hearing and speech sciences (Au D); language pathology (MA, PhD); neuroscience (PhD); speech (MA, PhD). *Accreditation:* ASHA (one or more programs are accredited). *Faculty:* 19 full-time (18 women), 13 part-time/adjunct (11 women). *Students:* 82 full-time (76 women), 18 part-time (all women); includes 20 minority (9 African Americans, 8 Asian Americans or Pacific Islanders, 3 Hispanic Americans), 2 international. 260 applicants, 46% accepted, 36 enrolled. In 2009, 23 master's, 11 doctorates awarded. *Degree requirements:* For master's, thesis optional; for doctorate, thesis/dissertation, written and oral exams. *Entrance requirements:* For master's, GRE General Test, minimum GPA of 3.5, 3 letters of recommendation; for doctorate, GRE General Test, minimum GPA of 3.5. Additional exam requirements/recommendations for international students: Required—TOEFL. *Application deadline:* For fall admission, 1/15 for domestic and international students. Applications are processed on a rolling basis. Application fee: $60. Electronic applications accepted. *Expenses:* Tuition, area resident: Part-time $471 per credit hour. Tuition, state resident: part-time $471 per credit hour. Tuition, nonresident: part-time $1016 per credit hour. Required fees: $337.04 per term. *Financial support:* In 2009–10, 3 fellowships with partial tuition reimbursements (averaging $10,848 per year), 2 research assistantships (averaging $15,614 per year), 34 teaching assistantships with tuition reimbursements (averaging $15,709 per year) were awarded; career-related internships or fieldwork, Federal Work-Study, scholarships/grants, and health care benefits also available. Support available to part-time students. Financial award applicants required to submit FAFSA. *Faculty research:* Speech perception, language acquisition, bilingualism, hearing loss. Total annual research expenditures: $491,296. *Unit head:* Dr. Nan B. Bernstein-Ratner, Chair, 301-405-4217, Fax: 301-314-2023, E-mail: nratner@umd.edu. *Application contact:* Dean of Graduate School, 301-405-0358, Fax: 301-314-9305.

University of Nebraska–Lincoln, Graduate College, College of Arts and Sciences, Department of Communication Studies, Lincoln, NE 68588. Offers instructional communication (MA, PhD); interpersonal communication (MA, PhD); marketing, communication studies, and advertising (MA, PhD); organizational communication (MA, PhD); rhetoric and culture (MA, PhD). *Degree requirements:* For master's, thesis optional; for doctorate, comprehensive exam, thesis/dissertation. *Entrance requirements:* For master's and doctorate, GRE General Test, writing sample. Additional exam requirements/recommendations for international students: Required—TOEFL (minimum score 600 paper-based; 250 computer-based). Electronic applications accepted. *Faculty research:* Message strategies, gender communication, political communication, organizational communication, instructional communication.

University of Nevada, Reno, Graduate School, College of Liberal Arts, Department of Speech Communications, Reno, NV 89557. Offers MA. *Degree requirements:* For master's, thesis optional. *Entrance requirements:* For master's, GRE General Test, minimum GPA of 2.75. Additional exam requirements/recommendations for international students: Required—TOEFL (minimum score 500 paper-based; 173 computer-based; 61 iBT), IELTS (minimum score 6). Electronic applications accepted. *Faculty research:* Rhetorical theory and criticism; communications/sex roles; judicial, legal, contextual, and behavioral approaches to communication theory.

University of South Carolina, The Graduate School, College of Education, Department of Instruction and Teacher Education, Program in Secondary Education, Columbia, SC 29208. Offers art education (IMA, MAT); business education (IMA, MAT); English (MAT); foreign language (MAT); health education (MAT); mathematics (MAT); science (IMA, MAT); secondary (Ed D); secondary education (MT, PhD); social studies (MAT); theatre and speech (MAT). IMA and MT offered jointly with the subject areas. *Accreditation:* NCATE. *Degree requirements:* For master's, comprehensive exam, thesis (for some programs), foreign language (MA); for doctorate, one foreign language, comprehensive exam, thesis/dissertation. *Entrance requirements:* For master's, GRE General Test or MAT, teaching certificate (IMA, M Ed), interview; for doctorate, GRE General Test or MAT, interview. *Faculty research:* Middle school programs, professional development, school collaboration.

University of Southern California, Graduate School, Annenberg School for Communication and Journalism, School of Communication, Program in Communication, Los Angeles, CA 90089. Offers communication (MA, PhD), including interpersonal and social dynamics (PhD), mass communication, technology, and public policy (PhD), organizational communication (PhD), rhetorical and cultural studies (PhD). *Degree requirements:* For doctorate, thesis/dissertation. *Entrance requirements:* For master's and doctorate, GRE General Test, resume, writing samples, 3 letters of recommendation, interest survey questionnaire, statement of purpose. Additional exam requirements/recommendations for international students: Required—TOEFL (minimum score 280 computer-based; 114 iBT); Recommended—TWE. Electronic applications accepted. *Expenses:* Tuition: Full-time $25,980; part-time $1315 per unit. Required fees: $554. One-time fee: $35 full-time. Full-time tuition and fees vary according to degree level and program. *Faculty research:* Computer-mediated communication, public health campaigns, communication democracy and the public sphere, new communication technologies in organizations, communication and community.

See Display on page 629 and Close-Up on page 685.

University of Southern Mississippi, Graduate School, College of Arts and Letters, Department of Speech Communication, Hattiesburg, MS 39406-0001. Offers MA, MS, PhD. *Faculty:* 9 full-time (2 women). *Students:* 15 full-time (9 women), 12 part-time (7 women); includes 5 minority (4 African Americans, 1 Hispanic American). Average age 32. 21 applicants, 52% accepted, 9 enrolled. In 2009, 4 master's, 4 doctorates awarded. *Degree requirements:* For master's, comprehensive exam, thesis optional; for doctorate, comprehensive exam, thesis/dissertation. *Entrance requirements:* For master's, GRE General Test, minimum GPA of 3.0 in last 60 hours and in major; for doctorate, GRE General Test, minimum GPA of 3.5. Additional exam requirements/recommendations for international students: Required—TOEFL. *Application deadline:* For fall admission, 3/1 priority date for domestic students, 3/1 for international students. Application fee: $35. *Expenses:* Tuition, state resident: full-time $5096; part-time $284 per hour. Tuition, nonresident: full-time $13,052; part-time $726 per hour. Required fees: $402. Tuition and fees vary according to course level and course load. *Financial support:* In 2009–10, 1 fellowship with full tuition reimbursement (averaging $12,000 per year), 8 teaching assistantships with full tuition reimbursements (averaging $13,500 per year) were awarded; research assistantships, Federal Work-Study, scholarships/grants, and unspecified assistantships also available. Financial award application deadline: 3/15; financial award applicants required to submit FAFSA. *Faculty research:* Persuasion and social influence, interpersonal communication, organizational communication, political communication, crisis communication. *Unit head:* Dr. Charles Tardy, Chair, 601-266-4271, Fax: 601-266-4275. *Application contact:* Dr. Lawrence Hosman, Graduate Coordinator, 601-266-4271, Fax: 601-266-4275.

The University of Tennessee, Graduate School, College of Communication and Information, Knoxville, TN 37996. Offers advertising (MS, PhD); broadcasting (MS, PhD); communications (MS, PhD); information sciences (MS, PhD); journalism (MS, PhD); public relations (MS, PhD); speech communication (MS, PhD). *Accreditation:* ACEJMC (one or more programs are accredited at the [master's] level). Part-time and evening/weekend programs available. Postbaccalaureate distance learning degree programs offered (no on-campus study). *Degree requirements:* For master's, thesis or alternative; for doctorate, thesis/dissertation. *Entrance requirements:* For master's and doctorate, GRE General Test, minimum GPA of 2.7. Additional exam requirements/recommendations for international students: Required—TOEFL. Electronic applications accepted. *Expenses:* Tuition, state resident: full-time $6826; part-time $380 per semester hour. Tuition, nonresident: full-time $21,844; part-time $1147 per semester hour. Tuition and fees vary according to program.

University of Wisconsin–Madison, Graduate School, College of Letters and Science, Department of Communicative Disorders, Madison, WI 53706-1380. Offers normal aspects of speech, language and hearing (MS, PhD); speech-language pathology (MS, PhD); MS/PhD. *Accreditation:* ASHA (one or more programs are accredited). *Degree requirements:* For doctorate, thesis/dissertation. *Entrance requirements:* For master's and doctorate, GRE. Electronic applications accepted. *Expenses:* Tuition, state resident: part-time $594 per credit. Tuition, nonresident: part-time $1504 per credit. Required fees: $65 per credit. Tuition and fees vary according to course load, program and reciprocity agreements. *Faculty research:* Language disorders in children and adults, disorders of speech production, intelligibility, fluency, hearing impairment, deafness.

University of Wisconsin–Stevens Point, College of Fine Arts and Communication, Division of Communication, Stevens Point, WI 54481-3897. Offers interpersonal communication (MA); mass communication (MA); organizational communication (MA); public relations (MA). Part-time programs available. *Students:* 7 full-time (3 women), 19 part-time (11 women). *Degree requirements:* For master's, thesis or alternative. *Entrance requirements:* For master's, GRE. Additional exam requirements/recommendations for international students: Required—TOEFL (minimum score 575 paper-based). *Application deadline:* For fall admission, 3/1 priority date for domestic students. Applications are processed on a rolling basis. Application fee: $45. *Expenses:* Tuition, state resident: full-time $7740; part-time $430 per credit hour. Tuition, nonresident: full-time $17,804; part-time $989 per credit hour. Tuition and fees vary according to course load and reciprocity agreements. *Financial support:* In 2009–10, 9 teaching assistantships were awarded; career-related internships or fieldwork, Federal Work-Study, institutionally sponsored loans, and unspecified assistantships also available. Support available to part-time students. Financial award application deadline: 5/1; financial award applicants required to submit FAFSA. *Faculty research:* Communication theory and research, film history. *Unit head:* Dr. James Haney, Chair, 715-346-3409, E-mail: jhaney@uwsp.edu. *Application contact:* Dr. Chris Sadler, Graduate Coordinator, 715-346-3898, E-mail: csadler@uwsp.edu.

University of Wisconsin–Superior, Graduate Division, Department of Communicating Arts, Superior, WI 54880-4500. Offers mass communication (MA); speech communication (MA); theater (MA). Part-time programs available. *Faculty:* 9 full-time (3 women), 1 (woman) part-time/adjunct. *Students:* 14 full-time (9 women), 5 part-time (3 women). Average age 30. 9 applicants, 100% accepted. In 2009, 7 master's awarded. *Degree requirements:* For master's, comprehensive exam, thesis or alternative, position paper or project. *Entrance requirements:* For master's, minimum GPA of 2.75. *Application deadline:* For fall admission, 4/1 priority date for domestic students; for spring admission, 10/15 priority date for domestic students. Applications are processed on a rolling basis. Application fee: $45. *Financial support:* Career-related internships or fieldwork, Federal Work-Study, institutionally sponsored loans, scholarships/grants, and tuition waivers (partial) available. Support available to part-time students. Financial award application deadline: 4/15; financial award applicants required to submit FAFSA. *Faculty research:* Multimedia technology, ethics in journalism, diversity, electronic portfolio assessment. *Unit head:* Dr. Martha Einerson, Program Coordinator, 715-394-8477, E-mail: meinerso@uwsuper.edu. *Application contact:* Sandy Wallgren, Program Assistant/Status Examiner, 715-394-8295, Fax: 715-394-8146, E-mail: swallgr1@uwsuper.edu.

Wake Forest University, Graduate School of Arts and Sciences, Department of Communication, Winston-Salem, NC 27109. Offers speech communication (MA). Part-time programs available. *Degree requirements:* For master's, one foreign language, thesis. *Entrance requirements:* For master's, GRE General Test, writing sample. Additional exam requirements/recommendations for international students: Required—TOEFL (minimum score 213 computer-based; 79 iBT). Electronic applications accepted.

Washington University in St. Louis, School of Medicine, Program in Audiology and Communication Sciences, St. Louis, MO 63110. Offers audiology (Au D); deaf education (MS); speech and hearing sciences (PhD). *Accreditation:* ASHA (one or more programs are accredited). *Faculty:* 22 full-time (12 women), 18 part-time/adjunct (12 women). *Students:* 74 full-time (72 women). Average age 24. 117 applicants, 21% accepted, 24 enrolled. In 2009, 14 master's, 9 doctorates awarded. *Degree requirements:* For master's, comprehensive exam, thesis, independent study project, oral exam; for doctorate, comprehensive exam, thesis/dissertation, capstone project, comprehensive exam. *Entrance requirements:* For master's, GRE General Test, minimum B average in undergraduate course work; for doctorate, GRE General Test, minimum B average. Additional exam requirements/recommendations for international students: Required—TOEFL (minimum score 600 paper-based; 250 computer-based; 100 iBT). *Application deadline:* For fall admission, 2/15 for domestic and international students. Application fee: $50 ($75 for international students). Electronic applications accepted. *Expenses:* Contact institution. *Financial support:* In 2009–10, 74 fellowships with tuition reimbursements were awarded; research assistantships with tuition reimbursements, teaching assistantships with tuition reimbursements, career-related internships or fieldwork, Federal Work-Study, institutionally sponsored loans, scholarships/grants, traineeships, health care benefits, tuition waivers (partial), and unspecified assistantships also available. Financial award application deadline: 2/15; financial award applicants required to submit FAFSA. *Faculty research:* Audiology, deaf education, speech and hearing sciences, hearing aids and cochlear implants, sensory neuroscience. *Unit head:* Dr. William W. Clark, Program Director, 314-747-0104, Fax: 314-747-0105. *Application contact:* Elizabeth A. Elliott, Manager, Financial Operations and Admissions, 314-747-0104, Fax: 314-747-0105, E-mail: elliottb@wustl.edu.

Wayne State University, College of Fine, Performing and Communication Arts, Department of Communication, Detroit, MI 48202. Offers communication studies (MA, PhD); public relations and organizational communication (MA); radio-TV-film (MA, PhD); speech communication (MA, PhD). *Degree requirements:* For master's, thesis, essay, or comprehensive exam; for doctorate, thesis/dissertation. *Entrance requirements:* For master's, minimum GPA of 3.0, sample of academic writing; for doctorate, GRE, minimum GPA of 3.3, MA; letters of recommendation; personal statement; sample of written scholarship. Additional exam requirements/recommendations for international students: Required—TOEFL (minimum score 550 paper-based; 213 computer-based); Recommended—TWE (minimum score 6). Electronic applications accepted. *Faculty research:* Rhetorical theory and criticism; mass media theory and research; argumentation; organizational communication; risk and crisis communication; interpersonal, family, and health communication.

Technical Communication

Boise State University, Graduate College, College of Arts and Sciences, Department of English, Program in Technical Communication, Boise, ID 83725-0399. Offers MA. Part-time programs available. *Degree requirements:* For master's, thesis. *Entrance requirements:* For master's, minimum GPA of 3.0. Electronic applications accepted. *Expenses:* Tuition, state resident: full-time $3106; part-time $209 per credit. Tuition, nonresident: part-time $284 per credit.

Bowling Green State University, Graduate College, College of Arts and Sciences, Department of English, Program in English, Bowling Green, OH 43403. Offers English (MA, PhD); literature (MA); rhetoric and writing (PhD); scientific and technical communication (MA). Part-time programs available. *Degree requirements:* For master's, thesis or alternative; for doctorate, comprehensive exam, thesis/dissertation, foreign language or proficiency in Old English. *Entrance requirements:* For master's and doctorate, GRE General Test. Additional exam requirements/recommendations for international students: Required—TOEFL. Electronic applications accepted. *Faculty research:* Postmodern literary theory, rhetorical theory, ethnic American literature, literature and culture, composition pedagogy.

Colorado State University, Graduate School, College of Liberal Arts, Department of Journalism and Technical Communication, Fort Collins, CO 80523-1785. Offers public communication and technology (MS, PhD); technical communication (MS). Part-time programs available. *Faculty:* 19 full-time (8 women). *Students:* 26 full-time (21 women), 38 part-time (28 women); includes 5 minority (1 American Indian/Alaska Native, 1 Asian American or Pacific Islander, 3 Hispanic Americans), 3 international. Average age 33. 60 applicants, 48% accepted, 15 enrolled. In 2009, 13 master's awarded. *Degree requirements:* For master's, variable foreign language requirement, comprehensive exam (for some programs), thesis (for some programs); for doctorate, variable foreign language requirement, comprehensive exam (for some programs), thesis/dissertation (for some programs). *Entrance requirements:* For master's, GRE General Test, samples of written work, letters of recommendation, resume or curriculum vitae, 3 writing/communication projects; for doctorate, GRE General Test, master's degree, minimum GPA of 3.0, scholarly/professional work, letters of recommendation, statement of career plans, resume. Additional exam requirements/recommendations for international students: Required—TOEFL (minimum score 600 paper-based; 250 computer-based). *Application deadline:* For fall admission, 2/15 priority date for domestic students, 12/15 priority date for international students; for spring admission, 6/15 priority date for domestic students. Applications are processed on a rolling basis. Application fee: $50. Electronic applications accepted. *Expenses:* Tuition, state resident: full-time $6434; part-time $359.10 per credit. Tuition, nonresident: full-time $18,116; part-time $1006.45 per credit. Required fees: $1496; $83 per credit. *Financial support:* In 2009–10, 21 students received support, including 21 teaching assistantships with partial tuition reimbursements available (averaging $9,428 per year); fellowships with partial tuition reimbursements available, research assistantships with full and partial tuition reimbursements available, career-related internships or fieldwork, Federal Work-Study, institutionally sponsored loans, scholarships/grants, traineeships, and unspecified assistantships also available. Support available to part-time students. Financial award application deadline: 3/1; financial award applicants required to submit FAFSA. *Faculty research:* Technical/science communication, public relations, health/risk communication, web/new media technologies, environmental communication. Total annual research expenditures: $133,759. *Unit head:* Dr. Greg Luft, Chair, 970-491-1979, Fax: 970-491-2908, E-mail: greg.luft@colostate.edu. *Application contact:* Dr. Craig Trumbo, Graduate Program Coordinator, 970-491-2077, Fax: 970-491-2908, E-mail: craig.trumbo@colostate.edu.

Drexel University, College of Arts and Sciences, Department of Culture and Communication, Program in Communication, Philadelphia, PA 19104-2875. Offers public communication (MS); science communication (MS); technical communication (MS). Part-time and evening/weekend programs available. *Degree requirements:* For master's, internship, professional portfolio. *Entrance requirements:* For master's, GRE or minimum GPA of 3.0. Additional exam requirements/recommendations for international students: Required—TOEFL. Electronic applications accepted.

Eastern Michigan University, Graduate School, College of Arts and Sciences, Department of English Language and Literature, Program in Written Communication, Ypsilanti, MI 48197. Offers technical communications (MA, Graduate Certificate); written communications (MA). Part-time and evening/weekend programs available. Postbaccalaureate distance learning degree programs offered (minimal on-campus study). *Students:* 7 full-time (5 women), 35 part-time (27 women); includes 2 minority (both African Americans). Average age 35. In 2009, 21 master's awarded. *Entrance requirements:* Additional exam requirements/recommendations for international students: Required—TOEFL. *Application deadline:* Applications are processed on a rolling basis. Application fee: $35. Tuition and fees vary according to course level. *Financial support:* Fellowships, research assistantships with full tuition reimbursements, teaching assistantships with full tuition reimbursements, career-related internships or fieldwork, Federal Work-Study, institutionally sponsored loans, scholarships/grants, tuition waivers (partial), and unspecified assistantships available. Support available to part-time students. Financial award applicants required to submit FAFSA. *Unit head:* Dr. Rebecca Sipe, Department Head, 734-487-4220, Fax: 734-483-9744, E-mail: rebecca.sipe@emich.edu. *Application contact:* Dr. Cheryl Cassidy, Program Advisor, 734-487-0150, Fax: 734-483-9744, E-mail: cheryl.cassidy@emich.edu.

Eastern Washington University, Graduate Studies, College of Arts and Letters, Department of English, Cheney, WA 99004-2431. Offers literature (MA); rhetoric, composition, and technical communication (MA); teaching English as a second language (MA). *Degree requirements:* For master's, comprehensive exam, thesis or alternative. *Entrance requirements:* For master's, GRE General Test, minimum GPA of 3.0. *Expenses:* Tuition, state resident: full-time $7476; part-time $249 per quarter hour. Tuition, nonresident: full-time $18,030; part-time $601 per quarter hour. Required fees: $3.50 per quarter hour. $142 per quarter.

Florida Institute of Technology, Graduate Programs, College of Psychology and Liberal Arts, Department of Humanities and Communication, Melbourne, FL 32901-6975. Offers technical and professional communication (MS). Part-time and evening/weekend programs available. *Faculty:* 4 full-time (all women). *Students:* 6 full-time (2 women), 11 part-time (9 women); includes 5 minority (2 African Americans, 1 American Indian/Alaska Native, 1 Asian American or Pacific Islander, 1 Hispanic American), 2 international. Average age 38. 4 applicants, 100% accepted, 2 enrolled. In 2009, 2 master's awarded. *Degree requirements:* For master's, comprehensive exam (for some programs), thesis optional. *Entrance requirements:* For master's, GRE (minimum score 1000 verbal and analytical), minimum GPA of 3.0, 2 letters of recommendation, discursive writing sample. Additional exam requirements/recommendations for international students: Required—TOEFL (minimum score 550 paper-based; 213 computer-based; 79 iBT). *Application deadline:* For fall admission, 4/1 for international students; for spring admission, 9/30 for international students. Applications are processed on a rolling basis. Application fee: $50. Electronic applications accepted. *Expenses:* Tuition: Part-time $1015 per credit. Tuition and fees vary according to campus/location and program. *Financial support:* Career-related internships or fieldwork and tuition remissions available. Support available to part-time students. Financial award application deadline: 3/1; financial award applicants required to submit FAFSA. *Faculty research:* Communication of astronomy in the seventeenth century, persuasion and patronage in seventeenth century work, technical and cross-cultural communication. *Unit head:* Dr. Robert A. Taylor, Department Head, 321-674-7384, Fax: 321-674-8109, E-mail: rotaylor@fit.edu. *Application contact:* Thomas M. Shea, Director of Graduate Admissions, 321-674-7577, Fax: 321-723-9468, E-mail: tshea@fit.edu.

Harvard University, Graduate School of Education, Master's Programs in Education, Cambridge, MA 02138. Offers arts in education (Ed M); education policy and management (Ed M); higher education (Ed M); human development and psychology (Ed M); international education policy (Ed M); language and literacy (Ed M); learning and teaching (Ed M); mid-career mathematics and science (teaching certificate) (Ed M); mind brain and education (Ed M); risk and prevention (Ed M); school leadership (Ed M); special studies (Ed M); teaching and curriculum (teaching certificate) (Ed M); technology innovation and education (Ed M). Part-time programs available. *Faculty:* 70 full-time (33 women), 36 part-time/adjunct (20 women). *Students:* 598 full-time (448 women), 76 part-time (60 women); includes 132 minority (40 African Americans, 2 American Indian/Alaska Native, 58 Asian Americans or Pacific Islanders, 32 Hispanic Americans), 103 international. Average age 28. 1,574 applicants, 58% accepted, 640 enrolled. In 2009, 556 master's awarded. *Entrance requirements:* For master's, GRE General Test, 3 letters of recommendation. Additional exam requirements/recommendations for international students: Required—TOEFL (minimum score 600 paper-based; 250 computer-based; 100 iBT), TWE (minimum score 5). *Application deadline:* For fall admission, 1/4 for domestic and international students. Application fee: $85. Electronic applications accepted. *Expenses:* Contact institution. *Financial support:* In 2009–10, 424 students received support, including 25 fellowships with full and partial tuition reimbursements available (averaging $15,890 per year); career-related internships or fieldwork, Federal Work-Study, institutionally sponsored loans, scholarships/grants, health care benefits, tuition waivers (full and partial), and unspecified assistantships also available. Support available to part-time students. Financial award application deadline: 2/1; financial award applicants required to submit FAFSA. *Faculty research:* Learning and development, educational leadership and organizations, educational policy analysis. Total annual research expenditures: $18.1 million. *Unit head:* Jennifer L. Petrallia, Assistant Dean for Master's Studies, 617-495-8445. *Application contact:* Information Contact, 617-495-3414, Fax: 617-496-3577, E-mail: gseadmissions@harvard.edu.

Lawrence Technological University, College of Arts and Sciences, Southfield, MI 48075-1058. Offers computer science (MS); educational technology (MET); science education (MSE); technical communication (MS). Part-time and evening/weekend programs available. *Faculty:* 14 full-time (6 women), 14 part-time/adjunct (4 women). *Students:* 6 full-time (3 women), 80 part-time (49 women); includes 19 minority (14 African Americans, 5 Asian Americans or Pacific Islanders), 12 international. Average age 35. 87 applicants, 57% accepted, 20 enrolled. In 2009, 34 master's awarded. *Degree requirements:* For master's, thesis (for some programs). *Entrance requirements:* For master's, GRE. Additional exam requirements/recommendations for international students: Required—TOEFL (minimum score 550 paper-based; 213 computer-based; 79 iBT). *Application deadline:* For fall admission, 8/1 priority date for domestic students, 6/1 for international students; for winter admission, 12/1 priority date for domestic students, 10/1 for international students; for spring admission, 5/1 priority date for domestic students, 3/1 for international students. Applications are processed on a rolling basis. Application fee: $50. Electronic applications accepted. *Expenses:* Tuition: Full-time $11,320; part-time $798 per credit hour. *Financial support:* Federal Work-Study available. Financial award application deadline: 4/1; financial award applicants required to submit FAFSA. *Unit head:* Dr. Hsiao-Ping Moore, Dean, 248-204-3500, Fax: 248-204-3518, E-mail: scidean@ltu.edu. *Application contact:* Jane Rohrback, Director of Admissions, 248-204-3160, Fax: 248-204-3188, E-mail: admissions@ltu.edu.

Michigan Technological University, Graduate School, College of Sciences and Arts, Department of Humanities, Program in Rhetoric and Technical Communication, Houghton, MI 49931. Offers MS, PhD. Part-time programs available. Terminal master's awarded for partial completion of doctoral program. *Degree requirements:* For master's, comprehensive exam; for doctorate, one foreign language, comprehensive exam, thesis/dissertation. *Entrance requirements:* Additional exam requirements/recommendations for international students: Required—TOEFL (minimum score 600 paper-based; 250 computer-based). Electronic applications accepted.

Minnesota State University Mankato, College of Graduate Studies, College of Arts and Humanities, Department of English, Mankato, MN 56001. Offers creative writing (MFA); English (MAT); English studies (MA); literature (MA); teaching English as a second language (MA, Certificate); technical communication (MA, Certificate). Part-time programs available. *Students:* 54 full-time (34 women), 114 part-time (78 women). *Degree requirements:* For master's, one foreign language, comprehensive exam, thesis or alternative. *Entrance requirements:* For master's, minimum GPA of 3.0 during previous 2 years, writing sample (MFA). Additional exam requirements/recommendations for international students: Required—TOEFL. *Application deadline:* Applications are processed on a rolling basis. Application fee: $40. Electronic applications accepted. *Expenses:* Tuition, state resident: full-time $5364. Tuition, nonresident: full-time $8314. *Financial support:* Research assistantships with full tuition reimbursements, teaching assistantships with full tuition reimbursements, career-related internships or fieldwork, Federal Work-Study, and unspecified assistantships available. Financial award application deadline: 3/15; financial award applicants required to submit FAFSA. *Faculty research:* Keats and Christianity. *Unit head:* Dr. John Banschbach, Chairperson, 507-389-2117. *Application contact:* 507-389-2321, E-mail: grad@mnsu.edu.

Montana Tech of The University of Montana, Graduate School, Department of Technical Communication, Butte, MT 59701-8997. Offers MS. Part-time programs available. *Faculty:* 5 full-time (2 women), 1 (woman) part-time/adjunct. *Students:* 8 full-time (6 women), 5 part-time (4 women). 11 applicants, 73% accepted, 3 enrolled. In 2009, 4 master's awarded. *Degree requirements:* For master's, project or thesis. *Entrance requirements:* For master's, GRE General Test, minimum GPA of 3.0. Additional exam requirements/recommendations for international students: Required—TOEFL (minimum score 525 paper-based; 195 computer-based; 71 iBT). *Application deadline:* For fall admission, 4/1 priority date for domestic students, 3/1 priority date for international students; for spring admission, 10/1 priority date for domestic students, 7/1 priority date for international students. Applications are processed on a rolling basis. Application fee: $30. Electronic applications accepted. *Expenses:* Tuition, state resident: full-time $5068; part-time $319 per credit. Tuition, nonresident: full-time $14,815; part-time $875 per credit. Tuition and fees vary according to course load and campus/location. *Financial support:* In 2009–10, 4 students received support, including 4 teaching assistantships with partial tuition reimbursements available (averaging $6,000 per year); research assistantships with partial tuition reimbursements available, career-related internships or fieldwork, tuition waivers (partial), and unspecified assistantships also available. Financial award application deadline: 4/1; financial award applicants required to submit FAFSA. *Faculty research:* Environmental concerns and the Big Hole River, history of Butte mining, African studies, multicultural communications. *Unit head:* Dr. Henrietta Shirk, Head, 406-496-4297, Fax: 406-496-4510, E-mail: hshirk@mtech.edu. *Application contact:* Cindy Dunstan, Administrator, Graduate School, 406-496-4304, Fax: 406-496-4710, E-mail: cdunstan@mtech.edu.

New Jersey Institute of Technology, Office of Graduate Studies, College of Science and Liberal Arts, Department of Humanities and Social Sciences, Program in Professional and Technical Communication, Newark, NJ 07102. Offers MS. Part-time and evening/weekend programs available. Terminal master's awarded for partial completion of doctoral program. *Degree requirements:* For master's, thesis or alternative. *Entrance requirements:* For master's, GRE General Test. Additional exam requirements/recommendations for international students: Required—TOEFL (minimum score 550 paper-based; 213 computer-based). Electronic applications accepted. *Faculty research:* Technology transfer, global sustainability, technology policy, professional ethics.

North Carolina State University, Graduate School, College of Humanities and Social Sciences, Department of English, Program in Technical Communication, Raleigh, NC 27695. Offers MS. *Degree requirements:* For master's, thesis optional. *Entrance requirements:* For master's, GRE General Test. Electronic applications accepted. *Faculty research:* Workplace writing, organizational socialization and power, integrated and multimedia documentation systems, technical communication management, usability testing theories.

Polytechnic Institute of NYU, Department of Humanities and Social Sciences, Major in Technical Communication, Brooklyn, NY 11201-2990. Offers Graduate Certificate. *Students:* 2

Technical Communication

Polytechnic Institute of NYU (continued)

full-time (1 woman), 2 part-time (0 women); includes 3 minority (2 African Americans, 1 Asian American or Pacific Islander). *Expenses:* Tuition: Full-time $21,492; part-time $1194 per credit hour. Required fees: $1160; $204 per course. *Unit head:* Prof. Teresa Feroli, Head, 718-260-3422, E-mail: tferoli@poly.edu. *Application contact:* Prof. Teresa Feroli, Head, 718-260-3422, E-mail: tferoli@poly.edu.

Rensselaer Polytechnic Institute, Graduate School, School of Humanities and Social Sciences, Department of Language, Literature, and Communication, Program in Technical Communication, Troy, NY 12180-3590. Offers MS. Part-time programs available. *Faculty:* 15 full-time (7 women), 1 (woman) part-time/adjunct. *Students:* 1 full-time (0 women), 3 part-time (all women). 5 applicants, 40% accepted, 2 enrolled. In 2009, 1 master's awarded. *Degree requirements:* For master's, thesis optional. *Entrance requirements:* For master's, GRE General Test, resume. Additional exam requirements/recommendations for international students: Required—TOEFL (minimum score 570 paper-based; 230 computer-based). *Application deadline:* For fall admission, 1/15 priority date for domestic students; for spring admission, 10/15 priority date for domestic students. Applications are processed on a rolling basis. Application fee: $75. Electronic applications accepted. *Expenses:* Tuition: Full-time $38,100. *Financial support:* In 2009–10, 1 teaching assistantship with full tuition reimbursement (averaging $16,500 per year) was awarded; fellowships, research assistantships, career-related internships or fieldwork and institutionally sponsored loans also available. Financial award application deadline: 1/15. *Faculty research:* Human-computer interaction; media design, theory and culture; visual communication; usability; professional and technical communication. *Unit head:* Prof. James P. Zappen, Head, 518-276-6468, Fax: 518-276-4092, E-mail: zappenj@rpi.edu. *Application contact:* Kathy A. Colman, Recruitment Coordinator, 518-276-6469, Fax: 518-276-4092, E-mail: colmak@rpi.edu.

Rochester Institute of Technology, Graduate Enrollment Services, College of Applied Science and Technology, Center for Multidisciplinary Studies, Program in Technical Information Design, Rochester, NY 14623-5603. Offers AC. Part-time programs available. Postbaccalaureate distance learning degree programs offered (no on-campus study). In 2009, 2 degrees awarded. *Entrance requirements:* Additional exam requirements/recommendations for international students: Required—TOEFL (minimum score 550 paper-based; 213 computer-based; 79 iBT), or IELTS (minimum score 6.5). *Application deadline:* For fall admission, 2/15 priority date for domestic and international students; for winter admission, 11/1 priority date for domestic students, 10/1 priority date for international students; for spring admission, 2/1 priority date for domestic students, 1/1 priority date for international students. Applications are processed on a rolling basis. Application fee: $50. Electronic applications accepted. *Expenses:* Tuition: Full-time $31,533; part-time $876 per credit hour. Required fees: $210. *Financial support:* Career-related internships or fieldwork and scholarships/grants available. Support available to part-time students. Financial award applicants required to submit FAFSA. *Unit head:* Thomas Moran, Program Chair, 585-475-4936, E-mail: tfmcad@rit.edu. *Application contact:* Diane Ellison, Assistant Vice President, Graduate Enrollment Services, 585-475-2229, Fax: 585-475-7164, E-mail: gradinfo@rit.edu.

Southern Polytechnic State University, School of Arts and Sciences, Department of English, Technical Communication, and Media Arts, Marietta, GA 30060-2896. Offers communications management (Graduate Certificate); content development (Graduate Certificate); information and instructional design (MSIID); information design and communication (MS); instructional design (Graduate Certificate); technical and professional communication (Graduate Certificate); visual communication and graphics (Graduate Certificate). Part-time and evening/weekend programs available. Postbaccalaureate distance learning degree programs offered (no on-campus study). *Faculty:* 4 full-time (3 women), 1 part-time/adjunct (0 women). *Students:* 5 full-time (all women), 50 part-time (32 women); includes 18 African Americans, 2 international. Average age 38. 32 applicants, 94% accepted, 26 enrolled. In 2009, 8 master's awarded. *Degree requirements:* For master's, thesis or internship; for Graduate Certificate, thesis optional, 18 hours completed through thesis option (6 hours), internship option (6 hours) or advanced coursework option (6 hours). *Entrance requirements:* For master's, GRE, statement of purpose, writing sample, professional recommendations, timed essay; for Graduate Certificate, writing sample, professional recommendations. Additional exam requirements/recommendations for international students: Required—TOEFL (minimum score 550 paper-based; 213 computer-based; 79 iBT), IELTS (minimum score 6.5). *Application deadline:* For fall admission, 5/1 priority date for domestic students, 7/1 priority date for international students; for spring admission, 9/1 priority date for domestic students, 11/1 priority date for international students. Applications are processed on a rolling basis. Application fee: $20. Electronic applications accepted. *Expenses:* Tuition, state resident: full-time $2896; part-time $181 per credit hour. Tuition, nonresident: full-time $11,552; part-time $722 per credit hour. Required fees: $1096; $1096 per year. *Financial support:* In 2009–10, 1 research assistantship with full tuition reimbursement (averaging $4,000 per year), 1 teaching assistantship with partial tuition reimbursement (averaging $4,000 per year) were awarded; career-related internships or fieldwork, Federal Work-Study, scholarships/grants, and unspecified assistantships also available. Support available to part-time students. Financial award application deadline: 5/1; financial award applicants required to submit FAFSA. *Faculty research:* Usability, user-centered design, instructional design, information architecture, information design. *Unit head:* Dr. Mark Nunes, Chair, 678-915-7202, Fax: 678-915-7425, E-mail: mnunes@spsu.edu. *Application contact:* Nikki Palamiotis, Director of Graduate Studies, 678-915-4276, Fax: 678-915-7292, E-mail: npalamio@spsu.edu.

Texas State University–San Marcos, Graduate School, College of Liberal Arts, Department of English, Program in Technical Communication, San Marcos, TX 78666. Offers MA. *Faculty:* 6 full-time (4 women). *Students:* 7 full-time (6 women), 18 part-time (14 women); includes 5 minority (1 African American, 1 Asian American or Pacific Islander, 3 Hispanic Americans). Average age 31. 11 applicants, 100% accepted, 9 enrolled. In 2009, 5 master's awarded. *Degree requirements:* For master's, comprehensive exam, thesis or alternative. *Entrance requirements:* For master's, course work in English, 3 letters of reference, at least 2 non-fiction papers (15 typed, double-spaced pages), 1 academic research paper. Additional exam requirements/recommendations for international students: Required—TOEFL (minimum score 550 paper-based; 213 computer-based). *Application deadline:* For fall admission, 6/15 priority date for domestic students, 6/1 for international students; for spring admission, 11/1 priority date for domestic students, 10/1 for international students. Applications are processed on a rolling basis. Application fee: $40 ($90 for international students). Electronic applications accepted. *Expenses:* Tuition, state resident: full-time $5784; part-time $241 per credit hour. Tuition, nonresident: part-time $551 per credit hour. Required fees: $1728; $48 per credit hour. $306. Tuition and fees vary according to course load. *Financial support:* In 2009–10, 16 students received support, including 1 teaching assistantship (averaging $5,206 per year); research assistantships, Federal Work-Study and institutionally sponsored loans also available. Support available to part-time students. Financial award application deadline: 4/1. *Unit head:* Dr. Libby Allison, Graduate Advisor, 512-245-2163, Fax: 512-245-8546, E-mail: ea10@txstate.edu. *Application contact:* Dr. Michael Willoughby, Dean of Graduate School, 512-245-2581, Fax: 512-245-8365, E-mail: gradcollege@txstate.edu.

University of Colorado Denver, College of Liberal Arts and Sciences, Department of Communication, Denver, CO 80217-3364. Offers communication (MA); technical communication (MS). Part-time and evening/weekend programs available. *Students:* 5 full-time (4 women), 11 part-time (7 women), 1 international. 14 applicants, 57% accepted, 3 enrolled. In 2009, 6 master's awarded. *Degree requirements:* For master's, comprehensive exam, thesis or alternative. *Entrance requirements:* For master's, GRE General Test. Additional exam requirements/recommendations for international students: Required—TOEFL (minimum score 525 paper-based; 197 computer-based). *Application deadline:* For fall admission, 6/1 for domestic students. Applications are processed on a rolling basis. Application fee: $50 ($75 for international students). Electronic applications accepted. *Financial support:* Fellowships with partial tuition reimbursements, research assistantships with partial tuition reimbursements, teaching assistantships, Federal Work-Study and institutionally sponsored loans available. Financial award application deadline: 4/1; financial award applicants required to submit FAFSA. *Unit head:* Dr. Stephen J. Hartnett, Chair, 303-556-2778, E-mail: stephen.hartnett@ucdenver.edu. *Application contact:* Dr. Stephen J. Hartnett, Chair, 303-556-2778, E-mail: stephen.hartnett@ucdenver.edu.

University of Houston–Downtown, College of Humanities and Social Sciences, Department of English, Houston, TX 77002. Offers professional writing and technical communication (MS). Part-time and evening/weekend programs available. *Faculty:* 5 full-time (3 women). *Students:* 4 full-time (all women), 18 part-time (14 women); includes 9 minority (7 African Americans, 1 Asian American or Pacific Islander, 1 Hispanic American). Average age 37. 5 applicants, 80% accepted, 4 enrolled. In 2009, 4 master's awarded. *Degree requirements:* For master's, thesis optional, graduation portfolio with oral defense. *Entrance requirements:* For master's, GRE (including Analytical Writing section), personal application statement, resume, writing sample, 3 letters of recommendation. Additional exam requirements/recommendations for international students: Required—TOEFL (minimum score 600 paper-based; 250 computer-based; 86 iBT). *Application deadline:* For fall admission, 5/1 for domestic and international students; for spring admission, 11/1 for domestic and international students. Application fee: $35 ($60 for international students). Electronic applications accepted. *Expenses:* Tuition, state resident: full-time $3150; part-time $175 per credit hour. Tuition, nonresident: full-time $7506; part-time $417 per credit hour. Required fees: $908; $322 per term. *Financial support:* Applicants required to submit FAFSA. *Faculty research:* Environmental rhetoric, instructional design, usability, assessment, presentation slides. *Unit head:* Dr. Robert Jarrett, Chair, 713-221-8013, Fax: 713-226-5205, E-mail: jarrettr@uhd.edu. *Application contact:* Dr. Michelle Moosally, Coordinator of MS in Professional Writing and Technical Communication and Professor, Department of English, 713-221-8013, Fax: 713-226-5205, E-mail: mspwtc@uhd.edu.

University of Nebraska at Omaha, Graduate Studies, College of Arts and Sciences, Department of English, Omaha, NE 68182. Offers advanced writing (Certificate); English (MA); teaching English to speakers of other languages (Certificate); technical communication (Certificate). Part-time and evening/weekend programs available. *Faculty:* 20 full-time (10 women). *Students:* 11 full-time (4 women), 59 part-time (43 women); includes 2 minority (1 African American, 1 Asian American or Pacific Islander), 3 international. Average age 32. 40 applicants, 68% accepted, 17 enrolled. In 2009, 13 master's, 8 other advanced degrees awarded. *Degree requirements:* For master's, comprehensive exam, thesis (for some programs). *Entrance requirements:* For master's, minimum GPA of 3.0, 3 letters of recommendation, writing sample. Additional exam requirements/recommendations for international students: Required—TOEFL (minimum score 600 paper-based; 250 computer-based; 100 iBT). *Application deadline:* For fall admission, 8/1 priority date for domestic students; for spring admission, 12/1 priority date for domestic students. Applications are processed on a rolling basis. Application fee: $45. Electronic applications accepted. *Financial support:* In 2009–10, 34 students received support; fellowships, teaching assistantships with tuition reimbursements available, Federal Work-Study, institutionally sponsored loans, scholarships/grants, tuition waivers (partial), and unspecified assistantships available. Support available to part-time students. Financial award application deadline: 3/1; financial award applicants required to submit FAFSA. *Unit head:* Dr. Susan Maher, Chairperson, 402-554-3636. *Application contact:* Dr. Joan Latchaw, Student Contact, 402-554-3636.

University of Washington, Graduate School, College of Engineering, Department of Human Centered Design and Engineering, Seattle, WA 98195-2315. Offers interdisciplinary Japanese (MSE); user-centered design (MS, PhD). Part-time and evening/weekend programs available. *Faculty:* 12 full-time (7 women), 6 part-time/adjunct (2 women). *Students:* 53 full-time (33 women), 56 part-time (28 women); includes 20 minority (4 African Americans, 13 Asian Americans or Pacific Islanders, 3 Hispanic Americans), 10 international. Average age 34. 109 applicants, 69% accepted, 55 enrolled. In 2009, 28 master's, 1 doctorate awarded. *Degree requirements:* For master's, thesis or alternative; for doctorate, comprehensive exam, thesis/dissertation. *Entrance requirements:* For master's and doctorate, GRE General Test, minimum GPA of 3.0. Additional exam requirements/recommendations for international students: Required—TOEFL (minimum score 580 paper-based; 237 computer-based; 70 iBT). *Application deadline:* For fall admission, 2/1 for domestic students, 11/15 priority date for international students. Applications are processed on a rolling basis. Application fee: $65. Electronic applications accepted. *Financial support:* In 2009–10, 1 student received support, including 15 research assistantships with full tuition reimbursements available (averaging $14,400 per year), 16 teaching assistantships with full tuition reimbursements available (averaging $14,400 per year); fellowships with full tuition reimbursements available, career-related internships or fieldwork, institutionally sponsored loans, and tuition waivers (full) also available. Financial award application deadline: 2/28; financial award applicants required to submit FAFSA. *Faculty research:* Human-computer interaction, communication design, user interface design and usability, new media design, comprehension processes. Total annual research expenditures: $1.5 million. *Unit head:* Dr. Jan Spyridakis, Professor and Chair, 206-685-1557, Fax: 206-543-8858, E-mail: jansp@u.washington.edu. *Application contact:* Gian Bruno, Academic Counselor, 206-543-1798, Fax: 206-543-8858, E-mail: gbruno@u.washington.edu.

University of Wisconsin–Milwaukee, Graduate School, College of Letters and Sciences, Department of English, Milwaukee, WI 53201-0413. Offers creative writing (PhD); English (MA); international technical communication (Certificate); linguistics (PhD); professional writing (PhD); professional writing and communication (Certificate); rhetoric and composition (PhD); MLIS/MA. *Faculty:* 38 full-time (19 women). *Students:* 107 full-time (64 women), 82 part-time (54 women); includes 13 minority (8 African Americans, 1 American Indian/Alaska Native, 2 Asian Americans or Pacific Islanders, 2 Hispanic Americans), 23 international. Average age 34. 193 applicants, 51% accepted, 31 enrolled. In 2009, 26 master's, 16 doctorates awarded. *Degree requirements:* For master's, thesis or alternative; for doctorate, one foreign language, thesis/dissertation. *Entrance requirements:* For master's, GRE General Test, GRE Subject Test; for doctorate, GRE. Additional exam requirements/recommendations for international students: Required—TOEFL (minimum score 550 paper-based; 79 iBT), IELTS (minimum score 6.5). *Application deadline:* For fall admission, 1/1 priority date for domestic students; for spring admission, 9/1 for domestic students. Applications are processed on a rolling basis. Application fee: $45 ($75 for international students). *Expenses:* Tuition, state resident: full-time $8800. Tuition, nonresident: full-time $20,760. Tuition and fees vary according to program and reciprocity agreements. *Financial support:* In 2009–10, 75 teaching assistantships were awarded; career-related internships or fieldwork and unspecified assistantships also available. Support available to part-time students. Financial award application deadline: 4/15. Total annual research expenditures: $41,495. *Unit head:* Tasha Oren, Representative, 414-229-4637, Fax: 414-229-2643, E-mail: tgoren@uwm.edu. *Application contact:* General Information Contact, 414-229-4982, Fax: 414-229-6967, E-mail: gradschool@uwm.edu.

AMERICAN UNIVERSITY
WASHINGTON, DC

AMERICAN UNIVERSITY

School of Communication

Programs of Study

American University's School of Communication (SOC) is a laboratory for professional education, communication research, and innovative production in journalism, film and media arts, and public communication, working across media platforms and with a focus on public affairs and public service. SOC offers graduate programs that prepare students for careers in traditional and emerging media. Students work closely with faculty in small, laboratory environments while pursuing professional opportunities in Washington, D.C.'s world-class media organizations, including Discovery Communications, *National Geographic, USA Today,* and *washingtonpost.com*. Most SOC faculty are practitioners who have won Oscars, Emmys, lifetime achievement awards, and other professional honors. A committed group of alumni also works with students individually in a unique mentoring program. All graduate programs emphasize writing, hands-on learning, and analysis of the social, legal, and economic challenges shaping today's communication industry.

SOC offers six full-time and three weekend master's degree programs. Full-time programs include the Master of Arts (M.A.) in journalism and public affairs (33 hours), with tracks in broadcast and print journalism and concentrations in economic, international, and public policy journalism; the M.A. in public communication (30 hours), with concentrations in arts, government, political, and public interest communication as well as corporate and international public relations; the M.A. in film and video (36 hours), with concentrations in film and video production, screenwriting, multimedia, and film history, theory, and criticism; the Master of Fine Arts (M.F.A.) in film and electronic media, a terminal degree that allows students to pursue collegiate-level teaching careers; the M.A. in international media (45 hours), a joint program with the School of International Service that offers a combination of theory, research, and professional production skills to provide a global media advantage; and the M.A. in political communication (36 hours), offered in partnership with the School of Public Affairs, is suitable for those seeking careers as politicians, policy-makers, political communication strategists, and campaign executives.

The weekend M.A. programs for working professionals include interactive journalism, public communication, and producing for film and video. Students move through the programs with a cohort of fellow students who meet every Saturday for twenty months.

Research Facilities

The SOC Friedheim Journalism Center (FJC) features two fully networked computer classrooms, each with twenty Macs configured for computer-assisted research and reporting, multimedia and Web authoring, and page layout and design. The FJC also contains a third, smaller lab with Mac and Windows computers for students' research, writing, and rich-media authoring. The School has three fully equipped Mac-based computer labs, all featuring state-of-the-art software applications for graphics production, digital imaging and compositing, layout and design, Web authoring, and digital video editing. A 109-seat theater is equipped with multiformat video projection and interactive videoconferencing capabilities. There are traditional black-and-white photographic darkroom facilities; small-, medium-, and large-format film cameras; high-quality digital scanning equipment; photo-quality color inkjet printing; and a growing collection of professional digital cameras, all dedicated for exclusive SOC-student use. A separate facility, the Media Production Center, houses a 40-foot by 40-foot, three-camera, high-definition television studio; the fully networked Ed Bliss Broadcast Newsroom; three digital audio studios; a large multiuse classroom; a field production equipment check-out facility; and thirteen digital video postproduction suites for Avid and Final Cut Pro editing.

Financial Aid

SOC offers merit-based financial aid awards on a competitive basis in all of its full-time graduate programs. Awards vary and may consist of tuition remission, stipend, teaching assistant or research assistant position, or a combination. In 2009–10, about 30 percent of SOC graduate students received merit-based financial aid. In addition to SOC-sponsored merit awards, the Journalism Division also offers prestigious fellowships in collaboration with the Center for Public Integrity, Bureau of National Affairs, and *USA Today*. American University offers need-based financial aid to students who qualify by filing the Free Application for Federal Student Aid (FAFSA) form.

Cost of Study

For the 2010–11 academic year, graduate tuition is $1299 per credit hour. Students may anticipate a 4 percent increase in tuition in each academic year. Full-time graduate study is considered to be at least 9 hours each semester; students in the full-time journalism and public communication programs usually complete 12 hours per semester. Special fees are charged for thesis processing, activities, and maintaining matriculation (if the student is not registered for courses). Courses requiring the use of production equipment or computer facilities typically incur additional lab fees.

Living and Housing Costs

Although many graduate students live off campus, the University has some graduate dormitory rooms for resident assistants. Housing application information is available on the University's Web site. The Off-Campus Housing Office maintains a referral file of rooms and apartments. Housing costs in Washington, D.C., are comparable to those in other major metropolitan areas.

Student Group

The SOC enrolls approximately 350 students in its graduate programs, divided more or less evenly among its full-time and weekend programs. Approximately 65 percent of the graduate students are women, 26 percent are members of minority groups, and 11 percent are international. All of the programs emphasize a strong liberal arts education as a requirement for admission, and none requires students to have majored in communication as undergraduates. Consequently, students selected in the competitive admission process come from diverse educational and professional backgrounds. Many students have worked professionally, and all have shown evidence of their professional and academic commitment.

Location

The School of Communication takes full advantage of the rich professional opportunities of Washington, D.C., as the nation's media capital as well as one of its largest production markets. Nationally recognized journalists, filmmakers, and public relations executives regularly serve as guest lecturers and adjunct professors. The city also offers the cultural resources of the Smithsonian Institution, the National Gallery of Art, the Kennedy Center for the Performing Arts, and the Library of Congress, plus a thriving artistic community of galleries and clubs.

The University and The School

Founded in 1893, American University (AU) is located on an 84-acre site in a residential area of northwest Washington that is accessible by Metro, the region's subway system. As a member of the Consortium of Universities of the Washington Metropolitan Area, AU offers its degree candidates the option of taking courses at other consortium universities for residence credit. SOC has educated communication professionals for forty years. Its journalism and public communication programs are accredited by the Accrediting Council for Education in Journalism and Mass Communications (ACEJMC), and its program in film and media arts is one of only fifteen U.S. programs accepted for membership in CILECT, the International Association of Film and Television Schools. The School's faculty members and alumni are working professionals who constitute a valuable network for graduating students seeking career advancement.

SOC is home to the Center for Social Media, Investigative Reporting Workshop, J-Lab: Institute for Interactive Journalism, Center for Environmental Filmmaking, and Foreign Correspondence Network.

Applying

Applicants must have earned a minimum GPA of 3.0 during their last 60 credits (two years) of undergraduate study for application to all graduate programs, except the M.A. in international media and the M.A. in political communication, which both require a minimum GPA of 3.3 in the last 60 credits of undergraduate study. GRE scores are required for applicants to full-time programs; GRE waivers may be granted to applicants with significant full-time, postbaccalaureate work experience. In addition, a 1,000-word statement of purpose, two letters of recommendation, a completed SOC graduate application form, and an application fee of $50 are required. Recommendations should be submitted on professional letterhead with a business card attached. International students who have learned English as a second language are required to score a minimum of 600 on the paper-based version, 250 on the computer-based version, or 100 on the Internet-based version of the TOEFL. SOC also accepts the IELTS exam for English proficiency from students with a minimum score of 7.0. The application deadline for fall admission into all full-time programs is June 1 (February 1 for merit award consideration). The film and video program admits students in the spring semester, with an application deadline of November 15. Weekend programs' priority deadline for applications is June 1; however, applications are accepted on a rolling admissions basis until the start of the fall semester in mid-August. Applications for financial aid should be submitted before February 1.

Correspondence and Information

Office of Graduate Programs
School of Communication
American University
4400 Massachusetts Avenue, NW
Washington, D.C. 20016-8017
Phone: 202-885-2040
E-mail: gradcomm@american.edu
Web site: http://www.american.edu/soc

American University

THE FACULTY

Larry Kirkman, Professor and Dean; M.A.T., Harvard.
Laird B. Anderson, Professor Emeritus; M.A., American. Journalism.
Patricia Aufderheide, Professor; Ph.D., Minnesota. Film and Media Arts.
Randall Blair, Associate Professor and Director, Weekend Producing for Film and Video Program; M.A., American. Film and Media Arts.
Kyle Brannon, Assistant Professor; M.F.A., American. Film and Electronic Media.
Carolyn Brown, Assistant Professor; M.A., Northern Arizona. Liberal Studies.
W. Joseph Campbell, Professor; Ph.D., North Carolina. Journalism.
Angie Chuang, Assistant Professor; M.A., Stanford. English Literature.
Wendell Cochran, Associate Professor; M.A., Missouri. Journalism.
John Doolittle, Associate Professor; Ph.D., Wisconsin–Madison. Journalism.
John Douglass, Associate Professor and Director, Film and Media Arts Division; M.A., American. Film and Media Arts.
Amy Eisman, Director, Writing Programs and Interactive Journalism Program; M.A., American. Journalism.
Larry Engel, Professor; M.F.A., Columbia. Film and Media Arts.
Wendy Melillo Farrill, Assistant Professor; M.A., Johns Hopkins. History, M.A., American. International Communication.
Declan Fahy, Assistant Professor; Ph.D., Dublin City. Communication.
Lauren Feldman, Assistant Professor; Ph.D., Pennsylvania. Communication.
William Gentile, Artist-in-Residence; M.A., Ohio State.
Joseph Graf, Assistant Professor; M.A., Ohio State. Public Communication.
Jane Hall, Associate Professor; M.S.J., Columbia. Journalism.
Sol Hart, Assistant Professor; Ph.D. candidate, Cornell. Communication.
Darrell Hayes, Assistant Professor and Director, Weekend Public Communication Program; M.A., Oklahoma. Public Communication.
Amy Hendrick, M.F.A., American. Film and Electronic Media.
Jerry Hendrix, Professor Emeritus; Ph.D., LSU. Public Communication.
Maria Ivancin, Assistant Professor; M.B.A., Illinois. Public Communication.
Leena Jayaswal, Associate Professor; M.F.A., Maryland Institute, College of Art. Film and Media Arts.
David Johnson, Assistant Professor; M.A., Texas A&M. Nautical Archaeology and Anthropology.
Iris Krasnow, Assistant Professor; M.A., Georgetown. Washington Journalism Semester.
Pallavi Kumar, Assistant Professor; M.A., Georgetown. Communication.
Charles Lewis, Professor; M.A., Johns Hopkins. Journalism.
Dotty Lynch, Executive-in-Residence; M.A., Fordham. Public Communication.
Brigid Maher, Assistant Professor; M.F.A., Northwestern. Film and Media Arts.
Sarah Menke-Fish, Assistant Professor; M.A., American. Film and Media Arts.
Kathryn Montgomery, Professor; Ph.D., UCLA. Public Communication.
Claudia Myers, Assistant Professor; M.F.A. Columbia. Film.
Matthew Nisbet, Assistant Professor; Ph.D., Cornell. Public Communication.
Jill Olmsted, Associate Professor and Director, Journalism Division; M.A., American. Journalism.
Chris Palmer, Distinguished-Film-Producer-in-Residence; M.A., Harvard. Film and Media Arts.
Lynne Perri, Journalist-in-Residence; M.S., Northwestern. Journalism.
Gemma Puglisi, Assistant Professor; M.A., Catholic University. Public Communication.
Rose Ann Robertson, Associate Dean; M.S., Southern Illinois. Journalism.
Rick Rockwell, Associate Professor; M.A., USC. Journalism.
Chris Simpson, Professor; M.A., Maryland. Journalism.
Rick Stack, Associate Professor; J.D., Missouri. Public Communication.
Leonard Steinhorn, Professor and Director, Public Communication Division; M.A., Johns Hopkins. Public Communication.
Margaret Stogner, Assistant Professor; M.A., Stanford. Film and Media Arts.
Rodger Streitmatter, Professor; Ph.D., American. Journalism.
John Watson, Associate Professor; J.D., Rutgers; Ph.D., North Carolina. Journalism.
Russell Williams, Artist-in-Residence; B.A., American. Film and Media Arts.
Lewis Wolfson, Professor Emeritus; M.S.J., Columbia; M.A., Harvard. Journalism.
Joanne Yamauchi, Professor Emeritus; Ph.D., Northwestern. Public Communication.
Rhonda Zaharna, Associate Professor; Ed.D., Columbia. Public Communication.
Anne Zelle, Professor Emeritus; M.A., Pius XII (Italy). Film and Media Arts.

BOSTON UNIVERSITY

College of Communication

Programs of Study

Boston University's College of Communication has three graduate departments: Film and Television; Mass Communication, Advertising, and Public Relations; and Journalism. Master of Science degree programs are available in advertising, broadcast journalism, business and economics journalism, journalism, mass communication, public relations, science journalism, television, and media ventures. A Master of Fine Arts is offered in film production, film studies, and screenwriting. The College also offers the following dual-degree programs: J.D./M.S. in mass communication and M.B.A./M.S. in media ventures.

The programs usually require three to four semesters of work. In several sequences, a creative project may be elected in place of a thesis. In the Department of Mass Communication, Advertising, and Public Relations, students may take a comprehensive exam in place of a thesis. A number of elective courses make up degree requirements within each program.

Summer internships are encouraged in all programs. Few summer courses are offered. Degree candidates must complete their work in seven years from the date of first course registration, or they may be required to satisfy additional requirements.

Research Facilities

The College provides opportunities for students to participate actively in ongoing research projects through part-time work and assistantships in the Communication Research Center, a research division organized to accept projects that have academic merit, do not compete directly with available commercial research facilities, and are in keeping with the objectives of the College. Physical facilities include a city room with an Associated Press wire service drop and a copy desk; VDTs; photo labs with fully equipped digital darkrooms; Ezratti HD Lab, recording, and broadcast facilities; Final Cut Studio; AVID editing suites; a closed-circuit TV center; complete film facilities; seminar rooms; and a reading room. The College has several computer labs and a state-of-the-art multimedia lab with both PCs and Macs. The University's Mugar Library has a substantial communication collection.

Financial Aid

The University offers various financial aid options to qualified students. These programs include merit scholarships ranging from $1000 to full tuition, the Federal Work-Study Program, and Federal Stafford Loans. Graduate assistantships are available through the individual departments. The stipends for scholarships and assistantships ranged from $1000 to $6000 per semester in 2009–10. Various loan programs and part-time jobs are also available. Students are urged to use their own initiative in finding support, since the resources of the graduate programs are limited; possible sources of aid include state agencies and private organizations. Library references and online searches are helpful information sources.

Cost of Study

Tuition was $37,910 for the 2009–10 academic year.

Living and Housing Costs

Most graduate students are advised to seek off-campus housing. Limited on-campus graduate housing is available. The cost for room and board is estimated to be about $12,000 for the nine-month academic year. The University maintains apartments for married full-time graduate students and their families.

Student Group

Of the 346 full- and part-time graduate students enrolling in fall 2010, 166 were returning to continue their studies, while 180 were beginning programs. There were several international students in the entering group, and many domestic students were from outside New England. Women make up 75 percent of the graduate class. Alumni of the College are found throughout the United States and in many other countries, practicing their communication skills in media, government, industry, social institutions, education, and private business.

Location

Boston, the largest city in New England and one of the largest media markets in the U.S., is a seaport whose character results from a rich blend of historical heritage, active cultural life, and contemporary growth in technology, medicine, and business. Greater Boston, with more than fifty colleges and universities, remains an unrivaled center of learning. Within the city's compact center are the Boston Common and the Public Garden, Faneuil Hall Marketplace, art galleries, Chinatown, and the Freedom Trail, along which are some of the most important landmarks in U.S. history. Admission to the Museum of Fine Arts is free for University students. The Boston Symphony Orchestra, the Opera Company of Boston, and many fine chamber and jazz groups offer annual seasons, as do dance and theater companies. Boston is the home of the New England Patriots, the Red Sox, the Celtics, and the Bruins.

The University and The College

Boston University is an independent, coeducational, nonsectarian university with an enrollment of about 29,000 full-time students and a faculty of more than 2,500. Its academic diversity meets the needs of one of the largest bodies of scholars in the world. Incorporated in 1869, the University today provides students with the advantages of a large, contemporary educational complex while maintaining many traditional priorities. Its sixteen schools and colleges respond to students' occupational needs and the increasingly specialized demands they face in the modern world. The main campus, on the south bank of the Charles River, occupies 64 acres just west of downtown Boston. The University's Medical Center is in the city's south end.

The College of Communication was founded in 1947 to provide professional education in public relations, journalism, broadcasting, and film. Graduate programs have been offered since the founding of the College. An integral part of the central campus, the College has its own building, lending a small-college atmosphere to its programs. The University is accredited by the New England Association of Schools and Colleges.

Applying

Applicants must have a bachelor's degree from an accredited college or university. Various majors are acceptable, but a strong background in social science and the humanities is considered desirable. Scores on the GRE General Test must be filed. M.B.A./M.S. media ventures students must file scores on the GMAT. Students applying to the J.D./M.S. in mass communication program must take the LSAT. International students must file TOEFL, in addition to the GRE scores; there are minimum score requirements, which can be found on the College's admissions Web site (http://www.bu.edu/com/grad/admissions). Consideration is given to academic performance, test scores, recommendations, writing samples, and evidence of motivation in respect to the selected major. Applications with credentials must be received at the College of Communication by February 1. Early applications are encouraged. Incomplete applications cannot be reviewed. Online applications are required; applications may be submitted online at http://www.bu.edu/com/grad.

Correspondence and Information

Graduate Services
College of Communication
Boston University
640 Commonwealth Avenue
Boston, Massachusetts 02215

Phone: 617-353-3481
800-992-6514 (toll-free)
Fax: 617-358-0399
E-mail: comgrad@bu.edu
Web site: http://www.bu.edu/com/grad

Boston University

THE FACULTY AND AREAS OF CONCENTRATION

The names of the full-time faculty members are listed below in conjunction with the department in which their major responsibilities lie. Many faculty members teach in several programs. The entire faculty teaches in both the undergraduate and graduate curricula of the College. In addition to possessing excellent academic credentials, most faculty members have had extensive experience as practitioners in their areas of specialization. The Dean of the College is Thomas E. Fiedler, B.S., M.S.

DEPARTMENT OF FILM AND TELEVISION. Paul Schneider, M.F.A., Chair; John Bernstein, B.A., Ph.D. (film); Raymond Carney, Ph.D. (American studies); Mary Jane Doherty, M.S. (visual studies); Roy Grundmann, Ph.D. (critical studies); Samuel Kauffmann, M.S. (film production); John R. Kelly, Ph.D. (radio, film, and television); Charles Merzbacher, M.F.A. (film production); Cathy Perron, M.S. (mass communication); Geoffrey Poister, Ph.D. (social science); Garland Waller, M.S. (broadcast journalism); Debbie Danielpour, A.B., M.A., M.F.A. (fiction and literature); Deborah Jaramillo, Ph.D. (radio, television, and film); Christophor Cavalieri, B.S.; Scott Thompson, M.F.A. (screenwriting).

Film Production. Mary Jane Doherty, Director. This two-year program provides thorough, hands-on training in all aspects of film production: scriptwriting, directing, cinematography, postproduction, and distribution. The emphasis is on narrative filmmaking. The curriculum includes courses in critical studies of film masterworks.

Screenwriting. John Bernstein, Director. This two-year program emphasizes a non-formulaic approach to screenwriting and requires students to understand and practice the art of screenwriting, to learn the fundamentals of dramatic production, to understand various models of film structure and film history, and to comprehend the role of the storyteller and the place of the screenplay in the dramatic tradition.

Film Studies. Roy Grundmann, Director. This two-year program prepares students to work as critics, historians, scholars, teachers, librarians, archivists, programmers, or exhibitors. Film studies majors, under faculty supervision, may pursue a variety of critical approaches to film.

Media Ventures. Cathy Perron, Director. This three-semester program is for students who have decided to pursue media careers in various telecommunications industries. There is also a five-semester dual-degree program in conjunction with the Graduate School of Management.

Television Production. Cathy Perron, Director. This three-semester program combines hands-on production experience with courses in the history and social impact of television and in television management to prepare students for careers in production, management, programming, marketing, teaching, and criticism.

DEPARTMENT OF JOURNALISM. Lou Ureneck, B.A. (English); Fred Bayles, B.S. (journalism); Keith Botsford, A.M.; Chris Daly, M.A. (American history); Anne Donohue, M.S. (broadcast journalism), M.A. (international relations); Jonathan Klarfeld, A.B. (English); H. Joachim Maitre, Ph.D. (literature); Robert Manoff, M.C.P. (urban studies); Elizabeth Mehren, M.J.; Sasha Norkin, M.S.; Safoura Rafeizadeh, M.F.A. (graphic design); Caryl Rivers, M.S. (journalism); Ellen Ruppel Shell, B.A. (biology); Frank H. Shorr, M.S. (broadcasting and film); Peter Smith, B.S.; Peter Southwick, B.A. (government); Douglas Starr, M.S. (science reporting); Susan Walker, B.A.; Mitchell Zuckoff, M.A. (journalism).

Journalism. Jonathan Klarfeld, Director. The program in journalism provides qualified students with an in-depth understanding of the press in its various aspects—its editorial and economic functions, its relation to other social institutions, and its limitations and responsibilities. Competence in research in mass communication problems is one area of emphasis. Another is proficiency in reporting, writing and editing, and other professional practices that prepare graduates for employment in the field. Graduate students may elect the traditional research thesis or a reporting project in a specialized area, designed for publication in the form of magazine articles or as an extended newspaper series.

Broadcast Journalism. The program provides a working knowledge of the organization and structure of broadcasting and its relationship to government, mastery of the techniques of television and radio newswriting, and a survey of the varied aspects of television news programming.

Business and Economics Journalism. Lou Ureneck, Director. This program combines journalism training with instruction in business and economics. Core courses include an introduction to business and economics reporting, advanced business writing, international business and economics reporting, and investigative techniques.

Science Journalism. Douglas Starr and Ellen Ruppel Shell, Co-Directors. This program prepares students to work as reporters, writers, and editors for scientific, engineering, or business newspapers and magazines. Students are also exposed to basic courses in audiovisual subjects, broadcast journalism, and publication management and may select advanced courses and directed-study projects in these professional areas. The three-semester, 48-credit program includes internships of the student's choice with various organizations, including a science news service, scientific and engineering newspapers and magazines, and scientific, industrial, and business institutions. In conjunction with their internships or course work, students also usually prepare a major science communication project for professional production or publication.

DEPARTMENT OF MASS COMMUNICATION, ADVERTISING, AND PUBLIC RELATIONS. T. Barton Carter, J.D. (law), Chair; Judith Austin, B.F.A.; Tobe Berkovitz, Ph.D. (theater arts, speech communication); Christopher Cakebread, Ph.D. (mass communication); John Carroll, A.B. (Latin, Greek, and English); Carolyn Clark, M.S. (marketing); Dorothy Clark, M.S. (mass communication); Jo O'Connor, M.S. (mass communication); Edward Downes, M.S. (journalism); Michel Elasmar, Ph.D. (mass communication); Thomas Fauls, M.S. (advertising); Hyun-Yeul Lee, Ph.D.; Joyce Macario, M.F.A. (graphic design); Peter Morrissey, B.S. (communication); Patrice Oppliger, Ph.D.; Susan Parenio, M.A. (English literature); John Verret, B.A. (economics); Tammy Vigil, Ph.D. (communication studies); H. Denis Wu, Ph.D.; Donald K. Wright, Ph.D.; James Shanahan, Ph.D.; Cheryl Ann Lambert, Ph.D. (public relations); Mina Tsay, Ph.D. (mass communications).

Advertising. The M.S. in advertising at Boston University is designed to prepare students to work in advertising agencies, media companies, and other marketing communications organizations. Some are prepared for doctoral-level studies. All students must take courses that provide a broad understanding of the advertising industry and of the role of communication in contemporary society. In addition, they focus on developing advertising campaigns or research skills. Students may choose one of three tracks: management track, creative track, or thesis track. The management track prepares students for careers in account management, media, account planning, or advertising research. The creative track prepares students for careers in art direction or copywriting. The thesis track prepares students for careers in marketing research or education.

Mass Communication. The mass communication program is designed to cover the broad range of professional communications studies and industries without specializing in any one area and to provide students with a strong understanding of communications theory, processes, and application, along with basic writing and media skills. Through this generalist approach, students are prepared to practice in such professional areas as advertising agencies, newspapers, publishing houses, television and radio stations, and nonprofit and government agencies. The program incorporates policy, planning, and management studies.

Public Relations. The program in public relations is designed to provide professional instruction for qualified students seeking careers in public relations for business, government, and nonprofit organizations. The program has three foundations: the theory and process of communication, the administrative and policy sciences, and research findings in communication and the social sciences. These foundations are interconnected by a body of knowledge drawn from the liberal arts, particularly the social sciences, and applied to the practical decisions and programs of public relations.

CUNY GRADUATE SCHOOL OF JOURNALISM

Master of Arts in Journalism

Programs of Study

The Master of Arts in Journalism program at the City University of New York (CUNY) Graduate School of Journalism is an intensive, full-time, three-semester course of study designed to train graduate students for a wide variety of careers in journalism. Through the 45-credit converged curriculum, all students learn to tell stories using print, broadcast, and interactive formats while undergoing rigorous instruction in the traditional skills, standards, and ethics of journalism. Classes are small and instruction is personalized.

Required courses in the first semester provide a solid grounding in the reporting, writing, broadcast, and interactive skills, as well as the legal and ethical values that all journalists must know. In the second semester, students may specialize in print, broadcast, or interactive journalism, but they are also free to mix and match media courses, depending on their interests and career goals. Also in the second semester, all students choose a subject concentration, selecting from arts and culture, business and economics, health and medicine, international, and urban reporting. Students take three courses in the concentration that build upon one another—one in the second semester and two in the third. The third semester also includes two media electives. In fall 2010, the School is scheduled to launch a program in entrepreneurial journalism that will add a fourth semester for participants.

To graduate, each student must complete a capstone project, which may be a significant print piece, broadcast project, or Web package. Students also participate in an 8–10 week paid summer internship between their second and third semesters to give them experience in a working news operation. They receive academic credit and a stipend of at least $3000.

Between the first and second semesters, the School offers optional enrichment seminars in its January Academy. Workshops include freelance writing, social media for journalists, and news photography. The School's Web-based NYCity News Service gives all students a chance to have their work distributed to professional media outlets. Broadcast students can also have their work aired on CUNY-TV, a 24-hour cable TV station that reaches 2 million viewers.

Research Facilities

The CUNY Graduate School of Journalism's state-of-the-art facility includes a 125-seat wireless newsroom, digital television and radio studios, editing suites equipped with Final Cut Pro video editing software, wireless classrooms, a café area, and student lounges. Students learn on the latest technology and are able to borrow a broad array of audio, video, and photography equipment to carry out their assignments.

The journalism library, known as the Research Center, features approximately 2,000 print volumes, more than 32,000 electronic books, 45 periodicals, over 100 electronic journals, and databases related to the field of journalism. Using the CUNY+ online catalog system, students, faculty, and staff have access to more than 4 million additional items via CUNY's open access policy.

Financial Aid

More than 80 percent of the students receive a tuition scholarship from the School, ranging from $2000 to full tuition during the first year. The need- and merit-based scholarships funded by supporters of the School include the Bloomberg Scholarship Fund, Chancellor's Scholarship Fund, Daniel Schorr Scholarship Fund, Julius Barnathan Fund, News Corporation Scholarship Fund, and Punch Sulzberger Scholarship Fund.

Approximately 75 percent of students take advantage of federal student loans to cover their living costs. Some students also qualify for federal work-study programs that pay them to work at the School while pursuing their degree. Some students continue to hold internships or part-time jobs during the academic year, but the School cautions against taking on more than 10 hours per week of outside work.

To be considered for a need-based scholarship from the School of Journalism, students must submit the Application for Financial Assistance and the Free Application for Federal Student Aid (FAFSA) by February 1 (can be filed online). To qualify for federal loan funding, students are also asked to complete the FAFSA by February 1.

Cost of Study

The tuition for New York State residents is $3680 per semester. Tuition for the entire three-semester program is $11,040, plus fees of $1795, bringing the three-semester total for tuition and fees to $12,835.

The tuition for non–New York State residents is $575 per credit. Assuming 15 credits per semester, the tuition is $8625 per semester. Out-of-state residents who are U.S. citizens or permanent residents may qualify for in-state tuition in their third semester if they become legal residents of New York State. If so, tuition for the entire three-semester program is $20,930 plus fees of $1795, bringing the three-semester total for tuition and fees to $22,725.

For international students, tuition for the entire three-semester program is $25,875, plus fees of $1795, bringing the three-semester total for tuition and fees to $27,670.

Living and Housing Costs

Estimated costs for room and board are about $17,000 for an academic year. To minimize expenses, many students live in the four boroughs outside Manhattan and share an apartment. Virtually all use public transportation. The Office of Admissions and Student Affairs can provide information about other housing options and connect students interested in shared living arrangements.

Student Group

Some 90 students are enrolled in the class of 2011, in addition to the 73 students on track to graduate in December 2010. About 42 percent are members of underrepresented minority groups and 61 percent are women. The average age is 26. Students come from a variety of backgrounds: the journalism profession, other fields, and undergraduate colleges. Although some had never produced a journalistic work before, all demonstrated an ability to write and think, a deep curiosity about the world, and a strong interest in making journalism their profession.

Location

The CUNY Graduate School of Journalism is housed at 219 West 40th Street, two blocks from Times Square, in the former home of the *New York Herald Tribune.* Located in the heart of the media capital of the world, the School is within a short walking distance of many of the nation's largest media companies. The headquarters for *The New York Times* are next door.

The School and The University

The CUNY J-School opened in August 2006 under the leadership of Dean Stephen B. Shepard, who served as editor-in-chief of *BusinessWeek* for more than twenty years. The School's Board of Advisers is made up of prominent media executives, including David Carey, president of Hearst Magazines; Connie Chung, television journalist and anchor; Les Hinton, CEO of Dow Jones & Co.; Howard Rubenstein, president of Rubenstein Associates; David Westin, president of ABC News; Mark Whitaker, Washington bureau chief of NBC News; Matthew Winkler, editor-in-chief of *Bloomberg News;* and Mortimer Zuckerman, chairman and publisher of the *New York Daily News* and *U.S. News & World Report.*

The Graduate School of Journalism operates under the aegis of the CUNY Graduate Center and is one of twenty-four institutions that comprise the City University of New York, the nation's largest urban university. The CUNY Graduate Center administers thirty-four doctoral and six master's programs as well as thirty research centers and institutes. The University's origins date back to 1847 to the Free Academy, which grew into City College. Throughout its history, the University has maintained a commitment to academic excellence and to providing access and opportunity to students from diverse ethnic and geographic backgrounds.

Applying

Applications are accepted for the fall semester only. A four-year undergraduate degree is required of all applicants. In general, students should have attained at least a minimum grade-point average of 3.0 in college, must submit scores for the Graduate Record Exam (GRE), and take CUNY tests. All international applicants, defined as those who hold or intend to apply for a nonimmigrant visa, are required to take the Test of English as a Foreign Language (TOEFL), including its writing component, the TWE. The deadline for all applications is December 17. The School uses an online application that can be accessed on its Web site. Students may mail supporting application materials to the CUNY Graduate School of Journalism, Office of Admissions, The Graduate Center, 365 Fifth Avenue, New York, New York 10016-4309.

Correspondence and Information

CUNY Graduate School of Journalism
219 West 40th Street
New York, New York 10018
Phone: 646-758-7700
E-mail: admissions@journalism.cuny.edu
Web site: http://www.journalism.cuny.edu

CUNY Graduate School of Journalism

THE FACULTY

The faculty is made up of veteran journalists from every media specialty and includes Pulitzer Prize, Emmy Award, and National Magazine Award winners. In addition to 11 full-time faculty members, at least 10 journalism professors from other CUNY colleges teach at the Graduate School of Journalism. Among those on the School's full-time faculty are Jeff Jarvis, an internationally known expert in online and collaborative media who heads the Interactive Journalism Program; Sarah Bartlett, a former writer and editor at *Fortune, BusinessWeek,* and *The New York Times* who directs the Urban Reporting Program; Peter Beinart, a senior political writer at The Daily Beast who previously served as editor of *The New Republic;* and Lonnie Isabel, former deputy managing editor of *Newsday* who oversees the International Reporting Program.

Adjunct Faculty

All adjunct instructors are experienced media professionals who continue to do outstanding work in newsrooms across the city as freelance journalists or as book authors. Among the organizations they work for are ABC News, *The Atlantic,* the BBC, Bloomberg News, NBC News, New York 1, *The New York Times,* and *The Washington Post*.

HAWAI'I PACIFIC UNIVERSITY

College of Communication

Program of Study

The Master of Arts in communication program (M.A./COM) provides students with an interdisciplinary approach integrating skills, theory, and knowledge. Students completing this Hawai'i Pacific University (HPU) program are prepared for careers ranging across the spectrum of business, marketing, advertising, mass media, public relations, entertainment, broadcast or print journalism, the Internet, or education. Technology is emphasized in each course so that graduates are prepared for rapid change in communication industries.

The M.A./COM requires a minimum of 39 semester hours of graduate work composed of 18 semester hours of core courses, 15 semester hours of electives, and 6 semester hours of writing a professional paper, project, or thesis. Assignments and internships use a pragmatic approach to develop marketable skills. Students apply what they learn in the classroom to actual problems faced by organizations and businesses.

Research Facilities

To support graduate studies, HPU's Meader and Atherton Libraries hold over 110,000 bound volumes, 350,000 microfiche items, and periodical subscriptions to 1,500 print titles and 30,000 electronic journals. Databases of public and state university libraries, legislative information, and business-oriented statistical data are also available in the library or online. Students can access HPU's library databases, course information, their academic information, and an e-mail account through Pipeline, the university's internal Web site for students. The University's accessible on-campus computer center houses more than 100 computers with specialized software to support graduate academic programs. HPU also provides free Wi-Fi so students can access Pipeline resources anywhere on campus using laptops. A significant number of online courses are available as well.

Financial Aid

The University participates in all federal financial aid programs designated for graduate students. These programs provide aid in the form of subsidized (need-based) and unsubsidized (non-need-based) Federal Stafford Student Loans. Through these loans, funds may be available to cover the student's entire cost of education. To apply for aid, students must submit the Free Application for Federal Student Aid (FAFSA) beginning January 1. Mailing of student award letters usually begins by the end of March. The University also offers several institutional graduate scholarships to new full-time, degree-seeking students. The Graduate Trustee Scholarship provides $6000 for two semesters, the Graduate Dean Scholarship provides $4000 for two semesters, and the Graduate Kokua Scholarship provides $2000 for two semesters. Priority consideration is given to those students who apply by the deadline.

Cost of Study

Tuition for graduate students enrolled in fall and spring semesters is determined on a per-credit basis; full-time status for a graduate student is 9 credits. Tuition for the optional winter and summer sessions is also determined on a per-credit basis. The estimated minimum funds needed for a nine-month academic year (September to May) based on 2010–11 school year expenses is $26,459. For the 2010–11 academic year, full-time tuition is $12,600 for most graduate degree programs, including the M.A./COM program. Books, supplies, and transportation cost $1885, and health insurance costs $880.

Living and Housing Costs

Most graduate students live in off-campus housing. The cost of living in off-campus apartments is approximately $11,094 for a double-occupancy room.

Student Group

University enrollment currently stands at more than 8,200. HPU is one of the most culturally diverse universities in America with students from all 50 U.S. states and more than 100 countries.

Location

Hawai'i Pacific University combines the excitement of an urban, downtown campus with the serenity of a residential campus. The main campus is ideally located in downtown Honolulu, the business and financial center of the Pacific. The downtown campus comprises six buildings in the center of Honolulu's business district and is home to the College of Business Administration and the College of Humanities and Social Sciences. Eight miles away, situated on 135 acres in Kaneohe, the windward Hawai'i Loa campus is the site of the College of Nursing and Health Sciences and the College of Natural and Computational Sciences. HPU is affiliated with the Oceanic Institute, an applied aquaculture research facility located on a 56-acre site at Makapu'u Point on the windward coast of Oahu, Hawaii. Students can conveniently travel between the three sites using the HPU shuttle service. There are also eight military campus programs located at Pearl Harbor, Barbers Point, Hickam Air Force Base, Schofield Barracks, Fort Shafter, Tripler Army Medical Center, Kaneohe Marine Corps Air Station, and Camp Smith.

The University

HPU is a private, nonprofit university with approximately 8,200 students. Founded in 1965, HPU prides itself on maintaining strong academic programs, small class sizes, individual attention to students, and a diverse faculty and student population. HPU is recognized as a "Best in the West" college by the Princeton Review and a "Best Buy" by *Barron's* business magazine. HPU offers more than fifty acclaimed undergraduate programs and thirteen distinguished graduate programs. The University has a faculty of more than 500, a student-faculty ratio of 15:1, and an average class size of fewer than 20 students. A wide range of counseling and other student support services are available. There are more than seventy student organizations on campus, including the Graduate Student Organization.

Applying

Students must have a baccalaureate degree from an accredited college or university in the United States or an equivalent degree from another country. Applicants should complete and forward a graduate admissions application, send in the $50 nonrefundable application fee, have official transcripts sent from all colleges or universities previously attended, and forward two letters of recommendation. A personal statement about the applicant's academic and career goals is required; submitting a resume is optional. Applicants who have taken the Graduate Record Examination (GRE) should have their scores sent directly to the Graduate Admissions Office. International students should submit scores of a recognized English proficiency test such as TOEFL. Admissions decisions are made on a rolling basis, and applicants are notified between one and two weeks after all documents have been submitted. Applicants are encouraged to submit their applications online.

Correspondence and Information

Graduate Admissions
Hawai'i Pacific University
1164 Bishop Street, #911
Honolulu, Hawaii 96813

Phone: 808-544-1135
866-GRAD-HPU (toll-free)
Fax: 808-544-0280
E-mail: graduate@hpu.edu
Web site: http://www.hpu.edu/hpumacom

Hawai'i Pacific University

THE FACULTY

John N. Barnum, Associate Professor of Communication; Ph.D., Texas at Austin.
Peter Britos, Associate Professor of Communication; Ph.D., USC.
Dale Burke, Instructor of Communication; D.Min., Ancilla Domini College.
Brian Cannon, Assistant Professor of Communication; Ph.D., Regent University (Virginia).
Katherine Clarke, Instructor of Communication; M.A., Denver.
Thomas Dowd, Instructor of Communication; M.A., California State, Northridge.
Steven Combs, Professor of Communication; Ph.D., USC.
Matthew George, Assistant Professor of Communication; Ph.D., Berkley.
John P. Hart, Professor of Communication; Ph.D., Kansas.
Serena Hashimoto, Associate Professor of Communication; Ph.D., European Graduate School (Switzerland).
Lowell Ing, Assistant Professor of Communication; M.F.A., CUNY, City College.
Anne Kennedy, Assistant Professor of Communication; Ph.D., Bowling Green State.
Laurence LeDoux, Assistant Professor of Communication; D.A., Oregon.
Marianne Luken, Instructor of Communication; M.I.A., School for International Training.
Malia Smith, Instructor of Communication; M.A., Hawai'i Pacific.
Penny Pence Smith, Assistant Professor of Communication; Ph.D., North Carolina at Chapel Hill.
Lewis Trusty, Instructor of Communication; M.A., USC.
James D. Whitfield, Professor of Communication; Ed.D., Texas Tech.
John Windrow, Instructor of Journalism; M.A., Missouri–Columbia.
Yanjun Zhao, Assistant Professor of Organizational Change; Ph.D., Nebraska–Lincoln.

POINT PARK UNIVERSITY

POINT PARK UNIVERSITY

Master of Arts in Journalism and Mass Communication

Program of Study

The graduate program in journalism and mass communication at Point Park University leads to the Master of Arts (M.A.) degree. The program admits students with a variety of undergraduate and professional backgrounds. The Point Park M.A. program, with opportunities such as working with the Innocence Institute of Western Pennsylvania and a news service tied to the *Pittsburgh Tribune-Review*, is exceptionally well designed for professionals already working, and planning to continue to work, for mass communication employers. Students may also apply to pursue a concurrent M.A./M.B.A. program, one of six in the nation. Other admitted students plan to enter a doctoral program, or a mass communication profession for the first time.

Full-time students may easily complete the program within two calendar years, and students who are both exceptionally able and extraordinarily motivated may complete the program in one calendar year. Courses are offered during three semesters: fall, spring, and summer. Part-time students, who traditionally compose the bulk of the graduate student body, may complete the program within three years. Writing a master's thesis is optional but highly recommended for students planning to pursue any doctoral degree.

The 36-credit program includes a core of four courses; up to three may be waived, based on courses in previous undergraduate programs, and/or relevant work experience, and replaced with electives. At least one course taken outside the School of Communication in a related area is required. Two courses are for independent student research, including a thesis option. All students will complete six to nine electives that allow a student to design their own significant concentrations in public relations, print journalism, television broadcasting (in a state-of-the-art TV studio and control room), and/or advertising. Students may petition for up to 9 credits (three courses) of graduate work at another institution to be accepted as transfer credits.

Research Facilities

The University's library is located in the University Center, a gloriously renovated historic building. The combined holdings number about 125,000 monographs, 16,640 periodical subscriptions, 37 online databases, 650 audio and videocassettes, and a total microform count of 20,000 volumes. The online catalog, wireless Internet access, and printers are available throughout the building.

Students are able to borrow material not held within the system and have it delivered to the University Center through the various interlibrary loan programs.

The library's journalism and mass communication collection, which is the most extensive in western Pennsylvania and the second largest in the state, exceeds those of most research universities in Pennsylvania and other states.

Financial Aid

Students may apply for financial aid, which is granted on the basis of need, and for various state and federal loans. International applicants may seek loans and scholarships from a number of home-country and international agencies. The School of Communication offers five graduate assistantships, including one working with the international scholarly journal *Journalism & Mass Communication Educator*. The assistant must be a full-time student in the program and be able to work in the School of Communication a minimum of 20 hours per week during fall and spring semesters.

Cost of Study

Tuition and fees for 2008–09 were $660 per credit. The cost of books and supplies averaged $350 per term.

Living and Housing Costs

Housing is available in the University's residence halls. The cost in 2008–09 was typically $4500 per term. Apartments are available to students within a short travel distance on Pittsburgh's effective mass transit system. A variety of meal plans are available at the campus student cafeteria.

Student Group

Enrollment in the graduate program in fall 2009 was about 75. Many were full-time. Most were employed full-time in the communications industry or elsewhere. Generally, a small contingent of international students adds an exciting multicultural flavor to the classes, which seldom exceed 15 students. For example, during 2008–09, the program hosted Fulbright students from Iraq and Russia, and other international students from countries such as Kenya and India.

Location

Pittsburgh is the nation's thirteenth-largest metropolitan area. In 2007, it was named the most livable city in the United States separately by *The Economist* magazine and by the *Places Rated Almanac* (Rand McNally method), and again by *The Economist* in 2009. Newspapers, radio and TV stations, and public relations and advertising agencies are within easy walking distance of the campus. The location is excellent for challenging graduate-level internships. Frequent association with professionals in the classroom, internships, part-time jobs, and freelancing often leads to full-time employment immediately after graduation.

The University

Point Park University is located in the Golden Triangle of downtown Pittsburgh. Founded in 1960, it has grown from a small business school to a four-year institution with graduate programs in journalism and mass communication, curriculum/instruction, engineering management, business administration, educational administration, criminal justice administration, acting/theater, organizational leadership, learning/training, secondary education certification, and environmental studies. It is accredited by the Middle States Association of Colleges and Schools and is a member of the Pittsburgh Council on Higher Education.

Applying

Applicants for the M.A. program must take the GRE if their undergraduate GPA falls below 2.75 overall and/or under 3.0 in their undergraduate major. Those whose first language is not English must take the TOEFL and the TWE. Students may be admitted for the fall, spring, or summer term.

Correspondence and Information

Point Park University
201 Wood Street
Pittsburgh, Pennsylvania 15222-1984
Phone: 412-392-3808
800-321-0129 (toll-free)
Fax: 412-392-6164
E-mail: ptenroll@pointpark.edu
Web site: http://www.pointpark.edu

Point Park University

THE FACULTY

In addition to the full-time faculty members listed below, the program utilizes qualified professionals who represent organizations engaged in the mass communication concentrations of the M.A. program.

Dane S. Claussen, Director; Ph.D., Georgia.
Tatyana Dumova, Ph.D., Bowling Green State.
David J. Fabilli, M.A., Youngstown State.
Helen M. Fallon, M.A., Duquesne.
Heather Starr Fiedler, Ph.D., Nova Southeastern.
Jan Getz, M.A., Miami (Ohio).
Steven Hallock, Ph.D., Ohio.
Timothy J. Hudson, Ph.D., Temple.
Anthony J. Moretti, Ph.D., Ohio.
William R. "Bill" Moushey Jr., M.S., Point Park.
Robert O'Gara, M.L.S., Duquesne.
Christopher Rolinson, M.A., Point Park.
Johan Yssel, D.Litt. et Phil., South Africa.

SYRACUSE UNIVERSITY

S. I. Newhouse School of Public Communications

Programs of Study

The Newhouse School offers programs leading to three graduate degrees: Master of Arts (M.A.), Master of Science (M.S.), and Doctor of Philosophy (Ph.D.). Candidates for the M.A. and M.S. degrees can major in advertising; arts journalism; broadcast and digital journalism; documentary film and history; magazine, newspaper, and online journalism; photography; media studies; public relations; or television-radio-film. A master's program in media management leading to an M.S. degree is offered jointly by the Newhouse School and the Whitman School of Management. A course of study in public diplomacy leading to an M.S. degree in public relations and an M.A. degree in international relations is offered jointly by the Newhouse School and the Maxwell School of Citizenship and Public Affairs. A Doctor of Philosophy is offered in mass communications. Newhouse also offers an interdisciplinary distance learning degree program for experienced public relations practitioners, leading to an M.S. in communications management.

Generally, the resident professional master's programs are completed in one calendar year and 36 credits are required. However, 36 to 42 credits are required for media management, 40 credits for broadcast and digital journalism, 39 credits for documentary film and history, 33 credits for photography, and a total of 58 credits for the public diplomacy course of study. Most students complete their studies by taking capstone courses. Television-radio-film students take comprehensive examinations, media studies students write theses, and photography students either write theses or complete special projects. In public relations, students either take a capstone course with a comprehensive examination or write theses.

The Ph.D. program in mass communications involves three years of academic work beyond the master's degree. Students must take a minimum of 60 credits beyond the master's level. A research dissertation is required of all doctoral candidates.

Research Facilities

The Newhouse School, housed in a 250,000-square-foot, three-building complex, is one of the world's most complete centers for the study of mass communications. An all-digital environment, Newhouse includes state-of-the-art classrooms, a 300-seat auditorium, a research center, a doctoral student suite and offices, a collaborative multimedia laboratory, an executive education wing, a café, and many spaces for formal and informal meetings and collaboration among students, faculty, and staff.

The School has several research areas, including the Bleier Center for Television and Popular Culture, the Carnegie Religion and Media Program, the Center for Digital Literacy, the Knight Chair in Political Reporting, and the Tully Center for Free Speech. In addition, students have access to the Transactional Records Access Clearinghouse (TRAC), a center devoted to assisting the news media in analyzing government documents through the use of computers. TRAC, which has an office complex at the School, is the leading research center for investigating and implementing new computer-assisted reporting techniques.

Financial Aid

There are University-wide competitions for McNair Fellowships and African American Fellowships. Newhouse annually awards one Deutsch Diversity Fellowship, two Turner Diversity Fellowships, and two Newhouse Foundation Fellowships for Minorities. These awards offer full tuition benefits as well as yearlong job placement after graduation. Several $10,000 Liu Foundation Multicultural Scholarships are awarded each year. The School awards a number of partial scholarships ranging from $5000 to $15,000. Instructional associates spend from 5 to 20 hours per week helping faculty members with classes or labs. They are paid $13 an hour and also receive partial-tuition scholarships. Need-based financial aid in the form of federal loans is also available.

Cost of Study

Tuition for graduate students is $1162 per credit for the 2010–11 academic year. Program fees range from $450 to $1050. Doctoral students are provided with a full-tuition scholarship and a stipend for work in teaching or research.

Living and Housing Costs

While extremely limited, University housing for single graduate students sharing an apartment costs approximately $12,000 for the calendar year. There are also numerous apartment complexes and rental houses that graduate students choose to live in. Many are within walking distance or on the bus line. Dependent on a number of factors, rent ranges from approximately $400 to $1000 per month.

Student Group

Each year, students with a variety of backgrounds are considered for admission to the graduate programs. A previous communications degree is not required. Programs are competitive, and admitted students typically have academic records and GRE scores well above average. Approximately 230 new students are enrolled each year, the majority of whom study full-time. About 15 percent of the graduate student population is international, and the male-female ratio is about 40:60.

Student Outcomes

The Newhouse School has a wide and varied alumni base. Many graduates are recognized as leaders in the various fields of public communications. The School operates a Career Development Center to assist students and alumni with career opportunities. A computerized Career Advisory Network has been established to provide an online database of alumni contacts in businesses throughout the world. Recruiters frequently conduct interviews at the Newhouse School, and current job listings are circulated regularly.

Location

SU is located in the city of Syracuse, the geographic center of New York State. Syracuse combines all the amenities of a major urban area with small-town charm and an affordable cost of living. The metropolitan area is home to more than half a million people who take advantage of an active social scene and the region's natural recreational resources. The city also offers students many opportunities to gain practical experience in the various fields of communications.

The University and The School

Syracuse University was founded in 1870 by the United Methodist Church, with assistance from the city of Syracuse. Privately endowed, coeducational, and nonsectarian, the University has grown from an original enrollment of 41 students to an overall enrollment of 19,638, which includes 5,682 graduate students. A member of both the Association of American Universities and the Council of Graduate Schools, Syracuse University is considered one of the nation's major institutions of higher learning. The Newhouse School is fully accredited by the Accrediting Council on Education in Journalism and Mass Communications and has an enrollment of approximately 1,800 undergraduate and 275 graduate students.

Applying

A complete application includes official transcripts, three letters of recommendation, personal statement, resume, GRE scores, TOEFL scores if applicable, and an application form. Additional requirements vary by program. Applications should be submitted online at https://apply.embark.com/grad/syracuse/. Newhouse professional master's programs begin in early July and the application deadline is February 1. To apply for merit aid, students need only check the appropriate boxes on the application form. Doctoral program applications are due by December 10.

Correspondence and Information

Graduate Records Office
S. I. Newhouse School of Public Communications
215 University Place
Syracuse, New York 13244-2100

Phone: 315-443-4039
Fax: 315-443-1834
E-mail: pcgrad@syr.edu
Web site: http://newhousemasters.syr.edu/

Syracuse University

THE FACULTY

Administration
Lorraine E. Branham, Dean.
Amy Falkner, Associate Dean for Academic Affairs.
Hubert Brown, Associate Dean for Research, Creativity, International Initiatives, and Diversity.
Rosanna Grassi, Associate Dean for Student Affairs.
Joel Kaplan, Associate Dean for Professional Graduate Studies.
Carol M. Liebler, Director of the Doctoral Program.
Lynn M. Vanderhoek, Assistant Dean for Advancement.
Karen McGee, Assistant Dean for Student Affairs.

Advertising
James Tsao, Professor and Chair; Ph.D., Temple. Advertising strategy, international advertising, Internet advertising.
Amy Falkner, Associate Professor; M.A., Syracuse. Media planning, advertising to gay and lesbian markets.
Jong-Hyuok Jung, Assistant Professor; Ph.D., Texas at Austin. Interactive advertising, consumer behavior.
Carla V. Lloyd, Associate Professor; Ph.D., Syracuse. Advertising media, copywriting.
Kevin O'Neill, Professor of Practice; M.A., Hollins. Advertising criticism, creative direction.
Ed Russell, Assistant Professor; M.S., Northwestern. Advertising strategies, campaigns.
Brian Sheehan, Associate Professor; M.A., Loyola Marymount. Advertising management, digital media.

Broadcast and Digital Journalism
Dona Hayes, Associate Professor and Chair; M.S., Syracuse. Broadcast news writing, reporting, production.
Hubert Brown, Associate Professor; M.A., Nebraska–Lincoln. Political reporting, writing.
Michael E. Cremedas, Associate Professor; Ph.D., Florida. Writing, reporting, production management.
Frank Currier, Professor of Practice; M.A., Missouri–Columbia. Radio news reporting, producing.
Barbara Croll Fought, Associate Professor; J.D., Detroit. Broadcast news writing, reporting.
E. Robert Lissit, Associate Professor; M.S., Northwestern. Broadcast news writing, producing.
Suzanne Lysak, Assistant Professor; B.S., Boston. Broadcast news producing and news management.
John Nicholson, Professor of Practice; B.S., Syracuse. Broadcast reporting.
Donald C. Torrance, Associate Professor; B.A., Alfred. Broadcast news writing, production.
Chris Tuohey, Assistant Professor; M.A., Ohio State. Broadcast news reporting.

Communications
Bradley W. Gorham, Associate Professor and Chair; Ph.D., Wisconsin–Madison. Media and society, media effects.
Courtney Barclay, Assistant Professor; Ph.D., Florida. Media law, online political communications, freedom of information.
Makana Chock, Assistant Professor; Ph.D., Cornell. Communications theory.
Roy Gutterman, Associate Professor; J.D., Syracuse. Communications law, legal affairs reporting.
Carol M. Liebler, Associate Professor; Ph.D., Wisconsin–Madison. Communications theory, methodology.
Jasmine McNealy, Assistant Professor; Ph.D., Florida. Media law issues.
David M. Rubin, Professor; Ph.D., Stanford. Communications law, media ethics, mass media and government.
Jay B. Wright, Professor; Ph.D., Syracuse. Communications law, ethics.

Magazine
Melissa Chessher, Associate Professor and Chair; M.A., Baylor. Magazine writing, editing.
Harriet Brown, Assistant Professor; M.F.A., Brooklyn. Magazine editing, science and medical journalism.
Aileen Gallagher; Assistant Professor; B.A., Syracuse. Multiplatform journalism, editing.
Robert E. Lloyd, Associate Professor; M.A., Syracuse. Newswriting and reporting, media and society.
Mark J. Obbie, Associate Professor; M.A., Missouri–Columbia. Magazine article writing and editing.

Multimedia Photography and Design
Anthony R. Golden, Associate Professor and Chair; Ph.D., Syracuse. Advertising and illustration photography.
Ken Harper, Assistant Professor; B.A., Western Kentucky. Multimedia content management systems.
Lawrence Mason Jr., Professor; Ph.D., Syracuse. Communications and society, photojournalism, multimedia.
Bruce Strong, Associate Professor; M.A., Ohio. Photojournalism, multimedia storytelling.
David C. Sutherland, Associate Professor; M.A., Western Kentucky. Photojournalism, graphics.
Sherri A. Taylor, Coordinator, Scholastic Programs; B.A., Baylor. Graphic design.

Newspaper and Online Journalism
Steve Davis, Associate Professor and Chair; B.J., Missouri–Columbia. Newswriting, reporting, impact of the Internet on politics.
Lorraine E. Branham, Professor; B.A., Temple. Ethics, diversity and media.
Joan A. Deppa, Associate Professor; Ph.D., Michigan State. Newswriting, reporting, computer graphics.
Elizabeth Lynne Flocke, Professor; Ph.D., Missouri–Columbia. Newswriting, communications law.
Seth Gitner, Assistant Professor; B.F.A., RIT. Multimedia journalism.
Roy Gutterman, Associate Professor; J.D., Syracuse. Communications law.
Joel Kaplan, Associate Professor; M.S., Illinois; M.S.L., Yale. Newswriting, investigative reporting, communications law.
Johanna Keller, Director, Goldring Program; Associate Professor; M.A., Antioch. Cultural journalism, arts criticism.
Stephen M. Masiclat, Director, Media Management Program; Associate Professor; M.P.S., Cornell. Graphics, multimedia, Web design.
Gustav Niebuhr, Associate Professor; M.A., Oxford. Religious journalism.
Francis Ward, Associate Professor; M.A., Syracuse. Newswriting, reporting.

Public Relations
Brenda J. Wrigley, Associate Professor and Chair; Ph.D., Syracuse. Gender and public relations, diversity issues.
Shannon Bowen, Associate Professor; Ph.D., Maryland. Ethics in corporate issues management, media ethics and terrorism, PR pedagogy.
Minjeong Kang, Assistant Professor; Ph.D., Syracuse. Public relations research.
Dennis F. Kinsey, Co-director, Public Diplomacy Program; Associate Professor; Ph.D., Stanford. Public relations theory, research.
Robert M. Kucharavy, Professor of Practice; M.A.L.A., Clark. Public relations management.
Maria P. Russell, Professor; M.A., Syracuse. Public relations management.
F. William Smullen III, Adjunct Professor; M.A., Syracuse. Government public relations, national security issues.
Sung-Un Yang, Assistant Professor; Ph.D., Maryland. Public relations research, organization-public relationships.

Television-Radio-Film
Michael Schoonmaker, Associate Professor and Chair; Ph.D., Syracuse. Television production, writing, media education.
Richard Breyer, Co-director, Documentary Film and History Program; Professor; M.A., NYU. Television production, documentary writing, production.
Fiona Chew, Associate Professor; Ph.D., Washington (Seattle). Television research.
Richard Dubin, Professor of Practice. Television writing, producing, and directing.
Larry Elin, Associate Professor; B.S., Syracuse. Television production, interactive media.
Tula Goenka, Associate Professor; M.S., Syracuse. Television production, writing.
Sharon R. Hollenback, Professor; Ph.D., Texas at Austin. Television writing, media and society.
Patricia H. Longstaff, Associate Professor; M.P.A., Harvard; J.D., Iowa. Communications law, new technologies.
Peter K. Moller, Professor; M.A., Pennsylvania. Television production, writing.
Douglas Quin, Associate Professor; Ph.D., Union (Ohio). Film sound, exhibit media design, acoustic ecology, bioacoustics.
Evan S. Smith, Associate Professor; M.S., Syracuse. Film business, scriptwriting.
Robert J. Thompson, Professor; Ph.D., Northwestern. Television criticism, production.
Roosevelt R. Wright Jr., Associate Professor; Ph.D., Syracuse. Radio programming, management.

Endowed Research Chairs
Frank Biocca, S. I. Newhouse Professor of Public Communications; Ph.D., Wisconsin–Madison. Mass communication, human-computer interaction, media psychology.
Charlotte Grimes, Knight Chair in Political Reporting; B.S., East Carolina. Media and politics, political reporting, journalism ethics.
Thomas R. Kennedy, Alexia Chair for Documentary Photography; B.S., Florida. Multimedia and visual storytelling.
Pamela J. Shoemaker, John Ben Snow Professor of Public Communications; Ph.D., Wisconsin–Madison. Communications theory and research, gatekeeping, news content.

UNIVERSITY OF SOUTHERN CALIFORNIA

Annenberg School for Communication & Journalism
School of Journalism
School of Communication
Programs In Communication, Journalism, Public Diplomacy, and Public Relations

Programs of Study

Through the School of Journalism and the School of Communication, the University of Southern California (USC) Annenberg School for Communication & Journalism offers master's degrees in communication management, global communication, journalism, public diplomacy, and strategic public relations and a Ph.D. in communication.

The School of Journalism, accredited by the Accrediting Council on Education of Journalism and Mass Communication (ACEJMC), places innovative multiplatform storytelling, pioneering digital and social networking opportunities, experimentation, and entrepreneurialism at the center of all that is taught. The School emphasizes hands-on training, writing, ethics, and professional practice. In the traditional two-year journalism programs, an innovative core curriculum teaches newswriting, reporting, and production across three media platforms. After completing the core curriculum, students concentrate on advanced course work. Student involvement is found in *Neon Tommy,* an online digital news site, *Annenberg TV News,* the award-winning day-of-air broadcasting operation; *Impact,* an outlet for long-form storytelling; and *Annenberg Radio News,* the day-of-air radio broadcast. The strategic public relations program equips students with the skills to succeed in agency, corporate, and nonprofit work. In the summer after the first year, students in journalism and strategic public relations may study and intern in Cape Town, Shanghai, or London. In the nine-month specialized journalism programs, students focus on journalism leadership and decision making while completing graduate course work in academic disciplines outside of journalism. In the specialized journalism (the arts) program, art practitioners and artists learn how to write for publications while advancing their academic exposure to the arts.

The School of Communication offers five master's degrees. Communication management students concentrate their studies in one of seven tracks: entertainment management, health and social change communication, marketing communication, information and communication technologies, international communication, organizational and strategic corporate communication, and communication law and policy. In addition, post-master's degree certificate programs are offered in the same tracks. Through the Charles Annenberg Weingarten Program on Online Communities (APOC), students explore the effects, impact, implementation, and management of social networking in different areas of society and business.

Global communication students live and study in two dynamic, multicultural media capitals of the world—first in London at the London School of Economics and Political Science (LSE) and the second year in Los Angeles at USC Annenberg.

Public diplomacy students study the impact of private activities—from popular culture to fashion to sports to news—on the national interests of organizations, corporations, and governments worldwide. As part of the degree program, students complete a summer field experience abroad or in the United States after completing their first year. In addition to the two-year program, a one-year master's degree is offered for mid-career professionals with five years or more of experience in public diplomacy, international relations, or international communication.

Students in the Ph.D. program in communication focus their critical studies of inquiry through concentrations in health and interpersonal communication; information and society; media, culture, and community; organizational communication; and rhetoric and political communication. Students acquire and demonstrate humanistic and behavioral knowledge of communication while acquiring the skills requisite to scholarly research in the discipline.

Research Facilities

The School is home to the Norman Lear Center for Entertainment Research, the Center for the Digital Future, and the Annenberg Center for Online Communities. It is also a partner with the Annenberg Center and the Schools of Cinema/Television and Engineering in USC's Integrated Media Systems Center, the nation's only university-based multimedia research center, which is funded by the National Science Foundation and the USC Center on Public Diplomacy (in partnership with the College of Letters, Arts, and Sciences).

The Strategic Public Relations Center plays a leading role in bridging the substantial gap between the public relations profession and the academic community that studies it. A host of centers affiliated with the School of Journalism may be explored on the USC Annenberg Web site.

Financial Aid

Merit scholarships for master's degree students in communication management, journalism, public diplomacy, and strategic public relations are awarded competitively based on the graduate admission application. All U.S. citizens and permanent residents are encouraged to apply for need-based federal financial aid. International students are eligible for merit scholarship consideration, and are required to submit a confidential statement of financial support. Ph.D. students receive full support for five years.

Cost of Study

For the 2010–11 academic year, the estimated cost for a full-time master's degree student (tuition and fees) is $27,776 and the estimated cost for a Ph.D. student is $33,216. The costs of housing, board, books, supplies, and personal expenses vary. For part-time graduate student estimates, please refer to the USC financial aid Web site at http://www.usc.edu/admission/fa/applying_receiving/graduates1/costs/html.

Living and Housing Costs

USC maintains a number of apartment buildings for graduate students only. Housing applications are sent to admitted students only. Rates for privately owned apartments near USC and elsewhere in greater Los Angeles are comparable to those in other large metropolitan areas. For more information on University housing options and rates, prospective students should visit http://housing.usc.edu.

Student Group

USC Annenberg enrolls approximately 560 graduate students. Thirty percent are international students. Some students enter the programs directly after earning the bachelor's degree; however, the majority of students have had some professional experience. The majority of Ph.D. students have completed a master's degree before enrolling at USC Annenberg. Most communication management students work or intern during the day, and many attend school part-time. Other master's degree and Ph.D. students attend daytime and evening classes. Graduate student organizations are active in this vibrant student-centered community.

Student Outcomes

School of Journalism graduates work at many of the nation's leading media and public relations organizations, such as ABC, CBS, NBC, CNN, Ketchum Public Relations, Manning Selvage & Lee, Weber Shandwick Worldwide, Ogilvy & Mather, EXPN, C-SPAN, CNBC, KMEX, Telemundo, KWHY, AOL, varity.com, LATimes.com, eCompanies, WashingtonPost.com, and the Associated Press. Communication management and global communication program graduates pursue careers in marketing communications and public relations, mass media, multimedia and interactive media management, media research and analysis, entertainment management, telecommunications, law and public policy, corporate communications, nonprofit management, and consulting. Graduates work at firms such as Warner Bros., FOXSports.com, GameSpot.com, AOL, McKinsey, KPMG, Nestlé USA, DIRECTV, MGM, Pacific Bell, and ABC TV.

The majority of Ph.D. graduates pursue careers in academia at such institutions as Georgetown University, Johns Hopkins University, Michigan State University, North Carolina State University, Northwestern University, City University of Hong Kong, Tokyo University, and the Universities of Illinois, Indiana, Texas at Austin, and Wisconsin. Ph.D. graduates also work in research, strategic analysis, and consulting with firms such as NuStats, the Pacific Telesis Group, Jet Propulsion Laboratory, and Frank Magid Associates.

Location

Los Angeles is a world capital of communication, entertainment, and multimedia. Many opportunities exist to contact and interact with alumni and other professionals and senior management, and for research in such areas as interactive media, radio/television/film, telecommunications, information systems, public and government policy, corporate communication, and marketing.

The School

Home to approximately 1,996 graduate and undergraduate students and 183 full-time faculty members, the USC Annenberg School is poised to tackle questions of our times with strategies and alternatives that serve the public good. The School's vibrant, intellectual community is enhanced by having Los Angeles as a neighborhood laboratory, providing critical exposure to new ideas, hands-on learning experiences, and professional opportunities. USC Annenberg offers professional academic advising, career development services, international programs, and a host of speaking series to compliment classroom instruction.

Applying

All applicants must complete the online USC Graduate Admission Application with required supplemental materials, including a professional resume, a statement of purpose, writing samples or scholarly writing, and letters of recommendation. Graduate Record Examinations (GRE) General Test scores are required for admission to all graduate degree programs, with two exceptions: the GRE is not required for admissions to the global communication degree program, and the GMAT is accepted in lieu of the GRE for admission to the communication management degree program. Proof of English language proficiency is required if the student's native language or language of instruction for their bachelor's degree is not English. Students must refer to the USC Annenberg Web site for graduate admission application guidelines for instructions.

In addition to the online USC graduate admission application, applicants to the M.A./M.Sc. in global communication program must complete the online LSE application.

Correspondence and Information

Admissions Office
Annenberg School for Communication
University of Southern California
3502 Watt Way, Suite 140
Los Angeles, California 90089-0281
Phone: 213-821-0770
Web site: http://www.annenberg.usc.edu

University of Southern California

THE FACULTY AND THEIR RESEARCH

School of Journalism

Daniel H. Birman, M.A., Lecturer. Nonfiction/documentary producer, executive producer for USC Annenberg's *Impact.*

Laura Castañeda, Ed.D., Associate Professor of Professional Practice and Assistant Director, School of Journalism. Former AP reporter, business reporter, coeditor, coauthor.

William Celis, M.S., Associate Professor. Author of *Battle Rock: The Struggle Over a One-Room School in America's Vanishing West.* Former education correspondent, reporter, columnist.

Serena Cha, M.S., Director and Faculty Adviser, Annenberg TV News. Former TV producer.

Dana Chinn, M.B.A., Lecturer. Senior consultant, Media Insight Group.

K. C. Cole, B.A., Professor. Science writer, columnist, editor, writer, author of seven books, including *The Universe and the Teacup: The Mathematics of Truth and Beauty.*

Marc Cooper, Lecturer and Associate Director, USC Annenberg Institute for Justice and Journalism. Senior editor, contributing editor, contributing writer, author of three nonfiction books, codirects the News21 project.

Norman Corwin, B.A., Visiting Professor and Writer-in-Residence. Radio/television dramatist and writer of five stage plays and nineteen books.

Geoffrey Cowan, L.L.B., University Professor and Annenberg Family Chair in Communication Leadership. Communication law attorney, Emmy Award–winning producer, playwright, newspaper columnist.

Ed Cray, B.A., Professor. Journalist, author of eighteen books.

Patricia Dean, M.S., Professor of Professional Practice and Associate Director, School of Journalism. Former senior executive producer and television program director, consumer investigative news producer, and news show and investigative unit producer. Codirects the News21 project.

Jennifer Floto, M.A., Associate Professor of Professional Practice. Former vice president/creative director of Ketchum Public Relations, former vice president/group manager for Manning Selvage & Lee, Los Angeles.

Félix Gutiérrez, Ph.D., Professor. Former senior vice president of Freedom Forum and Newseum, author/coauthor of five books and more than fifty scholarly articles and book chapters on Latinos and other racial/ethnic groups.

Jay T. Harris, B.A., Professor and Wallis Annenberg Chair in Journalism and Democracy. Formerly chairman and publisher of the *San Jose Mercury News;* vice president of operations for Knight-Ridder Inc.; executive editor, *Philadelphia Daily News;* national correspondent and columnist.

Robert Hernandez, B.A., Assistant Professor of Professional Practice. Former senior news director of development of the *Seattle Times*; Web designer and consultant for El Salvador's largest daily newspaper site, *La Prensa Gráfica*; Web producer for the *San Francisco Chronicle;* and online editor of the *San Francisco Examiner*.

Henry Jenkins, Ph.D., Provost's Professor of Communication, Journalism, and Cinematic Arts. Research: role of journalism in the digital age, new media technologies in educational settings, transmedia storytelling.

Jonathan Kotler, J.D., Associate Professor. Attorney, coauthor, former dean of USC Graduate School.

Josh Kun, Ph.D., Berkeley, Associate Professor. Author, director of the Popular Music Project at Norman Lear Center. Research: music, popular culture, U.S.-Mexico border, race.

Andrew Lih, M.S., Visiting Professor. New media researcher, consultant, former video and multimedia journalist for *Wall Street Journal Online*, and author of *The Wikipedia Revolution: How a Bunch of Nobodies Created the World's Greatest Encyclopedia.*

Judy Muller, B.A., Associate Professor. Commentator, author, former *ABC News* correspondent and *CBS News* correspondent and radio anchor.

Mary Murphy, B.A., Lecturer. Former reporter and news producer for *Entertainment Tonight,* contributing editor for the *Los Angeles Times Magazine,* and coauthor.

Bryce Nelson, M. Phil., Professor. Former reporter, spokesman for Christopher Commission, and Director of School of Journalism.

Geneva Overholser, M.S., Director, School of Journalism. Award-winning journalist and media scholar, former editor, syndicated columnist, coeditor.

Tim Page, B.A., Visiting Professor. Chief music critic and culture writer for the *Washington Post,* Grammy Award nominee, author, winner of Pulitzer Prize in Criticism (1997).

Michael Parks, B.A., Professor and Director, School of Journalism. Former editor, executive vice president, vice president of Times Mirror Co., bureau chief, winner of Pulitzer Prize in International Reporting (1987).

Larry Pryor, M.S., Associate Professor. Founding editor of *Online Journalism Review;* former *Los Angeles Times* Web-site editor and newspaper writer, editor, and reporter. Research: New media topics.

Richard Reeves, M.E., Lecturer. Author of eleven books, syndicated columnist, former chief correspondent, national editor, magazine columnist, chief political correspondent.

Joe Saltzman, M.S., Professor. News and documentary writer/reporter/producer, author, director of the Image of the Journalist in Popular Culture project.

Stacy Scholder, B.A. Associate Director, *Annenberg TV News.* Former television producer, executive producer, news producer.

Philip Seib, J.D., Professor. Author of numerous books, coeditor. Research: international communication issues related to new media technologies, democratization, war, terrorism.

Willa Seidenberg, B.A., Lecturer and Director, *Annenberg Radio News.* Former radio reporter, anchor, producer, TV news writer, coauthor.

Erna Smith, B.A. Author of several studies on race and the media, former reporter, editor, and copy editor at several newspapers. Research: diversity issues in journalism, journalism education.

Roberto Suro, M.S., Professor and Director, Master of Arts in Specialized Journalism Program. Newspaper print journalist in foreign, domestic, and Washington coverage; author; founding director, Pew Hispanic Center. Research: Hispanic population.

Jerry Swerling, M.S., Professor of Professional Practice and Director, Strategic Public Relations Center. Principal of Swerling & Associates, Communications Management and Organizational Consulting.

Burghardt Tenderich, Ph.D., Visiting Professor and Associate Director, Strategic Public Relations Center. Founding partner of TnT Initiatives, LLC; former vice president, public relations, at Siebel Systems; and senior vice president and partner at Applied Communication.

Sandy Tolan, Associate Professor. Radio and print journalist, author, producer of radio documentaries and features.

Jian Wang, Ph.D., Associate Professor. Author, former senior communications specialist for McKinsey & Company, and former consultant for Ketchum Public Relations.

Diane Winston, Ph.D., Associate Professor and Knight Chair in Media and Religion. Author, columnist, coeditor. Former newspaper reporter, television news writer, independent documentary filmmaker.

School of Communication

Jonathan D. Aronson, Ph.D., Professor. Cofounded Annenberg Research Network on International Communication. Research: communications policy, globalization, and international trade and trade negotiations. Former director, USC School of International Relations.

Sandra Ball-Rokeach, Ph.D., Associate Professor and Associate Dean for Faculty Affairs. Rockefeller and Fulbright Fellow. On editorial boards of a number of journals, coeditor of *Communication Research.* Research: transformation of urban communities.

Sarah Banet-Weiser, Ph.D., Associate Professor. Author and coeditor. Research: popular culture, media and consumer culture, with a focus on race, gender, and citizenship.

François Bar, Ph.D., Associate Professor and Director, Annenberg Research Network on International Communication. Research: continuing evolution of communication networks, including their deployment, regulation, and business use.

Daniela Baroffio-Bota, Ph.D., Senior Lecturer. Research: how feminism, U.S. militarism, and race in post-9/11 portrayals of female soldiers both consolidate traditional national ideologies and offer potential for resistance against patriarchal systems.

Manuel Castells, Ph.D., Professor and Wallis Annenberg Chair in Communication Technology and Society. Research: relationship between mass media, communication networks, and political power.

Peter Clarke, Ph.D., Professor. Author and former dean. Research: communication and health behavior; programs to improve the public's well-being, especially among underserved groups.

Michael J. Cody, Ph.D., Professor. Author and editor. Research: interpersonal communication and persuasion.

Jeffrey Cole, Ph.D., Research Professor and Director, Annenberg Center for the Digital Future. Research: effects of media policy, violence, and computer and Internet technology on all aspects of society. Founder/director of the twenty-country World Internet Project.

Geoffrey Cowan, L.L.B., University Professor and Annenberg Family Chair in Communication Leadership. Former director, *Voice of America;* communication law attorney; Emmy Award–winning producer, playwright, and newspaper columnist.

Nicholas Cull, Ph.D., Professor and Director, Master of Public Diplomacy Program. Author of numerous articles, including *Selling War,* one of *Choice* magazine's 10-best academic books of 1995.

Matthew Curtis, Ph.D., Lecturer. Research: how individuals and groups compare themselves to others in order to understand their role in work and social settings.

Daniel Durbin, Ph.D., Senior Lecturer. Research: rhetoric of sports, health, fitness, nutrition, and medicine; promotion of health, fitness, and medicine in popular-press advertising.

Robeson Taj P. Frazier, Ph.D., Assistant Professor. Research: race and ethnicity, comparative political economy, popular culture, sport, globalization, transnationalism and internationalism.

Janet Fulk, Ph.D., Professor. Author. Research: impact of communication systems on collaboration and knowledge distribution across boundaries of space, time, team, organization, and nation.

G. Thomas Goodnight, Ph.D., Professor and Director, Doctoral Studies. Deliberation and postwar society, science communication, argument and aesthetics, public discourse.

Jerrold Green, Ph.D., Research Professor. Formerly with the RAND Corporation, a partner in Best-Associates, a merchant banking firm.

Larry Gross, Ph.D., Professor and Director, School of Communication. Author and editor. Research: media and culture, art and communication, visual communication, media portrayals of minorities.

Thomas A. Hollihan, Ph.D., Professor. Research: arguments that shape public policy and political discourse; including issues of citizenship and community in the postmodern age.

Andrea B. Hollingshead, Ph.D., Associate Professor. Research: strategic communication, knowledge sharing, social influence, decision making in teams and online communities.

Yu Hong, Ph.D., Assistant Professor. Research: ICTs and development, political economy of global communication, China's information and communications industry, information labor.

Colleen Keough, Ph.D., Clinical Associate Professor. Strategic planning and financial management workshops in Central and Eastern Europe. Research: role of communications in conflict management.

Josh Kun, Ph.D., Associate Professor. Author of *Audiotopia;* directs the Popular Music Project at the Norman Lear Center. Research: music, popular culture, U.S.-Mexico border, race.

Randall Lake, Ph.D., Associate Professor. Writer. Research: contemporary rhetorical theory and practice, particularly political and public argumentation.

Ben Lee, Ph.D., Senior Lecturer. Sociologist and statistician. Research: human behavior in financial markets.

Kwan Min Lee, Ph.D., Assistant Professor. Author of "hot paper" in social sciences. Research: sociopsychological effects of new information and communication technologies, including human-computer and human-robot interaction.

Doe Mayer, Professor and Mary Pickford Chair, School of Cinematic Arts. Coauthor of *Creative Filmmaking From the Inside Out.* Research: practical international application of communication campaign strategies and designs for social issues and health-defined organizations.

Margaret McLaughlin, Ph.D., Professor. Key investigator at Integrated Media Systems Center. Research: use of virtual environments in delivery of health and social services.

Lynn C. Miller, Ph.D., Professor. Research: use of multidisciplinary approaches to create intelligent agents and virtual worlds for testing communication theory and enhancing health and educational outcomes.

Peter R. Monge, Ph.D., Professor. Coauthor and editor. Research: communication networks in a variety of social contexts, ecology of communication processes within organizational communities.

Sheila T. Murphy, Ph.D., Associate Professor. Research: relationship between emotion and cognition and their relative influence on judgments and beliefs, decision making, information processing, agenda setting, politics.

Stephen O'Leary, Ph.D., Associate Professor. Author. Research: religious communication, rhetorical theory, criticism.

Patricia Riley, Ph.D., Associate Professor and Director, M.A./M.Sc. in Global Communication Program. Author and consultant. Research: organizational communication, organizational politics, culture change, knowledge management.

Robert Scheer, Clinical Professor. Journalist and nationally syndicated columnist, author, editor, radio host.

Kenneth K. Sereno, Ph.D., Associate Professor. Research: communication theory, persuasion, interpersonal and family communication, humor's role in intimate relationships, effect of "clicker" technology in the classroom.

Christopher Smith, Ph.D., Senior Lecturer and Director, Johnson Communication Leadership Center. Research: modern financial markets and their impact on everyday culture, pop culture, entertainment's role in public diplomacy, convergence trends in media industries.

Stacy Smith, Ph.D., Associate Professor. Research: children's reactions to mass media, including developmental differences in emotional and cognitive processing; content patterns and effects of the media on youth.

Gordon Stables, Ph.D., Clinical Professor. Research: rhetoric and argumentation, policy debate and forensics, public debate surrounding the global war on terrorism.

Susan Resnick West, Ph.D. Author on performance appraisal, management of professional employees, and evaluation of strategic change efforts. Research: leadership, employee development, and evaluation to enable strategic change.

Dmitri Williams, Ph.D., Assistant Professor. Research: social and economic impacts of new media, with particular emphasis on video games and the Internet.

Ernest J. Wilson III, Ph.D., Professor and Walter Annenberg Chair in Communication. Research: politics of global sustainable innovation in high-tech industries, network inequality, China-Africa relations, and the role of culture in U.S. national security policy.

Section 17
Conflict Resolution and Mediation/Peace Studies

This section contains a directory of institutions offering graduate work in conflict resolution and mediation/peace studies. Additional information about programs listed in the directory but not augmented by an in-depth entry may be obtained by writing directly to the dean of a graduate school or chair of a department at the address given in the directory.

For programs offering related work, see also in this book *Political Science and International Affairs* and *Public, Regional, and Industrial Affairs.* In another guide in this series:

Graduate Programs in Business, Education, Health, Information Studies, Law & Social Work

See *Business Administration and Management* and *Law*

CONTENTS

Program Directory

Conflict Resolution and Mediation/Peace Studies 688

Close-Up

See:

American University—International Service 849

Conflict Resolution and Mediation/Peace Studies

Abilene Christian University, Graduate School, College of Arts and Sciences, Department of Conflict Resolution, Abilene, TX 79699-9100. Offers conflict resolution (Certificate); conflict resolution and reconciliation (MA). *Faculty:* 2 full-time (0 women), 3 part-time/adjunct (1 woman). *Students:* 14 full-time (9 women), 68 part-time (42 women); includes 10 minority (4 African Americans, 6 Hispanic Americans), 1 international. 80 applicants, 34% accepted, 23 enrolled. In 2009, 15 master's, 50 other advanced degrees awarded. *Application deadline:* For fall admission, 4/1 priority date for domestic students; for spring admission, 10/1 for domestic students. Applications are processed on a rolling basis. Application fee: $40. Electronic applications accepted. *Expenses:* Tuition: Full-time $11,520; part-time $640 per hour. Required fees: $1090; $53.50 per hour. $10 per term. Tuition and fees vary according to program. *Financial support:* In 2009–10, 60 students received support. Applicants required to submit FAFSA. *Unit head:* Dr. Garry P. Bailey, Graduate Adviser, 325-674-2015, Fax: 325-674-2427, E-mail: garrybailey@acu.edu. *Application contact:* William Horn, Graduate Admissions Counselor, 325-674-2656, Fax: 325-674-6717, E-mail: gradinfo@acu.edu.

American Public University System, AMU/APU Graduate Programs, Charles Town, WV 25414. Offers air warfare (MA Military Studies); American Revolution (MA Military Studies); business administration (MBA); Civil War (MA Military Studies); criminal justice (MA); defense management (MA Military Studies); emergency and disaster management (MA); environmental policy and management (MS); fire science management (MA); global engagement (MA); history (MA); homeland security (MA); humanities (MA); intelligence (MA Military Studies, MA Strategic Intelligence); international peace and conflict resolution (MA); international relations and conflict resolution (MA); joint warfare (MA Military Studies); land warfare international perspective (MA Military Studies); management (MA); military history (MA); military leadership (MA Military Studies); national security studies (MA); naval warfare international (MA Military Studies); naval warfare US (MA Military Studies); political science (MA); public administration (MA); public health (MA); security management (MA); space studies (MS); special ops/LIC (MA Military Studies); sports management (MA); transportation and logistics management (MA); transportation management (MA); unconventional warfare (MA Military Studies); World War II (MA Military Studies). Programs offered via distance learning only. Part-time and evening/weekend programs available. Postbaccalaureate distance learning degree programs offered (no on-campus study). *Faculty:* 10 full-time (3 women), 188 part-time/adjunct (57 women). *Students:* 340 full-time (98 women), 3,567 part-time (790 women); includes 615 minority (317 African Americans, 28 American Indian/Alaska Native, 85 Asian Americans or Pacific Islanders, 185 Hispanic Americans), 20 international. Average age 36. 2,123 applicants, 100% accepted, 893 enrolled. In 2009, 829 degrees awarded. *Degree requirements:* For master's, comprehensive exam. *Entrance requirements:* For master's, bachelor's degree or equivalent, minimum GPA of 2.7 in last 60 hours of course work. *Application deadline:* Applications are processed on a rolling basis. Application fee: $0. Electronic applications accepted. *Financial support:* Applicants required to submit FAFSA. *Faculty research:* Military history, criminal justice, management performance, national security. *Unit head:* Dr. Frank McCluskey, Provost, 877-468-6268, Fax: 304-724-3780. *Application contact:* Terry Grant, Director of Enrollment Management, 877-468-6268, Fax: 304-724-3780, E-mail: info@apus.edu.

American University, School of International Service, Washington, DC 20016-8071. Offers comparative and regional studies (Certificate); cross-cultural communication (Certificate); development management (MS); ethics, peace, and global affairs (MA); European studies (Certificate); global environmental policy (MA, Certificate); international affairs (MA), including comparative and regional studies, environmental policy, international economic policy, international politics, natural resources and sustainable development, U.S. foreign policy; international communication (MA, Certificate); international development (MA, Certificate); international development management (Certificate); international economic policy (Certificate); international economic relations (Certificate); international media (MA); international peace and conflict resolution (MA, Certificate); international relations (PhD); international service (MIS); peace building (Certificate); the Americas (Certificate); United States foreign policy (Certificate); JD/MA. Part-time and evening/weekend programs available. *Faculty:* 98 full-time (42 women), 48 part-time/adjunct (13 women). *Students:* 565 full-time (349 women), 329 part-time (189 women); includes 128 minority (44 African Americans, 2 American Indian/Alaska Native, 37 Asian Americans or Pacific Islanders, 45 Hispanic Americans), 102 international. Average age 27. 2,034 applicants, 63% accepted, 344 enrolled. In 2009, 326 master's, 6 doctorates, 9 other advanced degrees awarded. Terminal master's awarded for partial completion of doctoral program. *Degree requirements:* For master's, one foreign language, comprehensive exam, thesis or alternative; for doctorate, one foreign language, comprehensive exam, thesis/dissertation, research practicum; for Certificate, minimum 15 credit hours related course work. *Entrance requirements:* For master's, GRE, 24 credits of course work in related social sciences, minimum GPA of 3.5, 2 letters of recommendation, bachelor's degree, resume; for doctorate, GRE, 2 letters of recommendation, 24 credits in related social sciences; for Certificate, bachelor's degree. Additional exam requirements/recommendations for international students: Required—TOEFL (minimum score 600 paper-based; 250 computer-based; 100 iBT). *Application deadline:* For fall admission, 1/15 priority date for domestic students; for spring admission, 10/1 priority date for domestic students. Applications are processed on a rolling basis. Application fee: $50. *Expenses:* Tuition: Full-time $22,266; part-time $1237 per credit hour. Required fees: $430. Tuition and fees vary according to program. *Financial support:* Career-related internships or fieldwork, Federal Work-Study, and institutionally sponsored loans available. Financial award application deadline: 1/15. *Faculty research:* International intellectual property, international environmental issues, international law and legal order, international telecommunications/technology, international sustainable development. *Unit head:* Dr. Louis W. Goodman, Dean, 202-885-1600, Fax: 202-885-2494. *Application contact:* Yasmin Quianzon, Director of Graduate Admissions and Financial Aid, 202-885-2496, Fax: 202-885-1109.

See Close-Up on page 849.

The American University of Paris, Graduate Programs, Paris, France. Offers cross-cultural and sustainable business management (MA); cultural translation (MA); global communications (MA); global communications and civil society (MA); international affairs, conflict resolution and civil society development (MA); Middle East and Islamic studies (MA); Middle East and Islamic studies and international affairs (MA); public policy and international affairs (MA); public policy and international law (MA). *Faculty:* 14 full-time (3 women). *Students:* 143 full-time (109 women). 71 applicants, 92% accepted, 34 enrolled. *Degree requirements:* For master's, thesis. *Entrance requirements:* For master's, minimum undergraduate GPA of 3.0. *Application deadline:* For fall admission, 4/15 priority date for international students; for spring admission, 11/15 priority date for international students. Applications are processed on a rolling basis. Application fee: $75. Tuition charges are reported in euros. *Expenses:* Tuition: Full-time 23,460 euros. *Financial support:* Scholarships/grants available. Financial award applicants required to submit FAFSA. *Unit head:* Celeste Schenk, President, 33 1-40620659, E-mail: president@aup.fr. *Application contact:* International Admissions Counselor, 33 1-40620720, Fax: 33 1-47053432, E-mail: admissions@aup.edu.

Antioch University Midwest, Graduate Programs, Program in Conflict Analysis and Management, Yellow Springs, OH 45387-1609. Offers MA. Part-time and evening/weekend programs available. Postbaccalaureate distance learning degree programs offered (minimal on-campus study). *Faculty:* 1 full-time (0 women), 5 part-time/adjunct (3 women). *Students:* 21 full-time (16 women), 29 part-time (26 women); includes 16 minority (11 African Americans, 1 American Indian/Alaska Native, 3 Asian Americans or Pacific Islanders, 1 Hispanic American). Average age 42. 24 applicants, 83% accepted, 18 enrolled. In 2009, 13 master's awarded. *Degree requirements:* For master's, thesis or alternative. *Entrance requirements:* For master's, resume, 2 letters of reference. *Application deadline:* For fall admission, 8/15 for domestic and international students; for winter admission, 12/10 for domestic and international students; for spring admission, 3/8 for domestic and international students. Applications are processed on a rolling basis. Application fee: $50. Electronic applications accepted. *Expenses:* Contact institution. *Financial support:* Federal Work-Study available. Financial award applicants required to submit FAFSA. *Unit head:* Dr. Richard McGuigan, Chair, 937-769-1890, Fax: 937-769-1809, E-mail: rmcguigan@antioch.edu. *Application contact:* Rob McLaughlin, Enrollment Services Manager, 937-769-1816, Fax: 937-769-1804, E-mail: rmclaughlin@antioch.edu.

Arcadia University, Graduate Studies, Program in International Peace and Conflict Management, Glenside, PA 19038-3295. Offers MAIPCR. Part-time and evening/weekend programs available. *Students:* 54 full-time (40 women), 10 part-time (4 women); includes 3 minority (all African Americans), 6 international. Average age 27. In 2009, 10 master's awarded. *Degree requirements:* For master's, one foreign language. *Entrance requirements:* For master's, GRE. Additional exam requirements/recommendations for international students: Required—TOEFL. *Application deadline:* For fall admission, 4/1 priority date for domestic students. Application fee: $50. *Expenses:* Contact institution. *Unit head:* Dr. Warren Haffar, Director, 215-572-4094, Fax: 215-572-4049, E-mail: haffar@arcadia.edu. *Application contact:* 215-572-2910, Fax: 215-572-4049, E-mail: admiss@arcadia.edu.

Associated Mennonite Biblical Seminary, Graduate and Professional Programs, Elkhart, IN 46517-1999. Offers Christian formation (MA); divinity (M Div); mission and evangelism (MA); peace studies (MA); theological studies (MA, Certificate). *Accreditation:* ACIPE; ATS. Part-time programs available. *Degree requirements:* For master's, comprehensive exam, thesis optional; for M Div, integration paper. *Entrance requirements:* For M Div, master's, and Certificate, 3 letters of reference. Additional exam requirements/recommendations for international students: Required—TOEFL (minimum score 550 paper-based; 213 computer-based). Electronic applications accepted. *Faculty research:* Biblical studies, theology, church history, church leadership.

Baker University, School of Professional and Graduate Studies, Program in Conflict Management and Dispute Resolution, Baldwin City, KS 66006-0065. Offers MA. Part-time and evening/weekend programs available. *Entrance requirements:* Additional exam requirements/recommendations for international students: Required—TOEFL (minimum score 600 paper-based; 250 computer-based).

Bethany Theological Seminary, Graduate and Professional Programs, Richmond, IN 47374-4019. Offers biblical studies (MA Th); ministry studies (M Div); peace studies (M Div, MA Th); theological studies (MA Th, CATS); youth ministry (M Div). *Accreditation:* ACIPE; ATS. Part-time programs available. Postbaccalaureate distance learning degree programs offered (minimal on-campus study). *Degree requirements:* For master's, thesis. *Entrance requirements:* For M Div, letters of reference, minimum GPA of 2.75; for master's, letters of reference, minimum GPA of 3.0. Additional exam requirements/recommendations for international students: Required—TOEFL (minimum score 550 paper-based; 218 computer-based).

Brandeis University, Graduate School of Arts and Sciences, Program in Coexistence and Conflict, Waltham, MA 02454-9110. Offers MA, MA/MA. *Faculty:* 3 full-time (1 woman), 2 part-time/adjunct (1 woman). *Students:* 27 full-time (11 women); includes 2 minority (both African Americans), 22 international. 101 applicants, 59% accepted, 23 enrolled. In 2009, 12 master's awarded. *Degree requirements:* For master's, thesis, internship. *Entrance requirements:* For master's, 3 letters of recommendation, curriculum vitae or resume. Additional exam requirements/recommendations for international students: Required—TOEFL (minimum score 600 paper-based; 250 computer-based; 100 iBT); Recommended—IELTS (minimum score 7). *Application deadline:* For winter admission, 1/31 priority date for domestic and international students. Applications are processed on a rolling basis. Application fee: $75. Electronic applications accepted. *Financial support:* In 2009–10, 16 students received support. Tuition waivers (partial) available. Financial award application deadline: 4/15; financial award applicants required to submit FAFSA. *Faculty research:* Intercommunal conflicts, strategic intervention, conflict resolution, coexistence and conflict, international and inter-governmental organizations. *Unit head:* Dr. Mari Fitzduff, Director, 781-736-5001, Fax: 781-736-8561, E-mail: mfitzd@brandeis.edu. *Application contact:* Anne Gudaitis, Program Administrator, 781-736-8575, Fax: 781-736-8561, E-mail: gudaitis@brandeis.edu.

Brandeis University, Graduate School of Arts and Sciences, Program in Coexistence and Conflict and Sustainable International Development, Waltham, MA 02454-9110. Offers MA/MA.

California State University, Dominguez Hills, College of Arts and Humanities, Program in Negotiation, Conflict Resolution and Peacebuilding, Carson, CA 90747-0001. Offers MA. Part-time and evening/weekend programs available. Postbaccalaureate distance learning degree programs offered (no on-campus study). *Faculty:* 4 full-time (3 women), 2 part-time/adjunct (0 women). *Students:* 38 full-time (21 women), 160 part-time (104 women); includes 86 minority (55 African Americans, 1 American Indian/Alaska Native, 5 Asian Americans or Pacific Islanders, 25 Hispanic Americans). Average age 40. 177 applicants, 80% accepted, 59 enrolled. In 2009, 39 master's awarded. *Degree requirements:* For master's, portfolio. *Entrance requirements:* For master's, minimum GPA of 3.2, 3 letters of recommendation. *Application deadline:* For fall admission, 5/1 for domestic and international students; for spring admission, 12/1 for domestic and international students. Application fee: $55. Electronic applications accepted. *Expenses:* Tuition, nonresident: full-time $6696; part-time $372 per unit. Required fees: $5946; $1752 per semester. *Faculty research:* Ethnic conflict, mediator ethics, teacher training, global conflict resolution (including role of ombuds), optimal multicultural process. *Unit head:* Dr. A. Marco Turk, Professor and Director, 310-243-3237, Fax: 310-516-4268, E-mail: amturk@csudh.edu. *Application contact:* Penny Ann LaBaun, Administrative Coordinator, 310-243-3237, Fax: 310-516-4268, E-mail: plabaun@csudh.edu.

Cambridge College, School of Management, Cambridge, MA 02138-5304. Offers business negotiation and conflict resolution (M Mgt); general business (M Mgt); health care informatics (M Mgt); health care management (M Mgt); leadership in human and organizational dynamics (M Mgt); non-profit and public organization management (M Mgt); small business development (M Mgt); technology management (M Mgt). Part-time and evening/weekend programs available. *Faculty:* 4 full-time (3 women), 65 part-time/adjunct (32 women). *Students:* 297 full-time (178 women), 234 part-time (155 women); includes 217 minority (122 African Americans, 53 Asian Americans or Pacific Islanders, 42 Hispanic Americans), 135 international. Average age 39. In 2009, 259 master's awarded. *Degree requirements:* For master's, thesis, seminars. *Entrance requirements:* For master's, resume, 2 professional references. Additional exam requirements/recommendations for international students: Required—TOEFL (minimum score 550 paper-based; 213 computer-based; 79 iBT); Recommended—IELTS (minimum score 6). *Application deadline:* Applications are processed on a rolling basis. Application fee: $30. Electronic applications accepted. *Expenses:* Contact institution. *Financial support:* In 2009–10, 170 students received support. Career-related internships or fieldwork, Federal Work-Study, and scholarships/grants available. Financial award applicants required to submit FAFSA. *Faculty research:* Negotiation, mediation and conflict resolution; leadership; management of diverse organizations; case studies and simulation methodologies for management education, digital as a second language: social networking for digital immigrants. *Unit head:* Dr. Mary Ann Joseph, Acting Dean, 617-873-0227, E-mail: maryann.joseph@cambridgecollege.edu. *Application contact:* Stephen Lyons, Director of Enrollment, Graduate and N.I.T.E. Programs, 617-868-1000, Fax: 617-349-3561, E-mail: stephen.lyons@cambridgecollege.edu.

Conflict Resolution and Mediation/Peace Studies

Carleton University, Faculty of Graduate Studies, Faculty of Public Affairs and Management, Department of Law, Ottawa, ON K1S 5B6, Canada. Offers conflict resolution (Certificate); legal studies (MA). *Degree requirements:* For master's, thesis. *Entrance requirements:* For master's, honors degree. Additional exam requirements/recommendations for international students: Required—TOEFL. *Faculty research:* Legal and social theory; women, law, and gender relations; law, crime, and social order; political economy of law; international law.

Chaminade University of Honolulu, Graduate Services, Program in Education, Honolulu, HI 96816-1578. Offers social science via peace education (M Ed). Part-time and evening/weekend programs available. Postbaccalaureate distance learning degree programs offered (minimal on-campus study). *Degree requirements:* For master's, thesis or alternative. *Entrance requirements:* For master's, minimum GPA of 2.75, 3 letters of recommendation. Additional exam requirements/recommendations for international students: Required—TOEFL (minimum score 550 paper-based). *Faculty research:* Peace and curriculum education.

Colorado Technical University Colorado Springs, Graduate Studies, Program in Management, Colorado Springs, CO 80907-3896. Offers accounting (MBA, MSA); business administration (MBA); finance (MBA); human resources management (MBA); logistics/supply chain management (MBA); management (DM); marketing (MBA); mediation and dispute resolution (MBA); operations management (MBA); project management (MBA); technology management (MBA). Part-time and evening/weekend programs available. Postbaccalaureate distance learning degree programs offered. *Degree requirements:* For master's, thesis or alternative; for doctorate, thesis/dissertation. *Entrance requirements:* For doctorate, minimum graduate GPA of 3.0, 5 years of related work experience. *Faculty research:* Sexual harassment, performance evaluation, critical thinking.

Colorado Technical University Denver, Programs in Business Administration and Management, Greenwood Village, CO 80111. Offers accounting (MBA); business administration (MBA); business administration and management (EMBA); finance (MBA); human resource management (MBA); marketing (MBA); mediation and dispute resolution (MBA); operations management (MBA); project management (MBA); technology management (MBA). Part-time and evening/weekend programs available. *Degree requirements:* For master's, thesis or alternative. *Entrance requirements:* For master's, minimum undergraduate GPA of 3.0, resume.

Columbia College, Graduate Programs, Department of Human Relations, Columbia, SC 29203-5998. Offers human behavior and conflict management (MA); interpersonal relations/conflict management (Certificate); organizational behavior/conflict management (Certificate). Part-time and evening/weekend programs available. Postbaccalaureate distance learning degree programs offered (minimal on-campus study). *Faculty:* 3 part-time/adjunct (2 women). *Students:* 21 part-time (17 women); includes 7 minority (all African Americans). Average age 29. 26 applicants, 100% accepted. In 2009, 12 master's awarded. *Degree requirements:* For master's, thesis, practicum. *Entrance requirements:* For master's, GRE General Test, MAT, 2 letters of recommendation, minimum GPA of 3.2. Additional exam requirements/recommendations for international students: Required—TOEFL. *Application deadline:* For fall admission, 7/15 priority date for domestic students, 7/15 for international students. Applications are processed on a rolling basis. Application fee: $50. Electronic applications accepted. *Expenses:* Contact institution. *Financial support:* Available to part-time students. Application deadline: 7/1. *Faculty research:* Envisioning and the resolution of conflict, environmental conflict resolution, crisis negotiation. *Unit head:* Dr. Elaine Ferraro, Chair, 803-786-3687, Fax: 803-786-3790, E-mail: eferraro@colacoll.edu. *Application contact:* Carolyn Emeneker, Director of Graduate School and Evening College Admissions, 803-786-3766, Fax: 803-786-3674, E-mail: emeneker@colacoll.edu.

Columbia University, School of Continuing Education, Program in Negotiation and Conflict Resolution, New York, NY 10027. Offers MS. Part-time programs available. *Faculty:* 13 part-time/adjunct (5 women). *Students:* 18 full-time (13 women), 58 part-time (37 women); includes 25 minority (11 African Americans, 5 Asian Americans or Pacific Islanders, 9 Hispanic Americans), 7 international. Average age 36. 67 applicants, 88% accepted, 26 enrolled. *Entrance requirements:* For master's, 2 letters of recommendation, professional resume. *Application deadline:* For fall admission, 4/15 for domestic students. Application fee: $50. Electronic applications accepted. *Unit head:* Beth Fisher, Academic Director, 212-851-5956, E-mail: bf2017@columbia.edu. *Application contact:* Bryce Weinert, Admissions Adviser, 212-854-9666, E-mail: sce-apply@columbia.edu.

Cornell University, Graduate School, Graduate Fields of Architecture, Art and Planning, Field of Regional Science, Ithaca, NY 14853-0001. Offers environmental studies (MA, MS, PhD); international spatial problems (MA, MS, PhD); location theory (MA, MS, PhD); multiregional economic analysis (MA, MS, PhD); peace science (MA, MS, PhD); planning methods (MA, MS, PhD); urban and regional economics (MA, MS, PhD). *Faculty:* 22 full-time (5 women). *Students:* 21 full-time (8 women); includes 2 minority (1 African American, 1 Asian American or Pacific Islander), 18 international. Average age 35. 15 applicants, 53% accepted, 4 enrolled. In 2009, 1 master's, 4 doctorates awarded. Terminal master's awarded for partial completion of doctoral program. *Degree requirements:* For master's, thesis; for doctorate, comprehensive exam, thesis/dissertation. *Entrance requirements:* For master's and doctorate, GRE General Test, 2 letters of recommendation. Additional exam requirements/recommendations for international students: Required—TOEFL (minimum score 600 paper-based; 250 computer-based; 77 iBT). *Application deadline:* For fall admission, 1/15 priority date for domestic students. Application fee: $70. Electronic applications accepted. *Expenses:* Tuition: Full-time $29,500. Required fees: $70. Full-time tuition and fees vary according to degree level, program and student level. *Financial support:* In 2009–10, 7 students received support; fellowships with full tuition reimbursements available, research assistantships with full tuition reimbursements available, teaching assistantships with full tuition reimbursements available, institutionally sponsored loans, scholarships/grants, health care benefits, tuition waivers (full and partial), and unspecified assistantships available. Financial award applicants required to submit FAFSA. *Faculty research:* Urban and regional growth, spatial economics, formation of spatial patterns by socioeconomic systems, non-linear dynamics and complex systems, environmental-economic systems. *Unit head:* Director of Graduate Studies, 607-255-6848, Fax: 607-255-1971. *Application contact:* Graduate Field Assistant, 607-255-6848, Fax: 607-255-1971, E-mail: regsci@cornell.edu.

Creighton University, School of Law, Program in Negotiation and Dispute Resolution, Omaha, NE 68178. Offers MS, Certificate. Part-time and evening/weekend programs available. Postbaccalaureate distance learning degree programs offered (minimal on-campus study). *Faculty:* 5 full-time (1 woman), 13 part-time/adjunct (6 women). *Students:* 63 full-time (27 women), 50 part-time (25 women); includes 24 minority (11 African Americans, 8 Asian Americans or Pacific Islanders, 5 Hispanic Americans), 2 international. Average age 35. In 2009, 8 master's awarded. *Degree requirements:* For master's, thesis or alternative, practicum. *Entrance requirements:* For master's, GRE, MAT, or LSAT. Additional exam requirements/recommendations for international students: Required—TOEFL. *Application deadline:* Applications are processed on a rolling basis. Application fee: $50. Electronic applications accepted. *Expenses:* Tuition: Full-time $11,700; part-time $650 per credit hour. Required fees: $126 per semester. *Financial support:* Institutionally sponsored loans available. Financial award applicants required to submit FAFSA. *Faculty research:* Nationalism/identity and conflict; complex adaptive items and conflict engagement; history, memory and conflict; culture and conflict. *Unit head:* Prof. Arthur Pearlstein, Director and Professor of Law, 402-280-3853. *Application contact:* Prof. Jacqueline Font, Associate Director and Assistant Professor, 402-280-3883, E-mail: jnfont@creighton.edu.

Dallas Baptist University, College of Business, Business Administration Program, Dallas, TX 75211-9299. Offers accounting (MBA); business communication (MBA); conflict resolution management (MBA); e-business (MBA); entrepreneurship (MBA); finance (MBA); health care management (MBA); international business (MBA); leading the non-profit organization (MBA); management (MBA); management information systems (MBA); marketing (MBA); project management (MBA); technology and engineering management (MBA). *Accreditation:* ACBSP. Part-time and evening/weekend programs available. *Entrance requirements:* For master's, GMAT, minimum GPA of 3.0. Additional exam requirements/recommendations for international students: Required—TOEFL, IELTS. Electronic applications accepted. *Expenses:* Tuition: Full-time $10,674; part-time $593 per credit hour. *Faculty research:* Sports management, services marketing, retailing, strategic management, financial planning/investments.

Dallas Baptist University, College of Business, Management Program, Dallas, TX 75211-9299. Offers business communication (MA); conflict resolution management (MA); general management (MA); health care management (MA); human resource management (MA); performance management (MA). Part-time and evening/weekend programs available. *Entrance requirements:* For master's, GRE General Test, minimum GPA of 3.0. Additional exam requirements/recommendations for international students: Required—TOEFL, IELTS. Electronic applications accepted. *Expenses:* Tuition: Full-time $10,674; part-time $593 per credit hour. *Faculty research:* Organizational behavior, conflict personalities.

Duquesne University, Graduate School of Liberal Arts, Graduate Center for Social and Public Policy, Pittsburgh, PA 15282-0001. Offers conflict resolution and peace studies (Certificate); social and public policy (MA, Certificate). Part-time and evening/weekend programs available. *Faculty:* 15 full-time (3 women), 1 (woman) part-time/adjunct. *Students:* 40 full-time (26 women), 14 part-time (8 women); includes 5 minority (3 African Americans, 2 Hispanic Americans), 10 international. Average age 27. 31 applicants, 100% accepted, 19 enrolled. In 2009, 13 master's awarded. *Degree requirements:* For master's, thesis. *Entrance requirements:* For master's, GRE General Test. Additional exam requirements/recommendations for international students: Required—TOEFL. *Application deadline:* For fall admission, 4/30 priority date for domestic and international students; for spring admission, 11/1 priority date for domestic and international students. Applications are processed on a rolling basis. Electronic applications accepted. *Expenses:* Tuition: Part-time $851 per credit. Required fees: $81 per credit. *Financial support:* In 2009–10, 20 students received support, including 12 research assistantships with full and partial tuition reimbursements available (averaging $9,000 per year), 4 teaching assistantships with full and partial tuition reimbursements available (averaging $9,000 per year); career-related internships or fieldwork, institutionally sponsored loans, scholarships/grants, tuition waivers (full and partial), and unspecified assistantships also available. Support available to part-time students. Financial award application deadline: 5/1. *Faculty research:* Program evaluation, environmental policy, criminal justice policy, health care policy. Total annual research expenditures: $30,000. *Unit head:* Dr. Joseph Yenerall, Director, 412-396-6485, Fax: 412-396-5265, E-mail: socialpolicy@duq.edu. *Application contact:* Dr. Joseph Yenerall, Assistant to the Dean, 412-396-6485.

Eastern Mennonite University, Program in Conflict Transformation, Harrisonburg, VA 22802-2462. Offers MA, Graduate Certificate. Part-time programs available. *Faculty:* 7 full-time (3 women), 4 part-time/adjunct (0 women). *Students:* 39 full-time (22 women), 27 part-time (17 women); includes 6 minority (5 African Americans, 1 Asian American or Pacific Islander), 19 international. Average age 36. In 2009, 20 master's awarded. *Degree requirements:* For master's, practicum. *Entrance requirements:* For master's, minimum undergraduate GPA of 2.75. Additional exam requirements/recommendations for international students: Required—TOEFL (minimum score 550 paper-based; 213 computer-based). *Application deadline:* For fall admission, 2/15 priority date for domestic and international students. Applications are processed on a rolling basis. Application fee: $25. Electronic applications accepted. *Expenses:* Contact institution. *Financial support:* In 2009–10, 4 students received support. Scholarships/grants available. Financial award application deadline: 6/30; financial award applicants required to submit FAFSA. *Faculty research:* Restorative justice, negotiation, security in an age of terror, trauma recovery, development, peace building. *Unit head:* Dr. David Brubaker, Academic Director, 540-432-4423, Fax: 540-432-4449, E-mail: david.brubaker@emu.edu. *Application contact:* Janelle Myers-Benner, Administrative Assistant, 540-432-4986, Fax: 540-432-4449, E-mail: bennerj@emu.edu.

Florida International University, College of Education, Department of Educational Leadership and Policy Studies, Program in Conflict Resolution and Consensus Building, Miami, FL 33199. Offers Certificate. Part-time and evening/weekend programs available. *Entrance requirements:* Additional exam requirements/recommendations for international students: Required—TOEFL (minimum score 550 paper-based; 213 computer-based; 80 iBT), IELTS (minimum score 6.3). Electronic applications accepted. *Expenses:* Tuition, state resident: full-time $8008; part-time $4004 per year. Tuition, nonresident: full-time $20,104; part-time $10,052 per year. Required fees: $298; $149 per term. *Faculty research:* Workforce housing, labor conditions, labor organizations, workforce development.

Fresno Pacific University, Graduate Programs, Program in Peacemaking and Conflict Studies, Fresno, CA 93702-4709. Offers MA. Part-time and evening/weekend programs available. *Degree requirements:* For master's, thesis. *Entrance requirements:* For master's, GMAT, GRE, interview, 2 writing samples. Additional exam requirements/recommendations for international students: Required—TOEFL (minimum score 550 paper-based; 213 computer-based). Electronic applications accepted.

George Mason University, Institute for Conflict Analysis and Resolution, Fairfax, VA 22030. Offers conflict analysis and resolution (MS, PhD); conflict analysis and resolution advanced skills (Certificate); conflict analysis and resolution for collaborative leadership in community planning (Certificate); conflict analysis and resolution for prevention, reconstruction, and stabilization contexts (Certificate); environmental conflict resolution and collaboration (Certificate); world religions, diplomacy, and conflict resolution (Certificate). Part-time and evening/weekend programs available. *Faculty:* 22 full-time (10 women), 9 part-time/adjunct (6 women). *Students:* 80 full-time (45 women), 200 part-time (122 women); includes 41 minority (16 African Americans, 1 American Indian/Alaska Native, 9 Asian Americans or Pacific Islanders, 15 Hispanic Americans), 45 international. Average age 35. 410 applicants, 46% accepted, 112 enrolled. In 2009, 48 master's, 10 doctorates, 18 other advanced degrees awarded. *Degree requirements:* For master's, thesis optional; for doctorate, one foreign language, comprehensive exam, thesis/dissertation, oral defense of dissertation. *Entrance requirements:* For master's, 3 recommendation letters, resume; for doctorate, 3 recommendation letters, resume, expanded goals statement, writing sample. Additional exam requirements/recommendations for international students: Required—TOEFL (minimum score 575 paper-based; 230 computer-based; 88 iBT). *Application deadline:* For fall admission, 2/1 for domestic students. Application fee: $75. Electronic applications accepted. *Expenses:* Tuition, state resident: full-time $7568; part-time $315.33 per credit hour. Tuition, nonresident: full-time $21,704; part-time $904.33 per credit hour. Required fees: $2184; $91 per credit hour. *Financial support:* In 2009–10, 28 students received support, including 3 fellowships with full tuition reimbursements available (averaging $18,000 per year), 15 research assistantships with full and partial tuition reimbursements available (averaging $12,701 per year), 10 teaching assistantships with full and partial tuition reimbursements available (averaging $8,464 per year); career-related internships or fieldwork, Federal Work-Study, scholarships/grants, unspecified assistantships, and health care benefits (full-time research or teaching assistantship recipients) also available. Support available to part-time students. Financial award application deadline: 3/1; financial award applicants required to submit FAFSA. *Faculty research:* Preventive diplomacy, conflict/dispute resolution, peace/security, political violence, international terrorism. Total annual research expenditures: $535,838. *Unit head:* Andrea Bartoli, Director, 703-993-9716, Fax: 703-993-1302, E-mail: abartoli@gmu.edu. *Application contact:* Erin Ogilvie, Graduate Admissions and Student Services Director, 703-993-9683, E-mail: eogilvie@gmu.edu.

George Mason University, School of Public Policy, Program in Peace Operations, Arlington, VA 22201. Offers MNPS. Part-time programs available. *Faculty:* 61 full-time (14 women), 30 part-time/adjunct (4 women). *Students:* 20 full-time (11 women), 48 part-time (28 women); includes 4 minority (1 African American, 2 Asian Americans or Pacific Islanders, 1 Hispanic American), 5 international. 46 applicants, 67% accepted, 21 enrolled. In 2009, 23 master's awarded. *Degree requirements:* For master's, thesis or alternative. *Entrance requirements:* For master's, GRE (for students seeking merit-based scholarships), minimum undergraduate GPA of 3.0, 2 letters of recommendation, resume. Additional exam requirements/

Conflict Resolution and Mediation/Peace Studies

George Mason University (continued)
recommendations for international students: Required—TOEFL (minimum score 575 paper-based; 230 computer-based; 88 iBT). *Application deadline:* For fall admission, 6/1 priority date for domestic students, 5/1 priority date for international students; for spring admission, 12/1 priority date for domestic students, 11/1 priority date for international students. Applications are processed on a rolling basis. Application fee: $60. Electronic applications accepted. *Expenses:* Contact institution. *Financial support:* Career-related internships or fieldwork, Federal Work-Study, scholarships/grants, and tuition waivers (partial) available. Support available to part-time students. Financial award application deadline: 3/1; financial award applicants required to submit FAFSA. *Unit head:* Dr. Allison Frendak-Blume, Director, 703-993-8099, E-mail: spp@gmu.edu. *Application contact:* Leslie Metzger Levin, Assistant Dean of Graduate Admissions and Marketing, 703-993-8099, Fax: 703-993-4876, E-mail: lmetzger@gmu.edu.

Georgetown University, Graduate School of Arts and Sciences, Department of Government, Program in Conflict Resolution, Washington, DC 20057. Offers MA.

Georgetown University, Graduate School of Arts and Sciences, Edmund A. Walsh School of Foreign Service, Center for Peace and Security Studies, Washington, DC 20057. Offers security studies (MA); MA/JD; MA/PhD.

Hult International Business School, Program in International Relations—Hult London Campus, London, MA WC 1B 4JP, United Kingdom. Offers conflict resolution (MA); diplomacy (MA); international public law (MA); international relations (MA); Middle East international security (MA); politics (MA); security studies (MA); terrorism (MA); U.S. foreign policy (MA). Part-time programs available. *Entrance requirements:* Additional exam requirements/recommendations for international students: Required—TOEFL (minimum score 580 paper-based; 237 computer-based), TWE (minimum score 5). Electronic applications accepted. *Faculty research:* American foreign politics, Middle East, security studies.

Jones International University, School of Business, Centennial, CO 80112. Offers accounting (MBA); business communication (MABC); entrepreneurship (MABC, MBA); finance (MBA); global enterprise management (MBA); health care management (MBA); information security management (MBA); information technology management (MBA); leadership and influence (MABC); leading the customer-driven organization (MABC); negotiation and conflict management (MBA); project management (MABC, MBA). Program only offered online. Part-time and evening/weekend programs available. Postbaccalaureate distance learning degree programs offered (no on-campus study). *Degree requirements:* For master's, capstone project. *Entrance requirements:* For master's, minimum cumulative GPA of 2.5. Additional exam requirements/recommendations for international students: Recommended—TOEFL (minimum score 550 paper-based; 213 computer-based). Electronic applications accepted.

Kennesaw State University, College of Humanities and Social Sciences, Program in Conflict Management, Kennesaw, GA 30144-5591. Offers MSCM. Evening/weekend programs available. *Faculty:* 6 full-time (3 women). *Students:* 50 full-time (29 women); includes 15 minority (12 African Americans, 1 American Indian/Alaska Native, 1 Asian American or Pacific Islander, 1 Hispanic American), 4 international. Average age 38. 38 applicants, 71% accepted, 24 enrolled. In 2009, 27 master's awarded. *Entrance requirements:* For master's, GMAT, GRE, LSAT. Additional exam requirements/recommendations for international students: Required—TOEFL (minimum score 550 paper-based; 213 computer-based; 80 iBT), IELTS (minimum score 6). *Application deadline:* For fall admission, 6/1 for domestic and international students. Applications are processed on a rolling basis. Application fee: $60. Electronic applications accepted. *Expenses:* Tuition, state resident: full-time $2341; part-time $196 per credit hour. Tuition, nonresident: full-time $9396; part-time $783 per credit hour. Required fees: $573 per semester. *Financial support:* In 2009–10, 1 research assistantship with full tuition reimbursement (averaging $15,000 per year) was awarded; Federal Work-Study and unspecified assistantships also available. Support available to part-time students. Financial award application deadline: 6/15; financial award applicants required to submit FAFSA. *Unit head:* Dr. Linda Johnston, Director, 770-423-6299, Fax: 770-423-6312, E-mail: ljohnsto@kennesaw.edu. *Application contact:* Vilma Marquez, Admissions Counselor, 770-420-4377, Fax: 770-423-6885, E-mail: ksugrad@kennesaw.edu.

Lipscomb University, Institute for Conflict Management, Nashville, TN 37204-3951. Offers MA, Certificate. Part-time and evening/weekend programs available. *Faculty:* 1 full-time (0 women), 5 part-time/adjunct (1 woman). *Students:* 15 full-time (7 women), 20 part-time (13 women); includes 5 minority (all African Americans). Average age 41. 21 applicants, 57% accepted, 9 enrolled. In 2009, 4 master's, 3 other advanced degrees awarded. *Degree requirements:* For master's, completion of externship. *Entrance requirements:* For master's, GRE, GMAT, LSAT or equivalent, 3 years work experience. *Application deadline:* Applications are processed on a rolling basis. Application fee: $50 ($75 for international students). *Expenses:* Contact institution. *Unit head:* Dr. Larry Bridgesmith, Executive Director, 615-966-7145, Fax: 615-966-7143, E-mail: larry.bridgesmith@lipscomb.edu. *Application contact:* Sherri Guenther, Administrative Assistant, 615-966-7140, Fax: 615-966-7143, E-mail: sherri.guenther@lipscomb.edu.

Lipscomb University, MBA Program, Nashville, TN 37204-3951. Offers accounting (MBA); business administration (general) (MBA); conflict management (MBA); financial services (MBA); healthcare management (MBA); leadership (MBA); nonprofit management (MBA); sports administration (MBA); sustainable practice (MBA). *Accreditation:* ACBSP. Part-time and evening/weekend programs available. *Faculty:* 10 full-time (1 woman), 7 part-time/adjunct (2 women). *Students:* 43 full-time (23 women), 86 part-time (38 women); includes 23 minority (18 African Americans, 1 Asian American or Pacific Islander, 4 Hispanic Americans), 1 international. Average age 31. 95 applicants, 64% accepted, 35 enrolled. In 2009, 59 master's awarded. *Entrance requirements:* For master's, GMAT, interview, 2 references, resume. Additional exam requirements/recommendations for international students: Required—TOEFL (minimum score 570 paper-based; 230 computer-based). *Application deadline:* For fall admission, 2/1 for international students; for winter admission, 6/1 for international students. Applications are processed on a rolling basis. Application fee: $50 ($75 for international students). Electronic applications accepted. *Expenses:* Contact institution. *Financial support:* Career-related internships or fieldwork, Federal Work-Study, scholarships/grants, tuition waivers (partial), and unspecified assistantships available. Support available to part-time students. Financial award application deadline: 7/1; financial award applicants required to submit FAFSA. *Faculty research:* Impact of spirituality on organization commitment, leadership, psychological empowerment, training. *Unit head:* Dr. Mike Kendrick, Interim Chair of Graduate Business Studies, 615-966-1833, Fax: 615-966-1818, E-mail: mikekendrick@lipscomb.edu. *Application contact:* Emily Landsdell, 615-966-5284, E-mail: emily.lansdell@lipscomb.edu.

Montclair State University, The Graduate School, College of Humanities and Social Sciences, Department of Justice Studies, Montclair, NJ 07043-1624. Offers conflict management in the workplace (Certificate); dispute resolution (MA); governance, compliance and regulation (MA); intellectual property (MA); law and governance (MA); legal management, information and technology (MA); paralegal studies (Certificate). Part-time and evening/weekend programs available. *Faculty:* 10 full-time (8 women), 17 part-time/adjunct (10 women). *Students:* 9 full-time (6 women), 17 part-time (10 women). Average age 36. 15 applicants, 100% accepted, 8 enrolled. In 2009, 12 master's, 16 other advanced degrees awarded. *Degree requirements:* For master's, comprehensive exam, thesis or alternative. *Entrance requirements:* For master's, GRE General Test, 2 letters of recommendation; for Certificate, 2 letters of recommendation. Additional exam requirements/recommendations for international students: Required—TOEFL (minimum score 83 computer-based), or IELTS. *Application deadline:* For fall admission, 6/1 for international students; for spring admission, 10/1 for international students. Applications are processed on a rolling basis. Application fee: $60. Electronic applications accepted. *Expenses:* Tuition, area resident: Part-time $486.74 per credit. Tuition, state resident: part-time $486.74 per credit. Tuition, nonresident: part-time $751.34 per credit. Tuition and fees vary according to degree level and program. *Financial support:* Federal Work-Study and scholarships/grants available. Support available to part-time students. Financial award application deadline: 3/1. *Unit head:* Dr. Norma Connolly, Chairperson, 973-655-4152, E-mail: connolyn@mail.montclair.edu. *Application contact:* Amy Aiello, Director of Graduate Admissions and Operations, 973-655-4000, E-mail: graduate.school@montclair.edu.

National Defense University, College of International Security Affairs, Washington, DC 20319-5066. Offers strategic security studies (MA), including conflict management, counterterrorism, homeland defense/ security, international security studies. Part-time and evening/weekend programs available. *Degree requirements:* For master's, thesis. *Entrance requirements:* Additional exam requirements/recommendations for international students: Required—TOEFL.

National University, Academic Affairs, College of Letters and Sciences, Department of Professional Studies, La Jolla, CA 92037-1011. Offers forensic science (MFS), including criminalistics and investigation; public administration (MPA), including alternative dispute resolution, human resource management, organizational leadership, public finance. Part-time and evening/weekend programs available. Postbaccalaureate distance learning degree programs offered (no on-campus study). *Faculty:* 5 full-time (3 women), 27 part-time/adjunct (7 women). *Students:* 167 full-time (95 women), 246 part-time (133 women); includes 188 minority (71 African Americans, 2 American Indian/Alaska Native, 41 Asian Americans or Pacific Islanders, 74 Hispanic Americans). Average age 38. 284 applicants, 100% accepted, 206 enrolled. In 2009, 104 master's awarded. *Degree requirements:* For master's, thesis. *Entrance requirements:* For master's, interview, minimum GPA of 2.5. Additional exam requirements/recommendations for international students: Required—TOEFL (minimum score 550 paper-based; 213 computer-based; 79 iBT), IELTS (minimum score 6). *Application deadline:* Applications are processed on a rolling basis. Application fee: $60 ($65 for international students). Electronic applications accepted. *Expenses:* Tuition: Part-time $338 per quarter hour. *Financial support:* Career-related internships or fieldwork, institutionally sponsored loans, scholarships/grants, and tuition waivers (partial) available. Support available to part-time students. Financial award application deadline: 6/30; financial award applicants required to submit FAFSA. *Unit head:* Chandrika M. Kelso, Associate Professor and Chair, 858-642-8433, Fax: 858-642-8715, E-mail: ckelso@nu.edu. *Application contact:* Dominick Giovanniello, Associate Regional Dean—San Diego, 800-NAT-UNIV, Fax: 858-541-7792, E-mail: dgiovann@nu.edu.

National University, Academic Affairs, School of Business and Management, Department of Leadership and Business Administration, La Jolla, CA 92037-1011. Offers alternative dispute resolution (MBA); e-business (MBA); financial management (MBA); human resource management (MBA); human resources management (MA); international business (MBA); knowledge management (MS); marketing (MBA); organizational leadership (MBA, MS); technology management (MBA). Part-time and evening/weekend programs available. Postbaccalaureate distance learning degree programs offered (no on-campus study). *Faculty:* 4 full-time (2 women), 22 part-time/adjunct (9 women). *Students:* 95 full-time (56 women), 228 part-time (129 women); includes 63 African Americans, 24 Asian Americans or Pacific Islanders, 61 Hispanic Americans, 6 international. Average age 38. 191 applicants, 100% accepted, 131 enrolled. In 2009, 62 master's awarded. *Degree requirements:* For master's, thesis. *Entrance requirements:* For master's, interview, minimum GPA of 2.5. Additional exam requirements/recommendations for international students: Required—TOEFL (minimum score 550 paper-based; 213 computer-based; 79 iBT), IELTS (minimum score 6). *Application deadline:* Applications are processed on a rolling basis. Application fee: $60 ($65 for international students). Electronic applications accepted. *Expenses:* Tuition: Part-time $338 per quarter hour. *Financial support:* Career-related internships or fieldwork, institutionally sponsored loans, scholarships/grants, and tuition waivers (partial) available. Support available to part-time students. Financial award application deadline: 6/30; financial award applicants required to submit FAFSA. *Unit head:* Dr. George Drops, Chair and Professor, 858-642-8438, Fax: 858-642-8406, E-mail: gdrops@nu.edu. *Application contact:* Dominick Giovanniello, Associate Regional Dean—San Diego, 800-NAT-UNIV, Fax: 858-541-7792, E-mail: dgiovann@nu.edu.

New York University, School of Continuing and Professional Studies, Center for Global Affairs, New York, NY 10012-1019. Offers global affairs (MS), including environment/energy policy, human rights and humanitarian assistance, international law, dispute settlement, and institutions, international relations, peace building, private sector: international business, economics, and development, transnational security. Part-time and evening/weekend programs available. *Faculty:* 9 full-time (3 women), 31 part-time/adjunct (14 women). *Students:* 120 full-time (82 women), 179 part-time (121 women); includes 22 minority (1 American Indian/Alaska Native, 21 Asian Americans or Pacific Islanders), 27 international. Average age 30. 419 applicants, 59% accepted, 94 enrolled. In 2009, 86 master's awarded. *Degree requirements:* For master's, thesis. *Entrance requirements:* For master's, GRE General Test or GMAT (for recent graduates), 2 letters of recommendation, resume. Additional exam requirements/recommendations for international students: Required—TOEFL (minimum score 600 paper-based; 250 computer-based; 100 iBT), TWE. *Application deadline:* For fall admission, 2/1 priority date for domestic and international students; for spring admission, 10/15 priority date for domestic students, 8/15 priority date for international students. Applications are processed on a rolling basis. Application fee: $75. Electronic applications accepted. *Expenses:* Tuition: Full-time $30,528; part-time $1272 per credit. Required fees: $2177. *Financial support:* In 2009–10, 159 students received support, including 159 fellowships (averaging $2,932 per year); institutionally sponsored loans, scholarships/grants, and tuition waivers (partial) also available. Support available to part-time students. Financial award application deadline: 3/1; financial award applicants required to submit FAFSA. *Unit head:* Dr. Vera Jelinek, Assistant Dean and Director, 212-992-8380, Fax: 212-995-3638, E-mail: vera.jelinek@nyu.edu. *Application contact:* Mykellan Ledden, Associate Director, 212-992-8380, Fax: 212-995-3638, E-mail: mykellan.ledden@nyu.edu.

Norwich University, School of Graduate and Continuing Studies, Program in Diplomacy, Northfield, VT 05663. Offers international commerce (MA); international conflict management (MA); international terrorism (MA). Evening/weekend programs available. *Faculty:* 48 part-time/adjunct (8 women). *Students:* 798 full-time (233 women); includes 133 minority (55 African Americans, 23 Asian Americans or Pacific Islanders, 55 Hispanic Americans). Average age 38. 1,112 applicants, 77% accepted. In 2009, 145 master's awarded. *Degree requirements:* For master's, comprehensive exam, thesis optional. *Entrance requirements:* For master's, minimum undergraduate GPA of 2.75. Additional exam requirements/recommendations for international students: Required—TOEFL. *Application deadline:* For fall admission, 8/10 for domestic and international students; for winter admission, 11/7 for domestic and international students; for spring admission, 2/6 for domestic and international students. Application fee: $50. Electronic applications accepted. Full-time tuition and fees vary according to course level and course load. *Financial support:* Scholarships/grants available. Financial award applicants required to submit FAFSA. *Unit head:* Dr. Harold Kearsley, Program Director, 802-485-2730, E-mail: hkearsley@norwich.edu. *Application contact:* Lars Nielsen, Associate Program Director, 802-485-2853, Fax: 802-485-2533, E-mail: lnielsen@norwich.edu.

Nova Southeastern University, Graduate School of Humanities and Social Sciences, Department of Conflict Analysis and Resolution, Doctor of Conflict Analysis and Resolution Program, Fort Lauderdale, FL 33314-7796. Offers PhD, PhD/JD. Part-time and evening/weekend programs available. Postbaccalaureate distance learning degree programs offered (minimal on-campus study). *Faculty:* 10 full-time (5 women), 10 part-time/adjunct (4 women). *Students:* 137 full-time (76 women), 104 part-time (58 women); includes 115 minority (84 African Americans, 2 American Indian/Alaska Native, 3 Asian Americans or Pacific Islanders, 26 Hispanic Americans), 25 international. 75 applicants, 92% accepted, 38 enrolled. In 2009, 5 doctorates awarded. *Degree requirements:* For doctorate, comprehensive exam, thesis/dissertation, qualifying exam. *Entrance requirements:* For doctorate, interview, minimum GPA of 3.0. Additional exam requirements/recommendations for international students: Required—TOEFL. *Application deadline:* For fall admission, 7/1 priority date for domestic and international students; for winter admission, 11/1 priority date for domestic and international students; for spring admission, 5/1 priority date for domestic students, 3/1 priority date for international students. Applications are processed on a rolling basis. Application fee: $50. Electronic applications accepted. *Financial support:* In 2009–10, 144 students received support, including 7 research assistantships with partial tuition reimbursements available (averaging $15,600 per year), 3 teaching assistantships; career-related internships or fieldwork, Federal Work-Study, scholarships/grants, and unspecified assistantships also available. Financial award application deadline: 4/1; financial award applicants required to submit CSS PROFILE. *Faculty research:* International conflict, violence prevention, facilitation and mediation, communication and conflict. *Unit head:* Neil Katz, Chair, 954-262-3040, Fax: 954-262-3050, E-mail: kneil@nova.edu. *Application contact:* Marcia Arango, Student Recruitment Coordinator, 954-262-3006, Fax: 954-262-3968, E-mail: marango@nsu.nova.edu.

Nova Southeastern University, Graduate School of Humanities and Social Sciences, Department of Conflict Analysis and Resolution, Master's Program in Conflict Analysis and Resolution, Fort Lauderdale, FL 33314-7796. Offers MS, JD/MS. Part-time and evening/weekend programs available. Postbaccalaureate distance learning degree programs offered (minimal on-campus study). *Faculty:* 10 full-time (5 women), 10 part-time/adjunct (4 women). *Students:* 23 full-time (13 women), 47 part-time (37 women); includes 35 minority (18 African Americans, 2 Asian Americans or Pacific Islanders, 15 Hispanic Americans), 8 international. 67 applicants, 63% accepted, 40 enrolled. In 2009, 27 master's awarded. *Degree requirements:* For master's, comprehensive exam, thesis optional. *Entrance requirements:* For master's, interview, minimum GPA of 3.0, writing sample. Additional exam requirements/recommendations for international students: Required—TOEFL. Application fee: $50. *Faculty research:* International conflict, violence prevention, communication and conflict facilitation, mediation. *Unit head:* Neil Katz, Chair, 954-262-3040, Fax: 954-262-3968, E-mail: kneil@nova.edu. *Application contact:* Marcia Arango, Student Recruitment Coordinator, 954-262-3006, Fax: 954-262-3968, E-mail: marango@nsu.nova.edu.

Old Dominion University, College of Arts and Letters, Graduate Programs in International Studies, Norfolk, VA 23529. Offers conflict and cooperation (PhD), including women's studies certificate; U.S. foreign policy (MA), including modeling and simulation certificate. Part-time programs available. *Faculty:* 14 full-time (3 women). *Students:* 53 full-time (26 women), 44 part-time (17 women); includes 6 minority (3 African Americans, 3 Hispanic Americans), 29 international. Average age 32. 99 applicants, 54% accepted, 30 enrolled. In 2009, 18 master's, 5 doctorates awarded. Terminal master's awarded for partial completion of doctoral program. *Degree requirements:* For master's, one foreign language, comprehensive exam, thesis optional; for doctorate, one foreign language, comprehensive exam, thesis/dissertation. *Entrance requirements:* For master's, GRE General Test, sample of written work, 2 letters of recommendation; for doctorate, GRE General Test, sample of written work, 3 letters of recommendation. Additional exam requirements/recommendations for international students: Required—TOEFL (minimum score 570 paper-based; 230 computer-based). *Application deadline:* For fall admission, 3/15 for domestic students, 2/15 for international students; for spring admission, 10/15 for domestic and international students. Application fee: $40. Electronic applications accepted. *Expenses:* Tuition, state resident: full-time $8112; part-time $338 per credit. Tuition, nonresident: full-time $20,256; part-time $844 per credit. Required fees: $119 per semester. One-time fee: $50. *Financial support:* In 2009–10, 20 students received support, including 2 fellowships (averaging $13,000 per year), 9 research assistantships with tuition reimbursements available (averaging $11,000 per year), 9 teaching assistantships with tuition reimbursements available (averaging $11,000 per year); career-related internships or fieldwork, institutionally sponsored loans, scholarships/grants, and unspecified assistantships also available. Support available to part-time students. Financial award application deadline: 2/15; financial award applicants required to submit FAFSA. *Faculty research:* U. S. foreign policy, international security, transatlantic and transpacific relations, transnational issues, IPE and development. Total annual research expenditures: $330,391. *Unit head:* Dr. Regina Karp, Graduate Program Director, 757-683-5700, Fax: 757-683-5701, E-mail: rkarp@odu.edu. *Application contact:* Dr. Angelica Huizar, 757-683-3988, Fax: 757-683-5701, E-mail: ahuizar@odu.edu.

Pepperdine University, School of Law, Program in Dispute Resolution, Malibu, CA 90263. Offers LL M, MDR. *Degree requirements:* For master's, thesis. *Entrance requirements:* For master's, GRE General Test or LSAT. *Expenses:* Contact institution.

Portland State University, Graduate Studies, College of Liberal Arts and Sciences, Program in Conflict Resolution, Portland, OR 97207-0751. Offers MA, MS. *Degree requirements:* For master's, thesis or alternative, practicum. *Entrance requirements:* For master's, 3 letters of recommendation. Additional exam requirements/recommendations for international students: Required—TOEFL (minimum score 550 paper-based; 213 computer-based).

Regis University, College for Professional Studies, MA Program, Denver, CO 80221-1099. Offers criminology (MA); fine arts administration (Certificate); language and communication (MA); mediation (Certificate); psychology (MA); self-designed major (MA); social justice, peace, and reconciliation (Certificate); social science (MA); technical communication (Certificate). Program also offered in Henderson and Las Vegas (Summerlin), NV. Part-time and evening/weekend programs available. Postbaccalaureate distance learning degree programs offered (minimal on-campus study). *Degree requirements:* For master's, thesis, research project. *Entrance requirements:* For master's, resume, recommendations. Additional exam requirements/recommendations for international students: Required—TOEFL (minimum score 213 computer-based), TWE (minimum score 5). Electronic applications accepted. *Expenses:* Contact institution. *Faculty research:* Independent/nonresidential graduate study: new methods and models, adult learning and the capstone experience, Goal Setting, behavior of Adult students, Innovative Studies for Community Colleges.

Royal Roads University, Graduate Studies, Peace and Conflict Studies Program, Victoria, BC V9B 5Y2, Canada. Offers conflict analysis (G Dip); conflict analysis and management (MA); disaster and emergency management (MA); human security and peacebuilding (MA). Postbaccalaureate distance learning degree programs offered (minimal on-campus study). *Degree requirements:* For master's, thesis. *Entrance requirements:* For master's, 5-7 years of related work experience. Additional exam requirements/recommendations for international students: Required—TOEFL (paper-based 570; computer-based 233) or IELTS (paper-based 7) (recommended). Electronic applications accepted. *Faculty research:* Conflict analysis, ethno-political conflict reconciliation, international relations, displaced persons.

St. Edward's University, School of Education, Program in Teaching, Austin, TX 78704. Offers curriculum leadership (Certificate); instructional technology (Certificate); mentoring and supervision (Certificate); sports management (Certificate); teaching (MA), including conflict resolution, initial teacher certification, liberal arts, organization development and training, sports management, teacher leadership. Part-time and evening/weekend programs available. *Students:* 5 full-time (4 women), 36 part-time (26 women); includes 10 minority (1 African American, 9 Hispanic Americans). Average age 30. 23 applicants, 70% accepted, 12 enrolled. In 2009, 9 master's awarded. *Degree requirements:* For master's, minimum of 24 resident hours. *Entrance requirements:* For master's, GRE General Test, minimum GPA of 3.0 in last 60 hours or 2.75 overall. Additional exam requirements/recommendations for international students: Required—TOEFL (minimum score 550 paper-based; 213 computer-based; 79 iBT) or IELTS (minimum score 6). *Application deadline:* For fall admission, 7/1 for domestic and international students; for spring admission, 11/1 for domestic and international students. Applications are processed on a rolling basis. Application fee: $45 ($50 for international students). Electronic applications accepted. *Expenses:* Tuition: Full-time $14,922; part-time $829 per credit hour. Required fees: $50 per trimester. Full-time tuition and fees vary according to course load and program. *Financial support:* In 2009–10, 3 students received support. Scholarships/grants available. *Unit head:* Dr. David Hollier, Director, 512-448-8666, Fax: 512-428-1372, E-mail: davidrh@stedwards.edu. *Application contact:* Kay L. Arnold, Assistant Director of Admissions, 512-233-1636, Fax: 512-428-1032, E-mail: kayla@stedwards.edu.

St. Edward's University, School of Management and Business, Program in Human Services, Austin, TX 78704. Offers administration (Certificate); conflict resolution (Certificate); family mediation (Certificate); human services (MA), including administration, conflict resolution, human resource management, organization development and training, social and psychological services; mediation (Certificate); organization development and training (Certificate). Part-time and evening/weekend programs available. *Students:* 4 full-time (3 women), 51 part-time (43 women); includes 24 minority (9 African Americans, 2 Asian Americans or Pacific Islanders, 13 Hispanic Americans). Average age 34. 23 applicants, 96% accepted, 18 enrolled. In 2009, 19 master's awarded. *Degree requirements:* For master's, minimum of 24 resident hours. *Entrance requirements:* For master's, GRE General Test, GMAT, minimum GPA of 2.75 in last 60 hours of course work. Additional exam requirements/recommendations for international students: Required—TOEFL (minimum score 550 paper-based; 213 computer-based; 79 iBT) or IELTS (minimum score 6). *Application deadline:* For fall admission, 7/1 for domestic and international students; for spring admission, 11/1 for domestic and international students. Applications are processed on a rolling basis. Application fee: $45 ($50 for international students). Electronic applications accepted. *Expenses:* Tuition: Full-time $14,922; part-time $829 per credit hour. Required fees: $50 per trimester. Full-time tuition and fees vary according to course load and program. *Financial support:* In 2009–10, 2 students received support. Scholarships/grants available. *Faculty research:* Leadership development, organizational management, public policy. *Unit head:* Dr. Constance D. Porter, Director, 512-416-5827, Fax: 512-448-8492, E-mail: constanp@stedwards.edu. *Application contact:* Kay L. Arnold, Assistant Director of Admissions, 512-233-1636, Fax: 512-428-1032, E-mail: kayla@stedwards.edu.

Saint Paul University, Faculty of Human Sciences, Program in Conflict Studies, Ottawa, ON K1S 1C4, Canada. Offers MA. Part-time programs available. *Entrance requirements:* For master's, H=honors BA, B average.

Salisbury University, Graduate Division, Program in Conflict Analysis and Dispute Resolution, Salisbury, MD 21801-6837. Offers MA. *Faculty:* 3 full-time (0 women). *Students:* 17 full-time (12 women), 1 (woman) part-time; includes 2 minority (1 African American, 1 American Indian/Alaska Native), 1 international. Average age 32. 33 applicants, 67% accepted, 2 enrolled. *Expenses:* Tuition, area resident: Part-time $278 per credit hour. Tuition, state resident: part-time $278 per credit hour. Tuition, nonresident: part-time $574 per credit hour. Required fees: $57 per credit hour. *Financial support:* In 2009–10, 10 students received support. *Unit head:* Rob LaChance, Program Director, 410-677-0231, E-mail: rmlachance@salisbury.edu. *Application contact:* Rob LaChance, Program Director, 410-677-0231, E-mail: rmlachance@salisbury.edu.

SIT Graduate Institute, Graduate Programs, Master's Programs in Intercultural Service, Leadership, and Management, Program in Conflict Transformation, Brattleboro, VT 05302-0676. Offers MA.

Southern Methodist University, Annette Caldwell Simmons School of Education and Human Development, Department of Dispute Resolution and Counseling, Dallas, TX 75275. Offers counseling (MS); dispute resolution (MA, Certificate). Part-time programs available. *Faculty:* 6 full-time (2 women), 24 part-time/adjunct (11 women). *Students:* 5 full-time (all women), 207 part-time (165 women); includes 43 minority (18 African Americans, 8 Asian Americans or Pacific Islanders, 17 Hispanic Americans), 6 international. Average age 33. 103 applicants, 50% accepted, 46 enrolled. In 2009, 62 master's, 10 other advanced degrees awarded. *Degree requirements:* For master's, practica experience, 2 internships (counseling). *Entrance requirements:* For master's, minimum undergraduate GPA of 2.75 (for dispute resolution), 3.0 (for counseling); 3 letters of recommendation. Additional exam requirements/recommendations for international students: Required—TOEFL. *Application deadline:* For fall admission, 5/1 for domestic students; for spring admission, 12/1 for domestic students. Applications are processed on a rolling basis. Application fee: $75. Electronic applications accepted. *Unit head:* Dr. Tony Picchioni, Department Chair, 972-473-3408, Fax: 972-473-3425. *Application contact:* Cynthia McIntyre, Program Manager, 972-473-3431, Fax: 972-473-3425, E-mail: adr@smu.edu or counselingmaster@smu.edu.

Sullivan University, School of Business, Louisville, KY 40205. Offers business administration (MBA); collaborative leadership (MSCL); conflict management (MSCM); dispute resolution (MSDR); executive business administration (EMBA); human resource leadership (MSHRL); information technology (MSMIT); management and information technology (MBIT); pharmacy (Pharm D). Part-time programs available. Postbaccalaureate distance learning degree programs offered (no on-campus study). *Entrance requirements:* Additional exam requirements/recommendations for international students: Required—TOEFL.

Syracuse University, Maxwell School of Citizenship and Public Affairs, Program in Conflict Resolution, Syracuse, NY 13244. Offers CAS. *Students:* 1 (woman) part-time. Average age 42. 21 applicants, 95% accepted, 0 enrolled. In 2009, 48 CASs awarded. *Expenses:* Tuition: Full-time $26,808; part-time $1117 per credit. Required fees: $1024. *Unit head:* Catherine Gerard, Director, 315-443-2367, E-mail: parc@syr.edu. *Application contact:* Catherine Gerard, Director, 315-443-2367, E-mail: parc@syr.edu.

Syracuse University, Maxwell School of Citizenship and Public Affairs, Program in Post Conflict Reconstruction, Syracuse, NY 13244. Offers Certificate. *Expenses:* Tuition: Full-time $26,808; part-time $1117 per credit. Required fees: $1024. *Unit head:* Mitchel Wallerstein, Dean, 315-443-2253, Fax: 315-443-3385, E-mail: mwallers@syr.edu. *Application contact:* Lori Klish, Director of Graduate Admissions, 315-443-4492, E-mail: grad@syr.edu.

Tufts University, Fletcher School of Law and Diplomacy, Medford, MA 02155. Offers LL M, MA, MAHA, MALD, MIB, PhD, DVM/MA, JD/MALD, MALD/MA, MALD/MBA, MALD/MS, MD/MA. Postbaccalaureate distance learning degree programs offered (minimal on-campus study). *Faculty:* 34 full-time (7 women), 31 part-time/adjunct (8 women). *Students:* 443 full-time (224 women), 7 part-time (4 women); includes 51 minority (6 African Americans, 1 American Indian/Alaska Native, 26 Asian Americans or Pacific Islanders, 18 Hispanic Americans), 165 international. Average age 31. 1,866 applicants, 40% accepted, 292 enrolled. In 2009, 364 master's, 12 doctorates awarded. *Degree requirements:* For master's, one foreign language, thesis; for doctorate, one foreign language, comprehensive exam, thesis/dissertation, dissertation defense. *Entrance requirements:* For master's and doctorate, GMAT or GRE General Test. Additional exam requirements/recommendations for international students: Required—TOEFL (minimum score 600 paper-based; 250 computer-based; 100 iBT), IELTS (minimum score 7). *Application deadline:* For fall admission, 1/15 for domestic and international students; for spring admission, 10/15 for domestic and international students. Application fee: $70. Electronic applications accepted. *Expenses:* Contact institution. *Financial support:* Federal Work-Study, institutionally sponsored loans, scholarships/grants, and tuition waivers (partial) available. Financial award application deadline: 1/15; financial award applicants required to submit FAFSA. *Faculty research:* Negotiation and conflict resolution, international organizations, international business and economic law, security studies, development economics. *Unit head:* Stephen W. Bosworth, Dean, 617-627-3050, Fax: 617-627-3712. *Application contact:* Laurie A. Hurley, E-mail: fletcheradmissions@tufts.edu.

TUI University, College of Business Administration, Program in Business Administration, Cypress, CA 90630. Offers business administration (PhD); conflict and negotiation management (MBA); criminal justice administration (MBA); entrepreneurship (MBA); finance (MBA); general management (MBA); government accounting (MBA); human resource management (MBA); information security and digital assurance management (MBA); information technology management (MBA); international business (MBA); logistics management (MBA); marketing (MBA); project management (MBA); public management (MBA); quality management (MBA); strategic leadership (MBA). Part-time and evening/weekend programs available. Postbaccalaureate distance learning degree programs offered (no on-campus study). *Degree requirements:* For doctorate, comprehensive exam, thesis/dissertation, defense of dissertation. *Entrance requirements:* For master's, minimum GPA of 2.5 (students with GPA 3.0 or greater may transfer up to 30% of graduate level credits); for doctorate, minimum GPA of 3.4, curriculum vitae, course work in research methods or statistics. Additional exam requirements/recommendations for international students: Required—TOEFL. Electronic applications accepted.

Conflict Resolution and Mediation/Peace Studies

United Theological Seminary of the Twin Cities, Professional Program, New Brighton, MN 55112-2598. Offers advanced theological studies (Diploma); justice and peace studies (M Div, MA); leadership toward racial justice (MA, Certificate); leadership towards racial justice (M Div); Methodist studies (M Div, MA, Certificate); ministry (D Min); ministry renewal and professional development (Certificate); pastoral care and counseling (M Div, MA, MARL); religion and theology (MA); theological and religious studies (Certificate); theology and the arts (M Div, MA); urban ministry (M Div, MA, MARL); women's studies: religion, theology and ministry (MA); women's studies: religions, theology and ministry (M Div). *Accreditation:* ACIPE; ATS. Part-time and evening/weekend programs available. *Faculty:* 9 full-time (6 women), 22 part-time/adjunct (10 women). *Students:* 49 full-time (34 women), 105 part-time (68 women). Average age 47. 41 applicants, 98% accepted, 34 enrolled. In 2009, 24 first professional degrees, 5 master's, 2 doctorates, 2 other advanced degrees awarded. *Degree requirements:* For master's, thesis; for doctorate, comprehensive exam, thesis/dissertation; for M Div, integrative notebook, spiritual chronicle. *Entrance requirements:* For M Div and master's, minimum GPA of 2.75; strong analytical, reflective thinking and writing skills; vocational and academic goals compatible with those of Seminary; for doctorate, M Div or equivalent, minimum GPA of 3.0, 3 years experience in professional ministry; for other advanced degree, BA or equivalent life experience; strong analytical, reflective thinking and writing skills (Certificate); proficiency in English language, previous study of theology at a theological school, recommendation of student's denomination (Diploma). Additional exam requirements/recommendations for international students: Required—TOEFL (minimum score 550 paper-based). *Application deadline:* For fall admission, 7/1 priority date for domestic students, 11/1 priority date for international students; for winter admission, 11/1 priority date for domestic students; for spring admission, 11/15 priority date for domestic students. Applications are processed on a rolling basis. Application fee: $50. *Expenses:* Tuition: Full-time $11,502; part-time $426 per credit hour. Required fees: $295; $155 per term. One-time fee: $25. Tuition and fees vary according to course load, degree level and program. *Financial support:* In 2009–10, 120 students received support. Career-related internships or fieldwork, institutionally sponsored loans, and scholarships/grants available. Support available to part-time students. Financial award application deadline: 5/1; financial award applicants required to submit FAFSA. *Unit head:* Dr. Richard D. Weis, Dean of the Seminary, 651-255-6108 Ext. 108, Fax: 651-633-4315, E-mail: rweis@unitedseminary.edu. *Application contact:* Rev. Glen Herrington-Hall, Director of Admissions, 651-255-6107 Ext. 107, Fax: 651-633-4315, E-mail: gherrington-hall@unitedseminary.edu.

Universidad del Turabo, Graduate Programs, School of Social Sciences and Humanities, Programs in Public Affairs, Gurabo, PR 00778-3030. Offers arts administration (MPA); conflict and mediation studies (MPA); criminal justice studies (MPA); forensic science (MPA); human services administration (MPA). *Entrance requirements:* For master's, GRE, EXADEP, interview.

Université de Sherbrooke, Faculty of Law, Sherbrooke, QC J1K 2R1, Canada. Offers alternative dispute resolution (LL M, Diploma); biotechnology (LL B); business administration (LL B); business law (Diploma); health law (LL M, Diploma); law (LL B, LL D); legal management (Diploma); notarial law (DDN); transnational law (Diploma). Part-time and evening/weekend programs available. *Degree requirements:* For master's, thesis; for other advanced degree, one foreign language. *Entrance requirements:* For master's and other advanced degree, LL B. Electronic applications accepted.

University of Arkansas at Little Rock, Graduate School, College of Professional Studies, Program in Conflict Mediation, Little Rock, AR 72204-1099. Offers Graduate Certificate.

University of Baltimore, Graduate School, The Yale Gordon College of Liberal Arts, Program in Negotiations and Conflict Management, Baltimore, MD 21201-5779. Offers negotiations and conflict management (MS). Part-time and evening/weekend programs available. *Degree requirements:* For master's, thesis optional, internship. *Entrance requirements:* For master's, minimum GPA of 3.0. Additional exam requirements/recommendations for international students: Required—TOEFL (minimum score 550 paper-based; 213 computer-based). Electronic applications accepted. *Faculty research:* Communication and conflict, conflict management systems theory.

University of Bridgeport, International College, Bridgeport, CT 06604. Offers global development and peace (MA). Part-time and evening/weekend programs available. *Degree requirements:* For master's, thesis. *Entrance requirements:* Additional exam requirements/recommendations for international students: Recommended—TOEFL (minimum score 550 paper-based; 213 computer-based; 80 iBT), IELTS (minimum score 6.5).

University of Hawaii at Manoa, Graduate Division, College of Social Sciences, Spark M. Matsunaga Institute for Peace, Honolulu, HI 96822. Offers conflict resolution (Graduate Certificate). Part-time programs available. *Faculty:* 9 full-time (3 women), 8 part-time/adjunct (2 women). *Students:* 17 full-time (9 women), 10 part-time (6 women); includes 3 minority (all Asian Americans or Pacific Islanders), 9 international. Average age 34. 14 applicants, 71% accepted, 8 enrolled. In 2009, 12 Graduate Certificates awarded. *Entrance requirements:* For degree, GRE General Test. Additional exam requirements/recommendations for international students: Required—TOEFL (minimum score 540 paper-based; 207 computer-based; 76 iBT), IELTS (minimum score 5). *Application deadline:* For fall admission, 2/15 for domestic and international students; for spring admission, 9/30 for domestic and international students. Application fee: $60. *Expenses:* Tuition, state resident: full-time $8900; part-time $372 per credit. Tuition, nonresident: full-time $21,400; part-time $898 per credit. Required fees: $207 per semester. *Financial support:* In 2009–10, 1 student received support, including 2 fellowships (averaging $9,750 per year), 4 research assistantships (averaging $17,586 per year), 1 teaching assistantship (averaging $7,191 per year). *Application contact:* Dolores Foley, Chairperson, 808-956-6433, Fax: 808-956-9121, E-mail: dolores@hawaii.edu.

University of Massachusetts Amherst, Graduate School, College of Natural Sciences, Department of Psychology, Amherst, MA 01003. Offers clinical psychology (MS, PhD); cognitive psychology (MS, PhD); developmental science (MS, PhD); psychology of peace and violence (MS, PhD); social psychology (MS, PhD). *Accreditation:* APA (one or more programs are accredited). *Faculty:* 48 full-time (22 women). *Students:* 57 full-time (42 women), 13 part-time (10 women); includes 15 minority (6 African Americans, 6 Asian Americans or Pacific Islanders, 3 Hispanic Americans), 8 international. Average age 28. 381 applicants, 4% accepted, 11 enrolled. In 2009, 11 master's, 8 doctorates awarded. Terminal master's awarded for partial completion of doctoral program. *Degree requirements:* For master's, thesis; for doctorate, comprehensive exam, thesis/dissertation. *Entrance requirements:* For master's and doctorate, GRE General Test, 3 letters of recommendation. Additional exam requirements/recommendations for international students: Required—TOEFL (minimum score 550 paper-based; 213 computer-based; 80 iBT), IELTS (minimum score 6.5). *Application deadline:* For fall admission, 12/1 for domestic and international students. Applications are processed on a rolling basis. Application fee: $50 ($65 for international students). Electronic applications accepted. *Expenses:* Tuition, state resident: full-time $2640; part-time $110 per credit. Tuition, nonresident: full-time $9936; part-time $414 per credit. Tuition and fees vary according to course load. *Financial support:* In 2009–10, 8 fellowships with full tuition reimbursements (averaging $12,620 per year), 52 research assistantships with full tuition reimbursements (averaging $9,491 per year), 55 teaching assistantships with full tuition reimbursements (averaging $10,829 per year) were awarded; career-related internships or fieldwork, Federal Work-Study, scholarships/grants, traineeships, health care benefits, tuition waivers (full), and unspecified assistantships also available. Support available to part-time students. Financial award application deadline: 12/1. *Unit head:* Dr. Linda M. Isbell, Graduate Program Director, 413-545-2503, Fax: 413-545-0996. *Application contact:* Jean M. Ames, Supervisor of Admissions, 413-545-0722, Fax: 413-577-0010, E-mail: gradadm@grad.umass.edu.

University of Massachusetts Boston, Office of Graduate Studies, College of Public and Community Service, Program in Dispute Resolution, Boston, MA 02125-3393. Offers MA, Certificate. MA program accepts applications for fall admission only; Certificate program accepts applications for spring admission only. *Degree requirements:* For master's, practicum, final project. *Entrance requirements:* For master's, MAT or GRE, minimum GPA of 2.75; for Certificate, minimum GPA of 2.75. *Faculty research:* Mediation and negotiation, justice and conflict, cross-cultural mediation, environmental fairness, dispute resolution theory and ethics.

University of Missouri, Graduate School and School of Law, Program in Dispute Resolution, Columbia, MO 65211. Offers LL M. *Entrance requirements:* Additional exam requirements/recommendations for international students: Required—TOEFL (minimum score 600 paper-based; 250 computer-based; 100 iBT).

University of New Brunswick Fredericton, School of Graduate Studies, Policy Studies Program, Fredericton, NB E3B 5A3, Canada. Offers people, property and alternative dispute resolution (M Phil); philosophy politics and economics (M Phil); sustainable development (M Phil). Part-time programs available. *Faculty:* 6 full-time (2 women), 13 part-time/adjunct (2 women). *Students:* 8 full-time (3 women), 5 part-time (3 women). In 2009, 7 master's awarded. *Degree requirements:* For master's, thesis, report. *Entrance requirements:* For master's, minimum GPA of 3.5, BA; BA Honours. Additional exam requirements/recommendations for international students: Required—TOEFL (minimum score 600 paper-based; 250 computer-based; 100 iBT), TWE (minimum score 4), or IELTS (minimum score 7). Application fee: $50 Canadian dollars. Tuition and fees charges are reported in Canadian dollars. *Expenses:* Tuition, area resident: Full-time $5562 Canadian dollars; part-time $2781 Canadian dollars per year. Required fees: $49.75 Canadian dollars per term. *Financial support:* In 2009–10, 5 research assistantships (averaging $5,600 per year), 2 teaching assistantships (averaging $4,400 per year) were awarded. *Unit head:* Dr. Linda Eyre, Dean of Graduate Studies, 506-447-3044, Fax: 506-453-4817, E-mail: gradidst@unb.ca. *Application contact:* Janet Amurault, Graduate Secretary, 506-458-7558, Fax: 506-453-4817, E-mail: jamiraul@unb.ca.

University of New Haven, Graduate School, College of Arts and Sciences, Program in Industrial and Organizational Psychology, West Haven, CT 06516-1916. Offers conflict management (MA); human resource management (MA); industrial organizational psychology (MA); organizational development (MA); psychology of conflict management (Certificate). Part-time and evening/weekend programs available. *Faculty:* 5 full-time (3 women), 10 part-time/adjunct (5 women). *Students:* 97 full-time (59 women), 34 part-time (26 women); includes 20 minority (9 African Americans, 2 American Indian/Alaska Native, 2 Asian Americans or Pacific Islanders, 7 Hispanic Americans), 11 international. Average age 28. 85 applicants, 98% accepted, 48 enrolled. In 2009, 71 master's awarded. *Degree requirements:* For master's, thesis or alternative. *Entrance requirements:* Additional exam requirements/recommendations for international students: Required—TOEFL (minimum score 520 paper-based; 190 computer-based; 70 iBT); Recommended—IELTS (minimum score 5.5). *Application deadline:* For fall admission, 5/31 for international students; for winter admission, 10/15 for international students; for spring admission, 1/15 for international students. Applications are processed on a rolling basis. Application fee: $50. Electronic applications accepted. *Expenses:* Contact institution. *Financial support:* Research assistantships with partial tuition reimbursements, teaching assistantships with partial tuition reimbursements, career-related internships or fieldwork, Federal Work-Study, scholarships/grants, tuition waivers, and unspecified assistantships available. Support available to part-time students. Financial award applicants required to submit FAFSA. *Unit head:* Dr. Stuart D. Sidle, Coordinator, 203-932-7341. *Application contact:* Eloise Gormley, Information Contact, 203-932-7449.

The University of North Carolina at Greensboro, Graduate School, Program in Conflict Resolution, Greensboro, NC 27412-5001. Offers MA, Certificate. Electronic applications accepted.

University of Notre Dame, Graduate School, College of Arts and Letters, Division of Social Science, Joan B. Kroc Institute for International Peace Studies, Notre Dame, IN 46556. Offers MA, PhD. *Degree requirements:* For master's, one foreign language, comprehensive exam, thesis optional; for doctorate, one foreign language, comprehensive exam, thesis/dissertation. *Entrance requirements:* For master's, GRE General Test. Additional exam requirements/recommendations for international students: Required—TOEFL (minimum score 600 paper-based; 250 computer-based; 80 iBT). Electronic applications accepted. *Faculty research:* The role of international norms and institutions in peacemaking; the impact of religious, philosophical, and cultural influences on peace; the dynamics of intergroup conflict and conflict transformation; the promotion of social, economic, and environmental justice.

University of San Diego, Joan B. Kroc School of Peace Studies, San Diego, CA 92110-2492. Offers peace and justice studies (MA). *Faculty:* 2 full-time (1 woman), 1 part-time/adjunct (0 women). *Students:* 20 full-time (15 women); includes 3 minority (1 Asian American or Pacific Islander, 2 Hispanic Americans), 7 international. Average age 31. 60 applicants, 75% accepted, 20 enrolled. In 2009, 12 master's awarded. *Degree requirements:* For master's, capstone project. *Entrance requirements:* For master's, GRE General Test, minimum GPA of 3.0. Additional exam requirements/recommendations for international students: Required—TOEFL (minimum score 580 paper-based; 237 computer-based; 83 iBT), TWE. *Application deadline:* For fall admission, 2/15 for domestic and international students. Application fee: $45. Electronic applications accepted. *Expenses:* Tuition: Full-time $21,042; part-time $1169 per unit. Required fees: $224. Full-time tuition and fees vary according to course load and degree level. *Financial support:* In 2009–10, 20 students received support, including 9 fellowships; career-related internships or fieldwork, Federal Work-Study, institutionally sponsored loans, scholarships/grants, and unspecified assistantships also available. Support available to part-time students. Financial award application deadline: 4/1; financial award applicants required to submit FAFSA. *Faculty research:* Conflict analysis and resolution. *Unit head:* Fr. William Headley, Dean, E-mail: wheadley@sandiego.edu. *Application contact:* Dr. John Mosby, Associate Director of Graduate Admissions, 619-260-4524, Fax: 619-260-4158, E-mail: grads@sandiego.edu.

University of the Sacred Heart, Graduate Programs, Program in Systems of Justice, San Juan, PR 00914-0383. Offers human rights and anti-discriminatory processes (MASJ); mediation and transformation of conflicts (MASJ).

University of Victoria, Faculty of Graduate Studies, Faculty of Human and Social Development, School of Public Administration, Victoria, BC V8W 2Y2, Canada. Offers dispute resolution (MADR); public administration (MPA, PhD); MPA/LL B. Part-time and evening/weekend programs available. Postbaccalaureate distance learning degree programs offered. *Degree requirements:* For master's, thesis (for some programs), report; for doctorate, thesis/dissertation, candidacy exam. *Entrance requirements:* For master's, GMAT or GRE General Test, professional resume; for doctorate, GMAT or GRE General Test. Additional exam requirements/recommendations for international students: Required—TOEFL (minimum score 610 paper-based; 255 computer-based). Electronic applications accepted. *Faculty research:* Policy analysis, local government, performance management, energy markets, labor markets.

University of Wisconsin–Milwaukee, Graduate School, College of Letters and Sciences, Department of Communication, Milwaukee, WI 53201-0413. Offers communication (MA, PhD); mediation and negotiation (Certificate); rhetorical leadership (Certificate). Part-time programs available. *Faculty:* 19 full-time (11 women). *Students:* 17 full-time (14 women), 34 part-time (26 women); includes 4 minority (2 American Indian/Alaska Native, 2 Hispanic Americans), 7 international. Average age 30. 59 applicants, 68% accepted, 8 enrolled. In 2009, 13 master's awarded. *Degree requirements:* For master's, thesis or alternative; for doctorate, comprehensive exam. *Entrance requirements:* For master's, GRE General Test, minimum GPA of 3.0. Additional exam requirements/recommendations for international students: Required—TOEFL (minimum score 550 paper-based; 79 iBT), IELTS (minimum score 6). *Application deadline:* For fall admission, 1/1 priority date for domestic students; for spring admission, 9/1 for domestic students. Applications are processed on a rolling basis. Application fee: $45 ($75 for international students). *Expenses:* Tuition, state resident: full-time $8800. Tuition, nonresident: full-time $20,760. Tuition and fees vary according to program and reciprocity agreements. *Financial support:* In 2009–10, 30 teaching assistantships were awarded; career-related internships or fieldwork and unspecified assistantships also available. Support available to part-time students. Financial award application deadline: 4/15. *Unit head:* Mike R. Allen, Representative,

414-229-4261, Fax: 414-229-3859, E-mail: mikealle@uwm.edu. *Application contact:* General Information Contact, 414-229-4982, Fax: 414-229-6967, E-mail: gradschool@uwm.edu.

University of Wisconsin–Milwaukee, Graduate School, College of Letters and Sciences, Interdepartmental Program in Human Resources and Labor Relations, Milwaukee, WI 53201-0413. Offers human resources and labor relations (MHRLR); international human resources and labor relations (Certificate); mediation and negotiation (Certificate). Part-time programs available. *Students:* 14 full-time (10 women), 44 part-time (34 women); includes 12 minority (5 African Americans, 2 Asian Americans or Pacific Islanders, 5 Hispanic Americans), 2 international. Average age 31. 37 applicants, 51% accepted, 5 enrolled. In 2009, 22 master's awarded. *Entrance requirements:* For master's, GMAT or GRE General Test. Additional exam requirements/recommendations for international students: Required—TOEFL (minimum score 550 paper-based; 79 iBT), IELTS (minimum score 6.5). *Application deadline:* For fall admission, 1/1 priority date for domestic students; for spring admission, 9/1 for domestic students. Applications are processed on a rolling basis. Application fee: $45 ($75 for international students). *Expenses:* Tuition, state resident: full-time $8800. Tuition, nonresident: full-time $20,760. Tuition and fees vary according to program and reciprocity agreements. *Financial support:* Career-related internships or fieldwork available. Support available to part-time students. Financial award application deadline: 4/15. *Unit head:* Susan M. Donohue-Davies, Representative, 414-299-4009, Fax: 414-229-5915, E-mail: suedono@uwm.edu. *Application contact:* General Information Contact, 414-229-4982, Fax: 414-229-6967, E-mail: gradschool@uwm.edu.

Walden University, Graduate Programs, School of Public Policy and Administration, Minneapolis, MN 55401. Offers general program (MPA); government management (Post-baccalaureate Certificate); health policy (MPA); homeland security policy (MPA); interdisciplinary policy studies (MPA); law and public policy (MPA); local government management for sustainable communities (MPA); nonprofit management (Postbaccalaureate Certificate); nonprofit management and leadership (MPA, MS); policy analysis (MPA); public management and leadership (MPA); public policy and administration (PhD), including criminal justice, health services, homeland security policy and coordination, international nongovernmental organizations, law and public policy, local government management for sustainable communities, nonprofit management and leadership, public management and leadership, public policy, public safety management, terrorism, mediation, and peace; terrorism, mediation, and peace (MPA). Part-time and evening/weekend programs available. Postbaccalaureate distance learning degree programs offered (minimal on-campus study). *Faculty:* 7 full-time, 62 part-time/adjunct. *Students:* 1,468 full-time (941 women), 233 part-time (162 women); includes 852 minority (761 African Americans, 9 American Indian/Alaska Native, 19 Asian Americans or Pacific Islanders, 63 Hispanic Americans), 53 international. Average age 40. In 2009, 173 master's, 13 doctorates awarded. *Degree requirements:* For doctorate, thesis/dissertation, residency. *Entrance requirements:* For master's, bachelor's degree or equivalent in related field, minimum GPA of 2.5; for doctorate, master's degree or equivalent in related field; minimum GPA of 3.0; official transcripts; three years of related professional/academic experience (preferred); access to computer and Internet. Additional exam requirements/recommendations for international students: Required—TOEFL (minimum score 550 paper-based; 213 computer-based), IELTS (minimum score 6.5), or Michigan English Language Assessment Battery (minimum score 82). *Application deadline:* Applications are processed on a rolling basis. Application fee: $50. Electronic applications accepted. *Expenses:* Tuition: Full-time $13,665; part-time $560 per credit. Required fees: $1375. Tuition and fees vary according to course load, degree level and program. *Financial support:* In 2009–10, 207 students received support; fellowships with tuition reimbursements available, Federal Work-Study, scholarships/grants, unspecified assistantships, and family tuition reduction, active duty/veteran tuition reduction, group tuition reduction, interest-free payment plans available. Support available to part-time students. Financial award applicants required to submit FAFSA. *Unit head:* Dr. Mark Gordon, Associate Dean, 800-925-3368. *Application contact:* Jennifer Hall, Director of Enrollment, 866-4-WALDEN, E-mail: info@waldenu.edu.

Wayne State University, College of Fine, Performing and Communication Arts, Interdisciplinary Program in Dispute Resolution, Detroit, MI 48202. Offers MADR, Certificate, JD/MADR. *Entrance requirements:* For master's, GMAT, GRE General Test, or LSAT. Additional exam requirements/recommendations for international students: Required—TOEFL (minimum score 550 paper-based; 213 computer-based); Recommended—TWE (minimum score 6). Electronic applications accepted. *Faculty research:* Conflict resolution in higher education; workplace conflict and aggression; cultural diversity; domestic violence; intervention policies of major powers and small states.

Section 18
Criminology and Forensics

This section contains a directory of institutions offering graduate work in criminology and forensics, followed by an in-depth entry submitted by an institution that chose to prepare a detailed program description. Additional information about programs listed in the directory but not augmented by an in-depth entry may be obtained by writing directly to the dean of a graduate school or chair of a department at the address given in the directory.

For programs offering related work, see also in this book *Political Science and International Affairs, Psychology and Counseling,* and *Sociology, Anthropology, and Archaeology.* In another guide in this series:

Graduate Programs in Business, Education, Health, Information Studies, Law & Social Work

See *Law* and *Social Work*

CONTENTS

Program Directories

Criminal Justice and Criminology 696

Forensic Sciences 717

Close-Up

Nova Southeastern University 721

See also:

Adler School of Professional Psychology—Psychology 1047

Criminal Justice and Criminology

Adler School of Professional Psychology, Programs in Psychology, Chicago, IL 60601-7203. Offers art therapy (MA, Certificate); clinical hypnosis (Certificate); clinical psychology (Psy D); counseling (MA); counseling and organizational psychology (MA); forensic psychology (MA); gerontological counseling (MA); marriage and family counseling (MA); marriage and family therapy (Certificate); organizational psychology (MA); police psychology (MA); rehabilitation counseling (MA); sport and health psychology (MA); substance abuse counseling (Certificate); Psy D/Certificate; Psy D/MACAT; Psy D/MACP; Psy D/MAMFC; Psy D/MASAC. *Accreditation:* APA. Part-time and evening/weekend programs available. Postbaccalaureate distance learning degree programs offered (minimal on-campus study). *Faculty:* 41 full-time (21 women), 44 part-time/adjunct (19 women). *Students:* 551 full-time (441 women), 161 part-time (137 women). Average age 27.Terminal master's awarded for partial completion of doctoral program. *Degree requirements:* For master's, thesis or alternative, oral exam, practicum; for doctorate, thesis/dissertation, clinical exam, internship, oral exam, practicum, written qualifying exam. *Entrance requirements:* For master's, 12 semester hours in psychology, minimum GPA of 3.0; for doctorate, 18 semester hours in psychology, minimum GPA of 3.25; for Certificate, appropriate master's or doctoral degree. Additional exam requirements/recommendations for international students: Required—TOEFL (minimum score 550 paper-based; 213 computer-based; 79 iBT). *Application deadline:* For fall admission, 2/15 priority date for domestic students, 12/1 priority date for international students. Applications are processed on a rolling basis. Application fee: $50. Electronic applications accepted. *Expenses:* Tuition: Part-time $930 per credit. Required fees: $220 per term. *Financial support:* Career-related internships or fieldwork, Federal Work-Study, scholarships/grants, and tuition waivers (full and partial) available. Support available to part-time students. Financial award application deadline: 5/15; financial award applicants required to submit FAFSA. *Unit head:* Dr. Frank Gruba-McAllister, Vice President of Academic Affairs, 312-201-5900 Ext. 209, Fax: 312-201-5917. *Application contact:* Craig A. Hines, Associate Vice President of Admissions, 312-201-5900 Ext. 226, Fax: 312-201-5917, E-mail: chines@adler.edu.

See Close-Up on page 1047.

Albany State University, College of Arts and Humanities, Department of History, Political Science and Public Administration, Albany, GA 31705-2717. Offers community and economic development administration (MPA); criminal justice administration (MPA); fiscal management (MPA); general management (MPA); health administration and policy (MPA); human resources management (MPA); public policy (MPA); water resource management and policy (MPA). *Accreditation:* NASPAA. *Students:* 17 full-time (11 women), 43 part-time (29 women); includes 57 minority (56 African Americans, 1 Asian American or Pacific Islander). Average age 34. 21 applicants, 100% accepted, 17 enrolled. In 2009, 17 master's awarded. *Entrance requirements:* For master's, Graduate Record Examination (GRE) or Miller Analogies Test (MAT). *Application deadline:* For fall admission, 11/16 for domestic students, 9/16 for international students; for spring admission, 4/19 for domestic students, 2/19 for international students. Applications are processed on a rolling basis. Application fee: $20. Electronic applications accepted. *Expenses:* Tuition, state resident: full-time $2970; part-time $162 per credit hour. Tuition, nonresident: full-time $12,168; part-time $676 per credit hour. Required fees: $962; $75 per credit hour. *Financial support:* Application deadline: 6/30. *Faculty research:* Public policy, strategic public human resources and human capital management, diversity management in the public sector and collective bargaining and labor relations in the public sector, e-government and public sector information systems, public administration pedagogy and business process modeling simulation, funded research- community development, non profit organizations, civic engagement and civic participation, health care disparities among minorities and poverty. Total annual research expenditures: $26,000. *Unit head:* Dr. Peter Ngwafu, Director, 229-430-4873, Fax: 229-430-7895, E-mail: peter.ngwafu@asurams.edu. *Application contact:* Nicole Lane, Interim Graduate Admissions Officer, 229-430-4862, Fax: 229-430-6398, E-mail: nicole.lane@asurams.edu.

Albany State University, College of Sciences and Health Professions, Department of Criminal Justice and Forensic Science, Albany, GA 31705-2717. Offers corrections (MS); forensic science (MS); law enforcement (MS); public administration (MS). Part-time programs available. *Students:* 11 full-time (10 women), 43 part-time (29 women); includes 51 minority (50 African Americans, 1 Asian American or Pacific Islander). Average age 35. 18 applicants, 94% accepted, 10 enrolled. In 2009, 8 master's awarded. *Degree requirements:* For master's, comprehensive exam, thesis optional. *Entrance requirements:* For master's, GRE General Test or MAT, minimum GPA of 2.5, ASU Medical and Immunization Forms. Additional exam requirements/recommendations for international students: Required—TOEFL. *Application deadline:* For fall admission, 11/16 for domestic students, 9/16 for international students; for spring admission, 4/19 for domestic students, 2/19 for international students. Applications are processed on a rolling basis. Application fee: $20. Electronic applications accepted. *Expenses:* Tuition, state resident: full-time $2970; part-time $162 per credit hour. Tuition, nonresident: full-time $12,168; part-time $676 per credit hour. Required fees: $962; $75 per credit hour. *Financial support:* Application deadline: 6/30. *Faculty research:* Criminal alcoholic program, prevention of juvenile delinquency, police selection, constitutional issues. *Unit head:* Dr. Charles Ochie, Chair, 229-430-4864, Fax: 229-430-1676, E-mail: charles.ochie@asurams.edu. *Application contact:* Nicole Lane, Interim Graduate Admissions Officer, 229-430-4862, Fax: 229-430-6398, E-mail: nicole.lane@asurams.edu.

American Public University System, AMU/APU Graduate Programs, Charles Town, WV 25414. Offers air warfare (MA Military Studies); American Revolution (MA Military Studies); business administration (MBA); Civil War (MA Military Studies); criminal justice (MA); defense management (MA Military Studies); emergency and disaster management (MA); environmental policy and management (MS); fire science management (MA); global engagement (MA); history (MA); homeland security (MA); humanities (MA); intelligence (MA Military Studies, MA Strategic Intelligence); international peace and conflict resolution (MA); international relations and conflict resolution (MA); joint warfare (MA Military Studies); land warfare international perspective (MA Military Studies); management (MA); military history (MA); military leadership (MA Military Studies); national security studies (MA); naval warfare international (MA Military Studies); naval warfare US (MA Military Studies); political science (MA); public administration (MA); public health (MA); security management (MA); space studies (MS); special ops/LIC (MA Military Studies); sports management (MA); transportation and logistics management (MA); transportation management (MA); unconventional warfare (MA Military Studies); World War II (MA Military Studies). Programs offered via distance learning only. Part-time and evening/weekend programs available. Postbaccalaureate distance learning degree programs offered (no on-campus study). *Faculty:* 10 full-time (3 women), 188 part-time/adjunct (57 women). *Students:* 340 full-time (98 women), 3,567 part-time (790 women); includes 615 minority (317 African Americans, 28 American Indian/Alaska Native, 85 Asian Americans or Pacific Islanders, 185 Hispanic Americans), 20 international. Average age 36. 2,123 applicants, 100% accepted, 893 enrolled. In 2009, 829 degrees awarded. *Degree requirements:* For master's, comprehensive exam. *Entrance requirements:* For master's, bachelor's degree or equivalent, minimum GPA of 2.7 in last 60 hours of course work. *Application deadline:* Applications are processed on a rolling basis. Application fee: $0. Electronic applications accepted. *Financial support:* Applicants required to submit FAFSA. *Faculty research:* Military history, criminal justice, management performance, national security. *Unit head:* Dr. Frank McCluskey, Provost, 877-468-6268, Fax: 304-724-3780. *Application contact:* Terry Grant, Director of Enrollment Management, 877-468-6268, Fax: 304-724-3780, E-mail: info@apus.edu.

American University, School of Public Affairs, Department of Justice, Law and Society, Washington, DC 20016-8043. Offers MS, PhD, JD/MS. Part-time and evening/weekend programs available. *Faculty:* 24 full-time (13 women), 12 part-time/adjunct (5 women). *Students:* 28 full-time (20 women), 32 part-time (22 women); includes 9 minority (5 African Americans, 2 Asian Americans or Pacific Islanders, 2 Hispanic Americans), 1 international. Average age 27. 77 applicants, 62% accepted, 22 enrolled. In 2009, 26 master's, 1 doctorate awarded. *Degree requirements:* For master's, comprehensive exam, research; for doctorate, comprehensive exam, thesis/dissertation. *Entrance requirements:* For master's, GRE, 2 recommendations; for doctorate, GRE, minimum GPA of 3.2. Additional exam requirements/recommendations for international students: Required—TOEFL. *Application deadline:* For fall admission, 2/1 for domestic students; for spring admission, 11/1 for domestic students. Application fee: $55. *Expenses:* Tuition: Full-time $22,266; part-time $1237 per credit hour. Required fees: $430. Tuition and fees vary according to program. *Financial support:* Fellowships, research assistantships, teaching assistantships, career-related internships or fieldwork, Federal Work-Study, institutionally sponsored loans, and tuition waivers (full and partial) available. Financial award application deadline: 2/1. *Faculty research:* Mental health, court management. *Unit head:* Dr. Diedre Golash, Chair, 202-885-2955, E-mail: dgolash@american.edu. *Application contact:* Dr. Diedre Golash, Chair, 202-885-2955, E-mail: dgolash@american.edu.

American University of Puerto Rico, Program in Criminal Justice, Bayamón, PR 00960-2037. Offers MA. Evening/weekend programs available. *Faculty:* 9 part-time/adjunct (1 woman). *Students:* 18 full-time (12 women), 21 part-time (7 women); includes all Hispanic Americans. 20 applicants, 100% accepted, 18 enrolled. In 2009, 36 master's awarded. *Entrance requirements:* For master's, Entrance exam. *Application deadline:* For fall admission, 8/4 for domestic students; for winter admission, 10/18 for domestic students; for spring admission, 3/22 for domestic students. Applications are processed on a rolling basis. Application fee: $0. *Financial support:* Applicants required to submit FAFSA. *Application contact:* Information Contact, E-mail: oficnaadmisiones@aupr.edu.

Anderson University, Command College, Anderson, SC 29621-4035. Offers MA. Postbaccalaureate distance learning degree programs offered. *Entrance requirements:* For master's, minimum undergraduate GPA of 2.75, 5 years experience working in criminal justice field, resume.

Andrew Jackson University, Jeffrey D. Rubenstein College of Criminal Justice, Program in Criminal Justice, Birmingham, AL 35244. Offers MS. Part-time and evening/weekend programs available. Postbaccalaureate distance learning degree programs offered (no on-campus study). *Entrance requirements:* For master's, course work in calculus, statistics. Additional exam requirements/recommendations for international students: Required—TOEFL (minimum score 550 paper-based; 213 computer-based).

Anna Maria College, Graduate Division, Program in Criminal Justice, Paxton, MA 01612. Offers criminal justice (MS). Part-time and evening/weekend programs available. *Degree requirements:* For master's, capstone project or thesis. *Entrance requirements:* For master's, bachelor's degree in related field, minimum GPA of 2.7. Additional exam requirements/recommendations for international students: Required—TOEFL (minimum score 500 paper-based). Electronic applications accepted.

Anna Maria College, Graduate Division, Program in Justice Administration, Paxton, MA 01612. Offers MS. Part-time and evening/weekend programs available. *Degree requirements:* For master's, capstone project. *Entrance requirements:* Additional exam requirements/recommendations for international students: Required—TOEFL (minimum score 500 paper-based). Electronic applications accepted.

Anna Maria College, Graduate Division, Program in Security Management, Paxton, MA 01612. Offers MA. *Degree requirements:* For master's, thesis.

Appalachian State University, Cratis D. Williams Graduate School, Department of Government and Justice Studies, Boone, NC 28608. Offers criminal justice (MS); political science (MA), including American government, environmental politics and policy analysis, international relations; public administration (MPA), including public management, town, city and county management. Part-time programs available. Postbaccalaureate distance learning degree programs offered (no on-campus study). *Faculty:* 27 full-time (5 women), 12 part-time/adjunct (1 woman). *Students:* 65 full-time (26 women), 62 part-time (22 women); includes 6 minority (5 African Americans, 1 American Indian/Alaska Native), 1 international. 100 applicants, 93% accepted, 53 enrolled. In 2009, 45 master's awarded. *Degree requirements:* For master's, variable foreign language requirement, comprehensive exam, thesis optional. *Entrance requirements:* For master's, GRE General Test, 3 letters of recommendation. Additional exam requirements/recommendations for international students: Required—TOEFL (minimum score 570 paper-based; 230 computer-based; 79 iBT), IELTS (minimum score 6.5). *Application deadline:* For fall admission, 7/1 for domestic students, 2/1 for international students; for spring admission, 11/1 for domestic students, 7/1 for international students. Applications are processed on a rolling basis. Application fee: $50. Electronic applications accepted. *Expenses:* Tuition, state resident: full-time $2960. Tuition, nonresident: full-time $14,051. Required fees: $2320. *Financial support:* In 2009–10, 20 research assistantships (averaging $8,000 per year) were awarded; fellowships, teaching assistantships, career-related internships or fieldwork, Federal Work-Study, scholarships/grants, and unspecified assistantships also available. Financial award application deadline: 4/1; financial award applicants required to submit FAFSA. *Faculty research:* Campaign finance, emerging democracies, bureaucratic politics, judicial behavior, administration of justice. Total annual research expenditures: $320,000. *Unit head:* Dr. Brian Ellison, Chairperson, 828-262-3085, E-mail: ellisonba@appstate.edu. *Application contact:* Sandy Krause, Director of Admissions and Recruiting, 828-262-2130, Fax: 828-262-2709, E-mail: krausesl@appstate.edu.

Arizona State University, Graduate College, College of Public Programs, School of Criminology and Criminal Justice, Tempe, AZ 85287. Offers criminal justice (MA); criminology and criminal justice (MS, PhD). Part-time and evening/weekend programs available. *Degree requirements:* For master's, policy analysis project; for doctorate, thesis/dissertation. *Entrance requirements:* For master's, letters of recommendation, minimum 3.0 GPA; for doctorate, GRE, For master's, GRE (MS), 2 letters of recommendation, personal statement, resumé. Additional exam requirements/recommendations for international students: Required—TOEFL (minimum score 550 paper-based; 213 computer-based; 83 iBT). Electronic applications accepted.

Arkansas State University—Jonesboro, Graduate School, College of Humanities and Social Sciences, Department of Criminology, Sociology, and Geography, Jonesboro, State University, AR 72467. Offers criminal justice (MA, Certificate); sociology (MA); sociology education (SCCT). Part-time programs available. *Faculty:* 7 full-time (4 women). *Students:* 9 full-time (7 women), 32 part-time (23 women); includes 15 minority (all African Americans). Average age 33. 29 applicants, 59% accepted, 12 enrolled. In 2009, 7 master's awarded. *Degree requirements:* For master's, one foreign language, comprehensive exam, thesis or alternative; for other advanced degree, comprehensive exam. *Entrance requirements:* For master's, GRE General Test or MAT, appropriate bachelor's degree, letters of recommendation; for other advanced degree, GRE General Test or MAT, interview, master's degree, official transcript, immunization records. Additional exam requirements/recommendations for international students: Required—TOEFL (minimum score 550 paper-based; 213 computer-based; 79 iBT), IELTS (minimum score 6). *Application deadline:* For fall admission, 7/1 for domestic and international students; for spring admission, 11/15 for domestic students, 11/13 for international students. Applications are processed on a rolling basis. Application fee: $30 ($40 for international students). Electronic applications accepted. *Expenses:* Tuition, state resident: full-time $3744; part-time $208 per credit hour. Tuition, nonresident: full-time $9540; part-time $530 per credit hour. Required fees: $896; $47 per credit hour. $25 per term. One-time fee: $50. Tuition and fees vary according to course load and program. *Financial support:* In 2009–10, 8 students received support. Career-related internships or fieldwork, scholarships/grants, and unspecified assistantships available. Financial award application deadline: 7/1; financial award applicants required to submit FAFSA. *Unit head:* Dr. Anthony Troy Adams, Chair, 870-972-3705, Fax: 870-972-3694, E-mail: aadams@astate.edu. *Application contact:* Dr. Andrew Sustich, Dean of the Graduate School, 870-972-3029, Fax: 870-972-3857, E-mail: sustich@astate.edu.

Armstrong Atlantic State University, School of Graduate Studies, Program in Criminal Justice, Savannah, GA 31419-1997. Offers MS. Part-time and evening/weekend programs available. *Degree requirements:* For master's, comprehensive exam, thesis optional. *Entrance requirements:* For master's, GRE General Test or MAT, minimum GPA of 2.5, 2 letters of recommendation. Additional exam requirements/recommendations for international students: Required—TOEFL (minimum score 523 paper-based; 193 computer-based). Electronic applications accepted.

Auburn University Montgomery, School of Sciences, Department of Justice and Public Safety, Montgomery, AL 36124-4023. Offers MSJPS. Part-time and evening/weekend programs available. *Faculty:* 3 full-time (1 woman), 9 part-time/adjunct (2 women). *Students:* 21 full-time (16 women), 50 part-time (26 women); includes 48 minority (46 African Americans, 1 American Indian/Alaska Native, 1 Asian American or Pacific Islander). Average age 32. In 2009, 29 master's awarded. *Degree requirements:* For master's, comprehensive exam, thesis optional. *Entrance requirements:* For master's, GRE General Test or MAT. *Application deadline:* Applications are processed on a rolling basis. Electronic applications accepted. *Expenses:* Tuition, state resident: full-time $2841; part-time $225 per credit hour. Tuition, nonresident: full-time $8241; part-time $675 per credit hour. Required fees: $282; $8 per hour. $45 per term. *Financial support:* Career-related internships or fieldwork and scholarships/grants available. Support available to part-time students. Financial award application deadline: 3/1; financial award applicants required to submit FAFSA. *Faculty research:* Law enforcement, corrections, juvenile justice. *Unit head:* Dr. Gloria McPherson, Head, 334-244-3692, Fax: 334-244-3244, E-mail: gmcphers@mail.aum.edu. *Application contact:* Dr. Glen Ray, Acting Graduate Coordinator, 334-244-3590, Fax: 334-244-3826, E-mail: gray@mail.aum.edu.

Bayamón Central University, Graduate Programs, Program in Business Administration, Bayamón, PR 00960-1725. Offers accounting (MBA); finance (MBA); general business (MBA); management (MBA); management of security and protection (MBA); marketing (MBA). Part-time and evening/weekend programs available. *Degree requirements:* For master's, comprehensive exam (for some programs). *Entrance requirements:* For master's, EXADEP, bachelor's degree in business or related field.

Bellevue University, Graduate School, Bellevue, NE 68005-3098. Offers acquisition and contract management (MS); business administration (MBA); clinical counseling (MS); computer information systems (MS); healthcare administration (MA, MHA, MS), including healthcare administration (MHA), human services (MA, MS); human capital management (MS, PhD); instructional design and development (MS); leadership (MA); management (MA); management information systems (MS); organizational performance (MS); public administration (MPA); public health (MPH); security management (MS). Part-time and evening/weekend programs available. Postbaccalaureate distance learning degree programs offered (no on-campus study). *Degree requirements:* For master's, thesis or project. *Entrance requirements:* For master's, minimum GPA of 2.5 in last 60 hours. Additional exam requirements/recommendations for international students: Required—TOEFL (minimum score 538 paper-based; 200 computer-based).

Boise State University, Graduate College, College of Social Sciences and Public Affairs, Program in Criminal Justice Administration, Boise, ID 83725-0399. Offers MA. *Degree requirements:* For master's, thesis. *Entrance requirements:* For master's, minimum GPA of 3.0. Electronic applications accepted. *Expenses:* Tuition, state resident: full-time $3106; part-time $209 per credit. Tuition, nonresident: part-time $284 per credit.

Boston University, Metropolitan College, Program in Criminal Justice, Boston, MA 02215. Offers MCJ. Part-time and evening/weekend programs available. Postbaccalaureate distance learning degree programs offered (no on-campus study). *Faculty:* 5 full-time (1 woman), 5 part-time/adjunct (2 women). *Students:* 5 full-time (2 women), 383 part-time (228 women); includes 36 minority (13 African Americans, 3 American Indian/Alaska Native, 6 Asian Americans or Pacific Islanders, 14 Hispanic Americans), 12 international. Average age 33. 224 applicants, 97% accepted, 179 enrolled. In 2009, 272 master's awarded. *Degree requirements:* For master's, comprehensive exam. *Entrance requirements:* Additional exam requirements/recommendations for international students: Required—TOEFL (minimum score 590 paper-based; 243 computer-based; 84 iBT). *Application deadline:* For fall admission, 7/15 for domestic students, 7/15 priority date for international students; for spring admission, 12/15 for domestic students, 11/15 priority date for international students. Applications are processed on a rolling basis. Application fee: $70. Electronic applications accepted. *Expenses:* Tuition: Full-time $37,910; part-time $1184 per credit hour. Required fees: $386; $40 per semester. Part-time tuition and fees vary according to class time, course level, degree level and program. *Financial support:* In 2009–10, 10 research assistantships with partial tuition reimbursements (averaging $5,000 per year) were awarded; career-related internships or fieldwork, institutionally sponsored loans, tuition waivers (partial), and unspecified assistantships also available. Support available to part-time students. Financial award application deadline: 6/15; financial award applicants required to submit FAFSA. *Faculty research:* Criminal justice administration and planning, criminology, police, corrections, collective violence, juvenile issues. *Unit head:* Dr. Daniel P. LeClair, Chair, 617-353-3025, Fax: 617-358-3595, E-mail: dleclair@bu.edu. *Application contact:* Dr. Daniel P. LeClair, Chair, 617-353-3025, Fax: 617-358-3595, E-mail: dleclair@bu.edu.

Bowling Green State University, Graduate College, College of Health and Human Services, Program in Criminal Justice, Bowling Green, OH 43403. Offers MSCJ. Part-time and evening/weekend programs available. Postbaccalaureate distance learning degree programs offered (no on-campus study). *Degree requirements:* For master's, thesis or alternative. *Entrance requirements:* For master's, GRE General Test. Additional exam requirements/recommendations for international students: Required—TOEFL. Electronic applications accepted.

Bridgewater State University, School of Graduate Studies, School of Arts and Sciences, Department of Sociology, Program in Criminal Justice, Bridgewater, MA 02325-0001. Offers MS. *Entrance requirements:* For master's, GRE General Test.

Buffalo State College, State University of New York, The Graduate School, Faculty of Applied Science and Education, Department of Criminal Justice, Buffalo, NY 14222-1095. Offers MS. Part-time and evening/weekend programs available. *Degree requirements:* For master's, comprehensive exam, project. *Entrance requirements:* For master's, minimum GPA of 3.0. Additional exam requirements/recommendations for international students: Required—TOEFL (minimum score 550 paper-based; 213 computer-based).

California State University, Fresno, Division of Graduate Studies, College of Social Sciences, Department of Criminology, Fresno, CA 93740-8027. Offers MS. Part-time and evening/weekend programs available. *Degree requirements:* For master's, thesis or alternative. *Entrance requirements:* For master's, GRE General Test, minimum GPA of 3.0. Additional exam requirements/recommendations for international students: Required—TOEFL. Electronic applications accepted. *Faculty research:* Substance abuse, gangs vs. law enforcement, needs of female offenders, battered women, crime victims.

California State University, Long Beach, Graduate Studies, College of Health and Human Services, Department of Criminal Justice, Long Beach, CA 90840. Offers criminal justice (MS); emergency services administration (MS). Part-time programs available. *Faculty:* 8 full-time (5 women), 5 part-time/adjunct (1 woman). *Students:* 36 full-time (25 women), 16 part-time (11 women); includes 25 minority (5 African Americans, 8 Asian Americans or Pacific Islanders, 12 Hispanic Americans), 3 international. Average age 27. 118 applicants, 58% accepted, 22 enrolled. *Degree requirements:* For master's, comprehensive course or thesis. *Entrance requirements:* For master's, minimum GPA of 3.0. *Application deadline:* For fall admission, 5/1 for domestic students. Applications are processed on a rolling basis. Application fee: $55. Electronic applications accepted. *Expenses:* Required fees: $1802 per semester. Part-time tuition and fees vary according to course load. *Financial support:* Federal Work-Study, institutionally sponsored loans, and scholarships/grants available. Financial award application deadline: 3/2. *Unit head:* Dr. Henry F. Fradella, Chair, 562-985-2669, Fax: 562-985-8086, E-mail: hfradell@csulb.edu. *Application contact:* Dr. Connie Estrada Ireland, Graduate Advisor, 562-985-8711, Fax: 562-985-8086, E-mail: cireland@csulb.edu.

California State University, Los Angeles, Graduate Studies, College of Health and Human Services, Department of Criminal Justice and Criminalistics, Los Angeles, CA 90032-8530. Offers criminal justice (MS); criminalistics (MS). Part-time and evening/weekend programs available. *Faculty:* 4 full-time (3 women), 1 part-time/adjunct (0 women). *Students:* 23 full-time (17 women), 29 part-time (20 women); includes 23 minority (9 Asian Americans or Pacific Islanders, 14 Hispanic Americans), 1 international. Average age 28. 48 applicants, 98% accepted, 20 enrolled. In 2009, 15 master's awarded. *Degree requirements:* For master's, thesis. *Entrance requirements:* For master's, minimum GPA of 2.75. Additional exam requirements/recommendations for international students: Required—TOEFL (minimum score 500 paper-based; 173 computer-based). *Application deadline:* For fall admission, 5/1 for domestic and international students. Applications are processed on a rolling basis. Application fee: $55. *Financial support:* Federal Work-Study available. Support available to part-time students. Financial award application deadline: 3/1. *Unit head:* Dr. Joseph L. Peterson, Chair, 323-343-4610, Fax: 323-343-4646, E-mail: jpeters@calstatela.edu. *Application contact:* Dr. Cheryl L. Ney, Associate Vice President for Academic Affairs and Dean of Graduate Studies, 323-343-3820, Fax: 323-343-5653, E-mail: cney@cslanet.calstatela.edu.

California State University, Sacramento, Graduate Studies, College of Health and Human Services, Division of Criminal Justice, Sacramento, CA 95819. Offers MS. Part-time programs available. *Degree requirements:* For master's, thesis or alternative, writing proficiency exam. *Entrance requirements:* For master's, BA in criminal justice or equivalent, minimum GPA of 2.5 during previous 2 years of course work. Additional exam requirements/recommendations for international students: Required—TOEFL. Electronic applications accepted.

California State University, San Bernardino, Graduate Studies, College of Social and Behavioral Sciences, Department of Criminal Justice, San Bernardino, CA 92407-2397. Offers MA. Part-time programs available. *Faculty:* 6 full-time (4 women). *Students:* 20 full-time (13 women), 16 part-time (6 women); includes 16 minority (3 African Americans, 3 Asian Americans or Pacific Islanders, 10 Hispanic Americans). Average age 30. 41 applicants, 59% accepted, 12 enrolled. In 2009, 7 master's awarded. *Degree requirements:* For master's, comprehensive exam or thesis, advancement to candidacy. *Entrance requirements:* For master's, GRE General Test, minimum GPA of 3.0. *Application deadline:* For fall admission, 9/1 priority date for domestic students. Applications are processed on a rolling basis. Application fee: $55. *Financial support:* Research assistantships, career-related internships or fieldwork, Federal Work-Study, and institutionally sponsored loans available. Support available to part-time students. *Faculty research:* Crime seriousness, fear of crime, victimization, corrections management, crime correlates. *Unit head:* Dr. Larry Gaines, Chair, 909-537-5508, Fax: 909-537-7025, E-mail: lgaines@csusb.edu. *Application contact:* Olivia Rosas, Director of Admissions, 909-537-7577, Fax: 909-537-7034, E-mail: orosas@csusb.edu.

California State University, Stanislaus, College of Humanities and Social Sciences, Department of Criminal Justice, Turlock, CA 95382. Offers MA. Part-time programs available. *Degree requirements:* For master's, thesis optional. *Entrance requirements:* For master's, 3.0 minimum GPA, 3 letters of reference. *Faculty research:* Police gerontology services, hate crimes, juvenile justice, masculinities and modern society, nutrition and criminal behavior.

California University of Pennsylvania, School of Graduate Studies and Research, College of Liberal Arts, Department of Sociology/Criminal Justice, California, PA 15419-1394. Offers social science—criminal justice (MA). Part-time and evening/weekend programs available. *Degree requirements:* For master's, comprehensive exam, thesis optional. *Entrance requirements:* For master's, MAT, minimum GPA of 3.0. Additional exam requirements/recommendations for international students: Required—TOEFL (minimum score 550 paper-based; 213 computer-based; 80 iBT). Electronic applications accepted. *Faculty research:* Ethics and law, ethics in police practice, law and morality, police policy, St. Thomas Aquinas and crime.

Calumet College of Saint Joseph, Program in Public Safety Administration, Whiting, IN 46394-2195. Offers MS.

Capella University, School of Human Services, Minneapolis, MN 55402. Offers addictions counseling (Certificate); counseling studies (MS, PhD); criminal justice (MS, PhD, Certificate); diversity studies (Certificate); general human services (MS, PhD); health care administration (MS, PhD, Certificate); management of nonprofit agencies (MS, PhD, Certificate); marital, couple and family counseling/therapy (MS); marriage and family services (Certificate); mental health counseling (MS); professional counseling (Certificate); social and community services (MS, PhD, Certificate). Part-time and evening/weekend programs available. Postbaccalaureate distance learning degree programs offered (minimal on-campus study). Terminal master's awarded for partial completion of doctoral program. *Degree requirements:* For master's, thesis optional, integrative project; for doctorate, comprehensive exam, thesis/dissertation. *Entrance requirements:* Additional exam requirements/recommendations for international students: Required—TOEFL (minimum score 550 paper-based; 213 computer-based), TWE (minimum score 4). Electronic applications accepted. *Faculty research:* Compulsive and addictive behaviors, substance abuse, assessment of psychopathology and neuropsychology.

Capella University, School of Public Service Leadership, Minneapolis, MN 55402. Offers criminal justice (MS, PhD); emergency management (MS, PhD); general human services (MS, PhD); general public administration (MPA, DPA); gerontology (MS); health care administration (MS, PhD); health management and policy (MSPH); management of nonprofit agencies (MS, PhD); nurse educator (MS); public safety leadership (MS, PhD); social and community services (MS, PhD); social behavioral sciences (MSPH).

Caribbean University, Graduate School, Bayamón, PR 00960-0493. Offers administration and supervision (MA Ed); criminal justice (MA); curriculum and instruction (MA Ed), including elementary education, English education, history education, mathematics education, primary education, science education, Spanish education; education (PhD); gerontology (MSN); human resources (MBA); museology, archiving and art history (MA Ed); neonatal pediatrics (MSN); physical education (MA Ed); special education (MA Ed). *Entrance requirements:* For master's, interview, minimum GPA of 2.5.

Carnegie Mellon University, H. John Heinz III College, School of Information Systems and Management, Program in Information Security Policy and Management, Pittsburgh, PA 15213-3891. Offers MSISPM.

Central Connecticut State University, School of Graduate Studies, School of Arts and Sciences, Department of Criminology and Criminal Justice, New Britain, CT 06050-4010. Offers criminal justice (MS). Part-time and evening/weekend programs available. *Faculty:* 12 full-time (6 women), 19 part-time/adjunct (5 women). *Students:* 7 full-time (6 women), 38 part-time (19 women); includes 10 minority (7 African Americans, 3 Hispanic Americans). Average age 30. 30 applicants, 53% accepted, 14 enrolled. In 2009, 9 master's awarded. *Degree requirements:* For master's, comprehensive exam, thesis or alternative. *Entrance requirements:* For master's, minimum undergraduate GPA of 3.0. Additional exam requirements/recommendations for international students: Required—TOEFL. *Application deadline:* For fall admission, 5/1 for domestic students; for spring admission, 12/1 for domestic students. Applications are processed on a rolling basis. Application fee: $50. Electronic applications accepted. *Expenses:* Tuition, area resident: Full-time $4662; part-time $440 per credit. Tuition, state resident: full-time $6994; part-time $440 per credit. Tuition, nonresident: full-time $12,988; part-time $440 per credit. Required fees: $3606. One-time fee: $62 part-time. *Financial support:* In 2009–10, 5 students received support, including 4 research assistantships; career-related internships or fieldwork, Federal Work-Study, scholarships/grants, and unspecified assistantships also available. Support available to part-time students. Financial award application deadline: 3/1; financial award applicants required to submit FAFSA. *Unit head:* Dr. Raymond Tafrate, Chair, 860-832-3005. *Application contact:* Dr. Raymond Tafrate, Chair, 860-832-3005.

Criminal Justice and Criminology

Chaminade University of Honolulu, Graduate Services, Program in Criminal Justice Administration, Honolulu, HI 96816-1578. Offers criminal justice administration (MSCJA); homeland security (Certificate). Part-time and evening/weekend programs available. Post-baccalaureate distance learning degree programs offered (no on-campus study). *Degree requirements:* For master's, thesis optional. *Entrance requirements:* For master's, minimum undergraduate GPA of 3.0, 3 letters of recommendation. Additional exam requirements/recommendations for international students: Required—TOEFL (minimum score 550 paper-based). Electronic applications accepted. *Faculty research:* Penology, juvenile delinquency, multicultural and ethnic diversity in criminology, law enforcement administration and training, homeland security.

Charleston Southern University, Department of Criminal Justice, Charleston, SC 29423-8087. Offers MSCJ. Part-time and evening/weekend programs available. *Faculty:* 3 full-time (2 women), 1 part-time/adjunct (0 women). *Students:* 39 part-time (23 women); includes 16 minority (12 African Americans, 4 Hispanic Americans). Average age 31. 33 applicants, 85% accepted, 23 enrolled. In 2009, 10 master's awarded. *Degree requirements:* For master's, comprehensive exam, thesis optional. *Entrance requirements:* For master's, GRE or MAT, bachelor's degree in criminal justice. Additional exam requirements/recommendations for international students: Required—TOEFL (minimum score 550 paper-based; 213 computer-based; 79 iBT). *Application deadline:* Applications are processed on a rolling basis. Application fee: $30. *Expenses:* Tuition: Part-time $350 per credit hour. Required fees: $40 per semester. Tuition and fees vary according to program. *Financial support:* Research assistantships with full tuition reimbursements available. Financial award application deadline: 4/15; financial award applicants required to submit FAFSA. *Unit head:* Dr. Jacqueline Fish, Chair, 843-863-7131, Fax: 843-863-7198, E-mail: jfish@csuniv.edu. *Application contact:* Alison Harrison, Graduate Enrollment Counselor, 843-863-7534, Fax: 843-863-7070, E-mail: aharrison@csuniv.edu.

Chicago State University, School of Graduate and Professional Studies, College of Arts and Sciences, Department of Criminal Justice, Chicago, IL 60628. Offers MS. Part-time and evening/weekend programs available. *Entrance requirements:* For master's, minimum GPA of 2.75. *Faculty research:* Gang crime.

Clark Atlanta University, School of Arts and Sciences, Department of Criminal Justice, Atlanta, GA 30314. Offers MA. Part-time programs available. *Faculty:* 2 full-time (0 women), 1 (woman) part-time/adjunct. *Students:* 8 full-time (6 women); includes 7 minority (5 African Americans, 1 American Indian/Alaska Native, 1 Hispanic American). Average age 25. 10 applicants, 100% accepted, 8 enrolled. In 2009, 7 master's awarded. *Degree requirements:* For master's, one foreign language, comprehensive exam, thesis. *Entrance requirements:* For master's, GRE General Test, minimum GPA of 2.5. Additional exam requirements/recommendations for international students: Required—TOEFL (minimum score 500 paper-based; 173 computer-based). *Application deadline:* For fall admission, 4/1 for domestic and international students; for spring admission, 11/1 for domestic and international students. Applications are processed on a rolling basis. Application fee: $40 ($55 for international students). *Expenses:* Tuition: Full-time $12,240; part-time $680 per credit hour. Required fees: $710; $355 per semester. *Financial support:* Career-related internships or fieldwork, Federal Work-Study, scholarships/grants, and unspecified assistantships available. Support available to part-time students. Financial award application deadline: 4/30; financial award applicants required to submit FAFSA. *Faculty research:* Race and crime, black ex-offenders in the labor market. *Unit head:* Dr. Sandra Taylor, Chairperson, 404-880-8681, E-mail: staylor@cau.edu. *Application contact:* Michelle Clark-Davis, Graduate Program Admissions, 404-880-6605, E-mail: cauadmissions@cau.edu.

College of Saint Elizabeth, Program in Justice Studies, Morristown, NJ 07960-6989. Offers justice administration and public service (MA). Part-time and evening/weekend programs available. *Faculty:* 1 full-time (0 women). *Students:* 1 (woman) full-time, 8 part-time (5 women); includes 4 minority (all African Americans). Average age 34. 10 applicants, 80% accepted, 7 enrolled. *Expenses:* Tuition: Part-time $797 per credit hour. Required fees: $65 per credit hour. *Unit head:* Dr. James Ford. *Application contact:* Donna Tatarka, Dean of Admission, 973-290-4705, Fax: 973-290-4710, E-mail: dtatarka@cse.edu.

Colorado Technical University Colorado Springs, Graduate Studies, Program in Criminal Justice, Colorado Springs, CO 80907-3896. Offers MSM. Postbaccalaureate distance learning degree programs offered.

Colorado Technical University Denver, Program in Computer Science, Greenwood Village, CO 80111. Offers computer systems security (MSCS); database systems (MSCS); software engineering (MSCS). Part-time and evening/weekend programs available. *Degree requirements:* For master's, thesis or alternative. *Entrance requirements:* For master's, minimum undergraduate GPA of 3.0, resume.

Colorado Technical University Sioux Falls, Program in Criminal Justice, Sioux Falls, SD 57108. Offers MSM.

Columbia College, Master of Science in Criminal Justice Program, Columbia, MO 65216-0002. Offers MSCJ. Evening/weekend programs available. Postbaccalaureate distance learning degree programs offered (no on-campus study). *Faculty:* 4 full-time (0 women), 15 part-time/adjunct (6 women). *Students:* 117 full-time (68 women), 10 part-time (8 women); includes 33 minority (24 African Americans, 1 American Indian/Alaska Native, 1 Asian American or Pacific Islander, 7 Hispanic Americans), 2 international. Average age 37. 46 applicants, 65% accepted, 11 enrolled. In 2009, 18 master's awarded. *Degree requirements:* For master's, final exams, culminating experience (intensive writing seminar). *Entrance requirements:* For master's, 3 letters of recommendation, minimum cumulative undergraduate GPA of 3.0, resume. Additional exam requirements/recommendations for international students: Required—TOEFL (minimum score 550 paper-based; 213 computer-based; 79 iBT). *Application deadline:* For fall admission, 8/9 priority date for domestic and international students; for spring admission, 12/27 priority date for domestic and international students. Applications are processed on a rolling basis. Application fee: $55. Electronic applications accepted. *Expenses:* Tuition: Full-time $3588; part-time $299 per credit hour. Tuition and fees vary according to course load. *Financial support:* In 2009–10, 4 students received support. Federal Work-Study and scholarships/grants available. Financial award applicants required to submit FAFSA. *Faculty research:* Organized crime, policing in America. *Unit head:* Dr. Mike Lyman, Graduate Program Coordinator, 573-875-7472, E-mail: mlyman@ccis.edu. *Application contact:* Samantha White, Director of Admissions, 573-875-7352, Fax: 573-875-7506, E-mail: sjwhite@ccis.edu.

Columbia Southern University, College of Safety and Emergency Services, Orange Beach, AL 36561. Offers criminal justice (MS); environmental management (MS); occupational safety and health (MS); occupational safety and health/environmental management (MS). Part-time and evening/weekend programs available. Postbaccalaureate distance learning degree programs offered (no on-campus study). *Entrance requirements:* For master's, bachelor's degree from accredited/approved institution. Additional exam requirements/recommendations for international students: Required—TOEFL. Electronic applications accepted.

Columbus State University, Graduate Studies, College of Letters and Sciences, Master of Public Administration Program, Columbus, GA 31907-5645. Offers public administration (MPA), including government administration, health services administration, justice administration. Part-time and evening/weekend programs available. *Faculty:* 12 full-time (4 women), 12 part-time/adjunct (0 women). *Students:* 113 full-time (43 women), 209 part-time (63 women); includes 98 minority (86 African Americans, 4 American Indian/Alaska Native, 1 Asian American or Pacific Islander, 7 Hispanic Americans), 1 international. Average age 41. 84 applicants, 88% accepted, 58 enrolled. In 2009, 130 master's awarded. *Entrance requirements:* For master's, GRE General Test, minimum GPA of 2.75. Additional exam requirements/recommendations for international students: Required—TOEFL (minimum score 550 paper-based; 213 computer-based; 79 iBT). *Application deadline:* For fall admission, 5/1 priority date for domestic students, 5/1 for international students; for spring admission, 11/1 for domestic and international students. Applications are processed on a rolling basis. Application fee: $30. Electronic applications accepted. *Financial support:* In 2009–10, 71 students received support, including 6 research assistantships with partial tuition reimbursements available (averaging $3,000 per year); career-related internships or fieldwork, Federal Work-Study, institutionally sponsored loans, scholarships/grants, tuition waivers (partial), and unspecified assistantships also available. Support available to part-time students. Financial award application deadline: 5/1; financial award applicants required to submit FAFSA. *Unit head:* Dr. William Chappell, Program Director, 706-569-2891, E-mail: chappell_bill@colstate.edu. *Application contact:* Katie Thornton, Graduate Admissions Specialist, 706-568-2035, Fax: 706-568-2462, E-mail: thornton_katie@colstate.edu.

Concordia University, St. Paul, College of Business and Organizational Leadership, St. Paul, MN 55104-5494. Offers business and organizational leadership (MBA); criminal justice leadership (MA); health care management (MBA); human resources management (MA); leadership and management (MA). *Accreditation:* ACBSP. Evening/weekend programs available. Postbaccalaureate distance learning degree programs offered (minimal on-campus study). *Faculty:* 10 full-time (5 women), 19 part-time/adjunct (4 women). *Students:* 295 full-time (169 women), 3 part-time (2 women); includes 30 minority (19 African Americans, 2 American Indian/Alaska Native, 5 Asian Americans or Pacific Islanders, 4 Hispanic Americans), 3 international. Average age 32. In 2009, 114 master's awarded. *Application deadline:* Applications are processed on a rolling basis. Application fee: $50. Electronic applications accepted. *Financial support:* Applicants required to submit FAFSA. *Unit head:* Dr. Bruce Corrie, Dean, 651-641-8226, Fax: 651-641-8807, E-mail: corrie@csp.edu. *Application contact:* Kimberly Craig, Director of Graduate and Cohort Admission, 651-603-6223, Fax: 651-603-6320, E-mail: craig@csp.edu.

Coppin State University, Division of Graduate Studies, Division of Arts and Sciences, Department of Criminal Justice and Law Enforcement, Baltimore, MD 21216-3698. Offers criminal justice (MS). Part-time and evening/weekend programs available. *Degree requirements:* For master's, thesis optional. *Entrance requirements:* For master's, GRE, minimum GPA of 3.0.

Curry College, Graduate Studies, Program in Criminal Justice, Milton, MA 02186-9984. Offers MA. Part-time and evening/weekend programs available. *Faculty:* 5 full-time (1 woman), 5 part-time/adjunct (2 women). *Students:* 135 part-time (24 women). Average age 32. 32 applicants, 91% accepted, 29 enrolled. In 2009, 59 master's awarded. *Degree requirements:* For master's, thesis. *Entrance requirements:* For master's, MAT or GRE, resume, recommendations, interview. Additional exam requirements/recommendations for international students: Required—TOEFL (minimum score 550 paper-based; 213 computer-based; 80 iBT). *Application deadline:* For fall admission, 8/1 priority date for domestic students, 6/1 for international students; for winter admission, 10/1 for international students; for spring admission, 1/1 priority date for domestic students, 1/28 for international students. Applications are processed on a rolling basis. Application fee: $50. *Expenses:* Contact institution. *Unit head:* Dr. Rebecca Paynich, Director and Associate Professor, 617-333-2084, Fax: 617-979-3535. *Application contact:* John Bresnahan, Director of Graduate Enrollment and Student Services, 617-333-2243, Fax: 617-979-3535, E-mail: jbresnah0104@curry.edu.

Dallas Baptist University, College of Adult Education, Professional Development Program, Dallas, TX 75211-9299. Offers accounting (MA); church leadership (MA); counseling (MA); criminal justice (MA); English as a second language (MA); finance (MA); higher education (MA); leadership studies (MA); management (MA); management information systems (MA); marketing (MA); missions (MA). Part-time and evening/weekend programs available. *Entrance requirements:* For master's, minimum GPA of 3.0. Additional exam requirements/recommendations for international students: Required—TOEFL, IELTS. *Expenses:* Tuition: Full-time $10,674; part-time $593 per credit hour.

Defiance College, Program in Business Administration, Defiance, OH 43512-1610. Offers criminal justice (MBA); health care (MBA); leadership (MBA). Part-time and evening/weekend programs available. *Degree requirements:* For master's, thesis. *Entrance requirements:* For master's, minimum GPA of 2.5.

Delta State University, Graduate Programs, College of Arts and Sciences, Division of Social Sciences, Program in Criminal Justice, Cleveland, MS 38733-0001. Offers MS. Part-time programs available. Postbaccalaureate distance learning degree programs offered. *Degree requirements:* For master's, thesis or alternative. *Expenses:* Tuition, state resident: full-time $4450; part-time $247 per credit hour. Tuition, nonresident: full-time $11,520; part-time $640 per credit hour.

DeSales University, Graduate Division, Program in Criminal Justice, Center Valley, PA 18034-9568. Offers MACJ. Part-time programs available. Postbaccalaureate distance learning degree programs offered (no on-campus study). *Students:* 39 part-time. In 2009, 218 master's awarded. *Entrance requirements:* Additional exam requirements/recommendations for international students: Required—TOEFL. *Application deadline:* Applications are processed on a rolling basis. Application fee: $35. Electronic applications accepted. *Expenses:* Tuition: Full-time $17,500; part-time $665 per credit. Full-time tuition and fees vary according to program. Part-time tuition and fees vary according to course load. *Unit head:* Dr. Patrick McGrain, Director, 610-282-1100 Ext. 1584, Fax: 610-282-0787, E-mail: patrick.mcgrain@desales.edu. *Application contact:* Caryn Stopper, Director of Graduate Admissions, 610-282-1100 Ext. 1768, Fax: 610-282-0525, E-mail: caryn.stopper@desales.edu.

Drury University, Program in Criminology/Criminal Justice, Springfield, MO 65802. Offers criminal justice (MS); criminology (MA). Part-time and evening/weekend programs available. *Degree requirements:* For master's, thesis (for some programs). *Entrance requirements:* For master's, GMAT or MAT. Additional exam requirements/recommendations for international students: Required—TOEFL. Electronic applications accepted. *Expenses:* Contact institution. *Faculty research:* Gangs, fear of crime, social justice, social change and law, drug laws in Iran.

East Carolina University, Graduate School, College of Human Ecology, Department of Criminal Justice, Greenville, NC 27858-4353. Offers MS. Part-time and evening/weekend programs available. Postbaccalaureate distance learning degree programs offered (no on-campus study). *Degree requirements:* For master's, thesis, internship. *Entrance requirements:* For master's, GRE or MAT, bachelor's degree in criminal justice or related field. Additional exam requirements/recommendations for international students: Required—TOEFL. *Faculty research:* Corrections, policing, international criminal justice, terrorism.

East Central University, School of Graduate Studies, Department of Human Resources, Ada, OK 74820-6899. Offers administration (MSHR); counseling (MSHR); criminal justice (MSHR); rehabilitation counseling (MSHR). *Accreditation:* CORE. Part-time and evening/weekend programs available. *Degree requirements:* For master's, thesis optional. *Entrance requirements:* For master's, GRE General Test, MAT, minimum GPA of 2.5. Electronic applications accepted.

Eastern Kentucky University, The Graduate School, College of Justice and Safety, Program in Correctional and Juvenile Justice Studies, Richmond, KY 40475-3102. Offers MS. *Degree requirements:* For master's, comprehensive exam (for some programs), thesis (for some programs). *Entrance requirements:* For master's, GRE.

Eastern Kentucky University, The Graduate School, College of Justice and Safety, Program in Criminal Justice and Police Studies, Richmond, KY 40475-3102. Offers criminal justice (MS); criminal justice education (MS); police studies (MS). Part-time programs available. *Degree requirements:* For master's, thesis optional. *Entrance requirements:* For master's, GRE General Test, minimum GPA of 3.0.

Eastern Kentucky University, The Graduate School, College of Justice and Safety, Program in Loss Prevention and Safety, Richmond, KY 40475-3102. Offers MS. *Entrance requirements:* For master's, GRE.

Eastern Michigan University, Graduate School, College of Arts and Sciences, Department of Sociology, Anthropology and Criminology, Program in Criminology and Criminal Justice, Ypsilanti, MI 48197. Offers MA. *Students:* 2 full-time (both women), 29 part-time (18 women); includes 11 minority (8 African Americans, 1 American Indian/Alaska Native, 2 Hispanic Americans). Average age 31. In 2009, 5 master's awarded. Application fee: $35. Tuition and fees vary according to course level. *Application contact:* Dr. Donna Selman, Advisor, 734-487-0012, Fax: 734-487-9666, E-mail: dkillingb@emich.edu.

East Tennessee State University, School of Graduate Studies, College of Arts and Sciences, Department of Criminal Justice and Criminology, Johnson City, TN 37614. Offers MA. Part-time and evening/weekend programs available. *Degree requirements:* For master's, thesis or alternative. *Entrance requirements:* For master's, GRE General Test, minimum GPA of 3.0. Additional exam requirements/recommendations for international students: Required—TOEFL (minimum score 550 paper-based; 213 computer-based). *Faculty research:* Prisonization, peacemaking, sentencing decisions, family violence and sexual violence, juvenile justice.

Everest University, Graduate Programs, Jacksonville, FL 32256. Offers business (MBA); criminal justice (MS).

Everest University, Program in Criminal Justice, Tampa, FL 33619. Offers MS. Part-time and evening/weekend programs available. Postbaccalaureate distance learning degree programs offered (minimal on-campus study). *Faculty:* 2 part-time/adjunct (1 woman). *Students:* 1 (woman) full-time, 17 part-time (9 women); includes 10 minority (7 African Americans, 3 Hispanic Americans). Average age 40. In 2009, 1 master's awarded. *Degree requirements:* For master's, thesis optional, externship, research practicum. *Entrance requirements:* Additional exam requirements/recommendations for international students: Required—TOEFL (minimum score 550 paper-based; 213 computer-based). *Application deadline:* Applications are processed on a rolling basis. Application fee: $25. *Expenses:* Tuition: Full-time $12,120; part-time $505 per credit hour. Required fees: $60 per quarter. One-time fee: $245. *Financial support:* Institutionally sponsored loans and scholarships/grants available. *Unit head:* Seth Kanowitz, Chair, 813-621-0041 Ext. 219, Fax: 813-623-5769, E-mail: skanowitz@cci.edu. *Application contact:* Shandretta Pointer, Admissions Office, 813-621-0041 Ext. 106, Fax: 813-628-0919, E-mail: spointer@cci.edu.

Everest University, Program in Criminal Justice, Lakeland, FL 33801. Offers MS.

Everest University, Program in Criminal Justice, Pompano Beach, FL 33062. Offers MS.

Fairmont State University, Graduate Studies, Program in Criminal Justice, Fairmont, WV 26554. Offers MS. *Degree requirements:* For master's, thesis or comprehensive exam. *Entrance requirements:* For master's, GRE, minimum GPA of 3.0.

Fayetteville State University, Graduate School, Program in Criminal Justice, Fayetteville, NC 28301-4298. Offers MA. *Faculty:* 6 full-time (3 women). *Students:* 9 full-time (7 women), 22 part-time (11 women); includes 15 minority (all African Americans), 1 international. Average age 35. 9 applicants, 89% accepted, 8 enrolled. In 2009, 2 master's awarded. *Application deadline:* For fall admission, 4/15 for domestic students; for spring admission, 10/15 for domestic students. Application fee: $35. *Unit head:* Dr. Robert Brown, Interim Chair, 910-672-1478, Fax: 910-672-1908, E-mail: mbarlow@uncfsu.edu. *Application contact:* Katrina Hoffman, Associate Vice-Chancellor for Enrollment Management, 910-672-1374, Fax: 910-672-1470, E-mail: khoffma1@uncfsu.edu.

Ferris State University, College of Education and Human Services, School of Criminal Justice, Big Rapids, MI 49307. Offers criminal justice administration (MSCJ). Part-time and evening/weekend programs available. *Faculty:* 6 full-time (2 women), 1 part-time/adjunct (0 women). *Students:* 12 full-time (6 women), 44 part-time (24 women); includes 13 minority (12 African Americans, 1 American Indian/Alaska Native), 1 international. Average age 31. 12 applicants, 67% accepted, 7 enrolled. In 2009, 38 master's awarded. *Degree requirements:* For master's, comprehensive exam or thesis/dissertation. *Entrance requirements:* For master's, bachelor's degree in criminal justice or related field, minimum GPA of 3.0. Additional exam requirements/recommendations for international students: Required—TOEFL (minimum score 500 paper-based; 173 computer-based; 61 iBT). *Application deadline:* Applications are processed on a rolling basis. Application fee: $30. Electronic applications accepted. *Financial support:* In 2009–10, 2 research assistantships (averaging $4,800 per year) were awarded; Federal Work-Study and unspecified assistantships also available. Support available to part-time students. Financial award applicants required to submit FAFSA. *Faculty research:* Policy enactment, health and safety issues, criminological theory, juvenile justice, policy techniques, problem based learning. *Unit head:* Nancy L. Hogan, Graduate Program Coordinator, 231-591-5080, Fax: 231-591-3792, E-mail: hogann@ferris.edu. *Application contact:* Nancy L. Hogan, Assistant Professor, 231-591-5080, Fax: 231-591-3792, E-mail: hogann@ferris.edu.

Florida Agricultural and Mechanical University, Division of Graduate Studies, Research, and Continuing Education, College of Arts and Sciences, Division of History and Political Sciences, Program in Applied Social Science, Tallahassee, FL 32307-3200. Offers African American history (MASS); criminal justice (MASS); economics (MASS); history (MASS); political science (MASS); public administration (MASS); public management (MASS); social work (MASS); sociology (MASS). Part-time programs available. *Faculty:* 17 full-time (2 women). *Students:* 54 full-time (42 women), 4 part-time (2 women); includes 57 minority (all African Americans). In 2009, 14 master's awarded. *Degree requirements:* For master's, thesis optional. *Entrance requirements:* For master's, GRE General Test, minimum GPA of 3.0. *Application deadline:* For fall admission, 5/18 for domestic students, 12/18 for international students; for spring admission, 11/12 for domestic students, 5/12 for international students. Application fee: $20. *Financial support:* Fellowships, research assistantships, career-related internships or fieldwork, Federal Work-Study, and tuition waivers (full) available. Financial award application deadline: 4/1. *Faculty research:* Southern history, black history, election trends, presidential history. *Unit head:* Dr. Gary Paul, Director, 850-599-3447. *Application contact:* Dr. Chanta M. Haywood, Dean of Graduate Studies, Research, and Continuing Education, 850-599-3315, Fax: 850-599-3727.

Florida Atlantic University, College of Architecture, Urban and Public Affairs, School of Criminology and Criminal Justice, Boca Raton, FL 33431-0991. Offers MS. Part-time and evening/weekend programs available. Postbaccalaureate distance learning degree programs offered. *Faculty:* 13 full-time (4 women), 16 part-time/adjunct (2 women). *Students:* 9 full-time (6 women), 17 part-time (9 women); includes 10 minority (4 African Americans, 6 Hispanic Americans), 1 international. Average age 28. 32 applicants, 63% accepted, 9 enrolled. In 2009, 7 master's awarded. *Degree requirements:* For master's, thesis optional. *Entrance requirements:* For master's, GRE General Test, minimum GPA of 3.0, undergraduate course work in statistics and criminology. Additional exam requirements/recommendations for international students: Required—TOEFL (minimum score 550 paper-based; 213 computer-based). *Application deadline:* For fall admission, 7/1 priority date for domestic students, 2/15 for international students; for spring admission, 11/1 priority date for domestic students, 7/15 for international students. Applications are processed on a rolling basis. Application fee: $30. Electronic applications accepted. *Expenses:* Tuition, state resident: full-time $7055; part-time $293.94 per credit hour. Tuition, nonresident: full-time $22,096; part-time $920.66 per credit hour. *Financial support:* Research assistantships with partial tuition reimbursements, institutionally sponsored loans, scholarships/grants, and unspecified assistantships available. Financial award application deadline: 4/1. *Faculty research:* Restorative, justice corrections, logic modeling, criminal justice management, crime causation. *Unit head:* Dr. Gordon Bazemore, Chair, 561-297-3240. *Application contact:* Dr. Maria Schiff, Graduate Program Coordinator, 954-762-5638, Fax: 954-762-5673, E-mail: mschiff@fau.edu.

Florida Gulf Coast University, College of Professional Studies, Program in Criminal Justice Studies, Fort Myers, FL 33965-6565. Offers MS. *Faculty:* 32 full-time (11 women), 29 part-time/adjunct (12 women). *Students:* 7 full-time (4 women), 6 part-time (2 women); includes 4 minority (all Hispanic Americans). Average age 27. 10 applicants, 70% accepted, 6 enrolled. *Entrance requirements:* For master's, GRE General Test, minimum GPA of 3.0. Additional exam requirements/recommendations for international students: Required—TOEFL (minimum score 550 paper-based; 213 computer-based). *Application deadline:* For fall admission, 3/1 for domestic students; for spring admission, 11/1 for domestic students. Applications are processed on a rolling basis. Application fee: $30. Electronic applications accepted. *Unit head:* Tony Barringer, Chair, 239-590-7849, E-mail: tbarring@fgcu.edu. *Application contact:* Tony Barringer, Chair, 239-590-7849, E-mail: tbarring@fgcu.edu.

Florida Gulf Coast University, College of Professional Studies, Program in Public Administration, Fort Myers, FL 33965-6565. Offers criminal justice (MPA); environmental policy (MPA); general public administration (MPA); management (MPA). *Accreditation:* NASPAA. Part-time programs available. *Faculty:* 32 full-time (11 women), 29 part-time/adjunct (12 women). *Students:* 49 full-time (30 women), 19 part-time (12 women); includes 13 minority (4 African Americans, 2 Asian Americans or Pacific Islanders, 7 Hispanic Americans). Average age 35. 34 applicants, 68% accepted, 19 enrolled. In 2009, 14 master's awarded. *Entrance requirements:* For master's, GRE General Test, MAT, minimum GPA of 3.0. Additional exam requirements/recommendations for international students: Required—TOEFL (minimum score 550 paper-based; 213 computer-based). *Application deadline:* For fall admission, 7/1 priority date for domestic students; for spring admission, 11/15 for domestic students. Applications are processed on a rolling basis. Application fee: $30. Electronic applications accepted. *Financial support:* In 2009–10, 5 research assistantships were awarded; career-related internships or fieldwork and tuition waivers (full and partial) also available. Support available to part-time students. *Faculty research:* Personnel, public policy, public finance, housing policy. *Unit head:* Terry Busson, Chair, 239-590-7704, E-mail: tbusson@fgcu.edu. *Application contact:* Roger Green, Information Contact, 239-590-7838, Fax: 239-590-7846.

Florida International University, College of Arts and Sciences, Department of Criminal Justice, Miami, FL 33199. Offers MS. Part-time and evening/weekend programs available. *Faculty:* 11 full-time (4 women). *Students:* 87 full-time (52 women), 88 part-time (56 women); includes 140 minority (62 African Americans, 3 Asian Americans or Pacific Islanders, 75 Hispanic Americans), 3 international. Average age 31. 148 applicants, 51% accepted, 72 enrolled. In 2009, 23 master's awarded. *Degree requirements:* For master's, thesis optional. *Entrance requirements:* For master's, minimum undergraduate GPA of 3.0. Additional exam requirements/recommendations for international students: Required—TOEFL (minimum score 550 paper-based; 80 iBT). *Application deadline:* For fall admission, 6/1 for domestic students, 4/1 for international students; for spring admission, 10/1 for domestic students, 9/1 for international students. Applications are processed on a rolling basis. Application fee: $30. Electronic applications accepted. *Expenses:* Tuition, state resident: full-time $8008; part-time $4004 per year. Tuition, nonresident: full-time $20,104; part-time $10,052 per year. Required fees: $298; $149 per term. *Financial support:* Institutionally sponsored loans and scholarships/grants available. Financial award application deadline: 3/1; financial award applicants required to submit FAFSA. *Unit head:* Dr. Lisa Stolzenberg, Chair, 305-348-5890, Fax: 305-348-2503, E-mail: lisa.stolzenberg@fiu.edu. *Application contact:* Liga Replogle, Student Services Coordinator, 305-348-5890, Fax: 305-348-5848, E-mail: liga.replogle@fiu.edu.

Florida State University, The Graduate School, College of Criminology and Criminal Justice, Tallahassee, FL 32306-1127. Offers MA, MSC, PhD, MPA/MSC, MS/MSW. Part-time programs available. Postbaccalaureate distance learning degree programs offered (no on-campus study). *Faculty:* 21 full-time (4 women). *Students:* 82 full-time (48 women), 88 part-time (47 women); includes 28 minority (15 African Americans, 1 American Indian/Alaska Native, 5 Asian Americans or Pacific Islanders, 7 Hispanic Americans), 3 international. In 2009, 39 master's, 1 doctorate awarded. *Degree requirements:* For master's, thesis optional; for doctorate, comprehensive exam, thesis/dissertation. *Entrance requirements:* For master's, GRE General Test; for doctorate, GRE General Test, area paper or thesis. Additional exam requirements/recommendations for international students: Required—TOEFL (minimum score 600 paper-based; 260 computer-based; 100 iBT). *Application deadline:* For fall admission, 7/1 for domestic and international students; for spring admission, 11/1 for domestic and international students. Applications are processed on a rolling basis. Application fee: $30. Electronic applications accepted. *Expenses:* Tuition, state resident: full-time $7413. Tuition, nonresident: full-time $22,567. *Financial support:* In 2009–10, 1 fellowship with full tuition reimbursement (averaging $19,000 per year), 22 research assistantships with full tuition reimbursements (averaging $14,500 per year), 1 teaching assistantship with full tuition reimbursement (averaging $14,500 per year) were awarded; Federal Work-Study, institutionally sponsored loans, scholarships/grants, tuition waivers (partial), and unspecified assistantships also available. Financial award application deadline: 1/15; financial award applicants required to submit FAFSA. *Faculty research:* Criminological theory, criminal justice administration and planning, criminal justice evaluation, law and social control. *Unit head:* Dr. Thomas Blomberg, Dean, 850-644-7365, Fax: 850-644-9614. *Application contact:* Margarita Frankeberger, Graduate Student Coordinator, 850-644-7373, Fax: 850-644-9614, E-mail: mfrankeberger@fsu.edu.

George Mason University, College of Humanities and Social Sciences, Administration of Justice Department, Fairfax, VA 22030. Offers criminology, law and society (MA, PhD). *Faculty:* 22 full-time (14 women), 14 part-time/adjunct (3 women). *Students:* 11 full-time (7 women), 31 part-time (21 women); includes 5 minority (1 African American, 3 Asian Americans or Pacific Islanders, 1 Hispanic American), 2 international. Average age 29. 70 applicants, 59% accepted, 19 enrolled. In 2009, 3 master's, 1 doctorate awarded. *Degree requirements:* For master's, thesis; for doctorate, comprehensive exam, thesis/dissertation. *Entrance requirements:* For master's, personal goal statement, transcripts, 2 letters of recommendation; for doctorate, 2 letters of recommendation. Additional exam requirements/recommendations for international students: Required—TOEFL. *Application deadline:* For fall admission, 4/1 priority date for domestic students. Applications are processed on a rolling basis. Application fee: $75. Electronic applications accepted. *Expenses:* Tuition, state resident: full-time $7568; part-time $315.33 per credit hour. Tuition, nonresident: full-time $21,704; part-time $904.33 per credit hour. Required fees: $2184; $91 per credit hour. *Financial support:* In 2009–10, 12 students received support, including 2 fellowships with full tuition reimbursements available (averaging $18,000 per year), 9 research assistantships with full and partial tuition reimbursements available (averaging $13,428 per year), 2 teaching assistantships with full and partial tuition reimbursements available (averaging $12,000 per year); Federal Work-Study, scholarships/grants, unspecified assistantships, and health care benefits (full-time research or teaching assistantship recipients) also available. Support available to part-time students. Financial award application deadline: 3/1; financial award applicants required to submit FAFSA. *Faculty research:* Reducing violent crime in Trinidad and Tobago, wrongful convictions in capital cases, health and safety in incarcerated juveniles, impact of the war on terror on civil liberties. Total annual research expenditures: $4.8 million. *Unit head:* Jack Censer, Dean, 703-993-8715, Fax: 703-993-8714, E-mail: jcenser@gmu.edu. *Application contact:* Crystal Harris, Graduate Academic Advisor, 703-993-9417, E-mail: charri4@gmu.edu.

The George Washington University, Columbian College of Arts and Sciences, Department of Forensic Sciences, Washington, DC 20052. Offers crime scene investigation (MFS); forensic chemistry (MFS); forensic molecular biology (MFS); forensic toxicology (MFS); high-technology crime investigation (MFS); security management (MFS). High-technology crime investigation and security management programs offered in Arlington, VA. Part-time and evening/weekend programs available. *Faculty:* 6 full-time (1 woman), 28 part-time/adjunct (5 women). *Students:* 82 full-time (55 women), 54 part-time (35 women); includes 26 minority (12 African Americans, 2 American Indian/Alaska Native, 7 Asian Americans or Pacific Islanders, 5 Hispanic Americans), 10 international. Average age 28. 121 applicants, 81% accepted, 52 enrolled. In 2009, 80 master's awarded. *Degree requirements:* For master's, comprehensive exam. *Entrance requirements:* For master's, GRE General Test, minimum GPA of 3.0. Additional exam requirements/recommendations for international students: Required—TOEFL (minimum score 550 paper-based; 213 computer-based; 80 iBT). *Application deadline:* For fall admission, 1/16 priority date for international students; for spring admission, 10/1 priority date for domestic students, 9/1 priority date for international students. Applications are processed on a rolling basis. Application fee: $60. Electronic applications accepted. *Financial support:* In 2009–10,

Criminal Justice and Criminology

The George Washington University (continued)
19 students received support; fellowships with partial tuition reimbursements available, Federal Work-Study and tuition waivers available. *Unit head:* Dr. Walter F. Rowe, Chair, 202-994-1469, E-mail: wfrowe@gwu.edu. *Application contact:* Dr. Walter F. Rowe, Chair, 202-994-1469, E-mail: wfrowe@gwu.edu.

The George Washington University, Columbian College of Arts and Sciences, Department of Sociology, Program in Criminology, Washington, DC 20052. Offers MA. *Students:* 6 full-time (5 women), 4 part-time (all women); includes 1 minority (Hispanic American). Average age 25. 16 applicants, 56% accepted, 7 enrolled. In 2009, 1 master's awarded. *Degree requirements:* For master's, comprehensive exam. *Entrance requirements:* For master's, GRE General Test, minimum GPA of 3.0. Additional exam requirements/recommendations for international students: Required—TOEFL (minimum score 550 paper-based; 213 computer-based). *Application deadline:* For fall admission, 4/1 priority date for domestic and international students; for spring admission, 10/1 priority date for domestic and international students. Applications are processed on a rolling basis. Application fee: $60. Electronic applications accepted. *Financial support:* In 2009–10, fellowships with full tuition reimbursements (averaging $10,000 per year), teaching assistantships (averaging $5,000 per year) were awarded. Financial award application deadline: 2/1. *Unit head:* Ronald Weitzer, Director, 202-994-6895. *Application contact:* Information Contact, 202-994-6345, Fax: 202-994-3239, E-mail: soc@gwu.edu.

Georgia College & State University, Graduate School, College of Arts and Sciences, Department of Government and Sociology, Program in Criminal Justice, Milledgeville, GA 31061. Offers MS. Part-time and evening/weekend programs available. *Students:* 12 full-time (11 women), 7 part-time (5 women); includes 5 minority (all African Americans), 1 international. Average age 30. 9 applicants, 89% accepted, 7 enrolled. In 2009, 8 master's awarded. *Degree requirements:* For master's, comprehensive exam, thesis optional, capstone project. *Entrance requirements:* For master's, GRE or MAT, 3 letters of recommendation. Additional exam requirements/recommendations for international students: Required—TOEFL (minimum score 550 paper-based; 213 computer-based; 79 iBT). *Application deadline:* For fall admission, 7/1 for domestic students, 4/1 for international students; for spring admission, 11/15 for domestic students. Applications are processed on a rolling basis. Application fee: $40. Electronic applications accepted. *Expenses:* Tuition, area resident: Part-time $241 per credit hour. Tuition, state resident: full-time $4338. Tuition, nonresident: full-time $17,352; part-time $964 per credit hour. Required fees: $609 per semester. Tuition and fees vary according to course load and campus/location. *Financial support:* In 2009–10, 5 research assistantships with full tuition reimbursements were awarded; unspecified assistantships also available. Financial award applicants required to submit FAFSA. *Unit head:* Dr. Gerald Fisher, Graduate Coordinator, 478-445-0940, E-mail: gerald.fisher@gcsu.edu. *Application contact:* Dr. Gerald Fisher, Graduate Coordinator, 478-445-0940, E-mail: gerald.fisher@gcsu.edu.

Georgia State University, Andrew Young School of Policy Studies, Department of Public Management and Policy, Atlanta, GA 30303. Offers disaster management (Certificate); nonprofit management (Certificate); planning and economic development (Certificate); public administration (MPA), including criminal justice, management and finance, nonprofit management, planning and economic development, policy analysis and evaluation, public health; public policy (MPP, PhD), including disaster policy (MPP), nonprofit policy (MPP), planning and economic development policy (MPP), public finance policy (MPP), social policy (MPP); JD/MPA. *Accreditation:* NASPAA (one or more programs are accredited). Part-time and evening/weekend programs available. Terminal master's awarded for partial completion of doctoral program. *Degree requirements:* For master's, thesis optional; for doctorate, comprehensive exam, thesis/dissertation. *Entrance requirements:* For master's and doctorate, GRE General Test. Additional exam requirements/recommendations for international students: Required—TOEFL. Electronic applications accepted. *Faculty research:* Public management, policy analysis, public finance, planning and economic development, nonprofit leadership and policy.

Georgia State University, College of Health and Human Sciences, Department of Criminal Justice, Atlanta, GA 30302-3083. Offers MS. Part-time and evening/weekend programs available. *Degree requirements:* For master's, thesis optional. *Entrance requirements:* For master's, GRE General Test. Additional exam requirements/recommendations for international students: Required—TOEFL (minimum score 550 paper-based; 213 computer-based). Electronic applications accepted. *Faculty research:* Urban violence, family violence, social support and adolescent crime, policing issues, active offender crime.

Graduate School and University Center of the City University of New York, Graduate Studies, Program in Criminal Justice, New York, NY 10016-4039. Offers PhD. *Faculty:* 28 full-time (6 women). *Students:* 99 full-time (70 women), 5 part-time (2 women); includes 19 minority (9 African Americans, 1 Asian American or Pacific Islander, 9 Hispanic Americans), 14 international. Average age 36. 62 applicants, 23% accepted, 13 enrolled. In 2009, 17 doctorates awarded. *Degree requirements:* For doctorate, one foreign language, thesis/dissertation. *Entrance requirements:* For doctorate, GRE General Test, writing sample. Additional exam requirements/recommendations for international students: Required—TOEFL. *Application deadline:* For fall admission, 1/15 for domestic students. Application fee: $125. Electronic applications accepted. *Financial support:* In 2009–10, 70 students received support, including 54 fellowships, 5 teaching assistantships; research assistantships, career-related internships or fieldwork, Federal Work-Study, institutionally sponsored loans, and tuition waivers (full and partial) also available. Financial award application deadline: 2/1; financial award applicants required to submit FAFSA. *Unit head:* Dr. Karen Terry, Executive Officer, 212-237-8040, Fax: 212-237-8940, E-mail: kterry@jjay.cuny.edu. *Application contact:* Les Gribben, Director of Admissions, 212-817-7470, Fax: 212-817-1624, E-mail: lgribben@gc.cuny.edu.

Grambling State University, School of Graduate Studies and Research, College of Professional Studies, Program in Criminal Justice, Grambling, LA 71245. Offers MS. Part-time programs available. *Faculty:* 7 full-time (4 women), 1 part-time/adjunct (0 women). *Students:* 59 full-time (40 women), 29 part-time (17 women); includes 84 minority (83 African Americans, 1 Hispanic American). Average age 34. 28 applicants, 89% accepted, 20 enrolled. In 2009, 26 master's awarded. *Degree requirements:* For master's, comprehensive exam, thesis optional. *Entrance requirements:* For master's, GRE, minimum GPA of 2.5 on last degree and in four core courses. Additional exam requirements/recommendations for international students: Required—TOEFL (minimum score 500 paper-based; 173 computer-based; 61 iBT). *Application deadline:* For fall admission, 7/1 for domestic and international students; for spring admission, 12/1 for domestic and international students. Applications are processed on a rolling basis. Application fee: $20 ($30 for international students). Electronic applications accepted. *Expenses:* Tuition, state resident: full-time $2610. Tuition, nonresident: full-time $2610. *Financial support:* In 2009–10, 3 research assistantships (averaging $5,417 per year) were awarded; health care benefits, tuition waivers (full and partial), and unspecified assistantships also available. Financial award application deadline: 5/31; financial award applicants required to submit FAFSA. *Faculty research:* Corrections, terrorism, delinquency, complex organizations, post-modern theory. *Unit head:* Dr. Mahendra Singh, Department Head, Criminal Justice, 318-274-2526, Fax: 318-274-3101, E-mail: singhm@gram.edu. *Application contact:* Dr. Joyce Montgomery, Coordinator, 318-274-2876, Fax: 318-274-3101, E-mail: montgomeryj@gram.edu.

Grand Valley State University, College of Community and Public Service, School of Criminal Justice, Allendale, MI 49401-9403. Offers MS. Part-time and evening/weekend programs available. *Faculty:* 6 full-time (3 women), 6 part-time/adjunct (3 women). *Students:* 14 full-time (9 women), 14 part-time (5 women); includes 4 minority (1 African American, 1 American Indian/Alaska Native, 2 Hispanic Americans), 2 international. Average age 28. 20 applicants, 85% accepted, 12 enrolled. In 2009, 2 master's awarded. *Degree requirements:* For master's, thesis or alternative. *Entrance requirements:* For master's, minimum GPA of 3.0. Additional exam requirements/recommendations for international students: Required—TOEFL. *Application deadline:* For fall admission, 7/30 priority date for domestic students; for winter admission, 12/10 priority date for domestic students; for spring admission, 4/10 priority date for domestic students. Application fee: $30. *Expenses:* Tuition, state resident: part-time $471 per credit hour. Tuition, nonresident: part-time $646 per credit hour. Tuition and fees vary according to course level. *Financial support:* In 2009–10, 12 students received support, including 5 fellowships (averaging $3,587 per year), 9 research assistantships with full tuition reimbursements available (averaging $8,000 per year); career-related internships or fieldwork, Federal Work-Study, scholarships/grants, and unspecified assistantships also available. Support available to part-time students. Financial award application deadline: 5/1. *Faculty research:* Correctional administration, juvenile justice issues/gangs, women's issues, leadership, program/policy evaluation. *Unit head:* Dr. Carly Hilinski, Director, 616-331-7169, Fax: 616-331-7155, E-mail: hilinskc@gvsu.edu. *Application contact:* Dr. Carly Hilinski, Information Contact, 616-331-7169, Fax: 616-331-7155.

Hodges University, Graduate Programs, Naples, FL 34119. Offers business administration (MBA); computer information technology (MS); criminal justice (MCJ); education (MPS); information systems management (MIS); interdisciplinary (MPS); law (MPS); management (MSM); professional studies (MPS); psychology (MPS); public administration (MPA). Part-time and evening/weekend programs available. Postbaccalaureate distance learning degree programs offered (no on-campus study). *Faculty:* 14 full-time (4 women), 4 part-time/adjunct (3 women). *Students:* 37 full-time (28 women), 217 part-time (142 women); includes 76 minority (35 African Americans, 5 Asian Americans or Pacific Islanders, 36 Hispanic Americans). Average age 36. 92 applicants, 91% accepted, 81 enrolled. In 2009, 92 master's awarded. *Degree requirements:* For master's, comprehensive exam (for some programs), thesis (for some programs). *Entrance requirements:* For master's, in-house entrance exam. *Application deadline:* Applications are processed on a rolling basis. Application fee: $50. Electronic applications accepted. *Expenses:* Tuition: Full-time $16,605; part-time $615 per credit hour. Required fees: $570. *Financial support:* In 2009–10, 200 students received support. Federal Work-Study and scholarships/grants available. Financial award application deadline: 7/9; financial award applicants required to submit FAFSA. *Unit head:* Terry McMahan, President, 239-513-1122, Fax: 239-598-6253, E-mail: tmcmahan@hodges.edu. *Application contact:* Rita Lampus, Vice President of Student Enrollment Management, 239-513-1122, Fax: 239-598-6253, E-mail: rlampus@hodges.edu.

Holy Family University, Graduate School, School of Arts and Sciences, Philadelphia, PA 19114. Offers counseling psychology (MS); criminal justice (MA). Part-time and evening/weekend programs available. *Faculty:* 1 full-time (0 women), 4 part-time/adjunct (2 women). *Students:* 39 full-time (31 women), 137 part-time (108 women); includes 34 minority (18 African Americans, 2 Asian Americans or Pacific Islanders, 14 Hispanic Americans), 1 international. Average age 31. 111 applicants, 61% accepted, 45 enrolled. In 2009, 20 master's awarded. *Degree requirements:* For master's, comprehensive exam, thesis optional. *Entrance requirements:* For master's, MAT, interview, minimum GPA of 3.0. *Application deadline:* For fall admission, 7/1 priority date for domestic students; for winter admission, 11/1 for domestic students. Applications are processed on a rolling basis. Application fee: $25. *Expenses:* Tuition: Part-time $600 per credit. Required fees: $58 per semester. *Financial support:* Research assistantships with full and partial tuition reimbursements, Federal Work-Study available. Support available to part-time students. Financial award application deadline: 2/15; financial award applicants required to submit FAFSA. *Unit head:* Dr. Michael Markowitz, Dean, 267-341-3286, Fax: 215-827-0492, E-mail: mmarkowitz@holyfamily.edu. *Application contact:* Gidget Marie Montelibans, Graduate Admissions Counselor, 267-341-3558, Fax: 215-637-1478, E-mail: gmontelibano@holyfamily.edu.

Husson University, School of Graduate and Professional Studies, Program in Criminal Justice Administration, Bangor, ME 04401-2999. Offers MS.

Illinois State University, Graduate School, College of Applied Science and Technology, Department of Criminal Justice Sciences, Normal, IL 61790-2200. Offers MA, MS. *Degree requirements:* For master's, thesis or alternative. *Entrance requirements:* For master's, GRE General Test, minimum GPA of 2.6 in last 60 hours of course work. *Faculty research:* Graduate practicum for victim assistance and advocacy, graduate practicum in adult probation cases, graduate practicum in youth intervention program.

Indiana State University, School of Graduate Studies, College of Arts and Sciences, Department of Criminology and Criminal Justice, Terre Haute, IN 47809. Offers MA, MS. Part-time programs available. Postbaccalaureate distance learning degree programs offered (no on-campus study). *Degree requirements:* For master's, thesis (for some programs). *Entrance requirements:* For master's, minimum GPA of 2.75 in undergraduate work, 3.0 in previous graduate work. Additional exam requirements/recommendations for international students: Required—TOEFL (minimum score 550 paper-based). Electronic applications accepted. *Faculty research:* Violent crime, rape attitudes, classification of offenders, substance abuse, domestic violence.

Indiana Tech, Program in Police Administration, Fort Wayne, IN 46803-1297. Offers MS. Part-time and evening/weekend programs available. Postbaccalaureate distance learning degree programs offered (no on-campus study). *Entrance requirements:* For master's, application, 2 letters of recommendation, Bachelor's degree in Criminal Justice or related field with GPA of 2.5 or better. *Application deadline:* Applications are processed on a rolling basis. Application fee: $25. Electronic applications accepted. *Expenses:* Tuition: Full-time $5160; part-time $430 per credit hour. Tuition and fees vary according to degree level and program. *Financial support:* Applicants required to submit FAFSA. *Unit head:* Dr. Steven Hundersmarck, Director of the Center for Criminal Justice. *Application contact:* Steve Herendeen, Associate Vice President of CPS Admissions, 260-422-5561 Ext. 2121, Fax: 260-422-1518, E-mail: saherendeen@indianatech.edu.

Indiana University Bloomington, University Graduate School, College of Arts and Sciences, Department of Criminal Justice, Bloomington, IN 47405. Offers criminal justice (MA, PhD); criminology (MA, PhD); cross-cultural perspectives of crime and justice (MA, PhD); law and society (MA, PhD); psychology and the law (MA). Part-time programs available. *Faculty:* 15 full-time (5 women). *Students:* 41 full-time (23 women); includes 6 minority (3 African Americans, 2 American Indian/Alaska Native, 1 Hispanic American), 5 international. Average age 31. 31 applicants, 42% accepted, 9 enrolled. In 2009, 2 master's, 1 doctorate awarded. Terminal master's awarded for partial completion of doctoral program. *Degree requirements:* For master's, thesis optional; for doctorate, thesis/dissertation, foreign language or research practicum. *Entrance requirements:* For master's and doctorate, GRE General Test. Additional exam requirements/recommendations for international students: Required—TOEFL (minimum score 600 paper-based; 250 computer-based; 100 iBT). *Application deadline:* For fall admission, 1/15 for domestic students, 12/1 for international students. Application fee: $55 ($65 for international students). Electronic applications accepted. *Expenses:* Contact institution. *Financial support:* In 2009–10, 4 fellowships with full tuition reimbursements (averaging $25,000 per year), 3 research assistantships with full tuition reimbursements (averaging $11,721 per year), 21 teaching assistantships with full tuition reimbursements (averaging $11,721 per year) were awarded; Federal Work-Study, health care benefits, tuition waivers (full), and unspecified assistantships also available. Financial award application deadline: 1/15. *Faculty research:* Violence, crime, juveniles, psychology and law, cross-cultural studies. *Unit head:* Dr. Roger J. R. Levesque, Chair, 812-856-1210, E-mail: rlevesqu@indiana.edu. *Application contact:* Ruth Cord, Graduate Secretary, 812-856-4675, Fax: 812-855-5522, E-mail: rkapusti@indiana.edu.

Indiana University Northwest, School of Public and Environmental Affairs, Gary, IN 46408-1197. Offers criminal justice (MPA); environmental affairs (Graduate Certificate); health services administration (MPA); human services administration (MPA); nonprofit management (Graduate Certificate); public management (MPA, Graduate Certificate). *Accreditation:* NASPAA (one or more programs are accredited). Part-time programs available. *Faculty:* 5 full-time (3 women). *Students:* 19 full-time (14 women), 121 part-time (100 women); includes 100 minority (84 African Americans, 1 American Indian/Alaska Native, 1 Asian American or Pacific Islander, 14 Hispanic Americans). Average age 39. In 2009, 29 master's, 27 other advanced degrees awarded. *Entrance requirements:* For master's, GRE General Test or GMAT, letters of recommendation. *Application deadline:* For fall admission, 8/15 priority date for domestic students. Applications are processed on a rolling basis. Application fee: $25. *Financial support:* Career-related internships or fieldwork, Federal Work-Study, and tuition waivers (partial) available. Support available to part-time students. Financial award application deadline: 3/1. *Faculty research:* Employment in income security policies, evidence in criminal justice, equal employment law, social welfare policy and welfare reform, public finance in developing countries. *Unit head:* George Assibey-Mensah, Interim Dean/Division Director, 219-980-6695, Fax: 219-980-6737. *Application contact:* Sandra Hall Smith, Secretary, 219-980-6695, Fax: 219-980-6737, E-mail: shsmith@iun.edu.

Indiana University of Pennsylvania, School of Graduate Studies and Research, College of Health and Human Services, Department of Criminology, Doctoral Program in Criminology, Indiana, PA 15705-1087. Offers PhD. Part-time programs available. *Faculty:* 16 full-time (8 women). *Students:* 18 full-time (5 women), 31 part-time (17 women); includes 2 minority (both African Americans), 5 international. Average age 32. 37 applicants, 54% accepted, 12 enrolled. In 2009, 10 doctorates awarded. *Degree requirements:* For doctorate, one foreign language, comprehensive exam, thesis/dissertation. *Entrance requirements:* For doctorate, GRE, 3 letters of recommendation, writing sample, interview. Additional exam requirements/recommendations for international students: Required—TOEFL. *Application deadline:* For fall admission, 7/1 priority date for domestic students; for spring admission, 11/1 for domestic students. Applications are processed on a rolling basis. Application fee: $40. *Expenses:* Tuition, state resident: full-time $6666; part-time $370 per credit hour. Tuition, nonresident: full-time $10,666; part-time $593 per credit hour. Required fees: $813 per semester. *Financial support:* In 2009–10, 7 fellowships (averaging $1,554 per year), 14 research assistantships with full and partial tuition reimbursements (averaging $6,750 per year), 4 teaching assistantships with partial tuition reimbursements (averaging $1,844 per year) were awarded; Federal Work-Study also available. Support available to part-time students. Financial award application deadline: 3/15; financial award applicants required to submit FAFSA. *Unit head:* Dr. Jennifer Roberts, Graduate Coordinator, 724-357-5933, E-mail: jennifer.roberts@iup.edu. *Application contact:* Dr. Jacqueline Beck, Associate Dean, 724-357-2560, E-mail: jbeck@iup.edu.

Indiana University of Pennsylvania, School of Graduate Studies and Research, College of Health and Human Services, Department of Criminology, Master's Program in Criminology, Indiana, PA 15705-1087. Offers MA. Part-time and evening/weekend programs available. *Faculty:* 16 full-time (8 women). *Students:* 33 full-time (14 women), 86 part-time (36 women); includes 13 minority (6 African Americans, 1 American Indian/Alaska Native, 3 Asian Americans or Pacific Islanders, 3 Hispanic Americans), 2 international. Average age 32. 123 applicants, 60% accepted, 67 enrolled. In 2009, 42 master's awarded. *Degree requirements:* For master's, thesis optional. *Entrance requirements:* For master's, 2 letters of recommendation. Additional exam requirements/recommendations for international students: Required—TOEFL. *Application deadline:* For fall admission, 7/1 priority date for domestic students; for spring admission, 11/1 for domestic students. Applications are processed on a rolling basis. Application fee: $40. *Expenses:* Tuition, state resident: full-time $6666; part-time $370 per credit hour. Tuition, nonresident: full-time $10,666; part-time $593 per credit hour. Required fees: $813 per semester. *Financial support:* In 2009–10, 1 fellowship (averaging $500 per year), 8 research assistantships with full and partial tuition reimbursements (averaging $2,153 per year) were awarded; Federal Work-Study also available. Support available to part-time students. Financial award application deadline: 3/15; financial award applicants required to submit FAFSA. *Unit head:* Dr. Shannon Phaneuf, Graduate Coordinator, 724-357-5977, E-mail: shannon.phaneuf@iup.edu. *Application contact:* Dr. Jacqueline Beck, Associate Dean, 724-357-2560, E-mail: jbeck@iup.edu.

Indiana University–Purdue University Indianapolis, School of Public and Environmental Affairs, Indianapolis, IN 46202-2896. Offers health administration (MHA); public affairs (MPA), including criminal justice, environmental management, nonprofit management, policy analysis, public management; JD/MHA; MBA/MHA; MLS/NMC; MLS/PMC; MSN/MHA. *Accreditation:* CAHME (one or more programs are accredited); NASPAA. Part-time and evening/weekend programs available. *Faculty:* 17 full-time (6 women). *Students:* 126 full-time (71 women), 283 part-time (164 women); includes 58 minority (29 African Americans, 1 American Indian/Alaska Native, 17 Asian Americans or Pacific Islanders, 11 Hispanic Americans), 20 international. Average age 33. 255 applicants, 77% accepted, 136 enrolled. In 2009, 77 master's awarded. *Entrance requirements:* For master's, GRE General Test, minimum GPA of 3.0 (preferred). Additional exam requirements/recommendations for international students: Required—TOEFL. *Application deadline:* For fall admission, 7/15 priority date for domestic students; for spring admission, 11/15 for domestic students. Applications are processed on a rolling basis. Application fee: $55 ($65 for international students). *Financial support:* In 2009–10, 11 fellowships with full and partial tuition reimbursements (averaging $5,890 per year), 10 teaching assistantships (averaging $9,900 per year) were awarded; research assistantships with full and partial tuition reimbursements, career-related internships or fieldwork, Federal Work-Study, institutionally sponsored loans, and scholarships/grants also available. Support available to part-time students. Financial award application deadline: 3/1. *Faculty research:* Economic development, water and air quality, ethics, financing, organization design and structure. Total annual research expenditures: $1.9 million. *Unit head:* Dr. Greg Lindsey, Associate Dean, 317-274-4656, Fax: 317-274-5153. *Application contact:* 317-274-4656, Fax: 317-274-5153, E-mail: speainfo@speanet.iupui.edu.

Inter American University of Puerto Rico, Aguadilla Campus, Graduate School, Aguadilla, PR 00605. Offers accounting (MBA); business information systems (MBA); counseling psychology with an emphasis in family (MS); criminal justice (MA); educative management and leadership (MA); elementary education (MA); finance (MBA); human resources (MBA); industrial management (MBA); marketing (MBA). Part-time and evening/weekend programs available. *Degree requirements:* For master's, comprehensive exam. *Entrance requirements:* For master's, EXADEP, 2 letters of recommendation, minimum GPA of 2.5. Electronic applications accepted.

Inter American University of Puerto Rico, Metropolitan Campus, Graduate Programs, Program in Criminal Justice, San Juan, PR 00919-1293. Offers MA. Part-time and evening/weekend programs available. *Degree requirements:* For master's, comprehensive exam. *Entrance requirements:* For master's, GRE or EXADEP, interview. Electronic applications accepted.

Inter American University of Puerto Rico, Ponce Campus, Graduate School, Mercedita, PR 00715-1602. Offers accounting (MBA); biology (M Ed); chemistry (M Ed); criminal justice (MA); elementary education (M Ed); English as a Second Language (M Ed); finance (MBA); history (M Ed); human resources (MBA); marketing (MBA); mathematics (M Ed); Spanish (M Ed). *Entrance requirements:* For master's, minimum GPA of 2.5.

Iona College, School of Arts and Science, Program in Criminal Justice, New Rochelle, NY 10801-1890. Offers MS. Part-time and evening/weekend programs available. *Faculty:* 7 full-time (2 women), 3 part-time/adjunct (0 women). *Students:* 9 full-time (7 women), 16 part-time (8 women); includes 7 minority (3 African Americans, 4 Hispanic Americans). Average age 32. 20 applicants, 80% accepted, 5 enrolled. In 2009, 4 master's awarded. *Degree requirements:* For master's, thesis. *Entrance requirements:* For master's, minimum GPA of 2.75. Additional exam requirements/recommendations for international students: Required—TOEFL (minimum score 550 paper-based; 213 computer-based). *Application deadline:* Applications are processed on a rolling basis. Application fee: $50. Electronic applications accepted. *Expenses:* Tuition: Part-time $830 per credit. *Financial support:* Unspecified assistantships available. Financial award application deadline: 4/15; financial award applicants required to submit FAFSA. *Faculty research:* Police administration, victimology and criminal justice program evaluation. *Unit head:* Dr. Cathryn Lavery, Chair, 914-633-2597, E-mail: clavery@iona.edu. *Application contact:* Veronica Jarek-Prinz, Director of Graduate Admissions, 914-633-2420, Fax: 914-633-2277, E-mail: vjarekprinz@iona.edu.

Jackson State University, Graduate School, School of Liberal Arts, Center for Urban Affairs/Criminology and Justice Services, Jackson, MS 39217. Offers criminology and justice service (MA). Part-time and evening/weekend programs available. *Degree requirements:* For master's, comprehensive exam, thesis optional. *Entrance requirements:* For master's, GRE General Test. Additional exam requirements/recommendations for international students: Required—TOEFL.

Jacksonville State University, College of Graduate Studies and Continuing Education, College of Arts and Sciences, Department of Criminal Justice, Jacksonville, AL 36265-1602. Offers MS. Part-time and evening/weekend programs available. *Faculty:* 5 full-time (1 woman), 1 part-time/adjunct (0 women). *Students:* 10 full-time (6 women), 14 part-time (7 women); includes 9 minority (all African Americans). Average age 31. 10 applicants, 70% accepted, 5 enrolled. In 2009, 12 master's awarded. *Degree requirements:* For master's, comprehensive exam, thesis (for some programs). *Entrance requirements:* For master's, GRE General Test or MAT. *Application deadline:* Applications are processed on a rolling basis. Application fee: $30. Electronic applications accepted. *Financial support:* In 2009–10, 21 students received support. Available to part-time students. Application deadline: 4/1. *Unit head:* Richard Kania, Head, 256-782-5339, E-mail: rkania@jsu.edu. *Application contact:* Dr. Jean Pugliese, Associate Dean, 256-782-5329, Fax: 256-782-5321, E-mail: pugliese@jsu.edu.

John Jay College of Criminal Justice of the City University of New York, Graduate Studies, Program in Protection Management, New York, NY 10019-1093. Offers MS. Part-time and evening/weekend programs available. *Degree requirements:* For master's, thesis or alternative. *Entrance requirements:* For master's, minimum B average. Additional exam requirements/recommendations for international students: Required—TOEFL (minimum score 500 paper-based; 173 computer-based).

John Jay College of Criminal Justice of the City University of New York, Graduate Studies, Programs in Criminal Justice, New York, NY 10019-1093. Offers criminal justice (MA, PhD); criminology and deviance (PhD); forensic psychology (PhD); forensic science (PhD); law and philosophy (PhD); organizational behavior (PhD); public policy (PhD). Part-time and evening/weekend programs available. Terminal master's awarded for partial completion of doctoral program. *Degree requirements:* For master's, thesis or alternative; for doctorate, one foreign language, thesis/dissertation. *Entrance requirements:* For master's, GRE General Test, minimum B average; for doctorate, GRE General Test. Additional exam requirements/recommendations for international students: Required—TOEFL (minimum score 500 paper-based; 173 computer-based).

The Johns Hopkins University, School of Education, Division of Public Safety Leadership, Baltimore, MD 21218. Offers intelligence analysis (MS); management (MS). Part-time and evening/weekend programs available. *Faculty:* 10 full-time (3 women), 23 part-time/adjunct (7 women). *Students:* 159 full-time (47 women), 1 part-time (0 women); includes 55 minority (47 African Americans, 1 American Indian/Alaska Native, 3 Asian Americans or Pacific Islanders, 4 Hispanic Americans). Average age 39. 81 applicants, 75% accepted, 54 enrolled. In 2009, 110 master's awarded. *Entrance requirements:* For master's, minimum undergraduate GPA of 3.0, curriculum vitae/resume, interview, professional experience, endorsement letter (MS management). Additional exam requirements/recommendations for international students: Required—TOEFL (minimum score 600 paper-based; 250 computer-based; 100 iBT). *Application deadline:* For fall admission, 5/1 for international students; for spring admission, 10/15 for international students. Applications are processed on a rolling basis. Application fee: $0. Electronic applications accepted. *Financial support:* Scholarships/grants available. Support available to part-time students. Financial award application deadline: 6/1; financial award applicants required to submit FAFSA. *Faculty research:* Campus and school safety, prevention and effective response to violence against women, counterterrorism training, leadership development for public safety and homeland security executives. *Unit head:* Dr. Sheldon Greenberg, Associate Dean, 410-516-9900, Fax: 410-290-1061, E-mail: psl@jhu.edu. *Application contact:* Jennifer Shaffer, Director of Admissions, 410-516-9797, Fax: 410-516-9799, E-mail: educationinfo@jhu.edu.

Kaplan University, Davenport Campus, School of Criminal Justice, Davenport, IA 52807-2095. Offers corrections (MSCJ); global issues in criminal justice (MSCJ); law (MSCJ); leadership and executive management (MSCJ); policing (MSCJ). Part-time and evening/weekend programs available. Postbaccalaureate distance learning degree programs offered (no on-campus study). *Entrance requirements:* Additional exam requirements/recommendations for international students: Required—TOEFL (minimum score 550 paper-based; 218 computer-based; 80 iBT). Electronic applications accepted.

Kean University, College of Business and Public Administration, Program in Criminal Justice, Union, NJ 07083. Offers MA. Part-time and evening/weekend programs available. *Faculty:* 6 full-time (2 women). *Students:* 1 (woman) part-time. Average age 24. 1 applicant, 100% accepted, 1 enrolled. *Degree requirements:* For master's, thesis. *Entrance requirements:* For master's, GRE (minimum Analytic Writing score of 3.5), 3 reference letters, minimum GPA of 3.0, writing sample, official transcripts from all institutions attended. *Application deadline:* For fall admission, 5/1 for domestic students; for spring admission, 11/1 for domestic students. Application fee: $60 ($150 for international students). Electronic applications accepted. *Expenses:* Tuition, state resident: full-time $10,440; part-time $435 per credit. Tuition, nonresident: full-time $14,160; part-time $590 per credit. Required fees: $2642; $110 per credit. Part-time tuition and fees vary according to course load and degree level. *Financial support:* In 2009–10, research assistantships with full tuition reimbursements (averaging $3,263 per year); unspecified assistantships also available. *Unit head:* Dr. James Drylie, Program Coordinator, 908-737-4216, E-mail: jdrylie@kean.edu. *Application contact:* Dorothy Rowe, Pre-Admissions Coordinator, 908-737-5928, Fax: 908-737-5965, E-mail: drowe@kean.edu.

Keiser University, MA in Criminal Justice Program, Fort Lauderdale, FL 33309. Offers MA. Part-time programs available. Postbaccalaureate distance learning degree programs offered (no on-campus study). *Faculty:* 1 (woman) full-time, 5 part-time/adjunct (all women). *Students:* 8 full-time (5 women), 14 part-time (9 women); includes 8 minority (5 African Americans, 1 American Indian/Alaska Native, 2 Hispanic Americans). Average age 36. 19 applicants, 89% accepted, 13 enrolled. *Entrance requirements:* For master's, minimum GPA of 2.7 from an accredited college or university. Additional exam requirements/recommendations for international students: Required—TOEFL. *Application deadline:* Applications are processed on a rolling basis. Application fee: $50. Electronic applications accepted. *Financial support:* In 2009–10, 18 students received support. Federal Work-Study available. Financial award applicants required to submit FAFSA. *Unit head:* Dr. Sara Malmstrom, Dean of the Graduate School, 954-318-1620. *Application contact:* Manuel Christiansen, Associate Director of Admissions, 954-318-1620 Ext. 309, E-mail: mchristiansen@keiseruniversity.edu.

Kent State University, College of Arts and Sciences, Department of Justice Studies, Kent, OH 44242-0001. Offers MA. Part-time and evening/weekend programs available. *Degree requirements:* For master's, comprehensive exam, thesis optional. *Entrance requirements:* For master's, minimum GPA of 2.75. Additional exam requirements/recommendations for international students: Required—TOEFL. Electronic applications accepted. *Faculty research:* School violence, community policing.

Keuka College, Program in Criminal Justice Administration, Keuka Park, NY 14478-0098. Offers MS. Part-time and evening/weekend programs available. *Faculty:* 6 part-time/adjunct (2 women). *Students:* 9 full-time (6 women), 18 part-time (9 women); includes 1 minority (African American). 89 applicants, 100% accepted. In 2009, 9 master's awarded. *Application deadline:* For fall admission, 8/15 for domestic students; for winter admission, 12/15 for domestic students; for spring admission, 4/15 for domestic students. Application fee: $30. *Expenses:* Contact institution. *Unit head:* Dr. Tom Tremer, Program Director, 315-279-5672, E-mail: ttremer@mail.keuka.edu. *Application contact:* Claudine Ninestine, Director of Admissions, 315-279-5413, Fax: 315-279-5386, E-mail: admissions@mail.keuka.edu.

Lamar University, College of Graduate Studies, College of Arts and Sciences, Department of Sociology, Social Work, and Criminal Justice, Beaumont, TX 77710. Offers applied criminology (MS). Part-time programs available. *Faculty:* 3 full-time (0 women), 1 part-time/adjunct (0

Criminal Justice and Criminology

Lamar University (continued)
women). *Students:* 7 full-time (3 women), 7 part-time (3 women); includes 3 minority (2 African Americans, 1 Hispanic American). Average age 29. 24 applicants, 25% accepted, 6 enrolled. In 2009, 1 master's awarded. *Degree requirements:* For master's, thesis or alternative, applied projects. *Entrance requirements:* For master's, GRE General Test. Additional exam requirements/recommendations for international students: Required—TOEFL. *Application deadline:* For fall admission, 8/1 priority date for domestic students; for spring admission, 12/1 priority date for domestic students. Applications are processed on a rolling basis. Application fee: $25 ($50 for international students). *Financial support:* In 2009–10, 3 fellowships with partial tuition reimbursements (averaging $1,000 per year) were awarded; career-related internships or fieldwork, Federal Work-Study, and scholarships/grants also available. Support available to part-time students. Financial award application deadline: 4/1; financial award applicants required to submit FAFSA. *Faculty research:* Corrections, planning and evaluations, juveniles, terrorism, Mexican criminal justice. *Unit head:* Dr. Li-Chen J. Ma, Chair, 409-880-8545, Fax: 409-880-2324, E-mail: lma@lamar.edu. *Application contact:* Dr. J. Rick Altemose, Graduate Program Director, 409-880-8549, Fax: 409-880-2324, E-mail: altemosejr@hal.lamar.edu.

Lewis University, College of Arts and Sciences, Program in Criminal/Social Justice, Romeoville, IL 60446. Offers criminal/social justice (MS). Part-time and evening/weekend programs available. *Faculty:* 2 full-time (1 woman), 14 part-time/adjunct (2 women). *Students:* 11 full-time (7 women), 83 part-time (42 women); includes 35 minority (19 African Americans, 1 Asian American or Pacific Islander, 15 Hispanic Americans). Average age 31. In 2009, 38 master's awarded. *Entrance requirements:* For master's, bachelor's degree or a minimum of 12 related hours in criminal/social justice, 2 letters of recommendation, minimum GPA of 3.0, interview. Additional exam requirements/recommendations for international students: Required—TOEFL (minimum score 550 paper-based; 213 computer-based). *Application deadline:* For fall admission, 5/1 priority date for international students; for spring admission, 11/15 priority date for international students. Applications are processed on a rolling basis. Application fee: $40. Electronic applications accepted. *Expenses:* Tuition: Full-time $6480; part-time $720 per credit. One-time fee: $40. Tuition and fees vary according to course load, degree level and program. *Financial support:* Federal Work-Study, scholarships/grants, tuition waivers (full and partial), and unspecified assistantships available. Financial award application deadline: 5/1; financial award applicants required to submit FAFSA. *Faculty research:* Community policing, management, terrorism, biological warfare, drugs. *Unit head:* Dr. Calvin Edwards, Chair of Justice, Law and Public Safety Studies, 815-838-0500, Fax: 815-836-5870, E-mail: koloshsa@lewisu.edu. *Application contact:* Sarah Wiegman, Coordinator, 815-838-0500 Ext. 5686, Fax: 815-836-5870, E-mail: wiegmasa@lewisu.edu.

Lincoln University, School of Graduate Studies and Continuing Education, Jefferson City, MO 65102. Offers business administration (MBA), including accounting, entrepreneurship, management, public administration and policy; educational leadership (Ed S), including elementary leadership, secondary leadership, superintendency; guidance and counseling (M Ed), including community/agency counseling, elementary school, secondary school; history (MA); school administration and supervision (M Ed), including elementary school administration, secondary school administration, special education administration; school teaching (M Ed), including elementary school teaching, secondary school teaching; social science (MA), including history, political science, sociology; sociology (MA); sociology/criminal justice (MA). Part-time and evening/weekend programs available. *Students:* 52 full-time (27 women), 146 part-time (107 women); includes 40 minority (39 African Americans, 1 Asian American or Pacific Islander), 15 international. Average age 35. 76 applicants, 95% accepted, 46 enrolled. In 2009, 60 master's, 6 other advanced degrees awarded. *Degree requirements:* For master's and Ed S, comprehensive exam, thesis optional. *Entrance requirements:* For master's and Ed S, GRE, MAT or GMAT, minimum GPA of 2.75 in major, 2.5 overall; 3 letters of recommendation; minimum C average in English composition; personal statement of purpose. Additional exam requirements/recommendations for international students: Required—TOEFL (minimum score 500 paper-based; 173 computer-based; 61 iBT). *Application deadline:* For fall admission, 7/1 priority date for domestic and international students; for spring admission, 12/1 priority date for domestic and international students. Applications are processed on a rolling basis. Application fee: $20. *Expenses:* Tuition, state resident: full-time $4185; part-time $232.50 per credit hour. Tuition, nonresident: full-time $7767; part-time $431.50 per credit hour. Required fees: $270; $15 per credit hour. $20 per term. *Financial support:* Federal Work-Study and scholarships/grants available. Financial award application deadline: 4/1; financial award applicants required to submit FAFSA. *Faculty research:* Suicide prevention. *Unit head:* Dr. Linda S. Bickel, Dean, 573-681-5247, Fax: 573-681-5106, E-mail: gradschool@lincolnu.edu. *Application contact:* Irasema Steck, Administrative Assistant, 573-681-5247, Fax: 573-681-5106, E-mail: gradschool@lincolnu.edu.

Lindenwood University, Graduate Programs, College of Individualized Education, St. Charles, MO 63301-1695. Offers administration (MSA); business administration (MBA); communications (MA); criminal justice and administration (MS); gerontology (MA); health management (MS); human resource management (MS); information technology (MBA, Certificate); management (MSA); managing information technology (MS); marketing (MSA); writing (MFA). Part-time and evening/weekend programs available. *Faculty:* 15 full-time (8 women), 128 part-time/adjunct (53 women). *Students:* 679 full-time (432 women), 90 part-time (57 women); includes 138 minority (121 African Americans, 2 American Indian/Alaska Native, 5 Asian Americans or Pacific Islanders, 10 Hispanic Americans), 18 international. Average age 34. 223 applicants, 44% accepted, 87 enrolled. In 2009, 478 master's awarded. *Degree requirements:* For master's, thesis (for some programs), 1 colloquium per term. *Entrance requirements:* For master's, interview, minimum GPA of 3.0. Additional exam requirements/recommendations for international students: Required—TOEFL (minimum score 550 paper-based; 213 computer-based; 80 iBT). *Application deadline:* For fall admission, 10/2 priority date for domestic and international students; for winter admission, 1/8 priority date for domestic and international students; for spring admission, 4/8 priority date for domestic and international students. Applications are processed on a rolling basis. Application fee: $30 ($100 for international students). *Expenses:* Tuition: Full-time $12,960; part-time $370 per credit hour. Required fees: $340. One-time fee: $30 full-time. Tuition and fees vary according to course level and course load. *Financial support:* In 2009–10, 631 students received support. Career-related internships or fieldwork, institutionally sponsored loans, tuition waivers (partial), and unspecified assistantships available. Financial award application deadline: 6/30; financial award applicants required to submit FAFSA. *Unit head:* Dan Kemper, Dean, 636-949-4501, Fax: 636-949-4505, E-mail: dkemper@lindenwood.edu. *Application contact:* Brett Barger, Dean of Evening Admissions and Extension Campuses, 636-949-4934, Fax: 636-949-4109, E-mail: adultadmissions@lindenwood.edu.

Long Island University, Brentwood Campus, School of Public Service, Brentwood, NY 11717. Offers criminal justice (MS). Part-time and evening/weekend programs available.

Long Island University, C.W. Post Campus, College of Management, Department of Criminal Justice, Brookville, NY 11548-1300. Offers criminal justice (MS); fraud examination (MS); security administration (MS). Part-time and evening/weekend programs available. *Degree requirements:* For master's, thesis. *Entrance requirements:* For master's, minimum GPA of 3.0, background in criminal justice. Electronic applications accepted. *Faculty research:* Crime statistics, terrorism, women and law, policing.

Longwood University, Office of Graduate Studies, Department of Sociology, Anthropology, and Criminal Justice Studies, Farmville, VA 23909. Offers criminal justice (MS). Part-time and evening/weekend programs available. *Degree requirements:* For master's, comprehensive exam (for some programs), thesis (for some programs). *Entrance requirements:* For master's, minimum GPA of 2.75. Additional exam requirements/recommendations for international students: Required—TOEFL (minimum score 550 paper-based; 213 computer-based).

Loyola University Chicago, Graduate School, Department of Criminal Justice, Chicago, IL 60660. Offers MA. Part-time and evening/weekend programs available. *Faculty:* 8 full-time (1 woman), 12 part-time/adjunct (1 woman). *Students:* 12 full-time (7 women), 17 part-time (9 women); includes 7 minority (2 African Americans, 5 Hispanic Americans), 1 international. Average age 30. 20 applicants, 65% accepted, 7 enrolled. In 2009, 16 master's awarded. *Degree requirements:* For master's, thesis or alternative, comprehensive exams. *Entrance requirements:* For master's, GRE, minimum GPA of 3.0. Additional exam requirements/recommendations for international students: Required—TOEFL (minimum score 550 paper-based; 213 computer-based). *Application deadline:* For fall admission, 6/15 priority date for domestic students; for spring admission, 12/1 for domestic students. Applications are processed on a rolling basis. Application fee: $50. Electronic applications accepted. *Expenses:* Tuition: Full-time $14,220; part-time $790 per credit hour. Required fees: $60 per semester hour. Tuition and fees vary according to program. *Financial support:* In 2009–10, 1 student received support, including research assistantships with partial tuition reimbursements available (averaging $7,800 per year); career-related internships or fieldwork and scholarships/grants also available. Financial award application deadline: 2/1; financial award applicants required to submit FAFSA. *Faculty research:* Crime and delinquency causation, effectiveness and efficiency of criminal justice system. Total annual research expenditures: $120,000. *Unit head:* Dr. David Olson, Chair, 312-915-7563, Fax: 312-915-7650, E-mail: dolson1@luc.edu. *Application contact:* Dr. Loretta Stalans, Graduate Program Director, 312-915-7567, Fax: 312-915-7650, E-mail: lstalan@luc.edu.

Loyola University New Orleans, College of Social Sciences, Program in Criminal Justice, New Orleans, LA 70118-6195. Offers MCJ. Part-time and evening/weekend programs available. *Students:* 8 full-time (5 women), 25 part-time (12 women); includes 12 minority (9 African Americans, 1 Asian American or Pacific Islander, 2 Hispanic Americans). Average age 31. 15 applicants, 100% accepted, 11 enrolled. In 2009, 7 master's awarded. *Degree requirements:* For master's, comprehensive exam, research and practicum. *Entrance requirements:* For master's, GRE, resume, interview, letters of recommendation, work experience. Additional exam requirements/recommendations for international students: Required—TOEFL (minimum score 550 paper-based; 213 computer-based). *Application deadline:* For fall admission, 8/1 priority date for domestic and international students; for spring admission, 1/5 priority date for domestic and international students. Applications are processed on a rolling basis. Application fee: $20. Electronic applications accepted. *Expenses:* Contact institution. *Financial support:* In 2009–10, 3 research assistantships (averaging $4,333 per year) were awarded; scholarships/grants and unspecified assistantships also available. Financial award application deadline: 5/1; financial award applicants required to submit FAFSA. *Unit head:* Dr. William E. Thornton, Chair, Department of Criminal Justice, 504-865-2134, Fax: 504-865-3883, E-mail: thornton@loyno.edu. *Application contact:* David M. Aplin, Assistant to the Director, 504-865-3323, Fax: 504-865-3883, E-mail: daplin@loyno.edu.

Lynn University, College of Liberal Education, Boca Raton, FL 33431-5598. Offers applied psychology (MS); criminal justice administration (MS); emergency planning and administration (MS, Certificate). Part-time and evening/weekend programs available. Postbaccalaureate distance learning degree programs offered. *Entrance requirements:* For master's, GRE, resume, 2 letters of recommendation, minimum undergraduate GPA of 3.0. Additional exam requirements/recommendations for international students: Required—TOEFL (minimum score 550 paper-based; 213 computer-based). Application fee: $50. *Expenses:* Tuition: Part-time $580 per credit. One-time fee: $200 part-time. Part-time tuition and fees vary according to degree level. *Financial support:* Career-related internships or fieldwork, Federal Work-Study, institutionally sponsored loans, scholarships/grants, tuition waivers (full and partial), and unspecified assistantships available. Support available to part-time students. Financial award application deadline: 8/1; financial award applicants required to submit FAFSA. *Faculty research:* Terrorism, criminological theory, corrections, emergency planning. *Unit head:* Dr. Gregg Cox, Dean, 561-237-7210, E-mail: gcox@lynn.edu. *Application contact:* Dr. Larissa Baia, Assistant Director of Graduate Admissions, 561-237-7916, Fax: 561-237-7100, E-mail: admissionpm@lynn.edu.

Madonna University, School of Business, Livonia, MI 48150-1173. Offers business administration (MBA); international business (MSBA); leadership studies (MSBA); leadership studies in criminal justice (MSBA); quality and operations management (MSBA). Part-time and evening/weekend programs available. Postbaccalaureate distance learning degree programs offered (minimal on-campus study). *Degree requirements:* For master's, thesis (for some programs), foreign language proficiency (international business). *Entrance requirements:* For master's, GMAT, GRE General Test, minimum GPA of 3.0. Electronic applications accepted. *Faculty research:* Management, women in management, future studies.

Marshall University, Academic Affairs Division, College of Liberal Arts, Department of Criminal Justice, Huntington, WV 25755. Offers MS. Evening/weekend programs available. *Faculty:* 5 full-time (3 women), 13 part-time/adjunct (4 women). *Students:* 16 full-time (8 women), 2 part-time (0 women), 1 international. Average age 25. In 2009, 8 master's awarded. *Degree requirements:* For master's, thesis optional. *Entrance requirements:* For master's, GRE General Test. Application fee: $40. *Unit head:* Dr. Dru Bora, Chairperson, 304-696-3087, E-mail: bora@marshall.edu. *Application contact:* Dr. Dhruba Bora, Information Contact, 304-696-3087, Fax: 304-746-1902, E-mail: services@marshall.edu.

Marywood University, Academic Affairs, College of Liberal Arts and Sciences, Department of Social Sciences, Program in Criminal Justice, Scranton, PA 18509-1598. Offers MS. *Students:* 9 full-time (1 woman), 19 part-time (10 women); includes 4 minority (1 African American, 3 Hispanic Americans). Average age 30. In 2009, 3 master's awarded. *Entrance requirements:* Additional exam requirements/recommendations for international students: Required—TOEFL (minimum score 550 paper-based; 213 computer-based; 79 iBT). *Application deadline:* For fall admission, 4/1 priority date for domestic students, 3/31 priority date for international students; for spring admission, 11/1 priority date for domestic students, 8/31 priority date for international students. Applications are processed on a rolling basis. Application fee: $35. Electronic applications accepted. *Expenses:* Tuition: Part-time $715 per credit. Required fees: $270 per semester. Tuition and fees vary according to degree level, campus/location and program. *Financial support:* Career-related internships or fieldwork, scholarships/grants, and unspecified assistantships available. Support available to part-time students. Financial award application deadline: 6/30; financial award applicants required to submit FAFSA. *Application contact:* Tammy Manka, Assistant Director of Graduate Admissions, 866-279-9663, E-mail: tmanka@marywood.edu.

Mercyhurst College, Graduate Program, Program in Administration of Justice, Erie, PA 16546. Offers administration of justice (MS). Part-time and evening/weekend programs available. *Degree requirements:* For master's, thesis optional. *Entrance requirements:* For master's, GRE General Test, MAT, or minimum GPA of 3.0. Additional exam requirements/recommendations for international students: Required—TOEFL. Electronic applications accepted. *Faculty research:* Research methods, criminal justice administration, juvenile justice.

Mercyhurst College, Graduate Program, Program in Applied Intelligence, Erie, PA 16546. Offers MS, Certificate. *Entrance requirements:* For master's, GRE or MAT, interview. Additional exam requirements/recommendations for international students: Required—TOEFL. Electronic applications accepted.

Methodist University, School of Graduate Studies, Program in Justice Administration, Fayetteville, NC 28311-1498. Offers MJA. Part-time and evening/weekend programs available. *Faculty:* 3 full-time (0 women), 1 part-time/adjunct (0 women). *Students:* 27 part-time (11 women); includes 5 minority (all African Americans). 6 applicants, 100% accepted, 5 enrolled. In 2009, 2 master's awarded. *Entrance requirements:* For master's, bachelor's degree in criminal justice or related discipline with minimum overall GPA of 3.0 from accredited institution. Additional exam requirements/recommendations for international students: Required—TOEFL (minimum score 500 paper-based; 173 computer-based; 60 iBT). *Application deadline:* For fall admission, 7/15 for domestic and international students; for spring admission, 10/15 for domestic and international students. Application fee: $50. *Expenses:* Tuition: Full-time $26,895; part-time $698 per course. Required fees: $110; $600 per year. One-time fee: $1125 full-time; $175 part-time. Full-time tuition and fees vary according to program. Part-time tuition and fees vary according to campus/location. *Financial support:* In 2009–10, 9 students received support.

Available to part-time students. Application deadline: 8/10. *Unit head:* Dr. Darl H. Champion, Director, 800-488-7110 Ext. 7050, E-mail: champion@methodist.edu. *Application contact:* Kristine A. Thomas, Coordinator, 800-488-7110 Ext. 7268, E-mail: kathomas@methodist.edu.

Michigan State University, The Graduate School, College of Social Science, School of Criminal Justice, East Lansing, MI 48824. Offers criminal justice (MS, PhD); forensic science (MS); law enforcement intelligence and analysis (MS). Postbaccalaureate distance learning degree programs offered. *Faculty:* 25 full-time (8 women). *Students:* 88 full-time (46 women), 109 part-time (48 women); includes 21 minority (5 African Americans, 3 Asian Americans or Pacific Islanders, 13 Hispanic Americans), 18 international. Average age 30. 211 applicants, 43% accepted. In 2009, 38 master's, 1 doctorate awarded. *Entrance requirements:* Additional exam requirements/recommendations for international students: Required—TOEFL. Electronic applications accepted. *Expenses:* Tuition, state resident: part-time $478.25 per credit hour. Tuition, nonresident: part-time $966.50 per credit hour. Part-time tuition and fees vary according to program. *Financial support:* In 2009–10, 11 research assistantships with tuition reimbursements (averaging $6,151 per year), 34 teaching assistantships with tuition reimbursements (averaging $6,251 per year) were awarded; unspecified assistantships also available. Total annual research expenditures: $1.1 million. *Unit head:* Dr. Edmund F. McGarrell, Director, 517-355-2192, Fax: 517-432-1787, E-mail: mcgarrel@msu.edu. *Application contact:* Melissa Christle, Graduate Secretary, 517-353-7133, Fax: 517-432-1787, E-mail: burrier@msu.edu.

Middle Tennessee State University, College of Graduate Studies, College of Education and Behavioral Science, Department of Criminal Justice Administration, Murfreesboro, TN 37132. Offers MCJ. Part-time and evening/weekend programs available. Postbaccalaureate distance learning degree programs offered. *Faculty:* 6 full-time (2 women). *Students:* 3 full-time (0 women), 46 part-time (33 women); includes 27 minority (all African Americans). Average age 27. 61 applicants, 67% accepted, 41 enrolled. In 2009, 3 master's awarded. *Degree requirements:* For master's, one foreign language, comprehensive exam, thesis. *Entrance requirements:* For master's, GRE or MAT. Additional exam requirements/recommendations for international students: Required—TOEFL (minimum score 525 paper-based; 195 computer-based; 71 iBT) or IELTS (minimum score 6). *Application deadline:* For fall admission, 6/1 for domestic and international students. Applications are processed on a rolling basis. Application fee: $25 ($30 for international students). Electronic applications accepted. *Expenses:* Tuition, state resident: full-time $4404. Tuition, nonresident: full-time $10,956. *Financial support:* In 2009–10, 1 student received support. Institutionally sponsored loans available. Support available to part-time students. Financial award application deadline: 5/1; financial award applicants required to submit FAFSA. *Unit head:* Dr. Deborah Newman, Chair, 615-898-2630, Fax: 615-898-5614, E-mail: dnewman@mtsu.edu. *Application contact:* Dr. Michael Allen, Dean and Vice Provost for Research, 615-898-2840, Fax: 615-904-8020, E-mail: mallen@mtsu.edu.

Midwestern State University, Graduate Studies, College of Health Sciences and Human Services, Program in Health Services and Public Administration, Wichita Falls, TX 76308. Offers health services administration (MHA); public administration (MPA); public administration (administrative justice) (MPA); public administration (health services administration) with certificate (MPA); public administration (health services) (MPA). Part-time and evening/weekend programs available. *Degree requirements:* For master's, comprehensive exam, thesis. *Entrance requirements:* For master's, GRE. Additional exam requirements/recommendations for international students: Required—TOEFL (minimum score 550 paper-based; 213 computer-based). Electronic applications accepted. *Expenses:* Tuition, state resident: full-time $1620; part-time $90 per credit hour. Tuition, nonresident: full-time $2160; part-time $120 per credit hour. International tuition: $7506 full-time. Required fees: $3068.80; $145.60 per credit hour. $179 per semester.

Minot State University, Graduate School, Program in Criminal Justice, Minot, ND 58707-0002. Offers MS. *Degree requirements:* For master's, comprehensive exam, thesis. *Entrance requirements:* For master's, GRE General Test, bachelor's degree with a minor in criminal justice or related field, minimum GPA of 3.0. Additional exam requirements/recommendations for international students: Required—TOEFL. *Expenses:* Tuition, state resident: full-time $5720; part-time $283 per credit hour. Tuition, nonresident: full-time $5720; part-time $283 per credit hour. Required fees: $1034; $1034 per year. Tuition and fees vary according to course load, degree level and program. *Faculty research:* Sentencing, white-collar/organizational crime, juveniles, gender issues, policy analysis.

Mississippi College, Graduate School, College of Arts and Sciences, School of Humanities and Social Sciences, Department of History, Political Science, Administration of Justice, and Paralegal Studies, Clinton, MS 39058. Offers administration of justice (MSS); history (M Ed, MA, MSS); paralegal studies (Certificate); political science (MSS); social sciences (M Ed, MSS). Part-time programs available. *Faculty:* 4 full-time (0 women), 5 part-time/adjunct (1 woman). *Students:* 10 full-time (5 women), 27 part-time (10 women); includes 8 minority (all African Americans); 1 international. Average age 32. In 2009, 12 master's awarded. *Degree requirements:* For master's, one foreign language, comprehensive exam, thesis (for some programs). *Entrance requirements:* For master's, GRE or NTE, minimum GPA of 2.5. Additional exam requirements/recommendations for international students: Recommended—IELTS. *Application deadline:* For fall admission, 8/15 priority date for domestic students. Applications are processed on a rolling basis. Application fee: $30. Electronic applications accepted. *Expenses:* Tuition: Part-time $452 per credit hour. Required fees: $101 per semester. Tuition and fees vary according to degree level, campus/location, program and student level. *Financial support:* Teaching assistantships, Federal Work-Study, scholarships/grants, and unspecified assistantships available. Support available to part-time students. Financial award application deadline: 4/1; financial award applicants required to submit FAFSA. *Unit head:* Dr. Kirk Ford, Chair, 601-925-3326, E-mail: ford@mc.edu. *Application contact:* Elnora Lewis, Secretary, 601-925-3225, Fax: 601-925-3889, E-mail: lewis09@mc.edu.

Mississippi Valley State University, Department of Criminal Justice and Social Work, Itta Bena, MS 38941-1400. Offers criminal justice (MS). Part-time and evening/weekend programs available. *Degree requirements:* For master's, thesis optional. *Entrance requirements:* For master's, minimum GPA of 2.5. Electronic applications accepted. *Faculty research:* Police in the criminal justice system, the United States and international terrorism.

Missouri Southern State University, Program in Criminal Justice Administration, Joplin, MO 64801-1595. Offers MS. Postbaccalaureate distance learning degree programs offered. *Degree requirements:* For master's, thesis optional. *Entrance requirements:* For master's, minimum undergraduate GPA of 2.5.

Missouri State University, Graduate College, College of Humanities and Public Affairs, Department of Sociology, Anthropology, and Criminology, Springfield, MO 65897. Offers applied anthropology (MS); criminology (MS). Part-time programs available. *Faculty:* 20 full-time (6 women). *Students:* 31 full-time (10 women), 21 part-time (14 women); includes 4 minority (3 Asian Americans or Pacific Islanders, 1 Hispanic American). Average age 28. 25 applicants, 96% accepted, 19 enrolled. In 2009, 8 master's awarded. *Degree requirements:* For master's, comprehensive exam. *Entrance requirements:* For master's, GRE, minimum GPA of 3.0. Additional exam requirements/recommendations for international students: Required—TOEFL (minimum score 550 paper-based; 213 computer-based; 79 iBT). *Application deadline:* For fall admission, 7/20 priority date for domestic students, 5/1 for international students; for spring admission, 12/20 priority date for domestic students, 9/1 for international students. Applications are processed on a rolling basis. Application fee: $35 ($50 for international students). Electronic applications accepted. *Expenses:* Tuition, state resident: full-time $3852; part-time $214 per credit hour. Tuition, nonresident: full-time $7524; part-time $418 per credit hour. Required fees: $696; $172 per semester. Tuition and fees vary according to course level, course load, degree level and program. *Financial support:* Federal Work-Study, institutionally sponsored loans, scholarships/grants, and unspecified assistantships available. Financial award application deadline: 3/31; financial award applicants required to submit FAFSA. *Faculty research:* Youth delinquency, social theory, linguistic anthropology, forensic anthropology, homeland security. *Unit head:* Dr. Karl Kunkel, Head, 417-836-5640, Fax: 417-836-6416, E-mail: karlkunkel@missouristate.edu. *Application contact:* Eric Eckert, Coordinator of Admissions and Recruitment, 417-836-5331, Fax: 417-836-6888, E-mail: ericeckert@missouristate.edu.

Missouri State University, Graduate College, Interdisciplinary Program in Administrative Studies, Springfield, MO 65897. Offers applied communication (MS); criminal justice (MS); environmental management (MS); project management (MS); sports management (MS). Part-time and evening/weekend programs available. Postbaccalaureate distance learning degree programs offered (no on-campus study). *Students:* 17 full-time (11 women), 60 part-time (26 women); includes 6 minority (4 African Americans, 1 Asian American or Pacific Islander, 1 Hispanic American), 2 international. Average age 35. 24 applicants, 100% accepted, 19 enrolled. In 2009, 16 master's awarded. *Degree requirements:* For master's, comprehensive exam, thesis or alternative. *Entrance requirements:* For master's, GRE, GMAT, 3 years of work experience. Additional exam requirements/recommendations for international students: Required—TOEFL (minimum score 550 paper-based; 213 computer-based; 79 iBT). *Application deadline:* For fall admission, 7/20 priority date for domestic students; for spring admission, 12/20 priority date for domestic students. Applications are processed on a rolling basis. Application fee: $35 ($50 for international students). Electronic applications accepted. *Expenses:* Tuition, state resident: full-time $3852; part-time $214 per credit hour. Tuition, nonresident: full-time $7524; part-time $418 per credit hour. Required fees: $696; $172 per semester. Tuition and fees vary according to course level, course load, degree level and program. *Financial support:* In 2009–10, 1 teaching assistantship with full tuition reimbursement (averaging $7,340 per year) was awarded; career-related internships or fieldwork, Federal Work-Study, institutionally sponsored loans, scholarships/grants, and unspecified assistantships also available. Support available to part-time students. Financial award application deadline: 3/31; financial award applicants required to submit FAFSA. *Unit head:* John Bourhis, Director, 417-836-6390, E-mail: johnbourhis@missouristate.edu. *Application contact:* Eric Eckert, Coordinator of Graduate Admissions and Recruitment, 417-836-5331, Fax: 417-836-6200, E-mail: ericeckert@missouristate.edu.

Molloy College, Criminal Justice Program, Rockville Centre, NY 11571-5002. Offers MS. *Faculty:* 3 full-time (1 woman), 1 part-time/adjunct (0 women). *Students:* 19 full-time (8 women), 16 part-time (11 women); includes 11 African Americans, 1 American Indian/Alaska Native, 4 Hispanic Americans. Average age 32. In 2009, 8 master's awarded. *Expenses:* Tuition: Part-time $765 per credit. Required fees: $340 per semester. *Unit head:* Dr. John Eterno, Associate Dean/Director, 516-678-5000 Ext. 6135. *Application contact:* Alina Haitz, Interim Associate Dean/Director, 516-678-5000 Ext. 6399, Fax: 516-256-2247, E-mail: ahaitz@molloy.edu.

Monmouth University, Graduate School, Department of Criminal Justice, West Long Branch, NJ 07764-1898. Offers criminal justice administration (MA, Certificate); homeland security (Certificate). Part-time and evening/weekend programs available. *Faculty:* 3 full-time (0 women), 3 part-time/adjunct (2 women). *Students:* 21 full-time (11 women), 19 part-time (10 women); includes 7 minority (1 African American, 1 Asian American or Pacific Islander, 5 Hispanic Americans), 1 international. Average age 27. 36 applicants, 97% accepted, 23 enrolled. In 2009, 14 master's awarded. *Degree requirements:* For master's, comprehensive exam, thesis or alternative. *Entrance requirements:* For master's, minimum GPA of 3.0 in major, 2.5 overall. Additional exam requirements/recommendations for international students: Required—TOEFL (minimum score 550 paper-based; 213 computer-based; 79 iBT), IELTS (minimum score 5), Michigan English Language Assessment Battery (minimum score 77), Cambridge A, B, C. *Application deadline:* For fall admission, 7/15 priority date for domestic students, 6/1 for international students; for spring admission, 11/15 priority date for domestic students, 11/1 for international students. Applications are processed on a rolling basis. Application fee: $50. Electronic applications accepted. *Expenses:* Tuition: Part-time $773 per credit. Required fees: $157 per semester. *Financial support:* In 2009–10, 25 students received support, including 20 fellowships (averaging $1,915 per year), 2 research assistantships (averaging $6,668 per year); career-related internships or fieldwork, scholarships/grants, and unspecified assistantships also available. Support available to part-time students. Financial award applicants required to submit FAFSA. *Faculty research:* Violent crimes, criminal pathology, terrorism, computer crime, comparative criminal justice systems. *Unit head:* Dr. Gregory Coram, Director, 732-571-3448, Fax: 732-263-5148, E-mail: coram@monmouth.edu. *Application contact:* Kevin Roane, Director, Office of Graduate Admission, 732-571-3452, Fax: 732-263-5123, E-mail: gradadm@monmouth.edu.

Morehead State University, Graduate Programs, Caudill College of Arts, Humanities and Social Sciences, Department of Sociology, Social Work and Criminology, Morehead, KY 40351. Offers criminology (MA); general sociology (MA); gerontology (MA); sociology regional analysis (MA); sociology/chemical dependency (MA). Part-time and evening/weekend programs available. *Faculty:* 6 full-time (3 women), 1 (woman) part-time/adjunct. *Students:* 14 full-time (11 women), 18 part-time (12 women). Average age 34. 27 applicants, 78% accepted, 14 enrolled. In 2009, 5 master's awarded. *Degree requirements:* For master's, comprehensive exam, thesis (for some programs). *Entrance requirements:* For master's, GRE General Test, minimum GPA of 3.0 in sociology, 2.75 overall; 18 hours of course work in sociology, writing sample. Additional exam requirements/recommendations for international students: Required—TOEFL (minimum score 500 paper-based; 173 computer-based). *Application deadline:* For fall admission, 8/1 priority date for domestic and international students; for spring admission, 12/1 priority date for domestic and international students. Applications are processed on a rolling basis. Application fee: $30. Electronic applications accepted. *Expenses:* Tuition, state resident: full-time $6318; part-time $351 per credit hour. Tuition, nonresident: full-time $15,804; part-time $878 per credit hour. *Financial support:* In 2009–10, 4 teaching assistantships (averaging $10,000 per year) were awarded; career-related internships or fieldwork, Federal Work-Study, and unspecified assistantships also available. Financial award application deadline: 3/15; financial award applicants required to submit FAFSA. *Faculty research:* Death and dying; aging, drinking, and drugs; economic development; adult children of alcoholics. *Unit head:* Dr. Clarenda Phillips, Department Chair, 606-783-2434, Fax: 606-783-5070, E-mail: c.phillips@moreheadstate.edu. *Application contact:* Michelle Barber, Graduate Recruitment and Retention Assistant Director, 606-783-5127, Fax: 606-783-5061, E-mail: m.barber@moreheadstate.edu.

Mountain State University, Graduate Studies, Program in Criminal Justice Administration, Beckley, WV 25802-9003. Offers MCJA. Part-time and evening/weekend programs available. Postbaccalaureate distance learning degree programs offered (no on-campus study). *Faculty:* 7 full-time (2 women), 10 part-time/adjunct (4 women). *Students:* 28 full-time (15 women); includes 3 minority (all African Americans). Average age 41. 48 applicants, 48% accepted, 17 enrolled. In 2009, 6 master's awarded. *Degree requirements:* For master's, thesis or alternative. *Entrance requirements:* Additional exam requirements/recommendations for international students: Required—TOEFL (minimum score 550 paper-based; 213 computer-based); Recommended—IELTS (minimum score 6.5). *Application deadline:* For fall admission, 5/31 priority date for domestic and international students. Applications are processed on a rolling basis. Application fee: $25 ($50 for international students). Electronic applications accepted. *Expenses:* Tuition: Full-time $6450. Tuition and fees vary according to program. *Financial support:* Federal Work-Study, scholarships/grants, and unspecified assistantships available. Support available to part-time students. Financial award applicants required to submit FAFSA. *Unit head:* Dr. William White, Interim Dean, School of Graduate Studies/Dean, School of Leadership and Professional Services, 304-929-1658, Fax: 304-929-1637, E-mail: wwhite@mountainstate.edu. *Application contact:* Anita Diaz, Enrollment Coordinator of Graduate Studies, 304-461-3213, Fax: 304-929-1637, E-mail: adiaz@mountainstate.edu.

Mount Aloysius College, Criminal Justice Management in Correctional Administration Program, Cresson, PA 16630. Offers MA. *Entrance requirements:* For master's, GRE General Test. *Application deadline:* For fall admission, 8/1 for domestic students; for spring admission, 12/1 for domestic students. Applications are processed on a rolling basis. Application fee: $30. Electronic applications accepted. *Application contact:* Andrew D. Clouse, Associate Director of

Criminal Justice and Criminology

Mount Aloysius College (continued)
Admissions and Coordinator of Graduate Admissions, 814-886-6480, E-mail: aclouse@mtaloy.edu.

National University, Academic Affairs, College of Letters and Sciences, Department of Professional Studies, La Jolla, CA 92037-1011. Offers forensic science (MFS), including criminalistics and investigation; public administration (MPA), including alternative dispute resolution, human resource management, organizational leadership, public finance. Part-time and evening/weekend programs available. Postbaccalaureate distance learning degree programs offered (no on-campus study). *Faculty:* 5 full-time (3 women), 27 part-time/adjunct (7 women). *Students:* 167 full-time (95 women), 246 part-time (133 women); includes 188 minority (71 African Americans, 2 American Indian/Alaska Native, 41 Asian Americans or Pacific Islanders, 74 Hispanic Americans). Average age 38. 284 applicants, 100% accepted, 206 enrolled. In 2009, 104 master's awarded. *Degree requirements:* For master's, thesis. *Entrance requirements:* For master's, interview, minimum GPA of 2.5. Additional exam requirements/recommendations for international students: Required—TOEFL (minimum score 550 paper-based; 213 computer-based; 79 iBT), IELTS (minimum score 6). *Application deadline:* Applications are processed on a rolling basis. Application fee: $60 ($65 for international students). Electronic applications accepted. *Expenses:* Tuition: Part-time $338 per quarter hour. *Financial support:* Career-related internships or fieldwork, institutionally sponsored loans, scholarships/grants, and tuition waivers (partial) available. Support available to part-time students. Financial award application deadline: 6/30; financial award applicants required to submit FAFSA. *Unit head:* Chandrika M. Kelso, Associate Professor and Chair, 858-642-8433, Fax: 858-642-8715, E-mail: ckelso@nu.edu. *Application contact:* Dominick Giovanniello, Associate Regional Dean—San Diego, 800-NAT-UNIV, Fax: 858-541-7792, E-mail: dgiovann@nu.edu.

National University, Academic Affairs, School of Education, Department of Special Education, La Jolla, CA 92037-1011. Offers deaf and hard-of-hearing education (MS); juvenile justice special education (MS); special education (MS). Part-time and evening/weekend programs available. Postbaccalaureate distance learning degree programs offered (no on-campus study). *Degree requirements:* For master's, thesis (for some programs). *Entrance requirements:* For master's, interview, minimum GPA of 2.5. Additional exam requirements/recommendations for international students: Required—TOEFL (minimum score 550 paper-based; 213 computer-based; 79 iBT), IELTS (minimum score 6). *Application deadline:* Applications are processed on a rolling basis. Application fee: $60 ($65 for international students). Electronic applications accepted. *Expenses:* Tuition: Part-time $338 per quarter hour. *Financial support:* Career-related internships or fieldwork, institutionally sponsored loans, scholarships/grants, and tuition waivers (partial) available. Support available to part-time students. Financial award application deadline: 6/30; financial award applicants required to submit FAFSA. *Unit head:* Dr. Britt Ferguson, Department Chair, 858-642-8346, Fax: 858-642-8729, E-mail: mferguson@nu.edu. *Application contact:* Dr. Britt Ferguson, Department Chair, 858-642-8346, Fax: 858-642-8729, E-mail: mferguson@nu.edu.

New Jersey City University, Graduate Studies and Continuing Education, College of Professional Studies, Department of Criminal Justice, Jersey City, NJ 07305-1597. Offers criminal justice (MS); law enforcement (MS). Part-time and evening/weekend programs available. *Faculty:* 7. *Students:* 23 full-time (12 women), 27 part-time (14 women); includes 23 minority (9 African Americans, 1 Asian American or Pacific Islander, 13 Hispanic Americans), 1 international. Average age 30. In 2009, 9 master's awarded. *Degree requirements:* For master's, thesis or alternative. *Entrance requirements:* For master's, GRE General Test or MAT. Additional exam requirements/recommendations for international students: Required—TOEFL. *Application deadline:* For fall admission, 8/1 priority date for domestic students; for spring admission, 12/1 for domestic students. Applications are processed on a rolling basis. Application fee: $0. *Expenses:* Tuition, area resident: Part-time $456.75 per credit. Tuition, nonresident: part-time $842.55 per credit. Required fees: $65 per term. *Financial support:* Unspecified assistantships available. *Unit head:* Dr. Shirely Williams, Chairperson, 201-200-3492, E-mail: swilliams@njcu.edu. *Application contact:* Dr. Shirely Williams, Chairperson, 201-200-3492, E-mail: swilliams@njcu.edu.

New Mexico State University, Graduate School, College of Arts and Sciences, Department of Criminal Justice, Las Cruces, NM 88003-8001. Offers MCJ. Part-time and evening/weekend programs available. Postbaccalaureate distance learning degree programs offered (no on-campus study). *Faculty:* 10 full-time (5 women), 4 part-time/adjunct (3 women). *Students:* 44 full-time (28 women), 58 part-time (32 women); includes 44 minority (2 African Americans, 4 American Indian/Alaska Native, 2 Asian Americans or Pacific Islanders, 36 Hispanic Americans), 1 international. Average age 31. 61 applicants, 100% accepted, 39 enrolled. In 2009, 34 master's awarded. *Degree requirements:* For master's, comprehensive exam, thesis optional, oral and written exams. *Entrance requirements:* For master's, minimum GPA of 3.0. *Application deadline:* For fall admission, 4/1 priority date for domestic students; for spring admission, 11/1 priority date for domestic students. Applications are processed on a rolling basis. Application fee: $30 ($50 for international students). Electronic applications accepted. *Expenses:* Tuition, state resident: full-time $4080; part-time $223 per credit. Tuition, nonresident: full-time $14,256; part-time $647 per credit. Required fees: $1278; $639 per semester. *Financial support:* In 2009–10, 9 research assistantships with partial tuition reimbursements (averaging $12,733 per year), 2 teaching assistantships with partial tuition reimbursements (averaging $13,430 per year) were awarded; fellowships with partial tuition reimbursements, career-related internships or fieldwork, health care benefits, and unspecified assistantships also available. Financial award application deadline: 4/1. *Faculty research:* Juvenile justice, jails and prison administration, courts and legal decision making, victim studies, policy and evaluation research. *Unit head:* Dr. James R. Maupin, Head, 575-646-3316, Fax: 575-646-2827, E-mail: jmaupin@nmsu.edu. *Application contact:* James Maupin, Professor, 575-646-3316, Fax: 575-646-2827, E-mail: jmaupin@nmsu.edu.

Niagara University, Graduate Division of Arts and Sciences, Department of Criminal Justice, Niagara Falls, Niagara University, NY 14109. Offers criminal justice administration (MS). *Entrance requirements:* For master's, GRE. Additional exam requirements/recommendations for international students: Required—TOEFL.

Nichols College, Graduate Program in Business Administration, Dudley, MA 01571-5000. Offers business administration (MBA, MOL); security management (MBA); sport management (MBA). Part-time and evening/weekend programs available. Postbaccalaureate distance learning degree programs offered (no on-campus study). *Entrance requirements:* For master's, 2 letters of recommendation. Additional exam requirements/recommendations for international students: Required—TOEFL (minimum score 500 paper-based; 213 computer-based). Electronic applications accepted.

Norfolk State University, School of Graduate Studies, School of Liberal Arts, Department of Sociology, Program in Criminal Justice, Norfolk, VA 23504. Offers MA.

North Carolina Central University, Division of Academic Affairs, College of Behavioral and Social Sciences, Department of Criminal Justice, Durham, NC 27707-3129. Offers MS. Part-time and evening/weekend programs available. *Degree requirements:* For master's, one foreign language, comprehensive exam, thesis or alternative. *Entrance requirements:* For master's, GRE, minimum GPA of 3.0 in major, 2.5 overall. Additional exam requirements/recommendations for international students: Required—TOEFL.

North Dakota State University, College of Graduate and Interdisciplinary Studies, College of Arts, Humanities and Social Sciences, Department of Criminal Justice and Political Science, Fargo, ND 58108. Offers criminal justice (MS, PhD). Part-time programs available. *Faculty:* 3 full-time (1 woman). *Students:* 11 full-time (8 women), 3 part-time (0 women); includes 1 minority (Hispanic American), 1 international. Average age 25. 6 applicants, 67% accepted, 2 enrolled. In 2009, 1 master's awarded. Terminal master's awarded for partial completion of doctoral program. *Degree requirements:* For master's, thesis (for some programs); for doctorate, comprehensive exam, thesis/dissertation. *Entrance requirements:* For master's, minimum GPA of 3.0 in last 60 credit hours, approved bachelor's degree, course work in research methods and statistics; for doctorate, GRE General Test, minimum GPA of 3.0 over last 60 credit hours, 3 letters of recommendation. Additional exam requirements/recommendations for international students: Required—TOEFL (minimum score 525 paper-based; 197 computer-based; 71 iBT). *Application deadline:* For spring admission, 4/1 priority date for domestic students, 4/1 for international students. Applications are processed on a rolling basis. Application fee: $45 ($60 for international students). *Financial support:* In 2009–10, 6 research assistantships with tuition reimbursements (averaging $12,000 per year), 3 teaching assistantships with tuition reimbursements (averaging $6,000 per year) were awarded; career-related internships or fieldwork, institutionally sponsored loans, tuition waivers (full), and unspecified assistantships also available. Financial award application deadline: 4/1. *Faculty research:* Corrections, policing, drugs and crime, gender and crime, criminology. Total annual research expenditures: $150,000. *Unit head:* Dr. Kevin Thompson, Chair, 701-231-8938, Fax: 701-231-5877, E-mail: kevin.thompson@ndsu.edu. *Application contact:* Dr. Kevin Thompson, Chair, 701-231-8938, Fax: 701-231-5877, E-mail: kevin.thompson@ndsu.edu.

Northeastern State University, Graduate College, College of Liberal Arts, Program in Criminal Justice and Legal Studies, Tahlequah, OK 74464-2399. Offers criminal justice (MS). Part-time and evening/weekend programs available. *Degree requirements:* For master's, thesis optional, oral exam. *Entrance requirements:* For master's, MAT or GRE, minimum GPA of 2.5. Additional exam requirements/recommendations for international students: Required—TOEFL (minimum score 213 computer-based). Electronic applications accepted.

Northeastern University, College of Social Sciences and Humanities, School of Criminology and Criminal Justice, Boston, MA 02115-5096. Offers MS, PhD. Part-time and evening/weekend programs available. *Faculty:* 17 full-time (6 women), 11 part-time/adjunct (5 women). *Students:* 80 full-time (46 women), 12 part-time (6 women); includes 9 minority (5 African Americans, 1 American Indian/Alaska Native, 2 Asian Americans or Pacific Islanders, 1 Hispanic American), 12 international. 129 applicants, 62% accepted. In 2009, 21 master's awarded. *Degree requirements:* For master's, comprehensive exam, thesis optional. *Entrance requirements:* For master's and doctorate, GRE General Test. Additional exam requirements/recommendations for international students: Required—TOEFL. *Application deadline:* For fall admission, 3/1 for domestic students; for spring admission, 10/1 for domestic students. Applications are processed on a rolling basis. Application fee: $50. Electronic applications accepted. *Financial support:* In 2009–10, 12 teaching assistantships with full tuition reimbursements (averaging $13,654 per year) were awarded; research assistantships with full and partial tuition reimbursements, career-related internships or fieldwork, Federal Work-Study, and institutionally sponsored loans also available. Support available to part-time students. Financial award application deadline: 3/31; financial award applicants required to submit FAFSA. *Faculty research:* Juvenile justice, victimology, serial and mass murder, private security, criminology corrections, race and crime. *Unit head:* Jack McDevitt, Associate Dean, 617-373-2813, Fax: 617-373-8723. *Application contact:* Laurie A. Mastone, Assistant to the Director, 617-373-2813, Fax: 617-373-8723, E-mail: l.mastone@neu.edu.

Northern Arizona University, Graduate College, College of Social and Behavioral Sciences, Department of Criminology and Criminal Justice, Flagstaff, AZ 86011. Offers applied criminology (MS); criminal justice policy and planning (Certificate). Postbaccalaureate distance learning degree programs offered. *Faculty:* 16 full-time (9 women). *Students:* 19 full-time (16 women), 16 part-time (11 women); includes 8 minority (4 American Indian/Alaska Native, 4 Hispanic Americans), 1 international. Average age 30. 19 applicants, 95% accepted, 13 enrolled. In 2009, 3 master's awarded. *Degree requirements:* For master's, comprehensive exam, thesis, internship/practicum. *Entrance requirements:* For master's, minimum GPA of 3.0. Additional exam requirements/recommendations for international students: Required—TOEFL (minimum score 550 paper-based; 213 computer-based; 80 iBT), IELTS (minimum score 7), or a bachelor's degree from an English-speaking university and demonstrated proficiency. *Application deadline:* For fall admission, 3/15 priority date for domestic students, 9/1 priority date for international students; for spring admission, 10/15 priority date for domestic students. Applications are processed on a rolling basis. Application fee: $65. Electronic applications accepted. *Financial support:* In 2009–10, 6 teaching assistantships with partial tuition reimbursements (averaging $10,439 per year) were awarded; career-related internships or fieldwork, Federal Work-Study, scholarships/grants, health care benefits, tuition waivers (full and partial), and unspecified assistantships also available. Support available to part-time students. Financial award application deadline: 3/30; financial award applicants required to submit FAFSA. *Unit head:* Dr. Dennis Catlin, Chair, 928-523-7900, Fax: 928-523-6777, E-mail: dennis.catlin@nau.edu. *Application contact:* Dr. Luis Fernandez, Coordinator, 928-523-3710, Fax: 928-523-6777, E-mail: luis.fernandez@nau.edu.

Northern Michigan University, College of Graduate Studies, College of Professional Studies, Department of Criminal Justice, Marquette, MI 49855-5301. Offers MS. Part-time and evening/weekend programs available. *Entrance requirements:* For master's, minimum GPA of 3.0.

Nova Southeastern University, Criminal Justice Institute, Program in Criminal Justice, Fort Lauderdale, FL 33314-7796. Offers MS. *Faculty:* 41 part-time/adjunct (7 women). *Students:* 29 full-time (22 women), 140 part-time (93 women); includes 104 minority (73 African Americans, 1 American Indian/Alaska Native, 4 Asian Americans or Pacific Islanders, 26 Hispanic Americans). 41 applicants, 73% accepted, 30 enrolled. In 2009, 55 master's awarded. *Degree requirements:* For master's, comprehensive exam (for some programs), thesis optional. *Entrance requirements:* For master's, 3 letters of recommendation, minimum GPA of 2.5. *Application deadline:* For fall admission, 7/8 for domestic students; for winter admission, 1/8 for domestic students; for spring admission, 3/8 for domestic students. Application fee: $50. *Financial support:* Applicants required to submit FAFSA. *Unit head:* Dr. Tammy Kushner, Director, 954-262-7001, Fax: 954-937-7005, E-mail: kushner@nova.edu. *Application contact:* Russell Garner, Administrative Assistant, 954-262-7001, E-mail: cji@nova.edu.

See Close-Up on page 721.

Oklahoma City University, Petree College of Arts and Sciences, Division of Sociology and Justice Studies, Oklahoma City, OK 73106-1402. Offers applied sociology (MA), including nonprofit leadership; criminal justice (MCJ). Part-time and evening/weekend programs available. *Faculty:* 4 full-time (1 woman), 3 part-time/adjunct (2 women). *Students:* 11 full-time (8 women), 4 part-time (3 women); includes 3 minority (all African Americans), 1 international. Average age 31. 9 applicants, 89% accepted. In 2009, 7 master's awarded. *Degree requirements:* For master's, thesis optional. *Entrance requirements:* For master's, minimum GPA of 3.0, two letters of recommendation. Additional exam requirements/recommendations for international students: Required—TOEFL (minimum score 550 paper-based). *Application deadline:* For fall admission, 8/22 for domestic students; for spring admission, 1/15 for domestic students. Applications are processed on a rolling basis. Application fee: $30 ($70 for international students). *Expenses:* Contact institution. *Financial support:* Fellowships with partial tuition reimbursements, career-related internships or fieldwork available. Financial award application deadline: 8/1; financial award applicants required to submit FAFSA. *Faculty research:* Victims, police, corrections, security, women and crime. *Unit head:* Dr. Jody Horn, Director, 405-208-5247, Fax: 405-208-5447, E-mail: jhorn@okcu.edu. *Application contact:* Michelle Lockhart, Director, Admissions, 800-633-7242, Fax: 405-208-5916, E-mail: gadmissions@okcu.edu.

Old Dominion University, College of Arts and Letters, Program in Criminology and Criminal Justice, Norfolk, VA 23529. Offers PhD. Part-time and evening/weekend programs available. *Faculty:* 16 full-time (11 women). *Students:* 13 full-time (7 women), 2 part-time (1 woman); includes 3 minority (1 African American, 1 Asian American or Pacific Islander, 1 Hispanic American). Average age 34. 14 applicants, 57% accepted, 5 enrolled. *Degree requirements:* For doctorate, comprehensive exam, thesis/dissertation. *Entrance requirements:* For doctorate, GRE General Test, MA; minimum graduate GPA of 3.25; theory, methods, and statistics graduate coursework; letters of reference; writing sample. Additional exam requirements/recommendations for international students: Required—TOEFL. *Application deadline:* For fall admission, 2/15 for domestic and international students. Application fee: $40. Electronic applications accepted. *Expenses:* Tuition, state resident: full-time $8112; part-time $338 per credit. Tuition, nonresident: full-time $20,256; part-time $844 per credit. Required fees: $119 per semester. One-time fee: $50. *Financial support:* In 2009–10, 7 students received support, including 3 fellowships with full tuition reimbursements available (averaging $15,000 per year), 4 teaching assistantships with full tuition reimbursements available (averaging $15,000 per year). Financial award application deadline: 2/15. *Faculty research:* Inequality, crime and justice; domestic violence; community justice; criminological theory; methods; policing; courts and corrections; state crime. *Unit head:* Dr. Mona Danner, Graduate Program Director, 757-683-5931, Fax: 757-683-5634, E-mail: mdanner@odu.edu. *Application contact:* Dr. Robert Wojtowicz, Associate Dean, 757-683-6077, Fax: 757-683-5746, E-mail: rwojtowi@odu.edu.

Point Park University, School of Arts and Sciences, Department of Criminal Justice and Intelligence Studies, Pittsburgh, PA 15222-1984. Offers criminal justice administration (MS). Evening/weekend programs available. *Faculty:* 3 full-time, 4 part-time/adjunct. *Students:* 29 full-time (18 women), 4 part-time (all women); includes 21 minority (19 African Americans, 1 Asian American or Pacific Islander, 1 Hispanic American). Average age 32. 52 applicants, 60% accepted, 24 enrolled. In 2009, 17 master's awarded. *Degree requirements:* For master's, comprehensive exam (for some programs), thesis or alternative. *Entrance requirements:* For master's, minimum GPA of 2.75, resume, 2 letters of recommendation. Additional exam requirements/recommendations for international students: Required—TOEFL (minimum score 550 paper-based; 79 iBT). *Application deadline:* Applications are processed on a rolling basis. Application fee: $30. Electronic applications accepted. *Expenses:* Tuition: Full-time $11,880; part-time $660 per credit. Required fees: $486; $27 per credit. *Financial support:* In 2009–10, 29 students received support, including 2 research assistantships with full tuition reimbursements available (averaging $6,400 per year); scholarships/grants also available. Financial award application deadline: 4/15; financial award applicants required to submit FAFSA. *Unit head:* Dr. Lorelei Stein, Program Director, 412-392-6169, Fax: 412-392-3925, E-mail: lstein@pointpark.edu. *Application contact:* Lynn Ribar, Associate Director of Graduate and Adult Enrollment, 412-392-3908, Fax: 412-392-6164, E-mail: lribar@pointpark.edu.

Polytechnic Institute of NYU, Department of Computer Science and Engineering, Brooklyn, NY 11201-2990. Offers computer science (MS, PhD); cyber security (Graduate Certificate); software engineering (Graduate Certificate). Part-time and evening/weekend programs available. *Faculty:* 18 full-time (2 women), 7 part-time/adjunct (1 woman). *Students:* 225 full-time (58 women), 84 part-time (15 women); includes 35 minority (7 African Americans, 23 Asian Americans or Pacific Islanders, 5 Hispanic Americans), 226 international. Average age 26. 727 applicants, 65% accepted, 129 enrolled. In 2009, 76 master's, 2 doctorates awarded. *Degree requirements:* For master's, comprehensive exam (for some programs), thesis (for some programs); for doctorate, comprehensive exam, thesis/dissertation. *Entrance requirements:* For master's, BA or BS in computer science, mathematics, science, or engineering; working knowledge of a high-level program; for doctorate, GRE General Test, GRE Subject Test, qualifying exam, BA or BS in science, engineering, or management; MS or 1 year of graduate course work. Additional exam requirements/recommendations for international students: Required—TOEFL (minimum score 550 paper-based; 213 computer-based; 80 iBT); Recommended—IELTS (minimum score 6.5). *Application deadline:* For fall admission, 7/31 priority date for domestic students, 4/30 priority date for international students; for spring admission, 12/31 priority date for domestic students, 10/30 priority date for international students. Applications are processed on a rolling basis. Application fee: $75. Electronic applications accepted. *Expenses:* Tuition: Full-time $21,492; part-time $1194 per credit hour. Required fees: $1160; $204 per course. *Financial support:* In 2009–10, 6 fellowships with partial tuition reimbursements (averaging $2,220 per year), 22 research assistantships with tuition reimbursements (averaging $25,753 per year), 6 teaching assistantships with tuition reimbursements (averaging $35,131 per year) were awarded; institutionally sponsored loans, scholarships/grants, and unspecified assistantships also available. Support available to part-time students. Financial award applicants required to submit FAFSA. Total annual research expenditures: $2 million. *Unit head:* Dr. Keith W. Ross, Head, 718-260-3859, Fax: 718-260-3609, E-mail: ross@poly.edu. *Application contact:* JeanCarlo Bonilla, Director, Graduate Center, 718-260-3182, Fax: 718-260-3624, E-mail: gradinfo@poly.edu.

Polytechnic Institute of NYU, Westchester Graduate Center, Graduate Programs, Department of Computer Science and Engineering, Major in Cyber Security, Hawthorne, NY 10532-1507. Offers MS. *Students:* 10 part-time (3 women); includes 2 minority (1 African American, 1 Asian American or Pacific Islander). *Entrance requirements:* Additional exam requirements/recommendations for international students: Required—TOEFL (minimum score 550 paper-based; 213 computer-based; 80 iBT); Recommended—IELTS (minimum score 6.5). *Application deadline:* For fall admission, 7/31 priority date for domestic students, 4/30 priority date for international students; for spring admission, 12/31 priority date for domestic students, 11/30 priority date for international students. Applications are processed on a rolling basis. Application fee: $75. Electronic applications accepted. *Financial support:* Institutionally sponsored loans, scholarships/grants, and unspecified assistantships available. Support available to part-time students. *Unit head:* Dr. Keith W. Ross, Department Head, 718-260-3859, E-mail: ross@poly.edu. *Application contact:* JeanCarlo Bonilla, Director of Graduate Enrollment Management, 718-260-3182, Fax: 718-260-3624, E-mail: gradinfo@poly.edu.

Pontifical Catholic University of Puerto Rico, Institute of Graduate Studies in Behavioral Science and Community Affairs, Program in Criminology, Ponce, PR 00717-0777. Offers MA. Part-time and evening/weekend programs available. *Degree requirements:* For master's, thesis. *Entrance requirements:* For master's, EXADEP, 3 letters of recommendation, interview, minimum GPA of 2.75.

Pontificia Universidad Catolica Madre y Maestra, Graduate School, Santiago, Dominican Republic. Offers administration (M Adm); architecture of interiors (M Arch); architecture of tourist lodgings (M Arch); banking and financial management (M Mgmt); civil law (LL M); construction administration (ME); corporate business law (LL M); criminal procedure law (LL M); environmental engineering (ME, MEE); finance (M Mgmt); history applied to education (M Ed); human resources (EMBA); insurance (M Mgmt); international business (M Mgmt); labor law and Social Security (LL M); logistics management (ME); marketing (M Mgmt); renewable energy (ME); strategic cost management (M Mgmt). *Entrance requirements:* For master's, curriculum vitae, interview.

Portland State University, Graduate Studies, College of Urban and Public Affairs, Hatfield School of Government, Division of Criminology and Criminal Justice, Portland, OR 97207-0751. Offers MS, PhD. Part-time programs available. *Degree requirements:* For master's, thesis or alternative, comprehensive oral exam; for doctorate, comprehensive exam, thesis/dissertation, residency. *Entrance requirements:* For master's, minimum GPA of 3.0 in upper-division course work or 2.75 overall; for doctorate, GRE General Test. Additional exam requirements/recommendations for international students: Required—TOEFL (minimum score 550 paper-based; 213 computer-based). *Faculty research:* History of criminal justice, mental health issues, international terrorism, offender assessment, domestic violence.

Radford University, College of Graduate and Professional Studies, College of Humanities and Behavioral Sciences, Department of Criminal Justice, Radford, VA 24142. Offers MA, MS. Part-time programs available. *Faculty:* 10 full-time (5 women). *Students:* 16 full-time (11 women), 15 part-time (8 women); includes 3 minority (all African Americans). Average age 30. 36 applicants, 75% accepted, 23 enrolled. In 2009, 19 master's awarded. *Degree requirements:* For master's, comprehensive exam, thesis optional. *Entrance requirements:* For master's, GRE, minimum GPA of 2.9; 2 letters of reference; original writing sample. Additional exam requirements/recommendations for international students: Required—TOEFL (minimum score 550 paper-based; 213 computer-based; 79 iBT). *Application deadline:* For fall admission, 12/1 for international students; for spring admission, 7/1 for international students. Applications are processed on a rolling basis. Application fee: $50. Electronic applications accepted. *Expenses:* Tuition, state resident: full-time $5086; part-time $211 per credit hour. Tuition, nonresident: full-time $12,608; part-time $525 per credit hour. Required fees: $2508; $105 per credit hour. *Financial support:* In 2009–10, 8 students received support, including 8 research assistantships with partial tuition reimbursements available (averaging $8,000 per year); career-related internships or fieldwork, Federal Work-Study, institutionally sponsored loans, scholarships/grants, and unspecified assistantships also available. Financial award application deadline: 3/1; financial award applicants required to submit FAFSA. *Faculty research:* Capital punishment, crime mapping and analysis, elder abuse, guns and gun control, rural crime. *Unit head:* Dr. Mary Atwell, Chair, 540-831-6339, Fax: 540-831-6075, E-mail: matwell@radford.edu. *Application contact:* Graduate Admissions, 540-831-6431, Fax: 540-831-6061, E-mail: gradcollege@radford.edu.

Regis University, College for Professional Studies, MA Program, Denver, CO 80221-1099. Offers criminology (MA); fine arts administration (Certificate); language and communication (MA); mediation (Certificate); psychology (MA); self-designed major (MA); social justice, peace, and reconciliation (Certificate); social science (MA); technical communication (Certificate). Program also offered in Henderson and Las Vegas (Summerlin), NV. Part-time and evening/weekend programs available. Postbaccalaureate distance learning degree programs offered (minimal on-campus study). *Degree requirements:* For master's, thesis, research project. *Entrance requirements:* For master's, resume, recommendations. Additional exam requirements/recommendations for international students: Required—TOEFL (minimum score 213 computer-based), TWE (minimum score 5). Electronic applications accepted. *Expenses:* Contact institution. *Faculty research:* Independent/nonresidential graduate study: new methods and models, adult learning and the capstone experience, Goal Setting, behavior of Adult students, Innovative Studies for Community Colleges.

The Richard Stockton College of New Jersey, School of Graduate and Continuing Education, Program in Criminal Justice, Pomona, NJ 08240-0195. Offers MA. Part-time and evening/weekend programs available. *Degree requirements:* For master's, comprehensive exam (for some programs), thesis, student portfolio project. *Entrance requirements:* For master's, GRE General Test, minimum GPA of 3.0. Additional exam requirements/recommendations for international students: Required—TOEFL. *Expenses:* Tuition, state resident: part-time $497.36 per credit hour. Tuition, nonresident: part-time $765.61 per credit hour. Required fees: $129.12 per credit hour. Tuition and fees vary according to degree level. *Faculty research:* Homeland security, forensic psychology, corrections, sex crimes, violent crimes.

Rochester Institute of Technology, Graduate Enrollment Services, College of Liberal Arts, Department of Criminal Justice, Rochester, NY 14623-5603. Offers MS. Part-time programs available. *Students:* 2 full-time (both women), 2 part-time (both women). Average age 31. 2 applicants, 100% accepted, 2 enrolled. *Degree requirements:* For master's, thesis. *Entrance requirements:* For master's, GRE. Additional exam requirements/recommendations for international students: Required—TOEFL (minimum score 570 paper-based; 230 computer-based; 88 iBT), or IELTS (minimum score 6.5). Application fee: $50. *Expenses:* Tuition: Full-time $31,533; part-time $876 per credit hour. Required fees: $210. *Financial support:* In 2009–10, 4 students received support. Applicants required to submit FAFSA. *Faculty research:* Criminal justice policy; design, development of appropriate measures; collection and analysis of data using a wide range of methods. *Unit head:* John Klofas, Chair, 585-475-2432, E-mail: jmkgcj@rit.edu. *Application contact:* Diane Ellison, Assistant Vice President, Graduate Enrollment Services, 585-475-2229, Fax: 585-475-7164, E-mail: gradinfo@rit.edu.

Roger Williams University, School of Justice Studies, Bristol, RI 02809. Offers criminal justice (MS); MS/JD. Part-time and evening/weekend programs available. *Degree requirements:* For master's, comprehensive exam, thesis optional. *Entrance requirements:* For master's, 2 letters of recommendation. Additional exam requirements/recommendations for international students: Recommended—IELTS. Electronic applications accepted. *Expenses:* Contact institution.

Rowan University, Graduate School, College of Liberal Arts and Sciences, Program in Criminal Justice, Glassboro, NJ 08028-1701. Offers MA. Part-time and evening/weekend programs available. *Students:* 3 full-time (2 women), 9 part-time (4 women); includes 4 minority (2 African Americans, 2 Hispanic Americans). Average age 33. 7 applicants, 57% accepted, 3 enrolled. *Degree requirements:* For master's, thesis. *Entrance requirements:* For master's, GRE General Test. Additional exam requirements/recommendations for international students: Required—TOEFL. *Application deadline:* Applications are processed on a rolling basis. Application fee: $50. Electronic applications accepted. *Expenses:* Tuition, state resident: full-time $10,624; part-time $590 per semester hour. Tuition, nonresident: full-time $10,624; part-time $590 per semester hour. Required fees: $2320; $125 per semester hour. *Financial support:* Career-related internships or fieldwork, scholarships/grants, health care benefits, and unspecified assistantships available. *Unit head:* Dr. Mira Lalovic-Hand, Interim Associate Provost/Director of Graduate School, 856-256-5120, E-mail: lalovic-hand@rowan.edu. *Application contact:* Karen Haynes, Graduate Coordinator, 856-256-4052, Fax: 856-256-4436, E-mail: haynes@rowan.edu.

Rutgers, The State University of New Jersey, Camden, Graduate School of Arts and Sciences, Program in Criminal Justice, Camden, NJ 08102-1401. Offers MA, MPA/MA. Part-time and evening/weekend programs available. *Degree requirements:* For master's, comprehensive exam, thesis optional. *Entrance requirements:* For master's, GRE, 3 letters of recommendation. Additional exam requirements/recommendations for international students: Required—TOEFL, IELTS. Electronic applications accepted. *Faculty research:* Criminal justice policy, public management, children in criminal justice system, violence, gender and crime.

Rutgers, The State University of New Jersey, Newark, Graduate School, School of Criminal Justice, Program in Criminal Justice, Newark, NJ 07102. Offers PhD. *Entrance requirements:* For doctorate, GRE, minimum undergraduate B average.

Sacred Heart University, Graduate Programs, College of Arts and Sciences, Department of Criminal Justice, Fairfield, CT 06825-1000. Offers MA. Part-time programs available. *Faculty:* 4 full-time (1 woman). *Students:* 13 full-time (7 women), 27 part-time (13 women); includes 13 minority (9 African Americans, 1 Asian American or Pacific Islander, 3 Hispanic Americans), 1 international. Average age 30. 22 applicants, 100% accepted, 13 enrolled. In 2009, 9 master's awarded. *Degree requirements:* For master's, thesis optional. *Entrance requirements:* Additional exam requirements/recommendations for international students: Required—TOEFL (minimum score 550 paper-based; 213 computer-based). *Application deadline:* Applications are processed on a rolling basis. Application fee: $50 ($100 for international students). Electronic applications accepted. *Expenses:* Tuition: Full-time $24,000; part-time $650 per credit. Required fees: $248. *Financial support:* Career-related internships or fieldwork, institutionally sponsored loans and unspecified assistantships available. Support available to part-time students. Financial award applicants required to submit FAFSA. *Unit head:* Dr. Pearl Jacobs, Chair, 203-365-7764, E-mail: jacobsp@sacredheart.edu. *Application contact:* Alexis Haakonsen, Dean of Graduate Admissions, 203-365-4731, Fax: 203-365-4732, E-mail: haakonsena@sacredheart.edu.

St. Ambrose University, College of Arts and Sciences, Program in Criminal Justice, Davenport, IA 52803-2898. Offers criminal justice (MCJ); juvenile justice education (MCJ). Part-time and evening/weekend programs available. *Faculty:* 4 full-time (3 women), 4 part-time/adjunct (0 women). *Students:* 11 full-time (7 women), 20 part-time (11 women); includes 8 minority (2 American Indian/Alaska Native, 1 Asian American or Pacific Islander, 5 Hispanic Americans), 1 international. Average age 34. 17 applicants, 100% accepted, 17 enrolled. In 2009, 14 master's awarded. *Degree requirements:* For master's, thesis (for some programs), practicum or project. *Entrance requirements:* For master's, 2 years of work experience, 2 letters of recommendation, personal interview. Additional exam requirements/recommendations for international students: Required—TOEFL. *Application deadline:* For fall admission, 8/15 priority date for domestic students, 8/15 for international students; for spring admission, 11/1 for domestic and international students. Applications are processed on a rolling basis. Application fee: $25. Electronic applications accepted. *Expenses:* Tuition: Part-time $702 per credit hour.

Criminal Justice and Criminology

St. Ambrose University (continued)

Tuition and fees vary according to degree level, program and reciprocity agreements. *Financial support:* In 2009–10, 28 students received support, including 5 research assistantships with partial tuition reimbursements available (averaging $2,670 per year); career-related internships or fieldwork, scholarships/grants, and unspecified assistantships also available. Financial award application deadline: 3/15; financial award applicants required to submit FAFSA. *Faculty research:* Community policing. *Unit head:* Dr. Christopher C. Barnum, Acting Head, 563-333-6157, Fax: 563-333-6243, E-mail: barnumchristopherc@sau.edu. *Application contact:* Vivian F. Force, Administrative Assistant, 563-333-6166, Fax: 563-333-6243, E-mail: forcevivianf@sau.edu.

St. Cloud State University, School of Graduate Studies, College of Social Sciences, Department of Criminal Justice, Program in Criminal Justice, St. Cloud, MN 56301-4498. Offers criminal justice administration (MS). *Faculty:* 8 full-time (1 woman), 21 part-time/adjunct (5 women). *Students:* 48 full-time (34 women), 37 part-time (26 women); includes 5 minority (2 African Americans, 1 American Indian/Alaska Native, 2 Hispanic Americans), 3 international. *Unit head:* Dr. Robert Prout, Chairperson, 320-308-4101, Fax: 320-308-2993, E-mail: crimjustice@stcloudstate.edu. *Application contact:* Linda Lou Krueger, School of Graduate Studies, 320-308-2113, Fax: 320-308-5371, E-mail: lekrueger@stcloudstate.edu.

St. John's University, St. John's College of Liberal Arts and Sciences, Department of Sociology and Anthropology, Queens, NY 11439. Offers criminology and justice (MA); sociology (MA). Part-time and evening/weekend programs available. *Students:* 39 full-time (24 women), 25 part-time (16 women); includes 34 minority (16 African Americans, 7 Asian Americans or Pacific Islanders, 11 Hispanic Americans), 5 international. Average age 27. 67 applicants, 58% accepted, 31 enrolled. In 2009, 36 master's awarded. *Degree requirements:* For master's, comprehensive exam, thesis optional. *Entrance requirements:* For master's, 18 undergraduate credits in social services, minimum GPA of 3.0. Additional exam requirements/recommendations for international students: Required—TOEFL (minimum score 500 paper-based; 173 computer-based; 61 iBT), IELTS (minimum score 5.5). *Application deadline:* For fall admission, 5/1 priority date for domestic and international students; for spring admission, 11/1 priority date for domestic and international students. Applications are processed on a rolling basis. Application fee: $70. Electronic applications accepted. *Expenses:* Tuition: Full-time $16,290; part-time $905 per credit. Required fees: $300; $150 per semester. Tuition and fees vary according to program. *Financial support:* Research assistantships, career-related internships or fieldwork and scholarships/grants available. Support available to part-time students. Financial award application deadline: 3/1; financial award applicants required to submit FAFSA. *Faculty research:* Community studies and gentrification, global financial crisis, insurance fraud, globalization, immigration and human rights. *Unit head:* Dr. Dawn Esposito, Chair, 718-990-5667, E-mail: espositd@stjohns.edu. *Application contact:* Kathleen Davis, Director of Graduate Admission, 718-990-2790, Fax: 718-990-5686, E-mail: gradhelp@stjohns.edu.

Saint Joseph's University, College of Arts and Sciences, Department of Criminal Justice, Philadelphia, PA 19131-1395. Offers administration/police executive (MS); behavior analysis (MS, Post-Master's Certificate); criminal justice (MS, Post-Master's Certificate); criminology (MS); federal law (MS); intelligence and crime (MS); probation, parole, and corrections (MS). Part-time and evening/weekend programs available. Postbaccalaureate distance learning degree programs offered (no on-campus study). *Students:* 2 full-time (0 women), 302 part-time (193 women); includes 88 minority (64 African Americans, 1 American Indian/Alaska Native, 3 Asian Americans or Pacific Islanders, 20 Hispanic Americans), 2 international. Average age 33. In 2009, 86 master's awarded. *Degree requirements:* For master's, thesis. *Entrance requirements:* For master's, GRE General Test or minimum GPA of 3.0, 2 letters of recommendation. Additional exam requirements/recommendations for international students: Required—TOEFL (minimum score 550 paper-based; 213 computer-based; 79 iBT). *Application deadline:* For fall admission, 7/15 priority date for domestic students, 4/15 for international students; for winter admission, 1/15 for international students; for spring admission, 11/15 priority date for domestic students, 10/15 for international students. Applications are processed on a rolling basis. Application fee: $35. Electronic applications accepted. *Expenses:* Tuition: Part-time $729 per credit hour. Tuition and fees vary according to degree level and program. *Financial support:* Career-related internships or fieldwork and unspecified assistantships available. Financial award applicants required to submit FAFSA. *Unit head:* Patricia Griffin, Director, 610-660-1294, E-mail: pgriffin@sju.edu. *Application contact:* Kate McConnell, Director, Graduate College of Arts and Sciences Admissions and Retention, 610-660-3184, Fax: 610-660-3230, E-mail: kate.mconnell@sju.edu.

Saint Leo University, Graduate Business Studies, Saint Leo, FL 33574-6665. Offers accounting (MBA); business (MBA); criminal justice (MBA); health services management (MBA); human resource administration (MBA); information security management (MBA); marketing (MBA); sport business (MBA). Part-time and evening/weekend programs available. Postbaccalaureate distance learning degree programs offered (no on-campus study). *Faculty:* 31 full-time (5 women), 48 part-time/adjunct (17 women). *Students:* 1,433 full-time (856 women), 3 part-time (1 woman); includes 601 minority (429 African Americans, 8 American Indian/Alaska Native, 75 Asian Americans or Pacific Islanders, 89 Hispanic Americans), 11 international. Average age 37. In 2009, 405 master's awarded. *Entrance requirements:* For master's, GMAT (minimum score 500 if applicant does not have 5 years of professional work experience), bachelor's degree from regionally-accredited college or university with minimum GPA of 3.0 in the last 60 hours of coursework; 5 years of professional work experience; resume; 2 letters of recommendation. Additional exam requirements/recommendations for international students: Required—TOEFL (minimum score 550 paper-based; 213 computer-based; 80 iBT). *Application deadline:* For fall admission, 7/1 priority date for domestic students; for spring admission, 11/12 priority date for domestic students. Applications are processed on a rolling basis. Application fee: $75. Electronic applications accepted. *Expenses:* Contact institution. *Financial support:* In 2009–10, 1 student received support. Career-related internships or fieldwork, Federal Work-Study, and health care benefits available. Financial award application deadline: 3/1; financial award applicants required to submit FAFSA. *Unit head:* Dr. Robert Robertson, Director, 352-588-7390, Fax: 352-588-8585, E-mail: mba@saintleo.edu. *Application contact:* Jared Welling, Director, Graduate/Weekend and Evening Admission, 800-707-8846, Fax: 352-588-7873, E-mail: grad.admissions@saintleo.edu.

Saint Leo University, Graduate Studies in Criminal Justice, Saint Leo, FL 33574-6665. Offers criminal justice (MS); critical incident management (MS). Part-time and evening/weekend programs available. Postbaccalaureate distance learning degree programs offered (no on-campus study). *Faculty:* 6 full-time (1 woman), 9 part-time/adjunct (2 women). *Students:* 298 full-time (175 women), 1 (woman) part-time; includes 129 minority (109 African Americans, 1 American Indian/Alaska Native, 2 Asian Americans or Pacific Islanders, 17 Hispanic Americans). Average age 37. In 2009, 87 master's awarded. *Degree requirements:* For master's, comprehensive project. *Entrance requirements:* For master's, bachelor's degree from regionally-accredited college or university with minimum GPA of 3.0. Additional exam requirements/recommendations for international students: Required—TOEFL (minimum score 550 paper-based; 213 computer-based; 80 iBT). *Application deadline:* For fall admission, 7/1 priority date for domestic and international students; for spring admission, 11/1 priority date for domestic and international students. Applications are processed on a rolling basis. Application fee: $75. Electronic applications accepted. *Expenses:* Tuition: Part-time $1767 per course. Required fees: $115 per course. *Financial support:* Federal Work-Study and health care benefits available. *Unit head:* Dr. Robert Diemer, Director, 352-588-8974, Fax: 352-588-8289, E-mail: robert.diemer@saintleo.edu. *Application contact:* Jared Welling, Director, Graduate/Weekend and Evening Admission, 800-707-8846, Fax: 352-588-7873, E-mail: grad.admissions@saintleo.edu.

Saint Mary's University, Faculty of Arts, Program in Criminology, Halifax, NS B3H 3C3, Canada. Offers MA. Part-time programs available. *Faculty:* 14 full-time, 17 part-time/adjunct. *Degree requirements:* For master's, thesis. *Entrance requirements:* For master's, honors degree, official transcripts, sample of academic written work, 2 letters of recommendation. *Application deadline:* For fall admission, 2/1 for domestic students. Application fee: $35 Canadian dollars. Electronic applications accepted. *Expenses:* Contact institution. *Unit head:* Dr. Diane Crocker, Coordinator, 902-420-5871, Fax: 902-420-5121. *Application contact:* Dr. Diane Crocker, Coordinator, 902-420-5871, Fax: 902-420-5121.

Saint Peter's College, Program in Criminal Justice Administration, Jersey City, NJ 07306-5997. Offers MA. *Expenses:* Tuition: Part-time $971 per credit.

St. Thomas University, School of Business, Department of Management, Miami Gardens, FL 33054-6459. Offers accounting (MBA); general management (MSM, Certificate); health management (MBA, MSM, Certificate); human resource management (MBA, MSM, Certificate); international business (MBA, MIB, MSM, Certificate); justice administration (MSM, Certificate); management accounting (MSM, Certificate); public management (MSM, Certificate); sports administration (MS). Part-time and evening/weekend programs available. *Degree requirements:* For master's, comprehensive exam. *Entrance requirements:* For master's, interview, minimum GPA of 3.0 or GMAT. Additional exam requirements/recommendations for international students: Required—TOEFL (minimum score 550 paper-based; 213 computer-based; 79 iBT). Electronic applications accepted.

Salem State College, School of Graduate Studies, Program in Criminal Justice, Salem, MA 01970-5353. Offers MS. Part-time and evening/weekend programs available. *Students:* 2 full-time (both women), 15 part-time (9 women). Average age 29. 10 applicants, 90% accepted, 9 enrolled. In 2009, 4 master's awarded. *Entrance requirements:* For master's, GRE or MAT. Additional exam requirements/recommendations for international students: Required—TOEFL (minimum score 550 paper-based; 80 iBT), or IELTS (minimum score 5.5). *Application deadline:* For fall admission, 5/1 for domestic students; for spring admission, 10/1 for domestic students. Applications are processed on a rolling basis. Application fee: $50. *Expenses:* Tuition, state resident: full-time $2520; part-time $275 per credit hour. Tuition, nonresident: full-time $4140; part-time $365 per credit hour. Required fees: $2430. *Financial support:* In 2009–10, 6 students received support. Career-related internships or fieldwork, Federal Work-Study, scholarships/grants, and unspecified assistantships available. Support available to part-time students. Financial award application deadline: 5/1; financial award applicants required to submit FAFSA. *Unit head:* Kristen Kuehnle, Associate Professor, 978-542-6075, E-mail: kkuehnle@salemstate.edu. *Application contact:* Dr. Lee A. Brossoit, Assistant Dean of Graduate Admissions, 978-542-6673, Fax: 978-542-7215, E-mail: lbrossoit@salemstate.edu.

Salve Regina University, Graduate Studies, Programs in Administration of Justice, Newport, RI 02840-4192. Offers justice and homeland security (MS); law enforcement leadership (MS). Part-time and evening/weekend programs available. *Faculty:* 2 full-time (0 women), 9 part-time/adjunct (1 woman). *Students:* 26 full-time (14 women), 39 part-time (6 women); includes 2 minority (1 African American, 1 Hispanic American). Average age 30. 13 applicants, 69% accepted, 9 enrolled. In 2009, 17 master's awarded. *Entrance requirements:* For master's, GMAT, GRE General Test, or MAT. Additional exam requirements/recommendations for international students: Required—TOEFL (minimum score 600 paper-based; 250 computer-based; 100 iBT). *Application deadline:* For fall admission, 3/5 priority date for domestic students, 3/15 priority date for international students; for spring admission, 9/15 priority date for domestic students, 9/5 priority date for international students. Applications are processed on a rolling basis. Application fee: $60. Electronic applications accepted. *Expenses:* Tuition: Part-time $395 per credit. Part-time tuition and fees vary according to degree level. *Financial support:* Career-related internships or fieldwork and Federal Work-Study available. Support available to part-time students. Financial award application deadline: 3/1; financial award applicants required to submit FAFSA. *Unit head:* Dr. Daniel Knight, Director, 401-341-3255, E-mail: knightd@salve.edu. *Application contact:* Kelly Alverson, Graduate Admissions Counselor, 401-341-2153, Fax: 401-341-2973, E-mail: kelly.alverson@salve.edu.

Sam Houston State University, College of Criminal Justice, Huntsville, TX 77341. Offers criminal justice (MS, PhD); criminal justice and criminology (MA); criminal justice management (MS); forensic science (MS); security studies (MS); victim services management (MS). *Faculty:* 22 full-time (4 women). *Students:* 68 full-time (47 women), 170 part-time (69 women); includes 45 minority (10 African Americans, 1 American Indian/Alaska Native, 4 Asian Americans or Pacific Islanders, 30 Hispanic Americans), 34 international. Average age 33. 148 applicants, 88% accepted, 114 enrolled. In 2009, 46 master's, 6 doctorates awarded. *Degree requirements:* For master's, thesis (for some programs); for doctorate, comprehensive exam, thesis/dissertation. *Entrance requirements:* For master's, GRE General Test; for doctorate, GRE General Test, master's degree. Additional exam requirements/recommendations for international students: Required—TOEFL (minimum score 550 paper-based; 213 computer-based; 79 iBT). *Application deadline:* For fall admission, 8/1 for domestic students; for spring admission, 12/1 for domestic students. Applications are processed on a rolling basis. Application fee: $20. *Expenses:* Tuition, state resident: full-time $3690; part-time $205 per credit hour. Tuition, nonresident: full-time $8676; part-time $482 per credit hour. Required fees: $1474. Tuition and fees vary according to course load and campus/location. *Financial support:* Fellowships, research assistantships, teaching assistantships, career-related internships or fieldwork, Federal Work-Study, institutionally sponsored loans, and unspecified assistantships available. Support available to part-time students. Financial award application deadline: 5/31; financial award applicants required to submit FAFSA. *Unit head:* Dr. Vincent Webb, Dean, 936-294-1632, Fax: 936-294-1653, E-mail: vwebb@shsu.edu. *Application contact:* Doris Powell-Pratt, Advisor, 936-294-3637, Fax: 936-294-4055, E-mail: icc_dcp@shsu.edu.

San Diego State University, Graduate and Research Affairs, College of Professional Studies and Fine Arts, School of Public Affairs, Program in Criminal Justice Administration, San Diego, CA 92182. Offers MPA. Part-time programs available. *Entrance requirements:* For master's, GRE General Test, 2 letters of reference. Additional exam requirements/recommendations for international students: Required—TOEFL. Electronic applications accepted.

San Diego State University, Graduate and Research Affairs, College of Professional Studies and Fine Arts, School of Public Affairs, Program in Criminal Justice and Criminology, San Diego, CA 92182. Offers MS. *Entrance requirements:* For master's, GRE General Test, 2 letters of reference. Additional exam requirements/recommendations for international students: Required—TOEFL. Electronic applications accepted.

San Jose State University, Graduate Studies and Research, College of Applied Sciences and Arts, Department of Justice Studies, San Jose, CA 95192-0001. Offers MS. Part-time programs available. *Students:* 15 full-time (11 women), 22 part-time (18 women); includes 23 minority (1 African American, 1 American Indian/Alaska Native, 8 Asian Americans or Pacific Islanders, 13 Hispanic Americans), 1 international. Average age 30. 41 applicants, 61% accepted, 19 enrolled. In 2009, 8 master's awarded. *Degree requirements:* For master's, thesis or alternative. *Entrance requirements:* For master's, GRE or LSAT, minimum GPA of 3.0. Additional exam requirements/recommendations for international students: Required—TOEFL. *Application deadline:* For fall admission, 6/29 for domestic students; for spring admission, 11/30 for domestic students. Applications are processed on a rolling basis. Application fee: $59. Electronic applications accepted. *Financial support:* Career-related internships or fieldwork and institutionally sponsored loans available. Support available to part-time students. Financial award application deadline: 7/1; financial award applicants required to submit FAFSA. *Faculty research:* Employee stress, interagency cooperation, prison industries, application of death penalty sentences, sucrose ingestion and delinquency. *Unit head:* Dr. Mark Correia, Chair, 408-924-2940, Fax: 408-924-2953. *Application contact:* Dr. Mark Correia, Chair, 408-924-2940, Fax: 408-924-2953.

Seattle University, College of Arts and Sciences, Department of Criminal Justice, Seattle, WA 98122-1090. Offers MACJ.

Shippensburg University of Pennsylvania, School of Graduate Studies, College of Education and Human Services, Department of Criminal Justice, Shippensburg, PA 17257-2299. Offers administration of justice (MS), including juvenile justice. Part-time and evening/weekend programs available. *Degree requirements:* For master's, internship, practicum, or thesis. *Entrance requirements:* For master's, GRE or MAT (if GPA less than 2.75). Additional exam requirements/recommendations for international students: Required—TOEFL (minimum score 560 paper-based; 220 computer-based); Recommended—IELTS (minimum score 6). Electronic applications accepted.

Simon Fraser University, Graduate Studies, Faculty of Arts and Social Sciences, School of Criminology, Burnaby, BC V5A 1S6, Canada. Offers MA, PhD. *Degree requirements:* For master's, thesis; for doctorate, thesis/dissertation. *Entrance requirements:* For master's, minimum GPA of 3.0; for doctorate, minimum GPA of 3.5. Additional exam requirements/recommendations for international students: Required—TOEFL or IELTS. *Faculty research:* Media and crime, feminist jurisprudence, policy evaluation, penology, terrorism.

Simpson College, Department of Social Sciences, Indianola, IA 50125-1297. Offers criminal justice (MACJ). Evening/weekend programs available.

Southeast Missouri State University, School of Graduate Studies, Department of Criminal Justice and Sociology, Cape Girardeau, MO 63701-4799. Offers MS. Part-time and evening/weekend programs available. *Degree requirements:* For master's, comprehensive exam (for some programs), thesis or alternative. *Entrance requirements:* For master's, minimum undergraduate GPA of 2.5. Additional exam requirements/recommendations for international students: Required—TOEFL (minimum score 550 paper-based; 213 computer-based); Recommended—IELTS (minimum score 6). Electronic applications accepted. *Expenses:* Tuition, state resident: full-time $4266; part-time $237 per credit hour. Tuition, nonresident: full-time $7506; part-time $417 per credit hour. Required fees: $427; $427.

Southern Illinois University Carbondale, Graduate School, College of Liberal Arts, Administration of Justice Program, Carbondale, IL 62901-4701. Offers MA. *Degree requirements:* For master's, thesis optional. *Entrance requirements:* For master's, GRE General Test, minimum GPA of 2.7. Additional exam requirements/recommendations for international students: Required—TOEFL. *Faculty research:* Corrections, criminology, law enforcement, crime prevention, victims of crime.

Southern University and Agricultural and Mechanical College, Graduate School, Nelson Mandela School of Public Policy and Urban Affairs, Department of Criminal Justice, Baton Rouge, LA 70813. Offers MS. *Entrance requirements:* Additional exam requirements/recommendations for international students: Required—TOEFL (minimum score 525 paper-based; 193 computer-based).

South University, Graduate Programs, College of Business, Savannah, GA 31406. Offers corrections (MBA); entrepreneurship and small business (MBA); hospitality management (MBA); sustainability (MBA).

Southwestern College, Professional Studies Programs, Wichita, KS 67207. Offers business administration (MBA); leadership (MS); management (MS); security administration (MS); specialized ministries (MA). Part-time and evening/weekend programs available. Postbaccalaureate distance learning degree programs offered (minimal on-campus study). *Faculty:* 1 full-time (0 women), 26 part-time/adjunct (10 women). *Students:* 143 part-time (59 women); includes 25 minority (17 African Americans, 2 Asian Americans or Pacific Islanders, 6 Hispanic Americans). Average age 36. 33 applicants, 100% accepted, 28 enrolled. In 2009, 62 master's awarded. *Degree requirements:* For master's, practicum/capstone project. *Entrance requirements:* For master's, baccalaureate degree; minimum GPA of 2.5, 3.0 for MBA. Additional exam requirements/recommendations for international students: Required—TOEFL (minimum score 550 paper-based; 213 computer-based). *Application deadline:* For fall admission, 8/1 for domestic students; for spring admission, 12/1 for domestic students. Applications are processed on a rolling basis. Application fee: $0. Electronic applications accepted. *Financial support:* In 2009–10, 85 students received support. Federal Work-Study, tuition waivers (partial), and unspecified assistantships available. Financial award application deadline: 4/1; financial award applicants required to submit FAFSA. *Unit head:* Gail Cullen, Director of Academic Affairs, 888-684-5335 Ext. 203, Fax: 316-688-5218, E-mail: gail.cullen@sckans.edu. *Application contact:* Gail Cullen, Director of Academic Affairs, 888-684-5335 Ext. 203, Fax: 316-688-5218, E-mail: gail.cullen@sckans.edu.

Suffolk University, College of Arts and Sciences, Program in Crime and Justice Studies, Boston, MA 02108-2770. Offers MSCJS, MSCJS/JD, MSCJS/MPA, MSCJS/MSMHC. Part-time programs available. *Faculty:* 15 full-time (10 women). *Students:* 33 full-time (28 women), 34 part-time (25 women); includes 21 minority (9 African Americans, 2 Asian Americans or Pacific Islanders, 10 Hispanic Americans). Average age 26. 72 applicants, 76% accepted, 30 enrolled. In 2009, 32 master's awarded. *Entrance requirements:* For master's, 2 letters of recommendation, resume. Additional exam requirements/recommendations for international students: Required—TOEFL (minimum score 550 paper-based; 213 computer-based; 80 iBT). *Application deadline:* For fall admission, 6/15 priority date for domestic students, 6/15 for international students; for spring admission, 11/1 priority date for domestic students, 11/1 for international students. Applications are processed on a rolling basis. Application fee: $50. Electronic applications accepted. *Expenses:* Contact institution. *Financial support:* In 2009–10, 55 students received support, including 46 fellowships with partial tuition reimbursements available (averaging $6,208 per year); career-related internships or fieldwork, Federal Work-Study, and institutionally sponsored loans also available. Support available to part-time students. Financial award application deadline: 4/1; financial award applicants required to submit FAFSA. *Faculty research:* Restorative justice, anti-gang initiative, healthcare for female ex-offenders, violence against women, juvenile justice and the courts. *Unit head:* Dr. Donald Morton, Chairperson, 617-305-1990, Fax: 617-720-0490, E-mail: mscjs@suffolk.edu. *Application contact:* Judith Reynolds, Director of Graduate Admissions, 617-573-8302, Fax: 617-305-1733, E-mail: grad.admission@suffolk.edu.

Sul Ross State University, School of Professional Studies, Department of Criminal Justice, Alpine, TX 79832. Offers MS. *Entrance requirements:* For master's, GRE General Test, minimum GPA of 2.5 in last 60 hours of undergraduate work.

Tarleton State University, College of Graduate Studies, College of Liberal and Fine Arts, Department of Social Work, Sociology, and Criminal Justice, Stephenville, TX 76402. Offers criminal justice (MCJ). Part-time and evening/weekend programs available. *Degree requirements:* For master's, comprehensive exam (for some programs), thesis optional. *Entrance requirements:* For master's, GRE General Test, minimum GPA of 3.0. Additional exam requirements/recommendations for international students: Required—TOEFL (minimum score 550 paper-based; 213 computer-based; 80 iBT). Electronic applications accepted.

Temple University, Graduate School, College of Liberal Arts, Department of Criminal Justice, Philadelphia, PA 19122-6096. Offers MA, PhD. Part-time programs available. Terminal master's awarded for partial completion of doctoral program. *Degree requirements:* For master's, thesis optional; for doctorate, thesis/dissertation, qualifying exams. *Entrance requirements:* For master's, GRE General Test, minimum GPA of 3.0; for doctorate, GRE General Test. Additional exam requirements/recommendations for international students: Required—TOEFL (minimum score 550 paper-based; 213 computer-based; 79 iBT). Electronic applications accepted. *Faculty research:* Criminal justice policy formulation, courts, correctional alternatives, community crime prevention, juvenile justice.

Tennessee State University, The School of Graduate Studies and Research, College of Arts and Sciences, Department of Criminal Justice, Nashville, TN 37209-1561. Offers MCJ. *Degree requirements:* For master's, thesis. *Entrance requirements:* For master's, GRE General Test or MAT. Electronic applications accepted.

Texas A&M International University, Office of Graduate Studies and Research, College of Arts and Sciences, Department of Behavioral, Applied Sciences, and Criminal Justice, Laredo, TX 78041-1900. Offers counseling psychology (MACP); criminal justice (MS); psychology (MS); sociology (MA). *Faculty:* 8 full-time (3 women), 1 part-time/adjunct (0 women). *Students:* 13 full-time (8 women), 88 part-time (63 women); includes 94 minority (1 African American, 93 Hispanic Americans). Average age 30. 68 applicants, 69% accepted, 47 enrolled. In 2009, 14 master's awarded. *Degree requirements:* For master's, thesis (for some programs). *Entrance requirements:* For master's, GRE General Test. Additional exam requirements/recommendations for international students: Required—TOEFL (minimum score 550 paper-based; 213 computer-based). *Application deadline:* For fall admission, 4/30 priority date for domestic students; for spring admission, 11/30 for domestic students. Applications are processed on a rolling basis. Application fee: $25. *Financial support:* In 2009–10, 17 students received support, including 3 research assistantships, 1 teaching assistantship. Financial award application deadline: 11/1. *Unit head:* Dr. Roberto Heredia, Chair, 956-326-2637, Fax: 956-326-2459, E-mail: rheredia@tamiu.edu. *Application contact:* Rosie Espinoza-Dickinson, Director of Admissions, 956-326-2200, Fax: 956-326-2199, E-mail: enroll@tamiu.edu.

Texas Southern University, School of Public Affairs, Program in Administration of Justice, Houston, TX 77004-4584. Offers MS, PhD. *Faculty:* 3 full-time (1 woman), 1 part-time/adjunct (0 women). *Students:* 36 full-time (22 women), 13 part-time (3 women); includes 42 African Americans, 1 Asian American or Pacific Islander, 1 Hispanic American, 2 international. Average age 39. 21 applicants, 100% accepted, 18 enrolled. *Application deadline:* For fall admission, 7/1 for domestic and international students; for spring admission, 11/1 for domestic and international students. Applications are processed on a rolling basis. Application fee: $50 ($75 for international students). Electronic applications accepted. *Expenses:* Tuition, state resident: full-time $1805; part-time $100 per credit hour. Tuition, nonresident: full-time $6470; part-time $343 per credit hour. Tuition and fees vary according to course level, course load and degree level. *Financial support:* In 2009–10, 15 research assistantships (averaging $8,922 per year), 3 teaching assistantships (averaging $9,000 per year) were awarded; scholarships/grants and unspecified assistantships also available. *Unit head:* Dr. Daniel Abeyie, Chair, 713-313-4808, E-mail: georgesabeyide@tsu.edu. *Application contact:* Pinkie Cotton, Administrative Assistant, 713-313-7311, E-mail: cotton_pe@tsu.edu.

Texas State University–San Marcos, Graduate School, College of Applied Arts, Department of Criminal Justice, San Marcos, TX 78666. Offers MSCJ, PhD. Part-time and evening/weekend programs available. *Faculty:* 10 full-time (2 women). *Students:* 55 full-time (32 women), 75 part-time (39 women); includes 52 minority (13 African Americans, 3 Asian Americans or Pacific Islanders, 36 Hispanic Americans), 1 international. Average age 30. 88 applicants, 81% accepted, 53 enrolled. In 2009, 32 master's awarded. *Degree requirements:* For master's, comprehensive exam, thesis (for some programs); for doctorate, comprehensive exam, thesis/dissertation. *Entrance requirements:* For master's, bachelor's degree, minimum GPA of 3.0 in last 60 hours of course work; for doctorate, GRE (minimum combined Verbal and Quantitative score of 1000), master's degree in criminal justice or related field; minimum GPA of 3.5 in graduate courses; 3 letters of recommendation; personal/goals statement. Additional exam requirements/recommendations for international students: Required—TOEFL (minimum score 550 paper-based; 213 computer-based). *Application deadline:* For fall admission, 6/15 priority date for domestic students; for spring admission, 10/15 priority date for domestic students. Applications are processed on a rolling basis. Application fee: $40 ($90 for international students). Electronic applications accepted. *Expenses:* Tuition, state resident: full-time $5784; part-time $241 per credit hour. Tuition, nonresident: part-time $551 per credit hour. Required fees: $1728; $48 per credit hour. $306. Tuition and fees vary according to course load. *Financial support:* In 2009–10, 103 students received support, including 10 research assistantships (averaging $6,954 per year), 17 teaching assistantships (averaging $5,071 per year); Federal Work-Study and institutionally sponsored loans also available. Support available to part-time students. Financial award application deadline: 4/1; financial award applicants required to submit FAFSA. *Faculty research:* Geographic profiling, illegal crossing, criminal hunt pattern, reducing inmate rape, counterterrorism, displaced residents, TYC classify systems. Total annual research expenditures: $560,804. *Unit head:* Dr. Quint C. Thurman, Chair, 512-245-2174, Fax: 512-245-8063, E-mail: qt10@txstate.edu. *Application contact:* Dr. Joy Pollock, Advisor, 512-245-7706, Fax: 512-245-8063, E-mail: jp12@txstate.edu.

Texas State University–San Marcos, Graduate School, Interdisciplinary Studies Program in Criminal Justice, San Marcos, TX 78666. Offers MSIS. Part-time and evening/weekend programs available. *Degree requirements:* For master's, comprehensive exam, thesis optional. *Entrance requirements:* For master's, minimum GPA of 2.75 in last 60 hours of undergraduate work. Additional exam requirements/recommendations for international students: Required—TOEFL (minimum score 550 paper-based; 213 computer-based). *Application deadline:* For fall admission, 6/15 priority date for domestic students, 6/1 for international students; for spring admission, 10/15 priority date for domestic students, 10/1 for international students. Applications are processed on a rolling basis. Application fee: $40 ($90 for international students). *Expenses:* Tuition, state resident: full-time $5784; part-time $241 per credit hour. Tuition, nonresident: part-time $551 per credit hour. Required fees: $1728; $48 per credit hour. $306. Tuition and fees vary according to course load. *Financial support:* Application deadline: 4/1. *Unit head:* Dr. Donna Vandiver, Advisor, 512-245-2174, Fax: 512-245-2174, E-mail: dv14@txstate.edu. *Application contact:* Dr. J. Michael Willoughby, Dean of Graduate School, 512-245-2581, Fax: 512-245-8365, E-mail: gradcollege@txstate.edu.

Tiffin University, Program in Business Administration, Tiffin, OH 44883-2161. Offers general management (MBA); leadership (MBA); safety and security management (MBA); sports management (MBA). *Accreditation:* ACBSP. Part-time and evening/weekend programs available. Postbaccalaureate distance learning degree programs offered (no on-campus study). *Entrance requirements:* For master's, minimum undergraduate GPA of 2.5, work experience. Additional exam requirements/recommendations for international students: Required—TOEFL (minimum score 550 paper-based; 213 computer-based). Electronic applications accepted. *Faculty research:* Small business, executive development operations, research and statistical analysis, market research, management information systems.

Tiffin University, Program in Criminal Justice, Tiffin, OH 44883-2161. Offers crime analysis (MSCJ); criminal behavior (MSCJ); forensic psychology (MSCJ); homeland security administration (MSCJ); justice administration (MSCJ). Part-time and evening/weekend programs available. Postbaccalaureate distance learning degree programs offered (no on-campus study). *Degree requirements:* For master's, thesis optional. *Entrance requirements:* For master's, minimum undergraduate GPA of 2.5, work experience. Additional exam requirements/recommendations for international students: Required—TOEFL (minimum score 550 paper-based; 213 computer-based). Electronic applications accepted. *Faculty research:* Terrorism, intelligence, homeland security, guns and crime.

Trine University, Program in Criminal Justice, Angola, IN 46703-1764. Offers MS.

Troy University, Graduate School, College of Arts and Sciences, Program in Criminal Justice, Troy, AL 36082. Offers MS. Part-time and evening/weekend programs available. *Students:* 79 full-time (48 women), 293 part-time (182 women); includes 246 minority (231 African Americans, 6 American Indian/Alaska Native, 2 Asian Americans or Pacific Islanders, 7 Hispanic Americans). Average age 34. 180 applicants, 91% accepted. In 2009, 89 master's awarded. *Degree requirements:* For master's, comprehensive exam or thesis. *Entrance requirements:* For master's, GRE or MAT, minimum undergraduate GPA of 2.5. Additional exam requirements/recommendations for international students: Required—TOEFL (minimum score 523 paper-based; 193 computer-based; 70 iBT), IELTS (minimum score 6). *Application deadline:* Applications are processed on a rolling basis. Application fee: $50. Electronic applications accepted. *Financial support:* Available to part-time students. Applicants required to submit FAFSA. *Faculty research:* Crime victims, criminal justice personnel issues, disability issues in criminal justice. *Unit head:* Dr. Bill Grantham, Chairman, 334-670-3637, Fax: 334-670-3753, E-mail: bgranth@troy.edu. *Application contact:* Brenda K. Campbell, Director of Graduate Admissions, 334-670-3178, Fax: 334-670-3733, E-mail: bcamp@troy.edu.

Troy University, Graduate School, College of Arts and Sciences, Program in Public Administration, Troy, AL 36082. Offers education (MPA); environmental management (MPA);

Criminal Justice and Criminology

Troy University (continued)
government contracting (MPA); health care administration (MPA); justice administration (MPA); management information systems (MPA); national security affairs (MPA); nonprofit management (MPA); public human resources management (MPA); public management (MPA). *Accreditation:* NASPAA. Part-time and evening/weekend programs available. Postbaccalaureate distance learning degree programs offered (no on-campus study). *Students:* 239 full-time (161 women), 652 part-time (416 women); includes 596 minority (547 African Americans, 11 American Indian/Alaska Native, 6 Asian Americans or Pacific Islanders, 32 Hispanic Americans). Average age 34. 415 applicants, 80% accepted. In 2009, 247 master's awarded. *Degree requirements:* For master's, capstone course, research methodologies course. *Entrance requirements:* For master's, GRE, MAT or GMAT, minimum undergraduate GPA of 2.5, letter of recommendation. Additional exam requirements/recommendations for international students: Required—TOEFL (minimum score 523 paper-based; 193 computer-based; 70 iBT), IELTS (minimum score 6). *Application deadline:* Applications are processed on a rolling basis. Application fee: $50. Electronic applications accepted. *Financial support:* Available to part-time students. Applicants required to submit FAFSA. *Unit head:* Dr. Ellen Rosell, Chairman, 334-670-3758, Fax: 334-670-5647, E-mail: erosell@troy.edu. *Application contact:* Brenda K. Campbell, Director of Graduate Admissions, 334-670-3178, Fax: 334-670-3733, E-mail: bcamp@troy.edu.

Troy University, Graduate School, College of Business, Program in Business Administration, Troy, AL 36082. Offers accounting (EMBA, MBA); criminal justice (EMBA); finance (MBA); general management (EMBA); healthcare management (EMBA); information systems (EMBA, MBA); international economic development (MBA). *Accreditation:* ACBSP. Part-time and evening/weekend programs available. *Students:* 382 full-time (196 women), 732 part-time (457 women); includes 616 minority (483 African Americans, 14 American Indian/Alaska Native, 96 Asian Americans or Pacific Islanders, 23 Hispanic Americans). Average age 29. 869 applicants, 61% accepted. In 2009, 296 master's awarded. *Degree requirements:* For master's, thesis or alternative. *Entrance requirements:* For master's, GMAT (minimum score 500) or GRE General Test (minimum score 900), minimum GPA of 2.5; letter of recommendation. Additional exam requirements/recommendations for international students: Required—TOEFL (minimum score 523 paper-based; 193 computer-based; 70 iBT), IELTS (minimum score 6), or ACT Compass ESL (minimum score 270 on Listening, Reading, and Grammar with no individual score below 85 and a minimum score of 8 out of 12 on writing test). *Application deadline:* Applications are processed on a rolling basis. Application fee: $50. *Unit head:* Dr. Henry M. Findley, Interim Chair/Professor, 334-670-3271, Fax: 334-670-3599, E-mail: hfindley@troy.edu. *Application contact:* Brenda K. Campbell, Director of Graduate Admissions, 334-670-3178, Fax: 334-670-3733, E-mail: bcamp@troy.edu.

Troy University, Graduate School, College of Education, Program in Counseling and Psychology, Troy, AL 36082. Offers agency counsleing (Ed S); clinical mental health (MS); community counseling (MS, Ed S); corrections counseling (MS); rehabilitation counseling (MS); school psychology (MS, Ed S); school psychometry (MS); social service counseling (MS); student affairs counseling (MS); substance abuse counseling (MS). *Accreditation:* ACA; CORE; NCATE. Part-time and evening/weekend programs available. *Students:* 375 full-time (302 women), 753 part-time (642 women); includes 664 minority (610 African Americans, 8 American Indian/Alaska Native, 9 Asian Americans or Pacific Islanders, 37 Hispanic Americans). Average age 33. 493 applicants, 92% accepted. In 2009, 102 master's, 191 other advanced degrees awarded. *Degree requirements:* For master's, comprehensive exam, thesis. *Entrance requirements:* For master's, MAT, minimum GPA of 2.5. Additional exam requirements/recommendations for international students: Required—TOEFL (minimum score 523 paper-based; 193 computer-based; 70 iBT), IELTS (minimum score 6). *Application deadline:* Applications are processed on a rolling basis. Application fee: $50. Electronic applications accepted. *Unit head:* Dr. Andrew Creamer, Chair, 334-670-3350, Fax: 334-670-32961, E-mail: drcreamer@troy.edu. *Application contact:* Brenda K. Campbell, Director of Graduate Admissions, 334-670-3178, Fax: 334-670-3733, E-mail: bcamp@troy.edu.

Troy University, Graduate School, College of Education, Program in Postsecondary Education, Troy, AL 36082. Offers adult education (M Ed); biology (M Ed); criminal justice (M Ed); english (M Ed); foundations of education (M Ed); general science (M Ed); higher education administration (M Ed); history (M Ed); instructional technology (M Ed); mathematics (M Ed); music industry (M Ed); physical fitness (M Ed); political science (M Ed); public administration (M Ed); social science (M Ed); teaching english (M Ed). Also offered through the University College. *Accreditation:* NCATE. Part-time and evening/weekend programs available. *Students:* 267 full-time (192 women), 381 part-time (293 women); includes 326 minority (309 African Americans, 4 American Indian/Alaska Native, 5 Asian Americans or Pacific Islanders, 8 Hispanic Americans). Average age 34. 343 applicants, 90% accepted. In 2009, 480 master's awarded. *Degree requirements:* For master's, comprehensive exam, thesis. *Entrance requirements:* For master's, MAT (minimum score 385), minimum GPA of 2.5. Additional exam requirements/recommendations for international students: Required—TOEFL (minimum score 523 paper-based; 193 computer-based; 70 iBT), IELTS, or ACT Compass ESL (minimum score 270 on Listening, Reading, and Grammar with no individual score below 85 and a minimum score of 8 out of 12 on writing test). *Application deadline:* Applications are processed on a rolling basis. Application fee: $50. Electronic applications accepted. *Financial support:* Available to part-time students. Applicants required to submit FAFSA. *Unit head:* Dr. Andrew Creamer, Chair, 334-670-3350, E-mail: drcreamer@troy.edu. *Application contact:* Brenda K. Campbell, Director of Graduate Admissions, 334-670-3178, Fax: 334-670-3733, E-mail: bcamp@troy.edu.

TUI University, College of Business Administration, Program in Business Administration, Cypress, CA 90630. Offers business administration (PhD); conflict and negotiation management (MBA); criminal justice administration (MBA); entrepreneurship (MBA); finance (MBA); general management (MBA); government accounting (MBA); human resource management (MBA); information security and digital assurance management (MBA); information technology management (MBA); international business (MBA); logistics management (MBA); marketing (MBA); project management (MBA); public management (MBA); quality management (MBA); strategic leadership (MBA). Part-time and evening/weekend programs available. Postbaccalaureate distance learning degree programs offered (no on-campus study). *Degree requirements:* For doctorate, comprehensive exam, thesis/dissertation, defense of dissertation. *Entrance requirements:* For master's, minimum GPA of 2.5 (students with GPA 3.0 or greater may transfer up to 30% of graduate level credits); for doctorate, minimum GPA of 3.4, curriculum vitae, course work in research methods or statistics. Additional exam requirements/recommendations for international students: Required—TOEFL. Electronic applications accepted.

Universidad del Este, Graduate School, Carolina, PR 00984. Offers accounting (MBA); adult education (M Ed); agribusiness (MBA); bilingual education (M Ed); criminal justice and criminology (MA); early education (M Ed); elementary education (M Ed); human resources (MBA); information security management (MBA); information technology and Web business development (MBA); management (MBA); public policy (MPA); social work (MA), including clinical social work; special education (M Ed); strategic leadership (MBA); teaching English (M Ed); teaching Spanish (M Ed).

Universidad del Turabo, Graduate Programs, School of Social Sciences and Humanities, Programs in Public Affairs, Program in Criminal Justice Studies, Gurabo, PR 00778-3030. Offers MPA. *Faculty:* 2 full-time (1 woman), 8 part-time/adjunct (3 women). *Students:* 17 full-time (9 women), 11 part-time (8 women); includes 25 Hispanic Americans. Average age 32. 23 applicants, 83% accepted, 14 enrolled. In 2009, 9 master's awarded. *Entrance requirements:* For master's, GRE, EXADEP, interview. *Application deadline:* For fall admission, 8/5 for domestic students. Application fee: $25. *Financial support:* Institutionally sponsored loans available. *Unit head:* Dr. Marco A. Gil Dela Madrid, Dean, 787-743-7979. *Application contact:* Virginia Gonzalez, Admissions Officer, 787-746-3009.

Université de Montréal, Faculty of Arts and Sciences, School of Criminology, Montréal, QC H3C 3J7, Canada. Offers M Sc, PhD. Terminal master's awarded for partial completion of doctoral program. *Degree requirements:* For master's, thesis; for doctorate, thesis/dissertation, general exam. *Entrance requirements:* For master's, B Sc in criminology or the equivalent; for doctorate, M Sc in criminology or equivalent. Electronic applications accepted. *Faculty research:* Criminal behavior, criminality, prison population, victims of crime, female offender.

University at Albany, State University of New York, School of Criminal Justice, Albany, NY 12222-0001. Offers MA, PhD, MSW/MA. Part-time programs available. *Degree requirements:* For doctorate, thesis/dissertation. *Entrance requirements:* For master's and doctorate, GRE General Test. Additional exam requirements/recommendations for international students: Required—TOEFL (minimum score 550 paper-based; 213 computer-based). Electronic applications accepted. *Faculty research:* Causes of delinquency, comparative policing, world crime data, correctional policy, family violence.

The University of Alabama, Graduate School, College of Arts and Sciences, Department of Criminal Justice, Tuscaloosa, AL 35487. Offers MS. Part-time programs available. *Faculty:* 6 full-time (5 women). *Students:* 18 full-time (13 women), 2 part-time (both women); includes 5 minority (3 African Americans, 1 Asian American or Pacific Islander, 1 Hispanic American). Average age 26. 13 applicants, 54% accepted, 6 enrolled. In 2009, 23 master's awarded. *Degree requirements:* For master's, comprehensive exam, thesis or policy and practice course. *Entrance requirements:* For master's, GRE. Additional exam requirements/recommendations for international students: Required—TOEFL. *Application deadline:* For fall admission, 3/1 priority date for domestic and international students; for winter admission, 11/1 priority date for domestic and international students. Applications are processed on a rolling basis. Application fee: $50 ($60 for international students). Electronic applications accepted. *Expenses:* Tuition, state resident: full-time $7000. Tuition, nonresident: full-time $19,200. *Financial support:* In 2009–10, 1 fellowship (averaging $1,500 per year), 11 teaching assistantships with partial tuition reimbursements (averaging $5,145 per year) were awarded; institutionally sponsored loans, health care benefits, and unspecified assistantships also available. Financial award application deadline: 3/15. *Faculty research:* Domestic violence, AIDS research, youth and violence, gender crime, drugs and alcohol abuse, crime prevention. Total annual research expenditures: $54,114. *Unit head:* Dr. Ida Johnson, Interim Chair and Professor, 205-348-7795, Fax: 205-348-7178, E-mail: ijohnson@ua.edu. *Application contact:* Dr. Celia Lo, Professor, 205-348-3162, Fax: 205-348-7178, E-mail: clo@bama.ua.edu.

The University of Alabama at Birmingham, College of Arts and Sciences, Program in Criminal Justice, Birmingham, AL 35294. Offers MSCJ. Evening/weekend programs available. *Degree requirements:* For master's, thesis or alternative. *Entrance requirements:* For master's, GRE General Test or MAT. Electronic applications accepted.

The University of Alabama in Huntsville, School of Graduate Studies, Interdisciplinary Studies, Interdisciplinary Program in Information Assurance and Cybersecurity, Huntsville, AL 35899. Offers Certificate. Part-time and evening/weekend programs available. *Faculty:* 2 full-time (0 women), 2 part-time/adjunct (0 women). *Students:* 13 part-time (1 woman); includes 3 minority (2 African Americans, 1 American Indian/Alaska Native). Average age 38. 6 applicants, 67% accepted, 4 enrolled. In 2009, 10 Certificates awarded. *Entrance requirements:* For degree, GMAT, minimum GPA of 3.0. Additional exam requirements/recommendations for international students: Required—TOEFL (minimum score 550 paper-based; 213 computer-based; 62 iBT). *Application deadline:* For fall admission, 7/15 for domestic students, 4/1 for international students; for spring admission, 11/30 for domestic students, 9/1 for international students. Applications are processed on a rolling basis. Application fee: $40 ($50 for international students). Electronic applications accepted. *Expenses:* Tuition, state resident: part-time $355.75 per credit hour. Tuition, nonresident: part-time $847.10 per credit hour. Required fees: $210.80 per semester. Tuition and fees vary according to course load and program. *Financial support:* Career-related internships or fieldwork, Federal Work-Study, institutionally sponsored loans, scholarships/grants, health care benefits, and unspecified assistantships available. Support available to part-time students. Financial award application deadline: 4/1; financial award applicants required to submit FAFSA. *Unit head:* Dr. Debra Moriarity, Dean of Graduate Studies, 256-824-6002, Fax: 256-824-6405, E-mail: deangrad@uah.edu. *Application contact:* Jennifer Pettitt, College of Business Administration Director of Graduate Programs, 256-824-6681, Fax: 256-824-7572, E-mail: jennifer.pettitt@uah.edu.

University of Alaska Fairbanks, College of Liberal Arts, Department of Justice, Fairbanks, AK 99775-6120. Offers MA. Part-time programs available. Postbaccalaureate distance learning degree programs offered (no on-campus study). *Faculty:* 1 full-time (0 women). *Students:* 1 (woman) full-time, 16 part-time (8 women); includes 2 minority (both American Indian/Alaska Native). Average age 36. 10 applicants, 60% accepted, 6 enrolled. In 2009, 4 master's awarded. *Degree requirements:* For master's, comprehensive exam, thesis or alternative, oral defense. *Entrance requirements:* Additional exam requirements/recommendations for international students: Required—TOEFL (minimum score 550 paper-based; 213 computer-based; 80 iBT). *Application deadline:* For fall admission, 6/1 for domestic students, 3/1 for international students; for spring admission, 10/15 for domestic students, 9/1 for international students. Applications are processed on a rolling basis. Application fee: $60. Electronic applications accepted. *Expenses:* Tuition, state resident: full-time $7584; part-time $316 per credit. Tuition, nonresident: full-time $15,504; part-time $646 per credit. Required fees: $23 per credit. $135 per semester. Tuition and fees vary according to course level, course load and reciprocity agreements. *Financial support:* Federal Work-Study, scholarships/grants, and health care benefits available. Support available to part-time students. Financial award application deadline: 7/1; financial award applicants required to submit FAFSA. *Faculty research:* Substantive and procedural law, native Alaskans imprisoned in the Alaska State Department of Corrections, school violence, substance abuse in juveniles, community justice. *Unit head:* Dr. David M. Blurton, Department Chair, 907-474-5500, Fax: 907-474-6510, E-mail: fyjust@uaf.edu. *Application contact:* Dr. David M. Blurton, Department Chair, 907-474-5500, Fax: 907-474-6510, E-mail: fyjust@uaf.edu.

University of Alberta, Faculty of Graduate Studies and Research, Department of Sociology, Edmonton, AB T6G 2E1, Canada. Offers criminal justice (MA); demography (MA, PhD); sociology (MA, PhD). Part-time programs available. *Faculty:* 30 full-time (6 women), 8 part-time/adjunct (2 women). *Students:* 50 full-time (33 women), 33 part-time (21 women). 77 applicants, 34% accepted. In 2009, 8 master's, 11 doctorates awarded. *Degree requirements:* For master's, thesis (for some programs); for doctorate, thesis/dissertation. *Application deadline:* For fall admission, 3/1 for domestic students. Application fee: $60. Tuition and fees charges are reported in Canadian dollars. *Expenses:* Tuition, area resident: Full-time $4626 Canadian dollars; part-time $99.72 Canadian dollars per unit. International tuition: $8216 Canadian dollars full-time. Required fees: $3590 Canadian dollars; $99.72 Canadian dollars per unit. $215 Canadian dollars per term. *Financial support:* In 2009–10, 49 students received support, including 9 fellowships, 9 research assistantships, 17 teaching assistantships; career-related internships or fieldwork and scholarships/grants also available. Support available to part-time students. Financial award application deadline: 3/1. *Faculty research:* Criminology, knowledge and culture, methods and theory, population studies, stratification. *Unit head:* Dr. W. A. Johnston, Graduate Coordinator, 780-492-5236, Fax: 403-492-7196. *Application contact:* F. L. Van Reede, Graduate Program Coordinator, 403-492-5236, Fax: 403-492-7196, E-mail: socgrad2@ualberta.ca.

University of Arkansas at Little Rock, Graduate School, College of Professional Studies, Department of Criminal Justice, Little Rock, AR 72204-1099. Offers MA, MS, PhD. MS program is by distance education. Part-time and evening/weekend programs available. *Degree requirements:* For master's, thesis defense or written comprehensive exam; for doctorate, comprehensive exam, thesis/dissertation, research practicum. *Entrance requirements:* For master's, GRE General Test or MAT, interview, minimum GPA of 2.75; for doctorate, GRE General Test, minimum cumulative graduate GPA of 3.5; master's degree in criminology/criminal justice or closely related field; three courses in statistics and research methods at the master's level; transcripts; statement of purpose; career development plan; writing sample; two professional letters of recommendation. Additional exam requirements/recommendations for international students: Required—TOEFL (minimum score 550 paper-based; 213 computer-based; 79 iBT). *Faculty research:* Dissemination and analysis of behavioral science knowledge, leadership and managerial skills, philosophy of individual rights and humane treatment.

University of Baltimore, Graduate School, The Yale Gordon College of Liberal Arts, Division of Criminology, Criminal Justice, and Social Policy, Baltimore, MD 21201-5779. Offers criminal justice (MS); JD/MS. Part-time and evening/weekend programs available. *Degree requirements:* For master's, thesis or alternative. *Entrance requirements:* For master's, interview, minimum GPA of 2.8. Additional exam requirements/recommendations for international students: Required—TOEFL (minimum score 550 paper-based; 213 computer-based). Electronic applications accepted. *Faculty research:* Drugs and violence, police and community policing, women and crime, victimization, correction in community.

University of California, Irvine, Office of Graduate Studies, School of Social Ecology, Department of Criminology, Law and Society, Irvine, CA 92697. Offers MAS, PhD. *Students:* 87 full-time (53 women), 20 part-time (13 women); includes 32 minority (4 African Americans, 1 American Indian/Alaska Native, 10 Asian Americans or Pacific Islanders, 17 Hispanic Americans), 3 international. Average age 30. 124 applicants, 41% accepted, 36 enrolled. In 2009, 19 master's, 6 doctorates awarded. *Degree requirements:* For doctorate, thesis/dissertation, research project. *Entrance requirements:* For master's and doctorate, GRE General Test, minimum GPA of 3.0. Additional exam requirements/recommendations for international students: Required—TOEFL (minimum score 550 paper-based; 213 computer-based). *Application deadline:* For fall admission, 1/15 priority date for domestic and international students. Application fee: $70 ($90 for international students). Electronic applications accepted. *Financial support:* Fellowships, research assistantships with full tuition reimbursements, teaching assistantships, institutionally sponsored loans, traineeships, health care benefits, and unspecified assistantships available. Financial award application deadline: 3/1; financial award applicants required to submit FAFSA. *Faculty research:* White-collar and corporate crime; immigration, the poor, homelessness, and governmental regulation; sentencing, community corrections, and diversion; mathematical and scientific evidence in jury trials; legal and criminological theory development. *Unit head:* Valerie Jenness, Chair, 949-824-5575, E-mail: jenness@uci.edu. *Application contact:* Jill Vidas, Academic Counselor, 949-824-5918, Fax: 949-824-2056, E-mail: jjvidas@uci.edu.

University of Central Florida, College of Health and Public Affairs, Department of Criminal Justice and Legal Studies, Orlando, FL 32816. Offers corrections leadership (Certificate); crime analysis (Certificate); criminal justice (MS); juvenile justice leadership (Certificate); police leadership (Certificate). Part-time and evening/weekend programs available. *Faculty:* 36 full-time (13 women), 38 part-time/adjunct (8 women). *Students:* 84 full-time (58 women), 117 part-time (65 women); includes 68 minority (37 African Americans, 9 Asian Americans or Pacific Islanders, 22 Hispanic Americans), 2 international. Average age 29. 165 applicants, 82% accepted, 93 enrolled. In 2009, 81 master's, 19 other advanced degrees awarded. *Degree requirements:* For master's, thesis or alternative. *Entrance requirements:* For master's, GRE General Test, minimum GPA of 3.0. Additional exam requirements/recommendations for international students: Required—TOEFL. *Application deadline:* For fall admission, 7/15 for domestic students; for spring admission, 4/15 for domestic students. Electronic applications accepted. *Expenses:* Tuition, state resident: part-time $306.31 per credit hour. Tuition, nonresident: part-time $1099.01 per credit hour. Part-time tuition and fees vary according to degree level and program. *Financial support:* In 2009–10, 8 students received support, including 4 fellowships with partial tuition reimbursements available (averaging $10,000 per year), 1 research assistantship with partial tuition reimbursement available (averaging $6,400 per year), 3 teaching assistantships with partial tuition reimbursements available (averaging $6,400 per year); career-related internships or fieldwork, Federal Work-Study, institutionally sponsored loans, tuition waivers (partial), and unspecified assistantships also available. Financial award application deadline: 3/1; financial award applicants required to submit FAFSA. *Unit head:* Dr. Robert Langworthy, Chair, 407-823-5929, E-mail: rlangwor@mail.ucf.edu. *Application contact:* Dr. Robert Langworthy, Chair, 407-823-5929, E-mail: rlangwor@mail.ucf.edu.

University of Central Missouri, The Graduate School, College of Health and Human Services, Warrensburg, MO 64093. Offers criminal justice (MS); industrial hygiene (MS); occupational safety management (MS); physical education/exercise and sport science (MS); rural family nursing (MS); social gerontology (MS); sociology (MA); speech language pathology and audiology (MS). *Accreditation:* NCATE. Part-time programs available. Postbaccalaureate distance learning degree programs offered. *Faculty:* 53. *Students:* 169 full-time (107 women), 364 part-time (210 women); includes 65 minority (46 African Americans, 1 American Indian/Alaska Native, 5 Asian Americans or Pacific Islanders, 13 Hispanic Americans), 27 international. Average age 32. 236 applicants, 92% accepted, 211 enrolled. In 2009, 153 master's awarded. *Entrance requirements:* Additional exam requirements/recommendations for international students: Required—TOEFL (minimum score 550 paper-based; 79 computer-based). *Application deadline:* For fall admission, 6/1 priority date for domestic students, 5/1 for international students; for spring admission, 10/1 priority date for domestic students, 10/1 for international students. Applications are processed on a rolling basis. Application fee: $30 ($75 for international students). Electronic applications accepted. *Expenses:* Tuition, area resident: Part-time $245.80 per credit hour. Tuition, nonresident: part-time $491.60 per credit hour. Required fees: $24.20 per credit hour. Full-time tuition and fees vary according to course load, degree level, campus/location and reciprocity agreements. *Financial support:* Research assistantships with full and partial tuition reimbursements, teaching assistantships with full and partial tuition reimbursements, career-related internships or fieldwork, Federal Work-Study, scholarships/grants, and administrative and laboratory assistantships available. Support available to part-time students. Financial award application deadline: 3/1; financial award applicants required to submit FAFSA. *Unit head:* Dr. Rick Sluder, Dean, 660-543-4245, Fax: 660-543-4167, E-mail: sluder@ucmo.edu. *Application contact:* Laurie Delap, Admissions Coordinator, 660-543-4621, Fax: 660-543-4778, E-mail: gradinfo@ucmo.edu.

University of Central Oklahoma, College of Graduate Studies and Research, College of Liberal Arts, Department of Sociology, Criminal Justice and Substance Abuse Studies, Edmond, OK 73034-5209. Offers criminal justice management and administration (MA). Part-time programs available. *Entrance requirements:* Additional exam requirements/recommendations for international students: Required—TOEFL (minimum score 550 paper-based; 213 computer-based). Electronic applications accepted. *Expenses:* Tuition, state resident: full-time $4128; part-time $172 per credit hour. Tuition, nonresident: full-time $10,373; part-time $432.20 per credit hour. Required fees: $433.20; $18.05 per credit hour. *Faculty research:* Gender issues, violent offenders.

University of Cincinnati, Graduate School, College of Education, Criminal Justice, and Human Services, Division of Criminal Justice, Cincinnati, OH 45221. Offers MS, PhD. Part-time programs available. Postbaccalaureate distance learning degree programs offered (no on-campus study). *Degree requirements:* For master's, thesis or alternative; for doctorate, thesis/dissertation. *Entrance requirements:* For master's, GRE or MAT, minimum GPA of 3.0; for doctorate, minimum GPA of 3.5. Additional exam requirements/recommendations for international students: Required—TOEFL (minimum score 550 paper-based), OEPT 3. Electronic applications accepted.

University of Colorado at Colorado Springs, Graduate School, Graduate School of Public Affairs, Colorado Springs, CO 80933-7150. Offers criminal justice (MCJ); public administration (MPA). *Accreditation:* NASPAA. Part-time and evening/weekend programs available. *Faculty:* 7 full-time (2 women). *Students:* 36 full-time (19 women), 43 part-time (30 women); includes 14 minority (3 African Americans, 4 Asian Americans or Pacific Islanders, 7 Hispanic Americans). Average age 36. 34 applicants, 82% accepted, 24 enrolled. In 2009, 15 master's awarded. *Degree requirements:* For master's, internship (if no experience), capstone project. *Entrance requirements:* For master's, GRE General Test, GMAT, LSAT, minimum GPA of 3.0. *Application deadline:* For fall admission, 6/1 priority date for domestic students; for spring admission, 11/1 for domestic students. Applications are processed on a rolling basis. Application fee: $60 ($75 for international students). *Expenses:* Contact institution. *Financial support:* Career-related internships or fieldwork, Federal Work-Study, and scholarships/grants available. Support available to part-time students. Financial award application deadline: 3/1; financial award applicants required to submit FAFSA. *Unit head:* Dr. Terry Schwartz, Dean, 719-255-4047, Fax: 719-255-4183, E-mail: tschwart@uccs.edu. *Application contact:* Mary Lou Kartis, Program Assistant, 719-255-4182, Fax: 719-255-4183, E-mail: mkartis@uccs.edu.

University of Colorado Denver, Graduate School of Public Affairs, Program in Criminal Justice, Denver, CO 80217-3364. Offers MCJ. Part-time and evening/weekend programs available. *Students:* 8 full-time (7 women), 37 part-time (29 women); includes 13 minority (3 African Americans, 1 American Indian/Alaska Native, 2 Asian Americans or Pacific Islanders, 7 Hispanic Americans). 25 applicants, 76% accepted, 13 enrolled. In 2009, 18 master's awarded. *Degree requirements:* For master's, comprehensive exam, thesis optional. *Entrance requirements:* For master's, GRE General Test, minimum GPA of 3.0. Additional exam requirements/recommendations for international students: Required—TOEFL (minimum score 500 paper-based). *Application deadline:* For fall admission, 6/1 priority date for domestic students, 1/1 priority date for international students; for spring admission, 11/1 for domestic students, 5/1 for international students. Applications are processed on a rolling basis. Application fee: $50 ($60 for international students). *Financial support:* In 2009–10, 6 fellowships were awarded; research assistantships, teaching assistantships, career-related internships or fieldwork, Federal Work-Study, and institutionally sponsored loans also available. Support available to part-time students. Financial award application deadline: 4/1; financial award applicants required to submit FAFSA. *Unit head:* Dr. Mary Dodge, Director, 303-315-2086, Fax: 303-315-2229, E-mail: mary.dodge@ucdenver.edu. *Application contact:* Antoinette Sandoval, Student Service Specialist, 303-315-2487, Fax: 303-315-2229, E-mail: antoinette.sandoval@ucdenver.edu.

University of Delaware, College of Arts and Sciences, Department of Sociology and Criminology, Newark, DE 19716. Offers criminology (MA, PhD); sociology (MA, PhD). *Degree requirements:* For master's, thesis; for doctorate, comprehensive exam, thesis/dissertation. *Entrance requirements:* For master's and doctorate, GRE, 3 letters of recommendation. Additional exam requirements/recommendations for international students: Required—TOEFL. Electronic applications accepted. *Faculty research:* Sex and gender, criminology/deviance, theory, methods, collective behavior.

University of Denver, University College, Denver, CO 80208. Offers applied communication (MAS, MPS, Certificate); computer information systems (MAS, Certificate); environmental policy and management (MAS, Certificate); geographic information systems (MAS, Certificate); human resource administration (MPS, Certificate); knowledge and information technologies (MAS); liberal studies (MLS, Certificate); modern languages (MLS, Certificate); organizational leadership (MPS, Certificate); security management (Certificate); technology management (MAS, Certificate), including 21st century strategic management (MAS), international markets (MAS), project management (MAS), research and development management (MAS); telecommunications (MAS, Certificate), including broadband (MAS), telecommunications management and policy (MAS), telecommunications technology (MAS), wireless networks (MAS). Part-time and evening/weekend programs available. Postbaccalaureate distance learning degree programs offered (no on-campus study). *Faculty:* 160 part-time/adjunct (64 women). *Students:* 53 full-time (25 women), 984 part-time (551 women); includes 171 minority (72 African Americans, 10 American Indian/Alaska Native, 33 Asian Americans or Pacific Islanders, 56 Hispanic Americans), 75 international. Average age 36. 537 applicants, 96% accepted, 494 enrolled. In 2009, 229 master's, 109 Certificates awarded. *Entrance requirements:* Additional exam requirements/recommendations for international students: Required—TOEFL (minimum score 550 paper-based; 213 computer-based). *Application deadline:* Applications are processed on a rolling basis. Application fee: $75. Electronic applications accepted. *Expenses:* Contact institution. *Financial support:* Applicants required to submit FAFSA. *Unit head:* Dr. James Davis, Dean, 303-871-2291, Fax: 303-871-4047, E-mail: jdavis@du.edu. *Application contact:* Information Contact, 303-871-3155.

University of Detroit Mercy, College of Liberal Arts and Education, Department of Criminal Justice and Human Services, Program in Criminal Justice Studies, Detroit, MI 48221. Offers MA. Part-time and evening/weekend programs available. *Degree requirements:* For master's, thesis or alternative. *Entrance requirements:* For master's, minimum GPA of 2.75. *Faculty research:* Socialization and social control, law and correction practices.

University of Detroit Mercy, College of Liberal Arts and Education, Department of Criminal Justice and Human Services, Program in Security Administration, Detroit, MI 48221. Offers MS. Part-time and evening/weekend programs available. *Degree requirements:* For master's, thesis or alternative. *Entrance requirements:* For master's, minimum GPA of 2.75. *Faculty research:* Physical information and personnel security.

University of Florida, Graduate School, College of Liberal Arts and Sciences, Department of Criminology, Law and Society, Gainesville, FL 32611. Offers criminology and law (MA, PhD); MA/JD; MA/PhD.

University of Great Falls, Graduate Studies, Program in Criminal Justice, Great Falls, MT 59405. Offers MSM. Part-time and evening/weekend programs available. *Degree requirements:* For master's, thesis optional. *Entrance requirements:* For master's, GRE General Test or MAT, 3 letters of recommendation. Additional exam requirements/recommendations for international students: Required—TOEFL (minimum score 500 paper-based; 205 computer-based). Electronic applications accepted. *Faculty research:* Delinquency, domestic violence law.

University of Guelph, Graduate Program Services, College of Social and Applied Human Sciences, Department of Criminology and Criminal Justice Policy, Guelph, ON N1G 2W1, Canada. Offers MA. *Degree requirements:* For master's, thesis or major paper. *Entrance requirements:* For master's, minimum B+ average during previous 2 years of coursework. Electronic applications accepted.

University of Guelph, Graduate Program Services, College of Social and Applied Human Sciences, Department of Sociology and Anthropology, Guelph, ON N1G 2W1, Canada. Offers anthropology (MA); crime and criminal justice policy (MA); sociology (MA, PhD). *Degree requirements:* For master's, thesis or major paper; for doctorate, comprehensive exam, thesis/dissertation. *Entrance requirements:* For master's, minimum B+ average during previous 2 years of course work, honors BA or equivalent; for doctorate, must have an MA in Sociology, must have 80% or higher in graduate level studies. Additional exam requirements/recommendations for international students: Required—TOEFL (minimum score 550 paper-based; 213 computer-based; 89 iBT), IELTS (minimum score 6.5), TOEFL or IELTS. Electronic applications accepted. *Faculty research:* Rural and development sociology; education, employment, and the workplace; race, ethnicity, and native studies; criminology and deviance; social psychology.

University of Houston–Clear Lake, School of Human Sciences and Humanities, Programs in Human Sciences, Houston, TX 77058-1098. Offers behavioral sciences (MA), including criminology, cross cultural studies, general psychology, sociology; clinical psychology (MA); criminology (MA); cross cultural studies (MA); family therapy (MA); fitness and human performance (MA); school psychology (MA). *Accreditation:* AAMFT/COAMFTE. Part-time and evening/weekend programs available. Postbaccalaureate distance learning degree programs offered (minimal on-campus study). *Degree requirements:* For master's, thesis or alternative. *Entrance requirements:* For master's, GRE General Test. Additional exam requirements/recommendations for international students: Required—TOEFL (minimum score 550 paper-based; 213 computer-based). Electronic applications accepted. *Faculty research:* Smoking cessation, adolescent sexuality, white collar crime, serial murder, human factors/human computer interaction.

University of Houston–Downtown, College of Public Service, Department of Criminal Justice, Houston, TX 77002. Offers MS. Part-time and evening/weekend programs available. *Faculty:* 8 full-time (3 women). *Students:* 6 full-time (3 women), 63 part-time (32 women); includes 44 minority (19 African Americans, 3 Asian Americans or Pacific Islanders, 22 Hispanic Americans).

Criminal Justice and Criminology

University of Houston–Downtown (continued)
Average age 36. 26 applicants, 85% accepted, 22 enrolled. In 2009, 10 master's awarded. *Degree requirements:* For master's, thesis or project. *Entrance requirements:* For master's, GRE, MAT or GMAT, personal statement, 3 letters of recommendation. Additional exam requirements/recommendations for international students: Required—TOEFL (minimum score 550 paper-based; 213 computer-based; 79 iBT). *Application deadline:* For fall admission, 8/1 for domestic and international students; for spring admission, 11/15 for domestic and international students. Applications are processed on a rolling basis. Application fee: $35 ($60 for international students). Electronic applications accepted. *Expenses:* Tuition, state resident: full-time $3150; part-time $175 per credit hour. Tuition, nonresident: full-time $7506; part-time $417 per credit hour. Required fees: $908; $322 per term. *Financial support:* Federal Work-Study and scholarships/grants available. Financial award applicants required to submit FAFSA. *Faculty research:* Criminal justice education, issues in law enforcement, issues in security, adult probation, legal issues in prisons. *Unit head:* Dr. Clete Snell, Chair, 713-221-8943, Fax: 713-221-2726, E-mail: snellc@uhd.edu. *Application contact:* Dr. Traqina Emeka, Assistant Professor and Graduate Coordinator, 713-221-8282, Fax: 713-221-2726, E-mail: emekat@uhd.edu.

University of Houston–Downtown, College of Public Service, Master of Security Management for Executives Program, Houston, TX 77002. Offers MSM. Part-time and evening/weekend programs available. *Faculty:* 4 full-time (3 women), 1 part-time/adjunct (0 women). *Students:* 29 full-time (3 women); includes 9 minority (8 African Americans, 1 Hispanic American), 1 international. Average age 43. 14 applicants, 93% accepted, 13 enrolled. In 2009, 11 master's awarded. *Degree requirements:* For master's, capstone project. *Entrance requirements:* For master's, letter of intent, 3 letters of recommendation from supervisors indicating probability of applicant's success in program, proof of three years of paid work experience with supervisory or managerial responsibilities. Additional exam requirements/recommendations for international students: Required—TOEFL (minimum score 550 paper-based; 213 computer-based; 80 iBT). *Application deadline:* For fall admission, 8/10 for domestic and international students. Applications are processed on a rolling basis. Application fee: $35 ($60 for international students). Electronic applications accepted. *Expenses:* Tuition, state resident: full-time $3150; part-time $175 per credit hour. Tuition, nonresident: full-time $7506; part-time $417 per credit hour. Required fees: $908; $322 per term. *Financial support:* Federal Work-Study available. Financial award applicants required to submit FAFSA. *Unit head:* Dr. Beth Pelz, Dean, College of Public Service, 713-221-8194, Fax: 713-226-5274, E-mail: pelzb@uhd.edu. *Application contact:* John Presley, Executive Director, 713-221-5292, Fax: 713-226-5274, E-mail: presleyj@uhd.edu.

University of Illinois at Chicago, Graduate College, College of Liberal Arts and Sciences, Department of Criminal Justice, Chicago, IL 60607-7128. Offers MA, PhD. Evening/weekend programs available. *Degree requirements:* For master's, thesis. *Entrance requirements:* For master's, GRE General Test, minimum GPA of 3.0. Additional exam requirements/recommendations for international students: Required—TOEFL. Electronic applications accepted. *Faculty research:* Sentencing probation, police and court use of scientific evidence, community mediation and conflict resolution.

University of Louisiana at Monroe, Graduate School, College of Arts and Sciences, Program in Criminal Justice, Monroe, LA 71209-0001. Offers MA. Part-time and evening/weekend programs available. *Faculty:* 2 full-time (0 women). *Students:* 16 full-time (13 women), 17 part-time (10 women); includes 19 minority (all African Americans). Average age 30. In 2009, 6 master's awarded. *Degree requirements:* For master's, thesis (for some programs). *Entrance requirements:* For master's, GRE General Test, minimum GPA of 2.5. Additional exam requirements/recommendations for international students: Required—TOEFL (minimum score 500 paper-based; 173 computer-based; 61 iBT). *Application deadline:* For fall admission, 8/24 priority date for domestic students, 7/1 for international students; for winter admission, 12/14 priority date for domestic students; for spring admission, 1/19 for domestic students, 11/1 for international students. Applications are processed on a rolling basis. Application fee: $20 ($30 for international students). Electronic applications accepted. *Expenses:* Tuition, state resident: part-time $159 per credit hour. Tuition, nonresident: part-time $159 per credit hour. Required fees: $1300 per year. Tuition and fees vary according to course load. *Financial support:* In 2009–10, 3 research assistantships with full tuition reimbursements (averaging $2,500 per year) were awarded; career-related internships or fieldwork, Federal Work-Study, and unspecified assistantships also available. Financial award application deadline: 4/1; financial award applicants required to submit FAFSA. *Unit head:* Dr. Robert D. Hanser, Department Head, 318-342-1440, Fax: 318-342-1431, E-mail: hanser@ulm.edu. *Application contact:* Dr. Robert D. Hanser, Department Head, 318-342-1440, Fax: 318-342-1431, E-mail: hanser@ulm.edu.

University of Louisville, Graduate School, College of Arts and Sciences, Department of Justice Administration, Louisville, KY 40292. Offers MS. Part-time and evening/weekend programs available. Postbaccalaureate distance learning degree programs offered (no on-campus study). *Faculty:* 13 full-time (4 women), 5 part-time/adjunct (2 women). *Students:* 46 full-time (19 women), 48 part-time (24 women); includes 13 minority (12 African Americans, 1 Asian American or Pacific Islander). Average age 36. 43 applicants, 84% accepted, 23 enrolled. In 2009, 27 master's awarded. *Degree requirements:* For master's, comprehensive exam (for some programs), thesis (for some programs), professional paper. *Entrance requirements:* For master's, GRE General Test, 2 letters of recommendation. Additional exam requirements/recommendations for international students: Required—TOEFL (minimum score 550 paper-based; 213 computer-based; 79 iBT). *Application deadline:* For fall admission, 7/1 priority date for domestic and international students; for spring admission, 11/15 priority date for domestic and international students. Applications are processed on a rolling basis. Application fee: $50. Electronic applications accepted. *Financial support:* Research assistantships, health care benefits available. Financial award application deadline: 8/1; financial award applicants required to submit FAFSA. *Faculty research:* Applied research, program evaluation and policy analysis in criminal justice; juvenile sex offender research; theoretical criminology; crime analysis; organizational and leadership management. Total annual research expenditures: $137,442. *Unit head:* Dr. Deborah G. Keeling, Chair, 502-852-6567, Fax: 502-852-0065, E-mail: dgwilson@louisville.edu. *Application contact:* Libby Leggett, Director, Graduate Admissions, 502-852-3101, Fax: 502-852-6536, E-mail: gradadm@louisville.edu.

University of Management and Technology, Program in Criminal Justice, Arlington, VA 22209. Offers MS.

University of Maryland, College Park, Academic Affairs, College of Behavioral and Social Sciences, Department of Criminology and Criminal Justice, College Park, MD 20742. Offers MA, PhD, JD/MA. Part-time and evening/weekend programs available. *Faculty:* 21 full-time (8 women), 23 part-time/adjunct (10 women). *Students:* 65 full-time (45 women), 15 part-time (7 women); includes 7 minority (3 African Americans, 1 Asian American or Pacific Islander, 3 Hispanic Americans), 15 international. 136 applicants, 23% accepted, 13 enrolled. In 2009, 26 master's, 9 doctorates awarded. Terminal master's awarded for partial completion of doctoral program. *Degree requirements:* For master's, comprehensive exam, thesis optional; for doctorate, comprehensive exam, thesis/dissertation. *Entrance requirements:* For master's, GRE General Test, minimum GPA of 3.0, 3 letters of recommendation; for doctorate, GRE General Test. Additional exam requirements/recommendations for international students: Required—TOEFL. *Application deadline:* For fall admission, 12/15 for domestic students, 2/1 for international students. Applications are processed on a rolling basis. Application fee: $60. Electronic applications accepted. *Expenses:* Tuition, area resident: Part-time $471 per credit hour. Tuition, state resident: part-time $471 per credit hour. Tuition, nonresident: part-time $1016 per credit hour. Required fees: $337.04 per term. *Financial support:* In 2009–10, 3 fellowships with full tuition reimbursements (averaging $18,536 per year), 5 research assistantships with tuition reimbursements (averaging $16,132 per year), 31 teaching assistantships with tuition reimbursements (averaging $15,913 per year) were awarded; Federal Work-Study and scholarships/grants also available. Support available to part-time students. Financial award applicants required to submit FAFSA. *Faculty research:* Theory, crime prevention, death penalty, criminal justice technology, policy. Total annual research expenditures: $844,985. *Unit head:* Dr. Sally Simpson, Chair, 301-405-4699, Fax: 301-405-4733, E-mail: ssimpson@umd.edu. *Application contact:* Dean of Graduate School, 301-405-0358, Fax: 301-314-9305.

University of Maryland Eastern Shore, Graduate Programs, Department of Criminal Justice, Princess Anne, MD 21853-1299. Offers criminology and criminal justice (MS). Part-time and evening/weekend programs available. *Degree requirements:* For master's, comprehensive exam, thesis optional. *Entrance requirements:* For master's, GRE General Test, interview. Additional exam requirements/recommendations for international students: Required—TOEFL (minimum score 213 computer-based; 80 iBT).

University of Massachusetts Lowell, College of Arts and Sciences, Department of Criminal Justice and Criminology, Lowell, MA 01854-2881. Offers MA. Part-time and evening/weekend programs available. *Degree requirements:* For master's, thesis optional. *Entrance requirements:* For master's, GRE General Test or MAT. Electronic applications accepted. *Faculty research:* Family violence, criminal justice management, corrections, policing, delinquency.

University of Memphis, Graduate School, College of Arts and Sciences, Department of Criminology and Criminal Justice, Memphis, TN 38152. Offers MA. Part-time programs available. *Faculty:* 3 full-time (1 woman), 2 part-time/adjunct (0 women). *Students:* 8 full-time (6 women), 10 part-time (4 women); includes 4 minority (all African Americans). Average age 27. 11 applicants, 82% accepted, 5 enrolled. In 2009, 4 master's awarded. *Degree requirements:* For master's, comprehensive exam, thesis optional. *Entrance requirements:* For master's, GRE General Test, minimum GPA of 3.0. Additional exam requirements/recommendations for international students: Required—TOEFL. *Application deadline:* For fall admission, 6/1 for domestic students; for spring admission, 11/1 for domestic students. Application fee: $35 ($60 for international students). *Expenses:* Tuition, state resident: full-time $6246; part-time $347 per credit hour. Tuition, nonresident: full-time $15,894; part-time $883 per credit hour. Required fees: $1160. Full-time tuition and fees vary according to course load, degree level and program. *Financial support:* In 2009–10, 11 students received support; research assistantships with full tuition reimbursements available, teaching assistantships with full tuition reimbursements available, career-related internships or fieldwork, Federal Work-Study, institutionally sponsored loans, scholarships/grants, tuition waivers (partial), and unspecified assistantships available. Financial award application deadline: 2/15; financial award applicants required to submit FAFSA. *Faculty research:* Violence, crime prevention, crime analysis, survey research, crisis intervention. *Unit head:* Prof. W. Randolph Dupont, Chair, 901-678-2737, Fax: 901-678-5279, E-mail: rdupont@memphis.edu. *Application contact:* Dr. K. B. Turner, Coordinator of Graduate Studies, 901-678-2737, Fax: 901-678-5279, E-mail: kbturner@memphis.edu.

University of Minnesota, Duluth, Graduate School, College of Liberal Arts, Department of Sociology/Anthropology, Program in Criminology, Duluth, MN 55812-2496. Offers MA. Part-time and evening/weekend programs available. *Faculty:* 20 full-time (13 women). *Students:* 20 full-time (13 women). 12 applicants, 50% accepted, 6 enrolled. In 2009, 1 master's awarded. *Degree requirements:* For master's, thesis or alternative. *Entrance requirements:* For master's, minimum GPA of 3.0, letter of recommendation, personal statement. Additional exam requirements/recommendations for international students: Required—TOEFL. *Application deadline:* For fall admission, 7/15 for domestic students; for spring admission, 11/1 for domestic students. Applications are processed on a rolling basis. Application fee: $75 ($95 for international students). *Financial support:* In 2009–10, 1 teaching assistantship with full tuition reimbursement (averaging $13,065 per year) was awarded; research assistantships, tuition waivers (partial) also available. Financial award application deadline: 7/31. *Faculty research:* Restorative justice, juvenile delinquency, social justice, program evaluation. *Unit head:* Dr. Jeffrey Maahs, Director of Graduate Studies, 218-726-7395, Fax: 218-726-7395, E-mail: jmaahs@d.umn.edu. *Application contact:* Tami Vatalaro, Student Personnel Coordinator, 218-726-7523, Fax: 218-726-7759, E-mail: tvatalar@d.umn.edu.

University of Missouri–Kansas City, College of Arts and Sciences, Department of Criminal Justice and Criminology, Kansas City, MO 64110-2499. Offers MS. Part-time and evening/weekend programs available. *Faculty:* 7 full-time (4 women), 1 part-time/adjunct (0 women). *Students:* 6 full-time (4 women), 20 part-time (13 women); includes 5 minority (3 African Americans, 1 Asian American or Pacific Islander, 1 Hispanic American). Average age 27. 24 applicants, 58% accepted, 8 enrolled. In 2009, 1 master's awarded. *Degree requirements:* For master's, thesis optional. *Entrance requirements:* For master's, GRE, minimum GPA of 3.0 in major, 2.7 overall. Additional exam requirements/recommendations for international students: Required—TOEFL (minimum score 550 paper-based; 213 computer-based; 80 iBT). *Application deadline:* For fall admission, 3/1 for domestic and international students; for spring admission, 11/1 for domestic and international students. Applications are processed on a rolling basis. Application fee: $45 ($50 for international students). Electronic applications accepted. *Expenses:* Tuition, state resident: full-time $5378; part-time $299 per credit hour. Tuition, nonresident: full-time $13,881; part-time $771 per credit hour. Required fees: $641; $71 per credit hour. Tuition and fees vary according to course load and program. *Financial support:* In 2009–10, 3 research assistantships with full tuition reimbursements (averaging $10,667 per year), 2 teaching assistantships with full and partial tuition reimbursements (averaging $10,667 per year) were awarded; career-related internships or fieldwork, Federal Work-Study, institutionally sponsored loans, and tuition waivers (partial) also available. Support available to part-time students. Financial award application deadline: 3/1; financial award applicants required to submit FAFSA. *Faculty research:* Death penalty, community corrections, urban community and neighborhoods. Total annual research expenditures: $3,337. *Unit head:* Dr. Ken Novak, Chair, 816-235-1599, Fax: 816-235-5193, E-mail: novakk@umkc.edu. *Application contact:* Dr. Wayne L. Lucas, Graduate Advisor, 816-235-1598, Fax: 816-235-5193, E-mail: lucasw@umkc.edu.

University of Missouri–St. Louis, College of Arts and Sciences, Department of Criminology and Criminal Justice, St. Louis, MO 63121. Offers MA, PhD. *Faculty:* 13 full-time (6 women), 1 part-time/adjunct (0 women). *Students:* 32 full-time (18 women), 31 part-time (19 women); includes 9 minority (7 African Americans, 1 American Indian/Alaska Native, 1 Asian American or Pacific Islander), 3 international. Average age 30. In 2009, 11 master's, 3 doctorates awarded. *Degree requirements:* For doctorate, thesis/dissertation. *Entrance requirements:* For doctorate, GRE General Test, writing sample, 3 letters of recommendation. Additional exam requirements/recommendations for international students: Required—TOEFL (minimum score 550 paper-based; 213 computer-based). *Application deadline:* For fall admission, 4/1 priority date for domestic and international students. Applications are processed on a rolling basis. Application fee: $35 ($40 for international students). Electronic applications accepted. *Expenses:* Tuition, state resident: full-time $5377; part-time $297.70 per credit hour. Tuition, nonresident: full-time $13,882; part-time $771.20 per credit hour. Required fees: $220; $12.20 per credit hour. One-time fee: $12. Tuition and fees vary according to course level, campus/location and program. *Financial support:* In 2009–10, 8 research assistantships with full and partial tuition reimbursements (averaging $14,288 per year), 10 teaching assistantships with full and partial tuition reimbursements (averaging $13,500 per year) were awarded; fellowships with full tuition reimbursements, career-related internships or fieldwork also available. Financial award applicants required to submit FAFSA. *Faculty research:* Crime control, criminological theory, juvenile delinquency, violence, drugs. *Unit head:* Dr. Beth Huebner, Director of Graduate Studies, 314-516-5031, Fax: 314-516-5048, E-mail: huebner@umsl.edu. *Application contact:* 314-516-5458, Fax: 314-516-6996, E-mail: gradadm@umsl.edu.

The University of Montana, Graduate School, College of Arts and Sciences, Department of Sociology, Missoula, MT 59812-0002. Offers criminology (MA); rural and environmental change (MA); sociology (MA). *Entrance requirements:* For master's, GRE General Test. Additional exam requirements/recommendations for international students: Required—TOEFL. *Faculty research:* Housing, homelessness, hunger, infant mortality, work safety.

University of Nebraska at Omaha, Graduate Studies, College of Public Affairs and Community Service, Department of Criminal Justice, Omaha, NE 68182. Offers MA, MS, PhD. Part-time and evening/weekend programs available. *Faculty:* 20 full-time (11 women). *Students:*

20 full-time (16 women), 30 part-time (16 women); includes 5 minority (2 African Americans, 1 Asian American or Pacific Islander, 2 Hispanic Americans), 5 international. Average age 31. 44 applicants, 59% accepted, 12 enrolled. In 2009, 12 master's, 3 doctorates awarded. Terminal master's awarded for partial completion of doctoral program. *Degree requirements:* For master's, comprehensive exam, thesis (for some programs); for doctorate, comprehensive exam, thesis/dissertation. *Entrance requirements:* For master's, GRE General Test or MAT, previous course work in criminal justice, statistics, and research methods; minimum GPA of 3.0; for doctorate, GRE General Test, letters of recommendation, statement of intent. Additional exam requirements/recommendations for international students: Required—TOEFL (minimum score 550 paper-based; 213 computer-based; 80 iBT). *Application deadline:* For fall admission, 2/15 for domestic students; for spring admission, 12/1 priority date for domestic students. Applications are processed on a rolling basis. Application fee: $45. Electronic applications accepted. *Financial support:* In 2009–10, 34 students received support; research assistantships with tuition reimbursements available, teaching assistantships with tuition reimbursements available, career-related internships or fieldwork, Federal Work-Study, institutionally sponsored loans, scholarships/grants, tuition waivers (partial), and unspecified assistantships available. Support available to part-time students. Financial award application deadline: 3/1; financial award applicants required to submit FAFSA. *Unit head:* Dr. Candice Batten, Head, 402-554-2610. *Application contact:* Dr. William Wakefield, Student Contact, 402-554-2610.

University of Nevada, Las Vegas, Graduate College, Greenspun College of Urban Affairs, Department of Criminal Justice, Las Vegas, NV 89154-5009. Offers MA. Part-time programs available. *Faculty:* 12 full-time (5 women). *Students:* 20 full-time (17 women), 18 part-time (10 women); includes 5 minority (3 African Americans, 2 Hispanic Americans). Average age 30. 49 applicants, 43% accepted, 14 enrolled. In 2009, 10 master's awarded. *Degree requirements:* For master's, comprehensive exam (for some programs), thesis (for some programs). *Entrance requirements:* Additional exam requirements/recommendations for international students: Required—TOEFL (minimum score 550 paper-based; 213 computer-based; 80 iBT), IELTS (minimum score 7). *Application deadline:* For fall admission, 2/1 priority date for domestic and international students. Applications are processed on a rolling basis. Application fee: $60 ($95 for international students). Electronic applications accepted. *Financial support:* In 2009–10, 9 students received support, including 2 research assistantships with partial tuition reimbursements available (averaging $10,000 per year), 7 teaching assistantships with partial tuition reimbursements available (averaging $10,000 per year); institutionally sponsored loans, scholarships/grants, health care benefits, and unspecified assistantships also available. Financial award application deadline: 3/1. *Unit head:* Dr. Joel Lieberman, Chair/ Associate Professor, 702-895-0013, Fax: 702-895-0252, E-mail: joel.lieberman@unlv.edu. *Application contact:* Graduate College Admissions Evaluator, 702-895-3320, Fax: 702-895-4180, E-mail: gradcollege@unlv.edu.

University of Nevada, Reno, Graduate School, College of Liberal Arts, School of Social Research and Justice Studies, Department of Criminal Justice, Reno, NV 89557. Offers MA. *Degree requirements:* For master's, comprehensive exam, thesis optional. *Entrance requirements:* For master's, GRE or LSAT, undergraduate degree in criminal justice with minimum GPA of 3.0. Additional exam requirements/recommendations for international students: Required—TOEFL (minimum score 500 paper-based; 173 computer-based; 61 iBT), IELTS (minimum score 6). Electronic applications accepted. *Faculty research:* Criminal justice system, social policy interaction.

University of Nevada, Reno, Graduate School, College of Liberal Arts, School of Social Research and Justice Studies, Program in Justice Management, Reno, NV 89557. Offers MJM. Part-time programs available. Postbaccalaureate distance learning degree programs offered (no on-campus study). *Degree requirements:* For master's, thesis optional. *Entrance requirements:* For master's, minimum GPA of 2.75. Additional exam requirements/recommendations for international students: Required—TOEFL (minimum score 500 paper-based; 173 computer-based; 61 iBT), IELTS (minimum score 6). Electronic applications accepted. *Faculty research:* Justice administration, adult justice management, juvenile justice management.

University of New Haven, Graduate School, Henry C. Lee College of Criminal Justice and Forensic Sciences, Program in Criminal Justice, West Haven, CT 06516-1916. Offers crime analysis (MS); criminal justice management (MS); forensic computer investigation (MS, Certificate); forensic psychology (MS); victim advocacy and services management (Certificate); victimology (MS). Part-time and evening/weekend programs available. *Faculty:* 8 full-time (2 women), 10 part-time/adjunct (4 women). *Students:* 25 full-time (17 women), 37 part-time (26 women); includes 20 minority (12 African Americans, 1 Asian American or Pacific Islander, 7 Hispanic Americans), 1 international. Average age 25. 62 applicants, 85% accepted, 28 enrolled. In 2009, 30 master's awarded. *Degree requirements:* For master's, thesis or alternative. *Entrance requirements:* Additional exam requirements/recommendations for international students: Required—TOEFL (minimum score 520 paper-based; 190 computer-based; 70 iBT), IELTS (minimum score 5.5). *Application deadline:* For fall admission, 5/31 for international students; for winter admission, 10/15 for international students; for spring admission, 1/15 for international students. Applications are processed on a rolling basis. Application fee: $50. Electronic applications accepted. *Expenses:* Tuition: Part-time $700 per credit. Required fees: $45 per term. One-time fee: $390 part-time. *Financial support:* Research assistantships with partial tuition reimbursements, teaching assistantships with partial tuition reimbursements, career-related internships or fieldwork, Federal Work-Study, scholarships/grants, tuition waivers, and unspecified assistantships available. Support available to part-time students. Financial award applicants required to submit FAFSA. *Unit head:* Dr. James J. Cassidy, Coordinator, 203-932-7374. *Application contact:* Eloise Gormley, Director of Graduate Admissions, 203-932-7449, Fax: 203-932-7137, E-mail: gradinfo@newhaven.edu.

University of North Alabama, College of Arts and Sciences, Department of Social Work and Criminal Justice, Florence, AL 35632-0001. Offers criminal justice (MSCJ). Part-time and evening/weekend programs available. *Faculty:* 1 full-time (0 women), 2 part-time/adjunct (0 women). *Students:* 15 full-time (6 women), 11 part-time (8 women); includes 8 minority (6 African Americans, 2 Hispanic Americans). Average age 31. In 2009, 5 master's awarded. *Entrance requirements:* For master's, GRE General Test, MAT. *Application deadline:* For fall admission, 7/1 priority date for domestic students; for spring admission, 12/1 for domestic students. Applications are processed on a rolling basis. Application fee: $25. Electronic applications accepted. *Expenses:* Tuition, state resident: full-time $5040; part-time $210 per credit hour. Tuition, nonresident: full-time $10,080; part-time $420 per credit hour. Required fees: $906. *Unit head:* Dr. Joy Borah, Chair, 256-765-4531, E-mail: jsborah@una.edu. *Application contact:* Kim Mauldin, Director of Admissions, 256-765-4608, Fax: 256-765-4960, E-mail: komauldin@una.edu.

The University of North Carolina at Charlotte, Graduate School, College of Arts and Sciences, Department of Criminal Justice, Charlotte, NC 28223-0001. Offers MS. Part-time and evening/weekend programs available. *Faculty:* 13 full-time (7 women). *Students:* 7 full-time (3 women), 12 part-time (6 women); includes 2 minority (both African Americans). Average age 29. 20 applicants, 45% accepted, 5 enrolled. In 2009, 11 master's awarded. *Degree requirements:* For master's, thesis or comprehensive exam. *Entrance requirements:* For master's, GRE General Test or MAT, minimum GPA of 3.0 in undergraduate major, 2.75 overall. Additional exam requirements/recommendations for international students: Required—TOEFL (minimum score 557 paper-based; 220 computer-based; 83 iBT). *Application deadline:* For fall admission, 7/1 for domestic students, 5/1 for international students; for spring admission, 11/1 for domestic students, 10/1 for international students. Applications are processed on a rolling basis. Application fee: $55. Electronic applications accepted. *Financial support:* In 2009–10, 5 students received support, including 1 research assistantship (averaging $13,000 per year), 4 teaching assistantships (averaging $10,000 per year); career-related internships or fieldwork, Federal Work-Study, institutionally sponsored loans, scholarships/grants, and unspecified assistantships also available. Support available to part-time students. Financial award application deadline: 4/1; financial award applicants required to submit FAFSA. *Faculty research:* Social psychology, terrorism, and identity; diminished capacity mitigation in death penalty proceedings; effects of prenatal problems, family functioning, and neighborhood disadvantage in predicting violent offending; dynamic nature of the drug use/serious violence relationship; Chinese birth cohort: criminological implications. Total annual research expenditures: $185,828. *Unit head:* Dr. Vivian B. Lord, Chair, 704-687-2009, Fax: 704-687-3349, E-mail: vblord@uncc.edu. *Application contact:* Kathy B. Giddings, Director of Graduate Admissions, 704-687-5503, Fax: 704-687-3279, E-mail: gradadm@uncc.edu.

The University of North Carolina at Greensboro, Graduate School, College of Arts and Sciences, Department of Sociology, Greensboro, NC 27412-5001. Offers criminology (MA); sociology (MA). Part-time programs available. *Degree requirements:* For master's, comprehensive exam, thesis. *Entrance requirements:* For master's, GRE General Test. Additional exam requirements/recommendations for international students: Required—TOEFL. Electronic applications accepted.

The University of North Carolina Wilmington, College of Arts and Sciences, Department of Sociology and Criminology, Wilmington, NC 28403-3297. Offers criminology (MA); public sociology (MA). *Degree requirements:* For master's, comprehensive exam, thesis or internship. *Entrance requirements:* Additional exam requirements/recommendations for international students: Required—TOEFL (minimum score 550 paper-based; 217 computer-based; 79 iBT), IELTS (minimum score 6.5). Electronic applications accepted.

University of North Dakota, Graduate School, College of Arts and Sciences, Program in Criminal Justice, Grand Forks, ND 58202. Offers PhD. Part-time programs available. *Entrance requirements:* For doctorate, GRE General Test. Additional exam requirements/recommendations for international students: Required—TOEFL (minimum score 550 paper-based; 213 computer-based; 79 iBT), IELTS (minimum score 6.5). Electronic applications accepted.

University of Northern Iowa, Graduate College, College of Social and Behavioral Sciences, Department of Sociology, Anthropology and Criminology, Cedar Falls, IA 50614. Offers criminology (MA); sociology (MA). Part-time and evening/weekend programs available. *Students:* 16 full-time (12 women), 1 (woman) part-time; includes 2 minority (both American Indian/Alaska Native). 22 applicants, 59% accepted, 7 enrolled. In 2009, 2 master's awarded. *Degree requirements:* For master's, thesis. *Entrance requirements:* For master's, minimum GPA of 3.0. Additional exam requirements/recommendations for international students: Required—TOEFL (minimum score 500 paper-based; 180 computer-based; 61 iBT). *Application deadline:* For fall admission, 8/1 priority date for domestic students. Applications are processed on a rolling basis. Application fee: $30 ($50 for international students). Electronic applications accepted. *Financial support:* Career-related internships or fieldwork, Federal Work-Study, scholarships/grants, and tuition waivers (full and partial) available. Support available to part-time students. Financial award application deadline: 2/1. *Unit head:* Dr. Kent Sandstrom, Department Head/Professor, 319-273-2786, Fax: 319-273-7104, E-mail: kent.sandstrom@uni.edu. *Application contact:* Laurie S. Russell, Record Analyst, 319-273-2623, Fax: 319-273-6792, E-mail: laurie.russell@uni.edu.

University of North Florida, College of Arts and Sciences, Department of Criminology and Criminal Justice, Jacksonville, FL 32224. Offers criminal justice (MSCJ). *Faculty:* 7 full-time (4 women). *Students:* 9 full-time (8 women), 20 part-time (12 women); includes 5 minority (4 African Americans, 1 Asian American or Pacific Islander), 1 international. Average age 28. 20 applicants, 40% accepted, 4 enrolled. In 2009, 4 master's awarded. *Degree requirements:* For master's, comprehensive exam, thesis optional. *Entrance requirements:* For master's, GRE General Test, minimum GPA of 3.0 in last 60 hours, letters of recommendation. Additional exam requirements/recommendations for international students: Required—TOEFL (minimum score 500 paper-based; 173 computer-based). *Application deadline:* For fall admission, 7/1 priority date for domestic students, 5/1 for international students; for spring admission, 11/1 priority date for domestic students, 10/1 for international students. Applications are processed on a rolling basis. Application fee: $30. Electronic applications accepted. *Expenses:* Tuition, state resident: full-time $6649.20; part-time $277.05 per credit hour. Tuition, nonresident: full-time $22,970; part-time $957.08 per credit hour. Required fees: $985; $41.03 per credit hour. *Financial support:* In 2009–10, 24 students received support, including 1 teaching assistantship (averaging $5,556 per year). Financial award application deadline: 4/1; financial award applicants required to submit FAFSA. *Unit head:* Dr. Michael Hallett, Chair, 904-620-2850, E-mail: mhallett@unf.edu. *Application contact:* Kiersten Jarvis, Graduate Coordinator, The Graduate School, 904-620-1360, Fax: 904-620-1362, E-mail: kiersten.jarvis@unf.edu.

University of North Texas, Robert B. Toulouse School of Graduate Studies, College of Public Affairs and Community Service, Department of Criminal Justice, Denton, TX 76203-5017. Offers MS. Part-time and evening/weekend programs available. *Degree requirements:* For master's, comprehensive exam, thesis optional. *Entrance requirements:* For master's, GRE General Test, personal statement. Additional exam requirements/recommendations for international students: Required—proof of English language proficiency required for non-native English speakers; Recommended—TOEFL (minimum score 550 paper-based; 213 computer-based; 79 iBT). *Application deadline:* Applications are processed on a rolling basis. Application fee: $50 ($75 for international students). Electronic applications accepted. *Expenses:* Tuition, state resident: full-time $4298; part-time $239 per contact hour. Tuition, nonresident: full-time $9878; part-time $549 per contact hour. Required fees: $265 per contact hour. *Financial support:* Applicants required to submit FAFSA. *Faculty research:* Law enforcement administration/strategy, juvenile justice/delinquency, violent crime/victimization, terrorism, correction administration/issues, capital punishment, criminalistics. *Application contact:* Graduate Adviser, 940-565-4954, Fax: 940-565-2548.

University of Ottawa, Faculty of Graduate and Postdoctoral Studies, Faculty of Social Sciences, Department of Criminology, Ottawa, ON K1N 6N5, Canada. Offers MA, MCA, PhD. *Degree requirements:* For master's, thesis or alternative. *Entrance requirements:* For master's, honors bachelor's degree or equivalent, minimum B average. Electronic applications accepted. *Faculty research:* Creation and reform of criminal policies in Canada.

University of Pennsylvania, School of Arts and Sciences, Graduate Group in Criminology, Philadelphia, PA 19104. Offers MA, MS, PhD. *Faculty:* 15 full-time (3 women), 2 part-time/adjunct (1 woman). *Students:* 29 full-time (18 women), 6 part-time (4 women); includes 5 minority (1 African American, 2 Asian Americans or Pacific Islanders, 2 Hispanic Americans), 4 international. 95 applicants, 37% accepted, 30 enrolled. In 2009, 22 master's awarded. Application fee: $70. *Expenses:* Tuition: Full-time $25,660; part-time $4758 per course. Required fees: $2152; $270 per course. Tuition and fees vary according to course load, degree level and program. *Financial support:* Institutionally sponsored loans, scholarships/grants, traineeships, health care benefits, and unspecified assistantships available.

University of Phoenix, The Artemis School, College of Health and Human Services, Phoenix, AZ 85034-7209. Offers administration of justice and security (MS); community counseling (MSC); education (MHA); family nurse practitioner (MSN); gerontology (MHA); health administration (MHA); health care education (MSN); health care management (MBA, MSN); informatics (MHA); marriage, family, and child therapy (MSC); nursing (MSN); nursing for nurse practitioners (MSN); psychology (MS); MSN/MBA; MSN/MHA. *Accreditation:* AACN. Evening/weekend programs available. Postbaccalaureate distance learning degree programs offered. *Degree requirements:* For master's, thesis (for some programs). *Entrance requirements:* For master's, 3 years of work experience, minimum undergraduate GPA of 2.5, RN license. Additional exam requirements/recommendations for international students: Required—TOEFL (minimum score 550 paper-based; 213 computer-based; 79 iBT). Electronic applications accepted.

University of Phoenix–Atlanta Campus, The Artemis School, College of Health and Human Services, Sandy Springs, GA 30350-4153. Offers administration of justice and security (MS); health administration (MHA); health care management (MBA); nursing (MSN); nursing/health care education (MSN); MSN/MBA; MSN/MHA. Evening/weekend programs available. Postbaccalaureate distance learning degree programs offered. *Degree requirements:* For master's,

Criminal Justice and Criminology

University of Phoenix–Atlanta Campus (continued)
thesis (for some programs). *Entrance requirements:* For master's, minimum undergraduate GPA of 2.5, 3 years of work experience. Additional exam requirements/recommendations for international students: Required—TOEFL (minimum score 550 paper-based; 213 computer-based; 79 iBT). Electronic applications accepted.

University of Phoenix–Augusta Campus, College of Social and Behavioral Science, Augusta, GA 30909-4583. Offers administration of justice and security (MS).

University of Phoenix–Austin Campus, College of Social and Behavioral Science, Austin, TX 78759. Offers administration of justice and security (MS); psychology (MS). Postbaccalaureate distance learning degree programs offered.

University of Phoenix–Bay Area Campus, The Artemis School, College of Health and Human Services, Pleasanton, CA 94588-3677. Offers administration of justice and security (MS); family nurse practitioner (MSN); health care management (MBA); marriage, family and child therapy (MSC); nursing (MSN); nursing/health care education (MSN); MSN/MBA. Evening/weekend programs available. Postbaccalaureate distance learning degree programs offered (no on-campus study). *Degree requirements:* For master's, thesis (for some programs). *Entrance requirements:* For master's, minimum undergraduate GPA of 2.5, 3 years of work experience, RN license. Additional exam requirements/recommendations for international students: Required—TOEFL (minimum score 550 paper-based; 213 computer-based; 79 iBT). Electronic applications accepted.

University of Phoenix–Birmingham Campus, College of Social and Behavioral Science, Birmingham, AL 35244. Offers administration of justice and security (MS); psychology (MS).

University of Phoenix–Chattanooga Campus, College of Social and Behavioral Science, Chattanooga, TN 37421-3707. Offers administration of justice and security (MS); psychology (MSP). Postbaccalaureate distance learning degree programs offered.

University of Phoenix–Cheyenne Campus, College of Social and Behavioral Science, Cheyenne, WY 82009. Offers administration of justice and security (MS); psychology (MS). Postbaccalaureate distance learning degree programs offered.

University of Phoenix–Cincinnati Campus, The Artemis School, College of Health and Human Services, West Chester, OH 45069-4875. Offers administration of justice and security (MS); health care management (MBA); nursing (MSN); psychology (MS). Evening/weekend programs available. Postbaccalaureate distance learning degree programs offered. *Degree requirements:* For master's, thesis (for some programs). *Entrance requirements:* For master's, minimum undergraduate GPA of 2.5, 3 years of work experience. Additional exam requirements/recommendations for international students: Required—TOEFL (minimum score 550 paper-based; 79 iBT). Electronic applications accepted.

University of Phoenix–Cleveland Campus, The Artemis School, College of Health and Human Services, Independence, OH 44131-2194. Offers administration of justice and security (MS); health care management (MBA); nursing (MSN); psychology (MS). Evening/weekend programs available. Postbaccalaureate distance learning degree programs offered. *Degree requirements:* For master's, thesis (for some programs). *Entrance requirements:* For master's, minimum undergraduate GPA of 2.5, 3 years of work experience. Additional exam requirements/recommendations for international students: Required—TOEFL (minimum score 550 paper-based; 213 computer-based; 79 iBT). Electronic applications accepted.

University of Phoenix–Columbus Georgia Campus, The Artemis School, College of Health and Human Services, Columbus, GA 31904-6321. Offers administration of justice and security (MS); health administration (MHA); health care management (MBA); nursing (MSN). Postbaccalaureate distance learning degree programs offered. *Degree requirements:* For master's, thesis (for some programs). *Entrance requirements:* For master's, minimum undergraduate GPA of 2.5, 3 years of work experience. Additional exam requirements/recommendations for international students: Required—TOEFL (minimum score 550 paper-based; 213 computer-based; 79 iBT). Electronic applications accepted.

University of Phoenix–Columbus Ohio Campus, The Artemis School, College of Health and Human Services, Columbus, OH 43240-4032. Offers administration of justice and security (MS); health care management (MBA); nursing (MSN); psychology (MS). Evening/weekend programs available. Postbaccalaureate distance learning degree programs offered. *Degree requirements:* For master's, thesis (for some programs). *Entrance requirements:* For master's, minimum undergraduate GPA of 2.5, 3 years work experience. Additional exam requirements/recommendations for international students: Required—TOEFL (minimum score 550 paper-based; 213 computer-based; 79 iBT). Electronic applications accepted.

University of Phoenix–Dallas Campus, The Artemis School, College of Health and Human Services, Dallas, TX 75251-2009. Offers administration of justice and security (MS); health administration (MHA); health care management (MBA); psychology (MS). Postbaccalaureate distance learning degree programs offered. *Degree requirements:* For master's, thesis (for some programs). *Entrance requirements:* For master's, minimum undergraduate GPA of 2.5, 3 years of work experience. Additional exam requirements/recommendations for international students: Required—TOEFL (minimum score 550 paper-based; 213 computer-based; 79 iBT). Electronic applications accepted.

University of Phoenix–Denver Campus, The Artemis School, College of Health and Human Services, Lone Tree, CO 80124-5453. Offers administration of justice and security (MS); community counseling (MSC); health administration (MHA); health care management (MBA); marriage, family and child therapy (MSC); nursing (MSN); psychology (MS); MSN/MBA; MSN/MHA. Evening/weekend programs available. Postbaccalaureate distance learning degree programs offered. *Degree requirements:* For master's, thesis (for some programs). *Entrance requirements:* For master's, minimum undergraduate GPA of 2.5, 3 years work experience, RN license. Additional exam requirements/recommendations for international students: Required—TOEFL (minimum score 550 paper-based; 213 computer-based; 79 iBT). Electronic applications accepted.

University of Phoenix–Des Moines Campus, College of Social and Behavioral Science, Des Moines, IA 50266. Offers administration of justice and security (MS). Postbaccalaureate distance learning degree programs offered.

University of Phoenix–Harrisburg Campus, College of Social and Behavioral Science, Harrisburg, PA 17112. Offers administration of justice and security (MS); psychology (MS). Postbaccalaureate distance learning degree programs offered.

University of Phoenix–Hawaii Campus, The Artemis School, College of Health and Human Services, Honolulu, HI 96813-4317. Offers administration of justice and security (MS); community counseling (MSC); education (MHA); family nurse practitioner (MSN); gerontology (MHA); health administration (MHA); health care management (MBA); marriage, family and child therapy (MSC); nursing (MSN); nursing/health care education (MSN); psychology (MS); MSN/MBA. Evening/weekend programs available. *Degree requirements:* For master's, thesis (for some programs). *Entrance requirements:* For master's, minimum undergraduate GPA of 2.5, 3 years of work experience, RN license. Additional exam requirements/recommendations for international students: Required—TOEFL (minimum score 550 paper-based; 213 computer-based; 79 iBT). Electronic applications accepted.

University of Phoenix–Houston Campus, The Artemis School, College of Health and Human Services, Houston, TX 77079-2004. Offers administration of justice and security (MS); health administration (MHA); health care management (MBA); psychology (MS). Postbaccalaureate distance learning degree programs offered. *Degree requirements:* For master's, thesis (for some programs). *Entrance requirements:* For master's, minimum undergraduate GPA of 2.5, 3 years of work experience. Additional exam requirements/recommendations for international students: Required—TOEFL (minimum score 550 paper-based; 213 computer-based; 79 iBT). Electronic applications accepted.

University of Phoenix–Idaho Campus, The Artemis School, College of Health and Human Services, Meridian, ID 83642-3014. Offers administration of justice and security (MS); health administration (MHA); health care management (MBA); nursing (MSN); nursing/health care education (MSN); psychology (MS); MSN/MBA. Evening/weekend programs available. Postbaccalaureate distance learning degree programs offered. *Degree requirements:* For master's, thesis (for some programs). *Entrance requirements:* For master's, minimum undergraduate GPA of 2.5, 3 years of work experience. Additional exam requirements/recommendations for international students: Required—TOEFL (minimum score 550 paper-based; 213 computer-based). Electronic applications accepted.

University of Phoenix–Indianapolis Campus, The Artemis School, College of Health and Human Services, Indianapolis, IN 46250-932. Offers administration of justice and security (MS); health administration (MHA); health care management (MBA); nursing (MSN); nursing/health care education (MSN); psychology (MS); MSN/MBA; MSN/MHA. Evening/weekend programs available. Postbaccalaureate distance learning degree programs offered. *Degree requirements:* For master's, thesis. *Entrance requirements:* For master's, 3 years work experience, minimum undergraduate GPA of 2.5. Additional exam requirements/recommendations for international students: Required—TOEFL (minimum score 500 paper-based; 213 computer-based). Electronic applications accepted.

University of Phoenix–Jersey City Campus, College of Social and Behavioral Science, Jersey City, NJ 07310. Offers administration of justice and security (MS); psychology (MS). Postbaccalaureate distance learning degree programs offered.

University of Phoenix–Kansas City Campus, The Artemis School, College of Health and Human Services, Kansas City, MO 64131-4517. Offers administration of justice and security (MS); community counseling (MSC); health administration (MHA); health care management (MBA); nursing (MSN); MSN/MBA. Evening/weekend programs available. Postbaccalaureate distance learning degree programs offered. *Degree requirements:* For master's, thesis (for some programs). *Entrance requirements:* For master's, 3 years work experience, minimum undergraduate GPA of 2.5. Additional exam requirements/recommendations for international students: Required—TOEFL (minimum score 550 paper-based; 213 computer-based).

University of Phoenix–Las Vegas Campus, The Artemis School, College of Health and Human Services, Las Vegas, NV 89128. Offers administration of justice and security (MS); health administration (MHA); health care management (MBA); marriage, family, and child therapy (MSC); mental health counseling (MSC); nursing (MSN); nursing/health care education (MSN); psychology (MS); MSN/MBA; MSN/MHA. Postbaccalaureate distance learning degree programs offered. *Entrance requirements:* For master's, minimum undergraduate GPA of 2.5, 3 years of work experience. Additional exam requirements/recommendations for international students: Required—TOEFL (minimum score 550 paper-based; 213 computer-based; 79 iBT). Electronic applications accepted.

University of Phoenix–Louisiana Campus, The Artemis School, College of Health and Human Services, Metairie, LA 70001-2082. Offers administration of justice and security (MS); health administration (MHA); health care management (MBA); nursing (MSN); psychology (MS); MSN/MBA. Evening/weekend programs available. Postbaccalaureate distance learning degree programs offered (no on-campus study). *Degree requirements:* For master's, thesis (for some programs). *Entrance requirements:* For master's, minimum undergraduate GPA of 2.5, 3 years work experience, RN license. Additional exam requirements/recommendations for international students: Required—TOEFL (minimum score 550 paper-based; 213 computer-based; 79 iBT). Electronic applications accepted.

University of Phoenix–Maryland Campus, The Artemis School, College of Health and Human Services, Columbia, MD 21045-5424. Offers administration of justice and security (MS); health administration (MHA); health care education (MSN); health care management (MBA); nursing (MSN); psychology (MS); MSN/MBA; MSN/MHA. Evening/weekend programs available. *Degree requirements:* For master's, thesis (for some programs). *Entrance requirements:* For master's, minimum undergraduate GPA of 2.5, 3 years work experience. Additional exam requirements/recommendations for international students: Required—TOEFL (minimum score 550 paper-based; 213 computer-based; 79 iBT). Electronic applications accepted.

University of Phoenix–Memphis Campus, College of Social and Behavioral Science, Cordova, TN 38018. Offers administration of justice and security (MS).

University of Phoenix–Metro Detroit Campus, The Artemis School, College of Health and Human Services, Southfield, MI 48076. Offers administration of justice and security (MS); health administration (MHA); health care education (MSN); health care management (MBA); nursing (MSN); MSN/MBA. Evening/weekend programs available. *Degree requirements:* For master's, thesis (for some programs). *Entrance requirements:* For master's, minimum undergraduate GPA of 2.5, 3 years of work experience, RN license. Additional exam requirements/recommendations for international students: Required—TOEFL (minimum score 550 paper-based; 213 computer-based; 79 iBT). Electronic applications accepted.

University of Phoenix–New Mexico Campus, The Artemis School, College of Health and Human Services, Albuquerque, NM 87113-1570. Offers administration of justice and security (MS); health administration (MHA); health care education (MSN); health care management (MBA); marriage and family therapy (MSC); nursing (MSN); psychology (MS); MSN/MBA. Evening/weekend programs available. *Degree requirements:* For master's, thesis (for some programs). *Entrance requirements:* For master's, minimum undergraduate GPA of 2.5, 3 years of work experience, RN license. Additional exam requirements/recommendations for international students: Required—TOEFL (minimum score 550 paper-based; 213 computer-based; 79 iBT). Electronic applications accepted.

University of Phoenix–Northern Nevada Campus, College of Social and Behavioral Science, Reno, NV 89521-5862. Offers administration of justice and security (MS); marriage, family and child therapy (MSC); psychology (MS); school counseling (MSC).

University of Phoenix–Northern Virginia Campus, College of Social and Behavioral Science, Reston, VA 20190. Offers administration of justice and security (MS).

University of Phoenix–Northwest Arkansas Campus, College of Social and Behavioral Science, Rogers, AR 72756-9615. Offers administration of justice and security (MS).

University of Phoenix–Oklahoma City Campus, College of Health and Human Services, Oklahoma City, OK 73116-8244. Offers administration of justice and security (MS); health care management (MBA); nursing (MSN); psychology (MS).

University of Phoenix–Omaha Campus, College of Social and Behavioral Science, Omaha, NE 68154-5240. Offers administration of justice and security (MS).

University of Phoenix–Oregon Campus, The Artemis School, College of Health and Human Services, Tigard, OR 97223. Offers administration of justice and security (MS); health administration (MHA); health care management (MBA); nursing (MSN); psychology (MS); MSN/MBA. Evening/weekend programs available. *Degree requirements:* For master's, thesis (for some programs). *Entrance requirements:* For master's, minimum undergraduate GPA of 2.5, 3 years of work experience, current RN license (nursing). Additional exam requirements/recommendations for international students: Required—TOEFL (minimum score 550 paper-based; 213 computer-based; 79 iBT). Electronic applications accepted.

University of Phoenix–Philadelphia Campus, The Artemis School, College of Health and Human Services, Wayne, PA 19087-2121. Offers administration of justice and security (MS); health administration (MHA); health care education (MSN); health care management (MBA);

nursing (MSN); psychology (MS); MSN/MBA. Evening/weekend programs available. *Degree requirements:* For master's, thesis (for some programs). *Entrance requirements:* For master's, minimum undergraduate GPA of 2.5, 3 years work experience. Additional exam requirements/recommendations for international students: Required—TOEFL (minimum score 550 paper-based; 213 computer-based; 79 iBT). Electronic applications accepted.

University of Phoenix–Pittsburgh Campus, The Artemis School, College of Health and Human Services, Pittsburgh, PA 15276. Offers administration of justice and security (MS); health administration (MHA); health care education (MSN); health care management (MBA); nursing (MSN); psychology (MS); MSN/MBA; MSN/MHA. Evening/weekend programs available. *Degree requirements:* For master's, thesis (for some programs). *Entrance requirements:* For master's, minimum undergraduate GPA of 2.5, 3 years work experience, current RN license (nursing). Additional exam requirements/recommendations for international students: Required—TOEFL (minimum score 550 paper-based; 213 computer-based; 79 iBT). Electronic applications accepted.

University of Phoenix–Richmond Campus, The Artemis School, College of Health and Human Services, Richmond, VA 23230. Offers administration of justice and security (MS); health administration (MHA); health care education (MSN); health care management (MBA); nursing (MSN); psychology (MS); MSN/MBA; MSN/MHA. Evening/weekend programs available. *Degree requirements:* For master's, thesis (for some programs). *Entrance requirements:* For master's, minimum undergraduate GPA of 2.5, 3 years work experience, current RN license for nursing programs. Additional exam requirements/recommendations for international students: Required—TOEFL (minimum score 500 paper-based; 213 computer-based; 79 iBT). Electronic applications accepted.

University of Phoenix–Sacramento Valley Campus, The Artemis School, College of Health and Human Services, Sacramento, CA 95833-3632. Offers administration of justice and security (MS); community counseling (MSC); family nurse practitioner (MSN); health administration (MHA); health care education (MSN); health care management (MBA); marriage, family and child counseling (MSC); nursing (MSN); psychology (MS); MSN/MBA. Evening/weekend programs available. *Degree requirements:* For master's, thesis (for some programs). *Entrance requirements:* For master's, RN license, minimum undergraduate GPA of 2.5, 3 years work experience. Additional exam requirements/recommendations for international students: Required—TOEFL (minimum score 550 paper-based; 213 computer-based; 79 iBT). Electronic applications accepted.

University of Phoenix–St. Louis Campus, The Artemis School, College of Health and Human Services, St. Louis, MO 63043-4828. Offers administration of justice and security (MS); health administration (MHA); health care management (MBA); nursing (MSN); MSN/MBA; MSN/MHA. Evening/weekend programs available. *Degree requirements:* For master's, thesis (for some programs). *Entrance requirements:* For master's, minimum undergraduate GPA of 2.5, 3 years work experience. Additional exam requirements/recommendations for international students: Required—TOEFL (minimum score 550 paper-based; 213 computer-based; 79 iBT). Electronic applications accepted.

University of Phoenix–San Antonio Campus, College of Social and Behavioral Science, San Antonio, TX 78230. Offers administration of justice and security (MS); psychology (MS).

University of Phoenix–San Diego Campus, The Artemis School, College of Health and Human Services, San Diego, CA 92123. Offers administration of justice and security (MS); health care education (MSN); health care management (MBA); marriage, family and child counseling (MSC); marriage, family and child therapy (MSC); nursing (MSN); MSN/MBA. Evening/weekend programs available. *Degree requirements:* For master's, thesis (for some programs). *Entrance requirements:* For master's, minimum undergraduate GPA of 2.5, 3 years work experience, RN license. Additional exam requirements/recommendations for international students: Required—TOEFL (minimum score 550 paper-based; 213 computer-based; 79 iBT). Electronic applications accepted.

University of Phoenix–Savannah Campus, College of Social and Behavioral Science, Savannah, GA 31405-7400. Offers administration of justice and security (MS).

University of Phoenix–Southern Arizona Campus, The Artemis School, College of Health and Human Services, Tucson, AZ 85711. Offers administration of justice and security (MS); family nurse practitioner (MSN, Certificate); health administration (MHA); health care management (MBA); marriage, family and child therapy (MSC); nursing (MSN); psychology (MS). Evening/weekend programs available. *Degree requirements:* For master's, thesis (for some programs). *Entrance requirements:* For master's, minimum undergraduate GPA of 2.5, 3 years of work experience, RN license. Additional exam requirements/recommendations for international students: Required—TOEFL (minimum score 550 paper-based; 213 computer-based; 79 iBT). Electronic applications accepted.

University of Phoenix–Southern California Campus, The Artemis School, College of Health and Human Services, Costa Mesa, CA 92626. Offers administration of justice and security (MS); family nurse practitioner (MSN, Certificate); health administration (MHA); health care education (MSN); health care management (MBA); marriage, family and child therapy (MSC); nursing (MSN); psychology (MS); MSN/MBA; MSN/MHA. Evening/weekend programs available. *Degree requirements:* For master's, thesis (for some programs). *Entrance requirements:* For master's, minimum undergraduate GPA of 2.5, 3 years work experience, RN license. Additional exam requirements/recommendations for international students: Required—TOEFL (minimum score 550 paper-based; 213 computer-based; 79 iBT). Electronic applications accepted.

University of Phoenix–Southern Colorado Campus, The Artemis School, College of Health and Human Services, Colorado Springs, CO 80919-2335. Offers administration of justice and security (MS); community counseling (MSC); education (MHA); gerontology (MHA); health administration (MHA); health care management (MBA); marriage, family and child therapy (MSC); nursing (MSN); psychology (MS); MSN/MBA. Evening/weekend programs available. *Degree requirements:* For master's, thesis (for some programs). *Entrance requirements:* For master's, minimum undergraduate GPA of 2.5, 3 years of work experience, RN license. Additional exam requirements/recommendations for international students: Required—TOEFL (minimum score 550 paper-based; 213 computer-based; 79 iBT). Electronic applications accepted.

University of Phoenix–Springfield Campus, College of Social and Behavioral Science, Springfield, MO 65804-7211. Offers administration of justice and security (MS).

University of Phoenix–Tulsa Campus, College of Health and Human Services, Tulsa, OK 74134-1412. Offers administration of justice and security (MS); health care management (MBA); nursing (MSN); psychology (MS).

University of Phoenix–Western Washington Campus, College of Social and Behavioral Science, Tukwila, WA 98188. Offers administration of justice and security (MS).

University of Pittsburgh, Graduate School of Public and International Affairs, Doctoral Program in Public and International Affairs, Pittsburgh, PA 15260. Offers development policy (PhD); foreign and security policy (PhD); international political economy (PhD); public administration (PhD); public policy (PhD). *Accreditation:* NASPAA. Part-time programs available. *Faculty:* 28 full-time (8 women), 56 part-time/adjunct (20 women). *Students:* 11 full-time (4 women), 27 part-time (16 women); includes 4 minority (2 African Americans, 1 Asian American or Pacific Islander, 1 Hispanic American), 7 international. Average age 30. 63 applicants, 14% accepted, 5 enrolled. In 2009, 9 doctorates awarded. *Degree requirements:* For doctorate, comprehensive exam, thesis/dissertation. *Entrance requirements:* For doctorate, GRE, 3 letters of recommendation, resume, minimum GPA of 3.0, writing sample. Additional exam requirements/recommendations for international students: Required—TOEFL (minimum score 600 paper-based; 250 computer-based; 100 iBT), TWE (minimum score 4); Recommended—IELTS (minimum score 7). *Application deadline:* For fall admission, 2/1 for domestic students, 1/15 for international students. Application fee: $50. Electronic applications accepted. *Expenses:* Tuition, state resident: full-time $16,402; part-time $665 per credit. Tuition, nonresident: full-time $28,694; part-time $1175 per credit. Required fees: $690; $175 per term. Tuition and fees vary according to program. *Financial support:* In 2009–10, 17 students received support, including 6 fellowships (averaging $34,925 per year); scholarships/grants, tuition waivers (full and partial), and unspecified assistantships also available. Financial award application deadline: 2/1. *Faculty research:* International political economy, international development, public administration, public policy, foreign policy, international security policy. Total annual research expenditures: $357,117. *Unit head:* Dr. Kevin P. Kearns, Program Coordinator, 412-648-7621, Fax: 412-648-2605, E-mail: kkearns@pitt.edu. *Application contact:* Julie Korade, Program Administrator/Graduate Enrollment Counselor, 412-648-7640, Fax: 412-648-7641, E-mail: korade@pitt.edu.

University of Pittsburgh, School of Law, Master of Studies in Law Program, Pittsburgh, PA 15260. Offers business law (MSL), including commercial law, corporate law, general business law, international business, tax law; constitutional law (MSL); criminal law and justice (MSL); disabilities law (MSL); dispute resolution (MSL); education law (MSL); elder and estate planning law (MSL); employment and labor law (MSL); environment and real estate law (MSL); family law (MSL); general law and jurisprudence (MSL); health law (MSL); intellectual property and technology (MSL); international and comparative law (MSL); personal injury and civil litigation (MSL); regulatory law (MSL); self-designed (MSL); sports and entertainment law (MSL). Part-time programs available. *Faculty:* 43 full-time (16 women), 104 part-time/adjunct (30 women). *Students:* 3 full-time (2 women), 12 part-time (7 women); includes 3 minority (2 African Americans, 1 Asian American or Pacific Islander). Average age 31. 26 applicants, 58% accepted, 11 enrolled. In 2009, 9 master's awarded. *Entrance requirements:* Additional exam requirements/recommendations for international students: Required—TOEFL (minimum score 600 paper-based; 250 computer-based; 100 iBT). *Application deadline:* For fall admission, 6/30 for domestic students, 5/1 for international students. Applications are processed on a rolling basis. Application fee: $0. *Expenses:* Tuition, state resident: full-time $16,402; part-time $665 per credit. Tuition, nonresident: full-time $28,694; part-time $1175 per credit. Required fees: $690; $175 per term. Tuition and fees vary according to program. *Faculty research:* Law, health law, business law, contracts, intellectual property. *Unit head:* Prof. Alan Meisel, Director, 412-648-1384, Fax: 412-648-2649, E-mail: meisel@pitt.edu. *Application contact:* Bethann Pischke, Administrative Coordinator, 412-648-7120, Fax: 412-648-2649, E-mail: pischke@pitt.edu.

University of Regina, Faculty of Graduate Studies and Research, Faculty of Arts, Department of Justice Studies, Regina, SK S4S 0A2, Canada. Offers human justice (MA); justice studies (MA); police studies (MA). *Faculty:* 3 full-time (1 woman), 3 part-time/adjunct (1 woman). *Students:* 6 full-time (all women), 9 part-time (7 women). 14 applicants, 71% accepted. In 2009, 1 master's awarded. *Degree requirements:* For master's, thesis. *Entrance requirements:* Additional exam requirements/recommendations for international students: Required—TOEFL (minimum score 580 paper-based; 237 computer-based; 80 iBT). *Application deadline:* For fall admission, 3/31 for domestic students. Application fee: $90 ($100 for international students). Electronic applications accepted. *Financial support:* In 2009–10, 3 fellowships (averaging $19,000 per year), 1 research assistantship (averaging $16,910 per year), 3 teaching assistantships (averaging $6,650 per year) were awarded. *Unit head:* Dr. Jim Mulvale, Head, 306-585-4237, E-mail: jim.mulvale@uregina.ca. *Application contact:* Dr. Nick Jones, Program Coordinator, 306-585-5066, E-mail: nick.jones@uregina.ca.

University of South Africa, College of Law, Pretoria, South Africa. Offers correctional services management (M Tech); criminology (MA, PhD); law (LL M, LL D); penology (MA, PhD); police science (MA, PhD); policing (M Tech); security risk management (M Tech); social science in criminology (MA).

University of South Carolina, The Graduate School, College of Arts and Sciences, Department of Criminology and Criminal Justice, Columbia, SC 29208. Offers MA, PhD, JD/MA. Part-time and evening/weekend programs available. *Degree requirements:* For master's, comprehensive exam, thesis; for doctorate, comprehensive exam, thesis/dissertation. *Entrance requirements:* For master's and doctorate, GRE. Additional exam requirements/recommendations for international students: Required—TOEFL. Electronic applications accepted. *Faculty research:* Juvenile delinquency, substance abuse, policy development, minority issues, law enforcement services.

University of Southern Mississippi, Graduate School, College of Science and Technology, Department of Administration of Justice, Hattiesburg, MS 39406-0001. Offers administration of justice (PhD); corrections (MA, MS); juvenile justice (MA, MS); law enforcement (MA, MS). Part-time programs available. *Faculty:* 9 full-time (2 women), 2 part-time/adjunct (0 women). *Students:* 16 full-time (7 women), 24 part-time (17 women); includes 8 minority (7 African Americans, 1 Hispanic American), 1 international. Average age 34. 26 applicants, 38% accepted, 6 enrolled. In 2009, 14 master's awarded. *Degree requirements:* For master's, comprehensive exam, thesis; for doctorate, comprehensive exam, thesis/dissertation. *Entrance requirements:* For master's, GRE General Test, minimum GPA of 2.75 in last 2 years, 3.0 in field of study; for doctorate, GRE General Test, minimum GPA of 3.5. Additional exam requirements/recommendations for international students: Required—TOEFL. *Application deadline:* For fall admission, 3/15 priority date for domestic students, 3/15 for international students. Applications are processed on a rolling basis. Application fee: $35. *Expenses:* Tuition, state resident: full-time $5096; part-time $284 per hour. Tuition, nonresident: full-time $13,052; part-time $726 per hour. Required fees: $402. Tuition and fees vary according to course level and course load. *Financial support:* In 2009–10, 2 research assistantships with full tuition reimbursements (averaging $7,000 per year), 9 teaching assistantships with full tuition reimbursements (averaging $8,000 per year) were awarded; career-related internships or fieldwork, Federal Work-Study, and institutionally sponsored loans also available. Financial award application deadline: 3/15; financial award applicants required to submit FAFSA. *Faculty research:* Crime in the family, police training models, humanities and criminal justice. *Unit head:* Dr. Lisa Nored, Chair, 601-266-4509, Fax: 601-266-4391. *Application contact:* Tera Wright, Manager of Graduate Admissions, 601-266-4509, Fax: 601-266-4391.

University of South Florida, Graduate School, College of Behavioral and Community Sciences, Department of Criminology, Tampa, FL 33620-9951. Offers criminal justice administration (MA); criminology (MA, PhD). *Faculty:* 13 full-time (4 women), 3 part-time/adjunct (0 women). *Students:* 35 full-time (22 women), 67 part-time (36 women); includes 27 minority (15 African Americans, 5 Asian Americans or Pacific Islanders, 7 Hispanic Americans), 6 international. Average age 32. 151 applicants, 46% accepted, 44 enrolled. In 2009, 52 master's, 1 doctorate awarded. *Degree requirements:* For master's, comprehensive exam (for some programs), thesis (for some programs); for doctorate, comprehensive exam, thesis/dissertation. *Entrance requirements:* For master's, GRE General Test (criminology), 3 letters of recommendation, writing sample, minimum GPA of 3.0; for doctorate, GRE General Test, 3 letters of recommendation, statement of purpose, writing sample. Additional exam requirements/recommendations for international students: Required—TOEFL (minimum score 550 paper-based; 213 computer-based). *Application deadline:* For fall admission, 1/15 for domestic students, 1/2 for international students; for spring admission, 9/30 for domestic students, 6/1 for international students. Application fee: $30. Electronic applications accepted. *Financial support:* In 2009–10, 10 students received support, including teaching assistantships with tuition reimbursements available (averaging $21,078 per year). *Faculty research:* Criminal theory, drug abuse, violence, policing. Total annual research expenditures: $431,636. *Application contact:* Lorie Fridell, Director, 813-974-6862, Fax: 813-974-2803, E-mail: lfridell@bcs.usf.edu.

The University of Tennessee, Graduate School, College of Arts and Sciences, Department of Sociology, Knoxville, TN 37996. Offers criminology (MA, PhD); energy, environment, and resource policy (MA, PhD); political economy (MA, PhD). Part-time programs available. *Degree requirements:* For master's, thesis or alternative; for doctorate, thesis/dissertation. *Entrance*

Criminal Justice and Criminology

The University of Tennessee (continued)

requirements: For master's, GRE General Test, minimum GPA of 3.0; for doctorate, GRE General Test, minimum GPA of 3.5. Additional exam requirements/recommendations for international students: Required—TOEFL. Electronic applications accepted. *Expenses:* Tuition, state resident: full-time $6826; part-time $380 per semester hour. Tuition, nonresident: full-time $21,844; part-time $1147 per semester hour. Tuition and fees vary according to program.

The University of Tennessee at Chattanooga, Graduate School, College of Arts and Sciences, Department of Criminal Justice, Chattanooga, TN 37403. Offers MSCJ. Part-time and evening/weekend programs available. *Faculty:* 4 full-time (2 women). *Students:* 10 full-time (8 women), 11 part-time (7 women); includes 3 minority (all African Americans). Average age 29. 15 applicants, 80% accepted, 7 enrolled. In 2009, 15 master's awarded. *Degree requirements:* For master's, thesis optional, qualifying exams, internship. *Entrance requirements:* For master's, GRE General Test or MAT. Additional exam requirements/recommendations for international students: Required—TOEFL (minimum score 550 paper-based; 213 computer-based; 79 iBT), IELTS (minimum score 6). *Application deadline:* For fall admission, 8/1 priority date for domestic students, 6/1 for international students; for spring admission, 12/1 priority date for domestic students, 10/1 for international students. Applications are processed on a rolling basis. Application fee: $35. Electronic applications accepted. *Expenses:* Tuition, state resident: full-time $5404; part-time $300 per credit hour. Tuition, nonresident: full-time $16,702; part-time $928 per credit hour. Required fees: $1150; $130 per credit hour. *Financial support:* In 2009–10, 3 research assistantships with full and partial tuition reimbursements (averaging $5,500 per year), 2 teaching assistantships with full and partial tuition reimbursements (averaging $5,500 per year) were awarded; career-related internships or fieldwork, scholarships/grants, and unspecified assistantships also available. Support available to part-time students. *Faculty research:* Violence against women, crime prevention, police accountability, criminal justice privatization, public policy. *Unit head:* Dr. Helen M. Eigenberg, Chair, 423-425-4135, Fax: 423-425-2228, E-mail: helen-eigenberg@utc.edu. *Application contact:* Dr. Stephanie Bellar, Dean of Graduate Studies, 423-425-4666, Fax: 423-425-5223, E-mail: stephanie-bellar@utc.edu.

The University of Texas at Arlington, Graduate School, College of Liberal Arts, Department of Criminology and Criminal Justice, Arlington, TX 76019. Offers MA. Part-time and evening/weekend programs available. *Faculty:* 7 full-time (2 women), 1 part-time/adjunct (0 women). *Students:* 20 full-time (13 women), 59 part-time (30 women); includes 25 minority (21 African Americans, 4 Hispanic Americans), 1 international. 57 applicants, 98% accepted, 48 enrolled. In 2009, 14 master's awarded. *Degree requirements:* For master's, comprehensive exam, thesis or alternative. *Entrance requirements:* For master's, GRE General Test, minimum GPA of 3.0 in last 60 hours of undergraduate course work, 3 letters of recommendation. Additional exam requirements/recommendations for international students: Required—TOEFL (minimum score 550 paper-based; 213 computer-based). *Application deadline:* For fall admission, 6/16 for domestic students. Applications are processed on a rolling basis. Application fee: $35 ($50 for international students). *Financial support:* Career-related internships or fieldwork available. Financial award application deadline: 6/1; financial award applicants required to submit FAFSA. *Unit head:* Dr. Alejandro del Carmen, Chair, 817-272-3318, Fax: 817-272-5673, E-mail: adelcarmen@uta.edu. *Application contact:* Dr. Alejandro del Carmen, Chair, 817-272-3318, Fax: 817-272-5673, E-mail: adelcarmen@uta.edu.

The University of Texas at Dallas, School of Economic, Political and Policy Sciences, Program in Criminology, Richardson, TX 75080. Offers MS, PhD. Part-time and evening/weekend programs available. *Faculty:* 8 full-time (3 women), 3 part-time/adjunct (1 woman). *Students:* 40 full-time (20 women), 26 part-time (17 women); includes 23 minority (11 African Americans, 2 Asian Americans or Pacific Islanders, 10 Hispanic Americans). Average age 33. 35 applicants, 77% accepted, 20 enrolled. In 2009, 2 master's awarded. *Degree requirements:* For master's, thesis; for doctorate, thesis/dissertation. *Entrance requirements:* For master's and doctorate, GRE General Test, minimum GPA of 3.0 in upper-level course work in field. Additional exam requirements/recommendations for international students: Required—TOEFL (minimum score 550 paper-based; 213 computer-based). *Application deadline:* For fall admission, 7/15 for domestic students, 5/1 priority date for international students; for spring admission, 11/15 for domestic students, 9/1 priority date for international students. Applications are processed on a rolling basis. Application fee: $50 ($100 for international students). Electronic applications accepted. *Expenses:* Tuition, state resident: full-time $11,068; part-time $461 per credit hour. Tuition, nonresident: full-time $21,178; part-time $882 per credit hour. Tuition and fees vary according to course load. *Financial support:* In 2009–10, 2 research assistantships with full tuition reimbursements (averaging $14,437 per year), 12 teaching assistantships with full tuition reimbursements (averaging $11,400 per year) were awarded; career-related internships or fieldwork, Federal Work-Study, institutionally sponsored loans, scholarships/grants, and unspecified assistantships also available. Support available to part-time students. Financial award application deadline: 4/30; financial award applicants required to submit FAFSA. *Faculty research:* Urban policy, sexual orientation law, perception of crime, capital punishment, prison organizations, criminal justice policy, social dislocation, crime control policy. *Unit head:* Dr. James W. Marquart, Program Head, 972-883-4948, Fax: 972-883-2735, E-mail: marquart@utdallas.edu. *Application contact:* Dr. Denise Paquette Boots, Associate Program Head, 972-883-6468, Fax: 972-883-2735, E-mail: deniseboots@utdallas.edu.

The University of Texas at San Antonio, College of Public Policy, Department of Criminal Justice, San Antonio, TX 78249-0617. Offers justice policy (MS). Part-time and evening/weekend programs available. *Faculty:* 9 full-time (4 women). *Students:* 16 full-time (8 women), 46 part-time (24 women); includes 42 minority (5 African Americans, 3 Asian Americans or Pacific Islanders, 34 Hispanic Americans), 2 international. Average age 29. 23 applicants, 91% accepted, 18 enrolled. In 2009, 7 master's awarded. *Degree requirements:* For master's, comprehensive exam (for some programs), thesis (for some programs). *Entrance requirements:* For master's, GRE General Test, minimum GPA of 3.0 on last 60 hours. Additional exam requirements/recommendations for international students: Required—TOEFL (minimum score 500 paper-based; 173 computer-based; 61 iBT), IELTS (minimum score 5). *Application deadline:* For fall admission, 7/1 for domestic students, 4/1 for international students; for spring admission, 11/1 for domestic students, 9/1 for international students. Applications are processed on a rolling basis. Application fee: $45 ($80 for international students). Electronic applications accepted. *Expenses:* Tuition, state resident: full-time $3975; part-time $221 per contact hour. Tuition, nonresident: full-time $13,947; part-time $775 per contact hour. Required fees: $1853. *Financial support:* In 2009–10, 9 students received support, including 13 research assistantships (averaging $10,300 per year); career-related internships or fieldwork, scholarships/grants, tuition waivers, and unspecified assistantships also available. Support available to part-time students. *Faculty research:* Drug control policy, neighborhood patterns of violence, white collar and corporate crime, crime prevention, hispanic crime and delinquency. Total annual research expenditures: $26,782. *Unit head:* Dr. James M. Miller, Chair, 210-458-2537, Fax: 210-458-2680, E-mail: jm.miller@utsa.edu. *Application contact:* Roger Enriquez, Graduate Advisor, 210-458-2696, E-mail: roger.enriquez@utsa.edu.

The University of Texas at Tyler, College of Arts and Sciences, Department of Social Sciences, Tyler, TX 75799-0001. Offers criminal justice (MS); public administration (MPA); sociology (MS). Part-time and evening/weekend programs available. *Faculty:* 10 full-time (2 women). *Students:* 7 full-time (3 women), 21 part-time (14 women); includes 8 minority (5 African Americans, 2 American Indian/Alaska Native, 1 Asian American or Pacific Islander), 2 international. Average age 30. 6 applicants, 100% accepted, 6 enrolled. In 2009, 10 master's awarded. *Degree requirements:* For master's, comprehensive exam, thesis optional. *Entrance requirements:* For master's, GRE General Test, minimum GPA of 3.0. Additional exam requirements/recommendations for international students: Required—TOEFL (minimum score 79 computer-based). *Application deadline:* For fall admission, 8/17 priority date for domestic students, 7/1 priority date for international students; for spring admission, 12/21 priority date for domestic students, 11/1 priority date for international students. Applications are processed on a rolling basis. Application fee: $25 ($50 for international students). *Expenses:* Tuition, state resident: part-time $665 per semester hour. Tuition, nonresident: part-time $942 per semester hour. Part-time tuition and fees vary according to degree level and program. *Financial support:* In 2009–10, 1 fellowship (averaging $1,000 per year), 2 research assistantships, 2 teaching assistantships were awarded; career-related internships or fieldwork, Federal Work-Study, and scholarships/grants also available. Support available to part-time students. Financial award application deadline: 7/1; financial award applicants required to submit FAFSA. *Faculty research:* Urban segregation, minority business, violent crime, gender discrimination. *Unit head:* Dr. Ken Wink, Chair, 903-566-7434, Fax: 903-565-5537, E-mail: kwink@mail.uttyl.edu. *Application contact:* Dr. Ken Wink.

The University of Texas of the Permian Basin, Office of Graduate Studies, College of Arts and Sciences, Department of Social Sciences, Program in Criminal Justice Administration, Odessa, TX 79762-0001. Offers MS. Part-time and evening/weekend programs available. *Degree requirements:* For master's, comprehensive exam (for some programs), thesis (for some programs). *Entrance requirements:* For master's, GRE General Test, 3 letters of recommendation. Additional exam requirements/recommendations for international students: Required—TOEFL (minimum score 550 paper-based; 213 computer-based).

The University of Texas–Pan American, College of Social and Behavioral Sciences, Department of Criminal Justice, Edinburg, TX 78539. Offers MS. Part-time and evening/weekend programs available. Postbaccalaureate distance learning degree programs offered (no on-campus study). *Degree requirements:* For master's, comprehensive exam, applied project or thesis. *Entrance requirements:* For master's, minimum GPA of 2.75. *Expenses:* Tuition, state resident: full-time $3630.60; part-time $201.70 per credit hour. Tuition, nonresident: full-time $8617; part-time $478.70 per credit hour. Required fees: $806.50. *Faculty research:* Comparative criminal justice systems, death penalty, community policing, Hispanic women.

University of the Fraser Valley, Graduate Studies, Abbotsford, BC V2S 7M8, Canada. Offers criminal justice (MA). Evening/weekend programs available. *Faculty:* 5 full-time (1 woman), 2 part-time/adjunct (0 women). *Students:* 35 full-time (17 women), 12 part-time (9 women); includes 5 minority (all Asian Americans or Pacific Islanders). 23 applicants, 65% accepted, 13 enrolled. In 2009, 4 master's awarded. *Degree requirements:* For master's, thesis optional, major research paper. *Entrance requirements:* For master's, bachelor's degree and work experience in related field. Additional exam requirements/recommendations for international students: Recommended—TOEFL (minimum score 88 iBT), IELTS (minimum score 6.5), TWE. *Application deadline:* For fall admission, 1/31 priority date for domestic students, 4/1 priority date for international students; for winter admission, 9/30 priority date for domestic students, 10/1 priority date for international students; for spring admission, 12/31 priority date for domestic students, 2/1 priority date for international students. Application fee: $45 ($150 for international students). Electronic applications accepted. *Expenses:* Contact institution. *Financial support:* Research assistantships, health care benefits available. Financial award application deadline: 5/10. *Faculty research:* Human trafficking, illegal drug trade, criminal justice, criminology, safe schools. *Unit head:* Yvon Dandurand, Graduate Studies Committee Chair, 604-864-4654, E-mail: yvon.dandurand@ufv.ca. *Application contact:* Educational Advisors, 604-854-4528, Fax: 604-855-7614, E-mail: advising@ucfv.ca.

University of the Pacific, McGeorge School of Law, Sacramento, CA 95817. Offers advocacy (JD); criminal justice (JD); experiential law teaching (LL M); intellectual property (JD); international legal studies (JD); international water resources law (LL M, JSD); law (JD); public law and policy (JD); public policy and law (LL M); tax (JD); transnational business practice (LL M); JD/MBA; JD/MPPA. *Accreditation:* ABA. Part-time and evening/weekend programs available. *Faculty:* 55 full-time (24 women), 57 part-time/adjunct (18 women). *Students:* 697 full-time (343 women), 377 part-time (197 women); includes 301 minority (33 African Americans, 11 American Indian/Alaska Native, 163 Asian Americans or Pacific Islanders, 94 Hispanic Americans). Average age 24. 2,659 applicants, 43% accepted, 236 enrolled. In 2009, 254 first professional degrees, 51 master's awarded. *Degree requirements:* For master's, thesis (for some programs); for doctorate, thesis/dissertation. *Entrance requirements:* For JD, LSAT; for master's, JD; for doctorate, LL M. Additional exam requirements/recommendations for international students: Required—TOEFL (minimum score 600 paper-based; 250 computer-based; 100 iBT). *Application deadline:* For fall admission, 3/15 priority date for domestic students. Applications are processed on a rolling basis. Application fee: $50. Electronic applications accepted. *Expenses:* Contact institution. *Financial support:* In 2009–10, 887 students received support, including 1 fellowship, 114 research assistantships (averaging $1,839 per year), 12 teaching assistantships (averaging $953 per year); career-related internships or fieldwork, Federal Work-Study, institutionally sponsored loans, and scholarships/grants also available. Support available to part-time students. Financial award applicants required to submit FAFSA. *Faculty research:* International legal studies, public policy and law, advocacy, intellectual property law, taxation, criminal law. *Unit head:* Elizabeth Rindskopf Parker, Dean, 916-739-7151, E-mail: elizabeth@pacific.edu. *Application contact:* 916-739-7105, Fax: 916-739-7301, E-mail: mcgeorge@pacific.edu.

The University of Toledo, College of Graduate Studies, College of Health Science and Human Service, Division of Human Services, Department of Criminal Justice, Toledo, OH 43606-3390. Offers criminal justice (MA); juvenile justice (Certificate); severe behavioral spectrum (Certificate).

University of Toronto, School of Graduate Studies, Social Sciences Division, Centre for Criminology, Toronto, ON M5S 1A1, Canada. Offers MA, PhD. Part-time programs available. *Degree requirements:* For master's, research paper (optional); for doctorate, comprehensive exam, thesis/dissertation. *Entrance requirements:* For master's, 2 letters of reference, bachelor's degree in social science or humanities, minimum B+ average in last 2 years of undergraduate study; for doctorate, 2 letters of reference, MA in criminology or equivalent, minimum A– average. Additional exam requirements/recommendations for international students: Required—TOEFL (minimum score 580 paper-based; 237 computer-based), TWE (minimum score 5).

University of West Florida, College of Professional Studies, Department of Professional and Community Leadership, Program in Administration, Pensacola, FL 32514-5750. Offers acquisition and contract administration (MSA); biomedical/pharmaceutical (MSA); criminal justice administration (MSA); database administration (MSA); education leadership (MSA); healthcare administration (MSA); human performance technology (MSA); leadership (MSA); nursing administration (MSA); public administration (MSA); software engineering administration (MSA). Part-time and evening/weekend programs available. Postbaccalaureate distance learning degree programs offered (no on-campus study). *Students:* 33 full-time (21 women), 168 part-time (97 women); includes 53 minority (32 African Americans, 2 American Indian/Alaska Native, 5 Asian Americans or Pacific Islanders, 14 Hispanic Americans), 1 international. Average age 34. 103 applicants, 74% accepted, 64 enrolled. In 2009, 47 master's awarded. *Entrance requirements:* For master's, GRE General Test, letter of intent, names of references. Additional exam requirements/recommendations for international students: Required—TOEFL (minimum score 550 paper-based; 213 computer-based). *Application deadline:* For fall admission, 6/1 for domestic students, 5/15 for international students; for spring admission, 11/1 for domestic students, 10/1 for international students. Applications are processed on a rolling basis. Application fee: $30. *Expenses:* Tuition, state resident: full-time $4982; part-time $260 per credit hour. Tuition, nonresident: full-time $20,059; part-time $919 per credit hour. Required fees: $1247; $52 per credit hour. *Financial support:* Unspecified assistantships available. Financial award application deadline: 4/15; financial award applicants required to submit FAFSA. *Unit head:* Dr. Karen Rasmussen, Chairperson, 850-474-2301, Fax: 850-474-2804. *Application contact:* Terry McCray, Assistant Director of Graduate Admissions, 850-473-7718, Fax: 850-473-7714, E-mail: gradadmissions@uwf.edu.

University of West Florida, College of Professional Studies, School of Justice Studies and Social Work, Department of Justice Studies, Pensacola, FL 32514-5750. Offers criminal justice (MS). Part-time and evening/weekend programs available. *Faculty:* 4 full-time (2 women). *Students:* 8 full-time (3 women), 15 part-time (8 women); includes 1 Hispanic American. Average age 34. 16 applicants, 88% accepted, 12 enrolled. *Degree requirements:* For master's, thesis optional. *Entrance requirements:* For master's, GRE or MAT, 3 letters of recommendation.

Additional exam requirements/recommendations for international students: Required—TOEFL (minimum score 550 paper-based; 213 computer-based). *Application deadline:* For fall admission, 6/1 for domestic students, 5/1 for international students; for spring admission, 11/1 for domestic students, 10/1 for international students. Applications are processed on a rolling basis. Electronic applications accepted. *Expenses:* Tuition, state resident: full-time $4982; part-time $260 per credit hour. Tuition, nonresident: full-time $20,059; part-time $919 per credit hour. Required fees: $1247; $52 per credit hour. *Financial support:* In 2009–10, 4 research assistantships (averaging $3,280 per year), 2 teaching assistantships (averaging $3,760 per year) were awarded; unspecified assistantships also available. *Unit head:* Dr. Glenn Rohrer, Chair, 850-474-2154, E-mail: grohrer@uwf.edu. *Application contact:* Terry McCray, Assistant Director of Graduate Admissions, 850-473-7718, Fax: 850-473-7714, E-mail: gradadmissions@uwf.edu.

University of West Georgia, Graduate School, College of Arts and Sciences, Department of Sociology and Criminology, Carrollton, GA 30118. Offers criminology (MA); sociology (MA). Part-time and evening/weekend programs available. *Faculty:* 13 full-time (5 women), 5 part-time/adjunct (4 women). *Students:* 11 full-time (6 women), 8 part-time (4 women); includes 2 minority (both African Americans). Average age 30. 11 applicants, 82% accepted, 1 enrolled. In 2009, 3 master's awarded. *Degree requirements:* For master's, one foreign language, comprehensive exam (for some programs), thesis (for some programs). *Entrance requirements:* For master's, GRE General Test, minimum GPA of 2.5, references, intellectual biography. Additional exam requirements/recommendations for international students: Required—TOEFL. *Application deadline:* For fall admission, 7/17 for domestic students; for spring admission, 11/20 for domestic students. Applications are processed on a rolling basis. Application fee: $30. Electronic applications accepted. *Expenses:* Tuition, state resident: full-time $2952; part-time $164 per semester hour. Tuition, nonresident: full-time $11,808; part-time $656 per semester hour. Required fees: $42.90 per semester hour. $307 per semester. Tuition and fees vary according to course load. *Financial support:* In 2009–10, 8 students received support, including 7 research assistantships with full tuition reimbursements available (averaging $6,000 per year); career-related internships or fieldwork, scholarships/grants, and unspecified assistantships also available. Financial award application deadline: 7/1; financial award applicants required to submit FAFSA. *Faculty research:* Criminology, gangs, courts, policing, ethics, women's studies, methods. *Unit head:* Dr. N. Jane McCandless, Chair, 678-839-6505, Fax: 678-839-6506, E-mail: jmccandl@westga.edu. *Application contact:* Dr. Charles W. Clark, Dean, 678-839-6508, E-mail: cclark@westga.edu.

University of Windsor, Faculty of Graduate Studies, Faculty of Arts and Social Sciences, Department of Sociology and Anthropology, Windsor, ON N9B 3P4, Canada. Offers criminology (MA); sociology (MA); sociology-social justice (PhD). Part-time programs available. *Degree requirements:* For master's, thesis; for doctorate, comprehensive exam, thesis/dissertation. *Entrance requirements:* For master's, minimum B+ average; for doctorate, writing sample, minimum B+ average. Additional exam requirements/recommendations for international students: Required—TOEFL (minimum score 560 paper-based; 220 computer-based). Electronic applications accepted. *Faculty research:* Power and social change; criminology/deviance; social psychology; comparative development; race and ethnic relations; family, sex, and gender, social justice.

University of Wisconsin–Milwaukee, Graduate School, School of Social Welfare, Department of Criminal Justice, Milwaukee, WI 53201-0413. Offers administration (MS); corrections (MS); law enforcement (MS). Part-time programs available. *Faculty:* 7 full-time (2 women). *Students:* 16 full-time (8 women), 15 part-time (9 women); includes 6 minority (4 African Americans, 1 American Indian/Alaska Native, 1 Hispanic American). Average age 28. 16 applicants, 56% accepted, 6 enrolled. In 2009, 16 master's awarded. *Degree requirements:* For master's, thesis or alternative. *Entrance requirements:* For master's, GRE General Test, MAT. Additional exam requirements/recommendations for international students: Required—TOEFL (minimum score 550 paper-based; 79 iBT), IELTS (minimum score 6.5). *Application deadline:* For fall admission, 1/1 priority date for domestic students; for spring admission, 9/1 for domestic students. Applications are processed on a rolling basis. Application fee: $45 ($75 for international students). *Expenses:* Tuition, state resident: full-time $8800. Tuition, nonresident: full-time $20,760. Tuition and fees vary according to program and reciprocity agreements. *Financial support:* In 2009–10, 2 teaching assistantships were awarded; career-related internships or fieldwork and unspecified assistantships also available. Support available to part-time students. Financial award application deadline: 4/15. Total annual research expenditures: $172,614. *Unit head:* Steven Brandl, Representative, 414-229-5443, Fax: 414-229-5311, E-mail: sgb@uwm.edu. *Application contact:* General Information Contact, 414-229-4982, Fax: 414-229-6967, E-mail: gradschool@uwm.edu.

University of Wisconsin–Platteville, School of Graduate Studies, Distance Learning Center, Online Master of Science in Criminal Justice Program, Platteville, WI 53818-3099. Offers MS. Part-time and evening/weekend programs available. Postbaccalaureate distance learning degree programs offered (no on-campus study). *Students:* 6 full-time (all women), 73 part-time (34 women); includes 5 minority (1 African American, 2 American Indian/Alaska Native, 2 Hispanic Americans), 8 international. 20 applicants, 100% accepted, 20 enrolled. In 2009, 18 master's awarded. *Degree requirements:* For master's, thesis or alternative. *Entrance requirements:* Additional exam requirements/recommendations for international students: Required—TOEFL (minimum score 500 paper-based; 173 computer-based; 61 iBT). *Application deadline:* For fall admission, 7/1 priority date for domestic students; for spring admission, 11/1 priority date for domestic students. Applications are processed on a rolling basis. Application fee: $56. Electronic applications accepted. *Expenses:* Contact institution. *Financial support:* Scholarships/grants available. Support available to part-time students. *Unit head:* Dr. Cheryl Banachowski-Fuller, Coordinator, 608-342-1652, Fax: 608-342-1986, E-mail: banachoc@uwplatt.edu. *Application contact:* 608-342-1652, Fax: 608-342-1986, E-mail: criminaljstc@uwplatt.edu.

Upper Iowa University, Online Master's Programs, Fayette, IA 52142-1857. Offers accounting (MBA); corporate financial management (MBA); global business (MBA); health and human services (MPA); higher education administration (MHEA); homeland security (MPA); human resources management (MBA); justice administration (MPA); organizational development (MBA); public personnel management (MPA); quality management (MBA). MBA also available at Madison, WI campus. Part-time programs available. Postbaccalaureate distance learning degree programs offered (no on-campus study). *Faculty:* 3 full-time (0 women), 66 part-time/adjunct (27 women). *Students:* 723 full-time (442 women). *Degree requirements:* For master's, research project. *Entrance requirements:* For master's, GMAT, GRE, or minimum GPA of 2.7 during last 60 hours. Additional exam requirements/recommendations for international students: Required—TOEFL (minimum score 570 paper-based; 230 computer-based). *Application deadline:* Applications are processed on a rolling basis. Application fee: $50. Electronic applications accepted. *Expenses:* Tuition: Full-time $6948; part-time $386 per credit hour. *Financial support:* Available to part-time students. Applicants required to submit FAFSA. *Faculty research:* Total quality management, CQI, teams, organization culture and climate, management. *Application contact:* David Hannum, Admissions Advisor, 800-603-3756, E-mail: hannumd@uiu.edu.

Urbana University, College of Social and Behavioral Sciences, Urbana, OH 43078-2091. Offers criminal justice administration (MA). *Entrance requirements:* For master's, 3 letters of recommendation. *Expenses:* Tuition: Full-time $8550; part-time $475 per semester hour. Required fees: $950; $475 per semester. One-time fee: $25.

Utica College, Program in Economic Crime and Fraud Management, Utica, NY 13502-4892. Offers MBA. Part-time and evening/weekend programs available. Postbaccalaureate distance learning degree programs offered (minimal on-campus study). *Faculty:* 7 full-time (0 women). *Students:* 7 full-time (all women), 85 part-time (48 women); includes 11 minority (8 African Americans, 1 Asian American or Pacific Islander, 2 Hispanic Americans), 1 international. Average age 34. In 2009, 58 master's awarded. *Entrance requirements:* For master's, BS, minimum GPA of 3.0. Additional exam requirements/recommendations for international students: Required—TOEFL (minimum score 525 paper-based; 195 computer-based). *Application deadline:* Applications are processed on a rolling basis. Application fee: $50. Electronic applications accepted. *Expenses:* Contact institution. *Financial support:* Career-related internships or fieldwork, scholarships/grants, tuition waivers (partial), and unspecified assistantships available. Support available to part-time students. Financial award application deadline: 3/15; financial award applicants required to submit FAFSA. *Unit head:* Dr. R. Bruce McBride, Director of Economic Crime Graduate Programs, 315-792-3808, E-mail: rmcbride@utica.edu. *Application contact:* John D. Rowe, Director of Graduate Admissions, 315-792-3824, Fax: 315-792-3003, E-mail: jrowe@utica.edu.

Utica College, Program in Economic Crime Management, Utica, NY 13502-4892. Offers MS. Part-time programs available. Postbaccalaureate distance learning degree programs offered (minimal on-campus study). *Faculty:* 4 full-time (0 women). *Students:* 134 part-time (69 women); includes 15 minority (8 African Americans, 3 Asian Americans or Pacific Islanders, 4 Hispanic Americans), 3 international. Average age 36. In 2009, 10 master's awarded. *Degree requirements:* For master's, thesis. *Entrance requirements:* For master's, BS, minimum GPA of 3.0. Additional exam requirements/recommendations for international students: Required—TOEFL (minimum score 525 paper-based; 195 computer-based). *Application deadline:* Applications are processed on a rolling basis. Application fee: $50. Electronic applications accepted. *Expenses:* Contact institution. *Financial support:* Career-related internships or fieldwork, scholarships/grants, tuition waivers (partial), and unspecified assistantships available. Support available to part-time students. Financial award application deadline: 3/15; financial award applicants required to submit FAFSA. *Unit head:* Dr. R. Bruce McBride, Director of Economic Crime Graduate Programs, 315-792-3808, E-mail: rmcbride@utica.edu. *Application contact:* John D. Rowe, Director of Graduate Admissions, 315-792-3824, Fax: 315-792-3003, E-mail: jrowe@utica.edu.

Valdosta State University, Graduate School, Department of Sociology, Anthropology, and Criminal Justice, Valdosta, GA 31698. Offers criminal justice (MS); marriage and family therapy (MS); sociology (MS). *Accreditation:* AAMFT/COAMFTE. Part-time and evening/weekend programs available. *Degree requirements:* For master's, thesis or alternative, comprehensive written and/or oral exams. *Entrance requirements:* For master's, GRE General Test or MAT (sociology, marriage and family therapy), minimum GPA of 2.5. Additional exam requirements/recommendations for international students: Required—TOEFL (minimum score 523 paper-based; 193 computer-based). Electronic applications accepted. *Faculty research:* Police-civilian ride-along project.

Virginia College at Birmingham, Virginia College Online, Birmingham, AL 35209. Offers business administration (MBA); criminal justice (MCJ); cybersecurity (MC). Part-time and evening/weekend programs available. Postbaccalaureate distance learning degree programs offered (no on-campus study). *Financial support:* Military educational benefits available. Financial award applicants required to submit FAFSA. *Unit head:* Stan Banks, President, 877-207-1933, E-mail: vcoadm@vc.edu. *Application contact:* Christina Eschelman, Director of Admissions, 877-207-1933, E-mail: vcoadm@vc.edu.

Virginia Commonwealth University, Graduate School, College of Humanities and Sciences, Wilder School of Government and Public Affairs, Department of Criminal Justice, Richmond, VA 23284-9005. Offers MS, CCJA. Part-time and evening/weekend programs available. *Degree requirements:* For master's, thesis or comprehensive exam. *Entrance requirements:* For master's, GRE General Test, minimum GPA of 2.7.

Walden University, Graduate Programs, School of Counseling and Social Service, Minneapolis, MN 55401. Offers counselor education and supervision (PhD), including consultation, counseling and social change, forensic mental health counseling, general program, nonprofit management and leadership, trauma and crisis; human services (PhD), including clinical social work, counseling, criminal justice, family studies and intervention strategies, general program, human services administration, self-designed, social policy analysis and planning; marriage, couple, and family counseling (MS), including forensic counseling, trauma and crisis counseling; mental health counseling (MS), including forensic counseling. Part-time and evening/weekend programs available. Postbaccalaureate distance learning degree programs offered (minimal on-campus study). *Faculty:* 13 full-time, 78 part-time/adjunct. *Students:* 1,932 full-time (1,624 women), 210 part-time (181 women); includes 945 minority (817 African Americans, 24 American Indian/Alaska Native, 24 Asian Americans or Pacific Islanders, 80 Hispanic Americans), 34 international. Average age 39. In 2009, 55 master's, 5 doctorates awarded. *Degree requirements:* For master's, residency (for some programs); for doctorate, thesis/dissertation, residency. *Entrance requirements:* For master's, bachelor's degree or equivalent in related field, minimum GPA of 2.5; for doctorate, master's degree or equivalent in related field; minimum GPA of 3.0; official transcripts; three years' related professional/academic experience (preferred); access to computer and Internet. Additional exam requirements/recommendations for international students: Required—TOEFL (minimum score 550 paper-based; 213 computer-based), IELTS (minimum score 6.5), or Michigan English Language Assessment Battery (minimum score 82). *Application deadline:* Applications are processed on a rolling basis. Application fee: $50. Electronic applications accepted. *Expenses:* Tuition: Full-time $13,665; part-time $560 per credit. Required fees: $1375. Tuition and fees vary according to course load, degree level and program. *Financial support:* In 2009–10, 200 students received support; fellowships, Federal Work-Study, scholarships/grants, unspecified assistantships, and family tuition reduction, active duty/veteran tuition reduction, group tuition reduction, interest-free payment plans available. Support available to part-time students. Financial award applicants required to submit FAFSA. *Unit head:* Dr. Savitri Dixon-Saxon, Associate Dean, 800-925-3368. *Application contact:* Jennifer Hall, Director of Enrollment, 866-4-WALDEN, E-mail: info@waldenu.edu.

Walden University, Graduate Programs, School of Public Policy and Administration, Minneapolis, MN 55401. Offers general program (MPA); government management (Post-baccalaureate Certificate); health policy (MPA); homeland security policy (MPA); interdisciplinary policy studies (MPA); law and public policy (MPA); local government management for sustainable communities (MPA); nonprofit management (Postbaccalaureate Certificate); nonprofit management and leadership (MPA, MS); policy analysis (MPA); public management and leadership (MPA); public policy and administration (PhD), including criminal justice, health services, homeland security policy and coordination, international nongovernmental organizations, law and public policy, local government management for sustainable communities, nonprofit management and leadership, public management and leadership, public policy, public safety management, terrorism, mediation, and peace; terrorism, mediation, and peace (MPA). Part-time and evening/weekend programs available. Postbaccalaureate distance learning degree programs offered (minimal on-campus study). *Faculty:* 7 full-time, 62 part-time/adjunct. *Students:* 1,468 full-time (941 women), 233 part-time (162 women); includes 852 minority (761 African Americans, 9 American Indian/Alaska Native, 19 Asian Americans or Pacific Islanders, 63 Hispanic Americans), 53 international. Average age 40. In 2009, 173 master's, 13 doctorates awarded. *Degree requirements:* For doctorate, thesis/dissertation, residency. *Entrance requirements:* For master's, bachelor's degree or equivalent in related field, minimum GPA of 2.5; for doctorate, master's degree or equivalent in related field; minimum GPA of 3.0; official transcripts; three years of related professional/academic experience (preferred); access to computer and Internet. Additional exam requirements/recommendations for international students: Required—TOEFL (minimum score 550 paper-based; 213 computer-based), IELTS (minimum score 6.5), or Michigan English Language Assessment Battery (minimum score 82). *Application deadline:* Applications are processed on a rolling basis. Application fee: $50. Electronic applications accepted. *Expenses:* Tuition: Full-time $13,665; part-time $560 per credit. Required fees: $1375. Tuition and fees vary according to course load, degree level and program. *Financial support:* In 2009–10, 207 students received support; fellowships with tuition reimbursements available, Federal Work-Study, scholarships/grants, unspecified assistantships, and family tuition reduction, active duty/veteran tuition reduction, group tuition reduction, interest-free payment plans available. Support available to part-time students. Financial award applicants required to submit FAFSA. *Unit head:* Dr. Mark Gordon, Associate Dean, 800-925-3368. *Application contact:* Jennifer Hall, Director of Enrollment, 866-4-WALDEN, E-mail: info@waldenu.edu.

Criminal Justice and Criminology

Washburn University, School of Applied Studies, Department of Criminal Justice, Topeka, KS 66621. Offers MCJ. Part-time and evening/weekend programs available. Postbaccalaureate distance learning degree programs offered (minimal on-campus study). *Faculty:* 6 full-time (2 women), 2 part-time/adjunct (1 woman). *Students:* 21 full-time (11 women), 9 part-time (5 women); includes 7 minority (all African Americans). Average age 27. In 2009, 5 master's awarded. *Degree requirements:* For master's, thesis or alternative, continuous enrollment each fall and spring semester, completion of all program requirements within seven years of entry (MCJ). *Entrance requirements:* For master's, GRE (may be waived in certain situations), 3 letters of reference. Additional exam requirements/recommendations for international students: Required—TOEFL (minimum score 79 iBT). *Application deadline:* For fall admission, 4/1 priority date for domestic and international students; for spring admission, 11/1 priority date for domestic and international students. Applications are processed on a rolling basis. Application fee: $35. Electronic applications accepted. *Financial support:* In 2009–10, 23 students received support. Institutionally sponsored loans and scholarships/grants available. Support available to part-time students. Financial award application deadline: 3/1; financial award applicants required to submit FAFSA. *Faculty research:* Practitioner behavior, police management and training, field and institutional correction administration, terrorism, police training, sex slaves. *Unit head:* Dr. Gerald Bayens, Department Chair, 785-670-1411, Fax: 785-670-1027, E-mail: gerald.bayens@washburn.edu. *Application contact:* Dr. Phyllis E. Berry, MCJ Graduate Director, 785-670-2057, Fax: 785-670-1027, E-mail: phyllis.berry@washburn.edu.

Washington State University, Graduate School, College of Liberal Arts, Department of Political Science, Program in Criminal Justice, Pullman, WA 99164. Offers MA, PhD. *Faculty:* 8. *Students:* 24 full-time (11 women), 6 part-time (2 women); includes 4 minority (1 African American, 1 American Indian/Alaska Native, 1 Asian American or Pacific Islander, 1 Hispanic American), 3 international. Average age 32. 33 applicants, 58% accepted, 2 enrolled. In 2009, 15 master's, 5 doctorates awarded. *Degree requirements:* For master's, comprehensive exam (for some programs), thesis, oral exam; for doctorate, comprehensive exam, thesis/dissertation, oral or written exam. *Entrance requirements:* For master's and doctorate, GRE General Test, major in criminal justice, sociology, psychology, liberal arts, or a related field; strong writing and analytical skills; minimum GPA of 3.0. Additional exam requirements/recommendations for international students: Required—TOEFL, IELTS. *Application deadline:* For fall admission, 1/10 priority date for domestic and international students. Application fee: $50. Electronic applications accepted. *Financial support:* In 2009–10, 6 research assistantships with full and partial tuition reimbursements (averaging $13,917 per year), 7 teaching assistantships with full and partial tuition reimbursements (averaging $13,056 per year) were awarded; career-related internships or fieldwork, Federal Work-Study, institutionally sponsored loans, health care benefits, tuition waivers (partial), and teaching associateships also available. Financial award application deadline: 2/15; financial award applicants required to submit FAFSA. *Faculty research:* Community policing, community justice, corrections policy, crime prevention policy, criminal justice management. *Unit head:* Dr. Otwin Marenin, Interim Director, 509-335-2544, Fax: 509-335-7990, E-mail: siskeo@wsu.edu. *Application contact:* Graduate School Admissions, 800-GRADWSU, Fax: 509-335-1949, E-mail: gradsch@wsu.edu.

Washington State University Spokane, Graduate Programs, Program in Criminal Justice, Spokane, WA 99210. Offers MA, PhD. *Faculty:* 25. *Students:* 6 full-time (4 women), 4 part-time (1 woman). Average age 42. *Degree requirements:* For master's, comprehensive exam, thesis (for some programs); for doctorate, comprehensive exam, thesis/dissertation. *Entrance requirements:* For master's, GRE, minimum GPA of 3.0. Additional exam requirements/recommendations for international students: Required—TOEFL (minimum score 550 paper-based). *Application deadline:* For fall admission, 1/10 priority date for domestic students, 1/10 for international students; for spring admission, 7/1 priority date for domestic students, 7/1 for international students. Application fee: $50. *Expenses:* Tuition, state resident: part-time $423 per credit. Tuition, nonresident: part-time $1032 per credit. *Financial support:* In 2009–10, research assistantships (averaging $14,634 per year), teaching assistantships (averaging $13,383 per year) were awarded; fellowships also available. Financial award application deadline: 2/15. *Faculty research:* Community-oriented policing, crime, criminology theory, jury system, judicial evaluations, police performance. Total annual research expenditures: $443,591. *Unit head:* Dr. David Brody, Campus Academic Director, 509-358-7952, Fax: 509-358-7900, E-mail: brody@wsu.edu. *Application contact:* Graduate School Admissions, 800-GRADWSU, Fax: 509-335-1949, E-mail: gradsch@wsu.edu.

Wayland Baptist University, Graduate Programs, Program in Counseling, Plainview, TX 79072-6998. Offers counseling (MA); government administration (MPA); homeland security (MPA); justice administration (MPA). Part-time and evening/weekend programs available. Postbaccalaureate distance learning degree programs offered. *Faculty:* 9 full-time (2 women). *Students:* 71 part-time (58 women); includes 16 minority (5 African Americans, 1 American Indian/Alaska Native, 10 Hispanic Americans). Average age 34. 21 applicants, 90% accepted, 11 enrolled. In 2009, 16 master's awarded. *Degree requirements:* For master's, comprehensive exam. *Entrance requirements:* For master's, GRE, MAT. Additional exam requirements/recommendations for international students: Required—TOEFL (minimum score 500 paper-based; 173 computer-based; 61 iBT). *Application deadline:* Applications are processed on a rolling basis. Application fee: $50. Electronic applications accepted. *Expenses:* Tuition: Full-time $5796; part-time $322 per credit hour. Required fees: $782; $9 per credit hour. $60 per semester. Tuition and fees vary according to course load and campus/location. *Financial support:* Federal Work-Study, institutionally sponsored loans, and scholarships/grants available. Support available to part-time students. Financial award application deadline: 5/1; financial award applicants required to submit FAFSA. *Unit head:* Dr. Estelle Owens, Chairman, 806-291-1171, Fax: 806-291-1972, E-mail: owensest@wbu.edu. *Application contact:* Amanda Stanton, Graduate Studies, 806-291-3423, Fax: 806-291-1950, E-mail: stanton@wbu.edu.

Wayne State University, College of Liberal Arts and Sciences, Department of Criminal Justice, Detroit, MI 48202. Offers MS. *Degree requirements:* For master's, comprehensive exam, essay. *Entrance requirements:* For master's, GRE (if GPA is between 2.75 and 2.99), minimum GPA of 3.0 (resume and writing sample if less than 3.0), 2 letters of recommendation. Additional exam requirements/recommendations for international students: Required—TOEFL (minimum score 550 paper-based; 213 computer-based); Recommended—TWE (minimum score 6). Electronic applications accepted. *Faculty research:* Criminology, juvenile delinquency and justice, law, policing, corrections, social deviance.

Wayne State University, College of Liberal Arts and Sciences, Department of Political Science, Program in Public Administration, Detroit, MI 48202. Offers criminal justice (MPA); public administration (MPA). *Accreditation:* NASPAA. Evening/weekend programs available. *Entrance requirements:* For master's, GRE General Test. Additional exam requirements/recommendations for international students: Required—TOEFL (minimum score 550 paper-based; 213 computer-based); Recommended—TWE (minimum score 6). Electronic applications accepted. *Faculty research:* Urban politics, urban education, state administration.

Webber International University, Graduate School of Business, Babson Park, FL 33827-0096. Offers accounting (MBA); management (MBA); security management (MBA); sports management (MBA). Part-time and evening/weekend programs available. *Degree requirements:* For master's, thesis or alternative. *Entrance requirements:* For master's, previous course work in financial and managerial accounting. Additional exam requirements/recommendations for international students: Required—TOEFL. *Faculty research:* Finance strategy, market research, investments, intranet.

Webster University, George Herbert Walker School of Business and Technology, Department of Business, St. Louis, MO 63119-3194. Offers business (MA); business and organizational security management (MBA); computer resources and information management (MBA); environmental management (MBA); finance (MA, MBA); health services management (MBA); human resources development (MBA); human resources management (MBA); international business (MA, MBA); management and leadership (MBA); marketing (MBA); procurement and acquisitions management (MBA); telecommunications management (MBA). Part-time and evening/weekend programs available. Postbaccalaureate distance learning degree programs offered (no on-campus study). *Faculty:* 9 full-time, 430 part-time/adjunct. *Students:* 1,190 full-time (543 women), 4,226 part-time (2,159 women); includes 2,110 minority (1,448 African Americans, 20 American Indian/Alaska Native, 310 Asian Americans or Pacific Islanders, 332 Hispanic Americans), 2,176 international. Average age 34. In 2009, 2,021 master's awarded. *Degree requirements:* For master's, comprehensive exam (for some programs), thesis (for some programs). *Entrance requirements:* Additional exam requirements/recommendations for international students: Required—TOEFL. *Application deadline:* Applications are processed on a rolling basis. Application fee: $35 ($50 for international students). *Expenses:* Tuition: Part-time $565 per credit hour. Tuition and fees vary according to degree level, campus/location and program. *Financial support:* Federal Work-Study available. Support available to part-time students. Financial award application deadline: 4/1; financial award applicants required to submit FAFSA. *Unit head:* Dr. Debbie Psihountas, Chair, 314-246-7553 Ext. 7017, Fax: 314-968-7077, E-mail: buschair@webster.edu. *Application contact:* Matt Nolan, Assoc., V.P.—Enrollment Management / Dean of Admissions, Fax: 314-968-7116, E-mail: gadmit@webster.edu.

Webster University, George Herbert Walker School of Business and Technology, Department of Management, St. Louis, MO 63119-3194. Offers business and organizational security management (MA); computer resources and information management (MA); environmental management (MS); government contracting (Certificate); health care management (MA); health services management (MA); human resources development (MA); human resources management (MA); management (DM); management and leadership (MA); marketing (MA); nonprofit management (Certificate); procurement and acquisitions management (MA); public administration (MA); quality management (MA); space systems operations management (MS); telecommunications management (MA). Part-time and evening/weekend programs available. Postbaccalaureate distance learning degree programs offered (no on-campus study). *Faculty:* 16 full-time, 781 part-time/adjunct. *Students:* 1,369 full-time (610 women), 5,182 part-time (3,047 women); includes 3,460 minority (2,835 African Americans, 38 American Indian/Alaska Native, 169 Asian Americans or Pacific Islanders, 418 Hispanic Americans), 80 international. Average age 37. In 2009, 2,491 master's, 13 doctorates, 68 other advanced degrees awarded. *Degree requirements:* For master's, thesis (for some programs); for doctorate, thesis/dissertation, written exam. *Entrance requirements:* For doctorate, GMAT, 3 years of work experience, MBA. Additional exam requirements/recommendations for international students: Required—TOEFL. *Application deadline:* Applications are processed on a rolling basis. Application fee: $25 ($50 for international students). *Expenses:* Tuition: Part-time $565 per credit hour. Tuition and fees vary according to degree level, campus/location and program. *Financial support:* Federal Work-Study available. Support available to part-time students. Financial award application deadline: 4/1; financial award applicants required to submit FAFSA. *Unit head:* Jim Brasfield, Chair, 314-961-2660 Ext. 7063, Fax: 314-968-7077, E-mail: mgtchair@webster.edu. *Application contact:* Matt Nolan, Assoc. V.P.—Enrollment Management / Dean of Admissions, Fax: 314-968-7116, E-mail: gadmit@webster.edu.

West Chester University of Pennsylvania, Office of Graduate Studies, College of Business and Public Affairs, Department of Criminal Justice, West Chester, PA 19383. Offers criminal justice (MS). Part-time and evening/weekend programs available. *Students:* 14 full-time (5 women), 40 part-time (22 women); includes 10 minority (8 African Americans, 1 Asian American or Pacific Islander, 1 Hispanic American). Average age 25. 44 applicants, 95% accepted, 34 enrolled. In 2009, 23 master's awarded. *Degree requirements:* For master's, independent research project. *Entrance requirements:* For master's, MAT. Additional exam requirements/recommendations for international students: Required—TOEFL (minimum score 550 paper-based; 213 computer-based; 80 iBT). *Application deadline:* For fall admission, 4/15 priority date for domestic students, 3/15 for international students; for spring admission, 10/15 for domestic students, 9/1 for international students. Applications are processed on a rolling basis. Application fee: $35. Electronic applications accepted. *Expenses:* Tuition, state resident: full-time $6666; part-time $370 per credit. Tuition, nonresident: full-time $10,666; part-time $593 per credit. Required fees: $122.56 per credit. *Financial support:* In 2009–10, 3 research assistantships with full and partial tuition reimbursements (averaging $5,000 per year) were awarded; unspecified assistantships also available. Support available to part-time students. Financial award application deadline: 2/15; financial award applicants required to submit FAFSA. *Faculty research:* Criminal law, criminal procedure, constitutional interpretation. *Unit head:* Dr. Jana Nestlerode, Chair, 610-436-2647, E-mail: jnestlerode@wcupa.edu. *Application contact:* Dr. Mary P. Brewster, Graduate Coordinator, 610-436-2630, E-mail: mbrewster@wcupa.edu.

Western Connecticut State University, Division of Graduate Studies, Ancell School of Business, Program in Justice Administration, Danbury, CT 06810-6885. Offers MS. Part-time programs available. *Faculty:* 1 (woman) full-time. *Students:* 10 part-time (5 women); includes 2 minority (1 African American, 1 Hispanic American). Average age 31. 7 applicants, 71% accepted, 5 enrolled. *Degree requirements:* For master's, comprehensive exam or research project, completion of program within 6 years. *Entrance requirements:* For master's, GMAT, GRE, LSAT, or MAT. Additional exam requirements/recommendations for international students: Recommended—TOEFL (minimum score 550 paper-based; 213 computer-based; 79 iBT), IELTS (minimum score 6). *Application deadline:* For fall admission, 8/5 priority date for domestic students; for spring admission, 1/5 priority date for domestic students. Applications are processed on a rolling basis. Application fee: $50. *Expenses:* Tuition, state resident: full-time $5012; part-time $278 per credit hour. Tuition, nonresident: full-time $13,962; part-time $284 per credit hour. Required fees: $3886; $139 per credit hour. Full-time tuition and fees vary according to course load and program. Part-time tuition and fees vary according to course level, degree level and program. *Financial support:* Application deadline: 5/1. *Unit head:* Dr. Anthony G. Markert, Assistant Professor, 203-837-8469, Fax: 203-837-8527, E-mail: markerta@wcsu.edu. *Application contact:* Chris Shankle, Associate Director of Graduate Admissions, 203-837-9005, Fax: 203-837-8326, E-mail: shanklec@wcsu.edu.

Western Illinois University, School of Graduate Studies, College of Education and Human Services, School of Law Enforcement and Justice Administration, Macomb, IL 61455-1390. Offers law enforcement and justice administration (MA); police executive administration (Certificate). Part-time programs available. *Students:* 30 full-time (12 women), 46 part-time (15 women); includes 6 minority (4 African Americans, 2 Hispanic Americans). Average age 29. 16 applicants, 56% accepted. In 2009, 20 master's, 4 other advanced degrees awarded. *Degree requirements:* For master's, thesis or alternative. *Entrance requirements:* For master's, GRE or MAT, minimum GPA of 3.0. Additional exam requirements/recommendations for international students: Required—TOEFL (minimum score 520 paper-based; 190 computer-based; 68 iBT). *Application deadline:* Applications are processed on a rolling basis. Application fee: $30. Electronic applications accepted. *Expenses:* Tuition, state resident: full-time $4486; part-time $249.21 per credit hour. Tuition, nonresident: full-time $8972; part-time $498.42 per credit hour. Required fees: $72.62 per credit hour. *Financial support:* In 2009–10, 12 students received support, including 11 research assistantships with full tuition reimbursements available (averaging $7,280 per year), 1 teaching assistantship with full tuition reimbursement available (averaging $8,400 per year). Financial award applicants required to submit FAFSA. *Unit head:* Dr. Darrell Ross, Chairperson, 309-298-1038. *Application contact:* Evelyn Hoing, Assistant Director of Graduate Studies, 309-298-1806, Fax: 309-298-2345, E-mail: grad-office@wiu.edu.

Western Oregon University, Graduate Programs, College of Liberal Arts and Sciences, Division of Social Science, Monmouth, OR 97361-1394. Offers criminal justice (MA, MS). Part-time and evening/weekend programs available. *Degree requirements:* For master's, thesis optional, written exams. *Entrance requirements:* For master's, minimum GPA of 3.0. Additional exam requirements/recommendations for international students: Required—TOEFL (minimum score 550 paper-based; 213 computer-based; 79 iBT), IELTS (minimum score 6.5). *Faculty research:* Prison to community transition of adult felons, community justice, restorative justice, parole and probation.

Westfield State College, Division of Graduate and Continuing Education, Department of Criminal Justice, Westfield, MA 01086. Offers MS. Part-time and evening/weekend programs available. *Degree requirements:* For master's, comprehensive exam, thesis (for some programs). *Entrance requirements:* For master's, GRE General Test or MAT, minimum undergraduate GPA of 2.7.

West Texas A&M University, College of Education and Social Sciences, Department of History and Political Science, Program in Criminal Justice, Canyon, TX 79016-0001. Offers MA. Part-time and evening/weekend programs available. *Degree requirements:* For master's, comprehensive exam, thesis optional. *Entrance requirements:* For master's, GRE General Test. Additional exam requirements/recommendations for international students: Required—TOEFL (minimum score 550 paper-based). Electronic applications accepted. *Faculty research:* Racial profiling, changing nature of prisons, campus police and parking services.

Wichita State University, Graduate School, Fairmount College of Liberal Arts and Sciences, School of Community Affairs, Wichita, KS 67260. Offers criminal justice (MA); gerontology (MA). Part-time programs available. *Expenses:* Tuition, state resident: full-time $4247; part-time $235.95 per credit hour. Tuition, nonresident: full-time $11,171; part-time $620.60 per credit hour. Required fees: $34; $3.60 per credit hour. $17 per term. Tuition and fees vary according to campus/location and program. *Unit head:* Dr. Michael Birzer, Director, 316-978-7200, Fax: 316-978-3626, E-mail: michael.birzer@wichita.edu. *Application contact:* Dr. Michael Birzer, Director, 316-978-7200, Fax: 316-978-3626, E-mail: michael.birzer@wichita.edu.

Widener University, College of Arts and Sciences, Program in Criminal Justice, Chester, PA 19013-5792. Offers MA, Psy D/MA. Part-time and evening/weekend programs available. *Faculty:* 1 full-time (0 women), 2 part-time/adjunct (0 women). *Students:* 3 full-time (1 woman), 10 part-time (7 women); includes 3 minority (2 African Americans, 1 Asian American or Pacific Islander). Average age 31. 21 applicants, 90% accepted. In 2009, 1 master's awarded. *Degree requirements:* For master's, project. *Entrance requirements:* For master's, interview, minimum undergraduate GPA of 3.0. *Application deadline:* For fall admission, 3/1 priority date for domestic students. Applications are processed on a rolling basis. Application fee: $25 ($300 for international students). *Expenses:* Contact institution. *Financial support:* Career-related internships or fieldwork and institutionally sponsored loans available. Support available to part-time students. Financial award application deadline: 5/1. *Faculty research:* Criminal law and procedure, corrections, domestic violence. *Unit head:* Dr. William E. Harver, Director, 610-499-4554, Fax: 510-499-4605, E-mail: william.e.harver@widener.edu. *Application contact:* Christine M. Weist, Assistant to Associate Provost for Graduate Studies, 610-499-4351, Fax: 610-499-4277, E-mail: christine.m.weist@widener.edu.

Wilmington University, College of Social and Behavioral Sciences, New Castle, DE 19720-6491. Offers administration of human services (MS); administration of justice (MS); community counseling (MS). *Accreditation:* ACA. Part-time and evening/weekend programs available. *Entrance requirements:* Additional exam requirements/recommendations for international students: Required—TOEFL (minimum score 500 paper-based; 173 computer-based). Electronic applications accepted.

Wright State University, School of Graduate Studies, College of Liberal Arts, Program in Applied Behavioral Science, Dayton, OH 45435. Offers criminal justice and social problems (MA); international and comparative politics (MA). *Degree requirements:* For master's, thesis optional. *Entrance requirements:* Additional exam requirements/recommendations for international students: Required—TOEFL. *Faculty research:* Training and development, criminal justice and social problems, community systems, human factors, industrial/organizational psychology.

Xavier University, College of Social Sciences, Health and Education, Department of Criminal Justice, Cincinnati, OH 45207. Offers MS. Part-time and evening/weekend programs available. *Faculty:* 3 full-time (1 woman). *Students:* 6 full-time (all women), 11 part-time (5 women); includes 5 minority (4 African Americans, 1 Hispanic American). Average age 30. 17 applicants, 94% accepted, 7 enrolled. In 2009, 15 master's awarded. *Degree requirements:* For master's, comprehensive exam, thesis or alternative. *Entrance requirements:* For master's, MAT, GRE, or LSAT, minimum GPA of 2.7. Additional exam requirements/recommendations for international students: Required—TOEFL (minimum score 550 paper-based; 213 computer-based). *Application deadline:* For fall admission, 8/15 priority date for domestic students. Applications are processed on a rolling basis. Application fee: $35. Electronic applications accepted. *Expenses:* Tuition: Part-time $697 per credit hour. One-time fee: $35 part-time. *Financial support:* In 2009–10, 7 students received support. Career-related internships or fieldwork, scholarships/grants, and unspecified assistantships available. Support available to part-time students. Financial award applicants required to submit FAFSA. *Faculty research:* Women and crime, gun violence, homicide, crime policy, policing. *Unit head:* Dr. Y. Gail Hurst, Chair, 513-745-1070, Fax: 513-745-3220, E-mail: hurst@xavier.edu. *Application contact:* Roger Bosse, Interim Director of Graduate Studies, 513-745-3357, Fax: 513-745-1048, E-mail: bosse@xavier.edu.

Youngstown State University, Graduate School, Bitonte College of Health and Human Services, Department of Criminal Justice, Youngstown, OH 44555-0001. Offers MS. Part-time and evening/weekend programs available. *Degree requirements:* For master's, thesis optional. *Entrance requirements:* For master's, minimum GPA of 2.7. Additional exam requirements/recommendations for international students: Required—TOEFL. *Faculty research:* Police human resource allocation, police administration, computerized test development, criminal law.

Forensic Sciences

Albany State University, College of Sciences and Health Professions, Department of Criminal Justice and Forensic Science, Albany, GA 31705-2717. Offers corrections (MS); forensic science (MS); law enforcement (MS); public administration (MS). Part-time programs available. *Students:* 11 full-time (10 women), 43 part-time (29 women); includes 51 minority (50 African Americans, 1 Asian American or Pacific Islander). Average age 35. 18 applicants, 94% accepted, 10 enrolled. In 2009, 8 master's awarded. *Degree requirements:* For master's, comprehensive exam, thesis optional. *Entrance requirements:* For master's, GRE General Test or MAT, minimum GPA of 2.5, ASU Medical and Immunization Forms. Additional exam requirements/recommendations for international students: Required—TOEFL. *Application deadline:* For fall admission, 11/16 for domestic students, 9/16 for international students; for spring admission, 4/19 for domestic students, 2/19 for international students. Applications are processed on a rolling basis. Application fee: $20. Electronic applications accepted. *Expenses:* Tuition, state resident: full-time $2970; part-time $162 per credit hour. Tuition, nonresident: full-time $12,168; part-time $676 per credit hour. Required fees: $962; $75 per credit hour. *Financial support:* Application deadline: 6/30. *Faculty research:* Criminal alcoholic program, prevention of juvenile delinquency, police selection, constitutional issues. *Unit head:* Dr. Charles Ochie, Chair, 229-430-4864, Fax: 229-430-1676, E-mail: charles.ochie@asurams.edu. *Application contact:* Nicole Lane, Interim Graduate Admissions Officer, 229-430-4862, Fax: 229-430-6398, E-mail: nicole.lane@asurams.edu.

Alliant International University–Irvine, Center for Forensic Studies, Irvine, CA 92612. Offers Psy D.

Arcadia University, Graduate Studies, Program in Forensic Science, Glenside, PA 19038-3295. Offers MSFS. *Students:* 39 full-time (32 women), 1 part-time (0 women); includes 2 minority (1 African American, 1 Asian American or Pacific Islander), 1 international. Average age 23. In 2009, 13 master's awarded. Application fee: $50. *Expenses:* Tuition: Full-time $30,450; part-time $620 per credit hour. Required fees: $165. Tuition and fees vary according to program. *Unit head:* Larry Presley, Director, 215-572-4140. *Application contact:* Office of Enrollment Management, 215-572-2910, Fax: 215-572-4049, E-mail: admiss@arcadia.edu.

Cedar Crest College, Program in Forensic Science, Allentown, PA 18104-6196. Offers MS. *Degree requirements:* For master's, thesis. *Entrance requirements:* For master's, GRE. Electronic applications accepted. *Expenses:* Contact institution. *Faculty research:* Geotyping of low copy number DNA, presumptive and conformatory testing of GHB and GBL.

Chaminade University of Honolulu, Graduate Services, Program in Forensic Science, Honolulu, HI 96816-1578. Offers MSFS. Part-time programs available. *Degree requirements:* For master's, comprehensive exam, thesis or alternative. *Entrance requirements:* For master's, GRE, 2 letters of recommendation. Additional exam requirements/recommendations for international students: Required—TOEFL (minimum score 550 paper-based; 250 computer-based).

Duquesne University, Bayer School of Natural and Environmental Sciences, Program in Forensic Science and Law, Pittsburgh, PA 15282-0001. Offers MS. Part-time programs available. *Faculty:* 2 full-time (1 woman), 5 part-time/adjunct (2 women). *Students:* 19 full-time (16 women). Average age 23. 19 applicants, 100% accepted, 19 enrolled. In 2009, 26 master's awarded. *Degree requirements:* For master's, comprehensive exam. *Entrance requirements:* For master's, SAT or ACT, 1 recommendation form. *Application deadline:* For fall admission, 7/1 for domestic and international students. Applications are processed on a rolling basis. Application fee: $50. Electronic applications accepted. *Expenses:* Tuition: Part-time $851 per credit. Required fees: $81 per credit. *Financial support:* In 2009–10, 2 students received support, including 1 research assistantship, 1 teaching assistantship; career-related internships or fieldwork and unspecified assistantships also available. Financial award application deadline: 5/1. *Faculty research:* Extraction protocols, mass spectrometry, synthetic fiber analysis, synthetic polymer characterization, trace analysis. *Unit head:* Dr. Federick W. Fochtman, Director, 412-396-6373, E-mail: fochtman@duq.edu. *Application contact:* Val Lijewski, Academic Advisor, 412-396-1084, Fax: 412-396-1402, E-mail: lijewskski@duq.edu.

Florida Gulf Coast University, College of Professional Studies, Program in Criminal Forensic Studies, Fort Myers, FL 33965-6565. Offers MS. *Faculty:* 32 full-time (11 women), 29 part-time/adjunct (12 women). *Students:* 27 full-time (22 women), 19 part-time (15 women); includes 9 minority (2 African Americans, 2 American Indian/Alaska Native, 5 Hispanic Americans), 2 international. Average age 28. 26 applicants, 65% accepted, 13 enrolled. In 2009, 1 master's awarded. *Entrance requirements:* For master's, GRE General Test, minimum GPA 3.0. Additional exam requirements/recommendations for international students: Required—TOEFL (minimum score 550 paper-based; 213 computer-based). *Application deadline:* For fall admission, 4/1 for domestic students; for spring admission, 11/15 for domestic students. Applications are processed on a rolling basis. Application fee: $30. Electronic applications accepted. *Financial support:* Research assistantships, career-related internships or fieldwork and tuition waivers (full and partial) available. Support available to part-time students. *Unit head:* Dr. Kenneth Millar, Dean, 239-590-7724, Fax: 239-590-7846, E-mail: kmillar@fgcu.edu. *Application contact:* Dr. Kenneth Millar, Dean, 239-590-7724, Fax: 239-590-7846, E-mail: kmillar@fgcu.edu.

Florida International University, College of Arts and Sciences, Department of Chemistry, Program in Forensic Science, Miami, FL 33199. Offers MS. Part-time programs available. *Students:* 13 full-time (10 women), 3 part-time (all women); includes 4 minority (all Hispanic Americans), 6 international. Average age 25. 27 applicants, 26% accepted, 4 enrolled. In 2009, 5 master's awarded. *Degree requirements:* For master's, thesis optional. *Entrance requirements:* For master's, GRE, minimum GPA of 3.0, 3 letters of recommendation. Additional exam requirements/recommendations for international students: Required—TOEFL (minimum score 550 paper-based; 213 computer-based). *Application deadline:* For fall admission, 6/1 for domestic students, 4/1 for international students; for spring admission, 10/1 for domestic students, 9/1 for international students. Applications are processed on a rolling basis. Application fee: $30. Electronic applications accepted. *Expenses:* Tuition, state resident: full-time $8008; part-time $4004 per year. Tuition, nonresident: full-time $20,104; part-time $10,052 per year. Required fees: $298; $149 per term. *Financial support:* Research assistantships, teaching assistantships, institutionally sponsored loans and scholarships/grants available. Financial award application deadline: 3/1; financial award applicants required to submit FAFSA. *Unit head:* Dr. Stanislaw Wnuk, Chairperson, 305-348-2606, Fax: 305-348-3772, E-mail: stanislaw.wnuk@fiu.edu. *Application contact:* Nanett Rojas, Assistant Director of Graduate Admissions, 305-348-7442, Fax: 305-348-7441, E-mail: gradadm@fiu.edu.

George Mason University, Volgenau School of Information Technology and Engineering, Department of Electrical and Computer Engineering, Fairfax, VA 22030. Offers advanced networking protocols for telecommunications (Certificate); communications and networking (Certificate); computer engineering (MS); computer forensics (MS); electrical and computer engineering (PhD); electrical engineering (MS); network technology and applications (Certificate); networks, system integration and testing (Certificate); signal processing (Certificate); telecom systems modeling (Certificate); telecommunications (MS); telecommunications forensics and security (Certificate); VLSI design/manufacturing (Certificate); wireless communication (Certificate). Part-time and evening/weekend programs available. *Faculty:* 29 full-time (4 women), 37 part-time/adjunct (5 women). *Students:* 115 full-time (18 women), 308 part-time (46 women); includes 84 minority (17 African Americans, 51 Asian Americans or Pacific Islanders, 16 Hispanic Americans), 179 international. Average age 29. 461 applicants, 67% accepted, 105 enrolled. In 2009, 157 master's, 6 doctorates, 61 other advanced degrees awarded. *Degree requirements:* For master's, thesis optional; for doctorate, comprehensive exam, thesis or scholarly paper. *Entrance requirements:* For master's, GMAT or GRE General Test, letters of recommendation, resume; for doctorate, GRE/GMAT, personal goal statement, 2 transcripts, letter of recommendation. Additional exam requirements/recommendations for international students: Required—TOEFL. *Application deadline:* For fall admission, 7/15 priority date for domestic and international students; for spring admission, 12/2 for domestic students, 12/1 for international students. Applications are processed on a rolling basis. Application fee: $75. Electronic applications accepted. *Expenses:* Tuition, state resident: full-time $7568; part-time $315.33 per credit hour. Tuition, nonresident: full-time $21,704; part-time $904.33 per credit hour. Required fees: $2184; $91 per credit hour. *Financial support:* In 2009–10, 64 students received support, including 2 fellowships with full tuition reimbursements available (averaging $18,000 per year), 22 research assistantships with full and partial tuition reimbursements available (averaging $8,469 per year), 42 teaching assistantships with full and partial tuition reimbursements available (averaging $6,291 per year); career-related internships or fieldwork, Federal Work-Study, scholarships/grants, unspecified assistantships, and health care benefits (full-time research or teaching assistantship recipients) also available. Support available to part-time students. Financial award application deadline: 3/1; financial award applicants required to submit FAFSA. *Faculty research:* Communication networks, signal processing, system failure diagnosis, multiprocessors, material processing using microwave energy. Total annual

Forensic Sciences

George Mason University (continued)
research expenditures: $3 million. *Unit head:* Dr. Andre Manitius, Chairperson, 703-993-1569, Fax: 703-993-1601, E-mail: ece@gmu.edu. *Application contact:* Jessica Skinner, Associate Dean, 703-993-1569, E-mail: jskinne6@gmu.edu.

The George Washington University, Columbian College of Arts and Sciences, Department of Forensic Sciences, Washington, DC 20052. Offers crime scene investigation (MFS); forensic chemistry (MFS); forensic molecular biology (MFS); forensic toxicology (MFS); high-technology crime investigation (MFS); security management (MFS). High-technology crime investigation and security management programs offered in Arlington, VA. Part-time and evening/weekend programs available. *Faculty:* 6 full-time (1 woman), 28 part-time/adjunct (5 women). *Students:* 82 full-time (55 women), 54 part-time (35 women); includes 26 minority (12 African Americans, 2 American Indian/Alaska Native, 7 Asian Americans or Pacific Islanders, 5 Hispanic Americans), 10 international. Average age 28. 121 applicants, 81% accepted, 52 enrolled. In 2009, 80 master's awarded. *Degree requirements:* For master's, comprehensive exam. *Entrance requirements:* For master's, GRE General Test, minimum GPA of 3.0. Additional exam requirements/recommendations for international students: Required—TOEFL (minimum score 550 paper-based; 213 computer-based; 80 iBT). *Application deadline:* For fall admission, 1/16 priority date for international students; for spring admission, 10/1 priority date for domestic students, 9/1 priority date for international students. Applications are processed on a rolling basis. Application fee: $60. Electronic applications accepted. *Financial support:* In 2009–10, 19 students received support; fellowships with partial tuition reimbursements available, Federal Work-Study and tuition waivers available. *Unit head:* Dr. Walter F. Rowe, Chair, 202-994-1469, E-mail: wfrowe@gwu.edu. *Application contact:* Dr. Walter F. Rowe, Chair, 202-994-1469, E-mail: wfrowe@gwu.edu.

John Jay College of Criminal Justice of the City University of New York, Graduate Studies, Program in Forensic Computing, New York, NY 10019-1093. Offers MS. Part-time and evening/weekend programs available. *Degree requirements:* For master's, thesis or alternative. *Entrance requirements:* For master's, GRE General Test, minimum B average. Additional exam requirements/recommendations for international students: Required—TOEFL (minimum score 500 paper-based; 173 computer-based).

John Jay College of Criminal Justice of the City University of New York, Graduate Studies, Program in Forensic Science, New York, NY 10019-1093. Offers MS. Part-time and evening/weekend programs available. *Degree requirements:* For master's, thesis. *Entrance requirements:* For master's, GRE, minimum B average. Additional exam requirements/recommendations for international students: Required—TOEFL (minimum score 500 paper-based; 173 computer-based).

John Jay College of Criminal Justice of the City University of New York, Graduate Studies, Programs in Criminal Justice, New York, NY 10019-1093. Offers criminal justice (MA, PhD); criminology and deviance (PhD); forensic psychology (PhD); forensic science (PhD); law and philosophy (PhD); organizational behavior (PhD); public policy (PhD). Part-time and evening/weekend programs available. Terminal master's awarded for partial completion of doctoral program. *Degree requirements:* For master's, thesis or alternative; for doctorate, one foreign language, thesis/dissertation. *Entrance requirements:* For master's, GRE General Test, minimum B average; for doctorate, GRE General Test. Additional exam requirements/recommendations for international students: Required—TOEFL (minimum score 500 paper-based; 173 computer-based).

McGill University, Faculty of Graduate and Postdoctoral Studies, Faculty of Dentistry, Montréal, QC H3A 2T5, Canada. Offers forensic dentistry (Certificate); oral and maxillofacial surgery (M Sc, PhD).

Mercyhurst College, Graduate Program, Program in Forensic and Biological Anthropology, Erie, PA 16546. Offers MS. *Entrance requirements:* For master's, GRE or MAT, undergraduate degree in related field, interview. Additional exam requirements/recommendations for international students: Required—TOEFL.

Michigan State University, The Graduate School, College of Social Science, School of Criminal Justice, East Lansing, MI 48824. Offers criminal justice (MS, PhD); forensic science (MS); law enforcement intelligence and analysis (MS). Postbaccalaureate distance learning degree programs offered. *Faculty:* 25 full-time (8 women). *Students:* 88 full-time (46 women), 109 part-time (48 women); includes 21 minority (5 African Americans, 3 Asian Americans or Pacific Islanders, 13 Hispanic Americans), 18 international. Average age 30. 211 applicants, 43% accepted. In 2009, 38 master's, 1 doctorate awarded. *Entrance requirements:* Additional exam requirements/recommendations for international students: Required—TOEFL. Electronic applications accepted. *Expenses:* Tuition, state resident: part-time $478.25 per credit hour. Tuition, nonresident: part-time $966.50 per credit hour. Part-time tuition and fees vary according to program. *Financial support:* In 2009–10, 11 research assistantships with tuition reimbursements (averaging $6,151 per year), 34 teaching assistantships with tuition reimbursements (averaging $6,251 per year) were awarded; unspecified assistantships also available. Total annual research expenditures: $1.1 million. *Unit head:* Dr. Edmund F. McGarrell, Director, 517-355-2192, Fax: 517-432-1787, E-mail: mcgarrel@msu.edu. *Application contact:* Melissa Christle, Graduate Secretary, 517-353-7133, Fax: 517-432-1787, E-mail: burrier@msu.edu.

National University, Academic Affairs, College of Letters and Sciences, Department of Professional Studies, La Jolla, CA 92037-1011. Offers forensic science (MFS), including criminalistics and investigation; public administration (MPA), including alternative dispute resolution, human resource management, organizational leadership, public finance. Part-time and evening/weekend programs available. Postbaccalaureate distance learning degree programs offered (no on-campus study). *Faculty:* 5 full-time (3 women), 27 part-time/adjunct (7 women). *Students:* 167 full-time (95 women), 246 part-time (133 women); includes 188 minority (71 African Americans, 2 American Indian/Alaska Native, 41 Asian Americans or Pacific Islanders, 74 Hispanic Americans). Average age 38. 284 applicants, 100% accepted, 206 enrolled. In 2009, 104 master's awarded. *Degree requirements:* For master's, thesis. *Entrance requirements:* For master's, interview, minimum GPA of 2.5. Additional exam requirements/recommendations for international students: Required—TOEFL (minimum score 550 paper-based; 213 computer-based; 79 iBT), IELTS (minimum score 6). *Application deadline:* Applications are processed on a rolling basis. Application fee: $60 ($65 for international students). Electronic applications accepted. *Expenses:* Tuition: Part-time $338 per quarter hour. *Financial support:* Career-related internships or fieldwork, institutionally sponsored loans, scholarships/grants, and tuition waivers (partial) available. Support available to part-time students. Financial award application deadline: 6/30; financial award applicants required to submit FAFSA. *Unit head:* Chandrika M. Kelso, Associate Professor and Chair, 858-642-8433, Fax: 858-642-8715, E-mail: ckelso@nu.edu. *Application contact:* Dominick Giovanniello, Associate Regional Dean—San Diego, 800-NAT-UNIV, Fax: 858-541-7792, E-mail: dgiovann@nu.edu.

Nebraska Wesleyan University, University College, Program in Forensic Science, Lincoln, NE 68504-2796. Offers MFS. Part-time and evening/weekend programs available.

Oklahoma State University Center for Health Sciences, Graduate Program in Forensic Sciences, Tulsa, OK 74107-1898. Offers forensic DNA/molecular biology (MS); forensic examination of questioned documents (MFSA, Certificate); forensic pathology (MS); forensic psychology (MS); forensic sciences (MFSA); forensic toxicology (MS). Part-time and evening/weekend programs available. Postbaccalaureate distance learning degree programs offered (no on-campus study). *Degree requirements:* For master's, comprehensive exam (for some programs), thesis (for some programs). *Entrance requirements:* For master's, MAT (MFSA) or GRE General Test, professional experience (MFSA). Additional exam requirements/recommendations for international students: Required—TOEFL (minimum score 600 paper-based; 250 computer-based), TWE (minimum score 5). *Faculty research:* DNA typing, DNA polymorphism, identification through DNA, disease transmission, forensic dentistry, neurotoxicity of HIV, forensic toxicology method development, toxin detection and characterization.

Pace University, Dyson College of Arts and Sciences, Program in Forensic Science, New York, NY 10038. Offers MS. *Students:* 18 full-time (15 women), 35 part-time (31 women); includes 27 minority (11 African Americans, 10 Asian Americans or Pacific Islanders, 6 Hispanic Americans), 1 international. Average age 26. 46 applicants, 70% accepted, 14 enrolled. In 2009, 7 master's awarded. *Entrance requirements:* Additional exam requirements/recommendations for international students: Required—TOEFL. *Application deadline:* For fall admission, 8/1 priority date for domestic students; for spring admission, 12/1 priority date for domestic students. Application fee: $70. Electronic applications accepted. *Expenses:* Tuition: Part-time $954 per credit. Tuition and fees vary according to course load, degree level and program. *Financial support:* Application deadline: 2/15. *Unit head:* Dr. Demos Athanasopolous, Director, 212-346-1502. *Application contact:* Susan Ford-Goldschein, Director of Admissions, 212-346-1652, Fax: 212-346-1585, E-mail: gradnyc@pace.edu.

Philadelphia College of Osteopathic Medicine, Graduate and Professional Programs, Program in Forensic Medicine, Philadelphia, PA 19131-1694. Offers MS. *Entrance requirements:* For master's, minimum GPA of 3.0; coursework in biology, chemistry, anatomy and physiology.

Sam Houston State University, College of Criminal Justice, Huntsville, TX 77341. Offers criminal justice (MS, PhD); criminal justice and criminology (MA); criminal justice management (MS); forensic science (MS); security studies (MS); victim services management (MS). *Faculty:* 22 full-time (4 women). *Students:* 68 full-time (47 women), 170 part-time (69 women); includes 45 minority (10 African Americans, 1 American Indian/Alaska Native, 4 Asian Americans or Pacific Islanders, 30 Hispanic Americans), 34 international. Average age 33. 148 applicants, 88% accepted, 114 enrolled. In 2009, 46 master's, 6 doctorates awarded. *Degree requirements:* For master's, thesis (for some programs); for doctorate, comprehensive exam, thesis/dissertation. *Entrance requirements:* For master's, GRE General Test; for doctorate, GRE General Test, master's degree. Additional exam requirements/recommendations for international students: Required—TOEFL (minimum score 550 paper-based; 213 computer-based; 79 iBT). *Application deadline:* For fall admission, 8/1 for domestic students; for spring admission, 12/1 for domestic students. Applications are processed on a rolling basis. Application fee: $20. *Expenses:* Tuition, state resident: full-time $3690; part-time $205 per credit hour. Tuition, nonresident: full-time $8676; part-time $482 per credit hour. Required fees: $1474. Tuition and fees vary according to course load and campus/location. *Financial support:* Fellowships, research assistantships, teaching assistantships, career-related internships or fieldwork, Federal Work-Study, institutionally sponsored loans, and unspecified assistantships available. Support available to part-time students. Financial award application deadline: 5/31; financial award applicants required to submit FAFSA. *Unit head:* Dr. Vincent Webb, Dean, 936-294-1632, Fax: 936-294-1653, E-mail: vwebb@shsu.edu. *Application contact:* Doris Powell-Pratt, Advisor, 936-294-3637, Fax: 936-294-4055, E-mail: icc_dcp@shsu.edu.

Southeast Missouri State University, School of Graduate Studies, Department of Chemistry, Cape Girardeau, MO 63701-4799. Offers applied chemistry (MNS), including forensic chemistry. Part-time programs available. *Faculty:* 8 full-time (0 women). *Students:* 13 full-time (9 women), 6 part-time (3 women); includes 2 minority (both African Americans), 12 international. Average age 24. 25 applicants, 32% accepted. In 2009, 1 master's awarded. *Degree requirements:* For master's, comprehensive exam (for some programs), thesis (for some programs). *Entrance requirements:* For master's, GRE General Test, minimum GPA of 2.75 for last 30 semester hours of undergraduate science or math courses; 2 letters of recommendation; completed courses with associated labs in organic chemistry, analytical chemistry, chemistry instrumentation or quantitative analysis, and physical chemistry. Additional exam requirements/recommendations for international students: Required—TOEFL (minimum score 550 paper-based; 213 computer-based); Recommended—IELTS (minimum score 6). *Application deadline:* For fall admission, 8/1 for domestic students, 7/1 for international students; for spring admission, 11/21 for domestic students, 11/1 for international students. Applications are processed on a rolling basis. Application fee: $25 ($100 for international students). Electronic applications accepted. *Expenses:* Tuition, state resident: full-time $4266; part-time $237 per credit hour. Tuition, nonresident: full-time $7506; part-time $417 per credit hour. Required fees: $427; $427. *Financial support:* In 2009–10, 8 students received support, including 1 research assistantship with full tuition reimbursement available, 7 teaching assistantships with full tuition reimbursements available (averaging $7,600 per year); unspecified assistantships also available. Financial award applicants required to submit FAFSA. *Faculty research:* Crystallography, trace metal detection, electrochemistry of metalloporphyrins, organic reactions with supported reagents, synthesis of molecules of biological interest. *Unit head:* Dr. Philip W. Crawford, Chairperson and Professor, 573-651-2166, Fax: 573-986-6433, E-mail: pcrawford@semo.edu. *Application contact:* Marsha L. Arant, Senior Administrative Assistant, School of Graduate Studies, 573-651-2192, Fax: 573-651-2001, E-mail: marant@semo.edu.

Southern Utah University, College of Science, Program in Forensic Science, Cedar City, UT 84720-2498. Offers MS. *Faculty:* 4 part-time/adjunct (1 woman). *Students:* 1 part-time (0 women). In 2009, 16 master's awarded. *Application deadline:* Applications are processed on a rolling basis. Application fee: $50 ($65 for international students). Electronic applications accepted. *Unit head:* Dr. Robert Eves, Dean, 435-586-1934, Fax: 435-865-8550, E-mail: eves@suu.edu. *Application contact:* Barbara Rodriguez, Administrative Assistant, 435-586-7920, Fax: 435-865-8550, E-mail: rodriguez@suu.edu.

Stevenson University, Graduate and Professional Studies Programs, Program in Forensic Science, Stevenson, MD 21153. Offers MS. Partnership program with Maryland State Police Forensic Sciences Division. *Entrance requirements:* For master's, bachelor's degree in chemistry, biology, physics, or a related science with a minimum cumulative and science/math GPA of 3.2; course/lab work in general biology, general chemistry, organic chemistry, physics, cell biology, molecular genetics, analytical chemistry, instrumental analysis, human anatomy and physiology, biotechniques, and biochemistry.

Stevenson University, Graduate and Professional Studies Programs, Program in Forensic Studies, Stevenson, MD 21153. Offers forensic accounting (MS); forensic legal professional (MS); information technology (MS); interdisciplinary track (MS); investigations (MS). Postbaccalaureate distance learning degree programs offered (minimal on-campus study). *Degree requirements:* For master's, capstone course.

Syracuse University, College of Arts and Sciences, Program in Forensic Science, Syracuse, NY 13244. Offers MS. Part-time programs available. *Students:* 6 full-time (2 women), 1 (woman) part-time; includes 2 minority (1 African American, 1 Asian American or Pacific Islander). Average age 23. 21 applicants, 90% accepted, 7 enrolled. *Entrance requirements:* For master's, GRE General Test. Additional exam requirements/recommendations for international students: Required—TOEFL (minimum score 100 iBT). *Application deadline:* For fall admission, 2/1 priority date for domestic and international students. Applications are processed on a rolling basis. Application fee: $75. Electronic applications accepted. *Expenses:* Tuition: Full-time $26,808; part-time $1117 per credit. Required fees: $1024. *Financial support:* Application deadline: 1/1. *Unit head:* Dr. Michael Sponsler, Graduate Director, 315-443-4347, E-mail: sponsler@syr.edu. *Application contact:* Benjamin Zender, Information Contact, 315-443-0326, E-mail: brzender@syr.edu.

Towson University, College of Graduate Studies and Research, Program in Forensic Science, Towson, MD 21252-0001. Offers MS. *Entrance requirements:* For master's, minimum GPA of 3.0 for full admission, bachelor's in chemistry or forensic chemistry or related field.

Universidad del Turabo, Graduate Programs, School of Social Sciences and Humanities, Programs in Public Affairs, Program in Forensic Science, Gurabo, PR 00778-3030. Offers MPA. *Students:* 127 full-time (103 women), 31 part-time (26 women); includes 142 Hispanic Americans. Average age 28. 81 applicants, 73% accepted, 45 enrolled. In 2009, 29 master's awarded. *Unit head:* Dr. Marco A. Gil Dela Madrid, Dean, 787-743-7979. *Application contact:* Virginia Gonzalez, Admissions Officer, 787-746-3009.

Forensic Sciences

University at Albany, State University of New York, College of Arts and Sciences, Department of Biological Sciences, Albany, NY 12222-0001. Offers biodiversity, conservation, and policy (MS); ecology, evolution, and behavior (MS, PhD); forensic molecular biology (MS); molecular, cellular, developmental, and neural biology (MS, PhD). *Degree requirements:* For master's, one foreign language; for doctorate, one foreign language, thesis/dissertation. *Entrance requirements:* For master's and doctorate, GRE General Test. Additional exam requirements/recommendations for international students: Required—TOEFL (minimum score 550 paper-based; 213 computer-based). Electronic applications accepted. *Faculty research:* Interferon, neural development, RNA self-splicing, behavioral ecology, DNA repair enzymes.

University of California, Davis, Graduate Studies, Graduate Group in Forensic Science, Davis, CA 95616. Offers MS. *Degree requirements:* For master's, thesis. *Entrance requirements:* Additional exam requirements/recommendations for international students: Required—TOEFL (minimum score 550 paper-based; 213 computer-based), IELTS (minimum score 7). Electronic applications accepted.

University of Central Florida, College of Engineering and Computer Science, Interdisciplinary Program in Digital Forensics, Orlando, FL 32816. Offers MS. *Students:* 10 full-time (2 women), 22 part-time (4 women); includes 4 minority (1 African American, 2 Asian Americans or Pacific Islanders, 1 Hispanic American). *Degree requirements:* For master's, thesis optional. *Application deadline:* For fall admission, 7/15 for domestic students; for spring admission, 12/1 for domestic students. *Expenses:* Tuition, state resident: part-time $306.31 per credit hour. Tuition, nonresident: part-time $1099.01 per credit hour. Part-time tuition and fees vary according to degree level and program. *Financial support:* In 2009–10, 1 research assistantship (averaging $18,000 per year) was awarded. *Unit head:* Dr. Sheau-Dong Lang, Program Coordinator, 407-823-2474, Fax: 407-823-5419, E-mail: lang@eecs.ucf.edu. *Application contact:* Dr. Sheau-Dong Lang, Program Coordinator, 407-823-2474, Fax: 407-823-5419, E-mail: lang@eecs.ucf.edu.

University of Central Florida, College of Engineering and Computer Science, School of Electrical Engineering and Computer Science, Orlando, FL 32816. Offers computer engineering (MS Cp E, PhD), including computer engineering; computer science (MS, PhD); digital forensics (MS); electrical engineering (MSEE, PhD, Certificate), including communications systems (Certificate), electrical engineering (MSEE, PhD), electronic circuits (Certificate). Part-time and evening/weekend programs available. *Faculty:* 59 full-time (6 women), 5 part-time/adjunct (0 women). *Students:* 314 full-time (60 women), 302 part-time (47 women); includes 118 minority (24 African Americans, 2 American Indian/Alaska Native, 40 Asian Americans or Pacific Islanders, 52 Hispanic Americans), 202 international. Average age 29. 657 applicants, 57% accepted, 193 enrolled. In 2009, 106 master's, 25 doctorates awarded. *Degree requirements:* For master's, thesis or alternative; for doctorate, thesis/dissertation, departmental qualifying exam, candidacy exam. *Entrance requirements:* For master's, GRE General Test, minimum GPA of 3.0 in last 60 hours; for doctorate, GRE General Test, minimum GPA of 3.5 in last 60 hours. Additional exam requirements/recommendations for international students: Required—TOEFL. *Application deadline:* For fall admission, 7/15 priority date for domestic students; for spring admission, 12/1 priority date for domestic students. Application fee: $30. Electronic applications accepted. *Expenses:* Tuition, state resident: part-time $306.31 per credit hour. Tuition, nonresident: part-time $1099.01 per credit hour. Part-time tuition and fees vary according to degree level and program. *Financial support:* In 2009–10, 175 students received support, including 41 fellowships with partial tuition reimbursements available (averaging $8,800 per year), 153 research assistantships with partial tuition reimbursements available (averaging $9,700 per year), 43 teaching assistantships with partial tuition reimbursements available (averaging $8,700 per year); career-related internships or fieldwork, Federal Work-Study, institutionally sponsored loans, tuition waivers (partial), and unspecified assistantships also available. Financial award application deadline: 3/1; financial award applicants required to submit FAFSA. *Faculty research:* Communication theory, solid-state devices, electromagnetics, electro-optics, digital signal processing. *Unit head:* Dr. Issa Batarseh, Director, 407-823-0189, Fax: 407-823-5419, E-mail: batarseh@mail.ucf.edu. *Application contact:* Dr. Issa Batarseh, Director, 407-823-0189, Fax: 407-823-5419, E-mail: batarseh@mail.ucf.edu.

University of Central Florida, College of Health and Public Affairs, Department of Criminal Justice and Legal Studies, Orlando, FL 32816. Offers corrections leadership (Certificate); crime analysis (Certificate); criminal justice (MS); juvenile justice leadership (Certificate); police leadership (Certificate). Part-time and evening/weekend programs available. *Faculty:* 36 full-time (13 women), 38 part-time/adjunct (8 women). *Students:* 84 full-time (58 women), 117 part-time (65 women); includes 68 minority (37 African Americans, 9 Asian Americans or Pacific Islanders, 22 Hispanic Americans), 2 international. Average age 29. 165 applicants, 82% accepted, 93 enrolled. In 2009, 81 master's, 19 other advanced degrees awarded. *Degree requirements:* For master's, thesis or alternative. *Entrance requirements:* For master's, GRE General Test, minimum GPA of 3.0. Additional exam requirements/recommendations for international students: Required—TOEFL. *Application deadline:* For fall admission, 7/15 for domestic students; for spring admission, 4/15 for domestic students. Electronic applications accepted. *Expenses:* Tuition, state resident: part-time $306.31 per credit hour. Tuition, nonresident: part-time $1099.01 per credit hour. Part-time tuition and fees vary according to degree level and program. *Financial support:* In 2009–10, 8 students received support, including 4 fellowships with partial tuition reimbursements available (averaging $10,000 per year), 1 research assistantship with partial tuition reimbursement available (averaging $6,400 per year), 3 teaching assistantships with partial tuition reimbursements available (averaging $6,400 per year); career-related internships or fieldwork, Federal Work-Study, institutionally sponsored loans, tuition waivers (partial), and unspecified assistantships also available. Financial award application deadline: 3/1; financial award applicants required to submit FAFSA. *Unit head:* Dr. Robert Langworthy, Chair, 407-823-5929, E-mail: rlangwor@mail.ucf.edu. *Application contact:* Dr. Robert Langworthy, Chair, 407-823-5929, E-mail: rlangwor@mail.ucf.edu.

University of Central Florida, College of Sciences, Department of Chemistry, Orlando, FL 32816. Offers chemistry (PhD); computer forensics (Certificate); industrial chemistry (MS). Part-time and evening/weekend programs available. *Faculty:* 24 full-time (1 woman), 4 part-time/adjunct (1 woman). *Students:* 70 full-time (28 women), 12 part-time (4 women); includes 15 minority (2 African Americans, 5 Asian Americans or Pacific Islanders, 8 Hispanic Americans), 35 international. Average age 30. 91 applicants, 30% accepted, 7 enrolled. In 2009, 4 master's, 3 doctorates awarded. *Degree requirements:* For master's, thesis, final exam. *Entrance requirements:* For master's, GRE General Test, minimum GPA of 3.0 in last 60 hours. Additional exam requirements/recommendations for international students: Required—TOEFL. *Application deadline:* For fall admission, 7/15 for domestic students; for spring admission, 12/1 for domestic students. Application fee: $30. Electronic applications accepted. *Expenses:* Tuition, state resident: part-time $306.31 per credit hour. Tuition, nonresident: part-time $1099.01 per credit hour. Part-time tuition and fees vary according to degree level and program. *Financial support:* In 2009–10, 61 students received support, including 12 fellowships with partial tuition reimbursements available (averaging $5,000 per year), 19 research assistantships with partial tuition reimbursements available (averaging $11,600 per year), 39 teaching assistantships with partial tuition reimbursements available (averaging $11,600 per year); career-related internships or fieldwork, Federal Work-Study, institutionally sponsored loans, tuition waivers (partial), and unspecified assistantships also available. Financial award application deadline: 3/1; financial award applicants required to submit FAFSA. *Faculty research:* Physical and synthetic organic chemistry, lasers, polymers, biochemical action of pesticides, environmental analysis. *Unit head:* Dr. Kevin D. Belfield, Chair, 407-823-2246, Fax: 407-823-2252, E-mail: kbelfield@mail.ucf.edu. *Application contact:* Dr. Kevin D. Belfield, Chair, 407-823-2246, Fax: 407-823-2252, E-mail: kbelfield@mail.ucf.edu.

University of Florida, College of Pharmacy, Programs in Forensic Science, Gainesville, FL 32611. Offers forensic DNA and serology (MS, Certificate); forensic drug chemistry (MS, Certificate); forensic toxicology (MS, Certificate).

University of Illinois at Chicago, College of Pharmacy and Graduate College, Graduate Programs in Pharmacy, Program in Forensic Science, Chicago, IL 60607-7128. Offers MS. *Degree requirements:* For master's, thesis. *Entrance requirements:* For master's, GRE General Test. Additional exam requirements/recommendations for international students: Required—TOEFL. *Faculty research:* Interpretation of physical evidence, utilization of physical evidence, analytical toxicology of controlled substances, automated fingerprint systems, dye and ink characterizations.

University of Nevada, Las Vegas, Graduate College, Greenspun College of Urban Affairs, School of Social Work, Las Vegas, NV 89154-5032. Offers forensic social work (Advanced Certificate); social work (MSW); MSW/JD. *Accreditation:* CSWE. *Faculty:* 14 full-time (11 women), 11 part-time/adjunct (7 women). *Students:* 116 full-time (97 women), 66 part-time (51 women); includes 60 minority (20 African Americans, 2 American Indian/Alaska Native, 10 Asian Americans or Pacific Islanders, 28 Hispanic Americans), 1 international. Average age 34. 206 applicants, 45% accepted, 65 enrolled. In 2009, 66 master's, 3 other advanced degrees awarded. *Degree requirements:* For master's, comprehensive exam, thesis optional. *Entrance requirements:* Additional exam requirements/recommendations for international students: Required—TOEFL (minimum score 550 paper-based; 231 computer-based; 80 iBT), IELTS (minimum score 7). *Application deadline:* For fall admission, 2/1 priority date for domestic and international students. Applications are processed on a rolling basis. Application fee: $60 ($95 for international students). Electronic applications accepted. *Financial support:* In 2009–10, 4 students received support, including 4 teaching assistantships with partial tuition reimbursements available (averaging $10,000 per year); institutionally sponsored loans, scholarships/grants, health care benefits, and unspecified assistantships also available. Financial award application deadline: 3/1. *Faculty research:* Child welfare, mental health, substance abuse, youth services and wrap-around services, poverty and TANF. *Unit head:* Dr. Joanne Thompson, Director/ Professor, 702-895-0521, Fax: 702-895-4079, E-mail: joanne.thompson@unlv.edu. *Application contact:* Graduate College Admissions Evaluator, 702-895-3320, Fax: 702-895-4180, E-mail: gradcollege@unlv.edu.

University of New Haven, Graduate School, Henry C. Lee College of Criminal Justice and Forensic Sciences, Program in Criminal Justice, West Haven, CT 06516-1916. Offers crime analysis (MS); criminal justice management (MS); forensic computer investigation (MS, Certificate); forensic psychology (MS); victim advocacy and services management (Certificate); victimology (MS). Part-time and evening/weekend programs available. *Faculty:* 8 full-time (2 women), 10 part-time/adjunct (4 women). *Students:* 25 full-time (17 women), 37 part-time (26 women); includes 20 minority (12 African Americans, 1 Asian American or Pacific Islander, 7 Hispanic Americans), 1 international. Average age 25. 62 applicants, 85% accepted, 28 enrolled. In 2009, 30 master's awarded. *Degree requirements:* For master's, thesis or alternative. *Entrance requirements:* Additional exam requirements/recommendations for international students: Required—TOEFL (minimum score 520 paper-based; 190 computer-based; 70 iBT), IELTS (minimum score 5.5). *Application deadline:* For fall admission, 5/31 for international students; for winter admission, 10/15 for international students; for spring admission, 1/15 for international students. Applications are processed on a rolling basis. Application fee: $50. Electronic applications accepted. *Expenses:* Tuition: Part-time $700 per credit. Required fees: $45 per term. One-time fee: $390 part-time. *Financial support:* Research assistantships with partial tuition reimbursements, teaching assistantships with partial tuition reimbursements, career-related internships or fieldwork, Federal Work-Study, scholarships/grants, tuition waivers, and unspecified assistantships available. Support available to part-time students. Financial award applicants required to submit FAFSA. *Unit head:* Dr. James J. Cassidy, Coordinator, 203-932-7374. *Application contact:* Eloise Gormley, Director of Graduate Admissions, 203-932-7449, Fax: 203-932-7137, E-mail: gradinfo@newhaven.edu.

University of New Haven, Graduate School, Henry C. Lee College of Criminal Justice and Forensic Sciences, Program in Fire Science, West Haven, CT 06516-1916. Offers emergency management (Certificate); fire administration (MS); fire science technology (Certificate); fire/arson investigation (MS, Certificate); forensic science/fire science (Certificate); public safety management (MS); public safety management (Certificate). Part-time and evening/weekend programs available. *Faculty:* 2 full-time (0 women). *Students:* 14 part-time (4 women); includes 1 minority (Hispanic American), 1 international. Average age 33. 6 applicants, 83% accepted, 3 enrolled. In 2009, 6 master's, 4 other advanced degrees awarded. *Degree requirements:* For master's, thesis or alternative. *Entrance requirements:* Additional exam requirements/recommendations for international students: Required—TOEFL (minimum score 520 paper-based; 190 computer-based; 70 iBT); Recommended—IELTS (minimum score 5.5). *Application deadline:* For fall admission, 5/31 for international students; for winter admission, 10/15 for international students; for spring admission, 1/15 for international students. Applications are processed on a rolling basis. Application fee: $50. Electronic applications accepted. *Expenses:* Tuition: Part-time $700 per credit. Required fees: $45 per term. One-time fee: $390 part-time. *Financial support:* Research assistantships with partial tuition reimbursements, teaching assistantships with partial tuition reimbursements, career-related internships or fieldwork, Federal Work-Study, scholarships/grants, tuition waivers, and unspecified assistantships available. Support available to part-time students. Financial award applicants required to submit FAFSA. *Unit head:* Robert E. Massicotte, Director, 203-932-7424. *Application contact:* Eloise Gormley, Director of Graduate Admissions, 203-932-7449, Fax: 203-932-7137, E-mail: gradinfo@newhaven.edu.

University of New Haven, Graduate School, Henry C. Lee College of Criminal Justice and Forensic Sciences, Program in Forensic Science, West Haven, CT 06516-1916. Offers advanced investigation (MS, Certificate); criminalistics (MS, Certificate); fire science (MS). Part-time and evening/weekend programs available. *Faculty:* 6 full-time (1 woman), 2 part-time/adjunct (0 women). *Students:* 83 full-time (65 women), 20 part-time (9 women); includes 15 minority (8 African Americans, 3 Asian Americans or Pacific Islanders, 4 Hispanic Americans), 3 international. Average age 26. 124 applicants, 72% accepted, 47 enrolled. In 2009, 34 master's, 2 other advanced degrees awarded. *Degree requirements:* For master's, thesis or alternative. *Entrance requirements:* For master's, GRE. Additional exam requirements/recommendations for international students: Required—TOEFL (minimum score 520 paper-based; 190 computer-based; 70 iBT); Recommended—IELTS (minimum score 5.5). *Application deadline:* For fall admission, 5/31 for international students; for winter admission, 10/15 for international students; for spring admission, 1/15 for international students. Applications are processed on a rolling basis. Application fee: $50. Electronic applications accepted. *Expenses:* Tuition: Part-time $700 per credit. Required fees: $45 per term. One-time fee: $390 part-time. *Financial support:* Research assistantships with partial tuition reimbursements, teaching assistantships with partial tuition reimbursements, career-related internships or fieldwork, Federal Work-Study, scholarships/grants, tuition waivers, and unspecified assistantships available. Support available to part-time students. Financial award applicants required to submit FAFSA. *Unit head:* Dr. Timothy M. Palmbach, Coordinator, 203-932-7116. *Application contact:* Dr. Timothy M. Palmbach, Coordinator, 203-932-7116.

University of North Texas Health Science Center at Fort Worth, Graduate School of Biomedical Sciences, Fort Worth, TX 76107-2699. Offers anatomy and cell biology (MS, PhD); biochemistry and molecular biology (MS, PhD); biomedical sciences (MS, PhD); biotechnology (MS); forensic genetics (MS); integrative physiology (MS, PhD); medical science (MS); microbiology and immunology (MS, PhD); pharmacology (MS, PhD); science education (MS); DO/MS; DO/PhD. Terminal master's awarded for partial completion of doctoral program. *Degree requirements:* For master's, thesis; for doctorate, thesis/dissertation. *Entrance requirements:* For master's and doctorate, GRE General Test. Additional exam requirements/recommendations for international students: Required—TOEFL. *Expenses:* Contact institution. *Faculty research:* Alzheimer's disease, aging, eye diseases, cancer, cardiovascular disease.

University of Rhode Island, Graduate School, College of Arts and Sciences, Department of Computer Science and Statistics, Kingston, RI 02881. Offers applied mathematics (PhD), including computer science, statistics; computer science (MS, PhD); digital forensics (Graduate Certificate); statistics (MS). Part-time programs available. *Faculty:* 10 full-time (3 women), 3 part-time/adjunct (1 woman). *Students:* 18 full-time (5 women), 20 part-time (6 women); includes 4 minority (2 Asian Americans or Pacific Islanders, 2 Hispanic Americans), 7

Forensic Sciences

University of Rhode Island (continued)
international. In 2009, 7 master's awarded. *Degree requirements:* For master's, comprehensive exam (for some programs), thesis optional; for doctorate, comprehensive exam, thesis/dissertation. *Entrance requirements:* For master's and doctorate, GRE, 2 letters of recommendation. Additional exam requirements/recommendations for international students: Required—TOEFL (minimum score 550 paper-based; 213 computer-based). *Application deadline:* For fall admission, 7/15 for domestic students, 2/1 for international students; for spring admission, 11/15 for domestic students, 7/15 for international students. Application fee: $65. Electronic applications accepted. *Expenses:* Tuition, state resident: full-time $8828; part-time $490 per credit hour. Tuition, nonresident: full-time $22,100; part-time $1228 per credit hour. Required fees: $1118; $57 per semester. Tuition and fees vary according to program. *Financial support:* In 2009–10, 10 teaching assistantships with full and partial tuition reimbursements (averaging $11,094 per year) were awarded. Financial award application deadline: 2/1; financial award applicants required to submit FAFSA. *Faculty research:* Bioinformatics, computer and digital forensics, behavioral model of pedestrian dynamics, real-time distributed object computing, cryptography. Total annual research expenditures: $694,026. *Unit head:* Dr. James G. Kowalski, Chair, 401-874-2510, Fax: 401-874-4617, E-mail: kowalski@cs.uri.edu. *Application contact:* Dr. Victor Fay-Wolfe, Director of Graduate Studies, 401-874-2701, Fax: 401-874-4617, E-mail: wolfe@cs.uri.edu.

Virginia Commonwealth University, Graduate School, College of Humanities and Sciences, Department of Forensic Science, Richmond, VA 23284-9005. Offers MS.

West Virginia University, Eberly College of Arts and Sciences, Department of Biology, Morgantown, WV 26506. Offers cell and molecular biology (MS, PhD); environmental and evolutionary biology (MS, PhD); forensic biology (MS, PhD); genomic biology (MS, PhD); neurobiology (MS, PhD). Terminal master's awarded for partial completion of doctoral program. *Degree requirements:* For master's, thesis, final exam; for doctorate, thesis/dissertation, preliminary and final exams. *Entrance requirements:* For master's, GRE General Test, GRE Subject Test, minimum GPA of 3.0; for doctorate, GRE General Test, minimum GPA of 3.0. Additional exam requirements/recommendations for international students: Required—TOEFL. *Faculty research:* Environmental biology, genetic engineering, developmental biology, global change, biodiversity.

NOVA SOUTHEASTERN UNIVERSITY

Criminal Justice Institute

Programs of Study

The Nova Southeastern University (NSU) Criminal Justice Institute offers two online graduate degree programs: the Master of Science in criminal justice (36 credits required) and Master of Human Services in child protection (42 credits required). These programs challenge students to examine and understand complex theory and concerns surrounding behavioral issues, prevention, and intervention at the local, state, and federal levels. The program design begins with core courses that establish a foundation of knowledge, which is then augmented by several specialty tracks. These concentrations allow students to focus their studies in a particular area of interest and develop the advanced analytical skills necessary to become effective researchers and professionals within their chosen fields.

Courses are offered during three terms: fall, winter, and summer. The curriculum in each program consists of core specialization and elective courses. A typical student's time commitment is approximately 2 years in each program, averaging two courses per semester. Students who have more time to commit to studies may choose to take additional courses each semester in order to finish sooner.

Through online technology, students from agencies and professional environments all over the world share the classroom. For the past forty-six years, Nova Southeastern University has been a leader in innovative educational delivery. Online learning is immediate and intensely interactive. It allows learning to reach beyond traditional boundaries and promotes a spirited exchange of knowledge, experience, and perspective. Students are able to collaborate with professionals who are actively involved in the field and form close bonds with their peers as well as with their professors, who serve as valued guides and mentors. Typically, instructors are experts in their respective fields and guide their students in developing the skills necessary to reach their goals, including teaching, research, and professional employment.

Research Facilities

Nova Southeastern University has a complete library located on the main campus. It is accessible to all students in the master's degree program. The online format of the program enables students to conduct online research through the Internet and research service providers. The library has the capacity to house 1.4 million volumes of reference materials, making it the largest in Florida. The University Computing Center provides data processing facilities and services to meet the instructional, research, and administrative needs of the University and is available to qualified students for computer-oriented course work.

Financial Aid

Nova Southeastern University's Office of Student Financial Assistance administers comprehensive federal, state, institutional, and private financial aid programs. Students interested in receiving a financial aid packet should contact the Office of Student Financial Assistance at 954-262-3380 or 800-806-3680 (toll-free) or via the Internet at http://www.nova.edu/financialaid/index.html. It is recommended that students apply for financial aid well in advance of the date funds will be needed. Awards are made only for the academic year. Applications are generally available each January for the following academic year. Nova Southeastern University offers scholarships, Federal Stafford Student Loans, Federal Perkins Loans, and Federal Work-Study Program positions for students who meet eligibility requirements.

Cost of Study

Tuition costs $570 per credit hour. There is a registration fee of $50 per semester, books and supplies cost $80 to $200 per course, and a student services fee of $750 is assessed per year for full-time students and/or a prorated amount for part-time students. The application for degree fee is $75. Fees are subject to change without notice.

Living and Housing Costs

The degree programs offered through the NSU Criminal Justice Institute are completely online. The programs are available to qualified students around the world who have Internet access.

Student Group

While some students have an interest in pursuing a master's degree in this field without prior experience, most students enrolled in the program are employed in some capacity in their desired profession.

Location

The main campus of Nova Southeastern University is located on a 300-acre site in Fort Lauderdale, Florida. Fort Lauderdale is part of Broward County, a principal coastal area in south Florida, and a rapidly growing community for business, industrial, electronics, and computer opportunities. NSU is 10 miles inland from the Atlantic Ocean and is easily accessible from major highways, including I-75, I-95, I-595, the Sawgrass Expressway, and Florida's Turnpike. The climate is subtropical and has an average year-round temperature of 75 degrees. Natural areas for outdoor activities such as sailing, fishing, golf, tennis, and swimming are easily and quickly accessible from the University. With tourism as a major industry, Fort Lauderdale provides some of the best in shopping, dining, and cultural offerings, which include concerts, opera, ballet, museums, theater, and professional sporting events.

The University and The Institute

Nova Southeastern University is an independent, nonsectarian, fully accredited, coeducational university chartered by the state of Florida in 1964. As an acknowledged leader in field-based degree programs, NSU offers courses of study leading to bachelor's, master's, educational specialist, and doctoral degrees. Undergraduate and graduate programs are offered in allied health (physical therapy, physician assistant studies, and occupational therapy), business, computer sciences, criminal justice, dental medicine, education, human services, law, marine, medicine, medical education, optometry, osteopathic medicine, pharmacy, psychology, public administration, and social sciences. NSU has a total enrollment of more than 26,000 students, including over 6,220 undergraduates.

The Institute was established in 2001 to provide a supportive academic and professional environment for faculty members and graduate students utilizing the convenience of an online format.

Applying

To be admitted to the program, applicants must complete all parts of the admissions application form; submit an official transcript for each postsecondary school attended; provide a personal statement 150 to 300 words in length, indicating their goals in pursuing a degree at the graduate level; provide three letters of recommendation; and include a nonrefundable $50 application fee.

Correspondence and Information

Enrollment Processing Services (EPS)
Attention: Criminal Justice Institute
Nova Southeastern University
3301 College Avenue
P.O. Box 299000
Fort Lauderdale, Florida 33329-9905
Phone: 954-262-7001
800-541-NOVA (6682; toll-free)
E-mail: cji@nova.edu
Web site: http://www.cji.nova.edu

Nova Southeastern University

THE FACULTY AND THEIR RESEARCH

Catherine Arcabascio, Professor NSU Shephard Broad Law School and CJI Course Director; J.D., Boston College, 1987. Co-Founder and Director of the Florida Innocence Project.

Richard Beauchamp, Adjunct Professor; J.D., Stetson, 1984. Practices in the areas of insurance, real estate, commercial, and construction litigation and nursing home/health-care litigation.

Warren Brown, Adjunct Assistant Professor and Detective; Ph.D., Nova Southeastern, 2000; certified law enforcement officer. Conflict resolution, cultural diversity, defense tactics, hostage negotiation, drug abuse resistance education, gang resistance, investigation and interrogations.

Johnny Burris, Professor NSU Shephard Broad Law School and CJI Course Director; J.D., LL.M., Columbia, 1984. Criminal procedure, constitutional law, administrative law.

Frank De Piano, University Provost, Vice President of Academic Affairs, Chair, and CJI Course Director; Ph.D., South Carolina, 1980. Clinical psychology.

James Nardozzi, Adjunct Assistant Professor and Deputy Chief of Police; D.P.A., Nova Southeastern, 2003; certified law enforcement officer. Police administration and management, criminal investigation, white-collar crime, criminal justice.

Irving Rosenbaum, Vice Chancellor and Provost, Health Professions, and CJI Course Director; D.P.A., Nova Southeastern, 1984. Town administrator, city manager, consultant, research analyst, management analyst.

Rae Shearn, Esq., Adjunct Professor; former division chief prosecutor for Janet Reno. Currently, Shearn practices criminal defense in state and federal courts in the area of white-collar crime, complex RICO prosecutions, narcotic offenses, death-penalty litigation, and criminal defense for all other criminal prosecution.

Vincent Van Hasselt, Professor, CJI Course Director, and Professor for Center for Psychological Studies; Ph.D., Pittsburgh, 1979; certified law enforcement officer. Interpersonal violence, police psychology, criminal investigative analysis (psychological profiling), apprehension, interviewing and interrogation techniques, behavioral criminology.

George Yacoubian, Adjunct Assistant Professor and Director of Research; Ph.D., Madison, 2001. Drug treatment, drug prevention, drug-testing technology, genocide.

Section 19
Economics

This section contains a directory of institutions offering graduate work in economics, followed by in-depth entries submitted by institutions that chose to prepare detailed program descriptions. Additional information about programs listed in the directory but not augmented by an in-depth entry may be obtained by writing directly to the dean of a graduate school or chair of a department at the address given in the directory.

For programs offering related work, see also in this book *Family and Consumer Sciences, Political Science and International Affairs,* and *Public, Regional, and Industrial Affairs.* In the other guides in this series:

Graduate Programs in the Physical Sciences, Mathematics, Agricultural Sciences, the Environment & Natural Resources

See *Agricultural and Food Sciences* and *Mathematical Sciences*

Graduate Programs in Engineering & Applied Sciences

See *Computer Science and Information Technology; Geological, Mineral/Mining, and Petroleum Engineering;* and *Industrial Engineering*

Graduate Programs in Business, Education, Health, Information Studies, Law & Social Work

See *Business Administration and Management*

CONTENTS

Program Directories

Agricultural Economics and Agribusiness 724
Applied Economics 729
Economic Development 732
Economics 735
International Economics 756
Mineral Economics 757

Close-Up and Display

University of California, Riverside (Display) 747
The University of Texas at Dallas 759

See also:

Indiana University Bloomington—Public Affairs 1191

Agricultural Economics and Agribusiness

Alabama Agricultural and Mechanical University, School of Graduate Studies, School of Agricultural and Environmental Sciences, Department of Agribusiness, Huntsville, AL 35811. Offers MS. Part-time programs available. *Degree requirements:* For master's, thesis (for some programs). *Entrance requirements:* For master's, GRE General Test. Additional exam requirements/recommendations for international students: Required—TOEFL (minimum score 500 paper-based; 173 computer-based; 61 iBT). Electronic applications accepted. *Faculty research:* Farm economics.

Alcorn State University, School of Graduate Studies, School of Agriculture and Applied Science, Alcorn State, MS 39096-7500. Offers agricultural economics (MS Ag); agronomy (MS Ag); animal science (MS Ag). *Degree requirements:* For master's, thesis optional. *Faculty research:* Aquatic systems, dairy herd improvement, fruit production, alternative farming practices.

American University of Beirut, Graduate Programs, Faculty of Agricultural and Food Sciences, Beirut, Lebanon. Offers agricultural economics (MS); animal sciences (MS); ecosystem management (MSES); food technology (MS); irrigation (MS); mechanization (MS); nutrition (MS); plant protection (MS); plant science (MS); poultry science (MS); soils (MS). Part-time programs available. *Degree requirements:* For master's, one foreign language, comprehensive exam, thesis (for some programs). *Entrance requirements:* For master's, letter of recommendation. Additional exam requirements/recommendations for international students: Required—TOEFL (minimum score 600 paper-based; 250 computer-based; 100 iBT), IELTS (minimum score 7.5). *Faculty research:* Sustainable animal systems/agriculture; natural resource management; community nutrition, obesity and food safety; integrated pest management; ecosystem management.

Arizona State University, Graduate College, W.P. Carey School of Business, Morrison School of Management and Agribusiness, Tempe, AZ 85287. Offers agribusiness (MS). Part-time and evening/weekend programs available. *Degree requirements:* For master's, thesis, oral defense. *Entrance requirements:* For master's, GMAT, GRE General Test, MAT, minimum GPA of 3.0, 3 letters of recommendation, resume. Additional exam requirements/recommendations for international students: Required—TOEFL (minimum score 550 paper-based; 213 computer-based); Recommended—TWE. Electronic applications accepted. *Faculty research:* Agribusiness marketing, management and financial structuring.

Arizona State University, Graduate College, W.P. Carey School of Business, Program in Business Administration, Tempe, AZ 85287. Offers agribusiness (PhD); business administration (MBA); finance (MBA, PhD); health sector management (MBA); information systems (PhD); management (MBA, PhD); marketing (MBA, PhD); supply chain management (MBA, PhD); JD/MBA; MBA/M Arch; MBA/MHSM. *Accreditation:* AACSB. *Degree requirements:* For master's, thesis optional; for doctorate, thesis/dissertation. *Entrance requirements:* For master's, GMAT.

Auburn University, Graduate School, College of Agriculture, Department of Agricultural Economics and Rural Sociology, Auburn University, AL 36849. Offers agricultural economics (M Ag, MS); applied economics (PhD). Part-time programs available. *Faculty:* 18 full-time (3 women). *Students:* 28 full-time (9 women), 7 part-time (3 women); includes 2 minority (1 African American, 1 Asian American or Pacific Islander), 24 international. Average age 31. 55 applicants, 55% accepted, 9 enrolled. In 2009, 5 master's awarded. *Degree requirements:* For master's, thesis (for some programs); for doctorate, thesis/dissertation. *Entrance requirements:* For master's and doctorate, GRE General Test. *Application deadline:* For fall admission, 7/7 for domestic students; for spring admission, 11/24 for domestic students. Applications are processed on a rolling basis. Application fee: $50 ($60 for international students). Electronic applications accepted. *Expenses:* Tuition, state resident: full-time $6240. Tuition, nonresident: full-time $18,720. International tuition: $18,938 full-time. Required fees: $492. Tuition and fees vary according to course load, program and reciprocity agreements. *Financial support:* Research assistantships, teaching assistantships, Federal Work-Study available. Support available to part-time students. Financial award application deadline: 3/15; financial award applicants required to submit FAFSA. *Faculty research:* Farm management, agricultural marketing, production economics, resource economics, agricultural finance. *Unit head:* Dr. Curtis M. Jolly, Chair, 334-844-4800. *Application contact:* Dr. George Flowers, Dean of the Graduate School, 334-844-2125.

California Polytechnic State University, San Luis Obispo, College of Agriculture, Food and Environmental Sciences, Department of Agribusiness, San Luis Obispo, CA 93407. Offers MS. Part-time programs available. *Faculty:* 2 full-time (1 woman), 1 part-time/adjunct (0 women). *Students:* 4 full-time (1 woman), 3 part-time (1 woman). Average age 28. 9 applicants, 56% accepted, 4 enrolled. In 2009, 1 master's awarded. *Degree requirements:* For master's, comprehensive exam, thesis. *Entrance requirements:* For master's, GRE General Test (50th percentile), minimum GPA of 2.75 in last 90 quarter units of course work. Additional exam requirements/recommendations for international students: Required—TOEFL (minimum score 550 paper-based; 213 computer-based), or IELTS (minimum score 6). *Application deadline:* For fall admission, 2/1 for domestic students, 11/30 for international students; for winter admission, 11/1 for domestic students, 6/30 for international students; for spring admission, 2/1 for domestic students. Applications are processed on a rolling basis. Application fee: $55. Electronic applications accepted. *Expenses:* Tuition, nonresident: full-time $11,160; part-time $248 per unit. Required fees: $7134; $1553 per quarter. *Financial support:* Fellowships, research assistantships, teaching assistantships, career-related internships or fieldwork, Federal Work-Study, institutionally sponsored loans, scholarships/grants, and unspecified assistantships available. Support available to part-time students. Financial award application deadline: 3/2; financial award applicants required to submit FAFSA. *Faculty research:* Agribusiness management, commodity marketing, international and domestic agribusiness. *Unit head:* Dr. James Ahern, Graduate Coordinator, 805-756-5030, Fax: 805-756-5040, E-mail: jahern@calpoly.edu. *Application contact:* Dr. Mark Shelton, Associate Dean/Graduate Coordinator, 805-756-2161, Fax: 805-756-6577, E-mail: mshelton@calpoly.edu.

Colorado State University, Graduate School, College of Agricultural Sciences, Department of Agricultural and Resource Economics, Fort Collins, CO 80523-1172. Offers MS, PhD. Part-time programs available. Postbaccalaureate distance learning degree programs offered (minimal on-campus study). *Faculty:* 16 full-time (3 women). *Students:* 37 full-time (20 women), 13 part-time (6 women); includes 4 minority (1 American Indian/Alaska Native, 1 Asian American or Pacific Islander, 2 Hispanic Americans), 11 international. Average age 28. 70 applicants, 90% accepted, 16 enrolled. In 2009, 5 master's, 3 doctorates awarded. Terminal master's awarded for partial completion of doctoral program. *Degree requirements:* For master's, thesis; for doctorate, comprehensive exam, thesis/dissertation. *Entrance requirements:* For master's, GRE General Test, minimum GPA of 3.0, bachelor's degree, 3 letters of recommendation; for doctorate, GRE General Test, minimum GPA of 3.0, bachelor's degree, 3 letters of recommendation, statement of purpose. Additional exam requirements/recommendations for international students: Required—TOEFL (minimum score 550 paper-based; 213 computer-based; 80 iBT). Application fee: $50. Electronic applications accepted. *Expenses:* Tuition, state resident: full-time $6434; part-time $359.10 per credit. Tuition, nonresident: full-time $18,116; part-time $1006.45 per credit. Required fees: $1496; $83 per credit. *Financial support:* In 2009–10, 29 students received support, including 1 fellowship with partial tuition reimbursement available (averaging $32,500 per year), 22 research assistantships with full tuition reimbursements available (averaging $11,805 per year), 6 teaching assistantships with full tuition reimbursements available (averaging $8,565 per year); Federal Work-Study, unspecified assistantships, and first-year fellowships also available. *Faculty research:* Agricultural production economics, marketing and agribusiness economics, international development, natural resource economics, environmental economics. Total annual research expenditures: $2 million. *Unit head:* Stephen P. Davies, Chair, 970-491-6955, Fax: 970-491-2067, E-mail: stephen.davies@colostate.edu. *Application contact:* Barbara A. Brown, Program Assistant, 970-491-6955, Fax: 970-491-2067, E-mail: barbara.brown@colostate.edu.

Cornell University, Graduate School, Graduate Fields of Agriculture and Life Sciences, Field of International Agriculture and Rural Development, Ithaca, NY 14853-0001. Offers international agriculture and development (MPS). *Faculty:* 53 full-time (10 women). *Students:* 15 full-time (7 women); includes 5 minority (1 American Indian/Alaska Native, 2 Asian Americans or Pacific Islanders, 2 Hispanic Americans), 3 international. Average age 34. 23 applicants, 52% accepted, 6 enrolled. In 2009, 25 master's awarded. *Degree requirements:* For master's, project paper. *Entrance requirements:* For master's, GRE General Test (recommended), 2 years of development experience, 2 letters of recommendation. Additional exam requirements/recommendations for international students: Required—TOEFL (minimum score 550 paper-based; 213 computer-based; 77 iBT). *Application deadline:* For fall admission, 3/1 for domestic students. Application fee: $70. Electronic applications accepted. *Expenses:* Tuition: Full-time $29,500. Required fees: $70. Full-time tuition and fees vary according to degree level, program and student level. *Financial support:* In 2009–10, 4 students received support; fellowships with full tuition reimbursements available, research assistantships with full tuition reimbursements available, teaching assistantships with full tuition reimbursements available, institutionally sponsored loans, scholarships/grants, health care benefits, tuition waivers (full and partial), and unspecified assistantships available. Financial award applicants required to submit FAFSA. *Unit head:* Director of Graduate Studies, 607-255-3037, Fax: 607-255-1005. *Application contact:* Graduate Field Assistant, 607-255-3035, Fax: 607-255-1005, E-mail: mpsiard@cornell.edu.

Delaware Valley College, Program in Business Administration (MBA), Doylestown, PA 18901-2697. Offers accounting (MBA); food and agribusiness (MBA); general business (MBA); online global executive leadership (MBA). Part-time and evening/weekend programs available. Postbaccalaureate distance learning degree programs offered (no on-campus study). *Faculty:* 24 part-time/adjunct (10 women). *Students:* 25 full-time (16 women), 74 part-time (37 women); includes 7 minority (4 African Americans, 2 Asian Americans or Pacific Islanders, 1 Hispanic American). Average age 37. 18 applicants, 100% accepted, 18 enrolled. In 2009, 12 master's awarded. *Entrance requirements:* For master's, minimum undergraduate GPA of 3.0. *Application deadline:* Applications are processed on a rolling basis. Application fee: $50. *Expenses:* Contact institution. *Financial support:* Applicants required to submit FAFSA. *Unit head:* Thomas Kennedy, Director of MBA Program, 215-489-2322, E-mail: thomas.kennedy@delval.edu. *Application contact:* Pamela Heffner, Graduate and Continuing Studies Enrollment Manager, 215-489-4469, Fax: 215-489-4832, E-mail: pamela.heffner@deval.edu.

Florida Agricultural and Mechanical University, Division of Graduate Studies, Research, and Continuing Education, College of Engineering Science, Technology, and Agriculture, Division of Agricultural Sciences, Tallahassee, FL 32307-3200. Offers agribusiness (MS); animal science (MS); engineering technology (MS); entomology (MS); food science (MS); international programs (MS); plant science (MS). *Faculty:* 31 full-time (2 women). *Students:* 14 full-time (8 women), 8 part-time (4 women); includes 17 minority (16 African Americans, 1 Asian American or Pacific Islander), 3 international. In 2009, 7 master's awarded. *Degree requirements:* For master's, thesis. *Entrance requirements:* For master's, GRE General Test, minimum GPA of 3.0. Additional exam requirements/recommendations for international students: Required—TOEFL (minimum score 500 paper-based). *Application deadline:* For fall admission, 5/18 for domestic students, 12/18 for international students; for spring admission, 11/12 for domestic students, 5/12 for international students. Application fee: $20. *Financial support:* Application deadline: 2/15. *Unit head:* Dr. Mitwe N. Musingo, Graduate Coordinator, 850-561-2309, Fax: 850-599-8821. *Application contact:* Dr. Chanta M. Haywood, Dean of Graduate Studies, Research, and Continuing Education, 850-599-3315, Fax: 850-599-3727.

Illinois State University, Graduate School, College of Applied Science and Technology, Department of Agriculture, Normal, IL 61790-2200. Offers agribusiness (MS). *Degree requirements:* For master's, thesis optional. *Entrance requirements:* For master's, GRE General Test, minimum GPA of 3.0 in last 60 hours. *Faculty research:* Engineering-economic system models for rural ethanol production facilities, development and evaluation of a propane-fueled, production scale, on-site thermal destruction system C-FAR 2007; field scale evaluation and technology transfer of economically, ecologically systems; sound liquid swine manure treatment and application.

Instituto Centroamericano de Administración de Empresas, Graduate Programs, La Garita, Costa Rica. Offers agribusiness (MIAM); business administration (EMBA); economics and finance (MBA); industry and technology (MBA); sustainable development (MBA). *Degree requirements:* For master's, comprehensive exam, essay. *Entrance requirements:* For master's, GMAT or GRE General Test, fluency in Spanish, interview, letters of recommendation, minimum 1 year of work experience. Electronic applications accepted. *Faculty research:* Competitiveness, production.

Iowa State University of Science and Technology, Graduate College, College of Liberal Arts and Sciences, Department of Economics and College of Agriculture, Program in Agricultural Economics, Ames, IA 50011. Offers MS, PhD. *Faculty:* 28 full-time (3 women), 3 part-time/adjunct (all women). *Students:* 34 full-time (11 women), 8 part-time (5 women), 32 international. 70 applicants, 37% accepted, 7 enrolled. In 2009, 2 doctorates awarded. *Degree requirements:* For master's, thesis or alternative; for doctorate, thesis/dissertation. *Entrance requirements:* For master's and doctorate, GRE General Test. Additional exam requirements/recommendations for international students: Required—TOEFL (minimum score 570 paper-based; 88 iBT) or IELTS (minimum score 6.5). *Application deadline:* For fall admission, 1/20 priority date for domestic and international students. Application fee: $40 ($90 for international students). Electronic applications accepted. *Expenses:* Tuition, state resident: full-time $6716. Tuition, nonresident: full-time $8908. Tuition and fees vary according to course level, course load, program and student level. *Financial support:* In 2009–10, 16 research assistantships with full and partial tuition reimbursements (averaging $16,000 per year), 17 teaching assistantships with full and partial tuition reimbursements (averaging $16,000 per year) were awarded; fellowships, scholarships/grants, health care benefits, and unspecified assistantships also available. *Unit head:* Section Leader, 515-294-2702. *Application contact:* Dr. John Schroeter, Information Contact, 515-294-2702, E-mail: grad@econ.iastate.edu.

Iowa State University of Science and Technology, Graduate College, Interdisciplinary Programs, Program in Seed Technology and Business, Ames, IA 50011. Offers MS. Part-time and evening/weekend programs available. Postbaccalaureate distance learning degree programs offered (no on-campus study). *Students:* 19 part-time (3 women); includes 2 minority (1 Asian American or Pacific Islander, 1 Hispanic American), 5 international. *Degree requirements:* For master's, thesis or alternative. *Entrance requirements:* For master's, resume, 3 letters of recommendation. Additional exam requirements/recommendations for international students: Required—TOEFL (minimum score 570 paper-based; 85 iBT), IELTS (minimum score 6.5). *Application deadline:* For fall admission, 4/15 priority date for domestic students, 4/15 for international students. Application fee: $40 ($90 for international students). Electronic applications accepted. *Expenses:* Tuition, state resident: full-time $6716. Tuition, nonresident: full-time $8908. Tuition and fees vary according to course level, course load, program and student level. *Unit head:* Dr. Gary Munkvold, Supervisory Committee Chair, 515-294-8745. *Application contact:* Information Contact, 515-294-5836, Fax: 515-294-2592, E-mail: grad_admissions@iastate.edu.

Kansas State University, Graduate School, College of Agriculture, Department of Agricultural Economics, Manhattan, KS 66506. Offers MAB, MS, PhD. Part-time programs available. Postbaccalaureate distance learning degree programs offered (minimal on-campus study). *Faculty:* 26 full-time (1 woman), 2 part-time/adjunct (1 woman). *Students:* 42 full-time (17 women), 4 part-time (3 women). Average age 25. 53 applicants, 70% accepted, 12 enrolled. In 2009, 29 master's, 6 doctorates awarded. Terminal master's awarded for partial completion of doctoral program. *Degree requirements:* For master's, thesis or alternative, oral exam; for doctorate, thesis/dissertation, preliminary exams. *Entrance requirements:* For master's and doctorate, GRE General Test. Additional exam requirements/recommendations for international students: Required—TOEFL (minimum score 550 paper-based; 213 computer-based). *Application deadline:* For fall admission, 2/1 priority date for domestic and international students; for spring admission, 8/1 priority date for domestic and international students. Applications are processed on a rolling basis. Application fee: $40 ($55 for international students). Electronic applications accepted. *Financial support:* In 2009–10, 36 research assistantships (averaging $14,623 per year) were awarded; fellowships, teaching assistantships with partial tuition reimbursements, Federal Work-Study, institutionally sponsored loans, and scholarships/grants also available. Support available to part-time students. Financial award application deadline: 3/1; financial award applicants required to submit FAFSA. *Faculty research:* Livestock marketing, biofuels research, natural resources, agribusiness industry, international development and trade. Total annual research expenditures: $1.7 million. *Unit head:* Dr. David Lambert, Head, 785-532-4489, Fax: 785-532-6925, E-mail: labertd@ksu.edu. *Application contact:* Dr. John Crespi, Director, 785-532-3357, Fax: 785-532-6925, E-mail: jcrespi@agecon.ksu.edu.

Louisiana State University and Agricultural and Mechanical College, Graduate School, College of Agriculture, Department of Agricultural Economics and Agribusiness, Baton Rouge, LA 70803. Offers MS, PhD. *Faculty:* 22 full-time (0 women). *Students:* 35 full-time (10 women), 4 part-time (3 women); includes 1 African American, 1 Asian American or Pacific Islander, 24 international. Average age 29. 19 applicants, 53% accepted, 4 enrolled. In 2009, 9 doctorates awarded. *Degree requirements:* For master's, thesis (for some programs); for doctorate, thesis/dissertation. *Entrance requirements:* For master's and doctorate, GRE General Test, minimum GPA of 3.0. Additional exam requirements/recommendations for international students: Required—TOEFL (minimum score 550 paper-based; 213 computer-based; 79 iBT) or IELTS (minimum score 6.5). *Application deadline:* For fall admission, 1/25 priority date for domestic students, 5/15 for international students; for spring admission, 10/15 for international students. Applications are processed on a rolling basis. Application fee: $50 ($70 for international students). Electronic applications accepted. *Financial support:* In 2009–10, 37 students received support, including 34 research assistantships with partial tuition reimbursements available (averaging $15,673 per year); teaching assistantships with partial tuition reimbursements available, Federal Work-Study, institutionally sponsored loans, scholarships/grants, health care benefits, tuition waivers (full and partial), and unspecified assistantships also available. Support available to part-time students. Financial award applicants required to submit FAFSA. *Faculty research:* Natural and environmental economics, agribusiness, marketing, production economics, community economics, rural development. Total annual research expenditures: $10,733. *Unit head:* Dr. Gail L. Cramer, Head, 225-578-3282, Fax: 225-578-2716, E-mail: gcramer@agctr.lsu.edu. *Application contact:* Dr. Richard Kaemierczak, Graduate Coordinator, 225-578-2712, Fax: 225-578-2716, E-mail: rkazmierczak@agcenter.lsu.edu.

McGill University, Faculty of Graduate and Postdoctoral Studies, Faculty of Agricultural and Environmental Sciences, Department of Agricultural Economics, Montréal, QC H3A 2T5, Canada. Offers M Sc.

Michigan State University, The Graduate School, College of Agriculture and Natural Resources, Department of Agricultural, Food, and Resource Economics, East Lansing, MI 48824. Offers agricultural economics (MS, PhD); agricultural, food, and resource economics (MS, PhD). *Faculty:* 35 full-time (4 women). *Students:* 80 full-time (36 women), 7 part-time (2 women); includes 2 minority (1 African American, 1 American Indian/Alaska Native), 52 international. Average age 29. 141 applicants, 19% accepted. In 2009, 19 master's, 9 doctorates awarded. *Entrance requirements:* Additional exam requirements/recommendations for international students: Required—TOEFL (minimum score 550 paper-based; 213 computer-based), Michigan State University ELT (minimum score 85), Michigan Michigan English Language Assessment Battery (minimum score 83). *Application deadline:* Applications are processed on a rolling basis. Electronic applications accepted. *Expenses:* Tuition, state resident: part-time $478.25 per credit hour. Tuition, nonresident: part-time $966.50 per credit hour. Part-time tuition and fees vary according to program. *Financial support:* In 2009–10, 63 research assistantships with tuition reimbursements (averaging $7,315 per year), 1 teaching assistantship with tuition reimbursement (averaging $7,345 per year) were awarded. Total annual research expenditures: $9.2 million. *Unit head:* Dr. Steven D. Hanson, Chairperson, 517-355-4567, Fax: 517-432-1800, E-mail: hansons@msu.edu. *Application contact:* Debbie Conway, Graduate Secretary, 517-355-4563, Fax: 517-432-1800, E-mail: aecgrad@msu.edu.

Mississippi State University, College of Agriculture and Life Sciences, Department of Agricultural Economics, Mississippi State, MS 39762. Offers agribusiness management (MABM); agriculture (MS), including agricultural economics. Part-time programs available. *Faculty:* 15 full-time (1 woman). *Students:* 12 full-time (1 woman), 3 part-time (2 women); includes 1 minority (Asian American or Pacific Islander), 3 international. Average age 26. 14 applicants, 79% accepted, 8 enrolled. In 2009, 8 master's awarded. *Degree requirements:* For master's, thesis (for some programs), comprehensive oral or written exam, thesis defense. *Entrance requirements:* For master's, GRE, GMAT, minimum GPA of 3.0. Additional exam requirements/recommendations for international students: Required—TOEFL (minimum score 575 paper-based; 233 computer-based; 84 iBT); Recommended—IELTS (minimum score 7). *Application deadline:* For fall admission, 7/1 for domestic students, 5/1 for international students; for spring admission, 11/1 for domestic students, 9/1 for international students. Applications are processed on a rolling basis. Application fee: $40. Electronic applications accepted. *Expenses:* Tuition, state resident: full-time $2575.50; part-time $286.25 per credit hour. Tuition, nonresident: full-time $6510; part-time $723.50 per credit hour. Tuition and fees vary according to course load. *Financial support:* In 2009–10, 11 research assistantships with full tuition reimbursements (averaging $9,824 per year) were awarded; career-related internships or fieldwork, Federal Work-Study, institutionally sponsored loans, and unspecified assistantships also available. Financial award application deadline: 4/1; financial award applicants required to submit FAFSA. *Faculty research:* Production economics, policy, resource economics, international trade, agribusiness management. *Unit head:* Dr. Steven C. Turner, Head/Professor, 662-325-2049, Fax: 662-325-8777, E-mail: turner@aegcon.msstate.edu. *Application contact:* Dr. Stan Spurlock, Professor and Graduate Coordinator, 662-325-7995, Fax: 662-325-8777, E-mail: spurlock@agecon.msstate.edu.

New Mexico State University, Graduate School, College of Agricultural, Consumer and Environmental Sciences, Department of Agricultural Economics and Agricultural Business, Las Cruces, NM 88003-8001. Offers agribusiness (M Ag, MBA); agricultural economics (MS); economics (MA). Part-time programs available. *Faculty:* 8 full-time (2 women). *Students:* 14 full-time (7 women), 4 part-time (2 women); includes 2 minority (1 American Indian/Alaska Native, 1 Asian American or Pacific Islander), 6 international. Average age 28. 22 applicants, 82% accepted, 6 enrolled. In 2009, 6 master's awarded. *Degree requirements:* For master's, thesis (for some programs). *Entrance requirements:* For master's, previous course work in intermediate microeconomics, intermediate macroeconomics, college-level calculus, statistics. Additional exam requirements/recommendations for international students: Required—TOEFL. *Application deadline:* For fall admission, 7/1 priority date for domestic and international students; for spring admission, 11/1 priority date for domestic and international students. Applications are processed on a rolling basis. Application fee: $30 ($50 for international students). Electronic applications accepted. *Expenses:* Tuition, state resident: full-time $4080; part-time $223 per credit. Tuition, nonresident: full-time $14,256; part-time $647 per credit. Required fees: $1278; $639 per semester. *Financial support:* In 2009–10, 7 research assistantships (averaging $13,971 per year), 3 teaching assistantships (averaging $5,267 per year) were awarded; career-related internships or fieldwork and health care benefits also available. Financial award application deadline: 3/1. *Faculty research:* Natural resource policy, production economics and farm/ranch management, agribusiness and marketing, international marketing and trade, agricultural risk management. *Unit head:* Dr. Terry Crawford, Head, 575-646-3215, Fax: 575-646-3808, E-mail: crawford@nmsu.edu. *Application contact:* Dr. L. Allen Torell, Professor, 575-646-4732, Fax: 575-646-3808, E-mail: atorell@nmsu.edu.

North Carolina Agricultural and Technical State University, Graduate School, School of Agriculture and Environmental Sciences, Department of Agribusiness, Applied Economics, and Agriscience Education, Greensboro, NC 27411. Offers agricultural economics (MS); agricultural education (MS). *Accreditation:* NCATE. Part-time and evening/weekend programs available. *Degree requirements:* For master's, comprehensive exam, thesis or alternative, qualifying exam. *Entrance requirements:* For master's, GRE General Test, minimum GPA of 3.0. *Faculty research:* Aid for small farmers, agricultural technology resources, labor force mobility, agrology.

North Carolina State University, Graduate School, College of Agriculture and Life Sciences, Program in Agricultural and Resource Economics, Raleigh, NC 27695. Offers MS. Part-time programs available. *Degree requirements:* For master's, thesis. *Entrance requirements:* Additional exam requirements/recommendations for international students: Required—TOEFL. Electronic applications accepted. *Faculty research:* Resource economics, international economics, labor economics, econometrics, environmental economics.

North Dakota State University, College of Graduate and Interdisciplinary Studies, College of Agriculture, Food Systems, and Natural Resources, Department of Agribusiness and Applied Economics, Fargo, ND 58108. Offers agribusiness and applied economics (MS); international agribusiness (MS); natural resource management (MS). Part-time programs available. *Faculty:* 16 full-time (3 women), 5 part-time/adjunct (1 woman). *Students:* 16 full-time (5 women), 2 part-time (0 women); includes 3 African Americans, 4 Asian Americans or Pacific Islanders, 1 Hispanic American. Average age 24. 28 applicants, 68% accepted, 12 enrolled. In 2009, 13 master's awarded. *Degree requirements:* For master's, thesis. *Entrance requirements:* For master's, minimum GPA of 3.0. Additional exam requirements/recommendations for international students: Required—TOEFL (minimum score 525 paper-based; 225 computer-based; 71 iBT). *Application deadline:* For fall admission, 2/1 priority date for domestic students, 3/1 priority date for international students. Applications are processed on a rolling basis. Application fee: $45 ($60 for international students). Electronic applications accepted. *Financial support:* In 2009–10, 8 research assistantships with tuition reimbursements (averaging $14,520 per year) were awarded; Federal Work-Study and institutionally sponsored loans also available. Financial award application deadline: 4/15. *Faculty research:* Agribusiness, transportation, marketing, microeconomics, trade. Total annual research expenditures: $1 million. *Unit head:* Dr. Thomas I. Wahl, Chair, 701-231-7470, Fax: 701-231-7400. *Application contact:* Dr. Thomas I. Wahl, Chair, 701-231-7470, Fax: 701-231-7400.

Northwest Missouri State University, Graduate School, Melvin and Valorie Booth College of Business and Professional Studies, Department of Agriculture, Program in Agricultural Economics, Maryville, MO 64468-6001. Offers MBA. *Faculty:* 7 full-time (2 women). *Students:* 3 full-time (0 women). 3 applicants, 67% accepted, 1 enrolled. In 2009, 2 master's awarded. *Degree requirements:* For master's, comprehensive exam. *Entrance requirements:* For master's, GMAT, GRE, minimum GPA of 2.5. Additional exam requirements/recommendations for international students: Required—TOEFL (minimum score 550 paper-based; 213 computer-based). *Application deadline:* For fall admission, 7/1 for domestic and international students; for spring admission, 12/1 for domestic students, 11/15 for international students. Applications are processed on a rolling basis. Application fee: $0 ($50 for international students). *Expenses:* Tuition, state resident: part-time $296.34 per credit hour. Tuition, nonresident: part-time $510.43 per credit hour. *Financial support:* In 2009–10, research assistantships with full tuition reimbursements (averaging $6,000 per year), teaching assistantships with full tuition reimbursements (averaging $6,000 per year) were awarded. Financial award application deadline: 4/1; financial award applicants required to submit FAFSA. *Application contact:* Dr. Gregory Haddock, Dean of Graduate School, 660-562-1145, Fax: 660-562-1096, E-mail: gradsch@nwmissouri.edu.

The Ohio State University, Graduate School, College of Food, Agricultural, and Environmental Sciences, Department of Agricultural, Environmental, and Development Economics, Columbus, OH 43210. Offers agricultural economics and rural sociology (MS, PhD). *Faculty:* 32. *Students:* 62 full-time (30 women), 7 part-time (3 women); includes 3 minority (all Asian Americans or Pacific Islanders), 39 international. Average age 27. In 2009, 15 master's, 6 doctorates awarded. *Degree requirements:* For master's, thesis optional; for doctorate, thesis/dissertation. *Entrance requirements:* For master's and doctorate, GRE General Test. Additional exam requirements/recommendations for international students: Required—TOEFL (minimum score 550 paper-based; 213 computer-based) or IELTS (minimum score 7) or Michigan English Language Assessment Battery (minimum score 92). *Application deadline:* For fall admission, 8/15 priority date for domestic students, 7/1 priority date for international students; for winter admission, 12/1 priority date for domestic students, 11/1 priority date for international students; for spring admission, 3/1 priority date for domestic students, 2/1 priority date for international students. Applications are processed on a rolling basis. Application fee: $40 ($50 for international students). Electronic applications accepted. *Expenses:* Tuition, state resident: full-time $10,683. Tuition, nonresident: full-time $25,923. Tuition and fees vary according to course load and program. *Financial support:* Fellowships, research assistantships, teaching assistantships, Federal Work-Study and institutionally sponsored loans available. Support available to part-time students. *Unit head:* Mario Miranda, Graduate Studies Committee Chair, E-mail: miranda.4@osu.edu. *Application contact:* Graduate Admissions, 614-292-9444, Fax: 614-292-3895, E-mail: domestic.grad@osu.edu.

Oklahoma State University, College of Agricultural Science and Natural Resources, Department of Agricultural Economics, Stillwater, OK 74078. Offers M Ag, MS, PhD. *Faculty:* 35 full-time (8 women), 1 part-time/adjunct (0 women). *Students:* 46 full-time (14 women), 15 part-time (9 women); includes 4 minority (2 American Indian/Alaska Native, 1 Asian American or Pacific Islander, 1 Hispanic American), 32 international. Average age 29. 90 applicants, 48% accepted, 17 enrolled. In 2009, 15 master's, 4 doctorates awarded. *Degree requirements:* For master's, thesis or report, oral exam; for doctorate, comprehensive exam, thesis/dissertation. *Entrance requirements:* For master's and doctorate, GRE or GMAT. Additional exam requirements/recommendations for international students: Required—TOEFL (minimum score 550 paper-based; 79 iBT). *Application deadline:* For fall admission, 3/1 priority date for international students; for spring admission, 8/1 priority date for international students. Applications are processed on a rolling basis. Application fee: $40 ($75 for international students). Electronic applications accepted. *Expenses:* Tuition, state resident: full-time $3716; part-time $154.85 per credit hour. Tuition, nonresident: full-time $14,448; part-time $602 per credit hour. Required fees: $1772; $73.85 per credit hour. One-time fee: $50. Tuition and fees vary according to course load and campus/location. *Financial support:* In 2009–10, 45 research assistantships (averaging $14,279 per year), 2 teaching assistantships (averaging $13,008 per year) were awarded; career-related internships or fieldwork, Federal Work-Study, scholarships/grants, health care benefits, tuition waivers (partial), and unspecified assistantships also available. Support available to part-time students. Financial award application deadline: 3/1; financial award applicants required to submit FAFSA. *Faculty research:* Marketing and agribusiness, production and farm management, policy and natural resources, community and rural development, international trade and development. *Unit head:* Dr. Mike Woods, Head, 405-744-6161, Fax: 405-744-8210. *Application contact:* Dr. Gordon Emslie, Dean, 405-744-6368, Fax: 405-744-0355, E-mail: grad-i@okstate.edu.

Oregon State University, Graduate School, College of Agricultural Sciences, Department of Agricultural and Resource Economics, Corvallis, OR 97331. Offers agricultural and resource economics (M Agr, MAIS, MS, PhD); economics (MS, PhD). MS and PhD in economics offered through the University Graduate Faculty of Economics. Part-time programs available. *Faculty:* 9 full-time (2 women), 1 (woman) part-time/adjunct. *Students:* 19 full-time (9 women), 3 part-time (0 women); includes 2 minority (1 American Indian/Alaska Native, 1 Hispanic American), 12 international. Average age 29. In 2009, 1 master's, 4 doctorates awarded. Terminal master's awarded for partial completion of doctoral program. *Degree requirements:* For master's, thesis (for some programs); for doctorate, thesis/dissertation. *Entrance requirements:* For master's and doctorate, GRE General Test, minimum GPA of 3.0 in last 90 hours. Additional exam requirements/recommendations for international students: Required—TOEFL. *Application deadline:* For fall admission, 3/1 for domestic students. Applications are

Agricultural Economics and Agribusiness

Oregon State University (continued)

processed on a rolling basis. Application fee: $50. *Expenses:* Tuition, state resident: full-time $9774; part-time $362 per credit. Tuition, nonresident: full-time $15,849; part-time $587 per credit. Required fees: $1639. Full-time tuition and fees vary according to course load and program. *Financial support:* Fellowships, research assistantships, teaching assistantships, career-related internships or fieldwork, Federal Work-Study, and institutionally sponsored loans available. Support available to part-time students. Financial award application deadline: 2/1. *Faculty research:* Marine economics, environmental economics, effects of global climate change on agriculture, efficiency of agricultural markets, analysis of aquaculture development. *Unit head:* Dr. Gregory M. Perry, Department Head, 541-737-2942, Fax: 541-737-2563. *Application contact:* Kathy Carpenter, Administrative Assistant, 541-737-1398, Fax: 541-737-1441, E-mail: kathy.carpenter@orst.edu.

Penn State University Park, Graduate School, College of Agricultural Sciences, Department of Agricultural Economics and Rural Sociology, State College, University Park, PA 16802-1503. Offers MPS, MS, PhD.

Prairie View A&M University, College of Agriculture and Human Sciences, Prairie View, TX 77446-0519. Offers agricultural economics (MS); animal sciences (MS); interdisciplinary human sciences (MS); soil science (MS). Part-time and evening/weekend programs available. *Faculty:* 11 full-time (4 women). *Students:* 36 full-time (27 women), 40 part-time (29 women); includes 57 African Americans, 1 Hispanic American, 6 international. Average age 31. 147 applicants, 100% accepted. In 2009, 23 master's awarded. *Degree requirements:* For master's, comprehensive exam, thesis (for some programs), field placement. *Entrance requirements:* For master's, GRE General Test, minimum GPA of 2.45. Additional exam requirements/recommendations for international students: Required—TOEFL (minimum score 550 paper-based). *Application deadline:* For fall admission, 6/1 for domestic and international students; for spring admission, 10/1 for domestic and international students. Applications are processed on a rolling basis. Application fee: $50. *Expenses:* Tuition, state resident: full-time $2200. Tuition, nonresident: full-time $5600. Required fees: $1720. Tuition and fees vary according to course load. *Financial support:* In 2009–10, 57 students received support, including 8 fellowships with tuition reimbursements available (averaging $12,000 per year), 10 research assistantships with tuition reimbursements available (averaging $15,000 per year); career-related internships or fieldwork, Federal Work-Study, institutionally sponsored loans, scholarships/grants, tuition waivers (partial), and unspecified assistantships also available. Support available to part-time students. Financial award application deadline: 4/1; financial award applicants required to submit FAFSA. *Faculty research:* Domestic violence prevention, water quality, food growth regulators, wetland dynamics, biochemistry, obesity and nutrition, family therapy. Total annual research expenditures: $4 million. *Unit head:* Dr. Freddie Richards, Dean, 936-261-2528, Fax: 936-261-5143, E-mail: flrichards@pvamu.edu. *Application contact:* Dr. Richard W. Griffin, Interim Department Head, 936-261-5019, Fax: 936-261-5148, E-mail: rwgriffin@pvamu.edu.

Purdue University, Graduate School, College of Agriculture, Department of Agricultural Economics, West Lafayette, IN 47907. Offers agricultural economics (MS, PhD); food and agricultural business (EMBA). Part-time programs available. Terminal master's awarded for partial completion of doctoral program. *Degree requirements:* For master's, thesis (for some programs); for doctorate, thesis/dissertation. *Entrance requirements:* For master's and doctorate, GRE General Test. Additional exam requirements/recommendations for international students: Required—TOEFL, TWE (minimum score 4). Electronic applications accepted. *Faculty research:* Marketing, international trade, policy and development, production, resources.

Rutgers, The State University of New Jersey, New Brunswick, Graduate School-New Brunswick, Program in Food and Business Economics, Piscataway, NJ 08854-8097. Offers MS. *Degree requirements:* For master's, comprehensive exam, thesis or alternative. *Entrance requirements:* Additional exam requirements/recommendations for international students: Required—TOEFL. Electronic applications accepted. *Faculty research:* Science policy, land use, nutrition policy, food industry, international development.

Santa Clara University, Leavey School of Business, Program in Business Administration, Santa Clara, CA 95053. Offers accounting (MBA); entrepreneurship (MBA); executive MBA (EMBA); finance (MBA); food and agribusiness (MBA); international business (MBA); leading people and organizations (MBA); managing technology and innovation (MBA); marketing management (MBA); supply chain management (MBA). *Accreditation:* AACSB. Part-time and evening/weekend programs available. *Students:* 228 full-time (88 women), 838 part-time (265 women); includes 388 minority (17 African Americans, 2 American Indian/Alaska Native, 326 Asian Americans or Pacific Islanders, 43 Hispanic Americans), 218 international. Average age 31. 486 applicants, 77% accepted, 263 enrolled. In 2009, 317 master's awarded. *Degree requirements:* For master's, thesis or alternative. *Entrance requirements:* For master's, GMAT, GRE. Additional exam requirements/recommendations for international students: Required—TOEFL (minimum score 600 paper-based; 250 computer-based; 100 iBT). *Application deadline:* For fall admission, 6/1 for domestic and international students; for spring admission, 1/19 for domestic students, 1/17 for international students. Applications are processed on a rolling basis. Application fee: $75 ($100 for international students). Electronic applications accepted. *Expenses:* Contact institution. *Financial support:* Fellowships with partial tuition reimbursements, research assistantships with partial tuition reimbursements, career-related internships or fieldwork, Federal Work-Study, institutionally sponsored loans, scholarships/grants, health care benefits, and unspecified assistantships available. Support available to part-time students. Financial award applicants required to submit FAFSA. *Unit head:* Elizabeth B. Ford, Senior Assistant Dean, 408-554-2752, Fax: 408-554-4571, E-mail: eford@scu.edu. *Application contact:* Jennifer W. Taylor, Senior Director, 408-554-4539, Fax: 408-554-4571, E-mail: mbaadmissions@scu.edu.

South Carolina State University, School of Graduate Studies, Department of Accounting, Agribusiness and Economics, Orangeburg, SC 29117-0001. Offers agribusiness (MS); agribusiness and entrepreneurship (MBA). Part-time and evening/weekend programs available. *Degree requirements:* For master's, comprehensive exam, business plan. *Entrance requirements:* For master's, GMAT, minimum GPA of 2.8. Additional exam requirements/recommendations for international students: Required—TOEFL. Electronic applications accepted. *Expenses:* Tuition, state resident: part-time $470 per credit hour. Tuition, nonresident: part-time $924 per credit hour. *Faculty research:* Small farm income and profitability, agricultural credit, aquaculture, low-input sustainable agriculture, rural development.

Southern Illinois University Carbondale, Graduate School, College of Agriculture, Department of Agribusiness Economics, Carbondale, IL 62901-4701. Offers MS, MBA/MS. Part-time programs available. *Degree requirements:* For master's, thesis. *Entrance requirements:* For master's, minimum GPA of 2.7. Additional exam requirements/recommendations for international students: Required—TOEFL. *Faculty research:* Agricultural finance and credit, agribusiness management, resource use, rural area economic development, marketing and price analysis.

Texas A&M University, College of Agriculture and Life Sciences, Department of Agricultural Economics, College Station, TX 77843. Offers MAB, MS, PhD. Part-time programs available. *Faculty:* 25. *Students:* 161 full-time (64 women), 21 part-time (5 women); includes 10 minority (2 African Americans, 2 Asian Americans or Pacific Islanders, 6 Hispanic Americans), 112 international. Average age 29. In 2009, 19 master's, 7 doctorates awarded. Terminal master's awarded for partial completion of doctoral program. *Degree requirements:* For master's, comprehensive exam (for some programs), thesis (for some programs); for doctorate, comprehensive exam, thesis/dissertation. *Entrance requirements:* For master's and doctorate, GRE General Test. Additional exam requirements/recommendations for international students: Required—TOEFL. *Application deadline:* For fall admission, 3/1 for domestic students; for spring admission, 8/1 for domestic students. Applications are processed on a rolling basis. Application fee: $50 ($75 for international students). Electronic applications accepted. *Expenses:* Tuition, state resident: full-time $3991; part-time $221.74 per credit hour. Tuition, nonresident: full-time $9049; part-time $502.74 per credit hour. *Financial support:* Fellowships, research assistantships, teaching assistantships, career-related internships or fieldwork, Federal Work-Study, institutionally sponsored loans, and unspecified assistantships available. Financial award application deadline: 3/1; financial award applicants required to submit FAFSA. *Faculty research:* Production economics, agricultural finance, resources, marketing and policy, agribusiness. *Unit head:* A. Gene Nelson, Head, 979-845-2116, Fax: 979-862-1563, E-mail: nelsong@tamu.edu. *Application contact:* Vicki L. Heard, Graduate Admissions Supervisor, 979-845-5222, Fax: 979-862-1563, E-mail: vheard@tamu.edu.

Texas A&M University–Kingsville, College of Graduate Studies, College of Agriculture and Home Economics, Program in Agribusiness, Kingsville, TX 78363. Offers MS. *Degree requirements:* For master's, comprehensive exam, thesis or alternative. *Entrance requirements:* For master's, GRE General Test, minimum GPA of 3.0. Additional exam requirements/recommendations for international students: Required—TOEFL.

Texas Tech University, Graduate School, College of Agricultural Sciences and Natural Resources, Department of Agricultural and Applied Economics, Lubbock, TX 79409. Offers agribusiness (MAB); agricultural and applied economics (MS, PhD); JD/MS. Part-time programs available. *Faculty:* 12 full-time (0 women). *Students:* 40 full-time (18 women), 6 part-time (0 women); includes 1 minority (Hispanic American), 28 international. Average age 29. 53 applicants, 62% accepted, 6 enrolled. In 2009, 8 master's, 2 doctorates awarded. *Degree requirements:* For master's, thesis or alternative; for doctorate, thesis/dissertation. *Entrance requirements:* For master's and doctorate, GRE General Test. Additional exam requirements/recommendations for international students: Required—TOEFL (minimum score 550 paper-based; 213 computer-based). *Application deadline:* For fall admission, 3/1 priority date for international students; for spring admission, 11/1 priority date for international students. Applications are processed on a rolling basis. Application fee: $50 ($75 for international students). Electronic applications accepted. *Expenses:* Tuition, state resident: full-time $5100; part-time $213 per credit hour. Tuition, nonresident: full-time $11,748; part-time $490 per credit hour. Required fees: $2298; $50 per credit hour. $555 per semester. *Financial support:* In 2009–10, 13 research assistantships with partial tuition reimbursements (averaging $21,555 per year) were awarded; teaching assistantships with partial tuition reimbursements, Federal Work-Study and institutionally sponsored loans also available. Support available to part-time students. Financial award application deadline: 4/15; financial award applicants required to submit FAFSA. *Faculty research:* Economics of the United States cotton and textile industries, natural resource management in semi-arid climates, commodity policy analysis, international trade in agricultural products, agribusiness analysis. Total annual research expenditures: $1.3 million. *Unit head:* Dr. Eduardo Segarra, Chair, 806-742-2821, Fax: 806-742-1099, E-mail: eduardo.segarra@ttu.edu. *Application contact:* Dr. Tom Knight, Graduate Adviser, 806-742-2821, Fax: 806-742-1099, E-mail: tom.knight@ttu.edu.

Texas Tech University, Jerry S. Rawls College of Business Administration, Programs in Business Administration, Lubbock, TX 79409. Offers agricultural business (MBA); business administration (IMBA); entrepreneurship (MBA); finance (MBA); general business (MBA); health organization management (MBA); international business (MBA); management and leadership skills (MBA); management information systems (MBA); marketing (MBA); statistics (MBA); JD/MBA; MBA/M Arch; MBA/MA; MBA/MD; MBA/MS; MBA/Pharm D. Part-time and evening/weekend programs available. *Faculty:* 54 full-time (9 women), 5 part-time/adjunct (0 women). *Students:* 59 full-time (15 women), 487 part-time (148 women); includes 107 minority (24 African Americans, 4 American Indian/Alaska Native, 30 Asian Americans or Pacific Islanders, 49 Hispanic Americans), 51 international. Average age 30. 477 applicants, 81% accepted, 302 enrolled. In 2009, 185 master's awarded. *Degree requirements:* For master's, capstone course. *Entrance requirements:* For master's, GMAT, holistic review of academic credentials. Additional exam requirements/recommendations for international students: Required—TOEFL (minimum score 550 paper-based; 213 computer-based; 79 iBT). *Application deadline:* For fall admission, 4/1 priority date for domestic students, 1/15 priority date for international students; for spring admission, 9/1 priority date for domestic students, 7/15 priority date for international students. Applications are processed on a rolling basis. Application fee: $50 ($75 for international students). Electronic applications accepted. *Expenses:* Tuition, state resident: full-time $5100; part-time $213 per credit hour. Tuition, nonresident: full-time $11,748; part-time $490 per credit hour. Required fees: $2298; $50 per credit hour. $555 per semester. *Financial support:* In 2009–10, 13 research assistantships (averaging $8,000 per year) were awarded; teaching assistantships, career-related internships or fieldwork, Federal Work-Study, scholarships/grants, health care benefits, and unspecified assistantships also available. Support available to part-time students. Financial award applicants required to submit FAFSA. *Unit head:* Dr. W. Jay Conover, Director, 806-742-1546, Fax: 806-742-3958, E-mail: jay.conover@ttu.edu. *Application contact:* Cynthia D. Barnes, Director, Graduate Services Center, 806-742-3184, Fax: 806-742-3958, E-mail: ba_grad@ttu.edu.

Tropical Agriculture Research and Higher Education Center, Graduate School, Turrialba, Costa Rica. Offers agribusiness management (MS); agroforestry systems (PhD); ecological agriculture (MS); environmental socioeconomics (MS); forestry in tropical and subtropical zones (PhD); integrated watershed management (MS); management and conservation of tropical rainforests and biodiversity (MS); tropical agriculture (PhD); tropical agroforestry (MS). *Entrance requirements:* For master's, GRE, 2 years of related professional experience, letters of recommendation; for doctorate, GRE, 4 letters of recommendation, letter of support from employing organization, master's degree in agronomy, biological sciences, forestry, natural resources or related field. Additional exam requirements/recommendations for international students: Required—TOEFL (minimum score 550 paper-based; 213 computer-based). Electronic applications accepted. *Faculty research:* Biodiversity in fragmented landscapes, ecosystem management, integrated pest management, environmental livestock production, biotechnology carbon balances in diverse land uses.

Tuskegee University, Graduate Programs, College of Agricultural, Environmental and Natural Sciences, Department of Agricultural Sciences, Program in Agricultural and Resource Economics, Tuskegee, AL 36088. Offers MS. *Faculty:* 13 full-time (1 woman), 2 part-time/adjunct (1 woman). *Students:* 10 full-time (6 women), 1 (woman) part-time; includes 5 minority (all African Americans), 6 international. Average age 32. In 2009, 3 master's awarded. *Degree requirements:* For master's, thesis. *Entrance requirements:* For master's, GRE General Test. Additional exam requirements/recommendations for international students: Required—TOEFL (minimum score 500 paper-based; 69 computer-based). *Application deadline:* For fall admission, 7/15 for domestic students. Applications are processed on a rolling basis. Application fee: $25 ($35 for international students). *Expenses:* Tuition: Full-time $15,630; part-time $940 per credit hour. Required fees: $650. *Financial support:* Application deadline: 4/15. *Unit head:* Dr. P. K. Biswas, Head, 334-727-8446. *Application contact:* Dr. Robert L. Laney, Vice President/Director of Admissions and Enrollment Management, 334-727-8580, Fax: 334-727-5750, E-mail: planey@tuskegee.edu.

Universidad del Este, Graduate School, Carolina, PR 00984. Offers accounting (MBA); adult education (M Ed); agribusiness (MBA); bilingual education (M Ed); criminal justice and criminology (MA); early education (M Ed); elementary education (M Ed); human resources (MBA); information security management (MBA); information technology and Web business development (MBA); management (MBA); public policy (MPA); social work (MA), including clinical social work; special education (M Ed); strategic leadership (MBA); teaching English (M Ed); teaching Spanish (M Ed).

Université Laval, Faculty of Agricultural and Food Sciences, Department of Agricultural Economics and Consumer Sciences, Program in Agricultural Economics, Québec, QC G1K 7P4, Canada. Offers M Sc. Part-time programs available. *Degree requirements:* For master's, thesis (for some programs). *Entrance requirements:* For master's, knowledge of French. Electronic applications accepted.

University of Alberta, Faculty of Graduate Studies and Research, Department of Rural Economy, Edmonton, AB T6G 2E1, Canada. Offers agricultural economics (M Ag, M Sc, PhD); forest economics (M Ag, M Sc, PhD); rural sociology (M Ag, M Sc); MBA/M Ag. Part-time programs available. *Faculty:* 13 full-time (1 woman), 6 part-time/adjunct (0 women). *Students:* 31 full-time (13 women), 21 part-time (11 women). Average age 25. 35 applicants, 83% accepted. In 2009, 10 master's, 2 doctorates awarded. *Degree requirements:* For doctorate, thesis/dissertation. *Entrance requirements:* Additional exam requirements/recommendations for international students: Required—TOEFL. Application fee: $60. Tuition and fees charges are reported in Canadian dollars. *Expenses:* Tuition, area resident: Full-time $4626.24 Canadian dollars; part-time $99.72 Canadian dollars per unit. International tuition: $8216 Canadian dollars full-time. Required fees: $3589.92 Canadian dollars; $99.72 Canadian dollars per unit. $215 Canadian dollars per term. *Financial support:* In 2009–10, 4 fellowships, 12 research assistantships, 2 teaching assistantships were awarded; scholarships/grants also available. *Faculty research:* Agroforestry, development, extension education, marketing and trade, natural resources and environment, policy, production economics. Total annual research expenditures: $850,000. *Unit head:* Dr. V. Adamowicz, Graduate Coordinator, 403-492-4225, Fax: 403-492-0268. *Application contact:* Liz Bruce, Graduate Secretary, 780-492-4225, Fax: 780-492-0268, E-mail: rural.economy@ualberta.ca.

The University of Arizona, Graduate College, College of Agriculture and Life Sciences, Department of Agricultural and Resource Economics, Tucson, AZ 85721. Offers MS. *Faculty:* 8. *Students:* 19 full-time (5 women), 7 part-time (3 women); includes 2 minority (1 American Indian/Alaska Native, 1 Hispanic American), 13 international. Average age 29. 28 applicants, 29% accepted, 8 enrolled. In 2009, 15 master's awarded. *Degree requirements:* For master's, thesis or alternative. *Entrance requirements:* For master's, GRE General Test, 3 letters of recommendation, minimum GPA of 3.0. Additional exam requirements/recommendations for international students: Required—TOEFL. *Application deadline:* For fall admission, 2/1 for domestic and international students. Applications are processed on a rolling basis. Application fee: $75. Electronic applications accepted. *Expenses:* Tuition, state resident: full-time $9028. Tuition, nonresident: full-time $24,890. *Financial support:* In 2009–10, 8 research assistantships (averaging $15,338 per year), 7 teaching assistantships (averaging $15,336 per year) were awarded; career-related internships or fieldwork, institutionally sponsored loans, scholarships/grants, traineeships, health care benefits, tuition waivers (partial), and unspecified assistantships also available. Financial award application deadline: 3/1. *Faculty research:* Natural resources, international development trade, production and marketing, agricultural policy, rural development. Total annual research expenditures: $297,634. *Unit head:* Dr. Gary D. Thompson, Head, 520-621-6249, E-mail: garyt@ag.arizona.edu. *Application contact:* Nancy Smith, Graduate Coordinator, 520-621-2421, E-mail: garec@ag.arizona.edu.

University of Arkansas, Graduate School, Dale Bumpers College of Agricultural, Food and Life Sciences, Department of Agricultural Economics, Fayetteville, AR 72701-1201. Offers MS. *Students:* 30 full-time (14 women), 9 part-time (4 women); includes 5 minority (3 African Americans, 1 American Indian/Alaska Native, 1 Asian American or Pacific Islander), 15 international. In 2009, 16 master's awarded. *Degree requirements:* For master's, thesis optional. Application fee: $40 ($50 for international students). *Expenses:* Tuition, state resident: full-time $7355; part-time $356.58 per hour. Tuition, nonresident: full-time $17,401; part-time $775.17 per hour. Required fees: $1203. *Financial support:* In 2009–10, 10 research assistantships, 1 teaching assistantship were awarded; fellowships with tuition reimbursements, career-related internships or fieldwork and Federal Work-Study also available. Support available to part-time students. Financial award application deadline: 4/1; financial award applicants required to submit FAFSA. *Unit head:* Dr. Steve A. Halbrook, Chair, 479-575-2281, E-mail: halbrook@uark.edu. *Application contact:* Dr. Lucas Parsch, Graduate Coordinator, 479-575-2323, E-mail: lparsch@uark.edu.

The University of British Columbia, Faculty of Land and Food Systems, Agricultural Economics Program, Vancouver, BC V6T 1Z1, Canada. Offers M Sc. Part-time programs available. *Degree requirements:* For master's, thesis. *Entrance requirements:* Additional exam requirements/recommendations for international students: Required—TOEFL (minimum score 577 paper-based; 233 computer-based; 90 iBT), IELTS (minimum score 6.5). Electronic applications accepted. *Faculty research:* International development, natural resources and environmental economics, marketing and trade, agribusiness, food market analysis, applied econometrics.

University of California, Berkeley, Graduate Division, College of Natural Resources, Department of Agricultural and Resource Economics, Berkeley, CA 94720-1500. Offers PhD. *Students:* 72 full-time (35 women). Average age 30. 181 applicants, 14 enrolled. In 2009, 8 doctorates awarded. *Degree requirements:* For doctorate, thesis/dissertation, qualifying exam. *Entrance requirements:* For doctorate, GRE General Test, minimum GPA of 3.0, 3 letters of recommendation. *Application deadline:* For fall admission, 2/10 for domestic students. Application fee: $70 ($90 for international students). *Financial support:* Fellowships, research assistantships, teaching assistantships, institutionally sponsored loans, scholarships/grants, tuition waivers (full and partial), and unspecified assistantships available. Financial award applicants required to submit FAFSA. *Faculty research:* Agricultural economics and policy, environmental and resource economics and policy, international agricultural development and trade. *Unit head:* Prof. Larry Karp, Chair, 510-642-3345. *Application contact:* Gail T. Vawter, Student Affairs Officer, 510-642-3347, Fax: 510-643-8911, E-mail: gradadm@are.berkeley.edu.

University of California, Davis, Graduate Studies, Program in Agricultural and Resource Economics, Davis, CA 95616. Offers MS, PhD, MBA/MS. Terminal master's awarded for partial completion of doctoral program. *Degree requirements:* For master's, thesis optional; for doctorate, thesis/dissertation. *Entrance requirements:* For master's, GRE General Test, minimum GPA of 3.0; for doctorate, GRE General Test, minimum GPA of 3.3. Additional exam requirements/recommendations for international students: Required—TOEFL (minimum score 550 paper-based; 213 computer-based). Electronic applications accepted. *Faculty research:* Applied microeconomics, international trade, development, econometrics, environmental economics.

University of California, Santa Barbara, Graduate Division, Donald Bren School of Environmental Science and Management, Santa Barbara, CA 93106-5131. Offers MESM, PhD. *Faculty:* 18 full-time (4 women), 24 part-time/adjunct (7 women). *Students:* 187 full-time (112 women); includes 21 minority (1 African American, 1 American Indian/Alaska Native, 11 Asian Americans or Pacific Islanders, 8 Hispanic Americans), 15 international. Average age 27. 335 applicants, 61% accepted, 89 enrolled. In 2009, 63 master's, 8 doctorates awarded. *Degree requirements:* For master's, thesis optional, group project as student thesis; for doctorate, comprehensive exam, thesis/dissertation. *Entrance requirements:* For master's, GRE, 3 letters of recommendation, resume/curriculum vitae; for doctorate, GRE, 3 letters of recommendation, statement of purpose, personal achievements/contributions statement, resume/curriculum vitae, transcripts for post-secondary institutions attended. Additional exam requirements/recommendations for international students: Required—TOEFL (minimum score 550 paper-based; 213 computer-based; 80 iBT), or IELTS (minimum score 7). *Application deadline:* For fall admission, 1/10 priority date for domestic and international students. Application fee: $70 ($90 for international students). Electronic applications accepted. *Financial support:* In 2009–10, 68 students received support, including 44 fellowships with full and partial tuition reimbursements available (averaging $8,400 per year), 20 research assistantships with full and partial tuition reimbursements available (averaging $6,600 per year), 28 teaching assistantships with partial tuition reimbursements available (averaging $6,900 per year); career-related internships or fieldwork, Federal Work-Study, institutionally sponsored loans, scholarships/grants, health care benefits, and unspecified assistantships also available. Financial award application deadline: 12/15; financial award applicants required to submit FAFSA. *Faculty research:* Ecological processes, environmental politics and policy, sustainability, conservation science and planning, water resources management. *Unit head:* Dr. John Melack, Acting Dean, 805-893-3879, Fax: 805-893-6113, E-mail: melack@bren.ucsb.edu. *Application contact:* Kristen Robinson, Graduate Program Advisor, 805-893-7611, Fax: 805-893-6113, E-mail: gradasst@bren.ucsb.edu.

University of Connecticut, Graduate School, College of Agriculture and Natural Resources, Department of Agricultural and Resource Economics, Storrs, CT 06269. Offers MS, PhD. *Faculty:* 15 full-time (5 women). *Students:* 26 full-time (12 women), 6 part-time (4 women); includes 4 minority (1 Asian American or Pacific Islander, 3 Hispanic Americans), 19 international. Average age 32. 60 applicants, 18% accepted, 9 enrolled. In 2009, 8 master's, 7 doctorates awarded. Terminal master's awarded for partial completion of doctoral program. *Degree requirements:* For master's, comprehensive exam; for doctorate, thesis/dissertation. *Entrance requirements:* For master's and doctorate, GRE General Test. Additional exam requirements/recommendations for international students: Required—TOEFL (minimum score 550 paper-based; 213 computer-based). *Application deadline:* For fall admission, 2/1 priority date for domestic and international students; for spring admission, 11/1 for domestic students, 10/1 for international students. Applications are processed on a rolling basis. Application fee: $55. Electronic applications accepted. *Expenses:* Tuition, state resident: full-time $4725; part-time $525 per credit. Tuition, nonresident: full-time $12,267; part-time $1363 per credit. Required fees: $346 per semester. Tuition and fees vary according to course load. *Financial support:* In 2009–10, 15 research assistantships with full tuition reimbursements, 3 teaching assistantships with full tuition reimbursements were awarded; fellowships, Federal Work-Study, scholarships/grants, health care benefits, and unspecified assistantships also available. Financial award application deadline: 2/1; financial award applicants required to submit FAFSA. *Faculty research:* Food marketing, international agricultural development. *Unit head:* Rigoberto A. Lopez, Interim Department Head, 860-486-1921, Fax: 860-486-1932, E-mail: rlopez@canr.uconn.edu. *Application contact:* Farhed Shah, Chairperson, 860-486-4467, Fax: 860-486-1932, E-mail: farhed.shah@uconn.edu.

University of Delaware, College of Agriculture and Natural Resources, Department of Food and Resource Economics, Newark, DE 19716. Offers agricultural economics (MS); agriculture and technical education (MA); bioresources engineering (MS). Part-time programs available. *Degree requirements:* For master's, thesis. *Entrance requirements:* For master's, GRE General Test, 3 letters of recommendation. Additional exam requirements/recommendations for international students: Required—TOEFL (minimum score 550 paper-based; 213 computer-based). Electronic applications accepted. *Faculty research:* Experimental economics, environmental and resource economics, land use, law and economics.

University of Florida, Graduate School, College of Agricultural and Life Sciences, Department of Food and Resource Economics, Gainesville, FL 32611. Offers MAB, MS, PhD. *Degree requirements:* For master's, thesis optional; for doctorate, thesis/dissertation. *Entrance requirements:* For master's and doctorate, GRE General Test, minimum GPA of 3.0. Additional exam requirements/recommendations for international students: Required—TOEFL. Electronic applications accepted. *Faculty research:* Agribusiness management, production, environmental economics, international trade, economic development.

University of Georgia, Graduate School, College of Agricultural and Environmental Sciences, Department of Agricultural and Applied Economics, Athens, GA 30602. Offers agricultural economics (MAE, MS, PhD); environmental economics (MS). *Faculty:* 22 full-time (4 women), 1 part-time/adjunct (0 women). *Students:* 38 full-time (19 women), 7 part-time (1 woman); includes 4 minority (2 African Americans, 1 Asian American or Pacific Islander, 1 Hispanic American), 25 international. 45 applicants, 22% accepted, 9 enrolled. In 2009, 4 master's, 4 doctorates awarded. *Degree requirements:* For master's, thesis (MS); for doctorate, thesis/dissertation. *Entrance requirements:* For master's and doctorate, GRE General Test. *Application deadline:* For fall admission, 7/1 priority date for domestic students; for spring admission, 11/15 for domestic students. Application fee: $50. Electronic applications accepted. *Expenses:* Tuition, state resident: full-time $6000; part-time $250 per credit hour. Tuition, nonresident: full-time $20,904; part-time $871 per credit hour. Required fees: $730 per semester. *Financial support:* Fellowships, research assistantships, teaching assistantships, career-related internships or fieldwork and unspecified assistantships available. *Unit head:* Dr. Octavio A. Ramirez, Interim Head, 706-542-2481, Fax: 706-542-0739, E-mail: oramirez@agecon.uga.edu. *Application contact:* Dr. Michael E. Wetzstein, Graduate Coordinator, 706-543-0758, Fax: 706-542-0739, E-mail: mwetz@uga.edu.

University of Guelph, Graduate Program Services, College of Management and Economics, MBA Program, Guelph, ON N1G 2W1, Canada. Offers food and agribusiness management (MBA); hospitality and tourism management (MBA). Part-time and evening/weekend programs available. Postbaccalaureate distance learning degree programs offered (minimal on-campus study). *Entrance requirements:* For master's, minimum B-average, minimum of 3 years of relevant work experience. Additional exam requirements/recommendations for international students: Required—TOEFL (minimum score 550 paper-based; 213 computer-based). Electronic applications accepted. *Faculty research:* Marketing, operations management, business policy, financial management, organizational behavior.

University of Guelph, Graduate Program Services, Ontario Agricultural College, Department of Food, Agricultural and Resource Economics, Guelph, ON N1G 2W1, Canada. Offers agricultural economics (M Sc, PhD); collaborative international development studies (MA/M Sc); MA/M Sc. Part-time programs available. *Degree requirements:* For master's, thesis; for doctorate, comprehensive exam, thesis/dissertation. *Entrance requirements:* For master's, minimum B- average during previous 2 years of course work; for doctorate, minimum B standing in recognized master's degree. Additional exam requirements/recommendations for international students: Required—TOEFL (minimum score 550 paper-based; 213 computer-based), IELTS (minimum score 6.5). Electronic applications accepted. *Faculty research:* Agricultural policy, agribusiness, environmental economics, agricultural marketing, production economics.

University of Idaho, College of Graduate Studies, College of Agricultural and Life Sciences, Department of Agricultural Economics and Rural Sociology, Moscow, ID 83844-2282. Offers agricultural economics (MS); applied economics (MS), including agribusiness emphasis, agricultural economics emphasis. *Faculty:* 6 full-time, 4 part-time/adjunct. *Students:* 16 full-time. In 2009, 7 master's awarded. *Entrance requirements:* For master's, minimum GPA of 2.8. *Application deadline:* For fall admission, 8/1 for domestic students; for spring admission, 12/15 for domestic students. Application fee: $55 ($60 for international students). *Expenses:* Tuition, state resident: full-time $6120. Tuition, nonresident: full-time $17,712. *Financial support:* Research assistantships, teaching assistantships available. Financial award application deadline: 2/15. *Faculty research:* Crops: potatoes, blue grass; livestock: beef, dairy; rural and community development; natural resources and the environment; farm and ranch management. *Unit head:* Dr. Larry W. Van Tassell, Department Head, 208-885-7869, Fax: 208-885-5759. *Application contact:* Dr. Larry W. Van Tassell, Department Head, 208-885-7869, Fax: 208-885-5759.

University of Illinois at Urbana–Champaign, Graduate College, College of Agricultural, Consumer and Environmental Sciences, Department of Agricultural and Consumer Economics, Champaign, IL 61820. Offers MS, PhD. *Faculty:* 34 full-time (12 women). *Students:* 54 full-time (28 women), 23 part-time (10 women); includes 7 minority (4 African Americans, 3 Asian Americans or Pacific Islanders), 46 international. 89 applicants, 22% accepted, 12 enrolled. In 2009, 12 master's, 8 doctorates awarded. *Entrance requirements:* For master's, GRE, minimum GPA of 3.0; for doctorate, GRE, writing sample. Additional exam requirements/recommendations for international students: Required—TOEFL (minimum score 570 paper-based; 230 computer-based; 88 iBT), or IELTS (minimum score 6.5). *Application deadline:* Applications are processed on a rolling basis. Application fee: $60 ($75 for international students). Electronic applications accepted. *Financial support:* In 2009–10, 18 fellowships, 54 research assistantships, 30 teaching assistantships were awarded; tuition waivers (full and partial) also available. *Unit head:* Paul N. Ellinger, Head, 217-333-5503, Fax: 217-333-5538, E-mail: pellinge@illinois.edu. *Application contact:* Linda K. Foste, Administrative Assistant, 217-333-1830, Fax: 217-244-7088, E-mail: l-foste@illinois.edu.

University of Kentucky, Graduate School, College of Agriculture, Program in Agricultural Economics, Lexington, KY 40506-0032. Offers MS, PhD. *Degree requirements:* For master's,

Agricultural Economics and Agribusiness

University of Kentucky (continued)
comprehensive exam, thesis optional; for doctorate, comprehensive exam, thesis/dissertation. *Entrance requirements:* For master's, GRE General Test, minimum undergraduate GPA of 2.75; for doctorate, GRE General Test, minimum graduate GPA of 3.0. Additional exam requirements/recommendations for international students: Required—TOEFL (minimum score 550 paper-based; 213 computer-based). Electronic applications accepted. *Faculty research:* Food and agricultural marketing, agricultural and food policy, natural resources and environment, rural economic development.

University of Maine, Graduate School, College of Natural Sciences, Forestry, and Agriculture, Department of Resource Economics and Policy, Orono, ME 04469. Offers resource economics and policy (MS); resource utilization (MS). Part-time programs available. *Faculty:* 9 full-time (1 woman), 3 part-time/adjunct (1 woman). *Students:* 12 full-time (5 women), 3 part-time (all women); includes 1 minority (African American), 5 international. Average age 29. 21 applicants, 38% accepted, 6 enrolled. In 2009, 4 master's awarded. *Degree requirements:* For master's, thesis (for some programs). *Entrance requirements:* For master's, GRE General Test. Additional exam requirements/recommendations for international students: Required—TOEFL. *Application deadline:* For fall admission, 2/1 priority date for domestic students. Applications are processed on a rolling basis. Application fee: $65. Electronic applications accepted. *Financial support:* In 2009–10, 3 teaching assistantships with tuition reimbursements (averaging $12,790 per year) were awarded; career-related internships or fieldwork, Federal Work-Study, institutionally sponsored loans, scholarships/grants, and tuition waivers (full and partial) also available. Support available to part-time students. Financial award application deadline: 3/1. *Faculty research:* International trade, agricultural marketing, nonmarketing valuation, livestock health economics. *Unit head:* Dr. George Criner, Chair, 207-581-3151, Fax: 207-581-4278. *Application contact:* Scott G. Delcourt, Associate Dean of the Graduate School, 207-581-3291, Fax: 207-581-3232, E-mail: graduate@maine.edu.

University of Manitoba, Faculty of Graduate Studies, Faculty of Agricultural and Food Sciences, Department of Agribusiness and Agricultural Economics, Winnipeg, MB R3T 2N2, Canada. Offers agribusiness (M Sc, PhD). *Degree requirements:* For master's, thesis or alternative; for doctorate, thesis/dissertation.

University of Maryland, College Park, Academic Affairs, College of Agriculture and Natural Resources, Department of Agricultural and Resource Economics, College Park, MD 20742. Offers agriculture economics (MS, PhD); resource economics (MS, PhD). Part-time and evening/weekend programs available. *Faculty:* 22 full-time (5 women), 1 (woman) part-time/adjunct. *Students:* 65 full-time (24 women), 1 part-time (0 women); includes 2 minority (both Asian Americans or Pacific Islanders), 39 international. 188 applicants, 11% accepted, 8 enrolled. In 2009, 11 master's, 6 doctorates awarded. *Degree requirements:* For master's, variable foreign language requirement, thesis optional, oral exam; for doctorate, variable foreign language requirement, oral dissertation defense. *Entrance requirements:* For master's, GRE General Test, minimum GPA of 3.0, course work in microeconomics and calculus, 3 letters of recommendation; for doctorate, GRE General Test. Additional exam requirements/recommendations for international students: Required—TOEFL. *Application deadline:* For fall admission, 5/15 for domestic students, 2/1 for international students; for spring admission, 6/1 for international students. Applications are processed on a rolling basis. Application fee: $60 ($70 for international students). Electronic applications accepted. *Expenses:* Tuition, area resident: Part-time $471 per credit hour. Tuition, state resident: part-time $471 per credit hour. Tuition, nonresident: part-time $1016 per credit hour. Required fees: $337.04 per term. *Financial support:* In 2009–10, 43 research assistantships with tuition reimbursements (averaging $17,864 per year) were awarded; fellowships, teaching assistantships with tuition reimbursements, Federal Work-Study and scholarships/grants also available. Support available to part-time students. Financial award applicants required to submit FAFSA. *Faculty research:* Agricultural development, international trade, agricultural marketing, econometrics, farm management and production economics. Total annual research expenditures: $1.1 million. *Unit head:* Lars Olson, Chair, 301-405-7180, E-mail: ljolson@umd.edu. *Application contact:* Dean of Graduate School, 301-405-0376, Fax: 301-314-9305.

University of Massachusetts Amherst, Graduate School, Isenberg School of Management, Department of Resource Economics, Amherst, MA 01003. Offers MS, PhD. Part-time programs available. *Faculty:* 15 full-time (4 women). *Students:* 15 full-time (8 women), 5 part-time (3 women); includes 1 minority (African American), 7 international. Average age 28. 32 applicants, 34% accepted, 8 enrolled. In 2009, 6 master's, 4 doctorates awarded. Terminal master's awarded for partial completion of doctoral program. *Degree requirements:* For master's, thesis or alternative; for doctorate, comprehensive exam, thesis/dissertation. *Entrance requirements:* For master's and doctorate, GRE General Test. Additional exam requirements/recommendations for international students: Required—TOEFL (minimum score 550 paper-based; 213 computer-based; 80 iBT), IELTS (minimum score 6.5). *Application deadline:* For fall admission, 2/1 for domestic and international students. Applications are processed on a rolling basis. Application fee: $50 ($65 for international students). Electronic applications accepted. *Expenses:* Tuition, state resident: full-time $2640; part-time $110 per credit. Tuition, nonresident: full-time $9936; part-time $414 per credit. Tuition and fees vary according to course load. *Financial support:* In 2009–10, 13 research assistantships with full tuition reimbursements (averaging $8,329 per year), 16 teaching assistantships with full tuition reimbursements (averaging $10,296 per year) were awarded; fellowships, career-related internships or fieldwork, Federal Work-Study, scholarships/grants, traineeships, and unspecified assistantships also available. Support available to part-time students. Financial award application deadline: 2/1. *Unit head:* Dr. Nathalie Lavoie, Graduate Program Director, 413-545-5732, Fax: 413-545-5853. *Application contact:* Jean M. Ames, Supervisor of Admissions, 413-545-0722, Fax: 413-577-0010, E-mail: gradadm@grad.umass.edu.

University of Missouri, Graduate School, College of Agriculture, Food and Natural Resources, Department of Agricultural Economics, Columbia, MO 65211. Offers MS, PhD. *Faculty:* 53 full-time (13 women), 12 part-time/adjunct (5 women). *Students:* 25 full-time (13 women), 23 part-time (5 women); includes 4 minority (1 African American, 2 Asian Americans or Pacific Islanders, 1 Hispanic American), 21 international. Average age 30. 50 applicants, 38% accepted, 11 enrolled. In 2009, 3 master's, 3 doctorates awarded. *Degree requirements:* For doctorate, comprehensive exam, thesis/dissertation. *Entrance requirements:* For master's and doctorate, GRE General Test, minimum GPA of 3.0. Additional exam requirements/recommendations for international students: Required—TOEFL (minimum score 550 paper-based; 80 iBT). *Application deadline:* For fall admission, 2/15 priority date for domestic students; for winter admission, 9/15 for domestic students. Applications are processed on a rolling basis. Application fee: $45 ($60 for international students). Electronic applications accepted. *Financial support:* Research assistantships with tuition reimbursements, teaching assistantships with tuition reimbursements, institutionally sponsored loans available. *Unit head:* Dr. Michael Monson, Department Chair, E-mail: monsonm@missouri.edu. *Application contact:* Jody Pestle, Administrative Assistant, 573-882-3747, E-mail: pestlej@missouri.edu.

University of Nebraska–Lincoln, Graduate College, College of Agricultural Sciences and Natural Resources, Department of Agricultural Economics, Lincoln, NE 68588. Offers agribusiness (MBA); agricultural economics (MS, PhD); community development (M Ag). *Degree requirements:* For master's, thesis optional; for doctorate, comprehensive exam, thesis/dissertation. *Entrance requirements:* For master's and doctorate, GRE General Test. Additional exam requirements/recommendations for international students: Required—TOEFL (minimum score 550 paper-based; 213 computer-based). Electronic applications accepted. *Faculty research:* Marketing and agribusiness, production economics, resource law, international trade and development, rural policy and revitalization.

University of Nevada, Reno, Graduate School, College of Agriculture, Biotechnology and Natural Resources, Department of Resource Economics, Reno, NV 89557. Offers MS, PhD. Terminal master's awarded for partial completion of doctoral program. *Degree requirements:* For master's, thesis optional; for doctorate, thesis/dissertation. *Entrance requirements:* For master's, GRE General Test, minimum GPA of 2.75; for doctorate, GRE General Test, minimum GPA of 3.0. Additional exam requirements/recommendations for international students: Required—TOEFL (minimum score 500 paper-based; 173 computer-based; 61 iBT), IELTS (minimum score 6). Electronic applications accepted. *Faculty research:* Econometrics, environmental valuation, natural resource and environmental policy analysis, public lands management.

University of Puerto Rico, Mayagüez Campus, Graduate Studies, College of Agricultural Sciences, Department of Agricultural Economics, Mayagüez, PR 00681-9000. Offers MS. Part-time programs available. *Degree requirements:* For master's, comprehensive exam, thesis. *Entrance requirements:* For master's, bachelor's degree in agricultural economics or its equivalent. *Faculty research:* Farm management, agricultural development, agrimarketing, natural resource economics.

University of Saskatchewan, College of Graduate Studies and Research, College of Agriculture, Department of Agricultural Economics, Saskatoon, SK S7N 5A2, Canada. Offers M Ag, M Sc, MA, PhD, PGD. *Faculty:* 28. *Students:* 42. In 2009, 5 master's, 1 doctorate awarded. *Degree requirements:* For master's, thesis; for doctorate, comprehensive exam (for some programs), thesis/dissertation. *Entrance requirements:* Additional exam requirements/recommendations for international students: Required—TOEFL (minimum score 80 iBT); Recommended—IELTS (minimum score 6.5). *Application deadline:* For fall admission, 7/1 priority date for domestic students. Applications are processed on a rolling basis. Application fee: $75. Tuition and fees charges are reported in Canadian dollars. *Expenses:* Tuition, area resident: Full-time $3000 Canadian dollars; part-time $500 Canadian dollars per term. Required fees: $700 Canadian dollars; $100 Canadian dollars per term. *Financial support:* Fellowships, research assistantships, teaching assistantships available. Financial award application deadline: 1/31. *Unit head:* Dr. Lope Tabil, Head, 306-966-5305, Fax: 306-966-5334, E-mail: lope.tabil@usask.ca. *Application contact:* Dr. Oon-Doo Baik, Graduate Chair, 306-966-7618, Fax: 306-966-8413, E-mail: oon-doo.baik@usask.ca.

University of Saskatchewan, College of Graduate Studies and Research, Edwards School of Business, Program in Business Administration, Saskatoon, SK S7N 5A2, Canada. Offers agribusiness management (MBA); biotechnology management (MBA); health services management (MBA); indigenous management (MBA); international business management (MBA). Tuition and fees charges are reported in Canadian dollars. *Expenses:* Tuition, area resident: Full-time $3000 Canadian dollars; part-time $500 Canadian dollars per term. Required fees: $700 Canadian dollars; $100 Canadian dollars per term.

University of Vermont, Graduate College, College of Agriculture and Life Sciences, Department of Community Development and Applied Economics, Burlington, VT 05405. Offers community development and applied economics (MS); public administration (MPA). *Students:* 28 (18 women), 2 international. 42 applicants, 64% accepted, 10 enrolled. In 2009, 10 master's awarded. *Degree requirements:* For master's, thesis. *Entrance requirements:* For master's, GRE General Test. Additional exam requirements/recommendations for international students: Required—TOEFL (minimum score 550 paper-based; 213 computer-based; 80 iBT). *Application deadline:* For fall admission, 4/1 priority date for domestic students; for spring admission, 11/15 for domestic students. Applications are processed on a rolling basis. Application fee: $40. Electronic applications accepted. *Expenses:* Tuition, state resident: part-time $508 per credit hour. Tuition, nonresident: part-time $1281 per credit hour. *Financial support:* Fellowships, research assistantships, teaching assistantships, career-related internships or fieldwork available. Financial award application deadline: 3/1. *Faculty research:* Agricultural production and marketing. *Unit head:* Dr. J. Kolodinsky, Chairperson, 802-656-2001. *Application contact:* Dr. J. Kolodinsky, Chairperson, 802-656-2001.

University of Wisconsin–Madison, Graduate School, College of Agricultural and Life Sciences, Department of Agricultural and Applied Economics, Madison, WI 53706-1380. Offers MA, MS, PhD. Part-time programs available. *Degree requirements:* For doctorate, thesis/dissertation, preliminary exams. *Entrance requirements:* For master's and doctorate, GRE General Test. Additional exam requirements/recommendations for international students: Required—TOEFL. Electronic applications accepted. *Expenses:* Tuition, state resident: part-time $594 per credit. Tuition, nonresident: part-time $1504 per credit. Required fees: $65 per credit. Tuition and fees vary according to course load, program and reciprocity agreements. *Faculty research:* Environmental and resource economics, international development, state and local economics, food systems, markets and trade.

University of Wyoming, College of Agriculture, Department of Agricultural and Applied Economics, Laramie, WY 82070. Offers MS. Part-time programs available. *Degree requirements:* For master's, thesis (for some programs). *Entrance requirements:* For master's, GRE General Test, minimum GPA of 3.0. Additional exam requirements/recommendations for international students: Required—TOEFL. Electronic applications accepted. *Faculty research:* Farm management, agricultural markets, water economics, community development, agricultural business.

Virginia Polytechnic Institute and State University, Graduate School, College of Agriculture and Life Sciences, Department of Agricultural and Applied Economics, Blacksburg, VA 24061. Offers agribusiness (MS); agricultural economics (MS, PhD); applied economics (MS); developmental and international economics (PhD); econometrics (PhD); macro and micro economics (PhD); markets and industrial organizations (PhD); public and regional/urban economics (PhD); resource and environmental economics (PhD). *Faculty:* 22 full-time (5 women). *Students:* 33 full-time (18 women); includes 18 American Indian/Alaska Native, 1 Asian American or Pacific Islander, 1 international. Average age 28. 47 applicants, 43% accepted, 12 enrolled. In 2009, 13 master's, 3 doctorates awarded. *Entrance requirements:* For master's and doctorate, GRE, GMAT. Additional exam requirements/recommendations for international students: Required—TOEFL (minimum score 575 paper-based; 213 computer-based). *Application deadline:* For fall admission, 5/15 for international students; for spring admission, 10/15 for international students. Applications are processed on a rolling basis. Application fee: $65. Electronic applications accepted. *Expenses:* Tuition, area resident: Full-time $10,228; part-time $459 per credit hour. Tuition, nonresident: full-time $17,892; part-time $865 per credit hour. Required fees: $1966; $451 per semester. *Financial support:* In 2009–10, 1 fellowship with full tuition reimbursement (averaging $20,000 per year), 21 research assistantships with full tuition reimbursements (averaging $21,611 per year), 8 teaching assistantships with full tuition reimbursements (averaging $13,481 per year) were awarded; career-related internships or fieldwork, Federal Work-Study, scholarships/grants, and unspecified assistantships also available. Financial award application deadline: 1/15. *Faculty research:* Rural development. Total annual research expenditures: $2.3 million. *Unit head:* Dr. Kevin Boyle, Dean, 540-231-6301, Fax: 540-231-7417, E-mail: kjboyle@vt.edu. *Application contact:* Bradford Mills, Contact, 540-231-6461, Fax: 540-231-7417, E-mail: bfmills@vt.edu.

Washington State University, Graduate School, College of Agricultural, Human, and Natural Resource Sciences, School of Economic Sciences, Pullman, WA 99164. Offers agribusiness (MA, Certificate); agricultural economics (MA, PhD); applied economics (MA); economics (MA, PhD, Certificate), including applied economics (MA), economics (MA, PhD), international business economics (Certificate). Terminal master's awarded for partial completion of doctoral program. *Degree requirements:* For master's, comprehensive exam (for some programs), thesis (for some programs), oral exam; for doctorate, comprehensive exam, thesis/dissertation, oral exam, written exam, qualifying exams. *Entrance requirements:* For master's and doctorate, minimum GPA of 3.0, 3 letters of recommendation. Additional exam requirements/recommendations for international students: Required—TOEFL (minimum score 550 paper-based; 213 computer-based). Electronic applications accepted. *Faculty research:* Marketing, natural resources, production economics.

West Texas A&M University, College of Agriculture, Nursing, and Natural Sciences, Division of Agriculture, Emphasis in Agricultural Business and Economics, Canyon, TX 79016-0001. Offers MS. Part-time programs available. *Degree requirements:* For master's, comprehensive exam, thesis optional. *Entrance requirements:* For master's, GRE General Test. Additional exam requirements/recommendations for international students: Required—TOEFL (minimum score 550 paper-based). Electronic applications accepted. *Faculty research:* Utilizing expected revenue in selecting optimal marketing alternatives for fixed resource cow/calf operators in the Texas panhandle.

West Virginia University, Davis College of Agriculture, Forestry and Consumer Sciences, Division of Resource Management and Sustainable Development, Program in Agricultural and Resource Economics, Morgantown, WV 26506. Offers MS. Part-time programs available. *Degree requirements:* For master's, thesis optional. *Entrance requirements:* For master's, GRE General Test, minimum GPA of 2.5, 1 calculus course. Additional exam requirements/recommendations for international students: Required—TOEFL. *Faculty research:* Agricultural production and marketing, rural development, mineral and energy economics, economic development.

William Woods University, Graduate and Adult Studies, Fulton, MO 65251-1098. Offers administration (Ed S); agriculture (MBA); athletic/activities administration (M Ed); curriculum and instruction (M Ed); curriculum leadership (Ed S); elementary administration (M Ed); health management (MBA); human resources (MBA); principalship (Ed S); secondary administration (M Ed); special education director (M Ed). Evening/weekend programs available. *Degree requirements:* For master's, capstone course (MBA), action research (M Ed); for Ed S, field experience. *Entrance requirements:* For master's, 2 recommendations, resumé, BA/BS; teaching certification (M Ed); course work in economics and accounting (MBA); for Ed S, M Ed, 2 letters of recommendation, resume, teaching certification. Additional exam requirements/recommendations for international students: Required—TOEFL (minimum score 550 paper-based). Electronic applications accepted.

Applied Economics

American University, College of Arts and Sciences, Department of Economics, Washington, DC 20016-8029. Offers applied microeconomics (Certificate); economics (MA, PhD); international economic relations (Certificate). Part-time and evening/weekend programs available. *Faculty:* 27 full-time (10 women). *Students:* 55 full-time (23 women), 67 part-time (27 women); includes 15 minority (12 African Americans, 1 Asian American or Pacific Islander, 2 Hispanic Americans), 49 international. Average age 29. 156 applicants, 69% accepted, 34 enrolled. In 2009, 23 master's, 10 doctorates, 1 other advanced degree awarded. Terminal master's awarded for partial completion of doctoral program. *Degree requirements:* For master's, comprehensive exam, thesis or alternative; for doctorate, comprehensive exam, thesis/dissertation, 2 research seminars, field work. *Entrance requirements:* For master's and doctorate, GRE; for Certificate, bachelor's degree. Additional exam requirements/recommendations for international students: Required—TOEFL. *Application deadline:* For spring admission, 10/1 for domestic students. Applications are processed on a rolling basis. Application fee: $80. *Expenses:* Tuition: Full-time $22,266; part-time $1237 per credit hour. Required fees: $430. Tuition and fees vary according to program. *Financial support:* Fellowships, research assistantships with full and partial tuition reimbursements, teaching assistantships with full and partial tuition reimbursements, career-related internships or fieldwork, Federal Work-Study, institutionally sponsored loans, and tuition waivers (full and partial) available. Financial award application deadline: 2/1. *Faculty research:* Political economy, development, labor, gender. *Unit head:* Robert A. Blecker, Chair, 202-885-3767, Fax: 202-885-3790, E-mail: blecker@american.edu. *Application contact:* Kathleen Clowery, Director of Graduate Admissions, 202-885-3621, Fax: 202-885-1505, E-mail: clowery@american.edu.

Auburn University, Graduate School, College of Agriculture, Department of Agricultural Economics and Rural Sociology, Auburn University, AL 36849. Offers agricultural economics (M Ag, MS); applied economics (PhD). Part-time programs available. *Faculty:* 18 full-time (3 women). *Students:* 28 full-time (9 women), 7 part-time (3 women); includes 2 minority (1 African American, 1 Asian American or Pacific Islander), 24 international. Average age 31. 55 applicants, 55% accepted, 9 enrolled. In 2009, 5 master's awarded. *Degree requirements:* For master's, thesis (for some programs); for doctorate, thesis/dissertation. *Entrance requirements:* For master's and doctorate, GRE General Test. *Application deadline:* For fall admission, 7/7 for domestic students; for spring admission, 11/24 for domestic students. Applications are processed on a rolling basis. Application fee: $50 ($60 for international students). Electronic applications accepted. *Expenses:* Tuition, state resident: full-time $6240. Tuition, nonresident: full-time $18,720. International tuition: $18,938 full-time. Required fees: $492. Tuition and fees vary according to course load, program and reciprocity agreements. *Financial support:* Research assistantships, teaching assistantships, Federal Work-Study available. Support available to part-time students. Financial award application deadline: 3/15; financial award applicants required to submit FAFSA. *Faculty research:* Farm management, agricultural marketing, production economics, resource economics, agricultural finance. *Unit head:* Dr. Curtis M. Jolly, Chair, 334-844-4800. *Application contact:* Dr. George Flowers, Dean of the Graduate School, 334-844-2125.

Buffalo State College, State University of New York, The Graduate School, Faculty of Natural and Social Sciences, Department of Economics and Finance, Buffalo, NY 14222-1095. Offers applied economics (MA). *Degree requirements:* For master's, project. *Entrance requirements:* Additional exam requirements/recommendations for international students: Required—TOEFL (minimum score 550 paper-based; 213 computer-based).

Cornell University, Graduate School, Graduate Fields of Agriculture and Life Sciences, Graduate Field of Applied Economics and Management, Ithaca, NY 14853-0001. Offers MPS, MS, PhD. *Faculty:* 55 full-time (7 women). *Students:* 85 full-time (43 women); includes 8 minority (1 African American, 1 American Indian/Alaska Native, 5 Asian Americans or Pacific Islanders, 1 Hispanic American), 53 international. Average age 28. 278 applicants, 32% accepted, 39 enrolled. In 2009, 10 master's, 7 doctorates awarded. *Entrance requirements:* For master's and doctorate, GRE. Additional exam requirements/recommendations for international students: Required—TOEFL. *Expenses:* Tuition: Full-time $29,500. Required fees: $70. Full-time tuition and fees vary according to degree level, program and student level. *Financial support:* In 2009–10, 6 fellowships, 5 research assistantships, 6 teaching assistantships were awarded. *Application contact:* Graduate School Application Requests, Caldwell Hall, 607-255-5820.

Cornell University, Graduate School, Graduate Fields of Arts and Sciences, Field of Economics, Ithaca, NY 14853-0001. Offers applied economics (PhD); basic analytical economics (PhD); econometrics and economic statistics (PhD); economic development and planning (PhD); economic theory (PhD); industrial organization and control (PhD); international economics (PhD); labor economics (PhD); monetary and macroeconomics (PhD); public finance (PhD). *Faculty:* 89 full-time (13 women). *Students:* 93 full-time (34 women); includes 6 minority (2 African Americans, 3 Asian Americans or Pacific Islanders, 1 Hispanic American), 51 international. Average age 28. 625 applicants, 11% accepted, 21 enrolled. In 2009, 21 doctorates awarded. *Degree requirements:* For doctorate, comprehensive exam, thesis/dissertation. *Entrance requirements:* For doctorate, GRE General Test, 3 letters of recommendation. Additional exam requirements/recommendations for international students: Required—TOEFL (minimum score 550 paper-based; 213 computer-based; 77 iBT). *Application deadline:* For fall admission, 1/15 priority date for domestic students. Application fee: $70. Electronic applications accepted. *Expenses:* Tuition: Full-time $29,500. Required fees: $70. Full-time tuition and fees vary according to degree level, program and student level. *Financial support:* In 2009–10, 81 students received support, including 12 fellowships with full tuition reimbursements available, 2 teaching assistantships with full tuition reimbursements available; research assistantships with full tuition reimbursements available, institutionally sponsored loans, scholarships/grants, health care benefits, tuition waivers (full and partial), and unspecified assistantships also available. Financial award applicants required to submit FAFSA. *Faculty research:* Learning and games, economics of education, political economy, transfer payments, time series and nonparametrics. *Unit head:* Director of Graduate Studies, 607-255-4893, Fax: 607-255-2818. *Application contact:* Graduate Field Assistant, 607-255-4893, Fax: 607-255-2818, E-mail: econ_phd@cornell.edu.

Eastern Michigan University, Graduate School, College of Arts and Sciences, Department of Economics, Ypsilanti, MI 48197. Offers applied economics (MA); economics (MA); health economics (MA); international economics and development (MA); trade and development (MA). Part-time and evening/weekend programs available. Postbaccalaureate distance learning degree programs offered (minimal on-campus study). *Faculty:* 11 full-time (2 women). *Students:* 28 full-time (9 women), 29 part-time (12 women); includes 17 minority (12 African Americans, 1 American Indian/Alaska Native, 2 Asian Americans or Pacific Islanders, 2 Hispanic Americans), 12 international. Average age 31. 61 applicants, 67% accepted, 23 enrolled. In 2009, 22 master's awarded. *Degree requirements:* For master's, thesis or alternative. *Entrance requirements:* Additional exam requirements/recommendations for international students: Required—TOEFL. *Application deadline:* Applications are processed on a rolling basis. Application fee: $35. Tuition and fees vary according to course level. *Financial support:* Fellowships, research assistantships with full tuition reimbursements, teaching assistantships with full tuition reimbursements, career-related internships or fieldwork, Federal Work-Study, institutionally sponsored loans, scholarships/grants, tuition waivers (partial), and unspecified assistantships available. Support available to part-time students. Financial award applicants required to submit FAFSA. *Unit head:* Dr. Raouf S. Hanna, Department Head, 734-487-3395, Fax: 734-487-9666, E-mail: rhanna@emich.edu. *Application contact:* Dr. David Crary, Advisor, 734-487-0001, Fax: 734-487-9666, E-mail: david.crary@emich.edu.

Georgia Southern University, Jack N. Averitt College of Graduate Studies, College of Business Administration, School of Economic Development, Program in Applied Economics, Statesboro, GA 30460. Offers MS. Program is online. Part-time and evening/weekend programs available. Postbaccalaureate distance learning degree programs offered (no on-campus study). *Students:* 4 full-time (1 woman), 38 part-time (11 women); includes 6 minority (2 African Americans, 1 American Indian/Alaska Native, 1 Asian American or Pacific Islander, 2 Hispanic Americans), 2 international. Average age 33. 42 applicants, 90% accepted, 31 enrolled. *Entrance requirements:* For master's, GRE or GMAT, minimum GPA of 3.0. Additional exam requirements/recommendations for international students: Required—TOEFL (minimum score 550 paper-based; 213 computer-based; 80 iBT). *Application deadline:* For fall admission, 3/1 priority date for domestic and international students; for spring admission, 10/1 priority date for domestic students, 10/1 for international students. Applications are processed on a rolling basis. Application fee: $50. Electronic applications accepted. *Expenses:* Tuition, state resident: full-time $5040; part-time $210 per credit hour. Tuition, nonresident: full-time $20,136; part-time $839 per credit hour. Required fees: $1644. *Financial support:* In 2009–10, 18 students received support. Application deadline: 4/15. *Faculty research:* Theory of the firm, industrial organization, public economics, economic development and functioning of credit markets. *Unit head:* Dr. Godfrey Gibbison, Director, School of Economic Development, 912-478-0086, Fax: 912-478-0710, E-mail: ggibbiso@georgiasouthern.edu. *Application contact:* Dr. Charles Ziglar, Coordinator of Graduate Student Recruitment, 912-478-5635, Fax: 912-478-0740, E-mail: gradadmissions@georgiasouthern.edu.

HEC Montreal, School of Business Administration, Master of Science Programs in Administration, Program in Applied Economics, Montréal, QC H3T 2A7, Canada. Offers M Sc. All courses are given in French. Part-time programs available. *Students:* 22 full-time (6 women), 2 part-time (1 woman). 20 applicants, 70% accepted, 5 enrolled. In 2009, 7 master's awarded. *Degree requirements:* For master's, one foreign language, thesis. *Application deadline:* For fall admission, 3/14 for domestic students, 3/15 for international students; for winter admission, 9/15 for domestic and international students. Application fee: $77 Canadian dollars. Electronic applications accepted. Tuition and fees charges are reported in Canadian dollars. *Expenses:* Tuition, area resident: Part-time $65.60 Canadian dollars per credit. Tuition, state resident: full-time $2361.60 Canadian dollars; part-time $183.36 Canadian dollars per credit. Tuition, nonresident: full-time $6601 Canadian dollars; part-time $448.13 Canadian dollars per credit. International tuition: $16,132.68 Canadian dollars full-time. Required fees: $1254.15 Canadian dollars; $28.99 Canadian dollars per course. $91.68 Canadian dollars per term. Tuition and fees vary according to degree level and program. *Financial support:* Fellowships, research assistantships, teaching assistantships, scholarships/grants available. Financial award application deadline: 10/2. *Unit head:* Dr. Claude Laurin, Director, 514-340-6485, Fax: 514-340-5690, E-mail: claude.laurin@hec.ca. *Application contact:* Francine Blais, Administrative Director, 514-340-6112, Fax: 514-340-6411, E-mail: francine.blais@hec.ca.

The Johns Hopkins University, Zanvyl Krieger School of Arts and Sciences, Advanced Academic Programs, Program in Applied Economics, Baltimore, MD 21218-2699. Offers MA. Part-time and evening/weekend programs available. *Faculty:* 1 full-time (0 women), 32 part-time/adjunct (4 women). *Students:* 33 full-time (18 women), 280 part-time (118 women); includes 63 minority (14 African Americans, 2 American Indian/Alaska Native, 31 Asian Americans or Pacific Islanders, 16 Hispanic Americans), 36 international. Average age 28. 198 applicants, 58% accepted, 88 enrolled. In 2009, 67 master's awarded. *Degree requirements:* For master's, thesis (for some programs). *Entrance requirements:* For master's, minimum GPA of 3.0, coursework in microeconomics and macroeconomics. Additional exam requirements/recommendations for international students: Required—TOEFL (minimum score 250 computer-based; 100 iBT). *Application deadline:* For fall admission, 5/31 priority date for domestic students, 4/30 priority date for international students; for spring admission, 10/31 priority date for domestic and international students. Applications are processed on a rolling basis. Application fee: $75. Electronic applications accepted. *Financial support:* Applicants required to submit FAFSA. *Unit head:* Dr. Frank Weiss, Associate Program Chair, 202-452-0769, E-mail: fdweiss@jhu.edu. *Application contact:* Valana M. McMickens, Admissions Manager, 202-452-1941, Fax: 202-452-1970, E-mail: aapadmissions@jhu.edu.

Mississippi State University, College of Business, Department of Finance and Economics, MS State, MS 39762. Offers applied economics (PhD); business administration (PhD), including finance; economics (MA); finance (MSBA). Part-time programs available. *Faculty:* 13 full-time (2 women). *Students:* 15 full-time (4 women), 4 part-time (1 woman); includes 1 minority (African American), 11 international. Average age 31. 31 applicants, 23% accepted, 3 enrolled. In 2009, 2 master's, 3 doctorates awarded. Terminal master's awarded for partial completion of doctoral program. *Degree requirements:* For master's, comprehensive exam, thesis optional; for doctorate, comprehensive exam, thesis/dissertation. *Entrance requirements:* For master's and doctorate, GMAT, GRE General Test. Additional exam requirements/recommendations for international students: Required—TOEFL (minimum score 575 paper-based; 233 computer-based; 90 iBT); Recommended—IELTS (minimum score 6.5). *Application deadline:* For fall admission, 7/1 for domestic students, 5/1 for international students; for spring admission, 11/1

Applied Economics

Mississippi State University (continued)

for domestic students, 10/1 for international students. Applications are processed on a rolling basis. Application fee: $40. Electronic applications accepted. *Expenses:* Tuition, state resident: full-time $2575.50; part-time $286.25 per credit hour. Tuition, nonresident: full-time $6510; part-time $723.50 per credit hour. Tuition and fees vary according to course load. *Financial support:* In 2009–10, 5 teaching assistantships with tuition reimbursements (averaging $10,698 per year) were awarded; Federal Work-Study, scholarships/grants, health care benefits, and unspecified assistantships also available. Financial award application deadline: 4/1; financial award applicants required to submit FAFSA. *Faculty research:* Economics development, mergers, event studies, economic education, bank performance. Total annual research expenditures: $491,000. *Unit head:* Dr. Mike Highfield, Department Head, 662-325-3928, Fax: 662-325-1977, E-mail: mhighfield@cobilan.msstate.edu. *Application contact:* Dr. Benjamin F. Blair, Associate Professor/Graduate Coordinator, 662-325-1980, Fax: 662-325-1977, E-mail: bblair@cobilan.msstate.edu.

New York University, Graduate School of Arts and Science, Department of Economics, New York, NY 10012-1019. Offers applied economic analysis (Advanced Certificate); economics (MA, PhD); JD/MA; MD/PhD. Part-time and evening/weekend programs available. *Faculty:* 35 full-time (2 women). *Students:* 231 full-time (80 women), 38 part-time (9 women); includes 18 minority (1 African American, 16 Asian Americans or Pacific Islanders, 1 Hispanic American), 193 international. Average age 27. 1,344 applicants, 15% accepted, 78 enrolled. In 2009, 86 master's, 18 doctorates, 4 other advanced degrees awarded. Terminal master's awarded for partial completion of doctoral program. *Degree requirements:* For master's, thesis; for doctorate, one foreign language, thesis/dissertation, 4 qualifying exams. *Entrance requirements:* For master's and doctorate, GRE General Test; for Advanced Certificate, master's degree. Additional exam requirements/recommendations for international students: Required—TOEFL. *Application deadline:* For fall admission, 1/4 priority date for domestic students. Application fee: $90. *Expenses:* Tuition: Full-time $30,528; part-time $1272 per credit. Required fees: $2177. *Financial support:* Fellowships with tuition reimbursements, research assistantships with tuition reimbursements, teaching assistantships with tuition reimbursements, Federal Work-Study, institutionally sponsored loans, scholarships/grants, health care benefits, and unspecified assistantships available. Financial award application deadline: 1/4; financial award applicants required to submit FAFSA. *Faculty research:* Economic theory, experimental economics, growth and development, macroeconomics and finance, international trade and international finance. *Unit head:* Nicola Persico, Chair, 212-998-8900, Fax: 212-995-4186, E-mail: admissions@econ.nyu.edu. *Application contact:* Ennio Stacchetti, Director of Graduate Studies, 212-998-8900, Fax: 212-995-4186, E-mail: gsas.admissions@nyu.edu.

North Carolina Agricultural and Technical State University, Graduate School, School of Agriculture and Environmental Sciences, Department of Agribusiness, Applied Economics, and Agriscience Education, Greensboro, NC 27411. Offers agricultural economics (MS); agricultural education (MS). *Accreditation:* NCATE. Part-time and evening/weekend programs available. *Degree requirements:* For master's, comprehensive exam, thesis or alternative, qualifying exam. *Entrance requirements:* For master's, GRE General Test, minimum GPA of 3.0. *Faculty research:* Aid for small farmers, agricultural technology resources, labor force mobility, agrology.

Northeastern University, College of Social Sciences and Humanities, Department of Economics, Boston, MA 02115-5096. Offers MA, PhD. Part-time and evening/weekend programs available. *Faculty:* 17 full-time (2 women), 11 part-time/adjunct (6 women). *Students:* 74 full-time (41 women), 4 part-time (3 women); includes 1 African American, 4 Asian Americans or Pacific Islanders, 47 international. 197 applicants, 46% accepted, 32 enrolled. In 2009, 20 master's, 2 doctorates awarded. *Degree requirements:* For master's and doctorate, comprehensive exam. *Entrance requirements:* For master's, GRE. Additional exam requirements/recommendations for international students: Required—TOEFL. *Application deadline:* For fall admission, 8/1 for domestic students, 5/1 priority date for international students; for spring admission, 12/1 for domestic and international students. Applications are processed on a rolling basis. Application fee: $50. *Financial support:* In 2009–10, 13 teaching assistantships (averaging $15,667 per year) were awarded; Federal Work-Study, institutionally sponsored loans, tuition waivers (full and partial), and unspecified assistantships also available. Financial award application deadline: 2/1; financial award applicants required to submit FAFSA. *Faculty research:* U. S. labor markets, applied economics, microeconomic theory, macroeconomic theory, econometrics. *Unit head:* Dr. Steven Morrison, Chair, 617-373-2872, Fax: 617-373-3640, E-mail: econ@neu.edu. *Application contact:* Dr. Gregory Wassall, Graduate Coordinator, 617-373-2882, Fax: 617-373-3640, E-mail: econ@neu.edu.

Ohio University, Graduate College, College of Arts and Sciences, Department of Economics, Athens, OH 45701-2979. Offers applied economics (MA); financial economics (MFE). Part-time and evening/weekend programs available. *Faculty:* 15 full-time (3 women). *Students:* 56 full-time (20 women), 17 part-time (8 women); includes 10 minority (7 African Americans, 3 Asian Americans or Pacific Islanders), 33 international. 53 applicants, 57% accepted, 6 enrolled. In 2009, 49 master's awarded. *Degree requirements:* For master's, thesis or alternative. *Entrance requirements:* For master's, GRE or GMAT (recommended), minimum GPA of 3.0. Additional exam requirements/recommendations for international students: Required—TOEFL (minimum score 550 paper-based; 80 iBT) or IELTS Academic (minimum score 6.5). *Application deadline:* For fall admission, 2/15 priority date for domestic and international students; for winter admission, 12/1 for domestic students, 10/1 priority date for international students. Application fee: $50 ($55 for international students). Electronic applications accepted. *Expenses:* Tuition, state resident: full-time $7839; part-time $323 per quarter hour. Tuition, nonresident: full-time $15,831; part-time $654 per quarter hour. Required fees: $2931. *Financial support:* Research assistantships with full and partial tuition reimbursements, Federal Work-Study, tuition waivers (partial), and unspecified assistantships available. Financial award application deadline: 2/15. *Faculty research:* Macroeconomics, public finance, international economics and finance, monetary theory, healthcare economics. *Unit head:* Dr. Rosmary Rossiter, Chair, 740-593-2040, E-mail: rossiter@ohio.edu. *Application contact:* Dr. K. Doroodian, Graduate Chair, 740-593-2046, E-mail: doroodia@ohio.edu.

Old Dominion University, College of Business and Public Administration, Master's Program in Business Administration, Norfolk, VA 23529. Offers business and economic forecasting (MBA); financial analysis and valuation (MBA); information technology and enterprise integration (MBA); international business (MBA); maritime and port management (MBA); public administration (MBA). *Accreditation:* AACSB. Part-time and evening/weekend programs available. *Faculty:* 66 full-time (15 women), 6 part-time/adjunct (1 woman). *Students:* 81 full-time (27 women), 198 part-time (92 women); includes 46 minority (25 African Americans, 1 American Indian/Alaska Native, 13 Asian Americans or Pacific Islanders, 7 Hispanic Americans), 31 international. Average age 30. 169 applicants, 52% accepted, 61 enrolled. In 2009, 81 master's awarded. *Entrance requirements:* For master's, GMAT, letters of reference, resume, coursework in calculus. Additional exam requirements/recommendations for international students: Required—TOEFL (minimum score 550 paper-based; 213 computer-based; 80 iBT). *Application deadline:* For fall admission, 6/1 priority date for domestic students, 4/15 priority date for international students; for spring admission, 11/1 priority date for domestic students, 10/1 priority date for international students. Applications are processed on a rolling basis. Application fee: $50. Electronic applications accepted. *Expenses:* Tuition, state resident: full-time $8112; part-time $338 per credit. Tuition, nonresident: full-time $20,256; part-time $844 per credit. Required fees: $119 per semester. One-time fee: $50. *Financial support:* In 2009–10, 46 students received support, including 31 research assistantships with partial tuition reimbursements available (averaging $7,000 per year), 3 teaching assistantships with partial tuition reimbursements available (averaging $6,300 per year); career-related internships or fieldwork, scholarships/grants, and unspecified assistantships also available. Support available to part-time students. Financial award application deadline: 2/15; financial award applicants required to submit FAFSA. *Faculty research:* International business, buyer behavior, financial markets, strategy, operations research. *Unit head:* Dr. Bruce Rubin, Graduate Program Director, 757-683-3585, E-mail: mbainfo@odu.edu. *Application contact:* Shanna Wood, MBA Program Manager, 757-683-3585, Fax: 757-683-5750, E-mail: mbainfo@odu.edu.

Portland State University, Graduate Studies, College of Liberal Arts and Sciences, Department of Economics, Portland, OR 97207-0751. Offers applied economics (MA, MS); economics (PhD); general economics (MA, MS). Part-time programs available. *Degree requirements:* For master's, thesis optional; for doctorate, one foreign language, thesis/dissertation. *Entrance requirements:* For master's, minimum GPA of 3.0 in upper-division course work or 2.75 overall, course work in calculus. Additional exam requirements/recommendations for international students: Required—TOEFL (minimum score 550 paper-based; 213 computer-based). *Faculty research:* NAFTA, economies of transition, economics of Eastern Europe, artificial intelligence, comparative economic systems.

Roosevelt University, Graduate Division, College of Arts and Sciences, Department of Economics, Chicago, IL 60605. Offers applied economics (MA); economics (MA). Part-time and evening/weekend programs available. *Degree requirements:* For master's, thesis or alternative. *Entrance requirements:* For master's, minimum GPA of 2.7. *Faculty research:* Labor, gender issues, international trade and development, entrepreneurship, political economy and money.

St. Cloud State University, School of Graduate Studies, College of Social Sciences, Department of Economics, Program in Applied Economics, St. Cloud, MN 56301-4498. Offers MS. *Students:* 13 full-time (3 women), 5 part-time (2 women); includes 1 minority (African American), 12 international. 11 applicants, 73% accepted. In 2009, 6 master's awarded. *Unit head:* Dr. Patricia Hughes, Chairperson, 320-308-2076, E-mail: pahughes@stcloudstate.edu. *Application contact:* Linda Lou Krueger, School of Graduate Studies, 320-308-2113, Fax: 320-308-5371, E-mail: lekrueger@stcloudstate.edu.

San Jose State University, Graduate Studies and Research, College of Social Sciences, Department of Economics, San Jose, CA 95192-0001. Offers applied economics (MA); economics (MA). Part-time programs available. *Students:* 43 full-time (15 women), 33 part-time (11 women); includes 27 minority (1 African American, 18 Asian Americans or Pacific Islanders, 8 Hispanic Americans), 16 international. Average age 32. 94 applicants, 43% accepted, 29 enrolled. In 2009, 34 master's awarded. *Degree requirements:* For master's, comprehensive exam, thesis optional. *Entrance requirements:* For master's, GRE, minimum GPA of 3.0. *Application deadline:* For fall admission, 6/29 for domestic students; for spring admission, 11/30 for domestic students. Applications are processed on a rolling basis. Application fee: $59. Electronic applications accepted. *Financial support:* Teaching assistantships available. Financial award applicants required to submit FAFSA. *Unit head:* Dr. Lydia Ortega, Chair, 408-924-5400, Fax: 408-924-5406. *Application contact:* Dr. Lydia Ortega, Chair, 408-924-5400, Fax: 408-924-5406.

Southern Methodist University, Dedman College, Department of Economics, Dallas, TX 75205. Offers applied economics (MA); economics (MA, PhD); JD/MA. Part-time and evening/weekend programs available. *Faculty:* 17 full-time (4 women), 23 part-time/adjunct (9 women). *Students:* 47 full-time (22 women), 25 part-time (11 women); includes 9 minority (4 African Americans, 4 Asian Americans or Pacific Islanders, 1 Hispanic American), 33 international. Average age 27. 95 applicants, 78% accepted, 22 enrolled. In 2009, 17 master's, 5 doctorates awarded. Terminal master's awarded for partial completion of doctoral program. *Degree requirements:* For master's, thesis, oral qualifying exam; for doctorate, thesis/dissertation, written exams. *Entrance requirements:* For master's, GRE General Test or GMAT, 12 hours course work in economics, minimum GPA of 3.0, previous course work in calculus and statistics; for doctorate, GRE General Test, minimum GPA of 3.0; 3 semesters of course work in calculus; 1 semester each of course work in statistics and linear algebra. Additional exam requirements/recommendations for international students: Required—TOEFL (minimum score 550 paper-based; 213 computer-based). *Application deadline:* For fall admission, 2/1 priority date for domestic students; for spring admission, 11/30 priority date for domestic students. Applications are processed on a rolling basis. Application fee: $75. Electronic applications accepted. *Financial support:* In 2009–10, 23 students received support, including 1 fellowship with full tuition reimbursement available (averaging $16,000 per year), 1 research assistantship with full tuition reimbursement available (averaging $16,000 per year), 16 teaching assistantships with full tuition reimbursements available (averaging $16,000 per year). Financial award application deadline: 2/1; financial award applicants required to submit FAFSA. *Faculty research:* Economic theory, game theory, econometrics, international trade, labor. *Unit head:* Dr. Thomas Fomby, Chair, 214-768-2559, Fax: 214-768-2559, E-mail: tfomby@smu.edu. *Application contact:* Stephanie Hall, Information Contact, 214-768-2694, E-mail: eco@smu.edu.

Texas Tech University, Graduate School, College of Agricultural Sciences and Natural Resources, Department of Agricultural and Applied Economics, Lubbock, TX 79409. Offers agribusiness (MAB); agricultural and applied economics (MS, PhD); JD/MS. Part-time programs available. *Faculty:* 12 full-time (0 women). *Students:* 40 full-time (18 women), 6 part-time (0 women); includes 1 minority (Hispanic American), 28 international. Average age 29. 53 applicants, 62% accepted, 6 enrolled. In 2009, 8 master's, 2 doctorates awarded. *Degree requirements:* For master's, thesis or alternative; for doctorate, thesis/dissertation. *Entrance requirements:* For master's and doctorate, GRE General Test. Additional exam requirements/recommendations for international students: Required—TOEFL (minimum score 550 paper-based; 213 computer-based). *Application deadline:* For fall admission, 3/1 priority date for international students; for spring admission, 11/1 priority date for international students. Applications are processed on a rolling basis. Application fee: $50 ($75 for international students). Electronic applications accepted. *Expenses:* Tuition, state resident: full-time $5100; part-time $213 per credit hour. Tuition, nonresident: full-time $11,748; part-time $490 per credit hour. Required fees: $2298; $50 per credit hour. $555 per semester. *Financial support:* In 2009–10, 13 research assistantships with partial tuition reimbursements (averaging $21,555 per year) were awarded; teaching assistantships with partial tuition reimbursements, Federal Work-Study and institutionally sponsored loans also available. Support available to part-time students. Financial award application deadline: 4/15; financial award applicants required to submit FAFSA. *Faculty research:* Economics of the United States cotton and textile industries, natural resource management in semi-arid climates, commodity policy analysis, international trade in agricultural products, agribusiness analysis. Total annual research expenditures: $1.3 million. *Unit head:* Dr. Eduardo Segarra, Chair, 806-742-2821, Fax: 806-742-1099, E-mail: eduardo.segarra@ttu.edu. *Application contact:* Dr. Tom Knight, Graduate Adviser, 806-742-2821, Fax: 806-742-1099, E-mail: tom.knight@ttu.edu.

University of California, Santa Cruz, Division of Graduate Studies, Division of Social Sciences, Program in Applied Economics and Finance, Santa Cruz, CA 95064. Offers MS. *Degree requirements:* For master's, thesis or alternative, project. *Entrance requirements:* For master's, GRE General Test, GRE Subject Test. *Faculty research:* Economic decision-making skills for the design and operation of complex institutional systems.

University of Georgia, Graduate School, College of Agricultural and Environmental Sciences, Department of Agricultural and Applied Economics, Athens, GA 30602. Offers agricultural economics (MAE, MS, PhD); environmental economics (MS). *Faculty:* 22 full-time (4 women), 1 part-time/adjunct (0 women). *Students:* 38 full-time (19 women), 7 part-time (1 woman); includes 4 minority (2 African Americans, 1 Asian American or Pacific Islander, 1 Hispanic American), 25 international. 45 applicants, 22% accepted, 9 enrolled. In 2009, 4 master's, 4 doctorates awarded. *Degree requirements:* For master's, thesis (MS); for doctorate, thesis/dissertation. *Entrance requirements:* For master's and doctorate, GRE General Test. *Application deadline:* For fall admission, 7/1 priority date for domestic students; for spring admission, 11/15 for domestic students. Application fee: $50. Electronic applications accepted. *Expenses:* Tuition, state resident: full-time $6000; part-time $250 per credit hour. Tuition, nonresident: full-time $20,904; part-time $871 per credit hour. Required fees: $730 per semester. *Financial support:* Fellowships, research assistantships, teaching assistantships, career-related internships or fieldwork and unspecified assistantships available. *Unit head:* Dr. Octavio A. Ramirez, Interim Head, 706-542-2481, Fax: 706-542-0739, E-mail: oramirez@agecon.uga.edu. *Application* *contact:* Dr. Michael E. Wetzstein, Graduate Coordinator, 706-543-0758, Fax: 706-542-0739, E-mail: mwetz@uga.edu.

University of Idaho, College of Graduate Studies, College of Agricultural and Life Sciences, Department of Agricultural Economics and Rural Sociology, Moscow, ID 83844-2282. Offers agricultural economics (MS); applied economics (MS), including agribusiness emphasis, agricultural economics emphasis. *Faculty:* 6 full-time, 4 part-time/adjunct. *Students:* 16 full-time. In 2009, 7 master's awarded. *Entrance requirements:* For master's, minimum GPA of 2.8. *Application deadline:* For fall admission, 8/1 for domestic students; for spring admission, 12/15 for domestic students. Application fee: $55 ($60 for international students). *Expenses:* Tuition, state resident: full-time $6120. Tuition, nonresident: full-time $17,712. *Financial support:* Research assistantships, teaching assistantships available. Financial award application deadline: 2/15. *Faculty research:* Crops: potatoes, blue grass; livestock: beef, dairy; rural and community development; natural resources and the environment; farm and ranch management. *Unit head:* Dr. Larry W. Van Tassell, Department Head, 208-885-7869, Fax: 208-885-5759. *Application contact:* Dr. Larry W. Van Tassell, Department Head, 208-885-7869, Fax: 208-885-5759.

University of Michigan, Horace H. Rackham School of Graduate Studies, College of Literature, Science, and the Arts, Department of Economics, Program in Applied Economics, Ann Arbor, MI 48109. Offers AM. Part-time programs available. *Faculty:* 49 full-time (6 women). *Students:* 71 full-time (27 women); includes 52 minority (2 African Americans, 50 Asian Americans or Pacific Islanders). 253 applicants, 37% accepted, 31 enrolled. In 2009, 33 master's awarded. *Entrance requirements:* For master's, GRE General Test. Additional exam requirements/recommendations for international students: Required—TOEFL (minimum score 600 paper-based; 250 computer-based). *Application deadline:* For fall admission, 2/5 for domestic and international students. Application fee: $60 ($75 for international students). *Expenses:* Tuition, state resident: full-time $17,286; part-time $1099 per credit hour. Tuition, nonresident: full-time $34,944; part-time $2080 per credit hour. Required fees: $95 per semester. Tuition and fees vary according to course load, degree level and program. *Faculty research:* Econometric analysis transition, macro. *Unit head:* John Laitner, Director, 734-763-5316, Fax: 734-764-2769. *Application contact:* LaRue Cochran, Student Services Assistant, 734-763-5316, Fax: 734-764-2769, E-mail: larue@umich.edu.

University of Minnesota, Twin Cities Campus, Graduate School, College of Food, Agricultural and Natural Resource Sciences, Program in Applied Economics, Minneapolis, MN 55455-0213. Offers MS, PhD. *Degree requirements:* For master's, comprehensive exam, thesis; for doctorate, comprehensive exam, thesis/dissertation. *Entrance requirements:* For master's and doctorate, GRE, minimum GPA of 3.0 preferred. Additional exam requirements/recommendations for international students: Required—TOEFL (minimum score 550 paper-based; 213 computer-based; 79 iBT). Electronic applications accepted. *Faculty research:* Consumer behavior, household and labor, policy analysis and health, production and marketing, resource and environmental, trade and development.

University of Nevada, Reno, Graduate School, College of Agriculture, Biotechnology and Natural Resources, Department of Resource Economics, Reno, NV 89557. Offers MS, PhD. Terminal master's awarded for partial completion of doctoral program. *Degree requirements:* For master's, thesis optional; for doctorate, thesis/dissertation. *Entrance requirements:* For master's, GRE General Test, minimum GPA of 2.75; for doctorate, GRE General Test, minimum GPA of 3.0. Additional exam requirements/recommendations for international students: Required—TOEFL (minimum score 500 paper-based; 173 computer-based; 61 iBT), IELTS (minimum score 6). Electronic applications accepted. *Faculty research:* Econometrics, environmental valuation, natural resource and environmental policy analysis, public lands management.

University of New Brunswick Fredericton, School of Graduate Studies, Faculty of Arts, Department of Economics, Fredericton, NB E3B 5A3, Canada. Offers applied economics and finance (M Sc); economics (MA). Program in applied economics and finance offered at UNB Saint John Campus. *Faculty:* 10 full-time (1 woman), 3 part-time/adjunct (0 women). *Students:* 4 full-time (1 woman), 2 part-time (both women). In 2009, 6 master's awarded. *Entrance requirements:* For master's, GRE, minimum GPA of 3.0. Additional exam requirements/recommendations for international students: Required—TOEFL (minimum score 550 paper-based), TWE, or IELTS. *Application deadline:* 1/31 for domestic and international students. Applications are processed on a rolling basis. Application fee: $50 Canadian dollars. Tuition and fees charges are reported in Canadian dollars. *Expenses:* Tuition, area resident: Full-time $5562 Canadian dollars; part-time $2781 Canadian dollars per year. Required fees: $49.75 Canadian dollars per term. *Financial support:* In 2009–10, 2 research assistantships (averaging $16,000 per year) were awarded; scholarships/grants, health care benefits, and unspecified assistantships also available. Financial award application deadline: 1/31. *Faculty research:* Epidemiology and population health, micro/macro economics, economics of transportation, regional development. *Unit head:* Dr. Yuri Yevdokimov, Director of Graduate Studies, 506-447-3221, Fax: 506-453-4514, E-mail: yuri@unb.ca. *Application contact:* Lucina MacDonald, Graduate Secretary, 506-453-4828, Fax: 506-453-4514, E-mail: lmacdona@unb.ca.

The University of North Carolina at Greensboro, Graduate School, Bryan School of Business and Economics, Department of Economics, Program in Applied Economics, Greensboro, NC 27412-5001. Offers MA, MA/PhD. *Degree requirements:* For master's, comprehensive exam, thesis or alternative. *Entrance requirements:* For master's, GRE. Additional exam requirements/recommendations for international students: Required—TOEFL. Electronic applications accepted.

University of North Dakota, Graduate School, College of Business and Public Administration, Applied Economics Program, Grand Forks, ND 58202. Offers MSAE. *Degree requirements:* For master's, comprehensive exam, thesis or alternative. *Entrance requirements:* For master's, GRE General Test. Additional exam requirements/recommendations for international students: Required—TOEFL (minimum score 550 paper-based; 213 computer-based; 79 iBT), IELTS (minimum score 6.5).

University of North Texas, Robert B. Toulouse School of Graduate Studies, College of Public Affairs and Community Service, Institute of Applied Economics, Denton, TX 76203. Offers MS. Part-time programs available. *Degree requirements:* For master's, comprehensive exam, thesis or alternative. *Entrance requirements:* For master's, GRE General Test or GMAT, minimum B average in last 60 hours of course work. Additional exam requirements/recommendations for international students: Required—proof of English language proficiency required for non-native English speakers; Recommended—TOEFL (minimum score 550 paper-based; 213 computer-based; 79 iBT). *Application deadline:* Applications are processed on a rolling basis. Application fee: $50 ($75 for international students). Electronic applications accepted. *Expenses:* Tuition, state resident: full-time $4298; part-time $239 per contact hour. Tuition, nonresident: full-time $9878; part-time $549 per contact hour. Required fees: $265 per contact hour. *Financial support:* Research assistantships, career-related internships or fieldwork, Federal Work-Study, and tuition waivers (partial) available. Financial award applicants required to submit FAFSA. *Faculty research:* Economic/focal impact of sports and entertainment venues, economic development potential of stem cell research, state and local incentive programs, city and metropolitan area industrial targeting dispute resolution. *Application contact:* Graduate Adviser, 940-565-3437, Fax: 940-565-4658.

University of Pennsylvania, Wharton School, Program in Applied Economics, Philadelphia, PA 19104. Offers PhD. *Expenses:* Tuition: Full-time $25,660; part-time $4758 per course. Required fees: $2152; $270 per course. Tuition and fees vary according to course load, degree level and program.

University of Vermont, Graduate College, College of Agriculture and Life Sciences, Department of Community Development and Applied Economics, Burlington, VT 05405. Offers community development and applied economics (MS); public administration (MPA). *Students:* 28 (18 women), 2 international. 42 applicants, 64% accepted, 10 enrolled. In 2009, 10 master's awarded. *Degree requirements:* For master's, thesis. *Entrance requirements:* For master's, GRE General Test. Additional exam requirements/recommendations for international students: Required—TOEFL (minimum score 550 paper-based; 213 computer-based; 80 iBT). *Application deadline:* For fall admission, 4/1 priority date for domestic students; for spring admission, 11/15 for domestic students. Applications are processed on a rolling basis. Application fee: $40. Electronic applications accepted. *Expenses:* Tuition, state resident: part-time $508 per credit hour. Tuition, nonresident: part-time $1281 per credit hour. *Financial support:* Fellowships, research assistantships, teaching assistantships, career-related internships or fieldwork available. Financial award application deadline: 3/1. *Faculty research:* Agricultural production and marketing. *Unit head:* Dr. J. Kolodinsky, Chairperson, 802-656-2001. *Application contact:* Dr. J. Kolodinsky, Chairperson, 802-656-2001.

University of Wisconsin–Madison, Graduate School, College of Agricultural and Life Sciences, Department of Agricultural and Applied Economics, Madison, WI 53706-1380. Offers MA, MS, PhD. Part-time programs available. *Degree requirements:* For doctorate, thesis/dissertation, preliminary exams. *Entrance requirements:* For master's and doctorate, GRE General Test. Additional exam requirements/recommendations for international students: Required—TOEFL. Electronic applications accepted. *Expenses:* Tuition, state resident: part-time $594 per credit. Tuition, nonresident: part-time $1504 per credit. Required fees: $65 per credit. Tuition and fees vary according to course load, program and reciprocity agreements. *Faculty research:* Environmental and resource economics, international development, state and local economics, food systems, markets and trade.

University of Wyoming, College of Agriculture, Department of Agricultural and Applied Economics, Laramie, WY 82070. Offers MS. Part-time programs available. *Degree requirements:* For master's, thesis (for some programs). *Entrance requirements:* For master's, GRE General Test, minimum GPA of 3.0. Additional exam requirements/recommendations for international students: Required—TOEFL. Electronic applications accepted. *Faculty research:* Farm management, agricultural markets, water economics, community development, agricultural business.

Utah State University, School of Graduate Studies, College of Business and College of Agriculture, Department of Economics, Program in Applied Economics, Logan, UT 84322. Offers MS. Part-time programs available. *Degree requirements:* For master's, thesis optional. *Entrance requirements:* For master's, GRE General Test, minimum GPA of 3.0.

Virginia Polytechnic Institute and State University, Graduate School, College of Agriculture and Life Sciences, Department of Agricultural and Applied Economics, Blacksburg, VA 24061. Offers agribusiness (MS); agricultural economics (MS, PhD); applied economics (MS); developmental and international economics (PhD); econometrics (PhD); macro and micro economics (PhD); markets and industrial organizations (PhD); public and regional/urban economics (PhD); resource and environmental economics (PhD). *Faculty:* 22 full-time (5 women). *Students:* 33 full-time (18 women); includes 18 American Indian/Alaska Native, 1 Asian American or Pacific Islander, 1 international. Average age 28. 47 applicants, 43% accepted, 12 enrolled. In 2009, 13 master's, 3 doctorates awarded. *Entrance requirements:* For master's and doctorate, GRE, GMAT. Additional exam requirements/recommendations for international students: Required—TOEFL (minimum score 575 paper-based; 213 computer-based). *Application deadline:* For fall admission, 5/15 for international students; for spring admission, 10/15 for international students. Applications are processed on a rolling basis. Application fee: $65. Electronic applications accepted. *Expenses:* Tuition, area resident: Full-time $10,228; part-time $459 per credit hour. Tuition, nonresident: full-time $17,892; part-time $865 per credit hour. Required fees: $1966; $451 per semester. *Financial support:* In 2009–10, 1 fellowship with full tuition reimbursement (averaging $20,000 per year), 21 research assistantships with full tuition reimbursements (averaging $21,611 per year), 8 teaching assistantships with full tuition reimbursements (averaging $13,481 per year) were awarded; career-related internships or fieldwork, Federal Work-Study, scholarships/grants, and unspecified assistantships also available. Financial award application deadline: 1/15. *Faculty research:* Rural development. Total annual research expenditures: $2.3 million. *Unit head:* Dr. Kevin Boyle, Dean, 540-231-6301, Fax: 540-231-7417, E-mail: kjboyle@vt.edu. *Application contact:* Bradford Mills, Contact, 540-231-6461, Fax: 540-231-7417, E-mail: bfmills@vt.edu.

Washington State University, Graduate School, College of Agricultural, Human, and Natural Resource Sciences, School of Economic Sciences, Department of Economics, Pullman, WA 99164. Offers applied economics (MA); economics (MA, PhD); international business economics (Certificate). *Faculty:* 34. *Students:* 50 full-time (16 women), 6 part-time (2 women); includes 2 minority (1 American Indian/Alaska Native, 1 Hispanic American), 30 international. Average age 30. 233 applicants, 26% accepted, 26 enrolled. In 2009, 9 master's, 8 doctorates awarded. *Degree requirements:* For master's, comprehensive exam (for some programs), thesis (for some programs), oral exam; for doctorate, comprehensive exam, thesis/dissertation, oral exam, written exam, field exams. *Entrance requirements:* For master's, GRE General Test, Submit a statement of purpose, three letters of reference, copies of all transcripts, GRE scores and (for international students) TOEFL or IELTS scores.; for doctorate, GRE General Test or GMAT, Submit a statement of purpose, three letters of reference, copies of all transcripts, GRE scores and (for international students) TOEFL or IELTS scores. Additional exam requirements/recommendations for international students: Required—TOEFL, IELTS. *Application deadline:* For fall admission, 1/10 priority date for domestic students, 1/10 for international students. Applications are processed on a rolling basis. Application fee: $50. *Financial support:* In 2009–10, research assistantships (averaging $13,917 per year), 13 teaching assistantships (averaging $13,506 per year) were awarded; career-related internships or fieldwork, Federal Work-Study, institutionally sponsored loans, tuition waivers (partial), and teaching associateships also available. Financial award application deadline: 4/1; financial award applicants required to submit FAFSA. *Faculty research:* Economic theory and quantitative methods, applied microeconomics. Total annual research expenditures: $1 million. *Unit head:* Dr. Ron C. Mittelhammer, Director, 509-335-1706, Fax: 509-335-1173, E-mail: mittelha@wsu.edu. *Application contact:* Graduate School Admissions, 800-GRADWSU, Fax: 509-335-1949, E-mail: gradsch@wsu.edu.

Western Michigan University, Graduate College, College of Arts and Sciences, Department of Economics, Kalamazoo, MI 49008. Offers applied economics (MA, PhD). *Degree requirements:* For master's, thesis, oral or written exams; for doctorate, thesis/dissertation, oral exam, internship. *Entrance requirements:* For doctorate, GRE General Test.

Wright State University, School of Graduate Studies, Raj Soin College of Business, Department of Economics, Program in Social and Applied Economics, Dayton, OH 45435. Offers MS.

Economic Development

Albany State University, College of Arts and Humanities, Department of History, Political Science and Public Administration, Albany, GA 31705-2717. Offers community and economic development administration (MPA); criminal justice administration (MPA); fiscal management (MPA); general management (MPA); health administration and policy (MPA); human resources management (MPA); public policy (MPA); water resource management and policy (MPA). *Accreditation:* NASPAA. *Students:* 17 full-time (11 women), 43 part-time (29 women); includes 57 minority (56 African Americans, 1 Asian American or Pacific Islander). Average age 34. 21 applicants, 100% accepted, 17 enrolled. In 2009, 17 master's awarded. *Entrance requirements:* For master's, Graduate Record Examination (GRE) or Miller Analogies Test (MAT). *Application deadline:* For fall admission, 11/16 for domestic students, 9/16 for international students; for spring admission, 4/19 for domestic students, 2/19 for international students. Applications are processed on a rolling basis. Application fee: $20. Electronic applications accepted. *Expenses:* Tuition, state resident: full-time $2970; part-time $162 per credit hour. Tuition, nonresident: full-time $12,168; part-time $676 per credit hour. Required fees: $962; $75 per credit hour. *Financial support:* Application deadline: 6/30. *Faculty research:* Public policy, strategic public human resources and human capital management, diversity management in the public sector and collective bargaining and labor relations in the public sector, e-government and public sector information systems, public administration pedagogy and business process modeling simulation, funded research- community development, non profit organizations, civic engagement and civic participation, health care disparities among minorities and poverty. Total annual research expenditures: $26,000. *Unit head:* Dr. Peter Ngwafu, Director, 229-430-4873, Fax: 229-430-7895, E-mail: peter.ngwafu@asurams.edu. *Application contact:* Nicole Lane, Interim Graduate Admissions Officer, 229-430-4862, Fax: 229-430-6398, E-mail: nicole.lane@asurams.edu.

Boston University, Metropolitan College, Department of Administrative Sciences, Boston, MA 02215. Offers banking and financial management (MSM); business continuity in emergency management (MSM); economics development and tourism management (MSAS); electronic commerce, systems, and technology (MSAS); financial economics (MSAS); human resource management (MSM); innovation and technology (MSAS); insurance management (MSM); international market management (MSM); multinational commerce (MSAS); project management (MSM). *Accreditation:* AACSB. Part-time and evening/weekend programs available. Post-baccalaureate distance learning degree programs offered (no on-campus study). *Students:* 123 full-time (48 women), 204 part-time (92 women); includes 31 minority (10 African Americans, 1 American Indian/Alaska Native, 11 Asian Americans or Pacific Islanders, 9 Hispanic Americans), 146 international. Average age 30. In 2009, 154 master's awarded. *Degree requirements:* For master's, thesis optional. *Entrance requirements:* For master's, 1 year of work experience, minimum GPA of 3.0. Additional exam requirements/recommendations for international students: Required—TOEFL (minimum score 560 paper-based; 220 computer-based; 84 iBT). *Application deadline:* Applications are processed on a rolling basis. Application fee: $70. Electronic applications accepted. *Expenses:* Tuition: Full-time $37,910; part-time $1184 per credit hour. Required fees: $386; $40 per semester. Part-time tuition and fees vary according to class time, course level, degree level and program. *Financial support:* In 2009–10, 15 students received support, including 8 research assistantships (averaging $10,000 per year); career-related internships or fieldwork and Federal Work-Study also available. *Faculty research:* International business, innovative process. *Unit head:* Dr. Kip Becker, Chairman, 617-353-3016, E-mail: adminsc@bu.edu. *Application contact:* Lucille Dicker, Administrative Sciences Department, 617-353-3016, E-mail: adminsc@bu.edu.

Cape Breton University, Shannon School of Business, Sydney, NS B1P 6L2, Canada. Offers community economic development (MBA). *Faculty:* 12 full-time (2 women). *Students:* 162 full-time (90 women). 106 applicants, 81% accepted, 74 enrolled. In 2009, 1 master's awarded. *Degree requirements:* For master's, research project, research essay. *Entrance requirements:* For master's, interview, letters of reference. Additional exam requirements/recommendations for international students: Required—TOEFL. *Application deadline:* For spring admission, 5/31 for domestic students. Applications are processed on a rolling basis. *Expenses:* Contact institution. *Financial support:* Scholarships/grants and tuition waivers (full and partial) available. Financial award application deadline: 5/31. *Faculty research:* Community entrepreneurship, CED theory, transportation, governance, business and environmental issues in Canada. Total annual research expenditures: $20,000. *Unit head:* George Karaphillis, Director of the MBA Program, 902-563-1467, Fax: 902-563-1453, E-mail: george_karaphillis@cbu.ca. *Application contact:* Anne Michelle Chiasson, Program Coordinator, 902-563-1664, Fax: 902-563-1366, E-mail: anne_chiasson@cbu.ca.

Chicago State University, School of Graduate and Professional Studies, College of Arts and Sciences, Department of Geography, Sociology, Economics, and Anthropology, Chicago, IL 60628. Offers geography and economic development (MA). *Entrance requirements:* For master's, minimum GPA of 2.75.

Claremont Graduate University, Graduate Programs, School of Politics and Economics, Department of Economics, Claremont, CA 91711-6160. Offers business and financial economics (MA, PhD); economic development (Certificate); economics (PhD); industrial organization (PhD); international and development economics (PhD); international economics policy and development (MA); international money and finance (PhD); neuroeconomics (PhD); political economy and public policy (MA); public choice and public economics (PhD); MBA/PhD. Part-time programs available. *Faculty:* 5 full-time (0 women), 1 part-time/adjunct (0 women). *Students:* 103 full-time (25 women), 7 part-time (3 women); includes 16 minority (1 African American, 9 Asian Americans or Pacific Islanders, 6 Hispanic Americans), 62 international. Average age 33. In 2009, 15 master's, 8 doctorates awarded. *Entrance requirements:* For master's and doctorate, GRE General Test or GMAT. Additional exam requirements/recommendations for international students: Required—TOEFL (minimum score 550 paper-based; 213 computer-based; 80 iBT). *Application deadline:* For fall admission, 2/1 priority date for domestic students. Applications are processed on a rolling basis. Application fee: $60. Electronic applications accepted. *Expenses:* Tuition: Full-time $35,046; part-time $1524 per credit. Required fees: $161 per semester. *Financial support:* Fellowships, research assistantships, teaching assistantships, Federal Work-Study, institutionally sponsored loans, and scholarships/grants available. Support available to part-time students. Financial award application deadline: 2/15; financial award applicants required to submit FAFSA. *Faculty research:* International and financial economics, law and economics, regulation, public choice economics. *Unit head:* Paul Zak, Chair, 909-621-8788, Fax: 909-621-8545, E-mail: paul.zak@cgu.edu. *Application contact:* Lesa Hiben, Admissions Coordinator, 909-621-8699, Fax: 909-621-7545, E-mail: lesa.hiben@cga.edu.

Cleveland State University, College of Graduate Studies, Maxine Goodman Levin College of Urban Affairs, Program in Nonprofit Administration and Leadership, Cleveland, OH 44115. Offers geographic information systems (Certificate); local and urban management (Certificate); nonprofit administration and leadership (MNAL); nonprofit management (Certificate); urban economic development (Certificate). Part-time and evening/weekend programs available. *Degree requirements:* For master's, thesis or alternative, capstone course. *Entrance requirements:* For master's, GRE (minimum 40th percentile verbal and quantitative, 4.0 analytical writing), minimum GPA of 3.0. Additional exam requirements/recommendations for international students: Required—TOEFL (minimum score 525 paper-based; 197 computer-based; 65 iBT). Electronic applications accepted. *Faculty research:* Human resource management, volunteerism, performance measurement in nonprofits, government-nonprofit partnerships.

Cleveland State University, College of Graduate Studies, Maxine Goodman Levin College of Urban Affairs, Program in Urban Planning, Design, and Development, Cleveland, OH 44115. Offers geographic information systems (Certificate); local and urban management (Certificate); urban economic development (Certificate); urban planning, design, and development (MUPDD); urban real estate development and finance (Certificate); JD/MUPDD. *Accreditation:* ACSP. Part-time and evening/weekend programs available. *Degree requirements:* For master's, project or thesis. *Entrance requirements:* For master's, GRE General Test (minimum 50th percentile verbal and quantitative, 4.0 analytical writing), minimum GPA of 3.0. Additional exam requirements/recommendations for international students: Required—TOEFL (minimum score 525 paper-based; 197 computer-based; 65 iBT). Electronic applications accepted. *Faculty research:* Housing and neighborhood development, urban housing policy, environmental sustainability, economic development.

Cleveland State University, College of Graduate Studies, Maxine Goodman Levin College of Urban Affairs, Program in Urban Studies, Cleveland, OH 44115. Offers geographic information systems (Certificate); local and urban management (Certificate); nonprofit management (Certificate); urban economic development (Certificate); urban real estate development and finance (Certificate); urban studies (MS); urban studies and public affairs (PhD). Part-time and evening/weekend programs available. *Degree requirements:* For master's, thesis or alternative, exit project, capstone course; for doctorate, comprehensive exam, thesis/dissertation. *Entrance requirements:* For master's, GRE General Test, minimum GPA of 3.0; for doctorate, GRE General Test, minimum GPA of 3.5. Additional exam requirements/recommendations for international students: Required—TOEFL (minimum score 525 paper-based; 197 computer-based; 65 iBT). Electronic applications accepted. *Faculty research:* Environmental issues, economic development, urban and public policy, public management.

Concordia University, School of Graduate Studies, Faculty of Arts and Science, School of Community and Public Affairs, Montréal, QC H3G 1M8, Canada. Offers community economic development (Diploma).

Cornell University, Graduate School, Graduate Fields of Architecture, Art and Planning, Field of City and Regional Planning, Ithaca, NY 14853-0001. Offers city and regional planning (MRP, PhD); environmental planning and design (MRP, PhD); historic preservation planning (MA); international development planning (MRP, PhD); planning theory and systems analysis (MRP, PhD); regional economics and development planning (MRP, PhD); regional science (MRP, PhD); social and health systems planning (MRP, PhD); urban and regional theory (MRP, PhD); urban planning history (MRP, PhD). *Accreditation:* ACSP (one or more programs are accredited). *Faculty:* 32 full-time (11 women). *Students:* 127 full-time (70 women); includes 19 minority (5 African Americans, 8 Asian Americans or Pacific Islanders, 6 Hispanic Americans), 22 international. Average age 30. 331 applicants, 46% accepted, 68 enrolled. In 2009, 50 master's, 4 doctorates awarded. *Degree requirements:* For master's, thesis (MA); for doctorate, comprehensive exam, thesis/dissertation. *Entrance requirements:* For master's and doctorate, GRE General Test, 2 letters of recommendation. Additional exam requirements/recommendations for international students: Required—TOEFL (minimum score 600 paper-based; 250 computer-based; 77 iBT). *Application deadline:* For fall admission, 1/10 for domestic students. Application fee: $70. Electronic applications accepted. *Expenses:* Tuition: Full-time $29,500. Required fees: $70. Full-time tuition and fees vary according to degree level, program and student level. *Financial support:* In 2009–10, 24 students received support, including 3 teaching assistantships with full tuition reimbursements available; fellowships with full tuition reimbursements available, research assistantships with full tuition reimbursements available, institutionally sponsored loans, scholarships/grants, health care benefits, tuition waivers (full and partial), and unspecified assistantships also available. Financial award applicants required to submit FAFSA. *Faculty research:* Land use planning, economic development, international development, historic preservation, community development. *Unit head:* Director of Graduate Studies, 607-255-6848, Fax: 607-255-1971. *Application contact:* Graduate Field Assistant, 607-255-6848, Fax: 607-255-1971, E-mail: crp_admissions@cornell.edu.

Cornell University, Graduate School, Graduate Fields of Arts and Sciences, Field of Economics, Ithaca, NY 14853-0001. Offers applied economics (PhD); basic analytical economics (PhD); econometrics and economic statistics (PhD); economic development and planning (PhD); economic theory (PhD); industrial organization and control (PhD); international economics (PhD); labor economics (PhD); monetary and macroeconomics (PhD); public finance (PhD). *Faculty:* 89 full-time (13 women). *Students:* 93 full-time (34 women); includes 6 minority (2 African Americans, 3 Asian Americans or Pacific Islanders, 1 Hispanic American), 51 international. Average age 28. 625 applicants, 11% accepted, 21 enrolled. In 2009, 21 doctorates awarded. *Degree requirements:* For doctorate, comprehensive exam, thesis/dissertation. *Entrance requirements:* For doctorate, GRE General Test, 3 letters of recommendation. Additional exam requirements/recommendations for international students: Required—TOEFL (minimum score 550 paper-based; 213 computer-based; 77 iBT). *Application deadline:* For fall admission, 1/15 priority date for domestic students. Application fee: $70. Electronic applications accepted. *Expenses:* Tuition: Full-time $29,500. Required fees: $70. Full-time tuition and fees vary according to degree level, program and student level. *Financial support:* In 2009–10, 81 students received support, including 12 fellowships with full tuition reimbursements available, 2 teaching assistantships with full tuition reimbursements available; research assistantships with full tuition reimbursements available, institutionally sponsored loans, scholarships/grants, health care benefits, tuition waivers (full and partial), and unspecified assistantships also available. Financial award applicants required to submit FAFSA. *Faculty research:* Learning and games, economics of education, political economy, transfer payments, time series and nonparametrics. *Unit head:* Director of Graduate Studies, 607-255-4893, Fax: 607-255-2818. *Application contact:* Graduate Field Assistant, 607-255-4893, Fax: 607-255-2818, E-mail: econ_phd@cornell.edu.

Eastern Michigan University, Graduate School, College of Arts and Sciences, Department of Economics, Ypsilanti, MI 48197. Offers applied economics (MA); economics (MA); health economics (MA); international economics and development (MA); trade and development (MA). Part-time and evening/weekend programs available. Postbaccalaureate distance learning degree programs offered (minimal on-campus study). *Faculty:* 11 full-time (2 women). *Students:* 28 full-time (9 women), 29 part-time (12 women); includes 17 minority (12 African Americans, 1 American Indian/Alaska Native, 2 Asian Americans or Pacific Islanders, 2 Hispanic Americans), 12 international. Average age 31. 61 applicants, 67% accepted, 23 enrolled. In 2009, 22 master's awarded. *Degree requirements:* For master's, thesis or alternative. *Entrance requirements:* Additional exam requirements/recommendations for international students: Required—TOEFL. *Application deadline:* Applications are processed on a rolling basis. Application fee: $35. Tuition and fees vary according to course level. *Financial support:* Fellowships, research assistantships with full tuition reimbursements, teaching assistantships with full tuition reimbursements, career-related internships or fieldwork, Federal Work-Study, institutionally sponsored loans, scholarships/grants, tuition waivers (partial), and unspecified assistantships available. Support available to part-time students. Financial award applicants required to submit FAFSA. *Unit head:* Dr. Raouf S. Hanna, Department Head, 734-487-3395, Fax: 734-487-9666, E-mail: rhanna@emich.edu. *Application contact:* Dr. David Crary, Advisor, 734-487-0001, Fax: 734-487-9666, E-mail: david.crary@emich.edu.

Eastern University, School of Leadership and Development, St. Davids, PA 19087-3696. Offers economic development (MBA), including international development, urban development (MA, MBA); international development (MA), including global development, urban development (MA, MBA); nonprofit management (MS); organizational leadership (MA); M Div/MBA. Part-time and evening/weekend programs available. *Degree requirements:* For master's, thesis (for some programs). *Entrance requirements:* For master's, GMAT (MBA), minimum GPA of 2.5. *Expenses:* Contact institution. *Faculty research:* Micro-level economic development, China welfare and economic development, macroethics, micro- and macro-level economic development in transitional economics, organizational effectiveness.

East Tennessee State University, School of Graduate Studies, College of Business and Technology, Department of Economics, Finance, and Urban Studies, Johnson City, TN 37614. Offers city management (MCM); community development (MPM); general administration (MPM);

municipal service management (MPM); urban and regional economic development (MPM); urban and regional planning (MPM). *Degree requirements:* For master's, internship, oral defense of thesis, research report. *Entrance requirements:* For master's, GRE General Test, minimum GPA of 3.0. Additional exam requirements/recommendations for international students: Required—TOEFL (minimum score 550 paper-based; 213 computer-based).

Florida Atlantic University, College of Architecture, Urban and Public Affairs, School of Urban and Regional Planning, Boca Raton, FL 33431-0991. Offers economic development and tourism (Certificate); environmental planning (Certificate); sustainable community planning (Certificate); urban and regional planning (MURP); visual planning technology (Certificate). *Accreditation:* ACSP. Part-time and evening/weekend programs available. *Faculty:* 8 full-time (6 women), 1 (woman) part-time/adjunct. *Students:* 28 full-time (17 women), 12 part-time (4 women); includes 11 minority (2 African Americans, 1 Asian American or Pacific Islander, 8 Hispanic Americans), 3 international. Average age 31. 70 applicants, 47% accepted, 7 enrolled. In 2009, 14 master's awarded. *Entrance requirements:* For master's, GRE General Test, minimum GPA of 3.0. Additional exam requirements/recommendations for international students: Required—TOEFL. *Application deadline:* For fall admission, 7/1 priority date for domestic students, 2/15 for international students; for spring admission, 11/1 priority date for domestic students, 7/15 for international students. Applications are processed on a rolling basis. Application fee: $30. *Expenses:* Tuition, state resident: full-time $7055; part-time $293.94 per credit hour. Tuition, nonresident: full-time $22,096; part-time $920.66 per credit hour. *Financial support:* Fellowships with full tuition reimbursements, research assistantships, career-related internships or fieldwork, Federal Work-Study, institutionally sponsored loans, and tuition waivers (partial) available. Financial award application deadline: 4/1. *Faculty research:* Growth management, urban design, computer applications/geographical information systems, environmental planning. *Unit head:* Dr. Jaap Vos, Chair, 954-762-5653, Fax: 954-762-5673, E-mail: jvos@fau.edu. *Application contact:* Dr. Jaap Vos, Chair, 954-762-5653, Fax: 954-762-5673, E-mail: jvos@fau.edu.

Fordham University, Graduate School of Arts and Sciences, Program in International Political Economy and Development, New York, NY 10458. Offers MA, Certificate. Part-time and evening/weekend programs available. *Students:* 44 full-time (15 women), 18 part-time (10 women); includes 6 minority (1 African American, 1 American Indian/Alaska Native, 1 Asian American or Pacific Islander, 3 Hispanic Americans), 21 international. Average age 28. 213 applicants, 37% accepted, 36 enrolled. In 2009, 28 master's awarded. *Degree requirements:* For master's, comprehensive exam. *Entrance requirements:* For master's, GRE General Test. Additional exam requirements/recommendations for international students: Required—TOEFL (minimum score 600 paper-based; 250 computer-based). *Application deadline:* For fall admission, 1/4 priority date for domestic students; for spring admission, 11/1 for domestic students. Application fee: $70. Electronic applications accepted. *Financial support:* In 2009–10, 16 students received support, including 16 research assistantships with tuition reimbursements available (averaging $18,400 per year); career-related internships or fieldwork, institutionally sponsored loans, tuition waivers (full and partial), and unspecified assistantships also available. Financial award application deadline: 1/4; financial award applicants required to submit FAFSA. *Faculty research:* International economics, comparative international politics, international banking and finance, international development, emerging markets and country risk analysis. *Unit head:* Dr. Henry Schwalbenberg, Chair, 718-817-3866, Fax: 718-817-3518. *Application contact:* Charlene Dundie, Director of Graduate Admissions, 718-817-4420, Fax: 718-817-3566, E-mail: dundie@fordham.edu.

Georgetown University, Graduate School of Arts and Sciences, Department of Economics, Washington, DC 20057. Offers econometrics (PhD); economic development (PhD); economic theory (PhD); industrial organization (PhD); international macro and finance (PhD); international trade (PhD); labor economics (PhD); macroeconomics (PhD); public economics and political economics (PhD); MA/PhD; MS/MA. *Degree requirements:* For doctorate, comprehensive exam, thesis/dissertation. *Entrance requirements:* For doctorate, GRE General Test. Additional exam requirements/recommendations for international students: Required—TOEFL. *Faculty research:* International economics, economic development.

Georgia Institute of Technology, Graduate Studies and Research, College of Architecture, City and Regional Planning Program, Atlanta, GA 30332-0001. Offers city and regional planning (PhD); economic development (MCRP); environmental planning and management (MCRP); geographic information systems (MCRP); land and community development (MCRP); land use planning (MCRP); transportation (MCRP); urban design (MCRP); MCP/MSCE. *Accreditation:* ACSP. *Degree requirements:* For master's, thesis, internship. *Entrance requirements:* For master's, GRE General Test, minimum GPA of 2.7. Additional exam requirements/recommendations for international students: Required—TOEFL. Electronic applications accepted.

Georgia State University, Andrew Young School of Policy Studies, Department of Public Management and Policy, Atlanta, GA 30303. Offers disaster management (Certificate); nonprofit management (Certificate); planning and economic development (Certificate); public administration (MPA), including criminal justice, management and finance, nonprofit management, planning and economic development, policy analysis and evaluation, public health; public policy (MPP, PhD), including disaster policy (MPP), nonprofit policy (MPP), planning and economic development policy (MPP), public finance policy (MPP), social policy (MPP); JD/MPA. *Accreditation:* NASPAA (one or more programs are accredited). Part-time and evening/weekend programs available. Terminal master's awarded for partial completion of doctoral program. *Degree requirements:* For master's, thesis optional; for doctorate, comprehensive exam, thesis/dissertation. *Entrance requirements:* For master's and doctorate, GRE General Test. Additional exam requirements/recommendations for international students: Required—TOEFL. Electronic applications accepted. *Faculty research:* Public management, policy analysis, public finance, planning and economic development, nonprofit leadership and policy.

Indiana University Bloomington, School of Public and Environmental Affairs, Public Affairs Programs, Bloomington, IN 47405-7000. Offers comparative and international affairs (MPA); economic development (MPA); energy (MPA); environmental policy and natural resource management (MPA); information systems (MPA); local government management (MPA); nonprofit management (MPA); policy analysis (MPA); public financial administration (MPA); public management (MPA); sustainability and sustainable development (MPA); JD/MPA; MPA/MA; MPA/MIS; MPA/MLS; MSES/MPA. *Accreditation:* NASPAA (one or more programs are accredited). Part-time programs available. *Faculty:* 75 full-time (22 women), 91 part-time/adjunct (24 women). *Students:* 389 full-time (222 women), 45 part-time (24 women); includes 38 minority (18 African Americans, 1 American Indian/Alaska Native, 12 Asian Americans or Pacific Islanders, 7 Hispanic Americans), 72 international. Average age 26. 474 applicants, 206 enrolled. In 2009, 190 master's, 11 doctorates, 3 other advanced degrees awarded. Terminal master's awarded for partial completion of doctoral program. *Degree requirements:* For master's, thesis optional; for doctorate, comprehensive exam, thesis/dissertation or alternative, A thesis is required for the Public Affairs and Public Policy degree. *Entrance requirements:* For master's, GRE, LSAT (if also applying for the Law School), 3 letters of recommendation, resume or curriculum vitae; for doctorate, GRE General Test. Additional exam requirements/recommendations for international students: Required—TOEFL (minimum score 590 paper-based; 243 computer-based; 96 iBT). *Application deadline:* For fall admission, 2/1 priority date for domestic students, 12/1 priority date for international students; for spring admission, 9/1 for international students. Application fee: $55 ($65 for international students). Electronic applications accepted. *Financial support:* Fellowships with full tuition reimbursements, research assistantships with partial tuition reimbursements, teaching assistantships with partial tuition reimbursements, career-related internships or fieldwork, Federal Work-Study, institutionally sponsored loans, unspecified assistantships, and Service Corps programs available. Financial award application deadline: 2/1; financial award applicants required to submit FAFSA. *Faculty research:* Comparative and international affairs, environmental policy and resource management, policy analysis, public finance, public management, urban management, nonprofit management. *Unit head:* Dean John Graham, Dean, School of Public and Environmental Affairs, 812-855-1432, E-mail: grahamjd@indiana.edu. *Application contact:* Jennifer Medlin, Assistant Director of Admissions and Financial Aid, 812-855-3784, Fax: 812-856-3665, E-mail: jlmedlin@indiana.edu.

See Close-Up on page 1191.

New Mexico State University, Graduate School, College of Business, Department of Economics and International Business, Las Cruces, NM 88003-8001. Offers applied statistics (MS); economic development (DED); economics (MA). Part-time programs available. *Faculty:* 13 full-time (3 women), 1 part-time/adjunct (0 women). *Students:* 54 full-time (22 women), 15 part-time (4 women); includes 21 minority (4 African Americans, 1 Asian American or Pacific Islander, 16 Hispanic Americans), 29 international. Average age 31. 74 applicants, 85% accepted, 38 enrolled. In 2009, 23 master's awarded. *Degree requirements:* For master's, comprehensive exam, thesis or alternative; for doctorate, comprehensive exam, thesis/dissertation or alternative. *Entrance requirements:* For master's, minimum GPA of 3.0; for doctorate, appropriate master's degree. Additional exam requirements/recommendations for international students: Required—TOEFL. *Application deadline:* Applications are processed on a rolling basis. Application fee: $30 ($50 for international students). Electronic applications accepted. *Expenses:* Tuition, state resident: full-time $4080; part-time $223 per credit. Tuition, nonresident: full-time $14,256; part-time $647 per credit. Required fees: $1278; $639 per semester. *Financial support:* In 2009–10, 34 students received support, including 19 research assistantships (averaging $13,031 per year), 19 teaching assistantships (averaging $7,939 per year); fellowships, career-related internships or fieldwork, Federal Work-Study, and health care benefits also available. Support available to part-time students. Financial award application deadline: 3/1. *Faculty research:* Public utilities, environment, linear models, biological sampling, public policy, economics development. Total annual research expenditures: $400,000. *Unit head:* Dr. Anthony Popp, Graduate Adviser, 575-646-5198, Fax: 575-646-1915, E-mail: apopp@nmsu.edu. *Application contact:* Dr. Anthony Popp, Graduate Adviser, 575-646-5198, Fax: 575-646-1915, E-mail: apopp@nmsu.edu.

Southern New Hampshire University, School of Community Economic Development, Manchester, NH 03106-1045. Offers MA, MBA, MS, PhD. Part-time and evening/weekend programs available. *Degree requirements:* For master's, thesis or alternative, community project; for doctorate, comprehensive exam, thesis/dissertation, community project. *Entrance requirements:* For master's, 2 years of work experience, minimum GPA of 3.0, 2 letters of recommendation, review; for doctorate, 2 years of work experience, minimum GPA of 3.5, 3 letters of recommendation, research samples. Additional exam requirements/recommendations for international students: Required—TOEFL (minimum score 550 paper-based; 300 computer-based; 70 iBT). Electronic applications accepted. *Expenses:* Contact institution.

Troy University, Graduate School, College of Business, Program in Business Administration, Troy, AL 36082. Offers accounting (EMBA, MBA); criminal justice (EMBA); finance (MBA); general management (EMBA); healthcare management (EMBA); information systems (EMBA, MBA); international economic development (MBA). *Accreditation:* ACBSP. Part-time and evening/weekend programs available. *Students:* 382 full-time (196 women), 732 part-time (457 women); includes 616 minority (483 African Americans, 14 American Indian/Alaska Native, 96 Asian Americans or Pacific Islanders, 23 Hispanic Americans). Average age 29. 869 applicants, 61% accepted. In 2009, 296 master's awarded. *Degree requirements:* For master's, thesis or alternative. *Entrance requirements:* For master's, GMAT (minimum score 500) or GRE General Test (minimum score 900), minimum GPA of 2.5; letter of recommendation. Additional exam requirements/recommendations for international students: Required—TOEFL (minimum score 523 paper-based; 193 computer-based; 70 iBT), IELTS (minimum score 6), or ACT Compass ESL (minimum score 270 on Listening, Reading, and Grammar with no individual score below 85 and a minimum score of 8 out of 12 on writing test). *Application deadline:* Applications are processed on a rolling basis. Application fee: $50. *Unit head:* Dr. Henry M. Findley, Interim Chair/Professor, 334-670-3271, Fax: 334-670-3599, E-mail: hfindley@troy.edu. *Application contact:* Brenda K. Campbell, Director of Graduate Admissions, 334-670-3178, Fax: 334-670-3733, E-mail: bcamp@troy.edu.

University of Central Arkansas, Graduate School, College of Business Administration, Program in Community and Economic Development, Conway, AR 72035-0001. Offers MS. *Students:* 14 full-time (4 women), 12 part-time (7 women); includes 4 minority (3 African Americans, 1 Hispanic American), 8 international. Average age 31. 17 applicants, 94% accepted, 16 enrolled. In 2009, 6 master's awarded. *Degree requirements:* For master's, comprehensive exam, thesis. *Entrance requirements:* For master's, GRE General Test, minimum GPA of 2.7. Additional exam requirements/recommendations for international students: Required—TOEFL (minimum score 550 paper-based; 213 computer-based). *Application deadline:* For fall admission, 3/1 priority date for domestic students; for spring admission, 10/1 priority date for domestic students. Applications are processed on a rolling basis. Application fee: $25 ($40 for international students). *Expenses:* Contact institution. *Financial support:* Career-related internships or fieldwork, Federal Work-Study, and unspecified assistantships available. Financial award applicants required to submit FAFSA. *Unit head:* Dr. Lauren Maxwell, Coordinator, 501-450-5349. *Application contact:* Brenda Herring, Admissions Assistant, 501-450-5065, Fax: 501-450-5678, E-mail: bherring@uca.edu.

University of Houston–Victoria, School of Business Administration, Victoria, TX 77901-4450. Offers accounting (MBA); economic development and entrepreneurship (MS); finance (GMBA, MBA); general business (MBA); international business (MBA); management (GMBA, MBA); marketing (MBA). *Accreditation:* AACSB. Part-time and evening/weekend programs available. Postbaccalaureate distance learning degree programs offered (no on-campus study). *Entrance requirements:* For master's, GMAT. Additional exam requirements/recommendations for international students: Required—TOEFL (minimum score 550 paper-based; 213 computer-based). Electronic applications accepted. *Faculty research:* Economic development, marketing, finance.

University of Massachusetts Lowell, College of Arts and Sciences, Department of Regional Economic and Social Development, Lowell, MA 01854-2881. Offers MA, Graduate Certificate. Part-time programs available. *Entrance requirements:* For master's, GRE. Electronic applications accepted.

University of Miami, Graduate School, School of Business Administration, Department of Economics, Coral Gables, FL 33124. Offers economic development (MA, PhD); environmental economics (PhD); human resource economics (MA, PhD); international economics (MA, PhD); macroeconomics (PhD). Students admitted every two years in the fall semester. Terminal master's awarded for partial completion of doctoral program. *Degree requirements:* For master's, comprehensive exam; for doctorate, comprehensive exam, thesis/dissertation. *Entrance requirements:* For master's and doctorate, GRE General Test, minimum GPA of 3.0. Additional exam requirements/recommendations for international students: Required—TOEFL (minimum score 550 paper-based). *Faculty research:* International economics/trade, applied microeconomics, development.

University of Minnesota, Twin Cities Campus, Graduate School, Hubert H. Humphrey Institute of Public Affairs, Program in Public Policy, Minneapolis, MN 55455-0213. Offers advanced policy analysis methods (MPP); economic and community development (MPP); foreign policy (MPP); public and nonprofit leadership and management (MPP); science technology and environmental policy (MPP); social policy (MPP); women and public policy (MPP); JD/MPP; MPP/MS; MSW/MPP. Part-time programs available. *Faculty:* 33 full-time (14 women), 29 part-time/adjunct (15 women). *Students:* 165 full-time (107 women), 74 part-time (44 women); includes 41 minority (11 African Americans, 24 Asian Americans or Pacific Islanders, 6 Hispanic Americans). Average age 26. 345 applicants, 71% accepted, 109 enrolled. In 2009, 91 master's awarded. *Degree requirements:* For master's, thesis or alternative, internship or equivalent work experience. *Entrance requirements:* For master's, GRE General Test, minimum undergraduate GPA of 3.0. Additional exam requirements/recommendations for international students: Required—TOEFL (minimum score 600 paper-based; 250 computer-based; 100 iBT). *Application deadline:* For fall admission, 4/1 for domestic and international

Economic Development

University of Minnesota, Twin Cities Campus (continued)
students. Applications are processed on a rolling basis. Application fee: $55 ($75 for international students). Electronic applications accepted. *Financial support:* In 2009–10, 77 students received support, including fellowships with full and partial tuition reimbursements available (averaging $8,500 per year), research assistantships with full and partial tuition reimbursements available (averaging $5,270 per year), teaching assistantships with full and partial tuition reimbursements available (averaging $5,270 per year); career-related internships or fieldwork, Federal Work-Study, scholarships/grants, health care benefits, tuition waivers (full and partial), and unspecified assistantships also available. Financial award application deadline: 1/5. *Faculty research:* Social policy, public and non-profit management and leadership, community and economic development, foreign policy and international affairs, women and public policy. Total annual research expenditures: $5.1 million. *Unit head:* Dr. Maria Hanratty, Head, 612-624-3800, Fax: 612-626-0002, E-mail: hhhadmit@umn.edu. *Application contact:* Julie Harrold, Director of Admissions, 612-626-7229, Fax: 612-626-0002, E-mail: hhhadmit@umn.edu.

University of Minnesota, Twin Cities Campus, Graduate School, Hubert H. Humphrey Institute of Public Affairs, Program in Urban and Regional Planning, Minneapolis, MN 55455-0213. Offers environmental planning (MURP); housing and community development (MURP); land use and urban design (MURP); regional, economic and workforce development (MURP); transportation planning (MURP); JD/MURP; MURP/MLA; MURP/MS. *Accreditation:* ACSP (one or more programs are accredited). Part-time programs available. *Faculty:* 33 full-time (14 women), 29 part-time/adjunct (15 women). *Students:* 78 full-time (33 women), 26 part-time (9 women); includes 11 minority (3 African Americans, 8 Asian Americans or Pacific Islanders), 6 international. Average age 26. 136 applicants, 65% accepted, 47 enrolled. In 2009, 63 master's awarded. *Degree requirements:* For master's, thesis or alternative, internship or equivalent work experience. *Entrance requirements:* For master's, GRE General Test, minimum undergraduate GPA of 3.0. Additional exam requirements/recommendations for international students: Required—TOEFL (minimum score 600 paper-based; 250 computer-based; 100 iBT). *Application deadline:* For fall admission, 4/1 for domestic and international students. Applications are processed on a rolling basis. Application fee: $75 ($95 for international students). Electronic applications accepted. *Financial support:* In 2009–10, 26 students received support, including fellowships with full and partial tuition reimbursements available (averaging $8,500 per year), research assistantships with full and partial tuition reimbursements available (averaging $5,270 per year), teaching assistantships with full and partial tuition reimbursements available (averaging $5,270 per year); career-related internships or fieldwork, Federal Work-Study, scholarships/grants, health care benefits, tuition waivers (full and partial), and unspecified assistantships also available. Financial award application deadline: 1/5. *Faculty research:* Policy planning, resource allocation planning, regulatory planning, program planning, project planning. Total annual research expenditures: $5.1 million. *Unit head:* Dr. Ragui Assaad, Head, 612-624-3800, Fax: 612-626-0002, E-mail: hhhadmit@umn.edu. *Application contact:* Julie Harrold, Director of Admissions, 612-626-7229, Fax: 612-626-0002, E-mail: hhhadmit@umn.edu.

The University of North Carolina at Greensboro, Graduate School, College of Arts and Sciences, Department of Geography, Greensboro, NC 27412-5001. Offers applied geography (MA); geographic information science (Certificate); geography (PhD); urban and economic development (Certificate). *Degree requirements:* For master's, comprehensive exam, thesis or alternative. *Entrance requirements:* For master's, GRE General Test. Additional exam requirements/recommendations for international students: Required—TOEFL. Electronic applications accepted.

The University of North Carolina at Greensboro, Graduate School, College of Arts and Sciences, Department of Political Science, Greensboro, NC 27412-5001. Offers nonprofit management (Certificate); public affairs (MPA); urban and economic development (Certificate). *Accreditation:* NASPAA. *Degree requirements:* For master's, comprehensive exam. *Entrance requirements:* For master's, GRE General Test. Additional exam requirements/recommendations for international students: Required—TOEFL. Electronic applications accepted. *Faculty research:* U.S. Constitution, Canadian parliament, public management, ethical challenge of public service.

University of Southern California, Graduate School, College of Letters, Arts and Sciences, Department of Economics, Los Angeles, CA 90089. Offers economic development programming (MA, PhD); mathematical finance (MS); M Pl/MA; MA/JD. *Faculty:* 18 full-time (2 women), 14 part-time/adjunct (0 women). *Students:* 128 full-time (47 women), 6 part-time (2 women); includes 12 minority (1 African American, 8 Asian Americans or Pacific Islanders, 3 Hispanic Americans), 105 international. 355 applicants, 28% accepted, 32 enrolled. In 2009, 34 master's, 9 doctorates awarded. Terminal master's awarded for partial completion of doctoral program. *Degree requirements:* For master's, comprehensive exam, thesis optional; for doctorate, comprehensive exam, thesis/dissertation. *Entrance requirements:* For master's and doctorate, GRE. Additional exam requirements/recommendations for international students: Required—TOEFL (minimum score 93 iBT). *Application deadline:* For fall admission, 12/1 for domestic and international students; for spring admission, 11/1 for domestic and international students. Application fee: $85. *Expenses:* Tuition: Full-time $25,980; part-time $1315 per unit. Required fees: $554. One-time fee: $35 full-time. Full-time tuition and fees vary according to degree level and program. *Financial support:* In 2009–10, 61 students received support, including 14 fellowships with full tuition reimbursements available (averaging $21,000 per year), 4 research assistantships with full tuition reimbursements available (averaging $19,000 per year), 41 teaching assistantships with full tuition reimbursements available (averaging $19,000 per year). *Faculty research:* Applied micro/io, development, econometrics, finance, international finance, macroeconomic theory, microeconomic theory. *Unit head:* Prof. Simon Wilkie, Chair, 213-740-8335, Fax: 213-740-4595, E-mail: swilkie@usc.edu. *Application contact:* Morgan Ponder, Graduate Advisor, 213-740-3507, E-mail: ponder@usc.edu.

University of Southern Mississippi, Graduate School, College of Science and Technology, Department of Economic and Workforce Development, Hattiesburg, MS 39406-0001. Offers economic development (MS); human capital development (PhD); workforce training and development (MS). Part-time programs available. *Faculty:* 6 full-time (3 women). *Students:* 26 full-time (9 women), 48 part-time (30 women); includes 26 minority (25 African Americans, 1 Asian American or Pacific Islander), 2 international. Average age 41. 33 applicants, 39% accepted, 13 enrolled. In 2009, 23 master's awarded. *Degree requirements:* For master's, comprehensive exam, thesis optional, internships; for doctorate, comprehensive exam, thesis/dissertation. *Entrance requirements:* For master's, GMAT, GRE General Test, minimum GPA of 2.75 in last 60 hours; for doctorate, GMAT, GRE General Test, minimum GPA of 3.5. Additional exam requirements/recommendations for international students: Required—TOEFL. *Application deadline:* For fall admission, 8/1 for domestic students, 3/1 for international students; for spring admission, 1/3 for domestic and international students. Application fee: $35. Electronic applications accepted. *Expenses:* Tuition, state resident: full-time $5096; part-time $284 per hour. Tuition, nonresident: full-time $13,052; part-time $726 per hour. Required fees: $402. Tuition and fees vary according to course level and course load. *Financial support:* In 2009–10, 11 students received support, including 2 research assistantships with full tuition reimbursements available (averaging $13,000 per year), 6 teaching assistantships with full tuition reimbursements available (averaging $6,500 per year); career-related internships or fieldwork and Federal Work-Study also available. Financial award application deadline: 3/1; financial award applicants required to submit FAFSA. *Faculty research:* Economic development, international studies, geography. *Unit head:* Dr. Kenneth Malone, Chair, 601-266-4736, Fax: 601-266-6071, E-mail: ken.malone@usm.edu. *Application contact:* Dr. Cyndi Gaudet, Graduate Coordinator, 601-266-6519, Fax: 601-266-6071.

University of Waterloo, Graduate Studies, Faculty of Environmental Studies, Program in Local Economic Development, Waterloo, ON N2L 3G1, Canada. Offers MAES. Part-time programs available. *Degree requirements:* For master's, internship, research paper. Electronic applications accepted.

Vanderbilt University, Graduate School, Department of Economics, Nashville, TN 37240-1001. Offers economic development (MA); economics (MA, MAT, PhD); JD/PhD. *Faculty:* 44 full-time (7 women). *Students:* 111 full-time (45 women), 3 part-time (1 woman); includes 3 minority (all Asian Americans or Pacific Islanders), 80 international. Average age 27. 462 applicants, 31% accepted, 42 enrolled. In 2009, 30 master's, 9 doctorates awarded. Terminal master's awarded for partial completion of doctoral program. *Degree requirements:* For master's, thesis or alternative; for doctorate, thesis/dissertation, final and qualifying exams. *Entrance requirements:* For master's and doctorate, GRE General Test, GRE Subject Test (recommended). Additional exam requirements/recommendations for international students: Required—TOEFL (minimum score 570 paper-based; 230 computer-based; 88 iBT). *Application deadline:* For fall admission, 1/15 for domestic and international students; for spring admission, 11/1 for domestic students. Applications are processed on a rolling basis. Application fee: $0. Electronic applications accepted. *Financial support:* Fellowships with full and partial tuition reimbursements, teaching assistantships with full and partial tuition reimbursements, career-related internships or fieldwork, Federal Work-Study, institutionally sponsored loans, scholarships/grants, and health care benefits available. Financial award application deadline: 1/15; financial award applicants required to submit CSS PROFILE or FAFSA. *Faculty research:* Economic theory, applied fields, developmental economics, environmental economics, health economics and policy. *Unit head:* Tong Li, Chair, 615-322-3426, Fax: 615-343-8495, E-mail: tong.li@vanderbilt.edu. *Application contact:* Bill Collins, Director of Graduate Studies, 615-322-3428, Fax: 615-343-8495, E-mail: william.collins@vanderbilt.edu.

Virginia Polytechnic Institute and State University, Graduate School, College of Agriculture and Life Sciences, Department of Agricultural and Applied Economics, Blacksburg, VA 24061. Offers agribusiness (MS); agricultural economics (MS, PhD); applied economics (MS); developmental and international economics (PhD); econometrics (PhD); macro and micro economics (PhD); markets and industrial organizations (PhD); public and regional/urban economics (PhD); resource and environmental economics (PhD). *Faculty:* 22 full-time (5 women). *Students:* 33 full-time (18 women); includes 18 American Indian/Alaska Native, 1 Asian American or Pacific Islander, 1 international. Average age 28. 47 applicants, 43% accepted, 12 enrolled. In 2009, 13 master's, 3 doctorates awarded. *Entrance requirements:* For master's and doctorate, GRE, GMAT. Additional exam requirements/recommendations for international students: Required—TOEFL (minimum score 575 paper-based; 213 computer-based). *Application deadline:* For fall admission, 5/15 for international students; for spring admission, 10/15 for international students. Applications are processed on a rolling basis. Application fee: $65. Electronic applications accepted. *Expenses:* Tuition, area resident: Full-time $10,228; part-time $459 per credit hour. Tuition, nonresident: full-time $17,892; part-time $865 per credit hour. Required fees: $1966; $451 per semester. *Financial support:* In 2009–10, 1 fellowship with full tuition reimbursement (averaging $20,000 per year), 21 research assistantships with full tuition reimbursements (averaging $21,611 per year), 8 teaching assistantships with full tuition reimbursements (averaging $13,481 per year) were awarded; career-related internships or fieldwork, Federal Work-Study, scholarships/grants, and unspecified assistantships also available. Financial award application deadline: 1/15. *Faculty research:* Rural development. Total annual research expenditures: $2.3 million. *Unit head:* Dr. Kevin Boyle, Dean, 540-231-6301, Fax: 540-231-7417, E-mail: kjboyle@vt.edu. *Application contact:* Bradford Mills, Contact, 540-231-6461, Fax: 540-231-7417, E-mail: bfmills@vt.edu.

Virginia Polytechnic Institute and State University, Graduate School, College of Architecture and Urban Studies, School of Public and International Affairs, Blacksburg, VA 24061. Offers environmental planning and policy (MURP); government and international affairs (MPIA); housing, community and economic development (MURP); international development planning (MURP); land use and physical planning (MURP); planning, governance and globalization (PhD), including environmental planning and landscape analysis, physical planning and urban design, public and international affairs, urban and environmental design and planning; urban and regional planning (MURP). *Accreditation:* ACSP. *Faculty:* 27 full-time (11 women), 2 part-time/adjunct (1 woman). *Students:* 73 full-time (51 women), 65 part-time (39 women); includes 15 minority (4 African Americans, 1 American Indian/Alaska Native, 6 Asian Americans or Pacific Islanders, 4 Hispanic Americans), 10 international. Average age 29. 86 applicants, 67% accepted, 40 enrolled. In 2009, 26 master's, 1 doctorate awarded. *Entrance requirements:* Additional exam requirements/recommendations for international students: Required—TOEFL (minimum score 550 paper-based; 213 computer-based). *Application deadline:* For fall admission, 5/15 for international students; for spring admission, 10/15 for international students. Applications are processed on a rolling basis. Application fee: $45. Electronic applications accepted. *Financial support:* In 2009–10, 1 teaching assistantship with full tuition reimbursement (averaging $5,560 per year) was awarded; career-related internships or fieldwork, Federal Work-Study, scholarships/grants, and unspecified assistantships also available. Financial award application deadline: 4/1. *Faculty research:* Design theory, environmental planning, town planning, transportation planning. *Unit head:* Dr. John Randolph, Dean, 540-231-6971, Fax: 540-231-9938, E-mail: energy@vt.edu. *Application contact:* Krystal D. Wright, Information Contact, 540-231-*5683, Fax: 540-231-9938, E-mail: garch@vt.edu.

Wayne State University, College of Liberal Arts and Sciences, Interdisciplinary Program in Economic Development, Detroit, MI 48202. Offers Certificate. *Entrance requirements:* Additional exam requirements/recommendations for international students: Required—TOEFL (minimum score 550 paper-based; 213 computer-based); Recommended—TWE (minimum score 6). Electronic applications accepted.

West Virginia University, College of Business and Economics, Division of Economics and Finance, Morgantown, WV 26506. Offers business analysis (MA); developmental financial economics (PhD); environmental and resource economics (PhD); international economics (PhD); mathematical economics (MA); monetary economics (PhD); public finance (PhD); public policy (MA); regional and urban economics (PhD); statistics and economics (MA). Terminal master's awarded for partial completion of doctoral program. *Degree requirements:* For master's, thesis optional; for doctorate, comprehensive exam, thesis/dissertation. *Entrance requirements:* For master's and doctorate, GRE General Test, minimum GPA of 3.0; course work in intermediate microeconomics, intermediate macroeconomics, calculus, and statistics. Additional exam requirements/recommendations for international students: Required—TOEFL. Electronic applications accepted. *Faculty research:* Financial economics, regional/urban development, public economics, international trade/international finance/development economics, monetary economics.

Yale University, Graduate School of Arts and Sciences, Department of Economics, Program in International and Development Economics, New Haven, CT 06520. Offers MA. *Entrance requirements:* For master's, GRE General Test.

Economics

Albany State University, College of Arts and Humanities, Department of History, Political Science and Public Administration, Albany, GA 31705-2717. Offers community and economic development administration (MPA); criminal justice administration (MPA); fiscal management (MPA); general management (MPA); health administration and policy (MPA); human resources management (MPA); public policy (MPA); water resource management and policy (MPA). *Accreditation:* NASPAA. *Students:* 17 full-time (11 women), 43 part-time (29 women); includes 57 minority (56 African Americans, 1 Asian American or Pacific Islander). Average age 34. 21 applicants, 100% accepted, 17 enrolled. In 2009, 17 master's awarded. *Entrance requirements:* For master's, Graduate Record Examination (GRE) or Miller Analogies Test (MAT). *Application deadline:* For fall admission, 11/16 for domestic students, 9/16 for international students; for spring admission, 4/19 for domestic students, 2/19 for international students. Applications are processed on a rolling basis. Application fee: $20. Electronic applications accepted. *Expenses:* Tuition, state resident: full-time $2970; part-time $162 per credit hour. Tuition, nonresident: full-time $12,168; part-time $676 per credit hour. Required fees: $962; $75 per credit hour. *Financial support:* Application deadline: 6/30. *Faculty research:* Public policy, strategic public human resources and human capital management, diversity management in the public sector and collective bargaining and labor relations in the public sector, e-government and public sector information systems, public administration pedagogy and business process modeling simulation, funded research- community development, non profit organizations, civic engagement and civic participation, health care disparities among minorities and poverty. Total annual research expenditures: $26,000. *Unit head:* Dr. Peter Ngwafu, Director, 229-430-4873, Fax: 229-430-7895, E-mail: peter.ngwafu@asurams.edu. *Application contact:* Nicole Lane, Interim Graduate Admissions Officer, 229-430-4862, Fax: 229-430-6398, E-mail: nicole.lane@asurams.edu.

American University, College of Arts and Sciences, Department of Economics, Washington, DC 20016-8029. Offers applied microeconomics (Certificate); economics (MA, PhD); international economic relations (Certificate). Part-time and evening/weekend programs available. *Faculty:* 27 full-time (10 women). *Students:* 55 full-time (23 women), 67 part-time (27 women); includes 15 minority (12 African Americans, 1 Asian American or Pacific Islander, 2 Hispanic Americans), 49 international. Average age 29. 156 applicants, 69% accepted, 34 enrolled. In 2009, 23 master's, 10 doctorates, 1 other advanced degree awarded. Terminal master's awarded for partial completion of doctoral program. *Degree requirements:* For master's, comprehensive exam, thesis or alternative; for doctorate, comprehensive exam, thesis/dissertation, 2 research seminars, field work. *Entrance requirements:* For master's and doctorate, GRE; for Certificate, bachelor's degree. Additional exam requirements/recommendations for international students: Required—TOEFL. *Application deadline:* For spring admission, 10/1 for domestic students. Applications are processed on a rolling basis. Application fee: $80. *Expenses:* Tuition: Full-time $22,266; part-time $1237 per credit hour. Required fees: $430. Tuition and fees vary according to program. *Financial support:* Fellowships, research assistantships with full and partial tuition reimbursements, teaching assistantships with full and partial tuition reimbursements, career-related internships or fieldwork, Federal Work-Study, institutionally sponsored loans, and tuition waivers (full and partial) available. Financial award application deadline: 2/1. *Faculty research:* Political economy, development, labor, gender. *Unit head:* Robert A. Blecker, Chair, 202-885-3767, Fax: 202-885-3790, E-mail: blecker@american.edu. *Application contact:* Kathleen Clowery, Director of Graduate Admissions, 202-885-3621, Fax: 202-885-1505, E-mail: clowery@american.edu.

The American University in Cairo, Graduate Studies and Research, School of Business, Economics and Communication, Department of Economics, Cairo, Egypt. Offers MA. Part-time programs available. *Degree requirements:* For master's, thesis or alternative. *Entrance requirements:* For master's, GMAT. Additional exam requirements/recommendations for international students: Required—English entrance exam. Electronic applications accepted. *Faculty research:* Macro-economic policies, agricultural growth and rural credit markets, alleviation of poverty in Egypt.

American University of Beirut, Graduate Programs, Faculty of Arts and Sciences, Beirut, Lebanon. Offers anthropology (MA); Arabic language and literature (MA); archaeology (MA); biology (MS); chemistry (MS); computer science (MS); economics (MA); education (MA); English language (MA); English literature (MA); environmental policy planning (MSES); financial economics (MAFE); geology (MS); history (MA); mathematics (MA, MS); Middle Eastern studies (MA); philosophy (MA); physics (MS); political studies (MA); psychology (MA); public administration (MA); sociology (MA); statistics (MA, MS). Part-time programs available. *Degree requirements:* For master's, one foreign language, comprehensive exam, thesis (for some programs). *Entrance requirements:* For master's, GRE, letter of recommendation. Additional exam requirements/recommendations for international students: Required—TOEFL (minimum score 600 paper-based; 250 computer-based; 100 iBT), IELTS (minimum score 7.5). *Faculty research:* String theory and supergravity; computer graphics; algebra and number theory; popular Arabic literature; marine and freshwater biology; integrating science, math and technology.

Andrews University, School of Graduate Studies, School of Business, Graduate Programs in Business, Berrien Springs, MI 49104. Offers MBA, MSA. *Students:* 7 full-time (6 women), 12 part-time (6 women); includes 6 minority (4 African Americans, 1 Asian American or Pacific Islander, 1 Hispanic American), 5 international. Average age 27. 35 applicants, 46% accepted, 10 enrolled. In 2009, 7 master's awarded. *Entrance requirements:* For master's, GMAT. Additional exam requirements/recommendations for international students: Required—TOEFL (minimum score 550 paper-based). Application fee: $40. *Unit head:* Dr. Leonard K. Gashugi, Chair, 769-471-3429, E-mail: gashugi@andrews.edu. *Application contact:* Carolyn Hurst, Supervisor of Graduate Admission, 800-253-2874, Fax: 269-471-6321, E-mail: graduate@andrews.edu.

Arizona State University, Graduate College, W.P. Carey School of Business, Department of Economics, Tempe, AZ 85287. Offers PhD, JD/MS, MBA/MS. *Degree requirements:* For doctorate, thesis/dissertation. *Entrance requirements:* For doctorate, GRE.

Assumption College, Graduate School, Department of Business Studies, Worcester, MA 01609-1296. Offers accounting (MBA); business administration (CAGS); finance/economics (MBA); general business (MBA); human resources (MBA); international business (MBA); management (MBA); marketing (MBA); nonprofit leadership (MBA). Part-time and evening/weekend programs available. *Faculty:* 6 full-time (1 woman), 14 part-time/adjunct (2 women). *Students:* 19 full-time (11 women), 127 part-time (68 women); includes 22 minority (13 African Americans, 3 Asian Americans or Pacific Islanders, 6 Hispanic Americans). Average age 27. 88 applicants, 99% accepted. In 2009, 40 master's, 2 other advanced degrees awarded. *Entrance requirements:* For master's, 3 letters of recommendation, resume; for CAGS, 3 letters of recommendation, resume, essay. Additional exam requirements/recommendations for international students: Required—TOEFL (minimum score 540 paper-based; 200 computer-based; 76 iBT), IELTS (minimum score 6). *Application deadline:* For fall admission, 6/1 priority date for domestic students, 5/1 priority date for international students; for spring admission, 11/1 priority date for domestic students, 9/1 priority date for international students. Applications are processed on a rolling basis. Application fee: $30. Electronic applications accepted. *Expenses:* Tuition: Part-time $503 per credit. Required fees: $20 per semester. One-time fee: $100 part-time. Part-time tuition and fees vary according to campus/location. *Financial support:* In 2009–10, 47 students received support. Application deadline: 6/1. *Faculty research:* Workplace diversity, dynamics of team interaction, utilization of leased employees. *Unit head:* Michael Lewis, Director, 508-767-7372, Fax: 508-767-7252, E-mail: jhunter@assumption.edu. *Application contact:* Adrian O. Dumas, Director of Graduate Enrollment Management and Services, 508-767-7365, Fax: 508-767-7030, E-mail: adumas@assumption.edu.

Auburn University, Graduate School, College of Liberal Arts, Department of Economics, Auburn University, AL 36849. Offers MS. Part-time programs available. *Faculty:* 10 full-time (1 woman), 4 part-time/adjunct (0 women). *Students:* 15 full-time (3 women), 5 part-time (0 women), 2 international. Average age 26. 58 applicants, 45% accepted, 13 enrolled. In 2009, 11 master's awarded. *Degree requirements:* For master's, thesis. *Entrance requirements:* For master's, GMAT, GRE General Test. Additional exam requirements/recommendations for international students: Required—TOEFL. *Application deadline:* For fall admission, 7/7 for domestic students; for spring admission, 11/24 for domestic students. Applications are processed on a rolling basis. Application fee: $50 ($60 for international students). Electronic applications accepted. *Expenses:* Tuition, state resident: full-time $6240. Tuition, nonresident: full-time $18,720. International tuition: $18,938 full-time. Required fees: $492. Tuition and fees vary according to course load, program and reciprocity agreements. *Financial support:* Teaching assistantships, career-related internships or fieldwork and Federal Work-Study available. Support available to part-time students. Financial award application deadline: 3/15; financial award applicants required to submit FAFSA. *Unit head:* Dr. Barry Burkhart, Interim Chair, 334-844-2903. *Application contact:* Dr. George Flowers, Dean of the Graduate School, 334-844-2125.

Baylor University, Graduate School, Hankamer School of Business, Department of Economics, Waco, TX 76798. Offers economics (MS Eco); international economics (MA, MS). *Students:* 15 full-time (9 women), 1 part-time (0 women), 5 international. In 2009, 7 master's awarded. *Entrance requirements:* For master's, GMAT or GRE General Test. *Application deadline:* For fall admission, 8/1 for domestic students; for spring admission, 12/1 for domestic students. Applications are processed on a rolling basis. Application fee: $25. *Financial support:* Research assistantships, Federal Work-Study and institutionally sponsored loans available. Financial award application deadline: 4/1. *Faculty research:* Econometrics, international economics, private enterprise, comparative economic systems. *Unit head:* Dr. Steve Green, Chair, 254-710-4543, Fax: 254-710-3265, E-mail: steve_green@baylor.edu. *Application contact:* Susan Armstrong, Administrative Assistant, 254-710-6177, Fax: 254-710-1066, E-mail: susan_armstrong@baylor.edu.

Bernard M. Baruch College of the City University of New York, Zicklin School of Business, Department of Economics and Finance, Program in Economics, New York, NY 10010-5585. Offers MBA. Part-time and evening/weekend programs available. *Entrance requirements:* For master's, GMAT, 2 letters of recommendation, resume, 2 years of work experience. Additional exam requirements/recommendations for international students: Required—TOEFL (minimum score 590 paper-based; 243 computer-based), TWE (minimum score 5).

Boston College, Graduate School of Arts and Sciences, Department of Economics, Chestnut Hill, MA 02467-3800. Offers PhD. *Students:* 78 full-time (22 women); includes 6 minority (1 African American, 5 Asian Americans or Pacific Islanders), 56 international. 378 applicants, 10% accepted, 17 enrolled. In 2009, 4 doctorates awarded. *Degree requirements:* For doctorate, comprehensive exam, thesis/dissertation. *Entrance requirements:* For doctorate, GRE General Test, GRE Subject Test. Additional exam requirements/recommendations for international students: Required—TOEFL (minimum score 600 paper-based; 250 computer-based; 100 iBT). *Application deadline:* For fall admission, 1/2 for domestic and international students. Application fee: $70. Electronic applications accepted. *Financial support:* In 2009–10, fellowships (averaging $17,000 per year), research assistantships (averaging $18,000 per year), teaching assistantships (averaging $17,400 per year) were awarded; Federal Work-Study, scholarships/grants, and tuition waivers (full) also available. Support available to part-time students. Financial award application deadline: 3/1; financial award applicants required to submit FAFSA. *Faculty research:* Econometrics, international economics, public sector economics, monetary economics, urban economics. *Unit head:* Dr. Marvin Kraus, Chairperson, 617-552-3683. *Application contact:* Dr. Dick Tresch, Graduate Program Director, 617-552-3683, E-mail: richard.trusch@bc.edu.

Boston University, Graduate School of Arts and Sciences, Department of Economics, Boston, MA 02215. Offers economic policy (MAEP); economics (MA, PhD); political economy (MAPE); MBA/MA. *Students:* 230 full-time (93 women), 25 part-time (8 women); includes 17 minority (1 African American, 1 American Indian/Alaska Native, 9 Asian Americans or Pacific Islanders, 6 Hispanic Americans), 185 international. Average age 26. 1,029 applicants, 26% accepted, 117 enrolled. In 2009, 78 master's, 29 doctorates awarded. Terminal master's awarded for partial completion of doctoral program. *Degree requirements:* For master's, one foreign language, comprehensive exam; for doctorate, one foreign language, comprehensive exam, thesis/dissertation, qualifying exam. *Entrance requirements:* For master's and doctorate, GRE General Test, 3 letters of recommendation. Additional exam requirements/recommendations for international students: Required—TOEFL (minimum score 550 paper-based; 213 computer-based). *Application deadline:* For fall admission, 3/1 for domestic and international students. Application fee: $70. Electronic applications accepted. *Expenses:* Tuition: Full-time $37,910; part-time $1184 per credit hour. Required fees: $386; $40 per semester. Part-time tuition and fees vary according to class time, course level, degree level and program. *Financial support:* In 2009–10, 91 students received support, including 9 fellowships with full tuition reimbursements available (averaging $18,900 per year), 17 research assistantships with full and partial tuition reimbursements available (averaging $18,400 per year), 27 teaching assistantships with full tuition reimbursements available (averaging $18,400 per year); Federal Work-Study and scholarships/grants also available. Support available to part-time students. Financial award application deadline: 1/15; financial award applicants required to submit FAFSA. *Unit head:* Robert Margo, Chairman, 617-353-6819, Fax: 617-353-4449, E-mail: margora@bu.edu. *Application contact:* Andrew Campolieto, Graduate Program Administrator, 617-353-4454, Fax: 617-353-4449, E-mail: acamp@bu.edu.

Boston University, Metropolitan College, Department of Administrative Sciences, Boston, MA 02215. Offers banking and financial management (MSM); business continuity in emergency management (MSM); economics development and tourism management (MSAS); electronic commerce, systems, and technology (MSAS); financial economics (MSAS); human resource management (MSM); innovation and technology (MSAS); insurance management (MSM); international market management (MSM); multinational commerce (MSAS); project management (MSM). *Accreditation:* AACSB. Part-time and evening/weekend programs available. Post-baccalaureate distance learning degree programs offered (no on-campus study). *Students:* 123 full-time (48 women), 204 part-time (92 women); includes 31 minority (10 African Americans, 1 American Indian/Alaska Native, 11 Asian Americans or Pacific Islanders, 9 Hispanic Americans), 146 international. Average age 30. In 2009, 154 master's awarded. *Degree requirements:* For master's, thesis optional. *Entrance requirements:* For master's, 1 year of work experience, minimum GPA of 3.0. Additional exam requirements/recommendations for international students: Required—TOEFL (minimum score 560 paper-based; 220 computer-based; 84 iBT). *Application deadline:* Applications are processed on a rolling basis. Application fee: $70. Electronic applications accepted. *Expenses:* Tuition: Full-time $37,910; part-time $1184 per credit hour. Required fees: $386; $40 per semester. Part-time tuition and fees vary according to class time, course level, degree level and program. *Financial support:* In 2009–10, 15 students received support, including 8 research assistantships (averaging $10,000 per year); career-related internships or fieldwork and Federal Work-Study also available. *Faculty research:* International business, innovative process. *Unit head:* Dr. Kip Becker, Chairman, 617-353-3016, E-mail: adminsc@bu.edu. *Application contact:* Lucille Dicker, Administrative Sciences Department, 617-353-3016, E-mail: adminsc@bu.edu.

Bowling Green State University, Graduate College, College of Business Administration, Department of Economics, Bowling Green, OH 43403. Offers MA. Part-time programs available. *Degree requirements:* For master's, thesis or alternative. *Entrance requirements:* For master's, GRE General Test. Additional exam requirements/recommendations for international students: Required—TOEFL. Electronic applications accepted. *Faculty research:* Labor economics, monetary economics, economic education, mathematical economics.

Brandeis University, International Business School, Waltham, MA 02454-9110. Offers finance (MSF); international business (MBAi); international economics and finance (MA, PhD); inter-

Economics

Brandeis University (continued)

national finance/international economics (MBAi). Part-time and evening/weekend programs available. Terminal master's awarded for partial completion of doctoral program. *Degree requirements:* For master's, one foreign language, semester abroad; for doctorate, thesis/dissertation. *Entrance requirements:* For master's, GMAT or GRE General Test (MA), GMAT (MBAi, MSF); for doctorate, GRE General Test. Additional exam requirements/recommendations for international students: Required—TOEFL (minimum score 600 paper-based; 250 computer-based), IELTS (minimum score 7). Electronic applications accepted. *Faculty research:* International finance and business, trade policy, macroeconomics, Asian economic issues, developmental economics.

Brock University, Faculty of Graduate Studies, Faculty of Social Sciences, Program in Business Economics, St. Catharines, ON L2S 3A1, Canada. Offers MBE. *Degree requirements:* For master's, thesis or alternative. *Entrance requirements:* For master's, honours degree. Additional exam requirements/recommendations for international students: Required—TOEFL (minimum score 550 paper-based; 213 computer-based; 80 iBT), IELTS (minimum score 6.5), TWE (minimum score 4). Electronic applications accepted. *Faculty research:* Microeconomic theory, macroeconomics, econometrics, applied econometrics, economic development.

Brooklyn College of the City University of New York, Division of Graduate Studies, Department of Economics, Brooklyn, NY 11210-2889. Offers accounting (MS); economics (MA). Part-time and evening/weekend programs available. *Students:* 30 full-time (16 women), 161 part-time (85 women); includes 76 minority (56 African Americans, 15 Asian Americans or Pacific Islanders, 5 Hispanic Americans), 55 international. Average age 32. 109 applicants, 73% accepted, 61 enrolled. In 2009, 33 master's awarded. *Degree requirements:* For master's, comprehensive exam, thesis or alternative. *Entrance requirements:* For master's, GMAT (for MS), 2 letters of recommendation. Additional exam requirements/recommendations for international students: Required—TOEFL (minimum score 550 paper-based; 213 computer-based; 79 iBT). *Application deadline:* For fall admission, 3/1 priority date for domestic students, 2/1 priority date for international students; for spring admission, 11/1 priority date for domestic students, 10/1 priority date for international students. Applications are processed on a rolling basis. Application fee: $125. Electronic applications accepted. *Expenses:* Tuition, area resident: Full-time $7360; part-time $310 per credit hour. Tuition, state resident: full-time $7360; part-time $310 per credit hour. Tuition, nonresident: full-time $13,800; part-time $575 per credit hour. International tuition: $13,800 full-time. Required fees: $140.10 per semester. *Financial support:* Career-related internships or fieldwork, Federal Work-Study, institutionally sponsored loans, and scholarships/grants available. Support available to part-time students. Financial award application deadline: 5/1; financial award applicants required to submit FAFSA. *Faculty research:* Econometrics, environmental economics, microeconomics, macroeconomics, taxation. *Unit head:* Dr. Robert Bell, Chairperson, 718-951-5317, E-mail: rbell brooklyn.cuny.edu. *Application contact:* Hernan Sierra, Graduate Admissions Coordinator, 718-951-4536, Fax: 718-951-4506, E-mail: grads@brooklyn.cuny.edu.

Brown University, Graduate School, Department of Economics, Providence, RI 02912. Offers PhD. Terminal master's awarded for partial completion of doctoral program. *Degree requirements:* For doctorate, thesis/dissertation. *Entrance requirements:* For doctorate, GRE General Test.

Buffalo State College, State University of New York, The Graduate School, Faculty of Natural and Social Sciences, Department of Economics and Finance, Buffalo, NY 14222-1095. Offers applied economics (MA). *Degree requirements:* For master's, project. *Entrance requirements:* Additional exam requirements/recommendations for international students: Required—TOEFL (minimum score 550 paper-based; 213 computer-based).

California State Polytechnic University, Pomona, Academic Affairs, College of Letters, Arts, and Social Sciences, Program in Economics, Pomona, CA 91768-2557. Offers MS. Part-time programs available. *Students:* 11 full-time (2 women), 47 part-time (17 women); includes 31 minority (3 African Americans, 15 Asian Americans or Pacific Islanders, 13 Hispanic Americans), 12 international. Average age 29. 46 applicants, 63% accepted, 10 enrolled. In 2009, 9 master's awarded. *Degree requirements:* For master's, thesis or alternative. *Entrance requirements:* For master's, GRE General Test. *Application deadline:* For fall admission, 5/1 priority date for domestic students; for winter admission, 10/15 priority date for domestic students; for spring admission, 1/20 priority date for domestic students. Applications are processed on a rolling basis. Application fee: $55. Electronic applications accepted. *Expenses:* Tuition, nonresident: full-time $6696; part-time $248 per credit. Required fees: $5487; $3237 per term. Tuition and fees vary according to course load, degree level and program. *Financial support:* In 2009–10, 9 students received support. Federal Work-Study and institutionally sponsored loans available. Support available to part-time students. Financial award application deadline: 3/2; financial award applicants required to submit FAFSA. *Unit head:* Dr. Carsten Lange, Graduate Coordinator, 909-869-3843, E-mail: clange@csupomona.edu. *Application contact:* Scott J. Duncan, Director, Admissions, 909-869-3258, Fax: 909-869-4529, E-mail: sjduncan@csupomona.edu.

California State University, East Bay, Academic Programs and Graduate Studies, College of Business and Economics, Department of Economics, Hayward, CA 94542-3000. Offers economics (MA). Part-time and evening/weekend programs available. *Faculty:* 5 full-time (0 women), 1 part-time/adjunct (0 women). *Students:* 15 full-time (6 women), 39 part-time (16 women); includes 19 minority (4 African Americans, 11 Asian Americans or Pacific Islanders, 4 Hispanic Americans), 18 international. Average age 28. 71 applicants, 54% accepted, 19 enrolled. In 2009, 11 master's awarded. *Degree requirements:* For master's, comprehensive exam, project or thesis. *Entrance requirements:* For master's, GMAT, minimum GPA of 2.75 during previous 2 years of course work. Additional exam requirements/recommendations for international students: Required—TOEFL (minimum score 580 paper-based; 237 computer-based; 92 iBT). *Application deadline:* For fall admission, 6/30 for domestic and international students. Applications are processed on a rolling basis. Application fee: $55. Electronic applications accepted. *Financial support:* Career-related internships or fieldwork, Federal Work-Study, and institutionally sponsored loans available. Support available to part-time students. Financial award application deadline: 3/1; financial award applicants required to submit FAFSA. *Unit head:* Prof. Leo Kahane, Chair, 510-885-3369, Fax: 510-885-4796, E-mail: leo.kahane@csueastbay.edu. *Application contact:* Donna Wiley, Interim Associate Director, 510-885-2928, Fax: 510-885-4777, E-mail: donna.wiley@csueastbay.edu.

California State University, Fullerton, Graduate Studies, College of Business and Economics, Department of Economics, Fullerton, CA 92834-9480. Offers business economics (MBA); economics (MA). Part-time programs available. *Students:* 30 full-time (6 women), 16 part-time (3 women); includes 18 minority (2 African Americans, 8 Asian Americans or Pacific Islanders, 8 Hispanic Americans), 11 international. Average age 28. 63 applicants, 48% accepted, 23 enrolled. In 2009, 7 master's awarded. *Degree requirements:* For master's, thesis. *Entrance requirements:* For master's, GMAT, GRE General Test. Application fee: $55. *Expenses:* Tuition, nonresident: full-time $11,160; part-time $373 per credit. Required fees: $1440 per term. Tuition and fees vary according to course load, degree level and program. *Financial support:* Career-related internships or fieldwork, Federal Work-Study, institutionally sponsored loans, and scholarships/grants available. Support available to part-time students. Financial award application deadline: 3/1; financial award applicants required to submit FAFSA. *Faculty research:* Environmental and natural resource issues. *Unit head:* Dr. Morteza Rahmatian, Chair, 657-278-2228. *Application contact:* Admissions/Applications, 657-278-2371.

California State University, Long Beach, Graduate Studies, College of Liberal Arts, Department of Economics, Long Beach, CA 90840. Offers economics (MA); global logistics (MA). Part-time programs available. *Faculty:* 2 full-time (1 woman). *Students:* 15 full-time (5 women), 20 part-time (10 women); includes 11 minority (3 African Americans, 1 American Indian/Alaska Native, 4 Asian Americans or Pacific Islanders, 3 Hispanic Americans), 10 international. Average age 29. 78 applicants, 71% accepted, 17 enrolled. *Degree requirements:* For master's, comprehensive exam or thesis. *Entrance requirements:* For master's, GRE General Test, GRE Subject Test, minimum GPA of 3.0. *Application deadline:* For fall admission, 4/1 for domestic students. Applications are processed on a rolling basis. Application fee: $55. Electronic applications accepted. *Expenses:* Required fees: $1802 per semester. Part-time tuition and fees vary according to course load. *Financial support:* Federal Work-Study, institutionally sponsored loans, and scholarships/grants available. Financial award application deadline: 3/2. *Faculty research:* Trade and development, economic forecasting, resource economics. *Unit head:* Dr. Joseph P. Magaddino, Chair, 562-985-5061, Fax: 562-985-5804, E-mail: magaddin@csulb.edu. *Application contact:* Dr. Alejandra C. Edwards, Graduate Advisor, 562-985-5969, Fax: 562-985-5804, E-mail: acoxedwa@csulb.edu.

California State University, Los Angeles, Graduate Studies, College of Business and Economics, Department of Economics and Statistics, Los Angeles, CA 90032-8530. Offers analytical quantitative economics (MA); business economics (MA, MBA, MS); economics (MA). Part-time and evening/weekend programs available. *Faculty:* 3 full-time (0 women), 2 part-time/adjunct (0 women). *Students:* 13 full-time (4 women), 20 part-time (9 women); includes 15 minority (1 African American, 8 Asian Americans or Pacific Islanders, 6 Hispanic Americans), 11 international. Average age 27. 10 applicants, 100% accepted, 4 enrolled. In 2009, 10 master's awarded. *Degree requirements:* For master's, comprehensive exam or thesis. *Entrance requirements:* For master's, GMAT, minimum GPA of 2.5 during previous 2 years of course work. Additional exam requirements/recommendations for international students: Required—TOEFL (minimum score 550 paper-based; 213 computer-based). *Application deadline:* For fall admission, 5/1 for domestic and international students. Applications are processed on a rolling basis. Application fee: $55. Electronic applications accepted. *Financial support:* Career-related internships or fieldwork and Federal Work-Study available. Support available to part-time students. Financial award application deadline: 3/1. *Unit head:* Dr. Dang Tran, Chair, 323-343-2930, Fax: 323-343-5462, E-mail: dtran@calstatela.edu. *Application contact:* Dr. Cheryl L. Ney, Associate Vice President for Academic Affairs and Dean of Graduate Studies, 323-343-3820, Fax: 323-343-5653, E-mail: cney@cslanet.calstatela.edu.

Carleton University, Faculty of Graduate Studies, Faculty of Public Affairs and Management, Department of Economics, Ottawa, ON K1S 5B6, Canada. Offers MA, PhD. *Degree requirements:* For master's, thesis optional; for doctorate, comprehensive exam, thesis/dissertation. *Entrance requirements:* For master's, honors degree; for doctorate, master's degree. Additional exam requirements/recommendations for international students: Required—TOEFL. *Faculty research:* Monetary economics, economic development, public economics, industrial organization, international trade.

Carleton University, Faculty of Graduate Studies, Faculty of Public Affairs and Management, Institute of Political Economy, Ottawa, ON K1S 5B6, Canada. Offers MA, PhD. *Degree requirements:* For master's, thesis optional. *Entrance requirements:* For master's, honors degree. Additional exam requirements/recommendations for international students: Required—TOEFL. *Faculty research:* Relationships between economy and politics as they affect the political, social and cultural life of societies; historical processes whereby social change is located in the interaction of the economic, political and cultural, and ideological moments of social life.

Carnegie Mellon University, Tepper School of Business, Program in Economics, Pittsburgh, PA 15213-3891. Offers PhD. *Degree requirements:* For doctorate, thesis/dissertation. *Entrance requirements:* For doctorate, GMAT, GRE General Test. *Faculty research:* Research allocation under asymmetric information, monetary theory, estimation of rational expectations models.

Case Western Reserve University, Weatherhead School of Management, Department of Economics, Cleveland, OH 44106. Offers MBA. Part-time and evening/weekend programs available. *Entrance requirements:* For master's, GMAT. *Application deadline:* For fall admission, 4/15 priority date for domestic students. Applications are processed on a rolling basis. Application fee: $100. *Financial support:* Career-related internships or fieldwork, Federal Work-Study, institutionally sponsored loans, and tuition waivers (full and partial) available. Financial award application deadline: 5/1. *Faculty research:* Public finance and public choice, direct foreign investment, employment relationships, technical and institutional change, regional economics. *Unit head:* Sue Helper, Chairman, 216-368-4110, Fax: 216-368-5541, E-mail: sue.helper@case.edu. *Application contact:* Sue Helper, Chairman, 216-368-4110, Fax: 216-368-5541, E-mail: sue.helper@case.edu.

The Catholic University of America, School of Arts and Sciences, Department of Business and Economics, Washington, DC 20064. Offers international political economics (MA). Part-time programs available. *Faculty:* 7 full-time (2 women), 10 part-time/adjunct (5 women). *Students:* 1 part-time (0 women); minority (African American). Average age 30. In 2009, 26 master's awarded. *Degree requirements:* For master's, comprehensive exam. *Entrance requirements:* For master's, GRE General Test, 3 letters of recommendation. Additional exam requirements/recommendations for international students: Required—TOEFL (minimum score 580 paper-based; 237 computer-based). *Application deadline:* For fall admission, 8/1 priority date for domestic students, 7/15 for international students; for spring admission, 12/1 priority date for domestic students, 10/15 for international students. Applications are processed on a rolling basis. Application fee: $55. Electronic applications accepted. *Expenses:* Tuition: Full-time $31,740; part-time $1245 per credit hour. Required fees: $50; $25 per semester hour. One-time fee: $425. *Financial support:* Fellowships, research assistantships, teaching assistantships, Federal Work-Study, scholarships/grants, tuition waivers (full and partial), and unspecified assistantships available. Financial award application deadline: 2/1; financial award applicants required to submit FAFSA. *Faculty research:* Integrity of the marketing process, economics of energy and the environment, emerging markets, social change, international finance and economic development. Total annual research expenditures: $6,459. *Unit head:* Dr. Andrew V. Abela, Chair, 202-319-5235, Fax: 202-319-4426, E-mail: abela@cua.edu. *Application contact:* Julie Schwing, Director of Graduate Admissions, 202-319-5057, Fax: 202-319-6533, E-mail: cua-admissions@cua.edu.

Central European University, Graduate Studies, Department of Legal Studies, Budapest, Hungary. Offers comparative constitutional law (LL M); economic and legal studies (LL M, MA); human rights (LL M, MA); international business law (LL M); legal studies (SJD). Terminal master's awarded for partial completion of doctoral program. *Degree requirements:* For master's, one foreign language, thesis; for doctorate, one foreign language, comprehensive exam, thesis/dissertation. *Entrance requirements:* For master's and doctorate, LSAT, CEU admissions exams. Additional exam requirements/recommendations for international students: Required—TOEFL (minimum score 570 paper-based; 230 computer-based). Electronic applications accepted. *Expenses:* Contact institution. *Faculty research:* Institutional, constitutional and human rights in European Union law, biomedical law and reproductive rights, data protection law, Islamic banking and finance.

Central European University, Graduate Studies, School of Social Sciences and Humanities, Budapest, Hungary. Offers economics (MA, PhD); gender studies (MA, PhD); international relations and European studies (MA, PhD); mathematics and its applications (MS, PhD); medieval studies (MA, PhD); nationalism studies (MA, PhD); philosophy (MA, PhD); political science (MA, PhD); public policy (MA, PhD); sociology and social anthropology (MA, PhD). Terminal master's awarded for partial completion of doctoral program. *Degree requirements:* For master's, one foreign language, thesis; for doctorate, one foreign language, comprehensive exam, thesis/dissertation. *Entrance requirements:* For master's, interview; for doctorate, GRE, CEU subject test, interview. Additional exam requirements/recommendations for international students: Required—TOEFL (minimum score 570 paper-based; 230 computer-based). Electronic applications accepted. *Faculty research:* Civil society, fiscal decentralization, party politics, political philosophy (especially Liberalism, theory of Democracy).

Central Michigan University, College of Graduate Studies, College of Business Administration, Department of Economics, Mount Pleasant, MI 48859. Offers MA. Part-time programs available. *Degree requirements:* For master's, thesis or alternative. Electronic applications accepted.

Faculty research: Economic development, industrial organization, international trade, monetary theory, public choice/labor.

Chapman University, Graduate Studies, School of Law, Orange, CA 92866. Offers advocacy and dispute resolution (JD); entertainment law (JD); environmental, land use, and real estate (JD); international law (JD); law (LL M), including business law and economics, entertainment and media law, international and comparative law; prosecutorial science (LL M); tax law (JD); taxation (LL M); JD/MBA; JD/MFA. *Accreditation:* ABA. Part-time and evening/weekend programs available. *Faculty:* 56 full-time (21 women), 24 part-time/adjunct (4 women). *Students:* 535 full-time (260 women), 87 part-time (37 women); includes 126 minority (6 African Americans, 2 American Indian/Alaska Native, 79 Asian Americans or Pacific Islanders, 39 Hispanic Americans), 6 international. Average age 27. 2,996 applicants, 32% accepted, 226 enrolled. In 2009, 158 first professional degrees, 7 master's awarded. *Entrance requirements:* LSAT, minimum undergraduate GPA of 2.75. Additional exam requirements/recommendations for international students: Required—TOEFL (minimum score 600 paper-based; 213 computer-based; 80 iBT). *Application deadline:* For fall admission, 4/1 priority date for domestic students. Applications are processed on a rolling basis. Application fee: $65. Electronic applications accepted. *Expenses:* Contact institution. *Financial support:* Fellowships, Federal Work-Study and scholarships/grants available. Financial award application deadline: 6/30; financial award applicants required to submit FAFSA. *Unit head:* Dr. John Eastman, Dean, 714-628-2500. *Application contact:* Marissa Vargas, Admissions Recruiter/Financial Aid Counselor, 877-CHAPLAW, E-mail: mvargas@chapman.edu.

City College of the City University of New York, Graduate School, College of Liberal Arts and Science, Division of Social Science, Department of Economics, New York, NY 10031-9198. Offers MA. Part-time programs available. *Degree requirements:* For master's, comprehensive exam, proficiency in a foreign language or advanced statistics. *Entrance requirements:* Additional exam requirements/recommendations for international students: Required—TOEFL (minimum score 550 paper-based; 79 iBT). Electronic applications accepted. *Faculty research:* International economics, health, banking.

Claremont Graduate University, Graduate Programs, School of Politics and Economics, Department of Economics, Claremont, CA 91711-6160. Offers business and financial economics (MA, PhD); economic development (Certificate); economics (PhD); industrial organization (PhD); international and development economics (PhD); international economics policy and development (MA); international money and finance (PhD); neuroeconomics (PhD); political economy and public policy (MA); public choice and public economics (PhD); MBA/PhD. Part-time programs available. *Faculty:* 5 full-time (0 women), 1 part-time/adjunct (0 women). *Students:* 103 full-time (25 women), 7 part-time (3 women); includes 16 minority (1 African American, 9 Asian Americans or Pacific Islanders, 6 Hispanic Americans), 62 international. Average age 33. In 2009, 15 master's, 8 doctorates awarded. *Entrance requirements:* For master's and doctorate, GRE General Test or GMAT. Additional exam requirements/recommendations for international students: Required—TOEFL (minimum score 550 paper-based; 213 computer-based; 80 iBT). *Application deadline:* For fall admission, 2/1 priority date for domestic students. Applications are processed on a rolling basis. Application fee: $60. Electronic applications accepted. *Expenses:* Tuition: Full-time $35,046; part-time $1524 per credit. Required fees: $161 per semester. *Financial support:* Fellowships, research assistantships, teaching assistantships, Federal Work-Study, institutionally sponsored loans, and scholarships/grants available. Support available to part-time students. Financial award application deadline: 2/15; financial award applicants required to submit FAFSA. *Faculty research:* International and financial economics, law and economics, regulation, public choice economics. *Unit head:* Paul Zak, Chair, 909-621-8788, Fax: 909-621-8545, E-mail: paul.zak@cgu.edu. *Application contact:* Lesa Hiben, Admissions Coordinator, 909-621-8699, Fax: 909-621-7545, E-mail: lesa.hiben@cga.edu.

Claremont Graduate University, Graduate Programs, School of Politics and Economics, Department of Politics and Policy, Claremont, CA 91711-6160. Offers American politics (MA, PhD); comparative politics (PhD); international political economy (MA); international studies (MA); political philosophy (PhD); political science (PhD); politics, economics and business (MA); public policy (MA, PhD); world politics (PhD); MBA/PhD. Part-time programs available. *Faculty:* 8 full-time (3 women), 4 part-time/adjunct (0 women). *Students:* 163 full-time (68 women), 16 part-time (7 women); includes 29 minority (6 African Americans, 8 Asian Americans or Pacific Islanders, 15 Hispanic Americans), 40 international. Average age 32. In 2009, 23 master's, 19 doctorates awarded. Terminal master's awarded for partial completion of doctoral program. *Entrance requirements:* For master's and doctorate, GRE General Test. Additional exam requirements/recommendations for international students: Required—TOEFL (minimum score 550 paper-based; 213 computer-based; 80 iBT). *Application deadline:* For fall admission, 2/1 priority date for domestic students. Applications are processed on a rolling basis. Application fee: $60. Electronic applications accepted. *Expenses:* Tuition: Full-time $35,046; part-time $1524 per credit. Required fees: $161 per semester. *Financial support:* Fellowships, research assistantships, teaching assistantships, Federal Work-Study, institutionally sponsored loans, and scholarships/grants available. Support available to part-time students. Financial award application deadline: 2/15; financial award applicants required to submit FAFSA. *Faculty research:* Environmental policy, international debt, global democratization, Third World development, public sector discrimination. *Unit head:* Jennifer Merolla, Chair, 909-621-8696, Fax: 909-621-8545, E-mail: jennifer.merolla@cgu.edu. *Application contact:* Lesa Hiben, Admissions Coordinator, 909-621-8699, Fax: 909-621-7545, E-mail: lesa.hiben@cga.edu.

Clark Atlanta University, School of Business Administration, Department of Economics, Atlanta, GA 30314. Offers MA. Part-time programs available. *Degree requirements:* For master's, thesis optional. *Entrance requirements:* For master's, GRE General Test, minimum GPA of 2.5. Additional exam requirements/recommendations for international students: Required—TOEFL (minimum score 500 paper-based; 173 computer-based). *Application deadline:* For fall admission, 4/1 for domestic and international students; for spring admission, 11/1 for domestic and international students. Applications are processed on a rolling basis. Application fee: $40 ($55 for international students). Electronic applications accepted. *Expenses:* Tuition: Full-time $12,240; part-time $680 per credit hour. Required fees: $710; $355 per semester. *Financial support:* Career-related internships or fieldwork, Federal Work-Study, scholarships/grants, and unspecified assistantships available. Support available to part-time students. Financial award application deadline: 4/30; financial award applicants required to submit FAFSA. *Faculty research:* Minority energy demand. *Unit head:* Dr. Ajamu Nyomba, Chairperson, 404-880-6286, E-mail: anyomba@cau.edu. *Application contact:* Michelle Clark-Davis, Graduate Program Admissions, 404-880-6605, E-mail: cauadmissions@cau.edu.

Clark University, Graduate School, Department of Economics, Worcester, MA 01610-1477. Offers PhD. *Faculty:* 10 full-time (4 women), 1 (woman) part-time/adjunct. *Students:* 42 full-time (17 women); includes 4 minority (1 African American, 2 Asian Americans or Pacific Islanders, 1 Hispanic American), 29 international. Average age 28. 37 applicants, 49% accepted, 7 enrolled. In 2009, 6 doctorates awarded. *Degree requirements:* For doctorate, thesis/dissertation. *Entrance requirements:* For doctorate, GRE General Test. Additional exam requirements/recommendations for international students: Required—TOEFL. *Application deadline:* For fall admission, 2/1 priority date for domestic students. Applications are processed on a rolling basis. Application fee: $50. *Expenses:* Tuition: Full-time $34,900; part-time $4362.50 per course. *Financial support:* In 2009–10, fellowships with full and partial tuition reimbursements (averaging $12,000 per year), 2 research assistantships with full and partial tuition reimbursements (averaging $12,000 per year), 9 teaching assistantships with full and partial tuition reimbursements (averaging $12,000 per year) were awarded; career-related internships or fieldwork, institutionally sponsored loans, and tuition waivers (full and partial) also available. *Faculty research:* Public finance, economic development, industrial organization, international finance and trade, environmental regulation. Total annual research expenditures: $365,000. *Unit head:* Dr. Wayne Gray, Chair, 508-793-7226. *Application contact:* Cindy Rice, Department Secretary, 508-793-7226, Fax: 508-793-8849, E-mail: economics@clarku.edu.

Cleveland State University, College of Graduate Studies, College of Liberal Arts and Social Sciences, Department of Economics, Cleveland, OH 44115. Offers MA. Part-time and evening/weekend programs available. *Entrance requirements:* For master's, minimum GPA of 2.75; coursework in micro theory, macro theory, statistics, and calculus. Additional exam requirements/recommendations for international students: Required—TOEFL (minimum score 515 paper-based; 197 computer-based). Electronic applications accepted. *Faculty research:* Labor economics, health economics, energy, environment, economics of law, organization theory, industrial organization.

Cleveland State University, College of Graduate Studies, Maxine Goodman Levin College of Urban Affairs, Program in Nonprofit Administration and Leadership, Cleveland, OH 44115. Offers geographic information systems (Certificate); local and urban management (Certificate); nonprofit administration and leadership (MNAL); nonprofit management (Certificate); urban economic development (Certificate). Part-time and evening/weekend programs available. *Degree requirements:* For master's, thesis or alternative, capstone course. *Entrance requirements:* For master's, GRE (minimum 40th percentile verbal and quantitative, 4.0 analytical writing), minimum GPA of 3.0. Additional exam requirements/recommendations for international students: Required—TOEFL (minimum score 525 paper-based; 197 computer-based; 65 iBT). Electronic applications accepted. *Faculty research:* Human resource management, volunteerism, performance measurement in nonprofits, government-nonprofit partnerships.

Cleveland State University, College of Graduate Studies, Maxine Goodman Levin College of Urban Affairs, Program in Urban Planning, Design, and Development, Cleveland, OH 44115. Offers geographic information systems (Certificate); local and urban management (Certificate); urban economic development (Certificate); urban planning, design, and development (MUPDD); urban real estate development and finance (Certificate); JD/MUPDD. *Accreditation:* ACSP. Part-time and evening/weekend programs available. *Degree requirements:* For master's, project or thesis. *Entrance requirements:* For master's, GRE General Test (minimum 50th percentile verbal and quantitative, 4.0 analytical writing), minimum GPA of 3.0. Additional exam requirements/recommendations for international students: Required—TOEFL (minimum score 525 paper-based; 197 computer-based; 65 iBT). Electronic applications accepted. *Faculty research:* Housing and neighborhood development, urban housing policy, environmental sustainability, economic development.

Cleveland State University, College of Graduate Studies, Maxine Goodman Levin College of Urban Affairs, Program in Urban Studies, Cleveland, OH 44115. Offers geographic information systems (Certificate); local and urban management (Certificate); nonprofit management (Certificate); urban economic development (Certificate); urban real estate development and finance (Certificate); urban studies (MS); urban studies and public affairs (PhD). Part-time and evening/weekend programs available. *Degree requirements:* For master's, thesis or alternative, exit project, capstone course; for doctorate, comprehensive exam, thesis/dissertation. *Entrance requirements:* For master's, GRE General Test, minimum GPA of 3.0; for doctorate, GRE General Test, minimum GPA of 3.5. Additional exam requirements/recommendations for international students: Required—TOEFL (minimum score 525 paper-based; 197 computer-based; 65 iBT). Electronic applications accepted. *Faculty research:* Environmental issues, economic development, urban and public policy, public management.

Colorado State University, Graduate School, College of Liberal Arts, Department of Economics, Fort Collins, CO 80523-1771. Offers MA, PhD. Part-time programs available. *Faculty:* 14 full-time (5 women), 2 part-time/adjunct (1 woman). *Students:* 25 full-time (5 women), 33 part-time (10 women); includes 2 minority (both Hispanic Americans), 20 international. Average age 31. 72 applicants, 65% accepted, 16 enrolled. In 2009, 9 master's, 5 doctorates awarded. Terminal master's awarded for partial completion of doctoral program. *Degree requirements:* For master's, variable foreign language requirement, thesis or alternative; for doctorate, variable foreign language requirement, comprehensive exam, thesis/dissertation. *Entrance requirements:* For master's, GRE General Test (minimum score 1000 verbal and quantitative, 600 quantitative), minimum GPA of 3.0, letters of recommendation; for doctorate, GRE General Test (combined score of 1000 on Verbal and Quantitative sections with at least 600 on Quantitative section), minimum GPA of 3.0, letters of recommendation, statement of purpose. Additional exam requirements/recommendations for international students: Required—TOEFL. *Application deadline:* For fall admission, 1/31 priority date for domestic students. Applications are processed on a rolling basis. Application fee: $50. Electronic applications accepted. *Expenses:* Tuition, state resident: full-time $6434; part-time $359.10 per credit. Tuition, nonresident: full-time $18,116; part-time $1006.45 per credit. Required fees: $1496; $83 per credit. *Financial support:* In 2009–10, 18 students received support, including 18 teaching assistantships with full tuition reimbursements available (averaging $13,658 per year); fellowships, research assistantships, career-related internships or fieldwork, Federal Work-Study, institutionally sponsored loans, scholarships/grants, traineeships, and unspecified assistantships also available. Financial award application deadline: 3/1; financial award applicants required to submit FAFSA. *Faculty research:* Regional and development economics, political economy, international trade and investment, public finance, labor markets. Total annual research expenditures: $207,281. *Unit head:* Dr. Steven J. Shulman, Chair, 970-491-6940, Fax: 970-491-2925, E-mail: steven.shulman@colostate.edu. *Application contact:* Dr. Robert W. Kling, Coordinator of Graduate Studies, 970-491-5598, Fax: 970-491-2925, E-mail: robert.king@colostate.edu.

Columbia University, Graduate School of Arts and Sciences, Division of Social Sciences, Department of Economics, New York, NY 10027. Offers M Phil, MA, PhD, JD/MA, JD/PhD. *Degree requirements:* For master's, thesis or alternative; for doctorate, thesis/dissertation. *Entrance requirements:* For master's and doctorate, GRE General Test, GRE Subject Test, previous course work in mathematics. Additional exam requirements/recommendations for international students: Required—TOEFL. *Faculty research:* International trade.

Columbia University, Graduate School of Business, Doctoral Program in Business, New York, NY 10027. Offers business (PhD), including accounting, decision, risk, and operations, finance and economics, management, marketing. *Accreditation:* AACSB. *Faculty:* 149 full-time (23 women), 134 part-time/adjunct (16 women). *Students:* 91 full-time (37 women); includes 10 minority (8 Asian Americans or Pacific Islanders, 2 Hispanic Americans), 64 international. Average age 27. 758 applicants, 6% accepted, 20 enrolled. In 2009, 15 doctorates awarded. *Degree requirements:* For doctorate, comprehensive exam, thesis/dissertation, major field exam, research paper, thesis proposal. *Entrance requirements:* For doctorate, GMAT or GRE (finance), 2 letters of reference, resume. Additional exam requirements/recommendations for international students: Required—TOEFL. *Application deadline:* For fall admission, 1/1 for domestic and international students. Application fee: $75. Electronic applications accepted. *Expenses:* Contact institution. *Financial support:* In 2009–10, 91 students received support, including fellowships with full tuition reimbursements available (averaging $22,000 per year), research assistantships (averaging $4,000 per year); teaching assistantships, career-related internships or fieldwork, health care benefits, and tuition waivers (full) also available. *Faculty research:* Human decision making and behavioral research; real estate market and mortgage defaults; financial crisis and corporate governance; international business; security analysis and accounting. *Unit head:* Elizabeth Elam Chang, Administrative Director, 212-854-2836, Fax: 212-932-2359, E-mail: phdinfo@gsb.columbia.edu. *Application contact:* Elizabeth Elam Chang, Administrative Director, 212-854-2836, Fax: 212-932-2359, E-mail: phdinfo@gsb.columbia.edu.

Columbia University, Graduate School of Business, MBA Program, New York, NY 10027. Offers accounting (MBA); decision, risk, and operations (MBA); entrepreneurship (MBA); finance and economics (MBA); healthcare and pharmaceutical management (MBA); human resource management (MBA); international business (MBA); leadership and ethics (MBA); management (MBA); marketing (MBA); media (MBA); private equity (MBA); real estate (MBA); social enterprise (MBA); value investing (MBA); DDS/MBA; JD/MBA; MBA/MIA; MBA/MPH; MBA/MS; MD/MBA. *Faculty:* 149 full-time (23 women), 134 part-time/adjunct (16 women). *Students:* 1,293 full-time (435 women); includes 235 minority (65 African Americans, 4 American Indian/Alaska Native, 135 Asian Americans or Pacific Islanders, 31 Hispanic Americans), 417

Economics

Columbia University (continued)

international. Average age 28. 6,885 applicants, 15% accepted, 737 enrolled. In 2009, 696 master's awarded. *Entrance requirements:* For master's, GMAT, 2 letters of recommendation. Additional exam requirements/recommendations for international students: Required—TOEFL. *Application deadline:* For fall admission, 4/14 for domestic students, 3/3 for international students; for spring admission, 10/7 for domestic and international students. Applications are processed on a rolling basis. Application fee: $250. Electronic applications accepted. *Expenses:* Contact institution. *Financial support:* In 2009–10, 358 students received support, including 101 fellowships (averaging $23,250 per year); research assistantships, teaching assistantships, career-related internships or fieldwork, institutionally sponsored loans, and scholarships/grants also available. Financial award application deadline: 3/1; financial award applicants required to submit CSS PROFILE or FAFSA. *Faculty research:* Human decision making and behavioral research; real estate market and mortgage defaults; financial crisis and corporate governance; international business; security analysis and accounting. *Unit head:* Prof. Amir Ziv, Vice Dean of Students and the MBA Program, 212-854-3485, Fax: 212-932-0545, E-mail: az50@columbia.edu. *Application contact:* Mary J. Miller, Assistant Dean of Admissions, 212-854-1961, Fax: 212-662-6754, E-mail: apply@gsb.columbia.edu.

Concordia University, School of Graduate Studies, Faculty of Arts and Science, Department of Economics, Montréal, QC H3G 1M8, Canada. Offers MA, PhD, Diploma. *Degree requirements:* For master's, thesis or alternative, research paper; for doctorate, one foreign language, comprehensive exam, thesis/dissertation, research seminar. *Entrance requirements:* For master's and doctorate, honors degree in economics or equivalent. *Faculty research:* Trade and industrial adjustment, tax policy and reform, environmental policy, economics of migration, economics of telecommunications.

Cornell University, Graduate School, Graduate Fields of Architecture, Art and Planning, Field of Regional Science, Ithaca, NY 14853-0001. Offers environmental studies (MA, MS, PhD); international spatial problems (MA, MS, PhD); location theory (MA, MS, PhD); multiregional economic analysis (MA, MS, PhD); peace science (MA, MS, PhD); planning methods (MA, MS, PhD); urban and regional economics (MA, MS, PhD). *Faculty:* 22 full-time (5 women). *Students:* 21 full-time (8 women); includes 2 minority (1 African American, 1 Asian American or Pacific Islander), 18 international. Average age 35. 15 applicants, 53% accepted, 4 enrolled. In 2009, 1 master's, 4 doctorates awarded. Terminal master's awarded for partial completion of doctoral program. *Degree requirements:* For master's, thesis; for doctorate, comprehensive exam, thesis/dissertation. *Entrance requirements:* For master's and doctorate, GRE General Test, 2 letters of recommendation. Additional exam requirements/recommendations for international students: Required—TOEFL (minimum score 600 paper-based; 250 computer-based; 77 iBT). *Application deadline:* For fall admission, 1/15 priority date for domestic students. Application fee: $70. Electronic applications accepted. *Expenses:* Tuition: Full-time $29,500. Required fees: $70. Full-time tuition and fees vary according to degree level, program and student level. *Financial support:* In 2009–10, 7 students received support; fellowships with full tuition reimbursements available, research assistantships with full tuition reimbursements available, teaching assistantships with full tuition reimbursements available, institutionally sponsored loans, scholarships/grants, health care benefits, tuition waivers (full and partial), and unspecified assistantships available. Financial award applicants required to submit FAFSA. *Faculty research:* Urban and regional growth, spatial economics, formation of spatial patterns by socioeconomic systems, non-linear dynamics and complex systems, environmental-economic systems. *Unit head:* Director of Graduate Studies, 607-255-6848, Fax: 607-255-1971. *Application contact:* Graduate Field Assistant, 607-255-6848, Fax: 607-255-1971, E-mail: regsci@cornell.edu.

Cornell University, Graduate School, Graduate Fields of Arts and Sciences, Field of Economics, Ithaca, NY 14853-0001. Offers applied economics (PhD); basic analytical economics (PhD); econometrics and economic statistics (PhD); economic development and planning (PhD); economic theory (PhD); industrial organization and control (PhD); international economics (PhD); labor economics (PhD); monetary and macroeconomics (PhD); public finance (PhD). *Faculty:* 89 full-time (13 women). *Students:* 93 full-time (34 women); includes 6 minority (2 African Americans, 3 Asian Americans or Pacific Islanders, 1 Hispanic American), 51 international. Average age 28. 625 applicants, 11% accepted, 21 enrolled. In 2009, 21 doctorates awarded. *Degree requirements:* For doctorate, comprehensive exam, thesis/dissertation. *Entrance requirements:* For doctorate, GRE General Test, 3 letters of recommendation. Additional exam requirements/recommendations for international students: Required—TOEFL (minimum score 550 paper-based; 213 computer-based; 77 iBT). *Application deadline:* For fall admission, 1/15 priority date for domestic students. Application fee: $70. Electronic applications accepted. *Expenses:* Tuition: Full-time $29,500. Required fees: $70. Full-time tuition and fees vary according to degree level, program and student level. *Financial support:* In 2009–10, 81 students received support, including 12 fellowships with full tuition reimbursements available, 2 teaching assistantships with full tuition reimbursements available; research assistantships with full tuition reimbursements available, institutionally sponsored loans, scholarships/grants, health care benefits, tuition waivers (full and partial), and unspecified assistantships also available. Financial award applicants required to submit FAFSA. *Faculty research:* Learning and games, economics of education, political economy, transfer payments, time series and nonparametrics. *Unit head:* Director of Graduate Studies, 607-255-4893, Fax: 607-255-2818. *Application contact:* Graduate Field Assistant, 607-255-4893, Fax: 607-255-2818, E-mail: econ_phd@cornell.edu.

Dalhousie University, Faculty of Science, Department of Economics, Halifax, NS B3H 4R2, Canada. Offers MA, MDE, PhD. *Students:* 29 full-time (16 women), 12 part-time (5 women). 61 applicants, 49% accepted. In 2009, 5 master's, 1 doctorate awarded. *Degree requirements:* For master's, thesis; for doctorate, thesis/dissertation. *Entrance requirements:* For master's and doctorate, GRE (recommended). Additional exam requirements/recommendations for international students: Required—TOEFL, IELTS, CANTEST, CAEL, or Michigan English Language Assessment Battery. Application fee: $70. Electronic applications accepted. *Financial support:* In 2009–10, 8 fellowships (averaging $9,500 per year), 1 research assistantship (averaging $1,830 per year), 11 teaching assistantships (averaging $3,705 per year) were awarded; career-related internships or fieldwork, scholarships/grants, and health care benefits also available. *Faculty research:* Applied econometrics, industrial organization, labor and income distribution, economic theory (micro and macro), resource economics (fishing, forestry). Total annual research expenditures: $98,500. *Unit head:* Dr. Barry Lesser, Graduate Coordinator, 902-494-1682, Fax: 902-494-6917, E-mail: barry.lesser@dal.ca. *Application contact:* Monique Comeau, Chair, 902-494-2026, Fax: 902-494-6917, E-mail: economics@dal.ca.

DePaul University, Charles H. Kellstadt Graduate School of Business and College of Liberal Arts and Sciences, Department of Economics, Chicago, IL 60604-2287. Offers applied economics (MBA); business strategy (MBA); economics and policy analysis (MA); international business (MBA). Part-time and evening/weekend programs available. *Faculty:* 26 full-time (5 women), 21 part-time/adjunct (5 women). *Students:* 67 full-time (32 women), 28 part-time (16 women); includes 14 minority (3 African Americans, 6 Asian Americans or Pacific Islanders, 5 Hispanic Americans), 8 international. 47 applicants, 47 enrolled. In 2009, 7 master's awarded. *Degree requirements:* For master's, thesis optional. *Entrance requirements:* For master's, GMAT (MBA), GRE (MS). Additional exam requirements/recommendations for international students: Required—TOEFL. *Application deadline:* For fall admission, 7/1 for domestic students; for winter admission, 10/1 for domestic students; for spring admission, 2/1 for domestic students. Applications are processed on a rolling basis. Application fee: $40. Electronic applications accepted. *Expenses:* Tuition: Full-time $37,525; part-time $620 per credit hour. *Financial support:* In 2009–10, 3 students received support, including 2 research assistantships with partial tuition reimbursements available (averaging $9,999 per year). Support available to part-time students. *Faculty research:* Forensic economics, game theory sports, economics of education, banking in Poland and Thailand. *Unit head:* Dr. Thomas D. Donley, Chairperson, 312-362-8887, Fax: 312-362-5452, E-mail: tdonley@depaul.edu. *Application contact:* Gabriella Bucci, Director of Graduate Program in Economics, 773-362-6787, Fax: 312-362-5452, E-mail: gbucci@depaul.edu.

Drexel University, LeBow College of Business, Program in Business Administration, Philadelphia, PA 19104-2875. Offers business administration (MBA, PhD, APC), including accounting (MBA, PhD), decision sciences (PhD), economics (MBA, PhD), finance (MBA, PhD), legal studies (MBA), management (MBA), marketing (MBA, PhD), organizational sciences (PhD), quantitative methods (MBA), strategic management (PhD). *Accreditation:* AACSB. Part-time and evening/weekend programs available. Postbaccalaureate distance learning degree programs offered (minimal on-campus study). Terminal master's awarded for partial completion of doctoral program. *Entrance requirements:* For master's, GMAT, minimum GPA of 2.75; for doctorate, GMAT. Additional exam requirements/recommendations for international students: Required—TOEFL. Electronic applications accepted. *Faculty research:* Decision support systems, individual and group behavior, operations research, techniques and strategy.

Duke University, Graduate School, Department of Economics, Durham, NC 27708. Offers AM, PhD, JD/AM. *Faculty:* 49 full-time. *Students:* 171 full-time (68 women); includes 14 minority (4 African Americans, 7 Asian Americans or Pacific Islanders, 3 Hispanic Americans), 105 international. 823 applicants, 22% accepted, 63 enrolled. In 2009, 61 master's, 11 doctorates awarded. *Degree requirements:* For doctorate, thesis/dissertation. *Entrance requirements:* For master's and doctorate, GRE General Test. Additional exam requirements/recommendations for international students: Required—TOEFL (minimum score 550 paper-based; 213 computer-based; 83 iBT), IELTS (minimum score 7). *Application deadline:* For fall admission, 12/8 priority date for domestic students, 12/15 priority date for international students. Application fee: $75. Electronic applications accepted. *Financial support:* Fellowships, research assistantships, teaching assistantships, Federal Work-Study available. Financial award application deadline: 12/31. *Unit head:* Barbara Rossi, Director of Graduate Studies, Fax: 919-660-1891, E-mail: jennifer.counts@duke.edu. *Application contact:* Cynthia Robertson, Associate Dean for Enrollment Services, 919-684-3913, E-mail: grad-admissions@duke.edu.

East Carolina University, Graduate School, Thomas Harriot College of Arts and Sciences, Department of Economics, Greenville, NC 27858-4353. Offers applied resource economics (MS). Part-time programs available. *Degree requirements:* For master's, one foreign language, comprehensive exam. *Entrance requirements:* For master's, GRE General Test. Additional exam requirements/recommendations for international students: Required—TOEFL.

Eastern Illinois University, Graduate School, College of Sciences, Department of Economics, Charleston, IL 61920-3099. Offers MA. *Faculty:* 15 full-time (0 women). In 2009, 10 master's awarded. *Application deadline:* For fall admission, 3/31 priority date for domestic students. Applications are processed on a rolling basis. Application fee: $30. *Expenses:* Tuition, state resident: full-time $9434; part-time $239 per credit hour. Tuition, nonresident: full-time $23,774; part-time $717 per credit hour. Required fees: $802.63. *Financial support:* In 2009–10, research assistantships with tuition reimbursements (averaging $8,100 per year), 5 teaching assistantships with tuition reimbursements (averaging $8,100 per year) were awarded. *Unit head:* Dr. Linda Ghent, Chairperson, 217-581-5429, Fax: 217-581-5997, E-mail: lsghent@eiu.edu. *Application contact:* Dr. Mukti Upadhyay, Coordinator, 217-581-3812, Fax: 217-581-5997, E-mail: mpupadhyay@eiu.edu.

Eastern Michigan University, Graduate School, College of Arts and Sciences, Department of Economics, Ypsilanti, MI 48197. Offers applied economics (MA); economics (MA); health economics (MA); international economics and development (MA); trade and development (MA). Part-time and evening/weekend programs available. Postbaccalaureate distance learning degree programs offered (minimal on-campus study). *Faculty:* 11 full-time (2 women). *Students:* 28 full-time (9 women), 29 part-time (12 women); includes 17 minority (12 African Americans, 1 American Indian/Alaska Native, 2 Asian Americans or Pacific Islanders, 2 Hispanic Americans), 12 international. Average age 31. 61 applicants, 67% accepted, 23 enrolled. In 2009, 22 master's awarded. *Degree requirements:* For master's, thesis or alternative. *Entrance requirements:* Additional exam requirements/recommendations for international students: Required—TOEFL. *Application deadline:* Applications are processed on a rolling basis. Application fee: $35. Tuition and fees vary according to course level. *Financial support:* Fellowships, research assistantships with full tuition reimbursements, teaching assistantships with full tuition reimbursements, career-related internships or fieldwork, Federal Work-Study, institutionally sponsored loans, scholarships/grants, tuition waivers (partial), and unspecified assistantships available. Support available to part-time students. Financial award applicants required to submit FAFSA. *Unit head:* Dr. Raouf S. Hanna, Department Head, 734-487-3395, Fax: 734-487-9666, E-mail: rhanna@emich.edu. *Application contact:* Dr. David Crary, Advisor, 734-487-0001, Fax: 734-487-9666, E-mail: david.crary@emich.edu.

East Tennessee State University, School of Graduate Studies, College of Business and Technology, Department of Economics, Finance, and Urban Studies, Johnson City, TN 37614. Offers city management (MCM); community development (MPM); general administration (MPM); municipal service management (MPM); urban and regional economic development (MPM); urban and regional planning (MPM). *Degree requirements:* For master's, internship, oral defense of thesis, research report. *Entrance requirements:* For master's, GRE General Test, minimum GPA of 3.0. Additional exam requirements/recommendations for international students: Required—TOEFL (minimum score 550 paper-based; 213 computer-based).

Emory University, Graduate School of Arts and Sciences, Department of Economics, Atlanta, GA 30322-1100. Offers PhD. *Degree requirements:* For doctorate, comprehensive exam, thesis/dissertation. *Entrance requirements:* For doctorate, GRE General Test. Electronic applications accepted. *Faculty research:* Applied microeconomics, econometrics, public choice, macroeconomics, law and economics.

Florida Agricultural and Mechanical University, Division of Graduate Studies, Research, and Continuing Education, College of Arts and Sciences, Division of History and Political Sciences, Program in Applied Social Science, Tallahassee, FL 32307-3200. Offers African American history (MASS); criminal justice (MASS); economics (MASS); history (MASS); political science (MASS); public administration (MASS); public management (MASS); social work (MASS); sociology (MASS). Part-time programs available. *Faculty:* 17 full-time (2 women). *Students:* 54 full-time (42 women), 4 part-time (2 women); includes 57 minority (all African Americans). In 2009, 14 master's awarded. *Degree requirements:* For master's, thesis optional. *Entrance requirements:* For master's, GRE General Test, minimum GPA of 3.0. *Application deadline:* For fall admission, 5/18 for domestic students, 12/18 for international students; for spring admission, 11/12 for domestic students, 5/12 for international students. Application fee: $20. *Financial support:* Fellowships, research assistantships, career-related internships or fieldwork, Federal Work-Study, and tuition waivers (full) available. Financial award application deadline: 4/1. *Faculty research:* Southern history, black history, election trends, presidential history. *Unit head:* Dr. Gary Paul, Director, 850-599-3447. *Application contact:* Dr. Chanta M. Haywood, Dean of Graduate Studies, Research, and Continuing Education, 850-599-3315, Fax: 850-599-3727.

Florida Atlantic University, College of Business, Department of Economics, Boca Raton, FL 33431-0991. Offers MS. Part-time and evening/weekend programs available. *Faculty:* 13 full-time (3 women), 6 part-time/adjunct (0 women). *Students:* 16 full-time (5 women), 12 part-time (1 woman); includes 6 minority (1 African American, 1 Asian American or Pacific Islander, 4 Hispanic Americans), 5 international. Average age 33. 30 applicants, 50% accepted, 7 enrolled. In 2009, 15 master's awarded. *Degree requirements:* For master's, thesis optional. *Entrance requirements:* For master's, GMAT, GRE General Test, minimum GPA of 3.0. Additional exam requirements/recommendations for international students: Required—TOEFL (minimum score 600 paper-based; 250 computer-based). *Application deadline:* For fall admission, 7/1 priority date for domestic students, 2/15 priority date for international students; for winter admission, 11/1 priority date for domestic students, 8/15 priority date for international students; for spring admission, 4/1 priority date for domestic students, 1/15 priority date for international students. Applications are processed on a rolling basis. Application fee: $30. *Expenses:*

Tuition, state resident: full-time $7055; part-time $293.94 per credit hour. Tuition, nonresident: full-time $22,096; part-time $920.66 per credit hour. *Financial support:* Teaching assistantships with tuition reimbursements, tuition waivers (partial) and unspecified assistantships available. Financial award application deadline: 3/1. *Faculty research:* International trade and finance, decision making, monetary conditions, economic fluctuations and growth. *Unit head:* Dr. Charles Register, Chair, 561-297-4176, Fax: 561-297-2542, E-mail: register@fau.edu. *Application contact:* Dr. Eric P. Chiang, Graduate Director, 561-297-2947, Fax: 561-297-1315, E-mail: chiang@fau.edu.

Florida International University, College of Arts and Sciences, Department of Economics, Miami, FL 33199. Offers MA, PhD. Part-time and evening/weekend programs available. *Faculty:* 13 full-time (3 women), 1 part-time/adjunct (0 women). *Students:* 29 full-time (7 women), 6 part-time (2 women); includes 5 minority (all Hispanic Americans), 23 international. Average age 28. 78 applicants, 18% accepted, 13 enrolled. In 2009, 15 master's, 2 doctorates awarded. *Degree requirements:* For master's, thesis or alternative; for doctorate, comprehensive exam, thesis/dissertation. *Entrance requirements:* For master's, GRE, minimum GPA of 3.0, letters of recommendation; for doctorate, GRE General Test, 3 letters of recommendation, minimum GPA of 3.0. Additional exam requirements/recommendations for international students: Required—TOEFL (minimum score 550 paper-based; 80 iBT). *Application deadline:* For fall admission, 4/1 for domestic and international students. Application fee: $30. Electronic applications accepted. *Expenses:* Tuition, state resident: full-time $8008; part-time $4004 per year. Tuition, nonresident: full-time $20,104; part-time $10,052 per year. Required fees: $298; $149 per term. *Financial support:* Federal Work-Study, institutionally sponsored loans, and scholarships/grants available. Financial award application deadline: 3/1; financial award applicants required to submit FAFSA. *Faculty research:* Economic development, international economics, urban/regional economics, Latin American economics. *Unit head:* Dr. Peter Thompson, Chair, 305-348-2316, Fax: 305-348-1524, E-mail: peter.thompson2 @fiu.edu. *Application contact:* Dr. Cem Karayalcin, Graduate Director, 305-348-3285, Fax: 305-348-1524, E-mail: karayalc@fiu.edu.

Florida State University, The Graduate School, College of Social Sciences and Public Policy, Department of Economics, Tallahassee, FL 32306-2180. Offers MS, PhD, JD/MS. Part-time programs available. *Faculty:* 35 full-time (7 women), 5 part-time/adjunct (2 women). *Students:* 55 full-time (11 women), 8 part-time (3 women); includes 5 minority (1 African American, 1 Asian American or Pacific Islander, 3 Hispanic Americans), 14 international. Average age 26. 149 applicants, 48% accepted, 29 enrolled. In 2009, 25 master's, 6 doctorates awarded. Terminal master's awarded for partial completion of doctoral program. *Degree requirements:* For master's, thesis or alternative; for doctorate, thesis/dissertation, 2 comprehensive exams, workshops. *Entrance requirements:* For master's, GRE General Test, minimum GPA of 3.0, 3.4 on graduate work; minimum 1 course each in statistics and calculus; for doctorate, GRE General Test, minimum graduate GPA of 3.4; minimum 1 course each in statistics and linear algebra, 2 in calculus. Additional exam requirements/recommendations for international students: Required—TOEFL (minimum score 550 paper-based; 213 computer-based; 80 iBT). *Application deadline:* For fall admission, 7/1 priority date for domestic students, 5/1 priority date for international students; for spring admission, 11/1 priority date for domestic students, 9/1 priority date for international students. Applications are processed on a rolling basis. Application fee: $30. Electronic applications accepted. *Expenses:* Tuition, state resident: full-time $7413. Tuition, nonresident: full-time $22,567. *Financial support:* In 2009–10, 40 students received support, including 6 fellowships with full tuition reimbursements available (averaging $22,000 per year), 7 research assistantships with full tuition reimbursements available (averaging $13,500 per year), 22 teaching assistantships with full tuition reimbursements available (averaging $13,500 per year); scholarships/grants and tuition waivers also available. Financial award application deadline: 1/31; financial award applicants required to submit FAFSA. *Faculty research:* Labor, industrial organization, international, experimental/behavioral. Total annual research expenditures: $400,000. *Unit head:* Dr. Bruce L. Benson, Chairman, 850-644-5001, Fax: 850-644-4535, E-mail: bbenson@fsu.edu. *Application contact:* Dr. Thomas W. Zuehlke, Graduate Director, 850-644-7206, Fax: 850-644-4535, E-mail: tzuehlke@fsu.edu.

Fordham University, Graduate School of Arts and Sciences, Department of Economics, New York, NY 10458. Offers MA, PhD. Part-time and evening/weekend programs available. *Faculty:* 22 full-time (4 women). *Students:* 26 full-time (13 women), 71 part-time (23 women); includes 9 minority (1 American Indian/Alaska Native, 4 Asian Americans or Pacific Islanders, 4 Hispanic Americans), 33 international. Average age 30. 158 applicants, 42% accepted, 30 enrolled. In 2009, 22 master's, 6 doctorates awarded. Terminal master's awarded for partial completion of doctoral program. *Degree requirements:* For master's, comprehensive exam; for doctorate, comprehensive exam, thesis/dissertation. *Entrance requirements:* For master's and doctorate, GRE General Test. Additional exam requirements/recommendations for international students: Required—TOEFL (minimum score 600 paper-based; 250 computer-based). *Application deadline:* For fall admission, 1/4 priority date for domestic students; for spring admission, 11/1 for domestic students. Application fee: $70. Electronic applications accepted. *Financial support:* In 2009–10, 29 students received support, including 2 fellowships with tuition reimbursements available (averaging $22,225 per year), 10 research assistantships with tuition reimbursements available (averaging $16,290 per year), 17 teaching assistantships with tuition reimbursements available (averaging $12,593 per year); career-related internships or fieldwork, institutionally sponsored loans, tuition waivers (full and partial), and unspecified assistantships also available. Financial award application deadline: 1/4; financial award applicants required to submit FAFSA. *Faculty research:* Developmental economics, econometrics. Total annual research expenditures: $25,000. *Unit head:* Dr. Henry Schwalbenberg, Chair, 718-817-3866, Fax: 718-817-3518. *Application contact:* Charlene Dundie, Director of Graduate Admissions, 718-817-4420, Fax: 718-817-3566, E-mail: dundie@fordham.edu.

Fordham University, Graduate School of Arts and Sciences, Program in International Political Economy and Development, New York, NY 10458. Offers MA, Certificate. Part-time and evening/weekend programs available. *Students:* 44 full-time (15 women), 18 part-time (10 women); includes 6 minority (1 African American, 1 American Indian/Alaska Native, 1 Asian American or Pacific Islander, 3 Hispanic Americans), 21 international. Average age 28. 213 applicants, 37% accepted, 36 enrolled. In 2009, 28 master's awarded. *Degree requirements:* For master's, comprehensive exam. *Entrance requirements:* For master's, GRE General Test. Additional exam requirements/recommendations for international students: Required—TOEFL (minimum score 600 paper-based; 250 computer-based). *Application deadline:* For fall admission, 1/4 priority date for domestic students; for spring admission, 11/1 for domestic students. Application fee: $70. Electronic applications accepted. *Financial support:* In 2009–10, 16 students received support, including 16 research assistantships with tuition reimbursements available (averaging $18,400 per year); career-related internships or fieldwork, institutionally sponsored loans, tuition waivers (full and partial), and unspecified assistantships also available. Financial award application deadline: 1/4; financial award applicants required to submit FAFSA. *Faculty research:* International economics, comparative international politics, international banking and finance, international development, emerging markets and country risk analysis. *Unit head:* Dr. Henry Schwalbenberg, Chair, 718-817-3866, Fax: 718-817-3518. *Application contact:* Charlene Dundie, Director of Graduate Admissions, 718-817-4420, Fax: 718-817-3566, E-mail: dundie@fordham.edu.

George Mason University, College of Humanities and Social Sciences, Department of Economics, Fairfax, VA 22030. Offers economic systems design (Graduate Certificate); economics (MA, PhD). *Faculty:* 34 full-time (2 women), 14 part-time/adjunct (2 women). *Students:* 100 full-time (30 women), 106 part-time (20 women); includes 12 minority (1 African American, 6 Asian Americans or Pacific Islanders, 5 Hispanic Americans), 34 international. Average age 30. 273 applicants, 49% accepted, 58 enrolled. In 2009, 37 master's, 21 doctorates awarded. *Degree requirements:* For master's, thesis optional, 2 comprehensive exams; for doctorate, comprehensive exam, thesis/dissertation, 2 preliminary exams, field exams. *Entrance requirements:* For master's, GRE, course work in microeconomics and macroeconomics through intermediate level; for doctorate, GRE, 1 year of coursework in calculus, statistics; one semester each of matrix algebra and econometrics. Additional exam requirements/recommendations for international students: Required—TOEFL (minimum score 575 paper-based; 230 computer-based). *Application deadline:* For fall admission, 2/1 priority date for domestic students. Application fee: $75. Electronic applications accepted. *Expenses:* Tuition, state resident: full-time $7568; part-time $315.33 per credit hour. Tuition, nonresident: full-time $21,704; part-time $904.33 per credit hour. Required fees: $2184; $91 per credit hour. *Financial support:* In 2009–10, 56 students received support, including 3 fellowships with full tuition reimbursements available (averaging $18,000 per year), 34 research assistantships with full and partial tuition reimbursements available (averaging $14,401 per year), 20 teaching assistantships with full and partial tuition reimbursements available (averaging $5,721 per year); Federal Work-Study, scholarships/grants, unspecified assistantships, and health care benefits (full-time research or teaching assistantship recipients) also available. Support available to part-time students. *Faculty research:* Neuroeconomics, experimental economics (computer-based). Total annual research expenditures: $1.7 million. *Unit head:* Dr. Donald Boudreaux, Chairman, 703-993-1157, Fax: 703-993-1133, E-mail: dboudrea@gmu.edu. *Application contact:* Mary Jackson, Graduate Coordinator, 703-993-1135, E-mail: mjacksoq@gmu.edu.

Georgetown University, Graduate School of Arts and Sciences, Department of Economics, Washington, DC 20057. Offers econometrics (PhD); economic development (PhD); economic theory (PhD); industrial organization (PhD); international macro and finance (PhD); international trade (PhD); labor economics (PhD); macroeconomics (PhD); public economics and political economics (PhD); MA/PhD; MS/MA. *Degree requirements:* For doctorate, comprehensive exam, thesis/dissertation. *Entrance requirements:* For doctorate, GRE General Test. Additional exam requirements/recommendations for international students: Required—TOEFL. *Faculty research:* International economics, economic development.

The George Washington University, Columbian College of Arts and Sciences, Department of Economics, Washington, DC 20052. Offers MA, PhD. Part-time and evening/weekend programs available. *Faculty:* 21 full-time (5 women), 30 part-time/adjunct (10 women). *Students:* 49 full-time (25 women), 59 part-time (29 women); includes 11 minority (3 African Americans, 5 Asian Americans or Pacific Islanders, 3 Hispanic Americans), 62 international. Average age 30. 345 applicants, 54% accepted, 29 enrolled. In 2009, 14 master's, 5 doctorates awarded. Terminal master's awarded for partial completion of doctoral program. *Degree requirements:* For master's, comprehensive exam, thesis or alternative; for doctorate, thesis/dissertation, general exam. *Entrance requirements:* For master's and doctorate, GRE General Test, minimum GPA of 3.0. Additional exam requirements/recommendations for international students: Required—TOEFL (minimum score 550 paper-based; 213 computer-based; 80 iBT). *Application deadline:* For fall admission, 1/15 priority date for domestic and international students; for spring admission, 9/1 for international students. Applications are processed on a rolling basis. Application fee: $60. Electronic applications accepted. *Financial support:* In 2009–10, 25 students received support; fellowships with full tuition reimbursements available, teaching assistantships with tuition reimbursements available, Federal Work-Study available. Financial award application deadline: 1/15. *Unit head:* Robert F. Phillips, Chair, 202-994-8619, E-mail: rphil@gwu.edu. *Application contact:* Information Contact, 202-994-6150, Fax: 202-994-6147, E-mail: econgrad@gwu.edu.

Georgia Institute of Technology, Graduate Studies and Research, Ivan Allen College of Policy and International Affairs, School of Economics, Atlanta, GA 30332-0001. Offers MS. *Degree requirements:* For master's, thesis. *Entrance requirements:* For master's, GRE. Additional exam requirements/recommendations for international students: Required—TOEFL. *Faculty research:* Land use patterns in developing countries, office automation and productivity, dynamic modeling of financial markets.

Georgia State University, Andrew Young School of Policy Studies, Department of Economics, Atlanta, GA 30302-3083. Offers MA, PhD. MA offered through the College of Arts and Sciences. Part-time and evening/weekend programs available. Terminal master's awarded for partial completion of doctoral program. *Degree requirements:* For master's, thesis optional; for doctorate, comprehensive exam, thesis/dissertation. *Entrance requirements:* For master's, GRE; for doctorate, GRE General Test. Additional exam requirements/recommendations for international students: Required—TOEFL. Electronic applications accepted. *Faculty research:* Tax policy, economic growth and development, environmental economics, urban and regional economics, economics of science.

Georgia State University, J. Mack Robinson College of Business, Program in General Business Administration, Atlanta, GA 30302-3083. Offers accounting/information systems (MBA); economics (MBA, MS); enterprise risk management (MBA); general business (MBA); general business administration (EMBA, PMBA); information systems consulting (MBA); information systems risk management (MBA); international business and information technology (MBA); international entrepreneurship (MBA); MBA/JD. *Accreditation:* AACSB. Part-time and evening/weekend programs available. *Entrance requirements:* For master's, GMAT. Additional exam requirements/recommendations for international students: Required—TOEFL (minimum score 610 paper-based; 255 computer-based; 101 iBT). Electronic applications accepted.

Graduate School and University Center of the City University of New York, Graduate Studies, Program in Economics, New York, NY 10016-4039. Offers PhD. *Faculty:* 53 full-time (10 women). *Students:* 90 full-time (40 women), 2 part-time (1 woman); includes 7 minority (1 American Indian/Alaska Native, 4 Asian Americans or Pacific Islanders, 2 Hispanic Americans), 55 international. Average age 34. 61 applicants, 74% accepted, 12 enrolled. In 2009, 12 doctorates awarded. *Degree requirements:* For doctorate, thesis/dissertation. *Entrance requirements:* For doctorate, GRE General Test. Additional exam requirements/recommendations for international students: Required—TOEFL. *Application deadline:* For fall admission, 1/15 priority date for domestic students; for spring admission, 11/15 for domestic students. Application fee: $125. Electronic applications accepted. *Financial support:* In 2009–10, 63 students received support, including 51 fellowships, 10 teaching assistantships; research assistantships, career-related internships or fieldwork, Federal Work-Study, institutionally sponsored loans, and tuition waivers (full and partial) also available. Financial award application deadline: 2/1; financial award applicants required to submit FAFSA. *Unit head:* Dr. Thom Thurston, Executive Officer, 212-817-8256, Fax: 212-817-1514, E-mail: tthurston@gc.cuny.edu. *Application contact:* Les Gribben, Director of Admissions, 212-817-7470, Fax: 212-817-1624, E-mail: lgribben@gc.cuny.edu.

Harvard University, Graduate School of Arts and Sciences, Committee on Business Economics, Cambridge, MA 02138. Offers PhD. *Degree requirements:* For doctorate, thesis/dissertation. *Entrance requirements:* For doctorate, GMAT or GRE General Test. Additional exam requirements/recommendations for international students: Required—TOEFL. *Expenses:* Tuition: Full-time $33,696. Required fees: $1126. Full-time tuition and fees vary according to program.

Harvard University, Graduate School of Arts and Sciences, Department of Economics, Cambridge, MA 02138. Offers PhD. *Degree requirements:* For doctorate, thesis/dissertation, oral exam. *Entrance requirements:* For doctorate, GRE General Test, GRE Subject Test. Additional exam requirements/recommendations for international students: Required—TOEFL. *Expenses:* Tuition: Full-time $33,696. Required fees: $1126. Full-time tuition and fees vary according to program. *Faculty research:* Industrial organization, macromonetary issues, international economics.

Hawai'i Pacific University, College of Business Administration, Honolulu, HI 96813. Offers accounting/CPA (MBA); e-business (MBA); economics (MBA); finance (MBA); human resource management (MA, MBA); information systems (MBA, MSIS), including knowledge management (MSIS), software engineering (MSIS), telecommunications security (MSIS); international business (MBA); management (MBA); marketing (MBA); organizational change (MA, MBA); travel industry management (MBA). Part-time and evening/weekend programs available. *Faculty:* 15 full-time (5 women), 11 part-time/adjunct (4 women). *Students:* 206 full-time (107 women), 197 part-time (105 women); includes 136 minority (18 African Americans, 3 American Indian/Alaska Native, 98 Asian Americans or Pacific Islanders, 17 Hispanic Americans), 151 international. Average age 30. 235 applicants, 90% accepted, 127 enrolled. In 2009, 141 master's awarded. *Degree*

Economics

Hawai'i Pacific University (continued)
requirements: For master's, thesis. *Entrance requirements:* For master's, GMAT. Additional exam requirements/recommendations for international students: Recommended—TOEFL (minimum score 550 paper-based; 213 computer-based; 80 iBT), TWE (minimum score 5). *Application deadline:* For fall admission, 2/15 priority date for domestic students; for spring admission, 10/15 priority date for domestic students. Applications are processed on a rolling basis. Application fee: $50. Electronic applications accepted. *Expenses:* Tuition: Full-time $12,600; part-time $700 per credit hour. Tuition and fees vary according to program. *Financial support:* In 2009–10, 164 students received support; research assistantships, career-related internships or fieldwork, Federal Work-Study, scholarships/grants, and unspecified assistantships available. Support available to part-time students. Financial award application deadline: 3/1; financial award applicants required to submit FAFSA. *Faculty research:* Statistical control process as used by management, studies in comparative cross-cultural management styles, not-for-profit management. *Unit head:* Dr. Aytun Ozturk, Dean, 808-544-9301, Fax: 808-544-0283, E-mail: uozturk@hpu.edu. *Application contact:* Danny Lam, Assistant Director of Graduate Admissions, 808-544-1135, Fax: 808-544-0280, E-mail: graduate@hpu.edu.

Howard University, Graduate School, Department of Economics, Washington, DC 20059-0002. Offers MA, PhD. Part-time programs available. *Degree requirements:* For master's, comprehensive exam, thesis optional; for doctorate, one foreign language, comprehensive exam, thesis/dissertation. *Entrance requirements:* For master's, GRE General Test, minimum GPA of 3.0; for doctorate, GRE General Test, master's degree in economics or related field, minimum GPA of 3.0. Electronic applications accepted. *Faculty research:* Economic development, international trade, urban rentalization.

Hunter College of the City University of New York, Graduate School, School of Arts and Sciences, Department of Economics, New York, NY 10021-5085. Offers accounting (MS); economics (MA). Part-time and evening/weekend programs available. *Faculty:* 7 full-time (0 women), 6 part-time/adjunct (0 women). *Students:* 14 full-time (7 women), 40 part-time (22 women); includes 24 minority (5 African Americans, 16 Asian Americans or Pacific Islanders, 3 Hispanic Americans). Average age 29. 60 applicants, 35% accepted, 17 enrolled. In 2009, 33 master's awarded. *Degree requirements:* For master's, research paper or thesis. *Entrance requirements:* For master's, GMAT or GRE General Test, minimum GPA of 3.0, 18 credits of undergraduate course work in economics (9 in mathematics), 2 letters of recommendation (1 from a member of economics department). Additional exam requirements/recommendations for international students: Required—TOEFL. *Application deadline:* For fall admission, 4/1 for domestic students, 2/1 for international students; for spring admission, 11/1 for domestic students, 9/1 for international students. Application fee: $125. *Expenses:* Tuition, state resident: full-time $7360; part-time $310 per credit. Required fees: $250 per semester. *Financial support:* Fellowships, research assistantships, teaching assistantships, career-related internships or fieldwork, Federal Work-Study, institutionally sponsored loans, and tuition waivers (partial) available. Support available to part-time students. *Faculty research:* Earnings of immigrants and minority groups, taxation and the regional economy. *Unit head:* Dr. Marjorie P. Honig, Chairperson, 212-772-5400, Fax: 212-772-5398, E-mail: mhonig@hunter.cuny.edu. *Application contact:* Randall Filer, Professor/Advisor, 212-772-5399, Fax: 212-772-5398, E-mail: grad.econadvisor@hunter.cuny.edu.

Illinois State University, Graduate School, College of Arts and Sciences, Department of Economics, Normal, IL 61790-2200. Offers MA, MS. *Degree requirements:* For master's, thesis or alternative. *Entrance requirements:* For master's, GRE General Test, minimum GPA of 2.6 in last 60 hours of course work. *Faculty research:* Stevenson Center Graduate Assistantship in Community/Economic Development; the social, economic and educational correlates of rural school closure; Stevenson Center Americorps project.

Indiana University Bloomington, Kelley School of Business, Department of Business Economics and Public Policy, Bloomington, IN 47405-7000. Offers PhD. *Faculty:* 8 full-time (1 woman), 1 part-time/adjunct (0 women). *Students:* 20 applicants, 10% accepted, 2 enrolled. In 2009, 2 doctorates awarded. *Degree requirements:* For doctorate, comprehensive exam, thesis/dissertation. *Entrance requirements:* For doctorate, GRE or GMAT, bachelor's degree. Additional exam requirements/recommendations for international students: Required—TOEFL (minimum score 630 paper-based; 267 computer-based; 80 iBT). *Financial support:* Fellowships with full tuition reimbursements available. *Faculty research:* Industrial organization, pricing, environmental regulation and policy, information economics, economics of law and organization. *Unit head:* Dr. John W. Maxwell, Professor, 812-855-9219, Fax: 812-855-3354, E-mail: jwmax@indiana.edu. *Application contact:* Dr. Michael R. Baye, Bert Elwert Professor of Business Economics, 812-855-9219, Fax: 812-855-3354, E-mail: mbaye@indiana.edu.

Indiana University Bloomington, University Graduate School, College of Arts and Sciences, Department of Economics, Bloomington, IN 47405-7104. Offers MA, PhD. *Faculty:* 23 full-time (3 women). *Students:* 88 full-time (29 women), 2 part-time (0 women); includes 5 minority (1 African American, 2 Asian Americans or Pacific Islanders, 2 Hispanic Americans), 66 international. Average age 30. 178 applicants, 33% accepted, 24 enrolled. In 2009, 18 master's, 15 doctorates awarded. Terminal master's awarded for partial completion of doctoral program. *Degree requirements:* For master's, thesis optional, tool skill classes; for doctorate, comprehensive exam, thesis/dissertation, field exam, 3rd year paper, tool skill classes. *Entrance requirements:* For master's, GRE General Test, minimum one year of calculus; for doctorate, GRE General Test, minimum one year of calculus, semester of linear algebra. Additional exam requirements/recommendations for international students: Required—TOEFL (minimum score 600 paper-based; 250 computer-based; 100 iBT). *Application deadline:* For fall admission, 1/15 priority date for domestic students, 12/1 priority date for international students. Applications are processed on a rolling basis. Application fee: $55 ($65 for international students). Electronic applications accepted. *Financial support:* In 2009–10, 53 students received support, including 1 fellowship with full tuition reimbursement available (averaging $17,000 per year), 2 research assistantships with full tuition reimbursements available (averaging $15,500 per year), 32 teaching assistantships with full tuition reimbursements available (averaging $14,600 per year); institutionally sponsored loans and health care benefits also available. Financial award application deadline: 1/15. *Faculty research:* Games, experiments and organization, transition economics, growth and development, macroeconomics, econometrics. *Unit head:* Prof. Gerhard Glomm, Chair, 812-855-6160, Fax: 812-855-3736, E-mail: gglomm@indiana.edu. *Application contact:* Chris Cunningham, Graduate Services Assistant, 812-855-8453, Fax: 812-855-3736, E-mail: rcunning@indiana.edu.

Indiana University–Purdue University Indianapolis, School of Liberal Arts, Department of Economics, Indianapolis, IN 46202-2896. Offers MA, MA/MA. *Faculty:* 16 full-time (3 women). *Students:* 11 full-time (4 women), 10 part-time (6 women); includes 1 minority (Hispanic American), 12 international. Average age 26. 45 applicants, 58% accepted, 10 enrolled. In 2009, 7 master's awarded. *Entrance requirements:* For master's, GRE, minimum GPA of 3.0; courses in economic theory, statistics, calculus. Additional exam requirements/recommendations for international students: Required—TOEFL (minimum score 600 paper-based). *Application deadline:* For fall admission, 2/1 priority date for domestic and international students. Application fee: $55 ($65 for international students). *Financial support:* In 2009–10, 1 fellowship with partial tuition reimbursement (averaging $10,000 per year), 7 teaching assistantships (averaging $9,586 per year) were awarded; research assistantships with partial tuition reimbursements, career-related internships or fieldwork and health care benefits also available. *Faculty research:* Charitable giving. *Unit head:* Paul Carlin, Chair, 317-278-9236, E-mail: pcarlin@iupui.edu. *Application contact:* Natalie Harvey, Information Contact, 317-274-4756, Fax: 317-274-0097.

Instituto Centroamericano de Administración de Empresas, Graduate Programs, La Garita, Costa Rica. Offers agribusiness (MIAM); business administration (EMBA); economics and finance (MBA); industry and technology (MBA); sustainable development (MBA). *Degree requirements:* For master's, comprehensive exam, essay. *Entrance requirements:* For master's, GMAT or GRE General Test, fluency in Spanish, interview, letters of recommendation, minimum 1 year of work experience. Electronic applications accepted. *Faculty research:* Competitiveness, production.

Instituto Tecnológico y de Estudios Superiores de Monterrey, Campus Ciudad de México, Division of Business, Ciudad de Mexico, Mexico. Offers business administration (EMBA, MBA, PhD); economy (MBA); finance (MBA). Part-time and evening/weekend programs available. Postbaccalaureate distance learning degree programs offered (minimal on-campus study). *Entrance requirements:* For master's and doctorate, Instituto entrance exam. Additional exam requirements/recommendations for international students: Required—TOEFL.

Iowa State University of Science and Technology, Graduate College, College of Liberal Arts and Sciences, Department of Economics, Ames, IA 50011. Offers agricultural economics (MS, PhD); economics (MS, PhD); JD/MS; JD/PhD. *Faculty:* 45 full-time (7 women), 3 part-time/adjunct (all women). *Students:* 72 full-time (31 women), 16 part-time (11 women), 73 international. 313 applicants, 19% accepted, 17 enrolled. In 2009, 9 master's, 7 doctorates awarded. *Degree requirements:* For master's, thesis or alternative; for doctorate, thesis/dissertation. *Entrance requirements:* For master's and doctorate, GRE General Test. Additional exam requirements/recommendations for international students: Required—TOEFL (minimum score 550 paper-based; 88 iBT) or IELTS (minimum score 6.5). *Application deadline:* For fall admission, 1/20 priority date for domestic and international students. Application fee: $40 ($90 for international students). Electronic applications accepted. *Expenses:* Tuition, state resident: full-time $6716. Tuition, nonresident: full-time $8908. Tuition and fees vary according to course level, course load, program and student level. *Financial support:* In 2009–10, 22 research assistantships with full and partial tuition reimbursements (averaging $16,000 per year), 47 teaching assistantships with full and partial tuition reimbursements (averaging $16,000 per year) were awarded; fellowships, scholarships/grants, health care benefits, and unspecified assistantships also available. *Unit head:* Dr. GianCarlo Moschini, Chair, 515-294-6741, Fax: 515-294-7755, E-mail: grad@econ.iastate.edu. *Application contact:* Dr. John Schroeter, Information Contact, 515-294-2702, E-mail: grad@econ.iastate.edu.

The Johns Hopkins University, Zanvyl Krieger School of Arts and Sciences, Department of Economics, Baltimore, MD 21218-2699. Offers PhD. *Faculty:* 20 full-time (3 women), 9 part-time/adjunct (1 woman). *Students:* 64 full-time (33 women); includes 3 minority (all Asian Americans or Pacific Islanders), 45 international. Average age 26. 393 applicants, 3% accepted, 12 enrolled. In 2009, 4 doctorates awarded. Terminal master's awarded for partial completion of doctoral program. *Degree requirements:* For doctorate, comprehensive exam, thesis/dissertation. *Entrance requirements:* For doctorate, GRE General Test. Additional exam requirements/recommendations for international students: Required—TOEFL (minimum score 600 paper-based; 250 computer-based), IELTS. *Application deadline:* For fall admission, 1/2 priority date for domestic and international students. Applications are processed on a rolling basis. Application fee: $75. Electronic applications accepted. *Financial support:* In 2009–10, 7 fellowships (averaging $20,500 per year), 3 research assistantships (averaging $17,850 per year), 39 teaching assistantships (averaging $15,000 per year) were awarded. Financial award application deadline: 4/15; financial award applicants required to submit FAFSA. *Faculty research:* General economic theory, econometrics and mathematical economics, trade and development, game theory, urban economics. Total annual research expenditures: $521,538. *Unit head:* Prof. Joseph Harrington, Chair, 410-516-7615, Fax: 410-516-7600, E-mail: joe.harrington@jhu.edu. *Application contact:* Karen Allen, Graduate Admissions Coordinator, 410-516-7601, Fax: 410-516-7600, E-mail: econadmissions@jhu.edu.

Kansas State University, Graduate School, College of Arts and Sciences, Department of Economics, Manhattan, KS 66506. Offers MA, PhD. Part-time programs available. *Faculty:* 12 full-time (2 women), 3 part-time/adjunct (1 woman). *Students:* 51 full-time (15 women); includes 8 minority (3 African Americans, 1 American Indian/Alaska Native, 3 Asian Americans or Pacific Islanders, 1 Hispanic American), 22 international. Average age 29. 97 applicants, 72% accepted, 16 enrolled. In 2009, 9 master's, 5 doctorates awarded. Terminal master's awarded for partial completion of doctoral program. *Degree requirements:* For master's, thesis optional; for doctorate, comprehensive exam, thesis/dissertation. *Entrance requirements:* For master's, GRE (highly recommended), minimum GPA of 3.0; course work in microeconomics, macroeconomics, calculus and statistics; for doctorate, GRE (highly recommended), course work in microeconomics, macroecohomics, and calculus. Additional exam requirements/recommendations for international students: Required—TOEFL (minimum score 550 paper-based; 213 computer-based). *Application deadline:* For fall admission, 2/1 priority date for domestic and international students; for spring admission, 8/1 priority date for domestic and international students. Applications are processed on a rolling basis. Application fee: $40 ($55 for international students). Electronic applications accepted. *Financial support:* In 2009–10, 2 research assistantships (averaging $22,828 per year), 21 teaching assistantships with full tuition reimbursements (averaging $12,854 per year) were awarded; fellowships, career-related internships or fieldwork, institutionally sponsored loans, and scholarships/grants also available. Support available to part-time students. Financial award application deadline: 3/1; financial award applicants required to submit FAFSA. *Faculty research:* Macroeconomics, microeconomics and labor economics, development and growth, international economics, industrial organization. Total annual research expenditures: $32,310. *Unit head:* Dr. William Blankenau, Interim Head, 785-532-6340, Fax: 785-532-6919, E-mail: blankenw@ksu.edu. *Application contact:* Dr. Dong Li, Director, 785-532-4572, Fax: 785-532-6919, E-mail: dongli@ksu.edu.

Kent State University, Graduate School of Management, Master's Program in Economics, Kent, OH 44242-0001. Offers MA. Part-time programs available. *Faculty:* 9 full-time (1 woman), 2 part-time/adjunct (both women). *Students:* 17 full-time (7 women), 7 part-time (1 woman); includes 4 minority (1 African American, 2 Asian Americans or Pacific Islanders, 1 Hispanic American), 9 international. Average age 23. 28 applicants, 96% accepted, 18 enrolled. In 2009, 7 master's awarded. *Entrance requirements:* For master's, GMAT or GRE General Test, minimum GPA of 2.75. Additional exam requirements/recommendations for international students: Required—TOEFL (minimum score 550 paper-based; 213 computer-based; 79 iBT). *Application deadline:* For fall admission, 4/1 priority date for domestic students, 3/1 for international students; for spring admission, 12/15 for domestic students. Applications are processed on a rolling basis. Application fee: $30 ($60 for international students). Electronic applications accepted. *Financial support:* In 2009–10, 9 students received support, including 9 research assistantships with full tuition reimbursements available (averaging $5,025 per year); fellowships, Federal Work-Study also available. Financial award application deadline: 4/1; financial award applicants required to submit FAFSA. *Faculty research:* Macro and microeconomic theory, labor economics, international economics, quantitative methods. *Unit head:* Dr. Richard J. Kent, Chair and Professor, 330-672-2366, Fax: 330-672-9808, E-mail: rkent@kent.edu. *Application contact:* Louise M. Ditchey, Director, 330-672-2282, Fax: 330-672-7303, E-mail: gradbus@kent.edu.

Lakehead University, Graduate Studies, Faculty of Social Sciences and Humanities, Department of Economics, Thunder Bay, ON P7B 5E1, Canada. Offers MA. Part-time and evening/weekend programs available. *Degree requirements:* For master's, thesis or comprehensive exams, research papers. *Entrance requirements:* For master's, minimum B average. Additional exam requirements/recommendations for international students: Required—TOEFL. *Faculty research:* Public finance, economic history, mathematical economics, quantitative economics.

Lehigh University, College of Business and Economics, Department of Economics, Bethlehem, PA 18015. Offers economics (MS, PhD); health and bio-pharmaceutical economics (MS). Part-time programs available. *Faculty:* 10 full-time (3 women), 2 part-time/adjunct (0 women). *Students:* 37 full-time (17 women), 10 part-time (4 women); includes 3 minority (all Asian Americans or Pacific Islanders), 21 international. Average age 26. 97 applicants, 51% accepted, 14 enrolled. In 2009, 9 master's, 2 doctorates awarded. Terminal master's awarded for partial completion of doctoral program. *Degree requirements:* For master's, thesis optional; for doctorate, comprehensive exam, thesis/dissertation, proposal defense. *Entrance requirements:* For master's and doctorate, GMAT or GRE General Test. Additional exam requirements/recommendations for international students: Required—TOEFL (minimum score 600 paper-based; 250 computer-based; 94 iBT). *Application deadline:* For fall admission, 7/15 for domestic students; for spring admission, 12/1 for domestic students. Applications are processed on a rolling basis. Application fee: $100. Electronic applications accepted. *Expenses:* Contact institution. *Financial support:* In 2009–10, 3 fellowships with full tuition reimbursements (averaging $13,200 per year), 9 teaching assistantships with full tuition reimbursements (averaging $13,200 per year) were awarded; research assistantships with tuition reimbursements, scholarships/grants, health care benefits, tuition waivers (full and partial), and unspecified assistantships also available. Financial award application deadline: 1/15. *Faculty research:* Public finance, investments, applied econometrics, labor economics. Total annual research expenditures: $36,329. *Unit head:* Dr. Shin-Yi Chou, Director of PhD Program, 610-758-3444, Fax: 610-758-5283, E-mail: syc2@lehigh.edu. *Application contact:* Corinn McBride, Director of Recruitment and Admissions, 610-758-3418, Fax: 610-758-5283, E-mail: com207@lehigh.edu.

Long Island University, Brooklyn Campus, Richard L. Conolly College of Liberal Arts and Sciences, Department of Economics, Brooklyn, NY 11201-8423. Offers MA. Part-time and evening/weekend programs available. *Degree requirements:* For master's, thesis or alternative. *Entrance requirements:* For master's, 2 letters of recommendation. Additional exam requirements/recommendations for international students: Required—TOEFL (minimum score 550 paper-based; 173 computer-based). Electronic applications accepted.

Louisiana State University and Agricultural and Mechanical College, Graduate School, E. J. Ourso College of Business, Department of Economics, Baton Rouge, LA 70803. Offers MS, PhD. *Faculty:* 14 full-time (1 woman). *Students:* 30 full-time (12 women), 4 part-time (2 women), 26 international. Average age 29. 71 applicants, 18% accepted, 7 enrolled. In 2009, 5 master's, 1 doctorate awarded. Terminal master's awarded for partial completion of doctoral program. *Degree requirements:* For doctorate, thesis/dissertation. *Entrance requirements:* For master's and doctorate, GRE General Test, minimum GPA of 3.0. Additional exam requirements/recommendations for international students: Required—TOEFL (minimum score 550 paper-based; 213 computer-based; 79 iBT) or IELTS (minimum score 6.5). *Application deadline:* For fall admission, 1/25 priority date for domestic students, 5/15 for international students; for spring admission, 10/15 for international students. Applications are processed on a rolling basis. Application fee: $50 ($70 for international students). *Financial support:* In 2009–10, 31 students received support, including 2 fellowships (averaging $33,683 per year), 14 research assistantships with full and partial tuition reimbursements available (averaging $16,729 per year), 2 teaching assistantships with full and partial tuition reimbursements available (averaging $15,200 per year); Federal Work-Study, scholarships/grants, health care benefits, and unspecified assistantships also available. Support available to part-time students. Financial award application deadline: 6/15; financial award applicants required to submit FAFSA. *Faculty research:* Microeconomics, macroeconomics, econometrics, industrial organization, public finance, labor. Total annual research expenditures: $642,748. *Unit head:* Dr. Robert Newman, Chair, 225-578-3794, Fax: 225-578-3807, E-mail: eonewm@lsu.edu. *Application contact:* Dr. Arrendam Chanda, Graduate Director, 225-578-5211, Fax: 225-578-3807, E-mail: sarangi@lsu.edu.

Louisiana Tech University, Graduate School, College of Business, Department of Finance and Economics, Ruston, LA 71272. Offers business economics (MBA, DBA); finance (MBA, DBA). Part-time programs available. *Degree requirements:* For doctorate, thesis/dissertation. *Entrance requirements:* For master's and doctorate, GMAT.

Marquette University, Graduate School of Management, Department of Economics, Milwaukee, WI 53201-1881. Offers business economics (MSAE); financial economics (MSAE); international economics (MSAE). Part-time and evening/weekend programs available. *Faculty:* 13 full-time (4 women), 3 part-time/adjunct (0 women). *Students:* 28 full-time (8 women), 25 part-time (4 women); includes 4 minority (1 African American, 2 Asian Americans or Pacific Islanders, 1 Hispanic American), 14 international. Average age 25. 67 applicants, 81% accepted, 24 enrolled. In 2009, 9 master's awarded. *Degree requirements:* For master's, comprehensive exam, thesis or alternative, essay. *Entrance requirements:* For master's, GMAT or GRE General Test. Additional exam requirements/recommendations for international students: Required—TOEFL. Application fee: $40. *Financial support:* In 2009–10, 6 teaching assistantships were awarded; research assistantships, Federal Work-Study, institutionally sponsored loans, scholarships/grants, and tuition waivers (full and partial) also available. Support available to part-time students. Financial award application deadline: 2/15. *Faculty research:* Monetary and fiscal policy in open economy, housing and regional migration, political economy of taxation and state/local government. *Unit head:* Dr. David Clark, Chair, 414-288-3339, Fax: 414-288-5757. *Application contact:* Farrokh Nourzad, Information Contact, 414-288-3570.

Massachusetts Institute of Technology, School of Humanities, Arts, and Social Sciences, Department of Economics, Cambridge, MA 02139-4307. Offers SM, PhD. *Faculty:* 33 full-time (5 women), 1 part-time/adjunct (0 women). *Students:* 112 full-time (38 women), 2 part-time (0 women); includes 13 minority (3 African Americans, 9 Asian Americans or Pacific Islanders, 1 Hispanic American), 58 international. Average age 26. 714 applicants, 5% accepted, 20 enrolled. In 2009, 26 doctorates awarded. Terminal master's awarded for partial completion of doctoral program. *Degree requirements:* For doctorate, comprehensive exam, thesis/dissertation. *Entrance requirements:* For doctorate, GRE General Test. Additional exam requirements/recommendations for international students: Required—TOEFL (minimum score 600 paper-based; 250 computer-based; 100 iBT), IELTS (minimum score 7). *Application deadline:* For fall admission, 12/15 for domestic and international students. Application fee: $75. Electronic applications accepted. *Expenses:* Tuition: Full-time $37,510; part-time $585 per unit. Required fees: $272. *Financial support:* In 2009–10, 92 students received support, including 47 fellowships with tuition reimbursements available (averaging $34,787 per year), 1 research assistantship with tuition reimbursement available, 28 teaching assistantships with tuition reimbursements available (averaging $38,298 per year); Federal Work-Study, institutionally sponsored loans, scholarships/grants, health care benefits, and unspecified assistantships also available. *Faculty research:* Macroeconomics and international economics, economic theory, econometrics and statistical methods, applied microeconomics, labor/development economics. Total annual research expenditures: $2 million. *Unit head:* Prof. Ricardo Caballero, Department Head, 617-253-3361, Fax: 617-253-1330. *Application contact:* Peter Hoagland, Graduate Administrator, 617-253-8787, Fax: 617-253-1330, E-mail: econ-admit@mit.edu.

McGill University, Faculty of Graduate and Postdoctoral Studies, Faculty of Arts, Department of Economics, Montréal, QC H3A 2T5, Canada. Offers economics (MA, PhD); social statistics (MA).

McMaster University, School of Graduate Studies, Faculty of Social Sciences, Department of Economics, Hamilton, ON L8S 4M2, Canada. Offers MA, PhD. Part-time programs available. *Degree requirements:* For doctorate, comprehensive exam, thesis/dissertation. *Entrance requirements:* For master's, GRE (recommended), honors BA in economics; for doctorate, GRE (recommended), B+ average in a master's degree. Additional exam requirements/recommendations for international students: Required—TOEFL (minimum score 580 paper-based; 237 computer-based). *Faculty research:* Applied microeconomics, econometrics, health economics, labor economics, public finance.

Memorial University of Newfoundland, School of Graduate Studies, Department of Economics, St. John's, NL A1C 5S7, Canada. Offers MA. *Degree requirements:* For master's, thesis optional. *Entrance requirements:* For master's, honors degree (minimum 2nd class standing). *Faculty research:* Public sector economics, natural resource economics.

Miami University, Graduate School, Farmer School of Business, Department of Economics, Oxford, OH 45056. Offers MA. Part-time programs available. *Students:* 10 full-time (2 women), 1 part-time (0 women); includes 2 minority (both Asian Americans or Pacific Islanders), 3 international. *Entrance requirements:* For master's, GMAT, minimum undergraduate GPA of 3.0 during previous 2 years or 2.75 overall. Additional exam requirements/recommendations for international students: Required—TOEFL. Application fee: $50. *Expenses:* Tuition, state resident: full-time $11,280. Tuition, nonresident: full-time $24,912. Required fees: $516. *Financial support:* Fellowships with full tuition reimbursements, research assistantships, teaching assistantships, Federal Work-Study, health care benefits, tuition waivers (full), and unspecified assistantships available. Financial award application deadline: 3/1. *Unit head:* George Davis, Chair, 513-529-2836, Fax: 513-529-8047, E-mail: miamieco@muohio.edu. *Application contact:* Dr. Barnali Gupta, Director of Graduate Studies, 513-529-2856, E-mail: miamieco@muohio.edu.

Michigan State University, The Graduate School, College of Social Science, Department of Economics, East Lansing, MI 48824. Offers MA, PhD. *Faculty:* 42 full-time (7 women), 1 part-time/adjunct (0 women). *Students:* 78 full-time (19 women), 1 (woman) part-time; includes 6 minority (4 Asian Americans or Pacific Islanders, 2 Hispanic Americans), 48 international. Average age 29. 360 applicants, 9% accepted. In 2009, 11 master's, 13 doctorates awarded. *Entrance requirements:* Additional exam requirements/recommendations for international students: Required—TOEFL. Electronic applications accepted. *Expenses:* Tuition, state resident: part-time $478.25 per credit hour. Tuition, nonresident: part-time $966.50 per credit hour. Part-time tuition and fees vary according to program. *Financial support:* In 2009–10, 7 research assistantships with tuition reimbursements (averaging $6,849 per year), 43 teaching assistantships with tuition reimbursements (averaging $6,583 per year) were awarded. Total annual research expenditures: $73,455. *Unit head:* Dr. Carl Davidson, Chairperson, 517-355-5238, Fax: 517-432-1068, E-mail: davidso4@msu.edu. *Application contact:* Lori Jean Nichols, Graduate Secretary, 517-355-6579, Fax: 517-432-1068, E-mail: ecgrdsec@msu.edu.

Middle Tennessee State University, College of Graduate Studies, Jennings A. Jones College of Business, Department of Economics and Finance, Murfreesboro, TN 37132. Offers economics (MA, PhD). Part-time and evening/weekend programs available. Postbaccalaureate distance learning degree programs offered. *Faculty:* 20 full-time (3 women). *Students:* 10 full-time (3 women), 32 part-time (10 women); includes 18 minority (8 African Americans, 8 Asian Americans or Pacific Islanders, 2 Hispanic Americans). Average age 30. 30 applicants, 50% accepted, 15 enrolled. In 2009, 12 master's, 6 doctorates awarded. *Degree requirements:* For master's, thesis optional; for doctorate, comprehensive exam, thesis/dissertation. *Entrance requirements:* For master's and doctorate, GRE or MAT. Additional exam requirements/recommendations for international students: Required—TOEFL (minimum score 525 paper-based; 195 computer-based; 71 iBT) or IELTS (minimum score 6). *Application deadline:* For fall admission, 6/1 for domestic and international students. Applications are processed on a rolling basis. Application fee: $25 ($30 for international students). Electronic applications accepted. *Expenses:* Tuition, state resident: full-time $4404. Tuition, nonresident: full-time $10,956. *Financial support:* In 2009–10, 21 students received support. Institutionally sponsored loans available. Support available to part-time students. Financial award application deadline: 5/1; financial award applicants required to submit FAFSA. *Unit head:* Dr. Charles Baum, Chair, 615-898-2520, Fax: 615-898-5596, E-mail: cbaum@mtsu.edu. *Application contact:* Dr. Michael Allen, Dean and Vice Provost for Research, 615-898-2840, Fax: 615-904-8020, E-mail: mallen@mtsu.edu.

Mississippi State University, College of Business, Department of Finance and Economics, MS State, MS 39762. Offers applied economics (PhD); business administration (PhD), including finance; economics (MA); finance (MSBA). Part-time programs available. *Faculty:* 13 full-time (2 women). *Students:* 15 full-time (4 women), 4 part-time (1 woman); includes 1 minority (African American), 11 international. Average age 31. 31 applicants, 23% accepted, 3 enrolled. In 2009, 2 master's, 3 doctorates awarded. Terminal master's awarded for partial completion of doctoral program. *Degree requirements:* For master's, comprehensive exam, thesis optional; for doctorate, comprehensive exam, thesis/dissertation. *Entrance requirements:* For master's and doctorate, GMAT, GRE General Test. Additional exam requirements/recommendations for international students: Required—TOEFL (minimum score 575 paper-based; 233 computer-based; 90 iBT); Recommended—IELTS (minimum score 6.5). *Application deadline:* For fall admission, 7/1 for domestic students, 5/1 for international students; for spring admission, 11/1 for domestic students, 10/1 for international students. Applications are processed on a rolling basis. Application fee: $40. Electronic applications accepted. *Expenses:* Tuition, state resident: full-time $2575.50; part-time $286.25 per credit hour. Tuition, nonresident: full-time $6510; part-time $723.50 per credit hour. Tuition and fees vary according to course load. *Financial support:* In 2009–10, 5 teaching assistantships with tuition reimbursements (averaging $10,698 per year) were awarded; Federal Work-Study, scholarships/grants, health care benefits, and unspecified assistantships also available. Financial award application deadline: 4/1; financial award applicants required to submit FAFSA. *Faculty research:* Economics development, mergers, event studies, economic education, bank performance. Total annual research expenditures: $491,000. *Unit head:* Dr. Mike Highfield, Department Head, 662-325-3928, Fax: 662-325-1977, E-mail: mhighfield@cobilan.msstate.edu. *Application contact:* Dr. Benjamin F. Blair, Associate Professor/Graduate Coordinator, 662-325-1980, Fax: 662-325-1977, E-mail: bblair@cobilan.msstate.edu.

Montclair State University, The Graduate School, School of Business, Department of Economics and Finance, Montclair, NJ 07043-1624. Offers business economics (MBA); finance (MBA). Part-time and evening/weekend programs available. *Faculty:* 16 full-time (4 women), 3 part-time/adjunct (1 woman). *Students:* 24 full-time (9 women), 62 part-time (21 women). Average age 30. 44 applicants, 48% accepted, 16 enrolled. In 2009, 42 master's awarded. *Entrance requirements:* For master's, GRE General Test, 2 letters of recommendation, resume. Additional exam requirements/recommendations for international students: Required—TOEFL (minimum score 83 computer-based), or IELTS. *Application deadline:* For fall admission, 6/1 for international students; for spring admission, 10/1 for international students. Applications are processed on a rolling basis. Application fee: $60. Electronic applications accepted. *Expenses:* Tuition, area resident: Part-time $486.74 per credit. Tuition, state resident: part-time $486.74 per credit. Tuition, nonresident: part-time $751.34 per credit. Tuition and fees vary according to degree level and program. *Financial support:* In 2009–10, 4 research assistantships with full tuition reimbursements (averaging $7,000 per year) were awarded; Federal Work-Study, scholarships/grants, and unspecified assistantships also available. Support available to part-time students. Financial award application deadline: 3/1; financial award applicants required to submit FAFSA. *Unit head:* Dr. Richard Lord, Chair, 973-655-5255. *Application contact:* Amy Aiello, Director of Graduate Admissions and Operations, 973-655-5147, Fax: 973-655-7869, E-mail: graduate.school@montclair.edu.

Morgan State University, School of Graduate Studies, College of Liberal Arts, Department of Economics, Baltimore, MD 21251. Offers MA. *Degree requirements:* For master's, comprehensive exam. *Entrance requirements:* For master's, GRE. Additional exam requirements/recommendations for international students: Required—TOEFL (minimum score 550 paper-based; 213 computer-based).

Murray State University, College of Business and Public Affairs, Program in Economics, Murray, KY 42071. Offers MS. Part-time programs available. *Entrance requirements:* For master's, GRE General Test or GMAT, economics minor or equivalent, students may be conditionally admitted and fulfill undergraduate requirements. Additional exam requirements/recommendations for international students: Required—TOEFL. *Faculty research:* Economic education, public finance, economic development, banking, telecommunications systems management.

National University, Academic Affairs, School of Business and Management, Department of Accounting and Finance, La Jolla, CA 92037-1011. Offers accountancy (MS); corporate and international finance (MS). Part-time and evening/weekend programs available. Postbaccalaureate distance learning degree programs offered (no on-campus study). *Faculty:* 8 full-time (1 woman), 37 part-time/adjunct (10 women). *Students:* 67 full-time (32 women), 68 part-time (27 women); includes 41 minority (10 African Americans, 2 American Indian/Alaska Native, 13 Asian Americans or Pacific Islanders, 16 Hispanic Americans), 23 international. Average age 33. 145 applicants, 100% accepted, 75 enrolled. In 2009, 14 master's awarded. *Degree requirements:* For master's, thesis. *Entrance requirements:* For master's, interview, minimum GPA of 2.5. Additional exam requirements/recommendations for international students:

Economics

National University (continued)

Required—TOEFL (minimum score 550 paper-based; 213 computer-based; 79 iBT), IELTS (minimum score 6). *Application deadline:* Applications are processed on a rolling basis. Application fee: $60 ($65 for international students). Electronic applications accepted. *Expenses:* Tuition: Part-time $338 per quarter hour. *Financial support:* Career-related internships or fieldwork, institutionally sponsored loans, scholarships/grants, and tuition waivers (partial) available. Support available to part-time students. Financial award application deadline: 6/30; financial award applicants required to submit FAFSA. *Unit head:* Prof. Donald A. Schwartz, Chair and Associate Professor, 858-642-8420, Fax: 858-642-8740, E-mail: dschwartz@nu.edu. *Application contact:* Dominick Giovanniello, Associate Regional Dean—San Diego, 800-NAT-UNIV, Fax: 858-541-7792, E-mail: dgiovann@nu.edu.

New Mexico State University, Graduate School, College of Agricultural, Consumer and Environmental Sciences, Department of Agricultural Economics and Agricultural Business, Las Cruces, NM 88003-8001. Offers agribusiness (M Ag, MBA); agricultural economics (MS); economics (MA). Part-time programs available. *Faculty:* 8 full-time (2 women). *Students:* 14 full-time (7 women), 4 part-time (2 women); includes 2 minority (1 American Indian/Alaska Native, 1 Asian American or Pacific Islander), 6 international. Average age 28. 22 applicants, 82% accepted, 6 enrolled. In 2009, 6 master's awarded. *Degree requirements:* For master's, thesis (for some programs). *Entrance requirements:* For master's, previous course work in intermediate microeconomics, intermediate macroeconomics, college-level calculus, statistics. Additional exam requirements/recommendations for international students: Required—TOEFL. *Application deadline:* For fall admission, 7/1 priority date for domestic and international students; for spring admission, 11/1 priority date for domestic and international students. Applications are processed on a rolling basis. Application fee: $30 ($50 for international students). Electronic applications accepted. *Expenses:* Tuition, state resident: full-time $4080; part-time $223 per credit. Tuition, nonresident: full-time $14,256; part-time $647 per credit. Required fees: $1278; $639 per semester. *Financial support:* In 2009–10, 7 research assistantships (averaging $13,971 per year), 3 teaching assistantships (averaging $5,267 per year) were awarded; career-related internships or fieldwork and health care benefits also available. Financial award application deadline: 3/1. *Faculty research:* Natural resource policy, production economics and farm/ranch management, agribusiness and marketing, international marketing and trade, agricultural risk management. *Unit head:* Dr. Terry Crawford, Head, 575-646-3215, Fax: 575-646-3808, E-mail: crawford@nmsu.edu. *Application contact:* Dr. L. Allen Torell, Professor, 575-646-4732, Fax: 575-646-3808, E-mail: atorell@nmsu.edu.

New Mexico State University, Graduate School, College of Business, Department of Economics and International Business, Las Cruces, NM 88003-8001. Offers applied statistics (MS); economic development (DED); economics (MA). Part-time programs available. *Faculty:* 13 full-time (3 women), 1 part-time/adjunct (0 women). *Students:* 54 full-time (22 women), 15 part-time (4 women); includes 21 minority (4 African Americans, 1 Asian American or Pacific Islander, 16 Hispanic Americans), 29 international. Average age 31. 74 applicants, 85% accepted, 38 enrolled. In 2009, 23 master's awarded. *Degree requirements:* For master's, comprehensive exam, thesis or alternative; for doctorate, comprehensive exam, thesis/dissertation or alternative. *Entrance requirements:* For master's, minimum GPA of 3.0; for doctorate, appropriate master's degree. Additional exam requirements/recommendations for international students: Required—TOEFL. *Application deadline:* Applications are processed on a rolling basis. Application fee: $30 ($50 for international students). Electronic applications accepted. *Expenses:* Tuition, state resident: full-time $4080; part-time $223 per credit. Tuition, nonresident: full-time $14,256; part-time $647 per credit. Required fees: $1278; $639 per semester. *Financial support:* In 2009–10, 34 students received support, including 19 research assistantships (averaging $13,031 per year), 19 teaching assistantships (averaging $7,939 per year); fellowships, career-related internships or fieldwork, Federal Work-Study, and health care benefits also available. Support available to part-time students. Financial award application deadline: 3/1. *Faculty research:* Public utilities, environment, linear models, biological sampling, public policy, economics development. Total annual research expenditures: $400,000. *Unit head:* Dr. Anthony Popp, Graduate Adviser, 575-646-5198, Fax: 575-646-1915, E-mail: apopp@nmsu.edu. *Application contact:* Dr. Anthony Popp, Graduate Adviser, 575-646-5198, Fax: 575-646-1915, E-mail: apopp@nmsu.edu.

The New School: A University, The New School for Social Research, Department of Economics, New York, NY 10003. Offers economics (M Phil, MA, MS, DS Sc, PhD); global finance (MS); global political economy and finance (MA). Part-time and evening/weekend programs available. *Faculty:* 9 full-time (2 women). *Students:* 103 full-time (32 women), 55 part-time (12 women); includes 28 minority (9 African Americans, 12 Asian Americans or Pacific Islanders, 7 Hispanic Americans), 64 international. Average age 32. 138 applicants, 84% accepted, 41 enrolled. In 2009, 46 master's, 8 doctorates awarded. Terminal master's awarded for partial completion of doctoral program. *Degree requirements:* For master's, exam; for doctorate, one foreign language, thesis/dissertation, qualifying exam. *Entrance requirements:* For master's, GRE General Test; for doctorate, GRE General Test, MA. Additional exam requirements/recommendations for international students: Required—TOEFL (minimum score 600 paper-based; 250 computer-based; 100 iBT). *Application deadline:* For fall admission, 1/17 priority date for domestic students, 1/17 for international students; for spring admission, 10/15 priority date for domestic students, 10/15 for international students. Applications are processed on a rolling basis. Application fee: $50. Electronic applications accepted. *Financial support:* Fellowships, research assistantships, teaching assistantships, Federal Work-Study, scholarships/grants, tuition waivers (full and partial), and unspecified assistantships available. Support available to part-time students. Financial award application deadline: 3/1; financial award applicants required to submit FAFSA. *Faculty research:* Heterodox, history of economic thought, post-Keynesian, global political economy and finance. *Unit head:* Dr. Will Milberg, Chair, 212-229-5717 Ext. 3045, E-mail: milbergw@newschool.edu. *Application contact:* Robert MacDonald, Director of Admissions, 212-229-5710 Ext. 3007, Fax: 212-989-7102, E-mail: macdonar@newschool.edu.

New York University, Graduate School of Arts and Science, Department of Economics, New York, NY 10012-1019. Offers applied economic analysis (Advanced Certificate); economics (MA, PhD); JD/MA; MD/PhD. Part-time and evening/weekend programs available. *Faculty:* 35 full-time (2 women). *Students:* 231 full-time (80 women), 38 part-time (9 women); includes 18 minority (1 African American, 16 Asian Americans or Pacific Islanders, 1 Hispanic American), 193 international. Average age 27. 1,344 applicants, 15% accepted, 78 enrolled. In 2009, 86 master's, 18 doctorates, 4 other advanced degrees awarded. Terminal master's awarded for partial completion of doctoral program. *Degree requirements:* For master's, thesis; for doctorate, one foreign language, thesis/dissertation, 4 qualifying exams. *Entrance requirements:* For master's and doctorate, GRE General Test; for Advanced Certificate, master's degree. Additional exam requirements/recommendations for international students: Required—TOEFL. *Application deadline:* For fall admission, 1/4 priority date for domestic students. Application fee: $90. *Expenses:* Tuition: Full-time $30,528; part-time $1272 per credit. Required fees: $2177. *Financial support:* Fellowships with tuition reimbursements, research assistantships with tuition reimbursements, teaching assistantships with tuition reimbursements, Federal Work-Study, institutionally sponsored loans, scholarships/grants, health care benefits, and unspecified assistantships available. Financial award application deadline: 1/4; financial award applicants required to submit FAFSA. *Faculty research:* Economic theory, experimental economics, growth and development, macroeconomics and finance, international trade and international finance. *Unit head:* Nicola Persico, Chair, 212-998-8900, Fax: 212-995-4186, E-mail: admissions@econ.nyu.edu. *Application contact:* Ennio Stacchetti, Director of Graduate Studies, 212-998-8900, Fax: 212-995-4186, E-mail: gsas.admissions@nyu.edu.

New York University, Leonard N. Stern School of Business, Department of Economics, New York, NY 10012-1019. Offers MBA, PhD. *Expenses:* Tuition: Full-time $30,528; part-time $1272 per credit. Required fees: $2177. *Faculty research:* Applied macroeconomics, macroeconomics and macroeconomic policy, international financial markets, international trade and business, game theory.

North Carolina State University, Graduate School, College of Management and College of Agriculture and Life Sciences, Program in Economics, Raleigh, NC 27695. Offers M Econ, MA, PhD. Part-time programs available. Terminal master's awarded for partial completion of doctoral program. *Degree requirements:* For master's, thesis (for some programs); for doctorate, thesis/dissertation. *Entrance requirements:* For master's and doctorate, GRE General Test. Additional exam requirements/recommendations for international students: Required—TOEFL. Electronic applications accepted. *Faculty research:* Endogenous growth modeling, generalized methods of moments estimation, integration and trade, agricultural policy, path dependence and network externalities.

Northeastern University, College of Social Sciences and Humanities, Department of Economics, Boston, MA 02115-5096. Offers MA, PhD. Part-time and evening/weekend programs available. *Faculty:* 17 full-time (2 women), 11 part-time/adjunct (6 women). *Students:* 74 full-time (41 women), 4 part-time (3 women); includes 1 African American, 4 Asian Americans or Pacific Islanders, 47 international. 197 applicants, 46% accepted, 32 enrolled. In 2009, 20 master's, 2 doctorates awarded. *Degree requirements:* For master's and doctorate, comprehensive exam. *Entrance requirements:* For master's, GRE. Additional exam requirements/recommendations for international students: Required—TOEFL. *Application deadline:* For fall admission, 8/1 for domestic students, 5/1 priority date for international students; for spring admission, 12/1 for domestic and international students. Applications are processed on a rolling basis. Application fee: $50. *Financial support:* In 2009–10, 13 teaching assistantships (averaging $15,667 per year) were awarded; Federal Work-Study, institutionally sponsored loans, tuition waivers (full and partial), and unspecified assistantships also available. Financial award application deadline: 2/1; financial award applicants required to submit FAFSA. *Faculty research:* U. S. labor markets, applied economics, microeconomic theory, macroeconomic theory, econometrics. *Unit head:* Dr. Steven Morrison, Chair, 617-373-2872, Fax: 617-373-3640, E-mail: econ@neu.edu. *Application contact:* Dr. Gregory Wassall, Graduate Coordinator, 617-373-2882, Fax: 617-373-3640, E-mail: econ@neu.edu.

Northern Illinois University, Graduate School, College of Liberal Arts and Sciences, Department of Economics, De Kalb, IL 60115-2854. Offers MA, PhD. Part-time programs available. *Faculty:* 15 full-time (3 women). *Students:* 32 full-time (12 women), 12 part-time (7 women); includes 4 minority (2 African Americans, 2 Asian Americans or Pacific Islanders), 26 international. Average age 27. 86 applicants, 45% accepted, 11 enrolled. In 2009, 5 master's, 3 doctorates awarded. Terminal master's awarded for partial completion of doctoral program. *Degree requirements:* For master's, comprehensive exam, thesis or alternative; for doctorate, thesis/dissertation, candidacy exam, dissertation defense, research seminar. *Entrance requirements:* For master's, GRE General Test, minimum GPA of 2.75; for doctorate, GRE General Test, minimum GPA of 2.75 (undergraduate), 3.2 (graduate). Additional exam requirements/recommendations for international students: Required—TOEFL (minimum score 550 paper-based; 213 computer-based). *Application deadline:* For fall admission, 6/1 for domestic students, 5/1 for international students; for spring admission, 11/1 for domestic students, 10/1 for international students. Applications are processed on a rolling basis. Application fee: $30. Electronic applications accepted. *Expenses:* Tuition, state resident: full-time $6576; part-time $274 per credit hour. Tuition, nonresident: full-time $13,152; part-time $548 per credit hour. Required fees: $1813; $75.53 per credit hour. Part-time tuition and fees vary according to course load. *Financial support:* In 2009–10, 8 research assistantships with full tuition reimbursements, 21 teaching assistantships with full tuition reimbursements were awarded; fellowships with full tuition reimbursements, career-related internships or fieldwork, Federal Work-Study, scholarships/grants, tuition waivers (full), and unspecified assistantships also available. Support available to part-time students. Financial award applicants required to submit FAFSA. *Faculty research:* Unemployment, behavior under uncertainty, effect of debt on compensation and capital utilization, racial inequality of earnings. *Unit head:* Dr. Carl M. Campbell, Chair, 815-753-6974, Fax: 815-753-1019, E-mail: carlcamp@niu.edu. *Application contact:* Dr. Ardeshir Dalal, Director, Graduate Studies, 815-753-6966.

Northwestern University, The Graduate School, Judd A. and Marjorie Weinberg College of Arts and Sciences, Department of Economics, Evanston, IL 60208. Offers MA, PhD, JD/PhD. Admissions and degrees offered through The Graduate School. *Degree requirements:* For doctorate, thesis/dissertation, preliminary written exam. *Entrance requirements:* For doctorate, GRE General Test. Additional exam requirements/recommendations for international students: Required—TOEFL. *Faculty research:* Organization of industry, behavior of labor markets, effects of monetary policy, theory of markets.

Northwestern University, The Graduate School, Kellogg School of Management, Program in Managerial Economics and Strategy, Evanston, IL 60208. Offers PhD. Admissions and degree offered through The Graduate School. *Degree requirements:* For doctorate, comprehensive exam, thesis/dissertation. *Entrance requirements:* For doctorate, GMAT or GRE General Test. Additional exam requirements/recommendations for international students: Required—TOEFL. Electronic applications accepted. *Faculty research:* Competitive strategy and organization, managerial economics, decision sciences, game theory, operations management.

Oakland University, Graduate Study and Lifelong Learning, School of Business Administration, Department of Economics, Rochester, MI 48309-4401. Offers Certificate.

The Ohio State University, Graduate School, College of Social and Behavioral Sciences, School of Social and Behavioral Science, Department of Economics, Columbus, OH 43210. Offers MA, PhD. *Faculty:* 38. *Students:* 86 full-time (30 women), 30 part-time (7 women); includes 7 minority (1 African American, 5 Asian Americans or Pacific Islanders, 1 Hispanic American), 83 international. Average age 28. In 2009, 29 master's, 11 doctorates awarded. *Degree requirements:* For doctorate, thesis/dissertation. *Entrance requirements:* Additional exam requirements/recommendations for international students: Required—TOEFL (minimum score 600 paper-based; 250 computer-based). *Application deadline:* For fall admission, 8/15 priority date for domestic students, 7/1 priority date for international students; for winter admission, 12/1 priority date for domestic students, 11/1 priority date for international students; for spring admission, 3/1 priority date for domestic students, 2/1 priority date for international students. Applications are processed on a rolling basis. Application fee: $40 ($50 for international students). Electronic applications accepted. *Expenses:* Tuition, state resident: full-time $10,683. Tuition, nonresident: full-time $25,923. Tuition and fees vary according to course load and program. *Financial support:* Fellowships, research assistantships, teaching assistantships, Federal Work-Study and institutionally sponsored loans available. Support available to part-time students. *Unit head:* Hajime Miyazaki, Graduate Studies Committee Chair, 614-292-6701, Fax: 614-292-3906, E-mail: miyazaki.1@osu.edu. *Application contact:* 614-292-9444, Fax: 614-292-3895, E-mail: domestic.grad@osu.edu.

Ohio University, Graduate College, College of Arts and Sciences, Department of Economics, Athens, OH 45701-2979. Offers applied economics (MA); financial economics (MFE). Part-time and evening/weekend programs available. *Faculty:* 15 full-time (3 women). *Students:* 56 full-time (20 women), 17 part-time (8 women); includes 10 minority (7 African Americans, 3 Asian Americans or Pacific Islanders), 33 international. 53 applicants, 57% accepted, 6 enrolled. In 2009, 49 master's awarded. *Degree requirements:* For master's, thesis or alternative. *Entrance requirements:* For master's, GRE or GMAT (recommended), minimum GPA of 3.0. Additional exam requirements/recommendations for international students: Required—TOEFL (minimum score 550 paper-based; 80 iBT) or IELTS Academic (minimum score 6.5). *Application deadline:* For fall admission, 2/15 priority date for domestic and international students; for winter admission, 12/1 for domestic students, 10/1 priority date for international students. Application fee: $50 ($55 for international students). Electronic applications accepted. *Expenses:* Tuition, state resident: full-time $7839; part-time $323 per quarter hour. Tuition, nonresident: full-time $15,831; part-time $654 per quarter hour. Required fees: $2931. *Financial support:* Research assistantships with full and partial tuition reimbursements, Federal Work-Study, tuition waivers (partial), and unspecified assistantships available. Financial award application deadline: 2/15. *Faculty research:* Macroeconomics, public finance, international economics and finance, monetary theory, healthcare economics. *Unit head:* Dr. Rosmary Rossiter, Chair,

740-593-2040, E-mail: rossiter@ohio.edu. *Application contact:* Dr. K. Doroodian, Graduate Chair, 740-593-2046, E-mail: doroodia@ohio.edu.

Oklahoma State University, William S. Spears School of Business, Department of Economics and Legal Studies in Business, Stillwater, OK 74078. Offers MS, PhD. Part-time programs available. *Faculty:* 19 full-time (4 women), 3 part-time/adjunct (2 women). *Students:* 25 full-time (9 women), 17 part-time (7 women); includes 3 minority (1 African American, 2 American Indian/Alaska Native), 28 international. Average age 32. 43 applicants, 44% accepted, 11 enrolled. In 2009, 6 master's awarded. *Degree requirements:* For master's, thesis or alternative; for doctorate, comprehensive exam, thesis/dissertation. *Entrance requirements:* For master's and doctorate, GRE or GMAT. Additional exam requirements/recommendations for international students: Required—TOEFL (minimum score 550 paper-based; 79 iBT). *Application deadline:* For fall admission, 3/1 priority date for international students; for spring admission, 8/1 priority date for international students. Applications are processed on a rolling basis. Application fee: $40 ($75 for international students). Electronic applications accepted. *Expenses:* Tuition, state resident: full-time $3716; part-time $154.85 per credit hour. Tuition, nonresident: full-time $14,448; part-time $602 per credit hour. Required fees: $1772; $73.85 per credit hour. One-time fee: $50. Tuition and fees vary according to course load and campus/location. *Financial support:* In 2009–10, 23 teaching assistantships (averaging $16,264 per year) were awarded; career-related internships or fieldwork, Federal Work-Study, scholarships/grants, health care benefits, tuition waivers (partial), and unspecified assistantships also available. Support available to part-time students. Financial award application deadline: 3/1; financial award applicants required to submit FAFSA. *Faculty research:* Economics and legal studies in business regional economic modeling/econometrics, urban/regional economics, monetary economics, international trade/finance/development, environmental economics. *Unit head:* Dr. Jim Fain, Head, 405-744-5195, Fax: 405-744-5180. *Application contact:* Dr. Gordon Emslie, Dean, 405-744-6368, Fax: 405-744-0355, E-mail: grad-i@okstate.edu.

Oklahoma State University, William S. Spears School of Business, Department of Finance, Stillwater, OK 74078. Offers finance (PhD); quantitative financial economics (MS). Part-time programs available. *Faculty:* 14 full-time (2 women), 5 part-time/adjunct (0 women). *Students:* 21 full-time (9 women), 8 part-time (1 woman), 12 international. Average age 30. 60 applicants, 35% accepted, 6 enrolled. In 2009, 9 master's, 1 doctorate awarded. *Degree requirements:* For master's, thesis or alternative; for doctorate, comprehensive exam, thesis/dissertation. *Entrance requirements:* For master's and doctorate, GRE or GMAT. Additional exam requirements/recommendations for international students: Required—TOEFL (minimum score 550 paper-based; 79 iBT). *Application deadline:* For fall admission, 3/1 priority date for international students; for spring admission, 8/1 priority date for international students. Applications are processed on a rolling basis. Application fee: $40 ($75 for international students). Electronic applications accepted. *Expenses:* Tuition, state resident: full-time $3716; part-time $154.85 per credit hour. Tuition, nonresident: full-time $14,448; part-time $602 per credit hour. Required fees: $1772; $73.85 per credit hour. One-time fee: $50. Tuition and fees vary according to course load and campus/location. *Financial support:* In 2009–10, 14 research assistantships (averaging $9,552 per year), 3 teaching assistantships (averaging $32,656 per year) were awarded; career-related internships or fieldwork, Federal Work-Study, scholarships/grants, health care benefits, tuition waivers (partial), and unspecified assistantships also available. Support available to part-time students. Financial award application deadline: 3/1; financial award applicants required to submit FAFSA. *Faculty research:* Corporate risk management, derivatives banking, investments and securities issuance, corporate governance, banking. *Unit head:* Dr. John Polonchek, Head, 405-744-5199, Fax: 405-744-5180. *Application contact:* Dr. Gordon Emslie, Dean, 405-744-6368, Fax: 405-744-0355, E-mail: grad-i@okstate.edu.

Old Dominion University, College of Business and Public Administration, Program in Economics, Norfolk, VA 23529. Offers MA. Part-time and evening/weekend programs available. *Faculty:* 11 full-time (1 woman). *Students:* 13 full-time (4 women), 19 part-time (4 women); includes 8 minority (6 African Americans, 1 Asian American or Pacific Islander, 1 Hispanic American), 7 international. Average age 28. 36 applicants, 83% accepted, 17 enrolled. In 2009, 8 master's awarded. *Degree requirements:* For master's, comprehensive exam, thesis optional, independent research. *Entrance requirements:* For master's, GMAT or GRE General Test, minimum GPA of 2.5. Additional exam requirements/recommendations for international students: Required—TOEFL (minimum score 520 paper-based; 213 computer-based; 79 iBT). *Application deadline:* For fall admission, 8/1 priority date for domestic students; for spring admission, 10/1 priority date for domestic students. Applications are processed on a rolling basis. Application fee: $50. Electronic applications accepted. *Expenses:* Tuition, state resident: full-time $8112; part-time $338 per credit. Tuition, nonresident: full-time $20,256; part-time $844 per credit. Required fees: $119 per semester. One-time fee: $50. *Financial support:* In 2009–10, 4 students received support, including 4 teaching assistantships with tuition reimbursements available (averaging $12,000 per year); research assistantships with tuition reimbursements available, career-related internships or fieldwork, scholarships/grants, tuition waivers (partial), and unspecified assistantships also available. Financial award application deadline: 8/1; financial award applicants required to submit FAFSA. *Faculty research:* International economics, transportation, monetary economics, immigration, econometrics. *Unit head:* Dr. David Duden Selover, Graduate Program Director, 757-683-3541, Fax: 757-683-5639, E-mail: dselover@odu.edu. *Application contact:* Dr. Ali Ardalan, Associate Dean, 757-683-3520, Fax: 757-683-4076, E-mail: aardalan@odu.edu.

Oregon State University, Graduate School, College of Agricultural Sciences, Department of Agricultural and Resource Economics, Corvallis, OR 97331. Offers agricultural and resource economics (M Agr, MAIS, MS, PhD); economics (MS, PhD). MS and PhD in economics offered through the University Graduate Faculty of Economics. Part-time programs available. *Faculty:* 9 full-time (2 women), 1 (woman) part-time/adjunct. *Students:* 19 full-time (9 women), 3 part-time (0 women); includes 2 minority (1 American Indian/Alaska Native, 1 Hispanic American), 12 international. Average age 29. In 2009, 1 master's, 4 doctorates awarded. Terminal master's awarded for partial completion of doctoral program. *Degree requirements:* For master's, thesis (for some programs); for doctorate, thesis/dissertation. *Entrance requirements:* For master's and doctorate, GRE General Test, minimum GPA of 3.0 in last 90 hours. Additional exam requirements/recommendations for international students: Required—TOEFL. *Application deadline:* For fall admission, 3/1 for domestic students. Applications are processed on a rolling basis. Application fee: $50. *Expenses:* Tuition, state resident: full-time $9774; part-time $362 per credit. Tuition, nonresident: full-time $15,849; part-time $587 per credit. Required fees: $1639. Full-time tuition and fees vary according to course load and program. *Financial support:* Fellowships, research assistantships, teaching assistantships, career-related internships or fieldwork, Federal Work-Study, and institutionally sponsored loans available. Support available to part-time students. Financial award application deadline: 2/1. *Faculty research:* Marine economics, environmental economics, effects of global climate change on agriculture, efficiency of agricultural markets, analysis of aquaculture development. *Unit head:* Dr. Gregory M. Perry, Department Head, 541-737-2942, Fax: 541-737-2563. *Application contact:* Kathy Carpenter, Administrative Assistant, 541-737-1398, Fax: 541-737-1441, E-mail: kathy.carpenter@orst.edu.

Oregon State University, Graduate School, College of Liberal Arts, Department of Economics, Corvallis, OR 97331. Offers MA, MS, PhD. Part-time programs available. *Faculty:* 10 full-time (3 women), 2 part-time/adjunct (0 women). *Students:* 5 full-time (3 women), 2 part-time (1 woman), 5 international. Average age 30. In 2009, 3 master's, 3 doctorates awarded. Terminal master's awarded for partial completion of doctoral program. *Degree requirements:* For master's, thesis or alternative; for doctorate, thesis/dissertation. *Entrance requirements:* For master's and doctorate, GRE General Test, minimum GPA of 3.0 in last 90 hours. Additional exam requirements/recommendations for international students: Required—TOEFL. *Application deadline:* For fall admission, 3/1 priority date for domestic students. Applications are processed on a rolling basis. Application fee: $50. *Expenses:* Tuition, state resident: full-time $9774; part-time $362 per credit. Tuition, nonresident: full-time $15,849; part-time $587 per credit. Required fees: $1639. Full-time tuition and fees vary according to course load and program. *Financial support:* Research assistantships, teaching assistantships, career-related internships or fieldwork, Federal Work-Study, and institutionally sponsored loans available. Support available to part-time students. Financial award application deadline: 3/1. *Faculty research:* Applied microeconomics, applied econometrics. *Unit head:* Dr. Carlos Martins-Filho, Chair, 541-737-1476, Fax: 541-737-5917, E-mail: carlos.martins@oregonstate.edu. *Application contact:* Dr. Carlos Martins-Filho, Chair, 541-737-1476, Fax: 541-737-5917, E-mail: carlos.martins@oregonstate.edu.

Pace University, Lubin School of Business, Program in Business Economics, New York, NY 10038. Offers corporate economic planning (MBA); financial economics (MBA); international economics (MBA). Part-time and evening/weekend programs available. *Students:* 1 applicant, 0% accepted, 0 enrolled. *Entrance requirements:* For master's, GMAT. Additional exam requirements/recommendations for international students: Required—TOEFL. *Application deadline:* For fall admission, 7/31 priority date for domestic students; for spring admission, 11/30 for domestic students. Applications are processed on a rolling basis. Application fee: $70. Electronic applications accepted. *Expenses:* Tuition: Part-time $954 per credit. Tuition and fees vary according to course load, degree level and program. *Financial support:* Research assistantships, career-related internships or fieldwork and Federal Work-Study available. Support available to part-time students. Financial award applicants required to submit FAFSA. *Unit head:* Dr. Richard Lynn, Chairperson, 212-346-1817. *Application contact:* Susan Ford-Goldschein, Director of Admissions, 212-346-1652, Fax: 212-346-1585, E-mail: gradnyc@pace.edu.

Penn State University Park, Graduate School, College of the Liberal Arts, Department of Economics, State College, University Park, PA 16802-1503. Offers MA, PhD.

Pepperdine University, School of Public Policy, Malibu, CA 90263. Offers American politics (MPP); economics (MPP); international relations (MPP); public policy (MPP); state and local policy (MPP). *Faculty:* 7 full-time (2 women), 5 part-time/adjunct (0 women). *Students:* 117 full-time (62 women), 5 part-time (3 women); includes 30 minority (7 African Americans, 1 American Indian/Alaska Native, 10 Asian Americans or Pacific Islanders, 12 Hispanic Americans), 9 international. In 2009, 27 master's awarded. *Entrance requirements:* For master's, GRE, 2 letters of recommendation, resume. Additional exam requirements/recommendations for international students: Required—TOEFL. *Application deadline:* For fall admission, 4/15 for domestic students. Applications are processed on a rolling basis. Electronic applications accepted. *Expenses:* Tuition: Full-time $37,516; part-time $1310 per unit. Required fees: $80. *Financial support:* Research assistantships, teaching assistantships, institutionally sponsored loans and scholarships/grants available. Financial award application deadline: 5/1; financial award applicants required to submit FAFSA. *Unit head:* Dr. James R. Wilburn, Dean, 310-506-7490, Fax: 310-506-7494, E-mail: james.wilburn@pepperdine.edu. *Application contact:* Melinda E. van Hemert, Director of Recruitment and Career Services, 310-506-7492, Fax: 310-506-7494, E-mail: melinda.vanhemert@pepperdine.edu.

Peru State College, Graduate Programs, Program in Organizational Management, Peru, NE 68421. Offers MS. Program offered online only. Part-time programs available. *Degree requirements:* For master's, thesis (for some programs). *Expenses:* Contact institution. *Faculty research:* Emotional intelligence.

Portland State University, Graduate Studies, College of Liberal Arts and Sciences, Department of Economics, Portland, OR 97207-0751. Offers applied economics (MA, MS); economics (PhD); general economics (MA, MS). Part-time programs available. *Degree requirements:* For master's, thesis optional; for doctorate, one foreign language, thesis/dissertation. *Entrance requirements:* For master's, minimum GPA of 3.0 in upper-division course work or 2.75 overall, course work in calculus. Additional exam requirements/recommendations for international students: Required—TOEFL (minimum score 550 paper-based; 213 computer-based). *Faculty research:* NAFTA, economies of transition, economics of Eastern Europe, artificial intelligence, comparative economic systems.

Portland State University, Graduate Studies, Systems Science Program, Portland, OR 97207-0751. Offers computational intelligence (Certificate); computer modeling and simulation (Certificate); systems science (MS); systems science/anthropology (PhD); systems science/business administration (PhD); systems science/civil engineering (PhD); systems science/economics (PhD); systems science/engineering management (PhD); systems science/general (PhD); systems science/mathematical sciences (PhD); systems science/mechanical engineering (PhD); systems science/psychology (PhD); systems science/sociology (PhD). *Degree requirements:* For doctorate, variable foreign language requirement, thesis/dissertation. *Entrance requirements:* For master's, 2 letters of recommendation; for doctorate, GMAT, GRE General Test, minimum undergraduate GPA of 3.0. Additional exam requirements/recommendations for international students: Required—TOEFL. *Faculty research:* Systems theory and methodology, artificial intelligence neural networks, information theory, nonlinear dynamics/chaos, modeling and simulation.

Princeton University, Graduate School, Department of Economics, Princeton, NJ 08544-1019. Offers PhD. *Degree requirements:* For doctorate, thesis/dissertation. *Entrance requirements:* For doctorate, GRE General Test, GRE Subject Test (recommended), working knowledge of multivariate calculus and matrix algebra. Additional exam requirements/recommendations for international students: Required—TOEFL (minimum score 600 paper-based; 250 computer-based). Electronic applications accepted.

Princeton University, Graduate School, Program in Population Studies, Princeton, NJ 08544-1019. Offers demography (PhD, Certificate); economics and demography (PhD); public affairs and demography (PhD); sociology and demography (PhD). *Degree requirements:* For doctorate, thesis/dissertation. *Entrance requirements:* For doctorate, GRE General Test. Additional exam requirements/recommendations for international students: Required—TOEFL (minimum score 600 paper-based; 250 computer-based). Electronic applications accepted. *Faculty research:* Models, fertility, infant and child mortality, migration.

Providence College, Graduate Studies, School of Business, Providence, RI 02918. Offers accountancy (MBA); economics (MBA); entrepreneurship (MBA); finance (MBA); international business (MBA); management (MBA); marketing (MBA); not-for-profit (MBA); quantitative (MBA). Part-time and evening/weekend programs available. *Faculty:* 14 full-time (8 women), 7 part-time/adjunct (3 women). *Students:* 63 full-time (18 women), 46 part-time (19 women); includes 4 minority (2 African Americans, 2 Asian Americans or Pacific Islanders), 7 international. Average age 26. 43 applicants, 88% accepted. In 2009, 40 master's awarded. *Degree requirements:* For master's, thesis optional. *Entrance requirements:* For master's, GMAT. Additional exam requirements/recommendations for international students: Required—TOEFL (minimum score 550 paper-based; 213 computer-based; 80 iBT). *Application deadline:* For fall admission, 8/1 priority date for domestic and international students; for spring admission, 12/1 priority date for domestic and international students. Applications are processed on a rolling basis. Application fee: $55. *Expenses:* Contact institution. *Financial support:* In 2009–10, 34 research assistantships with full tuition reimbursements (averaging $8,400 per year) were awarded; Federal Work-Study, institutionally sponsored loans, and unspecified assistantships also available. Support available to part-time students. Financial award application deadline: 8/1; financial award applicants required to submit FAFSA. *Unit head:* Dr. MaryJane Lenon, Director, MBA Program, 401-865-2566, Fax: 401-865-2978, E-mail: mjlenon@providence.edu. *Application contact:* Katherine A. Follett, Administrative Coordinator, 401-865-2333, Fax: 401-865-2978, E-mail: kfollett@providence.edu.

Purdue University, Graduate School, Krannert School of Management, Doctoral Program in Economics, West Lafayette, IN 47907-2056. Offers PhD. *Students:* 41 full-time (19 women); includes 3 minority (1 African American, 2 Asian Americans or Pacific Islanders). Average age 26. 407 applicants, 5% accepted, 12 enrolled. In 2009, 6 doctorates awarded. *Degree requirements:* For doctorate, comprehensive exam, thesis/dissertation, dissertation proposal in 3rd year of study. *Entrance requirements:* For doctorate, GRE, Applicants must have

Economics

Purdue University (continued)

completed two semesters of calculus and one semester of linear algebra, as well as have demonstrated competence in undergraduate studies. Additional exam requirements/recommendations for international students: Required—TOEFL (minimum score 233 paper-based; 575 computer-based); Recommended—TWE. *Application deadline:* For fall admission, 2/15 priority date for domestic and international students. Application fee: $55. Electronic applications accepted. *Financial support:* In 2009–10, 2 fellowships with full and partial tuition reimbursements (averaging $25,000 per year), 29 research assistantships with partial tuition reimbursements (averaging $18,000 per year), 4 teaching assistantships with partial tuition reimbursements (averaging $18,000 per year) were awarded; institutionally sponsored loans, scholarships/grants, health care benefits, tuition waivers (partial), unspecified assistantships, and travel funds to present at a major conference also available. Financial award application deadline: 2/15. *Faculty research:* Econometrics, experimental economics, international economics, macroeconomic theory, industrial organization. *Unit head:* Dr. R. A. Cosier, Dean, 765-494-4366. *Application contact:* Krannert Ph.D. Admissions, 765-494-4375, E-mail: krannertphd@purdue.edu.

Regent University, Graduate School, Robertson School of Government, Virginia Beach, VA 23464. Offers american government (MA); global politics (MA); health care policy and administration (MA); international politics (MA); law and public policy (MA); Mid-East Politics (MA); political leadership and management (MA); political management (MA); political theory (MA); public administration (MA); public policy (MA); terrorism and homeland defense (MA); world economics and political development (MA); JD/MA; M Div/MA; M Ed/MA; MBA/MA. Part-time and evening/weekend programs available. Postbaccalaureate distance learning degree programs offered (minimal on-campus study). *Faculty:* 6 full-time (2 women), 11 part-time/adjunct (1 woman). *Students:* 77 full-time (55 women), 65 part-time (36 women); includes 47 minority (38 African Americans, 2 Asian Americans or Pacific Islanders, 7 Hispanic Americans), 4 international. Average age 30. 131 applicants, 65% accepted, 54 enrolled. In 2009, 51 master's awarded. *Degree requirements:* For master's, thesis optional, internship. *Entrance requirements:* For master's, GRE General Test or LSAT, minimum undergraduate GPA of 3.0, writing sample, resume, interview, references. Additional exam requirements/recommendations for international students: Required—TOEFL (minimum score 577 paper-based; 233 computer-based). *Application deadline:* For fall admission, 5/1 priority date for domestic students; for spring admission, 11/1 priority date for domestic students. Applications are processed on a rolling basis. Application fee: $50. Electronic applications accepted. *Expenses:* Contact institution. *Financial support:* In 2009–10, 130 students received support. Career-related internships or fieldwork, scholarships/grants, tuition waivers (full and partial), and unspecified assistantships available. Support available to part-time students. Financial award application deadline: 9/1; financial award applicants required to submit FAFSA. *Faculty research:* Education reform, political character issues, social capital concerns, administrative ethics, Biblical law and public policy. *Unit head:* Dr. Charles W. Dunn, Dean, 757-352-4322, Fax: 757-352-4643, E-mail: cwdunn@regent.edu. *Application contact:* Matthew Chadwick, Director of Admissions, 800-373-5504, Fax: 757-352-4381, E-mail: admissions@regent.edu.

Rensselaer Polytechnic Institute, Graduate School, School of Humanities and Social Sciences, Department of Economics, Program in Economics, Troy, NY 12180-3590. Offers MS. Part-time programs available. *Faculty:* 7 full-time (1 woman). *Students:* 11 full-time (7 women); includes 4 Asian Americans or Pacific Islanders, 3 Hispanic Americans. Average age 29. 30 applicants, 30% accepted, 2 enrolled.Terminal master's awarded for partial completion of doctoral program. *Degree requirements:* For master's, thesis. *Entrance requirements:* For master's, GRE General Test. Additional exam requirements/recommendations for international students: Required—TWE, TOEFL or IELTS. *Application deadline:* For fall admission, 1/15 priority date for domestic and international students. Applications are processed on a rolling basis. Application fee: $75. Electronic applications accepted. *Expenses:* Tuition: Full-time $38,100. *Financial support:* In 2009–10, 9 students received support, including 2 fellowships with full tuition reimbursements available (averaging $22,000 per year), 3 research assistantships with full tuition reimbursements available (averaging $17,500 per year), 4 teaching assistantships (averaging $17,500 per year); scholarships/grants and unspecified assistantships also available. Financial award application deadline: 1/15. *Faculty research:* Economic development and trade with a focus on technology, lifestyles, and environment; input-output analysis; pollution policy in the electric power sector; electricity market design; renewable energy integration in the power grid; experimental economics; law and economics; environmental economics; behavioral economics; technology change; applied econometrics. Total annual research expenditures: $100,000. *Unit head:* Prof. Faye Duchin, Professor/Director of PhD Program in Ecological Economics, 518-276-2038, Fax: 518-276-2235, E-mail: duchin@rpi.edu. *Application contact:* Betty Jean Kaufman, Administrative Assistant, 518-276-6387, Fax: 518-276-2235, E-mail: kaufmb@rpi.edu.

Rice University, Graduate Programs, School of Social Sciences, Department of Economics, Houston, TX 77251-1892. Offers MA, PhD. *Faculty:* 21 full-time (4 women), 5 part-time/adjunct (0 women). *Students:* 41 full-time (19 women); includes 2 minority (1 African American, 1 Hispanic American), 33 international. Average age 25. 222 applicants, 5% accepted, 8 enrolled. In 2009, 4 master's, 3 doctorates awarded. *Degree requirements:* For doctorate, comprehensive exam, thesis/dissertation. *Entrance requirements:* For doctorate, GRE. Additional exam requirements/recommendations for international students: Required—TOEFL (minimum score 600 paper-based; 90 iBT). *Application deadline:* For spring admission, 2/1 priority date for domestic students, 2/1 for international students. Application fee: $40. Electronic applications accepted. *Financial support:* In 2009–10, 35 students received support, including 35 fellowships with full tuition reimbursements available (averaging $15,000 per year); tuition waivers (full) also available. Financial award application deadline: 1/15. *Unit head:* Dr. Simon Grant, Professor and Director of Graduate Studies, 713-348-3332, Fax: 713-348-5278, E-mail: sgrant@rice.edu. *Application contact:* Altha D. Rodgers, Graduate Program Coordinator, 713-348-2289, Fax: 713-348-5278, E-mail: arodgers@rice.edu.

Roosevelt University, Graduate Division, College of Arts and Sciences, Department of Economics, Chicago, IL 60605. Offers applied economics (MA); economics (MA). Part-time and evening/weekend programs available. *Degree requirements:* For master's, thesis or alternative. *Entrance requirements:* For master's, minimum GPA of 2.7. *Faculty research:* Labor, gender issues, international trade and development, entrepreneurship, political economy and money.

Rutgers, The State University of New Jersey, Newark, Graduate School, Program in Economics, Newark, NJ 07102. Offers MA. *Entrance requirements:* For master's, GRE, minimum undergraduate B average.

Rutgers, The State University of New Jersey, Newark, Rutgers Business SchoolûNewark and New Brunswick, Department of Finance and Economics, Newark, NJ 07102. Offers MBA, MQF. *Entrance requirements:* For master's, GMAT (MBA), GRE General Test (MQF). Additional exam requirements/recommendations for international students: Required—TOEFL.

Rutgers, The State University of New Jersey, New Brunswick, Graduate School-New Brunswick, Program in Economics, Piscataway, NJ 08854-8097. Offers MA, PhD. Terminal master's awarded for partial completion of doctoral program. *Degree requirements:* For master's, comprehensive exam (for some programs), thesis or alternative; for doctorate, comprehensive exam, thesis/dissertation. *Entrance requirements:* For master's and doctorate, GRE General Test. Additional exam requirements/recommendations for international students: Required—TOEFL. Electronic applications accepted. *Faculty research:* Econometrics, microeconomics, macroeconomics, economichistory.

St. Cloud State University, School of Graduate Studies, College of Social Sciences, Department of Economics, St. Cloud, MN 56301-4498. Offers applied economics (MS); public and nonprofit institutions (MS). Part-time programs available. *Faculty:* 20 full-time (5 women), 1 part-time/adjunct (0 women). *Students:* 17 full-time (4 women), 11 part-time (8 women); includes 3 minority (all African Americans), 15 international. 17 applicants, 82% accepted, 0 enrolled. In 2009, 9 master's awarded. *Degree requirements:* For master's, thesis or alternative. *Entrance requirements:* For master's, GRE General Test, minimum GPA of 2.75. Additional exam requirements/recommendations for international students: Recommended—TOEFL (minimum score 550 paper-based; 213 computer-based), IELTS (minimum score 6.5). *Application deadline:* For fall admission, 6/1 priority date for domestic students, 4/1 for international students; for spring admission, 10/1 priority date for domestic students, 8/1 for international students. Applications are processed on a rolling basis. Application fee: $35. Electronic applications accepted. *Financial support:* Federal Work-Study, scholarships/grants, and unspecified assistantships available. *Unit head:* Dr. Patricia Hughes, Chairperson, 320-308-2076, Fax: 320-308-2228, E-mail: pahughes@stcloudstate.edu. *Application contact:* Linda Lou Krueger, School of Graduate Studies, 320-308-2113, Fax: 320-308-5371, E-mail: lekrueger@stcloudstate.edu.

San Diego State University, Graduate and Research Affairs, College of Arts and Letters, Department of Economics, San Diego, CA 92182. Offers MA. *Entrance requirements:* For master's, GRE General Test, 2 letters of recommendation. Additional exam requirements/recommendations for international students: Required—TOEFL. Electronic applications accepted. *Faculty research:* Financing public education, demand for alternative fuel vehicles, economics of the Gold Rush, interdependence of equity and economic efficiency, economics of welfare.

San Francisco State University, Division of Graduate Studies, College of Behavioral and Social Sciences, Department of Economics, San Francisco, CA 94132-1722. Offers MA.

San Jose State University, Graduate Studies and Research, College of Social Sciences, Department of Economics, San Jose, CA 95192-0001. Offers applied economics (MA); economics (MA). Part-time programs available. *Students:* 43 full-time (15 women), 33 part-time (11 women); includes 27 minority (1 African American, 18 Asian Americans or Pacific Islanders, 8 Hispanic Americans), 16 international. Average age 32. 94 applicants, 43% accepted, 29 enrolled. In 2009, 34 master's awarded. *Degree requirements:* For master's, comprehensive exam, thesis optional. *Entrance requirements:* For master's, GRE, minimum GPA of 3.0. *Application deadline:* For fall admission, 6/29 for domestic students; for spring admission, 11/30 for domestic students. Applications are processed on a rolling basis. Application fee: $59. Electronic applications accepted. *Financial support:* Teaching assistantships available. Financial award applicants required to submit FAFSA. *Unit head:* Dr. Lydia Ortega, Chair, 408-924-5400, Fax: 408-924-5406. *Application contact:* Dr. Lydia Ortega, Chair, 408-924-5400, Fax: 408-924-5406.

Simon Fraser University, Graduate Studies, Faculty of Arts and Social Sciences, Department of Economics, Burnaby, BC V5A 1S6, Canada. Offers MA, PhD. Evening/weekend programs available. *Degree requirements:* For doctorate, comprehensive exam, thesis/dissertation. *Entrance requirements:* For master's, GRE, minimum GPA of 3.0; for doctorate, GRE, minimum GPA of 3.5. Additional exam requirements/recommendations for international students: Required—TWE or IELTS. *Faculty research:* Industrial organization, public economics, econometrics, labor, macroeconomics.

South Dakota State University, Graduate School, College of Agriculture and Biological Sciences, Department of Economics, Brookings, SD 57007. Offers MS. *Degree requirements:* For master's, comprehensive exam, thesis (for some programs), oral exam. *Entrance requirements:* For master's, minimum GPA of 2.75. Additional exam requirements/recommendations for international students: Required—TOEFL (minimum score 550 paper-based; 213 computer-based; 79 iBT). *Faculty research:* Sustainable agriculture, rural finance, grain and livestock marketing, agricultural policy, applied economics.

Southern Illinois University Carbondale, Graduate School, College of Liberal Arts, Department of Economics, Carbondale, IL 62901-4701. Offers MA, MS, PhD. *Degree requirements:* For master's, thesis; for doctorate, thesis/dissertation. *Entrance requirements:* For master's, GRE General Test, minimum GPA of 2.7; for doctorate, GRE General Test, minimum GPA of 3.25. Additional exam requirements/recommendations for international students: Required—TOEFL. *Faculty research:* Advanced economic theory, applied microeconomics, economic development, finance, international economics, monetary theory and policy.

Southern Illinois University Edwardsville, Graduate Studies and Research, School of Business, Department of Economics and Finance, Edwardsville, IL 62026-0001. Offers MA, MS. Part-time and evening/weekend programs available. *Faculty:* 12 full-time (3 women). *Students:* 17 full-time (3 women), 10 part-time (3 women), 11 international. Average age 26. 61 applicants, 44% accepted. In 2009, 16 master's awarded. *Degree requirements:* For master's, thesis or alternative, final exam, portfolio. *Entrance requirements:* For master's, GMAT or GRE. Additional exam requirements/recommendations for international students: Required—TOEFL (minimum score 550 paper-based; 213 computer-based; 79 iBT), IELTS (minimum score 6.5). *Application deadline:* For fall admission, 7/23 for domestic students, 6/1 for international students; for spring admission, 12/11 for domestic students, 10/1 for international students. Applications are processed on a rolling basis. Application fee: $30. Electronic applications accepted. *Expenses:* Tuition, state resident: part-time $1252.50 per semester. Tuition, nonresident: part-time $3131.25 per semester. Required fees: $586.85 per semester. Tuition and fees vary according to course load. *Financial support:* In 2009–10, 1 fellowship with full tuition reimbursement (averaging $8,370 per year), 13 teaching assistantships with full tuition reimbursements (averaging $8,064 per year) were awarded; research assistantships with full tuition reimbursements, career-related internships or fieldwork, Federal Work-Study, institutionally sponsored loans, scholarships/grants, traineeships, and unspecified assistantships also available. Support available to part-time students. Financial award application deadline: 3/1; financial award applicants required to submit FAFSA. *Unit head:* Dr. Rik Hafer, Chair, 618-650-2542, E-mail: rhafer@siue.edu. *Application contact:* Dr. Ali Kutan, Director, 618-650-3473, E-mail: akutan@siue.edu.

Southern Methodist University, Dedman College, Department of Economics, Dallas, TX 75205. Offers applied economics (MA); economics (MA, PhD); JD/MA. Part-time and evening/weekend programs available. *Faculty:* 17 full-time (4 women), 23 part-time/adjunct (9 women). *Students:* 47 full-time (22 women), 25 part-time (11 women); includes 9 minority (4 African Americans, 4 Asian Americans or Pacific Islanders, 1 Hispanic American), 33 international. Average age 27. 95 applicants, 78% accepted, 22 enrolled. In 2009, 17 master's, 5 doctorates awarded. Terminal master's awarded for partial completion of doctoral program. *Degree requirements:* For master's, thesis, oral qualifying exam; for doctorate, thesis/dissertation, written exams. *Entrance requirements:* For master's, GRE General Test or GMAT, 12 hours course work in economics, minimum GPA of 3.0, previous course work in calculus and statistics; for doctorate, GRE General Test, minimum GPA of 3.0; 3 semesters of course work in calculus; 1 semester each of course work in statistics and linear algebra. Additional exam requirements/recommendations for international students: Required—TOEFL (minimum score 550 paper-based; 213 computer-based). *Application deadline:* For fall admission, 2/1 priority date for domestic students; for spring admission, 11/30 priority date for domestic students. Applications are processed on a rolling basis. Application fee: $75. Electronic applications accepted. *Financial support:* In 2009–10, 23 students received support, including 1 fellowship with full tuition reimbursement available (averaging $16,000 per year), 1 research assistantship with full tuition reimbursement available (averaging $16,000 per year), 16 teaching assistantships with full tuition reimbursements available (averaging $16,000 per year). Financial award application deadline: 2/1; financial award applicants required to submit FAFSA. *Faculty research:* Economic theory, game theory, econometrics, international trade, labor. *Unit head:* Dr. Thomas Fomby, Chair, 214-768-2559, Fax: 214-768-2559, E-mail: tfomby@smu.edu. *Application contact:* Stephanie Hall, Information Contact, 214-768-2694, E-mail: eco@smu.edu.

Stanford University, School of Humanities and Sciences, Department of Economics, Stanford, CA 94305-9991. Offers PhD. *Degree requirements:* For doctorate, thesis/dissertation, oral exam. *Entrance requirements:* For doctorate, GRE General Test. Additional exam requirements/recommendations for international students: Required—TOEFL. Electronic applications accepted. *Expenses:* Tuition: Full-time $37,380; part-time $2760 per quarter. Required fees: $501.

State University of New York at Binghamton, Graduate School, School of Arts and Sciences, Department of Economics, Binghamton, NY 13902-6000. Offers economics (MA, PhD); economics and finance (MA, PhD). *Faculty:* 23 full-time (4 women), 4 part-time/adjunct (0 women). *Students:* 43 full-time (16 women), 29 part-time (14 women); includes 7 minority (1 African American, 5 Asian Americans or Pacific Islanders, 1 Hispanic American), 52 international. Average age 29. 147 applicants, 67% accepted, 20 enrolled. In 2009, 16 master's, 7 doctorates awarded. Terminal master's awarded for partial completion of doctoral program. *Degree requirements:* For doctorate, thesis/dissertation. *Entrance requirements:* For master's and doctorate, GRE General Test. Additional exam requirements/recommendations for international students: Required—TOEFL (minimum score 550 paper-based; 213 computer-based; 80 iBT). *Application deadline:* For fall admission, 8/1 priority date for domestic and international students. Applications are processed on a rolling basis. Application fee: $60. Electronic applications accepted. *Financial support:* In 2009–10, 31 students received support, including 2 fellowships with full tuition reimbursements available (averaging $14,500 per year), 27 teaching assistantships with full tuition reimbursements available (averaging $14,500 per year); research assistantships, career-related internships or fieldwork, Federal Work-Study, institutionally sponsored loans, scholarships/grants, health care benefits, and unspecified assistantships also available. Financial award application deadline: 2/15; financial award applicants required to submit FAFSA. *Unit head:* Dr. Susan Wolcott, Chairperson, 607-777-2339, E-mail: swolcott@binghamton.edu. *Application contact:* Victoria Williams, Recruiting and Admissions Coordinator, 607-777-2151, Fax: 607-777-2501, E-mail: vwilliam@binghamton.edu.

Stony Brook University, State University of New York, Graduate School, College of Arts and Sciences, Department of Economics, Stony Brook, NY 11794. Offers MA, PhD. *Faculty:* 12 full-time (1 woman), 5 part-time/adjunct (0 women). *Students:* 45 full-time (28 women), 41 international. Average age 28. 139 applicants, 22% accepted. In 2009, 19 master's, 9 doctorates awarded. *Degree requirements:* For doctorate, comprehensive exam, thesis/dissertation. *Entrance requirements:* For master's and doctorate, GRE General Test. Additional exam requirements/recommendations for international students: Required—TOEFL. *Application deadline:* For fall admission, 1/15 for domestic students. Application fee: $60. *Expenses:* Tuition, state resident: full-time $8370; part-time $349 per credit. Tuition, nonresident: full-time $13,250; part-time $552 per credit. Required fees: $933. *Financial support:* In 2009–10, 1 research assistantship, 35 teaching assistantships were awarded; fellowships also available. *Faculty research:* Economic theory, game theory, econometrics, macroeconomics, applied microeconomics. Total annual research expenditures: $134,701. *Unit head:* Dr. William Dawes, Co-Chair, 631-632-7530. *Application contact:* Dr. Sandro Brusco, Director of Graduate Studies, 631-632-7548, E-mail: sbrusco@notes.cc.sunysb.edu.

Suffolk University, College of Arts and Sciences, Department of Economics, Boston, MA 02108-2770. Offers economic policy (MSEP); economics (MSE, PhD); international economics (MSIE); JD/MSIE. Part-time and evening/weekend programs available. *Faculty:* 13 full-time (3 women). *Students:* 24 full-time (7 women), 15 part-time (12 women); includes 2 minority (both Asian Americans or Pacific Islanders), 17 international. Average age 26. 103 applicants, 62% accepted, 26 enrolled. In 2009, 8 master's awarded. *Degree requirements:* For doctorate, comprehensive exam, thesis/dissertation. *Entrance requirements:* For master's, GRE General Test or GMAT, 2 letters of recommendation, resume; for doctorate, GRE General Test, 3 letters of recommendation. Additional exam requirements/recommendations for international students: Required—TOEFL (minimum score 550 paper-based; 213 computer-based; 80 iBT). *Application deadline:* For fall admission, 6/15 priority date for domestic students, 6/15 for international students; for spring admission, 11/1 priority date for domestic students, 11/1 for international students. Applications are processed on a rolling basis. Application fee: $50. Electronic applications accepted. *Expenses:* Contact institution. *Financial support:* In 2009–10, 32 students received support, including 21 fellowships with full and partial tuition reimbursements available (averaging $15,596 per year); career-related internships or fieldwork, Federal Work-Study, and institutionally sponsored loans also available. Support available to part-time students. Financial award application deadline: 4/1; financial award applicants required to submit FAFSA. *Faculty research:* Trade demands, fair tax, smoking, multinational firms, charitable giving, fair tax. *Unit head:* Dr. David Tuerck, Chairperson, 617-573-8259, Fax: 617-994-4216, E-mail: dtuerck@suffolk.edu. *Application contact:* Judith Reynolds, Director of Graduate Admissions, 617-573-8302, Fax: 617-305-1733, E-mail: grad.admission@suffolk.edu.

Syracuse University, Maxwell School of Citizenship and Public Affairs, Joint Program in Economics and International Relations, Syracuse, NY 13244. Offers MA/MA. Part-time programs available. *Students:* 10 full-time (7 women); includes 1 minority (Asian American or Pacific Islander), 5 international. Average age 26. 30 applicants, 67% accepted, 4 enrolled. *Entrance requirements:* Additional exam requirements/recommendations for international students: Required—TOEFL (minimum score 100 iBT). *Application deadline:* For fall admission, 2/1 priority date for domestic and international students. Application fee: $75. Electronic applications accepted. *Expenses:* Tuition: Full-time $26,808; part-time $1117 per credit. Required fees: $1024. *Financial support:* Fellowships with tuition reimbursements, research assistantships with tuition reimbursements, teaching assistantships with tuition reimbursements available. Financial award application deadline: 1/1. *Unit head:* Dr. Stuart Brown, Program Contact, 315-443-7097, Fax: 315-443-3385, E-mail: ssbrown@maxwell.syr.edu. *Application contact:* Dr. Stuart Brown, Program Contact, 315-443-7097, Fax: 315-443-3385, E-mail: ssbrown@maxwell.syr.edu.

Syracuse University, Maxwell School of Citizenship and Public Affairs, Program in Econometrics, Syracuse, NY 13244. Offers CAS. Part-time programs available. *Entrance requirements:* Additional exam requirements/recommendations for international students: Required—TOEFL (minimum score 100 iBT). *Application deadline:* For fall admission, 2/1 priority date for domestic and international students. Application fee: $75. *Expenses:* Tuition: Full-time $26,808; part-time $1117 per credit. Required fees: $1024. *Financial support:* Application deadline: 1/1. *Unit head:* Dr. Devashish Mitra, Chair, 315-443-3612, Fax: 315-443-3385, E-mail: dmitra@syr.edu. *Application contact:* Laura Sauta, Program Contact, 315-443-2414, E-mail: llsauta@maxwell.syr.edu.

Syracuse University, Maxwell School of Citizenship and Public Affairs, Program in Economics, Syracuse, NY 13244. Offers MA, PhD. *Students:* 47 full-time (21 women), 10 part-time (3 women); includes 3 minority (2 African Americans, 1 Asian American or Pacific Islander), 39 international. Average age 28. 283 applicants, 30% accepted, 20 enrolled. In 2009, 17 master's, 9 doctorates awarded. *Degree requirements:* For doctorate, comprehensive exam, thesis/dissertation. *Entrance requirements:* For master's and doctorate, GRE General Test. Additional exam requirements/recommendations for international students: Required—TOEFL (minimum score 100 iBT). *Application deadline:* For fall admission, 2/1 priority date for domestic and international students. Applications are processed on a rolling basis. Application fee: $75. Electronic applications accepted. *Expenses:* Tuition: Full-time $26,808; part-time $1117 per credit. Required fees: $1024. *Financial support:* Fellowships with full tuition reimbursements, research assistantships with full tuition reimbursements, teaching assistantships with full and partial tuition reimbursements, tuition waivers (partial) available. Financial award application deadline: 1/1. *Faculty research:* International economics, labor economics, public finance, urban economics. *Unit head:* Dr. Devashish Mitra, Chair, 315-443-3612, Fax: 315-443-3717. *Application contact:* Laura Sauta, Recruiting Contact, 315-443-2414.

Tarleton State University, College of Graduate Studies, College of Business Administration, Department of Accounting, Finance and Economics, Stephenville, TX 76402. Offers business administration (MBA). Part-time and evening/weekend programs available. *Degree requirements:* For master's, comprehensive exam. *Entrance requirements:* For master's, GRE or GMAT, minimum GPA of 3.0. Additional exam requirements/recommendations for international students: Required—TOEFL (minimum score 550 paper-based; 213 computer-based; 80 iBT). Electronic applications accepted.

Teachers College, Columbia University, Graduate Faculty of Education, Department of International and Transcultural Studies, Program in Economics and Education, New York, NY 10027-6696. Offers Ed M, MA, Ed D, PhD. *Faculty:* 3 full-time (0 women). *Students:* 151 full-time (14 women), 53 part-time (30 women); includes 27 minority (3 African Americans, 15 Asian Americans or Pacific Islanders, 9 Hispanic Americans), 27 international. Average age 30. 53 applicants, 74% accepted, 22 enrolled. In 2009, 11 master's, 4 doctorates awarded. *Degree requirements:* For doctorate, variable foreign language requirement, thesis/dissertation. *Entrance requirements:* For master's and doctorate, GRE. *Application deadline:* For fall admission, 5/15 for domestic students; for spring admission, 12/1 for domestic students. Application fee: $65. *Financial support:* Career-related internships or fieldwork, Federal Work-Study, institutionally sponsored loans, and tuition waivers (full and partial) available. Support available to part-time students. Financial award application deadline: 2/1. *Faculty research:* Education and economic growth, efficiency in education, training in education, labor and education policy, economic status of immigrant groups. *Unit head:* Dr. George Bond, Chair, 212-678-3947. *Application contact:* Deanna Ghozati, Assistant Director of Admission, 212-678-4018, Fax: 212-678-4171, E-mail: ghozati@tc.edu.

Texas A&M University, College of Liberal Arts, Department of Economics, College Station, TX 77843. Offers MS, PhD. Part-time programs available. *Faculty:* 15. *Students:* 124 full-time (46 women), 8 part-time (3 women); includes 3 minority (all Asian Americans or Pacific Islanders), 101 international. Average age 31. In 2009, 19 master's, 15 doctorates awarded. Terminal master's awarded for partial completion of doctoral program. *Degree requirements:* For master's, comprehensive exam, thesis optional; for doctorate, comprehensive exam, thesis/dissertation. *Entrance requirements:* For master's and doctorate, GRE General Test. Additional exam requirements/recommendations for international students: Required—TOEFL. *Application deadline:* For fall admission, 3/1 priority date for domestic students; for winter admission, 8/1 priority date for domestic students; for spring admission, 11/1 priority date for domestic students. Applications are processed on a rolling basis. Application fee: $50 ($75 for international students). Electronic applications accepted. *Expenses:* Tuition, state resident: full-time $3991; part-time $221.74 per credit hour. Tuition, nonresident: full-time $9049; part-time $502.74 per credit hour. *Financial support:* In 2009–10, fellowships (averaging $14,850 per year), research assistantships (averaging $12,380 per year), teaching assistantships (averaging $10,062 per year) were awarded; scholarships/grants, tuition waivers, and unspecified assistantships also available. Financial award application deadline: 2/1; financial award applicants required to submit FAFSA. *Faculty research:* Tax policy, state tax, labor, international economics, macroeconomics. *Unit head:* Dr. Larry Oliver, Head, 979-845-8541, E-mail: l-oliver@tamu.edu. *Application contact:* Christi Essix, Graduate Admissions Supervisor, 979-845-7376, Fax: 979-847-8557, E-mail: christi@econ.tamu.edu.

Texas A&M University–Commerce, Graduate School, College of Business and Technology, Department of Economics and Finance, Commerce, TX 75429-3011. Offers economics (MA, MS). Part-time programs available. *Degree requirements:* For master's, comprehensive exam, thesis (for some programs). *Entrance requirements:* For master's, GMAT or GRE General Test. Electronic applications accepted. *Faculty research:* Economic activity, forensic economics, volatility and finance, international economics.

Texas Tech University, Graduate School, College of Arts and Sciences, Department of Economics and Geography, Lubbock, TX 79409. Offers economics (MA, PhD). Part-time programs available. *Faculty:* 12 full-time (3 women), 1 part-time/adjunct (0 women). *Students:* 33 full-time (10 women), 8 part-time (3 women); includes 4 minority (1 Asian American or Pacific Islander, 3 Hispanic Americans), 32 international. Average age 31. 49 applicants, 65% accepted, 7 enrolled. In 2009, 7 master's, 3 doctorates awarded. *Degree requirements:* For master's, thesis or alternative; for doctorate, thesis/dissertation. *Entrance requirements:* For master's and doctorate, GRE General Test. Additional exam requirements/recommendations for international students: Required—TOEFL (minimum score 550 paper-based; 213 computer-based). *Application deadline:* For fall admission, 3/1 priority date for international students; for spring admission, 11/1 priority date for international students. Applications are processed on a rolling basis. Application fee: $50 ($75 for international students). Electronic applications accepted. *Expenses:* Tuition, state resident: full-time $5100; part-time $213 per credit hour. Tuition, nonresident: full-time $11,748; part-time $490 per credit hour. Required fees: $2298; $50 per credit hour. $555 per semester. *Financial support:* In 2009–10, 16 teaching assistantships with partial tuition reimbursements (averaging $12,967 per year) were awarded; research assistantships with partial tuition reimbursements, Federal Work-Study and institutionally sponsored loans also available. Support available to part-time students. Financial award application deadline: 4/15; financial award applicants required to submit FAFSA. *Faculty research:* Pensions and retirement, energy economics, monetary and international economics, labor economics; industrial organization. Total annual research expenditures: $110,954. *Unit head:* Dr. Klaus G. Becker, Chair, 806-742-2201 Ext. 231, Fax: 806-742-1137, E-mail: klaus.becker@ttu.edu. *Application contact:* Dr. Rashid Al-Hmoud, Graduate Advisor, 806-742-2201 Ext. 223, Fax: 806-742-1137, E-mail: rashid.al-hmoud@ttu.edu.

Trinity College, Graduate Programs, Department of Economics, Hartford, CT 06106-3100. Offers MA. Part-time and evening/weekend programs available. *Faculty:* 4 full-time (1 woman), 2 part-time/adjunct (0 women). *Students:* 22 part-time (4 women). Average age 38. In 2009, 8 master's awarded. *Degree requirements:* For master's, thesis optional, qualifying exam. *Entrance requirements:* For master's, minimum GPA of 3.0. *Application deadline:* For fall admission, 4/15 for domestic students; for spring admission, 11/15 for domestic students. Application fee: $50. *Expenses:* Tuition: Part-time $1700 per course. One-time fee: $75 full-time. *Financial support:* In 2009–10, 3 students received support; fellowships, tuition waivers (full) available. Support available to part-time students. Financial award application deadline: 4/1. *Unit head:* Dr. William Butos, Graduate Director, 860-297-2448. *Application contact:* Nicola Dawkins, Program Manager for Graduate Studies, 860-297-2151, Fax: 860-297-5179, E-mail: nicola.dawkins@trincoll.edu.

Tufts University, Graduate School of Arts and Sciences, Department of Economics, Medford, MA 02155. Offers MS. Part-time programs available. *Faculty:* 20 full-time, 15 part-time/adjunct. *Students:* 24 full-time (12 women); includes 3 minority (2 Asian Americans or Pacific Islanders, 1 Hispanic American), 13 international. Average age 27. 152 applicants, 39% accepted, 12 enrolled. In 2009, 10 master's awarded. *Degree requirements:* For master's, thesis optional. *Entrance requirements:* For master's, GRE General Test. Additional exam requirements/recommendations for international students: Required—TOEFL (minimum score 550 paper-based; 213 computer-based; 80 iBT). *Application deadline:* For fall admission, 2/15 for domestic students, 12/15 for international students. Applications are processed on a rolling basis. Application fee: $75. Electronic applications accepted. *Expenses:* Tuition: Full-time $38,096; part-time $3962 per credit. Required fees: $686; $40 per year. Tuition and fees vary according to course level, course load, degree level, program and student level. *Financial support:* Teaching assistantships with full and partial tuition reimbursements, Federal Work-Study, scholarships/grants, tuition waivers (partial), and unspecified assistantships available. Financial award application deadline: 2/15; financial award applicants required to submit FAFSA. *Unit head:* Enrico Spolaore, Chair, 617-627-3560, Fax: 617-627-3917. *Application contact:* Marcelo Bianconi, Graduate Advisor, 617-627-3560.

Tulane University, School of Liberal Arts, Department of Economics, New Orleans, LA 70118-5669. Offers MA, PhD. *Degree requirements:* For master's, thesis or alternative; for doctorate, one foreign language, thesis/dissertation. *Entrance requirements:* For master's, GRE General Test, minimum B average in undergraduate course work; for doctorate, GRE General Test. Additional exam requirements/recommendations for international students: Required—TOEFL. Electronic applications accepted. *Faculty research:* Economic development, public finance, labor economics, international and regional economics, industrial organization.

Universidad de las Américas–Puebla, Division of Graduate Studies, School of Social Sciences, Program in Economics, Puebla, Mexico. Offers economics (MA); finance (M Adm). Part-time and evening/weekend programs available. *Degree requirements:* For master's, one foreign language, thesis. *Faculty research:* Economic models (mathematics), industrial organization, assets and values market.

Economics

Université de Moncton, Faculty of Arts and Social Sciences, Department of Economics, Moncton, NB E1A 3E9, Canada. Offers MA. *Degree requirements:* For master's, one foreign language, thesis. *Entrance requirements:* For master's, minimum GPA of 3.0. *Faculty research:* Free trade, public finance, small and medium size businesses, regional development, demography and development.

Université de Montréal, Faculty of Arts and Sciences, Department of Economic Sciences, Montréal, QC H3C 3J7, Canada. Offers M Sc, PhD. *Degree requirements:* For master's, one foreign language, thesis; for doctorate, one foreign language, thesis/dissertation, general exam. Electronic applications accepted. *Faculty research:* Applied and economic theory, public choice, international trade, labor economics, industrial organization.

Université de Sherbrooke, Faculty of Letters and Human Sciences, Department of Economics, Sherbrooke, QC J1K 2R1, Canada. Offers MA. *Degree requirements:* For master's, thesis. *Faculty research:* Economic development, public finance, macroeconomics.

Université du Québec à Montréal, Graduate Programs, Program in Economics, Montréal, QC H3C 3P8, Canada. Offers M Sc, PhD. Part-time programs available. *Degree requirements:* For master's, thesis; for doctorate, thesis/dissertation. *Entrance requirements:* For master's, appropriate bachelor's degree or equivalent, proficiency in French; for doctorate, appropriate master's degree or equivalent, proficiency in French.

Université Laval, Faculty of Social Sciences, Department of Economics, Programs in Economics, Québec, QC G1K 7P4, Canada. Offers MA, PhD. Terminal master's awarded for partial completion of doctoral program. *Degree requirements:* For master's, thesis (for some programs); for doctorate, comprehensive exam, thesis/dissertation. *Entrance requirements:* For master's and doctorate, knowledge of French. Electronic applications accepted.

University at Albany, State University of New York, College of Arts and Sciences, Department of Economics, Albany, NY 12222-0001. Offers economics (MA, PhD); regulatory economics (Certificate). Part-time programs available. Terminal master's awarded for partial completion of doctoral program. *Degree requirements:* For doctorate, one foreign language, thesis/dissertation. *Entrance requirements:* For doctorate, GRE General Test, GRE Subject Test. Additional exam requirements/recommendations for international students: Required—TOEFL (minimum score 550 paper-based; 213 computer-based). Electronic applications accepted. *Faculty research:* Expectations of inflation and interest rates, diffusion of new technology, labor markets in developing countries, government deficits and international exchange markets.

University at Buffalo, the State University of New York, Graduate School, College of Arts and Sciences, Department of Economics, Buffalo, NY 14260. Offers economics (MA, MS, PhD); financial economics (Certificate); health services (Certificate); information and Internet economics (Certificate); international economics (Certificate); law and regulation (Certificate); urban and regional economics (Certificate). Part-time programs available. *Faculty:* 22 full-time (4 women), 2 part-time/adjunct (0 women). *Students:* 243 full-time (98 women); includes 19 minority (5 African Americans, 13 Asian Americans or Pacific Islanders, 1 Hispanic American), 183 international. Average age 25. 538 applicants, 44% accepted, 93 enrolled. In 2009, 83 master's, 6 doctorates, 5 other advanced degrees awarded. Terminal master's awarded for partial completion of doctoral program. *Degree requirements:* For master's, comprehensive exam; for doctorate, thesis/dissertation, field and theory exams. *Entrance requirements:* For master's and doctorate, GRE General Test. Additional exam requirements/recommendations for international students: Required—TOEFL (minimum score 550 paper-based; 213 computer-based; 79 iBT). *Application deadline:* For fall admission, 1/15 priority date for domestic and international students; for spring admission, 11/1 priority date for domestic and international students. Applications are processed on a rolling basis. Application fee: $50. Electronic applications accepted. *Financial support:* In 2009–10, 26 students received support, including 13 fellowships with full tuition reimbursements available (averaging $2,115 per year), 1 research assistantship with full tuition reimbursement available (averaging $13,220 per year), 12 teaching assistantships with full tuition reimbursements available (averaging $13,220 per year); Federal Work-Study, health care benefits, and unspecified assistantships also available. Financial award application deadline: 2/15; financial award applicants required to submit FAFSA. *Faculty research:* International economics, econometrics, applied economics, urban economics, economic growth and development. *Unit head:* Dr. Isaac Ehrlich, Chair, 716-645-8670, Fax: 716-645-2127, E-mail: mgtehrl@buffalo.edu. *Application contact:* Dr. Nagesh Revankar, Director of Graduate Studies, 716-645-2121 Ext. 428, Fax: 716-645-2127, E-mail: ecorevan@buffalo.edu.

The University of Akron, Graduate School, Buchtel College of Arts and Sciences, Department of Economics, Akron, OH 44325. Offers economics (MA). Part-time programs available. *Faculty:* 7 full-time (1 woman), 2 part-time/adjunct (1 woman). *Students:* 14 full-time (3 women), 1 (woman) part-time; includes 1 minority (African American), 5 international. Average age 25. 15 applicants, 73% accepted, 3 enrolled. In 2009, 3 master's awarded. *Degree requirements:* For master's, thesis optional. *Entrance requirements:* For master's, minimum GPA of 2.75, two letters of recommendation (preferably from academics). Additional exam requirements/recommendations for international students: Required—TOEFL (minimum score 550 paper-based; 213 computer-based; 79 iBT). *Application deadline:* Applications are processed on a rolling basis. Application fee: $30 ($40 for international students). Electronic applications accepted. *Expenses:* Tuition, state resident: full-time $6570; part-time $365 per credit hour. Tuition, nonresident: full-time $11,250; part-time $625 per credit hour. *Financial support:* In 2009–10, 14 teaching assistantships with full tuition reimbursements were awarded; institutionally sponsored loans also available. *Faculty research:* Regional economic performance, effects of addiction on labor market outcomes, programmatic assessment, regional trading arrangements, agriculture production in early twentieth century South. Total annual research expenditures: $97,583. *Unit head:* Dr. Michael Nelson, Chair, 330-972-7939, E-mail: nelson2@uakron.edu. *Application contact:* Dr. Sucharita Ghosh, Director of Graduate Studies, 330-972-7549, E-mail: sghosh@uakron.edu.

The University of Alabama, Graduate School, Manderson Graduate School of Business, Economics, Finance and Legal Studies Department, Tuscaloosa, AL 35487. Offers economics (MA, PhD); finance (MS, PhD). *Faculty:* 25 full-time (1 woman). *Students:* 75 full-time (20 women); includes 8 minority (5 African Americans, 3 Asian Americans or Pacific Islanders), 12 international. Average age 26. 224 applicants, 20% accepted, 34 enrolled. In 2009, 24 master's, 2 doctorates awarded. Terminal master's awarded for partial completion of doctoral program. *Median time to degree:* Of those who began their doctoral program in fall 2001, 99% received their degree in 8 years or less. *Degree requirements:* For master's, comprehensive exam (MA), thesis (MS); for doctorate, comprehensive exam, thesis/dissertation. *Entrance requirements:* For master's, GMAT, GRE; for doctorate, GRE or GMAT. Additional exam requirements/recommendations for international students: Required—TOEFL (minimum score 550 paper-based; 213 computer-based). *Application deadline:* For fall admission, 7/1 priority date for domestic students, 1/15 for international students; for spring admission, 11/1 priority date for domestic students, 6/1 for international students. Applications are processed on a rolling basis. Application fee: $50 ($60 for international students). Electronic applications accepted. *Expenses:* Tuition, state resident: full-time $7000. Tuition, nonresident: full-time $19,200. *Financial support:* In 2009–10, 10 fellowships (averaging $10,000 per year), 21 research assistantships with full and partial tuition reimbursements (averaging $12,000 per year), 15 teaching assistantships with full and partial tuition reimbursements (averaging $12,000 per year) were awarded; Federal Work-Study, institutionally sponsored loans, and unspecified assistantships also available. *Faculty research:* Taxation, futures market, monetary theory and policy, income distribution. *Unit head:* Prof. Billy P. Helms, Head, 205-348-8067, E-mail: bhelms@cba.ua.edu. *Application contact:* Debra F. Wheatley, 205-348-6683, Fax: 205-348-0590, E-mail: dwheatle@cba.ua.edu.

University of Alaska Fairbanks, School of Management, Department of Economics, Fairbanks, AK 99775-6080. Offers resource and applied economics (MS). Part-time programs available. *Faculty:* 7 full-time (1 woman), 1 part-time/adjunct (0 women). *Students:* 7 full-time (2 women), 9 part-time (1 woman); includes 3 minority (1 African American, 1 Asian American or Pacific Islander, 1 Hispanic American), 2 international. Average age 27. 16 applicants, 69% accepted, 8 enrolled. In 2009, 6 master's awarded. *Degree requirements:* For master's, comprehensive exam, thesis or alternative. *Entrance requirements:* Additional exam requirements/recommendations for international students: Required—TOEFL (minimum score 550 paper-based; 213 computer-based). *Application deadline:* For fall admission, 6/1 priority date for domestic students, 3/1 for international students; for spring admission, 10/15 priority date for domestic students, 9/1 for international students. Applications are processed on a rolling basis. Application fee: $60. Electronic applications accepted. *Expenses:* Tuition, state resident: full-time $7584; part-time $316 per credit. Tuition, nonresident: full-time $15,504; part-time $646 per credit. Required fees: $23 per credit. $135 per semester. Tuition and fees vary according to course level, course load and reciprocity agreements. *Financial support:* In 2009–10, 6 teaching assistantships (averaging $12,910 per year) were awarded; fellowships, research assistantships, career-related internships or fieldwork, Federal Work-Study, scholarships/grants, health care benefits, and unspecified assistantships also available. Support available to part-time students. Financial award application deadline: 2/15; financial award applicants required to submit FAFSA. *Faculty research:* Statistics; resource and agriculture economics; oil, gas, and energy; sustainability; public land management. *Unit head:* Gregory Goering, Economics Program Director, 907-474-5572, Fax: 907-474-5219, E-mail: gegoering@alaska.edu. *Application contact:* Gregory Goering, Economics Program Director, 907-474-5572, Fax: 907-474-5219, E-mail: gegoering@alaska.edu.

University of Alberta, Faculty of Graduate Studies and Research, Department of Economics, Edmonton, AB T6G 2E1, Canada. Offers economics (MA, PhD); economics and finance (MA); environmental and natural resource economics (PhD). Part-time programs available. *Faculty:* 25 full-time (5 women), 3 part-time/adjunct (0 women). *Students:* 33 full-time (7 women), 7 part-time (3 women). Average age 26. 112 applicants, 58% accepted, 22 enrolled. In 2009, 8 master's, 1 doctorate awarded. *Degree requirements:* For doctorate, thesis/dissertation. *Entrance requirements:* For master's and doctorate, GRE. Additional exam requirements/recommendations for international students: Required—TOEFL. *Application deadline:* For fall admission, 6/15 for domestic students. Applications are processed on a rolling basis. Tuition and fees charges are reported in Canadian dollars. *Expenses:* Tuition, area resident: Full-time $4626.24 Canadian dollars; part-time $99.72 Canadian dollars per unit. International tuition: $8216 Canadian dollars full-time. Required fees: $3589.92 Canadian dollars; $99.72 Canadian dollars per unit. $215 Canadian dollars per term. *Financial support:* In 2009–10, 19 students received support, including 6 research assistantships with partial tuition reimbursements available (averaging $14,300 per year), 5 teaching assistantships with partial tuition reimbursements available (averaging $11,200 per year); career-related internships or fieldwork and scholarships/grants also available. Financial award application deadline: 3/1. *Faculty research:* Public finance, international trade, industrial organization, Pacific Rim economics, monetary economics. *Unit head:* Henry van Egteren, Graduate Coordinator, 780-492-7634, Fax: 780-492-3300. *Application contact:* Audrey Jackson, Graduate Program Administrator, 780-492-7634, Fax: 780-492-3300, E-mail: econapps@ualberta.ca.

The University of Arizona, Graduate College, Eller College of Management, Department of Economics, Tucson, AZ 85721. Offers MA, PhD, JD/MA, JD/PhD. *Faculty:* 18. *Students:* 43 full-time (15 women), 13 part-time (5 women); includes 4 minority (1 African American, 2 Asian Americans or Pacific Islanders, 1 Hispanic American), 24 international. Average age 28. 237 applicants, 16% accepted, 21 enrolled. In 2009, 10 master's, 5 doctorates awarded. Terminal master's awarded for partial completion of doctoral program. *Degree requirements:* For master's, comprehensive exam; for doctorate, thesis/dissertation. *Entrance requirements:* For doctorate, GRE General Test, 3 letters of recommendation. Additional exam requirements/recommendations for international students: Required—TOEFL (minimum score 550 paper-based; 213 computer-based; 79 iBT). *Application deadline:* For fall admission, 2/1 for domestic and international students. Applications are processed on a rolling basis. Application fee: $75. Electronic applications accepted. *Expenses:* Tuition, state resident: full-time $9028. Tuition, nonresident: full-time $24,890. *Financial support:* In 2009–10, 3 research assistantships with full tuition reimbursements (averaging $15,176 per year), 33 teaching assistantships with full tuition reimbursements (averaging $14,705 per year) were awarded; Federal Work-Study, scholarships/grants, health care benefits, tuition waivers (partial), and unspecified assistantships also available. Financial award application deadline: 2/1. *Faculty research:* Applied microeconomics, experimental economics, economic history, microeconomic theory, property rights, industrial organization. Total annual research expenditures: $260,644. *Unit head:* Dr. Mark Walker, Head, 520-621-2821, Fax: 520-621-8450, E-mail: mwalker@eller.arizona.edu. *Application contact:* Lana Sooter, Information Contact, 520-621-2821, Fax: 520-621-8450, E-mail: lsooter@email.arizona.edu.

University of Arkansas, Graduate School, Sam M. Walton College of Business Administration, Department of Economics, Fayetteville, AR 72701-1201. Offers MA, PhD. *Students:* 13 full-time (2 women), 2 part-time (0 women), 5 international. In 2009, 4 master's awarded. *Degree requirements:* For doctorate, variable foreign language requirement, thesis/dissertation. *Entrance requirements:* For master's and doctorate, GRE General Test. Application fee: $40 ($50 for international students). *Expenses:* Tuition, state resident: full-time $7355; part-time $356.58 per hour. Tuition, nonresident: full-time $17,401; part-time $775.17 per hour. Required fees: $1203. *Financial support:* In 2009–10, 4 fellowships with tuition reimbursements, 9 research assistantships, 3 teaching assistantships were awarded; career-related internships or fieldwork and Federal Work-Study also available. Support available to part-time students. Financial award application deadline: 4/1; financial award applicants required to submit FAFSA. *Unit head:* Dr. Gary Ferrier, Chair, 479-575-3266, E-mail: gferrier@uark.edu. *Application contact:* Dr. Cary Deck, Graduate Coordinator, 479-575-6226, E-mail: cdeck@uark.edu.

The University of British Columbia, Faculty of Arts and Faculty of Graduate Studies, Department of Economics, Vancouver, BC V6T 1Z1, Canada. Offers MA, PhD. *Degree requirements:* For master's, thesis (for some programs); for doctorate, comprehensive exam, thesis/dissertation. *Entrance requirements:* For master's and doctorate, GRE General Test. Additional exam requirements/recommendations for international students: Required—TOEFL (minimum score 550 paper-based; 213 computer-based; 80 iBT). Electronic applications accepted. *Faculty research:* Economic theory, international economics, labor economics, public finance, economic development.

University of Calgary, Faculty of Graduate Studies, Faculty of Social Sciences, Department of Economics, Calgary, AB T2N 1N4, Canada. Offers M Ec, MA, PhD. Part-time and evening/weekend programs available. *Degree requirements:* For master's, thesis (for some programs); for doctorate, thesis/dissertation, candidacy exam. *Entrance requirements:* Additional exam requirements/recommendations for international students: Required—TOEFL. *Faculty research:* Energy economics, public finance/public choice, resource economics, international trade, monetary economics.

University of California, Berkeley, Graduate Division, College of Letters and Science, Department of Economics, Berkeley, CA 94720-1500. Offers PhD, JD/MA. *Students:* 144 full-time (42 women). Average age 29. 761 applicants, 21 enrolled. In 2009, 31 doctorates awarded. *Degree requirements:* For doctorate, thesis/dissertation, field exams, oral qualifying exam. *Entrance requirements:* For doctorate, GRE General Test, minimum GPA of 3.0, 3 letters of recommendation. Additional exam requirements/recommendations for international students: Required—TOEFL. *Application deadline:* For fall admission, 12/12 for domestic students. Application fee: $70 ($90 for international students). *Financial support:* Fellowships, research assistantships, teaching assistantships, unspecified assistantships available. *Unit head:* Prof. Gerard Roland, Chair, 510-642-3581, E-mail: ch_economics@ls.berkeley.edu. *Application contact:* Patrick G. Allen, Graduate Advisor, 510-642-0824, Fax: 510-642-6615, E-mail: gradofc@econ.berkeley.edu.

University of California, Davis, Graduate Studies, Program in Economics, Davis, CA 95616. Offers MA, PhD. Terminal master's awarded for partial completion of doctoral program. *Degree requirements:* For master's, comprehensive exam (for some programs), thesis (for some programs); for doctorate, thesis/dissertation. *Entrance requirements:* For master's, GRE General Test, minimum GPA of 3.0; for doctorate, GRE General Test, minimum GPA of 3.25. Additional exam requirements/recommendations for international students: Required—TOEFL (minimum score 550 paper-based; 213 computer-based). Electronic applications accepted. *Faculty research:* Applied microeconomics, macroeconomics, international studies, economic theory, economic history.

University of California, Irvine, Office of Graduate Studies, School of Social Sciences, Department of Economics, Irvine, CA 92697. Offers economics (MA, PhD); public choice (MA, PhD); transportation economics (MA, PhD). *Students:* 69 full-time (25 women); includes 14 Asian Americans or Pacific Islanders, 4 Hispanic Americans, 23 international. Average age 28. 218 applicants, 25% accepted, 20 enrolled. In 2009, 13 master's, 12 doctorates awarded. *Degree requirements:* For doctorate, thesis/dissertation. *Entrance requirements:* For master's and doctorate, GRE General Test, minimum GPA of 3.0. Additional exam requirements/recommendations for international students: Required—TOEFL (minimum score 550 paper-based; 213 computer-based). *Application deadline:* For fall admission, 1/15 priority date for domestic and international students. Applications are processed on a rolling basis. Application fee: $70 ($90 for international students). Electronic applications accepted. *Financial support:* Fellowships, research assistantships with full tuition reimbursements, teaching assistantships, institutionally sponsored loans, traineeships, health care benefits, and unspecified assistantships available. Financial award application deadline: 3/1; financial award applicants required to submit FAFSA. *Faculty research:* Econometrics, urban economics, applied microeconomics. *Unit head:* Michelle Garfinkel, Chair, 949-824-3190, E-mail: mrgarfin@uci.edu. *Application contact:* Diane Enriquez, Graduate Counselor, 949-824-5924, Fax: 949-824-3548, E-mail: dmvargas@uci.edu.

University of California, Los Angeles, Graduate Division, College of Letters and Science, Department of Economics, Los Angeles, CA 90034. Offers MA, PhD. *Students:* 107 full-time (28 women); includes 9 minority (1 African American, 6 Asian Americans or Pacific Islanders, 2 Hispanic Americans), 64 international. Average age 28. 372 applicants, 26% accepted, 19 enrolled. In 2009, 29 master's, 19 doctorates awarded. Terminal master's awarded for partial completion of doctoral program. *Degree requirements:* For master's, comprehensive exam; for doctorate, thesis/dissertation, oral and written qualifying exams. *Entrance requirements:* For master's, GRE General Test; for doctorate, GRE General Test, minimum undergraduate GPA of 3.0. *Application deadline:* For fall admission, 12/1 for domestic and international students. Application fee: $70 ($90 for international students). Electronic applications accepted. *Financial support:* In 2009–10, 78 fellowships with full and partial tuition reimbursements, 32 research assistantships with full and partial tuition reimbursements, 69 teaching assistantships with full and partial tuition reimbursements were awarded; Federal Work-Study, institutionally sponsored loans, scholarships/grants, health care benefits, tuition waivers (full and partial), and unspecified assistantships also available. Financial award application deadline: 3/1; financial award applicants required to submit FAFSA. *Unit head:* Dr. Roger Farmer, Chair, 310-825-1011. *Application contact:* Department Office, 310-206-1413, E-mail: bgarcia@econ.ucla.edu.

University of California, Riverside, Graduate Division, Department of Economics, Riverside, CA 92521-0102. Offers MA, PhD. *Faculty:* 22 full-time (5 women). *Students:* 59 full-time (25 women); includes 9 minority (2 African Americans, 5 Asian Americans or Pacific Islanders, 2 Hispanic Americans), 42 international. Average age 28. 164 applicants, 24% accepted, 17 enrolled. In 2009, 2 master's, 4 doctorates awarded. Terminal master's awarded for partial completion of doctoral program. *Degree requirements:* For master's, comprehensive exam; for doctorate, thesis/dissertation, qualifying exams. *Entrance requirements:* For master's and doctorate, GRE General Test, minimum GPA of 3.2. Additional exam requirements/recommendations for international students: Required—TOEFL (minimum score 550 paper-based; 213 computer-based; 80 iBT). *Application deadline:* For fall admission, 5/1 for domestic students, 2/1 for international students. Applications are processed on a rolling basis. Application fee: $85 ($100 for international students). Electronic applications accepted. *Financial support:* In 2009–10, fellowships with partial tuition reimbursements (averaging $12,000 per year), teaching assistantships with partial tuition reimbursements (averaging $16,500 per year) were awarded; research assistantships, career-related internships or fieldwork, institutionally sponsored loans, and tuition waivers (full and partial) also available. Financial award application deadline: 1/15; financial award applicants required to submit FAFSA. *Faculty research:* Advanced political economy; resource and environmental economics; advanced econometrics; labor economics; advanced microeconomics theory; advanced macroeconomics theory; development economics; economic history; international trade theory; money, credit and business cycles; public economics. *Unit head:* Dr. Aman Ullah, Chair, 951-827-1474, Fax: 951-827-5685, E-mail: econgrad@.ucr.edu. *Application contact:* Amanda Labagnara, Graduate Program Assistant, 951-827-1474, Fax: 951-827-5685, E-mail: econgrad@ucr.edu.

See Display below.

University of California, San Diego, Office of Graduate Studies, Department of Economics, La Jolla, CA 92093. Offers economics (PhD); economics and international affairs (PhD). *Degree requirements:* For doctorate, thesis/dissertation. *Entrance requirements:* For doctorate, GRE General Test. Electronic applications accepted. *Faculty research:* Microfoundations of macroeconomics, econometric model specification and testing, industrial organization.

University of California, San Diego, Office of Graduate Studies, Graduate School of International Relations and Pacific Studies, La Jolla, CA 92093. Offers economics and international affairs (PhD); Pacific international affairs (MPIA); political science and international affairs (PhD). *Degree requirements:* For master's, one foreign language; for doctorate, thesis/dissertation. *Entrance requirements:* For master's, GMAT or GRE General Test; for doctorate, GRE General Test. Additional exam requirements/recommendations for international students: Required—TOEFL (minimum score 550 paper-based; 213 computer-based). Electronic applications accepted. *Faculty research:* Pacific Rim as system and placement in global relations; studies in international economics, management and finance; analysis of patterns of policymaking in countries of the Pacific.

University of California, Santa Barbara, Graduate Division, College of Letters and Sciences, Division of Social Sciences, Department of Economics, Santa Barbara, CA 93106-9210. Offers business economics (MA); economics (PhD); MA/PhD. *Faculty:* 30 full-time (4 women), 14 part-time/adjunct (4 women). *Students:* 77 full-time (28 women). Average age 26. 276 applicants, 46% accepted, 34 enrolled. In 2009, 34 master's, 10 doctorates awarded. Terminal master's awarded for partial completion of doctoral program. *Degree requirements:* For master's, comprehensive exam, thesis; for doctorate, comprehensive exam, thesis/dissertation. *Entrance requirements:* For master's, GRE General Test, 3 letters of recommendation, resume/curriculum vitae; for doctorate, GRE General Test, 3 letters of recommendation, statement of purpose, personal achievements/contributions statement, resume/curriculum vitae, transcripts for post-secondary institutions attended. Additional exam requirements/recommendations for international students: Required—TOEFL (minimum score 550 paper-based; 213 computer-based; 80 iBT), or IELTS (minimum score 7). *Application deadline:* For fall admission, 12/1 priority date for domestic and international students. Application fee: $70 ($90 for international students). Electronic applications accepted. *Financial support:* In 2009–10, 30 students received support, including 29 fellowships with full and partial tuition reimbursements available (averaging $11,300 per year), 7 research assistantships with full and partial tuition reimbursements available (averaging $6,500 per year), 50 teaching assistantships with partial tuition reimbursements available (averaging $9,900 per year); Federal Work-Study, institutionally sponsored

Economics

University of California, Santa Barbara (continued)
loans, scholarships/grants, health care benefits, tuition waivers (full and partial), and unspecified assistantships also available. Support available to part-time students. Financial award application deadline: 12/1; financial award applicants required to submit FAFSA. *Faculty research:* Labor economics, econometrics, macroeconomic theory and policy, environmental and natural resources economics (EES), experimental and behavioral economics. *Unit head:* Prof. Perry Shapiro, Chair, Fax: 805-893-8830, E-mail: pxshap@econ.ucsb.edu. *Application contact:* Mark Patterson, Staff Graduate Advisor, 805-893-2205, Fax: 805-893-8830, E-mail: mark@econ.ucsb.edu.

University of California, Santa Barbara, Graduate Division, Donald Bren School of Environmental Science and Management, Santa Barbara, CA 93106-5131. Offers MESM, PhD. *Faculty:* 18 full-time (4 women), 24 part-time/adjunct (7 women). *Students:* 187 full-time (112 women); includes 21 minority (1 African American, 1 American Indian/Alaska Native, 11 Asian Americans or Pacific Islanders, 8 Hispanic Americans), 15 international. Average age 27. 335 applicants, 61% accepted, 89 enrolled. In 2009, 63 master's, 8 doctorates awarded. *Degree requirements:* For master's, thesis optional, group project as student thesis; for doctorate, comprehensive exam, thesis/dissertation. *Entrance requirements:* For master's, GRE, 3 letters of recommendation, resume/curriculum vitae; for doctorate, GRE, 3 letters of recommendation, statement of purpose, personal achievements/contributions statement, resume/curriculum vitae, transcripts for post-secondary institutions attended. Additional exam requirements/recommendations for international students: Required—TOEFL (minimum score 550 paper-based; 213 computer-based; 80 iBT), or IELTS (minimum score 7). *Application deadline:* For fall admission, 1/10 priority date for domestic and international students. Application fee: $70 ($90 for international students). Electronic applications accepted. *Financial support:* In 2009–10, 68 students received support, including 44 fellowships with full and partial tuition reimbursements available (averaging $8,400 per year), 20 research assistantships with full and partial tuition reimbursements available (averaging $6,600 per year), 28 teaching assistantships with partial tuition reimbursements available (averaging $6,900 per year); career-related internships or fieldwork, Federal Work-Study, institutionally sponsored loans, scholarships/grants, health care benefits, and unspecified assistantships also available. Financial award application deadline: 12/15; financial award applicants required to submit FAFSA. *Faculty research:* Ecological processes, environmental politics and policy, sustainability, conservation science and planning, water resources management. *Unit head:* Dr. John Melack, Acting Dean, 805-893-3879, Fax: 805-893-6113, E-mail: melack@bren.ucsb.edu. *Application contact:* Kristen Robinson, Graduate Program Advisor, 805-893-7611, Fax: 805-893-6113, E-mail: gradasst@bren.ucsb.edu.

University of California, Santa Cruz, Division of Graduate Studies, Division of Social Sciences, Program in International Economics, Santa Cruz, CA 95064. Offers PhD. *Degree requirements:* For doctorate, thesis/dissertation, 4 field exams, econometrics project. *Entrance requirements:* For doctorate, GRE General Test. *Faculty research:* Current and emerging issues in taxation, industrial policy, environmental regulation, market structure.

University of Central Arkansas, Graduate School, College of Business Administration, Program in Community and Economic Development, Conway, AR 72035-0001. Offers MS. *Students:* 14 full-time (4 women), 12 part-time (7 women); includes 4 minority (3 African Americans, 1 Hispanic American), 8 international. Average age 31. 17 applicants, 94% accepted, 16 enrolled. In 2009, 6 master's awarded. *Degree requirements:* For master's, comprehensive exam, thesis. *Entrance requirements:* For master's, GRE General Test, minimum GPA of 2.7. Additional exam requirements/recommendations for international students: Required—TOEFL (minimum score 550 paper-based; 213 computer-based). *Application deadline:* For fall admission, 3/1 priority date for domestic students; for spring admission, 10/1 priority date for domestic students. Applications are processed on a rolling basis. Application fee: $25 ($40 for international students). *Expenses:* Contact institution. *Financial support:* Career-related internships or fieldwork, Federal Work-Study, and unspecified assistantships available. Financial award applicants required to submit FAFSA. *Unit head:* Dr. Lauren Maxwell, Coordinator, 501-450-5349. *Application contact:* Brenda Herring, Admissions Assistant, 501-450-5065, Fax: 501-450-5678, E-mail: bherring@uca.edu.

University of Central Florida, College of Business Administration, Department of Economics, Orlando, FL 32816. Offers MS, PhD. Part-time and evening/weekend programs available. *Faculty:* 21 full-time (4 women), 2 part-time/adjunct (0 women). *Students:* 15 full-time (7 women), 9 part-time (4 women); includes 3 minority (all Asian Americans or Pacific Islanders), 11 international. In 2009, 5 master's awarded. *Degree requirements:* For master's, comprehensive exam, thesis or alternative. *Entrance requirements:* For master's, GMAT, minimum GPA of 3.0 in last 60 hours. Additional exam requirements/recommendations for international students: Required—TOEFL. *Application deadline:* For fall admission, 6/15 priority date for domestic students; for spring admission, 11/1 priority date for domestic students. Application fee: $30. Electronic applications accepted. *Expenses:* Tuition, state resident: part-time $306.31 per credit hour. Tuition, nonresident: part-time $1099.01 per credit hour. Part-time tuition and fees vary according to degree level and program. *Financial support:* In 2009–10, 2 fellowships with partial tuition reimbursements (averaging $17,000 per year), 8 research assistantships with partial tuition reimbursements (averaging $4,600 per year), 11 teaching assistantships with partial tuition reimbursements (averaging $5,600 per year) were awarded; career-related internships or fieldwork, Federal Work-Study, institutionally sponsored loans, tuition waivers (partial), and unspecified assistantships also available. Financial award application deadline: 3/1; financial award applicants required to submit FAFSA. *Unit head:* Dr. J. Wally Milon, Chair, 407-823-4429, E-mail: wally.milon@bus.ucf.edu. *Application contact:* Dr. J. Wally Milon, Chair, 407-823-4429, E-mail: wally.milon@bus.ucf.edu.

University of Chicago, Division of Social Sciences, Department of Economics, Chicago, IL 60637-1513. Offers PhD. *Students:* 173. In 2009, 17 doctorates awarded. *Degree requirements:* For doctorate, one foreign language, thesis/dissertation, written exams in 2 fields. *Entrance requirements:* For doctorate, GRE General Test. Additional exam requirements/recommendations for international students: Required—TOEFL, IELTS (minimum score 7). *Application deadline:* For fall admission, 12/28 for domestic and international students. Application fee: $100. Electronic applications accepted. *Financial support:* Fellowships, research assistantships, teaching assistantships, Federal Work-Study, institutionally sponsored loans, scholarships/grants, traineeships, health care benefits, and unspecified assistantships available. Financial award application deadline: 12/28; financial award applicants required to submit FAFSA. *Unit head:* Prof. Harald Uhlig, Chair, 773-702-9106. *Application contact:* Office of the Dean of Students, 773-702-8415, E-mail: admissions@ssd.uchicago.edu.

University of Cincinnati, Graduate School, McMicken College of Arts and Sciences, Department of Economics, Program in Applied Economics, Cincinnati, OH 45221. Offers MA. Part-time and evening/weekend programs available. *Degree requirements:* For master's, thesis optional. *Entrance requirements:* For master's, GRE General Test or GMAT, intermediate micro, macro theory, statistics, calculus. Additional exam requirements/recommendations for international students: Required—TOEFL. Electronic applications accepted. *Faculty research:* Econometrics, labor markets, pollution markets, transportation.

University of Colorado at Boulder, Graduate School, College of Arts and Sciences, Department of Economics, Boulder, CO 80309. Offers MA, PhD. *Faculty:* 30 full-time (7 women). *Students:* 70 full-time (28 women), 20 part-time (7 women); includes 5 minority (1 American Indian/Alaska Native, 3 Asian Americans or Pacific Islanders, 1 Hispanic American), 48 international. Average age 29. 157 applicants, 28% accepted, 24 enrolled. In 2009, 13 master's, 9 doctorates awarded. Terminal master's awarded for partial completion of doctoral program. *Degree requirements:* For master's, comprehensive exam, thesis or alternative; for doctorate, comprehensive exam, thesis/dissertation, preliminary exam. *Entrance requirements:* For master's, GRE General Test, minimum undergraduate GPA of 2.75; for doctorate, GRE General Test. Additional exam requirements/recommendations for international students: Required—TOEFL. *Application deadline:* For fall admission, 2/1 priority date for domestic students, 12/1 for international students. Applications are processed on a rolling basis. Application fee: $50 ($60 for international students). *Financial support:* In 2009–10, 17 fellowships with full tuition reimbursements (averaging $5,083 per year), 29 research assistantships with full tuition reimbursements (averaging $12,252 per year) were awarded; tuition waivers (full) also available. Financial award application deadline: 2/1; financial award applicants required to submit FAFSA. *Faculty research:* International, econometrics, public economics and natural resources and environmental economics, urban and regional economics, development economics, labor economics and demography, economic history. Total annual research expenditures: $373,584.

University of Colorado Denver, College of Liberal Arts and Sciences, Department of Economics, Denver, CO 80217-3364. Offers MA. Part-time and evening/weekend programs available. *Students:* 25 full-time (6 women), 27 part-time (10 women); includes 10 minority (6 Asian Americans or Pacific Islanders, 4 Hispanic Americans), 11 international. 57 applicants, 44% accepted, 20 enrolled. In 2009, 10 master's awarded. *Degree requirements:* For master's, thesis or alternative. *Entrance requirements:* For master's, GRE General Test, 15 hours of course work in economics, minimum GPA of 2.5. Additional exam requirements/recommendations for international students: Required—TOEFL (minimum score 525 paper-based; 197 computer-based). *Application deadline:* For fall admission, 6/1 for domestic students; for spring admission, 11/1 for domestic students. Applications are processed on a rolling basis. Application fee: $50 ($75 for international students). Electronic applications accepted. *Financial support:* Research assistantships, teaching assistantships, Federal Work-Study available. Financial award application deadline: 4/1; financial award applicants required to submit FAFSA. Total annual research expenditures: $85,986. *Unit head:* Dr. Laura Argys, Chair, 303-556-3949, Fax: 303-556-3547, E-mail: laura.argys@ucdenver.edu. *Application contact:* Christine Lukvec, Program Assistant, 303-315-2030, Fax: 303-315-2048, E-mail: christine.lukvec@ucdenver.edu.

University of Connecticut, Graduate School, College of Liberal Arts and Sciences, Department of Economics, Storrs, CT 06269-1063. Offers MA, PhD. *Faculty:* 32 full-time (4 women). *Students:* 66 full-time (26 women), 19 part-time (11 women); includes 7 minority (3 African Americans, 3 Asian Americans or Pacific Islanders, 1 Hispanic American), 52 international. Average age 29. 187 applicants, 17% accepted, 13 enrolled. In 2009, 12 master's, 6 doctorates awarded. Terminal master's awarded for partial completion of doctoral program. *Degree requirements:* For master's, comprehensive exam; for doctorate, thesis/dissertation. *Entrance requirements:* For master's and doctorate, GRE General Test, GRE Subject Test. Additional exam requirements/recommendations for international students: Required—TOEFL (minimum score 550 paper-based; 213 computer-based). *Application deadline:* For fall admission, 2/1 priority date for domestic and international students; for spring admission, 11/1 for domestic students, 10/1 for international students. Applications are processed on a rolling basis. Application fee: $55. Electronic applications accepted. *Expenses:* Tuition, state resident: full-time $4725; part-time $525 per credit. Tuition, nonresident: full-time $12,267; part-time $1363 per credit. Required fees: $346 per semester. Tuition and fees vary according to course load. *Financial support:* In 2009–10, 7 research assistantships with full tuition reimbursements, 39 teaching assistantships with full tuition reimbursements were awarded; fellowships, Federal Work-Study, scholarships/grants, health care benefits, and unspecified assistantships also available. Financial award application deadline: 2/1; financial award applicants required to submit FAFSA. *Unit head:* Prof. Dennis Heffley, Head, 860-486-4567, Fax: 860-486-4463. *Application contact:* Rosanne Fitzgerald, Graduate Program Coordinator, 860-486-4633, Fax: 860-486-4463, E-mail: rosanne.fitzgerald@uconn.edu.

University of Delaware, Alfred Lerner College of Business and Economics, Department of Economics, Newark, DE 19716. Offers economics (MA, MS, PhD); economics for entrepreneurship and educators (MA); MA/MBA. Part-time programs available. *Degree requirements:* For master's, comprehensive exam, thesis (for some programs), mathematics review exam, research project; for doctorate, comprehensive exam, thesis/dissertation, field exam. *Entrance requirements:* For master's, GMAT or GRE General Test, minimum GPA of 2.5; for doctorate, GRE General Test, minimum GPA of 3.5 in graduate economics course work. Additional exam requirements/recommendations for international students: Required—TOEFL (minimum score 550 paper-based; 225 computer-based). Electronic applications accepted. *Faculty research:* Applied quantitative economics, industrial organization, resource economics, monetary economics, labor economics.

University of Denver, Division of Arts, Humanities and Social Sciences, Department of Economics, Denver, CO 80208. Offers MA. Part-time programs available. *Faculty:* 5 full-time (1 woman), 5 part-time/adjunct (3 women). *Students:* 14 full-time (7 women), 2 part-time (1 woman); includes 6 minority (1 American Indian/Alaska Native, 3 Asian Americans or Pacific Islanders, 2 Hispanic Americans), 3 international. Average age 25. 38 applicants, 97% accepted, 7 enrolled. In 2009, 7 master's awarded. *Degree requirements:* For master's, thesis. *Entrance requirements:* For master's, GRE. Additional exam requirements/recommendations for international students: Required—TOEFL. *Application deadline:* Applications are processed on a rolling basis. Application fee: $50. Electronic applications accepted. *Expenses:* Tuition: Full-time $34,596; part-time $961 per quarter hour. Required fees: $4 per quarter hour. Tuition and fees vary according to course load, campus/location and program. *Financial support:* In 2009–10, 4 teaching assistantships with full and partial tuition reimbursements (averaging $6,000 per year) were awarded; career-related internships or fieldwork, Federal Work-Study, and scholarships/grants also available. Support available to part-time students. Financial award application deadline: 3/1; financial award applicants required to submit FAFSA. *Unit head:* Dr. Peter Ho, Chairperson, 303-871-2685. *Application contact:* Information Contact, 303-871-2685, E-mail: econ04@denver.du.edu.

University of Florida, Graduate School, Warrington College of Business Administration, Hough Graduate School of Business, Department of Economics, Gainesville, FL 32611. Offers MA, PhD. Terminal master's awarded for partial completion of doctoral program. *Degree requirements:* For master's, thesis optional; for doctorate, thesis/dissertation. *Entrance requirements:* Additional exam requirements/recommendations for international students: Required—TOEFL (minimum score 550 paper-based; 213 computer-based). Electronic applications accepted. *Faculty research:* Econometrics, international economics, industrial organization, public finance, economic theory.

University of Georgia, Graduate School, Terry College of Business, Department of Economics, Athens, GA 30602. Offers MA, PhD. *Faculty:* 12 full-time (0 women). *Students:* 24 full-time (5 women), 9 part-time (4 women); includes 6 minority (2 Asian Americans or Pacific Islanders, 4 Hispanic Americans), 13 international. 80 applicants, 28% accepted, 5 enrolled. In 2009, 4 master's, 6 doctorates awarded. *Degree requirements:* For master's, thesis; for doctorate, thesis/dissertation. *Entrance requirements:* For master's and doctorate, GRE General Test. *Application deadline:* For fall admission, 7/1 priority date for domestic students; for spring admission, 11/15 for domestic students. Application fee: $50. Electronic applications accepted. *Expenses:* Tuition, state resident: full-time $6000; part-time $250 per credit hour. Tuition, nonresident: full-time $20,904; part-time $871 per credit hour. Required fees: $730 per semester. *Financial support:* Fellowships, research assistantships, teaching assistantships available. *Unit head:* Dr. Christopher M. Cornwell, Head, 706-542-3670, Fax: 706-542-3376, E-mail: econdh@terry.uga.edu. *Application contact:* Dr. David B. Mustard, Graduate Coordinator, 706-542-3624, Fax: 706-542-3376, E-mail: econ-gc@terry.uga.edu.

University of Guelph, Graduate Program Services, College of Management and Economics, Department of Economics, Guelph, ON N1G 2W1, Canada. Offers MA, PhD. Part-time programs available. *Degree requirements:* For master's, thesis or alternative; for doctorate, comprehensive exam, thesis/dissertation. *Entrance requirements:* For master's, minimum B+ average during previous 2 years of course work; for doctorate, minimum A- average, MA in economics. Additional exam requirements/recommendations for international students: Required—TOEFL (minimum score 550 paper-based; 213 computer-based; 89 iBT), IELTS (minimum score 6.5). Electronic applications accepted. *Faculty research:* Resource and environmental economics, econometrics, labor economics, micro and macro economics.

University of Hawaii at Manoa, Graduate Division, College of Social Sciences, Department of Economics, Honolulu, HI 96822. Offers MA, PhD. Part-time programs available. *Faculty:* 20 full-time (3 women), 13 part-time/adjunct (3 women). *Students:* 45 full-time (26 women), 7 part-time (1 woman); includes 12 minority (all Asian Americans or Pacific Islanders), 31 international. Average age 27. 70 applicants, 67% accepted, 14 enrolled. In 2009, 7 master's, 4 doctorates awarded. Terminal master's awarded for partial completion of doctoral program. *Degree requirements:* For master's, thesis optional; for doctorate, comprehensive exam, thesis/dissertation. *Entrance requirements:* For master's and doctorate, GRE General Test. Additional exam requirements/recommendations for international students: Required—TOEFL (minimum score 500 paper-based; 173 computer-based; 61 iBT), IELTS (minimum score 5). *Application deadline:* For fall admission, 1/15 for domestic and international students; for spring admission, 8/1 for domestic and international students. Application fee: $60. *Expenses:* Tuition, state resident: full-time $8900; part-time $372 per credit. Tuition, nonresident: full-time $21,400; part-time $898 per credit. Required fees: $207 per semester. *Financial support:* In 2009–10, 6 fellowships (averaging $3,822 per year), 13 research assistantships (averaging $17,386 per year), 11 teaching assistantships (averaging $14,810 per year) were awarded. *Faculty research:* Trade, development, demography, labor, resource economics. Total annual research expenditures: $35,000. *Application contact:* Theresa Greaney, Graduate Chair, 808-956-2321, Fax: 808-956-4347, E-mail: greaney@hawaii.edu.

University of Houston, College of Liberal Arts and Social Sciences, Department of Economics, Houston, TX 77204. Offers MA, PhD. *Faculty:* 13 full-time (5 women), 1 (woman) part-time/adjunct. *Students:* 48 full-time (25 women), 3 part-time (all women); includes 8 minority (1 American Indian/Alaska Native, 4 Asian Americans or Pacific Islanders, 3 Hispanic Americans), 30 international. Average age 26. 111 applicants, 39% accepted, 17 enrolled. In 2009, 40 master's, 10 doctorates awarded. Terminal master's awarded for partial completion of doctoral program. *Degree requirements:* For master's, comprehensive exam, thesis optional; for doctorate, comprehensive exam, thesis/dissertation. *Entrance requirements:* For master's, GRE General Test, minimum GPA of 3.0, 3 letters of recommendation; for doctorate, GRE General Test, minimum GPA of 3.0, statement of purpose, three letters of recommendation. Additional exam requirements/recommendations for international students: Required—TOEFL (minimum score 550 paper-based; 79 iBT), IELTS (minimum score 6.5). *Application deadline:* For fall admission, 2/1 for domestic and international students. Electronic applications accepted. *Expenses:* Tuition, state resident: full-time $7676; part-time $320 per credit hour. Tuition, nonresident: full-time $14,324; part-time $597 per credit hour. Required fees: $3034. *Financial support:* In 2009–10, 2 research assistantships with full tuition reimbursements (averaging $12,300 per year), 36 teaching assistantships with full tuition reimbursements (averaging $12,300 per year) were awarded; career-related internships or fieldwork, Federal Work-Study, institutionally sponsored loans, scholarships/grants, health care benefits, and unspecified assistantships also available. Support available to part-time students. Financial award application deadline: 2/1. *Faculty research:* Econometrics, labor economics, international economics. *Unit head:* Dr. David Papell, Chairperson, 713-743-3800, Fax: 713-743-3798, E-mail: dpapell@uh.edu. *Application contact:* Amber Pozo, Academic Advisor, 713-743-8508, E-mail: apozo@central.uh.edu.

University of Illinois at Chicago, Graduate College, College of Liberal Arts and Sciences, Department of Economics, Chicago, IL 60607-7128. Offers MA, PhD, MBA/MA. Terminal master's awarded for partial completion of doctoral program. *Degree requirements:* For master's, comprehensive exam; for doctorate, thesis/dissertation. *Entrance requirements:* For master's and doctorate, GRE General Test, minimum GPA of 2.75. Additional exam requirements/recommendations for international students: Required—TOEFL. Electronic applications accepted. *Faculty research:* International, labor, and urban economics.

University of Illinois at Urbana–Champaign, Graduate College, College of Liberal Arts and Sciences, Department of Economics, Champaign, IL 61820. Offers economics (MS, PhD); policy economics (MS). *Faculty:* 26 full-time (3 women), 1 part-time/adjunct (0 women). *Students:* 199 full-time (83 women), 11 part-time (2 women); includes 8 minority (6 Asian Americans or Pacific Islanders, 2 Hispanic Americans), 180 international. 560 applicants, 21% accepted, 103 enrolled. In 2009, 53 master's, 7 doctorates awarded. Terminal master's awarded for partial completion of doctoral program. *Entrance requirements:* For master's, minimum GPA of 3.0; for doctorate, GRE General Test, minimum GPA of 3.3. Additional exam requirements/recommendations for international students: Required—TOEFL (minimum score 550 paper-based; 213 computer-based; 79 iBT). *Application deadline:* Applications are processed on a rolling basis. Application fee: $60 ($75 for international students). Electronic applications accepted. *Financial support:* In 2009–10, 21 fellowships, 14 research assistantships, 75 teaching assistantships were awarded; tuition waivers (full and partial) also available. *Unit head:* Dr. Geoffrey J. D. Hewings, Interim Head, 217-333-4740, Fax: 217-244-6678, E-mail: hewings@illinois.edu. *Application contact:* Carol Hartman, Assistant Director for Administration, 217-333-0120, Fax: 217-244-6678, E-mail: cbhartma@illinois.edu.

The University of Iowa, Henry B. Tippie College of Business, Department of Economics, Iowa City, IA 52242-1316. Offers PhD. *Faculty:* 17 full-time (3 women), 1 part-time/adjunct (0 women). *Students:* 32 full-time (8 women); includes 2 minority (both Asian Americans or Pacific Islanders), 23 international. Average age 27. 208 applicants, 10% accepted, 11 enrolled. In 2009, 6 doctorates awarded. *Degree requirements:* For doctorate, comprehensive exam, thesis/dissertation, thesis defense. *Entrance requirements:* For doctorate, GRE General Test. Additional exam requirements/recommendations for international students: Required—TOEFL (minimum score 600 paper-based; 250 computer-based; 100 iBT). *Application deadline:* For fall admission, 1/15 priority date for domestic and international students. Applications are processed on a rolling basis. Application fee: $60 ($85 for international students). Electronic applications accepted. *Financial support:* In 2009–10, 32 students received support, including 3 fellowships with full tuition reimbursements available (averaging $18,000 per year), 4 research assistantships with full tuition reimbursements available (averaging $16,600 per year), 25 teaching assistantships with full tuition reimbursements available (averaging $16,600 per year); institutionally sponsored loans, scholarships/grants, health care benefits, and unspecified assistantships also available. Financial award application deadline: 1/15. *Faculty research:* Political economy, macroeconomics, econometrics, game theory, economic development. *Unit head:* Prof. Srihari Govindan, Director/Executive Officer, 319-335-0829, Fax: 319-335-1956, E-mail: ravikumar@uiowa.edu. *Application contact:* Renea L. Jay, PhD Program Coordinator, 319-335-0830, Fax: 319-335-1956, E-mail: renea-jay@uiowa.edu.

The University of Kansas, Graduate Studies, College of Liberal Arts and Sciences, Department of Economics, Lawrence, KS 66045. Offers MA, PhD, JD/MA. Part-time programs available. *Faculty:* 18 full-time (2 women). *Students:* 89 full-time (32 women), 3 part-time (0 women); includes 3 minority (2 African Americans, 1 Hispanic American), 68 international. Average age 28. 134 applicants, 57% accepted, 31 enrolled. In 2009, 15 master's, 5 doctorates awarded. Terminal master's awarded for partial completion of doctoral program. *Degree requirements:* For master's, comprehensive exam, thesis optional; for doctorate, thesis/dissertation, qualifying exams. *Entrance requirements:* For doctorate, GRE. Additional exam requirements/recommendations for international students: Required—TOEFL, IELTS. *Application deadline:* For fall admission, 2/1 priority date for domestic and international students; for winter admission, 5/1 priority date for domestic and international students; for spring admission, 11/1 priority date for domestic and international students. Applications are processed on a rolling basis. Application fee: $45 ($55 for international students). Electronic applications accepted. *Expenses:* Tuition, state resident: full-time $6492; part-time $270.50 per credit hour. Tuition, nonresident: full-time $15,510; part-time $646.25 per credit hour. Required fees: $847; $70.56 per credit hour. Tuition and fees vary according to course load and program. *Financial support:* Fellowships with full tuition reimbursements, research assistantships with full tuition reimbursements, teaching assistantships with full tuition reimbursements, institutionally sponsored loans, scholarships/grants, health care benefits, and unspecified assistantships available. Financial award application deadline: 2/1. *Faculty research:* Macroeconomics, econometrics, industrial organization, microeconomics, economic development, international economics, financial economics. *Unit head:* Joseph Sicilian, Chair, 785-864-3501, Fax: 785-864-5270, E-mail: jsic@ku.edu. *Application contact:* Teri Chambers, Graduate Secretary, 785-864-3501, Fax: 785-864-5270, E-mail: econgrad@ku.edu.

University of Kentucky, Graduate School, Gatton College of Business and Economics, Program in Economics, Lexington, KY 40506-0032. Offers MS, PhD. *Degree requirements:* For master's, comprehensive exam; for doctorate, comprehensive exam, thesis/dissertation. *Entrance requirements:* For master's, GMAT, minimum undergraduate GPA of 2.75; for doctorate, GMAT, minimum undergraduate GPA of 3.0. Additional exam requirements/recommendations for international students: Required—TOEFL (minimum score 550 paper-based; 213 computer-based). Electronic applications accepted. *Faculty research:* Public economics, international economics and economic development, labor economics, environmental economics, industrial economics.

University of Lethbridge, School of Graduate Studies, Lethbridge, AB T1K 3M4, Canada. Offers accounting (MScM); addictions counseling (M Sc); agricultural biotechnology (M Sc); agricultural studies (M Sc, MA); anthropology (MA); archaeology (MA); art (MA, MFA); biochemistry (M Sc); biological sciences (M Sc); biomolecular science (PhD); biosystems and biodiversity (PhD); Canadian studies (MA); chemistry (M Sc); computer science (M Sc); computer science and geographical information science (M Sc); counseling psychology (M Ed); dramatic arts (MA); earth, space, and physical science (PhD); economics (MA); educational leadership (M Ed); English (MA); environmental science (M Sc); evolution and behavior (PhD); exercise science (M Sc); finance (MScM); French (MA); French/German (MA); French/Spanish (MA); general education (M Ed); general management (MScM); geography (M Sc, MA); German (MA); health science (M Sc); health sciences (MA); history (MA); human resource management and labour relations (MScM); individualized multidisciplinary (M Sc, MA); information systems (MScM); international management (MScM); kinesiology (M Sc, MA); management (M Sc, MA); marketing (MScM); mathematics (M Sc); music (M Mus, MA); Native American studies (MA); neuroscience (M Sc, PhD); new media (MA); nursing (M Sc); philosophy (MA); physics (M Sc); policy and strategy (MScM); political science (MA); psychology (M Sc, MA); religious studies (MA); social sciences (MA); sociology (MA); theatre and dramatic arts (MFA); theoretical and computational science (PhD); urban and regional studies (MA); women's studies (MA). Part-time and evening/weekend programs available. *Degree requirements:* For doctorate, comprehensive exam, thesis/dissertation. *Entrance requirements:* For master's, GMAT (M Sc in management), bachelor's degree in related field, minimum GPA of 3.0 during previous 20 graded semester courses, 2 years teaching or related experience (M Ed); for doctorate, master's degree, minimum graduate GPA of 3.5. Additional exam requirements/recommendations for international students: Required—TOEFL. *Faculty research:* Movement and brain plasticity, gibberellin physiology, photosynthesis, carbon cycling, molecular properties of main-group ring components.

University of Maine, Graduate School, College of Business, Public Policy and Health, Department of Economics, Orono, ME 04469. Offers economics (MA); financial economics (MA). Part-time programs available. *Faculty:* 4 full-time (2 women), 2 part-time/adjunct (1 woman). *Students:* 9 full-time (4 women), 2 part-time (1 woman), 3 international. Average age 35. 18 applicants, 61% accepted, 5 enrolled. In 2009, 6 master's awarded. *Degree requirements:* For master's, thesis optional. *Entrance requirements:* For master's, GRE General Test. Additional exam requirements/recommendations for international students: Required—TOEFL. *Application deadline:* For fall admission, 2/1 priority date for domestic students. Applications are processed on a rolling basis. Application fee: $65. Electronic applications accepted. *Financial support:* In 2009–10, 3 teaching assistantships with tuition reimbursements (averaging $12,790 per year) were awarded; career-related internships or fieldwork, Federal Work-Study, institutionally sponsored loans, and tuition waivers (full and partial) also available. Support available to part-time students. Financial award application deadline: 3/1. *Faculty research:* Health and marine resource economics, alternative political economy. *Unit head:* Dr. George Criner, Chair, 207-581-3150, Fax: 207-581-1953. *Application contact:* Scott G. Delcourt, Associate Dean of the Graduate School, 207-581-3291, Fax: 207-581-3232, E-mail: graduate@maine.edu.

University of Manitoba, Faculty of Graduate Studies, Faculty of Arts, Department of Economics, Winnipeg, MB R3T 2N2, Canada. Offers MA, PhD. *Degree requirements:* For master's, thesis or alternative; for doctorate, one foreign language, thesis/dissertation.

University of Maryland, Baltimore County, Graduate School, College of Arts, Humanities and Social Sciences, Department of Economics, Program in Economic Policy Analysis, Baltimore, MD 21250. Offers MA. Part-time and evening/weekend programs available. *Faculty:* 25 full-time (9 women), 2 part-time/adjunct (0 women). *Students:* 14 full-time (7 women), 11 part-time (2 women); includes 7 minority (2 African Americans, 1 American Indian/Alaska Native, 2 Asian Americans or Pacific Islanders, 2 Hispanic Americans), 6 international. Average age 27. 24 applicants, 67% accepted, 11 enrolled. In 2009, 9 master's awarded. *Degree requirements:* For master's, comprehensive exam, capstone research project. *Entrance requirements:* For master's, GRE General Test, undergraduate coursework in economic theory, econometrics, calculus. Additional exam requirements/recommendations for international students: Required—TOEFL. *Application deadline:* For fall admission, 7/1 priority date for domestic students, 3/1 priority date for international students; for spring admission, 1/1 priority date for domestic students, 9/15 priority date for international students. Applications are processed on a rolling basis. Application fee: $45. Electronic applications accepted. *Financial support:* In 2009–10, 4 students received support, including 5 research assistantships with full and partial tuition reimbursements available (averaging $11,324 per year); Federal Work-Study, health care benefits, tuition waivers (full and partial), and unspecified assistantships also available. Support available to part-time students. Financial award application deadline: 4/15; financial award applicants required to submit FAFSA. *Faculty research:* International trade policy analysis, health and hospital policy evaluation, environmental policy analysis, economics of education, economic growth and development. Total annual research expenditures: $50,000. *Unit head:* Dr. David F. Mitch, Professor of Economics and Graduate Director, Fax: 410-455-1054, E-mail: mitch@umbc.edu. *Application contact:* Dr. David F. Mitch, Professor of Economics and Graduate Director, Fax: 410-455-1054, E-mail: mitch@umbc.edu.

University of Maryland, Baltimore County, Graduate School, College of Arts, Humanities and Social Sciences, Department of Public Policy, Program in Public Policy, Baltimore, MD 21250. Offers economics (PhD); education (MPP, PhD); evaluation (MPP); health (MPP, PhD); legal (MPP, PhD); management (MPP, PhD); urban (MPP, PhD). Part-time and evening/weekend programs available. *Faculty:* 40 full-time (12 women), 2 part-time/adjunct (1 woman). *Students:* 57 full-time (34 women), 114 part-time (61 women); includes 47 minority (26 African Americans, 21 Hispanic Americans). Average age 33. 89 applicants, 47% accepted, 24 enrolled. In 2009, 12 master's, 5 doctorates awarded. Terminal master's awarded for partial completion of doctoral program. *Degree requirements:* For master's, thesis optional, public analysis paper; for doctorate, comprehensive exam, thesis/dissertation, comprehensive and field qualifying exams. *Entrance requirements:* For master's, GRE General Test, 3 academic letters of reference, transcripts, resume; for doctorate, GRE General Test, 3 academic letters of reference, transcripts, resume, research paper. Additional exam requirements/recommendations for international students: Required—TOEFL (minimum score 550 paper-based; 213 computer-based; 80 iBT). *Application deadline:* For fall admission, 1/15 priority date for domestic students, 1/1 priority date for international students; for spring admission, 11/1 priority date for domestic students, 5/1 priority date for international students. Applications are processed on a rolling basis. Application fee: $50. Electronic applications accepted. *Financial support:* In 2009–10, 32 students received support, including 1 fellowship (averaging $3,000 per year), 17 research assistantships with full tuition reimbursements available (averaging $17,400 per year); career-related internships or fieldwork, Federal Work-Study, scholarships/grants, health care benefits, and unspecified assistantships also available. Support available to part-time students. Financial award application deadline: 2/1; financial award applicants required to submit FAFSA. *Faculty research:* Health policy, education policy, urban policy, public management, evaluation and analytical method. *Unit head:* Dr. Donald Norris, Chair, 410-455-1455, E-mail: norris@umbc.edu. *Application contact:* Sally F. Helms, Administrator of Academic Affairs, 410-455-3202, Fax: 410-455-1172, E-mail: gradposi@umbc.edu.

Economics

University of Maryland, College Park, Academic Affairs, College of Behavioral and Social Sciences, Department of Economics, College Park, MD 20742. Offers MA, PhD. Part-time and evening/weekend programs available. *Faculty:* 49 full-time (18 women), 19 part-time/adjunct (4 women). *Students:* 131 full-time (44 women), 2 part-time (both women); includes 9 minority (2 African Americans, 3 Asian Americans or Pacific Islanders, 4 Hispanic Americans), 93 international. 642 applicants, 11% accepted, 29 enrolled. In 2009, 24 master's, 12 doctorates awarded. Terminal master's awarded for partial completion of doctoral program. *Degree requirements:* For master's, comprehensive exam, thesis optional; for doctorate, comprehensive exam, thesis/dissertation, exams. *Entrance requirements:* For master's, GRE General Test, minimum GPA of 3.0, course work in calculus and mathematics, 3 letters of recommendation; for doctorate, GRE General Test, calculus background. Additional exam requirements/recommendations for international students: Required—TOEFL. *Application deadline:* For fall admission, 1/15 for domestic and international students. Applications are processed on a rolling basis. Application fee: $60. Electronic applications accepted. *Expenses:* Tuition, area resident: Part-time $471 per credit hour. Tuition, state resident: part-time $471 per credit hour. Tuition, nonresident: part-time $1016 per credit hour. Required fees: $337.04 per term. *Financial support:* In 2009–10, 2 fellowships with partial tuition reimbursements (averaging $10,197 per year), 2 research assistantships with tuition reimbursements (averaging $18,223 per year), 90 teaching assistantships with tuition reimbursements (averaging $18,164 per year) were awarded; Federal Work-Study and scholarships/grants also available. Support available to part-time students. Financial award applicants required to submit FAFSA. *Faculty research:* International economics, natural resource and environmental economics, forecasting and policy analysis, economic growth, demography of inequality. Total annual research expenditures: $954,490. *Unit head:* Dr. Peter Murrell, Chairman, 301-405-3506, Fax: 301-405-4733, E-mail: pmurrell@umd.edu. *Application contact:* Dean of Graduate School, 301-405-0358, Fax: 301-314-9305.

University of Maryland, College Park, Academic Affairs, College of Behavioral and Social Sciences, Department of Government and Politics, College Park, MD 20742. Offers American politics (PhD); comparative politics (PhD); international relations (PhD); political economy (PhD); political theory (PhD). Part-time and evening/weekend programs available. *Faculty:* 54 full-time (17 women), 14 part-time/adjunct (5 women). *Students:* 124 full-time (56 women), 20 part-time (6 women); includes 20 minority (5 African Americans, 10 Asian Americans or Pacific Islanders, 5 Hispanic Americans), 22 international. 235 applicants, 18% accepted, 18 enrolled. In 2009, 16 doctorates awarded. *Degree requirements:* For doctorate, comprehensive exam, thesis/dissertation, written exams in 2 fields. *Entrance requirements:* For doctorate, GRE General Test, minimum GPA of 3.5, writing sample. Additional exam requirements/recommendations for international students: Required—TOEFL. *Application deadline:* For fall admission, 2/1 for domestic and international students. Applications are processed on a rolling basis. Application fee: $60. Electronic applications accepted. *Expenses:* Tuition, area resident: Part-time $471 per credit hour. Tuition, state resident: part-time $471 per credit hour. Tuition, nonresident: part-time $1016 per credit hour. Required fees: $337.04 per term. *Financial support:* In 2009–10, 10 fellowships with full tuition reimbursements (averaging $20,041 per year), 1 research assistantship with tuition reimbursement (averaging $15,924 per year), 67 teaching assistantships with tuition reimbursements (averaging $15,749 per year) were awarded; career-related internships or fieldwork, Federal Work-Study, scholarships/grants, and unspecified assistantships also available. Support available to part-time students. Financial award applicants required to submit FAFSA. *Faculty research:* International development/conflict, international security, post-communist society, public service, dynamics of conflict and conflict resolution. Total annual research expenditures: $2.9 million. *Unit head:* Dr. Mark Lichbach, Chairman, 301-405-4156, Fax: 301-314-9690, E-mail: mlichbac@umd.edu. *Application contact:* Dean of Graduate School, 301-405-0358, Fax: 301-314-9305.

University of Massachusetts Amherst, Graduate School, College of Social and Behavioral Sciences, Department of Economics, Amherst, MA 01003. Offers MA, PhD. Part-time programs available. *Faculty:* 23 full-time (5 women). *Students:* 69 full-time (32 women), 24 part-time (11 women); includes 8 minority (1 African American, 1 Asian American or Pacific Islander, 6 Hispanic Americans), 45 international. Average age 31. 166 applicants, 13% accepted, 12 enrolled. In 2009, 11 master's, 8 doctorates awarded. Terminal master's awarded for partial completion of doctoral program. *Degree requirements:* For master's, thesis or alternative; for doctorate, comprehensive exam, thesis/dissertation. *Entrance requirements:* For master's and doctorate, GRE General Test. Additional exam requirements/recommendations for international students: Required—TOEFL (minimum score 550 paper-based; 213 computer-based; 80 iBT), IELTS (minimum score 6.5). *Application deadline:* For fall admission, 1/15 for domestic and international students. Applications are processed on a rolling basis. Application fee: $50 ($65 for international students). Electronic applications accepted. *Expenses:* Tuition, state resident: full-time $2640; part-time $110 per credit. Tuition, nonresident: full-time $9936; part-time $414 per credit. Tuition and fees vary according to course load. *Financial support:* In 2009–10, 2 fellowships with full tuition reimbursements (averaging $7,625 per year), 16 research assistantships with full tuition reimbursements (averaging $4,257 per year), 59 teaching assistantships with full tuition reimbursements (averaging $10,107 per year) were awarded; career-related internships or fieldwork, Federal Work-Study, scholarships/grants, traineeships, health care benefits, tuition waivers (full), and unspecified assistantships also available. Support available to part-time students. Financial award application deadline: 1/15. *Unit head:* Dr. David M. Kotz, Graduate Program Director, 413-545-6352, Fax: 413-545-2921, E-mail: gradinfo@econs.umass.edu. *Application contact:* Jean M. Ames, Supervisor of Admissions, 413-545-0722, Fax: 413-577-0010, E-mail: gradadm@grad.umass.edu.

University of Massachusetts Lowell, College of Arts and Sciences, Department of Regional Economic and Social Development, Lowell, MA 01854-2881. Offers MA, Graduate Certificate. Part-time programs available. *Entrance requirements:* For master's, GRE. Electronic applications accepted.

University of Memphis, Graduate School, Fogelman College of Business and Economics, Department of Economics, Memphis, TN 38152. Offers MA, PhD. Part-time programs available. *Faculty:* 10 full-time (1 woman). *Students:* 2 full-time (1 woman), 3 part-time (0 women); includes 1 minority (Asian American or Pacific Islander), 1 international. Average age 28. 6 applicants, 83% accepted, 0 enrolled. In 2009, 3 master's awarded. *Degree requirements:* For master's, comprehensive exam, thesis or alternative; for doctorate, comprehensive exam, thesis/dissertation. *Entrance requirements:* For master's, GMAT or GRE General Test, previous course work in statistics, intermediate micro and macro theory; for doctorate, GMAT, interview, minimum GPA of 3.4. *Application deadline:* For fall admission, 8/1 for domestic students; for spring admission, 12/1 for domestic students. Application fee: $35 ($60 for international students). *Expenses:* Tuition, state resident: full-time $6246; part-time $347 per credit hour. Tuition, nonresident: full-time $15,894; part-time $883 per credit hour. Required fees: $1160. Full-time tuition and fees vary according to course load, degree level and program. *Financial support:* In 2009–10, 3 students received support; research assistantships with full tuition reimbursements available, teaching assistantships with full tuition reimbursements available, Federal Work-Study, scholarships/grants, and unspecified assistantships available. Financial award application deadline: 2/15; financial award applicants required to submit FAFSA. *Faculty research:* Tax research, medical economics, law and economics, labor economics, U.S. and Japanese economic relations. *Unit head:* Dr. William Smith, Interim Chair, 901-678-2785, E-mail: wtsmith@memphis.edu. *Application contact:* Dr. Pinaki Bose, Master's Program Coordinator, 901-678-5528, Fax: 901-678-4705, E-mail: psbose@memphis.edu.

University of Memphis, Graduate School, Fogelman College of Business and Economics, Program in Business Administration, Memphis, TN 38152. Offers accounting (MBA, PhD); economics (MBA, PhD); executive business administration (MBA); finance (PhD); finance, insurance, and real estate (MBA, MS); international business administration (IMBA); management (MBA, MS, PhD); management information systems (MBA, MS, PhD); management science (MBA); marketing (MBA, MS); marketing and supply chain management (PhD); real estate development (MS); JD/MBA. *Accreditation:* AACSB. *Faculty:* 44 full-time (9 women), 5 part-time/adjunct (0 women). *Students:* 263 full-time (106 women), 181 part-time (66 women); includes 70 minority (46 African Americans, 3 American Indian/Alaska Native, 16 Asian Americans or Pacific Islanders, 5 Hispanic Americans), 109 international. Average age 31. 374 applicants, 73% accepted, 119 enrolled. In 2009, 140 master's, 17 doctorates awarded. *Degree requirements:* For master's, comprehensive exam; for doctorate, comprehensive exam, thesis/dissertation. *Entrance requirements:* For master's, GMAT, resume; for doctorate, GMAT, interview, minimum GPA of 3.4, resume, letter of recommendation. Additional exam requirements/recommendations for international students: Required—TOEFL (minimum score 550 paper-based; 220 computer-based). *Application deadline:* For fall admission, 8/1 for domestic students; for spring admission, 12/1 for domestic students. Application fee: $35 ($60 for international students). *Expenses:* Tuition, state resident: full-time $6246; part-time $347 per credit hour. Tuition, nonresident: full-time $15,894; part-time $883 per credit hour. Required fees: $1160. Full-time tuition and fees vary according to course load, degree level and program. *Financial support:* In 2009–10, 164 students received support; research assistantships with full tuition reimbursements available, teaching assistantships with full tuition reimbursements available, career-related internships or fieldwork, Federal Work-Study, scholarships/grants, and unspecified assistantships available. Financial award application deadline: 2/15; financial award applicants required to submit FAFSA. *Faculty research:* Competitive business strategy, finance microstructures, supply chain management innovations, health care economics, litigation risks and corporate audits. *Unit head:* Rajiv Grover, Dean, 901-678-3759, E-mail: rgrover@memphis.edu. *Application contact:* Dr. Carol V. Danehower, Associate Dean for Programs, 901-678-5402, Fax: 901-678-3579, E-mail: fcbegp@memphis.edu.

University of Miami, Graduate School, School of Business Administration, Department of Economics, Coral Gables, FL 33124. Offers economic development (MA, PhD); environmental economics (PhD); human resource economics (MA, PhD); international economics (MA, PhD); macroeconomics (PhD). Students admitted every two years in the fall semester. Terminal master's awarded for partial completion of doctoral program. *Degree requirements:* For master's, comprehensive exam; for doctorate, comprehensive exam, thesis/dissertation. *Entrance requirements:* For master's and doctorate, GRE General Test, minimum GPA of 3.0. Additional exam requirements/recommendations for international students: Required—TOEFL (minimum score 550 paper-based). *Faculty research:* International economics/trade, applied microeconomics, development.

University of Michigan, Horace H. Rackham School of Graduate Studies, College of Literature, Science, and the Arts, Department of Economics, Ann Arbor, MI 48109. Offers applied economics (AM); economics (AM, PhD); public policy and economics (PhD); social work and economics (PhD); JD/PhD; MPP/AM. *Faculty:* 57 full-time (9 women). *Students:* 168 full-time (55 women); includes 23 minority (3 African Americans, 17 Asian Americans or Pacific Islanders, 3 Hispanic Americans), 55 international. Average age 27. 596 applicants, 23% accepted, 34 enrolled. In 2009, 42 master's, 21 doctorates awarded. Terminal master's awarded for partial completion of doctoral program. *Degree requirements:* For doctorate, oral defense of dissertation, preliminary exam. *Entrance requirements:* For master's and doctorate, GRE General Test. Additional exam requirements/recommendations for international students: Required—TOEFL (minimum score 600 paper-based; 250 computer-based; 100 iBT). *Application deadline:* For fall admission, 12/15 for domestic and international students. Application fee: $60 ($75 for international students). Electronic applications accepted. *Expenses:* Tuition, state resident: full-time $17,286; part-time $1099 per credit hour. Tuition, nonresident: full-time $34,944; part-time $2080 per credit hour. Required fees: $95 per semester. Tuition and fees vary according to course load, degree level and program. *Financial support:* In 2009–10, 118 students received support, including 40 fellowships with full tuition reimbursements available (averaging $16,000 per year), 18 research assistantships with full tuition reimbursements available (averaging $16,696 per year), 60 teaching assistantships with full tuition reimbursements available (averaging $16,696 per year); career-related internships or fieldwork and traineeships also available. Financial award application deadline: 12/15. *Faculty research:* Economic and econometrical analysis, industrial organization, international trade, public finance, development, health, labor, population standard, macro, theory. *Unit head:* Prof. Linda Tesar, Chair, 734-763-2254, Fax: 734-764-2769, E-mail: ltesar@umich.edu. *Application contact:* Prof. David Lam, Director of Graduate Studies, 734-763-9237, Fax: 734-764-2769, E-mail: davidl@umich.edu.

University of Minnesota, Twin Cities Campus, Graduate School, College of Liberal Arts, Department of Economics, Minneapolis, MN 55455. Offers PhD. *Faculty:* 25 full-time (5 women), 3 part-time/adjunct (1 woman). *Students:* 106 full-time (29 women), 8 part-time (3 women); includes 9 minority (6 Asian Americans or Pacific Islanders, 3 Hispanic Americans), 74 international. Average age 27. 395 applicants, 16% accepted, 21 enrolled. In 2009, 33 doctorates awarded. *Degree requirements:* For doctorate, thesis/dissertation, preliminary exams. *Entrance requirements:* For doctorate, GRE General Test. Additional exam requirements/recommendations for international students: Required—TOEFL (minimum score 600 paper-based; 250 computer-based; 100 iBT), IELTS (minimum score 7). *Application deadline:* For fall admission, 12/15 priority date for domestic and international students. Application fee: $75 ($95 for international students). Electronic applications accepted. *Financial support:* In 2009–10, 85 students received support, including fellowships with full tuition reimbursements available (averaging $21,000 per year), research assistantships with full tuition reimbursements available (averaging $15,500 per year), teaching assistantships with full tuition reimbursements available (averaging $15,300 per year); scholarships/grants and unspecified assistantships also available. Financial award application deadline: 12/15. *Faculty research:* Econometrics, macro and monetary economics, mathematical economics, industrial organization, applied micro theory. *Unit head:* Larry Jones, Chair, 612-625-6353, Fax: 612-624-0209. *Application contact:* Christopher Phelan, Director of Graduate Studies, 612-625-6833, Fax: 612-624-0209, E-mail: econdgs@econ.umn.edu.

University of Mississippi, Graduate School, College of Liberal Arts, Department of Economics, Oxford, University, MS 38677. Offers MA, PhD. *Faculty:* 16 full-time (7 women), 6 part-time/adjunct (2 women). *Students:* 16 full-time (5 women), 1 (woman) part-time; includes 3 minority (1 African American, 1 American Indian/Alaska Native, 1 Hispanic American), 6 international. In 2009, 5 master's, 3 doctorates awarded. *Application deadline:* For fall admission, 4/1 for domestic students; for spring admission, 10/1 for domestic students. Applications are processed on a rolling basis. Electronic applications accepted. *Financial support:* Scholarships/grants available. Financial award applicants required to submit FAFSA. *Unit head:* Dr. Jon Moen, Interim Chair, 662-915-6942, Fax: 662-915-6943, E-mail: jmoen@olemiss.edu. *Application contact:* Dr. Christy M. Wyandt, Associate Dean, 662-915-7474, Fax: 662-915-7577, E-mail: cwyandt@olemiss.edu.

University of Missouri, Graduate School, College of Arts and Sciences, Department of Economics, Columbia, MO 65211. Offers MA, PhD, JD/MA. *Faculty:* 25 full-time (7 women), 3 part-time/adjunct (1 woman). *Students:* 37 full-time (14 women), 30 part-time (15 women); includes 2 minority (1 African American, 1 Hispanic American), 54 international. Average age 29. 125 applicants, 34% accepted, 14 enrolled. In 2009, 11 master's, 4 doctorates awarded. Terminal master's awarded for partial completion of doctoral program. *Degree requirements:* For doctorate, comprehensive exam, thesis/dissertation. *Entrance requirements:* For master's, GRE General Test (minimum 700 quantitative, 400 verbal), minimum GPA of 3.0; bachelor's degree in any field; for doctorate, GRE General Test; min Q = 700; min V = 400, minimum GPA of 3.0. Additional exam requirements/recommendations for international students: Required—TOEFL (minimum score 550 paper-based; 213 computer-based; 79 iBT), IELTS (minimum score 6). *Application deadline:* For fall admission, 1/15 priority date for domestic students; for winter admission, 11/1 priority date for domestic students; for spring admission, 3/1 priority date for domestic students. Application fee: $45 ($60 for international students). Electronic applications accepted. *Financial support:* In 2009–10, 2 fellowships with full and partial tuition reimbursements, 6 research assistantships with full tuition reimbursements, 51 teaching assistantships with full tuition reimbursements were awarded; institutionally sponsored loans, health care benefits, and unspecified assistantships also available. *Unit head:* Dr. David Mandy, Department Chair, E-mail: mandyd@missouri.edu. *Application contact:* Lynne Riddell, 573-884-7989, E-mail: riddelll@missouri.edu.

University of Missouri–Kansas City, College of Arts and Sciences, Department of Economics, Kansas City, MO 64110-2499. Offers MA, PhD. PhD (interdisciplinary) offered through the School of Graduate Studies. Part-time and evening/weekend programs available. *Faculty:* 12 full-time (1 woman), 2 part-time/adjunct (0 women). *Students:* 19 full-time (6 women), 25 part-time (2 women); includes 7 minority (4 African Americans, 2 Asian Americans or Pacific Islanders, 1 Hispanic American), 9 international. Average age 32. 31 applicants, 81% accepted, 23 enrolled. In 2009, 8 master's awarded. *Degree requirements:* For doctorate, comprehensive exam, thesis/dissertation. *Entrance requirements:* For master's, GRE or minimum undergraduate GPA of 2.5; for doctorate, GRE, master's degree in economics or equivalent. Additional exam requirements/recommendations for international students: Required—TOEFL (minimum score 550 paper-based; 213 computer-based; 80 iBT). *Application deadline:* For fall admission, 2/1 priority date for domestic and international students; for spring admission, 9/1 priority date for domestic and international students. Applications are processed on a rolling basis. Application fee: $45 ($50 for international students). Electronic applications accepted. *Expenses:* Tuition, state resident: full-time $5378; part-time $299 per credit hour. Tuition, nonresident: full-time $13,881; part-time $771 per credit hour. Required fees: $641; $71 per credit hour. Tuition and fees vary according to course load and program. *Financial support:* In 2009–10, 23 teaching assistantships with partial tuition reimbursements (averaging $13,267 per year) were awarded; fellowships with partial tuition reimbursements, research assistantships with partial tuition reimbursements, career-related internships or fieldwork, Federal Work-Study, institutionally sponsored loans, and tuition waivers (full and partial) also available. Support available to part-time students. Financial award application deadline: 3/1; financial award applicants required to submit FAFSA. *Faculty research:* International trade, general theory, institutions/utilities, forensic economics, human resources. Total annual research expenditures: $184,804. *Unit head:* James Sturgeon, Chair, 816-235-2837, Fax: 816-238-2836, E-mail: sturgeonj@umkc.edu. *Application contact:* Fred Lee, Graduate Advisor, 816-235-2543, Fax: 816-238-2836, E-mail: leefs@umkc.edu.

University of Missouri–St. Louis, College of Arts and Sciences, Department of Economics, St. Louis, MO 63121. Offers general economics (MA), including business economics; managerial economics (Certificate). Part-time and evening/weekend programs available. *Faculty:* 10 full-time (3 women), 5 part-time/adjunct (3 women). *Students:* 13 full-time (6 women), 10 part-time (2 women); includes 4 minority (all African Americans), 1 international. Average age 31. 18 applicants, 78% accepted, 9 enrolled. In 2009, 6 master's awarded. *Entrance requirements:* For master's, GRE General Test, 2 letters of recommendation. Additional exam requirements/recommendations for international students: Required—TOEFL (minimum score 550 paper-based; 213 computer-based). *Application deadline:* For fall admission, 7/1 priority date for domestic and international students; for spring admission, 12/1 priority date for domestic and international students. Applications are processed on a rolling basis. Application fee: $35 ($40 for international students). Electronic applications accepted. *Expenses:* Tuition, state resident: full-time $5377; part-time $297.70 per credit hour. Tuition, nonresident: full-time $13,882; part-time $771.20 per credit hour. Required fees: $220; $12.20 per credit hour. One-time fee: $12. Tuition and fees vary according to course level, campus/location and program. *Financial support:* In 2009–10, 4 research assistantships with full and partial tuition reimbursements (averaging $5,000 per year) were awarded; teaching assistantships with full and partial tuition reimbursements. Financial award applicants required to submit FAFSA. *Faculty research:* Health economics, public policy analysis, econometrics, public choice, telecommunications and forensic economics. *Unit head:* Dr. Donald Kridel, Director of Graduate Studies, 314-516-5351, Fax: 314-516-5562, E-mail: kridel@umsl.edu. *Application contact:* 314-516-5458, Fax: 314-516-6996, E-mail: gradadm@umsl.edu.

The University of Montana, Graduate School, College of Arts and Sciences, Department of Economics, Missoula, MT 59812-0002. Offers MA. *Degree requirements:* For master's, thesis. *Entrance requirements:* For master's, GRE General Test. Additional exam requirements/recommendations for international students: Required—TOEFL (minimum score 525 paper-based; 197 computer-based). *Faculty research:* Resource economics, public policy, environmental economics, economic development, regional economics.

University of Nebraska at Omaha, Graduate Studies, College of Business Administration, Department of Economics, Omaha, NE 68182. Offers MA, MS. Part-time and evening/weekend programs available. *Faculty:* 10 full-time (2 women). *Students:* 25 full-time (8 women), 37 part-time (12 women); includes 10 minority (8 African Americans, 2 Asian Americans or Pacific Islanders), 30 international. Average age 29. 42 applicants, 62% accepted, 17 enrolled. In 2009, 23 master's awarded. *Degree requirements:* For master's, comprehensive exam, thesis (for some programs). *Entrance requirements:* For master's, minimum GPA of 3.0. Additional exam requirements/recommendations for international students: Required—TOEFL (minimum score 530 paper-based; 197 computer-based; 71 iBT). *Application deadline:* For fall admission, 7/1 priority date for domestic students; for spring admission, 12/15 priority date for domestic students. Applications are processed on a rolling basis. Application fee: $45. Electronic applications accepted. *Financial support:* In 2009–10, 23 students received support; research assistantships with tuition reimbursements available, Federal Work-Study, institutionally sponsored loans, scholarships/grants, and unspecified assistantships available. Support available to part-time students. Financial award application deadline: 3/1; financial award applicants required to submit FAFSA. *Faculty research:* Labor, economics of science, international development, monetary economics, econometrics. *Unit head:* Dr. Donald Baum, Graduate Chair, 402-554-2570. *Application contact:* Dr. Donald Baum, Graduate Chair, 402-554-2570.

University of Nebraska–Lincoln, Graduate College, College of Business Administration, Department of Economics, Lincoln, NE 68588. Offers MA, PhD, JD/MA. *Degree requirements:* For master's, thesis optional; for doctorate, comprehensive exam, thesis/dissertation. *Entrance requirements:* For master's and doctorate, GRE General Test. Additional exam requirements/recommendations for international students: Required—TOEFL (minimum score 550 paper-based; 213 computer-based). Electronic applications accepted. *Faculty research:* Applied microeconomics, economic education, international trade and finance, public finance, regional and institutional economics.

University of Nevada, Las Vegas, Graduate College, College of Business, Department of Economics, Las Vegas, NV 89154-6005. Offers MA. Part-time and evening/weekend programs available. *Faculty:* 16 full-time (1 woman), 1 part-time/adjunct (0 women). *Students:* 11 full-time (5 women), 14 part-time (2 women); includes 5 minority (2 African Americans, 2 Asian Americans or Pacific Islanders, 1 Hispanic American), 5 international. Average age 28. 36 applicants, 81% accepted, 12 enrolled. In 2009, 6 master's awarded. *Degree requirements:* For master's, thesis, oral defense of thesis. *Entrance requirements:* For master's, GRE General Test or GMAT. Additional exam requirements/recommendations for international students: Required—TOEFL (minimum score 550 paper-based; 213 computer-based; 80 iBT), IELTS (minimum score 7). *Application deadline:* For fall admission, 6/15 priority date for domestic students, 5/1 for international students; for spring admission, 11/15 priority date for domestic students, 10/1 for international students. Applications are processed on a rolling basis. Application fee: $60 ($95 for international students). Electronic applications accepted. *Financial support:* In 2009–10, 7 students received support, including 7 research assistantships with partial tuition reimbursements available (averaging $10,000 per year); institutionally sponsored loans, scholarships/grants, health care benefits, and unspecified assistantships also available. Financial award application deadline: 3/1. *Unit head:* Dr. Stephen Miller, Chair/Professor, 702-895-3969, Fax: 702-895-1354, E-mail: stephen.miller@unlv.edu. *Application contact:* Graduate College Admissions Evaluator, 702-895-3320, Fax: 702-895-4180, E-mail: gradcollege@unlv.edu.

University of Nevada, Reno, Graduate School, College of Business Administration, Department of Economics, Reno, NV 89557. Offers MA, MS. *Degree requirements:* For master's, thesis. *Entrance requirements:* For master's, GMAT or GRE, minimum GPA of 2.75. Additional exam requirements/recommendations for international students: Required—TOEFL (minimum score 500 paper-based; 173 computer-based; 61 iBT), IELTS (minimum score 6). Electronic applications accepted. *Faculty research:* Applied microeconomics, public finance, development, labor.

University of New Brunswick Fredericton, School of Graduate Studies, Faculty of Arts, Department of Economics, Fredericton, NB E3B 5A3, Canada. Offers applied economics and finance (M Sc); economics (MA). Program in applied economics and finance offered at UNB Saint John Campus. *Faculty:* 10 full-time (1 woman), 3 part-time/adjunct (0 women). *Students:* 4 full-time (1 woman), 2 part-time (both women). In 2009, 6 master's awarded. *Entrance requirements:* For master's, GRE, minimum GPA of 3.0. Additional exam requirements/recommendations for international students: Required—TOEFL (minimum score 550 paper-based), TWE, or IELTS. *Application deadline:* 1/31 for domestic and international students. Applications are processed on a rolling basis. Application fee: $50 Canadian dollars. Tuition and fees charges are reported in Canadian dollars. *Expenses:* Tuition, area resident: Full-time $5562 Canadian dollars; part-time $2781 Canadian dollars per year. Required fees: $49.75 Canadian dollars per term. *Financial support:* In 2009–10, 2 research assistantships (averaging $16,000 per year) were awarded; scholarships/grants, health care benefits, and unspecified assistantships also available. Financial award application deadline: 1/31. *Faculty research:* Epidemiology and population health, micro/macro economics, economics of transportation, regional development. *Unit head:* Dr. Yuri Yevdokimov, Director of Graduate Studies, 506-447-3221, Fax: 506-453-4514, E-mail: yuri@unb.ca. *Application contact:* Lucina MacDonald, Graduate Secretary, 506-453-4828, Fax: 506-453-4514, E-mail: lmacdona@unb.ca.

University of New Brunswick Fredericton, School of Graduate Studies, Policy Studies Program, Fredericton, NB E3B 5A3, Canada. Offers people, property and alternative dispute resolution (M Phil); philosophy politics and economics (M Phil); sustainable development (M Phil). Part-time programs available. *Faculty:* 6 full-time (2 women), 13 part-time/adjunct (2 women). *Students:* 8 full-time (3 women), 5 part-time (3 women). In 2009, 7 master's awarded. *Degree requirements:* For master's, thesis, report. *Entrance requirements:* For master's, minimum GPA of 3.5, BA; BA Honours. Additional exam requirements/recommendations for international students: Required—TOEFL (minimum score 600 paper-based; 250 computer-based; 100 iBT), TWE (minimum score 4), or IELTS (minimum score 7). Application fee: $50 Canadian dollars. Tuition and fees charges are reported in Canadian dollars. *Expenses:* Tuition, area resident: Full-time $5562 Canadian dollars; part-time $2781 Canadian dollars per year. Required fees: $49.75 Canadian dollars per term. *Financial support:* In 2009–10, 5 research assistantships (averaging $5,600 per year), 2 teaching assistantships (averaging $4,400 per year) were awarded. *Unit head:* Dr. Linda Eyre, Dean of Graduate Studies, 506-447-3044, Fax: 506-453-4817, E-mail: gradidst@unb.ca. *Application contact:* Janet Amurault, Graduate Secretary, 506-458-7558, Fax: 506-453-4817, E-mail: jamiraul@unb.ca.

University of New Hampshire, Graduate School, Whittemore School of Business and Economics, Department of Economics, Durham, NH 03824. Offers MA, PhD. Part-time programs available. *Faculty:* 13 full-time (4 women). *Students:* 33 full-time (12 women), 5 part-time (2 women), 16 international. Average age 28. 57 applicants, 60% accepted, 16 enrolled. In 2009, 12 master's, 1 doctorate awarded. Terminal master's awarded for partial completion of doctoral program. *Degree requirements:* For master's, thesis or alternative; for doctorate, one foreign language, thesis/dissertation. *Entrance requirements:* For master's and doctorate, GRE General Test. Additional exam requirements/recommendations for international students: Required—TOEFL (minimum score 550 paper-based; 213 computer-based; 80 iBT). *Application deadline:* For fall admission, 6/1 priority date for domestic students, 4/1 for international students; for spring admission, 11/1 for domestic students. Applications are processed on a rolling basis. Application fee: $65. Electronic applications accepted. *Expenses:* Tuition, state resident: full-time $10,380; part-time $577 per credit hour. Tuition, nonresident: full-time $24,350; part-time $1002 per credit hour. Required fees: $1550; $387.50 per semester. Tuition and fees vary according to course load and program. *Financial support:* In 2009–10, 32 students received support, including 1 fellowship, 30 teaching assistantships; research assistantships, career-related internships or fieldwork, Federal Work-Study, scholarships/grants, and tuition waivers (full and partial) also available. Support available to part-time students. Financial award application deadline: 2/15. *Faculty research:* Labor economics, international development, econometrics, finance, political economy. *Unit head:* Dr. Bruce Elmslie, Chair, 603-862-3357. *Application contact:* Sinthy Kounlasa, Administrative Assistant, 603-862-3457, E-mail: wsbe.grad@unh.edu.

University of New Mexico, Graduate School, College of Arts and Sciences, Department of Economics, Albuquerque, NM 87131-2039. Offers MA, PhD. Part-time programs available. *Faculty:* 13 full-time (5 women), 4 part-time/adjunct (1 woman). *Students:* 48 full-time (17 women), 14 part-time (4 women); includes 11 minority (1 African American, 3 American Indian/Alaska Native, 7 Hispanic Americans), 22 international. Average age 34. 60 applicants, 52% accepted, 16 enrolled. In 2009, 154 master's, 4 doctorates awarded. Terminal master's awarded for partial completion of doctoral program. *Degree requirements:* For master's, comprehensive exam, thesis (for some programs); for doctorate, comprehensive exam, thesis/dissertation. *Entrance requirements:* For master's and doctorate, GRE General Test, 3 letters of recommendation, letter of intent. Additional exam requirements/recommendations for international students: Required—TOEFL (minimum score 520 paper-based; 190 computer-based; 68 iBT). *Application deadline:* For fall admission, 3/1 priority date for domestic students, 3/1 for international students. Applications are processed on a rolling basis. Application fee: $50. Electronic applications accepted. *Expenses:* Tuition, state resident: full-time $2099; part-time $233.20 per credit hour. Tuition, nonresident: full-time $6650. Required fees: $25 per semester. Tuition and fees vary according to course load, program and reciprocity agreements. *Financial support:* In 2009–10, 18 students received support, including 2 fellowships with tuition reimbursements available (averaging $20,000 per year), 9 research assistantships with tuition reimbursements available (averaging $13,715 per year), 12 teaching assistantships (averaging $7,395 per year); career-related internships or fieldwork, Federal Work-Study, scholarships/grants, health care benefits, and unspecified assistantships also available. Support available to part-time students. Financial award application deadline: 3/1; financial award applicants required to submit FAFSA. *Faculty research:* Core theory, econometrics, public finance, international/development economics, labor/human resource economics, environmental/natural resource economics. Total annual research expenditures: $1.8 million. *Unit head:* Dr. Robert Berrens, Chair, 505-277-5304, Fax: 505-277-9445, E-mail: rberrens@unm.edu. *Application contact:* Shoshana Handel, Academic Advisor, 505-277-3056, Fax: 505-277-9445, E-mail: shandel@unm.edu.

University of New Orleans, Graduate School, College of Business Administration, Department of Economics and Finance, Program in Financial Economics, New Orleans, LA 70148. Offers PhD. Terminal master's awarded for partial completion of doctoral program. *Degree requirements:* For doctorate, one foreign language, comprehensive exam, thesis/dissertation, general exams. *Entrance requirements:* For doctorate, GRE General Test, minimum GPA of 3.0. Additional exam requirements/recommendations for international students: Required—TOEFL (minimum score 550 paper-based; 213 computer-based; 79 iBT). Electronic applications accepted. *Faculty research:* Urban and regional economics, economic development, monetary theory and policy, international finance.

The University of North Carolina at Chapel Hill, Graduate School, College of Arts and Sciences, Department of Economics, Chapel Hill, NC 27599. Offers MS, PhD. Terminal master's awarded for partial completion of doctoral program. *Degree requirements:* For master's, comprehensive exam, thesis or alternative; for doctorate, comprehensive exam, thesis/dissertation. *Entrance requirements:* For master's, GRE General Test, minimum GPA of 3.0; for doctorate, GRE General Test, minimum GPA of 3.5. Additional exam requirements/recommendations for international students: Required—TOEFL (minimum score 550 paper-based; 213 computer-based). Electronic applications accepted. *Faculty research:* Health economics, micro theory/IO, labor economics, economic history, financial econometrics.

The University of North Carolina at Charlotte, Graduate School, Belk College of Business, Department of Economics, Charlotte, NC 28223-0001. Offers MS. Part-time and evening/weekend programs available. *Faculty:* 18 full-time (4 women). *Students:* 29 full-time (13 women), 22 part-time (7 women); includes 4 African Americans, 1 Asian American or Pacific Islander, 2 Hispanic Americans, 21 international. Average age 27. 55 applicants, 89% accepted,

Economics

The University of North Carolina at Charlotte (continued)

20 enrolled. In 2009, 18 master's awarded. *Degree requirements:* For master's, thesis or project. *Entrance requirements:* For master's, GRE General Test, minimum undergraduate GPA of 3.0 in major, 2.8 overall. Additional exam requirements/recommendations for international students: Required—TOEFL (minimum score 557 paper-based; 220 computer-based; 83 iBT). *Application deadline:* For fall admission, 7/15 for domestic students, 5/1 for international students; for spring admission, 11/15 for domestic students, 10/1 for international students. Applications are processed on a rolling basis. Application fee: $55. Electronic applications accepted. *Financial support:* In 2009–10, 13 students received support, including 1 research assistantship (averaging $13,000 per year), 12 teaching assistantships (averaging $8,037 per year); career-related internships or fieldwork, institutionally sponsored loans, scholarships/grants, and unspecified assistantships also available. Support available to part-time students. Financial award application deadline: 4/1; financial award applicants required to submit FAFSA. *Faculty research:* Health care, taxation, energy, economic growth, monetary policy. *Unit head:* Dr. Rob Roy McGregor, Program Director, 704-687-7639, Fax: 704-687-6442, E-mail: rrmcgreg@uncc.edu. *Application contact:* Kathy B. Giddings, Director of Graduate Admissions, 704-687-5503, Fax: 704-687-3279, E-mail: gradadm@uncc.edu.

The University of North Carolina at Greensboro, Graduate School, Bryan School of Business and Economics, Department of Economics, Program in Economics, Greensboro, NC 27412-5001. Offers PhD. *Degree requirements:* For doctorate, comprehensive exam, thesis/dissertation. *Entrance requirements:* Additional exam requirements/recommendations for international students: Required—TOEFL. Electronic applications accepted.

University of North Texas, Robert B. Toulouse School of Graduate Studies, College of Arts and Sciences, Department of Economics, Denton, TX 76203. Offers economic research (MS); economics (MA, MS); labor and industrial relations (MS). Part-time and evening/weekend programs available. *Degree requirements:* For master's, comprehensive exam, thesis (for some programs). *Entrance requirements:* For master's, GMAT, GRE General Test, minimum GPA of 3.0, 2 letters of recommendation, 500-word essay. Additional exam requirements/recommendations for international students: Required—proof of English language proficiency required for non-native English speakers; Recommended—TOEFL (minimum score 550 paper-based; 213 computer-based). Application fee: $50 ($75 for international students). *Expenses:* Tuition, state resident: full-time $4298; part-time $239 per contact hour. Tuition, nonresident: full-time $9878; part-time $549 per contact hour. Required fees: $265 per contact hour. *Financial support:* In 2009–10, 25 students received support; fellowships with partial tuition reimbursements available, research assistantships with partial tuition reimbursements available, teaching assistantships with partial tuition reimbursements available, career-related internships or fieldwork, Federal Work-Study, and institutionally sponsored loans available. Support available to part-time students. Financial award application deadline: 4/1. *Faculty research:* Econometrics, international trade and development, immigration, telecommunications, micro enterprise development. *Application contact:* Graduate Adviser, 940-565-3442, Fax: 940-565-4426, E-mail: tieslau@unt.edu.

University of Notre Dame, Graduate School, College of Arts and Letters, Division of Social Science, Department of Economics and Econometrics, Notre Dame, IN 46556. Offers MA, PhD. Terminal master's awarded for partial completion of doctoral program. *Degree requirements:* For master's, comprehensive exam (for some programs), thesis optional; for doctorate, thesis/dissertation, candidacy exam. *Entrance requirements:* For doctorate, GRE General Test. Additional exam requirements/recommendations for international students: Required—TOEFL (minimum score 600 paper-based; 250 computer-based; 80 iBT). Electronic applications accepted.

University of Oklahoma, Graduate College, College of Arts and Sciences, Department of Economics, Norman, OK 73019. Offers MA, PhD. *Faculty:* 20 full-time (7 women), 3 part-time/adjunct (1 woman). *Students:* 49 full-time (14 women), 74 part-time (10 women); includes 22 minority (9 African Americans, 9 Asian Americans or Pacific Islanders, 4 Hispanic Americans), 21 international. 65 applicants, 82% accepted, 31 enrolled. In 2009, 36 master's, 1 doctorate awarded. Terminal master's awarded for partial completion of doctoral program. *Degree requirements:* For doctorate, 2 foreign languages, thesis/dissertation, general exams. *Entrance requirements:* For master's, GRE General Test, minimum GPA of 3.0 in last 60 hours of course work; for doctorate, GRE General Test. Additional exam requirements/recommendations for international students: Required—TOEFL (minimum score 550 paper-based; 213 computer-based). *Application deadline:* For fall admission, 1/15 for domestic and international students; for spring admission, 9/1 for domestic and international students. Applications are processed on a rolling basis. Application fee: $40 ($90 for international students). Electronic applications accepted. *Expenses:* Tuition, state resident: full-time $3744; part-time $156 per credit hour. Tuition, nonresident: full-time $13,577; part-time $565.70 per credit hour. Required fees: $2415; $90.10 per credit hour. *Financial support:* In 2009–10, 34 students received support, including 20 teaching assistantships with partial tuition reimbursements available (averaging $13,145 per year); scholarships/grants, health care benefits, and unspecified assistantships also available. Financial award applicants required to submit FAFSA. *Faculty research:* Industrial organization, international/macroeconomics, growth and development, public economics. Total annual research expenditures: $62,297. *Unit head:* Dr. Lex Holmes, Chair, 405-325-2861, Fax: 405-325-5842, E-mail: aholmes@ou.edu. *Application contact:* Cynthia Rogers, Graduate Liaison, 405-235-5843, Fax: 405-325-5842, E-mail: crogers@ou.edu.

University of Oregon, Graduate School, College of Arts and Sciences, Department of Economics, Eugene, OR 97403. Offers MA, MS, PhD. Terminal master's awarded for partial completion of doctoral program. *Degree requirements:* For master's, thesis or alternative; for doctorate, thesis/dissertation, qualifying exam. *Entrance requirements:* For master's and doctorate, GRE General Test, minimum GPA of 3.0. Additional exam requirements/recommendations for international students: Required—TOEFL. *Faculty research:* Labor economics, macroeconomics, international economics, industrial organization, public finance.

University of Ottawa, Faculty of Graduate and Postdoctoral Studies, Faculty of Social Sciences, Department of Economics, Ottawa, ON K1N 6N5, Canada. Offers MA, PhD. Part-time programs available. *Degree requirements:* For master's, thesis or alternative; for doctorate, comprehensive exam, thesis/dissertation. *Entrance requirements:* For master's, honors bachelor's degree or equivalent, minimum B average; for doctorate, master's degree, minimum B+ average. Electronic applications accepted. *Faculty research:* Public economics, industrial organizations, monetary economics, international economics, economic development.

University of Pennsylvania, School of Arts and Sciences, Graduate Group in Economics, Philadelphia, PA 19104. Offers AM, PhD, JD/AM, JD/PhD. *Faculty:* 37 full-time (5 women), 4 part-time/adjunct (0 women). *Students:* 125 full-time (38 women); includes 4 minority (all Asian Americans or Pacific Islanders), 87 international. 758 applicants, 13% accepted, 6 enrolled. In 2009, 17 master's, 22 doctorates awarded. *Degree requirements:* For doctorate, thesis/dissertation. *Entrance requirements:* For doctorate, GRE General Test. Additional exam requirements/recommendations for international students: Required—TOEFL. *Application deadline:* For fall admission, 12/1 priority date for domestic students. Application fee: $70. Electronic applications accepted. *Expenses:* Tuition: Full-time $25,660; part-time $4758 per course. Required fees: $2152; $270 per course. Tuition and fees vary according to course load, degree level and program. *Financial support:* Institutionally sponsored loans, scholarships/grants, traineeships, health care benefits, and unspecified assistantships available. Financial award application deadline: 12/15. *Faculty research:* Economic theory, econometrics, international economics, monetary/macroeconomics, applied microeconomics, empirical microeconomics.

University of Pittsburgh, Graduate School of Public and International Affairs, Doctoral Program in Public and International Affairs, Pittsburgh, PA 15260. Offers development policy (PhD); foreign and security policy (PhD); international political economy (PhD); public administration (PhD); public policy (PhD). *Accreditation:* NASPAA. Part-time programs available. *Faculty:* 28 full-time (8 women), 56 part-time/adjunct (20 women). *Students:* 11 full-time (4 women), 27 part-time (16 women); includes 4 minority (2 African Americans, 1 Asian American or Pacific Islander, 1 Hispanic American), 7 international. Average age 30. 63 applicants, 14% accepted, 5 enrolled. In 2009, 9 doctorates awarded. *Degree requirements:* For doctorate, comprehensive exam, thesis/dissertation. *Entrance requirements:* For doctorate, GRE, 3 letters of recommendation, resume, minimum GPA of 3.0, writing sample. Additional exam requirements/recommendations for international students: Required—TOEFL (minimum score 600 paper-based; 250 computer-based; 100 iBT), TWE (minimum score 4); Recommended—IELTS (minimum score 7). *Application deadline:* For fall admission, 2/1 for domestic students, 1/15 for international students. Application fee: $50. Electronic applications accepted. *Expenses:* Tuition, state resident: full-time $16,402; part-time $665 per credit. Tuition, nonresident: full-time $28,694; part-time $1175 per credit. Required fees: $690; $175 per term. Tuition and fees vary according to program. *Financial support:* In 2009–10, 17 students received support, including 6 fellowships (averaging $34,925 per year); scholarships/grants, tuition waivers (full and partial), and unspecified assistantships also available. Financial award application deadline: 2/1. *Faculty research:* International political economy, international development, public administration, public policy, foreign policy, international security policy. Total annual research expenditures: $357,117. *Unit head:* Dr. Kevin P. Kearns, Program Coordinator, 412-648-7621, Fax: 412-648-2605, E-mail: kkearns@pitt.edu. *Application contact:* Julie Korade, Program Administrator/Graduate Enrollment Counselor, 412-648-7640, Fax: 412-648-7641, E-mail: korade@pitt.edu.

University of Pittsburgh, Graduate School of Public and International Affairs, International Affairs Division, Pittsburgh, PA 15260. Offers global political economy (MPIA); human security (MPIA); security and intelligence studies (MPIA); JD/MPIA; MBA/MPIA; MID/MPIA; MPA/MPIA; MSIS/MPIA. Part-time and evening/weekend programs available. *Faculty:* 28 full-time (8 women), 56 part-time/adjunct (20 women). *Students:* 125 full-time (52 women), 19 part-time (11 women); includes 17 minority (10 African Americans, 4 Asian Americans or Pacific Islanders, 3 Hispanic Americans), 5 international. Average age 25. 270 applicants, 81% accepted, 79 enrolled. In 2009, 61 master's awarded. *Degree requirements:* For master's, thesis optional, internship, capstone seminar. *Entrance requirements:* For master's, GRE General Test, 3 letters of recommendation, resume, minimum GPA of 3.2. Additional exam requirements/recommendations for international students: Required—TOEFL (minimum score 550 paper-based; 213 computer-based), TWE (minimum score 4); Recommended—IELTS (minimum score 7). *Application deadline:* For fall admission, 3/1 for domestic students, 1/15 for international students; for spring admission, 11/1 for domestic students, 8/1 for international students. Application fee: $50. Electronic applications accepted. *Expenses:* Tuition, state resident: full-time $16,402; part-time $665 per credit. Tuition, nonresident: full-time $28,694; part-time $1175 per credit. Required fees: $690; $175 per term. Tuition and fees vary according to program. *Financial support:* In 2009–10, 45 students received support, including 6 fellowships (averaging $41,800 per year); career-related internships or fieldwork, scholarships/grants, tuition waivers (full and partial), and unspecified assistantships also available. Financial award application deadline: 2/1. *Faculty research:* International political economy, international security and intelligence, transnational organized crime, international trade, international finance, globalization, terrorism, multinational corporations and the global economy. Total annual research expenditures: $357,117. *Unit head:* Dr. Martin Staniland, Director, International Affairs and International Development Divisions, 412-648-7656, Fax: 412-648-2605, E-mail: mstan@pitt.edu. *Application contact:* Kelly C. McDevitt, Graduate Enrollment Counselor, 412-648-7640, Fax: 412-648-7641, E-mail: mcdevitt@pitt.edu.

University of Pittsburgh, School of Arts and Sciences, Department of Economics, Pittsburgh, PA 15260. Offers PhD. *Faculty:* 23 full-time (3 women). *Students:* 44 full-time (15 women); includes 23 minority (18 Asian Americans or Pacific Islanders, 5 Hispanic Americans). Average age 26. 290 applicants, 26% accepted, 12 enrolled. In 2009, 10 doctorates awarded. Terminal master's awarded for partial completion of doctoral program. *Degree requirements:* For doctorate, comprehensive exam, thesis/dissertation, comprehensive research paper. *Entrance requirements:* For doctorate, GRE, 3 letters of recommendation. Additional exam requirements/recommendations for international students: Required—TOEFL (minimum score 550 paper-based; 213 computer-based; 80 iBT), IELTS (minimum score 6.5). *Application deadline:* For fall admission, 1/15 for domestic and international students. Application fee: $50. Electronic applications accepted. *Expenses:* Tuition, state resident: full-time $16,402; part-time $665 per credit. Tuition, nonresident: full-time $28,694; part-time $1175 per credit. Required fees: $690; $175 per term. Tuition and fees vary according to program. *Financial support:* In 2009–10, 38 students received support, including 12 fellowships with full tuition reimbursements available (averaging $17,972 per year), 5 research assistantships with full tuition reimbursements available (averaging $15,675 per year), 21 teaching assistantships with full tuition reimbursements available (averaging $15,675 per year); institutionally sponsored loans, scholarships/grants, traineeships, health care benefits, and unspecified assistantships also available. Financial award application deadline: 1/15. *Faculty research:* Game theory, experimental economics, econometrics, labor, international trade. Total annual research expenditures: $2.1 million. *Unit head:* Dr. David N. De Jong, Department Chair, 412-648-2242, Fax: 41-648-7038, E-mail: dejong@pitt.edu. *Application contact:* Amy M. Linn, Graduate Program Administrator, 412-648-1399, Fax: 412-648-1793, E-mail: amlinn@pitt.edu.

University of Puerto Rico, Río Piedras, College of Social Sciences, Department of Economics, San Juan, PR 00931-3300. Offers MA. Part-time programs available. *Degree requirements:* For master's, comprehensive exam, thesis. *Entrance requirements:* For master's, GRE, PAEG, interview, minimum GPA of 3.0, letter of recommendation.

University of Regina, Faculty of Graduate Studies and Research, Johnson-Shoyama Graduate School of Public Policy, Regina, SK S4S 0A2, Canada. Offers economic analysis for public policy (Master's Certificate); non-profit management (Master's Certificate); public management (MPA, Master's Certificate); public policy (MPA, PhD, Master's Certificate). Part-time and evening/weekend programs available. *Faculty:* 6 full-time (3 women). *Students:* 51 full-time (24 women), 71 part-time (39 women). 113 applicants, 89% accepted. In 2009, 51 master's awarded. *Entrance requirements:* Additional exam requirements/recommendations for international students: Required—TOEFL (minimum score 580 paper-based; 237 computer-based; 80 iBT). *Application deadline:* Applications are processed on a rolling basis. Application fee: $90 ($100 for international students). Electronic applications accepted. *Expenses:* Contact institution. *Financial support:* In 2009–10, 7 fellowships (averaging $19,000 per year), 2 research assistantships (averaging $16,910 per year), 11 teaching assistantships (averaging $6,650 per year) were awarded. Financial award application deadline: 6/15. *Faculty research:* Public administration and policy. *Unit head:* Dr. Sylvain Charlebois, Associate Dean, 306-585-2695, E-mail: sylvain.charlebois@uregina.ca. *Application contact:* Elaine Groenendyk, Information Contact, 306-585-5462, E-mail: elaine.groenendyk@uregina.ca.

University of Rhode Island, Graduate School, College of the Environment and Life Sciences, Department of Environmental and Natural Resource Economics, Kingston, RI 02881. Offers MESM, MS, PhD. Part-time programs available. *Faculty:* 6 full-time (2 women), 2 part-time/adjunct (0 women). *Students:* 24 full-time (9 women), 8 part-time (4 women); includes 3 minority (1 African American, 2 Hispanic Americans), 11 international. In 2009, 4 master's, 4 doctorates awarded. *Degree requirements:* For master's, comprehensive exam (for some programs), thesis optional; for doctorate, comprehensive exam, thesis/dissertation. *Entrance requirements:* For master's, GRE, 2 letters of recommendation; for doctorate, GRE, 3 letters of recommendation. Additional exam requirements/recommendations for international students: Required—TOEFL (minimum score 550 paper-based; 213 computer-based). *Application deadline:* For fall admission, 7/15 for domestic students, 2/1 for international students; for spring admission, 11/15 for domestic students, 7/15 for international students. Application fee: $65. Electronic applications accepted. *Expenses:* Tuition, state resident: full-time $8828; part-time $490 per credit hour. Tuition, nonresident: full-time $22,100; part-time $1228 per credit hour. Required fees: $1118; $57 per semester. Tuition and fees vary according to program. *Financial support:* In 2009–10, 1 research assistantship with partial tuition reimbursement (averaging $6,947 per year), 6 teaching assistantships with full and partial tuition reimbursements (averaging $11,145 per year) were awarded. Financial award application deadline: 7/15; financial award applicants required to submit FAFSA. *Faculty research:* The Policy Simulation Laboratory utilizes computer technologies to help understand the consequences of policy actions, experimental economics. Total annual research expenditures: $654,763. *Unit head:* Dr. James L. Anderson, Chair, 401-874-4568, Fax: 401-874-4766, E-mail: jla@uri.edu. *Application contact:* Dr. Christopher M. Anderson, Director of Graduate Studies, 401-874-4587, Fax: 401-874-4766, E-mail: cma@uri.edu.

University of Rochester, The College, Arts and Sciences, Department of Economics, Rochester, NY 14627. Offers MA, PhD. *Degree requirements:* For doctorate, thesis/dissertation, qualifying exam. *Entrance requirements:* For doctorate, GRE General Test, GRE Subject Test (strongly recommended). Additional exam requirements/recommendations for international students: Required—TOEFL.

University of San Francisco, College of Arts and Sciences, Department of Economics, San Francisco, CA 94117-1080. Offers economics (MA); financial analysis (MS); international and development economics (MA); MS/MBA. Part-time and evening/weekend programs available. *Faculty:* 8 full-time (2 women), 9 part-time/adjunct (3 women). *Students:* 167 full-time (69 women), 6 part-time (2 women); includes 42 minority (5 African Americans, 26 Asian Americans or Pacific Islanders, 11 Hispanic Americans), 70 international. Average age 28. 627 applicants, 47% accepted, 96 enrolled. In 2009, 92 master's awarded. *Degree requirements:* For master's, comprehensive exam, thesis or alternative. *Entrance requirements:* For master's, GRE General Test (recommended), BA in economics (preferred). Additional exam requirements/recommendations for international students: Required—TOEFL. *Application deadline:* For fall admission, 7/15 priority date for domestic students; for spring admission, 12/15 for domestic students. Applications are processed on a rolling basis. Application fee: $55 ($65 for international students). *Expenses:* Tuition: Full-time $19,710; part-time $1095 per unit. Part-time tuition and fees vary according to degree level, campus/location and program. *Financial support:* In 2009–10, 96 students received support; fellowships, teaching assistantships, career-related internships or fieldwork available. Financial award application deadline: 3/2; financial award applicants required to submit FAFSA. *Faculty research:* Economic development, forecasting and planning, labor markets, Pacific Rim, financial markets. *Unit head:* Man-lui Lau, Chair, 415-422-2765, Fax: 415-422-5784. *Application contact:* Information Contact, 415-422-5135, Fax: 415-422-2217, E-mail: asgraduate@usfca.edu.

University of San Francisco, School of Business and Professional Studies, Masagung Graduate School of Management, Program in Business Administration, San Francisco, CA 94117-1080. Offers business economics (MBA); e-business (MBA); entrepreneurship (MBA); finance (MBA); international business (MBA); management (MBA); marketing (MBA); telecommunications management and policy (MBA); JD/MBA; MSN/MBA. *Accreditation:* AACSB. *Faculty:* 17 full-time (4 women), 16 part-time/adjunct (7 women). *Students:* 278 full-time (140 women), 18 part-time (10 women); includes 94 minority (5 African Americans, 1 American Indian/Alaska Native, 69 Asian Americans or Pacific Islanders, 19 Hispanic Americans), 53 international. Average age 30. 410 applicants, 70% accepted, 133 enrolled. In 2009, 137 master's awarded. *Entrance requirements:* For master's, GMAT, minimum undergraduate GPA of 3.2. Additional exam requirements/recommendations for international students: Required—TOEFL. *Application deadline:* For fall admission, 7/1 priority date for domestic students; for spring admission, 11/30 for domestic students. Applications are processed on a rolling basis. Application fee: $55 ($65 for international students). *Expenses:* Tuition: Full-time $19,710; part-time $1095 per unit. Part-time tuition and fees vary according to degree level, campus/location and program. *Financial support:* In 2009–10, 155 students received support; fellowships available. Financial award application deadline: 3/2; financial award applicants required to submit FAFSA. *Faculty research:* International financial markets, technology transfer licensing, international marketing, strategic planning. Total annual research expenditures: $50,000. *Unit head:* Kelly Brookes, Director, 415-422-2221, Fax: 415-422-6315. *Application contact:* Director, MBA Program, 415-422-2221, Fax: 415-422-6315, E-mail: mba@usfca.edu.

University of Saskatchewan, College of Graduate Studies and Research, College of Arts and Sciences, Department of Economics, Saskatoon, SK S7N 5A2, Canada. Offers MA, Diploma. *Faculty:* 20. *Students:* 27. In 2009, 10 master's awarded. *Degree requirements:* For master's, thesis (for some programs). *Entrance requirements:* Additional exam requirements/recommendations for international students: Required—TOEFL (minimum score 80 iBT); Recommended—IELTS (minimum score 6.5). *Application deadline:* For fall admission, 7/1 priority date for domestic students. Applications are processed on a rolling basis. Application fee: $75. Electronic applications accepted. Tuition and fees charges are reported in Canadian dollars. *Expenses:* Tuition, area resident: Full-time $3000 Canadian dollars; part-time $500 Canadian dollars per term. Required fees: $700 Canadian dollars; $100 Canadian dollars per term. *Financial support:* Fellowships, research assistantships, teaching assistantships available. Financial award application deadline: 1/31. *Unit head:* Dr. Donald Gilchrist, Head, 306-966-5198, Fax: 306-966-5232, E-mail: donald.gilchrist@usask.ca. *Application contact:* Dr. Joel Bruneau, Graduate Chair, 306-966-5198, Fax: 306-966-5232, E-mail: joel.bruneau@usask.ca.

University of South Africa, College of Economic and Management Sciences, Pretoria, South Africa. Offers accounting (D Admin, D Com); accounting science (DA); auditing (D Admin, D Com); business administration (M Tech); business economics (D Admin); business leadership (DBL); business management (D Admin, D Com); economic management analysis (M Tech); economics (D Admin, D Com, PhD); human resource development (M Tech); industrial psychology (D Admin, D Com, PhD); logistics (D Com); marketing (M Tech); public administration (D Admin, D Com, DPA, PhD); public management (M Tech); quantitative management (D Admin, D Com); real estate (M Tech); statistics (D Admin, PhD); tourism management (D Admin, D Com); transport economics (D Admin, D Com).

University of South Carolina, The Graduate School, Moore School of Business, Economics Program, Columbia, SC 29208. Offers MA, PhD, JD/MA. *Degree requirements:* For master's, comprehensive exam (for some programs), thesis; for doctorate, comprehensive exam, thesis/dissertation, qualifying exam. *Entrance requirements:* For master's, GMAT or GRE General Test, minimum GPA of 3.0; for doctorate, GRE General Test. Additional exam requirements/recommendations for international students: Required—TOEFL (minimum score 600 paper-based; 250 computer-based; 100 iBT). Electronic applications accepted. *Faculty research:* Monetary theory, labor economics, international economics, industrial organization.

University of Southern California, Graduate School, College of Letters, Arts and Sciences, Department of Economics, Los Angeles, CA 90089. Offers economic development programming (MA, PhD); mathematical finance (MS); M Pl/MA; MA/JD. *Faculty:* 18 full-time (2 women), 14 part-time/adjunct (0 women). *Students:* 128 full-time (47 women), 6 part-time (2 women); includes 12 minority (1 African American, 8 Asian Americans or Pacific Islanders, 3 Hispanic Americans), 105 international. 355 applicants, 28% accepted, 32 enrolled. In 2009, 34 master's, 9 doctorates awarded. Terminal master's awarded for partial completion of doctoral program. *Degree requirements:* For master's, comprehensive exam, thesis optional; for doctorate, comprehensive exam, thesis/dissertation. *Entrance requirements:* For master's and doctorate, GRE. Additional exam requirements/recommendations for international students: Required—TOEFL (minimum score 93 iBT). *Application deadline:* For fall admission, 12/1 for domestic and international students; for spring admission, 11/1 for domestic and international students. Application fee: $85. *Expenses:* Tuition: Full-time $25,980; part-time $1315 per unit. Required fees: $554. One-time fee: $35 full-time. Full-time tuition and fees vary according to degree level and program. *Financial support:* In 2009–10, 61 students received support, including 14 fellowships with full tuition reimbursements available (averaging $21,000 per year), 4 research assistantships with full tuition reimbursements available (averaging $19,000 per year), 41 teaching assistantships with full tuition reimbursements available (averaging $19,000 per year). *Faculty research:* Applied micro/io, development, econometrics, finance, international finance, macroeconomic theory, microeconomic theory. *Unit head:* Prof. Simon Wilkie, Chair, 213-740-8335, Fax: 213-740-4595, E-mail: swilkie@usc.edu. *Application contact:* Morgan Ponder, Graduate Advisor, 213-740-3507, E-mail: ponder@usc.edu.

University of Southern Mississippi, Graduate School, College of Science and Technology, Department of Economic and Workforce Development, Hattiesburg, MS 39406-0001. Offers economic development (MS); human capital development (PhD); workforce training and development (MS). Part-time programs available. *Faculty:* 6 full-time (3 women). *Students:* 26 full-time (9 women), 48 part-time (30 women); includes 26 minority (25 African Americans, 1 Asian American or Pacific Islander), 2 international. Average age 41. 33 applicants, 39% accepted, 13 enrolled. In 2009, 23 master's awarded. *Degree requirements:* For master's, comprehensive exam, thesis optional, internships; for doctorate, comprehensive exam, thesis/dissertation. *Entrance requirements:* For master's, GMAT, GRE General Test, minimum GPA of 2.75 in last 60 hours; for doctorate, GMAT, GRE General Test, minimum GPA of 3.5. Additional exam requirements/recommendations for international students: Required—TOEFL. *Application deadline:* For fall admission, 8/1 for domestic students, 3/1 for international students; for spring admission, 1/3 for domestic and international students. Application fee: $35. Electronic applications accepted. *Expenses:* Tuition, state resident: full-time $5096; part-time $284 per hour. Tuition, nonresident: full-time $13,052; part-time $726 per hour. Required fees: $402. Tuition and fees vary according to course level and course load. *Financial support:* In 2009–10, 11 students received support, including 2 research assistantships with full tuition reimbursements available (averaging $13,000 per year), 6 teaching assistantships with full tuition reimbursements available (averaging $6,500 per year); career-related internships or fieldwork and Federal Work-Study also available. Financial award application deadline: 3/1; financial award applicants required to submit FAFSA. *Faculty research:* Economic development, international studies, geography. *Unit head:* Dr. Kenneth Malone, Chair, 601-266-4736, Fax: 601-266-6071, E-mail: ken.malone@usm.edu. *Application contact:* Dr. Cyndi Gaudet, Graduate Coordinator, 601-266-6519, Fax: 601-266-6071.

University of South Florida, Graduate School, College of Arts and Sciences, Department of Economics, Tampa, FL 33620-9951. Offers MA, PhD. Part-time and evening/weekend programs available. *Faculty:* 13 full-time (1 woman), 1 part-time/adjunct (0 women). *Students:* 16 full-time (6 women), 9 part-time (4 women); includes 8 minority (3 African Americans, 1 Asian American or Pacific Islander, 4 Hispanic Americans), 3 international. Average age 32. 42 applicants, 50% accepted, 15 enrolled. In 2009, 10 master's awarded. *Degree requirements:* For master's, comprehensive exam; for doctorate, comprehensive exam, thesis/dissertation. *Entrance requirements:* For master's, GMAT, minimum GPA of 3.0 in last 60 hours of course work. Additional exam requirements/recommendations for international students: Required—TOEFL (minimum score 550 paper-based; 213 computer-based). *Application deadline:* For fall admission, 6/1 for domestic students, 1/2 for international students; for spring admission, 10/15 for domestic students, 6/1 for international students. Applications are processed on a rolling basis. Application fee: $30. *Financial support:* In 2009–10, teaching assistantships with tuition reimbursements (averaging $21,756 per year); unspecified assistantships also available. Financial award application deadline: 2/1; financial award applicants required to submit FAFSA. Total annual research expenditures: $105,942. *Unit head:* Dr. Kwabena Gyimah-Brempong, Chairperson, 813-974-4252, Fax: 813-974-6510, E-mail: kgyimah@coba.usf.edu. *Application contact:* Michael Loewy, Program Director, 813-974-4653, Fax: 813-974-6510, E-mail: mloewy@coba.usf.edu.

The University of Tampa, John H. Sykes College of Business, Tampa, FL 33606-1490. Offers accounting (MBA, MS); economics (MBA); entrepreneurship and innovation (MBA); finance (MBA, MS); information systems management (MBA); international business (MBA); management (MBA); marketing (MBA, MS); nonprofit management (MBA). *Accreditation:* AACSB. Part-time and evening/weekend programs available. *Faculty:* 62 full-time (22 women), 11 part-time/adjunct (4 women). *Students:* 240 full-time (101 women), 338 part-time (133 women); includes 95 minority (16 African Americans, 4 American Indian/Alaska Native, 24 Asian Americans or Pacific Islanders, 51 Hispanic Americans), 122 international. Average age 29. 564 applicants, 51% accepted, 186 enrolled. In 2009, 234 master's awarded. *Entrance requirements:* For master's, GMAT. Additional exam requirements/recommendations for international students: Required—TOEFL (minimum score 577 paper-based; 230 computer-based; 90 iBT), IELTS. *Application deadline:* For fall admission, 7/15 for domestic students, 6/1 for international students; for spring admission, 12/15 for domestic students, 11/1 for international students. Applications are processed on a rolling basis. Application fee: $40. Electronic applications accepted. *Expenses:* Tuition: Part-time $488 per credit hour. *Financial support:* In 2009–10, 332 students received support, including 71 research assistantships with full tuition reimbursements available (averaging $6,757 per year); career-related internships or fieldwork, scholarships/grants, and unspecified assistantships also available. Support available to part-time students. Financial award applicants required to submit FAFSA. *Faculty research:* Information systems, leadership, corporate governance, entrepreneurship, hedonic price estimation. *Unit head:* Dr. Don Morrill, Associate Dean, Graduate and Continuing Studies, 813-257-3557, E-mail: dmorrill@ut.edu. *Application contact:* Karen Full, Director of Admissions, Graduate and Continuing Studies, 813-257-3642, E-mail: kfull@ut.edu.

The University of Tennessee, Graduate School, College of Arts and Sciences, Department of Sociology, Knoxville, TN 37996. Offers criminology (MA, PhD); energy, environment, and resource policy (MA, PhD); political economy (MA, PhD). Part-time programs available. *Degree requirements:* For master's, thesis or alternative; for doctorate, thesis/dissertation. *Entrance requirements:* For master's, GRE General Test, minimum GPA of 3.0; for doctorate, GRE General Test, minimum GPA of 3.5. Additional exam requirements/recommendations for international students: Required—TOEFL. Electronic applications accepted. *Expenses:* Tuition, state resident: full-time $6826; part-time $380 per semester hour. Tuition, nonresident: full-time $21,844; part-time $1147 per semester hour. Tuition and fees vary according to program.

The University of Tennessee, Graduate School, College of Business Administration, Department of Economics, Knoxville, TN 37996. Offers MA, PhD. *Degree requirements:* For master's, thesis or alternative; for doctorate, thesis/dissertation. *Entrance requirements:* For master's and doctorate, GRE General Test or GMAT, minimum GPA of 2.7. Additional exam requirements/recommendations for international students: Required—TOEFL. Electronic applications accepted. *Expenses:* Tuition, state resident: full-time $6826; part-time $380 per semester hour. Tuition, nonresident: full-time $21,844; part-time $1147 per semester hour. Tuition and fees vary according to program.

The University of Texas at Arlington, Graduate School, College of Business, Economics Department, Arlington, TX 76019. Offers MA. Part-time and evening/weekend programs available. *Faculty:* 10 full-time (2 women). *Students:* 25 full-time (7 women), 16 part-time (2 women); includes 13 minority (5 African Americans, 4 Asian Americans or Pacific Islanders, 4 Hispanic Americans), 7 international. 43 applicants, 95% accepted, 22 enrolled. In 2009, 12 master's awarded. *Degree requirements:* For master's, thesis optional. *Entrance requirements:* For master's, GMAT or GRE General Test. Additional exam requirements/recommendations for international students: Required—TOEFL (minimum score 550 paper-based; 213 computer-based; 79 iBT). *Application deadline:* For fall admission, 6/5 for domestic students, 4/1 for international students; for spring admission, 10/15 for domestic students, 9/1 for international students. Applications are processed on a rolling basis. Application fee: $35 ($50 for international students). *Financial support:* In 2009–10, 1 fellowship (averaging $1,000 per year), research assistantships (averaging $6,000 per year), 14 teaching assistantships (averaging $13,000 per year) were awarded; career-related internships or fieldwork, scholarships/grants, and unspecified assistantships also available. Support available to part-time students. Financial award application deadline: 6/1; financial award applicants required to submit FAFSA. *Unit head:* Dr. Daniel Himarios, Chair, 817-272-2881, Fax: 817-272-2073, E-mail: himarios@uta.edu. *Application contact:* Dr. Roger Wehr, Graduate Advisor, 817-272-3287, Fax: 817-272-3145, E-mail: wehr@uta.edu.

The University of Texas at Austin, Graduate School, College of Liberal Arts, Department of Economics, Austin, TX 78712-1111. Offers MA, MS Econ, PhD. Part-time programs available. *Degree requirements:* For master's, thesis; for doctorate, comprehensive exam, thesis/dissertation. *Entrance requirements:* For master's and doctorate, GRE General Test, minimum GPA of 3.5 (based on upper-division undergraduate and graduate course work). Additional

Economics

The University of Texas at Austin (continued)
exam requirements/recommendations for international students: Required—TOEFL. Electronic applications accepted. *Faculty research:* Industrial organization, game theory, monetary economics, labor economics, public economics.

The University of Texas at Dallas, School of Economic, Political and Policy Sciences, Program in Economics, Richardson, TX 75080. Offers MS, PhD. Part-time and evening/weekend programs available. *Faculty:* 14 full-time (4 women). *Students:* 52 full-time (19 women), 15 part-time (4 women); includes 17 minority (6 African Americans, 10 Asian Americans or Pacific Islanders, 1 Hispanic American), 25 international. Average age 29. 93 applicants, 63% accepted, 34 enrolled. In 2009, 2 master's, 4 doctorates awarded. *Degree requirements:* For master's, internship; for doctorate, thesis/dissertation. *Entrance requirements:* For master's and doctorate, GRE General Test, minimum GPA of 3.0 in upper-level course work in field. Additional exam requirements/recommendations for international students: Required—TOEFL (minimum score 550 paper-based; 213 computer-based). *Application deadline:* For fall admission, 7/15 for domestic students, 5/1 priority date for international students; for spring admission, 11/15 for domestic students, 9/1 priority date for international students. Applications are processed on a rolling basis. Application fee: $50 ($100 for international students). Electronic applications accepted. *Expenses:* Tuition, state resident: full-time $11,068; part-time $461 per credit hour. Tuition, nonresident: full-time $21,178; part-time $882 per credit hour. Tuition and fees vary according to course load. *Financial support:* In 2009–10, 10 research assistantships with full tuition reimbursements (averaging $12,865 per year), 16 teaching assistantships with full tuition reimbursements (averaging $11,735 per year) were awarded; fellowships, career-related internships or fieldwork, Federal Work-Study, institutionally sponsored loans, scholarships/grants, and unspecified assistantships also available. Support available to part-time students. Financial award application deadline: 4/30; financial award applicants required to submit FAFSA. *Faculty research:* Economic base of distressed counties, analysis of nonprofits and their for-profit counterparts. *Unit head:* Dr. Daniel Arce, Program Head, 972-883-6857, Fax: 972-883-2735, E-mail: darce@utdallas.edu. *Application contact:* Dr. Nathan Berg, Associate Program Head, 972-883-2088, Fax: 972-883-2735, E-mail: nberg@utdallas.edu.

See Close-Up on page 759.

The University of Texas at Dallas, School of Economic, Political and Policy Sciences, Program in Public Policy and Political Economy, Richardson, TX 75080. Offers international political economy (MS); public policy (MPP); public policy and political economy (PhD). Part-time and evening/weekend programs available. *Faculty:* 16 full-time (4 women). *Students:* 49 full-time (25 women), 45 part-time (19 women); includes 28 minority (12 African Americans, 10 Asian Americans or Pacific Islanders, 6 Hispanic Americans), 19 international. Average age 36. 59 applicants, 68% accepted, 31 enrolled. In 2009, 5 master's, 8 doctorates awarded. *Degree requirements:* For doctorate, thesis/dissertation. *Entrance requirements:* For master's and doctorate, GRE General Test, minimum GPA of 3.0 in upper-level course work in field. Additional exam requirements/recommendations for international students: Required—TOEFL (minimum score 550 paper-based; 213 computer-based). *Application deadline:* For fall admission, 7/15 for domestic students, 5/1 priority date for international students; for spring admission, 11/15 for domestic students, 9/1 priority date for international students. Applications are processed on a rolling basis. Application fee: $50 ($100 for international students). Electronic applications accepted. *Expenses:* Tuition, state resident: full-time $11,068; part-time $461 per credit hour. Tuition, nonresident: full-time $21,178; part-time $882 per credit hour. Tuition and fees vary according to course load. *Financial support:* In 2009–10, 5 research assistantships with full tuition reimbursements (averaging $12,690 per year), 11 teaching assistantships with full tuition reimbursements (averaging $11,905 per year) were awarded; fellowships, career-related internships or fieldwork, Federal Work-Study, institutionally sponsored loans, and scholarships/grants also available. Support available to part-time students. Financial award application deadline: 4/30; financial award applicants required to submit FAFSA. *Faculty research:* New leadership development, gender and leadership, globalization and leadership opportunities in democracy. *Unit head:* Dr. Sheila Amin Gutierrez de Pineres, Program Head, 972-883-6228, Fax: 972-883-2735, E-mail: pineres@utdallas.edu. *Application contact:* Dr. Marie I. Chevrier, Associate Program Head, 972-883-2727, Fax: 972-883-2735, E-mail: chevrier@utdallas.edu.

See Close-Up on page 759.

The University of Texas at El Paso, Graduate School, College of Business Administration, Department of Economics and Finance, El Paso, TX 79968-0001. Offers economics (MS). Part-time and evening/weekend programs available. *Degree requirements:* For master's, thesis optional. *Entrance requirements:* For master's, GMAT, minimum GPA of 2.7. Additional exam requirements/recommendations for international students: Required—TOEFL. Electronic applications accepted.

The University of Texas at San Antonio, College of Business, Department of Economics, San Antonio, TX 78249-0617. Offers business economics (MBA); economics (MA). Part-time and evening/weekend programs available. *Faculty:* 7 full-time (3 women), 1 part-time/adjunct (0 women). *Students:* 8 full-time (2 women), 14 part-time (2 women); includes 7 minority (2 Asian Americans or Pacific Islanders, 5 Hispanic Americans), 2 international. Average age 30. 24 applicants, 71% accepted, 12 enrolled. In 2009, 6 master's awarded. *Degree requirements:* For master's, comprehensive exam (for some programs), thesis (for some programs). *Entrance requirements:* For master's, GMAT or GRE, minimum GPA of 3.0. Additional exam requirements/recommendations for international students: Required—TOEFL (minimum score 500 paper-based; 173 computer-based; 61 iBT), IELTS (minimum score 5). *Application deadline:* For fall admission, 7/1 for domestic students, 4/1 for international students; for spring admission, 11/1 for domestic students, 9/1 for international students. Application fee: $45 ($80 for international students). *Expenses:* Tuition, state resident: full-time $3975; part-time $221 per contact hour. Tuition, nonresident: full-time $13,947; part-time $775 per contact hour. Required fees: $1853. *Financial support:* In 2009–10, 4 students received support, including 3 research assistantships (averaging $10,400 per year), 11 teaching assistantships (averaging $7,055 per year); career-related internships or fieldwork, Federal Work-Study, scholarships/grants, and unspecified assistantships also available. Support available to part-time students. *Faculty research:* International economics, macroeconomics, microeconomics, econometrics, forecasting. Total annual research expenditures: $67,632. *Unit head:* Dr. Kenneth E. Weiher, Chair, 210-458-5315, Fax: 210-458-5837, E-mail: kweiher@utsa.edu. *Application contact:* Dr. Dorothy A. Flannagan, Dean of the Graduate School, 210-458-4330, Fax: 210-458-4332, E-mail: dorothy.flannagan@utsa.edu.

The University of Texas–Pan American, College of Business Administration, Program in International Business, Edinburg, TX 78539. Offers computer information systems (PhD); economics (PhD); finance (PhD); management (PhD); marketing (PhD). *Degree requirements:* For doctorate, comprehensive exam, thesis/dissertation. *Entrance requirements:* For doctorate, GMAT or GRE. Additional exam requirements/recommendations for international students: Required—TOEFL, IELTS. Electronic applications accepted. *Expenses:* Contact institution.

The University of Toledo, College of Graduate Studies, College of Arts and Sciences, Department of Economics, Toledo, OH 43606-3390. Offers MA. *Degree requirements:* For master's, comprehensive exam, paper or thesis. *Entrance requirements:* For master's, GRE General Test, minimum GPA of 2.75. Electronic applications accepted. *Faculty research:* Economic development.

The University of Toledo, College of Graduate Studies, College of Business Administration, Department of Finance and Business Economics, Toledo, OH 43606-3390. Offers MBA. Evening/weekend programs available. *Degree requirements:* For master's, thesis or alternative. *Entrance requirements:* For master's, GMAT. Additional exam requirements/recommendations for international students: Required—TOEFL. *Faculty research:* Financial management, banking, international finance, investments.

The University of Toledo, College of Graduate Studies, College of Education, Department of Curriculum and Instruction, Program in Education and Economics, Toledo, OH 43606-3390. Offers MAE.

University of Toronto, School of Graduate Studies, Social Sciences Division, Department of Economics, Toronto, ON M5S 1A1, Canada. Offers MA, MFE, PhD. Part-time programs available. *Degree requirements:* For doctorate, comprehensive exam, thesis/dissertation. *Entrance requirements:* For master's, GRE (for applicants without a degree from a Canadian university), minimum B average in final year, 2 letters of reference; for doctorate, GRE (for applicants without a degree from a Canadian university), master's degree in economics, minimum B+ average, 3 letters of reference. Additional exam requirements/recommendations for international students: Required—TOEFL (minimum score 580 paper-based; 237 computer-based), TWE (minimum score 5), IELTS (minimum score: 7) or Michigan English Language Assessment Battery (minimum score: 85).

University of Utah, The Graduate School, College of Social and Behavioral Science, Department of Economics, Salt Lake City, UT 84112-1107. Offers econometrics (M Stat); economics (M Phil, MA, MS, PhD). Part-time programs available. *Faculty:* 22 full-time (5 women). *Students:* 53 full-time (14 women), 45 part-time (11 women); includes 13 minority (5 Asian Americans or Pacific Islanders, 8 Hispanic Americans), 36 international. Average age 32. 132 applicants, 45% accepted, 20 enrolled. In 2009, 9 master's, 3 doctorates awarded. Terminal master's awarded for partial completion of doctoral program. *Degree requirements:* For master's, thesis or alternative, exam, oral presentation, research project; for doctorate, comprehensive exam, thesis/dissertation. *Entrance requirements:* For master's, GRE General Test, undergraduate course work in economics; for doctorate, GRE General Test, GRE Subject Test, minimum GPA of 3.0, course work in calculus and statistics. Additional exam requirements/recommendations for international students: Required—TOEFL (minimum score 500 paper-based; 173 computer-based) or IELTS (minimum score 5. *Application deadline:* For fall admission, 2/1 priority date for domestic and international students. Application fee: $55 ($65 for international students). *Expenses:* Tuition, state resident: full-time $4004; part-time $1674 per semester. Tuition, nonresident: full-time $14,134; part-time $5915 per semester. Required fees: $324 per semester. Tuition and fees vary according to course load, degree level and program. *Financial support:* In 2009–10, 41 students received support, including fellowships with full tuition reimbursements available (averaging $10,000 per year), 1 research assistantship (averaging $11,000 per year), 6 teaching assistantships (averaging $10,500 per year); career-related internships or fieldwork, Federal Work-Study, institutionally sponsored loans, health care benefits, tuition waivers (full and partial), and unspecified assistantships also available. Financial award application deadline: 2/1. *Faculty research:* History of economic thought, political economy, monetary economy, labor. Total annual research expenditures: $66,203. *Unit head:* Dr. Peter Philips, Chair, 801-581-7481, Fax: 801-585-5649, E-mail: philips@economics.utah.edu. *Application contact:* Tracey Farensworth, Academic Advisor, 801-581-7481, Fax: 801-585-5649, E-mail: tracey.farnsworth@economics.utah.edu.

University of Utah, The Graduate School, Interdepartmental Program in Statistics, Salt Lake City, UT 84112-1107. Offers biostatistics (MST); business (MST); econometrics (MST); educational psychology (MST); mathematics (MST); sociology (MST); statistics (M Stat). Part-time programs available. *Students:* 25 full-time (11 women), 15 part-time (6 women); includes 4 minority (3 Asian Americans or Pacific Islanders, 1 Hispanic American), 12 international. Average age 30. 59 applicants, 44% accepted, 12 enrolled. In 2009, 15 master's awarded. *Degree requirements:* For master's, comprehensive exam, projects. *Entrance requirements:* For master's, GMAT (business), GRE General Test (sociology and educational psychology), minimum GPA of 3.0; course work in calculus, matrix theory, statistics. Additional exam requirements/recommendations for international students: Required—TOEFL (minimum score 500 paper-based; 173 computer-based). *Application deadline:* For fall admission, 7/1 for domestic students, 4/1 for international students. Applications are processed on a rolling basis. Application fee: $55 ($65 for international students). *Expenses:* Tuition, state resident: full-time $4004; part-time $1674 per semester. Tuition, nonresident: full-time $14,134; part-time $5915 per semester. Required fees: $324 per semester. Tuition and fees vary according to course load, degree level and program. *Financial support:* Career-related internships or fieldwork available. *Faculty research:* Biostatistics, management, economics, educational psychology, mathematics. *Unit head:* Tariq Mughal, Chair, University Statistics Committee, 801-585-9547, E-mail: tariaq.mughal@business.utah.edu. *Application contact:* Laura Egbert, MSTAT Program Coordinator, 801-585-6853, E-mail: laura.demattia@utah.edu.

University of Victoria, Faculty of Graduate Studies, Faculty of Social Sciences, Department of Economics, Victoria, BC V8W 2Y2, Canada. Offers MA, PhD. Part-time programs available. *Degree requirements:* For master's, comprehensive exam (for some programs), thesis optional; for doctorate, comprehensive exam, thesis/dissertation, candidacy exam. *Entrance requirements:* For master's and doctorate, GRE. Additional exam requirements/recommendations for international students: Required—TOEFL (minimum score 575 paper-based; 233 computer-based), IELTS (minimum score 7). Electronic applications accepted. *Faculty research:* Industrial organization, cost/benefit, applied economics, econometrics, airline economics, health economics.

University of Virginia, College and Graduate School of Arts and Sciences, Department of Economics, Charlottesville, VA 22903. Offers MA, PhD, JD/MA. *Faculty:* 34 full-time (5 women), 2 part-time/adjunct (0 women). *Students:* 99 full-time (39 women); includes 3 Asian Americans or Pacific Islanders, 55 international. Average age 27. 417 applicants, 27% accepted, 27 enrolled. In 2009, 20 master's, 13 doctorates awarded. *Degree requirements:* For master's, comprehensive exam (for some programs), thesis (for some programs), thesis or comprehensive exam; for doctorate, comprehensive exam, thesis/dissertation. *Entrance requirements:* For master's and doctorate, GRE General Test. Additional exam requirements/recommendations for international students: Required—TOEFL (minimum score 600 paper-based; 250 computer-based; 90 iBT), IELTS (minimum score 7). *Application deadline:* For fall admission, 4/1 for domestic and international students. Applications are processed on a rolling basis. Application fee: $60. Electronic applications accepted. *Financial support:* Fellowships, research assistantships, teaching assistantships, tuition waivers (full and partial) available. Financial award application deadline: 2/1; financial award applicants required to submit FAFSA. *Faculty research:* Macroeconomics, public economics, labor, industrial organization, economic history. *Unit head:* Charlie Holt, Chair, 434-924-3177, Fax: 434-982-2904, E-mail: econ@virginia.edu. *Application contact:* Leora Friedburg, Director of Graduate Studies, E-mail: friedberg@virginia.edu.

University of Washington, Graduate School, College of Arts and Sciences, Department of Economics, Seattle, WA 98195. Offers PhD. Terminal master's awarded for partial completion of doctoral program. *Degree requirements:* For doctorate, comprehensive exam, thesis/dissertation. *Entrance requirements:* For doctorate, GRE General Test, minimum GPA of 3.0. Additional exam requirements/recommendations for international students: Required—TOEFL. Electronic applications accepted. *Faculty research:* Microeconomic theory; macroeconomic theory; econometrics; natural resource economics; international, development, and industrial organization.

University of Washington, Graduate School, School of Public Health, Department of Health Services, Seattle, WA 98195. Offers bioinformatics (PhD); cancer prevention and control (PhD); clinical research (MS); community oriented public health practice (MPH); economics or finance (PhD); evaluation sciences (PhD); executive program (MHA); health behavior and health promotion (PhD); health care and population health research (MPH); health policy analysis and process (PhD); health policy and analysis and process (MPH); health services (MS, PhD); health services administration (EMHA, MHA); in residence program (MHA); occupational health (PhD); population health and social determinants (PhD); social and behavioral sciences (MPH); sociology and demography (PhD); JD/MHA; MHA/MBA; MHA/MD; MHA/MPA; MPH/JD; MPH/MD; MPH/MN; MPH/MPA; MPH/MSD; MPH/MSW; MPH/PhD. Part-time and evening/weekend programs available. Postbaccalaureate distance learning degree programs offered (minimal on-campus study). *Faculty:* 52 full-time (24 women), 60 part-time/

adjunct (28 women). *Students:* 104 full-time (83 women), 100 part-time (76 women); includes 21 minority (6 African Americans, 1 American Indian/Alaska Native, 11 Asian Americans or Pacific Islanders, 3 Hispanic Americans), 6 international. Average age 34. 375 applicants, 17% accepted, 24 enrolled. In 2009, 33 master's awarded. Terminal master's awarded for partial completion of doctoral program. *Degree requirements:* For master's, thesis (for some programs), practicum (MPH); for doctorate, comprehensive exam, thesis/dissertation. *Entrance requirements:* For master's and doctorate, GRE General Test, minimum GPA of 3.0. Additional exam requirements/recommendations for international students: Required—TOEFL. *Application deadline:* For fall admission, 1/15 for domestic students, 11/1 for international students. Application fee: 50 Albanian leks. Electronic applications accepted. *Financial support:* In 2009–10, 64 students received support, including 10 fellowships with full and partial tuition reimbursements available (averaging $21,000 per year), 10 research assistantships with full and partial tuition reimbursements available (averaging $18,000 per year), 3 teaching assistantships with full and partial tuition reimbursements available (averaging $18,000 per year); career-related internships or fieldwork, Federal Work-Study, institutionally sponsored loans, and traineeships also available. Financial award application deadline: 2/28; financial award applicants required to submit FAFSA. *Faculty research:* Health promotion and disease prevention, maternal and child health, health services research design, program evaluation, health policy. Total annual research expenditures: $10.5 million. *Unit head:* Dr. Larry Kessler, Chair, 206-543-616-2930. *Application contact:* Kitty A. Andert, MPH/MS/PhD Program Manager, 206-616-2926, Fax: 206-543-3964, E-mail: kitander@u.washington.edu.

University of Waterloo, Graduate Studies, Faculty of Arts, Department of Economics, Waterloo, ON N2L 3G1, Canada. Offers MA, PhD. Part-time programs available. *Entrance requirements:* For master's, honors degree, minimum B average. Additional exam requirements/recommendations for international students: Required—TOEFL, TWE. Electronic applications accepted. *Faculty research:* Applied microeconomics, applied macroeconomics, public finance, international trade and finance, wage inflation and consumer problems.

The University of Western Ontario, Faculty of Graduate Studies, Social Sciences Division, Department of Economics, London, ON N6A 5B8, Canada. Offers MA, PhD. *Degree requirements:* For doctorate, thesis/dissertation. *Entrance requirements:* For master's, GRE, honours BA with B+ average. Additional exam requirements/recommendations for international students: Required—TOEFL.

University of Windsor, Faculty of Graduate Studies, Faculty of Science, Department of Economics, Windsor, ON N9B 3P4, Canada. Offers MA. Part-time programs available. *Degree requirements:* For master's, thesis or alternative. *Entrance requirements:* For master's, minimum B average. Additional exam requirements/recommendations for international students: Required—TOEFL (minimum score 560 paper-based; 220 computer-based). Electronic applications accepted. *Faculty research:* International trade, economic growth, microeconomic theory.

University of Wisconsin–Madison, Graduate School, College of Letters and Science, Department of Economics, Madison, WI 53706-1380. Offers PhD. *Degree requirements:* For doctorate, thesis/dissertation. *Entrance requirements:* For doctorate, GRE General Test, 3 semesters of course work in calculus, 1 semester of course work in algebra and mathematics/statistics. Electronic applications accepted. *Expenses:* Tuition, state resident: part-time $594 per credit. Tuition, nonresident: part-time $1504 per credit. Required fees: $65 per credit. Tuition and fees vary according to course load, program and reciprocity agreements.

University of Wisconsin–Milwaukee, Graduate School, College of Letters and Sciences, Department of Economics, Milwaukee, WI 53201-0413. Offers MA, PhD. *Faculty:* 20 full-time (2 women). *Students:* 64 full-time (24 women), 20 part-time (9 women); includes 3 minority (1 African American, 1 Asian American or Pacific Islander, 1 Hispanic American), 43 international. Average age 30. 96 applicants, 88% accepted, 20 enrolled. In 2009, 20 master's, 7 doctorates awarded. *Degree requirements:* For master's, comprehensive exam; for doctorate, comprehensive exam, thesis/dissertation. *Entrance requirements:* For master's, GRE General Test; for doctorate, GRE General Test, GRE Subject Test, minimum GPA of 3.0. Additional exam requirements/recommendations for international students: Required—TOEFL (minimum score 550 paper-based; 79 iBT), IELTS (minimum score 6.5). *Application deadline:* For fall admission, 1/1 priority date for domestic students; for spring admission, 9/1 for domestic students. Applications are processed on a rolling basis. Application fee: $45 ($75 for international students). *Expenses:* Tuition, state resident: full-time $8800. Tuition, nonresident: full-time $20,760. Tuition and fees vary according to program and reciprocity agreements. *Financial support:* In 2009–10, 28 teaching assistantships were awarded; career-related internships or fieldwork and unspecified assistantships also available. Support available to part-time students. Financial award application deadline: 4/15. Total annual research expenditures: $224,000. *Unit head:* Mohsen Bahmani-Oskooee, Representative, 414-229-4334, Fax: 414-229-3860, E-mail: bahmani@uwm.edu. *Application contact:* General Information Contact, 414-229-4982, Fax: 414-229-6967, E-mail: gradschool@uwm.edu.

University of Wyoming, College of Business, Department of Economics and Finance, Program in Economics, Laramie, WY 82070. Offers MS, PhD. Part-time programs available. *Degree requirements:* For master's, thesis; for doctorate, comprehensive exam, thesis/dissertation. *Entrance requirements:* For master's, GRE General Test or GMAT, minimum GPA of 3.0; for doctorate, GRE General Test, minimum GPA of 3.0. Additional exam requirements/recommendations for international students: Required—TOEFL (minimum score 525 paper-based; 197 computer-based). *Faculty research:* Resource and environmental economics, industrial organization, regulation.

University of Wyoming, College of Business, Department of Economics and Finance, Program in Economics and Finance, Laramie, WY 82070. Offers MS. *Degree requirements:* For master's, thesis. *Entrance requirements:* For master's, GRE, minimum GPA of 3.0. Additional exam requirements/recommendations for international students: Required—TOEFL (minimum score 540 paper-based; 207 computer-based; 76 iBT). *Faculty research:* Financial economics.

Utah State University, School of Graduate Studies, College of Business and College of Agriculture, Department of Economics, Logan, UT 84322. Offers applied economics (MS); economics (MA, MS, PhD). Terminal master's awarded for partial completion of doctoral program. *Degree requirements:* For master's, thesis (for some programs); for doctorate, comprehensive exam, thesis/dissertation. *Entrance requirements:* For master's, GRE General Test, GMAT, minimum GPA of 3.0, TOEFL for international; for doctorate, GRE General Test, minimum GPA of 3.0, TOEFL. Additional exam requirements/recommendations for international students: Required—TOEFL. Electronic applications accepted. *Faculty research:* Resource economics, economic theory, international trade, industrial organization, development.

Vanderbilt University, Graduate School, Department of Economics, Nashville, TN 37240-1001. Offers economic development (MA); economics (MA, MAT, PhD); JD/PhD. *Faculty:* 44 full-time (7 women). *Students:* 111 full-time (45 women), 3 part-time (1 woman); includes 3 minority (all Asian Americans or Pacific Islanders), 80 international. Average age 27. 462 applicants, 31% accepted, 42 enrolled. In 2009, 30 master's, 9 doctorates awarded. Terminal master's awarded for partial completion of doctoral program. *Degree requirements:* For master's, thesis or alternative; for doctorate, thesis/dissertation, final and qualifying exams. *Entrance requirements:* For master's and doctorate, GRE General Test, GRE Subject Test (recommended). Additional exam requirements/recommendations for international students: Required—TOEFL (minimum score 570 paper-based; 230 computer-based; 88 iBT). *Application deadline:* For fall admission, 1/15 for domestic and international students; for spring admission, 11/1 for domestic students. Applications are processed on a rolling basis. Application fee: $0. Electronic applications accepted. *Financial support:* Fellowships with full and partial tuition reimbursements, teaching assistantships with full and partial tuition reimbursements, career-related internships or fieldwork, Federal Work-Study, institutionally sponsored loans, scholarships/grants, and health care benefits available. Financial award application deadline: 1/15; financial award applicants required to submit CSS PROFILE or FAFSA. *Faculty research:* Economic theory, applied fields, developmental economics, environmental economics, health economics and policy. *Unit head:* Tong Li, Chair, 615-322-3426, Fax: 615-343-8495, E-mail: tong.li@vanderbilt.edu. *Application contact:* Bill Collins, Director of Graduate Studies, 615-322-3428, Fax: 615-343-8495, E-mail: william.collins@vanderbilt.edu.

Vanderbilt University, Vanderbilt University Law School, Nashville, TN 37203. Offers law (JD, LL M); law and economics (PhD); JD/M Div; JD/MA; JD/MBA; JD/MD; JD/MPP; JD/MTS; JD/PhD; LL M/MA. *Accreditation:* ABA. *Faculty:* 48 full-time (19 women), 75 part-time/adjunct (23 women). *Students:* 595 full-time (292 women); includes 77 minority (29 African Americans, 3 American Indian/Alaska Native, 22 Asian Americans or Pacific Islanders, 23 Hispanic Americans), 45 international. Average age 23. 4,850 applicants, 25% accepted, 195 enrolled. In 2009, 187 first professional degrees, 25 master's awarded. *Entrance requirements:* For JD, LSAT; for master's, foreign law degree. Additional exam requirements/recommendations for international students: Required—TOEFL. *Application deadline:* For fall admission, 3/15 for domestic and international students. Applications are processed on a rolling basis. Application fee: $50. Electronic applications accepted. *Expenses:* Contact institution. *Financial support:* In 2009–10, 393 students received support. Career-related internships or fieldwork, Federal Work-Study, institutionally sponsored loans, scholarships/grants, and health care benefits available. Financial award application deadline: 2/15; financial award applicants required to submit FAFSA. *Unit head:* G. Todd Morton, Assistant Dean for Admissions, 615-322-6452, Fax: 615-322-1531. *Application contact:* Admissions Office, 615-322-6452, Fax: 615-322-1531.

Virginia Commonwealth University, Graduate School, School of Business, Program in Economics, Richmond, VA 23284-9005. Offers MA, MBA, MS. *Degree requirements:* For master's, thesis optional. *Entrance requirements:* For master's, GRE General Test.

Virginia Polytechnic Institute and State University, Graduate School, College of Agriculture and Life Sciences, Department of Agricultural and Applied Economics, Blacksburg, VA 24061. Offers agribusiness (MS); agricultural economics (MS, PhD); applied economics (MS); developmental and international economics (PhD); econometrics (PhD); macro and micro economics (PhD); markets and industrial organizations (PhD); public and regional/urban economics (PhD); resource and environmental economics (PhD). *Faculty:* 22 full-time (5 women). *Students:* 33 full-time (18 women); includes 18 American Indian/Alaska Native, 1 Asian American or Pacific Islander, 1 international. Average age 28. 47 applicants, 43% accepted, 12 enrolled. In 2009, 13 master's, 3 doctorates awarded. *Entrance requirements:* For master's and doctorate, GRE, GMAT. Additional exam requirements/recommendations for international students: Required—TOEFL (minimum score 575 paper-based; 213 computer-based). *Application deadline:* For fall admission, 5/15 for international students; for spring admission, 10/15 for international students. Applications are processed on a rolling basis. Application fee: $65. Electronic applications accepted. *Expenses:* Tuition, area resident: Full-time $10,228; part-time $459 per credit hour. Tuition, nonresident: full-time $17,892; part-time $865 per credit hour. Required fees: $1966; $451 per semester. *Financial support:* In 2009–10, 1 fellowship with full tuition reimbursement (averaging $20,000 per year), 21 research assistantships with full tuition reimbursements (averaging $21,611 per year), 8 teaching assistantships with full tuition reimbursements (averaging $13,481 per year) were awarded; career-related internships or fieldwork, Federal Work-Study, scholarships/grants, and unspecified assistantships also available. Financial award application deadline: 1/15. *Faculty research:* Rural development. Total annual research expenditures: $2.3 million. *Unit head:* Dr. Kevin Boyle, Dean, 540-231-6301, Fax: 540-231-7417, E-mail: kjboyle@vt.edu. *Application contact:* Bradford Mills, Contact, 540-231-6461, Fax: 540-231-7417, E-mail: bfmills@vt.edu.

Virginia Polytechnic Institute and State University, Graduate School, College of Science, Department of Economics, Blacksburg, VA 24061. Offers PhD. *Faculty:* 15 full-time (2 women). *Students:* 23 full-time (9 women), 1 part-time (0 women); includes 20 American Indian/Alaska Native. Average age 29. 118 applicants, 8% accepted, 4 enrolled. In 2009, 5 doctorates awarded. *Entrance requirements:* For doctorate, GRE, GMAT. Additional exam requirements/recommendations for international students: Required—TOEFL (minimum score 500 paper-based; 213 computer-based). *Application deadline:* For fall admission, 5/15 for international students; for spring admission, 10/15 for international students. Applications are processed on a rolling basis. Application fee: $65. Electronic applications accepted. *Expenses:* Tuition, area resident: Full-time $10,228; part-time $459 per credit hour. Tuition, nonresident: full-time $17,892; part-time $865 per credit hour. Required fees: $1966; $451 per semester. *Financial support:* In 2009–10, 20 teaching assistantships with full tuition reimbursements (averaging $13,974 per year) were awarded; career-related internships or fieldwork, Federal Work-Study, scholarships/grants, and unspecified assistantships also available. Financial award application deadline: 1/15. Total annual research expenditures: $118,446. *Unit head:* Dr. Aris Spanos, Dean, 540-231-7981, Fax: 540-231-5097, E-mail: aris@vt.edu. *Application contact:* Richard Ashley, Information Contact, 540-231-6220, Fax: 540-231-5097, E-mail: ashleyr@vt.edu.

Virginia State University, School of Graduate Studies, Research, and Outreach, School of Liberal Arts and Education, Department of Economics, Petersburg, VA 23806-0001. Offers MA. *Degree requirements:* For master's, thesis optional. *Entrance requirements:* For master's, GRE General Test.

Washington State University, Graduate School, College of Agricultural, Human, and Natural Resource Sciences, School of Economic Sciences, Department of Economics, Pullman, WA 99164. Offers applied economics (MA); economics (MA, PhD); international business economics (Certificate). *Faculty:* 34. *Students:* 50 full-time (16 women), 6 part-time (2 women); includes 2 minority (1 American Indian/Alaska Native, 1 Hispanic American), 30 international. Average age 30. 233 applicants, 26% accepted, 26 enrolled. In 2009, 9 master's, 8 doctorates awarded. *Degree requirements:* For master's, comprehensive exam (for some programs), thesis (for some programs), oral exam; for doctorate, comprehensive exam, thesis/dissertation, oral exam, written exam, field exams. *Entrance requirements:* For master's, GRE General Test, Submit a statement of purpose, three letters of reference, copies of all transcripts, GRE scores and (for international students) TOEFL or IELTS scores.; for doctorate, GRE General Test or GMAT, Submit a statement of purpose, three letters of reference, copies of all transcripts, GRE scores and (for international students) TOEFL or IELTS scores. Additional exam requirements/recommendations for international students: Required—TOEFL, IELTS. *Application deadline:* For fall admission, 1/10 priority date for domestic students, 1/10 for international students. Applications are processed on a rolling basis. Application fee: $50. *Financial support:* In 2009–10, research assistantships (averaging $13,917 per year), 13 teaching assistantships (averaging $13,506 per year) were awarded; career-related internships or fieldwork, Federal Work-Study, institutionally sponsored loans, tuition waivers (partial), and teaching associateships also available. Financial award application deadline: 4/1; financial award applicants required to submit FAFSA. *Faculty research:* Economic theory and quantitative methods, applied microeconomics. Total annual research expenditures: $1 million. *Unit head:* Dr. Ron C. Mittelhammer, Director, 509-335-1706, Fax: 509-335-1173, E-mail: mittelha@wsu.edu. *Application contact:* Graduate School Admissions, 800-GRADWSU, Fax: 509-335-1949, E-mail: gradsch@wsu.edu.

Washington University in St. Louis, Graduate School of Arts and Sciences, Department of Economics, St. Louis, MO 63130-4899. Offers PhD. Terminal master's awarded for partial completion of doctoral program. *Degree requirements:* For doctorate, one foreign language, thesis/dissertation. *Entrance requirements:* For doctorate, GRE General Test, GRE Subject Test. Electronic applications accepted.

Wayne State University, College of Liberal Arts and Sciences, Department of Economics, Detroit, MI 48202. Offers MA, PhD, JD/MA. *Degree requirements:* For master's, thesis optional; for doctorate, thesis/dissertation. *Entrance requirements:* For master's, minimum GPA of 3.0; for doctorate, GRE, minimum GPA of 3.0. Additional exam requirements/recommendations for international students: Required—TOEFL (minimum score 550 paper-based; 213 computer-based); Recommended—TWE (minimum score 6). Electronic applications accepted. *Faculty research:* Health economics, international economics, macro economics, urban and labor economics, econometrics.

Economics

Wayne State University, College of Liberal Arts and Sciences, Interdisciplinary Program in Economic Development, Detroit, MI 48202. Offers Certificate. *Entrance requirements:* Additional exam requirements/recommendations for international students: Required—TOEFL (minimum score 550 paper-based; 213 computer-based); Recommended—TWE (minimum score 6). Electronic applications accepted.

West Chester University of Pennsylvania, Office of Graduate Studies, College of Business and Public Affairs, Department of Economics and Finance, West Chester, PA 19383. Offers business administration: economics-finance (MBA). Part-time and evening/weekend programs available. *Students:* 3 part-time (1 woman); includes 1 minority (Asian American or Pacific Islander). Average age 26. 1 applicant, 100% accepted, 1 enrolled. In 2009, 6 master's awarded. *Entrance requirements:* For master's, GMAT, statement of professional goals, resume, three letters of recommendation, interview . Additional exam requirements/recommendations for international students: Required—TOEFL (minimum score 550 paper-based; 213 computer-based; 80 iBT). *Application deadline:* For fall admission, 4/15 for domestic students, 3/15 for international students; for spring admission, 10/15 for domestic students, 9/1 for international students. Applications are processed on a rolling basis. Application fee: $35. Electronic applications accepted. *Expenses:* Tuition, state resident: full-time $6666; part-time $370 per credit. Tuition, nonresident: full-time $10,666; part-time $593 per credit. Required fees: $122.56 per credit. *Financial support:* In 2009–10, research assistantships with full and partial tuition reimbursements (averaging $5,000 per year); unspecified assistantships also available. Support available to part-time students. Financial award application deadline: 2/15; financial award applicants required to submit FAFSA. *Unit head:* Dr. Paul Christ, MBA Director and Graduate Coordinator, 610-425-5000, E-mail: pchrist@wcupa.edu. *Application contact:* Office of Graduate Studies, 610-436-2943, Fax: 610-436-2763, E-mail: gradstudy@wcupa.edu.

Western Illinois University, School of Graduate Studies, College of Business and Technology, Department of Economics, Macomb, IL 61455-1390. Offers MA, Certificate. Part-time programs available. *Students:* 31 full-time (8 women), 1 part-time (0 women); includes 5 minority (4 African Americans, 1 Asian American or Pacific Islander), 22 international. Average age 28. 19 applicants, 68% accepted. In 2009, 19 master's awarded. *Degree requirements:* For master's, thesis or alternative. *Entrance requirements:* Additional exam requirements/recommendations for international students: Required—TOEFL (minimum score 550 paper-based; 213 computer-based; 80 iBT). *Application deadline:* Applications are processed on a rolling basis. Application fee: $30. Electronic applications accepted. *Expenses:* Tuition, state resident: full-time $4486; part-time $249.21 per credit hour. Tuition, nonresident: full-time $8972; part-time $498.42 per credit hour. Required fees: $72.62 per credit hour. *Financial support:* In 2009–10, 12 students received support, including 12 research assistantships with full tuition reimbursements available (averaging $7,280 per year). Financial award applicants required to submit FAFSA. *Unit head:* Dr. Warren Jones, Chairperson, 309-298-1153. *Application contact:* Evelyn Hoing, Assistant Director of Graduate Studies, 309-298-1806, Fax: 309-298-2345, E-mail: grad-office@wiu.edu.

Western Michigan University, Graduate College, College of Arts and Sciences, Department of Economics, Kalamazoo, MI 49008. Offers applied economics (MA, PhD). *Degree requirements:* For master's, thesis, oral or written exams; for doctorate, thesis/dissertation, oral exam, internship. *Entrance requirements:* For doctorate, GRE General Test.

West Texas A&M University, College of Business, Department of Accounting, Economics, and Finance, Program in Finance and Economics, Canyon, TX 79016-0001. Offers MS. Part-time and evening/weekend programs available. Postbaccalaureate distance learning degree programs offered (minimal on-campus study). *Degree requirements:* For master's, comprehensive exam, thesis optional. *Entrance requirements:* For master's, GMAT. Additional exam requirements/recommendations for international students: Required—TOEFL (minimum score 550 paper-based). Electronic applications accepted. *Faculty research:* International trade composition, cycle of poverty, trade effects in Asian countries, structural problems in Japanese economy, reform and the US sugar program-Nebraska.

West Virginia University, College of Business and Economics, Division of Economics and Finance, Morgantown, WV 26506. Offers business analysis (MA); developmental financial economics (PhD); environmental and resource economics (PhD); international economics (PhD); mathematical economics (MA); monetary economics (PhD); public finance (PhD); public policy (MA); regional and urban economics (PhD); statistics and economics (MA). Terminal master's awarded for partial completion of doctoral program. *Degree requirements:* For master's, thesis optional; for doctorate, comprehensive exam, thesis/dissertation. *Entrance requirements:* For master's and doctorate, GRE General Test, minimum GPA of 3.0; course work in intermediate microeconomics, intermediate macroeconomics, calculus, and statistics. Additional exam requirements/recommendations for international students: Required—TOEFL. Electronic applications accepted. *Faculty research:* Financial economics, regional/urban development, public economics, international trade/international finance/development economics, monetary economics.

Wichita State University, Graduate School, W. Frank Barton School of Business, Department of Economics, Wichita, KS 67260. Offers business economics (MA); economic analysis (MA). Part-time and evening/weekend programs available. *Expenses:* Tuition, state resident: full-time $4247; part-time $235.95 per credit hour. Tuition, nonresident: full-time $11,171; part-time $620.60 per credit hour. Required fees: $34; $3.60 per credit hour. $17 per term. Tuition and fees vary according to campus/location and program. *Unit head:* Dr. Jen-Chi Cheng, Chair, 316-978-3220, Fax: 316-978-3845, E-mail: jenchi.cheng@wichita.edu. *Application contact:* Dr. Philip Hersch, Graduate Coordinator, 316-978-3220, Fax: 316-978-3845, E-mail: philip.hersch@wichita.edu.

Wilfrid Laurier University, Faculty of Graduate Studies, School of Business and Economics, Department of Economics, Waterloo, ON N2L 3C5, Canada. Offers MA. *Entrance requirements:* For master's, honors BA or the equivalent in economics, minimum B average in undergraduate course work. Additional exam requirements/recommendations for international students: Required—TOEFL (minimum score 230 computer-based; 89 iBT). Electronic applications accepted. *Faculty research:* Economic forecasting, economic policy analysis, industry and market studies, financial economics, strategic planning, public policy and business.

Wright State University, School of Graduate Studies, Raj Soin College of Business, Department of Economics, Dayton, OH 45435. Offers business economics (MBA); social and applied economics (MS); MBA/MS. *Entrance requirements:* For master's, GRE General Test. Additional exam requirements/recommendations for international students: Required—TOEFL.

Yale University, Graduate School of Arts and Sciences, Department of Economics, New Haven, CT 06520. Offers economics (PhD); international and development economics (MA). *Degree requirements:* For doctorate, thesis/dissertation. *Entrance requirements:* For master's, GRE General Test; for doctorate, GRE General Test, GRE Subject Test. *Faculty research:* Economic history of Western Europe, environmental economics, economic growth and development.

York University, Faculty of Graduate Studies, Faculty of Arts, Program in Economics, Toronto, ON M3J 1P3, Canada. Offers MA, PhD. Part-time programs available. *Degree requirements:* For doctorate, comprehensive exam, thesis/dissertation. Electronic applications accepted.

Youngstown State University, Graduate School, College of Liberal Arts and Social Sciences, Department of Economics, Youngstown, OH 44555-0001. Offers economics (MA); financial economics (MA). Part-time programs available. *Degree requirements:* For master's, comprehensive exam, thesis optional. *Entrance requirements:* For master's, minimum GPA of 2.7, 21 hours in economics. Additional exam requirements/recommendations for international students: Required—TOEFL. *Faculty research:* Forecasting, applied econometrics, labor economics, applied macroeconomics, industrial organization.

International Economics

Claremont Graduate University, Graduate Programs, School of Politics and Economics, Department of Economics, Claremont, CA 91711-6160. Offers business and financial economics (MA, PhD); economic development (Certificate); economics (PhD); industrial organization (PhD); international and development economics (PhD); international economics policy and development (MA); international money and finance (PhD); neuroeconomics (PhD); political economy and public policy (MA); public choice and public economics (PhD); MBA/PhD. Part-time programs available. *Faculty:* 5 full-time (0 women), 1 part-time/adjunct (0 women). *Students:* 103 full-time (25 women), 7 part-time (3 women); includes 16 minority (1 African American, 9 Asian Americans or Pacific Islanders, 6 Hispanic Americans), 62 international. Average age 33. In 2009, 15 master's, 8 doctorates awarded. *Entrance requirements:* For master's and doctorate, GRE General Test or GMAT. Additional exam requirements/recommendations for international students: Required—TOEFL (minimum score 550 paper-based; 213 computer-based; 80 iBT). *Application deadline:* For fall admission, 2/1 priority date for domestic students. Applications are processed on a rolling basis. Application fee: $60. Electronic applications accepted. *Expenses:* Tuition: Full-time $35,046; part-time $1524 per credit. Required fees: $161 per semester. *Financial support:* Fellowships, research assistantships, teaching assistantships, Federal Work-Study, institutionally sponsored loans, and scholarships/grants available. Support available to part-time students. Financial award application deadline: 2/15; financial award applicants required to submit FAFSA. *Faculty research:* International and financial economics, law and economics, regulation, public choice economics. *Unit head:* Paul Zak, Chair, 909-621-8788, Fax: 909-621-8545, E-mail: paul.zak@cgu.edu. *Application contact:* Lesa Hiben, Admissions Coordinator, 909-621-8699, Fax: 909-621-7545, E-mail: lesa.hiben@cga.edu.

Eastern Michigan University, Graduate School, College of Arts and Sciences, Department of Economics, Ypsilanti, MI 48197. Offers applied economics (MA); economics (MA); health economics (MA); international economics and development (MA); trade and development (MA). Part-time and evening/weekend programs available. Postbaccalaureate distance learning degree programs offered (minimal on-campus study). *Faculty:* 11 full-time (2 women). *Students:* 28 full-time (9 women), 29 part-time (12 women); includes 17 minority (12 African Americans, 1 American Indian/Alaska Native, 2 Asian Americans or Pacific Islanders, 2 Hispanic Americans), 12 international. Average age 31. 61 applicants, 67% accepted, 23 enrolled. In 2009, 22 master's awarded. *Degree requirements:* For master's, thesis or alternative. *Entrance requirements:* Additional exam requirements/recommendations for international students: Required—TOEFL. *Application deadline:* Applications are processed on a rolling basis. Application fee: $35. Tuition and fees vary according to course level. *Financial support:* Fellowships, research assistantships with full tuition reimbursements, teaching assistantships with full tuition reimbursements, career-related internships or fieldwork, Federal Work-Study, institutionally sponsored loans, scholarships/grants, tuition waivers (partial), and unspecified assistantships available. Support available to part-time students. Financial award applicants required to submit FAFSA. *Unit head:* Dr. Raouf S. Hanna, Department Head, 734-487-3395, Fax: 734-487-9666, E-mail: rhanna@emich.edu. *Application contact:* Dr. David Crary, Advisor, 734-487-0001, Fax: 734-487-9666, E-mail: david.crary@emich.edu.

Fordham University, Graduate School of Arts and Sciences, Program in International Political Economy and Development, New York, NY 10458. Offers MA, Certificate. Part-time and evening/weekend programs available. *Students:* 44 full-time (15 women); 18 part-time (10 women); includes 6 minority (1 African American, 1 American Indian/Alaska Native, 1 Asian American or Pacific Islander, 3 Hispanic Americans), 21 international. Average age 28. 213 applicants, 37% accepted, 36 enrolled. In 2009, 28 master's awarded. *Degree requirements:* For master's, comprehensive exam. *Entrance requirements:* For master's, GRE General Test. Additional exam requirements/recommendations for international students: Required—TOEFL (minimum score 600 paper-based; 250 computer-based). *Application deadline:* For fall admission, 1/4 priority date for domestic students; for spring admission, 11/1 for domestic students. Application fee: $70. Electronic applications accepted. *Financial support:* In 2009–10, 16 students received support, including 16 research assistantships with tuition reimbursements available (averaging $18,400 per year); career-related internships or fieldwork, institutionally sponsored loans, tuition waivers (full and partial), and unspecified assistantships also available. Financial award application deadline: 1/4; financial award applicants required to submit FAFSA. *Faculty research:* International economics, comparative international politics, international banking and finance, international development, emerging markets and country risk analysis. *Unit head:* Dr. Henry Schwalbenberg, Chair, 718-817-3866, Fax: 718-817-3518. *Application contact:* Charlene Dundie, Director of Graduate Admissions, 718-817-4420, Fax: 718-817-3566, E-mail: dundie@fordham.edu.

The Johns Hopkins University, Paul H. Nitze School of Advanced International Studies, Washington, DC 20036. Offers international development (MA, Certificate), including international economics (MA); international public policy (MIPP); international relations (PhD); international studies (Certificate); Japan studies (MA), including international economics; Korea Studies (MA), including international economics; South Asia studies (MA), including international economics; Southeast Asia studies (MA), including international economics; JD/MA; MBA/MA; MHS/MA. *Faculty:* 57 full-time (18 women), 125 part-time/adjunct (40 women). *Students:* 623 full-time (291 women), 38 part-time (17 women); includes 94 minority (11 African Americans, 55 Asian Americans or Pacific Islanders, 28 Hispanic Americans), 173 international. Average age 29. 1,444 applicants, 38% accepted, 212 enrolled. In 2009, 395 master's, 7 doctorates awarded. Terminal master's awarded for partial completion of doctoral program. *Degree requirements:* For master's, 2 core examinations, oral exam, proficiency in language other than native language (MA); for doctorate, 2 foreign languages, thesis/dissertation, 3 comprehensive exams, economics, quantitative and qualitative course, dissertation prospectus and defense. *Entrance requirements:* For master's, GMAT or GRE General Test, previous course work in economics, foreign language, undergraduate degree; for doctorate, GRE General Test, master's degree. Additional exam requirements/recommendations for international students: Required—TOEFL (minimum score 600 paper-based; 250 computer-based; 100 iBT), IELTS (minimum score 7), TOEFL (minimum score 600 paper-based; 250 computer-based; 100 iBT) or IELTS (minimum score 7). *Application deadline:* For fall admission, 1/7 for domestic and international students. Application fee: $85. Electronic applications accepted. *Expenses:* Contact institution. *Financial support:* In 2009–10, 450 students received support, including 450 fellowships (averaging $7,500 per year); teaching assistantships, career-related internships or fieldwork, Federal Work-Study, and scholarships/grants also available. Financial award application deadline: 2/15; financial award applicants required to submit FAFSA. *Faculty research:* Regional studies, international relations, international economics, energy and environment, international development. Total annual research expenditures: $7 million. *Unit* *head:* Sidney Jackson, Director of Admissions, 202-663-5700, Fax: 202-663-7788. *Application contact:* Admissions, 202-663-5700, Fax: 202-663-7788, E-mail: admissions.sais@jhu.edu.

The New School: A University, The New School for Social Research, Department of Economics, New York, NY 10003. Offers economics (M Phil, MA, MS, DS Sc, PhD); global finance (MS); global political economy and finance (MA). Part-time and evening/weekend programs available. *Faculty:* 9 full-time (2 women). *Students:* 103 full-time (32 women), 55 part-time (12 women); includes 28 minority (9 African Americans, 12 Asian Americans or Pacific Islanders, 7 Hispanic Americans), 64 international. Average age 32. 138 applicants, 84% accepted, 41 enrolled. In 2009, 46 master's, 8 doctorates awarded. Terminal master's awarded for partial completion of doctoral program. *Degree requirements:* For master's, exam; for doctorate, one foreign language, thesis/dissertation, qualifying exam. *Entrance requirements:* For master's, GRE General Test; for doctorate, GRE General Test, MA. Additional exam requirements/recommendations for international students: Required—TOEFL (minimum score 600 paper-based; 250 computer-based; 100 iBT). *Application deadline:* For fall admission, 1/17 priority date for domestic students, 1/17 for international students; for spring admission, 10/15 priority date for domestic students, 10/15 for international students. Applications are processed on a rolling basis. Application fee: $50. Electronic applications accepted. *Financial support:* Fellowships, research assistantships, teaching assistantships, Federal Work-Study, scholarships/grants, tuition waivers (full and partial), and unspecified assistantships available. Support available to part-time students. Financial award application deadline: 3/1; financial award applicants required to submit FAFSA. *Faculty research:* Heterodox, history of economic thought, post-Keynesian, global political economy and finance. *Unit head:* Dr. Will Milberg, Chair, 212-229-5717 Ext. 3045, E-mail: milbergw@newschool.edu. *Application contact:* Robert MacDonald, Director of Admissions, 212-229-5710 Ext. 3007, Fax: 212-989-7102, E-mail: macdonar@newschool.edu.

Regent University, Graduate School, Robertson School of Government, Virginia Beach, VA 23464. Offers american government (MA); global politics (MA); health care policy and administration (MA); international politics (MA); law and public policy (MA); Mid-East Politics (MA); political leadership and management (MA); political management (MA); political theory (MA); public administration (MA); public policy (MA); terrorism and homeland defense (MA); world economies and political development (MA); JD/MA; M Div/MA; M Ed/MA; MBA/MA. Part-time and evening/weekend programs available. Postbaccalaureate distance learning degree programs offered (minimal on-campus study). *Faculty:* 6 full-time (2 women), 11 part-time/adjunct (1 woman). *Students:* 77 full-time (55 women), 65 part-time (36 women); includes 47 minority (38 African Americans, 2 Asian Americans or Pacific Islanders, 7 Hispanic Americans), 4 international. Average age 30. 131 applicants, 65% accepted, 54 enrolled. In 2009, 51 master's awarded. *Degree requirements:* For master's, thesis optional, internship. *Entrance requirements:* For master's, GRE General Test or LSAT, minimum undergraduate GPA of 3.0, writing sample, resume, interview, references. Additional exam requirements/recommendations for international students: Required—TOEFL (minimum score 577 paper-based; 233 computer-based). *Application deadline:* For fall admission, 5/1 priority date for domestic students; for spring admission, 11/1 priority date for domestic students. Applications are processed on a rolling basis. Application fee: $50. Electronic applications accepted. *Expenses:* Contact institution. *Financial support:* In 2009–10, 130 students received support. Career-related internships or fieldwork, scholarships/grants, tuition waivers (full and partial), and unspecified assistantships available. Support available to part-time students. Financial award application deadline: 9/1; financial award applicants required to submit FAFSA. *Faculty research:* Education reform, political character issues, social capital concerns, administrative ethics, Biblical law and public policy. *Unit head:* Dr. Charles W. Dunn, Dean, 757-352-4322, Fax: 757-352-4643, E-mail: cwdunn@regent.edu. *Application contact:* Matthew Chadwick, Director of Admissions, 800-373-5504, Fax: 757-352-4381, E-mail: admissions@regent.edu.

University of Miami, Graduate School, School of Business Administration, Department of Economics, Coral Gables, FL 33124. Offers economic development (MA, PhD); environmental economics (PhD); human resource economics (MA, PhD); international economics (MA, PhD); macroeconomics (PhD). Students admitted every two years in the fall semester. Terminal master's awarded for partial completion of doctoral program. *Degree requirements:* For master's, comprehensive exam; for doctorate, comprehensive exam, thesis/dissertation. *Entrance requirements:* For master's and doctorate, GRE General Test, minimum GPA of 3.0. Additional exam requirements/recommendations for international students: Required—TOEFL (minimum score 550 paper-based). *Faculty research:* International economics/trade, applied microeconomics, development.

Valparaiso University, Graduate School, Program in International Economics and Finance, Valparaiso, IN 46383. Offers MS. Part-time and evening/weekend programs available. *Students:* 18 full-time (9 women), 4 part-time (2 women); includes 1 minority (Asian American or Pacific Islander), 17 international. Average age 23. *Entrance requirements:* For master's, 1 semester of college level calculus; 1 statistics or quantitative methods class; 2 semesters of introductory economics; 1 introductory accounting course; minimum undergraduate GPA of 3.0; 2 letters of recommendation. Additional exam requirements/recommendations for international students: Required—TOEFL (minimum score 550 paper-based; 213 computer-based; 80 iBT). Application fee: $30 ($50 for international students). *Financial support:* Available to part-time students. Applicants required to submit FAFSA. *Unit head:* Dr. David L. Rowland, Dean, Graduate Studies and Continuing Education/Associate Provost, 219-464-5313, Fax: 219-464-5381, E-mail: david.rowland@valpo.edu. *Application contact:* Jamie Haney, Coordinator of Graduate Admission, 219-464-5313, Fax: 219-464-5381, E-mail: jamie.haney@valpo.edu.

Virginia Polytechnic Institute and State University, Graduate School, College of Agriculture and Life Sciences, Department of Agricultural and Applied Economics, Blacksburg, VA 24061. Offers agribusiness (MS); agricultural economics (MS, PhD); applied economics (MS); developmental and international economics (PhD); econometrics (PhD); macro and micro economics (PhD); markets and industrial organizations (PhD); public and regional/urban economics (PhD); resource and environmental economics (PhD). *Faculty:* 22 full-time (5 women). *Students:* 33 full-time (18 women); includes 18 American Indian/Alaska Native, 1 Asian American or Pacific Islander, 1 international. Average age 28. 47 applicants, 43% accepted, 12 enrolled. In 2009, 13 master's, 3 doctorates awarded. *Entrance requirements:* For master's and doctorate, GRE, GMAT. Additional exam requirements/recommendations for international students: Required—TOEFL (minimum score 575 paper-based; 213 computer-based). *Application deadline:* For fall admission, 5/15 for international students; for spring admission, 10/15 for international students. Applications are processed on a rolling basis. Application fee: $65. Electronic applications accepted. *Expenses:* Tuition, area resident: Full-time $10,228; part-time $459 per credit hour. Tuition, nonresident: full-time $17,892; part-time $865 per credit hour. Required fees: $1966; $451 per semester. *Financial support:* In 2009–10, 1 fellowship with full tuition reimbursement (averaging $20,000 per year), 21 research assistantships with full tuition reimbursements (averaging $21,611 per year), 8 teaching assistantships with full tuition reimbursements (averaging $13,481 per year) were awarded; career-related internships or fieldwork, Federal Work-Study, scholarships/grants, and unspecified assistantships also available. Financial award application deadline: 1/15. *Faculty research:* Rural development. Total annual research expenditures: $2.3 million. *Unit head:* Dr. Kevin Boyle, Dean, 540-231-6301, Fax: 540-231-7417, E-mail: kjboyle@vt.edu. *Application contact:* Bradford Mills, Contact, 540-231-6461, Fax: 540-231-7417, E-mail: bfmills@vt.edu.

West Virginia University, College of Business and Economics, Division of Economics and Finance, Morgantown, WV 26506. Offers business analysis (MA); developmental financial economics (PhD); environmental and resource economics (PhD); international economics (PhD); mathematical economics (MA); monetary economics (PhD); public finance (PhD); public policy (MA); regional and urban economics (PhD); statistics and economics (MA). Terminal master's awarded for partial completion of doctoral program. *Degree requirements:* For master's, thesis optional; for doctorate, comprehensive exam, thesis/dissertation. *Entrance requirements:* For master's and doctorate, GRE General Test, minimum GPA of 3.0; course work in intermediate microeconomics, intermediate macroeconomics, calculus, and statistics. Additional exam requirements/recommendations for international students: Required—TOEFL. Electronic applications accepted. *Faculty research:* Financial economics, regional/urban development, public economics, international trade/international finance/development economics, monetary economics.

Yale University, Graduate School of Arts and Sciences, Department of Economics, Program in International and Development Economics, New Haven, CT 06520. Offers MA. *Entrance requirements:* For master's, GRE General Test.

Mineral Economics

Colorado School of Mines, Graduate School, Division of Economics and Business, Golden, CO 80401. Offers engineering and technology management (MS); mineral economics (MS, PhD). Part-time programs available. *Faculty:* 11 full-time (3 women), 6 part-time/adjunct (0 women). *Students:* 110 full-time (25 women), 18 part-time (3 women); includes 13 minority (4 African Americans, 1 American Indian/Alaska Native, 2 Asian Americans or Pacific Islanders, 6 Hispanic Americans), 32 international. Average age 30. 162 applicants, 92% accepted, 73 enrolled. In 2009, 47 master's, 2 doctorates awarded. *Degree requirements:* For master's, thesis (for some programs); for doctorate, comprehensive exam, thesis/dissertation. *Entrance requirements:* For master's and doctorate, GRE General Test. Additional exam requirements/recommendations for international students: Required—TOEFL (minimum score 550 paper-based; 213 computer-based; 80 iBT). *Application deadline:* For fall admission, 1/15 priority date for domestic and international students; for spring admission, 9/1 priority date for domestic and international students. Application fee: $50 ($70 for international students). Electronic applications accepted. *Expenses:* Tuition, state resident: full-time $10,584; part-time $588 per credit hour. Tuition, nonresident: full-time $24,750; part-time $1375 per credit hour. Required fees: $1654; $827.10 per semester. *Financial support:* In 2009–10, 25 students received support, including 3 fellowships with full tuition reimbursements available (averaging $20,000 per year), research assistantships with full tuition reimbursements available (averaging $20,000 per year), 22 teaching assistantships with full tuition reimbursements available (averaging $20,000 per year); scholarships/grants, health care benefits, and unspecified assistantships also available. Financial award application deadline: 1/15; financial award applicants required to submit FAFSA. *Faculty research:* International trade, resource and environmental economics, energy economics, operations research. Total annual research expenditures: $99,841. *Unit head:* Dr. Rod Eggert, Division Head, 303-273-3981, Fax: 303-273-3416, E-mail: reggert@mines.edu. *Application contact:* Kathleen A. Feighny, Administrative Faculty, 303-273-3979, Fax: 303-273-3416, E-mail: kfeighny@mines.edu.

Michigan Technological University, Graduate School, School of Business and Economics, Program in Applied Natural Resource Economics, Houghton, MI 49931. Offers MS. Part-time programs available. *Degree requirements:* For master's, comprehensive exam, thesis (for some programs). *Entrance requirements:* For master's, GRE. Additional exam requirements/recommendations for international students: Required—TOEFL (minimum score 550 paper-based; 213 computer-based). Electronic applications accepted.

The University of Texas at Austin, Graduate School, Cockrell School of Engineering, Department of Petroleum and Geosystems Engineering, Program in Energy and Earth Resources, Austin, TX 78712-1111. Offers MA. *Degree requirements:* For master's, thesis, seminar. *Entrance requirements:* For master's, GRE General Test. Additional exam requirements/recommendations for international students: Required—TOEFL. Electronic applications accepted.

THE UNIVERSITY OF TEXAS AT DALLAS

School of Economic, Political, and Policy Sciences

Programs of Study

The School of Economic, Political, and Policy Sciences (EPPS) at the University of Texas at Dallas (UT Dallas) offers Ph.D.s in criminology, economics, geospatial information sciences, political science, public affairs, and public policy and political economy (PPPE). It also offers master's degrees in applied sociology, criminology, economics, geospatial information sciences (in conjunction with the School of Natural Sciences), international political economy, public affairs, and public policy. Students receive education through lecture, internships, and workshop courses; a basic knowledge of statistics and computer skills is considered crucial.

EPPS offers a 36-hour M.S. program in applied sociology. This includes 12 hours of core courses in applied sociology, 15 hours of core courses, and 3 hours of internship. The program is designed for students interested in areas such as nonprofit organizations and federal, state, and local government philosophy. For more information, students should contact Judy Robertson (judy@utdallas.edu) or Dr. Richard Scotch (Richard.scotch@utdallas.edu).

The 36-hour Master of Science in criminology provides students with a coherent and intellectually challenging degree that prepares them to conduct interdisciplinary research on various aspects of criminology and/or criminal justice, depending on their specific areas of specialty. Students will be well prepared for analytical and administrative posts in international and domestic research and policy institutions, criminal justice organizations, and the private sector. For more information, students should contact Remona McLain (remonamc@utdallas.edu) or Dr. James Marquart (marquart@utdallas.edu).

The 36-hour M.S. in economics is aimed at students seeking to learn advanced economic theory and apply advanced economic tools to real socioeconomic problems. For more information, students should contact Judy Du (judy.du@utdallas.edu) or Dr. Daniel Arce (darce@utdallas.edu).

In addition, EPPS offers a 30-hour M.S. in geospatial information sciences (GIS). Offered jointly by the School of Economic, Political, and Policy Sciences and the School of Natural Sciences and Mathematics, it focuses on the use of geographic information systems. For more information, students should contact Rita Medford (rmedford@utdallas.edu) or Dr. Denis Dean (Denis.Dean@utdallas.edu).

The School also offers a 36-hour Master of Science in international political economy (IPE) that consists of three components, including required course work (18 hours), prescribed electives (12 hours), and free electives (6 hours). Moreover, students must demonstrate a foreign language proficiency equivalent to two years of study in one foreign language before graduation. For more information, students should contact Judy Robertson (judy@utdallas.edu) or Dr. Jennifer Holmes (jholmes@utdallas.edu).

The Master of Public Affairs (M.P.A.) degree is a 42-hour, interdisciplinary program that includes 21 hours of core courses and 18 hours of directed electives as well as an internship or workshop. It explores the interrelationship between economic, political, and social institutions. Students may emphasize course work in management, policy analysis, or applied technology. The curriculum places strong emphasis upon the development of computer and statistical skills that are necessary for successful performance in both the public and private sectors in the twenty-first century. For more information, students should contact Del Prisock (delfina@utdallas.edu) or Dr. Doug Kiel (dkiel@utdallas.edu).

The M.S. in public policy is an interdisciplinary 36-hour graduate degree designed to develop those skill sets critical for a career in which a solid understanding of the public policy process and the analysis and evaluation of public policies are essential. Specific skills include knowledge of the policy process and related ethical concerns, rigorous research skills that provide students with an essential grounding in statistical and data analysis and research design, and effective communication skills. Students will be prepared for analytical and administrative positions and responsibilities in a wide array of professional settings in the public, non-profit, and private sectors. For more information, students should contact Judy Robertson (judy@utdallas.edu) or Dr. Marie Chevrier (chevrier@utdallas.edu).

The Ph.D. degree in criminology is an interdisciplinary, research-oriented program that provides students with a coherent and intellectually challenging research degree that prepares them for an academic appointment as a university professor or an administrative appointment with oversight of research and development within criminal justice organizations. Graduates of the program will be competent to teach and conduct interdisciplinary research at both graduate and undergraduate levels in aspects of criminology and/or criminal justice, depending on their specific areas of specialty. They also will be well prepared for analytical and administrative posts in international and domestic research and policy institutions and in the private sector. For more information, students should contact Remona McLain (remonamc@utdallas.edu) or Dr. James Marquart (marquart@utdallas.edu).

The Ph.D. program in economics prepares students for careers in academics as well as research-oriented positions in the private and public sector. It provides cutting-edge education in micro and macroeconomic theory, rigorous training in mathematical and econometric techniques, and extensive exposure to various research areas in economics. Students complete a set of core courses, pass comprehensive exams in microeconomic and macroeconomic theory as well as econometrics, are certified in two research areas in economics, and submit and defend a dissertation. For more information, students should contact Judy Du (judy.du@utdallas.edu) or Dr. Daniel Arce (darce@utdallas.edu).

The Ph.D. program in geospatial information sciences, offered with the Schools of Natural Sciences and Mathematics as well as Engineering and Computer Science, offers advanced training in geographic information sciences and related fields. Students complete core courses and pass a qualifying exam before proceeding to the dissertation. For more information, students should contact Rita Medford (rmedford@utdallas.edu) or Dr. Denis Dean (Denis.Dean@utdallas.edu).

The Ph.D. in political science provides a rigorous, student-focused disciplinary program with multidisciplinary links. Students receive state-of-the-science graduate education in political methodology and the fields of democratization, globalization and international relations, institutions and processes, and public management and decision making. Students complete a set of core courses, course work in their designated major and minor fields, and examinations in the core courses and major and minor fields; students also write and defend a dissertation. For more information, students should contact Lynne Boyer (lynne.boyer@utdallas.edu) or Dr. Robert Lowry (robert.lowry@utdallas.edu).

The Ph.D. in public affairs is an interdisciplinary program that prepares graduates to assume positions in academe, research-producing organizations, or positions of administrative authority in public organizations. The degree is nontraditional in that it requires all students to conduct applied, field-based research as the foundation for the production of their dissertations. The Ph.D. program in public affairs is a cohort program, with entering cohorts beginning each fall semester. For more information, students should contact Del Prisock (delfina@utdallas.edu) or Dr. Doug Kiel (dkiel@utdallas.edu).

The Ph.D. in public policy and political economy is centered in critical thought and interdisciplinary research that explores the interaction of institutions, markets, and public policies. Students are expected to complete a set of core courses in topics related to public policy, including rigorous training in statistics and research design; students must also complete course work in two fields and a specialization and defend a dissertation. For more information, students should contact Judy Robertson (judy@utdallas.edu) or Dr. Sheila Pineres (pineres@utdallas.edu).

Research Facilities

The University of Texas at Dallas has advanced computing facilities. The School of Economic, Political, and Policy Sciences also houses the Bruton Center for Development Studies and the Center for Educational Studies and is affiliated with the Cecil and Ida Green Center for Science and Society. Students have access to the computing facilities in the School of Economic, Political, and Policy Sciences and the University's Computing Center. The School's two computing laboratories house over 30 computers that are network linked and equipped with major social science software packages, including E-Views, R, RATS, SPSS, and STATA. A computerized geographic information system, the LexisNexis Database, and WestLaw are also available for student use. The University's Computing Center provides personal computers and UNIX workstations. Many important data and reference materials are available online from professional associations or at UT–D via the Library's and School's memberships in the Inter-University Consortium for Political and Social Research (ICPSR), the Roper Center, the University Consortium for Geographic Information Science (UCGIS), and other organizations. The library has a substantial number of social science journals.

Financial Aid

The School of Economic, Political, and Policy Sciences (EPPS) provides teaching assistantships that range from $1100 to $1400, depending on experience. Students who are awarded a full-time, 20-hour assistantship receive in-state tuition waivers. The School also offers tuition waivers that cover all tuition for up to 12 credit hours. Teaching assistantships and graduate studies scholarships are competitive, with GRE scores and grades being important criteria in the selection process.

Cost of Study

Tuition and fees can be expected to be in the range of $8000 to $10,000 per year for full-time in-state students taking 9 hours per semester, including summers. Costs might be higher for international and out-of-state students. Students are eligible for teaching assistantships and graduate-studies scholarships, as detailed above.

Living and Housing Costs

On-campus housing is available at Waterview Park Apartments, with rents varying from $800 to $1200 per month.

Student Group

There are 6,000 graduate students and more than 8,000 undergraduates studying at UT–Dallas. UT-Dallas also has a varied international student body in both graduate and undergraduate programs of study.

Location

Richardson is located just north of Dallas and south of Plano in a pleasant suburban setting. It is near the high-technology corridor that is home to Ericsson, Nortel, and numerous other telecommunications companies.

The University

UT–Dallas was created in September 1969 by Act of the Sixty-First Texas Legislature, which provided for transfer of the privately funded Southwest Center for Advanced Studies (SCAS) to the state of Texas. Undergraduate and graduate programs grew rapidly. Today, UT–Dallas has a distinguished faculty that includes numerous members of the National Academy of Sciences and National Academy of Engineering.

Applying

Application for admission to the graduate school can be made for fall, spring, or summer. GRE scores are required for degree-seeking students, although applicants may be admitted provisionally as nondegree students. A combined verbal and quantitative GRE score of at least 1100 is recommended for doctoral students, and a combined score of at least 1000 is recommended for master's degree students.

Correspondence and Information

Euel Elliott, Associate Dean for Academic Programs
School of Economic, Political, and Policy Sciences
Box 830688
The University of Texas at Dallas
Richardson, Texas 75083-0688

E-mail: eelliott@utdallas.edu
Web site: http://epps.utdallas.edu/

The University of Texas at Dallas

THE FACULTY AND THEIR RESEARCH

Bobby C. Alexander, Associate Professor of Sociology; Ph.D. (religious studies/social-scientific study of religion), Columbia, 1985. Religious studies.

Sheila Amin Gutiérrez de Piñeres, Professor of Economics; Ph.D. (economics), Duke, 1992. Latin American development, trade policy.

Donald R. Arbuckle, Clinical Research Professor; Ph.D. (American civilizations), Pennsylvania. Public management, bureaucratic behavior, policymaking.

Daniel Arce, Professor of Economics; Ph.D. (economics), Illinois at Urbana-Champaign, 1992. Economics, defense economics.

Philip K. Armour, Associate Professor of Sociology; Ph.D. (sociology), Berkeley, 1979. Sociology of religion, medical sociology.

Paul Battaglio, Assistant Professor of Public Affairs; Ph.D. (public administration), Georgia, 2005. Comparative policy and administration, public human resource management, comparative political attitudes.

Ted Benavides, Senior Lecturer; M.P.A., SMU, 1994. Public management, human resources management.

Nathan Berg, Associate Professor of Economics; Ph.D. (economics), Kansas, 2001. Finance, behavioral economics.

Kurt J. Beron, Professor of Economics and Political Economy; Ph.D. (economics), North Carolina at Chapel Hill, 1985. Education policy, tax compliance, Internet economics.

Brian J. L. Berry, Lloyd Viel Berkner Regental Professor, Professor of Political Economy, and Dean; Ph.D. (geography), Washington (Seattle), 1958. Urban economics and geography, development, cycles of growth and decline.

Denise Paquette Boots, Assistant Professor; Ph.D. (criminology), South Florida, 2006. American correction systems, family and interpersonal violence, juvenile delinquency.

Patrick T. Brandt, Assistant Professor of Political Science; Ph.D. (political science), Indiana, 2001. Presidency, congressional behavior, time series analysis, Bayesian econometrics.

Timothy Bray, Clinical Assistant Professor of Criminology and Sociology; Ph.D. (criminology), Missouri–St. Louis, 2002. Criminology.

Thomas Brunell, Professor of Political Science; Ph.D. (political science), California, Irvine, 1997. Congressional behavior, congressional elections.

Anthony Champagne, Professor of Political Science; Ph.D. (political science), Illinois, 1973. Law and public policy, judicial politics.

Marie Isabelle Chevrier, Professor of Public Policy and Political Economy; Ph.D. (public policy), Harvard, 1991. Arms control, international negotiation.

Yongwan Chun, Clinical Assistant Professor of GIS; Ph.D. (GIS), Ohio State, 2007. Spatial analysis and modeling, spatial statistics.

Harold D. Clarke, Professor of Political Science and Program Head for Political Science; Ph.D. (political science), Duke, 1971. Electoral behavior, public opinion and political support.

Rachel Croson, Professor of Economics; Ph.D. (economics), Harvard, 1994. Economics, experimental economics, behavioral economics.

Chetan Dave, Assistant Professor of Economics; Ph.D. (economics), Pittsburgh, 2004. Macroeconomics, econometrics.

Kruti R. Dholakia, Clinical Assistant Professor of Political Economy and Associate Dean for Undergraduate Programs; Ph.D. (public policy and political economy), Texas at Dallas, 2006. Methodology, global economy, development economics, health policy.

Lloyd J. Dumas, Professor of Public Policy and Political Economy; Ph.D. (economics), Columbia, 1972. International security, economic conversion, human and technical reliability.

Catherine C. Eckel, Professor of Economics; Ph.D. (economics), Virginia, 1983. Experimental economics, risk and decision making, economic education.

Euel Elliott, Professor of Public Policy and Political Economy, Senior Associate Dean, and Director of Graduate Studies; Ph.D. (political science), Duke, 1987. Public policy (general), regulatory policy, electoral behavior, nonlinear dynamics.

Simon Fass, Associate Professor of Public Policy and Political Economy; Ph.D. (urban planning), UCLA, 1978. Economic and political development.

Daniel Griffith, Ashbel Smith Professor of Geography and Geospatial Sciences; Ph.D. (geography), Toronto, 1978. Spatial statistics, quantitative urban-economic geography, applied statistics.

Jeremy Hall, Assistant Professor of Public Affairs; Ph.D. (public administration), Kentucky, 2005. Human resource management, public budgeting.

Edward J. Harpham, Professor of Political Science and Political Economy and Director of Collegium V Honors Program; Ph.D. (government), Cornell, 1980. Political theory, public policy.

Wendy L. Hassett, Clinical Associate Professor; Ph.D. (public administration and public policy), Auburn, 2003. Public management, human resource development.

Karen Hayslett-McCall, Assistant Professor of Sociology; Ph.D. (sociology), Penn State, 2002. Criminology, spatial analysis of crime, crime and neighborhoods.

Donald A. Hicks, Professor of Public Policy and Political Economy and Vice Chairman, Bruton Center for Development Studies; Ph.D. (sociology), North Carolina at Chapel Hill, 1976. Urban and regional policy, technology innovation and diffusion.

Bruce Jacobs, Professor of Sociology and Criminology; Ph.D. (sociology), USC, 1994. Street offenders, drugs and crime, qualitative methods.

Paul A. Jargowsky, Professor of Sociology and of Public Policy and Political Economy; Ph.D. (public policy), Harvard, 1991. Welfare policy.

Linda Camp Keith, Associate Professor of Political Science; Ph.D. (political science), North Texas, 1999. Public law/judicial process, human rights.

L. Douglas Kiel, Professor of Public Administration; Ph.D. (political science), Oklahoma, 1986. Public administration, organizational change, productivity improvement, nonlinear dynamics.

Tom Kovandzic, Associate Professor of Criminology; Ph.D. (criminal justice and criminology), Florida State, 1999. Firearms and violence, criminal justice policy, quantitative methods, inequality and crime, and policing, with particular interest in use of econometric methods as a tool to evaluate criminal justice policy initiatives.

Murray Leaf, Professor of Public Policy and Political Economy; Ph.D. (social anthropology), Chicago, 1966. Comparative social and economic development.

Xin Li, Assistant Professor of Economics; Ph.D. (economics), Michigan, 2006. Public economics, labor economics, experimental economics, economics of the Internet.

Robert Lowry, Professor of Political Science and of Public Policy and Political Economy and Program Head for Political Science; Ph.D. (political science), Harvard, 1993. Institutions and organizations, methodology.

James W. Marquart, Professor of Criminology and Program Head for Criminology; Ph.D. (sociology), Texas A&M, 1983. Criminology, legal reform, victimology, health issues in prison populations, community-based corrections.

Susan McElroy, Associate Professor of Economics and Political Economy; Ph.D. (economics of education), Stanford, 1996. Education policy.

Robert Morris, Assistant Professor of Criminology; Ph.D. (criminology), Sam Houston State, 2007. White-collar offending over the life course, computer crime and computer deviance, identity theft, quantitative methods.

Stuart B. Murchison, Clinical Associate Professor of Geospatial Sciences and Geography; Ph.D. (geography), Utah, 1989. Remote sensing, global positioning systems.

James C. Murdoch, Professor of Economics and Program Head for Economics; Ph.D. (economics), Wyoming, 1982. Environmental policy, public goods provision, coalition theory.

Clint W. Peinhardt, Assistant Professor of Political Science; Ph.D. (political science), Michigan, 2004. International political economy, economic development and transition, formal modeling.

Fang Qiu, Associate Professor of Geospatial Sciences and Political Economy; Ph.D. (geography), South Carolina, 2000. Geographic information sciences (GIS), remote sensing.

Todd Sandler, Professor of Economics and Political Science; Ph.D. (economics), SUNY at Binghamton, 1971. International relations, public economics, collective action, theories of terrorism.

Richard K. Scotch, Professor of Sociology and of Public Policy and Political Economy; Ph.D. (sociology), Harvard, 1982. Social policy, health policy, disabilities policy.

Barry J. Seldon, Professor of Economics; Ph.D. (economics), Duke, 1985. Microeconomics, industrial organization, advertising.

Kevin Siqueira, Associate Professor of Economics; Ph.D. (economics), Iowa State, 1998. Public economics, environmental economics, microeconomic theory, game theory.

Sheryl Skaggs, Associate Professor of Sociology; Ph.D. (sociology), North Carolina State, 2001. Work, organizations and industry, social inequality.

Marianne C. Stewart, Professor of Political Science; Ph.D. (political science), Duke, 1986. Comparative politics, Anglo-American voting behavior, political participation.

Gregory S. Thielemann, Associate Professor of Political Economy; Ph.D. (political science), Rice, 1988. Southern politics, gay and lesbian politics.

Michael Tiefelsdorf, Associate Professor of Geography and Geospatial Sciences; Ph.D. (geography), Free University of Berlin, 1988. Spatial processes, spatial statistics, quantitative geography.

Paul E. Tracy, Professor of Sociology and of Public Policy and Political Economy; Ph.D. (sociology and criminology), Pennsylvania, 1978. Criminology, juvenile delinquency.

Nicholas Valcik, Clinical Assistant Professor of Public Affairs; Ph.D. (public affairs), Texas at Dallas, 2005. Facilities management, hazardous material safety.

Lynne Vieraitis, Associate Professor of Criminology; Ph.D. (criminal justice and criminology), Florida State, 2000. Inequality and crime, gender and crime, violence against women, theoretical criminology.

Douglas Watson, Professor of Public Administration and Program Head for Public Affairs; Ph.D. (public policy and public administration), Auburn, 1992. State and local government.

John L. Worrall, Professor of Criminology; Ph.D. (political science), Washington State, 1999. Crime central policy, legal issues in policing, methodology.

Section 20
Family and Consumer Sciences

This section contains a directory of institutions offering graduate work in family and consumer sciences. Additional information about programs listed in the directory but not augmented by an in-depth entry may be obtained by writing directly to the dean of a graduate school or chair of a department at the address given in the directory.

For programs offering related work, see also in this book *Economics, Psychology and Counseling,* and *Sociology, Anthropology, and Archaeology.* In another guide in this series:

Graduate Programs in Business, Education, Health, Information Studies, Law & Social Work
See *Social Work*

CONTENTS

Program Directories

Family and Consumer Sciences-General 762
Child and Family Studies 766
Child Development 774
Clothing and Textiles 776
Consumer Economics 778
Gerontology 781

Close-Ups

See:

Adler School of Professional Psychology—Psychology 1047
Fashion Institute of Technology—Fashion and Textile Studies 115

Family and Consumer Sciences-General

Alabama Agricultural and Mechanical University, School of Graduate Studies, School of Agricultural and Environmental Sciences, Department of Family and Consumer Sciences, Huntsville, AL 35811. Offers family and consumer sciences (MS); food science (MS, PhD). Part-time and evening/weekend programs available. *Degree requirements:* For master's, comprehensive exam, thesis optional; for doctorate, one foreign language, thesis/dissertation. *Entrance requirements:* For master's, GRE General Test; for doctorate, GRE General Test, MS. Additional exam requirements/recommendations for international students: Required—TOEFL (minimum score 500 paper-based; 173 computer-based; 61 iBT). Electronic applications accepted. *Faculty research:* Food biotechnology, nutrition, food microbiology, food engineering, food chemistry.

Appalachian State University, Cratis D. Williams Graduate School, Department of Family and Consumer Sciences, Boone, NC 28608. Offers child development (MA); family and consumer science (MA), including food and nutrition; family and consumer science education (MA). Part-time programs available. Postbaccalaureate distance learning degree programs offered (no on-campus study). *Faculty:* 12 full-time (10 women), 2 part-time/adjunct (1 woman). *Students:* 17 full-time (16 women), 15 part-time (all women); includes 2 minority (both African Americans), 1 international. 29 applicants, 83% accepted, 20 enrolled. In 2009, 6 master's awarded. *Degree requirements:* For master's, comprehensive exam, thesis optional. *Entrance requirements:* For master's, GRE General Test, 3 letters of recommendation. Additional exam requirements/recommendations for international students: Required—TOEFL (minimum score 550 paper-based; 230 computer-based; 79 iBT), IELTS (minimum score 6.5). *Application deadline:* For fall admission, 7/1 for domestic students, 2/1 for international students; for spring admission, 11/1 for domestic students, 7/1 for international students. Applications are processed on a rolling basis. Application fee: $50. Electronic applications accepted. *Expenses:* Tuition, state resident: full-time $2960. Tuition, nonresident: full-time $14,051. Required fees: $2320. *Financial support:* In 2009–10, 5 research assistantships (averaging $8,000 per year) were awarded; career-related internships or fieldwork, scholarships/grants, and unspecified assistantships also available. Financial award application deadline: 7/1; financial award applicants required to submit FAFSA. *Faculty research:* Food antioxidants, preschool curriculum, children with special needs, family child care, FCS curriculum content. *Unit head:* Dr. Sarah Jordan, Chairperson, 828-262-2661, E-mail: jordansr@appstate.edu. *Application contact:* Dr. Sandy Krause, Director of Graduate Admissions and Recruiting, 828-262-2130, E-mail: krausesl@appstate.edu.

Ball State University, Graduate School, College of Applied Science and Technology, Department of Family and Consumer Sciences, Muncie, IN 47306-1099. Offers MA, MS. *Entrance requirements:* For master's, resume. *Faculty research:* Maternal and infant nutrition, nutrition education.

Bowling Green State University, Graduate College, College of Education and Human Development, School of Family and Consumer Sciences, Bowling Green, OH 43403. Offers food and nutrition (MFCS); human development and family studies (MFCS). Part-time programs available. *Degree requirements:* For master's, thesis. *Entrance requirements:* For master's, GRE General Test, minimum GPA of 3.0. Additional exam requirements/recommendations for international students: Required—TOEFL. Electronic applications accepted. *Faculty research:* Public health, wellness, social issues and policies, ethnic foods, nutrition and aging.

California State University, Fresno, Division of Graduate Studies, College of Agricultural Sciences and Technology, Department of Child, Family and Consumer Sciences, Fresno, CA 93740-8027. Offers family and consumer sciences (MS). Currently not accepting applications. Part-time and evening/weekend programs available. *Degree requirements:* For master's, thesis (for some programs). *Entrance requirements:* For master's, GRE General Test, minimum GPA of 3.0 in last 60 hours. Additional exam requirements/recommendations for international students: Required—TOEFL. Electronic applications accepted.

California State University, Long Beach, Graduate Studies, College of Health and Human Services, Department of Family and Consumer Sciences, Long Beach, CA 90840. Offers family and consumer sciences (MA); nutritional science (MS), including food science, hospitality foodservice and hotel management, nutritional science. Part-time and evening/weekend programs available. *Faculty:* 5 full-time (all women). *Students:* 43 full-time (39 women), 56 part-time (54 women); includes 40 minority (4 African Americans, 22 Asian Americans or Pacific Islanders, 14 Hispanic Americans), 7 international. Average age 29. 6 applicants, 17% accepted, 1 enrolled. *Degree requirements:* For master's, comprehensive exam or thesis. *Entrance requirements:* For master's, GRE (MS), minimum GPA of 3.0. *Application deadline:* For fall admission, 5/1 for domestic students. Applications are processed on a rolling basis. Application fee: $55. Electronic applications accepted. *Expenses:* Required fees: $1802 per semester. Part-time tuition and fees vary according to course load. *Financial support:* Federal Work-Study, institutionally sponsored loans, and scholarships/grants available. Financial award application deadline: 3/2. *Faculty research:* School uniforms, consumer complaining behavior, nutrition and fitness education and behavior change, curriculum change, teaching experience of interns. *Unit head:* Dr. Wendy Reiboldt, Chair, 562-985-8250, Fax: 562-985-4414, E-mail: reiboldt@csulb.edu. *Application contact:* Dr. Jacqueline Lee, Graduate Coordinator, 562-985-4545, Fax: 562-985-4414, E-mail: jjlee@csulb.edu.

California State University, Northridge, Graduate Studies, College of Health and Human Development, Department of Family and Consumer Sciences, Northridge, CA 91330. Offers MS. Part-time and evening/weekend programs available. *Faculty:* 16 full-time (12 women), 37 part-time/adjunct (32 women). *Students:* 74 full-time (70 women), 106 part-time (97 women); includes 12 African Americans, 22 Asian Americans or Pacific Islanders, 30 Hispanic Americans, 15 international. Average age 31. 180 applicants, 64% accepted, 53 enrolled. In 2009, 29 master's awarded. *Degree requirements:* For master's, thesis, project, or comprehensive exam. *Entrance requirements:* For master's, GRE General Test or minimum GPA of 3.0. Additional exam requirements/recommendations for international students: Required—TOEFL. *Application deadline:* For fall admission, 11/30 for domestic students. Application fee: $55. *Financial support:* Teaching assistantships, career-related internships or fieldwork, Federal Work-Study, and institutionally sponsored loans available. Financial award application deadline: 3/1. *Unit head:* Dr. Alyce Akers, Chair, 818-677-3051. *Application contact:* Dr. Alyce Akers, Chair, 818-677-3051.

Central Michigan University, College of Graduate Studies, College of Education and Human Services, Department of Human Environmental Studies, Mount Pleasant, MI 48859. Offers apparel product development and merchandising technology (MS); human development and family studies (MA); nutrition and dietetics (MS). Part-time and evening/weekend programs available. *Degree requirements:* For master's, thesis or alternative. Electronic applications accepted. *Faculty research:* Human growth and development, family studies and human sexuality, human nutrition and dietetics, apparel and textile retailing, computer-aided design for apparel.

Central Washington University, Graduate Studies and Research, College of Education and Professional Studies, Department of Family and Consumer Sciences, Ellensburg, WA 98926. Offers family and consumer sciences education (MS); family studies (MS). Part-time programs available. *Faculty:* 14 full-time (9 women). *Students:* 11 full-time (10 women), 22 part-time (21 women); includes 1 minority (Asian American or Pacific Islander), 1 international. 9 applicants, 78% accepted, 7 enrolled. In 2009, 4 master's awarded. *Degree requirements:* For master's, thesis or alternative. *Entrance requirements:* For master's, minimum GPA of 3.0. Additional exam requirements/recommendations for international students: Required—TOEFL (minimum score 550 paper-based; 213 computer-based; 79 iBT). *Application deadline:* For fall admission, 2/1 priority date for domestic students; for winter admission, 10/1 for domestic students; for spring admission, 1/1 for domestic students. Applications are processed on a rolling basis. Application fee: $50. Electronic applications accepted. *Expenses:* Tuition, state resident: full-time $7353; part-time $245 per credit. Tuition, nonresident: full-time $16,383; part-time $546 per credit. Required fees: $882. Tuition and fees vary according to degree level. *Financial support:* In 2009–10, 1 research assistantship with full and partial tuition reimbursement (averaging $9,145 per year) was awarded; Federal Work-Study, health care benefits, and unspecified assistantships also available. Financial award application deadline: 3/1; financial award applicants required to submit FAFSA. *Unit head:* Dr. Jan Bowers, Chair, 509-963-2766, E-mail: bowersj@cwu.edu. *Application contact:* Justine Eason, Admissions Program Coordinator, 509-963-3103, Fax: 509-963-1799, E-mail: masters@cwu.edu.

Cornell University, Graduate School, Graduate Fields of Human Ecology, Ithaca, NY 14853-0001. Offers MA, MHA, MPS, MS, PhD. *Accreditation:* CAHME (one or more programs are accredited). *Faculty:* 150 full-time (64 women). *Students:* 130 full-time (86 women); includes 20 minority (4 African Americans, 13 Asian Americans or Pacific Islanders, 3 Hispanic Americans), 34 international. Average age 27. 280 applicants, 31% accepted, 58 enrolled. In 2009, 30 master's, 11 doctorates awarded. *Degree requirements:* For doctorate, comprehensive exam, thesis/dissertation. *Entrance requirements:* For master's and doctorate, GRE General Test. Additional exam requirements/recommendations for international students: Required—TOEFL. Application fee: $70. Electronic applications accepted. *Expenses:* Contact institution. *Financial support:* In 2009–10, 75 students received support, including 4 fellowships with full tuition reimbursements available, 19 teaching assistantships with full tuition reimbursements available; research assistantships with full tuition reimbursements available, institutionally sponsored loans, scholarships/grants, health care benefits, tuition waivers (full and partial), and unspecified assistantships also available. Financial award applicants required to submit FAFSA. *Application contact:* Graduate School Application Requests, Caldwell Hall, 607-255-5820.

Eastern Illinois University, Graduate School, Lumpkin College of Business and Applied Sciences, School of Family and Consumer Sciences, Charleston, IL 61920-3099. Offers dietetics (MS); family and consumer sciences (MS). Part-time programs available. *Faculty:* 12 full-time (10 women). *Students:* 34 full-time (33 women), 29 part-time (all women). In 2009, 40 master's awarded. *Degree requirements:* For master's, comprehensive exam. *Application deadline:* For fall admission, 3/31 priority date for domestic students. Applications are processed on a rolling basis. Application fee: $30. *Expenses:* Tuition, state resident: full-time $9434; part-time $239 per credit hour. Tuition, nonresident: full-time $23,774; part-time $717 per credit hour. Required fees: $802.63. *Financial support:* In 2009–10, 2 research assistantships with tuition reimbursements (averaging $8,100 per year), 6 teaching assistantships with tuition reimbursements (averaging $8,100 per year) were awarded; career-related internships or fieldwork also available. *Unit head:* Dr. James Painter, Chairperson, 217-581-6076, Fax: 217-581-6090, E-mail: jepainter@eiu.edu. *Application contact:* Dr. Lisa Taylor, Coordinator, 217-581-8584, Fax: 217-581-6090, E-mail: lmtaylor@eiu.edu.

Florida State University, The Graduate School, College of Human Sciences, Tallahassee, FL 32306-1490. Offers MS, PhD. *Accreditation:* AAMFT/COAMFTE. Part-time programs available. *Faculty:* 38 full-time (28 women). *Students:* 141 full-time (100 women), 49 part-time (40 women); includes 52 minority (28 African Americans, 8 Asian Americans or Pacific Islanders, 16 Hispanic Americans), 29 international. 175 applicants, 46% accepted, 49 enrolled. In 2009, 41 master's, 17 doctorates awarded. *Degree requirements:* For master's, comprehensive exam (for some programs), thesis optional; for doctorate, thesis/dissertation. *Entrance requirements:* For master's, GRE General Test, minimum upper-division GPA of 3.0; for doctorate, GRE General Test, minimum upper-division GPA of 3.0, master's degree. Additional exam requirements/recommendations for international students: Required—TOEFL (minimum score 570 paper-based; 80 iBT). *Application deadline:* For fall admission, 7/1 for domestic students, 5/1 for international students; for spring admission, 11/1 for domestic students, 12/1 for international students. Applications are processed on a rolling basis. Application fee: $30. Electronic applications accepted. *Expenses:* Tuition, state resident: full-time $7413. Tuition, nonresident: full-time $22,567. *Financial support:* In 2009–10, 107 students received support, including 1 fellowship with partial tuition reimbursement available (averaging $6,300 per year), 41 research assistantships with partial tuition reimbursements available (averaging $8,497 per year), 75 teaching assistantships with partial tuition reimbursements available (averaging $8,910 per year); career-related internships or fieldwork, Federal Work-Study, institutionally sponsored loans, scholarships/grants, and unspecified assistantships also available. Financial award application deadline: 1/15; financial award applicants required to submit FAFSA. *Faculty research:* Body composition, functional food, chronic disease and aging response; food safety, food allergy, and safety/quality detection methods; sports nutrition, energy balance and human performance; families at risk and relational interventions; parenting, martial process and family therapy. Total annual research expenditures: $1.9 million. *Unit head:* Dr. Billie J. Collier, Dean, 850-644-1281, Fax: 850-644-0700, E-mail: bcollier@fsu.edu. *Application contact:* Tara L. Hartman, Academic Program Specialist, 850-644-7221, Fax: 850-644-0700, E-mail: thartman@fsu.edu.

Fontbonne University, Graduate Programs, Department of Human Environmental Sciences, St. Louis, MO 63105-3098. Offers family and consumer sciences (MA). *Faculty:* 4 full-time (all women), 5 part-time/adjunct (all women). *Students:* 3 full-time (all women), 7 part-time (all women); includes 2 minority (both African Americans). Average age 37. In 2009, 1 master's awarded. *Degree requirements:* For master's, action paper/presentation portfolio. *Entrance requirements:* For master's, minimum GPA of 3.0. *Application deadline:* For fall admission, 8/8 priority date for domestic students; for spring admission, 1/8 priority date for domestic students. Application fee: $25. *Expenses:* Tuition: Part-time $562 per credit hour. *Financial support:* Application deadline: 4/1. *Faculty research:* Early intervention, public policy: children and families, program designer. *Unit head:* Cheryl Houston, Chairperson, 314-719-8020, Fax: 314-719-8615. *Application contact:* Dr. Janine Duncan, Director, Graduate Programs, 314-719-3639, Fax: 314-719-8015.

Illinois State University, Graduate School, College of Applied Science and Technology, Department of Family and Consumer Sciences, Normal, IL 61790-2200. Offers MA, MS. *Degree requirements:* For master's, thesis or alternative. *Entrance requirements:* For master's, GRE General Test, minimum GPA of 2.8 in last 60 hours of course work. *Faculty research:* Graduate practicum assistantships, startup for Jump Start of McLean County grant, providing low-income preschool children with early literacy experiences, generations of Hope-ICI replication.

Indiana State University, School of Graduate Studies, College of Arts and Sciences, Department of Family and Consumer Sciences, Terre Haute, IN 47809. Offers dietetics (MS); family and consumer sciences education (MS); inter-area option (MS). *Accreditation:* ADtA. Part-time programs available. *Degree requirements:* For master's, thesis optional. Electronic applications accepted.

Iowa State University of Science and Technology, Graduate College, College of Human Sciences, Program in Family and Consumer Sciences, Ames, IA 50011. Offers MFCS. *Students:* 5 full-time (all women), 40 part-time (29 women); includes 3 African Americans, 2 international. 16 applicants, 63% accepted, 6 enrolled. In 2009, 14 master's awarded. *Degree requirements:* For master's, thesis or alternative. *Entrance requirements:* For master's, GRE General Test. Additional exam requirements/recommendations for international students: Required—TOEFL (minimum score 550 paper-based; 79 iBT) or IELTS (minimum score 6.5). *Application deadline:* For fall admission, 4/15 priority date for domestic and international students; for spring admission, 10/15 priority date for domestic and international students. Application fee: $40 ($90 for international students). Electronic applications accepted. *Expenses:* Tuition, state resident: full-time $6716. Tuition, nonresident: full-time $8908. Tuition and fees vary according to course level, course load, program and student level. *Financial support:* In 2009–10, 1 research assistantship with full and partial tuition reimbursement (averaging $14,880 per year), 1 teaching assistantship with full and partial tuition reimbursement (averaging $14,880 per year) were awarded; scholarships/grants, health care benefits, and unspecified assistantships also available. *Unit head:* Dr. Carla Peterson, Supervisory Committee Chair, 515-294-7804, E-mail: mfcsinfo@iastate.edu. *Application contact:* Dr. Carla Peterson, Supervisory Committee Chair, 515-294-7804, E-mail: mfcsinfo@iastate.edu.

Kansas State University, Graduate School, College of Human Ecology, Manhattan, KS 66506. Offers MS, PhD. Part-time programs available. Postbaccalaureate distance learning degree programs offered. *Faculty:* 61 full-time (37 women), 7 part-time/adjunct (4 women). *Students:* 117 full-time (93 women), 191 part-time (112 women); includes 37 minority (23 African Americans, 2 American Indian/Alaska Native, 4 Asian Americans or Pacific Islanders, 8 Hispanic Americans), 33 international. 194 applicants, 68% accepted, 81 enrolled. In 2009, 66 master's, 14 doctorates awarded. *Degree requirements:* For master's, residency; for doctorate, thesis/dissertation, residency. *Application deadline:* For fall admission, 2/1 priority date for domestic and international students; for spring admission, 8/1 priority date for domestic and international students. Applications are processed on a rolling basis. Application fee: $40 ($55 for international students). Electronic applications accepted. *Financial support:* In 2009–10, 59 research assistantships (averaging $11,616 per year), 25 teaching assistantships with full and partial tuition reimbursements (averaging $11,412 per year) were awarded; career-related internships or fieldwork, Federal Work-Study, institutionally sponsored loans, scholarships/grants, and tuition waivers (full) also available. Support available to part-time students. Financial award application deadline: 3/1; financial award applicants required to submit FAFSA. *Faculty research:* Apparel and textiles, food service and hospitality management, life span human development, family life education and consultation, marriage and family therapy. Total annual research expenditures: $11.2 million. *Unit head:* Virginia Moxley, Dean, 785-532-5500, Fax: 785-532-5504, E-mail: moxley@ksu.edu. *Application contact:* Patricia Haas, Administrative Specialist, 785-532-5500, Fax: 785-532-5504, E-mail: haas@humec.ksu.edu.

Lamar University, College of Graduate Studies, College of Education and Human Development, Department of Family and Consumer Sciences, Beaumont, TX 77710. Offers family and consumer science (MS); vocational home economics (Certificate). Part-time and evening/weekend programs available. *Faculty:* 5 full-time (all women). *Students:* 11 full-time (all women), 6 part-time (all women); includes 6 minority (3 African Americans, 1 American Indian/Alaska Native, 1 Asian American or Pacific Islander, 1 Hispanic American). Average age 28. 17 applicants, 53% accepted, 3 enrolled. In 2009, 7 master's awarded. *Degree requirements:* For master's, thesis optional. *Entrance requirements:* For master's, GRE General Test. Additional exam requirements/recommendations for international students: Required—TOEFL. *Application deadline:* For fall admission, 8/1 for domestic students; for spring admission, 12/1 for domestic students. Applications are processed on a rolling basis. Application fee: $25 ($50 for international students). *Financial support:* In 2009–10, 3 students received support, including 3 teaching assistantships (averaging $5,000 per year); fellowships, research assistantships, career-related internships or fieldwork, Federal Work-Study, and institutionally sponsored loans also available. Support available to part-time students. Financial award application deadline: 4/1. *Faculty research:* Maternal and infant nutrition, eating disorders, sports nutrition, human sexuality, family violence. *Unit head:* Dr. Connie Ruiz, Chair, 409-880-8663, Fax: 409-880-8666. *Application contact:* Sandy Drane, Coordinator of Graduate Admissions, 409-880-8356, Fax: 409-880-8414, E-mail: gradmissions@hal.lamar.edu.

Louisiana State University and Agricultural and Mechanical College, Graduate School, College of Agriculture, School of Human Ecology, Baton Rouge, LA 70803. Offers MS, PhD. Part-time programs available. *Faculty:* 30 full-time (18 women), 1 part-time/adjunct (0 women). *Students:* 30 full-time (26 women), 16 part-time (14 women), 21 international. Average age 31. 28 applicants, 61% accepted, 8 enrolled. In 2009, 9 master's, 1 doctorate awarded. *Degree requirements:* For master's, thesis; for doctorate, thesis/dissertation. *Entrance requirements:* For master's and doctorate, GRE General Test, minimum GPA of 3.0. Additional exam requirements/recommendations for international students: Required—TOEFL (minimum score 550 paper-based; 213 computer-based; 79 iBT) or IELTS (minimum score 6.5). *Application deadline:* For fall admission, 1/25 priority date for domestic students, 5/15 for international students; for spring admission, 10/15 for international students. Applications are processed on a rolling basis. Application fee: $50 ($70 for international students). Electronic applications accepted. *Financial support:* In 2009–10, 34 students received support, including 12 research assistantships with full and partial tuition reimbursements available (averaging $15,492 per year), 10 teaching assistantships with full and partial tuition reimbursements available (averaging $9,760 per year); fellowships with full and partial tuition reimbursements available, career-related internships or fieldwork, Federal Work-Study, institutionally sponsored loans, scholarships/grants, health care benefits, and unspecified assistantships also available. Support available to part-time students. Financial award application deadline: 4/15; financial award applicants required to submit FAFSA. *Faculty research:* Nutrition for optimum health, textile and apparel production development, children's relationships with parents and caregivers, contextual influences on families. Total annual research expenditures: $103,525. *Unit head:* Dr. Karen Overstreet, 225-578-2282, Fax: 225-578-2697, E-mail: koverstreet@agcenter.lsu.edu. *Application contact:* Dr. Karen Overstreet, 225-578-2282, Fax: 225-578-2697, E-mail: koverstreet@agcenter.lsu.edu.

Louisiana Tech University, Graduate School, College of Applied and Natural Sciences, School for Human Ecology, Ruston, LA 71272. Offers dietetics (MS); human ecology (MS). Part-time programs available. *Degree requirements:* For master's, thesis or alternative, Registered Dietician Exam eligibility. *Entrance requirements:* For master's, GRE General Test.

Marshall University, Academic Affairs Division, College of Education and Human Services, Division of Human Development and Allied Technology, Department of Family and Consumer Sciences, Huntington, WV 25755. Offers MA. *Faculty:* 7 full-time (4 women), 15 part-time/adjunct (8 women). *Students:* 1 (woman) part-time. Average age 26. *Degree requirements:* For master's, thesis optional, comprehensive assessment. Application fee: $40. *Unit head:* Prof. Mary Mhango, Program Coordinator, 304-96-3535, E-mail: mhango@marshall.edu. *Application contact:* Information Contact, 304-746-1900, Fax: 304-746-1902, E-mail: services@marshall.edu.

Missouri State University, Graduate College, College of Natural and Applied Sciences, Department of Fashion and Interior Design, Springfield, MO 65897. Offers secondary education (MS Ed), including consumer sciences. Part-time programs available. *Faculty:* 2 full-time (both women), 1 (woman) part-time/adjunct. *Students:* 3 part-time (all women). Average age 47. 2 applicants, 50% accepted, 0 enrolled. *Degree requirements:* For master's, comprehensive exam, thesis or alternative. *Entrance requirements:* For master's, 9-12 teaching certification (MS Ed), minimum GPA of 3.0 (MNAS). Additional exam requirements/recommendations for international students: Required—TOEFL (minimum score 550 paper-based; 213 computer-based; 79 iBT). *Application deadline:* For fall admission, 7/20 priority date for domestic students, 5/1 for international students; for spring admission, 12/20 priority date for domestic students, 9/1 for international students. Applications are processed on a rolling basis. Application fee: $35 ($50 for international students). Electronic applications accepted. *Expenses:* Tuition, state resident: full-time $3852; part-time $214 per credit hour. Tuition, nonresident: full-time $7524; part-time $418 per credit hour. Required fees: $696; $172 per semester. Tuition and fees vary according to course level, course load, degree level and program. *Financial support:* Career-related internships or fieldwork, Federal Work-Study, institutionally sponsored loans, scholarships/grants, and unspecified assistantships available. Financial award application deadline: 3/31; financial award applicants required to submit FAFSA. *Unit head:* Dr. Paula Kemp, Head, 417-836-5497, Fax: 417-836-4341, E-mail: paulakemp@missouristate.edu. *Application contact:* Eric Eckert, Coordinator of Graduate Admissions and Recruitment, 417-836-5331, Fax: 417-836-6200, E-mail: ericeckert@missouristate.edu.

New Mexico State University, Graduate School, College of Agricultural, Consumer and Environmental Sciences, Department of Family and Consumer Sciences, Las Cruces, NM 88003-8001. Offers MS. Part-time programs available. *Faculty:* 12 full-time (10 women). *Students:* 33 full-time (27 women), 17 part-time (15 women); includes 30 minority (1 African American, 3 American Indian/Alaska Native, 1 Asian American or Pacific Islander, 25 Hispanic Americans), 4 international. Average age 32. 29 applicants, 93% accepted, 14 enrolled. In 2009, 25 master's awarded. *Degree requirements:* For master's, comprehensive exam (for some programs), thesis (for some programs), oral exam. *Entrance requirements:* For master's, GRE, 3 letters of reference, resume. Additional exam requirements/recommendations for international students: Required—TOEFL. *Application deadline:* For fall admission, 6/30 priority date for domestic students, 3/1 priority date for international students; for spring admission, 11/30 for domestic and international students. Applications are processed on a rolling basis. Application fee: $30 ($50 for international students). Electronic applications accepted. *Expenses:* Tuition, state resident: full-time $4080; part-time $223 per credit. Tuition, nonresident: full-time $14,256; part-time $647 per credit. Required fees: $1278; $639 per semester. *Financial support:* In 2009–10, 15 teaching assistantships (averaging $11,584 per year) were awarded; research assistantships, career-related internships or fieldwork, Federal Work-Study, scholarships/grants, health care benefits, and unspecified assistantships also available. Support available to part-time students. Financial award application deadline: 3/1. *Faculty research:* Work, stress, and family functioning; youth at risk; food product analysis; diet and health. *Unit head:* Dr. Martha Archuleta, Head, 575-646-3936, Fax: 575-646-1889, E-mail: maarchul@nmsu.edu. *Application contact:* Dr. Wanda A. Eastman, Coordinator, 575-646-1180, Fax: 575-646-1889, E-mail: wmorgan@nmsu.edu.

North Carolina Central University, Division of Academic Affairs, College of Behavioral and Social Sciences, Department of Human Sciences, Durham, NC 27707-3129. Offers family and consumer sciences (MS). Part-time and evening/weekend programs available. *Degree requirements:* For master's, one foreign language, comprehensive exam, thesis. *Entrance requirements:* For master's, GRE, minimum GPA of 3.0 in major, 2.5 overall. Additional exam requirements/recommendations for international students: Required—TOEFL.

North Dakota State University, College of Graduate and Interdisciplinary Studies, College of Human Development and Education, School of Education, Program in Family and Consumer Sciences Education, Fargo, ND 58108. Offers M Ed, MS. *Accreditation:* NCATE. Part-time programs available. *Faculty:* 1 (woman) full-time. *Students:* 1 (woman) full-time. Average age 40. 1 applicant, 100% accepted, 1 enrolled. In 2009, 2 master's awarded. *Degree requirements:* For master's, comprehensive exam, thesis or alternative. *Entrance requirements:* For master's, MAT. Additional exam requirements/recommendations for international students: Required—TOEFL. *Application deadline:* Applications are processed on a rolling basis. Application fee: $45 ($60 for international students). *Financial support:* Teaching assistantships, career-related internships or fieldwork and institutionally sponsored loans available. Financial award application deadline: 4/15. *Faculty research:* Needs of beginning teachers, learning styles and achievement, school-level variables and curriculum change. *Unit head:* Dr. William Martin, Chair, 701-231-7202, Fax: 701-231-7416, E-mail: william.martin@ndsu.edu. *Application contact:* Dr. Mari Borr, Assistant Professor, 701-231-7968, Fax: 701-231-9685, E-mail: mari.borr@ndsu.edu.

Ohio University, Graduate College, College of Health and Human Services, School of Human and Consumer Sciences, Athens, OH 45701-2979. Offers apparel, textiles, and merchandising (MS); child development and family life (MS); early childhood education (MS); family studies (MS); food and nutrition (MS). Part-time programs available. *Faculty:* 13 full-time (9 women), 5 part-time/adjunct (all women). *Students:* 18 full-time (14 women), 7 part-time (all women); includes 2 minority (1 African American, 1 Asian American or Pacific Islander), 3 international. 21 applicants, 81% accepted, 8 enrolled. In 2009, 6 master's awarded. *Degree requirements:* For master's, comprehensive exam (for some programs), thesis. *Entrance requirements:* For master's, GRE. Additional exam requirements/recommendations for international students: Required—TOEFL (minimum score 550 paper-based; 80 iBT) or IELTS Academic (minimum score 6.5). *Application deadline:* For fall admission, 3/1 priority date for domestic and international students. Applications are processed on a rolling basis. Application fee: $50 ($55 for international students). Electronic applications accepted. *Expenses:* Tuition, state resident: full-time $7839; part-time $323 per quarter hour. Tuition, nonresident: full-time $15,831; part-time $654 per quarter hour. Required fees: $2931. *Financial support:* Research assistantships, teaching assistantships, career-related internships or fieldwork, Federal Work-Study, institutionally sponsored loans, and unspecified assistantships available. Financial award application deadline: 3/15. *Faculty research:* Diversity, developmentally appropriate activities, death and dying, gerontology, sexuality education. *Unit head:* Dr. V. Ann Paulins, Director, 740-593-2880, Fax: 740-593-0289, E-mail: paulins@ohio.edu. *Application contact:* Dr. Annette Graham, Graduate Coordinator, 740-593-0700, E-mail: grahama@ohio.edu.

Oklahoma State University, College of Human Environmental Sciences, Dean of Human Environmental Sciences—MS in Family Financial Planning Program and PhD in HES, Stillwater, OK 74078. Offers human environmental sciences (MS, PhD), including family financial planning (MS). Part-time programs available. Postbaccalaureate distance learning degree programs offered. *Faculty:* 1 full-time (0 women). *Students:* 2 full-time (both women), 21 part-time (13 women); includes 2 minority (both African Americans), 1 international. Average age 37. 67 applicants, 48% accepted, 18 enrolled. In 2009, 1 master's awarded. *Degree requirements:* For master's, thesis or alternative, creative component; for doctorate, comprehensive exam, thesis/dissertation. *Entrance requirements:* For master's and doctorate, GRE or GMAT. Additional exam requirements/recommendations for international students: Required—TOEFL (minimum score 550 paper-based; 79 iBT). *Application deadline:* For fall admission, 3/1 priority date for international students; for spring admission, 8/1 priority date for international students. Applications are processed on a rolling basis. Application fee: $40 ($75 for international students). Electronic applications accepted. *Expenses:* Tuition, state resident: full-time $3716; part-time $154.85 per credit hour. Tuition, nonresident: full-time $14,448; part-time $602 per credit hour. Required fees: $1772; $73.85 per credit hour. One-time fee: $50. Tuition and fees vary according to course load and campus/location. *Financial support:* Career-related internships or fieldwork, Federal Work-Study, scholarships/grants, health care benefits, tuition waivers (partial), and unspecified assistantships available. Support available to part-time students. Financial award application deadline: 3/1; financial award applicants required to submit FAFSA. *Unit head:* Dr. Stephan Wilson, Dean, 405-744-5053, Fax: 405-744-7113. *Application contact:* Dr. Gordon Emslie, Dean, 405-744-6368, Fax: 405-744-0355, E-mail: grad-i@okstate.edu.

Oregon State University, Graduate School, College of Education, Program in Family and Consumer Sciences Education, Corvallis, OR 97331. Offers MAT, MS. Part-time programs available. In 2009, 1 master's awarded. *Degree requirements:* For master's, thesis (for some programs). *Entrance requirements:* For master's, NTE, California Basic Educational Skills Test, minimum GPA of 3.0 in last 90 hours of course work. Additional exam requirements/recommendations for international students: Required—TOEFL. *Application deadline:* For fall admission, 1/15 for domestic students. Application fee: $50. *Expenses:* Tuition, state resident: full-time $9774; part-time $362 per credit. Tuition, nonresident: full-time $15,849; part-time $587 per credit. Required fees: $1639. Full-time tuition and fees vary according to course load and program. *Financial support:* Fellowships, career-related internships or fieldwork, Federal Work-Study, and institutionally sponsored loans available. Support available to part-time students. Financial award application deadline: 2/1. *Faculty research:* Economy of time and methods. *Unit head:* Dr. Chris L. Ward, Coordinator, 541-737-1080, Fax: 541-737-2040, E-mail: chris.ward@oregonstate.edu. *Application contact:* Dr. Chris L. Ward, Coordinator, 541-737-1080, Fax: 541-737-2040, E-mail: chris.ward@oregonstate.edu.

Prairie View A&M University, College of Agriculture and Human Sciences, Prairie View, TX 77446-0519. Offers agricultural economics (MS); animal sciences (MS); interdisciplinary human sciences (MS); soil science (MS). Part-time and evening/weekend programs available. *Faculty:* 11 full-time (4 women). *Students:* 36 full-time (27 women), 40 part-time (29 women); includes 57 African Americans, 1 Hispanic American, 6 international. Average age 31. 147 applicants, 100% accepted. In 2009, 23 master's awarded. *Degree requirements:* For master's, comprehensive exam, thesis (for some programs), field placement. *Entrance requirements:* For master's, GRE General Test, minimum GPA of 2.45. Additional exam requirements/recommendations for international students: Required—TOEFL (minimum score 550 paper-based). *Application deadline:* For fall admission, 6/1 for domestic and international students; for spring admission, 10/1 for domestic and international students. Applications are processed

Family and Consumer Sciences-General

Prairie View A&M University (continued)

on a rolling basis. Application fee: $50. *Expenses:* Tuition, state resident: full-time $2200. Tuition, nonresident: full-time $5600. Required fees: $1720. Tuition and fees vary according to course load. *Financial support:* In 2009–10, 57 students received support, including 8 fellowships with tuition reimbursements available (averaging $12,000 per year), 10 research assistantships with tuition reimbursements available (averaging $15,000 per year); career-related internships or fieldwork, Federal Work-Study, institutionally sponsored loans, scholarships/grants, tuition waivers (partial), and unspecified assistantships also available. Support available to part-time students. Financial award application deadline: 4/1; financial award applicants required to submit FAFSA. *Faculty research:* Domestic violence prevention, water quality, food growth regulators, wetland dynamics, biochemistry, obesity and nutrition, family therapy. Total annual research expenditures: $4 million. *Unit head:* Dr. Freddie Richards, Dean, 936-261-2528, Fax: 936-261-5143, E-mail: flrichards@pvamu.edu. *Application contact:* Dr. Richard W. Griffin, Interim Department Head, 936-261-5019, Fax: 936-261-5148, E-mail: rwgriffin@pvamu.edu.

Purdue University, Graduate School, College of Consumer and Family Sciences, West Lafayette, IN 47907. Offers MS, PhD. Part-time programs available. *Degree requirements:* For doctorate, thesis/dissertation. *Entrance requirements:* Additional exam requirements/recommendations for international students: Required—TOEFL. Electronic applications accepted.

Queens College of the City University of New York, Division of Graduate Studies, Mathematics and Natural Sciences Division, Department of Family, Nutrition and Exercise Sciences, Flushing, NY 11367-1597. Offers home economics (MS Ed); physical education and exercise sciences (MS Ed). Part-time and evening/weekend programs available. *Faculty:* 12 full-time (7 women). *Students:* 13 full-time (all women), 68 part-time (44 women). 58 applicants, 78% accepted, 25 enrolled. In 2009, 9 master's awarded. *Degree requirements:* For master's, research project. *Entrance requirements:* For master's, minimum GPA of 3.0. Additional exam requirements/recommendations for international students: Required—TOEFL. *Application deadline:* For fall admission, 4/1 for domestic students; for spring admission, 11/1 for domestic students. Applications are processed on a rolling basis. Application fee: $125. *Expenses:* Tuition, state resident: full-time $7360; part-time $310 per credit. Tuition, nonresident: part-time $575 per credit. One-time fee: $195.25 full-time; $145.25 part-time. *Financial support:* Career-related internships or fieldwork, Federal Work-Study, institutionally sponsored loans, and tuition waivers (partial) available. Support available to part-time students. Financial award application deadline: 4/1; financial award applicants required to submit FAFSA. *Faculty research:* Exercise and environmental physiology, interdisciplinary approaches to school curricula using outdoor education, program development in cardiac rehabilitation and adult fitness, nutrition education. *Unit head:* Dr. Elizabeth Lowe, Chairperson, 718-997-4168. *Application contact:* Mario Caruso, Director of Graduate Admissions, 718-997-5200, Fax: 718-997-5193, E-mail: graduate_admissions@qc.edu.

Sam Houston State University, College of Humanities and Social Sciences, Department of Family and Consumer Sciences, Huntsville, TX 77341. Offers dietetics (MS); family and consumer sciences (MS). Part-time and evening/weekend programs available. *Faculty:* 5 full-time (all women). *Students:* 17 full-time (all women), 5 part-time (all women); includes 3 minority (1 American Indian/Alaska Native, 2 Hispanic Americans). Average age 26. 15 applicants, 93% accepted, 12 enrolled. In 2009, 9 master's awarded. *Entrance requirements:* For master's, GRE General Test, minimum GPA of 2.5. Additional exam requirements/recommendations for international students: Required—TOEFL (minimum score 550 paper-based; 213 computer-based; 79 iBT). *Application deadline:* For fall admission, 8/1 for domestic students; for spring admission, 12/1 for domestic students. Application fee: $20. *Expenses:* Tuition, state resident: full-time $3690; part-time $205 per credit hour. Tuition, nonresident: full-time $8676; part-time $482 per credit hour. Required fees: $1474. Tuition and fees vary according to course load and campus/location. *Financial support:* Teaching assistantships available. Financial award application deadline: 5/31; financial award applicants required to submit FAFSA. *Unit head:* Dr. Janis White, Chair, 936-294-1242, Fax: 936-294-4204, E-mail: jwhite@shsu.edu. *Application contact:* Dr. Claudia Sealey-Potts, Advisor, 936-294-1250, E-mail: clapotts@shsu.edu.

San Francisco State University, Division of Graduate Studies, College of Health and Human Services, Department of Consumer and Family Studies/Dietetics, San Francisco, CA 94132-1722. Offers family and consumer sciences (MA). Part-time programs available.

South Carolina State University, School of Graduate Studies, Department of Family and Consumer Sciences, Orangeburg, SC 29117-0001. Offers individual and family development (MS); nutritional sciences (MS). Part-time and evening/weekend programs available. *Degree requirements:* For master's, comprehensive exam, thesis optional, departmental qualifying exam. *Entrance requirements:* For master's, GRE, MAT, or NTE, minimum GPA of 2.7. Electronic applications accepted. *Expenses:* Tuition, state resident: part-time $470 per credit hour. Tuition, nonresident: part-time $924 per credit hour. *Faculty research:* Societal competence, relationship of parent-child interaction to adult, quality of well-being of rural elders.

South Dakota State University, Graduate School, College of Education and Human Sciences, Department of Human Development, Consumer and Family Sciences, Brookings, SD 57007. Offers MFCS. *Entrance requirements:* For master's, resume. Additional exam requirements/recommendations for international students: Required—TOEFL (minimum score 525 paper-based).

State University of New York College at Oneonta, Graduate Education, Division of Education, Department of Secondary Education, Oneonta, NY 13820-4015. Offers adolescence education (MS Ed); family and consumer science education (MS Ed). *Accreditation:* NCATE. Part-time and evening/weekend programs available. *Entrance requirements:* For master's, GRE General Test. *Application deadline:* For fall admission, 3/25 priority date for domestic students; for spring admission, 10/1 priority date for domestic students. Applications are processed on a rolling basis. Application fee: $50. *Expenses:* Tuition, state resident: part-time $349 per credit hour. Tuition, nonresident: full-time $12,870; part-time $552 per credit hour. Required fees: $1280; $15.85 per credit hour. *Unit head:* Dr. Dennis Banks, Chair, 607-436-3391, Fax: 607-436-2554, E-mail: banksdn@oneonta.edu. *Application contact:* Dr. Dennis Banks, Chair, 607-436-3391, Fax: 607-436-2554, E-mail: banksdn@oneonta.edu.

Stephen F. Austin State University, Graduate School, College of Education, Department of Human Sciences, Nacogdoches, TX 75962. Offers MS. *Degree requirements:* For master's, comprehensive exam, thesis or alternative. *Entrance requirements:* For master's, GRE General Test. Additional exam requirements/recommendations for international students: Required—TOEFL. *Faculty research:* Consumer economics, nutrition education, clothing and textiles, family, interior design.

Tennessee State University, The School of Graduate Studies and Research, School of Agriculture and Consumer Sciences, Nashville, TN 37209-1561. Offers agricultural sciences (MS), including agribusiness, agricultural education, animal science, plant science. Part-time and evening/weekend programs available. *Degree requirements:* For master's, thesis. *Entrance requirements:* For master's, GRE General Test, GRE Subject Test, MAT. *Faculty research:* Small farm economics, ornamental horticulture, beef cattle production, rural elderly.

Texas A&M University–Kingsville, College of Graduate Studies, College of Agriculture and Home Economics, Department of Human Sciences, Kingsville, TX 78363. Offers MS. Part-time and evening/weekend programs available. *Degree requirements:* For master's, comprehensive exam, thesis or alternative. *Entrance requirements:* For master's, GRE General Test, minimum GPA of 3.0. Additional exam requirements/recommendations for international students: Required—TOEFL. *Faculty research:* Mexican-American families, abuse in families, nontraditional students.

Texas Southern University, College of Liberal Arts and Behavioral Sciences, Department of Human Services and Consumer Sciences, Houston, TX 77004-4584. Offers MS. Part-time and evening/weekend programs available. *Faculty:* 2 full-time (both women). *Students:* 7 full-time (6 women), 25 part-time (23 women); includes all African Americans. Average age 34. 13 applicants, 100% accepted, 5 enrolled. In 2009, 10 master's awarded. *Degree requirements:* For master's, comprehensive exam, thesis (for some programs). *Entrance requirements:* For master's, GRE General Test, minimum GPA of 2.5. Additional exam requirements/recommendations for international students: Required—TOEFL. *Application deadline:* For fall admission, 7/1 for domestic and international students; for spring admission, 11/1 for domestic and international students. Applications are processed on a rolling basis. Application fee: $50 ($75 for international students). Electronic applications accepted. *Expenses:* Tuition, state resident: full-time $1805; part-time $100 per credit hour. Tuition, nonresident: full-time $6470; part-time $343 per credit hour. Tuition and fees vary according to course level, course load and degree level. *Financial support:* In 2009–10, 1 teaching assistantship (averaging $6,400 per year) was awarded; research assistantships, scholarships/grants and unspecified assistantships also available. Financial award application deadline: 5/1. *Faculty research:* Food radiation/food for space travel, adolescent parenting, gerontology/grandparenting. *Unit head:* Dr. Shirley R. Nealy, Chair, 713-313-7638, Fax: 713-313-7228, E-mail: nealy_sr@tsu.edu. *Application contact:* Dr. Gregory Maddox, Interim Dean of the Graduate School, 713-313-7011 Ext. 4410, Fax: 713-639-1876, E-mail: maddox_gh@tsu.edu.

Texas Tech University, Graduate School, College of Human Sciences, Lubbock, TX 79409. Offers MS, PhD, JD/MS, JD/MSA, MS/MBA, MS/MS. Part-time and evening/weekend programs available. Postbaccalaureate distance learning degree programs offered (minimal on-campus study). *Faculty:* 53 full-time (36 women), 1 part-time/adjunct (0 women). *Students:* 234 full-time (135 women), 100 part-time (68 women); includes 40 minority (8 African Americans, 2 American Indian/Alaska Native, 4 Asian Americans or Pacific Islanders, 26 Hispanic Americans), 82 international. Average age 31. 328 applicants, 64% accepted, 80 enrolled. In 2009, 63 master's, 26 doctorates awarded. Terminal master's awarded for partial completion of doctoral program. *Degree requirements:* For master's, thesis (for some programs); for doctorate, thesis/dissertation. *Entrance requirements:* For master's, GRE; for doctorate, GRE General Test. Additional exam requirements/recommendations for international students: Required—TOEFL (minimum score 550 paper-based; 213 computer-based). *Application deadline:* For fall admission, 3/1 priority date for domestic students; for spring admission, 11/1 priority date for domestic students. Applications are processed on a rolling basis. Application fee: $50 ($75 for international students). Electronic applications accepted. *Expenses:* Contact institution. *Financial support:* In 2009–10, 19 research assistantships with partial tuition reimbursements (averaging $25,790 per year), 48 teaching assistantships with partial tuition reimbursements (averaging $17,273 per year) were awarded; career-related internships or fieldwork, Federal Work-Study, institutionally sponsored loans, and scholarships/grants also available. Support available to part-time students. Financial award application deadline: 4/15; financial award applicants required to submit FAFSA. *Faculty research:* Substance abuse and recovery; the role of nutrition in the prevention of obesity; cancer and illness; the role of family factors in children's treatment response to cancer and serious illness; financial planning and credit management. Total annual research expenditures: $2.2 million. *Unit head:* Dr. Linda C. Hoover, Dean, 806-742-3031, Fax: 806-742-1849. *Application contact:* Dr. Lynn Huffman, Executive Associate Dean, 806-742-3031, Fax: 806-742-1849, E-mail: lynn.huffman@ttu.edu.

Tufts University, Graduate School of Arts and Sciences, Department of Child Development, Medford, MA 02155. Offers child development (MA, PhD, CAGS); early childhood education (MAT). Part-time programs available. *Faculty:* 16 full-time, 12 part-time/adjunct. *Students:* 66 (61 women). Average age 27. 113 applicants, 68% accepted, 35 enrolled. In 2009, 34 master's, 6 doctorates awarded. *Degree requirements:* For master's, thesis (for some programs); for doctorate, thesis/dissertation. *Entrance requirements:* For master's and doctorate, GRE General Test. Additional exam requirements/recommendations for international students: Required—TOEFL (minimum score 550 paper-based; 213 computer-based; 80 iBT). *Application deadline:* For fall admission, 1/15 for domestic students, 12/15 for international students. Applications are processed on a rolling basis. Application fee: $75. Electronic applications accepted. *Expenses:* Tuition: Full-time $38,096; part-time $3962 per credit. Required fees: $686; $40 per year. Tuition and fees vary according to course level, course load, degree level, program and student level. *Financial support:* Fellowships, research assistantships with full and partial tuition reimbursements, teaching assistantships with full and partial tuition reimbursements, Federal Work-Study, scholarships/grants, tuition waivers (partial), and unspecified assistantships available. Support available to part-time students. Financial award application deadline: 1/15; financial award applicants required to submit FAFSA. *Unit head:* Jayanthi Mistry, Chair, 617-627-3355. *Application contact:* Fred Rothbaum, Graduate Advisor, 617-627-3355.

The University of Alabama, Graduate School, College of Human Environmental Sciences, Tuscaloosa, AL 35487. Offers MA, MS, MSHES, PhD. Part-time and evening/weekend programs available. Postbaccalaureate distance learning degree programs offered (no on-campus study). *Faculty:* 29 full-time (21 women), 1 part-time/adjunct (0 women). *Students:* 157 full-time (116 women), 244 part-time (159 women); includes 99 minority (85 African Americans, 3 American Indian/Alaska Native, 6 Asian Americans or Pacific Islanders, 5 Hispanic Americans), 4 international. Average age 31. 337 applicants, 59% accepted, 150 enrolled. In 2009, 163 master's, 3 doctorates awarded. *Degree requirements:* For doctorate, thesis/dissertation. *Entrance requirements:* For master's, GRE General Test or MAT (minimum score: 50th percentile), minimum GPA of 3.0; for doctorate, GRE General Test or MAT, minimum GPA of 3.0. *Application deadline:* For fall admission, 7/6 for domestic students. Applications are processed on a rolling basis. Application fee: $50 ($60 for international students). Electronic applications accepted. *Expenses:* Tuition, state resident: full-time $7000. Tuition, nonresident: full-time $19,200. *Financial support:* In 2009–10, 2 research assistantships with full tuition reimbursements (averaging $9,000 per year) were awarded; fellowships with tuition reimbursements, teaching assistantships with full tuition reimbursements, career-related internships or fieldwork, Federal Work-Study, institutionally sponsored loans, and scholarships/grants also available. *Faculty research:* Students' use of credit; determinants of income differential: comparing Asians with blacks and whites; expenditure patterns of Chinese; racial and ethnic differences in the likelihood of charitable contributions; health insurance coverage and precautionary behavior savings. Total annual research expenditures: $1.1 million. *Unit head:* Dr. Milla D. Boschung, Dean, 205-348-6250, Fax: 205-348-1786, E-mail: mboschun@ches.ua.edu. *Application contact:* Dr. Milla D. Boschung, Dean, 205-348-6250, Fax: 205-348-1786, E-mail: mboschun@ches.ua.edu.

University of Alberta, Faculty of Graduate Studies and Research, Department of Human Ecology, Edmonton, AB T6G 2E1, Canada. Offers family ecology and practice (M Sc, PhD); textiles and clothing (M Sc, MA, PhD). Postbaccalaureate distance learning degree programs offered (no on-campus study). *Faculty:* 11 full-time (all women), 2 part-time/adjunct (both women). *Students:* 40 full-time (37 women), 15 part-time (all women). Average age 24. 25 applicants, 32% accepted. In 2009, 14 master's, 1 doctorate awarded. *Degree requirements:* For master's, thesis (for some programs); for doctorate, comprehensive exam, thesis/dissertation. *Entrance requirements:* For master's and doctorate, minimum GPA of 7.0 on a 9.0 scale. Additional exam requirements/recommendations for international students: Required—TOEFL (minimum score 580 paper-based; 237 computer-based). *Application deadline:* For fall admission, 2/1 for domestic students; for winter admission, 9/1 for domestic students. Application fee: $0. Tuition and fees charges are reported in Canadian dollars. *Expenses:* Tuition, area resident: Full-time $4626 Canadian dollars; part-time $99.72 Canadian dollars per unit. International tuition: $8216 Canadian dollars full-time. Required fees: $3590 Canadian dollars; $99.72 Canadian dollars per unit. $215 Canadian dollars per term. *Financial support:* In 2009–10, 3 research assistantships, 4 teaching assistantships were awarded; career-related internships or fieldwork, scholarships/grants, and tuition waivers also available. *Faculty research:* Families and aging, family and child poverty, paid and unpaid work of families, textiles and clothing, parent-child relationships. Total annual research expenditures: $1 million. *Unit head:* Dr. L. Capjack, Chair, 780-492-5230, Fax: 780-492-4821. *Application contact:* Linda Mirans, Administrative Assistant, 780-492-5230, Fax: 780-492-4821, E-mail: hec.grad@ualberta.ca.

The University of Arizona, Graduate College, College of Agriculture and Life Sciences, School of Family and Consumer Sciences, Tucson, AZ 85721. Offers MS, PhD. Part-time programs available. *Faculty:* 16. *Students:* 32 full-time (21 women), 7 part-time (5 women); includes 5 minority (2 African Americans, 1 Asian American or Pacific Islander, 2 Hispanic Americans), 12 international. Average age 33. 25 applicants, 44% accepted, 8 enrolled. In 2009, 1 master's, 3 doctorates awarded. *Entrance requirements:* For master's and doctorate, GRE General Test, minimum GPA of 3.0. Additional exam requirements/recommendations for international students: Required—TOEFL. *Application deadline:* Applications are processed on a rolling basis. Application fee: $75. *Expenses:* Tuition, state resident: full-time $9028. Tuition, nonresident: full-time $24,890. *Financial support:* In 2009–10, 19 research assistantships with full and partial tuition reimbursements (averaging $13,821 per year), 8 teaching assistantships with full and partial tuition reimbursements (averaging $13,778 per year) were awarded; fellowships, career-related internships or fieldwork, Federal Work-Study, institutionally sponsored loans, scholarships/grants, health care benefits, tuition waivers (full), and unspecified assistantships also available. Financial award application deadline: 3/1. *Faculty research:* Interpersonal relationships, human development, retailing management, consumer behaviors. Total annual research expenditures: $928,549. *Unit head:* Dr. Soyeon Shim, Director, 520-621-1075, Fax: 520-621-9445, E-mail: shim@ag.arizona.edu. *Application contact:* Mary Helen Scott, Program Coordinator, 520-621-5884, Fax: 520-621-9445, E-mail: mhscott@ag.arizona.edu.

University of Arkansas, Graduate School, Dale Bumpers College of Agricultural, Food and Life Sciences, School of Human Environmental Sciences, Fayetteville, AR 72701-1201. Offers MS. Part-time programs available. Postbaccalaureate distance learning degree programs offered (minimal on-campus study). *Students:* 2 full-time (both women), 17 part-time (16 women), 1 international. In 2009, 7 master's awarded. *Degree requirements:* For master's, comprehensive exam, thesis (for some programs). Application fee: $40 ($50 for international students). *Expenses:* Tuition, state resident: full-time $7355; part-time $356.58 per hour. Tuition, nonresident: full-time $17,401; part-time $775.17 per hour. Required fees: $1203. *Financial support:* In 2009–10, 9 research assistantships, 1 teaching assistantship were awarded; fellowships, Federal Work-Study also available. Support available to part-time students. Financial award application deadline: 4/1; financial award applicants required to submit FAFSA. *Unit head:* Dr. Mary Warnock, Department Head, 479-575-4305, E-mail: hesc@uark.edu. *Application contact:* Dr. Mary Warnock, Department Head, 479-575-4305, E-mail: hesc@uark.edu.

University of Central Arkansas, Graduate School, College of Health and Behavioral Sciences, Department of Family and Consumer Sciences, Conway, AR 72035-0001. Offers MS. *Faculty:* 1 (woman) full-time. *Students:* 39 full-time (36 women), 27 part-time (all women); includes 6 minority (5 African Americans, 1 Hispanic American), 1 international. Average age 28. 24 applicants, 96% accepted, 13 enrolled. In 2009, 38 master's awarded. *Degree requirements:* For master's, comprehensive exam, thesis optional. *Entrance requirements:* For master's, GRE General Test, minimum GPA of 2.7. Additional exam requirements/recommendations for international students: Required—TOEFL (minimum score 550 paper-based; 213 computer-based). *Application deadline:* For fall admission, 3/1 priority date for domestic students; for spring admission, 10/1 for domestic students. Applications are processed on a rolling basis. Application fee: $25 ($40 for international students). *Expenses:* Contact institution. *Financial support:* Career-related internships or fieldwork, scholarships/grants, and unspecified assistantships available. Support available to part-time students. Financial award application deadline: 2/15. *Faculty research:* Neurology, developmental disabilities, diet consequences. *Unit head:* Dr. Mary Harlan, Chairperson, 501-450-5950, Fax: 501-450-5958, E-mail: maryh@uca.edu. *Application contact:* Patti Hornor, Administrative Assistant, 501-450-5063, Fax: 501-450-5678, E-mail: pattih@uca.edu.

University of Central Oklahoma, College of Graduate Studies and Research, College of Education, Department of Human Environmental Sciences, Edmond, OK 73034-5209. Offers family and child studies (MS); family and consumer science education (MS); interior design (MS); nutrition-food management (MS). Part-time programs available. *Entrance requirements:* Additional exam requirements/recommendations for international students: Required—TOEFL (minimum score 550 paper-based; 213 computer-based). Electronic applications accepted. *Expenses:* Tuition, state resident: full-time $4128; part-time $172 per credit hour. Tuition, nonresident: full-time $10,373; part-time $432.20 per credit hour. Required fees: $433.20; $18.05 per credit hour. *Faculty research:* Dietetics and food science.

University of Florida, Graduate School, College of Agricultural and Life Sciences, Department of Family, Youth, and Community Sciences, Gainesville, FL 32611. Offers MFYCS, MS.

University of Georgia, Graduate School, College of Family and Consumer Sciences, Athens, GA 30602. Offers MAT, MFCS, MS, PhD. *Faculty:* 54 full-time (33 women). *Students:* 115 full-time (100 women), 36 part-time (28 women); includes 21 minority (18 African Americans, 3 Hispanic Americans), 16 international. 149 applicants, 47% accepted, 56 enrolled. In 2009, 29 master's, 6 doctorates awarded. *Degree requirements:* For doctorate, thesis/dissertation. *Entrance requirements:* For master's and doctorate, GRE General Test. *Application deadline:* For fall admission, 7/1 priority date for domestic students; for spring admission, 11/15 for domestic students. Application fee: $50. Electronic applications accepted. *Expenses:* Tuition, state resident: full-time $6000; part-time $250 per credit hour. Tuition, nonresident: full-time $20,904; part-time $871 per credit hour. Required fees: $730 per semester. *Financial support:* Fellowships, research assistantships, teaching assistantships, unspecified assistantships available. *Unit head:* Dr. Laura Dunn Jolly, Dean, 706-542-4879, Fax: 706-542-4862, E-mail: dean@fcs.uga.edu. *Application contact:* Director of Enrolled Student Services.

University of Houston, College of Technology, Department of Human Development and Consumer Science, Houston, TX 77204. Offers M Tech, MS. Part-time and evening/weekend programs available. *Faculty:* 3 full-time (2 women), 3 part-time/adjunct (1 woman). *Students:* 35 full-time (23 women), 56 part-time (36 women); includes 35 minority (22 African Americans, 4 Asian Americans or Pacific Islanders, 9 Hispanic Americans), 18 international. Average age 32. 41 applicants, 90% accepted, 30 enrolled. In 2009, 17 master's awarded. *Degree requirements:* For master's, project or thesis. *Entrance requirements:* For master's, GMAT, MAT. Additional exam requirements/recommendations for international students: Required—TOEFL (minimum score 550 paper-based; 79 iBT). *Application deadline:* For fall admission, 7/1 for domestic students, 4/1 for international students; for spring admission, 12/1 for domestic students, 10/1 for international students. Applications are processed on a rolling basis. Application fee: $75 ($150 for international students). Electronic applications accepted. *Expenses:* Tuition, state resident: full-time $7676; part-time $320 per credit hour. Tuition, nonresident: full-time $14,324; part-time $597 per credit hour. Required fees: $3034. *Financial support:* In 2009–10, 5 teaching assistantships with full tuition reimbursements (averaging $10,500 per year) were awarded. *Unit head:* Carole Goodson, Chairperson, 713-743-4046, Fax: 713-743-4033. *Application contact:* Tiffany Roosa, Academic Advisor, 713-743-2987, Fax: 713-743-4151, E-mail: troosa@uh.edu.

University of Manitoba, Faculty of Graduate Studies, Faculty of Human Ecology, Winnipeg, MB R3T 2N2, Canada. Offers M Sc. *Degree requirements:* For master's, thesis.

University of Maryland, College Park, Academic Affairs, School of Public Health, Department of Family Science, College Park, MD 20742. Offers family studies (PhD); marriage and family therapy (MS); maternal and child health (PhD). *Accreditation:* AAMFT/COAMFTE. Part-time and evening/weekend programs available. *Faculty:* 13 full-time (9 women), 14 part-time/adjunct (12 women). *Students:* 46 full-time (43 women), 2 part-time (both women); includes 13 minority (9 African Americans, 2 Asian Americans or Pacific Islanders, 2 Hispanic Americans), 3 international. 99 applicants, 15% accepted, 14 enrolled. In 2009, 7 master's, 4 doctorates awarded. *Degree requirements:* For master's, thesis or alternative; for doctorate, comprehensive exam, thesis/dissertation, oral defense. *Entrance requirements:* For master's, GRE General Test, minimum GPA of 3.0, 3 letters of recommendation; for doctorate, GRE General Test, minimum GPA of 3.0, 3 letters of recommendation, research sample. *Application deadline:* For fall admission, 12/1 for domestic and international students; for spring admission, 6/1 for international students. Applications are processed on a rolling basis. Application fee: $60. Electronic applications accepted. *Expenses:* Tuition, area resident: Part-time $471 per credit hour. Tuition, state resident: part-time $471 per credit hour. Tuition, nonresident: part-time $1016 per credit hour. Required fees: $337.04 per term. *Financial support:* In 2009–10, 6 fellowships with full and partial tuition reimbursements (averaging $10,021 per year), 40 teaching assistantships with tuition reimbursements (averaging $16,096 per year) were awarded; research assistantships with tuition reimbursements, career-related internships or fieldwork, Federal Work-Study, and scholarships/grants also available. Support available to part-time students. Financial award applicants required to submit FAFSA. *Faculty research:* Family life quality, interracial couples, child support, homeless families, family and child well-being. Total annual research expenditures: $346,806. *Unit head:* Elaine Anderson, Chairman, 301-405-4009, Fax: 301-314-9161, E-mail: eanders@umd.edu. *Application contact:* Dean of Graduate School, 301-405-0358.

University of Memphis, Graduate School, University College, Memphis, TN 38152. Offers liberal studies (MALS); merchandising and consumer science (MS), including consumer science and education; strategic leadership (MPS). Part-time and evening/weekend programs available. *Faculty:* 3 full-time (2 women), 3 part-time/adjunct (1 woman). *Students:* 30 full-time (19 women), 122 part-time (93 women); includes 91 minority (88 African Americans, 1 American Indian/Alaska Native, 1 Asian American or Pacific Islander, 1 Hispanic American), 1 international. Average age 40. 89 applicants, 74% accepted, 8 enrolled. In 2009, 41 master's awarded. *Degree requirements:* For master's, comprehensive exam, thesis (for some programs). *Entrance requirements:* For master's, MAT, GRE General Test (MS), interview (MALS). Additional exam requirements/recommendations for international students: Required—TOEFL (minimum score 550 paper-based; 210 computer-based). *Application deadline:* For fall admission, 7/1 for domestic students, 5/1 for international students; for spring admission, 11/1 for domestic students, 9/15 for international students. Applications are processed on a rolling basis. Application fee: $35 ($60 for international students). Electronic applications accepted. *Expenses:* Tuition, state resident: full-time $6246; part-time $347 per credit hour. Tuition, nonresident: full-time $15,894; part-time $883 per credit hour. Required fees: $1160. Full-time tuition and fees vary according to course load, degree level and program. *Financial support:* In 2009–10, 123 students received support; research assistantships with full tuition reimbursements available, teaching assistantships with tuition reimbursements available, Federal Work-Study, scholarships/grants, and unspecified assistantships available. Financial award application deadline: 2/15; financial award applicants required to submit FAFSA. *Faculty research:* Media ethics, history of psychiatry, public relations. *Unit head:* Dr. Dan Lattimore, Dean, 901-678-2991. *Application contact:* Dr. Herbert McCree, Coordinator of Graduate Studies, 901-678-4171, Fax: 901-678-3363, E-mail: hmccree@memphis.edu.

University of Mississippi, Graduate School, School of Applied Sciences, Department of Family and Consumer Sciences, Oxford, University, MS 38677. Offers MS. *Faculty:* 5 full-time (all women). *Students:* 19 full-time (16 women), 2 part-time (both women); includes 3 minority (2 African Americans, 1 Asian American or Pacific Islander). *Unit head:* Dr. Teresa Carithers, Chair, E-mail: carither@olemiss.edu. *Application contact:* Dr. Christy M. Wyandt, Associate Dean, 662-915-7474, Fax: 662-915-7577, E-mail: cwyandt@olemiss.edu.

University of Missouri, Graduate School, College of Human Environmental Science, Columbia, MO 65211. Offers MA, MS, PhD. Part-time programs available. *Degree requirements:* For doctorate, thesis/dissertation. *Entrance requirements:* For master's and doctorate, GRE General Test, minimum GPA of 3.0. Additional exam requirements/recommendations for international students: Required—TOEFL.

University of Nebraska–Lincoln, Graduate College, College of Education and Human Sciences, Department of Child, Youth and Family Studies, Lincoln, NE 68588. Offers child development/early childhood education (MS, PhD); child, youth and family studies (MS); family and consumer sciences education (MS, PhD); family financial planning (MS); family science (MS, PhD); gerontology (PhD); human sciences (PhD), including child, youth and family studies, gerontology, medical family therapy; marriage and family therapy (MS); medical family therapy (PhD); youth development (MS). *Accreditation:* AAMFT/COAMFTE (one or more programs are accredited). Postbaccalaureate distance learning degree programs offered. *Degree requirements:* For master's, thesis optional. *Entrance requirements:* For master's, GRE. Additional exam requirements/recommendations for international students: Required—TOEFL (minimum score 550 paper-based; 213 computer-based). Electronic applications accepted. *Faculty research:* Marriage and family therapy, child development/early childhood education, family financial management.

The University of North Carolina at Greensboro, Graduate School, School of Human Environmental Sciences, Greensboro, NC 27412-5001. Offers M Ed, MS, MSW, PhD, Certificate. *Degree requirements:* For master's, thesis (for some programs); for doctorate, thesis/dissertation. *Entrance requirements:* For master's and doctorate, GRE General Test. Additional exam requirements/recommendations for international students: Required—TOEFL. Electronic applications accepted. *Faculty research:* Impact of phosphate removal, protective clothing for pesticide workers, adolescent mothers, cancer prevention, immuno-stimulant effects.

University of Puerto Rico, Río Piedras, College of Education, Program in Family Ecology and Nutrition, San Juan, PR 00931-3300. Offers M Ed. Part-time programs available. *Degree requirements:* For master's, thesis. *Entrance requirements:* For master's, PAEG or GRE, minimum GPA of 3.0, letter of recommendation.

University of South Africa, College of Agriculture and Environmental Sciences, Pretoria, South Africa. Offers agriculture (MS); consumer science (MCS); environmental management (MA, MS, PhD); environmental science (MA, MS, PhD); geography (MA, MS, PhD); horticulture (M Tech); human ecology (MHE); life sciences (MS); nature conservation (M Tech).

The University of Tennessee, Graduate School, College of Education, Health and Human Sciences, Program in Human Ecology, Knoxville, TN 37996. Offers child and family studies (PhD); community health (PhD); nutrition science (PhD); retailing and consumer sciences (PhD); textile science (PhD). *Degree requirements:* For doctorate, thesis/dissertation. *Entrance requirements:* For doctorate, GRE General Test, minimum GPA of 2.7. Additional exam requirements/recommendations for international students: Required—TOEFL. Electronic applications accepted. *Expenses:* Tuition, state resident: full-time $6826; part-time $380 per semester hour. Tuition, nonresident: full-time $21,844; part-time $1147 per semester hour. Tuition and fees vary according to program.

The University of Tennessee at Martin, Graduate Programs, College of Agriculture and Applied Sciences, Department of Family and Consumer Sciences, Martin, TN 38238-1000. Offers dietetics (MSFCS); general family and consumer sciences (MSFCS). Part-time programs available. Postbaccalaureate distance learning degree programs offered (minimal on-campus study). *Faculty:* 6. *Students:* 47 (43 women). 5,430 applicants, 1% accepted, 23 enrolled. In 2009, 10 master's awarded. *Degree requirements:* For master's, comprehensive exam, thesis optional. *Entrance requirements:* For master's, GRE General Test, minimum GPA of 2.5. Additional exam requirements/recommendations for international students: Required—TOEFL (minimum score 525 paper-based; 197 computer-based; 71 iBT). *Application deadline:* For fall admission, 8/1 priority date for domestic students, 6/15 priority date for international students; for spring admission, 12/15 priority date for domestic students, 12/1 priority date for international students. Applications are processed on a rolling basis. Application fee: $30 ($130 for international students). Electronic applications accepted. *Expenses:* Tuition, state resident: full-time $6660; part-time $372 per hour. Tuition, nonresident: full-time $18,000; part-time $1005 per hour. *Financial support:* In 2009–10, 3 students received support, including 3 research assistantships with full tuition reimbursements available (averaging $7,234 per year); scholarships/grants and unspecified assistantships also available. Support available to part-time students. Financial award application deadline: 2/15; financial award applicants required to submit FAFSA. *Faculty research:* Children with developmental disabilities, regional food product

Family and Consumer Sciences-General

The University of Tennessee at Martin (continued)

development and marketing, parent education. *Unit head:* Dr. Lisa LeBleu, Coordinator, 731-881-7116, Fax: 731-881-7106, E-mail: llebleu@utm.edu. *Application contact:* Linda S. Arant, Student Services Specialist, 731-881-7012, Fax: 731-881-7499, E-mail: larant@utm.edu.

The University of Texas at Austin, Graduate School, College of Natural Sciences, School of Human Ecology, Austin, TX 78712-1111. Offers human development and family sciences (MA, PhD); nutritional sciences (MA, PhD), including nutrition (MA), nutritional sciences (PhD); textile and apparel technology (MS). *Degree requirements:* For master's, thesis; for doctorate, thesis/dissertation. *Entrance requirements:* For master's and doctorate, GRE General Test. Electronic applications accepted.

University of Wisconsin–Madison, Graduate School, School of Human Ecology, Madison, WI 53706-1380. Offers consumer behavior and family economics (MS, PhD); design studies (MFA, MS, PhD); human development and family studies (MS, PhD). *Degree requirements:* For master's, thesis (for some programs); for doctorate, comprehensive exam, thesis/dissertation. *Entrance requirements:* For master's, GRE General Test, portfolio (design studies), 3 letters of recommendation; for doctorate, GRE General Test. Additional exam requirements/recommendations for international students: Required—TOEFL (minimum score 580 paper-based; 237 computer-based). Electronic applications accepted. *Expenses:* Tuition, state resident: part-time $594 per credit. Tuition, nonresident: part-time $1504 per credit. Required fees: $65 per credit. Tuition and fees vary according to course load, program and reciprocity agreements.

University of Wisconsin–Stevens Point, College of Professional Studies, School of Health Promotion and Human Development, Program in Human and Community Resources, Stevens Point, WI 54481-3897. Offers MS. Part-time programs available. *Students:* 2 full-time (both women), 3 part-time (2 women); includes 2 African Americans. *Degree requirements:* For master's, thesis or alternative. *Entrance requirements:* For master's, minimum GPA of 2.75. *Application deadline:* For fall admission, 5/1 priority date for domestic students. Applications are processed on a rolling basis. Application fee: $45. *Expenses:* Tuition, state resident: full-time $7740; part-time $430 per credit hour. Tuition, nonresident: full-time $17,804; part-time $989 per credit hour. Tuition and fees vary according to course load and reciprocity agreements. *Financial support:* Research assistantships, teaching assistantships, Federal Work-Study available. Support available to part-time students. Financial award application deadline: 5/1; financial award applicants required to submit FAFSA. *Unit head:* Dr. Marty Loy, Head, 715-346-2830, Fax: 715-346-2720. *Application contact:* Dr. Jasia Steinmetz, Information Contact, 715-346-2830, Fax: 715-346-2720, E-mail: jsteinme@uwsp.edu.

Utah State University, School of Graduate Studies, College of Education and Human Services, Department of Family, Consumer, and Human Development, Logan, UT 84322. Offers family and human development (MFHD); family, consumer, and human development (MS, PhD), including adolescence/youth (MS), adult development/aging (MS), consumer science (MS), infancy/childhood (MS), marriage and family relations (MS), marriage and family therapy (MS). *Accreditation:* AAMFT/COAMFTE (one or more programs are accredited). Part-time and evening/weekend programs available. Postbaccalaureate distance learning degree programs offered (minimal on-campus study). *Degree requirements:* For master's, thesis; for doctorate, comprehensive exam, thesis/dissertation, competencies. *Entrance requirements:* For master's, GRE General Test or MAT, minimum GPA of 3.0, 3 letters of recommendation; for doctorate, GRE, minimum GPA of 3.0, 3 letters of recommendation. Additional exam requirements/recommendations for international students: Required—TOEFL. Electronic applications accepted. *Faculty research:* Marriage and family relations, adolescent problem behavior, family financial management, early literacy, mental health in the elderly, parent child attachment.

Western Michigan University, Graduate College, College of Education, Department of Family and Consumer Sciences, Program in Family and Consumer Sciences, Kalamazoo, MI 49008. Offers MA. *Faculty research:* Parenting education, kinship care, entrepreneurship, textiles and dress, nutrition.

Child and Family Studies

Arizona State University, Graduate College, College of Liberal Arts and Sciences, Division of Social Sciences, School of Social and Family Dynamics, Tempe, AZ 85287. Offers family and human development (MS, PhD); infant-family practice (MAS); marriage and family therapy (MAS); sociology (MA, PhD). *Degree requirements:* For master's, thesis or alternative; for doctorate, thesis/dissertation. *Entrance requirements:* For master's and doctorate, GRE.

Asbury University, School of Graduate and Professional Studies, Master of Social Work Program, Wilmore, KY 40390-1198. Offers child and family services (MSW). *Faculty:* 6 full-time (3 women). *Students:* 36 full-time (24 women); includes 2 African Americans, 1 Hispanic American, 1 international. 27 applicants, 81% accepted, 20 enrolled. *Degree requirements:* For master's, comprehensive exam, 954 praticum hours completed in agency. *Entrance requirements:* For master's, prerequisite courses in psychology, sociology, and statistics. Additional exam requirements/recommendations for international students: Required—TOEFL. *Application deadline:* Applications are processed on a rolling basis. Application fee: $25. Electronic applications accepted. *Expenses:* Contact institution. *Financial support:* Applicants required to submit FAFSA. *Faculty research:* Integration of faith and practice, survivors of family violence, program evaluation, cross-cultural counseling. *Unit head:* Dr. William Descoteaux, Program Director, 859-858-3511 Ext. 2206, Fax: 859-858-3921, E-mail: bill.descoteaux@asbury.edu. *Application contact:* Aaron D. Wilkinson, Coordinator of Admissions and Marketing, 859-858-3511 Ext. 25256, Fax: 859-858-3921, E-mail: aaron.wilkinson@asbury.edu.

Assumption College, Graduate School, Counseling Psychology Program, Worcester, MA 01609-1296. Offers child and family interventions (MA); cognitive and behavioral therapies (MA); counseling psychology (CAGS); general psychology (MA). Part-time and evening/weekend programs available. *Faculty:* 4 full-time (1 woman), 6 part-time/adjunct (2 women). *Students:* 50 full-time (42 women), 38 part-time (33 women); includes 9 minority (3 African Americans, 6 Hispanic Americans). Average age 24. 121 applicants, 86% accepted. In 2009, 20 master's, 2 other advanced degrees awarded. *Degree requirements:* For master's, comprehensive exam, internship, practicum, oral exam; for CAGS, comprehensive exam, oral exam. *Entrance requirements:* For master's, 3 letters of recommendation, resume; for CAGS, 3 letters of recommendation, resume, interview, essay. Additional exam requirements/recommendations for international students: Required—TOEFL (minimum score 540 paper-based; 200 computer-based; 76 iBT), IELTS (minimum score 6). *Application deadline:* For fall admission, 6/1 priority date for domestic students, 5/1 priority date for international students; for spring admission, 11/1 priority date for domestic students, 9/1 priority date for international students. Applications are processed on a rolling basis. Application fee: $30. Electronic applications accepted. *Expenses:* Tuition: Part-time $503 per credit. Required fees: $20 per semester. One-time fee: $100 part-time. Part-time tuition and fees vary according to campus/location. *Financial support:* In 2009–10, 19 fellowships with partial tuition reimbursements (averaging $6,808 per year), 2 teaching assistantships with full tuition reimbursements (averaging $9,940 per year) were awarded. Financial award application deadline: 3/1; financial award applicants required to submit FAFSA. *Faculty research:* Mood disorders, adjustment to life-threatening illness, perception of movement, socioemotional development of young children, discovery versus disclosure. *Unit head:* Dr. Leonard A. Doerfler, Director, 508-767-7549, Fax: 508-767-7263, E-mail: doerfler@assumption.edu. *Application contact:* Adrian O. Dumas, Director of Graduate Enrollment Management and Services, 508-767-7365, Fax: 508-767-7030, E-mail: adumas@assumption.edu.

Auburn University, Graduate School, College of Human Sciences, Department of Human Development and Family Studies, Auburn University, AL 36849. Offers MS, PhD. *Accreditation:* AAMFT/COAMFTE (one or more programs are accredited). Part-time programs available. *Faculty:* 20 full-time (12 women), 1 (woman) part-time/adjunct. *Students:* 28 full-time (24 women), 26 part-time (22 women); includes 18 minority (10 African Americans, 6 Asian Americans or Pacific Islanders, 2 Hispanic Americans), 6 international. Average age 28. 56 applicants, 55% accepted, 18 enrolled. In 2009, 15 master's, 2 doctorates awarded. *Degree requirements:* For master's, thesis, oral exam; for doctorate, thesis/dissertation. *Entrance requirements:* For master's, GRE General Test; for doctorate, GRE General Test, master's degree. *Application deadline:* For fall admission, 7/7 for domestic students; for spring admission, 11/24 for domestic students. Applications are processed on a rolling basis. Application fee: $50 ($60 for international students). *Expenses:* Tuition, state resident: full-time $6240. Tuition, nonresident: full-time $18,720. International tuition: $18,938 full-time. Required fees: $492. Tuition and fees vary according to course load, program and reciprocity agreements. *Financial support:* Research assistantships, teaching assistantships, Federal Work-Study available. Support available to part-time students. Financial award application deadline: 3/15; financial award applicants required to submit FAFSA. *Faculty research:* Family influences on personality and social development, parent-child relations, infancy, day care, parent education. *Unit head:* Dr. Leanne K. Lamke, Head, 334-844-4151, E-mail: mbradbar@humsci.auburn.edu. *Application contact:* Dr. George Flowers, Dean of the Graduate School, 334-844-2125.

Bank Street College of Education, Graduate School, Program in Child Life, New York, NY 10025. Offers MS. *Students:* 16 full-time (all women), 13 part-time (all women); includes 3 minority (1 African American, 1 Asian American or Pacific Islander, 1 Hispanic American). Average age 28. 38 applicants, 47% accepted, 14 enrolled. In 2009, 16 master's awarded. *Degree requirements:* For master's, thesis. *Entrance requirements:* For master's, interview and 100 hours of volunteer experience in a child life setting. Additional exam requirements/recommendations for international students: Required—TOEFL (minimum score 600 paper-based; 250 computer-based; 100 iBT), IELTS (minimum score 7). *Application deadline:* For fall admission, 3/1 priority date for domestic students; for spring admission, 11/1 priority date for domestic students. Applications are processed on a rolling basis. Application fee: $65. *Expenses:* Tuition: Part-time $1120 per credit. *Financial support:* Career-related internships or fieldwork, Federal Work-Study, scholarships/grants, and unspecified assistantships available. Support available to part-time students. Financial award application deadline: 4/15; financial award applicants required to submit FAFSA. *Faculty research:* Therapeutic play in child life setting, child advocacy, psychosocial and educational intervention with care of sick children. *Unit head:* Troy Pinkney-Ragsdale, Director, 212-875-4473, Fax: 212-875-4753, E-mail: tpinkneyragsdale@bankstreet.edu. *Application contact:* Troy Pinkney-Ragsdale, Director, 212-875-4473, Fax: 212-875-4753, E-mail: tpinkneyragsdale@bankstreet.edu.

Bank Street College of Education, Graduate School, Program in Infant and Family Development and Early Intervention, New York, NY 10025. Offers early childhood special and general education (MS Ed); early childhood special education (Ed M); infant and family development (MS Ed). *Students:* 16 full-time (all women), 29 part-time (all women); includes 7 minority (3 African Americans, 1 Asian American or Pacific Islander, 3 Hispanic Americans), 1 international. Average age 31. 21 applicants, 71% accepted, 10 enrolled. In 2009, 16 master's awarded. *Degree requirements:* For master's, thesis. *Entrance requirements:* For master's, interview. Additional exam requirements/recommendations for international students: Required—TOEFL (minimum score 600 paper-based; 250 computer-based; 100 iBT), IELTS (minimum score 7). *Application deadline:* For fall admission, 3/1 priority date for domestic students; for spring admission, 11/1 priority date for domestic students. Applications are processed on a rolling basis. Application fee: $65. *Expenses:* Tuition: Part-time $1120 per credit. *Financial support:* Career-related internships or fieldwork, Federal Work-Study, scholarships/grants, and unspecified assistantships available. Support available to part-time students. Financial award application deadline: 4/15; financial award applicants required to submit FAFSA. *Faculty research:* Early intervention, early attachment practice in infant and toddler childcare, parenting skills in adolescents. *Unit head:* Sue Cabary, Director, 212-875-4509, Fax: 212-875-4753, E-mail: scarbary@bankstreet.edu. *Application contact:* Ann Morgan, Director of Graduate Admissions, 212-875-4403, Fax: 212-875-4678, E-mail: amorgan@bankstreet.edu.

Bowling Green State University, Graduate College, College of Education and Human Development, School of Family and Consumer Sciences, Bowling Green, OH 43403. Offers food and nutrition (MFCS); human development and family studies (MFCS). Part-time programs available. *Degree requirements:* For master's, thesis. *Entrance requirements:* For master's, GRE General Test, minimum GPA of 3.0. Additional exam requirements/recommendations for international students: Required—TOEFL. Electronic applications accepted. *Faculty research:* Public health, wellness, social issues and policies, ethnic foods, nutrition and aging.

Brandeis University, The Heller School for Social Policy and Management, Program in Public Policy, Waltham, MA 02454-9110. Offers aging (MPP); behavioral health (MPP); children, youth and families (MPP); general social policy (MPP); health (MPP); poverty alleviation and development (MPP). Part-time programs available. *Entrance requirements:* Additional exam requirements/recommendations for international students: Required—TOEFL (minimum score 600 paper-based). Electronic applications accepted. *Faculty research:* Health policy, child and family policy, mental health policy, disability policy, aging policy, substance abuse, work, inequality and social change.

Brandeis University, The Heller School for Social Policy and Management, Program in Social Policy, Waltham, MA 02454-9110. Offers assets and inequalities (PhD); children, youth and families (PhD); health and behavioral health (PhD). *Degree requirements:* For doctorate, thesis/dissertation, qualifying paper, 2-year residency. *Entrance requirements:* For doctorate, GRE General Test.

Brigham Young University, Graduate Studies, College of Family, Home, and Social Sciences, Program in Marriage, Family and Human Development, Provo, UT 84602. Offers MS, PhD. *Accreditation:* AAMFT/COAMFTE. *Faculty:* 24 full-time (5 women). *Students:* 22 full-time (15 women); includes 1 minority (Asian American or Pacific Islander), 2 international. Average age 33. 27 applicants, 41% accepted, 8 enrolled. In 2009, 3 master's, 1 doctorate awarded. *Degree requirements:* For master's, thesis; for doctorate, comprehensive exam, thesis/dissertation, 2 publishable papers. *Entrance requirements:* For master's and doctorate, GRE General Test, minimum GPA of 3.0 in last 60 semester hours, letters of recommendation. Additional exam requirements/recommendations for international students: Required—TOEFL (minimum score 580 paper-based; 237 computer-based; 85 iBT), IELTS (minimum score 7). *Application deadline:* For fall admission, 1/10 for domestic and international students. Application fee: $50. Electronic applications accepted. *Expenses:* Tuition: Full-time $5580; part-time $301 per credit hour. Tuition and fees vary according to student's religious affiliation. *Financial support:* In 2009–10, 9 students received support, including 20 research assistantships with full and partial tuition reimbursements available (averaging $5,096 per year), 5 teaching assistantships with full and partial tuition reimbursements available (averaging $5,096 per year); scholarships/grants and unspecified assistantships also available. Financial award application deadline: 3/27. *Faculty research:* Family studies and family process; marriage; adolescence and emerging adulthood; adult development and aging; child development. *Unit head:* Dr. Richard Miller, Director, School of Life, 801-422-2069, Fax: 801-422-0230, E-mail: rick_miller@byu.edu. *Application contact:* Graduate Secretary, 801-422-2060, E-mail: mfhdgrad@byu.edu.

Brock University, Faculty of Graduate Studies, Faculty of Social Sciences, Program in Child and Youth Studies, St. Catharines, ON L2S 3A1, Canada. Offers MA. Part-time programs available. *Degree requirements:* For master's, thesis. *Entrance requirements:* For master's, honors BA. Additional exam requirements/recommendations for international students: Required—TOEFL (minimum score 550 paper-based; 213 computer-based; 80 iBT), IELTS (minimum score 6.5), TWE (minimum score 4). Electronic applications accepted. *Faculty research:* Cognitive mechanisms, youth resilience, developmental disabilities, parent-child interactions and communication.

California State University, Los Angeles, Graduate Studies, College of Health and Human Services, Department of Child and Family Studies, Los Angeles, CA 90032-8530. Offers child development (MA). Part-time and evening/weekend programs available. *Faculty:* 2 full-time (both women), 2 part-time/adjunct (both women). *Students:* 3 full-time (all women), 16 part-time (14 women); includes 11 minority (4 Asian Americans or Pacific Islanders, 7 Hispanic Americans). Average age 28. 14 applicants, 100% accepted, 3 enrolled. In 2009, 6 master's awarded. *Degree requirements:* For master's, comprehensive exam, project or thesis. *Entrance requirements:* Additional exam requirements/recommendations for international students: Required—TOEFL (minimum score 500 paper-based; 173 computer-based). *Application deadline:* For fall admission, 5/1 for domestic and international students. Applications are processed on a rolling basis. Application fee: $55. *Financial support:* Career-related internships or fieldwork and Federal Work-Study available. Support available to part-time students. Financial award application deadline: 3/1. *Faculty research:* Nutrition education, laundry product and fabric durability, computer usage in public school home economics. *Unit head:* Dr. Marlene Zepeda, Chair, 323-343-4590, Fax: 323-343-5019, E-mail: mzepeda@calstatela.edu. *Application contact:* Dr. Cheryl L. Ney, Associate Vice President for Academic Affairs and Dean of Graduate Studies, 323-343-3820, Fax: 323-343-5653, E-mail: cney@cslanet.calstatela.edu.

Capella University, Harold Abel School of Psychology, Minneapolis, MN 55402. Offers child and adolescent development (MS); clinical psychology (MS, Psy D); counseling psychology (MS); educational psychology (MS, PhD); evaluation, research, and measurement (MS); general psychology (MS, PhD); industrial/organizational psychology (MS, PhD); leadership coaching psychology (MS); organizational leader development (MS); school psychology (MS); sport psychology (MS). Part-time and evening/weekend programs available. Postbaccalaureate distance learning degree programs offered (minimal on-campus study). Terminal master's awarded for partial completion of doctoral program. *Degree requirements:* For master's, thesis optional, project; for doctorate, thesis/dissertation. *Entrance requirements:* For degree, master's degree in school psychology. Additional exam requirements/recommendations for international students: Required—TOEFL (minimum score 550 paper-based; 213 computer-based), TWE (minimum score 4); Recommended—IELTS. Electronic applications accepted.

Capella University, School of Human Services, Minneapolis, MN 55402. Offers addictions counseling (Certificate); counseling studies (MS, PhD); criminal justice (MS, PhD, Certificate); diversity studies (Certificate); general human services (MS, PhD); health care administration (MS, PhD, Certificate); management of nonprofit agencies (MS, PhD, Certificate); marital, couple and family counseling/therapy (MS); marriage and family services (Certificate); mental health counseling (MS); professional counseling (Certificate); social and community services (MS, PhD, Certificate). Part-time and evening/weekend programs available. Postbaccalaureate distance learning degree programs offered (minimal on-campus study). Terminal master's awarded for partial completion of doctoral program. *Degree requirements:* For master's, thesis optional, integrative project; for doctorate, comprehensive exam, thesis/dissertation. *Entrance requirements:* Additional exam requirements/recommendations for international students: Required—TOEFL (minimum score 550 paper-based; 213 computer-based), TWE (minimum score 4). Electronic applications accepted. *Faculty research:* Compulsive and addictive behaviors, substance abuse, assessment of psychopathology and neuropsychology.

Central Michigan University, College of Graduate Studies, College of Education and Human Services, Department of Human Environmental Studies, Mount Pleasant, MI 48859. Offers apparel product development and merchandising technology (MS); human development and family studies (MA); nutrition and dietetics (MS). Part-time and evening/weekend programs available. *Degree requirements:* For master's, thesis or alternative. Electronic applications accepted. *Faculty research:* Human growth and development, family studies and human sexuality, human nutrition and dietetics, apparel and textile retailing, computer-aided design for apparel.

Central Washington University, Graduate Studies and Research, College of Education and Professional Studies, Department of Family and Consumer Sciences, Ellensburg, WA 98926. Offers family and consumer sciences education (MS); family studies (MS). Part-time programs available. *Faculty:* 14 full-time (9 women). *Students:* 11 full-time (10 women), 22 part-time (21 women); includes 1 minority (Asian American or Pacific Islander), 1 international. 9 applicants, 78% accepted, 7 enrolled. In 2009, 4 master's awarded. *Degree requirements:* For master's, thesis or alternative. *Entrance requirements:* For master's, minimum GPA of 3.0. Additional exam requirements/recommendations for international students: Required—TOEFL (minimum score 550 paper-based; 213 computer-based; 79 iBT). *Application deadline:* For fall admission, 2/1 priority date for domestic students; for winter admission, 10/1 for domestic students; for spring admission, 1/1 for domestic students. Applications are processed on a rolling basis. Application fee: $50. Electronic applications accepted. *Expenses:* Tuition, state resident: full-time $7353; part-time $245 per credit. Tuition, nonresident: full-time $16,383; part-time $546 per credit. Required fees: $882. Tuition and fees vary according to degree level. *Financial support:* In 2009–10, 1 research assistantship with full and partial tuition reimbursement (averaging $9,145 per year) was awarded; Federal Work-Study, health care benefits, and unspecified assistantships also available. Financial award application deadline: 3/1; financial award applicants required to submit FAFSA. *Unit head:* Dr. Jan Bowers, Chair, 509-963-2766, E-mail: bowersj@cwu.edu. *Application contact:* Justine Eason, Admissions Program Coordinator, 509-963-3103, Fax: 509-963-1799, E-mail: masters@cwu.edu.

Colorado State University, Graduate School, College of Applied Human Sciences, Department of Human Development and Family Studies, Fort Collins, CO 80523-1570. Offers MS, PhD. *Accreditation:* AAMFT/COAMFTE. Part-time programs available. *Faculty:* 15 full-time (10 women). *Students:* 24 full-time (23 women), 12 part-time (10 women); includes 2 minority (1 African American, 1 Hispanic American), 3 international. Average age 29. 84 applicants, 33% accepted, 5 enrolled. In 2009, 6 master's awarded. Terminal master's awarded for partial completion of doctoral program. *Degree requirements:* For master's, thesis or alternative; for doctorate, comprehensive exam (for some programs), thesis/dissertation, competency exams. *Entrance requirements:* For master's, GRE General Test, minimum GPA of 3.0; course work in human development, family studies, and statistics; letters of recommendation; interview; BS/BA in human development and family studies or related field; for doctorate, GRE General Test (50th percentile on Verbal and Quantitative sections and 4.5 on Analytical Writing section), minimum GPA of 3.0; coursework in human development, family studies, and statistics; letters of recommendation; departmental application; interview; BS/BA or master's degree in related field. Additional exam requirements/recommendations for international students: Required—TOEFL (minimum score 550 paper-based; 213 computer-based; 80 iBT). *Application deadline:* For fall admission, 1/2 for domestic and international students. Applications are processed on a rolling basis. Application fee: $50. Electronic applications accepted. *Expenses:* Tuition, state resident: full-time $6434; part-time $359.10 per credit. Tuition, nonresident: full-time $18,116; part-time $1006.45 per credit. Required fees: $1496; $83 per credit. *Financial support:* In 2009–10, 23 students received support, including 1 fellowship (averaging $31,140 per year), 9 research assistantships with full and partial tuition reimbursements available (averaging $8,905 per year), 13 teaching assistantships with full and partial tuition reimbursements available (averaging $7,006 per year); career-related internships or fieldwork, Federal Work-Study, institutionally sponsored loans, scholarships/grants, health care benefits, and unspecified assistantships also available. Financial award application deadline: 3/1; financial award applicants required to submit FAFSA. *Faculty research:* Promoting resiliency and optimal development; gender, culture and diversity; gerontology/aging; child and adolescent health; disabilities. Total annual research expenditures: $898,742. *Unit head:* Dr. Lise Youngblade, Department Head, 970-491-5558, Fax: 970-491-7975, E-mail: lise.youngblade@colostate.edu. *Application contact:* Dr. Karen C. Barrett, Graduate Chair, 970-491-7382, Fax: 970-491-7975, E-mail: karen.barrett@colostate.edu.

Concordia University, School of Graduate Studies, Faculty of Arts and Science, Department of Education, Program in Child Study, Montréal, QC H3G 1M8, Canada. Offers MA. *Degree requirements:* For master's, one foreign language, thesis optional. *Entrance requirements:* For master's, minimum B average in undergraduate course work. *Faculty research:* Development and family relations, children and technology, cooperative learning strategies, exceptional children, second language acquisition.

Concordia University, St. Paul, College of Education, St. Paul, MN 55104-5494. Offers curriculum and instruction (MA Ed), including K-12 reading endorsement; differentiated instruction (MA Ed); early childhood education (MA Ed); educational leadership (MA Ed); family life education (MA); K-12 reading endorsement (Certificate); special education (Certificate); sports management (MA). *Accreditation:* NCATE. Evening/weekend programs available. Postbaccalaureate distance learning degree programs offered (minimal on-campus study). *Faculty:* 12 full-time (8 women), 59 part-time/adjunct (47 women). *Students:* 697 full-time (571 women), 13 part-time (12 women); includes 64 minority (31 African Americans, 1 American Indian/Alaska Native, 21 Asian Americans or Pacific Islanders, 11 Hispanic Americans), 1 international. Average age 34. In 2009, 402 master's, 29 other advanced degrees awarded. *Application deadline:* Applications are processed on a rolling basis. Application fee: $50. Electronic applications accepted. *Financial support:* Applicants required to submit FAFSA. *Unit head:* Dr. Donald Helmstetter, Dean, 651-641-8227, Fax: 651-641-8807, E-mail: helmstetter@csp.edu. *Application contact:* Kimberly Craig, Director of Graduate and Cohort Admission, 651-603-6223, Fax: 651-603-6320, E-mail: craig@csp.edu.

Concordia University Wisconsin, Graduate Programs, Department of Education, Program in Family Studies, Mequon, WI 53097-2402. Offers MS Ed. *Degree requirements:* For master's, comprehensive exam, thesis or alternative. *Entrance requirements:* For master's, minimum GPA of 3.0. Additional exam requirements/recommendations for international students: Required—TOEFL.

Cornell University, Graduate School, Graduate Fields of Human Ecology, Field of Human Development, Ithaca, NY 14853-0001. Offers developmental psychology (PhD), including cognitive development, developmental psychopathology, ecology of human development, social and personality development; human development and family studies (PhD), including ecology of human development, family studies and the life course. *Faculty:* 42 full-time (18 women). *Students:* 38 full-time (27 women); includes 3 minority (all Asian Americans or Pacific Islanders), 13 international. Average age 28. 81 applicants, 25% accepted, 12 enrolled. In 2009, 2 doctorates awarded. *Degree requirements:* For doctorate, comprehensive exam, thesis/dissertation, pre-doctoral research project, teaching experience. *Entrance requirements:* For doctorate, GRE General Test, 2 letters of recommendation. Additional exam requirements/recommendations for international students: Required—TOEFL (minimum score 550 paper-based; 213 computer-based; 77 iBT). *Application deadline:* For fall admission, 1/15 for domestic students. Application fee: $70. Electronic applications accepted. *Expenses:* Tuition: Full-time $29,500. Required fees: $70. Full-time tuition and fees vary according to degree level, program and student level. *Financial support:* In 2009–10, 26 students received support, including 2 fellowships with full tuition reimbursements available, 4 teaching assistantships with full tuition reimbursements available; research assistantships with full tuition reimbursements available, institutionally sponsored loans, scholarships/grants, health care benefits, tuition waivers (full and partial), and unspecified assistantships also available. Financial award applicants required to submit FAFSA. *Faculty research:* Cognitive development, developmental psychopathology, ecology of human development, family studies and the life course, social and personality development. *Unit head:* Director of Graduate Studies, 607-255-3181, Fax: 607-255-9856. *Application contact:* Graduate Field Assistant, 607-255-3181, Fax: 607-255-9856, E-mail: hdfs@cornell.edu.

East Carolina University, Graduate School, College of Human Ecology, Department of Child Development and Family Relations, Greenville, NC 27858-4353. Offers child development and family relations (MS); marriage and family therapy (MS). *Accreditation:* AAMFT/COAMFTE. Part-time programs available. *Degree requirements:* For master's, comprehensive exam, thesis optional. *Faculty research:* Child care quality, mental health delivery systems for children, family violence.

Eastern Michigan University, Graduate School, College of Health and Human Services, School of Social Work, Ypsilanti, MI 48197. Offers family and children's services (MSW); mental health and chemical dependency (MSW); services to the aging (MSW). *Accreditation:* CSWE. Part-time and evening/weekend programs available. *Faculty:* 20 full-time (16 women). *Students:* 34 full-time (30 women), 179 part-time (159 women); includes 69 minority (63 African Americans, 2 American Indian/Alaska Native, 2 Asian Americans or Pacific Islanders, 2 Hispanic Americans), 1 international. Average age 35. 220 applicants, 54% accepted, 99 enrolled. In 2009, 56 master's awarded. *Entrance requirements:* Additional exam requirements/recommendations for international students: Required—TOEFL. *Application deadline:* For fall admission, 1/15 priority date for domestic students. Applications are processed on a rolling basis. Application fee: $35. Tuition and fees vary according to course level. *Financial support:* Fellowships, research assistantships with full tuition reimbursements, teaching assistantships with full tuition reimbursements, career-related internships or fieldwork, Federal Work-Study, institutionally sponsored loans, scholarships/grants, tuition waivers (partial), and unspecified assistantships available. Support available to part-time students. Financial award applicants required to submit FAFSA. *Unit head:* Dr. Ann Alvarez, Director, 734-487-0393, Fax: 734-487-6832, E-mail: aalvare4@emich.edu. *Application contact:* Julie Harkema, Admissions Director, 734-487-4206, Fax: 734-487-6832, E-mail: jharkema@emich.edu.

Florida State University, The Graduate School, College of Human Sciences, Department of Family and Child Sciences, Tallahassee, FL 32306. Offers family and child sciences (MS); family relations (PhD); marriage and family therapy (PhD). *Accreditation:* AAMFT/COAMFTE. Part-time programs available. *Faculty:* 12 full-time (8 women), 2 part-time/adjunct (both women). *Students:* 34 full-time (28 women), 22 part-time (19 women); includes 20 minority (18 African Americans, 2 Asian Americans or Pacific Islanders), 2 international. 48 applicants, 31% accepted, 14 enrolled. In 2009, 2 master's, 6 doctorates awarded. *Degree requirements:* For master's, comprehensive exam, thesis optional; for doctorate, thesis/dissertation, preliminary examination; clinical examination (for marriage and family therapy). *Entrance requirements:* For master's and doctorate, GRE General Test, minimum GPA of 3.0. Additional exam requirements/recommendations for international students: Required—TOEFL (minimum score 80 iBT). *Application deadline:* For fall admission, 7/1 for domestic students, 5/1 for international students; for spring admission, 11/1 priority date for domestic students, 10/1 priority date for international students. Application fee: $30. Electronic applications accepted. *Expenses:* Tuition, state resident: full-time $7413. Tuition, nonresident: full-time $22,567. *Financial support:* In 2009–10, 25 students received support, including 1 fellowship with full tuition reimbursement available (averaging $15,000 per year), 6 research assistantships with full tuition reimbursements available (averaging $15,000 per year), 19 teaching assistantships with full tuition reimbursements available (averaging $15,000 per year); career-related internships or fieldwork, Federal Work-Study, institutionally sponsored loans, scholarships/grants, and unspecified

Child and Family Studies

Florida State University (continued)
assistantships also available. Financial award application deadline: 1/5; financial award applicants required to submit FAFSA. *Faculty research:* Family therapy, parent-child relations, distressed families and foster care, marital processes, relational interventions. *Unit head:* Dr. Kay Pasley, Chair, 850-644-3217, Fax: 850-644-3439, E-mail: kpasley@admin.fsu.edu. *Application contact:* Candy Tookes, Academic Support Assistant, 850-644-3217, Fax: 850-644-3439, E-mail: ctookes@admin.fsu.edu.

Indiana University Bloomington, School of Health, Physical Education and Recreation, Department of Applied Health Science, Bloomington, IN 47405-7000. Offers health behavior (PhD); health promotion (MS); human development/family studies (MS); nutrition science (MS); public health (MPH); safety management (MS); school and college health programs (MS). *Accreditation:* CEPH (one or more programs are accredited). *Faculty:* 24 full-time (12 women). *Students:* 131 full-time (92 women), 22 part-time (20 women); includes 35 minority (22 African Americans, 1 American Indian/Alaska Native, 5 Asian Americans or Pacific Islanders, 7 Hispanic Americans), 29 international. Average age 31. 118 applicants, 71% accepted, 52 enrolled. In 2009, 43 master's, 6 doctorates awarded. *Degree requirements:* For master's, thesis optional; for doctorate, thesis/dissertation. *Entrance requirements:* For master's, GRE (MS in nutrition science), 3 recommendations; for doctorate, GRE, 3 recommendations. Additional exam requirements/recommendations for international students: Required—TOEFL (minimum score 550 paper-based; 213 computer-based; 79 iBT). *Application deadline:* For fall admission, 4/30 priority date for domestic students, 12/1 priority date for international students; for spring admission, 11/15 priority date for domestic students, 9/1 priority date for international students. Application fee: $55 ($65 for international students). *Financial support:* In 2009–10, 80 students received support, including 12 fellowships (averaging $2,316 per year), 50 research assistantships with full and partial tuition reimbursements available (averaging $6,973 per year), 27 teaching assistantships with full and partial tuition reimbursements available (averaging $11,067 per year); career-related internships or fieldwork, Federal Work-Study, institutionally sponsored loans, scholarships/grants, tuition waivers (partial), and fee remissions also available. Financial award application deadline: 3/1. *Faculty research:* Cancer education, HIV/AIDS and drug education, public health, parent-child interactions, safety education. Total annual research expenditures: $2.8 million. *Unit head:* Dr. Mohammad R. Torabi, Chair, 812-855-4808, Fax: 812-855-3936, E-mail: torabi@indiana.edu. *Application contact:* Dr. Mohammad R. Torabi, Chair, 812-855-4808, Fax: 812-855-3936, E-mail: torabi@indiana.edu.

Indiana University–Purdue University Indianapolis, School of Liberal Arts, Department of Sociology, Indianapolis, IN 46202-2896. Offers family/gender studies (MA); medical sociology (MA); work/occupations (MA). *Faculty:* 17 full-time (8 women). *Students:* 13 full-time (8 women), 10 part-time (8 women), 3 international. Average age 29. 26 applicants, 73% accepted, 12 enrolled. In 2009, 5 master's awarded. Application fee: $55 ($65 for international students). *Financial support:* In 2009–10, 2 fellowships (averaging $9,500 per year), 2 teaching assistantships (averaging $6,309 per year) were awarded. *Unit head:* Carrie Foote, Director of Graduate Studies, 317-274-8981, E-mail: sociology@iupui.edu. *Application contact:* Director of Research and Graduate Programs, 317-274-8305.

Iowa State University of Science and Technology, Graduate College, College of Human Sciences, Department of Human Development and Family Studies, Ames, IA 50011. Offers human development and family studies (MFCS, MS, PhD). *Accreditation:* AAMFT/COAMFTE. *Faculty:* 23 full-time (18 women), 7 part-time/adjunct (5 women). *Students:* 62 full-time (54 women), 13 part-time (11 women); includes 6 minority (2 African Americans, 1 American Indian/Alaska Native, 3 Hispanic Americans), 12 international. 44 applicants, 82% accepted, 23 enrolled. In 2009, 11 master's, 3 doctorates awarded. *Degree requirements:* For master's, thesis; for doctorate, thesis/dissertation. *Entrance requirements:* For master's and doctorate, GRE General Test. Additional exam requirements/recommendations for international students: Required—TOEFL (minimum score 550 paper-based; 79 iBT) or IELTS (minimum score 6.5). *Application deadline:* For fall admission, 12/1 priority date for domestic and international students. Application fee: $40 ($90 for international students). Electronic applications accepted. *Expenses:* Tuition, state resident: full-time $6716. Tuition, nonresident: full-time $8908. Tuition and fees vary according to course level, course load, program and student level. *Financial support:* In 2009–10, 45 research assistantships with full and partial tuition reimbursements (averaging $14,880 per year), 11 teaching assistantships with full and partial tuition reimbursements (averaging $14,880 per year) were awarded; fellowships, scholarships/grants also available. *Faculty research:* Child development, early childhood education, family resource management and housing, life span studies. *Unit head:* Dr. Dianne Draper, Interim Chair, 515-294-6316, Fax: 515-294-2502, E-mail: hdfs-grad-adm@iastate.edu. *Application contact:* Dr. Dianne Draper, Interim Chair, 515-294-6316, Fax: 515-294-2502, E-mail: hdfs-grad-adm@iastate.edu.

Kansas State University, Graduate School, College of Human Ecology, Program in Human Ecology, Manhattan, KS 66506. Offers apparel and textiles (PhD); family life education and consultation (PhD); food service and hospitality management (PhD); lifespan and human development (PhD); marriage and family therapy (PhD); personal financial planning (PhD). *Faculty:* 3 full-time (all women). *Students:* 29 full-time (19 women), 43 part-time (23 women); includes 15 minority (13 African Americans, 1 American Indian/Alaska Native, 1 Asian American or Pacific Islander), 16 international. Average age 37. 29 applicants, 66% accepted, 16 enrolled. In 2009, 10 doctorates awarded. *Degree requirements:* For doctorate, thesis/dissertation. *Application deadline:* For fall admission, 2/1 priority date for domestic and international students; for spring admission, 8/1 priority date for domestic and international students. Applications are processed on a rolling basis. Application fee: $40 ($55 for international students). Electronic applications accepted. *Financial support:* Application deadline: 3/1. *Application contact:* Connie Fechter, Application Contact, 785-532-1473, Fax: 785-532-3796, E-mail: fechter@ksu.edu.

Kansas State University, Graduate School, College of Human Ecology, School of Family Studies and Human Services, Manhattan, KS 66506. Offers communication sciences and disorders (MS); early childhood education (MS); family studies (MS); life span human development (MS); marriage and family therapy (MS). *Accreditation:* AAMFT/COAMFTE; ASHA. Part-time programs available. *Faculty:* 25 full-time (15 women), 3 part-time/adjunct (2 women). *Students:* 76 full-time (67 women), 101 part-time (61 women); includes 17 minority (7 African Americans, 1 American Indian/Alaska Native, 2 Asian Americans or Pacific Islanders, 7 Hispanic Americans), 1 international. Average age 32. 117 applicants, 68% accepted, 47 enrolled. In 2009, 63 master's awarded. *Degree requirements:* For master's, thesis or alternative, oral exam, residency. *Entrance requirements:* For master's, GRE, minimum GPA of 3.0 in last 2 years of undergraduate study. Additional exam requirements/recommendations for international students: Required—TOEFL (minimum score 600 paper-based; 250 computer-based). *Application deadline:* For fall admission, 2/1 priority date for domestic and international students; for spring admission, 8/1 priority date for domestic and international students. Applications are processed on a rolling basis. Application fee: $40 ($55 for international students). Electronic applications accepted. *Financial support:* In 2009–10, 26 research assistantships (averaging $10,867 per year), 17 teaching assistantships with full and partial tuition reimbursements (averaging $11,635 per year) were awarded; Federal Work-Study, institutionally sponsored loans, scholarships/grants, and unspecified assistantships also available. Support available to part-time students. Financial award application deadline: 3/1; financial award applicants required to submit FAFSA. *Faculty research:* Health and security of military families, personal and family risk assessment and evaluation, disorders of communication and swallowing, families and health. Total annual research expenditures: $10.1 million. *Unit head:* Dr. Maurice McDonald, Head, 785-532-1472, E-mail: morey@ksu.edu. *Application contact:* Connie Fechter, Administrative Specialist, 785-532-1473, Fax: 785-532-5505, E-mail: fechter@ksu.edu.

Kent State University, Graduate School of Education, Health, and Human Services, School of Lifespan Development and Educational Sciences, Program in Family Studies, Kent, OH 44242-0001. Offers gerontology (MA); human development and family studies (MA). *Faculty:* 14 full-time (10 women), 9 part-time/adjunct (8 women). *Students:* 5 full-time (all women), 7 part-time (6 women); includes 1 minority (African American). 3 applicants, 100% accepted. In 2009, 2 master's awarded. Application fee: $30. *Financial support:* In 2009–10, 2 research assistantships (averaging $8,313 per year) were awarded. *Unit head:* Dr. Rhonda Richardson, Coordinator, 330-672-2026, E-mail: rrichard@kent.edu. *Application contact:* Nancy Miller, Academic Program Coordinator, 330-672-2576, Fax: 330-672-9162, E-mail: ogs@kent.edu.

Loma Linda University, School of Science and Technology, Department of Counseling and Family Science, Loma Linda, CA 92350. Offers MA, MS, DMFT, PhD, Certificate, MA/Certificate. *Degree requirements:* For master's, comprehensive exam, thesis optional; for doctorate, comprehensive exam, thesis/dissertation (for some programs). *Entrance requirements:* For master's, minimum GPA of 3.0; for doctorate, GRE. Additional exam requirements/recommendations for international students: Required—TOEFL (minimum score 550 paper-based; 213 computer-based), MTELP. Electronic applications accepted.

Miami University, Graduate School, School of Education and Allied Professions, Department of Family Studies and Social Work, Oxford, OH 45056. Offers child and family studies (MS). Part-time programs available. *Students:* 14 full-time (13 women), 3 part-time (all women); includes 6 minority (5 African Americans, 1 Hispanic American), 2 international. *Entrance requirements:* For master's, minimum undergraduate GPA of 3.0 during previous 2 years or 2.75 overall. Application fee: $50. *Expenses:* Tuition, state resident: full-time $11,280. Tuition, nonresident: full-time $24,912. Required fees: $516. *Financial support:* Fellowships, research assistantships, teaching assistantships, career-related internships or fieldwork, Federal Work-Study, health care benefits, tuition waivers (full), and unspecified assistantships available. Financial award application deadline: 3/1. *Unit head:* Dr. Gary Peterson, Chair, 513-529-2323, E-mail: petersgw@muohio.edu. *Application contact:* Dr. Charles Hennon, Director of Graduate Studies, 513-529-2323, E-mail: hennoncb@mushio.edu.

Michigan State University, The Graduate School, College of Social Science, Department of Family and Child Ecology, East Lansing, MI 48824. Offers child development (MA); community services (MS); family and child ecology (PhD); family studies (MA); marriage and family therapy (MA); youth development (MA). *Accreditation:* AAMFT/COAMFTE (one or more programs are accredited). *Faculty:* 19 full-time (14 women). *Students:* 64 full-time (54 women), 56 part-time (49 women); includes 18 minority (9 African Americans, 1 American Indian/Alaska Native, 5 Asian Americans or Pacific Islanders, 3 Hispanic Americans), 16 international. Average age 33. 52 applicants, 50% accepted. In 2009, 28 master's, 11 doctorates awarded. *Entrance requirements:* For master's, GRE General Test, minimum GPA of 3.0 in last 2 years of undergraduate course work, 3 letters of recommendation; for doctorate, GRE General Test, minimum GPA of 3.0, 3 letters of recommendation, background in behavioral sciences. Additional exam requirements/recommendations for international students: Required—TOEFL. Electronic applications accepted. *Expenses:* Tuition, state resident: part-time $478.25 per credit hour. Tuition, nonresident: part-time $966.50 per credit hour. Part-time tuition and fees vary according to program. *Financial support:* In 2009–10, 18 research assistantships with tuition reimbursements (averaging $6,363 per year), 10 teaching assistantships with tuition reimbursements (averaging $6,308 per year) were awarded. Total annual research expenditures: $216,042. *Unit head:* Dr. Karen Wampler, Chairperson, 517-355-7680, Fax: 517-432-2953, E-mail: kwampler@msu.edu. *Application contact:* Ruth Sedelmaier, Graduate Program Secretary, 517-353-5248, Fax: 517-432-3320, E-mail: sedelmai@msu.edu.

Middle Tennessee State University, College of Graduate Studies, College of Education and Behavioral Science, Department of Human Sciences, Murfreesboro, TN 37132. Offers child development and family studies (MS); nutrition and food science (MS). Part-time and evening/weekend programs available. Postbaccalaureate distance learning degree programs offered. *Faculty:* 7 full-time (all women). *Students:* 24 part-time (all women); includes 5 minority (4 African Americans, 1 Asian American or Pacific Islander). Average age 27. 22 applicants, 82% accepted, 18 enrolled. In 2009, 3 master's awarded. *Degree requirements:* For master's, comprehensive exam, thesis. *Entrance requirements:* For master's, GRE or MAT. Additional exam requirements/recommendations for international students: Required—TOEFL (minimum score 525 paper-based; 195 computer-based; 71 iBT) or IELTS (minimum score 6). *Application deadline:* For fall admission, 6/1 for domestic and international students. Applications are processed on a rolling basis. Application fee: $25 ($30 for international students). Electronic applications accepted. *Expenses:* Tuition, state resident: full-time $4404. Tuition, nonresident: full-time $10,956. *Financial support:* In 2009–10, 5 students received support. Application deadline: 5/1. *Faculty research:* Courtship relationships, feminist methodology and epistemology in family studies, school uniforms, body fat in elderly, asynchronous distance education. *Unit head:* Dr. Dellmar Walker, Chair, 615-898-2884. *Application contact:* Dr. Michael Allen, Dean and Vice Provost for Research, 615-898-2840, Fax: 615-904-8020, E-mail: mallen@mtsu.edu.

Missouri State University, Graduate College, College of Education, Department of Childhood Education and Family Studies, Program in Early Childhood and Family Development, Springfield, MO 65897. Offers MS. Part-time programs available. Postbaccalaureate distance learning degree programs offered. *Students:* 2 full-time (both women), 12 part-time (all women). Average age 27. 4 applicants, 100% accepted, 3 enrolled. In 2009, 5 master's awarded. *Entrance requirements:* For master's, GRE, minimum GPA of 3.0. Additional exam requirements/recommendations for international students: Required—TOEFL (minimum score 550 paper-based; 213 computer-based; 79 iBT). *Application deadline:* For fall admission, 7/20 priority date for domestic students, 5/1 for international students; for spring admission, 12/20 priority date for domestic students, 9/1 for international students. Applications are processed on a rolling basis. Application fee: $35 ($50 for international students). Electronic applications accepted. *Expenses:* Tuition, state resident: full-time $3852; part-time $214 per credit hour. Tuition, nonresident: full-time $7524; part-time $418 per credit hour. Required fees: $696; $172 per semester. Tuition and fees vary according to course level, course load, degree level and program. *Financial support:* Teaching assistantships, Federal Work-Study, institutionally sponsored loans, scholarships/grants, and unspecified assistantships available. Financial award application deadline: 3/31; financial award applicants required to submit FAFSA. *Unit head:* Dr. Joanna Brigden, Program Director, 417-836-8403, Fax: 417-836-8900, E-mail: cefs@missouristate.edu. *Application contact:* Eric Eckert, Coordinator of Admissions and Recruitment, 417-836-5331, Fax: 417-836-6200, E-mail: ericeckert@missouristate.edu.

Mount Saint Vincent University, Graduate Programs, Department of Child and Youth Study, Halifax, NS B3M 2J6, Canada. Offers MA. Part-time and evening/weekend programs available. *Degree requirements:* For master's, thesis. *Entrance requirements:* For master's, bachelor's degree in related field, minimum B+ average, professional experience. Electronic applications accepted.

Mount Saint Vincent University, Graduate Programs, Department of Family Studies and Gerontology, Halifax, NS B3M 2J6, Canada. Offers MA. Part-time programs available. Postbaccalaureate distance learning degree programs offered (minimal on-campus study). *Degree requirements:* For master's, thesis. *Entrance requirements:* For master's, minimum GPA of 3.0; course work in statistics, research methods, family and social theories.

North Dakota State University, College of Graduate and Interdisciplinary Studies, College of Human Development and Education, Department of Child Development and Family Science, Fargo, ND 58108. Offers child development and family science (MS); couple and family therapy (MS); family financial planning (MS); gerontology (MS, PhD). *Accreditation:* AAMFT/COAMFTE. Part-time and evening/weekend programs available. Postbaccalaureate distance learning degree programs offered (no on-campus study). *Faculty:* 12 full-time (7 women). *Students:* 26 full-time (25 women), 21 part-time (18 women); includes 1 African American, 2 international. 22 applicants, 64% accepted, 12 enrolled. In 2009, 12 master's awarded. *Degree requirements:* For master's, thesis or alternative; for doctorate, thesis/dissertation. *Entrance requirements:* Additional exam requirements/recommendations for international students: Required—TOEFL (minimum score 525 paper-based; 197 computer-based; 71 iBT). *Application deadline:* For fall admission, 2/1 for domestic and international students; for spring admission,

10/1 for domestic and international students. Application fee: $45 ($60 for international students). *Financial support:* In 2009–10, 17 students received support, including research assistantships with full tuition reimbursements available (averaging $3,000 per year), 17 teaching assistantships with full tuition reimbursements available (averaging $3,000 per year); career-related internships or fieldwork, Federal Work-Study, institutionally sponsored loans, and tuition waivers (full) also available. Financial award application deadline: 4/1. *Faculty research:* Family therapy, resilience, parenting, adolescent development, mental health. Total annual research expenditures: $333,582. *Unit head:* Dr. James Deal, Head, 701-231-7568, Fax: 701-231-9645, E-mail: jim_deal@ndsu.edu. *Application contact:* Theresa Anderson, Administrative Assistant, 701-231-8628, Fax: 701-231-9645, E-mail: theresa.anderson@ndsu.edu.

Northern Illinois University, Graduate School, College of Health and Human Sciences, School of Family, Consumer and Nutrition Sciences, De Kalb, IL 60115-2854. Offers applied family and child studies (MS); nutrition and dietetics (MS). *Accreditation:* AAMFT/COAMFTE. Part-time programs available. *Faculty:* 16 full-time (14 women), 2 part-time/adjunct (1 woman). *Students:* 55 full-time (49 women), 33 part-time (30 women); includes 11 minority (6 African Americans, 3 Asian Americans or Pacific Islanders, 2 Hispanic Americans), 2 international. Average age 26. In 2009, 28 degrees awarded. *Degree requirements:* For master's, comprehensive exam, internship, thesis (nutrition and dietetics). *Entrance requirements:* For master's, GRE General Test, minimum GPA of 2.75. Additional exam requirements/recommendations for international students: Required—TOEFL (minimum score 550 paper-based; 213 computer-based). *Application deadline:* For fall admission, 6/1 for domestic students, 5/1 for international students; for spring admission, 11/1 for domestic students, 10/1 for international students. Applications are processed on a rolling basis. Application fee: $30. Electronic applications accepted. *Expenses:* Tuition, state resident: full-time $6576; part-time $274 per credit hour. Tuition, nonresident: full-time $13,152; part-time $548 per credit hour. Required fees: $1813; $75.53 per credit hour. Part-time tuition and fees vary according to course load. *Financial support:* In 2009–10, 8 teaching assistantships with full tuition reimbursements were awarded; fellowships with full tuition reimbursements, research assistantships with full tuition reimbursements, career-related internships or fieldwork, Federal Work-Study, scholarships/grants, tuition waivers (full), and staff assistantships also available. Support available to part-time students. Financial award applicants required to submit FAFSA. *Faculty research:* Preliminary child development, hospitality administration in Asia, sports nutrition, eating disorders. *Unit head:* Dr. Laura Smart, Acting Chair, 815-753-1960, Fax: 815-753-1321, E-mail: lsmart@niu.edu. *Application contact:* Dr. Laura Smart, Acting Chair, 815-753-1960, Fax: 815-753-1321, E-mail: lsmart@niu.edu.

Nova Southeastern University, Fischler School of Education and Human Services, Programs in Human Services, Fort Lauderdale, FL 33314-7796. Offers child and youth studies (Ed D); child protection (MHS); education (MS), including human services; health professions education (MS); substance abuse counseling and education (MS). Part-time and evening/weekend programs available. *Students:* 1,867 full-time (1,442 women), 1,273 part-time (976 women); includes 1,866 minority (1,545 African Americans, 16 American Indian/Alaska Native, 48 Asian Americans or Pacific Islanders, 257 Hispanic Americans), 27 international. In 2009, 118 doctorates awarded. *Degree requirements:* For master's, thesis, practicum; for doctorate, thesis/dissertation, practicum. *Entrance requirements:* For master's, GRE or MAT, work experience in field, minimum GPA of 2.5; for doctorate, GRE or MAT, master's degree, minimum GPA of 3.0, work experience. Additional exam requirements/recommendations for international students: Recommended—TOEFL (minimum score 550 paper-based; 213 computer-based), IELTS (minimum score 6). *Application deadline:* Applications are processed on a rolling basis. Application fee: $50. Electronic applications accepted. *Expenses:* Contact institution. *Financial support:* Career-related internships or fieldwork and Federal Work-Study available. Support available to part-time students. Financial award application deadline: 4/15; financial award applicants required to submit FAFSA. *Unit head:* Dr. Elda Veloso, Associate Dean, 954-262-8538, Fax: 954-262-2917, E-mail: veloso@nova.edu. *Application contact:* Dr. Jennifer Quinones Nottingham, Dean of Student Affairs, 800-986-3223 Ext. 8500.

The Ohio State University, Graduate School, College of Education and Human Ecology, Department of Human Development and Family Science, Columbus, OH 43210. Offers M Ed, MS, PhD. *Faculty:* 24. *Students:* 20 full-time (18 women), 21 part-time (14 women); includes 5 minority (3 African Americans, 1 American Indian/Alaska Native, 1 Asian American or Pacific Islander), 11 international. Average age 27. In 2009, 3 master's, 5 doctorates awarded. *Degree requirements:* For master's, thesis optional; for doctorate, thesis/dissertation. *Entrance requirements:* For master's and doctorate, GRE General Test. Additional exam requirements/recommendations for international students: Required—TOEFL (minimum score 577 paper-based; 233 computer-based). *Application deadline:* For fall admission, 8/15 priority date for domestic students, 7/1 priority date for international students; for winter admission, 12/1 priority date for domestic students, 11/1 priority date for international students; for spring admission, 3/1 priority date for domestic students, 2/1 priority date for international students. Applications are processed on a rolling basis. Application fee: $40 ($50 for international students). Electronic applications accepted. *Expenses:* Tuition, state resident: full-time $10,683. Tuition, nonresident: full-time $25,923. Tuition and fees vary according to course load and program. *Financial support:* Fellowships, research assistantships, teaching assistantships, Federal Work-Study and institutionally sponsored loans available. Support available to part-time students. *Unit head:* Julianne Serovich, Chair, 614-292-5685, Fax: 614-292-4365, E-mail: jserovich@ehe.osu.edu. *Application contact:* 614-292-9444, Fax: 614-292-3895, E-mail: domestic.grad@osu.edu.

Ohio University, Graduate College, College of Health and Human Services, School of Human and Consumer Sciences, Athens, OH 45701-2979. Offers apparel, textiles, and merchandising (MS); child development and family life (MS); early childhood education (MS); family studies (MS); food and nutrition (MS). Part-time programs available. *Faculty:* 13 full-time (9 women), 5 part-time/adjunct (all women). *Students:* 18 full-time (14 women), 7 part-time (all women); includes 2 minority (1 African American, 1 Asian American or Pacific Islander), 3 international. 21 applicants, 81% accepted, 8 enrolled. In 2009, 6 master's awarded. *Degree requirements:* For master's, comprehensive exam (for some programs), thesis. *Entrance requirements:* For master's, GRE. Additional exam requirements/recommendations for international students: Required—TOEFL (minimum score 550 paper-based; 80 iBT) or IELTS Academic (minimum score 6.5). *Application deadline:* For fall admission, 3/1 priority date for domestic and international students. Applications are processed on a rolling basis. Application fee: $50 ($55 for international students). Electronic applications accepted. *Expenses:* Tuition, state resident: full-time $7839; part-time $323 per quarter hour. Tuition, nonresident: full-time $15,831; part-time $654 per quarter hour. Required fees: $2931. *Financial support:* Research assistantships, teaching assistantships, career-related internships or fieldwork, Federal Work-Study, institutionally sponsored loans, and unspecified assistantships available. Financial award application deadline: 3/15. *Faculty research:* Diversity, developmentally appropriate activities, death and dying, gerontology, sexuality education. *Unit head:* Dr. V. Ann Paulins, Director, 740-593-2880, Fax: 740-593-0289, E-mail: paulins@ohio.edu. *Application contact:* Dr. Annette Graham, Graduate Coordinator, 740-593-0700, E-mail: grahama@ohio.edu.

Oklahoma State University, College of Human Environmental Sciences, Department of Human Development and Family Science, Stillwater, OK 74078. Offers MS, PhD. *Accreditation:* AAMFT/COAMFTE (one or more programs are accredited). Postbaccalaureate distance learning degree programs offered. *Faculty:* 31 full-time (22 women), 4 part-time/adjunct (all women). *Students:* 30 full-time (21 women), 41 part-time (35 women); includes 8 minority (3 African Americans, 4 American Indian/Alaska Native, 1 Hispanic American), 5 international. Average age 32. 62 applicants, 40% accepted, 17 enrolled. In 2009, 15 master's, 4 doctorates awarded. *Degree requirements:* For master's, thesis (for some programs); for doctorate, comprehensive exam, thesis/dissertation. *Entrance requirements:* For master's and doctorate, GRE or GMAT. Additional exam requirements/recommendations for international students: Required—TOEFL (minimum score 550 paper-based; 79 iBT). *Application deadline:* For fall admission, 3/1 priority date for international students; for spring admission, 8/1 priority date for international students. Applications are processed on a rolling basis. Application fee: $40 ($75 for international students). Electronic applications accepted. *Expenses:* Tuition, state resident: full-time $3716; part-time $154.85 per credit hour. Tuition, nonresident: full-time $14,448; part-time $602 per credit hour. Required fees: $1772; $73.85 per credit hour. One-time fee: $50. Tuition and fees vary according to course load and campus/location. *Financial support:* In 2009–10, 30 research assistantships (averaging $8,943 per year), 17 teaching assistantships (averaging $8,821 per year) were awarded; career-related internships or fieldwork, Federal Work-Study, scholarships/grants, health care benefits, tuition waivers (partial), and unspecified assistantships also available. Support available to part-time students. Financial award application deadline: 3/1; financial award applicants required to submit FAFSA. *Faculty research:* Family relations and child development, consequences of adolescent parenting, family stress and coping, impacts of sexual abuse on families, children's social cognition and self-competence, gerontology and health care. *Unit head:* Dr. Sue Williams, Head, 405-744-5057, Fax: 405-744-2800. *Application contact:* Dr. Gordon Emslie, Dean, 405-744-6368, Fax: 405-744-0355, E-mail: grad-i@okstate.edu.

Oregon State University, Graduate School, College of Health and Human Sciences, Department of Human Development and Family Sciences, Corvallis, OR 97331. Offers gerontology (MAIS); human development and family studies (MS, PhD). *Faculty:* 11 full-time (7 women), 6 part-time/adjunct (2 women). *Students:* 28 full-time (20 women), 3 part-time (all women); includes 5 minority (3 Asian Americans or Pacific Islanders, 2 Hispanic Americans), 4 international. Average age 35. In 2009, 3 master's, 4 doctorates awarded. *Degree requirements:* For doctorate, thesis/dissertation. *Entrance requirements:* For master's and doctorate, GRE, minimum GPA of 3.0 in last 90 hours. Additional exam requirements/recommendations for international students: Required—TOEFL. *Application deadline:* Applications are processed on a rolling basis. Application fee: $50. *Expenses:* Tuition, state resident: full-time $9774; part-time $362 per credit. Tuition, nonresident: full-time $15,849; part-time $587 per credit. Required fees: $1639. Full-time tuition and fees vary according to course load and program. *Financial support:* Research assistantships, teaching assistantships, career-related internships or fieldwork, Federal Work-Study, and institutionally sponsored loans available. Support available to part-time students. Financial award application deadline: 2/1. *Unit head:* Dr. Carolyn Aldwin, Chair, 541-737-2024, Fax: 541-737-1076, E-mail: carolyn.aldwin@oregonstate.edu. *Application contact:* Dr. Carolyn Aldwin, Chair, 541-737-2024, Fax: 541-737-1076, E-mail: carolyn.aldwin@oregonstate.edu.

Oxford Graduate School, Graduate Programs, Dayton, TN 37321-6736. Offers family life education (M Litt); organizational leadership in nonprofits (M Litt); religion and society (D Phil).

Penn State University Park, Graduate School, College of Health and Human Development, Department of Human Development and Family Studies, State College, University Park, PA 16802-1503. Offers MS, PhD. *Unit head:* Dr. Steven H. Zarit, Head, 814-865-5260, Fax: 814-863-7963, E-mail: z67@psu.edu. *Application contact:* Dr. Douglas M. Teti, Professor in Charge of Graduate Program, 814-865-2644, E-mail: dmt16@psu.edu.

Purdue University, Graduate School, College of Consumer and Family Sciences, Department of Child Development and Family Studies, West Lafayette, IN 47907. Offers developmental studies (MS, PhD); family studies (MS, PhD); marriage and family therapy (MS, PhD). *Accreditation:* AAMFT/COAMFTE (one or more programs are accredited). Part-time programs available. Terminal master's awarded for partial completion of doctoral program. *Degree requirements:* For master's, thesis; for doctorate, thesis/dissertation. *Entrance requirements:* For master's and doctorate, GRE General Test. Additional exam requirements/recommendations for international students: Required—TWE. Electronic applications accepted. *Faculty research:* Inclusion of children with special needs, families as learning environments, relationships in child care, work-family relations, AIDS prevention.

Roberts Wesleyan College, Division of Social Work, Rochester, NY 14624-1997. Offers child and family practice (MSW); congregational and community practice (MSW); mental health practice (MSW). *Accreditation:* CSWE. *Entrance requirements:* For master's, minimum GPA of 2.75. *Faculty research:* Religion and social work, family studies, values and ethics.

Sage Graduate School, Graduate School, School of Health Sciences, Department of Psychology, Program in Community Psychology, Troy, NY 12180-4115. Offers child care and children's services (MA). Part-time and evening/weekend programs available. *Faculty:* 3 full-time (all women), 5 part-time/adjunct (3 women). *Students:* 8 full-time (7 women), 14 part-time (all women); includes 4 minority (2 African Americans, 1 Asian American or Pacific Islander, 1 Hispanic American). Average age 32. 14 applicants, 71% accepted, 10 enrolled. In 2009, 13 master's awarded. *Degree requirements:* For master's, thesis or alternative. *Entrance requirements:* For master's, minimum GPA of 2.75; 2 letters of reference; undergraduate courses in statistics, history, and systems of psychology; 3 other courses in behavioral science; resume. Additional exam requirements/recommendations for international students: Required—TOEFL (minimum score 550 paper-based; 213 computer-based). *Application deadline:* Applications are processed on a rolling basis. Application fee: $40. *Expenses:* Tuition: Full-time $10,620; part-time $590 per credit hour. *Financial support:* Fellowships, research assistantships, teaching assistantships, Federal Work-Study, scholarships/grants, and unspecified assistantships available. Support available to part-time students. Financial award application deadline: 3/1; financial award applicants required to submit FAFSA. *Unit head:* Dr. Bronna Romanoff, Director, 518-244-2260, E-mail: romanb@sage.edu. *Application contact:* Wendy D. Diefendorf, Director of Graduate and Adult Admission, 518-244-2443, Fax: 518-244-6880, E-mail: diefew@sage.edu.

St. Cloud State University, School of Graduate Studies, College of Education, Department of Child and Family Studies, St. Cloud, MN 56301-4498. Offers MS. *Faculty:* 6 full-time (5 women), 3 part-time/adjunct (all women). *Students:* 14 full-time (13 women), 28 part-time (all women); includes 4 minority (1 African American, 2 Asian Americans or Pacific Islanders, 1 Hispanic American). 5 applicants, 100% accepted. In 2009, 1 master's awarded. *Degree requirements:* For master's, thesis or alternative. *Entrance requirements:* For master's, GRE General Test, minimum GPA of 2.75. Additional exam requirements/recommendations for international students: Required—Michigan English Language Assessment Battery; Recommended—TOEFL (minimum score 550 paper-based; 213 computer-based), IELTS (minimum score 6.5). *Application deadline:* For fall admission, 6/1 for domestic students, 4/1 for international students; for spring admission, 10/1 for domestic students, 8/1 for international students. Applications are processed on a rolling basis. Application fee: $35. Electronic applications accepted. *Financial support:* Federal Work-Study, scholarships/grants, and unspecified assistantships available. Financial award application deadline: 3/1. *Unit head:* Dr. Glen Palm, Coordinator, 320-308-3969, E-mail: gfpalm@stcloudstate.edu. *Application contact:* Linda Lou Krueger, School of Graduate Studies, 320-308-2113, Fax: 320-308-5371, E-mail: lekrueger@stcloudstate.edu.

San Diego State University, Graduate and Research Affairs, College of Education, Department of Child and Family Development, San Diego, CA 92182. Offers child development (MS). Part-time programs available. *Degree requirements:* For master's, thesis. *Entrance requirements:* For master's, GRE General Test, 3 letters of recommendation, interview. Additional exam requirements/recommendations for international students: Required—TOEFL. Electronic applications accepted.

San Jose State University, Graduate Studies and Research, Connie L. Lurie College of Education, Department of Child and Adolescent Development, San Jose, CA 95192-0001. Offers MA. *Students:* 2 full-time (both women), 12 part-time (11 women); includes 5 minority (4 Asian Americans or Pacific Islanders, 1 Hispanic American). Average age 29. 19 applicants, 47% accepted, 5 enrolled. In 2009, 15 master's awarded. *Application deadline:* For fall admission, 6/29 for domestic students; for spring admission, 11/30 for domestic students. Applications are processed on a rolling basis. Application fee: $59. Electronic applications accepted. *Financial support:* Applicants required to submit FAFSA. *Unit head:* Dr. Toni Campbell, Chair, 408-924-3725, Fax: 408-924-3758. *Application contact:* Dr. Toni Campbell, Chair, 408-924-3725, Fax: 408-924-3758.

Child and Family Studies

South Carolina State University, School of Graduate Studies, Department of Family and Consumer Sciences, Orangeburg, SC 29117-0001. Offers individual and family development (MS); nutritional sciences (MS). Part-time and evening/weekend programs available. *Degree requirements:* For master's, comprehensive exam, thesis optional, departmental qualifying exam. *Entrance requirements:* For master's, GRE, MAT, or NTE, minimum GPA of 2.7. Electronic applications accepted. *Expenses:* Tuition, state resident: part-time $470 per credit hour. Tuition, nonresident: part-time $924 per credit hour. *Faculty research:* Societal competence, relationship of parent-child interaction to adult, quality of well-being of rural elders.

Spring Arbor University, School of Graduate and Professional Studies, Spring Arbor, MI 49283-9799. Offers counseling (MAC); family studies (MAFS); nursing (MSN); organizational management (MAOM). Part-time and evening/weekend programs available. Postbaccalaureate distance learning degree programs offered (no on-campus study). *Faculty:* 8 full-time (3 women), 99 part-time/adjunct (45 women). *Students:* 412 full-time (327 women), 420 part-time (351 women); includes 215 minority (182 African Americans, 2 American Indian/Alaska Native, 10 Asian Americans or Pacific Islanders, 21 Hispanic Americans), 3 international. Average age 40. In 2009, 257 master's awarded. *Entrance requirements:* For master's, minimum GPA of 3.0, interview, writing sample, 2 professional references. Additional exam requirements/recommendations for international students: Required—TOEFL (minimum score 550 paper-based; 220 computer-based). *Application deadline:* Applications are processed on a rolling basis. Application fee: $40. Electronic applications accepted. *Expenses:* Tuition: Full-time $5400; part-time $450 per credit hour. Required fees: $240; $150 per year. Tuition and fees vary according to course load and program. *Financial support:* Scholarships/grants available. Support available to part-time students. Financial award applicants required to submit FAFSA. *Unit head:* Dr. Robert Hamill, Dean of Graduate and Professional Studies, 517-750-1200 Ext. 1343, Fax: 517-750-6602, E-mail: rhamill@arbor.edu. *Application contact:* Greg Bentle, Coordinator of Graduate Recruitment, 517-750-6763, Fax: 517-750-6624, E-mail: gbentle@arbor.edu.

Stanford University, School of Education, Program in Psychological Studies in Education, Stanford, CA 94305-9991. Offers child and adolescent development (PhD); counseling psychology (PhD); educational psychology (PhD). *Degree requirements:* For doctorate, thesis/dissertation. *Entrance requirements:* For doctorate, GRE General Test. Electronic applications accepted. *Expenses:* Tuition: Full-time $37,380; part-time $2760 per quarter. Required fees: $501.

State University of New York at Oswego, Graduate Studies, School of Education, Department of Vocational Teacher Preparation, Oswego, NY 13126. Offers agriculture (MS Ed); business and marketing (MS Ed); family and consumer sciences (MS Ed); health careers (MS Ed); technical education (MS Ed); trade education (MS Ed). *Accreditation:* NCATE. Part-time and evening/weekend programs available. *Degree requirements:* For master's, thesis or alternative. *Entrance requirements:* Additional exam requirements/recommendations for international students: Required—TOEFL (minimum score 560 paper-based; 220 computer-based).

Syracuse University, College of Human Ecology, Program in Child and Family Studies, Syracuse, NY 13244. Offers MA, MS, PhD. *Accreditation:* AAMFT/COAMFTE (one or more programs are accredited). Part-time programs available. *Students:* 52 full-time (48 women), 4 part-time (all women); includes 10 minority (7 African Americans, 1 American Indian/Alaska Native, 1 Asian American or Pacific Islander, 1 Hispanic American), 13 international. Average age 36. 23 applicants, 83% accepted, 9 enrolled. In 2009, 8 master's, 2 doctorates awarded. *Degree requirements:* For master's, comprehensive exam (for some programs); for doctorate, thesis/dissertation. *Entrance requirements:* For master's and doctorate, GRE General Test. Additional exam requirements/recommendations for international students: Required—TOEFL (minimum score 100 iBT). *Application deadline:* For fall admission, 3/15 priority date for domestic students, 2/15 priority date for international students. Application fee: $75. Electronic applications accepted. *Expenses:* Tuition: Full-time $26,808; part-time $1117 per credit. Required fees: $1024. *Financial support:* Fellowships with full tuition reimbursements, research assistantships with tuition reimbursements, teaching assistantships with full and partial tuition reimbursements, tuition waivers (partial) available. Financial award application deadline: 1/1. *Unit head:* Dr. Ambika Krishnakumar, Chair, 315-443-4293, Fax: 315-443-9402. *Application contact:* Amy Pangborn, Information Contact, 315-443-5555, E-mail: inquire@hshp.syr.edu.

Texas State University–San Marcos, Graduate School, College of Applied Arts, Department of Family and Consumer Science, Program in Family and Child Studies, San Marcos, TX 78666. Offers MS. *Faculty:* 2 full-time (both women), 1 part-time/adjunct (0 women). *Students:* 22 full-time (19 women), 23 part-time (22 women); includes 9 minority (2 African Americans, 7 Hispanic Americans). Average age 26. 35 applicants, 89% accepted, 18 enrolled. In 2009, 7 master's awarded. *Degree requirements:* For master's, thesis (for some programs). *Entrance requirements:* For master's, minimum GPA of 3.0, three letters of reference, statement of interest and goals. Additional exam requirements/recommendations for international students: Required—TOEFL (minimum score 550 paper-based; 213 computer-based). *Application deadline:* For fall admission, 6/15 priority date for domestic students; for spring admission, 10/15 for domestic students. Applications are processed on a rolling basis. Application fee: $40 ($90 for international students). *Expenses:* Tuition, state resident: full-time $5784; part-time $241 per credit hour. Tuition, nonresident: part-time $551 per credit hour. Required fees: $1728; $48 per credit hour. $306. Tuition and fees vary according to course load. *Financial support:* In 2009–10, 33 students received support, including 2 research assistantships (averaging $5,076 per year), 10 teaching assistantships (averaging $5,089 per year). Financial award application deadline: 4/1. *Faculty research:* Healthy marriage. Total annual research expenditures: $513,572. *Unit head:* Dr. Michelle Toews, Graduate Adviser, 512-245-2155, Fax: 512-245-3829, E-mail: mt15@txstate.edu. *Application contact:* Dr. Michelle Toews, Graduate Adviser, 512-245-2155, Fax: 512-245-3829, E-mail: mt15@txstate.edu.

Texas Tech University, Graduate School, College of Human Sciences, Department of Human Development and Family Studies, Lubbock, TX 79409. Offers gerontology (MS); human development and family studies (MS, PhD). *Accreditation:* AAMFT/COAMFTE (one or more programs are accredited). Part-time programs available. *Faculty:* 19 full-time (15 women). *Students:* 42 full-time (35 women), 11 part-time (5 women); includes 6 minority (1 American Indian/Alaska Native, 1 Asian American or Pacific Islander, 4 Hispanic Americans), 14 international. Average age 33. 47 applicants, 62% accepted, 9 enrolled. In 2009, 7 master's, 5 doctorates awarded. *Degree requirements:* For master's, thesis; for doctorate, thesis/dissertation. *Entrance requirements:* For master's and doctorate, GRE General Test. Additional exam requirements/recommendations for international students: Required—TOEFL (minimum score 550 paper-based; 213 computer-based). *Application deadline:* For fall admission, 3/1 priority date for international students; for spring admission, 11/1 priority date for international students. Applications are processed on a rolling basis. Application fee: $50 ($75 for international students). Electronic applications accepted. *Expenses:* Tuition, state resident: full-time $5100; part-time $213 per credit hour. Tuition, nonresident: full-time $11,748; part-time $490 per credit hour. Required fees: $2298; $50 per credit hour. $555 per semester. *Financial support:* In 2009–10, 4 research assistantships with partial tuition reimbursements (averaging $25,450 per year), 21 teaching assistantships with partial tuition reimbursements (averaging $21,163 per year) were awarded; career-related internships or fieldwork, Federal Work-Study, institutionally sponsored loans, and scholarships/grants also available. Support available to part-time students. Financial award application deadline: 4/15; financial award applicants required to submit FAFSA. *Faculty research:* Parenting, marital and premarital relationships, adolescent risky behaviors, life span; child development. Total annual research expenditures: $60,398. *Unit head:* Malinda Colwell, Chair, 806-742-3000 Ext. 279, Fax: 806-742-0285, E-mail: malinda.colwell@ttu.edu. *Application contact:* Monya Castle, Graduate Secretary, 806-742-3000 Ext. 250, Fax: 806-742-0285, E-mail: monya.castle@ttu.edu.

Texas Woman's University, Graduate School, College of Professional Education, Department of Family Sciences, Denton, TX 76201. Offers child development (MS, PhD); counseling and development (MS); early childhood education (M Ed, MA, MS, Ed D); family studies (MS, PhD); family therapy (MS, PhD). *Accreditation:* ACA (one or more programs are accredited). Part-time and evening/weekend programs available. *Faculty:* 25 full-time (21 women), 4 part-time/adjunct (all women). *Students:* 111 full-time (105 women), 294 part-time (269 women); includes 149 minority (99 African Americans, 3 American Indian/Alaska Native, 7 Asian Americans or Pacific Islanders, 40 Hispanic Americans), 22 international. Average age 36. 179 applicants, 86% accepted, 72 enrolled. In 2009, 86 master's, 22 doctorates awarded. Terminal master's awarded for partial completion of doctoral program. *Degree requirements:* For master's, portfolio; for doctorate, comprehensive exam, thesis/dissertation. *Entrance requirements:* For master's, interview, letter of intent, curriculum vitae; for doctorate, interview, minimum GPA of 3.5 in last 60 hours of course work. Additional exam requirements/recommendations for international students: Required—TOEFL (minimum score 550 paper-based; 213 computer-based; 79 iBT). *Application deadline:* For fall admission, 2/15 priority date for domestic students, 3/1 for international students; for spring admission, 9/15 priority date for domestic students, 8/1 for international students. Applications are processed on a rolling basis. Application fee: $50. Electronic applications accepted. *Expenses:* Tuition, state resident: full-time $3564; part-time $198 per credit hour. Tuition, nonresident: full-time $8550; part-time $475 per credit hour. Required fees: $69.26 per credit hour. Tuition and fees vary according to course load. *Financial support:* In 2009–10, 96 students received support, including 13 research assistantships (averaging $10,746 per year), 7 teaching assistantships (averaging $10,746 per year); career-related internships or fieldwork, Federal Work-Study, institutionally sponsored loans, scholarships/grants, traineeships, health care benefits, and unspecified assistantships also available. Support available to part-time students. Financial award application deadline: 3/1; financial award applicants required to submit FAFSA. *Faculty research:* Parenting/parent education, distance education, play therapy, family sexuality, diversity, ANTHEM healthy marriages initiative. *Unit head:* Dr. Larry LeFlore, Chair, 940-898-2685, Fax: 940-898-2676, E-mail: famsci@twu.edu. *Application contact:* Samuel Wheeler, Assistant Director of Admissions, 940-898-3188, Fax: 940-898-3081, E-mail: wheelersr@twu.edu.

Towson University, College of Graduate Studies and Research, Program in Family-Professional Collaboration, Towson, MD 21252-0001. Offers Certificate.

Tufts University, Graduate School of Arts and Sciences, Department of Child Development, Medford, MA 02155. Offers child development (MA, PhD, CAGS); early childhood education (MAT). Part-time programs available. *Faculty:* 16 full-time, 12 part-time/adjunct. *Students:* 66 (61 women). Average age 27. 113 applicants, 68% accepted, 35 enrolled. In 2009, 34 master's, 6 doctorates awarded. *Degree requirements:* For master's, thesis (for some programs); for doctorate, thesis/dissertation. *Entrance requirements:* For master's and doctorate, GRE General Test. Additional exam requirements/recommendations for international students: Required—TOEFL (minimum score 550 paper-based; 213 computer-based; 80 iBT). *Application deadline:* For fall admission, 1/15 for domestic students, 12/15 for international students. Applications are processed on a rolling basis. Application fee: $75. Electronic applications accepted. *Expenses:* Tuition: Full-time $38,096; part-time $3962 per credit. Required fees: $686; $40 per year. Tuition and fees vary according to course level, course load, degree level, program and student level. *Financial support:* Fellowships, research assistantships with full and partial tuition reimbursements, teaching assistantships with full and partial tuition reimbursements, Federal Work-Study, scholarships/grants, tuition waivers (partial), and unspecified assistantships available. Support available to part-time students. Financial award application deadline: 1/15; financial award applicants required to submit FAFSA. *Unit head:* Jayanthi Mistry, Chair, 617-627-3355. *Application contact:* Fred Rothbaum, Graduate Advisor, 617-627-3355.

The University of Akron, Graduate School, College of Health Sciences and Human Services, School of Health and Human Services, Program in Child and Family Development, Akron, OH 44325. Offers child development (MA); family development (MA). *Students:* 5 full-time (all women), 5 part-time (all women); includes 3 minority (all African Americans). Average age 35. 3 applicants, 100% accepted, 1 enrolled. In 2009, 2 master's awarded. *Degree requirements:* For master's, comprehensive exam, project or thesis. *Entrance requirements:* For master's, GRE, minimum GPA of 2.75, letters of recommendation, resume. Additional exam requirements/recommendations for international students: Required—TOEFL (minimum score 550 paper-based; 213 computer-based; 79 iBT). *Application deadline:* For fall admission, 3/1 for domestic and international students; for spring admission, 10/1 for domestic and international students. Application fee: $30 ($40 for international students). Electronic applications accepted. *Expenses:* Tuition, state resident: full-time $6570; part-time $365 per credit hour. Tuition, nonresident: full-time $11,250; part-time $625 per credit hour. *Unit head:* Dr. Susan M. Witt, Coordinator, 330-972-7729, E-mail: susan8@uakron.edu. *Application contact:* Dr. Susan M. Witt, Coordinator, 330-972-7729, E-mail: susan8@uakron.edu.

The University of Akron, Graduate School, College of Health Sciences and Human Services, School of Health and Human Services, Program in Child Life, Akron, OH 44325. Offers MA. *Students:* 4 full-time (all women). Average age 29. 5 applicants, 20% accepted, 1 enrolled. In 2009, 1 master's awarded. *Degree requirements:* For master's, comprehensive exam, project or thesis. *Entrance requirements:* For master's, GRE, minimum GPA of 2.75, letters of recommendation, resume. Additional exam requirements/recommendations for international students: Required—TOEFL (minimum score 550 paper-based; 213 computer-based; 79 iBT). *Application deadline:* For fall admission, 3/1 for domestic and international students; for spring admission, 10/1 for domestic and international students. Application fee: $30 ($40 for international students). Electronic applications accepted. *Expenses:* Tuition, state resident: full-time $6570; part-time $365 per credit hour. Tuition, nonresident: full-time $11,250; part-time $625 per credit hour. *Unit head:* Dr. Susan Witt, Coordinator, 330-972-7723, E-mail: susan8@uakron.edu. *Application contact:* Dr. Susan Witt, Coordinator, 330-972-7723, E-mail: susan8@uakron.edu.

The University of Alabama, Graduate School, College of Human Environmental Sciences, Department of Human Development and Family Studies, Tuscaloosa, AL 35487. Offers MSHES. *Faculty:* 7 full-time (5 women). *Students:* 28 full-time (27 women), 8 part-time (all women); includes 11 minority (9 African Americans, 1 Asian American or Pacific Islander, 1 Hispanic American). Average age 27. 30 applicants, 57% accepted, 13 enrolled. In 2009, 13 degrees awarded. *Degree requirements:* For master's, thesis (for some programs). *Entrance requirements:* For master's, GRE General Test or MAT, minimum GPA of 3.0. Additional exam requirements/recommendations for international students: Required—TOEFL. *Application deadline:* For fall admission, 2/1 priority date for domestic and international students. Applications are processed on a rolling basis. Application fee: $50 ($60 for international students). Electronic applications accepted. *Expenses:* Tuition, state resident: full-time $7000. Tuition, nonresident: full-time $19,200. *Financial support:* In 2009–10, 10 students received support, including 1 fellowship with full tuition reimbursement available (averaging $15,000 per year), 4 research assistantships with full tuition reimbursements available (averaging $10,908 per year), 5 teaching assistantships (averaging $10,000 per year); career-related internships or fieldwork, Federal Work-Study, scholarships/grants, health care benefits, and unspecified assistantships also available. Financial award application deadline: 2/15. *Faculty research:* Parent/child relationships, preschool curricula and quality measures for child care programs, family strengths and adolescent behaviors, depression in mothers and infants, word association and word learning in young children. *Unit head:* Dr. Carroll M. Tingle, Chair, 205-348-6158, Fax: 205-348-8153, E-mail: ctingle@ches.ua.edu. *Application contact:* Dr. Maria Hernandez-Reif, Associate Professor, 205-348-5894, Fax: 205-348-8153, E-mail: mhernandez-reif@ches.ua.edu.

The University of Arizona, Graduate College, College of Education, Department of Disability and Psychoeducational Studies, Division of Family Studies and Human Development, Tucson, AZ 85721. Offers M Ed. *Faculty:* 17 full-time (9 women). *Students:* 23 full-time (20 women), 4 part-time (all women); includes 3 minority (1 American Indian/Alaska Native, 2 Hispanic Americans), 1 international. Average age 28. 30 applicants, 70% accepted, 14 enrolled. In 2009, 25 master's awarded. Terminal master's awarded for partial completion of doctoral program. *Entrance requirements:* Additional exam requirements/recommendations for international students: Required—TOEFL (minimum score 600 paper-based). *Application deadline:* For fall admission, 2/1 for domestic students. Applications are processed on a rolling basis.

Application fee: $65. *Expenses:* Tuition, state resident: full-time $9028. Tuition, nonresident: full-time $24,890. *Financial support:* In 2009–10, 4 research assistantships with full tuition reimbursements (averaging $12,828 per year), 4 teaching assistantships with full tuition reimbursements (averaging $12,378 per year) were awarded. *Unit head:* Dr. Ron Marx, Dean, 520-621-1081, E-mail: ronmarx@email.arizona.edu. *Application contact:* Cecilia Carlon, Administrative Assistant, 520-626-1248, E-mail: ccarlon@email.arizona.edu.

University of California, Santa Barbara, Graduate Division, Gevirtz Graduate School of Education, Santa Barbara, CA 93106-9490. Offers counseling, clinical and school psychology (PhD), including clinical psychology, counseling psychology, school psychology; education (M Ed, MA, PhD), including child and adolescent development (MA, PhD), cultural perspectives and comparative education (MA, PhD), educational leadership and organizations (MA, PhD), research methodology (MA, PhD), special education disabilities and risk studies (MA), special education, disabilities and risk studies (PhD), teaching (M Ed), teaching and learning (MA, PhD); educational leadership (Ed D); school psychology (M Ed); MA/PhD. *Accreditation:* APA (one or more programs are accredited). Postbaccalaureate distance learning degree programs offered (minimal on-campus study). *Faculty:* 42 full-time (20 women), 10 part-time/adjunct (4 women). *Students:* 390 full-time (303 women); includes 149 minority (14 African Americans, 3 American Indian/Alaska Native, 57 Asian Americans or Pacific Islanders, 75 Hispanic Americans), 16 international. Average age 31. 717 applicants, 40% accepted, 170 enrolled. In 2009, 140 master's, 46 doctorates awarded. Terminal master's awarded for partial completion of doctoral program. *Degree requirements:* For master's, comprehensive exam (for some programs), thesis (for some programs); for doctorate, comprehensive exam (for some programs), thesis/dissertation, qualifying exam. *Entrance requirements:* For master's, GRE, 3 letters of recommendation, resume/curriculum vitae; for doctorate, GRE, 3 letters of recommendation, statement of purpose, personal achievements/contributions statement, resume/curriculum vitae, transcripts for post-secondary institutions attended. Additional exam requirements/recommendations for international students: Required—TOEFL (minimum score 550 paper-based; 213 computer-based; 80 iBT) or IELTS (minimum score 7). Application fee: $70 ($90 for international students). Electronic applications accepted. *Financial support:* In 2009–10, 253 students received support, including 206 fellowships with full and partial tuition reimbursements available (averaging $5,000 per year), 62 research assistantships with full and partial tuition reimbursements available (averaging $6,200 per year), 87 teaching assistantships with partial tuition reimbursements available (averaging $6,500 per year); career-related internships or fieldwork, Federal Work-Study, institutionally sponsored loans, scholarships/grants, traineeships, health care benefits, and unspecified assistantships also available. Financial award applicants required to submit FAFSA. *Faculty research:* Professional development, early childhood development, school violence, literacy, science/math initiative. Total annual research expenditures: $4.4 million. *Unit head:* Dr. Jane Conoley, Chair, 805-893-2185, E-mail: jane-conoley@education.ucsb.edu. *Application contact:* Kathryn Marie Tucciarone, Student Affairs Officer, 805-893-2137, E-mail: katiet@education.ucsb.edu.

University of Central Florida, College of Health and Public Affairs, School of Social Work, Orlando, FL 32816. Offers aging studies (Certificate); children's services (Certificate); social work (MSW); social work administration (Certificate). *Accreditation:* CSWE. Part-time and evening/weekend programs available. *Faculty:* 16 full-time (11 women), 18 part-time/adjunct (14 women). *Students:* 149 full-time (129 women), 118 part-time (99 women); includes 91 minority (58 African Americans, 3 Asian Americans or Pacific Islanders, 30 Hispanic Americans), 4 international. Average age 31. 270 applicants, 80% accepted, 170 enrolled. In 2009, 79 master's, 10 other advanced degrees awarded. *Degree requirements:* For master's, thesis or alternative, field education. *Entrance requirements:* For master's, resume. Additional exam requirements/recommendations for international students: Required—TOEFL. *Application deadline:* For fall admission, 3/1 for domestic students. Application fee: $30. Electronic applications accepted. *Expenses:* Tuition, state resident: part-time $306.31 per credit hour. Tuition, nonresident: part-time $1099.01 per credit hour. Part-time tuition and fees vary according to degree level and program. *Financial support:* In 2009–10, 5 students received support, including 2 fellowships with partial tuition reimbursements available (averaging $10,000 per year), 1 research assistantship with partial tuition reimbursement available (averaging $7,100 per year), 2 teaching assistantships with partial tuition reimbursements available (averaging $3,200 per year); career-related internships or fieldwork, Federal Work-Study, institutionally sponsored loans, and unspecified assistantships also available. Financial award application deadline: 3/1; financial award applicants required to submit FAFSA. *Unit head:* Dr. John Ronnau, Director, 407-823-2114, Fax: 407-823-5697, E-mail: jronnau@mail.ucf.edu. *Application contact:* Dr. John Ronnau, Director, 407-823-2114, Fax: 407-823-5697, E-mail: jronnau@mail.ucf.edu.

University of Connecticut, Graduate School, College of Liberal Arts and Sciences, Department of Human Development and Family Studies, Storrs, CT 06269. Offers culture, health and human development (Graduate Certificate); human development and family studies (MA, PhD). *Accreditation:* AAMFT/COAMFTE (one or more programs are accredited). *Faculty:* 28 full-time (18 women). *Students:* 41 full-time (35 women), 11 part-time (10 women); includes 11 minority (2 African Americans, 5 Asian Americans or Pacific Islanders, 4 Hispanic Americans), 7 international. Average age 30. 61 applicants, 20% accepted, 5 enrolled. In 2009, 13 master's, 3 doctorates awarded. Terminal master's awarded for partial completion of doctoral program. *Degree requirements:* For master's, comprehensive exam; for doctorate, thesis/dissertation. *Entrance requirements:* For doctorate, GRE General Test. Additional exam requirements/recommendations for international students: Required—TOEFL (minimum score 550 paper-based; 213 computer-based). *Application deadline:* For fall admission, 2/1 priority date for domestic and international students; for spring admission, 11/1 for domestic students, 10/1 for international students. Applications are processed on a rolling basis. Application fee: $55. Electronic applications accepted. *Expenses:* Tuition, state resident: full-time $4725; part-time $525 per credit. Tuition, nonresident: full-time $12,267; part-time $1363 per credit. Required fees: $346 per semester. Tuition and fees vary according to course load. *Financial support:* In 2009–10, 16 research assistantships with full tuition reimbursements, 18 teaching assistantships with full tuition reimbursements were awarded; fellowships, career-related internships or fieldwork, Federal Work-Study, scholarships/grants, health care benefits, and unspecified assistantships also available. Financial award application deadline: 2/1; financial award applicants required to submit FAFSA. *Unit head:* Ronald M. Sabatelli, Head, 860-486-4726, Fax: 860-486-3452, E-mail: ronald.sabatelli@uconn.edu. *Application contact:* Nancy W. Sheehan, Chairperson, 860-486-4043, Fax: 860-486-3452, E-mail: nancy.w.sheehan@uconn.edu.

University of Delaware, College of Human Services, Education and Public Policy, Department of Individual and Family Studies, Newark, DE 19716. Offers human development and family studies (MS, PhD). Part-time programs available. Terminal master's awarded for partial completion of doctoral program. *Degree requirements:* For master's, thesis or alternative; for doctorate, comprehensive exam, thesis/dissertation. *Entrance requirements:* For master's and doctorate, GRE General Test, 3 letters of recommendation. Additional exam requirements/recommendations for international students: Required—TOEFL. Electronic applications accepted. *Faculty research:* Early childhood inclusive education, relationships, family risk and resilience, disability issues, program development and evaluation.

University of Denver, College of Education, Denver, CO 80208. Offers counseling psychology (MA, PhD); curriculum and instruction (MA, PhD, Certificate), including curriculum leadership (MA, PhD); educational administration and policy studies (Certificate); educational psychology (MA, PhD, Ed S), including child and family studies (MA, PhD), quantitative research methods (MA, PhD), school psychology (PhD, Ed S); higher education and adult studies (MA, PhD); library and information science (MLIS); library and information sciences (Certificate); school administration (PhD). *Accreditation:* ALA; APA (one or more programs are accredited). Part-time and evening/weekend programs available. Postbaccalaureate distance learning degree programs offered (no on-campus study). *Faculty:* 33 full-time (24 women), 62 part-time/adjunct (41 women). *Students:* 384 full-time (305 women), 453 part-time (336 women); includes 164 minority (47 African Americans, 8 American Indian/Alaska Native, 14 Asian Americans or Pacific Islanders, 95 Hispanic Americans), 20 international. Average age 34. 1,065 applicants, 59% accepted, 433 enrolled. In 2009, 206 master's, 38 doctorates, 117 other advanced degrees awarded. Terminal master's awarded for partial completion of doctoral program. *Degree requirements:* For master's, comprehensive exam; for doctorate, 2 foreign languages, comprehensive exam, thesis/dissertation. *Entrance requirements:* For master's and doctorate, GRE General Test or MAT. *Application deadline:* Applications are processed on a rolling basis. Application fee: $50. Electronic applications accepted. *Expenses:* Tuition: Full-time $34,596; part-time $961 per quarter hour. Required fees: $4 per quarter hour. Tuition and fees vary according to course load, campus/location and program. *Financial support:* In 2009–10, 78 teaching assistantships with full and partial tuition reimbursements (averaging $11,700 per year) were awarded; career-related internships or fieldwork, Federal Work-Study, institutionally sponsored loans, and scholarships/grants also available. Support available to part-time students. Financial award application deadline: 3/1; financial award applicants required to submit FAFSA. *Faculty research:* Parkinson's disease, personnel training, development and assessments, gifted education, service-learning, transportation, public schools. Total annual research expenditures: $340,000. *Unit head:* Dr. Gregory M. Anderson, Dean, 303-871-3665. *Application contact:* Janet Erickson, Director of Graduate Admission, 303-871-2485, E-mail: edinfo@du.edu.

University of Georgia, Graduate School, College of Education, Department of Elementary and Social Studies Education, Athens, GA 30602. Offers early childhood education (M Ed, MAT, PhD, Ed S), including child and family development (MAT); elementary education (PhD); middle school education (M Ed, PhD, Ed S); social studies education (M Ed, Ed D, PhD, Ed S). *Faculty:* 14 full-time (9 women). *Students:* 114 full-time (94 women), 130 part-time (112 women); includes 37 minority (20 African Americans, 1 American Indian/Alaska Native, 11 Asian Americans or Pacific Islanders, 5 Hispanic Americans), 9 international. 168 applicants, 57% accepted, 48 enrolled. In 2009, 75 master's, 9 doctorates, 12 other advanced degrees awarded. *Entrance requirements:* For master's and Ed S, GRE General Test or MAT; for doctorate, GRE General Test. *Application deadline:* For fall admission, 7/1 priority date for domestic students; for spring admission, 11/15 for domestic students. Application fee: $50. Electronic applications accepted. *Expenses:* Tuition, state resident: full-time $6000; part-time $250 per credit hour. Tuition, nonresident: full-time $20,904; part-time $871 per credit hour. Required fees: $730 per semester. *Financial support:* Fellowships, research assistantships, teaching assistantships, unspecified assistantships available. *Unit head:* Dr. Ronald L. VanSickle, Interim Head, 706-542-7265, Fax: 706-542-6506, E-mail: rvansick@uga.edu. *Application contact:* Dr. Ronald E. Butchart, Graduate Coordinator, 706-542-6490, Fax: 706-542-8996, E-mail: essegrad@uga.edu.

University of Georgia, Graduate School, College of Family and Consumer Sciences, Department of Child and Family Development, Athens, GA 30602. Offers child and family development (MS, PhD); early childhood education (MAT), including child and family development. *Accreditation:* AAMFT/COAMFTE (one or more programs are accredited). *Faculty:* 12 full-time (7 women). *Students:* 44 full-time (41 women), 15 part-time (14 women); includes 9 minority (7 African Americans, 2 Hispanic Americans), 5 international. 65 applicants, 43% accepted, 18 enrolled. In 2009, 7 master's, 3 doctorates awarded. *Degree requirements:* For master's, thesis (MS); for doctorate, thesis/dissertation. *Entrance requirements:* For master's and doctorate, GRE General Test. *Application deadline:* For fall admission, 7/1 priority date for domestic students; for spring admission, 11/15 for domestic students. Application fee: $50. Electronic applications accepted. *Expenses:* Tuition, state resident: full-time $6000; part-time $250 per credit hour. Tuition, nonresident: full-time $20,904; part-time $871 per credit hour. Required fees: $730 per semester. *Financial support:* Fellowships, research assistantships, teaching assistantships, unspecified assistantships available. *Unit head:* Dr. Leslie Gordon Simons, Interim Head, 706-542-4822, Fax: 706-542-4389, E-mail: lgsimons@uga.edu. *Application contact:* Graduate Coordinator.

University of Guelph, Graduate Program Services, College of Social and Applied Human Sciences, Department of Family Relations and Applied Nutrition, Guelph, ON N1G 2W1, Canada. Offers applied nutrition (MAN); family relations and human development (M Sc, PhD), including applied human nutrition, couple and family therapy (M Sc), family relations and human development. *Accreditation:* AAMFT/COAMFTE (one or more programs are accredited). Part-time programs available. *Degree requirements:* For master's, thesis (for some programs); for doctorate, comprehensive exam, thesis/dissertation. *Entrance requirements:* For master's, minimum B+ average; for doctorate, master's degree in family relations and human development or related field with a minimum B+ average or master's degree in applied human nutrition. Additional exam requirements/recommendations for international students: Required—TOEFL (minimum score 600 paper-based; 250 computer-based). Electronic applications accepted. *Faculty research:* Child and adolescent development, social gerontology, family roles and relations, couple and family therapy, applied human nutrition.

University of Illinois at Springfield, Graduate Programs, College of Education and Human Services, Program in Human Services, Springfield, IL 62703-5407. Offers alcoholism and substance abuse (MA); child and family services (MA); gerontology (MA); social services administration (MA). Part-time and evening/weekend programs available. Postbaccalaureate distance learning degree programs offered (no on-campus study). *Faculty:* 4 full-time (3 women), 1 (woman) part-time/adjunct. *Students:* 34 full-time (32 women), 91 part-time (76 women); includes 34 minority (31 African Americans, 1 American Indian/Alaska Native, 1 Asian American or Pacific Islander, 1 Hispanic American), 1 international. Average age 36. 76 applicants, 54% accepted, 33 enrolled. In 2009, 20 master's awarded. *Degree requirements:* For master's, internship; project or thesis. *Entrance requirements:* For master's, minimum undergraduate GPA of 3.0, 2 letters of recommendation. Additional exam requirements/recommendations for international students: Required—TOEFL (minimum score 500 paper-based; 176 computer-based; 61 iBT). Application fee: $50 ($60 for international students). Electronic applications accepted. *Expenses:* Tuition, state resident: full-time $6390; part-time $266.25 per credit hour. Tuition, nonresident: full-time $14,226; part-time $592.75 per credit hour. Required fees: $2044; $14.36 per credit hour. $722.50 per term. *Financial support:* In 2009–10, research assistantships with full tuition reimbursements (averaging $8,109 per year), teaching assistantships with full tuition reimbursements (averaging $8,109 per year) were awarded; career-related internships or fieldwork, scholarships/grants, health care benefits, and unspecified assistantships also available. Support available to part-time students. Financial award application deadline: 11/15. *Unit head:* Dr. Carolyn Peck, Program Administrator, 217-206-7577, Fax: 217-206-6775, E-mail: peck.carolyn@uis.edu. *Application contact:* Dr. Lynn Pardie, Office of Graduate Studies, 800-252-8533, Fax: 217-206-7623, E-mail: pardie.lynn@uis.edu.

University of Kentucky, Graduate School, College of Agriculture, Program in Family Studies, Human Development, and Resource Management, Lexington, KY 40506-0032. Offers MSFAM, PhD. *Accreditation:* AAMFT/COAMFTE. *Degree requirements:* For master's, comprehensive exam, thesis optional. *Entrance requirements:* For master's, GRE General Test, minimum undergraduate GPA of 2.75; for doctorate, GRE General Test, minimum undergraduate GPA of 3.0. Additional exam requirements/recommendations for international students: Required—TOEFL (minimum score 550 paper-based; 213 computer-based). Electronic applications accepted. *Faculty research:* Early childhood education, family therapy, family resource management and consumer studies, human development.

University of La Verne, College of Education and Organizational Leadership, Programs in Child Development/Child Life, La Verne, CA 91750-4443. Offers child development (MS); child life (MS). Part-time programs available. *Faculty:* 19 full-time (14 women), 35 part-time/adjunct (27 women). *Students:* 40 full-time (39 women), 36 part-time (34 women); includes 34 minority (3 African Americans, 10 Asian Americans or Pacific Islanders, 21 Hispanic Americans), 1 international. Average age 31. In 2009, 15 master's awarded. *Entrance requirements:* For master's, minimum GPA of 3.0, 3 letters of reference, writing sample. Additional exam requirements/recommendations for international students: Required—TOEFL (minimum score 550 paper-based; 213 computer-based). *Application deadline:* Applications are processed on a rolling basis. Application fee: $50. *Expenses:* Contact institution. *Financial support:* Institutionally sponsored loans, scholarships/grants, and unspecified assistantships available. Financial award

Child and Family Studies

University of La Verne (continued)
application deadline: 3/2; financial award applicants required to submit FAFSA. *Unit head:* Dr. Barbara Nicoll, Chairperson, 909-593-3511 Ext. 4632, Fax: 909-392-2710, E-mail: bnicoll@laverne.edu. *Application contact:* Christy Ranells, Program and Admission Specialist, 909-593-3511 Ext. 4644, Fax: 909-392-2761, E-mail: cranells@laverne.edu.

University of Manitoba, Faculty of Graduate Studies, Faculty of Human Ecology, Department of Family Social Sciences, Winnipeg, MB R3T 2N2, Canada. Offers M Sc. *Degree requirements:* For master's, thesis.

University of Maryland, College Park, Academic Affairs, School of Public Health, Department of Family Science, College Park, MD 20742. Offers family studies (PhD); marriage and family therapy (MS); maternal and child health (PhD). *Accreditation:* AAMFT/COAMFTE. Part-time and evening/weekend programs available. *Faculty:* 13 full-time (9 women), 14 part-time/adjunct (12 women). *Students:* 46 full-time (43 women), 2 part-time (both women); includes 13 minority (9 African Americans, 2 Asian Americans or Pacific Islanders, 2 Hispanic Americans), 3 international. 99 applicants, 15% accepted, 14 enrolled. In 2009, 7 master's, 4 doctorates awarded. *Degree requirements:* For master's, thesis or alternative; for doctorate, comprehensive exam, thesis/dissertation, oral defense. *Entrance requirements:* For master's, GRE General Test, minimum GPA of 3.0, 3 letters of recommendation; for doctorate, GRE General Test, minimum GPA of 3.0, 3 letters of recommendation, research sample. *Application deadline:* For fall admission, 12/1 for domestic and international students; for spring admission, 6/1 for international students. Applications are processed on a rolling basis. Application fee: $60. Electronic applications accepted. *Expenses:* Tuition, area resident: Part-time $471 per credit hour. Tuition, state resident: part-time $471 per credit hour. Tuition, nonresident: part-time $1016 per credit hour. Required fees: $337.04 per term. *Financial support:* In 2009–10, 6 fellowships with full and partial tuition reimbursements (averaging $10,021 per year), 40 teaching assistantships with tuition reimbursements (averaging $16,096 per year) were awarded; research assistantships with tuition reimbursements, career-related internships or fieldwork, Federal Work-Study, and scholarships/grants also available. Support available to part-time students. Financial award applicants required to submit FAFSA. *Faculty research:* Family life quality, interracial couples, child support, homeless families, family and child well-being. Total annual research expenditures: $346,806. *Unit head:* Elaine Anderson, Chairman, 301-405-4009, Fax: 301-314-9161, E-mail: eanders@umd.edu. *Application contact:* Dean of Graduate School, 301-405-0358.

University of Massachusetts Amherst, Graduate School, School of Education, Program in Education, Amherst, MA 01003. Offers bilingual, English as a second language, and multicultural education (M Ed, CAGS); child study and early education (M Ed); children, families and schools (Ed D, CAGS); early childhood and elementary teacher education (M Ed); education policy and leadership (CAGS); educational administration (M Ed, CAGS); educational policy and leadership (Ed D); higher education (M Ed, CAGS); international education (M Ed); language, literacy and culture (Ed D); learning, media and technology (M Ed, CAGS); mathematics, science, and learning technologies (Ed D); policy studies (M Ed); policy studies in education (CAGS); reading and writing (M Ed); research and evaluation methods (Ed D); school counselor education (M Ed, CAGS); school psychology (CAGS); science education (CAGS); secondary teacher education (M Ed); social justice education (M Ed, Ed D, CAGS); special education (M Ed, Ed D, CAGS). *Accreditation:* NCATE. Part-time programs available. Postbaccalaureate distance learning degree programs offered (minimal on-campus study). *Faculty:* 74 full-time (41 women). *Students:* 377 full-time (268 women), 347 part-time (232 women); includes 115 minority (59 African Americans, 2 American Indian/Alaska Native, 16 Asian Americans or Pacific Islanders, 38 Hispanic Americans), 108 international. Average age 35. 708 applicants, 68% accepted, 266 enrolled. In 2009, 183 master's, 17 doctorates awarded. Terminal master's awarded for partial completion of doctoral program. *Degree requirements:* For master's, thesis or alternative; for doctorate, comprehensive exam, thesis/dissertation. *Entrance requirements:* Additional exam requirements/recommendations for international students: Required—TOEFL (minimum score 550 paper-based; 213 computer-based; 80 iBT), IELTS (minimum score 6.5). *Application deadline:* For fall admission, 1/15 for domestic and international students. Applications are processed on a rolling basis. Application fee: $50 ($65 for international students). Electronic applications accepted. *Expenses:* Tuition, state resident: full-time $2640; part-time $110 per credit. Tuition, nonresident: full-time $9936; part-time $414 per credit. Tuition and fees vary according to course load. *Financial support:* In 2009–10, 1 fellowship with full tuition reimbursement (averaging $8,036 per year), 92 research assistantships with full tuition reimbursements (averaging $8,555 per year), 83 teaching assistantships with full tuition reimbursements (averaging $4,661 per year) were awarded; career-related internships or fieldwork, Federal Work-Study, scholarships/grants, traineeships, health care benefits, tuition waivers (full), and unspecified assistantships also available. Support available to part-time students. Financial award application deadline: 1/15. *Unit head:* Dr. Linda L. Griffin, Graduate Program Director, 413-545-6984, Fax: 413-545-2873. *Application contact:* Jean M. Ames, Supervisor of Admissions, 413-545-0722, Fax: 413-577-0010, E-mail: gradadm@grad.umass.edu.

University of Minnesota, Twin Cities Campus, Graduate School, College of Education and Human Development, Department of Family Social Science, Minneapolis, MN 55455-0213. Offers marriage and family therapy (MA, PhD). *Accreditation:* AAMFT/COAMFTE (one or more programs are accredited). *Faculty:* 16 full-time (12 women). *Students:* 52 full-time (42 women), 13 part-time (10 women); includes 12 minority (3 African Americans, 2 American Indian/Alaska Native, 5 Asian Americans or Pacific Islanders, 2 Hispanic Americans), 14 international. Average age 34. 22 applicants, 50% accepted, 9 enrolled. In 2009, 5 master's, 5 doctorates awarded. *Degree requirements:* For master's, thesis; for doctorate, thesis/dissertation. *Entrance requirements:* For master's and doctorate, GRE General Test, minimum undergraduate GPA of 3.0 (preferred). Additional exam requirements/recommendations for international students: Required—TOEFL. *Application deadline:* For fall admission, 12/15 for domestic students. Application fee: $55 ($75 for international students). *Financial support:* In 2009–10, 1 fellowship (averaging $22,500 per year), 69 research assistantships (averaging $25,877 per year), 15 teaching assistantships (averaging $26,130 per year) were awarded; career-related internships or fieldwork, Federal Work-Study, institutionally sponsored loans, and tuition waivers (partial) also available. Financial award application deadline: 6/30; financial award applicants required to submit FAFSA. *Faculty research:* Families and diversity, families and health, families and economic well-being, individuals and relationships across the lifespan. Total annual research expenditures: $1.2 million. *Unit head:* Dr. Jan McCulloch, Head, 612-624-1208, Fax: 612-625-4227, E-mail: jmccullo@che.umn.edu. *Application contact:* Roberta Daigle, Information Contact, 612-625-3116, E-mail: rdaigle@che.umn.edu.

University of Missouri, Graduate School, College of Human Environmental Science, Department of Human Development and Family Studies, Columbia, MO 65211. Offers MA, MS, PhD. *Entrance requirements:* For master's, GRE General Test, minimum GPA of 3.0. Additional exam requirements/recommendations for international students: Required—TOEFL (minimum score 550 paper-based; 213 computer-based; 80 iBT).

University of Nebraska–Lincoln, Graduate College, College of Education and Human Sciences, Department of Child, Youth and Family Studies, Lincoln, NE 68588. Offers child development/early childhood education (MS, PhD); child, youth and family studies (MS); family and consumer sciences education (MS, PhD); family financial planning (MS); family science (MS, PhD); gerontology (PhD); human sciences (PhD), including child, youth and family studies, gerontology, medical family therapy; marriage and family therapy (MS); medical family therapy (PhD); youth development (MS). *Accreditation:* AAMFT/COAMFTE (one or more programs are accredited). Postbaccalaureate distance learning degree programs offered. *Degree requirements:* For master's, thesis optional. *Entrance requirements:* For master's, GRE. Additional exam requirements/recommendations for international students: Required—TOEFL (minimum score 550 paper-based; 213 computer-based). Electronic applications accepted. *Faculty research:* Marriage and family therapy, child development/early childhood education, family financial management.

University of Nevada, Reno, Graduate School, College of Education, Department of Human Development and Family Studies, Reno, NV 89557. Offers MS. *Degree requirements:* For master's, thesis optional. *Entrance requirements:* For master's, GRE General Test, minimum GPA of 2.75. Additional exam requirements/recommendations for international students: Required—TOEFL (minimum score 500 paper-based; 173 computer-based; 61 iBT), IELTS (minimum score 6). Electronic applications accepted. *Faculty research:* Early childhood/adolescent development, family studies.

University of New Hampshire, Graduate School, School of Health and Human Services, Department of Family Studies, Durham, NH 03824. Offers family studies (MS); marriage and family therapy (MS). Program offered in fall only. *Accreditation:* AAMFT/COAMFTE. Part-time programs available. *Faculty:* 9 full-time (6 women). *Students:* 17 full-time (15 women), 8 part-time (all women); includes 3 minority (1 African American, 2 Asian Americans or Pacific Islanders). Average age 33. 18 applicants, 72% accepted, 7 enrolled. In 2009, 6 master's awarded. *Degree requirements:* For master's, thesis or alternative. *Entrance requirements:* For master's, GRE General Test. Additional exam requirements/recommendations for international students: Required—TOEFL (minimum score 550 paper-based; 213 computer-based; 80 iBT). *Application deadline:* For fall admission, 5/15 priority date for domestic students, 4/1 for international students. Applications are processed on a rolling basis. Application fee: $65. Electronic applications accepted. *Expenses:* Tuition, state resident: full-time $10,380; part-time $577 per credit hour. Tuition, nonresident: full-time $24,350; part-time $1002 per credit hour. Required fees: $1550; $387.50 per semester. Tuition and fees vary according to course load and program. *Financial support:* In 2009–10, 13 students received support, including 5 teaching assistantships; fellowships, research assistantships, career-related internships or fieldwork, Federal Work-Study, scholarships/grants, and tuition waivers (full and partial) also available. Support available to part-time students. Financial award application deadline: 2/15. *Unit head:* Dr. Kerry Kazura, Chairperson, 603-862-2135. *Application contact:* Matty Leighton, Administrative Assistant, 603-862-5021, E-mail: family.studies@unh.edu.

University of New Mexico, Graduate School, College of Education, Department of Individual, Family and Community Education, Program in Family Studies, Albuquerque, NM 87131-2039. Offers MA, PhD. Part-time and evening/weekend programs available. *Students:* 12 full-time (11 women), 10 part-time (all women); includes 11 minority (2 African Americans, 3 American Indian/Alaska Native, 1 Asian American or Pacific Islander, 5 Hispanic Americans), 1 international. Average age 39. 11 applicants, 64% accepted, 7 enrolled. *Degree requirements:* For master's, comprehensive exam, thesis (for some programs); for doctorate, comprehensive exam, thesis/dissertation. *Entrance requirements:* For master's, written paper, 3 letters of recommendation, personal statement, departmental application; for doctorate, GRE General Test, written paper, 3 letters of recommendation, personal statement, departmental application, interview. Additional exam requirements/recommendations for international students: Required—TOEFL (minimum score 550 paper-based; 213 computer-based). *Application deadline:* For fall admission, 3/15 priority date for domestic and international students; for spring admission, 10/15 priority date for domestic and international students. Applications are processed on a rolling basis. Application fee: $50. Electronic applications accepted. *Expenses:* Tuition, state resident: full-time $2099; part-time $233.20 per credit hour. Tuition, nonresident: full-time $6650. Required fees: $25 per semester. Tuition and fees vary according to course load, program and reciprocity agreements. *Financial support:* In 2009–10, 10 students received support, including 3 teaching assistantships with full and partial tuition reimbursements available (averaging $6,402 per year); research assistantships, scholarships/grants also available. Financial award application deadline: 3/1; financial award applicants required to submit FAFSA. *Faculty research:* Home, community and school relations; multicultural issues; parent-child interactions; grandparents as primary caretakers for grandchildren; fathering, early childhood evaluation, early childhood development, globalization and indigenous cultures. *Unit head:* Dr. Ziarat Hossain, Program Coordinator, 505-277-4162, Fax: 505-277-8361, E-mail: zhossain@unm.edu. *Application contact:* Cynthia Salas, Department Administrator, 505-277-4535, Fax: 505-277-8361, E-mail: divbse@unm.edu.

The University of North Carolina at Greensboro, Graduate School, School of Human Environmental Sciences, Department of Human Development and Family Studies, Greensboro, NC 27412-5001. Offers M Ed, MS, PhD. *Degree requirements:* For master's, one foreign language; for doctorate, one foreign language, thesis/dissertation. *Entrance requirements:* For master's and doctorate, GRE General Test. Additional exam requirements/recommendations for international students: Required—TOEFL. Electronic applications accepted. *Expenses:* Contact institution. *Faculty research:* Adolescent mothers, multi-handicapped, older adults.

University of North Texas, Robert B. Toulouse School of Graduate Studies, College of Education, Department of Educational Psychology, Program in Development and Family Studies, Denton, TX 76203. Offers MS, Certificate. Evening/weekend programs available. *Degree requirements:* For master's, comprehensive exam, thesis optional. *Entrance requirements:* For master's, GRE General Test, resume, references. Additional exam requirements/recommendations for international students; Required—proof of English language proficiency required for non-native English speakers; Recommended—TOEFL (minimum score 550 paper-based; 213 computer-based). *Application deadline:* Applications are processed on a rolling basis. Application fee: $50 ($75 for international students). Electronic applications accepted. *Expenses:* Tuition, state resident: full-time $4298; part-time $239 per contact hour. Tuition, nonresident: full-time $9878; part-time $549 per contact hour. Required fees: $265 per contact hour. *Financial support:* Teaching assistantships, career-related internships or fieldwork, Federal Work-Study, and institutionally sponsored loans available. Financial award applicants required to submit FAFSA. *Faculty research:* Parent-child issues, cognitive development, social development. *Application contact:* Becky Glover, Graduate Advisor, 940-565-4876, E-mail: becky.glover@unt.edu.

University of Rhode Island, Graduate School, College of Human Science and Services, Department of Human Development and Family Studies, Kingston, RI 02881. Offers college student personnel (MS); human development and family studies (MS); marriage and family therapy (MS). *Accreditation:* AAMFT/COAMFTE. Part-time programs available. *Faculty:* 14 full-time (11 women), 4 part-time/adjunct (2 women). *Students:* 36 full-time (31 women), 18 part-time (16 women); includes 11 minority (6 African Americans, 2 Asian Americans or Pacific Islanders, 3 Hispanic Americans). In 2009, 27 master's awarded. *Degree requirements:* For master's, comprehensive exam (for some programs), thesis optional. *Entrance requirements:* For master's, GRE or MAT, 2 letters of recommendation. Additional exam requirements/recommendations for international students: Required—TOEFL (minimum score 550 paper-based; 213 computer-based). Application fee: $65. Electronic applications accepted. *Expenses:* Tuition, state resident: full-time $8828; part-time $490 per credit hour. Tuition, nonresident: full-time $22,100; part-time $1228 per credit hour. Required fees: $1118; $57 per semester. Tuition and fees vary according to program. *Financial support:* In 2009–10, 3 research assistantships with full and partial tuition reimbursements (averaging $10,421 per year), 4 teaching assistantships with full and partial tuition reimbursements (averaging $7,443 per year) were awarded. Financial award applicants required to submit FAFSA. Total annual research expenditures: $833,866. *Unit head:* Dr. Jerome Adams, Chair, 401-874-5962, Fax: 401-874-4020, E-mail: jadams@uri.edu. *Application contact:* Dr. Jerome Adams, Chair, 401-874-5962, Fax: 401-874-4020, E-mail: jadams@uri.edu.

University of Southern California, Graduate School, School of Social Work, Los Angeles, CA 90089. Offers community organization, planning and administration (MSW); families and children (MSW); health (MSW); mental health (MSW); military social work and veterans services (MSW); older adults (MSW); public child welfare (MSW); school settings (MSW); social work (MSW, PhD); systems of mental illness recovery (MSW); work and life (MSW); JD/MSW; M Pl/MSW; MPA/MSW; MSW/MAJCS; MSW/MBA; MSW/MS. *Accreditation:* CSWE (one or more programs are accredited). Part-time programs available. Postbaccalaureate distance learning degree programs offered. *Faculty:* 72 full-time (50 women), 75 part-time/

adjunct (53 women). *Students:* 766 full-time (650 women), 155 part-time (131 women); includes 606 minority (132 African Americans, 3 American Indian/Alaska Native, 115 Asian Americans or Pacific Islanders, 356 Hispanic Americans), 37 international. 1,634 applicants, 49% accepted, 476 enrolled. In 2009, 288 master's, 7 doctorates awarded. *Degree requirements:* For doctorate, comprehensive exam, thesis/dissertation, qualifying exam/publishable paper. *Entrance requirements:* For doctorate, GRE General Test. Additional exam requirements/recommendations for international students: Recommended—TOEFL (minimum score 600 paper-based; 250 computer-based; 100 iBT). *Application deadline:* For fall admission, 3/15 for domestic and international students. Electronic applications accepted. *Expenses:* Tuition: Full-time $25,980; part-time $1315 per unit. Required fees: $554. One-time fee: $35 full-time. Full-time tuition and fees vary according to degree level and program. *Financial support:* In 2009–10, 738 students received support, including fellowships with full tuition reimbursements available (averaging $35,000 per year), teaching assistantships with full tuition reimbursements available (averaging $30,000 per year); Federal Work-Study and scholarships/grants also available. Financial award application deadline: 5/3; financial award applicants required to submit FAFSA. *Faculty research:* Military social work, homelessness, health disparities, school violence, depression and chronic diseases. *Unit head:* Dean Marilyn Flynn, Dean and Professor, 213-740-8311. *Application contact:* Janine M. Luzano, Director of Admissions and Financial Aid, 213-740-2013, Fax: 213-821-1235, E-mail: janinelu@usc.edu.

University of Southern Mississippi, Graduate School, College of Education and Psychology, Department of Child and Family Studies, Hattiesburg, MS 39406-0001. Offers child and family studies (MS); early intervention (MS); marriage and family therapy (MS). *Accreditation:* AAMFT/COAMFTE. Part-time programs available. *Faculty:* 7 full-time (3 women). *Students:* 28 full-time (all women), 37 part-time (all women); includes 18 minority (17 African Americans, 1 Asian American or Pacific Islander), 1 international. Average age 29. 57 applicants, 61% accepted, 34 enrolled. In 2009, 15 master's awarded. *Degree requirements:* For master's, comprehensive exam, thesis optional. *Entrance requirements:* For master's, GRE General Test, minimum GPA of 2.75 in last 60 hours. Additional exam requirements/recommendations for international students: Required—TOEFL. *Application deadline:* For fall admission, 3/1 priority date for domestic students, 3/1 for international students. Applications are processed on a rolling basis. Application fee: $35. Electronic applications accepted. *Expenses:* Tuition, state resident: full-time $5096; part-time $284 per hour. Tuition, nonresident: full-time $13,052; part-time $726 per hour. Required fees: $402. Tuition and fees vary according to course level and course load. *Financial support:* In 2009–10, 21 students received support, including 3 research assistantships with full tuition reimbursements available (averaging $7,300 per year); fellowships, career-related internships or fieldwork, Federal Work-Study, institutionally sponsored loans, scholarships/grants, and unspecified assistantships also available. Financial award application deadline: 3/15; financial award applicants required to submit FAFSA. *Faculty research:* School food service, teen pregnancy, diet and cholesterol metabolism. *Unit head:* Dr. Ann Blackwell, Chair, 601-266-5661, Fax: 601-266-4680. *Application contact:* Dr. Ann Blackwell, Chair, 601-266-5661, Fax: 601-266-4680.

The University of Tennessee, Graduate School, College of Education, Health and Human Sciences, Department of Child and Family Studies, Knoxville, TN 37996. Offers child and family studies (MS); early childhood education (MS). Part-time programs available. *Degree requirements:* For master's, thesis or alternative. *Entrance requirements:* For master's, GRE General Test, minimum GPA of 2.7. Additional exam requirements/recommendations for international students: Required—TOEFL. Electronic applications accepted. *Expenses:* Tuition, state resident: full-time $6826; part-time $380 per semester hour. Tuition, nonresident: full-time $21,844; part-time $1147 per semester hour. Tuition and fees vary according to program.

The University of Tennessee, Graduate School, College of Education, Health and Human Sciences, Program in Human Ecology, Knoxville, TN 37996. Offers child and family studies (PhD); community health (PhD); nutrition science (PhD); retailing and consumer sciences (PhD); textile science (PhD). *Degree requirements:* For doctorate, thesis/dissertation. *Entrance requirements:* For doctorate, GRE General Test, minimum GPA of 2.7. Additional exam requirements/recommendations for international students: Required—TOEFL. Electronic applications accepted. *Expenses:* Tuition, state resident: full-time $6826; part-time $380 per semester hour. Tuition, nonresident: full-time $21,844; part-time $1147 per semester hour. Tuition and fees vary according to program.

The University of Tennessee at Martin, Graduate Programs, College of Agriculture and Applied Sciences, Department of Family and Consumer Sciences, Martin, TN 38238-1000. Offers dietetics (MSFCS); general family and consumer sciences (MSFCS). Part-time programs available. Postbaccalaureate distance learning degree programs offered (minimal on-campus study). *Faculty:* 6. *Students:* 47 (43 women). 5,430 applicants, 1% accepted, 23 enrolled. In 2009, 10 master's awarded. *Degree requirements:* For master's, comprehensive exam, thesis optional. *Entrance requirements:* For master's, GRE General Test, minimum GPA of 2.5. Additional exam requirements/recommendations for international students; Required—TOEFL (minimum score 525 paper-based; 197 computer-based; 71 iBT). *Application deadline:* For fall admission, 8/1 priority date for domestic students, 6/15 priority date for international students; for spring admission, 12/15 priority date for domestic students, 12/1 priority date for international students. Applications are processed on a rolling basis. Application fee: $30 ($130 for international students). Electronic applications accepted. *Expenses:* Tuition, state resident: full-time $6660; part-time $372 per hour. Tuition, nonresident: full-time $18,000; part-time $1005 per hour. *Financial support:* In 2009–10, 3 students received support, including 3 research assistantships with full tuition reimbursements available (averaging $7,234 per year); scholarships/grants and unspecified assistantships also available. Support available to part-time students. Financial award application deadline: 2/15; financial award applicants required to submit FAFSA. *Faculty research:* Children with developmental disabilities, regional food product development and marketing, parent education. *Unit head:* Dr. Lisa LeBleu, Coordinator, 731-881-7116, Fax: 731-881-7106, E-mail: llebleu@utm.edu. *Application contact:* Linda S. Arant, Student Services Specialist, 731-881-7012, Fax: 731-881-7499, E-mail: larant@utm.edu.

The University of Texas at Austin, Graduate School, College of Natural Sciences, School of Human Ecology, Program in Human Development and Family Sciences, Austin, TX 78712-1111. Offers MA, PhD. *Degree requirements:* For master's, thesis; for doctorate, thesis/dissertation. *Entrance requirements:* For master's and doctorate, GRE General Test. Additional exam requirements/recommendations for international students: Required—TOEFL. Electronic applications accepted. *Faculty research:* Marriage and family relationships, parenting, impact of television on children, courtship, family policy.

The University of Texas at Dallas, School of Behavioral and Brain Sciences, Program in Psychological Sciences, Richardson, TX 75080. Offers early childhood disorders (MS); psychological sciences (MS, PhD). Part-time and evening/weekend programs available. *Faculty:* 30 full-time (14 women). *Students:* 41 full-time (32 women), 16 part-time (15 women); includes 15 minority (4 African Americans, 6 Asian Americans or Pacific Islanders, 5 Hispanic Americans), 10 international. Average age 30. 69 applicants, 38% accepted, 20 enrolled. In 2009, 12 master's awarded. *Degree requirements:* For master's, directed project or internship; for doctorate, thesis/dissertation. *Entrance requirements:* For master's and doctorate, GRE General Test, minimum GPA of 3.0 in upper-level course work. Additional exam requirements/recommendations for international students: Required—TOEFL (minimum score 550 paper-based; 213 computer-based). *Application deadline:* For fall admission, 7/15 for domestic students, 5/1 priority date for international students; for spring admission, 11/15 for domestic students, 9/1 priority date for international students. Applications are processed on a rolling basis. Application fee: $50 ($100 for international students). Electronic applications accepted. *Expenses:* Tuition, state resident: full-time $11,068; part-time $461 per credit hour. Tuition, nonresident: full-time $21,178; part-time $882 per credit hour. Tuition and fees vary according to course load. *Financial support:* In 2009–10, 3 research assistantships with full tuition reimbursements (averaging $12,168 per year), 15 teaching assistantships with full tuition reimbursements (averaging $10,882 per year) were awarded; fellowships, career-related internships or fieldwork, Federal Work-Study, scholarships/grants, and unspecified assistantships also available. Support available to part-time students. Financial award application deadline: 4/30; financial award applicants required to submit FAFSA. *Faculty research:* Social competence in normal and hyperactive youth, preschool number development, social-emotional development, family and peer relationships. *Unit head:* Dr. Melanie J. Spence, Head, PhD Programs, 972-883-2206, Fax: 972-883-2491, E-mail: mspence@utdallas.edu. *Application contact:* Dr. Robert D. Stillman, Program Head, 972-883-3106, Fax: 972-883-3022, E-mail: stillman@utdallas.edu.

University of Utah, The Graduate School, College of Social and Behavioral Science, Department of Family and Consumer Studies, Salt Lake City, UT 84112-0080. Offers human development and social policy (MS). Part-time and evening/weekend programs available. *Faculty:* 16 full-time (7 women), 1 (woman) part-time/adjunct. *Students:* 9 full-time (7 women), 5 part-time (all women), 1 international. Average age 36. 16 applicants, 38% accepted, 6 enrolled. In 2009, 2 master's awarded. *Degree requirements:* For master's, thesis optional. *Entrance requirements:* For master's, GRE General Test, minimum undergraduate GPA of 3.0, courses in research methods and statistics. Additional exam requirements/recommendations for international students: Required—TOEFL (minimum score 500 paper-based; 173 computer-based). *Application deadline:* For fall admission, 3/1 priority date for domestic and international students. Application fee: $55 ($65 for international students). Electronic applications accepted. *Expenses:* Tuition, state resident: full-time $4004; part-time $1674 per semester. Tuition, nonresident: full-time $14,134; part-time $5915 per semester. Required fees: $324 per semester. Tuition and fees vary according to course load, degree level and program. *Financial support:* In 2009–10, 10 students received support, including 1 research assistantship with partial tuition reimbursement available (averaging $5,500 per year), 9 teaching assistantships with partial tuition reimbursements available (averaging $5,500 per year). Financial award application deadline: 2/1. *Faculty research:* Social, physical and economic contexts of families and communities. Total annual research expenditures: $350,000. *Unit head:* Dr. Cheryl Wright, Chair, 801-581-7712, Fax: 801-581-5156, E-mail: cheryl.wright@fcs.utah.edu. *Application contact:* Dr. Marissa Diener, Graduate Director, 801-581-6521, E-mail: marissa.diener@fcs.utah.edu.

University of Victoria, Faculty of Graduate Studies, Faculty of Human and Social Development, School of Child and Youth Care, Victoria, BC V8W 2Y2, Canada. Offers MA, PhD. Part-time programs available. *Degree requirements:* For master's, thesis. *Entrance requirements:* For master's, resume, professional references, sample of academic writing. Additional exam requirements/recommendations for international students: Required—TOEFL (minimum score 575 paper-based; 233 computer-based), IELTS (minimum score 7). Electronic applications accepted.

University of Wisconsin–Madison, Graduate School, School of Human Ecology, Program in Human Development and Family Studies, Madison, WI 53706-1380. Offers MS, PhD. Part-time programs available. Terminal master's awarded for partial completion of doctoral program. *Degree requirements:* For master's, thesis; for doctorate, comprehensive exam, thesis/dissertation. *Entrance requirements:* For master's, GRE General Test, 3 letters of recommendation; for doctorate, GRE General Test, MS or MA, 3 letters of recommendation. Additional exam requirements/recommendations for international students: Required—TOEFL. Electronic applications accepted. *Expenses:* Tuition, state resident: part-time $594 per credit. Tuition, nonresident: part-time $1504 per credit. Required fees: $65 per credit. Tuition and fees vary according to course load, program and reciprocity agreements. *Faculty research:* Human development, adolescence, adulthood, prevention, intervention.

University of Wisconsin–Stout, Graduate School, College of Human Development, Program in Family Studies and Human Development, Menomonie, WI 54751. Offers MS. Part-time programs available. *Degree requirements:* For master's, thesis. *Entrance requirements:* For master's, minimum GPA of 2.75. Additional exam requirements/recommendations for international students: Required—TOEFL (minimum score 500 paper-based; 173 computer-based; 61 iBT). Electronic applications accepted. *Faculty research:* Diversity, work and family medical ethics, family policy, dementia and families.

Utah State University, School of Graduate Studies, College of Education and Human Services, Department of Family, Consumer, and Human Development, Logan, UT 84322. Offers family and human development (MFHD); family, consumer, and human development (MS, PhD), including adolescence/youth (MS), adult development/aging (MS), consumer science (MS), infancy/childhood (MS), marriage and family relations (MS), marriage and family therapy (MS). *Accreditation:* AAMFT/COAMFTE (one or more programs are accredited). Part-time and evening/weekend programs available. Postbaccalaureate distance learning degree programs offered (minimal on-campus study). *Degree requirements:* For master's, thesis; for doctorate, comprehensive exam, thesis/dissertation, competencies. *Entrance requirements:* For master's, GRE General Test or MAT, minimum GPA of 3.0, 3 letters of recommendation; for doctorate, GRE, minimum GPA of 3.0, 3 letters of recommendation. Additional exam requirements/recommendations for international students: Required—TOEFL. Electronic applications accepted. *Faculty research:* Marriage and family relations, adolescent problem behavior, family financial management, early literacy, mental health in the elderly, parent child attachment.

Vanderbilt University, Peabody College, Department of Psychology and Human Development, Nashville, TN 37240-1001. Offers child studies (M Ed). *Accreditation:* APA. Part-time programs available. *Faculty:* 28 full-time (15 women), 3 part-time/adjunct (1 woman). *Students:* 15 full-time (all women), 3 part-time (2 women); includes 5 minority (4 African Americans, 1 Hispanic American). Average age 25. 38 applicants, 50% accepted, 12 enrolled. In 2009, 13 master's awarded. *Degree requirements:* For master's, comprehensive exam, thesis optional. *Entrance requirements:* For master's, GRE General Test. Additional exam requirements/recommendations for international students: Required—TOEFL (minimum score 550 paper-based; 213 computer-based). *Application deadline:* For fall admission, 12/31 for domestic and international students; for spring admission, 11/1 for domestic and international students. Applications are processed on a rolling basis. Application fee: $0. Electronic applications accepted. *Financial support:* In 2009–10, 17 students received support, including 11 research assistantships with full and partial tuition reimbursements available, 1 teaching assistantship with full and partial tuition reimbursement available; fellowships with full and partial tuition reimbursements available, Federal Work-Study, institutionally sponsored loans, scholarships/grants, tuition waivers (partial), and unspecified assistantships also available. Financial award application deadline: 2/1; financial award applicants required to submit FAFSA. *Faculty research:* Cognitive, language and social development; stress, coping and emotion; quantitative methods and evaluation; clinical intervention and prevention; individual differences, disabilities and developmental psychopathology. *Unit head:* Dr. David Cole, Acting Chair, 615-322-8141, Fax: 615-343-9494, E-mail: david.cole@vanderbilt.edu. *Application contact:* Sharone Hall, Educational Coordinator, 615-343-4963, Fax: 615-343-9494, E-mail: sharone.k.hall@vanderbilt.edu.

Virginia Polytechnic Institute and State University, Graduate School, College of Liberal Arts and Human Sciences, Department of Human Development, Blacksburg, VA 24061. Offers adult development and aging (MS, PhD); adult learning and human resource development (MS, PhD); child development (MS, PhD); family studies (MS, PhD); marriage and family therapy (MS, PhD). *Accreditation:* AAMFT/COAMFTE (one or more programs are accredited). *Faculty:* 22 full-time (18 women). *Students:* 49 full-time (38 women), 64 part-time (44 women); includes 30 minority (1 African American, 7 American Indian/Alaska Native, 16 Asian Americans or Pacific Islanders, 6 Hispanic Americans), 2 international. Average age 34. 64 applicants, 34% accepted, 16 enrolled. In 2009, 10 master's, 14 doctorates awarded. *Entrance requirements:* For master's and doctorate, GRE, GMAT. Additional exam requirements/recommendations for international students: Required—TOEFL (minimum score 550 paper-based; 213 computer-based). *Application deadline:* For fall admission, 5/15 for international students; for spring admission, 10/15 for international students. Applications are processed on a rolling basis. Application fee: $65. Electronic applications accepted. *Expenses:* Tuition, area resident: Full-time $10,228; part-time $459 per credit hour. Tuition, nonresident: full-time $17,892; part-time $865 per credit hour. Required fees: $1966; $451 per semester. *Financial support:* In 2009–10, 7

Virginia Polytechnic Institute and State University (continued)
research assistantships with full tuition reimbursements (averaging $10,933 per year), 25 teaching assistantships with full tuition reimbursements (averaging $9,387 per year) were awarded; career-related internships or fieldwork, Federal Work-Study, scholarships/grants, and unspecified assistantships also available. Financial award application deadline: 1/15. *Faculty research:* Stress management, children's play, dual-career families, social cognition, relationships of elderly. Total annual research expenditures: $823,581. *Unit head:* Dr. Shannon E. Jarrott, Head, 540-231-4794, Fax: 540-231-7012, E-mail: sjarrott@vt.edu. *Application contact:* Mark Benson, Information Contact, 540-231-5720, Fax: 540-231-7012, E-mail: mbenson@vt.edu.

Walden University, Graduate Programs, School of Counseling and Social Service, Minneapolis, MN 55401. Offers counselor education and supervision (PhD), including consultation, counseling and social change, forensic mental health counseling, general program, nonprofit management and leadership, trauma and crisis; human services (PhD), including clinical social work, counseling, criminal justice, family studies and intervention strategies, general program, human services administration, self-designed, social policy analysis and planning; marriage, couple, and family counseling (MS), including forensic counseling, trauma and crisis counseling; mental health counseling (MS), including forensic counseling. Part-time and evening/weekend programs available. Postbaccalaureate distance learning degree programs offered (minimal on-campus study). *Faculty:* 13 full-time, 78 part-time/adjunct. *Students:* 1,932 full-time (1,624 women), 210 part-time (181 women); includes 945 minority (817 African Americans, 24 American Indian/Alaska Native, 24 Asian Americans or Pacific Islanders, 80 Hispanic Americans), 34 international. Average age 39. In 2009, 55 master's, 5 doctorates awarded. *Degree requirements:* For master's, residency (for some programs); for doctorate, thesis/dissertation, residency. *Entrance requirements:* For master's, bachelor's degree or equivalent in related field, minimum GPA of 2.5; for doctorate, master's degree or equivalent in related field; minimum GPA of 3.0; official transcripts; three years' related professional/academic experience (preferred); access to computer and Internet. Additional exam requirements/recommendations for international students: Required—TOEFL (minimum score 550 paper-based; 213 computer-based), IELTS (minimum score 6.5), or Michigan English Language Assessment Battery (minimum score 82). *Application deadline:* Applications are processed on a rolling basis. Application fee: $50. Electronic applications accepted. *Expenses:* Tuition: Full-time $13,665; part-time $560 per credit. Required fees: $1375. Tuition and fees vary according to course load, degree level and program. *Financial support:* In 2009–10, 200 students received support; fellowships, Federal Work-Study, scholarships/grants, unspecified assistantships, and family tuition reduction, active duty/veteran tuition reduction, group tuition reduction, interest-free payment plans available. Support available to part-time students. Financial award applicants required to submit FAFSA. *Unit head:* Dr. Savitri Dixon-Saxon, Associate Dean, 800-925-3368. *Application contact:* Jennifer Hall, Director of Enrollment, 866-4-WALDEN, E-mail: info@waldenu.edu.

Wayne State University, Graduate School, Interdisciplinary Program in Infant Mental Health, Detroit, MI 48202. Offers Certificate. *Entrance requirements:* For degree, concurrent admission to a master's or doctoral program, or master's degree; letters of reference. Additional exam requirements/recommendations for international students: Required—TOEFL (minimum score 550 paper-based; 213 computer-based); Recommended—TWE (minimum score 6). Electronic applications accepted. *Faculty research:* Infant mental health treatment, early intervention, child abuse and neglect, readiness, attachment.

West Virginia University, College of Human Resources and Education, Department of Technology, Learning and Culture, Program in Child Development and Family Studies, Morgantown, WV 26506. Offers MA. Part-time programs available. *Degree requirements:* For master's, thesis. *Entrance requirements:* For master's, GRE General Test, minimum GPA of 3.0, interview. Additional exam requirements/recommendations for international students: Required—TOEFL. Electronic applications accepted.

Wheelock College, Graduate Programs, Division of Child and Family Studies, Boston, MA 02215-4176. Offers family studies (MS); family support and parent education (MS); family, culture, and society (MS). Part-time programs available. Postbaccalaureate distance learning degree programs offered (minimal on-campus study). *Degree requirements:* For master's, comprehensive exam. Electronic applications accepted. *Faculty research:* Cross-cultural studies of parenting, effects of chronic illness on families, parenting education.

Child Development

Appalachian State University, Cratis D. Williams Graduate School, Department of Family and Consumer Sciences, Boone, NC 28608. Offers child development (MA); family and consumer science (MA), including food and nutrition; family and consumer science education (MA). Part-time programs available. Postbaccalaureate distance learning degree programs offered (no on-campus study). *Faculty:* 12 full-time (10 women), 2 part-time/adjunct (1 woman). *Students:* 17 full-time (16 women), 15 part-time (all women); includes 2 minority (both African Americans), 1 international. 29 applicants, 83% accepted, 20 enrolled. In 2009, 6 master's awarded. *Degree requirements:* For master's, comprehensive exam, thesis optional. *Entrance requirements:* For master's, GRE General Test, 3 letters of recommendation. Additional exam requirements/recommendations for international students: Required—TOEFL (minimum score 550 paper-based; 230 computer-based; 79 iBT), IELTS (minimum score 6.5). *Application deadline:* For fall admission, 7/1 for domestic students, 2/1 for international students; for spring admission, 11/1 for domestic students, 7/1 for international students. Applications are processed on a rolling basis. Application fee: $50. Electronic applications accepted. *Expenses:* Tuition, state resident: full-time $2960. Tuition, nonresident: full-time $14,051. Required fees: $2320. *Financial support:* In 2009–10, 5 research assistantships (averaging $8,000 per year) were awarded; career-related internships or fieldwork, scholarships/grants, and unspecified assistantships also available. Financial award application deadline: 7/1; financial award applicants required to submit FAFSA. *Faculty research:* Food antioxidants, preschool curriculum, children with special needs, family child care, FCS curriculum content. *Unit head:* Dr. Sarah Jordan, Chairperson, 828-262-2661, E-mail: jordansr@appstate.edu. *Application contact:* Dr. Sandy Krause, Director of Graduate Admissions and Recruiting, 828-262-2130, E-mail: krausesl@appstate.edu.

Arcadia University, Graduate Studies, Department of Education, Glenside, PA 19038-3295. Offers art education (M Ed, MA Ed); biology education (MA Ed); chemistry education (MA Ed); child development (CAS); computer education (M Ed, CAS); computer education 7–12 (MA Ed); early childhood education (M Ed, CAS), including individualized (M Ed), master teacher (M Ed), research in child development (M Ed); educational leadership (M Ed, CAS); educational psychology (CAS); elementary education (M Ed, CAS); English education (MA Ed); environmental education (MA Ed, CAS); history education (MA Ed); language arts (M Ed, CAS); mathematics education (M Ed, MA Ed, CAS); music education (MA Ed); psychology (MA Ed); pupil personnel services (CAS); reading (M Ed, CAS); school library science (M Ed); science education (M Ed, CAS); secondary education (M Ed, CAS); special education (M Ed, Ed D, CAS); theater arts (MA Ed); written communication (MA Ed). *Accreditation:* NASAD. Part-time and evening/weekend programs available. Postbaccalaureate distance learning degree programs offered (minimal on-campus study). *Faculty:* 12 full-time (8 women), 38 part-time/adjunct (26 women). *Students:* 89 full-time (74 women), 622 part-time (487 women); includes 112 minority (94 African Americans, 9 Asian Americans or Pacific Islanders, 9 Hispanic Americans), 2 international. Average age 32. In 2009, 257 master's, 4 doctorates awarded. *Application deadline:* Applications are processed on a rolling basis. Application fee: $40. Electronic applications accepted. *Expenses:* Tuition: Full-time $30,450; part-time $620 per credit hour. Required fees: $165. Tuition and fees vary according to program. *Financial support:* Career-related internships or fieldwork, tuition waivers (partial), and unspecified assistantships available. *Unit head:* Dr. Steven P. Gulkus. *Application contact:* 215-572-2925, Fax: 215-572-2126, E-mail: grad@arcadia.edu.

California State University, Los Angeles, Graduate Studies, College of Health and Human Services, Department of Child and Family Studies, Los Angeles, CA 90032-8530. Offers child development (MA). Part-time and evening/weekend programs available. *Faculty:* 2 full-time (both women), 2 part-time/adjunct (both women). *Students:* 3 full-time (all women), 16 part-time (14 women); includes 11 minority (4 Asian Americans or Pacific Islanders, 7 Hispanic Americans). Average age 28. 14 applicants, 100% accepted, 3 enrolled. In 2009, 6 master's awarded. *Degree requirements:* For master's, comprehensive exam, project or thesis. *Entrance requirements:* Additional exam requirements/recommendations for international students: Required—TOEFL (minimum score 500 paper-based; 173 computer-based). *Application deadline:* For fall admission, 5/1 for domestic and international students. Applications are processed on a rolling basis. Application fee: $55. *Financial support:* Career-related internships or fieldwork and Federal Work-Study available. Support available to part-time students. Financial award application deadline: 3/1. *Faculty research:* Nutrition education, laundry product and fabric durability, computer usage in public school home economics. *Unit head:* Dr. Marlene Zepeda, Chair, 323-343-4590, Fax: 323-343-5019, E-mail: mzepeda@calstatela.edu. *Application contact:* Dr. Cheryl L. Ney, Associate Vice President for Academic Affairs and Dean of Graduate Studies, 323-343-3820, Fax: 323-343-5653, E-mail: cney@cslanet.calstatela.edu.

California State University, San Bernardino, Graduate Studies, College of Social and Behavioral Sciences, Department of Psychology, San Bernardino, CA 92407-2397. Offers child development (MA), including psychology-life span; clinical/counseling psychology (MS), including clinical psychology; general/experimental psychology (MA), including psychology; industrial/organizational psychology (MS), including organizational psychology. *Faculty:* 20 full-time (8 women), 1 (woman) part-time/adjunct. *Students:* 85 full-time (67 women), 36 part-time (25 women); includes 47 minority (6 African Americans, 9 Asian Americans or Pacific Islanders, 32 Hispanic Americans), 8 international. Average age 28. 205 applicants, 51% accepted, 59 enrolled. In 2009, 36 master's awarded. *Degree requirements:* For master's, comprehensive exam, thesis (for some programs), advancement to candidacy. *Entrance requirements:* For master's, writing exam, minimum GPA of 3.0 in major. *Application deadline:* For fall admission, 8/31 priority date for domestic students. Application fee: $55. *Financial support:* Fellowships, research assistantships, teaching assistantships, career-related internships or fieldwork, Federal Work-Study, institutionally sponsored loans, and unspecified assistantships available. *Faculty research:* Perceptual development, human memory, psychopharmacology, psychology of women, language acquisition. *Unit head:* Dr. Mark S. Agars, Associate Dean, 909-537-5433, Fax: 909-537-7003, E-mail: magars@csusb.edu. *Application contact:* Stacy Brooks, Graduate Secretary, 909-537-5570, Fax: 909-537-7003, E-mail: sbrooks@csusb.edu.

California State University, Stanislaus, College of Human and Health Sciences, Department of Psychology, Turlock, CA 95382. Offers behavior analysis (MS); child development (Graduate Certificate); counseling (MS); psychology (MA, MS). Part-time programs available. *Degree requirements:* For master's, thesis. *Entrance requirements:* For master's, GRE General Test, minimum GPA of 3.0, 3 letters of reference. Additional exam requirements/recommendations for international students: Required—TOEFL (minimum score 550 paper-based; 213 computer-based). Electronic applications accepted. *Faculty research:* Hedonic tone judgement, syntax and autism, early literacy assessment and native and non-native languages.

East Carolina University, Graduate School, College of Human Ecology, Department of Child Development and Family Relations, Greenville, NC 27858-4353. Offers child development and family relations (MS); marriage and family therapy (MS). *Accreditation:* AAMFT/COAMFTE. Part-time programs available. *Degree requirements:* For master's, comprehensive exam, thesis optional. *Faculty research:* Child care quality, mental health delivery systems for children, family violence.

Erikson Institute, Academic Programs, Program in Child Development, Chicago, IL 60654. Offers MS. *Degree requirements:* For master's, comprehensive exam, internship. *Entrance requirements:* For master's, 3 letters of recommendation, minimum GPA of 2.75. Additional exam requirements/recommendations for international students: Required—TOEFL.

Michigan State University, The Graduate School, College of Social Science, Department of Family and Child Ecology, East Lansing, MI 48824. Offers child development (MA); community services (MS); family and child ecology (PhD); family studies (MA); marriage and family therapy (MA); youth development (MA). *Accreditation:* AAMFT/COAMFTE (one or more programs are accredited). *Faculty:* 19 full-time (14 women). *Students:* 64 full-time (54 women), 56 part-time (49 women); includes 18 minority (9 African Americans, 1 American Indian/Alaska Native, 5 Asian Americans or Pacific Islanders, 3 Hispanic Americans), 16 international. Average age 33. 52 applicants, 50% accepted. In 2009, 28 master's, 11 doctorates awarded. *Entrance requirements:* For master's, GRE General Test, minimum GPA of 3.0 in last 2 years of undergraduate course work, 3 letters of recommendation; for doctorate, GRE General Test, minimum GPA of 3.0, 3 letters of recommendation, background in behavioral sciences. Additional exam requirements/recommendations for international students: Required—TOEFL. Electronic applications accepted. *Expenses:* Tuition, state resident: part-time $478.25 per credit hour. Tuition, nonresident: part-time $966.50 per credit hour. Part-time tuition and fees vary according to program. *Financial support:* In 2009–10, 18 research assistantships with tuition reimbursements (averaging $6,363 per year), 10 teaching assistantships with tuition reimbursements (averaging $6,308 per year) were awarded. Total annual research expenditures: $216,042. *Unit head:* Dr. Karen Wampler, Chairperson, 517-355-7680, Fax: 517-432-2953, E-mail: kwampler@msu.edu. *Application contact:* Ruth Sedelmaier, Graduate Program Secretary, 517-353-5248, Fax: 517-432-3320, E-mail: sedelmai@msu.edu.

Middle Tennessee State University, College of Graduate Studies, College of Education and Behavioral Science, Department of Human Sciences, Murfreesboro, TN 37132. Offers child development and family studies (MS); nutrition and food science (MS). Part-time and evening/weekend programs available. Postbaccalaureate distance learning degree programs offered. *Faculty:* 7 full-time (all women). *Students:* 24 part-time (all women); includes 5 minority (4 African Americans, 1 Asian American or Pacific Islander). Average age 27. 22 applicants, 82% accepted, 18 enrolled. In 2009, 3 master's awarded. *Degree requirements:* For master's, comprehensive exam, thesis. *Entrance requirements:* For master's, GRE or MAT. Additional exam requirements/recommendations for international students: Required—TOEFL (minimum score 525 paper-based; 195 computer-based; 71 iBT) or IELTS (minimum score 6). *Application deadline:* For fall admission, 6/1 for domestic and international students. Applications are processed on a rolling basis. Application fee: $25 ($30 for international students). Electronic applications accepted. *Expenses:* Tuition, state resident: full-time $4404. Tuition, nonresident:

full-time $10,956. *Financial support:* In 2009–10, 5 students received support. Application deadline: 5/1. *Faculty research:* Courtship relationships, feminist methodology and epistemology in family studies, school uniforms, body fat in elderly, asynchronous distance education. *Unit head:* Dr. Dellmar Walker, Chair, 615-898-2884. *Application contact:* Dr. Michael Allen, Dean and Vice Provost for Research, 615-898-2840, Fax: 615-904-8020, E-mail: mallen@mtsu.edu.

North Dakota State University, College of Graduate and Interdisciplinary Studies, College of Human Development and Education, Department of Child Development and Family Science, Fargo, ND 58108. Offers child development and family science (MS); couple and family therapy (MS); family financial planning (MS); gerontology (MS, PhD). *Accreditation:* AAMFT/COAMFTE. Part-time and evening/weekend programs available. Postbaccalaureate distance learning degree programs offered (no on-campus study). *Faculty:* 12 full-time (7 women). *Students:* 26 full-time (25 women), 21 part-time (18 women); includes 1 African American, 2 international. 22 applicants, 64% accepted, 12 enrolled. In 2009, 12 master's awarded. *Degree requirements:* For master's, thesis or alternative; for doctorate, thesis/dissertation. *Entrance requirements:* Additional exam requirements/recommendations for international students: Required—TOEFL (minimum score 525 paper-based; 197 computer-based; 71 iBT). *Application deadline:* For fall admission, 2/1 for domestic and international students; for spring admission, 10/1 for domestic and international students. Application fee: $45 ($60 for international students). *Financial support:* In 2009–10, 17 students received support, including research assistantships with full tuition reimbursements available (averaging $3,000 per year), 17 teaching assistantships with full tuition reimbursements available (averaging $3,000 per year); career-related internships or fieldwork, Federal Work-Study, institutionally sponsored loans, and tuition waivers (full) also available. Financial award application deadline: 4/1. *Faculty research:* Family therapy, resilience, parenting, adolescent development, mental health. Total annual research expenditures: $333,582. *Unit head:* Dr. James Deal, Head, 701-231-7568, Fax: 701-231-9645, E-mail: jim_deal@ndsu.edu. *Application contact:* Theresa Anderson, Administrative Assistant, 701-231-8628, Fax: 701-231-9645, E-mail: theresa.anderson@ndsu.edu.

Ohio University, Graduate College, College of Health and Human Services, School of Human and Consumer Sciences, Athens, OH 45701-2979. Offers apparel, textiles, and merchandising (MS); child development and family life (MS); early childhood education (MS); family studies (MS); food and nutrition (MS). Part-time programs available. *Faculty:* 13 full-time (9 women), 5 part-time/adjunct (all women). *Students:* 18 full-time (14 women), 7 part-time (all women); includes 2 minority (1 African American, 1 Asian American or Pacific Islander), 3 international. 21 applicants, 81% accepted, 8 enrolled. In 2009, 6 master's awarded. *Degree requirements:* For master's, comprehensive exam (for some programs), thesis. *Entrance requirements:* For master's, GRE. Additional exam requirements/recommendations for international students: Required—TOEFL (minimum score 550 paper-based; 80 iBT) or IELTS Academic (minimum score 6.5). *Application deadline:* For fall admission, 3/1 priority date for domestic and international students. Applications are processed on a rolling basis. Application fee: $50 ($55 for international students). Electronic applications accepted. *Expenses:* Tuition, state resident: full-time $7839; part-time $323 per quarter hour. Tuition, nonresident: full-time $15,831; part-time $654 per quarter hour. Required fees: $2931. *Financial support:* Research assistantships, teaching assistantships, career-related internships or fieldwork, Federal Work-Study, institutionally sponsored loans, and unspecified assistantships available. Financial award application deadline: 3/15. *Faculty research:* Diversity, developmentally appropriate activities, death and dying, gerontology, sexuality education. *Unit head:* Dr. V. Ann Paulins, Director, 740-593-2880, Fax: 740-593-0289, E-mail: paulins@ohio.edu. *Application contact:* Dr. Annette Graham, Graduate Coordinator, 740-593-0700, E-mail: grahama@ohio.edu.

Purdue University, Graduate School, College of Consumer and Family Sciences, Department of Child Development and Family Studies, West Lafayette, IN 47907. Offers developmental studies (MS, PhD); family studies (MS, PhD); marriage and family therapy (MS, PhD). *Accreditation:* AAMFT/COAMFTE (one or more programs are accredited). Part-time programs available. Terminal master's awarded for partial completion of doctoral program. *Degree requirements:* For master's, thesis; for doctorate, thesis/dissertation. *Entrance requirements:* For master's and doctorate, GRE General Test. Additional exam requirements/recommendations for international students: Required—TWE. Electronic applications accepted. *Faculty research:* Inclusion of children with special needs, families as learning environments, relationships in child care, work-family relations, AIDS prevention.

Rutgers, The State University of New Jersey, Camden, Graduate School of Arts and Sciences, Program in Childhood Studies, Camden, NJ 08102-1401. Offers MA, PhD. Part-time and evening/weekend programs available. *Degree requirements:* For master's, thesis (for some programs). *Entrance requirements:* Additional exam requirements/recommendations for international students: Required—TOEFL, IELTS. *Faculty research:* Children's consumer culture, moral development, development of personality and social relations, children's literature, commodification of childhood.

San Diego State University, Graduate and Research Affairs, College of Education, Department of Child and Family Development, San Diego, CA 92182. Offers child development (MS). Part-time programs available. *Degree requirements:* For master's, thesis. *Entrance requirements:* For master's, GRE General Test, 3 letters of recommendation, interview. Additional exam requirements/recommendations for international students: Required—TOEFL. Electronic applications accepted.

Sarah Lawrence College, Graduate Studies, Program in Child Development, Bronxville, NY 10708-5999. Offers MA. Part-time programs available. *Faculty:* 7 part-time/adjunct (5 women). *Students:* 7 full-time (6 women), 9 part-time (all women); includes 5 minority (1 African American, 2 Asian Americans or Pacific Islanders, 2 Hispanic Americans). Average age 28. 76 applicants, 16% accepted, 5 enrolled. In 2009, 3 master's awarded. *Degree requirements:* For master's, thesis, fieldwork. *Entrance requirements:* For master's, minimum B average in undergraduate coursework. *Application deadline:* For fall admission, 2/1 for domestic and international students. Applications are processed on a rolling basis. Application fee: $60. *Expenses:* Tuition: Part-time $1161 per credit. Required fees: $232 per semester. Part-time tuition and fees vary according to course load, program and student level. *Financial support:* In 2009–10, 6 students received support, including 6 fellowships (averaging $5,667 per year); career-related internships or fieldwork and scholarships/grants also available. Support available to part-time students. Financial award application deadline: 3/1; financial award applicants required to submit FAFSA. *Unit head:* Barbara Schecter, Director, 914-395-2371. *Application contact:* Emanual Lomax, Director of Graduate Admissions, 914-395-2371, E-mail: sguma@mail.slc.edu.

Southern New Hampshire University, School of Education, Manchester, NH 03106-1045. Offers business education (MS); child development (M Ed); computer technology education (Certificate); curriculum and instruction (M Ed); education (M Ed, CAS); elementary education (M Ed); general special education (Certificate); school business administrator (Certificate); secondary education (M Ed); training and development (Certificate). Part-time and evening/weekend programs available. Postbaccalaureate distance learning degree programs offered (no on-campus study). *Degree requirements:* For master's, comprehensive exam (for some programs), thesis or alternative. *Entrance requirements:* For master's, PRAXIS I, minimum GPA of 2.75. Additional exam requirements/recommendations for international students: Required—TOEFL (minimum score 550 paper-based; 213 computer-based). Electronic applications accepted. *Expenses:* Contact institution.

Texas Woman's University, Graduate School, College of Professional Education, Department of Family Sciences, Denton, TX 76201. Offers child development (MS, PhD); counseling and development (MS); early childhood education (M Ed, MA, MS, Ed D); family studies (MS, PhD); family therapy (MS, PhD). *Accreditation:* ACA (one or more programs are accredited). Part-time and evening/weekend programs available. *Faculty:* 25 full-time (21 women), 4 part-time/adjunct (all women). *Students:* 111 full-time (105 women), 294 part-time (269 women); includes 149 minority (99 African Americans, 3 American Indian/Alaska Native, 7 Asian Americans or Pacific Islanders, 40 Hispanic Americans), 22 international. Average age 36. 179 applicants, 86% accepted, 72 enrolled. In 2009, 86 master's, 22 doctorates awarded. Terminal master's awarded for partial completion of doctoral program. *Degree requirements:* For master's, portfolio; for doctorate, comprehensive exam, thesis/dissertation. *Entrance requirements:* For master's, interview, letter of intent, curriculum vitae; for doctorate, interview, minimum GPA of 3.5 in last 60 hours of course work. Additional exam requirements/recommendations for international students: Required—TOEFL (minimum score 550 paper-based; 213 computer-based; 79 iBT). *Application deadline:* For fall admission, 2/15 priority date for domestic students, 3/1 for international students; for spring admission, 9/15 priority date for domestic students, 8/1 for international students. Applications are processed on a rolling basis. Application fee: $50. Electronic applications accepted. *Expenses:* Tuition, state resident: full-time $3564; part-time $198 per credit hour. Tuition, nonresident: full-time $8550; part-time $475 per credit hour. Required fees: $69.26 per credit hour. Tuition and fees vary according to course load. *Financial support:* In 2009–10, 96 students received support, including 13 research assistantships (averaging $10,746 per year), 7 teaching assistantships (averaging $10,746 per year); career-related internships or fieldwork, Federal Work-Study, institutionally sponsored loans, scholarships/grants, traineeships, health care benefits, and unspecified assistantships also available. Support available to part-time students. Financial award application deadline: 3/1; financial award applicants required to submit FAFSA. *Faculty research:* Parenting/parent education, distance education, play therapy, family sexuality, diversity, ANTHEM healthy marriages initiative. *Unit head:* Dr. Larry LeFlore, Chair, 940-898-2685, Fax: 940-898-2676, E-mail: famsci@twu.edu. *Application contact:* Samuel Wheeler, Assistant Director of Admissions, 940-898-3188, Fax: 940-898-3081, E-mail: wheelersr@twu.edu.

Tufts University, Graduate School of Arts and Sciences, Department of Child Development, Medford, MA 02155. Offers child development (MA, PhD, CAGS); early childhood education (MAT). Part-time programs available. *Faculty:* 16 full-time, 12 part-time/adjunct. *Students:* 66 (61 women). Average age 27. 113 applicants, 68% accepted, 35 enrolled. In 2009, 34 master's, 6 doctorates awarded. *Degree requirements:* For master's, thesis (for some programs); for doctorate, thesis/dissertation. *Entrance requirements:* For master's and doctorate, GRE General Test. Additional exam requirements/recommendations for international students: Required—TOEFL (minimum score 550 paper-based; 213 computer-based; 80 iBT). *Application deadline:* For fall admission, 1/15 for domestic students, 12/15 for international students. Applications are processed on a rolling basis. Application fee: $75. Electronic applications accepted. *Expenses:* Tuition: Full-time $38,096; part-time $3962 per credit. Required fees: $686; $40 per year. Tuition and fees vary according to course level, course load, degree level, program and student level. *Financial support:* Fellowships, research assistantships with full and partial tuition reimbursements, teaching assistantships with full and partial tuition reimbursements, Federal Work-Study, scholarships/grants, tuition waivers (partial), and unspecified assistantships available. Support available to part-time students. Financial award application deadline: 1/15; financial award applicants required to submit FAFSA. *Unit head:* Jayanthi Mistry, Chair, 617-627-3355. *Application contact:* Fred Rothbaum, Graduate Advisor, 617-627-3355.

The University of Akron, Graduate School, College of Health Sciences and Human Services, School of Health and Human Services, Program in Child and Family Development, Akron, OH 44325. Offers child development (MA); family development (MA). *Students:* 5 full-time (all women), 5 part-time (all women); includes 3 minority (all African Americans). Average age 35. 3 applicants, 100% accepted, 1 enrolled. In 2009, 2 master's awarded. *Degree requirements:* For master's, comprehensive exam, project or thesis. *Entrance requirements:* For master's, GRE, minimum GPA of 2.75, letters of recommendation, resume. Additional exam requirements/recommendations for international students: Required—TOEFL (minimum score 550 paper-based; 213 computer-based; 79 iBT). *Application deadline:* For fall admission, 3/1 for domestic and international students; for spring admission, 10/1 for domestic and international students. Application fee: $30 ($40 for international students). Electronic applications accepted. *Expenses:* Tuition, state resident: full-time $6570; part-time $365 per credit hour. Tuition, nonresident: full-time $11,250; part-time $625 per credit hour. *Unit head:* Dr. Susan M. Witt, Coordinator, 330-972-7729, E-mail: susan8@uakron.edu. *Application contact:* Dr. Susan M. Witt, Coordinator, 330-972-7729, E-mail: susan8@uakron.edu.

University of California, Davis, Graduate Studies, Graduate Group in Child Development, Davis, CA 95616. Offers MS. *Degree requirements:* For master's, comprehensive exam (for some programs), thesis (for some programs). *Entrance requirements:* For master's, GRE General Test, minimum GPA of 3.0. Additional exam requirements/recommendations for international students: Required—TOEFL (minimum score 550 paper-based; 213 computer-based). Electronic applications accepted. *Faculty research:* Cognitive development, socio-emotional development, early childhood.

University of La Verne, College of Education and Organizational Leadership, Programs in Child Development/Child Life, La Verne, CA 91750-4443. Offers child development (MS); child life (MS). Part-time programs available. *Faculty:* 19 full-time (14 women), 35 part-time/adjunct (27 women). *Students:* 40 full-time (39 women), 36 part-time (34 women); includes 34 minority (3 African Americans, 10 Asian Americans or Pacific Islanders, 21 Hispanic Americans), 1 international. Average age 31. In 2009, 15 master's awarded. *Entrance requirements:* For master's, minimum GPA of 3.0, 3 letters of reference, writing sample. Additional exam requirements/recommendations for international students: Required—TOEFL (minimum score 550 paper-based; 213 computer-based). *Application deadline:* Applications are processed on a rolling basis. Application fee: $50. *Expenses:* Contact institution. *Financial support:* Institutionally sponsored loans, scholarships/grants, and unspecified assistantships available. Financial award application deadline: 3/2; financial award applicants required to submit FAFSA. *Unit head:* Dr. Barbara Nicoll, Chairperson, 909-593-3511 Ext. 4632, Fax: 909-392-2710, E-mail: bnicoll@laverne.edu. *Application contact:* Christy Ranells, Program and Admission Specialist, 909-593-3511 Ext. 4644, Fax: 909-392-2761, E-mail: cranells@laverne.edu.

University of Minnesota, Twin Cities Campus, Graduate School, College of Education and Human Development, Institute of Child Development, Minneapolis, MN 55455-0213. Offers child psychology (MA, PhD); early childhood education (M Ed, MA, PhD); school psychology (MA, PhD). *Faculty:* 17 full-time (7 women). *Students:* 108 full-time (99 women), 34 part-time (32 women); includes 13 minority (2 African Americans, 3 American Indian/Alaska Native, 5 Asian Americans or Pacific Islanders, 3 Hispanic Americans), 11 international. Average age 31. 149 applicants, 29% accepted, 37 enrolled. In 2009, 45 master's, 7 doctorates awarded. *Financial support:* In 2009–10, 26 fellowships (averaging $24,044 per year), 23 research assistantships with full tuition reimbursements (averaging $26,058 per year), 39 teaching assistantships with full tuition reimbursements (averaging $27,413 per year) were awarded. *Faculty research:* Developmental affective and cognitive neuroscience; developmental psychopathology; intervention and prevention science; social and emotional development; cognitive, language, and perceptual development. Total annual research expenditures: $3.8 million. *Unit head:* Dr. Nicki Crick, Director, 612-625-8879, Fax: 612-624-6373, E-mail: crick001@umn.edu. *Application contact:* Claudia Johnston, Information Contact, 612-624-2576, Fax: 612-624-6373, E-mail: johnstc@staff.tc.umn.edu.

University of Nebraska–Lincoln, Graduate College, College of Education and Human Sciences, Department of Child, Youth and Family Studies, Lincoln, NE 68588. Offers child development/early childhood education (MS, PhD); child, youth and family studies (MS); family and consumer sciences education (MS, PhD); family financial planning (MS); family science (MS, PhD); gerontology (PhD); human sciences (PhD), including child, youth and family studies, gerontology, medical family therapy; marriage and family therapy (MS); medical family therapy (PhD); youth development (MS). *Accreditation:* AAMFT/COAMFTE (one or more programs are accredited). Postbaccalaureate distance learning degree programs offered. *Degree requirements:* For master's, thesis optional. *Entrance requirements:* For master's, GRE. Additional exam requirements/recommendations for international students: Required—TOEFL (minimum score 550 paper-based; 213 computer-based). Electronic applications accepted. *Faculty research:* Marriage and family therapy, child development/early childhood education, family financial management.

Child Development

The University of North Carolina at Charlotte, Graduate School, College of Education, Department of Special Education and Child Development, Charlotte, NC 28223-0001. Offers special education (M Ed, PhD), including academically gifted (M Ed), behavioral—emotional handicaps (M Ed), cross-categorical disabilities (M Ed), learning disabilities (M Ed), mental handicaps (M Ed), severe and profound handicaps (M Ed). Part-time programs available. *Faculty:* 25 full-time (17 women), 5 part-time/adjunct (4 women). *Students:* 20 full-time (19 women), 141 part-time (130 women); includes 13 African Americans, 3 American Indian/Alaska Native, 2 Hispanic Americans, 2 international. Average age 35. 17 applicants, 94% accepted, 12 enrolled. In 2009, 19 master's, 22 doctorates awarded. *Degree requirements:* For doctorate, comprehensive exam, thesis/dissertation, portfolio, qualifying exam. *Entrance requirements:* For master's, GRE or MAT; for doctorate, GRE or MAT, 3 letters of reference, resume or curriculum vitae, minimum GPA of 3.5, master's degree in special education or related field, 3 years of teaching experience. Additional exam requirements/recommendations for international students: Required—TOEFL (minimum score 557 paper-based; 220 computer-based; 83 iBT), TOEFL (minimum score 550 paper-based; 220 computer-based) or Michigan English Language Assessment Battery. *Application deadline:* For fall admission, 7/15 for domestic students, 5/1 for international students; for spring admission, 11/15 for domestic students, 10/1 for international students. Application fee: $55. *Financial support:* In 2009–10, 18 students received support, including 9 research assistantships (averaging $12,299 per year), 9 teaching assistantships (averaging $14,165 per year). Financial award application deadline: 4/1; financial award applicants required to submit FAFSA. *Faculty research:* Transition to adulthood and self-determination, teaching reading and other academic skills to students with disabilities, alternate assessment, early intervention, preschool education. Total annual research expenditures: $3.2 million. *Unit head:* David Gilmore, Unit Head, 704-687-8186, Fax: 704-687-2916. *Application contact:* Kathy B. Giddings, Director of Graduate Admissions, 704-687-5503, Fax: 704-687-3279, E-mail: gradadm@uncc.edu.

The University of Tennessee at Martin, Graduate Programs, College of Agriculture and Applied Sciences, Department of Family and Consumer Sciences, Martin, TN 38238-1000. Offers dietetics (MSFCS); general family and consumer sciences (MSFCS). Part-time programs available. Postbaccalaureate distance learning degree programs offered (minimal on-campus study). *Faculty:* 6. *Students:* 47 (43 women). 5,430 applicants, 1% accepted, 23 enrolled. In 2009, 10 master's awarded. *Degree requirements:* For master's, comprehensive exam, thesis optional. *Entrance requirements:* For master's, GRE General Test, minimum GPA of 2.5. Additional exam requirements/recommendations for international students: Required—TOEFL (minimum score 525 paper-based; 197 computer-based; 71 iBT). *Application deadline:* For fall admission, 8/1 priority date for domestic students, 6/15 priority date for international students; for spring admission, 12/15 priority date for domestic students, 12/1 priority date for international students. Applications are processed on a rolling basis. Application fee: $30 ($130 for international students). Electronic applications accepted. *Expenses:* Tuition, state resident: full-time $6660; part-time $372 per hour. Tuition, nonresident: full-time $18,000; part-time $1005 per hour. *Financial support:* In 2009–10, 3 students received support, including 3 research assistantships with full tuition reimbursements available (averaging $7,234 per year); scholarships/grants and unspecified assistantships also available. Support available to part-time students. Financial award application deadline: 2/15; financial award applicants required to submit FAFSA. *Faculty research:* Children with developmental disabilities, regional food product development and marketing, parent education. *Unit head:* Dr. Lisa LeBleu, Coordinator, 731-881-7116, Fax: 731-881-7106, E-mail: llebleu@utm.edu. *Application contact:* Linda S. Arant, Student Services Specialist, 731-881-7012, Fax: 731-881-7499, E-mail: larant@utm.edu.

The University of Texas at Austin, Graduate School, College of Natural Sciences, School of Human Ecology, Austin, TX 78712-1111. Offers human development and family sciences (MA, PhD); nutritional sciences (MA, PhD), including nutrition (MA), nutritional sciences (PhD); textile and apparel technology (MS). *Degree requirements:* For master's, thesis; for doctorate, thesis/dissertation. *Entrance requirements:* For master's and doctorate, GRE General Test. Electronic applications accepted.

University of Wyoming, College of Agriculture, Department of Family and Consumer Sciences, Laramie, WY 82070. Offers early childhood development (MS); family and consumer sciences (MS); food science and human nutrition (MS). Part-time programs available. *Degree requirements:* For master's, thesis, project. *Entrance requirements:* For master's, GRE General Test or MCAT, minimum GPA of 3.0. Additional exam requirements/recommendations for international students: Required—TOEFL (minimum score 540 paper-based; 207 computer-based; 76 iBT). Electronic applications accepted. *Faculty research:* Asthma, obesity and healthy weights, nutrition concerns of children with special health care needs, food product development, food safety, postpartum health, exercise nutrition.

Virginia Polytechnic Institute and State University, Graduate School, College of Liberal Arts and Human Sciences, Department of Human Development, Blacksburg, VA 24061. Offers adult development and aging (MS, PhD); adult learning and human resource development (MS, PhD); child development (MS, PhD); family studies (MS, PhD); marriage and family therapy (MS, PhD). *Accreditation:* AAMFT/COAMFTE (one or more programs are accredited). *Faculty:* 22 full-time (18 women). *Students:* 49 full-time (38 women), 64 part-time (44 women); includes 30 minority (1 African American, 7 American Indian/Alaska Native, 16 Asian Americans or Pacific Islanders, 6 Hispanic Americans), 2 international. Average age 34. 64 applicants, 34% accepted, 16 enrolled. In 2009, 10 master's, 14 doctorates awarded. *Entrance requirements:* For master's and doctorate, GRE, GMAT. Additional exam requirements/recommendations for international students: Required—TOEFL (minimum score 550 paper-based; 213 computer-based). *Application deadline:* For fall admission, 5/15 for international students; for spring admission, 10/15 for international students. Applications are processed on a rolling basis. Application fee: $65. Electronic applications accepted. *Expenses:* Tuition, area resident: Full-time $10,228; part-time $459 per credit hour. Tuition, nonresident: full-time $17,892; part-time $865 per credit hour. Required fees: $1966; $451 per semester. *Financial support:* In 2009–10, 7 research assistantships with full tuition reimbursements (averaging $10,933 per year), 25 teaching assistantships with full tuition reimbursements (averaging $9,387 per year) were awarded; career-related internships or fieldwork, Federal Work-Study, scholarships/grants, and unspecified assistantships also available. Financial award application deadline: 1/15. *Faculty research:* Stress management, children's play, dual-career families, social cognition, relationships of elderly. Total annual research expenditures: $823,581. *Unit head:* Dr. Shannon E. Jarrott, Head, 540-231-4794, Fax: 540-231-7012, E-mail: sjarrott@vt.edu. *Application contact:* Mark Benson, Information Contact, 540-231-5720, Fax: 540-231-7012, E-mail: mbenson@vt.edu.

Whittier College, Graduate Programs, Department of Education and Child Development, Whittier, CA 90608-0634. Offers educational administration (MA Ed); elementary education (MA Ed); secondary education (MA Ed). Part-time and evening/weekend programs available. *Degree requirements:* For master's, thesis. *Entrance requirements:* For master's, GRE General Test, MAT, minimum GPA of 3.5, academic writing sample.

Clothing and Textiles

Academy of Art University, Graduate Program, School of Fashion, San Francisco, CA 94105-3410. Offers fashion design (MFA); fashion merchandising (MFA); fashion textiles (MFA); knitwear (MFA). Part-time programs available. Postbaccalaureate distance learning degree programs offered (no on-campus study). *Degree requirements:* For master's, thesis, final review. *Entrance requirements:* For master's, minimum GPA of 3.0, portfolio. Electronic applications accepted.

Auburn University, Graduate School, College of Human Sciences, Department of Consumer Affairs, Auburn University, AL 36849. Offers apparel and textiles (MS). Part-time programs available. *Faculty:* 14 full-time (all women), 1 (woman) part-time/adjunct. *Students:* 5 full-time (4 women), 7 part-time (6 women); includes 3 minority (2 African Americans, 1 Hispanic American), 5 international. Average age 28. 16 applicants, 69% accepted, 3 enrolled. In 2009, 8 master's awarded. *Degree requirements:* For master's, thesis (for some programs). *Entrance requirements:* For master's, GRE General Test. *Application deadline:* For fall admission, 7/7 for domestic students; for spring admission, 11/24 for domestic students. Applications are processed on a rolling basis. Application fee: $50 ($60 for international students). Electronic applications accepted. *Expenses:* Tuition, state resident: full-time $6240. Tuition, nonresident: full-time $18,720. International tuition: $18,938 full-time. Required fees: $492. Tuition and fees vary according to course load, program and reciprocity agreements. *Financial support:* Fellowships, research assistantships, teaching assistantships, career-related internships or fieldwork and Federal Work-Study available. Support available to part-time students. Financial award application deadline: 3/15; financial award applicants required to submit FAFSA. *Faculty research:* Merchandising, consumer behavior, international marketing of textiles and apparel, apparel product development. Total annual research expenditures: $875,000. *Unit head:* Dr. Carol L. Warfield, Head, 334-844-4084, E-mail: cwarfiel@humsci.auburn.edu. *Application contact:* Dr. George Flowers, Dean of the Graduate School, 334-844-2125.

Central Michigan University, College of Graduate Studies, College of Education and Human Services, Department of Human Environmental Studies, Mount Pleasant, MI 48859. Offers apparel product development and merchandising technology (MS); human development and family studies (MA); nutrition and dietetics (MS). Part-time and evening/weekend programs available. *Degree requirements:* For master's, thesis or alternative. Electronic applications accepted. *Faculty research:* Human growth and development, family studies and human sexuality, human nutrition and dietetics, apparel and textile retailing, computer-aided design for apparel.

Cornell University, Graduate School, Graduate Fields of Human Ecology, Field of Textiles, Ithaca, NY 14853-0001. Offers apparel design (MA, MPS); fiber science (MS, PhD); polymer science (MS, PhD); textile science (MS, PhD). *Faculty:* 17 full-time (7 women). *Students:* 21 full-time (16 women); includes 1 minority (Hispanic American), 12 international. Average age 30. 26 applicants, 19% accepted, 3 enrolled. In 2009, 1 master's, 4 doctorates awarded. *Degree requirements:* For master's, thesis (MA, MS), project paper (MPS); for doctorate, comprehensive exam, thesis/dissertation. *Entrance requirements:* For master's, GRE General Test, 2 letters of recommendation, portfolio (functional apparel design); for doctorate, GRE General Test, 2 letters of recommendation. Additional exam requirements/recommendations for international students: Required—TOEFL (minimum score 600 paper-based; 250 computer-based; 77 iBT). *Application deadline:* For fall admission, 3/1 for domestic students; for spring admission, 10/1 for domestic students. Application fee: $70. Electronic applications accepted. *Expenses:* Tuition: Full-time $29,500. Required fees: $70. Full-time tuition and fees vary according to degree level, program and student level. *Financial support:* In 2009–10, 19 students received support, including 2 teaching assistantships with full tuition reimbursements available; fellowships with full tuition reimbursements available, research assistantships with full tuition reimbursements available, institutionally sponsored loans, scholarships/grants, health care benefits, tuition waivers (full and partial), and unspecified assistantships also available. Financial award applicants required to submit FAFSA. *Faculty research:* Apparel design, consumption, mass customization, 3-D body scanning. *Unit head:* Director of Graduate Studies, 607-255-3151, Fax: 607-255-1093. *Application contact:* Graduate Field Assistant, 607-255-3151, Fax: 607-255-1093, E-mail: textiles_grad@cornell.edu.

Eastern Michigan University, Graduate School, College of Technology, School of Technology Studies, Program in Apparel, Textile Merchandising, Ypsilanti, MI 48197. Offers MS. Part-time and evening/weekend programs available. Postbaccalaureate distance learning degree programs offered (minimal on-campus study). *Students:* 8 full-time (4 women), 10 part-time (all women); includes 5 minority (3 African Americans, 1 Asian American or Pacific Islander, 1 Hispanic American), 7 international. Average age 30. In 2009, 2 master's awarded. *Entrance requirements:* Additional exam requirements/recommendations for international students: Required—TOEFL. *Application deadline:* Applications are processed on a rolling basis. Application fee: $35. Tuition and fees vary according to course level. *Financial support:* Fellowships, research assistantships with full tuition reimbursements, teaching assistantships with full tuition reimbursements, career-related internships or fieldwork, Federal Work-Study, institutionally sponsored loans, scholarships/grants, tuition waivers (partial), and unspecified assistantships available. Support available to part-time students. Financial award applicants required to submit FAFSA. *Unit head:* Dr. Subhas Ghosh, Program Coordinator, 734-487-2476, Fax: 734-487-7690, E-mail: sghosh@emich.edu. *Application contact:* Dr. Subhas Ghosh, Program Coordinator, 734-487-2476, Fax: 734-487-7690, E-mail: sghosh@emich.edu.

Fashion Institute of Technology, School of Graduate Studies, Programs in Fashion and Textile Studies: History, Theory, and Museum Practice, New York, NY 10001-5992. Offers MA. *Accreditation:* NASAD. *Degree requirements:* For master's, one foreign language, thesis, internship. *Entrance requirements:* For master's, GRE General Test or GRE Subject Test, previous course work in art history and chemistry, 4 semesters of a foreign language. Additional exam requirements/recommendations for international students: Required—TOEFL (minimum score 550 paper-based; 213 computer-based). Electronic applications accepted. *Expenses:* Tuition, state resident: full-time $8198; part-time $342 per credit. Tuition, nonresident: full-time $12,972; part-time $541 per credit. Required fees: $450.

See Close-Up on page 115.

Iowa State University of Science and Technology, Graduate College, College of Human Sciences, Department of Apparel, Education Studies, and Hospitality Management, Program in Textiles and Clothing, Ames, IA 50011. Offers MFCS, MS, PhD. *Students:* 29 full-time (21 women), 2 part-time (both women); includes 5 minority (3 African Americans, 1 Asian American or Pacific Islander, 1 Hispanic American), 21 international. In 2009, 2 master's, 2 doctorates awarded. *Degree requirements:* For master's, thesis; for doctorate, thesis/dissertation. *Entrance requirements:* For master's and doctorate, GRE General Test. Additional exam requirements/recommendations for international students: Required—TOEFL (minimum score 550 paper-based; 79 iBT) or IELTS (minimum score 6.5). *Application deadline:* For fall admission, 2/1 priority date for domestic and international students. Applications are processed on a rolling basis. Application fee: $40 ($90 for international students). Electronic applications accepted. *Expenses:* Tuition, state resident: full-time $6716. Tuition, nonresident: full-time $8908. Tuition and fees vary according to course level, course load, program and student level. *Financial support:* In 2009–10, 11 research assistantships with full and partial tuition reimbursements (averaging $14,750 per year), 10 teaching assistantships with full and partial tuition reimbursements (averaging $14,750 per year) were awarded; scholarships/grants also available. *Unit head:* Dr. Ann Marie Fiore, Director of Graduate Education, 515-294-9303, E-mail: amfiore@iastate.edu. *Application contact:* Dr. Ann Marie Fiore, Director of Graduate Education, 515-294-9303, E-mail: amfiore@iastate.edu.

Kansas State University, Graduate School, College of Human Ecology, Department of Apparel, Textiles, and Interior Design, Manhattan, KS 66506. Offers design (MS); general apparel and textile (MS); marketing (MS); merchandising (MS); product development (MS). *Faculty:* 10 full-time (8 women), 1 (woman) part-time/adjunct. *Students:* 7 full-time (5 women), 15 part-time (12 women); includes 3 minority (1 African American, 1 Asian American or Pacific Islander, 1 Hispanic American). Average age 29. 13 applicants, 85% accepted, 7 enrolled. In 2009, 3 master's awarded. *Degree requirements:* For master's, thesis optional, residency. *Entrance requirements:* For master's, GRE General Test, minimum undergraduate GPA of 3.0. Additional exam requirements/recommendations for international students: Required—TOEFL (minimum score 600 paper-based; 250 computer-based). *Application deadline:* For fall admission, 2/1 priority date for domestic and international students; for spring admission, 8/1 priority date for domestic and international students. Applications are processed on a rolling basis. Application fee: $40 ($55 for international students). Electronic applications accepted. *Financial support:* In 2009–10, 3 research assistantships (averaging $14,460 per year), 5 teaching assistantships with full tuition reimbursements (averaging $10,590 per year) were awarded; career-related internships or fieldwork, Federal Work-Study, institutionally sponsored loans, and scholarships/grants also available. Support available to part-time students. Financial award application deadline: 3/1; financial award applicants required to submit FAFSA. *Faculty research:* Apparel marketing and consumer behavior, protective and functional clothing and textiles, social and environmental responsibility, apparel design, new product development. Total annual research expenditures: $40,303. *Unit head:* Jana Hawley, Head, 785-532-6993, Fax: 785-532-3796, E-mail: hawleyj@ksu.edu. *Application contact:* Gina Jackson, Application Contact, 785-532-6693, Fax: 785-532-3796, E-mail: gjackson@ksu.edu.

Kansas State University, Graduate School, College of Human Ecology, Program in Human Ecology, Manhattan, KS 66506. Offers apparel and textiles (PhD); family life education and consultation (PhD); food service and hospitality management (PhD); lifespan and human development (PhD); marriage and family therapy (PhD); personal financial planning (PhD). *Faculty:* 3 full-time (all women). *Students:* 29 full-time (19 women), 43 part-time (23 women); includes 15 minority (13 African Americans, 1 American Indian/Alaska Native, 1 Asian American or Pacific Islander), 16 international. Average age 37. 29 applicants, 66% accepted, 16 enrolled. In 2009, 10 doctorates awarded. *Degree requirements:* For doctorate, thesis/dissertation. *Application deadline:* For fall admission, 2/1 priority date for domestic and international students; for spring admission, 8/1 priority date for domestic and international students. Applications are processed on a rolling basis. Application fee: $40 ($55 for international students). Electronic applications accepted. *Financial support:* Application deadline: 3/1. *Application contact:* Connie Fechter, Application Contact, 785-532-1473, Fax: 785-532-3796, E-mail: fechter@ksu.edu.

North Carolina State University, Graduate School, College of Textiles, Program in Textile Technology Management, Raleigh, NC 27695. Offers PhD. *Degree requirements:* For doctorate, one foreign language, thesis/dissertation, cumulative exams. *Entrance requirements:* For doctorate, GRE or GMAT. Electronic applications accepted. *Faculty research:* Niche markets, supply chain, globalization, logistics.

The Ohio State University, Graduate School, College of Education and Human Ecology, Program in Textiles and Clothing, Columbus, OH 43210. Offers MS, PhD. *Faculty:* 8. *Students:* 8 full-time (all women), 8 part-time (7 women); includes 1 minority (Asian American or Pacific Islander), 10 international. Average age 34. In 2009, 2 master's, 1 doctorate awarded. *Degree requirements:* For master's, thesis optional; for doctorate, thesis/dissertation. *Entrance requirements:* For master's and doctorate, GRE General Test. Additional exam requirements/recommendations for international students: Required—TOEFL (minimum score 577 paper-based; 233 computer-based). *Application deadline:* For fall admission, 8/15 priority date for domestic students, 7/1 priority date for international students; for winter admission, 12/1 priority date for domestic students, 11/1 priority date for international students; for spring admission, 3/1 priority date for domestic students, 2/1 priority date for international students. Applications are processed on a rolling basis. Application fee: $40 ($50 for international students). Electronic applications accepted. *Expenses:* Tuition, state resident: full-time $10,683. Tuition, nonresident: full-time $25,923. Tuition and fees vary according to course load and program. *Financial support:* Fellowships, research assistantships, teaching assistantships, Federal Work-Study, institutionally sponsored loans, and unspecified assistantships available. Support available to part-time students. *Unit head:* Leslie D. Stoel, Graduate Studies Committee Chair, 614-292-8594, Fax: 614-292-2581, E-mail: stoel.1@osu.edu. *Application contact:* 614-292-9444, Fax: 614-292-3895, E-mail: domestic.grad@osu.edu.

Ohio University, Graduate College, College of Health and Human Services, School of Human and Consumer Sciences, Athens, OH 45701-2979. Offers apparel, textiles, and merchandising (MS); child development and family life (MS); early childhood education (MS); family studies (MS); food and nutrition (MS). Part-time programs available. *Faculty:* 13 full-time (9 women), 5 part-time/adjunct (all women). *Students:* 18 full-time (14 women), 7 part-time (all women); includes 2 minority (1 African American, 1 Asian American or Pacific Islander), 3 international. 21 applicants, 81% accepted, 8 enrolled. In 2009, 6 master's awarded. *Degree requirements:* For master's, comprehensive exam (for some programs), thesis. *Entrance requirements:* For master's, GRE. Additional exam requirements/recommendations for international students: Required—TOEFL (minimum score 550 paper-based; 80 iBT) or IELTS Academic (minimum score 6.5). *Application deadline:* For fall admission, 3/1 priority date for domestic and international students. Applications are processed on a rolling basis. Application fee: $50 ($55 for international students). Electronic applications accepted. *Expenses:* Tuition, state resident: full-time $7839; part-time $323 per quarter hour. Tuition, nonresident: full-time $15,831; part-time $654 per quarter hour. Required fees: $2931. *Financial support:* Research assistantships, teaching assistantships, career-related internships or fieldwork, Federal Work-Study, institutionally sponsored loans, and unspecified assistantships available. Financial award application deadline: 3/15. *Faculty research:* Diversity, developmentally appropriate activities, death and dying, gerontology, sexuality education. *Unit head:* Dr. V. Ann Paulins, Director, 740-593-2880, Fax: 740-593-0289, E-mail: paulins@ohio.edu. *Application contact:* Dr. Annette Graham, Graduate Coordinator, 740-593-0700, E-mail: grahama@ohio.edu.

Oklahoma State University, College of Human Environmental Sciences, Department of Design, Housing and Merchandising, Stillwater, OK 74078. Offers MS, PhD. *Faculty:* 16 full-time (12 women), 4 part-time/adjunct (3 women). *Students:* 11 full-time (8 women), 20 part-time (18 women); includes 3 minority (1 African American, 1 Asian American or Pacific Islander, 1 Hispanic American), 10 international. Average age 32. 23 applicants, 43% accepted, 7 enrolled. In 2009, 6 master's, 1 doctorate awarded. *Degree requirements:* For master's, thesis (for some programs); for doctorate, comprehensive exam, thesis/dissertation. *Entrance requirements:* For master's and doctorate, GRE or GMAT. Additional exam requirements/recommendations for international students: Required—TOEFL (minimum score 550 paper-based; 79 iBT). *Application deadline:* For fall admission, 3/1 priority date for international students; for spring admission, 8/1 priority date for international students. Applications are processed on a rolling basis. Application fee: $40 ($75 for international students). Electronic applications accepted. *Expenses:* Tuition, state resident: full-time $3716; part-time $154.85 per credit hour. Tuition, nonresident: full-time $14,448; part-time $602 per credit hour. Required fees: $1772; $73.85 per credit hour. One-time fee: $50. Tuition and fees vary according to course load and campus/location. *Financial support:* In 2009–10, 13 research assistantships (averaging $11,781 per year), 7 teaching assistantships (averaging $14,158 per year) were awarded; career-related internships or fieldwork, Federal Work-Study, scholarships/grants, health care benefits, tuition waivers (partial), and unspecified assistantships also available. Support available to part-time students. Financial award application deadline: 3/1; financial award applicants required to submit FAFSA. *Faculty research:* Environmental sciences design, housing and merchandising; creativity and physical environment; product development, production and evaluation; experimental learning and critical thinking; technology strategies and assessment; customer expectation and satisfaction. *Unit head:* Dr. Randall Russ, Interim Head, 405-744-5049, Fax: 405-744-6910. *Application contact:* Dr. Gordon Emslie, Dean, 405-744-6368, Fax: 405-744-0355, E-mail: grad-i@okstate.edu.

Oregon State University, Graduate School, College of Health and Human Sciences, Department of Design and Human Environment, Corvallis, OR 97331. Offers MA, MAIS, MS, PhD. *Faculty:* 10 full-time (all women), 1 (woman) part-time/adjunct. *Students:* 22 full-time (21 women), 2 part-time (both women); includes 2 minority (1 Asian American or Pacific Islander, 1 Hispanic American), 7 international. Average age 32. In 2009, 6 master's, 4 doctorates awarded. Terminal master's awarded for partial completion of doctoral program. *Degree requirements:* For master's, thesis or alternative; for doctorate, thesis/dissertation. *Entrance requirements:* For master's and doctorate, GRE General Test, minimum GPA of 3.0 in last 90 hours. Additional exam requirements/recommendations for international students: Required—TOEFL. *Application deadline:* For fall admission, 2/1 priority date for domestic students. Application fee: $50. *Expenses:* Tuition, state resident: full-time $9774; part-time $362 per credit. Tuition, nonresident: full-time $15,849; part-time $587 per credit. Required fees: $1639. Full-time tuition and fees vary according to course load and program. *Financial support:* Research assistantships, teaching assistantships, career-related internships or fieldwork, Federal Work-Study, and institutionally sponsored loans available. Support available to part-time students. Financial award application deadline: 2/1. *Unit head:* Dr. Leslie D. Burns, Chair, 541-737-0983, Fax: 541-737-0993, E-mail: leslie.burns@oregonstate.edu. *Application contact:* Dr. Elaine Pedersen, Chair, Graduate Committee, 541-737-0984, Fax: 541-737-0993, E-mail: pedersee@oregonstate.edu.

Philadelphia University, School of Engineering and Textiles, Program in Fashion Apparel Studies, Philadelphia, PA 19144. Offers MS. Part-time programs available. *Entrance requirements:* For master's, GRE or GMAT, minimum GPA of 2.8. Additional exam requirements/recommendations for international students: Required—TOEFL (minimum score 550 paper-based; 213 computer-based; 79 iBT). Electronic applications accepted.

Purdue University, Graduate School, College of Consumer and Family Sciences, Department of Consumer Sciences and Retailing, West Lafayette, IN 47907. Offers consumer behavior (MS, PhD); family and consumer economics (MS, PhD); retail management (MS, PhD); textile science (MS, PhD). Part-time programs available. *Degree requirements:* For master's, thesis; for doctorate, thesis/dissertation. *Entrance requirements:* For master's and doctorate, GMAT or GRE General Test. Additional exam requirements/recommendations for international students: Required—TOEFL. Electronic applications accepted. *Faculty research:* Family financial resources, retail management and patronage, chemical analysis of textile dyes and finishes.

South Dakota State University, Graduate School, College of Education and Human Sciences, Department of Apparel Merchandising and Interior Design, Brookings, SD 57007. Offers MFCS. Part-time and evening/weekend programs available. Postbaccalaureate distance learning degree programs offered. *Entrance requirements:* Additional exam requirements/recommendations for international students: Required—TOEFL (minimum score 550 paper-based; 213 computer-based; 79 iBT). *Faculty research:* Rural internet shopping, professional development in apparel merchandising, gender, aesthetics.

The University of Akron, Graduate School, College of Health Sciences and Human Services, School of Health and Human Services, Program in Clothing, Textiles and Interiors, Akron, OH 44325. Offers MA. *Students:* 5 full-time (4 women), 1 (woman) part-time; includes 1 minority (African American). Average age 34. 6 applicants, 67% accepted, 1 enrolled. In 2009, 2 master's awarded. *Degree requirements:* For master's, comprehensive exam, thesis or project. *Entrance requirements:* For master's, GRE, minimum GPA of 2.75, letters of recommendation, resume. Additional exam requirements/recommendations for international students: Required—TOEFL (minimum score 550 paper-based; 213 computer-based; 79 iBT). *Application deadline:* For fall admission, 3/1 for domestic and international students; for spring admission, 10/1 for domestic and international students. Application fee: $30 ($40 for international students). Electronic applications accepted. *Expenses:* Tuition, state resident: full-time $6570; part-time $365 per credit hour. Tuition, nonresident: full-time $11,250; part-time $625 per credit hour. *Unit head:* Dr. Sandra Buckland, Associate Professor, 330-972-8090, E-mail: skb@uakron.edu. *Application contact:* Dr. Sandra Buckland, Associate Professor, 330-972-8090, E-mail: skb@uakron.edu.

The University of Alabama, Graduate School, College of Human Environmental Sciences, Department of Clothing, Textiles, and Interior Design, Tuscaloosa, AL 35487. Offers MSHES. *Faculty:* 5 full-time (all women). *Students:* 1 (woman) full-time. Average age 55. *Degree requirements:* For master's, comprehensive exam, thesis optional. *Entrance requirements:* For master's, GRE General Test or MAT, minimum GPA of 3.0. *Application deadline:* For fall admission, 7/6 for domestic students. Applications are processed on a rolling basis. Application fee: $50 ($60 for international students). *Expenses:* Tuition, state resident: full-time $7000. Tuition, nonresident: full-time $19,200. *Financial support:* In 2009–10, 1 research assistantship with full tuition reimbursement (averaging $8,100 per year), 2 teaching assistantships with full tuition reimbursements (averaging $8,100 per year) were awarded; fellowships, career-related internships or fieldwork, Federal Work-Study, and scholarships/grants also available. Financial award application deadline: 3/15. *Faculty research:* Archeological textiles, textile science, material culture, social psychology, international trade. *Unit head:* Dr. Carolyn Callis, Chair and Associate Professor, 205-348-6176, Fax: 205-348-0022, E-mail: ccallis@ches.ua.edu. *Application contact:* Dr. Carolyn Callis, Chair and Associate Professor, 205-348-6176, Fax: 205-348-0022, E-mail: ccallis@ches.ua.edu.

University of Alberta, Faculty of Graduate Studies and Research, Department of Human Ecology, Edmonton, AB T6G 2E1, Canada. Offers family ecology and practice (M Sc, PhD); textiles and clothing (M Sc, MA, PhD). Postbaccalaureate distance learning degree programs offered (no on-campus study). *Faculty:* 11 full-time (all women), 2 part-time/adjunct (both women). *Students:* 40 full-time (37 women), 15 part-time (all women). Average age 24. 25 applicants, 32% accepted. In 2009, 14 master's, 1 doctorate awarded. *Degree requirements:* For master's, thesis (for some programs); for doctorate, comprehensive exam, thesis/dissertation. *Entrance requirements:* For master's and doctorate, minimum GPA of 7.0 on a 9.0 scale. Additional exam requirements/recommendations for international students: Required—TOEFL (minimum score 580 paper-based; 237 computer-based). *Application deadline:* For fall admission, 2/1 for domestic students; for winter admission, 9/1 for domestic students. Application fee: $0. Tuition and fees charges are reported in Canadian dollars. *Expenses:* Tuition, area resident: Full-time $4626 Canadian dollars; part-time $99.72 Canadian dollars per unit. International tuition: $8216 Canadian dollars full-time. Required fees: $3590 Canadian dollars; $99.72 Canadian dollars per unit. $215 Canadian dollars per term. *Financial support:* In 2009–10, 3 research assistantships, 4 teaching assistantships were awarded; career-related internships or fieldwork, scholarships/grants, and tuition waivers also available. *Faculty research:* Families and aging, family and child poverty, paid and unpaid work of families, textiles and clothing, parent-child relationships. Total annual research expenditures: $1 million. *Unit head:* Dr. L. Capjack, Chair, 780-492-5230, Fax: 780-492-4821. *Application contact:* Linda Mirans, Administrative Assistant, 780-492-5230, Fax: 780-492-4821, E-mail: hec.grad@ualberta.ca.

University of California, Davis, Graduate Studies, Graduate Group in Textiles, Davis, CA 95616. Offers MS. *Degree requirements:* For master's, comprehensive exam (for some programs), thesis (for some programs). *Entrance requirements:* For master's, GRE General Test, minimum GPA of 3.0. Additional exam requirements/recommendations for international students: Required—TOEFL (minimum score 550 paper-based; 213 computer-based). Electronic applications accepted. *Faculty research:* Fiber science, social psychology, consumer psychology, chemical and physical properties of fibrous and polymeric materials.

University of Delaware, College of Arts and Sciences, Department of Fashion and Apparel Studies, Newark, DE 19716. Offers MS.

University of Georgia, Graduate School, College of Family and Consumer Sciences, Department of Textiles, Merchandising, and Interiors, Athens, GA 30602. Offers historic costume and textiles (MS); merchandising/international trade (MS); textile analysis (PhD); textile chemical processes (PhD); textile products and standards (PhD); textile science (MS). *Faculty:* 13 full-time (9 women). *Students:* 18 full-time (15 women), 6 part-time (all women); includes 3

Clothing and Textiles

University of Georgia (continued)
minority (2 African Americans, 1 Hispanic American), 6 international. 20 applicants, 50% accepted, 9 enrolled. In 2009, 5 master's awarded. *Degree requirements:* For master's, thesis; for doctorate, thesis/dissertation. *Entrance requirements:* For master's and doctorate, GRE General Test. *Application deadline:* For fall admission, 7/1 priority date for domestic students; for spring admission, 11/15 for domestic students. Application fee: $50. Electronic applications accepted. *Expenses:* Tuition, state resident: full-time $6000; part-time $250 per credit hour. Tuition, nonresident: full-time $20,904; part-time $871 per credit hour. Required fees: $730 per semester. *Financial support:* Fellowships, research assistantships, teaching assistantships, unspecified assistantships available. *Unit head:* Dr. Patricia K. Hunt-Hurst, Department Head, 706-542-4888, Fax: 706-542-0410, E-mail: phunt@fcs.uga.edu. *Application contact:* Dr. Patricia K. Hunt-Hurst, Department Head, 706-542-4888, Fax: 706-542-0410, E-mail: phunt@fcs.uga.edu.

University of Kentucky, Graduate School, College of Design, Program in Interior Design, Merchandising, and Textiles, Lexington, KY 40506-0032. Offers MAIDM, MSIDM. *Degree requirements:* For master's, comprehensive exam, thesis optional. *Entrance requirements:* For master's, GRE General Test, minimum undergraduate GPA of 2.75. Additional exam requirements/recommendations for international students: Required—TOEFL (minimum score 550 paper-based; 213 computer-based). Electronic applications accepted. *Faculty research:* Interior design, apparel merchandising, textile evaluation, creativity in design, social-psychological aspects of dress and interiors.

University of Manitoba, Faculty of Graduate Studies, Faculty of Human Ecology, Department of Textile Sciences, Winnipeg, MB R3T 2N2, Canada. Offers M Sc. *Degree requirements:* For master's, thesis.

University of Minnesota, Twin Cities Campus, Graduate School, College of Design, Department of Design, Housing, and Apparel, Minneapolis, MN 55455-0213. Offers apparel (MA, MS, PhD); design communication (MA, MS, PhD); housing studies (MA, MS, PhD, Postbaccalaureate Certificate); interactive design (MFA); interior design (MA, MS, PhD). Part-time programs available. *Degree requirements:* For master's and Postbaccalaureate Certificate, comprehensive exam, thesis (for some programs); for doctorate, comprehensive exam, thesis/dissertation. *Entrance requirements:* For master's, GRE General Test, minimum GPA of 3.0 (preferred), portfolio, 3 letters of recommendation; for doctorate, GRE General Test, minimum GPA of 3.0 (preferred), portfolio, 3 letters of recommendation, writing sample; for Post-baccalaureate Certificate, GRE General Test, minimum GPA of 3.0 (preferred). Additional exam requirements/recommendations for international students: Required—TOEFL (minimum score 550 paper-based; 213 computer-based; 79 iBT). Electronic applications accepted. *Faculty research:* Housing policy and community development; consumer behavior; interactive design; design history; social, cultural, and behavioral issues related to designed environments.

University of Missouri, Graduate School, College of Human Environmental Science, Department of Textile and Apparel Management, Columbia, MO 65211. Offers MA, MS. *Entrance requirements:* For master's, GRE General Test, minimum GPA of 3.0. Additional exam requirements/recommendations for international students: Required—TOEFL (minimum score 550 paper-based; 213 computer-based; 79 iBT).

University of Nebraska–Lincoln, Graduate College, College of Education and Human Sciences, Department of Textiles, Clothing and Design, Lincoln, NE 68588. Offers human sciences (PhD), including textiles, clothing and design (MS, PhD); merchandising (MS); textile history/quilt studies (MA); textile science (MS); textile-apparel (MA); textiles, clothing and design (MA, MS), including textiles, clothing and design (MS, PhD). Part-time programs available. Postbaccalaureate distance learning degree programs offered (minimal on-campus study). *Degree requirements:* For master's, thesis optional. *Entrance requirements:* For master's, GRE General Test. Additional exam requirements/recommendations for international students: Required—TOEFL (minimum score 550 paper-based; 213 computer-based). Electronic applications accepted. *Faculty research:* Merchandising, textile science, fiber arts, textile history, quilt studies.

University of North Texas, Robert B. Toulouse School of Graduate Studies, School of Merchandising and Hospitality Management, Denton, TX 76203. Offers hospitality management (MS); merchandising (MS). Part-time programs available. Postbaccalaureate distance learning degree programs offered (no on-campus study). *Degree requirements:* For master's, comprehensive exam, thesis or alternative. *Entrance requirements:* For master's, GRE General Test or GMAT, minimum GPA of 2.8, course work in major area, 3 references, resume. Additional exam requirements/recommendations for international students: Required—proof of English language proficiency required for non-native English speakers; Recommended—TOEFL (minimum score 550 paper-based; 213 computer-based; 79 iBT). *Application deadline:* Applications are processed on a rolling basis. Application fee: $50 ($75 for international students). Electronic applications accepted. *Expenses:* Tuition, state resident: full-time $4298; part-time $239 per contact hour. Tuition, nonresident: full-time $9878; part-time $549 per contact hour. Required fees: $265 per contact hour. *Financial support:* Fellowships, research assistantships, teaching assistantships, career-related internships or fieldwork, Federal Work-Study, and institutionally sponsored loans available. Financial award application deadline: 4/1; financial award applicants required to submit FAFSA. *Faculty research:* Management, hospitality, merchandising, globalization, consumer behavior and experiences. *Application contact:* Coordinator, 940-565-4757, Fax: 940-565-4348, E-mail: kennon@smhm.unt.edu.

University of Rhode Island, Graduate School, College of Human Science and Services, Department of Textiles, Fashion Merchandising and Design, Kingston, RI 02881. Offers MS. Part-time programs available. *Faculty:* 8 full-time (7 women). *Students:* 6 full-time (all women), 8 part-time (all women), 1 international. In 2009, 7 master's awarded. *Degree requirements:* For master's, comprehensive exam (for some programs), thesis optional. *Entrance requirements:* For master's, GRE, 2 letters of recommendation. Additional exam requirements/recommendations for international students: Required—TOEFL (minimum score 550 paper-based; 213 computer-based). *Application deadline:* For fall admission, 7/15 for domestic students, 2/1 for international students; for spring admission, 11/15 for domestic students, 7/15 for international students. Application fee: $65. Electronic applications accepted. *Expenses:* Tuition, state resident: full-time $8828; part-time $490 per credit hour. Tuition, nonresident: full-time $22,100; part-time $1228 per credit hour. Required fees: $1118; $57 per semester. Tuition and fees vary according to program. *Financial support:* In 2009–10, 2 teaching assistantships with partial tuition reimbursements (averaging $6,947 per year) were awarded. Financial award application deadline: 7/15; financial award applicants required to submit FAFSA. Total annual research expenditures: $14,355. *Unit head:* Dr. Linda Welters, Chair, 401-874-4525, Fax: 401-874-2581, E-mail: lwelters@uri.edu. *Application contact:* Dr. Linda Welters, Chair, 401-874-4525, Fax: 401-874-2581, E-mail: lwelters@uri.edu.

The University of Tennessee, Graduate School, College of Education, Health and Human Sciences, Department of Consumer and Industry Services Management, Program in Consumer Services Management, Knoxville, TN 37996. Offers retail and consumer sciences (MS); textile science (MS). Part-time programs available. *Degree requirements:* For master's, thesis or alternative. *Entrance requirements:* For master's, GRE General Test, minimum GPA of 2.7. Additional exam requirements/recommendations for international students: Required—TOEFL. Electronic applications accepted. *Expenses:* Tuition, state resident: full-time $6826; part-time $380 per semester hour. Tuition, nonresident: full-time $21,844; part-time $1147 per semester hour. Tuition and fees vary according to program.

The University of Tennessee, Graduate School, College of Education, Health and Human Sciences, Program in Human Ecology, Knoxville, TN 37996. Offers child and family studies (PhD); community health (PhD); nutrition science (PhD); retailing and consumer sciences (PhD); textile science (PhD). *Degree requirements:* For doctorate, thesis/dissertation. *Entrance requirements:* For doctorate, GRE General Test, minimum GPA of 2.7. Additional exam requirements/recommendations for international students: Required—TOEFL. Electronic applications accepted. *Expenses:* Tuition, state resident: full-time $6826; part-time $380 per semester hour. Tuition, nonresident: full-time $21,844; part-time $1147 per semester hour. Tuition and fees vary according to program.

Virginia Polytechnic Institute and State University, Graduate School, College of Liberal Arts and Human Sciences, Department of Apparel, Housing, and Resource Management, Blacksburg, VA 24061. Offers apparel business and economics (MS, PhD); apparel product design and analysis (MS, PhD); apparel quality analysis (MS, PhD); consumer studies (MS, PhD); family financial management (MS, PhD); household equipment (MS, PhD); housing (MS, PhD); interior design (MS, PhD); resource management (MS, PhD). *Faculty:* 14 full-time (all women). *Students:* 10 full-time (9 women), 5 part-time (all women); includes 9 minority (1 African American, 6 American Indian/Alaska Native, 1 Asian American or Pacific Islander, 1 Hispanic American). Average age 34. 6 applicants. In 2009, 3 master's, 5 doctorates awarded. *Entrance requirements:* For master's and doctorate, GRE, GMAT. Additional exam requirements/recommendations for international students: Required—TOEFL (minimum score 550 paper-based; 213 computer-based). *Application deadline:* For fall admission, 5/15 for international students; for spring admission, 10/15 for international students. Applications are processed on a rolling basis. Application fee: $65. Electronic applications accepted. *Expenses:* Tuition, area resident: Full-time $10,228; part-time $459 per credit hour. Tuition, nonresident: full-time $17,892; part-time $865 per credit hour. Required fees: $1966; $451 per semester. *Financial support:* In 2009–10, 6 teaching assistantships with full tuition reimbursements (averaging $13,546 per year) were awarded; career-related internships or fieldwork, Federal Work-Study, scholarships/grants, and unspecified assistantships also available. Financial award application deadline: 1/15. *Faculty research:* Housing for elderly, affordable housing, household time use, phosphate laundry study, economic well-living. Total annual research expenditures: $27,151. *Unit head:* Dr. LuAnn R. Gaskill, Dean, 540-231-4781, Fax: 540-231-3250, E-mail: lagaskil@vt.edu. *Application contact:* Julia Beemish, Information Contact, 540-231-8881, Fax: 540-231-3250, E-mail: jbeamish@vt.edu.

Washington State University, Graduate School, College of Agricultural, Human, and Natural Resource Sciences, Department of Apparel, Merchandising, Design, and Textiles, Pullman, WA 99164. Offers apparel, merchandising, design and textiles (MA); interdisciplinary (PhD); interior design (MA). Part-time programs available. *Faculty:* 8. *Students:* 6 full-time (all women), 4 part-time (all women); includes 1 minority (Asian American or Pacific Islander), 2 international. Average age 33. 10 applicants, 20% accepted, 1 enrolled. In 2009, 3 master's awarded. *Degree requirements:* For master's, comprehensive exam (for some programs), thesis, oral exam; for doctorate, comprehensive exam, thesis/dissertation. *Entrance requirements:* For master's, GRE, minimum GPA of 3.0, 3 writing samples, 3 letters of recommendation, portfolio. Additional exam requirements/recommendations for international students: Required—TOEFL, IELTS. *Application deadline:* For fall admission, 1/11 priority date for domestic students, 1/10 for international students; for spring admission, 7/1 for domestic and international students. Applications are processed on a rolling basis. Application fee: $50. Electronic applications accepted. *Financial support:* In 2009–10, research assistantships with full and partial tuition reimbursements (averaging $14,634 per year), 5 teaching assistantships with full and partial tuition reimbursements (averaging $13,383 per year) were awarded; career-related internships or fieldwork, Federal Work-Study, institutionally sponsored loans, and scholarships/grants also available. Financial award application deadline: 2/15; financial award applicants required to submit FAFSA. *Faculty research:* Product development, design theory, cultural diversity, computer design accessibility. *Unit head:* Dr. Karen K. Leonas, Department Chair, 509-335-1233, Fax: 509-355-7299, E-mail: kleonas@wsu.edu. *Application contact:* Graduate School Admissions, 800-GRADWSU, Fax: 509-335-1949, E-mail: gradsch@wsu.edu.

Consumer Economics

California State University, Long Beach, Graduate Studies, College of Health and Human Services, Department of Family and Consumer Sciences, Long Beach, CA 90840. Offers family and consumer sciences (MA); nutritional science (MS), including food science, hospitality foodservice and hotel management, nutritional science. Part-time and evening/weekend programs available. *Faculty:* 5 full-time (all women). *Students:* 43 full-time (39 women), 56 part-time (54 women); includes 40 minority (4 African Americans, 22 Asian Americans or Pacific Islanders, 14 Hispanic Americans), 7 international. Average age 29. 6 applicants, 17% accepted, 1 enrolled. *Degree requirements:* For master's, comprehensive exam or thesis. *Entrance requirements:* For master's, GRE (MS), minimum GPA of 3.0. *Application deadline:* For fall admission, 5/1 for domestic students. Applications are processed on a rolling basis. Application fee: $55. Electronic applications accepted. *Expenses:* Required fees: $1802 per semester. Part-time tuition and fees vary according to course load. *Financial support:* Federal Work-Study, institutionally sponsored loans, and scholarships/grants available. Financial award application deadline: 3/2. *Faculty research:* School uniforms, consumer complaining behavior, nutrition and fitness education and behavior change, curriculum change, teaching experience of interns. *Unit head:* Dr. Wendy Reiboldt, Chair, 562-985-8250, Fax: 562-985-4414, E-mail: reiboldt@csulb.edu. *Application contact:* Dr. Jacqueline Lee, Graduate Coordinator, 562-985-4545, Fax: 562-985-4414, E-mail: jjlee@csulb.edu.

Colorado State University, Graduate School, College of Applied Human Sciences, Department of Design and Merchandising, Fort Collins, CA 80523-1574. Offers MS. Part-time programs available. Postbaccalaureate distance learning degree programs offered (no on-campus study). *Faculty:* 13 full-time (10 women). *Students:* 17 full-time (all women), 20 part-time (all women); includes 7 minority (1 African American, 2 American Indian/Alaska Native, 2 Asian Americans or Pacific Islanders, 2 Hispanic Americans), 3 international. Average age 31. 36 applicants, 78% accepted, 20 enrolled. In 2009, 7 master's awarded. *Degree requirements:* For master's, thesis (for some programs). *Entrance requirements:* For master's, GRE General Test, minimum GPA of 3.0, resume, portfolio (if applicable to area of study), letters of recommendation. Additional exam requirements/recommendations for international students: Required—TOEFL (minimum score 550 paper-based; 213 computer-based; 80 iBT). *Application deadline:* For fall admission, 4/1 priority date for domestic and international students; for spring admission, 11/1 priority date for domestic and international students. Applications are processed on a rolling basis. Application fee: $50. Electronic applications accepted. *Expenses:* Tuition, state resident: full-time $6434; part-time $359.10 per credit. Tuition, nonresident: full-time $18,116; part-time $1006.45 per credit. Required fees: $1496; $83 per credit. *Financial support:* In 2009–10, 10 students received support, including 10 teaching assistantships with full and partial tuition reimbursements available (averaging $6,245 per year); fellowships, research assistantships with partial tuition reimbursements available, career-related internships or fieldwork, Federal

Work-Study, institutionally sponsored loans, scholarships/grants, traineeships, and unspecified assistantships also available. Support available to part-time students. Financial award application deadline: 3/1; financial award applicants required to submit FAFSA. *Faculty research:* Consumer and textile end use, apparel design, consumer behavior, interior design, historic costume and textiles. Total annual research expenditures: $219,367. *Unit head:* Dr. Mary A. Littrell, Head, 970-491-7890, Fax: 970-491-4855, E-mail: mary.littrell@colostate.edu. *Application contact:* Dr. Jen Ogle, Graduate Coordinator, 970-491-3794, Fax: 970-491-4855, E-mail: jennifer.ogle@colostate.edu.

Cornell University, Graduate School, Graduate Fields of Human Ecology, Field of Policy Analysis and Management, Ithaca, NY 14853-0001. Offers consumer policy (PhD); evaluation (PhD); family and social welfare policy (PhD); health administration (MHA); health management and policy (PhD). *Faculty:* 40 full-time (17 women). *Students:* 51 full-time (27 women); includes 13 minority (4 African Americans, 8 Asian Americans or Pacific Islanders, 1 Hispanic American), 7 international. Average age 26. 130 applicants, 38% accepted, 31 enrolled. In 2009, 25 master's, 5 doctorates awarded. *Degree requirements:* For master's, thesis; for doctorate, thesis/dissertation. *Entrance requirements:* For master's, GRE General Test or GMAT, 2 letters of recommendation; for doctorate, GRE General Test, 2 letters of recommendation. Additional exam requirements/recommendations for international students: Required—TOEFL (minimum score 550 paper-based; 213 computer-based; 77 iBT). *Application deadline:* For fall admission, 1/15 for domestic students. Application fee: $70. Electronic applications accepted. *Expenses:* Tuition: Full-time $29,500. Required fees: $70. Full-time tuition and fees vary according to degree level, program and student level. *Financial support:* In 2009–10, 17 students received support, including 1 fellowship with full and partial tuition reimbursement available, 8 teaching assistantships with full and partial tuition reimbursements available; research assistantships with full and partial tuition reimbursements available, institutionally sponsored loans, scholarships/grants, health care benefits, tuition waivers (full and partial), and unspecified assistantships also available. Financial award applicants required to submit FAFSA. *Faculty research:* Health policy, family policy, social welfare policy, program evaluation, consumer policy. *Unit head:* Director of Graduate Studies, 607-255-7772. *Application contact:* Graduate Field Assistant, 607-255-7772, Fax: 607-255-4071, E-mail: pam_phd@cornell.edu.

Eastern Illinois University, Graduate School, Lumpkin College of Business and Applied Sciences, School of Family and Consumer Sciences, Charleston, IL 61920-3099. Offers dietetics (MS); family and consumer sciences (MS). Part-time programs available. *Faculty:* 12 full-time (10 women). *Students:* 34 full-time (33 women), 29 part-time (all women). In 2009, 40 master's awarded. *Degree requirements:* For master's, comprehensive exam. *Application deadline:* For fall admission, 3/31 priority date for domestic students. Applications are processed on a rolling basis. Application fee: $30. *Expenses:* Tuition, state resident: full-time $9434; part-time $239 per credit hour. Tuition, nonresident: full-time $23,774; part-time $717 per credit hour. Required fees: $802.63. *Financial support:* In 2009–10, 2 research assistantships with tuition reimbursements (averaging $8,100 per year), 6 teaching assistantships with tuition reimbursements (averaging $8,100 per year) were awarded; career-related internships or fieldwork also available. *Unit head:* Dr. James Painter, Chairperson, 217-581-6076, Fax: 217-581-6090, E-mail: jepainter@eiu.edu. *Application contact:* Dr. Lisa Taylor, Coordinator, 217-581-8584, Fax: 217-581-6090, E-mail: lmtaylor@eiu.edu.

Indiana State University, School of Graduate Studies, College of Arts and Sciences, Department of Family and Consumer Sciences, Terre Haute, IN 47809. Offers dietetics (MS); family and consumer sciences education (MS); inter-area option (MS). *Accreditation:* ADtA. Part-time programs available. *Degree requirements:* For master's, thesis optional. Electronic applications accepted.

Iowa State University of Science and Technology, Graduate College, College of Human Sciences, Department of Apparel, Education Studies, and Hospitality Management, Program in Family and Consumer Sciences Education and Studies, Ames, IA 50011. Offers M Ed, MS, PhD. *Students:* 20 part-time (18 women); includes 3 minority (all African Americans), 3 international. In 2009, 3 master's, 7 doctorates awarded. *Degree requirements:* For master's, thesis (for some programs); for doctorate, thesis/dissertation. *Entrance requirements:* For master's and doctorate, GRE General Test. Additional exam requirements/recommendations for international students: Required—TOEFL (minimum score 550 paper-based; 213 computer-based; 80 iBT) or IELTS (minimum score 6.5). Application fee: $40 ($90 for international students). *Expenses:* Tuition, state resident: full-time $6716. Tuition, nonresident: full-time $8908. Tuition and fees vary according to course level, course load, program and student level. *Financial support:* Research assistantships with full and partial tuition reimbursements, teaching assistantships with full and partial tuition reimbursements, scholarships/grants available. *Unit head:* Dr. Robert Bosselman, Director of Graduate Education, 515-294-7474. *Application contact:* Dr. Robert Bosselman, Director of Graduate Education, 515-294-7474.

Kansas State University, Graduate School, College of Human Ecology, Program in Human Ecology, Manhattan, KS 66506. Offers apparel and textiles (PhD); family life education and consultation (PhD); food service and hospitality management (PhD); lifespan and human development (PhD); marriage and family therapy (PhD); personal financial planning (PhD). *Faculty:* 3 full-time (all women). *Students:* 29 full-time (19 women), 43 part-time (23 women); includes 15 minority (13 African Americans, 1 American Indian/Alaska Native, 1 Asian American or Pacific Islander), 16 international. Average age 37. 29 applicants, 66% accepted, 16 enrolled. In 2009, 10 doctorates awarded. *Degree requirements:* For doctorate, thesis/dissertation. *Application deadline:* For fall admission, 2/1 priority date for domestic and international students; for spring admission, 8/1 priority date for domestic and international students. Applications are processed on a rolling basis. Application fee: $40 ($55 for international students). Electronic applications accepted. *Financial support:* Application deadline: 3/1. *Application contact:* Connie Fechter, Application Contact, 785-532-1473, Fax: 785-532-3796, E-mail: fechter@ksu.edu.

Montana State University, College of Graduate Studies, College of Education, Health, and Human Development, Department of Health and Human Development, Bozeman, MT 59717. Offers health and human development (MS), including counseling, exercise and nutrition sciences, family and consumer sciences, family financial planning, health promotion and education. *Accreditation:* ACA. Part-time programs available. Postbaccalaureate distance learning degree programs offered (no on-campus study). *Faculty:* 27 full-time (18 women), 7 part-time/adjunct (6 women). *Students:* 54 full-time (47 women), 18 part-time (15 women); includes 1 minority (Hispanic American). Average age 30. 32 applicants, 34% accepted, 10 enrolled. In 2009, 26 master's awarded. *Degree requirements:* For master's, comprehensive exam. *Entrance requirements:* For master's, GRE General Test. Additional exam requirements/recommendations for international students: Required—TOEFL (minimum score 550 paper-based; 213 computer-based). *Application deadline:* For fall admission, 7/15 priority date for domestic students, 5/15 priority date for international students; for spring admission, 12/1 priority date for domestic students, 10/1 priority date for international students. Applications are processed on a rolling basis. Application fee: $30. Electronic applications accepted. *Expenses:* Tuition, state resident: full-time $5635; part-time $3492 per year. Tuition, nonresident: full-time $17,212; part-time $7865.10 per year. Required fees: $1441; $153.15 per credit. Tuition and fees vary according to course load and program. *Financial support:* In 2009–10, 24 students received support, including 7 research assistantships (averaging $1,000 per year), 17 teaching assistantships with full tuition reimbursements available (averaging $8,000 per year). Financial award application deadline: 3/1; financial award applicants required to submit FAFSA. *Faculty research:* Gait analysis, cancer prevention, obesity prevention, energy expenditure, decision making. Total annual research expenditures: $2.8 million. *Unit head:* Dr. Tim Dunnagan, Head, 404-994-3242, Fax: 404-994-2013, E-mail: dunnagan@montana.edu. *Application contact:* Dr. Carl Fox.

North Dakota State University, College of Graduate and Interdisciplinary Studies, College of Human Development and Education, Department of Child Development and Family Science, Fargo, ND 58108. Offers child development and family science (MS); couple and family therapy (MS); family financial planning (MS); gerontology (MS, PhD). *Accreditation:* AAMFT/COAMFTE. Part-time and evening/weekend programs available. Postbaccalaureate distance learning degree programs offered (no on-campus study). *Faculty:* 12 full-time (7 women). *Students:* 26 full-time (25 women), 21 part-time (18 women); includes 1 African American, 2 international. 22 applicants, 64% accepted, 12 enrolled. In 2009, 12 master's awarded. *Degree requirements:* For master's, thesis or alternative; for doctorate, thesis/dissertation. *Entrance requirements:* Additional exam requirements/recommendations for international students: Required—TOEFL (minimum score 525 paper-based; 197 computer-based; 71 iBT). *Application deadline:* For fall admission, 2/1 for domestic and international students; for spring admission, 10/1 for domestic and international students. Application fee: $45 ($60 for international students). *Financial support:* In 2009–10, 17 students received support, including research assistantships with full tuition reimbursements available (averaging $3,000 per year), 17 teaching assistantships with full tuition reimbursements available (averaging $3,000 per year); career-related internships or fieldwork, Federal Work-Study, institutionally sponsored loans, and tuition waivers (full) also available. Financial award application deadline: 4/1. *Faculty research:* Family therapy, resilience, parenting, adolescent development, mental health. Total annual research expenditures: $333,582. *Unit head:* Dr. James Deal, Head, 701-231-7568, Fax: 701-231-9645, E-mail: jim_deal@ndsu.edu. *Application contact:* Theresa Anderson, Administrative Assistant, 701-231-8628, Fax: 701-231-9645, E-mail: theresa.anderson@ndsu.edu.

The Ohio State University, Graduate School, College of Education and Human Ecology, Program in Family Resource Management, Columbus, OH 43210. Offers MS, PhD. *Faculty:* 10. *Students:* 7 full-time (5 women), 4 part-time (3 women); includes 1 minority (Asian American or Pacific Islander), 7 international. Average age 28. In 2009, 5 doctorates awarded. *Degree requirements:* For master's, thesis optional; for doctorate, thesis/dissertation. *Entrance requirements:* For master's and doctorate, GRE General Test. Additional exam requirements/recommendations for international students: Required—TOEFL (minimum score 577 paper-based; 233 computer-based). *Application deadline:* For fall admission, 8/15 priority date for domestic students, 7/1 priority date for international students; for winter admission, 12/1 priority date for domestic students, 11/1 priority date for international students; for spring admission, 3/1 priority date for domestic students, 2/1 priority date for international students. Applications are processed on a rolling basis. Application fee: $40 ($50 for international students). Electronic applications accepted. *Expenses:* Tuition, state resident: full-time $10,683. Tuition, nonresident: full-time $25,923. Tuition and fees vary according to course load and program. *Financial support:* Fellowships, research assistantships, teaching assistantships, Federal Work-Study and institutionally sponsored loans available. Support available to part-time students. *Unit head:* Catherine P. Montalto, Graduate Studies Committee Chair, 614-292-4571, Fax: 614-292-2581, E-mail: montalto.2@osu.edu. *Application contact:* 614-292-9444, Fax: 614-292-3895, E-mail: domestic.grad@osu.edu.

Oklahoma State University, College of Human Environmental Sciences, Dean of Human Environmental Sciences—MS in Family Financial Planning Program and PhD in HES, Stillwater, OK 74078. Offers human environmental sciences (MS, PhD), including family financial planning (MS). Part-time programs available. Postbaccalaureate distance learning degree programs offered. *Faculty:* 1 full-time (0 women). *Students:* 2 full-time (both women), 21 part-time (13 women); includes 2 minority (both African Americans), 1 international. Average age 37. 67 applicants, 48% accepted, 18 enrolled. In 2009, 1 master's awarded. *Degree requirements:* For master's, thesis or alternative, creative component; for doctorate, comprehensive exam, thesis/dissertation. *Entrance requirements:* For master's and doctorate, GRE or GMAT. Additional exam requirements/recommendations for international students: Required—TOEFL (minimum score 550 paper-based; 79 iBT). *Application deadline:* For fall admission, 3/1 priority date for international students; for spring admission, 8/1 priority date for international students. Applications are processed on a rolling basis. Application fee: $40 ($75 for international students). Electronic applications accepted. *Expenses:* Tuition, state resident: full-time $3716; part-time $154.85 per credit hour. Tuition, nonresident: full-time $14,448; part-time $602 per credit hour. Required fees: $1772; $73.85 per credit hour. One-time fee: $50. Tuition and fees vary according to course load and campus/location. *Financial support:* Career-related internships or fieldwork, Federal Work-Study, scholarships/grants, health care benefits, tuition waivers (partial), and unspecified assistantships available. Support available to part-time students. Financial award application deadline: 3/1; financial award applicants required to submit FAFSA. *Unit head:* Dr. Stephan Wilson, Dean, 405-744-5053, Fax: 405-744-7113. *Application contact:* Dr. Gordon Emslie, Dean, 405-744-6368, Fax: 405-744-0355, E-mail: grad-i@okstate.edu.

Purdue University, Graduate School, College of Consumer and Family Sciences, Department of Consumer Sciences and Retailing, West Lafayette, IN 47907. Offers consumer behavior (MS, PhD); family and consumer economics (MS, PhD); retail management (MS, PhD); textile science (MS, PhD). Part-time programs available. *Degree requirements:* For master's, thesis; for doctorate, thesis/dissertation. *Entrance requirements:* For master's and doctorate, GMAT or GRE General Test. Additional exam requirements/recommendations for international students: Required—TOEFL. Electronic applications accepted. *Faculty research:* Family financial resources, retail management and patronage, chemical analysis of textile dyes and finishes.

State University of New York at Oswego, Graduate Studies, School of Education, Department of Vocational Teacher Preparation, Oswego, NY 13126. Offers agriculture (MS Ed); business and marketing (MS Ed); family and consumer sciences (MS Ed); health careers (MS Ed); technical education (MS Ed); trade education (MS Ed). *Accreditation:* NCATE. Part-time and evening/weekend programs available. *Degree requirements:* For master's, thesis or alternative. *Entrance requirements:* Additional exam requirements/recommendations for international students: Required—TOEFL (minimum score 560 paper-based; 220 computer-based).

Texas Tech University, Graduate School, College of Human Sciences, Department of Applied and Professional Studies, Division of Personal Financial Planning, Lubbock, TX 79409. Offers MS, PhD, JD/MS, MS/MBA, MS/MS. Part-time programs available. *Students:* 75 full-time (21 women), 18 part-time (7 women); includes 19 minority (6 African Americans, 13 Hispanic Americans), 13 international. Average age 29. 89 applicants, 78% accepted, 22 enrolled. In 2009, 26 master's, 2 doctorates awarded. *Degree requirements:* For master's, thesis or alternative; for doctorate, thesis/dissertation. *Entrance requirements:* For doctorate, GRE General Test, GMAT. Additional exam requirements/recommendations for international students: Required—TOEFL (minimum score 550 paper-based; 213 computer-based). *Application deadline:* For fall admission, 3/1 priority date for international students; for spring admission, 11/1 priority date for international students. Applications are processed on a rolling basis. Application fee: $50 ($75 for international students). *Expenses:* Tuition, state resident: full-time $5100; part-time $213 per credit hour. Tuition, nonresident: full-time $11,748; part-time $490 per credit hour. Required fees: $2298; $50 per credit hour. $555 per semester. *Financial support:* Research assistantships, teaching assistantships, career-related internships or fieldwork, Federal Work-Study, and institutionally sponsored loans available. Support available to part-time students. Financial award application deadline: 4/15; financial award applicants required to submit FAFSA. *Faculty research:* Financial risk tolerance, determinants of success on CFP exam, financial literacy, retirement planning. *Unit head:* Dr. Vickie Hampton, Director, 806-742-5050 Ext. 272, Fax: 806-742-5033, E-mail: vickie.hampton@ttu.edu. *Application contact:* Dr. Vickie Hampton, Director, 806-742-5050 Ext. 272, Fax: 806-742-5033, E-mail: vickie.hampton@ttu.edu.

Université Laval, Faculty of Agricultural and Food Sciences, Department of Agricultural Economics and Consumer Sciences, Program in Consumer Sciences, Québec, QC G1K 7P4, Canada. Offers Diploma. Part-time programs available. *Entrance requirements:* For degree, knowledge of French and English. Electronic applications accepted.

The University of Alabama, Graduate School, College of Human Environmental Sciences, Department of Consumer Sciences, Tuscaloosa, AL 35487-0158. Offers MS. Part-time and evening/weekend programs available. Postbaccalaureate distance learning degree programs offered (minimal on-campus study). *Faculty:* 7 full-time (4 women). *Students:* 1 part-time (0 women). Average age 43. 5 applicants, 20% accepted, 1 enrolled. *Degree requirements:* For

Consumer Economics

The University of Alabama (continued)

master's, capstone. *Entrance requirements:* For master's, minimum GPA of 3.0. Additional exam requirements/recommendations for international students: Required—TOEFL. *Application deadline:* For fall admission, 7/1 priority date for domestic and international students; for winter admission, 1/1 priority date for domestic and international students. Applications are processed on a rolling basis. Application fee: $50 ($60 for international students). Electronic applications accepted. *Expenses:* Tuition, state resident: full-time $7000. Tuition, nonresident: full-time $19,200. *Financial support:* In 2009–10, 1 research assistantship (averaging $8,100 per year), 1 teaching assistantship (averaging $8,100 per year) were awarded; fellowships also available. Financial award application deadline: 3/15. *Faculty research:* Consumer economics, financial planning. *Unit head:* Dr. Milla Dailey Boschung, Department Chair, 205-348-6250, Fax: 205-348-3789, E-mail: mboschun@ches.ua.edu. *Application contact:* Dr. Cliff A. Robb, Assistant Professor, 205-348-6178, Fax: 205-348-8721, E-mail: crobb@ches.ua.edu.

University of Georgia, Graduate School, College of Family and Consumer Sciences, Department of Housing and Consumer Economics, Athens, GA 30602. Offers MS, PhD. Part-time programs available. *Faculty:* 16 full-time (8 women). *Students:* 18 full-time (11 women), 12 part-time (5 women); includes 8 minority (7 African Americans, 1 Asian American or Pacific Islander). 16 applicants, 63% accepted, 6 enrolled. In 2009, 3 master's, 2 doctorates awarded. *Degree requirements:* For master's, thesis; for doctorate, thesis/dissertation. *Entrance requirements:* For master's and doctorate, GRE General Test. Additional exam requirements/recommendations for international students: Required—TOEFL (minimum score 575 paper-based; 230 computer-based). *Application deadline:* For fall admission, 7/1 for domestic students, 2/1 for international students; for spring admission, 11/15 for domestic students. Application fee: $50. Electronic applications accepted. *Expenses:* Tuition, state resident: full-time $6000; part-time $250 per credit hour. Tuition, nonresident: full-time $20,904; part-time $871 per credit hour. Required fees: $730 per semester. *Financial support:* In 2009–10, 10 students received support; fellowships, research assistantships, teaching assistantships, unspecified assistantships available. Financial award application deadline: 2/1. *Faculty research:* Demographics, consumer decision making, home ownership counseling, financial management, economics of divorce and poverty. *Unit head:* Dr. Anne L. Sweaney, Head, 706-542-4877, Fax: 706-542-4397, E-mail: asweaney@fcs.uga.edu. *Application contact:* Dr. Anne L. Sweaney, Head, 706-542-4877, Fax: 706-542-4397, E-mail: asweaney@fcs.uga.edu.

University of Guelph, Graduate Program Services, College of Management and Economics, Department of Marketing and Consumer Studies, Guelph, ON N1G 2W1, Canada. Offers M Sc. *Degree requirements:* For master's, thesis. *Entrance requirements:* For master's, GMAT or GRE General Test, minimum B average during previous 2 years of course work. Additional exam requirements/recommendations for international students: Required—TOEFL (minimum score 575 paper-based; 213 computer-based). Electronic applications accepted. *Faculty research:* Marketing, quality management, consumer economics, housing and real estate management, problem gambling.

University of Idaho, College of Graduate Studies, College of Agricultural and Life Sciences, Margaret Ritchie School of Family and Consumer Sciences, Moscow, ID 83844-3183. Offers MS. *Faculty:* 9 full-time. *Students:* 11 full-time, 14 part-time. In 2009, 2 master's awarded. *Degree requirements:* For master's, thesis. *Entrance requirements:* For master's, minimum GPA of 2.8. *Application deadline:* For fall admission, 8/1 for domestic students; for spring admission, 12/15 for domestic students. Application fee: $55 ($60 for international students). *Expenses:* Tuition, state resident: full-time $6120. Tuition, nonresident: full-time $17,712. *Financial support:* Research assistantships, teaching assistantships available. Financial award application deadline: 2/15. *Faculty research:* Food and nutrition; clothing, textiles and design; child, family and consumer studies; early childhood development. *Unit head:* Dr. Sandra Evenson, Interim Chair, 208-885-6546. *Application contact:* Dr. Sandra Evenson, Interim Chair, 208-885-6546.

University of Illinois at Urbana–Champaign, Graduate College, College of Agricultural, Consumer and Environmental Sciences, Department of Agricultural and Consumer Economics, Champaign, IL 61820. Offers MS, PhD. *Faculty:* 34 full-time (12 women). *Students:* 54 full-time (28 women), 23 part-time (10 women); includes 7 minority (4 African Americans, 3 Asian Americans or Pacific Islanders), 46 international. 89 applicants, 22% accepted, 12 enrolled. In 2009, 12 master's, 8 doctorates awarded. *Entrance requirements:* For master's, GRE, minimum GPA of 3.0; for doctorate, GRE, writing sample. Additional exam requirements/recommendations for international students: Required—TOEFL (minimum score 570 paper-based; 230 computer-based; 88 iBT), or IELTS (minimum score 6.5). *Application deadline:* Applications are processed on a rolling basis. Application fee: $60 ($75 for international students). Electronic applications accepted. *Financial support:* In 2009–10, 18 fellowships, 54 research assistantships, 30 teaching assistantships were awarded; tuition waivers (full and partial) also available. *Unit head:* Paul N. Ellinger, Head, 217-333-5503, Fax: 217-333-5538, E-mail: pellinge@illinois.edu. *Application contact:* Linda K. Foste, Administrative Assistant, 217-333-1830, Fax: 217-244-7088, E-mail: l-foste@illinois.edu.

University of Missouri, Graduate School, College of Human Environmental Science, Department of Personal Financial Planning, Columbia, MO 65211. Offers MS. *Entrance requirements:* For master's, GRE General Test, minimum GPA of 3.0. Additional exam requirements/recommendations for international students: Required—TOEFL (minimum score 550 paper-based; 213 computer-based; 79 iBT).

University of Nebraska–Lincoln, Graduate College, College of Education and Human Sciences, Department of Child, Youth and Family Studies, Lincoln, NE 68588. Offers child development/early childhood education (MS, PhD); child, youth and family studies (MS); family and consumer sciences education (MS, PhD); family financial planning (MS); family science (MS, PhD); gerontology (PhD); human sciences (PhD), including child, youth and family studies, gerontology, medical family therapy; marriage and family therapy (MS); medical family therapy (PhD); youth development (MS). *Accreditation:* AAMFT/COAMFTE (one or more programs are accredited). Postbaccalaureate distance learning degree programs offered. *Degree requirements:* For master's, thesis optional. *Entrance requirements:* For master's, GRE. Additional exam requirements/recommendations for international students: Required—TOEFL (minimum score 550 paper-based; 213 computer-based). Electronic applications accepted. *Faculty research:* Marriage and family therapy, child development/early childhood education, family financial management.

University of South Carolina, The Graduate School, College of Hospitality, Retail, and Sport Management, Department of Retailing, Columbia, SC 29208. Offers MR. Part-time programs available. *Degree requirements:* For master's, comprehensive exam, internship or thesis. *Entrance requirements:* For master's, GMAT or GRE General Test, minimum GPA of 3.0. Additional exam requirements/recommendations for international students: Required—TOEFL (minimum score 80 iBT). Electronic applications accepted. *Faculty research:* Retail technology, retail strategy, international retailing.

The University of Tennessee, Graduate School, College of Education, Health and Human Sciences, Department of Consumer and Industry Services Management, Program in Consumer Services Management, Knoxville, TN 37996. Offers retail and consumer sciences (MS); textile science (MS). Part-time programs available. *Degree requirements:* For master's, thesis or alternative. *Entrance requirements:* For master's, GRE General Test, minimum GPA of 2.7. Additional exam requirements/recommendations for international students: Required—TOEFL. Electronic applications accepted. *Expenses:* Tuition, state resident: full-time $6826; part-time $380 per semester hour. Tuition, nonresident: full-time $21,844; part-time $1147 per semester hour. Tuition and fees vary according to program.

The University of Tennessee, Graduate School, College of Education, Health and Human Sciences, Program in Human Ecology, Knoxville, TN 37996. Offers child and family studies (PhD); community health (PhD); nutrition science (PhD); retailing and consumer sciences (PhD); textile science (PhD). *Degree requirements:* For doctorate, thesis/dissertation. *Entrance requirements:* For doctorate, GRE General Test, minimum GPA of 2.7. Additional exam requirements/recommendations for international students: Required—TOEFL. Electronic applications accepted. *Expenses:* Tuition, state resident: full-time $6826; part-time $380 per semester hour. Tuition, nonresident: full-time $21,844; part-time $1147 per semester hour. Tuition and fees vary according to program.

University of Utah, The Graduate School, College of Social and Behavioral Science, Department of Family and Consumer Studies, Salt Lake City, UT 84112-0080. Offers human development and social policy (MS). Part-time and evening/weekend programs available. *Faculty:* 16 full-time (7 women), 1 (woman) part-time/adjunct. *Students:* 9 full-time (7 women), 5 part-time (all women), 1 international. Average age 36. 16 applicants, 38% accepted, 6 enrolled. In 2009, 2 master's awarded. *Degree requirements:* For master's, thesis optional. *Entrance requirements:* For master's, GRE General Test, minimum undergraduate GPA of 3.0, courses in research methods and statistics. Additional exam requirements/recommendations for international students: Required—TOEFL (minimum score 500 paper-based; 173 computer-based). *Application deadline:* For fall admission, 3/1 priority date for domestic and international students. Application fee: $55 ($65 for international students). Electronic applications accepted. *Expenses:* Tuition, state resident: full-time $4004; part-time $1674 per semester. Tuition, nonresident: full-time $14,134; part-time $5915 per semester. Required fees: $324 per semester. Tuition and fees vary according to course load, degree level and program. *Financial support:* In 2009–10, 10 students received support, including 1 research assistantship with partial tuition reimbursement available (averaging $5,500 per year), 9 teaching assistantships with partial tuition reimbursements available (averaging $5,500 per year). Financial award application deadline: 2/1. *Faculty research:* Social, physical and economic contexts of families and communities. Total annual research expenditures: $350,000. *Unit head:* Dr. Cheryl Wright, Chair, 801-581-7712, Fax: 801-581-5156, E-mail: cheryl.wright@fcs.utah.edu. *Application contact:* Dr. Marissa Diener, Graduate Director, 801-581-6521, E-mail: marissa.diener@fcs.utah.edu.

University of Wisconsin–Madison, Graduate School, School of Human Ecology, Program in Consumer Behavior and Family Economics, Madison, WI 53706-1380. Offers MS, PhD. *Degree requirements:* For master's, thesis; for doctorate, comprehensive exam, thesis/dissertation. *Entrance requirements:* For master's and doctorate, GRE General Test, 3 letters of recommendation. Additional exam requirements/recommendations for international students: Required—TOEFL (minimum score 580 paper-based; 237 computer-based). Electronic applications accepted. *Expenses:* Tuition, state resident: part-time $594 per credit. Tuition, nonresident: part-time $1504 per credit. Required fees: $65 per credit. Tuition and fees vary according to course load, program and reciprocity agreements. *Faculty research:* Economic well-being of elderly, finance, financial planning, health care policy, consumer behavior.

University of Wyoming, College of Agriculture, Department of Family and Consumer Sciences, Laramie, WY 82070. Offers early childhood development (MS); family and consumer sciences (MS); food science and human nutrition (MS). Part-time programs available. *Degree requirements:* For master's, thesis, project. *Entrance requirements:* For master's, GRE General Test or MCAT, minimum GPA of 3.0. Additional exam requirements/recommendations for international students: Required—TOEFL (minimum score 540 paper-based; 207 computer-based; 76 iBT). Electronic applications accepted. *Faculty research:* Asthma, obesity and healthy weights, nutrition concerns of children with special health care needs, food product development, food safety, postpartum health, exercise nutrition.

Utah State University, School of Graduate Studies, College of Agriculture, Department of Agricultural Systems Technology and Education, Logan, UT 84322. Offers agricultural systems technology (MS), including agricultural extension education, agricultural mechanization, international agricultural extension, secondary and postsecondary agricultural education; family and consumer sciences education (MS). Part-time programs available. Postbaccalaureate distance learning degree programs offered (minimal on-campus study). *Degree requirements:* For master's, comprehensive exam (for some programs), thesis (for some programs). *Entrance requirements:* For master's, GRE General Test, MAT, BS in agricultural education, agricultural extension, or related agricultural or science discipline; minimum GPA of 3.0. Additional exam requirements/recommendations for international students: Required—TOEFL. *Faculty research:* Extension and adult education; structures and environment; low-input agriculture; farm safety, systems, and mechanizations.

Virginia Polytechnic Institute and State University, Graduate School, College of Liberal Arts and Human Sciences, Department of Apparel, Housing, and Resource Management, Blacksburg, VA 24061. Offers apparel business and economics (MS, PhD); apparel product design and analysis (MS, PhD); apparel quality analysis (MS, PhD); consumer studies (MS, PhD); family financial management (MS, PhD); household equipment (MS, PhD); housing (MS, PhD); interior design (MS, PhD); resource management (MS, PhD). *Faculty:* 14 full-time (all women). *Students:* 10 full-time (9 women), 5 part-time (all women); includes 9 minority (1 African American, 6 American Indian/Alaska Native, 1 Asian American or Pacific Islander, 1 Hispanic American). Average age 34. 6 applicants. In 2009, 3 master's, 5 doctorates awarded. *Entrance requirements:* For master's and doctorate, GRE, GMAT. Additional exam requirements/recommendations for international students: Required—TOEFL (minimum score 550 paper-based; 213 computer-based). *Application deadline:* For fall admission, 5/15 for international students; for spring admission, 10/15 for international students. Applications are processed on a rolling basis. Application fee: $65. Electronic applications accepted. *Expenses:* Tuition, area resident: Full-time $10,228; part-time $459 per credit hour. Tuition, nonresident: full-time $17,892; part-time $865 per credit hour. Required fees: $1966; $451 per semester. *Financial support:* In 2009–10, 6 teaching assistantships with full tuition reimbursements (averaging $13,546 per year) were awarded; career-related internships or fieldwork, Federal Work-Study, scholarships/grants, and unspecified assistantships also available. Financial award application deadline: 1/15. *Faculty research:* Housing for elderly, affordable housing, household time use, phosphate laundry study, economic well-living. Total annual research expenditures: $27,151. *Unit head:* Dr. LuAnn R. Gaskill, Dean, 540-231-4781, Fax: 540-231-3250, E-mail: lagaskil@vt.edu. *Application contact:* Julia Beemish, Information Contact, 540-231-8881, Fax: 540-231-3250, E-mail: jbeamish@vt.edu.

Gerontology

Abilene Christian University, Graduate School, College of Arts and Sciences, Department of Sociology and Family Studies, Program in Gerontology, Abilene, TX 79699-9100. Offers MS, Certificate. *Faculty:* 3 part-time/adjunct (0 women). *Students:* 2 full-time (both women), 1 (woman) part-time; includes 2 minority (1 African American, 1 Hispanic American), 1 international. 2 applicants, 100% accepted, 1 enrolled. In 2009, 2 master's, 1 other advanced degree awarded. *Degree requirements:* For master's, comprehensive exam. *Entrance requirements:* For master's, GRE General Test or MAT. *Application deadline:* For fall admission, 4/1 priority date for domestic students; for spring admission, 11/1 for domestic students. Applications are processed on a rolling basis. Application fee: $40 ($45 for international students). Electronic applications accepted. *Expenses:* Tuition: Full-time $11,520; part-time $640 per hour. Required fees: $1090; $53.50 per hour. $10 per term. Tuition and fees vary according to program. *Financial support:* In 2009–10, 3 students received support. Career-related internships or fieldwork and Federal Work-Study available. Support available to part-time students. Financial award application deadline: 4/1; financial award applicants required to submit FAFSA. *Unit head:* Dr. Charlie D. Pruett, Director of the Center for Aging, 325-674-2350, Fax: 325-674-6804, E-mail: pruettc@acu.edu. *Application contact:* William Horn, Graduate Admissions Counselor, 325-674-2656, Fax: 325-674-6717, E-mail: gradinfo@acu.edu.

Adelphi University, School of Education, Program in Physical Education and Human Performance Science, Garden City, NY 11530-0701. Offers aging (Certificate); physical/educational human performance science (MA). Part-time and evening/weekend programs available. *Students:* 39 full-time (20 women), 107 part-time (42 women); includes 12 minority (6 African Americans, 3 Asian Americans or Pacific Islanders, 3 Hispanic Americans), 4 international. Average age 29. In 2009, 60 master's awarded. *Degree requirements:* For master's, internship. *Entrance requirements:* For master's, 3 letters of recommendation, resume. Additional exam requirements/recommendations for international students: Required—TOEFL (minimum score 550 paper-based; 213 computer-based; 80 iBT). *Application deadline:* For fall admission, 4/1 for international students; for spring admission, 11/1 for international students. Applications are processed on a rolling basis. Application fee: $50. Electronic applications accepted. *Expenses:* Tuition: Full-time $28,340; part-time $830 per credit. Required fees: $600; $250 per credit. Full-time tuition and fees vary according to course load and program. *Financial support:* Fellowships, research assistantships with full and partial tuition reimbursements, teaching assistantships, career-related internships or fieldwork, Federal Work-Study, institutionally sponsored loans, and tuition waivers (full) available. Support available to part-time students. Financial award application deadline: 2/15; financial award applicants required to submit FAFSA. *Faculty research:* Physical education for the handicapped, sport sociology, sport pedagogy. *Unit head:* Dr. Stephen J. Virgilio, Chair, 516-877-4262, E-mail: virgilio@adelphi.edu. *Application contact:* Christine Murphy, Director of Admissions, 516-877-3050, Fax: 516-877-3039, E-mail: graduateadmissions@adelphi.edu.

Adler School of Professional Psychology, Programs in Psychology, Chicago, IL 60601-7203. Offers art therapy (MA, Certificate); clinical hypnosis (Certificate); clinical psychology (Psy D); counseling (MA); counseling and organizational psychology (MA); forensic psychology (MA); gerontological counseling (MA); marriage and family counseling (MA); marriage and family therapy (Certificate); organizational psychology (MA); police psychology (MA); rehabilitation counseling (MA); sport and health psychology (MA); substance abuse counseling (Certificate); Psy D/Certificate; Psy D/MACAT; Psy D/MACP; Psy D/MAMFC; Psy D/MASAC. *Accreditation:* APA. Part-time and evening/weekend programs available. Postbaccalaureate distance learning degree programs offered (minimal on-campus study). *Faculty:* 41 full-time (21 women), 44 part-time/adjunct (19 women). *Students:* 551 full-time (441 women), 161 part-time (137 women). Average age 27.Terminal master's awarded for partial completion of doctoral program. *Degree requirements:* For master's, thesis or alternative, oral exam, practicum; for doctorate, thesis/dissertation, clinical exam, internship, oral exam, practicum, written qualifying exam. *Entrance requirements:* For master's, 12 semester hours in psychology, minimum GPA of 3.0; for doctorate, 18 semester hours in psychology, minimum GPA of 3.25; for Certificate, appropriate master's or doctoral degree. Additional exam requirements/recommendations for international students: Required—TOEFL (minimum score 550 paper-based; 213 computer-based; 79 iBT). *Application deadline:* For fall admission, 2/15 priority date for domestic students, 12/1 priority date for international students. Applications are processed on a rolling basis. Application fee: $50. Electronic applications accepted. *Expenses:* Tuition: Part-time $930 per credit. Required fees: $220 per term. *Financial support:* Career-related internships or fieldwork, Federal Work-Study, scholarships/grants, and tuition waivers (full and partial) available. Support available to part-time students. Financial award application deadline: 5/15; financial award applicants required to submit FAFSA. *Unit head:* Dr. Frank Gruba-McAllister, Vice President of Academic Affairs, 312-201-5900 Ext. 209, Fax: 312-201-5917. *Application contact:* Craig A. Hines, Associate Vice President of Admissions, 312-201-5900 Ext. 226, Fax: 312-201-5917, E-mail: chines@adler.edu.

See Close-Up on page 1047.

Alliant International University–Los Angeles, California School of Professional Psychology, Program in Marital and Family Therapy, Alhambra, CA 91803-1360. Offers biofeedback (MA); chemical dependency (MA); gerontology (MA); Latin American family therapy (MA). *Accreditation:* AAMFT/COAMFTE.

Appalachian State University, Cratis D. Williams Graduate School, Department of Sociology, Boone, NC 28608. Offers gerontology (MA). Part-time programs available. *Faculty:* 10 full-time (2 women), 1 (woman) part-time/adjunct. *Students:* 5 full-time (2 women), 15 part-time (11 women); includes 1 minority (Hispanic American). 15 applicants, 100% accepted, 13 enrolled. In 2009, 4 master's awarded. *Degree requirements:* For master's, comprehensive exam, thesis optional. *Entrance requirements:* For master's, GRE General Test, 3 letters of recommendation. Additional exam requirements/recommendations for international students: Required—TOEFL (minimum score 570 paper-based; 230 computer-based), IELTS (minimum score 6.5). *Application deadline:* For fall admission, 7/1 for domestic students, 2/1 for international students; for spring admission, 11/1 for domestic students, 7/1 for international students. Applications are processed on a rolling basis. Application fee: $50. Electronic applications accepted. *Expenses:* Tuition, state resident: full-time $2960. Tuition, nonresident: full-time $14,051. Required fees: $2320. *Financial support:* In 2009–10, 3 research assistantships (averaging $8,000 per year) were awarded; fellowships with partial tuition reimbursements, teaching assistantships, career-related internships or fieldwork, Federal Work-Study, scholarships/grants, and unspecified assistantships also available. Financial award application deadline: 4/1; financial award applicants required to submit FAFSA. *Faculty research:* Aging, criminology, deviance. Total annual research expenditures: $722,000. *Unit head:* Dr. Ed Folts, Chairman, 828-262-2293, E-mail: foltswe@appstate.edu. *Application contact:* Dr. Ed Rosenberg, Graduate Program Director, 828-262-2293, E-mail: rosenberge@appstate.edu.

Arizona State University, Graduate College, School of Aging and Lifespan Development, Tempe, AZ 85287. Offers aging and lifespan development (MS); gerontology (Certificate). Part-time and evening/weekend programs available. *Degree requirements:* For master's, applied project. *Entrance requirements:* For master's, 3 letters of recommendation; for Certificate, 2 letters of recommendation. Additional exam requirements/recommendations for international students: Required—TOEFL (minimum score 550 paper-based; 213 computer-based; 83 iBT). Electronic applications accepted.

Arkansas State University—Jonesboro, Graduate School, College of Nursing and Health Professions, Department of Physical Therapy, Jonesboro, State University, AR 72467. Offers aging studies (Certificate); health sciences (MS); health sciences education (Certificate); physical therapy (DPT). *Accreditation:* APTA. Part-time programs available. *Faculty:* 8 full-time (4 women), 1 (woman) part-time/adjunct. *Students:* 49 full-time (31 women), 26 part-time (19 women); includes 12 minority (all African Americans), 5 international. Average age 28. 53 applicants, 70% accepted, 32 enrolled. In 2009, 22 master's awarded. *Degree requirements:* For master's, comprehensive exam; for doctorate, comprehensive exam, thesis/dissertation. *Entrance requirements:* For master's, GRE General Test, Allied Health Profession Admissions Test, writing exam, appropriate bachelor's degree, letters of reference, resume, writing sample; for doctorate, GRE, Allied Health Professions Admissions Test, appropriate bachelor's or master's degree, letters of reference, resume, official transcript, volunteer experience, criminal background check, immunization records. Additional exam requirements/recommendations for international students: Required—TOEFL (minimum score 550 paper-based; 213 computer-based; 79 iBT), IELTS (minimum score 6). *Application deadline:* For fall admission, 3/1 for domestic and international students. Applications are processed on a rolling basis. Application fee: $50. Electronic applications accepted. *Expenses:* Contact institution. *Financial support:* In 2009–10, 7 students received support; fellowships, career-related internships or fieldwork, scholarships/grants, and unspecified assistantships available. Financial award application deadline: 7/1; financial award applicants required to submit FAFSA. *Unit head:* Dr. Patricia King, Chair, 870-972-3591, Fax: 870-972-3652, E-mail: pking@astate.edu. *Application contact:* Dr. Andrew Sustich, Dean of the Graduate School, 870-972-3029, Fax: 870-972-3857, E-mail: sustich@astate.edu.

A.T. Still University of Health Sciences, School of Health Management, Kirksville, MO 63501. Offers geriatric healthcare (MGH); health administration (MHA); health education (MH Ed, DH Ed); public health (MPH). Part-time and evening/weekend programs available. Postbaccalaureate distance learning degree programs offered (minimal on-campus study). *Faculty:* 12 full-time (6 women), 31 part-time/adjunct (12 women). *Students:* 84 full-time (59 women), 503 part-time (340 women); includes 179 minority (103 African Americans, 11 American Indian/Alaska Native, 37 Asian Americans or Pacific Islanders, 28 Hispanic Americans). Average age 32. 179 applicants, 100% accepted, 98 enrolled. In 2009, 98 master's, 22 doctorates awarded. *Degree requirements:* For master's, thesis (for some programs), integrated terminal project; for doctorate, thesis/dissertation. *Entrance requirements:* For master's, minimum GPA of 2.5, bachelor's degree or equivalent from U.S. institution; for doctorate, minimum GPA of 2.5, master's or terminal degree, employment. Additional exam requirements/recommendations for international students: Required—TOEFL (minimum score 550 paper-based; 213 computer-based; 80 iBT). *Application deadline:* For fall admission, 8/7 for domestic and international students; for winter admission, 10/23 for domestic and international students; for spring admission, 2/5 for domestic and international students. Applications are processed on a rolling basis. Application fee: $60. Electronic applications accepted. *Expenses:* Contact institution. *Financial support:* In 2009–10, 408 students received support. Application deadline: 5/1. *Unit head:* Dr. Kimberly O'Reilly, Interim Dean, 660-626-2820, Fax: 660-626-2826, E-mail: koreilley@atsu.edu. *Application contact:* Sarah Spencer, Director of Recruitment, 660-626-2820 Ext. 2669, Fax: 660-626-2826, E-mail: sbartlett@atsu.edu.

Ball State University, Graduate School, College of Applied Science and Technology, Fisher Institute for Wellness, Program in Applied Gerontology, Muncie, IN 47306-1099. Offers MA.

Bethel University, Graduate School, Program in Gerontology, St. Paul, MN 55112-6999. Offers gerontology (MA). Part-time and evening/weekend programs available. *Faculty:* 1 full-time (0 women), 2 part-time/adjunct (both women). *Students:* 24 full-time (20 women), 1 (woman) part-time; includes 1 minority (Asian American or Pacific Islander). Average age 45. 18 applicants, 67% accepted, 11 enrolled. In 2009, 9 master's awarded. *Degree requirements:* For master's, thesis or alternative, project, practicum. *Entrance requirements:* For master's, interview, 3 years of work experience, minimum GPA of 3.0, letters of reference. Additional exam requirements/recommendations for international students: Required—TOEFL (minimum score 550 paper-based; 213 computer-based; 80 iBT). *Application deadline:* For fall admission, 7/15 priority date for domestic students; for spring admission, 5/1 priority date for domestic students. Applications are processed on a rolling basis. Application fee: $25. Electronic applications accepted. *Expenses:* Tuition: Full-time $7920; part-time $440 per credit. One-time fee: $25. Tuition and fees vary according to course load, degree level and program. *Financial support:* Applicants required to submit FAFSA. *Unit head:* Dr. Diane L. Dahl, Assistant Dean, 651-635-8000, Fax: 651-635-8004, E-mail: diane-dahl@bethel.edu. *Application contact:* Michael Price, Director of Admissions, 651-635-8000, Fax: 651-635-8004, E-mail: m-price@bethel.edu.

California State University, Fullerton, Graduate Studies, College of Humanities and Social Sciences, Program in Gerontology, Fullerton, CA 92834-9480. Offers MS. Part-time programs available. *Students:* 9 full-time (all women), 18 part-time (16 women); includes 8 minority (4 Asian Americans or Pacific Islanders, 4 Hispanic Americans), 2 international. Average age 38. 16 applicants, 56% accepted, 8 enrolled. In 2009, 21 master's awarded. *Expenses:* Tuition, nonresident: full-time $11,160; part-time $373 per credit. Required fees: $1440 per term. Tuition and fees vary according to course load, degree level and program. *Financial support:* Career-related internships or fieldwork, Federal Work-Study, institutionally sponsored loans, and scholarships/grants available. Financial award application deadline: 3/1; financial award applicants required to submit FAFSA. *Unit head:* Dr. Joseph Weber, Coordinator, 657-278-7057. *Application contact:* Admissions/Applications, 657-278-2371.

California State University, Long Beach, Graduate Studies, College of Health and Human Services, Program in Gerontology, Long Beach, CA 90840. Offers MS. Part-time programs available. *Faculty:* 6 full-time (1 woman). *Students:* 16 full-time (13 women), 30 part-time (28 women); includes 26 minority (3 African Americans, 12 Asian Americans or Pacific Islanders, 11 Hispanic Americans), 4 international. Average age 32. 18 applicants, 56% accepted, 9 enrolled. *Degree requirements:* For master's, thesis optional. *Application deadline:* For fall admission, 7/1 for domestic students. Applications are processed on a rolling basis. Application fee: $55. Electronic applications accepted. *Expenses:* Required fees: $1802 per semester. Part-time tuition and fees vary according to course load. *Financial support:* Federal Work-Study, institutionally sponsored loans, and scholarships/grants available. Financial award application deadline: 3/2. *Unit head:* Dr. Barbara White, Director, 562-985-1582, Fax: 562-985-4414, E-mail: bwhite@csulb.edu. *Application contact:* Dr. Barbara White, Director, 562-985-1582, Fax: 562-985-4414, E-mail: bwhite@csulb.edu.

California State University, Stanislaus, College of Humanities and Social Sciences, Department of Sociology, Turlock, CA 95382. Offers gerontology (Certificate). *Entrance requirements:* For degree, minimum GPA of 2.5.

Capella University, School of Public Service Leadership, Minneapolis, MN 55402. Offers criminal justice (MS, PhD); emergency management (MS, PhD); general human services (MS, PhD); general public administration (MPA, DPA); gerontology (MS); health care administration (MS, PhD); health management and policy (MSPH); management of nonprofit agencies (MS, PhD); nurse educator (MS); public safety leadership (MS, PhD); social and community services (MS, PhD); social behavioral sciences (MSPH).

Chestnut Hill College, School of Graduate Studies, Program in Administration of Human Services, Philadelphia, PA 19118-2693. Offers administration of human services (MS); adult and aging services (CAS); leadership development (CAS). Part-time and evening/weekend programs available. *Degree requirements:* For master's, special projects or internship. *Entrance requirements:* For master's, GRE General Test or MAT, 100 volunteer hours or 1 year work-related human services experience, statement of professional goals, writing sample, transcripts, letters of recommendation; for CAS, GRE or MAT, letters of recommendation. Additional exam requirements/recommendations for international students: Required—TOEFL (minimum score 500 paper-based; 213 computer-based).

Cleveland State University, College of Graduate Studies, College of Science, Department of Psychology, Cleveland, OH 44115. Offers adult development and aging (PhD); clinical psychology (MA); consumer/industrial research (MA); diversity management (MA); experimental research psychology (MA); school psychology (Psy S). *Degree requirements:* For master's, comprehensive

Gerontology

Cleveland State University (continued)
exam (for some programs), thesis (for some programs); for doctorate, comprehensive exam, thesis/dissertation; for Psy S, internship. *Entrance requirements:* For master's and doctorate, GRE General Test. Additional exam requirements/recommendations for international students: Required—TOEFL (minimum score 525 paper-based; 197 computer-based). Electronic applications accepted. *Faculty research:* Cognitive and social psychology, consumer psychology, clinical psychology, school psychology, aging.

The College of New Rochelle, Graduate School, Division of Human Services, Program in Gerontology, New Rochelle, NY 10805-2308. Offers MS, Certificate. Part-time and evening/weekend programs available. *Degree requirements:* For master's, fieldwork, internship. *Entrance requirements:* For master's, interview, minimum GPA of 3.0, writing sample.

Concordia University Chicago, College of Graduate and Innovative Programs, Program in Gerontology, River Forest, IL 60305-1499. Offers MA. Part-time and evening/weekend programs available. *Degree requirements:* For master's, comprehensive exam, thesis. *Entrance requirements:* For master's, minimum GPA of 2.9. Additional exam requirements/recommendations for international students: Required—TOEFL (minimum score 550 paper-based; 195 computer-based). Electronic applications accepted.

Dominican University of California, Graduate Programs, School of Health and Natural Sciences, Program in Nursing, San Rafael, CA 94901-2298. Offers geriatric and nurse educator (MS); integrated health practices (clinical nursing specialist) (MS). *Accreditation:* AACN. Part-time and evening/weekend programs available. *Degree requirements:* For master's, thesis. *Entrance requirements:* For master's, minimum GPA of 3.0; clinical experience; course work in nursing research and statistics; CPR certification; professional liability and malpractice insurance; interview. Additional exam requirements/recommendations for international students: Required—TOEFL (minimum score 550 paper-based; 213 computer-based). Electronic applications accepted.

Eastern Illinois University, Graduate School, Lumpkin College of Business and Applied Sciences, Program in Gerontology, Charleston, IL 61920-3099. Offers MA. *Faculty:* 7 full-time (3 women). In 2009, 10 master's awarded. *Application deadline:* For fall admission, 3/31 priority date for domestic students. Applications are processed on a rolling basis. Application fee: $30. *Expenses:* Tuition, state resident: full-time $9434; part-time $239 per credit hour. Tuition, nonresident: full-time $23,774; part-time $717 per credit hour. Required fees: $802.63. *Financial support:* In 2009–10, research assistantships with tuition reimbursements (averaging $8,100 per year), 4 teaching assistantships with tuition reimbursements (averaging $8,100 per year) were awarded; career-related internships or fieldwork and institutionally sponsored loans also available. *Unit head:* Dr. James Painter, Chairperson, 217-581-6076, Fax: 217-581-6090, E-mail: jepainter@eiu.edu. *Application contact:* Dr. Jackie Frank, Coordinator, 217-581-6076, Fax: 217-581-6090, E-mail: jbfrank@eiu.edu.

Eastern Michigan University, Graduate School, College of Arts and Sciences, Department of Sociology, Anthropology and Criminology, Ypsilanti, MI 48197. Offers criminology and criminal justice (MA); gerontology–dementia (Graduate Certificate); sociology (MA), including schools, society and violence, sociology, sociology—family specialty. Part-time and evening/weekend programs available. Postbaccalaureate distance learning degree programs offered (minimal on-campus study). *Faculty:* 17 full-time (7 women). *Students:* 9 full-time (7 women), 58 part-time (43 women); includes 26 minority (20 African Americans, 1 American Indian/Alaska Native, 1 Asian American or Pacific Islander, 4 Hispanic Americans), 1 international. Average age 34. 47 applicants, 81% accepted, 24 enrolled. In 2009, 11 master's, 7 other advanced degrees awarded. *Degree requirements:* For master's, thesis optional. *Entrance requirements:* Additional exam requirements/recommendations for international students: Required—TOEFL. *Application deadline:* Applications are processed on a rolling basis. Application fee: $35. Tuition and fees vary according to course level. *Financial support:* Fellowships, research assistantships with full tuition reimbursements, teaching assistantships with full tuition reimbursements, career-related internships or fieldwork, Federal Work-Study, institutionally sponsored loans, scholarships/grants, tuition waivers (partial), and unspecified assistantships available. Support available to part-time students. Financial award applicants required to submit FAFSA. *Unit head:* Dr. Peter Wood, Head, 734-487-0012, Fax: 734-487-9666, E-mail: peter.wood@emich.edu. *Application contact:* Dr. Peter Wood, Head, 734-487-0012, Fax: 734-487-9666, E-mail: peter.wood@emich.edu.

East Tennessee State University, School of Graduate Studies, College of Public and Allied Health, Department of Public Health, Johnson City, TN 37614. Offers community health (MPH); epidemiology (Certificate); gerontology (Certificate); health care management (Certificate); public health (MPH); public health administration (MPH). *Accreditation:* CEPH. Part-time programs available. *Degree requirements:* For master's, comprehensive exam, thesis optional. *Entrance requirements:* For master's, GRE General Test, 2 years of community health experience. Additional exam requirements/recommendations for international students: Required—TOEFL (minimum score 550 paper-based; 213 computer-based). *Faculty research:* Rural health issues, youth and adolescent health, health of the elderly, environmental epidemiology, spatial analysis of data.

Emory University, Nell Hodgson Woodruff School of Nursing, Atlanta, GA 30322-1100. Offers adult and elder health advanced practice nursing (MSN), including acute care, adult nurse practitioner, gerontological nurse practitioner; emergency nurse practitioner (MSN); family nurse practitioner (MSN); family nurse-midwife (MSN); nurse midwifery (MSN); pediatric nurse practitioner acute and primary care (MSN); public health nursing leadership (MSN); women's health nurse practitioner (MSN); women's health title x (MSN); women's health/adult health nurse practitioner (MSN); MSN/MPH. *Accreditation:* AACN; ACNM/DOA (one or more programs are accredited). Part-time programs available. *Faculty:* 30 full-time (29 women), 11 part-time/adjunct (10 women). *Students:* 110 full-time (106 women), 53 part-time (51 women); includes 49 minority (35 African Americans, 2 American Indian/Alaska Native, 10 Asian Americans or Pacific Islanders, 2 Hispanic Americans), 4 international. Average age 32. 182 applicants, 63% accepted, 86 enrolled. In 2009, 81 master's awarded. *Entrance requirements:* For master's, GRE General Test or MAT, minimum GPA of 3.0, BS in nursing from an accredited institution, RN license and additional course work, 3 letters of recommendation. Additional exam requirements/recommendations for international students: Required—TOEFL (minimum score 600 paper-based; 100 iBT). *Application deadline:* For fall admission, 1/15 priority date for domestic and international students; for spring admission, 10/1 priority date for domestic and international students. Applications are processed on a rolling basis. Application fee: $50. Electronic applications accepted. *Expenses:* Contact institution. *Financial support:* In 2009–10, 14 fellowships (averaging $28,000 per year) were awarded; career-related internships or fieldwork, Federal Work-Study, institutionally sponsored loans, and scholarships/grants also available. Support available to part-time students. Financial award application deadline: 3/1; financial award applicants required to submit CSS PROFILE or FAFSA. *Faculty research:* Older adult falls and injuries, minority health issues, cardiac symptoms and quality of life, bio-ethics and decision making, menopausal issues. *Unit head:* Dr. Linda McCauley, Dean, 404-727-7976, Fax: 404-727-9800, E-mail: linda.mccauley@emory.edu. *Application contact:* Katie Kennedy, Associate Director for Admission and Financial Aid, 404-727-7980, Fax: 404-727-8509, E-mail: admit@nursing.emory.edu.

Gannon University, School of Graduate Studies, College of Humanities, Education, and Social Sciences, School of Humanities, Program in Gerontology, Erie, PA 16541-0001. Offers Certificate. Part-time and evening/weekend programs available. *Entrance requirements:* For degree, interview. Additional exam requirements/recommendations for international students: Required—TOEFL (minimum score 79 iBT). *Application deadline:* Applications are processed on a rolling basis. Application fee: $25. Electronic applications accepted. *Expenses:* Tuition: Full-time $13,590; part-time $755 per credit. Required fees: $524; $17 per credit. Tuition and fees vary according to course load, degree level, campus/location and program. *Financial support:* Career-related internships or fieldwork available. Financial award application deadline: 7/1; financial award applicants required to submit FAFSA. *Unit head:* Charles Murphy, Director, 814-871-7542, E-mail: murphy001@gannon.edu. *Application contact:* Kara Morgan, Assistant Director of Graduate Admissions, 814-871-5831, Fax: 814-871-5827, E-mail: graduate@gannon.edu.

George Mason University, College of Health and Human Services, Department of Global and Community Health, Fairfax, VA 22030. Offers biostatistics (Certificate); epidemiology (Certificate); epidemiology and biostatistics (MS); gerontology (Certificate); global health (MS, Certificate); nutrition (Certificate); public health (MPH, Certificate); rehabilitation science (Certificate). *Faculty:* 14 full-time (8 women), 12 part-time/adjunct (8 women). *Students:* 93 full-time (75 women), 106 part-time (92 women); includes 87 minority (46 African Americans, 1 American Indian/Alaska Native, 31 Asian Americans or Pacific Islanders, 9 Hispanic Americans), 22 international. Average age 31. 269 applicants, 69% accepted, 146 enrolled. In 2009, 17 master's, 2 other advanced degrees awarded. *Degree requirements:* For master's, comprehensive exam (for some programs), thesis or practicum. *Entrance requirements:* For master's, GRE, BA with minimum GPA of 3.0, 2 letters of recommendation. Additional exam requirements/recommendations for international students: Required—TOEFL. *Application deadline:* For fall admission, 4/1 priority date for domestic students, 4/1 for international students; for spring admission, 11/1 for domestic and international students. Applications are processed on a rolling basis. Application fee: $75. Electronic applications accepted. *Expenses:* Tuition, state resident: full-time $7568; part-time $315.33 per credit hour. Tuition, nonresident: full-time $21,704; part-time $904.33 per credit hour. Required fees: $2184; $91 per credit hour. *Financial support:* In 2009–10, 4 students received support, including 2 research assistantships with full and partial tuition reimbursements available (averaging $3,500 per year), 2 teaching assistantships with full and partial tuition reimbursements available (averaging $2,790 per year); Federal Work-Study, scholarships/grants, unspecified assistantships, and research awards, health care benefits health care benefits (full-time research or teaching assistantship recipients) also available. Support available to part-time students. Financial award application deadline: 3/1. *Faculty research:* Providing introductory and advanced degrees in health-related disciplines centered in global and community issues, health issues and the needs of affected populations at the regional and global level. *Unit head:* Dr. Shirley S. Travis, Dean, 703-993-1918. *Application contact:* Allan Weiss, Office Manager, 703-993-3126, E-mail: aweiss2@gmu.edu.

Georgia State University, College of Arts and Sciences, Gerontology Institute, Atlanta, GA 30302-3083. Offers MA. Part-time programs available. *Degree requirements:* For master's, thesis, internship. *Entrance requirements:* For master's, GRE, 3 letters of reference, resume. Additional exam requirements/recommendations for international students: Required—TOEFL, TWE. Electronic applications accepted. *Faculty research:* Long-term care; assisted living; aging families and grandparenting; mental health, caregiving and well-being; health, exercise and rehabilitation; images of aging; and work, retirement, and economics of aging.

Hofstra University, School of Education, Health, and Human Services, Department of Counseling, Research, Special Education and Rehabilitation, Program in Gerontology, Hempstead, NY 11549. Offers MS, Advanced Certificate. Part-time programs available. *Students:* 4 full-time (3 women), 8 part-time (all women); includes 4 minority (3 African Americans, 1 Asian American or Pacific Islander), 1 international. Average age 41. 13 applicants, 92% accepted, 6 enrolled. In 2009, 5 master's awarded. *Degree requirements:* For master's, thesis optional, internship. *Entrance requirements:* For master's, interview, letter of recommendation; for Advanced Certificate, letter of recommendation, interview. Additional exam requirements/recommendations for international students: Required—TOEFL (minimum score 550 paper-based; 213 computer-based; 80 iBT). *Application deadline:* Applications are processed on a rolling basis. Application fee: $60. Electronic applications accepted. *Expenses:* Tuition: Full-time $16,200; part-time $900 per credit hour. Required fees: $970; $145 per term. Tuition and fees vary according to program. *Financial support:* In 2009–10, 7 students received support, including 4 fellowships with full and partial tuition reimbursements available (averaging $2,563 per year); research assistantships with full and partial tuition reimbursements available, career-related internships or fieldwork, Federal Work-Study, institutionally sponsored loans, scholarships/grants, and tuition waivers (full and partial) also available. Support available to part-time students. Financial award applicants required to submit FAFSA. *Faculty research:* Elder abuse, geropsychology, environmental gerontology, later life education. *Unit head:* Dr. Jeffrey P. Rosenfield, Director, 516-463-5752, Fax: 516-463-6184, E-mail: cprjzr@hofstra.edu. *Application contact:* Carol Drummer, Dean of Graduate Admissions, 516-463-4876, Fax: 516-463-4664, E-mail: gradstudent@hofstra.edu.

Kent State University, Graduate School of Education, Health, and Human Services, School of Lifespan Development and Educational Sciences, Program in Family Studies, Kent, OH 44242-0001. Offers gerontology (MA); human development and family studies (MA). *Faculty:* 14 full-time (10 women), 9 part-time/adjunct (8 women). *Students:* 5 full-time (all women), 7 part-time (6 women); includes 1 minority (African American). 3 applicants, 100% accepted. In 2009, 2 master's awarded. Application fee: $30. *Financial support:* In 2009–10, 2 research assistantships (averaging $8,313 per year) were awarded. *Unit head:* Dr. Rhonda Richardson, Coordinator, 330-672-2026, E-mail: rrichard@kent.edu. *Application contact:* Nancy Miller, Academic Program Coordinator, 330-672-2576, Fax: 330-672-9162, E-mail: ogs@kent.edu.

Lakehead University, Graduate Studies, Department of History, Thunder Bay, ON P7B 5E1, Canada. Offers gerontology (MA); history (MA); women's studies (MA). Part-time programs available. *Degree requirements:* For master's, one foreign language, thesis. *Entrance requirements:* For master's, minimum B average. Additional exam requirements/recommendations for international students: Required—TOEFL. *Faculty research:* Canadian history, British history, Russian/German history, women's studies.

Lakehead University, Graduate Studies, Faculty of Education, Thunder Bay, ON P7B 5E1, Canada. Offers educational studies (PhD); gerontology (M Ed); women's studies (M Ed). Part-time and evening/weekend programs available. *Degree requirements:* For master's, project or thesis. *Entrance requirements:* For master's, minimum B average. Additional exam requirements/recommendations for international students: Required—TOEFL. *Faculty research:* Art education, AIDS education, language arts education, gerontology, women's studies.

Lakehead University, Graduate Studies, Faculty of Social Sciences and Humanities, Department of Sociology, Thunder Bay, ON P7B 5E1, Canada. Offers gerontology (MA); health services and policy research (MA); sociology (MA); women's studies (MA). Part-time and evening/weekend programs available. *Degree requirements:* For master's, research project or thesis. *Entrance requirements:* For master's, minimum B average. Additional exam requirements/recommendations for international students: Required—TOEFL. *Faculty research:* Sociology of medicine, cultural and social change, health human resources, gerontology, women's studies.

Lakehead University, Graduate Studies, Gerontology Collaborative Program-Northern Educational Center for Aging and Health, Thunder Bay, ON P7B 5E1, Canada. Offers specialization gerontology (M Ed, M Sc, MA, MSW). Part-time programs available. *Degree requirements:* For master's, thesis (for some programs). *Entrance requirements:* Additional exam requirements/recommendations for international students: Required—TOEFL. *Faculty research:* Integrated health information systems.

Lakehead University, Graduate Studies, School of Kinesiology, Thunder Bay, ON P7B 5E1, Canada. Offers kinesiology (M Sc); kinesiology and gerontology (M Sc). Part-time programs available. *Degree requirements:* For master's, thesis. *Entrance requirements:* For master's, minimum B average. Additional exam requirements/recommendations for international students: Required—TOEFL. *Faculty research:* Social psychology and physical education, sport history, sports medicine, exercise physiology, gerontology.

Lakehead University, Graduate Studies, School of Social Work, Thunder Bay, ON P7B 5E1, Canada. Offers gerontology (MSW); social work (MSW); women's studies (MSW). Part-time programs available. *Degree requirements:* For master's, thesis or project. *Entrance requirements:*

For master's, minimum B average. Additional exam requirements/recommendations for international students: Required—TOEFL. *Faculty research:* Clinical psychology, social work and practice theory, long-term care, health care for frail elderly, women's studies.

Lindenwood University, Graduate Programs, College of Individualized Education, St. Charles, MO 63301-1695. Offers administration (MSA); business administration (MBA); communications (MA); criminal justice and administration (MS); gerontology (MA); health management (MS); human resource management (MS); information technology (MBA, Certificate); management (MSA); managing information technology (MS); marketing (MSA); writing (MFA). Part-time and evening/weekend programs available. *Faculty:* 15 full-time (8 women), 128 part-time/adjunct (53 women). *Students:* 679 full-time (432 women), 90 part-time (57 women); includes 138 minority (121 African Americans, 2 American Indian/Alaska Native, 5 Asian Americans or Pacific Islanders, 10 Hispanic Americans), 18 international. Average age 34. 223 applicants, 44% accepted, 87 enrolled. In 2009, 478 master's awarded. *Degree requirements:* For master's, thesis (for some programs), 1 colloquium per term. *Entrance requirements:* For master's, interview, minimum GPA of 3.0. Additional exam requirements/recommendations for international students: Required—TOEFL (minimum score 550 paper-based; 213 computer-based; 80 iBT). *Application deadline:* For fall admission, 10/2 priority date for domestic and international students; for winter admission, 1/8 priority date for domestic and international students; for spring admission, 4/8 priority date for domestic and international students. Applications are processed on a rolling basis. Application fee: $30 ($100 for international students). *Expenses:* Tuition: Full-time $12,960; part-time $370 per credit hour. Required fees: $340. One-time fee: $30 full-time. Tuition and fees vary according to course level and course load. *Financial support:* In 2009–10, 631 students received support. Career-related internships or fieldwork, institutionally sponsored loans, tuition waivers (partial), and unspecified assistantships available. Financial award application deadline: 6/30; financial award applicants required to submit FAFSA. *Unit head:* Dan Kemper, Dean, 636-949-4501, Fax: 636-949-4505, E-mail: dkemper@lindenwood.edu. *Application contact:* Brett Barger, Dean of Evening Admissions and Extension Campuses, 636-949-4934, Fax: 636-949-4109, E-mail: adultadmissions@lindenwood.edu.

Long Island University, C.W. Post Campus, College of Management, Department of Health Care and Public Administration, Brookville, NY 11548-1300. Offers gerontology (Certificate); health care administration (MPA); health care administration/gerontology (MPA); nonprofit management (MPA, Certificate); public administration (MPA). *Accreditation:* NASPAA (one or more programs are accredited). Part-time and evening/weekend programs available. *Degree requirements:* For master's, thesis. *Entrance requirements:* For master's, GMAT, minimum GPA of 2.5; for Certificate, minimum GPA of 2.5. Electronic applications accepted. *Faculty research:* Critical issues in sexuality, social work in religious communities, gerontological social work.

Long Island University, Rockland Graduate Campus, Graduate School, Programs in Health and Public Administration, Orangeburg, NY 10962. Offers gerontology (Advanced Certificate); health administration (MPA); public administration (MPA). *Faculty:* 1 full-time (0 women), 5 part-time/adjunct (3 women). *Students:* 2 full-time (1 woman), 25 part-time (19 women). In 2009, 8 master's awarded. *Entrance requirements:* For master's, GRE General Test. *Application deadline:* Applications are processed on a rolling basis. Application fee: $30. *Expenses:* Tuition: Part-time $930 per credit. Required fees: $200 per semester. *Financial support:* Applicants required to submit FAFSA. *Unit head:* Prof. Patricia Latona, Program Director, 845-359-7200 Ext. 5410, Fax: 845-359-7248, E-mail: patricia.latona@liu.edu. *Application contact:* Peter S. Reiner, Director of Admissions and Marketing, 845-359-7200, Fax: 845-359-7248, E-mail: peter.reiner@liu.edu.

Marywood University, Academic Affairs, College of Health and Human Services, Department of Nursing and Public Administration, Program in Gerontology, Scranton, PA 18509-1598. Offers MS. *Students:* 4 full-time (all women), 2 international. Average age 24. In 2009, 1 master's awarded. *Entrance requirements:* Additional exam requirements/recommendations for international students: Required—TOEFL (minimum score 550 paper-based; 213 computer-based; 79 iBT). *Application deadline:* For fall admission, 4/1 for domestic students, 3/31 for international students; for spring admission, 11/1 for domestic students, 8/31 for international students. Applications are processed on a rolling basis. Application fee: $35. Electronic applications accepted. *Expenses:* Tuition: Part-time $715 per credit. Required fees: $270 per semester. Tuition and fees vary according to degree level, campus/location and program. *Financial support:* Career-related internships or fieldwork, scholarships/grants, and unspecified assistantships available. Support available to part-time students. Financial award application deadline: 6/30; financial award applicants required to submit FAFSA. *Faculty research:* Dementia. *Application contact:* Tammy Manka, Assistant Director of Graduate Admissions, 866-279-9663, E-mail: tmanka@marywood.edu.

Miami University, Graduate School, College of Arts and Sciences, Department of Sociology and Gerontology, Oxford, OH 45056. Offers gerontology (MGS); social gerontology (PhD). Part-time programs available. *Students:* 28 full-time (21 women), 6 part-time (4 women); includes 2 minority (1 African American, 1 Asian American or Pacific Islander), 8 international. *Entrance requirements:* For master's, GRE General Test, minimum undergraduate GPA of 3.0 during previous 2 years or 2.75 overall; for doctorate, GRE, minimum undergraduate GPA of 3.0 during previous 2 years or 2.75 overall. Additional exam requirements/recommendations for international students: Required—TOEFL. Application fee: $50. *Expenses:* Tuition, state resident: full-time $11,280. Tuition, nonresident: full-time $24,912. Required fees: $516. *Financial support:* Fellowships, research assistantships, teaching assistantships, career-related internships or fieldwork, Federal Work-Study, institutionally sponsored loans, health care benefits, tuition waivers (full), and unspecified assistantships available. Financial award application deadline: 3/1; financial award applicants required to submit FAFSA. *Unit head:* Dr. Suzanne R. Kunkel, Director, Scripps Gerontology Center, 513-529-2914, Fax: 513-529-1476, E-mail: scripps@muohio.edu. *Application contact:* Dr. Lisa Groger, Director of Graduate Programs, 513-529-2914, Fax: 513-529-1476, E-mail: scripps@muohio.edu.

Middle Tennessee State University, College of Graduate Studies, Program in Gerontology, Murfreesboro, TN 37132. Offers Graduate Certificate. Part-time and evening/weekend programs available. Postbaccalaureate distance learning degree programs offered. *Students:* 1 (woman) full-time, 3 part-time (all women); includes 3 minority (all African Americans). *Entrance requirements:* Additional exam requirements/recommendations for international students: Required—TOEFL (minimum score 525 paper-based; 195 computer-based; 71 iBT) or IELTS (minimum score 6). *Expenses:* Tuition, state resident: full-time $4404. Tuition, nonresident: full-time $10,956. *Financial support:* Application deadline: 5/1. *Unit head:* Dr. Brandon Wallace, Program Director, 615-898-5976, E-mail: jbwallae@mtsu.edu. *Application contact:* Dr. Michael Allen, Dean and Vice Provost for Research, 615-898-2840, Fax: 615-904-8020, E-mail: mallen@mtsu.edu.

Minnesota State University Mankato, College of Graduate Studies, College of Social and Behavioral Sciences, Program in Gerontology, Mankato, MN 56001. Offers MS, Certificate. *Students:* 4 full-time (3 women), 5 part-time (all women). *Degree requirements:* For master's, comprehensive exam, thesis. *Entrance requirements:* For master's, GRE, minimum GPA of 3.0 during previous 2 years, letters of recommendation. Additional exam requirements/recommendations for international students: Required—TOEFL. *Application deadline:* For fall admission, 7/1 priority date for domestic students; for spring admission, 11/1 for domestic students. Applications are processed on a rolling basis. Application fee: $40. Electronic applications accepted. *Expenses:* Tuition, state resident: full-time $5364. Tuition, nonresident: full-time $8314. *Financial support:* Federal Work-Study and unspecified assistantships available. Support available to part-time students. Financial award application deadline: 3/15; financial award applicants required to submit FAFSA. *Unit head:* Dr. Don Ebel, Director, 507-389-5188. *Application contact:* 507-389-2321, E-mail: grad@mnsu.edu.

Morehead State University, Graduate Programs, Caudill College of Arts, Humanities and Social Sciences, Department of Sociology, Social Work and Criminology, Morehead, KY 40351. Offers criminology (MA); general sociology (MA); gerontology (MA); sociology regional analysis (MA); sociology/chemical dependency (MA). Part-time and evening/weekend programs available. *Faculty:* 6 full-time (3 women), 1 (woman) part-time/adjunct. *Students:* 14 full-time (11 women), 18 part-time (12 women). Average age 34. 27 applicants, 78% accepted, 14 enrolled. In 2009, 5 master's awarded. *Degree requirements:* For master's, comprehensive exam, thesis (for some programs). *Entrance requirements:* For master's, GRE General Test, minimum GPA of 3.0 in sociology, 2.75 overall; 18 hours of course work in sociology, writing sample. Additional exam requirements/recommendations for international students: Required—TOEFL (minimum score 500 paper-based; 173 computer-based). *Application deadline:* For fall admission, 8/1 priority date for domestic and international students; for spring admission, 12/1 priority date for domestic and international students. Applications are processed on a rolling basis. Application fee: $30. Electronic applications accepted. *Expenses:* Tuition, state resident: full-time $6318; part-time $351 per credit hour. Tuition, nonresident: full-time $15,804; part-time $878 per credit hour. *Financial support:* In 2009–10, 4 teaching assistantships (averaging $10,000 per year) were awarded; career-related internships or fieldwork, Federal Work-Study, and unspecified assistantships also available. Financial award application deadline: 3/15; financial award applicants required to submit FAFSA. *Faculty research:* Death and dying; aging, drinking, and drugs; economic development; adult children of alcoholics. *Unit head:* Dr. Clarenda Phillips, Department Chair, 606-783-2434, Fax: 606-783-5070, E-mail: c.phillips@moreheadstate.edu. *Application contact:* Michelle Barber, Graduate Recruitment and Retention Assistant Director, 606-783-5127, Fax: 606-783-5061, E-mail: m.barber@moreheadstate.edu.

Mount Saint Vincent University, Graduate Programs, Department of Family Studies and Gerontology, Halifax, NS B3M 2J6, Canada. Offers MA. Part-time programs available. Postbaccalaureate distance learning degree programs offered (minimal on-campus study). *Degree requirements:* For master's, thesis. *Entrance requirements:* For master's, minimum GPA of 3.0; course work in statistics, research methods, family and social theories.

North Dakota State University, College of Graduate and Interdisciplinary Studies, College of Human Development and Education, Department of Child Development and Family Science, Fargo, ND 58108. Offers child development and family science (MS); couple and family therapy (MS); family financial planning (MS); gerontology (MS, PhD). *Accreditation:* AAMFT/COAMFTE. Part-time and evening/weekend programs available. Postbaccalaureate distance learning degree programs offered (no on-campus study). *Faculty:* 12 full-time (7 women). *Students:* 26 full-time (25 women), 21 part-time (18 women); includes 1 African American, 2 international. 22 applicants, 64% accepted, 12 enrolled. In 2009, 12 master's awarded. *Degree requirements:* For master's, thesis or alternative; for doctorate, thesis/dissertation. *Entrance requirements:* Additional exam requirements/recommendations for international students: Required—TOEFL (minimum score 525 paper-based; 197 computer-based; 71 iBT). *Application deadline:* For fall admission, 2/1 for domestic and international students; for spring admission, 10/1 for domestic and international students. Application fee: $45 ($60 for international students). *Financial support:* In 2009–10, 17 students received support, including research assistantships with full tuition reimbursements available (averaging $3,000 per year), 17 teaching assistantships with full tuition reimbursements available (averaging $3,000 per year); career-related internships or fieldwork, Federal Work-Study, institutionally sponsored loans, and tuition waivers (full) also available. Financial award application deadline: 4/1. *Faculty research:* Family therapy, resilience, parenting, adolescent development, mental health. Total annual research expenditures: $333,582. *Unit head:* Dr. James Deal, Head, 701-231-7568, Fax: 701-231-9645, E-mail: jim_deal@ndsu.edu. *Application contact:* Theresa Anderson, Administrative Assistant, 701-231-8628, Fax: 701-231-9645, E-mail: theresa.anderson@ndsu.edu.

Northeastern Illinois University, Graduate College, College of Arts and Sciences, Department of Gerontology, Program in Gerontology, Chicago, IL 60625-4699. Offers MA. Part-time and evening/weekend programs available. *Degree requirements:* For master's, comprehensive exam, paper and project or thesis, practicum. *Entrance requirements:* For master's, 15 hours in social sciences (3 hours in gerontology), 1 course in research methods or statistics, minimum GPA of 2.75. Additional exam requirements/recommendations for international students: Required—TOEFL (minimum score 550 paper-based; 213 computer-based; 80 iBT). Electronic applications accepted. *Faculty research:* Later life development, cultural diversity, humanities and aging, elder abuse, AIDS and aging, computer training.

Oregon Health & Science University, School of Nursing, Program in Nursing Education, Portland, OR 97239-3098. Offers MN; MS, Post Master's Certificate. Tuition and fees vary according to course level, course load, degree level, program and reciprocity agreements.

Oregon State University, Graduate School, College of Health and Human Sciences, Department of Human Development and Family Sciences, Program in Gerontology, Corvallis, OR 97331. Offers MAIS. *Degree requirements:* For master's, thesis optional. *Entrance requirements:* For master's, GRE, minimum GPA of 3.0 in last 90 hours. Additional exam requirements/recommendations for international students: Required—TOEFL. *Application deadline:* For fall admission, 1/15 for domestic students. Application fee: $50. *Expenses:* Tuition, state resident: full-time $9774; part-time $362 per credit. Tuition, nonresident: full-time $15,849; part-time $587 per credit. Required fees: $1639. Full-time tuition and fees vary according to course load and program. *Financial support:* Research assistantships, teaching assistantships, career-related internships or fieldwork, Federal Work-Study, and institutionally sponsored loans available. Support available to part-time students. Financial award application deadline: 2/1. *Faculty research:* Aging/families, social/psychological aspects of aging, osteoporosis, nutrition, disease and aging. *Unit head:* Dr. Karen Hooker, Director, 541-737-4336, Fax: 541-737-1076, E-mail: hookerk@oregonstate.edu. *Application contact:* Dr. Karen Hooker, Director, 541-737-4336, Fax: 541-737-1076, E-mail: hookerk@oregonstate.edu.

Portland State University, Graduate Studies, College of Urban and Public Affairs, School of Community Health, Institute on Aging, Portland, OR 97207-0751. Offers Certificate. Part-time programs available.

Rochester Institute of Technology, Graduate Enrollment Services, College of Applied Science and Technology, Department of Hospitality and Service Management, Rochester, NY 14623-5603. Offers health systems administration (MS, AC), including elements of health care leadership (AC), health information resources (AC), health systems administration (MS), health systems administration executive leader (MS), health systems-finance (AC), senior living management (AC); hospitality-tourism management (MS); human resources development (MS); service leadership and innovation (MS). Part-time and evening/weekend programs available. Postbaccalaureate distance learning degree programs offered (no on-campus study). *Students:* 40 full-time (27 women), 95 part-time (62 women); includes 21 minority (16 African Americans, 2 American Indian/Alaska Native, 3 Hispanic Americans), 27 international. Average age 33. 152 applicants, 67% accepted, 54 enrolled. In 2009, 60 master's, 3 other advanced degrees awarded. *Degree requirements:* For master's, thesis or alternative. *Entrance requirements:* For master's and AC, minimum GPA of 3.0. Additional exam requirements/recommendations for international students: Required—TOEFL (minimum score 550 paper-based; 213 computer-based; 79 iBT), or IELTS (minimum score 6.5). *Application deadline:* For fall admission, 2/15 priority date for domestic and international students; for winter admission, 11/1 priority date for domestic students, 10/1 priority date for international students; for spring admission, 2/1 priority date for domestic students, 1/1 priority date for international students. Applications are processed on a rolling basis. Application fee: $50. Electronic applications accepted. *Expenses:* Tuition: Full-time $31,533; part-time $876 per credit hour. Required fees: $210. *Financial support:* In 2009–10, 82 students received support; research assistantships with partial tuition reimbursements available, teaching assistantships with partial tuition reimbursements available, career-related internships or fieldwork, scholarships/grants, and unspecified assistantships available. Support available to part-time students. Financial award applicants required to submit FAFSA. *Faculty research:* Investment criterion in hotel development, legal impacts on meeting/conference planning, tourism marketing systems, computers in the food industry. *Unit head:* Dr. Linda Underhill, Interim Co-Chair, 585-475-2867, Fax: 585-475-

Gerontology

Rochester Institute of Technology (continued)
5099, E-mail: lmuism@rit.edu. *Application contact:* Diane Ellison, Assistant Vice President, Graduate Enrollment Services, 585-475-2229, Fax: 585-475-7164, E-mail: gradinfo@rit.edu.

Sacred Heart University, Graduate Programs, College of Education and Health Professions, Program in Geriatric Health and Wellness, Fairfield, CT 06825-1000. Offers MS. Part-time and evening/weekend programs available. Postbaccalaureate distance learning degree programs offered. *Faculty:* 6 full-time (4 women). *Students:* 12 part-time (9 women); includes 3 minority (2 African Americans, 1 Asian American or Pacific Islander). Average age 35. 11 applicants, 100% accepted, 10 enrolled. *Entrance requirements:* Additional exam requirements/recommendations for international students: Required—TOEFL (minimum score 550 paper-based; 213 computer-based; 75 iBT). *Application deadline:* Applications are processed on a rolling basis. Application fee: $50 ($100 for international students). Electronic applications accepted. *Expenses:* Contact institution. *Financial support:* Applicants required to submit FAFSA. *Unit head:* Dr. Michelle Lusardi, Director, 203-365-4721. *Application contact:* Kathy Dilks, Assistant Dean of Graduate Admissions, Health Professions, 203-396-8259, Fax: 203-365-4732, E-mail: gradstudies@sacredheart.edu.

Sage Graduate School, Graduate School, School of Management, Program in Health Services Administration, Troy, NY 12180-4115. Offers dietetic internship (Certificate); gerontology (MS). Part-time and evening/weekend programs available. *Faculty:* 4 full-time (2 women), 6 part-time/adjunct (0 women). *Students:* 7 full-time (6 women), 19 part-time (15 women); includes 4 minority (2 African Americans, 2 Hispanic Americans). Average age 29. 16 applicants. In 2009, 5 master's awarded. *Entrance requirements:* For master's, minimum GPA of 2.75, resume, 2 letters of recommendation. Additional exam requirements/recommendations for international students: Required—TOEFL (minimum score 550 paper-based; 213 computer-based). Application fee: $40. *Expenses:* Tuition: Full-time $10,620; part-time $590 per credit hour. *Financial support:* Fellowships, research assistantships, Federal Work-Study, scholarships/grants, and unspecified assistantships available. Support available to part-time students. Financial award application deadline: 3/1; financial award applicants required to submit FAFSA. *Unit head:* Dr. Kimberly Fredricks, Program Director, 518-292-1700, Fax: 518-292-5414, E-mail: fredek1@sage.edu. *Application contact:* Wendy D. Diefendorf, Director of Graduate and Adult Admission, 518-244-2443, Fax: 518-244-6880, E-mail: diefew@sage.edu.

St. Cloud State University, School of Graduate Studies, College of Social Sciences, Program in Gerontology, St. Cloud, MN 56301-4498. Offers MS. Part-time programs available. *Faculty:* 8 full-time (5 women). *Students:* 13 full-time (9 women), 5 part-time (4 women); includes 2 minority (both African Americans). 5 applicants, 100% accepted. In 2009, 1 master's awarded. *Degree requirements:* For master's, thesis or alternative. *Entrance requirements:* For master's, GRE General Test, minimum GPA of 2.75. Additional exam requirements/recommendations for international students: Required—Michigan English Language Assessment Battery; Recommended—TOEFL (minimum score 550 paper-based; 213 computer-based), IELTS (minimum score 6.5). *Application deadline:* For fall admission, 6/1 priority date for domestic students, 6/1 for international students; for spring admission, 10/1 priority date for domestic students, 10/1 for international students. Applications are processed on a rolling basis. Application fee: $35. Electronic applications accepted. *Financial support:* Federal Work-Study, scholarships/grants, and unspecified assistantships available. Financial award application deadline: 3/1. *Unit head:* Dr. Phyllis Greenberg, Coordinator, 320-308-3947, E-mail: pgreenberg@stcloudstate.edu. *Application contact:* Linda Lou Krueger, School of Graduate Studies, 320-308-2113, Fax: 320-308-5371, E-mail: lekrueger@stcloudstate.edu.

Saint Joseph College, Department of Gerontology, West Hartford, CT 06117-2700. Offers human development/gerontology (MA, Certificate). Part-time and evening/weekend programs available. *Students:* 3 full-time (all women), 22 part-time (20 women); includes 7 minority (4 African Americans, 1 Asian American or Pacific Islander, 2 Hispanic Americans). *Entrance requirements:* For master's, 2 letters of recommendation. *Application deadline:* Applications are processed on a rolling basis. Application fee: $50. Electronic applications accepted. *Expenses:* Tuition: Part-time $595 per credit. Required fees: $30 per credit. Tuition and fees vary according to program. *Financial support:* Career-related internships or fieldwork and unspecified assistantships available. Support available to part-time students. Financial award applicants required to submit FAFSA. *Application contact:* Graduate Admissions Office, 860-231-5261, E-mail: graduate@sjc.edu.

Saint Joseph's University, College of Arts and Sciences, Program in Gerontological Services, Philadelphia, PA 19131-1395. Offers gerontological counseling (MS); gerontological services (Post-Master's Certificate); human services administration (MS). Part-time and evening/weekend programs available. *Students:* 2 full-time (0 women), 8 part-time (all women); includes 2 minority (both African Americans), 2 international. Average age 34. In 2009, 5 master's awarded. *Entrance requirements:* For master's, 2 letters of recommendation. Additional exam requirements/recommendations for international students: Required—TOEFL (minimum score 550 paper-based; 213 computer-based; 79 iBT). *Application deadline:* For fall admission, 7/15 priority date for domestic students, 4/15 for international students; for winter admission, 7/15 for international students; for spring admission, 11/15 priority date for domestic students, 10/15 for international students. Applications are processed on a rolling basis. Application fee: $35. Electronic applications accepted. *Expenses:* Tuition: Part-time $729 per credit hour. Tuition and fees vary according to degree level and program. *Financial support:* Fellowships available. Financial award applicants required to submit FAFSA. *Unit head:* Dr. Catherine Murray, Director, 610-660-1805, E-mail: cmurray@sju.edu. *Application contact:* Kate McConnell, Director, Graduate College of Arts and Sciences Admissions and Retention, 610-660-3184, Fax: 610-660-3230, E-mail: kate.mcconnell@sju.edu.

San Diego State University, Graduate and Research Affairs, College of Health and Human Services, Department of Gerontology, San Diego, CA 92182. Offers MS. Part-time and evening/weekend programs available. *Degree requirements:* For master's, thesis. *Entrance requirements:* For master's, GRE General Test. Additional exam requirements/recommendations for international students: Required—TOEFL. Electronic applications accepted.

San Francisco State University, Division of Graduate Studies, College of Health and Human Services, Gerontology Program, San Francisco, CA 94132-1722. Offers geriatric care management (MA); health, wellness and aging (MA); long-term care administration (MA). Part-time programs available.

San Jose State University, Graduate Studies and Research, College of Applied Sciences and Arts, Department of Health Science, San Jose, CA 95192-0001. Offers applied social gerontology (Certificate); community health education (MPH). *Accreditation:* CEPH (one or more programs are accredited). Postbaccalaureate distance learning degree programs offered. *Students:* 26 full-time (21 women), 51 part-time (45 women); includes 42 minority (6 African Americans, 1 American Indian/Alaska Native, 16 Asian Americans or Pacific Islanders, 19 Hispanic Americans), 3 international. Average age 33. 121 applicants, 24% accepted, 25 enrolled. In 2009, 11 master's awarded. *Entrance requirements:* For master's, GRE General Test. *Application deadline:* For fall admission, 6/29 for domestic students; for spring admission, 11/30 for domestic students. Applications are processed on a rolling basis. Application fee: $59. Electronic applications accepted. *Financial support:* Career-related internships or fieldwork, Federal Work-Study, and institutionally sponsored loans available. Support available to part-time students. Financial award applicants required to submit FAFSA. *Faculty research:* Behavioral science in occupational and health care settings, epidemiology in health care settings. *Unit head:* Dr. Kathleen Roe, Chair, 408-924-2976, Fax: 408-924-2979. *Application contact:* Dr. Kathleen Roe, Chair, 408-924-2976, Fax: 408-924-2979.

Shippensburg University of Pennsylvania, School of Graduate Studies, College of Education and Human Services, Department of Social Work and Gerontology, Shippensburg, PA 17257-2299. Offers aging (Certificate); social work (MSW). Part-time and evening/weekend programs available. Postbaccalaureate distance learning degree programs offered. *Degree requirements:* For master's, thesis, practicum. *Entrance requirements:* For master's, GRE or MAT, 3 letters of reference; resume; minimum GPA of 2.8; course work in human biology, economics, government/political science, psychology, sociology/anthropology and statistics. Additional exam requirements/recommendations for international students: Required—TOEFL (minimum score 560 paper-based; 220 computer-based); Recommended—IELTS (minimum score 6). Electronic applications accepted.

Simon Fraser University, Graduate Studies, Faculty of Arts and Social Sciences, Department of Gerontology, Burnaby, BC V5A 1S6, Canada. Offers MA, PhD. *Degree requirements:* For master's, thesis (for some programs). *Entrance requirements:* For master's, minimum GPA of 3.5. Additional exam requirements/recommendations for international students: Required—TOEFL or IELTS. *Faculty research:* Aging and the built environment, health promotion and aging.

Texas A&M University–Kingsville, College of Graduate Studies, College of Arts and Sciences, Department of Psychology and Sociology, Kingsville, TX 78363. Offers gerontology (MS); psychology (MA, MS); sociology (MA, MS). Part-time and evening/weekend programs available. *Degree requirements:* For master's, comprehensive exam, thesis or alternative. *Entrance requirements:* For master's, GRE General Test, minimum GPA of 2.5. Additional exam requirements/recommendations for international students: Required—TOEFL. *Faculty research:* Hispanic female voting behavior, attitudes toward criminal justice, immigration of aged into south Texas, folk medicine.

Texas Tech University, Graduate School, College of Human Sciences, Department of Human Development and Family Studies, Lubbock, TX 79409. Offers gerontology (MS); human development and family studies (MS, PhD). *Accreditation:* AAMFT/COAMFTE (one or more programs are accredited). Part-time programs available. *Faculty:* 19 full-time (15 women). *Students:* 42 full-time (35 women), 11 part-time (5 women); includes 6 minority (1 American Indian/Alaska Native, 1 Asian American or Pacific Islander, 4 Hispanic Americans), 14 international. Average age 33. 47 applicants, 62% accepted, 9 enrolled. In 2009, 7 master's, 5 doctorates awarded. *Degree requirements:* For master's, thesis; for doctorate, thesis/dissertation. *Entrance requirements:* For master's and doctorate, GRE General Test. Additional exam requirements/recommendations for international students: Required—TOEFL (minimum score 550 paper-based; 213 computer-based). *Application deadline:* For fall admission, 3/1 priority date for international students; for spring admission, 11/1 priority date for international students. Applications are processed on a rolling basis. Application fee: $50 ($75 for international students). Electronic applications accepted. *Expenses:* Tuition, state resident: full-time $5100; part-time $213 per credit hour. Tuition, nonresident: full-time $11,748; part-time $490 per credit hour. Required fees: $2298; $50 per credit hour. $555 per semester. *Financial support:* In 2009–10, 4 research assistantships with partial tuition reimbursements (averaging $25,450 per year), 21 teaching assistantships with partial tuition reimbursements (averaging $21,163 per year) were awarded; career-related internships or fieldwork, Federal Work-Study, institutionally sponsored loans, and scholarships/grants also available. Support available to part-time students. Financial award application deadline: 4/15; financial award applicants required to submit FAFSA. *Faculty research:* Parenting, marital and premarital relationships, adolescent risky behaviors, life span; child development. Total annual research expenditures: $60,398. *Unit head:* Malinda Colwell, Chair, 806-742-3000 Ext. 279, Fax: 806-742-0285, E-mail: malinda.colwell@ttu.edu. *Application contact:* Monya Castle, Graduate Secretary, 806-742-3000 Ext. 250, Fax: 806-742-0285, E-mail: monya.castle@ttu.edu.

Towson University, College of Graduate Studies and Research, Program in Applied Gerontology, Towson, MD 21252-0001. Offers MS, Certificate. *Entrance requirements:* For master's, minimum of 9 credits of upper-level related coursework, 2 letters of recommendation; for Certificate, minimum of 9 credits of upper-level related coursework. Electronic applications accepted.

Université de Montréal, Faculty of Medicine, Program in Specialized Studies, Montréal, QC H3C 3J7, Canada. Offers anesthesia (DESS); diagnostic radiology (DESS); family medicine (DESS); gastroenterology (DESS); geriatry (DESS); intensive care (DESS); medical biochemistry (DESS); medical genetics (DESS); medicine (DESS); microbiology and infectious diseases (DESS); nuclear medicine (DESS); obstetrics and gynecology (DESS); ophthalmology (DESS); pediatrics (DESS); pneumology (DESS); psychiatry (DESS); radiology-oncology (DESS); rheumatology (DESS); surgery (DESS). *Entrance requirements:* For degree, proficiency in French. Electronic applications accepted.

Université de Sherbrooke, Faculty of Letters and Human Sciences, Department of Psychology, Sherbrooke, QC J1K 2R1, Canada. Offers gerontology (MA). *Degree requirements:* For master's, thesis. *Faculty research:* Human relations.

Université Laval, Faculty of Medicine, Post-Professional Programs in Medical Studies, Québec, QC G1K 7P4, Canada. Offers anatomy–pathology (DESS); anesthesiology (DESS); cardiology (DESS); care of older people (Diploma); clinical research (DESS); community health (DESS); dermatology (DESS); diagnostic radiology (DESS); emergency medicine (Diploma); family medicine (DESS); general surgery (DESS); geriatrics (DESS); hematology (DESS); internal medicine (DESS); maternal and fetal medicine (Diploma); medical biochemistry (DESS); medical microbiology and infectious diseases (DESS); medical oncology (DESS); nephrology (DESS); neurology (DESS); neurosurgery (DESS); obstetrics and gynecology (DESS); ophthalmology (DESS); orthopedic surgery (DESS); oto-rhino-laryngology (DESS); palliative medicine (Diploma); pediatrics (DESS); plastic surgery (DESS); psychiatry (DESS); pulmonary medicine (DESS); radiology–oncology (DESS); thoracic surgery (DESS); urology (DESS). *Degree requirements:* For other advanced degree, comprehensive exam. *Entrance requirements:* For degree, knowledge of French. Electronic applications accepted.

University of Arkansas at Little Rock, Graduate School, College of Arts, Humanities, and Social Science, Program in Gerontology, Little Rock, AR 72204-1099. Offers Graduate Certificate.

University of Central Florida, College of Health and Public Affairs, School of Social Work, Orlando, FL 32816. Offers aging studies (Certificate); children's services (Certificate); social work (MSW); social work administration (Certificate). *Accreditation:* CSWE. Part-time and evening/weekend programs available. *Faculty:* 16 full-time (11 women), 18 part-time/adjunct (14 women). *Students:* 149 full-time (129 women), 118 part-time (99 women); includes 91 minority (58 African Americans, 3 Asian Americans or Pacific Islanders, 30 Hispanic Americans), 4 international. Average age 31. 270 applicants, 80% accepted, 170 enrolled. In 2009, 79 master's, 10 other advanced degrees awarded. *Degree requirements:* For master's, thesis or alternative, field education. *Entrance requirements:* For master's, resume. Additional exam requirements/recommendations for international students: Required—TOEFL. *Application deadline:* For fall admission, 3/1 for domestic students. Application fee: $30. Electronic applications accepted. *Expenses:* Tuition, state resident: part-time $306.31 per credit hour. Tuition, nonresident: part-time $1099.01 per credit hour. Part-time tuition and fees vary according to degree level and program. *Financial support:* In 2009–10, 5 students received support, including 2 fellowships with partial tuition reimbursements available (averaging $10,000 per year), 1 research assistantship with partial tuition reimbursement available (averaging $7,100 per year), 2 teaching assistantships with partial tuition reimbursements available (averaging $3,200 per year); career-related internships or fieldwork, Federal Work-Study, institutionally sponsored loans, and unspecified assistantships also available. Financial award application deadline: 3/1; financial award applicants required to submit FAFSA. *Unit head:* Dr. John Ronnau, Director, 407-823-2114, Fax: 407-823-5697, E-mail: jronnau@mail.ucf.edu. *Application contact:* Dr. John Ronnau, Director, 407-823-2114, Fax: 407-823-5697, E-mail: jronnau@mail.ucf.edu.

University of Central Missouri, The Graduate School, College of Health and Human Services, Warrensburg, MO 64093. Offers criminal justice (MS); industrial hygiene (MS); occupational safety management (MS); physical education/exercise and sport science (MS); rural family nursing (MS); social gerontology (MS); sociology (MA); speech language pathology and audiology (MS). *Accreditation:* NCATE. Part-time programs available. Postbaccalaureate distance learning degree programs offered. *Faculty:* 53. *Students:* 169 full-time (107 women), 364 part-time (210 women); includes 65 minority (46 African Americans, 1 American Indian/Alaska Native, 5 Asian Americans or Pacific Islanders, 13 Hispanic Americans), 27 international. Average age 32. 236 applicants, 92% accepted, 211 enrolled. In 2009, 153 master's awarded. *Entrance requirements:* Additional exam requirements/recommendations for international students: Required—TOEFL (minimum score 550 paper-based; 79 computer-based). *Application deadline:* For fall admission, 6/1 priority date for domestic students, 5/1 for international students; for spring admission, 10/1 priority date for domestic students, 10/1 for international students. Applications are processed on a rolling basis. Application fee: $30 ($75 for international students). Electronic applications accepted. *Expenses:* Tuition, area resident: Part-time $245.80 per credit hour. Tuition, nonresident: part-time $491.60 per credit hour. Required fees: $24.20 per credit hour. Full-time tuition and fees vary according to course load, degree level, campus/location and reciprocity agreements. *Financial support:* Research assistantships with full and partial tuition reimbursements, teaching assistantships with full and partial tuition reimbursements, career-related internships or fieldwork, Federal Work-Study, scholarships/grants, and administrative and laboratory assistantships available. Support available to part-time students. Financial award application deadline: 3/1; financial award applicants required to submit FAFSA. *Unit head:* Dr. Rick Sluder, Dean, 660-543-4245, Fax: 660-543-4167, E-mail: sluder@ucmo.edu. *Application contact:* Laurie Delap, Admissions Coordinator, 660-543-4621, Fax: 660-543-4778, E-mail: gradinfo@ucmo.edu.

University of Central Oklahoma, College of Graduate Studies and Research, College of Education, Department of Occupational and Technical Education, Program in Adult Education, Edmond, OK 73034-5209. Offers community services (M Ed); gerontology (M Ed). *Accreditation:* NCATE. Part-time programs available. *Entrance requirements:* For master's, GRE General Test. Additional exam requirements/recommendations for international students: Required—TOEFL (minimum score 550 paper-based; 213 computer-based). Electronic applications accepted. *Expenses:* Tuition, state resident: full-time $4128; part-time $172 per credit hour. Tuition, nonresident: full-time $10,373; part-time $432.20 per credit hour. Required fees: $433.20; $18.05 per credit hour.

University of Georgia, College of Public Health, Institute of Gerontology, Athens, GA 30602. Offers Certificate. *Faculty:* 2 full-time (1 woman). *Students:* 3 part-time (all women). 3 applicants, 67% accepted. *Expenses:* Tuition, state resident: full-time $6000; part-time $250 per credit hour. Tuition, nonresident: full-time $20,904; part-time $871 per credit hour. Required fees: $730 per semester. *Unit head:* Dr. Leonard W. Poon, Director, 706-425-3222, E-mail: lpoon@geron.uga.edu. *Application contact:* Dr. Anne H. Glass, Graduate Coordinator, 706-425-3222, E-mail: aglass@geron.uga.edu.

University of Illinois at Springfield, Graduate Programs, College of Education and Human Services, Program in Human Services, Springfield, IL 62703-5407. Offers alcoholism and substance abuse (MA); child and family services (MA); gerontology (MA); social services administration (MA). Part-time and evening/weekend programs available. Postbaccalaureate distance learning degree programs offered (no on-campus study). *Faculty:* 4 full-time (3 women), 1 (woman) part-time/adjunct. *Students:* 34 full-time (32 women), 91 part-time (76 women); includes 34 minority (31 African Americans, 1 American Indian/Alaska Native, 1 Asian American or Pacific Islander, 1 Hispanic American), 1 international. Average age 36. 76 applicants, 54% accepted, 33 enrolled. In 2009, 20 master's awarded. *Degree requirements:* For master's, internship; project or thesis. *Entrance requirements:* For master's, minimum undergraduate GPA of 3.0, 2 letters of recommendation. Additional exam requirements/recommendations for international students: Required—TOEFL (minimum score 500 paper-based; 176 computer-based; 61 iBT). Application fee: $50 ($60 for international students). Electronic applications accepted. *Expenses:* Tuition, state resident: full-time $6390; part-time $266.25 per credit hour. Tuition, nonresident: full-time $14,226; part-time $592.75 per credit hour. Required fees: $2044; $14.36 per credit hour. $722.50 per term. *Financial support:* In 2009–10, research assistantships with full tuition reimbursements (averaging $8,109 per year), teaching assistantships with full tuition reimbursements (averaging $8,109 per year) were awarded; career-related internships or fieldwork, scholarships/grants, health care benefits, and unspecified assistantships also available. Support available to part-time students. Financial award application deadline: 11/15. *Unit head:* Dr. Carolyn Peck, Program Administrator, 217-206-7577, Fax: 217-206-6775, E-mail: peck.carolyn@uis.edu. *Application contact:* Dr. Lynn Pardie, Office of Graduate Studies, 800-252-8533, Fax: 217-206-7623, E-mail: pardie.lynn@uis.edu.

University of Indianapolis, Graduate Programs, Center for Aging and Community, Indianapolis, IN 46227-3697. Offers gerontology (MS, Certificate). Part-time and evening/weekend programs available. Postbaccalaureate distance learning degree programs offered. *Students:* 20 part-time (17 women); includes 2 minority (both African Americans), 1 international. Average age 37. *Degree requirements:* For master's, capstone course. *Entrance requirements:* For master's, 3 letters of recommendation. Additional exam requirements/recommendations for international students: Required—TOEFL (minimum score 550 paper-based; 213 computer-based). *Application deadline:* Applications are processed on a rolling basis. Application fee: $50. *Financial support:* Career-related internships or fieldwork, Federal Work-Study, scholarships/grants, and tuition waivers (full and partial) available. Support available to part-time students. *Unit head:* Dr. Ellen Miller, Executive Director, 317-791-5930, Fax: 317-791-5945, E-mail: emiller@uindy.edu. *Application contact:* Tamora Wolske, Academic Program Director, 317-791-5930, Fax: 317-791-5945, E-mail: wolsketl@uindy.edu.

University of Indianapolis, Graduate Programs, School of Nursing, Indianapolis, IN 46227-3697. Offers family practice (post-RN) (MSN); gerontological nurse practitioner (MSN); nurse-midwifery (MSN); nursing (MSN); nursing administration (MSN); nursing education (MSN); MBA/MSN. *Accreditation:* AACN; ACNM. *Faculty:* 4 full-time (3 women), 2 part-time/adjunct (both women). *Students:* 27 full-time (26 women), 118 part-time (109 women); includes 10 minority (6 African Americans, 1 American Indian/Alaska Native, 1 Asian American or Pacific Islander, 2 Hispanic Americans), 2 international. Average age 38. *Entrance requirements:* For master's, minimum GPA of 3.0, interview, letters of recommendation, resume, IN nursing license, 1 year professional practice. Additional exam requirements/recommendations for international students: Required—TOEFL (minimum score 550 paper-based; 213 computer-based). *Application deadline:* For fall admission, 8/1 for domestic students; for winter admission, 12/15 for domestic students; for spring admission, 4/15 for domestic students. Applications are processed on a rolling basis. Application fee: $50. *Financial support:* Federal Work-Study available. *Unit head:* Dr. Anne Thomas, Dean, 317-788-3206, E-mail: athomas@uindy.edu. *Application contact:* T. C. Crum, Information Contact, 317-788-2128, Fax: 317-788-3542, E-mail: tcrum@uindy.edu.

The University of Kansas, Graduate Studies, College of Liberal Arts and Sciences, Program in Gerontology, Lawrence, KS 66045. Offers MA, PhD, Graduate Certificate. *Students:* 10 applicants, 20% accepted, 0 enrolled. In 2009, 1 doctorate awarded. *Degree requirements:* For master's, thesis; for doctorate, comprehensive exam, thesis/dissertation, written preliminary exam. *Entrance requirements:* For master's and doctorate, GRE, 3 letters of reference. Additional exam requirements/recommendations for international students: Required—TOEFL. *Application deadline:* For fall admission, 2/1 priority date for domestic and international students. Applications are processed on a rolling basis. Application fee: $45 ($55 for international students). Electronic applications accepted. *Expenses:* Tuition, state resident: full-time $6492; part-time $270.50 per credit hour. Tuition, nonresident: full-time $15,510; part-time $646.25 per credit hour. Required fees: $847; $70.56 per credit hour. Tuition and fees vary according to course load and program. *Financial support:* Fellowships with full tuition reimbursements, research assistantships with full tuition reimbursements, career-related internships or fieldwork, traineeships, and unspecified assistantships available. Financial award application deadline: 1/15. *Faculty research:* Communication and aging, work and retirement, family studies, cognitive aging, exercise and disability. *Unit head:* David J. Ekerdt, Center Director, 785-864-4130, Fax: 785-864-2666, E-mail: gerontology@ku.edu. *Application contact:* Susan Kemper, Graduate Adviser, 785-864-0748, E-mail: skemper@ku.edu.

University of Kentucky, Graduate School, College of Public Health, Program in Gerontology, Lexington, KY 40506-0032. Offers PhD. *Degree requirements:* For doctorate, comprehensive exam, thesis/dissertation. *Entrance requirements:* For doctorate, GRE General Test, minimum undergraduate GPA of 2.75, graduate 3.0. Additional exam requirements/recommendations for international students: Required—TOEFL (minimum score 550 paper-based; 213 computer-based). Electronic applications accepted.

University of La Verne, College of Business and Public Management, Program in Gerontology, La Verne, CA 91750-4443. Offers gerontology (Certificate); gerontology administration (MS). Part-time programs available. *Faculty:* 22 full-time (11 women), 41 part-time/adjunct (8 women). *Students:* 13 full-time (11 women), 25 part-time (24 women); includes 16 minority (9 African Americans, 3 Asian Americans or Pacific Islanders, 4 Hispanic Americans). Average age 43. In 2009, 11 master's awarded. *Entrance requirements:* For master's, minimum GPA of 2.5. Additional exam requirements/recommendations for international students: Required—TOEFL (minimum score 550 paper-based; 213 computer-based). *Application deadline:* Applications are processed on a rolling basis. Application fee: $50. *Expenses:* Contact institution. *Financial support:* Institutionally sponsored loans available. Financial award application deadline: 3/2; financial award applicants required to submit FAFSA. *Unit head:* Joan Branin, Chairperson, 909-593-3511 Ext. 4247, E-mail: jbranin@laverne.edu. *Application contact:* Barbara Cox, Program and Admissions Specialist, 909-593-3511 Ext. 4004, Fax: 909-392-2761, E-mail: bcox@laverne.edu.

University of Louisiana at Monroe, Graduate School, College of Arts and Sciences, Program in Gerontology, Monroe, LA 71209-0001. Offers MA, CGS. *Faculty:* 2 full-time (1 woman), 3 part-time/adjunct (all women). *Students:* 14 full-time (13 women), 21 part-time (20 women); includes 14 minority (all African Americans), 1 international. Average age 35. In 2009, 4 master's awarded. *Degree requirements:* For master's, thesis (for some programs), internship. *Entrance requirements:* For master's, GRE General Test, minimum GPA of 2.75. Additional exam requirements/recommendations for international students: Required—TOEFL (minimum score 500 paper-based; 173 computer-based; 61 iBT). *Application deadline:* For fall admission, 8/24 priority date for domestic students, 7/1 for international students; for winter admission, 12/14 priority date for domestic students; for spring admission, 1/19 for domestic students, 11/1 for international students. Applications are processed on a rolling basis. Application fee: $20 ($30 for international students). Electronic applications accepted. *Expenses:* Tuition, state resident: part-time $159 per credit hour. Tuition, nonresident: part-time $159 per credit hour. Required fees: $1300 per year. Tuition and fees vary according to course load. *Financial support:* In 2009–10, 4 research assistantships with full tuition reimbursements (averaging $2,500 per year) were awarded; career-related internships or fieldwork, Federal Work-Study, and unspecified assistantships also available. Financial award application deadline: 4/1; financial award applicants required to submit FAFSA. *Unit head:* Dr. James Bulot, Unit Head, 318-342-1465, Fax: 318-342-1431, E-mail: bulot@ulm.edu. *Application contact:* Paul Karlowitz, Assistant Dean, 318-342-1758, Fax: 318-342-1755, E-mail: karlowitz@ulm.edu.

University of Louisville, Graduate School, Raymond A. Kent School of Social Work, Louisville, KY 40292-0001. Offers marriage and family therapy (PMC); social work (MSSW, PhD), including alcohol and drug counseling (MSSW), gerontology (MSSW), school social work (MSSW). *Accreditation:* AAMFT/COAMFTE; CSWE (one or more programs are accredited). Part-time and evening/weekend programs available. *Faculty:* 23 full-time (15 women), 38 part-time/adjunct (21 women). *Students:* 279 full-time (221 women), 64 part-time (52 women); includes 79 minority (70 African Americans, 2 American Indian/Alaska Native, 2 Asian Americans or Pacific Islanders, 5 Hispanic Americans), 5 international. Average age 32. 288 applicants, 74% accepted, 145 enrolled. In 2009, 137 master's, 4 doctorates awarded. *Degree requirements:* For doctorate, comprehensive exam, thesis/dissertation. *Entrance requirements:* For master's, GRE or minimum GPA of 2.75; for doctorate, GRE General Test, interview, writing sample. Additional exam requirements/recommendations for international students: Required—TOEFL (minimum score 550 paper-based; 213 computer-based; 79 iBT). *Application deadline:* For fall admission, 7/31 for domestic and international students. Applications are processed on a rolling basis. Application fee: $50. Electronic applications accepted. *Financial support:* In 2009–10, 70 students received support, including 9 research assistantships with full tuition reimbursements available (averaging $19,000 per year), 1 teaching assistantship (averaging $19,000 per year); Federal Work-Study, institutionally sponsored loans, scholarships/grants, health care benefits, and unspecified assistantships also available. Support available to part-time students. Financial award application deadline: 5/15; financial award applicants required to submit FAFSA. *Faculty research:* Child welfare, substance abuse, gerontology, family functioning, health behavior. Total annual research expenditures: $2.8 million. *Unit head:* Dr. Terry Singer, Dean, 502-852-6402, Fax: 502-852-0422, E-mail: terry.singer@louisville.edu. *Application contact:* Libby Leggett, Director, Graduate Admissions, 502-852-3101, Fax: 502-852-6536, E-mail: gradadm@louisville.edu.

University of Maryland, Baltimore, Graduate School, Graduate Program in Life Sciences, Program in Gerontology, Baltimore, MD 21201. Offers PhD. *Students:* 6 full-time (all women), 3 part-time (2 women); includes 2 minority (both African Americans). Average age 31. 9 applicants, 33% accepted, 1 enrolled. *Degree requirements:* For doctorate, comprehensive exam, thesis/dissertation. *Entrance requirements:* For doctorate, GRE General Test. Additional exam requirements/recommendations for international students: Required—TOEFL (minimum score 550 paper-based; 80 iBT), or IELTS (minimum score 7). *Application deadline:* For fall admission, 1/15 for domestic and international students. Application fee: $50. Electronic applications accepted. *Expenses:* Tuition, state resident: full-time $7290; part-time $405 per credit hour. Tuition, nonresident: full-time $12,780; part-time $710 per credit hour. Required fees: $774; $10 per credit hour. $297 per semester. Tuition and fees vary according to course load, degree level and program. *Financial support:* Fellowships, research assistantships available. Financial award applicants required to submit FAFSA. *Unit head:* Dr. Denise Orwig, Professor and Program Director, 410-706-4926. *Application contact:* Justine Golden, Coordinator.

University of Maryland, Baltimore, School of Medicine, Department of Epidemiology and Preventive Medicine, Baltimore, MD 21201. Offers biostatistics (MS); clinical research (MS); epidemiology (PhD); epidemiology and preventive medicine (MPH, MS); gerontology (PhD); human genetics and genomic (MS, PhD); molecular epidemiology (PhD); toxicology (MS, PhD); JD/MS; MD/PhD; MS/PhD. *Accreditation:* CEPH. Part-time programs available. *Students:* 64 full-time (42 women), 60 part-time (40 women); includes 40 minority (17 African Americans, 19 Asian Americans or Pacific Islanders, 4 Hispanic Americans), 16 international. Average age 31. 207 applicants, 48% accepted, 50 enrolled. In 2009, 24 master's, 9 doctorates awarded. *Entrance requirements:* For master's and doctorate, GRE General Test, minimum GPA of 3.0. Additional exam requirements/recommendations for international students: Required—TOEFL; Recommended—IELTS. *Application deadline:* For fall admission, 1/15 for domestic and international students. Application fee: $50. Electronic applications accepted. *Expenses:* Tuition, state resident: full-time $7290; part-time $405 per credit hour. Tuition, nonresident: full-time $12,780; part-time $710 per credit hour. Required fees: $774; $10 per credit hour. $297 per semester. Tuition and fees vary according to course load, degree level and program. *Financial support:* In 2009–10, research assistantships with partial tuition reimbursements (averaging $25,000 per year); fellowships also available. Financial award application deadline: 3/1. *Unit head:* Dr. Patricia Langenberg, Program Director, 410-706-3251, Fax: 410-706-8013. *Application contact:* Rachael Holmes, Academic Coordinator, 410-706-8492, Fax: 410-706-4225, E-mail: rholmes@epi.umaryland.edu.

University of Maryland, Baltimore County, Graduate School, Erickson School of Aging Studies, Baltimore, MD 21228. Offers management of aging services (MA). *Faculty:* 3 full-time (1 woman), 16 part-time/adjunct (6 women). *Students:* 25 full-time (21 women), 11 part-time (7 women); includes 5 African Americans, 2 Hispanic Americans. Average age 43. 28 applicants, 46% accepted, 13 enrolled. In 2009, 23 master's awarded. *Application deadline:* Applications are processed on a rolling basis. Electronic applications accepted. *Financial support:* Applicants required to submit FAFSA. *Unit head:* Dr. Janet C. Rutledge, Interim Vice Provost for Graduate

Gerontology

University of Maryland, Baltimore County (continued)

Education, 410-455-2199. *Application contact:* Kathryn Nee, Coordinator of Domestic Admissions, 410-455-2944, E-mail: nee@umbc.edu.

University of Maryland, Baltimore County, Graduate School, Program in Gerontology, Baltimore, MD 21201. Offers aging policy for the elderly (PhD); epidemiology of aging (PhD); social, cultural, and behavioral sciences (PhD). Part-time programs available. *Faculty:* 19 part-time/adjunct (13 women). *Students:* 18 full-time (14 women), 8 part-time (all women); includes 7 minority (5 African Americans, 2 Asian Americans or Pacific Islanders). Average age 34. 26 applicants, 19% accepted, 4 enrolled. In 2009, 3 doctorates awarded. *Degree requirements:* For doctorate, comprehensive exam, thesis/dissertation. *Entrance requirements:* For doctorate, GRE General Test. Additional exam requirements/recommendations for international students: Required—TOEFL, TWE. *Application deadline:* For spring admission, 1/15 for domestic and international students. Application fee: $45. Electronic applications accepted. *Financial support:* In 2009–10, 6 fellowships with full tuition reimbursements (averaging $22,314 per year), 5 research assistantships with full tuition reimbursements (averaging $21,008 per year) were awarded; teaching assistantships with full tuition reimbursements, career-related internships or fieldwork, scholarships/grants, traineeships, health care benefits, tuition waivers (partial), and unspecified assistantships also available. Financial award application deadline: 2/1; financial award applicants required to submit FAFSA. *Faculty research:* Aging and health policy, behavioral aspects of aging, caregiving, LTC, epidemiology of aging. Total annual research expenditures: $39.5 million. *Unit head:* Dr. Leslie Morgan, Co-Director, 410-455-2074, Fax: 410-455-1154, E-mail: lmorgan@umbc.edu. *Application contact:* Justine Golden, Academic Coordinator, 410-706-4926, Fax: 410-706-4433, E-mail: jgold002@umaryland.edu.

University of Massachusetts Boston, Office of Graduate Studies, John W. McCormack Graduate School of Policy Studies, Program in Gerontology, Boston, MA 02125-3393. Offers gerontology (MS, PhD, Certificate); gerontology research (MA); management in aging services (MA). Part-time programs available. *Degree requirements:* For doctorate, comprehensive exam, thesis/dissertation. *Entrance requirements:* For doctorate, GRE General Test, minimum GPA of 3.0. *Faculty research:* Aging with a chronic disability, pension policy and social security system, elderly minorities, health services research, living arrangements.

University of Missouri–St. Louis, College of Arts and Sciences, Program in Gerontology, St. Louis, MO 63121. Offers gerontology (MS, Certificate); long term care administration (Certificate). Part-time and evening/weekend programs available. *Faculty:* 5 full-time (3 women), 8 part-time/adjunct (6 women). *Students:* 6 full-time (2 women), 13 part-time (12 women); includes 3 minority (all African Americans), 1 international. Average age 40. In 2009, 6 master's awarded. *Entrance requirements:* For master's, 3 letters of recommendation. Additional exam requirements/recommendations for international students: Required—TOEFL (minimum score 550 paper-based; 213 computer-based). *Application deadline:* For fall admission, 7/1 priority date for domestic and international students; for spring admission, 12/1 priority date for domestic and international students. Applications are processed on a rolling basis. Application fee: $35 ($40 for international students). Electronic applications accepted. *Expenses:* Tuition, state resident: full-time $5377; part-time $297.70 per credit hour. Tuition, nonresident: full-time $13,882; part-time $771.20 per credit hour. Required fees: $220; $12.20 per credit hour. One-time fee: $12. Tuition and fees vary according to course level, campus/location and program. *Financial support:* In 2009–10, 1 research assistantship with full and partial tuition reimbursement (averaging $5,625 per year) was awarded; career-related internships or fieldwork and Federal Work-Study also available. Financial award applicants required to submit FAFSA. *Faculty research:* Health care policy, social support and stress, retirement policy health behavior, ethnic differences in aging. *Unit head:* Thomas Meuser, Director, 314-516-5421, Fax: 314-516-5210, E-mail: meusert@umsl.edu. *Application contact:* 314-516-5458, Fax: 314-516-6996, E-mail: gradadm@umsl.edu.

University of Nebraska at Omaha, Graduate Studies, College of Education, Department of Counseling, Omaha, NE 68182. Offers community counseling (MA, MS); counseling gerontology (MA, MS); school counseling (MA, MS); student affairs practice in higher education (MA, MS). *Accreditation:* ACA (one or more programs are accredited); NCATE. Part-time and evening/weekend programs available. *Faculty:* 5 full-time (1 woman). *Students:* 34 full-time (28 women), 152 part-time (128 women); includes 14 minority (10 African Americans, 1 Asian American or Pacific Islander, 3 Hispanic Americans). Average age 29. 50 applicants, 38% accepted, 13 enrolled. In 2009, 46 master's awarded. *Degree requirements:* For master's, comprehensive exam, thesis (for some programs). *Entrance requirements:* For master's, GRE General Test, MAT, department test, interview, minimum GPA of 3.0. Additional exam requirements/recommendations for international students: Required—TOEFL (minimum score 550 paper-based; 213 computer-based; 80 iBT). *Application deadline:* For fall admission, 3/1 for domestic students; for spring admission, 10/1 for domestic students. Applications are processed on a rolling basis. Application fee: $45. Electronic applications accepted. *Financial support:* In 2009–10, 79 students received support, including 2 research assistantships with tuition reimbursements available; fellowships, Federal Work-Study, institutionally sponsored loans, scholarships/grants, tuition waivers (partial), and unspecified assistantships also available. Support available to part-time students. Financial award application deadline: 3/1; financial award applicants required to submit FAFSA. *Unit head:* Dr. Jeanette Seaberry, Chairperson, 402-554-2727. *Application contact:* Penny Harmoney, Director, Graduate Studies, 402-554-2341, Fax: 402-554-3143, E-mail: graduate@unomaha.edu.

University of Nebraska at Omaha, Graduate Studies, College of Public Affairs and Community Service, Department of Gerontology, Omaha, NE 68182. Offers gerontology (Certificate); social gerontology (MA). Part-time and evening/weekend programs available. *Faculty:* 5 full-time (2 women). *Students:* 2 full-time (both women), 10 part-time (8 women), 1 international. Average age 36. 12 applicants, 42% accepted, 1 enrolled. In 2009, 1 other advanced degree awarded. *Degree requirements:* For master's, comprehensive exam, thesis. *Entrance requirements:* For master's, GRE General Test, MAT, minimum GPA of 3.0, writing sample, letters of recommendation. Additional exam requirements/recommendations for international students: Required—TOEFL (minimum score 550 paper-based; 213 computer-based; 80 iBT). *Application deadline:* For fall admission, 7/1 priority date for domestic students; for spring admission, 12/1 priority date for domestic students. Applications are processed on a rolling basis. Application fee: $45. Electronic applications accepted. *Financial support:* In 2009–10, 5 students received support; fellowships, career-related internships or fieldwork, Federal Work-Study, institutionally sponsored loans, scholarships/grants, and tuition waivers (partial) available. Support available to part-time students. Financial award application deadline: 3/1; financial award applicants required to submit FAFSA. *Unit head:* Dr. Karl Kosloski, Chairperson, 402-554-2272. *Application contact:* Penny Harmoney, Director, Graduate Studies, 402-554-2341, Fax: 402-554-3143, E-mail: graduate@unomaha.edu.

University of Nebraska–Lincoln, Graduate College, College of Education and Human Sciences, Department of Child, Youth and Family Studies, Lincoln, NE 68588. Offers child development/early childhood education (MS, PhD); child, youth and family studies (MS); family and consumer sciences education (MS, PhD); family financial planning (MS); family science (MS, PhD); gerontology (PhD); human sciences (PhD), including child, youth and family studies, gerontology, medical family therapy; marriage and family therapy (MS); medical family therapy (PhD); youth development (MS). *Accreditation:* AAMFT/COAMFTE (one or more programs are accredited). Postbaccalaureate distance learning degree programs offered. *Degree requirements:* For master's, thesis optional. *Entrance requirements:* For master's, GRE. Additional exam requirements/recommendations for international students: Required—TOEFL (minimum score 550 paper-based; 213 computer-based). Electronic applications accepted. *Faculty research:* Marriage and family therapy, child development/early childhood education, family financial management.

University of New England, Westbrook College of Health Professions, School of Social Work, Biddeford, ME 04005-9526. Offers addictions counseling (Certificate); gerontology (Certificate); social work (MSW). *Accreditation:* CSWE. Part-time programs available. *Faculty:* 12 full-time (8 women), 4 part-time/adjunct (all women). *Students:* 159 full-time (134 women), 2 part-time (both women); includes 6 minority (5 African Americans, 1 American Indian/Alaska Native), 3 international. In 2009, 44 master's awarded. *Degree requirements:* For master's, field internships. *Entrance requirements:* Additional exam requirements/recommendations for international students: Required—TOEFL (minimum score 550 paper-based; 213 computer-based). *Application deadline:* For fall admission, 1/15 priority date for domestic students; for spring admission, 3/31 priority date for domestic students, 3/31 for international students. Applications are processed on a rolling basis. Application fee: $40. Electronic applications accepted. *Financial support:* In 2009–10, 40 students received support. Scholarships/grants and tuition waivers (partial) available. Financial award application deadline: 5/1; financial award applicants required to submit FAFSA. *Faculty research:* Domestic violence, solution-focused practice, empowerment models, adverse childhood experiences. *Unit head:* Martha Wilson, Director, 207-221-4513, E-mail: mwilson@une.edu. *Application contact:* Stacy Gato, Assistant Director of Graduate Admissions, 207-221-4225, Fax: 207-221-4898, E-mail: gradadmissions@une.edu.

The University of North Carolina at Charlotte, Graduate School, College of Arts and Sciences, Program in Gerontology, Charlotte, NC 28223-0001. Offers MA. Part-time programs available. *Faculty:* 1 (woman) part-time/adjunct. *Students:* 9 full-time (all women), 13 part-time (10 women); includes 7 minority (6 African Americans, 1 Hispanic American), 3 international. Average age 29. 11 applicants, 91% accepted, 9 enrolled. In 2009, 5 master's awarded. *Degree requirements:* For master's, thesis optional. *Entrance requirements:* For master's, GRE or MAT. Additional exam requirements/recommendations for international students: Required—TOEFL (minimum score 557 paper-based; 220 computer-based; 83 iBT). *Application deadline:* For fall admission, 7/1 for domestic students, 5/1 for international students; for spring admission, 11/1 for domestic students, 10/1 for international students. Applications are processed on a rolling basis. Application fee: $55. Electronic applications accepted. *Financial support:* In 2009–10, 3 students received support, including 1 research assistantship (averaging $5,000 per year), 2 teaching assistantships (averaging $9,000 per year); career-related internships or fieldwork, institutionally sponsored loans, scholarships/grants, and unspecified assistantships also available. Support available to part-time students. Financial award application deadline: 4/1; financial award applicants required to submit FAFSA. *Faculty research:* Rural older adults; person-centered dementia care; formal and informal systems of care; health care issues: gay, lesbian, and African American aging. *Unit head:* Dr. Dena Shenk, Director, 704-687-4349, Fax: 704-687-4347, E-mail: dshenk@uncc.edu. *Application contact:* Kathy B. Giddings, Director of Graduate Admissions, 704-687-5503, Fax: 704-687-3279, E-mail: gradadm@uncc.edu.

The University of North Carolina at Greensboro, Graduate School, Program in Gerontology, Greensboro, NC 27412-5001. Offers MS, Certificate, MS/MBA. Electronic applications accepted.

The University of North Carolina Wilmington, College of Arts and Sciences, Department of Health and Applied Human Sciences, Wilmington, NC 28403-3297. Offers applied gerontology (MS). Part-time programs available. Postbaccalaureate distance learning degree programs offered. *Degree requirements:* For master's, comprehensive exam, thesis or alternative. *Entrance requirements:* For master's, GRE, minimum undergraduate B average. Additional exam requirements/recommendations for international students: Required—TOEFL (minimum score 550 paper-based; 217 computer-based; 79 iBT), IELTS (minimum score 6.5).

University of Northern Colorado, Graduate School, College of Natural and Health Sciences, School of Human Sciences, Program in Gerontology, Greeley, CO 80639. Offers MA. Part-time programs available. *Faculty:* 2 full-time (both women). *Students:* 8 full-time (7 women), 2 part-time (both women); includes 1 minority (Hispanic American). Average age 33. 7 applicants, 86% accepted, 6 enrolled. In 2009, 4 master's awarded. *Degree requirements:* For master's, comprehensive exam. *Entrance requirements:* For master's, GRE General Test or MAT, 2 letters of recommendation. *Application deadline:* Applications are processed on a rolling basis. Application fee: $50 ($60 for international students). Electronic applications accepted. *Expenses:* Tuition, state resident: full-time $5770; part-time $320.55 per credit hour. Tuition, nonresident: full-time $13,847; part-time $769.27 per credit hour. Required fees: $948.78; $52.72 per credit. *Financial support:* Fellowships, research assistantships, teaching assistantships, unspecified assistantships available. Financial award application deadline: 3/1; financial award applicants required to submit FAFSA. *Unit head:* Dr. Susan Collins, Program Coordinator, 970-351-2403. *Application contact:* Linda Sisson, Graduate Student Admission Coordinator, 970-351-1807, Fax: 970-351-2371, E-mail: linda.sisson@unco.edu.

University of North Florida, Brooks College of Health, Department of Public Health, Jacksonville, FL 32224. Offers community health (MPH); geriatric management (MSH); health administration (MHA); health behavior research and evaluation (Certificate); nutrition (MSH); rehabilitation counseling (MS). *Accreditation:* CEPH; CORE. Part-time and evening/weekend programs available. *Faculty:* 23 full-time (17 women). *Students:* 118 full-time (91 women), 82 part-time (61 women); includes 42 minority (23 African Americans, 8 Asian Americans or Pacific Islanders, 11 Hispanic Americans), 9 international. Average age 31. 192 applicants, 26% accepted, 23 enrolled. In 2009, 69 master's awarded. *Degree requirements:* For master's, thesis optional. *Entrance requirements:* For master's, GRE General Test (MSH, MS, MPH); GMAT or GRE General Test (MHA), minimum GPA of 3.0 in last 60 hours. Additional exam requirements/recommendations for international students: Required—TOEFL (minimum score 500 paper-based; 173 computer-based). *Application deadline:* For fall admission, 7/1 priority date for domestic students, 5/1 for international students; for spring admission, 11/1 priority date for domestic students, 10/1 for international students. Applications are processed on a rolling basis. Application fee: $30. Electronic applications accepted. *Expenses:* Tuition, state resident: full-time $6649.20; part-time $277.05 per credit hour. Tuition, nonresident: full-time $22,970; part-time $957.08 per credit hour. Required fees: $985; $41.03 per credit hour. *Financial support:* In 2009–10, 99 students received support, including 1 teaching assistantship (averaging $1,004 per year); research assistantships, career-related internships or fieldwork, Federal Work-Study, scholarships/grants, and tuition waivers (partial) also available. Support available to part-time students. Financial award application deadline: 4/1; financial award applicants required to submit FAFSA. *Faculty research:* Dietary supplements; alcohol, tobacco, and other drug use prevention; turnover among health professionals; aging; psychosocial aspects of disabilities. Total annual research expenditures: $335,106. *Unit head:* Dr. JoAnn Nolin, Chair, 904-620-2840, Fax: 904-620-2848, E-mail: jnolin@unf.edu. *Application contact:* Heather Kenney, Director of Advising, 904-620-2810, Fax: 904-620-1030, E-mail: heather.kenney@unf.edu.

University of North Texas, Robert B. Toulouse School of Graduate Studies, College of Public Affairs and Community Service, Department of Applied Gerontology, Denton, TX 76203. Offers aging (Certificate); applied gerontology (PhD); general studies in aging (MA, MS); long term care, senior housing, and aging services (MA, MS). Part-time and evening/weekend programs available. Postbaccalaureate distance learning degree programs offered (minimal on-campus study). *Faculty:* 5 full-time (1 woman). *Students:* 20 full-time (13 women), 16 part-time (15 women); includes 14 minority (10 African Americans, 2 Asian Americans or Pacific Islanders, 2 Hispanic Americans), 3 international. Average age 40. 9 applicants, 56% accepted, 4 enrolled. In 2009, 5 master's, 1 doctorate awarded. *Degree requirements:* For master's, comprehensive exam (for some programs), thesis, internship; capstone; for doctorate, one foreign language, comprehensive exam, thesis/dissertation. *Entrance requirements:* For master's and doctorate, GRE General Test. Additional exam requirements/recommendations for international students: Required—proof of English language proficiency required for non-native English speakers; Recommended—TOEFL (minimum score 550 paper-based; 213 computer-based; 79 iBT). *Application deadline:* For fall admission, 7/15 for domestic students; for spring admission, 11/15 for domestic students. Applications are processed on a rolling basis. Application fee: $50 ($75 for international students). *Expenses:* Tuition, state resident: full-time $4298; part-time $239 per contact hour. Tuition, nonresident: full-time $9878; part-time $549 per contact hour. Required fees: $265 per contact hour. *Financial support:* In 2009–10, 22 students received support, including 12 fellowships (averaging $6,750 per year), 3 research assistantships (averaging $4,800 per year), 1 teaching assistantship (averaging $5,100 per year); career-related internships or fieldwork, Federal Work-Study, institutionally sponsored loans, and scholarships/grants also available. Financial award application deadline: 6/1; financial award applicants required to submit FAFSA. *Faculty research:* Minority aging, housing for the elderly, aging and developmental disability, caregiving, public policy and aging. *Unit head:* Dr. Keith W. Turner, Chair, 940-565-2765, Fax: 940-565-4370, E-mail: keith.turner@unt.edu. *Application contact:* Keith Turner, Graduate Advisor, 940-565-2765, Fax: 940-565-4370, E-mail: gerontology@unt.edu.

University of Phoenix, The Artemis School, College of Health and Human Services, Phoenix, AZ 85034-7209. Offers administration of justice and security (MS); community counseling (MSC); education (MHA); family nurse practitioner (MSN); gerontology (MHA); health administration (MHA); health care education (MSN); health care management (MBA, MSN); informatics (MHA); marriage, family, and child therapy (MSC); nursing (MSN); nursing for nurse practitioners (MSN); psychology (MS); MSN/MBA; MSN/MHA. *Accreditation:* AACN. Evening/weekend programs available. Postbaccalaureate distance learning degree programs offered. *Degree requirements:* For master's, thesis (for some programs). *Entrance requirements:* For master's, 3 years of work experience, minimum undergraduate GPA of 2.5, RN license. Additional exam requirements/recommendations for international students: Required—TOEFL (minimum score 550 paper-based; 213 computer-based; 79 iBT). Electronic applications accepted.

University of Phoenix–Birmingham Campus, College of Health and Human Services, Birmingham, AL 35244. Offers education (MHA); gerontology (MHA); health administration (MHA); health care management (MBA); informatics (MHA); nursing (MSN); nursing/health care education (MSN); MSN/MBA; MSN/MHA.

University of Phoenix–Central Valley Campus, College of Health and Human Services, Fresno, CA 93720-1562. Offers education (MHA); gerontology (MHA); health administration (MHA); health care management (MBA); nursing (MSN); MSN/MBA.

University of Phoenix–Chattanooga Campus, College of Health and Human Services, Chattanooga, TN 37421-3707. Offers education (MHA); gerontology (MHA); health administration (MHA); health care management (MBA).

University of Phoenix–Hawaii Campus, The Artemis School, College of Health and Human Services, Honolulu, HI 96813-4317. Offers administration of justice and security (MS); community counseling (MSC); education (MHA); family nurse practitioner (MSN); gerontology (MHA); health administration (MHA); health care management (MBA); marriage, family and child therapy (MSC); nursing (MSN); nursing/health care education (MSN); psychology (MS); MSN/MBA. Evening/weekend programs available. *Degree requirements:* For master's, thesis (for some programs). *Entrance requirements:* For master's, minimum undergraduate GPA of 2.5, 3 years of work experience, RN license. Additional exam requirements/recommendations for international students: Required—TOEFL (minimum score 550 paper-based; 213 computer-based; 79 iBT). Electronic applications accepted.

University of Phoenix–Phoenix Campus, The Artemis School, College of Health and Human Services, Phoenix, AZ 85040-1958. Offers community counseling (MSC); education (MHA); family nurse practitioner (MSN); gerontology (MHA); health administration (MHA); health care education (MSN); health care management (MBA); informatics (MHA); marriage, family, and child therapy (MSC); nurse practitioner (Certificate); nursing (MSN); nursing health care education (Certificate); psychology (MS); MSN/MBA; MSN/MHA. Evening/weekend programs available. *Degree requirements:* For master's, thesis (for some programs). *Entrance requirements:* For master's, 3 years of work experience in field, minimum undergraduate GPA of 2.5, RN license. Additional exam requirements/recommendations for international students: Required—TOEFL (minimum score 550 paper-based; 213 computer-based; 79 iBT). Electronic applications accepted.

University of Phoenix–Southern Colorado Campus, The Artemis School, College of Health and Human Services, Colorado Springs, CO 80919-2335. Offers administration of justice and security (MS); community counseling (MSC); education (MHA); gerontology (MHA); health administration (MHA); health care management (MBA); marriage, family and child therapy (MSC); nursing (MSN); psychology (MS); MSN/MBA. Evening/weekend programs available. *Degree requirements:* For master's, thesis (for some programs). *Entrance requirements:* For master's, minimum undergraduate GPA of 2.5, 3 years of work experience, RN license. Additional exam requirements/recommendations for international students: Required—TOEFL (minimum score 550 paper-based; 213 computer-based; 79 iBT). Electronic applications accepted.

University of Pittsburgh, Graduate School of Public Health, Department of Behavioral and Community Health Science, Pittsburgh, PA 15260. Offers behavioral and community health sciences (MPH, Dr PH); lesbian, gay, bisexual and transgender health and wellness (Certificate); minority health and health disparities (Certificate); program evaluation (Certificate); public health and aging (Certificate); public health preparedness (Certificate); MID/MPH; MPH/MPA; MPH/MSW; MPH/PhD. *Accreditation:* CAHME (one or more programs are accredited). Part-time programs available. *Faculty:* 17 full-time (8 women), 13 part-time/adjunct (3 women). *Students:* 86 full-time (66 women), 46 part-time (37 women); includes 27 minority (20 African Americans, 1 American Indian/Alaska Native, 4 Asian Americans or Pacific Islanders, 2 Hispanic Americans), 7 international. Average age 30. 235 applicants, 74% accepted, 46 enrolled. In 2009, 30 master's, 5 doctorates awarded. *Degree requirements:* For master's, thesis; for doctorate, comprehensive exam, thesis/dissertation, preliminary exams. *Entrance requirements:* For master's and Certificate, GRE; for doctorate, GRE, master's degree in public health or related field. Additional exam requirements/recommendations for international students: Required—TOEFL (minimum score 550 paper-based; 213 computer-based; 80 iBT). *Application deadline:* For fall admission, 5/1 priority date for domestic students, 4/1 for international students; for winter admission, 9/1 for international students; for spring admission, 10/1 priority date for domestic students, 2/1 for international students. Applications are processed on a rolling basis. Application fee: $95. Electronic applications accepted. *Expenses:* Tuition, state resident: full-time $16,402; part-time $665 per credit. Tuition, nonresident: full-time $28,694; part-time $1175 per credit. Required fees: $690; $175 per term. Tuition and fees vary according to program. *Financial support:* In 2009–10, 21 students received support, including 1 fellowship with full tuition reimbursement available (averaging $20,976 per year), 19 research assistantships with full and partial tuition reimbursements available (averaging $12,300 per year), 2 teaching assistantships with full tuition reimbursements available (averaging $15,065 per year); unspecified assistantships also available. *Faculty research:* Maternal and child health, program evaluation, community-based participatory research, minority health and health disparities, aging. Total annual research expenditures: $1.7 million. *Unit head:* Dr. Ronald D. Stall, Chairman, 412-624-7933, Fax: 412-648-5975, E-mail: rstall@pitt.edu. *Application contact:* Natalie C. Arnold, Recruitment and Academic Affairs Administrator, 412-624-3107, Fax: 412-624-5510, E-mail: narnold@pitt.edu.

University of Pittsburgh, School of Social Work, Pittsburgh, PA 15260. Offers gerontology (Certificate); social work (MSW, PhD); M Div/MSW; MPA/MSW; MPH/PhD; MPIA/MSW; MSW/JD; MSW/MAJCS; MSW/MPH. *Accreditation:* CSWE (one or more programs are accredited). Part-time programs available. *Faculty:* 21 full-time (12 women), 35 part-time/adjunct (29 women). *Students:* 392 full-time (325 women), 242 part-time (200 women); includes 114 minority (83 African Americans, 2 American Indian/Alaska Native, 15 Asian Americans or Pacific Islanders, 14 Hispanic Americans). Average age 28. 500 applicants, 86% accepted, 255 enrolled. In 2009, 174 master's, 4 doctorates awarded. *Degree requirements:* For master's, practicum; for doctorate, comprehensive exam, thesis/dissertation; for Certificate, thesis. *Entrance requirements:* For master's, minimum QPA of 3.0, course work in statistics; for doctorate, GRE, MSW or related degree, course work in statistics. Additional exam requirements/recommendations for international students: Required—TOEFL (minimum score 550 paper-based; 213 computer-based; 80 iBT). *Application deadline:* For fall admission, 5/1 for domestic and international students. Applications are processed on a rolling basis. Application fee: $40 ($50 for international students). Electronic applications accepted. *Expenses:* Tuition, state resident: full-time $16,402; part-time $665 per credit. Tuition, nonresident: full-time $28,694; part-time $1175 per credit. Required fees: $690; $175 per term. Tuition and fees vary according to program. *Financial support:* In 2009–10, 213 students received support, including 1 research assistantship with full tuition reimbursement available (averaging $11,830 per year), 3 teaching assistantships with full tuition reimbursements available (averaging $15,065 per year); fellowships, career-related internships or fieldwork, institutionally sponsored loans, scholarships/grants, traineeships, tuition waivers (full), and unspecified assistantships also available. Financial award application deadline: 3/31; financial award applicants required to submit FAFSA. *Faculty research:* Mental health services research, child abuse and neglect, geriatrics, criminal justice race issues. Total annual research expenditures: $595,476. *Unit head:* Dr. Larry E. Davis, Dean, 412-624-6304, Fax: 412-624-6323, E-mail: ledavis@pitt.edu. *Application contact:* Philip Mack, Director of Admissions, 412-624-6346, Fax: 412-624-6323, E-mail: psm8@pitt.edu.

University of Puerto Rico, Medical Sciences Campus, Graduate School of Public Health, Program in Gerontology, San Juan, PR 00936-5067. Offers MPH, Certificate. Part-time and evening/weekend programs available. *Entrance requirements:* For master's, GRE, previous course work in social sciences, biology, psychology, and algebra.

University of Regina, Faculty of Graduate Studies and Research, Faculty of Arts, Program in Gerontology, Regina, SK S4S 0A2, Canada. Offers M Sc, MA. *Faculty:* 10 full-time (3 women). *Students:* 5 full-time (3 women), 2 part-time (both women). 7 applicants, 57% accepted. *Degree requirements:* For master's, thesis. *Entrance requirements:* Additional exam requirements/recommendations for international students: Required—TOEFL (minimum score 580 paper-based; 237 computer-based; 80 iBT). *Application deadline:* For fall admission, 3/31 for domestic students. Application fee: $90 ($100 for international students). Electronic applications accepted. *Financial support:* Fellowships, research assistantships, teaching assistantships available. *Unit head:* Dr. David Malloy, Program Coordinator, 306-337-3181. *Application contact:* Dr. David Malloy, Program Coordinator, 306-337-3181.

University of Rhode Island, Graduate School, College of Nursing, Kingston, RI 02881. Offers administration (MS); clinical nurse leader (MS); clinical specialist in gerontology (MS); clinical specialist in psychiatric/mental health (MS); family nurse practitioner (MS); gerontological nurse practitioner (MS); nursing (DNP, PhD); nursing education (MS). *Accreditation:* AACN; ACNM/DOA (one or more programs are accredited). Part-time programs available. *Faculty:* 28 full-time (27 women), 3 part-time/adjunct (all women). *Students:* 21 full-time (20 women), 74 part-time (71 women); includes 3 minority (1 African American, 2 Asian Americans or Pacific Islanders), 5 international. In 2009, 29 master's, 2 doctorates awarded. *Degree requirements:* For master's, comprehensive exam; for doctorate, comprehensive exam, thesis/dissertation. *Entrance requirements:* For master's, GRE or MAT, 2 letters of recommendation, scholarly papers; for doctorate, GRE, 3 letters of recommendation, scholarly papers. Additional exam requirements/recommendations for international students: Required—TOEFL (minimum score 550 paper-based; 213 computer-based). *Application deadline:* For fall admission, 4/15 for domestic students, 2/1 for international students; for spring admission, 11/15 for domestic students, 7/15 for international students. Application fee: $65. Electronic applications accepted. *Expenses:* Tuition, state resident: full-time $8828; part-time $490 per credit hour. Tuition, nonresident: full-time $22,100; part-time $1228 per credit hour. Required fees: $1118; $57 per semester. Tuition and fees vary according to program. *Financial support:* In 2009–10, 3 teaching assistantships with full and partial tuition reimbursements (averaging $8,428 per year) were awarded. Financial award application deadline: 4/15; financial award applicants required to submit FAFSA. *Faculty research:* Group intervention for grieving women in prison, translating Best Practice in non-drug interventions for postoperative pain management, further development and testing of the pain assessment inventory, preschool motor and functional performance of two cohorts, neuroactivation of brain motor areas in preterm children. Total annual research expenditures: $926,949. *Unit head:* Dr. Dayle Joseph, Dean, 401-874-2766, Fax: 401-874-2061, E-mail: dayle@uri.edu. *Application contact:* Dr. Mary C. Sullivan, Director of Graduate Studies, 401-874-5339, Fax: 401-874-2061, E-mail: mcsullivan@uri.edu.

University of South Alabama, Graduate School, College of Arts and Sciences, Program in Gerontology, Mobile, AL 36688-0002. Offers Certificate. Part-time programs available. *Entrance requirements:* For degree, GRE General Test. *Expenses:* Tuition, state resident: part-time $218 per contact hour. Required fees: $1102 per year.

University of South Carolina, The Graduate School, Program in Gerontology, Columbia, SC 29208. Offers Certificate. Part-time programs available. *Degree requirements:* For Certificate, practicum. Electronic applications accepted.

University of Southern California, Graduate School, Davis School of Gerontology, Los Angeles, CA 90089. Offers MASM, MS, PhD, Graduate Certificate, DDS/MS, JD/MS, M Pl/MS, MBA/MS, MHA/MS, MPA/MS, MS/MA, MS/MSW, Pharm D/MS. Part-time and evening/weekend programs available. Postbaccalaureate distance learning degree programs offered (no on-campus study). *Faculty:* 15 full-time (5 women), 8 part-time/adjunct (4 women). *Students:* 81 full-time (58 women), 35 part-time (27 women); includes 32 minority (6 African Americans, 1 American Indian/Alaska Native, 15 Asian Americans or Pacific Islanders, 10 Hispanic Americans), 10 international. 96 applicants, 63% accepted, 55 enrolled. In 2009, 24 master's, 4 doctorates, 7 other advanced degrees awarded. *Degree requirements:* For master's, thesis or alternative; for doctorate, comprehensive exam, thesis/dissertation. *Entrance requirements:* For master's and doctorate, GRE. Additional exam requirements/recommendations for international students: Required—TOEFL (minimum score 100 iBT). *Application deadline:* For fall admission, 2/1 priority date for domestic and international students; for spring admission, 10/1 priority date for domestic and international students. Applications are processed on a rolling basis. Application fee: $85. Electronic applications accepted. *Expenses:* Tuition: Full-time $25,980; part-time $1315 per unit. Required fees: $554. One-time fee: $35 full-time. Full-time tuition and fees vary according to degree level and program. *Financial support:* In 2009–10, 90 students received support, including 4 fellowships with full tuition reimbursements available (averaging $30,000 per year), 14 research assistantships with full tuition reimbursements available (averaging $19,000 per year), 2 teaching assistantships (averaging $19,000 per year); scholarships/grants also available. Financial award application deadline: 3/15. *Faculty research:* Sex steroids and Alzheimer's disease, memory, cognition and brain plasticity, environment and injury prevention, antioxidants, stress and aging, inflammation and aging, euthanasia, caloric restriction and chemotherapy, biodemographic of aging, health outcomes research, families and intergenerational relatives, care-giving of elderly. *Unit head:* Maria Henke, Assistant Dean, 213-740-5156, Fax: 213- 740-7069, E-mail: mhenke@usc.edu. *Application contact:* Jim deVera, Student Advisor, 213-740-1729, Fax: 213- 740-7069, E-mail: edevera@usc.edu.

University of Southern California, Graduate School, School of Social Work, Los Angeles, CA 90089. Offers community organization, planning and administration (MSW); families and children (MSW); health (MSW); mental health (MSW); military social work and veterans services (MSW); older adults (MSW); public child welfare (MSW); school settings (MSW); social work (MSW, PhD); systems of mental illness recovery (MSW); work and life (MSW); JD/MSW; M Pl/MSW; MPA/MSW; MSW/MAJCS; MSW/MBA; MSW/MS. *Accreditation:* CSWE (one or more programs are accredited). Part-time programs available. Postbaccalaureate distance learning degree programs offered. *Faculty:* 72 full-time (50 women), 75 part-time/adjunct (53 women). *Students:* 766 full-time (650 women), 155 part-time (131 women); includes 606 minority (132 African Americans, 3 American Indian/Alaska Native, 115 Asian Americans or Pacific Islanders, 356 Hispanic Americans), 37 international. 1,634 applicants, 49% accepted, 476 enrolled. In 2009, 288 master's, 7 doctorates awarded. *Degree requirements:* For doctorate, comprehensive exam, thesis/dissertation, qualifying exam/publishable paper. *Entrance requirements:* For doctorate, GRE General Test. Additional exam requirements/recommendations for international students: Recommended—TOEFL (minimum score 600 paper-based; 250 computer-based; 100 iBT). *Application deadline:* For fall admission, 3/15 for domestic and international students. Electronic applications accepted. *Expenses:* Tuition: Full-time $25,980;

Gerontology

University of Southern California (continued)

part-time $1315 per unit. Required fees: $554. One-time fee: $35 full-time. Full-time tuition and fees vary according to degree level and program. *Financial support:* In 2009–10, 738 students received support, including fellowships with full tuition reimbursements available (averaging $35,000 per year), teaching assistantships with full tuition reimbursements available (averaging $30,000 per year); Federal Work-Study and scholarships/grants also available. Financial award application deadline: 5/3; financial award applicants required to submit FAFSA. *Faculty research:* Military social work, homelessness, health disparities, school violence, depression and chronic diseases. *Unit head:* Dean Marilyn Flynn, Dean and Professor, 213-740-8311. *Application contact:* Janine M. Luzano, Director of Admissions and Financial Aid, 213-740-2013, Fax: 213-821-1235, E-mail: janinelu@usc.edu.

University of South Florida, Graduate School, College of Behavioral and Community Sciences, Department of Aging Studies, Tampa, FL 33620-9951. Offers aging studies (PhD); gerontology (MA). Part-time and evening/weekend programs available. *Faculty:* 12 full-time (8 women). *Students:* 23 full-time (20 women), 12 part-time (all women); includes 6 minority (3 African Americans, 3 Hispanic Americans), 4 international. Average age 32. 29 applicants, 31% accepted, 6 enrolled. In 2009, 10 master's, 3 doctorates awarded. *Degree requirements:* For master's, comprehensive exam, thesis; for doctorate, comprehensive exam, thesis/dissertation. *Entrance requirements:* For master's, GRE General Test, minimum GPA of 3.0 in last 60 hours; for doctorate, GRE General Test, minimum GPA of 3.25, letter of recommendation. Additional exam requirements/recommendations for international students: Required—TOEFL (minimum score 550 paper-based; 213 computer-based). *Application deadline:* For fall admission, 2/1 priority date for domestic students, 1/2 priority date for international students. Application fee: $30. Electronic applications accepted. *Financial support:* In 2009–10, teaching assistantships with tuition reimbursements (averaging $14,223 per year). Financial award application deadline: 2/3. *Faculty research:* Minorities, caregiving, guardianship, Alzheimer's disease, cognitive aging. Total annual research expenditures: $871,972. *Unit head:* Cathy L. McEvoy, Director, 813-974-2414, Fax: 813-974-9754, E-mail: cmcevoy@cas.usf.edu. *Application contact:* Amy Woodberry, Staff Assistant, 813-974-2419, Fax: 813-974-9754, E-mail: amwoodbu@chuma1.cas.usf.edu.

The University of Tennessee, Graduate School, College of Education, Health and Human Sciences, Program in Public Health, Knoxville, TN 37996. Offers community health education (MPH); gerontology (MPH); health planning/administration (MPH); MS/MPH. *Accreditation:* CEPH. *Degree requirements:* For master's, thesis optional. *Entrance requirements:* For master's, minimum GPA of 2.7. Additional exam requirements/recommendations for international students: Required—TOEFL. Electronic applications accepted. *Expenses:* Tuition, state resident: full-time $6826; part-time $380 per semester hour. Tuition, nonresident: full-time $21,844; part-time $1147 per semester hour. Tuition and fees vary according to program.

The University of Toledo, College of Graduate Studies, College of Medicine, Biomedical Science Programs, Program in Gerontology, Toledo, OH 43606-3390. Offers contemporary gerontological practice (Certificate).

University of Utah, The Graduate School, College of Nursing, Gerontology Interdisciplinary Program, Salt Lake City, UT 84112. Offers MS, Certificate. *Accreditation:* AACN. Part-time programs available. *Faculty:* 2 full-time (0 women), 1 (woman) part-time/adjunct. *Students:* 3 full-time (all women), 12 part-time (9 women); includes 2 minority (1 Asian American or Pacific Islander, 1 Hispanic American), 1 international. Average age 38. 7 applicants, 57% accepted, 4 enrolled. In 2009, 5 master's awarded. *Degree requirements:* For master's, thesis optional. *Entrance requirements:* For master's, minimum undergraduate GPA of 3.0. Additional exam requirements/recommendations for international students: Required—TOEFL (minimum score 500 paper-based; 173 computer-based). *Application deadline:* For fall admission, 4/1 priority date for domestic and international students. Applications are processed on a rolling basis. Application fee: $75 ($85 for international students). Electronic applications accepted. *Expenses:* Contact institution. *Financial support:* In 2009–10, 10 students received support, including 20 fellowships with partial tuition reimbursements available, 2 research assistantships; teaching assistantships, scholarships/grants also available. Financial award application deadline: 4/1. *Faculty research:* Spousal bereavement, family caregiving, healthy promotion and self-care, environmental issues, geriatric care management, technology and aging. Total annual research expenditures: $104,232. *Unit head:* Dr. Scott D. Wright, Director, 801-793-5752, E-mail: scott.wright@nurs.utah.edu. *Application contact:* Mirela Rankovic, Administrative Assistant, 801-581-8273, Fax: 801-581-4642, E-mail: mirela.rankovic@nurs.utah.edu.

University of West Florida, College of Professional Studies, Division of Health, Leisure, and Exercise Science, Community Health Education, Pensacola, FL 32514-5750. Offers aging studies (MS); promotion and worksite wellness (MS); psycho-social (MS). Part-time and evening/weekend programs available. *Faculty:* 2 full-time (1 woman), 1 (woman) part-time/adjunct. *Students:* 7 full-time (6 women), 7 part-time (all women); includes 4 minority (1 African American, 1 American Indian/Alaska Native, 1 Asian American or Pacific Islander, 1 Hispanic American), 1 international. Average age 34. 7 applicants, 86% accepted, 5 enrolled. In 2009, 13 master's awarded. *Degree requirements:* For master's, thesis or alternative. *Entrance requirements:* For master's, GRE General Test, minimum GPA of 3.0. Additional exam requirements/recommendations for international students: Required—TOEFL (minimum score 550 paper-based; 213 computer-based). *Application deadline:* For fall admission, 6/1 for domestic students, 5/15 for international students; for spring admission, 11/1 for domestic students, 10/1 for international students. Applications are processed on a rolling basis. Application fee: $30. *Expenses:* Tuition, state resident: full-time $4982; part-time $260 per credit hour. Tuition, nonresident: full-time $20,059; part-time $919 per credit hour. Required fees: $1247; $52 per credit hour. *Financial support:* Research assistantships, teaching assistantships, unspecified assistantships available. *Unit head:* Dr. John Todorovich, Chairperson, 850-473-7248, Fax: 850-474-2106. *Application contact:* Terry McCray, Assistant Director of Graduate Admissions, 850-473-7718, Fax: 850-473-7714, E-mail: gradadmissions@uwf.edu.

University of Wisconsin–Milwaukee, Graduate School, School of Social Welfare, Department of Social Work, Milwaukee, WI 53201-0413. Offers applied gerontology (Certificate); marriage and family therapy (Certificate); non-profit management (Certificate); social work (MSW, PhD). *Accreditation:* CSWE. Part-time programs available. *Faculty:* 18 full-time (11 women). *Students:* 173 full-time (157 women), 101 part-time (92 women); includes 55 minority (38 African Americans, 2 American Indian/Alaska Native, 7 Asian Americans or Pacific Islanders, 8 Hispanic Americans). Average age 31. 303 applicants, 62% accepted, 93 enrolled. In 2009, 105 master's awarded. *Degree requirements:* For master's, thesis or alternative. *Entrance requirements:* For doctorate, GRE, bachelor's degree. Additional exam requirements/recommendations for international students: Required—TOEFL (minimum score 550 paper-based; 79 iBT), IELTS (minimum score 6.5). *Application deadline:* For fall admission, 1/1 priority date for domestic students; for spring admission, 9/1 for domestic students. Applications are processed on a rolling basis. Application fee: $45 ($75 for international students). *Expenses:* Tuition, state resident: full-time $8800. Tuition, nonresident: full-time $20,760. Tuition and fees vary according to program and reciprocity agreements. *Financial support:* In 2009–10, 3 fellowships, 4 teaching assistantships were awarded; research assistantships, career-related internships or fieldwork and unspecified assistantships also available. Support available to part-time students. Financial award application deadline: 4/15. Total annual research expenditures: $806,977. *Unit head:* Deborah Padgett, Representative, 414-229-4851, Fax: 414-229-5311, E-mail: dpadgett@uwm.edu. *Application contact:* Steve McMurtry, General Information Contact, 414-229-2249, Fax: 414-229-6967, E-mail: mcmurtry@uwm.edu.

Valparaiso University, Graduate School, Programs in Liberal Studies, Concentration in Gerontology, Valparaiso, IN 46383. Offers MALS, Post-Master's Certificate, JD/MALS. Part-time and evening/weekend programs available. *Students:* 2 full-time (both women), 1 (woman) part-time. Average age 47. *Entrance requirements:* For master's, minimum GPA of 3.0. Additional exam requirements/recommendations for international students: Required—TOEFL (minimum score 550 paper-based; 213 computer-based; 80 iBT). *Application deadline:* Applications are processed on a rolling basis. Application fee: $30 ($50 for international students). Electronic applications accepted. *Financial support:* Available to part-time students. Applicants required to submit FAFSA. *Unit head:* Dr. David L. Rowland, Dean, Graduate Studies and Continuing Education/Associate Provost, 219-464-5313, Fax: 219-464-5381, E-mail: david.rowland@valpo.edu. *Application contact:* Jamie Haney, Coordinator of Graduate Admission, 219-464-5313, Fax: 219-464-5381, E-mail: jamie.haney@valpo.edu.

Virginia Commonwealth University, Graduate School, School of Allied Health Professions, Department of Gerontology, Richmond, VA 23284-9005. Offers aging studies (CAS); gerontology (MS). *Entrance requirements:* For master's, GRE General Test or MAT. *Faculty research:* Alzheimer's disease, age-related alcoholism and suicide, pain perception, curriculum development and evaluation in gerontology/geriatrics.

Virginia Commonwealth University, Graduate School, School of Allied Health Professions, Department of Health Administration, Doctoral Program in Health Related Sciences, Richmond, VA 23284-9005. Offers clinical laboratory sciences (PhD); gerontology (PhD); health administration (PhD); nurse anesthesia (PhD); occupational therapy (PhD); physical therapy (PhD); radiation sciences (PhD); rehabilitation leadership (PhD).

Virginia Polytechnic Institute and State University, Graduate School, College of Liberal Arts and Human Sciences, Department of Human Development, Blacksburg, VA 24061. Offers adult development and aging (MS, PhD); adult learning and human resource development (MS, PhD); child development (MS, PhD); family studies (MS, PhD); marriage and family therapy (MS, PhD). *Accreditation:* AAMFT/COAMFTE (one or more programs are accredited). *Faculty:* 22 full-time (18 women). *Students:* 49 full-time (38 women), 64 part-time (44 women); includes 30 minority (1 African American, 7 American Indian/Alaska Native, 16 Asian Americans or Pacific Islanders, 6 Hispanic Americans), 2 international. Average age 34. 64 applicants, 34% accepted, 16 enrolled. In 2009, 10 master's, 14 doctorates awarded. *Entrance requirements:* For master's and doctorate, GRE, GMAT. Additional exam requirements/recommendations for international students: Required—TOEFL (minimum score 550 paper-based; 213 computer-based). *Application deadline:* For fall admission, 5/15 for international students; for spring admission, 10/15 for international students. Applications are processed on a rolling basis. Application fee: $65. Electronic applications accepted. *Expenses:* Tuition, area resident: Full-time $10,228; part-time $459 per credit hour. Tuition, nonresident: full-time $17,892; part-time $865 per credit hour. Required fees: $1966; $451 per semester. *Financial support:* In 2009–10, 7 research assistantships with full tuition reimbursements (averaging $10,933 per year), 25 teaching assistantships with full tuition reimbursements (averaging $9,387 per year) were awarded; career-related internships or fieldwork, Federal Work-Study, scholarships/grants, and unspecified assistantships also available. Financial award application deadline: 1/15. *Faculty research:* Stress management, children's play, dual-career families, social cognition, relationships of elderly. Total annual research expenditures: $823,581. *Unit head:* Dr. Shannon E. Jarrott, Head, 540-231-4794, Fax: 540-231-7012, E-mail: sjarrott@vt.edu. *Application contact:* Mark Benson, Information Contact, 540-231-5720, Fax: 540-231-7012, E-mail: mbenson@vt.edu.

Wayne State University, Graduate School, Interdisciplinary Program in Gerontology, Detroit, MI 48202. Offers Certificate. *Entrance requirements:* For degree, letters of reference; interview. Additional exam requirements/recommendations for international students: Required—TOEFL (minimum score 550 paper-based; 213 computer-based); Recommended—TWE (minimum score 6). Electronic applications accepted. *Faculty research:* Aging and health, cognitive and neuroscience, aging and disability, minority aging, human factors and aging.

Webster University, College of Arts and Sciences, Department of Behavioral and Social Sciences, Program in Gerontology, St. Louis, MO 63119-3194. Offers MA. Part-time programs available. *Entrance requirements:* Additional exam requirements/recommendations for international students: Required—TOEFL. *Expenses:* Tuition: Part-time $565 per credit hour. Tuition and fees vary according to degree level, campus/location and program.

West Chester University of Pennsylvania, Office of Graduate Studies, College of Arts and Sciences, Department of Anthropology and Sociology, West Chester, PA 19383. Offers gerontology (Certificate); long term health care (MSA). Part-time and evening/weekend programs available. *Students:* 1 (woman) full-time, 2 part-time (both women). Average age 38. 4 applicants, 100% accepted, 1 enrolled. *Degree requirements:* For master's, comprehensive exam. *Entrance requirements:* For master's, MAT, GRE, or GMAT, interview, resume, 2 letters of reference. Additional exam requirements/recommendations for international students: Required—TOEFL (minimum score 550 paper-based; 213 computer-based; 80 iBT). *Application deadline:* For fall admission, 4/15 priority date for domestic students, 3/15 for international students; for spring admission, 10/15 for domestic students, 9/1 for international students. Applications are processed on a rolling basis. Application fee: $35. Electronic applications accepted. *Expenses:* Tuition, state resident: full-time $6666; part-time $370 per credit. Tuition, nonresident: full-time $10,666; part-time $593 per credit. Required fees: $122.56 per credit. *Financial support:* In 2009–10, research assistantships with full tuition reimbursements (averaging $5,000 per year); unspecified assistantships also available. Support available to part-time students. Financial award application deadline: 2/15; financial award applicants required to submit FAFSA. *Faculty research:* West African communities in the U.S., life long learning-distance education, comparative religions. *Unit head:* Dr. Douglas McConatha, Chair and Graduate Coordinator, 610-436-2556, E-mail: dmcconatha@wcupa.edu. *Application contact:* Dr. Douglas McConatha, Chair and Graduate Coordinator, 610-436-2556, E-mail: dmcconatha@wcupa.edu.

Wichita State University, Graduate School, Fairmount College of Liberal Arts and Sciences, School of Community Affairs, Wichita, KS 67260. Offers criminal justice (MA); gerontology (MA). Part-time programs available. *Expenses:* Tuition, state resident: full-time $4247; part-time $235.95 per credit hour. Tuition, nonresident: full-time $11,171; part-time $620.60 per credit hour. Required fees: $34; $3.60 per credit hour. $17 per term. Tuition and fees vary according to campus/location and program. *Unit head:* Dr. Michael Birzer, Director, 316-978-7200, Fax: 316-978-3626, E-mail: michael.birzer@wichita.edu. *Application contact:* Dr. Michael Birzer, Director, 316-978-7200, Fax: 316-978-3626, E-mail: michael.birzer@wichita.edu.

Wilmington University, College of Health Professions, New Castle, DE 19720-6491. Offers adult nurse practitioner (MSN); family nurse practitioner (MSN); gerontology (MSN); leadership (MSN); nursing (MSN); women's nurse practitioner (MSN). *Accreditation:* AACN. Part-time programs available. *Degree requirements:* For master's, thesis. *Entrance requirements:* For master's, BSN, RN license, interview, 3 letters of recommendation. Additional exam requirements/recommendations for international students: Required—TOEFL (minimum score 500 paper-based; 173 computer-based). Electronic applications accepted. *Faculty research:* Outcomes assessment, student writing ability.

Section 21
Geography

This section contains a directory of institutions offering graduate work in geography. Additional information about programs listed in the directory but not augmented by an in-depth entry may be obtained by writing directly to the dean of a graduate school or chair of a department at the address given in the directory.

For programs offering related work, see also in this book *Area and Cultural Studies* and *Humanities*. In another guide in this series:

Graduate Programs in the Physical Sciences, Mathematics, Agricultural Sciences, the Environment & Natural Resources

See *Geosciences*

CONTENTS

Program Directories

Geographic Information Systems 790
Geography 794

Close-Up

See:

The University of Texas at Dallas—Economic, Political, and Policy Sciences 759

Geographic Information Systems

Acadia University, Faculty of Pure and Applied Science, Program in Applied Geomatics, Wolfville, NS B4P 2R6, Canada. Offers M Sc. Program jointly offered with Nova Scotia Community College. *Students:* 6 full-time (2 women). 6 applicants, 83% accepted, 5 enrolled. In 2009, 3 master's awarded. *Degree requirements:* For master's, thesis optional. *Entrance requirements:* Additional exam requirements/recommendations for international students: Required—TOEFL (minimum score 580 paper-based; 237 computer-based; 93 iBT), IELTS (minimum score 6.5). *Application deadline:* For fall admission, 2/1 for domestic and international students. Applications are processed on a rolling basis. Application fee: $50. *Financial support:* Research assistantships, teaching assistantships, scholarships/grants and unspecified assistantships available. Financial award application deadline: 2/1. *Unit head:* Dr. Ian Spooner, Coordinator, 902-585-1312, E-mail: ian.spooner@acadiau.ca. *Application contact:* Dr. Ian Spooner, Coordinator, 902-585-1312, E-mail: ian.spooner@acadiau.ca.

Appalachian State University, Cratis D. Williams Graduate School, Department of Geography and Planning, Boone, NC 28608. Offers geography (MA), including GIS, planning. Part-time programs available. Postbaccalaureate distance learning degree programs offered (no on-campus study). *Faculty:* 12 full-time (2 women), 3 part-time/adjunct (1 woman). *Students:* 25 full-time (9 women), 15 part-time (7 women). 21 applicants, 81% accepted, 13 enrolled. In 2009, 10 master's awarded. *Degree requirements:* For master's, comprehensive exam, thesis or alternative. *Entrance requirements:* For master's, GRE General Test, 3 letters of recommendation. Additional exam requirements/recommendations for international students: Required—TOEFL (minimum score 570 paper-based; 230 computer-based; 79 iBT), IELTS (minimum score 6.5). *Application deadline:* For fall admission, 7/1 for domestic students, 2/1 for international students; for spring admission, 11/1 for domestic students, 7/1 for international students. Applications are processed on a rolling basis. Application fee: $50. Electronic applications accepted. *Expenses:* Tuition, state resident: full-time $2960. Tuition, nonresident: full-time $14,051. Required fees: $2320. *Financial support:* In 2009–10, 10 research assistantships (averaging $7,500 per year) were awarded; fellowships, teaching assistantships, career-related internships or fieldwork, Federal Work-Study, scholarships/grants, and unspecified assistantships also available. Financial award application deadline: 4/1; financial award applicants required to submit FAFSA. *Faculty research:* Global change, climatology, production cartography, geographic information systems, North Carolina geography, Latin America. Total annual research expenditures: $85,000. *Unit head:* Dr. James Young, Chairperson, 828-262-3000, Fax: 828-262-3067. *Application contact:* Dr. Kathleen Schroeder, Graduate Program Director, 828-262-3000.

Arizona State University, Graduate College, College of Liberal Arts and Sciences, Division of Social Sciences, School of Geographical Sciences, Tempe, AZ 85287. Offers geographic education (MAS); geographic information systems (MAS); geography (MA, PhD). *Degree requirements:* For master's, thesis; for doctorate, thesis/dissertation. *Entrance requirements:* For master's and doctorate, GRE.

Boston University, Graduate School of Arts and Sciences, Department of Geography and Environment, Boston, MA 02215. Offers energy and environmental analysis (MA); environmental remote sensing and GIs (MA); geography (MA); geography and environment (PhD); international relations and environmental policy (MA). *Students:* 50 full-time (22 women), 15 part-time (6 women); includes 2 minority (1 Asian American or Pacific Islander, 1 Hispanic American), 19 international. Average age 30. 64 applicants, 23% accepted, 5 enrolled. In 2009, 4 master's, 6 doctorates awarded. Terminal master's awarded for partial completion of doctoral program. *Degree requirements:* For master's, one foreign language, comprehensive exam, thesis; for doctorate, one foreign language, comprehensive exam, thesis/dissertation. *Entrance requirements:* For master's and doctorate, GRE General Test, GRE Subject Test, 3 letters of recommendation. Additional exam requirements/recommendations for international students: Required—TOEFL (minimum score 600 paper-based; 250 computer-based). *Application deadline:* For fall admission, 7/1 for domestic and international students; for spring admission, 11/15 for domestic and international students. Application fee: $70. Electronic applications accepted. *Expenses:* Tuition: Full-time $37,910; part-time $1184 per credit hour. Required fees: $386; $40 per semester. Part-time tuition and fees vary according to class time, course level, degree level and program. *Financial support:* In 2009–10, 33 students received support, including 2 fellowships with full tuition reimbursements available (averaging $18,900 per year), 20 research assistantships with full tuition reimbursements available (averaging $18,400 per year), 11 teaching assistantships with full tuition reimbursements available (averaging $18,400 per year); Federal Work-Study and unspecified assistantships also available. Support available to part-time students. Financial award application deadline: 1/15; financial award applicants required to submit FAFSA. Total annual research expenditures: $1.2 million. *Unit head:* Robert Kaufmann, Chairman, 617-353-3940, Fax: 617-353-8399, E-mail: kaufmann@bu.edu. *Application contact:* Christopher DeVits, Graduate Program Coordinator, 617-353-7554, Fax: 617-353-8399, E-mail: cdevits@bu.edu.

Clark University, Graduate School, Department of Geography, Program in Geographic Information Science, Worcester, MA 01610-1477. Offers MA. *Students:* 4 full-time (1 woman). Average age 22. 4 applicants, 100% accepted, 4 enrolled. In 2009, 3 master's awarded. *Application deadline:* For fall admission, 12/31 priority date for domestic students. Application fee: $50. *Expenses:* Tuition: Full-time $34,900; part-time $4362.50 per course. *Unit head:* Dr. Anthony Lee Bebbington, Director, 508-793-7336. *Application contact:* Christine Silva, Admission Coordinator, 508-793-7337, Fax: 508-793-8881, E-mail: geography@clarku.edu.

Clark University, Graduate School, Department of International Development, Community, and Environment, Program in Geographic Information Science for Development and Environment, Worcester, MA 01610-1477. Offers MA. *Faculty:* 2 full-time (1 woman). *Students:* 32 full-time (17 women); includes 2 minority (1 African American, 1 Asian American or Pacific Islander), 19 international. Average age 26. 50 applicants, 80% accepted, 23 enrolled. In 2009, 7 master's awarded. *Degree requirements:* For master's, thesis. *Entrance requirements:* For master's, 3 references, resume or curriculum vitae. Additional exam requirements/recommendations for international students: Required—TOEFL (minimum score 575 paper-based; 233 computer-based; 90 iBT) or IELTS (minimum score 6.5). *Application deadline:* For fall admission, 1/15 for domestic students. Application fee: $50. *Expenses:* Tuition: Full-time $34,900; part-time $4362.50 per course. *Financial support:* Fellowships, institutionally sponsored loans and scholarships/grants available. *Faculty research:* Land-use change, the effects of environmental influences on child health and development, quantitative methods, watershed management, brownfields redevelopment, human/environment interactions, biodiversity conservation, climate change. *Unit head:* Department of International Development, Community, and Environment, 508-793-7201, Fax: 508-793-8820. *Application contact:* Paula Hall, Department of International Development, Community, and Environment Graduate Admissions Office, 508-793-7205, E-mail: idce@clarku.edu.

Cleveland State University, College of Graduate Studies, Maxine Goodman Levin College of Urban Affairs, Program in Environmental Studies, Cleveland, OH 44115. Offers environmental studies (MAES); geographic information systems (Certificate); urban real estate development and finance (Certificate); JD/MAES. Part-time and evening/weekend programs available. *Degree requirements:* For master's, thesis or alternative, exit project. *Entrance requirements:* For master's, GRE General Test (minimum score: verbal and quantitative 40th percentile, analytical writing 4.0), minimum GPA of 3.0. Additional exam requirements/recommendations for international students: Required—TOEFL (minimum score 525 paper-based; 197 computer-based; 65 iBT). Electronic applications accepted. *Faculty research:* Environmental policy and administration, environmental planning, geographic information systems (GIS), nonprofit management.

Cleveland State University, College of Graduate Studies, Maxine Goodman Levin College of Urban Affairs, Program in Nonprofit Administration and Leadership, Cleveland, OH 44115. Offers geographic information systems (Certificate); local and urban management (Certificate); nonprofit administration and leadership (MNAL); nonprofit management (Certificate); urban economic development (Certificate). Part-time and evening/weekend programs available. *Degree requirements:* For master's, thesis or alternative, capstone course. *Entrance requirements:* For master's, GRE (minimum 40th percentile verbal and quantitative, 4.0 analytical writing), minimum GPA of 3.0. Additional exam requirements/recommendations for international students: Required—TOEFL (minimum score 525 paper-based; 197 computer-based; 65 iBT). Electronic applications accepted. *Faculty research:* Human resource management, volunteerism, performance measurement in nonprofits, government-nonprofit partnerships.

Cleveland State University, College of Graduate Studies, Maxine Goodman Levin College of Urban Affairs, Program in Public Administration, Cleveland, OH 44115. Offers geographic information systems (Certificate); local and urban management (Certificate); non-profit management (Certificate); public administration (MPA); urban real estate development (Certificate); JD/MPA. *Accreditation:* NASPAA. Part-time and evening/weekend programs available. *Degree requirements:* For master's, thesis or alternative, capstone course. *Entrance requirements:* For master's, GRE General Test (minimum 40th percentile verbal and quantitative, 4.0 writing), minimum GPA of 3.0. Additional exam requirements/recommendations for international students: Required—TOEFL (minimum score 525 paper-based; 197 computer-based; 65 iBT). Electronic applications accepted. *Faculty research:* Health care administration, public management, economic development, city management, nonprofit management.

Cleveland State University, College of Graduate Studies, Maxine Goodman Levin College of Urban Affairs, Program in Urban Planning, Design, and Development, Cleveland, OH 44115. Offers geographic information systems (Certificate); local and urban management (Certificate); urban economic development (Certificate); urban planning, design, and development (MUPDD); urban real estate development and finance (Certificate); JD/MUPDD. *Accreditation:* ACSP. Part-time and evening/weekend programs available. *Degree requirements:* For master's, project or thesis. *Entrance requirements:* For master's, GRE General Test (minimum 50th percentile verbal and quantitative, 4.0 analytical writing), minimum GPA of 3.0. Additional exam requirements/recommendations for international students: Required—TOEFL (minimum score 525 paper-based; 197 computer-based; 65 iBT). Electronic applications accepted. *Faculty research:* Housing and neighborhood development, urban housing policy, environmental sustainability, economic development.

Cleveland State University, College of Graduate Studies, Maxine Goodman Levin College of Urban Affairs, Program in Urban Studies, Cleveland, OH 44115. Offers geographic information systems (Certificate); local and urban management (Certificate); nonprofit management (Certificate); urban economic development (Certificate); urban real estate development and finance (Certificate); urban studies (MS); urban studies and public affairs (PhD). Part-time and evening/weekend programs available. *Degree requirements:* For master's, thesis or alternative, exit project, capstone course; for doctorate, comprehensive exam, thesis/dissertation. *Entrance requirements:* For master's, GRE General Test, minimum GPA of 3.0; for doctorate, GRE General Test, minimum GPA of 3.5. Additional exam requirements/recommendations for international students: Required—TOEFL (minimum score 525 paper-based; 197 computer-based; 65 iBT). Electronic applications accepted. *Faculty research:* Environmental issues, economic development, urban and public policy, public management.

Eastern Michigan University, Graduate School, College of Arts and Sciences, Department of Geography and Geology, Program in Geographic Information Systems, Ypsilanti, MI 48197. Offers geographic information systems (MS); GIS educator (Graduate Certificate); GIS professional (Graduate Certificate); GIS-planning (MS). *Students:* 20 full-time (9 women), 33 part-time (11 women); includes 1 minority (African American), 24 international. Average age 30. In 2009, 11 master's, 2 other advanced degrees awarded. Application fee: $35. Tuition and fees vary according to course level. *Application contact:* Dr. Hugh Semple, Program Advisor, 734-487-0218, Fax: 734-487-6979, E-mail: hsemple@emich.edu.

Florida State University, The Graduate School, College of Social Sciences and Public Policy, Department of Geography, Tallahassee, FL 32306. Offers geographic information science (MS); geography (MA, MS, PhD). *Faculty:* 9 full-time (2 women), 3 part-time/adjunct (1 woman). *Students:* 67 full-time (24 women), 27 part-time (14 women); includes 12 minority (4 African Americans, 1 American Indian/Alaska Native, 3 Asian Americans or Pacific Islanders, 4 Hispanic Americans), 7 international. Average age 28. 51 applicants, 59% accepted, 27 enrolled. In 2009, 31 master's, 4 doctorates awarded. Terminal master's awarded for partial completion of doctoral program. *Degree requirements:* For master's, thesis (for some programs); for doctorate, comprehensive exam, thesis/dissertation. *Entrance requirements:* For master's and doctorate, GRE General Test, minimum GPA of 3.0. Additional exam requirements/recommendations for international students: Required—TOEFL. *Application deadline:* For fall admission, 1/15 priority date for domestic students, 12/15 priority date for international students; for spring admission, 11/1 for domestic students, 9/15 for international students. Applications are processed on a rolling basis. Application fee: $30. Electronic applications accepted. *Expenses:* Tuition, state resident: full-time $7413. Tuition, nonresident: full-time $22,567. *Financial support:* In 2009–10, 26 students received support, including 5 research assistantships with full tuition reimbursements available (averaging $13,000 per year), 21 teaching assistantships with full tuition reimbursements available (averaging $13,000 per year); fellowships with full tuition reimbursements available, career-related internships or fieldwork, Federal Work-Study, institutionally sponsored loans, scholarships/grants, health care benefits, and unspecified assistantships also available. Financial award application deadline: 1/15; financial award applicants required to submit FAFSA. *Faculty research:* Society-nature interactions, geographic information science, environmental studies, hazards, remote sensing. Total annual research expenditures: $197,475. *Unit head:* Dr. Victor Mesev, Chair, 850-645-2498, Fax: 850-644-5913. *Application contact:* Dr. Mark Horner, Graduate Director, 850-644-8377, Fax: 850-644-5193, E-mail: mhorner@fsu.edu.

George Mason University, College of Science, Department of Earth Systems and Geoinformation Sciences, Fairfax, VA 22030. Offers MS, PhD, Certificate. *Expenses:* Tuition, state resident: full-time $7568; part-time $315.33 per credit hour. Tuition, nonresident: full-time $21,704; part-time $904.33 per credit hour. Required fees: $2184; $91 per credit hour.

George Mason University, College of Science, Department of Geography, Fairfax, VA 22030. Offers geographic and cartographic sciences (MS). *Degree requirements:* For master's, thesis optional. *Entrance requirements:* For master's, GRE General Test, minimum GPA of 3.0 in last 60 hours; BS or BA in geography, cartography, or related field. Electronic applications accepted. *Expenses:* Tuition, state resident: full-time $7568; part-time $315.33 per credit hour. Tuition, nonresident: full-time $21,704; part-time $904.33 per credit hour. Required fees: $2184; $91 per credit hour.

Georgia Institute of Technology, Graduate Studies and Research, College of Architecture, City and Regional Planning Program, Atlanta, GA 30332-0001. Offers city and regional planning (PhD); economic development (MCRP); environmental planning and management (MCRP); geographic information systems (MCRP); land and community development (MCRP); land use planning (MCRP); transportation (MCRP); urban design (MCRP); MCP/MSCE. *Accreditation:* ACSP. *Degree requirements:* For master's, thesis, internship. *Entrance requirements:* For master's, GRE General Test, minimum GPA of 2.7. Additional exam requirements/recommendations for international students: Required—TOEFL. Electronic applications accepted.

Georgia State University, College of Arts and Sciences, Department of Geosciences, Program in Geographic Information Systems, Atlanta, GA 30302-3083. Offers Certificate. Part-time programs available. *Entrance requirements:* Additional exam requirements/recommendations for international students: Required—TOEFL. Electronic applications accepted. *Faculty research:* Cartography, remote sensing.

Geographic Information Systems

Hunter College of the City University of New York, Graduate School, School of Arts and Sciences, Department of Geography, New York, NY 10021-5085. Offers analytical geography (MA); earth system science (MA); environmental and social issues (MA); geographic information science (Certificate); geographic information systems (MA); teaching earth science (MA). Part-time and evening/weekend programs available. *Faculty:* 12 full-time (5 women), 4 part-time/adjunct (0 women). *Students:* 17 full-time (16 women), 20 part-time (19 women); includes 9 minority (1 African American, 1 American Indian/Alaska Native, 4 Asian Americans or Pacific Islanders, 3 Hispanic Americans). Average age 31. 13 applicants, 92% accepted, 9 enrolled. In 2009, 10 master's, 3 other advanced degrees awarded. *Degree requirements:* For master's, comprehensive exam or thesis. *Entrance requirements:* For master's, GRE General Test, minimum B average in major, B- overall; 18 credits of course work in geography; 2 letters of recommendation; for Certificate, minimum B average in major, B- overall. Additional exam requirements/recommendations for international students: Required—TOEFL. *Application deadline:* For fall admission, 4/1 for domestic students; for spring admission, 11/1 for domestic students. Applications are processed on a rolling basis. Application fee: $125. *Expenses:* Tuition, state resident: full-time $7360; part-time $310 per credit. Required fees: $250 per semester. *Financial support:* In 2009–10, 1 fellowship (averaging $3,000 per year), 2 research assistantships (averaging $10,000 per year), 10 teaching assistantships (averaging $6,000 per year) were awarded; career-related internships or fieldwork, Federal Work-Study, institutionally sponsored loans, and unspecified assistantships also available. Financial award application deadline: 3/1. *Faculty research:* Urban geography, economic geography, geographic information science, demographic methods, climate change. *Unit head:* Prof. William Solecki, Chair, 212-772-4536, Fax: 212-772-5268, E-mail: wsolecki@hunter.cuny.edu. *Application contact:* Prof. Marianna Pavlovskaya, Graduate Adviser, 212-772-5320, Fax: 212-772-5268, E-mail: mpavlov@geo.hunter.cuny.edu.

Idaho State University, Office of Graduate Studies, College of Arts and Sciences, Department of Geosciences, Pocatello, ID 83209-8072. Offers geographic information science (MS); geology (MNS, MS); geology emphasis environmental geoscience (MS); geophysics/hydrology/geology (MS); geotechnology (Postbaccalaureate Certificate). Part-time programs available. *Faculty:* 8 full-time (1 woman). *Students:* 25 full-time (12 women), 20 part-time (6 women); includes 1 minority (Asian American or Pacific Islander), 4 international. Average age 33. In 2009, 7 master's, 2 other advanced degrees awarded. *Degree requirements:* For master's, comprehensive exam, thesis, oral colloquium; for Postbaccalaureate Certificate, thesis optional, minimum 19 credits. *Entrance requirements:* For master's, GRE General Test (minimum 50th percentile in 2 sections), 3 letters of recommendation; for Postbaccalaureate Certificate, GRE General Test, 3 letters of recommendation, bachelor's degree, statement of goals. Additional exam requirements/recommendations for international students: Required—TOEFL (minimum score 550 paper-based; 213 computer-based; 80 iBT). *Application deadline:* For fall admission, 7/1 for domestic students, 6/1 for international students; for spring admission, 12/1 for domestic students, 11/1 for international students. Applications are processed on a rolling basis. Application fee: $55. Electronic applications accepted. *Expenses:* Tuition, state resident: full-time $3318; part-time $297 per credit hour. Tuition, nonresident: full-time $13,120; part-time $437 per credit hour. Required fees: $2530. Tuition and fees vary according to program. *Financial support:* In 2009–10, 20 research assistantships with full and partial tuition reimbursements (averaging $9,713 per year), 7 teaching assistantships with full and partial tuition reimbursements (averaging $10,841 per year) were awarded; career-related internships or fieldwork, Federal Work-Study, institutionally sponsored loans, scholarships/grants, health care benefits, tuition waivers (full and partial), and unspecified assistantships also available. Support available to part-time students. Financial award application deadline: 1/1; financial award applicants required to submit FAFSA. *Faculty research:* Quantitative field mapping and sampling: microscopic, geochemical, and isotopic analysis of rocks, minerals and water; remote sensing, geographic information systems, and global positioning systems: environmental and watershed management; surficial and fluvial processes: landscape change; regional tectonics, structural geology; planetary geology. *Unit head:* Dr. David Rodgers, Chairman, 208-282-3365, Fax: 208-282-4414, E-mail: rodgdavi@isu.edu. *Application contact:* Tami Carson, Graduate School Technical Records Specialist, 208-282-2150, Fax: 208-282-4847, E-mail: carstami@isu.edu.

Indiana University–Purdue University Indianapolis, School of Liberal Arts, Department of Geography, Indianapolis, IN 46202-2896. Offers geographic information systems (MS, Certificate). *Students:* 8 part-time (4 women); includes 1 Asian American or Pacific Islander. Average age 31. 10 applicants, 60% accepted, 5 enrolled. *Entrance requirements:* For master's, GRE, minimum GPA of 3.0. Application fee: $55 ($65 for international students). *Financial support:* In 2009–10, 2 fellowships (averaging $9,000 per year), 1 teaching assistantship (averaging $7,067 per year) were awarded. *Unit head:* Robert W. White, Dean, School of Liberal Arts, 317-274-8448. *Application contact:* Joyce Haibe, Department Secretary, 317-274-8877, E-mail: geogdept@iupui.edu.

Minnesota State University Mankato, College of Graduate Studies, College of Social and Behavioral Sciences, Department of Geography, Mankato, MN 56001. Offers geography (MS); GIS (Certificate). Part-time programs available. *Students:* 5 full-time (2 women), 21 part-time (8 women). *Degree requirements:* For master's, one foreign language, comprehensive exam. *Entrance requirements:* For master's, GRE General Test (if GPA less than 2.8 for the last 2 years), minimum GPA of 3.0 during previous 2 years. *Application deadline:* For fall admission, 7/1 priority date for domestic students; for spring admission, 11/1 for domestic students. Applications are processed on a rolling basis. Application fee: $40. Electronic applications accepted. *Expenses:* Tuition, state resident: full-time $5364. Tuition, nonresident: full-time $8314. *Financial support:* Research assistantships, teaching assistantships with full tuition reimbursements, career-related internships or fieldwork, Federal Work-Study, institutionally sponsored loans, and unspecified assistantships available. Support available to part-time students. Financial award application deadline: 3/15; financial award applicants required to submit FAFSA. *Unit head:* Dr. Donald Friend, Chairperson, 507-389-2617. *Application contact:* 507-389-2321, E-mail: grad@mnsu.edu.

Montclair State University, The Graduate School, College of Science and Mathematics, Department of Earth and Environmental Studies, Montclair, NJ 07043-1624. Offers earth science (Certificate); environmental management (MA, D Env M); environmental studies (MS), including environmental education, environmental health, environmental management, environmental science; geographic information science (Certificate); geoscience (MS, Certificate), including geoscience (MS), water resource management (Certificate). Part-time and evening/weekend programs available. *Faculty:* 16 full-time (2 women), 13 part-time/adjunct (4 women). *Students:* 36 full-time (17 women), 60 part-time (26 women). Average age 34. 42 applicants, 60% accepted, 17 enrolled. In 2009, 11 degrees awarded. *Degree requirements:* For master's, comprehensive exam, thesis or alternative; for doctorate, thesis/dissertation. *Entrance requirements:* For master's, GRE General Test, 2 letters of recommendation; for doctorate, GRE General Test, 3 letters of recommendation. Additional exam requirements/recommendations for international students: Required—TOEFL (minimum score 83 computer-based), or IELTS. *Application deadline:* For fall admission, 6/1 for international students; for spring admission, 10/1 for international students. Applications are processed on a rolling basis. Application fee: $60. Electronic applications accepted. *Expenses:* Tuition, area resident: Part-time $486.74 per credit. Tuition, state resident: part-time $486.74 per credit. Tuition, nonresident: part-time $751.34 per credit. Tuition and fees vary according to degree level and program. *Financial support:* In 2009–10, 3 fellowships (averaging $15,000 per year), 12 research assistantships with full tuition reimbursements (averaging $8,500 per year), 11 teaching assistantships with full tuition reimbursements (averaging $15,000 per year) were awarded; Federal Work-Study, scholarships/grants, and unspecified assistantships also available. Support available to part-time students. Financial award application deadline: 3/1; financial award applicants required to submit FAFSA. *Faculty research:* Antarctica, carbon pools, contaminated sediments, wetlands. *Unit head:* Dr. Duke Ophori, Chairperson, 973-655-7558. *Application contact:* Amy Aiello, Director of Graduate Admissions and Operations, 973-655-5147, Fax: 973-655-7869, E-mail: graduate.school@montclair.edu.

North Carolina State University, Graduate School, College of Natural Resources, Department of Parks, Recreation and Tourism Management, Raleigh, NC 27695. Offers natural resource management (MPRTM, MS); park and recreation management (MPRTM, MS); parks, recreation and tourism management (PhD); recreational sport management (MPRTM, MS); spatial information science (MPRTM, MS); tourism policy and development (MPRTM, MS). *Degree requirements:* For master's, thesis (for some programs); for doctorate, thesis/dissertation. *Entrance requirements:* For master's and doctorate, GRE General Test. Additional exam requirements/recommendations for international students: Required—TOEFL. Electronic applications accepted. *Faculty research:* Tourism policy and development, spatial information systems, natural resource management, recreational sports management, park and recreation management.

Northern Arizona University, Graduate College, College of Social and Behavioral Sciences, Department of Geography, Planning, and Recreation, Flagstaff, AZ 86011. Offers applied geographic information science (MS); geographic information systems (Certificate); rural geography (MA). Postbaccalaureate distance learning degree programs offered. *Faculty:* 15 full-time (7 women). *Students:* 14 full-time (10 women), 11 part-time (7 women); includes 3 minority (1 American Indian/Alaska Native, 2 Hispanic Americans). Average age 32. 14 applicants, 71% accepted, 7 enrolled. In 2009, 5 master's awarded. *Degree requirements:* For master's, thesis. *Entrance requirements:* For master's, GRE General Test. Additional exam requirements/recommendations for international students: Required—TOEFL (minimum score 550 paper-based; 213 computer-based; 80 iBT), IELTS (minimum score 7). *Application deadline:* For fall admission, 2/15 priority date for domestic students, 9/1 for international students; for spring admission, 10/15 for domestic students. Applications are processed on a rolling basis. Application fee: $65. Electronic applications accepted. *Financial support:* In 2009–10, 7 teaching assistantships with partial tuition reimbursements (averaging $10,439 per year) were awarded; career-related internships or fieldwork, Federal Work-Study, health care benefits, tuition waivers (full and partial), and unspecified assistantships also available. Support available to part-time students. Financial award application deadline: 3/30. *Unit head:* Dr. Pamela Foti, Chair, 928-523-6196, Fax: 928-523-2275, E-mail: pam.foti@nau.edu. *Application contact:* Alan Lew, Coordinator, 928-523-6567, E-mail: alan.lew@nau.edu.

Northwest Missouri State University, Graduate School, College of Arts and Sciences, Department of Geology/Geography, Program in Geographic Information Sciences, Maryville, MO 64468-6001. Offers MS, Certificate. Part-time programs available. *Faculty:* 11 full-time (2 women). *Students:* 6 full-time (2 women), 96 part-time (37 women); includes 8 minority (1 African American, 4 Asian Americans or Pacific Islanders, 3 Hispanic Americans). 23 applicants, 52% accepted, 8 enrolled. In 2009, 11 master's awarded. *Degree requirements:* For master's, comprehensive exam, thesis. *Entrance requirements:* For master's, GRE General Test, 2 letters of recommendation, writing sample, minimum undergraduate GPA of 2.5. Additional exam requirements/recommendations for international students: Required—TOEFL (minimum score 550 paper-based; 213 computer-based). *Application deadline:* For fall admission, 4/15 for domestic and international students. Application fee: $0 ($50 for international students). *Expenses:* Tuition, state resident: part-time $296.34 per credit hour. Tuition, nonresident: part-time $510.43 per credit hour. *Financial support:* In 2009–10, 2 research assistantships (averaging $6,000 per year) were awarded. Financial award application deadline: 4/1; financial award applicants required to submit FAFSA. *Unit head:* Dr. Patricia Drews, Head, 660-562-1273, E-mail: drews@nwmissouri.edu. *Application contact:* Dr. Gregory Haddock, Dean of Graduate School, 660-562-1145, Fax: 660-562-1096, E-mail: gradsch@nwmissouri.edu.

Saint Louis University, Graduate School, College of Education and Public Service and Graduate School, Department of Public Policy Studies, St. Louis, MO 63103-2097. Offers geographic information systems (Certificate); organizational development (Certificate); public administration (MAPA); public policy analysis (PhD); urban affairs (MAUA); urban planning and real estate development (MUPRED). *Accreditation:* NASPAA. Part-time programs available. *Degree requirements:* For master's, comprehensive exam (for some programs), thesis (for some programs); for doctorate, comprehensive exam, thesis/dissertation, preliminary exams. *Entrance requirements:* For master's, GMAT, GRE General Test, or LSAT, letters of recommendation, resume; for doctorate, GMAT, GRE General Test, or LSAT, letters of recommendation, resumé, interview, transcripts, goal statement. Additional exam requirements/recommendations for international students: Required—TOEFL (minimum score 525 paper-based; 194 computer-based). Electronic applications accepted. *Faculty research:* Urban politics, brown fields, e-government, and administration, evaluation research, community development, electronic government and governance.

Saint Mary's University of Minnesota, Schools of Graduate and Professional Programs, Graduate School of Business and Technology, Geographic Information Science Program, Winona, MN 55987-1399. Offers MS, Certificate. *Unit head:* Dr. David McConville, Director, 507-457-1542, Fax: 507-457-1633, E-mail: dmcconvi@smumn.edu. *Application contact:* Jami Spitzer, Information Contact, 507-457-7500, E-mail: jspitzer@smumn.edu.

Salisbury University, Graduate Division, Master of Science in Geographic Information Systems Management Program, Salisbury, MD 21801-6837. Offers MS. Part-time programs available. Postbaccalaureate distance learning degree programs offered (minimal on-campus study). *Faculty:* 2 full-time (0 women). *Students:* 4 full-time (0 women), 9 part-time (1 woman); includes 2 minority (both African Americans). Average age 30. 15 applicants, 87% accepted, 11 enrolled. In 2009, 7 master's awarded. *Degree requirements:* For master's, cooperative project. *Entrance requirements:* For master's, GRE (for recent graduates), GIS and administration experience. Additional exam requirements/recommendations for international students: Required—TOEFL (minimum score 550 paper-based; 213 computer-based). *Application deadline:* For fall admission, 2/15 for domestic students. Application fee: $45. Electronic applications accepted. *Expenses:* Tuition, area resident: Part-time $278 per credit hour. Tuition, state resident: part-time $278 per credit hour. Tuition, nonresident: part-time $574 per credit hour. Required fees: $57 per credit hour. *Financial support:* In 2009–10, 5 students received support. *Faculty research:* GIS in local governments, parallel applications of GIS, GIS and vulnerability, GIS and crime analysis. *Unit head:* Dr. Michael Scott, Director, 410-543-6456, Fax: 410-548-4506, E-mail: msscott@salisbury.edu. *Application contact:* Susan Parks, Program Management Specialist, 410-543-6460, Fax: 410-548-4506, E-mail: slparks@salisbury.edu.

San Jose State University, Graduate Studies and Research, College of Social Sciences, Department of Geography, San Jose, CA 95192-0001. Offers geographic information science (Certificate); geography (MA). *Students:* 1 full-time (0 women), 13 part-time (6 women); includes 3 minority (2 Asian Americans or Pacific Islanders, 1 Hispanic American). Average age 39. 10 applicants, 50% accepted, 2 enrolled. In 2009, 5 master's awarded. *Entrance requirements:* For master's, minimum GPA of 3.0. *Application deadline:* For fall admission, 6/29 for domestic students; for spring admission, 11/30 for domestic students. Applications are processed on a rolling basis. Application fee: $59. Electronic applications accepted. *Financial support:* Applicants required to submit FAFSA. *Unit head:* Dr. Richard Taketa, Chair, 408-924-5425, E-mail: rtaketa@email.sjsu.edu. *Application contact:* Dr. Richard Taketa, Chair, 408-924-5425, E-mail: rtaketa@email.sjsu.edu.

Texas State University–San Marcos, Graduate School, College of Liberal Arts, Department of Geography, Program in Environmental Geography, Geography Education, and Geographic Information Science, San Marcos, TX 78666. Offers environmental geography (PhD); geography education (PhD); information science (PhD). Part-time programs available. *Students:* 46 full-time (22 women), 25 part-time (12 women); includes 16 minority (3 African Americans, 7 Asian Americans or Pacific Islanders, 6 Hispanic Americans), 3 international. Average age 39. 23 applicants, 83% accepted, 8 enrolled. In 2009, 6 doctorates awarded. *Degree requirements:* For doctorate, thesis/dissertation. *Entrance requirements:* For doctorate, GRE General Test, minimum GPA of 3.5, master's degree in geography, demonstrated scholarly research. Additional exam requirements/recommendations for international students: Required—TOEFL (minimum score 550 paper-based; 213 computer-based). *Application deadline:* For fall admission, 6/15 priority date for domestic students, 6/1 for international students; for spring admission, 10/15 priority date for domestic students, 10/1 for international students. Applications are processed on a rolling basis. Application fee: $40 ($90 for international students). Electronic applications

Geographic Information Systems

Texas State University–San Marcos (continued)

accepted. *Expenses:* Tuition, state resident: full-time $5784; part-time $241 per credit hour. Tuition, nonresident: part-time $551 per credit hour. Required fees: $1728; $48 per credit hour. $306. Tuition and fees vary according to course load. *Financial support:* In 2009–10, 60 students received support, including 17 research assistantships (averaging $10,552 per year), 26 teaching assistantships (averaging $9,874 per year); career-related internships or fieldwork, Federal Work-Study, and institutionally sponsored loans also available. Support available to part-time students. Financial award application deadline: 4/1; financial award applicants required to submit FAFSA. *Unit head:* Dr. David Butler, Graduate Adviser, 512-245-2170, Fax: 512-245-8353, E-mail: db25@txstate.edu. *Application contact:* Dr. J. Michael Willoughby, Dean of Graduate School, 512-245-2581, Fax: 512-245-8365, E-mail: gradcollege@txstate.edu.

Texas State University–San Marcos, Graduate School, College of Liberal Arts, Department of Geography, Program in Geographic Information Science, San Marcos, TX 78666. Offers MAG. Part-time and evening/weekend programs available. *Faculty:* 6 full-time (2 women). *Students:* 5 full-time (3 women), 7 part-time (5 women); includes 2 minority (1 African American, 1 Hispanic American). Average age 31. 5 applicants, 80% accepted, 4 enrolled. In 2009, 10 master's awarded. *Degree requirements:* For master's, comprehensive exam. *Entrance requirements:* For master's, GRE General Test, minimum GPA of 3.0 in last 60 hours of course work, letter of interest, 2 letters of recommendation, curriculum vitae/resume. Additional exam requirements/recommendations for international students: Required—TOEFL (minimum score 550 paper-based; 213 computer-based). *Application deadline:* For fall admission, 6/15 priority date for domestic students, 6/1 for international students; for spring admission, 10/15 priority date for domestic students, 10/1 for international students. Applications are processed on a rolling basis. Application fee: $40 ($90 for international students). Electronic applications accepted. *Expenses:* Tuition, state resident: full-time $5784; part-time $241 per credit hour. Tuition, nonresident: part-time $551 per credit hour. Required fees: $1728; $48 per credit hour. $306. Tuition and fees vary according to course load. *Financial support:* In 2009–10, 5 students received support, including 1 teaching assistantship (averaging $5,850 per year); research assistantships, career-related internships or fieldwork, Federal Work-Study, institutionally sponsored loans, and scholarships/grants also available. Support available to part-time students. Financial award application deadline: 4/1; financial award applicants required to submit FAFSA. *Unit head:* Dr. David Butler, Graduate Adviser, 512-245-2170, Fax: 512-245-8353, E-mail: db25@txstate.edu. *Application contact:* Dr. J. Michael Willoughby, Dean of Graduate School, 512-245-2581, Fax: 512-245-8365, E-mail: gradcollege@txstate.edu.

Université du Québec à Montréal, Graduate Programs, Program in Geographical Information Systems, Montréal, QC H3C 3P8, Canada. Offers Diploma. Part-time programs available. *Entrance requirements:* For degree, appropriate bachelor's degree or equivalent, proficiency in French.

Université Laval, Faculty of Administrative Sciences, Programs in Business Administration, Québec, QC G1K 7P4, Canada. Offers accounting (MBA); agri-food management (MBA); electronic business (MBA, Diploma); factory management and logistics (MBA); finance (MBA); firm management (MBA); geomatic management (MBA); information technology management (MBA); international management (MBA); management (MBA); management accounting (MBA, Diploma); marketing (MBA); modeling and organizational decision (MBA); occupational health and safety management (MBA); pharmacy management (MBA); social and environmental responsibility (MBA); technological entrepreneurship (Diploma). *Accreditation:* AACSB. Part-time and evening/weekend programs available. Postbaccalaureate distance learning degree programs offered (no on-campus study). *Entrance requirements:* For master's and Diploma, knowledge of French and English. Electronic applications accepted.

University at Albany, State University of New York, College of Arts and Sciences, Department of Geography and Planning, Program in Geography, Albany, NY 12222-0001. Offers geographic information systems and spatial analysis (Certificate); geography (MA). *Degree requirements:* For master's, thesis or alternative. *Entrance requirements:* Additional exam requirements/recommendations for international students: Required—TOEFL (minimum score 550 paper-based; 213 computer-based). Electronic applications accepted. *Faculty research:* Remote sensing, cultural/social geography, urban geography.

University at Buffalo, the State University of New York, Graduate School, College of Arts and Sciences, Department of Geography, Buffalo, NY 14260. Offers earth systems science (MA); economic geography and international business and world trade (MA); environmental and earth systems science (MS); environmental modeling and analysis (MA); geographic information science (MA, Certificate); geographic information systems and science (MS); geography (MA, PhD); urban and regional geography (MA); MA/MBA. *Faculty:* 14 full-time (6 women), 2 part-time/adjunct (0 women). *Students:* 63 full-time (16 women), 32 part-time (8 women); includes 31 minority (3 African Americans, 26 Asian Americans or Pacific Islanders, 2 Hispanic Americans), 3 international. Average age 29. 154 applicants, 42% accepted, 24 enrolled. In 2009, 18 master's, 6 doctorates awarded. *Degree requirements:* For master's, thesis (for some programs), project; for doctorate, thesis/dissertation. *Entrance requirements:* For master's, GRE General Test, minimum GPA of 2.9; for doctorate, GRE General Test, minimum GPA of 3.0. Additional exam requirements/recommendations for international students: Required—TOEFL (minimum score 550 paper-based; 213 computer-based; 79 iBT). *Application deadline:* For fall admission, 7/1 priority date for domestic students, 1/10 priority date for international students; for spring admission, 12/1 priority date for domestic students, 10/1 priority date for international students. Applications are processed on a rolling basis. Application fee: $75. Electronic applications accepted. *Financial support:* In 2009–10, 19 students received support, including 6 fellowships with full tuition reimbursements available (averaging $4,333 per year), 14 teaching assistantships with full tuition reimbursements available (averaging $13,361 per year); research assistantships with full tuition reimbursements available, career-related internships or fieldwork, Federal Work-Study, institutionally sponsored loans, traineeships, health care benefits, and unspecified assistantships also available. Financial award application deadline: 1/10. *Faculty research:* International business and world trade, geographic information systems and cartography, transportation, urban and regional analysis, physical and environmental geography. Total annual research expenditures: $944,614. *Unit head:* Dr. Peter Rogerson, Chairman, 716-645-0473, Fax: 716-645-2329, E-mail: rogerson@buffalo.edu. *Application contact:* Betsy Abraham, Graduate Secretary, 716-645-0471, Fax: 716-645-2329, E-mail: babraham@buffalo.edu.

The University of Akron, Graduate School, Buchtel College of Arts and Sciences, Department of Geography and Planning, Program in Geographic Information Science, Akron, OH 44325. Offers MS. *Students:* 1 full-time (0 women), 1 part-time (0 women). Average age 35. 12 applicants, 83% accepted. In 2009, 9 master's awarded. *Entrance requirements:* For master's, two letters of recommendation; statement of purpose. Additional exam requirements/recommendations for international students: Required—TOEFL (minimum score 550 paper-based; 213 computer-based; 79 iBT). *Application deadline:* Applications are processed on a rolling basis. Electronic applications accepted. *Expenses:* Tuition, state resident: full-time $6570; part-time $365 per credit hour. Tuition, nonresident: full-time $11,250; part-time $625 per credit hour. *Unit head:* Dr. Linda Barrett, Graduate Director, 330-972-6120, E-mail: barrettr@uakron.edu. *Application contact:* Dr. Linda Barrett, Graduate Director, 330-972-6120, E-mail: barrettr@uakron.edu.

University of Central Arkansas, Graduate School, College of Liberal Arts, Department of Geography, Conway, AR 72035-0001. Offers geographic information systems (MGIS, Certificate). Part-time programs available. Postbaccalaureate distance learning degree programs offered (minimal on-campus study). *Faculty:* 3 full-time (0 women). *Students:* 2 full-time (1 woman), 17 part-time (3 women); includes 3 minority (1 African American, 1 Asian American or Pacific Islander, 1 Hispanic American). Average age 36. 7 applicants, 100% accepted, 6 enrolled. *Entrance requirements:* Additional exam requirements/recommendations for international students: Required—TOEFL (minimum score 550 paper-based; 213 computer-based). *Application deadline:* For fall admission, 3/1 priority date for domestic and international students; for spring admission, 10/1 priority date for domestic and international students. Applications are processed on a rolling basis. Application fee: $25 ($50 for international students). *Expenses:* Tuition, state resident: full-time $5136; part-time $214 per credit hour. Required fees: $379.50; $127 per term. Tuition and fees vary according to course level, course load and campus/location. *Financial support:* Applicants required to submit FAFSA. *Unit head:* Dr. Brooks Green, Chairperson, 501-450-5636, Fax: 501-450-5185, E-mail: brooksg@uca.edu. *Application contact:* Brenda Herring, Admissions Assistant, 501-450-5065, Fax: 501-450-5678, E-mail: bherring@uca.edu.

University of Colorado Denver, College of Engineering and Applied Science, Department of Civil Engineering, Denver, CO 80217-3364. Offers civil engineering (MS, PhD); geographic information systems (M Eng). Part-time and evening/weekend programs available. *Students:* 22 full-time (5 women), 139 part-time (39 women); includes 31 minority (11 African Americans, 11 Asian Americans or Pacific Islanders, 9 Hispanic Americans), 15 international. 83 applicants, 64% accepted, 36 enrolled. In 2009, 35 master's, 6 doctorates awarded. *Degree requirements:* For master's, comprehensive exam, thesis or alternative; for doctorate, comprehensive exam, thesis/dissertation. *Entrance requirements:* For master's and doctorate, GRE. Additional exam requirements/recommendations for international students: Required—TOEFL (minimum score 525 paper-based; 197 computer-based). *Application deadline:* For fall admission, 4/1 for domestic students; for spring admission, 10/1 for domestic students. Applications are processed on a rolling basis. Application fee: $50 ($75 for international students). Electronic applications accepted. *Financial support:* Research assistantships, teaching assistantships, career-related internships or fieldwork and Federal Work-Study available. Financial award application deadline: 4/1; financial award applicants required to submit FAFSA. *Unit head:* Dr. Nien-Yin Chang, Acting Chair, 303-556-2810, Fax: 303-556-2368, E-mail: nien.chang@ucdenver.edu. *Application contact:* Mindy Gewuerz, Program Assistant, 303-556-6712, Fax: 303-556-2368, E-mail: mindy.gewuerz@ucdenver.edu.

University of Connecticut, Graduate School, College of Liberal Arts and Sciences, Department of Geography, Storrs, CT 06269. Offers geographic information systems (Certificate); geography (MS, PhD). *Faculty:* 13 full-time (5 women). *Students:* 25 full-time (2 women), 12 part-time (4 women); includes 4 minority (3 Asian Americans or Pacific Islanders, 1 Hispanic American), 6 international. Average age 30. 35 applicants, 29% accepted, 6 enrolled. In 2009, 3 master's, 1 doctorate, 5 other advanced degrees awarded. *Degree requirements:* For master's, comprehensive exam; for doctorate, thesis/dissertation. *Entrance requirements:* For master's and doctorate, GRE General Test. Additional exam requirements/recommendations for international students: Required—TOEFL (minimum score 550 paper-based; 213 computer-based). *Application deadline:* For fall admission, 2/1 priority date for domestic and international students; for spring admission, 11/1 for domestic students, 10/1 for international students. Applications are processed on a rolling basis. Application fee: $55. Electronic applications accepted. *Expenses:* Tuition, state resident: full-time $4725; part-time $525 per credit. Tuition, nonresident: full-time $12,267; part-time $1363 per credit. Required fees: $346 per semester. Tuition and fees vary according to course load. *Financial support:* In 2009–10, 5 research assistantships with full tuition reimbursements, 16 teaching assistantships with full tuition reimbursements were awarded; fellowships, Federal Work-Study, scholarships/grants, health care benefits, and unspecified assistantships also available. Financial award application deadline: 2/1; financial award applicants required to submit FAFSA. *Unit head:* Jeffrey Osleeb, Head, 860-486-6977, Fax: 860-486-1348, E-mail: jeffrey.osleeb@uconn.edu. *Application contact:* Dean Hanink, Interim Graduate Program Director, 860-486-3450, Fax: 860-486-1348, E-mail: dean.hanink@uconn.edu.

University of Denver, University College, Denver, CO 80208. Offers applied communication (MAS, MPS, Certificate); computer information systems (MAS, Certificate); environmental policy and management (MAS, Certificate); geographic information systems (MAS, Certificate); human resource administration (MPS, Certificate); knowledge and information technologies (MAS); liberal studies (MLS, Certificate); modern languages (MLS, Certificate); organizational leadership (MPS, Certificate); security management (Certificate); technology management (MAS, Certificate), including 21st century strategic management (MAS), international markets (MAS), project management (MAS), research and development management (MAS); telecommunications (MAS, Certificate), including broadband (MAS), telecommunications management and policy (MAS), telecommunications technology (MAS), wireless networks (MAS). Part-time and evening/weekend programs available. Postbaccalaureate distance learning degree programs offered (no on-campus study). *Faculty:* 160 part-time/adjunct (64 women). *Students:* 53 full-time (25 women), 984 part-time (551 women); includes 171 minority (72 African Americans, 10 American Indian/Alaska Native, 33 Asian Americans or Pacific Islanders, 56 Hispanic Americans), 75 international. Average age 36. 537 applicants, 96% accepted, 494 enrolled. In 2009, 229 master's, 109 Certificates awarded. *Entrance requirements:* Additional exam requirements/recommendations for international students: Required—TOEFL (minimum score 550 paper-based; 213 computer-based). *Application deadline:* Applications are processed on a rolling basis. Application fee: $75. Electronic applications accepted. *Expenses:* Contact institution. *Financial support:* Applicants required to submit FAFSA. *Unit head:* Dr. James Davis, Dean, 303-871-2291, Fax: 303-871-4047, E-mail: jdavis@du.edu. *Application contact:* Information Contact, 303-871-3155.

University of Lethbridge, School of Graduate Studies, Lethbridge, AB T1K 3M4, Canada. Offers accounting (MScM); addictions counseling (M Sc); agricultural biotechnology (M Sc); agricultural studies (M Sc, MA); anthropology (MA); archaeology (MA); art (MA, MFA); biochemistry (M Sc); biological sciences (M Sc); biomolecular science (PhD); biosystems and biodiversity (PhD); Canadian studies (MA); chemistry (M Sc); computer science (M Sc); computer science and geographical information science (M Sc); counseling psychology (M Ed); dramatic arts (MA); earth, space, and physical science (PhD); economics (MA); educational leadership (M Ed); English (MA); environmental science (M Sc); evolution and behavior (PhD); exercise science (M Sc); finance (MScM); French (MA); French/German (MA); French/Spanish (MA); general education (M Ed); general management (MScM); geography (M Sc, MA); German (MA); health science (M Sc); health sciences (MA); history (MA); human resource management and labour relations (MScM); individualized multidisciplinary (M Sc, MA); information systems (MScM); international management (MScM); kinesiology (M Sc, MA); management (M Sc, MA); marketing (MScM); mathematics (M Sc); music (M Mus, MA); Native American studies (MA); neuroscience (M Sc, PhD); new media (MA); nursing (M Sc); philosophy (MA); physics (M Sc); policy and strategy (MScM); political science (MA); psychology (M Sc, MA); religious studies (MA); social sciences (MA); sociology (MA); theatre and dramatic arts (MFA); theoretical and computational science (PhD); urban and regional studies (MA); women's studies (MA). Part-time and evening/weekend programs available. *Degree requirements:* For doctorate, comprehensive exam, thesis/dissertation. *Entrance requirements:* For master's, GMAT (M Sc in management), bachelor's degree in related field, minimum GPA of 3.0 during previous 20 graded semester courses, 2 years teaching or related experience (M Ed); for doctorate, master's degree, minimum graduate GPA of 3.5. Additional exam requirements/recommendations for international students: Required—TOEFL. *Faculty research:* Movement and brain plasticity, gibberellin physiology, photosynthesis, carbon cycling, molecular properties of main-group ring components.

University of Maryland, Baltimore County, Graduate School, College of Arts, Humanities and Social Sciences, Department of Geography and Environmental Systems, Program in Geographic Information Systems, Baltimore, MD 21250. Offers MPS, Certificate. Part-time and evening/weekend programs available. *Faculty:* 10 part-time/adjunct (3 women). *Students:* 2 full-time (1 woman), 29 part-time (7 women); includes 11 minority (2 African Americans, 7 Asian Americans or Pacific Islanders, 2 Hispanic Americans), 2 international. Average age 31. 9 applicants, 89% accepted, 7 enrolled. *Entrance requirements:* Additional exam requirements/recommendations for international students: Required—TOEFL. *Application deadline:* For fall admission, 6/1 for domestic and international students; for spring admission, 11/1 for domestic and international students. Applications are processed on a rolling basis. Application fee: $70. Electronic applications accepted. *Faculty research:* Enterprise GIS. *Unit head:* Dr. Sandy Parker, Chair, 410-455-2002, E-mail: eparker@umbc.edu. *Application contact:* Kathryn Nee, Coordinator of Domestic Admissions, 410-455-2944, E-mail: nee@umbc.edu.

University of Minnesota, Twin Cities Campus, Graduate School, College of Liberal Arts, Program in Geographic Information Science, Minneapolis, MN 55455-0213. Offers MGIS. Part-time programs available. *Faculty:* 14 full-time (1 woman), 3 part-time/adjunct (0 women). *Students:* 44 full-time (18 women), 15 part-time (2 women); includes 1 minority (Asian American or Pacific Islander), 6 international. 21 applicants, 71% accepted, 8 enrolled. In 2009, 7 master's awarded. *Degree requirements:* For master's, comprehensive exam, capstone project. *Entrance requirements:* For master's, minimum GPA of 3.0; course work in college-level math, statistics, and computer programming. Additional exam requirements/recommendations for international students: Required—TOEFL (minimum score 600 paper-based; 250 computer-based; 100 iBT). *Application deadline:* For fall admission, 1/30 for domestic students; for spring admission, 9/1 for domestic students. Application fee: $55 ($75 for international students). *Expenses:* Contact institution. *Financial support:* In 2009–10, 13 students received support, including 10 research assistantships with full and partial tuition reimbursements available, 3 teaching assistantships with full and partial tuition reimbursements available; career-related internships or fieldwork and unspecified assistantships also available. *Faculty research:* Geographic information science and society, spatial analysis and modeling, spatial databases, remote sensing, geovisualization. *Unit head:* Dr. Paul V. Bolstad, Co-Director, 612-624-9711, Fax: 612-625-5212, E-mail: pbolstad@umn.edu. *Application contact:* Dr. Susanna A. McMaster, Associate Program Director, 612-624-1498, Fax: 612-624-1044, E-mail: mcmas002@umn.edu.

The University of Montana, Graduate School, College of Arts and Sciences, Department of Geography, Missoula, MT 59812-0002. Offers geography (MA), including cartography and GIS, community and environmental planning. *Entrance requirements:* For master's, GRE General Test. Additional exam requirements/recommendations for international students: Required—TOEFL.

University of New Haven, Graduate School, College of Arts and Sciences, Program in Environmental Sciences, West Haven, CT 06516-1916. Offers environmental ecology (Certificate); environmental geoscience (MS); environmental health and management (MS); environmental science (MS); geographical information systems (Certificate). Part-time and evening/weekend programs available. *Faculty:* 6 full-time (3 women), 8 part-time/adjunct (2 women). *Students:* 8 full-time (5 women), 21 part-time (9 women); includes 2 minority (both African Americans), 4 international. Average age 27. 28 applicants, 79% accepted, 4 enrolled. In 2009, 7 master's, 5 other advanced degrees awarded. *Degree requirements:* For master's, thesis or alternative. *Entrance requirements:* Additional exam requirements/recommendations for international students: Required—TOEFL (minimum score 520 paper-based; 190 computer-based; 70 iBT); Recommended—IELTS (minimum score 5.5). *Application deadline:* For fall admission, 5/31 for international students; for winter admission, 10/15 for international students; for spring admission, 1/15 for international students. Applications are processed on a rolling basis. Application fee: $50. Electronic applications accepted. *Expenses:* Tuition: Part-time $700 per credit. Required fees: $45 per term. One-time fee: $390 part-time. *Financial support:* Research assistantships with partial tuition reimbursements, teaching assistantships with partial tuition reimbursements, career-related internships or fieldwork, Federal Work-Study, scholarships/grants, tuition waivers, and unspecified assistantships available. Support available to part-time students. Financial award applicants required to submit FAFSA. *Faculty research:* Mapping and assessing geological and living resources in Long Island Sound, geology, San Salvador Island, Bahamas. *Unit head:* Dr. Roman Zajac, Coordinator, 203-932-7108. *Application contact:* Eloise Gormley, Director of Graduate Admissions, 203-932-7449, Fax: 203-932-7137, E-mail: gradinfo@newhaven.edu.

The University of North Carolina at Greensboro, Graduate School, College of Arts and Sciences, Department of Geography, Greensboro, NC 27412-5001. Offers applied geography (MA); geographic information science (Certificate); geography (PhD); urban and economic development (Certificate). *Degree requirements:* For master's, comprehensive exam, thesis or alternative. *Entrance requirements:* For master's, GRE General Test. Additional exam requirements/recommendations for international students: Required—TOEFL. Electronic applications accepted.

University of Pittsburgh, School of Arts and Sciences, Department of Geology and Planetary Science, Pittsburgh, PA 15260-3332. Offers geographical information systems (PM Sc); geology and planetary science (MS, PhD). Part-time programs available. *Faculty:* 9 full-time (1 woman), 4 part-time/adjunct (1 woman). *Students:* 27 full-time (15 women), 7 part-time (4 women), 1 international. Average age 30. 38 applicants, 24% accepted, 6 enrolled. In 2009, 1 doctorate awarded. *Degree requirements:* For master's, thesis, oral thesis defense; for doctorate, comprehensive exam, thesis/dissertation, oral dissertation defense. *Entrance requirements:* For master's and doctorate, GRE General Test. Additional exam requirements/recommendations for international students: Required—TOEFL (minimum score 550 paper-based; 213 computer-based; 80 iBT). *Application deadline:* For fall admission, 2/1 priority date for domestic students, 2/1 for international students. Application fee: $50. Electronic applications accepted. *Expenses:* Tuition, state resident: full-time $16,402; part-time $665 per credit. Tuition, nonresident: full-time $28,694; part-time $1175 per credit. Required fees: $690; $175 per term. Tuition and fees vary according to program. *Financial support:* In 2009–10, 25 students received support, including 2 fellowships with full tuition reimbursements available (averaging $14,400 per year), 13 research assistantships with full and partial tuition reimbursements available (averaging $14,400 per year), 10 teaching assistantships with full and partial tuition reimbursements available (averaging $15,065 per year); career-related internships or fieldwork, Federal Work-Study, institutionally sponsored loans, scholarships/grants, and tuition waivers (full and partial) also available. Support available to part-time students. Financial award application deadline: 2/1; financial award applicants required to submit FAFSA. *Faculty research:* Geographical information systems, hydrology, low temperature geochemistry, volcanology, paleoclimatology. Total annual research expenditures: $1.2 million. *Unit head:* Dr. Thomas Anderson, Chair, 412-624-8783, Fax: 412-624-3914, E-mail: bstewart@pitt.edu. *Application contact:* Dr. Brian W. Stewart, Graduate Adviser, 412-624-8883, Fax: 412-624-3914, E-mail: taco@pitt.edu.

University of Redlands, College of Arts and Sciences, Program in Geographic Information Systems, Redlands, CA 92373-0999. Offers MS. *Entrance requirements:* For master's, 2 years of professional experience using GIS or 2 university-level GIS courses plus internship, minimum undergraduate GPA of 3.0, 2 letters of recommendation. Additional exam requirements/recommendations for international students: Required—TOEFL (minimum score 550 paper-based; 210 computer-based); Recommended—IELTS (minimum score 5.5). Electronic applications accepted. *Expenses:* Contact institution.

University of Southern California, Graduate School, College of Letters, Arts and Sciences, Department of Geography, Los Angeles, CA 90089. Offers geographic information science and technology (MS, Graduate Certificate); geography (PhD). Part-time programs available. Post-baccalaureate distance learning degree programs offered (minimal on-campus study). *Faculty:* 3 full-time (0 women), 5 part-time/adjunct (2 women). *Students:* 29 full-time (14 women), 9 part-time (1 woman); includes 9 minority (1 African American, 3 American Indian/Alaska Native, 2 Asian Americans or Pacific Islanders, 3 Hispanic Americans), 7 international. 4 applicants, 100% accepted, 3 enrolled. In 2009, 3 doctorates, 22 other advanced degrees awarded. Terminal master's awarded for partial completion of doctoral program. *Degree requirements:* For master's, thesis; for doctorate, thesis/dissertation. *Entrance requirements:* For master's and doctorate, GRE. Additional exam requirements/recommendations for international students: Required—TOEFL (minimum score 600 paper-based; 250 computer-based; 100 iBT). *Application deadline:* Applications are processed on a rolling basis. Application fee: $85. Electronic applications accepted. *Expenses:* Tuition: Full-time $25,980; part-time $1315 per unit. Required fees: $554. One-time fee: $35 full-time. Full-time tuition and fees vary according to degree level and program. *Financial support:* In 2009–10, 18 students received support, including 9 fellowships with full tuition reimbursements available (averaging $19,715 per year), 1 research assistantship with full tuition reimbursement available (averaging $18,800 per year), 8 teaching assistantships with full tuition reimbursements available (averaging $18,800 per year); health care benefits and unspecified assistantships also available. *Faculty research:* Public heath, environmental modeling, natural hazards, landscape dynamics, geomorphology, geographic information science, urban geography and nature-society relations, GIS. *Unit head:* Dr. John P. Wilson, Chair, 213-740-1908, E-mail: jpwilson@usc.edu. *Application contact:* Kate A. Kelsey, Student Program Advisor, 213-740-8298, Fax: 213-740-0056, E-mail: kkelsey@usc.edu.

The University of Texas at Dallas, School of Economic, Political and Policy Sciences, Program in Geospatial Sciences, Richardson, TX 75080. Offers MS, PhD. Part-time and evening/weekend programs available. *Faculty:* 7 full-time (1 woman), 1 part-time/adjunct (0 women). *Students:* 17 full-time (5 women), 24 part-time (9 women); includes 4 minority (1 African American, 2 Asian Americans or Pacific Islanders, 1 Hispanic American), 19 international. Average age 35. 18 applicants, 44% accepted, 5 enrolled. In 2009, 17 master's awarded. *Degree requirements:* For master's, internship; for doctorate, thesis/dissertation. *Entrance requirements:* For master's and doctorate, GRE General Test, minimum GPA of 3.0 in upper-level coursework in field. Additional exam requirements/recommendations for international students: Required—TOEFL (minimum score 550 paper-based; 213 computer-based). *Application deadline:* For fall admission, 7/15 for domestic students, 5/1 priority date for international students; for spring admission, 11/15 for domestic students, 9/1 priority date for international students. Applications are processed on a rolling basis. Application fee: $50 ($100 for international students). Electronic applications accepted. *Expenses:* Tuition, state resident: full-time $11,068; part-time $461 per credit hour. Tuition, nonresident: full-time $21,178; part-time $882 per credit hour. Tuition and fees vary according to course load. *Financial support:* In 2009–10, 2 research assistantships with full tuition reimbursements (averaging $19,149 per year), 9 teaching assistantships with full tuition reimbursements (averaging $12,200 per year) were awarded; fellowships, career-related internships or fieldwork, Federal Work-Study, institutionally sponsored loans, scholarships/grants, and unspecified assistantships also available. Support available to part-time students. Financial award application deadline: 4/30; financial award applicants required to submit FAFSA. *Faculty research:* Neighborhood evaluation using geographical information systems, urban and regional development, spatial analysis, demographics patterns. *Unit head:* Dr. Denis Dean, Program Head, 972-883-6852, Fax: 972-883-2735, E-mail: djd081000@utdallas.edu. *Application contact:* Dr. Daniel A. Griffith, Associate Program Head, 972-883-4950, Fax: 972-883-2735, E-mail: dagriffith@utdallas.edu.

See Close-Up on page 759.

The University of Toledo, College of Graduate Studies, College of Arts and Sciences, Department of Geography and Planning, Toledo, OH 43606-3390. Offers geographic information systems and applied geographics (Certificate); geography (MA); planning (MA). Part-time programs available. *Degree requirements:* For master's, thesis. *Entrance requirements:* For master's, GRE General Test. Electronic applications accepted.

University of Wisconsin–Madison, Graduate School, College of Letters and Science, Department of Geography, Madison, WI 53706-1380. Offers cartography and geographic information systems (MS); geographic information systems (Certificate); geography (MS, PhD). Part-time programs available. *Degree requirements:* For master's, thesis; for doctorate, thesis/dissertation; for Certificate, internship. *Entrance requirements:* For master's and doctorate, GRE General Test, minimum GPA of 3.25. Electronic applications accepted. *Expenses:* Tuition, state resident: part-time $594 per credit. Tuition, nonresident: part-time $1504 per credit. Required fees: $65 per credit. Tuition and fees vary according to course load, program and reciprocity agreements. *Faculty research:* Physical geography, urban/historical geography, people-environment, history of cartography, GIS.

University of Wisconsin–Milwaukee, Graduate School, School of Architecture and Urban Planning, Department of Urban Planning, Milwaukee, WI 53201-0413. Offers geographic information systems (Certificate); real estate development (Certificate); urban planning (MUP); M Arch/MUP; MPA/MUP; MUP/MS. *Accreditation:* ACSP. Part-time programs available. *Faculty:* 4 full-time (1 woman). *Students:* 29 full-time (11 women), 5 part-time (3 women), 2 international. Average age 28. 52 applicants, 71% accepted, 13 enrolled. In 2009, 22 master's awarded. *Degree requirements:* For master's, comprehensive exam, thesis or alternative. *Entrance requirements:* For master's, GRE General Test. Additional exam requirements/recommendations for international students: Required—TOEFL (minimum score 550 paper-based; 213 computer-based; 79 iBT), IELTS (minimum score 6.5). *Application deadline:* For fall admission, 1/1 priority date for domestic students; for spring admission, 9/1 for domestic students. Applications are processed on a rolling basis. Application fee: $45 ($75 for international students). *Expenses:* Tuition, state resident: full-time $8800. Tuition, nonresident: full-time $20,760. Tuition and fees vary according to program and reciprocity agreements. *Financial support:* In 2009–10, 3 teaching assistantships were awarded; career-related internships or fieldwork and unspecified assistantships also available. Support available to part-time students. Financial award application deadline: 4/15. Total annual research expenditures: $4,667. *Unit head:* Joan Simuncak, Representative, 414-229-4015, Fax: 414-229-6976, E-mail: joanarch@uwm.edu. *Application contact:* General Information Contact, 414-229-4982, Fax: 414-229-6967, E-mail: gradschool@uwm.edu.

Virginia Commonwealth University, Graduate School, College of Humanities and Sciences, Wilder School of Government and Public Affairs, Department of Urban Studies and Planning, Program in Geographic Information Systems, Richmond, VA 23284-9005. Offers Certificate.

Virginia Polytechnic Institute and State University, Graduate School, College of Natural Resources, Program in Geospatial and Environmental Analysis, Blacksburg, VA 24061. Offers PhD.

West Chester University of Pennsylvania, Office of Graduate Studies, College of Business and Public Affairs, Department of Geography and Planning, West Chester, PA 19383. Offers geographic technology (Certificate); geography (MA); regional planning (MSA). Part-time and evening/weekend programs available. *Students:* 3 full-time (0 women), 27 part-time (9 women); includes 5 minority (3 African Americans, 1 Asian American or Pacific Islander, 1 Hispanic American), 1 international. Average age 28. 13 applicants, 100% accepted, 9 enrolled. In 2009, 11 master's, 5 other advanced degrees awarded. *Degree requirements:* For master's, comprehensive exam, thesis optional. *Entrance requirements:* For master's, GRE, GMAT, or MAT, minimum GPA of 2.8, resume, two letters of recommendation; for Certificate, minimum GPA of 2.8, resume, two letters of recommendation. Additional exam requirements/recommendations for international students: Required—TOEFL (minimum score 550 paper-based; 213 computer-based; 80 iBT). *Application deadline:* For fall admission, 4/15 priority date for domestic students, 3/15 for international students; for spring admission, 10/15 for domestic students, 9/1 for international students. Applications are processed on a rolling basis. Application fee: $35. Electronic applications accepted. *Expenses:* Tuition, state resident: full-time $6666; part-time $370 per credit. Tuition, nonresident: full-time $10,666; part-time $593 per credit. Required fees: $122.56 per credit. *Financial support:* In 2009–10, 6 research assistantships with full and partial tuition reimbursements (averaging $5,000 per year) were awarded; unspecified assistantships also available. Support available to part-time students. Financial award application deadline: 2/15; financial award applicants required to submit FAFSA. *Faculty research:* Environmental education, land use/suburban planning, landscapes of Catalunya. *Unit head:* Dr. Joan Welch, Chair and Graduate Coordinator, 610-436-2940, E-mail: jwelch@wcupa.edu. *Application contact:* Dr. Dottie Ives Dewey, MSA Graduate Coordinator, 610-436-2746, E-mail: divesdewey@wcupa.edu.

Western Illinois University, School of Graduate Studies, College of Arts and Sciences, Department of Biological Sciences, Macomb, IL 61455-1390. Offers biological sciences (MS); environmental geographic information systems (Certificate); zoo and aquarium studies (Certificate). Part-time programs available. *Students:* 62 full-time (43 women), 28 part-time (17 women); includes 6 minority (2 African Americans, 2 Asian Americans or Pacific Islanders, 2 Hispanic Americans), 10 international. Average age 26. 53 applicants, 72% accepted. In 2009, 25 master's, 15 other advanced degrees awarded. *Degree requirements:* For master's, thesis or alternative. *Entrance requirements:* Additional exam requirements/recommendations for international students: Required—TOEFL (minimum score 550 paper-based; 213 computer-

Geographic Information Systems

Western Illinois University (continued)

based; 80 iBT). *Application deadline:* Applications are processed on a rolling basis. Application fee: $30. Electronic applications accepted. *Expenses:* Tuition, state resident: full-time $4486; part-time $249.21 per credit hour. Tuition, nonresident: full-time $8972; part-time $498.42 per credit hour. Required fees: $72.62 per credit hour. *Financial support:* In 2009–10, 34 students received support, including 16 research assistantships with full tuition reimbursements available (averaging $7,280 per year), 18 teaching assistantships with full tuition reimbursements available (averaging $8,400 per year). Financial award applicants required to submit FAFSA. *Unit head:* Dr. Michael Romano, Chairperson, 309-298-1546. *Application contact:* Evelyn Hoing, Assistant Director of Graduate Studies, 309-298-1806, Fax: 309-298-2345, E-mail: grad-office@wiu.edu.

Western Illinois University, School of Graduate Studies, College of Arts and Sciences, Department of Geography, Macomb, IL 61455-1390. Offers community development (Certificate); environmental GIS (Certificate); geography (MA). Part-time programs available. *Students:* 13 full-time (5 women), 5 part-time (2 women); includes 3 minority (1 African American, 2 Asian Americans or Pacific Islanders), 2 international. Average age 32. 9 applicants, 67% accepted. In 2009, 9 master's, 7 other advanced degrees awarded. *Degree requirements:* For master's, thesis or alternative. *Entrance requirements:* Additional exam requirements/recommendations for international students: Required—TOEFL (minimum score 550 paper-based; 213 computer-based; 80 iBT). *Application deadline:* Applications are processed on a rolling basis. Application fee: $30. Electronic applications accepted. *Expenses:* Tuition, state resident: full-time $4486; part-time $249.21 per credit hour. Tuition, nonresident: full-time $8972; part-time $498.42 per credit hour. Required fees: $72.62 per credit hour. *Financial support:* In 2009–10, 9 students received support, including 9 research assistantships with full tuition reimbursements available (averaging $7,280 per year). Financial award applicants required to submit FAFSA. *Unit head:* Dr. Sam Thompson, Chairperson, 309-298-1648. *Application contact:* Evelyn Hoing, Assistant Director of Graduate Studies, 309-298-1806, Fax: 309-298-2345, E-mail: grad-office@wiu.edu.

West Virginia University, Eberly College of Arts and Sciences, Department of Geology and Geography, Program in Geography, Morgantown, WV 26506. Offers energy and environmental resources (MA); geographic information systems (PhD); geography-regional development (PhD); GIS/cartographic analysis (MA); regional development (MA). Part-time programs available. *Degree requirements:* For master's, thesis, oral and written exams; for doctorate, comprehensive exam, thesis/dissertation, oral and written exams. *Entrance requirements:* For master's and doctorate, GRE General Test, minimum GPA of 3.0. Additional exam requirements/recommendations for international students: Required—TOEFL. Electronic applications accepted. *Faculty research:* Space, place and development, geographic information science, environmental geography.

Geography

Appalachian State University, Cratis D. Williams Graduate School, Department of Geography and Planning, Boone, NC 28608. Offers geography (MA), including GIS, planning. Part-time programs available. Postbaccalaureate distance learning degree programs offered (no on-campus study). *Faculty:* 12 full-time (2 women), 3 part-time/adjunct (1 woman). *Students:* 25 full-time (9 women), 15 part-time (7 women). 21 applicants, 81% accepted, 13 enrolled. In 2009, 10 master's awarded. *Degree requirements:* For master's, comprehensive exam, thesis or alternative. *Entrance requirements:* For master's, GRE General Test, 3 letters of recommendation. Additional exam requirements/recommendations for international students: Required—TOEFL (minimum score 570 paper-based; 230 computer-based; 79 iBT), IELTS (minimum score 6.5). *Application deadline:* For fall admission, 7/1 for domestic students, 2/1 for international students; for spring admission, 11/1 for domestic students, 7/1 for international students. Applications are processed on a rolling basis. Application fee: $50. Electronic applications accepted. *Expenses:* Tuition, state resident: full-time $2960. Tuition, nonresident: full-time $14,051. Required fees: $2320. *Financial support:* In 2009–10, 10 research assistantships (averaging $7,500 per year) were awarded; fellowships, teaching assistantships, career-related internships or fieldwork, Federal Work-Study, scholarships/grants, and unspecified assistantships also available. Financial award application deadline: 4/1; financial award applicants required to submit FAFSA. *Faculty research:* Global change, climatology, production cartography, geographic information systems, North Carolina geography, Latin America. Total annual research expenditures: $85,000. *Unit head:* Dr. James Young, Chairperson, 828-262-3000, Fax: 828-262-3067. *Application contact:* Dr. Kathleen Schroeder, Graduate Program Director, 828-262-3000.

Arizona State University, Graduate College, College of Liberal Arts and Sciences, Division of Social Sciences, School of Geographical Sciences, Tempe, AZ 85287. Offers geographic education (MAS); geographic information systems (MAS); geography (MA, PhD). *Degree requirements:* For master's, thesis; for doctorate, thesis/dissertation. *Entrance requirements:* For master's and doctorate, GRE.

Auburn University, Graduate School, College of Sciences and Mathematics, Department of Geology and Geography, Auburn University, AL 36849. Offers geography (MS); geology (MS). Part-time programs available. *Faculty:* 14 full-time (2 women), 1 part-time/adjunct (0 women). *Students:* 13 full-time (3 women), 8 part-time (3 women), 4 international. Average age 28. 25 applicants, 56% accepted, 7 enrolled. In 2009, 5 master's awarded. *Degree requirements:* For master's, computer language or geographic information systems, field camp. *Entrance requirements:* For master's, GRE General Test. *Application deadline:* For fall admission, 7/7 for domestic students; for spring admission, 11/24 for domestic students. Applications are processed on a rolling basis. Application fee: $50 ($60 for international students). Electronic applications accepted. *Expenses:* Tuition, state resident: full-time $6240. Tuition, nonresident: full-time $18,720. International tuition: $18,938 full-time. Required fees: $492. Tuition and fees vary according to course load, program and reciprocity agreements. *Financial support:* Research assistantships, teaching assistantships, Federal Work-Study available. Support available to part-time students. Financial award application deadline: 3/15; financial award applicants required to submit FAFSA. *Faculty research:* Empirical magma dynamics and melt migration, ore mineralogy, role of terrestrial plant biomass in deposition, metamorphic petrology and isotope geochemistry, reef development, crinoid topology. *Unit head:* Dr. Charles E. Savrda, Chair, 334-844-4282. *Application contact:* Dr. George Flowers, Dean of the Graduate School, 334-844-2125.

Boston University, Graduate School of Arts and Sciences, Department of Geography and Environment, Boston, MA 02215. Offers energy and environmental analysis (MA); environmental remote sensing and GIs (MA); geography (MA); geography and environment (PhD); international relations and environmental policy (MA). *Students:* 50 full-time (22 women), 15 part-time (6 women); includes 2 minority (1 Asian American or Pacific Islander, 1 Hispanic American), 19 international. Average age 30. 64 applicants, 23% accepted, 5 enrolled. In 2009, 4 master's, 6 doctorates awarded. Terminal master's awarded for partial completion of doctoral program. *Degree requirements:* For master's, one foreign language, comprehensive exam, thesis; for doctorate, one foreign language, comprehensive exam, thesis/dissertation. *Entrance requirements:* For master's and doctorate, GRE General Test, GRE Subject Test, 3 letters of recommendation. Additional exam requirements/recommendations for international students: Required—TOEFL (minimum score 600 paper-based; 250 computer-based). *Application deadline:* For fall admission, 7/1 for domestic and international students; for spring admission, 11/15 for domestic and international students. Application fee: $70. Electronic applications accepted. *Expenses:* Tuition: Full-time $37,910; part-time $1184 per credit hour. Required fees: $386; $40 per semester. Part-time tuition and fees vary according to class time, course level, degree level and program. *Financial support:* In 2009–10, 33 students received support, including 2 fellowships with full tuition reimbursements available (averaging $18,900 per year), 20 research assistantships with full tuition reimbursements available (averaging $18,400 per year), 11 teaching assistantships with full tuition reimbursements available (averaging $18,400 per year); Federal Work-Study and unspecified assistantships also available. Support available to part-time students. Financial award application deadline: 1/15; financial award applicants required to submit FAFSA. Total annual research expenditures: $1.2 million. *Unit head:* Robert Kaufmann, Chairman, 617-353-3940, Fax: 617-353-8399, E-mail: kaufmann@bu.edu. *Application contact:* Christopher DeVits, Graduate Program Coordinator, 617-353-7554, Fax: 617-353-8399, E-mail: cdevits@bu.edu.

Brigham Young University, Graduate Studies, College of Family, Home, and Social Sciences, Department of Geography, Provo, UT 84602-1001. Offers MS. *Faculty:* 9 full-time (0 women), 1 part-time/adjunct (0 women). *Students:* 4 full-time (1 woman); includes 1 minority (Hispanic American). Average age 26. *Expenses:* Tuition: Full-time $5580; part-time $301 per credit hour. Tuition and fees vary according to student's religious affiliation. *Faculty research:* Global studies, physical environment, urban planning, travel and tourism, geospatial intelligence, geographic information systems. *Unit head:* Dr. J. Matthew Shumway, Chair, 801-422-2707, Fax: 801-422-0266, E-mail: jms7@byu.edu. *Application contact:* Adviser, 801-422-4541, Fax: 801-378-5238, E-mail: gradstudies@byu.edu.

Brock University, Faculty of Graduate Studies, Faculty of Social Sciences, Program in Geography, St. Catharines, ON L2S 3A1, Canada. Offers MA. Part-time programs available. *Degree requirements:* For master's, thesis optional. *Entrance requirements:* For master's, honors degree. Additional exam requirements/recommendations for international students: Required—TOEFL (minimum score 550 paper-based; 213 computer-based; 80 iBT), IELTS (minimum score 6.5), TWE (minimum score 4).

California State University, Chico, Graduate School, College of Behavioral and Social Sciences, Department of Geography and Planning, Program in Geography, Chico, CA 95929-0722. Offers MA. Part-time programs available. *Students:* 2 full-time (1 woman), 5 part-time (3 women); includes 2 minority (1 American Indian/Alaska Native, 1 Hispanic American). Average age 36. 4 applicants, 100% accepted, 1 enrolled. In 2009, 1 master's awarded. *Entrance requirements:* For master's, GRE General Test, 2 letters of recommendation. Additional exam requirements/recommendations for international students: Required—TOEFL (minimum score 550 paper-based; 213 computer-based; 80 iBT), IELTS (minimum score 6.5). *Application deadline:* For fall admission, 3/1 priority date for domestic students, 3/1 for international students; for spring admission, 9/15 priority date for domestic students, 9/15 for international students. Applications are processed on a rolling basis. Application fee: $55. Electronic applications accepted. *Unit head:* Dr. Dean Fairbanks, Graduate Coordinator, 530-898-5780. *Application contact:* Dr. Paul Melcon, Graduate Coordinator, 530-898-6871.

California State University, East Bay, Academic Programs and Graduate Studies, College of Letters, Arts, and Social Sciences, Department of Geography and Environmental Studies, Hayward, CA 94542-3000. Offers geography (MA). Part-time programs available. *Faculty:* 6 full-time (1 woman). *Students:* 11 full-time (6 women), 8 part-time (5 women); includes 6 minority (1 African American, 5 Asian Americans or Pacific Islanders). Average age 36. 7 applicants, 57% accepted, 3 enrolled. In 2009, 3 master's awarded. *Degree requirements:* For master's, variable foreign language requirement, project or thesis. *Entrance requirements:* For master's, GRE, minimum GPA of 3.0 in field. Additional exam requirements/recommendations for international students: Required—TOEFL (minimum score 550 paper-based; 213 computer-based). *Application deadline:* For fall admission, 6/30 for domestic and international students; for winter admission, 10/31 for domestic students; for spring admission, 11/30 for domestic and international students. Applications are processed on a rolling basis. Application fee: $55. Electronic applications accepted. *Financial support:* Fellowships, teaching assistantships, career-related internships or fieldwork, Federal Work-Study, institutionally sponsored loans, and scholarships/grants available. Support available to part-time students. Financial award application deadline: 3/1; financial award applicants required to submit FAFSA. *Unit head:* Dr. David Larson, Chair, 510-885-3193 Ext. 3193, Fax: 510-885-2353, E-mail: david.larson@csueastbay.edu. *Application contact:* Donna Wiley, Interim Associate Director, 510-885-2928, Fax: 510-885-4777, E-mail: donna.wiley@csueastbay.edu.

California State University, Fullerton, Graduate Studies, College of Humanities and Social Sciences, Department of Geography, Fullerton, CA 92834-9480. Offers MA. Part-time programs available. *Students:* 9 full-time (5 women), 15 part-time (5 women); includes 4 minority (2 Asian Americans or Pacific Islanders, 2 Hispanic Americans), 1 international. Average age 32. 18 applicants, 83% accepted, 10 enrolled. In 2009, 6 master's awarded. *Degree requirements:* For master's, comprehensive exam or thesis. *Entrance requirements:* For master's, minimum GPA of 3.0, 18 undergraduate credits in field. Application fee: $55. *Expenses:* Tuition, nonresident: full-time $11,160; part-time $373 per credit. Required fees: $1440 per term. Tuition and fees vary according to course load, degree level and program. *Financial support:* Career-related internships or fieldwork, Federal Work-Study, institutionally sponsored loans, and scholarships/grants available. Support available to part-time students. Financial award application deadline: 3/1; financial award applicants required to submit FAFSA. *Faculty research:* Human geography, physical geography. *Unit head:* Dr. John Carroll, Chair, 657-278-3161. *Application contact:* Admissions/Applications, 657-278-2371.

California State University, Long Beach, Graduate Studies, College of Liberal Arts, Department of Geography, Long Beach, CA 90840. Offers MA. Part-time programs available. *Faculty:* 7 full-time (3 women). *Students:* 14 full-time (9 women), 21 part-time (10 women); includes 5 minority (1 African American, 2 Asian Americans or Pacific Islanders, 2 Hispanic Americans), 2 international. Average age 30. 32 applicants, 63% accepted, 16 enrolled. *Degree requirements:* For master's, thesis. *Application deadline:* For fall admission, 4/15 for domestic students; for spring admission, 10/15 for domestic students. Applications are processed on a rolling basis. Application fee: $55. Electronic applications accepted. *Expenses:* Required fees: $1802 per semester. Part-time tuition and fees vary according to course load. *Financial support:* Career-related internships or fieldwork, Federal Work-Study, institutionally sponsored loans, and scholarships/grants available. Financial award application deadline: 3/2. *Faculty research:* Demography, geographic information systems, world landforms and societies. *Unit head:* Dr. Vincent J. Del Casino, Chair, 562-985-4977, Fax: 562-985-8993, E-mail: vdelcasi@csulb.edu. *Application contact:* Dr. Christine Rodrigue, Graduate Advisor, 562-985-2358, Fax: 562-985-8993, E-mail: rodrigue@csulb.edu.

California State University, Los Angeles, Graduate Studies, College of Natural and Social Sciences, Department of Geography and Urban Analysis, Los Angeles, CA 90032-8530. Offers geography (MA). Part-time and evening/weekend programs available. *Faculty:* 5 full-time (1 woman), 1 part-time/adjunct (0 women). *Students:* 10 full-time (2 women), 13 part-time (4 women); includes 10 minority (1 African American, 3 Asian Americans or Pacific Islanders, 6

Hispanic Americans), 4 international. Average age 33. 8 applicants, 100% accepted, 4 enrolled. In 2009, 9 master's awarded. *Degree requirements:* For master's, one foreign language, comprehensive exam or thesis. *Entrance requirements:* Additional exam requirements/recommendations for international students: Required—TOEFL (minimum score 500 paper-based; 173 computer-based). *Application deadline:* For fall admission, 5/1 for domestic and international students. Applications are processed on a rolling basis. Application fee: $55. Electronic applications accepted. *Financial support:* Career-related internships or fieldwork and Federal Work-Study available. Support available to part-time students. Financial award application deadline: 3/1. *Faculty research:* Technique focus–air photography, cartography, locational analysis. *Unit head:* Dr. Ali Modarres, Chair, 323-343-2220, Fax: 323-343-6494, E-mail: amodarr@calstatela.edu. *Application contact:* Dr. Cheryl L. Ney, Associate Vice President for Academic Affairs and Dean of Graduate Studies, 323-343-3820, Fax: 323-343-5653, E-mail: cney@cslanet.calstatela.edu.

California State University, Northridge, Graduate Studies, College of Social and Behavioral Sciences, Department of Geography, Northridge, CA 91330. Offers MA. Part-time programs available. *Faculty:* 11 full-time (3 women), 13 part-time/adjunct (6 women). *Students:* 20 full-time (11 women), 31 part-time (12 women); includes 1 African American, 3 Asian Americans or Pacific Islanders, 3 Hispanic Americans, 1 international. Average age 35. 46 applicants, 80% accepted, 22 enrolled. In 2009, 8 master's awarded. *Degree requirements:* For master's, one foreign language, thesis. *Entrance requirements:* For master's, GRE General Test or minimum GPA of 3.0. Additional exam requirements/recommendations for international students: Required—TOEFL. *Application deadline:* For fall admission, 11/30 for domestic students. Application fee: $55. *Financial support:* Teaching assistantships available. Financial award application deadline: 3/1. *Unit head:* Darrick Danta, Chair, 818-677-3532. *Application contact:* Dr. Edward Jackiewicz, Graduate Advisor, 818-677-4565.

Carleton University, Faculty of Graduate Studies, Faculty of Arts and Social Sciences, Department of Geography and Environmental Studies, Ottawa, ON K1S 5B6, Canada. Offers geography (M Sc, MA, PhD). *Degree requirements:* For master's, thesis, seminar; for doctorate, one foreign language, thesis/dissertation, 2 comprehensive exams. *Entrance requirements:* For master's, honors degree; for doctorate, master's degree in geography. Additional exam requirements/recommendations for international students: Required—TOEFL. *Faculty research:* Human dimensions of global environmental change, winter environments, population studies, historical geography, globalization.

Central Connecticut State University, School of Graduate Studies, School of Arts and Sciences, Department of Geography, New Britain, CT 06050-4010. Offers MS. Part-time and evening/weekend programs available. *Faculty:* 10 full-time (4 women), 10 part-time/adjunct (1 woman). *Students:* 8 full-time (3 women), 14 part-time (5 women); includes 5 minority (1 African American, 1 American Indian/Alaska Native, 2 Asian Americans or Pacific Islanders, 1 Hispanic American), 1 international. Average age 32. 14 applicants, 36% accepted, 3 enrolled. In 2009, 9 master's awarded. *Degree requirements:* For master's, comprehensive exam, thesis or alternative. *Entrance requirements:* For master's, minimum undergraduate GPA of 2.7. Additional exam requirements/recommendations for international students: Required—TOEFL. *Application deadline:* For fall admission, 7/1 for domestic students; for spring admission, 12/1 for domestic students. Applications are processed on a rolling basis. Application fee: $50. Electronic applications accepted. *Expenses:* Tuition, area resident: Full-time $4662; part-time $440 per credit. Tuition, state resident: full-time $6994; part-time $440 per credit. Tuition, nonresident: full-time $12,988; part-time $440 per credit. Required fees: $3606. One-time fee: $62 part-time. *Financial support:* In 2009–10, 6 students received support, including 3 research assistantships; career-related internships or fieldwork, Federal Work-Study, scholarships/grants, and unspecified assistantships also available. Support available to part-time students. Financial award application deadline: 3/1; financial award applicants required to submit FAFSA. *Faculty research:* Regional planning, environmental protection, tourism, computer mapping and geographic information systems. *Unit head:* Dr. Xiaoping Shen, Chair, 860-832-2785. *Application contact:* Dr. Xiaoping Shen, Chair, 860-832-2785.

Chicago State University, School of Graduate and Professional Studies, College of Arts and Sciences, Department of Geography, Sociology, Economics, and Anthropology, Chicago, IL 60628. Offers geography and economic development (MA). *Entrance requirements:* For master's, minimum GPA of 2.75.

Clark University, Graduate School, Department of Geography, Worcester, MA 01610-1477. Offers geographic information science (MA); geography (PhD). *Faculty:* 16 full-time (5 women), 1 part-time/adjunct (0 women). *Students:* 49 full-time (23 women); includes 1 minority (African American), 23 international. Average age 29. 96 applicants, 21% accepted, 12 enrolled. In 2009, 3 master's, 11 doctorates awarded. *Degree requirements:* For doctorate, thesis/dissertation. *Entrance requirements:* For doctorate, GRE General Test. Additional exam requirements/recommendations for international students: Required—TOEFL. *Application deadline:* For fall admission, 12/31 priority date for domestic students. Applications are processed on a rolling basis. Application fee: $50. *Expenses:* Tuition: Full-time $34,900; part-time $4362.50 per course. *Financial support:* In 2009–10, 5 fellowships with full tuition reimbursements (averaging $15,700 per year), 14 research assistantships with full tuition reimbursements (averaging $15,700 per year), 15 teaching assistantships with full tuition reimbursements (averaging $15,700 per year) were awarded; career-related internships or fieldwork and tuition waivers (full) also available. *Faculty research:* Global environmental change, geographic information systems, natural and technological hazards, water resources, urbanization. Total annual research expenditures: $2 million. *Unit head:* Dr. Anthony Bebbington, Director, 508-793-7336. *Application contact:* Christine Silva, Admission Coordinator, 508-793-7337, Fax: 508-793-8881, E-mail: geography@clarku.edu.

Concordia University, School of Graduate Studies, Faculty of Arts and Science, Department of Geography, Planning and Environment, Montréal, QC H3G 1M8, Canada. Offers environmental impact assessment (Diploma); geography, urban and environmental studies (M Sc).

Concordia University, School of Graduate Studies, Faculty of Arts and Science, Department of Political Science, Montréal, QC H3G 1M8, Canada. Offers political science (PhD); public policy and public administration (MA), including geography. *Degree requirements:* For master's, one foreign language, comprehensive exam, thesis optional, internship. *Entrance requirements:* For master's, honors degree or equivalent. Additional exam requirements/recommendations for international students: Required—TOEFL. *Faculty research:* International public policy and administration, Quebec public administration, public policy and social/political theory, geography and public policy, public administration and decision making.

Concord University, Graduate Studies, Athens, WV 24712-1000. Offers behavioral science (M Ed); educational leadership and supervision (M Ed); geography (M Ed); health promotion (M Ed); reading specialist (M Ed); social studies (M Ed). Postbaccalaureate distance learning degree programs offered. *Entrance requirements:* For master's, GRE or MAT, baccalaureate degree with minimum GPA of 2.5 GPA from regionally accredited institution; teaching license; 2 letters of recommendation.

East Carolina University, Graduate School, Thomas Harriot College of Arts and Sciences, Department of Geography, Greenville, NC 27858-4353. Offers MA. Part-time and evening/weekend programs available. *Degree requirements:* For master's, one foreign language, comprehensive exam, thesis optional. *Entrance requirements:* For master's, GRE General Test. Additional exam requirements/recommendations for international students: Required—TOEFL.

Eastern Michigan University, Graduate School, College of Arts and Sciences, Department of Geography and Geology, Programs in Geography and Geology, Ypsilanti, MI 48197. Offers geography (MA, MS); water resources (Graduate Certificate). Part-time and evening/weekend programs available. Postbaccalaureate distance learning degree programs offered (minimal on-campus study). *Degree requirements:* For master's, thesis optional. *Entrance requirements:* Additional exam requirements/recommendations for international students: Required—TOEFL. *Application deadline:* Applications are processed on a rolling basis. Application fee: $35. Tuition and fees vary according to course level. *Financial support:* Fellowships, research assistantships with full tuition reimbursements, teaching assistantships with full tuition reimbursements, career-related internships or fieldwork, Federal Work-Study, institutionally sponsored loans, traineeships, and unspecified assistantships available. Support available to part-time students. Financial award applicants required to submit FAFSA. *Application contact:* Dr. Andrew Nazzaro, Program Advisor, 734-487-0218, Fax: 734-487-6979, E-mail: andrew.nazzaro@emich.edu.

Florida Atlantic University, Charles E. Schmidt College of Science, Department of Geosciences, Program in Geography, Boca Raton, FL 33431-0991. Offers MA. Part-time programs available. *Students:* 4 full-time (1 woman), 5 part-time (2 women); includes 2 minority (both Hispanic Americans), 1 international. Average age 37. 3 applicants, 67% accepted, 1 enrolled. In 2009, 5 master's awarded. *Degree requirements:* For master's, thesis (for some programs). *Entrance requirements:* For master's, GRE General Test, minimum GPA of 3.0. *Application deadline:* For fall admission, 3/15 priority date for domestic students, 3/15 for international students; for spring admission, 10/15 for domestic and international students. Applications are processed on a rolling basis. Application fee: $30. Electronic applications accepted. *Expenses:* Tuition, state resident: full-time $7055; part-time $293.94 per credit hour. Tuition, nonresident: full-time $22,096; part-time $920.66 per credit hour. *Financial support:* Research assistantships with partial tuition reimbursements, teaching assistantships with partial tuition reimbursements, career-related internships or fieldwork, Federal Work-Study, institutionally sponsored loans, and unspecified assistantships available. Financial award application deadline: 4/15. *Faculty research:* Remote sensing/digital images, location-allocation modeling, analysis of less-developed countries, historical settlement patterns, urban form. *Unit head:* Dr. Russell Ivy, Chair, 561-297-3295, Fax: 561-297-2745, E-mail: ivy@fau.edu. *Application contact:* Dr. David Warburton, Graduate Coordinator, 561-297-3312, Fax: 561-297-2745, E-mail: warburto@fau.edu.

Florida State University, The Graduate School, College of Social Sciences and Public Policy, Department of Geography, Tallahassee, FL 32306. Offers geographic information science (MS); geography (MA, MS, PhD). *Faculty:* 9 full-time (2 women), 3 part-time/adjunct (1 woman). *Students:* 67 full-time (24 women), 27 part-time (14 women); includes 12 minority (4 African Americans, 1 American Indian/Alaska Native, 3 Asian Americans or Pacific Islanders, 4 Hispanic Americans), 7 international. Average age 28. 51 applicants, 59% accepted, 27 enrolled. In 2009, 31 master's, 4 doctorates awarded. Terminal master's awarded for partial completion of doctoral program. *Degree requirements:* For master's, thesis (for some programs); for doctorate, comprehensive exam, thesis/dissertation. *Entrance requirements:* For master's and doctorate, GRE General Test, minimum GPA of 3.0. Additional exam requirements/recommendations for international students: Required—TOEFL. *Application deadline:* For fall admission, 1/15 priority date for domestic students, 12/15 priority date for international students; for spring admission, 11/1 for domestic students, 9/15 for international students. Applications are processed on a rolling basis. Application fee: $30. Electronic applications accepted. *Expenses:* Tuition, state resident: full-time $7413. Tuition, nonresident: full-time $22,567. *Financial support:* In 2009–10, 26 students received support, including 5 research assistantships with full tuition reimbursements available (averaging $13,000 per year), 21 teaching assistantships with full tuition reimbursements available (averaging $13,000 per year); fellowships with full tuition reimbursements available, career-related internships or fieldwork, Federal Work-Study, institutionally sponsored loans, scholarships/grants, health care benefits, and unspecified assistantships also available. Financial award application deadline: 1/15; financial award applicants required to submit FAFSA. *Faculty research:* Society-nature interactions, geographic information science, environmental studies, hazards, remote sensing. Total annual research expenditures: $197,475. *Unit head:* Dr. Victor Mesev, Chair, 850-645-2498, Fax: 850-644-5913. *Application contact:* Dr. Mark Horner, Graduate Director, 850-644-8377, Fax: 850-644-5193, E-mail: mhorner@fsu.edu.

Fort Hays State University, Graduate School, College of Arts and Sciences, Department of Geosciences, Program in Geosciences, Hays, KS 67601-4099. Offers geography (MS); geology (MS). *Degree requirements:* For master's, comprehensive exam, thesis. *Entrance requirements:* For master's, GRE General Test. Additional exam requirements/recommendations for international students: Required—TOEFL (minimum score 550 paper-based; 213 computer-based). Electronic applications accepted. *Faculty research:* Cretaceous and late Cenozoic stratigraphy, sedimentation, paleontology.

George Mason University, College of Science, Department of Geography, Fairfax, VA 22030. Offers geographic and cartographic sciences (MS). *Degree requirements:* For master's, thesis optional. *Entrance requirements:* For master's, GRE General Test, minimum GPA of 3.0 in last 60 hours; BS or BA in geography, cartography, or related field. Electronic applications accepted. *Expenses:* Tuition, state resident: full-time $7568; part-time $315.33 per credit hour. Tuition, nonresident: full-time $21,704; part-time $904.33 per credit hour. Required fees: $2184; $91 per credit hour.

The George Washington University, Columbian College of Arts and Sciences, Department of Geography, Washington, DC 20052. Offers MA. *Faculty:* 8 full-time (4 women), 15 part-time/adjunct (4 women). *Students:* 11 full-time (5 women), 8 part-time (3 women); includes 3 minority (1 American Indian/Alaska Native, 2 Hispanic Americans), 1 international. Average age 26. 18 applicants, 78% accepted, 9 enrolled. In 2009, 7 master's awarded. *Degree requirements:* For master's, comprehensive exam, thesis or alternative. *Entrance requirements:* For master's, GRE General Test, BA in geography or related field, minimum GPA of 3.0. Additional exam requirements/recommendations for international students: Required—TOEFL (minimum score 550 paper-based; 213 computer-based; 80 iBT). *Application deadline:* For fall admission, 4/1 priority date for domestic students, 1/15 priority date for international students; for spring admission, 10/1 priority date for domestic students, 9/1 priority date for international students. Applications are processed on a rolling basis. Application fee: $60. Electronic applications accepted. *Financial support:* In 2009–10, 10 students received support; fellowships with tuition reimbursements available, teaching assistantships with tuition reimbursements available, Federal Work-Study, institutionally sponsored loans, and tuition waivers available. Financial award application deadline: 1/15. *Unit head:* Dr. Marie Price, Chair, 202-994-6187. *Application contact:* Information Contact, 202-994-6185, Fax: 202-994-2484.

Georgia State University, College of Arts and Sciences, Department of Geosciences, Program in Geography, Atlanta, GA 30302-3083. Offers MA. Part-time programs available. *Degree requirements:* For master's, one foreign language, thesis or alternative, written and oral exams. *Entrance requirements:* For master's, GRE General Test. Additional exam requirements/recommendations for international students: Required—TOEFL. Electronic applications accepted. *Faculty research:* Urban economics, biogeography, cartography, GIS, environmental.

Hunter College of the City University of New York, Graduate School, School of Arts and Sciences, Department of Geography, New York, NY 10021-5085. Offers analytical geography (MA); earth system science (MA); environmental and social issues (MA); geographic information science (Certificate); geographic information systems (MA); teaching earth science (MA). Part-time and evening/weekend programs available. *Faculty:* 12 full-time (5 women), 4 part-time/adjunct (0 women). *Students:* 17 full-time (16 women), 20 part-time (19 women); includes 9 minority (1 African American, 1 American Indian/Alaska Native, 4 Asian Americans or Pacific Islanders, 3 Hispanic Americans). Average age 31. 13 applicants, 92% accepted, 9 enrolled. In 2009, 10 master's, 3 other advanced degrees awarded. *Degree requirements:* For master's, comprehensive exam or thesis. *Entrance requirements:* For master's, GRE General Test, minimum B average in major, B- overall; 18 credits of course work in geography; 2 letters of recommendation; for Certificate, minimum B average in major, B- overall. Additional exam requirements/recommendations for international students: Required—TOEFL. *Application deadline:* For fall admission, 4/1 for domestic students; for spring admission, 11/1 for domestic students. Applications are processed on a rolling basis. Application fee: $125. *Expenses:*

Geography

Hunter College of the City University of New York (continued)
Tuition, state resident: full-time $7360; part-time $310 per credit. Required fees: $250 per semester. *Financial support:* In 2009–10, 1 fellowship (averaging $3,000 per year), 2 research assistantships (averaging $10,000 per year), 10 teaching assistantships (averaging $6,000 per year) were awarded; career-related internships or fieldwork, Federal Work-Study, institutionally sponsored loans, and unspecified assistantships also available. Financial award application deadline: 3/1. *Faculty research:* Urban geography, economic geography, geographic information science, demographic methods, climate change. *Unit head:* Prof. William Solecki, Chair, 212-772-4536, Fax: 212-772-5268, E-mail: wsolecki@hunter.cuny.edu. *Application contact:* Prof. Marianna Pavlovskaya, Graduate Adviser, 212-772-5320, Fax: 212-772-5268, E-mail: mpavlov@geo.hunter.cuny.edu.

Indiana State University, School of Graduate Studies, College of Arts and Sciences, Department of Geography, Geology and Anthropology, Terre Haute, IN 47809. Offers geography (MA); geology (MS); physical geography (PhD). *Degree requirements:* For master's, thesis or alternative; for doctorate, comprehensive exam, thesis/dissertation, departmental qualifying exam. *Entrance requirements:* For doctorate, GRE General Test. Additional exam requirements/recommendations for international students: Required—TOEFL (minimum score 550 paper-based). Electronic applications accepted.

Indiana University Bloomington, University Graduate School, College of Arts and Sciences, Department of Geography, Bloomington, IN 47405-7000. Offers MA, MAT, MS, PhD, MSES/MA, MSES/MS. *Faculty:* 13 full-time (5 women), 15 part-time/adjunct (1 woman). *Students:* 23 full-time (13 women), 3 part-time (2 women); includes 1 minority (Hispanic American), 8 international. Average age 31. 40 applicants, 45% accepted, 6 enrolled. In 2009, 5 master's, 5 doctorates awarded. *Degree requirements:* For master's, comprehensive exam, thesis; for doctorate, comprehensive exam, thesis/dissertation. *Entrance requirements:* For master's and doctorate, GRE General Test, minimum GPA of 3.0. Additional exam requirements/recommendations for international students: Required—TOEFL (minimum score 620 paper-based; 260 computer-based; 104 iBT). *Application deadline:* For fall admission, 2/15 priority date for domestic students, 12/15 priority date for international students; for spring admission, 11/15 priority date for domestic students, 11/1 priority date for international students. Application fee: $55 ($65 for international students). Electronic applications accepted. *Financial support:* In 2009–10, 17 students received support, including 1 fellowship with full tuition reimbursement available (averaging $22,150 per year), 2 research assistantships with full tuition reimbursements available (averaging $15,000 per year), 17 teaching assistantships with full tuition reimbursements available (averaging $12,901 per year); health care benefits also available. Financial award application deadline: 2/15; financial award applicants required to submit FAFSA. *Faculty research:* Synoptic climatology, urban and regional modeling, regional development, hydrology and statistical climatology, migration, atmospheric science, GIS human environment interaction, human geography. Total annual research expenditures: $2 million. *Unit head:* Dr. Scott Robeson, Chair and Professor, 812-855-6303, Fax: 812-855-1661, E-mail: srobeson@indiana.edu. *Application contact:* Susan White, Graduate Secretary, 812-855-6303, Fax: 812-855-1661, E-mail: suswhite@indiana.edu.

Indiana University of Pennsylvania, School of Graduate Studies and Research, College of Humanities and Social Sciences, Department of Geography and Regional Planning, Program in Geography, Indiana, PA 15705-1087. Offers MA, MS. Part-time programs available. *Faculty:* 10 full-time (1 woman). *Students:* 24 full-time (4 women), 2 part-time (1 woman); includes 1 minority (Asian American or Pacific Islander), 2 international. Average age 28. 25 applicants, 64% accepted, 15 enrolled. In 2009, 7 master's awarded. *Degree requirements:* For master's, thesis optional. *Entrance requirements:* For master's, GRE, 2 letters of recommendation. Additional exam requirements/recommendations for international students: Required—TOEFL. *Application deadline:* For fall admission, 7/1 priority date for domestic students; for spring admission, 11/1 for domestic students. Applications are processed on a rolling basis. Application fee: $40. *Expenses:* Tuition, state resident: full-time $6666; part-time $370 per credit hour. Tuition, nonresident: full-time $10,666; part-time $593 per credit hour. Required fees: $813 per semester. *Financial support:* In 2009–10, 157 research assistantships with full and partial tuition reimbursements (averaging $4,554 per year) were awarded; Federal Work-Study also available. Support available to part-time students. Financial award application deadline: 3/15; financial award applicants required to submit FAFSA. *Unit head:* Dr. Kevin Patrick, E-mail: kevin.patrick@iup.edu. *Application contact:* Dr. John E. Benhart, Chairperson, 724-357-2250, E-mail: jbenhart@iup.edu.

The Johns Hopkins University, G. W. C. Whiting School of Engineering, Department of Geography and Environmental Engineering, Baltimore, MD 21218-2699. Offers MA, MS, MSE, PhD. *Faculty:* 15 full-time (4 women), 4 part-time/adjunct (0 women). *Students:* 55 full-time (25 women), 5 part-time (4 women); includes 4 minority (1 African American, 1 Asian American or Pacific Islander, 2 Hispanic Americans), 29 international. Average age 27. 118 applicants, 73% accepted, 25 enrolled. In 2009, 27 master's, 7 doctorates awarded. Terminal master's awarded for partial completion of doctoral program. *Degree requirements:* For master's, thesis (for some programs), 1 year full-time residency; for doctorate, comprehensive exam, thesis/dissertation, oral exam, 2 year full-time residency. *Entrance requirements:* For master's and doctorate, GRE General Test. Additional exam requirements/recommendations for international students: Required—TOEFL (minimum score 670 paper-based; 300 computer-based; 120 iBT); Recommended—IELTS. *Application deadline:* For fall admission, 1/15 priority date for domestic and international students. Applications are processed on a rolling basis. Application fee: $75. Electronic applications accepted. *Financial support:* In 2009–10, 3 fellowships with full tuition reimbursements (averaging $27,000 per year), 24 research assistantships with full tuition reimbursements (averaging $24,000 per year) were awarded; teaching assistantships with full tuition reimbursements, Federal Work-Study, institutionally sponsored loans, scholarships/grants, health care benefits, tuition waivers (partial), and unspecified assistantships also available. *Faculty research:* Environmental engineering; environmental chemistry; water resources engineering; systems analysis and economics for public decision making; geomorphology, hydrology and ecology. Total annual research expenditures: $1.2 million. *Unit head:* Dr. Edward J. Bouwer, Chair, 410-516-7102, Fax: 410-516-8996, E-mail: bouwer@jhu.edu. *Application contact:* Dr. Edward J. Bouwer, Chair, 410-516-7102, Fax: 410-516-8996, E-mail: bouwer@jhu.edu.

Kansas State University, Graduate School, College of Arts and Sciences, Department of Geography, Manhattan, KS 66506. Offers MA, PhD. *Faculty:* 12 full-time (3 women), 1 part-time/adjunct (0 women). *Students:* 32 full-time (14 women), 13 part-time (4 women); includes 2 minority (both Asian Americans or Pacific Islanders), 3 international. Average age 28. 32 applicants, 56% accepted, 12 enrolled. In 2009, 3 master's, 2 doctorates awarded. *Degree requirements:* For master's, thesis optional, oral exam; for doctorate, one foreign language, thesis/dissertation. *Entrance requirements:* For master's and doctorate, GRE General Test, minimum GPA of 3.0. *Application deadline:* For fall admission, 2/1 priority date for domestic and international students; for spring admission, 8/1 priority date for domestic and international students. Applications are processed on a rolling basis. Application fee: $40 ($55 for international students). Electronic applications accepted. *Financial support:* In 2009–10, 7 research assistantships (averaging $13,351 per year), 17 teaching assistantships with full tuition reimbursements (averaging $12,476 per year) were awarded; Federal Work-Study, institutionally sponsored loans, and scholarships/grants also available. Support available to part-time students. Financial award application deadline: 3/1; financial award applicants required to submit FAFSA. *Faculty research:* Human environment interaction, health and population, culture and landscape, physical geography, geospatial analysis and applications. Total annual research expenditures: $441,795. *Unit head:* Richard Marston, Head, 785-532-5412, Fax: 785-532-7310, E-mail: rmarston@ksu.edu. *Application contact:* Kevin Blake, Director, 785-532-3406, Fax: 785-532-7310, E-mail: kblake@ksu.edu.

Kent State University, College of Arts and Sciences, Department of Geography, Kent, OH 44242-0001. Offers MA, PhD. Part-time programs available. *Degree requirements:* For master's, thesis optional; for doctorate, comprehensive exam, thesis/dissertation. *Entrance requirements:* For master's and doctorate, GRE, minimum GPA of 3.0. Additional exam requirements/recommendations for international students: Required—TOEFL. Electronic applications accepted.

Louisiana State University and Agricultural and Mechanical College, Graduate School, College of Arts and Sciences, Department of Geography and Anthropology, Baton Rouge, LA 70803. Offers anthropology (MA); geography (MA, MS, PhD). Part-time programs available. *Faculty:* 30 full-time (11 women), 1 part-time/adjunct (0 women). *Students:* 63 full-time (32 women), 25 part-time (14 women); includes 4 minority (1 African American, 3 Hispanic Americans), 19 international. Average age 31. 68 applicants, 71% accepted, 15 enrolled. In 2009, 8 master's, 5 doctorates awarded. Terminal master's awarded for partial completion of doctoral program. *Degree requirements:* For master's, 2 foreign languages, thesis (for some programs); for doctorate, 2 foreign languages, thesis/dissertation. *Entrance requirements:* For master's and doctorate, GRE General Test, minimum GPA of 3.0. Additional exam requirements/recommendations for international students: Required—TOEFL (minimum score 550 paper-based; 213 computer-based; 79 iBT) or IELTS (minimum score 6.5). *Application deadline:* For fall admission, 1/25 priority date for domestic students, 5/15 for international students; for spring admission, 10/15 for international students. Applications are processed on a rolling basis. Application fee: $50 ($70 for international students). Electronic applications accepted. *Financial support:* In 2009–10, 73 students received support, including 2 fellowships with full tuition reimbursements available (averaging $33,473 per year), 17 research assistantships with full and partial tuition reimbursements available (averaging $16,266 per year), 30 teaching assistantships with full and partial tuition reimbursements available (averaging $13,013 per year); career-related internships or fieldwork, health care benefits, and unspecified assistantships also available. Financial award application deadline: 3/1; financial award applicants required to submit FAFSA. *Faculty research:* Cultural, coastal, climate, geographic information systems-geography, cultural, linguistics, archaeology-anthropology. Total annual research expenditures: $731,204. *Unit head:* Dr. Patrick A. Hesp, Chair, 225-578-5942, Fax: 225-578-4420, E-mail: gachair@lsu.edu. *Application contact:* Dr. Helen Regis, Graduate Adviser, 225-578-6171, Fax: 225-578-4420, E-mail: hregis1@lsu.edu.

Marshall University, Academic Affairs Division, College of Liberal Arts, Department of Geography, Huntington, WV 25755. Offers MA, MS. *Faculty:* 5 full-time (1 woman), 9 part-time/adjunct (2 women). *Students:* 12 full-time (5 women), 4 part-time (1 woman), 1 international. Average age 29. In 2009, 8 master's awarded. *Degree requirements:* For master's, thesis optional. Application fee: $40. *Unit head:* Larry Jarrett, Chairperson, 304-696-2886, E-mail: jarrettl@marshall.edu. *Application contact:* Information Contact, 304-746-1900, Fax: 304-746-1902, E-mail: services@marshall.edu.

McGill University, Faculty of Graduate and Postdoctoral Studies, Faculty of Science, Department of Geography, Montréal, QC H3A 2T5, Canada. Offers geography (M Sc, MA, PhD); neo-tropical environment (MA, PhD); social statistics (MA).

McMaster University, School of Graduate Studies, Faculty of Science, School of Geography and Earth Sciences, Hamilton, ON L8S 4M2, Canada. Offers geochemistry (PhD); geology (M Sc, PhD); human geography (MA, PhD); physical geography (M Sc, PhD). Part-time programs available. Terminal master's awarded for partial completion of doctoral program. *Degree requirements:* For master's, thesis; for doctorate, comprehensive exam, thesis/dissertation. *Entrance requirements:* For master's, minimum B+ average. Additional exam requirements/recommendations for international students: Required—TOEFL (minimum score 550 paper-based; 213 computer-based).

Memorial University of Newfoundland, School of Graduate Studies, Department of Geography, St. John's, NL A1C 5S7, Canada. Offers M Sc, MA, PhD. *Degree requirements:* For master's, thesis; for doctorate, comprehensive exam, thesis/dissertation, seminar, oral defense of thesis. *Entrance requirements:* For master's, 2nd class degree; for doctorate, master's degree. Electronic applications accepted. *Faculty research:* Cultural/historical geography, physical geography, economic geography, cartography, geographical information systems.

Miami University, Graduate School, College of Arts and Sciences, Department of Geography, Oxford, OH 45056. Offers MA. Part-time programs available. *Students:* 18 full-time (10 women), 2 part-time (0 women); includes 2 minority (both African Americans), 6 international. *Entrance requirements:* For master's, minimum undergraduate GPA of 3.0 during previous 2 years or 2.75 overall. Additional exam requirements/recommendations for international students: Required—TOEFL. Application fee: $50. *Expenses:* Tuition, state resident: full-time $11,280. Tuition, nonresident: full-time $24,912. Required fees: $516. *Financial support:* Fellowships with full tuition reimbursements, research assistantships, teaching assistantships, career-related internships or fieldwork, Federal Work-Study, institutionally sponsored loans, health care benefits, tuition waivers (full), and unspecified assistantships available. Financial award application deadline: 3/1; financial award applicants required to submit FAFSA. *Unit head:* Dr. Bill Renwick, Chair, 513-529-5010, Fax: 513-529-1948, E-mail: renwicwh@muohio.edu. *Application contact:* Dr. Bruce D'Arcus, Graduate Studies Advisor, 513-529-1521, E-mail: darcusb@muohio.edu.

Michigan State University, The Graduate School, College of Social Science, Department of Geography, East Lansing, MI 48824. Offers geographic information science (MS); geography (MS, PhD). *Faculty:* 27 full-time (8 women). *Students:* 50 full-time (24 women), 10 part-time (2 women); includes 3 minority (1 African American, 2 Hispanic Americans), 21 international. Average age 31. 60 applicants, 47% accepted. In 2009, 11 master's, 4 doctorates awarded. *Degree requirements:* For master's, comprehensive exam, thesis (for some programs), presentation of poster/paper or oral defense of thesis; for doctorate, comprehensive exam, thesis/dissertation, presentation of poster/paper, presentation and defense of dissertation proposal, oral exam in defense of dissertation. *Entrance requirements:* Additional exam requirements/recommendations for international students: Required—TOEFL (minimum score 600 paper-based; 250 computer-based). Electronic applications accepted. *Expenses:* Tuition, state resident: part-time $478.25 per credit hour. Tuition, nonresident: part-time $966.50 per credit hour. Part-time tuition and fees vary according to program. *Financial support:* In 2009–10, 17 research assistantships with tuition reimbursements (averaging $6,328 per year), 13 teaching assistantships with tuition reimbursements (averaging $6,621 per year) were awarded. Total annual research expenditures: $1.3 million. *Unit head:* Dr. Richard E. Groop, Chairperson, 517-432-4748, Fax: 517-432-1671, E-mail: groop@msu.edu. *Application contact:* Sharon Ruggles, Graduate Secretary, 517-355-4650, Fax: 517-432-1671, E-mail: geo@msu.edu.

Minnesota State University Mankato, College of Graduate Studies, College of Social and Behavioral Sciences, Department of Geography, Mankato, MN 56001. Offers geography (MS); GIS (Certificate). Part-time programs available. *Students:* 5 full-time (2 women), 21 part-time (8 women). *Degree requirements:* For master's, one foreign language, comprehensive exam. *Entrance requirements:* For master's, GRE General Test (if GPA less than 2.8 for the last 2 years), minimum GPA of 3.0 during previous 2 years. *Application deadline:* For fall admission, 7/1 priority date for domestic students; for spring admission, 11/1 for domestic students. Applications are processed on a rolling basis. Application fee: $40. Electronic applications accepted. *Expenses:* Tuition, state resident: full-time $5364. Tuition, nonresident: full-time $8314. *Financial support:* Research assistantships, teaching assistantships with full tuition reimbursements, career-related internships or fieldwork, Federal Work-Study, institutionally sponsored loans, and unspecified assistantships available. Support available to part-time students. Financial award application deadline: 3/15; financial award applicants required to submit FAFSA. *Unit head:* Dr. Donald Friend, Chairperson, 507-389-2617. *Application contact:* 507-389-2321, E-mail: grad@mnsu.edu.

Missouri State University, Graduate College, College of Natural and Applied Sciences, Department of Geography, Geology, and Planning, Springfield, MO 65897. Offers geospatial sciences (MS); natural and applied science (MNAS), including geography, geology and planning; secondary education (MS Ed), including earth science, geography. *Accreditation:* ACSP. Part-time and evening/weekend programs available. *Faculty:* 20 full-time (4 women). *Students:*

19 full-time (10 women), 12 part-time (5 women); includes 1 minority (American Indian/Alaska Native), 1 international. Average age 29. 19 applicants, 100% accepted, 13 enrolled. In 2009, 4 master's awarded. *Degree requirements:* For master's, comprehensive exam, thesis (for some programs). *Entrance requirements:* For master's, GRE General Test (MS, MNAS), minimum undergraduate GPA of 3.0 (MS, MNAS), 9-12 teacher certification (MS Ed). Additional exam requirements/recommendations for international students: Required—TOEFL (minimum score 550 paper-based; 213 computer-based; 79 iBT). *Application deadline:* For fall admission, 7/20 priority date for domestic students, 5/1 for international students; for spring admission, 12/20 priority date for domestic students, 9/1 for international students. Applications are processed on a rolling basis. Application fee: $35 ($50 for international students). Electronic applications accepted. *Expenses:* Tuition, state resident: full-time $3852; part-time $214 per credit hour. Tuition, nonresident: full-time $7524; part-time $418 per credit hour. Required fees: $696; $172 per semester. Tuition and fees vary according to course level, course load, degree level and program. *Financial support:* In 2009–10, 7 research assistantships with full tuition reimbursements (averaging $8,933 per year), 8 teaching assistantships with full tuition reimbursements (averaging $8,236 per year) were awarded; career-related internships or fieldwork, Federal Work-Study, institutionally sponsored loans, scholarships/grants, and unspecified assistantships also available. Financial award application deadline: 3/31; financial award applicants required to submit FAFSA. *Faculty research:* Stratigraphy and ancient meteorite impacts, environmental geochemistry of karst, hyperspectral image processing, water quality, small town planning. *Unit head:* Dr. Thomas Plymate, Head, 417-836-5800, Fax: 417-836-6934, E-mail: tomplymate@missouristate.edu. *Application contact:* Eric Eckert, Coordinator of Graduate Admissions and Recruitment, 417-836-5331, Fax: 417-836-6200, E-mail: ericeckert@missouristate.edu.

New Mexico State University, Graduate School, College of Arts and Sciences, Department of Geography, Las Cruces, NM 88003-8001. Offers MAG. Part-time programs available. *Faculty:* 6 full-time (2 women). *Students:* 15 full-time (6 women), 11 part-time (3 women); includes 4 minority (all Hispanic Americans). Average age 33. 17 applicants, 100% accepted, 13 enrolled. In 2009, 3 master's awarded. *Degree requirements:* For master's, thesis or alternative. *Entrance requirements:* For master's, GRE General Test, previous course work in geography, map use, and physical geography. Additional exam requirements/recommendations for international students: Required—TOEFL. *Application deadline:* For fall admission, 7/1 priority date for domestic students; for spring admission, 11/1 for domestic students. Applications are processed on a rolling basis. Application fee: $30 ($50 for international students). Electronic applications accepted. *Expenses:* Tuition, state resident: full-time $4080; part-time $223 per credit. Tuition, nonresident: full-time $14,256; part-time $647 per credit. Required fees: $1278; $639 per semester. *Financial support:* In 2009–10, 1 research assistantship (averaging $15,800 per year), 6 teaching assistantships (averaging $7,917 per year) were awarded; career-related internships or fieldwork and health care benefits also available. Financial award application deadline: 3/1. *Faculty research:* Landscape ecology, land use, geomorphology, Latin America and the U.S.-Mexico border, geographic information systems. *Unit head:* Dr. John Wright, Head, 575-646-3509, Fax: 575-646-7430, E-mail: jowright@nmsu.edu. *Application contact:* Dr. Daniel Dugas, Assistant Professor, 575-646-3509, Fax: 575-646-7430, E-mail: ddugas@nmsu.edu.

Northeastern Illinois University, Graduate College, College of Arts and Sciences, Department of Geography, Environmental Studies and Economics, Program in Geography and Environmental Studies, Chicago, IL 60625-4699. Offers MA. Part-time and evening/weekend programs available. *Degree requirements:* For master's, comprehensive exam, thesis optional. *Entrance requirements:* For master's, undergraduate minor in geography or environmental studies, minimum GPA of 2.75. Additional exam requirements/recommendations for international students: Required—TOEFL (minimum score 550 paper-based; 213 computer-based; 80 iBT). Electronic applications accepted. *Faculty research:* Segregation and urbanization of minority groups in the Chicago area, scale dependence and parameterization in nonpoint source pollution modeling, ecological land classification and mapping, ecosystem restoration, soil-vegetation relationships.

Northern Arizona University, Graduate College, College of Social and Behavioral Sciences, Department of Geography, Planning, and Recreation, Flagstaff, AZ 86011. Offers applied geographic information science (MS); geographic information systems (Certificate); rural geography (MA). Postbaccalaureate distance learning degree programs offered. *Faculty:* 15 full-time (7 women). *Students:* 14 full-time (10 women), 11 part-time (7 women); includes 3 minority (1 American Indian/Alaska Native, 2 Hispanic Americans). Average age 32. 14 applicants, 71% accepted, 7 enrolled. In 2009, 5 master's awarded. *Degree requirements:* For master's, thesis. *Entrance requirements:* For master's, GRE General Test. Additional exam requirements/recommendations for international students: Required—TOEFL (minimum score 550 paper-based; 213 computer-based; 80 iBT), IELTS (minimum score 7). *Application deadline:* For fall admission, 2/15 priority date for domestic students, 9/1 for international students; for spring admission, 10/15 for domestic students. Applications are processed on a rolling basis. Application fee: $65. Electronic applications accepted. *Financial support:* In 2009–10, 7 teaching assistantships with partial tuition reimbursements (averaging $10,439 per year) were awarded; career-related internships or fieldwork, Federal Work-Study, health care benefits, tuition waivers (full and partial), and unspecified assistantships also available. Support available to part-time students. Financial award application deadline: 3/30. *Unit head:* Dr. Pamela Foti, Chair, 928-523-6196, Fax: 928-523-2275, E-mail: pam.foti@nau.edu. *Application contact:* Alan Lew, Coordinator, 928-523-6567, E-mail: alan.lew@nau.edu.

Northern Illinois University, Graduate School, College of Liberal Arts and Sciences, Department of Geography, De Kalb, IL 60115-2854. Offers MS. Part-time programs available. *Faculty:* 8 full-time (2 women). *Students:* 26 full-time (9 women), 8 part-time (5 women); includes 1 minority (African American), 2 international. Average age 25. 28 applicants, 75% accepted, 12 enrolled. In 2009, 8 master's awarded. *Degree requirements:* For master's, comprehensive exam, thesis optional, research seminar. *Entrance requirements:* For master's, GRE General Test, minimum GPA of 2.75. Additional exam requirements/recommendations for international students: Required—TOEFL (minimum score 550 paper-based; 213 computer-based). *Application deadline:* For fall admission, 2/1 priority date for domestic students, 5/1 for international students; for spring admission, 10/1 priority date for domestic students, 10/1 for international students. Applications are processed on a rolling basis. Application fee: $30. Electronic applications accepted. *Expenses:* Tuition, state resident: full-time $6576; part-time $274 per credit hour. Tuition, nonresident: full-time $13,152; part-time $548 per credit hour. Required fees: $1813; $75.53 per credit hour. Part-time tuition and fees vary according to course load. *Financial support:* In 2009–10, 10 research assistantships with full tuition reimbursements, 12 teaching assistantships with full tuition reimbursements were awarded; fellowships with full tuition reimbursements, career-related internships or fieldwork, Federal Work-Study, scholarships/grants, tuition waivers (full), and unspecified assistantships also available. Support available to part-time students. Financial award applicants required to submit FAFSA. *Faculty research:* Synoptic meteorology, human impacts on soil properties, plant soil relationships, hydrological cycle, climate variability. *Unit head:* Dr. Andrew Krmenec, Chair, 815-753-6826, Fax: 815-753-6872, E-mail: akrmenec@niu.edu. *Application contact:* Dr. Fahui Wang, Coordinator of Graduate Studies, 815-753-6842, E-mail: fwang@niu.edu.

Northwest Missouri State University, Graduate School, College of Arts and Sciences, Department of Geology/Geography, Maryville, MO 64468-6001. Offers geographic information sciences (MS, Certificate). Part-time programs available. *Faculty:* 11 full-time (2 women). *Students:* 6 full-time (2 women), 96 part-time (37 women); includes 8 minority (1 African American, 4 Asian Americans or Pacific Islanders, 3 Hispanic Americans). 23 applicants, 52% accepted, 8 enrolled. In 2009, 11 master's awarded. *Degree requirements:* For master's, comprehensive exam, thesis. *Entrance requirements:* For master's, GRE General Test, 2 letters of recommendation, writing sample, minimum undergraduate GPA of 2.5. *Application deadline:* For fall admission, 4/15 for domestic and international students. Application fee: $0 ($50 for international students). *Expenses:* Tuition, state resident: part-time $296.34 per credit hour. Tuition, nonresident: part-time $510.43 per credit hour. *Financial support:* In 2009–10, 2 research assistantships were awarded. Financial award application deadline: 4/1; financial award applicants required to submit FAFSA. *Unit head:* Greg Haddock, Chairperson, 660-562-1719. *Application contact:* Dr. Gregory Haddock, Dean of Graduate School, 660-562-1145, Fax: 660-562-1096, E-mail: gradsch@nwmissouri.edu.

The Ohio State University, Graduate School, College of Social and Behavioral Sciences, School of Social and Behavioral Science, Department of Geography, Columbus, OH 43210. Offers atmospheric sciences (MS, PhD); geography (MA, PhD). *Faculty:* 24. *Students:* 40 full-time (15 women), 9 part-time (3 women); includes 1 minority (Asian American or Pacific Islander), 16 international. Average age 28. In 2009, 12 master's, 11 doctorates awarded. *Degree requirements:* For doctorate, variable foreign language requirement, thesis/dissertation. *Entrance requirements:* Additional exam requirements/recommendations for international students: Recommended—TOEFL (minimum score 600 paper-based; 250 computer-based). *Application deadline:* For fall admission, 8/15 priority date for domestic students, 7/1 priority date for international students; for winter admission, 12/1 priority date for domestic students, 11/1 priority date for international students; for spring admission, 3/1 priority date for domestic students, 2/1 priority date for international students. Applications are processed on a rolling basis. Application fee: $40 ($50 for international students). Electronic applications accepted. *Expenses:* Tuition, state resident: full-time $10,683. Tuition, nonresident: full-time $25,923. Tuition and fees vary according to course load and program. *Financial support:* Fellowships, research assistantships, teaching assistantships, Federal Work-Study and institutionally sponsored loans available. Support available to part-time students. *Unit head:* Mei-Po Kwan, Graduate Studies Committee Chair, 614-292-2514, Fax: 614-292-6213, E-mail: kwan.8@osu.edu. *Application contact:* 614-292-9444, Fax: 614-292-3895, E-mail: domestic.grad@osu.edu.

Ohio University, Graduate College, College of Arts and Sciences, Department of Geography, Athens, OH 45701-2979. Offers MA. Part-time programs available. *Faculty:* 13 full-time (6 women), 6 part-time/adjunct (0 women). *Students:* 22 full-time (11 women), 3 part-time (2 women); includes 2 minority (1 American Indian/Alaska Native, 1 Hispanic American), 1 international. 18 applicants, 56% accepted, 10 enrolled. In 2009, 7 master's awarded. *Degree requirements:* For master's, thesis or alternative. *Entrance requirements:* For master's, GRE General Test, minimum GPA of 3.0. Additional exam requirements/recommendations for international students: Required—TOEFL (minimum score 600 paper-based; 100 iBT) or IELTS Academic (minimum score 8). *Application deadline:* For fall admission, 2/15 priority date for domestic and international students. Application fee: $50 ($55 for international students). Electronic applications accepted. *Expenses:* Tuition, state resident: full-time $7839; part-time $323 per quarter hour. Tuition, nonresident: full-time $15,831; part-time $654 per quarter hour. Required fees: $2931. *Financial support:* Research assistantships with full tuition reimbursements, teaching assistantships with full tuition reimbursements, Federal Work-Study, institutionally sponsored loans, tuition waivers (partial), and unspecified assistantships available. Financial award application deadline: 2/15. *Faculty research:* Environmental geography, cartography and geographic information systems, cultural ecology, area studies, historical geography. Total annual research expenditures: $81,622. *Unit head:* Dr. Timothy G. Anderson, Graduate Chair, 740-593-1138, Fax: 740-593-1139, E-mail: anderstl@ohio.edu. *Application contact:* Dr. Geoffrey Buckley, Graduate Chair, 740-593-1143, Fax: 740-593-1139, E-mail: buckleyg@ohio.edu.

Oklahoma State University, College of Arts and Sciences, Department of Geography, Stillwater, OK 74078. Offers MS, PhD. *Faculty:* 14 full-time (4 women). *Students:* 13 full-time (3 women), 23 part-time (6 women); includes 4 minority (1 American Indian/Alaska Native, 2 Asian Americans or Pacific Islanders, 1 Hispanic American), 11 international. Average age 31. 32 applicants, 47% accepted, 3 enrolled. In 2009, 5 master's awarded. *Degree requirements:* For master's, thesis or alternative; for doctorate, comprehensive exam, thesis/dissertation. *Entrance requirements:* For master's and doctorate, GRE. Additional exam requirements/recommendations for international students: Required—TOEFL (minimum score 550 paper-based; 79 iBT). *Application deadline:* For fall admission, 3/1 priority date for international students; for spring admission, 8/1 priority date for international students. Applications are processed on a rolling basis. Application fee: $40 ($75 for international students). Electronic applications accepted. *Expenses:* Tuition, state resident: full-time $3716; part-time $154.85 per credit hour. Tuition, nonresident: full-time $14,448; part-time $602 per credit hour. Required fees: $1772; $73.85 per credit hour. One-time fee: $50. Tuition and fees vary according to course load and campus/location. *Financial support:* In 2009–10, 11 research assistantships (averaging $13,845 per year), 17 teaching assistantships (averaging $15,560 per year) were awarded; career-related internships or fieldwork, Federal Work-Study, scholarships/grants, health care benefits, tuition waivers (partial), and unspecified assistantships also available. Support available to part-time students. Financial award application deadline: 3/1; financial award applicants required to submit FAFSA. *Faculty research:* Cultural ecology, resource management, historical/cultural geography, central Asia, geographic information systems. *Unit head:* Dr. Dale R. Lightfoot, Head, 405-744-6250, Fax: 405-744-5620. *Application contact:* Dr. Gordon Emslie, Dean, 405-744-6368, Fax: 405-744-0355, E-mail: grad-i@okstate.edu.

Oregon State University, Graduate School, College of Science, Department of Geosciences, Program in Geography, Corvallis, OR 97331. Offers MA, MAIS, MS, PhD. Part-time programs available. *Students:* 22 full-time (9 women), 7 part-time (3 women), 2 international. Average age 34. In 2009, 10 master's awarded. Terminal master's awarded for partial completion of doctoral program. *Degree requirements:* For master's, variable foreign language requirement, thesis optional; for doctorate, one foreign language, thesis/dissertation. *Entrance requirements:* For master's and doctorate, GRE General Test, GRE Subject Test, minimum GPA of 3.0 in last 90 hours. Additional exam requirements/recommendations for international students: Required—TOEFL. *Application deadline:* For fall admission, 2/1 for domestic students. Applications are processed on a rolling basis. Application fee: $50. *Expenses:* Tuition, state resident: full-time $9774; part-time $362 per credit. Tuition, nonresident: full-time $15,849; part-time $587 per credit. Required fees: $1639. Full-time tuition and fees vary according to course load and program. *Financial support:* Fellowships, research assistantships, teaching assistantships, Federal Work-Study and institutionally sponsored loans available. Support available to part-time students. Financial award application deadline: 2/1. *Faculty research:* Resources, physical geography, cartography, remote sensing. *Unit head:* Dr. Lawrence C. Becker, Director, 541-737-9504, E-mail: beckerla@geo.oregonstate.edu. *Application contact:* Dr. Julia A. Jones, Professor, 541-737-1224, Fax: 541-737-1200, E-mail: jonesj@geo.oregonstate.edu.

Penn State University Park, Graduate School, College of Earth and Mineral Sciences, Department of Geography, State College, University Park, PA 16802-1503. Offers MS, PhD.

Portland State University, Graduate Studies, College of Liberal Arts and Sciences, Department of Geography, Portland, OR 97207-0751. Offers MA, MAT, MS, MST, PhD. Part-time programs available. *Degree requirements:* For master's, thesis (for some programs). *Entrance requirements:* For master's, GRE General Test, minimum GPA of 3.0 in upper-division course work or 2.75 overall, 3 letters of recommendation. Additional exam requirements/recommendations for international students: Required—TOEFL (minimum score 550 paper-based; 213 computer-based). *Faculty research:* Geographic information systems, natural lands, Latin American subsistence farming, climatic change, urban perspectives.

Queen's University at Kingston, School of Graduate Studies and Research, Faculty of Arts and Sciences, Department of Geography, Kingston, ON K7L 3N6, Canada. Offers M Sc, MA, PhD. *Degree requirements:* For master's, thesis; for doctorate, comprehensive exam, thesis/dissertation. *Entrance requirements:* Additional exam requirements/recommendations for international students: Required—TOEFL. *Faculty research:* Urban and economic geography, historical-cultural geography, earth system science.

Rutgers, The State University of New Jersey, New Brunswick, Graduate School-New Brunswick, Program in Geography, Piscataway, NJ 08854-8097. Offers MA, MS, PhD. Terminal master's awarded for partial completion of doctoral program. *Degree requirements:* For master's, thesis or alternative; for doctorate, comprehensive exam, thesis/dissertation. *Entrance requirements:* For master's and doctorate, GRE General Test. Additional exam requirements/

Geography

Rutgers, The State University of New Jersey, New Brunswick (continued)
recommendations for international students: Required—TOEFL. *Faculty research:* Urban social theory, climate, political biology, hazards, economic development.

St. Cloud State University, School of Graduate Studies, College of Social Sciences, Department of Geography, St. Cloud, MN 56301-4498. Offers MS. *Faculty:* 9 full-time (0 women). *Students:* 11 full-time (1 woman), 5 part-time (1 woman), 1 international. 4 applicants, 100% accepted. In 2009, 2 master's awarded. *Degree requirements:* For master's, comprehensive exam (for some programs), thesis or alternative. *Entrance requirements:* For master's, GRE General Test, minimum GPA of 2.75. Additional exam requirements/recommendations for international students: Required—Michigan English Language Assessment Battery; Recommended—TOEFL (minimum score 550 paper-based; 213 computer-based), IELTS (minimum score 6.5). *Application deadline:* For fall admission, 6/1 priority date for domestic students, 4/1 for international students; for spring admission, 10/1 priority date for domestic students, 8/1 for international students. Applications are processed on a rolling basis. Application fee: $35. Electronic applications accepted. *Financial support:* Federal Work-Study, scholarships/grants, and unspecified assistantships available. Financial award application deadline: 3/1. *Unit head:* Dr. Lewis Wixon, Chairperson, 320-308-3160, Fax: 320-308-5198. *Application contact:* Linda Lou Krueger, School of Graduate Studies, 320-308-2113, Fax: 320-308-5371, E-mail: lekrueger@stcloudstate.edu.

Salem State College, School of Graduate Studies, Program in Geo-Information Science, Salem, MA 01970-5353. Offers geo-information science (MS). Part-time and evening/weekend programs available. *Students:* 1 full-time (0 women), 9 part-time (4 women), 5 international. Average age 37. 4 applicants, 100% accepted, 4 enrolled. In 2009, 6 master's awarded. *Degree requirements:* For master's, thesis optional. *Entrance requirements:* For master's, GRE or MAT. Additional exam requirements/recommendations for international students: Required—TOEFL (minimum score 550 paper-based; 80 iBT), or IELTS (minimum score 5.5). *Application deadline:* For fall admission, 5/1 for domestic students; for spring admission, 10/1 for domestic students. Applications are processed on a rolling basis. Application fee: $50. *Expenses:* Tuition, state resident: full-time $2520; part-time $275 per credit hour. Tuition, nonresident: full-time $4140; part-time $365 per credit hour. Required fees: $2430. *Financial support:* In 2009–10, 5 students received support. Career-related internships or fieldwork, Federal Work-Study, scholarships/grants, and unspecified assistantships available. Support available to part-time students. Financial award application deadline: 5/1; financial award applicants required to submit FAFSA. *Unit head:* Dr. Keith Ratner, Coordinator, 978-542-6075, E-mail: kratner@salemstate.edu. *Application contact:* Dr. Lee A. Brossoit, Assistant Dean of Graduate Admissions, 978-542-6675, Fax: 978-542-7215, E-mail: lbrossoit@salemstate.edu.

San Diego State University, Graduate and Research Affairs, College of Arts and Letters, Department of Geography, San Diego, CA 92182. Offers MA, PhD. *Degree requirements:* For master's, thesis; for doctorate, thesis/dissertation. *Entrance requirements:* For master's, GRE General Test, bachelor's degree in related field, 3 letters of recommendation. Additional exam requirements/recommendations for international students: Required—TOEFL. Electronic applications accepted. *Faculty research:* Physical geography, human geography, biogeography, environmental resources, geographic analysis.

San Francisco State University, Division of Graduate Studies, College of Behavioral and Social Sciences, Department of Geography and Human Environmental Studies, San Francisco, CA 94132-1722. Offers geography (MA), including resource management and environmental planning.

San Jose State University, Graduate Studies and Research, College of Social Sciences, Department of Geography, San Jose, CA 95192-0001. Offers geographic information science (Certificate); geography (MA). *Students:* 1 full-time (0 women), 13 part-time (6 women); includes 3 minority (2 Asian Americans or Pacific Islanders, 1 Hispanic American). Average age 39. 10 applicants, 50% accepted, 2 enrolled. In 2009, 5 master's awarded. *Entrance requirements:* For master's, minimum GPA of 3.0. *Application deadline:* For fall admission, 6/29 for domestic students; for spring admission, 11/30 for domestic students. Applications are processed on a rolling basis. Application fee: $59. Electronic applications accepted. *Financial support:* Applicants required to submit FAFSA. *Unit head:* Dr. Richard Taketa, Chair, 408-924-5425, E-mail: rtaketa@email.sjsu.edu. *Application contact:* Dr. Richard Taketa, Chair, 408-924-5425, E-mail: rtaketa@email.sjsu.edu.

Shippensburg University of Pennsylvania, School of Graduate Studies, College of Education and Human Services, Department of Teacher Education, Shippensburg, PA 17257-2299. Offers curriculum and instruction (M Ed), including biology, early childhood education, elementary education, English, foreign languages, geography/earth science, history, mathematics, middle school education; reading (M Ed). *Accreditation:* NCATE. Part-time and evening/weekend programs available. *Degree requirements:* For master's, comprehensive exam (for some programs), thesis optional, practicum or internship (for some programs). *Entrance requirements:* For master's, MAT (if GPA less than 2.75), interview, 3 letters of recommendation, writing sample of teaching background and future goals. Additional exam requirements/recommendations for international students: Required—TOEFL (minimum score 560 paper-based; 220 computer-based); Recommended—IELTS (minimum score 6). Electronic applications accepted.

Simon Fraser University, Graduate Studies, Faculty of Arts and Social Sciences, Department of Geography, Burnaby, BC V5A 1S6, Canada. Offers M Sc, MA, PhD. *Degree requirements:* For master's, one foreign language, thesis or alternative; for doctorate, one foreign language, thesis/dissertation, qualifying exams. *Entrance requirements:* For master's, minimum GPA of 3.0; for doctorate, minimum GPA of 3.5. Additional exam requirements/recommendations for international students: Required—TOEFL or IELTS. Electronic applications accepted. *Faculty research:* Theoretical and systematic aspects of geography, ginseng research, geographic information sciences, tourism and community planning, geomorphology.

South Dakota State University, Graduate School, College of Arts and Science, Department of Geography, Brookings, SD 57007. Offers MS. Part-time programs available. *Degree requirements:* For master's, thesis, oral exam. *Entrance requirements:* Additional exam requirements/recommendations for international students: Required—TOEFL (minimum score 525 paper-based; 197 computer-based; 71 iBT). *Faculty research:* Contemporary agriculture and rural land use, geography of Indian casino gambling, geography of illegal drug trade, geography of crop circles.

Southern Illinois University Carbondale, Graduate School, College of Liberal Arts, Department of Geography, Carbondale, IL 62901-4701. Offers MS, PhD. *Degree requirements:* For master's, thesis; for doctorate, thesis/dissertation. *Entrance requirements:* For master's, minimum GPA of 2.7; for doctorate, minimum GPA of 3.25. Additional exam requirements/recommendations for international students: Required—TOEFL. *Faculty research:* Natural resources management emphasizing water resources and environmental quality of air, water, and land systems.

Southern Illinois University Edwardsville, Graduate Studies and Research, College of Arts and Sciences, Department of Geography, Edwardsville, IL 62026-0001. Offers MS. Part-time and evening/weekend programs available. *Faculty:* 13 full-time (5 women). *Students:* 10 full-time (5 women), 20 part-time (12 women); includes 3 minority (1 American Indian/Alaska Native, 2 Hispanic Americans), 1 international. Average age 26. 26 applicants, 62% accepted. In 2009, 6 master's awarded. *Degree requirements:* For master's, thesis (for some programs), final exam. *Entrance requirements:* For master's, GRE. Additional exam requirements/recommendations for international students: Required—TOEFL (minimum score 550 paper-based; 213 computer-based; 79 iBT), IELTS (minimum score 6.5). *Application deadline:* For fall admission, 7/23 for domestic students, 6/1 for international students; for spring admission, 12/11 for domestic students, 10/1 for international students. Applications are processed on a rolling basis. Application fee: $30. Electronic applications accepted. *Expenses:* Tuition, state resident: part-time $1252.50 per semester. Tuition, nonresident: part-time $3131.25 per semester. Required fees: $586.85 per semester. Tuition and fees vary according to course load. *Financial support:* In 2009–10, 1 fellowship with full tuition reimbursement (averaging $8,370 per year), 8 teaching assistantships with full tuition reimbursements (averaging $8,064 per year) were awarded; research assistantships with full tuition reimbursements, career-related internships or fieldwork, Federal Work-Study, institutionally sponsored loans, scholarships/grants, traineeships, and unspecified assistantships also available. Support available to part-time students. Financial award application deadline: 3/1; financial award applicants required to submit FAFSA. *Unit head:* Dr. Shunfu Hu, Chair, 618-650-2090, E-mail: shu@siue.edu. *Application contact:* Dr. Michael Starr, Director, 618-650-2492, E-mail: mstarr@siue.edu.

State University of New York at Binghamton, Graduate School, School of Arts and Sciences, Department of Geography, Binghamton, NY 13902-6000. Offers MA. *Faculty:* 7 full-time (2 women), 1 part-time/adjunct (0 women). *Students:* 14 full-time (8 women), 5 part-time (1 woman); includes 4 minority (1 Asian American or Pacific Islander, 3 Hispanic Americans), 7 international. Average age 29. 20 applicants, 90% accepted, 8 enrolled. In 2009, 11 master's awarded. *Degree requirements:* For master's, one foreign language, thesis (for some programs), oral and written exams. *Entrance requirements:* For master's, GRE General Test, GRE Subject Test. Additional exam requirements/recommendations for international students: Required—TOEFL (minimum score 550 paper-based; 213 computer-based; 80 iBT). *Application deadline:* For fall admission, 5/15 priority date for domestic and international students; for spring admission, 10/15 priority date for domestic and international students. Applications are processed on a rolling basis. Application fee: $60. Electronic applications accepted. *Financial support:* In 2009–10, 13 students received support, including 1 fellowship with full tuition reimbursement available (averaging $10,000 per year), 10 teaching assistantships with full tuition reimbursements available (averaging $10,000 per year); research assistantships with full tuition reimbursements available, career-related internships or fieldwork, Federal Work-Study, institutionally sponsored loans, scholarships/grants, health care benefits, and unspecified assistantships also available. Financial award application deadline: 2/15; financial award applicants required to submit FAFSA. *Unit head:* Dr. Norah Henry, Chairperson, 607-777-2615, E-mail: nhenry@binghamton.edu. *Application contact:* Victoria Williams, Recruiting and Admissions Coordinator, 607-777-2151, Fax: 607-777-2501, E-mail: vwilliam@binghamton.edu.

Syracuse University, Maxwell School of Citizenship and Public Affairs, Program in Geography, Syracuse, NY 13244. Offers MA, PhD. Part-time and evening/weekend programs available. *Students:* 34 full-time (20 women), 4 part-time (3 women); includes 7 minority (3 African Americans, 2 Asian Americans or Pacific Islanders, 2 Hispanic Americans), 6 international. Average age 31. 62 applicants, 48% accepted, 5 enrolled. In 2009, 3 master's, 2 doctorates awarded. *Degree requirements:* For master's, thesis or alternative; for doctorate, thesis/dissertation. *Entrance requirements:* For master's and doctorate, GRE General Test. Additional exam requirements/recommendations for international students: Required—TOEFL (minimum score 100 iBT). *Application deadline:* For fall admission, 2/1 priority date for domestic and international students. Application fee: $75. Electronic applications accepted. *Expenses:* Tuition: Full-time $26,808; part-time $1117 per credit. Required fees: $1024. *Financial support:* Fellowships with full tuition reimbursements, research assistantships with full tuition reimbursements, teaching assistantships with full and partial tuition reimbursements, tuition waivers (partial) available. Financial award application deadline: 1/1. *Unit head:* Dr. Tod Rutherford, Chair, 315-443-2605, Fax: 315-443-4227, E-mail: trutherf@syr.edu. *Application contact:* Chris Chapman, Recruiting Contact, 315-443-2605, E-mail: cmchapma@maxwell.syr.edu.

Temple University, Graduate School, College of Liberal Arts, Department of Geography and Urban Studies, Philadelphia, PA 19122-6096. Offers geography (MA); urban studies (MA). *Degree requirements:* For master's, comprehensive exam, thesis or alternative. *Entrance requirements:* For master's, GRE General Test, minimum GPA of 3.0. Additional exam requirements/recommendations for international students: Required—TOEFL (minimum score 550 paper-based; 213 computer-based; 79 iBT). Electronic applications accepted. *Faculty research:* Environmental issues, urban political economy, poverty and unemployment, neighborhood development, African and Asian urbanization, housing, computer cartography.

Texas A&M University, College of Geosciences, Department of Geography, College Station, TX 77843. Offers MS, PhD. Part-time programs available. *Faculty:* 14. *Students:* 69 full-time (31 women), 17 part-time (4 women); includes 6 minority (2 African Americans, 4 Asian Americans or Pacific Islanders), 28 international. Average age 34. In 2009, 9 master's, 7 doctorates awarded. *Degree requirements:* For master's, thesis optional; for doctorate, thesis/dissertation. *Entrance requirements:* For master's and doctorate, GRE General Test. Additional exam requirements/recommendations for international students: Required—TOEFL. *Application deadline:* For fall admission, 3/1 priority date for domestic students; for spring admission, 10/1 for domestic students. Applications are processed on a rolling basis. Application fee: $50 ($75 for international students). Electronic applications accepted. *Expenses:* Tuition, state resident: full-time $3991; part-time $221.74 per credit hour. Tuition, nonresident: full-time $9049; part-time $502.74 per credit hour. *Financial support:* Fellowships, research assistantships, teaching assistantships, career-related internships or fieldwork, Federal Work-Study, and institutionally sponsored loans available. Financial award application deadline: 3/1; financial award applicants required to submit FAFSA. *Faculty research:* Geomorphology, historical geography, urban-economic geography, geographic education and technology, human-environment interaction. *Unit head:* Head, 979-845-7188. *Application contact:* Graduate Advisor, 979-845-7154, Fax: 979-862-4487, E-mail: growe@geog.tamu.edu.

Texas State University–San Marcos, Graduate School, College of Liberal Arts, Department of Geography, Program in Environmental Geography, Geography Education, and Geography Information Science, San Marcos, TX 78666. Offers environmental geography (PhD); geography education (PhD); information science (PhD). Part-time programs available. *Students:* 46 full-time (22 women), 25 part-time (12 women); includes 16 minority (3 African Americans, 7 Asian Americans or Pacific Islanders, 6 Hispanic Americans), 3 international. Average age 39. 23 applicants, 83% accepted, 8 enrolled. In 2009, 6 doctorates awarded. *Degree requirements:* For doctorate, thesis/dissertation. *Entrance requirements:* For doctorate, GRE General Test, minimum GPA of 3.5, master's degree in geography, demonstrated scholarly research. Additional exam requirements/recommendations for international students: Required—TOEFL (minimum score 550 paper-based; 213 computer-based). *Application deadline:* For fall admission, 6/15 priority date for domestic students, 6/1 for international students; for spring admission, 10/15 priority date for domestic students, 10/1 for international students. Applications are processed on a rolling basis. Application fee: $40 ($90 for international students). Electronic applications accepted. *Expenses:* Tuition, state resident: full-time $5784; part-time $241 per credit hour. Tuition, nonresident: part-time $551 per credit hour. Required fees: $1728; $48 per credit hour. $306. Tuition and fees vary according to course load. *Financial support:* In 2009–10, 60 students received support, including 17 research assistantships (averaging $10,552 per year), 26 teaching assistantships (averaging $9,874 per year); career-related internships or fieldwork, Federal Work-Study, and institutionally sponsored loans also available. Support available to part-time students. Financial award application deadline: 4/1; financial award applicants required to submit FAFSA. *Unit head:* Dr. David Butler, Graduate Adviser, 512-245-2170, Fax: 512-245-8353, E-mail: db25@txstate.edu. *Application contact:* Dr. J. Michael Willoughby, Dean of Graduate School, 512-245-2581, Fax: 512-245-8365, E-mail: gradcollege@txstate.edu.

Texas State University–San Marcos, Graduate School, College of Liberal Arts, Department of Geography, Program in Geography, San Marcos, TX 78666. Offers applied geography (MAG); geography (MS). Part-time and evening/weekend programs available. *Faculty:* 5 full-time (1 woman), 2 part-time/adjunct (0 women). *Students:* 30 full-time (18 women), 29 part-time (15 women); includes 3 minority (2 Asian Americans or Pacific Islanders, 1 Hispanic American), 1 international. Average age 32. 16 applicants, 88% accepted, 11 enrolled. In 2009, 14 master's awarded. *Degree requirements:* For master's, comprehensive exam, thesis (for some programs). *Entrance requirements:* For master's, GRE General Test, minimum GPA of 3.0 in last 60 hours of course work, letter of interest, 2 letters of recommendation, curriculum vitae/resume. Additional exam requirements/recommendations for international students: Required—TOEFL (minimum score 550 paper-based; 213 computer-based). *Application deadline:* For fall admission,

6/15 priority date for domestic students, 6/1 for international students; for spring admission, 10/15 priority date for domestic students, 10/1 for international students. Applications are processed on a rolling basis. Application fee: $40 ($90 for international students). Electronic applications accepted. *Expenses:* Tuition, state resident: full-time $5784; part-time $241 per credit hour. Tuition, nonresident: part-time $551 per credit hour. Required fees: $1728; $48 per credit hour. $306. Tuition and fees vary according to course load. *Financial support:* In 2009–10, 26 students received support, including 6 research assistantships (averaging $5,716 per year), 11 teaching assistantships (averaging $5,443 per year); career-related internships or fieldwork, Federal Work-Study, and institutionally sponsored loans also available. Support available to part-time students. Financial award application deadline: 4/1; financial award applicants required to submit FAFSA. *Faculty research:* Applied cartography and geographic information systems, physical and environmental studies, land/area development and management. *Unit head:* Dr. David Butler, Graduate Adviser, 512-245-2170, Fax: 512-245-8353, E-mail: db25@txstate.edu. *Application contact:* Dr. J. Michael Willoughby, Dean of Graduate School, 512-245-2581, Fax: 512-245-8365, E-mail: gradcollege@txstate.edu.

Texas State University–San Marcos, Graduate School, College of Liberal Arts, Department of Geography, Program in Land/Area Studies, San Marcos, TX 78666. Offers MAG. Part-time and evening/weekend programs available. *Faculty:* 5 full-time (0 women), 1 part-time/adjunct (0 women). *Students:* 4 full-time (1 woman), 12 part-time (4 women); includes 2 minority (both Hispanic Americans). Average age 29. 6 applicants, 100% accepted, 5 enrolled. In 2009, 3 master's awarded. *Degree requirements:* For master's, comprehensive exam. *Entrance requirements:* For master's, GRE General Test, minimum GPA of 3.0 in last 60 hours of course work, letter of interest, 2 letters of recommendation, curriculum vitae/resume. Additional exam requirements/recommendations for international students: Required—TOEFL (minimum score 550 paper-based; 213 computer-based). *Application deadline:* For fall admission, 6/15 priority date for domestic students, 6/1 for international students; for spring admission, 10/15 priority date for domestic students, 10/1 for international students. Applications are processed on a rolling basis. Application fee: $40 ($90 for international students). Electronic applications accepted. *Expenses:* Tuition, state resident: full-time $5784; part-time $241 per credit hour. Tuition, nonresident: part-time $551 per credit hour. Required fees: $1728; $48 per credit hour. $306. Tuition and fees vary according to course load. *Financial support:* In 2009–10, 3 students received support; research assistantships, teaching assistantships, career-related internships or fieldwork, Federal Work-Study, institutionally sponsored loans, and scholarships/grants available. Support available to part-time students. Financial award application deadline: 4/1; financial award applicants required to submit FAFSA. *Unit head:* Dr. David Butler, Graduate Adviser, 512-245-2170, Fax: 512-245-8353, E-mail: db25@txstate.edu. *Application contact:* Dr. J. Michael Willoughby, Dean of Graduate School, 512-245-2581, Fax: 512-245-8365, E-mail: gradcollege@txstate.edu.

Towson University, College of Graduate Studies and Research, Program in Geography and Environmental Planning, Towson, MD 21252-0001. Offers MA. Part-time and evening/weekend programs available. *Degree requirements:* For master's, thesis optional. *Entrance requirements:* For master's, 9 credits of course work in geography, minimum GPA of 3.0 in geography, 2 narrative letters of recomendation. Additional exam requirements/recommendations for international students: Required—TOEFL. Electronic applications accepted. *Faculty research:* Geographic information systems, regional planning, hazards, development issues, urban fluvial systems.

Trent University, Graduate Studies, Program in Applications of Modeling in the Natural and Social Sciences, Peterborough, ON K9J 7B8, Canada. Offers applications of modeling in the natural and social sciences (MA); biology (M Sc, PhD); chemistry (M Sc); computer studies (M Sc); geography (M Sc, PhD); physics (M Sc). Part-time programs available. *Degree requirements:* For master's, thesis. *Entrance requirements:* For master's, honours degree. *Faculty research:* Computation of heat transfer, atmospheric physics, statistical mechanics, stress and coping, evolutionary ecology.

Trent University, Graduate Studies, Program in Environmental and Life Sciences and Program in Applications of Modeling in the Natural and Social Sciences, Department of Geography, Peterborough, ON K9J 7B8, Canada. Offers M Sc, PhD. Part-time programs available. *Degree requirements:* For master's, thesis; for doctorate, thesis/dissertation. *Entrance requirements:* For master's, honors degree; for doctorate, master's degree. *Faculty research:* Hydrometeorology, snow and ice, urban hydrology, fluvial geomorphology.

Université de Montréal, Faculty of Arts and Sciences, Department of Geography, Montréal, QC H3C 3J7, Canada. Offers environment and durable development (DESS); geography (M Sc, PhD, DESS); geomatical and spatial analysis (Certificate). *Degree requirements:* For master's, 2 foreign languages, thesis (for some programs); for doctorate, 3 foreign languages, thesis/dissertation, general exam. *Entrance requirements:* For master's, bachelor's degree in related field; for doctorate, MA in geography or related field. Electronic applications accepted. *Faculty research:* Cartography, palynology, geomorphology, economic geography, regional and urban development.

Université de Sherbrooke, Faculty of Letters and Human Sciences, Department of Geography and Remote Sensing, Sherbrooke, QC J1K 2R1, Canada. Offers M Sc, PhD. *Degree requirements:* For master's, one foreign language, thesis; for doctorate, thesis/dissertation. *Faculty research:* Cartography.

Université du Québec à Montréal, Graduate Programs, Program in Geography, Montréal, QC H3C 3P8, Canada. Offers M Sc. Part-time programs available. *Degree requirements:* For master's, thesis optional. *Entrance requirements:* For master's, appropriate bachelor's degree or equivalent and proficiency in French.

Université Laval, Faculty of Forestry and Geomatics, Department of Geography, Program in Geographical Sciences, Québec, QC G1K 7P4, Canada. Offers M Sc Geogr, PhD. Terminal master's awarded for partial completion of doctoral program. *Degree requirements:* For master's, thesis; for doctorate, comprehensive exam, thesis/dissertation. *Entrance requirements:* For master's, knowledge of French; for doctorate, knowledge of French, knowledge of a second language. Electronic applications accepted.

University at Albany, State University of New York, College of Arts and Sciences, Department of Geography and Planning, Program in Geography, Albany, NY 12222-0001. Offers geographic information systems and spatial analysis (Certificate); geography (MA). *Degree requirements:* For master's, thesis or alternative. *Entrance requirements:* Additional exam requirements/recommendations for international students: Required—TOEFL (minimum score 550 paper-based; 213 computer-based). Electronic applications accepted. *Faculty research:* Remote sensing, cultural/social geography, urban geography.

University at Buffalo, the State University of New York, Graduate School, College of Arts and Sciences, Department of Geography, Buffalo, NY 14260. Offers earth systems science (MA); economic geography and international business and world trade (MA); environmental and earth systems science (MS); environmental modeling and analysis (MA); geographic information science (MA, Certificate); geographic information systems and science (MS); geography (MA, PhD); urban and regional geography (MA); MA/MBA. *Faculty:* 14 full-time (6 women), 2 part-time/adjunct (0 women). *Students:* 63 full-time (16 women), 32 part-time (8 women); includes 31 minority (3 African Americans, 26 Asian Americans or Pacific Islanders, 2 Hispanic Americans), 3 international. Average age 29. 154 applicants, 42% accepted, 24 enrolled. In 2009, 18 master's, 6 doctorates awarded. *Degree requirements:* For master's, thesis (for some programs), project; for doctorate, thesis/dissertation. *Entrance requirements:* For master's, GRE General Test, minimum GPA of 2.9; for doctorate, GRE General Test, minimum GPA of 3.0. Additional exam requirements/recommendations for international students: Required—TOEFL (minimum score 550 paper-based; 213 computer-based; 79 iBT). *Application deadline:* For fall admission, 7/1 priority date for domestic students, 1/10 priority date for international students; for spring admission, 12/1 priority date for domestic students, 10/1 priority date for international students. Applications are processed on a rolling basis. Application fee: $75. Electronic applications accepted. *Financial support:* In 2009–10, 19 students received support, including 6 fellowships with full tuition reimbursements available (averaging $4,333 per year), 14 teaching assistantships with full tuition reimbursements available (averaging $13,361 per year); research assistantships with full tuition reimbursements available, career-related internships or fieldwork, Federal Work-Study, institutionally sponsored loans, traineeships, health care benefits, and unspecified assistantships also available. Financial award application deadline: 1/10. *Faculty research:* International business and world trade, geographic information systems and cartography, transportation, urban and regional analysis, physical and environmental geography. Total annual research expenditures: $944,614. *Unit head:* Dr. Peter Rogerson, Chairman, 716-645-0473, Fax: 716-645-2329, E-mail: rogerson@buffalo.edu. *Application contact:* Betsy Abraham, Graduate Secretary, 716-645-0471, Fax: 716-645-2329, E-mail: babraham@buffalo.edu.

The University of Akron, Graduate School, Buchtel College of Arts and Sciences, Department of Geography and Planning, Akron, OH 44325. Offers geographic information science (MS); urban planning (MA). Part-time and evening/weekend programs available. *Faculty:* 5 full-time (1 woman), 7 part-time/adjunct (2 women). *Students:* 37 full-time (12 women), 3 part-time (1 woman); includes 3 minority (1 African American, 1 Asian American or Pacific Islander, 1 Hispanic American), 11 international. Average age 27. 26 applicants, 88% accepted, 14 enrolled. In 2009, 13 master's awarded. *Degree requirements:* For master's, thesis optional. *Entrance requirements:* For master's, minimum GPA of 2.75, 2 letters of recommendation. Additional exam requirements/recommendations for international students: Required—TOEFL (minimum score 550 paper-based; 213 computer-based; 79 iBT). *Application deadline:* Applications are processed on a rolling basis. Application fee: $30 ($40 for international students). Electronic applications accepted. *Expenses:* Tuition, state resident: full-time $6570; part-time $365 per credit hour. Tuition, nonresident: full-time $11,250; part-time $625 per credit hour. *Financial support:* In 2009–10, 1 research assistantship with full and partial tuition reimbursement, 30 teaching assistantships with full and partial tuition reimbursements were awarded; career-related internships or fieldwork, Federal Work-Study, institutionally sponsored loans, scholarships/grants, and unspecified assistantships also available. *Faculty research:* Geographic information sciences; urban and regional planning; human geography especially cultural, political, and urban; regional geography, especially Native America, Asia, and Middle East. Total annual research expenditures: $135,890. *Unit head:* Dr. Charles Monroe, Interim Chair, 330-972-8033, E-mail: monroe@uakron.edu. *Application contact:* Dr. Linda Barrett, Director of Graduate Studies, 330-972-6120, Fax: 330-972-6080, E-mail: barrett@uakron.edu.

The University of Alabama, Graduate School, College of Arts and Sciences, Department of Geography, Tuscaloosa, AL 35487. Offers MS. Part-time programs available. *Faculty:* 11 full-time (2 women). *Students:* 21 full-time (13 women), 5 part-time (1 woman); includes 1 minority (African American), 3 international. Average age 26. 22 applicants, 64% accepted, 11 enrolled. In 2009, 6 degrees awarded. *Degree requirements:* For master's, comprehensive exam, thesis or alternative. *Entrance requirements:* For master's, GRE, minimum GPA of 3.0. Additional exam requirements/recommendations for international students: Required—TOEFL. *Application deadline:* For fall admission, 2/15 priority date for domestic students, 2/1 priority date for international students; for spring admission, 10/1 priority date for domestic and international students. Applications are processed on a rolling basis. Application fee: $50 ($60 for international students). Electronic applications accepted. *Expenses:* Tuition, state resident: full-time $7000. Tuition, nonresident: full-time $19,200. *Financial support:* In 2009–10, 16 students received support, including fellowships (averaging $12,500 per year), 3 research assistantships with full tuition reimbursements available (averaging $10,908 per year), 15 teaching assistantships with full tuition reimbursements available (averaging $10,908 per year); career-related internships or fieldwork, health care benefits, and unspecified assistantships also available. Financial award application deadline: 2/15. *Faculty research:* Land use, regional and urban planning, geographic information systems, forest ecology, environmental management, geomorphology, climatology. Total annual research expenditures: $3,429. *Unit head:* Prof. Bobby Wilson, Chair, 205-348-5047, Fax: 205-348-2278, E-mail: bmwilson@bama.ua.edu. *Application contact:* Information Contact, 205-348-5047, Fax: 205-348-2278.

University of Alaska Fairbanks, School of Natural Resources and Agricultural Sciences, Fairbanks, AK 99775-7140. Offers natural resource and sustainability (PhD); natural resource management (MS); natural resource management and geography (MS). Part-time programs available. *Faculty:* 20 full-time (3 women), 2 part-time/adjunct (1 woman). *Students:* 31 full-time (21 women), 18 part-time (7 women); includes 2 minority (1 American Indian/Alaska Native, 1 Asian American or Pacific Islander), 5 international. Average age 32. 49 applicants, 45% accepted, 16 enrolled. In 2009, 7 master's, 3 doctorates awarded. *Degree requirements:* For master's, comprehensive exam, thesis or alternative. *Entrance requirements:* For master's, GRE General Test. Additional exam requirements/recommendations for international students: Required—TOEFL (minimum score 550 paper-based; 213 computer-based). *Application deadline:* For fall admission, 6/1 for domestic students, 3/1 for international students; for spring admission, 10/15 for domestic students, 9/1 for international students. Applications are processed on a rolling basis. Application fee: $60. Electronic applications accepted. *Expenses:* Tuition, state resident: full-time $7584; part-time $316 per credit. Tuition, nonresident: full-time $15,504; part-time $646 per credit. Required fees: $23 per credit. $135 per semester. Tuition and fees vary according to course level, course load and reciprocity agreements. *Financial support:* In 2009–10, 16 research assistantships (averaging $10,412 per year), 2 teaching assistantships (averaging $9,472 per year) were awarded; fellowships, career-related internships or fieldwork, Federal Work-Study, scholarships/grants, health care benefits, and unspecified assistantships also available. Support available to part-time students. Financial award application deadline: 2/15; financial award applicants required to submit FAFSA. *Faculty research:* Conservation biology, soil/water conservation, land use policy and planning in the arctic and subarctic, forest ecosystem management, subarctic agricultural production. Total annual research expenditures: $5.8 million. *Unit head:* Dr. Carol E. Lewis, Dean, 907-474-7083, Fax: 907-474-6567, E-mail: fysnras@uaf.edu. *Application contact:* Veazey David, Director of Enrollment Management, 907-474-5276, Fax: 907-474-6567, E-mail: dave.veazey@alaska.edu.

The University of Arizona, Graduate College, College of Social and Behavioral Sciences, Department of Geography and Regional Development, Tucson, AZ 85721. Offers geography (MA, PhD). Part-time programs available. *Faculty:* 10 full-time (4 women). *Students:* 35 full-time (19 women), 46 part-time (21 women); includes 8 minority (2 African Americans, 1 American Indian/Alaska Native, 5 Hispanic Americans), 14 international. Average age 33. 107 applicants, 29% accepted, 14 enrolled. In 2009, 7 master's, 4 doctorates awarded. Terminal master's awarded for partial completion of doctoral program. *Degree requirements:* For master's, thesis or additional course work; for doctorate, variable foreign language requirement, thesis/dissertation. *Entrance requirements:* For master's, GRE General Test, 2 letters of recommendation; for doctorate, GRE General Test, statement of purpose, 2 letters of recommendation, master's degree. Additional exam requirements/recommendations for international students: Required—TOEFL (minimum score 550 paper-based; 213 computer-based; 79 iBT). *Application deadline:* For fall admission, 1/15 for domestic and international students. Application fee: $65. Electronic applications accepted. *Expenses:* Tuition, state resident: full-time $9028. Tuition, nonresident: full-time $24,890. *Financial support:* In 2009–10, 7 research assistantships with full tuition reimbursements (averaging $14,914 per year), 27 teaching assistantships with full tuition reimbursements (averaging $15,083 per year) were awarded; career-related internships or fieldwork, scholarships/grants, health care benefits, and unspecified assistantships also available. Financial award application deadline: 2/1. *Faculty research:* Population, Latin America, Anglo America, the former Soviet Union, Middle East. Total annual research expenditures: $514,629. *Unit head:* Dr. John Paul Jones, Department Head, 520-621-1652, Fax: 520-621-2889, E-mail: jpjones@email.arizona.edu. *Application contact:* Linda Koski, Information Contact, 520-621-1652, Fax: 520-621-2889, E-mail: lkoski@email.arizona.edu.

University of Arkansas, Graduate School, J. William Fulbright College of Arts and Sciences, Department of Geosciences, Program in Geography, Fayetteville, AR 72701-1201. Offers MA. Part-time programs available. *Students:* 8 full-time (2 women), 16 part-time (4 women); includes

Geography

University of Arkansas (continued)
3 minority (2 American Indian/Alaska Native, 1 Asian American or Pacific Islander), 1 international. In 2009, 4 master's awarded. *Degree requirements:* For master's, thesis. Application fee: $40 ($50 for international students). *Expenses:* Tuition, state resident: full-time $7355; part-time $356.58 per hour. Tuition, nonresident: full-time $17,401; part-time $775.17 per hour. Required fees: $1203. *Financial support:* In 2009–10, 2 research assistantships, 4 teaching assistantships were awarded; fellowships, career-related internships or fieldwork and Federal Work-Study also available. Support available to part-time students. Financial award application deadline: 4/1; financial award applicants required to submit FAFSA. *Unit head:* Dr. Ralph Davis, Chair, 479-575-3355, Fax: 479-575-3469, E-mail: ralphd@uark.edu. *Application contact:* Dr. Tom Graff, Graduate Coordinator, 479-575-3878, E-mail: tgraff@uark.edu.

The University of British Columbia, Faculty of Arts and Faculty of Graduate Studies, Department of Geography, Vancouver, BC V6T 1Z2, Canada. Offers M Sc, MA, PhD. Part-time programs available. Terminal master's awarded for partial completion of doctoral program. *Degree requirements:* For master's, thesis; for doctorate, comprehensive exam, thesis/dissertation. *Entrance requirements:* For master's and doctorate, minimum B average, 2nd class honors, upper division (class II, division I). Additional exam requirements/recommendations for international students: Required—TOEFL (minimum score 600 paper-based; 250 computer-based; 100 iBT). Electronic applications accepted. *Faculty research:* Earth system science, environmental geography, historical geography, social geography, urban geography.

University of Calgary, Faculty of Graduate Studies, Faculty of Social Sciences, Department of Geography, Calgary, AB T2N 1N4, Canada. Offers M Sc, MA, MGIS, PhD. Part-time programs available. *Degree requirements:* For master's, thesis, departmental conference; for doctorate, thesis/dissertation, candidacy exam, departmental conference. *Entrance requirements:* For master's, minimum undergraduate GPA of 3.0 during last 2 years; for doctorate, minimum GPA of 3.0 during previous 2 years, master's degree. Additional exam requirements/recommendations for international students: Required—TOEFL (minimum score 550 paper-based; 213 computer-based). Electronic applications accepted. *Faculty research:* Geographic information systems, remote sensing, geomorphology, earth system processes, urban and required environmental health research.

University of California, Berkeley, Graduate Division, College of Letters and Science, Department of Geography, Berkeley, CA 94720-1500. Offers PhD. *Students:* 56 full-time (29 women). Average age 32. 101 applicants, 10 enrolled. In 2009, 7 doctorates awarded. *Degree requirements:* For doctorate, thesis/dissertation, qualifying exam. *Entrance requirements:* For doctorate, GRE General Test, minimum GPA of 3.0, 3 letters of recommendation. *Application deadline:* For fall admission, 12/12 for domestic students. Application fee: $70 ($90 for international students). Electronic applications accepted. *Financial support:* Fellowships, research assistantships, teaching assistantships, unspecified assistantships available. *Unit head:* Prof. Kurt Cuffey, Chair, 510-642-3903, Fax: 510-642-3370, E-mail: ch_geography@ls.berkeley.edu. *Application contact:* Carol Page, Graduate Assistant for Admission, 510-642-3904, Fax: 510-642-3370, E-mail: carolpage@socrates.berkeley.edu.

University of California, Davis, Graduate Studies, Graduate Group in Geography, Davis, CA 95616. Offers MA, PhD. Terminal master's awarded for partial completion of doctoral program. *Degree requirements:* For master's, comprehensive exam (for some programs), thesis (for some programs); for doctorate, thesis/dissertation. *Entrance requirements:* For master's, GRE General Test, minimum GPA of 3.0; for doctorate, GRE General Test, master's degree, minimum GPA of 3.0. Additional exam requirements/recommendations for international students: Required—TOEFL (minimum score 550 paper-based; 213 computer-based). Electronic applications accepted. *Faculty research:* Cultural agrosystems, mountain society habitat and South Asia.

University of California, Los Angeles, Graduate Division, College of Letters and Science, Department of Geography, Los Angeles, CA 90095. Offers MA, PhD. *Students:* 49 full-time (22 women); includes 8 minority (1 African American, 3 Asian Americans or Pacific Islanders, 4 Hispanic Americans), 10 international. Average age 31. 68 applicants, 28% accepted, 10 enrolled. In 2009, 2 master's, 4 doctorates awarded. Terminal master's awarded for partial completion of doctoral program. *Degree requirements:* For master's, thesis; for doctorate, thesis/dissertation, oral and written qualifying exams. *Entrance requirements:* For master's, GRE General Test, minimum GPA of 3.3; for doctorate, GRE General Test, minimum undergraduate GPA of 3.3, sample of research writing or thesis. *Application deadline:* For fall admission, 12/31 for domestic and international students. Application fee: $60 ($80 for international students). Electronic applications accepted. *Financial support:* In 2009–10, 33 fellowships with full and partial tuition reimbursements, 12 research assistantships with full and partial tuition reimbursements, 33 teaching assistantships with full and partial tuition reimbursements were awarded; Federal Work-Study, institutionally sponsored loans, scholarships/grants, health care benefits, tuition waivers (full and partial), and unspecified assistantships also available. Financial award application deadline: 3/1; financial award applicants required to submit FAFSA. *Unit head:* Dr. David Rigby, Chair, 310-206-5536. *Application contact:* Department Office, 310-825-1071, E-mail: gradapps@geog.ucla.edu.

University of California, Santa Barbara, Graduate Division, College of Letters and Sciences, Division of Mathematics, Life, and Physical Sciences, Department of Geography, Santa Barbara, CA 93106-4060. Offers cognitive science (PhD); geography (MA); quantitative methods in the social sciences (PhD); transportation (PhD); MA/PhD. *Students:* 67 full-time (33 women). Average age 30. 92 applicants, 28% accepted, 15 enrolled. In 2009, 3 master's, 13 doctorates awarded. *Degree requirements:* For master's, comprehensive exam (for some programs), thesis; for doctorate, comprehensive exam, thesis/dissertation. *Entrance requirements:* For master's, GRE General Test, 3 letters of recommendation, resume/curriculum vitae; for doctorate, GRE General Test, 3 letters of recommendation, statement of purpose, personal achievements/contributions statement, resume/curriculum vitae, transcripts for post-secondary institutions attended. Additional exam requirements/recommendations for international students: Required—TOEFL (minimum score 550 paper-based; 213 computer-based; 80 iBT) or IELTS (minimum score 7). *Application deadline:* For fall admission, 2/1 for domestic and international students. Application fee: $70 ($90 for international students). Electronic applications accepted. *Financial support:* In 2009–10, 59 students received support, including 36 fellowships with full and partial tuition reimbursements available (averaging $10,700 per year), 29 research assistantships with full and partial tuition reimbursements available (averaging $8,600 per year), 31 teaching assistantships with partial tuition reimbursements available (averaging $8,000 per year); Federal Work-Study, institutionally sponsored loans, scholarships/grants, health care benefits, and unspecified assistantships also available. Financial award applicants required to submit FAFSA. *Faculty research:* Earth system science, human environment relations, modeling, measurement and computation, quantitative methods in social sciences. *Unit head:* Dr. Oliver Chadwick, Chair, 805-893-4223, E-mail: oac@geog.ucsb.edu. *Application contact:* Graduate Program Assistant, 805-893-3663, Fax: 805-893-3146, E-mail: grad_assistant@geog.ucsb.edu.

University of Central Arkansas, Graduate School, College of Liberal Arts, Department of Geography, Conway, AR 72035-0001. Offers geographic information systems (MGIS, Certificate). Part-time programs available. Postbaccalaureate distance learning degree programs offered (minimal on-campus study). *Faculty:* 3 full-time (0 women). *Students:* 2 full-time (1 woman), 17 part-time (3 women); includes 3 minority (1 African American, 1 Asian American or Pacific Islander, 1 Hispanic American). Average age 36. 7 applicants, 100% accepted, 6 enrolled. *Entrance requirements:* Additional exam requirements/recommendations for international students: Required—TOEFL (minimum score 550 paper-based; 213 computer-based). *Application deadline:* For fall admission, 3/1 priority date for domestic and international students; for spring admission, 10/1 priority date for domestic and international students. Applications are processed on a rolling basis. Application fee: $25 ($50 for international students). *Expenses:* Tuition, state resident: full-time $5136; part-time $214 per credit hour. Required fees: $379.50; $127 per term. Tuition and fees vary according to course level, course load and campus/location. *Financial support:* Applicants required to submit FAFSA. *Unit head:* Dr. Brooks Green, Chairperson, 501-450-5636, Fax: 501-450-5185, E-mail: brooksg@uca.edu. *Application contact:* Brenda Herring, Admissions Assistant, 501-450-5065, Fax: 501-450-5678, E-mail: bherring@uca.edu.

University of Cincinnati, Graduate School, McMicken College of Arts and Sciences, Department of Geography, Cincinnati, OH 45221. Offers MA, PhD. Terminal master's awarded for partial completion of doctoral program. *Degree requirements:* For master's, thesis optional; for doctorate, one foreign language, comprehensive exam, thesis/dissertation. *Entrance requirements:* For master's and doctorate, GRE General Test. Additional exam requirements/recommendations for international students: Required—TOEFL. Electronic applications accepted. *Faculty research:* Urban-economics, GIS, physical-environmental.

University of Colorado at Boulder, Graduate School, College of Arts and Sciences, Department of Geography, Boulder, CO 80309. Offers MA, PhD. Part-time programs available. *Faculty:* 21 full-time (6 women). *Students:* 57 full-time (25 women), 16 part-time (5 women); includes 1 minority (Asian American or Pacific Islander), 12 international. Average age 31. 135 applicants, 12% accepted, 16 enrolled. In 2009, 10 master's, 2 doctorates awarded. Terminal master's awarded for partial completion of doctoral program. *Degree requirements:* For master's, thesis; for doctorate, one foreign language, comprehensive exam, thesis/dissertation. *Entrance requirements:* For master's, GRE General Test, minimum undergraduate GPA of 3.0; for doctorate, GRE General Test. *Application deadline:* For fall admission, 1/15 priority date for domestic students, 12/1 for international students. Application fee: $50 ($60 for international students). *Financial support:* In 2009–10, 19 fellowships (averaging $11,176 per year), 14 research assistantships with tuition reimbursements (averaging $15,971 per year) were awarded. Financial award application deadline: 1/15. *Faculty research:* Physical geography, human geography, environmental society relations, technical geography, GIS and cartography. Total annual research expenditures: $28.4 million.

University of Colorado at Colorado Springs, Graduate School, College of Letters, Arts and Sciences, Department of Geography and Environmental Studies, Colorado Springs, CO 80933-7150. Offers MA. Part-time programs available. *Faculty:* 11 full-time (2 women), 1 part-time/adjunct (0 women). *Students:* 11 full-time (2 women), 6 part-time (2 women); includes 1 minority (Hispanic American). Average age 36. 13 applicants, 85% accepted, 8 enrolled. In 2009, 3 master's awarded. *Degree requirements:* For master's, thesis (for some programs). *Entrance requirements:* For master's, GRE. *Application deadline:* For fall admission, 4/1 for domestic students. Application fee: $60. *Expenses:* Tuition, state resident: full-time $8922; part-time $639 per credit hour. Tuition, nonresident: full-time $19,372; part-time $1154 per credit hour. Tuition and fees vary according to course level, course load, degree level, program, reciprocity agreements and student level. *Financial support:* Federal Work-Study and scholarships/grants available. Support available to part-time students. Financial award application deadline: 3/1; financial award applicants required to submit FAFSA. *Faculty research:* Natural hazard mitigation and policy issues, applied geography, geographic information systems, population geography. *Unit head:* Dr. Robert Larkin, Associate Professor, 719-255-4053, Fax: 719-255-4066, E-mail: rlarkin@uccs.edu. *Application contact:* Mary McGill, Program Assistant, 719-255-3016, E-mail: mmcgill@uccs.edu.

University of Connecticut, Graduate School, College of Liberal Arts and Sciences, Department of Geography, Storrs, CT 06269. Offers geographic information systems (Certificate); geography (MS, PhD). *Faculty:* 13 full-time (5 women). *Students:* 25 full-time (2 women), 12 part-time (4 women); includes 4 minority (3 Asian Americans or Pacific Islanders, 1 Hispanic American), 6 international. Average age 30. 35 applicants, 29% accepted, 6 enrolled. In 2009, 3 master's, 1 doctorate, 5 other advanced degrees awarded. *Degree requirements:* For master's, comprehensive exam; for doctorate, thesis/dissertation. *Entrance requirements:* For master's and doctorate, GRE General Test. Additional exam requirements/recommendations for international students: Required—TOEFL (minimum score 550 paper-based; 213 computer-based). *Application deadline:* For fall admission, 2/1 priority date for domestic and international students; for spring admission, 11/1 for domestic students, 10/1 for international students. Applications are processed on a rolling basis. Application fee: $55. Electronic applications accepted. *Expenses:* Tuition, state resident: full-time $4725; part-time $525 per credit. Tuition, nonresident: full-time $12,267; part-time $1363 per credit. Required fees: $346 per semester. Tuition and fees vary according to course load. *Financial support:* In 2009–10, 5 research assistantships with full tuition reimbursements, 16 teaching assistantships with full tuition reimbursements were awarded; fellowships, Federal Work-Study, scholarships/grants, health care benefits, and unspecified assistantships also available. Financial award application deadline: 2/1; financial award applicants required to submit FAFSA. *Unit head:* Jeffrey Osleeb, Head, 860-486-6977, Fax: 860-486-1348, E-mail: jeffrey.osleeb@uconn.edu. *Application contact:* Dean Hanink, Interim Graduate Program Director, 860-486-3450, Fax: 860-486-1348, E-mail: dean.hanink@uconn.edu.

University of Delaware, College of Arts and Sciences, Department of Geography, Newark, DE 19716. Offers climatology (PhD); geography (MA, MS). *Degree requirements:* For master's, thesis; for doctorate, thesis/dissertation. *Entrance requirements:* For master's and doctorate, GRE General Test. Additional exam requirements/recommendations for international students: Required—TOEFL. Electronic applications accepted. *Faculty research:* Permafrost, Glaciers, Climatology, Physical Geography, Human Geography.

University of Denver, Faculty of Natural Sciences and Mathematics, Department of Geography, Denver, CO 80208. Offers MA, MS, PhD. Part-time programs available. *Faculty:* 12 full-time (4 women), 1 part-time/adjunct (0 women). *Students:* 11 full-time (3 women), 36 part-time (14 women); includes 1 minority (Asian American or Pacific Islander), 3 international. Average age 33. 52 applicants, 77% accepted, 22 enrolled. In 2009, 8 master's awarded. Terminal master's awarded for partial completion of doctoral program. *Degree requirements:* For master's, thesis or alternative; for doctorate, one foreign language, thesis/dissertation. *Entrance requirements:* For master's, GRE General Test; for doctorate, GRE General Test, MA. Additional exam requirements/recommendations for international students: Required—TOEFL. *Application deadline:* Applications are processed on a rolling basis. Application fee: $50. Electronic applications accepted. *Expenses:* Tuition: Full-time $34,596; part-time $961 per quarter hour. Required fees: $4 per quarter hour. Tuition and fees vary according to course load, campus/location and program. *Financial support:* In 2009–10, 14 teaching assistantships with full and partial tuition reimbursements (averaging $17,000 per year) were awarded; research assistantships with full and partial tuition reimbursements, career-related internships or fieldwork, Federal Work-Study, institutionally sponsored loans, and scholarships/grants also available. Support available to part-time students. Financial award application deadline: 3/1; financial award applicants required to submit FAFSA. *Faculty research:* Transportation and land use, fluvial geography and water resources, climatology, geographic information systems, biogeography. Total annual research expenditures: $158,000. *Unit head:* Dr. Andrew Goetz, Chair, 303-871-2201. *Application contact:* Information Contact, 303-871-2201, E-mail: kescobar@du.edu.

University of Florida, Graduate School, College of Liberal Arts and Sciences, Department of Geography, Gainesville, FL 32611. Offers MA, MS, PhD. *Degree requirements:* For master's, variable foreign language requirement, thesis (for some programs); for doctorate, thesis/dissertation. *Entrance requirements:* For master's and doctorate, GRE General Test, minimum GPA of 3.0. Additional exam requirements/recommendations for international students: Required—TOEFL (minimum score 550 paper-based; 213 computer-based). Electronic applications accepted. *Faculty research:* Economic development, physical geography, hydrology, climatology, tropical agriculture.

University of Georgia, Graduate School, College of Arts and Sciences, Department of Geography, Athens, GA 30602. Offers MA, MS, PhD. *Faculty:* 21 full-time (7 women), 1 part-time/adjunct (0 women). *Students:* 47 full-time (17 women), 13 part-time (6 women); includes 4 minority (2 African Americans, 2 Asian Americans or Pacific Islanders), 12 international. 60 applicants, 53% accepted, 13 enrolled. In 2009, 12 master's, 4 doctorates awarded. *Degree requirements:* For master's, one foreign language, thesis; for doctorate, one foreign language, thesis/dissertation. *Entrance requirements:* For master's and doctorate, GRE General

Test. *Application deadline:* For fall admission, 7/1 priority date for domestic students; for spring admission, 11/15 for domestic students. Application fee: $50. Electronic applications accepted. *Expenses:* Tuition, state resident: full-time $6000; part-time $250 per credit hour. Tuition, nonresident: full-time $20,904; part-time $871 per credit hour. Required fees: $730 per semester. *Financial support:* Fellowships, research assistantships, teaching assistantships, unspecified assistantships available. *Unit head:* Dr. George A. Brook, Head, 706-542-2322, Fax: 706-542-2388, E-mail: gabrook@uga.edu. *Application contact:* Dr. David S. Leigh, Graduate Coordinator, 706-542-2346, E-mail: dleigh@uga.edu.

University of Guelph, Graduate Program Services, College of Social and Applied Human Sciences, Department of Geography, Guelph, ON N1G 2W1, Canada. Offers M Sc, MA, PhD. Part-time programs available. *Degree requirements:* For master's, thesis (for some programs); for doctorate, comprehensive exam, thesis/dissertation. *Entrance requirements:* For master's, minimum B average during previous 2 years of course work; for doctorate, minimum A-average. Additional exam requirements/recommendations for international students: Required—TOEFL (minimum score 550 paper-based; 213 computer-based). Electronic applications accepted. *Faculty research:* Rural resource evaluation, environmental analysis, biophysical process, rural settlement and land use, resource assessment.

University of Hawaii at Manoa, Graduate Division, College of Social Sciences, Department of Geography, Honolulu, HI 96822. Offers geography (MA, PhD); ocean policy (Graduate Certificate). Part-time programs available. *Faculty:* 19 full-time (5 women), 10 part-time/adjunct (3 women). *Students:* 45 full-time (18 women), 7 part-time (3 women); includes 10 minority (9 Asian Americans or Pacific Islanders, 1 Hispanic American), 13 international. Average age 31. 34 applicants, 38% accepted, 12 enrolled. In 2009, 7 master's, 3 doctorates awarded. *Degree requirements:* For master's, one foreign language, comprehensive exam, thesis; for doctorate, one foreign language, comprehensive exam, thesis/dissertation. *Entrance requirements:* For master's, GRE General Test; for doctorate, GRE General Test, sample of written work. Additional exam requirements/recommendations for international students: Required—TOEFL (minimum score 500 paper-based; 173 computer-based; 61 iBT), IELTS (minimum score 5). *Application deadline:* For fall admission, 1/15 for domestic and international students. Applications are processed on a rolling basis. Application fee: $60. *Expenses:* Tuition, state resident: full-time $8900; part-time $372 per credit. Tuition, nonresident: full-time $21,400; part-time $898 per credit. Required fees: $207 per semester. *Financial support:* In 2009–10, 1 student received support, including 7 fellowships (averaging $2,157 per year), 11 research assistantships (averaging $18,670 per year), 9 teaching assistantships (averaging $15,505 per year); career-related internships or fieldwork, Federal Work-Study, institutionally sponsored loans, and tuition waivers (full) also available. Financial award application deadline: 3/1. *Faculty research:* Physical geography, human geography, methodology. Total annual research expenditures: $740,000. *Application contact:* Matthew McGranaghan, Graduate Chair, 808-956-8465, Fax: 808-956-3512, E-mail: matt@hawaii.edu.

University of Idaho, College of Graduate Studies, College of Science, Department of Geography, Moscow, ID 83844-2282. Offers geography (MS, PhD). *Faculty:* 8 full-time, 2 part-time/adjunct. *Students:* 17 full-time, 5 part-time. In 2009, 2 master's, 4 doctorates awarded. *Degree requirements:* For doctorate, one foreign language, thesis/dissertation. *Entrance requirements:* For master's, minimum GPA of 2.8; for doctorate, minimum undergraduate GPA of 2.8, graduate 3.0. *Application deadline:* For fall admission, 8/1 for domestic students; for spring admission, 12/15 for domestic students. Application fee: $55 ($60 for international students). *Expenses:* Tuition, state resident: full-time $6120. Tuition, nonresident: full-time $17,712. *Financial support:* Research assistantships, teaching assistantships available. Financial award application deadline: 2/15. *Faculty research:* Land cover land use changes, rural development, geographic trade models, climate change and effects on ecosystems, migration and regional development. *Unit head:* Dr. Harley E. Johansen, Head, 208-885-6216. *Application contact:* Dr. Harley E. Johansen, Head, 208-885-6216.

University of Illinois at Chicago, Graduate College, College of Liberal Arts and Sciences, Department of Anthropology, Program in Environmental and Urban Geography, Chicago, IL 60607-7128. Offers environmental studies (MA); urban geography (MA). Part-time programs available. *Degree requirements:* For master's, thesis. *Entrance requirements:* For master's, GRE General Test, minimum GPA of 2.75. Additional exam requirements/recommendations for international students: Required—TOEFL. Electronic applications accepted.

University of Illinois at Urbana–Champaign, Graduate College, College of Liberal Arts and Sciences, School of Earth, Society and Environment, Department of Geography, Champaign, IL 61820. Offers MA, MS, PhD. *Faculty:* 14 full-time (2 women), 1 part-time/adjunct (0 women). *Students:* 26 full-time (11 women), 14 part-time (4 women); includes 4 minority (1 African American, 2 Asian Americans or Pacific Islanders, 1 Hispanic American), 12 international. 51 applicants, 20% accepted, 9 enrolled. In 2009, 6 master's awarded. *Entrance requirements:* For master's, GRE, minimum GPA of 3.0; for doctorate, GRE, minimum GPA of 3.5. Additional exam requirements/recommendations for international students: Required—TOEFL. *Application deadline:* Applications are processed on a rolling basis. Application fee: $60 ($75 for international students). Electronic applications accepted. *Financial support:* In 2009–10, 14 fellowships, 12 research assistantships, 16 teaching assistantships were awarded; tuition waivers (full and partial) also available. *Unit head:* Bruce Rhoads, Head, 217-333-1322, Fax: 217-244-1785, E-mail: brhoads@illinois.edu. *Application contact:* Susan Etter, Office Support Specialist, 217-244-3488, Fax: 217-244-1785, E-mail: etter1@illinois.edu.

The University of Iowa, Graduate College, College of Liberal Arts and Sciences, Department of Geography, Iowa City, IA 52242-1316. Offers MA, PhD. *Degree requirements:* For master's, thesis optional, exam; for doctorate, comprehensive exam, thesis/dissertation. *Entrance requirements:* For master's and doctorate, GRE General Test, minimum GPA of 3.0. Additional exam requirements/recommendations for international students: Required—TOEFL (minimum score 550 paper-based; 213 computer-based; 81 iBT). Electronic applications accepted.

The University of Kansas, Graduate Studies, College of Liberal Arts and Sciences, Department of Geography, Lawrence, KS 66045-7613. Offers atmospheric science (MS); geography (MA, PhD); MUP/MA. Part-time programs available. *Students:* 74 full-time (27 women), 16 part-time (2 women); includes 4 minority (1 African American, 3 American Indian/Alaska Native), 13 international. Average age 32. 58 applicants, 59% accepted, 15 enrolled. In 2009, 10 master's, 6 doctorates awarded. *Degree requirements:* For master's, comprehensive exam, thesis, thesis defense; for doctorate, one foreign language, comprehensive exam, thesis/dissertation, dissertation defense. *Entrance requirements:* For master's, GRE General Test, 3 letters of reference; for doctorate, GRE General Test, 3 letters of reference, transcripts, statement of interests. Additional exam requirements/recommendations for international students: Required—TOEFL. *Application deadline:* For fall admission, 1/15 for domestic students, 1/15 priority date for international students; for spring admission, 11/1 for domestic students, 10/1 for international students. Applications are processed on a rolling basis. Application fee: $45 ($55 for international students). Electronic applications accepted. *Expenses:* Tuition, state resident: full-time $6492; part-time $270.50 per credit hour. Tuition, nonresident: full-time $15,510; part-time $646.25 per credit hour. Required fees: $847; $70.56 per credit hour. Tuition and fees vary according to course load and program. *Financial support:* Fellowships with full tuition reimbursements, research assistantships with full tuition reimbursements, teaching assistantships with full and partial tuition reimbursements, unspecified assistantships available. Financial award application deadline: 1/15. *Faculty research:* Physical geography, techniques (cartography, GIS, remote sensing), cultural/regional geography, atmospheric science. *Unit head:* Terry Slocum, Chair, 785-864-5146, Fax: 785-864-5378, E-mail: t-slocum@ku.edu. *Application contact:* Stephen Egbert, Graduate Director, 785-864-4252, Fax: 785-864-5378, E-mail: s-egbert@ku.edu.

University of Kentucky, Graduate School, College of Arts and Sciences, Program in Geography, Lexington, KY 40506-0032. Offers MA, PhD. *Degree requirements:* For master's, comprehensive exam, thesis optional; for doctorate, one foreign language, comprehensive exam, thesis/dissertation. *Entrance requirements:* For master's, GRE General Test, minimum undergraduate GPA of 2.75; for doctorate, GRE General Test, minimum graduate GPA of 3.0. Additional exam requirements/recommendations for international students: Required—TOEFL (minimum score 550 paper-based; 213 computer-based). Electronic applications accepted. *Faculty research:* Cultural, industrial, medical, political, social, population, and transportation geography; geographic analysis; Third World (especially Southeast Asia theory); Eastern Europe.

University of Lethbridge, School of Graduate Studies, Lethbridge, AB T1K 3M4, Canada. Offers accounting (MScM); addictions counseling (M Sc); agricultural biotechnology (M Sc); agricultural studies (M Sc, MA); anthropology (MA); archaeology (MA); art (MA, MFA); biochemistry (M Sc); biological sciences (M Sc); biomolecular science (PhD); biosystems and biodiversity (PhD); Canadian studies (MA); chemistry (M Sc); computer science (M Sc); computer science and geographical information science (M Sc); counseling psychology (M Ed); dramatic arts (MA); earth, space, and physical science (PhD); economics (MA); educational leadership (M Ed); English (MA); environmental science (M Sc); evolution and behavior (PhD); exercise science (M Sc); finance (MScM); French (MA); French/German (MA); French/Spanish (MA); general education (M Ed); general management (MScM); geography (M Sc, MA); German (MA); health science (M Sc); health sciences (MA); history (MA); human resource management and labour relations (MScM); individualized multidisciplinary (M Sc, MA); information systems (MScM); international management (MScM); kinesiology (M Sc, MA); management (M Sc, MA); marketing (MScM); mathematics (M Sc); music (M Mus, MA); Native American studies (MA); neuroscience (M Sc, PhD); new media (MA); nursing (M Sc); philosophy (MA); physics (M Sc); policy and strategy (MScM); political science (MA); psychology (M Sc, MA); religious studies (MA); social sciences (MA); sociology (MA); theatre and dramatic arts (MFA); theoretical and computational science (PhD); urban and regional studies (MA); women's studies (MA). Part-time and evening/weekend programs available. *Degree requirements:* For doctorate, comprehensive exam, thesis/dissertation. *Entrance requirements:* For master's, GMAT (M Sc in management), bachelor's degree in related field, minimum GPA of 3.0 during previous 20 graded semester courses, 2 years teaching or related experience (M Ed); for doctorate, master's degree, minimum graduate GPA of 3.5. Additional exam requirements/recommendations for international students: Required—TOEFL. *Faculty research:* Movement and brain plasticity, gibberellin physiology, photosynthesis, carbon cycling, molecular properties of main-group ring components.

University of Louisville, Graduate School, College of Arts and Sciences, Department of Geography and Geosciences, Louisville, KY 40292-0001. Offers applied geography (MS). *Students:* 2 full-time (0 women), 4 part-time (2 women). Average age 35. 7 applicants, 86% accepted, 6 enrolled. *Unit head:* Dr. Keith R. Mountain, Chair, 502-852-2692, E-mail: krmoun01@gwise.louisville.edu. *Application contact:* Libby Leggett, Director, Graduate Admissions, 502-852-3101, Fax: 502-852-6536, E-mail: gradadm@louisville.edu.

University of Manitoba, Faculty of Graduate Studies, Clayton H. Riddell Faculty of Environment, Earth, and Resources, Department of Environment and Geography, Winnipeg, MB R3T 2N2, Canada. Offers environment (M Env); environment and geography (M Sc); geography (MA, PhD). *Degree requirements:* For master's, thesis; for doctorate, one foreign language, thesis/dissertation.

University of Maryland, Baltimore County, Graduate School, College of Arts, Humanities and Social Sciences, Department of Geography and Environmental Systems, Program in Geography and Environmental Systems, Baltimore, MD 21250. Offers MS, PhD. *Faculty:* 11 full-time (4 women), 6 part-time/adjunct (1 woman). *Students:* 18 full-time (12 women), 4 part-time (3 women); includes 2 African Americans, 1 Asian American or Pacific Islander, 2 international. Average age 32. 32 applicants, 28% accepted, 7 enrolled.Terminal master's awarded for partial completion of doctoral program. *Degree requirements:* For master's, thesis optional, annual faculty evaluation, research paper; for doctorate, comprehensive exam, thesis/dissertation, annual faculty evaluation, qualifying exams, proposal and dissertation defense. *Entrance requirements:* For master's and doctorate, GRE, minimum GPA of 3.0 overall, 3.3 in major. Additional exam requirements/recommendations for international students: Required—TOEFL (minimum score 550 paper-based; 213 computer-based; 80 iBT). *Application deadline:* For fall admission, 2/1 for domestic and international students. Application fee: $50. Electronic applications accepted. *Financial support:* In 2009–10, 15 students received support, including 1 fellowship with full tuition reimbursement available (averaging $30,000 per year), 8 research assistantships with full tuition reimbursements available (averaging $18,392 per year), 6 teaching assistantships with full tuition reimbursements available (averaging $18,392 per year); scholarships/grants, traineeships, and unspecified assistantships also available. Financial award application deadline: 2/1. *Faculty research:* Watershed processes, climate and weather systems; ecology and biogeography; landscape ecology and land-use change; human geography, urban sustainability and environmental health; environmental policy; geographic information science and remote sensing. *Unit head:* Dr. Christopher M. Swan, Graduate Program Director, 410-455-2002, E-mail: gpd.ges@umbc.edu. *Application contact:* Kathryn Nee, Coordinator of Domestic Admissions, 410-455-2944, E-mail: nee@umbc.edu.

University of Maryland, College Park, Academic Affairs, College of Behavioral and Social Sciences, Department of Geography, College Park, MD 20742. Offers MA, PhD, MA/MLS. Part-time and evening/weekend programs available. *Faculty:* 44 full-time (14 women), 5 part-time/adjunct (3 women). *Students:* 70 full-time (32 women), 6 part-time (4 women); includes 14 minority (6 African Americans, 5 Asian Americans or Pacific Islanders, 3 Hispanic Americans), 23 international. 61 applicants, 38% accepted, 18 enrolled. In 2009, 4 master's, 4 doctorates awarded. Terminal master's awarded for partial completion of doctoral program. *Degree requirements:* For master's, thesis, oral exam; for doctorate, comprehensive exam, thesis/dissertation. *Entrance requirements:* For master's, GRE General Test, minimum GPA of 3.0, 3 letters of recommendation; for doctorate, GRE General Test. Additional exam requirements/recommendations for international students: Required—TOEFL, TWE. *Application deadline:* For fall admission, 1/15 for domestic students, 2/1 for international students. Applications are processed on a rolling basis. Application fee: $60. Electronic applications accepted. *Expenses:* Tuition, area resident: Part-time $471 per credit hour. Tuition, state resident: part-time $471 per credit hour. Tuition, nonresident: part-time $1016 per credit hour. Required fees: $337.04 per term. *Financial support:* In 2009–10, 8 fellowships with full and partial tuition reimbursements (averaging $18,403 per year), 12 research assistantships with tuition reimbursements (averaging $16,983 per year), 42 teaching assistantships with tuition reimbursements (averaging $16,559 per year) were awarded; Federal Work-Study and scholarships/grants also available. Support available to part-time students. Financial award applicants required to submit FAFSA. *Faculty research:* Cartography and automated mapping, environmental systems analysis, metropolitan analysis and planning, historical and human geography, coastal geomorphology. Total annual research expenditures: $6.6 million. *Unit head:* Sam Goward, Interim Chair, 301-405-4050, Fax: 301-314-9299, E-mail: sgoward@umd.edu. *Application contact:* Dean of Graduate School, 301-405-0358, Fax: 301-314-9305.

University of Maryland, College Park, Academic Affairs, Program in Geography, Library, and Information Services, College Park, MD 20742. Offers MA/MLS. *Application deadline:* For fall admission, 1/15 for domestic and international students. Applications are processed on a rolling basis. Application fee: $60. Electronic applications accepted. *Expenses:* Tuition, area resident: Part-time $471 per credit hour. Tuition, state resident: part-time $471 per credit hour. Tuition, nonresident: part-time $1016 per credit hour. Required fees: $337.04 per term. *Financial support:* Fellowships, research assistantships, teaching assistantships available. Financial award application deadline: 2/1; financial award applicants required to submit FAFSA. *Unit head:* Dr. Diane Barlow, Associate Dean, 301-405-2042, Fax: 301-314-9145, E-mail: dbarlow@umd.edu. *Application contact:* Dean of Graduate School, 301-405-0376, Fax: 301-314-9305.

University of Massachusetts Amherst, Graduate School, College of Natural Sciences, Department of Geosciences, Program in Geography, Amherst, MA 01003. Offers MS. Part-time programs available. *Students:* 7 full-time (3 women), 3 part-time (1 woman); includes 2 minority (1 American Indian/Alaska Native, 1 Hispanic American), 1 international. Average age 35. 18 applicants, 56% accepted, 5 enrolled. In 2009, 3 master's awarded. *Degree requirements:*

Geography

University of Massachusetts Amherst (continued)

For master's, thesis optional. *Entrance requirements:* For master's, GRE General Test. Additional exam requirements/recommendations for international students: Required—TOEFL (minimum score 550 paper-based; 213 computer-based; 80 iBT), IELTS (minimum score 6.5). *Application deadline:* For fall admission, 2/1 for domestic and international students; for spring admission, 10/1 for domestic and international students. Applications are processed on a rolling basis. Application fee: $50 ($65 for international students). Electronic applications accepted. *Expenses:* Tuition, state resident: full-time $2640; part-time $110 per credit. Tuition, nonresident: full-time $9936; part-time $414 per credit. Tuition and fees vary according to course load. *Financial support:* Fellowships, research assistantships, teaching assistantships, career-related internships or fieldwork, Federal Work-Study, scholarships/grants, traineeships, health care benefits, tuition waivers (full), and unspecified assistantships available. Support available to part-time students. Financial award application deadline: 2/1. *Unit head:* Dr. Piper R. Gaubatz, Graduate Program Director, 413-545-2286, Fax: 413-545-1200. *Application contact:* Jean M. Ames, Supervisor of Admissions, 413-545-0722, Fax: 413-577-0010, E-mail: gradadm@grad.umass.edu.

University of Miami, Graduate School, College of Arts and Sciences, Department of Geography and Regional Studies, Coral Gables, FL 33124. Offers geography (MA). Part-time programs available. *Degree requirements:* For master's, thesis. *Entrance requirements:* For master's, GRE, 3 letters of recommendation, official transcripts. Additional exam requirements/recommendations for international students: Required—TOEFL. Electronic applications accepted. *Faculty research:* Urbanization, globalization, environmental change.

University of Missouri, Graduate School, College of Arts and Sciences, Department of Geography, Columbia, MO 65211. Offers MA. *Faculty:* 12 full-time (3 women). *Students:* 11 full-time (8 women), 4 part-time (2 women), 3 international. Average age 27. 18 applicants, 56% accepted, 5 enrolled. In 2009, 3 master's awarded. *Entrance requirements:* For master's, GRE General Test (minimum score 1000 verbal and quantitative), minimum GPA of 3.0. Additional exam requirements/recommendations for international students: Required—TOEFL (minimum score 500 paper-based; 173 computer-based; 61 iBT). *Application deadline:* For fall admission, 2/15 priority date for domestic students; for winter admission, 10/1 priority date for domestic students; for spring admission, 4/1 priority date for domestic students. Applications are processed on a rolling basis. Application fee: $45 ($60 for international students). Electronic applications accepted. *Financial support:* In 2009–10, 3 fellowships with full tuition reimbursements, 2 research assistantships with full tuition reimbursements, 6 teaching assistantships with full tuition reimbursements were awarded; institutionally sponsored loans, health care benefits, and unspecified assistantships also available. *Unit head:* Dr. Joseph Hobbs, Department Chair, E-mail: hobbsj@missouri.edu. *Application contact:* Dina Weaver, 573-882-8370, E-mail: weaverdr@missouri.edu.

The University of Montana, Graduate School, College of Arts and Sciences, Department of Geography, Missoula, MT 59812-0002. Offers geography (MA), including cartography and GIS, community and environmental planning. *Entrance requirements:* For master's, GRE General Test. Additional exam requirements/recommendations for international students: Required—TOEFL.

University of Nebraska at Omaha, Graduate Studies, College of Arts and Sciences, Department of Geography and Geology, Omaha, NE 68182. Offers geographic information science (Certificate); geography (MA). Part-time programs available. *Faculty:* 11 full-time (3 women). *Students:* 5 full-time (1 woman), 15 part-time (4 women); includes 2 minority (both African Americans), 4 international. Average age 37. 24 applicants, 63% accepted, 10 enrolled. In 2009, 8 master's, 5 other advanced degrees awarded. *Degree requirements:* For master's, comprehensive exam, thesis (for some programs). *Entrance requirements:* For master's, GRE, minimum GPA of 3.0, 15 undergraduate geography hours, resume. Additional exam requirements/recommendations for international students: Required—TOEFL (minimum score 550 paper-based; 213 computer-based; 80 iBT). *Application deadline:* For fall admission, 3/1 priority date for domestic students; for spring admission, 12/1 priority date for domestic students. Applications are processed on a rolling basis. Application fee: $45. Electronic applications accepted. *Financial support:* In 2009–10, 12 students received support; fellowships, research assistantships with tuition reimbursements available, teaching assistantships with tuition reimbursements available, Federal Work-Study, institutionally sponsored loans, scholarships/grants, tuition waivers (partial), and unspecified assistantships available. Support available to part-time students. Financial award application deadline: 3/1; financial award applicants required to submit FAFSA. *Unit head:* Dr. Jeffrey Peake, Chairperson, 402-554-2662. *Application contact:* Penny Harmoney, Director, Graduate Studies, 402-554-2341, Fax: 402-554-3143, E-mail: graduate@unomaha.edu.

University of Nebraska–Lincoln, Graduate College, College of Arts and Sciences, Department of Anthropology and Geography, Program in Geography, Lincoln, NE 68588. Offers MA, PhD. *Degree requirements:* For master's, thesis optional; for doctorate, comprehensive exam, thesis/dissertation. *Entrance requirements:* For master's and doctorate, GRE General Test. Additional exam requirements/recommendations for international students: Required—TOEFL (minimum score 550 paper-based; 213 computer-based). Electronic applications accepted. *Faculty research:* Climatology, historical-cultural geography, geographic information systems/cartography/remote sensing, human geography, Great Plains studies.

University of Nevada, Reno, Graduate School, College of Science, Mackay School of Earth Sciences and Engineering, Department of Geography, Program in Geography, Reno, NV 89557. Offers MS, PhD. Terminal master's awarded for partial completion of doctoral program. *Degree requirements:* For master's, comprehensive exam, thesis; for doctorate, comprehensive exam, thesis/dissertation. *Entrance requirements:* For master's and doctorate, GRE General Test, minimum GPA of 2.75. Additional exam requirements/recommendations for international students: Required—TOEFL (minimum score 500 paper-based; 173 computer-based; 61 iBT), IELTS (minimum score 6). Electronic applications accepted. *Faculty research:* Natural resources, education, climatology, biogeography, ethnic/cultural geography.

University of New Mexico, Graduate School, College of Arts and Sciences, Department of Geography, Albuquerque, NM 87131-2039. Offers MS. Part-time programs available. *Faculty:* 7 full-time (2 women), 1 (woman) part-time/adjunct. *Students:* 7 full-time (4 women), 5 part-time (1 woman); includes 2 minority (both Hispanic Americans). Average age 33. 8 applicants, 63% accepted, 4 enrolled. In 2009, 4 master's awarded. *Degree requirements:* For master's, comprehensive exam (for some programs), thesis (for some programs). *Entrance requirements:* For master's, GRE. Additional exam requirements/recommendations for international students: Required—TOEFL. *Application deadline:* For fall admission, 2/1 priority date for domestic students, 1/1 priority date for international students; for spring admission, 11/15 for domestic and international students. Application fee: $50. Electronic applications accepted. *Expenses:* Tuition, state resident: full-time $2099; part-time $233.20 per credit hour. Tuition, nonresident: full-time $6650. Required fees: $25 per semester. Tuition and fees vary according to course load, program and reciprocity agreements. *Financial support:* In 2009–10, 3 students received support, including 3 research assistantships with full tuition reimbursements available (averaging $14,000 per year), 3 teaching assistantships with full tuition reimbursements available (averaging $14,000 per year); health care benefits and tuition waivers (full and partial) also available. Financial award applicants required to submit FAFSA. *Faculty research:* Geographic information science, environmental management. Total annual research expenditures: $94,525. *Unit head:* Dr. Richard P. Santos, Interim Chair, 505-277-5041, Fax: 505-277-3614, E-mail: santos@unm.edu. *Application contact:* Dr. Jazmin Knight, Department Administrator, 505-277-5041, Fax: 505-277-3614, E-mail: jkknight@unm.edu.

University of New Orleans, Graduate School, College of Liberal Arts, Department of Geography, New Orleans, LA 70148. Offers MA. *Entrance requirements:* For master's, GRE General Test. Additional exam requirements/recommendations for international students: Required—TOEFL (minimum score 550 paper-based; 213 computer-based; 79 iBT). Electronic applications accepted.

The University of North Carolina at Chapel Hill, Graduate School, College of Arts and Sciences, Department of Geography, Chapel Hill, NC 27599. Offers MA, PhD. *Degree requirements:* For master's, one foreign language, comprehensive exam, thesis; for doctorate, 2 foreign languages, comprehensive exam, thesis/dissertation. *Entrance requirements:* For master's and doctorate, GRE General Test, minimum GPA of 3.0. *Faculty research:* Geographic information systems, climatology, hydrology, population research, Latino immigration.

The University of North Carolina at Charlotte, Graduate School, College of Arts and Sciences, Department of Geography and Earth Sciences, Charlotte, NC 28223-0001. Offers earth sciences (MS), including climatology and hydrology, environmental systems analysis, solid earth sciences; geography (MA), including community planning, location analysis, transportation studies, urban regional analysis; geography and urban and regional analysis (PhD). Part-time and evening/weekend programs available. *Faculty:* 25 full-time (8 women), 1 part-time/adjunct (0 women). *Students:* 40 full-time (20 women), 30 part-time (10 women); includes 3 African Americans, 17 international. Average age 29. 27 applicants, 78% accepted, 11 enrolled. In 2009, 11 master's awarded. *Degree requirements:* For master's, comprehensive exam, project. *Entrance requirements:* For master's, GRE General Test or MAT, Doppelt Mathematical Reasoning Test, minimum GPA of 3.0 in undergraduate major, 2.75 overall. Additional exam requirements/recommendations for international students: Required—TOEFL (minimum score 557 paper-based; 220 computer-based; 83 iBT). *Application deadline:* For fall admission, 7/1 for domestic students, 5/1 for international students; for spring admission, 11/1 for domestic students, 10/1 for international students. Applications are processed on a rolling basis. Application fee: $55. Electronic applications accepted. *Financial support:* In 2009–10, 29 students received support, including 1 fellowship (averaging $12,251 per year), 11 research assistantships (averaging $12,385 per year), 17 teaching assistantships (averaging $7,748 per year); career-related internships or fieldwork, institutionally sponsored loans, scholarships/grants, and unspecified assistantships also available. Support available to part-time students. Financial award application deadline: 4/1; financial award applicants required to submit FAFSA. *Faculty research:* Location analysis, applications of GIS technology, community planning and development, regional economic modeling, retail geography. Total annual research expenditures: $720,387. *Unit head:* Dr. Harrison Campbell, Graduate Coordinator, 704-687-5997, Fax: 704-687-3182, E-mail: hscampbe@uncc.edu. *Application contact:* Kathy B. Giddings, Director of Graduate Admissions, 704-687-5503, Fax: 704-687-3279, E-mail: gradadm@uncc.edu.

The University of North Carolina at Greensboro, Graduate School, College of Arts and Sciences, Department of Geography, Greensboro, NC 27412-5001. Offers applied geography (MA); geographic information science (Certificate); geography (PhD); urban and economic development (Certificate). *Degree requirements:* For master's, comprehensive exam, thesis or alternative. *Entrance requirements:* For master's, GRE General Test. Additional exam requirements/recommendations for international students: Required—TOEFL. Electronic applications accepted.

University of North Dakota, Graduate School, College of Arts and Sciences, Department of Geography, Grand Forks, ND 58202. Offers MA, MS. Part-time programs available. *Degree requirements:* For master's, comprehensive exam, thesis or alternative. *Entrance requirements:* For master's, minimum GPA of 3.0. Additional exam requirements/recommendations for international students: Required—TOEFL (minimum score 550 paper-based; 213 computer-based; 79 iBT), IELTS (minimum score 6.5). Electronic applications accepted. *Faculty research:* Regional and urban development, environmental geography, geographic education, geographic techniques.

University of Northern Iowa, Graduate College, College of Social and Behavioral Sciences, Department of Geography, Cedar Falls, IA 50614. Offers MA. Part-time programs available. *Students:* 8 full-time (2 women), 6 part-time (3 women); includes 2 minority (both African Americans), 5 international. 16 applicants, 69% accepted, 5 enrolled. In 2009, 4 master's awarded. *Degree requirements:* For master's, thesis or alternative. *Entrance requirements:* For master's, minimum GPA of 3.0; 2 letters of recommendation; brief statement about professional interests and career objectives. Additional exam requirements/recommendations for international students: Required—TOEFL (minimum score 500 paper-based; 180 computer-based; 61 iBT). *Application deadline:* For fall admission, 8/1 priority date for domestic students. Applications are processed on a rolling basis. Application fee: $30 ($50 for international students). Electronic applications accepted. *Financial support:* Career-related internships or fieldwork, Federal Work-Study, scholarships/grants, and tuition waivers (full and partial) available. Support available to part-time students. Financial award application deadline: 2/1. *Unit head:* Dr. Patrick P. Pease, Department Head/Associate Professor, 319-273-2772, Fax: 319-273-7103, E-mail: patrick.pease@uni.edu. *Application contact:* Laurie S. Russell, Record Analyst, 319-273-2623, Fax: 319-273-6792, E-mail: laurie.russell@uni.edu.

University of North Texas, Robert B. Toulouse School of Graduate Studies, College of Arts and Sciences, Department of Geography, Denton, TX 76203. Offers MS. Part-time programs available. *Degree requirements:* For master's, comprehensive exam (for some programs), thesis (for some programs). *Entrance requirements:* For master's, GRE General Test, BA/BS. Additional exam requirements/recommendations for international students: Required—proof of English language proficiency required for non-native English speakers; Recommended—TOEFL (minimum score 550 paper-based; 213 computer-based; 79 iBT). Application fee: $50 ($75 for international students). Electronic applications accepted. *Expenses:* Tuition, state resident: full-time $4298; part-time $239 per contact hour. Tuition, nonresident: full-time $9878; part-time $549 per contact hour. Required fees: $265 per contact hour. *Financial support:* Fellowships with full and partial tuition reimbursements, teaching assistantships, career-related internships or fieldwork, health care benefits, and tuition waivers (partial) available. Financial award application deadline: 4/15; financial award applicants required to submit FAFSA. *Faculty research:* Environmental monitoring and modeling, health and economic geography, environmental archaeology. Total annual research expenditures: $800,000. *Application contact:* Graduate Adviser/Coordinator, 940-565-2721, Fax: 940-369-7550.

University of Oklahoma, Graduate College, College of Atmospheric and Geographic Sciences, Department of Geography, Norman, OK 73019. Offers MA, PhD. Part-time programs available. *Faculty:* 13 full-time (2 women), 2 part-time/adjunct (1 woman). *Students:* 26 full-time (13 women), 13 part-time (3 women); includes 2 minority (both American Indian/Alaska Native), 11 international. 20 applicants, 65% accepted, 9 enrolled. In 2009, 6 master's, 3 doctorates awarded. Terminal master's awarded for partial completion of doctoral program. *Degree requirements:* For master's, thesis, oral and written exams; for doctorate, one foreign language, thesis/dissertation, general exams. *Entrance requirements:* For master's, GRE, minimum GPA of 3.0, writing sample, 3 letters of recommendation. Additional exam requirements/recommendations for international students: Required—TOEFL (minimum score 550 paper-based; 213 computer-based). *Application deadline:* For fall admission, 2/1 for domestic students, 4/1 for international students; for spring admission, 12/1 for domestic students, 9/1 for international students. Applications are processed on a rolling basis. Application fee: $40 ($90 for international students). Electronic applications accepted. *Expenses:* Tuition, state resident: full-time $3744; part-time $156 per credit hour. Tuition, nonresident: full-time $13,577; part-time $565.70 per credit hour. Required fees: $2415; $90.10 per credit hour. *Financial support:* In 2009–10, 32 students received support, including 5 fellowships with full tuition reimbursements available (averaging $5,000 per year), 14 teaching assistantships with partial tuition reimbursements available (averaging $14,845 per year); career-related internships or fieldwork, Federal Work-Study, scholarships/grants, health care benefits, and unspecified assistantships also available. Financial award application deadline: 2/1; financial award applicants required to submit FAFSA. *Faculty research:* Renewable energy, sustainability, and environmental policy; hydroclimatic variability, landscape change, and fluvial process; natural hazards and response; Latin America (environment and social movements); indigenous peoples, colonialism, and post-colonialism. Total annual research expenditures: $573,944. *Unit head:* Aondover Tarhule, Acting Chair, 405-325-5325, Fax: 405-325-6090, E-mail: atarhule@ou.edu. *Application contact:* Dr. Karl Offen, Associate Professor/Graduate Liaison, 405-325-3912, Fax: 405-325-6090, E-mail: koffen@ou.edu.

University of Oregon, Graduate School, College of Arts and Sciences, Department of Geography, Eugene, OR 97403. Offers MA, MS, PhD. *Degree requirements:* For master's, one foreign language, thesis; for doctorate, one foreign language, thesis/dissertation. *Entrance requirements:* For master's and doctorate, GRE General Test, minimum GPA of 3.0. Additional exam requirements/recommendations for international students: Required—TOEFL. *Faculty research:* Place-name research, past climates, quaternary environments, plant diffusions, population redistributions.

University of Ottawa, Faculty of Graduate and Postdoctoral Studies, Faculty of Arts, Department of Geography, Ottawa, ON K1N 6N5, Canada. Offers M Geog, M Sc, MA, PhD. *Degree requirements:* For master's, one foreign language, thesis; for doctorate, one foreign language, comprehensive exam, thesis/dissertation. *Entrance requirements:* For master's, honors degree or equivalent, minimum B average; for doctorate, master's degree, minimum B+ average. Electronic applications accepted. *Faculty research:* The physical geography of cold environment; space, place and society, environmental change.

University of Prince Edward Island, Faculty of Arts, Charlottetown, PE C1A 4P3, Canada. Offers island studies (MA). Part-time programs available. *Degree requirements:* For master's, thesis. *Entrance requirements:* Additional exam requirements/recommendations for international students: Required—TOEFL (minimum score 550 paper-based; 213 computer-based; 80 iBT), Canadian Academic English Language Assessment, Michigan English Language Assessment Battery, Canadian Test of English for Scholars and Trainees. *Faculty research:* International island studies.

University of Regina, Faculty of Graduate Studies and Research, Faculty of Arts, Department of Geography, Regina, SK S4S 0A2, Canada. Offers M Sc, MA, PhD. *Faculty:* 12 full-time (3 women), 2 part-time/adjunct (both women). *Students:* 4 full-time (2 women), 2 part-time (both women). 11 applicants, 64% accepted. *Degree requirements:* For master's, thesis. *Entrance requirements:* Additional exam requirements/recommendations for international students: Required—TOEFL (minimum score 580 paper-based; 237 computer-based; 80 iBT). *Application deadline:* Applications are processed on a rolling basis. Application fee: $90 ($100 for international students). Electronic applications accepted. *Financial support:* In 2009–10, 1 fellowship (averaging $19,000 per year), 1 research assistantship (averaging $16,910 per year), 1 teaching assistantship (averaging $6,650 per year) were awarded; scholarships/grants also available. Financial award application deadline: 6/15. *Faculty research:* Cultural, historical, economic, rural, and urban geography; cartography; resource management; hydrology. *Unit head:* Dr. Bernard Thraves, Graduate Program Coordinator, 306-585-4104, E-mail: bernard.thraves@uregina.ca. *Application contact:* Dr. Joe Piwowar, Graduate Program Coordinator, 306-585-5273, E-mail: joe.piwowar@uregina.ca.

University of Saskatchewan, College of Graduate Studies and Research, College of Arts and Sciences, Department of Geography, Saskatoon, SK S7N 5A2, Canada. Offers M Sc, MA, PhD. *Faculty:* 26. *Students:* 48. In 2009, 4 master's, 3 doctorates awarded. *Degree requirements:* For master's, thesis; for doctorate, comprehensive exam (for some programs), thesis/dissertation. *Entrance requirements:* Additional exam requirements/recommendations for international students: Required—TOEFL (minimum score 80 iBT); Recommended—IELTS (minimum score 6.5). *Application deadline:* For fall admission, 7/1 priority date for domestic students. Applications are processed on a rolling basis. Application fee: $75. Electronic applications accepted. Tuition and fees charges are reported in Canadian dollars. *Expenses:* Tuition, area resident: Full-time $3000 Canadian dollars; part-time $500 Canadian dollars per term. Required fees: $700 Canadian dollars; $100 Canadian dollars per term. *Financial support:* Fellowships, research assistantships, teaching assistantships available. Financial award application deadline: 1/31. *Unit head:* Dr. Alec Aitken, Acting Head, 306-966-5671, Fax: 306-966-5680, E-mail: archibald@sask.usask.ca. *Application contact:* Dr. Bram Nobel, Graduate Chair, 306-966-5656, Fax: 306-966-5680, E-mail: bram.nobel@usask.ca.

University of South Africa, College of Agriculture and Environmental Sciences, Pretoria, South Africa. Offers agriculture (MS); consumer science (MCS); environmental management (MA, MS, PhD); environmental science (MA, MS, PhD); geography (MA, MS, PhD); horticulture (M Tech); human ecology (MHE); life sciences (MS); nature conservation (M Tech).

University of South Carolina, The Graduate School, College of Arts and Sciences, Department of Geography, Columbia, SC 29208. Offers geography (MA, MS, PhD); geography education (IMA). IMA and MAT offered in cooperation with the College of Education. Part-time programs available. *Degree requirements:* For master's, comprehensive exam, thesis (for some programs); for doctorate, comprehensive exam, thesis/dissertation. *Entrance requirements:* For master's, GRE General Test; for doctorate, GRE General Test, master's degree. Electronic applications accepted. *Faculty research:* Geographic information processing; economic, cultural, physical, and environmental geography.

University of Southern California, Graduate School, College of Letters, Arts and Sciences, Department of Geography, Los Angeles, CA 90089. Offers geographic information science and technology (MS, Graduate Certificate); geography (PhD). Part-time programs available. Postbaccalaureate distance learning degree programs offered (minimal on-campus study). *Faculty:* 3 full-time (0 women), 5 part-time/adjunct (2 women). *Students:* 29 full-time (14 women), 9 part-time (1 woman); includes 9 minority (1 African American, 3 American Indian/Alaska Native, 2 Asian Americans or Pacific Islanders, 3 Hispanic Americans), 7 international. 4 applicants, 100% accepted, 3 enrolled. In 2009, 3 doctorates, 22 other advanced degrees awarded. Terminal master's awarded for partial completion of doctoral program. *Degree requirements:* For master's, thesis; for doctorate, thesis/dissertation. *Entrance requirements:* For master's and doctorate, GRE. Additional exam requirements/recommendations for international students: Required—TOEFL (minimum score 600 paper-based; 250 computer-based; 100 iBT). *Application deadline:* Applications are processed on a rolling basis. Application fee: $85. Electronic applications accepted. *Expenses:* Tuition: Full-time $25,980; part-time $1315 per unit. Required fees: $554. One-time fee: $35 full-time. Full-time tuition and fees vary according to degree level and program. *Financial support:* In 2009–10, 18 students received support, including 9 fellowships with full tuition reimbursements available (averaging $19,715 per year), 1 research assistantship with full tuition reimbursement available (averaging $18,800 per year), 8 teaching assistantships with full tuition reimbursements available (averaging $18,800 per year); health care benefits and unspecified assistantships also available. *Faculty research:* Public heath, environmental modeling, natural hazards, landscape dynamics, geomorphology, geographic information science, urban geography and nature-society relations, GIS. *Unit head:* Dr. John P. Wilson, Chair, 213-740-1908, E-mail: jpwilson@usc.edu. *Application contact:* Kate A. Kelsey, Student Program Advisor, 213-740-8298, Fax: 213-740-0056, E-mail: kkelsey@usc.edu.

University of Southern Mississippi, Graduate School, College of Science and Technology, Department of Geography and Geology, Hattiesburg, MS 39406-0001. Offers geography (MS, PhD); geology (MS). Part-time programs available. *Faculty:* 11 full-time (2 women), 1 part-time/adjunct (0 women). *Students:* 16 full-time (7 women), 15 part-time (3 women); includes 1 minority (African American). Average age 34. 9 applicants, 89% accepted, 7 enrolled. In 2009, 2 master's awarded. *Degree requirements:* For master's, comprehensive exam, thesis (for some programs), internships; for doctorate, comprehensive exam, thesis/dissertation. *Entrance requirements:* For master's, GMAT, GRE General Test, minimum GPA of 3.0. Additional exam requirements/recommendations for international students: Required—TOEFL. *Application deadline:* For fall admission, 3/15 for domestic and international students; for spring admission, 1/3 for domestic students. Applications are processed on a rolling basis. Application fee: $35. Electronic applications accepted. *Expenses:* Tuition, state resident: full-time $5096; part-time $284 per hour. Tuition, nonresident: full-time $13,052; part-time $726 per hour. Required fees: $402. Tuition and fees vary according to course level and course load. *Financial support:* In 2009–10, 1 research assistantship with tuition reimbursement (averaging $18,000 per year), 8 teaching assistantships with full tuition reimbursements (averaging $8,632 per year) were awarded; fellowships with full tuition reimbursements, career-related internships or fieldwork, Federal Work-Study, and institutionally sponsored loans also available. Financial award application deadline: 3/15; financial award applicants required to submit FAFSA. *Faculty research:* City and regional planning, geographic techniques, physical geography, human geography. *Unit head:* Dr. Clifton Dixon, Chair, 601-266-4729, Fax: 601-266-6219, E-mail: c.dixon@usm.edu. *Application contact:* Dr. Gail Russell, Graduate Coordinator, 601-266-6519, Fax: 601-266-6219.

University of South Florida, Graduate School, College of Arts and Sciences, Department of Geography, Tampa, FL 33620-9951. Offers MA, PhD. Part-time and evening/weekend programs available. *Faculty:* 18 full-time (6 women). *Students:* 15 full-time (7 women), 12 part-time (4 women); includes 5 minority (2 African Americans, 1 Asian American or Pacific Islander, 2 Hispanic Americans). Average age 32. 54 applicants, 46% accepted, 18 enrolled. In 2009, 8 master's awarded. *Degree requirements:* For master's, comprehensive exam, thesis; for doctorate, comprehensive exam, thesis/dissertation. *Entrance requirements:* For master's, GRE General Test, minimum GPA of 3.0 in last 60 hours of course work. Additional exam requirements/recommendations for international students: Required—TOEFL (minimum score 550 paper-based; 213 computer-based). *Application deadline:* For fall admission, 2/15 for domestic students, 1/2 for international students; for spring admission, 10/15 for domestic students, 6/1 for international students. Application fee: $30. *Financial support:* In 2009–10, teaching assistantships with tuition reimbursements (averaging $23,269 per year); unspecified assistantships also available. Financial award application deadline: 3/1. *Faculty research:* Natural hazards, geographic information systems models, soil contamination, urban geography and social theory. Total annual research expenditures: $70,617. *Unit head:* Dr. Robert Brinkmann, Associate Professor/Chair, 813-974-4939, Fax: 813-974-4808, E-mail: rbrinkmann@cas.usf.edu. *Application contact:* Philip Van Beynen, Program Director, 813-974-3026, Fax: 813-974-4808, E-mail: vanbeynen@cas.usf.edu.

The University of Tennessee, Graduate School, College of Arts and Sciences, Department of Geography, Knoxville, TN 37996. Offers MS, PhD. *Degree requirements:* For master's, thesis or alternative; for doctorate, thesis/dissertation. *Entrance requirements:* For master's and doctorate, GRE General Test, minimum GPA of 2.7. Additional exam requirements/recommendations for international students: Required—TOEFL. Electronic applications accepted. *Expenses:* Tuition, state resident: full-time $6826; part-time $380 per semester hour. Tuition, nonresident: full-time $21,844; part-time $1147 per semester hour. Tuition and fees vary according to program.

The University of Texas at Austin, Graduate School, College of Liberal Arts, Department of Geography and the Environment, Austin, TX 78712-1111. Offers MA, PhD, MSCRP/PhD. *Degree requirements:* For master's, thesis or alternative; for doctorate, thesis/dissertation. *Entrance requirements:* For master's and doctorate, GRE General Test. Additional exam requirements/recommendations for international students: Required—TOEFL. Electronic applications accepted. *Faculty research:* Cultural and historical geography, environmental and physical geography, human-environment interactions, electronic technology and hypermedia, international area studies.

The University of Toledo, College of Graduate Studies, College of Arts and Sciences, Department of Geography and Planning, Toledo, OH 43606-3390. Offers geographic information systems and applied geographics (Certificate); geography (MA); planning (MA). Part-time programs available. *Degree requirements:* For master's, thesis. *Entrance requirements:* For master's, GRE General Test. Electronic applications accepted.

University of Toronto, School of Graduate Studies, Social Sciences Division, Department of Geography, Toronto, ON M5S 1A1, Canada. Offers geography (M Sc, MA, PhD); planning (M Sc Pl); urban design studies (MUD). Part-time programs available. *Degree requirements:* For master's, thesis optional; for doctorate, thesis/dissertation. *Entrance requirements:* For master's, bachelor's degree or equivalent in geography or a closely related field, minimum B+ average in each of 2 final years of degree, 3 letters of reference; for doctorate, master of geography degree, minimum A–average.

University of Utah, The Graduate School, College of Social and Behavioral Science, Department of Geography, Salt Lake City, UT 84112-9155. Offers MA, MS, PhD. Part-time programs available. *Faculty:* 12 full-time (3 women), 2 part-time/adjunct (both women). *Students:* 25 full-time (13 women), 25 part-time (11 women); includes 3 minority (1 Asian American or Pacific Islander, 2 Hispanic Americans), 14 international. Average age 34. 54 applicants, 43% accepted, 10 enrolled. In 2009, 7 master's, 1 doctorate awarded. *Degree requirements:* For master's, variable foreign language requirement, thesis or alternative, 6 research hours; for doctorate, comprehensive exam, thesis/dissertation, 14 research hours. *Entrance requirements:* For master's and doctorate, GRE General Test, minimum undergraduate GPA of 3.0. Additional exam requirements/recommendations for international students: Required—TOEFL (minimum score 500 paper-based; 173 computer-based; 61 iBT), IELTS (minimum score 5). *Application deadline:* For fall admission, 1/20 priority date for domestic students, 1/20 for international students. Application fee: $55 ($65 for international students). Electronic applications accepted. *Expenses:* Tuition, state resident: full-time $4004; part-time $1674 per semester. Tuition, nonresident: full-time $14,134; part-time $5915 per semester. Required fees: $324 per semester. Tuition and fees vary according to course load, degree level and program. *Financial support:* In 2009–10, 27 students received support, including 2 fellowships with full tuition reimbursements available (averaging $24,000 per year), 9 research assistantships with full tuition reimbursements available (averaging $11,000 per year), 12 teaching assistantships with full tuition reimbursements available (averaging $11,000 per year); career-related internships or fieldwork, Federal Work-Study, scholarships/grants, health care benefits, and unspecified assistantships also available. Financial award application deadline: 2/15; financial award applicants required to submit FAFSA. *Faculty research:* Urban geography, earth system science, geographic information systems, remote sensing, hazards. Total annual research expenditures: $831,298. *Unit head:* Dr. George F. Hepner, Chair, 801-581-8218, Fax: 801-581-8219, E-mail: george.hepner@geog.utah.edu. *Application contact:* Dr. Philip E. Dennison, Director of Graduate Studies, 801-581-8218, Fax: 801-581-8219, E-mail: dennison@geog.utah.edu.

University of Victoria, Faculty of Graduate Studies, Faculty of Social Sciences, Department of Geography, Victoria, BC V8W 2Y2, Canada. Offers M Sc, MA, PhD. Part-time programs available. *Degree requirements:* For master's, thesis; for doctorate, comprehensive exam, thesis/dissertation, candidacy exam. *Entrance requirements:* For master's, minimum B+ average in undergraduate course work; for doctorate, master's degree. Additional exam requirements/recommendations for international students: Required—TOEFL (minimum score 575 paper-based; 233 computer-based), IELTS (minimum score 7). Electronic applications accepted. *Faculty research:* Resources and protected areas, remote sensing and forestry, geographic information systems and cartography, urban regional planning, physical climatology.

University of Washington, Graduate School, College of Arts and Sciences, Department of Geography, Seattle, WA 98195. Offers MA, PhD. *Degree requirements:* For master's, thesis; for doctorate, thesis/dissertation. *Entrance requirements:* For master's and doctorate, GRE General Test. Additional exam requirements/recommendations for international students: Required—TOEFL. Electronic applications accepted. *Faculty research:* Globalization and social theory, nature and society, regional economic development, urban patterns and processes, geographic information systems.

University of Waterloo, Graduate Studies, Faculty of Environmental Studies, Department of Geography, Waterloo, ON N2L 3G1, Canada. Offers MA, PhD. *Degree requirements:* For master's, thesis optional; for doctorate, one foreign language, comprehensive exam, thesis/dissertation. *Entrance requirements:* For master's, honors degree, minimum B average; for

Geography

University of Waterloo (continued)
doctorate, master's degree, minimum A- average. Additional exam requirements/ recommendations for international students: Required—TOEFL, TWE. Electronic applications accepted. *Faculty research:* Urban economic geography; physical geography; resource management; cultural, regional, historical geography; spatial data.

The University of Western Ontario, Faculty of Graduate Studies, Social Sciences Division, Department of Geography, London, ON N6A 5B8, Canada. Offers M Sc, MA, PhD. *Degree requirements:* For master's, thesis; for doctorate, thesis/dissertation. *Entrance requirements:* For master's, GRE, honors degree, minimum B average; for doctorate, honors degree, minimum B average. Additional exam requirements/recommendations for international students: Required—TOEFL.

University of Wisconsin–Madison, Graduate School, College of Letters and Science, Department of Geography, Madison, WI 53706-1380. Offers cartography and geographic information systems (MS); geographic information systems (Certificate); geography (MS, PhD). Part-time programs available. *Degree requirements:* For master's, thesis; for doctorate, thesis/ dissertation; for Certificate, internship. *Entrance requirements:* For master's and doctorate, GRE General Test, minimum GPA of 3.25. Electronic applications accepted. *Expenses:* Tuition, state resident: part-time $594 per credit. Tuition, nonresident: part-time $1504 per credit. Required fees: $65 per credit. Tuition and fees vary according to course load, program and reciprocity agreements. *Faculty research:* Physical geography, urban/historical geography, people-environment, history of cartography, GIS.

University of Wisconsin–Milwaukee, Graduate School, College of Letters and Sciences, Department of Geography, Milwaukee, WI 53201-0413. Offers MA, MS, PhD, MLIS/MA. *Faculty:* 13 full-time (6 women). *Students:* 15 full-time (8 women), 13 part-time (6 women); includes 3 minority (2 Asian Americans or Pacific Islanders, 1 Hispanic American), 10 international. Average age 30. 32 applicants, 44% accepted, 6 enrolled. In 2009, 3 master's, 4 doctorates awarded. *Degree requirements:* For master's, comprehensive exam, thesis; for doctorate, thesis/dissertation. *Entrance requirements:* For master's and doctorate, GRE. Additional exam requirements/recommendations for international students: Required—TOEFL (minimum score 550 paper-based; 79 iBT), IELTS (minimum score 6.5). *Application deadline:* For fall admission, 1/1 priority date for domestic students; for spring admission, 9/1 for domestic students. Applications are processed on a rolling basis. Application fee: $45 ($75 for international students). *Expenses:* Tuition, state resident: full-time $8800. Tuition, nonresident: full-time $20,760. Tuition and fees vary according to program and reciprocity agreements. *Financial support:* In 2009–10, 2 research assistantships, 17 teaching assistantships were awarded; career-related internships or fieldwork and unspecified assistantships also available. Support available to part-time students. Financial award application deadline: 4/15. Total annual research expenditures: $209,958. *Unit head:* Rina Ghose, Representative, 414-229-4797, Fax: 414-229-3981, E-mail: rghose@uwm.edu. *Application contact:* General Information Contact, 414-229-4982, Fax: 414-229-6967, E-mail: gradschool@uwm.edu.

University of Wyoming, College of Arts and Sciences, Department of Geography, Laramie, WY 82070. Offers geography (MA, MP, MST); geography/water resources (MA); rural planning and natural resources (MP), including community and regional planning and natural resources. Postbaccalaureate distance learning degree programs offered (minimal on-campus study). *Degree requirements:* For master's, thesis optional. *Entrance requirements:* For master's, GRE General Test, minimum GPA of 3.0. Additional exam requirements/recommendations for international students: Required—TOEFL. Electronic applications accepted. *Faculty research:* Landscape ecology, landscape change, public land management, rural and small town planning, GIS.

Utah State University, School of Graduate Studies, College of Natural Resources, Department of Environment and Society, Logan, UT 84322. Offers bioregional planning (MS); geography (MA, MS); human dimensions of ecosystem science and management (MS, PhD); recreation resource management (MS, PhD). *Degree requirements:* For master's, comprehensive exam, thesis (for some programs). *Entrance requirements:* For master's and doctorate, GRE General Test, minimum GPA of 3.0. Additional exam requirements/recommendations for international students: Required—TOEFL. Electronic applications accepted. *Faculty research:* Geographic information systems/geographic and environmental education, bioregional planning, natural resource and environmental policy, outdoor recreation and tourism, natural resource and environmental management.

Virginia Polytechnic Institute and State University, Graduate School, College of Natural Resources, Department of Geography, Blacksburg, VA 24061. Offers MS, PhD. *Faculty:* 9 full-time (4 women), 1 part-time/adjunct (0 women). *Students:* 12 full-time (9 women), 4 part-time (1 woman); includes 2 minority (both American Indian/Alaska Native). Average age 29. 15 applicants, 53% accepted, 6 enrolled. In 2009, 11 master's awarded. *Entrance requirements:* For master's and doctorate, GRE, GMAT. Additional exam requirements/ recommendations for international students: Required—TOEFL (minimum score 550 paper-based; 213 computer-based). *Application deadline:* For fall admission, 5/15 for international students; for spring admission, 10/15 for international students. Applications are processed on a rolling basis. Application fee: $65. Electronic applications accepted. *Expenses:* Tuition, area resident: Full-time $10,228; part-time $459 per credit hour. Tuition, nonresident: full-time $17,892; part-time $865 per credit hour. Required fees: $1966; $451 per semester. *Financial support:* In 2009–10, 1 research assistantship with full tuition reimbursement (averaging $7,662 per year), 7 teaching assistantships with full tuition reimbursements (averaging $14,086 per year) were awarded; career-related internships or fieldwork, Federal Work-Study, scholarships/grants, and unspecified assistantships also available. Financial award application deadline: 1/15. *Faculty research:* Third World development, geographical information systems, remote sensing, critical geopolitics, medical geography. Total annual research expenditures: $93,158. *Unit head:* Dr. Laurence W. Carstensen, Dean, 540-231-5116, Fax: 540-231-2089, E-mail: carstens@vt.edu. *Application contact:* Karen Bland, Information Contact, 540-231-6886, Fax: 540-231-2089.

Wayne State University, College of Liberal Arts and Sciences, Department of Geography and Urban Planning, Detroit, MI 48202. Offers geography (MA); urban planning (MUP). Evening/ weekend programs available. *Entrance requirements:* For master's, minimum 3.0 GPA, 2 letters of recommendation. Additional exam requirements/recommendations for international students: Required—TOEFL (minimum score 550 paper-based; 213 computer-based); Recommended—TWE (minimum score 6). Electronic applications accepted. *Faculty research:* Housing and community development, urban and regional economic development, urban development and land use, transportation policy and planning, environmental policy and planning.

Wayne State University, College of Liberal Arts and Sciences, Program in Geography, Detroit, MI 48202. Offers MA. *Entrance requirements:* For master's, GRE General Test. Additional exam requirements/recommendations for international students: Required—TOEFL (minimum score 550 paper-based; 213 computer-based); Recommended—TWE (minimum score 6). Electronic applications accepted.

West Chester University of Pennsylvania, Office of Graduate Studies, College of Business and Public Affairs, Department of Geography and Planning, West Chester, PA 19383. Offers geographic technology (Certificate); geography (MA); regional planning (MSA). Part-time and evening/weekend programs available. *Students:* 3 full-time (0 women), 27 part-time (9 women); includes 5 minority (3 African Americans, 1 Asian American or Pacific Islander, 1 Hispanic American), 1 international. Average age 28. 13 applicants, 100% accepted, 9 enrolled. In 2009, 11 master's, 5 other advanced degrees awarded. *Degree requirements:* For master's, comprehensive exam, thesis optional. *Entrance requirements:* For master's, GRE, GMAT, or MAT, minimum GPA of 2.8, resume, two letters of recommendation; for Certificate, minimum GPA of 2.8, resume, two letters of recommendation. Additional exam requirements/ recommendations for international students: Required—TOEFL (minimum score 550 paper-based; 213 computer-based; 80 iBT). *Application deadline:* For fall admission, 4/15 priority date for domestic students, 3/15 for international students; for spring admission, 10/15 for domestic students, 9/1 for international students. Applications are processed on a rolling basis. Application fee: $35. Electronic applications accepted. *Expenses:* Tuition, state resident: full-time $6666; part-time $370 per credit. Tuition, nonresident: full-time $10,666; part-time $593 per credit. Required fees: $122.56 per credit. *Financial support:* In 2009–10, 6 research assistantships with full and partial tuition reimbursements (averaging $5,000 per year) were awarded; unspecified assistantships also available. Support available to part-time students. Financial award application deadline: 2/15; financial award applicants required to submit FAFSA. *Faculty research:* Environmental education, land use/suburban planning, landscapes of Catalunya. *Unit head:* Dr. Joan Welch, Chair and Graduate Coordinator, 610-436-2940, E-mail: jwelch@wcupa.edu. *Application contact:* Dr. Dottie Ives Dewey, MSA Graduate Coordinator, 610-436-2746, E-mail: divesdewey@wcupa.edu.

Western Illinois University, School of Graduate Studies, College of Arts and Sciences, Department of Geography, Macomb, IL 61455-1390. Offers community development (Certificate); environmental GIS (Certificate); geography (MA). Part-time programs available. *Students:* 13 full-time (5 women), 5 part-time (2 women); includes 3 minority (1 African American, 2 Asian Americans or Pacific Islanders), 2 international. Average age 32. 9 applicants, 67% accepted. In 2009, 9 master's, 7 other advanced degrees awarded. *Degree requirements:* For master's, thesis or alternative. *Entrance requirements:* Additional exam requirements/recommendations for international students: Required—TOEFL (minimum score 550 paper-based; 213 computer-based; 80 iBT). *Application deadline:* Applications are processed on a rolling basis. Application fee: $30. Electronic applications accepted. *Expenses:* Tuition, state resident: full-time $4486; part-time $249.21 per credit hour. Tuition, nonresident: full-time $8972; part-time $498.42 per credit hour. Required fees: $72.62 per credit hour. *Financial support:* In 2009–10, 9 students received support, including 9 research assistantships with full tuition reimbursements available (averaging $7,280 per year). Financial award applicants required to submit FAFSA. *Unit head:* Dr. Sam Thompson, Chairperson, 309-298-1648. *Application contact:* Evelyn Hoing, Assistant Director of Graduate Studies, 309-298-1806, Fax: 309-298-2345, E-mail: grad-office@wiu.edu.

Western Kentucky University, Graduate Studies, Ogden College of Science and Engineering, Department of Geography and Geology, Bowling Green, KY 42101. Offers MAE, MS. *Degree requirements:* For master's, comprehensive exam, thesis or alternative. *Entrance requirements:* For master's, GRE General Test, minimum GPA of 2.75. Additional exam requirements/ recommendations for international students: Required—TOEFL (minimum score 555 paper-based; 213 computer-based; 79 iBT). *Expenses:* Tuition, state resident: full-time $4160; part-time $416 per credit hour. Tuition, nonresident: full-time $9550; part-time $506 per credit hour. Tuition and fees vary according to campus/location and reciprocity agreements. *Faculty research:* Hydroclimatology, electronic data sets, groundwater, sinkhole liquification potential, meteorological analysis.

Western Michigan University, Graduate College, College of Arts and Sciences, Department of Geography, Kalamazoo, MI 49008. Offers geographic information science (Graduate Certificate); geography (MA). *Degree requirements:* For master's, thesis, internship.

Western Washington University, Graduate School, Huxley College of the Environment, Department of Environmental Studies, Program in Geography, Bellingham, WA 98225-5996. Offers MS. *Entrance requirements:* Additional exam requirements/recommendations for international students: Required—TOEFL (minimum score 567 paper-based; 227 computer-based). Electronic applications accepted.

West Virginia University, Eberly College of Arts and Sciences, Department of Geology and Geography, Program in Geography, Morgantown, WV 26506. Offers energy and environmental resources (MA); geographic information systems (PhD); geography-regional development (PhD); GIS/cartographic analysis (MA); regional development (MA). Part-time programs available. *Degree requirements:* For master's, thesis, oral and written exams; for doctorate, comprehensive exam, thesis/dissertation, oral and written exams. *Entrance requirements:* For master's and doctorate, GRE General Test, minimum GPA of 3.0. Additional exam requirements/ recommendations for international students: Required—TOEFL. Electronic applications accepted. *Faculty research:* Space, place and development, geographic information science, environmental geography.

Wilfrid Laurier University, Faculty of Graduate Studies, Faculty of Arts, Department of Geography and Environmental Studies, Waterloo, ON N2L 3C5, Canada. Offers M Sc, MA, MES, PhD. *Degree requirements:* For master's, thesis optional; for doctorate, thesis/dissertation. *Entrance requirements:* For master's, honors BA in geography, minimum B average in undergraduate course work; honors BSc with minimum B+ or honors BES or BA in physical geography, environmental or earth sciences or the equivalent; for doctorate, MA in geography, minimum A-average. Additional exam requirements/recommendations for international students: Required—TOEFL (minimum score 230 computer-based; 89 iBT). Electronic applications accepted. *Faculty research:* Resources management, urban/economic/physical/cultural/earth surfaces/geomatics/historical/regional, spatial data handling.

York University, Faculty of Graduate Studies, Faculty of Arts and Faculty of Science and Engineering, Program in Geography, Toronto, ON M3J 1P3, Canada. Offers M Sc, MA, PhD. Part-time programs available. *Degree requirements:* For master's, thesis or alternative; for doctorate, comprehensive exam, thesis/dissertation. Electronic applications accepted.

Section 22
Military and Defense Studies

This section contains a directory of institutions offering graduate work in military and defense studies, followed by an in-depth entry submitted by an institution that chose to prepare a detailed program description. Additional information about programs listed in the directory but not augmented by an in-depth entry may be obtained by writing directly to the dean of a graduate school or chair of a department at the address given in the directory.

For programs offering related work, see also in this book *History* and *Political Science and International Affairs.*

CONTENTS

Program Directories

Military and Defense Studies 806
National Security 807

Close-Up

Hawai'i Pacific University 809

Military and Defense Studies

American Public University System, AMU/APU Graduate Programs, Charles Town, WV 25414. Offers air warfare (MA Military Studies); American Revolution (MA Military Studies); business administration (MBA); Civil War (MA Military Studies); criminal justice (MA); defense management (MA Military Studies); emergency and disaster management (MA); environmental policy and management (MS); fire science management (MA); global engagement (MA); history (MA); homeland security (MA); humanities (MA); intelligence (MA Military Studies, MA Strategic Intelligence); international peace and conflict resolution (MA); international relations and conflict resolution (MA); joint warfare (MA Military Studies); land warfare international perspective (MA Military Studies); management (MA); military history (MA); military leadership (MA Military Studies); national security studies (MA); naval warfare international (MA Military Studies); naval warfare US (MA Military Studies); political science (MA); public administration (MA); public health (MA); security management (MA); space studies (MS); special ops/LIC (MA Military Studies); sports management (MA); transportation and logistics management (MA); transportation management (MA); unconventional warfare (MA Military Studies); World War II (MA Military Studies). Programs offered via distance learning only. Part-time and evening/weekend programs available. Postbaccalaureate distance learning degree programs offered (no on-campus study). *Faculty:* 10 full-time (3 women), 188 part-time/adjunct (57 women). *Students:* 340 full-time (98 women), 3,567 part-time (790 women); includes 615 minority (317 African Americans, 28 American Indian/Alaska Native, 85 Asian Americans or Pacific Islanders, 185 Hispanic Americans), 20 international. Average age 36. 2,123 applicants, 100% accepted, 893 enrolled. In 2009, 829 degrees awarded. *Degree requirements:* For master's, comprehensive exam. *Entrance requirements:* For master's, bachelor's degree or equivalent, minimum GPA of 2.7 in last 60 hours of course work. *Application deadline:* Applications are processed on a rolling basis. Application fee: $0. Electronic applications accepted. *Financial support:* Applicants required to submit FAFSA. *Faculty research:* Military history, criminal justice, management performance, national security. *Unit head:* Dr. Frank McCluskey, Provost, 877-468-6268, Fax: 304-724-3780. *Application contact:* Terry Grant, Director of Enrollment Management, 877-468-6268, Fax: 304-724-3780, E-mail: info@apus.edu.

Austin Peay State University, College of Graduate Studies, College of Arts and Letters, Department of History and Philosophy, Clarksville, TN 37044. Offers military history (MA). Part-time programs available. Postbaccalaureate distance learning degree programs offered (minimal on-campus study). *Faculty:* 6 full-time (0 women), 4 part-time/adjunct (1 woman). *Students:* 17 full-time (5 women), 27 part-time (4 women); includes 4 minority (1 African American, 3 Asian Americans or Pacific Islanders). Average age 35. 40 applicants, 98% accepted, 18 enrolled. In 2009, 4 master's awarded. *Degree requirements:* For master's, comprehensive exam, thesis optional. *Entrance requirements:* For master's, GRE General Test, minimum undergraduate GPA of 2.75, 3 letters of recommendation, bachelor's degree. Additional exam requirements/recommendations for international students: Required—TOEFL (minimum score 500 paper-based; 173 computer-based). *Application deadline:* For fall admission, 7/27 priority date for domestic students; for spring admission, 12/17 priority date for domestic students. Applications are processed on a rolling basis. Application fee: $25. Electronic applications accepted. *Expenses:* Tuition, state resident: full-time $6160; part-time $608 per credit hour. Tuition, nonresident: full-time $17,080; part-time $854 per credit hour. Required fees: $1224; $61.20 per credit hour. *Financial support:* In 2009–10, 3 students received support, including 3 research assistantships with full tuition reimbursements available (averaging $5,184 per year); career-related internships or fieldwork, Federal Work-Study, institutionally sponsored loans, scholarships/grants, and unspecified assistantships also available. Support available to part-time students. Financial award application deadline: 3/1; financial award applicants required to submit FAFSA. *Unit head:* Dr. Dewey Browder, Chair, 931-221-7919, Fax: 931-221-9917, E-mail: browderd@apsu.edu. *Application contact:* Dr. Dixie Dennis, Dean, College of Graduate Studies, 931-221-7662, Fax: 931-221-7641, E-mail: dennisdi@apsu.edu.

The George Washington University, Elliott School of International Affairs, Program in Security Policy Studies, Washington, DC 20052. Offers MA, JD/MA. Part-time and evening/weekend programs available. *Students:* 63 full-time (24 women), 63 part-time (22 women); includes 18 minority (1 African American, 15 Asian Americans or Pacific Islanders, 2 Hispanic Americans), 5 international. Average age 27. 252 applicants, 49% accepted, 42 enrolled. In 2009, 50 master's awarded. *Degree requirements:* For master's, one foreign language, capstone project. *Entrance requirements:* For master's, GRE General Test, 2 semesters of introductory economics, 2 years of a modern foreign language or 1 semester of statistics. Additional exam requirements/recommendations for international students: Required—TOEFL. *Application deadline:* For fall admission, 2/1 for domestic students; for spring admission, 10/1 for domestic students. Application fee: $60. Electronic applications accepted. *Financial support:* In 2009–10, 22 students received support; fellowships with tuition reimbursements available, research assistantships with tuition reimbursements available, career-related internships or fieldwork, Federal Work-Study, institutionally sponsored loans, and tuition waivers (full) available. Financial award application deadline: 1/15; financial award applicants required to submit FAFSA. *Faculty research:* U. S. arms transfer policies, military balance in the Third World, U. S. foreign policy, technology and security policy. *Unit head:* Joanna Spear, Director, 202-994-1088, E-mail: jspear@gwu.edu. *Application contact:* Jeff V. Miles, Director of Graduate Admissions, 202-994-7050, Fax: 202-994-9537, E-mail: esiagrad@gwu.edu.

Hawai'i Pacific University, College of Humanities and Social Sciences, Program in Diplomacy and Military Studies, Honolulu, HI 96813. Offers MA. *Faculty:* 3 full-time (0 women), 1 part-time/adjunct (0 women). *Students:* 35 full-time (16 women), 52 part-time (17 women); includes 23 minority (4 African Americans, 1 American Indian/Alaska Native, 14 Asian Americans or Pacific Islanders, 4 Hispanic Americans), 8 international. Average age 32. 54 applicants, 93% accepted, 25 enrolled. In 2009, 15 master's awarded. *Expenses:* Tuition: Full-time $12,600; part-time $700 per credit hour. Tuition and fees vary according to program. *Unit head:* Dr. William Potter, Associate Vice President and Dean, 808-544-0228, Fax: 808-544-1424, E-mail: wpotter@hpu.edu. *Application contact:* Danny Lam, Assistant Director of Graduate Admissions, 808-544-1135, Fax: 808-544-0280, E-mail: graduate@hpu.edu.

See Close-Up on page 809.

The Institute of World Politics, Graduate Programs in National Security, Intelligence, and International Affairs, Washington, DC 20036. Offers American foreign policy (Certificate); comparative political culture (Certificate); counterintelligence (Certificate); democracy building (Certificate); intelligence (Certificate); international politics (Certificate); national security affairs (Certificate); public diplomacy and political warfare (Certificate); statecraft and national security affairs (MA); statecraft and world politics (MA); strategic intelligence studies (MA). Part-time and evening/weekend programs available. *Degree requirements:* For master's, comprehensive exam, thesis optional. *Entrance requirements:* For master's, GRE General Test. Additional exam requirements/recommendations for international students: Required—TOEFL. Electronic applications accepted. *Faculty research:* Intelligence, national security, statecraft.

The Johns Hopkins University, School of Education, Division of Public Safety Leadership, Baltimore, MD 21218. Offers intelligence analysis (MS); management (MS). Part-time and evening/weekend programs available. *Faculty:* 10 full-time (3 women), 23 part-time/adjunct (7 women). *Students:* 159 full-time (47 women), 1 part-time (0 women); includes 55 minority (47 African Americans, 1 American Indian/Alaska Native, 3 Asian Americans or Pacific Islanders, 4 Hispanic Americans). Average age 39. 81 applicants, 75% accepted, 54 enrolled. In 2009, 110 master's awarded. *Entrance requirements:* For master's, minimum undergraduate GPA of 3.0, curriculum vitae/resume, interview, professional experience, endorsement letter (MS management). Additional exam requirements/recommendations for international students: Required—TOEFL (minimum score 600 paper-based; 250 computer-based; 100 iBT). *Application deadline:* For fall admission, 5/1 for international students; for spring admission, 10/15 for international students. Applications are processed on a rolling basis. Application fee: $0. Electronic applications accepted. *Financial support:* Scholarships/grants available. Support available to part-time students. Financial award application deadline: 6/1; financial award applicants required to submit FAFSA. *Faculty research:* Campus and school safety, prevention and effective response to violence against women, counterterrorism training, leadership development for public safety and homeland security executives. *Unit head:* Dr. Sheldon Greenberg, Associate Dean, 410-516-9900, Fax: 410-290-1061, E-mail: psl@jhu.edu. *Application contact:* Jennifer Shaffer, Director of Admissions, 410-516-9797, Fax: 410-516-9799, E-mail: educationinfo@jhu.edu.

The Judge Advocate General's School, U.S. Army, Graduate Programs, Charlottesville, VA 22903-1781. Offers military law (LL M). Only active duty military lawyers attend this school. *Accreditation:* ABA. *Degree requirements:* For master's, thesis optional. *Entrance requirements:* For master's, active duty military lawyer, international military officer, or DOD civilian attorney, JD or LL B. *Faculty research:* Criminal law, administrative and civil law, contract law, international law, legal research and writing.

Missouri State University, Graduate College, College of Humanities and Public Affairs, Department of Defense and Strategic Studies, Fairfax, VA 22031. Offers MS. Part-time programs available. *Faculty:* 1 full-time (0 women), 24 part-time/adjunct (1 woman). *Students:* 36 full-time (13 women), 26 part-time (4 women); includes 2 minority (1 Asian American or Pacific Islander, 1 Hispanic American), 1 international. Average age 28. 39 applicants, 97% accepted, 25 enrolled. In 2009, 20 master's awarded. *Degree requirements:* For master's, comprehensive exam, thesis or alternative. *Entrance requirements:* For master's, GRE, minimum GPA of 2.75, 3 letters of recommendation. Additional exam requirements/recommendations for international students: Required—TOEFL (minimum score 550 paper-based; 213 computer-based; 79 iBT). *Application deadline:* For fall admission, 7/20 priority date for domestic students, 5/1 for international students; for spring admission, 12/20 priority date for domestic students, 9/1 for international students. Applications are processed on a rolling basis. Application fee: $35 ($50 for international students). Electronic applications accepted. *Expenses:* Tuition, state resident: full-time $3852; part-time $214 per credit hour. Tuition, nonresident: full-time $7524; part-time $418 per credit hour. Required fees: $696; $172 per semester. Tuition and fees vary according to course level, course load, degree level and program. *Financial support:* Career-related internships or fieldwork, Federal Work-Study, institutionally sponsored loans, and scholarships/grants available. Financial award application deadline: 3/31; financial award applicants required to submit FAFSA. *Faculty research:* Middle East, terrorism, arms control, U.S.-Soviet military balance, Strategic Defense Initiative. *Unit head:* Dr. Keith Payne, Head, 703-218-3565, Fax: 703-218-3568, E-mail: kbpayne@missouristate.edu. *Application contact:* Dr. Keith Payne, Head, 703-218-3565, Fax: 703-218-3568, E-mail: kbpayne@missouristate.edu.

National Defense Intelligence College, Graduate Program, Washington, DC 20340-5100. Offers MSSI. Open only to federal government employees. Part-time and evening/weekend programs available. *Degree requirements:* For master's, thesis. *Entrance requirements:* For master's, MAT, authorized nomination. *Faculty research:* Law and intelligence, intelligence and higher education, low-intensity conflict, intelligence information systems.

National Defense University, Industrial College of the Armed Forces, Washington, DC 20319-5066. Offers national resource strategy (MS). Open only to Department of Defense employees and specific federal agencies. *Degree requirements:* For master's, comprehensive exam. *Entrance requirements:* Additional exam requirements/recommendations for international students: Required—TOEFL. *Faculty research:* Industrial base and relation to national security, acquisition and relation to national security, resourcing the national security strategy.

National Defense University, Joint Advanced Warfighting School, Norfolk, AB 23511. Offers joint campaign planning and strategy (MS). Open only to Department of Defense employees and specific federal agencies. *Degree requirements:* For master's, thesis. *Entrance requirements:* For master's, Phase 1 JPME. *Faculty research:* Irregular warfare, national policy and strategy, international organizations and policies, modern military history and applications of lessons learned, historical military leadership relating to present-day environments.

National Defense University, National War College, Washington, DC 20319-5066. Offers national security strategy (MS). Open only to Department of Defense employees and specific federal agencies. *Degree requirements:* For master's, comprehensive exam. *Entrance requirements:* Additional exam requirements/recommendations for international students: Required—TOEFL. *Faculty research:* National security policy, regional security, US national security strategy, US military, strategy.

Naval Postgraduate School, Graduate Programs, Department of Computer Science, Program in Modeling of Virtual Environments and Simulations, Monterey, CA 93943. Offers MS, PhD. Program only open to commissioned officers of the United States and friendly nations and selected United States federal civilian employees. Part-time programs available. *Degree requirements:* For master's, thesis; for doctorate, one foreign language, thesis/dissertation.

Naval Postgraduate School, Graduate Programs, Department of Defense Analysis, Monterey, CA 93943. Offers defense analysis (MS); joint information operations (MS); special operations (MS). Program only open to commissioned officers of the United States and friendly nations and selected United States federal civilian employees. Part-time programs available. *Degree requirements:* For master's, thesis.

Naval Postgraduate School, Graduate Programs, Program in Undersea Warfare, Monterey, CA 93943. Offers applied science (MS); electrical engineering (MS); engineering acoustics (MS); operations research (MS); physical oceanography (MS). Program only open to commissioned officers of the United States and friendly nations and selected United States federal civilian employees. Part-time programs available. *Degree requirements:* For master's, thesis.

Naval Postgraduate School, Graduate Programs, School of Business and Public Policy, Monterey, CA 93943. Offers contract management (MS); defense-focused business administration (MBA); executive business administration (MBA); leadership and human resource development (MS); management (MS); program management (MS); systems engineering management (MS). Program only open to commissioned officers of the United States and friendly nations and selected United States federal civilian employees. *Accreditation:* AACSB; NASPAA. Part-time programs available. Postbaccalaureate distance learning degree programs offered (minimal on-campus study). *Degree requirements:* For master's, thesis.

Norwich University, School of Graduate and Continuing Studies, Program in Military History, Northfield, VT 05663. Offers race and gender in military history (MA); U. S. military history (MA). Evening/weekend programs available. *Faculty:* 33 part-time/adjunct (2 women). *Students:* 531 full-time (85 women); includes 30 minority (3 African Americans, 6 American Indian/Alaska Native, 6 Asian Americans or Pacific Islanders, 15 Hispanic Americans). Average age 42. 736 applicants, 80% accepted, 531 enrolled. In 2009, 503 master's awarded. *Entrance requirements:* For master's, minimum undergraduate GPA of 2.75. Additional exam requirements/recommendations for international students: Required—TOEFL (minimum score 550 paper-based; 212 computer-based; 83 iBT). *Application deadline:* For fall admission, 8/10 for domestic and international students; for winter admission, 11/7 for domestic and international students; for spring admission, 2/6 for domestic and international students. Application fee: $50. Electronic applications accepted. Full-time tuition and fees vary according to course level and course load. *Financial support:* Scholarships/grants available. Financial award applicants required to submit FAFSA. *Unit head:* Dr. James Erhman, Program Director, 802-485-2567, Fax: 802-485-2533. *Application contact:* Lars Nielsen, Administrative Director, 802-485-2853, Fax: 802-485-2533, E-mail: lnielsen@norwich.edu.

Royal Military College of Canada, Division of Graduate Studies and Research, Continuing Studies, Department of History, Kingston, ON K7K 7B4, Canada. Offers defense management and policy (MA); history (PhD); war studies (MA). *Degree requirements:* For master's, thesis.

Entrance requirements: For master's, honours degree with second-class standing; for doctorate, master's degree. Electronic applications accepted.

School of Advanced Air and Space Studies, Program in Airpower Art and Science, Maxwell AFB, AL 36112-6424. Offers MA. Available to active duty military officers only. *Degree requirements:* For master's, comprehensive exam, thesis. *Entrance requirements:* For master's, less than 16 years total of active commissioned service; master's degree or undergraduate degree with a minimum GPA of 2.75. Additional exam requirements/recommendations for international students: Required—TOEFL. *Faculty research:* Military history, political science, international relations, social history, technology.

United States Army Command and General Staff College, Graduate Program, Fort Leavenworth, KS 66027-2301. Offers military art and science (MMAS). Only career military officers are selected to attend United States Army Command and General Staff College; Graduate Program is voluntary for first-year students, but mandatory for second-year students.

University of Calgary, Faculty of Graduate Studies, Centre for Military and Strategic Studies, Calgary, AB T2N 1N4, Canada. Offers MSS, PhD. PhD offered in special cases only. Part-time programs available. *Degree requirements:* For master's, thesis; for doctorate, comprehensive exam, thesis/dissertation. *Entrance requirements:* For master's, minimum GPA of 3.4. Additional exam requirements/recommendations for international students: Recommended—TOEFL (minimum score 550 paper-based). *Faculty research:* Military history, Israeli studies, strategic studies, int'l relations, Arctic security.

University of Detroit Mercy, College of Liberal Arts and Education, Department of Criminal Justice and Human Services, Detroit, MI 48221. Offers criminal justice (MA); intelligence analysis (MS); security administration (MS).

University of Pittsburgh, Graduate School of Public and International Affairs, International Affairs Division, Pittsburgh, PA 15260. Offers global political economy (MPIA); human security (MPIA); security and intelligence studies (MPIA); JD/MPIA; MBA/MPIA; MID/MPIA; MPA/MPIA; MSIS/MPIA. Part-time and evening/weekend programs available. *Faculty:* 28 full-time (8 women), 56 part-time/adjunct (20 women). *Students:* 125 full-time (52 women), 19 part-time (11 women); includes 17 minority (10 African Americans, 4 Asian Americans or Pacific Islanders, 3 Hispanic Americans), 5 international. Average age 25. 270 applicants, 81% accepted, 79 enrolled. In 2009, 61 master's awarded. *Degree requirements:* For master's, thesis optional, internship, capstone seminar. *Entrance requirements:* For master's, GRE General Test, 3 letters of recommendation, resume, minimum GPA of 3.2. Additional exam requirements/recommendations for international students: Required—TOEFL (minimum score 550 paper-based; 213 computer-based), TWE (minimum score 4); Recommended—IELTS (minimum score 7). *Application deadline:* For fall admission, 3/1 for domestic students, 1/15 for international students; for spring admission, 11/1 for domestic students, 8/1 for international students. Application fee: $50. Electronic applications accepted. *Expenses:* Tuition, state resident: full-time $16,402; part-time $665 per credit. Tuition, nonresident: full-time $28,694; part-time $1175 per credit. Required fees: $690; $175 per term. Tuition and fees vary according to program. *Financial support:* In 2009–10, 45 students received support, including 6 fellowships (averaging $41,800 per year); career-related internships or fieldwork, scholarships/grants, tuition waivers (full and partial), and unspecified assistantships also available. Financial award application deadline: 2/1. *Faculty research:* International political economy, international security and intelligence, transnational organized crime, international trade, international finance, globalization, terrorism, multinational corporations and the global economy. Total annual research expenditures: $357,117. *Unit head:* Dr. Martin Staniland, Director, International Affairs and International Development Divisions, 412-648-7656, Fax: 412-648-2605, E-mail: mstan@pitt.edu. *Application contact:* Kelly C. McDevitt, Graduate Enrollment Counselor, 412-648-7640, Fax: 412-648-7641, E-mail: mcdevitt@pitt.edu.

The University of Texas at El Paso, Graduate School, Institute for Policy and Economic Development, El Paso, TX 79968-0001. Offers border administration (Certificate); homeland security (Certificate); intelligence and national security (MS, Certificate); leadership studies (MA); public administration (MPA). *Accreditation:* NASPAA. Part-time and evening/weekend programs available. *Students:* 187 (57 women); includes 124 minority (19 African Americans, 1 American Indian/Alaska Native, 5 Asian Americans or Pacific Islanders, 99 Hispanic Americans), 5 international. 142 applicants, 77% accepted. In 2009, 76 master's awarded. *Degree requirements:* For master's, thesis optional. *Entrance requirements:* For master's, GRE, Statement of Purpose, Letters of Recommendation. Additional exam requirements/recommendations for international students: Required—TOEFL; Recommended—IELTS. *Application deadline:* For fall admission, 8/1 for domestic students, 3/1 for international students; for spring admission, 10/1 for domestic students, 9/1 for international students. Applications are processed on a rolling basis. Application fee: $45 ($80 for international students). Electronic applications accepted. *Financial support:* Fellowships with partial tuition reimbursements, research assistantships with partial tuition reimbursements, teaching assistantships with partial tuition reimbursements, institutionally sponsored loans, scholarships/grants, health care benefits, tuition waivers (partial), and unspecified assistantships available. Support available to part-time students. Financial award application deadline: 3/15; financial award applicants required to submit FAFSA. *Unit head:* Dr. Dennis Soden, Director, 915-747-7974, Fax: 915-747-7948, E-mail: desoden@utep.edu. *Application contact:* Dr. Patricia D. Witherspoon, Dean of the Graduate School, 915-747-5491, Fax: 915-747-5788, E-mail: withersp@utep.edu.

University of West Florida, College of Arts and Sciences: Arts, Department of History, Pensacola, FL 32514-5750. Offers historic preservation (MA); history (MA); military history (MA); public history (MA). Part-time and evening/weekend programs available. *Faculty:* 5 full-time (1 woman), 1 part-time/adjunct (0 women). *Students:* 14 full-time (6 women), 23 part-time (12 women); includes 5 minority (2 African Americans, 1 American Indian/Alaska Native, 1 Asian American or Pacific Islander, 1 Hispanic American). Average age 31. 26 applicants, 73% accepted, 9 enrolled. In 2009, 10 master's awarded. *Degree requirements:* For master's, thesis or alternative. *Entrance requirements:* For master's, GRE General Test, minimum GPA of 3.0, minimum 15 hours of upper-level history courses. Additional exam requirements/recommendations for international students: Required—TOEFL (minimum score 550 paper-based; 213 computer-based). *Application deadline:* For fall admission, 6/1 for domestic students, 5/15 for international students; for spring admission, 11/1 for domestic students, 10/1 for international students. Applications are processed on a rolling basis. Application fee: $30. *Expenses:* Tuition, state resident: full-time $4982; part-time $260 per credit hour. Tuition, nonresident: full-time $20,059; part-time $919 per credit hour. Required fees: $1247; $52 per credit hour. *Financial support:* In 2009–10, 2 teaching assistantships with partial tuition reimbursements (averaging $5,000 per year) were awarded; unspecified assistantships also available. Financial award application deadline: 4/15; financial award applicants required to submit FAFSA. *Unit head:* Dr. John J. Clune, Chairperson, 850-474-2680. *Application contact:* Terry McCray, Assistant Director of Graduate Admissions, 850-473-7718, Fax: 850-473-7714, E-mail: gradadmissions@uwf.edu.

National Security

American Public University System, AMU/APU Graduate Programs, Charles Town, WV 25414. Offers air warfare (MA Military Studies); American Revolution (MA Military Studies); business administration (MBA); Civil War (MA Military Studies); criminal justice (MA); defense management (MA Military Studies); emergency and disaster management (MA); environmental policy and management (MS); fire science management (MA); global engagement (MA); history (MA); homeland security (MA); humanities (MA); intelligence (MA Military Studies, MA Strategic Intelligence); international peace and conflict resolution (MA); international relations and conflict resolution (MA); joint warfare (MA Military Studies); land warfare international perspective (MA Military Studies); management (MA); military history (MA); military leadership (MA Military Studies); national security studies (MA); naval warfare international (MA Military Studies); naval warfare US (MA Military Studies); political science (MA); public administration (MA); public health (MA); security management (MA); space studies (MS); special ops/LIC (MA Military Studies); sports management (MA); transportation and logistics management (MA); transportation management (MA); unconventional warfare (MA Military Studies); World War II (MA Military Studies). Programs offered via distance learning only. Part-time and evening/weekend programs available. Postbaccalaureate distance learning degree programs offered (no on-campus study). *Faculty:* 10 full-time (3 women), 188 part-time/adjunct (57 women). *Students:* 340 full-time (98 women), 3,567 part-time (790 women); includes 615 minority (317 African Americans, 28 American Indian/Alaska Native, 85 Asian Americans or Pacific Islanders, 185 Hispanic Americans), 20 international. Average age 36. 2,123 applicants, 100% accepted, 893 enrolled. In 2009, 829 degrees awarded. *Degree requirements:* For master's, comprehensive exam. *Entrance requirements:* For master's, bachelor's degree or equivalent, minimum GPA of 2.7 in last 60 hours of course work. *Application deadline:* Applications are processed on a rolling basis. Application fee: $0. Electronic applications accepted. *Financial support:* Applicants required to submit FAFSA. *Faculty research:* Military history, criminal justice, management performance, national security. *Unit head:* Dr. Frank McCluskey, Provost, 877-468-6268, Fax: 304-724-3780. *Application contact:* Terry Grant, Director of Enrollment Management, 877-468-6268, Fax: 304-724-3780, E-mail: info@apus.edu.

California State University, San Bernardino, Graduate Studies, College of Social and Behavioral Sciences, National Security Studies Program, San Bernardino, CA 92407-2397. Offers MA. Part-time and evening/weekend programs available. *Students:* 60 full-time (13 women), 14 part-time (4 women); includes 27 minority (5 African Americans, 8 Asian Americans or Pacific Islanders, 14 Hispanic Americans), 2 international. Average age 29. 52 applicants, 71% accepted, 26 enrolled. In 2009, 15 master's awarded. *Degree requirements:* For master's, comprehensive exam. *Entrance requirements:* For master's, minimum GPA of 2.5. *Application deadline:* Applications are processed on a rolling basis. Application fee: $55. *Financial support:* Career-related internships or fieldwork, Federal Work-Study, institutionally sponsored loans, and unspecified assistantships available. Support available to part-time students. *Faculty research:* Strategy, arms control, defense policy, terrorism, U.S. foreign policy, operations analysis. *Unit head:* Dr. Mark Clark, Director, 909-537-5534, Fax: 909-537-7018, E-mail: mtclark@csusb.edu. *Application contact:* Olivia Rosas, Director of Admissions, 909-537-7577, Fax: 909-537-7034, E-mail: orosas@csusb.edu.

Hult International Business School, Program in International Relations—Hult London Campus, London, MA WC 1B 4JP, United Kingdom. Offers conflict resolution (MA); diplomacy (MA); international public law (MA); international relations (MA); Middle East international security (MA); politics (MA); security studies (MA); terrorism (MA); U.S. foreign policy (MA). Part-time programs available. *Entrance requirements:* Additional exam requirements/recommendations for international students: Required—TOEFL (minimum score 580 paper-based; 237 computer-based), TWE (minimum score 5). Electronic applications accepted. *Faculty research:* American foreign politics, Middle East, security studies.

The Institute of World Politics, Graduate Programs in National Security, Intelligence, and International Affairs, Washington, DC 20036. Offers American foreign policy (Certificate); comparative political culture (Certificate); counterintelligence (Certificate); democracy building (Certificate); intelligence (Certificate); international politics (Certificate); national security affairs (Certificate); public diplomacy and political warfare (Certificate); statecraft and national security affairs (MA); statecraft and world politics (MA); strategic intelligence studies (MA). Part-time and evening/weekend programs available. *Degree requirements:* For master's, comprehensive exam, thesis optional. *Entrance requirements:* For master's, GRE General Test. Additional exam requirements/recommendations for international students: Required—TOEFL. Electronic applications accepted. *Faculty research:* Intelligence, national security, statecraft.

Kansas State University, Graduate School, College of Arts and Sciences, Department of History, Manhattan, KS 66506. Offers history (MA); security studies (MA, PhD). Part-time programs available. *Faculty:* 19 full-time (8 women), 1 part-time/adjunct (0 women). *Students:* 74 full-time (13 women), 62 part-time (14 women); includes 3 minority (1 African American, 2 Asian Americans or Pacific Islanders), 2 international. Average age 29. 86 applicants, 72% accepted, 41 enrolled. In 2009, 19 master's, 5 doctorates awarded. *Degree requirements:* For master's, thesis (for some programs); for doctorate, one foreign language, thesis/dissertation, qualifying exam. *Entrance requirements:* For master's, GRE General Test or MAT, minimum undergraduate GPA of 3.0; for doctorate, GRE General Test or MAT. Additional exam requirements/recommendations for international students: Required—TOEFL (minimum score 600 paper-based). *Application deadline:* For fall admission, 2/1 priority date for domestic and international students; for spring admission, 8/1 priority date for domestic and international students. Applications are processed on a rolling basis. Application fee: $40 ($55 for international students). Electronic applications accepted. *Financial support:* In 2009–10, 7 research assistantships (averaging $18,104 per year), 12 teaching assistantships with full tuition reimbursements (averaging $8,954 per year) were awarded; career-related internships or fieldwork, Federal Work-Study, institutionally sponsored loans, and scholarships/grants also available. Support available to part-time students. Financial award application deadline: 3/1; financial award applicants required to submit FAFSA. *Faculty research:* Environmental history, history of Christianity, American social history, history of war and society, history of international relations and diplomacy. Total annual research expenditures: $16,186. *Unit head:* Louise Breen, Head, 785-532-0365, Fax: 785-532-7004, E-mail: breen@ksu.edu. *Application contact:* Louise Breen, Recruiting Program Director, 785-532-0365, Fax: 785-532-7004, E-mail: breen@ksu.edu.

National Defense University, College of International Security Affairs, Washington, DC 20319-5066. Offers strategic security studies (MA), including conflict management, counterterrorism, homeland defense/ security, international security studies. Part-time and evening/weekend programs available. *Degree requirements:* For master's, thesis. *Entrance requirements:* Additional exam requirements/recommendations for international students: Required—TOEFL.

National Defense University, National War College, Washington, DC 20319-5066. Offers national security strategy (MS). Open only to Department of Defense employees and specific federal agencies. *Degree requirements:* For master's, comprehensive exam. *Entrance requirements:* Additional exam requirements/recommendations for international students: Required—TOEFL. *Faculty research:* National security policy, regional security, US national security strategy, US military, strategy.

Naval Postgraduate School, Graduate Programs, Department of National Security Affairs, Monterey, CA 93943. Offers intelligence (MA); international relations (MA); political science (MA); regional security education (MA); security building (MA); security studies (MA). Program only open to commissioned officers of the United States and friendly nations and selected

National Security

Naval Postgraduate School (continued)
United States federal civilian employees. Part-time programs available. *Degree requirements:* For master's, thesis.

Naval War College, Program in National Security and Strategic Studies, Newport, RI 02841-1207. Offers MA. Program open only to full-time military personnel.

New York University, School of Continuing and Professional Studies, Center for Global Affairs, New York, NY 10012-1019. Offers global affairs (MS), including environment/energy policy, human rights and humanitarian assistance, international law, dispute settlement, and institutions, international relations, peace building, private sector: international business, economics, and development, transnational security. Part-time and evening/weekend programs available. *Faculty:* 9 full-time (3 women), 31 part-time/adjunct (14 women). *Students:* 120 full-time (82 women), 179 part-time (121 women); includes 22 minority (1 American Indian/Alaska Native, 21 Asian Americans or Pacific Islanders), 27 international. Average age 30. 419 applicants, 59% accepted, 94 enrolled. In 2009, 86 master's awarded. *Degree requirements:* For master's, thesis. *Entrance requirements:* For master's, GRE General Test or GMAT (for recent graduates), 2 letters of recommendation, resume. Additional exam requirements/recommendations for international students: Required—TOEFL (minimum score 600 paper-based; 250 computer-based; 100 iBT), TWE. *Application deadline:* For fall admission, 2/1 priority date for domestic and international students; for spring admission, 10/15 priority date for domestic students, 8/15 priority date for international students. Applications are processed on a rolling basis. Application fee: $75. Electronic applications accepted. *Expenses:* Tuition: Full-time $30,528; part-time $1272 per credit. Required fees: $2177. *Financial support:* In 2009–10, 159 students received support, including 159 fellowships (averaging $2,932 per year); institutionally sponsored loans, scholarships/grants, and tuition waivers (partial) also available. Support available to part-time students. Financial award application deadline: 3/1; financial award applicants required to submit FAFSA. *Unit head:* Dr. Vera Jelinek, Assistant Dean and Director, 212-992-8380, Fax: 212-995-3638, E-mail: vera.jelinek@nyu.edu. *Application contact:* Mykellan Ledden, Associate Director, 212-992-8380, Fax: 212-995-3638, E-mail: mykellan.ledden@nyu.edu.

Texas A&M University, George Bush School of Government and Public Service, College Station, TX 77843. Offers advanced international affairs (Certificate); homeland security (Certificate); international affairs (MPIA), including international economics and development, national security affairs; nonprofit management (Certificate); public service and administration (MPSA), including public management, public policy analysis. *Accreditation:* NASPAA. *Faculty:* 51. *Students:* 209 full-time (97 women), 93 part-time (43 women); includes 48 minority (15 African Americans, 5 Asian Americans or Pacific Islanders, 28 Hispanic Americans), 19 international. Average age 24. In 2009, 87 master's awarded. *Degree requirements:* For master's, summer internship. *Entrance requirements:* For master's, GRE (preferred) or GMAT. *Application deadline:* For fall admission, 1/24 for domestic and international students. Application fee: $50 ($75 for international students). Electronic applications accepted. *Expenses:* Tuition, state resident: full-time $3991; part-time $221.74 per credit hour. Tuition, nonresident: full-time $9049; part-time $502.74 per credit hour. *Financial support:* In 2009–10, fellowships (averaging $11,000 per year), research assistantships (averaging $11,250 per year) were awarded; career-related internships or fieldwork, Federal Work-Study, and institutionally sponsored loans also available. Financial award application deadline: 2/1; financial award applicants required to submit FAFSA. *Faculty research:* Public policy, presidential studies, public leadership, economic policy, social policy. *Unit head:* A. Benton Cocanougher, Interim Dean, 979-862-8842, E-mail: bushschool@tamu.edu. *Application contact:* Kathryn Meyer, Recruitment and Placement Officer, 979-458-4767, Fax: 979-845-4155, E-mail: admissions@bushschool.tamu.edu.

Trinity (Washington) University, School of Professional Studies, Washington, DC 20017-1094. Offers business administration (MBA); communication (MA); international security studies (MA); organizational management (MSA), including federal program management, human resource management, nonprofit management, organizational development, public and community health. Part-time and evening/weekend programs available. *Degree requirements:* For master's, thesis (for some programs), capstone project (MSA). *Entrance requirements:* For master's, minimum GPA of 2.5. Additional exam requirements/recommendations for international students: Required—TOEFL (minimum score 550 paper-based; 213 computer-based).

Troy University, Graduate School, College of Arts and Sciences, Program in International Relations, Troy, AL 36082. Offers national security affairs (MS), including global studies, national security affairs, regional affairs. Part-time and evening/weekend programs available. Postbaccalaureate distance learning degree programs offered (no on-campus study). *Students:* 78 full-time (35 women), 336 part-time (135 women); includes 120 minority (50 African Americans, 4 American Indian/Alaska Native, 32 Asian Americans or Pacific Islanders, 34 Hispanic Americans). Average age 32. 307 applicants, 86% accepted. In 2009, 136 master's awarded. *Degree requirements:* For master's, comprehensive exam or thesis. *Entrance requirements:* For master's, GRE, MAT, or GMAT, minimum undergraduate GPA of 2.5. Additional exam requirements/recommendations for international students: Required—TOEFL (minimum score 523 paper-based; 193 computer-based; 70 iBT), IELTS (minimum score 6). *Application deadline:* Applications are processed on a rolling basis. Application fee: $50. Electronic applications accepted. *Financial support:* Available to part-time students. Applicants required to submit FAFSA. *Faculty research:* Elections, religion and world politics, terrorism. *Unit head:* Dr. Charles Krupnick, Department Chairman, 334-670-5968, Fax: 334-670-5647, E-mail: ckrupnick@troy.edu. *Application contact:* Brenda K. Campbell, Director of Graduate Admissions, 334-670-3178, Fax: 334-670-3733, E-mail: bcamp@troy.edu.

Troy University, Graduate School, College of Arts and Sciences, Program in Public Administration, Troy, AL 36082. Offers education (MPA); environmental management (MPA); government contracting (MPA); health care administration (MPA); justice administration (MPA); management information systems (MPA); national security affairs (MPA); nonprofit management (MPA); public human resources management (MPA); public management (MPA). *Accreditation:* NASPAA. Part-time and evening/weekend programs available. Postbaccalaureate distance learning degree programs offered (no on-campus study). *Students:* 239 full-time (161 women), 652 part-time (416 women); includes 596 minority (547 African Americans, 11 American Indian/Alaska Native, 6 Asian Americans or Pacific Islanders, 32 Hispanic Americans). Average age 34. 415 applicants, 80% accepted. In 2009, 247 master's awarded. *Degree requirements:* For master's, capstone course, research methodologies course. *Entrance requirements:* For master's, GRE, MAT or GMAT, minimum undergraduate GPA of 2.5, letter of recommendation. Additional exam requirements/recommendations for international students: Required—TOEFL (minimum score 523 paper-based; 193 computer-based; 70 iBT), IELTS (minimum score 6). *Application deadline:* Applications are processed on a rolling basis. Application fee: $50. Electronic applications accepted. *Financial support:* Available to part-time students. Applicants required to submit FAFSA. *Unit head:* Dr. Ellen Rosell, Chairman, 334-670-3758, Fax: 334-670-5647, E-mail: erosell@troy.edu. *Application contact:* Brenda K. Campbell, Director of Graduate Admissions, 334-670-3178, Fax: 334-670-3733, E-mail: bcamp@troy.edu.

University of New Haven, Graduate School, Henry C. Lee College of Criminal Justice and Forensic Sciences, National Security and Public Safety Program, West Haven, CT 06516-1916. Offers information protection and security (MS); national security (Certificate); national security administration (Certificate). Part-time and evening/weekend programs available. *Faculty:* 8 full-time (2 women), 5 part-time/adjunct (0 women). *Students:* 34 full-time (10 women), 39 part-time (21 women); includes 19 minority (4 African Americans, 1 American Indian/Alaska Native, 4 Asian Americans or Pacific Islanders, 10 Hispanic Americans), 4 international. Average age 32. 39 applicants, 100% accepted, 33 enrolled. In 2009, 51 master's, 5 other advanced degrees awarded. *Entrance requirements:* Additional exam requirements/recommendations for international students: Required—TOEFL (minimum score 520 paper-based; 190 computer-based; 70 iBT); Recommended—IELTS (minimum score 5.5). *Application deadline:* For fall admission, 5/31 for international students; for winter admission, 10/15 for international students; for spring admission, 1/15 for international students. Applications are processed on a rolling basis. Application fee: $50. Electronic applications accepted. *Expenses:* Tuition: Part-time $700 per credit. Required fees: $45 per term. One-time fee: $390 part-time. *Financial support:* Research assistantships with partial tuition reimbursements, teaching assistantships with partial tuition reimbursements, career-related internships or fieldwork, Federal Work-Study, scholarships/grants, tuition waivers, and unspecified assistantships available. Support available to part-time students. Financial award applicants required to submit FAFSA. *Unit head:* Dr. William L. Tafoya, Dean, 203-932-7260. *Application contact:* Eloise Gormley, Director of Graduate Admissions, 203-932-7449, Fax: 203-932-7137, E-mail: gradinfo@newhaven.edu.

University of Pittsburgh, Graduate School of Public and International Affairs, Public Policy and Management Program for Mid-Career Professionals, Pittsburgh, PA 15260. Offers development planning (MPPM); international development (MPPM); international political economy (MPPM); international security studies (MPPM); management of non profit organizations (MPPM); metropolitan management and regional development (MPPM); policy analysis and evaluation (MPPM). Part-time programs available. *Faculty:* 28 full-time (8 women), 56 part-time/adjunct (20 women). *Students:* 3 full-time (0 women), 39 part-time (21 women); includes 2 minority (both African Americans), 1 international. Average age 38. 48 applicants, 75% accepted, 19 enrolled. In 2009, 17 master's awarded. *Degree requirements:* For master's, thesis optional, capstone seminar. *Entrance requirements:* For master's, 2 letters of recommendation, resume, 5 years of supervisory or budgetary experience. Additional exam requirements/recommendations for international students: Required—TOEFL (minimum score 600 paper-based; 250 computer-based; 100 iBT), TWE (minimum score 4); Recommended—IELTS (minimum score 7). *Application deadline:* For fall admission, 6/1 priority date for domestic students, 2/15 for international students; for spring admission, 1/1 priority date for domestic students, 8/1 for international students. Applications are processed on a rolling basis. Application fee: $50. Electronic applications accepted. *Expenses:* Tuition, state resident: full-time $16,402; part-time $665 per credit. Tuition, nonresident: full-time $28,694; part-time $1175 per credit. Required fees: $690; $175 per term. Tuition and fees vary according to program. *Financial support:* In 2009–10, 10 students received support. Institutionally sponsored loans, scholarships/grants, and tuition waivers (partial) available. Support available to part-time students. Financial award application deadline: 2/1. *Faculty research:* Nonprofit management, urban and regional affairs, policy analysis and evaluation, security and intelligence studies, global political economy, nongovernmental organizations, civil society, development planning and environmental sustainability, human security. Total annual research expenditures: $357,117. *Unit head:* Dr. George Dougherty, Director, Executive Education, 412-648-7603, Fax: 412-648-2605, E-mail: gwdjr@pitt.edu. *Application contact:* Michael T. Rizzi, Associate Director of Student Services, 412-648-7640, Fax: 412-648-7641, E-mail: rizzim@pitt.edu.

The University of Texas at El Paso, Graduate School, Institute for Policy and Economic Development, El Paso, TX 79968-0001. Offers border administration (Certificate); homeland security (Certificate); intelligence and national security (MS, Certificate); leadership studies (MA); public administration (MPA). *Accreditation:* NASPAA. Part-time and evening/weekend programs available. *Students:* 187 (57 women); includes 124 minority (19 African Americans, 1 American Indian/Alaska Native, 5 Asian Americans or Pacific Islanders, 99 Hispanic Americans), 5 international. 142 applicants, 77% accepted. In 2009, 76 master's awarded. *Degree requirements:* For master's, thesis optional. *Entrance requirements:* For master's, GRE, Statement of Purpose, Letters of Recommendation. Additional exam requirements/recommendations for international students: Required—TOEFL; Recommended—IELTS. *Application deadline:* For fall admission, 8/1 for domestic students, 3/1 for international students; for spring admission, 10/1 for domestic students, 9/1 for international students. Applications are processed on a rolling basis. Application fee: $45 ($80 for international students). Electronic applications accepted. *Financial support:* Fellowships with partial tuition reimbursements, research assistantships with partial tuition reimbursements, teaching assistantships with partial tuition reimbursements, institutionally sponsored loans, scholarships/grants, health care benefits, tuition waivers (partial), and unspecified assistantships available. Support available to part-time students. Financial award application deadline: 3/15; financial award applicants required to submit FAFSA. *Unit head:* Dr. Dennis Soden, Director, 915-747-7974, Fax: 915-747-7948, E-mail: desoden@utep.edu. *Application contact:* Dr. Patricia D. Witherspoon, Dean of the Graduate School, 915-747-5491, Fax: 915-747-5788, E-mail: withersp@utep.edu.

Virginia Polytechnic Institute and State University, VT Online, Blacksburg, VA 24061. Offers aerospace engineering (MS); business information systems (Graduate Certificate); career and technical education (MS); computer engineering (M Eng, MS); decision support systems (Graduate Certificate); eLearning leadership (MA); electrical engineering (M Eng, MS); engineering administration (MEA); environmental politics and policy (Graduate Certificate); foundations of political analysis (Graduate Certificate); health product risk management (Graduate Certificate); information policy and society (Graduate Certificate); information security (Graduate Certificate); instructional technology (MA); liberal arts (Graduate Certificate); life sciences: health product risk management (MS); natural resources (MNR, Graduate Certificate); networking (Graduate Certificate); nonprofit and nongovernmental organization management (Graduate Certificate); ocean engineering (MS); political science (MA); security studies (Graduate Certificate); software development (Graduate Certificate).

HAWAI'I PACIFIC UNIVERSITY

Diplomacy and Military Studies Program

Program of Study

Hawai'i Pacific University's (HPU's) Master of Arts in diplomacy and military studies (M.A./DMS) is designed to provide students with an interdisciplinary view of the role of diplomacy and the military in world affairs from both historical and contemporary perspectives. The program combines courses in history, art history, literature, philosophy, anthropology, international relations, strategic studies, and political science to acquaint students with different approaches and methods in the study of diplomacy and the military.

The M.A./DMS program is an excellent opportunity for those wishing to explore the complex relationships of politics, society, and the military. It is a useful degree for those who are either professional military officers or those who work in a variety of government positions. It is also outstanding preparation for more advanced graduate studies in history, political science, or international relations.

The M.A./DMS requires a minimum of 42 semester hours of graduate work: 12 semester hours of core courses, 12 semester hours of electives in diplomatic and military history, 12 semester hours of supporting field electives, and 6 semester hours of capstone courses. Unlike other similar programs, which have a focus on the United States and Europe, the M.A./DMS integrates a variety of courses in Asia and the Pacific, as well as courses of a comparative nature.

The core classes are drawn from the disciplines of history, interdisciplinary humanities, philosophy, and political science and provide students with the historical, ethical, and practical background necessary to understand fully the multifaceted character of the military. They are also intended to give students a sound introduction to the fundamental literature dealing with the history of foreign relations and the military.

Research Facilities

To support graduate studies, HPU's Meader and Atherton Libraries hold more than 110,000 bound volumes, 350,000 microfiche items, and periodical subscriptions to 1,500 print titles and 30,000 electronic journals. Databases of public and state university libraries, legislative information, and business-oriented statistical data are also available in the library or online. Students can access HPU's library databases, course information, their academic information, and an e-mail account through Pipeline, the university's internal Web site for students. The University's accessible on-campus computer center houses more than 100 computers with specialized software to support graduate academic programs. HPU also provides free Wi-Fi so that students can access Pipeline resources anywhere on campus using laptops. A significant number of online courses are available.

Financial Aid

The University participates in all federal financial aid programs designated for graduate students. These programs provide aid in the form of subsidized (need-based) and unsubsidized (non-need-based) Federal Stafford Student Loans. Through these loans, funds may be available to cover a student's entire cost of education. To apply for aid, students must submit the Free Application for Federal Student Aid (FAFSA) beginning January 1. Mailing of student award letters usually begins by the end of March. The University also offers several types of institutional graduate scholarships to new full-time, degree-seeking students. The Graduate Trustee Scholarship provides $6000 for two semesters, the Graduate Dean Scholarship provides $4000 for two semesters, and the Graduate Kokua Scholarship provides $2000 for two semesters. Priority consideration is given to those students who apply by the deadline.

Cost of Study

Tuition for graduate students enrolled in fall and spring semesters is determined on a per-credit basis; full-time status for a graduate student is 9 credits. Tuition for the optional winter and summer sessions is also determined on a per-credit basis. The estimated minimum funds needed for a nine-month academic year (September to May) based on 2010–11 school year expenses is $26,459. For the 2010–11 academic year, full-time tuition is $12,600 for most graduate degree programs, including the M.A./DMS program. Books, supplies, and transportation cost $1885, and health insurance costs $880.

Living and Housing Costs

Most graduate students live in off-campus housing. The cost of living in off-campus apartments is approximately $11,094 for a double-occupancy room.

Student Group

University enrollment currently stands at more than 8,200. HPU is one of the most culturally diverse universities in America with students from all 50 U.S. states and more than 100 countries.

Location

Hawai'i Pacific University combines the excitement of an urban, downtown campus with the serenity of a residential campus. The main campus is ideally located in downtown Honolulu, the business and financial center of the Pacific. The downtown campus comprises six buildings in the center of Honolulu's business district and is home to the College of Business Administration and the College of Humanities and Social Sciences. Eight miles away, situated on 135 acres in Kaneohe, the windward Hawai'i Loa campus is the site of the College of Nursing and Health Sciences and the College of Natural and Computational Sciences. HPU is affiliated with the Oceanic Institute, an applied aquaculture research facility located on a 56-acre site at Makapu'u Point on the windward coast of Oahu, Hawaii. Students can conveniently travel between the three sites using the HPU shuttle service. There are also eight military campus programs located at Pearl Harbor, Barbers Point, Hickam Air Force Base, Schofield Barracks, Fort Shafter, Tripler Army Medical Center, Kaneohe Marine Corps Air Station, and Camp Smith.

The University

HPU is a private, nonprofit university with approximately 8,200 students. Founded in 1965, HPU prides itself on maintaining strong academic programs, small class sizes, individual attention to students, and a diverse faculty and student population. HPU is recognized as a "Best in the West" college by the Princeton Review and a "Best Buy" by *Barron's* business magazine. HPU offers more than fifty acclaimed undergraduate programs and thirteen distinguished graduate programs. The University has a faculty of more than 500, a student-faculty ratio of 15:1, and an average class size of fewer than 20 students. A wide range of counseling and other student support services are available. There are more than seventy student organizations on campus, including the Graduate Student Organization.

Applying

Students must have a baccalaureate degree from an accredited college or university in the United States or an equivalent degree from another country. Applicants should complete and forward a graduate admissions application, send in the $50 nonrefundable application fee, have official transcripts sent from all colleges or universities previously attended, and forward two letters of recommendation. A personal statement about the applicant's academic and career goals is required; submitting a resume is optional. Applicants who have taken the Graduate Record Examination (GRE) should have their scores sent directly to the Graduate Admissions Office. International students should submit scores of a recognized English proficiency test such as TOEFL. Admissions decisions are made on a rolling basis, and applicants are notified between one and two weeks after all documents have been submitted. Applicants are encouraged to submit their applications online.

Correspondence and Information

Graduate Admissions
Hawai'i Pacific University
1164 Bishop Street, #911
Honolulu, Hawaii 96813

Phone: 808-544-1135
866-GRAD-HPU (toll-free)
Fax: 808-544-0280
E-mail: graduate@hpu.edu
Web site: http://www.hpu.edu/hpumadms

Hawai'i Pacific University

THE FACULTY

Pierre Asselin, Associate Professor of History; Ph.D., Hawai'i at Manoa.
Patrick Bratton, Assistant Professor of Political Science; Ph.D., Catholic University.
Grace Cheng, Associate Professor of Political Science; Ph.D., Hawai'i.
Allison Gough, Associate Professor of History; Ph.D., Ohio State.
Russell Hart, Associate Professor of History; Ph.D., Ohio State.
Carlos Juarez, Professor of Political Science; Ph.D., UCLA.
James Primm, Associate Professor of Political Science; Ph.D., Hawai'i.
George Satterfield, Associate Professor of History; Ph.D., Illinois at Urbana-Champaign.

Section 23
Political Science and International Affairs

This section contains a directory of institutions offering graduate work in political science and international affairs, followed by in-depth entries submitted by institutions that chose to prepare detailed program descriptions. Additional information about programs listed in the directory but not augmented by an in-depth entry may be obtained by writing directly to the dean of a graduate school or chair of a department at the address given in the directory.

For programs offering related work, see also in this book *Area and Cultural Studies, History, Language and Literature,* and *Public, Regional, and Industrial Affairs.* In another guide in this series:

Graduate Programs in Business, Education, Health, Information Studies, Law & Social Work

See *International Business*

CONTENTS

Program Directories

International Affairs 812
International Development 824
International Trade Policy 826
Political Science 827

Close-Ups and Display

American University 849
Missouri State University 851
Global Studies (Display) 817
Monterey Institute of International Studies 853
Seton Hall University 855
Villanova University 857

See also:

Indiana University Bloomington—Public Affairs 1191
University of Southern California—Communication and Journalism 685
The University of Texas at Dallas—Economic, Political, and Policy Sciences 759

International Affairs

Alliant International University–México City, International Studies Division, Mexico City, Mexico. Offers international relations (MA).

Alliant International University–México City, Marshall Goldsmith School of Management, Mexico City, Mexico. Offers international business administration (MIBA); international relations (MA). Part-time and evening/weekend programs available. *Entrance requirements:* For master's, GMAT, minimum GPA of 3.0. Additional exam requirements/recommendations for international students: Required—TOEFL (minimum score 550 paper-based; 213 computer-based), TWE (minimum score 5). Electronic applications accepted. *Faculty research:* Environmental impact and business in Mexico.

Alliant International University–México City, Programs in Arts and Science, Mexico City, Mexico. Offers counseling psychology (MA); international relations (MA). Part-time programs available. *Degree requirements:* For master's, thesis optional. *Entrance requirements:* For master's, GRE General Test, letters of recommendation. Additional exam requirements/recommendations for international students: Required—TOEFL. Electronic applications accepted.

Alliant International University–San Diego, Marshall Goldsmith School of Management, International Studies Division, San Diego, CA 92131-1799. Offers international relations (MA). Part-time programs available. *Degree requirements:* For master's, thesis. *Entrance requirements:* For master's, GRE, minimum GPA of 2.5, letters of recommendation. Additional exam requirements/recommendations for international students: Required—TOEFL (minimum score 550 paper-based).

American Graduate School in Paris, Program in International Relations and Diplomacy, Paris, France. Offers MA, PhD.

American Public University System, AMU/APU Graduate Programs, Charles Town, WV 25414. Offers air warfare (MA Military Studies); American Revolution (MA Military Studies); business administration (MBA); Civil War (MA Military Studies); criminal justice (MA); defense management (MA Military Studies); emergency and disaster management (MA); environmental policy and management (MS); fire science management (MA); global engagement (MA); history (MA); homeland security (MA); humanities (MA); intelligence (MA Military Studies, MA Strategic Intelligence); international peace and conflict resolution (MA); international relations and conflict resolution (MA); joint warfare (MA Military Studies); land warfare international perspective (MA Military Studies); management (MA); military history (MA); military leadership (MA Military Studies); national security studies (MA); naval warfare international (MA Military Studies); naval warfare US (MA Military Studies); political science (MA); public administration (MA); public health (MA); security management (MA); space studies (MS); special ops/LIC (MA Military Studies); sports management (MA); transportation and logistics management (MA); transportation management (MA); unconventional warfare (MA Military Studies); World War II (MA Military Studies). Programs offered via distance learning only. Part-time and evening/weekend programs available. Postbaccalaureate distance learning degree programs offered (no on-campus study). *Faculty:* 10 full-time (3 women), 188 part-time/adjunct (57 women). *Students:* 340 full-time (98 women), 3,567 part-time (790 women); includes 615 minority (317 African Americans, 28 American Indian/Alaska Native, 85 Asian Americans or Pacific Islanders, 185 Hispanic Americans), 20 international. Average age 36. 2,123 applicants, 100% accepted, 893 enrolled. In 2009, 829 degrees awarded. *Degree requirements:* For master's, comprehensive exam. *Entrance requirements:* For master's, bachelor's degree or equivalent, minimum GPA of 2.7 in last 60 hours of course work. *Application deadline:* Applications are processed on a rolling basis. Application fee: $0. Electronic applications accepted. *Financial support:* Applicants required to submit FAFSA. *Faculty research:* Military history, criminal justice, management performance, national security. *Unit head:* Dr. Frank McCluskey, Provost, 877-468-6268, Fax: 304-724-3780. *Application contact:* Terry Grant, Director of Enrollment Management, 877-468-6268, Fax: 304-724-3780, E-mail: info@apus.edu.

American University, College of Arts and Sciences, Department of Economics, Washington, DC 20016-8029. Offers applied microeconomics (Certificate); economics (MA, PhD); international economic relations (Certificate). Part-time and evening/weekend programs available. *Faculty:* 27 full-time (10 women). *Students:* 55 full-time (23 women), 67 part-time (27 women); includes 15 minority (12 African Americans, 1 Asian American or Pacific Islander, 2 Hispanic Americans), 49 international. Average age 29. 156 applicants, 69% accepted, 34 enrolled. In 2009, 23 master's, 10 doctorates, 1 other advanced degree awarded. Terminal master's awarded for partial completion of doctoral program. *Degree requirements:* For master's, comprehensive exam, thesis or alternative; for doctorate, comprehensive exam, thesis/dissertation, 2 research seminars, field work. *Entrance requirements:* For master's and doctorate, GRE; for Certificate, bachelor's degree. Additional exam requirements/recommendations for international students: Required—TOEFL. *Application deadline:* For spring admission, 10/1 for domestic students. Applications are processed on a rolling basis. Application fee: $80. *Expenses:* Tuition: Full-time $22,266; part-time $1237 per credit hour. Required fees: $430. Tuition and fees vary according to program. *Financial support:* Fellowships, research assistantships with full and partial tuition reimbursements, teaching assistantships with full and partial tuition reimbursements, career-related internships or fieldwork, Federal Work-Study, institutionally sponsored loans, and tuition waivers (full and partial) available. Financial award application deadline: 2/1. *Faculty research:* Political economy, development, labor, gender. *Unit head:* Robert A. Blecker, Chair, 202-885-3767, Fax: 202-885-3790, E-mail: blecker@american.edu. *Application contact:* Kathleen Clowery, Director of Graduate Admissions, 202-885-3621, Fax: 202-885-1505, E-mail: clowery@american.edu.

American University, School of International Service, Washington, DC 20016-8071. Offers comparative and regional studies (Certificate); cross-cultural communication (Certificate); development management (MS); ethics, peace, and global affairs (MA); European studies (Certificate); global environmental policy (MA, Certificate); international affairs (MA), including comparative and regional studies, environmental policy, international economic policy, international politics, natural resources and sustainable development, U.S. foreign policy; international communication (MA, Certificate); international development (MA, Certificate); international development management (Certificate); international economic policy (Certificate); international economic relations (Certificate); international media (MA); international peace and conflict resolution (MA, Certificate); international relations (PhD); international service (MIS); peace building (Certificate); the Americas (Certificate); United States foreign policy (Certificate); JD/MA. Part-time and evening/weekend programs available. *Faculty:* 98 full-time (42 women), 48 part-time/adjunct (13 women). *Students:* 565 full-time (349 women), 329 part-time (189 women); includes 128 minority (44 African Americans, 2 American Indian/Alaska Native, 37 Asian Americans or Pacific Islanders, 45 Hispanic Americans), 102 international. Average age 27. 2,034 applicants, 63% accepted, 344 enrolled. In 2009, 326 master's, 6 doctorates, 9 other advanced degrees awarded. Terminal master's awarded for partial completion of doctoral program. *Degree requirements:* For master's, one foreign language, comprehensive exam, thesis or alternative; for doctorate, one foreign language, comprehensive exam, thesis/dissertation, research practicum; for Certificate, minimum 15 credit hours related course work. *Entrance requirements:* For master's, GRE, 24 credits of course work in related social sciences, minimum GPA of 3.5, 2 letters of recommendation, bachelor's degree, resume; for doctorate, GRE, 2 letters of recommendation, 24 credits in related social sciences; for Certificate, bachelor's degree. Additional exam requirements/recommendations for international students: Required—TOEFL (minimum score 600 paper-based; 250 computer-based; 100 iBT). *Application deadline:* For fall admission, 1/15 priority date for domestic students; for spring admission, 10/1 priority date for domestic students. Applications are processed on a rolling basis. Application fee: $50. *Expenses:* Tuition: Full-time $22,266; part-time $1237 per credit hour. Required fees: $430. Tuition and fees vary according to program. *Financial support:* Career-related internships or fieldwork, Federal Work-Study, and institutionally sponsored loans available. Financial award application deadline: 1/15. *Faculty research:* International intellectual property, international environmental issues, international law and legal order, international telecommunications/technology, international sustainable development. *Unit head:* Dr. Louis W. Goodman, Dean, 202-885-1600, Fax: 202-885-2494. *Application contact:* Yasmin Quianzon, Director of Graduate Admissions and Financial Aid, 202-885-2496, Fax: 202-885-1109.

See Close-Up on page 849.

The American University of Paris, Graduate Programs, Paris, France. Offers cross-cultural and sustainable business management (MA); cultural translation (MA); global communications (MA); global communications and civil society (MA); international affairs, conflict resolution and civil society development (MA); Middle East and Islamic studies (MA); Middle East and Islamic studies and international affairs (MA); public policy and international affairs (MA); public policy and international law (MA). *Faculty:* 14 full-time (3 women). *Students:* 143 full-time (109 women). 71 applicants, 92% accepted, 34 enrolled. *Degree requirements:* For master's, thesis. *Entrance requirements:* For master's, minimum undergraduate GPA of 3.0. *Application deadline:* For fall admission, 4/15 priority date for international students; for spring admission, 11/15 priority date for international students. Applications are processed on a rolling basis. Application fee: $75. Tuition charges are reported in euros. *Expenses:* Tuition: Full-time 23,460 euros. *Financial support:* Scholarships/grants available. Financial award applicants required to submit FAFSA. *Unit head:* Celeste Schenk, President, 33 1-40620659, E-mail: president@aup.fr. *Application contact:* International Admissions Counselor, 33 1-40620720, Fax: 33 1-47053432, E-mail: admissions@aup.edu.

Appalachian State University, Cratis D. Williams Graduate School, Department of Government and Justice Studies, Boone, NC 28608. Offers criminal justice (MS); political science (MA), including American government, environmental politics and policy analysis, international relations; public administration (MPA), including public management, town, city and county management. Part-time programs available. Postbaccalaureate distance learning degree programs offered (no on-campus study). *Faculty:* 27 full-time (5 women), 12 part-time/adjunct (1 woman). *Students:* 65 full-time (26 women), 62 part-time (22 women); includes 6 minority (5 African Americans, 1 American Indian/Alaska Native), 1 international. 100 applicants, 93% accepted, 53 enrolled. In 2009, 45 master's awarded. *Degree requirements:* For master's, variable foreign language requirement, comprehensive exam, thesis optional. *Entrance requirements:* For master's, GRE General Test, 3 letters of recommendation. Additional exam requirements/recommendations for international students: Required—TOEFL (minimum score 570 paper-based; 230 computer-based; 79 iBT), IELTS (minimum score 6.5). *Application deadline:* For fall admission, 7/1 for domestic students, 2/1 for international students; for spring admission, 11/1 for domestic students, 7/1 for international students. Applications are processed on a rolling basis. Application fee: $50. Electronic applications accepted. *Expenses:* Tuition, state resident: full-time $2960. Tuition, nonresident: full-time $14,051. Required fees: $2320. *Financial support:* In 2009–10, 20 research assistantships (averaging $8,000 per year) were awarded; fellowships, teaching assistantships, career-related internships or fieldwork, Federal Work-Study, scholarships/grants, and unspecified assistantships also available. Financial award application deadline: 4/1; financial award applicants required to submit FAFSA. *Faculty research:* Campaign finance, emerging democracies, bureaucratic politics, judicial behavior, administration of justice. Total annual research expenditures: $320,000. *Unit head:* Dr. Brian Ellison, Chairperson, 828-262-3085, E-mail: ellisonba@appstate.edu. *Application contact:* Sandy Krause, Director of Admissions and Recruiting, 828-262-2130, Fax: 828-262-2709, E-mail: krausesl@appstate.edu.

Arcadia University, Graduate Studies, Program in International Relations and Diplomacy, Glenside, PA 19038-3295. Offers MA. In 2009, 9 master's awarded. *Expenses:* Tuition: Full-time $30,450; part-time $620 per credit hour. Required fees: $165. Tuition and fees vary according to program. *Unit head:* Dr. Eileen Servidio-Delabre, President, 33-1-47-20-00-94. *Application contact:* Office of Enrollment Management, 215-572-2910, Fax: 215-572-4049, E-mail: admiss@arcadia.edu.

Baylor University, Graduate School, College of Arts and Sciences, Department of Political Science, Waco, TX 76798. Offers international studies (MA); political science (MA, PhD); public policy and administration (MPPA); JD/MPPA. *Students:* 28 full-time (8 women), 1 part-time (0 women), 3 international. In 2009, 5 master's, 1 doctorate awarded. *Entrance requirements:* For master's, GRE General Test. *Application deadline:* Applications are processed on a rolling basis. Application fee: $25. *Financial support:* Research assistantships, career-related internships or fieldwork, Federal Work-Study, and institutionally sponsored loans available. Financial award application deadline: 3/1. *Unit head:* Dr. David Corey, Graduate Program Director, 254-710-3161, Fax: 254-710-3122, E-mail: david_d_corey@baylor.edu. *Application contact:* Jenice Langston, Administrative Assistant, 254-710-3161, Fax: 254-710-3870, E-mail: jenice_langston@baylor.edu.

Baylor University, Graduate School, Hankamer School of Business, Department of Economics, Waco, TX 76798. Offers economics (MS Eco); international economics (MA, MS). *Students:* 15 full-time (9 women), 1 part-time (0 women), 5 international. In 2009, 7 master's awarded. *Entrance requirements:* For master's, GMAT or GRE General Test. *Application deadline:* For fall admission, 8/1 for domestic students; for spring admission, 12/1 for domestic students. Applications are processed on a rolling basis. Application fee: $25. *Financial support:* Research assistantships, Federal Work-Study and institutionally sponsored loans available. Financial award application deadline: 4/1. *Faculty research:* Econometrics, international economics, private enterprise, comparative economic systems. *Unit head:* Dr. Steve Green, Chair, 254-710-4543, Fax: 254-710-3265, E-mail: steve_green@baylor.edu. *Application contact:* Susan Armstrong, Administrative Assistant, 254-710-6177, Fax: 254-710-1066, E-mail: susan_armstrong@baylor.edu.

Boston University, Graduate School of Arts and Sciences, Department of Geography and Environment, Boston, MA 02215. Offers energy and environmental analysis (MA); environmental remote sensing and GIs (MA); geography (MA); geography and environment (PhD); international relations and environmental policy (MA). *Students:* 50 full-time (22 women), 15 part-time (6 women); includes 2 minority (1 Asian American or Pacific Islander, 1 Hispanic American), 19 international. Average age 30. 64 applicants, 23% accepted, 5 enrolled. In 2009, 4 master's, 6 doctorates awarded. Terminal master's awarded for partial completion of doctoral program. *Degree requirements:* For master's, one foreign language, comprehensive exam, thesis; for doctorate, one foreign language, comprehensive exam, thesis/dissertation. *Entrance requirements:* For master's and doctorate, GRE General Test, GRE Subject Test, 3 letters of recommendation. Additional exam requirements/recommendations for international students: Required—TOEFL (minimum score 600 paper-based; 250 computer-based). *Application deadline:* For fall admission, 7/1 for domestic and international students; for spring admission, 11/15 for domestic and international students. Application fee: $70. Electronic applications accepted. *Expenses:* Tuition: Full-time $37,910; part-time $1184 per credit hour. Required fees: $386; $40 per semester. Part-time tuition and fees vary according to class time, course level, degree level and program. *Financial support:* In 2009–10, 33 students received support, including 2 fellowships with full tuition reimbursements available (averaging $18,900 per year), 20 research assistantships with full tuition reimbursements available (averaging $18,400 per year), 11 teaching assistantships with full tuition reimbursements available (averaging $18,400 per year); Federal Work-Study and unspecified assistantships also available. Support available to part-time students. Financial award application deadline: 1/15; financial award applicants required to submit FAFSA. Total annual research expenditures: $1.2 million. *Unit head:* Robert Kaufmann, Chairman, 617-353-3940, Fax: 617-353-8399, E-mail: kaufmann@bu.edu. *Application contact:* Christopher DeVits, Graduate Program Coordinator, 617-353-7554, Fax: 617-353-8399, E-mail: cdevits@bu.edu.

Boston University, Graduate School of Arts and Sciences, Department of International Relations, Boston, MA 02215. Offers African studies (Certificate); international relations (MA); international relations and environmental policy management (MA); international relations and international communication (MA); JD/MA; MBA/MA. *Students:* 66 full-time (41 women), 16 part-time (10 women); includes 7 minority (3 African Americans, 3 Asian Americans or Pacific Islanders, 1 Hispanic American), 16 international. Average age 27. 417 applicants, 59% accepted, 50 enrolled. In 2009, 43 master's awarded. *Degree requirements:* For master's, one foreign language, comprehensive exam, thesis. *Entrance requirements:* For master's, GRE General Test, 3 letters of recommendation; for Certificate, GRE General Test. Additional exam requirements/recommendations for international students: Required—TOEFL (minimum score 600 paper-based; 250 computer-based). *Application deadline:* For fall admission, 4/15 for domestic and international students; for spring admission, 10/15 for domestic and international students. Application fee: $70. Electronic applications accepted. *Expenses:* Tuition: Full-time $37,910; part-time $1184 per credit hour. Required fees: $386; $40 per semester. Part-time tuition and fees vary according to class time, course level, degree level and program. *Financial support:* In 2009–10, 17 students received support. Federal Work-Study, scholarships/grants, and unspecified assistantships available. Support available to part-time students. Financial award application deadline: 1/15; financial award applicants required to submit FAFSA. *Unit head:* Dr. Erik Goldstein, Chairman, 617-353-9280, Fax: 617-353-9290, E-mail: goldstee@bu.edu. *Application contact:* Michael Williams, Graduate Program Administrator, 617-353-9349, Fax: 617-353-9290, E-mail: mawillia@bu.edu.

Brandeis University, Graduate School of Arts and Sciences, Graduate Program in Global Studies, Waltham, MA 02454-9110. Offers MA. Part-time programs available. *Faculty:* 8 full-time (3 women). *Students:* 10 full-time (6 women), 1 part-time (0 women); includes 4 minority (3 Asian Americans or Pacific Islanders, 1 Hispanic American), 1 international. 32 applicants, 66% accepted, 11 enrolled. *Degree requirements:* For master's, thesis. *Entrance requirements:* For master's, GRE, official transcript(s), 2 recommendation letters, CV or resume, statement of purpose, writing sample. Additional exam requirements/recommendations for international students: Required—TOEFL (minimum score 600 paper-based; 250 computer-based; 100 iBT); Recommended—IELTS (minimum score 7). *Application deadline:* Applications are processed on a rolling basis. Application fee: $75. Electronic applications accepted. *Financial support:* In 2009–10, 7 teaching assistantships (averaging $3,200 per year) were awarded; scholarships/grants and unspecified assistantships also available. Support available to part-time students. Financial award application deadline: 4/15; financial award applicants required to submit FAFSA. *Faculty research:* Globalization, civil society and human rights, communications and media,culture and globalization, global and regional governance, global environment, global health, immigration, social justice and gender. *Unit head:* Prof. Richard J. Parmentier, Director, 781-736-2220, E-mail: rparmentier@brandeis.edu. *Application contact:* Mangok Bol, Department Administrator, 781-736-2234, Fax: 781-736-2232, E-mail: mbol@brandeis.edu.

Brandeis University, International Business School, Waltham, MA 02454-9110. Offers finance (MSF); international business (MBAi); international economics and finance (MA, PhD); international finance/international economics (MBAi). Part-time and evening/weekend programs available. Terminal master's awarded for partial completion of doctoral program. *Degree requirements:* For master's, one foreign language, semester abroad; for doctorate, thesis/dissertation. *Entrance requirements:* For master's, GMAT or GRE General Test (MA), GMAT (MBAi, MSF); for doctorate, GRE General Test. Additional exam requirements/recommendations for international students: Required—TOEFL (minimum score 600 paper-based; 250 computer-based), IELTS (minimum score 7). Electronic applications accepted. *Faculty research:* International finance and business, trade policy, macroeconomics, Asian economic issues, developmental economics.

Brock University, Faculty of Graduate Studies, Faculty of Social Sciences, Program in Political Science, St. Catharines, ON L2S 3A1, Canada. Offers Canadian politics (MA); comparative politics (MA); international relations (MA); political theory or philosophy (MA); public policy (MA). Part-time programs available. *Degree requirements:* For master's, thesis optional. *Entrance requirements:* For master's, honors degree. Additional exam requirements/recommendations for international students: Required—TOEFL (minimum score 550 paper-based; 213 computer-based; 80 iBT), IELTS (minimum score 6.5), TWE (minimum score 4). Electronic applications accepted. *Faculty research:* Public administration reform, economic and social justice, politics of societies, Canadian politics, international relations.

Brooklyn College of the City University of New York, Division of Graduate Studies, Department of Political Science, Brooklyn, NY 11210-2889. Offers international affairs (MA); political science (MA, PhD); political science, urban policy and administration (MA). Part-time and evening/weekend programs available. *Students:* 24 full-time (13 women), 168 part-time (98 women); includes 99 minority (70 African Americans, 13 Asian Americans or Pacific Islanders, 16 Hispanic Americans), 29 international. Average age 30. 123 applicants, 87% accepted, 79 enrolled. In 2009, 46 master's awarded. *Degree requirements:* For master's, comprehensive exam (for some programs), thesis or alternative, foreign language exam (for international affairs program). *Entrance requirements:* For master's, 2 letters of recommendation, personal statement. Additional exam requirements/recommendations for international students: Required—TOEFL (minimum score 500 paper-based; 173 computer-based; 61 iBT). *Application deadline:* For fall admission, 5/1 for domestic and international students; for spring admission, 12/12 for domestic students, 11/1 for international students. *Expenses:* Tuition, area resident: Full-time $7360; part-time $310 per credit hour. Tuition, state resident: full-time $7360; part-time $310 per credit hour. Tuition, nonresident: full-time $13,800; part-time $575 per credit hour. International tuition: $13,800 full-time. Required fees: $140.10 per semester. *Financial support:* Career-related internships or fieldwork and Federal Work-Study available. Support available to part-time students. Financial award application deadline: 5/1; financial award applicants required to submit FAFSA. *Faculty research:* Ethics and politics, politics of criminal justice, Western Europe, international law and politics, labor politics. *Unit head:* Dr. Noel Anderson, Acting Chairperson, 718-951-5306, E-mail: anderson@brooklyn.cuny.edu. *Application contact:* Hernan Sierra, Graduate Admissions Coordinator, 718-951-4536, Fax: 718-951-4506, E-mail: grads@brooklyn.cuny.edu.

California State University, Fresno, Division of Graduate Studies, College of Social Sciences, Department of Political Science, Program in International Relations, Fresno, CA 93740-8027. Offers MA. Part-time and evening/weekend programs available. *Degree requirements:* For master's, one foreign language, thesis or alternative. *Entrance requirements:* For master's, GRE General Test, minimum GPA of 3.0. Additional exam requirements/recommendations for international students: Required—TOEFL. Electronic applications accepted.

California State University, Sacramento, Graduate Studies, College of Social Sciences and Interdisciplinary Studies, International Affairs Graduate Program, Sacramento, CA 95819. Offers MA. Part-time programs available. *Degree requirements:* For master's, one foreign language, thesis or alternative, writing proficiency exam. *Entrance requirements:* For master's, GRE General Test, appropriate bachelor's degree, minimum GPA of 3.0 in last 2 years of course work. Additional exam requirements/recommendations for international students: Required—TOEFL. Electronic applications accepted.

California State University, Stanislaus, College of Humanities and Social Sciences, Department of History, Turlock, CA 95382. Offers history (MA); international relations (MA); secondary school teachers (MA). Part-time programs available. *Degree requirements:* For master's, one foreign language, comprehensive exam, thesis or alternative. *Entrance requirements:* For master's, GRE General Test, minimum undergraduate GPA of 3.0. Additional exam requirements/recommendations for international students: Required—TOEFL (minimum score 550 paper-based; 213 computer-based). Electronic applications accepted. *Faculty research:* History of Ancient Greece, history and ecology of the central valley, acculturation and gender.

Carleton University, Faculty of Graduate Studies, Faculty of Public Affairs and Management, Norman Paterson School of International Affairs, Ottawa, ON K1S 5B6, Canada. Offers MA, PhD. Part-time programs available. *Degree requirements:* For master's, one foreign language, comprehensive exam, thesis optional. *Entrance requirements:* For master's, honors degree. Additional exam requirements/recommendations for international students: Required—TOEFL. *Faculty research:* International conflict, development, political economy, conflict analysis.

The Catholic University of America, School of Arts and Sciences, Department of Business and Economics, Washington, DC 20064. Offers international political economics (MA). Part-time programs available. *Faculty:* 7 full-time (2 women), 10 part-time/adjunct (5 women). *Students:* 1 part-time (0 women); minority (African American). Average age 30. In 2009, 26 master's awarded. *Degree requirements:* For master's, comprehensive exam. *Entrance requirements:* For master's, GRE General Test, 3 letters of recommendation. Additional exam requirements/recommendations for international students: Required—TOEFL (minimum score 580 paper-based; 237 computer-based). *Application deadline:* For fall admission, 8/1 priority date for domestic students, 7/15 for international students; for spring admission, 12/1 priority date for domestic students, 10/15 for international students. Applications are processed on a rolling basis. Application fee: $55. Electronic applications accepted. *Expenses:* Tuition: Full-time $31,740; part-time $1245 per credit hour. Required fees: $50; $25 per semester hour. One-time fee: $425. *Financial support:* Fellowships, research assistantships, teaching assistantships, Federal Work-Study, scholarships/grants, tuition waivers (full and partial), and unspecified assistantships available. Financial award application deadline: 2/1; financial award applicants required to submit FAFSA. *Faculty research:* Integrity of the marketing process, economics of energy and the environment, emerging markets, social change, international finance and economic development. Total annual research expenditures: $6,459. *Unit head:* Dr. Andrew V. Abela, Chair, 202-319-5235, Fax: 202-319-4426, E-mail: abela@cua.edu. *Application contact:* Julie Schwing, Director of Graduate Admissions, 202-319-5057, Fax: 202-319-6533, E-mail: cua-admissions@cua.edu.

The Catholic University of America, School of Arts and Sciences, Department of Politics, Washington, DC 20064. Offers American government (MA, PhD); Congressional and presidential studies (MA); international affairs (MA); international political economics (MA); political theory (MA, PhD); world politics (MA, PhD); MA/JD. Part-time programs available. *Faculty:* 13 full-time (1 woman), 8 part-time/adjunct (0 women). *Students:* 31 full-time (8 women), 73 part-time (21 women); includes 13 minority (5 African Americans, 4 Asian Americans or Pacific Islanders, 4 Hispanic Americans), 10 international. Average age 30. 120 applicants, 66% accepted, 30 enrolled. In 2009, 32 master's, 7 doctorates awarded. *Degree requirements:* For master's, one foreign language, comprehensive exam, thesis or alternative; for doctorate, variable foreign language requirement, comprehensive exam, thesis/dissertation. *Entrance requirements:* For master's, GRE General Test, 3 letters of recommendation, minimum GPA of 3.0; for doctorate, GRE General Test, statement of purpose, official copies of academic transcripts, three letters of recommendation, minimum GPA of 3.0. Additional exam requirements/recommendations for international students: Required—TOEFL (minimum score 580 paper-based; 237 computer-based). *Application deadline:* For fall admission, 8/1 priority date for domestic students, 7/15 for international students; for spring admission, 12/1 priority date for domestic students, 10/15 for international students. Applications are processed on a rolling basis. Application fee: $55. Electronic applications accepted. *Expenses:* Tuition: Full-time $31,740; part-time $1245 per credit hour. Required fees: $50; $25 per semester hour. One-time fee: $425. *Financial support:* Fellowships, research assistantships, teaching assistantships, Federal Work-Study, scholarships/grants, tuition waivers (full and partial), and unspecified assistantships available. Financial award application deadline: 2/1; financial award applicants required to submit FAFSA. *Faculty research:* Political philosophy, American political institutions and processes, political economy, international relations, U.S. political leadership since 1789. *Unit head:* Dr. Philip Henderson, Chair, 202-319-6226, Fax: 202-319-6289, E-mail: hendersp@cua.edu. *Application contact:* Julie Schwing, Director of Graduate Admissions, 202-319-5057, Fax: 202-319-6533, E-mail: cua-admissions@cua.edu.

Central Connecticut State University, School of Graduate Studies, School of Arts and Sciences, Program in International Area Studies, New Britain, CT 06050-4010. Offers international studies (MS). Part-time and evening/weekend programs available. *Students:* 16 full-time (5 women), 22 part-time (14 women); includes 9 minority (6 African Americans, 1 Asian American or Pacific Islander, 2 Hispanic Americans), 1 international. Average age 33. 27 applicants, 56% accepted, 14 enrolled. In 2009, 5 master's awarded. *Degree requirements:* For master's, comprehensive exam, thesis or alternative. *Entrance requirements:* For master's, minimum undergraduate GPA of 2.7. Additional exam requirements/recommendations for international students: Required—TOEFL. *Application deadline:* For fall admission, 5/1 for domestic students; for spring admission, 12/1 for domestic students. Applications are processed on a rolling basis. Application fee: $50. Electronic applications accepted. *Expenses:* Tuition, area resident: Full-time $4662; part-time $440 per credit. Tuition, state resident: full-time $6994; part-time $440 per credit. Tuition, nonresident: full-time $12,988; part-time $440 per credit. Required fees: $3606. One-time fee: $62 part-time. *Financial support:* In 2009–10, 4 students received support, including 2 research assistantships; career-related internships or fieldwork, Federal Work-Study, scholarships/grants, and unspecified assistantships also available. Support available to part-time students. Financial award application deadline: 3/1; financial award applicants required to submit FAFSA. *Unit head:* Dr. Evelyn Newman Phillips, Program Director, 860-832-2617. *Application contact:* Dr. Evelyn Newman Phillips, Program Director, 860-832-2617.

Central European University, Graduate Studies, School of Social Sciences and Humanities, Budapest, Hungary. Offers economics (MA, PhD); gender studies (MA, PhD); international relations and European studies (MA, PhD); mathematics and its applications (MS, PhD); medieval studies (MA, PhD); nationalism studies (MA, PhD); philosophy (MA, PhD); political science (MA, PhD); public policy (MA, PhD); sociology and social anthropology (MA, PhD). Terminal master's awarded for partial completion of doctoral program. *Degree requirements:* For master's, one foreign language, thesis; for doctorate, one foreign language, comprehensive exam, thesis/dissertation. *Entrance requirements:* For master's, interview; for doctorate, GRE, CEU subject test, interview. Additional exam requirements/recommendations for international students: Required—TOEFL (minimum score 570 paper-based; 230 computer-based). Electronic applications accepted. *Faculty research:* Civil society, fiscal decentralization, party politics, political philosophy (especially Liberalism, theory of Democracy).

Central Michigan University, Central Michigan University Off-Campus Programs, Program in Administration, Mount Pleasant, MI 48859. Offers acquisitions administration (MSA, Certificate); general administration (MSA, Certificate); health services administration (MSA, Certificate); human resources administration (MSA, Certificate); information resource management (MSA, Certificate); international administration (MSA, Certificate); leadership (MSA, Certificate); public administration (MSA, Certificate); vehicle design and manufacturing administration (MSA, Certificate). Part-time and evening/weekend programs available. Postbaccalaureate distance learning degree programs offered (no on-campus study). *Students:* Average age 38. *Entrance requirements:* For master's, minimum GPA of 2.7 in major. *Application deadline:* Applications are processed on a rolling basis. Application fee: $50. Electronic applications accepted. *Financial support:* Scholarships/grants available. Support available to part-time students. Financial award applicants required to submit FAFSA. *Unit head:* Dr. Nana Korsah, Director, MSA Programs, 989-774-6525, E-mail: korsa1na@cmich.edu. *Application contact:* 877-268-4636, E-mail: cmuoffcampus@cmich.edu.

Chapman University, Graduate Studies, Wilkinson College of Humanities and Social Sciences, International Studies Program, Orange, CA 92866. Offers MA. Part-time and evening/weekend programs available. *Faculty:* 12 full-time (5 women). *Students:* 12 full-time (8 women); includes 9 minority (2 African Americans, 2 Asian Americans or Pacific Islanders, 5 Hispanic Americans). Average age 24. 22 applicants, 91% accepted, 12 enrolled. *Entrance requirements:* For master's, GRE, 2 letters of recommendation. Additional exam requirements/recommendations for international students: Required—TOEFL (minimum score 550 paper-based; 213 computer-based; 80 iBT). Application fee: $50. Tuition and fees vary according to course load, degree level and program. *Financial support:* Fellowships, Federal Work-Study

International Affairs

Chapman University (continued)
and scholarships/grants available. Financial award applicants required to submit FAFSA. *Unit head:* Dr. James Coyle, Director, 714-744-7074, E-mail: coyle@chapman.edu. *Application contact:* Priscilla Garcia Powers, Graduate Admission Counselor, 714-997-6711, E-mail: pgarcia@chapman.edu.

City College of the City University of New York, Graduate School, College of Liberal Arts and Science, Division of Social Science, Program in International Relations, New York, NY 10031-9198. Offers MA. Part-time programs available. *Degree requirements:* For master's, one foreign language, thesis. *Entrance requirements:* For master's, GRE, 3 letters of recommendation. Additional exam requirements/recommendations for international students: Required—TOEFL (minimum score 600 paper-based; 100 iBT). Electronic applications accepted. *Faculty research:* International finance, international economics, European diplomatic history, area studies, international politics and diplomacy.

Claremont Graduate University, Graduate Programs, School of Politics and Economics, Department of Politics and Policy, Claremont, CA 91711-6160. Offers American politics (MA, PhD); comparative politics (PhD); international political economy (MA); international studies (MA); political philosophy (PhD); political science (PhD); politics, economics and business (MA); public policy (MA, PhD); world politics (PhD); MBA/PhD. Part-time programs available. *Faculty:* 8 full-time (3 women), 4 part-time/adjunct (0 women). *Students:* 163 full-time (68 women), 16 part-time (7 women); includes 29 minority (6 African Americans, 8 Asian Americans or Pacific Islanders, 15 Hispanic Americans), 40 international. Average age 32. In 2009, 23 master's, 19 doctorates awarded. Terminal master's awarded for partial completion of doctoral program. *Entrance requirements:* For master's and doctorate, GRE General Test. Additional exam requirements/recommendations for international students: Required—TOEFL (minimum score 550 paper-based; 213 computer-based; 80 iBT). *Application deadline:* For fall admission, 2/1 priority date for domestic students. Applications are processed on a rolling basis. Application fee: $60. Electronic applications accepted. *Expenses:* Tuition: Full-time $35,046; part-time $1524 per credit. Required fees: $161 per semester. *Financial support:* Fellowships, research assistantships, teaching assistantships, Federal Work-Study, institutionally sponsored loans, and scholarships/grants available. Support available to part-time students. Financial award application deadline: 2/15; financial award applicants required to submit FAFSA. *Faculty research:* Environmental policy, international debt, global democratization, Third World development, public sector discrimination. *Unit head:* Jennifer Merolla, Chair, 909-621-8696, Fax: 909-621-8545, E-mail: jennifer.merolla@cgu.edu. *Application contact:* Lesa Hiben, Admissions Coordinator, 909-621-8699, Fax: 909-621-7545, E-mail: lesa.hiben@cga.edu.

Colorado School of Mines, Graduate School, Division of Liberal Arts and International Studies, Golden, CO 80401. Offers international political economy (Graduate Certificate); liberal arts and international studies (MIPER); science and technology policy (Graduate Certificate). Part-time programs available. *Faculty:* 20 full-time (8 women), 26 part-time/adjunct (14 women). *Students:* 16 full-time (7 women), 5 part-time (2 women); includes 4 minority (2 Asian Americans or Pacific Islanders, 2 Hispanic Americans), 6 international. Average age 28. 13 applicants, 92% accepted, 9 enrolled. In 2009, 10 master's awarded. *Degree requirements:* For master's, thesis (for some programs). *Entrance requirements:* For master's, GRE. Additional exam requirements/recommendations for international students: Required—TOEFL (minimum score 550 paper-based; 213 computer-based; 80 iBT). *Application deadline:* For fall admission, 1/15 priority date for domestic and international students; for spring admission, 9/1 priority date for domestic and international students. Application fee: $50 ($70 for international students). Electronic applications accepted. *Expenses:* Tuition, state resident: full-time $10,584; part-time $588 per credit hour. Tuition, nonresident: full-time $24,750; part-time $1375 per credit hour. Required fees: $1654; $827.10 per semester. *Financial support:* In 2009–10, 9 students received support, including fellowships with full tuition reimbursements available (averaging $20,000 per year), research assistantships with full tuition reimbursements available (averaging $20,000 per year), 9 teaching assistantships with full tuition reimbursements available (averaging $20,000 per year); scholarships/grants, health care benefits, and unspecified assistantships also available. Financial award application deadline: 1/15. Total annual research expenditures: $38,822. *Unit head:* Dr. James Jesudason, Director, 303-273-3425, Fax: 303-273-3751, E-mail: jjesudas@mines.edu. *Application contact:* Connie Warren, Program Assistant, 303-273-3590, Fax: 303-273-3751, E-mail: cwarren@mines.edu.

Columbia University, School of International and Public Affairs, Program in International Affairs, New York, NY 10027. Offers MIA, JD/MIA, MBA/MIA, MIA/MS, MPH/MIA, MSJ/MIA. *Degree requirements:* For master's, one foreign language. *Entrance requirements:* For master's, GRE General Test. Additional exam requirements/recommendations for international students: Required—TOEFL (minimum score 600 paper-based; 250 computer-based; 100 iBT). Electronic applications accepted.

Concordia University, School of Business and Professional Studies, Irvine, CA 92612-3299. Offers business administration: business practice (MBA); international studies (MA). Part-time and evening/weekend programs available. Postbaccalaureate distance learning degree programs offered. *Faculty:* 4 full-time (0 women), 18 part-time/adjunct (3 women). *Students:* 84 full-time (32 women), 50 part-time (30 women); includes 38 minority (5 African Americans, 1 American Indian/Alaska Native, 21 Asian Americans or Pacific Islanders, 11 Hispanic Americans), 13 international. Average age 30. 36 applicants, 81% accepted, 22 enrolled. In 2009, 67 master's awarded. *Degree requirements:* For master's, capstone project or thesis. *Entrance requirements:* For master's, resume, 2 references, interview (MBA). Additional exam requirements/recommendations for international students: Required—TOEFL. *Application deadline:* For fall admission, 8/1 for domestic students, 6/1 for international students; for spring admission, 1/1 for domestic students, 11/1 for international students. Application fee: $50 ($125 for international students). Electronic applications accepted. *Expenses:* Contact institution. *Financial support:* In 2009–10, 95 students received support. Tuition waivers (full and partial) and unspecified assistantships available. Financial award applicants required to submit FAFSA. *Unit head:* Dr. Timothy Peters, Dean, 949-854-8002 Ext. 1333, E-mail: tim.peters@cui.edu. *Application contact:* Aaron Stewart, Assistant Director of Graduate and Adult Admissions, 949-854-8002 Ext. 1343, Fax: 949-854-6894, E-mail: aaron.stewart@cui.edu.

Cornell University, Graduate School, Graduate Fields of Arts and Sciences, Field of Government, Ithaca, NY 14853-0001. Offers American politics (PhD); comparative politics (PhD); international relations (PhD); political methodology (PhD); political thought (PhD); public policy (PhD). *Faculty:* 58 full-time (19 women). *Students:* 65 full-time (35 women); includes 9 minority (1 African American, 1 American Indian/Alaska Native, 2 Asian Americans or Pacific Islanders, 5 Hispanic Americans), 20 international. Average age 29. 317 applicants, 7% accepted, 11 enrolled. In 2009, 14 doctorates awarded. *Degree requirements:* For doctorate, comprehensive exam, thesis/dissertation. *Entrance requirements:* For doctorate, GRE General Test, sample of written work, 3 letters of recommendation. Additional exam requirements/recommendations for international students: Required—TOEFL (minimum score 550 paper-based; 213 computer-based; 77 iBT). *Application deadline:* For fall admission, 1/15 for domestic students. Application fee: $70. Electronic applications accepted. *Expenses:* Tuition: Full-time $29,500. Required fees: $70. Full-time tuition and fees vary according to degree level, program and student level. *Financial support:* In 2009–10, 60 students received support, including 10 fellowships with full tuition reimbursements available; research assistantships with full tuition reimbursements available, teaching assistantships with full tuition reimbursements available, institutionally sponsored loans, scholarships/grants, health care benefits, tuition waivers (full and partial), and unspecified assistantships also available. Financial award applicants required to submit FAFSA. *Faculty research:* Political theory, American politics, comparative politics, international relations, methodology. *Unit head:* Director of Graduate Studies, 607-255-3567, Fax: 607-255-4530. *Application contact:* Graduate Field Assistant, 607-255-3567, Fax: 607-255-4530, E-mail: cu_govt@cornell.edu.

Creighton University, Graduate School, College of Arts and Sciences, Program in International Relations, Omaha, NE 68178-0001. Offers MA. Part-time and evening/weekend programs available. *Faculty:* 10 full-time (3 women). *Students:* 7 full-time (4 women), 14 part-time (4 women), 3 international. Average age 29. 15 applicants, 67% accepted, 10 enrolled. In 2009, 5 master's awarded. *Degree requirements:* For master's, one foreign language, thesis optional. *Entrance requirements:* For master's, GRE General Test, 3 letters of recommendation. Additional exam requirements/recommendations for international students: Required—TOEFL (minimum score 550 paper-based; 213 computer-based; 80 iBT). *Application deadline:* For fall admission, 3/1 priority date for domestic and international students; for winter admission, 12/1 priority date for domestic students, 7/1 priority date for international students; for spring admission, 4/1 priority date for domestic students, 9/1 priority date for international students. Applications are processed on a rolling basis. Application fee: $50. Electronic applications accepted. *Expenses:* Tuition: Full-time $11,700; part-time $650 per credit hour. Required fees: $126 per semester. *Financial support:* In 2009–10, 4 fellowships with full and partial tuition reimbursements (averaging $10,438 per year) were awarded; research assistantships with tuition reimbursements, health care benefits also available. Support available to part-time students. Financial award application deadline: 5/1; financial award applicants required to submit FAFSA. *Unit head:* Dr. Terry Clark, Chair, 402-280-4712, E-mail: tclark@creighton.edu. *Application contact:* Taunya Plater, Senior Program Coordinator, 402-280-2870, Fax: 402-280-2899, E-mail: taunyaplater@creighton.edu.

East Carolina University, Graduate School, Thomas Harriot College of Arts and Sciences, Program in International Studies, Greenville, NC 27858-4353. Offers MA. Part-time programs available. *Degree requirements:* For master's, comprehensive exam. *Entrance requirements:* For master's, GRE General Test. Additional exam requirements/recommendations for international students: Required—TOEFL.

Fairleigh Dickinson University, Metropolitan Campus, University College: Arts, Sciences, and Professional Studies, School of History, Political and International Studies, Program in International Studies, Teaneck, NJ 07666-1914. Offers MA. *Students:* 6 full-time (3 women), 8 part-time (6 women), 3 international. Average age 31. 11 applicants, 55% accepted, 2 enrolled. In 2009, 3 master's awarded. *Application deadline:* Applications are processed on a rolling basis. Application fee: $40. *Application contact:* Susan Brooman, University Director of Graduate Admissions, 201-692-2554, Fax: 201-692-2560, E-mail: globaleducation@fdu.edu.

Florida Agricultural and Mechanical University, Division of Graduate Studies, Research, and Continuing Education, College of Engineering Science, Technology, and Agriculture, Division of Agricultural Sciences, Tallahassee, FL 32307-3200. Offers agribusiness (MS); animal science (MS); engineering technology (MS); entomology (MS); food science (MS); international programs (MS); plant science (MS). *Faculty:* 31 full-time (2 women). *Students:* 14 full-time (8 women), 8 part-time (4 women); includes 17 minority (16 African Americans, 1 Asian American or Pacific Islander), 3 international. In 2009, 7 master's awarded. *Degree requirements:* For master's, thesis. *Entrance requirements:* For master's, GRE General Test, minimum GPA of 3.0. Additional exam requirements/recommendations for international students: Required—TOEFL (minimum score 500 paper-based). *Application deadline:* For fall admission, 5/18 for domestic students, 12/18 for international students; for spring admission, 11/12 for domestic students, 5/12 for international students. Application fee: $20. *Financial support:* Application deadline: 2/15. *Unit head:* Dr. Mitwe N. Musingo, Graduate Coordinator, 850-561-2309, Fax: 850-599-8821. *Application contact:* Dr. Chanta M. Haywood, Dean of Graduate Studies, Research, and Continuing Education, 850-599-3315, Fax: 850-599-3727.

Florida International University, College of Arts and Sciences, Department of Politics and International Relations, Miami, FL 33199. Offers international relations (MA, PhD), including international studies; political science (MA, PhD). Fall admission only for PhD. Part-time and evening/weekend programs available. *Faculty:* 26 full-time (7 women). *Students:* 56 full-time (20 women), 42 part-time (23 women); includes 38 minority (11 African Americans, 1 American Indian/Alaska Native, 6 Asian Americans or Pacific Islanders, 20 Hispanic Americans), 24 international. Average age 30. 125 applicants, 19% accepted, 20 enrolled. In 2009, 30 master's, 5 doctorates awarded. *Degree requirements:* For master's, one foreign language, thesis optional; for doctorate, one foreign language, comprehensive exam, thesis/dissertation. *Entrance requirements:* For master's and doctorate, GRE General Test, minimum GPA of 3.0, letters of recommendation. Additional exam requirements/recommendations for international students: Required—TOEFL (minimum score 550 paper-based; 80 iBT). *Application deadline:* For fall admission, 3/15 for domestic and international students; for spring admission, 8/15 for domestic and international students. Application fee: $30. Electronic applications accepted. *Expenses:* Tuition, state resident: full-time $8008; part-time $4004 per year. Tuition, nonresident: full-time $20,104; part-time $10,052 per year. Required fees: $298; $149 per term. *Financial support:* Institutionally sponsored loans, scholarships/grants, and unspecified assistantships available. Financial award application deadline: 3/1; financial award applicants required to submit FAFSA. *Unit head:* Dr. Richard Olsen, Chair, 305-348-2556, Fax: 305-348-6138, E-mail: pir@fiu.edu. *Application contact:* Dr. Ronald Cox, Director of Graduate Studies, 305-348-2556, Fax: 305-348-6138, E-mail: pir@fiu.edu.

Florida State University, The Graduate School, College of Social Sciences and Public Policy, Program in International Affairs, Tallahassee, FL 32306. Offers MA, MS, JD/MA, JD/MS. Part-time programs available. *Students:* 47 full-time (24 women), 55 part-time (28 women); includes 23 minority (9 African Americans, 1 American Indian/Alaska Native, 2 Asian Americans or Pacific Islanders, 11 Hispanic Americans), 12 international. Average age 25. 130 applicants, 97% accepted, 55 enrolled. In 2009, 36 master's awarded. *Degree requirements:* For master's, one foreign language, comprehensive exam, thesis optional. *Entrance requirements:* For master's, GRE General Test, minimum GPA of 3.0. Additional exam requirements/recommendations for international students: Required—TOEFL (minimum score 550 paper-based; 213 computer-based; 80 iBT). *Application deadline:* For fall admission, 7/1 for domestic students; for spring admission, 7/1 for domestic students. Applications are processed on a rolling basis. Application fee: $30. *Expenses:* Tuition, state resident: full-time $7413. Tuition, nonresident: full-time $22,567. *Financial support:* In 2009–10, 5 students received support, including 5 research assistantships with full tuition reimbursements available (averaging $5,000 per year); career-related internships or fieldwork, Federal Work-Study, institutionally sponsored loans, and unspecified assistantships also available. Financial award application deadline: 2/1; financial award applicants required to submit FAFSA. *Unit head:* Dr. Lee K. Metcalf, Director, 850-644-7327, Fax: 850-645-4981, E-mail: lmetcalf@fsu.edu. *Application contact:* Patty Lollis, Academic Program Specialist, 850-644-4418, Fax: 850-645-4981, E-mail: plollis@fsu.edu.

Fordham University, Graduate School of Arts and Sciences, Program in International Political Economy and Development, New York, NY 10458. Offers MA, Certificate. Part-time and evening/weekend programs available. *Students:* 44 full-time (15 women), 18 part-time (10 women); includes 6 minority (1 African American, 1 American Indian/Alaska Native, 1 Asian American or Pacific Islander, 3 Hispanic Americans), 21 international. Average age 28. 213 applicants, 37% accepted, 36 enrolled. In 2009, 28 master's awarded. *Degree requirements:* For master's, comprehensive exam. *Entrance requirements:* For master's, GRE General Test. Additional exam requirements/recommendations for international students: Required—TOEFL (minimum score 600 paper-based; 250 computer-based). *Application deadline:* For fall admission, 1/4 priority date for domestic students; for spring admission, 11/1 for domestic students. Application fee: $70. Electronic applications accepted. *Financial support:* In 2009–10, 16 students received support, including 16 research assistantships with tuition reimbursements available (averaging $18,400 per year); career-related internships or fieldwork, institutionally sponsored loans, tuition waivers (full and partial), and unspecified assistantships also available. Financial award application deadline: 1/4; financial award applicants required to submit FAFSA. *Faculty research:* International economics, comparative international politics, international banking and finance, international development, emerging markets and country risk analysis. *Unit head:* Dr. Henry Schwalbenberg, Chair, 718-817-3866, Fax: 718-817-3518. *Application contact:* Charlene Dundie, Director of Graduate Admissions, 718-817-4420, Fax: 718-817-3566, E-mail: dundie@fordham.edu.

George Mason University, School of Public Policy, Program in International Commerce and Policy, Fairfax, VA 22030. Offers MA. Part-time programs available. *Faculty:* 61 full-time (14 women), 30 part-time/adjunct (4 women). *Students:* 69 full-time (39 women), 170 part-time (95 women); includes 37 minority (9 African Americans, 10 Asian Americans or Pacific Islanders, 18 Hispanic Americans), 25 international. 183 applicants, 73% accepted, 77 enrolled. In 2009, 96 master's awarded. *Degree requirements:* For master's, thesis or alternative. *Entrance requirements:* For master's, GRE (for students seeking merit-based scholarships), minimum undergraduate GPA of 3.0, 2 letters of recommendation, resume. Additional exam requirements/recommendations for international students: Required—TOEFL (minimum score 575 paper-based; 230 computer-based; 88 iBT). *Application deadline:* For fall admission, 6/1 priority date for domestic students, 5/1 priority date for international students; for spring admission, 12/1 priority date for domestic students, 11/1 priority date for international students. Applications are processed on a rolling basis. Application fee: $60. Electronic applications accepted. *Expenses:* Contact institution. *Financial support:* Career-related internships or fieldwork, Federal Work-Study, scholarships/grants, and tuition waivers (partial) available. Support available to part-time students. Financial award application deadline: 3/1; financial award applicants required to submit FAFSA. *Unit head:* Dr. Kenneth Reinert, Director, 703-993-8099, E-mail: spp@gmu.edu. *Application contact:* Leslie Metzger Levin, Assistant Dean, Graduate Admissions and Marketing, 703-993-8099, Fax: 703-993-4876, E-mail: lmetzger@gmu.edu.

Georgetown University, Graduate School of Arts and Sciences, BMW Center for German and European Studies, Washington, DC 20057. Offers MA, MA/JD, MA/PhD. *Degree requirements:* For master's, 2 foreign languages, comprehensive exam. *Entrance requirements:* For master's, GRE General Test. Additional exam requirements/recommendations for international students: Required—TOEFL. *Faculty research:* Trans-Atlantic relations, European Union, German and European Studies.

Georgetown University, Graduate School of Arts and Sciences, Department of Government, Washington, DC 20057. Offers American government (MA, PhD); comparative government (PhD); conflict resolution (MA); democracy and governance (MA); international law and government (MA); international relations (PhD); political theory (PhD); MA/PhD. Terminal master's awarded for partial completion of doctoral program. *Degree requirements:* For master's, one foreign language, comprehensive exam; for doctorate, one foreign language, comprehensive exam, thesis/dissertation. *Entrance requirements:* For master's, GRE General Test, minimum B average; for doctorate, GRE General Test, MA. Additional exam requirements/recommendations for international students: Required—TOEFL. *Faculty research:* Western Europe, Latin America, the Middle East, political theory, international relations and law, methodology, American politics and institutions.

Georgetown University, Graduate School of Arts and Sciences, Edmund A. Walsh School of Foreign Service, Washington, DC 20057. Offers foreign service (MS); security studies (MA); JD/MS; MA/JD; MA/PhD; MBA/MS; MS/MA. *Degree requirements:* For master's, one foreign language, comprehensive exam. *Entrance requirements:* For master's, GRE General Test, 3 semesters of undergraduate course work in economics. Additional exam requirements/recommendations for international students: Required—TOEFL. *Faculty research:* International business diplomacy, political risk analysis, foreign policy decision making, intercultural perspectives on contemporary issues.

Georgetown University, Graduate School of Arts and Sciences, School of Continuing Studies, Washington, DC 20057. Offers American studies (MALS); Catholic studies (MALS); classical civilizations (MALS); ethics and the professions (MALS); human resources management (MPS); humanities (MALS); individualized study (MALS); international affairs (MALS); Islam and Muslim-Christian relations (MALS); journalism (MPS); liberal studies (DLS); literature and society (MALS); medieval and early modern European studies (MALS); public relations (MPS); real estate (MPS); religious studies (MALS); social and public policy (MALS); sports industry management (MPS); the theory and practice of American democracy (MALS); visual culture (MALS). *Entrance requirements:* Additional exam requirements/recommendations for international students: Required—TOEFL.

Georgetown University, Law Center, Washington, DC 20001. Offers general (LL M); global health law (LL M); international and comparative law (LL M); international business and economic law (LL M); international legal studies (LL M); law (JD, SJD); securities and financial regulation (LL M); taxation (LL M); JD/LL M; JD/MA; JD/MBA; JD/MPH; JD/PhD. *Accreditation:* ABA. Part-time and evening/weekend programs available. *Degree requirements:* For master's, thesis; for doctorate, thesis/dissertation. *Entrance requirements:* For JD, LSAT; for master's and doctorate, JD, LL B, or first law degree earned in country of origin. Additional exam requirements/recommendations for international students: Required—TOEFL. *Expenses:* Contact institution. *Faculty research:* Constitutional law, legal history, jurisprudence.

The George Washington University, Elliott School of International Affairs, Program in International Affairs, Washington, DC 20052. Offers MA, JD/MA, MBA/MA, MPH/MA. Part-time and evening/weekend programs available. *Faculty:* 52 full-time (11 women), 88 part-time/adjunct (23 women). *Students:* 270 full-time (156 women), 95 part-time (60 women); includes 47 minority (7 African Americans, 23 Asian Americans or Pacific Islanders, 17 Hispanic Americans), 55 international. Average age 26. 816 applicants, 60% accepted, 179 enrolled. In 2009, 124 master's awarded. *Degree requirements:* For master's, one foreign language, capstone project. *Entrance requirements:* For master's, GRE General Test, 2 years of a modern foreign language, 2 semesters of introductory economics. Additional exam requirements/recommendations for international students: Required—TOEFL. *Application deadline:* For fall admission, 2/1 for domestic students; for spring admission, 10/1 for domestic students. Application fee: $60. Electronic applications accepted. *Financial support:* In 2009–10, 61 students received support; fellowships with tuition reimbursements available, research assistantships with tuition reimbursements available, career-related internships or fieldwork, Federal Work-Study, institutionally sponsored loans, and tuition waivers (full) available. Financial award application deadline: 1/15; financial award applicants required to submit FAFSA. *Faculty research:* Area studies, international economics, national security policy studies, international economic development, Sino-Soviet studies. *Unit head:* Dr. Karl F. Inderfurth, Director, 202-994-2619, E-mail: ambkfi@gwu.edu. *Application contact:* Jeff V. Miles, Director of Graduate Admissions, 202-994-7050, Fax: 202-994-9537, E-mail: esiagrad@gwu.edu.

The George Washington University, Elliott School of International Affairs, Program in International Policy and Practice, Washington, DC 20052. Offers MIPP. Part-time and evening/weekend programs available. *Students:* 11 full-time (3 women), 26 part-time (13 women); includes 8 minority (2 African Americans, 4 Asian Americans or Pacific Islanders, 2 Hispanic Americans), 9 international. Average age 38. 72 applicants, 76% accepted, 20 enrolled. In 2009, 26 master's awarded. *Degree requirements:* For master's, one foreign language, capstone project. *Entrance requirements:* For master's, GRE (recommended), advanced degree or 8 years experience plus BA. Additional exam requirements/recommendations for international students: Required—TOEFL. *Application deadline:* For fall admission, 2/1 for domestic students; for spring admission, 10/1 for domestic students. Application fee: $60. Electronic applications accepted. *Financial support:* In 2009–10, 13 students received support; fellowships with tuition reimbursements available, research assistantships with tuition reimbursements available, career-related internships or fieldwork, Federal Work-Study, institutionally sponsored loans, and tuition waivers available. Financial award application deadline: 1/15; financial award applicants required to submit FAFSA. *Unit head:* Dr. Chris Kojm, Director, 202-994-7969, E-mail: ckojm@gwu.edu. *Application contact:* Jeff V. Miles, Director of Graduate Admissions, 202-994-7050, Fax: 202-994-9537, E-mail: esiagrad@gwu.edu.

The George Washington University, Elliott School of International Affairs, Program in International Studies, Washington, DC 20052. Offers MIS.

Georgia Institute of Technology, Graduate Studies and Research, Ivan Allen College of Policy and International Affairs, Sam Nunn School of International Affairs, Atlanta, GA 30332-0001. Offers MS Int A, PhD. *Degree requirements:* For master's, one foreign language. *Entrance requirements:* Additional exam requirements/recommendations for international students: Required—TOEFL. Electronic applications accepted. *Faculty research:* International political economy, international security, Asian and European studies.

Harvard University, Graduate School of Arts and Sciences, Department of Government, Cambridge, MA 02138. Offers political science (PhD), including American politics, comparative politics, international relations, political thought, quantitative methods. *Degree requirements:* For doctorate, one foreign language, thesis/dissertation, general exams. *Entrance requirements:* For doctorate, GRE General Test. Additional exam requirements/recommendations for international students: Required—TOEFL. *Expenses:* Tuition: Full-time $33,696. Required fees: $1126. Full-time tuition and fees vary according to program.

Harvard University, Law School, Professional Programs in Law, Cambridge, MA 02138. Offers international and comparative law (JD); law and business (JD); law and government (JD); law and social change (JD); law, science and technology (JD); JD/MALD; JD/MBA; JD/MPH; JD/MPP; JD/PhD. *Accreditation:* ABA. *Degree requirements:* For JD, 3rd year paper. *Entrance requirements:* LSAT. *Expenses:* Tuition: Full-time $33,696. Required fees: $1126. Full-time tuition and fees vary according to program. *Faculty research:* Constitutional law, voting rights law, cyber law.

Hult International Business School, Program in International Relations—Hult London Campus, London, MA WC 1B 4JP, United Kingdom. Offers conflict resolution (MA); diplomacy (MA); international public law (MA); international relations (MA); Middle East international security (MA); politics (MA); security studies (MA); terrorism (MA); U.S. foreign policy (MA). Part-time programs available. *Entrance requirements:* Additional exam requirements/recommendations for international students: Required—TOEFL (minimum score 580 paper-based; 237 computer-based), TWE (minimum score 5). Electronic applications accepted. *Faculty research:* American foreign politics, Middle East, security studies.

Hult International Business School, Program in International Relations—Hult San Francisco Campus, San Francisco, CA 94133. Offers MA.

Indiana University Bloomington, School of Public and Environmental Affairs, Public Affairs Programs, Bloomington, IN 47405-7000. Offers comparative and international affairs (MPA); economic development (MPA); energy (MPA); environmental policy and natural resource management (MPA); information systems (MPA); local government management (MPA); nonprofit management (MPA); policy analysis (MPA); public financial administration (MPA); public management (MPA); sustainability and sustainable development (MPA); JD/MPA; MPA/MA; MPA/MIS; MPA/MLS; MSES/MPA. *Accreditation:* NASPAA (one or more programs are accredited). Part-time programs available. *Faculty:* 75 full-time (22 women), 91 part-time/adjunct (24 women). *Students:* 389 full-time (222 women), 45 part-time (24 women); includes 38 minority (18 African Americans, 1 American Indian/Alaska Native, 12 Asian Americans or Pacific Islanders, 7 Hispanic Americans), 72 international. Average age 26. 474 applicants, 206 enrolled. In 2009, 190 master's, 11 doctorates, 3 other advanced degrees awarded. Terminal master's awarded for partial completion of doctoral program. *Degree requirements:* For master's, thesis optional; for doctorate, comprehensive exam, thesis/dissertation or alternative, A thesis is required for the Public Affairs and Public Policy degree. *Entrance requirements:* For master's, GRE, LSAT (if also applying for the Law School), 3 letters of recommendation, resume or curriculum vitae; for doctorate, GRE General Test. Additional exam requirements/recommendations for international students: Required—TOEFL (minimum score 590 paper-based; 243 computer-based; 96 iBT). *Application deadline:* For fall admission, 2/1 priority date for domestic students, 12/1 priority date for international students; for spring admission, 9/1 for international students. Application fee: $55 ($65 for international students). Electronic applications accepted. *Financial support:* Fellowships with full tuition reimbursements, research assistantships with partial tuition reimbursements, teaching assistantships with partial tuition reimbursements, career-related internships or fieldwork, Federal Work-Study, institutionally sponsored loans, unspecified assistantships, and Service Corps programs available. Financial award application deadline: 2/1; financial award applicants required to submit FAFSA. *Faculty research:* Comparative and international affairs, environmental policy and resource management, policy analysis, public finance, public management, urban management, nonprofit management. *Unit head:* Dean John Graham, Dean, School of Public and Environmental Affairs, 812-855-1432, E-mail: grahamjd@indiana.edu. *Application contact:* Jennifer Medlin, Assistant Director of Admissions and Financial Aid, 812-855-3784, Fax: 812-856-3665, E-mail: jlmedlin@indiana.edu.

See Close-Up on page 1191.

Instituto Tecnológico y de Estudios Superiores de Monterrey, Campus Ciudad Obregón, Program in International Relations, Ciudad Obregón, Mexico. Offers MIR.

The Johns Hopkins University, Paul H. Nitze School of Advanced International Studies, Washington, DC 20036. Offers international development (MA, Certificate), including international economics (MA); international public policy (MIPP); international relations (PhD); international studies (Certificate); Japan studies (MA), including international economics; Korea Studies (MA), including international economics; South Asia studies (MA), including international economics; Southeast Asia studies (MA), including international economics; JD/MA; MBA/MA; MHS/MA. *Faculty:* 57 full-time (18 women), 125 part-time/adjunct (40 women). *Students:* 623 full-time (291 women), 38 part-time (17 women); includes 94 minority (11 African Americans, 55 Asian Americans or Pacific Islanders, 28 Hispanic Americans), 173 international. Average age 29. 1,444 applicants, 38% accepted, 212 enrolled. In 2009, 395 master's, 7 doctorates awarded. Terminal master's awarded for partial completion of doctoral program. *Degree requirements:* For master's, 2 core examinations, oral exam, proficiency in language other than native language (MA); for doctorate, 2 foreign languages, thesis/dissertation, 3 comprehensive exams, economics, quantitative and qualitative course, dissertation prospectus and defense. *Entrance requirements:* For master's, GMAT or GRE General Test, previous course work in economics, foreign language, undergraduate degree; for doctorate, GRE General Test, master's degree. Additional exam requirements/recommendations for international students: Required—TOEFL (minimum score 600 paper-based; 250 computer-based; 100 iBT), IELTS (minimum score 7), TOEFL (minimum score 600 paper-based; 250 computer-based; 100 iBT) or IELTS (minimum score 7). *Application deadline:* For fall admission, 1/7 for domestic and international students. Application fee: $85. Electronic applications accepted. *Expenses:* Contact institution. *Financial support:* In 2009–10, 450 students received support, including 450 fellowships (averaging $7,500 per year); teaching assistantships, career-related internships or fieldwork, Federal Work-Study, and scholarships/grants also available. Financial award application deadline: 2/15; financial award applicants required to submit FAFSA. *Faculty research:* Regional studies, international relations, international economics, energy and environment, international development. Total annual research expenditures: $7 million. *Unit head:* Sidney Jackson, Director of Admissions, 202-663-5700, Fax: 202-663-7788. *Application contact:* Admissions, 202-663-5700, Fax: 202-663-7788, E-mail: admissions.sais@jhu.edu.

Kansas State University, Graduate School, College of Arts and Sciences, Department of Political Science, Manhattan, KS 66506. Offers political science (MA), including international service, political science; public administration (MPA). Part-time programs available. *Faculty:* 16 full-time (4 women). *Students:* 41 full-time (18 women), 6 part-time (3 women); includes 6 minority (3 American Indian/Alaska Native, 3 Asian Americans or Pacific Islanders), 6 international. Average age 28. 37 applicants, 81% accepted, 30 enrolled. In 2009, 19 master's awarded. *Degree requirements:* For master's, thesis or alternative. *Entrance requirements:* For master's, GRE (recommended), minimum GPA of 3.0. Additional exam requirements/recommendations for international students: Required—TOEFL (minimum score 550 paper-based; 213 computer-based). *Application deadline:* For fall admission, 2/1 priority date for domestic and international students; for spring admission, 8/1 priority date for domestic and international students. Applications are processed on a rolling basis. Application fee: $40 ($55 for international students). Electronic applications accepted. *Financial support:* In 2009–10, 3 research assistantships (averaging $20,126 per year), 9 teaching assistantships with tuition reimbursements (averaging $10,500 per year) were awarded; fellowships, career-related intern-

International Affairs

Kansas State University (continued)

ships or fieldwork, Federal Work-Study, institutionally sponsored loans, and scholarships/grants also available. Support available to part-time students. Financial award application deadline: 3/1; financial award applicants required to submit FAFSA. *Faculty research:* Armed conflict, civil military relations, comparative public administration and policy, electoral competition, legislative studies. Total annual research expenditures: $30,909. *Unit head:* Jeff Pickering, Head, 785-532-0454, Fax: 785-532-2339, E-mail: jjp@ksu.edu. *Application contact:* James Franke, Director, 785-532-0451, Fax: 785-532-2339, E-mail: jfranke@ksu.edu.

Kentucky State University, College of Professional Studies, Frankfort, KY 40601. Offers business administration (MBA), including accounting, finance, management, marketing; public administration (MPA), including human resource management, international administration and development, management information systems, nonprofit management; special education (MA). Part-time and evening/weekend programs available. Postbaccalaureate distance learning degree programs offered (minimal on-campus study). *Faculty:* 11 full-time (3 women), 2 part-time/adjunct (both women). *Students:* 79 full-time (51 women), 66 part-time (34 women); includes 88 minority (85 African Americans, 2 Asian Americans or Pacific Islanders, 1 Hispanic American), 4 international. Average age 34. 92 applicants, 75% accepted, 52 enrolled. In 2009, 32 master's awarded. *Degree requirements:* For master's, comprehensive exam, thesis optional. *Entrance requirements:* For master's, GMAT, GRE. Additional exam requirements/recommendations for international students: Required—TOEFL (minimum score 525 paper-based; 173 computer-based). *Application deadline:* For fall admission, 7/1 priority date for domestic students, 4/15 priority date for international students; for spring admission, 11/15 priority date for domestic students, 8/1 priority date for international students. Applications are processed on a rolling basis. Application fee: $30 ($100 for international students). Electronic applications accepted. *Expenses:* Tuition, state resident: full-time $5634; part-time $313 per credit hour. Tuition, nonresident: full-time $14,598; part-time $811 per credit hour. Required fees: $450; $25 per credit hour. *Financial support:* In 2009–10, 113 students received support, including 4 research assistantships (averaging $14,035 per year); career-related internships or fieldwork, scholarships/grants, tuition waivers (partial), and unspecified assistantships also available. Financial award application deadline: 4/15; financial award applicants required to submit FAFSA. *Unit head:* Dr. Gashaw Lake, Dean, College of Professional Studies, 502-597-6105, Fax: 502-597-6715, E-mail: gashaw.lake@kysu.edu. *Application contact:* Cedric Cunningham, Administrative Assistant, Office of Graduate Studies, 502-597-6536, E-mail: cedric.cunningham@kysu.edu.

Lebanese American University, School of Arts and Sciences, Beirut, Lebanon. Offers computer science (MS); international affairs (MA).

Lesley University, Graduate School of Arts and Social Sciences, Program in Intercultural Relations, Cambridge, MA 02138-2790. Offers MA, CAGS. Part-time and evening/weekend programs available. *Degree requirements:* For master's, one foreign language, internship, practicum; for CAGS, one foreign language, thesis. *Entrance requirements:* For master's, interview; for CAGS, interview, master's degree. Additional exam requirements/recommendations for international students: Required—TOEFL (minimum score 550 paper-based; 213 computer-based; 80 iBT). *Faculty research:* Sociolinguistics, cross-cultural feminist theory, immigration and diaspora, intercultural business training.

Lindenwood University, Graduate Programs, School of Humanities, St. Charles, MO 63301-1695. Offers American studies (MA); international studies (MA). Part-time programs available. *Faculty:* 4 full-time (2 women), 5 part-time/adjunct (1 woman). *Students:* 11 full-time (4 women), 8 part-time (6 women); includes 1 minority (African American), 9 international. Average age 30. 8 applicants, 6 enrolled. In 2009, 2 master's awarded. *Entrance requirements:* For master's, minimum GPA of 2.5, 2 letters of recommendation. Additional exam requirements/recommendations for international students: Required—TOEFL (minimum score 550 paper-based; 213 computer-based; 80 iBT). *Application deadline:* For fall admission, 8/27 priority date for domestic and international students; for spring admission, 1/28 for domestic students, 1/28 priority date for international students. Applications are processed on a rolling basis. Application fee: $30 ($100 for international students). Electronic applications accepted. *Expenses:* Tuition: Full-time $12,960; part-time $370 per credit hour. Required fees: $340. One-time fee: $30 full-time. Tuition and fees vary according to course level and course load. *Financial support:* In 2009–10, 19 students received support. Career-related internships or fieldwork, institutionally sponsored loans, tuition waivers (partial), and unspecified assistantships available. Financial award application deadline: 6/30; financial award applicants required to submit FAFSA. *Unit head:* Dr. Ana Schnellmann, Dean, 636-949-4873, E-mail: aschnellmann@lindenwood.edu. *Application contact:* Brett Barger, Dean of Evening Admissions and Extension Campuses, 636-949-4934, Fax: 636-949-4109, E-mail: adultadmissions@lindenwood.edu.

Long Island University, Brooklyn Campus, Richard L. Conolly College of Liberal Arts and Sciences, Program in Social Science, Brooklyn, NY 11201-8423. Offers history (MS); United Nations studies (Certificate). Part-time and evening/weekend programs available. *Entrance requirements:* For master's, 2 letters of recommendation. Additional exam requirements/recommendations for international students: Required—TOEFL (minimum score 500 paper-based; 173 computer-based). Electronic applications accepted.

Long Island University, C.W. Post Campus, College of Liberal Arts and Sciences, Department of Political Science/International Studies, Brookville, NY 11548-1300. Offers MA. Part-time and evening/weekend programs available. *Degree requirements:* For master's, comprehensive exam, thesis or alternative. *Entrance requirements:* For master's, GRE. Electronic applications accepted. *Faculty research:* International relations, Middle Eastern politics, political philosophy.

Marquette University, Graduate School, College of Arts and Sciences, Department of Political Science/International Affairs, Milwaukee, WI 53201-1881. Offers international affairs (MA), including comparative politics, international political economy, international politics; political science (MA), including American politics, comparative politics, international politics, political philosophy; JD/MA. Part-time programs available. *Faculty:* 15 full-time (3 women), 5 part-time/adjunct (3 women). *Students:* 18 full-time (11 women), 9 part-time (6 women), 5 international. Average age 26. 71 applicants, 51% accepted, 11 enrolled. In 2009, 14 master's awarded. *Degree requirements:* For master's, comprehensive exam, thesis optional. *Entrance requirements:* For master's, GRE General Test. Additional exam requirements/recommendations for international students: Required—TOEFL. Application fee: $40. *Financial support:* In 2009–10, 5 research assistantships were awarded; Federal Work-Study, institutionally sponsored loans, scholarships/grants, and tuition waivers (full and partial) also available. Support available to part-time students. Financial award application deadline: 2/15. *Faculty research:* Public opinion and electoral behavior, public policy analysis, Congress and the Presidency, judicial behavior, political system transitions. *Unit head:* Dr. Duane Swank, Chair, 414-288-3418, Fax: 414-288-3360. *Application contact:* Dr. Lowell Barrington, Director of Graduate Studies, 414-288-6842, Fax: 414-288-3360.

McMaster University, School of Graduate Studies, Faculty of Humanities and Faculty of Social Sciences, Institute on Globalization and the Human Condition, Hamilton, ON L8S 4M2, Canada. Offers globalization studies (MA).

McMaster University, School of Graduate Studies, Faculty of Social Sciences, Department of Political Science, Hamilton, ON L8S 4M2, Canada. Offers international relations (PhD); political science (MA); public and the global economy (MA); public policy (PhD); public policy and administration (MA). Part-time programs available. *Degree requirements:* For master's, thesis or alternative. *Entrance requirements:* For master's, minimum B+ average. Additional exam requirements/recommendations for international students: Required—TOEFL (minimum score 580 paper-based; 237 computer-based). *Faculty research:* Organizational theory, internationalization of public policy, water resource policies, political interest intermediation, comparative politics.

Missouri State University, Graduate College, College of Humanities and Public Affairs, Department of Political Science, Program in Global Studies, Springfield, MO 65897. Offers MGS. Part-time programs available. *Students:* 25 full-time (7 women), 5 part-time (2 women); includes 6 minority (2 African Americans, 3 Asian Americans or Pacific Islanders, 1 Hispanic American), 6 international. Average age 30. 20 applicants, 90% accepted, 8 enrolled. In 2009, 13 master's awarded. *Degree requirements:* For master's, 2 foreign languages, comprehensive exam, thesis or alternative. *Entrance requirements:* For master's, GRE, minimum GPA of 3.0. Additional exam requirements/recommendations for international students: Required—TOEFL (minimum score 550 paper-based; 213 computer-based; 79 iBT). *Application deadline:* For fall admission, 7/20 priority date for domestic students, 5/1 for international students; for spring admission, 12/20 priority date for domestic students, 9/1 for international students. Applications are processed on a rolling basis. Application fee: $35 ($50 for international students). Electronic applications accepted. *Expenses:* Tuition, state resident: full-time $3852; part-time $214 per credit hour. Tuition, nonresident: full-time $7524; part-time $418 per credit hour. Required fees: $696; $172 per semester. Tuition and fees vary according to course level, course load, degree level and program. *Financial support:* In 2009–10, 1 research assistantship with full tuition reimbursement (averaging $9,730 per year), 2 teaching assistantships with full tuition reimbursements (averaging $7,340 per year) were awarded; Federal Work-Study, institutionally sponsored loans, scholarships/grants, and unspecified assistantships also available. Support available to part-time students. Financial award application deadline: 3/31; financial award applicants required to submit FAFSA. *Faculty research:* U.S.-China policy, Eastern European politics, South American political reform, landmine use policy. *Unit head:* Dr. Beat Kernen, Graduate Director, 417-836-6957, Fax: 417-836-6655, E-mail: beatkernen@missouristate.edu. *Application contact:* Eric Eckert, Coordinator of Graduate Admissions and Recruitment, 417-836-5331, Fax: 417-836-6200, E-mail: ericeckert@missouristate.edu.

See Display on page 817 and Close-Up on page 851.

Monterey Institute of International Studies, Graduate School of International Policy and Management, Program in International Policy Studies, Monterey, CA 93940-2691. Offers MA. *Students:* 224 full-time (123 women), 10 part-time (6 women); includes 27 minority (6 African Americans, 2 American Indian/Alaska Native, 8 Asian Americans or Pacific Islanders, 11 Hispanic Americans), 52 international. Average age 27. In 2009, 118 master's awarded. *Degree requirements:* For master's, one foreign language. *Entrance requirements:* For master's, minimum GPA of 3.0, proficiency in a foreign language. Additional exam requirements/recommendations for international students: Required—TOEFL (minimum score 550 paper-based; 213 computer-based; 80 iBT). *Application deadline:* For fall admission, 3/15 priority date for domestic and international students; for spring admission, 10/1 priority date for domestic and international students. Applications are processed on a rolling basis. Application fee: $50. Electronic applications accepted. *Expenses:* Tuition: Full-time $31,000; part-time $1500 per credit. Required fees: $56. *Financial support:* Application deadline: 3/15. *Application contact:* 831-647-4123, Fax: 831-647-6405, E-mail: admit@miis.edu.

See Close-Up on page 853.

Morgan State University, School of Graduate Studies, College of Liberal Arts, Department of World Languages and International Studies, Baltimore, MD 21251. Offers international studies (MA). Part-time and evening/weekend programs available. *Degree requirements:* For master's, one foreign language, comprehensive exam, thesis. *Entrance requirements:* For master's, GRE. Additional exam requirements/recommendations for international students: Required—TOEFL (minimum score 550 paper-based; 213 computer-based).

Naval Postgraduate School, Graduate Programs, Department of National Security Affairs, Monterey, CA 93943. Offers intelligence (MA); international relations (MA); political science (MA); regional security education (MA); security building (MA); security studies (MA). Program only open to commissioned officers of the United States and friendly nations and selected United States federal civilian employees. Part-time programs available. *Degree requirements:* For master's, thesis.

New England College, Program in Management, Henniker, NH 03242-3293. Offers accounting (MSA); healthcare administration (MS); international relations (MA); marketing management (MS); nonprofit leadership (MS); project management (MS); strategic leadership (MS). Part-time and evening/weekend programs available. *Degree requirements:* For master's, independent research project. Electronic applications accepted.

The New School: A University, The New School for General Studies, Program in International Affairs, New York, NY 10011. Offers MA, MS. Part-time and evening/weekend programs available. *Faculty:* 12 full-time (5 women). *Students:* 252 full-time (186 women), 132 part-time (90 women); includes 83 minority (28 African Americans, 1 American Indian/Alaska Native, 17 Asian Americans or Pacific Islanders, 37 Hispanic Americans), 68 international. Average age 29. 445 applicants, 79% accepted, 149 enrolled. In 2009, 107 master's awarded. *Degree requirements:* For master's, thesis or practicum. *Entrance requirements:* Additional exam requirements/recommendations for international students: Required—TOEFL (minimum score 600 paper-based; 250 computer-based; 100 iBT). *Application deadline:* For fall admission, 1/15 priority date for domestic and international students; for spring admission, 10/15 priority date for domestic and international students. Applications are processed on a rolling basis. Application fee: $50. Electronic applications accepted. *Financial support:* Federal Work-Study, scholarships/grants, and tuition waivers (full and partial) available. Support available to part-time students. Financial award application deadline: 3/1; financial award applicants required to submit FAFSA. *Unit head:* Dr. Michael Cohen, Director, 212-206-3524, Fax: 212-645-0661, E-mail: cohenm2@newschool.edu. *Application contact:* Robert MacDonald, Director of Admissions, 212-229-5710 Ext. 3007, Fax: 212-989-3887, E-mail: macdonar@newschool.edu.

New York University, Graduate School of Arts and Science, Department of Politics, New York, NY 10012-1019. Offers political campaign management (MA); politics (MA, PhD); JD/MA; MBA/MA. Part-time programs available. *Faculty:* 30 full-time (4 women). *Students:* 186 full-time (92 women), 56 part-time (37 women); includes 27 minority (3 African Americans, 13 Asian Americans or Pacific Islanders, 11 Hispanic Americans), 118 international. Average age 28. 633 applicants, 42% accepted, 97 enrolled. In 2009, 78 master's, 5 doctorates awarded. Terminal master's awarded for partial completion of doctoral program. *Degree requirements:* For master's, one foreign language, thesis or alternative; for doctorate, 2 foreign languages, comprehensive exam, thesis/dissertation. *Entrance requirements:* For master's, GRE General Test; for doctorate, GRE General Test, master's degree in political science, minimum GPA of 2.5. Additional exam requirements/recommendations for international students: Required—TOEFL. *Application deadline:* For fall admission, 12/18 priority date for domestic students. Application fee: $90. *Expenses:* Tuition: Full-time $30,528; part-time $1272 per credit. Required fees: $2177. *Financial support:* Fellowships with tuition reimbursements, teaching assistantships with tuition reimbursements, career-related internships or fieldwork, Federal Work-Study, and institutionally sponsored loans available. Financial award application deadline: 12/18; financial award applicants required to submit FAFSA. *Faculty research:* Comparative politics, democratic theory and practice, rational choice, political economy, international relations. *Unit head:* Michael Gilligan, Director of Ph.D. program, 212-998-8500, Fax: 212-995-4184, E-mail: politics.phd@nyu.edu. *Application contact:* Shinasi Rama, Director Master's Program, 212-998-8500, Fax: 212-995-4184, E-mail: politics.masters@nyu.edu.

New York University, Robert F. Wagner Graduate School of Public Service, Program in Public Administration, New York, NY 10012-1019. Offers public administration (PhD); public and nonprofit management and policy (MPA, Advanced Certificate), including developmental administration (Advanced Certificate), financial management and public finance, human resources management (Advanced Certificate), international administration (Advanced Certificate), management (MPA), management for public and nonprofit organizations (Advanced Certificate), public policy analysis, quantitative analysis and computer applications (Advanced Certificate), urban public policy (Advanced Certificate); JD/MPA; MBA/MPA; MPA/MA. *Accreditation:* NASPAA (one or more programs are accredited). Part-time and evening/weekend programs available. *Faculty:* 31 full-time (13 women), 33 part-time/adjunct (16 women). *Students:* 363 full-time (270 women), 228 part-time (171 women); includes 146 minority (46

African Americans, 64 Asian Americans or Pacific Islanders, 36 Hispanic Americans), 76 international. Average age 28. 1,117 applicants, 57% accepted, 225 enrolled. In 2009, 236 master's, 3 doctorates awarded. *Degree requirements:* For master's, thesis or alternative, capstone/end event; for doctorate, one foreign language, thesis/dissertation. *Entrance requirements:* For master's, minimum undergraduate GPA of 3.0; for doctorate, GMAT or GRE General Test, minimum GPA of 3.5. Additional exam requirements/recommendations for international students: Required—TOEFL (minimum score 600 paper-based; 250 computer-based; 100 iBT), TWE (minimum score 4). *Application deadline:* For fall admission, 6/1 for domestic students, 1/15 for international students; for spring admission, 11/15 for domestic students, 10/1 for international students. Applications are processed on a rolling basis. Application fee: $80. Electronic applications accepted. *Expenses:* Contact institution. *Financial support:* In 2009–10, 155 students received support, including 150 fellowships (averaging $11,335 per year), 5 research assistantships with full tuition reimbursements available (averaging $22,440 per year); career-related internships or fieldwork, Federal Work-Study, institutionally sponsored loans, scholarships/grants, health care benefits, and unspecified assistantships also available. Support available to part-time students. Financial award application deadline: 12/1; financial award applicants required to submit FAFSA. *Unit head:* Katty Jones, Director, Program Services, 212-998-7411, Fax: 212-995-4164, E-mail: katty.jones@nyu.edu. *Application contact:* Christopher Alexander, Administrative Aide, Enrollment, 212-998-7414, Fax: 212-995-4611, E-mail: wagner.admissions@nyu.edu.

New York University, School of Continuing and Professional Studies, Center for Global Affairs, New York, NY 10012-1019. Offers global affairs (MS), including environment/energy policy, human rights and humanitarian assistance, international law, dispute settlement, and institutions, international relations, peace building, private sector: international business, economics, and development, transnational security. Part-time and evening/weekend programs available. *Faculty:* 9 full-time (3 women), 31 part-time/adjunct (14 women). *Students:* 120 full-time (82 women), 179 part-time (121 women); includes 22 minority (1 American Indian/Alaska Native, 21 Asian Americans or Pacific Islanders), 27 international. Average age 30. 419 applicants, 59% accepted, 94 enrolled. In 2009, 86 master's awarded. *Degree requirements:* For master's, thesis. *Entrance requirements:* For master's, GRE General Test or GMAT (for recent graduates), 2 letters of recommendation, resume. Additional exam requirements/recommendations for international students: Required—TOEFL (minimum score 600 paper-based; 250 computer-based; 100 iBT), TWE. *Application deadline:* For fall admission, 2/1 priority date for domestic and international students; for spring admission, 10/15 priority date for domestic students, 8/15 priority date for international students. Applications are processed on a rolling basis. Application fee: $75. Electronic applications accepted. *Expenses:* Tuition: Full-time $30,528; part-time $1272 per credit. Required fees: $2177. *Financial support:* In 2009–10, 159 students received support, including 159 fellowships (averaging $2,932 per year); institutionally sponsored loans, scholarships/grants, and tuition waivers (partial) also available. Support available to part-time students. Financial award application deadline: 3/1; financial award applicants required to submit FAFSA. *Unit head:* Dr. Vera Jelinek, Assistant Dean and Director, 212-992-8380, Fax: 212-995-3638, E-mail: vera.jelinek@nyu.edu. *Application contact:* Mykellan Ledden, Associate Director, 212-992-8380, Fax: 212-995-3638, E-mail: mykellan.ledden@nyu.edu.

North Carolina State University, Graduate School, College of Humanities and Social Sciences, School of Public and International Affairs, Program in International Studies, Raleigh, NC 27695. Offers MIS. *Degree requirements:* For master's, thesis optional. *Entrance requirements:* For master's, GRE General Test, minimum GPA of 3.0 during previous 2 years. Electronic applications accepted. *Faculty research:* Global environmental policy and climate change, drug policy and the Caribbean, U.S. national security politics, local responses to globalization, the political economy of the European Union.

Northeastern University, College of Social Sciences and Humanities, Department of Political Science, Boston, MA 02115-5096. Offers political science (MA); public administration (MPA, Certificate), including development administration (MPA), health administration and policy (MPA), state and local government (MPA), urban studies (Certificate); public and international affairs (PhD). Part-time and evening/weekend programs available. *Faculty:* 22 full-time (4 women), 10 part-time/adjunct (1 woman). *Students:* 10 full-time (3 women), 62 part-time (28 women); includes 7 minority (2 African Americans, 2 American Indian/Alaska Native, 2 Asian Americans or Pacific Islanders, 1 Hispanic American), 11 international. Average age 30. 129 applicants, 69% accepted, 24 enrolled. In 2009, 28 master's, 3 doctorates awarded. *Degree requirements:* For master's, thesis optional; for doctorate, thesis/dissertation. *Entrance requirements:* For master's, GRE General Test. Additional exam requirements/recommendations for international students: Required—TOEFL. *Application deadline:* Applications are processed on a rolling basis. Application fee: $50. *Financial support:* In 2009–10, 12 fellowships, 3 research assistantships with tuition reimbursements, 18 teaching assistantships with tuition reimbursements (averaging $14,035 per year) were awarded; career-related internships or fieldwork, Federal Work-Study, tuition waivers (full and partial), and unspecified assistantships also available. Support available to part-time students. Financial award application deadline: 2/1; financial award applicants required to submit FAFSA. *Faculty research:* Presidency, public opinion, Congress, democratization, national identity. *Unit head:* Dr. John Portz, Chair, 617-373-2796, Fax: 617-373-5311, E-mail: gradpolisci@neu.edu. *Application contact:* Brynn Thompson, Graduate Programs Assistant, 617-373-4404, Fax: 617-373-5311, E-mail: gradpolisci@neu.edu.

Northwestern University, The Graduate School, Center for International and Comparative Studies, Evanston, IL 60208. Offers Certificate.

Northwestern University, Law School, Chicago, IL 60611-3069. Offers executive (LL M); international human rights (LL M); law (JD, LL M); tax (LL M in Tax); two-year accelerated (JD); JD/LL M; JD/MBA; JD/PhD; LL M/Certificate. *Accreditation:* ABA. *Entrance requirements:* For JD, LSAT, 1 letter of recommendation, resume; for master's, law degree or equivalent, letter of recommendation, resume. Additional exam requirements/recommendations for international students: Required—TOEFL. Electronic applications accepted. *Expenses:* Contact institution. *Faculty research:* Constitutional law, corporate law, international law, law and social policy, ethical studies.

Norwich University, School of Graduate and Continuing Studies, Program in Diplomacy, Northfield, VT 05663. Offers international commerce (MA); international conflict management (MA); international terrorism (MA). Evening/weekend programs available. *Faculty:* 48 part-time/adjunct (8 women). *Students:* 798 full-time (233 women); includes 133 minority (55 African Americans, 23 Asian Americans or Pacific Islanders, 55 Hispanic Americans). Average age 38. 1,112 applicants, 77% accepted. In 2009, 145 master's awarded. *Degree requirements:* For master's, comprehensive exam, thesis optional. *Entrance requirements:* For master's, minimum undergraduate GPA of 2.75. Additional exam requirements/recommendations for international students: Required—TOEFL. *Application deadline:* For fall admission, 8/10 for domestic and international students; for winter admission, 11/7 for domestic and international students; for spring admission, 2/6 for domestic and international students. Application fee: $50. Electronic applications accepted. Full-time tuition and fees vary according to course level and course load. *Financial support:* Scholarships/grants available. Financial award applicants required to submit FAFSA. *Unit head:* Dr. Harold Kearsley, Program Director, 802-485-2730, E-mail: hkearsley@norwich.edu. *Application contact:* Lars Nielsen, Associate Program Director, 802-485-2853, Fax: 802-485-2533, E-mail: lnielsen@norwich.edu.

Ohio University, Graduate College, Center for International Studies, Program in Communications and Development Studies, Athens, OH 45701-2979. Offers MA. Part-time programs

International Affairs

Ohio University (continued)

available. *Faculty:* 13 full-time (5 women), 4 part-time/adjunct (2 women). *Students:* 30 full-time (17 women), 2 part-time (1 woman); includes 2 minority (both African Americans), 22 international. Average age 30. 45 applicants, 49% accepted, 12 enrolled. In 2009, 13 master's awarded. *Degree requirements:* For master's, one foreign language, thesis optional, internship. *Entrance requirements:* For master's, minimum GPA of 3.0. Additional exam requirements/recommendations for international students: Required—TOEFL (minimum score 550 paper-based; 213 computer-based; 80 iBT), IELTS (minimum score 6.5). *Application deadline:* For fall admission, 1/1 for domestic and international students. Application fee: $50 ($55 for international students). Electronic applications accepted. *Expenses:* Tuition, state resident: full-time $7839; part-time $323 per quarter hour. Tuition, nonresident: full-time $15,831; part-time $654 per quarter hour. Required fees: $2931. *Financial support:* In 2009–10, 19 students received support, including research assistantships with full tuition reimbursements available (averaging $11,499 per year); Federal Work-Study, institutionally sponsored loans, and tuition waivers (partial) also available. Financial award application deadline: 1/1. *Faculty research:* National development processes, public relations and participatory research, audio and video production, health communication, urban development. *Unit head:* Dr. Rafael Obregon, Director, E-mail: obregon@ohio.edu. *Application contact:* Joan Kraynanski, Administrative Assistant, 740-593-1840, Fax: 740-593-1837, E-mail: kraynans@ohio.edu.

Oklahoma State University, Graduate College, Stillwater, OK 74078. Offers environmental science (MS); international studies (MS); natural and applied science (MS); photonics (PhD); plant science (PhD). Programs are interdisciplinary. *Faculty:* 2 full-time (0 women). *Students:* 82 full-time (47 women), 156 part-time (75 women); includes 49 minority (15 African Americans, 17 American Indian/Alaska Native, 10 Asian Americans or Pacific Islanders, 7 Hispanic Americans), 68 International. Average age 32. 779 applicants, 68% accepted, 87 enrolled. In 2009, 77 master's, 8 doctorates awarded. *Degree requirements:* For master's, thesis (for some programs); for doctorate, comprehensive exam, thesis/dissertation. *Entrance requirements:* For master's and doctorate, GRE or GMAT. Additional exam requirements/recommendations for international students: Required—TOEFL (minimum score 550 paper-based; 79 iBT). *Application deadline:* For fall admission, 3/1 priority date for international students; for spring admission, 8/1 priority date for international students. Applications are processed on a rolling basis. Application fee: $40 ($75 for international students). Electronic applications accepted. *Expenses:* Tuition, state resident: full-time $3716; part-time $154.85 per credit hour. Tuition, nonresident: full-time $14,448; part-time $602 per credit hour. Required fees: $1772; $73.85 per credit hour. One-time fee: $50. Tuition and fees vary according to course load and campus/location. *Financial support:* In 2009–10, 2 research assistantships (averaging $10,200 per year) were awarded; career-related internships or fieldwork, Federal Work-Study, scholarships/grants, health care benefits, tuition waivers (partial), and unspecified assistantships also available. Support available to part-time students. Financial award application deadline: 3/1; financial award applicants required to submit FAFSA. *Unit head:* Dr. Gordon Emslie, Dean, 405-744-6368, Fax: 405-744-0355, E-mail: grad-i@okstate.edu. *Application contact:* Dr. Susan Mathew, Coordinator of Admissions, 405-744-6368, Fax: 405-744-0355, E-mail: grad-i@okstate.edu.

Old Dominion University, College of Arts and Letters, Graduate Programs in International Studies, Norfolk, VA 23529. Offers conflict and cooperation (PhD), including women's studies certificate; U.S. foreign policy (MA), including modeling and simulation certificate. Part-time programs available. *Faculty:* 14 full-time (3 women). *Students:* 53 full-time (26 women), 44 part-time (17 women); includes 6 minority (3 African Americans, 3 Hispanic Americans), 29 international. Average age 32. 99 applicants, 54% accepted, 30 enrolled. In 2009, 18 master's, 5 doctorates awarded. Terminal master's awarded for partial completion of doctoral program. *Degree requirements:* For master's, one foreign language, comprehensive exam, thesis optional; for doctorate, one foreign language, comprehensive exam, thesis/dissertation. *Entrance requirements:* For master's, GRE General Test, sample of written work, 2 letters of recommendation; for doctorate, GRE General Test, sample of written work, 3 letters of recommendation. Additional exam requirements/recommendations for international students: Required—TOEFL (minimum score 570 paper-based; 230 computer-based). *Application deadline:* For fall admission, 3/15 for domestic students, 2/15 for international students; for spring admission, 10/15 for domestic and international students. Application fee: $40. Electronic applications accepted. *Expenses:* Tuition, state resident: full-time $8112; part-time $338 per credit. Tuition, nonresident: full-time $20,256; part-time $844 per credit. Required fees: $119 per semester. One-time fee: $50. *Financial support:* In 2009–10, 20 students received support, including 2 fellowships (averaging $13,000 per year), 9 research assistantships with tuition reimbursements available (averaging $11,000 per year), 9 teaching assistantships with tuition reimbursements available (averaging $11,000 per year); career-related internships or fieldwork, institutionally sponsored loans, scholarships/grants, and unspecified assistantships also available. Support available to part-time students. Financial award application deadline: 2/15; financial award applicants required to submit FAFSA. *Faculty research:* U. S. foreign policy, international security, transatlantic and transpacific relations, transnational issues, IPE and development. Total annual research expenditures: $330,391. *Unit head:* Dr. Regina Karp, Graduate Program Director, 757-683-5700, Fax: 757-683-5701, E-mail: rkarp@odu.edu. *Application contact:* Dr. Angelica Huizar, 757-683-3988, Fax: 757-683-5701, E-mail: ahuizar@odu.edu.

Pepperdine University, School of Public Policy, Malibu, CA 90263. Offers American politics (MPP); economics (MPP); international relations (MPP); public policy (MPP); state and local policy (MPP). *Faculty:* 7 full-time (2 women), 5 part-time/adjunct (0 women). *Students:* 117 full-time (62 women), 5 part-time (3 women); includes 30 minority (7 African Americans, 1 American Indian/Alaska Native, 10 Asian Americans or Pacific Islanders, 12 Hispanic Americans), 9 international. In 2009, 27 master's awarded. *Entrance requirements:* For master's, GRE, 2 letters of recommendation, resume. Additional exam requirements/recommendations for international students: Required—TOEFL. *Application deadline:* For fall admission, 4/15 for domestic students. Applications are processed on a rolling basis. Electronic applications accepted. *Expenses:* Tuition: Full-time $37,516; part-time $1310 per unit. Required fees: $80. *Financial support:* Research assistantships, teaching assistantships, institutionally sponsored loans and scholarships/grants available. Financial award application deadline: 5/1; financial award applicants required to submit FAFSA. *Unit head:* Dr. James R. Wilburn, Dean, 310-506-7490, Fax: 310-506-7494, E-mail: james.wilburn@pepperdine.edu. *Application contact:* Melinda E. van Hemert, Director of Recruitment and Career Services, 310-506-7492, Fax: 310-506-7494, E-mail: melinda.vanhemert@pepperdine.edu.

Princeton University, Graduate School, Woodrow Wilson School of Public and International Affairs, Princeton, NJ 08544-1019. Offers public affairs (MPA, PhD); public policy (MPP); JD/MPA. Terminal master's awarded for partial completion of doctoral program. *Degree requirements:* For master's, internship; for doctorate, one foreign language, thesis/dissertation. *Entrance requirements:* For master's, GRE General Test, original policy memo; for doctorate, GRE General Test. Additional exam requirements/recommendations for international students: Required—TOEFL (minimum score 600 paper-based; 250 computer-based). Electronic applications accepted.

Queen's University at Kingston, School of Graduate Studies and Research, Faculty of Arts and Sciences, Department of Political Studies, Kingston, ON K7L 3N6, Canada. Offers Canadian politics (PhD); comparative politics (PhD); gender and politics (PhD); international relations (PhD); political theory (PhD). *Degree requirements:* For master's, thesis or alternative; for doctorate, one foreign language, thesis/dissertation, qualifying exams. *Entrance requirements:* Additional exam requirements/recommendations for international students: Required—TOEFL (minimum score 600 paper-based; 250 computer-based). *Faculty research:* Canadian politics, comparative politics, political thought, international politics, women and politics.

Regent's American College London, Webster Graduate School, London, United Kingdom. Offers business (MBA); finance (MS); human resources (MA); information technology management (MA); international business (MA); international non-governmental organizations (MA); international relations (MA); management and leadership (MA); marketing (MA). Part-time programs available.

Regent University, Graduate School, Robertson School of Government, Virginia Beach, VA 23464. Offers american government (MA); global politics (MA); health care policy and administration (MA); international politics (MA); law and public policy (MA); Mid-East Politics (MA); political leadership and management (MA); political management (MA); political theory (MA); public administration (MA); public policy (MA); terrorism and homeland defense (MA); world economies and political development (MA); JD/MA; M Div/MA; M Ed/MA; MBA/MA. Part-time and evening/weekend programs available. Postbaccalaureate distance learning degree programs offered (minimal on-campus study). *Faculty:* 6 full-time (2 women), 11 part-time/adjunct (1 woman). *Students:* 77 full-time (55 women), 65 part-time (36 women); includes 47 minority (38 African Americans, 2 Asian Americans or Pacific Islanders, 7 Hispanic Americans), 4 international. Average age 30. 131 applicants, 65% accepted, 54 enrolled. In 2009, 51 master's awarded. *Degree requirements:* For master's, thesis optional, internship. *Entrance requirements:* For master's, GRE General Test or LSAT, minimum undergraduate GPA of 3.0, writing sample, resume, interview, references. Additional exam requirements/recommendations for international students: Required—TOEFL (minimum score 577 paper-based; 233 computer-based). *Application deadline:* For fall admission, 5/1 priority date for domestic students; for spring admission, 11/1 priority date for domestic students. Applications are processed on a rolling basis. Application fee: $50. Electronic applications accepted. *Expenses:* Contact institution. *Financial support:* In 2009–10, 130 students received support. Career-related internships or fieldwork, scholarships/grants, tuition waivers (full and partial), and unspecified assistantships available. Support available to part-time students. Financial award application deadline: 9/1; financial award applicants required to submit FAFSA. *Faculty research:* Education reform, political character issues, social capital concerns, administrative ethics, Biblical law and public policy. *Unit head:* Dr. Charles W. Dunn, Dean, 757-352-4322, Fax: 757-352-4643, E-mail: cwdunn@regent.edu. *Application contact:* Matthew Chadwick, Director of Admissions, 800-373-5504, Fax: 757-352-4381, E-mail: admissions@regent.edu.

Richmond, The American International University in London, MA in International Relations Program, Richmond, United Kingdom. Offers MA. Part-time programs available. *Entrance requirements:* Additional exam requirements/recommendations for international students: Required—TOEFL, IELTS. *Application deadline:* For fall admission, 3/31 priority date for domestic students. Applications are processed on a rolling basis. Electronic applications accepted. Tuition charges are reported in British pounds. *Expenses:* Tuition: Full-time 15,000 British pounds. Full-time tuition and fees vary according to program. *Financial support:* Application deadline: 3/1. *Unit head:* Dr. James D. Boys, Director, (44) 207-368-8458, E-mail: james.boys@richmond.ac.uk. *Application contact:* Mark Kopenski, Vice President and Dean of Enrollment, (44) 208-332-8252, Fax: (44) 208-332-1596, E-mail: ma@richmond.ac.uk.

Rutgers, The State University of New Jersey, Camden, Graduate School of Arts and Sciences, Department of Public Policy and Administration, Camden, NJ 08102-1401. Offers education policy and leadership (MPA); international public service and development (MPA); public management (MPA); JD/MPA; MPA/MA. *Accreditation:* NASPAA. Part-time and evening/weekend programs available. *Degree requirements:* For master's, directed study, research workshop. *Entrance requirements:* For master's, GRE General Test, GMAT or LSAT, 3 letters of recommendation; resume. Additional exam requirements/recommendations for international students: Required—TOEFL (minimum score 550 paper-based; 213 computer-based), IELTS. Electronic applications accepted. *Faculty research:* Nonprofit management, county and municipal administration, health and human services, government communication, administrative law, educational finance.

Rutgers, The State University of New Jersey, Newark, Graduate School, Division of Global Affairs, Newark, NJ 07102. Offers MS, PhD. Part-time and evening/weekend programs available. *Degree requirements:* For master's, one foreign language, thesis optional. *Entrance requirements:* For master's and doctorate, GRE General Test, minimum B average. Electronic applications accepted. *Faculty research:* International organizations, diplomacy, world history, international political economy, global environment.

Rutgers, The State University of New Jersey, Newark, Graduate School, Program in Political Science, Newark, NJ 07102. Offers American political system (MA); international relations (MA); JD/MA. Part-time and evening/weekend programs available. *Degree requirements:* For master's, comprehensive exam, thesis optional. *Entrance requirements:* For master's, GRE, minimum undergraduate B average. Electronic applications accepted. *Faculty research:* Policymaking and policy evaluation in the United States; government and politics in Europe, Middle East, Asia, Africa, and Latin America.

Rutgers, The State University of New Jersey, New Brunswick, Graduate School-New Brunswick, Department of Political Science, Piscataway, NJ 08854-8097. Offers American politics (PhD); comparative politics (PhD); international relations (PhD); political theory (PhD); public law (PhD); women and politics (PhD). *Degree requirements:* For doctorate, one foreign language, comprehensive exam, thesis/dissertation. *Entrance requirements:* For doctorate, GRE General Test. Additional exam requirements/recommendations for international students: Required—TOEFL.

St. John Fisher College, School of Arts and Sciences, Program in International Studies, Rochester, NY 14618-3597. Offers MS. Part-time and evening/weekend programs available. *Faculty:* 6 full-time (0 women), 2 part-time/adjunct (0 women). *Students:* 7 full-time (2 women), 26 part-time (14 women); includes 4 minority (2 African Americans, 1 American Indian/Alaska Native, 1 Hispanic American). Average age 28. 18 applicants, 83% accepted, 12 enrolled. In 2009, 12 master's awarded. *Degree requirements:* For master's, research project. *Entrance requirements:* For master's, 2 letters of recommendation, personal statement, current resume. Additional exam requirements/recommendations for international students: Required—TOEFL (minimum score 575 paper-based; 233 computer-based; 80 iBT). *Application deadline:* Applications are processed on a rolling basis. Application fee: $30. Electronic applications accepted. *Expenses:* Tuition: Part-time $680 per credit hour. Required fees: $25 per semester. Tuition and fees vary according to degree level and program. *Financial support:* In 2009–10, 22 students received support. Federal Work-Study and scholarships/grants available. Financial award applicants required to submit FAFSA. *Faculty research:* International relations, international affairs, international economics, Chinese politics. *Unit head:* Dr. David Baronov, Program Director, 585-385-8220, E-mail: dbaronov@sjfc.edu. *Application contact:* Jose Perales, Director of Graduate Admissions, 585-385-8067, E-mail: jperales@sjfc.edu.

St. John's University, College of Professional Studies, Department of Mass Communications, Queens, NY 11439. Offers international communications (MS). *Students:* 26 full-time (19 women); includes 18 minority (3 African Americans, 15 Hispanic Americans). Average age 23. 37 applicants, 92% accepted, 26 enrolled. *Degree requirements:* For master's, one foreign language, thesis optional. *Entrance requirements:* For master's, GRE, official transcript showing conferral of bachelor's degree, 3 letters of recommendation, proficiency in a foreign language. Additional exam requirements/recommendations for international students: Required—TOEFL (minimum score 500 paper-based; 173 computer-based; 61 iBT), IELTS (minimum score 5.5). *Application deadline:* For fall admission, 5/1 priority date for domestic and international students; for spring admission, 11/1 priority date for domestic and international students. Applications are processed on a rolling basis. Application fee: $70. Electronic applications accepted. *Expenses:* Tuition: Full-time $16,290; part-time $905 per credit. Required fees: $300; $150 per semester. Tuition and fees vary according to program. *Unit head:* Prof. Thomas McCarthy, Acting Chair, 718-990-7399, E-mail: mccartht@stjohns.edu. *Application contact:* Kathleen Davis, Director of Graduate Admission, 718-990-2790, Fax: 718-990-5686, E-mail: gradhelp@stjohns.edu.

St. Mary's University, Graduate School, Department of Political Science, Interdisciplinary Program in International Relations, San Antonio, TX 78228-8507. Offers MA, JD/MA. Part-time programs available. Postbaccalaureate distance learning degree programs offered (no on-campus study). *Degree requirements:* For master's, one foreign language, comprehensive exam. *Entrance requirements:* For master's, GRE General Test. Additional exam requirements/recommendations for international students: Required—TOEFL (minimum score 550 paper-based; 213 computer-based; 80 iBT). Electronic applications accepted. *Expenses:* Tuition: Full-time $8004. Required fees: $536. One-time fee: $5 full-time. Full-time tuition and fees vary according to program. *Faculty research:* Eastern Europe, Soviet Union, Balkans, modern Asia, Latin America.

Salve Regina University, Graduate Studies, Program in International Relations, Newport, RI 02840-4192. Offers homeland security (Certificate); international relations (MA, Certificate). Part-time and evening/weekend programs available. Postbaccalaureate distance learning degree programs offered (minimal on-campus study). *Faculty:* 3 full-time (0 women), 5 part-time/adjunct (2 women). *Students:* 11 full-time (6 women), 62 part-time (25 women); includes 3 minority (all Hispanic Americans), 1 international. Average age 34. 66 applicants, 56% accepted, 35 enrolled. In 2009, 35 master's awarded. *Entrance requirements:* For master's, GMAT, GRE General Test, MAT or LSAT. Additional exam requirements/recommendations for international students: Required—TOEFL (minimum score 600 paper-based; 250 computer-based; 100 iBT), IELTS. *Application deadline:* For fall admission, 3/15 priority date for domestic and international students; for spring admission, 9/15 priority date for domestic and international students. Applications are processed on a rolling basis. Application fee: $60. Electronic applications accepted. *Expenses:* Tuition: Part-time $395 per credit. Part-time tuition and fees vary according to degree level. *Financial support:* Career-related internships or fieldwork and Federal Work-Study available. Support available to part-time students. Financial award application deadline: 3/1; financial award applicants required to submit FAFSA. *Unit head:* Dr. Symeon Giannakos, Director, 401-341-3177, Fax: 401-341-2993, E-mail: symeon.giannakos@salve.edu. *Application contact:* Kelly Alverson, Graduate Admissions Counselor, 401-341-2153, Fax: 401-341-2973, E-mail: kelly.alverson@salve.edu.

San Francisco State University, Division of Graduate Studies, College of Behavioral and Social Sciences, Department of International Relations, San Francisco, CA 94132-1722. Offers MA.

Schiller International University, Graduate Programs, London, Program in International Relations and Diplomacy, London, United Kingdom. Offers MA. Part-time programs available. *Degree requirements:* For master's, thesis optional, GMAT before graduation. *Entrance requirements:* For master's, 1 year of undergraduate economics, 1 foreign language. Additional exam requirements/recommendations for international students: Required—TOEFL (minimum score 550 paper-based; 213 computer-based).

Schiller International University, Program in International Relations and Diplomacy, Paris, France. Offers MA. Part-time and evening/weekend programs available. *Degree requirements:* For master's, one foreign language, final comprehensive exam or thesis. *Entrance requirements:* For master's, undergraduate mathematics (strongly advised). Additional exam requirements/recommendations for international students: Required—TOEFL (minimum score 550 paper-based; 213 computer-based).

Seton Hall University, Whitehead School of Diplomacy and International Relations, South Orange, NJ 07079-2697. Offers MA, JD/MA, MA/MA, MBA/MA, MPA/MA. Part-time and evening/weekend programs available. *Faculty:* 16 full-time (5 women), 21 part-time/adjunct (8 women). *Students:* 250. Average age 26. In 2009, 106 master's awarded. *Degree requirements:* For master's, thesis (for some programs), research project, internship. *Entrance requirements:* For master's, GMAT, GRE, or LSAT, minimum GPA of 3.2. Additional exam requirements/recommendations for international students: Required—TOEFL (minimum score 600 paper-based; 250 computer-based; 100 iBT). *Application deadline:* For fall admission, 5/1 priority date for domestic students. Applications are processed on a rolling basis. Application fee: $50. Electronic applications accepted. *Financial support:* Research assistantships with full and partial tuition reimbursements, career-related internships or fieldwork, scholarships/grants, tuition waivers (full and partial), and unspecified assistantships available. *Faculty research:* International economics and development, global health, United Nations conflict negotiation and conflict management. *Unit head:* Dr. Ursula Sanjamino, Associate Dean, 973-313-6210, Fax: 973-275-2519, E-mail: sanjamur@shu.edu. *Application contact:* Dr. Catherine Ruby, Director of Graduate Admissions, 973-275-2142, Fax: 973-275-2519, E-mail: rubycath@shu.edu.

See Close-Up on page 855.

SIT Graduate Institute, Graduate Programs, Master's Programs in Intercultural Service, Leadership, and Management, Brattleboro, VT 05302-0676. Offers conflict transformation (MA); intercultural service, leadership, and management (MA); international education (MA); management (MS); social justice in intercultural relations (MA); sustainable development (MA). Postbaccalaureate distance learning degree programs offered (minimal on-campus study). *Degree requirements:* For master's, one foreign language, thesis. *Entrance requirements:* For master's, 3 letters of reference. Additional exam requirements/recommendations for international students: Required—TOEFL. *Faculty research:* Intercultural communication, conflict resolution, advising and training, world issues, international business.

Stanford University, School of Humanities and Sciences, Program in International Policy Studies, Stanford, CA 94305-9991. Offers MA. *Degree requirements:* For master's, thesis optional. *Entrance requirements:* For master's, GRE General Test. Additional exam requirements/recommendations for international students: Required—TOEFL. Electronic applications accepted. *Expenses:* Tuition: Full-time $37,380; part-time $2760 per quarter. Required fees: $501.

Syracuse University, Maxwell School of Citizenship and Public Affairs, International Relations/Public Administration Joint Program, Syracuse, NY 13244. Offers MPA/MA. *Students:* 27 full-time (15 women), 2 part-time (1 woman); includes 10 minority (4 African Americans, 3 Asian Americans or Pacific Islanders, 3 Hispanic Americans), 3 international. Average age 26. 141 applicants, 65% accepted, 19 enrolled. *Entrance requirements:* Additional exam requirements/recommendations for international students: Required—TOEFL (minimum score 100 iBT). *Application deadline:* For fall admission, 2/1 priority date for domestic and international students. Application fee: $75. Electronic applications accepted. *Expenses:* Tuition: Full-time $26,808; part-time $1117 per credit. Required fees: $1024. *Financial support:* Fellowships with tuition reimbursements, research assistantships with tuition reimbursements, teaching assistantships with tuition reimbursements available. Financial award application deadline: 1/1; financial award applicants required to submit FAFSA. *Unit head:* Donald Planty, Chair and Ambassador, 315-443-2306. *Application contact:* Nell Bartkowiak, Director, International Relations, 315-443-9340, E-mail: nsbartko@syr.edu.

Syracuse University, Maxwell School of Citizenship and Public Affairs, Joint Program in Economics and International Relations, Syracuse, NY 13244. Offers MA/MA. Part-time programs available. *Students:* 10 full-time (7 women); includes 1 minority (Asian American or Pacific Islander), 5 international. Average age 26. 30 applicants, 67% accepted, 4 enrolled. *Entrance requirements:* Additional exam requirements/recommendations for international students: Required—TOEFL (minimum score 100 iBT). *Application deadline:* For fall admission, 2/1 priority date for domestic and international students. Application fee: $75. Electronic applications accepted. *Expenses:* Tuition: Full-time $26,808; part-time $1117 per credit. Required fees: $1024. *Financial support:* Fellowships with tuition reimbursements, research assistantships with tuition reimbursements, teaching assistantships with tuition reimbursements available. Financial award application deadline: 1/1. *Unit head:* Dr. Stuart Brown, Program Contact, 315-443-7097, Fax: 315-443-3385, E-mail: ssbrown@maxwell.syr.edu. *Application contact:* Dr. Stuart Brown, Program Contact, 315-443-7097, Fax: 315-443-3385, E-mail: ssbrown@maxwell.syr.edu.

Syracuse University, Maxwell School of Citizenship and Public Affairs, Program in Public Diplomacy, Syracuse, NY 13244. Offers MS/MA. *Students:* 18 full-time (15 women); includes 3 minority (1 African American, 2 Asian Americans or Pacific Islanders), 4 international. Average age 25. 40 applicants, 73% accepted, 18 enrolled. *Entrance requirements:* Additional exam requirements/recommendations for international students: Required—TOEFL (minimum score 100 iBT). *Application deadline:* For fall admission, 2/1 for domestic students, 2/1 priority date for international students. Application fee: $75. Electronic applications accepted. *Expenses:* Tuition: Full-time $26,808; part-time $1117 per credit. Required fees: $1024. *Financial support:* Application deadline: 1/1. *Unit head:* Dr. Dennis Kinsey, Director, 315-443-1944, E-mail: publicdiplomacy@syr.edu. *Application contact:* Martha Coria, Program Contact, 315-443-5749, Fax: 315-443-1834, E-mail: pcgrad@syr.edu.

Syracuse University, S. I. Newhouse School of Public Communications and Maxwell School of Citizenship and Public Affairs, Program in Public Diplomacy, Syracuse, NY 13244. Offers MS/MA. *Students:* 34 full-time (22 women); includes 5 minority (1 African American, 3 Asian Americans or Pacific Islanders, 1 Hispanic American), 9 international. Average age 25. 90 applicants, 57% accepted, 17 enrolled. *Entrance requirements:* Additional exam requirements/recommendations for international students: Required—TOEFL (minimum score 100 iBT). *Application deadline:* For fall admission, 2/1 priority date for domestic and international students. Application fee: $75. Electronic applications accepted. *Expenses:* Tuition: Full-time $26,808; part-time $1117 per credit. Required fees: $1024. *Financial support:* Fellowships with tuition reimbursements, research assistantships with tuition reimbursements, teaching assistantships with tuition reimbursements, tuition waivers (partial) available. Financial award application deadline: 2/1. *Unit head:* Dr. Dennis Kinsey, Director, 315-443-1944, E-mail: publicdiplomacy@syr.edu. *Application contact:* Martha Coria, Graduate Records Office, 315-443-5749, Fax: 315-443-1834, E-mail: pcgrad@syr.edu.

Texas A&M University, George Bush School of Government and Public Service, College Station, TX 77843. Offers advanced international affairs (Certificate); homeland security (Certificate); international affairs (MPIA), including international economics and development, national security affairs; nonprofit management (Certificate); public service and administration (MPSA), including public management, public policy analysis. *Accreditation:* NASPAA. *Faculty:* 51. *Students:* 209 full-time (97 women), 93 part-time (43 women); includes 48 minority (15 African Americans, 5 Asian Americans or Pacific Islanders, 28 Hispanic Americans), 19 international. Average age 24. In 2009, 87 master's awarded. *Degree requirements:* For master's, summer internship. *Entrance requirements:* For master's, GRE (preferred) or GMAT. *Application deadline:* For fall admission, 1/24 for domestic and international students. Application fee: $50 ($75 for international students). Electronic applications accepted. *Expenses:* Tuition, state resident: full-time $3991; part-time $221.74 per credit hour. Tuition, nonresident: full-time $9049; part-time $502.74 per credit hour. *Financial support:* In 2009–10, fellowships (averaging $11,000 per year), research assistantships (averaging $11,250 per year) were awarded; career-related internships or fieldwork, Federal Work-Study, and institutionally sponsored loans also available. Financial award application deadline: 2/1; financial award applicants required to submit FAFSA. *Faculty research:* Public policy, presidential studies, public leadership, economic policy, social policy. *Unit head:* A. Benton Cocanougher, Interim Dean, 979-862-8842, E-mail: bushschool@tamu.edu. *Application contact:* Kathryn Meyer, Recruitment and Placement Officer, 979-458-4767, Fax: 979-845-4155, E-mail: admissions@bushschool.tamu.edu.

Texas State University–San Marcos, Graduate School, Program in International Studies, San Marcos, TX 78666. Offers MA. *Students:* 17 full-time (6 women), 22 part-time (13 women); includes 7 minority (all Hispanic Americans), 6 international. Average age 29. 19 applicants, 100% accepted, 15 enrolled. In 2009, 2 master's awarded. *Degree requirements:* For master's, comprehensive exam, thesis optional. *Entrance requirements:* For master's, minimum GPA of 3.0 on last 60 hours of undergraduate work, 2- to 5-page essay, 2 letters of reference. Additional exam requirements/recommendations for international students: Required—TOEFL (minimum score 550 paper-based; 213 computer-based). *Application deadline:* For fall admission, 6/15 priority date for domestic students, 6/1 for international students; for spring admission, 10/15 priority date for domestic students, 10/1 for international students. Applications are processed on a rolling basis. Application fee: $40 ($90 for international students). *Expenses:* Tuition, state resident: full-time $5784; part-time $241 per credit hour. Tuition, nonresident: part-time $551 per credit hour. Required fees: $1728; $48 per credit hour. $306. Tuition and fees vary according to course load. *Financial support:* In 2009–10, 29 students received support, including 1 research assistantship (averaging $4,928 per year), 2 teaching assistantships (averaging $5,076 per year). Financial award application deadline: 4/1; financial award applicants required to submit FAFSA. *Unit head:* Dr. Dennis Dunn, Head, 512-245-2339, E-mail: dd05@txstate.edu. *Application contact:* Dr. J. Michael Willoughby, Dean of Graduate School, 512-245-2581, Fax: 512-245-8365, E-mail: gradcollege@txstate.edu.

Troy University, Graduate School, College of Arts and Sciences, Program in International Relations, Troy, AL 36082. Offers national security affairs (MS), including global studies, national security affairs, regional affairs. Part-time and evening/weekend programs available. Postbaccalaureate distance learning degree programs offered (no on-campus study). *Students:* 78 full-time (35 women), 336 part-time (135 women); includes 120 minority (50 African Americans, 4 American Indian/Alaska Native, 32 Asian Americans or Pacific Islanders, 34 Hispanic Americans). Average age 32. 307 applicants, 86% accepted. In 2009, 136 master's awarded. *Degree requirements:* For master's, comprehensive exam or thesis. *Entrance requirements:* For master's, GRE, MAT, or GMAT, minimum undergraduate GPA of 2.5. Additional exam requirements/recommendations for international students: Required—TOEFL (minimum score 523 paper-based; 193 computer-based; 70 iBT), IELTS (minimum score 6). *Application deadline:* Applications are processed on a rolling basis. Application fee: $50. Electronic applications accepted. *Financial support:* Available to part-time students. Applicants required to submit FAFSA. *Faculty research:* Elections, religion and world politics, terrorism. *Unit head:* Dr. Charles Krupnick, Department Chairman, 334-670-5968, Fax: 334-670-5647, E-mail: ckrupnick@troy.edu. *Application contact:* Brenda K. Campbell, Director of Graduate Admissions, 334-670-3178, Fax: 334-670-3733, E-mail: bcamp@troy.edu.

Tufts University, Fletcher School of Law and Diplomacy, Medford, MA 02155. Offers LL M, MA, MAHA, MALD, MIB, PhD, DVM/MA, JD/MALD, MALD/MA, MALD/MBA, MALD/MS, MD/MA. Postbaccalaureate distance learning degree programs offered (minimal on-campus study). *Faculty:* 34 full-time (7 women), 31 part-time/adjunct (8 women). *Students:* 443 full-time (224 women), 7 part-time (4 women); includes 51 minority (6 African Americans, 1 American Indian/Alaska Native, 26 Asian Americans or Pacific Islanders, 18 Hispanic Americans), 165 international. Average age 31. 1,866 applicants, 40% accepted, 292 enrolled. In 2009, 364 master's, 12 doctorates awarded. *Degree requirements:* For master's, one foreign language, thesis; for doctorate, one foreign language, comprehensive exam, thesis/dissertation, dissertation defense. *Entrance requirements:* For master's and doctorate, GMAT or GRE General Test. Additional exam requirements/recommendations for international students: Required—TOEFL (minimum score 600 paper-based; 250 computer-based; 100 iBT), IELTS (minimum score 7). *Application deadline:* For fall admission, 1/15 for domestic and international students; for spring admission, 10/15 for domestic and international students. Application fee: $70. Electronic applications accepted. *Expenses:* Contact institution. *Financial support:* Federal Work-Study, institutionally sponsored loans, scholarships/grants, and tuition waivers (partial) available. Financial award application deadline: 1/15; financial award applicants required to submit FAFSA. *Faculty research:* Negotiation and conflict resolution, international organizations, international business and economic law, security studies, development economics. *Unit head:* Stephen W. Bosworth, Dean, 617-627-3050, Fax: 617-627-3712. *Application contact:* Laurie A. Hurley, E-mail: fletcheradmissions@tufts.edu.

United States International University, School of Arts and Sciences, Nairobi, Kenya. Offers counseling psychology (MA); international relations (MA). Part-time and evening/weekend programs available. *Degree requirements:* For master's, thesis, practicum. *Entrance requirements:* For master's, GRE General Test, 2 letters of recommendation, resume. Additional exam requirements/recommendations for international students: Required—TOEFL (minimum score 550 paper-based; 213 computer-based). *Faculty research:* Trauma in children, African intellectualism, psychological assessment tools.

International Affairs

Universidad de las Americas, A.C., Program in International Organizations and Institutions, Mexico City, Mexico. Offers MA.

Université de Montréal, Faculty of Arts and Sciences, Programs in International Studies, Montréal, QC H3C 3J7, Canada.

Université Laval, Québec Institute for Advanced International Studies, Program in International Relations, Québec, QC G1K 7P4, Canada. Offers MA, PhD. *Degree requirements:* For master's, thesis (for some programs). *Entrance requirements:* For master's, English exam, French exam. Electronic applications accepted.

University of Bridgeport, International College, Bridgeport, CT 06604. Offers global development and peace (MA). Part-time and evening/weekend programs available. *Degree requirements:* For master's, thesis. *Entrance requirements:* Additional exam requirements/recommendations for international students: Recommended—TOEFL (minimum score 550 paper-based; 213 computer-based; 80 iBT), IELTS (minimum score 6.5).

The University of British Columbia, Institute of Asian Research, Vancouver, BC V6T 1Z2, Canada. Offers MAPPS. *Degree requirements:* For master's, thesis optional. *Entrance requirements:* Additional exam requirements/recommendations for international students: Required—TOEFL (minimum score 600 paper-based; 250 computer-based; 100 iBT), GRE (recommended). Electronic applications accepted. *Faculty research:* Social cohesion, globalization, social safety nets, policy research, research and development alliances, knowledge-based workshops on Asia-Pacific studies.

University of California, Berkeley, Graduate Division, Group in International and Area Studies, Berkeley, CA 94720-1500. Offers MA, PhD, JD/MA, MBA/MA, MJ/MA. *Students:* 7 full-time (3 women). Average age 32. In 2009, 6 master's awarded. Application fee: $70 ($90 for international students). *Unit head:* Prof. John Lie, Chair, 510-642-0656, E-mail: iasone@berkeley.edu. *Application contact:* Prof. John Lie, Chair, 510-642-0656, E-mail: iasone@berkeley.edu.

University of California, Berkeley, Graduate Division, Haas School of Business and Group in International and Area Studies, MBA/MA Program in International and Area Studies, Berkeley, CA 94720-1500. Offers MBA/MA. *Accreditation:* AACSB. *Students:* 1 full-time (0 women). *Entrance requirements:* Additional exam requirements/recommendations for international students: Required—TOEFL. Application fee: $200. *Financial support:* Fellowships with full tuition reimbursements, research assistantships, teaching assistantships with partial tuition reimbursements, career-related internships or fieldwork, scholarships/grants, and unspecified assistantships available. Financial award application deadline: 3/1; financial award applicants required to submit FAFSA. *Unit head:* Julia Hwang, Director, MBA Program, 510-642-1405, Fax: 510-643-6659, E-mail: julia_hwang@haas.berkeley.edu. *Application contact:* 510-642-1405, Fax: 510-643-6659.

University of California, San Diego, Office of Graduate Studies, Department of Economics, La Jolla, CA 92093. Offers economics (PhD); economics and international affairs (PhD). *Degree requirements:* For doctorate, thesis/dissertation. *Entrance requirements:* For doctorate, GRE General Test. Electronic applications accepted. *Faculty research:* Microfoundations of macroeconomics, econometric model specification and testing, industrial organization.

University of California, San Diego, Office of Graduate Studies, Department of Political Science, La Jolla, CA 92093. Offers Latin American studies (MA); political science (PhD); political science and international affairs (PhD). *Entrance requirements:* For master's and doctorate, GRE General Test. Electronic applications accepted.

University of California, San Diego, Office of Graduate Studies, Graduate School of International Relations and Pacific Studies, La Jolla, CA 92093. Offers economics and international affairs (PhD); Pacific international affairs (MPIA); political science and international affairs (PhD). *Degree requirements:* For master's, one foreign language; for doctorate, thesis/dissertation. *Entrance requirements:* For master's, GMAT or GRE General Test; for doctorate, GRE General Test. Additional exam requirements/recommendations for international students: Required—TOEFL (minimum score 550 paper-based; 213 computer-based). Electronic applications accepted. *Faculty research:* Pacific Rim as system and placement in global relations; studies in international economics, management and finance; analysis of patterns of policymaking in countries of the Pacific.

University of California, Santa Barbara, Graduate Division, College of Letters and Sciences, Division of Humanities and Fine Arts, Department of English, Santa Barbara, CA 93106-3170. Offers English (PhD); feminist studies (PhD); global studies (PhD); MA/PhD. *Faculty:* 26 full-time (13 women), 17 part-time/adjunct (12 women). *Students:* 81 full-time (43 women). Average age 30. 151 applicants, 19% accepted, 13 enrolled. In 2009, 12 doctorates awarded. Terminal master's awarded for partial completion of doctoral program. *Degree requirements:* For doctorate, one foreign language, comprehensive exam, thesis/dissertation. *Entrance requirements:* For doctorate, GRE General Test, GRE Subject Test (literature), sample of written work, 3 letters of recommendation, resume/curriculum vitae. Additional exam requirements/recommendations for international students: Required—TOEFL (minimum score 550 paper-based; 213 computer-based; 80 iBT) or IELTS (minimum score 7). *Application deadline:* For fall admission, 12/15 for domestic and international students. Application fee: $70 ($90 for international students). Electronic applications accepted. *Financial support:* In 2009–10, 70 students received support, including 32 fellowships with full and partial tuition reimbursements available (averaging $10,800 per year), 6 research assistantships with full and partial tuition reimbursements available (averaging $4,200 per year), 54 teaching assistantships with partial tuition reimbursements available (averaging $10,800 per year); Federal Work-Study, institutionally sponsored loans, scholarships/grants, health care benefits, tuition waivers (full and partial), and unspecified assistantships also available. Financial award application deadline: 12/15; financial award applicants required to submit FAFSA. *Faculty research:* Renaissance literature, eighteenth century literature, American literature, race and ethnic studies, literature and theory of technology/media/information. *Unit head:* Prof. Alan Liu, Chair, 805-893-3478, Fax: 805-893-4622, E-mail: ayliu@english.ucsb.edu. *Application contact:* Chelsea Houdyshell, Staff Graduate Advisor, 805-893-2639, Fax: 805-893-4622, E-mail: chelsea@english.ucsb.edu.

University of California, Santa Barbara, Graduate Division, College of Letters and Sciences, Division of Humanities and Fine Arts, Department of History, Santa Barbara, CA 93106-9410. Offers feminist studies (PhD); global studies (PhD); public history (PhD); MA/PhD. *Faculty:* 40 full-time (17 women), 11 part-time/adjunct (6 women). *Students:* 120 full-time (62 women). Average age 34. 130 applicants, 38% accepted, 22 enrolled. In 2009, 9 doctorates awarded. Terminal master's awarded for partial completion of doctoral program. *Degree requirements:* For doctorate, variable foreign language requirement, comprehensive exam, thesis/dissertation. *Entrance requirements:* For doctorate, GRE, 3 letters of recommendation, resume/curriculum vitae. Additional exam requirements/recommendations for international students: Required—TOEFL (minimum score 550 paper-based; 213 computer-based; 80 iBT) or IELTS (minimum score 7). *Application deadline:* For fall admission, 12/5 for domestic and international students. Application fee: $70 ($90 for international students). Electronic applications accepted. *Financial support:* In 2009–10, 94 students received support, including 53 fellowships with full and partial tuition reimbursements available (averaging $8,600 per year), 2 research assistantships with full and partial tuition reimbursements available (averaging $7,400 per year), 70 teaching assistantships with partial tuition reimbursements available (averaging $9,400 per year); Federal Work-Study, institutionally sponsored loans, scholarships/grants, traineeships, health care benefits, tuition waivers (full and partial), and unspecified assistantships also available. Financial award application deadline: 12/5; financial award applicants required to submit FAFSA. *Faculty research:* Europe, U. S., Latin America, Africa, Middle East, East Asia. *Unit head:* Kenneth J. Moure, Chair, 805-893-2993, Fax: 805-893-8795, E-mail: moure@history.ucrb.edu. *Application contact:* Prof. Sharon Farmer, Director of Graduate Studies, 805-893-2543, Fax: 805-893-8795, E-mail: farmer@history.ucsb.edu.

University of California, Santa Barbara, Graduate Division, College of Letters and Sciences, Division of Humanities and Fine Arts, Department of Religious Studies, Santa Barbara, CA 93106-3130. Offers European Medieval studies (PhD); feminist studies (PhD); global studies (PhD); religious studies (MA, PhD); MA/PhD. *Faculty:* 18 full-time (8 women), 11 part-time/adjunct (5 women). *Students:* 86 full-time (33 women). Average age 31. 151 applicants, 31% accepted, 17 enrolled. In 2009, 7 master's, 6 doctorates awarded. Terminal master's awarded for partial completion of doctoral program. *Degree requirements:* For master's, one foreign language, comprehensive exam (for some programs), thesis (for some programs); for doctorate, one foreign language, thesis/dissertation. *Entrance requirements:* For master's, GRE General Test; for doctorate, GRE General Test, MA in related field, 3 letters of recommendation, statement of purpose, personal achievements/contributions statement, resume/curriculum vitae, transcripts for post-secondary institutions attended. Additional exam requirements/recommendations for international students: Required—TOEFL (minimum score 550 paper-based; 213 computer-based; 80 iBT) or IELTS (minimum score 7). *Application deadline:* For fall admission, 12/1 for domestic and international students. Application fee: $70 ($90 for international students). Electronic applications accepted. *Financial support:* In 2009–10, 67 students received support, including 29 fellowships with full and partial tuition reimbursements available (averaging $12,600 per year), 5 research assistantships with full and partial tuition reimbursements available (averaging $7,900 per year), 46 teaching assistantships with partial tuition reimbursements available (averaging $8,400 per year); career-related internships or fieldwork, Federal Work-Study, institutionally sponsored loans, scholarships/grants, traineeships, health care benefits, tuition waivers (full and partial), and unspecified assistantships also available. Financial award application deadline: 12/1; financial award applicants required to submit FAFSA. *Faculty research:* Religion and politics, religion and violence, contemporary spirituality, religious traditions, theoretical approaches to the study of religion, area studies. *Unit head:* Prof. Catherine L. Albanese, Chair, 805-893-3564, Fax: 805-893-2059, E-mail: albanese@religion.ucsb.edu. *Application contact:* Sally J. Lombrozo, Graduate Program Assistant, 805-893-2744, Fax: 805-893-2059, E-mail: lombrozo@religion.ucsb.edu.

University of California, Santa Barbara, Graduate Division, College of Letters and Sciences, Division of Social Sciences, Department of Anthropology, Santa Barbara, CA 93106-3210. Offers European archaeology (MA); global studies (PhD); North American archeology (MA); sociocultural anthropology (MA); South American archaeology (MA); MA/PhD. *Faculty:* 13 full-time (2 women), 2 part-time/adjunct (both women). *Students:* 57 full-time (36 women). Average age 31. 64 applicants, 41% accepted, 11 enrolled. In 2009, 7 master's, 3 doctorates awarded. Terminal master's awarded for partial completion of doctoral program. *Degree requirements:* For master's, comprehensive exam, thesis; for doctorate, comprehensive exam, thesis/dissertation. *Entrance requirements:* For master's, GRE General Test, sample of written work, 3 letters of recommendation, resume/curriculum vitae; for doctorate, GRE General Test, sample of written work, 3 letters of recommendation, statement of purpose, personal achievements/contributions statement, resume/curriculum vitae, transcripts for post-secondary institutions attended. Additional exam requirements/recommendations for international students: Required—TOEFL (minimum score 550 paper-based; 213 computer-based; 80 iBT) or IELTS (minimum score 7). *Application deadline:* For fall admission, 12/1 for domestic and international students. Application fee: $70 ($90 for international students). Electronic applications accepted. *Financial support:* In 2009–10, 51 students received support, including 47 fellowships with full and partial tuition reimbursements available (averaging $4,000 per year), 9 research assistantships with full and partial tuition reimbursements available (averaging $7,400 per year), 30 teaching assistantships with partial tuition reimbursements available (averaging $10,500 per year); career-related internships or fieldwork, Federal Work-Study, institutionally sponsored loans, scholarships/grants, traineeships, health care benefits, and unspecified assistantships also available. Financial award application deadline: 3/1; financial award applicants required to submit FAFSA. *Faculty research:* Archaeology, bioarchaeology, biosocial anthropology, evolutionary ecology, evolutionary psychology, sociocultural anthropology. *Unit head:* Prof. Katharina Schreiber, Chair, 805-893-2519, Fax: 805-893-8707, E-mail: kschreiber@anth.ucsb.edu. *Application contact:* Robin Roe, Graduate Program Assistant, 805-893-2516, Fax: 805-893-8707, E-mail: roe@anth.ucsb.edu.

University of California, Santa Barbara, Graduate Division, College of Letters and Sciences, Division of Social Sciences, Department of Global and International Studies, Santa Barbara, CA 93106-7065. Offers MA. *Faculty:* 7 full-time (1 woman), 9 part-time/adjunct (5 women). *Students:* 22 full-time (18 women). Average age 27. 69 applicants, 45% accepted, 18 enrolled. In 2009, 15 master's awarded. *Degree requirements:* For master's, one foreign language, comprehensive exam (for some programs), thesis or alternative, internship/study abroad. *Entrance requirements:* For master's, GRE, 2 years of a second language with B grade or better, 3 letters of recommendation, resume/curriculum vitae. Additional exam requirements/recommendations for international students: Required—TOEFL (minimum score 550 paper-based; 213 computer-based; 80 iBT) or IELTS. *Application deadline:* For fall admission, 12/15 for domestic and international students. Application fee: $70 ($90 for international students). Electronic applications accepted. *Financial support:* In 2009–10, 25 fellowships with full and partial tuition reimbursements (averaging $4,700 per year), 27 teaching assistantships with partial tuition reimbursements (averaging $5,400 per year) were awarded; career-related internships or fieldwork, Federal Work-Study, institutionally sponsored loans, scholarships/grants, health care benefits, tuition waivers (partial), unspecified assistantships, and travel support for internships also available. Financial award applicants required to submit FAFSA. *Faculty research:* Globalization, NGO/non-profit organizations, world system theory, international/global conflict resolution, international/global ethics. *Unit head:* Prof. Giles Gunn, Chair, 805-893-4299, Fax: 805-893-8003, E-mail: ggunn@global.ucsb.edu. *Application contact:* Jessea Gay Marie, Graduate Program Advisor/Internship Assistance Officer, 805-893-4668, Fax: 805-893-8003, E-mail: jmarie@global.ucsb.edu.

University of California, Santa Barbara, Graduate Division, College of Letters and Sciences, Division of Social Sciences, Department of Sociology, Santa Barbara, CA 93106-9430. Offers global studies (PhD); human development (PhD); language, interaction and social organization (PhD); technology and society (PhD); women's studies (PhD); MA/PhD. *Faculty:* 35 full-time (14 women). *Students:* 77 full-time (50 women). Average age 30. 155 applicants, 9% accepted, 8 enrolled. In 2009, 10 doctorates awarded. Terminal master's awarded for partial completion of doctoral program. *Degree requirements:* For doctorate, comprehensive exam, thesis/dissertation. *Entrance requirements:* For doctorate, GRE General Test, sample of written work, 3 letters of recommendation, resume/curriculum vitae. Additional exam requirements/recommendations for international students: Required—TOEFL (minimum score 550 paper-based; 213 computer-based; 80 iBT), or IELTS. *Application deadline:* For fall admission, 12/10 for domestic students. Application fee: $70 ($90 for international students). Electronic applications accepted. *Financial support:* In 2009–10, 69 students received support, including 50 fellowships with full tuition reimbursements available (averaging $7,900 per year), 6 research assistantships with full and partial tuition reimbursements available (averaging $2,600 per year), 53 teaching assistantships with partial tuition reimbursements available (averaging $9,200 per year); career-related internships or fieldwork, Federal Work-Study, institutionally sponsored loans, scholarships/grants, health care benefits, and unspecified assistantships also available. Financial award applicants required to submit FAFSA. *Faculty research:* Conversation analysis, social movements, human sexuality, urban sociology, race and ethnic relations. *Unit head:* Prof. Verta Taylor, Chair, 805-893-3118, Fax: 805-893-3324, E-mail: grad-soc@soc.ucsb.edu. *Application contact:* Ra Thea, Graduate Staff Advisor, 805-893-3328, Fax: 805-893-3324, E-mail: grad-soc@soc.ucsb.edu.

University of California, Santa Cruz, Division of Graduate Studies, Division of Social Sciences, Program in International Economics, Santa Cruz, CA 95064. Offers PhD. *Degree requirements:* For doctorate, thesis/dissertation, 4 field exams, econometrics project. *Entrance requirements:* For doctorate, GRE General Test. *Faculty research:* Current and emerging issues in taxation, industrial policy, environmental regulation, market structure.

University of Central Oklahoma, College of Graduate Studies and Research, College of Liberal Arts, Department of Political Science, Program in International Affairs, Edmond, OK

73034-5209. Offers MA. Part-time programs available. *Entrance requirements:* Additional exam requirements/recommendations for international students: Required—TOEFL (minimum score 550 paper-based; 213 computer-based). Electronic applications accepted. *Expenses:* Tuition, state resident: full-time $4128; part-time $172 per credit hour. Tuition, nonresident: full-time $10,373; part-time $432.20 per credit hour. Required fees: $433.20; $18.05 per credit hour. *Faculty research:* Korean and Japanese politics.

University of Chicago, Division of Social Sciences, Committee on International Relations, Chicago, IL 60637-1513. Offers AM, MBA/AM. Part-time programs available. *Students:* 58. In 2009, 45 master's awarded. *Degree requirements:* For master's, thesis. *Entrance requirements:* For master's, GRE General Test. Additional exam requirements/recommendations for international students: Required—TOEFL. *Application deadline:* For fall admission, 1/4 for domestic and international students. Application fee: $55. Electronic applications accepted. *Financial support:* Federal Work-Study, institutionally sponsored loans, and scholarships/grants available. Financial award application deadline: 1/4. *Unit head:* Prof. Mark Bradley, Chair, 773-702-8078. *Application contact:* Office of the Dean of Students, 773-702-8415, E-mail: admissions@ssd.uchicago.edu.

University of Colorado at Boulder, Graduate School, College of Arts and Sciences, Department of Political Science, Boulder, CO 80309. Offers international affairs (MA); political science (MA, PhD); public policy (MA). *Faculty:* 25 full-time (8 women). *Students:* 55 full-time (27 women), 8 part-time (5 women); includes 7 minority (2 American Indian/Alaska Native, 1 Asian American or Pacific Islander, 4 Hispanic Americans), 6 international. Average age 30. 179 applicants, 9% accepted, 13 enrolled. In 2009, 12 master's, 7 doctorates awarded. Terminal master's awarded for partial completion of doctoral program. *Degree requirements:* For master's, comprehensive exam, thesis; for doctorate, one foreign language, thesis/dissertation. *Entrance requirements:* For master's, GRE General Test, minimum undergraduate GPA of 3.0; for doctorate, GRE General Test, minimum GPA of 3.5 (undergraduate), 3.0 (graduate). *Application deadline:* For fall admission, 12/31 priority date for domestic students, 12/31 for international students. Application fee: $50 ($60 for international students). *Financial support:* In 2009–10, 10 fellowships (averaging $2,060 per year), 41 research assistantships (averaging $12,087 per year) were awarded; Federal Work-Study also available. Financial award application deadline: 12/31. *Faculty research:* American government and politics, comparative politics, international relations, public policy, law and politics, political philosophy, empirical theory and methodology. Total annual research expenditures: $180,188.

University of Connecticut, Graduate School, College of Liberal Arts and Sciences, Field of International Studies, Program in International Studies, Storrs, CT 06269. Offers MA. *Faculty:* 42 full-time (21 women). *Students:* 3 full-time (all women), 4 part-time (3 women), 3 international. Average age 27. 12 applicants, 33% accepted, 1 enrolled. In 2009, 3 master's awarded. *Degree requirements:* For master's, comprehensive exam. *Entrance requirements:* For master's, GRE General Test. Additional exam requirements/recommendations for international students: Required—TOEFL (minimum score 550 paper-based; 213 computer-based). *Application deadline:* For fall admission, 2/1 priority date for domestic and international students; for spring admission, 11/1 for domestic students, 10/1 for international students. Applications are processed on a rolling basis. Electronic applications accepted. *Expenses:* Tuition, state resident: full-time $4725; part-time $525 per credit. Tuition, nonresident: full-time $12,267; part-time $1363 per credit. Required fees: $346 per semester. Tuition and fees vary according to course load. *Financial support:* In 2009–10, 2 research assistantships with full tuition reimbursements were awarded; teaching assistantships with full tuition reimbursements, Federal Work-Study, scholarships/grants, health care benefits, and unspecified assistantships also available. Financial award application deadline: 2/1. *Unit head:* M. Elizabeth Mahan, Director, 860-486-2908, Fax: 860-486-2963, E-mail: elizabeth.mahan@uconn.edu. *Application contact:* M. Elizabeth Mahan, Director, 860-486-2908, Fax: 860-486-2963, E-mail: elizabeth.mahan@uconn.edu.

University of Delaware, College of Arts and Sciences, Department of Political Science and International Relations, Newark, DE 19716. Offers MA, PhD. Terminal master's awarded for partial completion of doctoral program. *Degree requirements:* For master's, research paper; for doctorate, one foreign language, comprehensive exam, thesis/dissertation. *Entrance requirements:* For master's and doctorate, GRE General Test, minimum GPA of 3.2 in major, 3.0 overall. Additional exam requirements/recommendations for international students: Required—TOEFL (minimum score 600 paper-based). Electronic applications accepted. *Faculty research:* Social constructivism. international migration, international security, democratization, human rights.

University of Denver, Josef Korbel School of International Studies, Denver, CO 80208. Offers MA, PhD. Part-time programs available. *Faculty:* 30 full-time (7 women), 28 part-time/adjunct (12 women). *Students:* 425 full-time (254 women), 57 part-time (32 women); includes 53 minority (7 African Americans, 2 American Indian/Alaska Native, 19 Asian Americans or Pacific Islanders, 25 Hispanic Americans), 31 international. Average age 27. 944 applicants, 79% accepted, 287 enrolled. In 2009, 171 master's, 7 doctorates awarded. *Degree requirements:* For master's, one foreign language, thesis; for doctorate, one foreign language, thesis/dissertation. *Entrance requirements:* For master's and doctorate, GRE General Test. Additional exam requirements/recommendations for international students: Required—TOEFL. *Application deadline:* For fall admission, 1/15 priority date for domestic students, 12/1 priority date for international students; for winter admission, 10/15 priority date for domestic and international students. Applications are processed on a rolling basis. Application fee: $60. Electronic applications accepted. *Expenses:* Tuition: Full-time $34,596; part-time $961 per quarter hour. Required fees: $4 per quarter hour. Tuition and fees vary according to course load, campus/location and program. *Financial support:* In 2009–10, 7 teaching assistantships with full and partial tuition reimbursements (averaging $10,000 per year) were awarded; career-related internships or fieldwork, Federal Work-Study, institutionally sponsored loans, and scholarships/grants also available. Support available to part-time students. Financial award applicants required to submit FAFSA. *Faculty research:* Human rights and international security, international politics and economics, economic-social and political development, international technology analysis and management, economic-social and political development. *Unit head:* Brad Miller, Director of Graduate Admissions, 303-871-2544. *Application contact:* Office of Graduate Admissions, 303-871-2544, E-mail: korbeladm@du.edu.

University of Florida, Graduate School, College of Liberal Arts and Sciences, Department of Political Science, Program in International Relations, Gainesville, FL 32611. Offers MA, MAT. Part-time programs available. Terminal master's awarded for partial completion of doctoral program. *Degree requirements:* For master's, variable foreign language requirement, thesis or alternative. *Entrance requirements:* For master's, GRE General Test, minimum GPA of 3.0. Additional exam requirements/recommendations for international students: Required—TOEFL (minimum score 550 paper-based; 213 computer-based). Electronic applications accepted. *Faculty research:* American and comparative foreign policy, North-South relations, international political economy.

University of Indianapolis, Graduate Programs, College of Arts and Sciences, Department of History and Political Science, Indianapolis, IN 46227-3697. Offers history (MA); international relations (MA). Part-time and evening/weekend programs available. *Faculty:* 5 full-time (1 woman). *Students:* 10 full-time (2 women), 17 part-time (10 women); includes 2 minority (1 African American, 1 Hispanic American), 4 international. Average age 28. *Degree requirements:* For master's, thesis optional. *Entrance requirements:* For master's, GRE Subject Test, minimum GPA of 3.0, 3 letters of recommendation. Additional exam requirements/recommendations for international students: Required—TOEFL (minimum score 550 paper-based; 213 computer-based). *Application deadline:* Applications are processed on a rolling basis. Application fee: $30. Electronic applications accepted. *Financial support:* Federal Work-Study, scholarships/grants, and tuition waivers (full and partial) available. Support available to part-time students. Financial award application deadline: 5/1; financial award applicants required to submit FAFSA. *Unit head:* Dr. Lawrence Sondhaus, Chairperson, 317-788-2196, Fax: 317-788-3480, E-mail: sondhaus@uindy.edu. *Application contact:* Dr. Lawrence Sondhaus, Chairperson, 317-788-2196, Fax: 317-788-3480, E-mail: sohdhaus@uindy.edu.

The University of Kansas, Graduate Studies, College of Liberal Arts and Sciences, Global and International Studies Program, Lawrence, KS 66045. Offers MA. Part-time and evening/weekend programs available. *Students:* 14 full-time (4 women), 34 part-time (17 women); includes 4 minority (3 Asian Americans or Pacific Islanders, 1 Hispanic American), 1 international. Average age 31. 17 applicants, 47% accepted, 7 enrolled. In 2009, 14 master's awarded. *Degree requirements:* For master's, one foreign language, thesis or exam. *Entrance requirements:* For master's, GRE, minimum GPA of 3.0, 3 letters of reference, curriculum vitae. Additional exam requirements/recommendations for international students: Required—TOEFL. *Application deadline:* For fall admission, 5/1 priority date for domestic and international students; for spring admission, 11/15 priority date for domestic and international students. Applications are processed on a rolling basis. Application fee: $45 ($55 for international students). Electronic applications accepted. *Expenses:* Tuition, state resident: full-time $6492; part-time $270.50 per credit hour. Tuition, nonresident: full-time $15,510; part-time $646.25 per credit hour. Required fees: $847; $70.56 per credit hour. Tuition and fees vary according to course load and program. *Financial support:* Scholarships/grants available. *Faculty research:* Globalization, environmental sociology. *Unit head:* Dr. Eric Hanley, Program Director, 913-897-8510, Fax: 913-897-8491, E-mail: hanley@ku.edu. *Application contact:* Dr. Eric Hanley, Program Director, 913-897-8510, Fax: 913-897-8491, E-mail: hanley@ku.edu.

University of Kentucky, Graduate School, Patterson School of Diplomacy and International Commerce, Lexington, KY 40506-0027. Offers MA. *Degree requirements:* For master's, one foreign language, comprehensive exam, statistics. *Entrance requirements:* For master's, GRE General Test, minimum undergraduate GPA of 3.0. Additional exam requirements/recommendations for international students: Required—TOEFL (minimum score 550 paper-based; 213 computer-based; 79 iBT). Electronic applications accepted. *Faculty research:* International relations, foreign and defense policy, cross-cultural negotiation, international science and technology, diplomacy, international economics and development, geopolitical modeling.

University of Miami, Graduate School, College of Arts and Sciences, Department of International Studies, Coral Gables, FL 33124. Offers MA, PhD. *Degree requirements:* For master's, one foreign language, comprehensive exam; for doctorate, one foreign language, comprehensive exam, thesis/dissertation. *Entrance requirements:* For master's, GRE General Test, minimum GPA of 3.0; for doctorate, GRE General Test. Additional exam requirements/recommendations for international students: Required—TOEFL. Electronic applications accepted. *Faculty research:* Latin American studies, international economics, international security and conflict, comparative development, international health policy.

University of Miami, Graduate School, Program in International Administration, Coral Gables, FL 33124. Offers MAIA. Part-time and evening/weekend programs available. *Degree requirements:* For master's, practicum. *Entrance requirements:* For master's, GRE General Test. Additional exam requirements/recommendations for international students: Required—TOEFL (minimum score 550 paper-based; 213 computer-based), IELTS (minimum score 6.5). Electronic applications accepted.

University of Northern British Columbia, Office of Graduate Studies, Prince George, BC V2N 4Z9, Canada. Offers business administration (Diploma); community health science (M Sc); disability management (MA); education (M Ed); first nations studies (MA); gender studies (MA); history (MA); interdisciplinary studies (MA); international studies (MA); mathematical, computer and physical sciences (M Sc); natural resources and environmental studies (M Sc, MA, MNRES, PhD); political science (MA); psychology (M Sc, PhD); social work (MSW). Part-time and evening/weekend programs available. Postbaccalaureate distance learning degree programs offered (no on-campus study). *Degree requirements:* For master's, thesis; for doctorate, thesis/dissertation. *Entrance requirements:* For master's, GRE, minimum B average in undergraduate course work; for doctorate, candidacy exam, minimum A average in graduate course work.

University of Oklahoma, Graduate College, School of International and Area Studies, Norman, OK 73019-0390. Offers international studies (MA), including global affairs, global management. *Faculty:* 17 full-time (5 women), 1 part-time/adjunct (0 women). *Students:* 15 full-time (10 women), 4 part-time (2 women); includes 3 minority (1 Asian American or Pacific Islander, 2 Hispanic Americans). 13 applicants, 69% accepted, 5 enrolled. In 2009, 2 master's awarded. *Degree requirements:* For master's, one foreign language, thesis optional. *Entrance requirements:* For master's, GMAT or GRE. Additional exam requirements/recommendations for international students: Required—TOEFL (minimum score 550 paper-based; 213 computer-based). *Application deadline:* For fall admission, 2/15 for domestic students, 4/1 for international students; for spring admission, 10/15 for domestic students, 9/1 for international students. Applications are processed on a rolling basis. Application fee: $40 ($90 for international students). Electronic applications accepted. *Expenses:* Tuition, state resident: full-time $3744; part-time $156 per credit hour. Tuition, nonresident: full-time $13,577; part-time $565.70 per credit hour. Required fees: $2415; $90.10 per credit hour. *Financial support:* In 2009–10, 19 students received support, including 7 research assistantships (averaging $11,302 per year), 6 teaching assistantships with partial tuition reimbursements available (averaging $13,590 per year); tuition waivers (full) and unspecified assistantships also available. Financial award applicants required to submit FAFSA. *Faculty research:* Political economy, foreign policy, linguistics, environmental affairs, international law. Total annual research expenditures: $379,964. *Unit head:* Mark Fraizer, Director, 405-325-1584, Fax: 405-325-7738, E-mail: markfrazier@ou.edu. *Application contact:* Mitchell Smith, Associate Professor, 405-325-8893, Fax: 405-325-0718, E-mail: mps@ou.edu.

University of Oregon, Graduate School, College of Arts and Sciences, Program in International Studies, Eugene, OR 97403. Offers MA. Part-time programs available. *Degree requirements:* For master's, one foreign language, thesis, internship. *Entrance requirements:* For master's, minimum GPA of 3.0. Additional exam requirements/recommendations for international students: Required—TOEFL. *Faculty research:* International development studies; environmental studies; cross-cultural communications; planning, public policy, and management; several world regions.

University of Pennsylvania, School of Arts and Sciences, Graduate Group in International Studies, Philadelphia, PA 19104. Offers AM. *Students:* 17 full-time (8 women); includes 6 minority (2 African Americans, 3 Asian Americans or Pacific Islanders, 1 Hispanic American), 5 international. In 2009, 57 master's awarded. Application fee: $70. *Expenses:* Tuition: Full-time $25,660; part-time $4758 per course. Required fees: $2152; $270 per course. Tuition and fees vary according to course load, degree level and program.

University of Pittsburgh, Graduate School of Public and International Affairs, Doctoral Program in Public and International Affairs, Pittsburgh, PA 15260. Offers development policy (PhD); foreign and security policy (PhD); international political economy (PhD); public administration (PhD); public policy (PhD). *Accreditation:* NASPAA. Part-time programs available. *Faculty:* 28 full-time (8 women), 56 part-time/adjunct (20 women). *Students:* 11 full-time (4 women), 27 part-time (16 women); includes 4 minority (2 African Americans, 1 Asian American or Pacific Islander, 1 Hispanic American), 7 international. Average age 30. 63 applicants, 14% accepted, 5 enrolled. In 2009, 9 doctorates awarded. *Degree requirements:* For doctorate, comprehensive exam, thesis/dissertation. *Entrance requirements:* For doctorate, GRE, 3 letters of recommendation, resume, minimum GPA of 3.0, writing sample. Additional exam requirements/recommendations for international students: Required—TOEFL (minimum score 600 paper-based; 250 computer-based; 100 iBT), TWE (minimum score 4); Recommended—IELTS (minimum score 7). *Application deadline:* For fall admission, 2/1 for domestic students, 1/15 for international students. Application fee: $50. Electronic applications accepted. *Expenses:* Tuition, state resident: full-time $16,402; part-time $665 per credit. Tuition, nonresident: full-time $28,694; part-time $1175 per credit. Required fees: $690; $175 per term. Tuition and fees vary

International Affairs

University of Pittsburgh (continued)
according to program. *Financial support:* In 2009–10, 17 students received support, including 6 fellowships (averaging $34,925 per year); scholarships/grants, tuition waivers (full and partial), and unspecified assistantships also available. Financial award application deadline: 2/1. *Faculty research:* International political economy, international development, public administration, public policy, foreign policy, international security policy. Total annual research expenditures: $357,117. *Unit head:* Dr. Kevin P. Kearns, Program Coordinator, 412-648-7621, Fax: 412-648-2605, E-mail: kkearns@pitt.edu. *Application contact:* Julie Korade, Program Administrator/Graduate Enrollment Counselor, 412-648-7640, Fax: 412-648-7641, E-mail: korade@pitt.edu.

University of Pittsburgh, Graduate School of Public and International Affairs, International Affairs Division, Pittsburgh, PA 15260. Offers global political economy (MPIA); human security (MPIA); security and intelligence studies (MPIA); JD/MPIA; MBA/MPIA; MID/MPIA; MPA/MPIA; MSIS/MPIA. Part-time and evening/weekend programs available. *Faculty:* 28 full-time (8 women), 56 part-time/adjunct (20 women). *Students:* 125 full-time (52 women), 19 part-time (11 women); includes 17 minority (10 African Americans, 4 Asian Americans or Pacific Islanders, 3 Hispanic Americans), 5 international. Average age 25. 270 applicants, 81% accepted, 79 enrolled. In 2009, 61 master's awarded. *Degree requirements:* For master's, thesis optional, internship, capstone seminar. *Entrance requirements:* For master's, GRE General Test, 3 letters of recommendation, resume, minimum GPA of 3.2. Additional exam requirements/recommendations for international students: Required—TOEFL (minimum score 550 paper-based; 213 computer-based), TWE (minimum score 4); Recommended—IELTS (minimum score 7). *Application deadline:* For fall admission, 3/1 for domestic students, 1/15 for international students; for spring admission, 11/1 for domestic students, 8/1 for international students. Application fee: $50. Electronic applications accepted. *Expenses:* Tuition, state resident: full-time $16,402; part-time $665 per credit. Tuition, nonresident: full-time $28,694; part-time $1175 per credit. Required fees: $690; $175 per term. Tuition and fees vary according to program. *Financial support:* In 2009–10, 45 students received support, including 6 fellowships (averaging $41,800 per year); career-related internships or fieldwork, scholarships/grants, tuition waivers (full and partial), and unspecified assistantships also available. Financial award application deadline: 2/1. *Faculty research:* International political economy, international security and intelligence, transnational organized crime, international trade, international finance, globalization, terrorism, multinational corporations and the global economy. Total annual research expenditures: $357,117. *Unit head:* Dr. Martin Staniland, Director, International Affairs and International Development Divisions, 412-648-7656, Fax: 412-648-2605, E-mail: mstan@pitt.edu. *Application contact:* Kelly C. McDevitt, Graduate Enrollment Counselor, 412-648-7640, Fax: 412-648-7641, E-mail: mcdevitt@pitt.edu.

University of Pittsburgh, Katz Graduate School of Business, MBA/Master of Public and International Affairs Dual-Degree Program, Pittsburgh, PA 15260. Offers MBA/MPIA. Part-time and evening/weekend programs available. *Students:* 22 applicants, 59% accepted, 7 enrolled. *Entrance requirements:* Additional exam requirements/recommendations for international students: Required—TOEFL (minimum score 600 paper-based; 250 computer-based; 100 iBT), or IELTS. *Application deadline:* For fall admission, 7/1 for domestic and international students; for winter admission, 11/1 for domestic and international students; for spring admission, 3/1 for domestic and international students. Applications are processed on a rolling basis. Application fee: $50. Electronic applications accepted. *Expenses:* Tuition, state resident: full-time $16,402; part-time $665 per credit. Tuition, nonresident: full-time $28,694; part-time $1175 per credit. Required fees: $690; $175 per term. Tuition and fees vary according to program. *Financial support:* In 2009–10, 3 students received support. Career-related internships or fieldwork, institutionally sponsored loans, and scholarships/grants available. Financial award application deadline: 6/1; financial award applicants required to submit FAFSA. *Unit head:* William T. Valenta, Assistant Dean/Director of MBA Programs, 412-648-1610, Fax: 412-648-1659, E-mail: wtvalenta@katz.pitt.edu. *Application contact:* Cliff McCormick, Director of MBA Admissions, 412-648-1700, Fax: 412-648-1659, E-mail: mba@katz.pitt.edu.

University of Pittsburgh, University Center for International Studies, Pittsburgh, PA 15260. Offers African studies (Certificate); Asian studies (Certificate); European Union studies (Certificate); global studies (Certificate); Latin American studies (Certificate); Russian and East European studies (Certificate); West European studies (Certificate). *Students:* 332 (129 women); includes 31 minority (7 African Americans, 10 Asian Americans or Pacific Islanders, 14 Hispanic Americans), 136 international. In 2009, 59 Certificates awarded. *Degree requirements:* For Certificate, one foreign language, study abroad. *Application deadline:* Applications are processed on a rolling basis. *Expenses:* Tuition, state resident: full-time $16,402; part-time $665 per credit. Tuition, nonresident: full-time $28,694; part-time $1175 per credit. Required fees: $690; $175 per term. Tuition and fees vary according to program. *Unit head:* Lawrence F. Feick, Director, 412-648-7374, Fax: 412-624-4672, E-mail: feick@pitt.edu. *Application contact:* Information Contact, 412-624-4141, E-mail: graduate@pitt.edu.

University of Rhode Island, Graduate School, College of Arts and Sciences, Department of Political Science, Kingston, RI 02881. Offers political science (MA), including American politics, comparative government, international relations, public policy; public policy and administration (MPA); MLIS/MPA. Part-time programs available. *Faculty:* 10 full-time (4 women), 1 part-time/adjunct (0 women). *Students:* 17 full-time (11 women), 44 part-time (28 women); includes 9 minority (4 African Americans, 1 Asian American or Pacific Islander, 4 Hispanic Americans). In 2009, 29 master's awarded. *Degree requirements:* For master's, comprehensive exam (for some programs), thesis optional. *Entrance requirements:* For master's, GRE, GMAT or MAT, 2 letters of recommendation. Additional exam requirements/recommendations for international students: Required—TOEFL (minimum score 550 paper-based; 213 computer-based). *Application deadline:* For fall admission, 2/1 for international students; for spring admission, 7/15 for international students. Application fee: $65. Electronic applications accepted. *Expenses:* Tuition, state resident: full-time $8828; part-time $490 per credit hour. Tuition, nonresident: full-time $22,100; part-time $1228 per credit hour. Required fees: $1118; $57 per semester. Tuition and fees vary according to program. *Financial support:* In 2009–10, 4 teaching assistantships with full tuition reimbursements (averaging $13,894 per year) were awarded. Financial award applicants required to submit FAFSA. *Unit head:* Dr. Gerry Tyler, Chairperson, 401-874-4053, Fax: 401-874-4072, E-mail: gtyler@uri.edu. *Application contact:* Dr. Gerry Tyler, Chairperson, 401-874-4053, Fax: 401-874-4072, E-mail: gtyler@uri.edu.

University of San Diego, College of Arts and Sciences, Department of Political Science and International Relations, San Diego, CA 92110-2492. Offers international relations (MA); JD/MA. Part-time and evening/weekend programs available. *Faculty:* 1 (woman) full-time, 4 part-time/adjunct (0 women). *Students:* 8 full-time (5 women), 10 part-time (4 women); includes 3 minority (1 American Indian/Alaska Native, 1 Asian American or Pacific Islander, 1 Hispanic American), 1 international. Average age 26. 54 applicants, 44% accepted, 7 enrolled. In 2009, 13 master's awarded. *Degree requirements:* For master's, comprehensive exam. *Entrance requirements:* For master's, GRE General Test, minimum GPA of 3.1. Additional exam requirements/recommendations for international students: Required—TOEFL (minimum score 580 paper-based; 237 computer-based; 83 iBT), TWE. *Application deadline:* For fall admission, 8/31 for domestic and international students; for spring admission, 1/15 for domestic students, 11/15 for international students. Applications are processed on a rolling basis. Application fee: $45. Electronic applications accepted. *Expenses:* Tuition: Full-time $21,042; part-time $1169 per unit. Required fees: $224. Full-time tuition and fees vary according to course load and degree level. *Financial support:* In 2009–10, 14 students received support. Federal Work-Study, institutionally sponsored loans, and unspecified assistantships available. Support available to part-time students. Financial award application deadline: 4/1; financial award applicants required to submit FAFSA. *Faculty research:* International security, U. S.-Mexican border politics, Latin American politics, African politics, Soviet politics. *Unit head:* Dr. Emily Edmonds-Poli, Graduate Program Director, 619-260-7802, Fax: 619-260-6840, E-mail: edmonds@sandiego.edu. *Application contact:* Dr. John Mosby, Associate Director of Graduate Admissions, 619-260-4524, Fax: 619-260-4158, E-mail: grads@sandiego.edu.

University of San Francisco, College of Arts and Sciences, Department of Economics, San Francisco, CA 94117-1080. Offers economics (MA); financial analysis (MS); international and development economics (MA); MS/MBA. Part-time and evening/weekend programs available. *Faculty:* 8 full-time (2 women), 9 part-time/adjunct (3 women). *Students:* 167 full-time (69 women), 6 part-time (2 women); includes 42 minority (5 African Americans, 26 Asian Americans or Pacific Islanders, 11 Hispanic Americans), 70 international. Average age 28. 627 applicants, 47% accepted, 96 enrolled. In 2009, 92 master's awarded. *Degree requirements:* For master's, comprehensive exam, thesis or alternative. *Entrance requirements:* For master's, GRE General Test (recommended), BA in economics (preferred). Additional exam requirements/recommendations for international students: Required—TOEFL. *Application deadline:* For fall admission, 7/15 priority date for domestic students; for spring admission, 12/15 for domestic students. Applications are processed on a rolling basis. Application fee: $55 ($65 for international students). *Expenses:* Tuition: Full-time $19,710; part-time $1095 per unit. Part-time tuition and fees vary according to degree level, campus/location and program. *Financial support:* In 2009–10, 96 students received support; fellowships, teaching assistantships, career-related internships or fieldwork available. Financial award application deadline: 3/2; financial award applicants required to submit FAFSA. *Faculty research:* Economic development, forecasting and planning, labor markets, Pacific Rim, financial markets. *Unit head:* Man-lui Lau, Chair, 415-422-2765, Fax: 415-422-5784. *Application contact:* Information Contact, 415-422-5135, Fax: 415-422-2217, E-mail: asgraduate@usfca.edu.

University of San Francisco, College of Arts and Sciences, International Studies Program, San Francisco, CA 94117-1080. Offers MA. *Faculty:* 3 full-time (2 women). *Students:* 21 full-time (14 women); includes 5 minority (1 African American, 2 Asian Americans or Pacific Islanders, 2 Hispanic Americans), 1 international. Average age 27. 61 applicants, 54% accepted, 21 enrolled. *Expenses:* Tuition: Full-time $19,710; part-time $1095 per unit. Part-time tuition and fees vary according to degree level, campus/location and program. *Financial support:* In 2009–10, 19 students received support. *Unit head:* Prof. Anne Bartlett, Program Director, 415-422-5101. *Application contact:* Information Contact, 415-422-5135, Fax: 415-422-2217, E-mail: asgraduate@usfca.edu.

University of South Carolina, The Graduate School, College of Arts and Sciences, Department of Political Science, Program in International Studies, Columbia, SC 29208. Offers MA, PhD. Part-time programs available. Terminal master's awarded for partial completion of doctoral program. *Degree requirements:* For master's, one foreign language, thesis or alternative; for doctorate, one foreign language, comprehensive exam, thesis/dissertation. *Entrance requirements:* For master's, GRE General Test, minimum GPA of 3.3; for doctorate, GRE General Test, minimum GPA of 3.5. Additional exam requirements/recommendations for international students: Required—TOEFL. Electronic applications accepted. *Faculty research:* International relations, international organization, foreign policy, comparative politics.

University of Southern California, Graduate School, Annenberg School for Communication and Journalism, School of Communication, Program in Public Diplomacy, Los Angeles, CA 90089. Offers MPD. *Degree requirements:* For master's, thesis. *Entrance requirements:* For master's, GRE, resume, writing samples, recommendation letters. Additional exam requirements/recommendations for international students: Required—TOEFL (minimum score 280 computer-based; 114 iBT). Electronic applications accepted. *Expenses:* Tuition: Full-time $25,980; part-time $1315 per unit. Required fees: $554. One-time fee: $35 full-time. Full-time tuition and fees vary according to degree level and program.

See Display on page 629 and Close-Up on page 685.

University of Southern California, Graduate School, College of Letters, Arts and Sciences, Department of Political Science, Los Angeles, CA 90089. Offers politics and international relations (PhD). *Faculty:* 38 full-time (13 women). *Students:* 60 full-time (28 women), 1 (woman) part-time; includes 19 minority (1 African American, 1 American Indian/Alaska Native, 9 Asian Americans or Pacific Islanders, 8 Hispanic Americans), 25 international. 122 applicants, 13% accepted, 8 enrolled. In 2009, 14 doctorates awarded. *Degree requirements:* For doctorate, one foreign language, comprehensive exam. *Entrance requirements:* For doctorate, GRE (minimum score 1000). *Application deadline:* For fall admission, 12/1 for domestic and international students. Application fee: $85. Electronic applications accepted. *Expenses:* Tuition: Full-time $25,980; part-time $1315 per unit. Required fees: $554. One-time fee: $35 full-time. Full-time tuition and fees vary according to degree level and program. *Financial support:* In 2009–10, 44 students received support, including 13 fellowships with full tuition reimbursements available (averaging $22,755 per year), 7 research assistantships with full tuition reimbursements available (averaging $19,000 per year), 24 teaching assistantships with full tuition reimbursements available (averaging $19,000 per year); tuition waivers (full and partial) also available. *Faculty research:* Comparative politics, political communication, American politics, international political economy, race and ethnicity. Total annual research expenditures: $136,000. *Unit head:* Prof. Ann N. Crigler, 213-740-6998, Fax: 213-740-8893, E-mail: acrigler@college.usc.edu. *Application contact:* Alex Venegas, Program Advisor, 213-740-1695, Fax: 213-740-8893, E-mail: venegasa@college.usc.edu.

University of Southern California, Graduate School, School of Policy, Planning, and Development, Master of International Public Policy and Management Program, Los Angeles, CA 90089. Offers MPPM. *Faculty:* 51 full-time (12 women), 74 part-time/adjunct (26 women). *Students:* 38 full-time (25 women), 17 part-time (13 women); includes 13 minority (2 African Americans, 6 Asian Americans or Pacific Islanders, 5 Hispanic Americans), 41 international. 111 applicants, 66% accepted, 33 enrolled. In 2009, 39 master's awarded. *Entrance requirements:* Additional exam requirements/recommendations for international students: Required—TOEFL (minimum score 527 paper-based; 197 computer-based; 71 iBT). *Application deadline:* For fall admission, 4/1 for domestic and international students. Applications are processed on a rolling basis. Application fee: $85. Electronic applications accepted. *Expenses:* Contact institution. *Faculty research:* International development, economic development, social policy problems, issues of developing countries, international and comparative. Total annual research expenditures: $5 million. *Unit head:* Dr. Joyce Mann, Director, 213-740-0547, Fax: 213-821-1331, E-mail: joyceman@usc.edu. *Application contact:* Marisol R. Gonzalez, Director of Recruitment and Admission, 213-740-0550, Fax: 213-740-7573, E-mail: marisolr@usc.edu.

University of Southern Mississippi, Graduate School, College of Arts and Letters, Department of Political Science, International Development, and International Affairs, Hattiesburg, MS 39406-0001. Offers international development (PhD); political science (MA, MS). Part-time programs available. *Faculty:* 14 full-time (2 women). *Students:* 23 full-time (11 women), 59 part-time (21 women); includes 20 minority (13 African Americans, 1 American Indian/Alaska Native, 1 Asian American or Pacific Islander, 5 Hispanic Americans), 5 international. Average age 36. 28 applicants, 39% accepted, 9 enrolled. In 2009, 8 master's, 1 doctorate awarded. *Degree requirements:* For master's, comprehensive exam, thesis (for some programs). *Entrance requirements:* For master's, GRE General Test, minimum GPA of 2.75 in last 2 years, 3.0 in field of study. *Application deadline:* For fall admission, 3/1 priority date for domestic students, 3/1 for international students. Applications are processed on a rolling basis. Application fee: $35. *Expenses:* Tuition, state resident: full-time $5096; part-time $284 per hour. Tuition, nonresident: full-time $13,052; part-time $726 per hour. Required fees: $402. Tuition and fees vary according to course level and course load. *Financial support:* In 2009–10, 4 research assistantships with full and partial tuition reimbursements (averaging $9,000 per year), 8 teaching assistantships with full tuition reimbursements (averaging $7,000 per year) were awarded; career-related internships or fieldwork, Federal Work-Study, scholarships/grants, and unspecified assistantships also available. Financial award application deadline: 3/15; financial award applicants required to submit FAFSA. *Faculty research:* American politics, international politics, political theory, comparative politics, public law. *Unit head:* Dr. Thomas Lansford, Interim Chair, 601-266-4310. *Application contact:* Dr. Robert Pauley, Graduate Coordinator, 601-266-4310, Fax: 601-266-4172.

University of South Florida, Graduate School, College of Arts and Sciences, Department of Government and International Affairs, Tampa, FL 33620-9951. Offers Latin American Caribbean and Latino Studies (MA); government (PhD); political science (MA); public administration (MPA). Part-time and evening/weekend programs available. *Faculty:* 19 full-time (4 women), 1 (woman) part-time/adjunct. *Students:* 31 full-time (16 women), 76 part-time (37 women); includes 28 minority (16 African Americans, 1 American Indian/Alaska Native, 4 Asian Americans or Pacific Islanders, 7 Hispanic Americans), 3 international. Average age 32. 126 applicants, 38% accepted, 24 enrolled. In 2009, 28 master's awarded. *Degree requirements:* For master's, comprehensive exam, thesis; for doctorate, comprehensive exam, thesis/dissertation. *Entrance requirements:* For master's, GRE (minimum score 470 verbal, 470 quantitative), minimum GPA of 3.0 in last 60 hours of course work. Additional exam requirements/recommendations for international students: Required—TOEFL (minimum score 550 paper-based; 213 computer-based). *Application deadline:* For fall admission, 2/15 for domestic students, 1/2 for international students; for spring admission, 10/15 for domestic students, 6/1 for international students. Applications are processed on a rolling basis. Application fee: $30. Electronic applications accepted. *Financial support:* In 2009–10, teaching assistantships with tuition reimbursements (averaging $24,000 per year); unspecified assistantships also available. Financial award application deadline: 4/1. *Unit head:* Dr. Mohsen Milani, Chairperson, 813-974-2384, Fax: 813-974-0832, E-mail: milani@chuma1.cas.usf.edu. *Application contact:* Dr. Stephen Tauber, Graduate Coordinator, 813-974-0781, Fax: 813-974-0832, E-mail: stauber@chuma1.cas.usf.edu.

University of the Pacific, McGeorge School of Law, Sacramento, CA 95817. Offers advocacy (JD); criminal justice (JD); experiential law teaching (LL M); intellectual property (JD); international legal studies (JD); international water resources law (LL M, JSD); law (JD); public law and policy (JD); public policy and law (LL M); tax (JD); transnational business practice (LL M); JD/MBA; JD/MPPA. *Accreditation:* ABA. Part-time and evening/weekend programs available. *Faculty:* 55 full-time (24 women), 57 part-time/adjunct (18 women). *Students:* 697 full-time (343 women), 377 part-time (197 women); includes 301 minority (33 African Americans, 11 American Indian/Alaska Native, 163 Asian Americans or Pacific Islanders, 94 Hispanic Americans). Average age 24. 2,659 applicants, 43% accepted, 236 enrolled. In 2009, 254 first professional degrees, 51 master's awarded. *Degree requirements:* For master's, thesis (for some programs); for doctorate, thesis/dissertation. *Entrance requirements:* For JD, LSAT; for master's, JD; for doctorate, LL M. Additional exam requirements/recommendations for international students: Required—TOEFL (minimum score 600 paper-based; 250 computer-based; 100 iBT). *Application deadline:* For fall admission, 3/15 priority date for domestic students. Applications are processed on a rolling basis. Application fee: $50. Electronic applications accepted. *Expenses:* Contact institution. *Financial support:* In 2009–10, 887 students received support, including 1 fellowship, 114 research assistantships (averaging $1,839 per year), 12 teaching assistantships (averaging $953 per year); career-related internships or fieldwork, Federal Work-Study, institutionally sponsored loans, and scholarships/grants also available. Support available to part-time students. Financial award applicants required to submit FAFSA. *Faculty research:* International legal studies, public policy and law, advocacy, intellectual property law, taxation, criminal law. *Unit head:* Elizabeth Rindskopf Parker, Dean, 916-739-7151, E-mail: elizabeth@pacific.edu. *Application contact:* 916-739-7105, Fax: 916-739-7301, E-mail: mcgeorge@pacific.edu.

University of the Pacific, School of International Studies, Program in Intercultural Relations, Stockton, CA 95211-0197. Offers MA. *Faculty:* 7 full-time (4 women), 3 part-time/adjunct (0 women). In 2009, 9 master's awarded. *Entrance requirements:* Additional exam requirements/recommendations for international students: Required—TOEFL (minimum score 475 paper-based; 150 computer-based). Application fee: $75. *Financial support:* Application deadline: 3/1. *Unit head:* Dr. Cynthia Weick, Dean, 209-946-2650, E-mail: mensign@pacific.edu. *Application contact:* Office of Graduate Admissions, 209-946-2344.

University of Utah, The Graduate School, College of Social and Behavioral Science, Program in International Affairs and Global Enterprise, Salt Lake City, UT 84112-1107. Offers MS. Part-time programs available. *Faculty:* 1 part-time/adjunct (0 women). *Students:* 12 full-time (7 women), 5 part-time (2 women); includes 2 minority (both Hispanic Americans), 4 international. Average age 29. 22 applicants, 50% accepted, 10 enrolled. *Degree requirements:* For master's, one foreign language, comprehensive exam, thesis optional, major research paper. *Entrance requirements:* For master's, GMAT, LSAT, or GRE, Must have completed the following as undergrad: Undergrad Statistics, Microeconomics Theory & Macroeconomics Theory. Additional exam requirements/recommendations for international students: Required—TOEFL (minimum score 233 computer-based; 90 iBT). *Application deadline:* For fall admission, 3/1 for domestic and international students; for spring admission, 9/1 for domestic and international students. Applications are processed on a rolling basis. Application fee: $55 ($65 for international students). *Expenses:* Tuition, state resident: full-time $4004; part-time $1674 per semester. Tuition, nonresident: full-time $14,134; part-time $5915 per semester. Required fees: $324 per semester. Tuition and fees vary according to course load, degree level and program. *Financial support:* In 2009–10, 2 students received support. Unspecified assistantships available. *Faculty research:* East Asian economies. *Unit head:* J. Steven Ott, Dean, 801-581-6781, Fax: 801-585-5081, E-mail: jsott@csbs.utah.edu. *Application contact:* Stephen E. Reynolds, Associate Dean, 801-581-8620, Fax: 801-585-5081, E-mail: stephen.reynolds@csbs.utah.edu.

University of Virginia, College and Graduate School of Arts and Sciences, Department of Politics, Program in Foreign Affairs, Charlottesville, VA 22903. Offers MA, PhD. *Students:* 51 full-time (22 women); includes 4 minority (all Asian Americans or Pacific Islanders), 15 international. Average age 29. 106 applicants, 34% accepted, 12 enrolled. In 2009, 6 master's, 9 doctorates awarded. *Degree requirements:* For master's, one foreign language, 2 research/statistics courses or thesis; for doctorate, variable foreign language requirement, thesis/dissertation, 2 research/statistics courses. *Entrance requirements:* For master's and doctorate, GRE General Test, long writing sample; 2 letters of recommendation. Additional exam requirements/recommendations for international students: Required—TOEFL (minimum score 600 paper-based; 250 computer-based; 90 iBT), IELTS (minimum score 7). *Application deadline:* For fall admission, 12/4 for domestic and international students. Applications are processed on a rolling basis. Application fee: $60. Electronic applications accepted. *Financial support:* Fellowships, teaching assistantships available. Financial award application deadline: 12/4; financial award applicants required to submit FAFSA. *Unit head:* Jeffrey W. Legro, Chair, 434-924-3192, Fax: 434-924-3359. *Application contact:* Jeffrey W. Legro, Chair, 434-924-3192, Fax: 434-924-3359.

University of Washington, Graduate School, College of Arts and Sciences, Henry M. Jackson School of International Studies, Seattle, WA 98195. Offers China studies (MAIS); comparative religion (MAIS); international studies (MAIS); Japan studies (MAIS); Korea studies (MAIS); Middle East studies (MAIS); Russian, East European and Central Asian studies (MAIS), including Central Asian studies, East European studies, Russian studies; South Asian studies (MAIS); Southeast Asian studies (MAIS); JD/MAIS; MBA/MAIS; MFR/MAIS; MMA/MAIS; MPA/MAIS; MPH/MAIS. *Students:* 164 full-time (80 women); includes 24 minority (4 African Americans, 1 American Indian/Alaska Native, 17 Asian Americans or Pacific Islanders, 2 Hispanic Americans), 16 international. 295 applicants, 62% accepted, 64 enrolled. In 2009, 42 master's awarded. *Entrance requirements:* For master's, GRE General Test, minimum GPA of 3.0. Additional exam requirements/recommendations for international students: Required—TOEFL (minimum score 500 paper-based; 213 computer-based; 92 iBT), or IELTS (minimum score 7). *Application deadline:* For fall admission, 12/30 for domestic students, 12/1 for international students. Application fee: $75. Electronic applications accepted. *Financial support:* Fellowships with full and partial tuition reimbursements, research assistantships with full and partial tuition reimbursements, teaching assistantships with full and partial tuition reimbursements, career-related internships or fieldwork, Federal Work-Study, institutionally sponsored loans, scholarships/grants, tuition waivers (full and partial), and summer language study awards available. Financial award application deadline: 12/30; financial award applicants required to submit FAFSA. *Unit head:* Prof. Resat Kasaba, Director, 206-543-4373. *Application contact:* 206-543-6001, Fax: 206-616-3170, E-mail: jsisinfo@uw.edu.

University of Waterloo, Graduate Studies, Faculty of Arts, Department of Political Science, Global Governance Program, Waterloo, ON N2L 3G1, Canada. Offers MA, PhD. *Entrance requirements:* For doctorate, MA. Additional exam requirements/recommendations for international students: Required—TOEFL. Electronic applications accepted. *Faculty research:* Global political economy, global environment, peace and security, global justice and human rights, multilateral institutions and diplomacy.

University of Wyoming, College of Arts and Sciences, Program in International Studies, Laramie, WY 82070. Offers international peace corps (MA); international studies (MA). Part-time programs available. *Degree requirements:* For master's, one foreign language, thesis. *Entrance requirements:* For master's, GRE General Test, minimum GPA of 3.0. Additional exam requirements/recommendations for international students: Required—TOEFL (minimum score 525 paper-based; 195 computer-based). Electronic applications accepted. *Faculty research:* International political economy, comparative social institutions, foreign policy, economic development.

Virginia Polytechnic Institute and State University, Graduate School, College of Architecture and Urban Studies, School of Public and International Affairs, Blacksburg, VA 24061. Offers environmental planning and policy (MURP); government and international affairs (MPIA); housing, community and economic development (MURP); international development planning (MURP); land use and physical planning (MURP); planning, governance and globalization (PhD), including environmental planning and landscape analysis, physical planning and urban design, public and international affairs, urban and environmental design and planning; urban and regional planning (MURP). *Accreditation:* ACSP. *Faculty:* 27 full-time (11 women), 2 part-time/adjunct (1 woman). *Students:* 73 full-time (51 women), 65 part-time (39 women); includes 15 minority (4 African Americans, 1 American Indian/Alaska Native, 6 Asian Americans or Pacific Islanders, 4 Hispanic Americans), 10 international. Average age 29. 86 applicants, 67% accepted, 40 enrolled. In 2009, 26 master's, 1 doctorate awarded. *Entrance requirements:* Additional exam requirements/recommendations for international students: Required—TOEFL (minimum score 550 paper-based; 213 computer-based). *Application deadline:* For fall admission, 5/15 for international students; for spring admission, 10/15 for international students. Applications are processed on a rolling basis. Application fee: $45. Electronic applications accepted. *Financial support:* In 2009–10, 1 teaching assistantship with full tuition reimbursement (averaging $5,560 per year) was awarded; career-related internships or fieldwork, Federal Work-Study, scholarships/grants, and unspecified assistantships also available. Financial award application deadline: 4/1. *Faculty research:* Design theory, environmental planning, town planning, transportation planning. *Unit head:* Dr. John Randolph, Dean, 540-231-6971, Fax: 540-231-9938, E-mail: energy@vt.edu. *Application contact:* Krystal D. Wright, Information Contact, 540-231-*5683, Fax: 540-231-9938, E-mail: garch@vt.edu.

Walden University, Graduate Programs, School of Public Policy and Administration, Minneapolis, MN 55401. Offers general program (MPA); government management (Post-baccalaureate Certificate); health policy (MPA); homeland security policy (MPA); interdisciplinary policy studies (MPA); law and public policy (MPA); local government management for sustainable communities (MPA); nonprofit management (Postbaccalaureate Certificate); nonprofit management and leadership (MPA, MS); policy analysis (MPA); public management and leadership (MPA); public policy and administration (PhD), including criminal justice, health services, homeland security policy and coordination, international nongovernmental organizations, law and public policy, local government management for sustainable communities, nonprofit management and leadership, public management and leadership, public policy, public safety management, terrorism, mediation, and peace; terrorism, mediation, and peace (MPA). Part-time and evening/weekend programs available. Postbaccalaureate distance learning degree programs offered (minimal on-campus study). *Faculty:* 7 full-time, 62 part-time/adjunct. *Students:* 1,468 full-time (941 women), 233 part-time (162 women); includes 852 minority (761 African Americans, 9 American Indian/Alaska Native, 19 Asian Americans or Pacific Islanders, 63 Hispanic Americans), 53 international. Average age 40. In 2009, 173 master's, 13 doctorates awarded. *Degree requirements:* For doctorate, thesis/dissertation, residency. *Entrance requirements:* For master's, bachelor's degree or equivalent in related field, minimum GPA of 2.5; for doctorate, master's degree or equivalent in related field; minimum GPA of 3.0; official transcripts; three years of related professional/academic experience (preferred); access to computer and Internet. Additional exam requirements/recommendations for international students: Required—TOEFL (minimum score 550 paper-based; 213 computer-based), IELTS (minimum score 6.5), or Michigan English Language Assessment Battery (minimum score 82). *Application deadline:* Applications are processed on a rolling basis. Application fee: $50. Electronic applications accepted. *Expenses:* Tuition: Full-time $13,665; part-time $560 per credit. Required fees: $1375. Tuition and fees vary according to course load, degree level and program. *Financial support:* In 2009–10, 207 students received support; fellowships with tuition reimbursements available, Federal Work-Study, scholarships/grants, unspecified assistantships, and family tuition reduction, active duty/veteran tuition reduction, group tuition reduction, interest-free payment plans available. Support available to part-time students. Financial award applicants required to submit FAFSA. *Unit head:* Dr. Mark Gordon, Associate Dean, 800-925-3368. *Application contact:* Jennifer Hall, Director of Enrollment, 866-4-WALDEN, E-mail: info@waldenu.edu.

Washington State University, Graduate School, College of Liberal Arts, Edward R. Murrow College of Communication, Pullman, WA 99164. Offers health communications (MA, PhD); intercultural and international communications (MA, PhD); media and society (MA, PhD); media process and effects (MA, PhD); organizational communications (MA, PhD). *Degree requirements:* For master's, comprehensive exam (for some programs), thesis optional, oral exam; for doctorate, comprehensive exam, thesis/dissertation. *Entrance requirements:* For master's, GRE General Test, minimum GPA of 3.25, 3 letters of recommendation; for doctorate, GRE General Test, minimum undergraduate GPA of 3.25, graduate 3.5; MA in communication; 3 letters of recommendation. Additional exam requirements/recommendations for international students: Required—TOEFL (minimum score 580 paper-based; 237 computer-based). Electronic applications accepted. *Faculty research:* Advocacy communication, mediated communication in decision making, communication technology policy and effects, multicultural and international psychology and physiology of communication.

Webster University, College of Arts and Sciences, Department of History, Politics and International Relations, Program in International Relations, St. Louis, MO 63119-3194. Offers MA. Part-time and evening/weekend programs available. *Degree requirements:* For master's, thesis optional. *Expenses:* Tuition: Part-time $565 per credit hour. Tuition and fees vary according to degree level, campus/location and program. *Faculty research:* International organizations, international political economy, politics of development, environmental law, Latin American law.

West Virginia University, Eberly College of Arts and Sciences, Department of Political Science, Morgantown, WV 26506. Offers American public policy and politics (MA); international and comparative public policy and politics (MA); political science (PhD); public policy analysis (PhD). Terminal master's awarded for partial completion of doctoral program. *Degree requirements:* For master's, thesis optional; for doctorate, comprehensive exam, thesis/dissertation. *Entrance requirements:* For master's, GRE General Test, minimum GPA of 2.75; for doctorate, GRE General Test, minimum GPA of 3.0. Additional exam requirements/recommendations for international students: Required—TOEFL. *Faculty research:* Public policy, research methods, foreign policy analysis, judicial politics, environmental and energy policy.

Wilfrid Laurier University, Faculty of Graduate Studies, Faculty of Arts and School of Business and Economics, Global Governance Program, Waterloo, ON N2L 3C5, Canada. Offers PhD. *Degree requirements:* For doctorate, thesis/dissertation. *Entrance requirements:* For doctorate, MA in political science, history, economics, international development studies, international peace studies, globalization studies, environmental studies or related field with minimum A-. Additional exam requirements/recommendations for international students: Required—TOEFL (minimum score 230 computer-based; 89 iBT). Electronic applications accepted. *Faculty research:* Global political economy, global environment, conflict and security, global justice and human rights, multilateral institutions and diplomacy.

Wilfrid Laurier University, Faculty of Graduate Studies, Faculty of Arts and School of Business and Economics, International Public Policy Program, Waterloo, ON N2L 3C5, Canada.

International Affairs

Wilfrid Laurier University (continued)
Offers MIPP. *Entrance requirements:* For master's, honours BA with minimum B average. Additional exam requirements/recommendations for international students: Required—TOEFL (minimum score 230 computer-based; 89 iBT). Electronic applications accepted. *Faculty research:* International environmental policy, international economic relations, human security, global governance.

Yale University, Graduate School of Arts and Sciences, Department of Economics, Program in International and Development Economics, New Haven, CT 06520. Offers MA. *Entrance requirements:* For master's, GRE General Test.

Yale University, Graduate School of Arts and Sciences, Graduate Program in International Relations, New Haven, CT 06520. Offers MA, JD/MA, M E Sc/MA, MBA/MA, MEM/MA, MF/MA, MFS/MA, MPH/MA. *Faculty:* 230. *Students:* 47 full-time (24 women); includes 6 minority (1 African American, 1 American Indian/Alaska Native, 4 Asian Americans or Pacific Islanders), 15 international. Average age 27. 293 applicants, 18% accepted, 21 enrolled. In 2009, 21 master's awarded. *Degree requirements:* For master's, one foreign language, research paper, summer project. *Entrance requirements:* For master's, GRE General Test, previous course work in microeconomics and macroeconomics, professional experience (preferred). Additional exam requirements/recommendations for international students: Required—TOEFL (minimum score 610 paper-based; 253 computer-based; 102 iBT), or IELTS (minimum score 7.5). *Application deadline:* For fall admission, 1/2 for domestic and international students. Application fee: $95. Electronic applications accepted. *Financial support:* In 2009–10, 32 students received support, including 9 fellowships with full and partial tuition reimbursements available (averaging $10,833 per year), 32 teaching assistantships (averaging $7,190 per year); research assistantships, career-related internships or fieldwork, institutionally sponsored loans, scholarships/grants, tuition waivers (full and partial), unspecified assistantships, and competitive fellowships for summer research also available. Financial award application deadline: 1/2. *Faculty research:* International security studies, global health, international economic development, political economy, policy studies. *Unit head:* Prof. Cheryl Doss, Director of Graduate Studies, 203-432-3418, Fax: 203-432-9886, E-mail: international.relations@yale.edu. *Application contact:* Alice J. Kustenbauder, Registrar, 203-432-3418, Fax: 203-432-9886, E-mail: international.relations@yale.edu.

York University, Faculty of Graduate Studies, Glendon College, Program in Public and International Affairs, Toronto, ON M3J 1P3, Canada. Offers MA.

International Development

American University, School of International Service, Washington, DC 20016-8071. Offers comparative and regional studies (Certificate); cross-cultural communication (Certificate); development management (MS); ethics, peace, and global affairs (MA); European studies (Certificate); global environmental policy (MA, Certificate); international affairs (MA), including comparative and regional studies, environmental policy, international economic policy, international politics, natural resources and sustainable development, U.S. foreign policy; international communication (MA, Certificate); international development (MA, Certificate); international development management (Certificate); international economic policy (Certificate); international economic relations (Certificate); international media (MA); international peace and conflict resolution (MA, Certificate); international relations (PhD); international service (MIS); peace building (Certificate); the Americas (Certificate); United States foreign policy (Certificate); JD/MA. Part-time and evening/weekend programs available. *Faculty:* 98 full-time (42 women), 48 part-time/adjunct (13 women). *Students:* 565 full-time (349 women), 329 part-time (189 women); includes 128 minority (44 African Americans, 2 American Indian/Alaska Native, 37 Asian Americans or Pacific Islanders, 45 Hispanic Americans), 102 international. Average age 27. 2,034 applicants, 63% accepted, 344 enrolled. In 2009, 326 master's, 6 doctorates, 9 other advanced degrees awarded. Terminal master's awarded for partial completion of doctoral program. *Degree requirements:* For master's, one foreign language, comprehensive exam, thesis or alternative; for doctorate, one foreign language, comprehensive exam, thesis/dissertation, research practicum; for Certificate, minimum 15 credit hours related course work. *Entrance requirements:* For master's, GRE, 24 credits of course work in related social sciences, minimum GPA of 3.5, 2 letters of recommendation, bachelor's degree, resume; for doctorate, GRE, 2 letters of recommendation, 24 credits in related social sciences; for Certificate, bachelor's degree. Additional exam requirements/recommendations for international students: Required—TOEFL (minimum score 600 paper-based; 250 computer-based; 100 iBT). *Application deadline:* For fall admission, 1/15 priority date for domestic students; for spring admission, 10/1 priority date for domestic students. Applications are processed on a rolling basis. Application fee: $50. *Expenses:* Tuition: Full-time $22,266; part-time $1237 per credit hour. Required fees: $430. Tuition and fees vary according to program. *Financial support:* Career-related internships or fieldwork, Federal Work-Study, and institutionally sponsored loans available. Financial award application deadline: 1/15. *Faculty research:* International intellectual property, international environmental issues, international law and legal order, international telecommunications/technology, international sustainable development. *Unit head:* Dr. Louis W. Goodman, Dean, 202-885-1600, Fax: 202-885-2494. *Application contact:* Yasmin Quianzon, Director of Graduate Admissions and Financial Aid, 202-885-2496, Fax: 202-885-1109.

See Close-Up on page 849.

Andrews University, School of Graduate Studies, College of Arts and Sciences, Department of Behavioral Science, Program in International Development, Berrien Springs, MI 49104. Offers MSA. Postbaccalaureate distance learning degree programs offered. *Students:* 9 full-time (7 women), 3 part-time (all women); includes 5 minority (2 African Americans, 1 Asian American or Pacific Islander, 2 Hispanic Americans), 5 international. Average age 31. 17 applicants, 47% accepted, 4 enrolled. In 2009, 3 master's awarded. *Entrance requirements:* For master's, GRE General Test. Additional exam requirements/recommendations for international students: Required—TOEFL (minimum score 550 paper-based). Application fee: $40. *Unit head:* Dr. Duane C. McBride, Director, 269-471-3152. *Application contact:* Carolyn Hurst, Supervisor of Graduate Admission, 800-253-2874, Fax: 269-471-6321, E-mail: graduate@andrews.edu.

Athabasca University, Centre for Integrated Studies, Athabasca, AB T9S 3A3, Canada. Offers adult education (MA); community studies (MA); cultural studies (MA); educational studies (MA); global change (MA); work, organization, and leadership (MA). Part-time and evening/weekend programs available. Postbaccalaureate distance learning degree programs offered (no on-campus study). *Faculty:* 10 full-time (4 women), 12 part-time/adjunct (9 women). *Students:* 705 part-time. Average age 35. 195 applicants, 38 enrolled. In 2009, 52 master's awarded. *Degree requirements:* For master's, project. *Entrance requirements:* Additional exam requirements/recommendations for international students: Required—TOEFL (minimum score 560 paper-based; 220 computer-based). *Application deadline:* For fall admission, 3/1 for domestic and international students; for winter admission, 9/1 for domestic and international students. Application fee: $80. Electronic applications accepted. *Expenses:* Tuition: Part-time $16,500 per degree program. Required fees: $200 per year. One-time fee: $80 part-time. *Faculty research:* Women's history, literature and culture studies, sustainable development, labor and education. *Unit head:* Dr. Michael Gismondi, Program Director, 780-675-6218, Fax: 780-675-6921, E-mail: mikeg@athabascau.ca. *Application contact:* Derek Stovin, Program Administrator, 780-675-6236, Fax: 780-675-6921, E-mail: dereks@athabascau.ca.

Brandeis University, The Heller School for Social Policy and Management, Program in Sustainable International Development, Waltham, MA 02454-9110. Offers international development (MA); sustainable development (MA). *Degree requirements:* For master's, 2nd year fieldwork or internship. *Entrance requirements:* For master's, 3 letters of recommendation, curriculum vitae or resume. Additional exam requirements/recommendations for international students: Required—TOEFL, IELTS. Electronic applications accepted. *Expenses:* Contact institution. *Faculty research:* Water resource management, human rights, biosphere management, rural development, public policy and governance.

Clark University, Graduate School, Department of International Development, Community, and Environment, Program in International Development and Social Change, Worcester, MA 01610-1477. Offers MA. *Faculty:* 9 full-time (6 women), 1 (woman) part-time/adjunct. *Students:* 47 full-time (30 women), 15 part-time (13 women); includes 6 minority (5 African Americans, 1 Hispanic American), 21 international. 160 applicants, 79% accepted, 38 enrolled. In 2009, 39 master's awarded. *Degree requirements:* For master's, thesis. *Entrance requirements:* For master's, 3 references, resume or curriculum vitae. Additional exam requirements/recommendations for international students: Required—TOEFL (minimum score 575 paper-based; 233 computer-based; 90 iBT) or IELTS (minimum score 6.5). *Application deadline:* For fall admission, 1/15 for domestic students. Application fee: $50. *Expenses:* Tuition: Full-time $34,900; part-time $4362.50 per course. *Financial support:* Fellowships, institutionally sponsored loans and scholarships/grants available. *Faculty research:* Community action research, gender analysis, land-use planning, geographic information systems, HIV and AIDS, global health and social justice, environmental health, climate change and sustainability. *Unit head:* Department of International Development, Community, and Environment, 508-793-7201, Fax: 508-793-8820. *Application contact:* Paula Hall, Department of International Development, Community, and Environment Graduate Admissions Office, 508-793-7205, E-mail: idce@clarku.edu.

Cornell University, Graduate School, Graduate Fields of Arts and Sciences, Field of International Development, Ithaca, NY 14853-0001. Offers development policy (MPS); international nutrition (MPS); international planning (MPS); international population (MPS); science and technology policy (MPS). *Faculty:* 54 full-time (18 women). *Students:* 1 (woman) full-time, all international. Average age 33. 31 applicants, 42% accepted, 1 enrolled. In 2009, 15 master's awarded. *Degree requirements:* For master's, project paper. *Entrance requirements:* For master's, GRE General Test (recommended), 2 academic recommendations, 2 years of development experience. Additional exam requirements/recommendations for international students: Required—TOEFL (minimum score 77 iBT). *Application deadline:* Applications are processed on a rolling basis. Application fee: $70. Electronic applications accepted. *Expenses:* Tuition: Full-time $29,500. Required fees: $70. Full-time tuition and fees vary according to degree level, program and student level. *Financial support:* In 2009–10, 1 student received support; fellowships with full tuition reimbursements available, research assistantships with full tuition reimbursements available, teaching assistantships with full tuition reimbursements available, institutionally sponsored loans, scholarships/grants, health care benefits, tuition waivers (full and partial), and unspecified assistantships available. Financial award applicants required to submit FAFSA. *Faculty research:* Development policy, international nutrition, international planning, science and technology policy, international population. *Unit head:* Director of Graduate Studies, 607-255-3037, Fax: 607-255-1005. *Application contact:* Graduate Field Assistant, 607-255-0831, Fax: 607-255-1005, E-mail: mpsid@cornell.edu.

Dalhousie University, Faculty of Arts and Social Science, Department of International Development Studies, Halifax, NS B3H 4R2, Canada. Offers MA. In 2009, 2 master's awarded. *Entrance requirements:* Additional exam requirements/recommendations for international students: Required—TOEFL, IELTS, CANTEST, CAEL, or Michigan English Language Assessment Battery. *Application deadline:* For fall admission, 6/1 for domestic students, 4/1 for international students; for winter admission, 10/31 for domestic students, 8/31 for international students; for spring admission, 2/28 for domestic students, 12/31 for international students. Application fee: $70. Electronic applications accepted. *Financial support:* Career-related internships or fieldwork, scholarships/grants, and health care benefits available. *Unit head:* Dr. Nissim Mannathukkaren, Graduate Coordinator, 902-494-3814, Fax: 902-494-2105, E-mail: idsgrad@dal.ca. *Application contact:* Graduate Administrator, 902-494-3814, Fax: 902-494-2105, E-mail: idsgrad@dal.ca.

Duke University, Graduate School, Duke Sanford Institute of Public Policy, Master of International Development Policy Program, Durham, NC 27708-0237. Offers AM, Certificate. *Degree requirements:* For master's, internship, project. *Entrance requirements:* For master's, minimum 3 years of professional experience in a development-related field. Additional exam requirements/recommendations for international students: Required—TOEFL (minimum score 550 paper-based; 213 computer-based; 83 iBT), IELTS (minimum score 7). Electronic applications accepted. *Expenses:* Contact institution.

Eastern University, School of Leadership and Development, St. Davids, PA 19087-3696. Offers economic development (MBA), including international development, urban development (MA, MBA); international development (MA), including global development, urban development (MA, MBA); nonprofit management (MS); organizational leadership (MA); M Div/MBA. Part-time and evening/weekend programs available. *Degree requirements:* For master's, thesis (for some programs). *Entrance requirements:* For master's, GMAT (MBA), minimum GPA of 2.5. *Expenses:* Contact institution. *Faculty research:* Micro-level economic development, China welfare and economic development, macroethics, micro- and macro-level economic development in transitional economics, organizational effectiveness.

Fordham University, Graduate School of Arts and Sciences, Program in International Political Economy and Development, New York, NY 10458. Offers MA, Certificate. Part-time and evening/weekend programs available. *Students:* 44 full-time (15 women), 18 part-time (10 women); includes 6 minority (1 African American, 1 American Indian/Alaska Native, 1 Asian American or Pacific Islander, 3 Hispanic Americans), 21 international. Average age 28. 213 applicants, 37% accepted, 36 enrolled. In 2009, 28 master's awarded. *Degree requirements:* For master's, comprehensive exam. *Entrance requirements:* For master's, GRE General Test. Additional exam requirements/recommendations for international students: Required—TOEFL (minimum score 600 paper-based; 250 computer-based). *Application deadline:* For fall admission, 1/4 priority date for domestic students; for spring admission, 11/1 for domestic students. Application fee: $70. Electronic applications accepted. *Financial support:* In 2009–10, 16 students received support, including 16 research assistantships with tuition reimbursements available (averaging $18,400 per year); career-related internships or fieldwork, institutionally sponsored loans, tuition waivers (full and partial), and unspecified assistantships also available. Financial award application deadline: 1/4; financial award applicants required to submit FAFSA. *Faculty research:* International economics, comparative international politics, international banking and finance, international development, emerging markets and country risk analysis. *Unit head:* Dr. Henry Schwalbenberg, Chair, 718-817-3866, Fax: 718-817-3518. *Application contact:* Charlene Dundie, Director of Graduate Admissions, 718-817-4420, Fax: 718-817-3566, E-mail: dundie@fordham.edu.

The George Washington University, Columbian College of Arts and Sciences, Department of Anthropology, Concentration in International Development, Washington, DC 20052. Offers MA.

The George Washington University, Columbian College of Arts and Sciences, Trachtenberg School of Public Policy and Public Administration, Programs in Public Administration, Washington, DC 20052. Offers budget and public finance (MPA); federal policy, politics, and management (MPA); international development management (MPA); managing public organizations (MPA); managing state and local governments (MPA); nonprofit management (MPA); policy analysis and evaluation (MPA); public administration (MPA); public-private policy and management (MPA). *Accreditation:* NASPAA. Part-time programs available. *Faculty:* 16 full-time (5 women), 4 part-time/adjunct (1 woman). *Students:* 58 full-time (39 women), 55 part-time (37 women); includes 18 minority (5 African Americans, 9 Asian Americans or Pacific Islanders, 4 Hispanic Americans), 7 international. Average age 28. 206 applicants, 66% accepted, 41 enrolled. In 2009, 55 master's awarded. *Entrance requirements:* For master's, GRE General Test. Additional exam requirements/recommendations for international students: Required—TOEFL (minimum score 600 paper-based; 250 computer-based; 100 iBT). *Application deadline:* For fall admission, 1/15 priority date for domestic students, 1/15 for international students; for spring admission, 10/1 for domestic students, 9/1 for international students. Applications are processed on a rolling basis. Application fee: $60. Electronic applications accepted. *Financial support:* In 2009–10, 28 students received support; fellowships, teaching assistantships, career-related internships or fieldwork, Federal Work-Study, and tuition waivers available. Financial award application deadline: 1/15. *Faculty research:* Regulatory reform, policy and program evaluation, ethics and public management, managing not-for-profits, policy-making in the White House and Congress. *Unit head:* Dr. Lori Brainard, Director, 202-994-6295, E-mail: brainard@gwu.edu. *Application contact:* Bethany Pope, 202-994-6662, E-mail: tspppa@gwu.edu.

The George Washington University, Elliott School of International Affairs, Program in International Development Studies, Washington, DC 20052. Offers MA, JD/MA, MPH/MA. *Students:* 71 full-time (58 women), 14 part-time (9 women); includes 6 minority (4 Asian Americans or Pacific Islanders, 2 Hispanic Americans), 7 international. Average age 27. 351 applicants, 47% accepted, 45 enrolled. In 2009, 37 master's awarded. *Degree requirements:* For master's, one foreign language, capstone project. *Entrance requirements:* For master's, GRE General Test, 2 years (or the equivalent) of a modern foreign language, introductory course in microeconomics, 1 semester of statistics. Additional exam requirements/recommendations for international students: Required—TOEFL. *Application deadline:* For fall admission, 2/1 for domestic students; for spring admission, 10/1 for domestic students. Application fee: $60. Electronic applications accepted. *Financial support:* In 2009–10, 27 students received support; fellowships with tuition reimbursements available, research assistantships with tuition reimbursements available, career-related internships or fieldwork, Federal Work-Study, institutionally sponsored loans, and tuition waivers available. Financial award application deadline: 1/15; financial award applicants required to submit FAFSA. *Faculty research:* Development, anthropology, health and development, political science, education. *Unit head:* Sean Roberts, 202-994-7739, E-mail: seanrr@gwu.edu. *Application contact:* Jeff V. Miles, Director of Graduate Admissions, 202-994-7050, Fax: 202-994-9537, E-mail: esiagrad@gwu.edu.

Harvard University, John F. Kennedy School of Government, Master in Public Administration/International Development Program, Cambridge, MA 02138. Offers MPAID. *Students:* 141 full-time (52 women), 5 part-time (2 women); includes 12 minority (9 Asian Americans or Pacific Islanders, 3 Hispanic Americans), 98 international. Average age 29. 349 applicants, 30% accepted, 76 enrolled. In 2009, 52 master's awarded. *Entrance requirements:* For master's, GMAT or GRE General Test (joint Business School applicants), one course each in microeconomics and macroeconomics; two college-level calculus courses (one must contain multivariable calculus); bachelor's degree; 2-3 years of professional experience in development (strongly encouraged). Additional exam requirements/recommendations for international students: Required—TOEFL (minimum score 600 paper-based; 250 computer-based; 100 iBT). *Application deadline:* For fall admission, 1/2 for domestic students. Application fee: $80. Electronic applications accepted. *Expenses:* Tuition: Full-time $33,696. Required fees: $1126. Full-time tuition and fees vary according to program. *Financial support:* Fellowships, research assistantships, teaching assistantships, career-related internships or fieldwork, Federal Work-Study, institutionally sponsored loans, scholarships/grants, health care benefits, and unspecified assistantships available. Financial award application deadline: 2/6; financial award applicants required to submit CSS PROFILE or FAFSA. *Unit head:* Carol Finney, Director, 617-495-7799, E-mail: carol_finney@harvard.edu. *Application contact:* 617-495-2133, E-mail: mpaid_program@hks.harvard.edu.

Hope International University, School of Graduate and Professional Studies, Program in Business Administration, Fullerton, CA 92831-3138. Offers business administration (MBA); educational administration (MSM); international development (MBA, MSM); management (MBA); nonprofit management (MBA). Part-time programs available. Postbaccalaureate distance learning degree programs offered (no on-campus study). *Degree requirements:* For master's, comprehensive exam (for some programs), thesis (for some programs), project. *Entrance requirements:* For master's, minimum GPA of 3.0; 2 references. Additional exam requirements/recommendations for international students: Required—TOEFL (minimum score 550 paper-based; 213 computer-based; 86 iBT); Recommended—IELTS (minimum score 6.5). Electronic applications accepted. *Expenses:* Contact institution.

The Johns Hopkins University, Paul H. Nitze School of Advanced International Studies, Washington, DC 20036. Offers international development (MA, Certificate), including international economics (MA); international public policy (MIPP); international relations (PhD); international studies (Certificate); Japan studies (MA), including international economics; Korea Studies (MA), including international economics; South Asia studies (MA), including international economics; Southeast Asia studies (MA), including international economics; JD/MA; MBA/MA; MHS/MA. *Faculty:* 57 full-time (18 women), 125 part-time/adjunct (40 women). *Students:* 623 full-time (291 women), 38 part-time (17 women); includes 94 minority (11 African Americans, 55 Asian Americans or Pacific Islanders, 28 Hispanic Americans), 173 international. Average age 29. 1,444 applicants, 38% accepted, 212 enrolled. In 2009, 305 master's, 7 doctorates awarded. Terminal master's awarded for partial completion of doctoral program. *Degree requirements:* For master's, 2 core examinations, oral exam, proficiency in language other than native language (MA); for doctorate, 2 foreign languages, thesis/dissertation, 3 comprehensive exams, economics, quantitative and qualitative course, dissertation prospectus and defense. *Entrance requirements:* For master's, GMAT or GRE General Test, previous course work in economics, foreign language, undergraduate degree; for doctorate, GRE General Test, master's degree. Additional exam requirements/recommendations for international students: Required—TOEFL (minimum score 600 paper-based; 250 computer-based; 100 iBT), IELTS (minimum score 7), TOEFL (minimum score 600 paper-based; 250 computer-based; 100 iBT) or IELTS (minimum score 7). *Application deadline:* For fall admission, 1/7 for domestic and international students. Application fee: $85. Electronic applications accepted. *Expenses:* Contact institution. *Financial support:* In 2009–10, 450 students received support, including 450 fellowships (averaging $7,500 per year); teaching assistantships, career-related internships or fieldwork, Federal Work-Study, and scholarships/grants also available. Financial award application deadline: 2/15; financial award applicants required to submit FAFSA. *Faculty research:* Regional studies, international relations, international economics, energy and environment, international development. Total annual research expenditures: $7 million. *Unit head:* Sidney Jackson, Director of Admissions, 202-663-5700, Fax: 202-663-7788. *Application contact:* Admissions, 202-663-5700, Fax: 202-663-7788, E-mail: admissions.sais@jhu.edu.

Lehigh University, College of Education, Program in Comparative and International Education, Bethlehem, PA 18015. Offers comparative and international education (MA); globalization and educational change (M Ed); international counseling (Certificate); international development in education (Certificate); special education (Certificate); TESOL (Certificate). Part-time and evening/weekend programs available. Postbaccalaureate distance learning degree programs offered (no on-campus study). *Faculty:* 2 full-time (1 woman). *Students:* 9 full-time (6 women), 40 part-time (39 women); includes 3 minority (2 African Americans, 1 Hispanic American), 10 international. Average age 36. 46 applicants, 67% accepted, 18 enrolled. In 2009, 11 master's awarded. *Degree requirements:* For master's, thesis (MA). *Entrance requirements:* For master's, 2 letters of recommendation. Additional exam requirements/recommendations for international students: Required—TOEFL (minimum score 600 paper-based; 250 computer-based; 93 iBT). *Application deadline:* For fall admission, 5/15 for domestic and international students; for spring admission, 11/1 for domestic and international students. Applications are processed on a rolling basis. Application fee: $65. Electronic applications accepted. *Financial support:* In 2009–10, 4 students received support, including 4 research assistantships with full and partial tuition reimbursements available (averaging $13,000 per year). Financial award application deadline: 3/15. *Faculty research:* Gender equity in education, post-socialist education transformation, educational borrowing, comparing education systems, education policy and globalization. *Unit head:* Dr. Alexander W. Wiseman, Coordinator, 610-758-5740, Fax: 610-758-6223, E-mail: aww207@lehigh.edu. *Application contact:* Donna M. Johnson, Coordinator, 610-758-3231, Fax: 610-758-6223, E-mail: dmj4@lehigh.edu.

McGill University, Faculty of Graduate and Postdoctoral Studies, Desautels Faculty of Management, Montréal, QC H3A 2T5, Canada. Offers administration (PhD); entrepreneurial studies (MBA); finance (MBA); general management (Post Master's Certificate); information systems (MBA); international business (exchange program) (MBA); international Master's program in practicing management (MM); management (MBA); management for development (MBA); manufacturing management (MMM); marketing (MBA); operations management (MBA); public accountancy (Diploma); strategic management (MBA); MBA/LL B; MD/MBA.

Ohio University, Graduate College, Center for International Studies, Program in International Development Studies, Athens, OH 45701-2979. Offers MA. Part-time programs available. *Students:* 23 full-time (15 women), 2 part-time (1 woman); includes 2 minority (both African Americans), 16 international. Average age 29. 91 applicants, 53% accepted, 14 enrolled. In 2009, 18 master's awarded. *Degree requirements:* For master's, one foreign language, thesis optional. *Entrance requirements:* For master's, minimum GPA of 3.0. Additional exam requirements/recommendations for international students: Required—TOEFL (minimum score 550 paper-based; 213 computer-based; 80 iBT), IELTS (minimum score 6.5). *Application deadline:* For fall admission, 1/1 for domestic and international students. Application fee: $50 ($55 for international students). Electronic applications accepted. *Expenses:* Tuition, state resident: full-time $7839; part-time $323 per quarter hour. Tuition, nonresident: full-time $15,831; part-time $654 per quarter hour. Required fees: $2931. *Financial support:* In 2009–10, 21 students received support; research assistantships with full tuition reimbursements available, career-related internships or fieldwork, Federal Work-Study, institutionally sponsored loans, tuition waivers (partial), and unspecified assistantships available. Financial award application deadline: 1/1. *Faculty research:* Problems and issues in social, economic, political, health and environmental development. *Unit head:* Dr. Jieli Li, Director, E-mail: lij@ohio.edu. *Application contact:* Joan Kraynanski, Administrative Assistant, 740-593-1840, Fax: 740-593-1837, E-mail: kraynans@ohio.edu.

Rutgers, The State University of New Jersey, Camden, Graduate School of Arts and Sciences, Department of Public Policy and Administration, Camden, NJ 08102-1401. Offers education policy and leadership (MPA); international public service and development (MPA); public management (MPA); JD/MPA; MPA/MA. *Accreditation:* NASPAA. Part-time and evening/weekend programs available. *Degree requirements:* For master's, directed study, research workshop. *Entrance requirements:* For master's, GRE General Test, GMAT or LSAT, 3 letters of recommendation; resume. Additional exam requirements/recommendations for international students: Required—TOEFL (minimum score 550 paper-based; 213 computer-based), IELTS. Electronic applications accepted. *Faculty research:* Nonprofit management, county and municipal administration, health and human services, government communication, administrative law, educational finance.

Saint Mary's University, Faculty of Arts, International Development Studies Program, Halifax, NS B3H 3C3, Canada. Offers MA, Graduate Diploma. Part-time programs available. *Faculty:* 15 full-time, 13 part-time/adjunct. *Degree requirements:* For master's, thesis. *Entrance requirements:* For master's, honors degree. *Application deadline:* For fall admission, 3/1 for domestic students. Application fee: $35. *Financial support:* Fellowships available. *Faculty research:* Dynamics of global development, gender and development, policy analysis, models and strategies for development, Latin American and Caribbean development. *Unit head:* Dr. Anthony H. O'Malley, Coordinator, 902-491-6221. *Application contact:* Dr. Anthony H. O'Malley, Coordinator, 902-491-6221.

Texas A&M University, George Bush School of Government and Public Service, College Station, TX 77843. Offers advanced international affairs (Certificate); homeland security (Certificate); international affairs (MPIA), including international economics and development, national security affairs; nonprofit management (Certificate); public service and administration (MPSA), including public management, public policy analysis. *Accreditation:* NASPAA. *Faculty:* 51. *Students:* 209 full-time (97 women), 93 part-time (43 women); includes 48 minority (15 African Americans, 5 Asian Americans or Pacific Islanders, 28 Hispanic Americans), 19 international. Average age 24. In 2009, 87 master's awarded. *Degree requirements:* For master's, summer internship. *Entrance requirements:* For master's, GRE (preferred) or GMAT. *Application deadline:* For fall admission, 1/24 for domestic and international students. Application fee: $50 ($75 for international students). Electronic applications accepted. *Expenses:* Tuition, state resident: full-time $3991; part-time $221.74 per credit hour. Tuition, nonresident: full-time $9049; part-time $502.74 per credit hour. *Financial support:* In 2009–10, fellowships (averaging $11,000 per year), research assistantships (averaging $11,250 per year) were awarded; career-related internships or fieldwork, Federal Work-Study, and institutionally sponsored loans also available. Financial award application deadline: 2/1; financial award applicants required to submit FAFSA. *Faculty research:* Public policy, presidential studies, public leadership, economic policy, social policy. *Unit head:* A. Benton Cocanougher, Interim Dean, 979-862-8842, E-mail: bushschool@tamu.edu. *Application contact:* Kathryn Meyer, Recruitment and Placement Officer, 979-458-4767, Fax: 979-845-4155, E-mail: admissions@bushschool.tamu.edu.

Tufts University, Fletcher School of Law and Diplomacy, Medford, MA 02155. Offers LL M, MA, MAHA, MALD, MIB, PhD, DVM/MA, JD/MALD, MALD/MA, MALD/MBA, MALD/MS, MD/MA. Postbaccalaureate distance learning degree programs offered (minimal on-campus study). *Faculty:* 34 full-time (7 women), 31 part-time/adjunct (8 women). *Students:* 443 full-time (224 women), 7 part-time (4 women); includes 51 minority (6 African Americans, 1 American Indian/Alaska Native, 26 Asian Americans or Pacific Islanders, 18 Hispanic Americans), 165 international. Average age 31. 1,866 applicants, 40% accepted, 292 enrolled. In 2009, 364 master's, 12 doctorates awarded. *Degree requirements:* For master's, one foreign language, thesis; for doctorate, one foreign language, comprehensive exam, thesis/dissertation, dissertation defense. *Entrance requirements:* For master's and doctorate, GMAT or GRE General Test. Additional exam requirements/recommendations for international students: Required—TOEFL (minimum score 600 paper-based; 250 computer-based; 100 iBT), IELTS (minimum score 7). *Application deadline:* For fall admission, 1/15 for domestic and international students; for spring admission, 10/15 for domestic and international students. Application fee: $70. Electronic applications accepted. *Expenses:* Contact institution. *Financial support:* Federal Work-Study, institutionally sponsored loans, scholarships/grants, and tuition waivers (partial) available. Financial award application deadline: 1/15; financial award applicants required to submit FAFSA. *Faculty research:* Negotiation and conflict resolution, international organizations, international business and economic law, security studies, development economics. *Unit head:* Stephen W. Bosworth, Dean, 617-627-3050, Fax: 617-627-3712. *Application contact:* Laurie A. Hurley, E-mail: fletcheradmissions@tufts.edu.

Tufts University, Graduate School of Arts and Sciences, Department of Urban and Environmental Policy and Planning, Medford, MA 02155. Offers community development (MA); environmental policy (MA); health and human welfare (MA); housing policy (MA); international environment/development policy (MA); public policy (MPP); MA/MS; MALD/MA. *Accreditation:* ACSP (one or more programs are accredited). Part-time programs available. *Faculty:* 11 full-time, 9 part-time/adjunct. *Students:* 133 (83 women); includes 26 minority (15 African Americans, 5 Asian Americans or Pacific Islanders, 6 Hispanic Americans), 2 international.

International Development

Tufts University (continued)

Average age 27. 200 applicants, 63% accepted, 53 enrolled. In 2009, 44 master's awarded. *Degree requirements:* For master's, thesis, internship. *Entrance requirements:* For master's, GRE General Test. Additional exam requirements/recommendations for international students: Required—TOEFL (minimum score 550 paper-based; 213 computer-based; 80 iBT). *Application deadline:* For fall admission, 1/15 for domestic students, 12/15 for international students. Applications are processed on a rolling basis. Application fee: $75. Electronic applications accepted. *Expenses:* Contact institution. *Financial support:* Teaching assistantships with partial tuition reimbursements, career-related internships or fieldwork, Federal Work-Study, scholarships/grants, tuition waivers (partial), and unspecified assistantships available. Support available to part-time students. Financial award application deadline: 1/15; financial award applicants required to submit FAFSA. *Unit head:* Julian Agyeman, Chair, 617-627-3394, Fax: 617-627-3377. *Application contact:* Ann Urosevich, Department Administrator, 617-627-3394.

Tulane University, School of Liberal Arts, The Payson Center for International Development and Technology Transfer, New Orleans, LA 70118-5669. Offers international development (MS, PhD). Part-time programs available. *Degree requirements:* For master's, comprehensive exam (for some programs), thesis optional; for doctorate, comprehensive exam, thesis/dissertation. *Entrance requirements:* For master's, GRE General Test, minimum B average in undergraduate course work. Additional exam requirements/recommendations for international students: Required—TOEFL. Electronic applications accepted. *Faculty research:* Third World development.

University of Florida, Graduate School, College of Liberal Arts and Sciences, Department of Political Science, Gainesville, FL 32611. Offers international development policy and administration (MA, Certificate); international relations (MA, MAT); political campaigning (MA, Certificate); political science (MA, MAT, PhD); public affairs (MA, Certificate); JD/MA. Part-time programs available. Terminal master's awarded for partial completion of doctoral program. *Degree requirements:* For master's, variable foreign language requirement, thesis or alternative; for doctorate, variable foreign language requirement, thesis/dissertation. *Entrance requirements:* For master's and doctorate, GRE General Test, minimum GPA of 3.0. Additional exam requirements/recommendations for international students: Required—TOEFL (minimum score 550 paper-based; 213 computer-based). Electronic applications accepted. *Faculty research:* U.S. political development, religion and politics, environmental politics and policy, developing societies, international relations.

University of Guelph, Graduate Program Services, Collaborative International Development Studies, Guelph, ON N1G 2W1, Canada. Offers M Eng, M Sc, MA, MBA, PhD. Part-time programs available. *Degree requirements:* For master's, thesis (for some programs), seminar; for doctorate, comprehensive exam (for some programs), thesis/dissertation. *Entrance requirements:* For master's, honour's degree with courses in economics, social science, and empirical methods. *Faculty research:* Transformation of developing societies, regional differences, national and international processes of development, long-term change.

University of Minnesota, Twin Cities Campus, Graduate School, Hubert H. Humphrey Institute of Public Affairs, Program in International Development, Minneapolis, MN 55455-0213. Offers MDP. Program jointly administered with Interdisciplinary Center for the Study of Global Change (ICGC).

University of Ottawa, Faculty of Graduate and Postdoctoral Studies, Program in Globalization and International Development, Ottawa, ON K1N 6N5, Canada. Offers MA. *Degree requirements:* For master's, thesis or alternative. *Entrance requirements:* For master's, honours bachelor's degree or equivalent, minimum B average.

University of Pittsburgh, Graduate School of Public and International Affairs, Division of International Development, Pittsburgh, PA 15260. Offers development planning and environmental sustainability (MID); human security (MID); nongovernmental organizations and civil society (MID); MID/JD; MID/MBA; MID/MPH; MID/MPIA; MID/MSIS; MID/MSW. Part-time programs available. *Faculty:* 28 full-time (8 women), 56 part-time/adjunct (20 women). *Students:* 47 full-time (34 women), 4 part-time (3 women); includes 8 minority (3 African Americans, 2 Asian Americans or Pacific Islanders, 3 Hispanic Americans), 4 international. Average age 25. 123 applicants, 87% accepted, 37 enrolled. In 2009, 26 master's awarded. *Degree requirements:* For master's, thesis optional, internship, capstone seminar. *Entrance requirements:* For master's, GRE General Test, 3 letters of recommendation, minimum GPA of 3.2. Additional exam requirements/recommendations for international students: Required—TOEFL (minimum score 550 paper-based; 213 computer-based; 80 iBT), TWE (minimum score 4); Recommended—IELTS (minimum score 7). *Application deadline:* For fall admission, 2/1 for domestic students, 1/5 for international students; for spring admission, 11/1 for domestic students, 8/1 for international students. Application fee: $50. Electronic applications accepted. *Expenses:* Tuition, state resident: full-time $16,402; part-time $665 per credit. Tuition, nonresident: full-time $28,694; part-time $1175 per credit. Required fees: $690; $175 per term. Tuition and fees vary according to program. *Financial support:* In 2009–10, 27 students received support, including 4 fellowships (averaging $30,000 per year); scholarships/grants, tuition waivers (full and partial), and unspecified assistantships also available. Financial award application deadline: 2/1. *Faculty research:* Nongovernmental organizations, religion and civil society, international development, development economics and policy, human rights and development, humanitarian intervention, ethnic conflict and civil war, post-conflict peace building, corruption and transnational governance, civil society and public affairs, political constraints on rural development. Total annual research expenditures: $357,117. *Unit head:* Dr. Louis Picard, Director, 412-648-7659, Fax: 412-648-2605, E-mail: picard@pitt.edu. *Application contact:* Elizabeth Hruby, Graduate Enrollment Counselor, 412-648-7640, Fax: 412-648-7641, E-mail: eah44@pitt.edu.

University of Pittsburgh, Graduate School of Public and International Affairs, Public Policy and Management Program for Mid-Career Professionals, Pittsburgh, PA 15260. Offers development planning (MPPM); international development (MPPM); international political economy (MPPM); international security studies (MPPM); management of non profit organizations (MPPM); metropolitan management and regional development (MPPM); policy analysis and evaluation (MPPM). Part-time programs available. *Faculty:* 28 full-time (8 women), 56 part-time/adjunct (20 women). *Students:* 3 full-time (0 women), 39 part-time (21 women); includes 2 minority (both African Americans), 1 international. Average age 38. 48 applicants, 75% accepted, 19 enrolled. In 2009, 17 master's awarded. *Degree requirements:* For master's, thesis optional, capstone seminar. *Entrance requirements:* For master's, 2 letters of recommendation, resume, 5 years of supervisory or budgetary experience. Additional exam requirements/recommendations for international students: Required—TOEFL (minimum score 600 paper-based; 250 computer-based; 100 iBT), TWE (minimum score 4); Recommended—IELTS (minimum score 7). *Application deadline:* For fall admission, 6/1 priority date for domestic students, 2/15 for international students; for spring admission, 1/1 priority date for domestic students, 8/1 for international students. Applications are processed on a rolling basis. Application fee: $50. Electronic applications accepted. *Expenses:* Tuition, state resident: full-time $16,402; part-time $665 per credit. Tuition, nonresident: full-time $28,694; part-time $1175 per credit. Required fees: $690; $175 per term. Tuition and fees vary according to program. *Financial support:* In 2009–10, 10 students received support. Institutionally sponsored loans, scholarships/grants, and tuition waivers (partial) available. Support available to part-time students. Financial award application deadline: 2/1. *Faculty research:* Nonprofit management, urban and regional affairs, policy analysis and evaluation, security and intelligence studies, global political economy, nongovernmental organizations, civil society, development planning and environmental sustainability, human security. Total annual research expenditures: $357,117. *Unit head:* Dr. George Dougherty, Director, Executive Education, 412-648-7603, Fax: 412-648-2605, E-mail: gwdjr@pitt.edu. *Application contact:* Michael T. Rizzi, Associate Director of Student Services, 412-648-7640, Fax: 412-648-7641, E-mail: rizzim@pitt.edu.

University of San Francisco, College of Arts and Sciences, Department of Economics, Program in International and Development Economics, San Francisco, CA 94117-1080. Offers MA. *Faculty:* 8 full-time (2 women), 9 part-time/adjunct (3 women). *Students:* 40 full-time (15 women), 3 part-time (1 woman); includes 8 minority (1 African American, 4 Asian Americans or Pacific Islanders, 3 Hispanic Americans), 11 international. Average age 28. 143 applicants, 43% accepted, 20 enrolled. In 2009, 17 master's awarded. *Expenses:* Tuition: Full-time $19,710; part-time $1095 per unit. Part-time tuition and fees vary according to degree level, campus/location and program. *Financial support:* In 2009–10, 27 students received support. *Unit head:* Dr. Elizabeth Katz, Co-Director, 415-422-2711, Fax: 415-422-6983. *Application contact:* Information Contact, 415-422-5135, Fax: 415-422-6983, E-mail: asgraduate@usfca.edu.

University of Southern Mississippi, Graduate School, College of Arts and Letters, Department of Political Science, International Development, and International Affairs, Hattiesburg, MS 39406-0001. Offers international development (PhD); political science (MA, MS). Part-time programs available. *Faculty:* 14 full-time (2 women). *Students:* 23 full-time (11 women), 59 part-time (21 women); includes 20 minority (13 African Americans, 1 American Indian/Alaska Native, 1 Asian American or Pacific Islander, 5 Hispanic Americans), 5 international. Average age 36. 28 applicants, 39% accepted, 9 enrolled. In 2009, 8 master's, 1 doctorate awarded. *Degree requirements:* For master's, comprehensive exam, thesis (for some programs). *Entrance requirements:* For master's, GRE General Test, minimum GPA of 2.75 in last 2 years, 3.0 in field of study. *Application deadline:* For fall admission, 3/1 priority date for domestic students, 3/1 for international students. Applications are processed on a rolling basis. Application fee: $35. *Expenses:* Tuition, state resident: full-time $5096; part-time $284 per hour. Tuition, nonresident: full-time $13,052; part-time $726 per hour. Required fees: $402. Tuition and fees vary according to course level and course load. *Financial support:* In 2009–10, 4 research assistantships with full and partial tuition reimbursements (averaging $9,000 per year), 8 teaching assistantships with full tuition reimbursements (averaging $7,000 per year) were awarded; career-related internships or fieldwork, Federal Work-Study, scholarships/grants, and unspecified assistantships also available. Financial award application deadline: 3/15; financial award applicants required to submit FAFSA. *Faculty research:* American politics, international politics, political theory, comparative politics, public law. *Unit head:* Dr. Thomas Lansford, Interim Chair, 601-266-4310. *Application contact:* Dr. Robert Pauley, Graduate Coordinator, 601-266-4310, Fax: 601-266-4172.

Virginia Polytechnic Institute and State University, Graduate School, College of Architecture and Urban Studies, School of Public and International Affairs, Blacksburg, VA 24061. Offers environmental planning and policy (MURP); government and international affairs (MPIA); housing, community and economic development (MURP); international development planning (MURP); land use and physical planning (MURP); planning, governance and globalization (PhD), including environmental planning and landscape analysis, physical planning and urban design, public and international affairs, urban and environmental design and planning; urban and regional planning (MURP). *Accreditation:* ACSP. *Faculty:* 27 full-time (11 women), 2 part-time/adjunct (1 woman). *Students:* 73 full-time (51 women), 65 part-time (39 women); includes 15 minority (4 African Americans, 1 American Indian/Alaska Native, 6 Asian Americans or Pacific Islanders, 4 Hispanic Americans), 10 international. Average age 29. 86 applicants, 67% accepted, 40 enrolled. In 2009, 26 master's, 1 doctorate awarded. *Entrance requirements:* Additional exam requirements/recommendations for international students: Required—TOEFL (minimum score 550 paper-based; 213 computer-based). *Application deadline:* For fall admission, 5/15 for international students; for spring admission, 10/15 for international students. Applications are processed on a rolling basis. Application fee: $45. Electronic applications accepted. *Financial support:* In 2009–10, 1 teaching assistantship with full tuition reimbursement (averaging $5,560 per year) was awarded; career-related internships or fieldwork, Federal Work-Study, scholarships/grants, and unspecified assistantships also available. Financial award application deadline: 4/1. *Faculty research:* Design theory, environmental planning, town planning, transportation planning. *Unit head:* Dr. John Randolph, Dean, 540-231-6971, Fax: 540-231-9938, E-mail: energy@vt.edu. *Application contact:* Krystal D. Wright, Information Contact, 540-231-*5683, Fax: 540-231-9938, E-mail: garch@vt.edu.

International Trade Policy

The George Washington University, Elliott School of International Affairs, Program in International Trade and Investment Policy, Washington, DC 20052. Offers MA, JD/MA, MBA/MA. Part-time and evening/weekend programs available. *Students:* 36 full-time (21 women), 13 part-time (10 women); includes 7 minority (1 African American, 3 Asian Americans or Pacific Islanders, 3 Hispanic Americans), 9 international. Average age 26. 93 applicants, 73% accepted, 23 enrolled. In 2009, 19 master's awarded. *Degree requirements:* For master's, one foreign language, capstone project. *Entrance requirements:* For master's, GRE General Test, 2 years of a modern foreign language, 2 semesters of introductory economics. Additional exam requirements/recommendations for international students: Required—TOEFL. *Application deadline:* For fall admission, 2/1 for domestic students; for spring admission, 10/1 for domestic students. Application fee: $60. Electronic applications accepted. *Financial support:* In 2009–10, 11 students received support; fellowships with tuition reimbursements available, research assistantships with tuition reimbursements available, career-related internships or fieldwork, Federal Work-Study, institutionally sponsored loans, and tuition waivers available. Financial award application deadline: 1/15. *Unit head:* Steven Suranovic, Director, 202-994-7579, Fax: 202-994-5477, E-mail: smsuran@gwu.edu. *Application contact:* Jeff V. Miles, Director of Graduate Admissions, 202-994-7050, Fax: 202-994-9537, E-mail: esiagrad@gwu.edu.

Monterey Institute of International Studies, Graduate School of International Policy and Management, Program in International Trade Policy, Monterey, CA 93940-2691. Offers MA. *Students:* 13 full-time (6 women), 3 part-time (1 woman); includes 3 minority (2 African Americans, 1 Asian American or Pacific Islander), 4 international. Average age 27. In 2009, 17 master's awarded. *Degree requirements:* For master's, one foreign language. *Entrance requirements:* For master's, minimum GPA of 3.0, proficiency in a foreign language. Additional exam requirements/recommendations for international students: Required—TOEFL (minimum score 550 paper-based; 213 computer-based; 80 iBT). *Application deadline:* For fall admission, 3/15 priority date for domestic and international students; for spring admission, 10/1 priority date for domestic and international students. Applications are processed on a rolling basis. Application fee: $50. Electronic applications accepted. *Expenses:* Tuition: Full-time $31,000; part-time $1500 per credit. Required fees: $56. *Financial support:* Application deadline: 3/15. *Application contact:* 831-647-4123, Fax: 831-647-6405, E-mail: admit@miis.edu.

See Close-Up on page 853.

Political Science

Acadia University, Faculty of Arts, Department of Political Science, Wolfville, NS B4P 2R6, Canada. Offers MA. *Faculty:* 7 full-time (2 women), 1 part-time/adjunct (0 women). *Students:* 1 full-time (0 women), 5 part-time (2 women). Average age 26. 9 applicants, 56% accepted, 2 enrolled. In 2009, 1 master's awarded. *Degree requirements:* For master's, thesis. *Entrance requirements:* For master's, honors degree or equivalent. Additional exam requirements/recommendations for international students: Required—TOEFL (minimum score 580 paper-based; 237 computer-based; 93 iBT), IELTS (minimum score 6.5). *Application deadline:* For fall admission, 2/1 priority date for domestic and international students. Applications are processed on a rolling basis. Application fee: $50. *Financial support:* In 2009–10, 1 student received support; teaching assistantships available. Financial award application deadline: 2/1. *Faculty research:* Atlantic Canada, international relations and organization, human rights, Canadian politics, political thought, technology. *Unit head:* Dr. Malcolm Grieve, Head, 902-585-1507, Fax: 902-585-1070, E-mail: malcolm.grieve@acadiau.ca. *Application contact:* Danielle Fraser, Administrative Secretary, 902-585-1506, Fax: 902-585-1070, E-mail: polisci@acadiau.ca.

American Public University System, AMU/APU Graduate Programs, Charles Town, WV 25414. Offers air warfare (MA Military Studies); American Revolution (MA Military Studies); business administration (MBA); Civil War (MA Military Studies); criminal justice (MA); defense management (MA Military Studies); emergency and disaster management (MA); environmental policy and management (MS); fire science management (MA); global engagement (MA); history (MA); homeland security (MA); humanities (MA); intelligence (MA Military Studies, MA Strategic Intelligence); international peace and conflict resolution (MA); international relations and conflict resolution (MA); joint warfare (MA Military Studies); land warfare international perspective (MA Military Studies); management (MA); military history (MA); military leadership (MA Military Studies); national security studies (MA); naval warfare international (MA Military Studies); naval warfare US (MA Military Studies); political science (MA); public administration (MA); public health (MA); security management (MA); space studies (MS); special ops/LIC (MA Military Studies); sports management (MA); transportation and logistics management (MA); transportation management (MA); unconventional warfare (MA Military Studies); World War II (MA Military Studies). Programs offered via distance learning only. Part-time and evening/weekend programs available. Postbaccalaureate distance learning degree programs offered (no on-campus study). *Faculty:* 10 full-time (3 women), 188 part-time/adjunct (57 women). *Students:* 340 full-time (98 women), 3,567 part-time (790 women); includes 615 minority (317 African Americans, 28 American Indian/Alaska Native, 85 Asian Americans or Pacific Islanders, 185 Hispanic Americans), 20 international. Average age 36. 2,123 applicants, 100% accepted, 893 enrolled. In 2009, 829 degrees awarded. *Degree requirements:* For master's, comprehensive exam. *Entrance requirements:* For master's, bachelor's degree or equivalent, minimum GPA of 2.7 in last 60 hours of course work. *Application deadline:* Applications are processed on a rolling basis. Application fee: $0. Electronic applications accepted. *Financial support:* Applicants required to submit FAFSA. *Faculty research:* Military history, criminal justice, management performance, national security. *Unit head:* Dr. Frank McCluskey, Provost, 877-468-6268, Fax: 304-724-3780. *Application contact:* Terry Grant, Director of Enrollment Management, 877-468-6268, Fax: 304-724-3780, E-mail: info@apus.edu.

American University, School of Communication, Program in Political Communication, Washington, DC 20016-8001. Offers MA. Part-time programs available. *Degree requirements:* For master's, comprehensive exam, thesis or alternative. *Entrance requirements:* For master's, GRE General Test. Additional exam requirements/recommendations for international students: Required—TOEFL (minimum score 600 paper-based; 250 computer-based). *Application deadline:* For fall admission, 2/1 priority date for domestic students, 4/1 for international students. Applications are processed on a rolling basis. Application fee: $50. *Expenses:* Tuition: Full-time $22,266; part-time $1237 per credit hour. Required fees: $430. Tuition and fees vary according to program. *Financial support:* Career-related internships or fieldwork, Federal Work-Study, institutionally sponsored loans, scholarships/grants, tuition waivers (partial), and unspecified assistantships available. Financial award application deadline: 2/1. *Faculty research:* Polling and public opinion, political polling, advocacy communication, entertainment and politics, communication research and management, political communication theory, campaign ethics. *Unit head:* Dean Larry Kirkman, Dean, 202-885-2058, Fax: 202-885-2099, E-mail: larry@american.edu. *Application contact:* Sharmeen Ahsan-Bracciale, Graduate Admissions Office, 202-885-2040, Fax: 202-885-2019, E-mail: gradcomm@american.edu.

American University, School of Public Affairs, Department of Government, Washington, DC 20016-8130. Offers political science (MA, PhD), including American politics (MA), comparative politics (MA); women, policy and political leadership (Certificate). Part-time and evening/weekend programs available. *Faculty:* 33 full-time (16 women), 25 part-time/adjunct (3 women). *Students:* 59 full-time (34 women), 35 part-time (15 women); includes 8 minority (1 African American, 1 American Indian/Alaska Native, 2 Asian Americans or Pacific Islanders, 4 Hispanic Americans), 7 international. Average age 27. 158 applicants, 63% accepted, 38 enrolled. In 2009, 21 master's, 4 doctorates, 4 other advanced degrees awarded. Terminal master's awarded for partial completion of doctoral program. *Degree requirements:* For master's, comprehensive exam; for doctorate, comprehensive exam, thesis/dissertation. *Entrance requirements:* For master's, GRE, 2 recommendations; for doctorate, GRE, statement of purpose; 3 recommendations; for Certificate, bachelor's degree. Additional exam requirements/recommendations for international students: Required—TOEFL. *Application deadline:* For fall admission, 2/1 for domestic students; for spring admission, 11/1 for domestic students. Application fee: $55. *Expenses:* Tuition: Full-time $22,266; part-time $1237 per credit hour. Required fees: $430. Tuition and fees vary according to program. *Financial support:* Fellowships, research assistantships, teaching assistantships, career-related internships or fieldwork and institutionally sponsored loans available. Financial award application deadline: 2/1. *Faculty research:* Political leadership, interest groups, politics of regulation, public law, political behavior. *Unit head:* Dr. Candice Nelson, Chair, 202-885-2338, E-mail: cnelson@american.edu. *Application contact:* Dr. Candice Nelson, Chair, 202-885-2338, E-mail: cnelson@american.edu.

The American University in Cairo, Graduate Studies and Research, School of Humanities and Social Sciences, Department of Political Science, Cairo, Egypt. Offers MA. *Degree requirements:* For master's, thesis. *Entrance requirements:* Additional exam requirements/recommendations for international students: Required—English entrance exam and/or TOEFL. Electronic applications accepted. *Faculty research:* African and Middle East politics, international relations, development of human rights, international law.

The American University of Athens, The School of Graduate Studies, Athens, Greece. Offers biomedical sciences (MS); business (MBA); business communication (MA); computer sciences (MS); engineering and applied sciences (MS); politics and policy making (MA); systems engineering (MS); telecommunications (MS). *Entrance requirements:* For master's, resum&e, 2 recommendation letters. Additional exam requirements/recommendations for international students: Required—TOEFL (minimum score 550 paper-based; 213 computer-based). *Faculty research:* Nanotechnology, environmental sciences, rock mechanics, human skin studies, Monte Carlo algorithms and software.

American University of Beirut, Graduate Programs, Faculty of Arts and Sciences, Beirut, Lebanon. Offers anthropology (MA); Arabic language and literature (MA); archaeology (MA); biology (MS); chemistry (MS); computer science (MS); economics (MA); education (MA); English language (MA); English literature (MA); environmental policy planning (MSES); financial economics (MAFE); geology (MS); history (MA); mathematics (MA, MS); Middle Eastern studies (MA); philosophy (MA); physics (MS); political studies (MA); psychology (MA); public administration (MA); sociology (MA); statistics (MA, MS). Part-time programs available. *Degree requirements:* For master's, one foreign language, comprehensive exam, thesis (for some programs). *Entrance requirements:* For master's, GRE, letter of recommendation. Additional exam requirements/recommendations for international students: Required—TOEFL (minimum score 600 paper-based; 250 computer-based; 100 iBT), IELTS (minimum score 7.5). *Faculty research:* String theory and supergravity; computer graphics; algebra and number theory; popular Arabic literature; marine and freshwater biology; integrating science, math and technology.

Appalachian State University, Cratis D. Williams Graduate School, Department of Government and Justice Studies, Boone, NC 28608. Offers criminal justice (MS); political science (MA), including American government, environmental politics and policy analysis, international relations; public administration (MPA), including public management, town, city and county management. Part-time programs available. Postbaccalaureate distance learning degree programs offered (no on-campus study). *Faculty:* 27 full-time (5 women), 12 part-time/adjunct (1 woman). *Students:* 65 full-time (26 women), 62 part-time (22 women); includes 6 minority (5 African Americans, 1 American Indian/Alaska Native), 1 international. 100 applicants, 93% accepted, 53 enrolled. In 2009, 45 master's awarded. *Degree requirements:* For master's, variable foreign language requirement, comprehensive exam, thesis optional. *Entrance requirements:* For master's, GRE General Test, 3 letters of recommendation. Additional exam requirements/recommendations for international students: Required—TOEFL (minimum score 570 paper-based; 230 computer-based; 79 iBT), IELTS (minimum score 6.5). *Application deadline:* For fall admission, 7/1 for domestic students, 2/1 for international students; for spring admission, 11/1 for domestic students, 7/1 for international students. Applications are processed on a rolling basis. Application fee: $50. Electronic applications accepted. *Expenses:* Tuition, state resident: full-time $2960. Tuition, nonresident: full-time $14,051. Required fees: $2320. *Financial support:* In 2009–10, 20 research assistantships (averaging $8,000 per year) were awarded; fellowships, teaching assistantships, career-related internships or fieldwork, Federal Work-Study, scholarships/grants, and unspecified assistantships also available. Financial award application deadline: 4/1; financial award applicants required to submit FAFSA. *Faculty research:* Campaign finance, emerging democracies, bureaucratic politics, judicial behavior, administration of justice. Total annual research expenditures: $320,000. *Unit head:* Dr. Brian Ellison, Chairperson, 828-262-3085, E-mail: ellisonba@appstate.edu. *Application contact:* Sandy Krause, Director of Admissions and Recruiting, 828-262-2130, Fax: 828-262-2709, E-mail: krausesl@appstate.edu.

Arizona State University, Graduate College, College of Liberal Arts and Sciences, Division of Social Sciences, Department of Political Science, Tempe, AZ 85287. Offers MA, PhD. *Degree requirements:* For master's, thesis or alternative; for doctorate, thesis/dissertation. *Entrance requirements:* For master's and doctorate, GRE.

Arkansas State University—Jonesboro, Graduate School, College of Humanities and Social Sciences, Department of Political Science, Jonesboro, State University, AR 72467. Offers political science (MA); political science education (SCCT); public administration (MPA). *Accreditation:* NASPAA (one or more programs are accredited). Part-time programs available. *Faculty:* 8 full-time (3 women), 1 (woman) part-time/adjunct. *Students:* 24 full-time (8 women), 21 part-time (11 women); includes 12 minority (11 African Americans, 1 American Indian/Alaska Native), 7 international. Average age 32. 27 applicants, 89% accepted, 21 enrolled. In 2009, 17 master's awarded. *Degree requirements:* For master's, comprehensive exam, thesis or alternative; for SCCT, comprehensive exam. *Entrance requirements:* For master's, GRE General Test or MAT, GMAT, appropriate bachelor's degree, letters of recommendation; for SCCT, GRE General Test or MAT, GMAT, interview, master's degree, official transcript, letters of recommendation, immunization records. Additional exam requirements/recommendations for international students: Required—TOEFL (minimum score 550 paper-based; 213 computer-based; 79 iBT), IELTS (minimum score 6). *Application deadline:* For fall admission, 7/1 for domestic and international students; for spring admission, 11/15 for domestic students, 11/13 for international students. Applications are processed on a rolling basis. Application fee: $30 ($40 for international students). Electronic applications accepted. *Expenses:* Tuition, state resident: full-time $3744; part-time $208 per credit hour. Tuition, nonresident: full-time $9540; part-time $530 per credit hour. Required fees: $896; $47 per credit hour. $25 per term. One-time fee: $50. Tuition and fees vary according to course load and program. *Financial support:* In 2009–10, 11 students received support; teaching assistantships, career-related internships or fieldwork, scholarships/grants, and unspecified assistantships available. Financial award application deadline: 7/1; financial award applicants required to submit FAFSA. *Unit head:* Dr. Richard Wang, Chair, 870-972-3048, Fax: 870-972-2720, E-mail: rwang@astate.edu. *Application contact:* Dr. Andrew Sustich, Dean of the Graduate School, 870-972-3029, Fax: 870-972-3857, E-mail: sustich@astate.edu.

Ashland University, College of Arts and Sciences, Program in American History and Government, Ashland, OH 44805-3702. Offers MAHG. Part-time programs available. *Faculty:* 5 full-time (0 women), 33 part-time/adjunct (2 women). *Students:* 57 full-time (25 women), 69 part-time (27 women); includes 7 minority (1 African American, 1 Asian American or Pacific Islander, 5 Hispanic Americans). Average age 39. 98 applicants, 72% accepted, 49 enrolled. In 2009, 5 master's awarded. *Degree requirements:* For master's, capstone project or thesis. *Entrance requirements:* For master's, minimum undergraduate GPA of 2.75, 3.0 graduate. *Application deadline:* Applications are processed on a rolling basis. Application fee: $30. Electronic applications accepted. *Expenses:* Contact institution. *Financial support:* In 2009–10, 45 students received support. Application deadline: 4/15. *Faculty research:* American founding, United States Civil War, Progressive Era. *Unit head:* Dr. Peter W. Schramm, Executive Director, Ashbrook Center, 419-289-5411, Fax: 419-289-5425, E-mail: pschramm@ashland.edu. *Application contact:* Christian A. Pascarella, Associate Director, 419-289-5411, Fax: 419-289-5425, E-mail: cpascare@ashland.edu.

Auburn University, Graduate School, College of Liberal Arts, Department of Political Science, Auburn University, AL 36849. Offers public administration (MPA, PhD); MPA/MCP. Part-time programs available. *Faculty:* 22 full-time (8 women), 3 part-time/adjunct (1 woman). *Students:* 35 full-time (17 women), 34 part-time (18 women); includes 13 minority (9 African Americans, 2 Asian Americans or Pacific Islanders, 2 Hispanic Americans), 9 international. Average age 33. 57 applicants, 54% accepted, 24 enrolled. In 2009, 13 master's, 6 doctorates awarded. *Degree requirements:* For doctorate, thesis/dissertation. *Entrance requirements:* For master's, GRE General Test, minimum GPA of 3.0 in political science, 2.5 overall; for doctorate, GRE General Test. *Application deadline:* For fall admission, 7/7 for domestic students; for spring admission, 11/24 for domestic students. Applications are processed on a rolling basis. Application fee: $50 ($60 for international students). Electronic applications accepted. *Expenses:* Tuition, state resident: full-time $6240. Tuition, nonresident: full-time $18,720. International tuition: $18,938 full-time. Required fees: $492. Tuition and fees vary according to course load, program and reciprocity agreements. *Financial support:* Fellowships, research assistantships, teaching assistantships, career-related internships or fieldwork and Federal Work-Study available. Support available to part-time students. Financial award application deadline: 3/15; financial award applicants required to submit FAFSA. *Faculty research:* Policy evaluation, political economy, privatization, participation, election administration. Total annual research expenditures: $200,000. *Unit head:* Dr. Gerard Gryski, Chair, 334-844-5370. *Application contact:* Dr. George Flowers, Dean of the Graduate School, 334-844-2125.

Auburn University Montgomery, School of Sciences, Department of Public Administration and Political Science, Montgomery, AL 36124-4023. Offers MPA, MPS, PhD. *Accreditation:* NASPAA (one or more programs are accredited). Part-time and evening/weekend programs available. *Faculty:* 6 full-time (1 woman), 4 part-time/adjunct (1 woman). *Students:* 31 full-time (22 women), 118 part-time (79 women); includes 68 minority (60 African Americans, 5 Asian Americans or Pacific Islanders, 3 Hispanic Americans), 3 international. Average age 32. In 2009, 22 master's awarded. *Degree requirements:* For master's, comprehensive exam; for doctorate, thesis/dissertation. *Entrance requirements:* For master's, GRE General Test or MAT; for doctorate, GRE General Test. *Application deadline:* Applications are processed on a rolling basis. Electronic applications accepted. *Expenses:* Tuition, state resident: full-time $2841; part-time $225 per credit hour. Tuition, nonresident: full-time $8241; part-time $675 per

Political Science

Auburn University Montgomery (continued)

credit hour. Required fees: $282; $8 per hour. $45 per term. *Financial support:* In 2009–10, 1 research assistantship was awarded; career-related internships or fieldwork and scholarships/grants also available. Support available to part-time students. Financial award application deadline: 3/1; financial award applicants required to submit FAFSA. *Unit head:* Dr. Thomas Vocino, Head, 334-244-3696, Fax: 334-244-3826, E-mail: vocino@mail.aum.edu. *Application contact:* Dr. Glen Ray, Acting Graduate Coordinator, 334-244-3590, Fax: 334-244-3826, E-mail: gray@mail.aum.edu.

Augusta State University, Graduate Studies, College of Arts and Sciences, Department of Political Science, Augusta, GA 30904-2200. Offers MPA. Part-time and evening/weekend programs available. *Degree requirements:* For master's, comprehensive exam, thesis. *Entrance requirements:* For master's, GRE General Test. Electronic applications accepted. *Faculty research:* Political behavior, administrative law, political participation, human resources administration.

Ball State University, Graduate School, College of Sciences and Humanities, Department of Political Science, Program in Political Science, Muncie, IN 47306-1099. Offers MA. *Faculty research:* Survey research, public policy.

Baylor University, Graduate School, College of Arts and Sciences, Department of Political Science, Waco, TX 76798. Offers international studies (MA); political science (MA, PhD); public policy and administration (MPPA); JD/MPPA. *Students:* 28 full-time (8 women), 1 part-time (0 women), 3 international. In 2009, 5 master's, 1 doctorate awarded. *Entrance requirements:* For master's, GRE General Test. *Application deadline:* Applications are processed on a rolling basis. Application fee: $25. *Financial support:* Research assistantships, career-related internships or fieldwork, Federal Work-Study, and institutionally sponsored loans available. Financial award application deadline: 3/1. *Unit head:* Dr. David Corey, Graduate Program Director, 254-710-3161, Fax: 254-710-3122, E-mail: david_d_corey@baylor.edu. *Application contact:* Jenice Langston, Administrative Assistant, 254-710-3161, Fax: 254-710-3870, E-mail: jenice_langston@baylor.edu.

Baylor University, Graduate School, College of Arts and Sciences, J. M. Dawson Institute of Church-State Studies, Waco, TX 76798. Offers MA, PhD. *Students:* 33 full-time (12 women), 6 part-time (2 women); includes 8 minority (1 American Indian/Alaska Native, 3 Asian Americans or Pacific Islanders, 4 Hispanic Americans), 7 international. In 2009, 5 master's, 3 doctorates awarded. *Degree requirements:* For master's, thesis, oral exam; for doctorate, one foreign language, thesis/dissertation, preliminary exams. *Entrance requirements:* For master's, GRE General Test; for doctorate, GRE General Test, MA or equivalent. *Application deadline:* For fall admission, 3/1 for domestic students. Applications are processed on a rolling basis. Application fee: $25. *Financial support:* Fellowships, research assistantships, teaching assistantships, Federal Work-Study and institutionally sponsored loans available. Financial award application deadline: 3/1. *Faculty research:* Religion and politics, religion and public education, religious freedom and international politics, First Amendment jurisprudence. *Unit head:* Dr. Christopher Marsh, Graduate Program Director, 254-710-4412, Fax: 254-710-1571, E-mail: chris_marsh@baylor.edu. *Application contact:* Suzanne Seller, Administrative Assistant, 254-710-1510, Fax: 254-710-1571, E-mail: suzanne_sellers@baylor.edu.

Boston College, Graduate School of Arts and Sciences, Department of Political Science, Chestnut Hill, MA 02467-3800. Offers MA, PhD. *Students:* 50 full-time (22 women); includes 3 minority (1 Asian American or Pacific Islander, 2 Hispanic Americans), 8 international. 212 applicants, 31% accepted, 15 enrolled. In 2009, 10 master's, 7 doctorates awarded. Terminal master's awarded for partial completion of doctoral program. *Degree requirements:* For master's, thesis or alternative; for doctorate, one foreign language, thesis/dissertation. *Entrance requirements:* For master's and doctorate, GRE General Test. Additional exam requirements/recommendations for international students: Required—TOEFL (minimum score 600 paper-based; 250 computer-based; 100 iBT). *Application deadline:* For fall admission, 1/2 for domestic and international students. Application fee: $70. Electronic applications accepted. *Financial support:* In 2009–10, fellowships with full tuition reimbursements (averaging $18,350 per year), research assistantships with full tuition reimbursements (averaging $18,350 per year), teaching assistantships with full tuition reimbursements (averaging $18,350 per year) were awarded; Federal Work-Study and scholarships/grants also available. Support available to part-time students. Financial award application deadline: 3/1; financial award applicants required to submit FAFSA. *Faculty research:* Political theory, American politics, international politics. *Unit head:* Dr. Susan Shell, Chairperson, 617-552-4161, E-mail: susan.shell@bc.edu. *Application contact:* Dr. Christopher Kelly, Graduate Program Director, 617-552-1565, E-mail: christopher.kelly@bc.edu.

Boston University, Graduate School of Arts and Sciences, Department of Political Science, Boston, MA 02215. Offers MA, PhD. *Students:* 63 full-time (21 women), 2 part-time (1 woman); includes 5 minority (3 African Americans, 2 Asian Americans or Pacific Islanders), 22 international. Average age 32. 156 applicants, 25% accepted, 14 enrolled. In 2009, 2 master's, 2 doctorates awarded. Terminal master's awarded for partial completion of doctoral program. *Degree requirements:* For master's, one foreign language; for doctorate, 2 foreign languages, comprehensive exam, thesis/dissertation. *Entrance requirements:* For master's and doctorate, GRE General Test, 3 letters of recommendation. Additional exam requirements/recommendations for international students: Required—TOEFL (minimum score 600 paper-based; 250 computer-based). *Application deadline:* For fall admission, 12/1 for domestic and international students. Application fee: $70. Electronic applications accepted. *Expenses:* Tuition: Full-time $37,910; part-time $1184 per credit hour. Required fees: $386; $40 per semester. Part-time tuition and fees vary according to class time, course level, degree level and program. *Financial support:* In 2009–10, 17 students received support, including 1 fellowship with full tuition reimbursement available (averaging $18,900 per year), 11 teaching assistantships with full tuition reimbursements available (averaging $18,400 per year); career-related internships or fieldwork, Federal Work-Study, and stipends also available. Support available to part-time students. Financial award application deadline: 12/1; financial award applicants required to submit FAFSA. *Unit head:* Walter Connor, Chairman, 617-353-7003, Fax: 617-353-5508, E-mail: wdconnor@bu.edu. *Application contact:* Linda Simons, Graduate Program Coordinator, 617-353-2541, Fax: 617-353-5508, E-mail: pograd@bu.edu.

Bowling Green State University, Graduate College, College of Arts and Sciences, Department of Political Science, Program in Political Science, Bowling Green, OH 43403. Offers MA/MA. *Entrance requirements:* Additional exam requirements/recommendations for international students: Required—TOEFL. Electronic applications accepted.

Brandeis University, Graduate School of Arts and Sciences, Department of Politics, Waltham, MA 02454-9110. Offers MA, PhD. Part-time programs available. *Faculty:* 14 full-time (3 women). *Students:* 27 full-time (15 women), 4 international. 46 applicants, 20% accepted, 3 enrolled. In 2009, 1 master's, 2 doctorates awarded. Terminal master's awarded for partial completion of doctoral program. *Degree requirements:* For master's, thesis; for doctorate, one foreign language, comprehensive exam, thesis/dissertation. *Entrance requirements:* For master's and doctorate, GRE General Test, sample of written work, resume, 3 letters of recommendation. Additional exam requirements/recommendations for international students: Required—TOEFL (minimum score 600 paper-based; 250 computer-based; 100 iBT); Recommended—IELTS (minimum score 7). *Application deadline:* For fall admission, 1/15 for domestic and international students. Application fee: $75. Electronic applications accepted. *Financial support:* In 2009–10, 13 students received support, including 11 fellowships with full tuition reimbursements available (averaging $20,000 per year), 2 teaching assistantships with partial tuition reimbursements available (averaging $3,200 per year); scholarships/grants, health care benefits, tuition waivers (full and partial), and unspecified assistantships also available. Financial award application deadline: 2/1; financial award applicants required to submit FAFSA. *Faculty research:* American institutions, international law and foreign policy, political theory, comparative politics, European politics. *Unit head:* Prof. Daniel Kryder, Director of Graduate Studies, 781-736-2778, Fax: 781-736-2777, E-mail: kryder@brandeis.edu. *Application contact:* Rosanne Colocouris, Department Administrator, 781-736-2755, Fax: 781-736-2777, E-mail: colocour@brandeis.edu.

Brigham Young University, Graduate Studies, College of Family, Home, and Social Sciences, Department of Political Science–Public Policy, Provo, UT 84602. Offers MPP, JD/MPP. *Faculty:* 4 full-time (0 women), 3 part-time/adjunct (1 woman). *Students:* 16 full-time (7 women); includes 4 minority (1 African American, 1 American Indian/Alaska Native, 1 Asian American or Pacific Islander, 1 Hispanic American). Average age 26. 31 applicants, 58% accepted, 9 enrolled. In 2009, 4 master's awarded. *Degree requirements:* For master's, internship. *Entrance requirements:* For master's, GRE. Additional exam requirements/recommendations for international students: Required—TOEFL (minimum score 580 paper-based; 237 computer-based; 85 iBT). *Application deadline:* For fall admission, 3/1 priority date for domestic and international students. Application fee: $50. Electronic applications accepted. *Expenses:* Tuition: Full-time $5580; part-time $301 per credit hour. Tuition and fees vary according to student's religious affiliation. *Financial support:* In 2009–10, 13 students received support, including 7 research assistantships with full and partial tuition reimbursements available (averaging $2,456 per year), 1 teaching assistantship with full and partial tuition reimbursement available (averaging $2,500 per year); fellowships also available. Financial award application deadline: 3/1. *Faculty research:* Welfare, environment, and health policy issues; U. S. elections. *Unit head:* Dr. Sven E. Wilson, Graduate Program Director, 801-422-9018, Fax: 801-422-0224, E-mail: sven_wilson@byu.edu. *Application contact:* Jessica A. McArthur, Graduate Secretary, 801-422-7146, Fax: 801-422-0224, E-mail: publicpolicy@byu.edu.

Brigham Young University, Graduate Studies, Marriott School of Management, Master of Public Administration Program, Provo, UT 84602. Offers finance (MPA); human resources (MPA); local government (MPA); nonprofit management (MPA); JD/MPA. *Faculty:* 10 full-time (4 women), 18 part-time/adjunct (1 woman). *Students:* 128 full-time (54 women); includes 26 minority (3 African Americans, 13 Asian Americans or Pacific Islanders, 10 Hispanic Americans). Average age 27. 136 applicants, 66% accepted, 62 enrolled. In 2009, 53 master's awarded. *Entrance requirements:* For master's, GRE, GMAT, minimum GPA of 3.0. Additional exam requirements/recommendations for international students: Required—TOEFL (minimum score 580 paper-based; 85 iBT), IELTS (minimum score 7). *Application deadline:* For fall admission, 2/1 for domestic and international students. Application fee: $50. Electronic applications accepted. *Expenses:* Tuition: Full-time $5580; part-time $301 per credit hour. Tuition and fees vary according to student's religious affiliation. *Financial support:* In 2009–10, 96 students received support. Career-related internships or fieldwork and scholarships/grants available. Financial award application deadline: 4/15; financial award applicants required to submit FAFSA. *Faculty research:* Taxes, budgeting, nonprofit, ethics, decision modeling, work balance, organizational behavior. *Unit head:* Dr. David W. Hart, Director, 801-422-4221, Fax: 801-422-0311, E-mail: mpa@byu.edu. *Application contact:* Catherine Cooper, Director of Student Services, E-mail: mpa@byu.edu.

Brock University, Faculty of Graduate Studies, Faculty of Social Sciences, Program in Political Science, St. Catharines, ON L2S 3A1, Canada. Offers Canadian politics (MA); comparative politics (MA); international relations (MA); political theory or philosophy (MA); public policy (MA). Part-time programs available. *Degree requirements:* For master's, thesis optional. *Entrance requirements:* For master's, honors degree. Additional exam requirements/recommendations for international students: Required—TOEFL (minimum score 550 paper-based; 213 computer-based; 80 iBT), IELTS (minimum score 6.5), TWE (minimum score 4). Electronic applications accepted. *Faculty research:* Public administration reform, economic and social justice, politics of societies, Canadian politics, international relations.

Brooklyn College of the City University of New York, Division of Graduate Studies, Department of Political Science, Brooklyn, NY 11210-2889. Offers international affairs (MA); political science (MA, PhD); political science, urban policy and administration (MA). Part-time and evening/weekend programs available. *Students:* 24 full-time (13 women), 168 part-time (98 women); includes 99 minority (70 African Americans, 13 Asian Americans or Pacific Islanders, 16 Hispanic Americans), 29 international. Average age 30. 123 applicants, 87% accepted, 79 enrolled. In 2009, 46 master's awarded. *Degree requirements:* For master's, comprehensive exam (for some programs), thesis or alternative, foreign language exam (for international affairs program). *Entrance requirements:* For master's, 2 letters of recommendation, personal statement. Additional exam requirements/recommendations for international students: Required—TOEFL (minimum score 500 paper-based; 173 computer-based; 61 iBT). *Application deadline:* For fall admission, 5/1 for domestic and international students; for spring admission, 12/12 for domestic students, 11/1 for international students. *Expenses:* Tuition, area resident: Full-time $7360; part-time $310 per credit hour. Tuition, state resident: full-time $7360; part-time $310 per credit hour. Tuition, nonresident: full-time $13,800; part-time $575 per credit hour. International tuition: $13,800 full-time. Required fees: $140.10 per semester. *Financial support:* Career-related internships or fieldwork and Federal Work-Study available. Support available to part-time students. Financial award application deadline: 5/1; financial award applicants required to submit FAFSA. *Faculty research:* Ethics and politics, politics of criminal justice, Western Europe, international law and politics, labor politics. *Unit head:* Dr. Noel Anderson, Acting Chairperson, 718-951-5306, E-mail: anderson@brooklyn.cuny.edu. *Application contact:* Hernan Sierra, Graduate Admissions Coordinator, 718-951-4536, Fax: 718-951-4506, E-mail: grads@brooklyn.cuny.edu.

Brown University, Graduate School, Department of Political Science, Providence, RI 02912. Offers PhD, MA/PhD. *Degree requirements:* For doctorate, thesis/dissertation. *Entrance requirements:* For doctorate, GRE General Test.

California Polytechnic State University, San Luis Obispo, College of Liberal Arts, Department of Political Science, San Luis Obispo, CA 93407. Offers MPP. Part-time programs available. *Faculty:* 4 full-time (2 women). *Students:* 25 full-time (18 women), 13 part-time (3 women); includes 9 minority (1 Asian American or Pacific Islander, 8 Hispanic Americans). Average age 31. 50 applicants, 68% accepted, 16 enrolled. In 2009, 11 master's awarded. *Degree requirements:* For master's, thesis or alternative. *Entrance requirements:* For master's, minimum GPA of 2.75 in last 90 quarter units of course work, three letters of recommendation. Additional exam requirements/recommendations for international students: Required—TOEFL (minimum score 550 paper-based; 213 computer-based), or IELTS (minimum score 6). *Application deadline:* For fall admission, 2/15 for domestic students, 11/30 for international students; for winter admission, 6/30 for international students. Application fee: $55. *Expenses:* Tuition, nonresident: full-time $11,160; part-time $248 per unit. Required fees: $7134; $1553 per quarter. *Financial support:* Career-related internships or fieldwork, Federal Work-Study, and scholarships/grants available. Support available to part-time students. Financial award application deadline: 3/2; financial award applicants required to submit FAFSA. *Faculty research:* Public policy analysis, public finance, policy internship. *Unit head:* Dr. Elizabeth Lowham, Graduate Coordinator, 805-756-2919, Fax: 805-756-7168, E-mail: elowham@calpoly.edu. *Application contact:* Dr. Elizabeth Lowham, Graduate Coordinator, 805-756-2919, Fax: 805-756-7168, E-mail: elowham@calpoly.edu.

California State University, Chico, Graduate School, College of Behavioral and Social Sciences, Department of Political Science, Program in Political Science, Chico, CA 95929-0722. Offers MA. Part-time programs available. *Students:* 16 full-time (11 women), 13 part-time (4 women); includes 5 minority (1 African American, 1 Asian American or Pacific Islander, 3 Hispanic Americans), 3 international. Average age 30. 27 applicants, 81% accepted, 13 enrolled. In 2009, 5 master's awarded. *Entrance requirements:* For master's, 2 letters of recommendation. Additional exam requirements/recommendations for international students: Required—TOEFL (minimum score 550 paper-based; 213 computer-based; 80 iBT), IELTS (minimum score 6.5). *Application deadline:* For fall admission, 3/1 priority date for domestic students, 3/1 for international students; for spring admission, 9/15 priority date for domestic students, 9/15 for international students. Applications are processed on a rolling basis. Application fee: $55. Electronic applications accepted. *Financial support:* Career-related internships or fieldwork available. *Unit head:* Dr. Charles Turner, Graduate Coordinator, 530-898-5960. *Application contact:* Dr. Charles Turner, Graduate Coordinator, 530-898-5960.

California State University, Fullerton, Graduate Studies, College of Humanities and Social Sciences, Division of Politics, Administration, and Justice, Fullerton, CA 92834-9480. Offers political science (MA); public administration (MPA). *Accreditation:* NASPAA (one or more programs are accredited). Part-time programs available. *Students:* 28 full-time (17 women), 144 part-time (68 women); includes 89 minority (5 African Americans, 1 American Indian/Alaska Native, 33 Asian Americans or Pacific Islanders, 50 Hispanic Americans), 3 international. Average age 30. 165 applicants, 47% accepted, 46 enrolled. In 2009, 62 master's awarded. *Degree requirements:* For master's, comprehensive exam, project or thesis. *Entrance requirements:* For master's, minimum GPA of 2.5 in last 60 units of course work, 12 units of course work in social sciences. Application fee: $55. *Expenses:* Tuition, nonresident: full-time $11,160; part-time $373 per credit. Required fees: $1440 per term. Tuition and fees vary according to course load, degree level and program. *Financial support:* Career-related internships or fieldwork, Federal Work-Study, institutionally sponsored loans, and scholarships/grants available. Support available to part-time students. Financial award application deadline: 3/1; financial award applicants required to submit FAFSA. *Faculty research:* Emergency management plans. *Unit head:* Dr. Phil Gianos, Chair, 657-278-3521. *Application contact:* Admissions/Applications, 657-278-2371.

California State University, Long Beach, Graduate Studies, College of Liberal Arts, Department of Political Science, Long Beach, CA 90840. Offers MA. Part-time programs available. *Faculty:* 7 full-time (2 women), 1 part-time/adjunct (0 women). *Students:* 12 full-time (7 women), 24 part-time (12 women); includes 12 minority (3 Asian Americans or Pacific Islanders, 9 Hispanic Americans). Average age 27. 48 applicants, 40% accepted, 9 enrolled. *Degree requirements:* For master's, one foreign language, comprehensive exam or thesis. *Entrance requirements:* For master's, GRE General Test, minimum GPA of 3.0 in field. *Application deadline:* For fall admission, 4/1 for domestic students. Applications are processed on a rolling basis. Application fee: $55. Electronic applications accepted. *Expenses:* Required fees: $1802 per semester. Part-time tuition and fees vary according to course load. *Financial support:* In 2009–10, 6 students received support; teaching assistantships, Federal Work-Study, institutionally sponsored loans, and scholarships/grants available. Financial award application deadline: 3/2. *Faculty research:* Social welfare policy, international political economy, Marxism, voting behavior. *Unit head:* Dr. Teresa Wright, Chair, 562-985-4704, Fax: 562-985-4979, E-mail: twright@csulb.edu. *Application contact:* Dr. Liesl Haas, Graduate Advisor, 562-985-5860, Fax: 562-985-4979, E-mail: lhaas@csulb.edu.

California State University, Los Angeles, Graduate Studies, College of Natural and Social Sciences, Department of Political Science, Los Angeles, CA 90032-8530. Offers political science (MA); public administration (MS). Part-time and evening/weekend programs available. *Faculty:* 5 full-time (1 woman), 4 part-time/adjunct (2 women). *Students:* 13 full-time (5 women), 110 part-time (69 women); includes 69 minority (7 African Americans, 12 Asian Americans or Pacific Islanders, 50 Hispanic Americans), 14 international. Average age 31. 73 applicants, 100% accepted, 28 enrolled. In 2009, 20 master's awarded. *Degree requirements:* For master's, comprehensive exam or thesis. *Entrance requirements:* Additional exam requirements/recommendations for international students: Required—TOEFL (minimum score 500 paper-based; 173 computer-based). *Application deadline:* For fall admission, 5/1 for domestic and international students. Applications are processed on a rolling basis. Application fee: $55. Electronic applications accepted. *Financial support:* Career-related internships or fieldwork and Federal Work-Study available. Support available to part-time students. Financial award application deadline: 3/1. *Faculty research:* Government; public policy and law; international, political, and economic relations; comparative politics. *Unit head:* Dr. Scott Bowman, Chair, 323-343-2248, Fax: 323-343-6452, E-mail: sbowman@calstatela.edu. *Application contact:* Dr. Cheryl L. Ney, Associate Vice President for Academic Affairs and Dean of Graduate Studies, 323-343-3820, Fax: 323-343-5653, E-mail: cney@cslanet.calstatela.edu.

California State University, Northridge, Graduate Studies, College of Social and Behavioral Sciences, Department of Political Science, Northridge, CA 91330. Offers MA. *Faculty:* 16 full-time (7 women), 8 part-time/adjunct (2 women). *Students:* 14 full-time (6 women), 26 part-time (11 women); includes 9 minority (1 African American, 2 Asian Americans or Pacific Islanders, 6 Hispanic Americans), 3 international. Average age 32. 539 applicants, 82% accepted, 13 enrolled. In 2009, 112 master's awarded. *Degree requirements:* For master's, comprehensive exam. *Entrance requirements:* For master's, GRE (if cumulative undergraduate GPA less than 3.0), 2 letters of recommendation. Additional exam requirements/recommendations for international students: Required—TOEFL. *Application deadline:* For fall admission, 11/30 for domestic students. Application fee: $55. *Financial support:* Application deadline: 3/1. *Unit head:* Dr. Martin Saiz, Chair, 818-677-3488, E-mail: martin.saiz@csun.edu. *Application contact:* Dr. Martin Saiz, Chair, 818-677-3488, E-mail: martin.saiz@csun.edu.

California State University, Sacramento, Graduate Studies, College of Social Sciences and Interdisciplinary Studies, Department of Government, Sacramento, CA 95819. Offers MA. Part-time programs available. *Degree requirements:* For master's, thesis or alternative, writing proficiency exam. *Entrance requirements:* For master's, GRE General Test, minimum GPA of 3.0 during previous 2 years. Additional exam requirements/recommendations for international students: Required—TOEFL. Electronic applications accepted.

Carleton University, Faculty of Graduate Studies, Faculty of Public Affairs and Management, Department of Political Science, Ottawa, ON K1S 5B6, Canada. Offers MA, PhD. *Degree requirements:* For master's, one foreign language, comprehensive exam, thesis optional; for doctorate, one foreign language, comprehensive exam, thesis/dissertation. *Entrance requirements:* For master's, honors degree in political science, minimum B average; for doctorate, master's degree in political science. Additional exam requirements/recommendations for international students: Required—TOEFL. *Faculty research:* Canadian politics, comparative politics, international relations, public administration and policy analysis, political theory.

Carleton University, Faculty of Graduate Studies, Faculty of Public Affairs and Management, Institute of Political Economy, Ottawa, ON K1S 5B6, Canada. Offers MA, PhD. *Degree requirements:* For master's, thesis optional. *Entrance requirements:* For master's, honors degree. Additional exam requirements/recommendations for international students: Required—TOEFL. *Faculty research:* Relationships between economy and politics as they affect the political, social and cultural life of societies; historical processes whereby social change is located in the interaction of the economic, political and cultural, and ideological moments of social life.

Case Western Reserve University, School of Graduate Studies, Department of Political Science, Cleveland, OH 44106. Offers MA, PhD. Part-time programs available. *Faculty:* 10 full-time (4 women), 1 part-time/adjunct (0 women). *Students:* 1 (woman) full-time. 17 applicants, 12% accepted, 0 enrolled. In 2009, 2 master's awarded. Terminal master's awarded for partial completion of doctoral program. *Degree requirements:* For master's, comprehensive exam; for doctorate, thesis/dissertation. *Entrance requirements:* For master's, GRE General Test, 18 hours in political science; for doctorate, GRE General Test, master's degree in political science. Additional exam requirements/recommendations for international students: Required—TOEFL (minimum score 550 paper-based; 213 computer-based; 79 iBT). *Application deadline:* For fall admission, 5/1 priority date for domestic students; for spring admission, 11/1 for domestic students. Applications are processed on a rolling basis. Application fee: $50. Electronic applications accepted. *Financial support:* Federal Work-Study available. Financial award application deadline: 2/15; financial award applicants required to submit FAFSA. *Faculty research:* American cultural politics and policy, Western and Eastern European governments, African politics in international affairs, American legislative and presidential politics, women and politics, Southern politics. *Unit head:* Joseph White, Chairman, 216-368-2426, Fax: 216-368-4681, E-mail: joseph.white@case.edu. *Application contact:* Sharon Skowronski, Department Assistant, 216-368-2424, Fax: 216-368-4681, E-mail: sxs22@po.cwru.edu.

The Catholic University of America, School of Arts and Sciences, Department of Politics, Washington, DC 20064. Offers American government (MA, PhD); Congressional and presidential studies (MA); international affairs (MA); international political economics (MA); political theory (MA, PhD); world politics (MA, PhD); MA/JD. Part-time programs available. *Faculty:* 13 full-time (1 woman), 8 part-time/adjunct (0 women). *Students:* 31 full-time (8 women), 73 part-time (21 women); includes 13 minority (5 African Americans, 4 Asian Americans or Pacific Islanders, 4 Hispanic Americans), 10 international. Average age 30. 120 applicants, 66% accepted, 30 enrolled. In 2009, 32 master's, 7 doctorates awarded. *Degree requirements:* For master's, one foreign language, comprehensive exam, thesis or alternative; for doctorate, variable foreign language requirement, comprehensive exam, thesis/dissertation. *Entrance requirements:* For master's, GRE General Test, 3 letters of recommendation, minimum GPA of 3.0; for doctorate, GRE General Test, statement of purpose, official copies of academic transcripts, three letters of recommendation, minimum GPA of 3.0. Additional exam requirements/recommendations for international students: Required—TOEFL (minimum score 580 paper-based; 237 computer-based). *Application deadline:* For fall admission, 8/1 priority date for domestic students, 7/15 for international students; for spring admission, 12/1 priority date for domestic students, 10/15 for international students. Applications are processed on a rolling basis. Application fee: $55. Electronic applications accepted. *Expenses:* Tuition: Full-time $31,740; part-time $1245 per credit hour. Required fees: $50; $25 per semester hour. One-time fee: $425. *Financial support:* Fellowships, research assistantships, teaching assistantships, Federal Work-Study, scholarships/grants, tuition waivers (full and partial), and unspecified assistantships available. Financial award application deadline: 2/1; financial award applicants required to submit FAFSA. *Faculty research:* Political philosophy, American political institutions and processes, political economy, international relations, U.S. political leadership since 1789. *Unit head:* Dr. Philip Henderson, Chair, 202-319-6226, Fax: 202-319-6289, E-mail: hendersp@cua.edu. *Application contact:* Julie Schwing, Director of Graduate Admissions, 202-319-5057, Fax: 202-319-6533, E-mail: cua-admissions@cua.edu.

Central European University, Graduate Studies, School of Social Sciences and Humanities, Budapest, Hungary. Offers economics (MA, PhD); gender studies (MA, PhD); international relations and European studies (MA, PhD); mathematics and its applications (MS, PhD); medieval studies (MA, PhD); nationalism studies (MA, PhD); philosophy (MA, PhD); political science (MA, PhD); public policy (MA, PhD); sociology and social anthropology (MA, PhD). Terminal master's awarded for partial completion of doctoral program. *Degree requirements:* For master's, one foreign language, thesis; for doctorate, one foreign language, comprehensive exam, thesis/dissertation. *Entrance requirements:* For master's, interview; for doctorate, GRE, CEU subject test, interview. Additional exam requirements/recommendations for international students: Required—TOEFL (minimum score 570 paper-based; 230 computer-based). Electronic applications accepted. *Faculty research:* Civil society, fiscal decentralization, party politics, political philosophy (especially Liberalism, theory of Democracy).

Central Michigan University, Central Michigan University Off-Campus Programs, Program in Public Administration, Mount Pleasant, MI 48859. Offers public management (MPA); state and local government (MPA). Part-time and evening/weekend programs available. *Entrance requirements:* For master's, minimum GPA of 2.8. Additional exam requirements/recommendations for international students: Required—TOEFL. Electronic applications accepted. *Financial support:* Scholarships/grants available. Support available to part-time students. *Unit head:* Dr. Lawrence Sych, Program Director, 989-774-3316, E-mail: sych1l@cmich.edu. *Application contact:* 877-268-4636, E-mail: cmuoffcampus@cmich.edu.

Central Michigan University, College of Graduate Studies, College of Humanities and Social and Behavioral Sciences, Department of Political Science, Program in Political Science, Mount Pleasant, MI 48859. Offers political science (MA), including American concentration, comparative/international concentration. Part-time programs available. *Degree requirements:* For master's, thesis or alternative. Electronic applications accepted.

Central Michigan University, College of Graduate Studies, College of Humanities and Social and Behavioral Sciences, Department of Political Science, Program in Public Administration, Mount Pleasant, MI 48859. Offers professional development in public administration (Graduate Certificate); public administration (MPA), including cognate courses option; public management (MPA); state and local government (MPA). Part-time programs available. *Degree requirements:* For master's, thesis or alternative. Electronic applications accepted.

Claremont Graduate University, Graduate Programs, School of Politics and Economics, Department of Politics and Policy, Claremont, CA 91711-6160. Offers American politics (MA, PhD); comparative politics (PhD); international political economy (MA); international studies (MA); political philosophy (PhD); political science (PhD); politics, economics and business (MA); public policy (MA, PhD); world politics (PhD); MBA/PhD. Part-time programs available. *Faculty:* 8 full-time (3 women), 4 part-time/adjunct (0 women). *Students:* 163 full-time (68 women), 16 part-time (7 women); includes 29 minority (6 African Americans, 8 Asian Americans or Pacific Islanders, 15 Hispanic Americans), 40 international. Average age 32. In 2009, 23 master's, 19 doctorates awarded. Terminal master's awarded for partial completion of doctoral program. *Entrance requirements:* For master's and doctorate, GRE General Test. Additional exam requirements/recommendations for international students: Required—TOEFL (minimum score 550 paper-based; 213 computer-based; 80 iBT). *Application deadline:* For fall admission, 2/1 priority date for domestic students. Applications are processed on a rolling basis. Application fee: $60. Electronic applications accepted. *Expenses:* Tuition: Full-time $35,046; part-time $1524 per credit. Required fees: $161 per semester. *Financial support:* Fellowships, research assistantships, teaching assistantships, Federal Work-Study, institutionally sponsored loans, and scholarships/grants available. Support available to part-time students. Financial award application deadline: 2/15; financial award applicants required to submit FAFSA. *Faculty research:* Environmental policy, international debt, global democratization, Third World development, public sector discrimination. *Unit head:* Jennifer Merolla, Chair, 909-621-8696, Fax: 909-621-8545, E-mail: jennifer.merolla@cgu.edu. *Application contact:* Lesa Hiben, Admissions Coordinator, 909-621-8699, Fax: 909-621-7545, E-mail: lesa.hiben@cga.edu.

Clark Atlanta University, School of Arts and Sciences, Department of Political Science, Atlanta, GA 30314. Offers MA, PhD. Part-time programs available. *Faculty:* 5 full-time (0 women), 1 part-time/adjunct (0 women). *Students:* 4 full-time (3 women), 40 part-time (19 women); includes 40 minority (all African Americans), 1 international. Average age 40. 16 applicants, 63% accepted, 4 enrolled. In 2009, 1 master's, 3 doctorates awarded. Terminal master's awarded for partial completion of doctoral program. *Degree requirements:* For master's, one foreign language, comprehensive exam, thesis; for doctorate, 2 foreign languages, comprehensive exam, thesis/dissertation. *Entrance requirements:* For master's, GRE General Test, minimum GPA of 2.5; for doctorate, GRE General Test, minimum graduate GPA of 3.0. Additional exam requirements/recommendations for international students: Required—TOEFL (minimum score 500 paper-based; 173 computer-based). *Application deadline:* For fall admission, 4/1 for domestic and international students; for spring admission, 11/1 for domestic and international students. Applications are processed on a rolling basis. Application fee: $40 ($55 for international students). *Expenses:* Tuition: Full-time $12,240; part-time $680 per credit hour. Required fees: $710; $355 per semester. *Financial support:* In 2009–10, 12 fellowships, 4 teaching assistantships were awarded; scholarships/grants and unspecified assistantships also available. Financial award application deadline: 4/30; financial award applicants required to submit FAFSA. *Faculty research:* Public policy and education, rural politics, women and state economic programs, reconstruction after war in Africa, environmental policies. *Unit head:* Dr. Fragano Ledgister, Chairperson, 404-880-8737, Fax: 404-880-8717, E-mail: fledgister@cau.edu. *Application contact:* Michelle Clark-Davis, Graduate Program Admissions, 404-880-6605, E-mail: cauadmissions@cau.edu.

The College of Saint Rose, Graduate Studies, School of Arts and Humanities, Program in History/Political Science, Albany, NY 12203-1419. Offers MA. Part-time and evening/weekend programs available. *Degree requirements:* For master's, final paper/project, thesis or comprehensive exam. *Entrance requirements:* For master's, minimum undergraduate GPA of

Political Science

The College of Saint Rose (continued)

3.0, 12 undergraduate credits in US history and/or political science. Additional exam requirements/recommendations for international students: Required—TOEFL (minimum score 550 paper-based; 213 computer-based). Electronic applications accepted.

Colorado State University, Graduate School, College of Liberal Arts, Department of Political Science, Fort Collins, CO 80523-1782. Offers MA, PhD. Part-time programs available. *Faculty:* 17 full-time (8 women), 1 (woman) part-time/adjunct. *Students:* 20 full-time (10 women), 26 part-time (11 women); includes 1 minority (African American), 1 international. Average age 30. 39 applicants, 85% accepted, 15 enrolled. In 2009, 7 master's, 2 doctorates awarded. *Degree requirements:* For master's, variable foreign language requirement, comprehensive exam (for some programs), thesis (for some programs); for doctorate, variable foreign language requirement, comprehensive exam (for some programs), thesis/dissertation (for some programs). *Entrance requirements:* For master's, GRE General Test (minimum score 1050 verbal and quantitative), minimum GPA of 3.0, BA/BS, letters of recommendation; for doctorate, GRE General Test (minimum combined score of 1200 on Verbal and Quantitative sections), minimum GPA of 3.5, 15-page writing sample, MA/MS or at least 24 credits in a master's program, letters of recommendation. Additional exam requirements/recommendations for international students: Required—TOEFL (minimum score 600 paper-based; 250 computer-based). *Application deadline:* For fall admission, 2/15 priority date for domestic and international students; for spring admission, 10/15 priority date for domestic students, 8/1 priority date for international students. Applications are processed on a rolling basis. Application fee: $50. Electronic applications accepted. *Expenses:* Tuition, state resident: full-time $6434; part-time $359.10 per credit. Tuition, nonresident: full-time $18,116; part-time $1006.45 per credit. Required fees: $1496; $83 per credit. *Financial support:* In 2009–10, 27 students received support, including 1 research assistantship (averaging $16,524 per year), 26 teaching assistantships with full tuition reimbursements available (averaging $13,787 per year); fellowships, career-related internships or fieldwork, Federal Work-Study, institutionally sponsored loans, scholarships/grants, traineeships, and unspecified assistantships also available. Financial award application deadline: 3/1; financial award applicants required to submit FAFSA. *Faculty research:* Environmental politics and policy, international relations, politics of developing nations, state and local politics and administration, political behavior. *Unit head:* Dr. Robert Duffy, Chair, 970-491-6225, Fax: 970-491-2490, E-mail: robert.duffy@colostate.edu. *Application contact:* Dr. Sandra K. Davis, Coordinator, 970-491-5281, Fax: 970-491-2490, E-mail: sandra.davis@colostate.edu.

Columbia University, Graduate School of Arts and Sciences, Division of Social Sciences, Department of Political Science, New York, NY 10027. Offers M Phil, MA, PhD, JD/MA, JD/PhD. *Degree requirements:* For master's, one foreign language; for doctorate, 2 foreign languages, thesis/dissertation. *Entrance requirements:* For master's and doctorate, GRE General Test. Additional exam requirements/recommendations for international students: Required—TOEFL. *Faculty research:* Comparative politics, American government, international relations.

Concordia University, School of Graduate Studies, Faculty of Arts and Science, Department of Political Science, Montréal, QC H3G 1M8, Canada. Offers political science (PhD); public policy and public administration (MA), including geography. *Degree requirements:* For master's, one foreign language, comprehensive exam, thesis optional, internship. *Entrance requirements:* For master's, honors degree or equivalent. Additional exam requirements/recommendations for international students: Required—TOEFL. *Faculty research:* International public policy and administration, Quebec public administration, public policy and social/political theory, geography and public policy, public administration and decision making.

Converse College, School of Education and Graduate Studies, Program in Liberal Arts, Spartanburg, SC 29302-0006. Offers English (MLA); history (MLA); political science (MLA). *Degree requirements:* For master's, capstone paper. *Entrance requirements:* For master's, minimum GPA of 3.0, 2 recommendations.

Cornell University, Graduate School, Graduate Fields of Arts and Sciences, Field of Government, Ithaca, NY 14853-0001. Offers American politics (PhD); comparative politics (PhD); international relations (PhD); political methodology (PhD); political thought (PhD); public policy (PhD). *Faculty:* 58 full-time (19 women). *Students:* 65 full-time (35 women); includes 9 minority (1 African American, 1 American Indian/Alaska Native, 2 Asian Americans or Pacific Islanders, 5 Hispanic Americans), 20 international. Average age 29. 317 applicants, 7% accepted, 11 enrolled. In 2009, 14 doctorates awarded. *Degree requirements:* For doctorate, comprehensive exam, thesis/dissertation. *Entrance requirements:* For doctorate, GRE General Test, sample of written work, 3 letters of recommendation. Additional exam requirements/recommendations for international students: Required—TOEFL (minimum score 550 paper-based; 213 computer-based; 77 iBT). *Application deadline:* For fall admission, 1/15 for domestic students. Application fee: $70. Electronic applications accepted. *Expenses:* Tuition: Full-time $29,500. Required fees: $70. Full-time tuition and fees vary according to degree level, program and student level. *Financial support:* In 2009–10, 60 students received support, including 10 fellowships with full tuition reimbursements available; research assistantships with full tuition reimbursements available, teaching assistantships with full tuition reimbursements available, institutionally sponsored loans, scholarships/grants, health care benefits, tuition waivers (full and partial), and unspecified assistantships also available. Financial award applicants required to submit FAFSA. *Faculty research:* Political theory, American politics, comparative politics, international relations, methodology. *Unit head:* Director of Graduate Studies, 607-255-3567, Fax: 607-255-4530. *Application contact:* Graduate Field Assistant, 607-255-3567, Fax: 607-255-4530, E-mail: cu_govt@cornell.edu.

Dalhousie University, Faculty of Arts and Social Science, Department of Political Science, Halifax, NS B3H 4R2, Canada. Offers MA, PhD. *Entrance requirements:* Additional exam requirements/recommendations for international students: Required—TOEFL, IELTS, CANTEST, CAEL, or Michigan English Language Assessment Battery. *Application deadline:* For fall admission, 6/1 for domestic students, 4/1 for international students; for winter admission, 10/31 for domestic students, 8/31 for international students; for spring admission, 2/28 for domestic students, 12/31 for international students. Application fee: $70. Electronic applications accepted. *Financial support:* Career-related internships or fieldwork, scholarships/grants, and health care benefits available. *Faculty research:* Canadian political behavior and institutions, international politics, foreign policy, African politics, liberalism and modern political theory. *Unit head:* Dr. Louise Carbert, Graduate Coordinator, 902-494-6628, Fax: 902-494-3825, E-mail: psadmin@dal.ca. *Application contact:* Karen Watts, Graduate Adminstrator, 902-494-2396, Fax: 902-494-3825, E-mail: psadmin@dal.ca.

Duke University, Graduate School, Department of Political Science, Durham, NC 27708. Offers AM, PhD, JD/AM, JD/PhD. *Faculty:* 40 full-time. *Students:* 103 full-time (35 women); includes 12 minority (4 African Americans, 1 American Indian/Alaska Native, 2 Asian Americans or Pacific Islanders, 5 Hispanic Americans), 36 international. 369 applicants, 19% accepted, 31 enrolled. In 2009, 14 master's, 8 doctorates awarded. Terminal master's awarded for partial completion of doctoral program. *Degree requirements:* For doctorate, 2 foreign languages, thesis/dissertation. *Entrance requirements:* For master's and doctorate, GRE General Test. Additional exam requirements/recommendations for international students: Required—TOEFL (minimum score 550 paper-based; 213 computer-based; 83 iBT), IELTS (minimum score 7). *Application deadline:* For fall admission, 12/8 priority date for domestic and international students. Application fee: $75. Electronic applications accepted. *Financial support:* Fellowships, research assistantships, teaching assistantships, Federal Work-Study available. Financial award application deadline: 12/31. *Unit head:* Ward Michael, Director of Graduate Studies, Fax: 919-660-4327, E-mail: knigh021@duke.edu. *Application contact:* Cynthia Robertson, Associate Dean for Enrollment Services, 919-684-3913, E-mail: grad-admissions@duke.edu.

East Carolina University, Graduate School, Thomas Harriot College of Arts and Sciences, Department of Political Science, Greenville, NC 27858-4353. Offers public administration (MPA). *Accreditation:* NASPAA. Part-time and evening/weekend programs available. *Degree requirements:* For master's, one foreign language, comprehensive exam. *Entrance requirements:* For master's, GRE General Test. Additional exam requirements/recommendations for international students: Required—TOEFL.

Eastern Illinois University, Graduate School, College of Sciences, Department of Political Science, Charleston, IL 61920-3099. Offers MA. *Faculty:* 11 full-time (2 women). In 2009, 11 master's awarded. *Application deadline:* For fall admission, 3/31 priority date for domestic students. Applications are processed on a rolling basis. Application fee: $30. *Expenses:* Tuition, state resident: full-time $9434; part-time $239 per credit hour. Tuition, nonresident: full-time $23,774; part-time $717 per credit hour. Required fees: $802.63. *Financial support:* In 2009–10, research assistantships with tuition reimbursements (averaging $8,100 per year), 4 teaching assistantships with tuition reimbursements (averaging $8,100 per year) were awarded. *Unit head:* Dr. Jeff Ashley, Chairperson, 217-581-8418, E-mail: jsashley@eiu.edu. *Application contact:* Dr. Ryan Hendrickson, Coordinator, 217-581-6224, E-mail: rchendrickson@eiu.edu.

Eastern Kentucky University, The Graduate School, College of Arts and Sciences, Department of Government, Program in Political Science, Richmond, KY 40475-3102. Offers MA. *Entrance requirements:* For master's, GRE General Test, minimum GPA of 2.5.

East Stroudsburg University of Pennsylvania, Graduate School, College of Arts and Sciences, Department of Political Science, East Stroudsburg, PA 18301-2999. Offers M Ed, MA. Part-time and evening/weekend programs available. *Faculty:* 8 full-time (3 women). *Students:* 24 full-time (16 women), 30 part-time (18 women); includes 10 minority (8 African Americans, 2 Hispanic Americans), 1 international. Average age 32. In 2009, 20 master's awarded. *Degree requirements:* For master's, variable foreign language requirement, comprehensive exam, thesis or alternative. *Entrance requirements:* Additional exam requirements/recommendations for international students: Required—TOEFL (minimum score 560 paper-based; 220 computer-based; 83 iBT). *Application deadline:* For fall admission, 7/31 priority date for domestic students, 5/1 priority date for international students; for spring admission, 11/30 for domestic students, 10/1 for international students. Applications are processed on a rolling basis. Application fee: $50. *Financial support:* In 2009–10, 17 research assistantships with full and partial tuition reimbursements (averaging $1,618 per year) were awarded; Federal Work-Study and institutionally sponsored loans also available. Financial award application deadline: 3/1; financial award applicants required to submit FAFSA. *Unit head:* Dr. Patricia Crotty, Graduate Coordinator, 570-422-3271, Fax: 570-422-3506, E-mail: pcrotty@po-box.esu.edu. *Application contact:* Kevin Quintero, Graduate Admissions Coordinator, 570-422-3890, Fax: 570-422-2711, E-mail: kquintero@po-box.esu.edu.

Emory University, Graduate School of Arts and Sciences, Department of Political Science, Atlanta, GA 30322-1100. Offers PhD. *Degree requirements:* For doctorate, comprehensive exam, thesis/dissertation. *Entrance requirements:* For doctorate, GRE General Test, minimum GPA of 3.0. Additional exam requirements/recommendations for international students: Required—TOEFL. Electronic applications accepted. *Faculty research:* Post-Soviet politics, comparative politics, international politics, judicial politics and methodology, American national political institutions.

Fairleigh Dickinson University, Metropolitan Campus, University College: Arts, Sciences, and Professional Studies, School of History, Political and International Studies, Program in Political Science, Teaneck, NJ 07666-1914. Offers MA. *Students:* 3 part-time (1 woman). Average age 34. 2 applicants, 100% accepted, 1 enrolled. In 2009, 2 master's awarded. *Application deadline:* Applications are processed on a rolling basis. Application fee: $40. *Application contact:* Susan Brooman, University Director of Graduate Admissions, 201-692-2554, Fax: 201-692-2560, E-mail: globaleducation@fdu.edu.

Fayetteville State University, Graduate School, Department of Geography, History and Political Science, Fayetteville, NC 28301-4298. Offers history (MA); political science (MA). Part-time and evening/weekend programs available. *Faculty:* 4 full-time (0 women). *Students:* 1 full-time (0 women), 6 part-time (2 women); includes 2 minority (both African Americans). Average age 40. 1 applicant, 100% accepted, 1 enrolled. In 2009, 2 master's awarded. *Degree requirements:* For master's, comprehensive exam, internship. *Entrance requirements:* For master's, GRE General Test. *Application deadline:* For fall admission, 4/15 for domestic students; for spring admission, 10/15 for domestic students. Applications are processed on a rolling basis. Application fee: $35. Electronic applications accepted. *Unit head:* Dr. Adeguke Ademiluyi, Chairperson, 910-672-1137, E-mail: aademiluyi@uncfsu.edu. *Application contact:* Roxie Shabazz, Associate Vice-Chancellor for Enrollment Management, 910-672-1784, Fax: 910-672-2209, E-mail: rshabazz@uncfsu.edu.

Florida Agricultural and Mechanical University, Division of Graduate Studies, Research, and Continuing Education, College of Arts and Sciences, Division of History and Political Sciences, Program in Applied Social Science, Tallahassee, FL 32307-3200. Offers African American history (MASS); criminal justice (MASS); economics (MASS); history (MASS); political science (MASS); public administration (MASS); public management (MASS); social work (MASS); sociology (MASS). Part-time programs available. *Faculty:* 17 full-time (2 women). *Students:* 54 full-time (42 women), 4 part-time (2 women); includes 57 minority (all African Americans). In 2009, 14 master's awarded. *Degree requirements:* For master's, thesis optional. *Entrance requirements:* For master's, GRE General Test, minimum GPA of 3.0. *Application deadline:* For fall admission, 5/18 for domestic students, 12/18 for international students; for spring admission, 11/12 for domestic students, 5/12 for international students. Application fee: $20. *Financial support:* Fellowships, research assistantships, career-related internships or fieldwork, Federal Work-Study, and tuition waivers (full) available. Financial award application deadline: 4/1. *Faculty research:* Southern history, black history, election trends, presidential history. *Unit head:* Dr. Gary Paul, Director, 850-599-3447. *Application contact:* Dr. Chanta M. Haywood, Dean of Graduate Studies, Research, and Continuing Education, 850-599-3315, Fax: 850-599-3727.

Florida Atlantic University, Dorothy F. Schmidt College of Arts and Letters, Department of Political Science, Boca Raton, FL 33431-0991. Offers MA, MAT. Part-time programs available. *Faculty:* 15 full-time (3 women), 6 part-time/adjunct (1 woman). *Students:* 9 full-time (5 women), 24 part-time (7 women); includes 6 minority (1 African American, 2 Asian Americans or Pacific Islanders, 3 Hispanic Americans), 1 international. Average age 31. 29 applicants, 59% accepted, 8 enrolled. In 2009, 10 master's awarded. *Degree requirements:* For master's, one foreign language, thesis or alternative. *Entrance requirements:* For master's, GRE General Test, minimum GPA of 3.0 during last 60 hours of course work. *Application deadline:* For fall admission, 7/1 for domestic students, 2/15 for international students; for spring admission, 11/1 for domestic students, 7/15 for international students. Applications are processed on a rolling basis. Application fee: $30. Electronic applications accepted. *Expenses:* Tuition, state resident: full-time $7055; part-time $293.94 per credit hour. Tuition, nonresident: full-time $22,096; part-time $920.66 per credit hour. *Financial support:* Research assistantships, teaching assistantships with partial tuition reimbursements, career-related internships or fieldwork, Federal Work-Study, and institutionally sponsored loans available. Support available to part-time students. Financial award application deadline: 4/16. *Faculty research:* Public policy, comparative policy affecting women, Congress, international system, urban policy. *Unit head:* Dr. Timothy Lenz, Chair, 561-297-3212, Fax: 561-297-2997, E-mail: lenz@fau.edu. *Application contact:* Dr. Robert Rabil, Director of Graduate Studies, 561-297-3215, Fax: 561-297-2997, E-mail: rrabil@fau.edu.

Florida International University, College of Arts and Sciences, Department of Politics and International Relations, Program of Political Science, Miami, FL 33199. Offers MA, PhD. Part-time and evening/weekend programs available. *Students:* 21 full-time (6 women), 9 part-time (4 women); includes 12 minority (4 African Americans, 8 Hispanic Americans), 9 international. Average age 29. 29 applicants, 34% accepted, 9 enrolled. In 2009, 12 master's, 3 doctorates awarded. *Degree requirements:* For master's, one foreign language, thesis or alternative, research project; for doctorate, one foreign language, comprehensive exam, thesis/dissertation. *Entrance requirements:* For master's, GRE General Test, minimum GPA of 3.2, 2 letters of recommendation; for doctorate, GRE General Test, minimum GPA of 3.2 (undergraduate), 3.25 (graduate), 2 letters of recommendation; Masters Thesis or other major paper. Additional exam requirements/recommendations for international students: Required—TOEFL (minimum score 550 paper-based; 80 iBT). *Application deadline:* For fall admission, 3/15 for domestic and international students. Application fee: $30. Electronic applications accepted. *Expenses:* Tuition, state resident: full-time $8008; part-time $4004 per year. Tuition, nonresident: full-time $20,104; part-time $10,052 per year. Required fees: $298; $149 per term. *Financial support:* Institutionally sponsored loans and scholarships/grants available. Financial award application deadline: 3/1; financial award applicants required to submit FAFSA. *Unit head:* Dr. Richard Olson, Chair, Politics and International Relations, 305-348-2556, Fax: 305-348-6138, E-mail: pir@fiu.edu. *Application contact:* Dr. Ronald Cox, Director of Graduate Studies, 305-348-2556, Fax: 305-348-6138, E-mail: pir@fiu.edu.

Florida State University, The Graduate School, College of Social Sciences and Public Policy, Department of Political Science, Tallahassee, FL 32306-2230. Offers MA, MS, PhD. Part-time programs available. *Faculty:* 27 full-time (4 women). *Students:* 60 full-time (19 women), 51 part-time (21 women); includes 15 minority (3 African Americans, 4 Asian Americans or Pacific Islanders, 8 Hispanic Americans), 6 international. Average age 24. 149 applicants, 49% accepted, 54 enrolled. In 2009, 45 master's, 5 doctorates awarded. Terminal master's awarded for partial completion of doctoral program. *Degree requirements:* For master's, thesis optional; for doctorate, comprehensive exam, thesis/dissertation. *Entrance requirements:* For master's, GRE General Test, minimum undergraduate GPA of 3.0; for doctorate, GRE General Test, minimum graduate GPA of 3.5, undergraduate 3.0. Additional exam requirements/recommendations for international students: Required—TOEFL (minimum score 600 paper-based; 100 iBT). *Application deadline:* For fall admission, 1/15 priority date for domestic and international students. Applications are processed on a rolling basis. Application fee: $30. Electronic applications accepted. *Expenses:* Tuition, state resident: full-time $7413. Tuition, nonresident: full-time $22,567. *Financial support:* In 2009–10, 35 students received support, including 2 fellowships with full tuition reimbursements available (averaging $18,000 per year), 29 research assistantships with full tuition reimbursements available (averaging $17,000 per year), 7 teaching assistantships with full tuition reimbursements available (averaging $17,000 per year); Federal Work-Study, institutionally sponsored loans, scholarships/grants, and unspecified assistantships also available. Financial award application deadline: 1/15; financial award applicants required to submit FAFSA. *Faculty research:* American government, international relations, comparative government, public policy. Total annual research expenditures: $317,000. *Unit head:* Dr. Charles Barrilleaux, Director of Graduate Studies, 850-644-7643, Fax: 850-644-1367, E-mail: cbarrile@fsu.edu. *Application contact:* Jerry Fisher, Academic Coordinator, 850-644-7305, Fax: 850-644-1367, E-mail: jfisher@admin.fsu.edu.

Fordham University, Graduate School of Arts and Sciences, Department of Political Science, New York, NY 10458. Offers elections and campaign management (MA). Part-time and evening/weekend programs available. *Faculty:* 18 full-time (2 women). *Students:* 5 full-time (0 women), 5 part-time (3 women); includes 1 minority (Hispanic American), 3 international. Average age 30. 33 applicants, 76% accepted, 5 enrolled. In 2009, 8 master's awarded. *Degree requirements:* For master's, comprehensive exam. *Entrance requirements:* For master's, GRE General Test. Additional exam requirements/recommendations for international students: Required—TOEFL (minimum score 600 paper-based; 250 computer-based). *Application deadline:* For fall admission, 1/4 priority date for domestic students; for spring admission, 11/1 for domestic students. Application fee: $70. Electronic applications accepted. *Financial support:* In 2009–10, 5 students received support, including 5 research assistantships with tuition reimbursements available (averaging $14,720 per year); institutionally sponsored loans, tuition waivers (full and partial), and unspecified assistantships also available. Financial award application deadline: 1/4; financial award applicants required to submit FAFSA. *Faculty research:* Protest in emerging democracies, impact of religion on presidential elections, increasing partisan polarization in U.S. politics, comparative urban development, democracy vs. authoritarianism in the Middle East, election and campaign management. *Unit head:* Dr. Bruce Berg, Chair, 718-817-3950, Fax: 718-817-3972, E-mail: berg@fordham.edu. *Application contact:* Charlene Dundie, Director of Graduate Admissions, 718-817-4420, Fax: 718-817-3566, E-mail: dundie@fordham.edu.

Fordham University, Graduate School of Arts and Sciences, Program in International Political Economy and Development, Program in Elections and Campaign Management, New York, NY 10458. Offers MA. *Students:* 9 full-time (3 women), 22 part-time (7 women); includes 7 minority (3 African Americans, 4 Hispanic Americans), 2 international. 37 applicants, 86% accepted, 14 enrolled. In 2009, 13 master's awarded. Application fee: $70. *Unit head:* Dr. Costas Panagopoulos, Director, 718-817-3967. *Application contact:* Charlene Dundie, Director of Graduate Admissions, 718-817-4420, Fax: 718-817-3566, E-mail: dundie@fordham.edu.

George Mason University, College of Humanities and Social Sciences, Department of Public and International Affairs, Fairfax, VA 22030. Offers association management (Certificate); biodefense (MS, PhD); critical analysis and strategic responses to terrorism (Certificate); nonprofit management (Certificate); political science (MA, PhD); public administration (MPA); public management (Certificate). *Accreditation:* NASPAA (one or more programs are accredited). *Faculty:* 37 full-time (14 women), 34 part-time/adjunct (7 women). *Students:* 115 full-time (62 women), 323 part-time (182 women); includes 60 minority (29 African Americans, 1 American Indian/Alaska Native, 18 Asian Americans or Pacific Islanders, 12 Hispanic Americans), 21 international. Average age 31. 458 applicants, 60% accepted, 129 enrolled. In 2009, 147 master's, 2 doctorates, 6 other advanced degrees awarded. *Entrance requirements:* For master's, GRE General Test, minimum GPA of 3.0 in last 60 hours of course work. Additional exam requirements/recommendations for international students: Required—TOEFL. *Application deadline:* For fall admission, 3/1 priority date for domestic students; for spring admission, 10/15 for domestic students. Application fee: $75. Electronic applications accepted. *Expenses:* Tuition, state resident: full-time $7568; part-time $315.33 per credit hour. Tuition, nonresident: full-time $21,704; part-time $904.33 per credit hour. Required fees: $2184; $91 per credit hour. *Financial support:* In 2009–10, 27 students received support, including 3 fellowships with full tuition reimbursements available (averaging $18,000 per year), 10 research assistantships with full and partial tuition reimbursements available (averaging $11,033 per year), 14 teaching assistantships with full and partial tuition reimbursements available (averaging $9,213 per year); Federal Work-Study, scholarships/grants, unspecified assistantships, and health care benefits (full-time research or teaching assistantship recipients) also available. Support available to part-time students. Financial award application deadline: 3/1; financial award applicants required to submit FAFSA. *Faculty research:* The Rehnquist Court and economic liberties; intersection of economic development with high-tech industry, telecommunications, and entrepreneurism; political economy of development; violence, terrorism and U.S. foreign policy; international security issues. Total annual research expenditures: $429,868. *Unit head:* Dr. Robert Dudley, Chair, 703-993-1400, Fax: 703-993-1399, E-mail: rdudley@gmu.edu. *Application contact:* Peg Koback, Information Contact, 703-993-9466, E-mail: mkoback@gmu.edu.

Georgetown University, Graduate School of Arts and Sciences, Department of Government, Program in Democracy and Governance, Washington, DC 20057. Offers MA.

Georgetown University, Graduate School of Arts and Sciences, School of Continuing Studies, Washington, DC 20057. Offers American studies (MALS); Catholic studies (MALS); classical civilizations (MALS); ethics and the professions (MALS); human resources management (MPS); humanities (MALS); individualized study (MALS); international affairs (MALS); Islam and Muslim-Christian relations (MALS); journalism (MPS); liberal studies (DLS); literature and society (MALS); medieval and early modern European studies (MALS); public relations (MPS); real estate (MPS); religious studies (MALS); social and public policy (MALS); sports industry management (MPS); the theory and practice of American democracy (MALS); visual culture (MALS). *Entrance requirements:* Additional exam requirements/recommendations for international students: Required—TOEFL.

The George Washington University, College of Professional Studies, Graduate School of Political Management, Program in Legislative Affairs, Washington, DC 20052. Offers MA. Part-time and evening/weekend programs available. *Students:* 33 full-time (11 women), 55 part-time (30 women); includes 21 minority (9 African Americans, 3 American Indian/Alaska Native, 3 Asian Americans or Pacific Islanders, 6 Hispanic Americans). Average age 31. 67 applicants, 94% accepted, 52 enrolled. In 2009, 27 master's awarded. *Degree requirements:* For master's, comprehensive exam. *Entrance requirements:* For master's, GRE General Test, minimum GPA of 3.0. Additional exam requirements/recommendations for international students: Required—TOEFL (minimum score 550 paper-based; 213 computer-based). *Application deadline:* For fall admission, 4/1 priority date for domestic and international students; for spring admission, 10/1 priority date for domestic and international students. Applications are processed on a rolling basis. Application fee: $60. Electronic applications accepted. *Financial support:* Application deadline: 2/1. *Unit head:* Dr. Steven E. Billet, Director, 202-994-6000, E-mail: sbillet@gwu.edu. *Application contact:* Information Contact, 202-994-6000, Fax: 202-994-6006, E-mail: gspmmail@gwu.edu.

The George Washington University, Columbian College of Arts and Sciences, Department of Political Science, Washington, DC 20052. Offers MA, PhD. Part-time and evening/weekend programs available. *Faculty:* 28 full-time (8 women). *Students:* 41 full-time (18 women), 43 part-time (16 women); includes 9 minority (8 Asian Americans or Pacific Islanders, 1 Hispanic American), 17 international. Average age 30. 368 applicants, 27% accepted, 20 enrolled. In 2009, 6 master's, 6 doctorates awarded. Terminal master's awarded for partial completion of doctoral program. *Degree requirements:* For master's, one foreign language, comprehensive exam, thesis or alternative; for doctorate, 2 foreign languages, thesis/dissertation, general exam. *Entrance requirements:* For master's and doctorate, GRE General Test, minimum GPA of 3.0. Additional exam requirements/recommendations for international students: Required—TOEFL (minimum score 550 paper-based; 213 computer-based; 80 iBT). *Application deadline:* For fall admission, 1/15 priority date for domestic students; for spring admission, 10/1 priority date for domestic students. Applications are processed on a rolling basis. Application fee: $60. Electronic applications accepted. *Financial support:* In 2009–10, 43 students received support; fellowships with tuition reimbursements available, teaching assistantships with tuition reimbursements available, Federal Work-Study and tuition waivers available. *Unit head:* Christopher J. Deering, Chair, 202-994-6564, E-mail: rocket@gwu.edu. *Application contact:* Christopher J. Deering, Chair, 202-994-6564, E-mail: rocket@gwu.edu.

The George Washington University, Elliott School of International Affairs, Program in Security Policy Studies, Washington, DC 20052. Offers MA, JD/MA. Part-time and evening/weekend programs available. *Students:* 63 full-time (24 women), 63 part-time (22 women); includes 18 minority (1 African American, 15 Asian Americans or Pacific Islanders, 2 Hispanic Americans), 5 international. Average age 27. 252 applicants, 49% accepted, 42 enrolled. In 2009, 50 master's awarded. *Degree requirements:* For master's, one foreign language, capstone project. *Entrance requirements:* For master's, GRE General Test, 2 semesters of introductory economics, 2 years of a modern foreign language or 1 semester of statistics. Additional exam requirements/recommendations for international students: Required—TOEFL. *Application deadline:* For fall admission, 2/1 for domestic students; for spring admission, 10/1 for domestic students. Application fee: $60. Electronic applications accepted. *Financial support:* In 2009–10, 22 students received support; fellowships with tuition reimbursements available, research assistantships with tuition reimbursements available, career-related internships or fieldwork, Federal Work-Study, institutionally sponsored loans, and tuition waivers (full) available. Financial award application deadline: 1/15; financial award applicants required to submit FAFSA. *Faculty research:* U. S. arms transfer policies, military balance in the Third World, U. S. foreign policy, technology and security policy. *Unit head:* Joanna Spear, Director, 202-994-1088, E-mail: jspear@gwu.edu. *Application contact:* Jeff V. Miles, Director of Graduate Admissions, 202-994-7050, Fax: 202-994-9537, E-mail: esiagrad@gwu.edu.

Georgia State University, College of Arts and Sciences, Department of Political Science, Atlanta, GA 30302-3083. Offers MA, PhD. Part-time and evening/weekend programs available. Terminal master's awarded for partial completion of doctoral program. *Degree requirements:* For master's, thesis or alternative, exam; for doctorate, one foreign language, thesis/dissertation, exam. *Entrance requirements:* For master's, GRE General Test, 2 letters of recommendation; for doctorate, GRE General Test, 3 letters of recommendation, writing sample. Additional exam requirements/recommendations for international students: Required—TOEFL. Electronic applications accepted. *Faculty research:* International politics, American politics, comparative politics, public administration, international political economy.

Governors State University, College of Arts and Sciences, Program in Political and Justice Studies, University Park, IL 60466-0975. Offers MA. Part-time and evening/weekend programs available. *Degree requirements:* For master's, thesis or alternative. *Entrance requirements:* For master's, bachelor's degree in related field.

Graduate School and University Center of the City University of New York, Graduate Studies, Program in Political Science, New York, NY 10016-4039. Offers MA, PhD. *Faculty:* 56 full-time (10 women). *Students:* 129 full-time (60 women), 28 part-time (15 women); includes 19 minority (6 African Americans, 1 American Indian/Alaska Native, 3 Asian Americans or Pacific Islanders, 9 Hispanic Americans), 31 international. Average age 34. 214 applicants, 29% accepted, 30 enrolled. In 2009, 14 master's, 11 doctorates awarded. Terminal master's awarded for partial completion of doctoral program. *Degree requirements:* For master's, one foreign language, thesis; for doctorate, one foreign language, thesis/dissertation. *Entrance requirements:* For master's and doctorate, GRE General Test. Additional exam requirements/recommendations for international students: Required—TOEFL. *Application deadline:* For fall admission, 2/1 for domestic students. Application fee: $125. Electronic applications accepted. *Financial support:* In 2009–10, 90 students received support, including 82 fellowships, 6 research assistantships, 7 teaching assistantships; career-related internships or fieldwork, Federal Work-Study, institutionally sponsored loans, and tuition waivers (full and partial) also available. Financial award application deadline: 2/1; financial award applicants required to submit FAFSA. *Unit head:* Dr. Joan Tronto, Executive Officer, 212-817-8671, Fax: 212-817-1532. *Application contact:* Les Gribben, Director of Admissions, 212-817-7470, Fax: 212-817-1624, E-mail: lgribben@gc.cuny.edu.

Grambling State University, School of Graduate Studies and Research, College of Arts and Sciences, Program in Public Administration, Grambling, LA 71270. Offers health service administration (MPA); human resource management (MPA); public management (MPA); state and local government (MPA). *Accreditation:* NASPAA. Part-time programs available. *Faculty:* 5 full-time (2 women), 2 part-time/adjunct (0 women). *Students:* 25 full-time (16 women), 14 part-time (12 women); includes 32 minority (all African Americans), 5 international. Average age 29. 30 applicants, 53% accepted, 11 enrolled. In 2009, 12 master's awarded. *Degree requirements:* For master's, comprehensive exam (for some programs), thesis optional. *Entrance requirements:* For master's, GRE, minimum GPA of 2.75 on last degree. Additional exam requirements/recommendations for international students: Required—TOEFL (minimum score 500 paper-based; 173 computer-based; 61 iBT). *Application deadline:* For fall admission, 7/1 for domestic and international students; for spring admission, 12/1 for domestic and international students. Applications are processed on a rolling basis. Application fee: $20 ($30 for international students). Electronic applications accepted. *Expenses:* Tuition, state resident: full-time $2610. Tuition, nonresident: full-time $2610. *Financial support:* In 2009–10, 6 research assistantships (averaging $5,958 per year) were awarded; health care benefits, tuition waivers (full), and unspecified assistantships also available. Financial award application deadline: 5/31. *Unit head:* Dr. Rose Harris, Director, 318-274-2310, Fax: 318-274-3427, E-mail: harrisr@gram.edu. *Application contact:* Sarah Dennis, Admissions Coordinator, 318-274-2319, Fax: 318-274-3427, E-mail: denniss@alpha0.gram.edu.

Harvard University, Graduate School of Arts and Sciences, Committee on Political Economy and Government, Cambridge, MA 02138. Offers PhD. *Entrance requirements:* For doctorate, GRE General Test or GMAT. Additional exam requirements/recommendations for international students: Required—TOEFL. *Expenses:* Tuition: Full-time $33,696. Required fees: $1126. Full-time tuition and fees vary according to program.

Political Science

Harvard University, Graduate School of Arts and Sciences, Department of Government, Cambridge, MA 02138. Offers political science (PhD), including American politics, comparative politics, international relations, political thought, quantitative methods. *Degree requirements:* For doctorate, one foreign language, thesis/dissertation, general exams. *Entrance requirements:* For doctorate, GRE General Test. Additional exam requirements/recommendations for international students: Required—TOEFL. *Expenses:* Tuition: Full-time $33,696. Required fees: $1126. Full-time tuition and fees vary according to program.

Harvard University, John F. Kennedy School of Government, Cambridge, MA 02138. Offers MPA, MPAID, MPP, MPPUP, PhD, JD/MPAID, MBA/MPAID, MD/MPAID, JD/MPP, MBA/MPP, MD/MPP. *Accreditation:* NASPAA. *Students:* 907 full-time (375 women), 62 part-time (25 women); includes 195 minority (46 African Americans, 12 American Indian/Alaska Native, 85 Asian Americans or Pacific Islanders, 52 Hispanic Americans), 381 international. Average age 31. 2,953 applicants, 32% accepted, 613 enrolled. In 2009, 508 master's awarded. *Degree requirements:* For doctorate, thesis/dissertation. *Entrance requirements:* For master's, GMAT or GRE General Test; for doctorate, GRE General Test. Additional exam requirements/recommendations for international students: Required—TOEFL (minimum score 600 paper-based; 250 computer-based; 100 iBT), TWE. Application fee: $80. Electronic applications accepted. *Expenses:* Tuition: Full-time $33,696. Required fees: $1126. Full-time tuition and fees vary according to program. *Financial support:* Fellowships, research assistantships, teaching assistantships, career-related internships or fieldwork, Federal Work-Study, institutionally sponsored loans, scholarships/grants, and unspecified assistantships available. Support available to part-time students. Financial award applicants required to submit CSS PROFILE or FAFSA. *Unit head:* Dr. David Ellwood, Dean, 617-495-1122. *Application contact:* 617-495-1155, Fax: 617-496-1165, E-mail: hks_admissions@harvard.edu.

Howard University, Graduate School, Department of Political Science, Program in Political Science, Washington, DC 20059-0002. Offers MA, PhD. *Degree requirements:* For master's, comprehensive exam. *Entrance requirements:* For master's, GRE General Test, minimum GPA of 3.0; for doctorate, GRE General Test, minimum GPA of 2.8.

Hult International Business School, Program in International Relations—Hult London Campus, London, MA WC 1B 4JP, United Kingdom. Offers conflict resolution (MA); diplomacy (MA); international public law (MA); international relations (MA); Middle East international security (MA); politics (MA); security studies (MA); terrorism (MA); U.S. foreign policy (MA). Part-time programs available. *Entrance requirements:* Additional exam requirements/recommendations for international students: Required—TOEFL (minimum score 580 paper-based; 237 computer-based), TWE (minimum score 5). Electronic applications accepted. *Faculty research:* American foreign politics, Middle East, security studies.

Idaho State University, Office of Graduate Studies, College of Arts and Sciences, Department of Political Science, Pocatello, ID 83209-8073. Offers political science (MA, DA); public administration (MPA). Part-time programs available. *Faculty:* 7 full-time (1 woman). *Students:* 36 full-time (15 women), 27 part-time (13 women); includes 2 minority (1 African American, 1 Asian American or Pacific Islander). Average age 36. In 2009, 9 master's, 2 doctorates awarded. *Degree requirements:* For master's, comprehensive exam, thesis optional; for doctorate, comprehensive exam, thesis/dissertation, teaching internship. *Entrance requirements:* For master's, GRE General Test, minimum GPA of 3.0 in last 2 years of undergraduate study, 3 letters of recommendation; for doctorate, GRE General Test, major field of American politics, minimum GPA of 3.0 in last 2 years of undergraduate study, 3 letters of recommendation. Additional exam requirements/recommendations for international students: Required—TOEFL (minimum score 550 paper-based; 213 computer-based; 80 iBT). *Application deadline:* For fall admission, 7/1 for domestic students, 6/1 for international students; for spring admission, 12/1 for domestic students, 11/1 for international students. Applications are processed on a rolling basis. Application fee: $55. Electronic applications accepted. *Expenses:* Tuition, state resident: full-time $3318; part-time $297 per credit hour. Tuition, nonresident: full-time $13,120; part-time $437 per credit hour. Required fees: $2530. Tuition and fees vary according to program. *Financial support:* In 2009–10, 9 teaching assistantships with full and partial tuition reimbursements (averaging $10,841 per year) were awarded; fellowships with full and partial tuition reimbursements, career-related internships or fieldwork, Federal Work-Study, institutionally sponsored loans, scholarships/grants, health care benefits, tuition waivers (full and partial), and unspecified assistantships also available. Support available to part-time students. Financial award application deadline: 1/1; financial award applicants required to submit FAFSA. *Faculty research:* International affairs, environmental policy, decision making, Constitution, executive/legislative relations. *Unit head:* Dr. Wayne Gabardi, Chairman, 208-282-4536, Fax: 208-282-4833, E-mail: gabawayn@isu.edu. *Application contact:* Tami Carson, Graduate School Technical Records Specialist, 208-282-2150, Fax: 208-282-4847, E-mail: carstami@isu.edu.

Illinois State University, Graduate School, College of Arts and Sciences, Department of Politics and Government, Normal, IL 61790-2200. Offers MA, MS. *Degree requirements:* For master's, thesis or alternative. *Entrance requirements:* For master's, GRE General Test, minimum GPA of 3.0 in last 60 hours of course work, 15 hours of course work in political science. *Faculty research:* Political tolerance in a democracy under external threats: a survey of public opinion.

Indiana State University, School of Graduate Studies, College of Arts and Sciences, Department of Political Science, Terre Haute, IN 47809. Offers political science (MA, MS); public administration (MPA). *Degree requirements:* For master's, thesis (for some programs). *Entrance requirements:* For master's, GRE or minimum undergraduate GPA of 2.75, 18 semester hours of course work in political science. Additional exam requirements/recommendations for international students: Required—TOEFL (minimum score 550 paper-based). Electronic applications accepted.

Indiana University Bloomington, University Graduate School, College of Arts and Sciences, Department of Political Science, Bloomington, IN 47405-7000. Offers MA, PhD. *Faculty:* 26 full-time (9 women). *Students:* 90 full-time (35 women), 1 part-time (0 women); includes 9 minority (4 African Americans, 5 Asian Americans or Pacific Islanders), 18 international. Average age 31. 138 applicants, 20% accepted, 11 enrolled. In 2009, 6 master's, 6 doctorates awarded. Terminal master's awarded for partial completion of doctoral program. *Degree requirements:* For master's, thesis, 30 credit hours; for doctorate, comprehensive exam, thesis/dissertation. *Entrance requirements:* For master's, GRE, personal statement, transcripts, 3 letters of recommendation; for doctorate, GRE, sample of written work, 3 letters of recommendation. Additional exam requirements/recommendations for international students: Required—TOEFL (minimum score 640 paper-based; 273 computer-based; 112 iBT). *Application deadline:* For fall admission, 1/15 for domestic students, 12/1 for international students. Application fee: $55 ($65 for international students). Electronic applications accepted. *Financial support:* In 2009–10, 56 students received support, including 10 fellowships with full tuition reimbursements available (averaging $16,000 per year), 6 research assistantships with full tuition reimbursements available (averaging $15,542 per year), 13 teaching assistantships with full tuition reimbursements available (averaging $15,542 per year); Federal Work-Study, institutionally sponsored loans, scholarships/grants, health care benefits, and unspecified assistantships also available. Financial award application deadline: 2/26. *Faculty research:* American politics, international relations, public policy, political theory, comparative politics, theory and methodology. Total annual research expenditures: $291,773. *Unit head:* Russell Hanson, Chair, 812-855-1209, Fax: 812-855-2027, E-mail: hansonr@indiana.edu. *Application contact:* Sharon LaRoche, Graduate Secretary, 812-855-1208, Fax: 812-855-2027, E-mail: laroches@indiana.edu.

Indiana University of Pennsylvania, School of Graduate Studies and Research, College of Humanities and Social Sciences, Department of Political Science, Indiana, PA 15705-1087. Offers public affairs (MA). Part-time programs available. *Faculty:* 5 full-time (3 women). *Students:* 8 full-time (1 woman), 3 part-time (2 women), 5 international. Average age 34. 15 applicants, 47% accepted, 4 enrolled. In 2009, 5 master's awarded. *Degree requirements:* For master's, thesis optional. *Entrance requirements:* For master's, GRE, 2 letters of recommendation. Additional exam requirements/recommendations for international students: Required—TOEFL. *Application deadline:* For fall admission, 7/1 priority date for domestic students; for spring admission, 11/1 for domestic students. Applications are processed on a rolling basis. Application fee: $40. *Expenses:* Tuition, state resident: full-time $6666; part-time $370 per credit hour. Tuition, nonresident: full-time $10,666; part-time $593 per credit hour. Required fees: $813 per semester. *Financial support:* In 2009–10, 8 research assistantships with full and partial tuition reimbursements (averaging $3,400 per year) were awarded; Federal Work-Study also available. Support available to part-time students. Financial award application deadline: 3/15; financial award applicants required to submit FAFSA. *Unit head:* Dr. Steven Jackson, Chairperson, 724-357-2776, E-mail: sjackson@iup.edu. *Application contact:* Dr. David Chambers, Graduate Coordinator, 724-357-2776, E-mail: chambers@iup.edu.

Indiana University–Purdue University Indianapolis, School of Liberal Arts, Department of Political Science, Indianapolis, IN 46202-2896. Offers MA, Certificate. *Students:* 4 full-time (1 woman), 7 part-time (5 women); includes 3 minority (2 African Americans, 1 Hispanic American). Average age 28. 11 applicants, 55% accepted, 5 enrolled. *Unit head:* John McCormick, Chair, 317-274-7387. *Application contact:* Director of Research and Graduate Programs, 317-274-8305.

Institute for Christian Studies, Graduate Programs, Toronto, ON M5T 1R4, Canada. Offers education (M Phil F, PhD); history of philosophy (M Phil F, PhD); philosophical aesthetics (M Phil F, PhD); philosophy of religion (M Phil F, PhD); political theory (M Phil F, PhD); systematic philosophy (M Phil F, PhD); theology (M Phil F, PhD); worldview studies (MWS). Part-time programs available. Postbaccalaureate distance learning degree programs offered (minimal on-campus study). *Degree requirements:* For master's, one foreign language, thesis; for doctorate, 2 foreign languages, thesis/dissertation. *Entrance requirements:* For master's and doctorate, philosophy background. Additional exam requirements/recommendations for international students: Required—TOEFL (minimum score 600 paper-based; 250 computer-based). *Faculty research:* Human rights, anthropology of self, medieval discourse, gender and body, post-modern thought; biblical hermeneutics, creational aesthetics, ecumenism, epistemology, political theory and public policy, relational psychotherapy.

The Institute of World Politics, Graduate Programs in National Security, Intelligence, and International Affairs, Washington, DC 20036. Offers American foreign policy (Certificate); comparative political culture (Certificate); counterintelligence (Certificate); democracy building (Certificate); intelligence (Certificate); international politics (Certificate); national security affairs (Certificate); public diplomacy and political warfare (Certificate); statecraft and national security affairs (MA); statecraft and world politics (MA); strategic intelligence studies (MA). Part-time and evening/weekend programs available. *Degree requirements:* For master's, comprehensive exam, thesis optional. *Entrance requirements:* For master's, GRE General Test. Additional exam requirements/recommendations for international students: Required—TOEFL. Electronic applications accepted. *Faculty research:* Intelligence, national security, statecraft.

Iowa State University of Science and Technology, Graduate College, College of Liberal Arts and Sciences, Department of Political Science, Ames, IA 50011. Offers political science (MA); public administration (MPA); JD/MA. *Accreditation:* NASPAA. *Faculty:* 12 full-time (3 women), 5 part-time/adjunct (3 women). *Students:* 32 full-time (16 women), 40 part-time (17 women); includes 4 minority (all Asian Americans or Pacific Islanders), 11 international. 38 applicants, 79% accepted, 20 enrolled. In 2009, 15 master's awarded. *Degree requirements:* For master's, thesis (for some programs). *Entrance requirements:* For master's, GRE General Test, GMAT or LSAT. Additional exam requirements/recommendations for international students: Required—TOEFL (minimum score 570 paper-based; 80 iBT) or IELTS (minimum score 6.5). *Application deadline:* For fall admission, 1/1 priority date for domestic and international students; for spring admission, 10/1 for domestic and international students. Applications are processed on a rolling basis. Application fee: $40 ($90 for international students). Electronic applications accepted. *Expenses:* Tuition, state resident: full-time $6716. Tuition, nonresident: full-time $8908. Tuition and fees vary according to course level, course load, program and student level. *Financial support:* In 2009–10, 17 research assistantships with full and partial tuition reimbursements (averaging $13,500 per year), 2 teaching assistantships with full and partial tuition reimbursements (averaging $13,990 per year) were awarded; fellowships, scholarships/grants, health care benefits, and unspecified assistantships also available. *Unit head:* Dr. James M. McCormick, Chair, 515-294-8682, Fax: 515-294-1003, E-mail: polsc@iastate.edu. *Application contact:* Dr. Mack Shelley, Director of Graduate Education, 515-294-1075, E-mail: polsci@iastate.edu.

Jackson State University, Graduate School, School of Liberal Arts, Department of Political Science, Jackson, MS 39217. Offers MA. Part-time and evening/weekend programs available. *Degree requirements:* For master's, comprehensive exam, thesis or alternative. *Entrance requirements:* For master's, GRE General Test. Additional exam requirements/recommendations for international students: Required—TOEFL.

Jacksonville State University, College of Graduate Studies and Continuing Education, College of Arts and Sciences, Department of Political Science, Jacksonville, AL 36265-1602. Offers MPA. Part-time and evening/weekend programs available. *Degree requirements:* For master's, comprehensive exam, thesis (for some programs). *Entrance requirements:* For master's, GRE General Test or MAT. Electronic applications accepted.

James Madison University, The Graduate School, College of Arts and Letters, Department of Political Science, Program in Political Science, Harrisonburg, VA 22807. Offers MA. Part-time programs available. *Students:* 17 full-time (11 women); includes 1 minority (Asian American or Pacific Islander). Average age 27. *Entrance requirements:* For master's, GRE General Test, GRE Writing Test, 2 letters of recommendation; resume; goals, language proficiency and policy interest statements. Additional exam requirements/recommendations for international students: Required—TOEFL. *Application deadline:* For fall admission, 5/1 priority date for domestic students; for spring admission, 9/1 priority date for domestic students. Applications are processed on a rolling basis. Application fee: $55. Electronic applications accepted. *Expenses:* Tuition, area resident: Part-time $305 per credit hour. Tuition, state resident: part-time $305 per credit hour. Tuition, nonresident: part-time $890 per credit hour. *Financial support:* Application deadline: 3/1. *Unit head:* Dr. Jessica Adolino, Academic Unit Head, 540-568-6149, E-mail: adolinjr@jmu.edu. *Application contact:* Dr. B. Douglas Skelley, Graduate Coordinator, 540-568-6149.

The Johns Hopkins University, Zanvyl Krieger School of Arts and Sciences, Advanced Academic Programs, Program in Government, Baltimore, MD 21218-2699. Offers government (MA); national securities study (Certificate); MA/MBA. Part-time and evening/weekend programs available. *Faculty:* 4 full-time (2 women), 35 part-time/adjunct (5 women). *Students:* 206 full-time (94 women), 240 part-time (103 women); includes 96 minority (39 African Americans, 3 American Indian/Alaska Native, 21 Asian Americans or Pacific Islanders, 33 Hispanic Americans), 13 international. Average age 29. 144 applicants, 73% accepted, 92 enrolled. In 2009, 85 master's awarded. *Degree requirements:* For master's, thesis. *Entrance requirements:* For master's, minimum GPA of 3.0. Additional exam requirements/recommendations for international students: Required—TOEFL (minimum score 250 computer-based; 100 iBT). *Application deadline:* For fall admission, 5/31 priority date for domestic students, 4/30 priority date for international students; for spring admission, 10/31 priority date for domestic and international students. Applications are processed on a rolling basis. Application fee: $75. Electronic applications accepted. *Financial support:* Applicants required to submit FAFSA. *Unit head:* Dr. Kathy Wagner, Associate Program Chair, 202-452-1953, E-mail: kwagner@jhu.edu. *Application contact:* Valana M. McMickens, Admissions Manager, 202-452-1941, Fax: 202-452-1970, E-mail: aapadmissions@jhu.edu.

The Johns Hopkins University, Zanvyl Krieger School of Arts and Sciences, Department of Political Science, Baltimore, MD 21218-2699. Offers MA, PhD. *Faculty:* 20 full-time (6 women), 3 part-time/adjunct (0 women). *Students:* 60 full-time (28 women); includes 8 minority (1 African American, 1 American Indian/Alaska Native, 6 Asian Americans or Pacific Islanders),

20 international. Average age 29. 201 applicants, 11% accepted, 22 enrolled. In 2009, 3 master's, 3 doctorates awarded. *Degree requirements:* For doctorate, one foreign language, comprehensive exam, thesis/dissertation. *Entrance requirements:* For doctorate, GRE General Test. Additional exam requirements/recommendations for international students: Required—TOEFL (minimum score 600 paper-based; 250 computer-based; 100 iBT), IELTS. *Application deadline:* For fall admission, 1/15 for domestic and international students. Application fee: $75. Electronic applications accepted. *Financial support:* In 2009–10, 54 students received support, including 23 fellowships with full tuition reimbursements available (averaging $17,000 per year), 31 teaching assistantships with full tuition reimbursements available (averaging $17,000 per year); research assistantships with full tuition reimbursements available, Federal Work-Study and institutionally sponsored loans also available. Financial award application deadline: 4/15; financial award applicants required to submit FAFSA. *Faculty research:* American politics, comparative politics, international relations, political theory, urban politics. Total annual research expenditures: $104,641. *Unit head:* Dr. Richard Katz, Chair, 410-516-7534, Fax: 410-516-5515, E-mail: richard.katz@jhu.edu. *Application contact:* Barbara Hall, Academic Program Coordinator, 410-516-7540, Fax: 410-516-5515, E-mail: bhall@jhu.edu.

Kansas State University, Graduate School, College of Arts and Sciences, Department of Political Science, Manhattan, KS 66506. Offers political science (MA), including international service, political science; public administration (MPA). Part-time programs available. *Faculty:* 16 full-time (4 women). *Students:* 41 full-time (18 women), 6 part-time (3 women); includes 6 minority (3 American Indian/Alaska Native, 3 Asian Americans or Pacific Islanders), 6 international. Average age 28. 37 applicants, 81% accepted, 30 enrolled. In 2009, 19 master's awarded. *Degree requirements:* For master's, thesis or alternative. *Entrance requirements:* For master's, GRE (recommended), minimum GPA of 3.0. Additional exam requirements/recommendations for international students: Required—TOEFL (minimum score 550 paper-based; 213 computer-based). *Application deadline:* For fall admission, 2/1 priority date for domestic and international students; for spring admission, 8/1 priority date for domestic and international students. Applications are processed on a rolling basis. Application fee: $40 ($55 for international students). Electronic applications accepted. *Financial support:* In 2009–10, 3 research assistantships (averaging $20,126 per year), 9 teaching assistantships with tuition reimbursements (averaging $10,500 per year) were awarded; fellowships, career-related internships or fieldwork, Federal Work-Study, institutionally sponsored loans, and scholarships/grants also available. Support available to part-time students. Financial award application deadline: 3/1; financial award applicants required to submit FAFSA. *Faculty research:* Armed conflict, civil military relations, comparative public administration and policy, electoral competition, legislative studies. Total annual research expenditures: $30,909. *Unit head:* Jeff Pickering, Head, 785-532-0454, Fax: 785-532-2339, E-mail: jjp@ksu.edu. *Application contact:* James Franke, Director, 785-532-0451, Fax: 785-532-2339, E-mail: jfranke@ksu.edu.

Kaplan University, Davenport Campus, School of Legal Studies, Davenport, IA 52807-2095. Offers health care delivery (MS); pathway to paralegal (Postbaccalaureate Certificate); state and local government (MS). Part-time and evening/weekend programs available. Postbaccalaureate distance learning degree programs offered (no on-campus study). *Entrance requirements:* Additional exam requirements/recommendations for international students: Required—TOEFL (minimum score 550 paper-based; 218 computer-based; 80 iBT).

Kean University, College of Humanities and Social Sciences, Program in Political Science, Union, NJ 07083. Offers MA. Part-time and evening/weekend programs available. *Faculty:* 10 full-time (1 woman). *Students:* 2 full-time (1 woman), 8 part-time (2 women); includes 5 minority (1 African American, 1 Asian American or Pacific Islander, 3 Hispanic Americans). Average age 30. 4 applicants, 75% accepted, 0 enrolled. In 2009, 8 master's awarded. *Degree requirements:* For master's, comprehensive exam, thesis. *Entrance requirements:* For master's, GRE General Test, minimum GPA of 3.0, 3 letters of recommendation. *Application deadline:* For fall admission, 5/1 for domestic students; for spring admission, 11/1 for domestic students. Application fee: $60 ($150 for international students). Electronic applications accepted. *Expenses:* Tuition, state resident: full-time $10,440; part-time $435 per credit. Tuition, nonresident: full-time $14,160; part-time $590 per credit. Required fees: $2642; $110 per credit. Part-time tuition and fees vary according to course load and degree level. *Financial support:* In 2009–10, 1 research assistantship with full tuition reimbursement (averaging $3,263 per year) was awarded; unspecified assistantships also available. *Unit head:* Dr. Larry Chang, Program Coordinator, 908-737-3998, E-mail: lchang@kean.edu. *Application contact:* Steven Koch, Pre-Admissions Coordinator, 908-737-5924, Fax: 908-737-5965, E-mail: skoch@kean.edu.

Kent State University, College of Arts and Sciences, Department of Political Science, Kent, OH 44242-0001. Offers political science (MA); public administration (MPA); public policy (PhD). Part-time programs available. Postbaccalaureate distance learning degree programs offered. *Degree requirements:* For master's, thesis optional; for doctorate, 2 foreign languages, thesis/dissertation. *Entrance requirements:* For master's, GRE General Test, minimum GPA of 2.75; for doctorate, GRE General Test, minimum GPA of 3.0. Additional exam requirements/recommendations for international students: Required—TOEFL. Electronic applications accepted.

Lamar University, College of Graduate Studies, College of Arts and Sciences, Department of Political Science, Beaumont, TX 77710. Offers public administration (MPA). Part-time programs available. *Faculty:* 3 full-time (1 woman). *Students:* 8 full-time (3 women), 6 part-time (1 woman); includes 5 minority (2 African Americans, 1 Asian American or Pacific Islander, 2 Hispanic Americans), 1 international. Average age 26. 18 applicants, 56% accepted, 8 enrolled. In 2009, 4 master's awarded. *Entrance requirements:* For master's, GRE General Test. Additional exam requirements/recommendations for international students: Required—TOEFL. *Application deadline:* For fall admission, 8/1 for domestic students; for spring admission, 12/1 for domestic students. Applications are processed on a rolling basis. Application fee: $25 ($50 for international students). *Financial support:* Fellowships, research assistantships, teaching assistantships, career-related internships or fieldwork, Federal Work-Study, and institutionally sponsored loans available. Financial award application deadline: 4/1. *Faculty research:* Political activities of administrators, administrative response to Hurricane Rita, budgeting, environmental politics, urban planning. *Unit head:* Dr. Glenn Utter, Chair, 409-880-8526, Fax: 409-880-8710. *Application contact:* Dr. Terri Davis, Director, 409-880-8533, Fax: 409-880-1710, E-mail: davistb@hal.lamar.edu.

Lehigh University, College of Arts and Sciences, Department of Political Science, Bethlehem, PA 18015. Offers politics and policy (MA). Part-time programs available. *Faculty:* 11 full-time (6 women). *Students:* 13 full-time (8 women), 2 part-time (both women), 2 international. Average age 26. 22 applicants, 59% accepted, 8 enrolled. In 2009, 6 master's awarded. *Degree requirements:* For master's, comprehensive exam (for some programs), thesis optional. *Entrance requirements:* For master's, GRE General Test. Additional exam requirements/recommendations for international students: Required—TOEFL (minimum score 560 paper-based; 223 computer-based). *Application deadline:* For fall admission, 7/15 for domestic and international students; for spring admission, 12/1 for domestic and international students. Applications are processed on a rolling basis. Application fee: $65. Electronic applications accepted. *Financial support:* In 2009–10, 11 students received support, including 2 teaching assistantships with full tuition reimbursements available; fellowships, research assistantships, career-related internships or fieldwork and tuition waivers (partial) also available. Financial award application deadline: 1/15. *Faculty research:* American politics and institutions, comparative politics, public policy, policy analysis. *Unit head:* Dr. Richard K. Matthews, Chairman, 610-758-3340, Fax: 610-758-3348, E-mail: rm02@lehigh.edu. *Application contact:* Dr. Frank L. Davis, Director, Graduate Studies, 610-758-5987, Fax: 610-758-3348, E-mail: fld1@lehigh.edu.

Lincoln University, School of Graduate Studies and Continuing Education, Jefferson City, MO 65102. Offers business administration (MBA), including accounting, entrepreneurship, management, public administration and policy; educational leadership (Ed S), including elementary leadership, secondary leadership, superintendency; guidance and counseling (M Ed), including community/agency counseling, elementary school, secondary school; history (MA); school administration and supervision (M Ed), including elementary school administration, secondary school administration, special education administration; school teaching (M Ed), including elementary school teaching, secondary school teaching; social science (MA), including history, political science, sociology; sociology (MA); sociology/criminal justice (MA). Part-time and evening/weekend programs available. *Students:* 52 full-time (27 women), 146 part-time (107 women); includes 40 minority (39 African Americans, 1 Asian American or Pacific Islander), 15 international. Average age 35. 76 applicants, 95% accepted, 46 enrolled. In 2009, 60 master's, 6 other advanced degrees awarded. *Degree requirements:* For master's and Ed S, comprehensive exam, thesis optional. *Entrance requirements:* For master's and Ed S, GRE, MAT or GMAT, minimum GPA of 2.75 in major, 2.5 overall; 3 letters of recommendation; minimum C average in English composition; personal statement of purpose. Additional exam requirements/recommendations for international students: Required—TOEFL (minimum score 500 paper-based; 173 computer-based; 61 iBT). *Application deadline:* For fall admission, 7/1 priority date for domestic and international students; for spring admission, 12/1 priority date for domestic and international students. Applications are processed on a rolling basis. Application fee: $20. *Expenses:* Tuition, state resident: full-time $4185; part-time $232.50 per credit hour. Tuition, nonresident: full-time $7767; part-time $431.50 per credit hour. Required fees: $270; $15 per credit hour. $20 per term. *Financial support:* Federal Work-Study and scholarships/grants available. Financial award application deadline: 4/1; financial award applicants required to submit FAFSA. *Faculty research:* Suicide prevention. *Unit head:* Dr. Linda S. Bickel, Dean, 573-681-5247, Fax: 573-681-5106, E-mail: gradschool@lincolnu.edu. *Application contact:* Irasema Steck, Administrative Assistant, 573-681-5247, Fax: 573-681-5106, E-mail: gradschool@lincolnu.edu.

Long Island University, Brooklyn Campus, Richard L. Conolly College of Liberal Arts and Sciences, Department of Political Science, Brooklyn, NY 11201-8423. Offers MA. Part-time and evening/weekend programs available. *Degree requirements:* For master's, thesis or alternative. *Entrance requirements:* For master's, 2 letters of recommendation. Additional exam requirements/recommendations for international students: Required—TOEFL (minimum score 550 paper-based; 173 computer-based). Electronic applications accepted.

Long Island University, C.W. Post Campus, College of Liberal Arts and Sciences, Department of Political Science/International Studies, Brookville, NY 11548-1300. Offers MA. Part-time and evening/weekend programs available. *Degree requirements:* For master's, comprehensive exam, thesis or alternative. *Entrance requirements:* For master's, GRE. Electronic applications accepted. *Faculty research:* International relations, Middle Eastern politics, political philosophy.

Louisiana State University and Agricultural and Mechanical College, Graduate School, College of Arts and Sciences, Department of Political Science, Baton Rouge, LA 70803. Offers MA, PhD. *Faculty:* 25 full-time (6 women). *Students:* 49 full-time (19 women), 10 part-time (6 women); includes 7 minority (2 African Americans, 2 Asian Americans or Pacific Islanders, 3 Hispanic Americans), 7 international. Average age 29. 58 applicants, 64% accepted, 16 enrolled. In 2009, 10 master's, 4 doctorates awarded. Terminal master's awarded for partial completion of doctoral program. *Degree requirements:* For master's, thesis or alternative; for doctorate, one foreign language, thesis/dissertation. *Entrance requirements:* For master's and doctorate, GRE General Test, minimum GPA of 3.0. Additional exam requirements/recommendations for international students: Required—TOEFL (minimum score 550 paper-based; 213 computer-based; 79 iBT) or IELTS (minimum score 6.5). *Application deadline:* For fall admission, 2/15 priority date for domestic students, 5/15 for international students; for spring admission, 10/15 for domestic and international students. Application fee: $50 ($70 for international students). Electronic applications accepted. *Financial support:* In 2009–10, 45 students received support, including 4 fellowships with full and partial tuition reimbursements available (averaging $29,222 per year), 4 research assistantships with full and partial tuition reimbursements available (averaging $15,912 per year), 23 teaching assistantships with full and partial tuition reimbursements available (averaging $11,718 per year); Federal Work-Study, institutionally sponsored loans, health care benefits, tuition waivers (full), and unspecified assistantships also available. Financial award application deadline: 3/1; financial award applicants required to submit FAFSA. *Faculty research:* American government and policy, political theory, international relations and comparative politics. Total annual research expenditures: $187,925. *Unit head:* Dr. Greg Stoner, Chair, 225-578-2141, Fax: 225-578-2540. *Application contact:* Dr. Kathleen Bratton, Director of Graduate Studies, 225-578-1912, Fax: 225-578-2540, E-mail: bratton@lsu.edu.

Loyola University Chicago, Graduate School, Department of Political Science, Chicago, IL 60660. Offers MA, PhD. Part-time and evening/weekend programs available. *Faculty:* 18 full-time (2 women), 1 (woman) part-time/adjunct. *Students:* 29 full-time (14 women), 10 part-time (2 women); includes 2 minority (1 African American, 1 Hispanic American), 2 international. Average age 29. 87 applicants, 37% accepted, 13 enrolled. In 2009, 8 master's awarded. *Degree requirements:* For master's, thesis or alternative; for doctorate, variable foreign language requirement, comprehensive exam, thesis/dissertation. *Entrance requirements:* For master's and doctorate, GRE General Test. *Application deadline:* For fall admission, 6/1 for domestic students; for spring admission, 10/1 for domestic students. Applications are processed on a rolling basis. Application fee: $50. Electronic applications accepted. *Expenses:* Tuition: Full-time $14,220; part-time $790 per credit hour. Required fees: $60 per semester hour. Tuition and fees vary according to program. *Financial support:* In 2009–10, 5 fellowships with full tuition reimbursements (averaging $14,000 per year), 5 research assistantships with full tuition reimbursements (averaging $14,000 per year) were awarded; Federal Work-Study, institutionally sponsored loans, scholarships/grants, tuition waivers (partial), and unspecified assistantships also available. Financial award application deadline: 2/15; financial award applicants required to submit FAFSA. *Faculty research:* American parties and elections, state and local politics, American political institutions, international political economy, modern and contemporary political thought. *Unit head:* Prof. Peter M. Sanchez, Chair, 773-508-8658, Fax: 773-508-3131, E-mail: psanche@luc.edu. *Application contact:* Prof. Peter M. Sanchez, Chair, 773-508-8658, Fax: 773-508-3131, E-mail: psanche@luc.edu.

Marquette University, Graduate School, College of Arts and Sciences, Department of Political Science/International Affairs, Milwaukee, WI 53201-1881. Offers international affairs (MA), including comparative politics, international political economy, international politics; political science (MA), including American politics, comparative politics, international politics, political philosophy; JD/MA. Part-time programs available. *Faculty:* 15 full-time (3 women), 5 part-time/adjunct (3 women). *Students:* 18 full-time (11 women), 9 part-time (6 women), 5 international. Average age 26. 71 applicants, 51% accepted, 11 enrolled. In 2009, 14 master's awarded. *Degree requirements:* For master's, comprehensive exam, thesis optional. *Entrance requirements:* For master's, GRE General Test. Additional exam requirements/recommendations for international students: Required—TOEFL. Application fee: $40. *Financial support:* In 2009–10, 5 research assistantships were awarded; Federal Work-Study, institutionally sponsored loans, scholarships/grants, and tuition waivers (full and partial) also available. Support available to part-time students. Financial award application deadline: 2/15. *Faculty research:* Public opinion and electoral behavior, public policy analysis, Congress and the Presidency, judicial behavior, political system transitions. *Unit head:* Dr. Duane Swank, Chair, 414-288-3418, Fax: 414-288-3360. *Application contact:* Dr. Lowell Barrington, Director of Graduate Studies, 414-288-6842, Fax: 414-288-3360.

Marshall University, Academic Affairs Division, College of Liberal Arts, Department of Political Science, Huntington, WV 25755. Offers MA. *Faculty:* 7 full-time (3 women), 5 part-time/adjunct (2 women). *Students:* 13 full-time (5 women), 3 part-time (2 women); includes 1 minority (American Indian/Alaska Native), 1 international. Average age 25. In 2009, 4 master's awarded. *Degree requirements:* For master's, thesis optional. *Entrance requirements:* For master's, GRE General Test. Application fee: $40. *Unit head:* Dr. MaryBeth Beller, Chairperson, 304-696-2763, Fax: 304-696-3245, E-mail: beller@marshall.edu. *Application contact:* Graduate Admissions, 304-746-1900, Fax: 304-746-1902, E-mail: services@marshall.edu.

Massachusetts Institute of Technology, School of Humanities, Arts, and Social Sciences, Department of Political Science, Cambridge, MA 02139-4307. Offers SM, PhD. *Faculty:* 24

Political Science

Massachusetts Institute of Technology (continued)
full-time (8 women). *Students:* 68 full-time (22 women); includes 7 minority (4 Asian Americans or Pacific Islanders, 3 Hispanic Americans), 17 international. Average age 29. 429 applicants, 12% accepted, 28 enrolled. In 2009, 7 master's, 7 doctorates awarded. Terminal master's awarded for partial completion of doctoral program. *Degree requirements:* For master's, thesis; for doctorate, one foreign language, comprehensive exam, thesis/dissertation. *Entrance requirements:* For master's and doctorate, GRE General Test. Additional exam requirements/recommendations for international students: Required—TOEFL (minimum score 600 paper-based; 250 computer-based; 100 iBT), IELTS (minimum score 7). *Application deadline:* For fall admission, 12/31 for domestic and international students. Application fee: $75. Electronic applications accepted. *Expenses:* Tuition: Full-time $37,510; part-time $585 per unit. Required fees: $272. *Financial support:* In 2009–10, 58 students received support, including 15 fellowships with tuition reimbursements available (averaging $27,495 per year), 27 research assistantships with tuition reimbursements available (averaging $28,337 per year), 10 teaching assistantships with tuition reimbursements available (averaging $30,666 per year); Federal Work-Study, institutionally sponsored loans, scholarships/grants, health care benefits, and unspecified assistantships also available. *Faculty research:* International security, American politics, political economy, ethnic conflict and politics, democratization. Total annual research expenditures: $1.5 million. *Unit head:* Prof. Charles Stewart, Department Head, 617-253-5262, Fax: 617-258-6164. *Application contact:* Graduate Administrator, 617-253-8336, Fax: 617-258-6164, E-mail: twarog@mit.edu.

McGill University, Faculty of Graduate and Postdoctoral Studies, Faculty of Arts, Department of Political Science, Montréal, QC H3A 2T5, Canada. Offers MA, PhD.

McMaster University, School of Graduate Studies, Faculty of Social Sciences, Department of Political Science, Hamilton, ON L8S 4M2, Canada. Offers international relations (PhD); political science (MA); public and the global economy (MA); public policy (PhD); public policy and administration (MA). Part-time programs available. *Degree requirements:* For master's, thesis or alternative. *Entrance requirements:* For master's, minimum B+ average. Additional exam requirements/recommendations for international students: Required—TOEFL (minimum score 580 paper-based; 237 computer-based). *Faculty research:* Organizational theory, internationalization of public policy, water resource policies, political interest intermediation, comparative politics.

Memorial University of Newfoundland, School of Graduate Studies, Department of Political Science, St. John's, NL A1C 5S7, Canada. Offers MA. Part-time and evening/weekend programs available. *Degree requirements:* For master's, thesis optional. *Entrance requirements:* For master's, minimum 2nd class bachelor's degree. Electronic applications accepted. *Faculty research:* Comparative politics, Canadian government and politics, Newfoundland politics, and the politics of multi-level systems.

Miami University, Graduate School, College of Arts and Sciences, Department of Political Science, Oxford, OH 45056. Offers MA. *Students:* 18 full-time (7 women), 1 part-time (0 women); includes 2 minority (both African Americans), 2 international. *Entrance requirements:* For master's, GRE General Test, minimum undergraduate GPA of 3.0 during previous 2 years or 2.75 overall. Additional exam requirements/recommendations for international students: Required—TOEFL. Application fee: $50. *Expenses:* Tuition, state resident: full-time $11,280. Tuition, nonresident: full-time $24,912. Required fees: $516. *Financial support:* Fellowships with full tuition reimbursements, research assistantships with full tuition reimbursements, teaching assistantships with full tuition reimbursements, Federal Work-Study, institutionally sponsored loans, health care benefits, tuition waivers (full), and unspecified assistantships available. Financial award application deadline: 3/1; financial award applicants required to submit FAFSA. *Faculty research:* Constitutional rights and liberties, American foreign policy, world regional politics, public management, political philosophy, parties and interest groups, international law. *Unit head:* Dr. Abdoulaye Saine, Interim Chair, 513-529-2000, E-mail: political@muohio.edu. *Application contact:* Dr. Steven DeLue, Director of Graduate Studies, 513-529-2000, E-mail: political@muohio.edu.

Michigan State University, The Graduate School, College of Social Science, Department of Political Science, East Lansing, MI 48824. Offers political science (MA, PhD); public policy (MPP). *Faculty:* 31 full-time (6 women). *Students:* 70 full-time (26 women), 8 part-time (4 women); includes 7 minority (4 African Americans, 1 Asian American or Pacific Islander, 2 Hispanic Americans), 26 international. Average age 29. 126 applicants, 34% accepted. In 2009, 19 master's, 4 doctorates awarded. *Degree requirements:* For master's, practicum; for doctorate, comprehensive exam, presentation of dissertation. *Entrance requirements:* Additional exam requirements/recommendations for international students: Required—TOEFL. Electronic applications accepted. *Expenses:* Tuition, state resident: part-time $478.25 per credit hour. Tuition, nonresident: part-time $966.50 per credit hour. Part-time tuition and fees vary according to program. *Financial support:* In 2009–10, 19 research assistantships with tuition reimbursements (averaging $6,581 per year), 30 teaching assistantships with tuition reimbursements (averaging $6,461 per year) were awarded. Total annual research expenditures: $419,116. *Unit head:* Dr. Richard C. Hula, Chairperson, 517-355-6590, Fax: 517-432-1091, E-mail: rhula@msu.edu. *Application contact:* Karen Battin, Graduate Programs Assistant, 517-355-2167, Fax: 517-432-1091, E-mail: battink@msu.edu.

Midwestern State University, Graduate Studies, College of Humanities and Social Sciences, Department of Political Science, Wichita Falls, TX 76308. Offers MA. *Degree requirements:* For master's, one foreign language, comprehensive exam. *Entrance requirements:* For master's, GRE General Test. Additional exam requirements/recommendations for international students: Required—TOEFL (minimum score 550 paper-based; 213 computer-based). Electronic applications accepted. *Expenses:* Tuition, state resident: full-time $1620; part-time $90 per credit hour. Tuition, nonresident: full-time $2160; part-time $120 per credit hour. International tuition: $7506 full-time. Required fees: $3068.80; $145.60 per credit hour. $179 per semester.

Mississippi College, Graduate School, College of Arts and Sciences, School of Humanities and Social Sciences, Department of History, Political Science, Administration of Justice, and Paralegal Studies, Clinton, MS 39058. Offers administration of justice (MSS); history (M Ed, MA, MSS); paralegal studies (Certificate); political science (MSS); social sciences (M Ed, MSS). Part-time programs available. *Faculty:* 4 full-time (0 women), 5 part-time/adjunct (1 woman). *Students:* 10 full-time (5 women), 27 part-time (10 women); includes 8 minority (all African Americans), 1 international. Average age 32. In 2009, 12 master's awarded. *Degree requirements:* For master's, one foreign language, comprehensive exam, thesis (for some programs). *Entrance requirements:* For master's, GRE or NTE, minimum GPA of 2.5. Additional exam requirements/recommendations for international students: Recommended—IELTS. *Application deadline:* For fall admission, 8/15 priority date for domestic students. Applications are processed on a rolling basis. Application fee: $30. Electronic applications accepted. *Expenses:* Tuition: Part-time $452 per credit hour. Required fees: $101 per semester. Tuition and fees vary according to degree level, campus/location, program and student level. *Financial support:* Teaching assistantships, Federal Work-Study, scholarships/grants, and unspecified assistantships available. Support available to part-time students. Financial award application deadline: 4/1; financial award applicants required to submit FAFSA. *Unit head:* Dr. Kirk Ford, Chair, 601-925-3326, E-mail: ford@mc.edu. *Application contact:* Elnora Lewis, Secretary, 601-925-3225, Fax: 601-925-3889, E-mail: lewis09@mc.edu.

Mississippi State University, College of Arts and Sciences, Department of Political Science and Public Administration, Mississippi State, MS 39762. Offers political science (MA); public policy and administration (MPPA, PhD). *Accreditation:* NASPAA (one or more programs are accredited). Evening/weekend programs available. Postbaccalaureate distance learning degree programs offered (no on-campus study). *Faculty:* 14 full-time (4 women). *Students:* 67 full-time (35 women), 44 part-time (33 women); includes 40 minority (37 African Americans, 1 American Indian/Alaska Native, 2 Asian Americans or Pacific Islanders), 4 international. Average age 30. 85 applicants, 60% accepted, 39 enrolled. In 2009, 28 master's, 2 doctorates awarded. *Degree requirements:* For master's, thesis optional, comprehensive oral or written exam; for doctorate, thesis/dissertation, comprehensive oral and written exam. *Entrance requirements:* For master's, GRE, minimum GPA of 3.0 on the last two years of undergraduate courses or graduate work; for doctorate, GRE General Test, minimum graduate GPA of 3.35. Additional exam requirements/recommendations for international students: Required—TOEFL (minimum score 600 paper-based; 250 computer-based; 100 iBT); Recommended—IELTS (minimum score 7.5). *Application deadline:* For fall admission, 8/1 priority date for domestic students, 5/1 for international students; for spring admission, 12/1 priority date for domestic students, 9/1 for international students. Applications are processed on a rolling basis. Application fee: $40. Electronic applications accepted. *Expenses:* Tuition, state resident: full-time $2575.50; part-time $286.25 per credit hour. Tuition, nonresident: full-time $6510; part-time $723.50 per credit hour. Tuition and fees vary according to course load. *Financial support:* In 2009–10, 5 research assistantships (averaging $14,451 per year), 6 teaching assistantships with full tuition reimbursements (averaging $9,030 per year) were awarded; Federal Work-Study, institutionally sponsored loans, scholarships/grants, and unspecified assistantships also available. Financial award application deadline: 4/15. *Faculty research:* American politics, international relations, state and local government, comparative government, public administration. Total annual research expenditures: $879,000. *Unit head:* Dr. KC Morrison, Department Head, 662-325-2711, Fax: 662-325-2716, E-mail: kcmorrison@ps.msstate.edu. *Application contact:* Dr. Doug Goodman, Associate Professor and Graduate Coordinator, 662-325-7856, Fax: 662-325-2716, E-mail: dg114@ps.msstate.edu.

Missouri State University, Graduate College, College of Humanities and Public Affairs, Department of Political Science, Springfield, MO 65897. Offers global studies (MGS); public administration (MPA). Part-time programs available. *Faculty:* 15 full-time (1 woman). *Students:* 43 full-time (13 women), 15 part-time (6 women); includes 7 minority (2 African Americans, 4 Asian Americans or Pacific Islanders, 1 Hispanic American), 8 international. Average age 29. 31 applicants, 84% accepted, 10 enrolled. In 2009, 31 master's awarded. *Degree requirements:* For master's, variable foreign language requirement, comprehensive exam, thesis or alternative. *Entrance requirements:* For master's, GRE, minimum GPA of 3.0. Additional exam requirements/recommendations for international students: Required—TOEFL (minimum score 550 paper-based; 213 computer-based; 79 iBT). *Application deadline:* For fall admission, 7/20 priority date for domestic students, 5/1 for international students; for spring admission, 12/20 priority date for domestic students, 9/1 for international students. Applications are processed on a rolling basis. Application fee: $35 ($50 for international students). Electronic applications accepted. *Expenses:* Tuition, state resident: full-time $3852; part-time $214 per credit hour. Tuition, nonresident: full-time $7524; part-time $418 per credit hour. Required fees: $696; $172 per semester. Tuition and fees vary according to course level, course load, degree level and program. *Financial support:* In 2009–10, 2 research assistantships with full tuition reimbursements (averaging $8,535 per year), 2 teaching assistantships with full tuition reimbursements (averaging $7,340 per year) were awarded; career-related internships or fieldwork, Federal Work-Study, scholarships/grants, and unspecified assistantships also available. Support available to part-time students. Financial award application deadline: 3/31; financial award applicants required to submit FAFSA. *Unit head:* Dr. George Connor, Acting Head, 417-836-5630, Fax: 417-836-6655, E-mail: georgeconnor@missouristate.edu. *Application contact:* Dr. George Connor, Acting Head, 417-836-5630, Fax: 417-836-6655, E-mail: georgeconnor@missouristate.edu.

Montclair State University, The Graduate School, College of Humanities and Social Sciences, Department of Political Science and Law, Montclair, NJ 07043-1624. Offers law and governance (MA). Part-time and evening/weekend programs available. *Faculty:* 13 full-time (6 women), 22 part-time/adjunct (7 women). *Students:* 15 full-time (9 women), 22 part-time (16 women). Average age 33. 15 applicants, 53% accepted, 3 enrolled. In 2009, 12 master's awarded. *Degree requirements:* For master's, thesis or comprehensive exam. *Entrance requirements:* For master's, GRE, minimum cumulative GPA of 2.75 for undergraduate work. Additional exam requirements/recommendations for international students: Required—TOEFL (minimum score 83 computer-based), or IELTS. *Expenses:* Tuition, area resident: Part-time $486.74 per credit. Tuition, state resident: part-time $486.74 per credit. Tuition, nonresident: part-time $751.34 per credit. Tuition and fees vary according to degree level and program. *Financial support:* In 2009–10, 1 research assistantship with full tuition reimbursement (averaging $7,000 per year) was awarded; Federal Work-Study, scholarships/grants, and unspecified assistantships also available. Support available to part-time students. Financial award application deadline: 3/1. *Unit head:* Dr. William Berlin, Chair, 973-655-7576, E-mail: berlinw@mail.montclair.edu. *Application contact:* Amy Aiello, Director of Graduate Admissions and Operations, 973-655-5147, Fax: 973-655-7869, E-mail: graduate.school@montclair.edu.

Naval Postgraduate School, Graduate Programs, Department of National Security Affairs, Monterey, CA 93943. Offers intelligence (MA); international relations (MA); political science (MA); regional security education (MA); security building (MA); security studies (MA). Program only open to commissioned officers of the United States and friendly nations and selected United States federal civilian employees. Part-time programs available. *Degree requirements:* For master's, thesis.

New Mexico State University, Graduate School, College of Arts and Sciences, Department of Government, Las Cruces, NM 88003-8001. Offers MA, MPA. *Accreditation:* NASPAA (one or more programs are accredited). Part-time and evening/weekend programs available. *Faculty:* 9 full-time (5 women), 2 part-time/adjunct (1 woman). *Students:* 31 full-time (16 women), 16 part-time (6 women); includes 17 minority (1 African American, 1 Asian American or Pacific Islander, 15 Hispanic Americans), 5 international. Average age 31. 30 applicants, 97% accepted, 19 enrolled. In 2009, 7 master's awarded. *Degree requirements:* For master's, comprehensive exam (for some programs), thesis optional. *Entrance requirements:* For master's, GRE (if GPA less than 3.0), writing sample, 3 letters of recommendation, resume. Additional exam requirements/recommendations for international students: Required—TOEFL (minimum score 530 paper-based; 197 computer-based). *Application deadline:* Applications are processed on a rolling basis. Application fee: $30 ($50 for international students). Electronic applications accepted. *Expenses:* Tuition, state resident: full-time $4080; part-time $223 per credit. Tuition, nonresident: full-time $14,256; part-time $647 per credit. Required fees: $1278; $639 per semester. *Financial support:* In 2009–10, 3 research assistantships (averaging $11,850 per year), 11 teaching assistantships with tuition reimbursements (averaging $5,745 per year) were awarded; career-related internships or fieldwork, Federal Work-Study, scholarships/grants, health care benefits, and unspecified assistantships also available. Support available to part-time students. Financial award application deadline: 3/1. *Faculty research:* U.S./Mexico border studies, public administration and policy, international relations, Latin America, American politics and theory. *Unit head:* Dr. Nancy Baker, Head, 575-646-4935, Fax: 575-646-2052, E-mail: nbaker@nmsu.edu. *Application contact:* Rona M. Lujan, Department Secretary, 575-646-4734, Fax: 575-646-2052, E-mail: rona@nmsu.edu.

The New School: A University, The New School for Social Research, Department of Political Science, New York, NY 10003. Offers M Phil, MA, DS Sc, PhD. Part-time programs available. *Faculty:* 14 full-time (7 women). *Students:* 118 full-time (48 women), 22 part-time (12 women); includes 18 minority (7 African Americans, 3 Asian Americans or Pacific Islanders, 8 Hispanic Americans), 52 international. Average age 33. 163 applicants, 61% accepted, 22 enrolled. In 2009, 22 master's, 8 doctorates awarded. Terminal master's awarded for partial completion of doctoral program. *Degree requirements:* For master's, thesis; for doctorate, one foreign language, comprehensive exam, thesis/dissertation, two methodology courses, PhD seminar, field seminars. *Entrance requirements:* For master's, GRE General Test; for doctorate, GRE General Test, MA. Additional exam requirements/recommendations for international students: Required—TOEFL (minimum score 600 paper-based; 250 computer-based; 100 iBT). *Application deadline:* For fall admission, 1/17 priority date for domestic and international students; for spring admission, 10/15 priority date for domestic and international students. Applications are processed on a rolling basis. Application fee: $50. Electronic applications accepted. *Financial support:* Fellowships, research assistantships, teaching assistantships, Federal Work-Study, scholarships/grants, tuition waivers (full and partial), and unspecified assistantships available. Support available to part-time students. Financial award application deadline: 3/1; financial award applicants required to submit FAFSA. *Faculty research:* Democratic transitions and institution; race, class and gender; immigration and incorporation. *Unit head:* Dr. Nancy Fraser, Chair, 212-229-5747 Ext. 3089, Fax: 212-229-5315. *Application contact:* Robert MacDonald, Director of Admissions, 212-229-5710 Ext. 3007, Fax: 212-989-7102, E-mail: macdonar@newschool.edu.

New York University, Graduate School of Arts and Science, Department of Politics, New York, NY 10012-1019. Offers political campaign management (MA); politics (MA, PhD); JD/MA; MBA/MA. Part-time programs available. *Faculty:* 30 full-time (4 women). *Students:* 186 full-time (92 women), 56 part-time (37 women); includes 27 minority (3 African Americans, 13 Asian Americans or Pacific Islanders, 11 Hispanic Americans), 118 international. Average age 28. 633 applicants, 42% accepted, 97 enrolled. In 2009, 78 master's, 5 doctorates awarded. Terminal master's awarded for partial completion of doctoral program. *Degree requirements:* For master's, one foreign language, thesis or alternative; for doctorate, 2 foreign languages, comprehensive exam, thesis/dissertation. *Entrance requirements:* For master's, GRE General Test; for doctorate, GRE General Test, master's degree in political science, minimum GPA of 2.5. Additional exam requirements/recommendations for international students: Required—TOEFL. *Application deadline:* For fall admission, 12/18 priority date for domestic students. Application fee: $90. *Expenses:* Tuition: Full-time $30,528; part-time $1272 per credit. Required fees: $2177. *Financial support:* Fellowships with tuition reimbursements, teaching assistantships with tuition reimbursements, career-related internships or fieldwork, Federal Work-Study, and institutionally sponsored loans available. Financial award application deadline: 12/18; financial award applicants required to submit FAFSA. *Faculty research:* Comparative politics, democratic theory and practice, rational choice, political economy; international relations. *Unit head:* Michael Gilligan, Director of Ph.D. program, 212-998-8500, Fax: 212-995-4184, E-mail: politics.phd@nyu.edu. *Application contact:* Shinasi Rama, Director Master's Program, 212-998-8500, Fax: 212-995-4184, E-mail: politics.masters@nyu.edu.

Northeastern Illinois University, Graduate College, College of Arts and Sciences, Department of Political Science, Program in Political Science, Chicago, IL 60625-4699. Offers MA. Part-time and evening/weekend programs available. *Degree requirements:* For master's, comprehensive exam, thesis optional. *Entrance requirements:* For master's, minimum GPA of 2.75. Additional exam requirements/recommendations for international students: Required—TOEFL (minimum score 550 paper-based; 213 computer-based; 80 iBT). Electronic applications accepted. *Faculty research:* Chinese politics, Latin American democratization, Jewish feminism, administration and delegation.

Northeastern University, College of Social Sciences and Humanities, Department of Political Science, Boston, MA 02115-5096. Offers political science (MA); public administration (MPA, Certificate), including development administration (MPA), health administration and policy (MPA), state and local government (MPA), urban studies (Certificate); public and international affairs (PhD). Part-time and evening/weekend programs available. *Faculty:* 22 full-time (4 women), 10 part-time/adjunct (1 woman). *Students:* 10 full-time (3 women), 62 part-time (28 women); includes 7 minority (2 African Americans, 2 American Indian/Alaska Native, 2 Asian Americans or Pacific Islanders, 1 Hispanic American), 11 international. Average age 30. 129 applicants, 69% accepted, 24 enrolled. In 2009, 28 master's, 3 doctorates awarded. *Degree requirements:* For master's, thesis optional; for doctorate, thesis/dissertation. *Entrance requirements:* For master's, GRE General Test. Additional exam requirements/recommendations for international students: Required—TOEFL. *Application deadline:* Applications are processed on a rolling basis. Application fee: $50. *Financial support:* In 2009–10, 12 fellowships, 3 research assistantships with tuition reimbursements, 18 teaching assistantships with tuition reimbursements (averaging $14,035 per year) were awarded; career-related internships or fieldwork, Federal Work-Study, tuition waivers (full and partial), and unspecified assistantships also available. Support available to part-time students. Financial award application deadline: 2/1; financial award applicants required to submit FAFSA. *Faculty research:* Presidency, public opinion, Congress, democratization, national identity. *Unit head:* Dr. John Portz, Chair, 617-373-2796, Fax: 617-373-5311, E-mail: gradpolisci@neu.edu. *Application contact:* Brynn Thompson, Graduate Programs Assistant, 617-373-4404, Fax: 617-373-5311, E-mail: gradpolisci@neu.edu.

Northern Arizona University, Graduate College, College of Social and Behavioral Sciences, Department of Politics and International Affairs, Program in Political Science, Flagstaff, AZ 86011. Offers political science (MA, PhD); public management (Certificate). *Faculty:* 23 full-time (9 women). *Students:* 25 full-time (12 women), 18 part-time (9 women); includes 12 minority (2 African Americans, 2 American Indian/Alaska Native, 2 Asian Americans or Pacific Islanders, 6 Hispanic Americans), 5 international. Average age 35. 29 applicants, 76% accepted, 15 enrolled. In 2009, 4 master's, 2 doctorates awarded. *Degree requirements:* For master's, thesis optional; for doctorate, one foreign language, thesis/dissertation. *Entrance requirements:* For master's, minimum GPA of 3.0; for doctorate, GRE General Test. Additional exam requirements/recommendations for international students: Required—TOEFL (minimum score 550 paper-based; 213 computer-based; 80 iBT), IELTS (minimum score 7), or a bachelor's degree from an English-speaking university and demonstrated proficiency. *Application deadline:* For fall admission, 2/15 priority date for domestic students. Applications are processed on a rolling basis. Application fee: $65. Electronic applications accepted. *Financial support:* In 2009–10, 12 teaching assistantships with partial tuition reimbursements (averaging $11,300 per year) were awarded; tuition waivers (full and partial) also available. Financial award application deadline: 3/30. *Unit head:* Dr. Lori Poloni-Staudinger, Graduate Coordinator, 928-523-6546, E-mail: lori.poloni-staudinger@nau.edu. *Application contact:* Susan Bemus, Secretary, 928-523-6979, E-mail: political.science@nau.edu.

Northern Illinois University, Graduate School, College of Liberal Arts and Sciences, Department of Political Science, De Kalb, IL 60115-2854. Offers political science (MA, PhD); public administration (MPA). Part-time and evening/weekend programs available. *Faculty:* 24 full-time (5 women), 8 part-time/adjunct (2 women). *Students:* 86 full-time (27 women), 84 part-time (29 women); includes 18 minority (11 African Americans, 1 Asian American or Pacific Islander, 6 Hispanic Americans), 20 international. Average age 31. 91 applicants, 56% accepted, 30 enrolled. In 2009, 11 master's, 8 doctorates awarded. Terminal master's awarded for partial completion of doctoral program. *Degree requirements:* For master's, comprehensive exam, thesis optional; for doctorate, variable foreign language requirement, thesis/dissertation, candidacy exam, dissertation defense. *Entrance requirements:* For master's, GRE General Test, minimum GPA of 2.75, 9 hours of course work in political science; for doctorate, GRE General Test, minimum GPA of 2.75 (undergraduate), 3.2 (graduate); undergraduate major in related field. Additional exam requirements/recommendations for international students: Required—TOEFL (minimum score 550 paper-based; 213 computer-based). *Application deadline:* For fall admission, 3/1 priority date for domestic students, 5/1 for international students; for spring admission, 11/1 for domestic students, 10/1 for international students. Applications are processed on a rolling basis. Application fee: $30. Electronic applications accepted. *Expenses:* Tuition, state resident: full-time $6576; part-time $274 per credit hour. Tuition, nonresident: full-time $13,152; part-time $548 per credit hour. Required fees: $1813; $75.53 per credit hour. Part-time tuition and fees vary according to course load. *Financial support:* In 2009–10, 4 research assistantships with full tuition reimbursements, 22 teaching assistantships with full tuition reimbursements were awarded; fellowships with full tuition reimbursements, career-related internships or fieldwork, Federal Work-Study, scholarships/grants, tuition waivers (full), and unspecified assistantships also available. Support available to part-time students. Financial award applicants required to submit FAFSA. *Faculty research:* Terrorism and dynamics of trade; U.S. foreign policy, political economy of development, biopolitical theory, women and politics. *Unit head:* Dr. Christopher Jones, Chair, 815-753-7040, Fax: 815-753-6302. *Application contact:* Dr. Dwight King, Director, Graduate Studies, 815-753-7054, E-mail: dking@niu.edu.

Northwestern University, The Graduate School, Judd A. and Marjorie Weinberg College of Arts and Sciences, Department of Political Science, Evanston, IL 60208. Offers MA, PhD, JD/PhD. Admissions and degrees offered through The Graduate School. Terminal master's awarded for partial completion of doctoral program. *Degree requirements:* For master's, thesis or alternative; for doctorate, thesis/dissertation, qualifying exams. *Entrance requirements:* For master's and doctorate, GRE General Test, sample of written work. Additional exam requirements/recommendations for international students: Required—TOEFL. *Faculty research:* Formal theory/formal political economy, political economy of development/state-business relations, labor market institutions and welfare policy, public opinion and political behavior, feminist political theory.

The Ohio State University, Graduate School, College of Social and Behavioral Sciences, School of Social and Behavioral Science, Department of Political Science, Columbus, OH 43210. Offers MA, PhD. *Faculty:* 40. *Students:* 38 full-time (16 women), 54 part-time (19 women); includes 11 minority (5 African Americans, 2 Asian Americans or Pacific Islanders, 4 Hispanic Americans), 24 international. Average age 28. In 2009, 17 master's, 12 doctorates awarded. *Degree requirements:* For master's, thesis optional; for doctorate, thesis/dissertation. *Entrance requirements:* For master's and doctorate, GRE General Test. Additional exam requirements/recommendations for international students: Recommended—TOEFL (minimum score 620 paper-based; 260 computer-based). *Application deadline:* For fall admission, 8/15 priority date for domestic students, 7/1 priority date for international students; for winter admission, 12/1 priority date for domestic students, 11/1 priority date for international students; for spring admission, 3/1 priority date for domestic students, 2/1 priority date for international students. Applications are processed on a rolling basis. Application fee: $40 ($50 for international students). Electronic applications accepted. *Expenses:* Tuition, state resident: full-time $10,683. Tuition, nonresident: full-time $25,923. Tuition and fees vary according to course load and program. *Financial support:* Fellowships, research assistantships, teaching assistantships, Federal Work-Study and institutionally sponsored loans available. Support available to part-time students. *Faculty research:* American, comparative, and international politics; political theory. *Unit head:* Dr. Kathleen M. McGraw, Graduate Studies Committee Chair, 614-292-2880, Fax: 614-292-1146, E-mail: mcgraw.36@osu.edu. *Application contact:* 614-292-9444, Fax: 614-292-3895, E-mail: domestic.grad@osu.edu.

Ohio University, Graduate College, College of Arts and Sciences, Department of Political Science, Athens, OH 45701-2979. Offers political science (MA); public administration (MPA). Part-time and evening/weekend programs available. *Faculty:* 24 full-time (8 women). *Students:* 98 full-time (50 women), 11 part-time (2 women); includes 10 minority (7 African Americans, 1 Asian American or Pacific Islander, 2 Hispanic Americans), 19 international. 116 applicants, 83% accepted, 51 enrolled. In 2009, 32 master's awarded. *Degree requirements:* For master's, comprehensive exam, thesis or alternative. *Entrance requirements:* For master's, GRE General Test, minimum GPA of 3.0. Additional exam requirements/recommendations for international students: Required—TOEFL (minimum score 550 paper-based; 80 iBT) or IELTS Academic (minimum score 6.5). *Application deadline:* For fall admission, 2/15 priority date for domestic and international students. Applications are processed on a rolling basis. Application fee: $50 ($55 for international students). Electronic applications accepted. *Expenses:* Tuition, state resident: full-time $7839; part-time $323 per quarter hour. Tuition, nonresident: full-time $15,831; part-time $654 per quarter hour. Required fees: $2931. *Financial support:* Research assistantships with full tuition reimbursements, teaching assistantships with full tuition reimbursements, career-related internships or fieldwork, Federal Work-Study, institutionally sponsored loans, and tuition waivers (partial) available. Financial award application deadline: 2/15. *Faculty research:* International relations, Latin American politics, public policy, economic development, political theory. *Unit head:* Dr. John Gilliom, Chair, 740-593-4368, Fax: 740-593-0394. *Application contact:* Dr. Judith Millesen, Graduate Director, 740-593-4381, Fax: 740-593-0394.

Oklahoma State University, College of Arts and Sciences, Department of Political Science, Stillwater, OK 74078. Offers fire and emergency management administration (MS, PhD); political science (MA). *Faculty:* 19 full-time (5 women), 5 part-time/adjunct (1 woman). *Students:* 27 full-time (4 women), 54 part-time (8 women); includes 10 minority (2 African Americans, 6 American Indian/Alaska Native, 1 Asian American or Pacific Islander, 1 Hispanic American), 20 international. Average age 35. 77 applicants, 45% accepted, 27 enrolled. In 2009, 22 master's awarded. *Degree requirements:* For master's, comprehensive exam, thesis or creative component; for doctorate, comprehensive exam, thesis/dissertation. *Entrance requirements:* For master's, GRE; for doctorate, GRE. Additional exam requirements/recommendations for international students: Required—TOEFL (minimum score 550 paper-based; 79 iBT). *Application deadline:* For fall admission, 3/1 priority date for international students; for spring admission, 8/1 priority date for international students. Applications are processed on a rolling basis. Application fee: $40 ($75 for international students). Electronic applications accepted. *Expenses:* Tuition, state resident: full-time $3716; part-time $154.85 per credit hour. Tuition, nonresident: full-time $14,448; part-time $602 per credit hour. Required fees: $1772; $73.85 per credit hour. One-time fee: $50. Tuition and fees vary according to course load and campus/location. *Financial support:* In 2009–10, 3 research assistantships (averaging $11,090 per year), 11 teaching assistantships (averaging $10,767 per year) were awarded; career-related internships or fieldwork, Federal Work-Study, scholarships/grants, health care benefits, tuition waivers (partial), and unspecified assistantships also available. Support available to part-time students. Financial award application deadline: 3/1; financial award applicants required to submit FAFSA. *Faculty research:* Fire and emergency management, environmental dispute resolution, voting and elections, women and politics, urban politics. *Unit head:* Dr. James Scott, Head, 405-744-5569, Fax: 405-744-6534. *Application contact:* Dr. Gordon Emslie, Dean, 405-744-6368, Fax: 405-744-0355, E-mail: grad-i@okstate.edu.

Penn State University Park, Graduate School, College of the Liberal Arts, Department of Political Science, State College, University Park, PA 16802-1503. Offers MA, PhD. *Unit head:* Dr. Donna Bahry, Head, 814-863-1449, E-mail: dlb46@psu.edu. *Application contact:* Dr. Donna Bahry, Head, 814-863-1449, E-mail: dlb46@psu.edu.

Pepperdine University, School of Public Policy, Malibu, CA 90263. Offers American politics (MPP); economics (MPP); international relations (MPP); public policy (MPP); state and local policy (MPP). *Faculty:* 7 full-time (2 women), 5 part-time/adjunct (0 women). *Students:* 117 full-time (62 women), 5 part-time (3 women); includes 30 minority (7 African Americans, 1 American Indian/Alaska Native, 10 Asian Americans or Pacific Islanders, 12 Hispanic Americans), 9 international. In 2009, 27 master's awarded. *Entrance requirements:* For master's, GRE, 2 letters of recommendation, resume. Additional exam requirements/recommendations for international students: Required—TOEFL. *Application deadline:* For fall admission, 4/15 for domestic students. Applications are processed on a rolling basis. Electronic applications accepted. *Expenses:* Tuition: Full-time $37,516; part-time $1310 per unit. Required fees: $80. *Financial support:* Research assistantships, teaching assistantships, institutionally sponsored loans and scholarships/grants available. Financial award application deadline: 5/1; financial award applicants required to submit FAFSA. *Unit head:* Dr. James R. Wilburn, Dean, 310-506-7490, Fax: 310-506-7494, E-mail: james.wilburn@pepperdine.edu. *Application contact:* Melinda E. van Hemert, Director of Recruitment and Career Services, 310-506-7492, Fax: 310-506-7494, E-mail: melinda.vanhemert@pepperdine.edu.

Portland State University, Graduate Studies, College of Urban and Public Affairs, Hatfield School of Government, Division of Political Science, Portland, OR 97207-0751. Offers MA, MAT, MS, MST, PhD. Part-time programs available. *Degree requirements:* For master's, one foreign language, comprehensive exam, thesis; for doctorate, comprehensive exam, thesis/dissertation, residency. *Entrance requirements:* For master's, GRE General Test or MAT, minimum GPA of 3.1, 2 letters of recommendation; for doctorate, GRE General Test. Additional exam requirements/recommendations for international students: Required—TOEFL (minimum score 550 paper-based; 213 computer-based). *Faculty research:* Congress, presidency, political reform, international environment, hate speech.

Princeton University, Graduate School, Department of Politics, Princeton, NJ 08544-1019. Offers political philosophy (PhD); politics (PhD). *Degree requirements:* For doctorate, comprehensive exam, thesis/dissertation, teaching experience. *Entrance requirements:* For doctorate, GRE General Test, sample of written work, letters of recommendation. Additional exam requirements/recommendations for international students: Required—TOEFL (minimum

Political Science

Princeton University (continued)
score 600 paper-based; 250 computer-based). Electronic applications accepted. *Faculty research:* American politics, comparative politics, formal and quantitative methods, international relations, public law, political theory.

Purdue University, Graduate School, College of Liberal Arts, Department of Political Science, West Lafayette, IN 47907. Offers MA, PhD. Part-time and evening/weekend programs available. Terminal master's awarded for partial completion of doctoral program. *Degree requirements:* For doctorate, 2 foreign languages, thesis/dissertation. *Entrance requirements:* For master's and doctorate, GRE General Test, minimum GPA of 3.0. Additional exam requirements/recommendations for international students: Required—TOEFL. Electronic applications accepted. *Faculty research:* American politics, comparative politics, political theory, public policy/public administration, international relations.

Queen's University at Kingston, School of Graduate Studies and Research, Faculty of Arts and Sciences, Department of Political Studies, Kingston, ON K7L 3N6, Canada. Offers Canadian politics (PhD); comparative politics (PhD); gender and politics (PhD); international relations (PhD); political theory (PhD). *Degree requirements:* For master's, thesis or alternative; for doctorate, one foreign language, thesis/dissertation, qualifying exams. *Entrance requirements:* Additional exam requirements/recommendations for international students: Required—TOEFL (minimum score 600 paper-based; 250 computer-based). *Faculty research:* Canadian politics, comparative politics, political thought, international politics, women and politics.

Regent University, Graduate School, Robertson School of Government, Virginia Beach, VA 23464. Offers american government (MA); global politics (MA); health care policy and administration (MA); international politics (MA); law and public policy (MA); Mid-East Politics (MA); political leadership and management (MA); political management (MA); political theory (MA); public administration (MA); public policy (MA); terrorism and homeland defense (MA); world economies and political development (MA); JD/MA; M Div/MA; M Ed/MA; MBA/MA. Part-time and evening/weekend programs available. Postbaccalaureate distance learning degree programs offered (minimal on-campus study). *Faculty:* 6 full-time (2 women), 11 part-time/adjunct (1 woman). *Students:* 77 full-time (55 women), 65 part-time (36 women); includes 47 minority (38 African Americans, 2 Asian Americans or Pacific Islanders, 7 Hispanic Americans), 4 international. Average age 30. 131 applicants, 65% accepted, 54 enrolled. In 2009, 51 master's awarded. *Degree requirements:* For master's, thesis optional, internship. *Entrance requirements:* For master's, GRE General Test or LSAT, minimum undergraduate GPA of 3.0, writing sample, resume, interview, references. Additional exam requirements/recommendations for international students: Required—TOEFL (minimum score 577 paper-based; 233 computer-based). *Application deadline:* For fall admission, 5/1 priority date for domestic students; for spring admission, 11/1 priority date for domestic students. Applications are processed on a rolling basis. Application fee: $50. Electronic applications accepted. *Expenses:* Contact institution. *Financial support:* In 2009–10, 130 students received support. Career-related internships or fieldwork, scholarships/grants, tuition waivers (full and partial), and unspecified assistantships available. Support available to part-time students. Financial award application deadline: 9/1; financial award applicants required to submit FAFSA. *Faculty research:* Education reform, political character issues, social capital concerns, administrative ethics, Biblical law and public policy. *Unit head:* Dr. Charles W. Dunn, Dean, 757-352-4322, Fax: 757-352-4643, E-mail: cwdunn@regent.edu. *Application contact:* Matthew Chadwick, Director of Admissions, 800-373-5504, Fax: 757-352-4381, E-mail: admissions@regent.edu.

Rice University, Graduate Programs, School of Social Sciences, Department of Political Science, Houston, TX 77251-1892. Offers PhD. *Faculty:* 20 full-time (4 women), 1 part-time/adjunct (0 women). *Students:* 28 full-time (7 women); includes 7 minority (3 African Americans, 2 Asian Americans or Pacific Islanders, 2 Hispanic Americans), 9 international. Average age 26. 77 applicants, 8% accepted, 6 enrolled. In 2009, 2 doctorates awarded. Terminal master's awarded for partial completion of doctoral program. *Degree requirements:* For doctorate, comprehensive exam, thesis/dissertation, and 42 hours of coursework. *Entrance requirements:* For doctorate, GRE General Test. Additional exam requirements/recommendations for international students: Required—TOEFL (minimum score 600 paper-based; 250 computer-based; 90 iBT). *Application deadline:* For fall admission, 2/1 priority date for domestic and international students. Application fee: $70. Electronic applications accepted. *Financial support:* In 2009–10, 26 students received support, including 14 fellowships with full tuition reimbursements available (averaging $18,000 per year), 5 research assistantships with full tuition reimbursements available (averaging $18,000 per year), 9 teaching assistantships with full tuition reimbursements available (averaging $18,000 per year); career-related internships or fieldwork, Federal Work-Study, scholarships/grants, traineeships, health care benefits, and unspecified assistantships also available. Financial award application deadline: 2/1; financial award applicants required to submit FAFSA. *Faculty research:* Comparative government in Western Europe and the former Soviet Union, international relations, Congress and public policy in American government, minority politics. Total annual research expenditures: $547,359. *Unit head:* Dr. Mark P. Jones, Chairman, 713-348-4842 Ext. 2107, Fax: 713-348-5273, E-mail: mpjones@rice.edu. *Application contact:* Elizabeth A. Franks, Administrative Coordinator, 713-348-4842 Ext. 6308, Fax: 713-348-5273, E-mail: eaf1@rice.edu.

Roosevelt University, Graduate Division, College of Arts and Sciences, Department of Political Science and Public Administration, Program in Political Science, Chicago, IL 60605. Offers MA. Part-time and evening/weekend programs available. *Degree requirements:* For master's, thesis or alternative. *Entrance requirements:* For master's, minimum GPA of 2.7. *Faculty research:* Metropolitan social movements, American politics, comparative politics, political theory.

Rutgers, The State University of New Jersey, Newark, Graduate School, Program in Political Science, Newark, NJ 07102. Offers American political system (MA); international relations (MA); JD/MA. Part-time and evening/weekend programs available. *Degree requirements:* For master's, comprehensive exam, thesis optional. *Entrance requirements:* For master's, GRE, minimum undergraduate B average. Electronic applications accepted. *Faculty research:* Policymaking and policy evaluation in the United States; government and politics in Europe, Middle East, Asia, Africa, and Latin America.

Rutgers, The State University of New Jersey, New Brunswick, Graduate School-New Brunswick, Department of Political Science, Piscataway, NJ 08854-8097. Offers American politics (PhD); comparative politics (PhD); international relations (PhD); political theory (PhD); public law (PhD); women and politics (PhD). *Degree requirements:* For doctorate, one foreign language, comprehensive exam, thesis/dissertation. *Entrance requirements:* For doctorate, GRE General Test. Additional exam requirements/recommendations for international students: Required—TOEFL.

St. John's University, St. John's College of Liberal Arts and Sciences, Department of Government and Politics, Program in Government and Politics, Queens, NY 11439. Offers MA, Adv C, JD/MA. Part-time and evening/weekend programs available. *Students:* 57 full-time (31 women), 52 part-time (29 women); includes 33 minority (13 African Americans, 1 American Indian/Alaska Native, 7 Asian Americans or Pacific Islanders, 12 Hispanic Americans), 5 international. Average age 26. 147 applicants, 61% accepted, 50 enrolled. In 2009, 32 master's, 18 other advanced degrees awarded. *Degree requirements:* For master's, comprehensive exam, thesis optional. *Entrance requirements:* For master's, minimum GPA of 3.0. Additional exam requirements/recommendations for international students: Required—TOEFL (minimum score 500 paper-based; 173 computer-based; 61 iBT), IELTS (minimum score 5.5). *Application deadline:* For fall admission, 5/1 priority date for domestic and international students; for spring admission, 11/1 priority date for domestic and international students. Applications are processed on a rolling basis. Application fee: $70. Electronic applications accepted. *Expenses:* Tuition: Full-time $16,290; part-time $905 per credit. Required fees: $300; $150 per semester. Tuition and fees vary according to program. *Financial support:* Research assistantships, scholarships/grants available. Support available to part-time students. Financial award application deadline: 3/1; financial award applicants required to submit FAFSA. *Unit head:* Dr. Luba Racanska, Chair, 718-990-6329, E-mail: racanskl@stjohns.edu. *Application contact:* Kathleen Davis, Director of Graduate Admissions, 718-990-2790, Fax: 718-990-5686, E-mail: gradhelp@stjohns.edu.

St. John's University, St. John's College of Liberal Arts and Sciences, Department of Government and Politics and Division of Library and Information Science, Program in Government Information Specialist, Queens, NY 11439. Offers MA/MLS. Part-time and evening/weekend programs available. *Students:* 1 (woman) full-time. Average age 23. 3 applicants, 33% accepted, 0 enrolled. *Entrance requirements:* Additional exam requirements/recommendations for international students: Required—TOEFL (minimum score 500 paper-based; 173 computer-based; 61 iBT), IELTS (minimum score 5.5). *Application deadline:* For fall admission, 5/1 priority date for domestic and international students; for spring admission, 11/1 priority date for domestic and international students. Applications are processed on a rolling basis. Application fee: $70. *Expenses:* Tuition: Full-time $16,290; part-time $905 per credit. Required fees: $300; $150 per semester. Tuition and fees vary according to program. *Financial support:* Research assistantships, career-related internships or fieldwork and scholarships/grants available. Support available to part-time students. Financial award application deadline: 3/1; financial award applicants required to submit FAFSA. *Unit head:* Dr. Luba Racanska, Chair, 718-990-6329, E-mail: racanskl@stjohns.edu. *Application contact:* Kathleen Davis, Director of Graduate Admission, 718-990-2790, Fax: 718-990-5686, E-mail: gradhelp@stjohns.edu.

Saint Louis University, Graduate School, College of Arts and Sciences and Graduate School, Department of Political Science, St. Louis, MO 63103-2097. Offers MA. Part-time programs available. *Entrance requirements:* For master's, GRE or LSAT, letters of recommendation, resume, writing sample. Additional exam requirements/recommendations for international students: Required—TOEFL (minimum score 525 paper-based; 194 computer-based). Electronic applications accepted. *Faculty research:* Part of Asia, Africa, Latin America, and Russia; international political economy; diplomacy and international organization; theories of democracy and justice; American political institutions.

St. Mary's University, Graduate School, Department of Political Science, San Antonio, TX 78228-8507. Offers international relations (MA); political communications and applied science (MA); political science (MA); public administration (MPA), including inter-American administration, public management; JD/MA; JD/MPA. Part-time programs available. *Degree requirements:* For master's, one foreign language, comprehensive exam. *Entrance requirements:* For master's, GRE General Test. Additional exam requirements/recommendations for international students: Required—TOEFL (minimum score 550 paper-based; 213 computer-based; 80 iBT). Electronic applications accepted. *Expenses:* Tuition: Full-time $8004. Required fees: $536. One-time fee: $5 full-time. Full-time tuition and fees vary according to program. *Faculty research:* Voting rights, natural resources and urban policy, comparative politics and international relations.

Sam Houston State University, College of Humanities and Social Sciences, Department of Political Science, Huntsville, TX 77341. Offers political science (MA); public administration (MPA). Evening/weekend programs available. *Faculty:* 8 full-time (5 women). *Students:* 6 full-time (4 women), 23 part-time (14 women); includes 3 minority (1 Asian American or Pacific Islander, 2 Hispanic Americans), 4 international. Average age 31. 18 applicants, 94% accepted, 13 enrolled. In 2009, 9 master's awarded. *Degree requirements:* For master's, thesis or alternative. *Entrance requirements:* For master's, GRE General Test. Additional exam requirements/recommendations for international students: Required—TOEFL (minimum score 550 paper-based; 213 computer-based; 79 iBT). *Application deadline:* For fall admission, 8/1 for domestic students; for spring admission, 12/1 for domestic students. Applications are processed on a rolling basis. Application fee: $20. *Expenses:* Tuition, state resident: full-time $3690; part-time $205 per credit hour. Tuition, nonresident: full-time $8676; part-time $482 per credit hour. Required fees: $1474. Tuition and fees vary according to course load and campus/location. *Financial support:* Research assistantships, teaching assistantships, career-related internships or fieldwork and institutionally sponsored loans available. Support available to part-time students. Financial award application deadline: 5/31; financial award applicants required to submit FAFSA. *Unit head:* Dr. Rhonda Callaway, Chair, 936-294-4108, Fax: 936-294-4172, E-mail: rlc005@shsu.edu. *Application contact:* Dr. Tamara Waggener, Advisor, 936-294-1466, E-mail: pol_taw@shsu.edu.

San Diego State University, Graduate and Research Affairs, College of Arts and Letters, Department of Political Science, San Diego, CA 92182. Offers MA. Part-time programs available. *Degree requirements:* For master's, thesis. *Entrance requirements:* For master's, GRE General Test, minimum GPA of 3.0, 2 letters of reference. Additional exam requirements/recommendations for international students: Required—TOEFL. Electronic applications accepted.

San Francisco State University, Division of Graduate Studies, College of Behavioral and Social Sciences, Department of Political Science, San Francisco, CA 94132-1722. Offers MA.

Simon Fraser University, Graduate Studies, Faculty of Arts and Social Sciences, Department of Political Science, Burnaby, BC V5A 1S6, Canada. Offers MA, PhD. *Degree requirements:* For master's, thesis (for some programs); for doctorate, one foreign language, comprehensive exam, thesis/dissertation. *Entrance requirements:* For master's, minimum GPA of 3.0; for doctorate, minimum GPA of 3.67, master's in political science. Additional exam requirements/recommendations for international students: Required—TOEFL or IELTS. *Faculty research:* Theory, comparative government, public policy and administration, federalism, international relations, Canadian politics.

Sonoma State University, School of Social Sciences, Department of Political Science, Rohnert Park, CA 94928. Offers public administration (MPA). Part-time and evening/weekend programs available. *Faculty:* 2 full-time (0 women), 1 (woman) part-time/adjunct. *Students:* 6 full-time (1 woman), 45 part-time (31 women); includes 7 minority (1 African American, 3 Asian Americans or Pacific Islanders, 3 Hispanic Americans). Average age 34. 25 applicants, 76% accepted, 7 enrolled. In 2009, 12 master's awarded. *Degree requirements:* For master's, thesis or alternative. *Entrance requirements:* For master's, GRE General Test, minimum GPA of 3.0. Additional exam requirements/recommendations for international students: Required—TOEFL (minimum score 500 paper-based; 173 computer-based). *Application deadline:* For fall admission, 11/30 for domestic students; for spring admission, 8/31 for domestic students. Application fee: $55. *Expenses:* Tuition, nonresident: full-time $11,160. Required fees: $6226. Full-time tuition and fees vary according to course load. *Financial support:* Research assistantships, teaching assistantships, career-related internships or fieldwork and Federal Work-Study available. Support available to part-time students. Financial award application deadline: 3/2; financial award applicants required to submit FAFSA. *Unit head:* Dr. Diane Parness, Chair, 707-664-2179. *Application contact:* Dr. Donald Dixon, Graduate Program Coordinator, 707-664-2179, Fax: 707-664-3920, E-mail: dixon@sonoma.edu.

Southern Connecticut State University, School of Graduate Studies, School of Arts and Sciences, Department of Political Science, New Haven, CT 06515-1355. Offers MS. Part-time and evening/weekend programs available. *Faculty:* 6 full-time. *Students:* 8 full-time (3 women), 21 part-time (9 women); includes 4 minority (all African Americans). 17 applicants, 29% accepted, 4 enrolled. In 2009, 6 master's awarded. *Degree requirements:* For master's, thesis or alternative. *Entrance requirements:* For master's, interview. *Application deadline:* For fall admission, 7/15 priority date for domestic students. Applications are processed on a rolling basis. Application fee: $50. Electronic applications accepted. Tuition and fees vary according to program. *Financial support:* Application deadline: 4/15. *Unit head:* Dr. Arthur Paulson, Chairperson, 203-392-5657, Fax: 203-392-5670, E-mail: paulsona1@southernct.edu. *Application contact:* Dr. John Critzer, Graduate Coordinator, 203-392-5658, Fax: 203-392-5670, E-mail: critzerj1@southernct.edu.

Southern Illinois University Carbondale, Graduate School, College of Liberal Arts, Department of Political Science, Program in Political Science, Carbondale, IL 62901-4701. Offers MA, PhD, JD/PhD. Part-time programs available. *Degree requirements:* For doctorate, thesis/

dissertation. *Entrance requirements:* For master's, GRE General Test, minimum GPA of 2.7; for doctorate, GRE General Test, minimum GPA of 3.5. Additional exam requirements/recommendations for international students: Required—TOEFL. *Faculty research:* Public law, international relations, comparative government, American government.

Southern University and Agricultural and Mechanical College, Graduate School, Nelson Mandela School of Public Policy and Urban Affairs, Department of Political Science and Geography, Baton Rouge, LA 70813. Offers social sciences (MA). *Degree requirements:* For master's, thesis. *Entrance requirements:* For master's, GMAT or GRE General Test, minimum GPA of 3.0. Additional exam requirements/recommendations for international students: Required—TOEFL. *Faculty research:* Redistricting, comparative studies, environmental politics, political geography, mayoral elections.

Stanford University, School of Humanities and Sciences, Department of Political Science, Stanford, CA 94305-9991. Offers MA, PhD. Terminal master's awarded for partial completion of doctoral program. *Degree requirements:* For doctorate, one foreign language, thesis/dissertation, oral exam. *Entrance requirements:* For master's and doctorate, GRE General Test. Additional exam requirements/recommendations for international students: Required—TOEFL. Electronic applications accepted. *Expenses:* Tuition: Full-time $37,380; part-time $2760 per quarter. Required fees: $501.

State University of New York at Binghamton, Graduate School, School of Arts and Sciences, Department of Political Science, Binghamton, NY 13902-6000. Offers political science (MA, PhD); public policy (MA, PhD). *Faculty:* 13 full-time (4 women), 1 part-time/adjunct (0 women). *Students:* 30 full-time (8 women), 21 part-time (12 women); includes 3 minority (all African Americans), 20 international. Average age 29. 56 applicants, 55% accepted, 11 enrolled. In 2009, 9 master's, 3 doctorates awarded. Terminal master's awarded for partial completion of doctoral program. *Degree requirements:* For master's, thesis or alternative, written exam; for doctorate, 2 foreign languages, thesis/dissertation, written exam. *Entrance requirements:* For master's and doctorate, GRE General Test, GRE Subject Test. Additional exam requirements/recommendations for international students: Required—TOEFL (minimum score 550 paper-based; 213 computer-based; 80 iBT). *Application deadline:* For fall admission, 2/15 priority date for domestic and international students. Applications are processed on a rolling basis. Application fee: $60. Electronic applications accepted. *Financial support:* In 2009 10, 30 students received support, including 1 fellowship with full tuition reimbursement available (averaging $15,000 per year), 3 research assistantships with full tuition reimbursements available (averaging $15,000 per year), 19 teaching assistantships with full tuition reimbursements available (averaging $15,000 per year); career-related internships or fieldwork, Federal Work-Study, institutionally sponsored loans, scholarships/grants, health care benefits, tuition waivers (full), and unspecified assistantships also available. Financial award application deadline: 2/15; financial award applicants required to submit FAFSA. *Unit head:* Dr. Benjamin Fordham, Chairperson, 607-777-4398, E-mail: bfordham@binghamton.edu. *Application contact:* Victoria Williams, Recruiting and Admissions Coordinator, 607-777-2151, Fax: 607-777-2501, E-mail: vwilliam@binghamton.edu.

Stony Brook University, State University of New York, Graduate School, College of Arts and Sciences, Department of Political Science, Stony Brook, NY 11794. Offers political science (MA, PhD); public policy (MAPP); public policy and urban development (MA). Evening/weekend programs available. *Faculty:* 16 full-time (3 women), 1 part-time/adjunct (0 women). *Students:* 64 full-time (19 women), 16 part-time (9 women); includes 22 minority (11 African Americans, 7 Asian Americans or Pacific Islanders, 4 Hispanic Americans), 11 international. Average age 27. 125 applicants, 52% accepted. In 2009, 36 master's, 3 doctorates awarded. *Degree requirements:* For doctorate, thesis/dissertation. *Entrance requirements:* For master's and doctorate, GRE General Test. *Application deadline:* For fall admission, 1/15 for domestic students. Application fee: $60. *Expenses:* Tuition, state resident: full-time $8370; part-time $349 per credit. Tuition, nonresident: full-time $13,250; part-time $552 per credit. Required fees: $933. *Financial support:* In 2009–10, 32 teaching assistantships were awarded; fellowships, research assistantships also available. Total annual research expenditures: $93,902. *Unit head:* Dr. Jeffrey Segal, Chair, 631-632-7640. *Application contact:* Dr. Charles Taber, Director, 631-632-7667, Fax: 631-632-4116, E-mail: charles.taber@stonybrook.edu.

Suffolk University, College of Arts and Sciences, Department of Government, Boston, MA 02108-2770. Offers international relations (MSPS); political science (MSPS); professional politics (MSPS, CAGS); MPA/MSPS. Part-time and evening/weekend programs available. *Faculty:* 11 full-time (5 women), 15 part-time/adjunct (8 women). *Students:* 16 full-time (11 women), 15 part-time (2 women); includes 5 minority (4 African Americans, 1 Hispanic American), 4 international. Average age 28. 65 applicants, 86% accepted, 26 enrolled. In 2009, 27 master's awarded. *Degree requirements:* For master's, thesis optional. *Entrance requirements:* For master's, GRE General Test or MAT, 2 letters of recommendation, resume. Additional exam requirements/recommendations for international students: Required—TOEFL (minimum score 550 paper-based; 213 computer-based; 80 iBT). *Application deadline:* For fall admission, 6/15 priority date for domestic students, 6/15 for international students; for spring admission, 11/1 priority date for domestic students, 11/1 for international students. Applications are processed on a rolling basis. Application fee: $50. Electronic applications accepted. *Expenses:* Contact institution. *Financial support:* In 2009–10, 30 students received support, including 26 fellowships with full and partial tuition reimbursements available (averaging $6,036 per year); career-related internships or fieldwork, Federal Work-Study, and institutionally sponsored loans also available. Support available to part-time students. Financial award application deadline: 4/1; financial award applicants required to submit FAFSA. *Faculty research:* Political parties, women in politics, Canadian politics, public policy, legislative policies. *Unit head:* Dr. John Berg, Chairperson, 617-573-8126, Fax: 617-367-4623, E-mail: jberg@suffolk.edu. *Application contact:* Judith Reynolds, Director of Graduate Admissions, 617-573-8302, Fax: 617-305-1733, E-mail: grad.admission@suffolk.edu.

Sul Ross State University, School of Arts and Sciences, Department of Behavioral and Social Sciences, Program in Political Science, Alpine, TX 79832. Offers MA. Part-time and evening/weekend programs available. *Degree requirements:* For master's, thesis optional. *Entrance requirements:* For master's, GRE General Test, minimum undergraduate GPA of 2.5 in last 60 hours. *Faculty research:* Local government, state government, borderland studies, British studies.

Syracuse University, Maxwell School of Citizenship and Public Affairs, Program in E-Government Management and Leadership, Syracuse, NY 13244. Offers CAS. Part-time programs available. *Entrance requirements:* For degree, Must be matriculated in a SU degree program. Additional exam requirements/recommendations for international students: Required—TOEFL (minimum score 100 iBT). *Application deadline:* For fall admission, 2/1 priority date for domestic and international students. Application fee: $75. Electronic applications accepted. *Expenses:* Tuition: Full-time $26,808; part-time $1117 per credit. Required fees: $1024. *Unit head:* Margaret Lane, Director of Executive Education, 315-443-8708, E-mail: melane@syr.edu. *Application contact:* Margaret Lane, Director of Executive Education, 315-443-8708, E-mail: melane@syr.edu.

Syracuse University, Maxwell School of Citizenship and Public Affairs, Program in Political Science, Syracuse, NY 13244. Offers MA, PhD. *Students:* 70 full-time (34 women), 6 part-time (5 women); includes 3 minority (1 African American, 2 Hispanic Americans), 31 international. Average age 30. 141 applicants, 18% accepted, 12 enrolled. In 2009, 9 master's, 6 doctorates awarded. *Degree requirements:* For doctorate, thesis/dissertation. *Entrance requirements:* For master's and doctorate, GRE General Test. Additional exam requirements/recommendations for international students: Required—TOEFL (minimum score 100 iBT). *Application deadline:* For fall admission, 2/1 priority date for domestic and international students. Application fee: $75. Electronic applications accepted. *Expenses:* Tuition: Full-time $26,808; part-time $1117 per credit. Required fees: $1024. *Financial support:* Fellowships with full and partial tuition reimbursements, research assistantships with full tuition reimbursements, teaching assistantships with full and partial tuition reimbursements, tuition waivers (partial) available. Financial award application deadline: 1/1. *Unit head:* Dr. Mark Rupert, Chair, 315-443-2416, Fax: 315-443-9082, E-mail: polisci@maxwell.syr.edu. *Application contact:* Candy Brooks, Recruiting Contact, 315-443-2416, E-mail: cbrooks01@syr.edu.

Tarleton State University, College of Graduate Studies, College of Liberal and Fine Arts, Department of Social Sciences, Stephenville, TX 76402. Offers history (MA); political science (MA). Part-time and evening/weekend programs available. Postbaccalaureate distance learning degree programs offered (minimal on-campus study). *Degree requirements:* For master's, variable foreign language requirement, comprehensive exam, thesis optional. *Entrance requirements:* For master's, GRE General Test, minimum GPA of 3.0. Additional exam requirements/recommendations for international students: Required—TOEFL (minimum score 550 paper-based; 213 computer-based; 80 iBT). Electronic applications accepted.

Teachers College, Columbia University, Graduate Faculty of Education, Department of Organization and Leadership, Program in Politics and Education, New York, NY 10027-6696. Offers Ed M, MA, Ed D, PhD. *Faculty:* 2 part-time/adjunct. *Students:* 16 full-time (12 women), 25 part-time (13 women); includes 11 minority (5 African Americans, 4 Asian Americans or Pacific Islanders, 2 Hispanic Americans), 2 international. Average age 30. 437 applicants, 5% accepted, 11 enrolled. In 2009, 10 master's, 1 doctorate awarded. *Degree requirements:* For doctorate, thesis/dissertation. *Application deadline:* For fall admission, 5/15 for domestic students. Application fee: $65. *Financial support:* Career-related internships or fieldwork, Federal Work-Study, institutionally sponsored loans, and tuition waivers (full and partial) available. Support available to part-time students. Financial award application deadline: 2/1. *Faculty research:* Urban and social programs in education. *Unit head:* Warner Burke, Chair, 212-678-3258. *Application contact:* Debbie Lesperance, Assistant Director of Admission, 212-678-3710, Fax: 212-678-4171.

Temple University, Graduate School, College of Liberal Arts, Department of Political Science, Philadelphia, PA 19122-6096. Offers MA, PhD. Part-time programs available. Terminal master's awarded for partial completion of doctoral program. *Degree requirements:* For master's, comprehensive exam; for doctorate, thesis/dissertation, preliminary and oral exams. *Entrance requirements:* For master's and doctorate, GRE General Test, minimum GPA of 3.0. Additional exam requirements/recommendations for international students: Required—TOEFL (minimum score 550 paper-based; 213 computer-based; 79 iBT). Electronic applications accepted. *Faculty research:* American politics, international politics, comparative politics, political theory, urban politics, public policy.

Texas A&M International University, Office of Graduate Studies and Research, College of Arts and Sciences, Department of Social Sciences, Laredo, TX 78041-1900. Offers history (MA); political science (MA); public administration (MPA). *Faculty:* 9 full-time (3 women). *Students:* 11 full-time (4 women), 52 part-time (25 women); includes 61 minority (all Hispanic Americans), 2 international. Average age 32. 37 applicants. In 2009, 15 master's awarded. *Degree requirements:* For master's, thesis (for some programs). *Entrance requirements:* For master's, GRE General Test. Additional exam requirements/recommendations for international students: Required—TOEFL (minimum score 550 paper-based; 213 computer-based). *Application deadline:* For fall admission, 4/30 priority date for domestic students; for spring admission, 11/30 for domestic students. Applications are processed on a rolling basis. Application fee: $25. *Financial support:* In 2009–10, 14 students received support, including 2 research assistantships, 3 teaching assistantships. Financial award application deadline: 11/1. *Unit head:* Dr. Mohammed Ben-Ruwin, Chair, 956-328-2632, E-mail: mbenruwin@tamiu.edu. *Application contact:* Rosie Espinoza-Dickinson, Director of Admissions, 956-326-2200, Fax: 956-326-2199, E-mail: enroll@tamiu.edu.

Texas A&M University, College of Liberal Arts, Department of Political Science, College Station, TX 77843. Offers MA, PhD. *Faculty:* 24. *Students:* 47 full-time (27 women), 9 part-time (2 women); includes 12 minority (7 African Americans, 1 American Indian/Alaska Native, 2 Asian Americans or Pacific Islanders, 2 Hispanic Americans), 12 international. Average age 30. In 2009, 6 master's, 11 doctorates awarded. *Degree requirements:* For master's, thesis optional; for doctorate, comprehensive exam, thesis/dissertation. *Entrance requirements:* For master's and doctorate, GRE General Test, minimum GPA of 3.4. Additional exam requirements/recommendations for international students: Required—TOEFL. *Application deadline:* For fall admission, 12/20 for domestic and international students. Application fee: $50 ($75 for international students). Electronic applications accepted. *Expenses:* Tuition, state resident: full-time $3991; part-time $221.74 per credit hour. Tuition, nonresident: full-time $9049; part-time $502.74 per credit hour. *Financial support:* In 2009–10, fellowships (averaging $3,000 per year), research assistantships (averaging $15,600 per year) were awarded; institutionally sponsored loans and assistant lecturer positions also available. Financial award application deadline: 12/20; financial award applicants required to submit FAFSA. *Faculty research:* American politics, international relations, comparative politics, political theory, public policy. *Unit head:* Dr. James Rogers, Head, 979-845-2905, E-mail: rogers@tamu.edu. *Application contact:* Dr. Cary J. Nederman, Graduate Advisor, 979-845-4845, Fax: 979-845-4845, E-mail: nederman@polisci.tamu.edu.

Texas A&M University–Kingsville, College of Graduate Studies, College of Arts and Sciences, Program in History and Political Science, Kingsville, TX 78363. Offers MA, MS. Part-time and evening/weekend programs available. *Degree requirements:* For master's, comprehensive exam, thesis or alternative. *Entrance requirements:* For master's, GRE General Test. Additional exam requirements/recommendations for international students: Required—TOEFL.

Texas State University–San Marcos, Graduate School, College of Liberal Arts, Department of Political Science, Program in Political Science, San Marcos, TX 78666. Offers M Ed, MA. Part-time and evening/weekend programs available. *Faculty:* 11 full-time (3 women), 1 part time/adjunct (0 women). *Students:* 38 full-time (17 women), 36 part-time (15 women); includes 19 minority (4 African Americans, 2 Asian Americans or Pacific Islanders, 13 Hispanic Americans). Average age 29. 42 applicants, 95% accepted, 23 enrolled. In 2009, 15 master's awarded. *Degree requirements:* For master's, comprehensive exam, thesis (for some programs). *Entrance requirements:* For master's, minimum GPA of 2.9 in last 60 hours of course work. Additional exam requirements/recommendations for international students: Required—TOEFL (minimum score 550 paper-based; 213 computer-based). *Application deadline:* For fall admission, 6/15 priority date for domestic students, 6/1 priority date for international students; for spring admission, 10/15 priority date for domestic students, 10/1 priority date for international students. Applications are processed on a rolling basis. Application fee: $40 ($90 for international students). Electronic applications accepted. *Expenses:* Tuition, state resident: full-time $5784; part-time $241 per credit hour. Tuition, nonresident: part-time $551 per credit hour. Required fees: $1728; $48 per credit hour. $306. Tuition and fees vary according to course load. *Financial support:* In 2009–10, 33 students received support, including 1 research assistantship (averaging $5,053 per year), 9 teaching assistantships (averaging $5,327 per year); career-related internships or fieldwork, Federal Work-Study, and institutionally sponsored loans also available. Support available to part-time students. Financial award application deadline: 4/1; financial award applicants required to submit FAFSA. *Faculty research:* Religion in American public life, international humanitarian and refugee policy, judicial biography and history, citizenship and ethics, business and government policy making. *Unit head:* Dr. Cecilia Castillio, Graduate Adviser, 512-245-2143, Fax: 512-345-7815, E-mail: cr09@txstate.edu. *Application contact:* Dr. J. Michael Willoughby, Dean of Graduate School, 512-245-2581, Fax: 512-245-8365, E-mail: gradcollege@txstate.edu.

Texas State University–San Marcos, Graduate School, Interdisciplinary Studies in Political Science, San Marcos, TX 78666. Offers MAIS. *Students:* 1 part-time (0 women). Average age 35. 1 applicant, 100% accepted, 1 enrolled. *Degree requirements:* For master's, comprehensive exam, thesis optional. *Entrance requirements:* For master's, minimum GPA of 2.9 or GRE (minimum combined score of 900 Verbal and Quantitative preferred). Additional exam requirements/recommendations for international students: Required—TOEFL (minimum score 550 paper-based; 213 computer-based). *Application deadline:* For fall admission, 6/15 priority date for domestic students, 6/1 for international students; for spring admission, 10/15 priority

Political Science

Texas State University–San Marcos (continued)
date for domestic students, 10/1 for international students. Applications are processed on a rolling basis. Application fee: $40 ($90 for international students). *Expenses:* Tuition, state resident: full-time $5784; part-time $241 per credit hour. Tuition, nonresident: part-time $551 per credit hour. Required fees: $1728; $48 per credit hour. $306. Tuition and fees vary according to course load. *Financial support:* Application deadline: 4/1. *Unit head:* Dr. Cecilia Castillio, Graduate Advisor, 512-245-3255, Fax: 512-345-7815, E-mail: cr09@txstate.edu. *Application contact:* Dr. J. Michael Willoughby, Dean of Graduate School, 512-245-2581, Fax: 512-245-8365, E-mail: gradcollege@txstate.edu.

Texas Tech University, Graduate School, College of Arts and Sciences, Department of Political Science, Lubbock, TX 79409. Offers political science (MA, PhD); public administration (MPA); JD/MPA; MPA/MA. *Accreditation:* NASPAA (one or more programs are accredited). Part-time programs available. *Faculty:* 13 full-time (3 women). *Students:* 62 full-time (28 women), 16 part-time (4 women); includes 14 minority (1 African American, 2 American Indian/Alaska Native, 2 Asian Americans or Pacific Islanders, 9 Hispanic Americans), 12 international. Average age 28. 103 applicants, 53% accepted, 23 enrolled. In 2009, 29 master's, 1 doctorate awarded. *Degree requirements:* For master's, thesis or alternative; for doctorate, thesis/dissertation. *Entrance requirements:* For master's and doctorate, GRE General Test. Additional exam requirements/recommendations for international students: Required—TOEFL (minimum score 550 paper-based; 213 computer-based). *Application deadline:* For fall admission, 3/1 priority date for international students; for spring admission, 11/1 priority date for international students. Applications are processed on a rolling basis. Application fee: $50 ($75 for international students). Electronic applications accepted. *Expenses:* Tuition, state resident: full-time $5100; part-time $213 per credit hour. Tuition, nonresident: full-time $11,748; part-time $490 per credit hour. Required fees: $2298; $50 per credit hour. $555 per semester. *Financial support:* In 2009–10, 7 teaching assistantships with partial tuition reimbursements (averaging $14,691 per year) were awarded; research assistantships with partial tuition reimbursements, Federal Work-Study and institutionally sponsored loans also available. Support available to part-time students. Financial award application deadline: 4/15; financial award applicants required to submit FAFSA. *Faculty research:* State politics, American institutions and behavior, Asian politics, international and comparative political relations and economics, public administration and organizations. Total annual research expenditures: $18,150. *Unit head:* Dr. Dennis Patterson, Chair, 806-742-3121, Fax: 806-742-0850, E-mail: dennis.patterson@ttu.edu. *Application contact:* Dr. Frank Thames, Associate Chair, 806-742-4049, Fax: 806-742-0850, E-mail: frank.thames@ttu.edu.

Texas Woman's University, Graduate School, College of Arts and Sciences, Department of History and Government, Denton, TX 76201. Offers government (MA); history (MA). Part-time and evening/weekend programs available. *Faculty:* 10 full-time (3 women), 1 (woman) part-time/adjunct. *Students:* 7 full-time (5 women), 28 part-time (23 women); includes 8 minority (4 African Americans, 1 American Indian/Alaska Native, 3 Hispanic Americans), 2 international. Average age 36. 11 applicants, 55% accepted, 6 enrolled. In 2009, 12 master's awarded. *Degree requirements:* For master's, comprehensive exam, thesis. *Entrance requirements:* For master's, GRE (waived if completed a graduate degree), minimum GPA of 3.3, writing sample/portfolio. Additional exam requirements/recommendations for international students: Required—TOEFL (minimum score 550 paper-based; 213 computer-based; 79 iBT). *Application deadline:* For fall admission, 7/1 priority date for domestic students, 3/1 for international students; for spring admission, 12/1 priority date for domestic students, 7/1 for international students. Applications are processed on a rolling basis. Application fee: $50. Electronic applications accepted. *Expenses:* Tuition, state resident: full-time $3564; part-time $198 per credit hour. Tuition, nonresident: full-time $8550; part-time $475 per credit hour. Required fees: $69.26 per credit hour. Tuition and fees vary according to course load. *Financial support:* In 2009–10, 9 students received support, including 14 research assistantships (averaging $9,684 per year), 1 teaching assistantship (averaging $9,684 per year); career-related internships or fieldwork, Federal Work-Study, institutionally sponsored loans, scholarships/grants, traineeships, health care benefits, and unspecified assistantships also available. Support available to part-time students. Financial award application deadline: 3/1; financial award applicants required to submit FAFSA. *Faculty research:* Recent American history, civil liberties, military history, legal studies, women and politics. *Unit head:* Dr. Mark Kessler, Chair, 940-898-2133, Fax: 940-898-2130, E-mail: historygov@twu.edu. *Application contact:* Samuel Wheeler, Assistant Director of Admissions, 940-898-3188, Fax: 940-898-3081, E-mail: wheelersr@twu.edu.

Troy University, Graduate School, College of Education, Program in Postsecondary Education, Troy, AL 36082. Offers adult education (M Ed); biology (M Ed); criminal justice (M Ed); english (M Ed); foundations of education (M Ed); general science (M Ed); higher education administration (M Ed); history (M Ed); instructional technology (M Ed); mathematics (M Ed); music industry (M Ed); physical fitness (M Ed); political science (M Ed); public administration (M Ed); social science (M Ed); teaching english (M Ed). Also offered through the University College. *Accreditation:* NCATE. Part-time and evening/weekend programs available. *Students:* 267 full-time (192 women), 381 part-time (293 women); includes 326 minority (309 African Americans, 4 American Indian/Alaska Native, 5 Asian Americans or Pacific Islanders, 8 Hispanic Americans). Average age 34. 343 applicants, 90% accepted. In 2009, 480 master's awarded. *Degree requirements:* For master's, comprehensive exam, thesis. *Entrance requirements:* For master's, MAT (minimum score 385), minimum GPA of 2.5. Additional exam requirements/recommendations for international students: Required—TOEFL (minimum score 523 paper-based; 193 computer-based; 70 iBT), IELTS, or ACT Compass ESL (minimum score 270 on Listening, Reading, and Grammar with no individual score below 85 and a minimum score of 8 out of 12 on writing test). *Application deadline:* Applications are processed on a rolling basis. Application fee: $50. Electronic applications accepted. *Financial support:* Available to part-time students. Applicants required to submit FAFSA. *Unit head:* Dr. Andrew Creamer, Chair, 334-670-3350, E-mail: drcreamer@troy.edu. *Application contact:* Brenda K. Campbell, Director of Graduate Admissions, 334-670-3178, Fax: 334-670-3733, E-mail: bcamp@troy.edu.

Tulane University, School of Liberal Arts, Department of Political Science, New Orleans, LA 70118-5669. Offers MA, PhD, MA/JD. *Degree requirements:* For master's, one foreign language, thesis optional, seminar; for doctorate, 2 foreign languages, thesis/dissertation. *Entrance requirements:* For master's, GRE General Test, minimum B average in undergraduate course work; for doctorate, GRE General Test. Additional exam requirements/recommendations for international students: Required—TOEFL. Electronic applications accepted.

Université de Montréal, Faculty of Arts and Sciences, Department of Political Science, Montréal, QC H3C 3J7, Canada. Offers M Sc, PhD. *Degree requirements:* For master's, thesis; for doctorate, thesis/dissertation, general exam. *Entrance requirements:* For master's, minimum GPA of 2.8; for doctorate, master's degree, minimum GPA of 3.0. Electronic applications accepted.

Université du Québec à Montréal, Graduate Programs, Program in Political Science, Montréal, QC H3C 3P8, Canada. Offers MA, PhD. Part-time programs available. *Degree requirements:* For master's, thesis; for doctorate, thesis/dissertation. *Entrance requirements:* For master's, appropriate bachelor's degree or equivalent, proficiency in French; for doctorate, appropriate master's degree or equivalent, proficiency in French.

Université Laval, Faculty of Social Sciences, Department of Political Science, Program in Policy Analysis, Québec, QC G1K 7P4, Canada. Offers MA. *Degree requirements:* For master's, thesis (for some programs). *Entrance requirements:* For master's, knowledge of French, comprehension of written English. Electronic applications accepted.

Université Laval, Faculty of Social Sciences, Department of Political Science, Programs in Political Science, Québec, QC G1K 7P4, Canada. Offers MA, PhD. Terminal master's awarded for partial completion of doctoral program. *Degree requirements:* For master's, thesis (for some programs); for doctorate, comprehensive exam, thesis/dissertation. *Entrance requirements:* For master's, knowledge of French; for doctorate, knowledge of French, comprehension of written English. Electronic applications accepted.

University at Albany, State University of New York, Nelson A. Rockefeller College of Public Affairs and Policy, Department of Political Science, Albany, NY 12222-0001. Offers MA, PhD. *Degree requirements:* For doctorate, one foreign language, thesis/dissertation. *Entrance requirements:* For doctorate, GRE General Test. Additional exam requirements/recommendations for international students: Required—TOEFL (minimum score 550 paper-based; 213 computer-based). Electronic applications accepted.

University at Buffalo, the State University of New York, Graduate School, College of Arts and Sciences, Department of Political Science, Buffalo, NY 14260. Offers MA, PhD. *Faculty:* 13 full-time (3 women), 8 part-time/adjunct (3 women). *Students:* 42 full-time (11 women), 5 part-time (2 women); includes 4 minority (3 Asian Americans or Pacific Islanders, 1 Hispanic American), 7 international. Average age 27. 58 applicants, 48% accepted, 17 enrolled. In 2009, 7 master's, 2 doctorates awarded. Terminal master's awarded for partial completion of doctoral program. *Degree requirements:* For master's, thesis or alternative, paper, project; for doctorate, comprehensive exam, thesis/dissertation. *Entrance requirements:* For master's, GRE General Test, minimum GPA of 3.0; for doctorate, GRE General Test, minimum GPA of 3.3. Additional exam requirements/recommendations for international students: Required—TOEFL (minimum score 550 paper-based; 213 computer-based; 79 iBT). *Application deadline:* For fall admission, 6/1 priority date for domestic students, 3/1 for international students; for spring admission, 11/1 priority date for domestic students, 10/1 for international students. Applications are processed on a rolling basis. Application fee: $75. Electronic applications accepted. *Financial support:* In 2009–10, 11 students received support, including 3 fellowships with full tuition reimbursements available (averaging $16,800 per year), 11 teaching assistantships with full tuition reimbursements available (averaging $10,400 per year); research assistantships, career-related internships or fieldwork, Federal Work-Study, health care benefits, tuition waivers (partial), and unspecified assistantships also available. Financial award application deadline: 2/1; financial award applicants required to submit FAFSA. *Faculty research:* American politics, public law, comparative politics, international politics. *Unit head:* Dr. James Campbell, Chairman, 716-645-8452, Fax: 716-645-2166, E-mail: jcampbel@buffalo.edu. *Application contact:* Mary E. OBrien, Graduate Coordinator, 716-645-3441, Fax: 716-645-2166, E-mail: meobrien@buffalo.edu.

The University of Akron, Graduate School, Buchtel College of Arts and Sciences, Department of Political Science, Akron, OH 44325. Offers applied politics (MA); political science (MA); JD/MAP. Part-time programs available. *Faculty:* 12 full-time (2 women), 14 part-time/adjunct (4 women). *Students:* 41 full-time (14 women), 30 part-time (12 women); includes 7 minority (4 African Americans, 2 Asian Americans or Pacific Islanders, 1 Hispanic American), 2 international. Average age 28. 40 applicants, 88% accepted, 21 enrolled. In 2009, 23 master's awarded. *Degree requirements:* For master's, comprehensive exam, essay, seminars (political science), portfolio (applied politics). *Entrance requirements:* For master's, minimum GPA of 2.75, letters of recommendation. Additional exam requirements/recommendations for international students: Required—TOEFL (minimum score 550 paper-based; 213 computer-based; 79 iBT). *Application deadline:* Applications are processed on a rolling basis. Application fee: $30 ($40 for international students). Electronic applications accepted. *Expenses:* Tuition, state resident: full-time $6570; part-time $365 per credit hour. Tuition, nonresident: full-time $11,250; part-time $625 per credit hour. *Financial support:* In 2009–10, 4 research assistantships with full tuition reimbursements, 9 teaching assistantships with full tuition reimbursements were awarded. *Faculty research:* Public opinion and public policy, applied/electrical politics, international/comparative politics, the politics of criminal justice, conflict management. Total annual research expenditures: $75,888. *Unit head:* Dr. James McHugh, Chair, 330-972-6291, E-mail: mchugh@uakron.edu. *Application contact:* Dr. Ronald Gelleny, Graduate Director, 330-972-7406, E-mail: gelleny@uakron.edu.

The University of Alabama, Graduate School, College of Arts and Sciences, Department of Political Science, Tuscaloosa, AL 35487. Offers political science (MA, PhD); public administration (MPA). Part-time programs available. *Faculty:* 15 full-time (4 women). *Students:* 50 full-time (18 women), 13 part-time (7 women); includes 12 minority (6 African Americans, 1 American Indian/Alaska Native, 2 Asian Americans or Pacific Islanders, 3 Hispanic Americans), 6 international. Average age 29. 70 applicants, 44% accepted, 21 enrolled. In 2009, 3 master's, 3 doctorates awarded. Terminal master's awarded for partial completion of doctoral program. *Median time to degree:* Of those who began their doctoral program in fall 2001, 100% received their degree in 8 years or less. *Degree requirements:* For master's, thesis optional; for doctorate, comprehensive exam, thesis/dissertation. *Entrance requirements:* For master's and doctorate, GRE (minimum score: 1000), minimum undergraduate GPA of 3.0. Additional exam requirements/recommendations for international students: Required—TOEFL. *Application deadline:* For fall admission, 6/30 for domestic and international students; for spring admission, 10/15 for domestic and international students. Applications are processed on a rolling basis. Application fee: $50 ($60 for international students). Electronic applications accepted. *Expenses:* Tuition, state resident: full-time $7000. Tuition, nonresident: full-time $19,200. *Financial support:* In 2009–10, 15 students received support, including teaching assistantships with full tuition reimbursements available (averaging $10,908 per year); fellowships, career-related internships or fieldwork and Federal Work-Study also available. Financial award application deadline: 2/15. *Faculty research:* American politics, comparative politics, international relations, public administration, political theory. Total annual research expenditures: $20,223. *Unit head:* Dr. Carol A. Cassel, Chair and Professor, 205-348-5981, Fax: 205-348-5298, E-mail: ccassel@tenhoor.as.ua.edu. *Application contact:* Dr. Joseph Smith, Graduate Advisor, 205-348-3806, Fax: 205-348-5248, E-mail: josmith@bama.ua.edu.

University of Alberta, Faculty of Graduate Studies and Research, Department of Political Science, Edmonton, AB T6G 2E1, Canada. Offers MA, PhD. Part-time programs available. *Faculty:* 21 full-time (7 women), 8 part-time/adjunct (4 women). *Students:* 33 full-time (18 women), 24 part-time (7 women). *Degree requirements:* For master's, thesis (for some programs); for doctorate, one foreign language, thesis/dissertation. *Entrance requirements:* Additional exam requirements/recommendations for international students: Required—TOEFL. *Application deadline:* For fall admission, 1/15 for domestic students. Application fee: $60. Tuition and fees charges are reported in Canadian dollars. *Expenses:* Tuition, area resident: Full-time $4626 Canadian dollars; part-time $99.72 Canadian dollars per unit. International tuition: $8216 Canadian dollars full-time. Required fees: $3590 Canadian dollars; $99.72 Canadian dollars per unit. $215 Canadian dollars per term. *Financial support:* In 2009–10, 15 students received support, including 8 teaching assistantships; scholarships/grants also available. *Faculty research:* Canadian politics, international relations, globalization, classical and contemporary political theory, gender and politics. *Unit head:* Dr. L. Harder, Graduate Coordinator, 780-492-4771, Fax: 403-492-2586. *Application contact:* Scott Jensen, Graduate Secretary, 403-492-4771, Fax: 403-492-2586, E-mail: psgrad@ualberta.ca.

The University of Arizona, Graduate College, College of Social and Behavioral Sciences, Department of Political Science, Tucson, AZ 85721. Offers MA, PhD. *Faculty:* 21 full-time (8 women). *Students:* 24 full-time (14 women), 9 part-time (5 women); includes 2 minority (1 African American, 1 Hispanic American), 7 international. Average age 30. 63 applicants, 6% accepted, 4 enrolled. In 2009, 4 master's, 1 doctorate awarded. Terminal master's awarded for partial completion of doctoral program. *Degree requirements:* For master's, thesis or alternative; for doctorate, variable foreign language requirement, comprehensive exam, thesis/dissertation. *Entrance requirements:* For master's, GRE General Test, minimum GPA of 3.2, 3 letters of recommendation, writing sample; for doctorate, GRE General Test, minimum GPA of 3.2, 3 letters of recommendation, statement of purpose, writing sample. Additional exam requirements/recommendations for international students: Required—TOEFL (minimum score 550 paper-based; 213 computer-based; 79 iBT). *Application deadline:* For fall admission, 1/15 for domestic and international students. Applications are processed on a rolling basis. Application fee: $65. Electronic applications accepted. *Expenses:* Tuition, state resident: full-time $9028. Tuition, nonresident: full-time $24,890. *Financial support:* In 2009–10, 2 research assistantships with full tuition reimbursements (averaging $13,742 per year), 23 teaching assistantships with full tuition reimbursements (averaging $13,088 per year) were awarded; institutionally sponsored loans, scholarships/grants, health care benefits, tuition waivers (full), and unspecified assistantships also available. Financial award application deadline: 3/6. *Faculty research:* Voting behavior, political participation, Soviet domestic and Sino-Soviet relations, presidential leadership and congressional behavior. Total annual research expenditures: $50,514. *Unit head:* Dr. William Dixon, Head, 520-621-5728, Fax: 520-621-5051, E-mail: dixonw@email.arizona.edu. *Application contact:* Victoria Healey, Coordinator, 520-621-7601, Fax: 520-621-5051, E-mail: vhealey@email.arizona.edu.

University of Arkansas, Graduate School, J. William Fulbright College of Arts and Sciences, Department of Political Science, Program in Political Science, Fayetteville, AR 72701-1201. Offers MA. *Students:* 15 full-time (8 women), 6 part-time (3 women); includes 2 minority (both African Americans), 3 international. In 2009, 11 master's awarded. *Degree requirements:* For master's, thesis or alternative. *Entrance requirements:* For master's, GRE General Test. Application fee: $40 ($50 for international students). *Expenses:* Tuition, state resident: full-time $7355; part-time $356.58 per hour. Tuition, nonresident: full-time $17,401; part-time $775.17 per hour. Required fees: $1203. *Financial support:* In 2009–10, 1 research assistantship, 2 teaching assistantships were awarded; fellowships, career-related internships or fieldwork and Federal Work-Study also available. Support available to part-time students. Financial award application deadline: 4/1; financial award applicants required to submit FAFSA. *Unit head:* Dr. Margaret Reid, Graduate Coordinator, 479-575-3356, E-mail: mreid@uark.edu. *Application contact:* Dr. Andrew Dowdle, Graduate Coordinator, 479-575-6445, E-mail: adowdle@uark.edu.

The University of British Columbia, Faculty of Arts and Faculty of Graduate Studies, Department of Political Science, Vancouver, BC V6T 1Z1, Canada. Offers MA, PhD. Part-time programs available. *Degree requirements:* For master's, thesis; for doctorate, comprehensive exam, thesis/dissertation. *Entrance requirements:* For master's, BA in political science; for doctorate, GRE, BA and MA in political science. Additional exam requirements/recommendations for international students: Required—TOEFL (minimum score 580 paper-based; 237 computer-based), TWE (minimum score 5). Electronic applications accepted. *Faculty research:* Canadian politics, international relations, political theory, comparative politics, public policy.

University of Calgary, Faculty of Graduate Studies, Faculty of Social Sciences, Department of Political Science, Calgary, AB T2N 1N4, Canada. Offers MA, PhD. *Degree requirements:* For master's, thesis; for doctorate, one foreign language, comprehensive exam, thesis/dissertation, prospectus, oral and written candidacy exams. *Entrance requirements:* For master's, minimum GPA of 3.4; for doctorate, minimum GPA of 3.7. Additional exam requirements/recommendations for international students: Required—TOEFL (minimum score 620 paper-based; 260 computer-based). Electronic applications accepted. *Faculty research:* Canadian politics, international relations, comparative politics, theory, public policy.

University of California, Berkeley, Graduate Division, College of Letters and Science, Charles and Louise Travers Department of Political Science, Berkeley, CA 94720-1500. Offers PhD. *Faculty:* 44 full-time, 1 part-time/adjunct. *Students:* 150 full-time (60 women). Average age 31. 428 applicants, 20 enrolled. In 2009, 18 doctorates awarded. *Degree requirements:* For doctorate, thesis/dissertation, oral qualifying exams. *Entrance requirements:* For doctorate, GRE General Test, minimum GPA of 3.0, 3 letters of recommendation. *Application deadline:* For fall admission, 12/2 for domestic students. Application fee: $70 ($90 for international students). Electronic applications accepted. *Financial support:* Fellowships, research assistantships, teaching assistantships, unspecified assistantships available. *Unit head:* Prof. Paul Pierson, Chair, 510-643-4408, E-mail: ch_politicalscience@ls.berkeley.edu. *Application contact:* Janet Eva Newhall, Information Contact, 510-643-4408, E-mail: pscadmit@berkeley.edu.

University of California, Davis, Graduate Studies, Program in Political Science, Davis, CA 95616. Offers MA, PhD. Terminal master's awarded for partial completion of doctoral program. *Degree requirements:* For master's, thesis; for doctorate, thesis/dissertation. *Entrance requirements:* For master's and doctorate, GRE General Test, minimum GPA of 3.0, writing sample. Additional exam requirements/recommendations for international students: Required—TOEFL (minimum score 550 paper-based; 213 computer-based). Electronic applications accepted. *Faculty research:* American government and politics, political theory, comparative politics, international relations, public law.

University of California, Irvine, Office of Graduate Studies, School of Social Sciences, Department of Political Science, Irvine, CA 92697. Offers political psychology (PhD); political sciences (PhD); public choice (PhD). *Students:* 75 full-time (34 women), 5 part-time (1 woman); includes 3 African Americans, 11 Asian Americans or Pacific Islanders, 6 Hispanic Americans, 3 international. Average age 29. 153 applicants, 20% accepted, 15 enrolled. In 2009, 9 doctorates awarded. *Degree requirements:* For doctorate, thesis/dissertation. *Entrance requirements:* For doctorate, GRE General Test, minimum GPA of 3.0. Additional exam requirements/recommendations for international students: Required—TOEFL (minimum score 550 paper-based; 213 computer-based). *Application deadline:* For fall admission, 1/15 priority date for domestic students, 1/15 for international students. Applications are processed on a rolling basis. Application fee: $70 ($90 for international students). Electronic applications accepted. *Financial support:* Fellowships, research assistantships with full tuition reimbursements, teaching assistantships, institutionally sponsored loans, traineeships, health care benefits, and unspecified assistantships available. Financial award application deadline: 3/1; financial award applicants required to submit FAFSA. *Faculty research:* Political behavior, political economy, international relations. *Unit head:* Katherine Tate, Chair, 949-824-4012, E-mail: ktate@uci.edu. *Application contact:* Diane Enriquez, Graduate Counselor, 949-824-5924, Fax: 949-824-3548, E-mail: dmvargas@uci.edu.

University of California, Los Angeles, Graduate Division, College of Letters and Science, Department of Political Science, Los Angeles, CA 90095. Offers MA, PhD. *Students:* 145 full-time (60 women); includes 32 minority (7 African Americans, 10 Asian Americans or Pacific Islanders, 15 Hispanic Americans), 25 international. Average age 30. 314 applicants, 20% accepted, 19 enrolled. In 2009, 12 master's, 12 doctorates awarded. *Degree requirements:* For master's, comprehensive exam; for doctorate, one foreign language, thesis/dissertation, oral and written qualifying exams. *Entrance requirements:* For master's, GRE General Test, minimum GPA of 3.0, sample of written work; for doctorate, GRE General Test, minimum undergraduate GPA of 3.0, sample of written work. *Application deadline:* For fall admission, 12/15 for domestic and international students. Application fee: $70 ($90 for international students). Electronic applications accepted. *Financial support:* In 2009–10, 81 fellowships with full tuition reimbursements, 36 research assistantships with full tuition reimbursements, 86 teaching assistantships with full tuition reimbursements were awarded; Federal Work-Study, institutionally sponsored loans, scholarships/grants, health care benefits, tuition waivers (full and partial), and unspecified assistantships also available. Financial award application deadline: 3/1; financial award applicants required to submit FAFSA. *Unit head:* Dr. Edmond Keller, Chair, 310-206-1307. *Application contact:* Joseph Brown, Graduate Advisor, 310-825-3372, Fax: 310-825-0778, E-mail: joseph@polisci.ucla.edu.

University of California, Riverside, Graduate Division, Department of Political Science, Riverside, CA 92521-0102. Offers MA, PhD. Part-time programs available. Terminal master's awarded for partial completion of doctoral program. *Degree requirements:* For master's, comprehensive exams or thesis; for doctorate, thesis/dissertation, qualifying exams. *Entrance requirements:* For master's and doctorate, GRE General Test, minimum GPA of 3.2. Additional exam requirements/recommendations for international students: Required—TOEFL (minimum score 550 paper-based; 213 computer-based; 80 iBT). Electronic applications accepted. *Faculty research:* American politics, mass political behavior, comparative politics, international relations, political theory.

University of California, San Diego, Office of Graduate Studies, Department of Political Science, La Jolla, CA 92093. Offers Latin American studies (MA); political science (PhD); political science and international affairs (PhD). *Entrance requirements:* For master's and doctorate, GRE General Test. Electronic applications accepted.

University of California, San Diego, Office of Graduate Studies, Graduate School of International Relations and Pacific Studies, La Jolla, CA 92093. Offers economics and international affairs (PhD); Pacific international affairs (MPIA); political science and international affairs (PhD). *Degree requirements:* For master's, one foreign language; for doctorate, thesis/dissertation. *Entrance requirements:* For master's, GMAT or GRE General Test; for doctorate, GRE General Test. Additional exam requirements/recommendations for international students: Required—TOEFL (minimum score 550 paper-based; 213 computer-based). Electronic applications accepted. *Faculty research:* Pacific Rim as system and placement in global relations; studies in international economics, management and finance; analysis of patterns of policymaking in countries of the Pacific.

University of California, Santa Barbara, Graduate Division, College of Letters and Sciences, Division of Social Sciences, Department of Political Science, Santa Barbara, CA 93106-9420. Offers political science (MA); women's studies (PhD); MA/PhD. Part-time programs available. *Faculty:* 22 full-time (10 women), 5 part-time/adjunct (2 women). *Students:* 51 full-time (22 women). Average age 30. 94 applicants, 32% accepted, 7 enrolled. In 2009, 9 master's, 4 doctorates awarded. Terminal master's awarded for partial completion of doctoral program. *Degree requirements:* For master's, comprehensive exam (for some programs), thesis optional; for doctorate, one foreign language, comprehensive exam, thesis/dissertation. *Entrance requirements:* For master's, GRE General Test, minimum undergraduate GPA of 3.0, 3 letters of recommendation, resume/curriculum vitae; for doctorate, GRE General Test, master's degree with minimum GPA of 3.0, 3 letters of recommendation, statement of purpose, personal achievements/contributions statement, resume/curriculum vitae, transcripts for post-secondary institutions attended. Additional exam requirements/recommendations for international students: Required—TOEFL (minimum score 600 paper-based; 250 computer-based; 100 iBT), or IELTS. *Application deadline:* For fall admission, 1/1 priority date for domestic and international students. Application fee: $70 ($90 for international students). Electronic applications accepted. *Financial support:* In 2009–10, 43 students received support, including 25 fellowships with full tuition reimbursements available (averaging $8,200 per year), 42 teaching assistantships with partial tuition reimbursements available (averaging $8,900 per year); Federal Work-Study, institutionally sponsored loans, scholarships/grants, and health care benefits also available. Financial award applicants required to submit FAFSA. *Faculty research:* American politics, comparative politics, international relations, political theory, methodology. *Unit head:* Dr. John Woolley, Chair, 805-893-3432, Fax: 805-893-3309, E-mail: woolley@polsci.ucsb.edu. *Application contact:* Linda James, Staff Graduate Advisor, 805-893-3626, Fax: 805-893-3309, E-mail: james@polsci.ucsb.edu.

University of California, Santa Cruz, Division of Graduate Studies, Division of Social Sciences, Politics Department, Santa Cruz, CA 95064. Offers PhD. *Entrance requirements:* Additional exam requirements/recommendations for international students: Required—TOEFL. Electronic applications accepted.

University of Central Florida, College of Sciences, Department of Political Science, Orlando, FL 32816. Offers MA. Part-time and evening/weekend programs available. *Faculty:* 22 full-time (6 women), 7 part-time/adjunct (1 woman). *Students:* 35 full-time (17 women), 30 part-time (11 women); includes 11 minority (1 African American, 10 Hispanic Americans), 3 international. Average age 27. 54 applicants, 74% accepted, 18 enrolled. In 2009, 1 master's awarded. *Degree requirements:* For master's, comprehensive exam, thesis. *Entrance requirements:* For master's, GRE General Test, minimum GPA of 3.0 in last 60 hours. Additional exam requirements/recommendations for international students: Required—TOEFL. *Application deadline:* For fall admission, 7/15 for domestic students; for spring admission, 12/1 for domestic students. Application fee: $30. Electronic applications accepted. *Expenses:* Tuition, state resident: part-time $306.31 per credit hour. Tuition, nonresident: part-time $1099.01 per credit hour. Part-time tuition and fees vary according to degree level and program. *Financial support:* In 2009–10, 8 students received support, including 3 fellowships with partial tuition reimbursements available (averaging $6,900 per year), 6 teaching assistantships with partial tuition reimbursements available (averaging $7,700 per year); career-related internships or fieldwork, Federal Work-Study, institutionally sponsored loans, tuition waivers (partial), and unspecified assistantships also available. Financial award application deadline: 3/1; financial award applicants required to submit FAFSA. *Faculty research:* Environment, presidential campaigning, term limits for elected officials. *Unit head:* Dr. Roger Handberg, Chair, 407-823-2608, Fax: 407-823-0051. *Application contact:* Dr. Roger Handberg, Chair, 407-823-2608, Fax: 407-823-0051.

University of Central Oklahoma, College of Graduate Studies and Research, College of Liberal Arts, Department of Political Science, Program in Political Science, Edmond, OK 73034-5209. Offers MA. Part-time programs available. *Entrance requirements:* Additional exam requirements/recommendations for international students: Required—TOEFL (minimum score 550 paper-based; 213 computer-based). Electronic applications accepted. *Expenses:* Tuition, state resident: full-time $4128; part-time $172 per credit hour. Tuition, nonresident: full-time $10,373; part-time $432.20 per credit hour. Required fees: $433.20; $18.05 per credit hour. *Faculty research:* U. S. Congress.

University of Chicago, Division of Social Sciences, Department of Political Science, Chicago, IL 60637-1513. Offers PhD. *Students:* 144. In 2009, 16 doctorates awarded. *Degree requirements:* For doctorate, one foreign language, thesis/dissertation, exam, qualifying paper. *Entrance requirements:* For doctorate, GRE General Test. Additional exam requirements/recommendations for international students: Required—TOEFL, IELTS (minimum score 7). *Application deadline:* For fall admission, 12/10 for domestic and international students. Application fee: $55. Electronic applications accepted. *Financial support:* Fellowships, research assistantships, teaching assistantships, Federal Work-Study, institutionally sponsored loans, scholarships/grants, traineeships, health care benefits, and unspecified assistantships available. Financial award application deadline: 12/10. *Faculty research:* Political philosophy, international political economy, strategic studies, public policy and race relations, comparative politics (China, Middle East, Soviet Union, Africa, India, Japan). *Unit head:* Prof. Bernard Harcourt, Chair, 773-702-6708. *Application contact:* Office of the Dean of Students, 773-702-8415.

University of Cincinnati, Graduate School, McMicken College of Arts and Sciences, Department of Political Science, Cincinnati, OH 45221. Offers MA, PhD. Terminal master's awarded for partial completion of doctoral program. *Degree requirements:* For master's, thesis (for some programs); for doctorate, thesis/dissertation. *Entrance requirements:* For master's and doctorate, GRE General Test, GRE Subject Test. Additional exam requirements/recommendations for international students: Required—TOEFL. Electronic applications accepted. *Faculty research:* International security, methodology, American politics, comparative politics.

University of Colorado at Boulder, Graduate School, College of Arts and Sciences, Department of Political Science, Boulder, CO 80309. Offers international affairs (MA); political science (MA, PhD); public policy (MA). *Faculty:* 25 full-time (8 women). *Students:* 55 full-time (27 women), 8 part-time (5 women); includes 7 minority (2 American Indian/Alaska Native, 1 Asian American or Pacific Islander, 4 Hispanic Americans), 6 international. Average age 30. 179 applicants, 9% accepted, 13 enrolled. In 2009, 12 master's, 7 doctorates awarded. Terminal master's awarded for partial completion of doctoral program. *Degree requirements:* For master's, comprehensive exam, thesis; for doctorate, one foreign language, thesis/dissertation. *Entrance requirements:* For master's, GRE General Test, minimum undergraduate GPA of 3.0; for doctorate, GRE General Test, minimum GPA of 3.5 (undergraduate), 3.0 (graduate). *Application deadline:* For fall admission, 12/31 priority date for domestic students, 12/31 for international students. Application fee: $50 ($60 for international students). *Financial support:* In 2009–10, 10 fellowships (averaging $2,060 per year), 41 research assistantships (averaging $12,087 per year) were awarded; Federal Work-Study also available. Financial award application deadline: 12/31. *Faculty research:* American government and politics, comparative politics, international relations, public policy, law and politics, political philosophy, empirical theory and methodology. Total annual research expenditures: $180,188.

Political Science

University of Colorado Denver, College of Liberal Arts and Sciences, Department of Political Science, Denver, CO 80217-3364. Offers MA. Part-time and evening/weekend programs available. *Students:* 11 full-time (1 woman), 43 part-time (23 women); includes 11 minority (2 African Americans, 4 American Indian/Alaska Native, 5 Hispanic Americans), 5 international. 40 applicants, 75% accepted, 6 enrolled. In 2009, 23 master's awarded. *Degree requirements:* For master's, thesis or alternative. *Entrance requirements:* For master's, GRE, 18 hours of course work in political science. Additional exam requirements/recommendations for international students: Required—TOEFL (minimum score 525 paper-based; 197 computer-based). *Application deadline:* For fall admission, 6/1 for domestic students; for spring admission, 11/1 for domestic students. Applications are processed on a rolling basis. Application fee: $50 ($75 for international students). Electronic applications accepted. *Financial support:* Research assistantships, teaching assistantships, Federal Work-Study available. Financial award application deadline: 4/1; financial award applicants required to submit FAFSA. *Faculty research:* Palestinian peace process, post-Soviet governmental corruption, gender/racial/ethnic politics in the U.S.A., U.S. immigration. *Unit head:* Jana Everett, Chair, 303-556-3515, Fax: 303-556-4861, E-mail: jana.everett@ucdenver.edu. *Application contact:* Cory Gruebele, Program Assistant, 303-556-3556, Fax: 303-556-6041, E-mail: corwin.lydel.gruebele@ucdenver.edu.

University of Connecticut, Graduate School, College of Liberal Arts and Sciences, Department of Political Science, Storrs, CT 06269. Offers MA, PhD. *Faculty:* 36 full-time (11 women). *Students:* 52 full-time (22 women), 18 part-time (2 women); includes 7 minority (3 African Americans, 1 Asian American or Pacific Islander, 3 Hispanic Americans), 12 international. Average age 32. 103 applicants, 11% accepted, 6 enrolled. In 2009, 8 master's, 7 doctorates awarded. Terminal master's awarded for partial completion of doctoral program. *Degree requirements:* For master's, comprehensive exam; for doctorate, 2 foreign languages, thesis/dissertation. *Entrance requirements:* For master's and doctorate, GRE General Test. Additional exam requirements/recommendations for international students: Required—TOEFL (minimum score 550 paper-based; 213 computer-based). *Application deadline:* For fall admission, 2/1 priority date for domestic and international students; for spring admission, 11/1 for domestic students, 10/1 for international students. Applications are processed on a rolling basis. Application fee: $55. Electronic applications accepted. *Expenses:* Tuition, state resident: full-time $4725; part-time $525 per credit. Tuition, nonresident: full-time $12,267; part-time $1363 per credit. Required fees: $346 per semester. Tuition and fees vary according to course load. *Financial support:* In 2009–10, 14 research assistantships with full tuition reimbursements, 29 teaching assistantships with full tuition reimbursements were awarded; fellowships, career-related internships or fieldwork, Federal Work-Study, scholarships/grants, health care benefits, and unspecified assistantships also available. Financial award application deadline: 2/1; financial award applicants required to submit FAFSA. *Unit head:* Prof. Howard L. Reiter, Head, 860-486-2440, Fax: 860-486-3347, E-mail: howard.reiter@uconn.edu. *Application contact:* Prof. John Garry Clifford, Director of Graduate Studies, 860-486-2079, Fax: 860-486-3347, E-mail: john.clifford@uconn.edu.

University of Dallas, Braniff Graduate School of Liberal Arts, Institute of Philosophic Studies, Doctoral Program in Politics, Irving, TX 75062-4736. Offers PhD. *Faculty:* 5 full-time (1 woman). *Students:* 24 full-time (5 women); includes 3 minority (1 American Indian/Alaska Native, 1 Asian American or Pacific Islander, 1 Hispanic American), 4 international. Average age 30. 17 applicants, 59% accepted, 6 enrolled. In 2009, 2 doctorates awarded. *Degree requirements:* For doctorate, 2 foreign languages, comprehensive exam, thesis/dissertation. *Entrance requirements:* For doctorate, GRE General Test. Additional exam requirements/recommendations for international students: Required—TOEFL. *Application deadline:* For fall admission, 2/15 priority date for domestic students. Application fee: $50. *Expenses:* Tuition: Full-time $10,080; part-time $560 per credit hour. Required fees: $50 per term. Tuition and fees vary according to program. *Financial support:* In 2009–10, 18 students received support. Scholarships/grants available. Financial award application deadline: 2/15. *Faculty research:* Classical, medieval, and modern political philosophy; American political thought and institutions; politics and literature. *Unit head:* Dr. Richard Dougherty, Chair, 972-721-5043, Fax: 972-721-4007, E-mail: alvarez@udallas.edu. *Application contact:* Graduate Coordinator, 972-721-5106, Fax: 972-721-5280, E-mail: graduate@acad.udallas.edu.

University of Dallas, Braniff Graduate School of Liberal Arts, Master's Program in Politics, Irving, TX 75062-4736. Offers M Pol, MA. Part-time programs available. *Faculty:* 6 full-time (1 woman). *Students:* 11 full-time (3 women), 5 part-time (2 women); includes 2 minority (1 Asian American or Pacific Islander, 1 Hispanic American). Average age 24. 11 applicants, 100% accepted, 6 enrolled. In 2009, 2 master's awarded. *Degree requirements:* For master's, one foreign language, comprehensive exam, thesis. *Entrance requirements:* For master's, GRE General Test. Additional exam requirements/recommendations for international students: Required—TOEFL. *Application deadline:* For fall admission, 2/15 priority date for domestic students; for spring admission, 11/15 for domestic students. Applications are processed on a rolling basis. Application fee: $50. *Expenses:* Tuition: Full-time $10,080; part-time $560 per credit hour. Required fees: $50 per term. Tuition and fees vary according to program. *Financial support:* In 2009–10, 15 students received support. Scholarships/grants available. Financial award application deadline: 2/15. *Faculty research:* Classical, medieval, and modern political philosophy; American political thought and institutions; politics and literature. *Unit head:* Dr. Richard Dougherty, Chair, 972-721-5043, Fax: 972-721-4007, E-mail: doughr@udallas.edu. *Application contact:* Graduate Coordinator, 972-721-5106, Fax: 972-721-5280, E-mail: graduate@acad.udallas.edu.

University of Delaware, College of Arts and Sciences, Department of Political Science and International Relations, Newark, DE 19716. Offers MA, PhD. Terminal master's awarded for partial completion of doctoral program. *Degree requirements:* For master's, research paper; for doctorate, one foreign language, comprehensive exam, thesis/dissertation. *Entrance requirements:* For master's and doctorate, GRE General Test, minimum GPA of 3.2 in major, 3.0 overall. Additional exam requirements/recommendations for international students: Required—TOEFL (minimum score 600 paper-based). Electronic applications accepted. *Faculty research:* Social constructivism. international migration, international security, democratization, human rights.

University of Florida, Graduate School, College of Liberal Arts and Sciences, Department of Political Science, Gainesville, FL 32611. Offers international development policy and administration (MA, Certificate); international relations (MA, MAT); political campaigning (MA, Certificate); political science (MA, MAT, PhD); public affairs (MA, Certificate); JD/MA. Part-time programs available. Terminal master's awarded for partial completion of doctoral program. *Degree requirements:* For master's, variable foreign language requirement, thesis or alternative; for doctorate, variable foreign language requirement, thesis/dissertation. *Entrance requirements:* For master's and doctorate, GRE General Test, minimum GPA of 3.0. Additional exam requirements/recommendations for international students: Required—TOEFL (minimum score 550 paper-based; 213 computer-based). Electronic applications accepted. *Faculty research:* U.S. political development, religion and politics, environmental politics and policy, developing societies, international relations.

University of Georgia, School of Public and International Affairs, Program in Political Science, Athens, GA 30602. Offers MA, PhD. *Faculty:* 16 full-time (3 women). *Students:* 63 full-time (18 women), 21 part-time (10 women); includes 3 minority (all Hispanic Americans), 22 international. 148 applicants, 20% accepted, 26 enrolled. In 2009, 14 master's, 5 doctorates awarded. *Degree requirements:* For master's, one foreign language, thesis; for doctorate, one foreign language, thesis/dissertation. *Entrance requirements:* For master's and doctorate, GRE General Test. *Application deadline:* For fall admission, 7/1 priority date for domestic students; for spring admission, 11/15 for domestic students. Application fee: $50. Electronic applications accepted. *Expenses:* Tuition, state resident: full-time $6000; part-time $250 per credit hour. Tuition, nonresident: full-time $20,904; part-time $871 per credit hour. Required fees: $730 per semester. *Financial support:* Fellowships, research assistantships, teaching assistantships, unspecified assistantships available. *Unit head:* Dr. John A. Maltese, Head, 706-542-2057, Fax: 706-542-4421, E-mail: jmaltese@uga.edu. *Application contact:* Dr. Audrey A. Haynes, Graduate Coordinator, 706-542-2933, Fax: 706-542-4421, E-mail: polaah@uga.edu.

University of Guelph, Graduate Program Services, College of Social and Applied Human Sciences, Department of Political Science, Guelph, ON N1G 2W1, Canada. Offers comparative politics (MA); international development (MA); political science (MA); public policy and public administration (MA); the Americas (Canada emphasis) (MA). MA in public policy and public administration offered in collaboration with Department of Political Science of McMaster University. *Degree requirements:* For master's, thesis or paper. *Entrance requirements:* For master's, minimum B average during previous 2 years of course work, 4 year Honours Degree in Political Science. Additional exam requirements/recommendations for international students: Required—TOEFL. Electronic applications accepted. *Faculty research:* Political ethics, constitutional power.

University of Hawaii at Manoa, Graduate Division, College of Social Sciences, Department of Political Science, Honolulu, HI 96822. Offers MA, PhD. Part-time programs available. *Faculty:* 25 full-time (7 women), 10 part-time/adjunct (6 women). *Students:* 95 full-time (40 women), 33 part-time (16 women); includes 38 minority (1 African American, 34 Asian Americans or Pacific Islanders, 3 Hispanic Americans), 33 international. Average age 31. 142 applicants, 35% accepted, 32 enrolled. In 2009, 21 master's, 10 doctorates awarded. Terminal master's awarded for partial completion of doctoral program. *Degree requirements:* For master's, thesis optional; for doctorate, comprehensive exam, thesis/dissertation. *Entrance requirements:* Additional exam requirements/recommendations for international students: Required—TOEFL (minimum score 540 paper-based; 207 computer-based; 76 iBT), IELTS (minimum score 5). *Application deadline:* For fall admission, 2/1 for domestic students, 1/15 for international students. Application fee: $60. *Expenses:* Tuition, state resident: full-time $8900; part-time $372 per credit. Tuition, nonresident: full-time $21,400; part-time $898 per credit. Required fees: $207 per semester. *Financial support:* In 2009–10, 4 students received support, including 16 fellowships (averaging $4,486 per year), 13 research assistantships (averaging $15,915 per year), 13 teaching assistantships (averaging $15,466 per year); career-related internships or fieldwork, Federal Work-Study, and institutionally sponsored loans also available. Support available to part-time students. Financial award application deadline: 3/1. *Faculty research:* Asia/Pacific, political economy, human rights, futures, postmodernism. Total annual research expenditures: $24,000. *Application contact:* Debora Halbert, Graduate Chair, 808-956-8357, Fax: 808-956-6877, E-mail: halbert@hawaii.edu.

University of Houston, College of Liberal Arts and Social Sciences, Department of Political Science, Houston, TX 77204. Offers MA, PhD. Part-time and evening/weekend programs available. *Faculty:* 20 full-time (4 women), 4 part-time/adjunct (1 woman). *Students:* 46 full-time (18 women), 59 part-time (33 women); includes 18 minority (9 African Americans, 2 Asian Americans or Pacific Islanders, 7 Hispanic Americans), 16 international. Average age 33. 124 applicants, 41% accepted, 40 enrolled. In 2009, 16 master's, 4 doctorates awarded. Terminal master's awarded for partial completion of doctoral program. *Degree requirements:* For master's, thesis optional; for doctorate, thesis/dissertation. *Entrance requirements:* For master's and doctorate, GRE. Additional exam requirements/recommendations for international students: Required—TOEFL (minimum score 550 paper-based; 213 computer-based; 79 iBT). *Application deadline:* For fall admission, 2/15 for domestic and international students; for spring admission, 10/1 for domestic and international students. Application fee: $0 ($75 for international students). *Expenses:* Tuition, state resident: full-time $7676; part-time $320 per credit hour. Tuition, nonresident: full-time $14,324; part-time $597 per credit hour. Required fees: $3034. *Financial support:* In 2009–10, 2 fellowships with full tuition reimbursements (averaging $12,850 per year), 27 teaching assistantships with full tuition reimbursements (averaging $12,850 per year) were awarded; career-related internships or fieldwork, Federal Work-Study, institutionally sponsored loans, scholarships/grants, health care benefits, and unspecified assistantships also available. Support available to part-time students. Financial award application deadline: 2/1. *Faculty research:* American politics, political theory, judicial process, public policy, comparative politics. *Unit head:* Dr. Harrell Rodgers, Chairperson, 713-743-3890, Fax: 713-743-3927, E-mail: hrodgers@uh.edu. *Application contact:* Edward Manouelian, Graduate Advisor, 713-743-3939, E-mail: eemanoue@central.uh.edu.

University of Idaho, College of Graduate Studies, College of Letters, Arts and Social Sciences, Department of Political Science and Public Affairs Research, Program in Political Science, Moscow, ID 83844-2282. Offers MA, PhD. *Students:* 8 full-time, 7 part-time. In 2009, 2 master's, 1 doctorate awarded. *Degree requirements:* For doctorate, thesis/dissertation. *Entrance requirements:* For master's, minimum GPA of 2.8; for doctorate, minimum undergraduate GPA of 2.8, 3.0 graduate. *Application deadline:* For fall admission, 8/1 for domestic students; for spring admission, 12/15 for domestic students. Application fee: $55 ($60 for international students). *Expenses:* Tuition, state resident: full-time $6120. Tuition, nonresident: full-time $17,712. *Financial support:* Application deadline: 2/15. *Unit head:* Dr. Donald W. Crowley, Chair, 208-885-6328. *Application contact:* Dr. Donald W. Crowley, Chair, 208-885-6328.

University of Illinois at Chicago, Graduate College, College of Liberal Arts and Sciences, Department of Political Science, Chicago, IL 60607-7128. Offers MA, PhD. Part-time programs available. Terminal master's awarded for partial completion of doctoral program. *Degree requirements:* For master's, thesis or comprehensive exam. *Entrance requirements:* For master's, GRE General Test, minimum GPA of 3.0. Additional exam requirements/recommendations for international students: Required—TOEFL. Electronic applications accepted. *Faculty research:* Policy analysis/national urban politics and policy, electoral behavior.

University of Illinois at Springfield, Graduate Programs, College of Public Affairs and Administration, Department of Political Science, Springfield, IL 62703-5407. Offers MA. Part-time and evening/weekend programs available. *Faculty:* 11 full-time (2 women), 2 part-time/adjunct (1 woman). *Students:* 17 full-time (7 women), 32 part-time (8 women); includes 9 minority (7 African Americans, 1 Asian American or Pacific Islander, 1 Hispanic American). Average age 29. 35 applicants, 77% accepted, 18 enrolled. In 2009, 22 master's awarded. *Degree requirements:* For master's, comprehensive exam, participant/observer case study, or thesis. *Entrance requirements:* Additional exam requirements/recommendations for international students: Required—TOEFL (minimum score 500 paper-based; 176 computer-based; 61 iBT). *Application deadline:* Applications are processed on a rolling basis. Application fee: $50 ($60 for international students). Electronic applications accepted. *Expenses:* Tuition, state resident: full-time $6390; part-time $266.25 per credit hour. Tuition, nonresident: full-time $14,226; part-time $592.75 per credit hour. Required fees: $2044; $14.36 per credit hour. $722.50 per term. *Financial support:* In 2009–10, research assistantships with full tuition reimbursements (averaging $8,109 per year), teaching assistantships with full tuition reimbursements (averaging $8,109 per year) were awarded; career-related internships or fieldwork, Federal Work-Study, scholarships/grants, health care benefits, and unspecified assistantships also available. Support available to part-time students. Financial award application deadline: 11/15; financial award applicants required to submit FAFSA. *Unit head:* Dr. Jason Pierceson, Program Administrator, 217-206-7842, E-mail: jpier2@uis.edu. *Application contact:* Dr. Lynn Pardie, Office of Graduate Studies, 800-252-8533, Fax: 217-206-7623, E-mail: pardie.lynn@uis.edu.

University of Illinois at Urbana–Champaign, Graduate College, College of Liberal Arts and Sciences, Department of Political Science, Champaign, IL 61820. Offers MA, PhD, PhD/JD. *Faculty:* 30 full-time (10 women), 5 part-time/adjunct (1 woman). *Students:* 67 full-time (31 women), 4 part-time (3 women); includes 10 minority (2 African Americans, 6 Asian Americans or Pacific Islanders, 2 Hispanic Americans), 12 international. 134 applicants, 7% accepted, 9 enrolled. In 2009, 15 master's, 5 doctorates awarded. *Entrance requirements:* For master's, GRE General Test, minimum GPA of 3.0; for doctorate, GRE General Test, writing sample, minimum GPA of 3.0. Additional exam requirements/recommendations for international students: Required—TOEFL (minimum score 79 iBT). *Application deadline:* Applications are processed on a rolling basis. Application fee: $60 ($75 for international students). Electronic applications accepted. *Financial support:* In 2009–10, 55 fellowships, 24 research assistantships, 42 teaching assistantships were awarded; tuition waivers (full and partial) also available. *Unit head:* William T. Bernhard, Head, 217-333-2602, Fax: 217-244-5712, E-mail: bernhard@illinois.edu. *Application contact:* Brenda R. Stamm, Office Administrator, 217-333-3880, Fax: 217-244-5712, E-mail: stamm@illinois.edu.

The University of Iowa, Graduate College, College of Liberal Arts and Sciences, Department of Political Science, Iowa City, IA 52242-1316. Offers MA, PhD. *Degree requirements:* For master's, thesis optional, exam; for doctorate, comprehensive exam, thesis/dissertation. *Entrance requirements:* For master's and doctorate, GRE General Test, minimum GPA of 3.0. Additional exam requirements/recommendations for international students: Required—TOEFL (minimum score 600 paper-based; 250 computer-based; 100 iBT). Electronic applications accepted.

The University of Kansas, Graduate Studies, College of Liberal Arts and Sciences, Department of Political Science, Lawrence, KS 66045. Offers MA, PhD. Part-time programs available. *Students:* 59 full-time (17 women), 7 part-time (4 women); includes 5 minority (1 African American, 1 American Indian/Alaska Native, 2 Asian Americans or Pacific Islanders, 1 Hispanic American), 15 international. Average age 30. 85 applicants, 54% accepted, 17 enrolled. In 2009, 5 master's awarded. Terminal master's awarded for partial completion of doctoral program. *Degree requirements:* For master's, comprehensive exam, thesis or alternative; for doctorate, comprehensive exam, thesis/dissertation, research skills. *Entrance requirements:* For master's, GRE General Test, 3 letters of recommendation, curriculum vitae; for doctorate, GRE General Test, 3 letters of recommendation, transcripts, personal statement, curriculum vitae. Additional exam requirements/recommendations for international students: Required—TOEFL. *Application deadline:* For fall admission, 1/9 priority date for domestic and international students. Application fee: $55 ($60 for international students). Electronic applications accepted. *Expenses:* Tuition, state resident: full-time $6492; part-time $270.50 per credit hour. Tuition, nonresident: full-time $15,510; part-time $646.25 per credit hour. Required fees: $847; $70.56 per credit hour. Tuition and fees vary according to course load and program. *Financial support:* Fellowships with full tuition reimbursements, research assistantships, teaching assistantships with full tuition reimbursements, scholarships/grants, health care benefits, and unspecified assistantships available. Financial award application deadline: 1/9. *Faculty research:* Public policy, political economy and development, political institutions and organized interests, international conflict and cooperation. *Unit head:* Elaine Sharp, Chair, 785-864-3523, Fax: 785-864-5700, E-mail: esharp@ku.edu. *Application contact:* Prof. Paul E. Johnson, Graduate Director, 785-864-3523, Fax: 785-864-5700, E-mail: pauljohn@ku.edu.

University of Kentucky, Graduate School, College of Arts and Sciences, Program in Political Science, Lexington, KY 40506-0032. Offers MA, PhD. *Degree requirements:* For master's, comprehensive exam, thesis optional; for doctorate, comprehensive exam, thesis/dissertation. *Entrance requirements:* For master's, GRE General Test, minimum undergraduate GPA of 2.75; for doctorate, GRE General Test, minimum graduate GPA of 3.0. Additional exam requirements/recommendations for international students: Required—TOEFL (minimum score 550 paper-based; 213 computer-based). Electronic applications accepted. *Faculty research:* International political economy, critical policy studies, regional conflict and integration, race and American politics, media studies.

University of Lethbridge, School of Graduate Studies, Lethbridge, AB T1K 3M4, Canada. Offers accounting (MScM); addictions counseling (M Sc); agricultural biotechnology (M Sc); agricultural studies (M Sc, MA); anthropology (MA); archaeology (MA); art (MA, MFA); biochemistry (M Sc); biological sciences (M Sc); biomolecular science (PhD); biosystems and biodiversity (PhD); Canadian studies (MA); chemistry (M Sc); computer science (M Sc); computer science and geographical information science (M Sc); counseling psychology (M Ed); dramatic arts (MA); earth, space, and physical science (PhD); economics (MA); educational leadership (M Ed); English (MA); environmental science (M Sc); evolution and behavior (PhD); exercise science (M Sc); finance (MScM); French (MA); French/German (MA); French/Spanish (MA); general education (M Ed); general management (MScM); geography (M Sc, MA); German (MA); health science (M Sc); health sciences (MA); history (MA); human resource management and labour relations (MScM); individualized multidisciplinary (M Sc, MA); information systems (MScM); international management (MScM); kinesiology (M Sc, MA); management (M Sc, MA); marketing (MScM); mathematics (M Sc); music (M Mus, MA); Native American studies (MA); neuroscience (M Sc, PhD); new media (MA); nursing (M Sc); philosophy (MA); physics (M Sc); policy and strategy (MScM); political science (MA); psychology (M Sc, MA); religious studies (MA); social sciences (MA); sociology (MA); theatre and dramatic arts (MFA); theoretical and computational science (PhD); urban and regional studies (MA); women's studies (MA). Part-time and evening/weekend programs available. *Degree requirements:* For doctorate, comprehensive exam, thesis/dissertation. *Entrance requirements:* For master's, GMAT (M Sc in management), bachelor's degree in related field, minimum GPA of 3.0 during previous 20 graded semester courses, 2 years teaching or related experience (M Ed); for doctorate, master's degree, minimum graduate GPA of 3.5. Additional exam requirements/recommendations for international students: Required—TOEFL. *Faculty research:* Movement and brain plasticity, gibberellin physiology, photosynthesis, carbon cycling, molecular properties of main-group ring components.

University of Louisville, Graduate School, College of Arts and Sciences, Department of Political Science, Louisville, KY 40292-0001. Offers MA. Part-time and evening/weekend programs available. *Faculty:* 13 full-time (5 women), 3 part-time/adjunct (0 women). *Students:* 18 full-time (8 women), 9 part-time (6 women); includes 1 minority (African American). Average age 27. 20 applicants, 80% accepted, 12 enrolled. In 2009, 6 master's awarded. *Degree requirements:* For master's, thesis or directed research paper. *Entrance requirements:* For master's, GRE General Test, 2 academic letters of recommendation. Additional exam requirements/recommendations for international students: Required—TOEFL. *Application deadline:* For fall admission, 8/1 for domestic and international students; for winter admission, 8/1 for domestic students; for spring admission, 12/1 for domestic and international students. Applications are processed on a rolling basis. Application fee: $30 ($40 for international students). *Financial support:* Research assistantships available. Financial award application deadline: 6/1. *Faculty research:* International law, politics of east Asia, comparative political systems, environmental policy, international relations. Total annual research expenditures: $45,000. *Unit head:* Dr. Ronald K. Vogel, Chair, 502-852-3312, Fax: 502-852-7923, E-mail: ron.vogel@louisvile.edu. *Application contact:* Libby Leggett, Director, Graduate Admissions, 502-852-3101, Fax: 502-852-6536, E-mail: gradadm@louisville.edu.

University of Manitoba, Faculty of Graduate Studies, Faculty of Arts, Department of Political Studies, Winnipeg, MB R3T 2N2, Canada. Offers political studies (MA); public administration (MPA). *Degree requirements:* For master's, one foreign language, thesis or alternative.

University of Maryland, College Park, Academic Affairs, College of Behavioral and Social Sciences, Department of Government and Politics, College Park, MD 20742. Offers American politics (PhD); comparative politics (PhD); international relations (PhD); political economy (PhD); political theory (PhD). Part-time and evening/weekend programs available. *Faculty:* 54 full-time (17 women), 14 part-time/adjunct (5 women). *Students:* 124 full-time (56 women), 20 part-time (6 women); includes 20 minority (5 African Americans, 10 Asian Americans or Pacific Islanders, 5 Hispanic Americans), 22 international. 235 applicants, 18% accepted, 18 enrolled. In 2009, 16 doctorates awarded. *Degree requirements:* For doctorate, comprehensive exam, thesis/dissertation, written exams in 2 fields. *Entrance requirements:* For doctorate, GRE General Test, minimum GPA of 3.5, writing sample. Additional exam requirements/recommendations for international students: Required—TOEFL. *Application deadline:* For fall admission, 2/1 for domestic and international students. Applications are processed on a rolling basis. Application fee: $60. Electronic applications accepted. *Expenses:* Tuition, area resident: Part-time $471 per credit hour. Tuition, state resident: part-time $471 per credit hour. Tuition, nonresident: part-time $1016 per credit hour. Required fees: $337.04 per term. *Financial support:* In 2009–10, 10 fellowships with full tuition reimbursements (averaging $20,041 per year), 1 research assistantship with tuition reimbursement (averaging $15,924 per year), 67 teaching assistantships with tuition reimbursements (averaging $15,749 per year) were awarded; career-related internships or fieldwork, Federal Work-Study, scholarships/grants, and unspecified assistantships also available. Support available to part-time students. Financial award applicants required to submit FAFSA. *Faculty research:* International development/conflict, international security, post-communist society, public service, dynamics of conflict and conflict resolution. Total annual research expenditures: $2.9 million. *Unit head:* Dr. Mark Lichbach, Chairman, 301-405-4156, Fax: 301-314-9690, E-mail: mlichbac@umd.edu. *Application contact:* Dean of Graduate School, 301-405-0358, Fax: 301-314-9305.

University of Massachusetts Amherst, Graduate School, College of Social and Behavioral Sciences, Department of Political Science, Amherst, MA 01003. Offers MA, PhD. Part-time programs available. *Faculty:* 35 full-time (12 women). *Students:* 30 full-time (11 women), 32 part-time (14 women); includes 3 minority (1 African American, 2 Hispanic Americans), 14 international. Average age 30. 139 applicants, 17% accepted, 10 enrolled. In 2009, 7 master's, 3 doctorates awarded. Terminal master's awarded for partial completion of doctoral program. *Degree requirements:* For master's, one foreign language, thesis or alternative; for doctorate, one foreign language, comprehensive exam, thesis/dissertation. *Entrance requirements:* For master's and doctorate, GRE General Test, writing sample, 3 letters of recommendation. Additional exam requirements/recommendations for international students: Required—TOEFL (minimum score 550 paper-based; 213 computer-based; 80 iBT), IELTS (minimum score 6.5). *Application deadline:* For fall admission, 1/15 for domestic and international students. Applications are processed on a rolling basis. Application fee: $50 ($65 for international students). Electronic applications accepted. *Expenses:* Tuition, state resident: full-time $2640; part-time $110 per credit. Tuition, nonresident: full-time $9936; part-time $414 per credit. Tuition and fees vary according to course load. *Financial support:* In 2009–10, 3 fellowships with full tuition reimbursements (averaging $3,919 per year), 33 research assistantships with full tuition reimbursements (averaging $5,998 per year), 41 teaching assistantships with full tuition reimbursements (averaging $10,976 per year) were awarded; career-related internships or fieldwork, Federal Work-Study, scholarships/grants, traineeships, health care benefits, tuition waivers (full), and unspecified assistantships also available. Support available to part-time students. Financial award application deadline: 1/15. *Unit head:* Dr. Frederic C. Schaffer, Graduate Program Director, 413-545-0410, Fax: 413-545-3349. *Application contact:* Jean M. Ames, Supervisor of Admissions, 413-545-0722, Fax: 413-577-0010, E-mail: gradadm@grad.umass.edu.

University of Massachusetts Boston, Office of Graduate Studies, Division of Continuing Education and John W. McCormack Graduate School of Policy Studies, Program in Women in Politics and Government, Boston, MA 02125-3393. Offers Certificate. Part-time and evening/weekend programs available. *Degree requirements:* For Certificate, practicum, final project. *Entrance requirements:* For degree, interview, minimum GPA of 2.75.

University of Massachusetts Boston, Office of Graduate Studies, John W. McCormack Graduate School of Policy Studies, Boston, MA 02125-3393. Offers gerontology (MA, MS, PhD, Certificate), including gerontology (MS, PhD, Certificate), gerontology research (MA), management in aging services (MA); public affairs (MS); public policy (PhD); women in politics and government (Certificate). Certificate program in women in politics and government offered jointly with Division of Continuing Education. Part-time and evening/weekend programs available. *Degree requirements:* For doctorate, thesis/dissertation; for Certificate, practicum, final project. *Entrance requirements:* For doctorate, GRE General Test; for Certificate, interview, minimum GPA of 2.5.

University of Memphis, Graduate School, College of Arts and Sciences, Department of Political Science, Memphis, TN 38152. Offers MA. *Faculty:* 5 full-time (2 women). *Students:* 14 full-time (10 women), 2 part-time (1 woman); includes 2 minority (1 African American, 1 Asian American or Pacific Islander). Average age 27. 10 applicants, 100% accepted, 3 enrolled. In 2009, 8 master's awarded. *Degree requirements:* For master's, comprehensive exam, thesis or alternative, internship. *Entrance requirements:* For master's, GRE General Test or GMAT, minimum GPA of 3.0. *Application deadline:* For fall admission, 8/1 for domestic students; for spring admission, 12/1 for domestic students. Applications are processed on a rolling basis. Application fee: $35 ($60 for international students). *Expenses:* Tuition, state resident: full-time $6246; part-time $347 per credit hour. Tuition, nonresident: full-time $15,894; part-time $883 per credit hour. Required fees: $1160. Full-time tuition and fees vary according to course load, degree level and program. *Financial support:* In 2009–10, 10 students received support; research assistantships with full tuition reimbursements available, Federal Work-Study, scholarships/grants, and unspecified assistantships available. Financial award application deadline: 2/15; financial award applicants required to submit FAFSA. *Faculty research:* Political philosophy, comparative judicial studies, conflict studies, legislative studies, foreign policy. *Unit head:* Dr. Robert Blanton, Interim Chair, 901-678-2395, Fax: 901-678-2983, E-mail: rblanton@memphis.edu. *Application contact:* Dr. David Richards, Graduate Studies Coordinator, 901-678-3348, Fax: 901-678-2983, E-mail: drich1@memphis.edu.

University of Miami, Graduate School, College of Arts and Sciences, Department of Political Science, Coral Gables, FL 33124. Offers MPA, MPA/MPH. Part-time and evening/weekend programs available. *Degree requirements:* For master's, thesis optional. *Entrance requirements:* For master's, GRE General Test. Additional exam requirements/recommendations for international students: Required—TOEFL.

University of Michigan, Horace H. Rackham School of Graduate Studies, College of Literature, Science, and the Arts, Department of Political Science, Ann Arbor, MI 48109. Offers political science (AM, PhD); social work and political science (PhD); JD/AM. Terminal master's awarded for partial completion of doctoral program. *Degree requirements:* For master's, thesis; for doctorate, comprehensive exam, thesis/dissertation, oral defense of dissertation, preliminary exam. *Entrance requirements:* For master's and doctorate, GRE General Test. Additional exam requirements/recommendations for international students: Required—TOEFL. Electronic applications accepted. *Expenses:* Tuition, state resident: full-time $17,286; part-time $1099 per credit hour. Tuition, nonresident: full-time $34,944; part-time $2080 per credit hour. Required fees: $95 per semester. Tuition and fees vary according to course load, degree level and program. *Faculty research:* Political theory, American politics, world politics, comparative politics, methodology, public law.

University of Minnesota, Twin Cities Campus, Graduate School, College of Liberal Arts, Department of Political Science, Minneapolis, MN 55455-0213. Offers PhD. *Faculty:* 32 full-time (12 women), 4 part-time/adjunct (0 women). *Students:* 59 full-time (21 women), 17 part-time (7 women); includes 22 minority (7 African Americans, 2 American Indian/Alaska Native, 9 Asian Americans or Pacific Islanders, 4 Hispanic Americans). Average age 30. 206 applicants, 10% accepted, 8 enrolled. In 2009, 16 doctorates awarded. *Degree requirements:* For doctorate, thesis/dissertation, 1 foreign language or statistics. *Entrance requirements:* For doctorate, GRE. Additional exam requirements/recommendations for international students: Required—TOEFL; Recommended—IELTS. *Application deadline:* For fall admission, 12/15 for domestic and international students. Application fee: $75 ($95 for international students). Electronic applications accepted. *Financial support:* In 2009–10, 57 students received support, including 15 fellowships with full tuition reimbursements available (averaging $18,000 per year), 6 research assistantships with full tuition reimbursements available (averaging $18,000 per year), 36 teaching assistantships with full tuition reimbursements available (averaging $18,000 per year); health care benefits also available. Financial award application deadline: 12/15. *Faculty research:* American politics, comparative politics, international relations, political theory, research methodology. Total annual research expenditures: $292,993. *Unit head:* Raymond D. Duvall, Chair, 612-624-4144, Fax: 612-626-7599, E-mail: rduvall@umn.edu. *Application contact:* Judith Mitchell, Assistant to Director of Graduate Studies, 612-624-4144, Fax: 612-626-7599, E-mail: papply@umn.edu.

University of Mississippi, Graduate School, College of Liberal Arts, Department of Political Science, Oxford, University, MS 38677. Offers MA, PhD. *Faculty:* 17 full-time (4 women), 3 part-time/adjunct (1 woman). *Students:* 17 full-time (8 women), 4 part-time (3 women), 2 international. In 2009, 2 master's, 1 doctorate awarded. *Degree requirements:* For doctorate,

Political Science

University of Mississippi (continued)

thesis/dissertation. *Entrance requirements:* For master's, GRE General Test, minimum GPA of 3.0; for doctorate, GRE General Test. Additional exam requirements/recommendations for international students: Required—TOEFL. *Application deadline:* For fall admission, 2/15 for domestic students; for spring admission, 10/1 for domestic students. Applications are processed on a rolling basis. Application fee: $25. Electronic applications accepted. *Financial support:* Scholarships/grants available. Financial award application deadline: 3/1; financial award applicants required to submit FAFSA. *Unit head:* Dr. Richard G. Forgette, Chairman, 662-915-7401, Fax: 662-915-7808, E-mail: rforgett@olemiss.edu. *Application contact:* Dr. Christy M. Wyandt, Associate Dean, 662-915-7474, Fax: 662-915-7577, E-mail: cwyandt@olemiss.edu.

University of Missouri, Graduate School, College of Arts and Sciences, Department of Political Science, Columbia, MO 65211. Offers MA, PhD. *Faculty:* 16 full-time (3 women). *Students:* 51 full-time (18 women), 16 part-time (10 women); includes 3 minority (1 American Indian/Alaska Native, 1 Asian American or Pacific Islander, 1 Hispanic American), 19 international. Average age 28. 48 applicants, 63% accepted, 16 enrolled. In 2009, 5 master's, 2 doctorates awarded. Terminal master's awarded for partial completion of doctoral program. *Degree requirements:* For doctorate, one foreign language, comprehensive exam, thesis/dissertation. *Entrance requirements:* For master's, GRE General Test (minimum combined score 1000 Verbal and Quantitative), minimum GPA of 3.0 in last 60 hours and in political science courses; at least 12 hours of upper-level course work in political science; for doctorate, GRE General Test (minimum combined score 1200 Verbal and Quantitative), minimum GPA of 3.0 in last 60 hours and in political science courses; at least 12 hours of upper-level course work in political science. Additional exam requirements/recommendations for international students: Required—TOEFL (minimum score 570 paper-based; 240 computer-based; 88 iBT). *Application deadline:* For fall admission, 2/1 priority date for domestic students; for winter admission, 10/6 for domestic students. Applications are processed on a rolling basis. Application fee: $45 ($60 for international students). Electronic applications accepted. *Financial support:* In 2009–10, 5 fellowships with full tuition reimbursements, 22 research assistantships with full tuition reimbursements, 33 teaching assistantships with full tuition reimbursements were awarded; institutionally sponsored loans, health care benefits, and unspecified assistantships also available. *Faculty research:* American politics, comparative politics, international relations, public policy and administration. *Unit head:* Dr. John Petrocik, Department Chair, E-mail: petrocikj@missouri.edu. *Application contact:* Dana Davis, Administrative Assistant, 573-882-2062, E-mail: davisdana@missouri.edu.

University of Missouri–Kansas City, College of Arts and Sciences, Department of Political Science, Kansas City, MO 64110-2499. Offers MA, PhD. PhD (interdisciplinary) offered through the School of Graduate Studies. Part-time and evening/weekend programs available. *Faculty:* 6 full-time (2 women), 6 part-time/adjunct (1 woman). *Students:* 6 full-time (2 women), 7 part-time (2 women); includes 2 minority (1 African American, 1 Hispanic American). Average age 37. 7 applicants, 43% accepted, 3 enrolled. In 2009, 2 master's awarded. Terminal master's awarded for partial completion of doctoral program. *Degree requirements:* For master's, thesis optional; for doctorate, thesis/dissertation. *Entrance requirements:* For master's, GRE, minimum GPA of 3.0, course work in political science, 2 letters of recommendation; for doctorate, GRE, minimum GPA of 3.0, MA in political science or related area, writing sample. Additional exam requirements/recommendations for international students: Required—TOEFL (minimum score 550 paper-based; 213 computer-based; 80 iBT). *Application deadline:* For fall admission, 4/1 priority date for domestic and international students; for spring admission, 11/1 priority date for domestic and international students. Applications are processed on a rolling basis. Application fee: $45 ($50 for international students). Electronic applications accepted. *Expenses:* Tuition, state resident: full-time $5378; part-time $299 per credit hour. Tuition, nonresident: full-time $13,881; part-time $771 per credit hour. Required fees: $641; $71 per credit hour. Tuition and fees vary according to course load and program. *Financial support:* In 2009–10, 1 research assistantship (averaging $5,700 per year), 1 teaching assistantship with partial tuition reimbursement (averaging $27,300 per year) were awarded; career-related internships or fieldwork and institutionally sponsored loans also available. Financial award application deadline: 3/1; financial award applicants required to submit FAFSA. *Faculty research:* Sex and gender, Chinese politics, voting behavior, politics of presidency and social security, public law. *Unit head:* Dr. Harris Mirkin, Chair, 816-235-2792, Fax: 816-235-5594, E-mail: mirkinh@umkc.edu. *Application contact:* Dr. Harris Mirkin, Chair, 816-235-2792, Fax: 816-235-5594, E-mail: mirkinh@umkc.edu.

University of Missouri–St. Louis, College of Arts and Sciences, Department of Political Science, St. Louis, MO 63121. Offers American politics (MA); comparative politics (MA); international politics (MA); political process and behavior (MA); political science (PhD); public administration and public policy (MA); urban and regional politics (MA). Part-time and evening/weekend programs available. *Faculty:* 19 full-time (7 women), 1 (woman) part-time/adjunct. *Students:* 12 full-time (7 women), 35 part-time (17 women); includes 12 minority (8 African Americans, 1 American Indian/Alaska Native, 3 Asian Americans or Pacific Islanders), 2 international. Average age 35. 30 applicants, 57% accepted, 9 enrolled. In 2009, 6 master's, 2 doctorates awarded. Terminal master's awarded for partial completion of doctoral program. *Degree requirements:* For master's, thesis optional; for doctorate, thesis/dissertation. *Entrance requirements:* For master's, GRE General Test, 2 letters of recommendation; for doctorate, GRE General Test, 3 letters of recommendation. Additional exam requirements/recommendations for international students: Required—TOEFL (minimum score 550 paper-based; 213 computer-based). *Application deadline:* For fall admission, 2/15 priority date for domestic and international students; for spring admission, 10/15 priority date for domestic and international students. Applications are processed on a rolling basis. Application fee: $35 ($40 for international students). Electronic applications accepted. *Expenses:* Tuition, state resident: full-time $5377; part-time $297.70 per credit hour. Tuition, nonresident: full-time $13,882; part-time $771.20 per credit hour. Required fees: $220; $12.20 per credit hour. One-time fee: $12. Tuition and fees vary according to course level, campus/location and program. *Financial support:* In 2009–10, 10 research assistantships with full and partial tuition reimbursements (averaging $10,800 per year), 5 teaching assistantships with full and partial tuition reimbursements (averaging $10,800 per year) were awarded; fellowships, career-related internships or fieldwork also available. Support available to part-time students. Financial award application deadline: 3/15; financial award applicants required to submit FAFSA. *Faculty research:* Public policy, urban politics and administration, American government. *Unit head:* Dr. Barbara Graham, Director of Graduate Studies, 314-516-5522, Fax: 314-516-5268, E-mail: umslpolisci@umsl.edu. *Application contact:* 314-516-5458, Fax: 314-516-6996, E-mail: gradadm@umsl.edu.

The University of Montana, Graduate School, College of Arts and Sciences, Department of Political Science, Program in Political Science, Missoula, MT 59812-0002. Offers MA. *Degree requirements:* For master's, thesis. *Entrance requirements:* For master's, GRE General Test.

University of Nebraska at Omaha, Graduate Studies, College of Arts and Sciences, Department of Political Science, Omaha, NE 68182. Offers MS. Part-time and evening/weekend programs available. *Faculty:* 11 full-time (4 women). *Students:* 6 full-time (1 woman), 15 part-time (8 women); includes 1 minority (American Indian/Alaska Native), 2 international. Average age 31. 13 applicants, 77% accepted, 6 enrolled. In 2009, 12 master's awarded. *Degree requirements:* For master's, comprehensive exam, thesis (for some programs). *Entrance requirements:* For master's, 15 undergraduate political science hours, minimum undergraduate GPA of 3.0, 2 letters of recommendation. Additional exam requirements/recommendations for international students: Required—TOEFL (minimum score 500 paper-based; 173 computer-based; 61 iBT). *Application deadline:* For fall admission, 3/15 priority date for domestic students; for spring admission, 11/1 priority date for domestic students. Applications are processed on a rolling basis. Application fee: $45. Electronic applications accepted. *Financial support:* In 2009–10, 10 students received support; fellowships, research assistantships, teaching assistantships, Federal Work-Study, scholarships/grants, tuition waivers (partial), and unspecified assistantships available. Financial award application deadline: 3/1; financial award applicants required to submit FAFSA. *Unit head:* Dr. Loree Bykerk, Chairperson, 402-554-2624. *Application contact:* Dr. Randall Adkins, Student Contact, 402-554-2624.

University of Nebraska–Lincoln, Graduate College, College of Arts and Sciences, Department of Political Science, Lincoln, NE 68588. Offers political science (MA, PhD); public policy analysis (Graduate Certificate). *Degree requirements:* For master's, thesis optional; for doctorate, variable foreign language requirement, comprehensive exam, thesis/dissertation. *Entrance requirements:* For master's and doctorate, GRE General Test, writing sample. Additional exam requirements/recommendations for international students: Required—TOEFL (minimum score 600 paper-based; 250 computer-based). Electronic applications accepted. *Faculty research:* Public policy; comparative politics; international relations; political theory, behavior, and methodology; American politics.

University of Nevada, Las Vegas, Graduate College, College of Liberal Arts, Department of Political Science, Las Vegas, NV 89154-5029. Offers ethics and policy studies (MA); political science (PhD). Part-time programs available. *Faculty:* 13 full-time (3 women), 1 (woman) part-time/adjunct. *Students:* 13 full-time (6 women), 10 part-time (3 women); includes 5 minority (1 African American, 2 Asian Americans or Pacific Islanders, 2 Hispanic Americans). Average age 30. 17 applicants, 53% accepted, 6 enrolled. In 2009, 6 master's awarded. *Degree requirements:* For master's, comprehensive exam (for some programs), thesis (for some programs); for doctorate, comprehensive exam, thesis/dissertation, oral examination. *Entrance requirements:* For master's and doctorate, GRE General Test. Additional exam requirements/recommendations for international students: Required—TOEFL (minimum score 550 paper-based; 213 computer-based; 80 iBT), IELTS (minimum score 7). *Application deadline:* For fall admission, 2/1 priority date for domestic and international students; for spring admission, 10/1 priority date for domestic and international students. Applications are processed on a rolling basis. Application fee: $60 ($95 for international students). Electronic applications accepted. *Financial support:* In 2009–10, 10 students received support, including 10 research assistantships with partial tuition reimbursements available (averaging $10,725 per year); institutionally sponsored loans, scholarships/grants, health care benefits, and unspecified assistantships also available. Financial award application deadline: 3/1. *Faculty research:* Global political economy, global health and environmental policy, religion and politics, state and local politics and policy, classical political theory. *Unit head:* Dr. Mehran Tamadonfar, Chair/Associate Professor, 702-895-5258, Fax: 702-895-1065, E-mail: mehran.tamadorfar@unlv.edu. *Application contact:* Graduate College Admissions Evaluator, 702-895-3320, Fax: 702-895-4180, E-mail: gradcollege@unlv.edu.

University of Nevada, Reno, Graduate School, College of Liberal Arts, Department of Political Science, Program in Political Science, Reno, NV 89557. Offers MA, PhD. Terminal master's awarded for partial completion of doctoral program. *Degree requirements:* For master's, comprehensive exam, oral exam/thesis or professional paper; for doctorate, thesis/dissertation, 2 field exams, oral exam. *Entrance requirements:* For master's, GRE General Test, GMAT, LSAT, minimum GPA of 2.75; for doctorate, GRE General Test, GMAT, LSAT, minimum GPA of 3.0. Additional exam requirements/recommendations for international students: Required—TOEFL (minimum score 500 paper-based; 173 computer-based; 61 iBT), IELTS (minimum score 6). Electronic applications accepted. *Faculty research:* Analysis of political processes, institutions, and policies.

University of New Brunswick Fredericton, School of Graduate Studies, Faculty of Arts, Department of Political Science, Fredericton, NB E3B 5A3, Canada. Offers MA. Part-time programs available. *Faculty:* 6 full-time (2 women), 1 part-time/adjunct (0 women). *Students:* 14 full-time (5 women), 2 part-time (both women). In 2009, 3 master's awarded. *Degree requirements:* For master's, thesis (for some programs). *Entrance requirements:* For master's, minimum cumulative GPA of 3.3, 42 credit hours of course work in political science. *Application deadline:* For fall admission, 3/1 priority date for domestic students. Application fee: $50 Canadian dollars. Electronic applications accepted. Tuition and fees charges are reported in Canadian dollars. *Expenses:* Tuition, area resident: Full-time $5562 Canadian dollars; part-time $2781 Canadian dollars per year. Required fees: $49.75 Canadian dollars per term. *Financial support:* In 2009–10, 4 research assistantships (averaging $12,540 per year), 2 teaching assistantships (averaging $3,145 per year) were awarded. *Faculty research:* Canadian politics, political theory, public policy, gender and politics, international studies. *Unit head:* Dr. Joanne Wright, Director of Graduate Studies, 506-458-7422, Fax: 506-453-4755, E-mail: jwright@unb.ca. *Application contact:* Deborah Sloan, Graduate Secretary, 506-453-4826, Fax: 506-453-4755, E-mail: dsloan@unb.ca.

University of New Hampshire, Graduate School, College of Liberal Arts, Department of Political Science, Program in Political Science, Durham, NH 03824. Offers MA. Part-time programs available. *Faculty:* 15 full-time. *Students:* 11 full-time (3 women), 9 part-time (3 women); includes 4 minority (1 African American, 2 American Indian/Alaska Native, 1 Asian American or Pacific Islander). Average age 29. 23 applicants, 83% accepted, 9 enrolled. In 2009, 8 master's awarded. *Degree requirements:* For master's, thesis. *Entrance requirements:* For master's, GRE General Test. Additional exam requirements/recommendations for international students: Required—TOEFL (minimum score 550 paper-based; 213 computer-based; 80 iBT). *Application deadline:* For fall admission, 6/1 priority date for domestic students, 4/1 for international students; for spring admission, 12/1 for domestic students. Applications are processed on a rolling basis. Application fee: $65. Electronic applications accepted. *Expenses:* Tuition, state resident: full-time $10,380; part-time $577 per credit hour. Tuition, nonresident: full-time $24,350; part-time $1002 per credit hour. Required fees: $1550; $387.50 per semester. Tuition and fees vary according to course load and program. *Financial support:* In 2009–10, 4 students received support, including 3 teaching assistantships; fellowships, research assistantships, career-related internships or fieldwork, Federal Work-Study, scholarships/grants, and tuition waivers (full and partial) also available. Support available to part-time students. Financial award application deadline: 2/15. *Unit head:* Dr. Dante Scala, Chairperson, 603-862-3225. *Application contact:* Janis Marshal, Administrative Assistant, 603-862-1750, E-mail: mpa.ma.political.science.grad@unh.edu.

University of New Mexico, Graduate School, College of Arts and Sciences, Department of Political Science, Albuquerque, NM 87131-2039. Offers MA, PhD. Part-time programs available. *Faculty:* 15 full-time (6 women), 5 part-time/adjunct (2 women). *Students:* 32 full-time (12 women), 4 part-time (1 woman); includes 9 minority (1 African American, 1 Asian American or Pacific Islander, 7 Hispanic Americans), 4 international. Average age 32. 38 applicants, 39% accepted, 10 enrolled. In 2009, 6 master's, 2 doctorates awarded. Terminal master's awarded for partial completion of doctoral program. *Degree requirements:* For master's, comprehensive exam, thesis optional; for doctorate, comprehensive exam, thesis/dissertation, field research paper, minimum cumulative GPA of 3.5. *Entrance requirements:* For master's and doctorate, GRE General Test, 3 letters of recommendation, writing sample, letter of intent. Additional exam requirements/recommendations for international students: Required—TOEFL. *Application deadline:* For fall admission, 1/15 priority date for domestic and international students. Application fee: $50. Electronic applications accepted. *Expenses:* Tuition, state resident: full-time $2099; part-time $233.20 per credit hour. Tuition, nonresident: full-time $6650. Required fees: $25 per semester. Tuition and fees vary according to course load, program and reciprocity agreements. *Financial support:* In 2009–10, 10 students received support, including 5 research assistantships with tuition reimbursements available (averaging $14,634 per year), 7 teaching assistantships with tuition reimbursements available (averaging $14,634 per year); scholarships/grants, health care benefits, and unspecified assistantships also available. Financial award application deadline: 1/15; financial award applicants required to submit FAFSA. *Faculty research:* Latin American politics, American politics, comparative politics, public policy, international relations, methodology. Total annual research expenditures: $250,000. *Unit head:* Dr. Mark Peceny, Chair, 505-277-5104, Fax: 505-277-2821, E-mail: markpec@unm.edu. *Application contact:* Beth Leahy, Graduate Program Assistant, 505-277-5104, Fax: 505-288-2821, E-mail: bleahy@unm.edu.

University of New Orleans, Graduate School, College of Liberal Arts, Department of Political Science, New Orleans, LA 70148. Offers political science (MA, PhD); public administration

(MPA). Evening/weekend programs available. *Degree requirements:* For master's, one foreign language, thesis or alternative; for doctorate, one foreign language, thesis/dissertation. *Entrance requirements:* For master's, GRE General Test; for doctorate, GRE General Test, GRE Subject Test. Additional exam requirements/recommendations for international students: Required—TOEFL (minimum score 550 paper-based; 213 computer-based; 79 iBT). Electronic applications accepted. *Faculty research:* Judicial politics, public policy, voting rights, Southern politics, presidential-congressional relations.

The University of North Carolina at Chapel Hill, Graduate School, College of Arts and Sciences, Department of Political Science, Program in Political Science, Chapel Hill, NC 27599. Offers MA, PhD. *Degree requirements:* For master's, comprehensive exam, thesis; for doctorate, one foreign language, comprehensive exam, thesis/dissertation. *Entrance requirements:* For master's and doctorate, GRE General Test, GRE Subject Test, minimum GPA of 3.0.

The University of North Carolina at Greensboro, Graduate School, College of Arts and Sciences, Department of Political Science, Greensboro, NC 27412-5001. Offers nonprofit management (Certificate); public affairs (MPA); urban and economic development (Certificate). *Accreditation:* NASPAA. *Degree requirements:* For master's, comprehensive exam. *Entrance requirements:* For master's, GRE General Test. Additional exam requirements/recommendations for international students: Required—TOEFL. Electronic applications accepted. *Faculty research:* U.S. Constitution, Canadian parliament, public management, ethical challenge of public service.

University of Northern British Columbia, Office of Graduate Studies, Prince George, BC V2N 4Z9, Canada. Offers business administration (Diploma); community health science (M Sc); disability management (MA); education (M Ed); first nations studies (MA); gender studies (MA); history (MA); interdisciplinary studies (MA); international studies (MA); mathematical, computer and physical sciences (M Sc); natural resources and environmental studies (M Sc, MA, MNRES, PhD); political science (MA); psychology (M Sc, PhD); social work (MSW). Part-time and evening/weekend programs available. Postbaccalaureate distance learning degree programs offered (no on-campus study). *Degree requirements:* For master's, thesis; for doctorate, thesis/dissertation. *Entrance requirements:* For master's, GRE, minimum B average in undergraduate course work; for doctorate, candidacy exam, minimum A average in graduate course work.

University of Northern Iowa, Graduate College, College of Social and Behavioral Sciences, Department of Political Science, Cedar Falls, IA 50614. Offers MA. *Entrance requirements:* For master's, minimum GPA of 3.0. Additional exam requirements/recommendations for international students: Required—TOEFL (minimum score 500 paper-based; 180 computer-based; 61 iBT). *Unit head:* Dr. Michael Licari, Head, 319-273-6048, Fax: 319-273-7103, E-mail: michael.licari@uni.edu. *Application contact:* Laurie S. Russell, Record Analyst, 319-273-2623, Fax: 319-273-6792, E-mail: laurie.russell@uni.edu.

University of North Texas, Robert B. Toulouse School of Graduate Studies, College of Arts and Sciences, Department of Political Science, Denton, TX 76203. Offers MA, MS, PhD. Part-time and evening/weekend programs available. *Degree requirements:* For master's, variable foreign language requirement, thesis; for doctorate, variable foreign language requirement, comprehensive exam, thesis/dissertation. *Entrance requirements:* For master's, GRE General Test, minimum GPA of 3.0, 3 letters of recommendation; for doctorate, GRE General Test, minimum GPA of 3.0, 3 letters of recommendation, statement of interest. Additional exam requirements/recommendations for international students: Required—proof of English language proficiency; Recommended—TOEFL (minimum score 550 paper-based; 213 computer-based; 79 iBT). Application fee: $50 ($75 for international students). *Expenses:* Tuition, state resident: full-time $4298; part-time $239 per contact hour. Tuition, nonresident: full-time $9878; part-time $549 per contact hour. Required fees: $265 per contact hour. *Financial support:* In 2009–10, 35 students received support; fellowships with full tuition reimbursements available, research assistantships with partial tuition reimbursements available, teaching assistantships with partial tuition reimbursements available, career-related internships or fieldwork, Federal Work-Study, and institutionally sponsored loans available. Financial award applicants required to submit FAFSA. *Faculty research:* Political parties, international conflict, judicial politics, comparative politics. *Application contact:* Graduate Advisor, 940-565-2315, Fax: 940-565-4818, E-mail: paolino@unt.edu.

University of Notre Dame, Graduate School, College of Arts and Letters, Division of Social Science, Department of Political Science, Notre Dame, IN 46556. Offers PhD. *Degree requirements:* For doctorate, one foreign language, comprehensive exam, thesis/dissertation, candidacy exam. *Entrance requirements:* For doctorate, GRE General Test. Additional exam requirements/recommendations for international students: Required—TOEFL (minimum score 600 paper-based; 250 computer-based; 80 iBT). Electronic applications accepted. *Faculty research:* American government, comparative politics, international relations, political theory.

University of Oklahoma, Graduate College, College of Arts and Sciences, Department of Political Science, Program in Political Science, Norman, OK 73019-0390. Offers MA, PhD. *Students:* 31 full-time (12 women), 23 part-time (11 women); includes 2 minority (both Asian Americans or Pacific Islanders), 10 international. 32 applicants, 41% accepted, 7 enrolled. In 2009, 3 master's, 4 doctorates awarded. Terminal master's awarded for partial completion of doctoral program. *Degree requirements:* For master's, thesis or alternative; for doctorate, thesis/dissertation, language or quantitative techniques. *Entrance requirements:* For master's and doctorate, GRE General Test, 3 letters of recommendation. Additional exam requirements/recommendations for international students: Required—TOEFL (minimum score 600 paper-based; 250 computer-based). *Application deadline:* For fall admission, 2/1 for domestic and international students; for spring admission, 10/15 for domestic students, 9/1 for international students. Applications are processed on a rolling basis. Application fee: $40 ($90 for international students). Electronic applications accepted. *Expenses:* Tuition, state resident: full-time $3744; part-time $156 per credit hour. Tuition, nonresident: full-time $13,577; part-time $565.70 per credit hour. Required fees: $2415; $90.10 per credit hour. *Financial support:* In 2009–10, 46 students received support. Tuition waivers (partial) and unspecified assistantships available. *Faculty research:* American politics; institutions, processes and political behavior; democratization; international security; terrorism; knowledge utilization in the policy process; comparative administration systems. *Application contact:* Mitchell P. Smith, Graduate Programs Director, 405-325-8893, Fax: 405-325-0718, E-mail: mps@ou.edu.

University of Oregon, Graduate School, College of Arts and Sciences, Department of Political Science, Eugene, OR 97403. Offers MA, MS, PhD. Terminal master's awarded for partial completion of doctoral program. *Degree requirements:* For master's, thesis or alternative; for doctorate, thesis/dissertation. *Entrance requirements:* For master's and doctorate, GRE General Test, minimum GPA of 3.0. Additional exam requirements/recommendations for international students: Required—TOEFL. *Faculty research:* Public policy, public choice, comparative politics, political economy, international relations.

University of Ottawa, Faculty of Graduate and Postdoctoral Studies, Faculty of Social Sciences, Department of Political Studies, Ottawa, ON K1N 6N5, Canada. Offers MA, PhD. *Degree requirements:* For master's, thesis or alternative, fluency in English and French; for doctorate, comprehensive exam, thesis/dissertation. *Entrance requirements:* For master's, honors bachelor's degree or equivalent, minimum B average; for doctorate, master's degree, minimum B+ average. Electronic applications accepted. *Faculty research:* Political thought and analysis of ideologies, Canadian and Québécois policies, international and comparative policies.

University of Pennsylvania, School of Arts and Sciences, Graduate Group in Political Science, Philadelphia, PA 19104. Offers AM, PhD, MGA/AM. *Faculty:* 36 full-time (12 women), 4 part-time/adjunct (1 woman). *Students:* 57 full-time (24 women), 8 part-time (3 women); includes 4 minority (2 African Americans, 1 Asian American or Pacific Islander, 1 Hispanic American), 21 international. 284 applicants, 11% accepted, 13 enrolled. In 2009, 8 master's, 1 doctorate awarded. Terminal master's awarded for partial completion of doctoral program. *Degree requirements:* For doctorate, one foreign language, thesis/dissertation. *Entrance requirements:* For master's and doctorate, GRE General Test. Additional exam requirements/recommendations for international students: Required—TOEFL. *Application deadline:* For fall admission, 12/1 priority date for domestic students. Application fee: $70. Electronic applications accepted. *Expenses:* Tuition: Full-time $25,660; part-time $4758 per course. Required fees: $2152; $270 per course. Tuition and fees vary according to course load, degree level and program. *Financial support:* Fellowships, research assistantships, teaching assistantships, institutionally sponsored loans, scholarships/grants, traineeships, health care benefits, and unspecified assistantships available. Financial award application deadline: 12/15.

University of Pittsburgh, Graduate School of Public and International Affairs, International Affairs Division, Pittsburgh, PA 15260. Offers global political economy (MPIA); human security (MPIA); security and intelligence studies (MPIA); JD/MPIA; MBA/MPIA; MID/MPIA; MPA/MPIA; MSIS/MPIA. Part-time and evening/weekend programs available. *Faculty:* 28 full-time (8 women), 56 part-time/adjunct (20 women). *Students:* 125 full-time (52 women), 19 part-time (11 women); includes 17 minority (10 African Americans, 4 Asian Americans or Pacific Islanders, 3 Hispanic Americans), 5 international. Average age 25. 270 applicants, 81% accepted, 79 enrolled. In 2009, 61 master's awarded. *Degree requirements:* For master's, thesis optional, internship, capstone seminar. *Entrance requirements:* For master's, GRE General Test, 3 letters of recommendation, resume, minimum GPA of 3.2. Additional exam requirements/recommendations for international students: Required—TOEFL (minimum score 550 paper-based; 213 computer-based), TWE (minimum score 4); Recommended—IELTS (minimum score 7). *Application deadline:* For fall admission, 3/1 for domestic students, 1/15 for international students; for spring admission, 11/1 for domestic students, 8/1 for international students. Application fee: $50. Electronic applications accepted. *Expenses:* Tuition, state resident: full-time $16,402; part-time $665 per credit. Tuition, nonresident: full-time $28,694; part-time $1175 per credit. Required fees: $690; $175 per term. Tuition and fees vary according to program. *Financial support:* In 2009–10, 45 students received support, including 6 fellowships (averaging $41,800 per year); career-related internships or fieldwork, scholarships/grants, tuition waivers (full and partial), and unspecified assistantships also available. Financial award application deadline: 2/1. *Faculty research:* International political economy, international security and intelligence, transnational organized crime, international trade, international finance, globalization, terrorism, multinational corporations and the global economy. Total annual research expenditures: $357,117. *Unit head:* Dr. Martin Staniland, Director, International Affairs and International Development Divisions, 412-648-7656, Fax: 412-648-2605, E-mail: mstan@pitt.edu. *Application contact:* Kelly C. McDevitt, Graduate Enrollment Counselor, 412-648-7640, Fax: 412-648-7641, E-mail: mcdevitt@pitt.edu.

University of Pittsburgh, Graduate School of Public and International Affairs, Public Policy and Management Program for Mid-Career Professionals, Pittsburgh, PA 15260. Offers development planning (MPPM); international development (MPPM); international political economy (MPPM); international security studies (MPPM); management of non profit organizations (MPPM); metropolitan management and regional development (MPPM); policy analysis and evaluation (MPPM). Part-time programs available. *Faculty:* 28 full-time (8 women), 56 part-time/adjunct (20 women). *Students:* 3 full-time (0 women), 39 part-time (21 women); includes 2 minority (both African Americans), 1 international. Average age 38. 48 applicants, 75% accepted, 19 enrolled. In 2009, 17 master's awarded. *Degree requirements:* For master's, thesis optional, capstone seminar. *Entrance requirements:* For master's, 2 letters of recommendation, resume, 5 years of supervisory or budgetary experience. Additional exam requirements/recommendations for international students: Required—TOEFL (minimum score 600 paper-based; 250 computer-based; 100 iBT), TWE (minimum score 4); Recommended—IELTS (minimum score 7). *Application deadline:* For fall admission, 6/1 priority date for domestic students, 2/15 for international students; for spring admission, 1/1 priority date for domestic students, 8/1 for international students. Applications are processed on a rolling basis. Application fee: $50. Electronic applications accepted. *Expenses:* Tuition, state resident: full-time $16,402; part-time $665 per credit. Tuition, nonresident: full-time $28,694; part-time $1175 per credit. Required fees: $690; $175 per term. Tuition and fees vary according to program. *Financial support:* In 2009–10, 10 students received support. Institutionally sponsored loans, scholarships/grants, and tuition waivers (partial) available. Support available to part-time students. Financial award application deadline: 2/1. *Faculty research:* Nonprofit management, urban and regional affairs, policy analysis and evaluation, security and intelligence studies, global political economy, nongovernmental organizations, civil society, development planning and environmental sustainability, human security. Total annual research expenditures: $357,117. *Unit head:* Dr. George Dougherty, Director, Executive Education, 412-648-7603, Fax: 412-648-2605, E-mail: gwdjr@pitt.edu. *Application contact:* Michael T. Rizzi, Associate Director of Student Services, 412-648-7640, Fax: 412-648-7641, E-mail: rizzim@pitt.edu.

University of Pittsburgh, School of Arts and Sciences, Department of Political Science, Pittsburgh, PA 15260. Offers MA, PhD. Part-time programs available. *Faculty:* 26 full-time (9 women), 4 part-time/adjunct (0 women). *Students:* 47 full-time (22 women), 1 part-time (0 women); includes 17 minority (6 Asian Americans or Pacific Islanders, 11 Hispanic Americans), 5 international. Average age 30. 109 applicants, 12% accepted, 9 enrolled. In 2009, 3 master's, 6 doctorates awarded. Terminal master's awarded for partial completion of doctoral program. *Degree requirements:* For master's, comprehensive exam; for doctorate, comprehensive exam, thesis/dissertation. *Entrance requirements:* For master's and doctorate, GRE General Test, minimum QPA of 3.0. Additional exam requirements/recommendations for international students: Required—TOEFL. *Application deadline:* For fall admission, 1/1 for domestic and international students. Applications are processed on a rolling basis. Application fee: $50. Electronic applications accepted. *Expenses:* Tuition, state resident: full-time $16,402; part-time $665 per credit. Tuition, nonresident: full-time $28,694; part-time $1175 per credit. Required fees: $690; $175 per term. Tuition and fees vary according to program. *Financial support:* In 2009–10, 28 students received support, including 15 fellowships with full tuition reimbursements available (averaging $17,972 per year), 2 research assistantships with full tuition reimbursements available (averaging $17,230 per year), 14 teaching assistantships with full tuition reimbursements available (averaging $15,010 per year); tuition waivers (partial) also available. Financial award application deadline: 1/1. *Unit head:* Prof. Barry Ames, Chairman, 412-648-7290, Fax: 412-648-7277, E-mail: barrya@pitt.edu. *Application contact:* Prof. David Barker, Director of Graduate Students, 412-648-7275, Fax: 412-648-7277, E-mail: dbarker@pitt.edu.

University of Regina, Faculty of Graduate Studies and Research, Faculty of Arts, Department of Philosophy, Regina, SK S4S 0A2, Canada. Offers philosophy (MA); social and political thought (MA). *Faculty:* 9 full-time (3 women). *Students:* 1 (woman) full-time, 2 part-time (0 women). 2 applicants, 50% accepted. *Degree requirements:* For master's, thesis. *Entrance requirements:* Additional exam requirements/recommendations for international students: Required—TOEFL (minimum score 580 paper-based; 237 computer-based; 80 iBT). *Application deadline:* Applications are processed on a rolling basis. Application fee: $90 ($100 for international students). Electronic applications accepted. *Financial support:* Fellowships, research assistantships, teaching assistantships, scholarships/grants available. Financial award application deadline: 6/15. *Faculty research:* History of philosophy, ethics, aesthetics, metaphysics, epistemology. *Unit head:* Dr. Eldon Soifer, Head, 306-585-4301, Fax: 306-585-4827, E-mail: eldon.soifer@uregina.ca. *Application contact:* Dr. Eldon Soifer, Head, 306-585-4301, Fax: 306-585-4827, E-mail: eldon.soifer@uregina.ca.

University of Regina, Faculty of Graduate Studies and Research, Faculty of Arts, Department of Political Science, Regina, SK S4S 0A2, Canada. Offers MA. Part-time programs available. *Faculty:* 10 full-time (3 women), 1 (woman) part-time/adjunct. *Students:* 9 full-time (4 women), 5 part-time (3 women). 12 applicants, 67% accepted. In 2009, 4 master's awarded. *Degree requirements:* For master's, thesis. *Entrance requirements:* Additional exam requirements/recommendations for international students: Required—TOEFL (minimum score 580 paper-based; 237 computer-based; 80 iBT). *Application deadline:* For fall admission, 3/15 for domestic students. Applications are processed on a rolling basis. Application fee: $90 ($100 for international students). Electronic applications accepted. *Financial support:* In 2009–10, 4 fellowships (averaging $19,000 per year), 1 research assistantship (averaging $16,910 per year), 3

Political Science

University of Regina (continued)

teaching assistantships (averaging $6,650 per year) were awarded; scholarships/grants also available. Financial award application deadline: 6/15. *Faculty research:* Canadian politics, comparative politics, international politics. *Unit head:* Dr. Jeremy Rayner, Head, 306-585-5679, Fax: 306-585-4815, E-mail: jeremy.rayner@uregina.ca. *Application contact:* Dr. Yuchao Zhu, Graduate Coordinator, 306-585-4060, E-mail: yuchao.zhu@uregina.ca.

University of Regina, Faculty of Graduate Studies and Research, Faculty of Arts, Program in Social and Political Thought, Regina, SK S4S 0A2, Canada. Offers MA. *Faculty:* 9 full-time (3 women). *Students:* 2 full-time (1 woman), 3 part-time (1 woman). 2 applicants, 100% accepted. In 2009, 2 master's awarded. *Degree requirements:* For master's, thesis. *Entrance requirements:* Additional exam requirements/recommendations for international students: Required—TOEFL (minimum score 580 paper-based; 237 computer-based; 80 iBT). *Application deadline:* For fall admission, 3/15 for domestic students. Application fee: $90 ($100 for international students). Electronic applications accepted. *Financial support:* In 2009–10, 1 fellowship (averaging $19,000 per year) was awarded; research assistantships, teaching assistantships. *Unit head:* Dr. Shadia Drury, Program Coordinator, 306-585-4073, E-mail: shadia.drury@uregina.ca. *Application contact:* Dr. Shadia Drury, Program Coordinator, 306-585-4073, E-mail: shadia.drury@uregina.ca.

University of Rhode Island, Graduate School, College of Arts and Sciences, Department of Political Science, Kingston, RI 02881. Offers political science (MA), including American politics, comparative government, international relations, public policy; public policy and administration (MPA); MLIS/MPA. Part-time programs available. *Faculty:* 10 full-time (4 women), 1 part-time/adjunct (0 women). *Students:* 17 full-time (11 women), 44 part-time (28 women); includes 9 minority (4 African Americans, 1 Asian American or Pacific Islander, 4 Hispanic Americans). In 2009, 29 master's awarded. *Degree requirements:* For master's, comprehensive exam (for some programs), thesis optional. *Entrance requirements:* For master's, GRE, GMAT or MAT, 2 letters of recommendation. Additional exam requirements/recommendations for international students: Required—TOEFL (minimum score 550 paper-based; 213 computer-based). *Application deadline:* For fall admission, 2/1 for international students; for spring admission, 7/15 for international students. Application fee: $65. Electronic applications accepted. *Expenses:* Tuition, state resident: full-time $8828; part-time $490 per credit hour. Tuition, nonresident: full-time $22,100; part-time $1228 per credit hour. Required fees: $1118; $57 per semester. Tuition and fees vary according to program. *Financial support:* In 2009–10, 4 teaching assistantships with full tuition reimbursements (averaging $13,894 per year) were awarded. Financial award applicants required to submit FAFSA. *Unit head:* Dr. Gerry Tyler, Chairperson, 401-874-4053, Fax: 401-874-4072, E-mail: gtyler@uri.edu. *Application contact:* Dr. Gerry Tyler, Chairperson, 401-874-4053, Fax: 401-874-4072, E-mail: gtyler@uri.edu.

University of Rochester, The College, Arts and Sciences, Department of Political Science, Rochester, NY 14627. Offers MA, PhD, MPH/MS, MS/PhD. Terminal master's awarded for partial completion of doctoral program. *Degree requirements:* For doctorate, thesis/dissertation, qualifying exam. *Entrance requirements:* For master's and doctorate, GRE General Test. Additional exam requirements/recommendations for international students: Required—TOEFL.

University of Saskatchewan, College of Graduate Studies and Research, College of Arts and Sciences, Department of Political Studies, Saskatoon, SK S7N 5A2, Canada. Offers MA. *Faculty:* 19. *Students:* 24. In 2009, 6 master's awarded. *Degree requirements:* For master's, thesis. *Entrance requirements:* Additional exam requirements/recommendations for international students: Required—TOEFL (minimum score 80 iBT); Recommended—IELTS (minimum score 6.5). *Application deadline:* For fall admission, 7/1 priority date for domestic students. Applications are processed on a rolling basis. Application fee: $75. Electronic applications accepted. Tuition and fees charges are reported in Canadian dollars. *Expenses:* Tuition, area resident: Full-time $3000 Canadian dollars; part-time $500 Canadian dollars per term. Required fees: $700 Canadian dollars; $100 Canadian dollars per term. *Financial support:* Fellowships, research assistantships, teaching assistantships available. Financial award application deadline: 1/31. *Unit head:* Dr. Peter Phillips, Acting Head, 306-966-5208, Fax: 306-966-5250, E-mail: pter.phillips@usask.ca. *Application contact:* Dr. Hans Michelmann, Graduate Chair, 306-966-5219, Fax: 306-966-6400, E-mail: hans.michelmann@usask.ca.

University of South Africa, College of Human Sciences, Pretoria, South Africa. Offers adult education (M Ed); African languages (MA, PhD); African politics (MA, PhD); Afrikaans (MA, PhD); ancient history (MA, PhD); ancient Near Eastern studies (MA, PhD); anthropology (MA, PhD); applied linguistics (MA); Arabic (MA, PhD); archaeology (MA); art history (MA); Biblical archaeology (MA); Biblical studies (M Th, D Th, PhD); Christian spirituality (M Th, D Th); church history (M Th, D Th); classical studies (MA, PhD); clinical psychology (MA); communication (MA, PhD); comparative education (M Ed, Ed D); consulting psychology (D Admin, D Com, PhD); curriculum studies (M Ed, Ed D); development studies (M Admin, MA, D Admin, PhD); didactics (M Ed, Ed D); education (M Tech); education management (M Ed, Ed D); educational psychology (M Ed); English (MA); environmental education (M Ed); French (MA, PhD); German (MA, PhD); Greek (MA); guidance and counseling (M Ed); health studies (MA, PhD), including health sciences education (MA), health services management (MA), medical and surgical nursing science (critical care general) (MA), midwifery and neonatal nursing science (MA), trauma and emergency care (MA); history (MA, PhD); history of education (Ed D); inclusive education (M Ed, Ed D); information and communications technology policy and regulation (MA); information science (MA, MIS, PhD); international politics (MA, PhD); Islamic studies (MA, PhD); Italian (MA, PhD); Judaica (MA, PhD); linguistics (MA, PhD); mathematical education (M Ed); mathematics education (MA); missiology (M Th, D Th); modern Hebrew (MA, PhD); musicology (MA, MMus, D Mus, PhD); natural science education (M Ed); New Testament (M Th, D Th); Old Testament (D Th); pastoral therapy (M Th, D Th); philosophy (MA); philosophy of education (M Ed, Ed D); politics (MA, PhD); Portuguese (MA, PhD); practical theology (M Th, D Th); psychology (MA, MS, PhD); psychology of education (M Ed, Ed D); public health (MA); religious studies (MA, D Th, PhD); Romance languages (MA); Russian (MA, PhD); Semitic languages (MA, PhD); social behavior studies in HIV/AIDS (MA); social science (mental health) (MA); social science in development studies (MA); social science in psychology (MA); social science in social work (MA); social science in sociology (MA); social work (MSW, DSW, PhD); socio-education (M Ed, Ed D); sociolinguistics (MA); sociology (MA, PhD); Spanish (MA, PhD); systematic theology (M Th, D Th); TESOL (teaching English to speakers of other languages) (MA); theological ethics (M Th, D Th); theory of literature (MA, PhD); urban ministries (D Th); urban ministry (M Th).

University of South Carolina, The Graduate School, College of Arts and Sciences, Department of Political Science, Program in Political Science, Columbia, SC 29208. Offers MA, PhD. Part-time programs available. Terminal master's awarded for partial completion of doctoral program. *Degree requirements:* For master's, one foreign language, thesis; for doctorate, one foreign language, comprehensive exam, thesis/dissertation. *Entrance requirements:* For master's and doctorate, GRE General Test, minimum GPA of 3.5. Additional exam requirements/recommendations for international students: Required—TOEFL. Electronic applications accepted. *Faculty research:* American government and politics, comparative politics, political theory, international politics, public administration and policy.

The University of South Dakota, Graduate School, College of Arts and Sciences, Department of Political Science, Vermillion, SD 57069-2390. Offers American political institutions (PhD); political science (MA); public administration (MPA, PhD); public policy (PhD); JD/MA; JD/MPA. *Accreditation:* NASPAA (one or more programs are accredited). Part-time programs available. Postbaccalaureate distance learning degree programs offered. *Degree requirements:* For master's, comprehensive exam, thesis (for some programs). *Entrance requirements:* For master's, GRE or LSAT (MPA), GRE General Test (MA), minimum GPA of 2.7. Additional exam requirements/recommendations for international students: Required—TOEFL (minimum score 550 paper-based; 213 computer-based; 79 iBT). Electronic applications accepted.

University of Southern California, Graduate School, Annenberg School for Communication and Journalism, School of Communication, Program in Public Diplomacy, Los Angeles, CA 90089. Offers MPD. *Degree requirements:* For master's, thesis. *Entrance requirements:* For master's, GRE, resume, writing samples, recommendation letters. Additional exam requirements/recommendations for international students: Required—TOEFL (minimum score 280 computer-based; 114 iBT). Electronic applications accepted. *Expenses:* Tuition: Full-time $25,980; part-time $1315 per unit. Required fees: $554. One-time fee: $35 full-time. Full-time tuition and fees vary according to degree level and program.

See Close-Up on page 685.

University of Southern California, Graduate School, College of Letters, Arts and Sciences, Department of Political Science, Los Angeles, CA 90089. Offers politics and international relations (PhD). *Faculty:* 38 full-time (13 women). *Students:* 60 full-time (28 women), 1 (woman) part-time; includes 19 minority (1 African American, 1 American Indian/Alaska Native, 9 Asian Americans or Pacific Islanders, 8 Hispanic Americans), 25 international. 122 applicants, 13% accepted, 8 enrolled. In 2009, 14 doctorates awarded. *Degree requirements:* For doctorate, one foreign language, comprehensive exam. *Entrance requirements:* For doctorate, GRE (minimum score 1000). *Application deadline:* For fall admission, 12/1 for domestic and international students. Application fee: $85. Electronic applications accepted. *Expenses:* Tuition: Full-time $25,980; part-time $1315 per unit. Required fees: $554. One-time fee: $35 full-time. Full-time tuition and fees vary according to degree level and program. *Financial support:* In 2009–10, 44 students received support, including 13 fellowships with full tuition reimbursements available (averaging $22,755 per year), 7 research assistantships with full tuition reimbursements available (averaging $19,000 per year), 24 teaching assistantships with full tuition reimbursements available (averaging $19,000 per year); tuition waivers (full and partial) also available. *Faculty research:* Comparative politics, political communication, American politics, international political economy, race and ethnicity. Total annual research expenditures: $136,000. *Unit head:* Prof. Ann N. Crigler, 213-740-6998, Fax: 213-740-8893, E-mail: acrigler@college.usc.edu. *Application contact:* Alex Venegas, Program Advisor, 213-740-1695, Fax: 213-740-8893, E-mail: venegasa@college.usc.edu.

University of Southern Mississippi, Graduate School, College of Arts and Letters, Department of Political Science, International Development, and International Affairs, Hattiesburg, MS 39406-0001. Offers international development (PhD); political science (MA, MS). Part-time programs available. *Faculty:* 14 full-time (2 women). *Students:* 23 full-time (11 women), 59 part-time (21 women); includes 20 minority (13 African Americans, 1 American Indian/Alaska Native, 1 Asian American or Pacific Islander, 5 Hispanic Americans), 5 international. Average age 36. 28 applicants, 39% accepted, 9 enrolled. In 2009, 8 master's, 1 doctorate awarded. *Degree requirements:* For master's, comprehensive exam, thesis (for some programs). *Entrance requirements:* For master's, GRE General Test, minimum GPA of 2.75 in last 2 years, 3.0 in field of study. *Application deadline:* For fall admission, 3/1 priority date for domestic students, 3/1 for international students. Applications are processed on a rolling basis. Application fee: $35. *Expenses:* Tuition, state resident: full-time $5096; part-time $284 per hour. Tuition, nonresident: full-time $13,052; part-time $726 per hour. Required fees: $402. Tuition and fees vary according to course level and course load. *Financial support:* In 2009–10, 4 research assistantships with full and partial tuition reimbursements (averaging $9,000 per year), 8 teaching assistantships with full tuition reimbursements (averaging $7,000 per year) were awarded; career-related internships or fieldwork, Federal Work-Study, scholarships/grants, and unspecified assistantships also available. Financial award application deadline: 3/15; financial award applicants required to submit FAFSA. *Faculty research:* American politics, international politics, political theory, comparative politics, public law. *Unit head:* Dr. Thomas Lansford, Interim Chair, 601-266-4310. *Application contact:* Dr. Robert Pauley, Graduate Coordinator, 601-266-4310, Fax: 601-266-4172.

University of South Florida, Graduate School, College of Arts and Sciences, Department of Government and International Affairs, Tampa, FL 33620-9951. Offers Latin American Caribbean and Latino Studies (MA); government (PhD); political science (MA); public administration (MPA). Part-time and evening/weekend programs available. *Faculty:* 19 full-time (4 women), 1 (woman) part-time/adjunct. *Students:* 31 full-time (16 women), 76 part-time (37 women); includes 28 minority (16 African Americans, 1 American Indian/Alaska Native, 4 Asian Americans or Pacific Islanders, 7 Hispanic Americans), 3 international. Average age 32. 126 applicants, 38% accepted, 24 enrolled. In 2009, 28 master's awarded. *Degree requirements:* For master's, comprehensive exam, thesis; for doctorate, comprehensive exam, thesis/dissertation. *Entrance requirements:* For master's, GRE (minimum score 470 verbal, 470 quantitative), minimum GPA of 3.0 in last 60 hours of course work. Additional exam requirements/recommendations for international students: Required—TOEFL (minimum score 550 paper-based; 213 computer-based). *Application deadline:* For fall admission, 2/15 for domestic students, 1/2 for international students; for spring admission, 10/15 for domestic students, 6/1 for international students. Applications are processed on a rolling basis. Application fee: $30. Electronic applications accepted. *Financial support:* In 2009–10, teaching assistantships with tuition reimbursements (averaging $24,000 per year); unspecified assistantships also available. Financial award application deadline: 4/1. *Unit head:* Dr. Mohsen Milani, Chairperson, 813-974-2384, Fax: 813-974-0832, E-mail: milani@chuma1.cas.usf.edu. *Application contact:* Dr. Stephen Tauber, Graduate Coordinator, 813-974-0781, Fax: 813-974-0832, E-mail: stauber@chuma1.cas.usf.edu.

The University of Tennessee, Graduate School, College of Arts and Sciences, Department of Political Science, Program in Political Science, Knoxville, TN 37996. Offers MA, PhD. Part-time programs available. *Degree requirements:* For master's, thesis or alternative; for doctorate, one foreign language, thesis/dissertation. *Entrance requirements:* For master's and doctorate, GRE General Test, minimum GPA of 2.7. Additional exam requirements/recommendations for international students: Required—TOEFL. Electronic applications accepted. *Expenses:* Tuition, state resident: full-time $6826; part-time $380 per semester hour. Tuition, nonresident: full-time $21,844; part-time $1147 per semester hour. Tuition and fees vary according to program.

The University of Tennessee, Graduate School, College of Arts and Sciences, Department of Sociology, Knoxville, TN 37996. Offers criminology (MA, PhD); energy, environment, and resource policy (MA, PhD); political economy (MA, PhD). Part-time programs available. *Degree requirements:* For master's, thesis or alternative; for doctorate, thesis/dissertation. *Entrance requirements:* For master's, GRE General Test, minimum GPA of 3.0; for doctorate, GRE General Test, minimum GPA of 3.5. Additional exam requirements/recommendations for international students: Required—TOEFL. Electronic applications accepted. *Expenses:* Tuition, state resident: full-time $6826; part-time $380 per semester hour. Tuition, nonresident: full-time $21,844; part-time $1147 per semester hour. Tuition and fees vary according to program.

The University of Texas at Arlington, Graduate School, College of Liberal Arts, Department of Political Science, Arlington, TX 76019. Offers MA. Part-time and evening/weekend programs available. *Faculty:* 15 full-time (5 women), 1 part-time/adjunct (0 women). *Students:* 14 full-time (10 women), 17 part-time (13 women); includes 11 minority (5 African Americans, 1 American Indian/Alaska Native, 5 Hispanic Americans). 19 applicants, 95% accepted, 13 enrolled. In 2009, 13 master's awarded. *Degree requirements:* For master's, comprehensive exam, thesis optional. *Entrance requirements:* For master's, GRE, minimum GPA of 3.0 in last 60 hours of course work. Additional exam requirements/recommendations for international students: Required—TOEFL (minimum score 550 paper-based; 213 computer-based). *Application deadline:* For fall admission, 6/16 for domestic students. Applications are processed on a rolling basis. Application fee: $35 ($50 for international students). *Financial support:* In 2009–10, 2 students received support, including 2 teaching assistantships (averaging $5,000 per year); career-related internships or fieldwork, institutionally sponsored loans, and scholarships/grants also available. Support available to part-time students. Financial award application deadline: 6/1; financial award applicants required to submit FAFSA. *Unit head:* Dr. Rebecca Deen, Chair, 817-272-2991, Fax: 817-272-2525, E-mail: deen@uta.edu. *Application contact:* Dr. Brent Boyea, Graduate Advisor, 817-272-2991, E-mail: boyea@uta.edu.

The University of Texas at Austin, Graduate School, College of Liberal Arts, Department of Government, Austin, TX 78712-1111. Offers PhD. *Degree requirements:* For doctorate, comprehensive exam, thesis/dissertation. *Entrance requirements:* For doctorate, GRE General Test. Electronic applications accepted.

The University of Texas at Brownsville, Graduate Studies, College of Liberal Arts, Department of Government, Brownsville, TX 78520-4991. Offers MAIS. Part-time and evening/weekend programs available. *Degree requirements:* For master's, comprehensive exam, thesis optional. *Entrance requirements:* For master's, GRE General Test. Additional exam requirements/recommendations for international students: Required—TOEFL.

The University of Texas at Dallas, School of Economic, Political and Policy Sciences, Program in Political Science, Richardson, TX 75080. Offers constitutional law (MA); legislative studies (MA); political science (MA, PhD). Part-time and evening/weekend programs available. *Faculty:* 12 full-time (2 women). *Students:* 42 full-time (15 women), 21 part-time (10 women); includes 21 minority (4 African Americans, 2 American Indian/Alaska Native, 9 Asian Americans or Pacific Islanders, 6 Hispanic Americans), 5 international. Average age 33. 37 applicants, 65% accepted, 21 enrolled. In 2009, 18 master's, 3 doctorates awarded. *Degree requirements:* For doctorate, thesis/dissertation. *Entrance requirements:* For master's and doctorate, GRE General Test, minimum GPA of 3.0 in upper-level course work in field. Additional exam requirements/recommendations for international students: Required—TOEFL (minimum score 550 paper-based; 213 computer-based). *Application deadline:* For fall admission, 7/15 for domestic students, 5/1 priority date for international students; for spring admission, 11/15 for domestic students, 9/1 priority date for international students. Applications are processed on a rolling basis. Application fee: $50 ($100 for international students). Electronic applications accepted. *Expenses:* Tuition, state resident: full-time $11,068; part-time $461 per credit hour. Tuition, nonresident: full-time $21,178; part-time $882 per credit hour. Tuition and fees vary according to course load. *Financial support:* In 2009–10, 4 research assistantships with full tuition reimbursements (averaging $12,600 per year), 15 teaching assistantships with full tuition reimbursements (averaging $11,880 per year) were awarded; fellowships, career-related internships or fieldwork, Federal Work-Study, institutionally sponsored loans, and scholarships/grants also available. Support available to part-time students. Financial award application deadline: 4/30; financial award applicants required to submit FAFSA. *Faculty research:* Judicial politics and Congressional history, forecasting conflict, political violence and terrorism, elections and representation, international disputes. *Unit head:* Dr. Robert C. Lowry, Program Head, 972-883-6720, Fax: 972-883-2735, E-mail: robert.lowry@utdallas.edu. *Application contact:* Dr. Thomas L. Brunell, Associate Program Head, 972-883-4963, Fax: 972-883-2735, E-mail: tbrunell@utdallas.edu.

The University of Texas at Dallas, School of Economic, Political and Policy Sciences, Program in Public Policy and Political Economy, Richardson, TX 75080. Offers international political economy (MS); public policy (MPP); public policy and political economy (PhD). Part-time and evening/weekend programs available. *Faculty:* 16 full-time (4 women). *Students:* 49 full-time (25 women), 45 part-time (19 women); includes 28 minority (12 African Americans, 10 Asian Americans or Pacific Islanders, 6 Hispanic Americans), 19 international. Average age 36. 59 applicants, 68% accepted, 31 enrolled. In 2009, 5 master's, 8 doctorates awarded. *Degree requirements:* For doctorate, thesis/dissertation. *Entrance requirements:* For master's and doctorate, GRE General Test, minimum GPA of 3.0 in upper-level course work in field. Additional exam requirements/recommendations for international students: Required—TOEFL (minimum score 550 paper-based; 213 computer-based). *Application deadline:* For fall admission, 7/15 for domestic students, 5/1 priority date for international students; for spring admission, 11/15 for domestic students, 9/1 priority date for international students. Applications are processed on a rolling basis. Application fee: $50 ($100 for international students). Electronic applications accepted. *Expenses:* Tuition, state resident: full-time $11,068; part-time $461 per credit hour. Tuition, nonresident: full-time $21,178; part-time $882 per credit hour. Tuition and fees vary according to course load. *Financial support:* In 2009–10, 5 research assistantships with full tuition reimbursements (averaging $12,690 per year), 11 teaching assistantships with full tuition reimbursements (averaging $11,905 per year) were awarded; fellowships, career-related internships or fieldwork, Federal Work-Study, institutionally sponsored loans, and scholarships/grants also available. Support available to part-time students. Financial award application deadline: 4/30; financial award applicants required to submit FAFSA. *Faculty research:* New leadership development, gender and leadership, globalization and leadership opportunities in democracy. *Unit head:* Dr. Sheila Amin Gutierrez de Pineres, Program Head, 972-883-6228, Fax: 972-883-2735, E-mail: pineres@utdallas.edu. *Application contact:* Dr. Marie I. Chevrier, Associate Program Head, 972-883-2727, Fax: 972-883-2735, E-mail: chevrier@utdallas.edu.

See Close-Up on page 759.

The University of Texas at El Paso, Graduate School, College of Liberal Arts, Department of Political Science, El Paso, TX 79968-0001. Offers MA. Part-time and evening/weekend programs available. *Students:* 25 (10 women); includes 14 minority (2 African Americans, 12 Hispanic Americans), 4 international. Average age 34. In 2009, 8 master's awarded. *Degree requirements:* For master's, thesis optional. *Entrance requirements:* For master's, GRE, minimum GPA of 3.0, letters of recommendation. Additional exam requirements/recommendations for international students: Required—TOEFL; Recommended—IELTS. *Application deadline:* For fall admission, 8/1 priority date for domestic students, 3/1 for international students; for spring admission, 11/1 priority date for domestic students, 9/1 for international students. Applications are processed on a rolling basis. Application fee: $45 ($80 for international students). Electronic applications accepted. *Financial support:* In 2009–10, research assistantships with partial tuition reimbursements (averaging $18,625 per year), 10 teaching assistantships with partial tuition reimbursements (averaging $14,900 per year) were awarded; fellowships with partial tuition reimbursements, institutionally sponsored loans, scholarships/grants, health care benefits, tuition waivers (partial), and unspecified assistantships also available. Support available to part-time students. Financial award application deadline: 3/15; financial award applicants required to submit FAFSA. *Unit head:* Dr. Gregory D. Schmidt, Chair, 915-747-5227, Fax: 915-747-6616, E-mail: gdschmidt@utep.edu. *Application contact:* Dr. Patricia D. Witherspoon, Dean of the Graduate School, 915-747-5491, Fax: 915-747-5788, E-mail: withersp@utep.edu.

The University of Texas at San Antonio, College of Liberal and Fine Arts, Department of Political Science and Geography, San Antonio, TX 78249-0617. Offers political science (MA). Part-time and evening/weekend programs available. *Faculty:* 10 full-time (3 women). *Students:* 24 full-time (12 women), 27 part-time (16 women); includes 31 minority (3 African Americans, 28 Hispanic Americans), 1 international. Average age 29. 46 applicants, 57% accepted, 18 enrolled. In 2009, 6 master's awarded. *Degree requirements:* For master's, comprehensive exam (for some programs), thesis (for some programs). *Entrance requirements:* For master's, GRE General Test. Additional exam requirements/recommendations for international students: Required—TOEFL (minimum score 500 paper-based; 173 computer-based; 61 iBT), IELTS (minimum score 5). *Application deadline:* For fall admission, 7/1 for domestic students, 4/1 for international students; for spring admission, 11/1 for domestic students, 9/1 for international students. Applications are processed on a rolling basis. Application fee: $45 ($80 for international students). Electronic applications accepted. *Expenses:* Tuition, state resident: full-time $3975; part-time $221 per contact hour. Tuition, nonresident: full-time $13,947; part-time $775 per contact hour. Required fees: $1853. *Financial support:* In 2009–10, 2 students received support, including 13 research assistantships (averaging $9,543 per year), 7 teaching assistantships (averaging $7,980 per year); scholarships/grants, tuition waivers, and unspecified assistantships also available. Support available to part-time students. Total annual research expenditures: $3,185. *Unit head:* Dr. Mansour El-Kikhia, Chair, 210-458-5600, Fax: 210-458-5615, E-mail: mansour.elkikhia@utsa.edu. *Application contact:* Amy E. Jasperson, Graduate Advisor, 210-458-5431, E-mail: amy.jasperson@utsa.edu.

The University of Texas at Tyler, College of Arts and Sciences, Department of Political Science, Tyler, TX 75799-0001. Offers MA. Part-time and evening/weekend programs available. *Faculty:* 4 full-time (1 woman). *Students:* 5 full-time (3 women), 4 part-time (1 woman); includes 1 African American. Average age 33. 7 applicants, 100% accepted, 3 enrolled. In 2009, 3 master's awarded. *Degree requirements:* For master's, comprehensive exam, thesis optional. *Entrance requirements:* Additional exam requirements/recommendations for international students: Required—TOEFL (minimum score 79 computer-based). *Application deadline:* For fall admission, 8/17 priority date for domestic students, 7/1 priority date for international students; for spring admission, 12/21 priority date for domestic students, 11/1 priority date for international students. Application fee: $25 ($50 for international students). *Expenses:* Tuition, state resident: part-time $665 per semester hour. Tuition, nonresident: part-time $942 per semester hour. Part-time tuition and fees vary according to degree level and program. *Financial support:* In 2009–10, fellowships (averaging $500 per year), 1 teaching assistantship (averaging $6,750 per year) were awarded; scholarships/grants also available. Financial award application deadline: 7/1. *Faculty research:* American politics, comparative politics, international relations, political theory and philosophy. *Unit head:* Dr. Marcus Stadelmann, Head, 903-566-7412, Fax: 903-565-5537, E-mail: mstadelmann@uttyler.edu. *Application contact:* Dr. Randy LeBlanc, Information Contact, 903-566-7415, E-mail: rlblanc@uttyler.edu.

The University of Texas of the Permian Basin, Office of Graduate Studies, College of Arts and Sciences, Department of Social Sciences, Odessa, TX 79762-0001. Offers criminal justice administration (MS); political science (MPA). Part-time and evening/weekend programs available. *Degree requirements:* For master's, comprehensive exam (for some programs), thesis (for some programs). *Entrance requirements:* For master's, GRE General Test. Additional exam requirements/recommendations for international students: Required—TOEFL (minimum score 550 paper-based; 213 computer-based).

The University of Toledo, College of Graduate Studies, College of Arts and Sciences, Department of Political Science and Public Administration, Program in Political Science, Toledo, OH 43606-3390. Offers MA. *Degree requirements:* For master's, thesis. *Entrance requirements:* For master's, GRE General Test, GRE Subject Test, minimum GPA of 2.7. Electronic applications accepted. *Faculty research:* Economic policy, development, Third World, Eastern Europe, Africa.

University of Toronto, School of Graduate Studies, Social Sciences Division, Department of Political Science, Toronto, ON M5S 1A1, Canada. Offers MA, PhD. Part-time programs available. *Degree requirements:* For master's, thesis optional; for doctorate, one foreign language, thesis/dissertation, reading competency in a language other than English. *Entrance requirements:* For master's, 3 letters of recommendation, writing sample; for doctorate, 4 letters of recommendation, writing sample.

University of Utah, The Graduate School, College of Humanities, Program in Middle East Studies, Salt Lake City, UT 84112. Offers anthropology (MA); Arabic (MA, PhD); Arabic and linguistics (MA, PhD); Hebrew (MA); history (MA, PhD); Persian (MA, PhD); political science (MA, PhD); Turkish (MA). *Students:* 24 full-time (8 women), 19 part-time (9 women), 13 international. Average age 33. 33 applicants, 48% accepted, 10 enrolled. In 2009, 8 master's, 2 doctorates awarded. Terminal master's awarded for partial completion of doctoral program. *Degree requirements:* For master's, 2 foreign languages, comprehensive exam, thesis optional; for doctorate, 3 foreign languages, comprehensive exam, thesis/dissertation. *Entrance requirements:* For master's, GRE General Test, minimum GPA of 3.2; for doctorate, GRE General Test, MA in Middle East studies or equivalent, minimum GPA of 3.2. Additional exam requirements/recommendations for international students: Required—TOEFL (minimum score 580 paper-based; 237 computer-based; 92 iBT). *Application deadline:* For fall admission, 1/15 priority date for domestic and international students; for spring admission, 9/15 priority date for domestic and international students. Application fee: $55 ($65 for international students). Electronic applications accepted. *Expenses:* Tuition, state resident: full-time $4004; part-time $1674 per semester. Tuition, nonresident: full-time $14,134; part-time $5915 per semester. Required fees: $324 per semester. Tuition and fees vary according to course load, degree level and program. *Financial support:* In 2009–10, 19 students received support, including 15 fellowships with full tuition reimbursements available (averaging $14,000 per year), 3 teaching assistantships with full tuition reimbursements available (averaging $12,000 per year); unspecified assistantships also available. Financial award application deadline: 1/15. *Faculty research:* Arabic linguistics; Islamic studies; Middle Eastern history; political science; Judaic studies; anthropology; Arabic, Persian, Hebrew, and Turkish language and literature. *Unit head:* Dr. Bahman Baktiari, Director, 801-581-6181, Fax: 801-581-6183, E-mail: b.baktiari@utah.edu. *Application contact:* Peter von Sivers, Director of Graduate Studies, 801-581-9028, Fax: 801-581-6183, E-mail: peter.vonsivers@utah.edu.

University of Utah, The Graduate School, College of Social and Behavioral Science, Department of Political Science, Program in Political Science, Salt Lake City, UT 84112-1107. Offers MA, MS, PhD. Part-time programs available. *Students:* 18 full-time (9 women), 41 part-time (13 women); includes 7 minority (1 African American, 2 Asian Americans or Pacific Islanders, 4 Hispanic Americans), 12 international. Average age 34. 55 applicants, 40% accepted, 3 enrolled. In 2009, 7 master's, 1 doctorate awarded. Terminal master's awarded for partial completion of doctoral program. *Degree requirements:* For master's, variable foreign language requirement, thesis or research paper; for doctorate, variable foreign language requirement, comprehensive exam, thesis/dissertation. *Entrance requirements:* For master's and doctorate, GRE General Test, minimum GPA of 3.2. Additional exam requirements/recommendations for international students: Required—TOEFL (minimum score 580 paper-based; 237 computer-based; 92 iBT). *Application deadline:* For fall admission, 1/15 priority date for domestic and international students; for spring admission, 10/1 for domestic and international students. Application fee: $55 ($65 for international students). *Expenses:* Tuition, state resident: full-time $4004; part-time $1674 per semester. Tuition, nonresident: full-time $14,134; part-time $5915 per semester. Required fees: $324 per semester. Tuition and fees vary according to course load, degree level and program. *Financial support:* In 2009–10, 15 students received support, including 10 teaching assistantships with full tuition reimbursements available (averaging $11,500 per year); fellowships with full tuition reimbursements available, research assistantships with full tuition reimbursements available, career-related internships or fieldwork also available. Financial award application deadline: 1/15; financial award applicants required to submit FAFSA. *Faculty research:* Middle East politics, environmental politics, democratic theory, political participation, Latin-American politics. *Unit head:* Dr. Matthew Burbank, Chair, 801-581-6312, E-mail: mburbank@poli-sci.utah.edu. *Application contact:* Mary Ann Underwood, Graduate Coordinator, 801-581-8608, Fax: 801-585-6492, E-mail: maryann.underwood@poli-sci.utah.edu.

University of Victoria, Faculty of Graduate Studies, Faculty of Social Sciences, Department of Political Science, Victoria, BC V8W 2Y2, Canada. Offers MA, PhD. Part-time programs available. *Degree requirements:* For master's, thesis; for doctorate, thesis/dissertation, candidacy exam. *Entrance requirements:* For master's, minimum B+ average in last 2 years of undergraduate course work. Additional exam requirements/recommendations for international students: Required—TOEFL (minimum score 600 paper-based; 250 computer-based). Electronic applications accepted. *Faculty research:* Political theory, political parties, international political economy, comparative public policy, British Columbian politics.

University of Virginia, College and Graduate School of Arts and Sciences, Department of Politics, Program in Government, Charlottesville, VA 22903. Offers MA, PhD, JD/MA, MBA/MA. *Students:* 28 full-time (9 women), 3 part-time (2 women); includes 1 minority (African American), 7 international. Average age 29. 64 applicants, 48% accepted, 6 enrolled. In 2009, 2 master's, 4 doctorates awarded. *Degree requirements:* For master's, 2 research/statistics courses or thesis; for doctorate, variable foreign language requirement, thesis/dissertation, 2 research/statistics courses. *Entrance requirements:* For master's and doctorate, GRE General Test, long writing sample; 2 letters of recommendation. Additional exam requirements/recommendations for international students: Required—TOEFL (minimum score 600 paper-based; 250 computer-based; 90 iBT), IELTS (minimum score 7). *Application deadline:* For fall admission, 12/4 for domestic and international students. Applications are processed on a

Political Science

University of Virginia (continued)

rolling basis. Application fee: $60. Electronic applications accepted. *Financial support:* Fellowships, teaching assistantships available. Financial award application deadline: 12/4; financial award applicants required to submit FAFSA. *Unit head:* Jeffrey W. Legro, Chair, 434-924-3192, Fax: 434-924-3159. *Application contact:* Jeffrey W. Legro, Chair, 434-924-3192, Fax: 434-924-3159.

University of Washington, Graduate School, College of Arts and Sciences, Department of Political Science, Seattle, WA 98195. Offers MA, PhD. *Degree requirements:* For doctorate, thesis/dissertation. *Entrance requirements:* For master's and doctorate, GRE General Test, minimum GPA of 3.0. Additional exam requirements/recommendations for international students: Required—TOEFL. Electronic applications accepted. *Faculty research:* American politics, comparative politics, international relations, political theory, political economy.

University of Waterloo, Graduate Studies, Faculty of Arts, Department of Political Science, Global Governance Program, Waterloo, ON N2L 3G1, Canada. Offers MA, PhD. *Entrance requirements:* For doctorate, MA. Additional exam requirements/recommendations for international students: Required—TOEFL. Electronic applications accepted. *Faculty research:* Global political economy, global environment, peace and security, global justice and human rights, multilateral institutions and diplomacy.

The University of Western Ontario, Faculty of Graduate Studies, Social Sciences Division, Department of Political Science, London, ON N6A 5B8, Canada. Offers MA, MPA, PhD. Part-time programs available. *Degree requirements:* For master's, thesis; for doctorate, comprehensive exam, thesis/dissertation. *Entrance requirements:* For master's, minimum B average, honors BA in political science or equivalent, sample of written work; for doctorate, MA in political science or equivalent. *Faculty research:* Political theory, Canadian politics, local government, comparative politics, international relations.

University of West Florida, College of Arts and Sciences: Arts, Department of Government, Pensacola, FL 32514-5750. Offers political science (MA), including public administration, security and diplomacy. Part-time and evening/weekend programs available. *Faculty:* 2 full-time (0 women), 1 part-time/adjunct (0 women). *Students:* 6 full-time (1 woman), 8 part-time (3 women); includes 3 minority (all Hispanic Americans). Average age 31. 12 applicants, 67% accepted, 5 enrolled. In 2009, 9 master's awarded. *Degree requirements:* For master's, thesis or alternative. *Entrance requirements:* For master's, GRE General Test, minimum GPA of 3.0. Additional exam requirements/recommendations for international students: Required—TOEFL (minimum score 550 paper-based; 213 computer-based). *Application deadline:* For fall admission, 6/1 for domestic students, 5/15 for international students; for spring admission, 11/1 for domestic students, 10/1 for international students. Applications are processed on a rolling basis. Application fee: $30. *Expenses:* Tuition, state resident: full-time $4982; part-time $260 per credit hour. Tuition, nonresident: full-time $20,059; part-time $919 per credit hour. Required fees: $1247; $52 per credit hour. *Financial support:* In 2009–10, 1 teaching assistantship with partial tuition reimbursement (averaging $5,000 per year) was awarded; unspecified assistantships also available. Financial award application deadline: 4/15; financial award applicants required to submit FAFSA. *Faculty research:* Political campaigns, elections, law enforcement, growth management. *Unit head:* Dr. Alfred Cuzan, Chairperson, 850-474-2337, E-mail: govt@uwf.edu. *Application contact:* Terry McCray, Assistant Director of Graduate Admissions, 850-473-7718, Fax: 850-473-7714, E-mail: gradadmissions@uwf.edu.

University of Windsor, Faculty of Graduate Studies, Faculty of Arts and Social Sciences, Department of Political Science, Windsor, ON N9B 3P4, Canada. Offers MA. Part-time programs available. *Entrance requirements:* For master's, minimum B+ average. Additional exam requirements/recommendations for international students: Required—TOEFL (minimum score 600 paper-based; 250 computer-based). Electronic applications accepted. *Faculty research:* Canadian politics and government, local government, comparative political Canadian public administration, public policy.

University of Wisconsin–Madison, Graduate School, College of Letters and Science, Department of Political Science, Madison, WI 53706-1380. Offers PhD. *Degree requirements:* For doctorate, thesis/dissertation. *Entrance requirements:* For doctorate, GRE General Test. Electronic applications accepted. *Expenses:* Tuition, state resident: part-time $594 per credit. Tuition, nonresident: part-time $1504 per credit. Required fees: $65 per credit. Tuition and fees vary according to course load, program and reciprocity agreements. *Faculty research:* Comparative politics, American politics, international relations, political theory, political methodology.

University of Wisconsin–Milwaukee, Graduate School, College of Letters and Sciences, Department of Political Science, Milwaukee, WI 53201-0413. Offers MA, PhD. *Faculty:* 21 full-time (6 women). *Students:* 32 full-time (13 women), 18 part-time (8 women); includes 5 minority (1 African American, 1 Asian American or Pacific Islander, 3 Hispanic Americans), 7 international. Average age 29. 67 applicants, 55% accepted, 12 enrolled. In 2009, 8 master's, 3 doctorates awarded. *Degree requirements:* For master's, thesis or alternative; for doctorate, one foreign language, thesis/dissertation. *Entrance requirements:* For master's and doctorate, GRE General Test, minimum GPA of 3.0. Additional exam requirements/recommendations for international students: Required—TOEFL (minimum score 550 paper-based; 79 iBT), IELTS (minimum score 6.5). *Application deadline:* For fall admission, 1/1 priority date for domestic students; for spring admission, 9/1 for domestic students. Applications are processed on a rolling basis. Application fee: $45 ($75 for international students). *Expenses:* Tuition, state resident: full-time $8800. Tuition, nonresident: full-time $20,760. Tuition and fees vary according to program and reciprocity agreements. *Financial support:* In 2009–10, 1 research assistantship, 21 teaching assistantships were awarded; career-related internships or fieldwork and unspecified assistantships also available. Support available to part-time students. Financial award application deadline: 4/15. Total annual research expenditures: $3,951. *Unit head:* John Bohte, Representative, 414-229-4328, Fax: 414-229-5021, E-mail: jbohte@uwm.edu. *Application contact:* General Information Contact, 414-229-4982, Fax: 414-229-6967, E-mail: gradschool@uwm.edu.

University of Wyoming, College of Arts and Sciences, Department of Political Science, Program in Political Science, Laramie, WY 82070. Offers MA. Part-time programs available. *Degree requirements:* For master's, thesis or alternative. *Entrance requirements:* For master's, GRE General Test, bachelor's degree in political science, minimum GPA of 3.0. Additional exam requirements/recommendations for international students: Required—TOEFL (minimum score 525 paper-based; 195 computer-based). Electronic applications accepted. *Faculty research:* American government, public law, judicial politics, political theory, international relations.

Utah State University, School of Graduate Studies, College of Humanities, Arts and Social Sciences, Department of Political Science, Logan, UT 84322. Offers MA, MS. Part-time programs available. *Degree requirements:* For master's, one foreign language, thesis. *Entrance requirements:* For master's, GRE General Test, minimum GPA of 3.0. Additional exam requirements/recommendations for international students: Required—TOEFL. *Faculty research:* Political parties; social choice; international political economics; foreign policy; politics, markets, and public policy.

Vanderbilt University, Graduate School, Department of Political Science, Nashville, TN 37240-1001. Offers MA, MAT, PhD. *Faculty:* 31 full-time (14 women). *Students:* 36 full-time (18 women), 2 part-time (0 women); includes 6 minority (3 African Americans, 3 Hispanic Americans), 12 international. Average age 31. 135 applicants, 11% accepted, 8 enrolled. In 2009, 6 master's, 5 doctorates awarded. Terminal master's awarded for partial completion of doctoral program. *Degree requirements:* For master's, thesis; for doctorate, thesis/dissertation, final and qualifying exams. *Entrance requirements:* For master's and doctorate, GRE General Test, writing sample. Additional exam requirements/recommendations for international students: Required—TOEFL (minimum score 570 paper-based; 230 computer-based; 88 iBT). *Application deadline:* For fall admission, 1/15 for domestic and international students. Application fee: $0. Electronic applications accepted. *Financial support:* Fellowships with full tuition reimbursements, research assistantships with full tuition reimbursements, teaching assistantships with full tuition reimbursements, Federal Work-Study, institutionally sponsored loans, scholarships/grants, and health care benefits available. Financial award application deadline: 1/15; financial award applicants required to submit CSS PROFILE or FAFSA. *Faculty research:* American politics, comparative politics, international politics, political theory, political culture and life. *Unit head:* Bruce Oppenheimer, Interim Chair, 615-322-6222, Fax: 615-343-6003, E-mail: bruce.i.oppenheimer@vanderbilt.edu. *Application contact:* Jonathan Hiskey, Director of Graduate Studies, 615-322-6236, Fax: 615-343-6003, E-mail: j.hiskey@vanderbilt.edu.

Villanova University, Graduate School of Liberal Arts and Sciences, Department of Political Science, Program in Political Science, Villanova, PA 19085-1699. Offers MA. Part-time programs available. *Students:* 18 full-time (9 women), 25 part-time (7 women); includes 8 minority (1 African American, 6 Asian Americans or Pacific Islanders, 1 Hispanic American), 1 international. Average age 27. 37 applicants, 86% accepted, 13 enrolled. In 2009, 24 master's awarded. *Degree requirements:* For master's, comprehensive exam, thesis or alternative. *Entrance requirements:* For master's, GRE, minimum GPA of 3.0. Additional exam requirements/recommendations for international students: Required—TOEFL. *Application deadline:* For fall admission, 2/1 priority date for domestic and international students; for spring admission, 11/15 priority date for domestic students, 10/15 priority date for international students. Applications are processed on a rolling basis. Application fee: $50. Electronic applications accepted. *Expenses:* Tuition: Part-time $630 per credit. Required fees: $60 per credit. Part-time tuition and fees vary according to degree level and program. *Financial support:* Scholarships/grants and unspecified assistantships available. Financial award application deadline: 3/15; financial award applicants required to submit FAFSA. *Unit head:* Dr. Markus Kreuzer, Director, 610-519-4710. *Application contact:* Dr. Adele Lindenmeyr, Information Contact, 610-519-7093, E-mail: matthew.kerbel@villanova.edu.

See Close-Up on page 857.

Virginia Commonwealth University, Graduate School, College of Humanities and Sciences, Wilder School of Government and Public Affairs, Richmond, VA 23284-9005. Offers MA, MPA, MS, MURP, PhD, CASR, CCJA, CPM, CURP, Certificate, Graduate Certificate, JD/MURP, MSW/Certificate.

Virginia Polytechnic Institute and State University, Graduate School, College of Liberal Arts and Human Sciences, Department of Political Science, Blacksburg, VA 24061. Offers MA. *Faculty:* 21 full-time (6 women), 1 (woman) part-time/adjunct. *Students:* 46 full-time (18 women), 40 part-time (19 women); includes 14 minority (2 African Americans, 9 American Indian/Alaska Native, 1 Asian American or Pacific Islander, 2 Hispanic Americans), 3 international. Average age 32. 64 applicants, 59% accepted, 28 enrolled. In 2009, 18 master's awarded. *Entrance requirements:* For master's, GRE, GMAT. Additional exam requirements/recommendations for international students: Required—TOEFL (minimum score 550 paper-based; 213 computer-based). *Application deadline:* For fall admission, 5/15 for international students; for spring admission, 10/15 for international students. Applications are processed on a rolling basis. Application fee: $65. Electronic applications accepted. *Expenses:* Tuition, area resident: Full-time $10,228; part-time $459 per credit hour. Tuition, nonresident: full-time $17,892; part-time $865 per credit hour. Required fees: $1966; $451 per semester. *Financial support:* In 2009–10, 14 teaching assistantships with full tuition reimbursements (averaging $11,192 per year) were awarded; career-related internships or fieldwork, Federal Work-Study, scholarships/grants, and unspecified assistantships also available. Financial award application deadline: 1/15. *Faculty research:* Comparative politics, international relations, American government and politics, research methods. Total annual research expenditures: $931. *Unit head:* Dr. Ilja A. Luciak, Dean, 540-231-6571, Fax: 540-231-6078, E-mail: iluciak@vt.edu. *Application contact:* Tim Luke, Information Contact, 540-231-6633, Fax: 540-231-6078, E-mail: twluke@vt.edu.

Virginia Polytechnic Institute and State University, VT Online, Blacksburg, VA 24061. Offers aerospace engineering (MS); business information systems (Graduate Certificate); career and technical education (MS); computer engineering (M Eng, MS); decision support systems (Graduate Certificate); eLearning leadership (MA); electrical engineering (M Eng, MS); engineering administration (MEA); environmental politics and policy (Graduate Certificate); foundations of political analysis (Graduate Certificate); health product risk management (Graduate Certificate); information policy and society (Graduate Certificate); information security (Graduate Certificate); instructional technology (MA); liberal arts (Graduate Certificate); life sciences: health product risk management (MS); natural resources (MNR, Graduate Certificate); networking (Graduate Certificate); nonprofit and nongovernmental organization management (Graduate Certificate); ocean engineering (MS); political science (MA); security studies (Graduate Certificate); software development (Graduate Certificate).

Washington State University, Graduate School, College of Liberal Arts, Department of Political Science, Program in Political Science, Pullman, WA 99164. Offers MA, PhD. Terminal master's awarded for partial completion of doctoral program. *Degree requirements:* For master's, comprehensive exam (for some programs), thesis, oral exam; for doctorate, comprehensive exam, thesis/dissertation, oral exam, written exam. *Entrance requirements:* For master's, GRE General Test, minimum GPA of 3.0; for doctorate, GRE General Test, minimum GPA of 3.5. Additional exam requirements/recommendations for international students: Required—TOEFL. Electronic applications accepted. *Faculty research:* Political psychology and image theory, grass roots environmental policy, federal juvenile policy.

Washington University in St. Louis, Graduate School of Arts and Sciences, Department of Political Science, St. Louis, MO 63130-4899. Offers political economy and public policy (MA); political science (PhD). Terminal master's awarded for partial completion of doctoral program. *Degree requirements:* For master's, thesis or alternative; for doctorate, thesis/dissertation. *Entrance requirements:* For master's and doctorate, GRE General Test. Electronic applications accepted.

Wayne State University, College of Liberal Arts and Sciences, Department of Political Science, Program in Political Science, Detroit, MI 48202. Offers MA, PhD, JD/MA. *Degree requirements:* For doctorate, thesis/dissertation. *Entrance requirements:* For master's, GRE General Test, minimum GPA of 3.0; for doctorate, GRE General Test, minimum GPA of 3.0, 3 letters of recommendation. Additional exam requirements/recommendations for international students: Required—TOEFL (minimum score 550 paper-based; 213 computer-based); Recommended—TWE (minimum score 6). Electronic applications accepted. *Faculty research:* Political theory and thought, international relations, American politics, comparative politics, public policy, public administration, urban politics.

West Chester University of Pennsylvania, Office of Graduate Studies, College of Business and Public Affairs, Department of Political Science, West Chester, PA 19383. Offers administration (Certificate); human resource management (MSA, Certificate); individualized (MSA); non profit administration (Certificate); nonprofit administration (MSA); public administration (MSA); training and development (MSA). Part-time and evening/weekend programs available. *Students:* 3 full-time (2 women), 42 part-time (31 women); includes 8 minority (6 African Americans, 2 Hispanic Americans), 2 international. Average age 28. 28 applicants, 96% accepted, 11 enrolled. In 2009, 12 master's awarded. *Degree requirements:* For master's, comprehensive exam (for some programs). *Entrance requirements:* For master's, GMAT, GRE General Test, or MAT; for Certificate, GMAT, GRE General Test, or MAT, statement of professional goals, resume, two letters of reference. Additional exam requirements/recommendations for international students: Required—TOEFL (minimum score 550 paper-based; 213 computer-based; 80 iBT). *Application deadline:* For fall admission, 4/15 priority date for domestic students, 3/15 for international students; for spring admission, 10/15 for domestic students, 9/1 for international students. Applications are processed on a rolling basis. Application fee: $35. Electronic applications accepted. *Expenses:* Tuition, state resident: full-time $6666; part-time $370 per credit. Tuition, nonresident: full-time $10,666; part-time $593 per credit. Required fees: $122.56 per credit. *Financial support:* In 2009–10, 5 research assistantships with full and partial tuition reimbursements (averaging $5,000 per year) were awarded; unspecified assistantships also available. Support available to part-time students. Financial award application deadline: 2/15; financial award applicants required to submit FAFSA. *Unit head:* Dr. Christopher Fiorentino, Dean, College of Business and Public Affairs, 610-436-2930, E-mail: cfiorentino@wcupa.edu. *Application contact:* Dr. Lorraine Bernotsky, Graduate Coordinator, 610-738-0576, E-mail: lbernotsky@wcupa.edu.

Western Illinois University, School of Graduate Studies, College of Arts and Sciences, Department of Political Science, Macomb, IL 61455-1390. Offers political science (MA); public and non-profit management (Certificate). Part-time programs available. *Students:* 22 full-time (9 women), 3 part-time (1 woman); includes 4 minority (2 African Americans, 2 Hispanic Americans), 6 international. Average age 26. 20 applicants, 70% accepted. In 2009, 10 master's, 1 other advanced degree awarded. *Degree requirements:* For master's, comprehensive exam, thesis or alternative. *Entrance requirements:* Additional exam requirements/recommendations for international students: Required—TOEFL (minimum score 550 paper-based; 213 computer-based; 80 iBT). *Application deadline:* Applications are processed on a rolling basis. Application fee: $30. Electronic applications accepted. *Expenses:* Tuition, state resident: full-time $4486; part-time $249.21 per credit hour. Tuition, nonresident: full-time $8972; part-time $498.42 per credit hour. Required fees: $72.62 per credit hour. *Financial support:* In 2009–10, 15 students received support, including 15 research assistantships with full tuition reimbursements available (averaging $7,280 per year). Financial award applicants required to submit FAFSA. *Unit head:* Dr. Richard Hardy, Chairperson, 309-298-1055. *Application contact:* Evelyn Hoing, Assistant Director of Graduate Studies, 309-298-1806, Fax: 309-298-2345, E-mail: grad-office@wiu.edu.

Western Kentucky University, Graduate Studies, Potter College of Arts and Letters, Department of Political Science, Bowling Green, KY 42101. Offers MPA. Part-time and evening/weekend programs available. *Degree requirements:* For master's, comprehensive exam, final exam. *Entrance requirements:* For master's, GRE General Test, minimum GPA of 2.75. Additional exam requirements/recommendations for international students: Required—TOEFL (minimum score 555 paper-based; 213 computer-based; 79 iBT). *Expenses:* Tuition, state resident: full-time $4160; part-time $416 per credit hour. Tuition, nonresident: full-time $9550; part-time $506 per credit hour. Tuition and fees vary according to campus/location and reciprocity agreements. *Faculty research:* Role of non-profits, comparative policy analysis, social welfare policy, rural administration, ethics and bureaucracy.

Western Michigan University, Graduate College, College of Arts and Sciences, Department of Political Science, Program in Political Science, Kalamazoo, MI 49008. Offers MA, PhD. *Degree requirements:* For master's, thesis optional, oral exams; for doctorate, thesis/dissertation, oral exam. *Entrance requirements:* For doctorate, GRE General Test.

Western Washington University, Graduate School, College of Humanities and Social Sciences, Department of Political Science, Bellingham, WA 98225-5996. Offers MA. Part-time programs available. *Degree requirements:* For master's, comprehensive exam, thesis (for some programs). *Entrance requirements:* For master's, GRE General Test, minimum GPA of 3.0 in last 60 semester hours or last 90 quarter hours. Additional exam requirements/recommendations for international students: Required—TOEFL (minimum score 567 paper-based; 227 computer-based). Electronic applications accepted. *Faculty research:* Elections, environment, identity, international relations.

West Texas A&M University, College of Education and Social Sciences, Department of History and Political Science, Program in Political Science, Canyon, TX 79016-0001. Offers MA. Part-time and evening/weekend programs available. *Degree requirements:* For master's, comprehensive exam, thesis optional. *Entrance requirements:* For master's, GRE General Test. Additional exam requirements/recommendations for international students: Required—TOEFL (minimum score 550 paper-based). Electronic applications accepted. *Faculty research:* American government, public administration, state and local government, international politics.

West Virginia University, Eberly College of Arts and Sciences, Department of Political Science, Morgantown, WV 26506. Offers American public policy and politics (MA); international and comparative public policy and politics (MA); political science (PhD); public policy analysis (PhD). Terminal master's awarded for partial completion of doctoral program. *Degree requirements:* For master's, thesis optional; for doctorate, comprehensive exam, thesis/dissertation. *Entrance requirements:* For master's, GRE General Test, minimum GPA of 2.75; for doctorate, GRE General Test, minimum GPA of 3.0. Additional exam requirements/recommendations for international students: Required—TOEFL. *Faculty research:* Public policy, research methods, foreign policy analysis, judicial politics, environmental and energy policy.

Wilfrid Laurier University, Faculty of Graduate Studies, Faculty of Arts, Department of Political Science, Waterloo, ON N2L 3C5, Canada. Offers MA. *Degree requirements:* For master's, thesis optional. *Entrance requirements:* For master's, honors bachelor's degree or the equivalent in political science, minimum B average in undergraduate course work. Additional exam requirements/recommendations for international students: Required—TOEFL (minimum score 230 computer-based; 89 iBT). Electronic applications accepted. *Faculty research:* Political behavior/political psychology, Canadian political studies, comparative, politics/relations, public opinion and electoral studies, international.

Yale University, Graduate School of Arts and Sciences, Department of Political Science, New Haven, CT 06520. Offers PhD. *Degree requirements:* For doctorate, one foreign language, thesis/dissertation. *Entrance requirements:* For doctorate, GRE General Test. *Faculty research:* U.N. and international security.

York University, Faculty of Graduate Studies, Faculty of Arts, Program in Political Science, Toronto, ON M3J 1P3, Canada. Offers MA, PhD. Part-time programs available. *Degree requirements:* For master's, thesis or alternative; for doctorate, one foreign language, comprehensive exam, thesis/dissertation. Electronic applications accepted.

York University, Faculty of Graduate Studies, Faculty of Arts, Program in Social and Political Thought, Toronto, ON M3J 1P3, Canada. Offers MA, PhD. Part-time programs available. *Degree requirements:* For master's, one foreign language, thesis or alternative, oral exams; for doctorate, one foreign language, comprehensive exam, thesis/dissertation. Electronic applications accepted.

AMERICAN UNIVERSITY
WASHINGTON, DC

AMERICAN UNIVERSITY

School of International Service

Programs of Study

A founding member of the Association of Professional Schools of International Affairs, American University's (AU) School of International Service (SIS) is the largest and most-applied-to school of international affairs in the United States. SIS offers the following two-year standard master's programs: comparative and regional studies, global environmental politics, international communication, international development, international economic relations, international politics, international peace and conflict resolution, and U.S. foreign policy.

SIS also offers a one-year executive master's program (Master of International Service) for midcareer professionals with five to seven years of work experience, preferably in international affairs, and a Ph.D. program in international relations. In addition, the School has dual-degree programs with Ritsumeikan University in Japan, Korea University and Sookmyung Women's University in Korea, and the University of Peace in Costa Rica. Joint-degree programs in international media, ethics, peace, and global affairs and dual J.D./M.A., M.A./M.B.A., M.A./M.A.T., and M.A./M.T.S. programs are also available on the American University campus.

Within the graduate curriculum, students can tailor their programs to reflect their special interest and career paths and are encouraged to integrate professional experience, including internships. General M.A. degree requirements include 39–42 credit hours of approved graduate course work, a comprehensive examination, demonstration of research and writing skills through completion of a master's thesis, substantial research paper requirement or research practicum, and proficiency in a modern foreign language. General Ph.D. degree requirements include 72 credit hours of approved graduate course work consisting of 60 hours of course credits and 12 credit hours of independent dissertation supervision.

Teaching styles at SIS are highly collegial. The curriculum is distinguished by linking theory and practice and addressing emerging issues both conceptually and empirically. SIS students have the opportunity to participate in cutting-edge faculty-led research projects and are constantly challenged to care about the moral, philosophical, and practical implications of an increasingly interdependent world.

The University's nationally recognized Career Center and SIS partner with domestic and international employers to offer substantive internship experiences for which students may earn academic credit. SIS students have interned and worked at such organizations as the International Monetary Fund, Amnesty International, Global Fund for Women, U.N. Higher Commissioner for Refugees, the U.S. Department of State, the World Bank, Search for Common Ground, foreign embassies, and many others.

Research Facilities

The School of International Service offers research opportunities through a number of research programs and centers, such as the Center for Asian Studies, the Center for Global Peace, Intercultural Management Institute, Center for Human Rights, Peacebuilding and Development Institute, and Public International Law and Policy Program.

During the summer, SIS also offers specialized study tours to sites including Belgium, China, the Galapagos Islands, India, Israel and Palestine, Korea, Malaysia, Mexico, South Africa, and the United Arab Emirates; students on these tours are encouraged to pursue self-designed research in conjunction with a faculty adviser.

The American University's Bender Library and Learning Resources Center house more than 780,000 titles, as well as journals, film/video/multimedia recordings, and microforms. The library also contains special collections in music, mathematics, Japanese materials, and broadcast journalism. The library provides online access to 2,000 other member libraries. The University is also ranked by Intel as one of the top ten most unwired college campuses and was selected as T-Mobile's first HotSpot WiFi Internet campus.

Financial Aid

SIS offers merit-based awards to a limited number of eligible domestic and international graduate students upon notification of admission. Only full-time students are eligible to receive merit-based assistance. These awards are highly competitive and require that the recipient follow American University academic regulations and remain in good academic standing. The award amounts and types vary but can include partial- to full-tuition remission and/or a monthly stipend and/or a research assistantship with a faculty member. All admitted Ph.D. students are fully funded for their course work during their study at SIS. Students should note that all required application materials need to be received by the posted deadline in order to be considered for merit-based aid.

Cost of Study

Tuition for the 2010–11 academic year is $23,382, based on two semesters of full-time enrollment, 9 credits/semester, at the rate of $1299 per credit. Fees are $1930, which includes an SIS fee of $750 per semester for full-time students (registering for 9 credits or above) or $500 per semester for part-time students (registering for 6 to 8 credits), plus $300 for other estimated University fees. Students should anticipate an increase of 5 to 8 percent for each succeeding academic year.

Living and Housing Costs

Washington, D.C., is a diverse and eclectic city with many options for graduate students looking for housing. The best place to start searching is the American University Housing and Dining Web site (http://www.american.edu/ocl/housing/), where information about housing in Washington, D.C., and current postings for a variety of accommodations are listed. Some students choose to live on their own, renting a studio or one-bedroom apartment in the AU neighborhood or in one of the many centers around the city; others opt for group housing, sharing costs with several people in a house or apartment. Washington, D.C., has plenty of options from which to choose. There are many resources for finding housing in the city, including the American University Housing and Dining Programs (http://www.american.edu/ocl/housing/), Apartment Search (http://www.apartmentsearch.com), craigslist–Washington D.C. (http://www.washingtondc.craigslist.org), Off Campus Network (http://www.offcampusnetwork.com/index.asp), Washington City Paper classifieds (http://www.washingtoncitypaper.com/class/classifieds.html), Washington Post classifieds (http://www.washingtonpost.com), Washington D.C. ForRent (http://www.washingtondc.forrent.com), Washington D.C. Convention and Visitors Bureau (http://www.2chambers.com/tourist5.htm), and Washington Metropolitan Transit Authority (http://www.wmata.com).

Student Group

With a graduate student body of more than 800, SIS is the largest and most-applied-to school of international affairs in the U.S. A very diverse student body is composed of about 20 percent international students from more than 130 countries, and an additional 25 percent are members of domestic minority groups.

Location

American University is located in northwest Washington, D.C., home to some 192 foreign embassies, chanceries, and the headquarters of many international organizations. In addition, the Smithsonian Institution, National Institutes of Health, John F. Kennedy Center for the Performing Arts, National Archives, Brookings Institute, World Bank, and Library of Congress are all just a short distance from the campus. There are also a host of research and internship sites related to each field, including the Office of European Union Commission, Organization of American States, TransAfrica Forum, and Asia Society.

The University and The School

American University was chartered by an Act of the United States Congress in 1893. The first graduate students were admitted in 1914, and President Woodrow Wilson officially dedicated the University on May 27, 1914. Today, as a premiere global university, American University has more than 11,000 students enrolled and attracts students from all fifty states, the District of Columbia, Puerto Rico and the territories, and nearly 150 other countries.

During the Cold War, U.S. President Dwight Eisenhower was aware that the world needed to prepare for a time when the U.S.-Soviet rivalry no longer dominated foreign policy. He encouraged thirteen university presidents, including AU's Hurst Anderson, to incorporate human-focused international affairs into higher education. Anderson and the Methodist Bishop of Washington shared a similar vision: a school predicated on service to the global community. Eisenhower embraced the idea and spoke at the School's groundbreaking ceremony in 1957. The School of International Service opened in 1958 to an inaugural class of 80 students from thirty-six countries.

Applying

To be considered for admission to the master's programs, all applicants must possess a bachelor's degree or its equivalent from an accredited institution and submit the application form; a resume; a statement of purpose; two letters of recommendation (three for the Ph.D. program); official transcripts; official test scores, such as GRE scores and/or TOEFL/IELTS/Pearson's Test scores (if applicable, for international students); and a $50 application fee. GRE scores are required for all Ph.D. applicants. The minimum TOEFL requirement for international students is 100 on the iBT, 250 on the CBT, or 600 on the PBT. The minimum IELTS requirement is 7.0. The minimum Pearson's Test requirement is 68. International students who have not graduated (or will not graduate before coming to AU if admitted) from an English-speaking university are not required to take the GRE but do need to take the TOEFL/IELTS/Pearson's. The M.A. application deadline for spring semester is October 1 for domestic students and September 15 for international students; the M.A. application deadline for fall semester is January 15 for all applicants. The Ph.D. application deadline is January 1. All application materials must reach the Graduate Admissions Office by the deadline if students wish to be considered for merit-based financial aid.

Correspondence and Information

Office of Graduate Admissions
School of International Service
American University
4400 Massachusetts Avenue, NW
Washington, D.C. 20016-8071

Phone: 202-885-1646
Fax: 202-885-1109
E-mail: sisgrad@american.edu
Web site: http://www.american.edu/sis

American University

THE FACULTY AND THEIR RESEARCH

The diversity of SIS faculty members exemplifies the multidisciplinary and cross-cultural aspects of international relations. Bringing cutting-edge research into their classrooms, the faculty members use a variety of interactive approaches, such as simulations and case studies, in their teaching. The School regularly appoints adjunct and visiting professors and benefits from their expertise in the field of international relations.

Comparative and Regional Studies: Michelle Egan, Director
Global Environmental Politics: Paul Wapner, Director
International Communication: Nanette Levinson, Director
International Development: David Hirschmann, Director
International Economic Relations: Tamar Gutner, Interim Director
International Peace and Conflict Resolution: Ronald Fisher, Director
International Politics: Tamar Gutner, Director
U.S. Foreign Policy: Shoon Murray, Director

MISSOURI STATE UNIVERSITY

Department of Political Science
Master of Global Studies

Program of Study

The Department of Political Science offers a Master of Global Studies (M.G.S.) degree to meet the growing societal and occupational needs in a highly competitive and yet increasingly interdependent world. The main mission of the M.G.S. program is to produce well-rounded and educated persons who understand and appreciate the diversity and complexity of international affairs and the role of global citizenship and who can bring imaginative and creative problem-solving skills to problems faced by the global community.

The M.G.S. is designed to equip students with skills in areas such as quantitative analysis, policy analysis, foreign languages, communication, and problem solving that allow them to pursue careers in both public and private-sector agencies in an international environment. The M.G.S. also prepares students to continue their education at the doctoral level in international relations, political science, or other related fields.

Students enrolled in the M.G.S. program must complete a series of core courses that have been crafted to provide them with a firm foundation in international affairs. These courses include seminars in international relations theory, international organizations, international political economy, comparative politics, foreign policy decision making, and comparative public administration. In addition to the core curriculum, each student selects a cognate field and specializes in it. These fields include international relations and comparative politics, international economics and business, public administration, and national security. The student completes a total of 15 to 18 hours in his or her cognate field. Students also must either complete an independent research project supervised by a faculty member or opt for the 6-hour thesis option, whereby the student writes a full-fledged thesis. Finally, students must complete the equivalent of two years of training in a modern foreign language. Those students who earn a grade point average of less than 3.75 in the program must pass a comprehensive exam composed of both written and oral assessments. This exam is designed to measure the extent to which these students have absorbed the core body of knowledge included in the curriculum.

Students are encouraged to enroll in an internship. In the past, students have secured positions in internships in locations ranging from the local area to Japan. Students may receive 3 hours of credit for the internship, and it may be counted in the cognate field portion of the program requirements. Graduate students enrolled in the M.G.S. program also participate in numerous international conferences and a wide variety of other academic-related events. Such activities play a critical role in helping students learn about the global community (and help make them more competitive job candidates after graduation).

The M.G.S. program also encourages students to participate in study-abroad trips. Past study tours have included China, Africa, the Middle East, and various European countries, including Russia.

Research Facilities

Missouri State University libraries have comprehensive electronic resources, including an online catalog, electronic indexes and full-text resources, and Internet accessibility. The University is a member of the Center for Research Libraries and is both a U.S. and United Nations document depository (the only UN depository in Missouri).

Financial Aid

Graduate assistantships are awarded on a competitive basis in the Department and elsewhere on campus. The Department typically awards up to five graduate assistantships per year to students in the M.G.S. program. All students applying for a graduate assistantship must have their GRE scores (verbal and quantitative) on file at the time of application. Each award is granted for an academic year. A stipend and a waiver of tuition accompany the assistantship. Student research grants of up to $2000 are available to students who wish to conduct research in East Asia.

Cost of Study

Missouri residents pay $2304 for 9 hours plus approximately $348 in fees; nonresidents pay $4140 for 9 hours plus approximately $348 in fees.

Living and Housing Costs

Graduate student housing with meal plans costs between $7420 and $9590 per person; without a meal plan, it costs between $6604 and $8774. A twelve-month family meal plan can be purchased for $1230 per semester. Two-bedroom apartments in the community rent for approximately $540 a month.

Student Group

The total enrollment at Missouri State University is approximately 22,000 students, of whom 16 percent are graduate students. Students come from across the United States and from more than sixty countries. There are 40 students enrolled in the M.G.S. program. Students in the program come from the surrounding area, the state of Missouri, across the U.S., and from many other nations.

Student Outcomes

The M.G.S. program enjoys a record of nearly 100 percent in placing its graduates in Ph.D. programs in America and abroad. Graduates have been admitted to the American University, Cambridge University, University of New Mexico, Catholic University, University of Southern California, University of Missouri, University of Northern Illinois, University of North Texas, University of South Carolina, Indiana University, and University of Essex. It is noteworthy that many of these students have received prestigious and highly competitive scholarships and/or graduate assistantships.

A vast majority of graduates who have opted for a career have managed to secure employment in prestigious organizations. Government placements include the Department of Defense, the U.S. Diplomatic Corp, the Federal Bureau of Investigation, the United Nations in New York City, and UN branch offices in various countries overseas. Opportunities in the private sector have included Television Tokyo, Strategic Forecasting Inc., and InDiv Export Management Company. Some international students who have earned the M.G.S. degree have found employment with their respective home governments or with international businesses.

Location

Missouri State University is located in Springfield, the third-largest city in Missouri, with a metropolitan service region of 400,000. Located in the heart of the Ozarks recreational area, the University is within easy driving distance of numerous lakes, streams, and parks. The community of Springfield is supported by an industrial/manufacturing base and an expanding service industry in tourism, with people drawn by the natural beauty and recreation of the Ozarks and the musical attractions in nearby Branson. Springfield has an extensive health and medical economy serving southwest Missouri, northwest Arkansas, southeast Kansas, and northeast Oklahoma.

The University

Missouri State University, founded in 1905, is a multicampus metropolitan university system with a statewide mission in public affairs. The University offers more than 150 undergraduate majors and forty-three graduate programs, many of which are the strongest of their kind in the state. The students experience college life at its best, with NCAA Division I athletics and more than 250 student organizations.

Applying

Individuals interested in applying to the M.G.S. program may obtain an application from the Graduate College, Carrington Hall, Room 306, Missouri State University, 901 South National, Springfield, Missouri 65897 (417-836-5335). Downloadable forms and an online application are provided at the Graduate College Web site at http://graduate.missouristate.edu/admissions.htm/. International students must also follow all directions as outlined on the Graduate College Web site at http://graduate.missouristate.edu/international.htm/.

Correspondence and Information

Dr. Dennis Hickey
M.G.S. Program Director
Missouri State University
901 South National
Springfield, Missouri 65897
Phone: 417-836-5850
E-mail: dennishickey@missouristate.edu
Web site: http://polsci.missouristate.edu/mgs/

Missouri State University

THE FACULTY AND THEIR RESEARCH

M.G.S. faculty members are student oriented. They are also among the most productive and visible faculty at MSU. M.G.S. faculty members have published a string of policy-relevant publications (books and articles) focusing on international affairs. As a consequence, M.G.S. faculty have been asked to provide testimony before the U.S. Congress and served as consultants to various agencies and departments within the executive branch of the national government. Moreover, they are regularly invited to appear on local television and radio programs and have made appearances on national or international television broadcasts including the Voice of America's *Issues & Opinions* (a television program broadcast into China) and China Central Television (CCTV). With respect to the print media, faculty members have contributed opinion pieces to many of the world's major newspapers, including the *China Daily, Wall Street Journal, Los Angeles Times, Chicago Tribune, Taipei Times,* and *Kansas City Star.* Not surprisingly, the M.G.S. program has hosted a number of important international conferences. Students are strongly encouraged to participate in these events.

Dennis Hickey, Professor and Director of the M.G.S. program; Ph.D., Texas. Dr. Hickey's research and teaching interests include international relations, Asian politics, national security, and American foreign policy. During the spring semester of 2008, Dr. Hickey was a Fulbright Exchange Scholar at the China Foreign Affairs University in Beijing, China. His most recent book, *Foreign Policy Making in Taiwan: From Principle to Pragmatism,* was published by Routledge in 2007. (dennishickey@missouristate.edu)

Gabriel Ondetti, Associate Professor; Ph.D., North Carolina at Chapel Hill. Dr. Ondetti's teaching and research interests include Latin American politics and international political economy. His current research focuses on the impact of democracy on redistributive policies in Latin America. In spring 2008 he published *Land, Protest, and Politics: The Landless Movement and the Struggle for Agrarian Reform in Brazil* (Penn State Press). (gabrielondetti@missouristate.edu)

Indira Palacios-Valladares, Full-Time Instructor; Ph.D., North Carolina at Chapel Hill. Dr. Palacios-Valladares's teaching and research interests include Latin American politics and labor issues and comparative politics. She has a forthcoming publication entitled *Industrial Relations after Pinochet: Firm-Level Unionism and Collective Bargaining Outcomes in Chile.* (indirapalacios@missouristate.edu)

David Romano, Assistant Professor and Strong Chair of Middle Eastern Politics; Ph.D., Toronto. Dr. Romano's research and teaching interests include Middle Eastern politics, nationalism, and social movements. He published *The Kurdish Nationalist Movement* in 2006 with Cambridge University Press and he writes a weekly column for *Rudaw*, a Kurdish newspaper in Iraq.

Monterey Institute of International Studies
A Graduate School of Middlebury College

MONTEREY INSTITUTE OF INTERNATIONAL STUDIES

Graduate School of International Policy and Management

Programs of Study

The Graduate School of International Policy and Management (GSIPM) offers four, two-year professional master's degree programs: the Master of Arts in international policy studies (MAIPS), the Master of Arts in nonproliferation and terrorism studies, the Master of Public Administration (M.P.A.), and the Master of Arts in international environmental policy (MAIEP). In addition to these policy related degrees, the Institute also offers an M.B.A. in international management. Degree students are eligible to take courses from the M.B.A. program, which will allow them to develop a unique, cross-disciplinary curriculum.

The MAIPS program combines language and policy studies to train students for careers in the public, nonprofit, or private sectors in cross-cultural settings. The curriculum includes courses in policy analysis, economics, quantitative analysis, international relations, comparative politics, area studies, and language, with an in-depth focus on specific policy problems or sectors.

Within the MAIPS program, GSIPM offers three specialized tracks: international development, international trade, and conflict resolution. Many students will focus these tracks on more specific areas, such as international negotiation, international norms/humans rights/justice, or international organizations/nonprofit management.

The M.P.A. program focuses on the knowledge, professional skills, and leadership abilities needed to effectively help local, national, and global organizations build or improve community developments. The curriculum includes courses in public and nonprofit management, organizational theory, data analysis, budgeting, accounting, and program evaluation.

The MAIEP program responds to the growing need for policymakers to address environmental problems with international dimensions, such as biodiversity protection, climate-change policy, sustainable development, renewable energy, water and air quality, coastal watersheds, and marine policy. Courses include the scientific foundations of environmental policy, international environmental law and policy, environmental economics, and conflict management.

In addition to the degree programs, the Graduate School of International Policy and Management offers stand-alone certificate programs structured around defined clusters of courses that examine specific policy areas: nonproliferation studies, conflict resolution, international environmental policy, and international trade policy.

Research Facilities

Internships and research opportunities are available through the Institute's James Martin Center for Nonproliferation Studies; the Center for East Asian Studies; the Monterey Center for Humanitarian Assistance, Development, and Security; and the Monterey Terrorism Research and Education Program.

The William Tell Coleman Library includes 95,000 volumes, more than 500 print periodicals, over 50 online databases, more than 400 academic journals, about thirty-five newspapers, and approximately 15,000 electronic books. One third of the collection is in languages other than English.

Innovative and challenging curricula at the Institute require appropriate facilities and cutting-edge technology. Classrooms vary in size from large halls where plenary sessions with simultaneous interpretation can be held to smaller classrooms and labs befitting seminar-style classes for 5 to 15 students.

The Max Kade Digital Media Commons is a fully equipped digital media and learning center. It provides multimedia classrooms and conference rooms with state-of-the-art technology, including a multimedia resource center and the campus Teaching and Learning Collaborative.

Financial Aid

Candidates with a minimum grade point average of 3.3 on a 4.0 scale (or equivalent) are considered for merit scholarships ranging from $4000.to $15,000 per year. Veterans of military service or orphans/dependants of veterans may be eligible for veteran's benefits, some of which may cover the full cost of tuition. Other scholarships may be awarded by outside foundations.

Under the Federal Stafford Loan program, students may borrow up to $8500 in subsidized loans or $20,500 in unsubsidized loans, less any subsidized amount. Graduate PLUS Loans cover the cost of college minus other financial aid resources. The Federal Work-Study Program allows students to work up to $3000 per academic year, working a maximum of 20 hours per week.

Cost of Study

Tuition and fees for 2010–11 are $32,056.

Living and Housing Costs

The estimated variable expenses for books, supplies, housing, food, local transportation, personal expenses, and health insurance is $17,792.

Student Group

Institute enrollment is approximately 800. About one-third of the students are from outside the United States, representing more than sixty countries. More than 90 percent of students from the U.S. have worked or studied abroad. More than fifty languages are spoken by students on campus. Language classes are regularly offered in English, Spanish, Arabic, French, Russian, Japanese, Chinese (Mandarin), and German. Other languages are offered by request.

Student Outcomes

The School's graduates are prepared for careers in policy research, project coordination, and management. They apply those skills in a wide range of settings and organizations, such as international development (UNDP, World Bank), environmental protection (UNEP, World Wildlife Fund), intergovernmental organizations (World Trade Organization, United Nations), national governments (Japan, China, Kazakhstan, Russia, India), the U.S. government (Departments of State, Energy, and Commerce; USAID; DIA; CIA), and international NGOs (Save the Children, Mercy Corps).

Location

The Monterey Institute is situated in one of the most spectacular natural environments in the world. The Monterey Peninsula is 130 miles south of San Francisco on California's central coast, surrounded by ocean and mountains. Silicon Valley is only a short drive away. With a population of 100,000, the area combines a variety of rich cultural resources and agricultural activities.

The Institute

Established in 1955 with summer classes in language and culture, the Monterey Institute of Foreign Studies was the first institute dedicated to the then-revolutionary concept that a living language should be taught as such: French in French, German in German, etc. Year-round degree programs began in 1961. By 1979, the Institute had grown to international distinction and was renamed the Monterey Institute of International Studies.

The Monterey Institute is an affiliate of Middlebury College. Founded in 1800, Middlebury is one of the country's top liberal arts colleges. It offers students a broad curriculum embracing the arts, humanities, literature, foreign languages, social sciences, and natural sciences. The affiliation further enriches the curriculum, creates a bicoastal presence, and offers valuable connections to build greater global connection.

Applying

The Monterey Institute of International Studies has a rolling application process and allows students to begin in both fall and spring semesters. The priority deadlines for applicants who wish to be considered for merit-based scholarships are October 1 for the spring semester, and December 1, February 1, or March 15 for the fall semester.

Prospective students are required to have a U.S. bachelor's degree or the equivalent from an accredited college/university and a minimum GPA of 3.0 on a 4.0 scale. Applicants with a GPA below 3.0 should submit a GRE score; otherwise, a GRE score is optional. In order to complete the application process, prospective students are required to submit the following: a completed application form, a personal statement (600 words), a resume/CV, official transcripts from all colleges attended, two letters of recommendation, and a nonrefundable $50 application fee.

Nonnative English speakers must also provide a TOEFL or IELTS score. The minimum TOEFL requirements are as follows: Paper-based test, 550, test of written English, 4.0; Computer-based test: 213, test of written English: 4.0; Internet-based test: 80, test of written English: 23, no other subscores below 19. The IELTS minimum is 6.5 overall with no subscore below 6.0 on the Academic module. International students should apply three months before enrollment to allow enough time for the visa process.

Correspondence and Information

Admissions Office
Monterey Institute of International Studies
460 Pierce Street
Monterey, California 93940
Phone: 831-647-4123
800-824-7235 (toll-free within the United States)
Fax: 831-647-6405
E-mail: admit@miis.edu
Web site: http://www.miis.edu

Monterey Institute of International Studies

THE FULL-TIME FACULTY AND THEIR RESEARCH

Tsuneo Akaha, Professor and Director, Center for East Asian Studies; Ph.D. (political science), USC. Dr. Akaha teaches courses on security in Northeast Asia and public policy in Japan, especially foreign and environmental.

William Arrocha, Assistant Professor; Ph.D. (international relations), Queen's at Kingston. Dr. Arrocha teaches courses on international political economy, trade policy with special reference to NAFTA, and politics of Mexico.

Mahabat Baimyrzaeva; Ph.D. (public administration), USC. Professor Baimyrzaeva teaches courses in public administration, management, policy, and international development.

Jeffrey M. Bale, Assistant Professor and Director, Monterey Terrorism Research and Education Program (MonTREP); Ph.D. (European history), Berkeley. Dr. Bale teaches courses in terrorism and security issues.

Jan Knippers Black, Professor; Ph.D. (international studies), American. Dr. Black teaches courses on Latin American politics and development (media, foreign policy, women, and human rights).

Fernando DePaolis, Assistant Professor; Ph.D. (regional analysis), UCLA. Dr. DePaolis teaches courses on regional analysis, data analysis, and the labor and income effects of trade policies.

Stephen Garrett, Professor; Ph.D. (international affairs), Virginia. Dr. Garrett spent academic year 1978–79 in Bangkok, Thailand, as a senior lecturer on a Fulbright Fellowship and was appointed to the Gordon Paul Smith Chair of International Policy Studies in 1988–89. Dr. Garrett teaches courses on ethics and force in international relations, comparative approaches to transitional justice, and humanitarian intervention.

Gordon Hahn, Professor; Ph.D. (political science), Boston University. Dr. Hahn is the author of *Russia's Islamic Threat* (Yale University Press, 2007), and numerous scholarly and analytical articles on politics, Islam, and jihadism in Russia. Dr. Hahn teaches courses within the terrorism program.

Pushpa Iyer, Assistant Professor; Ph.D. (conflict analysis and resolution), George Mason. Dr. Iyer teaches courses in conflict resolution, identity conflicts, civil wars, peace processes and non-state armed actors.

Nuket Kardam, Associate Professor; Ph.D. (political science), Michigan State. Dr. Kardam teaches courses on international organizations, organization behavior, and women and civil society in Islamic countries, especially Turkey.

Sharad Joshi, Associate Professor; Ph.D., Pittsburgh. Dr. Sharad Joshi is a researcher in the Monterey Terrorism Research and Education Program (MonTREP). Dr. Joshi teaches courses on terrorism and international security.

Jeffrey Langholz, Professor; Ph.D. (natural resource policy and management), Cornell. Dr. Langholz teaches courses on natural resource policy and management, international environmental policy, and sustainable development.

Edward J. Laurance, Professor; Ph.D. (international relations), Pennsylvania. Dr. Laurance has served as a consultant to the UN Department of Disarmament Affairs since 1992. He also cofounded the International Action Network on Small Arms, the largest transnational small arms NGO. Dr. Laurance teaches courses on international organizations, multilateral problem solving, and small arms control.

Beryl Levinger, Distinguished Professor of Nonprofit Management; Ph.D. (educational planning), Alabama. Dr. Levinger teaches courses on nonprofit organization and management, and human capacity building.

Wei Liang, Professor; Ph.D. USC. Dr. Liang teaches courses in international trade negotiation, international relations, international political economy, and Asian studies.

Robert McCleery, Professor; Ph.D. (economics), Stanford. Dr. McCleery teaches courses on international economics, quantitative analysis for trade policy, and economic development, especially East Asia and Mexico.

Philip Murphy, Associate Professor; Ph.D. (political science), Pittsburgh. Dr. Murphy teaches course work in quantitative methods and public policy analysis.

William Potter, Professor and Director, Center for Russian and Eurasian Studies and the James Martin Center for Nonproliferation Studies; Ph.D. (political science), Michigan. Dr. Potter teaches courses on disarmament and nonproliferation of weapons of mass destruction.

Moyara de Moraes Ruehsen, Associate Professor; Ph.D. (international economics and Middle Eastern studies), Johns Hopkins. Dr. Ruehsen teaches courses on international economics, illegal markets, and data analysis.

Jason Scorse, Assistant Professor; Ph.D. (environmental economics and policy), Berkeley. Dr. Scorse teaches courses on environmental and resource economics, sustainable development, international trade, and international economics.

Sheikh Shahnawaz, Assistant Professor; Ph.D. (economics), USC. Dr. Shahnawaz teaches courses on trade services, international economics, and the political economy of the Middle East.

Fred Wehling, Assistant Professor; Ph.D. (political science), UCLA. Dr. Wehling teaches courses on international security, fissile material control, terrorism with nuclear/chemical/biological/radiological weapons, and nuclear nonproliferation

Jim Williams, Associate Professor; Ph.D., M.S. (energy and resources) Berkeley. Prior to coming to the Monterey Institute, Dr. Williams worked at Energy and Environmental Economics (E3) where he was lead analyst on the E3 team modeling implementation of California's Global Warming Solutions Act (AB32) for California state agencies. Dr. Williams teaches courses on energy and climate change policy.

Jing-dong Yuan, Associate Professor; Ph.D. (political science), Queen's at Kingston. Dr. Yuan teaches courses on Chinese security and foreign policy, Chinese politics, arms control, East Asia security, Sino-Indian relations, and Sino-U.S. relations.

Lyuba Zarsky, Associate Professor; Ph.D. (economics), Massachusetts Amherst. Dr. Zarsky teaches courses in trade, sustainable development, globalization, environmental governance, development economics, and macroeconomics of sustainable development.

WHITEHEAD SCHOOL OF DIPLOMACY AND INTERNATIONAL RELATIONS
SETON HALL UNIVERSITY

SETON HALL UNIVERSITY

The Whitehead School of Diplomacy and International Relations

Programs of Study

The John C. Whitehead School of Diplomacy and International Relations educates students from around the world to bring diplomatic skills and a solid understanding of international affairs to careers in public service, business, law, and the nonprofit sector. The only school of its kind in the United States to share a unique link with the United Nations Association of the USA, the Whitehead School of Diplomacy exposes students to the policymakers and practitioners addressing today's worldwide concerns. Innovative graduate and undergraduate degree programs, taught by a distinguished faculty of scholars and professionals, prepare students to be effective and ethical leaders in their professional careers. The Whitehead School of Diplomacy is an affiliate member of the Association of Professional Schools of International Affairs (APSIA).

The graduate curriculum combines interdisciplinary global studies with research methodology and policy analysis, culminating in a professional internship and significant research project. The School's Director of Internships and Career Development works closely with students to tailor their internships to their specific career goals. To attain the M.A. degree, students complete a total of 45 credit hours, satisfying core curriculum requirements, and two specializations. Students select from an array of functional and regional specializations structuring their academic studies according to their particular interests, career goals, and backgrounds. Functional specializations include foreign policy analysis, global health and human security, global negotiation and conflict management, international economics and development, international law and human rights, international organizations, and international security. Regional specializations in Africa, Asia, Europe, Latin America and the Caribbean, and the Middle East are also available.

Joint graduate degree programs combine an M.A. in diplomacy and international relations with a J.D., an M.B.A., an M.P.A. (with a focus on government or nonprofit management), an M.A. in Asian studies, or an M.A. in strategic communications.

At the Whitehead School, graduate students of diverse cultural, educational, and professional backgrounds form an international academic community. The graduate program fosters leadership and civic responsibility and sharpens analytical and practical skills. Small classes create a supportive environment that encourages mentoring relationships. An active graduate student association takes on a variety of projects and activities. Graduate assistantships, scholarships, and positions on the student-edited *Whitehead Journal of Diplomacy and International Relations* are awarded on a competitive basis.

Research Facilities

Walsh Library is a state-of-the-art facility built in 1994. In addition to housing print materials, library services include expert research support, bibliographic searching with online text retrieval (also available remotely), extensive CD-ROM databases, and interlibrary borrowing. As a U.N. depository, optical disk technology makes available up-to-date documentation from the United Nations. The library's computer labs and study carrels are all Internet-linked and offer wireless Internet.

Financial Aid

In addition to federal loan and work-study programs, the Whitehead School of Diplomacy may award graduate assistantships and scholarships to full-time students who exhibit high academic and professional potential. The School's Office of Internships and Career Development guides students' career development activities.

Cost of Study

In 2010–11, tuition is $946 per credit. Full-time students pay $305 per semester in University and technology fees; part-time students pay $185.

Living and Housing Costs

On-campus housing is not available for graduate students. Housing and living costs in South Orange and surrounding towns are comparable to most suburban cities, with studio and one-bedroom apartments renting for $750 to $1000 per month. The member organization of graduate students, the Graduate Diplomacy Council, supports an online housing database on the University's online posting board. This forum helps students to find roommates and discuss various apartment buildings and neighborhoods in the area.

Student Group

Approximately 250 full-time graduate students are enrolled in the program. Students come from throughout the United States and nearly forty countries. Their diverse backgrounds are a tremendous asset, offering students a truly international experience. The student body includes recent college graduates as well as midcareer professionals from various disciplines. The School's graduate student association organizes academic, professional, and social events and serves as a support network for mentoring new students.

Location

Nestled on 58 acres in the suburban town of South Orange, New Jersey, Seton Hall is just 14 miles from New York City.

The University and The School

For 150 years, Seton Hall University has been a catalyst for leadership, developing the whole student—mind, heart, and spirit. Seton Hall combines the resources of a large university with the personal attention of a small liberal arts college. Composed of 5,200 undergraduate students and 4,800 graduate students, Seton Hall is a Catholic university that embraces students of all races and religions, challenging each to better the world through integrity, compassion, and a commitment to serving others.

Through a unique alliance with the United Nations Association of the USA, the Whitehead School of Diplomacy and International Relations provides students with a link to the United Nations system, the diplomatic community, nongovernmental organizations, and global business. A continuous exchange of people and ideas between the School and the U.N. brings students in direct contact with policymakers and practitioners and exposes them to ongoing opportunities to foster professional growth and development. The curriculum is enhanced by the perspectives and insights of practitioners from all sectors of the international community who participate in panel discussions, video conferences, and as adjunct professors and guest lecturers.

Beyond the classroom, the Whitehead School actively promotes dialogue on critical global issues. A prestigious World Leaders Forum has brought to the campus thought-provoking lectures and discussions with former Prime Minister of Great Britain and Northern Ireland Tony Blair, former Polish President Lech Walesa, former Soviet President Mikhail Gorbachev, United Nations Secretary-General Kofi Annan, Iranian President Mohammad Khatami, former Prime Minister of Israel Shimon Peres, and many others.

Applying

The Whitehead School of Diplomacy and International Relations selects students from around the world who have completed undergraduate degrees in a variety of disciplines, and whose academic record, international experience, or professional achievements and personal goals show promise of leadership. English proficiency is a requirement, and students whose education was not in English are required to submit TOEFL scores. Applications are evaluated on a rolling basis, and students may begin the program in September, January, or May. Students applying to the dual-degree programs should submit separate applications to each school.

Correspondence and Information

Catherine Ruby, Ph.D., Director
Office of Graduate Admissions
The Whitehead School of Diplomacy and International Relations
Seton Hall University
400 South Orange Avenue
South Orange, New Jersey 07079
Phone: 973-275-2515
Fax: 973-275-2519
E-mail: diplomat@shu.edu
Web site: http://diplomacy.shu.edu

Seton Hall University

THE FACULTY

Administrative Organization

Ambassador John K. Menzies, Ph.D., Dean.
Courtney Smith, Ph.D., Associate Dean of Academic Affairs.
Ursula Sanjamino, Ph.D., Associate Dean of Graduate Studies.
Elizabeth Bakes, M.A., Assistant Dean of External Affairs.
Catherine Ruby, Ph.D., Director of Graduate Admissions.

Faculty

Margarita Balmaceda, Associate Professor; Ph.D., Princeton. Central and Eastern Europe, security and energy policy.
Assefaw Bariagaber, Professor; Ph.D., Southern Illinois. Ethno-political analysis, refugee policy, Africa.
Martin Edwards, Assistant Professor; Ph.D., Rutgers. International organizations and international political economy.
Omer Gokcekus, Professor; Ph.D., Duke. Interest groups and trade policy, organizational architecture and corruption.
Benjamin Goldfrank, Assistant Professor; Ph.D., Berkeley. Comparative analysis of Latin American politics, sub-national governments, participatory budgeting, political parties.
Yinan He, Assistant Professor; Ph.D., M.I.T. Security studies.
Yanzhong Huang, Associate Professor; Ph.D., Chicago. Global health studies, U.S.-China relations, Chinese politics.
Fredline M'Cormack-Hale; Ph.D., Florida. African Studies, non-governmental organizations, democratization.
Philip Moremen, Associate Professor; J.D., UCLA; Ph.D., Tufts (Fletcher). International law, environmental policy.
Ann Marie Murphy, Assistant Professor; Ph.D., Columbia. Comparative foreign policy.
Jesse Russell, Assistant Professor; Ph.D., California, Santa Barbara. International relations theory, research methods.
Courtney Smith, Associate Professor; Ph.D., Ohio State. United Nations studies.
Yui Suzuki, Assistant Professor; Ph.D., Michigan. International macro/finance, economic development and transition, macroeconomics and international trade.
Zheng Wang, Assistant Professor; Ph.D., George Mason. Negotiation and conflict management.
Elizabeth Wilson; J.D., Harvard; Ph.D., Pennsylvania. International law, human rights.

Distinguished Adjunct Faculty Members

Ambassador Marc Grossman, former U.S. Under Secretary of State for Political Affairs.
Ambassador Ahmad Kamal, M.A., former Permanent Representative of Pakistan to the United Nations.
Ambassador Laszlo Molnar, Ph.D., former Permanent Representative of Hungary to the United Nations.
Ambassador Slavi Pachovski, J.D., Ph.D., former Permanent Representative of Bulgaria to the United Nations.

VILLANOVA UNIVERSITY

Graduate Studies
Liberal Arts and Sciences
Department of Political Science

Program of Study

The Department of Political Science at Villanova University offers two graduate programs: the Master of Arts (M.A.) in political science and the Master of Public Administration (M.P.A.).

The M.A. program features courses on American government, comparative government, international relations, and political theory. A degree requires ten courses and a capstone oral exam that involves the defense of the student's portfolio or eight courses and a 6-credit thesis. All students pursuing the M.A. must complete PSC 7000 and one course from each of the three concentrations: American government, international relations, and political philosophy.

The M.P.A. is a 36- to 39-credit program, designed to prepare students for management careers in the public and nonprofit sectors. Required courses provide students with knowledge of public administration theory and history, statistical analysis and research methods, organization theory and design, and how to manage financial and human resources in order to be successful in their careers. Elective courses include 3-credit and 1-credit courses. The M.P.A. program is fully accredited by the National Association of Schools of Public Affairs and Administration (NASPAA).

Both graduate programs also offer graduate certificates (five courses or 15 credits are required) for students not seeking a master's degree or for those looking for a specialization within their degree. Both graduate degree programs admit part-time students. Class size ranges from 4 to 20 students, with the average around 12. Courses meet for 2 hours once per week in the evening.

Research Facilities

The Falvey Memorial Library provides resources and facilities for study and research by students and faculty members, with a book capacity of more than half a million volumes. The Office of University Information Technologies (UNIT) provides data and voice communication, computing services, and access to remote computing and information services over the Internet. Student computer laboratories throughout campus are open 24 hours a day.

Financial Aid

Financial support (tuition remission and/or stipends) is available through the political science department in the form of graduate assistantships and tuition scholarships. Loan programs and need-based financial aid are available through the Office of Financial Assistance, Kennedy Hall, Villanova University, Villanova, Pennsylvania 19085; telephone: 610-519-4010.

Cost of Study

Graduate tuition is $650 per credit hour in 2010–11. In addition, there is a University fee of $60 each semester.

Living and Housing Costs

Various affordable housing possibilities are available near the Villanova University campus or are easily accessible by public transportation. Housing costs vary in accordance with the option chosen. Room and board for a single graduate student may average about $8000 for a twelve-month period. Villanova University does not provide on-campus housing for graduate students.

Student Group

Students in the M.A. and M.P.A. programs combine a variety of academic backgrounds, professional interests, and personal aims. The M.A. program enrolls 40 to 50 students per year, and the M.P.A. program enrolls 50 to 60 students per year. The ratio of men to women is 1:1. About 20 percent of the students in both programs are international. The majority of students in both programs are part-time.

Student Outcomes

Recent graduates of both programs have been admitted to doctoral programs at schools such as Cornell, Penn, Emory, Johns Hopkins, Duke, Maryland, Michigan, NYU, and Penn State. Others attend law schools, such as Georgetown, George Washington, Seton Hall, and Villanova. Graduates also pursue public service careers in the national, state, and local governments and with nonprofit organizations.

Location

Villanova University provides a tranquil setting for study and reflection. Situated on the historic Main Line, a western suburb of Philadelphia, Villanova is located on Lancaster Avenue (Route 30), 2 minutes from the Blue Route (Route 476) and 5 minutes from the Pennsylvania Turnpike, Schuylkill Expressway, and Route 202. Philadelphia's revitalized Center City is 25 minutes away by train, and historic Valley Forge and the Brandywine Valley are easily accessible by car. Villanova is within easy driving distance of several other premier institutions of higher learning, including Bryn Mawr, Haverford, and Swarthmore Colleges; Temple University; and the University of Pennsylvania. With ample parking and mass transit stops right on University grounds, the campus allows for easy travel by car, bus, or train.

The University

Villanova University is an institute rich in history and tradition. For more than 150 years, Villanova has been directed by one of the oldest teaching orders of the Catholic Church, the Order of St. Augustine. From modest beginnings on a country estate of a Revolutionary War officer, the University has seen significant growth in its student population as well as its position as a leading coeducational institute of higher learning.

Applying

Applications for admission and financial aid are available from the Office of Graduate Studies. Applications should be sent to the Office of Graduate Studies, College of Liberal Arts and Sciences, Villanova University, 800 Lancaster Avenue, Villanova, Pennsylvania 19085. Completed applications include an application for admission, nonrefundable application fee of $50, official postsecondary academic transcripts, and GRE scores (General Test only), three letters of recommendation, and a two-page narrative explaining anticipated career objectives and reasons for seeking admission. No interviews are necessary. Applicants from non-English-speaking countries must submit TOEFL scores, a credentials evaluation, and financial certification. Applications are considered on a rolling basis. Financial aid decisions are made by April 15. Only applicants seeking full-time admission are considered for financial aid.

Correspondence and Information

Director of Graduate Studies (specify M.A. or M.P.A. or both)
Department of Political Science
Villanova University
Villanova, Pennsylvania 19085

Phone: 610-519-4710
Fax: 610-519-7487
Web site: http://www.villanova.edu/artsci/psc/graduate

Villanova University

THE FACULTY AND THEIR RESEARCH

David Barrett, Ph.D., Notre Dame. National security policy, intelligence policy, foreign policy formation.
Lara Brown, Ph.D., UCLA. Presidents, elections, political parties, congress.
Kail C. Ellis, O.S.A., Dean, College of Arts and Sciences; Ph.D., Catholic University. Comparative politics of Arab states.
Lowell S. Gustafson, Associate Dean; Ph.D., Virginia. Latin American politics, international political economy, theories of international relations.
John R. Johannes, Vice President for Academic Affairs; Ph.D., Harvard. American government, congress.
Christine Kelleher Palus, Ph.D., North Carolina at Chapel Hill. American politics, state and local government, urban politics, research methods.
Matthew R. Kerbel, Ph.D., Michigan. Political communications, the presidency.
Marcus L. Kreuzer, Ph.D., Columbia. Parties, comparative political economy, democratization, European politics.
Robert W. Langran, Ph.D., Bryn Mawr. Constitutional development, constitutional law, civil rights and civil liberties, congress, government and business, women and politics.
Robert A. Maranto, Ph.D., Minnesota. Public policy, public administration, American government.
Colleen A. Sheehan, Ph.D., Claremont. American political theory.
Thomas W. Smith, Associate Dean, Ph.D., Notre Dame. Ancient political theory, religion and politics.
Joseph E. Thompson, Ph.D., Catholic University. International relations, American foreign policy, comparative politics, Ireland.
A. Maria Toyoda, Chair, Ph.D., Georgetown. East Asia, comparative politics.
Catherine E. Warrick, Ph.D., Georgetown. Comparative politics, Middle East, South Asia, gender and Islamic politics.
Craig Wheeland, Associate Vice President for Academic Affairs; Ph.D., Penn State. Public administration, urban politics, intergovernmental management.
Catherine Wilson, Ph.D., Pennsylvania. Public administration, nonprofit management, immigration, religion and politics.

Section 24
Psychology and Counseling

This section contains a directory of institutions offering graduate work in psychology and counseling, followed by in-depth entries submitted by institutions that chose to prepare detailed program descriptions. Additional information about programs listed in the directory but not augmented by an in-depth entry may be obtained by writing directly to the dean of a graduate school or chair of a department at the address given in the directory.

For programs offering related work, see also in this book *Criminology and Forensics, Family and Consumer Sciences,* and *Sociology, Anthropology, and Archaeology.* In the other guides in this series:

Graduate Programs in the Biological Sciences

See *Biological and Biomedical Sciences; Genetics, Developmental Biology, and Reproductive Biology; Neuroscience and Neurobiology;* and *Pharmacology and Toxicology*

Graduate Programs in Business, Education, Health, Information Studies, Law & Social Work

See *Education, Nursing (Psychiatric Nursing), Pharmacy and Pharmaceutical Sciences, Public Health,* and *Social Work*

CONTENTS

Program Directories

Psychology—General 860
Addictions/Substance Abuse Counseling 900
Clinical Psychology 904
Cognitive Sciences 925
Counseling Psychology 931
Developmental Psychology 956
Experimental Psychology 961
Forensic Psychology 968
Genetic Counseling 970
Health Psychology 971
Human Development 975
Industrial and Organizational Psychology 983
Marriage and Family Therapy 992
Psychoanalysis and Psychotherapy 1005
Rehabilitation Counseling 1005
School Psychology 1012
Social Psychology 1031
Sport Psychology 1043
Thanatology 1045
Transpersonal and Humanistic Psychology 1045

Close-Ups

Adler School of Professional Psychology 1047
Argosy University, Atlanta 1049
Argosy University, Chicago 1051
Argosy University, Dallas 1053
Argosy University, Denver 1055
Argosy University, Hawai'i 1057
Argosy University, Inland Empire 1059
Argosy University, Los Angeles 1061
Argosy University, Nashville 1063
Argosy University, Orange County 1065
Argosy University, Phoenix 1067
Argosy University, Salt Lake City 1069
Argosy University, San Diego 1071
Argosy University, San Francisco Bay Area 1073
Argosy University, Sarasota 1075
Argosy University, Schaumburg 1077
Argosy University, Seattle 1079
Argosy University, Tampa 1081
Argosy University, Twin Cities 1083
Argosy University, Washington DC 1085
Felician College 1087
Florida Institute of Technology 1089
Philadelphia College of Osteopathic Medicine 1091
Rutgers, The State University of New Jersey, Newark 1093
South University (Columbia Campus) 1095
South University (Montgomery Campus) 1097
South University (Richmond Campus) 1099
South University (Savannah Campus) 1101
South University (Virginia Beach Campus) 1103
South University (West Palm Beach Campus) 1105
Villanova University 1107

Psychology—General

Abilene Christian University, Graduate School, College of Arts and Sciences, Department of Psychology, Program in Psychology, Abilene, TX 79699-9100. Offers MS. *Students:* 2 part-time (1 woman). 2 applicants, 50% accepted, 0 enrolled. In 2009, 2 master's awarded. *Degree requirements:* For master's, comprehensive exam, thesis optional. *Entrance requirements:* For master's, GRE General Test. *Application deadline:* For fall admission, 4/1 priority date for domestic students; for spring admission, 11/1 for domestic students. Applications are processed on a rolling basis. Application fee: $40. Electronic applications accepted. *Expenses:* Tuition: Full-time $11,520; part-time $640 per hour. Required fees: $1090; $53.50 per hour. $10 per term. Tuition and fees vary according to program. *Financial support:* Federal Work-Study available. Support available to part-time students. Financial award application deadline: 4/1; financial award applicants required to submit FAFSA. *Unit head:* Dr. Robert McKelvain, Graduate Advisor, 325-674-2286, Fax: 325-674-6968, E-mail: mckelvainr@acu.edu. *Application contact:* William Horn, Graduate Admissions Counselor, 325-674-2656, Fax: 325-674-6717, E-mail: gradinfo@acu.edu.

Acadia University, Faculty of Pure and Applied Science, Department of Psychology, Wolfville, NS B4P 2R6, Canada. Offers clinical psychology (M Sc). *Faculty:* 12 full-time (6 women), 11 part-time/adjunct (5 women). *Students:* 8 full-time (7 women). Average age 26. 44 applicants, 20% accepted, 5 enrolled. In 2009, 4 master's awarded. *Degree requirements:* For master's, thesis. *Entrance requirements:* For master's, GRE General Test, GRE Subject Test, honors degree or equivalent. Additional exam requirements/recommendations for international students: Required—TOEFL (minimum score 580 paper-based; 237 computer-based; 93 iBT), IELTS (minimum score 6.5). *Application deadline:* For fall admission, 2/1 priority date for domestic students, 2/1 for international students. Applications are processed on a rolling basis. Application fee: $50. *Financial support:* Teaching assistantships, career-related internships or fieldwork, scholarships/grants, and unspecified assistantships available. Financial award application deadline: 2/1. *Faculty research:* Social psychology, job stress, psychotherapy, cognition perception, development. *Unit head:* Dr. Peter McLeod, Head, 902-585-1301, Fax: 902-585-1078, E-mail: peter.mcleod@acadiau.ca. *Application contact:* Dr. Peter Horvath, Information Contact, 902-585-1200, Fax: 902-585-1078, E-mail: peter.horvath@acadiau.ca.

Adelphi University, Derner Institute of Advanced Psychological Studies, Garden City, NY 11530-0701. Offers clinical psychology (PhD); general psychology (MA); mental health counseling (MA); school psychology (MA). *Accreditation:* APA (one or more programs are accredited). Part-time programs available. *Faculty:* 25 full-time (11 women), 72 part-time/adjunct (44 women). *Students:* 186 full-time (145 women), 118 part-time (100 women); includes 58 minority (26 African Americans, 15 Asian Americans or Pacific Islanders, 17 Hispanic Americans), 14 international. Average age 29. 605 applicants, 33% accepted, 96 enrolled. In 2009, 82 master's, 12 doctorates awarded. *Degree requirements:* For master's, comprehensive exam; for doctorate, thesis/dissertation, research (second year), 1 year internship. *Entrance requirements:* For master's, 3 letters of recommendation, minimum GPA of 3.0; for doctorate, GRE General Test, GRE Subject Test, interview; resume; undergraduate course work in psychology, experimental psychology, statistics, developmental psychology, and abnormal psychology. Additional exam requirements/recommendations for international students: Required—TOEFL (minimum score 550 paper-based; 213 computer-based; 80 iBT). *Application deadline:* For fall admission, 4/1 priority date for domestic students, 5/1 priority date for international students; for spring admission, 11/1 priority date for international students. Application fee: $50. Electronic applications accepted. *Expenses:* Contact institution. *Financial support:* In 2009–10, 77 research assistantships with full and partial tuition reimbursements (averaging $5,527 per year) were awarded; teaching assistantships, career-related internships or fieldwork, Federal Work-Study, institutionally sponsored loans, and unspecified assistantships also available. Financial award application deadline: 2/15; financial award applicants required to submit FAFSA. *Faculty research:* Psychoanalytic processes, trauma and resilience, personality disorders, program evaluation, psychotherapy process. *Unit head:* Dr. Jeau Lau Chin, Dean, 516-877-4800, E-mail: chin@adelphi.edu. *Application contact:* Christine Murphy, Director of Admissions, 516-877-3050, Fax: 516-877-3039, E-mail: graduateadmissions@adelphi.edu.

Adler School of Professional Psychology, Programs in Psychology, Chicago, IL 60601-7203. Offers art therapy (MA, Certificate); clinical hypnosis (Certificate); clinical psychology (Psy D); counseling (MA); counseling and organizational psychology (MA); forensic psychology (MA); gerontological counseling (MA); marriage and family counseling (MA); marriage and family therapy (Certificate); organizational psychology (MA); police psychology (MA); rehabilitation counseling (MA); sport and health psychology (MA); substance abuse counseling (Certificate); Psy D/Certificate; Psy D/MACAT; Psy D/MACP; Psy D/MAMFC; Psy D/MASAC. *Accreditation:* APA. Part-time and evening/weekend programs available. Postbaccalaureate distance learning degree programs offered (minimal on-campus study). *Faculty:* 41 full-time (21 women), 44 part-time/adjunct (19 women). *Students:* 551 full-time (441 women), 161 part-time (137 women). Average age 27.Terminal master's awarded for partial completion of doctoral program. *Degree requirements:* For master's, thesis or alternative, oral exam, practicum; for doctorate, thesis/dissertation, clinical exam, internship, oral exam, practicum, written qualifying exam. *Entrance requirements:* For master's, 12 semester hours in psychology, minimum GPA of 3.0; for doctorate, 18 semester hours in psychology, minimum GPA of 3.25; for Certificate, appropriate master's or doctoral degree. Additional exam requirements/recommendations for international students: Required—TOEFL (minimum score 550 paper-based; 213 computer-based; 79 iBT). *Application deadline:* For fall admission, 2/15 priority date for domestic students, 12/1 priority date for international students. Applications are processed on a rolling basis. Application fee: $50. Electronic applications accepted. *Expenses:* Tuition: Part-time $930 per credit. Required fees: $220 per term. *Financial support:* Career-related internships or fieldwork, Federal Work-Study, scholarships/grants, and tuition waivers (full and partial) available. Support available to part-time students. Financial award application deadline: 5/15; financial award applicants required to submit FAFSA. *Unit head:* Dr. Frank Gruba-McAllister, Vice President of Academic Affairs, 312-201-5900 Ext. 209, Fax: 312-201-5917. *Application contact:* Craig A. Hines, Associate Vice President of Admissions, 312-201-5900 Ext. 226, Fax: 312-201-5917, E-mail: chines@adler.edu.

See Close-Up on page 1047.

Alabama Agricultural and Mechanical University, School of Graduate Studies, School of Education, Department of Counseling and Special Education, Huntsville, AL 35811. Offers communicative disorders (M Ed, MS); psychology and counseling (MS, Ed S), including clinical psychology (MS), counseling and guidance, counseling psychology (MS), personnel management (MS), psychometry (MS), school psychology (MS); special education (M Ed, MS). *Accreditation:* CORE; NCATE. Part-time and evening/weekend programs available. *Degree requirements:* For master's, comprehensive exam. *Entrance requirements:* For master's, GRE General Test. Additional exam requirements/recommendations for international students: Required—TOEFL (minimum score 500 paper-based; 173 computer-based; 61 iBT). *Faculty research:* Increasing numbers of minorities in special education and speech-language pathology.

Alliant International University–Fresno, California School of Professional Psychology, Fresno, CA 93727. Offers PhD, Psy D. *Accreditation:* APA. *Degree requirements:* For doctorate, thesis/dissertation. *Entrance requirements:* For doctorate, interview, 3.0 GPA, letters of recommendation. *Faculty research:* Child and family, body image, psychoanalysis, neuropsychology, teaching of psychology.

Alliant International University–Los Angeles, California School of Professional Psychology, Alhambra, CA 91803-1360. Offers MA, PhD, Psy D. *Accreditation:* APA. *Degree requirements:* For doctorate, comprehensive exam, thesis/dissertation. *Entrance requirements:* For doctorate, interview, minimum GPA of 3.0 in psychology and overall, letters of recommendation. Additional exam requirements/recommendations for international students: Required—TOEFL (minimum score 600 paper-based; 250 computer-based), TWE (minimum score 5). Electronic applications accepted. *Faculty research:* Family therapy, pregnancy-related issues, multi-cultural psychology, post-traumatic stress.

Alliant International University–Sacramento, California School of Professional Psychology, Sacramento, CA 95825. Offers MA, Psy D. Electronic applications accepted.

Alliant International University–San Diego, California School of Professional Psychology, San Diego, CA 92131-1799. Offers MA, PhD, Psy D. *Accreditation:* APA. Part-time programs available. *Degree requirements:* For doctorate, thesis/dissertation. *Entrance requirements:* For doctorate, interview, minimum GPA of 3.0 in both psychology and overall. *Faculty research:* Native American studies, cross-cultural family therapy, families.

Alliant International University–San Francisco, California School of Professional Psychology, San Francisco, CA 94133-1221. Offers Post-Doctoral MS, PhD, Psy D, Certificate. *Accreditation:* APA (one or more programs are accredited). *Degree requirements:* For doctorate, comprehensive exam, thesis/dissertation. *Entrance requirements:* For master's and doctorate, interview, minimum GPA of 3.0. Additional exam requirements/recommendations for international students: Required—TOEFL (minimum score 600 paper-based; 250 computer-based), TWE (minimum score 5). Electronic applications accepted. *Faculty research:* Multicultural issues, lesbian/gay/bisexual/transgender issues, health psychology, family systems, substance abuse.

American International College, School of Arts, Education and Sciences, Department of Psychology, Springfield, MA 01109-3189. Offers clinical psychology (MA); educational psychology (MA, Ed D); forensic psychology (MS). Part-time and evening/weekend programs available. *Degree requirements:* For master's, comprehensive exam (for some programs), thesis (for some programs); practicum. *Entrance requirements:* For master's, minimum GPA of 3.0; for doctorate, GRE General Test, interview. Additional exam requirements/recommendations for international students: Required—TOEFL. Electronic applications accepted. *Expenses:* Tuition: Full-time $12,510; part-time $695 per credit hour. Required fees: $35 per term.

American University, College of Arts and Sciences, Department of Psychology, Program in Behavior, Cognition, and Neuroscience, Washington, DC 22016-8062. Offers psychology (PhD), including behavior, cognition and neuroscience. *Students:* 8 full-time (5 women), 16 part-time (12 women); includes 4 minority (1 African American, 2 Asian Americans or Pacific Islanders, 1 Hispanic American), 3 international. Average age 28. 26 applicants, 23% accepted, 4 enrolled. *Degree requirements:* For doctorate, comprehensive exam, thesis/dissertation, 2 lab rotations, 2 tools of research. *Entrance requirements:* For doctorate, GRE General Test, GRE Subject Test, 3 recommendations. Additional exam requirements/recommendations for international students: Required—TOEFL. *Application deadline:* For fall admission, 1/1 for domestic students. Application fee: $80. *Expenses:* Tuition: Full-time $22,266; part-time $1237 per credit hour. Required fees: $430. Tuition and fees vary according to program. *Financial support:* Fellowships, research assistantships, teaching assistantships, career-related internships or fieldwork, Federal Work-Study, institutionally sponsored loans, and tuition waivers (full and partial) available. Support available to part-time students. Financial award application deadline: 2/1. *Faculty research:* Psychophysics, drug discrimination learning, choice behavior, conditioning and learning, olfaction and taste. *Application contact:* Sara Holland, Senior Administrative Assistant, 202-885-1717, Fax: 202-885-1023.

American University, College of Arts and Sciences, Department of Psychology, Program in Clinical Psychology, Washington, DC 22016-8062. Offers psychology (PhD), including clinical psychology. *Accreditation:* APA. *Students:* 23 full-time (19 women), 20 part-time (17 women); includes 9 minority (3 African Americans, 1 Asian American or Pacific Islander, 5 Hispanic Americans). Average age 29. 215 applicants, 5% accepted, 7 enrolled. In 2009, 7 doctorates awarded. *Degree requirements:* For doctorate, comprehensive exam, thesis/dissertation, internship. *Entrance requirements:* For doctorate, GRE General Test, GRE Subject Test, recommendations. Additional exam requirements/recommendations for international students: Required—TOEFL. *Application deadline:* For fall admission, 1/1 for domestic students. Application fee: $80. *Expenses:* Tuition: Full-time $22,266; part-time $1237 per credit hour. Required fees: $430. Tuition and fees vary according to program. *Financial support:* Fellowships, research assistantships, teaching assistantships, career-related internships or fieldwork, Federal Work-Study, institutionally sponsored loans, tuition waivers (full and partial), and unspecified assistantships available. Support available to part-time students. Financial award application deadline: 2/1. *Faculty research:* Depression, eating disorders, anxiety disorders, addictions, behavior therapy. *Application contact:* Sara Holland, Senior Administrative Assistant, 202-885-1717, Fax: 202-885-1023.

American University of Beirut, Graduate Programs, Faculty of Arts and Sciences, Beirut, Lebanon. Offers anthropology (MA); Arabic language and literature (MA); archaeology (MA); biology (MS); chemistry (MS); computer science (MS); economics (MA); education (MA); English language (MA); English literature (MA); environmental policy planning (MSES); financial economics (MAFE); geology (MS); history (MA); mathematics (MA, MS); Middle Eastern studies (MA); philosophy (MA); physics (MS); political studies (MA); psychology (MA); public administration (MA); sociology (MA); statistics (MA, MS). Part-time programs available. *Degree requirements:* For master's, one foreign language, comprehensive exam, thesis (for some programs). *Entrance requirements:* For master's, GRE, letter of recommendation. Additional exam requirements/recommendations for international students: Required—TOEFL (minimum score 600 paper-based; 250 computer-based; 100 iBT), IELTS (minimum score 7.5). *Faculty research:* String theory and supergravity; computer graphics; algebra and number theory; popular Arabic literature; marine and freshwater biology; integrating science, math and technology.

Andrews University, School of Graduate Studies, School of Education, Department of Educational and Counseling Psychology, Berrien Springs, MI 49104. Offers community counseling (MA); counseling psychology (PhD); educational and developmental psychology (MA, Ed D, PhD), including educational and developmental psychology (MA), educational psychology (Ed D, PhD); school counseling (MA); school psychology (Ed S); special education (MS). *Accreditation:* ACA (one or more programs are accredited). Part-time programs available. *Students:* 57 full-time (40 women), 40 part-time (23 women); includes 40 minority (22 African Americans, 2 Asian Americans or Pacific Islanders, 16 Hispanic Americans), 12 international. Average age 33. 75 applicants, 51% accepted, 27 enrolled. In 2009, 15 master's, 2 doctorates, 6 other advanced degrees awarded. Terminal master's awarded for partial completion of doctoral program. *Degree requirements:* For master's, thesis optional; for doctorate, thesis/dissertation. *Entrance requirements:* For master's, GRE Subject Test, minimum GPA of 2.6; for doctorate, GRE General Test, MA, minimum GPA of 3.5, sample of research. Additional exam requirements/recommendations for international students: Required—TOEFL (minimum score 550 paper-based). *Application deadline:* Applications are processed on a rolling basis. Application fee: $40. *Faculty research:* Testing methods, temperament, African-American studies, counseling process, multicultural issues. *Unit head:* Dr. Rudi Bailey, Chair, 269-471-3473. *Application contact:* Carolyn Hurst, Supervisor of Graduate Admission, 800-253-2874, Fax: 269-471-6321, E-mail: graduate@andrews.edu.

Angelo State University, College of Graduate Studies, College of Liberal and Fine Arts, Department of Psychology, Sociology and Social Work, San Angelo, TX 76909. Offers psychology (MS), including counseling psychology, general psychology, industrial and organizational psychology. Part-time and evening/weekend programs available. *Faculty:* 8 full-time (2 women). *Students:* 33 full-time (22 women), 14 part-time (11 women); includes 10 minority (2 African Americans, 1 Asian American or Pacific Islander, 7 Hispanic Americans). Average age 29. 46 applicants, 78% accepted, 26 enrolled. In 2009, 23 master's awarded. *Degree requirements:* For master's, comprehensive exam, thesis optional. *Entrance requirements:* For master's, GRE General Test. Additional exam requirements/recommendations for international students: Required—TOEFL or IELTS. *Application deadline:* For fall admission, 7/15 priority date for domestic students, 6/10 for international students; for spring admission, 12/1 priority date for domestic students, 11/1 for international students. Applications are processed on a rolling basis. Application fee: $40 ($50 for international students). Electronic applications accepted. *Expenses:* Tuition, state resident: full-time $3396; part-time $142 per credit hour. Tuition, nonresident: full-time $10,152; part-time $423 per credit hour. Required fees: $1786; $36.25 per credit hour. $494 per semester. Full-time tuition and fees vary according to course load, degree level and program. *Financial support:* In 2009–10, 44 students received support, including 3 teaching assistantships (averaging $10,251 per year); career-related internships or fieldwork, Federal Work-Study, scholarships/grants, and unspecified assistantships also available. Support available to part-time students. Financial award application deadline: 3/1; financial award applicants required to submit FAFSA. *Faculty research:* Toddlers use of actors' intentions to learn verbs. Total annual research expenditures: $116,915. *Unit head:* Dr. William B. Davidson, Department Head, 325-942-2068 Ext. 248, Fax: 325-942-2290, E-mail: bill.davidson@angelo.edu. *Application contact:* Theresa Fortin, Graduate Admissions Assistant, 325-942-2169, Fax: 325-942-2194, E-mail: theresa.fortin@angelo.edu.

Antioch University Los Angeles, Graduate Programs, Program in Psychology, Culver City, CA 90230. Offers clinical psychology (MA); psychology (MA). Part-time programs available. *Degree requirements:* For master's, thesis (for some programs), internship. *Entrance requirements:* For master's, interview. Additional exam requirements/recommendations for international students: Required—TOEFL. *Faculty research:* Creativity and humor, ethnic humor, adult development, Jungian theory, psychoanalytic theory.

Antioch University Midwest, Graduate Programs, Individualized Liberal and Professional Studies Program, Yellow Springs, OH 45387-1609. Offers liberal and professional studies (MA), including counseling, creative writing, education, film studies, liberal studies, management, modern literature, psychology, theatre, visual arts. Part-time and evening/weekend programs available. Postbaccalaureate distance learning degree programs offered (minimal on-campus study). *Faculty:* 1 full-time (0 women), 2 part-time/adjunct (1 woman). *Students:* 23 full-time (13 women), 41 part-time (30 women); includes 13 minority (11 African Americans, 2 Hispanic Americans). Average age 40. 21 applicants, 76% accepted, 15 enrolled. In 2009, 24 master's awarded. *Degree requirements:* For master's, thesis or alternative. *Entrance requirements:* For master's, resume, 2 letters of reference. *Application deadline:* For fall admission, 8/1 for domestic students; for winter admission, 12/1 for domestic students; for spring admission, 3/10 for domestic students. Applications are processed on a rolling basis. Application fee: $50. Electronic applications accepted. *Expenses:* Contact institution. *Financial support:* Federal Work-Study available. Financial award applicants required to submit FAFSA. *Unit head:* Dr. Jon Saari, Chair, 937-769-1879, Fax: 937-769-1807, E-mail: jsaari@antioch.edu. *Application contact:* Seth Gordon, Assistant Director of Admissions, 937-769-1800 Ext. 1825, Fax: 937-769-1804, E-mail: sgordon@antioch.edu.

Antioch University New England, Graduate School, Department of Applied Psychology, Keene, NH 03431-3552. Offers autism spectrum disorders (Certificate); clinical mental health counseling (MA); dance/movement therapy and counseling (M Ed, MA); marriage and family therapy (MA, PhD). *Degree requirements:* For master's, internship, practicum. *Entrance requirements:* For master's, previous course work and work experience in psychology. Additional exam requirements/recommendations for international students: Required—TOEFL (minimum score 600 paper-based; 250 computer-based). Electronic applications accepted. *Expenses:* Contact institution. *Faculty research:* Diversity, descendents of survivors of the Holocaust and American slavery.

Antioch University Santa Barbara, Program in Psychology, Santa Barbara, CA 93101-1581. Offers MA. Part-time and evening/weekend programs available. *Degree requirements:* For master's, internship. *Entrance requirements:* Additional exam requirements/recommendations for international students: Required—TOEFL (minimum score 550 paper-based; 213 computer-based). Electronic applications accepted.

Antioch University Seattle, Graduate Programs, Program in Psychology, Seattle, WA 98121-1814. Offers MA, Psy D. Part-time and evening/weekend programs available. *Degree requirements:* For master's, internship. Electronic applications accepted. *Faculty research:* Trauma and post-traumatic stress disorders, workplace harassment and violence, multicultural issues and diversity.

Appalachian State University, Cratis D. Williams Graduate School, Department of Psychology, Boone, NC 28608. Offers clinical health psychology (MA); general experimental psychology (MA); industrial and organizational psychology (MA). Part-time programs available. *Faculty:* 31 full-time (11 women). *Students:* 51 full-time (37 women), 13 part-time (10 women); includes 4 minority (2 African Americans, 2 Asian Americans or Pacific Islanders), 2 international. 181 applicants, 25% accepted, 26 enrolled. In 2009, 22 master's, 7 other advanced degrees awarded. *Degree requirements:* For master's and MS/Specialist, comprehensive exam, thesis optional, GRE Subject Test exit exam. *Entrance requirements:* For master's and MS/Specialist, GRE General Test, 3 letters of recommendation. Additional exam requirements/recommendations for international students: Required—TOEFL (minimum score 550 paper-based; 230 computer-based; 79 iBT), or IELTS (minimum score 6.5). *Application deadline:* For fall admission, 3/1 for domestic students, 2/1 for international students. Applications are processed on a rolling basis. Application fee: $50. Electronic applications accepted. *Expenses:* Tuition, state resident: full-time $2960. Tuition, nonresident: full-time $14,051. Required fees: $2320. *Financial support:* In 2009–10, 34 research assistantships (averaging $4,000 per year), 25 teaching assistantships (averaging $4,000 per year) were awarded; fellowships, career-related internships or fieldwork, Federal Work-Study, scholarships/grants, and unspecified assistantships also available. Financial award application deadline: 4/1; financial award applicants required to submit FAFSA. *Faculty research:* Eating disorders, school-based consultations, organizational behavior management, brain mechanisms of sound localization, parenting styles. Total annual research expenditures: $114,200. *Unit head:* Dr. James Denniston, Chair, 828-262-2272, Fax: 828-262-2272, E-mail: dennistonjc@appstate.edu. *Application contact:* Dr. Denise Martz, Graduate Coordinator, 828-262-2715, E-mail: martzdm@appstate.edu.

Arcadia University, Graduate Studies, Department of Education, Glenside, PA 19038-3295. Offers art education (M Ed, MA Ed); biology education (MA Ed); chemistry education (MA Ed); child development (CAS); computer education (M Ed, CAS); computer education 7–12 (MA Ed); early childhood education (M Ed, CAS), including individualized (M Ed), master teacher (M Ed), research in child development (M Ed); educational leadership (M Ed, CAS); educational psychology (CAS); elementary education (M Ed, CAS); English education (MA Ed); environmental education (MA Ed, CAS); history education (MA Ed); language arts (M Ed, CAS); mathematics education (M Ed, MA Ed, CAS); music education (MA Ed); psychology (MA Ed); pupil personnel services (CAS); reading (M Ed, CAS); school library science (M Ed); science education (M Ed, CAS); secondary education (M Ed, CAS); special education (M Ed, Ed D, CAS); theater arts (MA Ed); written communication (MA Ed). *Accreditation:* NASAD. Part-time and evening/weekend programs available. Postbaccalaureate distance learning degree programs offered (minimal on-campus study). *Faculty:* 12 full-time (8 women), 38 part-time/adjunct (26 women). *Students:* 89 full-time (74 women), 622 part-time (487 women); includes 112 minority (94 African Americans, 9 Asian Americans or Pacific Islanders, 9 Hispanic Americans), 2 international. Average age 32. In 2009, 257 master's, 4 doctorates awarded. *Application deadline:* Applications are processed on a rolling basis. Application fee: $40. Electronic applications accepted. *Expenses:* Tuition: Full-time $30,450; part-time $620 per credit hour. Required fees: $165. Tuition and fees vary according to program. *Financial support:* Career-related internships or fieldwork, tuition waivers (partial), and unspecified assistantships available. *Unit head:* Dr. Steven P. Gulkus. *Application contact:* 215-572-2925, Fax: 215-572-2126, E-mail: grad@arcadia.edu.

Arcadia University, Graduate Studies, Department of Psychology, Glenside, PA 19038-3295. Offers community counseling (MACP); school counseling (MACP). Part-time programs available. *Faculty:* 4 full-time (2 women), 6 part-time/adjunct (4 women). *Students:* 30 full-time (26 women), 30 part-time (23 women); includes 6 minority (5 African Americans, 1 Asian American or Pacific Islander), 1 international. Average age 27. In 2009, 3 master's awarded. *Degree requirements:* For master's, practicum. *Entrance requirements:* For master's, GRE General Test or MAT. *Application deadline:* Applications are processed on a rolling basis. Application fee: $50. *Expenses:* Tuition: Full-time $30,450; part-time $620 per credit hour. Required fees: $165. Tuition and fees vary according to program. *Financial support:* Research assistantships, career-related internships or fieldwork and unspecified assistantships available. Support available to part-time students. Financial award application deadline: 8/15. *Unit head:* Dr. Eleonora Bartoli, Director, 215-572-4693. *Application contact:* 215-572-2925, Fax: 215-572-2126, E-mail: grad@arcadia.edu.

Argosy University, Atlanta, College of Psychology and Behavioral Sciences, Atlanta, GA 30328. Offers clinical psychology (MA, Psy D, Postdoctoral Respecialization Certificate), including child and family psychology (Psy D), general adult clinical (Psy D), health psychology (Psy D), neuropsychology/geropsychology (Psy D); community counseling (MA), including marriage and family therapy; counselor education and supervision (Ed D); forensic psychology (MA); industrial organizational psychology (MA); marriage and family therapy (Certificate); sport-exercise psychology (MA). *Accreditation:* APA.

See Close-Up on page 1049.

Argosy University, Chicago, College of Psychology and Behavioral Sciences, Chicago, IL 60601. Offers clinical psychology (MA, Psy D), including child and adolescent psychology (Psy D), client-centered and experiential psychotherapies (Psy D), diversity and multicultural psychology (Psy D), family psychology (Psy D), forensic psychology (Psy D), health psychology (Psy D), neuropsychology (Psy D), organizational consulting (Psy D), psychoanalytic psychology (Psy D), psychology and spirituality (Psy D); community counseling (MA); counseling psychology (Ed D), including counselor education and supervision; counselor education and supervision (Ed D); industrial organizational psychology (MA). *Accreditation:* APA (one or more programs are accredited). Postbaccalaureate distance learning degree programs offered (minimal on-campus study).

See Close-Up on page 1051.

Argosy University, Dallas, College of Psychology and Behavioral Sciences, Farmers Branch, TX 75244. Offers MA, Ed D, Psy D.

See Close-Up on page 1053.

Argosy University, Denver, College of Psychology and Behavioral Sciences, Denver, CO 80231. Offers clinical mental health counseling (MA); clinical psychology (MA, Psy D); counseling psychology (Ed D); counselor education and supervision (Ed D); forensic psychology (MA); industrial organizational psychology (MA); marriage and family therapy (MA, DMFT).

See Close-Up on page 1055.

Argosy University, Hawai'i, College of Psychology and Behavioral Sciences, Honolulu, HI 96813. Offers MA, MS, Ed D, Psy D, Certificate, Postdoctoral Respecialization Certificate. *Accreditation:* APA.

See Close-Up on page 1057.

Argosy University, Inland Empire, College of Psychology and Behavioral Sciences, San Bernardino, CA 92408. Offers clinical psychology/marriage and family therapy (MA); counseling psychology (Ed D); counseling psychology/marriage and family therapy (MA); forensic psychology (MA); industrial organizational psychology (MA); sport-exercise psychology (MA).

See Close-Up on page 1059.

Argosy University, Los Angeles, College of Psychology and Behavioral Sciences, Santa Monica, CA 90045. Offers clinical psychology/marriage and family therapy (MA); counseling psychology (Ed D); counseling psychology/marriage and family therapy (MA); forensic psychology (MA).

See Close-Up on page 1061.

Argosy University, Nashville, College of Psychology and Behavioral Sciences, Nashville, TN 37214. Offers counselor education and supervision (Ed D); mental health counseling (MA).

See Close-Up on page 1063.

Argosy University, Orange County, College of Psychology and Behavioral Sciences, Orange, CA 92868. Offers MA, Ed D, Psy D. *Accreditation:* APA. Part-time and evening/weekend programs available. *Faculty:* 8 full-time (5 women), 19 part-time/adjunct (6 women). *Students:* 160 full-time (118 women), 41 part-time (30 women). Average age 30. 217 applicants, 69 enrolled. In 2009, 6 master's, 2 doctorates awarded. *Degree requirements:* For master's, comprehensive exam; for doctorate, comprehensive exam, thesis/dissertation. *Entrance requirements:* For master's and doctorate, 3 letters of recommendation, interview, resume. Additional exam requirements/recommendations for international students: Required—TOEFL. *Application deadline:* Applications are processed on a rolling basis. Application fee: $50. Electronic applications accepted. *Financial support:* In 2009–10, 15 students received support. Career-related internships or fieldwork, Federal Work-Study, institutionally sponsored loans, and scholarships/grants available. Support available to part-time students. Financial award applicants required to submit FAFSA. *Faculty research:* The psychological aspects of infertility medicine, depression, psychoanalytic therapy, experiential approaches to teaching. *Unit head:* Dr. Gary Bruss, Dean, 800-716-9598, Fax: 714-437-1284, E-mail: gbruss@argosy.edu. *Application contact:* Mark Betz, Director of Admissions, 800-716-9598, Fax: 714-437-1697, E-mail: mbetz@argosy.edu.

See Close-Up on page 1065.

Argosy University, Phoenix, College of Psychology and Behavioral Sciences, Phoenix, AZ 85021. Offers MA, Psy D.

See Close-Up on page 1067.

Argosy University, Salt Lake City, College of Psychology and Behavioral Sciences, Draper, UT 84020. Offers counseling psychology (Ed D); counselor education and supervision (Ed D); forensic psychology (MA); marriage and family therapy (MA, DMFT); mental health counseling (MA).

See Close-Up on page 1069.

Argosy University, San Diego, College of Psychology and Behavioral Sciences, San Diego, CA 92108. Offers clinical psychology/marriage and family therapy (MA); counseling psychology (Ed D); counseling psychology/marriage and family therapy (MA); forensic psychology (MA).

See Close-Up on page 1071.

Argosy University, San Francisco Bay Area, College of Psychology and Behavioral Sciences, Alameda, CA 94501. Offers clinical psychology (MA, Psy D); counseling psychology (MA, Ed D); forensic psychology (MA); sport-exercise psychology (MA). *Accreditation:* APA (one or more programs are accredited).

See Close-Up on page 1073.

Argosy University, Sarasota, College of Psychology and Behavioral Sciences, Sarasota, FL 34235. Offers community counseling (MA); counseling psychology (Ed D); counselor education and supervision (Ed D); forensic psychology (MA); marriage and family therapy (MA); mental health counseling (MA); pastoral community counseling (Ed D).

See Close-Up on page 1075.

Psychology—General

Argosy University, Schaumburg, College of Psychology and Behavioral Sciences, Schaumburg, IL 60173-5403. Offers clinical health psychology (Post-Graduate Certificate); clinical psychology (MA, Psy D), including child and family psychology (Psy D), clinical health psychology (Psy D), diversity and multicultural psychology (Psy D), forensic psychology (Psy D), neuropsychology (Psy D); community counseling (MA); counseling psychology (Ed D), including counselor education and supervision; counselor education and supervision (Ed D); forensic psychology (Post-Graduate Certificate); industrial organizational psychology (MA). *Accreditation:* ACA; APA.

See Close-Up on page 1077.

Argosy University, Seattle, College of Psychology and Behavioral Sciences, Seattle, WA 98121. Offers MA, Ed D, Psy D, Postdoctoral Respecialization Certificate.

See Close-Up on page 1079.

Argosy University, Tampa, College of Psychology and Behavioral Sciences, Tampa, FL 33607. Offers clinical psychology (MA, Psy D), including clinical psychology; counselor education and supervision (Ed D); industrial organizational psychology (MA); marriage and family therapy (MA); mental health counseling (MA).

See Close-Up on page 1081.

Argosy University, Twin Cities, College of Psychology and Behavioral Sciences, Eagan, MN 55121. Offers clinical psychology (MA, Psy D), including child and family psychology (Psy D), forensic psychology (Psy D), health and neuropsychology (Psy D), trauma (Psy D); forensic counseling (Post-Graduate Certificate); forensic psychology (MA); industrial organizational psychology (MA); marriage and family therapy (MA, DMFT), including forensic counseling (MA). *Accreditation:* APA.

See Close-Up on page 1083.

Argosy University, Washington DC, College of Psychology and Behavioral Sciences, Arlington, VA 22209. Offers clinical psychology (MA, Psy D), including child and family psychology (Psy D), diversity and multicultural psychology (Psy D), forensic psychology (Psy D), health and neuropsychology (Psy D); community counseling (MA); counseling psychology (Ed D), including counselor education and supervision; counselor education and supervision (Ed D); forensic psychology (MA). *Accreditation:* APA.

See Close-Up on page 1085.

Arizona State University, Graduate College, College of Liberal Arts and Sciences, Division of Natural Sciences, Department of Psychology, Tempe, AZ 85287. Offers behavioral neuroscience (PhD); clinical psychology (PhD); cognition, action and perception (PhD); developmental psychology (PhD); quantitative psychology (PhD); social psychology (PhD). *Accreditation:* APA. *Degree requirements:* For doctorate, thesis/dissertation. *Entrance requirements:* For doctorate, GRE General Test, GRE Subject Test.

Arizona State University, Graduate College, College of Technology and Innovation, Applied Psychology Program, Tempe, AZ 85287. Offers MS. *Degree requirements:* For master's, thesis or applied project with oral defense. *Entrance requirements:* For master's, GRE, 3 letters of recommendation, minimum GPA of 3.0. Additional exam requirements/recommendations for international students: Required—TOEFL (minimum score 550 paper-based; 213 computer-based; 83 iBT); Recommended—TWE. Electronic applications accepted.

Arkansas Tech University, Graduate College, College of Arts and Humanities, Russellville, AR 72801. Offers communication (MLA); English (M Ed, MA); fine arts (MLA); history (MA); multi-media journalism (MA); psychology (MS); social science (MLA); Spanish (MA, MLA); teaching English as a second language (MA, MLA). Part-time programs available. *Students:* 39 full-time (30 women), 80 part-time (63 women); includes 11 minority (3 African Americans, 1 American Indian/Alaska Native, 1 Asian American or Pacific Islander, 6 Hispanic Americans), 23 international. Average age 33. In 2009, 70 master's awarded. *Degree requirements:* For master's, comprehensive exam (for some programs), thesis (for some programs), project. *Entrance requirements:* For master's, GRE General Test or MAT. Additional exam requirements/recommendations for international students: Required—TOEFL (minimum score 550 paper-based; 213 computer-based; 79 iBT), IELTS (minimum score 6). *Application deadline:* For fall admission, 3/1 priority date for domestic students, 5/1 priority date for international students; for spring admission, 10/1 priority date for domestic and international students. Applications are processed on a rolling basis. Application fee: $0 ($50 for international students). Electronic applications accepted. *Expenses:* Tuition, state resident: full-time $3438; part-time $191 per hour. Tuition, nonresident: full-time $6876; part-time $382 per hour. Required fees: $482; $9 per credit hour. $140 per semester. Tuition and fees vary according to course load. *Financial support:* In 2009–10, teaching assistantships with full tuition reimbursements (averaging $4,000 per year); research assistantships, career-related internships or fieldwork, Federal Work-Study, scholarships/grants, health care benefits, and unspecified assistantships also available. Support available to part-time students. Financial award application deadline: 4/15; financial award applicants required to submit FAFSA. *Unit head:* Dr. Micheal Tarver, Dean, 479-968-0274, Fax: 479-964-0812, E-mail: mtarver@atu.edu. *Application contact:* Dr. Mary B. Gunter, Dean of Graduate College, 479-968-0398, Fax: 479-964-0542, E-mail: graduate.school@atu.edu.

Assumption College, Graduate School, Counseling Psychology Program, Worcester, MA 01609-1296. Offers child and family interventions (MA); cognitive and behavioral therapies (MA); counseling psychology (CAGS); general psychology (MA). Part-time and evening/weekend programs available. *Faculty:* 4 full-time (1 woman), 6 part-time/adjunct (2 women). *Students:* 50 full-time (42 women), 38 part-time (33 women); includes 9 minority (3 African Americans, 6 Hispanic Americans). Average age 24. 121 applicants, 86% accepted. In 2009, 20 master's, 2 other advanced degrees awarded. *Degree requirements:* For master's, comprehensive exam, internship, practicum, oral exam; for CAGS, comprehensive exam, oral exam. *Entrance requirements:* For master's, 3 letters of recommendation, resume; for CAGS, 3 letters of recommendation, resume, interview, essay. Additional exam requirements/recommendations for international students: Required—TOEFL (minimum score 540 paper-based; 200 computer-based; 76 iBT), IELTS (minimum score 6). *Application deadline:* For fall admission, 6/1 priority date for domestic students, 5/1 priority date for international students; for spring admission, 11/1 priority date for domestic students, 9/1 priority date for international students. Applications are processed on a rolling basis. Application fee: $30. Electronic applications accepted. *Expenses:* Tuition: Part-time $503 per credit. Required fees: $20 per semester. One-time fee: $100 part-time. Part-time tuition and fees vary according to campus/location. *Financial support:* In 2009–10, 19 fellowships with partial tuition reimbursements (averaging $6,808 per year), 2 teaching assistantships with full tuition reimbursements (averaging $9,940 per year) were awarded. Financial award application deadline: 3/1; financial award applicants required to submit FAFSA. *Faculty research:* Mood disorders, adjustment to life-threatening illness, perception of movement, socioemotional development of young children, discovery versus disclosure. *Unit head:* Dr. Leonard A. Doerfler, Director, 508-767-7549, Fax: 508-767-7263, E-mail: doerfler@assumption.edu. *Application contact:* Adrian O. Dumas, Director of Graduate Enrollment Management and Services, 508-767-7365, Fax: 508-767-7030, E-mail: adumas@assumption.edu.

Athabasca University, Graduate Centre for Applied Psychology, Athabasca, AB T9S 3A3, Canada. Offers art therapy (MC); career counseling (MC); counseling (Advanced Certificate); counseling psychology (MC); school counseling (MC). *Faculty:* 5 full-time (2 women). *Students:* 210 part-time. Average age 35. 117 applicants, 15 enrolled. In 2009, 36 master's, 1 Advanced Certificate awarded. *Application deadline:* For fall admission, 3/1 for domestic and international students. Application fee: $80. *Expenses:* Tuition: Part-time $16,500 per degree program. Required fees: $200 per year. One-time fee: $80 part-time. *Unit head:* Dr. Trevor Gilbert, Chair, 866-242-8768, Fax: 780-675-6186, E-mail: trevorg@athabascau.ca. *Application contact:* Information Contact, 800-788-9041, Fax: 780-675-6437.

Auburn University, Graduate School, College of Liberal Arts, Department of Psychology, Auburn University, AL 36849. Offers applied behavior analysis in developmental disabilities (MS); clinical psychology (PhD); experimental psychology (PhD); industrial/organizational psychology (PhD). *Accreditation:* APA (one or more programs are accredited). Part-time programs available. *Faculty:* 24 full-time (7 women), 4 part-time/adjunct (3 women). *Students:* 36 full-time (28 women), 57 part-time (33 women); includes 15 minority (6 African Americans, 4 Asian Americans or Pacific Islanders, 5 Hispanic Americans). Average age 26. 293 applicants, 9% accepted, 19 enrolled. In 2009, 20 master's, 11 doctorates awarded. *Degree requirements:* For doctorate, thesis/dissertation. *Entrance requirements:* For master's, GRE General Test, GRE Subject Test, minimum GPA of 3.25 in psychology, 3.0 overall; for doctorate, GRE General Test, GRE Subject Test. *Application deadline:* For fall admission, 7/7 for domestic students; for spring admission, 11/24 for domestic students. Applications are processed on a rolling basis. Application fee: $50 ($60 for international students). Electronic applications accepted. *Expenses:* Tuition, state resident: full-time $6240. Tuition, nonresident: full-time $18,720. International tuition: $18,938 full-time. Required fees: $492. Tuition and fees vary according to course load, program and reciprocity agreements. *Financial support:* Research assistantships, teaching assistantships, Federal Work-Study available. Support available to part-time students. Financial award application deadline: 3/15; financial award applicants required to submit FAFSA. *Faculty research:* Clinical psychology, learning, industrial psychology, organizational psychology. Total annual research expenditures: $200,000. *Unit head:* Dr. Barry Burkhart, Chair, 334-844-4412. *Application contact:* Dr. George Flowers, Dean of the Graduate School, 334-844-2125.

Auburn University Montgomery, School of Sciences, Department of Psychology, Montgomery, AL 36124-4023. Offers MSPG. Part-time and evening/weekend programs available. *Faculty:* 4 full-time (2 women), 1 part-time/adjunct (0 women). *Students:* 17 full-time (13 women), 10 part-time (7 women); includes 10 minority (9 African Americans, 1 Asian American or Pacific Islander), 1 international. Average age 27. In 2009, 4 master's awarded. *Degree requirements:* For master's, comprehensive exam, thesis optional. *Entrance requirements:* For master's, GRE General Test or MAT. *Application deadline:* Applications are processed on a rolling basis. Electronic applications accepted. *Expenses:* Tuition, state resident: full-time $2841; part-time $225 per credit hour. Tuition, nonresident: full-time $8241; part-time $675 per credit hour. Required fees: $282; $8 per hour. $45 per term. *Financial support:* In 2009–10, 7 teaching assistantships were awarded; career-related internships or fieldwork and scholarships/grants also available. Support available to part-time students. Financial award application deadline: 3/1; financial award applicants required to submit FAFSA. *Faculty research:* Community service, diagnosis, behavior modification. *Unit head:* Dr. Peter Zachar, Chair, 334-244-3311, Fax: 334-244-3826, E-mail: pzachar@mail.aum.edu. *Application contact:* Dr. Steve LoBello, Graduate Coordinator, 334-244-3309, Fax: 334-244-3826, E-mail: slobello@mail.aum.edu.

Augusta State University, Graduate Studies, College of Arts and Sciences, Department of Psychology, Augusta, GA 30904-2200. Offers MS. Part-time programs available. *Degree requirements:* For master's, thesis optional, written/oral exam. *Entrance requirements:* For master's, GRE General Test, minimum GPA of 2.5, bachelor's degree in psychology or equivalent course work. *Faculty research:* Developmental, cognitive, gender and aging issues, consumer behavior, conditioned taste aversions, circadian rhythms, use of slang and offensive language.

Austin Peay State University, College of Graduate Studies, College of Behavioral and Health Sciences, Department of Psychology, Clarksville, TN 37044. Offers counseling (MS); counseling and guidance (Ed S); psychology (MA). Part-time programs available. Postbaccalaureate distance learning degree programs offered (no on-campus study). *Faculty:* 12 full-time (7 women), 1 (woman) part-time/adjunct. *Students:* 56 full-time (45 women), 27 part-time (21 women); includes 13 minority (8 African Americans, 1 Asian American or Pacific Islander, 4 Hispanic Americans), 1 international. Average age 29. 47 applicants, 96% accepted, 32 enrolled. In 2009, 23 master's awarded. *Degree requirements:* For master's, comprehensive exam, thesis (for some programs). *Entrance requirements:* For master's, GRE General Test, minimum undergraduate GPA of 2.5, 3 letters of recommendation, bachelor's degree. Additional exam requirements/recommendations for international students: Required—TOEFL (minimum score 500 paper-based; 173 computer-based). *Application deadline:* For fall admission, 3/27 priority date for domestic students; for spring admission, 11/1 priority date for domestic students. Applications are processed on a rolling basis. Application fee: $25. Electronic applications accepted. *Expenses:* Tuition, state resident: full-time $6160; part-time $608 per credit hour. Tuition, nonresident: full-time $17,080; part-time $854 per credit hour. Required fees: $1224; $61.20 per credit hour. *Financial support:* In 2009–10, 12 students received support, including 12 research assistantships with full tuition reimbursements available (averaging $5,184 per year); career-related internships or fieldwork, Federal Work-Study, institutionally sponsored loans, scholarships/grants, and unspecified assistantships also available. Support available to part-time students. Financial award application deadline: 3/1; financial award applicants required to submit FAFSA. *Unit head:* Dr. Samuel Fung, Chair, 931-221-7233, Fax: 931-221-6267, E-mail: fungs@apsu.edu. *Application contact:* Dr. Dixie Dennis, Dean, College of Graduate Studies, 931-221-7662, Fax: 931-221-7641, E-mail: dennisdi@apsu.edu.

Avila University, Department of Psychology, Kansas City, MO 64145-1698. Offers counseling psychology (MS); general psychology (MS). Part-time and evening/weekend programs available. *Faculty:* 6 full-time (5 women), 12 part-time/adjunct (7 women). *Students:* 125 full-time (101 women), 30 part-time (23 women); includes 32 minority (24 African Americans, 4 Asian Americans or Pacific Islanders, 4 Hispanic Americans), 8 international. Average age 32. 76 applicants, 79% accepted, 48 enrolled. In 2009, 36 master's awarded. *Degree requirements:* For master's, capstone project. *Entrance requirements:* For master's, minimum GPA of 3.0 in last 60 hours, 2 letters of recommendation. Additional exam requirements/recommendations for international students: Required—TOEFL. *Application deadline:* Applications are processed on a rolling basis. Application fee: $0. *Expenses:* Tuition: Full-time $8622; part-time $479 per credit hour. Required fees: $432; $24 per credit hour. Tuition and fees vary according to program. *Financial support:* In 2009–10, 132 students received support. Career-related internships or fieldwork, scholarships/grants, and unspecified assistantships available. Support available to part-time students. Financial award applicants required to submit FAFSA. *Faculty research:* Neuro/biofeedback, emotional regulation, perception, mindful wellness, trauma and restorative justice. *Unit head:* Shirlene Hess, Director of Graduate Psychology, 816-501-2969, Fax: 816-501-2455, E-mail: shirlene.hess@avila.edu. *Application contact:* Beth Brown, Administrative Assistant, 816-501-3698, Fax: 816-501-2455, E-mail: gradpsych@avila.edu.

Azusa Pacific University, School of Behavioral and Applied Sciences, Department of Graduate Psychology, Azusa, CA 91702-7000. Offers clinical psychology (MA, Psy D), including family therapy (MA). *Accreditation:* APA (one or more programs are accredited). Part-time and evening/weekend programs available. *Degree requirements:* For master's, comprehensive exam, 250 hours of clinical experience, individual and group therapy. *Entrance requirements:* For master's, interview, minimum GPA of 3.0, Minnesota Multiphasic Personality Inventory. Additional exam requirements/recommendations for international students: Required—TOEFL (minimum score 600 paper-based).

Ball State University, Graduate School, College of Sciences and Humanities, Department of Psychological Science, Muncie, IN 47306-1099. Offers clinical psychology (MA); cognitive and social processes (MA).

Barry University, School of Arts and Sciences, Department of Psychology, Miami Shores, FL 33161-6695. Offers clinical psychology (MS); school psychology (MS, SSP). Part-time and evening/weekend programs available. *Degree requirements:* For master's, thesis, practicum. *Entrance requirements:* For master's, GRE General Test, minimum GPA of 3.0, course work in psychology. Electronic applications accepted. *Faculty research:* Closed head injury, memory and aging, infant/mother interaction, evolutionary aspects of behavior, gender roles.

Bayamón Central University, Graduate Programs, Program in Psychology, Bayamón, PR 00960-1725. Offers MA. Part-time and evening/weekend programs available. *Degree requirements:* For master's, comprehensive exam. *Entrance requirements:* For master's, EXADEP, bachelor's degree in psychology or related field.

Baylor University, Graduate School, College of Arts and Sciences, Department of Psychology and Neuroscience, Program in Psychology, Waco, TX 76798. Offers MA, PhD. *Students:* 17 full-time (11 women); includes 1 minority (Hispanic American), 1 international. In 2009, 4 master's awarded. *Degree requirements:* For doctorate, comprehensive exam. *Entrance requirements:* For master's and doctorate, GRE General Test. *Application deadline:* Applications are processed on a rolling basis. Application fee: $25. *Unit head:* Dr. Matthew Stanford, Graduate Program Director, 254-710-2236, Fax: 254-710-3033, E-mail: matthew_stanford@baylor.edu. *Application contact:* Barbara Prisco, Graduate Coordinator, 254-757-0535, Fax: 254-710-3033, E-mail: barbara_prisco@baylor.edu.

Biola University, Rosemead School of Psychology, La Mirada, CA 90639-0001. Offers MA, PhD, Psy D. *Accreditation:* APA. Terminal master's awarded for partial completion of doctoral program. *Degree requirements:* For master's, thesis, internship; for doctorate, comprehensive exam, thesis/dissertation, internship. *Entrance requirements:* For master's and doctorate, GRE General Test, GRE Subject Test, Minnesota Multiphasic Personality Inventory, interview, 30 undergraduate credits in psychology. Additional exam requirements/recommendations for international students: Required—TOEFL (minimum score 250 computer-based). *Expenses:* Contact institution. *Faculty research:* Integration of psychology and theology, practice of psychotherapy, therapy process and outcomes.

Boston College, Graduate School of Arts and Sciences, Department of Psychology, Chestnut Hill, MA 02467-3800. Offers MA, PhD. *Students:* 21 full-time (17 women); includes 1 minority (Asian American or Pacific Islander), 2 international. 250 applicants, 3% accepted, 6 enrolled. In 2009, 5 master's, 10 doctorates awarded. *Degree requirements:* For doctorate, thesis/dissertation, fieldwork. *Entrance requirements:* For master's, GRE General Test; for doctorate, GRE General Test, GRE Subject Test. Additional exam requirements/recommendations for international students: Required—TOEFL (minimum score 600 paper-based; 250 computer-based; 100 iBT). *Application deadline:* For fall admission, 1/2 for domestic and international students. Application fee: $75. Electronic applications accepted. *Financial support:* In 2009–10, fellowships with full tuition reimbursements (averaging $19,500 per year), research assistantships with full tuition reimbursements (averaging $19,500 per year), teaching assistantships with full tuition reimbursements (averaging $19,500 per year) were awarded; career-related internships or fieldwork also available. Support available to part-time students. Financial award application deadline: 3/1; financial award applicants required to submit FAFSA. *Faculty research:* Social, cognitive, and biological processes. *Unit head:* Dr. James Russell, Chairperson, 617-552-4100, E-mail: james.russell@bc.edu. *Application contact:* Dr. Jon Horvitz, Graduate Program Director, 617-552-2999, E-mail: jon.horvitz@bc.edu.

Boston Graduate School of Psychoanalysis, Master's Program—New York, New York, NY 10011. Offers MA. Part-time programs available. *Entrance requirements:* For master's, interview, writing sample.

Boston University, Graduate School of Arts and Sciences, Department of Psychology, Boston, MA 02215. Offers MA, PhD. *Accreditation:* APA (one or more programs are accredited). *Students:* 128 full-time (99 women), 13 part-time (12 women); includes 24 minority (7 African Americans, 1 American Indian/Alaska Native, 12 Asian Americans or Pacific Islanders, 4 Hispanic Americans), 24 international. Average age 27. 936 applicants, 17% accepted, 55 enrolled. In 2009, 64 master's, 16 doctorates awarded. Terminal master's awarded for partial completion of doctoral program. *Degree requirements:* For master's, one foreign language, comprehensive exam; for doctorate, one foreign language, comprehensive exam, thesis/dissertation. *Entrance requirements:* For master's and doctorate, GRE General Test. Additional exam requirements/recommendations for international students: Required—TOEFL. *Application deadline:* For fall admission, 12/1 for domestic and international students. Application fee: $70. Electronic applications accepted. *Expenses:* Tuition: Full-time $37,910; part-time $1184 per credit hour. Required fees: $386; $40 per semester. Part-time tuition and fees vary according to class time, course level, degree level and program. *Financial support:* In 2009–10, 85 students received support, including 4 fellowships (averaging $18,900 per year), 56 research assistantships with full tuition reimbursements available (averaging $18,400 per year), 23 teaching assistantships with full and partial tuition reimbursements available (averaging $18,400 per year); career-related internships or fieldwork, Federal Work-Study, and unspecified assistantships also available. Support available to part-time students. Financial award application deadline: 12/1; financial award applicants required to submit FAFSA. *Unit head:* Michael Lyons, Chairman, 617-353-3820, Fax: 617-353-6933, E-mail: mlyons@bu.edu. *Application contact:* Michael Lyons, Chairman, 617-353-3820, Fax: 617-353-6933, E-mail: mlyons@bu.edu.

Bowling Green State University, Graduate College, College of Arts and Sciences, Department of Psychology, Bowling Green, OH 43403. Offers clinical psychology (MA, PhD); developmental psychology (MA, PhD); experimental psychology (MA, PhD); industrial/organizational psychology (MA, PhD); quantitative psychology (MA, PhD). *Accreditation:* APA (one or more programs are accredited). *Degree requirements:* For doctorate, thesis/dissertation. *Entrance requirements:* For doctorate, GRE General Test, GRE Subject Test. Additional exam requirements/recommendations for international students: Required—TOEFL. Electronic applications accepted. *Faculty research:* Personnel psychology, developmental-mathematical models, behavioral medication, brain process, child/adolescent social cognition.

Brandeis University, Graduate School of Arts and Sciences, Department of Psychology, Waltham, MA 02454-9110. Offers brain, body and behavior (PhD); cognitive neuroscience (PhD); general psychology (MA); social/developmental psychology (PhD). Part-time programs available. *Faculty:* 16 full-time (4 women), 3 part-time/adjunct (2 women). *Students:* 35 full-time (27 women), 1 (woman) part-time; includes 2 minority (both Asian Americans or Pacific Islanders), 7 international. Average age 26. 121 applicants, 31% accepted, 13 enrolled. In 2009, 9 master's, 3 doctorates awarded. *Degree requirements:* For doctorate, comprehensive exam, thesis/dissertation. *Entrance requirements:* For master's, GRE General Test, GRE Subject Test (recommended), 3 letters of recommendation, statement of purpose; for doctorate, GRE General Test, GRE Subject Test (recommended), 3 letters of recommendation. Additional exam requirements/recommendations for international students: Required—TOEFL (minimum score 600 paper-based; 250 computer-based; 100 iBT); Recommended—IELTS (minimum score 7). *Application deadline:* For fall admission, 1/15 for domestic and international students. Applications are processed on a rolling basis. Application fee: $75. Electronic applications accepted. *Financial support:* In 2009–10, 16 fellowships with full tuition reimbursements (averaging $20,000 per year), 3 research assistantships with full tuition reimbursements (averaging $20,000 per year), 9 teaching assistantships with partial tuition reimbursements (averaging $3,200 per year) were awarded; institutionally sponsored loans, scholarships/grants, traineeships, health care benefits, tuition waivers (full), and unspecified assistantships also available. Support available to part-time students. Financial award applicants required to submit FAFSA. *Faculty research:* Development, cognition, social aging, perception, social/developmental psychology, cognitive neuroscience, brain, body and behavior, motor control, visual perception, taste physiology and psychophysics, memory, learning, aggression, emotion, personality and cognition in adulthood and old age, social relations and health, stereotypes and nonverbal communication. *Unit head:* Prof. Paul DiZio, Director of Graduate Studies, 781-736-3300, Fax: 781-736-3291, E-mail: dizio@brandeis.edu. *Application contact:* Donna J. Coletti, Graduate Admissions Coordinator, 781-736-3303, Fax: 781-736-3291, E-mail: coletti@brandeis.edu.

Brenau University, Graduate Programs, School of Health and Science, Gainesville, GA 30501. Offers family nurse practitioner (MSN); nurse educator (MSN); nursing management (MSN); occupational therapy (MS); psychology (MS). *Accreditation:* AOTA; NLN. Part-time and evening/weekend programs available. *Faculty:* 14 full-time (12 women), 6 part-time/adjunct (5 women). *Students:* 97 full-time (92 women), 92 part-time (84 women); includes 46 minority (37 African Americans, 2 American Indian/Alaska Native, 2 Asian Americans or Pacific Islanders, 5 Hispanic Americans), 2 international. Average age 34. 168 applicants, 50% accepted, 68 enrolled. In 2009, 35 master's awarded. *Degree requirements:* For master's, comprehensive exam (for some programs), thesis (for some programs), clinical practicum hours. *Entrance requirements:* For master's, GRE General Test or MAT (for some programs), interview, writing sample, references (for some programs). Additional exam requirements/recommendations for international students: Required—TOEFL (minimum score 500 paper-based). *Application deadline:* Applications are processed on a rolling basis. Application fee: $35. Electronic applications accepted. *Expenses:* Contact institution. *Financial support:* In 2009–10, 32 students received support. Scholarships/grants and traineeships available. Support available to part-time students. Financial award application deadline: 7/15; financial award applicants required to submit FAFSA. *Unit head:* Dr. Gale Starich, Dean, 777-718-5305, Fax: 770-297-5929, E-mail: gstarich@brenau.edu. *Application contact:* Christina White, Admissions Coordinator, 770-718-5320, Fax: 770-770-5338, E-mail: cwhite@brenau.edu.

Bridgewater State University, School of Graduate Studies, School of Arts and Sciences, Department of Psychology, Bridgewater, MA 02325-0001. Offers MA. Part-time and evening/weekend programs available. *Entrance requirements:* For master's, GRE General Test.

Brigham Young University, Graduate Studies, College of Family, Home, and Social Sciences, Department of Psychology, Provo, UT 84602. Offers clinical psychology (PhD); general psychology (MS); psychology (PhD), including applied social psychology, behavioral neurobiology. *Accreditation:* APA (one or more programs are accredited). *Faculty:* 27 full-time (5 women). *Students:* 90 full-time (30 women); includes 7 minority (3 African Americans, 4 Hispanic Americans), 8 international. Average age 24. 91 applicants, 20% accepted, 18 enrolled. In 2009, 9 master's, 14 doctorates awarded. *Degree requirements:* For master's, thesis; for doctorate, comprehensive exam, thesis/dissertation, publishable paper. *Entrance requirements:* For master's and doctorate, GRE General Test, minimum GPA of 3.0 in last 60 hours of upper division course work. Additional exam requirements/recommendations for international students: Required—TOEFL. *Application deadline:* For fall admission, 1/5 for domestic students. Application fee: $50. Electronic applications accepted. *Expenses:* Tuition: Full-time $5580; part-time $301 per credit hour. Tuition and fees vary according to student's religious affiliation. *Financial support:* In 2009–10, 85 students received support, including 20 research assistantships with partial tuition reimbursements available (averaging $10,000 per year), 30 teaching assistantships with partial tuition reimbursements available (averaging $10,000 per year); fellowships, career-related internships or fieldwork, scholarships/grants, tuition waivers (partial), and unspecified assistantships also available. Financial award application deadline: 5/31. *Faculty research:* Psychotherapy process, Alzheimer's disease/dementia, psychology and law, health, psychology, developmental. Total annual research expenditures: $1 million. *Unit head:* Dr. Ramona Hopkins, Chair, 801-422-1170, Fax: 801-422-0602, E-mail: ramona_hopkins@byu.edu. *Application contact:* Karen A. Christensen, Coordinator of Student Programs, 801-422-4560, Fax: 801-422-0602, E-mail: karen_christensen@byu.edu.

Brock University, Faculty of Graduate Studies, Faculty of Social Sciences, Program in Psychology, St. Catharines, ON L2S 3A1, Canada. Offers behavioral neuroscience (MA, PhD); life span development (MA, PhD); social personality (MA, PhD). Part-time programs available. *Degree requirements:* For master's, thesis; for doctorate, thesis/dissertation. *Entrance requirements:* For master's, GRE, honors degree; for doctorate, GRE, master's degree. Additional exam requirements/recommendations for international students: Required—TOEFL (minimum score 550 paper-based; 213 computer-based; 80 iBT), IELTS (minimum score 6.5), TWE (minimum score 4). Electronic applications accepted. *Faculty research:* Social personality, behavioral neuroscience, life-span development.

Brooklyn College of the City University of New York, Division of Graduate Studies, Department of Psychology, Brooklyn, NY 11210-2889. Offers experimental psychology (MA); industrial and organizational psychology (MA), including human relations, organizational behavior; mental health counseling (MA); psychology (PhD). Part-time programs available. *Students:* 89 full-time (74 women), 131 part-time (97 women); includes 83 minority (52 African Americans, 11 Asian Americans or Pacific Islanders, 20 Hispanic Americans), 17 international. Average age 30. 322 applicants, 55% accepted, 98 enrolled. In 2009, 62 master's awarded. *Degree requirements:* For master's, comprehensive exam, thesis (for some programs). *Entrance requirements:* For master's, minimum GPA of 3.0, 2 letters of recommendation, essay; for doctorate, GRE. Additional exam requirements/recommendations for international students: Required—TOEFL (minimum score 520 paper-based; 190 computer-based; 69 iBT). *Application deadline:* For fall admission, 3/1 for domestic students, 2/1 for international students; for spring admission, 11/1 for domestic students, 10/1 for international students. Applications are processed on a rolling basis. Application fee: $125. Electronic applications accepted. *Expenses:* Tuition, area resident: Full-time $7360; part-time $310 per credit hour. Tuition, state resident: full-time $7360; part-time $310 per credit hour. Tuition, nonresident: full-time $13,800; part-time $575 per credit hour. International tuition: $13,800 full-time. Required fees: $140.10 per semester. *Financial support:* Career-related internships or fieldwork, Federal Work-Study, institutionally sponsored loans, scholarships/grants, and tuition waivers (partial) available. Support available to part-time students. Financial award application deadline: 5/1; financial award applicants required to submit FAFSA. *Unit head:* Dr. Margaret-Ellen Pipe, Chairperson, 718-951-5601, Fax: 718-951-4814, E-mail: mepipe@brooklyn.cuny.edu. *Application contact:* Hernan Sierra, Graduate Admissions Coordinator, 718-951-4536, Fax: 718-951-4506, E-mail: grads@brooklyn.cuny.edu.

Brown University, Graduate School, Department of Psychology, Providence, RI 02912. Offers behavioral neuroscience (PhD); cognitive processes (PhD); sensation and perception (PhD); social/developmental (PhD); MS/PhD. *Degree requirements:* For doctorate, thesis/dissertation. *Entrance requirements:* For doctorate, GRE General Test, GRE Subject Test.

Bryn Mawr College, Graduate School of Arts and Sciences, Department of Psychology, Bryn Mawr, PA 19010-2899. Offers clinical developmental psychology (PhD). Part-time programs available. *Degree requirements:* For doctorate, one foreign language, comprehensive exam, thesis/dissertation. *Entrance requirements:* For doctorate, GRE General Test. Additional exam requirements/recommendations for international students: Required—TOEFL (minimum score 600 paper-based; 250 computer-based). *Expenses:* Tuition: Full-time $31,340. Required fees: $430.

Bucknell University, Graduate Studies, College of Arts and Sciences, Department of Psychology, Lewisburg, PA 17837. Offers MA, MS. Part-time programs available. *Degree requirements:* For master's, thesis. *Entrance requirements:* For master's, GRE General Test, GRE Subject Test, minimum GPA of 2.8. Additional exam requirements/recommendations for international students: Required—TOEFL.

Caldwell College, Graduate Studies, Program in Applied Behavior Analysis, Caldwell, NJ 07006-6195. Offers MA, PhD. *Entrance requirements:* For master's, GRE, minimum GPA of 3.0, writing sample. Additional exam requirements/recommendations for international students: Required—TOEFL (minimum score 580 paper-based; 237 computer-based).

California Coast University, Program in Psychology, Santa Ana, CA 92701. Offers MS. Part-time and evening/weekend programs available. Postbaccalaureate distance learning degree programs offered (no on-campus study). Application fee: $75. *Application contact:* Christi Okuma, 714-547-9625, Fax: 714-547-5777, E-mail: ccu@calcoast.edu.

California Institute of Integral Studies, School of Consciousness and Transformation, San Francisco, CA 94103. Offers creative inquiry (MFA); cultural anthropology and social transformation (MA); East-West psychology (MA, PhD); integrative health studies (MA); philosophy and religion (MA, PhD), including Asian and comparative studies, philosophy, cosmology, and consciousness, women's spirituality; social and cultural anthropology (PhD); transformative leadership (MA); transformative studies (PhD); writing and consciousness (MFA).

Psychology—General

California Institute of Integral Studies (continued)

Part-time and evening/weekend programs available. Postbaccalaureate distance learning degree programs offered (minimal on-campus study). *Students:* 334 full-time (218 women), 126 part-time (77 women); includes 116 minority (40 African Americans, 4 American Indian/Alaska Native, 42 Asian Americans or Pacific Islanders, 30 Hispanic Americans). Average age 38. 265 applicants, 90% accepted, 149 enrolled. In 2009, 64 master's, 22 doctorates awarded. Terminal master's awarded for partial completion of doctoral program. *Degree requirements:* For master's, comprehensive exam (for some programs), thesis optional; for doctorate, comprehensive exam, thesis/dissertation, 1 foreign language (Asian comparative studies). *Entrance requirements:* For master's, minimum GPA of 3.0, letters of recommendation, writing sample; for doctorate, master's degree, minimum GPA of 3.0, letters of recommendation, writing sample. Additional exam requirements/recommendations for international students: Required—TOEFL. *Application deadline:* For fall admission, 2/1 priority date for domestic and international students; for spring admission, 10/15 priority date for domestic and international students. Applications are processed on a rolling basis. Application fee: $65. Electronic applications accepted. *Expenses:* Tuition: Full-time $15,300; part-time $850 per credit hour. Required fees: $110 per semester. Tuition and fees vary according to degree level. *Financial support:* In 2009–10, 330 students received support; research assistantships, teaching assistantships, career-related internships or fieldwork, Federal Work-Study, scholarships/grants, and tuition waivers (partial) available. Support available to part-time students. Financial award application deadline: 4/15; financial award applicants required to submit FAFSA. *Faculty research:* Altered states of consciousness, dreams, cosmology, postcolonial studies, integrative health studies. *Application contact:* Allyson Werner, Associate Director of Admissions, 415-575-6155, Fax: 415-575-1268.

California Institute of Integral Studies, School of Professional Psychology, San Francisco, CA 94103. Offers clinical psychology (Psy D); community mental health (MA); drama therapy (MA); expressive arts therapy (MA); integral counseling psychology (MA); integral counseling psychology–weekend (MA); somatic psychology (MA). *Accreditation:* APA. Part-time programs available. *Students:* 639 full-time (483 women), 53 part-time (43 women); includes 148 minority (32 African Americans, 2 American Indian/Alaska Native, 62 Asian Americans or Pacific Islanders, 52 Hispanic Americans). Average age 38. 476 applicants, 71% accepted, 202 enrolled. In 2009, 136 master's, 21 doctorates awarded. *Degree requirements:* For master's, comprehensive exam; for doctorate, comprehensive exam, thesis/dissertation. *Entrance requirements:* For master's, minimum GPA of 3.0, letters of recommendation, writing sample; for doctorate, GRE, MA in psychology or social work with appropriate practical experience for advanced standing, or BA with a minimum GPA of 3.1; letters of recommendation; writing sample. Additional exam requirements/recommendations for international students: Required—TOEFL. *Application deadline:* For fall admission, 2/1 priority date for domestic and international students; for spring admission, 10/15 priority date for domestic and international students. Applications are processed on a rolling basis. Application fee: $65. Electronic applications accepted. *Expenses:* Tuition: Full-time $15,300; part-time $850 per credit hour. Required fees: $110 per semester. Tuition and fees vary according to degree level. *Financial support:* In 2009–10, 677 students received support; research assistantships with tuition reimbursements available, teaching assistantships with tuition reimbursements available, career-related internships or fieldwork, Federal Work-Study, scholarships/grants, and tuition waivers (partial) available. Support available to part-time students. Financial award application deadline: 4/15; financial award applicants required to submit FAFSA. *Faculty research:* Somatic psychology, comparative psychology, art therapy, transpersonal psychology, eco-psychology. *Application contact:* David Townes, Senior Admissions Counselor, 415-575-6152, Fax: 415-575-1268, E-mail: dtownes@ciis.edu.

California Lutheran University, Graduate Studies, Department of Psychology, Thousand Oaks, CA 91360-2787. Offers clinical psychology (MS, Psy D); marital and family therapy (MS). Part-time programs available. *Degree requirements:* For master's, thesis or comprehensive exams; for doctorate, internship. *Entrance requirements:* For master's, GRE General Test, interview, minimum GPA of 3.0.

California Polytechnic State University, San Luis Obispo, College of Liberal Arts, Department of Psychology and Child Development, San Luis Obispo, CA 93407. Offers psychology (MS). Part-time programs available. *Faculty:* 3 full-time (2 women), 1 (woman) part-time/adjunct. *Students:* 33 full-time (29 women), 13 part-time (12 women); includes 6 minority (all Hispanic Americans), 1 international. Average age 29. 65 applicants, 42% accepted, 19 enrolled. In 2009, 11 master's awarded. *Degree requirements:* For master's, comprehensive exam, thesis (for some programs). *Entrance requirements:* For master's, GRE General Test, minimum GPA of 3.0 in last 90 quarter units of course work, 4 letters of recommendation, interview. Additional exam requirements/recommendations for international students: Required—TOEFL (minimum score 550 paper-based; 213 computer-based), or IELTS (minimum score 6). *Application deadline:* For fall admission, 12/1 for domestic students, 11/30 for international students. Application fee: $55. Electronic applications accepted. *Expenses:* Tuition, nonresident: full-time $11,160; part-time $248 per unit. Required fees: $7134; $1553 per quarter. *Financial support:* Career-related internships or fieldwork, Federal Work-Study, and institutionally sponsored loans available. Support available to part-time students. Financial award application deadline: 3/2; financial award applicants required to submit FAFSA. *Faculty research:* Eating disorders, mood disorders, neuropsychology, forensic psychology, group therapy. *Unit head:* Dr. Kelly Moreno, Graduate Coordinator, 805-756-2805, Fax: 805-756-1134, E-mail: kmoreno@calpoly.edu. *Application contact:* Margaret Booker, Administrative Analyst, 805-756-2456, Fax: 805-756-1134, E-mail: mbooker@calpoly.edu.

California State Polytechnic University, Pomona, Academic Affairs, College of Letters, Arts, and Social Sciences, Program in Psychology, Pomona, CA 91768-2557. Offers MS. Part-time programs available. *Students:* 23 full-time (19 women), 4 part-time (all women); includes 11 minority (1 African American, 6 Asian Americans or Pacific Islanders, 4 Hispanic Americans), 2 international. Average age 28. 94 applicants, 17% accepted, 15 enrolled. In 2009, 15 master's awarded. *Degree requirements:* For master's, thesis or alternative. *Application deadline:* For fall admission, 4/15 for domestic students. Applications are processed on a rolling basis. Application fee: $55. Electronic applications accepted. *Expenses:* Tuition, nonresident: full-time $6696; part-time $248 per credit. Required fees: $5487; $3237 per term. Tuition and fees vary according to course load, degree level and program. *Financial support:* Application deadline: 3/2. *Unit head:* Dr. Jeffery Mio, Director of Graduate Studies, 909-869-3899, E-mail: jsmio@csupomona.edu. *Application contact:* Scott J. Duncan, Director, Admissions, 909-869-3258, Fax: 909-869-4529, E-mail: sjduncan@csupomona.edu.

California State University, Bakersfield, Division of Graduate Studies, School of Humanities and Social Sciences, Program in Psychology, Bakersfield, CA 93311. Offers MA. Part-time programs available. *Degree requirements:* For master's, comprehensive exam, thesis. *Entrance requirements:* For master's, GRE General Test, 3 letters of recommendation.

California State University, Chico, Graduate School, College of Behavioral and Social Sciences, Department of Psychology, Program in Psychological Science, Chico, CA 95929-0722. Offers MA. *Students:* 11 full-time (5 women), 10 part-time (2 women); includes 3 minority (1 Asian American or Pacific Islander, 2 Hispanic Americans), 1 international. Average age 30. 26 applicants, 62% accepted, 8 enrolled. In 2009, 15 master's awarded. *Degree requirements:* For master's, thesis or alternative. *Entrance requirements:* For master's, GRE General Test or MAT, 3 letters of recommendation on departmental form. Additional exam requirements/recommendations for international students: Required—TOEFL (minimum score 550 paper-based; 213 computer-based; 80 iBT), IELTS (minimum score 6.5). *Application deadline:* For fall admission, 3/1 for domestic and international students. Application fee: $55. *Unit head:* Dr. Linda Kline, Graduate Coordinator, 530-898-6263. *Application contact:* Dr. Linda Kline, Graduate Coordinator, 530-898-6263.

California State University, Dominguez Hills, College of Natural and Behavioral Sciences, Program in Psychology, Carson, CA 90747-0001. Offers clinical psychology (MA). Part-time and evening/weekend programs available. *Faculty:* 7 full-time (5 women), 1 (woman) part-time/adjunct. *Students:* 35 full-time (30 women), 15 part-time (13 women); includes 32 minority (10 African Americans, 1 Asian American or Pacific Islander, 21 Hispanic Americans), 1 international. Average age 32. 46 applicants, 74% accepted, 22 enrolled. In 2009, 5 master's awarded. Terminal master's awarded for partial completion of doctoral program. *Degree requirements:* For master's, comprehensive exam, thesis optional. *Entrance requirements:* For master's, GRE General Test or MAT, interview, minimum GPA of 3.0, prerequisite psychology courses. Additional exam requirements/recommendations for international students: Required—TOEFL (minimum score 550 paper-based). *Application deadline:* For fall admission, 3/1 for domestic and international students. Application fee: $55. Electronic applications accepted. *Expenses:* Tuition, nonresident: full-time $6696; part-time $372 per unit. Required fees: $5946; $1752 per semester. *Faculty research:* Culture and health, neuropsychology and HIV, psychohistory of the Holocaust, community and adolescents, malingering. *Unit head:* Dr. Ramona Davis, Chair, 310-243-3474, E-mail: rdavis@csudh.edu. *Application contact:* Dr. Karen I. Mason, Coordinator, 310-243-3642, Fax: 310-516-3642, E-mail: kmason@csudh.edu.

California State University, Fresno, Division of Graduate Studies, College of Science and Mathematics, Department of Psychology, Fresno, CA 93740-8027. Offers MA, MS. *Degree requirements:* For master's, thesis. *Entrance requirements:* For master's, GRE General Test, GRE Subject Test, minimum GPA of 3.0. Additional exam requirements/recommendations for international students: Required—TOEFL. Electronic applications accepted. *Faculty research:* Oncology prediction, parenting stress, wellness, aging and memory, retrieval inhibition, anger, minority mental health.

California State University, Fullerton, Graduate Studies, College of Humanities and Social Sciences, Department of Psychology, Fullerton, CA 92834-9480. Offers clinical/community psychology (MS); psychology (MA). Part-time programs available. *Students:* 17 full-time (9 women), 29 part-time (18 women); includes 20 minority (2 African Americans, 13 Asian Americans or Pacific Islanders, 5 Hispanic Americans), 3 international. Average age 26. 140 applicants, 31% accepted, 36 enrolled. In 2009, 19 master's awarded. *Degree requirements:* For master's, thesis. *Entrance requirements:* For master's, GRE General Test, GRE Subject Test, undergraduate major in psychology or related field. Application fee: $55. *Expenses:* Tuition, nonresident: full-time $11,160; part-time $373 per credit. Required fees: $1440 per term. Tuition and fees vary according to course load, degree level and program. *Financial support:* Career-related internships or fieldwork, Federal Work-Study, institutionally sponsored loans, and scholarships/grants available. Support available to part-time students. Financial award application deadline: 3/1; financial award applicants required to submit FAFSA. *Unit head:* Dr. Daniel Kee, Chair, 657-278-3514. *Application contact:* Admissions/Applications, 657-278-2371.

California State University, Long Beach, Graduate Studies, College of Liberal Arts, Department of Psychology, Long Beach, CA 90840. Offers human factors (MS); industrial/organizational psychology (MS); psychology (MA). Part-time and evening/weekend programs available. *Faculty:* 14 full-time (3 women), 4 part-time/adjunct (2 women). *Students:* 41 full-time (30 women), 19 part-time (12 women); includes 23 minority (5 African Americans, 8 Asian Americans or Pacific Islanders, 10 Hispanic Americans). Average age 26. 161 applicants, 25% accepted, 34 enrolled. *Degree requirements:* For master's, comprehensive exam, thesis. *Entrance requirements:* For master's, GRE General Test, GRE Subject Test. *Application deadline:* For fall admission, 3/1 for domestic students. Applications are processed on a rolling basis. Application fee: $55. Electronic applications accepted. *Expenses:* Required fees: $1802 per semester. Part-time tuition and fees vary according to course load. *Financial support:* Federal Work-Study, institutionally sponsored loans, and scholarships/grants available. Financial award application deadline: 3/2. *Faculty research:* Physiological psychology, social and personality psychology, community-clinical psychology, industrial-organizational psychology, developmental psychology. *Unit head:* Dr. Kenneth Green, Chair, 562-985-5049, Fax: 562-985-8004, E-mail: kgreen@csulb.edu. *Application contact:* Dr. Kenneth Green, Chair, 562-985-5049, Fax: 562-985-8004, E-mail: kgreen@csulb.edu.

California State University, Los Angeles, Graduate Studies, College of Natural and Social Sciences, Department of Psychology, Los Angeles, CA 90032-8530. Offers MA, MS. Part-time and evening/weekend programs available. *Faculty:* 7 full-time (2 women), 4 part-time/adjunct (2 women). *Students:* 39 full-time (33 women), 60 part-time (50 women); includes 48 minority (10 African Americans, 13 Asian Americans or Pacific Islanders, 25 Hispanic Americans), 12 international. Average age 29. 148 applicants, 100% accepted, 33 enrolled. In 2009, 34 master's awarded. *Degree requirements:* For master's, comprehensive exam or thesis. *Entrance requirements:* Additional exam requirements/recommendations for international students: Required—TOEFL (minimum score 500 paper-based; 173 computer-based). *Application deadline:* For fall admission, 5/1 for domestic and international students. Applications are processed on a rolling basis. Application fee: $55. Electronic applications accepted. *Financial support:* Career-related internships or fieldwork and Federal Work-Study available. Support available to part-time students. Financial award application deadline: 3/1. *Faculty research:* Binaural resolution of the size of an acoustic array, response and generalization of matching to sample in children. *Unit head:* Dr. Fary Cachelin, Chair, 323-343-2250, Fax: 323-343-2281, E-mail: fcachel@calstatela.edu. *Application contact:* Dr. Cheryl L. Ney, Associate Vice President for Academic Affairs and Dean of Graduate Studies, 323-343-3820, Fax: 323-343-5653, E-mail: cney@cslanet.calstatela.edu.

California State University, Northridge, Graduate Studies, College of Social and Behavioral Sciences, Department of Psychology, Northridge, CA 91330. Offers clinical psychology (MA); general-experimental psychology (MA); human factors and applied experimental psychology (MA). *Faculty:* 27 full-time (16 women), 19 part-time/adjunct (8 women). *Students:* 67 full-time (42 women), 25 part-time (19 women); includes 33 minority (2 African Americans, 9 Asian Americans or Pacific Islanders, 22 Hispanic Americans), 4 international. Average age 27. 173 applicants, 19% accepted, 29 enrolled. In 2009, 18 master's awarded. *Degree requirements:* For master's, thesis. *Entrance requirements:* For master's, GRE General Test, GRE Subject Test, minimum GPA of 3.0, letters of recommendation. Additional exam requirements/recommendations for international students: Required—TOEFL. *Application deadline:* For fall admission, 11/30 for domestic students. Application fee: $55. *Financial support:* Application deadline: 3/1. *Unit head:* Dr. Carrie Saetermoe, Chair, 818-677-3506. *Application contact:* Dr. Carrie Saetermoe, Chair, 818-677-3506.

California State University, Sacramento, Graduate Studies, College of Social Sciences and Interdisciplinary Studies, Department of Psychology, Sacramento, CA 95819. Offers counseling psychology (MA). Part-time programs available. *Degree requirements:* For master's, thesis, writing proficiency exam. *Entrance requirements:* For master's, GRE Subject Test, minimum GPA of 3.0 during previous 2 years. Additional exam requirements/recommendations for international students: Required—TOEFL. Electronic applications accepted.

California State University, San Bernardino, Graduate Studies, College of Social and Behavioral Sciences, Department of Psychology, San Bernardino, CA 92407-2397. Offers child development (MA), including psychology-life span; clinical/counseling psychology (MS), including clinical psychology; general/experimental psychology (MA), including psychology; industrial/organizational psychology (MS), including organizational psychology. *Faculty:* 20 full-time (8 women), 1 (woman) part-time/adjunct. *Students:* 85 full-time (67 women), 36 part-time (25 women); includes 47 minority (6 African Americans, 9 Asian Americans or Pacific Islanders, 32 Hispanic Americans), 8 international. Average age 28. 205 applicants, 51% accepted, 59 enrolled. In 2009, 36 master's awarded. *Degree requirements:* For master's, comprehensive exam, thesis (for some programs), advancement to candidacy. *Entrance requirements:* For master's, writing exam, minimum GPA of 3.0 in major. *Application deadline:* For fall admission, 8/31 priority date for domestic students. Application fee: $55. *Financial support:* Fellowships, research assistantships, teaching assistantships, career-related internships or fieldwork, Federal Work-Study, institutionally sponsored loans, and unspecified assistantships available. *Faculty research:* Perceptual development, human memory, psychopharmacology, psychology of women, language acquisition. *Unit head:* Dr. Mark S. Agars,

Associate Dean, 909-537-5433, Fax: 909-537-7003, E-mail: magars@csusb.edu. *Application contact:* Stacy Brooks, Graduate Secretary, 909-537-5570, Fax: 909-537-7003, E-mail: sbrooks@csusb.edu.

California State University, San Marcos, College of Arts and Sciences, Program in Psychology, San Marcos, CA 92096-0001. Offers MA. *Degree requirements:* For master's, thesis. *Entrance requirements:* For master's, GRE General Test, GRE Subject Test (recommended), 3 letters of recommendation. Additional exam requirements/recommendations for international students: Required—TOEFL (minimum score 550 paper-based). *Faculty research:* Psychopharmacology, recovery from major surgery, computer literacy in children, neuropsychology of hemispheric differences, conservation psychology.

California State University, Stanislaus, College of Human and Health Sciences, Department of Psychology, Turlock, CA 95382. Offers behavior analysis (MS); child development (Graduate Certificate); counseling (MS); psychology (MA, MS). Part-time programs available. *Degree requirements:* For master's, thesis. *Entrance requirements:* For master's, GRE General Test, minimum GPA of 3.0, 3 letters of reference. Additional exam requirements/recommendations for international students: Required—TOEFL (minimum score 550 paper-based; 213 computer-based). Electronic applications accepted. *Faculty research:* Hedonic tone judgement, syntax and autism, early literacy assessment and native and non-native languages.

Cambridge College, School of Psychology and Counseling, Cambridge, MA 02138-5304. Offers addiction counseling (M Ed); alcohol & drug counseling (Certificate); counseling psychology (M Ed, CAGS); counseling psychology: forensic counseling (M Ed); marriage and family therapy (M Ed); mental health and addiction counseling (M Ed); mental health counseling (M Ed); mental health counseling for school guidance counselors (Post Master's Certificate); psychological studies (M Ed); school adjustment and mental health counseling (M Ed); school adjustment, mental health and addiction counseling (M Ed); school guidance counselor (M Ed); trauma studies (Certificate). Part-time and evening/weekend programs available. *Faculty:* 5 full-time (2 women), 87 part-time/adjunct (50 women). *Students:* 501 full-time (395 women), 307 part-time (245 women); includes 382 minority (295 African Americans, 2 American Indian/Alaska Native, 6 Asian Americans or Pacific Islanders, 79 Hispanic Americans), 4 international. Average age 38. In 2009, 237 master's, 15 other advanced degrees awarded. *Degree requirements:* For master's, thesis, practicum/internship; for other advanced degree, thesis, practicum/internship. *Entrance requirements:* For master's, resume, 2 professional references; for other advanced degree, official transcripts, documents for transfer credit evaluation, resume, written personal statement/essay, 2 professional references, health insurance, immunizations form. Additional exam requirements/recommendations for international students: Required—TOEFL (minimum score 550 paper-based; 213 computer-based; 79 iBT); Recommended—IELTS (minimum score 6). *Application deadline:* Applications are processed on a rolling basis. Application fee: $30. Electronic applications accepted. *Expenses:* Contact institution. *Financial support:* In 2009–10, 686 students received support. Career-related internships or fieldwork, Federal Work-Study, and scholarships/grants available. Financial award applicants required to submit FAFSA. *Unit head:* Dr. Niti Seth, Dean, 617-873-0208, Fax: 617-349-3561, E-mail: nseth@cambridgecollege.edu. *Application contact:* Stephen Lyons, Director of Enrollment, Graduate and N.I.T.E. Programs, 617-868-1000, Fax: 617-349-3561, E-mail: stephen.lyons@cambridgecollege.edu.

Cameron University, Office of Graduate Studies, Program in Behavioral Sciences, Lawton, OK 73505-6377. Offers MS. Part-time and evening/weekend programs available. *Degree requirements:* For master's, comprehensive exam, thesis optional. *Entrance requirements:* Additional exam requirements/recommendations for international students: Required—TOEFL (minimum score 550 paper-based; 213 computer-based). Electronic applications accepted. *Faculty research:* Student burnout, attention deficit hyperactivity disorder, group decision making, counseling outcomes, smoking cessation.

Capella University, Harold Abel School of Psychology, Minneapolis, MN 55402. Offers child and adolescent development (MS); clinical psychology (MS, Psy D); counseling psychology (MS); educational psychology (MS, PhD); evaluation, research, and measurement (MS); general psychology (MS, PhD); industrial/organizational psychology (MS, PhD); leadership coaching psychology (MS); organizational leader development (MS); school psychology (MS); sport psychology (MS). Part-time and evening/weekend programs available. Postbaccalaureate distance learning degree programs offered (minimal on-campus study). Terminal master's awarded for partial completion of doctoral program. *Degree requirements:* For master's, thesis optional, project; for doctorate, thesis/dissertation. *Entrance requirements:* For degree, master's degree in school psychology. Additional exam requirements/recommendations for international students: Required—TOEFL (minimum score 550 paper-based; 213 computer-based), TWE (minimum score 4); Recommended—IELTS. Electronic applications accepted.

Cardinal Stritch University, College of Arts and Sciences, Department of Psychology, Milwaukee, WI 53217-3985. Offers clinical psychology (MA). Part-time and evening/weekend programs available. *Degree requirements:* For master's, thesis, portfolio, clinical practicum. *Entrance requirements:* For master's, GRE General Test, GRE Subject Test (psychology), interview, minimum GPA of 3.0, 3 letters of recommendation.

Carleton University, Faculty of Graduate Studies, Faculty of Arts and Social Sciences, Department of Psychology, Ottawa, ON K1S 5B6, Canada. Offers neuroscience (M Sc); psychology (MA, PhD). Part-time programs available. *Degree requirements:* For master's, thesis; for doctorate, comprehensive exam, thesis/dissertation. *Entrance requirements:* For master's, honors degree; for doctorate, GRE, master's degree. Additional exam requirements/recommendations for international students: Required—TOEFL. *Faculty research:* Behavioral neuroscience, social and personality psychology, cognitive/perception, developmental psychology, computer user research and evaluation, forensic psychology, health psychology.

Carlos Albizu University, Graduate Programs, San Juan, PR 00901. Offers clinical psychology (MS, PhD, Psy D); general psychology (PhD); industrial/organizational psychology (MS, PhD); speech and language pathology (MS). *Accreditation:* APA (one or more programs are accredited). Part-time and evening/weekend programs available. Terminal master's awarded for partial completion of doctoral program. *Degree requirements:* For master's, one foreign language, comprehensive exam, thesis; for doctorate, one foreign language, comprehensive exam, thesis/dissertation, written qualifying exams. *Entrance requirements:* For master's, GRE General Test or EXADEP, interview; minimum GPA of 3.0 (industrial/organizational psychology), 3.25 (speech and language pathology); for doctorate, GRE General Test or EXADEP, interview; minimum GPA of 3.0 (industrial/organizational psychology), 3.25 (PhD and Psy D in clinical psychology). *Faculty research:* Psychotherapeutic techniques for Hispanics, psychology of the aged, school dropouts, stress, violence.

Carlos Albizu University, Miami Campus, Graduate Programs, Miami, FL 33172-2209. Offers clinical psychology (Psy D); entrepreneurship (MBA); exceptional student education (MS); industrial/organizational psychology (MS); marriage and family therapy (MS); mental health counseling (MS); nonprofit management (MBA); organizational management (MBA); psychology (MS); school counseling (MS); teaching English as a second language (MS). *Accreditation:* APA. Part-time and evening/weekend programs available. *Faculty:* 23 full-time (13 women), 41 part-time/adjunct (21 women). *Students:* 529 full-time (420 women), 171 part-time (139 women); includes 551 minority (55 African Americans, 1 American Indian/Alaska Native, 5 Asian Americans or Pacific Islanders, 490 Hispanic Americans). Average age 37. 278 applicants, 57% accepted, 142 enrolled. In 2009, 139 master's, 26 doctorates awarded. Terminal master's awarded for partial completion of doctoral program. *Degree requirements:* For master's, one foreign language, comprehensive exam, integrative project (MBA), research project (exceptional student education, teaching English as a second language); for doctorate, one foreign language, comprehensive exam, internship, project. *Entrance requirements:* For master's, 3 letters of recommendation, interview, minimum GPA of 3.0, resume; for doctorate, 3 letters of recommendation, minimum GPA of 3.0, resume, interview. *Application deadline:* For fall admission, 8/1 priority date for domestic students; for spring admission, 11/30 priority date for domestic students. Applications are processed on a rolling basis. Application fee: $50. Electronic applications accepted. *Expenses:* Tuition: Full-time $9090; part-time $505 per credit hour. Required fees: $298 per term. Tuition and fees vary according to course load, degree level and program. *Financial support:* In 2009–10, 127 students received support. Federal Work-Study, scholarships/grants, and tuition discounts available. Financial award application deadline: 6/1; financial award applicants required to submit FAFSA. *Faculty research:* Psychotherapy, forensic psychology, neuropsychology, marketing strategy, entrepreneurship, special education. *Unit head:* Dr. Carmen S. Roca, Chancellor, 305-593-1223 Ext. 120, Fax: 305-629-8052, E-mail: croca@albizu.edu. *Application contact:* Annalye Alonso, Secretary, 305-593-1223 Ext. 137, Fax: 305-593-1854, E-mail: aalonso@albizu.edu.

Carnegie Mellon University, College of Humanities and Social Sciences, Department of Psychology, Pittsburgh, PA 15213-3891. Offers cognitive neuroscience (PhD); cognitive psychology (PhD); developmental psychology (PhD); social/personality/health psychology (PhD). *Degree requirements:* For doctorate, comprehensive exam, thesis/dissertation. *Entrance requirements:* For doctorate, GRE General Test. Additional exam requirements/recommendations for international students: Required—TOEFL. *Faculty research:* Artificial intelligence, stress and the immune system, children's learning strategies, neural basis of cognition.

Case Western Reserve University, School of Graduate Studies, Department of Psychology, Cleveland, OH 44106. Offers clinical psychology (PhD); experimental psychology (PhD). *Accreditation:* APA. Part-time programs available. *Degree requirements:* For doctorate, thesis/dissertation, internship. *Entrance requirements:* For doctorate, GRE General Test, GRE Subject Test. Additional exam requirements/recommendations for international students: Required—TOEFL (minimum score 550 paper-based; 213 computer-based; 79 iBT). Electronic applications accepted. *Faculty research:* Adolescent suicide, cognitive processing, repressive responses, visual perception, impact of HIV infection, neuropsychology.

Castleton State College, Division of Graduate Studies, Department of Psychology, Castleton, VT 05735. Offers forensic psychology (MA). *Degree requirements:* For master's, thesis. *Entrance requirements:* For master's, GRE General Test, minimum undergraduate GPA of 3.5, previous course work in research methodology and statistics. Additional exam requirements/recommendations for international students: Required—TOEFL. *Expenses:* Tuition, state resident: full-time $10,290; part-time $429 per credit. Tuition, nonresident: full-time $15,420; part-time $643 per credit. One-time fee: $200 full-time. *Faculty research:* Psychology and law, juvenile delinquency, criminal psychology, correctional psychology, police psychology.

The Catholic University of America, School of Arts and Sciences, Department of Psychology, Washington, DC 20064. Offers applied experimental psychology (PhD); clinical psychology (PhD); general psychology (MA); human factors (MA); MA/JD. *Accreditation:* APA (one or more programs are accredited). Part-time programs available. *Faculty:* 12 full-time (6 women), 3 part-time/adjunct (0 women). *Students:* 40 full-time (25 women), 38 part-time (33 women); includes 14 minority (5 African Americans, 4 Asian Americans or Pacific Islanders, 5 Hispanic Americans), 1 international. Average age 29. 200 applicants, 36% accepted, 25 enrolled. In 2009, 16 master's, 6 doctorates awarded. *Degree requirements:* For master's, comprehensive exam, thesis (for some programs); for doctorate, comprehensive exam, thesis/dissertation. *Entrance requirements:* For master's, GRE General Test, 3 letters of recommendation; for doctorate, GRE General Test, GRE Subject Test, statement of purpose, official copies of academic transcripts, three letters of recommendation. Additional exam requirements/recommendations for international students: Required—TOEFL (minimum score 580 paper-based; 237 computer-based). *Application deadline:* For fall admission, 8/1 priority date for domestic students, 7/15 for international students; for spring admission, 12/1 priority date for domestic students, 10/15 for international students. Applications are processed on a rolling basis. Application fee: $55. Electronic applications accepted. *Expenses:* Tuition: Full-time $31,740; part-time $1245 per credit hour. Required fees: $50; $25 per semester hour. One-time fee: $425. *Financial support:* Fellowships, research assistantships, teaching assistantships, Federal Work-Study, scholarships/grants, tuition waivers (full and partial), and unspecified assistantships available. Financial award application deadline: 2/1; financial award applicants required to submit FAFSA. *Faculty research:* Clinical psychology, applied cognitive science, psychopathology, cognitive neuroscience, psychotherapy. Total annual research expenditures: $409,988. *Unit head:* Dr. Marc M. Sebrechts, Chair, 202-319-5757, Fax: 202-319-6263, E-mail: sebrechts@cua.edu. *Application contact:* Julie Schwing, Director of Graduate Admissions, 202-319-5057, Fax: 202-319-6533, E-mail: cua-admissions@cua.edu.

Central Connecticut State University, School of Graduate Studies, School of Arts and Sciences, Department of Psychology, New Britain, CT 06050-4010. Offers community psychology (MA); general psychology (MA); health psychology (MA). Part-time and evening/weekend programs available. *Faculty:* 20 full-time (13 women), 22 part-time/adjunct (7 women). *Students:* 21 full-time (19 women), 31 part-time (27 women); includes 9 minority (4 African Americans, 5 Hispanic Americans). Average age 27. 49 applicants, 43% accepted, 17 enrolled. In 2009, 8 master's awarded. *Degree requirements:* For master's, comprehensive exam, thesis or alternative. *Entrance requirements:* For master's, minimum undergraduate GPA of 2.7, essay. Additional exam requirements/recommendations for international students: Required—TOEFL. *Application deadline:* For fall admission, 4/25 for domestic students; for spring admission, 12/1 for domestic students. Applications are processed on a rolling basis. Application fee: $50. Electronic applications accepted. *Expenses:* Tuition, area resident: Full-time $4662; part-time $440 per credit. Tuition, state resident: full-time $6994; part-time $440 per credit. Tuition, nonresident: full-time $12,988; part-time $440 per credit. Required fees: $3606. One-time fee: $62 part-time. *Financial support:* In 2009–10, 8 students received support, including 6 research assistantships; career-related internships or fieldwork, Federal Work-Study, scholarships/grants, and unspecified assistantships also available. Support available to part-time students. Financial award application deadline: 3/1; financial award applicants required to submit FAFSA. *Faculty research:* Clinical psychology, general psychology, child development, cognitive development, drugs/behavior. *Unit head:* Dr. Laura Bowman, Chair, 860-832-3100. *Application contact:* Dr. Laura Bowman, Chair, 860-832-3100.

Central Michigan University, College of Graduate Studies, College of Humanities and Social and Behavioral Sciences, Department of Psychology, Mount Pleasant, MI 48859. Offers clinical psychology (MA, PhD); experimental psychology (MS, PhD), including applied experimental psychology (PhD), experimental psychology (MS); industrial and organizational psychology (MA, PhD); neuroscience (MS, PhD); school psychology (PhD, S Psy S), including psychological services (S Psy S), school psychology (PhD). *Accreditation:* APA (one or more programs are accredited). Terminal master's awarded for partial completion of doctoral program. *Degree requirements:* For master's, thesis or alternative; for doctorate, thesis/dissertation; for S Psy S, thesis. *Entrance requirements:* For doctorate, GRE. Electronic applications accepted. *Faculty research:* Experimental psychology; clinical psychology; industrial/organizational psychology; school psychology; neuroscience.

Central Washington University, Graduate Studies and Research, College of the Sciences, Department of Psychology, Ellensburg, WA 98926. Offers experimental psychology (MS); mental health counseling (MS); school counseling (M Ed); school psychology (M Ed). Evening/weekend programs available. *Faculty:* 32 full-time (16 women). *Students:* 64 full-time (38 women), 17 part-time (11 women); includes 8 minority (1 African American, 2 American Indian/Alaska Native, 5 Hispanic Americans). 90 applicants, 59% accepted, 53 enrolled. In 2009, 23 master's awarded. *Degree requirements:* For master's, thesis. *Entrance requirements:* For master's, GRE General Test, minimum GPA of 3.0. Additional exam requirements/recommendations for international students: Required—TOEFL (minimum score 550 paper-based; 213 computer-based; 79 iBT). *Application deadline:* For fall admission, 2/1 for domestic students. Application fee: $50. *Expenses:* Tuition, state resident: full-time $7353; part-time $245 per credit. Tuition, nonresident: full-time $16,383; part-time $546 per credit. Required fees: $882. Tuition and fees vary according to degree level. *Financial support:* In 2009–10, 16 research assistantships with full and partial tuition reimbursements (averaging $9,145 per year) were awarded; career-related internships or fieldwork, Federal Work-Study, health care

Psychology—General

Central Washington University (continued)

benefits, and unspecified assistantships also available. Financial award application deadline: 3/1; financial award applicants required to submit FAFSA. *Unit head:* Dr. Stephanie Stein, Chair, 509-963-2381. *Application contact:* Justine Eason, Admissions Program Coordinator, 509-963-3103, Fax: 509-963-1799, E-mail: masters@cwu.edu.

Chestnut Hill College, School of Graduate Studies, Division of Psychology, Philadelphia, PA 19118-2693. Offers clinical and counseling psychology (MA, MS, CAS); clinical psychology (Psy D). Part-time and evening/weekend programs available. *Degree requirements:* For master's, thesis optional, practica; for doctorate, comprehensive exam, thesis/dissertation, internship, practica, clinical competency exam. *Entrance requirements:* For master's, GRE General Test, writing sample, letters of recommendation; for doctorate, GRE General Test, master's degree in clinical counseling or closely related field, transcripts, letters of recommendation, statement of professional goals, writing sample; for CAS, GRE General Test, official transcripts, letters of recommendation, statement of professional goals, writing sample. Additional exam requirements/recommendations for international students: Required—TOEFL (minimum score 500 paper-based; 213 computer-based). *Faculty research:* Adolescent development, trauma and sexual abuse, cultural diversity, family psychology and family therapy, psychodynamic therapy.

The Chicago School of Professional Psychology, Program in Applied Behavior Analysis, Chicago, IL 60610. Offers applied behavior analysis (Psy D); clinical psychology (applied behavior analysis specialization) (MA). *Students:* 104 full-time (88 women), 26 part-time (22 women); includes 17 African Americans, 4 Asian Americans or Pacific Islanders, 10 Hispanic Americans, 4 international. 105 applicants, 94% accepted, 59 enrolled. In 2009, 10 master's awarded. *Degree requirements:* For master's, thesis, practicum; for doctorate, thesis/dissertation, practicum. *Entrance requirements:* For doctorate, GRE. Additional exam requirements/recommendations for international students: Required—TOEFL. *Financial support:* In 2009–10, research assistantships (averaging $6,000 per year), teaching assistantships (averaging $6,000 per year) were awarded; Federal Work-Study, institutionally sponsored loans, and scholarships/grants also available. Financial award application deadline: 3/1; financial award applicants required to submit FAFSA. *Unit head:* Dr. Charles Merbitz, Department Chair, 312-329-6628, E-mail: cmerbitz@thechicagoschool.edu. *Application contact:* Andrea Schmoyer, Director of Admission, 312-329-6666, Fax: 312-644-3333, E-mail: admissions@thechicagoschool.edu.

The Chicago School of Professional Psychology, Program in Business Psychology, Chicago, IL 60610. Offers Psy D. *Students:* 63 full-time (35 women), 4 part-time (all women); includes 17 minority (10 African Americans, 4 Asian Americans or Pacific Islanders, 3 Hispanic Americans), 1 international. 33 applicants, 76% accepted, 19 enrolled. *Degree requirements:* For doctorate, thesis/dissertation optional. *Entrance requirements:* For doctorate, GRE. Additional exam requirements/recommendations for international students: Required—TOEFL. *Financial support:* In 2009–10, research assistantships (averaging $6,000 per year), teaching assistantships (averaging $6,000 per year) were awarded; Federal Work-Study and institutionally sponsored loans also available. Financial award application deadline: 3/1; financial award applicants required to submit FAFSA. *Unit head:* Dr. Ilianna Kwaske, Department Chair, 312-467-8601, E-mail: ikwaske@thechicagoschool.edu. *Application contact:* Andrea Schmoyer, Director of Admission, 312-329-6666, Fax: 312-644-3333, E-mail: admissions@thechicagoschool.edu.

The Chicago School of Professional Psychology, Program in Clinical Psychology, Chicago, IL 60610. Offers applied behavior analysis (MA); clinical psychology (Psy D); counseling (MA). *Students:* 341 full-time (268 women), 10 part-time (7 women); includes 52 minority (22 African Americans, 2 American Indian/Alaska Native, 15 Asian Americans or Pacific Islanders, 13 Hispanic Americans), 16 international. 452 applicants, 54% accepted, 106 enrolled. In 2009, 71 doctorates awarded. *Degree requirements:* For master's, thesis (for some programs); for doctorate, comprehensive exam, thesis/dissertation. *Entrance requirements:* For master's, minimum undergraduate GPA of 3.0, 1 course in psychology, 1 course in either statistics or research methods; for doctorate, GRE, 18 hours of psychology credit (including courses in statistics, normal psychology and human development); minimum GPA of 3.2. Additional exam requirements/recommendations for international students: Required—TOEFL. Electronic applications accepted. *Financial support:* In 2009–10, fellowships with partial tuition reimbursements (averaging $10,000 per year), research assistantships (averaging $6,000 per year), teaching assistantships (averaging $6,000 per year) were awarded; Federal Work-Study, institutionally sponsored loans, and scholarships/grants also available. Financial award application deadline: 3/1; financial award applicants required to submit FAFSA. *Unit head:* Dr. James Galezewski, Department Chair, 312-467-2169, E-mail: jgalezewski@thechicagoschool.edu. *Application contact:* Andrea Schmoyer, Director of Admission, 312-329-6666, Fax: 312-644-3333, E-mail: admissions@thechicagoschool.edu.

The Chicago School of Professional Psychology at Downtown Los Angeles, Applied Behavior Analysis, Los Angeles, CA 90017. Offers Psy D. *Students:* 35 full-time (28 women), 4 part-time (3 women); includes 18 minority (4 African Americans, 1 American Indian/Alaska Native, 5 Asian Americans or Pacific Islanders, 8 Hispanic Americans). 61 applicants, 97% accepted. *Unit head:* Dr. Rachel Findel-Pyles, Lead Faculty, 312-342-2492, E-mail: rtarbox@thechicagoschool.edu. *Application contact:* Heather LaBelle, Director of Admissions, 213-615-7200, Fax: 213-627-1985, E-mail: admissions@thechicagoschool.edu.

The Chicago School of Professional Psychology at Downtown Los Angeles, Clinical Psychology, Los Angeles, CA 90017. Offers applied behavior analysis (MA); clinical psychology (Psy D); marital and family therapy (MA). *Students:* 196 full-time (168 women), 8 part-time (6 women); includes 75 minority (23 African Americans, 1 American Indian/Alaska Native, 23 Asian Americans or Pacific Islanders, 28 Hispanic Americans), 1 international. 152 applicants, 94% accepted, 57 enrolled. *Application contact:* Heather LaBelle, Director of Admissions, 213-615-7200, Fax: 213-627-1985, E-mail: admissions@thechicagoschool.edu.

The Chicago School of Professional Psychology at Irvine, Psychology, Irvine, CA 92612. Offers generalist (Psy D); psychodynamic psychotherapy (Psy D). *Students:* 9 full-time (7 women); includes 4 minority (1 American Indian/Alaska Native, 1 Asian American or Pacific Islander, 2 Hispanic Americans). *Unit head:* Dr. Terry Webster, Lead Faculty, E-mail: twebster@thechicagoschool.edu. *Application contact:* Betty Vu, Director of Admissions, 949-737-5460, Fax: 949-737-5467, E-mail: admissions@thechicagoschool.edu.

The Chicago School of Professional Psychology at Westwood, Psychology, Los Angeles, CA 90024. Offers generalist (Psy D); psychodynamic psychotherapy (Psy D). *Students:* 40 full-time (33 women); includes 13 minority (6 African Americans, 2 Asian Americans or Pacific Islanders, 5 Hispanic Americans). *Application contact:* Heather LaBelle, Director of Admissions, 310-208-4240, Fax: 310-208-0684, E-mail: admissions@thechicagoschool.edu.

The Chicago School of Professional Psychology: Online, International Psychology, Chicago, IL 60654. Offers PhD. *Students:* 22 part-time (14 women); includes 2 minority (1 Asian American or Pacific Islander, 1 Hispanic American), 1 international. *Unit head:* Dr. Robert Clark, Department Chair, 312-467-2513, E-mail: rclark@thechicagoschool.edu. *Application contact:* Pari Pinyo, Director of Online Admission, 312-329-6666, Fax: 312-644-3333, E-mail: admissions@thechicagoschool.edu.

The Chicago School of Professional Psychology: Online, Psychology, Chicago, IL 60654. Offers child and adolescent psychology (MA); generalist (MA); gerontology (MA); international psychology (MA); organizational leadership (MA); sport and exercise psychology (MA). *Students:* 142 part-time (113 women); includes 25 minority (9 African Americans, 1 American Indian/Alaska Native, 5 Asian Americans or Pacific Islanders, 10 Hispanic Americans), 1 international. *Unit head:* Dr. Ilianna Kwaske, Dean of Academic Affairs, 312-467-8601, E-mail: ikwaske@thechicagoschool.edu. *Application contact:* Pari Pinyo, Director of Online Admissions, 312-329-6666, Fax: 312-644-3333, E-mail: admissions@thechicagoschool.edu.

The Citadel, The Military College of South Carolina, Citadel Graduate College, Department of Psychology, Charleston, SC 29409. Offers psychology (MA), including clinical counseling; school psychology (Ed S), including school psychology. Part-time and evening/weekend programs available. *Faculty:* 10 full-time (3 women), 2 part-time/adjunct (1 woman). *Students:* 69 full-time (58 women), 62 part-time (56 women); includes 7 minority (4 African Americans, 1 Asian American or Pacific Islander, 2 Hispanic Americans), 1 international. Average age 27. In 2009, 16 master's, 14 other advanced degrees awarded. *Degree requirements:* For master's, comprehensive exam, thesis optional; for Ed S, comprehensive exam, thesis, internship. *Entrance requirements:* For master's, GRE (minimum score 1000) or MAT (minimum score 410), minimum undergraduate GPA of 3.0; 2 letters of reference; for Ed S, GRE (minimum 1000) or MAT with prior permission (minimum 410), minimum undergraduate or graduate GPA of 3.0; 2 letters of reference. Additional exam requirements/recommendations for international students: Required—TOEFL (minimum score 550 paper-based; 213 computer-based). *Application deadline:* For fall admission, 3/15 for domestic students. Application fee: $30. Electronic applications accepted. *Expenses:* Tuition, state resident: part-time $400 per credit hour. Tuition, nonresident: part-time $657 per credit hour. Required fees: $40 per term. *Financial support:* Research assistantships, career-related internships or fieldwork, health care benefits, and unspecified assistantships available. Support available to part-time students. Financial award application deadline: 7/1; financial award applicants required to submit FAFSA. *Faculty research:* Ostracism and social exclusion, bullying, social concerns of special-needs children, childhood obesity, phantom limb pain, validation of psychological tests, perfectionism, school-based interventions with at-risk children. *Unit head:* Dr. P. Michael Politano, Department Head, 843-953-5230, Fax: 843-953-6797, E-mail: politanom@citadel.edu. *Application contact:* Dr. William G. Johnson, Program Director, 843-953-6827, Fax: 843-953-6769, E-mail: will.johnson@citadel.edu.

City College of the City University of New York, Graduate School, College of Liberal Arts and Science, Division of Social Science, Department of Psychology, New York, NY 10031-9198. Offers clinical psychology (PhD); experimental cognition (PhD); general psychology (MA); mental health counseling (MA). *Accreditation:* APA (one or more programs are accredited). Part-time programs available. *Degree requirements:* For master's, one foreign language, comprehensive exam, thesis. *Entrance requirements:* For master's, GRE. Additional exam requirements/recommendations for international students: Required—TOEFL (minimum score 550 paper-based; 79 iBT). Electronic applications accepted. *Faculty research:* Social/personality psychology, physiological psychology, cognition and development.

Claremont Graduate University, Graduate Programs, School of Behavioral and Organizational Sciences, Department of Psychology, Claremont, CA 91711-6160. Offers advanced study in evaluation (Certificate); cognitive psychology (MA, PhD); developmental psychology (MA, PhD); evaluation and applied research methods (MA, PhD); health behavior research and evaluation (MA, PhD); human resource development and evaluation (MA); industrial/organizational psychology (MA, PhD); organizational behavior (MA, PhD); organizational psychology (MA, PhD); social psychology (MA, PhD); MBA/PhD. Part-time programs available. *Faculty:* 17 full-time (7 women), 1 part-time/adjunct (0 women). *Students:* 231 full-time (155 women), 25 part-time (18 women); includes 62 minority (13 African Americans, 1 American Indian/Alaska Native, 31 Asian Americans or Pacific Islanders, 17 Hispanic Americans), 21 international. Average age 30. In 2009, 37 master's, 12 doctorates, 8 other advanced degrees awarded. Terminal master's awarded for partial completion of doctoral program. *Entrance requirements:* For master's and doctorate, GRE General Test. Additional exam requirements/recommendations for international students: Required—TOEFL (minimum score 550 paper-based; 213 computer-based; 80 iBT). *Application deadline:* For fall admission, 1/15 priority date for domestic students. Applications are processed on a rolling basis. Application fee: $60. Electronic applications accepted. *Expenses:* Tuition: Full-time $35,046; part-time $1524 per credit. Required fees: $161 per semester. *Financial support:* Fellowships, research assistantships, teaching assistantships, Federal Work-Study, institutionally sponsored loans, scholarships/grants, and tuition waivers (full and partial) available. Support available to part-time students. Financial award application deadline: 2/15; financial award applicants required to submit FAFSA. *Faculty research:* Social intervention, diversity in organizations, eyewitness memory, aging and cognition, drug policy. *Unit head:* Stewart Donaldson, Dean, 909-607-9001, Fax: 909-621-8905, E-mail: stewart.donaldson@cgu.edu. *Application contact:* Paul Thomas, Director, External Affairs, 909-607-9016, Fax: 909-621-8905, E-mail: paul.thomas@cgu.edu.

Clark University, Graduate School, Department of Psychology, Worcester, MA 01610-1477. Offers clinical psychology (PhD); developmental psychology (PhD); social-personality psychology (PhD). *Accreditation:* APA. *Faculty:* 17 full-time (10 women), 1 (woman) part-time/adjunct. *Students:* 46 full-time (36 women); includes 6 minority (1 African American, 1 Asian American or Pacific Islander, 4 Hispanic Americans), 7 international. Average age 29. 175 applicants, 10% accepted, 9 enrolled. In 2009, 10 doctorates awarded. *Degree requirements:* For doctorate, thesis/dissertation. *Entrance requirements:* For doctorate, GRE General Test. Additional exam requirements/recommendations for international students: Required—TOEFL. *Application deadline:* For fall admission, 12/28 priority date for domestic students. Applications are processed on a rolling basis. Application fee: $50. *Expenses:* Tuition: Full-time $34,900; part-time $4362.50 per course. *Financial support:* In 2009–10, 2 fellowships with full tuition reimbursements (averaging $15,700 per year), 11 research assistantships with full tuition reimbursements (averaging $15,700 per year), 15 teaching assistantships with full tuition reimbursements (averaging $15,700 per year) were awarded; career-related internships or fieldwork and tuition waivers (full and partial) also available. *Faculty research:* Development of psychological processes in sociocultural context, conceptualizing and reasoning, symbolization, psychotherapy, metaphor, emotions and personalities. Total annual research expenditures: $1.5 million. *Unit head:* Dr. Marianne Wiser, Chair, 508-793-7273. *Application contact:* Peggy Moskowitz, Graduate School Secretary, 508-793-7274, Fax: 508-793-7265, E-mail: psychology@clarku.edu.

Clemson University, Graduate School, College of Business and Behavioral Science, Department of Psychology, Program in Applied Psychology, Clemson, SC 29634. Offers MS. *Students:* 8 full-time (all women), 1 part-time (0 women). Average age 27. 40 applicants, 5% accepted, 2 enrolled. In 2009, 4 master's awarded. *Degree requirements:* For master's, thesis, internship. *Entrance requirements:* For master's, GRE General Test, 18 hours of course work in psychology. Additional exam requirements/recommendations for international students: Required—TOEFL. *Application deadline:* For fall admission, 12/15 for domestic students, 4/15 for international students; for spring admission, 9/15 for international students. Applications are processed on a rolling basis. Application fee: $70 ($80 for international students). Electronic applications accepted. *Expenses:* Contact institution. *Financial support:* In 2009–10, 6 students received support, including 1 fellowship with full and partial tuition reimbursement available (averaging $9,000 per year), 1 research assistantship with partial tuition reimbursement available (averaging $12,310 per year), 5 teaching assistantships with partial tuition reimbursements available (averaging $11,200 per year); career-related internships or fieldwork, institutionally sponsored loans, scholarships/grants, health care benefits, and unspecified assistantships also available. Support available to part-time students. Financial award application deadline: 3/15; financial award applicants required to submit FAFSA. *Faculty research:* Personnel selection and validation; performance evaluation; training, motivation and decision making; human factors; TOEFL. *Unit head:* Dr. Patrick Raymark, Chair, 864-656-4715, Fax: 864-656-0358, E-mail: praymar@clemson.edu. *Application contact:* Dr. Robert Sinclair, Graduate Program Coordinator, 864-656-3931, Fax: 864-656-0358, E-mail: rsincla@clemson.edu.

Clemson University, Graduate School, College of Business and Behavioral Science, Department of Psychology, Program in Human Factors Psychology, Clemson, SC 29634. Offers PhD. *Students:* 13 full-time (6 women), 2 part-time (both women). Average age 28. 25 applicants, 8% accepted, 1 enrolled. *Degree requirements:* For doctorate, thesis/dissertation. *Entrance requirements:* For doctorate, GRE General Test. Additional exam requirements/recommendations for international students: Required—TOEFL. *Application deadline:* For fall admission, 12/15 for domestic students. Applications are processed on a rolling basis. Application fee: $70 ($80 for international students). Electronic applications accepted. *Expenses:* Contact institution. *Financial support:* In 2009–10, 12 students received support, including 6 research assistantships with partial tuition reimbursements available (averaging $14,217 per year), 6 teaching assistantships with partial tuition reimbursements available (averaging $13,417 per year); fellowships with full and partial tuition reimbursements available, career-related internships or fieldwork, institutionally sponsored loans, scholarships/grants, health care benefits, and unspecified assistantships also available. Support available to part-time students. *Unit head:* Dr. Patrick Raymark, Chair, 864-656-4715, Fax: 864-656-0358, E-mail: praymar@clemson.edu. *Application contact:* Dr. Robert Sinclair, 864-656-3931, Fax: 864-656-0358, E-mail: rsincla@clemson.edu.

Cleveland State University, College of Graduate Studies, College of Science, Department of Psychology, Cleveland, OH 44115. Offers adult development and aging (PhD); clinical psychology (MA); consumer/industrial research (MA); diversity management (MA); experimental research psychology (MA); school psychology (Psy S). *Degree requirements:* For master's, comprehensive exam (for some programs), thesis (for some programs); for doctorate, comprehensive exam, thesis/dissertation; for Psy S, internship. *Entrance requirements:* For master's and doctorate, GRE General Test. Additional exam requirements/recommendations for international students: Required—TOEFL (minimum score 525 paper-based; 197 computer-based). Electronic applications accepted. *Faculty research:* Cognitive and social psychology, consumer psychology, clinical psychology, school psychology, aging.

The College at Brockport, State University of New York, School of Science and Mathematics, Department of Psychology, Brockport, NY 14420-2997. Offers MA. Part-time programs available. *Students:* 22 full-time (15 women), 4 part-time (3 women); includes 2 minority (1 Asian American or Pacific Islander, 1 Hispanic American). 34 applicants, 44% accepted, 14 enrolled. In 2009, 7 master's awarded. *Degree requirements:* For master's, thesis optional. *Entrance requirements:* For master's, GRE General Test, letters of recommendation, interview, minimum GPA of 3.0. Additional exam requirements/recommendations for international students: Required—TOEFL (minimum score 550 paper-based; 213 computer-based; 79 iBT). *Application deadline:* For fall admission, 4/1 priority date for domestic and international students. Application fee: $50. Electronic applications accepted. *Expenses:* Tuition, state resident: full-time $8370; part-time $349 per credit. Tuition, nonresident: full-time $13,250; part-time $522 per credit. *Financial support:* In 2009–10, 2 teaching assistantships with full tuition reimbursements (averaging $6,000 per year) were awarded; Federal Work-Study, scholarships/grants, and unspecified assistantships also available. Support available to part-time students. Financial award application deadline: 3/15; financial award applicants required to submit FAFSA. *Faculty research:* Positive psychology, decision-making and applied behavior analysis, family processes and close relationships, cognition and neuropsychology, social/personality and industrial/organizational psychology. *Unit head:* Dr. Melissa M. Brown, Chairperson, 585-395-2488, Fax: 585-395-2116, E-mail: mmbrown@brockport.edu. *Application contact:* Dr. Janet Gillespie, Graduate Director, 585-395-2433, Fax: 585-395-2116, E-mail: jgillesp@brockport.edu.

College of Saint Elizabeth, Department of Psychology, Morristown, NJ 07960-6989. Offers counseling psychology (MA); forensic psychology (MA); student affairs in higher education (Certificate). Part-time and evening/weekend programs available. *Faculty:* 5 full-time (2 women), 10 part-time/adjunct (9 women). *Students:* 23 full-time (19 women), 73 part-time (67 women); includes 25 minority (12 African Americans, 2 Asian Americans or Pacific Islanders, 11 Hispanic Americans), 2 international. Average age 32. 104 applicants, 58% accepted, 47 enrolled. In 2009, 10 master's awarded. *Degree requirements:* For master's, thesis or alternative, portfolio. *Entrance requirements:* For master's, minimum GPA of 3.0, BA in psychology (preferred), 12 credits of course work in psychology. *Application deadline:* For fall admission, 4/14 priority date for domestic students; for spring admission, 11/15 for domestic students. Applications are processed on a rolling basis. Application fee: $35. Electronic applications accepted. *Expenses:* Tuition: Part-time $797 per credit hour. Required fees: $65 per credit hour. *Financial support:* Career-related internships or fieldwork, tuition waivers (partial), and unspecified assistantships available. Support available to part-time students. Financial award application deadline: 3/15; financial award applicants required to submit FAFSA. *Faculty research:* Family systems, dissociative identity disorder, multicultural counseling, outcomes assessment. *Unit head:* Dr. Valerie Scott, Director of the Graduate Program in Counseling Psychology, 973-290-4102, Fax: 973-290-4676, E-mail: vscott@cse.edu. *Application contact:* Donna Tatarka, Dean of Admission, 973-290-4705, Fax: 973-290-4710, E-mail: dtatarka@cse.edu.

College of St. Joseph, Graduate Programs, Division of Psychology and Human Services, Rutland, VT 05701-3899. Offers alcohol and substance abuse counseling (MS); clinical mental health counseling (MS); clinical psychology (MS); community counseling (MS); school guidance counseling (MS). Part-time and evening/weekend programs available. *Degree requirements:* For master's, comprehensive exam, thesis. *Entrance requirements:* For master's, 2 letters of reference, interview. Electronic applications accepted. *Expenses:* Tuition: Full-time $13,500; part-time $350 per credit. Required fees: $45 per term. One-time fee: $445. Tuition and fees vary according to program.

Colorado State University, Graduate School, College of Natural Sciences, Department of Psychology, Fort Collins, CO 80523-1876. Offers MS, PhD. *Accreditation:* APA. Post-baccalaureate distance learning degree programs offered (no on-campus study). *Faculty:* 25 full-time (12 women), 2 part-time/adjunct (0 women). *Students:* 65 full-time (45 women), 49 part-time (33 women); includes 25 minority (1 African American, 5 American Indian/Alaska Native, 10 Asian Americans or Pacific Islanders, 9 Hispanic Americans), 2 international. Average age 28. 359 applicants, 6% accepted, 20 enrolled. In 2009, 12 master's, 16 doctorates awarded. Terminal master's awarded for partial completion of doctoral program. *Degree requirements:* For master's, comprehensive exam (for some programs), thesis (for some programs); for doctorate, comprehensive exam, thesis/dissertation. *Entrance requirements:* For master's, GRE General Test, GRE Subject Test, minimum GPA of 3.0; transcripts; 3 letters of recommendation; resume or curriculum vitae; statement of interest; sample of scientific writing (for some areas of study); for doctorate, GRE General Test, GRE Subject Test, minimum GPA of 3.0; 3 letters of recommendation; resume or curriculum vitae; sample of scientific writing (for some areas of study). Additional exam requirements/recommendations for international students: Required—TOEFL (minimum score 550 paper-based; 213 computer-based; 80 iBT). *Application deadline:* For fall admission, 9/15 priority date for domestic and international students; for spring admission, 1/15 priority date for domestic and international students. Applications are processed on a rolling basis. Application fee: $50. Electronic applications accepted. *Expenses:* Tuition, state resident: full-time $6434; part-time $359.10 per credit. Tuition, nonresident: full-time $18,116; part-time $1006.45 per credit. Required fees: $1496; $83 per credit. *Financial support:* In 2009–10, 76 students received support, including 3 fellowships (averaging $39,567 per year), 17 research assistantships with full tuition reimbursements available (averaging $6,853 per year), 56 teaching assistantships with full tuition reimbursements available (averaging $10,434 per year); health care benefits also available. Financial award application deadline: 1/15; financial award applicants required to submit FAFSA. *Faculty research:* Environmental psychology, cognitive learning, health psychology, counseling and clinical issues, industrial and organizational psychology. Total annual research expenditures: $4.3 million. *Unit head:* Dr. Ernest L. Chavez, Chair and Professor, 970-491-6364, Fax: 970-491-1032, E-mail: ernest.chavez@colostate.edu. *Application contact:* Joanne Moran, Program Assistant I, 970-491-7298, Fax: 970-491-1032, E-mail: joanne.moran@colostate.edu.

Columbia University, Graduate School of Arts and Sciences, Division of Natural Sciences, Department of Psychology, New York, NY 10027. Offers experimental psychology (M Phil, MA, PhD); psychobiology (M Phil, MA, PhD); social psychology (M Phil, MA, PhD); JD/MA; JD/PhD; MD/PhD. *Degree requirements:* For master's, thesis; for doctorate, thesis/dissertation. *Entrance requirements:* For master's and doctorate, GRE General Test. Additional exam requirements/recommendations for international students: Required—TOEFL.

Concordia University, School of Graduate Studies, Faculty of Arts and Science, Department of Psychology, Program in Psychology (General), Montréal, QC H3G 1M8, Canada. Offers MA, PhD. *Degree requirements:* For master's, comprehensive exam, thesis; for doctorate, comprehensive exam, thesis/dissertation. *Entrance requirements:* For master's, GRE General Test, GRE Subject Test, honors degree in psychology or equivalent; for doctorate, master's degree in psychology. *Faculty research:* Appetitive motivation and drug dependence, human information processing, psychology of physical activity.

Concordia University Chicago, College of Graduate and Innovative Programs, Program in Psychology, River Forest, IL 60305-1499. Offers MA. Part-time and evening/weekend programs available. *Degree requirements:* For master's, comprehensive exam, thesis optional. *Entrance requirements:* For master's, minimum GPA of 2.9. Additional exam requirements/recommendations for international students: Required—TOEFL (minimum score 550 paper-based; 195 computer-based). Electronic applications accepted. *Faculty research:* Lutheran high school counseling research.

Concordia University Wisconsin, Graduate Programs, Department of Psychology, Mequon, WI 53097-2402. Offers professional counseling (MPC).

Concord University, Graduate Studies, Athens, WV 24712-1000. Offers behavioral science (M Ed); educational leadership and supervision (M Ed); geography (M Ed); health promotion (M Ed); reading specialist (M Ed); social studies (M Ed). Postbaccalaureate distance learning degree programs offered. *Entrance requirements:* For master's, GRE or MAT, baccalaureate degree with minimum GPA of 2.5 GPA from regionally accredited institution; teaching license; 2 letters of recommendation.

Connecticut College, Graduate School, Department of Psychology, New London, CT 06320-4196. Offers MA. Part-time programs available. *Degree requirements:* For master's, comprehensive exam (for some programs), thesis. *Entrance requirements:* For master's, GRE General Test. Additional exam requirements/recommendations for international students: Required—TOEFL (minimum score 600 paper-based). *Expenses:* Tuition: Full-time $11,480; part-time $1640 per course. *Faculty research:* Behavioral medicine, personality-social psychology, clinical, neuroscience/psychobiology.

Cornell University, Graduate School, Graduate Fields of Arts and Sciences, Field of Psychology, Ithaca, NY 14853-0001. Offers biopsychology (PhD); human experimental psychology (PhD); personality and social psychology (PhD). *Faculty:* 49 full-time (17 women). *Students:* 37 full-time (24 women); includes 5 minority (1 African American, 2 Asian Americans or Pacific Islanders, 2 Hispanic Americans), 10 international. Average age 29. 221 applicants, 4% accepted, 8 enrolled. In 2009, 3 doctorates awarded. *Degree requirements:* For doctorate, comprehensive exam, thesis/dissertation, 2 semesters of teaching experience. *Entrance requirements:* For doctorate, GRE General Test, 3 letters of recommendation. Additional exam requirements/recommendations for international students: Required—TOEFL (minimum score 550 paper-based; 213 computer-based; 77 iBT). *Application deadline:* For fall admission, 12/15 for domestic students. Application fee: $70. Electronic applications accepted. *Expenses:* Tuition: Full-time $29,500. Required fees: $70. Full-time tuition and fees vary according to degree level, program and student level. *Financial support:* In 2009–10, 36 students received support, including 6 fellowships with full tuition reimbursements available, 2 teaching assistantships with full tuition reimbursements available; research assistantships with full tuition reimbursements available, institutionally sponsored loans, scholarships/grants, health care benefits, tuition waivers (full and partial), and unspecified assistantships also available. Financial award applicants required to submit FAFSA. *Faculty research:* Sensory and perceptual systems, social cognition, cognitive development, quantitative and computational modeling, behavioral neuroscience. *Unit head:* Director of Graduate Studies, 607-255-6364, Fax: 607-255-8433. *Application contact:* Graduate Field Assistant, 607-255-3834, Fax: 607-255-8433, E-mail: psychapp@cornell.edu.

Dalhousie University, Faculty of Science, Department of Psychology, Halifax, NS B3H 4R2, Canada. Offers clinical psychology (PhD); psychology (M Sc, PhD); psychology/neuroscience (M Sc, PhD). *Accreditation:* APA (one or more programs are accredited). *Faculty:* 30 full-time (8 women), 34 part-time/adjunct (14 women). *Students:* 56 full-time (35 women); includes 2 minority (both Asian Americans or Pacific Islanders). 200 applicants, 8% accepted. In 2009, 8 master's, 7 doctorates awarded. *Degree requirements:* For master's, thesis; for doctorate, thesis/dissertation. *Entrance requirements:* For doctorate, GRE General Test. Additional exam requirements/recommendations for international students: Required—TOEFL, IELTS, CANTEST, CAEL, or Michigan English Language Assessment Battery. Application fee: $70. Electronic applications accepted. *Financial support:* In 2009–10, 19 fellowships, 26 teaching assistantships (averaging $1,853 per year) were awarded; career-related internships or fieldwork, scholarships/grants, and health care benefits also available. Financial award application deadline: 2/1. *Faculty research:* Physiological psychology, psychology of learning, learning and behavior, forensic clinical health psychology, development perception and cognition. Total annual research expenditures: $1.9 million. *Unit head:* Dr. Tracy Taylor-Helmick, Graduate Coordinator, 902-494-3001, Fax: 902-494-6585, E-mail: tracy.taylor.helmick@dal.ca. *Application contact:* Mary Macconnachie, Graduate Secretary, 902-494-3839, Fax: 902-494-6585, E-mail: mary.macconnachie@dal.ca.

Dartmouth College, Arts and Sciences Graduate Programs, Department of Psychological and Brain Sciences, Hanover, NH 03755. Offers cognitive neuroscience (PhD); psychology (PhD). *Faculty:* 20 full-time (6 women). *Students:* 32 full-time (16 women); includes 4 minority (1 African American, 2 Asian Americans or Pacific Islanders, 1 Hispanic American), 8 international. Average age 26. 88 applicants, 15% accepted, 8 enrolled. In 2009, 1 doctorate awarded. *Degree requirements:* For doctorate, thesis/dissertation. *Entrance requirements:* For doctorate, GRE General Test, GRE Subject Test. Additional exam requirements/recommendations for international students: Required—TOEFL. *Application deadline:* For fall admission, 1/15 priority date for domestic students. Application fee: $40. *Financial support:* In 2009–10, 24 students received support, including fellowships with full tuition reimbursements available (averaging $23,832 per year), research assistantships with full tuition reimbursements available (averaging $23,832 per year), teaching assistantships (averaging $23,832 per year); institutionally sponsored loans, traineeships, tuition waivers (full), and unspecified assistantships also available. *Faculty research:* Behavioral neuroscience, cognitive neuroscience, cognitive science, social/personality psychology. *Unit head:* Dr. Howard C. Hughes, Chair, 603-646-3181, Fax: 603-646-1419, E-mail: howard.hughes@dartmouth.edu. *Application contact:* Nancy Tenney, Department Administrator, 603-646-3181, E-mail: nancy.tenney@dartmouth.edu.

DePaul University, College of Liberal Arts and Sciences, Department of Psychology, Chicago, IL 60604-2287. Offers clinical psychology (MA, PhD), including child clinical psychology, community clinical psychology; experimental psychology (MA, PhD); general psychology (MS); industrial/organizational psychology (MA, PhD); MA/PhD. *Accreditation:* APA (one or more programs are accredited). *Faculty:* 31 full-time (19 women), 6 part-time/adjunct (4 women). *Students:* 59 full-time (36 women), 54 part-time (35 women); includes 26 minority (10 African Americans, 5 Asian Americans or Pacific Islanders, 11 Hispanic Americans), 2 international. Average age 28. 332 applicants, 14% accepted, 23 enrolled. In 2009, 14 master's, 17 doctorates awarded. *Degree requirements:* For master's, thesis, oral exam; for doctorate, comprehensive exam, thesis/dissertation, oral and written exams. *Entrance requirements:* For master's and doctorate, GRE General Test, GRE Subject Test, 32 quarter hours of course work in psychology, 3 letters of recommendation. Additional exam requirements/recommendations for international students: Required—TOEFL. Application fee: $40. Electronic applications accepted. *Expenses:* Tuition: Full-time $37,525; part-time $620 per credit hour. *Financial support:* In 2009–10, 48 students received support, including 35 research assistantships with full tuition reimbursements available (averaging $11,800 per year), 13 teaching assistantships with full tuition reimbursements available (averaging $11,800 per year); career-related internships or fieldwork, scholarships/grants, traineeships, tuition waivers (full and partial), and unspecified assistantships also available. Financial award application deadline: 1/10. *Faculty research:* Adolescent stress and depression, minority adolescents sexuality, public policy, community influences in child adjustment. *Unit head:* Dr. Christopher B. Keys, Chairman, 773-325-7887, Fax: 773-325-7888. *Application contact:* Alison Pereida Knapp, Graduate Admissions Assistant, 773-325-7887, Fax: 773-325-7888.

Psychology—General

Drexel University, College of Arts and Sciences, Department of Psychology, Philadelphia, PA 19104-2875. Offers clinical psychology (PhD), including clinical psychology, forensic psychology, health psychology, neuropsychology; law-psychology (PhD); psychology (MS); JD/PhD. *Accreditation:* APA (one or more programs are accredited). *Degree requirements:* For doctorate, thesis/dissertation, internship. *Entrance requirements:* For doctorate, GRE General Test. Additional exam requirements/recommendations for international students: Required—TOEFL. Electronic applications accepted. *Expenses:* Contact institution. *Faculty research:* Neurosciences, rehabilitation psychology, cognitive science, neurological assessment.

Duke University, Graduate School, Department of Psychology, Durham, NC 27708-0586. Offers biological psychology (PhD); clinical psychology (PhD); cognitive psychology (PhD); developmental psychology (PhD); experimental psychology (PhD); health psychology (PhD); human social development (PhD); JD/MA. *Accreditation:* APA (one or more programs are accredited). *Faculty:* 40 full-time. *Students:* 92 full-time (70 women); includes 13 minority (5 African Americans, 2 Asian Americans or Pacific Islanders, 6 Hispanic Americans), 14 international. 478 applicants, 8% accepted, 21 enrolled. In 2009, 10 doctorates awarded. *Degree requirements:* For doctorate, thesis/dissertation. *Entrance requirements:* For doctorate, GRE General Test. Additional exam requirements/recommendations for international students: Required—TOEFL (minimum score 550 paper-based; 213 computer-based; 83 iBT), IELTS (minimum score 7). *Application deadline:* For fall admission, 12/8 priority date for domestic and international students. Application fee: $75. Electronic applications accepted. *Financial support:* Fellowships, research assistantships, teaching assistantships, career-related internships or fieldwork and Federal Work-Study available. Financial award application deadline: 12/31. *Unit head:* Melanie Bonner, Director of Graduate Studies, Fax: 919-660-5715, E-mail: morrell@duke.edu. *Application contact:* Cynthia Robertson, Associate Dean for Enrollment Services, 919-684-3913, E-mail: grad-admissions@duke.edu.

Duquesne University, Graduate School of Liberal Arts, Department of Psychology, Pittsburgh, PA 15282-0001. Offers clinical psychology (PhD). *Accreditation:* APA. *Faculty:* 14 full-time (5 women). *Students:* 49 full-time (24 women); includes 1 minority (Hispanic American), 8 international. Average age 25. 111 applicants, 6% accepted, 5 enrolled. In 2009, 9 doctorates awarded. *Degree requirements:* For doctorate, comprehensive exam, thesis/dissertation. *Entrance requirements:* For doctorate, GRE General Test, MA in psychology. Additional exam requirements/recommendations for international students: Required—TOEFL. *Application deadline:* For fall admission, 12/15 for domestic and international students. Electronic applications accepted. *Expenses:* Tuition: Part-time $851 per credit. Required fees: $81 per credit. *Financial support:* In 2009–10, 1 research assistantship with full tuition reimbursement (averaging $13,000 per year), 14 teaching assistantships with full tuition reimbursements (averaging $13,000 per year) were awarded; fellowships with full tuition reimbursements, career-related internships or fieldwork, scholarships/grants, tuition waivers (partial), and unspecified assistantships also available. Financial award application deadline: 5/1. *Faculty research:* Emotion, language motivation, imagination, development. *Unit head:* Dr. Daniel Burston, Chair, 412-396-5067. *Application contact:* Dr. Daniel Buston, Chair, 412-396-5067.

East Carolina University, Graduate School, Thomas Harriot College of Arts and Sciences, Department of Psychology, Program in General Psychology, Greenville, NC 27858-4353. Offers MA. *Degree requirements:* For master's, one foreign language, comprehensive exam, thesis. *Entrance requirements:* For master's, GRE General Test, GRE Subject Test. Additional exam requirements/recommendations for international students: Required—TOEFL.

East Central University, School of Graduate Studies, Department of Psychology, Ada, OK 74820-6899. Offers MSPS. Part-time and evening/weekend programs available. *Entrance requirements:* For master's, GRE General Test, MAT. Electronic applications accepted.

Eastern Illinois University, Graduate School, College of Sciences, Department of Psychology, Charleston, IL 61920-3099. Offers clinical psychology (MA); school psychology (SSP). *Faculty:* 18 full-time (4 women). In 2009, 10 master's, 11 other advanced degrees awarded. *Degree requirements:* For master's, comprehensive exam; for SSP, thesis. *Entrance requirements:* For master's and SSP, GRE General Test. *Application deadline:* For fall admission, 3/31 priority date for domestic students. Applications are processed on a rolling basis. Application fee: $30. *Expenses:* Tuition, state resident: full-time $9434; part-time $239 per credit hour. Tuition, nonresident: full-time $23,774; part-time $717 per credit hour. Required fees: $802.63. *Financial support:* In 2009–10, research assistantships with tuition reimbursements (averaging $8,100 per year), 9 teaching assistantships with tuition reimbursements (averaging $8,100 per year) were awarded; career-related internships or fieldwork also available. *Unit head:* Dr. John H. Mace, Chairperson, 217-581-2127, Fax: 217-581-6764, E-mail: jhmace@eiu.edu. *Application contact:* Bill Elliott, Assistant Dean of Graduate and International Admissions, 217-581-7489, Fax: 217-581-6020, E-mail: wjelliott@eiu.edu.

Eastern Kentucky University, The Graduate School, College of Arts and Sciences, Department of Psychology, Richmond, KY 40475-3102. Offers clinical psychology (MS); industrial/organizational psychology (MS); school psychology (Psy S). Part-time programs available. *Entrance requirements:* For master's and Psy S, GRE General Test, minimum GPA of 2.5. *Faculty research:* Autism, social psychology, parenting, assessment of depression/anxiety, reading.

Eastern Michigan University, Graduate School, College of Arts and Sciences, Department of Psychology, Ypsilanti, MI 48197. Offers clinical behavioral psychology (MS); clinical psychology (MS, PhD); experimental psychology (MS). *Accreditation:* APA. *Faculty:* 24 full-time (14 women). *Students:* 44 full-time (34 women), 46 part-time (34 women); includes 9 minority (2 African Americans, 4 Asian Americans or Pacific Islanders, 3 Hispanic Americans), 4 international. Average age 27. 181 applicants, 19% accepted, 33 enrolled. In 2009, 17 master's, 12 doctorates awarded. *Degree requirements:* For master's, 600 hour practicum; for doctorate, 1500-hour practicum; 2000 hour internship. *Entrance requirements:* For master's and doctorate, GRE. *Application deadline:* For fall admission, 2/15 for domestic students. Application fee: $35. Tuition and fees vary according to course level. *Financial support:* In 2009–10, 33 fellowships (averaging $15,000 per year) were awarded. *Unit head:* Dr. Carol Freedman-Doan, Interim Department Head, 734-487-1155, Fax: 734-487-6553, E-mail: cfreedman@emich.edu. *Application contact:* Dawn Stentzel, Graduate Secretary, 734-487-1155, Fax: 734-487-6553.

Eastern Washington University, Graduate Studies, College of Social and Behavioral Sciences, Department of Psychology, Cheney, WA 99004-2431. Offers clinical psychology (MS); experimental psychology (MS); psychology (MS); school psychology (MS). *Degree requirements:* For master's, comprehensive exam, thesis or alternative. *Entrance requirements:* For master's, GRE General Test, minimum GPA of 3.0. *Expenses:* Tuition, state resident: full-time $7476; part-time $249 per quarter hour. Tuition, nonresident: full-time $18,030; part-time $601 per quarter hour. Required fees: $3.50 per quarter hour. $142 per quarter.

East Tennessee State University, School of Graduate Studies, College of Arts and Sciences, Department of Psychology, Johnson City, TN 37614. Offers clinical psychology (MA); general psychology (MA). *Degree requirements:* For master's, thesis, oral exams. *Entrance requirements:* For master's, GRE General Test, GRE Subject Test, minimum GPA of 3.0. Additional exam requirements/recommendations for international students: Required—TOEFL (minimum score 550 paper-based; 213 computer-based). *Faculty research:* Language acquisition, recovery of brain function after injury or damage, violence in domestic relationships and road rage, reasons for living, unhealthy tanning behaviors.

Edinboro University of Pennsylvania, School of Graduate Studies and Research, School of Liberal Arts, Department of Psychology, Edinboro, PA 16444. Offers clinical psychology (MA). *Students:* Part-time and evening/weekend programs available. *Faculty:* 3 full-time (all women). *Students:* 14 full-time (13 women), 2 part-time (both women). Average age 26. In 2009, 4 master's awarded. *Degree requirements:* For master's, comprehensive exam, thesis or alternative, project. *Entrance requirements:* For master's, GRE or MAT, minimum QPA of 2.5. *Application deadline:* For fall admission, 3/15 priority date for domestic students. Applications are processed on a rolling basis. Application fee: $30. Electronic applications accepted. *Expenses:* Tuition, state resident: full-time $6666; part-time $370 per credit. Tuition, nonresident: full-time $10,666; part-time $593 per credit. Required fees: $2206.28. One-time fee: $204 part-time. *Financial support:* In 2009–10, 3 research assistantships with full and partial tuition reimbursements (averaging $4,050 per year) were awarded; career-related internships or fieldwork, Federal Work-Study, scholarships/grants, and unspecified assistantships also available. Support available to part-time students. Financial award application deadline: 2/15; financial award applicants required to submit FAFSA.

Emory University, Graduate School of Arts and Sciences, Department of Psychology, Atlanta, GA 30322-1100. Offers clinical psychology (PhD); cognition and development (PhD); neuroscience and animal behavior (PhD). *Accreditation:* APA. *Degree requirements:* For doctorate, comprehensive exam, thesis/dissertation. *Entrance requirements:* For doctorate, GRE General Test, minimum GPA of 3.25. Additional exam requirements/recommendations for international students: Required—TOEFL. Electronic applications accepted. *Faculty research:* Neuroscience and animal behavior; adult and child psychopathology, cognition development assessment.

Emporia State University, School of Graduate Studies, The Teachers College, Department of Psychology, Art Therapy, Rehabilitation and Mental Health Counseling, Program in Psychology, Emporia, KS 66801-5087. Offers general psychology (MS); industrial/organizational psychology (MS). Part-time programs available. *Students:* 10 full-time (6 women), 12 part-time (7 women); includes 1 minority (Hispanic American), 5 international. 4 applicants, 100% accepted, 4 enrolled. In 2009, 2 master's awarded. *Degree requirements:* For master's, comprehensive exam or thesis, internship. *Entrance requirements:* For master's, GRE General Test or MAT, graduate essay exam, appropriate bachelor's degree, letters of recommendation. Additional exam requirements/recommendations for international students: Required—TOEFL (minimum score 520 paper-based; 133 computer-based; 68 iBT). *Application deadline:* For fall admission, 6/1 priority date for domestic students; for spring admission, 10/1 for domestic students. Applications are processed on a rolling basis. Application fee: $30 ($75 for international students). Electronic applications accepted. *Expenses:* Tuition, state resident: full-time $4154; part-time $173 per credit hour. Tuition, nonresident: full-time $12,864; part-time $536 per credit hour. Required fees: $948; $58 per credit hour. Tuition and fees vary according to campus/location. *Financial support:* Career-related internships or fieldwork, Federal Work-Study, institutionally sponsored loans, health care benefits, and unspecified assistantships available. Financial award application deadline: 3/15; financial award applicants required to submit FAFSA. *Faculty research:* Driving under the influence (DUI) personality, lifestyles and imposter phenomenon. *Unit head:* Dr. Brian W. Schrader, Chair, 620-341-5317, E-mail: bschrade@emporia.edu. *Application contact:* Mary Sewell, Admissions Coordinator, 800-950-GRAD, Fax: 620-341-5909, E-mail: msewell@emporia.edu.

Evangel University, Department of Psychology, Springfield, MO 65802. Offers clinical psychology (MS); counseling psychology (MS). Part-time programs available. *Faculty:* 3 full-time (2 women), 2 part-time/adjunct (1 woman). *Students:* 19 full-time (13 women), 14 part-time (12 women). Average age 27. 17 applicants, 100% accepted, 15 enrolled. In 2009, 6 master's awarded. *Degree requirements:* For master's, comprehensive exam, thesis optional. *Entrance requirements:* For master's, GRE General Test or MAT, minimum undergraduate GPA of 3.0, undergraduate major or minor in psychology. Additional exam requirements/recommendations for international students: Required—TOEFL (minimum score 550 paper-based; 213 computer-based). *Application deadline:* For fall admission, 2/1 priority date for domestic students; for spring admission, 10/15 priority date for domestic students. Applications are processed on a rolling basis. Application fee: $25. Electronic applications accepted. *Financial support:* In 2009–10, 6 students received support. Career-related internships or fieldwork, scholarships/grants, and unspecified assistantships available. Support available to part-time students. Financial award application deadline: 3/1; financial award applicants required to submit FAFSA. *Unit head:* Dr. Grant Jones, Chair, 417-865-2815 Ext. 8619, E-mail: jonesg@evangel.edu. *Application contact:* Charity H. Fahlstrom, Admissions Representative, Graduate and Professional Studies, 417-865-2815 Ext. 7227, Fax: 417-575-5484, E-mail: fahlstromc@evangel.edu.

Fairfield University, Graduate School of Education and Allied Professions, Department of Psychological and Educational Consultation, Fairfield, CT 06824-5195. Offers applied psychology (MA), including foundations of advanced psychology, human services, industrial/organizational/personnel; media/educational technology (MA); school media specialist (MA); school psychology (MA, CAS); special education (MA, CAS). Part-time and evening/weekend programs available. *Degree requirements:* For master's, comprehensive exam, thesis optional. *Entrance requirements:* For master's, PRAXIS I (PPST), minimum QPA of 3.0, 2 recommendations, resume. Additional exam requirements/recommendations for international students: Required—TOEFL (minimum score 550 paper-based; 213 computer-based; 80 iBT). Electronic applications accepted. *Faculty research:* Child neuropsychology, disabilities, effect of pre-treatment orientation on treatment, autism, technology in business and classroom, collaboration with schools, communities and industry.

Fairleigh Dickinson University, College at Florham, Maxwell Becton College of Arts and Sciences, Department of Psychology, Madison, NJ 07940-1099. Offers counseling (MA); industrial/organizational psychology (MA); organizational behavior (MA, Certificate), including organizational behavior (MA), organizational leadership (Certificate); MA/MBA. *Students:* 66 full-time (46 women), 91 part-time (62 women), 1 international. Average age 32. 113 applicants, 70% accepted, 37 enrolled. In 2009, 55 master's awarded. *Application deadline:* Applications are processed on a rolling basis. Application fee: $40. *Unit head:* Dr. Diane Wentworth, Chairperson, 973-443-8548. *Application contact:* Susan Brooman, University Director, Graduate Admissions, 973-443-8905, Fax: 973-443-8088, E-mail: grad@fdu.edu.

Fairleigh Dickinson University, Metropolitan Campus, University College: Arts, Sciences, and Professional Studies, School of Psychology, Teaneck, NJ 07666-1914. Offers clinical psychology (MA, PhD); clinical psychopharmacology (MA); forensic psychology (MA); general-theoretical psychology (MA, Certificate); school psychology (MA, Psy D). *Accreditation:* APA (one or more programs are accredited). *Students:* 204 full-time (151 women), 44 part-time (32 women), 6 international. Average age 32. 189 applicants, 72% accepted, 74 enrolled. In 2009, 57 master's, 27 doctorates awarded. *Application deadline:* Applications are processed on a rolling basis. Application fee: $40. *Application contact:* Susan Brooman, University Director of Graduate Admissions, 201-692-2554, Fax: 201-692-2560, E-mail: globaleducation@fdu.edu.

Fayetteville State University, Graduate School, Program in Psychology, Fayetteville, NC 28301-4298. Offers MA. Part-time and evening/weekend programs available. *Faculty:* 10 full-time (4 women). *Students:* 18 full-time (16 women), 18 part-time (16 women); includes 23 minority (19 African Americans, 2 American Indian/Alaska Native, 1 Asian American or Pacific Islander, 1 Hispanic American). Average age 31. 5 applicants, 100% accepted, 5 enrolled. In 2009, 8 master's awarded. *Degree requirements:* For master's, comprehensive exam, internship. *Application deadline:* For fall admission, 4/15 for domestic students. Applications are processed on a rolling basis. Application fee: $35. Electronic applications accepted. *Faculty research:* Coping strategies, reasons for living, hypnosis, cultural differences in expression of emotions, ethics, morals, stress, adult development. *Unit head:* Dr. Thomas Van Cantfort, Head, 910-672-1413, Fax: 910-672-1043, E-mail: tvancantfort@uncfsu.edu. *Application contact:* Katrina Hoffman, Associate Vice-Chancellor for Enrollment Management, 910-672-1374, Fax: 910-672-1470, E-mail: khoffma1@uncfsu.edu.

Fielding Graduate University, Graduate Programs, School of Psychology, Santa Barbara, CA 93105-3538. Offers clinical psychology (PhD); clinical psychology respecialization (Post-Doctoral Certificate); media psychology (PhD); media psychology and social change (MA); neuropsychology (Post-Doctoral Certificate). *Accreditation:* APA. Postbaccalaureate distance learning degree programs offered (minimal on-campus study). *Faculty:* 31 full-time (17 women), 10 part-time/adjunct (6 women). *Students:* 509 full-time (380 women), 104 part-time (71 women); includes 126 minority (34 African Americans, 8 American Indian/Alaska Native, 28 Asian Americans or Pacific Islanders, 56 Hispanic Americans), 20 international. Average age

43. 337 applicants, 47% accepted, 96 enrolled. In 2009, 2 master's, 43 doctorates, 18 other advanced degrees awarded. Terminal master's awarded for partial completion of doctoral program. *Degree requirements:* For master's, thesis or alternative, capstone project; for doctorate, comprehensive exam, thesis/dissertation. *Entrance requirements:* For doctorate, writing sample, minimum GPA of 3.0, 3 letters of recommendation, resume. *Application deadline:* For fall admission, 2/23 for domestic and international students; for spring admission, 8/25 for domestic and international students. Application fee: $75. Electronic applications accepted. *Expenses:* Contact institution. *Financial support:* In 2009–10, 403 students received support. Scholarships/grants and health care benefits available. Support available to part-time students. Financial award application deadline: 5/15; financial award applicants required to submit FAFSA. *Unit head:* Dr. Raymond Trybus, Dean, 805-898-2909, E-mail: rtrybus@fielding.edu. *Application contact:* Kathryn Romero, Admission Counselor, 800-340-1099, Fax: 805-687-9793, E-mail: kromero@fielding.edu.

Fisk University, Division of Graduate Studies, Department of Psychology, Nashville, TN 37208-3051. Offers clinical psychology (MA); psychology (MA). *Faculty:* 4 full-time (2 women), 1 (woman) part-time/adjunct. *Students:* 6 full-time (2 women), 9 part-time (8 women); all minorities (14 African Americans, 1 Hispanic American). Average age 26. 9 applicants, 44% accepted, 4 enrolled. In 2009, 1 master's awarded. *Degree requirements:* For master's, thesis. *Entrance requirements:* For master's, GRE General Test, GRE Subject Test, minimum GPA of 3.0. *Application deadline:* For fall admission, 6/1 priority date for domestic students. Applications are processed on a rolling basis. Application fee: $50. Electronic applications accepted. *Expenses:* Tuition: Full-time $16,848; part-time $936 per credit hour. Required fees: $1510; $465 per semester. *Financial support:* In 2009–10, 5 students received support, including 3 fellowships (averaging $17,060 per year); research assistantships, teaching assistantships with partial tuition reimbursements available, traineeships, tuition waivers (full and partial), and unspecified assistantships also available. *Faculty research:* Ethnic and gender identity, development, female adolescent development, juvenile delinquency prevention. *Unit head:* Dr. Sheila Peters, Chair, 615-329-8617, E-mail: speters@fisk.edu. *Application contact:* Keith Chandler, Dean of Admission, 615-329-8819, Fax: 615-329-8774, E-mail: kchandler@fisk.edu.

Florida Agricultural and Mechanical University, Division of Graduate Studies, Research, and Continuing Education, College of Arts and Sciences, Department of Psychology, Tallahassee, FL 32307-3200. Offers community psychology (MS); school psychology (MS). *Faculty:* 6 full-time (2 women). *Students:* 39 full-time (32 women), 23 part-time (16 women); includes 60 minority (all African Americans), 1 international. In 2009, 14 master's awarded. *Degree requirements:* For master's, thesis. *Entrance requirements:* For master's, GRE General Test, minimum GPA of 3.0. Additional exam requirements/recommendations for international students: Required—TOEFL. *Application deadline:* For fall admission, 5/18 for domestic students, 12/18 for international students; for spring admission, 11/12 for domestic students, 5/12 for international students. Application fee: $20. *Financial support:* Fellowships, research assistantships, career-related internships or fieldwork, Federal Work-Study, institutionally sponsored loans, and tuition waivers (partial) available. *Unit head:* Dr. Yvonne Bell, Chairperson, 850-599-3468, Fax: 850-561-2540, E-mail: yvonne.bell@famu.edu. *Application contact:* Dr. Chanta M. Haywood, Dean of Graduate Studies, Research, and Continuing Education, 850-599-3315, Fax: 850-599-3727.

Florida Atlantic University, Charles E. Schmidt College of Science, Department of Psychology, Boca Raton, FL 33431-0991. Offers MA, PhD. *Faculty:* 26 full-time (8 women), 6 part-time/adjunct (2 women). *Students:* 60 full-time (36 women), 16 part-time (11 women); includes 13 minority (2 African Americans, 1 American Indian/Alaska Native, 4 Asian Americans or Pacific Islanders, 6 Hispanic Americans), 6 international. Average age 30. 124 applicants, 45% accepted, 7 enrolled. In 2009, 14 master's, 1 doctorate awarded. Terminal master's awarded for partial completion of doctoral program. *Degree requirements:* For master's, one foreign language, thesis or alternative; for doctorate, one foreign language, comprehensive exam, thesis/dissertation. *Entrance requirements:* For master's and doctorate, GRE General Test, minimum GPA of 3.0 during previous 2 years. *Application deadline:* For fall admission, 5/1 for domestic students, 5/15 for international students. Application fee: $30. Electronic applications accepted. *Expenses:* Tuition, state resident: full-time $7055; part-time $293.94 per credit hour. Tuition, nonresident: full-time $22,096; part-time $920.66 per credit hour. *Financial support:* Research assistantships with partial tuition reimbursements, teaching assistantships with partial tuition reimbursements, Federal Work-Study, institutionally sponsored loans, scholarships/grants, and unspecified assistantships available. Financial award application deadline: 3/1; financial award applicants required to submit FAFSA. *Faculty research:* Cognition, psychobiology, developmental psychology, social psychology, neuroscience. *Unit head:* Dr. David L. Wolgin, Chair, 561-297-3366, Fax: 561-297-2160, E-mail: wolgindl@fau.edu. *Application contact:* Dr. David F. Bjorklund, Graduate Program Coordinator, 561-297-3368, Fax: 561-297-2160, E-mail: dbjorklu@fau.edu.

Florida Institute of Technology, Graduate Programs, College of Psychology and Liberal Arts, School of Psychology, Melbourne, FL 32901-6975. Offers applied behavior analysis (MS); applied behavior analysis and organizational behavior management (MS, PhD); clinical psychology (Psy D); industrial/organizational psychology (MS, PhD); organizational behavior management (MS). *Accreditation:* APA (one or more programs are accredited). Part-time programs available. *Faculty:* 24 full-time (11 women), 6 part-time/adjunct (1 woman). *Students:* 210 full-time (169 women), 4 part-time (2 women); includes 31 minority (8 African Americans, 6 Asian Americans or Pacific Islanders, 17 Hispanic Americans), 21 international. Average age 27. 195 applicants, 59% accepted, 55 enrolled. In 2009, 30 master's, 3 doctorates awarded. Terminal master's awarded for partial completion of doctoral program. *Degree requirements:* For master's, comprehensive exam (for some programs), thesis (for some programs), BCBA certification, final exam; for doctorate, comprehensive exam, thesis/dissertation, internship, full time resident of school for 4 years (8 semesters, 3 summers). *Entrance requirements:* For master's, GRE General Test, 3 letters of recommendation, minimum GPA of 3.0, resume; for doctorate, GRE General Test, GRE Subject Test (psychology), 3 letters of recommendation, minimum GPA of 3.2, resume, statement of objectives. Additional exam requirements/recommendations for international students: Required—TOEFL (minimum score 550 paper-based; 213 computer-based; 79 iBT). *Application deadline:* For fall admission, 1/15 for domestic and international students. Applications are processed on a rolling basis. Application fee: $50. Electronic applications accepted. *Expenses:* Tuition: Part-time $1015 per credit. Tuition and fees vary according to campus/location and program. *Financial support:* In 2009–10, 19 students received support, including 14 research assistantships with full and partial tuition reimbursements available (averaging $4,079 per year), 5 teaching assistantships with full and partial tuition reimbursements available (averaging $7,002 per year); fellowships with full and partial tuition reimbursements available, career-related internships or fieldwork, institutionally sponsored loans, tuition waivers (partial), unspecified assistantships, and tuition remissions also available. Support available to part-time students. Financial award application deadline: 3/1; financial award applicants required to submit FAFSA. *Faculty research:* Addictions, neuropsychology, child abuse, assessment, psychological trauma. Total annual research expenditures: $836,475. *Unit head:* Dr. Mary Beth Kenkel, Dean, 321-674-8142, Fax: 321-674-7105, E-mail: mkenkel@fit.edu. *Application contact:* Thomas M. Shea, Director of Graduate Admissions, 321-674-7577, Fax: 321-723-9468, E-mail: tshea@fit.edu.

See Close-Up on page 1089.

Florida International University, College of Arts and Sciences, Department of Psychology, Miami, FL 33199. Offers MS, PhD. Programs only admit for Fall. Part-time and evening/weekend programs available. *Faculty:* 25 full-time (11 women). *Students:* 91 full-time (67 women), 36 part-time (28 women); includes 74 minority (12 African Americans, 4 Asian Americans or Pacific Islanders, 58 Hispanic Americans), 13 international. Average age 30. 198 applicants, 19% accepted, 38 enrolled. In 2009, 20 master's, 8 doctorates awarded. Terminal master's awarded for partial completion of doctoral program. *Degree requirements:* For master's, thesis; for doctorate, comprehensive exam, thesis/dissertation. *Entrance requirements:* For master's, GRE General Test, minimum GPA of 3.0, resume, 3 letters of recommendation; for doctorate, GRE General Test, 3 letters of recommendation, resume, letter of intent, two writing samples, minimum GPA of 3.0. Additional exam requirements/recommendations for international students: Required—TOEFL (minimum score 550 paper-based; 80 iBT). *Application deadline:* For fall admission, 12/15 for domestic and international students. Application fee: $30. Electronic applications accepted. *Expenses:* Tuition, state resident: full-time $8008; part-time $4004 per year. Tuition, nonresident: full-time $20,104; part-time $10,052 per year. Required fees: $298; $149 per term. *Financial support:* Institutionally sponsored loans and scholarships/grants available. Financial award application deadline: 3/1. *Faculty research:* Legal psychology, organizational and industrial psychology, child behavior psychology. *Unit head:* Dr. Mary Levitt, Chair, 305-348-2880, Fax: 305-348-3879, E-mail: mary.levitt@fiu.edu. *Application contact:* Lara Wilson, Senior Secretary, 305-348-2881, Fax: 305-348-3879, E-mail: lara.wilson@fiu.edu.

Florida State University, The Graduate School, College of Arts and Sciences, Department of Psychology, Tallahassee, FL 32306. Offers applied behavior analysis (MS); clinical psychology (PhD); cognitive psychology (PhD); developmental psychology (PhD); neuroscience (PhD); social psychology (PhD). *Accreditation:* APA (one or more programs are accredited). *Faculty:* 45 full-time (18 women). *Students:* 170 full-time (113 women), 6 part-time (4 women); includes 26 minority (8 African Americans, 1 American Indian/Alaska Native, 6 Asian Americans or Pacific Islanders, 11 Hispanic Americans), 2 international. Average age 26. 439 applicants, 16% accepted, 47 enrolled. In 2009, 22 master's, 13 doctorates awarded. Terminal master's awarded for partial completion of doctoral program. *Degree requirements:* For master's, comprehensive exam; for doctorate, thesis/dissertation, preliminary exam. *Entrance requirements:* For master's and doctorate, GRE General Test, minimum GPA of 3.0. Additional exam requirements/recommendations for international students: Required—TOEFL (minimum score 550 paper-based; 213 computer-based; 80 iBT). Application fee: $30. Electronic applications accepted. *Expenses:* Tuition, state resident: full-time $7413. Tuition, nonresident: full-time $22,567. *Financial support:* In 2009–10, 147 students received support, including 30 fellowships with full tuition reimbursements available (averaging $18,000 per year), 72 research assistantships with full tuition reimbursements available (averaging $18,000 per year), 45 teaching assistantships with full tuition reimbursements available (averaging $15,000 per year); career-related internships or fieldwork, Federal Work-Study, institutionally sponsored loans, scholarships/grants, traineeships, health care benefits, and unspecified assistantships also available. Financial award applicants required to submit FAFSA. Total annual research expenditures: $6 million. *Unit head:* Dr. Janet Kistner, Chairman, 850-644-2040, Fax: 850-644-7739, E-mail: kistner@psy.fsu.edu. *Application contact:* Cherie P. Miller, Graduate Program Assistant, 850-644-2499, Fax: 850-644-7739, E-mail: grad-info@psy.fsu.edu.

Fordham University, Graduate School of Arts and Sciences, Department of Psychology, New York, NY 10458. Offers applied developmental psychology (PhD); clinical psychology (PhD); psychometrics (PhD). Terminal master's awarded for partial completion of doctoral program. *Degree requirements:* For doctorate, comprehensive exam, thesis/dissertation. *Entrance requirements:* For doctorate, GRE General Test, GRE Subject Test. Additional exam requirements/recommendations for international students: Required—TOEFL (minimum score 600 paper-based; 250 computer-based). Electronic applications accepted.

Fort Hays State University, Graduate School, College of Arts and Sciences, Department of Psychology, Hays, KS 67601-4099. Offers psychology (MS); school psychology (Ed S). *Degree requirements:* For master's and Ed S, comprehensive exam, thesis. *Entrance requirements:* For master's, GRE General Test. Additional exam requirements/recommendations for international students: Required—TOEFL (minimum score 550 paper-based; 213 computer-based). Electronic applications accepted. *Faculty research:* Memory, learning, motivation, clinical and experimental psychology, history and systems of psychological stressors in rural environments.

Framingham State College, Division of Graduate and Continuing Education, Program in Counseling Psychology, Framingham, MA 01701-9101. Offers MA. Part-time and evening/weekend programs available.

Francis Marion University, Graduate Programs, Department of Psychology, Florence, SC 29502-0547. Offers applied psychology (MS), including clinical/counseling, school psychology; school psychology (MS). Part-time and evening/weekend programs available. *Faculty:* 10 full-time (4 women), 5 part-time/adjunct (4 women). *Students:* 16 full-time (15 women), 19 part-time (18 women); includes 6 minority (all African Americans). Average age 35. 44 applicants, 55% accepted, 8 enrolled. In 2009, 19 degrees awarded. *Degree requirements:* For master's, internship. *Entrance requirements:* For master's, GRE General Test. *Application deadline:* For fall admission, 3/15 for domestic students; for spring admission, 10/15 for domestic students. Applications are processed on a rolling basis. Application fee: $30. *Expenses:* Tuition, state resident: full-time $8345; part-time $417.25 per semester hour. Tuition, nonresident: full-time $16,690; part-time $814.50 per semester hour. Required fees: $335; $12.25 per semester hour. $30 per semester. *Financial support:* In 2009–10, 13 students received support, including 1 research assistantship (averaging $7,000 per year), 3 teaching assistantships (averaging $8,000 per year); career-related internships or fieldwork, unspecified assistantships, and scholarships with out-of-state waivers also available. Support available to part-time students. Financial award application deadline: 3/1; financial award applicants required to submit FAFSA. *Faculty research:* Parenting and family relationships, child development, applied behavioral analysis, posttraumatic stress disorder, clinical psychology in adults. *Unit head:* Dr. John R. Hester, Chair, 843-661-1635, Fax: 843-661-1628. *Application contact:* Jennifer Taylor, Administrative Assistant, 843-661-1378, Fax: 843-661-1628.

Frostburg State University, Graduate School, College of Liberal Arts and Sciences, Department of Psychology, Frostburg, MD 21532-1099. Offers counseling psychology (MS). Part-time and evening/weekend programs available. *Faculty:* 6 full-time (3 women), 2 part-time/adjunct (both women). *Students:* 33 full-time (31 women), 4 part-time (all women); includes 1 minority (African American), 3 international. Average age 26. 38 applicants, 29% accepted, 9 enrolled. In 2009, 10 master's awarded. *Degree requirements:* For master's, internship. *Entrance requirements:* For master's, GRE General Test or MAT, interview, minimum GPA of 3.0, resume. Additional exam requirements/recommendations for international students: Required—TOEFL. *Application deadline:* For fall admission, 2/1 for domestic students. Applications are processed on a rolling basis. Application fee: $30. Electronic applications accepted. *Expenses:* Tuition, state resident: full-time $5706; part-time $317 per credit hour. Tuition, nonresident: full-time $6948; part-time $386 per credit hour. Required fees: $1476; $82 per credit hour. $11 per term. One-time fee: $30 full-time. *Financial support:* In 2009–10, 7 research assistantships with full tuition reimbursements (averaging $5,000 per year) were awarded; career-related internships or fieldwork and Federal Work-Study also available. Financial award application deadline: 4/1; financial award applicants required to submit FAFSA. *Unit head:* Dr. Kevin Peterson, Chair, 301-687-4193, E-mail: kpeterson@frostburg.edu. *Application contact:* Vickie Mazer, Director, Graduate Services, 301-687-7053, Fax: 301-687-4597, E-mail: vmmazer@frostburg.edu.

Fuller Theological Seminary, Graduate School of Psychology, Pasadena, CA 91182. Offers MA, MS, PhD, Psy D, Certificate. *Accreditation:* APA (one or more programs are accredited). Terminal master's awarded for partial completion of doctoral program. *Degree requirements:* For master's, practicum; for doctorate, thesis/dissertation, internships. *Entrance requirements:* For master's, GRE General Test; for doctorate, GRE General Test, GRE Subject Test, interview. Additional exam requirements/recommendations for international students: Required—TOEFL. *Faculty research:* Psychology of religion, depression, shame, psychoneuroimmunology, marital intimacy, sex roles, psychoanalytic theory, men's issues, family relations.

Gallaudet University, The Graduate School, College of Arts and Sciences, Department of Psychology, Washington, DC 20002-3625. Offers clinical psychology (PhD); school psychology (MA, Psy S), including developmental psychology (MA), school psychology (Psy S). *Accreditation:* APA (one or more programs are accredited). *Degree requirements:* For master's,

Psychology—General

Gallaudet University (continued)
thesis optional; for doctorate, thesis/dissertation. *Entrance requirements:* For master's, GRE General Test or MAT; for doctorate, GRE General Test or MAT, interview. Electronic applications accepted.

Gardner-Webb University, Graduate School, School of Psychology, Boiling Springs, NC 28017. Offers mental health counseling (MA); school counseling (MA). Part-time and evening/weekend programs available. *Faculty:* 7 full-time (4 women), 1 part-time/adjunct (0 women). *Students:* 71 part-time (60 women); includes 16 minority (13 African Americans, 3 Hispanic Americans). Average age 36. In 2009, 27 master's awarded. *Degree requirements:* For master's, comprehensive exam. *Entrance requirements:* For master's, GRE General Test, MAT, minimum GPA of 2.7. *Application deadline:* For fall admission, 7/1 priority date for domestic students. Applications are processed on a rolling basis. Application fee: $25. Electronic applications accepted. *Expenses:* Tuition: Part-time $305 per credit hour. *Financial support:* Unspecified assistantships available. *Unit head:* Dr. David Carscaddon, Chair, 704-406-4437, Fax: 704-406-4329, E-mail: dcarscaddon@gardner-webb.edu. *Application contact:* Dr. Jackson Rainer, Dean, Graduate School, 704-406-4724, Fax: 704-406-4329, E-mail: gradschool@gardner-webb.edu.

Geneva College, Program in Counseling, Beaver Falls, PA 15010-3599. Offers marriage and family (MA); mental health (MA); school counseling (MA). *Accreditation:* ACA. Part-time and evening/weekend programs available. *Faculty:* 5 full-time (2 women), 2 part-time/adjunct (1 woman). *Students:* 28 full-time (21 women), 21 part-time (17 women); includes 6 minority (5 African Americans, 1 Asian American or Pacific Islander). Average age 26. 32 applicants, 97% accepted, 18 enrolled. In 2009, 11 master's awarded. *Degree requirements:* For master's, comprehensive exam, internship. *Entrance requirements:* For master's, GRE General Test or MAT, minimum GPA of 3.0 (preferred), letters of recommendation, faith statement. Additional exam requirements/recommendations for international students: Required—TOEFL. *Application deadline:* For fall admission, 7/1 priority date for domestic students; for spring admission, 11/1 priority date for domestic students. Applications are processed on a rolling basis. Application fee: $50 ($100 for international students). Electronic applications accepted. *Expenses:* Tuition: Full-time $11,250; part-time $625 per credit. Tuition and fees vary according to program. *Financial support:* In 2009–10, 8 teaching assistantships (averaging $3,500 per year) were awarded; career-related internships or fieldwork and unspecified assistantships also available. Financial award applicants required to submit FAFSA. *Unit head:* Dr. Carol Luce, Director, 724-847-6622, Fax: 724-847-6101, E-mail: cbluce@geneva.edu. *Application contact:* JoAnn Westover, Graduate Program Manager, 724-847-6697, E-mail: counseling@geneva.edu.

George Fox University, Graduate Department of Clinical Psychology, Newberg, OR 97132-2697. Offers MA, Psy D. *Accreditation:* APA. *Faculty:* 7 full-time (3 women), 4 part-time/adjunct (1 woman). *Students:* 86 full-time (60 women), 14 part-time (7 women); includes 9 minority (1 American Indian/Alaska Native, 5 Asian Americans or Pacific Islanders, 3 Hispanic Americans). Average age 29. 70 applicants, 56% accepted, 21 enrolled. In 2009, 18 master's, 19 doctorates awarded. *Degree requirements:* For master's, comprehensive exam, 60 semester hours of required and elective courses; for doctorate, thesis/dissertation, internship. *Entrance requirements:* For master's and doctorate, GRE General Test, bachelor's degree from regionally-accredited university or college, minimum undergraduate GPA of 3.0 during previous 2 years, interview. Additional exam requirements/recommendations for international students: Required—TOEFL (minimum score 577 paper-based; 233 computer-based; 90 iBT). *Application deadline:* For fall admission, 1/15 priority date for domestic and international students. Application fee: $40. Electronic applications accepted. *Expenses:* Contact institution. *Financial support:* Scholarships/grants available. Financial award application deadline: 5/15; financial award applicants required to submit FAFSA. *Faculty research:* Psychological assessment, impact of psychological services on medical outcome, spirituality and wellness, effectiveness of clinical training and supervision, shame. *Unit head:* Dr. Wayne Adams, Professor/Chairperson, 800-765-4369 Ext. 2372, E-mail: wadams@georgefox.edu. *Application contact:* Adina McConaughey, Admission Counselor, 800-631-0921 Ext. 2263, Fax: 503-554-2263, E-mail: psyd@georgefox.edu.

George Mason University, College of Humanities and Social Sciences, Department of Psychology, Fairfax, VA 22030. Offers aviation psychology (Certificate); cognitive neuroscience (Certificate); psychology (MA, PhD); school psychology (Certificate); usability (Certificate). *Accreditation:* APA. *Faculty:* 48 full-time (20 women), 14 part-time/adjunct (8 women). *Students:* 98 full-time (64 women), 133 part-time (94 women); includes 27 minority (8 African Americans, 13 Asian Americans or Pacific Islanders, 6 Hispanic Americans), 8 international. Average age 28. 598 applicants, 23% accepted, 70 enrolled. In 2009, 60 master's, 24 doctorates, 11 other advanced degrees awarded. Terminal master's awarded for partial completion of doctoral program. *Degree requirements:* For master's, comprehensive exam, thesis (for biopsychology); for doctorate, comprehensive exam, thesis/dissertation, 2nd year project. *Entrance requirements:* For master's, GRE General Test, minimum GPA of 3.25 in last 60 hours of course work, undergraduate course work in psychology, 3 letters of recommendation, resume; for doctorate, GRE General Test, minimum undergraduate GPA of 3.5, 3 letters of recommendation, resume, expanded goals statement. Additional exam requirements/recommendations for international students: Required—TOEFL (minimum score 575 paper-based; 230 computer-based; 88 iBT). *Application deadline:* For fall admission, 3/1 priority date for domestic students; for spring admission, 10/15 for domestic students. Application fee: $75. Electronic applications accepted. *Expenses:* Tuition, state resident: full-time $7568; part-time $315.33 per credit hour. Tuition, nonresident: full-time $21,704; part-time $904.33 per credit hour. Required fees: $2184; $91 per credit hour. *Financial support:* In 2009–10, 105 students received support, including 3 fellowships with full tuition reimbursements available (averaging $18,000 per year), 67 research assistantships with full and partial tuition reimbursements available (averaging $7,530 per year), 59 teaching assistantships with full and partial tuition reimbursements available (averaging $3,699 per year); career-related internships or fieldwork, scholarships/grants, traineeships, tuition waivers (partial), unspecified assistantships, and health care benefits (full-time research or teaching assistantship recipients) also available. Financial award application deadline: 3/1; financial award applicants required to submit FAFSA. *Faculty research:* Applied developmental psychology, biopsychology, clinical psychology, human factors/applied cognition psychology, industrial/organizational psychology, school psychology. Total annual research expenditures: $4.1 million. *Unit head:* Dr. Deborah Boehm-Davis, Chairperson, 703-993-1398, Fax: 703-993-1359, E-mail: dbdavis@gmu.edu. *Application contact:* Darby Wiggins, Graduate Program Assistant, 703-993-1548, E-mail: dwiggin3@gmu.edu.

Georgetown University, Graduate School of Arts and Sciences, Department of Psychology, Washington, DC 20057. Offers PhD, JD/MPP. *Degree requirements:* For doctorate, thesis/dissertation. *Entrance requirements:* For doctorate, GRE General Test, GRE Subject Test. Additional exam requirements/recommendations for international students: Required—TOEFL.

The George Washington University, Columbian College of Arts and Sciences, Department of Psychology, Washington, DC 20052. Offers applied social psychology (PhD); clinical psychology (PhD); cognitive neuroscience (PhD). *Accreditation:* APA. Part-time and evening/weekend programs available. *Faculty:* 27 full-time (15 women), 25 part-time/adjunct (14 women). *Students:* 117 full-time (94 women), 89 part-time (73 women); includes 56 minority (16 African Americans, 2 American Indian/Alaska Native, 23 Asian Americans or Pacific Islanders, 15 Hispanic Americans), 4 international. Average age 28. 787 applicants, 6% accepted, 43 enrolled. In 2009, 49 doctorates awarded. *Degree requirements:* For doctorate, thesis/dissertation or alternative, general exam. *Entrance requirements:* For doctorate, GRE General Test, minimum GPA of 3.0. Additional exam requirements/recommendations for international students: Required—TOEFL (minimum score 550 paper-based; 213 computer-based; 80 iBT). *Application deadline:* For fall admission, 1/15 for domestic and international students. Application fee: $60. *Financial support:* In 2009–10, 62 students received support; fellowships with tuition reimbursements available, teaching assistantships with tuition reimbursements available, career-related internships or fieldwork, Federal Work-Study, and tuition waivers available. *Unit head:* Dr. Paul Poppen, Chair, 202-994-6324, E-mail: pjp@gwu.edu. *Application contact:* Information Contact, 202-994-6320, Fax: 202-994-1602, E-mail: psydept@gwu.edu.

The George Washington University, Columbian College of Arts and Sciences, Program in Professional Psychology, Washington, DC 20052. Offers Psy D. *Accreditation:* APA. *Entrance requirements:* For doctorate, GRE General Test, interview, minimum GPA of 3.0. Additional exam requirements/recommendations for international students: Required—TOEFL (minimum score 550 paper-based; 213 computer-based; 80 iBT). Electronic applications accepted.

Georgia Institute of Technology, Graduate Studies and Research, College of Sciences, School of Psychology, Atlanta, GA 30332-0001. Offers human computer interaction (MSHCI); psychology (MS, MS Psy, PhD), including engineering psychology (PhD), experimental psychology (PhD), industrial/organizational psychology (PhD). Terminal master's awarded for partial completion of doctoral program. *Degree requirements:* For master's, thesis; for doctorate, thesis/dissertation. *Entrance requirements:* For master's and doctorate, GRE General Test, GRE Subject Test, minimum GPA of 3.0. Additional exam requirements/recommendations for international students: Required—TOEFL. Electronic applications accepted. *Faculty research:* Experimental, industrial-organizational, and engineering psychology; cognitive aging and processes; leadership; human factors.

Georgia Southern University, Jack N. Averitt College of Graduate Studies, College of Liberal Arts and Social Sciences, Department of Psychology, Statesboro, GA 30460. Offers MS, Psy D. *Students:* 32 full-time (18 women), 2 part-time (both women); includes 3 minority (2 African Americans, 1 Asian American or Pacific Islander). Average age 25. 40 applicants, 50% accepted, 14 enrolled. In 2009, 7 master's awarded. Terminal master's awarded for partial completion of doctoral program. *Degree requirements:* For master's, comprehensive exam, thesis (for some programs), terminal exam; for doctorate, comprehensive exam, thesis/dissertation, clinical qualifying exam, practicum, internship. *Entrance requirements:* For master's, GRE General Test, minimum GPA of 3.0, introductory courses in psychology and statistics, letters of recommendation; for doctorate, GRE General Test; GRE Subject Test (if no undergraduate degree in psychology), minimum undergraduate GPA of 3.25; 3 letters of reference; statement of purpose. Additional exam requirements/recommendations for international students: Required—TOEFL (minimum score 550 paper-based; 213 computer-based; 80 iBT). *Application deadline:* For fall admission, 1/15 priority date for domestic students, 1/15 for international students. Applications are processed on a rolling basis. Application fee: $50. Electronic applications accepted. *Expenses:* Tuition, state resident: full-time $5040; part-time $210 per credit hour. Tuition, nonresident: full-time $20,136; part-time $839 per credit hour. Required fees: $1644. *Financial support:* In 2009–10, 30 students received support, including fellowships with partial tuition reimbursements available (averaging $12,000 per year), research assistantships with partial tuition reimbursements available (averaging $7,200 per year), teaching assistantships with partial tuition reimbursements available (averaging $7,200 per year); career-related internships or fieldwork, Federal Work-Study, scholarships/grants, tuition waivers (partial), and unspecified assistantships also available. Support available to part-time students. Financial award application deadline: 4/15; financial award applicants required to submit FAFSA. *Faculty research:* Psychology of religion, health and psychological response to illness, psychology and law, adult and child attachment. Total annual research expenditures: $50,396. *Unit head:* Dr. John Murray, Chair, 912-478-5539, Fax: 912-478-0751, E-mail: jmurray@georgiasouthern.edu. *Application contact:* Dr. Charles Ziglar, Coordinator for Graduate Student Recruitment, 912-478-5635, Fax: 912-478-0740, E-mail: gradadmissions@georgiasouthern.edu.

Georgia State University, College of Arts and Sciences, Department of Psychology, Atlanta, GA 30302-3083. Offers MA, PhD. *Accreditation:* APA (one or more programs are accredited). *Degree requirements:* For master's, thesis; for doctorate, comprehensive exam, thesis/dissertation. *Entrance requirements:* For doctorate, GRE General Test, departmental supplemental form. Additional exam requirements/recommendations for international students: Required—TOEFL. Electronic applications accepted. *Faculty research:* Social psychology, developmental and comparative psychology, neuropsychology, clinical psychology, neuropsychology.

Golden Gate University, Ageno School of Business, San Francisco, CA 94105-2968. Offers accounting (MBA); business administration (EMBA, MBA, PMBA, DBA); finance (MBA, MS, Certificate); financial planning (MS, Certificate); human resource management (MBA, MS); human resources management (Certificate); information systems (MS); information technology (MBA); information technology management (Certificate); integrated marketing and communications (MS, Certificate); international business (MBA); management (MBA); marketing (MBA, MS, Certificate); operations management (Certificate); psychology (MA, Certificate); public relations (MS, Certificate); JD/MBA. Part-time and evening/weekend programs available. *Faculty:* 16 full-time (4 women), 241 part-time/adjunct (72 women). *Students:* 380 full-time (193 women), 750 part-time (414 women); includes 480 minority (98 African Americans, 2 American Indian/Alaska Native, 298 Asian Americans or Pacific Islanders, 82 Hispanic Americans), 166 international. Average age 33. 681 applicants, 78% accepted, 270 enrolled. In 2009, 550 master's, 13 doctorates awarded. *Degree requirements:* For doctorate, thesis/dissertation. *Entrance requirements:* For master's, GMAT (MBA), minimum GPA of 2.5 (MS). Additional exam requirements/recommendations for international students: Required—TOEFL. *Application deadline:* For fall admission, 5/15 for international students; for winter admission, 1/15 for international students; for spring admission, 9/15 for international students. Applications are processed on a rolling basis. Application fee: $70 ($110 for international students). Electronic applications accepted. *Expenses:* Contact institution. *Financial support:* Career-related internships or fieldwork, Federal Work-Study, institutionally sponsored loans, and scholarships/grants available. Support available to part-time students. Financial award applicants required to submit FAFSA. *Unit head:* Terry Connelly, Dean, 415-442-6519, Fax: 415-442-5369. *Application contact:* Angela Melero, Enrollment Services, 415-442-7800, Fax: 415-442-7807, E-mail: info@ggu.edu.

Governors State University, College of Education, Program in Psychology, University Park, IL 60466-0975. Offers MA. Part-time and evening/weekend programs available. *Degree requirements:* For master's, thesis or alternative, practicum. *Entrance requirements:* For master's, GRE or MAT.

Graduate School and University Center of the City University of New York, Graduate Studies, Program in Psychology, New York, NY 10016-4039. Offers basic applied neurocognition (PhD); biopsychology (PhD); clinical psychology (PhD); developmental psychology (PhD); environmental psychology (PhD); experimental psychology (PhD); industrial psychology (PhD); learning processes (PhD); neuropsychology (PhD); psychology (PhD); social personality (PhD). *Faculty:* 119 full-time (40 women). *Students:* 559 full-time (414 women), 1 part-time (0 women); includes 101 minority (34 African Americans, 25 Asian Americans or Pacific Islanders, 42 Hispanic Americans), 57 international. Average age 33. 750 applicants, 16% accepted, 84 enrolled. In 2009, 54 doctorates awarded. *Degree requirements:* For doctorate, one foreign language, thesis/dissertation. *Entrance requirements:* For doctorate, GRE General Test. Additional exam requirements/recommendations for international students: Required—TOEFL. *Application deadline:* For fall admission, 12/15 priority date for domestic students. Application fee: $125. Electronic applications accepted. *Financial support:* In 2009–10, 371 students received support, including 340 fellowships, 34 research assistantships, 33 teaching assistantships; career-related internships or fieldwork, Federal Work-Study, institutionally sponsored loans, and tuition waivers (full and partial) also available. Financial award application deadline: 2/1; financial award applicants required to submit FAFSA. *Unit head:* Dr. Joseph Glick, Executive Officer, 212-817-8706, Fax: 212-817-1533, E-mail: jglick@gc.cuny.edu. *Application contact:* Les Gribben, Director of Admissions, 212-817-7470, Fax: 212-817-1624, E-mail: lgribben@gc.cuny.edu.

Hardin-Simmons University, Graduate School, Cynthia Ann Parker College of Liberal Arts, Department of Psychology, Abilene, TX 79698-0001. Offers family psychology (MA). Part-time programs available. *Faculty:* 6 full-time (2 women). *Students:* 12 full-time (8 women), 6 part-time (5 women); includes 2 minority (both Hispanic Americans). Average age 25. 10 applicants, 90% accepted, 9 enrolled. In 2009, 7 master's awarded. *Degree requirements:* For master's, comprehensive exam, clinical experience, project. *Entrance requirements:* For master's, 21 semester hours of course work in psychology (18 in upper division classes); minimum undergraduate GPA of 3.0 in major, 2.7 overall; writing sample; letters of recommendation. Additional exam requirements/recommendations for international students: Required—TOEFL (minimum score 550 paper-based; 213 computer-based; 75 iBT). *Application deadline:* For fall admission, 8/15 priority date for domestic students, 4/1 for international students; for spring admission, 1/5 priority date for domestic students, 9/1 for international students. Applications are processed on a rolling basis. Application fee: $50. *Expenses:* Tuition: Full-time $11,430; part-time $635 per credit hour. Required fees: $650; $110 per semester. Tuition and fees vary according to degree level. *Financial support:* In 2009–10, 14 students received support, including 16 fellowships (averaging $900 per year); career-related internships or fieldwork and scholarships/grants also available. Support available to part-time students. Financial award application deadline: 6/30; financial award applicants required to submit FAFSA. *Faculty research:* Spirituality in marriage, intimacy and sexuality in marriage, sex education in the church, role of faith in marital satisfaction, family stress management. *Unit head:* Dr. Doug Thomas, Head, 325-670-1534, Fax: 325-670-1458, E-mail: dthomas@hsutx.edu. *Application contact:* Dr. Gary Stanlake, Dean of Graduate Studies, 325-670-1298, Fax: 325-670-1564, E-mail: gradoff@hsutx.edu.

Harvard University, Graduate School of Arts and Sciences, Department of Psychology, Cambridge, MA 02138. Offers psychology (PhD), including behavior and decision analysis, cognition, developmental psychology, experimental psychology, personality, psychobiology, psychopathology; social psychology (PhD). *Accreditation:* APA. *Degree requirements:* For doctorate, thesis/dissertation, general exams. *Entrance requirements:* For doctorate, GRE General Test. Additional exam requirements/recommendations for international students: Required—TOEFL. *Expenses:* Tuition: Full-time $33,696. Required fees: $1126. Full-time tuition and fees vary according to program.

Hodges University, Graduate Programs, Naples, FL 34119. Offers business administration (MBA); computer information technology (MS); criminal justice (MCJ); education (MPS); information systems management (MIS); interdisciplinary (MPS); law (MPS); management (MSM); professional studies (MPS); psychology (MPS); public administration (MPA). Part-time and evening/weekend programs available. Postbaccalaureate distance learning degree programs offered (no on-campus study). *Faculty:* 14 full-time (4 women), 4 part-time/adjunct (3 women). *Students:* 37 full-time (28 women), 217 part-time (142 women); includes 76 minority (35 African Americans, 5 Asian Americans or Pacific Islanders, 36 Hispanic Americans). Average age 36. 92 applicants, 91% accepted, 81 enrolled. In 2009, 92 master's awarded. *Degree requirements:* For master's, comprehensive exam (for some programs), thesis (for some programs). *Entrance requirements:* For master's, in-house entrance exam. *Application deadline:* Applications are processed on a rolling basis. Application fee: $50. Electronic applications accepted. *Expenses:* Tuition: Full-time $16,605; part-time $615 per credit hour. Required fees: $570. *Financial support:* In 2009–10, 200 students received support. Federal Work-Study and scholarships/grants available. Financial award application deadline: 7/9; financial award applicants required to submit FAFSA. *Unit head:* Terry McMahan, President, 239-513-1122, Fax: 239-598-6253, E-mail: tmcmahan@hodges.edu. *Application contact:* Rita Lampus, Vice President of Student Enrollment Management, 239-513-1122, Fax: 239-598-6253, E-mail: rlampus@hodges.edu.

Hofstra University, College of Liberal Arts and Sciences, Department of Psychology, Hempstead, NY 11549. Offers applied organizational psychology (PhD); clinical psychology (PhD); industrial/organizational psychology (MA); school-community psychology (Psy D). Part-time and evening/weekend programs available. *Faculty:* 32 full-time (10 women), 11 part-time/adjunct (3 women). *Students:* 173 full-time (122 women), 39 part-time (26 women); includes 36 minority (11 African Americans, 21 Asian Americans or Pacific Islanders, 4 Hispanic Americans), 3 international. Average age 27. 341 applicants, 31% accepted, 63 enrolled. In 2009, 50 master's, 44 doctorates awarded. Terminal master's awarded for partial completion of doctoral program. *Degree requirements:* For master's, comprehensive exam, thesis optional, internship; for doctorate, comprehensive exam, thesis/dissertation, 1st year qualifying examination, 2nd year research project, successful practicum/externship placements, written presentation and successful oral defense of dissertation, completion of full-time internship. *Entrance requirements:* For master's, GRE, interview; for doctorate, GRE General Test, GRE Subject Test (psychology), letters of recommendation, interview, essay. Additional exam requirements/recommendations for international students: Required—TOEFL (minimum score 550 paper-based; 213 computer-based; 80 iBT). *Application deadline:* For fall admission, 1/15 priority date for domestic and international students. Application fee: $60. Electronic applications accepted. *Expenses:* Tuition: Full-time $16,200; part-time $900 per credit hour. Required fees: $970; $145 per term. Tuition and fees vary according to program. *Financial support:* In 2009–10, 108 students received support, including 99 fellowships with full and partial tuition reimbursements available (averaging $7,095 per year), 9 research assistantships with full and partial tuition reimbursements available (averaging $4,767 per year); career-related internships or fieldwork, Federal Work-Study, institutionally sponsored loans, scholarships/grants, tuition waivers (full and partial), unspecified assistantships, and some externship placements offer support stipends also available. Support available to part-time students. Financial award applicants required to submit FAFSA. *Faculty research:* Cognitive-behavioral psychology; childhood and adult trauma; occupational and organizational health; visual cognition and language; neuropsychology of attention and emotion. Total annual research expenditures: $130,000. *Unit head:* Dr. Charles F. Levinthal, Chairperson, 516-463-5627, Fax: 516-463-6052, E-mail: psycfl@hofstra.edu. *Application contact:* Carol Drummer, Dean of Graduate Admissions, 516-463-4876, Fax: 516-463-4664, E-mail: gradstudent@hofstra.edu.

Hood College, Graduate School, Programs in Human Sciences, Frederick, MD 21701-8575. Offers human sciences (MA), including psychology; thanatology (MA, Certificate). Part-time and evening/weekend programs available. *Faculty:* 6 full-time (3 women), 6 part-time/adjunct (3 women). *Students:* 13 full-time (11 women), 86 part-time (77 women); includes 16 minority (11 African Americans, 2 American Indian/Alaska Native, 2 Asian Americans or Pacific Islanders, 1 Hispanic American), 2 international. Average age 35. 54 applicants, 89% accepted, 26 enrolled. In 2009, 42 master's, 31 other advanced degrees awarded. *Degree requirements:* For master's, comprehensive exam, capstone/research project. *Entrance requirements:* For master's, minimum GPA of 2.75. Additional exam requirements/recommendations for international students: Required—TOEFL (minimum score 575 paper-based; 231 computer-based; 89 iBT). *Application deadline:* For fall admission, 7/15 for domestic and international students; for spring admission, 12/15 for domestic and international students. Applications are processed on a rolling basis. Application fee: $35. Electronic applications accepted. *Expenses:* Tuition: Full-time $6480; part-time $360 per credit. Required fees: $100; $50 per term. *Financial support:* Applicants required to submit FAFSA. *Faculty research:* Mind-body medicine and multicultural healing, the New Orleans jazz funeral, death practices in African-American culture, bereavement theories and gender differences, Piaget's theory of cognitive development as a formal mathematical model. *Unit head:* Dr. Dana G. Cable, Director, 301-696-3758, Fax: 301-696-3597, E-mail: cable@hood.edu. *Application contact:* Dr. Allen P. Flora, Dean of Graduate School, 301-696-3811, Fax: 301-696-3597, E-mail: gofurther@hood.edu.

Houston Baptist University, College of Education and Behavioral Sciences, Program in Psychology, Houston, TX 77074-3298. Offers MAP. Part-time and evening/weekend programs available. *Degree requirements:* For master's, comprehensive exam. *Entrance requirements:* For master's, GRE General Test, minimum GPA of 3.0. Additional exam requirements/recommendations for international students: Required—TOEFL (minimum score 550 paper-based; 213 computer-based).

Howard University, Graduate School, Department of Psychology, Washington, DC 20059-0002. Offers clinical psychology (PhD); developmental psychology (PhD); experimental psychology (PhD); neuropsychology (PhD); personality psychology (PhD); psychology (MS); social psychology (PhD). *Accreditation:* APA (one or more programs are accredited). Part-time programs available. *Degree requirements:* For master's, thesis; for doctorate, comprehensive exam, thesis/dissertation, qualifying exam. *Entrance requirements:* For master's, GRE General Test, minimum GPA of 2.5, bachelor's degree in psychology or related field; for doctorate, GRE General Test, minimum GPA of 3.0. *Faculty research:* Personality and psychophysiology, educational and social development of African-American children, child and adult psychopathology.

Humboldt State University, Graduate Studies, College of Professional Studies, Department of Psychology, Arcata, CA 95521-8299. Offers psychology (MA), including academic research, counseling, school psychology. *Students:* 60 full-time (45 women), 10 part-time (6 women); includes 13 minority (2 African Americans, 1 American Indian/Alaska Native, 3 Asian Americans or Pacific Islanders, 7 Hispanic Americans), 1 international. Average age 29. 64 applicants, 38% accepted, 21 enrolled. In 2009, 16 master's awarded. *Degree requirements:* For master's, thesis. *Entrance requirements:* For master's, appropriate bachelor's degree, minimum GPA of 2.5. Additional exam requirements/recommendations for international students: Required—TOEFL (minimum score 500 paper-based; 173 computer-based). *Application deadline:* For fall admission, 2/15 for domestic and international students. Applications are processed on a rolling basis. Application fee: $55. *Expenses:* Tuition, nonresident: full-time $8928. Required fees: $6102. Tuition and fees vary according to program. *Financial support:* Career-related internships or fieldwork available. Financial award application deadline: 3/1; financial award applicants required to submit FAFSA. *Faculty research:* School psychology, counseling, eating disorders, mood induction, depression. *Unit head:* Dr. Brent Duncan, Chair, 707-826-3755, Fax: 707-826-4993, E-mail: bbd1@humboldt.edu. *Application contact:* Dr. Chris Aberson, Coordinator, 707-826-3670, Fax: 707-826-4993, E-mail: cla18@humboldt.edu.

Hunter College of the City University of New York, Graduate School, School of Arts and Sciences, Department of Psychology, New York, NY 10021-5085. Offers applied and evaluative psychology (MA); biopsychology and comparative psychology (MA); social, cognitive, and developmental psychology (MA). Part-time and evening/weekend programs available. *Faculty:* 18 full-time (9 women), 2 part-time/adjunct (0 women). *Students:* 12 full-time (10 women), 68 part-time (56 women); includes 13 minority (2 African Americans, 3 Asian Americans or Pacific Islanders, 8 Hispanic Americans). Average age 28. 122 applicants, 37% accepted, 24 enrolled. In 2009, 15 master's awarded. *Degree requirements:* For master's, comprehensive exam, thesis. *Entrance requirements:* For master's, GRE General Test, minimum 12 credits of course work in psychology, including statistics and experimental psychology; 2 letters of recommendation. Additional exam requirements/recommendations for international students: Required—TOEFL. *Application deadline:* For fall admission, 4/1 for domestic students, 2/1 for international students; for spring admission, 11/1 for domestic students, 9/1 for international students. Applications are processed on a rolling basis. Application fee: $125. *Expenses:* Tuition, state resident: full-time $7360; part-time $310 per credit. Required fees: $250 per semester. *Financial support:* Federal Work-Study, scholarships/grants, and tuition waivers (partial) available. Support available to part-time students. *Faculty research:* Personality, cognitive and linguistic development, hormonal and neural control of behavior, gender and culture, social cognition of health and attitudes. *Unit head:* Dr. Jeffrey Parsons, Chairperson, 212-772-5550, Fax: 212-772-5620, E-mail: jeffrey.parsons@hunter.cuny.edu. *Application contact:* Martin Braun, Acting Program Director, 212-772-4482, Fax: 212-650-3336, E-mail: cbraun@hunter.cuny.edu.

Idaho State University, Office of Graduate Studies, College of Arts and Sciences, Department of Psychology, Pocatello, ID 83209-8112. Offers clinical psychology (PhD); psychology (MS). *Accreditation:* APA (one or more programs are accredited). Part-time programs available. *Faculty:* 10 full-time (6 women). *Students:* 28 full-time (18 women), 12 part-time (11 women); includes 4 minority (2 Asian Americans or Pacific Islanders, 2 Hispanic Americans), 2 international. Average age 34. In 2009, 8 master's, 4 doctorates awarded. *Degree requirements:* For master's, comprehensive exam, thesis, active participation in the research process; for doctorate, comprehensive exam, thesis/dissertation, 1 year full-time clinical internship. *Entrance requirements:* For master's, GRE General Test, GRE Subject Test, BS in psychology, minimum GPA of 3.0 in last 2 years of undergraduate courses; for doctorate, GRE General Test, GRE Subject Test, MS in psychology, recommendation from Clinical Admissions Committee. Additional exam requirements/recommendations for international students: Required—TOEFL (minimum score 550 paper-based; 213 computer-based; 80 iBT). *Application deadline:* For fall admission, 7/1 for domestic students, 6/1 for international students; for spring admission, 12/1 for domestic students, 11/1 for international students. Applications are processed on a rolling basis. Application fee: $55. Electronic applications accepted. *Expenses:* Tuition, state resident: full-time $3318; part-time $297 per credit hour. Tuition, nonresident: full-time $13,120; part-time $437 per credit hour. Required fees: $2530. Tuition and fees vary according to program. *Financial support:* In 2009–10, 10 research assistantships with full and partial tuition reimbursements (averaging $9,960 per year), 17 teaching assistantships with full and partial tuition reimbursements (averaging $10,841 per year) were awarded; career-related internships or fieldwork, Federal Work-Study, institutionally sponsored loans, scholarships/grants, traineeships, health care benefits, tuition waivers (full and partial), and unspecified assistantships also available. Support available to part-time students. Financial award application deadline: 1/1; financial award applicants required to submit FAFSA. *Faculty research:* Substance abuse, sexual decision making, trauma, behavioral pharmacology, developmental psychopathology, working memory and strategies, goal setting, person perception, developmental psychobiology, parent-child interactions. *Unit head:* Dr. Shannon Lynch, Interim Chair, 208-282-2462, Fax: 208-282-4832, E-mail: lyncshan@isu.edu. *Application contact:* Tami Carson, Graduate School Technical Records Specialist, 208-282-2150, Fax: 208-282-4847, E-mail: carstami@isu.edu.

Illinois Institute of Technology, Graduate College, Institute of Psychology, Chicago, IL 60616-3793. Offers clinical psychology (PhD); industrial/organizational psychology (PhD); personnel/human resource development (MS); psychology (MS); rehabilitation counseling (MS); rehabilitation counselor education (PhD). *Accreditation:* APA (one or more programs are accredited); CORE. Part-time and evening/weekend programs available. *Faculty:* 19 full-time (8 women), 5 part-time/adjunct (all women). *Students:* 118 full-time (88 women), 82 part-time (62 women); includes 33 minority (10 African Americans, 1 American Indian/Alaska Native, 14 Asian Americans or Pacific Islanders, 8 Hispanic Americans), 24 international. Average age 29. 281 applicants, 33% accepted, 28 enrolled. In 2009, 37 master's, 13 doctorates awarded. Terminal master's awarded for partial completion of doctoral program. *Degree requirements:* For master's, thesis (for some programs); for doctorate, comprehensive exam, thesis/dissertation, 96-108 credit hours, internship for Clinical and I/O specializations. *Entrance requirements:* For master's, GRE General Test, minimum high school GPA of 3.0, official transcripts, 3 letters of recommendation, personal statement; for doctorate, GRE General Test, minimum high school GPA of 3.0, official transcriptions, 3 letters of recommendation, personal statement. Additional exam requirements/recommendations for international students: Required—TOEFL (minimum score 550 paper-based; 80 iBT). *Application deadline:* For fall admission, 2/15 for domestic and international students. Application fee: $40. Electronic applications accepted. *Expenses:* Tuition: Full-time $17,550; part-time $888 per credit hour. Required fees: $850; $7.50 per credit hour. One-time fee: $50 full-time. Full-time tuition and fees vary according to program. *Financial support:* In 2009–10, 39 fellowships with partial tuition reimbursements (averaging $2,798 per year), 1 research assistantship with partial tuition reimbursement, 24 teaching assistantships with partial tuition reimbursements (averaging $4,405 per year) were awarded; career-related internships or fieldwork, Federal Work-Study, institutionally sponsored loans, scholarships/grants, traineeships, health care benefits, tuition waivers (partial), and unspecified assistantships also available. Support available to part-time students. Financial award application deadline: 1/15; financial award applicants required to submit FAFSA. *Faculty research:* Stigma and mental illness, depression, couples communication, leadership, psychometric theory. Total annual research expenditures: $426,090. *Unit head:* Dr. M. Ellen Mitchell, Dean, 312-567-3362, Fax: 312-567-3493, E-mail: mitchelle@iit.edu. *Application contact:* Institute of Psychology Graduate Admissions, 312-567-3500, Fax: 312-567-3493, E-mail: psychology@iit.edu.

Illinois State University, Graduate School, College of Arts and Sciences, Department of Psychology, Normal, IL 61790-2200. Offers psychology (MA, MS), including clinical psychology, counseling psychology, developmental psychology, educational psychology, experimental

Psychology—General

Illinois State University (continued)
psychology, measurement-evaluation, organizational-industrial psychology; school psychology (PhD, SSP). *Accreditation:* APA. *Degree requirements:* For master's, thesis or alternative; for doctorate, variable foreign language requirement, thesis/dissertation, 2 terms of residency, internship, practicum. *Entrance requirements:* For master's, GRE General Test, GRE Subject Test, minimum GPA of 3.0 in last 60 hours of course work; for doctorate, GRE General Test. *Faculty research:* Comprehensive evaluation system for the central region professional development grant, Illinois school psychology internship consortium, for children's sake.

Immaculata University, College of Graduate Studies, Department of Psychology, Immaculata, PA 19345. Offers clinical psychology (Psy D); counseling psychology (MA, Certificate), including school guidance counselor (Certificate), school psychologist (Certificate). *Accreditation:* APA. Part-time and evening/weekend programs available. *Degree requirements:* For master's, comprehensive exam, thesis optional; for doctorate, comprehensive exam, thesis/dissertation. *Entrance requirements:* For master's, GRE General Test or MAT, minimum GPA of 3.0; for doctorate, GRE General Test, minimum GPA of 3.5. Additional exam requirements/recommendations for international students: Required—TOEFL, IELTS. *Faculty research:* Supervision ethics, psychology of teaching, gender.

Indiana State University, School of Graduate Studies, College of Arts and Sciences, Department of Psychology, Terre Haute, IN 47809. Offers clinical psychology (Psy D); general psychology (MA, MS). *Accreditation:* APA (one or more programs are accredited). Terminal master's awarded for partial completion of doctoral program. *Degree requirements:* For master's, thesis (for some programs); for doctorate, comprehensive exam, thesis/dissertation, internship, professional research project. *Entrance requirements:* For master's, GRE General Test, 12 semester hours of course work in psychology, minimum GPA of 2.75; for doctorate, GRE General Test, minimum GPA of 3.0. Additional exam requirements/recommendations for international students: Required—TOEFL (minimum score 550 paper-based). Electronic applications accepted.

Indiana University Bloomington, University Graduate School, College of Arts and Sciences, Department of Criminal Justice, Bloomington, IN 47405. Offers criminal justice (MA, PhD); criminology (MA, PhD); cross-cultural perspectives of crime and justice (MA, PhD); law and society (MA, PhD); psychology and the law (MA). Part-time programs available. *Faculty:* 15 full-time (5 women). *Students:* 41 full-time (23 women); includes 6 minority (3 African Americans, 2 American Indian/Alaska Native, 1 Hispanic American), 5 international. Average age 31. 31 applicants, 42% accepted, 9 enrolled. In 2009, 2 master's, 1 doctorate awarded. Terminal master's awarded for partial completion of doctoral program. *Degree requirements:* For master's, thesis optional; for doctorate, thesis/dissertation, foreign language or research practicum. *Entrance requirements:* For master's and doctorate, GRE General Test. Additional exam requirements/recommendations for international students: Required—TOEFL (minimum score 600 paper-based; 250 computer-based; 100 iBT). *Application deadline:* For fall admission, 1/15 for domestic students, 12/1 for international students. Application fee: $55 ($65 for international students). Electronic applications accepted. *Expenses:* Contact institution. *Financial support:* In 2009–10, 4 fellowships with full tuition reimbursements (averaging $25,000 per year), 3 research assistantships with full tuition reimbursements (averaging $11,721 per year), 21 teaching assistantships with full tuition reimbursements (averaging $11,721 per year) were awarded; Federal Work-Study, health care benefits, tuition waivers (full), and unspecified assistantships also available. Financial award application deadline: 1/15. *Faculty research:* Violence, crime, juveniles, psychology and law, cross-cultural studies. *Unit head:* Dr. Roger J. R. Levesque, Chair, 812-856-1210, E-mail: rlevesqu@indiana.edu. *Application contact:* Ruth Cord, Graduate Secretary, 812-856-4675, Fax: 812-855-5522, E-mail: rkapusti@indiana.edu.

Indiana University Bloomington, University Graduate School, College of Arts and Sciences, Department of Psychological and Brain Sciences, Bloomington, IN 47405-7000. Offers biology and behavior (PhD); clinical science (PhD); cognitive psychology (PhD); developmental psychology (PhD); psychological and brain sciences (MA); social psychology (PhD). *Accreditation:* APA (one or more programs are accredited). *Faculty:* 53 full-time (16 women). *Students:* 92 full-time (51 women); includes 12 minority (4 African Americans, 4 Asian Americans or Pacific Islanders, 4 Hispanic Americans), 19 international. Average age 28. 239 applicants, 10% accepted, 15 enrolled. In 2009, 3 master's, 13 doctorates awarded. *Degree requirements:* For doctorate, comprehensive exam, thesis/dissertation, 1st and 2nd year projects, 1 year as associate instructor, qualifying exam, student teaching. *Entrance requirements:* For doctorate, GRE. Additional exam requirements/recommendations for international students: Required—TOEFL (minimum score 550 paper-based; 213 computer-based). *Application deadline:* For fall admission, 12/15 for domestic students, 12/1 for international students. Application fee: $55 ($65 for international students). Electronic applications accepted. *Financial support:* In 2009–10, 25 fellowships with full tuition reimbursements (averaging $23,000 per year), 11 research assistantships with full tuition reimbursements (averaging $17,850 per year), 7 teaching assistantships with full tuition reimbursements (averaging $17,850 per year) were awarded; scholarships/grants, health care benefits, and unspecified assistantships also available. *Unit head:* Dr. Linda B. Smith, Chair, 812-855-3991, Fax: 812-855-4691, E-mail: smith4@indiana.edu. *Application contact:* Patricia G. Crouch, Academic Services Coordinator, 812-855-4528, Fax: 812-855-4691, E-mail: pcrouch@indiana.edu.

Indiana University of Pennsylvania, School of Graduate Studies and Research, College of Natural Sciences and Mathematics, Department of Psychology, Indiana, PA 15705-1087. Offers clinical psychology (Psy D); psychology (MA). *Accreditation:* APA (one or more programs are accredited). Part-time programs available. *Faculty:* 14 full-time (8 women). *Students:* 41 full-time (33 women), 17 part-time (16 women); includes 2 minority (both Hispanic Americans). Average age 28. 109 applicants, 8% accepted, 9 enrolled. In 2009, 8 master's, 15 doctorates awarded. Terminal master's awarded for partial completion of doctoral program. *Degree requirements:* For doctorate, comprehensive exam, thesis/dissertation, internship, practicum. *Entrance requirements:* For master's, GRE General Test; for doctorate, GRE General Test, minimum GPA of 3.0, interview, letters of recommendation. Additional exam requirements/recommendations for international students: Required—TOEFL. *Application deadline:* For fall admission, 1/10 for domestic students. Applications are processed on a rolling basis. Application fee: $40. *Expenses:* Tuition, state resident: full-time $6666; part-time $370 per credit hour. Tuition, nonresident: full-time $10,666; part-time $593 per credit hour. Required fees: $813 per semester. *Financial support:* In 2009–10, 3 fellowships (averaging $2,667 per year), 39 research assistantships with full and partial tuition reimbursements (averaging $4,018 per year), 1 teaching assistantship (averaging $21,536 per year) were awarded; Federal Work-Study and scholarships/grants also available. Financial award application deadline: 3/15; financial award applicants required to submit FAFSA. *Unit head:* Dr. Mary Lou Zanich, Chairperson, 724-357-2426, E-mail: mtzanich@iup.edu. *Application contact:* Dr. Donald Robertson, Graduate Coordinator, 724-357-4522, E-mail: durobert@iup.edu.

Indiana University–Purdue University Indianapolis, School of Science, Department of Psychology, Indianapolis, IN 46202-3275. Offers clinical rehabilitation psychology (MS); industrial/organizational psychology (MS); psychobiology of addictions (MS, PhD). *Accreditation:* APA (one or more programs are accredited). *Faculty:* 10 full-time (2 women). *Students:* 50 full-time (45 women), 11 part-time (9 women); includes 7 minority (4 African Americans, 2 Asian Americans or Pacific Islanders, 1 Hispanic American), 3 international. Average age 28. 132 applicants, 17% accepted, 22 enrolled. In 2009, 7 master's awarded. Terminal master's awarded for partial completion of doctoral program. *Degree requirements:* For master's, thesis; for doctorate, thesis/dissertation. *Entrance requirements:* For master's, GRE General Test, minimum undergraduate GPA of 3.0; for doctorate, GRE General Test, GRE Subject Test (clinical rehabilitation psychology), minimum undergraduate GPA of 3.2. *Application deadline:* For fall admission, 1/1 priority date for domestic students. Application fee: $55 ($65 for international students). *Financial support:* In 2009–10, 5 fellowships with partial tuition reimbursements (averaging $12,218 per year), 23 teaching assistantships with partial tuition reimbursements (averaging $7,553 per year) were awarded; research assistantships with partial tuition reimbursements, career-related internships or fieldwork, Federal Work-Study, and institutionally sponsored loans also available. Financial award application deadline: 3/1; financial award applicants required to submit FAFSA. *Faculty research:* Psychiatric rehabilitation, chronic stress, neurological research, language and cognitive development in infants, alcoholism and psychopathology. *Unit head:* Dr. J. Gregor Fetterman, Chairman, 317-274-6945, Fax: 317-274-6756, E-mail: gfetter@iupui.edu. *Application contact:* Dr. J. Gregor Fetterman, Chairman, 317-274-6945, Fax: 317-274-6756, E-mail: gfetter@iupui.edu.

Indiana University South Bend, College of Liberal Arts and Sciences, South Bend, IN 46634-7111. Offers applied mathematics and computer science (MS); applied psychology (MA); English (MA); liberal studies (MLS). Part-time and evening/weekend programs available. *Faculty:* 79 full-time (33 women). *Students:* 27 full-time (10 women), 83 part-time (55 women); includes 17 minority (10 African Americans, 2 American Indian/Alaska Native, 2 Asian Americans or Pacific Islanders, 3 Hispanic Americans), 10 international. Average age 36. In 2009, 24 master's awarded. *Degree requirements:* For master's, thesis (for some programs). *Entrance requirements:* For master's, minimum GPA of 3.0. Additional exam requirements/recommendations for international students: Required—TOEFL. *Application deadline:* For fall admission, 7/31 priority date for domestic students, 7/1 priority date for international students; for spring admission, 3/31 priority date for domestic students, 11/1 priority date for international students. Applications are processed on a rolling basis. Application fee: $46 ($58 for international students). *Financial support:* In 2009–10, 5 students received support, including 5 teaching assistantships; Federal Work-Study also available. Support available to part-time students. *Faculty research:* Artificial intelligence, bioinformatics, English language and literature, creative writing, computer networks. Total annual research expenditures: $127,000. *Unit head:* Dr. Lynn R. Williams, Dean, 574-520-4322, Fax: 574-520-4528, E-mail: lwilliam@iusb.edu. *Application contact:* Dr. Lynn R. Williams, Dean, 574-520-4322, Fax: 574-520-4528, E-mail: lwilliam@iusb.edu.

Institute of Transpersonal Psychology, Global Online Programs, Palo Alto, CA 94303. Offers psychology (PhD); transpersonal psychology (MTP); transpersonal studies (Certificate). Postbaccalaureate distance learning degree programs offered (minimal on-campus study). Terminal master's awarded for partial completion of doctoral program. *Degree requirements:* For master's, thesis (for some programs); for doctorate, thesis/dissertation. *Entrance requirements:* For master's and doctorate, bachelor's degree. Additional exam requirements/recommendations for international students: Required—TOEFL. *Expenses:* Contact institution.

Institute of Transpersonal Psychology, Low-Residency Programs, Palo Alto, CA 94303. Offers counseling psychology (online) (MA); spiritual guidance (MA); women's spirituality (MA). Postbaccalaureate distance learning degree programs offered (minimal on-campus study).

Institute of Transpersonal Psychology, Residential Programs, Palo Alto, CA 94303. Offers counseling psychology (MA); spiritually oriented clinical psychology (Psy D); transpersonal psychology (MA, PhD). Part-time and evening/weekend programs available. Terminal master's awarded for partial completion of doctoral program. *Degree requirements:* For doctorate, thesis/dissertation. *Entrance requirements:* For master's and doctorate, bachelor's degree.

Instituto Tecnologico de Santo Domingo, Graduate School, Santo Domingo, Dominican Republic. Offers applied linguistics (MA); construction administration (M Mgmt); corporate finance (M Mgmt); education (M Ed); engineering (M Eng), including data telecommunications, industrial engineering, logistics and supply chain, maintenance engineering, sanitary and environmental engineering, structural engineering; environmental science (M En S), including environmental education, environmental management, marine and coastal ecosystems, natural resources management; family therapy (MA); food science and technology (MS); human development (MA); human resources administration (M Mgmt); international business (M Mgmt); labor risks (M Mgmt); management (M Mgmt); marketing (M Mgmt); mathematics (MS); organizational development (M Mgmt); planning and taxation (M Mgmt); psychology (MA); social science (M Ed); upper management (M Mgmt). *Entrance requirements:* For master's, birth certificate, minimum GPA of 2.0.

Inter American University of Puerto Rico, Metropolitan Campus, Graduate Programs, Program in Psychology, San Juan, PR 00919-1293. Offers counseling psychology (MA, PhD); industrial/organizational psychology (MA, PhD); labor relations (MA); school psychology (MA, PhD). *Degree requirements:* For master's, comprehensive exam. *Entrance requirements:* For master's, GRE or EXADEP, interview. Electronic applications accepted.

Inter American University of Puerto Rico, San Germán Campus, Graduate Studies Center, Program in Psychology, San Germán, PR 00683-5008. Offers counseling psychology (MA, PhD); school psychology (MA, PhD). Part-time and evening/weekend programs available. *Degree requirements:* For master's, comprehensive exam, thesis; for doctorate, comprehensive exam, thesis/dissertation. *Entrance requirements:* For master's, GRE General Test or EXADEP, minimum GPA of 3.0; for doctorate, GRE, EXADEP or MAT, minimum GPA of 3.0.

Iona College, School of Arts and Science, Department of Psychology, New Rochelle, NY 10801-1890. Offers experimental psychology (MA); industrial-organizational psychology (MA); mental health counseling (MA); psychology (MA); school psychology (MA). Part-time and evening/weekend programs available. *Faculty:* 14 full-time (8 women), 10 part-time/adjunct (8 women). *Students:* 74 full-time (58 women), 46 part-time (34 women); includes 28 minority (13 African Americans, 1 American Indian/Alaska Native, 3 Asian Americans or Pacific Islanders, 11 Hispanic Americans), 1 international. Average age 25. 186 applicants, 61% accepted, 44 enrolled. In 2009, 35 master's awarded. *Degree requirements:* For master's, thesis. *Entrance requirements:* For master's, GRE or minimum GPA of 3.0. Additional exam requirements/recommendations for international students: Required—TOEFL (minimum score 550 paper-based; 213 computer-based). *Application deadline:* Applications are processed on a rolling basis. Application fee: $50. Electronic applications accepted. *Expenses:* Tuition: Part-time $830 per credit. *Financial support:* Career-related internships or fieldwork, tuition waivers (partial), and unspecified assistantships available. Support available to part-time students. Financial award application deadline: 4/15; financial award applicants required to submit FAFSA. *Unit head:* Dr. Paul Greene, Chair, 914-633-2048, E-mail: pgreene@iona.edu. *Application contact:* Veronica Jarek-Prinz, Director of Graduate Admissions, 914-633-2420, Fax: 914-633-2277, E-mail: vjarekprinz@iona.edu.

Iowa State University of Science and Technology, Graduate College, College of Liberal Arts and Sciences, Department of Psychology, Ames, IA 50011. Offers cognitive psychology (PhD); counseling psychology (PhD); social psychology (PhD). *Accreditation:* APA. *Faculty:* 25 full-time (8 women), 8 part-time/adjunct (4 women). *Degree requirements:* For doctorate, comprehensive exam, thesis/dissertation. *Entrance requirements:* For doctorate, GRE General Test, GRE Subject Test (psychology), 3 letters of recommendation. Additional exam requirements/recommendations for international students: Required—TOEFL (minimum score 560 paper-based; 220 computer-based). *Application deadline:* For fall admission, 1/2 priority date for domestic and international students. Application fee: $30 ($70 for international students). Electronic applications accepted. *Expenses:* Tuition, state resident: full-time $6716. Tuition, nonresident: full-time $8908. Tuition and fees vary according to course level, course load, program and student level. *Financial support:* In 2009–10, fellowships with full tuition reimbursements (averaging $14,055 per year), research assistantships with full tuition reimbursements (averaging $12,200 per year), teaching assistantships with full tuition reimbursements (averaging $12,200 per year) were awarded; scholarships/grants, health care benefits, and unspecified assistantships also available. *Faculty research:* Counseling psychology, cognitive psychology, social psychology, health psychology, psychology and public policy. *Unit head:* Carolyn Cutrona, Chair, 515-294-0283, Fax: 515-294-6424, E-mail: ccutrona@iastate.edu. *Application contact:* Ann Schmidt, Graduate Admissions Secretary, 515-294-1743, Fax: 515-294-6424, E-mail: psychadm@iastate.edu.

Jackson State University, Graduate School, School of Liberal Arts, Department of Psychology, Jackson, MS 39217. Offers clinical psychology (PhD). *Accreditation:* APA. *Degree requirements:* For doctorate, comprehensive exam, thesis/dissertation. *Entrance requirements:* For doctorate, MAT, GRE.

Jacksonville State University, College of Graduate Studies and Continuing Education, College of Arts and Sciences, Department of Psychology, Jacksonville, AL 36265-1602. Offers MS. Part-time and evening/weekend programs available. *Degree requirements:* For master's, comprehensive exam, thesis (for some programs). *Entrance requirements:* For master's, GRE General Test or MAT. Electronic applications accepted.

James Madison University, The Graduate School, College of Integrated Science and Technology, Department of Graduate Psychology, Harrisonburg, VA 22807. Offers assessment and measurement (PhD); clinical mental health counseling (M Ed, MA, Ed S); college student personnel administration (M Ed); combined-integrated clinical and school psychology (Psy D); psychological sciences (MA); school counseling (Ed S); school psychology (M Ed, MA, Ed S), including school counseling (M Ed, Ed S), school psychology (MA, Ed S). *Accreditation:* ACA (one or more programs are accredited); APA (one or more programs are accredited). Part-time and evening/weekend programs available. *Faculty:* 34 full-time (19 women), 18 part-time/adjunct (12 women). *Students:* 115 full-time (83 women), 43 part-time (35 women); includes 18 minority (12 African Americans, 3 Asian Americans or Pacific Islanders, 3 Hispanic Americans), 4 international. Average age 27. In 2009, 44 master's, 14 doctorates, 27 other advanced degrees awarded. *Degree requirements:* For doctorate, thesis/dissertation; for Ed S, thesis. *Entrance requirements:* For master's, GRE General Test, GRE Subject Test; for doctorate, GRE General Test. Additional exam requirements/recommendations for international students: Required—TOEFL. *Application deadline:* For fall admission, 2/1 priority date for domestic students; for spring admission, 9/1 for domestic students. Applications are processed on a rolling basis. Application fee: $55. Electronic applications accepted. *Expenses:* Tuition, area resident: Part-time $305 per credit hour. Tuition, state resident: part-time $305 per credit hour. Tuition, nonresident: part-time $890 per credit hour. *Financial support:* In 2009–10, 91 students received support, including 3 teaching assistantships with full tuition reimbursements available (averaging $8,664 per year); research assistantships, career-related internships or fieldwork and Federal Work-Study also available. Financial award application deadline: 3/1; financial award applicants required to submit FAFSA. *Unit head:* Sheena J. Rogers, Academic Unit Head, 540-568-6439, Fax: 540-568-3322, E-mail: rogerssj@cisat.jmu.edu. *Application contact:* Sheena J. Rogers, Academic Unit Head, 540-568-6439, Fax: 540-568-3322, E-mail: rogerssj@cisat.jmu.edu.

John F. Kennedy University, Graduate School of Holistic Studies, Department of Integral Studies, Program in Integral Psychology, Pleasant Hill, CA 94523-4817. Offers dream studies (Certificate); integral psychology (MA); life coaching (Certificate). Part-time and evening/weekend programs available.

John F. Kennedy University, Graduate School of Professional Psychology, Pleasant Hill, CA 94523-4817. Offers MA, Psy D, Certificate. *Accreditation:* APA. Part-time and evening/weekend programs available. *Degree requirements:* For master's, thesis or alternative. *Entrance requirements:* For master's, interview. Additional exam requirements/recommendations for international students: Required—TOEFL.

The Johns Hopkins University, Zanvyl Krieger School of Arts and Sciences, Department of Psychological and Brain Sciences, Baltimore, MD 21218. Offers PhD. *Faculty:* 16 full-time (8 women), 8 part-time/adjunct (1 woman). *Students:* 27 full-time (13 women); includes 4 minority (1 African American, 3 Asian Americans or Pacific Islanders), 6 international. Average age 26. 91 applicants, 14% accepted, 7 enrolled. In 2009, 6 doctorates awarded. *Median time to degree:* Of those who began their doctoral program in fall 2001, 100% received their degree in 8 years or less. *Degree requirements:* For doctorate, thesis/dissertation, research project, teaching experience. *Entrance requirements:* For doctorate, GRE General Test, GRE Subject Test. Additional exam requirements/recommendations for international students: Required—TOEFL (minimum score 600 paper-based; 250 computer-based; 100 iBT), IELTS. *Application deadline:* For fall admission, 12/15 priority date for domestic students, 12/15 for international students. Application fee: $75. Electronic applications accepted. *Financial support:* In 2009–10, 8 fellowships with partial tuition reimbursements (averaging $25,333 per year), 18 teaching assistantships with full tuition reimbursements (averaging $25,333 per year) were awarded; Federal Work-Study, tuition waivers (full), and unspecified assistantships also available. Financial award application deadline: 4/15; financial award applicants required to submit FAFSA. *Faculty research:* Biopsychology, cognitive psychology, cognitive neuroscience, developmental psychology, neurobiology. Total annual research expenditures: $2.5 million. *Unit head:* Dr. Steven Yantis, Chair, 410-516-5328, Fax: 410-516-4478, E-mail: psychair@jhu.edu. *Application contact:* Hope Stein, Admissions Coordinator, 410-516-6175, Fax: 410-516-4478, E-mail: hope.stein@jhu.edu.

Kansas State University, Graduate School, College of Arts and Sciences, Department of Psychology, Manhattan, KS 66506. Offers MS, PhD. Part-time programs available. *Faculty:* 14 full-time (5 women), 6 part-time/adjunct (1 woman). *Students:* 8 full-time (3 women), 33 part-time (24 women). Average age 29. 112 applicants, 38% accepted, 22 enrolled. In 2009, 12 master's, 6 doctorates awarded. *Degree requirements:* For master's, thesis or alternative; for doctorate, thesis/dissertation, preliminary exam. *Entrance requirements:* For master's, GRE General Test, minimum undergraduate GPA of 3.0; for doctorate, GRE General Test, minimum GPA of 3.0. Additional exam requirements/recommendations for international students: Required—TOEFL (minimum score 600 paper-based; 250 computer-based). *Application deadline:* For fall admission, 2/1 priority date for domestic and international students; for spring admission, 8/1 priority date for domestic and international students. Applications are processed on a rolling basis. Application fee: $40 ($55 for international students). Electronic applications accepted. *Financial support:* In 2009–10, 4 research assistantships (averaging $11,660 per year), 15 teaching assistantships with full tuition reimbursements (averaging $10,702 per year) were awarded; career-related internships or fieldwork, institutionally sponsored loans, and scholarships/grants also available. Support available to part-time students. Financial award application deadline: 3/1; financial award applicants required to submit FAFSA. *Faculty research:* Personal and occupational health, neurological bases of drug use and abuse, measurement and reduction of prejudice, judgment and decision making, visual perception. Total annual research expenditures: $333,324. *Unit head:* Jerry Frieman, Head, 785-532-0607, Fax: 785-532-5401, E-mail: frieman@ksu.edu. *Application contact:* Clive Fullagar, Director, 785-532-0608, Fax: 785-532-5401, E-mail: fullagar@ksu.edu.

Kean University, College of Humanities and Social Sciences, Program in Psychology, Union, NJ 07083. Offers human behavior and organizational psychology (MA); psychological services (MA). Part-time and evening/weekend programs available. *Faculty:* 15 full-time (13 women). *Students:* 14 full-time (10 women), 35 part-time (30 women); includes 20 minority (11 African Americans, 2 Asian Americans or Pacific Islanders, 7 Hispanic Americans), 2 international. Average age 30. 28 applicants, 82% accepted, 15 enrolled. In 2009, 15 master's awarded. *Degree requirements:* For master's, comprehensive exam, thesis, research. *Entrance requirements:* For master's, GRE General Test, minimum GPA of 3.0, 2 letters of recommendation, interview, 12 credits in psychology. *Application deadline:* For fall admission, 5/1 for domestic students; for spring admission, 11/1 for domestic students. Application fee: $60 ($150 for international students). Electronic applications accepted. *Expenses:* Tuition, state resident: full-time $10,440; part-time $435 per credit. Tuition, nonresident: full-time $14,160; part-time $590 per credit. Required fees: $2642; $110 per credit. Part-time tuition and fees vary according to course load and degree level. *Financial support:* In 2009–10, 1 research assistantship with full tuition reimbursement (averaging $3,263 per year) was awarded; unspecified assistantships also available. *Unit head:* Dr. Joanne Walsh, Program Coordinator, 908-737-5870, E-mail: jwalsh@kean.edu. *Application contact:* Reenat Hasan, Pre-Admissions Coordinator, 908-737-5923, Fax: 908-737-5965, E-mail: rhasan@exchange.kean.edu.

Kent State University, College of Arts and Sciences, Department of Psychology, Kent, OH 44242-0001. Offers clinical psychology (MA, PhD); experimental psychology (MA, PhD). *Accreditation:* APA (one or more programs are accredited). *Degree requirements:* For master's, thesis; for doctorate, thesis/dissertation. *Entrance requirements:* For master's, GRE, minimum GPA of 3.0, minimum 18 semester hours in psychology with one course in statistics and one experimental course with a lab component; for doctorate, GRE, minimum GPA of 3.0. Additional exam requirements/recommendations for international students: Required—TOEFL (minimum score 525 paper-based), Michigan English Language Assessment Battery (minimum score: 77).

Lakehead University, Graduate Studies, Department of Psychology, Thunder Bay, ON P7B 5E1, Canada. Offers clinical psychology (PhD); experimental psychology (MA). Part-time and evening/weekend programs available. *Degree requirements:* For master's, thesis optional; for doctorate, thesis/dissertation, 2 comprehensive exams, internship. *Entrance requirements:* For master's, GRE, honors degree in psychology, advanced course work in statistics, minimum B average; for doctorate, GRE, minimum B average. Additional exam requirements/recommendations for international students: Required—TOEFL. *Faculty research:* Chaos theory, health psychology, counseling psychology, gerontology, women's studies.

Lamar University, College of Graduate Studies, College of Arts and Sciences, Department of Psychology, Beaumont, TX 77710. Offers community/clinical psychology (MS); industrial/organizational psychology (MS). Part-time programs available. *Faculty:* 6 full-time (3 women). *Students:* 14 full-time (10 women), 11 part-time (5 women); includes 4 minority (2 African Americans, 2 Hispanic Americans), 1 international. Average age 25. 34 applicants, 18% accepted, 4 enrolled. In 2009, 1 master's awarded. *Degree requirements:* For master's, thesis, practicum. *Entrance requirements:* For master's, GRE General Test, minimum GPA of 2.75 in last 60 hours of undergraduate course work. Additional exam requirements/recommendations for international students: Required—TOEFL. *Application deadline:* For fall admission, 8/1 for domestic students; for spring admission, 12/1 for domestic students. Application fee: $25 ($50 for international students). *Financial support:* In 2009–10, 12 students received support, including 3 teaching assistantships (averaging $4,500 per year); fellowships, research assistantships, career-related internships or fieldwork, Federal Work-Study, scholarships/grants, and tuition waivers (partial) also available. Support available to part-time students. Financial award application deadline: 4/1. *Faculty research:* Groupthink, health psychology, school psychology, behavioral neuroscience. *Application contact:* Assistant Dean, 409-880-7978, E-mail: westgate@hal.lamar.edu.

La Salle University, School of Arts and Sciences, Program in Psychology, Philadelphia, PA 19141-1199. Offers clinical psychology (Psy D); family psychology (Psy D); rehabilitation psychology (Psy D). Part-time and evening/weekend programs available. *Entrance requirements:* For doctorate, GRE, minimum GPA of 3.0. *Expenses:* Contact institution. *Faculty research:* Cognitive therapy, attribution theory, treatment of addiction.

Laurentian University, School of Graduate Studies and Research, Programme in Psychology, Sudbury, ON P3E 2C6, Canada. Offers applied psychology (MA); experimental psychology (MA).

Lehigh University, College of Arts and Sciences, Department of Psychology, Bethlehem, PA 18015. Offers human cognition and development (MS, PhD). *Faculty:* 13 full-time (7 women). *Students:* 14 full-time (11 women), 1 (woman) part-time, 4 international. Average age 27. 56 applicants, 14% accepted, 3 enrolled. In 2009, 5 master's awarded. *Degree requirements:* For master's, thesis; for doctorate, comprehensive exam, thesis/dissertation. *Entrance requirements:* For doctorate, GRE General Test. Additional exam requirements/recommendations for international students: Required—TOEFL. *Application deadline:* For fall admission, 1/15 for domestic and international students. Application fee: $75. Electronic applications accepted. *Expenses:* Contact institution. *Financial support:* In 2009–10, 15 students received support, including 1 fellowship with full tuition reimbursement available (averaging $22,000 per year), 3 research assistantships with full tuition reimbursements available (averaging $17,400 per year), 11 teaching assistantships with full tuition reimbursements available (averaging $17,400 per year); scholarships/grants, tuition waivers (full and partial), and unspecified assistantships also available. Financial award application deadline: 1/15. *Faculty research:* Cognition, memory, language, and their development; prosocial cognition, emotion, and action; conflict and cooperation between and within groups; self-control of cognition and emotion; optimizing developmental and relational outcomes. Total annual research expenditures: $142,283. *Unit head:* Diane Hyland, Chairperson, 610-758-3631, Fax: 610-758-6277, E-mail: dthl@lehigh.edu. *Application contact:* Dr. Michael Gill, Program Director, 610-758-3630, Fax: 610-758-6277, E-mail: inpsy@lehigh.edu.

Lesley University, Graduate School of Arts and Social Sciences, Cambridge, MA 02138-2790. Offers clinical mental health counseling (MA), including expressive therapies counseling, holistic counseling, school and community counseling; counseling psychology (MA, CAGS), including professional counseling (MA), school counseling (MA); creative arts in learning (CAGS); creative writing (MFA); ecological teaching and learning (MS); environmental education (MS); expressive therapies (MA, PhD, CAGS), including art (MA), dance (MA), expressive therapies, music (MA); independent studies (CAGS); independent study (MA); intercultural relations (MA, CAGS); interdisciplinary studies (MA), including individualized studies, integrative holistic health, women's studies; urban environmental leadership (MA); visual arts (MFA). Part-time and evening/weekend programs available. Postbaccalaureate distance learning degree programs offered (minimal on-campus study). *Degree requirements:* For master's, internship, practicum, thesis (expressive therapies); for doctorate, thesis/dissertation, arts apprenticeship, field placement; for CAGS, thesis, internship (counseling psychology, expressive therapies). *Entrance requirements:* For master's, MAT (counseling psychology), interview, writing samples, art portfolio; for doctorate, GRE or MAT; for CAGS, interview, master's degree. Additional exam requirements/recommendations for international students: Required—TOEFL (minimum score 550 paper-based; 213 computer-based; 80 iBT). Electronic applications accepted. *Faculty research:* Psychotherapy and culture; psychotherapy and psychological trauma; women's issues in art, teaching and psychotherapy; community based art, psycho-spiritual inquiry.

Lewis & Clark College, Graduate School of Education and Counseling, Department of Counseling Psychology, Portland, OR 97219-7899. Offers addictions treatment (MA, MS); community counseling (MA, MS); marriage, couple and family therapy (MA, MS); psychological and cultural studies (MA, MS); school psychology (Ed S). Part-time and evening/weekend programs available. *Faculty:* 11 full-time (7 women), 22 part-time/adjunct (15 women). *Students:* 103 full-time (87 women), 146 part-time (115 women); includes 22 minority (3 African Americans, 9 Asian Americans or Pacific Islanders, 10 Hispanic Americans), 3 international. Average age 31. 157 applicants, 78% accepted, 75 enrolled. In 2009, 69 master's, 13 other advanced degrees awarded. *Degree requirements:* For master's, thesis proposal (MS). *Entrance requirements:* For master's, GRE General Test, minimum undergraduate GPA of 2.75. Additional exam requirements/recommendations for international students: Required—TOEFL (minimum score 575 paper-based; 233 computer-based). *Application deadline:* For fall admission, 2/1 priority date for domestic and international students; for spring admission, 10/1 priority date for domestic and international students. Application fee: $50. Electronic applications accepted. *Expenses:* Tuition: Part-time $713 per semester hour. Tuition and fees vary according to course level and campus/location. *Financial support:* In 2009–10, 230 students received support. Career-related internships or fieldwork, Federal Work-Study, institutionally sponsored loans, scholarships/grants, health care benefits, and tuition waivers (partial) available. Support available to part-time students. Financial award application deadline: 3/1; financial award applicants required to submit FAFSA. *Unit head:* Dr. Tod Sloan, Chair, 503-768-6060, Fax: 503-768-6065, E-mail: cpsy@lclark.edu. *Application contact:* Becky Haas, Director of Admissions, 503-768-6200, Fax: 503-768-6205, E-mail: gseadmit@lclark.edu.

Lipscomb University, Program in Counseling, Nashville, TN 37204-3951. Offers counseling psychology (Certificate); professional counseling (MS); psychology (MS). Part-time and evening/weekend programs available. Postbaccalaureate distance learning degree programs offered

Psychology—General

Lipscomb University (continued)
(minimal on-campus study). *Faculty:* 4 full-time (0 women), 13 part-time/adjunct (6 women). *Students:* 67 full-time (48 women), 39 part-time (26 women); includes 16 minority (9 African Americans, 1 American Indian/Alaska Native, 2 Asian Americans or Pacific Islanders, 4 Hispanic Americans), 1 international. Average age 30. 72 applicants, 82% accepted, 42 enrolled. *Entrance requirements:* For master's, GRE, resume, 3 reference letters, minimum GPA of 3.0. Application fee: $50. Electronic applications accepted. *Expenses:* Tuition: Full-time $16,002; part-time $889 per credit hour. Tuition and fees vary according to program. *Faculty research:* Cognitive psychology, neuroscience, health psychology, grief issues. *Unit head:* Dr. Jake Morris, Graduate Program Director and Professor of Psychology, E-mail: jake.morris@lipscomb.edu. *Application contact:* Elena Zemmel, Administrative Assistant, 615-966-5906, E-mail: elena.zemmel@lipscomb.edu.

Loma Linda University, School of Science and Technology, Department of Psychology, Loma Linda, CA 92350. Offers PhD, Psy D. *Accreditation:* APA. *Degree requirements:* For doctorate, comprehensive exam, thesis/dissertation. *Entrance requirements:* For doctorate, GRE General Test. Additional exam requirements/recommendations for international students: Required—TOEFL (minimum score 550 paper-based; 213 computer-based), MTELP. Electronic applications accepted.

Long Island University, Brooklyn Campus, Richard L. Conolly College of Liberal Arts and Sciences, Department of Psychology, Brooklyn, NY 11201-8423. Offers clinical psychology (PhD); psychology (MA). *Accreditation:* APA (one or more programs are accredited). Part-time and evening/weekend programs available. Terminal master's awarded for partial completion of doctoral program. *Degree requirements:* For master's, thesis or alternative; for doctorate, thesis/dissertation. *Entrance requirements:* For master's, GRE Subject Test, GRE General Test, 2 letters of recommendation; for doctorate, GRE Subject Test, GRE General Test. Additional exam requirements/recommendations for international students: Required—TOEFL (minimum score 500 paper-based; 173 computer-based). Electronic applications accepted.

Long Island University, C.W. Post Campus, College of Liberal Arts and Sciences, Department of Psychology, Brookville, NY 11548-1300. Offers clinical psychology (Psy D); psychology (MA). *Accreditation:* APA. Part-time programs available. *Degree requirements:* For master's, thesis; for doctorate, thesis/dissertation, internship. *Entrance requirements:* For master's, GRE General Test, GRE Subject Test, minimum GPA of 3.0 in psychology, 2.8 overall; for doctorate, GRE General Test, GRE Subject Test, bachelor's degree in psychology, minimum GPA of 3.25. Electronic applications accepted. *Faculty research:* Visual perception, animal learning, attachment, neuropsychology, developmental disabilities, severe mental illness.

Loras College, Graduate Division, Program in Applied Psychology, Dubuque, IA 52004-0178. Offers MA. Part-time and evening/weekend programs available. *Degree requirements:* For master's, comprehensive exam, thesis (for some programs). *Entrance requirements:* For master's, Ohio State University Psychological Test or GRE General Test, minimum undergraduate GPA of 2.75.

Louisiana State University and Agricultural and Mechanical College, Graduate School, College of Arts and Sciences, Department of Psychology, Baton Rouge, LA 70803. Offers biological psychology (MA, PhD); clinical psychology (MA, PhD); cognitive psychology (MA, PhD); developmental psychology (MA, PhD); industrial/organizational psychology (MA, PhD); school psychology (MA, PhD). *Accreditation:* APA (one or more programs are accredited). *Faculty:* 27 full-time (10 women). *Students:* 94 full-time (68 women), 17 part-time (12 women); includes 14 minority (6 African Americans, 2 American Indian/Alaska Native, 2 Asian Americans or Pacific Islanders, 4 Hispanic Americans), 3 international. Average age 27. 232 applicants, 18% accepted, 29 enrolled. In 2009, 13 master's, 14 doctorates awarded. Terminal master's awarded for partial completion of doctoral program. *Degree requirements:* For master's, thesis; for doctorate, thesis/dissertation, 1 year internship. *Entrance requirements:* For master's and doctorate, GRE General Test, minimum GPA of 3.0. Additional exam requirements/recommendations for international students: Required—TOEFL (minimum score 550 paper-based; 213 computer-based; 79 iBT) or IELTS (minimum score 6.5). *Application deadline:* For fall admission, 1/15 for domestic and international students. Applications are processed on a rolling basis. Application fee: $50 ($70 for international students). Electronic applications accepted. *Financial support:* In 2009–10, 108 students received support, including 5 fellowships (averaging $26,974 per year), 2 research assistantships with partial tuition reimbursements available (averaging $18,000 per year), 74 teaching assistantships with partial tuition reimbursements available (averaging $14,751 per year); career-related internships or fieldwork, Federal Work-Study, institutionally sponsored loans, scholarships/grants, health care benefits, and tuition waivers (full and partial) also available. Financial award applicants required to submit FAFSA. *Faculty research:* Clinical psychology, autism, anxiety, addition, neuropsychology, school psychology, cognitive psychology, experimental psychology. Total annual research expenditures: $1 million. *Unit head:* Dr. Robert Matthews, Chair, 225-578-8745, Fax: 225-578-4125, E-mail: psmath@lsu.edu. *Application contact:* Dr. Jason Hicks, Coordinator of Graduate Studies, 225-578-4109, Fax: 225-578-4125, E-mail: jhicks@lsu.edu.

Louisiana Tech University, Graduate School, College of Education, Department of Behavioral Sciences and Psychology, Ruston, LA 71272. Offers counseling (MA); counseling psychology (PhD); industrial/organizational psychology (MA); special education (MA). *Accreditation:* APA (one or more programs are accredited). Part-time programs available. *Degree requirements:* For master's, thesis or alternative; for doctorate, thesis/dissertation. *Entrance requirements:* For master's and doctorate, GRE General Test.

Loyola University Chicago, Graduate School, Department of Psychology, Chicago, IL 60660. Offers applied social psychology (MA, PhD); clinical psychology (MA, PhD); developmental psychology (MA, PhD); human perception (MS). *Accreditation:* APA (one or more programs are accredited). *Faculty:* 27 full-time (12 women), 1 part-time/adjunct (0 women). *Students:* 97 full-time (79 women), 8 part-time (all women); includes 18 minority (9 African Americans, 1 American Indian/Alaska Native, 3 Asian Americans or Pacific Islanders, 5 Hispanic Americans), 6 international. Average age 29. 423 applicants, 7% accepted, 22 enrolled. In 2009, 12 master's, 12 doctorates awarded. Terminal master's awarded for partial completion of doctoral program. *Degree requirements:* For master's, comprehensive exam, thesis; for doctorate, comprehensive exam, thesis/dissertation. *Entrance requirements:* For master's and doctorate, GRE General Test, GRE Subject Test. Application fee: $50. Electronic applications accepted. *Expenses:* Tuition: Full-time $14,220; part-time $790 per credit hour. Required fees: $60 per semester hour. Tuition and fees vary according to program. *Financial support:* In 2009–10, 7 fellowships with full tuition reimbursements (averaging $12,000 per year), 24 research assistantships with full tuition reimbursements (averaging $12,000 per year), 10 teaching assistantships with full tuition reimbursements (averaging $12,000 per year) were awarded; career-related internships or fieldwork, Federal Work-Study, scholarships/grants, and traineeships also available. Financial award applicants required to submit FAFSA. *Faculty research:* Cognitive development, hearing and vision, attitude and prejudice, child and family, AIDS and health promotion. Total annual research expenditures: $2.5 million. *Unit head:* Dr. R. Scott Tindale, Chair, 773-508-3014, E-mail: rtindal@luc.edu. *Application contact:* Ron Martin, Assistant Director of Enrollment Management, 312-915-8950, Fax: 312-915-8905, E-mail: gradapp@luc.edu.

Loyola University Maryland, Graduate Programs, College of Arts and Sciences, Department of Psychology, Baltimore, MD 21210-2699. Offers clinical psychology (MS, Psy D, CAS); counseling psychology (MS, CAS). *Accreditation:* APA. Part-time and evening/weekend programs available. *Entrance requirements:* For master's, doctorate, and CAS, GRE General Test, GRE Subject Test (recommended). Additional exam requirements/recommendations for international students: Required—TOEFL (minimum score 550 paper-based; 213 computer-based).

Lynn University, College of Liberal Education, Boca Raton, FL 33431-5598. Offers applied psychology (MS); criminal justice administration (MS); emergency planning and administration (MS, Certificate). Part-time and evening/weekend programs available. Postbaccalaureate distance learning degree programs offered. *Entrance requirements:* For master's, GRE, resume, 2 letters of recommendation, minimum undergraduate GPA of 3.0. Additional exam requirements/recommendations for international students: Required—TOEFL (minimum score 550 paper-based; 213 computer-based). Application fee: $50. *Expenses:* Tuition: Part-time $580 per credit. One-time fee: $200 part-time. Part-time tuition and fees vary according to degree level. *Financial support:* Career-related internships or fieldwork, Federal Work-Study, institutionally sponsored loans, scholarships/grants, tuition waivers (full and partial), and unspecified assistantships available. Support available to part-time students. Financial award application deadline: 8/1; financial award applicants required to submit FAFSA. *Faculty research:* Terrorism, criminological theory, corrections, emergency planning. *Unit head:* Dr. Gregg Cox, Dean, 561-237-7210, E-mail: gcox@lynn.edu. *Application contact:* Dr. Larissa Baia, Assistant Director of Graduate Admissions, 561-237-7916, Fax: 561-237-7100, E-mail: admissionpm@lynn.edu.

Madonna University, Department of Psychology, Livonia, MI 48150-1173. Offers clinical psychology (MSCP). Part-time and evening/weekend programs available. *Degree requirements:* For master's, thesis or alternative. *Entrance requirements:* Additional exam requirements/recommendations for international students: Required—TOEFL. Electronic applications accepted.

Mansfield University of Pennsylvania, Graduate Studies, Program in Organizational Leadership, Mansfield, PA 16933. Offers MA. Postbaccalaureate distance learning degree programs offered. *Expenses:* Tuition, state resident: full-time $6666; part-time $370 per credit. Tuition, nonresident: full-time $10,666; part-time $593 per credit. Required fees: $1388. *Unit head:* Dr. Peter Chiaramonte, Director, 570-662-4344, E-mail: pchiaram@mansfield.edu. *Application contact:* Christina Hale, Assistant Director of Enrollment Management/Graduate Admissions, 570-662-4812, Fax: 570-662-4121, E-mail: chale@mansfield.edu.

Marietta College, Program in Psychology, Marietta, OH 45750-4000. Offers MAP.

Marist College, Graduate Programs, School of Social and Behavioral Sciences, Poughkeepsie, NY 12601-1387. Offers counseling psychology (MA); education (M Ed); education psychology (MA); school psychology (MA, Adv C). Part-time and evening/weekend programs available. *Degree requirements:* For master's, thesis optional. *Entrance requirements:* For master's, GRE General Test, letters of recommendation, minimum undergraduate GPA of 3.0, interview. Additional exam requirements/recommendations for international students: Required—TOEFL (minimum score 550 paper-based; 213 computer-based; 80 iBT); Recommended—IELTS (minimum score 6.5). Electronic applications accepted. *Expenses:* Tuition: Full-time $12,510; part-time $695 per credit hour. *Faculty research:* AIDS prevention, educational intervention, humanistic counseling research, aging and development, neuroimaging.

Marquette University, Graduate School, College of Arts and Sciences, Department of Psychology, Milwaukee, WI 53201-1881. Offers clinical psychology (MS); psychology (PhD). *Accreditation:* APA. Part-time programs available. *Faculty:* 17 full-time (8 women), 3 part-time/adjunct (1 woman). *Students:* 34 full-time (25 women), 14 part-time (7 women); includes 4 minority (2 African Americans, 1 American Indian/Alaska Native, 1 Hispanic American), 2 international. Average age 27. 107 applicants, 10% accepted, 8 enrolled. In 2009, 6 master's, 5 doctorates awarded. *Degree requirements:* For master's, comprehensive exam, thesis or alternative; for doctorate, thesis/dissertation, internship, qualifying exam. *Entrance requirements:* For master's, GRE General Test, GRE Subject Test, MAT; for doctorate, GRE General Test, GRE Subject Test, sample of scholarly writing. Additional exam requirements/recommendations for international students: Required—TOEFL. *Application deadline:* For fall admission, 2/15 for domestic students. Application fee: $40. *Financial support:* In 2009–10, 3 research assistantships, 16 teaching assistantships were awarded; career-related internships or fieldwork, Federal Work-Study, institutionally sponsored loans, scholarships/grants, and tuition waivers (full and partial) also available. Support available to part-time students. Financial award application deadline: 2/15. *Faculty research:* Mental imagery, moral development, organizational behavior, depression, psychotherapy outcomes. *Unit head:* Dr. Mike Wierzbicki, Chair, 414-288-7218, Fax: 414-288-5333. *Application contact:* Dr. Steve Saunders, Information Contact, 414-288-7459.

Marshall University, Academic Affairs Division, College of Liberal Arts, Department of Psychology, Huntington, WV 25755. Offers clinical psychology (MA); general psychology (MA); industrial and organizational psychology (MA); psychology (Psy D). *Accreditation:* APA. *Faculty:* 13 full-time (4 women), 1 part-time/adjunct (0 women). *Students:* 101 full-time (71 women), 19 part-time (14 women); includes 6 minority (4 African Americans, 2 Hispanic Americans), 4 international. Average age 29. In 2009, 33 master's, 3 doctorates awarded. *Degree requirements:* For master's, thesis optional. *Entrance requirements:* For master's, GRE General Test or MAT. *Application deadline:* For fall admission, 3/1 for domestic students; for spring admission, 11/1 for domestic students. Application fee: $40. *Financial support:* Teaching assistantships with tuition reimbursements available. *Unit head:* Dr. Steven Mewaldt, Chairperson, 304-696-27tt, E-mail: mewaldt@marshall.edu. *Application contact:* Graduate Admissions, 304-746-1900, Fax: 304-746-1902, E-mail: services@marshall.edu.

Martin University, Division of Psychology, Indianapolis, IN 46218-3867. Offers community psychology (MS). Part-time and evening/weekend programs available. *Degree requirements:* For master's, thesis. *Entrance requirements:* For master's, GRE General Test, GRE Subject Test.

Marywood University, Academic Affairs, Reap College of Education and Human Development, Department of Psychology and Counseling, Program in Psychology, Scranton, PA 18509-1598. Offers clinical services (MA); general theoretical (MA). *Students:* 23 full-time (16 women), 20 part-time (16 women); includes 2 minority (both Hispanic Americans). Average age 26. 62 applicants, 66% accepted. In 2009, 30 master's awarded. *Entrance requirements:* Additional exam requirements/recommendations for international students: Required—TOEFL (minimum score 550 paper-based; 213 computer-based; 79 iBT). *Application deadline:* For fall admission, 4/1 priority date for domestic students, 3/30 priority date for international students; for spring admission, 11/1 priority date for domestic students, 8/31 priority date for international students. Applications are processed on a rolling basis. Application fee: $35. Electronic applications accepted. *Expenses:* Tuition: Part-time $715 per credit. Required fees: $270 per semester. Tuition and fees vary according to degree level, campus/location and program. *Financial support:* Career-related internships or fieldwork, scholarships/grants, and unspecified assistantships available. Support available to part-time students. Financial award application deadline: 6/30; financial award applicants required to submit FAFSA. *Faculty research:* Personality disorders, counselor training, preschool development, self-esteem measurement, family dynamics. *Unit head:* Dr. Edward Crawley, Chairperson, 570-348-6211 Ext. 2325, E-mail: crawley@marywood.edu. *Application contact:* Tammy Manka, Assistant Director of Graduate Admissions, 866-279-9663, E-mail: tmanka@marywood.edu.

Massachusetts School of Professional Psychology, Graduate Programs, Boston, MA 02132. Offers clinical psychology (Psy D); clinical psychopharmacology (Post-Doctoral MS); counseling psychology (MA); executive coaching (Graduate Certificate); forensic psychology (MA); organizational psychology (MA); respecialization in clinical psychology (Certificate); MA/CAGS. *Accreditation:* APA. *Degree requirements:* For master's, comprehensive exam; for doctorate, thesis/dissertation. *Entrance requirements:* For doctorate, GRE General Test. Additional exam requirements/recommendations for international students: Required—TOEFL (minimum score 550 paper-based; 213 computer-based). Electronic applications accepted.

McGill University, Faculty of Graduate and Postdoctoral Studies, Faculty of Medicine, Department of Psychiatry, Montréal, QC H3A 2T5, Canada. Offers M Sc.

McGill University, Faculty of Graduate and Postdoctoral Studies, Faculty of Science, Department of Psychology, Montréal, QC H3A 2T5, Canada. Offers clinical psychology (PhD); experimental psychology (M Sc, MA, PhD). *Accreditation:* APA (one or more programs are accredited).

McMaster University, School of Graduate Studies, Faculty of Science, Department of Psychology, Hamilton, ON L8S 4M2, Canada. Offers M Sc, PhD. *Degree requirements:* For doctorate, comprehensive exam, thesis/dissertation. *Entrance requirements:* For doctorate, GRE General Test, honors degree, minimum B+ average. Additional exam requirements/recommendations for international students: Required—TOEFL (minimum score 550 paper-based; 213 computer-based).

McNeese State University, Doré School of Graduate Studies, Burton College of Education, Department of Psychology, Lake Charles, LA 70609. Offers addiction treatment (MA); applied behavior analysis (MA); counseling psychology (MA); general/experimental psychology (MA). Evening/weekend programs available. *Faculty:* 6 full-time (3 women). *Students:* 34 full-time (24 women), 30 part-time (22 women); includes 10 minority (7 African Americans, 1 Asian American or Pacific Islander, 2 Hispanic Americans), 2 international. In 2009, 18 master's awarded. *Entrance requirements:* For master's, GRE. *Application deadline:* For fall admission, 5/15 priority date for domestic and international students; for spring admission, 10/15 priority date for domestic and international students. Applications are processed on a rolling basis. Application fee: $20 ($30 for international students). *Expenses:* Tuition, area resident: Full-time $2556. Tuition, state resident: full-time $2556. Required fees: $1031. Tuition and fees vary according to course load. *Financial support:* Application deadline: 5/1. *Unit head:* Dr. Dena L. Matzenbacher, Head, 337-475-5457, Fax: 337-562-4115, E-mail: dena@mcneese.edu. *Application contact:* Dr. George F. Mead, Interim Dean of Dore' School of Graduate Studies, 337-475-5396, Fax: 337-475-5397, E-mail: admissions@mcneese.edu.

Medaille College, Programs in Psychology, Buffalo, NY 14214-2695. Offers mental health counseling (MA); psychology (MA). Part-time and evening/weekend programs available. *Faculty:* 4 full-time (2 women), 9 part-time/adjunct (6 women). *Students:* 223 full-time (188 women); includes 45 minority (42 African Americans, 1 Asian American or Pacific Islander, 2 Hispanic Americans). Average age 31. 51 applicants, 45% accepted, 22 enrolled. In 2009, 74 master's awarded. *Degree requirements:* For master's, comprehensive exam (for some programs), thesis (for some programs). *Entrance requirements:* For master's, GRE General Test (psychology), minimum GPA of 2.75 (psychology). Additional exam requirements/recommendations for international students: Required—TOEFL (minimum score 550 paper-based; 213 computer-based). *Application deadline:* Applications are processed on a rolling basis. Application fee: $35. Electronic applications accepted. *Financial support:* In 2009–10, 90 students received support. Federal Work-Study available. Financial award applicants required to submit FAFSA. *Faculty research:* Schizophrenia, Parkinson's Disease, eyewitness testimony, methodology. *Unit head:* Dr. Judith Horowitz, Dean of Adult and Graduate Studies, 716-880-2229, Fax: 716-884-0291, E-mail: jhorowitz@medaille.edu. *Application contact:* Jacqueline Matheny, Executive Director of Marketing and Enrollment, 716-932-2541, Fax: 716-632-1811, E-mail: jmatheny@medaille.edu.

Memorial University of Newfoundland, School of Graduate Studies, Department of Psychology, St. John's, NL A1C 5S7, Canada. Offers applied social psychology (MASP); experimental psychology (M Sc, PhD). Part-time programs available. *Degree requirements:* For master's, workterms (MASP), thesis (M Sc); for doctorate, comprehensive exam, thesis/dissertation, oral thesis defense. *Entrance requirements:* For master's, GRE, honors bachelor's degree of high second class standing or equivalent; for doctorate, GRE, master's or honors degree. Electronic applications accepted. *Faculty research:* Behavioral neuroscience, cognition, theory and research on abnormal behavior.

Mercy College, School of Social and Behavioral Sciences, Program in Psychology, Dobbs Ferry, NY 10522-1189. Offers MS. Part-time and evening/weekend programs available. Postbaccalaureate distance learning degree programs offered (minimal on-campus study). *Students:* 17 full-time (14 women), 16 part-time (10 women); includes 19 minority (7 African Americans, 2 American Indian/Alaska Native, 1 Asian American or Pacific Islander, 9 Hispanic Americans). Average age 32. 61 applicants, 38% accepted, 14 enrolled. In 2009, 11 master's awarded. *Degree requirements:* For master's, written comprehensive exam or 6 credit thesis. *Entrance requirements:* For master's, BA in psychology, sociology, behavioral science or education; interview; letters of recommendation; minimum GPA of 3.0; resume; 3- to 5-page essay stating reason for pursuing master's degree in psychology. Additional exam requirements/recommendations for international students: Required—TOEFL (minimum score 600 paper-based; 250 computer-based; 100 iBT). *Application deadline:* For fall admission, 8/1 for international students. Applications are processed on a rolling basis. Application fee: $40. Electronic applications accepted. *Expenses:* Tuition: Full-time $13,158; part-time $731 per credit. Required fees: $500. Tuition and fees vary according to degree level and program. *Financial support:* Career-related internships or fieldwork, Federal Work-Study, scholarships/grants, and unspecified assistantships available. Support available to part-time students. Financial award applicants required to submit FAFSA. *Unit head:* Dr. Barbara Melamed, Program Director, 914-674-7345, E-mail: bmelamed@mercy.edu. *Application contact:* Dr. Barbara Melamed, Program Director, 914-674-7345, E-mail: bmelamed@mercy.edu.

Metropolitan State University, College of Professional Studies, St. Paul, MN 55106-5000. Offers psychology (MA). Part-time and evening/weekend programs available. *Degree requirements:* For master's, thesis. *Entrance requirements:* For master's, resume, letters of reference, minimum GPA of 3.0. Additional exam requirements/recommendations for international students: Required—TOEFL (minimum score 550 paper-based; 213 computer-based). *Expenses:* Tuition, state resident: full-time $5520; part-time $276 per credit hour. Tuition, nonresident: full-time $11,040; part-time $552 per credit hour. Required fees: $209; $10 per credit hour. Tuition and fees vary according to degree level.

Miami University, Graduate School, College of Arts and Sciences, Department of Psychology, Oxford, OH 45056. Offers PhD. *Accreditation:* APA. *Students:* 75 full-time (45 women), 3 part-time (1 woman); includes 8 minority (3 African Americans, 4 Asian Americans or Pacific Islanders, 1 Hispanic American), 5 international. *Degree requirements:* For doctorate, comprehensive exam, thesis/dissertation. *Entrance requirements:* For doctorate, GRE General Test, minimum GPA of 2.75 (undergraduate), 3.0 (graduate). Additional exam requirements/recommendations for international students: Required—TOEFL. Application fee: $50. *Expenses:* Tuition, state resident: full-time $11,280. Tuition, nonresident: full-time $24,912. Required fees: $516. *Financial support:* Fellowships with full tuition reimbursements, research assistantships with full tuition reimbursements, teaching assistantships with full tuition reimbursements, career-related internships or fieldwork, Federal Work-Study, health care benefits, tuition waivers (full), and unspecified assistantships available. Financial award application deadline: 3/1. *Unit head:* Dr. Carl Paternite, Chair, 513-529-2400, Fax: 513-529-2420, E-mail: paternce@muohio.edu. *Application contact:* Pam Turner, Senior Program Assistant, Graduate Program, 513-529-7224, Fax: 513-529-2420, E-mail: turnerpr@muohio.edu.

Michigan School of Professional Psychology, Programs in Humanistic and Clinical Psychology, Farmington Hills, MI 48334. Offers MA, Psy D. *Students:* 111 full-time (92 women), 3 part-time (all women); includes 20 minority (13 African Americans, 7 Asian Americans or Pacific Islanders). Average age 38. *Degree requirements:* For master's, thesis, practicum; for doctorate, thesis/dissertation, internship, practicum. *Entrance requirements:* For master's, 1 year of work experience, interview, minimum GPA of 3.0, curriculum vitae, personal essay, bachelor's degree, 3 letters of recommendation; for doctorate, 3 years of work experience, 2 interviews, minimum graduate GPA of 3.0, scholarly writing sample, curriculum vitae, personal essay, MA, 3 letters of recommendation. Additional exam requirements/recommendations for international students: Required—TOEFL. *Application deadline:* For fall admission, 1/15 priority date for domestic students. Applications are processed on a rolling basis. Application fee: $75. Electronic applications accepted. *Financial support:* Application deadline: 6/30. *Faculty research:* Qualitative research, existential-phenomenological psychology, applications to clinical practice. *Unit head:* Dr. Kerry Moustakas, President, 248-476-1122, Fax: 248-476-1125, E-mail: kmoustakas@mispp.edu. *Application contact:* Linda Potter-Gallant, Admissions Advisor, 248-476-1122 Ext. 117, Fax: 248-476-1125, E-mail: lpgallant@mispp.edu.

Michigan State University, The Graduate School, College of Social Science, Department of Psychology, East Lansing, MI 48824. Offers MA, PhD. *Accreditation:* APA (one or more programs are accredited). *Faculty:* 53 full-time (25 women). *Students:* 94 full-time (64 women), 5 part-time (all women); includes 13 minority (3 African Americans, 1 American Indian/Alaska Native, 5 Asian Americans or Pacific Islanders, 4 Hispanic Americans), 14 international. Average age 27. 268 applicants, 6% accepted. In 2009, 19 master's, 15 doctorates awarded. *Entrance requirements:* Additional exam requirements/recommendations for international students: Required—TOEFL (minimum score 550 paper-based; 213 computer-based), Michigan State University ELT (minimum score 85), Michigan Michigan English Language Assessment Battery (minimum score 83). Electronic applications accepted. *Expenses:* Tuition, state resident: part-time $478.25 per credit hour. Tuition, nonresident: part-time $966.50 per credit hour. Part-time tuition and fees vary according to program. *Financial support:* In 2009–10, 52 research assistantships with tuition reimbursements (averaging $6,604 per year), 29 teaching assistantships with tuition reimbursements (averaging $6,508 per year) were awarded. Financial award applicants required to submit FAFSA. Total annual research expenditures: $3.2 million. *Unit head:* Dr. Neal Schmitt, Chairperson, 517-355-9563, Fax: 517-432-2476, E-mail: schmitt@msu.edu. *Application contact:* Julie Detwiler, Graduate Program Administrator, 517-353-5258, Fax: 517-432-2476, E-mail: detwiler@msu.edu.

Middle Tennessee State University, College of Graduate Studies, College of Education and Behavioral Science, Department of Psychology, Program in Psychology, Murfreesboro, TN 37132. Offers MA. Part-time and evening/weekend programs available. Postbaccalaureate distance learning degree programs offered. *Students:* 23 full-time (19 women), 87 part-time (67 women); includes 15 minority (6 African Americans, 7 Asian Americans or Pacific Islanders, 2 Hispanic Americans). 141 applicants, 64% accepted, 90 enrolled. In 2009, 33 master's awarded. *Degree requirements:* For master's, one foreign language, comprehensive exam, thesis. *Entrance requirements:* For master's, GRE. Additional exam requirements/recommendations for international students: Required—TOEFL (minimum score 525 paper-based; 195 computer-based; 71 iBT) or IELTS (minimum score 6). *Application deadline:* For fall admission, 6/1 for domestic and international students. Applications are processed on a rolling basis. Application fee: $25 ($30 for international students). Electronic applications accepted. *Expenses:* Tuition, state resident: full-time $4404. Tuition, nonresident: full-time $10,956. *Financial support:* Application deadline: 5/1. *Unit head:* Dr. Dennis Papini, Chair, 615-898-2706, Fax: 615-898-5027. *Application contact:* Dr. Michael Allen, Dean and Vice Provost for Research, 615-898-2840, Fax: 615-904-8020, E-mail: mallen@mtsu.edu.

Midwestern State University, Graduate Studies, College of Humanities and Social Sciences, Department of Psychology, Wichita Falls, TX 76308. Offers MA. Part-time and evening/weekend programs available. *Degree requirements:* For master's, one foreign language, comprehensive exam, thesis optional. *Entrance requirements:* For master's, GRE General Test, 3 recommendation forms. Additional exam requirements/recommendations for international students: Required—TOEFL (minimum score 550 paper-based; 213 computer-based). Electronic applications accepted. *Expenses:* Tuition, state resident: full-time $1620; part-time $90 per credit hour. Tuition, nonresident: full-time $2160; part-time $120 per credit hour. International tuition: $7506 full-time. Required fees: $3068.80; $145.60 per credit hour. $179 per semester. *Faculty research:* Personality disorders, child sexual abuse and sexual coercion, educational psychology.

Millersville University of Pennsylvania, College of Graduate and Professional Studies, School of Education, Department of Psychology, Millersville, PA 17551-0302. Offers school counseling (M Ed); school psychology (MS), including clinical psychology, school psychology. Part-time programs available. *Faculty:* 18 full-time (12 women), 9 part-time/adjunct (5 women). *Students:* 54 full-time (44 women), 79 part-time (69 women); includes 7 minority (3 African Americans, 1 Asian American or Pacific Islander, 3 Hispanic Americans), 1 international. Average age 29. 81 applicants, 49% accepted, 27 enrolled. In 2009, 46 master's awarded. *Degree requirements:* For master's, comprehensive exam, thesis optional. *Entrance requirements:* For master's, GRE, 3 letters of recommendation, interview (in-person). Additional exam requirements/recommendations for international students: Required—TOEFL (minimum score 500 paper-based; 183 computer-based; 65 iBT) or IELTS (minimum score 6). *Application deadline:* For fall admission, 1/15 for domestic and international students; for winter admission, 10/1 for domestic and international students; for spring admission, 10/1 for domestic and international students. Application fee: $40 ($50 for international students). Electronic applications accepted. *Expenses:* Tuition, state resident: full-time $6666; part-time $370 per credit. Tuition, nonresident: full-time $10,666; part-time $593 per credit. Required fees: $1578.50; $76.25 per credit. One-time fee: $60 part-time. Tuition and fees vary according to course load. *Financial support:* In 2009–10, 54 students received support, including 54 research assistantships with full and partial tuition reimbursements available (averaging $4,008 per year); institutionally sponsored loans and unspecified assistantships also available. Support available to part-time students. Financial award application deadline: 3/15; financial award applicants required to submit FAFSA. *Unit head:* Dr. Helena Tuleya-Payne, Chair, 717-872-3925, Fax: 717-871-2480, E-mail: helena.tuleya-payne@millersville.edu. *Application contact:* Dr. Victor S. DeSantis, Dean of Graduate and Professional Studies, 717-872-3099, Fax: 717-872-3453, E-mail: victor.desantis@millersville.edu.

Minnesota State University Mankato, College of Graduate Studies, College of Social and Behavioral Sciences, Department of Psychology, Mankato, MN 56001. Offers clinical psychology (MA); industrial/organizational psychology (MA); school psychology (Psy D). Part-time programs available. *Students:* 51 full-time (32 women), 3 part-time (1 woman). *Degree requirements:* For master's, one foreign language, comprehensive exam, thesis (for some programs). *Entrance requirements:* For master's, GRE General Test, GRE Subject Test (clinical psychology), minimum GPA of 3.0 during previous 2 years, 3 letters of reference. Additional exam requirements/recommendations for international students: Required—TOEFL. *Application deadline:* For fall admission, 1/1 priority date for domestic students. Applications are processed on a rolling basis. Application fee: $40. Electronic applications accepted. *Expenses:* Tuition, state resident: full-time $5364. Tuition, nonresident: full-time $8314. *Financial support:* Research assistantships, teaching assistantships with full tuition reimbursements, career-related internships or fieldwork, Federal Work-Study, institutionally sponsored loans, and unspecified assistantships available. Support available to part-time students. Financial award application deadline: 3/15; financial award applicants required to submit FAFSA. *Faculty research:* Professional competency in hospitals, mood disturbance, 360-degree feedback, employee selection, planning fallacy. *Unit head:* Dr. Barry Ries, Chairperson, 507-389-2724. *Application contact:* 507-389-2321, E-mail: grad@mnsu.edu.

Mississippi State University, College of Arts and Sciences, Department of Psychology, Mississippi State, MS 39762. Offers cognitive science (PhD); psychology (MS), including clinical psychology, experimental psychology. *Faculty:* 13 full-time (5 women). *Students:* 40 full-time (26 women), 4 part-time (3 women); includes 3 minority (2 African Americans, 1 Asian American or Pacific Islander), 3 international. Average age 26. 69 applicants, 46% accepted, 20 enrolled. In 2009, 11 master's awarded. Terminal master's awarded for partial completion of doctoral program. *Degree requirements:* For master's, comprehensive exam, thesis; for doctorate, thesis/dissertation, qualifying exam, comprehensive written and oral exam. *Entrance requirements:* For master's, GRE General Test, minimum GPA of 2.75 on last two years of undergraduate courses; for doctorate, GRE General Test, proficiency in at least 1 computer language. Additional exam requirements/recommendations for international students: Required—TOEFL (minimum score 475 paper-based; 153 computer-based; 53 iBT); Recommended—IELTS (minimum score 4.5). *Application deadline:* For fall admission, 1/15 priority date for domestic students, 5/1 for international students; for spring admission, 11/1 priority date for domestic students, 9/1 for international students. Applications are processed on a rolling basis. Application fee: $40. Electronic applications accepted. *Expenses:* Tuition, state resident: full-time $2575.50; part-time $286.25 per credit hour. Tuition, nonresident: full-time $6510; part-time $723.50 per credit hour. Tuition and fees vary according to course load. *Financial support:* In 2009–10, 7 research assistantships with full tuition reimbursements (averaging $11,132 per year), 15 teaching assistantships with full tuition reimbursements (averaging

Psychology—General

Mississippi State University (continued)
$9,023 per year) were awarded; career-related internships or fieldwork, Federal Work-Study, institutionally sponsored loans, scholarships/grants, and unspecified assistantships also available. Financial award application deadline: 4/1; financial award applicants required to submit FAFSA. *Faculty research:* Personality type, alcoholism, blindness and low vision, mental retardation, language comprehension. Total annual research expenditures: $2.2 million. *Unit head:* Dr. Stephen B. Klein, Department Head, 662-325-3202, Fax: 662-325-7212, E-mail: sbkl@ra.msstate.edu. *Application contact:* Dr. Keven J. Armstrong, Graduate Coordinator, 662-325-3202, Fax: 662-325-7212, E-mail: grad@psychology.msstate.edu.

Missouri State University, Graduate College, College of Health and Human Services, Department of Psychology, Springfield, MO 65897. Offers psychology (MS), including clinical, experimental, industrial/organizational. *Faculty:* 26 full-time (11 women), 1 part-time/adjunct (0 women). *Students:* 44 full-time (28 women), 5 part-time (3 women); includes 2 minority (1 African American, 1 Hispanic American). Average age 26. 63 applicants, 56% accepted, 22 enrolled. In 2009, 21 master's awarded. *Degree requirements:* For master's, comprehensive exam, thesis. *Entrance requirements:* For master's, GRE General Test, GRE Subject Test, minimum GPA of 3.25 in major, 3.0 overall; 20 hours of course work in psychology (experimental and statistics). Additional exam requirements/recommendations for international students: Required—TOEFL (minimum score 550 paper-based; 213 computer-based; 79 iBT). *Application deadline:* For fall admission, 3/1 priority date for domestic and international students. Application fee: $35 ($50 for international students). Electronic applications accepted. *Expenses:* Tuition, state resident: full-time $3852; part-time $214 per credit hour. Tuition, nonresident: full-time $7524; part-time $418 per credit hour. Required fees: $696; $172 per semester. Tuition and fees vary according to course level, course load, degree level and program. *Financial support:* In 2009–10, 7 research assistantships with full tuition reimbursements (averaging $8,023 per year), 3 teaching assistantships with full tuition reimbursements (averaging $9,730 per year) were awarded; career-related internships or fieldwork, Federal Work-Study, institutionally sponsored loans, scholarships/grants, and unspecified assistantships also available. Financial award application deadline: 3/31; financial award applicants required to submit FAFSA. *Faculty research:* Work-family conflict, child forensic psychology, sports psychology, body image assessment, visual learning. *Unit head:* Dr. Robert G. Jones, Head, 417-836-5797, Fax: 417-836-8330, E-mail: psychology@missouristate.edu. *Application contact:* Eric Eckert, Coordinator of Admissions and Recruitment, 417-836-5331, Fax: 417-836-6200, E-mail: ericeckert@missouristate.edu.

Monmouth University, Graduate School, Department of Psychology, West Long Branch, NJ 07764-1898. Offers mental health counseling (MS); psychological counseling (MA, PMC). *Accreditation:* ACA. Part-time and evening/weekend programs available. *Faculty:* 6 full-time (2 women), 6 part-time/adjunct (all women). *Students:* 126 full-time (110 women), 124 part-time (103 women); includes 45 minority (20 African Americans, 2 American Indian/Alaska Native, 10 Asian Americans or Pacific Islanders, 13 Hispanic Americans), 1 international. Average age 30. 169 applicants, 95% accepted, 98 enrolled. In 2009, 54 master's awarded. *Degree requirements:* For master's, thesis optional, fieldwork. *Entrance requirements:* For master's, GRE General Test, minimum GPA of 3.0 in major, 24 credits in psychology. Additional exam requirements/recommendations for international students: Required—TOEFL (minimum score 550 paper-based; 213 computer-based; 79 iBT), IELTS (minimum score 5), Michigan English Language Assessment Battery (minimum score 77), Cambridge A, B, C. *Application deadline:* For fall admission, 7/15 priority date for domestic students, 6/1 for international students; for spring admission, 11/15 priority date for domestic students, 11/1 for international students. Applications are processed on a rolling basis. Application fee: $50. Electronic applications accepted. *Expenses:* Tuition: Part-time $773 per credit. Required fees: $157 per semester. *Financial support:* In 2009–10, 159 students received support, including 149 fellowships (averaging $1,946 per year), 12 research assistantships (averaging $10,848 per year); career-related internships or fieldwork, scholarships/grants, and unspecified assistantships also available. Support available to part-time students. Financial award applicants required to submit FAFSA. *Faculty research:* Violent crime, single parenting, the African-American male, counseling older women, successful behavior for under-achieving youth. *Unit head:* Dr. George Kapalka, Director, 732-263-5583, Fax: 732-263-5159, E-mail: gkapalka@monmouth.edu. *Application contact:* Kevin Roane, Director, Office of Graduate Admission, 732-571-3452, Fax: 732-263-5123, E-mail: gradadm@monmouth.edu.

Montana State University, College of Graduate Studies, College of Letters and Science, Department of Psychology, Bozeman, MT 59717. Offers MS. Part-time programs available. *Faculty:* 9 full-time (3 women), 2 part-time/adjunct (1 woman). *Students:* 5 full-time (2 women), 4 part-time (3 women). Average age 26. 13 applicants, 31% accepted, 4 enrolled. In 2009, 4 master's awarded. *Degree requirements:* For master's, comprehensive exam, thesis (for some programs). *Entrance requirements:* For master's, GRE General Test. Additional exam requirements/recommendations for international students: Required—TOEFL (minimum score 550 paper-based; 213 computer-based). *Application deadline:* For fall admission, 7/15 priority date for domestic students, 5/15 priority date for international students; for spring admission, 12/1 priority date for domestic students, 10/1 priority date for international students. Applications are processed on a rolling basis. Application fee: $30. Electronic applications accepted. *Expenses:* Tuition, state resident: full-time $5635; part-time $3492 per year. Tuition, nonresident: full-time $17,212; part-time $7865.10 per year. Required fees: $1441; $153.15 per credit. Tuition and fees vary according to course load and program. *Financial support:* In 2009–10, 9 students received support, including 10 teaching assistantships with full tuition reimbursements available (averaging $10,244 per year); unspecified assistantships also available. Financial award application deadline: 3/1; financial award applicants required to submit FAFSA. *Faculty research:* Psychological study of social cognitive, neuro and eating behaviors. Total annual research expenditures: $69,277. *Unit head:* Dr. Ruth Striegel-Moore, Department Head, 406-994-5174, Fax: 406-994-3804, E-mail: ruth.striegelmoore@montana.edu. *Application contact:* Dr. Carl A. Fox, Vice Provost for Graduate Education, 406-994-4145, Fax: 406-994-7433, E-mail: gradstudy@montana.edu.

Montana State University Billings, College of Arts and Sciences, Department of Psychology, Billings, MT 59101-0298. Offers MS. Part-time programs available. *Degree requirements:* For master's, thesis optional. *Entrance requirements:* For master's, GRE General Test, 3 letters of recommendation, resume.

Montclair State University, The Graduate School, College of Humanities and Social Sciences, Department of Psychology, Montclair, NJ 07043-1624. Offers educational psychology (MA), including child/adolescent clinical psychology, clinical psychology for Spanish/English bilinguals; psychology (MA, Certificate), including industrial and organizational psychology (MA); school psychologist (Certificate). Part-time and evening/weekend programs available. *Faculty:* 29 full-time (14 women), 26 part-time/adjunct (14 women). *Students:* 37 full-time (27 women), 33 part-time (23 women). Average age 27. 72 applicants, 47% accepted, 20 enrolled. In 2009, 7 master's awarded. *Degree requirements:* For master's, comprehensive exam, thesis or alternative. *Entrance requirements:* For master's, GRE General Test, 2 letters of recommendation. Additional exam requirements/recommendations for international students: Required—TOEFL (minimum score 83 computer-based), or IELTS. *Application deadline:* For fall admission, 2/1 for domestic and international students; for spring admission, 10/1 for domestic and international students. Applications are processed on a rolling basis. Application fee: $60. Electronic applications accepted. *Expenses:* Tuition, area resident: Part-time $486.74 per credit. Tuition, state resident: part-time $486.74 per credit. Tuition, nonresident: part-time $751.34 per credit. Tuition and fees vary according to degree level and program. *Financial support:* In 2009–10, 17 research assistantships with full tuition reimbursements (averaging $7,000 per year) were awarded; Federal Work-Study, scholarships/grants, and unspecified assistantships also available. Support available to part-time students. Financial award application deadline: 3/1; financial award applicants required to submit FAFSA. *Faculty research:* Engaged learning, academic and civic development. Total annual research expenditures: $10,000. *Unit head:* Dr. Peter Vietze, Chairperson, 973-655-5201. *Application contact:* Amy Aiello, Director of Admissions and Operations, 973-655-5147, Fax: 973-655-7869, E-mail: graduate.school@montclair.edu.

Morehead State University, Graduate Programs, College of Science and Technology, Department of Psychology, Morehead, KY 40351. Offers clinical/counseling psychology (MS); general/experimental psychology (MS). Part-time and evening/weekend programs available. *Faculty:* 7 full-time (2 women). *Students:* 32 full-time (23 women), 2 part-time (1 woman), 1 international. Average age 25. 39 applicants, 51% accepted, 19 enrolled. In 2009, 12 master's awarded. *Degree requirements:* For master's, comprehensive exam, thesis optional. *Entrance requirements:* For master's, GRE General Test, 18 undergraduate hours in psychology, minimum GPA of 3.0, 3 letters of recommendation. Additional exam requirements/recommendations for international students: Required—TOEFL (minimum score 500 paper-based; 173 computer-based). *Application deadline:* For fall admission, 8/1 priority date for domestic and international students; for spring admission, 12/1 for domestic students, 12/1 priority date for international students. Applications are processed on a rolling basis. Application fee: $30. Electronic applications accepted. *Expenses:* Tuition, state resident: full-time $6318; part-time $351 per credit hour. Tuition, nonresident: full-time $15,804; part-time $878 per credit hour. *Financial support:* In 2009–10, 26 research assistantships (averaging $10,000 per year) were awarded; career-related internships or fieldwork, Federal Work-Study, and unspecified assistantships also available. Financial award application deadline: 3/15; financial award applicants required to submit FAFSA. *Faculty research:* Mood induction effects, serotonin receptor activity, stress, perceptual processes. *Unit head:* Dr. Laurie Couch, Interim Department Chair, 606-783-2950. *Application contact:* Michelle Barber, Graduate Recruitment and Retention Assistant Director, 606-783-5127, Fax: 606-783-5061, E-mail: m.barber@moreheadstate.edu.

Morgan State University, School of Graduate Studies, College of Liberal Arts, Department of Psychology, Baltimore, MD 21251. Offers psychometrics (MS, PhD). *Entrance requirements:* For master's and doctorate, GRE.

Mountain State University, Graduate Studies, Program in Psychology, Beckley, WV 25802-9003. Offers MA. *Expenses:* Tuition: Full-time $6450. Tuition and fees vary according to program. *Unit head:* Dr. Judith Halle, Dean, School of Health Sciences, 304-929-1327, E-mail: jhalle@mountainstate.edu. *Application contact:* Anita Diaz, Enrollment Coordinator of Graduate Studies, 304-461-3213, Fax: 304-929-1637, E-mail: adiaz@mountainstate.edu.

Mount Aloysius College, Program in Psychology, Cresson, PA 16630-1999. Offers MS. *Entrance requirements:* For master's, GRE General Test. *Application contact:* Andrew D. Clouse, Associate Director of Admissions and Coordinator of Graduate Admissions, 814-886-6480, Fax: 814-886-6480, E-mail: aclouse@mtaloy.edu.

Mount Holyoke College, Department of Psychology and Education, South Hadley, MA 01075. Offers MA.

Mount St. Mary's College, Graduate Division, Program in Counseling Psychology, Los Angeles, CA 90049-1599. Offers counseling psychology (MS); marriage and family therapy (MS); psychology (MS). Part-time and evening/weekend programs available. *Faculty:* 3 full-time (2 women), 6 part-time/adjunct (5 women). *Students:* 43 full-time (38 women), 4 part-time (3 women); includes 10 minority (1 African American, 2 Asian Americans or Pacific Islanders, 7 Hispanic Americans). Average age 31. In 2009, 12 master's awarded. *Degree requirements:* For master's, research project. *Entrance requirements:* For master's, minimum GPA of 3.0. *Application deadline:* For fall admission, 7/15 for domestic students; for spring admission, 11/15 for domestic students. *Expenses:* Tuition: Part-time $730 per unit. Part-time tuition and fees vary according to degree level and program. *Financial support:* Institutionally sponsored loans and tuition waivers (partial) available. Support available to part-time students. Financial award application deadline: 3/15; financial award applicants required to submit FAFSA. *Unit head:* Dr. Gregory Travis, Director, Graduate Psychology, 213-477-2654, E-mail: gtravis@msmc.la.edu. *Application contact:* Director of Graduate Admission.

Murray State University, College of Humanities and Fine Arts, Program in Psychology, Murray, KY 42071. Offers clinical psychology (MA, MS); psychology (MA, MS). Part-time programs available. *Degree requirements:* For master's, one foreign language, comprehensive exam (for some programs), thesis. *Entrance requirements:* For master's, GRE General Test. Additional exam requirements/recommendations for international students: Required—TOEFL.

National-Louis University, College of Arts and Sciences, Program in Psychology, Chicago, IL 60603. Offers community psychology (PhD); cultural psychology (MA); health psychology (MA); human development (MA); organizational psychology (MA); psychology (Certificate), including general, health, human development, organizational, psychological assessment. Part-time and evening/weekend programs available. *Degree requirements:* For master's, thesis, internship (health psychology). *Entrance requirements:* For master's, GRE General Test, MAT, or Watson-Glaser Critical Thinking Appraisal, interview, minimum GPA of 3.0; for Certificate, GRE, MAT, or Watson-Glaser Critical Thinking Appraisal, interview, minimum GPA of 3.0, undergraduate course work in psychology. *Expenses:* Tuition: Full-time $17,160; part-time $715 per semester hour. Tuition and fees vary according to course load, degree level, campus/location and program. *Faculty research:* Human development, personality theory, abnormal psychology.

National University, Academic Affairs, College of Letters and Sciences, Department of Psychology, La Jolla, CA 92037-1011. Offers counseling psychology (MA); human behavior (MA). Part-time and evening/weekend programs available. Postbaccalaureate distance learning degree programs offered (no on-campus study). *Faculty:* 15 full-time (8 women), 66 part-time/adjunct (40 women). *Students:* 421 full-time (340 women), 443 part-time (356 women); includes 343 minority (118 African Americans, 4 American Indian/Alaska Native, 47 Asian Americans or Pacific Islanders, 174 Hispanic Americans), 6 international. Average age 36. 585 applicants, 100% accepted, 320 enrolled. In 2009, 226 master's awarded. *Degree requirements:* For master's, thesis (for some programs). *Entrance requirements:* For master's, interview, minimum GPA of 2.5. Additional exam requirements/recommendations for international students: Required—TOEFL (minimum score 550 paper-based; 213 computer-based; 79 iBT), IELTS (minimum score 6). *Application deadline:* Applications are processed on a rolling basis. Application fee: $60 ($65 for international students). Electronic applications accepted. *Expenses:* Tuition: Part-time $338 per quarter hour. *Financial support:* Career-related internships or fieldwork, institutionally sponsored loans, scholarships/grants, and tuition waivers (partial) available. Support available to part-time students. Financial award application deadline: 6/30; financial award applicants required to submit FAFSA. *Unit head:* Dr. Maureen O'Hara, Chair and Professor, 858-642-8464, Fax: 858-642-8715, E-mail: mohara@nu.edu. *Application contact:* Dominick Giovanniello, Associate Regional Dean—San Diego, 800-NAT-UNIV, Fax: 858-541-7792, E-mail: dgiovann@nu.edu.

New Mexico Highlands University, Graduate Studies, College of Arts and Sciences, Department of Behavioral Sciences, Las Vegas, NM 87701. Offers psychology (MS), including clinical psychology, general psychology. Part-time programs available. *Degree requirements:* For master's, comprehensive exam, thesis or alternative. *Entrance requirements:* For master's, minimum undergraduate GPA of 3.0. Additional exam requirements/recommendations for international students: Required—TOEFL (minimum score 540 paper-based; 207 computer-based). *Faculty research:* Southwest Native American resettlement development, community-level interventions, neurochemistry of personality, comparative criminal justice, social theory and activism.

New Mexico State University, Graduate School, College of Arts and Sciences, Department of Psychology, Las Cruces, NM 88003-8001. Offers MA, PhD. Part-time programs available. *Faculty:* 13 full-time (3 women). *Students:* 39 full-time (19 women), 9 part-time (5 women); includes 5 minority (1 Asian American or Pacific Islander, 4 Hispanic Americans), 5 international. Average age 30. 49 applicants, 49% accepted, 20 enrolled. In 2009, 2 master's, 5 doctorates awarded. *Degree requirements:* For master's, thesis; for doctorate, comprehensive exam, thesis/dissertation. *Entrance requirements:* For master's, GRE General Test, letters of recommendation, curriculum vitae; for doctorate, GRE General Test, letters of recommendation, master's thesis or proposal, curriculum vitae. *Application deadline:* For fall admission, 2/1 priority date for domestic students, 2/1 for international students. Applications are processed on a rolling basis. Application fee: $30 ($50 for international students). Electronic applications accepted. *Expenses:* Tuition, state resident: full-time $4080; part-time $223 per credit. Tuition, nonresident: full-time $14,256; part-time $647 per credit. Required fees: $1278; $639 per semester. *Financial support:* In 2009–10, 5 research assistantships with partial tuition reimbursements (averaging $7,980 per year), 31 teaching assistantships with partial tuition reimbursements (averaging $7,193 per year) were awarded; fellowships, career-related internships or fieldwork, Federal Work-Study, and health care benefits also available. Support available to part-time students. Financial award application deadline: 2/15. *Faculty research:* Engineering, cognitive and social psychology; human/computer interaction; cognitive science. *Unit head:* Dr. James E. McDonald, Head, 575-646-5130, Fax: 575-646-6212, E-mail: jemcdon@nmsu.edu. *Application contact:* Dr. Laura J. Madson, Associate Professor/Chair of Graduate Committee, 575-646-6207, Fax: 575-646-6212, E-mail: lmadson@nmsu.edu.

The New School: A University, The New School for Social Research, Department of Psychology, New York, NY 10011. Offers clinical psychology (PhD); cognitive, social and developmental psychology (PhD); general psychology (MA). *Accreditation:* APA (one or more programs are accredited). Part-time programs available. *Faculty:* 13 full-time (5 women). *Students:* 172 full-time (130 women), 105 part-time (87 women); includes 49 minority (13 African Americans, 1 American Indian/Alaska Native, 15 Asian Americans or Pacific Islanders, 20 Hispanic Americans), 41 international. Average age 30. 299 applicants, 80% accepted, 76 enrolled. In 2009, 74 master's, 17 doctorates awarded. Terminal master's awarded for partial completion of doctoral program. *Degree requirements:* For master's, comprehensive exam (for some programs), thesis (for some programs); for doctorate, thesis/dissertation, qualifying exam. *Entrance requirements:* For master's, GRE General Test; for doctorate, GRE General Test, MA. Additional exam requirements/recommendations for international students: Required—TOEFL (minimum score 600 paper-based; 250 computer-based; 100 iBT). *Application deadline:* For fall admission, 1/17 priority date for domestic and international students; for spring admission, 10/15 priority date for domestic and international students. Applications are processed on a rolling basis. Application fee: $50. Electronic applications accepted. *Financial support:* Fellowships, research assistantships, teaching assistantships, Federal Work-Study, scholarships/grants, tuition waivers (full and partial), and unspecified assistantships available. Support available to part-time students. Financial award application deadline: 3/1; financial award applicants required to submit FAFSA. *Faculty research:* Consciousness, memory, language, perceptions, psychopathology. *Unit head:* Dr. McWelling Todman, Chair, 212-229-5727 Ext. 3258, E-mail: todmanm@newschool.edu. *Application contact:* Robert MacDonald, Director of Admissions, 212-229-5727 Ext. 3007, Fax: 212-989-7102, E-mail: macdonar@newschool.edu.

New York University, Graduate School of Arts and Science, Department of Psychology, New York, NY 10012-1019. Offers cognition and perception (PhD); community psychology (PhD); general psychology (MA); industrial/organizational psychology (MA); psychotherapy and psychoanalysis (Advanced Certificate); social/personality psychology (PhD). Part-time programs available. *Students:* 151 full-time (94 women), 273 part-time (192 women); includes 59 minority (13 African Americans, 1 American Indian/Alaska Native, 27 Asian Americans or Pacific Islanders, 18 Hispanic Americans), 62 international. Average age 32. 748 applicants, 46% accepted, 122 enrolled. In 2009, 100 master's, 11 doctorates, 8 other advanced degrees awarded. Terminal master's awarded for partial completion of doctoral program. *Degree requirements:* For master's, comprehensive exam, thesis or alternative; for doctorate, thesis/dissertation. *Entrance requirements:* For master's, GRE General Test, minimum GPA of 3.0; for doctorate, GRE General Test, GRE Subject Test; for Advanced Certificate, doctoral degree, minimum GPA of 3.0. Additional exam requirements/recommendations for international students: Required—TOEFL. *Application deadline:* For fall admission, 12/18 for domestic students. Application fee: $90. *Expenses:* Tuition: Full-time $30,528; part-time $1272 per credit. Required fees: $2177. *Financial support:* Fellowships with tuition reimbursements, research assistantships with tuition reimbursements, teaching assistantships with tuition reimbursements, career-related internships or fieldwork, Federal Work-Study, institutionally sponsored loans, scholarships/grants, traineeships, health care benefits, and unspecified assistantships available. Financial award application deadline: 12/18; financial award applicants required to submit FAFSA. *Faculty research:* Vision, memory, social cognition, social and cognitive development, relationships. *Unit head:* Madeline Heilman, Director of Ph.D. Program, 212-998-7900, Fax: 212-995-4018, E-mail: psychq@psych.nyu.edu. *Application contact:* Barry Cohen, Director of M.A. Program, 212-998-7900, Fax: 212-995-4018, E-mail: psychq@psych.nyu.edu.

New York University, Steinhardt School of Culture, Education, and Human Development, Department of Applied Psychology, Programs in Educational and Developmental Psychology, New York, NY 10012-1019. Offers educational psychology (MA); human development and social intervention (MA); psychological development (PhD); psychology and social intervention (PhD). *Accreditation:* APA (one or more programs are accredited). Part-time programs available. *Students:* 48 full-time (42 women), 36 part-time (30 women); includes 24 minority (9 African Americans, 4 Asian Americans or Pacific Islanders, 11 Hispanic Americans), 11 international. Average age 29. 233 applicants, 30% accepted, 26 enrolled. In 2009, 29 master's, 9 doctorates awarded. *Degree requirements:* For master's, thesis (for some programs); for doctorate, thesis/dissertation. *Entrance requirements:* For doctorate, GRE General Test, interview. Additional exam requirements/recommendations for international students: Required—TOEFL. *Application deadline:* For fall admission, 12/15 priority date for domestic and international students. Applications are processed on a rolling basis. Application fee: $75. Electronic applications accepted. *Expenses:* Tuition: Full-time $30,528; part-time $1272 per credit. Required fees: $2177. *Financial support:* Teaching assistantships with partial tuition reimbursements, career-related internships or fieldwork, Federal Work-Study, institutionally sponsored loans, and tuition waivers (partial) available. Support available to part-time students. Financial award application deadline: 2/1; financial award applicants required to submit FAFSA. *Faculty research:* High risk children and youth; child and adolescent developments; families and schooling; infant cognition; exploration, language, and symbolic play in toddlerhood. *Unit head:* Dr. LaRue Allen, Director, 212-998-5555, Fax: 212-995-4358. *Application contact:* 212-998-5030, Fax: 212-995-4328, E-mail: steinhardt.gradadmissions@nyu.edu.

Norfolk State University, School of Graduate Studies, School of Liberal Arts, Department of Psychology, Norfolk, VA 23504. Offers community/clinical psychology (MA); psychology (Psy D). Psy D offered through the Virginia Consortium for Professional Psychology; for information call 757-431-4950. Part-time programs available. *Degree requirements:* For master's, comprehensive exam, thesis or alternative; for doctorate, comprehensive exam, thesis/dissertation. *Entrance requirements:* For master's, minimum GPA of 2.7.

North Carolina Central University, Division of Academic Affairs, College of Behavioral and Social Sciences, Department of Psychology, Durham, NC 27707-3129. Offers MA. Part-time and evening/weekend programs available. *Degree requirements:* For master's, one foreign language, comprehensive exam, thesis. *Entrance requirements:* For master's, GRE, minimum GPA of 3.0 in major, 2.5 overall. Additional exam requirements/recommendations for international students: Required—TOEFL. *Faculty research:* Aggression, hypertension, faces, anger, teaching.

North Carolina State University, Graduate School, College of Humanities and Social Sciences, Department of Psychology, Raleigh, NC 27695. Offers developmental psychology (PhD); ergonomics and experimental psychology (PhD); industrial/organizational psychology (PhD); psychology in the public interest (PhD); school psychology (PhD). *Accreditation:* APA. *Degree requirements:* For doctorate, comprehensive exam, thesis/dissertation. *Entrance requirements:* For doctorate, GRE General Test, GRE Subject Test (industrial/organizational psychology), MAT (recommended), minimum GPA of 3.0 in major. Electronic applications accepted. *Faculty research:* Cognitive and social development (human factors, families, the workplace, community issues and health, aging).

Northcentral University, Graduate Studies, Prescott Valley, AZ 86314. Offers business (MBA, DBA, PhD, CAGS); education (M Ed, Ed D, PhD, CAGS); marriage and family therapy (MA, PhD); psychology (MA, PhD, CAGS). Evening/weekend programs available. Postbaccalaureate distance learning degree programs offered (no on-campus study). *Students:* 8,148 full-time (4,063 women); includes 984 minority (646 African Americans, 54 American Indian/Alaska Native, 125 Asian Americans or Pacific Islanders, 159 Hispanic Americans). Average age 43. In 2009, 271 master's, 189 doctorates, 13 other advanced degrees awarded. *Entrance requirements:* For master's, Bachelor's degree from regionally accredited institution & current resume; for doctorate and CAGS, A conferred master's from a regionally accredited university. Additional exam requirements/recommendations for international students: Required—TOEFL (minimum score 95 computer-based), IELTS (minimum score 7), Pearson Test of English (minimum score 65). *Application deadline:* Applications are processed on a rolling basis. Application fee: $75. *Expenses:* Tuition: Part-time $560 per credit. Part-time tuition and fees vary according to degree level and program. *Financial support:* Scholarships/grants available. *Unit head:* Dr. Barnaby Barratt, Provost and Professor of Psychology, 888-327-2877, Fax: 928-759-6381, E-mail: bbarratt@ncu.edu. *Application contact:* Kevin Lustig, Director of Admissions, 480-478-7490, Fax: 928-759-6285, E-mail: klustig@ncu.edu.

North Dakota State University, College of Graduate and Interdisciplinary Studies, College of Science and Mathematics, Department of Psychology, Fargo, ND 58108. Offers clinical psychology (MS); cognitive and visual neuroscience (PhD); health and social psychology (PhD); psychology (MS). *Faculty:* 18 full-time (4 women), 2 part-time/adjunct (1 woman). *Students:* 36 full-time (27 women); includes 4 minority (1 African American, 2 Asian Americans or Pacific Islanders, 1 Hispanic American), 1 international. Average age 24. 48 applicants, 33% accepted, 10 enrolled. In 2009, 3 master's, 1 doctorate awarded. *Degree requirements:* For master's, thesis; for doctorate, thesis/dissertation. *Entrance requirements:* For master's and doctorate, GRE General Test, GRE Subject Test. Additional exam requirements/recommendations for international students: Required—TOEFL (minimum score 525 paper-based; 197 computer-based; 71 iBT). *Application deadline:* For fall admission, 3/1 for domestic and international students. Application fee: $45 ($60 for international students). Electronic applications accepted. *Financial support:* In 2009–10, 36 students received support, including 2 fellowships with full tuition reimbursements available (averaging $16,000 per year), 23 research assistantships with full tuition reimbursements available (averaging $16,000 per year), 11 teaching assistantships with full tuition reimbursements available (averaging $6,000 per year); career-related internships or fieldwork, Federal Work-Study, institutionally sponsored loans, tuition waivers (full and partial), and unspecified assistantships also available. Support available to part-time students. Financial award application deadline: 3/1. *Faculty research:* Cognition science, neuropsychology, group behavior, applied behavior analysis, behavior therapy. Total annual research expenditures: $2 million. *Unit head:* Dr. Paul D. Rokke, Chair, 701-231-8622, Fax: 701-231-8426, E-mail: paul.rokke@ndsu.edu. *Application contact:* Dr. Paul D. Rokke, Chair, 701-231-8622, Fax: 701-231-8426, E-mail: paul.rokke@ndsu.edu.

Northeastern State University, Graduate College, College of Education, Department of Psychology and Counseling, Tahlequah, OK 74464-2399. Offers counseling psychology (MS); school counseling (M Ed). Part-time and evening/weekend programs available. *Degree requirements:* For master's, thesis (for some programs), written and oral examinations. *Entrance requirements:* For master's, GRE, minimum GPA of 2.5.

Northeastern University, Bouvé College of Health Sciences Graduate School, Department of Counseling and Applied Educational Psychology, Boston, MA 02115-5096. Offers applied behavior analysis (MS); college student development and counseling (MS, CAGS); counseling psychology (MS, PhD, CAGS); school psychology (PhD, CAGS). *Accreditation:* APA (one or more programs are accredited). Part-time and evening/weekend programs available. *Faculty:* 20 full-time (12 women), 17 part-time/adjunct (8 women). *Students:* 353 full-time (308 women), 51 part-time (42 women). 452 applicants, 24% accepted. In 2009, 95 master's, 10 doctorates, 25 other advanced degrees awarded. *Degree requirements:* For doctorate, comprehensive exam, thesis/dissertation, qualifying exams; for CAGS, comprehensive exam. *Entrance requirements:* For master's and CAGS, GRE General Test or MAT; for doctorate, GRE General Test. Additional exam requirements/recommendations for international students: Required—TOEFL (minimum score 100 iBT). *Application deadline:* Applications are processed on a rolling basis. Application fee: $50. Electronic applications accepted. *Financial support:* Research assistantships, teaching assistantships with full tuition reimbursements, career-related internships or fieldwork, Federal Work-Study, scholarships/grants, tuition waivers (partial), and unspecified assistantships available. Support available to part-time students. Financial award application deadline: 3/1; financial award applicants required to submit FAFSA. *Faculty research:* Early intervention, career development and choice, crisis intervention, family systems, bilingual education in special education, eating disorders. *Unit head:* Dr. Y. Barr Chung, Chairman, 617-373-8120, Fax: 617-373-8892, E-mail: y.chunk@neu.edu. *Application contact:* Margaret Schnabel, Director of Graduate Admissions, 617-373-2708, E-mail: bouvegrad@neu.edu.

Northern Arizona University, Graduate College, College of Social and Behavioral Sciences, Department of Psychology, Flagstaff, AZ 86011. Offers applied health psychology (MA); clinical psychology (MA); general psychology (MA); teaching of psychology (MA). Part-time programs available. *Faculty:* 20 full-time (10 women). *Students:* 26 full-time (15 women), 6 part-time (all women); includes 4 minority (1 American Indian/Alaska Native, 3 Hispanic Americans), 2 international. Average age 30. 58 applicants, 41% accepted, 16 enrolled. In 2009, 4 master's awarded. *Degree requirements:* For master's, comprehensive exam (for some programs), thesis (for some programs), oral defense. *Entrance requirements:* For master's, GRE General Test. Additional exam requirements/recommendations for international students: Required—TOEFL (minimum score 550 paper-based; 213 computer-based; 80 iBT), IELTS (minimum score 7), or a bachelor's degree from an English-speaking university and demonstrated proficiency. *Application deadline:* For fall admission, 2/15 priority date for domestic students, 9/1 priority date for international students. Applications are processed on a rolling basis. Application fee: $65. Electronic applications accepted. *Financial support:* In 2009–10, 12 teaching assistantships with partial tuition reimbursements (averaging $10,439 per year) were awarded; career-related internships or fieldwork, Federal Work-Study, institutionally sponsored loans, scholarships/grants, health care benefits, tuition waivers (full and partial), and unspecified assistantships also available. Support available to part-time students. Financial award application deadline: 3/30; financial award applicants required to submit FAFSA. *Unit head:* Dr. Laurie Dickson, Chair, 928-523-0575, Fax: 928-523-6777, E-mail: laurie.dickson@nau.edu. *Application contact:* Dr. Steven Barger, Graduate Coordinator, 928-523-1829, Fax: 928-523-6777, E-mail: steven.barger@nau.edu.

Northern Illinois University, Graduate School, College of Liberal Arts and Sciences, Department of Psychology, De Kalb, IL 60115-2854. Offers MA, PhD. *Accreditation:* APA (one or more programs are accredited). *Faculty:* 26 full-time (11 women), 5 part-time/adjunct (1 woman). *Students:* 117 full-time (81 women), 14 part-time (7 women); includes 19 minority (3 African Americans, 4 American Indian/Alaska Native, 7 Asian Americans or Pacific Islanders, 5 Hispanic Americans), 5 international. Average age 28. 376 applicants, 14% accepted, 36 enrolled. In 2009, 26 master's, 19 doctorates awarded. *Degree requirements:* For master's, comprehensive exam, thesis optional; for doctorate, thesis/dissertation, candidacy exam, dissertation defense. *Entrance requirements:* For master's, GRE General Test, minimum GPA of 3.0 for last 2 years of undergraduate work; for doctorate, GRE General Test, minimum undergraduate GPA of 2.75, graduate 3.2; master's degree with research thesis. Additional exam requirements/recommendations for international students: Required—TOEFL (minimum score 550 paper-based; 213 computer-based). *Application deadline:* For fall admission, 3/1 for domestic students, 5/1 for international students; for spring admission, 11/1 for domestic students, 10/1 for international students. Applications are processed on a rolling basis. Application fee: $30. Electronic applications accepted. *Expenses:* Tuition, state resident: full-time $6576; part-time $274 per credit hour. Tuition, nonresident: full-time $13,152; part-time $548 per credit hour. Required fees: $1813; $75.53 per credit hour. Part-time tuition and fees vary according to course load. *Financial support:* In 2009–10, 41 research assistantships with full tuition reimbursements, 52 teaching assistantships with full tuition reimbursements were awarded;

Psychology—General

Northern Illinois University (continued)
fellowships with full tuition reimbursements, career-related internships or fieldwork, Federal Work-Study, scholarships/grants, tuition waivers (full), and staff assistantships also available. Support available to part-time students. Financial award applicants required to submit FAFSA. *Faculty research:* Neglect syndrome, ADHD, workplace discrimination, adolescent suicide, social dilemmas. *Unit head:* Dr. Gregory A. Waas, Chair, 815-753-7065, E-mail: gwaas@niu.edu. *Application contact:* Dr. Gregory A. Waas, Chair, 815-753-7065, E-mail: gwaas@niu.edu.

Northern Michigan University, College of Graduate Studies, College of Arts and Sciences, Department of Psychology, Marquette, MI 49855-5301. Offers MS. Part-time and evening/weekend programs available. *Degree requirements:* For master's, thesis (for some programs). *Entrance requirements:* For master's, GRE, minimum GPA of 3.0.

Northwestern State University of Louisiana, Graduate Studies and Research, Department of Psychology, Natchitoches, LA 71497. Offers clinical psychology (MS). *Degree requirements:* For master's, comprehensive exam, thesis or alternative. *Entrance requirements:* For master's, GRE General Test, GRE Subject Test, minimum undergraduate GPA of 2.5.

Northwestern University, The Graduate School, Judd A. and Marjorie Weinberg College of Arts and Sciences, Department of Psychology, Evanston, IL 60208. Offers brain, behavior and cognition (PhD); clinical psychology (PhD); cognitive psychology (PhD); personality (PhD); social psychology (PhD); JD/PhD. Admissions and degrees offered through The Graduate School. *Accreditation:* APA (one or more programs are accredited). Part-time programs available. *Degree requirements:* For doctorate, thesis/dissertation. *Entrance requirements:* For doctorate, GRE General Test, GRE Subject Test. Additional exam requirements/recommendations for international students: Required—TOEFL. Electronic applications accepted. *Faculty research:* Memory and higher order cognition, anxiety and depression, effectiveness of psychotherapy, social cognition, molecular basis of memory.

Northwest Missouri State University, Graduate School, College of Education and Human Services, Department of Psychology and Sociology, Maryville, MO 64468-6001. Offers guidance and counseling (MS Ed). Part-time programs available. *Faculty:* 8 full-time (6 women). *Students:* 6 full-time (5 women), 28 part-time (25 women); includes 1 minority (Asian American or Pacific Islander). 25 applicants, 80% accepted, 15 enrolled. In 2009, 8 master's awarded. *Degree requirements:* For master's, comprehensive exam, thesis. *Entrance requirements:* For master's, GRE General Test, minimum undergraduate GPA of 2.5, 3.0 in major; writing sample. Additional exam requirements/recommendations for international students: Required—TOEFL (minimum score 550 paper-based; 213 computer-based). *Application deadline:* For fall admission, 3/1 for domestic and international students. Applications are processed on a rolling basis. Application fee: $0 ($50 for international students). Electronic applications accepted. *Expenses:* Tuition, state resident: part-time $296.34 per credit hour. Tuition, nonresident: part-time $510.43 per credit hour. *Financial support:* In 2009–10, 4 research assistantships with full tuition reimbursements (averaging $6,000 per year) were awarded; unspecified assistantships also available. Financial award application deadline: 4/1; financial award applicants required to submit FAFSA. *Unit head:* Dr. Jackie Kibler, Chairperson, 660-562-1852. *Application contact:* Dr. Gregory Haddock, Dean of Graduate School, 660-562-1145, Fax: 660-562-1096, E-mail: gradsch@nwmissouri.edu.

Northwest University, College of Social and Behavioral Sciences, Kirkland, WA 98033. Offers counseling psychology (MA, Psy D); international care and community development (MA). Evening/weekend programs available. *Faculty:* 5 full-time (2 women), 11 part-time/adjunct (5 women). *Students:* 87 full-time (68 women), 30 part-time (26 women); includes 17 minority (5 African Americans, 6 Asian Americans or Pacific Islanders, 6 Hispanic Americans), 2 international. 156 applicants, 86% accepted, 77 enrolled. In 2009, 39 master's awarded. *Entrance requirements:* For master's, 3 character references. Additional exam requirements/recommendations for international students: Required—TOEFL (minimum score 580 paper-based; 237 computer-based). *Application deadline:* For fall admission, 12/1 priority date for domestic and international students; for spring admission, 4/1 priority date for domestic and international students. Applications are processed on a rolling basis. Application fee: $75. *Expenses:* Contact institution. *Financial support:* Career-related internships or fieldwork, health care benefits, and international student scholarships available. Financial award application deadline: 6/30. *Unit head:* Dr. William Herkelrath, Dean, 425-889-5328, Fax: 425-739-4602, E-mail: william.herkelrath@northwestu.edu. *Application contact:* Jon Troll, Director of Student Services, 425-889-5249, Fax: 425-739-4602, E-mail: jon.troll@northwestu.edu.

Notre Dame de Namur University, Division of Academic Affairs, College of Arts and Sciences, Department of Clinical Psychology and Gerontology, Belmont, CA 94002-1908. Offers clinical psychology (MS); clinical psychology: marital and family therapy (MS). Part-time and evening/weekend programs available. *Faculty:* 2 full-time (both women), 6 part-time/adjunct (5 women). *Students:* 29 full-time (25 women), 65 part-time (56 women); includes 31 minority (5 African Americans, 11 Asian Americans or Pacific Islanders, 15 Hispanic Americans), 1 international. Average age 35. 26 applicants, 81% accepted, 16 enrolled. In 2009, 27 master's awarded. *Entrance requirements:* For master's, interview, minimum GPA of 2.5. Additional exam requirements/recommendations for international students: Required—TOEFL (minimum score 550 paper-based; 213 computer-based; 79 iBT). *Application deadline:* For fall admission, 8/1 priority date for domestic students; for spring admission, 12/1 priority date for domestic students. Applications are processed on a rolling basis. Application fee: $60. Electronic applications accepted. *Expenses:* Tuition: Part-time $720 per credit. Required fees: $35 per semester hour. *Financial support:* Career-related internships or fieldwork available. Support available to part-time students. Financial award applicants required to submit FAFSA. *Unit head:* Dr. Nusha Askari, Chair, 650-508-3728, E-mail: naskari@ndnu.edu. *Application contact:* Candace Hallmark, Associate Director of Admissions, 650-508-3592, Fax: 650-508-3426, E-mail: grad.admit@ndnu.edu.

Nova Southeastern University, Center for Psychological Studies, Fort Lauderdale, FL 33314-7796. Offers MS, PhD, Psy D, Psy S, SPS. *Accreditation:* APA (one or more programs are accredited). Postbaccalaureate distance learning degree programs offered. *Faculty:* 34 full-time (11 women), 68 part-time/adjunct (32 women). *Students:* 854 full-time (716 women), 698 part-time (622 women); includes 644 minority (265 African Americans, 2 American Indian/Alaska Native, 39 Asian Americans or Pacific Islanders, 338 Hispanic Americans), 41 international. 1,433 applicants, 49% accepted, 520 enrolled. In 2009, 348 master's, 80 doctorates, 24 other advanced degrees awarded. Terminal master's awarded for partial completion of doctoral program. *Degree requirements:* For master's, comprehensive exam, 3 practica; for doctorate, thesis/dissertation, clinical internship, competency exam; for other advanced degree, comprehensive exam, internship. *Entrance requirements:* For doctorate, GRE General Test, GRE Subject Test (recommended), minimum undergraduate GPA of 3.0; for other advanced degree, GRE General Test. Additional exam requirements/recommendations for international students: Required—TOEFL (minimum score 550 paper-based; 213 computer-based). *Application deadline:* Applications are processed on a rolling basis. Application fee: $50. Electronic applications accepted. *Expenses:* Contact institution. *Financial support:* In 2009–10, 5 research assistantships, 34 teaching assistantships (averaging $1,000 per year) were awarded; career-related internships or fieldwork, Federal Work-Study, institutionally sponsored loans, scholarships/grants, and unspecified assistantships also available. Support available to part-time students. Financial award application deadline: 4/1. *Faculty research:* Clinical and child clinical psychology, geriatrics, interpersonal violence. *Unit head:* Karen Grosby, Deah, 954-262-5701, Fax: 954-262-3859, E-mail: grosby@nova.edu. *Application contact:* Carlos Perez, Enrollment Management, 954-262-5790, Fax: 954-262-3893, E-mail: cpsinfo@cps.nova.edu.

The Ohio State University, Graduate School, College of Social and Behavioral Sciences, School of Social and Behavioral Science, Department of Psychology, Columbus, OH 43210. Offers behavioral neuroscience (PhD); clinical psychology (PhD); cognitive psychology (PhD); developmental psychology (PhD); mental retardation and developmental disabilities (PhD); psychology (MA); quantitative psychology (PhD); social psychology (PhD). *Accreditation:* APA (one or more programs are accredited). *Faculty:* 60. *Students:* 88 full-time (59 women), 47 part-time (31 women); includes 20 minority (7 African Americans, 1 American Indian/Alaska Native, 5 Asian Americans or Pacific Islanders, 7 Hispanic Americans), 20 international. Average age 27. In 2009, 15 master's, 20 doctorates awarded. *Degree requirements:* For doctorate, thesis/dissertation. *Entrance requirements:* For master's and doctorate, GRE General Test. Additional exam requirements/recommendations for international students: Required—TOEFL (minimum score 600 paper-based; 250 computer-based). *Application deadline:* For fall admission, 12/31 for domestic students, 11/30 for international students. Applications are processed on a rolling basis. Application fee: $40 ($50 for international students). Electronic applications accepted. *Expenses:* Tuition, state resident: full-time $10,683. Tuition, nonresident: full-time $25,923. Tuition and fees vary according to course load and program. *Financial support:* Fellowships, research assistantships, teaching assistantships available. *Unit head:* Michael Vasey, Graduate Studies Committee Chair, E-mail: vasey.1@osu.edu. *Application contact:* 614-292-9444, Fax: 614-292-3895, E-mail: domestic.grad@osu.edu.

Ohio University, Graduate College, College of Arts and Sciences, Department of Psychology, Athens, OH 45701-2979. Offers clinical psychology (PhD); experimental psychology (PhD); organizational psychology (PhD). *Accreditation:* APA. *Faculty:* 23 full-time (10 women), 6 part-time/adjunct (3 women). *Students:* 70 full-time (45 women), 22 part-time (16 women); includes 11 minority (3 African Americans, 6 Asian Americans or Pacific Islanders, 2 Hispanic Americans), 10 international. 193 applicants, 11% accepted, 15 enrolled. In 2009, 14 doctorates awarded. *Degree requirements:* For doctorate, one foreign language, comprehensive exam, thesis/dissertation. *Entrance requirements:* For doctorate, GRE General Test, GRE Subject Test. Additional exam requirements/recommendations for international students: Required—TOEFL (minimum score 550 paper-based; 80 iBT) or IELTS Academic (minimum score 6.5). *Application deadline:* For fall admission, 1/1 for domestic and international students. Application fee: $50 ($55 for international students). Electronic applications accepted. *Expenses:* Tuition, state resident: full-time $7839; part-time $323 per quarter hour. Tuition, nonresident: full-time $15,831; part-time $654 per quarter hour. Required fees: $2931. *Financial support:* Fellowships with full tuition reimbursements, research assistantships with full tuition reimbursements, teaching assistantships with full tuition reimbursements, career-related internships or fieldwork, Federal Work-Study, institutionally sponsored loans, traineeships, tuition waivers (partial), and unspecified assistantships available. Financial award application deadline: 1/15. *Faculty research:* Health, cognitive, child clinical, and social psychology. Total annual research expenditures: $11.2 million. *Unit head:* Dr. Bruce Carlson, Head, 740-593-1077, Fax: 740-593-0053, E-mail: carlsonb@ohio.edu. *Application contact:* Karyl Jones, Administrative Secretary, 740-593-1090, Fax: 740-593-0579, E-mail: psychology@ohio.edu.

Oklahoma State University, College of Arts and Sciences, Department of Psychology, Stillwater, OK 74078. Offers clinical psychology (PhD); general psychology (MS); lifespan development psychology (PhD). *Accreditation:* APA (one or more programs are accredited). *Faculty:* 26 full-time (12 women). *Students:* 36 full-time (23 women), 15 part-time (8 women); includes 8 minority (2 African Americans, 3 American Indian/Alaska Native, 3 Hispanic Americans), 2 international. Average age 28. 120 applicants, 9% accepted, 7 enrolled. In 2009, 10 master's, 9 doctorates awarded. *Degree requirements:* For master's, thesis or alternative; for doctorate, comprehensive exam, thesis/dissertation. *Entrance requirements:* For master's and doctorate, GRE General Test. Additional exam requirements/recommendations for international students: Required—TOEFL (minimum score 550 paper-based; 79 iBT). *Application deadline:* For fall admission, 3/1 priority date for international students; for spring admission, 8/1 priority date for international students. Applications are processed on a rolling basis. Application fee: $40 ($75 for international students). Electronic applications accepted. *Expenses:* Tuition, state resident: full-time $3716; part-time $154.85 per credit hour. Tuition, nonresident: full-time $14,448; part-time $602 per credit hour. Required fees: $1772; $73.85 per credit hour. One-time fee: $50. Tuition and fees vary according to course load and campus/location. *Financial support:* In 2009–10, 16 research assistantships (averaging $13,215 per year), 29 teaching assistantships (averaging $13,370 per year) were awarded; career-related internships or fieldwork, Federal Work-Study, scholarships/grants, health care benefits, tuition waivers (partial), and unspecified assistantships also available. Support available to part-time students. Financial award application deadline: 3/1; financial award applicants required to submit FAFSA. *Unit head:* Dr. Larry Mullins, Head, 405-744-6028, Fax: 405-744-8067. *Application contact:* Dr. Gordon Emslie, Dean, 405-744-6368, Fax: 405-744-0355, E-mail: grad-i@okstate.edu.

Old Dominion University, College of Sciences, Doctoral Program in Psychology, Norfolk, VA 23529. Offers applied experimental psychology (PhD); human factors psychology (PhD); industrial/organizational psychology (PhD). *Faculty:* 21 full-time (9 women). *Students:* 24 full-time (17 women), 12 part-time (8 women); includes 2 minority (both Hispanic Americans), 1 international. Average age 29. 60 applicants, 15% accepted, 9 enrolled. In 2009, 4 doctorates awarded. *Degree requirements:* For doctorate, thesis/dissertation, candidacy exam. *Entrance requirements:* For doctorate, GRE General Test, GRE Subject Test, 3 recommendation letters. Additional exam requirements/recommendations for international students: Required—TOEFL (minimum score 550 paper-based). *Application deadline:* For winter admission, 1/5 for domestic and international students. Application fee: $40. Electronic applications accepted. *Expenses:* Tuition, state resident: full-time $8112; part-time $338 per credit. Tuition, nonresident: full-time $20,256; part-time $844 per credit. Required fees: $119 per semester. One-time fee: $50. *Financial support:* In 2009–10, 13 students received support, including 2 fellowships with full tuition reimbursements available (averaging $18,000 per year), research assistantships with full tuition reimbursements available (averaging $12,000 per year), 11 teaching assistantships with full tuition reimbursements available (averaging $12,000 per year). Financial award application deadline: 1/15. *Faculty research:* Human factors, industrial psychology, organizational psychology, applied experimental (health, developmental, quantitative). Total annual research expenditures: $493,384. *Unit head:* Dr. Brian Porter, Graduate Program Director, 757-683-4458, Fax: 757-683-5087, E-mail: bporter@odu.edu. *Application contact:* Dr. Brian Porter, Graduate Program Director, 757-683-4458, Fax: 757-683-5087, E-mail: bporter@odu.edu.

Old Dominion University, College of Sciences, Program in Psychology, Norfolk, VA 23529. Offers MS. Part-time programs available. *Faculty:* 20 full-time (9 women). *Students:* 12 full-time (10 women), 4 part-time (1 woman); includes 2 minority (1 African American, 1 Asian American or Pacific Islander). Average age 26. 28 applicants, 61% accepted, 7 enrolled. In 2009, 9 master's awarded. *Degree requirements:* For master's, comprehensive exam, thesis optional. *Entrance requirements:* For master's, GRE General Test, minimum GPA of 3.0 in major, previous course work in psychology. Additional exam requirements/recommendations for international students: Required—TOEFL. *Application deadline:* For fall admission, 5/15 for domestic and international students. Applications are processed on a rolling basis. Application fee: $40. Electronic applications accepted. *Expenses:* Tuition, state resident: full-time $8112; part-time $338 per credit. Tuition, nonresident: full-time $20,256; part-time $844 per credit. Required fees: $119 per semester. One-time fee: $50. *Financial support:* In 2009–10, 7 students received support, including research assistantships with partial tuition reimbursements available (averaging $9,000 per year), 7 teaching assistantships with partial tuition reimbursements available (averaging $9,000 per year); career-related internships or fieldwork, scholarships/grants, and tuition waivers (partial) also available. Financial award application deadline: 2/15; financial award applicants required to submit FAFSA. *Faculty research:* Social psychology, developmental psychology, physiopsychology, clinical psychology, industrial/organizational psychology. *Unit head:* Dr. Louis H. Janda, Graduate Program Director, 757-683-4211, Fax: 757-683-5087, E-mail: ljanda@odu.edu. *Application contact:* Dr. Louis H. Janda, Graduate Program Director, 757-683-4211, Fax: 757-683-5087, E-mail: ljanda@odu.edu.

Our Lady of the Lake University of San Antonio, School of Professional Studies, Program in Psychology, San Antonio, TX 78207-4689. Offers counseling psychology (MS, Psy D); marriage and family therapy (MS); school psychology (MS). *Accreditation:* APA (one or more programs are accredited). Part-time and evening/weekend programs available. *Students:* 111

full-time (90 women), 84 part-time (75 women); includes 118 minority (19 African Americans, 1 American Indian/Alaska Native, 4 Asian Americans or Pacific Islanders, 94 Hispanic Americans), 5 international. Average age 30. In 2009, 42 master's, 3 doctorates awarded. *Degree requirements:* For master's, comprehensive exam, thesis optional, practicum; for doctorate, thesis/dissertation, internship, qualifying exam. *Entrance requirements:* For master's and doctorate, GRE General Test or MAT, interview. Additional exam requirements/recommendations for international students: Required—TOEFL. *Application deadline:* For fall admission, 3/1 priority date for domestic and international students. Applications are processed on a rolling basis. Application fee: $25 ($50 for international students). Electronic applications accepted. *Expenses:* Tuition: Full-time $12,330; part-time $685 per contact hour. Required fees: $139; $12 per contact hour. $57 per semester. Tuition and fees vary according to campus/location. *Financial support:* Research assistantships, teaching assistantships, career-related internships or fieldwork available. Support available to part-time students. Financial award application deadline: 4/15. *Faculty research:* Marriage and family therapy, supervision, cross-cultural counseling, violence. *Unit head:* Dr. Joan Biever, Chair, 210-434-6711, E-mail: jbiever@lake.ollusa.edu. *Application contact:* 210-434-6711, Fax: 210-431-4036, E-mail: gradadm@lake.ollusa.edu.

Pace University, Dyson College of Arts and Sciences, Department of Psychology, Program in Psychology, New York, NY 10038. Offers MA. *Students:* 28 full-time (23 women), 6 part-time (3 women); includes 7 minority (2 African Americans, 1 Asian American or Pacific Islander, 4 Hispanic Americans), 6 international. Average age 25. 71 applicants, 76% accepted, 11 enrolled. In 2009, 22 master's awarded. *Entrance requirements:* Additional exam requirements/recommendations for international students: Required—TOEFL. *Application deadline:* For fall admission, 7/31 priority date for domestic students; for spring admission, 11/30 for domestic students. Applications are processed on a rolling basis. Application fee: $70. Electronic applications accepted. *Expenses:* Tuition: Part-time $954 per credit. Tuition and fees vary according to course load, degree level and program. *Unit head:* Dr. Barbara Mowder, Director, 212-346-1506. *Application contact:* Susan Ford-Goldschein, Director of Graduate Admissions, 212-346-1652, Fax: 212-346-1585, E-mail: gradnyc@pace.edu.

Pacifica Graduate Institute, Graduate Programs, Carpinteria, CA 93013. Offers clinical psychology (PhD); counseling psychology (MA); depth psychology (MA, PhD); mythological studies (MA, PhD). Terminal master's awarded for partial completion of doctoral program. *Degree requirements:* For master's, thesis (for some programs), practicum; for doctorate, comprehensive exam, thesis/dissertation, internship. *Entrance requirements:* For master's, resume, 3 letters of recommendation, writing sample, interview; for doctorate, resumé, 4 letters of recommendation, writing sample, interview. Additional exam requirements/recommendations for international students: Required—TOEFL. *Faculty research:* Imaginal and archetypal theory; post-Colonial psychoanalytic and Jungian theory; myth literature as it applies to the theory and practice of psychology.

Pacific University, School of Professional Psychology, Forest Grove, OR 97116-1797. Offers clinical psychology (MS, Psy D); counseling psychology (MA). *Accreditation:* APA (one or more programs are accredited). Part-time programs available. *Degree requirements:* For master's, comprehensive exam (for some programs), thesis (for some programs); for doctorate, comprehensive exam, thesis/dissertation. *Entrance requirements:* For master's, course work in introductory psychology, statistics, and abnormal psychology; minimum GPA of 3.0; for doctorate, GRE General Test, minimum GPA of 3.0, undergraduate course work in psychology, minimum GPA of 3.1 in last 2 years. Additional exam requirements/recommendations for international students: Required—TOEFL (minimum score 600 paper-based; 105 computer-based). Electronic applications accepted. *Expenses:* Contact institution. *Faculty research:* Neuropsychological assessment, assessment and treatment of anxiety, forensic psychology, cross-cultural psychology, child and adolescent psychopathology.

Palo Alto University, Distance Learning Program in Psychology, Palo Alto, CA 94303-4232. Offers MS. Postbaccalaureate distance learning degree programs offered (no on-campus study). *Entrance requirements:* For master's, GRE General Test. Additional exam requirements/recommendations for international students: Required—TOEFL (minimum score 550 paper-based; 220 computer-based). Electronic applications accepted. *Expenses:* Tuition: Full-time $33,009; part-time $916 per credit hour. Required fees: $1243 per quarter.

Palo Alto University, Program in Clinical Psychology, Palo Alto, CA 94303-4232. Offers PhD, JD/PhD, MBA/PhD. *Degree requirements:* For doctorate, comprehensive exam, thesis/dissertation, 2000 hour clinical internship, oral clinical competency exam. *Entrance requirements:* For doctorate, GRE General Test, BA or MA in psychology or related area, minimum undergraduate GPA of 3.0, 3.3 graduate. Additional exam requirements/recommendations for international students: Required—TOEFL. Electronic applications accepted. *Expenses:* Tuition: Full-time $33,009; part-time $916 per credit hour. Required fees: $1243 per quarter. *Faculty research:* Child/family studies, health psychology, neuropsychology, personality development, assessment.

Penn State Harrisburg, Graduate School, School of Behavioral Sciences and Education, Middletown, PA 17057-4898. Offers M Ed, MA, D Ed. Part-time and evening/weekend programs available. *Financial support:* Career-related internships or fieldwork available. *Unit head:* Dr. William D. Milheim, Director, 717-948-6205, Fax: 717-948-6209, E-mail: wdm2@psu.edu. *Application contact:* Dr. Robert W. Coffman, Director of Admissions, 717-948-6214, E-mail: rwc11@psu.edu.

Penn State University Park, Graduate School, College of the Liberal Arts, Department of Psychology, State College, University Park, PA 16802-1503. Offers MS, PhD. *Accreditation:* APA (one or more programs are accredited). *Unit head:* Dr. Melvin M. Mark, Interim Head, 814-865-9515, Fax: 814-863-7002, E-mail: m5m@psu.edu. *Application contact:* Dr. Melvin M. Mark, Interim Head, 814-865-9515, Fax: 814-863-7002, E-mail: m5m@psu.edu.

Pepperdine University, Graduate School of Education and Psychology, Division of Psychology, Malibu, CA 90263. Offers clinical psychology (MA, Psy D), including clinical psychology, clinical psychology (daytime) (MA), clinical psychology (evening) (MA); psychology (MA). Part-time and evening/weekend programs available. *Faculty:* 26 full-time (14 women), 78 part-time/adjunct (51 women). *Students:* 409 full-time (342 women), 523 part-time (449 women); includes 263 minority (75 African Americans, 7 American Indian/Alaska Native, 81 Asian Americans or Pacific Islanders, 100 Hispanic Americans), 20 international. *Entrance requirements:* For master's and doctorate, GRE General Test. Additional exam requirements/recommendations for international students: Required—TOEFL. *Application deadline:* For fall admission, 2/1 for domestic students. Applications are processed on a rolling basis. Application fee: $55. *Expenses:* Contact institution. *Financial support:* Research assistantships, teaching assistantships, career-related internships or fieldwork and scholarships/grants available. Support available to part-time students. Financial award application deadline: 7/1; financial award applicants required to submit FAFSA. *Unit head:* Dr. Robert deMayo, Associate Dean, 310-568-5747, E-mail: robert.demayo@pepperdine.edu. *Application contact:* Brenden Wysocki, Admissions Manager, 310-568-5786.

Philadelphia College of Osteopathic Medicine, Graduate and Professional Programs, Department of Psychology, Philadelphia, PA 19131-1694. Offers clinical psychology (Psy D); counseling and clinical health psychology (MS); organizational leadership and development (MS); psychology (Certificate, Post-Doctoral Certificate); school psychology (MS, Psy D, Ed S). *Accreditation:* APA. *Degree requirements:* For master's, thesis; for doctorate, comprehensive exam, thesis/dissertation, final project, fieldwork. *Entrance requirements:* For master's, GRE or MAT, minimum GPA of 3.0; course work in biology, chemistry, English, physics; for other advanced degree, PRAXIS. *Faculty research:* Depression in primary care, integrated primary care, geriatric mental health.

See Close-Up on page 1091.

Pittsburg State University, Graduate School, College of Education, Department of Psychology and Counseling, Program in Psychology, Pittsburg, KS 66762. Offers MS. *Degree requirements:* For master's, thesis or alternative. *Entrance requirements:* For master's, GRE General Test, minimum GPA of 2.8. *Expenses:* Tuition, state resident: full-time $4212; part-time $176 per credit. Tuition, nonresident: full-time $11,530; part-time $480 per credit. Required fees: $940; $43 per credit. Tuition and fees vary according to course level, course load, degree level, campus/location, reciprocity agreements and student level.

Polytechnic Institute of NYU, Department of Humanities and Social Sciences, Major in Environment-Behavior Studies, Brooklyn, NY 11201-2990. Offers MS, Graduate Certificate. Part-time and evening/weekend programs available. *Students:* 1 applicant, 0% accepted. *Degree requirements:* For master's, comprehensive exam (for some programs), thesis (for some programs). *Entrance requirements:* Additional exam requirements/recommendations for international students: Required—TOEFL (minimum score 550 paper-based; 213 computer-based; 80 iBT); Recommended—IELTS (minimum score 6.5). *Application deadline:* For fall admission, 7/31 priority date for domestic students, 4/30 priority date for international students; for spring admission, 12/31 priority date for domestic students, 11/30 priority date for international students. Applications are processed on a rolling basis. Application fee: $55. Electronic applications accepted. *Expenses:* Tuition: Full-time $21,492; part-time $1194 per credit hour. Required fees: $1160; $204 per course. *Financial support:* Institutionally sponsored loans, scholarships/grants, and unspecified assistantships available. Support available to part-time students. *Unit head:* Prof. Teresa Feroli, Head, 718-260-3422, E-mail: tferoli@poly.edu. *Application contact:* JeanCarlo Bonilla, Director of Graduate Enrollment Management, 718-260-3182, Fax: 718-260-3624, E-mail: gradinfo@poly.edu.

Pontifical Catholic University of Puerto Rico, Institute of Graduate Studies in Behavioral Science and Community Affairs, Ponce, PR 00717-0777. Offers clinical psychology (MA, MS, PhD, Psy D); clinical social work (MSW); criminology (MA); industrial psychology (MS, PhD); psychology (PhD); public administration (MA); vocational rehabilitation counseling (MSS). Part-time and evening/weekend programs available. *Degree requirements:* For master's, thesis; for doctorate, comprehensive exam, thesis/dissertation. *Entrance requirements:* For master's, EXADEP, GRE General Test, 3 letters of recommendation, interview, minimum GPA of 2.75.

Portland State University, Graduate Studies, College of Liberal Arts and Sciences, Department of Psychology, Portland, OR 97207-0751. Offers MA, MS, PhD. *Degree requirements:* For master's, variable foreign language requirement, thesis; for doctorate, variable foreign language requirement, comprehensive exam, thesis/dissertation. *Entrance requirements:* For master's, GRE General Test, minimum GPA of 3.0 in upper-division course work or 2.75 overall, 3 letters of recommendation. Additional exam requirements/recommendations for international students: Required—TOEFL (minimum score 550 paper-based; 213 computer-based). *Faculty research:* Organizational psychology, work and the family, quantitative psychology, decision making, psychosocial factors affecting health.

Portland State University, Graduate Studies, Systems Science Program, Portland, OR 97207-0751. Offers computational intelligence (Certificate); computer modeling and simulation (Certificate); systems science (MS); systems science/anthropology (PhD); systems science/business administration (PhD); systems science/civil engineering (PhD); systems science/economics (PhD); systems science/engineering management (PhD); systems science/general (PhD); systems science/mathematical sciences (PhD); systems science/mechanical engineering (PhD); systems science/psychology (PhD); systems science/sociology (PhD). *Degree requirements:* For doctorate, variable foreign language requirement, thesis/dissertation. *Entrance requirements:* For master's, 2 letters of recommendation; for doctorate, GMAT, GRE General Test, minimum undergraduate GPA of 3.0. Additional exam requirements/recommendations for international students: Required—TOEFL. *Faculty research:* Systems theory and methodology, artificial intelligence neural networks, information theory, nonlinear dynamics/chaos, modeling and simulation.

Princeton University, Graduate School, Department of Psychology, Princeton, NJ 08544-1019. Offers neuroscience (PhD); psychology (PhD). *Degree requirements:* For doctorate, thesis/dissertation. *Entrance requirements:* For doctorate, GRE General Test, GRE Subject Test. Additional exam requirements/recommendations for international students: Required—TOEFL (minimum score 550 paper-based). Electronic applications accepted.

Purdue University, Graduate School, College of Liberal Arts, Department of Psychological Sciences, West Lafayette, IN 47907. Offers PhD. *Accreditation:* APA. *Entrance requirements:* For doctorate, GRE General Test. Additional exam requirements/recommendations for international students: Required—TOEFL. Electronic applications accepted. *Faculty research:* Career development of women in science, development of friendships during childhood and adolescence, social competence, human information processing.

Queens College of the City University of New York, Division of Graduate Studies, Mathematics and Natural Sciences Division, Department of Psychology, Flushing, NY 11367-1597. Offers clinical behavioral applications in mental health settings (MA); psychology (MA). Part-time programs available. *Faculty:* 27 full-time (13 women). *Students:* 16 full-time (12 women), 84 part-time (74 women). 134 applicants, 47% accepted, 48 enrolled. In 2009, 17 master's awarded. *Degree requirements:* For master's, comprehensive exam, thesis or alternative. *Entrance requirements:* For master's, GRE, minimum GPA of 3.0. Additional exam requirements/recommendations for international students: Required—TOEFL. *Application deadline:* For fall admission, 4/1 for domestic students; for spring admission, 11/1 for domestic students. Applications are processed on a rolling basis. Application fee: $125. *Expenses:* Tuition, state resident: full-time $7360; part-time $310 per credit. Tuition, nonresident: part-time $575 per credit. One-time fee: $195.25 full-time; $145.25 part-time. *Financial support:* Career-related internships or fieldwork, Federal Work-Study, institutionally sponsored loans, and tuition waivers (partial) available. Support available to part-time students. Financial award application deadline: 4/1; financial award applicants required to submit FAFSA. *Unit head:* Dr. Richard Bodnar, Chairperson, 718-997-3200. *Application contact:* Dr. Philip Ramsey, Graduate Adviser, 718-997-3200, E-mail: philip_ramsey@qc.edu.

Queen's University at Kingston, School of Graduate Studies and Research, Faculty of Arts and Sciences, Department of Psychology, Kingston, ON K7L 3N6, Canada. Offers brain behavior and cognitive science (MA, PhD); clinical psychology (MA, PhD); developmental psychology (MA, PhD); social personality psychology (MA, PhD). *Accreditation:* APA (one or more programs are accredited). *Degree requirements:* For master's, thesis; for doctorate, comprehensive exam, thesis/dissertation. *Entrance requirements:* For master's and doctorate, GRE General Test. Additional exam requirements/recommendations for international students: Required—TOEFL. *Faculty research:* Human development, social, personality, behavioral neuroscience, forensic.

Radford University, College of Graduate and Professional Studies, College of Humanities and Behavioral Sciences, Program in Psychology, Radford, VA 24142. Offers clinical psychology (MA, MS); experimental psychology (MA); general psychology (MS); industrial/organizational psychology (MA, MS). Part-time programs available. *Faculty:* 21 full-time (9 women), 6 part-time/adjunct (2 women). *Students:* 44 full-time (25 women), 1 (woman) part-time; includes 5 minority (3 African Americans, 2 Asian Americans or Pacific Islanders), 1 international. Average age 25. 110 applicants, 65% accepted, 22 enrolled. In 2009, 31 master's awarded. *Degree requirements:* For master's, comprehensive exam, thesis (for some programs). *Entrance requirements:* For master's, GRE, minimum GPA of 3.0; 3 letters of reference; essay. Additional exam requirements/recommendations for international students: Required—TOEFL (minimum score 550 paper-based; 213 computer-based; 79 iBT). *Application deadline:* For fall admission, 2/15 priority date for domestic students, 12/1 for international students. Applications are processed on a rolling basis. Application fee: $50. Electronic applications accepted. *Expenses:* Tuition, state resident: full-time $5086; part-time $211 per credit hour. Tuition, nonresident: full-time $12,608; part-time $525 per credit hour. Required fees: $2508; $105 per credit hour. *Financial support:* In 2009–10, 34 students received support, including 20 research assistant-

Psychology—General

Radford University (continued)
ships with partial tuition reimbursements available (averaging $8,000 per year), 14 teaching assistantships with partial tuition reimbursements available (averaging $8,700 per year); career-related internships or fieldwork, institutionally sponsored loans, scholarships/grants, and unspecified assistantships also available. Financial award application deadline: 3/1; financial award applicants required to submit FAFSA. *Unit head:* Dr. Hilary M. Lips, Chair, 540-831-5387, Fax: 540-831-6113, E-mail: hlips@radford.edu. *Application contact:* Graduate Admissions Office, 540-831-5431, Fax: 540-831-6061, E-mail: gradcollege@radford.edu.

Regis University, College for Professional Studies, MA Program, Denver, CO 80221-1099. Offers criminology (MA); fine arts administration (Certificate); language and communication (MA); mediation (Certificate); psychology (MA); self-designed major (MA); social justice, peace, and reconciliation (Certificate); social science (MA); technical communication (Certificate). Program also offered in Henderson and Las Vegas (Summerlin), NV. Part-time and evening/weekend programs available. Postbaccalaureate distance learning degree programs offered (minimal on-campus study). *Degree requirements:* For master's, thesis, research project. *Entrance requirements:* For master's, resume, recommendations. Additional exam requirements/recommendations for international students: Required—TOEFL (minimum score 213 computer-based), TWE (minimum score 5). Electronic applications accepted. *Expenses:* Contact institution. *Faculty research:* Independent/nonresidential graduate study: new methods and models, adult learning and the capstone experience, Goal Setting, behavior of Adult students, Innovative Studies for Community Colleges.

Rhode Island College, School of Graduate Studies, Faculty of Arts and Sciences, Department of Psychology, Providence, RI 02908-1991. Offers MA. Part-time and evening/weekend programs available. *Faculty:* 4 full-time (all women). *Students:* 5 full-time (4 women), 7 part-time (6 women). Average age 30. In 2009, 1 master's awarded. *Degree requirements:* For master's, comprehensive exam. *Entrance requirements:* For master's, GRE or MAT, 3 letters of recommendation. Additional exam requirements/recommendations for international students: Recommended—TOEFL (minimum score 550 paper-based; 213 computer-based; 79 iBT). *Application deadline:* For fall admission, 4/1 for domestic students; for spring admission, 11/1 for domestic students. Applications are processed on a rolling basis. Application fee: $50. *Expenses:* Tuition, state resident: full-time $7440; part-time $310 per credit hour. Tuition, nonresident: full-time $14,784; part-time $616 per credit hour. Required fees: $552; $20 per credit. $70 per term. *Financial support:* In 2009–10, 2 teaching assistantships with full tuition reimbursements (averaging $4,550 per year) were awarded; Federal Work-Study, scholarships/grants, health care benefits, and unspecified assistantships also available. Support available to part-time students. Financial award application deadline: 5/15; financial award applicants required to submit FAFSA. *Unit head:* Dr. Thomas Malloy, Chair, 401-456-8015. *Application contact:* Graduate Studies, 401-456-8700.

Rice University, Graduate Programs, School of Humanities, Department of Religious Studies, Houston, TX 77251-1892. Offers African religions (PhD); African-American religions (PhD); contemplative studies (PhD); ghosticism, esotericism, mysticism (PhD); Islam (PhD); Jewish thought and philosophy (PhD); modern Christianity in thought and popular culture (PhD); psychology of religion (PhD); the Bible and beyond (PhD). *Faculty:* 11 full-time (3 women), 2 part-time/adjunct (both women). *Students:* 37 full-time (13 women); includes 10 minority (9 African Americans, 1 Asian American or Pacific Islander), 9 international. Average age 31. 42 applicants, 14% accepted, 6 enrolled. In 2009, 2 doctorates awarded. *Degree requirements:* For doctorate, 2 foreign languages, comprehensive exam, thesis/dissertation. *Entrance requirements:* For doctorate, GRE, letters of recommendation, writing sample. Additional exam requirements/recommendations for international students: Required—TOEFL (minimum score 600 paper-based; 90 iBT). *Application deadline:* For fall admission, 1/1 for domestic students, 1/15 for international students. Application fee: $70. Electronic applications accepted. *Financial support:* In 2009–10, 14 fellowships (averaging $15,900 per year) were awarded. Financial award application deadline: 5/15; financial award applicants required to submit FAFSA. *Faculty research:* Origins and historical development of Islam, history of Christianity, the study of comparative religion, African-American religion, religion and culture. Total annual research expenditures: $46,514. *Unit head:* Prof. William B. Parsons, Associate Professor, Religious Studies, 713-348-2712, Fax: 713-348-5486, E-mail: pars@rice.edu. *Application contact:* Sylvia Louie, Senior Department Coordinator, 713-348-5201, Fax: 713-348-5486, E-mail: reli@rice.edu.

Rice University, Graduate Programs, School of Social Sciences, Department of Psychology, Houston, TX 77251-1892. Offers cognitive sciences (MA, PhD); industrial-organizational/social psychology (MA, PhD); psychology (MA, PhD). *Faculty:* 16 full-time (6 women), 26 part-time/adjunct (13 women). *Students:* 44 full-time (29 women); includes 12 minority (3 African Americans, 3 Asian Americans or Pacific Islanders, 6 Hispanic Americans), 9 international. Average age 29. 146 applicants, 7% accepted, 7 enrolled. In 2009, 6 master's, 7 doctorates awarded. Terminal master's awarded for partial completion of doctoral program. *Degree requirements:* For master's, thesis; for doctorate, thesis/dissertation. *Entrance requirements:* For doctorate, GRE General Test, minimum GPA of 3.0. Additional exam requirements/recommendations for international students: Required—TOEFL. *Application deadline:* For fall admission, 1/15 priority date for domestic and international students. Applications are processed on a rolling basis. Application fee: $35. Electronic applications accepted. *Financial support:* In 2009–10, 29 students received support, including 25 fellowships with full tuition reimbursements available (averaging $18,500 per year), 5 research assistantships with full tuition reimbursements available (averaging $18,500 per year); career-related internships or fieldwork, Federal Work-Study, institutionally sponsored loans, scholarships/grants, health care benefits, tuition waivers (full), and unspecified assistantships also available. Financial award application deadline: 1/15; financial award applicants required to submit FAFSA. *Faculty research:* Cognitive, cognitive neuropsychology, human factors, human-computer interaction, industrial-organizational psychology. Total annual research expenditures: $754,120. *Unit head:* Dr. James L. Dannemiller, Chairman, 713-348-4850, Fax: 713-348-5221, E-mail: psyc@rice.edu. *Application contact:* Lanita K. Martin, Coordinator, 713-348-4850, Fax: 713-348-5221, E-mail: psyc@rice.edu.

Richmont Graduate University, Graduate Programs, Atlanta, GA 30327. Offers Christian psychological studies (MS); marriage and family therapy (MA); professional counseling (MA).

Rochester Institute of Technology, Graduate Enrollment Services, College of Liberal Arts, Department of Psychology, Rochester, NY 14623-5603. Offers MS. Part-time programs available. *Students:* 51 full-time (45 women), 10 part-time (6 women); includes 2 minority (1 African American, 1 Asian American or Pacific Islander), 1 international. Average age 28. 71 applicants, 54% accepted, 20 enrolled. In 2009, 19 master's awarded. *Degree requirements:* For master's, thesis. *Entrance requirements:* For master's, GRE, minimum GPA of 3.0. Additional exam requirements/recommendations for international students: Required—TOEFL (minimum score 580 paper-based; 237 computer-based; 92 iBT) or IELTS (minimum score 7). *Application deadline:* For fall admission, 2/1 priority date for domestic and international students; for winter admission, 11/1 for domestic and international students; for spring admission, 2/1 for domestic and international students. Applications are processed on a rolling basis. Application fee: $50. Electronic applications accepted. *Expenses:* Tuition: Full-time $31,533; part-time $876 per credit hour. Required fees: $210. *Financial support:* Research assistantships with partial tuition reimbursements, teaching assistantships with partial tuition reimbursements, career-related internships or fieldwork, scholarships/grants, and unspecified assistantships available. Support available to part-time students. Financial award applicants required to submit FAFSA. *Unit head:* Dr. Andrew Herbert, Chair, 585-475-4554, Fax: 585-475-7120, E-mail: psychdept@rit.edu. *Application contact:* Diane Ellison, Assistant Vice President, Graduate Enrollment Services, 585-475-2229, Fax: 585-475-7164, E-mail: gradinfo@rit.edu.

Roosevelt University, Graduate Division, College of Arts and Sciences, Department of Psychology, Program in Psychology, Chicago, IL 60605. Offers Psy D.

Rosalind Franklin University of Medicine and Science, College of Health Professions, Department of Psychology, North Chicago, IL 60064-3095. Offers clinical counseling (MS); psychology (MS, PhD). *Accreditation:* APA. *Faculty:* 7 full-time (1 woman), 6 part-time/adjunct (1 woman). *Students:* 71 full-time (57 women); includes 10 minority (3 African Americans, 5 Asian Americans or Pacific Islanders, 2 Hispanic Americans), 4 international. 78 applicants, 31% accepted, 22 enrolled. Terminal master's awarded for partial completion of doctoral program. *Degree requirements:* For master's, capstone experience. *Entrance requirements:* For master's, minimum GPA of 3.0, bachelor's degree (preferably in related subject); for doctorate, GRE, minimum GPA of 3.0, bachelor's or master's degree. Additional exam requirements/recommendations for international students: Required—TOEFL. *Application deadline:* For fall admission, 9/1 for domestic students. Applications are processed on a rolling basis. Application fee: $50. *Financial support:* In 2009–10, 14 fellowships with partial tuition reimbursements (averaging $10,000 per year), 3 research assistantships with partial tuition reimbursements (averaging $10,000 per year), 6 teaching assistantships (averaging $10,000 per year) were awarded; career-related internships or fieldwork and Federal Work-Study also available. *Faculty research:* Anxiety, pain, psychopathy, epilepsy, neuropsychology. *Unit head:* Dr. John E. Calamari, Professor and Chairman, 847-578-8747, Fax: 847-578-8765, E-mail: john.calamari@rosalindfranklin.edu. *Application contact:* Melissa Knox, Admissions Officer, 847-578-8772, Fax: 847-775-6559, E-mail: melissa.knox@rosalindfranklin.edu.

Rowan University, Graduate School, College of Liberal Arts and Sciences, Department of Psychology, Glassboro, NJ 08028-1701. Offers applied behavioral analysis (MA); clinical mental health counseling (MA); mental health counseling (MA). Part-time and evening/weekend programs available. *Faculty:* 18 full-time (13 women), 4 part-time/adjunct (1 woman). *Students:* 23 full-time (19 women), 41 part-time (36 women); includes 7 minority (5 African Americans, 2 Asian Americans or Pacific Islanders). Average age 30. 66 applicants, 48% accepted, 31 enrolled. In 2009, 10 master's awarded. *Degree requirements:* For master's, thesis. *Entrance requirements:* For master's, GRE General Test. Additional exam requirements/recommendations for international students: Required—TOEFL. *Application deadline:* Applications are processed on a rolling basis. Electronic applications accepted. *Expenses:* Tuition, state resident: full-time $10,624; part-time $590 per semester hour. Tuition, nonresident: full-time $10,624; part-time $590 per semester hour. Required fees: $2320; $125 per semester hour. *Financial support:* Career-related internships or fieldwork, scholarships/grants, health care benefits, and unspecified assistantships available. *Unit head:* Dr. Mira Lalovic-Hand, Interim Associate Provost/Director of Graduate School, 856-256-5120, E-mail: lalovic-hand@rowan.edu. *Application contact:* Karen Haynes, Graduate Coordinator, 856-256-4052, Fax: 856-256-4436, E-mail: haynes@rowan.edu.

Rowan University, Graduate School, College of Liberal Arts and Sciences, Program in Mental Health Counseling and Applied Psychology, Glassboro, NJ 08028-1701. Offers MA. Part-time and evening/weekend programs available. *Students:* 8 full-time (all women), 21 part-time (18 women); includes 4 minority (3 African Americans, 1 Asian American or Pacific Islander). Average age 31. 32 applicants, 72% accepted, 22 enrolled. In 2009, 31 master's awarded. *Degree requirements:* For master's, thesis. *Entrance requirements:* For master's, GRE General Test. Additional exam requirements/recommendations for international students: Required—TOEFL. *Application deadline:* Applications are processed on a rolling basis. Application fee: $50. Electronic applications accepted. *Expenses:* Tuition, state resident: full-time $10,624; part-time $590 per semester hour. Tuition, nonresident: full-time $10,624; part-time $590 per semester hour. Required fees: $2320; $125 per semester hour. *Financial support:* Career-related internships or fieldwork, scholarships/grants, health care benefits, and unspecified assistantships available. *Unit head:* Dr. Mira Lalovic-Hand, Interim Associate Provost/Director of Graduate School, 856-256-5120, E-mail: lalovic-hand@rowan.edu. *Application contact:* Karen Haynes, Graduate Coordinator, 856-256-4052, Fax: 856-256-4436, E-mail: haynes@rowan.edu.

Rutgers, The State University of New Jersey, Camden, Graduate School of Arts and Sciences, Program in Psychology, Camden, NJ 08102-1401. Offers MA. Part-time and evening/weekend programs available. *Degree requirements:* For master's, thesis. *Entrance requirements:* For master's, GRE, 3 letters of recommendation; prerequisite course work in introductory psychology, statistics and experimental psychology. Additional exam requirements/recommendations for international students: Required—TOEFL, IELTS. Electronic applications accepted. *Faculty research:* Cognitive psychology, sexuality, health psychology, personality psychology, clinical psychology.

Rutgers, The State University of New Jersey, Newark, Graduate School, Program in Psychology, Newark, NJ 07102. Offers cognitive neuroscience (PhD); cognitive science (PhD); perception (PhD); psychobiology (PhD); social cognition (PhD). *Degree requirements:* For doctorate, comprehensive exam, thesis/dissertation. *Entrance requirements:* For doctorate, GRE General Test, GRE Subject Test, minimum undergraduate B average. Electronic applications accepted. *Faculty research:* Visual perception (luminance, motion), neuroendocrine mechanisms in behavior (reproduction, pain), attachment theory, connectionist modeling of cognition.

See Close-Up on page 1093.

Rutgers, The State University of New Jersey, New Brunswick, Graduate School-New Brunswick, Program in Psychology, Piscataway, NJ 08854-8097. Offers behavioral neuroscience (PhD); clinical psychology (PhD); cognitive psychology (PhD); interdisciplinary health psychology (PhD); social psychology (PhD). *Accreditation:* APA. *Degree requirements:* For doctorate, comprehensive exam, thesis/dissertation. *Entrance requirements:* For doctorate, GRE General Test, 3 letters of recommendation. Additional exam requirements/recommendations for international students: Required—TOEFL (minimum score 577 paper-based; 233 computer-based). Electronic applications accepted. *Faculty research:* Learning and memory, behavioral ecology, hormones and behavior, psychopharmacology, anxiety disorders.

Rutgers, The State University of New Jersey, New Brunswick, Graduate School of Applied and Professional Psychology, Piscataway, NJ 08854-8097. Offers Psy M, Psy D. *Accreditation:* APA (one or more programs are accredited). *Degree requirements:* For doctorate, comprehensive exam, thesis/dissertation, 1 year internship. *Entrance requirements:* For doctorate, GRE General Test, GRE Subject Test, bachelor's degree in psychology or equivalent. Additional exam requirements/recommendations for international students: Required—TOEFL. Electronic applications accepted. *Expenses:* Contact institution. *Faculty research:* Organizational psychology, behavior modification, long- and short-term dynamic therapy, school psychology, addictive behaviors.

Sage Graduate School, Graduate School, School of Health Sciences, Department of Psychology, Troy, NY 12180-4115. Offers community psychology (MA), including child care and children's services, community counseling, community health education, community psychology, general psychology; counseling and community psychology (MA). Part-time and evening/weekend programs available. *Faculty:* 3 full-time (all women), 5 part-time/adjunct (3 women). *Students:* 35 full-time (33 women), 55 part-time (51 women); includes 14 minority (8 African Americans, 1 American Indian/Alaska Native, 1 Asian American or Pacific Islander, 4 Hispanic Americans). Average age 28. 78 applicants, 46% accepted, 21 enrolled. In 2009, 29 master's awarded. *Degree requirements:* For master's, thesis or alternative. *Entrance requirements:* For master's, GRE General Test. Additional exam requirements/recommendations for international students: Required—TOEFL (minimum score 550 paper-based; 213 computer-based). *Application deadline:* Applications are processed on a rolling basis. Application fee: $40. *Expenses:* Tuition: Full-time $10,620; part-time $590 per credit hour. *Financial support:* Fellowships, research assistantships, Federal Work-Study, scholarships/grants, and unspecified assistantships available. Support available to part-time students. Financial award application deadline: 3/1; financial award applicants required to submit FAFSA. *Faculty research:* Effectiveness of arts integration programs in elementary/secondary schools, literacy-based substance abuse program, outcome evaluation of program to increase college entry among urban youth. *Unit head:* Dr. Jean Poppei, Chair, 518-244-2076, Fax: 518-244-4545, E-mail:

poppei@sage.edu. *Application contact:* Wendy D. Diefendorf, Director of Graduate and Adult Admission, 518-244-2443, Fax: 518-244-6880, E-mail: diefew@sage.edu.

St. Cloud State University, School of Graduate Studies, College of Education, Department of Counselor Education, Higher Education, and Educational Psychology, St. Cloud, MN 56301-4498. Offers college counseling and student development (MS); higher education administration (MS, Ed D); rehabilitation counseling (MS); school counseling (MS). *Faculty:* 12 full-time (5 women). *Students:* 77 full-time (52 women), 89 part-time (56 women); includes 14 minority (3 African Americans, 3 American Indian/Alaska Native, 8 Asian Americans or Pacific Islanders), 13 international. 67 applicants, 82% accepted. In 2009, 17 master's awarded. *Degree requirements:* For master's, thesis or alternative. *Entrance requirements:* For master's, GRE General Test, minimum GPA of 2.75. Additional exam requirements/recommendations for international students: Required—Michigan English Language Assessment Battery; Recommended—TOEFL (minimum score 550 paper-based; 213 computer-based), IELTS (minimum score 6.5). *Application deadline:* Applications are processed on a rolling basis. Application fee: $35. Electronic applications accepted. *Financial support:* Career-related internships or fieldwork, Federal Work-Study, scholarships/grants, and unspecified assistantships available. Financial award application deadline: 3/1. *Unit head:* Dr. Steve Hoorer, Chairperson, 320-308-4089, Fax: 320-308-4082, E-mail: smhoover@stcloudstate.edu. *Application contact:* Linda Lou Krueger, School of Graduate Studies, 320-308-2113, Fax: 320-308-5371, E-mail: lekrueger@stcloudstate.edu.

St. Cloud State University, School of Graduate Studies, College of Education, Department of Educational Leadership and Community Psychology, Program in Applied Behavior Analysis, St. Cloud, MN 56301-4498. Offers MS. Part-time programs available. Postbaccalaureate distance learning degree programs offered (no on-campus study). *Faculty:* 2 full-time (1 woman). *Students:* 27 full-time (19 women), 85 part-time (71 women); includes 19 minority (1 American Indian/Alaska Native, 16 Asian Americans or Pacific Islanders, 2 Hispanic Americans), 5 international. Average age 27. 74 applicants, 57% accepted. In 2009, 16 master's awarded. *Degree requirements:* For master's, comprehensive exam (for some programs), thesis or alternative. *Entrance requirements:* For master's, GRE General Test, minimum GPA of 2.75. Additional exam requirements/recommendations for international students: Required—Michigan English Language Assessment Battery; Recommended—TOEFL (minimum score 550 paper-based; 213 computer-based), IELTS (minimum score 6.5). *Application deadline:* For fall admission, 4/1 for domestic and international students. Applications are processed on a rolling basis. Application fee: $35. *Financial support:* Career-related internships or fieldwork, Federal Work-Study, scholarships/grants, and unspecified assistantships available. Financial award application deadline: 3/1; financial award applicants required to submit FAFSA. *Unit head:* Dr. Kimberly Schulze, Coordinator, 320-308-4155. *Application contact:* Linda Lou Krueger, School of Graduate Studies, 320-308-2113, Fax: 320-308-5371, E-mail: lekrueger@stcloudstate.edu.

St. John's University, St. John's College of Liberal Arts and Sciences, Department of Psychology, Queens, NY 11439. Offers clinical psychology (PhD), including clinical psychology-child, clinical psychology-general; general experimental psychology (MA); school psychology (MS, Psy D). *Accreditation:* APA (one or more programs are accredited). Part-time and evening/weekend programs available. *Students:* 208 full-time (176 women), 61 part-time (54 women); includes 46 minority (12 African Americans, 12 Asian Americans or Pacific Islanders, 22 Hispanic Americans), 12 international. Average age 27. 502 applicants, 25% accepted, 64 enrolled. In 2009, 40 master's, 35 doctorates awarded. *Degree requirements:* For master's, comprehensive exam, thesis optional; for doctorate, comprehensive exam, thesis/dissertation, internship. *Entrance requirements:* For master's, GRE, minimum GPA of 3.0, 2 writing samples; for doctorate, GRE General Test, GRE Subject Test, interview. Additional exam requirements/recommendations for international students: Required—TOEFL (minimum score 500 paper-based; 173 computer-based; 61 iBT), IELTS (minimum score 5.5). *Application deadline:* For fall admission, 1/15 priority date for domestic and international students; for spring admission, 11/1 priority date for domestic and international students. Applications are processed on a rolling basis. Application fee: $70. Electronic applications accepted. *Expenses:* Contact institution. *Financial support:* Fellowships, research assistantships, career-related internships or fieldwork, scholarships/grants, and unspecified assistantships available. Support available to part-time students. Financial award application deadline: 3/1; financial award applicants required to submit FAFSA. *Faculty research:* Clinical psychology, school psychology, developmental psychopathology, risky behaviors and health, cognitive behavior treatments for trauma. Total annual research expenditures: $900,000. *Unit head:* Dr. Raymond DiGiuseppe, Chair, 718-990-1955, E-mail: digiuser@stjohns.edu. *Application contact:* Kathleen Davis, Director of Graduate Admissions, 718-990-2790, Fax: 718-990-5686, E-mail: gradhelp@stjohns.edu.

Saint Joseph's University, College of Arts and Sciences, Department of Criminal Justice, Philadelphia, PA 19131-1395. Offers administration/police executive (MS); behavior analysis (MS, Post-Master's Certificate); criminal justice (MS, Post-Master's Certificate); criminology (MS); federal law (MS); intelligence and crime (MS); probation, parole, and corrections (MS). Part-time and evening/weekend programs available. Postbaccalaureate distance learning degree programs offered (no on-campus study). *Students:* 2 full-time (0 women), 302 part-time (193 women); includes 88 minority (64 African Americans, 1 American Indian/Alaska Native, 3 Asian Americans or Pacific Islanders, 20 Hispanic Americans), 2 international. Average age 33. In 2009, 86 master's awarded. *Degree requirements:* For master's, thesis. *Entrance requirements:* For master's, GRE General Test or minimum GPA of 3.0, 2 letters of recommendation. Additional exam requirements/recommendations for international students: Required—TOEFL (minimum score 550 paper-based; 213 computer-based; 79 iBT). *Application deadline:* For fall admission, 7/15 priority date for domestic students, 4/15 for international students; for winter admission, 1/15 for international students; for spring admission, 11/15 priority date for domestic students, 10/15 for international students. Applications are processed on a rolling basis. Application fee: $35. Electronic applications accepted. *Expenses:* Tuition: Part-time $729 per credit hour. Tuition and fees vary according to degree level and program. *Financial support:* Career-related internships or fieldwork and unspecified assistantships available. Financial award applicants required to submit FAFSA. *Unit head:* Patricia Griffin, Director, 610-660-1294, E-mail: pgriffin@sju.edu. *Application contact:* Kate McConnell, Director, Graduate College of Arts and Sciences Admissions and Retention, 610-660-3184, Fax: 610-660-3230, E-mail: kate.mconnell@sju.edu.

Saint Joseph's University, College of Arts and Sciences, Department of Psychology, Philadelphia, PA 19131-1395. Offers MS. Evening/weekend programs available. *Students:* 27 full-time (19 women), 8 part-time (all women); includes 6 minority (5 African Americans, 1 Asian American or Pacific Islander), 2 international. Average age 24. In 2009, 19 master's awarded. *Entrance requirements:* For master's, GRE General Test, 2 letters of recommendation, application, official transcripts, personal statement, psychology insert. Additional exam requirements/recommendations for international students: Required—TOEFL (minimum score 550 paper-based; 213 computer-based; 79 iBT). *Application deadline:* For fall admission, 3/1 priority date for domestic and international students; for winter admission, 1/15 for international students; for spring admission, 11/15 for domestic students, 10/15 for international students. Application fee: $35. Electronic applications accepted. *Expenses:* Tuition: Part-time $729 per credit hour. Tuition and fees vary according to degree level and program. *Financial support:* Teaching assistantships, unspecified assistantships available. Financial award applicants required to submit FAFSA. *Faculty research:* Early child care and development, preschool quality. Total annual research expenditures: $374,500. *Unit head:* Dr. Jodi Mindell, Director, 610-660-1806, E-mail: jmindell@sju.edu. *Application contact:* Kate McConnell, Director, Graduate College of Arts and Sciences Admissions and Retention, 610-660-3184, Fax: 610-660-3230, E-mail: kate.mcconnell@sju.edu.

Saint Louis University, Graduate School, College of Arts and Sciences and Graduate School, Department of Psychology, St. Louis, MO 63103-2097. Offers clinical psychology (MS-R, PhD); experimental psychology (MS-R, PhD); industrial-organizational psychology (PhD); psychology (PhD). *Accreditation:* APA (one or more programs are accredited). Part-time programs available. *Degree requirements:* For master's, comprehensive exam, thesis; for doctorate, thesis/dissertation, clinical internship (for clinical psychology PhD). *Entrance requirements:* For master's, GRE General Test, interview, letters of recommendation, resume; for doctorate, GRE General Test, interview, letters of recommendation, resumé, transcripts, goal statement. Additional exam requirements/recommendations for international students: Required—TOEFL (minimum score 550 paper-based; 213 computer-based). Electronic applications accepted. *Faculty research:* Violence and trauma; neural basis of learning and memory function; eating disorders; body image and health behavior; prejudice, stereotyping, and victimization; memory, cognitive aging and language processing.

Saint Mary's University, Faculty of Science, Department of Psychology, Halifax, NS B3H 3C3, Canada. Offers applied psychology (M Sc, PhD), including industrial/organizational psychology (M Sc). Part-time programs available. *Degree requirements:* For master's, thesis, 500-hour internship; for doctorate, comprehensive exam, thesis/dissertation, research project. *Entrance requirements:* For master's and doctorate, GRE General Test. *Application deadline:* For fall admission, 2/1 for domestic students. Application fee: $35. *Financial support:* Fellowships, research assistantships, teaching assistantships, career-related internships or fieldwork and scholarships/grants available. Support available to part-time students. *Faculty research:* Assessment, health psychology, social psychology, cognition. *Unit head:* Dr. Victor Catano, Chairperson, 902-420-5845. *Application contact:* Dr. Mark Fleming, Graduate Program Coordinator, 902-420-5273, E-mail: mark.fleming@smu.ca.

St. Mary's University, Graduate School, Department of Psychology, San Antonio, TX 78228-8507. Offers clinical psychology (MA, MS); industrial/organizational psychology (MA, MS). Part-time programs available. *Degree requirements:* For master's, comprehensive exam. *Entrance requirements:* For master's, GRE General Test, letters of recommendation, work experience. Additional exam requirements/recommendations for international students: Required—TOEFL (minimum score 550 paper-based; 213 computer-based; 80 iBT). Electronic applications accepted. *Expenses:* Tuition: Full-time $8004. Required fees: $536. One-time fee: $5 full-time. Full-time tuition and fees vary according to program.

Saint Xavier University, Graduate Studies, School of Arts and Sciences, Department of Psychology, Chicago, IL 60655-3105. Offers adult counseling (Certificate); child/adolescent counseling (Certificate); core counseling (Certificate); counseling psychology (MA). Part-time and evening/weekend programs available. *Entrance requirements:* For master's, GRE General Test, minimum GPA of 3.0, interview. *Expenses:* Tuition: Part-time $743 per credit hour. Required fees: $135 per semester.

Salem State College, School of Graduate Studies, Program in Counseling and Psychological Services, Salem, MA 01970-5353. Offers MS. Part-time and evening/weekend programs available. *Students:* 41 full-time (32 women), 41 part-time (31 women); includes 7 minority (1 African American, 6 Hispanic Americans), 2 international. Average age 33. 22 applicants, 95% accepted, 21 enrolled. In 2009, 19 master's awarded. *Entrance requirements:* For master's, GRE or MAT. Additional exam requirements/recommendations for international students: Required—TOEFL (minimum score 550 paper-based; 80 iBT), or IELTS (minimum score 5.5). *Application deadline:* For fall admission, 5/1 for domestic students; for spring admission, 10/1 for domestic students. Applications are processed on a rolling basis. Application fee: $50. *Expenses:* Tuition, state resident: full-time $2520; part-time $275 per credit hour. Tuition, nonresident: full-time $4140; part-time $365 per credit hour. Required fees: $2430. *Financial support:* In 2009–10, 6 students received support. Career-related internships or fieldwork, Federal Work-Study, scholarships/grants, and unspecified assistantships available. Support available to part-time students. Financial award application deadline: 5/1; financial award applicants required to submit FAFSA. *Unit head:* Dr. Patrice Miller, Coordinator, 978-542-6075, Fax: 978-542-6596, E-mail: pmiller@salemstate.edu. *Application contact:* Dr. Lee A. Brossoit, Assistant Dean of Graduate Admissions, 978-542-6673, Fax: 978-542-7215, E-mail: lbrossoit@salemstate.edu.

Sam Houston State University, College of Humanities and Social Sciences, Department of Psychology and Philosophy, Huntsville, TX 77341. Offers clinical psychology (PhD); psychology (MA). *Accreditation:* APA. Part-time programs available. *Faculty:* 13 full-time (5 women), 1 part-time/adjunct (0 women). *Students:* 61 full-time (46 women), 27 part-time (21 women); includes 21 minority (8 African Americans, 3 Asian Americans or Pacific Islanders, 10 Hispanic Americans), 3 international. Average age 26. 113 applicants, 29% accepted, 24 enrolled. In 2009, 20 master's, 4 doctorates awarded. *Degree requirements:* For master's, thesis. *Entrance requirements:* For master's, GRE General Test or MAT, minimum GPA of 3.0. Additional exam requirements/recommendations for international students: Required—TOEFL (minimum score 550 paper-based; 213 computer-based; 79 iBT). *Application deadline:* For fall admission, 8/1 for domestic students; for spring admission, 12/1 for domestic students. Applications are processed on a rolling basis. Application fee: $20. *Expenses:* Tuition, state resident: full-time $3690; part-time $205 per credit hour. Tuition, nonresident: full-time $8676; part-time $482 per credit hour. Required fees: $1474. Tuition and fees vary according to course load and campus/location. *Financial support:* Research assistantships, teaching assistantships, career-related internships or fieldwork and institutionally sponsored loans available. Support available to part-time students. Financial award application deadline: 5/31; financial award applicants required to submit FAFSA. *Unit head:* Dr. Christopher Wilson, Chair, 936-294-3052, Fax: 936-294-3798, E-mail: psy_dcw@shsu.edu. *Application contact:* Dr. Jeffrey Anastasi, Coordinator, 936-294-3049, Fax: 936-294-3798, E-mail: jsa001@shsu.edu.

San Diego State University, Graduate and Research Affairs, College of Sciences, Department of Psychology, San Diego, CA 92182. Offers clinical psychology (MS, PhD); industrial and organizational psychology (MS); program evaluation (MS); psychology (MA). *Accreditation:* APA (one or more programs are accredited). Terminal master's awarded for partial completion of doctoral program. *Degree requirements:* For master's, thesis, oral exam; for doctorate, thesis/dissertation. *Entrance requirements:* For master's, GRE General Test, GRE Subject Test, 3 letters of recommendation; for doctorate, GRE General Test, GRE Subject Test, minimum GPA of 3.0, 3 letters of recommendation. Additional exam requirements/recommendations for international students: Required—TOEFL. Electronic applications accepted.

San Francisco State University, Division of Graduate Studies, College of Behavioral and Social Sciences, Department of Psychology, San Francisco, CA 94132-1722. Offers MA, MS.

San Jose State University, Graduate Studies and Research, College of Social Sciences, Department of Psychology, San Jose, CA 95192-0001. Offers clinical psychology (MS); experimental psychology (MA); industrial/organizational psychology (MS); psychology (MA). *Students:* 51 full-time (37 women), 20 part-time (14 women); includes 18 minority (1 African American, 1 American Indian/Alaska Native, 12 Asian Americans or Pacific Islanders, 4 Hispanic Americans), 6 international. Average age 28. 153 applicants, 20% accepted, 26 enrolled. In 2009, 17 master's awarded. *Degree requirements:* For master's, comprehensive exam, thesis (for some programs). *Entrance requirements:* For master's, GRE General Test, minimum GPA of 3.0. *Application deadline:* For fall admission, 6/29 for domestic students; for spring admission, 11/30 for domestic students. Applications are processed on a rolling basis. Application fee: $59. Electronic applications accepted. *Financial support:* Teaching assistantships, career-related internships or fieldwork and institutionally sponsored loans available. Financial award application deadline: 3/1; financial award applicants required to submit FAFSA. *Faculty research:* Drug and alcohol abuse, neurohormonal mechanisms in motion sickness, behavior modification, sleep research, genetics. *Unit head:* Dr. Sheila Bienenfeld, Chair, 408-924-5642, Fax: 408-924-5605. *Application contact:* Dr. Sheila Bienenfeld, Chair, 408-924-5642, Fax: 408-924-5605.

Saybrook University, Graduate College of Psychology and Humanistic Studies, San Francisco, CA 94111-1920. Offers clinical psychology (Psy D); human science (MA, PhD), including consciousness and spirituality, humanistic and transpersonal psychology, integrative health studies, organizational systems, social transformation, transformative social change (MA); organizational systems (MA, PhD), including consciousness and spirituality, humanistic and transpersonal psychology, integrative health studies, leadership of sustainable systems (MA),

Psychology—General

Saybrook University (continued)
organizational systems, social transformation; psychology (MA, PhD), including clinical psychology (PhD), consciousness and spirituality, creativity studies (MA), humanistic and transpersonal psychology, integrative health studies, Jungian studies, marriage and family therapy (MA), organizational systems, social transformation. Postbaccalaureate distance learning degree programs offered (minimal on-campus study). Terminal master's awarded for partial completion of doctoral program. *Degree requirements:* For master's, thesis or alternative; for doctorate, thesis/dissertation. Electronic applications accepted. *Faculty research:* Humanistic theory, health studies, organizational systems, consciousness and spirituality, social transformation.

Saybrook University, LIOS Graduate College, San Francisco, CA 94111-1920. Offers leadership and organization development (MA); systems counseling (MA). *Degree requirements:* For master's, thesis (for some programs), oral exams. *Entrance requirements:* For master's, bachelor's degree from an accredited university or college.

The School of Professional Psychology at Forest Institute, Graduate Programs, Springfield, MO 65807. Offers clinical psychology (MA, Psy D); counseling psychology (MA); marriage and family therapy (MA, PGC). *Accreditation:* AAMFT/COAMFTE; APA (one or more programs are accredited). *Faculty:* 18 full-time (9 women), 18 part-time/adjunct (10 women). *Students:* 214 full-time (144 women), 46 part-time (35 women); includes 35 minority (11 African Americans, 9 American Indian/Alaska Native, 5 Asian Americans or Pacific Islanders, 10 Hispanic Americans), 3 international. Average age 28. 176 applicants, 69% accepted, 45 enrolled. In 2009, 35 master's, 31 doctorates awarded. Terminal master's awarded for partial completion of doctoral program. *Degree requirements:* For master's, thesis, practicum; for doctorate, comprehensive exam, thesis/dissertation, internship, practicum. *Entrance requirements:* For master's, GRE General Test, interview, minimum GPA of 3.0, 12 hours in psychology; for doctorate, GRE General Test, interview, minimum GPA of 3.0, 18 hours in psychology. Additional exam requirements/recommendations for international students: Required—TOEFL (minimum score 550 paper-based; 213 computer-based). *Application deadline:* For fall admission, 1/15 priority date for domestic and international students; for spring admission, 8/1 priority date for domestic and international students. Applications are processed on a rolling basis. Application fee: $50. Electronic applications accepted. *Expenses:* Tuition: Full-time $23,625; part-time $675 per credit hour. Required fees: $275 per semester. Tuition and fees vary according to course load and program. *Financial support:* In 2009–10, 59 students received support, including 5 fellowships with partial tuition reimbursements available (averaging $7,200 per year), 11 teaching assistantships (averaging $100 per year); career-related internships or fieldwork, Federal Work-Study, scholarships/grants, tuition waivers (partial), and unspecified assistantships also available. Financial award applicants required to submit FAFSA. *Faculty research:* Forensics/corrections, marriage and family therapy, child and adolescent, integrated health care, neuropsychology. *Unit head:* Dr. Mark E. Skrade, President, 417-823-3477, Fax: 417-823-3442, E-mail: mskrade@forest.edu. *Application contact:* Bethany Ritter, Admissions Counselor, 417-823-3477, Fax: 417-823-3442, E-mail: britter@forest.edu.

Seattle University, College of Arts and Sciences, Department of Psychology, Seattle, WA 98122-1090. Offers existential and phenomenological therapeutic psychology (MA Psych). *Degree requirements:* For master's, thesis. *Entrance requirements:* For master's, interview, minimum GPA of 3.0, previous undergraduate course work in psychology. *Faculty research:* Healing, transformations in relationships, therapy, dialogical research.

Seton Hall University, College of Arts and Sciences, Department of Psychology, South Orange, NJ 07079-2697. Offers experimental psychology (MS), including behavioral neuroscience. Part-time and evening/weekend programs available. *Faculty:* 12 full-time (7 women). *Students:* 14 full-time (7 women); includes 3 minority (2 Asian Americans or Pacific Islanders, 1 Hispanic American). Average age 25. 28 applicants, 71% accepted, 10 enrolled. In 2009, 5 master's awarded. *Entrance requirements:* For master's, GRE. Additional exam requirements/recommendations for international students: Required—TOEFL. *Application deadline:* For fall admission, 7/1 priority date for domestic and international students. Applications are processed on a rolling basis. Application fee: $50. Electronic applications accepted. *Financial support:* Research assistantships, teaching assistantships with full tuition reimbursements, career-related internships or fieldwork, Federal Work-Study, scholarships/grants, and unspecified assistantships available. Financial award applicants required to submit FAFSA. *Faculty research:* Behavioral neuroscience, cognitive psychology, social psychology, perception/motor skills, memory, depression, anxiety. *Unit head:* Dr. Susan A. Nolan, Chair, 973-761-9484, Fax: 973-275-5829, E-mail: nolansus@shu.edu. *Application contact:* Dr. Janine P. Buckner, Director of Graduate Studies, 973-761-9484, Fax: 973-275-5829, E-mail: buckneja@shu.edu.

Seton Hall University, College of Education and Human Services, Department of Professional Psychology and Family Therapy, South Orange, NJ 07079-2697. Offers counseling psychology (MA, PhD); marriage and family therapy (MS, PhD, Ed S); psychological studies (MA); school psychology (Ed S). *Accreditation:* APA. Part-time and evening/weekend programs available. Postbaccalaureate distance learning degree programs offered (minimal on-campus study). *Faculty:* 17 full-time (8 women). *Students:* 88 full-time (73 women), 287 part-time (233 women); includes 82 minority (47 African Americans, 1 American Indian/Alaska Native, 11 Asian Americans or Pacific Islanders, 23 Hispanic Americans), 11 international. Average age 34. 336 applicants, 51% accepted, 108 enrolled. In 2009, 108 master's, 6 doctorates, 38 other advanced degrees awarded. Terminal master's awarded for partial completion of doctoral program. *Degree requirements:* For master's, comprehensive exam, case study; for doctorate, comprehensive exam, thesis/dissertation, internship; for Ed S, comprehensive exam, internship. *Entrance requirements:* For master's, GRE or MAT; for doctorate, GRE, interview; for Ed S, GRE or MAT, interview. *Application deadline:* For fall admission, 2/15 for domestic students. Applications are processed on a rolling basis. Application fee: $50. *Financial support:* In 2009–10, 4 research assistantships with full tuition reimbursements (averaging $4,500 per year) were awarded; career-related internships or fieldwork also available. Financial award application deadline: 2/1. *Faculty research:* Counseling process, ethics, family systems, child pathology. *Unit head:* Dr. Laura Palmer, Chair, 973-761-9450, E-mail: palmerla@shu.edu. *Application contact:* Information Contact, 973-761-9451.

Shippensburg University of Pennsylvania, School of Graduate Studies, College of Arts and Sciences, Department of Psychology, Shippensburg, PA 17257-2299. Offers MS. Part-time and evening/weekend programs available. *Degree requirements:* For master's, thesis optional. *Entrance requirements:* For master's, GRE Subject Test (psychology), minimum GPA of 2.75, 1 course in statistics, 6 undergraduate credit hours in psychology. Additional exam requirements/recommendations for international students: Required—TOEFL (minimum score 560 paper-based; 220 computer-based); Recommended—IELTS (minimum score 6). Electronic applications accepted.

Simmons College, College of Arts and Sciences Graduate Studies, Program in Behavior Analysis, Boston, MA 02115. Offers MS, PhD. Part-time programs available. *Students:* 49 full-time (46 women), 74 part-time (64 women); includes 10 minority (4 African Americans, 3 Asian Americans or Pacific Islanders, 3 Hispanic Americans), 5 international. 44 applicants, 89% accepted, 30 enrolled. In 2009, 23 master's, 1 doctorate awarded. *Degree requirements:* For doctorate, thesis/dissertation. *Application deadline:* For fall admission, 8/1 for domestic and international students; for winter admission, 12/15 for domestic and international students; for spring admission, 5/1 for domestic and international students. Applications are processed on a rolling basis. Application fee: $35. Electronic applications accepted. *Expenses:* Contact institution. *Faculty research:* Verbal behavior for children with autism spectrum disorder, stimulus equivalence for teaching academic skills, analysis and treatment of obesity and health related issues, innovative pedagogy in higher education, organizational behavior management. *Unit head:* Michael J. Cameron, Chair, 617-521-2569, E-mail: michael.cameron@simmons.edu. *Application contact:* Kristen Haack, Director, CAS Graduate Studies Admission, 617-521-2917, Fax: 617-521-3058, E-mail: gsa@simmons.edu.

Simon Fraser University, Graduate Studies, Faculty of Arts and Social Sciences, Department of Psychology, Burnaby, BC V5A 1S6, Canada. Offers MA, PhD. *Accreditation:* APA (one or more programs are accredited). *Degree requirements:* For master's, thesis; for doctorate, thesis/dissertation. *Entrance requirements:* For master's and doctorate, GRE, minimum GPA of 3.5. Additional exam requirements/recommendations for international students: Required—TOEFL or IELTS. *Expenses:* Contact institution. *Faculty research:* Social cognition/biological neuropsychology, theory and methods.

Southeastern Baptist Theological Seminary, Graduate and Professional Programs, Wake Forest, NC 27588-1889. Offers advanced biblical studies (M Div); Christian education (M Div, MACE); Christian ethics (PhD); Christian ministry (M Div); Christian planting (M Div); church music (MACM); counseling (MACO); evangelism (PhD); language (M Div); ministry (D Min); New Testament (PhD); Old Testament (PhD); philosophy (PhD); theology (Th M, PhD); women's studies (M Div). *Accreditation:* ACIPE; ATS (one or more programs are accredited). *Degree requirements:* For master's, thesis (for some programs), oral exam; for doctorate, thesis/dissertation, fieldwork; for M Div, supervised ministry. *Entrance requirements:* For master's, Cooperative English Test, minimum GPA of 2.0, M Div or equivalent (Th M); for doctorate, GRE General Test or MAT, Cooperative English Test, M Div or equivalent, 3 years of professional experience.

Southeastern Louisiana University, College of Arts, Humanities and Social Sciences, Department of Psychology, Hammond, LA 70402. Offers MA. Part-time programs available. *Faculty:* 5 full-time (1 woman). *Students:* 14 full-time (11 women), 10 part-time (7 women); includes 1 minority (Asian American or Pacific Islander), 3 international. Average age 24. 32 applicants, 50% accepted, 7 enrolled. In 2009, 4 master's awarded. *Degree requirements:* For master's, comprehensive exam, thesis. *Entrance requirements:* For master's, GRE (minimum combined score 950), minimum GPA of 3.0, 18 undergraduate hours in psychology/educational psychology, 3 letters of reference. Additional exam requirements/recommendations for international students: Required—TOEFL (minimum score 500 paper-based; 173 computer-based; 61 iBT). *Application deadline:* For fall admission, 7/15 priority date for domestic students, 6/1 priority date for international students; for spring admission, 12/1 priority date for domestic students, 10/1 priority date for international students. Applications are processed on a rolling basis. Application fee: $20 ($30 for international students). Electronic applications accepted. *Expenses:* Tuition, state resident: full-time $3086; part-time $225 per credit hour. Tuition, nonresident: part-time $529 per credit hour. Required fees: $1195. Tuition and fees vary according to course level and course load. *Financial support:* In 2009–10, 10 students received support, including 10 research assistantships (averaging $8,655 per year); career-related internships or fieldwork, Federal Work-Study, institutionally sponsored loans, and administrative assistantship also available. Support available to part-time students. Financial award application deadline: 5/1; financial award applicants required to submit FAFSA. *Faculty research:* Social cognition, police lineup identification, body image, cross-cultural parenting strategy, organizational performance. *Unit head:* Dr. Matt Rossano, Department Head, 985-549-2154, Fax: 985-549-6892, E-mail: mrossano@selu.edu. *Application contact:* Sandra Meyers, Graduate Admissions Analyst, 985-549-5620, Fax: 985-549-5632, E-mail: admissions@selu.edu.

Southern Adventist University, School of Education and Psychology, Collegedale, TN 37315-0370. Offers clinical mental health counseling (MS); inclusive education (MS Ed); instructional leadership (MS Ed); literacy education (MS Ed); outdoor teacher education (MS Ed); school counseling (MS). *Accreditation:* NCATE. Part-time and evening/weekend programs available. *Faculty:* 4 full-time (2 women), 8 part-time/adjunct (5 women). *Students:* 33 full-time (15 women), 17 part-time (13 women); includes 16 minority (7 African Americans, 9 Hispanic Americans). Average age 30. In 2009, 23 master's awarded. *Degree requirements:* For master's, comprehensive exam (for some programs), thesis optional, position paper (MS), portfolio (MS Ed in outdoor teacher education). *Entrance requirements:* For master's, interview (MS); 9 semester hours of upper division course work in psychology or related field, including 1 course in psychology research or statistics; 9 semester hours of education (MS Ed). Additional exam requirements/recommendations for international students: Required—TOEFL (minimum score 600 paper-based; 250 computer-based; 100 iBT). *Application deadline:* For fall admission, 7/1 priority date for domestic students, 6/1 priority date for international students; for winter admission, 11/1 priority date for domestic students, 10/1 priority date for international students; for spring admission, 4/1 priority date for domestic students, 3/1 priority date for international students. Applications are processed on a rolling basis. Application fee: $25. Electronic applications accepted. *Expenses:* Tuition: Full-time $13,149; part-time $487 per credit hour. *Financial support:* In 2009–10, 7 students received support, including 1 research assistantship with full tuition reimbursement available (averaging $15,000 per year), 5 teaching assistantships with full tuition reimbursements available (averaging $15,000 per year); career-related internships or fieldwork, scholarships/grants, tuition waivers (partial), and unspecified assistantships also available. Support available to part-time students. Financial award application deadline: 4/1; financial award applicants required to submit FAFSA. *Unit head:* Dr. Wesley Taylor, Dean, 423-236-2444, Fax: 423-236-1765, E-mail: jwtv@southern.edu. *Application contact:* Mikhaile Spence, Information Contact, 423-236-2496, Fax: 423-236-1765, E-mail: maspence@southern.edu.

Southern California Seminary, Graduate and Professional Programs, El Cajon, CA 92019. Offers biblical studies (MA); counseling psychology (MACP); psychology (Psy D); religious studies (MRS); theology (M Div). Part-time and evening/weekend programs available. Postbaccalaureate distance learning degree programs offered (minimal on-campus study). *Degree requirements:* For master's, thesis (for some programs); for doctorate, thesis/dissertation; for M Div, 2 foreign languages. *Entrance requirements:* For doctorate, master's degree in psychology. Additional exam requirements/recommendations for international students: Required—TOEFL (minimum score 550 paper-based). Electronic applications accepted.

Southern Connecticut State University, School of Graduate Studies, School of Arts and Sciences, Department of Psychology, New Haven, CT 06515-1355. Offers MA. Part-time and evening/weekend programs available. *Faculty:* 6 full-time, 1 part-time/adjunct. *Students:* 16 full-time (14 women), 25 part-time (21 women); includes 6 minority (4 African Americans, 2 Hispanic Americans). 64 applicants, 45% accepted, 17 enrolled. In 2009, 21 master's awarded. *Degree requirements:* For master's, thesis or alternative. *Entrance requirements:* For master's, interview, previous course work in psychology. *Application deadline:* For fall admission, 5/15 priority date for domestic students. Applications are processed on a rolling basis. Application fee: $50. Electronic applications accepted. Tuition and fees vary according to program. *Financial support:* Teaching assistantships available. Financial award application deadline: 4/15; financial award applicants required to submit FAFSA. *Unit head:* Dr. Claire Novosad, Chairperson, 203-392-6863, Fax: 203-392-6805, E-mail: novosadc1@southernct.edu. *Application contact:* Dr. William Hauselt, Coordinator, 203-392-6874, Fax: 203-392-6805, E-mail: hauseltw1@southernct.edu.

Southern Illinois University Carbondale, Graduate School, College of Education, Department of Behavior Analysis and Therapy, Carbondale, IL 62901-4701. Offers MS.

Southern Illinois University Carbondale, Graduate School, College of Liberal Arts, Department of Psychology, Carbondale, IL 62901-4701. Offers clinical psychology (MA, MS, PhD); counseling psychology (MA, MS, PhD); experimental psychology (MA, MS, PhD). *Accreditation:* APA (one or more programs are accredited). *Degree requirements:* For master's, thesis; for doctorate, thesis/dissertation. *Entrance requirements:* For master's, GRE General Test, GRE Subject Test, minimum GPA of 2.7; for doctorate, GRE General Test, GRE Subject Test, minimum GPA of 3.25. Additional exam requirements/recommendations for international students: Required—TOEFL. *Faculty research:* Developmental neuropsychology; smoking, affect, and cognition; personality measurement; vocational psychology; program evaluation.

Southern Illinois University Edwardsville, Graduate Studies and Research, School of Education, Department of Psychology, Edwardsville, IL 62026-0001. Offers clinical child and school psychology (MS); clinical-adult psychology (MA); industrial-organizational psychology (MA); school psychology (SD). Part-time programs available. *Faculty:* 19 full-time (9 women).

Students: 51 full-time (44 women), 38 part-time (28 women); includes 4 minority (1 African American, 2 Asian Americans or Pacific Islanders, 1 Hispanic American), 2 international. Average age 26. 160 applicants, 26% accepted. In 2009, 23 master's, 7 other advanced degrees awarded. *Degree requirements:* For master's, thesis (for some programs), research paper; for SD, thesis. *Entrance requirements:* For master's, GRE. Additional exam requirements/recommendations for international students: Required—TOEFL (minimum score 550 paper-based; 213 computer-based; 79 iBT), IELTS (minimum score 6.5). *Application deadline:* For fall admission, 2/1 for domestic and international students. Application fee: $30. Electronic applications accepted. *Expenses:* Tuition, state resident: part-time $1252.50 per semester. Tuition, nonresident: part-time $3131.25 per semester. Required fees: $586.85 per semester. Tuition and fees vary according to course load. *Financial support:* In 2009–10, 1 fellowship with full tuition reimbursement (averaging $8,370 per year), 3 research assistantships with full tuition reimbursements (averaging $8,064 per year), 42 teaching assistantships with full tuition reimbursements (averaging $8,064 per year) were awarded; career-related internships or fieldwork, Federal Work-Study, institutionally sponsored loans, scholarships/grants, traineeships, and unspecified assistantships also available. Support available to part-time students. Financial award application deadline: 3/1; financial award applicants required to submit FAFSA. *Unit head:* Dr. Lynn Bartels, Co-Chair, 618-650-2202, E-mail: lbartel@siue.edu. *Application contact:* Dr. Lynn Bartels, Co-Chair, 618-650-2202, E-mail: lbartel@siue.edu.

Southern Methodist University, Dedman College, Department of Psychology, Dallas, TX 75275. Offers clinical psychology (PhD). *Faculty:* 16 full-time (6 women), 7 part-time/adjunct (all women). *Students:* 24 full-time (21 women); includes 5 minority (1 American Indian/Alaska Native, 4 Hispanic Americans), 1 international. Average age 29. 80 applicants, 10% accepted, 5 enrolled. In 2009, 1 doctorate awarded. Terminal master's awarded for partial completion of doctoral program. *Degree requirements:* For doctorate, comprehensive exam, thesis/dissertation, oral exam, practicum, research presentation and publication. *Entrance requirements:* For doctorate, GRE General Test, minimum GPA of 3.4. Additional exam requirements/recommendations for international students: Required—TOEFL (minimum score 550 paper-based). *Application deadline:* For fall admission, 12/1 priority date for domestic and international students. Application fee: $75. Electronic applications accepted. *Financial support:* In 2009–10, 23 students received support, including 23 research assistantships with full tuition reimbursements available (averaging $14,000 per year); career-related internships or fieldwork, institutionally sponsored loans, health care benefits, and unspecified assistantships also available. Financial award application deadline: 12/1; financial award applicants required to submit FAFSA. *Faculty research:* Experimental, social, developmental, and cognitive psychology; anger/violence; mood disorders; depression and anxiety; family assessment and development; chronic pain and mental health. *Unit head:* Dr. Ernest Jouriles, Chair, 214-768-2360, Fax: 214-768-3910, E-mail: ejourile@mail.smu.edu. *Application contact:* Dr. Robert B. Hampson, Director of Graduate Studies, 214-768-2734, Fax: 214-768-3910, E-mail: rhampson@smu.edu.

Southern Nazarene University, Graduate College, School of Psychology, Bethany, OK 73008. Offers counseling psychology (MSCP); marriage and family therapy (MA). *Degree requirements:* For master's, thesis optional. *Entrance requirements:* For master's, English proficiency exam, minimum GPA of 3.0 in last 60 hours/major, 2.7 overall.

Southern New Hampshire University, School of Liberal Arts, Manchester, NH 03106-1045. Offers clinical services for adults psychiatric disabilities (Certificate); clinical services for children and adolescents with psychiatric disabilities (Certificate); clinical services for persons with co-occurring substance abuse and psychiatric disabilities (Certificate); community mental health (MS); fiction writing (MFA); non-fiction writing (MFA); teaching English as a foreign language (MS). Part-time and evening/weekend programs available. *Degree requirements:* For master's, one foreign language, thesis. *Entrance requirements:* For master's, minimum GPA of 2.75: MS-TEFL, 3.0: MFA. Additional exam requirements/recommendations for international students: Required—TOEFL (minimum score 550 paper-based; 213 computer-based; 79 iBT), IELTS (minimum score 6.5), TWE (minimum score 5). Electronic applications accepted. *Expenses:* Contact institution. *Faculty research:* Action research, state of the art practice in behavioral health services, wraparound approaches to working with youth, learning styles.

Southern Oregon University, Graduate Studies, College of Arts and Sciences, Department of Psychology, Ashland, OR 97520. Offers mental health counseling (MAP). Part-time programs available. *Degree requirements:* For master's, thesis, portfolio and oral defense. *Entrance requirements:* For master's, GRE General Test, minimum GPA of 3.0. Electronic applications accepted.

Southern University and Agricultural and Mechanical College, Graduate School, College of Sciences, Department of Psychology, Baton Rouge, LA 70813. Offers rehabilitation counseling (MS). *Degree requirements:* For master's, comprehensive exam, thesis optional. *Entrance requirements:* For master's, GMAT or GRE General Test. Additional exam requirements/recommendations for international students: Required—TOEFL (minimum score 525 paper-based; 193 computer-based). *Faculty research:* Cultural diversity, professional preparation and participation of minorities, needs and satisfaction of students with disabilities, prediction model for rehabilitation outcome, diabetes.

Southwestern College, Program in Psychodrama and Action Methods, Santa Fe, NM 87502-4788. Offers Certificate. *Entrance requirements:* For degree, 3 letters of reference. *Application deadline:* Applications are processed on a rolling basis. Application fee: $25. *Unit head:* Kate Cook, Director, 877-471-5756, Fax: 877-471-4071. *Application contact:* Dru Phoenix, Director of Admissions, 505-471-5756 Ext. 26, Fax: 505-471-4071, E-mail: admissions@swc.edu.

Spalding University, Graduate Studies, College of Social Sciences and Humanities, School of Professional Psychology, Louisville, KY 40203-2188. Offers clinical psychology (MA, Psy D). *Accreditation:* APA (one or more programs are accredited). Part-time programs available. *Faculty:* 9 full-time (5 women), 12 part-time/adjunct (3 women). *Students:* 100 full-time (76 women), 47 part-time (35 women); includes 16 minority (3 African Americans, 2 American Indian/Alaska Native, 7 Asian Americans or Pacific Islanders, 4 Hispanic Americans), 1 international. Average age 30. 122 applicants, 46% accepted, 34 enrolled. In 2009, 14 master's, 16 doctorates awarded. Terminal master's awarded for partial completion of doctoral program. *Degree requirements:* For master's, comprehensive exam; for doctorate, thesis/dissertation. *Entrance requirements:* For master's, GRE General Test, 18 hours of undergraduate course work in psychology, interview; for doctorate, GRE General Test, interview, 18 hours of coursework in psychology. Additional exam requirements/recommendations for international students: Required—TOEFL (minimum score 535 paper-based; 203 computer-based). *Application deadline:* For fall admission, 1/15 for domestic students, 2/15 for international students. Application fee: $30. *Expenses:* Tuition: Full-time $11,340; part-time $630 per credit hour. Tuition and fees vary according to program. *Financial support:* In 2009–10, 112 students received support, including 41 research assistantships with partial tuition reimbursements available (averaging $4,831 per year); career-related internships or fieldwork, Federal Work-Study, scholarships/grants, and unspecified assistantships also available. Financial award application deadline: 3/15; financial award applicants required to submit FAFSA. *Faculty research:* Substance abuse, prayer research, end-of-life issues, complementary and alternative medicine, research methodology and statistical inference. *Unit head:* Dr. Steven Katsikas, Chair, 502-585-9911 Ext. 2700, E-mail: skatsikas@spalding.edu. *Application contact:* Elizabeth A. Simpson, Administrative Assistant, 502-585-7127, Fax: 502-585-7159, E-mail: esimpson@spalding.edu.

Stanford University, School of Humanities and Sciences, Department of Psychology, Stanford, CA 94305-9991. Offers PhD. *Degree requirements:* For doctorate, thesis/dissertation, oral exam. *Entrance requirements:* For doctorate, GRE General Test, GRE Subject Test. Additional exam requirements/recommendations for international students: Required—TOEFL. Electronic applications accepted. *Expenses:* Tuition: Full-time $37,380; part-time $2760 per quarter. Required fees: $501.

State University of New York at Binghamton, Graduate School, School of Arts and Sciences, Department of Psychology, Binghamton, NY 13902-6000. Offers behavioral neuroscience (MA, PhD); clinical psychology (MA, PhD); cognitive and behavioral science (MA, PhD). *Accreditation:* APA (one or more programs are accredited). *Faculty:* 27 full-time (11 women), 7 part-time/adjunct (2 women). *Students:* 48 full-time (33 women), 34 part-time (25 women); includes 10 minority (3 African Americans, 1 Asian American or Pacific Islander, 6 Hispanic Americans), 3 international. Average age 27. 253 applicants, 5% accepted, 10 enrolled. In 2009, 14 master's, 12 doctorates awarded. Terminal master's awarded for partial completion of doctoral program. *Degree requirements:* For master's, thesis; for doctorate, thesis/dissertation, departmental qualifying exam. *Entrance requirements:* For master's and doctorate, GRE General Test, GRE Subject Test. Additional exam requirements/recommendations for international students: Required—TOEFL (minimum score 550 paper-based; 213 computer-based; 80 iBT). *Application deadline:* Applications are processed on a rolling basis. Application fee: $60. Electronic applications accepted. *Financial support:* In 2009–10, 64 students received support, including 6 fellowships with full tuition reimbursements available (averaging $17,500 per year), 16 research assistantships with full tuition reimbursements available (averaging $17,500 per year), 35 teaching assistantships with full tuition reimbursements available (averaging $17,500 per year); career-related internships or fieldwork, Federal Work-Study, institutionally sponsored loans, scholarships/grants, health care benefits, and unspecified assistantships also available. Financial award application deadline: 2/15; financial award applicants required to submit FAFSA. *Unit head:* Dr. Celia Klin, Chair, 607-777-4991, E-mail: cklin@binghamton.edu. *Application contact:* Victoria Williams, Recruiting and Admissions Coordinator, 607-777-2151, Fax: 607-777-2501, E-mail: vwilliam@binghamton.edu.

State University of New York at New Paltz, Graduate School, School of Liberal Arts and Sciences, Department of Psychology, New Paltz, NY 12561. Offers mental health counseling (MS); psychology (MA); school counseling (MS). Part-time and evening/weekend programs available. *Faculty:* 11 full-time (8 women), 1 (woman) part-time/adjunct. *Students:* 40 full-time (33 women), 11 part-time (7 women); includes 3 minority (1 African American, 1 Asian American or Pacific Islander, 1 Hispanic American), 3 international. Average age 26. 113 applicants, 44% accepted, 33 enrolled. In 2009, 24 master's awarded. *Degree requirements:* For master's, comprehensive exam, thesis. *Entrance requirements:* For master's, GRE General Test, minimum GPA of 3.0. Additional exam requirements/recommendations for international students: Required—TOEFL (minimum score 550 paper-based; 213 computer-based; 80 iBT), IELTS (minimum score 6.5). *Application deadline:* For fall admission, 1/20 priority date for domestic and international students; for spring admission, 11/15 for domestic and international students. Application fee: $50. Electronic applications accepted. *Financial support:* In 2009–10, 7 students received support, including 6 teaching assistantships with partial tuition reimbursements available (averaging $5,000 per year); career-related internships or fieldwork, Federal Work-Study, institutionally sponsored loans, traineeships, tuition waivers (full), and unspecified assistantships also available. Financial award application deadline: 8/1; financial award applicants required to submit FAFSA. *Faculty research:* Disaster mental health, women's objectification, mate selection, cultural psychology, achievement motivation. *Unit head:* Dr. Glenn Geher, Chair, 845-257-3091, E-mail: geherg@newpaltz.edu. *Application contact:* Dr. Jonathan Raskin, Coordinator, 845-257-3471, E-mail: raskinj@newpaltz.edu.

State University of New York at Plattsburgh, Faculty of Arts and Science, Department of Psychology, Plattsburgh, NY 12901-2681. Offers school psychology (MA, CAS). Part-time programs available. *Faculty:* 4 full-time (1 woman), 2 part-time/adjunct (both women). *Students:* 20 full-time (19 women), 10 part-time (7 women); includes 5 minority (2 Asian Americans or Pacific Islanders, 3 Hispanic Americans), 2 international. Average age 26. 24 applicants, 88% accepted, 11 enrolled. In 2009, 15 master's, 8 other advanced degrees awarded. *Degree requirements:* For master's, thesis, internship. *Entrance requirements:* For master's, GRE General Test, minimum GPA of 3.0. Additional exam requirements/recommendations for international students: Required—TOEFL (minimum score 550 paper-based; 213 computer-based; 79 iBT). *Application deadline:* For fall admission, 2/15 priority date for domestic students. Applications are processed on a rolling basis. Application fee: $75. *Expenses:* Tuition, state resident: full-time $8370; part-time $349 per credit hour. Tuition, nonresident: full-time $13,250; part-time $552 per credit hour. Required fees: $1130. *Financial support:* Federal Work-Study available. Support available to part-time students. Financial award application deadline: 4/15; financial award applicants required to submit FAFSA. *Faculty research:* Alzheimer's disease, adolescent behavior, intellectual assessment, learning disabilities, reading skill acquisition. *Unit head:* Dr. Wendy Braje, Chair, 518-564-3383, E-mail: brajewl@plattsburgh.edu. *Application contact:* Marguerite Adelman, Assistant Director, Graduate Admissions, 518-564-4723, Fax: 518-564-4722, E-mail: adelmaml@plattsburgh.edu.

Stephen F. Austin State University, Graduate School, College of Liberal Arts, Department of Psychology, Nacogdoches, TX 75962. Offers MA. *Degree requirements:* For master's, comprehensive exam, thesis. *Entrance requirements:* For master's, GRE General Test. Additional exam requirements/recommendations for international students: Required—TOEFL.

Stony Brook University, State University of New York, Graduate School, College of Arts and Sciences, Department of Psychology, Stony Brook, NY 11794. Offers biopsychology (PhD); clinical psychology (PhD); cognitive/experimental psychology (PhD); social and health psychology (PhD). *Accreditation:* APA. *Faculty:* 31 full-time (13 women), 1 (woman) part-time/adjunct. *Students:* 96 full-time (70 women); includes 17 minority (2 African Americans, 8 Asian Americans or Pacific Islanders, 7 Hispanic Americans), 11 international. Average age 27. 477 applicants, 6% accepted. In 2009, 23 doctorates awarded. *Degree requirements:* For doctorate, thesis/dissertation. *Entrance requirements:* For doctorate, GRE General Test, GRE Subject Test. Additional exam requirements/recommendations for international students: Required—TOEFL. *Application deadline:* For fall admission, 1/15 for domestic students. Application fee: $60. *Expenses:* Tuition, state resident: full-time $8370; part-time $349 per credit. Tuition, nonresident: full-time $13,250; part-time $552 per credit. Required fees: $933. *Financial support:* In 2009–10, 20 research assistantships, 53 teaching assistantships were awarded; fellowships, career-related internships or fieldwork also available. *Faculty research:* Behavior therapy, memory and cognition, child and family studies, quantitative methods, health psychology. Total annual research expenditures: $4.3 million. *Unit head:* Dr. Nancy Squires, Chair, 631-632-7855, Fax: 631-632-7876, E-mail: nancy.squires@stonybrook.edu. *Application contact:* Graduate Director, 631-632-7855, Fax: 631-632-7876.

Suffolk University, College of Arts and Sciences, Department of Psychology, Boston, MA 02108-2770. Offers clinical psychology (PhD). *Accreditation:* APA. *Faculty:* 19 full-time (11 women). *Students:* 37 full-time (33 women), 2 part-time (both women); includes 1 Asian American or Pacific Islander, 3 Hispanic Americans, 2 international. Average age 26. 252 applicants, 10% accepted, 13 enrolled. In 2009, 14 doctorates awarded. *Degree requirements:* For doctorate, thesis/dissertation, practicum. *Entrance requirements:* For doctorate, GRE General Test or MAT, 2 letters of recommendation, resume. Additional exam requirements/recommendations for international students: Required—TOEFL (minimum score 550 paper-based; 213 computer-based; 80 iBT). *Application deadline:* For fall admission, 12/15 for domestic and international students. Applications are processed on a rolling basis. Application fee: $50. Electronic applications accepted. *Expenses:* Contact institution. *Financial support:* In 2009–10, 39 students received support, including 38 fellowships with full and partial tuition reimbursements available (averaging $19,539 per year); career-related internships or fieldwork, Federal Work-Study, and institutionally sponsored loans also available. Support available to part-time students. Financial award application deadline: 4/1; financial award applicants required to submit FAFSA. *Faculty research:* Olfaction decision-making in substance-dependent individuals, ego development, experiential avoidance in generalized anxiety disorder. *Unit head:* Dr. Krisanne Bursik, Chairperson, 617-573-8293, Fax: 617-367-2924, E-mail: kbursik@suffolk.edu. *Application contact:* Judith Reynolds, Director of Graduate Admissions, 617-573-8302, Fax: 617-305-1733, E-mail: grad.admission@suffolk.edu.

Sul Ross State University, School of Arts and Sciences, Department of Behavioral and Social Sciences, Program in Psychology, Alpine, TX 79832. Offers MA. *Entrance requirements:* For master's, GRE General Test, minimum GPA of 2.5 in last 60 hours of undergraduate work.

Psychology—General

Temple University, Graduate School, College of Liberal Arts, Department of Psychology, Philadelphia, PA 19122-6096. Offers clinical psychology (PhD); cognitive psychology (PhD); developmental psychology (PhD); social psychology (PhD). *Accreditation:* APA. *Degree requirements:* For doctorate, thesis/dissertation. *Entrance requirements:* For doctorate, GRE General Test, minimum GPA of 3.0. Additional exam requirements/recommendations for international students: Required—TOEFL (minimum score 550 paper-based; 213 computer-based; 79 iBT). Electronic applications accepted.

Tennessee State University, The School of Graduate Studies and Research, College of Education, Department of Psychology, Nashville, TN 37209-1561. Offers counseling and guidance (MS), including counseling, elementary school counseling, organizational counseling, secondary school counseling; counseling psychology (PhD); psychology (MS, PhD); school psychology (MS, PhD). *Accreditation:* APA. *Degree requirements:* For doctorate, thesis/dissertation (for some programs). *Entrance requirements:* For master's, GRE General Test or MAT; for doctorate, GRE General Test or MAT, minimum GPA of 3.25, work experience. Electronic applications accepted.

Texas A&M International University, Office of Graduate Studies and Research, College of Arts and Sciences, Department of Behavioral, Applied Sciences, and Criminal Justice, Laredo, TX 78041-1900. Offers counseling psychology (MACP); criminal justice (MS); psychology (MS); sociology (MA). *Faculty:* 8 full-time (3 women), 1 part-time/adjunct (0 women). *Students:* 13 full-time (8 women), 88 part-time (63 women); includes 94 minority (1 African American, 93 Hispanic Americans). Average age 30. 68 applicants, 69% accepted, 47 enrolled. In 2009, 14 master's awarded. *Degree requirements:* For master's, thesis (for some programs). *Entrance requirements:* For master's, GRE General Test. Additional exam requirements/recommendations for international students: Required—TOEFL (minimum score 550 paper-based; 213 computer-based). *Application deadline:* For fall admission, 4/30 priority date for domestic students; for spring admission, 11/30 for domestic students. Applications are processed on a rolling basis. Application fee: $25. *Financial support:* In 2009–10, 17 students received support, including 3 research assistantships, 1 teaching assistantship. Financial award application deadline: 11/1. *Unit head:* Dr. Roberto Heredia, Chair, 956-326-2637, Fax: 956-326-2459, E-mail: rheredia@tamiu.edu. *Application contact:* Rosie Espinoza-Dickinson, Director of Admissions, 956-326-2200, Fax: 956-326-2199, E-mail: enroll@tamiu.edu.

Texas A&M University, College of Liberal Arts, Department of Psychology, College Station, TX 77843. Offers behavioral and cellular neuroscience (MS, PhD); clinical psychology (MS, PhD); cognitive psychology (MS, PhD); developmental psychology (MS, PhD); industrial/organizational psychology (MS, PhD); social psychology (MS, PhD). *Accreditation:* APA (one or more programs are accredited). *Faculty:* 36. *Students:* 84 full-time (58 women), 6 part-time (5 women); includes 26 minority (6 African Americans, 3 Asian Americans or Pacific Islanders, 17 Hispanic Americans), 6 international. In 2009, 12 master's, 8 doctorates awarded. *Degree requirements:* For master's, thesis; for doctorate, comprehensive exam (for some programs), thesis/dissertation. *Entrance requirements:* For master's and doctorate, GRE General Test. Additional exam requirements/recommendations for international students: Required—TOEFL. *Application deadline:* For fall admission, 1/5 for domestic and international students. Application fee: $50 ($75 for international students). Electronic applications accepted. *Expenses:* Tuition, state resident: full-time $3991; part-time $221.74 per credit hour. Tuition, nonresident: full-time $9049; part-time $502.74 per credit hour. *Financial support:* Fellowships with partial tuition reimbursements, research assistantships with partial tuition reimbursements, teaching assistantships with partial tuition reimbursements, career-related internships or fieldwork, institutionally sponsored loans, health care benefits, and unspecified assistantships available. Financial award application deadline: 1/5; financial award applicants required to submit FAFSA. *Unit head:* Dr. Les Morey, Head, 979-845-2581, Fax: 979-845-4727, E-mail: lmorey@psych.tamu.edu. *Application contact:* Sharon Starr, Graduate Admissions Supervisor, 979-458-1710, Fax: 979-845-4727, E-mail: gradadv@psyc.tamu.edu.

Texas A&M University–Commerce, Graduate School, College of Education and Human Services, Department of Psychology and Special Education, Commerce, TX 75429-3011. Offers cognition and instruction (PhD); psychology (MA, MS); special education (M Ed, MA, MS). Part-time programs available. Terminal master's awarded for partial completion of doctoral program. *Degree requirements:* For master's, comprehensive exam, thesis (for some programs); for doctorate, thesis/dissertation, departmental qualifying exam. *Entrance requirements:* For master's, GRE General Test; for doctorate, GRE General Test, 3 letters of recommendation. Electronic applications accepted. *Faculty research:* Human learning, study skills, multicultural bilingual, diversity and special education, educationally handicapped.

Texas A&M University–Corpus Christi, Graduate Studies and Research, College of Liberal Arts, Program in Psychology, Corpus Christi, TX 78412-5503. Offers MA. Part-time and evening/weekend programs available. *Degree requirements:* For master's, comprehensive exam, thesis (for some programs). *Entrance requirements:* For master's, GRE General Test. Additional exam requirements/recommendations for international students: Required—TOEFL. Electronic applications accepted.

Texas A&M University–Kingsville, College of Graduate Studies, College of Arts and Sciences, Department of Psychology and Sociology, Kingsville, TX 78363. Offers gerontology (MS); psychology (MA, MS); sociology (MA, MS). Part-time and evening/weekend programs available. *Degree requirements:* For master's, comprehensive exam, thesis or alternative. *Entrance requirements:* For master's, GRE General Test, minimum GPA of 2.5. Additional exam requirements/recommendations for international students: Required—TOEFL. *Faculty research:* Hispanic female voting behavior, attitudes toward criminal justice, immigration of aged into south Texas, folk medicine.

Texas A&M University–Texarkana, Graduate Studies and Research, College of Health and Behavioral Sciences, Texarkana, TX 75505-5518. Offers counseling psychology (MS). Part-time and evening/weekend programs available. *Degree requirements:* For master's, comprehensive exam (for some programs), thesis or alternative. *Entrance requirements:* For master's, minimum GPA of 3.0 in last 60 hours of bachelor's degree. Additional exam requirements/recommendations for international students: Required—TOEFL. Electronic applications accepted.

Texas Christian University, College of Science and Engineering, Department of Psychology, Fort Worth, TX 76129-0002. Offers experimental psychology (PhD), including cognitive psychology, learning, neuropsychology, social psychology; psychology (MA, MS). *Degree requirements:* For master's, thesis; for doctorate, thesis/dissertation. *Entrance requirements:* For master's and doctorate, GRE General Test. Additional exam requirements/recommendations for international students: Required—TOEFL. *Application deadline:* For fall admission, 3/1 for domestic and international students; for spring admission, 12/1 for domestic students. Applications are processed on a rolling basis. Application fee: $50. *Expenses:* Tuition: Full-time $17,640; part-time $980 per credit hour. Tuition and fees vary according to program. *Financial support:* In 2009–10, 20 students received support; teaching assistantships with full tuition reimbursements available, unspecified assistantships available. Financial award application deadline: 3/1. *Unit head:* Dr. Charles Lord, Graduate Director, 817-257-7410, E-mail: c.lord@tcu.edu. *Application contact:* Marilyn Eudaly, Department Manager, 817-257-6437.

Texas Southern University, College of Liberal Arts and Behavioral Sciences, Department of Psychology, Houston, TX 77004-4584. Offers MA. *Faculty:* 5 full-time (2 women). *Students:* 39 full-time (32 women), 33 part-time (28 women); includes 61 African Americans, 3 Hispanic Americans, 1 international. Average age 33. 31 applicants, 94% accepted, 23 enrolled. In 2009, 12 master's awarded. *Application deadline:* For fall admission, 7/1 for domestic and international students; for spring admission, 11/1 for domestic and international students. Applications are processed on a rolling basis. Application fee: $50. Electronic applications accepted. *Expenses:* Tuition, state resident: full-time $1805; part-time $100 per credit hour. Tuition, nonresident: full-time $6470; part-time $343 per credit hour. Tuition and fees vary according to course level, course load and degree level. *Financial support:* Research assistantships, teaching assistantships, scholarships/grants and unspecified assistantships available. *Unit head:* Dr. Leon H. Belcher, Chair, 713-313-7062, E-mail: belcher_lh@tsu.edu. *Application contact:* Dr. Gregory Maddox, Interim Dean of the Graduate School, 713-313-7011 Ext. 4410, Fax: 713-639-1876, E-mail: maddox_gh@tsu.edu.

Texas State University–San Marcos, Graduate School, College of Liberal Arts, Department of Psychology, San Marcos, TX 78666. Offers health psychology (MA). *Faculty:* 13 full-time (6 women), 1 part-time/adjunct (0 women). *Students:* 32 full-time (26 women), 11 part-time (9 women); includes 14 minority (2 Asian Americans or Pacific Islanders, 12 Hispanic Americans). Average age 27. 38 applicants, 68% accepted, 15 enrolled. In 2009, 16 master's awarded. *Degree requirements:* For master's, comprehensive exam, thesis (for some programs). *Entrance requirements:* For master's, GRE General Test, minimum GPA of 3.0 in last 60 hours, in psychology, and in psychology core courses; 3 letters of recommendation; statement of purpose. Additional exam requirements/recommendations for international students: Required—TOEFL (minimum score 550 paper-based; 213 computer-based). *Application deadline:* For fall admission, 3/15 for domestic and international students. Applications are processed on a rolling basis. Application fee: $40 ($90 for international students). Electronic applications accepted. *Expenses:* Tuition, state resident: full-time $5784; part-time $241 per credit hour. Tuition, nonresident: part-time $551 per credit hour. Required fees: $1728; $48 per credit hour. $306. Tuition and fees vary according to course load. *Financial support:* In 2009–10, 26 students received support, including 2 research assistantships (averaging $5,467 per year), 14 teaching assistantships (averaging $2,946 per year). Financial award application deadline: 4/1. *Faculty research:* Gaze interaction, stress and alcohol. Total annual research expenditures: $67,834. *Unit head:* Dr. Maria Czyzewska, Graduate Advisor, 512-245-2526, Fax: 512-245-3153, E-mail: mc07@txstate.edu. *Application contact:* Dr. Michael Willoughby, Dean of Graduate College, 512-245-2581, Fax: 512-245-8365, E-mail: gradcollege@txstate.edu.

Texas State University–San Marcos, Graduate School, Interdisciplinary Studies Program in Educational Administration and Psychological Services, San Marcos, TX 78666. Offers MAIS. *Degree requirements:* For master's, comprehensive exam. *Application deadline:* For fall admission, 6/15 priority date for domestic students; for spring admission, 10/15 priority date for domestic students. Applications are processed on a rolling basis. Application fee: $40 ($90 for international students). *Expenses:* Tuition, state resident: full-time $5784; part-time $241 per credit hour. Tuition, nonresident: part-time $551 per credit hour. Required fees: $1728; $48 per credit hour. $306. Tuition and fees vary according to course load. *Financial support:* Application deadline: 4/1. *Unit head:* Dr. Stan Carpenter, Dean, 512-245-2575, Fax: 512-245-8345, E-mail: sc33@txstate.edu. *Application contact:* Dr. J. Michael Willoughby, Dean of Graduate School, 512-245-2581, Fax: 512-245-8365, E-mail: gradcollege@txstate.edu.

Texas State University–San Marcos, Graduate School, Interdisciplinary Studies Program in Psychology, San Marcos, TX 78666. Offers MAIS. *Degree requirements:* For master's, comprehensive exam. *Application deadline:* For fall admission, 6/15 priority date for domestic students; for spring admission, 10/15 priority date for domestic students. Applications are processed on a rolling basis. Application fee: $40 ($90 for international students). *Expenses:* Tuition, state resident: full-time $5784; part-time $241 per credit hour. Tuition, nonresident: part-time $551 per credit hour. Required fees: $1728; $48 per credit hour. $306. Tuition and fees vary according to course load. *Financial support:* Application deadline: 4/1. *Unit head:* Dr. Francisco Barrios, Advisor, 512-245-3159, E-mail: fb12@txstate.edu. *Application contact:* Dr. J. Michael Willoughby, Dean of Graduate School, 512-245-2581, Fax: 512-245-8365, E-mail: gradcollege@txstate.edu.

Texas Tech University, Graduate School, College of Arts and Sciences, Department of Psychology, Lubbock, TX 79409. Offers clinical psychology (PhD); counseling psychology (MA, PhD); experimental psychology (MA, PhD); psychology (MA, PhD). *Accreditation:* APA (one or more programs are accredited). Part-time programs available. *Faculty:* 25 full-time (11 women). *Students:* 96 full-time (69 women), 16 part-time (10 women); includes 13 minority (5 African Americans, 8 Hispanic Americans), 7 international. Average age 28. 248 applicants, 13% accepted, 18 enrolled. In 2009, 11 master's, 12 doctorates awarded. *Degree requirements:* For doctorate, thesis/dissertation. *Entrance requirements:* For master's and doctorate, GRE General Test, GRE Subject Test. Additional exam requirements/recommendations for international students: Required—TOEFL (minimum score 550 paper-based; 213 computer-based). *Application deadline:* For fall admission, 3/1 priority date for international students; for spring admission, 11/1 priority date for international students. Applications are processed on a rolling basis. Application fee: $50 ($75 for international students). Electronic applications accepted. *Expenses:* Tuition, state resident: full-time $5100; part-time $213 per credit hour. Tuition, nonresident: full-time $11,748; part-time $490 per credit hour. Required fees: $2298; $50 per credit hour. $555 per semester. *Financial support:* In 2009–10, 1 research assistantship with partial tuition reimbursement (averaging $11,742 per year), 69 teaching assistantships with partial tuition reimbursements (averaging $20,157 per year) were awarded; career-related internships or fieldwork, Federal Work-Study, and institutionally sponsored loans also available. Support available to part-time students. Financial award application deadline: 4/15; financial award applicants required to submit FAFSA. *Faculty research:* Failure/success in relationships, peer rejection in school, stress and coping, group processes, clinical and health psychology. Total annual research expenditures: $144,070. *Unit head:* Dr. Susan S. Hendrick, Chair, 806-742-3711 Ext. 224, Fax: 806-742-0818, E-mail: s.hendrick@ttu.edu. *Application contact:* Dr. Lee M. Cohen, Director of Clinical Program, 806-742-3711 Ext. 254, Fax: 806-742-0818, E-mail: lee.cohen@ttu.edu.

Texas Woman's University, Graduate School, College of Arts and Sciences, Department of Psychology and Philosophy, Denton, TX 76201. Offers counseling psychology (MA, PhD); school psychology (PhD, SSP). *Accreditation:* APA (one or more programs are accredited). *Faculty:* 15 full-time (9 women). *Students:* 66 full-time (55 women), 53 part-time (48 women); includes 24 minority (9 African Americans, 1 American Indian/Alaska Native, 7 Asian Americans or Pacific Islanders, 7 Hispanic Americans), 2 international. Average age 30. 105 applicants, 100% accepted, 11 enrolled. In 2009, 18 master's, 12 doctorates awarded. Terminal master's awarded for partial completion of doctoral program. *Degree requirements:* For master's, thesis; for doctorate, comprehensive exam, thesis/dissertation, internship, residency. *Entrance requirements:* For master's, GRE (minimum score 500 verbal, 500 quantitative), BA/BS or 18 hours in psychology, minimum GPA of 3.5 in undergraduate psychology classes, 3 letters of reference; for doctorate, GRE (Verbal 500, Quantitative 500, Analytical 4), 3 letters of reference; minimum overall and psychology undergraduate GPA of 3.0; BS/BA in psychology or 18 hours of required psychology classes, essay. Additional exam requirements/recommendations for international students: Required—TOEFL (minimum score 550 paper-based; 213 computer-based; 79 iBT). *Application deadline:* For fall admission, 12/15 priority date for domestic and international students. Applications are processed on a rolling basis. Application fee: $50. Electronic applications accepted. *Expenses:* Tuition, state resident: full-time $3564; part-time $198 per credit hour. Tuition, nonresident: full-time $8550; part-time $475 per credit hour. Required fees: $69.26 per credit hour. Tuition and fees vary according to course load. *Financial support:* In 2009–10, 49 students received support, including 14 research assistantships (averaging $10,746 per year), 10 teaching assistantships (averaging $10,746 per year); career-related internships or fieldwork, Federal Work-Study, institutionally sponsored loans, scholarships/grants, traineeships, health care benefits, and unspecified assistantships also available. Support available to part-time students. Financial award application deadline: 3/1; financial award applicants required to submit FAFSA. *Faculty research:* Women's anger, pre-school assessments, body image dysfunction, traumatic stress, classical ethics, mental health and behavioral needs of adolescents in alternative education. *Unit head:* Dr. Dan Miller, Chair, 940-898-2303, Fax: 940-898-2301, E-mail: dmiller@twu.edu. *Application contact:* Samuel Wheeler, Assistant Director of Admissions, 940-898-3188, Fax: 940-898-3081, E-mail: wheelersr@twu.edu.

Trevecca Nazarene University, Graduate Division, Graduate Psychology Programs, Nashville, TN 37210-2877. Offers clinical counseling (Ed D); counseling (MA); counseling psychology (MA); marriage and family therapy (MMFT). Part-time and evening/weekend programs available. *Faculty:* 5 full-time (1 woman), 14 part-time/adjunct (7 women). *Students:* 244 full-time (188 women), 47 part-time (34 women); includes 60 minority (55 African Americans, 1 American

Indian/Alaska Native, 1 Asian American or Pacific Islander, 3 Hispanic Americans), 1 international. Average age 31. In 2009, 75 master's awarded. *Degree requirements:* For master's, comprehensive exam; for doctorate, comprehensive exam, thesis/dissertation. *Entrance requirements:* For master's, GRE General Test or MAT, minimum GPA of 2.7, 2 reference assessment forms; for doctorate, GRE, minimum GPA of 3.25, 3 recommendation forms, 400-word letter of intent, interview. Additional exam requirements/recommendations for international students: Required—TOEFL (minimum score 550 paper-based; 213 computer-based). *Application deadline:* Applications are processed on a rolling basis. *Expenses:* Contact institution. *Financial support:* Applicants required to submit FAFSA. *Unit head:* Dr. Peter Wilson, Director, 615-248-1384, Fax: 615-248-1662, E-mail: pwilson@trevecca.edu. *Application contact:* Heather Ambrefe, Department Secretary, 615-248-1384, Fax: 615-248-1662, E-mail: admissions_psy@trevecca.edu.

Tufts University, Graduate School of Arts and Sciences, Department of Psychology, Medford, MA 02155. Offers MS, PhD. *Faculty:* 18 full-time, 7 part-time/adjunct. *Students:* 38 full-time (23 women); includes 4 minority (2 African Americans, 1 Asian American or Pacific Islander, 1 Hispanic American), 6 international. Average age 27. 150 applicants, 9% accepted, 9 enrolled. In 2009, 6 master's, 6 doctorates awarded. Terminal master's awarded for partial completion of doctoral program. *Degree requirements:* For master's, thesis; for doctorate, one foreign language, thesis/dissertation. *Entrance requirements:* For master's and doctorate, GRE General Test, GRE Subject Test. Additional exam requirements/recommendations for international students: Required—TOEFL (minimum score 550 paper-based; 213 computer-based; 80 iBT). *Application deadline:* For fall admission, 12/15 for domestic and international students. Applications are processed on a rolling basis. Application fee: $75. Electronic applications accepted. *Expenses:* Tuition: Full-time $38,096; part-time $3962 per credit. Required fees: $686; $40 per year. Tuition and fees vary according to course level, course load, degree level, program and student level. *Financial support:* Fellowships, research assistantships with full tuition reimbursements, teaching assistantships with full tuition reimbursements, Federal Work-Study, scholarships/grants, tuition waivers (partial), and unspecified assistantships available. Support available to part-time students. Financial award application deadline: 1/15; financial award applicants required to submit FAFSA. *Unit head:* Robert Cook, Chair, 617-627-2546. *Application contact:* Holly Taylor, Graduate Advisor, 617-627-3523, Fax: 617-627-3181.

Tulane University, School of Science and Engineering, Department of Psychology, New Orleans, LA 70118-5669. Offers MS, PhD. *Accreditation:* APA (one or more programs are accredited). Terminal master's awarded for partial completion of doctoral program. *Degree requirements:* For master's, variable foreign language requirement, thesis; for doctorate, thesis/dissertation. *Entrance requirements:* For master's, GRE General Test, minimum B average in undergraduate course work; for doctorate, GRE General Test. Additional exam requirements/recommendations for international students: Required—TOEFL. Electronic applications accepted. *Faculty research:* Hormones and behavior, aggression, personnel selection, cognitive development, stereotyping, diabetes.

Uniformed Services University of the Health Sciences, School of Medicine, Graduate Programs in the Biomedical Sciences and Public Health, Department of Medical and Clinical Psychology, Bethesda, MD 20814. Offers clinical psychology (PhD); medical and clinical psychology (clinical/dual track) (PhD); medical and clinical psychology (research track) (PhD). Clinical psychology available to active duty military only. *Accreditation:* APA. *Faculty:* 8 full-time (3 women), 42 part-time/adjunct (13 women). *Students:* 24 full-time (14 women); includes 2 minority (1 African American, 1 Hispanic American). Average age 27. 69 applicants, 16% accepted, 8 enrolled. In 2009, 3 doctorates awarded. Terminal master's awarded for partial completion of doctoral program. *Degree requirements:* For doctorate, comprehensive exam, thesis/dissertation, qualifying exam. *Entrance requirements:* For doctorate, GRE General Test, minimum GPA of 3.0, U.S. citizenship. Additional exam requirements/recommendations for international students: Required—TOEFL. *Application deadline:* For fall admission, 1/15 priority date for domestic and international students. Applications are processed on a rolling basis. Application fee: $0. Electronic applications accepted. *Financial support:* In 2009–10, fellowships with full tuition reimbursements (averaging $26,000 per year); career-related internships or fieldwork, scholarships/grants, health care benefits, and tuition waivers (full) also available. *Faculty research:* Addictive and appetitive behavior, psychopharmacology, stress and eating, obesity, health. *Unit head:* Dr. Andrew M. Waters, Graduate Program Director, 301-295-9675, Fax: 301-295-3034, E-mail: andrew.waters@usuhs.mil. *Application contact:* Elena Marina Sherman, Graduate Program Coordinator, 301-295-3913, Fax: 301-295-6772, E-mail: elena.sherman@usuhs.mil.

Union College, Graduate Programs, Department of Psychology, Barbourville, KY 40906-1499. Offers clinical psychology (MA); counseling psychology (MA); school psychology (MA).

Union Institute & University, MA Program in Psychology and Counseling, Brattleboro, VT 05301. Offers clinical mental health counseling (MA); clinical psychology (MA); counseling psychology (MA); developmental psychology (MA); educational psychology (MA); organizational psychology (MA). Postbaccalaureate distance learning degree programs offered (minimal on-campus study). *Faculty:* 2 full-time (1 woman), 8 part-time/adjunct (2 women). *Students:* 57 full-time (50 women), 20 part-time (16 women); includes 4 minority (1 African American, 3 Hispanic Americans). Average age 41. In 2009, 23 master's awarded. *Degree requirements:* For master's, thesis, internship (depending on concentration). *Application deadline:* Applications are processed on a rolling basis. Electronic applications accepted. Tuition and fees vary according to course load, degree level, campus/location and program. *Unit head:* Dr. Nicholas Young, Director, 802-257-8911, E-mail: nick.young@myunion.edu. *Application contact:* Diane Robinson, Director of Admissions, Brattleboro, 800-336-6794, E-mail: diane.robinson@myunion.edu.

Union Institute & University, Master of Arts Program–Online, Montpelier, VT 05602. Offers creativity studies (MA); education (MA); health and wellness (MA); history and culture (MA); leadership, public policy, and social issues (MA); literature and writing (MA); psychology (MA). Part-time programs available. Postbaccalaureate distance learning degree programs offered (no on-campus study). *Faculty:* 3 full-time (1 woman), 16 part-time/adjunct (11 women). *Students:* 27 full-time (23 women), 113 part-time (84 women); includes 30 minority (22 African Americans, 2 American Indian/Alaska Native, 1 Asian American or Pacific Islander, 5 Hispanic Americans). Average age 40. In 2009, 26 master's awarded. *Degree requirements:* For master's, thesis. *Application deadline:* Applications are processed on a rolling basis. Application fee: $50. Electronic applications accepted. *Expenses:* Contact institution. *Financial support:* Career-related internships or fieldwork and tuition waivers available. Financial award applicants required to submit FAFSA. *Unit head:* Dr. Brian Webb, Program Director, 802-828-8777, E-mail: brian.webb@tui.edu. *Application contact:* Kathleen Murphy, Interim Director of Admissions—Montpelier, 888-828-8575, E-mail: admissions@myunion.edu.

Universidad de las Americas, A.C., Program in Psychology, Mexico City, Mexico. Offers family therapy (MA).

Universidad de las Américas–Puebla, Division of Graduate Studies, School of Social Sciences, Program in Psychology, Puebla, Mexico. Offers MA. Part-time and evening/weekend programs available. *Degree requirements:* For master's, one foreign language, thesis. *Entrance requirements:* For master's, minimum B+ average. *Faculty research:* Testing, social hemispheric specialization, clinical psychology.

Université de Montréal, Faculty of Arts and Sciences, Department of Psychology, Montréal, QC H3C 3J7, Canada. Offers M Sc, PhD. Terminal master's awarded for partial completion of doctoral program. *Degree requirements:* For master's, one foreign language, thesis; for doctorate, one foreign language, thesis/dissertation, general exam. Electronic applications accepted. *Faculty research:* Vision, marital counseling, memory.

Université de Sherbrooke, Faculty of Letters and Human Sciences, Department of Psychology, Sherbrooke, QC J1K 2R1, Canada. Offers gerontology (MA). *Degree requirements:* For master's, thesis. *Faculty research:* Human relations.

Université du Québec à Montréal, Graduate Programs, Program in Psychology, Montréal, QC H3C 3P8, Canada. Offers D Ps, PhD. Part-time programs available. *Degree requirements:* For doctorate, thesis/dissertation. *Entrance requirements:* For doctorate, appropriate master's degree or equivalent, proficiency in French.

Université du Québec à Trois-Rivières, Graduate Programs, Program in Psychology, Trois-Rivières, QC G9A 5H7, Canada. Offers PhD, Certificate. Part-time programs available. *Degree requirements:* For doctorate, thesis/dissertation. *Entrance requirements:* For doctorate, appropriate master's degree, proficiency in French. *Faculty research:* Child and family development, gerontology, mental health.

Université Laval, Faculty of Social Sciences, School of Psychology, Programs in Psychology, Québec, QC G1K 7P4, Canada. Offers clinical psychology (PhD); community psychology (PhD); psychology (PhD, Psy D). *Degree requirements:* For doctorate, comprehensive exam, thesis/dissertation. *Entrance requirements:* For doctorate, comprehension of written English, knowledge of French, interview. Electronic applications accepted.

University at Albany, State University of New York, College of Arts and Sciences, Department of Psychology, Albany, NY 12222-0001. Offers autism (Certificate); biopsychology (PhD); clinical psychology (PhD); general/experimental psychology (PhD); industrial/organizational psychology (PhD); psychology (MA); social/personality psychology (PhD). *Accreditation:* APA (one or more programs are accredited). *Degree requirements:* For doctorate, thesis/dissertation. *Entrance requirements:* For doctorate, GRE General Test, GRE Subject Test. Additional exam requirements/recommendations for international students: Required—TOEFL (minimum score 550 paper-based; 213 computer-based). Electronic applications accepted.

University at Buffalo, the State University of New York, Graduate School, College of Arts and Sciences, Department of Psychology, Buffalo, NY 14260. Offers behavioral neuroscience (PhD); clinical psychology (PhD); cognitive psychology (PhD); general psychology (MA); social-personality psychology (PhD). *Accreditation:* APA (one or more programs are accredited). *Faculty:* 32 full-time (12 women), 8 part-time/adjunct (6 women). *Students:* 94 full-time (64 women), 7 part-time (2 women); includes 5 minority (2 African Americans, 3 Hispanic Americans), 12 international. Average age 27. 353 applicants, 11% accepted. In 2009, 18 master's, 7 doctorates awarded. Terminal master's awarded for partial completion of doctoral program. *Degree requirements:* For master's, project; for doctorate, thesis/dissertation. *Entrance requirements:* For master's and doctorate, GRE General Test. Additional exam requirements/recommendations for international students: Required—TOEFL (minimum score 550 paper-based; 213 computer-based; 79 iBT). *Application deadline:* For fall admission, 1/5 for domestic and international students. Application fee: $50. Electronic applications accepted. *Financial support:* In 2009–10, 81 students received support, including 20 fellowships with full tuition reimbursements available (averaging $14,400 per year), 1 research assistantship with full tuition reimbursement available (averaging $10,400 per year), 38 teaching assistantships with full tuition reimbursements available (averaging $10,400 per year); career-related internships or fieldwork, Federal Work-Study, institutionally sponsored loans, scholarships/grants, and tuition waivers (partial) also available. Financial award application deadline: 1/5; financial award applicants required to submit FAFSA. *Faculty research:* Neural, endocrine, and molecular bases of behavior; adult mood and anxiety disorders; relationship dysfunction; attention deficit/hyperactivity disorder; psycho-linguistics. Total annual research expenditures: $7.9 million. *Unit head:* Dr. Paul A. Luce, Chair, 716-645-3650 Ext. 203, Fax: 716-645-3801, E-mail: psychair@acsu.buffalo.edu. *Application contact:* Michele Nowacki, Coordinator of Admissions, 716-645-3650 Ext. 209, Fax: 716-645-3801, E-mail: psych@acsu.buffalo.edu.

The University of Akron, Graduate School, Buchtel College of Arts and Sciences, Department of Psychology, Akron, OH 44325. Offers counseling psychology (MA, PhD); industrial/organizational psychology (MA, PhD); psychology (MA). *Accreditation:* APA (one or more programs are accredited). *Faculty:* 20 full-time (9 women), 8 part-time/adjunct (4 women). *Students:* 59 full-time (47 women), 29 part-time (23 women); includes 8 minority (4 African Americans, 3 Asian Americans or Pacific Islanders, 1 Hispanic American), 7 international. Average age 28. 125 applicants, 12% accepted, 4 enrolled. In 2009, 11 master's, 9 doctorates awarded. Terminal master's awarded for partial completion of doctoral program. *Degree requirements:* For master's, thesis or specialty exam; for doctorate, one foreign language, comprehensive exam, thesis/dissertation. *Entrance requirements:* For master's, GRE General Test, GRE Subject Test, minimum GPA of 2.75, 3.0 in psychology courses; letters of recommendation; curriculum vitae; for doctorate, GRE General Test, GRE Subject Test, minimum graduate GPA of 3.25, letters of recommendation, personal statement, curriculum vitae. Additional exam requirements/recommendations for international students: Required—TOEFL (minimum score 550 paper-based; 213 computer-based; 79 iBT). *Application deadline:* For fall admission, 1/15 for domestic and international students. Application fee: $30 ($40 for international students). Electronic applications accepted. *Expenses:* Tuition, state resident: full-time $6570; part-time $365 per credit hour. Tuition, nonresident: full-time $11,250; part-time $625 per credit hour. *Financial support:* In 2009–10, 2 research assistantships with full tuition reimbursements, 46 teaching assistantships with full tuition reimbursements were awarded; career-related internships or fieldwork, Federal Work-Study, and institutionally sponsored loans also available. *Faculty research:* Social cognitive determinants of behavior, the application of psychological principles to the workplace and career planning/development, the psychological processes of aging. Total annual research expenditures: $428,599. *Unit head:* Dr. Paul Levy, Chair, 330-972-8367, E-mail: plevy@uakron.edu. *Application contact:* Dr. Paul Levy, Chair, 330-972-8367, E-mail: plevy@uakron.edu.

The University of Alabama, Graduate School, College of Arts and Sciences, Department of Psychology, Tuscaloosa, AL 35487. Offers clinical psychology (PhD); experimental psychology (PhD). *Accreditation:* APA. *Faculty:* 22 full-time (9 women), 2 part-time/adjunct (both women). *Students:* 77 full-time (60 women), 19 part-time (11 women); includes 13 minority (6 African Americans, 3 Asian Americans or Pacific Islanders, 4 Hispanic Americans), 4 international. Average age 27. 266 applicants, 10% accepted, 16 enrolled. In 2009, 14 doctorates awarded. *Median time to degree:* Of those who began their doctoral program in fall 2001, 78% received their degree in 8 years or less. *Degree requirements:* For doctorate, thesis/dissertation, internship for clinical students. *Entrance requirements:* For doctorate, GRE. Additional exam requirements/recommendations for international students: Required—TOEFL (minimum score 550 paper-based). *Application deadline:* For fall admission, 12/1 for domestic and international students. Application fee: $50 ($60 for international students). Electronic applications accepted. *Expenses:* Tuition, state resident: full-time $7000. Tuition, nonresident: full-time $19,200. *Financial support:* In 2009–10, 73 students received support, including 12 fellowships with full tuition reimbursements available (averaging $15,000 per year), 34 research assistantships with full and partial tuition reimbursements available (averaging $11,142 per year), 26 teaching assistantships with tuition reimbursements available (averaging $11,142 per year); career-related internships or fieldwork, institutionally sponsored loans, scholarships/grants, health care benefits, and unspecified assistantships also available. Financial award application deadline: 12/1. *Faculty research:* Cognitive development/disability, child clinical, psychology and law, health/aging, social psychology. Total annual research expenditures: $2.1 million. *Unit head:* Dr. Beverly E. Thorn, Chair, 205-348-1919, Fax: 205-348-8648, E-mail: bthorn@bama.ua.edu. *Application contact:* Colett Thomas, Information Contact, 205-348-1913, Fax: 205-348-8648, E-mail: cthomas@as.ua.edu.

The University of Alabama at Birmingham, College of Arts and Sciences, Program in Psychology, Birmingham, AL 35294. Offers MA, PhD. *Accreditation:* APA (one or more programs are accredited). Electronic applications accepted. *Faculty research:* Biological basis of behavior structure, function of the nervous system.

The University of Alabama in Huntsville, School of Graduate Studies, College of Liberal Arts, Department of Psychology, Huntsville, AL 35899. Offers MA. Part-time and evening/weekend programs available. *Faculty:* 6 full-time (3 women). *Students:* 9 full-time (6 women), 2 part-time (both women). Average age 24. 13 applicants, 69% accepted, 6 enrolled. In 2009, 6 master's awarded. *Degree requirements:* For master's, comprehensive exam, thesis or

Psychology—General

The University of Alabama in Huntsville (continued)

alternative, oral and written exams. *Entrance requirements:* For master's, GRE General Test, 15 hours of course work in psychology, minimum GPA of 3.25, sample of written work. Additional exam requirements/recommendations for international students: Required—TOEFL (minimum score 500 paper-based; 173 computer-based; 62 iBT). *Application deadline:* For fall admission, 7/15 for domestic students, 4/1 for international students; for spring admission, 11/30 for domestic students, 9/1 for international students. Applications are processed on a rolling basis. Application fee: $40 ($50 for international students). Electronic applications accepted. *Expenses:* Tuition, state resident: part-time $355.75 per credit hour. Tuition, nonresident: part-time $847.10 per credit hour. Required fees: $210.80 per semester. Tuition and fees vary according to course load and program. *Financial support:* In 2009–10, 7 students received support, including 2 teaching assistantships with full tuition reimbursements available (averaging $8,460 per year); career-related internships or fieldwork, Federal Work-Study, institutionally sponsored loans, scholarships/grants, health care benefits, tuition waivers, and unspecified assistantships also available. Support available to part-time students. Financial award application deadline: 4/1; financial award applicants required to submit FAFSA. *Faculty research:* Personal and social cognition, development and aging, human factors, perception, biological psychology: hormones and behavior. Total annual research expenditures: $290,663. *Unit head:* Dr. Jeffrey Neuschatz, Assistant Chair, 256-824-2321, Fax: 256-824-2387, E-mail: neuschaj@uah.edu. *Application contact:* Kathy Biggs, Graduate Studies Admissions Manager, 256-824-6199, Fax: 256-824-6405, E-mail: deangrad@uah.edu.

University of Alaska Anchorage, College of Arts and Sciences, Department of Psychology, Anchorage, AK 99508. Offers clinical psychology (MS); clinical-community psychology with rural-indigenous emphasis (PhD). Part-time programs available. *Degree requirements:* For master's, thesis. *Entrance requirements:* For master's, GRE General Test, GRE Subject Test, interview, references; for doctorate, interview, bachelor's or master's degree in psychology. Additional exam requirements/recommendations for international students: Required—TOEFL (minimum score 550 paper-based; 213 computer-based). *Faculty research:* Substance abuse, childhood autism, biofeedback, psychological assessment, mental health in Native Alaskans.

University of Alaska Fairbanks, College of Liberal Arts, Department of Psychology, Fairbanks, AK 99775-6480. Offers clinical-community psychology (PhD), including rural cross-cultural emphasis. *Faculty:* 10 full-time (5 women), 3 part-time/adjunct (1 woman). *Students:* 4 full-time (1 woman), 20 part-time (17 women); includes 8 minority (1 African American, 5 American Indian/Alaska Native, 2 Hispanic Americans), 1 international. Average age 35. 34 applicants, 32% accepted, 9 enrolled. In 2009, 1 doctorate awarded. *Degree requirements:* For doctorate, comprehensive exam, thesis/dissertation, oral exam, oral defense. *Entrance requirements:* For doctorate, disclosure statement. Additional exam requirements/recommendations for international students: Required—TOEFL (minimum score 550 paper-based; 213 computer-based; 80 iBT). *Application deadline:* For fall admission, 12/15 for domestic and international students. Application fee: $60. *Expenses:* Tuition, state resident: full-time $7584; part-time $316 per credit. Tuition, nonresident: full-time $15,504; part-time $646 per credit. Required fees: $23 per credit. $135 per semester. Tuition and fees vary according to course level, course load and reciprocity agreements. *Financial support:* In 2009–10, 2 fellowships (averaging $15,270 per year), 7 research assistantships (averaging $16,089 per year), 8 teaching assistantships (averaging $15,611 per year) were awarded; career-related internships or fieldwork, Federal Work-Study, scholarships/grants, health care benefits, and unspecified assistantships also available. Support available to part-time students. Financial award application deadline: 7/1; financial award applicants required to submit FAFSA. *Faculty research:* Clinical and community psychology; rural, indigenous, and cultural psychology. *Unit head:* Dr. Dani Sheppard, Department Chair, 907-474-7007, Fax: 907-474-5781, E-mail: fypsych@uaf.edu. *Application contact:* Dr. Dani Sheppard, Department Chair, 907-474-7007, Fax: 907-474-5781, E-mail: fypsych@uaf.edu.

University of Alberta, Faculty of Graduate Studies and Research, Department of Psychology, Edmonton, AB T6G 2E1, Canada. Offers M Sc, MA, PhD. *Faculty:* 32 full-time (9 women), 1 part-time/adjunct (0 women). *Students:* 38 full-time (26 women). Average age 30. 40 applicants, 45% accepted, 12 enrolled. In 2009, 10 doctorates awarded. Terminal master's awarded for partial completion of doctoral program. *Degree requirements:* For master's, thesis (for some programs); for doctorate, thesis/dissertation. *Entrance requirements:* For master's and doctorate, GRE. Additional exam requirements/recommendations for international students: Required—TOEFL (minimum score 550 paper-based; 213 computer-based). *Application deadline:* For fall admission, 1/15 priority date for domestic students. Electronic applications accepted. Tuition and fees charges are reported in Canadian dollars. *Expenses:* Tuition, area resident: Full-time $4626 Canadian dollars; part-time $99.72 Canadian dollars per unit. International tuition: $8216 Canadian dollars full-time. Required fees: $3590 Canadian dollars; $99.72 Canadian dollars per unit. $215 Canadian dollars per term. *Financial support:* In 2009–10, 35 students received support, including 9 research assistantships with full and partial tuition reimbursements available (averaging $18,000 per year), 26 teaching assistantships with full and partial tuition reimbursements available (averaging $18,000 per year); career-related internships or fieldwork and scholarships/grants also available. Financial award application deadline: 1/15. *Faculty research:* Animal behavior processes; cognitive, social and perceptual processes; development and aging; neuroscience. Total annual research expenditures: $2.5 million. *Unit head:* Dr. Peter Dixon, Graduate Coordinator, 780-492-0969, Fax: 780-492-1768, E-mail: peter.dixon@ualberta.ca. *Application contact:* Donalee Campbell, Graduate Program Assistant, 780-492-0969, Fax: 780-492-1768, E-mail: psygrad@ualberta.ca.

The University of Arizona, Graduate College, College of Social and Behavioral Sciences, Department of Psychology, Tucson, AZ 85721. Offers MA, PhD. *Accreditation:* APA (one or more programs are accredited). *Faculty:* 27 full-time (10 women). *Students:* 43 full-time (27 women), 50 part-time (32 women); includes 14 minority (1 American Indian/Alaska Native, 3 Asian Americans or Pacific Islanders, 10 Hispanic Americans), 16 international. Average age 30. 364 applicants, 4% accepted, 11 enrolled. In 2009, 11 master's, 8 doctorates awarded. *Degree requirements:* For doctorate, comprehensive exam, thesis/dissertation. *Entrance requirements:* For master's, GRE General Test, 3 letters of recommendation, statement of purpose; for doctorate, GRE General Test, 3 letters of recommendation. Additional exam requirements/recommendations for international students: Required—TOEFL (minimum score 550 paper-based; 213 computer-based; 79 iBT). *Application deadline:* For fall admission, 12/15 for domestic and international students. Applications are processed on a rolling basis. Application fee: $65. Electronic applications accepted. *Expenses:* Tuition, state resident: full-time $9028. Tuition, nonresident: full-time $24,890. *Financial support:* In 2009–10, 17 research assistantships with full tuition reimbursements (averaging $14,412 per year), 54 teaching assistantships with full tuition reimbursements (averaging $13,709 per year) were awarded; scholarships/grants, health care benefits, and unspecified assistantships also available. Financial award application deadline: 1/1; financial award applicants required to submit FAFSA. *Faculty research:* Cognitive neuroscience, aging, law and psychology, psycholinguistics, family psychology. Total annual research expenditures: $5 million. *Unit head:* Dr. Alfred W. Kaszniak, Head, 520-621-5149, Fax: 520-621-9306, E-mail: kaszniak@u.arizona.edu. *Application contact:* Beth Owens, Information Contact, 520-621-7456, Fax: 520-621-9306, E-mail: psycgrad@u.arizona.edu.

University of Arkansas, Graduate School, J. William Fulbright College of Arts and Sciences, Department of Psychology, Fayetteville, AR 72701-1201. Offers MA, PhD. *Accreditation:* APA (one or more programs are accredited). *Students:* 32 full-time (23 women), 10 part-time (3 women); includes 1 minority (Hispanic American), 1 international. In 2009, 4 master's, 11 doctorates awarded. *Degree requirements:* For master's, thesis; for doctorate, variable foreign language requirement, thesis/dissertation. *Entrance requirements:* For doctorate, GRE General Test, GRE Subject Test. Application fee: $40 ($50 for international students). *Expenses:* Tuition, state resident: full-time $7355; part-time $356.58 per hour. Tuition, nonresident: full-time $17,401; part-time $775.17 per hour. Required fees: $1203. *Financial support:* In 2009–10, 27 fellowships with tuition reimbursements, 30 research assistantships, 7 teaching assistantships were awarded; career-related internships or fieldwork, Federal Work-Study, and traineeships also available. Support available to part-time students. Financial award application deadline: 4/1; financial award applicants required to submit FAFSA. *Unit head:* Dr. Doug Behrend, Department Chairperson, 479-575-4256, Fax: 479-575-3219, E-mail: psycapp@uark.edu. *Application contact:* Dr. Doug Behrend, Department Chairperson, 479-575-4256, Fax: 479-575-3219, E-mail: psycapp@uark.edu.

University of Arkansas at Little Rock, Graduate School, College of Arts, Humanities, and Social Science, Department of Psychology, Little Rock, AR 72204-1099. Offers applied psychology (MAP). Part-time and evening/weekend programs available. *Entrance requirements:* For master's, GRE General Test, minimum GPA of 2.7. *Faculty research:* Psychological methods and theories in business industry, government, and organizations; personnel program evaluation; training; affirmative action; organizational analysis and development.

University of Baltimore, Graduate School, The Yale Gordon College of Liberal Arts, Program in Applied Psychology, Baltimore, MD 21201-5779. Offers applied psychology (MS), including counseling, industrial and organizational psychology, psychological applications. Part-time and evening/weekend programs available. *Degree requirements:* For master's, thesis optional. *Entrance requirements:* For master's, GRE, minimum GPA of 3.0. Additional exam requirements/recommendations for international students: Required—TOEFL (minimum score 550 paper-based; 213 computer-based). Electronic applications accepted. *Expenses:* Contact institution. *Faculty research:* Participatory decision making, counter productive workplace behavior, organizational consulting, substance abuse treatment, cognitive functioning in head injured.

The University of British Columbia, Faculty of Arts and Faculty of Graduate Studies, Department of Psychology, Vancouver, BC V6T 1Z4, Canada. Offers behavioral neuroscience (MA, PhD); clinical psychology (MA, PhD); cognitive science (MA, PhD); developmental psychology (MA, PhD); health psychology (MA, PhD); quantitative methods (MA, PhD); social/personality psychology (MA, PhD). *Accreditation:* APA (one or more programs are accredited). Terminal master's awarded for partial completion of doctoral program. *Degree requirements:* For master's, thesis; for doctorate, comprehensive exam, thesis/dissertation. *Entrance requirements:* For master's and doctorate, GRE General Test. Additional exam requirements/recommendations for international students: Required—TOEFL (minimum score 550 paper-based; 230 computer-based; 80 iBT). Electronic applications accepted. *Faculty research:* Clinical, developmental, social/personality, cognition, behavioral neuroscience.

University of Calgary, Faculty of Graduate Studies, Faculty of Social Sciences, Department of Psychology, Calgary, AB T2N 1N4, Canada. Offers clinical psychology (M Sc, PhD); psychology (M Sc, PhD). *Degree requirements:* For master's, thesis; for doctorate, thesis/dissertation. *Entrance requirements:* For master's, GRE General Test, bachelor's degree in psychology, minimum GPA of 3.4. Additional exam requirements/recommendations for international students: Required—TOEFL (minimum score 550 paper-based; 213 computer-based). Electronic applications accepted. *Faculty research:* Cognition and cognitive development, social psychology, theoretical psychology, perception, aging.

University of California, Berkeley, Graduate Division, College of Letters and Science, Department of Psychology, Berkeley, CA 94720-1500. Offers PhD. *Accreditation:* APA. *Students:* 108 full-time (62 women). Average age 29. 610 applicants, 16 enrolled. In 2009, 13 doctorates awarded. *Degree requirements:* For doctorate, thesis/dissertation, qualifying exam. *Entrance requirements:* For doctorate, GRE General Test, GRE Subject Test, minimum GPA of 3.0, 3 letters of recommendation. *Application deadline:* For fall admission, 12/3 for domestic students. Application fee: $70 ($90 for international students). Electronic applications accepted. *Financial support:* Unspecified assistantships available. *Unit head:* Prof. Stephen Hinshaw, Chair, 510-642-5292, E-mail: psychgradinfo@berkeley.edu. *Application contact:* Michael Ortt, Graduate Admissions Officer, 510-642-1382, Fax: 510-642-5293, E-mail: psychgradinfo@berkeley.edu.

University of California, Davis, Graduate Studies, Program in Psychology, Davis, CA 95616. Offers PhD. *Degree requirements:* For doctorate, thesis/dissertation. *Entrance requirements:* For doctorate, GRE General Test, GRE Subject Test, minimum GPA of 3.0. Additional exam requirements/recommendations for international students: Required—TOEFL (minimum score 550 paper-based; 213 computer-based). Electronic applications accepted. *Faculty research:* Social personality, perception, cognition, psychobiology.

University of California, Irvine, Office of Graduate Studies, School of Social Ecology, Department of Psychology and Social Behavior, Irvine, CA 92697. Offers PhD. *Students:* 62 full-time (43 women); includes 14 minority (2 African Americans, 11 Asian Americans or Pacific Islanders, 1 Hispanic American), 1 international. Average age 28. 204 applicants, 9% accepted, 8 enrolled. In 2009, 12 doctorates awarded. *Degree requirements:* For doctorate, thesis/dissertation, research project. *Entrance requirements:* For doctorate, GRE General Test, minimum GPA of 3.0. Additional exam requirements/recommendations for international students: Required—TOEFL (minimum score 550 paper-based; 213 computer-based). *Application deadline:* For fall admission, 12/15 priority date for domestic and international students. Applications are processed on a rolling basis. Application fee: $70 ($90 for international students). Electronic applications accepted. *Financial support:* Fellowships, research assistantships with full tuition reimbursements, teaching assistantships, institutionally sponsored loans, traineeships, health care benefits, and unspecified assistantships available. Financial award application deadline: 3/1; financial award applicants required to submit FAFSA. *Faculty research:* Psychosocial development in children, adolescents, and adults; gerontology, childhood behavior disorders, and developmental psychopathology; sex differences; attitude change; social psychology. *Unit head:* Chuansheng Chen, Chair, 949-824-4184, E-mail: ksrook@uci.edu. *Application contact:* Jill Vidas, Academic Counselor, 949-824-5918, Fax: 949-824-2056, E-mail: jjvidas@uci.edu.

University of California, Irvine, Office of Graduate Studies, School of Social Sciences, Department of Cognitive Science, Irvine, CA 92697. Offers psychology (PhD). *Students:* 55 full-time (20 women), 1 part-time (0 women); includes 6 Asian Americans or Pacific Islanders, 8 Hispanic Americans, 6 international. Average age 28. 75 applicants, 21% accepted, 8 enrolled. In 2009, 10 doctorates awarded. *Degree requirements:* For doctorate, thesis/dissertation. *Entrance requirements:* For doctorate, GRE General Test, minimum GPA of 3.0. Additional exam requirements/recommendations for international students: Required—TOEFL (minimum score 550 paper-based; 213 computer-based). *Application deadline:* For fall admission, 1/15 priority date for domestic and international students. Applications are processed on a rolling basis. Application fee: $70 ($90 for international students). Electronic applications accepted. *Financial support:* Fellowships, research assistantships with full tuition reimbursements, teaching assistantships, institutionally sponsored loans, traineeships, health care benefits, and unspecified assistantships available. Financial award application deadline: 3/1; financial award applicants required to submit FAFSA. *Faculty research:* Mathematical psychology, visual and auditory perception, cognitive development, problem solving, experimental psychology. *Unit head:* Charles (Ted) Wright, Chair, 949-824-7589, Fax: 949-824-2307, E-mail: cewright@uci.edu. *Application contact:* Diane Enriquez, Graduate Counselor, 949-824-5924, Fax: 949-824-3548, E-mail: dmvargas@uci.edu.

University of California, Los Angeles, Graduate Division, College of Letters and Science, Department of Psychology, Los Angeles, CA 90034. Offers MA, PhD. *Accreditation:* APA (one or more programs are accredited). *Students:* 179 full-time (122 women); includes 38 minority (7 African Americans, 19 Asian Americans or Pacific Islanders, 12 Hispanic Americans), 9 international. Average age 27. 635 applicants, 7% accepted, 29 enrolled. In 2009, 36 master's, 18 doctorates awarded. Terminal master's awarded for partial completion of doctoral program. *Degree requirements:* For master's, comprehensive exam; for doctorate, thesis/dissertation, oral and written qualifying exams, teaching experience. *Entrance requirements:* For master's, GRE General Test, GRE Subject Test, minimum GPA of 3.0; for doctorate, GRE General Test, GRE Subject Test, MAT, minimum undergraduate GPA of 3.0. Additional exam requirements/recommendations for international students: Required—TOEFL. Application fee: $70 ($90 for international students). Electronic applications accepted. *Financial support:* In 2009–10, 125 fellowships with full and partial tuition reimbursements, 77 research assistantships with full and partial tuition reimbursements, 114 teaching assistantships with full and partial tuition reimbursements were awarded; Federal Work-Study, institutionally sponsored loans, scholarships/grants, health care benefits, tuition waivers (full and partial), and unspecified assistantships also available. Financial award application deadline: 3/1; financial award applicants required to submit FAFSA. *Unit head:* Dr. Bruce Baker, Chair, 310-825-2288. *Application contact:* Department Office, 310-825-2617, E-mail: gradadm@psych.ucla.edu.

University of California, Riverside, Graduate Division, Department of Psychology, Riverside, CA 92521-0102. Offers MA, PhD. *Accreditation:* APA. *Degree requirements:* For doctorate, comprehensive exam, thesis/dissertation, 3 quarters of teaching experience, qualifying exams. *Entrance requirements:* For doctorate, GRE General Test, minimum GPA of 3.2. Additional exam requirements/recommendations for international students: Required—TOEFL (minimum score 550 paper-based; 213 computer-based; 80 iBT). Electronic applications accepted. *Faculty research:* Neuroscience, personality and social psychology, developmental psychology, cognition, health psychology, quantitative psychology.

University of California, San Diego, Office of Graduate Studies, Department of Psychology, La Jolla, CA 92093. Offers PhD. *Degree requirements:* For doctorate, thesis/dissertation. *Entrance requirements:* For doctorate, GRE General Test. Electronic applications accepted.

University of California, San Diego, Office of Graduate Studies, Interdisciplinary Program in Cognitive Science, La Jolla, CA 92093. Offers cognitive science/anthropology (PhD); cognitive science/communication (PhD); cognitive science/computer science and engineering (PhD); cognitive science/linguistics (PhD); cognitive science/neuroscience (PhD); cognitive science/philosophy (PhD); cognitive science/psychology (PhD); cognitive science/sociology (PhD). Admissions offered through affiliated departments. *Degree requirements:* For doctorate, thesis/dissertation. *Entrance requirements:* For doctorate, GRE General Test, acceptance into one of the eight participating departments. *Faculty research:* Language and cognition, philosophy of mind, visual perception, biological anthropology, sociolinguistics.

University of California, Santa Barbara, Graduate Division, College of Letters and Sciences, Division of Mathematics, Life, and Physical Sciences, Department of Psychology, Santa Barbara, CA 93106-9660. Offers MA, PhD. *Faculty:* 30 full-time (10 women), 1 (woman) part-time/adjunct. *Students:* 75 full-time (43 women). Average age 27. 229 applicants, 10% accepted, 9 enrolled. In 2009, 4 master's, 7 doctorates awarded. Terminal master's awarded for partial completion of doctoral program. *Degree requirements:* For master's, thesis; for doctorate, comprehensive exam, thesis/dissertation, teaching assistant training, progress report, papers, mini-convention presentation, 1 quarter of student teaching or teaching assistant class with section lab. *Entrance requirements:* For doctorate, GRE General Test, 3 letters of recommendation, resume/curriculum vitae. Additional exam requirements/recommendations for international students: Required—TOEFL (minimum score 550 paper-based; 213 computer-based; 80 iBT) or IELTS (minimum score 7). *Application deadline:* For fall admission, 12/1 for domestic and international students. Application fee: $70 ($90 for international students). Electronic applications accepted. *Financial support:* In 2009–10, 74 students received support, including 60 fellowships with full and partial tuition reimbursements available (averaging $4,800 per year), 29 research assistantships with full and partial tuition reimbursements available (averaging $8,200 per year), 45 teaching assistantships with partial tuition reimbursements available (averaging $8,000 per year); Federal Work-Study, institutionally sponsored loans, scholarships/grants, health care benefits, and unspecified assistantships also available. Financial award application deadline: 12/15; financial award applicants required to submit FAFSA. *Faculty research:* Social psychology; developmental and evolutionary psychology; neuroscience and behavior; cognition, perception and cognitive neuroscience. Total annual research expenditures: $6 million. *Unit head:* Dr. F. Gregory Ashby, Chair, 805-893-2130, Fax: 805-893-4303, E-mail: ashby@psych.ucsb.edu. *Application contact:* Sondra Gordon, Staff Graduate Advisor, 805-893-2793, Fax: 805-893-4303, E-mail: gordon@psych.ucsb.edu.

University of California, Santa Cruz, Division of Graduate Studies, Division of Social Sciences, Program in Psychology, Santa Cruz, CA 95064. Offers PhD. *Degree requirements:* For doctorate, thesis/dissertation, qualifying exam. *Entrance requirements:* For doctorate, GRE General Test. *Faculty research:* Cognitive psychology, human information processing, sensation perceptions, psychobiology.

University of Central Arkansas, Graduate School, College of Health and Behavioral Sciences, Department of Counseling and Psychology, Conway, AR 72035-0001. Offers community service counseling (MS); counseling psychology (MS); school psychology (MS, PhD). *Accreditation:* APA. *Faculty:* 17 full-time (4 women). *Students:* 64 full-time (54 women), 45 part-time (39 women); includes 3 minority (1 American Indian/Alaska Native, 1 Asian American or Pacific Islander, 1 Hispanic American), 1 international. Average age 27. 41 applicants, 80% accepted, 32 enrolled. In 2009, 35 master's awarded. Terminal master's awarded for partial completion of doctoral program. *Degree requirements:* For master's, comprehensive exam, thesis optional, internship; for doctorate, comprehensive exam, thesis/dissertation, internship. *Entrance requirements:* For master's, GRE General Test, minimum GPA of 2.75; for doctorate, GRE General Test, minimum GPA of 3.25. Additional exam requirements/recommendations for international students: Required—TOEFL (minimum score 550 paper-based; 213 computer-based). *Application deadline:* For fall admission, 3/1 priority date for domestic students; for spring admission, 10/1 priority date for domestic students. Applications are processed on a rolling basis. Application fee: $25 ($50 for international students). *Expenses:* Tuition, state resident: full-time $5136; part-time $214 per credit hour. Required fees: $379.50; $127 per term. Tuition and fees vary according to course level, course load and campus/location. *Financial support:* In 2009–10, 17 research assistantships with partial tuition reimbursements (averaging $6,000 per year) were awarded; career-related internships or fieldwork, Federal Work-Study, scholarships/grants, tuition waivers (partial), and unspecified assistantships also available. Support available to part-time students. Financial award application deadline: 6/30; financial award applicants required to submit FAFSA. *Unit head:* Dr. David Skotko, Chair, 501-450-3175, Fax: 501-450-5424, E-mail: davids@uca.edu. *Application contact:* Patti Hornor, Administrative Assistant, 501-450-5063, Fax: 501-450-5678, E-mail: pattih@uca.edu.

University of Central Florida, College of Sciences, Department of Psychology, Orlando, FL 32816. Offers applied experimental and human factors psychology (MA, PhD); clinical psychology (MA, MS, PhD); industrial/organizational psychology (MS, PhD). *Accreditation:* APA. Part-time and evening/weekend programs available. *Faculty:* 45 full-time (19 women), 5 part-time/adjunct (1 woman). *Students:* 139 full-time (95 women), 12 part-time (8 women); includes 29 minority (4 African Americans, 7 Asian Americans or Pacific Islanders, 18 Hispanic Americans), 3 international. Average age 27. 452 applicants, 22% accepted, 50 enrolled. In 2009, 28 master's, 18 doctorates awarded. *Degree requirements:* For doctorate, thesis/dissertation, candidacy exam. *Entrance requirements:* For master's, GRE General Test, minimum GPA of 3.0 in last 60 hours. Additional exam requirements/recommendations for international students: Required—TOEFL. *Application deadline:* For fall admission, 2/15 for domestic students. Application fee: $30. Electronic applications accepted. *Expenses:* Tuition, state resident: part-time $306.31 per credit hour. Tuition, nonresident: part-time $1099.01 per credit hour. Part-time tuition and fees vary according to degree level and program. *Financial support:* In 2009–10, 71 students received support, including 17 fellowships with partial tuition reimbursements available (averaging $4,520 per year), 29 research assistantships with partial tuition reimbursements available (averaging $10,100 per year), 41 teaching assistantships with partial tuition reimbursements available (averaging $5,700 per year); career-related internships or fieldwork, Federal Work-Study, institutionally sponsored loans, tuition waivers (partial), and unspecified assistantships also available. Financial award application deadline: 3/1; financial award applicants required to submit FAFSA. *Faculty research:* Professional ethical decision making, electronic selection systems, psychometrics. *Unit head:* Dr. Robert Dipboye, Chair, 407-823-2216, E-mail: rdipboye@mail.ucf.edu. *Application contact:* Dr. Robert Dipboye, Chair, 407-823-2216, E-mail: rdipboye@mail.ucf.edu.

University of Central Missouri, The Graduate School, College of Arts, Humanities and Social Sciences, Warrensburg, MO 64093. Offers English (MA); history (MA); mass communication (MA); music (MA); psychology (MS); speech communication (MA); teaching english as a second language (MA); theatre (MA). Part-time programs available. *Faculty:* 82. *Students:* 60 full-time (35 women), 101 part-time (61 women); includes 11 minority (5 African Americans, 3 Asian Americans or Pacific Islanders, 3 Hispanic Americans), 17 international. Average age 30. 80 applicants, 80% accepted, 58 enrolled. In 2009, 51 master's awarded. *Entrance requirements:* Additional exam requirements/recommendations for international students: Required—TOEFL (minimum score 550 paper-based; 79 computer-based). *Application deadline:* For fall admission, 6/1 priority date for domestic students, 5/1 for international students; for spring admission, 10/1 priority date for domestic students, 10/1 for international students. Applications are processed on a rolling basis. Application fee: $30 ($75 for international students). Electronic applications accepted. *Expenses:* Tuition, area resident: Part-time $245.80 per credit hour. Tuition, nonresident: part-time $491.60 per credit hour. Required fees: $24.20 per credit hour. Full-time tuition and fees vary according to course load, degree level, campus/location and reciprocity agreements. *Financial support:* Research assistantships with full and partial tuition reimbursements, teaching assistantships with full and partial tuition reimbursements, career-related internships or fieldwork, Federal Work-Study, scholarships/grants, and administrative and laboratory assistantships available. Support available to part-time students. Financial award application deadline: 3/1; financial award applicants required to submit FAFSA. *Unit head:* Dr. Gersham Nelson, Dean, 660-543-4750, Fax: 660-543-8271, E-mail: nelson@ucmo.edu. *Application contact:* Laurie Delap, Admissions Coordinator, 660-543-4621, Fax: 660-543-4778, E-mail: gradinfo@ucmo.edu.

University of Central Oklahoma, College of Graduate Studies and Research, College of Education, Department of Psychology, Program in General Psychology, Edmond, OK 73034-5209. Offers MA. *Degree requirements:* For master's, thesis. *Entrance requirements:* For master's, GRE General Test. Additional exam requirements/recommendations for international students: Required—TOEFL (minimum score 550 paper-based; 213 computer-based). Electronic applications accepted. *Expenses:* Tuition, state resident: full-time $4128; part-time $172 per credit hour. Tuition, nonresident: full-time $10,373; part-time $432.20 per credit hour. Required fees: $433.20; $18.05 per credit hour.

University of Chicago, Division of Social Sciences, Department of Psychology, Chicago, IL 60637-1513. Offers PhD. *Students:* 53. In 2009, 7 doctorates awarded. *Degree requirements:* For doctorate, one foreign language, thesis/dissertation, exams. *Entrance requirements:* For doctorate, GRE General Test, GRE Subject Test. Additional exam requirements/recommendations for international students: Required—TOEFL, IELTS (minimum score 7). *Application deadline:* For fall admission, 12/10 for domestic and international students. Application fee: $55. Electronic applications accepted. *Financial support:* Fellowships, research assistantships, teaching assistantships, Federal Work-Study, institutionally sponsored loans, scholarships/grants, traineeships, health care benefits, and unspecified assistantships available. Financial award application deadline: 12/10. *Unit head:* Prof. Susan C. Levine, Chair, 773-702-8829. *Application contact:* Office of the Dean of Students, 773-702-8415, E-mail: admissions@ssd.uchicago.edu.

University of Cincinnati, Graduate School, McMicken College of Arts and Sciences, Department of Psychology, Cincinnati, OH 45221. Offers clinical psychology (PhD); experimental psychology (PhD). *Accreditation:* APA. *Degree requirements:* For doctorate, comprehensive exam, thesis/dissertation. *Entrance requirements:* For doctorate, GRE General Test. Additional exam requirements/recommendations for international students: Required—TOEFL. *Faculty research:* Neuropsychology, human factors, health.

University of Colorado at Boulder, Graduate School, College of Arts and Sciences, Department of Psychology and Neuroscience, Boulder, CO 80309. Offers MA, PhD. *Accreditation:* APA (one or more programs are accredited). *Faculty:* 39 full-time (13 women). *Students:* 117 full-time (63 women), 15 part-time (8 women); includes 3 minority (1 African American, 2 Hispanic Americans), 5 international. Average age 29. 521 applicants, 4% accepted, 20 enrolled. In 2009, 21 master's, 15 doctorates awarded. *Degree requirements:* For master's, comprehensive exam; for doctorate, thesis/dissertation. *Entrance requirements:* For master's, GRE General Test, minimum undergraduate GPA of 2.75; for doctorate, GRE General Test. *Application deadline:* For fall admission, 1/1 for domestic students, 12/1 for international students. Application fee: $50 ($60 for international students). *Financial support:* In 2009–10, 33 fellowships (averaging $13,156 per year), 41 research assistantships (averaging $13,718 per year) were awarded; tuition waivers (full) also available. Financial award application deadline: 1/1. *Faculty research:* Clinical psychology, behavioral genetics, behavioral neuroscience, cognitive psychology, social psychology. Total annual research expenditures: $16.1 million.

University of Colorado at Colorado Springs, Graduate School, College of Letters, Arts and Sciences, Department of Psychology, Colorado Springs, CO 80933-7150. Offers MA, PhD. *Accreditation:* APA. Part-time programs available. *Faculty:* 18 full-time (10 women), 1 part-time/adjunct (0 women). *Students:* 36 full-time (28 women), 8 part-time (6 women); includes 8 minority (2 African Americans, 2 Asian Americans or Pacific Islanders, 4 Hispanic Americans). Average age 28. 65 applicants, 45% accepted, 14 enrolled. In 2009, 6 master's, 2 doctorates awarded. *Degree requirements:* For master's, thesis; for doctorate, comprehensive exam, thesis/dissertation. *Entrance requirements:* For master's, GRE, BA in psychology or equivalent background; minimum GPA of 3.0. *Application deadline:* For fall admission, 1/1 for domestic students. Applications are processed on a rolling basis. *Expenses:* Tuition, state resident: full-time $8922; part-time $639 per credit hour. Tuition, nonresident: full-time $19,372; part-time $1154 per credit hour. Tuition and fees vary according to course level, course load, degree level, program, reciprocity agreements and student level. *Financial support:* Research assistantships, teaching assistantships, career-related internships or fieldwork, Federal Work-Study, and scholarships/grants available. Support available to part-time students. Financial award application deadline: 3/1; financial award applicants required to submit FAFSA. *Faculty research:* Aging, social psychology, learning and memory, personality disorders, psychology and law. *Unit head:* Dr. Kelli Klebe, Chair, 719-255-4181, Fax: 719-255-4166, E-mail: kklebe@uccs.edu. *Application contact:* Dr. Hasker Davis, Graduate Student Advisor, 719-255-4148, Fax: 719-255-4166, E-mail: hdavis@uccs.edu.

University of Colorado Denver, College of Liberal Arts and Sciences, Department of Psychology, Denver, CO 80217-3364. Offers MA. Part-time and evening/weekend programs available. *Students:* 13 full-time (8 women), 9 part-time (8 women); includes 4 minority (1 African American, 3 Asian Americans or Pacific Islanders). 76 applicants, 12% accepted, 8 enrolled. In 2009, 11 master's awarded. *Degree requirements:* For master's, comprehensive exam, thesis or alternative. *Entrance requirements:* For master's, GRE General Test, GRE Subject Test, minimum GPA of 2.75. Additional exam requirements/recommendations for international students: Required—TOEFL (minimum score 525 paper-based; 197 computer-based). *Application deadline:* For fall admission, 3/1 for domestic students. Applications are processed on a rolling basis. Application fee: $50 ($75 for international students). Electronic applications accepted. *Financial support:* Research assistantships, teaching assistantships, career-related internships or fieldwork, Federal Work-Study, and scholarships/grants available. Financial award application deadline: 4/1; financial award applicants required to submit FAFSA. *Faculty research:* Organizational behavior, body image perception, professional ethics, infant perception and cognition, charismatic leadership. *Unit head:* Dr. Allison Bashe, Program Director, 303-556-2669, Fax: 303-556-3520, E-mail: allison.bashe@ucdenver.edu. *Application contact:* Gay Freebern, Program Assistant, 303-556-8565, Fax: 303-556-3520, E-mail: gay.freebern@ucdenver.edu.

University of Connecticut, Graduate School, College of Liberal Arts and Sciences, Department of Psychology, Storrs, CT 06269. Offers behavioral neuroscience (PhD); biopsychology (PhD); clinical psychology (MA, PhD); cognition and instruction (PhD); developmental psychology (MA, PhD); ecological psychology (PhD); experimental psychology (PhD); general psychology

Psychology—General

University of Connecticut (continued)
(MA, PhD); health psychology (Graduate Certificate); industrial/organizational psychology (PhD); language and cognition (PhD); neuroscience (PhD); occupational health psychology (Graduate Certificate); social psychology (MA, PhD). *Accreditation:* APA. *Faculty:* 59 full-time (26 women). *Students:* 194 full-time (133 women), 24 part-time (12 women); includes 48 minority (12 African Americans, 21 Asian Americans or Pacific Islanders, 15 Hispanic Americans), 25 international. Average age 28. 585 applicants, 4% accepted, 14 enrolled. In 2009, 22 master's, 24 doctorates awarded. Terminal master's awarded for partial completion of doctoral program. *Degree requirements:* For master's, comprehensive exam; for doctorate, thesis/dissertation. *Entrance requirements:* For master's and doctorate, GRE General Test, GRE Subject Test. Additional exam requirements/recommendations for international students: Required—TOEFL (minimum score 550 paper-based; 213 computer-based). *Application deadline:* For fall admission, 2/1 priority date for domestic and international students; for spring admission, 11/1 for domestic students, 10/1 for international students. Applications are processed on a rolling basis. Application fee: $55. Electronic applications accepted. *Expenses:* Tuition, state resident: full-time $4725; part-time $525 per credit. Tuition, nonresident: full-time $12,267; part-time $1363 per credit. Required fees: $346 per semester. Tuition and fees vary according to course load. *Financial support:* In 2009–10, 109 research assistantships with full tuition reimbursements, 72 teaching assistantships with full tuition reimbursements were awarded; fellowships, career-related internships or fieldwork, Federal Work-Study, scholarships/grants, health care benefits, and unspecified assistantships also available. Financial award application deadline: 2/1; financial award applicants required to submit FAFSA. *Unit head:* Charles A. Lowe, Head, 860-486-3517, Fax: 860-486-2760, E-mail: charles.lowe@uconn.edu. *Application contact:* Charles A. Lowe, Head, 860-486-3517, Fax: 860-486-2760, E-mail: charles.lowe@uconn.edu.

University of Dallas, Braniff Graduate School of Liberal Arts, Program in Psychology, Irving, TX 75062-4736. Offers M Psych, MA. Part-time programs available. *Faculty:* 4 full-time (1 woman), 1 (woman) part-time/adjunct. *Students:* 13 full-time (10 women), 1 (woman) part-time; includes 4 minority (all Hispanic Americans). Average age 30. 9 applicants, 100% accepted, 8 enrolled. In 2009, 3 master's awarded. *Degree requirements:* For master's, one foreign language, comprehensive exam (for some programs), thesis (for some programs). *Entrance requirements:* Additional exam requirements/recommendations for international students: Required—TOEFL. *Application deadline:* For fall admission, 2/15 priority date for domestic students; for spring admission, 11/15 for domestic students. Application fee: $50. *Expenses:* Tuition: Full-time $10,080; part-time $560 per credit hour. Required fees: $50 per term. Tuition and fees vary according to program. *Financial support:* In 2009–10, 14 students received support. Scholarships/grants available. *Unit head:* Dr. Scott Churchill, Chairman, 972-721-5106, Fax: 972-721-4034. *Application contact:* Graduate Coordinator, 972-721-5106, Fax: 972-721-5280, E-mail: graduate@acad.udallas.edu.

University of Dayton, Graduate School, College of Arts and Sciences, Department of Psychology, Dayton, OH 45469-1300. Offers clinical psychology (MA); general psychology (MA). *Faculty:* 18 full-time (5 women), 2 part-time/adjunct (1 woman). *Students:* 27 full-time (22 women), 1 (woman) part-time; includes 7 minority (4 African Americans, 1 American Indian/Alaska Native, 2 Hispanic Americans), 1 international. Average age 25. 34 applicants, 35% accepted, 5 enrolled. In 2009, 17 master's awarded. *Degree requirements:* For master's, thesis. *Entrance requirements:* For master's, GRE General Test, GRE Subject Test (recommended). Additional exam requirements/recommendations for international students: Required—TOEFL (minimum score 550 paper-based; 213 computer-based; 80 iBT). *Application deadline:* For fall admission, 3/1 priority date for domestic students, 2/1 priority date for international students. Application fee: $0 ($50 for international students). Electronic applications accepted. *Expenses:* Tuition: Full-time $8412; part-time $701 per credit hour. Required fees: $325; $65 per course. $25 per semester. Tuition and fees vary according to course load, degree level and program. *Financial support:* In 2009–10, 27 students received support, including 9 research assistantships with full tuition reimbursements available (averaging $9,980 per year); institutionally sponsored loans, traineeships, and tuition waivers (partial) also available. Financial award application deadline: 3/1; financial award applicants required to submit FAFSA. *Faculty research:* Cognitive processes, television and children, interpersonal process, modes and mechanisms of therapy. *Unit head:* Dr. David W. Biers, Chair, 937-229-2713, Fax: 937-229-3900, E-mail: biers@udayton.edu. *Application contact:* Graduate Admissions, 937-229-4411, Fax: 937-229-4729, E-mail: gradadmission@udayton.edu.

University of Delaware, College of Arts and Sciences, Department of Psychology, Newark, DE 19716. Offers behavioral neuroscience (PhD); clinical psychology (PhD); cognitive psychology (PhD); social psychology (PhD). *Accreditation:* APA. *Degree requirements:* For doctorate, thesis/dissertation. *Entrance requirements:* For doctorate, GRE General Test. Additional exam requirements/recommendations for international students: Required—TOEFL (minimum score 600 paper-based; 250 computer-based). Electronic applications accepted. *Faculty research:* Emotion development, neural and cognitive aspects of memory, neural control of feeding, intergroup relations, social cognition and communication.

University of Denver, Division of Arts, Humanities and Social Sciences, Department of Psychology, Denver, CO 80208. Offers MA, PhD. *Accreditation:* APA (one or more programs are accredited). *Faculty:* 21 full-time (9 women), 4 part-time/adjunct (2 women). *Students:* 29 full-time (26 women), 3 part-time (all women); includes 5 minority (4 Asian Americans or Pacific Islanders, 1 Hispanic American), 2 international. Average age 27. 289 applicants, 7% accepted, 8 enrolled. In 2009, 4 master's, 8 doctorates awarded. *Degree requirements:* For doctorate, thesis/dissertation. *Entrance requirements:* For master's and doctorate, GRE General Test. Additional exam requirements/recommendations for international students: Required—TOEFL. *Application deadline:* Applications are processed on a rolling basis. Application fee: $50. Electronic applications accepted. *Expenses:* Tuition: Full-time $34,596; part-time $961 per quarter hour. Required fees: $4 per quarter hour. Tuition and fees vary according to course load, campus/location and program. *Financial support:* In 2009–10, 13 research assistantships with full and partial tuition reimbursements (averaging $15,000 per year), 23 teaching assistantships with full and partial tuition reimbursements (averaging $14,400 per year) were awarded; career-related internships or fieldwork, Federal Work-Study, institutionally sponsored loans, and scholarships/grants also available. Support available to part-time students. Financial award application deadline: 1/1; financial award applicants required to submit FAFSA. *Faculty research:* Developmental neuropsychology, self-esteem and peer relationships, child abuse and neglect, marital and family interactions, adolescent peer and romantic relationships. Total annual research expenditures: $3.9 million. *Unit head:* Dr. Ralph J. Roberts, Chairperson, 303-871-3803. *Application contact:* Paula Houghtaling, Information Contact, 303-871-3803, E-mail: info@psy.du.edu.

University of Denver, Graduate School of Professional Psychology, Denver, CO 80208. Offers clinical psychology (Psy D); psychology (MA). *Accreditation:* APA. *Faculty:* 14 full-time (7 women), 32 part-time/adjunct (15 women). *Students:* 203 full-time (161 women), 26 part-time (22 women); includes 24 minority (6 African Americans, 2 American Indian/Alaska Native, 7 Asian Americans or Pacific Islanders, 9 Hispanic Americans), 4 international. Average age 26. 524 applicants, 38% accepted, 114 enrolled. In 2009, 74 master's, 36 doctorates awarded. *Degree requirements:* For doctorate, paper, internship. *Entrance requirements:* For master's and doctorate, GRE General Test. Additional exam requirements/recommendations for international students: Required—TOEFL. *Application deadline:* For fall admission, 1/5 for domestic students. Application fee: $50. Electronic applications accepted. *Expenses:* Tuition: Full-time $34,596; part-time $961 per quarter hour. Required fees: $4 per quarter hour. Tuition and fees vary according to course load, campus/location and program. *Financial support:* In 2009–10, 36 teaching assistantships with full and partial tuition reimbursements (averaging $3,500 per year) were awarded; career-related internships or fieldwork, Federal Work-Study, institutionally sponsored loans, scholarships/grants, and clinical assistantships also available. Support available to part-time students. Financial award application deadline: 3/1; financial award applicants required to submit FAFSA. *Unit head:* Dr. Peter Buirski, Dean, 303-871-2382. *Application contact:* Admissions, 303-871-3873, Fax: 303-871-4220, E-mail: gsppinfo@du.edu.

University of Detroit Mercy, College of Liberal Arts and Education, Department of Psychology, Detroit, MI 48221. Offers clinical psychology (MA, PhD); industrial/organizational psychology (MA); school psychology (Spec). *Accreditation:* APA. Evening/weekend programs available. *Degree requirements:* For doctorate, departmental qualifying exam. *Faculty research:* Gerontology.

University of Florida, Graduate School, College of Liberal Arts and Sciences, Department of Psychology, Gainesville, FL 32611. Offers behavior analysis (PhD); behavioral neuroscience (MS, PhD); cognitive and sensory processes (PhD); counseling psychology (PhD); developmental psychology (PhD); social psychology (MS, PhD); JD/PhD. *Degree requirements:* For master's, thesis or alternative; for doctorate, thesis/dissertation. *Entrance requirements:* For master's and doctorate, GRE General Test, minimum GPA of 3.0. Additional exam requirements/recommendations for international students: Required—TOEFL (minimum score 550 paper-based; 213 computer-based). Electronic applications accepted. *Faculty research:* Experimental analysis of behavior, psychobiology, cognition and sensory processes, counseling psychology, social psychology, developmental psychology.

University of Georgia, Graduate School, College of Arts and Sciences, Department of Psychology, Athens, GA 30602. Offers MS, PhD. *Accreditation:* APA (one or more programs are accredited). *Faculty:* 38 full-time (15 women), 3 part-time/adjunct (2 women). *Students:* 102 full-time (73 women), 7 part-time (all women); includes 14 minority (8 African Americans, 4 Asian Americans or Pacific Islanders, 2 Hispanic Americans), 8 international. 288 applicants, 16% accepted, 27 enrolled. In 2009, 22 master's, 18 doctorates awarded. *Degree requirements:* For master's, thesis; for doctorate, one foreign language, thesis/dissertation. *Entrance requirements:* For master's and doctorate, GRE General Test. Additional exam requirements/recommendations for international students: Required—TOEFL. *Application deadline:* For fall admission, 12/1 for domestic students; for spring admission, 11/15 for domestic students. Application fee: $50. Electronic applications accepted. *Expenses:* Tuition, state resident: full-time $6000; part-time $250 per credit hour. Tuition, nonresident: full-time $20,904; part-time $871 per credit hour. Required fees: $730 per semester. *Financial support:* Fellowships, research assistantships, teaching assistantships, unspecified assistantships available. *Unit head:* Dr. Patricia H. Miller, Head, 706-542-2174, Fax: 706-542-3275, E-mail: phmiller@uga.edu. *Application contact:* Dr. Billy R. Hammond, Graduate Coordinator, 706-542-4812, Fax: 706-542-3275, E-mail: bhammond@uga.edu.

University of Guelph, Graduate Program Services, College of Social and Applied Human Sciences, Department of Psychology, Guelph, ON N1G 2W1, Canada. Offers applied social psychology (MA, PhD); clinical psychology applied development emphasis (PhD); clinical psychology applied developmental emphasis (MA); industrial/organizational psychology (MA, PhD); neuroscience and applied cognitive science (MA, PhD). *Degree requirements:* For master's, thesis; for doctorate, comprehensive exam, thesis/dissertation. *Entrance requirements:* For master's, GRE General Test, GRE Subject Test, minimum B+ average during previous 2 years of course work; for doctorate, GRE General Test, GRE Subject Test, minimum A- average. Additional exam requirements/recommendations for international students: Required—TOEFL (minimum score 89 iBT). Electronic applications accepted. *Faculty research:* Organizational psychology, reading comprehension and mathematical ability, drug addiction and relapse, gender issues and culture, memory, clinical psychology.

University of Hartford, College of Arts and Sciences, Department of Psychology, West Hartford, CT 06117-1599. Offers clinical practices (MA, Psy D), including clinical practices (Psy D), psychology (MA); general experimental psychology (MA); organizational behavior (MS); school psychology (MS). *Accreditation:* APA. Part-time programs available. *Degree requirements:* For master's, comprehensive exam, thesis (for some programs). *Entrance requirements:* For master's, GRE General Test, GRE Subject Test, minimum GPA of 3.0; for doctorate, GRE General Test, GRE Subject Test. Additional exam requirements/recommendations for international students: Required—TOEFL (minimum score 550 paper-based; 213 computer-based). Electronic applications accepted. *Expenses:* Contact institution.

University of Hawaii at Manoa, Graduate Division, College of Social Sciences, Department of Psychology, Honolulu, HI 96822. Offers clinical psychology (PhD); community and cultural psychology (PhD); community and culture (MA); psychology (MA, PhD, Graduate Certificate). *Accreditation:* APA (one or more programs are accredited). Part-time programs available. *Faculty:* 27 full-time (10 women), 17 part-time/adjunct (1 woman). *Students:* 70 full-time (52 women), 18 part-time (13 women); includes 27 minority (2 African Americans, 1 American Indian/Alaska Native, 21 Asian Americans or Pacific Islanders, 3 Hispanic Americans), 14 international. Average age 28. 202 applicants, 10% accepted, 16 enrolled. In 2009, 5 master's, 9 doctorates, 1 other advanced degree awarded. Terminal master's awarded for partial completion of doctoral program. *Degree requirements:* For master's, comprehensive exam, thesis; for doctorate, comprehensive exam, thesis/dissertation. *Entrance requirements:* For master's and doctorate, GRE General Test, GRE Subject Test. Additional exam requirements/recommendations for international students: Required—TOEFL (minimum score 600 paper-based; 250 computer-based; 100 iBT), IELTS (minimum score 7). *Application deadline:* For fall admission, 1/1 for domestic and international students. Application fee: $60. *Expenses:* Tuition, state resident: full-time $8900; part-time $372 per credit. Tuition, nonresident: full-time $21,400; part-time $898 per credit. Required fees: $207 per semester. *Financial support:* In 2009–10, 6 students received support, including 6 fellowships (averaging $3,969 per year), 41 research assistantships (averaging $17,740 per year), 14 teaching assistantships (averaging $14,802 per year); career-related internships or fieldwork, institutionally sponsored loans, and tuition waivers (full and partial) also available. Financial award application deadline: 1/1. *Faculty research:* Cross-cultural psychology, health psychology, marine mammals, child/adult psychopathology. Total annual research expenditures: $1.3 million. *Application contact:* Catherine Sophian, Graduate Chair, 808-956-8414, Fax: 808-956-4700, E-mail: csophian@hawaii.edu.

University of Houston, College of Liberal Arts and Social Sciences, Department of Psychology, Houston, TX 77204. Offers MA, PhD. *Accreditation:* APA (one or more programs are accredited). *Faculty:* 31 full-time (14 women), 4 part-time/adjunct (2 women). *Students:* 116 full-time (89 women), 19 part-time (15 women); includes 28 minority (6 African Americans, 8 Asian Americans or Pacific Islanders, 14 Hispanic Americans), 15 international. Average age 27. 401 applicants, 7% accepted, 30 enrolled. In 2009, 33 master's, 15 doctorates awarded. *Degree requirements:* For master's, comprehensive exam, thesis; for doctorate, comprehensive exam, thesis/dissertation. *Entrance requirements:* For master's, GRE, Career statement, letters of recommendation (3); for doctorate, GRE General Test, 3 letters of recommendation. Additional exam requirements/recommendations for international students: Required—TOEFL (minimum score 550 paper-based; 79 iBT). *Application deadline:* For fall admission, 1/15 for domestic students, 12/1 for international students. Application fee: $40 ($75 for international students). Electronic applications accepted. *Expenses:* Tuition, state resident: full-time $7676; part-time $320 per credit hour. Tuition, nonresident: full-time $14,324; part-time $597 per credit hour. Required fees: $3034. *Financial support:* In 2009–10, 15 fellowships with full tuition reimbursements (averaging $11,200 per year), 13 research assistantships with full tuition reimbursements (averaging $10,050 per year), 76 teaching assistantships with full tuition reimbursements (averaging $10,250 per year) were awarded; career-related internships or fieldwork, Federal Work-Study, institutionally sponsored loans, scholarships/grants, health care benefits, and unspecified assistantships also available. Support available to part-time students. Financial award application deadline: 2/1; financial award applicants required to submit FAFSA. *Faculty research:* Health psychology, depression, child/family process, organizational effectiveness, close relationships. *Unit head:* Dr. David Francis, Chairperson, 713-743-8588, E-mail: dfrancis@uh.edu. *Application contact:* Patti Tolar, Program Manager, 713-743-8500, E-mail: ptolar@uh.edu.

University of Houston–Clear Lake, School of Human Sciences and Humanities, Programs in Human Sciences, Houston, TX 77058-1098. Offers behavioral sciences (MA), including criminology, cross cultural studies, general psychology, sociology; clinical psychology (MA); criminology (MA); cross cultural studies (MA); family therapy (MA); fitness and human performance (MA); school psychology (MA). *Accreditation:* AAMFT/COAMFTE. Part-time and evening/weekend programs available. Postbaccalaureate distance learning degree programs offered (minimal on-campus study). *Degree requirements:* For master's, thesis or alternative. *Entrance requirements:* For master's, GRE General Test. Additional exam requirements/recommendations for international students: Required—TOEFL (minimum score 550 paper-based; 213 computer-based). Electronic applications accepted. *Faculty research:* Smoking cessation, adolescent sexuality, white collar crime, serial murder, human factors/human computer interaction.

University of Houston–Victoria, School of Arts and Sciences, Program in Psychology, Victoria, TX 77901-4450. Offers counseling psychology (MA); school psychology (MA). Part-time and evening/weekend programs available. Postbaccalaureate distance learning degree programs offered. *Degree requirements:* For master's, project or thesis. *Entrance requirements:* For master's, GRE General Test. Additional exam requirements/recommendations for international students: Required—TOEFL (minimum score 550 paper-based; 213 computer-based). Electronic applications accepted.

University of Idaho, College of Graduate Studies, College of Letters, Arts and Social Sciences, Department of Psychology and Communication Studies, Moscow, ID 83844-2282. Offers psychology (MS). *Faculty:* 9 full-time, 6 part-time/adjunct. *Students:* 19 full-time (5 women), 11 part-time (6 women). In 2009, 11 master's awarded. *Entrance requirements:* For master's, GRE, minimum GPA of 2.8. *Application deadline:* For fall admission, 8/1 for domestic students; for spring admission, 12/15 for domestic students. Application fee: $55 ($60 for international students). *Expenses:* Tuition, state resident: full-time $6120. Tuition, nonresident: full-time $17,712. *Financial support:* Fellowships, research assistantships, teaching assistantships available. Financial award application deadline: 2/15. *Faculty research:* Clinical, experimental, and cognitive psychology. *Unit head:* Dr. Richard D. Locke, Chair, 208-885-6324. *Application contact:* Dr. Richard D. Locke, Chair, 208-885-6324.

University of Illinois at Chicago, Graduate College, College of Liberal Arts and Sciences, Department of Psychology, Chicago, IL 60607-7128. Offers PhD. *Accreditation:* APA. *Degree requirements:* For doctorate, thesis/dissertation, departmental qualifying exam. *Entrance requirements:* For doctorate, GRE General Test, minimum GPA of 2.75. Additional exam requirements/recommendations for international students: Required—TOEFL. Electronic applications accepted.

University of Illinois at Urbana–Champaign, Graduate College, College of Liberal Arts and Sciences, Department of Psychology, Champaign, IL 61820. Offers MA, MS, PhD. *Accreditation:* APA (one or more programs are accredited). *Faculty:* 53 full-time (18 women), 3 part-time/adjunct (2 women). *Students:* 171 full-time (109 women), 5 part-time (3 women); includes 32 minority (8 African Americans, 2 American Indian/Alaska Native, 14 Asian Americans or Pacific Islanders, 8 Hispanic Americans), 48 international. 588 applicants, 10% accepted, 30 enrolled. In 2009, 18 master's, 26 doctorates awarded. *Entrance requirements:* For master's and doctorate, GRE General Test, minimum GPA of 3.0. Additional exam requirements/recommendations for international students: Required—TOEFL (minimum score 79 iBT), or IELTS (minimum score 6.5). *Application deadline:* Applications are processed on a rolling basis. Application fee: $60 ($75 for international students). Electronic applications accepted. *Financial support:* In 2009–10, 35 fellowships with full tuition reimbursements, 83 research assistantships with full tuition reimbursements, 92 teaching assistantships with full tuition reimbursements were awarded; tuition waivers (full) also available. *Unit head:* Dr. David E. Irwin, Head, 217-333-0632, Fax: 217-244-5876, E-mail: irwin@illinois.edu. *Application contact:* Lori Hendricks, Administrative Aide, 217-333-2169, Fax: 217-244-5876, E-mail: lahendri@illinois.edu.

University of Indianapolis, Graduate Programs, School of Psychological Sciences, Indianapolis, IN 46227-3697. Offers clinical psychology (Psy D); clinical psychology/mental health counseling (MA). *Accreditation:* APA. *Faculty:* 6 full-time (1 woman), 1 (woman) part-time/adjunct. *Students:* 107 full-time (96 women), 63 part-time (51 women); includes 8 minority (6 African Americans, 1 Asian American or Pacific Islander, 1 Hispanic American), 7 international. Average age 27. *Degree requirements:* For master's, practicum; for doctorate, comprehensive exam, thesis/dissertation, 1200 hours of clinical practicum, 2000 hour internship. *Entrance requirements:* For master's, GRE, 3 letters of recommendation; for doctorate, GRE, minimum GPA of 3.0, 18 hours of course work in psychology, 3 letters of recommendation. Additional exam requirements/recommendations for international students: Required—TOEFL (minimum score 550 paper-based; 213 computer-based). *Application deadline:* For fall admission, 2/25 for domestic students. Application fee: $50. *Financial support:* Federal Work-Study available. *Unit head:* Dr. E. John McIlvried, Dean, 317-788-3274, Fax: 317-788-3480, E-mail: jmcilvried@uindy.edu. *Application contact:* Dr. E. John McIlvried, Associate Provost for Graduate and International Programs, 317-788-3274, E-mail: jmcilvried@uindy.edu.

The University of Iowa, Graduate College, College of Education, Department of Psychological and Quantitative Foundations, Iowa City, IA 52242-1316. Offers counseling psychology (PhD); educational measurement and statistics (MA, PhD); educational psychology (MA, PhD); school psychology (PhD, Ed S); JD/PhD. *Accreditation:* APA. *Degree requirements:* For master's, thesis optional, exam; for doctorate, comprehensive exam, thesis/dissertation; for Ed S, exam. *Entrance requirements:* For master's, doctorate, and Ed S, GRE General Test, minimum GPA of 3.0. Additional exam requirements/recommendations for international students: Required—TOEFL (minimum score 550 paper-based; 213 computer-based; 81 iBT). Electronic applications accepted.

The University of Iowa, Graduate College, College of Liberal Arts and Sciences, Department of Psychology, Iowa City, IA 52242-1316. Offers neural and behavioral sciences (PhD); psychology (MA, PhD). *Degree requirements:* For master's, thesis optional, exam; for doctorate, comprehensive exam, thesis/dissertation. *Entrance requirements:* For master's and doctorate, GRE General Test, minimum GPA of 3.0. Additional exam requirements/recommendations for international students: Required—TOEFL (minimum score 550 paper-based; 213 computer-based; 81 iBT). Electronic applications accepted.

The University of Kansas, Graduate Studies, College of Liberal Arts and Sciences, Department of Applied Behavioral Science, Lawrence, KS 66045. Offers applied behavioral science (MA); behavioral psychology (PhD). *Faculty:* 17. *Students:* 53 full-time (37 women), 2 part-time (both women); includes 4 minority (1 African American, 2 Asian Americans or Pacific Islanders, 1 Hispanic American), 4 international. Average age 32. 57 applicants, 25% accepted, 10 enrolled. In 2009, 3 master's, 4 doctorates awarded. Terminal master's awarded for partial completion of doctoral program. *Degree requirements:* For master's, thesis; for doctorate, comprehensive exam, thesis/dissertation, comprehensive oral and written exams, journal reviews. *Entrance requirements:* For master's and doctorate, departmental application, curriculum vitae, 3 letters of recommendation. Additional exam requirements/recommendations for international students: Required—TOEFL. *Application deadline:* For fall admission, 12/15 priority date for domestic and international students. Applications are processed on a rolling basis. Application fee: $45 ($55 for international students). Electronic applications accepted. *Expenses:* Tuition, state resident: full-time $6492; part-time $270.50 per credit hour. Tuition, nonresident: full-time $15,510; part-time $646.25 per credit hour. Required fees: $847; $70.56 per credit hour. Tuition and fees vary according to course load and program. *Financial support:* Fellowships, research assistantships with full and partial tuition reimbursements, teaching assistantships with full and partial tuition reimbursements, career-related internships or fieldwork, traineeships, tuition waivers (full), and unspecified assistantships available. Financial award application deadline: 12/15; financial award applicants required to submit CSS PROFILE or FAFSA. *Faculty research:* Early childhood, developmental disabilities, community health and development, adults with disabilities, applied behavior analysis. *Unit head:* Dr. Edward K. Morris, Chair, 785-864-4840, Fax: 785-864-5202, E-mail: ekm@ku.edu. *Application contact:* Dr. Gregory J. Madden, Graduate Director, 785-864-4840, Fax: 785-864-5202, E-mail: gmadden@ku.edu.

The University of Kansas, Graduate Studies, College of Liberal Arts and Sciences, Department of Psychology, Lawrence, KS 66045. Offers clinical child psychology (MA, PhD); clinical health and rehabilitation (PhD); cognitive (PhD); developmental (PhD); quantitative (PhD); social (MA). *Accreditation:* APA (one or more programs are accredited). *Faculty:* 27 full-time (8 women), 9 part-time/adjunct (4 women). *Students:* 85 full-time (62 women), 11 part-time (9 women); includes 13 minority (4 African Americans, 1 American Indian/Alaska Native, 6 Asian Americans or Pacific Islanders, 2 Hispanic Americans), 7 international. Average age 27. 185 applicants, 15% accepted, 17 enrolled. In 2009, 13 master's, 10 doctorates awarded. *Degree requirements:* For master's, thesis; for doctorate, variable foreign language requirement, comprehensive exam, thesis/dissertation. *Entrance requirements:* For doctorate, GRE General Test, minimum GPA of 3.0; undergraduate degree with 15 hours of course work in psychology, vita, writing sample (Clinical Program Only). Additional exam requirements/recommendations for international students: Required—TOEFL. *Application deadline:* For fall admission, 12/1 for domestic and international students. Application fee: $45 ($55 for international students). Electronic applications accepted. *Expenses:* Tuition, state resident: full-time $6492; part-time $270.50 per credit hour. Tuition, nonresident: full-time $15,510; part-time $646.25 per credit hour. Required fees: $847; $70.56 per credit hour. Tuition and fees vary according to course load and program. *Financial support:* Fellowships with full tuition reimbursements, research assistantships with partial tuition reimbursements, teaching assistantships with full and partial tuition reimbursements, career-related internships or fieldwork and unspecified assistantships available. Financial award application deadline: 12/1; financial award applicants required to submit FAFSA. *Faculty research:* Information processing in depression, rape and other forms of sexual coerciom, motions on physical function, processes of memory and understanding text, social stigmas and hostile group environments. *Unit head:* Dr. Ruth Ann Atchley, Chair, 785-864-9821, Fax: 785-864-5696, E-mail: ratchley@ku.edu. *Application contact:* Cathy L. O'Keefe, Graduate Admissions Officer, 785-864-4195, Fax: 785-864-5696, E-mail: psycgrad@ku.edu.

University of Kentucky, Graduate School, College of Arts and Sciences, Program in Psychology, Lexington, KY 40506-0032. Offers clinical psychology (MA); experimental psychology (MA). *Accreditation:* APA (one or more programs are accredited). *Degree requirements:* For master's, comprehensive exam, thesis; for doctorate, comprehensive exam, thesis/dissertation. *Entrance requirements:* For master's, GRE General Test, minimum undergraduate GPA of 2.75; for doctorate, GRE General Test, minimum graduate GPA of 3.0. Additional exam requirements/recommendations for international students: Required—TOEFL (minimum score 550 paper-based; 213 computer-based). Electronic applications accepted. *Faculty research:* Psychopharmacology and teratology, behavioral neuroscience, social psychology, cognitive psychology, development and developmental psychobiology.

University of La Verne, College of Arts and Sciences, Department of Psychology, La Verne, CA 91750-4443. Offers clinical-community psychology (Psy D); counseling (MS), including counseling, marriage and family therapy. *Accreditation:* APA (one or more programs are accredited). Part-time programs available. *Faculty:* 12 full-time (5 women), 22 part-time/adjunct (14 women). *Students:* 83 full-time (73 women), 108 part-time (96 women); includes 115 minority (28 African Americans, 13 Asian Americans or Pacific Islanders, 74 Hispanic Americans). Average age 29. In 2009, 36 master's, 15 doctorates awarded. *Degree requirements:* For master's, thesis, competency exam, personal psychotherapy; for doctorate, thesis/dissertation, clinical internship, competency exams, practicum, personal psychotherapy. *Entrance requirements:* For master's, minimum undergraduate GPA of 3.0, 3 letters of recommendation, interview; for doctorate, minimum GPA of 3.25 undergraduate, 3.65 graduate; 3 recommendations; interview; curriculum vitae. Additional exam requirements/recommendations for international students: Required—TOEFL (minimum score 600 paper-based; 250 computer-based). *Application deadline:* Applications are processed on a rolling basis. *Expenses:* Contact institution. *Financial support:* Career-related internships or fieldwork, institutionally sponsored loans, and scholarships/grants available. Financial award application deadline: 3/2; financial award applicants required to submit FAFSA. *Faculty research:* Developmental therapy and counseling. *Unit head:* Dr. Glenn Gamst, Department Chair, 909-593-3511 Ext. 4176, E-mail: ggamst@laverne.edu. *Application contact:* Connie Hamlow, Admissions Information Specialist, 909-593-3511 Ext. 4519, Fax: 909-392-2761, E-mail: gradadmission@laverne.edu.

University of Lethbridge, School of Graduate Studies, Lethbridge, AB T1K 3M4, Canada. Offers accounting (MScM); addictions counseling (M Sc); agricultural biotechnology (M Sc); agricultural studies (M Sc, MA); anthropology (MA); archaeology (MA); art (MA, MFA); biochemistry (M Sc); biological sciences (M Sc); biomolecular science (PhD); biosystems and biodiversity (PhD); Canadian studies (MA); chemistry (M Sc); computer science (M Sc); computer science and geographical information science (M Sc); counseling psychology (M Ed); dramatic arts (MA); earth, space, and physical science (PhD); economics (MA); educational leadership (M Ed); English (MA); environmental science (M Sc); evolution and behavior (PhD); exercise science (M Sc); finance (MScM); French (MA); French/German (MA); French/Spanish (MA); general education (M Ed); general management (MScM); geography (M Sc, MA); German (MA); health science (M Sc); health sciences (MA); history (MA); human resource management and labour relations (MScM); individualized multidisciplinary (M Sc, MA); information systems (MScM); international management (MScM); kinesiology (M Sc, MA); management (M Sc, MA); marketing (MScM); mathematics (M Sc); music (M Mus, MA); Native American studies (MA); neuroscience (M Sc, PhD); new media (MA); nursing (M Sc); philosophy (MA); physics (M Sc); policy and strategy (MScM); political science (MA); psychology (M Sc, MA); religious studies (MA); social sciences (MA); sociology (MA); theatre and dramatic arts (MFA); theoretical and computational science (PhD); urban and regional studies (MA); women's studies (MA). Part-time and evening/weekend programs available. *Degree requirements:* For doctorate, comprehensive exam, thesis/dissertation. *Entrance requirements:* For master's, GMAT (M Sc in management), bachelor's degree in related field, minimum GPA of 3.0 during previous 20 graded semester courses, 2 years teaching or related experience (M Ed); for doctorate, master's degree, minimum graduate GPA of 3.5. Additional exam requirements/recommendations for international students: Required—TOEFL. *Faculty research:* Movement and brain plasticity, gibberellin physiology, photosynthesis, carbon cycling, molecular properties of main-group ring components.

University of Louisiana at Lafayette, College of Liberal Arts, Department of Psychology, Program in Psychology, Lafayette, LA 70504. Offers MS. *Degree requirements:* For master's, comprehensive exam, thesis (for some programs). *Entrance requirements:* For master's, GRE General Test. Additional exam requirements/recommendations for international students: Required—TOEFL (minimum score 550 paper-based; 213 computer-based).

University of Louisiana at Monroe, Graduate School, College of Education and Human Development, Department of Psychology, Monroe, LA 71209-0001. Offers general psychology (MS); school psychology (MS, SSP). Part-time and evening/weekend programs available. *Faculty:* 9 full-time (2 women), 3 part-time/adjunct (1 woman). *Students:* 18 full-time (12 women), 10 part-time (5 women); includes 5 minority (4 African Americans, 1 Asian American or Pacific Islander). Average age 28. In 2009, 5 master's, 2 other advanced degrees awarded. *Degree requirements:* For master's, thesis; for SSP, comprehensive exam, thesis, field and practicum experiences (400 hours), internship (1250 hours). *Entrance requirements:* For master's, minimum GPA of 2.75 or GRE General Test; for SSP, GRE General Test, minimum GPA of 3.25. Additional exam requirements/recommendations for international students: Required—TOEFL (minimum score 500 paper-based; 173 computer-based; 61 iBT). *Application deadline:* For fall admission, 8/22 priority date for domestic students, 7/1 for international students; for winter admission, 12/14 priority date for domestic students; for spring admission, 1/19 for domestic students, 11/1 for international students. Applications are processed on a rolling basis. Application fee: $20 ($30 for international students). Electronic applications accepted. *Expenses:* Tuition, state resident: part-time $159 per credit hour. Tuition, nonresident: part-time $159 per credit hour. Required fees: $1300 per year. Tuition and fees vary according to course load. *Financial support:* In 2009–10, 9 research assistantships with full tuition reimbursements (averaging $2,500 per year) were awarded; career-related internships or fieldwork, Federal Work-Study, and unspecified assistantships also available. Financial award

Psychology—General

University of Louisiana at Monroe (continued)
application deadline: 4/1; financial award applicants required to submit FAFSA. *Faculty research:* Identity development comparison, alcohol and drug problems. *Unit head:* Dr. David Williamson, Head, 318-342-1331, Fax: 318-342-1352, E-mail: williamson@ulm.edu. *Application contact:* Dr. David Williamson, Head, 318-342-1331, Fax: 318-342-1352, E-mail: williamson@ulm.edu.

University of Louisville, Graduate School, College of Arts and Sciences, Department of Psychological and Brain Sciences, Louisville, KY 40292-0001. Offers clinical psychology (PhD); experimental psychology (PhD). *Accreditation:* APA. *Faculty:* 22 full-time (9 women), 4 part-time/adjunct (1 woman). *Students:* 68 full-time (49 women); includes 6 minority (3 African Americans, 2 Asian Americans or Pacific Islanders, 1 Hispanic American), 7 international. Average age 30. 194 applicants, 8% accepted, 4 enrolled. In 2009, 11 doctorates awarded. *Degree requirements:* For doctorate, thesis/dissertation, preliminary exam, research, internship. *Entrance requirements:* For doctorate, GRE General Test. Additional exam requirements/recommendations for international students: Required—TOEFL. *Application deadline:* For fall admission, 12/1 for domestic students, 11/1 for international students. Application fee: $50. Electronic applications accepted. *Financial support:* In 2009–10, 36 students received support, including 7 fellowships (averaging $22,000 per year), 29 teaching assistantships (averaging $22,000 per year); career-related internships or fieldwork also available. *Faculty research:* Health psychology, geropsychology, psychopathology, cognitive and development science, neuroscience and neuropsychology, vision and hearing. *Unit head:* Dr. Suzanne Meeks, Chair, 502-852-6068, Fax: 502-852-8904, E-mail: smeeks@louisville.edu. *Application contact:* Mary E. Leggett, Director, Graduate Admissions, 502-852-3101, Fax: 502-852-6536, E-mail: gradadm@louisville.edu.

University of Maine, Graduate School, College of Liberal Arts and Sciences, Department of Psychology, Orono, ME 04469. Offers clinical psychology (PhD); developmental psychology (MA); experimental psychology (MA, PhD); social psychology (MA). *Accreditation:* APA (one or more programs are accredited). *Faculty:* 17 full-time (8 women), 7 part-time/adjunct (3 women). *Students:* 27 full-time (16 women), 9 part-time (7 women); includes 2 minority (1 Asian American or Pacific Islander, 1 Hispanic American), 1 international. Average age 28. 134 applicants, 8% accepted, 7 enrolled. In 2009, 3 master's, 3 doctorates awarded. *Degree requirements:* For master's, thesis; for doctorate, thesis/dissertation. *Entrance requirements:* For master's and doctorate, GRE General Test, GRE Subject Test. Additional exam requirements/recommendations for international students: Required—TOEFL. *Application deadline:* For fall admission, 2/1 priority date for domestic students. Applications are processed on a rolling basis. Application fee: $65. Electronic applications accepted. *Financial support:* In 2009–10, 3 research assistantships with tuition reimbursements (averaging $14,063 per year), 21 teaching assistantships with tuition reimbursements (averaging $12,790 per year) were awarded; Federal Work-Study, institutionally sponsored loans, and tuition waivers (full and partial) also available. Financial award application deadline: 3/1. *Faculty research:* Social development, hypertension and aging, attitude change, self-confidence in achievement situations, health psychology. *Unit head:* Dr. Michael Robbins, Chair, 207-581-2051, Fax: 207-581-6128. *Application contact:* Scott G. Delcourt, Associate Dean of the Graduate School, 207-581-3291, Fax: 207-581-3232, E-mail: graduate@maine.edu.

University of Manitoba, Faculty of Graduate Studies, Faculty of Arts, Department of Psychology, Winnipeg, MB R3T 2N2, Canada. Offers clinical psychology (PhD); psychology (MA, PhD); school psychology (MA). *Accreditation:* APA (one or more programs are accredited). *Degree requirements:* For master's, thesis; for doctorate, one foreign language, thesis/dissertation. *Entrance requirements:* For master's and doctorate, GRE General Test.

University of Mary Hardin-Baylor, Graduate Studies in Counseling and Psychology, Belton, TX 76513. Offers community counseling (MA); marriage and family Christian counseling (MA); psychology and counseling (MA); school counseling and psychology (MA). Part-time and evening/weekend programs available. *Degree requirements:* For master's, comprehensive exam. *Entrance requirements:* For master's, GRE General Test, minimum GPA of 3.0 in last 60 hours or 2.75 overall. Electronic applications accepted.

University of Maryland, Baltimore County, Graduate School, College of Arts, Humanities and Social Sciences, Department of Psychology, Baltimore, MD 21250. Offers applied developmental psychology (PhD); human services psychology (MA, PhD), including applied behavioral analysis (MA), human services psychology/clinical (PhD); industrial organizational psychology (MPS); psychology (MPS). *Accreditation:* APA (one or more programs are accredited). *Faculty:* 24 full-time (9 women), 11 part-time/adjunct (4 women). *Students:* 97 full-time (84 women), 35 part-time (28 women); includes 35 minority (12 African Americans, 15 Asian Americans or Pacific Islanders, 8 Hispanic Americans). Average age 29. 151 applicants, 28% accepted, 22 enrolled. In 2009, 23 master's, 13 doctorates awarded. Terminal master's awarded for partial completion of doctoral program. *Degree requirements:* For master's, thesis or alternative; for doctorate, comprehensive exam, thesis/dissertation. *Entrance requirements:* For master's, GRE General Test; for doctorate, GRE General Test, GRE Subject Test. Additional exam requirements/recommendations for international students: Required—TOEFL. *Application deadline:* For fall admission, 12/1 for domestic and international students. Application fee: $70. Electronic applications accepted. *Financial support:* In 2009–10, fellowships with full and partial tuition reimbursements (averaging $22,000 per year), 21 research assistantships with full and partial tuition reimbursements (averaging $14,857 per year), 42 teaching assistantships with full and partial tuition reimbursements (averaging $14,857 per year) were awarded; career-related internships or fieldwork, Federal Work-Study, health care benefits, tuition waivers (full and partial), and unspecified assistantships also available. Financial award application deadline: 3/1; financial award applicants required to submit FAFSA. *Faculty research:* Prevention and treatment of behavior problems, early intervention, cultural contexts, applications to education, behavioral medicine. Total annual research expenditures: $2.3 million. *Unit head:* Dr. Linda Baker, Chair, 410-455-2415, Fax: 410-455-1055, E-mail: baker@umbc.edu. *Application contact:* Nicole Mooney, Program Management Specialist, 410-455-2567, Fax: 410-455-1055, E-mail: psycdept@umbc.edu.

University of Maryland, College Park, Academic Affairs, College of Behavioral and Social Sciences, Department of Psychology, College Park, MD 20742. Offers clinical psychology (PhD); developmental psychology (PhD); experimental psychology (PhD); industrial psychology (MA, MS, PhD); social psychology (PhD). *Accreditation:* APA (one or more programs are accredited). *Faculty:* 71 full-time (35 women), 8 part-time/adjunct (4 women). *Students:* 82 full-time (67 women); includes 13 minority (2 African Americans, 4 Asian Americans or Pacific Islanders, 7 Hispanic Americans), 12 international. 568 applicants, 4% accepted, 8 enrolled. In 2009, 13 master's, 10 doctorates awarded. *Degree requirements:* For master's, thesis; for doctorate, variable foreign language requirement, comprehensive exam, thesis/dissertation. *Entrance requirements:* For master's and doctorate, GRE General Test, GRE Subject Test, minimum GPA of 3.5, research and/or work experience, 3 letters of recommendation. *Application deadline:* For fall admission, 12/1 for domestic and international students. Applications are processed on a rolling basis. Application fee: $60. Electronic applications accepted. *Expenses:* Tuition, area resident: Part-time $471 per credit hour. Tuition, state resident: part-time $471 per credit hour. Tuition, nonresident: part-time $1016 per credit hour. Required fees: $337.04 per term. *Financial support:* In 2009–10, 11 fellowships with full and partial tuition reimbursements (averaging $19,195 per year), 5 research assistantships (averaging $17,734 per year), 45 teaching assistantships with tuition reimbursements (averaging $17,116 per year) were awarded; career-related internships or fieldwork, Federal Work-Study, and scholarships/grants also available. Support available to part-time students. Financial award applicants required to submit FAFSA. *Faculty research:* Social stereotyping and prejudice, anxiety disorders, auditory neuroethology, counseling and social psychology. Total annual research expenditures: $3.8 million. *Unit head:* Thomas S. Wallsten, Chair, 301-405-3562, Fax: 301-314-9566, E-mail: twallst@umd.edu. *Application contact:* Dean of Graduate School, 301-405-0358, Fax: 301-314-9305.

University of Massachusetts Amherst, Graduate School, College of Natural Sciences, Department of Psychology, Amherst, MA 01003. Offers clinical psychology (MS, PhD); cognitive psychology (MS, PhD); developmental science (MS, PhD); psychology of peace and violence (MS, PhD); social psychology (MS, PhD). *Accreditation:* APA (one or more programs are accredited). *Faculty:* 48 full-time (22 women). *Students:* 57 full-time (42 women), 13 part-time (10 women); includes 15 minority (6 African Americans, 6 Asian Americans or Pacific Islanders, 3 Hispanic Americans), 8 international. Average age 28. 381 applicants, 4% accepted, 11 enrolled. In 2009, 11 master's, 8 doctorates awarded. Terminal master's awarded for partial completion of doctoral program. *Degree requirements:* For master's, thesis; for doctorate, comprehensive exam, thesis/dissertation. *Entrance requirements:* For master's and doctorate, GRE General Test, 3 letters of recommendation. Additional exam requirements/recommendations for international students: Required—TOEFL (minimum score 550 paper-based; 213 computer-based; 80 iBT), IELTS (minimum score 6.5). *Application deadline:* For fall admission, 12/1 for domestic and international students. Applications are processed on a rolling basis. Application fee: $50 ($65 for international students). Electronic applications accepted. *Expenses:* Tuition, state resident: full-time $2640; part-time $110 per credit. Tuition, nonresident: full-time $9936; part-time $414 per credit. Tuition and fees vary according to course load. *Financial support:* In 2009–10, 8 fellowships with full tuition reimbursements (averaging $12,620 per year), 52 research assistantships with full tuition reimbursements (averaging $9,491 per year), 55 teaching assistantships with full tuition reimbursements (averaging $10,829 per year) were awarded; career-related internships or fieldwork, Federal Work-Study, scholarships/grants, traineeships, health care benefits, tuition waivers (full), and unspecified assistantships also available. Support available to part-time students. Financial award application deadline: 12/1. *Unit head:* Dr. Linda M. Isbell, Graduate Program Director, 413-545-2503, Fax: 413-545-0996. *Application contact:* Jean M. Ames, Supervisor of Admissions, 413-545-0722, Fax: 413-577-0010, E-mail: gradadm@grad.umass.edu.

University of Massachusetts Dartmouth, Graduate School, College of Arts and Sciences, Department of Psychology, North Dartmouth, MA 02747-2300. Offers behavior analyst (Post-baccalaureate Certificate); clinical psychology (MA); general psychology (MA). Part-time programs available. *Faculty:* 18 full-time (9 women), 8 part-time/adjunct (4 women). *Students:* 19 full-time (15 women), 39 part-time (30 women); includes 5 minority (3 African Americans, 2 Hispanic Americans), 1 international. Average age 29. 91 applicants, 51% accepted, 30 enrolled. In 2009, 7 master's awarded. *Degree requirements:* For master's, thesis (for some programs). *Entrance requirements:* For master's, GRE General Test, minimum GPA of 2.75, 3 letters of recommendation. Additional exam requirements/recommendations for international students: Required—TOEFL (minimum score 500 paper-based). *Application deadline:* For fall admission, 3/31 for domestic students, 1/31 for international students. Application fee: $40 ($60 for international students). Electronic applications accepted. *Expenses:* Tuition, state resident: full-time $2071; part-time $86.29 per credit. Tuition, nonresident: full-time $8099; part-time $337.46 per credit. Required fees: $9446. Tuition and fees vary according to class time, course load and reciprocity agreements. *Financial support:* In 2009–10, 1 research assistantship with full tuition reimbursement (averaging $10,000 per year), 9 teaching assistantships with full tuition reimbursements (averaging $3,500 per year) were awarded; career-related internships or fieldwork, Federal Work-Study, and unspecified assistantships also available. Support available to part-time students. Financial award application deadline: 3/1; financial award applicants required to submit FAFSA. *Faculty research:* Nonverbal communication, behavioral medicine, psychotherapy, intimate relationships, learning. Total annual research expenditures: $62,000. *Unit head:* Dr. Paul Donnelly, Director, Clinical Psychology, 508-999-8334, E-mail: pdonnelly@umassd.edu. *Application contact:* Elan Turcotte-Shamski, Graduate Admissions Officer, 508-999-8604, Fax: 508-999-8183, E-mail: graduate@umassd.edu.

University of Massachusetts Lowell, College of Arts and Sciences, Department of Psychology, Lowell, MA 01854-2881. Offers community social psychology (MA). Part-time programs available. *Degree requirements:* For master's, thesis optional. *Entrance requirements:* For master's, GRE General Test or MAT. Electronic applications accepted. *Faculty research:* Domestic violence, youth sports, teen pregnancy, substance abuse, family and work roles.

University of Memphis, Graduate School, College of Arts and Sciences, Department of Psychology, Memphis, TN 38152-3230. Offers psychology (MS, PhD), including clinical (PhD), experimental (PhD), general psychology (MS), school (PhD); school psychology (MA, Ed S); MS/PhD. *Faculty:* 28 full-time (9 women), 4 part-time/adjunct (0 women). *Students:* 115 full-time (81 women), 22 part-time (15 women); includes 23 minority (15 African Americans, 1 American Indian/Alaska Native, 4 Asian Americans or Pacific Islanders, 3 Hispanic Americans), 7 international. Average age 27. 220 applicants, 15% accepted, 29 enrolled. In 2009, 31 master's, 9 doctorates awarded. *Degree requirements:* For master's, comprehensive exam (for some programs), thesis (for some programs), 37 credit hours (MA); 33 credit hours with thesis or 36 with exam (MS); for doctorate, comprehensive exam (for some programs), thesis/dissertation, 80 semester hours, major area paper; clinical: 1 year placement and 1 year internship; internship (school psychology). *Entrance requirements:* For master's, GRE; for doctorate, GRE (minimum combined score of 1100), minimum GPA of 2.75, 18 hours of undergraduate psychology courses, transcripts, personal statement, letters of recommendation; for Ed S, GRE (minimum combined score of 1100), minimum GPA of 2.75, 18 hours of undergraduate psychology courses, letters of recommendation. Additional exam requirements/recommendations for international students: Required—TOEFL. *Application deadline:* For fall admission, 12/5 for domestic students. Applications are processed on a rolling basis. Application fee: $35 ($60 for international students). Electronic applications accepted. *Expenses:* Tuition, state resident: full-time $6246; part-time $347 per credit hour. Tuition, nonresident: full-time $15,894; part-time $883 per credit hour. Required fees: $1160. Full-time tuition and fees vary according to course load, degree level and program. *Financial support:* In 2009–10, 66 students received support; fellowships with full tuition reimbursements available, research assistantships with full tuition reimbursements available, teaching assistantships with full tuition reimbursements available, Federal Work-Study, scholarships/grants, tuition waivers (partial), and unspecified assistantships available. Financial award application deadline: 2/15; financial award applicants required to submit FAFSA. *Faculty research:* Clinical health; school, child and family research; psychotherapy research; cognitive and behavioral neuroscience research; industrial-organizational research. *Unit head:* Dr. Robert Cohen, Coordinator of Graduate Programs, 901-678-4679, Fax: 901-678-2579, E-mail: rcohen@memphis.edu. *Application contact:* Lynell Connable, Graduate Secretary, 901-678-4340, Fax: 901-678-2579, E-mail: dconnabl@memphis.edu.

University of Miami, Graduate School, College of Arts and Sciences, Department of Psychology, Coral Gables, FL 33124. Offers adult clinical (PhD); behavioral neuroscience (PhD); child clinical (PhD); developmental psychology (PhD); health clinical (PhD); psychology (MS). *Accreditation:* APA (one or more programs are accredited). *Degree requirements:* For doctorate, comprehensive exam, thesis/dissertation. *Entrance requirements:* For doctorate, GRE General Test, minimum GPA of 3.5. Additional exam requirements/recommendations for international students: Required—TOEFL. Electronic applications accepted. *Faculty research:* Behavioral factors in cardiovascular disease and cancer adult psychopathology, developmental disabilities, social and emotional development, mechanisms of coping.

University of Michigan, Horace H. Rackham School of Graduate Studies, College of Literature, Science, and the Arts, Department of Psychology, Ann Arbor, MI 48451. Offers biopsychology (PhD); clinical psychology (PhD); cognition and perception (PhD); developmental psychology (PhD); personality and social contexts (PhD); social psychology (PhD). *Accreditation:* APA. *Faculty:* 87 full-time (40 women), 28 part-time/adjunct (16 women). *Students:* 147 full-time (101 women); includes 40 minority (15 African Americans, 2 American Indian/Alaska Native, 18 Asian Americans or Pacific Islanders, 5 Hispanic Americans), 25 international. Average age 27. 621 applicants, 10% accepted, 37 enrolled. In 2009, 25 doctorates awarded. *Degree requirements:* For doctorate, comprehensive exam, thesis/dissertation, oral defense of dissertation, preliminary exam. *Entrance requirements:* For doctorate, GRE General Test. Additional exam requirements/recommendations for international students: Required—TOEFL. *Application deadline:* For fall admission, 12/1 for domestic and international students. Application fee: $60

($75 for international students). Electronic applications accepted. *Expenses:* Tuition, state resident: full-time $17,286; part-time $1099 per credit hour. Tuition, nonresident: full-time $34,944; part-time $2080 per credit hour. Required fees: $95 per semester. Tuition and fees vary according to course load, degree level and program. *Financial support:* In 2009–10, 133 students received support, including 52 fellowships with full tuition reimbursements available (averaging $20,900 per year), 16 research assistantships with full tuition reimbursements available (averaging $20,900 per year), 79 teaching assistantships with full tuition reimbursements available (averaging $16,694 per year); career-related internships or fieldwork also available. Financial award application deadline: 4/15. *Unit head:* Prof. Theresa Lee, Chair, 734-764-7429. *Application contact:* Laurie Brannan, Psychology Student Academic Affairs, 731-764-2580, Fax: 734-615-7584, E-mail: psych.saa@umich.edu.

University of Michigan, Horace H. Rackham School of Graduate Studies, College of Literature, Science, and the Arts, Department of Women's Studies, Ann Arbor, MI 48109. Offers English and women's studies (PhD); history and women's studies (PhD); lesbian, gay, bisexual, transgender, queer (LGBTQ) studies (Certificate); psychology and women's studies (PhD); sociology and women's studies (PhD); women's studies (Certificate). *Faculty:* 74 full-time (66 women). *Students:* 68 full-time (63 women); includes 21 minority (7 African Americans, 1 American Indian/Alaska Native, 8 Asian Americans or Pacific Islanders, 5 Hispanic Americans), 12 international. Average age 31. 119 applicants, 9% accepted, 7 enrolled. In 2009, 5 doctorates, 8 other advanced degrees awarded. *Degree requirements:* For doctorate, variable foreign language requirement, comprehensive exam (for some programs), thesis/dissertation. *Entrance requirements:* For doctorate, GRE General Test, previous undergraduate course work in women's studies. *Application deadline:* For fall admission, 12/1 for domestic and international students. Application fee: $60 ($75 for international students). Electronic applications accepted. *Expenses:* Tuition, state resident: full-time $17,286; part-time $1099 per credit hour. Tuition, nonresident: full-time $34,944; part-time $2080 per credit hour. Required fees: $95 per semester. Tuition and fees vary according to course load, degree level and program. *Financial support:* In 2009–10, 34 students received support, including 19 fellowships with full tuition reimbursements available (averaging $16,000 per year), 15 teaching assistantships with full and partial tuition reimbursements available (averaging $16,135 per year); career-related internships or fieldwork, institutionally sponsored loans, scholarships/grants, traineeships, health care benefits, and unspecified assistantships also available. *Faculty research:* Gender issues; LGBTQ studies; sexuality; women and science; global feminism. *Unit head:* Anne Herrmann, Chair, 734-763-2047, Fax: 734-647-4943, E-mail: anneh@umich.edu. *Application contact:* Aimee Germain, Graduate Program Coordinator, 734-763-2047, Fax: 734-647-4943, E-mail: wsdgradInquiry@umich.edu.

University of Michigan, Horace H. Rackham School of Graduate Studies, Combined Program in Education and Psychology, Ann Arbor, MI 48109. Offers PhD. *Faculty:* 20 part-time/adjunct (9 women). *Students:* 30 full-time (21 women); includes 14 minority (8 African Americans, 2 Asian Americans or Pacific Islanders, 4 Hispanic Americans), 5 international. Average age 28. 47 applicants, 19% accepted, 7 enrolled. In 2009, 3 doctorates awarded. *Degree requirements:* For doctorate, thesis/dissertation, independent research project, preliminary exam, oral defense of dissertation. *Entrance requirements:* For doctorate, GRE General Test with Analytical Writing Test. Additional exam requirements/recommendations for international students: Required—TOEFL (minimum score 600 paper-based; 250 computer-based; 100 iBT). *Application deadline:* For fall admission, 12/5 for domestic and international students. Application fee: $60 ($75 for international students). Electronic applications accepted. *Expenses:* Tuition, state resident: full-time $17,286; part-time $1099 per credit hour. Tuition, nonresident: full-time $34,944; part-time $2080 per credit hour. Required fees: $95 per semester. Tuition and fees vary according to course load, degree level and program. *Financial support:* In 2009–10, 28 students received support, including 15 fellowships with full tuition reimbursements available (averaging $26,304 per year), 8 research assistantships with full tuition reimbursements available (averaging $25,189 per year), 8 teaching assistantships with full tuition reimbursements available (averaging $27,303 per year); institutionally sponsored loans, scholarships/grants, traineeships, tuition waivers, and unspecified assistantships also available. Financial award application deadline: 12/5. *Faculty research:* Human development in context of schools, families, communities; cognitive and learning sciences; motivation and self-regulated learning; culture, ethnicity, social and class influences on learning and motivation. *Unit head:* Tabbye M. Chavous, Director, 734-647-0626, Fax: 734-615-2164, E-mail: tchavous@umich.edu. *Application contact:* Janie Knieper, Administrative Specialist, 734-647-0626, Fax: 734-615-2164, E-mail: cpep@umich.edu.

University of Minnesota, Twin Cities Campus, Graduate School, College of Liberal Arts, Department of Psychology, Minneapolis, MN 55455-0213. Offers biological psychopathology (PhD); clinical psychology (PhD); cognitive and biological psychology (PhD); counseling psychology (PhD); industrial/organizational psychology (PhD); personality, individual differences, and behavior genetics (PhD); quantitative/psychometric methods (PhD); school psychology (PhD); social psychology (PhD). *Accreditation:* APA. *Degree requirements:* For doctorate, comprehensive exam, thesis/dissertation. *Entrance requirements:* For doctorate, GRE General Test, GRE Subject Test (recommended), 12 credits of upper-level psychology courses, including a course in statistics or psychological measurement. Additional exam requirements/recommendations for international students: Required—TOEFL (minimum score 550 paper-based; 213 computer-based; 79 iBT).

University of Mississippi, Graduate School, College of Liberal Arts, Department of Psychology, Oxford, University, MS 38677. Offers clinical psychology (PhD); experimental psychology (PhD); psychology (MA). *Accreditation:* APA (one or more programs are accredited). *Faculty:* 18 full-time (8 women), 2 part-time/adjunct (both women). *Students:* 52 full-time (38 women), 6 part-time (4 women); includes 10 minority (7 African Americans, 1 American Indian/Alaska Native, 1 Asian American or Pacific Islander, 1 Hispanic American), 1 international. In 2009, 3 master's, 6 doctorates awarded. *Degree requirements:* For master's, thesis; for doctorate, thesis/dissertation. *Entrance requirements:* For master's, GRE General Test, minimum GPA of 3.0; for doctorate, GRE General Test. Additional exam requirements/recommendations for international students: Required—TOEFL. *Application deadline:* For fall admission, 1/15 for domestic students; for spring admission, 10/1 for domestic students. Applications are processed on a rolling basis. Application fee: $25. Electronic applications accepted. *Financial support:* Scholarships/grants available. Financial award application deadline: 3/1; financial award applicants required to submit FAFSA. *Unit head:* Dr. Michael T. Allen, Chairman, 662-915-5190, Fax: 662-915-5398, E-mail: mta1@olemiss.edu. *Application contact:* Dr. Christy M. Wyandt, Associate Dean, 662-915-7474, Fax: 662-915-7577, E-mail: cwyandt@olemiss.edu.

University of Missouri, Graduate School, College of Arts and Sciences, Department of Psychological Sciences, Columbia, MO 65211. Offers MA, MS, PhD. *Accreditation:* APA (one or more programs are accredited). *Faculty:* 45 full-time (16 women), 5 part-time/adjunct (2 women). *Students:* 61 full-time (34 women), 21 part-time (16 women); includes 10 minority (2 African Americans, 3 Asian Americans or Pacific Islanders, 5 Hispanic Americans), 11 international. Average age 27. 232 applicants, 9% accepted, 12 enrolled. In 2009, 7 master's, 5 doctorates awarded. Terminal master's awarded for partial completion of doctoral program. *Degree requirements:* For doctorate, comprehensive exam, thesis/dissertation. *Entrance requirements:* For master's, GRE General Test, minimum GPA of 3.0; for doctorate, GRE General Test; subject test strongly recommended, minimum GPA of 3.0. Additional exam requirements/recommendations for international students: Required—TOEFL (minimum score 500 paper-based; 173 computer-based; 61 iBT). *Application deadline:* For fall admission, 12/1 priority date for domestic students. Applications are processed on a rolling basis. Application fee: $45 ($60 for international students). Electronic applications accepted. *Financial support:* In 2009–10, 23 fellowships with full tuition reimbursements, 16 research assistantships with full tuition reimbursements, 37 teaching assistantships with full tuition reimbursements were awarded; career-related internships or fieldwork, institutionally sponsored loans, traineeships, health care benefits, and unspecified assistantships also available. *Faculty research:* Clinical psychology, cognition and neuroscience, developmental psychology, quantitative psychology and social/personality psychology, as well as a dual program in child clinical & developmental psychology. *Unit head:* Dr. Ann Bettencourt, Department Chair, E-mail: bettencourta@missouri.edu. *Application contact:* Linda Jacobs, Office Support Staff IV, 573-882-0838, E-mail: jacobsl@missouri.edu.

University of Missouri–Kansas City, College of Arts and Sciences, Department of Psychology, Kansas City, MO 64110-2499. Offers clinical psychology (PhD); community psychology (PhD); health psychology (PhD); psychology (MA). PhD (interdisciplinary) offered through the School of Graduate Studies. *Accreditation:* APA. *Faculty:* 12 full-time (9 women), 3 part-time/adjunct (2 women). *Students:* 15 full-time (12 women), 7 part-time (6 women); includes 2 minority (1 African American, 1 Hispanic American). Average age 31. 86 applicants, 3% accepted, 3 enrolled. In 2009, 4 master's, 4 doctorates awarded. Terminal master's awarded for partial completion of doctoral program. *Degree requirements:* For master's, thesis; for doctorate, comprehensive exam, thesis/dissertation, residency. *Entrance requirements:* For master's, GRE, minimum GPA of 3.5, letter of recommendation; for doctorate, GRE, minimum GPA of 3.25. Additional exam requirements/recommendations for international students: Required—TOEFL (minimum score 550 paper-based; 213 computer-based; 80 iBT). *Application deadline:* For fall admission, 1/15 for domestic and international students. Applications are processed on a rolling basis. Application fee: $45 ($50 for international students). Electronic applications accepted. *Expenses:* Tuition, state resident: full-time $5378; part-time $299 per credit hour. Tuition, nonresident: full-time $13,881; part-time $771 per credit hour. Required fees: $641; $71 per credit hour. Tuition and fees vary according to course load and program. *Financial support:* In 2009–10, 18 research assistantships (averaging $11,500 per year), 3 teaching assistantships (averaging $8,000 per year) were awarded; career-related internships or fieldwork, Federal Work-Study, and institutionally sponsored loans also available. Support available to part-time students. Financial award application deadline: 3/1; financial award applicants required to submit FAFSA. *Faculty research:* HIV/AIDS research group, psycho-oncology, sensory and cognitive neuroscience, cognitive psychophysiology, obesity and related metabolic disorders. Total annual research expenditures: $673,228. *Unit head:* Dr. Tamera Murdock, Chairperson/Professor, 816-235-1318, Fax: 816-235-1062, E-mail: murdockt@umkc.edu. *Application contact:* Dr. Lisa Terre, Director, Graduate Programs, 816-235-1318, Fax: 816-235-1062, E-mail: terrel@umkc.edu.

University of Missouri–St. Louis, College of Arts and Sciences, Department of Psychology, St. Louis, MO 63121. Offers behavioral neuroscience (PhD); clinical psychology respecialization (Certificate); community psychology (PhD); general psychology (MA); industrial/organizational psychology (PhD). *Accreditation:* APA (one or more programs are accredited). Evening/weekend programs available. *Faculty:* 21 full-time (10 women), 5 part-time/adjunct (3 women). *Students:* 35 full-time (29 women), 39 part-time (30 women); includes 4 minority (1 American Indian/Alaska Native, 1 Asian American or Pacific Islander, 2 Hispanic Americans). Average age 28. 208 applicants, 9% accepted, 13 enrolled. In 2009, 16 master's, 6 doctorates awarded. Terminal master's awarded for partial completion of doctoral program. *Degree requirements:* For master's, thesis; for doctorate, thesis/dissertation. *Entrance requirements:* For master's and doctorate, GRE General Test, GRE Subject Test, 3 letters of recommendation. Additional exam requirements/recommendations for international students: Required—TOEFL (minimum score 550 paper-based; 213 computer-based). *Application deadline:* For fall admission, 1/15 for domestic and international students. Application fee: $35 ($40 for international students). Electronic applications accepted. *Expenses:* Tuition, state resident: full-time $5377; part-time $297.70 per credit hour. Tuition, nonresident: full-time $13,882; part-time $771.20 per credit hour. Required fees: $220; $12.20 per credit hour. One-time fee: $12. Tuition and fees vary according to course level, campus/location and program. *Financial support:* In 2009–10, 7 research assistantships with full and partial tuition reimbursements (averaging $10,600 per year), 20 teaching assistantships with full and partial tuition reimbursements (averaging $9,788 per year) were awarded; fellowships with full tuition reimbursements also available. Financial award applicants required to submit FAFSA. *Faculty research:* Bereavement and loss, neuroscience, post-traumatic stress disorder, conflict and negotiation, social psychology. *Unit head:* Dr. George Taylor, Chair, 314-516-5391, Fax: 314-516-5392, E-mail: umslpsychology@msx.umsl.edu. *Application contact:* 314-516-5458, Fax: 314-516-6996, E-mail: gradadm@umsl.edu.

The University of Montana, Graduate School, College of Arts and Sciences, Department of Psychology, Missoula, MT 59812-0002. Offers clinical psychology (PhD); experimental psychology (PhD), including animal behavior psychology, developmental psychology; school psychology (MA, PhD, Ed S). *Accreditation:* APA (one or more programs are accredited). Terminal master's awarded for partial completion of doctoral program. *Degree requirements:* For master's, thesis; for doctorate, thesis/dissertation. *Entrance requirements:* For master's, doctorate, and Ed S, GRE General Test. Additional exam requirements/recommendations for international students: Required—TOEFL.

University of Nebraska at Omaha, Graduate Studies, College of Arts and Sciences, Department of Psychology, Omaha, NE 68182. Offers developmental psychology (PhD); industrial/organizational psychology (MS, PhD); psychobiology (PhD); psychology (MA); school psychology (MS, Ed S). Part-time programs available. *Faculty:* 18 full-time (8 women). *Students:* 44 full-time (36 women), 23 part-time (18 women); includes 3 minority (1 African American, 1 Asian American or Pacific Islander, 1 Hispanic American), 2 international. Average age 26. 116 applicants, 34% accepted, 28 enrolled. In 2009, 30 master's, 5 other advanced degrees awarded. *Degree requirements:* For master's, comprehensive exam, thesis (for some programs). *Entrance requirements:* For master's, GRE General Test, GRE Subject Test, previous course work in psychology, including statistics and a laboratory course; minimum GPA of 3.0, 3 letters of recommendation; for doctorate, GRE General Test. Additional exam requirements/recommendations for international students: Required—TOEFL (minimum score 500 paper-based; 173 computer-based; 61 iBT). *Application deadline:* For fall admission, 1/5 for domestic students. Application fee: $45. Electronic applications accepted. *Financial support:* In 2009–10, 44 students received support; fellowships, research assistantships with tuition reimbursements available, teaching assistantships with tuition reimbursements available, career-related internships or fieldwork, Federal Work-Study, institutionally sponsored loans, scholarships/grants, tuition waivers (partial), and unspecified assistantships available. Support available to part-time students. Financial award application deadline: 3/1; financial award applicants required to submit FAFSA. *Unit head:* Dr. Kenneth Deffenbacher, Chairperson, 402-554-2592. *Application contact:* Dr. Joseph Brown, Student Contact, 402-554-2592.

University of Nebraska–Lincoln, Graduate College, College of Arts and Sciences, Department of Psychology, Lincoln, NE 68588. Offers biopsychology (PhD); clinical psychology (PhD); cognitive psychology (PhD); developmental psychology (PhD); psychology (MA); social/personality psychology (PhD); JD/MA; JD/PhD. *Accreditation:* APA (one or more programs are accredited). *Degree requirements:* For master's, thesis optional; for doctorate, comprehensive exam, thesis/dissertation. *Entrance requirements:* For master's and doctorate, GRE General Test. Additional exam requirements/recommendations for international students: Required—TOEFL (minimum score 550 paper-based; 213 computer-based). Electronic applications accepted. *Faculty research:* Law and psychology, rural mental health, chronic mental illness, neuropsychology, child clinical psychology.

University of Nevada, Las Vegas, Graduate College, College of Liberal Arts, Department of Psychology, Las Vegas, NV 89154-5030. Offers PhD. *Accreditation:* APA. Part-time programs available. *Faculty:* 22 full-time (9 women), 4 part-time/adjunct (2 women). *Students:* 60 full-time (44 women), 18 part-time (12 women); includes 9 minority (3 African Americans, 2 American Indian/Alaska Native, 2 Asian Americans or Pacific Islanders, 2 Hispanic Americans), 3 international. Average age 32. 96 applicants, 11% accepted, 11 enrolled. In 2009, 10 doctorates awarded. *Degree requirements:* For doctorate, comprehensive exam, thesis/dissertation, oral defense of dissertation. *Entrance requirements:* For doctorate, GRE General and Subject Tests. Additional exam requirements/recommendations for international students: Required—TOEFL (minimum score 550 paper-based; 213 computer-based; 80 iBT), IELTS (minimum score 7). *Application deadline:* For fall admission, 12/15 priority date for domestic students, 5/1 for international students. Applications are processed on a rolling basis. Application fee: $60 ($95 for international students). Electronic applications accepted. *Financial support:* In 2009–10,

Psychology—General

University of Nevada, Las Vegas (continued)
55 students received support, including 10 research assistantships with partial tuition reimbursements available (averaging $12,000 per year), 45 teaching assistantships with partial tuition reimbursements available (averaging $12,000 per year); institutionally sponsored loans, scholarships/grants, health care benefits, and unspecified assistantships also available. Financial award application deadline: 3/1. *Faculty research:* Childhood anxiety disorders, text comprehension, infant face recognition, auditory perception in schizophrenia, treatment of substance abuse. *Unit head:* Dr. Mark Ashcraft, Chair/ Professor, 702-895-3305, Fax: 702-895-0195, E-mail: mark.ashcraft@unlv.edu. *Application contact:* Graduate College Admissions Evaluator, 702-895-3320, Fax: 702-895-4180, E-mail: gradcollege@unlv.edu.

University of Nevada, Reno, Graduate School, College of Liberal Arts, Department of Psychology, Reno, NV 89557. Offers behavior analysis (MA, PhD); clinical psychology (MA, PhD); cognitive brain science (MA, PhD). *Accreditation:* APA (one or more programs are accredited). Terminal master's awarded for partial completion of doctoral program. *Degree requirements:* For master's, thesis optional; for doctorate, thesis/dissertation. *Entrance requirements:* For master's, GRE General Test, GRE Subject Test, minimum GPA of 2.75; for doctorate, GRE General Test, GRE Subject Test, minimum GPA of 3.0. Additional exam requirements/recommendations for international students: Required—TOEFL (minimum score 500 paper-based; 173 computer-based; 61 iBT), IELTS (minimum score 6). Electronic applications accepted. *Faculty research:* Cognitive psychology, social psychological theory, animal and human intelligence, psychotherapy outcome, perception.

University of New Brunswick Fredericton, School of Graduate Studies, Faculty of Arts, Department of Psychology, Fredericton, NB E3B 5A3, Canada. Offers clinical (PhD); experimental (MA). Part-time programs available. *Faculty:* 14 full-time (9 women). *Students:* 25 full-time (20 women), 2 part-time (both women). In 2009, 4 doctorates awarded. *Degree requirements:* For doctorate, comprehensive exam, thesis/dissertation. *Entrance requirements:* For doctorate, GRE General Test, GRE Subject Test, minimum GPA of 3.7. Additional exam requirements/recommendations for international students: Required—TOEFL (minimum score 600 paper-based). *Application deadline:* For fall admission, 1/15 priority date for domestic and international students. Application fee: $50 Canadian dollars. Tuition and fees charges are reported in Canadian dollars. *Expenses:* Tuition, area resident: Full-time $5562 Canadian dollars; part-time $2781 Canadian dollars per year. Required fees: $49.75 Canadian dollars per term. *Financial support:* In 2009–10, 8 fellowships (averaging $35,000 per year), 15 research assistantships (averaging $11,000 per year), 15 teaching assistantships (averaging $4,000 per year) were awarded. Financial award application deadline: 1/15. *Faculty research:* Depression, adolescence, human sexuality, family violence, autism. *Unit head:* Dr. Daniel Voyer, Director of Graduate Studies, 506-453-7974, Fax: 506-447-3063, E-mail: psycdogs@unb.ca. *Application contact:* Theresa Mills, Graduate Secretary, 506-453-4707, Fax: 506-447-3063, E-mail: tmills@unb.ca.

University of New Brunswick Saint John, Department of Psychology, Saint John, NB E2L 4L5, Canada. Offers applied and experimental psychology (PhD); clinical psychology (PhD); experimental psychology (MA). Part-time programs available. *Faculty:* 9 full-time (4 women). *Students:* 4 full-time (2 women), 1 (woman) part-time. In 2009, 3 master's, 1 doctorate awarded. *Degree requirements:* For master's, thesis. *Entrance requirements:* For master's, GRE General and Subject Tests, honours thesis. Additional exam requirements/recommendations for international students: Required—TOEFL (minimum score 550 paper-based), TWE. *Application deadline:* For fall admission, 2/1 for domestic students. Application fee: $50. *Financial support:* In 2009–10, 4 research assistantships (averaging $9,000 per year), 4 teaching assistantships (averaging $4,500 per year) were awarded; unspecified assistantships also available. Support available to part-time students. Financial award application deadline: 2/1. *Faculty research:* Psychopharmacology and addictions, forensic psychology and criminal justice, interpersonal relations, perception and graphical perception, lie detection. *Unit head:* Dr. Lily Both, Director of Graduate Studies, 506-648-5769, Fax: 506-648-5780, E-mail: lboth@unbsj.ca. *Application contact:* Frances Stevens, Secretary, 506-648-5640, Fax: 506-648-5780, E-mail: fstevens@unb.ca.

University of New Hampshire, Graduate School, College of Liberal Arts, Department of Psychology, Durham, NH 03824. Offers PhD. *Faculty:* 23 full-time (7 women). *Students:* 24 full-time (17 women), 6 part-time (4 women), 2 international. Average age 27. 86 applicants, 17% accepted, 6 enrolled. In 2009, 5 doctorates awarded. *Degree requirements:* For doctorate, thesis/dissertation. *Entrance requirements:* For doctorate, GRE General Test, GRE Subject Test. Additional exam requirements/recommendations for international students: Required—TOEFL (minimum score 550 paper-based; 213 computer-based; 80 iBT). *Application deadline:* For fall admission, 6/15 priority date for domestic students, 4/15 for international students; for spring admission, 12/1 for domestic students. Applications are processed on a rolling basis. Application fee: $65. Electronic applications accepted. *Expenses:* Tuition, state resident: full-time $10,380; part-time $577 per credit hour. Tuition, nonresident: full-time $24,350; part-time $1002 per credit hour. Required fees: $1550; $387.50 per semester. Tuition and fees vary according to course load and program. *Financial support:* In 2009–10, 29 students received support, including 2 fellowships, 27 teaching assistantships; research assistantships, career-related internships or fieldwork, Federal Work-Study, scholarships/grants, and tuition waivers (full and partial) also available. Support available to part-time students. Financial award application deadline: 2/15. *Faculty research:* History of psychology; cognition and perception; learning, developmental, physiological, and social psychology. *Unit head:* Dr. Robert Mair, Chairperson, 603-862-3198. *Application contact:* Donna Hardy, Administrative Assistant, 603-862-3167, E-mail: psychology.ph.d@unh.edu.

University of New Mexico, Graduate School, College of Arts and Sciences, Department of Psychology, Albuquerque, NM 87131-2039. Offers clinical psychology (MS, PhD); psychology (PhD). *Accreditation:* APA (one or more programs are accredited). *Faculty:* 28 full-time (12 women), 8 part-time/adjunct (2 women). *Students:* 71 full-time (51 women), 8 part-time (5 women); includes 11 minority (all Hispanic Americans), 9 international. Average age 31. 159 applicants, 9% accepted, 12 enrolled. In 2009, 12 master's, 7 doctorates awarded. Terminal master's awarded for partial completion of doctoral program. *Degree requirements:* For master's, thesis; for doctorate, comprehensive exam, thesis/dissertation, pre-doctoral internship. *Entrance requirements:* For doctorate, GRE General Test, GRE Subject Test (psychology), minimum GPA of 3.0. Additional exam requirements/recommendations for international students: Required—TOEFL. *Application deadline:* For fall admission, 1/15 priority date for domestic and international students. Applications are processed on a rolling basis. Application fee: $50. Electronic applications accepted. *Expenses:* Tuition, state resident: full-time $2099; part-time $233.20 per credit hour. Tuition, nonresident: full-time $6650. Required fees: $25 per semester. Tuition and fees vary according to course load, program and reciprocity agreements. *Financial support:* In 2009–10, 39 students received support, including research assistantships with full and partial tuition reimbursements available (averaging $13,445 per year), teaching assistantships with full and partial tuition reimbursements available (averaging $13,445 per year); fellowships, career-related internships or fieldwork, Federal Work-Study, institutionally sponsored loans, scholarships/grants, health care benefits, tuition waivers (full and partial), and unspecified assistantships also available. Financial award application deadline: 3/1; financial award applicants required to submit FAFSA. *Faculty research:* Addictions, clinical, cognition, brain and behavior, developmental, evolutionary, functional neuroimaging, health psychology, learning and memory, neuropsychology. Total annual research expenditures: $953,743. *Unit head:* Dr. Jane Ellen Smith, Chair, 505-277-4121, Fax: 505-277-1394, E-mail: janellen@unm.edu. *Application contact:* Program Advisement Coordinator, 505-277-5009, Fax: 505-277-1394.

University of New Orleans, Graduate School, College of Sciences, Department of Psychology, New Orleans, LA 70148. Offers MS, PhD. *Degree requirements:* For doctorate, thesis/dissertation. *Entrance requirements:* For doctorate, GRE General Test, minimum GPA of 3.0, 21 hours of course work in psychology. Additional exam requirements/recommendations for international students: Required—TOEFL (minimum score 550 paper-based; 213 computer-based; 79 iBT). Electronic applications accepted. *Faculty research:* Biofeedback, visual and auditory perception, psychopharmacology, neuropeptides.

The University of North Carolina at Chapel Hill, Graduate School, College of Arts and Sciences, Department of Psychology, Chapel Hill, NC 27599. Offers biological psychology (PhD); clinical psychology (PhD); cognitive psychology (PhD); developmental psychology (PhD); quantitative psychology (PhD); social psychology (PhD). *Accreditation:* APA. *Degree requirements:* For doctorate, comprehensive exam, thesis/dissertation. *Entrance requirements:* For doctorate, GRE General Test, minimum GPA of 3.0. Electronic applications accepted. *Faculty research:* Expressed emotion, cognitive development, social cognitive neuroscience, human memory personality.

The University of North Carolina at Charlotte, Graduate School, College of Arts and Sciences, Department of Psychology, Charlotte, NC 28223-0001. Offers community/clinical psychology (MA); health psychology (PhD); industrial/organizational psychology (MA); organizational science (PhD). Part-time programs available. *Faculty:* 30 full-time (12 women), 1 part-time/adjunct (0 women). *Students:* 41 full-time (34 women), 23 part-time (20 women); includes 7 African Americans, 1 Asian American or Pacific Islander, 6 Hispanic Americans. Average age 28. 279 applicants, 10% accepted, 15 enrolled. In 2009, 21 master's awarded. *Degree requirements:* For master's, thesis. *Entrance requirements:* For master's, GRE General Test, GRE Subject Test, minimum GPA of 3.0 in undergraduate major, 2.8 overall. Additional exam requirements/recommendations for international students: Required—TOEFL (minimum score 557 paper-based; 220 computer-based; 83 iBT). *Application deadline:* Applications are processed on a rolling basis. Application fee: $55. Electronic applications accepted. *Financial support:* In 2009–10, 40 students received support, including 8 research assistantships (averaging $17,750 per year), 30 teaching assistantships (averaging $10,754 per year); career-related internships or fieldwork, Federal Work-Study, institutionally sponsored loans, scholarships/grants, and administrative assistantships also available. Support available to part-time students. Financial award application deadline: 4/1; financial award applicants required to submit FAFSA. *Faculty research:* Health psychology, industrial-organizational psychology, cognitive science. Total annual research expenditures: $476,892. *Unit head:* Dr. Brian L. Cutler, Chair, 704-687-4731, Fax: 704-687-3096, E-mail: blcutler@uncc.edu. *Application contact:* Kathy B. Giddings, Director of Graduate Admissions, 704-687-5503, Fax: 704-687-3279, E-mail: gradadm@uncc.edu.

The University of North Carolina at Greensboro, Graduate School, College of Arts and Sciences, Department of Psychology, Greensboro, NC 27412-5001. Offers clinical psychology (MA, PhD); cognitive psychology (MA, PhD); developmental psychology (MA, PhD); social psychology (MA, PhD). *Accreditation:* APA (one or more programs are accredited). Terminal master's awarded for partial completion of doctoral program. *Degree requirements:* For master's, comprehensive exam, thesis; for doctorate, one foreign language, thesis/dissertation, preliminary exam. *Entrance requirements:* For master's and doctorate, GRE General Test. Additional exam requirements/recommendations for international students: Required—TOEFL. Electronic applications accepted. *Faculty research:* Sensory and perceptual determinants; evoked potential: disorders, deafness, and development.

The University of North Carolina Wilmington, College of Arts and Sciences, Department of Psychology, Wilmington, NC 28403-3297. Offers MA. Part-time programs available. *Degree requirements:* For master's, comprehensive exam, thesis. *Entrance requirements:* For master's, GRE General Test, GRE Subject Test, minimum B average in undergraduate major. Additional exam requirements/recommendations for international students: Required—TOEFL (minimum score 550 paper-based; 217 computer-based; 79 iBT), IELTS (minimum score 6.5).

University of North Dakota, Graduate School, College of Arts and Sciences, Department of Psychology, Grand Forks, ND 58202. Offers clinical psychology (PhD); counseling psychology (PhD); experimental psychology (PhD); forensic psychology (MA, MS); psychology (MA). *Accreditation:* APA (one or more programs are accredited). *Degree requirements:* For master's, thesis, final exam; for doctorate, comprehensive exam, thesis/dissertation, internship, final exam. *Entrance requirements:* For master's, GRE General Test, GRE Subject Test, minimum GPA of 3.0; for doctorate, GRE General Test, GRE Subject Test, minimum GPA of 3.5. Additional exam requirements/recommendations for international students: Required—TOEFL (minimum score 550 paper-based; 213 computer-based; 79 iBT), IELTS (minimum score 6.5). Electronic applications accepted. *Faculty research:* Developmental psychology, clinical social psychology, educational psychology, personality disorders.

University of Northern British Columbia, Office of Graduate Studies, Prince George, BC V2N 4Z9, Canada. Offers business administration (Diploma); community health science (M Sc); disability management (MA); education (M Ed); first nations studies (MA); gender studies (MA); history (MA); interdisciplinary studies (MA); international studies (MA); mathematical, computer and physical sciences (M Sc); natural resources and environmental studies (M Sc, MA, MNRES, PhD); political science (MA); psychology (M Sc, PhD); social work (MSW). Part-time and evening/weekend programs available. Postbaccalaureate distance learning degree programs offered (no on-campus study). *Degree requirements:* For master's, thesis; for doctorate, thesis/dissertation. *Entrance requirements:* For master's, GRE, minimum B average in undergraduate course work; for doctorate, candidacy exam, minimum A average in graduate course work.

University of Northern Colorado, Graduate School, College of Education and Behavioral Sciences, School of Psychological Sciences, Greeley, CO 80639. Offers MA, PhD. Part-time programs available. *Faculty:* 15 full-time (6 women). *Students:* 23 full-time (11 women), 16 part-time (14 women); includes 3 minority (1 Asian American or Pacific Islander, 2 Hispanic Americans), 8 international. Average age 33. 11 applicants, 91% accepted, 8 enrolled. In 2009, 6 master's, 4 doctorates awarded. *Degree requirements:* For master's, comprehensive exam, thesis or alternative; for doctorate, comprehensive exam, thesis/dissertation. *Entrance requirements:* For master's and doctorate, GRE General Test, letters of recommendation. *Application deadline:* Applications are processed on a rolling basis. Application fee: $50 ($60 for international students). Electronic applications accepted. *Expenses:* Tuition, state resident: full-time $5770; part-time $320.55 per credit hour. Tuition, nonresident: full-time $13,847; part-time $769.27 per credit hour. Required fees: $948.78; $52.72 per credit. *Financial support:* In 2009–10, 5 research assistantships (averaging $3,418 per year), 8 teaching assistantships (averaging $4,898 per year) were awarded; fellowships, unspecified assistantships also available. Financial award application deadline: 3/1; financial award applicants required to submit FAFSA. *Unit head:* Dr. Mark Alcorn, Director, 970-351-2957, Fax: 970-351-1103. *Application contact:* Linda Sisson, Graduate Student Admission Coordinator, 970-351-1807, Fax: 970-351-2371, E-mail: linda.sisson@unco.edu.

University of Northern Iowa, Graduate College, College of Social and Behavioral Sciences, Department of Psychology, Cedar Falls, IA 50614. Offers MA. Part-time programs available. *Students:* 33 full-time (19 women); includes 1 minority (African American), 2 international. 97 applicants, 34% accepted, 18 enrolled. In 2009, 13 master's awarded. *Degree requirements:* For master's, comprehensive exam, thesis. *Entrance requirements:* For master's, GRE, minimum GPA of 3.0, 3 letters of recommendation. Additional exam requirements/recommendations for international students: Required—TOEFL (minimum score 500 paper-based; 180 computer-based; 61 iBT). *Application deadline:* For fall admission, 4/30 for domestic students. Applications are processed on a rolling basis. Application fee: $30 ($50 for international students). Electronic applications accepted. *Financial support:* Career-related internships or fieldwork, Federal Work-Study, and tuition waivers (full and partial) available. Support available to part-time students. Financial award application deadline: 2/1. *Unit head:* Dr. Carolyn Hildebrandt, Interim Department Head/Professor, 319-273-7179, Fax: 319-273-6188, E-mail: carolyn.hildebrandt@uni.edu. *Application contact:* Laurie S. Russell, Record Analyst, 319-273-2623, Fax: 319-273-6792, E-mail: laurie.russell@uni.edu.

University of North Florida, College of Arts and Sciences, Department of Psychology, Jacksonville, FL 32224. Offers counseling psychology (MAC); general psychology (MA). Part-time and evening/weekend programs available. *Faculty:* 14 full-time (5 women). *Students:* 61 full-time (37 women), 7 part-time (5 women); includes 10 minority (4 African Americans, 1 American Indian/Alaska Native, 5 Hispanic Americans). Average age 27. 110 applicants, 25% accepted, 15 enrolled. In 2009, 15 master's awarded. *Degree requirements:* For master's, comprehensive exam, thesis optional, practicum. *Entrance requirements:* For master's, GRE General Test, 2 letters of recommendation, minimum GPA of 3.0 in last 60 hours of course work. Additional exam requirements/recommendations for international students: Required—TOEFL (minimum score 500 paper-based; 173 computer-based). *Application deadline:* For fall admission, 6/1 priority date for domestic students, 4/1 for international students. Applications are processed on a rolling basis. Application fee: $30. Electronic applications accepted. *Expenses:* Tuition, state resident: full-time $6649.20; part-time $277.05 per credit hour. Tuition, nonresident: full-time $22,970; part-time $957.08 per credit hour. Required fees: $985; $41.03 per credit hour. *Financial support:* In 2009–10, 45 students received support, including 3 research assistantships (averaging $2,476 per year), 4 teaching assistantships (averaging $3,499 per year); Federal Work-Study and tuition waivers (partial) also available. Support available to part-time students. Financial award application deadline: 4/1; financial award applicants required to submit FAFSA. *Faculty research:* Sensory perception, social cognition, sexual behavior, evolutionary psychology, psychology and law. Total annual research expenditures: $89,642. *Unit head:* Dr. Michael Toglia, Chair, 904-620-1624, E-mail: m.toglia@unf.edu. *Application contact:* Dr. Randy Russac, Graduate Coordinator for General Psychology, 904-620-2807, Fax: 904-620-3814, E-mail: rrussac@unf.edu.

University of North Texas, Robert B. Toulouse School of Graduate Studies, College of Arts and Sciences, Department of Psychology, Denton, TX 76203-5017. Offers clinical psychology (PhD); counseling psychology (MA, MS, PhD); experimental psychology (MA, MS, PhD); health psychology and behavioral medicine (PhD). *Accreditation:* APA (one or more programs are accredited). Terminal master's awarded for partial completion of doctoral program. *Degree requirements:* For master's, comprehensive exam, thesis or alternative; for doctorate, one foreign language, comprehensive exam, thesis/dissertation. *Entrance requirements:* For master's and doctorate, GRE General Test, interview. Additional exam requirements/recommendations for international students: Required—proof of English language proficiency required for non-native English speakers; Recommended—TOEFL (minimum score 550 paper-based; 213 computer-based; 79 iBT). *Application deadline:* Applications are processed on a rolling basis. Application fee: $50 ($75 for international students). Electronic applications accepted. *Expenses:* Tuition, state resident: full-time $4298; part-time $239 per contact hour. Tuition, nonresident: full-time $9878; part-time $549 per contact hour. Required fees: $265 per contact hour. *Financial support:* Fellowships, research assistantships, teaching assistantships, career-related internships or fieldwork, Federal Work-Study, and institutionally sponsored loans available. Financial award applicants required to submit FAFSA. *Application contact:* Graduate Coordinator, 940-565-2671, Fax: 940-565-4682, E-mail: amym@unt.edu.

University of North Texas, Robert B. Toulouse School of Graduate Studies, College of Public Affairs and Community Service, Department of Behavior Analysis, Denton, TX 76203. Offers MS. *Accreditation:* APA. *Degree requirements:* For master's, thesis. *Entrance requirements:* For master's, GRE General Test. Additional exam requirements/recommendations for international students: Required—proof of English language proficiency required for non-native English speakers; Recommended—TOEFL (minimum score 550 paper-based; 213 computer-based; 79 iBT). *Application deadline:* Applications are processed on a rolling basis. Application fee: $50 ($75 for international students). Electronic applications accepted. *Expenses:* Tuition, state resident: full-time $4298; part-time $239 per contact hour. Tuition, nonresident: full-time $9878; part-time $549 per contact hour. Required fees: $265 per contact hour. *Financial support:* Fellowships, teaching assistantships, career-related internships or fieldwork, Federal Work-Study, scholarships/grants, and tuition waivers (partial) available. Support available to part-time students. Financial award applicants required to submit FAFSA. *Faculty research:* Human operant research, applied behavior analysis, animal training, autism. *Application contact:* Graduate Advisor, 940-369-7961, Fax: 940-565-2467, E-mail: manish.vaidya@unt.edu.

University of Notre Dame, Graduate School, College of Arts and Letters, Division of Social Science, Department of Psychology, Notre Dame, IN 46556. Offers cognitive psychology (PhD); counseling psychology (PhD); developmental psychology (PhD); quantitative psychology (PhD). *Accreditation:* APA. *Degree requirements:* For doctorate, comprehensive exam, thesis/dissertation, candidacy exam. *Entrance requirements:* For doctorate, GRE General Test, GRE Subject Test (strongly recommended). Additional exam requirements/recommendations for international students: Required—TOEFL (minimum score 600 paper-based; 250 computer-based; 80 iBT). Electronic applications accepted. *Faculty research:* Cognitive and socio-emotional development, statistical methods and quantitative models applicable to psychology, interpersonal relations, life span development and developmental delay, childhood depression, structural equation and dynamical systems.

University of Oklahoma, Graduate College, College of Arts and Sciences, Department of Psychology, Norman, OK 73019. Offers organizational dynamics (MS); psychology (MS, PhD). *Faculty:* 24 full-time (12 women), 1 part-time/adjunct (0 women). *Students:* 72 full-time (34 women), 34 part-time (21 women); includes 15 minority (5 African Americans, 5 American Indian/Alaska Native, 1 Asian American or Pacific Islander, 4 Hispanic Americans), 5 international. 75 applicants, 28% accepted, 17 enrolled. In 2009, 17 master's, 10 doctorates awarded. Terminal master's awarded for partial completion of doctoral program. *Degree requirements:* For master's, thesis or alternative; for doctorate, thesis/dissertation, general exam. *Entrance requirements:* For master's, GRE General Test, GRE Subject Test, minimum GPA of 3.0, 3 letters of recommendation; for doctorate, GRE General Test, GRE Subject Test, 3 letters of recommendation. Additional exam requirements/recommendations for international students: Required—TOEFL (minimum score 550 paper-based; 213 computer-based). *Application deadline:* For fall admission, 4/1 priority date for domestic students, 4/1 for international students; for spring admission, 11/1 for domestic students, 9/1 for international students. Applications are processed on a rolling basis. Application fee: $40 ($90 for international students). Electronic applications accepted. *Expenses:* Tuition, state resident: full-time $3744; part-time $156 per credit hour. Tuition, nonresident: full-time $13,577; part-time $565.70 per credit hour. Required fees: $2415; $90.10 per credit hour. *Financial support:* In 2009–10, 75 students received support, including 16 fellowships with full tuition reimbursements available (averaging $5,742 per year), 9 research assistantships with partial tuition reimbursements available (averaging $12,876 per year), 38 teaching assistantships with partial tuition reimbursements available (averaging $13,951 per year); scholarships/grants, health care benefits, and unspecified assistantships also available. Financial award application deadline: 3/1; financial award applicants required to submit FAFSA. *Faculty research:* Industrial organizational psychology including leadership and creativity; cognitive psychology with an emphasis in modeling, memory, and decision science; quantitative methods (measurement, modeling, and statistics); social psychology (self and stereotype thinking); personality and animal behavior. Total annual research expenditures: $1.6 million. *Unit head:* Dr. Jorge Mendoza, Chair, 405-325-4511, Fax: 405-325-4737, E-mail: jmendoza@ou.edu. *Application contact:* Kathryn Paine, Graduate Admissions Coordinator, 405-325-4512, Fax: 405-325-4737, E-mail: kpaine@ou.edu.

University of Oregon, Graduate School, College of Arts and Sciences, Department of Psychology, Eugene, OR 97403. Offers clinical psychology (PhD); cognitive psychology (MA, MS, PhD); developmental psychology (MA, MS, PhD); physiological psychology (MA, MS, PhD); psychology (MA, MS, PhD); social/personality psychology (MA, MS, PhD). *Accreditation:* APA (one or more programs are accredited). Terminal master's awarded for partial completion of doctoral program. *Degree requirements:* For doctorate, thesis/dissertation. *Entrance requirements:* For master's, GRE General Test, minimum GPA of 3.0; for doctorate, GRE General Test. Additional exam requirements/recommendations for international students: Required—TOEFL.

University of Ottawa, Faculty of Graduate and Postdoctoral Studies, Faculty of Social Sciences, School of Psychology, Ottawa, ON K1N 6N5, Canada. Offers PhD. *Accreditation:* APA. *Degree requirements:* For doctorate, thesis/dissertation. *Entrance requirements:* For doctorate, minimum B+ average. Electronic applications accepted. *Faculty research:* Behavioral neuroscience, social psychology, developmental psychology, cognition.

University of Pennsylvania, School of Arts and Sciences, Graduate Group in Psychology, Philadelphia, PA 19104. Offers PhD. *Accreditation:* APA. *Faculty:* 64 full-time (20 women), 10 part-time/adjunct (3 women). *Students:* 51 full-time (31 women), 1 (woman) part-time; includes 3 minority (2 Asian Americans or Pacific Islanders, 1 Hispanic American), 11 international. 443 applicants, 5% accepted, 8 enrolled. In 2009, 10 doctorates awarded. *Degree requirements:* For doctorate, thesis/dissertation. *Entrance requirements:* For doctorate, GRE General Test, GRE Subject Test. Additional exam requirements/recommendations for international students: Required—TOEFL. *Application deadline:* For fall admission, 12/1 priority date for domestic students. Application fee: $70. Electronic applications accepted. *Expenses:* Tuition: Full-time $25,660; part-time $4758 per course. Required fees: $2152; $270 per course. Tuition and fees vary according to course load, degree level and program. *Financial support:* In 2009–10, 10 fellowships, 2 research assistantships, 20 teaching assistantships were awarded; institutionally sponsored loans, scholarships/grants, traineeships, health care benefits, and unspecified assistantships also available. Financial award application deadline: 12/15. *Faculty research:* Cognitive psychology, sensation and perception, biological psychology, clinical psychology, social psychology.

University of Phoenix, The Artemis School, College of Health and Human Services, Phoenix, AZ 85034-7209. Offers administration of justice and security (MS); community counseling (MSC); education (MHA); family nurse practitioner (MSN); gerontology (MHA); health administration (MHA); health care education (MSN); health care management (MBA, MSN); informatics (MHA); marriage, family, and child therapy (MSC); nursing (MSN); nursing for nurse practitioners (MSN); psychology (MS); MSN/MBA; MSN/MHA. *Accreditation:* AACN. Evening/weekend programs available. Postbaccalaureate distance learning degree programs offered. *Degree requirements:* For master's, thesis (for some programs). *Entrance requirements:* For master's, 3 years of work experience, minimum undergraduate GPA of 2.5, RN license. Additional exam requirements/recommendations for international students: Required—TOEFL (minimum score 550 paper-based; 213 computer-based; 79 iBT). Electronic applications accepted.

University of Phoenix–Austin Campus, College of Social and Behavioral Science, Austin, TX 78759. Offers administration of justice and security (MS); psychology (MS). Postbaccalaureate distance learning degree programs offered.

University of Phoenix–Birmingham Campus, College of Social and Behavioral Science, Birmingham, AL 35244. Offers administration of justice and security (MS); psychology (MS).

University of Phoenix–Chattanooga Campus, College of Social and Behavioral Science, Chattanooga, TN 37421-3707. Offers administration of justice and security (MS); psychology (MSP). Postbaccalaureate distance learning degree programs offered.

University of Phoenix–Cheyenne Campus, College of Social and Behavioral Science, Cheyenne, WY 82009. Offers administration of justice and security (MS); psychology (MS). Postbaccalaureate distance learning degree programs offered.

University of Phoenix–Cincinnati Campus, The Artemis School, College of Health and Human Services, West Chester, OH 45069-4875. Offers administration of justice and security (MS); health care management (MBA); nursing (MSN); psychology (MS). Evening/weekend programs available. Postbaccalaureate distance learning degree programs offered. *Degree requirements:* For master's, thesis (for some programs). *Entrance requirements:* For master's, minimum undergraduate GPA of 2.5, 3 years of work experience. Additional exam requirements/recommendations for international students: Required—TOEFL (minimum score 550 paper-based; 79 iBT). Electronic applications accepted.

University of Phoenix–Cleveland Campus, The Artemis School, College of Health and Human Services, Independence, OH 44131-2194. Offers administration of justice and security (MS); health care management (MBA); nursing (MSN); psychology (MS). Evening/weekend programs available. Postbaccalaureate distance learning degree programs offered. *Degree requirements:* For master's, thesis (for some programs). *Entrance requirements:* For master's, minimum undergraduate GPA of 2.5, 3 years of work experience. Additional exam requirements/recommendations for international students: Required—TOEFL (minimum score 550 paper-based; 213 computer-based; 79 iBT). Electronic applications accepted.

University of Phoenix–Columbus Ohio Campus, The Artemis School, College of Health and Human Services, Columbus, OH 43240-4032. Offers administration of justice and security (MS); health care management (MBA); nursing (MSN); psychology (MS). Evening/weekend programs available. Postbaccalaureate distance learning degree programs offered. *Degree requirements:* For master's, thesis (for some programs). *Entrance requirements:* For master's, minimum undergraduate GPA of 2.5, 3 years work experience. Additional exam requirements/recommendations for international students: Required—TOEFL (minimum score 550 paper-based; 213 computer-based; 79 iBT). Electronic applications accepted.

University of Phoenix–Dallas Campus, The Artemis School, College of Health and Human Services, Dallas, TX 75251-2009. Offers administration of justice and security (MS); health administration (MHA); health care management (MBA); psychology (MS). Postbaccalaureate distance learning degree programs offered. *Degree requirements:* For master's, thesis (for some programs). *Entrance requirements:* For master's, minimum undergraduate GPA of 2.5, 3 years of work experience. Additional exam requirements/recommendations for international students: Required—TOEFL (minimum score 550 paper-based; 213 computer-based; 79 iBT). Electronic applications accepted.

University of Phoenix–Denver Campus, The Artemis School, College of Health and Human Services, Lone Tree, CO 80124-5453. Offers administration of justice and security (MS); community counseling (MSC); health administration (MHA); health care management (MBA); marriage, family and child therapy (MSC); nursing (MSN); psychology (MS); MSN/MBA; MSN/MHA. Evening/weekend programs available. Postbaccalaureate distance learning degree programs offered. *Degree requirements:* For master's, thesis (for some programs). *Entrance requirements:* For master's, minimum undergraduate GPA of 2.5, 3 years work experience, RN license. Additional exam requirements/recommendations for international students: Required—TOEFL (minimum score 550 paper-based; 213 computer-based; 79 iBT). Electronic applications accepted.

University of Phoenix–Harrisburg Campus, College of Social and Behavioral Science, Harrisburg, PA 17112. Offers administration of justice and security (MS); psychology (MS). Postbaccalaureate distance learning degree programs offered.

University of Phoenix–Hawaii Campus, The Artemis School, College of Health and Human Services, Honolulu, HI 96813-4317. Offers administration of justice and security (MS); community counseling (MSC); education (MHA); family nurse practitioner (MSN); gerontology (MHA); health administration (MHA); health care management (MBA); marriage, family and child therapy (MSC); nursing (MSN); nursing/health care education (MSN); psychology (MS); MSN/MBA. Evening/weekend programs available. *Degree requirements:* For master's, thesis (for some programs). *Entrance requirements:* For master's, minimum undergraduate GPA of 2.5, 3 years of work experience, RN license. Additional exam requirements/recommendations for international students: Required—TOEFL (minimum score 550 paper-based; 213 computer-based; 79 iBT). Electronic applications accepted.

University of Phoenix–Houston Campus, The Artemis School, College of Health and Human Services, Houston, TX 77079-2004. Offers administration of justice and security (MS); health administration (MHA); health care management (MBA); psychology (MS). Postbaccalaureate distance learning degree programs offered. *Degree requirements:* For master's, thesis (for some programs). *Entrance requirements:* For master's, minimum undergraduate GPA of 2.5, 3

Psychology—General

University of Phoenix–Houston Campus (continued)
years of work experience. Additional exam requirements/recommendations for international students: Required—TOEFL (minimum score 550 paper-based; 213 computer-based; 79 iBT). Electronic applications accepted.

University of Phoenix–Idaho Campus, The Artemis School, College of Health and Human Services, Meridian, ID 83642-3014. Offers administration of justice and security (MS); health administration (MHA); health care management (MBA); nursing (MSN); nursing/health care education (MSN); psychology (MS); MSN/MBA. Evening/weekend programs available. Postbaccalaureate distance learning degree programs offered. *Degree requirements:* For master's, thesis (for some programs). *Entrance requirements:* For master's, minimum undergraduate GPA of 2.5, 3 years of work experience. Additional exam requirements/recommendations for international students: Required—TOEFL (minimum score 550 paper-based; 213 computer-based). Electronic applications accepted.

University of Phoenix–Indianapolis Campus, The Artemis School, College of Health and Human Services, Indianapolis, IN 46250-932. Offers administration of justice and security (MS); health administration (MHA); health care management (MBA); nursing (MSN); nursing/health care education (MSN); psychology (MS); MSN/MBA; MSN/MHA. Evening/weekend programs available. Postbaccalaureate distance learning degree programs offered. *Degree requirements:* For master's, thesis. *Entrance requirements:* For master's, 3 years work experience, minimum undergraduate GPA of 2.5. Additional exam requirements/recommendations for international students: Required—TOEFL (minimum score 500 paper-based; 213 computer-based). Electronic applications accepted.

University of Phoenix–Jersey City Campus, College of Social and Behavioral Science, Jersey City, NJ 07310. Offers administration of justice and security (MS); psychology (MS). Postbaccalaureate distance learning degree programs offered.

University of Phoenix–Las Vegas Campus, The Artemis School, College of Health and Human Services, Las Vegas, NV 89128. Offers administration of justice and security (MS); health administration (MHA); health care management (MBA); marriage, family, and child therapy (MSC); mental health counseling (MSC); nursing (MSN); nursing/health care education (MSN); psychology (MS); MSN/MBA; MSN/MHA. Postbaccalaureate distance learning degree programs offered. *Entrance requirements:* For master's, minimum undergraduate GPA of 2.5, 3 years of work experience. Additional exam requirements/recommendations for international students: Required—TOEFL (minimum score 550 paper-based; 213 computer-based; 79 iBT). Electronic applications accepted.

University of Phoenix–Louisiana Campus, The Artemis School, College of Health and Human Services, Metairie, LA 70001-2082. Offers administration of justice and security (MS); health administration (MHA); health care management (MBA); nursing (MSN); psychology (MS); MSN/MBA. Evening/weekend programs available. Postbaccalaureate distance learning degree programs offered (no on-campus study). *Degree requirements:* For master's, thesis (for some programs). *Entrance requirements:* For master's, minimum undergraduate GPA of 2.5, 3 years work experience, RN license. Additional exam requirements/recommendations for international students: Required—TOEFL (minimum score 550 paper-based; 213 computer-based; 79 iBT). Electronic applications accepted.

University of Phoenix–Maryland Campus, The Artemis School, College of Health and Human Services, Columbia, MD 21045-5424. Offers administration of justice and security (MS); health administration (MHA); health care education (MSN); health care management (MBA); nursing (MSN); psychology (MS); MSN/MBA; MSN/MHA. Evening/weekend programs available. *Degree requirements:* For master's, thesis (for some programs). *Entrance requirements:* For master's, minimum undergraduate GPA of 2.5, 3 years work experience. Additional exam requirements/recommendations for international students: Required—TOEFL (minimum score 550 paper-based; 213 computer-based; 79 iBT). Electronic applications accepted.

University of Phoenix–New Mexico Campus, The Artemis School, College of Health and Human Services, Albuquerque, NM 87113-1570. Offers administration of justice and security (MS); health administration (MHA); health care education (MSN); health care management (MBA); marriage and family therapy (MSC); nursing (MSN); psychology (MS); MSN/MBA. Evening/weekend programs available. *Degree requirements:* For master's, thesis (for some programs). *Entrance requirements:* For master's, minimum undergraduate GPA of 2.5, 3 years of work experience, RN license. Additional exam requirements/recommendations for international students: Required—TOEFL (minimum score 550 paper-based; 213 computer-based; 79 iBT). Electronic applications accepted.

University of Phoenix–Northern Nevada Campus, College of Social and Behavioral Science, Reno, NV 89521-5862. Offers administration of justice and security (MS); marriage, family and child therapy (MSC); psychology (MS); school counseling (MSC).

University of Phoenix–Oklahoma City Campus, College of Health and Human Services, Oklahoma City, OK 73116-8244. Offers administration of justice and security (MS); health care management (MBA); nursing (MSN); psychology (MS).

University of Phoenix–Oregon Campus, The Artemis School, College of Health and Human Services, Tigard, OR 97223. Offers administration of justice and security (MS); health administration (MHA); health care management (MBA); nursing (MSN); psychology (MS); MSN/MBA. Evening/weekend programs available. *Degree requirements:* For master's, thesis (for some programs). *Entrance requirements:* For master's, minimum undergraduate GPA of 2.5, 3 years of work experience, current RN license (nursing). Additional exam requirements/recommendations for international students: Required—TOEFL (minimum score 550 paper-based; 213 computer-based; 79 iBT). Electronic applications accepted.

University of Phoenix–Philadelphia Campus, The Artemis School, College of Health and Human Services, Wayne, PA 19087-2121. Offers administration of justice and security (MS); health administration (MHA); health care education (MSN); health care management (MBA); nursing (MSN); psychology (MS); MSN/MBA. Evening/weekend programs available. *Degree requirements:* For master's, thesis (for some programs). *Entrance requirements:* For master's, minimum undergraduate GPA of 2.5, 3 years work experience. Additional exam requirements/recommendations for international students: Required—TOEFL (minimum score 550 paper-based; 213 computer-based; 79 iBT). Electronic applications accepted.

University of Phoenix–Phoenix Campus, The Artemis School, College of Health and Human Services, Phoenix, AZ 85040-1958. Offers community counseling (MSC); education (MHA); family nurse practitioner (MSN); gerontology (MHA); health administration (MHA); health care education (MSN); health care management (MBA); informatics (MHA); marriage, family, and child therapy (MSC); nurse practitioner (Certificate); nursing (MSN); nursing health care education (Certificate); psychology (MS); MSN/MBA; MSN/MHA. Evening/weekend programs available. *Degree requirements:* For master's, thesis (for some programs). *Entrance requirements:* For master's, 3 years of work experience in field, minimum undergraduate GPA of 2.5, RN license. Additional exam requirements/recommendations for international students: Required—TOEFL (minimum score 550 paper-based; 213 computer-based; 79 iBT). Electronic applications accepted.

University of Phoenix–Pittsburgh Campus, The Artemis School, College of Health and Human Services, Pittsburgh, PA 15276. Offers administration of justice and security (MS); health administration (MHA); health care education (MSN); health care management (MBA); nursing (MSN); psychology (MS); MSN/MBA; MSN/MHA. Evening/weekend programs available. *Degree requirements:* For master's, thesis (for some programs). *Entrance requirements:* For master's, minimum undergraduate GPA of 2.5, 3 years work experience, current RN license (nursing). Additional exam requirements/recommendations for international students: Required—TOEFL (minimum score 550 paper-based; 213 computer-based; 79 iBT). Electronic applications accepted.

University of Phoenix–Richmond Campus, The Artemis School, College of Health and Human Services, Richmond, VA 23230. Offers administration of justice and security (MS); health administration (MHA); health care education (MSN); health care management (MBA); nursing (MSN); psychology (MS); MSN/MBA; MSN/MHA. Evening/weekend programs available. *Degree requirements:* For master's, thesis (for some programs). *Entrance requirements:* For master's, minimum undergraduate GPA of 2.5, 3 years work experience, current RN license for nursing programs. Additional exam requirements/recommendations for international students: Required—TOEFL (minimum score 500 paper-based; 213 computer-based; 79 iBT). Electronic applications accepted.

University of Phoenix–Sacramento Valley Campus, The Artemis School, College of Health and Human Services, Sacramento, CA 95833-3632. Offers administration of justice and security (MS); community counseling (MSC); family nurse practitioner (MSN); health administration (MHA); health care education (MSN); health care management (MBA); marriage, family and child counseling (MSC); nursing (MSN); psychology (MS); MSN/MBA. Evening/weekend programs available. *Degree requirements:* For master's, thesis (for some programs). *Entrance requirements:* For master's, RN license, minimum undergraduate GPA of 2.5, 3 years work experience. Additional exam requirements/recommendations for international students: Required—TOEFL (minimum score 550 paper-based; 213 computer-based; 79 iBT). Electronic applications accepted.

University of Phoenix–San Antonio Campus, College of Social and Behavioral Science, San Antonio, TX 78230. Offers administration of justice and security (MS); psychology (MS).

University of Phoenix–Southern Arizona Campus, The Artemis School, College of Health and Human Services, Tucson, AZ 85711. Offers administration of justice and security (MS); family nurse practitioner (MSN, Certificate); health administration (MHA); health care management (MBA); marriage, family and child therapy (MSC); nursing (MSN); psychology (MS). Evening/weekend programs available. *Degree requirements:* For master's, thesis (for some programs). *Entrance requirements:* For master's, minimum undergraduate GPA of 2.5, 3 years of work experience, RN license. Additional exam requirements/recommendations for international students: Required—TOEFL (minimum score 550 paper-based; 213 computer-based; 79 iBT). Electronic applications accepted.

University of Phoenix–Southern California Campus, The Artemis School, College of Health and Human Services, Costa Mesa, CA 92626. Offers administration of justice and security (MS); family nurse practitioner (MSN, Certificate); health administration (MHA); health care education (MSN); health care management (MBA); marriage, family and child therapy (MSC); nursing (MSN); psychology (MS); MSN/MBA; MSN/MHA. Evening/weekend programs available. *Degree requirements:* For master's, thesis (for some programs). *Entrance requirements:* For master's, minimum undergraduate GPA of 2.5, 3 years work experience, RN license. Additional exam requirements/recommendations for international students: Required—TOEFL (minimum score 550 paper-based; 213 computer-based; 79 iBT). Electronic applications accepted.

University of Phoenix–Southern Colorado Campus, The Artemis School, College of Health and Human Services, Colorado Springs, CO 80919-2335. Offers administration of justice and security (MS); community counseling (MSC); education (MHA); gerontology (MHA); health administration (MHA); health care management (MBA); marriage, family and child therapy (MSC); nursing (MSN); psychology (MS); MSN/MBA. Evening/weekend programs available. *Degree requirements:* For master's, thesis (for some programs). *Entrance requirements:* For master's, minimum undergraduate GPA of 2.5, 3 years of work experience, RN license. Additional exam requirements/recommendations for international students: Required—TOEFL (minimum score 550 paper-based; 213 computer-based; 79 iBT). Electronic applications accepted.

University of Phoenix–Tulsa Campus, College of Health and Human Services, Tulsa, OK 74134-1412. Offers administration of justice and security (MS); health care management (MBA); nursing (MSN); psychology (MS).

University of Pittsburgh, School of Arts and Sciences, Department of Psychology, Pittsburgh, PA 15260. Offers MS, PhD. *Accreditation:* APA (one or more programs are accredited). *Faculty:* 39 full-time (16 women), 8 part-time/adjunct (4 women). *Students:* 100 full-time (87 women); includes 12 minority (2 African Americans, 6 Asian Americans or Pacific Islanders, 4 Hispanic Americans), 10 international. 339 applicants, 6% accepted, 12 enrolled. In 2009, 8 master's, 5 doctorates awarded. Terminal master's awarded for partial completion of doctoral program. *Degree requirements:* For master's, comprehensive exam, thesis; for doctorate, comprehensive exam, thesis/dissertation. *Entrance requirements:* For doctorate, GRE General Test, minimum GPA of 3.0. Additional exam requirements/recommendations for international students: Required—TOEFL, TOEFL (minimum score 550 paper-based; 213 computer-based) or IELTS (minimum score 7). *Application deadline:* For fall admission, 12/1 for domestic and international students. Application fee: $50. Electronic applications accepted. *Expenses:* Tuition, state resident: full-time $16,402; part-time $665 per credit. Tuition, nonresident: full-time $28,694; part-time $1175 per credit. Required fees: $690; $175 per term. Tuition and fees vary according to program. *Financial support:* In 2009–10, 100 students received support, including 18 fellowships with full tuition reimbursements available (averaging $17,972 per year), 35 research assistantships with full tuition reimbursements available (averaging $13,600 per year), 34 teaching assistantships with full tuition reimbursements available (averaging $15,675 per year); career-related internships or fieldwork, scholarships/grants, traineeships, health care benefits, and unspecified assistantships also available. Financial award application deadline: 12/1. *Faculty research:* Behavioral medicine and psychoneuroimmunology; learning, reasoning and memory; psychopathology and behavioral problems; social cognition; social influence and group processes; social and cognitive development. Total annual research expenditures: $16.5 million. *Unit head:* Dr. Daniel S. Shaw, Chairman, 412-624-4501, Fax: 412-624-4428, E-mail: casey@pitt.edu. *Application contact:* Maria Milleville, Graduate Program Administrator, 412-624-4502, Fax: 412-624-4428, E-mail: psygrad@pitt.edu.

University of Puerto Rico, Río Piedras, College of Social Sciences, Department of Psychology, San Juan, PR 00931-3300. Offers clinical psychology (MA); industrial organizational psychology (MA); investigative academic psychology (MA); psychology (PhD); social-community psychology (MA). Part-time programs available. *Degree requirements:* For master's, comprehensive exam, thesis; for doctorate, comprehensive exam, thesis/dissertation, internship. *Entrance requirements:* For master's, GRE or PAEG, interview, minimum GPA of 3.0; for doctorate, GRE or PAEG, interview, master's degree, minimum GPA of 3.0. *Faculty research:* Intervention on Depressed Latino Youth, biosychosocial training.

University of Regina, Faculty of Graduate Studies and Research, Faculty of Arts, Department of Psychology, Regina, SK S4S 0A2, Canada. Offers clinical psychology (MA, PhD); experimental and applied psychology (MA, PhD). *Faculty:* 18 full-time (10 women). *Students:* 57 full-time (40 women), 5 part-time (all women). 54 applicants, 30% accepted. In 2009, 6 master's, 5 doctorates awarded. *Degree requirements:* For master's, thesis; for doctorate, comprehensive exam, thesis/dissertation. *Entrance requirements:* For master's, GRE General Test, GRE Subject Test; for doctorate, GRE General Test, GRE Subject Test (optional for students who hold a master's degree from a Canadian university). Additional exam requirements/recommendations for international students: Required—TOEFL (minimum score 580 paper-based; 237 computer-based; 80 iBT). *Application deadline:* For fall admission, 2/15 for domestic students. Application fee: $90 ($100 for international students). Electronic applications accepted. *Financial support:* In 2009–10, 23 fellowships (averaging $19,000 per year), 3 research assistantships (averaging $16,910 per year), 10 teaching assistantships (averaging $6,650 per year) were awarded; career-related internships or fieldwork and scholarships/grants also available. Financial award application deadline: 6/15. *Faculty research:* Clinical, experimental and applied psychology. *Unit head:* Dr. William E. Smythe, Head, 306-585-4157, Fax: 306-585-5429, E-mail: william.smythe@uregina.ca. *Application contact:* Dr. Dongyan Blachford, Associate Dean, 306-585-5186, Fax: 306-337-2444, E-mail: dongyan.blachford@uregina.ca.

University of Rhode Island, Graduate School, College of Arts and Sciences, Department of Psychology, Kingston, RI 02881. Offers behavioral science (PhD); clinical psychology (MA, PhD); school psychology (MS, PhD). *Accreditation:* APA (one or more programs are accredited). Part-time programs available. *Faculty:* 25 full-time (10 women), 5 part-time/adjunct (1 woman). *Students:* 72 full-time (56 women), 33 part-time (27 women); includes 20 minority (7 African Americans, 6 Asian Americans or Pacific Islanders, 7 Hispanic Americans), 4 international. In 2009, 12 master's, 11 doctorates awarded. *Degree requirements:* For master's, comprehensive exam, thesis optional; for doctorate, thesis/dissertation. *Entrance requirements:* For master's and doctorate, GRE, 3 letters of recommendation. Additional exam requirements/recommendations for international students: Required—TOEFL (minimum score 550 paper-based; 213 computer-based). Application fee: $65. Electronic applications accepted. *Expenses:* Tuition, state resident: full-time $8828; part-time $490 per credit hour. Tuition, nonresident: full-time $22,100; part-time $1228 per credit hour. Required fees: $1118; $57 per semester. Tuition and fees vary according to program. *Financial support:* In 2009–10, 3 research assistantships with full and partial tuition reimbursements (averaging $8,519 per year), 20 teaching assistantships with full and partial tuition reimbursements (averaging $12,364 per year) were awarded. Financial award applicants required to submit FAFSA. Total annual research expenditures: $4.6 million. *Unit head:* Dr. Patricia Morokoff, Chairperson, 401-874-4239, Fax: 401-874-2157, E-mail: morokoff@uri.edu. *Application contact:* Dr. Patricia Morokoff, Chairperson, 401-874-4239, Fax: 401-874-2157, E-mail: morokoff@uri.edu.

University of Rochester, The College, Arts and Sciences, Department of Clinical and Social Sciences in Psychology, Rochester, NY 14627. Offers clinical psychology (PhD); developmental psychology (PhD); psychology (MA); social-personality psychology (PhD). *Accreditation:* APA (one or more programs are accredited). Terminal master's awarded for partial completion of doctoral program. *Degree requirements:* For doctorate, thesis/dissertation, qualifying exam. *Entrance requirements:* For doctorate, GRE General Test. Additional exam requirements/recommendations for international students: Required—TOEFL.

University of Saint Francis, Graduate School, Department of Psychology and Counseling, Fort Wayne, IN 46808-3994. Offers general psychology (MS); mental health counseling (MS); pastoral counseling (MS); school counseling (MS Ed). Part-time and evening/weekend programs available. *Entrance requirements:* For master's, interview, minimum undergraduate GPA of 3.0.

University of Saint Mary, Graduate Programs, Program in Psychology, Leavenworth, KS 66048-5082. Offers MA. Part-time and evening/weekend programs available. *Degree requirements:* For master's, thesis. *Entrance requirements:* For master's, minimum undergraduate GPA of 2.75.

University of St. Thomas, Graduate Studies, Graduate School of Professional Psychology, St. Paul, MN 55105-1096. Offers counseling psychology (MA, Psy D); marriage and family psychology (MA, Certificate). *Accreditation:* APA. Part-time and evening/weekend programs available. *Faculty:* 11 full-time (5 women), 13 part-time/adjunct (6 women). *Students:* 68 full-time (54 women), 141 part-time (113 women); includes 21 minority (5 African Americans, 13 Asian Americans or Pacific Islanders, 3 Hispanic Americans), 4 international. Average age 29. 578 applicants, 42% accepted. In 2009, 22 master's, 11 doctorates awarded. *Degree requirements:* For master's, comprehensive exam, practicum; for doctorate, comprehensive exam, thesis/dissertation, qualifying exam, practicum, internship. *Entrance requirements:* For master's, GRE, minimum GPA of 2.75, letters of recommendation, personal statement; for doctorate, GRE, minimum GPA of 3.2, letters of recommendation, personal statement. Additional exam requirements/recommendations for international students: Required—TOEFL (minimum score 550 paper-based; 213 computer-based; 80 iBT). *Application deadline:* For fall admission, 3/1 priority date for domestic students; for winter admission, 2/1 priority date for domestic students; for spring admission, 9/15 priority date for domestic students, 3/1 for international students. Application fee: $50. *Expenses:* Contact institution. *Financial support:* In 2009–10, 2 fellowships (averaging $5,000 per year) were awarded; research assistantships, institutionally sponsored loans and scholarships/grants also available. Support available to part-time students. Financial award application deadline: 8/1; financial award applicants required to submit FAFSA. *Faculty research:* Elderly, eating disorders, anxiety, family. *Unit head:* Dr. Christopher S. Vye, Associate Dean, 651-962-4666, Fax: 651-962-4666, E-mail: bnolan@stthomas.edu. *Application contact:* Laurie Dupont, Administrative Assistant, 651-962-4669, Fax: 651-962-4651, E-mail: ldupont@stthomas.edu.

University of Saskatchewan, College of Graduate Studies and Research, College of Arts and Sciences, Department of Psychology, Saskatoon, SK S7N 5A2, Canada. Offers MA, PhD. *Accreditation:* APA (one or more programs are accredited). *Faculty:* 43. *Students:* 86. In 2009, 6 master's, 5 doctorates awarded. *Degree requirements:* For master's, thesis; for doctorate, comprehensive exam (for some programs), thesis/dissertation. *Entrance requirements:* Additional exam requirements/recommendations for international students: Required—TOEFL (minimum score 80 iBT); Recommended—IELTS (minimum score 6.5). *Application deadline:* For fall admission, 7/1 priority date for domestic students. Applications are processed on a rolling basis. Application fee: $75. Electronic applications accepted. Tuition and fees charges are reported in Canadian dollars. *Expenses:* Tuition, area resident: Full-time $3000 Canadian dollars; part-time $500 Canadian dollars per term. Required fees: $700 Canadian dollars; $100 Canadian dollars per term. *Financial support:* Fellowships, research assistantships, teaching assistantships available. Financial award application deadline: 1/31. *Unit head:* Dr. Valerie Tompson, Head, 306-966-6701, Fax: 306-966-6630, E-mail: valerie.thompson@usask.ca. *Application contact:* Dr. Linda McMullen, Graduate Chair, 306-966-6668, Fax: 306-966-6630, E-mail: linda.mcmullen@usask.ca.

University of South Africa, College of Human Sciences, Pretoria, South Africa. Offers adult education (M Ed); African languages (MA, PhD); African politics (MA, PhD); Afrikaans (MA, PhD); ancient history (MA, PhD); ancient Near Eastern studies (MA, PhD); anthropology (MA, PhD); applied linguistics (MA); Arabic (MA, PhD); archaeology (MA); art history (MA); Biblical archaeology (MA); Biblical studies (M Th, D Th, PhD); Christian spirituality (M Th, D Th); church history (M Th, D Th); classical studies (MA, PhD); clinical psychology (MA); communication (MA, PhD); comparative education (M Ed, Ed D); consulting psychology (D Admin, D Com, PhD); curriculum studies (M Ed, Ed D); development studies (M Admin, MA, D Admin, PhD); didactics (M Ed, Ed D); education (M Tech); education management (M Ed, Ed D); educational psychology (M Ed); English (MA); environmental education (M Ed); French (MA, PhD); German (MA, PhD); Greek (MA); guidance and counseling (M Ed); health studies (MA, PhD), including health sciences education (MA), health services management (MA), medical and surgical nursing science (critical care general) (MA), midwifery and neonatal nursing science (MA), trauma and emergency care (MA); history (MA, PhD); history of education (Ed D); inclusive education (M Ed, Ed D); information and communications technology policy and regulation (MA); information science (MA, MIS, PhD); international politics (MA, PhD); Islamic studies (MA, PhD); Italian (MA, PhD); Judaica (MA, PhD); linguistics (MA, PhD); mathematical education (M Ed); mathematics education (MA); missiology (M Th, D Th); modern Hebrew (MA, PhD); musicology (MA, MMus, D Mus, PhD); natural science education (M Ed); New Testament (M Th, D Th); Old Testament (D Th); pastoral therapy (M Th, D Th); philosophy (MA); philosophy of education (M Ed, Ed D); politics (MA, PhD); Portuguese (MA, PhD); practical theology (M Th, D Th); psychology (MA, MS, PhD); psychology of education (M Ed, Ed D); public health (MA); religious studies (MA, D Th, PhD); Romance languages (MA); Russian (MA, PhD); Semitic languages (MA, PhD); social behavior studies in HIV/AIDS (MA); social science (mental health) (MA); social science in development studies (MA); social science in psychology (MA); social science in social work (MA); social science in sociology (MA); social work (MSW, DSW, PhD); socio-education (M Ed, Ed D); sociolinguistics (MA); sociology (MA, PhD); Spanish (MA, PhD); systematic theology (M Th, D Th); TESOL (teaching English to speakers of other languages) (MA); theological ethics (M Th, D Th); theory of literature (MA, PhD); urban ministries (D Th); urban ministry (M Th).

University of South Alabama, Graduate School, College of Arts and Sciences, Department of Psychology, Mobile, AL 36688-0002. Offers MS. Part-time and evening/weekend programs available. *Degree requirements:* For master's, comprehensive exam, thesis optional. *Entrance requirements:* For master's, GRE General Test, GRE Subject Test (recommended), minimum GPA of 3.0, major in psychology or equivalent. *Expenses:* Tuition, state resident: part-time $218 per contact hour. Required fees: $1102 per year. *Faculty research:* Language acquisition and development.

University of South Carolina, The Graduate School, College of Arts and Sciences, Department of Psychology, Columbia, SC 29208. Offers clinical/community psychology (MA, PhD), including clinical/community psychology (PhD), general psychology (MA); experimental psychology (MA, PhD); school psychology (PhD). *Accreditation:* APA (one or more programs are accredited). Terminal master's awarded for partial completion of doctoral program. *Degree requirements:* For master's, thesis; for doctorate, comprehensive exam, thesis/dissertation. *Entrance requirements:* For master's and doctorate, GRE General Test. Additional exam requirements/recommendations for international students: Required—TOEFL. Electronic applications accepted. *Faculty research:* Developmental cognitive neuroscience, alcohol and drug addictions, reading and language processing, child and family, prevention.

The University of South Dakota, Graduate School, College of Arts and Sciences, Department of Psychology, Vermillion, SD 57069-2390. Offers clinical psychology (MA, PhD); human factors (MA, PhD). *Accreditation:* APA (one or more programs are accredited). *Degree requirements:* For master's, comprehensive exam, thesis; for doctorate, comprehensive exam, thesis/dissertation. *Entrance requirements:* For master's, GRE, minimum GPA of 2.7; for doctorate, GRE General Test, GRE Subject Test, minimum GPA of 2.7. Additional exam requirements/recommendations for international students: Required—TOEFL (minimum score 550 paper-based; 213 computer-based; 79 iBT). Electronic applications accepted. *Faculty research:* Human-computer interactions, perceptual-cognitive processing, medical psychology, depression, moral psychology.

University of Southern California, Graduate School, College of Letters, Arts and Sciences, Department of Psychology, Los Angeles, CA 90089. Offers brain and cognitive science (PhD); clinical science (PhD); developmental psychology (PhD); human behavior (MHB); psychology (MA); quantitative methods (PhD); social psychology (PhD); PhD/MPH. *Accreditation:* APA. *Faculty:* 34 full-time (10 women), 17 part-time/adjunct (7 women). *Students:* 107 full-time (73 women); includes 38 minority (6 African Americans, 21 Asian Americans or Pacific Islanders, 11 Hispanic Americans), 19 international. 430 applicants, 6% accepted, 13 enrolled. In 2009, 17 master's, 12 doctorates awarded. *Degree requirements:* For doctorate, comprehensive exam, thesis/dissertation, one-year internship (for clinical science students). *Entrance requirements:* For doctorate, GRE. Additional exam requirements/recommendations for international students: Recommended—TOEFL (minimum score 600 paper-based; 250 computer-based; 100 iBT). *Application deadline:* For fall admission, 12/1 for domestic and international students. Application fee: $95. Electronic applications accepted. *Expenses:* Tuition: Full-time $25,980; part-time $1315 per unit. Required fees: $554. One-time fee: $35 full-time. Full-time tuition and fees vary according to degree level and program. *Financial support:* In 2009–10, 80 students received support, including 16 fellowships with full tuition reimbursements available (averaging $22,500 per year), 22 research assistantships with full tuition reimbursements available (averaging $19,000 per year), 38 teaching assistantships with full tuition reimbursements available (averaging $19,000 per year); career-related internships or fieldwork, scholarships/grants, traineeships, and health care benefits also available. *Faculty research:* Affective neuroscience; children and families; vision, culture and ethnicity; intergroup relations; aggression and violence; language and reading development; substance abuse. *Unit head:* Dr. Margaret Gatz, Chair and Professor, 213-740-2203, Fax: 213-746-9028, E-mail: gatz@usc.edu. *Application contact:* Irene Takaragawa, Graduate Advisor, 213-740-2205, E-mail: itakarag@usc.edu.

University of Southern Mississippi, Graduate School, College of Education and Psychology, Department of Psychology, Hattiesburg, MS 39406-0001. Offers clinical psychology (MA, PhD); counseling psychology (PhD); experimental psychology (MA, PhD); psychology (MS); school psychology (MA, PhD). *Accreditation:* APA (one or more programs are accredited). *Faculty:* 32 full-time (9 women). *Students:* 104 full-time (80 women), 29 part-time (19 women); includes 14 minority (7 African Americans, 2 Asian Americans or Pacific Islanders, 5 Hispanic Americans), 7 international. Average age 29. 225 applicants, 16% accepted, 30 enrolled. In 2009, 23 master's, 13 doctorates awarded. Terminal master's awarded for partial completion of doctoral program. *Degree requirements:* For master's, comprehensive exam, thesis; for doctorate, comprehensive exam, thesis/dissertation. *Entrance requirements:* For master's, GRE General Test, minimum GPA of 3.0; for doctorate, GRE General Test, interview, minimum GPA of 3.0. Additional exam requirements/recommendations for international students: Required—TOEFL. *Application deadline:* For fall admission, 3/1 priority date for domestic students, 3/1 for international students. Applications are processed on a rolling basis. Application fee: $35. *Expenses:* Tuition, state resident: full-time $5096; part-time $284 per hour. Tuition, nonresident: full-time $13,052; part-time $726 per hour. Required fees: $402. Tuition and fees vary according to course level and course load. *Financial support:* In 2009–10, 48 research assistantships with full tuition reimbursements (averaging $8,802 per year), 48 teaching assistantships with full tuition reimbursements (averaging $6,500 per year) were awarded; career-related internships or fieldwork, Federal Work-Study, and institutionally sponsored loans also available. Financial award application deadline: 3/15; financial award applicants required to submit FAFSA. *Faculty research:* Dolphin cognition, sleep, neuropsychology, health-related behaviors, psychopathology. Total annual research expenditures: $101,200. *Unit head:* Dr. Joesph Olmi, Chair, 601-266-4177, Fax: 601-266-5580. *Application contact:* Dr. Heather Sterling-Turner, Graduate Coordinator, 601-266-4177, Fax: 601-266-5580.

University of South Florida, Graduate School, College of Arts and Sciences, Department of Psychology, Tampa, FL 33620-9951. Offers clinical psychology (PhD); cognitive and neural sciences (PhD); industrial-organizational psychology (PhD). *Accreditation:* APA. *Faculty:* 32 full-time (9 women). *Students:* 98 full-time (55 women), 21 part-time (13 women); includes 16 minority (3 African Americans, 7 Asian Americans or Pacific Islanders, 6 Hispanic Americans), 11 international. Average age 32. 437 applicants, 8% accepted, 24 enrolled. In 2009, 24 doctorates awarded. *Degree requirements:* For doctorate, comprehensive exam, thesis/dissertation, internship. *Entrance requirements:* For doctorate, GRE General Test, minimum GPA of 3.0 in last 60 hours of course work. Additional exam requirements/recommendations for international students: Required—TOEFL (minimum score 550 paper-based; 213 computer-based). *Application deadline:* For fall admission, 12/1 for domestic and international students. Application fee: $30. Electronic applications accepted. *Expenses:* Contact institution. *Financial support:* In 2009–10, teaching assistantships with tuition reimbursements (averaging $27,086 per year); tuition waivers (partial) and unspecified assistantships also available. Financial award applicants required to submit FAFSA. *Faculty research:* Clinical, cognitive, neuroscience, social, industrial/organizational. Total annual research expenditures: $4.7 million. *Unit head:* Michael Brannick, Chairperson, 813-974-0478, Fax: 813-974-4617, E-mail: mbrannick@usf.edu. *Application contact:* William Sacco, Program Director, 813-974-0375, Fax: 813-974-4617, E-mail: sacco@cas.usf.edu.

The University of Tennessee, Graduate School, College of Arts and Sciences, Department of Psychology, Knoxville, TN 37996. Offers clinical psychology (PhD); experimental psychology (MA, PhD); psychology (MA). *Accreditation:* APA (one or more programs are accredited). Terminal master's awarded for partial completion of doctoral program. *Degree requirements:* For master's, thesis; for doctorate, thesis/dissertation. *Entrance requirements:* For master's and doctorate, GRE General Test, GRE Subject Test, minimum GPA of 2.7. Additional exam requirements/recommendations for international students: Required—TOEFL. Electronic applications accepted. *Expenses:* Tuition, state resident: full-time $6826; part-time $380 per semester

Psychology—General

The University of Tennessee (continued)

hour. Tuition, nonresident: full-time $21,844; part-time $1147 per semester hour. Tuition and fees vary according to program.

The University of Tennessee at Chattanooga, Graduate School, College of Arts and Sciences, Department of Psychology, Chattanooga, TN 37403. Offers industrial/organizational psychology (MS); research psychology (MS). Part-time and evening/weekend programs available. *Faculty:* 6 full-time (1 woman). *Students:* 39 full-time (24 women), 5 part-time (3 women); includes 7 minority (4 African Americans, 2 Asian Americans or Pacific Islanders, 1 Hispanic American), 1 international. Average age 29. 75 applicants, 85% accepted, 16 enrolled. In 2009, 21 master's awarded. *Degree requirements:* For master's, thesis (for some programs), practicum (industrial/organizational psychology). *Entrance requirements:* For master's, GRE General Test, minimum GPA of 2.5 on all undergraduate coursework or 3.0 in senior year. Additional exam requirements/recommendations for international students: Required—TOEFL (minimum score 550 paper-based; 213 computer-based; 79 iBT), IELTS (minimum score 6). *Application deadline:* For fall admission, 8/1 priority date for domestic students, 6/1 for international students; for spring admission, 12/1 priority date for domestic students, 10/1 for international students. Applications are processed on a rolling basis. Application fee: $35. Electronic applications accepted. *Expenses:* Tuition, state resident: full-time $5404; part-time $300 per credit hour. Tuition, nonresident: full-time $16,702; part-time $928 per credit hour. Required fees: $1150; $130 per credit hour. *Financial support:* In 2009–10, 20 research assistantships with full and partial tuition reimbursements (averaging $5,500 per year) were awarded; career-related internships or fieldwork, scholarships/grants, and unspecified assistantships also available. Support available to part-time students. *Faculty research:* Decision processes, philosophical psychology, memory, social cognition, employee selection. Total annual research expenditures: $35,031. *Unit head:* Dr. Paul J. Watson, Department Head, 423-425-4262, Fax: 423-425-4284, E-mail: paul-watson@utc.edu. *Application contact:* Dr. Stephanie Bellar, Dean of Graduate Studies, 423-425-4666, Fax: 423-425-5223, E-mail: stephanie-bellar@utc.edu.

The University of Texas at Arlington, Graduate School, College of Science, Department of Psychology, Arlington, TX 76019. Offers experimental psychology (PhD); health psychology (PhD); industrial organizational psychology (MS); psychology (MS). Part-time programs available. *Faculty:* 16 full-time (5 women), 1 part-time/adjunct (0 women). *Students:* 62 full-time (41 women), 10 part-time (7 women); includes 13 minority (5 African Americans, 2 Asian Americans or Pacific Islanders, 6 Hispanic Americans), 7 international. 72 applicants, 90% accepted, 22 enrolled. In 2009, 16 master's, 6 doctorates awarded. Terminal master's awarded for partial completion of doctoral program. *Degree requirements:* For master's, comprehensive exam or thesis; for doctorate, thesis/dissertation (for some programs). *Entrance requirements:* For master's and doctorate, GRE General Test, minimum GPA of 3.0 in last 60 hours of course work. Additional exam requirements/recommendations for international students: Required—TOEFL (minimum score 550 paper-based; 213 computer-based). *Application deadline:* For fall admission, 6/16 for domestic students. Applications are processed on a rolling basis. Application fee: $35 ($50 for international students). *Financial support:* In 2009–10, 4 fellowships (averaging $1,000 per year), 2 research assistantships with tuition reimbursements (averaging $15,000 per year), 28 teaching assistantships with tuition reimbursements (averaging $15,000 per year) were awarded; career-related internships or fieldwork, Federal Work-Study, institutionally sponsored loans, scholarships/grants, traineeships, tuition waivers (partial), and unspecified assistantships also available. Financial award application deadline: 6/1; financial award applicants required to submit FAFSA. *Unit head:* Dr. Robert Gatchel, Chair, 817-272-2281, Fax: 817-272-2364, E-mail: gatchel@uta.edu. *Application contact:* Dr. Jared Kenworthy, Graduate Advisor, 817-272-2281, Fax: 817-272-2364, E-mail: kenworthy@uta.edu.

The University of Texas at Austin, Graduate School, College of Liberal Arts, Department of Psychology, Austin, TX 78712-1111. Offers PhD. *Accreditation:* APA. *Degree requirements:* For doctorate, thesis/dissertation. *Entrance requirements:* For doctorate, GRE General Test. Electronic applications accepted. *Faculty research:* Behavioral neuroscience, sensory neuroscience, evolutionary psychology, cognitive processes in psychopathology, cognitive processes and their development.

The University of Texas at Brownsville, Graduate Studies, College of Liberal Arts, Department of Behavioral Sciences, Brownsville, TX 78520-4991. Offers MAIS. Part-time and evening/weekend programs available. *Degree requirements:* For master's, thesis or comprehensive exam. *Entrance requirements:* For master's, GRE General Test. Additional exam requirements/recommendations for international students: Required—TOEFL. *Faculty research:* Memory, socio-political structure of South America, cartography of Mexico and Central America, family economic structure of Spain.

The University of Texas at Dallas, School of Behavioral and Brain Sciences, Program in Psychological Sciences, Richardson, TX 75080. Offers early childhood disorders (MS); psychological sciences (MS, PhD). Part-time and evening/weekend programs available. *Faculty:* 30 full-time (14 women). *Students:* 41 full-time (32 women), 16 part-time (15 women); includes 15 minority (4 African Americans, 6 Asian Americans or Pacific Islanders, 5 Hispanic Americans), 10 international. Average age 30. 69 applicants, 38% accepted, 20 enrolled. In 2009, 12 master's awarded. *Degree requirements:* For master's, directed project or internship; for doctorate, thesis/dissertation. *Entrance requirements:* For master's and doctorate, GRE General Test, minimum GPA of 3.0 in upper-level course work. Additional exam requirements/recommendations for international students: Required—TOEFL (minimum score 550 paper-based; 213 computer-based). *Application deadline:* For fall admission, 7/15 for domestic students, 5/1 priority date for international students; for spring admission, 11/15 for domestic students, 9/1 priority date for international students. Applications are processed on a rolling basis. Application fee: $50 ($100 for international students). Electronic applications accepted. *Expenses:* Tuition, state resident: full-time $11,068; part-time $461 per credit hour. Tuition, nonresident: full-time $21,178; part-time $882 per credit hour. Tuition and fees vary according to course load. *Financial support:* In 2009–10, 3 research assistantships with full tuition reimbursements (averaging $12,168 per year), 15 teaching assistantships with full tuition reimbursements (averaging $10,882 per year) were awarded; fellowships, career-related internships or fieldwork, Federal Work-Study, scholarships/grants, and unspecified assistantships also available. Support available to part-time students. Financial award application deadline: 4/30; financial award applicants required to submit FAFSA. *Faculty research:* Social competence in normal and hyperactive youth, preschool number development, social-emotional development, family and peer relationships. *Unit head:* Dr. Melanie J. Spence, Head, PhD Programs, 972-883-2206, Fax: 972-883-2491, E-mail: mspence@utdallas.edu. *Application contact:* Dr. Robert D. Stillman, Program Head, 972-883-3106, Fax: 972-883-3022, E-mail: stillman@utdallas.edu.

The University of Texas at El Paso, Graduate School, College of Liberal Arts, Department of Psychology, El Paso, TX 79968-0001. Offers clinical psychology (MA); experimental psychology (MA); psychology (PhD). Part-time and evening/weekend programs available. *Students:* 47 (28 women); includes 20 minority (1 Asian American or Pacific Islander, 19 Hispanic Americans), 6 international. Average age 34. In 2009, 11 master's, 5 doctorates awarded. *Degree requirements:* For master's, thesis; for doctorate, thesis/dissertation. *Entrance requirements:* For master's, GRE, letters of recommendation; for doctorate, GRE, Statement of Purpose, Letters of Recommendation. Additional exam requirements/recommendations for international students: Required—TOEFL; Recommended—IELTS. *Application deadline:* For fall admission, 8/1 for domestic students, 3/1 for international students; for spring admission, 11/1 for domestic students, 9/1 for international students. Applications are processed on a rolling basis. Application fee: $45 ($80 for international students). Electronic applications accepted. *Financial support:* In 2009–10, research assistantships with partial tuition reimbursements (averaging $18,625 per year), teaching assistantships with partial tuition reimbursements (averaging $14,900 per year) were awarded; fellowships with partial tuition reimbursements, institutionally sponsored loans, scholarships/grants, health care benefits, tuition waivers (partial), and unspecified assistantships also available. Support available to part-time students. Financial award application deadline: 3/15; financial award applicants required to submit FAFSA. *Unit head:* Dr. Edward Casta?eda, Chair, 915-747-5551, Fax: 915-747-6553, E-mail: ecastaneda9@utep.edu. *Application contact:* Dr. Patricia D. Witherspoon, Dean of the Graduate School, 915-747-5491, Fax: 915-747-5788, E-mail: withersp@utep.edu.

The University of Texas at San Antonio, College of Liberal and Fine Arts, Department of Psychology, San Antonio, TX 78249-0617. Offers MS. Part-time and evening/weekend programs available. *Faculty:* 11 full-time (7 women), 2 part-time/adjunct (0 women). *Students:* 28 full-time (21 women), 13 part-time (8 women); includes 19 minority (2 African Americans, 3 Asian Americans or Pacific Islanders, 14 Hispanic Americans), 2 international. Average age 27. 50 applicants, 66% accepted, 25 enrolled. In 2009, 8 master's awarded. *Degree requirements:* For master's, comprehensive exam (for some programs), thesis (for some programs). *Entrance requirements:* For master's, GRE General Test, minimum GPA of 3.0 in last 60 hours and in all psychology courses. Additional exam requirements/recommendations for international students: Required—TOEFL (minimum score 500 paper-based; 173 computer-based; 61 iBT), IELTS (minimum score 5). *Application deadline:* For fall admission, 7/1 for domestic students, 4/1 for international students; for spring admission, 11/1 for domestic students, 9/1 for international students. Applications are processed on a rolling basis. Application fee: $45 ($80 for international students). Electronic applications accepted. *Expenses:* Tuition, state resident: full-time $3975; part-time $221 per contact hour. Tuition, nonresident: full-time $13,947; part-time $775 per contact hour. Required fees: $1853. *Financial support:* In 2009–10, 6 students received support, including 12 research assistantships (averaging $10,714 per year), 4 teaching assistantships (averaging $9,200 per year); career-related internships or fieldwork, scholarships/grants, tuition waivers, and unspecified assistantships also available. Support available to part-time students. Total annual research expenditures: $201,776. *Unit head:* Dr. Robert W. Fuhrman, Chair, 210-458-4372, Fax: 210-458-7352, E-mail: rfuhrman@utsa.edu. *Application contact:* Dr. Stella Garcia-Lopez, Graduate Advisor, 210-458-5731, E-mail: stella.lopez@utsa.edu.

The University of Texas at Tyler, College of Education and Psychology, Department of Psychology and Counseling, Tyler, TX 75799-0001. Offers clinical psychology (MS), including neuropsychology, school psychology; counseling psychology (MA), including general, marriage and family; interdisciplinary studies (MSIS); school counseling (MA). Part-time and evening/weekend programs available. *Faculty:* 11 full-time (3 women). *Students:* 80 full-time (63 women), 46 part-time (38 women); includes 5 minority (3 African Americans, 1 American Indian/Alaska Native, 1 Hispanic American). Average age 29. 64 applicants, 77% accepted, 28 enrolled. In 2009, 36 master's awarded. *Degree requirements:* For master's, comprehensive exam, thesis optional. *Entrance requirements:* For master's, GRE General Test, minimum GPA of 3.0. Additional exam requirements/recommendations for international students: Required—TOEFL (minimum score 79 computer-based). *Application deadline:* For fall admission, 8/17 priority date for domestic students, 7/1 priority date for international students; for spring admission, 12/21 priority date for domestic students, 11/1 priority date for international students. Application fee: $25 ($50 for international students). Electronic applications accepted. *Expenses:* Tuition, state resident: part-time $665 per semester hour. Tuition, nonresident: part-time $942 per semester hour. Part-time tuition and fees vary according to degree level and program. *Financial support:* In 2009–10, fellowships with partial tuition reimbursements (averaging $3,000 per year), research assistantships (averaging $5,000 per year), teaching assistantships (averaging $1,500 per year) were awarded; career-related internships or fieldwork, Federal Work-Study, and institutionally sponsored loans also available. Support available to part-time students. Financial award application deadline: 7/1. *Faculty research:* Neuropsychology, child abuse, psychometric properties of psychological instruments, maternal behavior, clinical practice issues, victimization of women, post-traumatic stress disorder. *Unit head:* Dr. Charles B. Barke, Chair/Professor, 903-565-5875, Fax: 903-565-5560, E-mail: cbarke@uttyler.edu. *Application contact:* Dr. Charles Barke.

The University of Texas of the Permian Basin, Office of Graduate Studies, College of Arts and Sciences, Department of Psychology, Odessa, TX 79762-0001. Offers applied research psychology (MA); clinical psychology (MA). Part-time and evening/weekend programs available. *Degree requirements:* For master's, comprehensive exam, thesis, practicum. *Entrance requirements:* For master's, GRE General Test, 3 letters of recommendation. Additional exam requirements/recommendations for international students: Required—TOEFL (minimum score 550 paper-based; 213 computer-based).

The University of Texas–Pan American, College of Social and Behavioral Sciences, Department of Psychology and Anthropology, Edinburg, TX 78539. Offers psychology (MA), including clinical psychology, experimental psychology. Part-time and evening/weekend programs available. *Degree requirements:* For master's, comprehensive exam, thesis optional, internship. *Entrance requirements:* For master's, GRE, letters of recommendation. Additional exam requirements/recommendations for international students: Required—TOEFL. Electronic applications accepted. *Expenses:* Tuition, state resident: full-time $3630.60; part-time $201.70 per credit hour. Tuition, nonresident: full-time $8617; part-time $478.70 per credit hour. Required fees: $806.50. *Faculty research:* Biofeedback, acculturation, health, stress/trauma, neuropsychological assessment, false memories, children's theory of mind.

University of the Pacific, College of the Pacific, Department of Psychology, Stockton, CA 95211-0197. Offers MA. *Faculty:* 8 full-time (5 women), 1 (woman) part-time/adjunct. *Students:* 13 part-time (8 women); includes 4 minority (2 Asian Americans or Pacific Islanders, 2 Hispanic Americans), 2 international. Average age 25. 18 applicants, 44% accepted, 5 enrolled. In 2009, 5 master's awarded. *Degree requirements:* For master's, thesis. *Entrance requirements:* For master's, GRE General Test. Additional exam requirements/recommendations for international students: Required—TOEFL (minimum score 475 paper-based; 150 computer-based). *Application deadline:* For fall admission, 3/1 priority date for domestic students. Applications are processed on a rolling basis. Application fee: $75. *Financial support:* In 2009–10, 7 teaching assistantships were awarded; institutionally sponsored loans also available. Support available to part-time students. Financial award application deadline: 3/1; financial award applicants required to submit FAFSA. *Unit head:* Dr. Carolynn Kohn, Chairperson, 209-946-2133, E-mail: rhannon@pacific.edu. *Application contact:* Information Contact, 209-946-2261.

University of the Rockies, Graduate Programs, Colorado Springs, CO 80903. Offers MA, Psy D.

The University of Toledo, College of Graduate Studies, College of Arts and Sciences, Department of Psychology, Toledo, OH 43606-3390. Offers behavioral (PhD), including cognitive, psychobiology and learning, social; clinical psychology (PhD); experimental psychology (MA). *Accreditation:* APA. *Degree requirements:* For master's, thesis; for doctorate, one foreign language, thesis/dissertation. *Entrance requirements:* For master's and doctorate, GRE General Test, GRE Subject Test. *Faculty research:* Neural taste response.

University of Toronto, School of Graduate Studies, Life Sciences Division, Department of Psychology, Toronto, ON M5S 1A1, Canada. Offers MA, PhD. *Accreditation:* APA (one or more programs are accredited). *Degree requirements:* For master's, thesis; for doctorate, thesis/dissertation, oral exam. *Entrance requirements:* For master's, minimum A– average in last two years, 6 full courses in psychology, laboratory experience; for doctorate, minimum A– average, research experience.

University of Tulsa, Graduate School, College of Arts and Sciences, Department of Psychology, Tulsa, OK 74104-3189. Offers clinical psychology (MA, PhD); industrial/organizational psychology (MA, PhD); JD/MA. *Accreditation:* APA (one or more programs are accredited). Part-time programs available. *Faculty:* 13 full-time (5 women), 1 (woman) part-time/adjunct. *Students:* 43 full-time (33 women), 25 part-time (20 women); includes 7 minority (2 African Americans, 1 American Indian/Alaska Native, 1 Asian American or Pacific Islander, 3 Hispanic Americans), 2 international. Average age 28. 122 applicants, 33% accepted, 15 enrolled. In 2009, 4 master's, 8 doctorates awarded. Terminal master's awarded for partial completion of doctoral program.

Degree requirements: For doctorate, comprehensive exam, thesis/dissertation. *Entrance requirements:* For master's and doctorate, GRE General Test. Additional exam requirements/recommendations for international students: Required—TOEFL (minimum score 575 paper-based; 231 computer-based; 91 iBT), IELTS (minimum score 6.5). Application fee: $40. Electronic applications accepted. *Expenses:* Tuition: Full-time $16,182; part-time $899 per credit hour. Required fees: $4 per credit hour. Tuition and fees vary according to course load. *Financial support:* In 2009–10, 45 students received support, including 12 fellowships with full and partial tuition reimbursements available (averaging $2,843 per year), 11 research assistantships with full and partial tuition reimbursements available (averaging $8,974 per year), 32 teaching assistantships with full and partial tuition reimbursements available (averaging $11,395 per year); career-related internships or fieldwork, Federal Work-Study, scholarships/grants, health care benefits, tuition waivers (full and partial), and unspecified assistantships also available. Support available to part-time students. Financial award application deadline: 2/1; financial award applicants required to submit FAFSA. *Faculty research:* Traumatic stress studies, randomized control trials of exposure treatments, pain modulation, neuropsychological assessment of health/mental health, psychological assessment, psychometrics, ethics, longitudinal assessment of child development, trauma and journalism, MMPI studies, personnel testing and selection, training, performance appraisal, organizational development, job attitudes and motivation, leadership. Total annual research expenditures: $3.9 million. *Unit head:* Dr. Judy Berry, Chairperson, 918-631-2834, Fax: 918-631-2833, E-mail: judy-berry@utulsa.edu. *Application contact:* Graduate School, 918-631-2336, Fax: 918-631-2156, E-mail: grad@utulsa.edu.

University of Utah, The Graduate School, College of Social and Behavioral Science, Department of Psychology, Salt Lake City, UT 84112. Offers clinical psychology (PhD); psychology (PhD). *Accreditation:* APA. *Faculty:* 32 full-time (15 women), 1 part-time/adjunct (0 women). *Students:* 48 full-time (33 women), 12 part-time (8 women); includes 5 minority (4 Asian Americans or Pacific Islanders, 1 Hispanic American), 4 international. Average age 30. 249 applicants, 6% accepted, 15 enrolled. In 2009, 12 doctorates awarded. *Degree requirements:* For doctorate, thesis/dissertation. *Entrance requirements:* For doctorate, GRE General Test. Additional exam requirements/recommendations for international students: Required—TOEFL (minimum score 500 paper-based; 173 computer-based). *Application deadline:* For fall admission, 12/15 for domestic and international students. Applications are processed on a rolling basis. Application fee: $55 ($65 for international students). Electronic applications accepted. *Expenses:* Tuition, state resident: full-time $4004; part-time $1674 per semester. Tuition, nonresident: full-time $14,134; part-time $5915 per semester. Required fees: $324 per semester. Tuition and fees vary according to course load, degree level and program. *Financial support:* In 2009–10, 46 students received support, including 4 fellowships with full tuition reimbursements available (averaging $11,000 per year), 21 research assistantships with full tuition reimbursements available (averaging $11,000 per year), 26 teaching assistantships with full tuition reimbursements available (averaging $11,000 per year); career-related internships or fieldwork also available. Financial award applicants required to submit FAFSA. *Faculty research:* Cognitive neuroscience, health, social cognition, psychopathology, cognitive and social development. Total annual research expenditures: $1.7 million. *Unit head:* Dr. Cynthia A. Berg, Chair, 801-581-8925, Fax: 801-581-5841, E-mail: cynthia.berg@psych.utah.edu. *Application contact:* Nancy Seegmiller, Administrative Assistant, 801-581-8925, Fax: 801-581-5841, E-mail: nancy.seegmiller@psych.utah.edu.

University of Vermont, Graduate College, College of Arts and Sciences, Department of Psychology, Burlington, VT 05405. Offers clinical psychology (PhD); psychology (PhD). *Accreditation:* APA. *Students:* 54 (44 women); includes 6 minority (1 African American, 1 Asian American or Pacific Islander, 4 Hispanic Americans), 3 international. 231 applicants, 5% accepted, 7 enrolled. In 2009, 5 doctorates awarded. *Degree requirements:* For doctorate, thesis/dissertation. *Entrance requirements:* For doctorate, GRE General Test. Additional exam requirements/recommendations for international students: Required—TOEFL (minimum score 550 paper-based; 213 computer-based; 80 iBT). *Application deadline:* For fall admission, 12/1 for domestic students. Application fee: $40. Electronic applications accepted. *Expenses:* Tuition, state resident: part-time $508 per credit hour. Tuition, nonresident: part-time $1281 per credit hour. *Financial support:* Fellowships, research assistantships, teaching assistantships available. Financial award application deadline: 2/1. *Unit head:* Dr. William Falls, Chairperson, 802-656-2670. *Application contact:* Dr. Rex Forehand, Coordinator, 802-656-2670.

University of Victoria, Faculty of Graduate Studies, Faculty of Social Sciences, Department of Psychology, Victoria, BC V8W 2Y2, Canada. Offers clinical psychology (PhD); clinical psychology (neuropsychology) (M Sc); cognition and brain science (M Sc, PhD); experimental neuropsychology (M Sc, PhD); individualized study (M Sc, PhD); life span development psychology (PhD); life span developmental psychology (M Sc); social psychology (M Sc, PhD). *Accreditation:* APA (one or more programs are accredited). *Degree requirements:* For master's, thesis; for doctorate, thesis/dissertation, candidacy exam. *Entrance requirements:* For master's and doctorate, GRE General Test. Additional exam requirements/recommendations for international students: Required—TOEFL (minimum score 600 paper-based; 250 computer-based). Electronic applications accepted. *Faculty research:* Life span development psychology and aging, behavioral neuroscience, cognitive psychology, behavioral psychology, environmental psychology.

University of Virginia, College and Graduate School of Arts and Sciences, Department of Psychology, Charlottesville, VA 22903. Offers MA, PhD. *Accreditation:* APA (one or more programs are accredited). *Faculty:* 37 full-time (10 women), 3 part-time/adjunct (2 women). *Students:* 82 full-time (57 women), 1 part-time (0 women); includes 7 minority (6 African Americans, 1 Asian American or Pacific Islander), 8 international. Average age 27. 495 applicants, 7% accepted, 17 enrolled. In 2009, 13 master's, 17 doctorates awarded. *Degree requirements:* For master's, pre-dissertation research project; for doctorate, comprehensive exam, thesis/dissertation. *Entrance requirements:* For master's and doctorate, GRE General Test, 3 or more letters of recommendation. Additional exam requirements/recommendations for international students: Required—TOEFL (minimum score 600 paper-based; 250 computer-based; 90 iBT), IELTS (minimum score 7). *Application deadline:* For fall admission, 12/1 for domestic and international students. Applications are processed on a rolling basis. Application fee: $60. Electronic applications accepted. *Financial support:* Fellowships, research assistantships, teaching assistantships available. Financial award applicants required to submit FAFSA. *Unit head:* Dennis R. Proffitt, Chair, 434-982-4750, Fax: 434-982-4766, E-mail: psy-dept@virginia.edu. *Application contact:* Debbie Snow, Psychology Department Admission Secretary, 434-982-4750, Fax: 434-982-4766, E-mail: dsnow@virginia.edu.

University of Washington, Graduate School, College of Arts and Sciences, Department of Psychology, Seattle, WA 98195. Offers animal behavior (PhD); child psychology (PhD); clinical psychology (PhD); cognition and perception (PhD); developmental psychology (PhD); quantitative psychology (PhD); social psychology and personality (PhD). *Accreditation:* APA. *Degree requirements:* For doctorate, thesis/dissertation. *Entrance requirements:* For doctorate, GRE General Test, minimum GPA of 3.0. Electronic applications accepted. *Faculty research:* Addictive behaviors, artificial intelligence, child psychopathology, mechanisms and development of vision, physiology of ingestive behaviors.

University of Waterloo, Graduate Studies, Faculty of Arts, Department of Psychology, Waterloo, ON N2L 3G1, Canada. Offers MA, MA Sc, PhD. *Accreditation:* APA (one or more programs are accredited). Terminal master's awarded for partial completion of doctoral program. *Degree requirements:* For master's, thesis (for some programs); for doctorate, thesis/dissertation. *Entrance requirements:* For master's, GRE, honors degree in psychology, minimum B average; for doctorate, GRE, master's degree in psychology, minimum B average. Additional exam requirements/recommendations for international students: Required—TOEFL, TWE. Electronic applications accepted. *Faculty research:* Memory and attention, attitudes and behavior in the workplace, object recognition, judgment and decision making, communication and knowledge in toddlers.

The University of Western Ontario, Faculty of Graduate Studies, Biosciences Division, Department of Psychology, London, ON N6A 5B8, Canada. Offers MA, PhD. *Degree requirements:* For master's, thesis; for doctorate, thesis/dissertation. *Entrance requirements:* For master's, minimum B average during last 2 years; for doctorate, MA in psychology. Additional exam requirements/recommendations for international students: Required—TOEFL. *Faculty research:* Clinical, applied and social/personality psychology; psychobiology; cognitive processes.

University of West Florida, College of Arts and Sciences: Arts, Department of Psychology, Pensacola, FL 32514-5750. Offers counseling (MA); counseling-licensed mental health counselor (MA); general (MA); industrial-organizational (MA). Part-time programs available. *Faculty:* 10 full-time (3 women), 2 part-time/adjunct (1 woman). *Students:* 69 full-time (50 women), 45 part-time (35 women); includes 14 minority (11 African Americans, 1 Asian American or Pacific Islander, 2 Hispanic Americans), 5 international. Average age 27. 124 applicants, 60% accepted, 34 enrolled. In 2009, 16 master's awarded. *Degree requirements:* For master's, thesis (for some programs). *Entrance requirements:* For master's, GRE General Test, GRE Subject Test, minimum GPA of 3.0. Additional exam requirements/recommendations for international students: Required—TOEFL (minimum score 550 paper-based; 213 computer-based). *Application deadline:* For fall admission, 6/1 for domestic students, 5/15 for international students; for spring admission, 11/1 for domestic students, 10/1 for international students. Applications are processed on a rolling basis. Application fee: $30. *Expenses:* Tuition, state resident: full-time $4982; part-time $260 per credit hour. Tuition, nonresident: full-time $20,059; part-time $919 per credit hour. Required fees: $1247; $52 per credit hour. *Financial support:* In 2009–10, 3 research assistantships with partial tuition reimbursements (averaging $3,760 per year), 3 teaching assistantships with partial tuition reimbursements (averaging $5,000 per year) were awarded; career-related internships or fieldwork and unspecified assistantships also available. Financial award application deadline: 4/15; financial award applicants required to submit FAFSA. *Faculty research:* Prose recall, brain imaging, peak performance, biofeedback and pain control, comparable worth. Total annual research expenditures: $15,000. *Unit head:* Dr. Laura Koppes, Chairperson, 850-474-3493. *Application contact:* Terry McCray, Assistant Director of Graduate Admissions, 850-473-7718, Fax: 850-473-7714, E-mail: gradadmissions@uwf.edu.

University of West Georgia, Graduate School, College of Arts and Sciences, Department of Psychology, Carrollton, GA 30118. Offers individual, organizational, and community transformation: consciousness and society (Psy D); psychology (MA). Part-time programs available. *Faculty:* 14 full-time (2 women). *Students:* 55 full-time (33 women), 18 part-time (10 women); includes 10 minority (7 African Americans, 3 Hispanic Americans), 2 international. Average age 32. 59 applicants, 46% accepted, 13 enrolled. In 2009, 14 master's awarded. Terminal master's awarded for partial completion of doctoral program. *Degree requirements:* For master's, one foreign language, comprehensive exam, thesis optional; for doctorate, comprehensive exam, thesis/dissertation. *Entrance requirements:* For master's, GRE General Test, interview, minimum GPA of 2.5, written statement; for doctorate, GRE or MAT, interview, written statement. *Application deadline:* For fall admission, 7/17 for domestic students; for spring admission, 11/20 for domestic students. Applications are processed on a rolling basis. Application fee: $30. Electronic applications accepted. *Expenses:* Tuition, state resident: full-time $2952; part-time $164 per semester hour. Tuition, nonresident: full-time $11,808; part-time $656 per semester hour. Required fees: $42.90 per semester hour. $307 per semester. Tuition and fees vary according to course load. *Financial support:* In 2009–10, 12 students received support, including 12 research assistantships with full tuition reimbursements available (averaging $3,000 per year); career-related internships or fieldwork, tuition waivers (full), and unspecified assistantships also available. Support available to part-time students. Financial award application deadline: 7/1; financial award applicants required to submit FAFSA. *Faculty research:* Creativity, inspiration and consciousness; symbolism and metaphor in psychotherapy; spirituality of children; feminism and culture; mind/body connection. Total annual research expenditures: $30,000. *Unit head:* Dr. Donadrian Lawrence Rice, Chair, 678-839-6510, Fax: 678-839-0611, E-mail: drice@westga.edu. *Application contact:* Dr. Charles W. Clark, Dean, 678-839-6508, E-mail: cclark@westga.edu.

University of Windsor, Faculty of Graduate Studies, Faculty of Arts and Social Sciences, Department of Psychology, Windsor, ON N9B 3P4, Canada. Offers adult clinical (MA, PhD); applied social psychology (MA, PhD); child clinical (MA, PhD); clinical neuropsychology (MA, PhD). *Accreditation:* APA (one or more programs are accredited). *Degree requirements:* For master's, thesis; for doctorate, comprehensive exam, thesis/dissertation. *Entrance requirements:* For master's, GRE General Test, GRE Subject Test in psychology, minimum B average; for doctorate, GRE General Test, GRE Subject Test in psychology, master's degree. Additional exam requirements/recommendations for international students: Required—TOEFL (minimum score 600 paper-based; 250 computer-based). Electronic applications accepted. *Faculty research:* Gambling, suicidology, emotional competence, psychotherapy and trauma.

University of Wisconsin–Eau Claire, College of Arts and Sciences, Department of Psychology, Eau Claire, WI 54702-4004. Offers school psychology (MSE, Ed S). Part-time programs available. *Faculty:* 17 full-time (9 women). *Students:* 18 full-time (16 women), 10 part-time (7 women), 2 international. Average age 24. 46 applicants, 39% accepted, 16 enrolled. In 2009, 8 master's, 6 other advanced degrees awarded. *Degree requirements:* For master's, comprehensive exam, thesis, National Certified School Psychologist Professional Exam, written exam, externship. *Entrance requirements:* For master's, GRE, minimum undergraduate GPA of 3.0; courses in exceptional children and youth, statistics, psychopathology, and theories of counseling. Additional exam requirements/recommendations for international students: Required—TOEFL (minimum score 550 paper-based; 213 computer-based; 79 iBT). *Application deadline:* For fall admission, 3/1 priority date for domestic students, 6/1 priority date for international students; for spring admission, 11/1 priority date for international students. Applications are processed on a rolling basis. Application fee: $56. Electronic applications accepted. *Expenses:* Tuition, state resident: full-time $6705.90; part-time $372.55 per credit. Tuition, nonresident: full-time $16,771; part-time $931.74 per credit. Required fees: $925.50; $51.19 per credit. One-time fee: $56. *Financial support:* In 2009–10, 21 students received support, including 5 fellowships (averaging $1,100 per year); Federal Work-Study and unspecified assistantships also available. Financial award application deadline: 3/1; financial award applicants required to submit FAFSA. *Unit head:* Dr. Lori Bica, Chair, 715-836-5733, Fax: 715-836-2214, E-mail: bicala@uwec.edu. *Application contact:* Kristina Anderson, Director of Admissions, 715-836-5415, Fax: 715-836-2409, E-mail: admissions@uwec.edu.

University of Wisconsin–La Crosse, Office of University Graduate Studies, College of Liberal Studies, Department of Psychology, La Crosse, WI 54601-3742. Offers school psychology (MS Ed, Ed S); student affairs administration (MS Ed). *Faculty:* 19 full-time (12 women). *Students:* 56 full-time (49 women), 68 part-time (55 women); includes 9 minority (1 African American, 1 American Indian/Alaska Native, 3 Asian Americans or Pacific Islanders, 4 Hispanic Americans), 1 international. Average age 27. 160 applicants, 39% accepted, 48 enrolled. In 2009, 50 master's awarded. *Degree requirements:* For master's, thesis, seminar, or comprehensive exams. *Entrance requirements:* For master's, GRE General Test, minimum GPA of 2.85, interview, writing sample, resume. Additional exam requirements/recommendations for international students: Required—TOEFL (minimum score 550 paper-based; 213 computer-based; 79 iBT). Application fee: $56. Electronic applications accepted. *Financial support:* In 2009–10, 6 research assistantships with partial tuition reimbursements (averaging $7,227 per year) were awarded; career-related internships or fieldwork, Federal Work-Study, institutionally sponsored loans, scholarships/grants, health care benefits, and unspecified assistantships also available. Support available to part-time students. *Unit head:* Dr. Emily Johnson, Chair, 608-785-6888, Fax: 608-785-8443, E-mail: johnson.emil@uwlax.edu. *Application contact:* Kathryn Kiefer, Director of Admissions, 608-785-8939, E-mail: admissions@uwlax.edu.

University of Wisconsin–Madison, Graduate School, College of Letters and Science, Department of Psychology, Madison, WI 53706-1380. Offers biology of brain and behavior (PhD); clinical psychology (PhD); cognitive neurosciences (PhD); developmental psychology

Psychology—General

University of Wisconsin–Madison (continued)
(PhD); perception (PhD); psychology (PhD); social and personality psychology (PhD). *Accreditation:* APA. *Degree requirements:* For doctorate, comprehensive exam, thesis/dissertation. *Entrance requirements:* For doctorate, GRE General Test, minimum undergraduate GPA of 3.0. Additional exam requirements/recommendations for international students: Required—TOEFL. Electronic applications accepted. *Expenses:* Tuition, state resident: part-time $594 per credit. Tuition, nonresident: part-time $1504 per credit. Required fees: $65 per credit. Tuition and fees vary according to course load, program and reciprocity agreements.

University of Wisconsin–Milwaukee, Graduate School, College of Letters and Sciences, Department of Psychology, Milwaukee, WI 53201-0413. Offers clinical psychology (MS, PhD); psychology (MS, PhD). *Accreditation:* APA (one or more programs are accredited). *Faculty:* 23 full-time (6 women). *Students:* 54 full-time (32 women), 17 part-time (11 women); includes 12 minority (3 African Americans, 2 Asian Americans or Pacific Islanders, 7 Hispanic Americans), 4 international. Average age 28. 162 applicants, 14% accepted, 11 enrolled. In 2009, 14 master's, 11 doctorates awarded. *Degree requirements:* For master's, thesis; for doctorate, variable foreign language requirement, thesis/dissertation. *Entrance requirements:* For master's and doctorate, GRE General Test, GRE Subject Test. Additional exam requirements/recommendations for international students: Required—TOEFL (minimum score 550 paper-based; 79 iBT), IELTS (minimum score 6.5). *Application deadline:* For fall admission, 1/1 priority date for domestic students; for spring admission, 9/1 for domestic students. Applications are processed on a rolling basis. Application fee: $45 ($75 for international students). *Expenses:* Tuition, state resident: full-time $8800. Tuition, nonresident: full-time $20,760. Tuition and fees vary according to program and reciprocity agreements. *Financial support:* In 2009–10, 2 research assistantships, 42 teaching assistantships were awarded; career-related internships or fieldwork and unspecified assistantships also available. Support available to part-time students. Financial award application deadline: 4/15. Total annual research expenditures: $1.4 million. *Unit head:* Hobart Davies, Representative, 414-229-6594, Fax: 414-229-5219, E-mail: hobart@uwm.edu. *Application contact:* Susan Lima, General Information Contact, 414-229-4359, Fax: 414-229-6967, E-mail: suelima@uwm.edu.

University of Wisconsin–Oshkosh, The Office of Graduate Studies, College of Letters and Science, Department of Psychology, Oshkosh, WI 54901. Offers experimental psychology (MS); industrial/organizational psychology (MS). *Degree requirements:* For master's, thesis. *Entrance requirements:* For master's, GRE, 10 semester hours of undergraduate course work in psychology. Additional exam requirements/recommendations for international students: Required—TOEFL (minimum score 550 paper-based; 213 computer-based; 79 iBT). Electronic applications accepted. *Faculty research:* Performance evaluation, training, biological bases of behavior, tactile perception, aging.

University of Wisconsin–Stout, Graduate School, College of Human Development, Program in Applied Psychology, Menomonie, WI 54751. Offers MS. Part-time programs available. *Degree requirements:* For master's, thesis. *Entrance requirements:* For master's, GRE General Test, GRE Subject Test, minimum GPA of 3.0, 15 semester credits of undergraduate course work in psychology, 8 semester credits in research methods and statistics. Additional exam requirements/recommendations for international students: Required—TOEFL (minimum score 500 paper-based; 173 computer-based; 61 iBT). Electronic applications accepted. *Faculty research:* Health complementary therapies, motivation, group dynamics, social reasoning, stress.

University of Wisconsin–Whitewater, School of Graduate Studies, College of Letters and Sciences, Department of Psychology, Whitewater, WI 53190-1790. Offers school psychology (MS Ed, Ed S). Part-time and evening/weekend programs available. Postbaccalaureate distance learning degree programs offered (no on-campus study). *Degree requirements:* For master's, comprehensive exam or thesis. *Entrance requirements:* For master's, MAT or GRE, interview, minimum GPA of 3.0, 3 letters of recommendation. Additional exam requirements/recommendations for international students: Required—TOEFL (minimum score 550 paper-based; 213 computer-based). Electronic applications accepted. *Faculty research:* School violence/youth violence; anger/aggression interventions; women's mental health; pedagogy of empathy, social psychology, and personality.

University of Wyoming, College of Arts and Sciences, Department of Psychology, Laramie, WY 82070. Offers MA, MS, PhD. *Accreditation:* APA (one or more programs are accredited). Terminal master's awarded for partial completion of doctoral program. *Degree requirements:* For master's, thesis; for doctorate, comprehensive exam, thesis/dissertation. *Entrance requirements:* For master's and doctorate, GRE General Test, GRE Subject Test, minimum GPA of 3.0. Additional exam requirements/recommendations for international students: Required—TOEFL. *Faculty research:* Child development, health psychology, psychology and law, social psychology, mood/anxiety disorders.

Utah State University, School of Graduate Studies, College of Education and Human Services, Department of Psychology, Logan, UT 84322. Offers clinical/counseling/school psychology (PhD); research and evaluation methodology (PhD); school counseling (MS); school psychology (MS). *Accreditation:* APA (one or more programs are accredited). Part-time and evening/weekend programs available. Postbaccalaureate distance learning degree programs offered (no on-campus study). Terminal master's awarded for partial completion of doctoral program. *Degree requirements:* For master's, thesis (for some programs); for doctorate, thesis/dissertation. *Entrance requirements:* For master's, GRE General Test (school psychology), MAT (school counseling), minimum GPA of 3.5; for doctorate, GRE General Test, minimum GPA of 3.5. Additional exam requirements/recommendations for international students: Required—TOEFL. *Faculty research:* Hearing loss detection in infancy, ADHD, eating disorders, domestic violence, neuropsychology, bilingual/Spanish speaking students/parents.

Valdosta State University, Graduate School, Department of Psychology and Counseling, Valdosta, GA 31698. Offers clinical/counseling psychology (MS); industrial/organizational psychology (MS); school counseling (M Ed, Ed S); school psychology (Ed S). Part-time and evening/weekend programs available. *Degree requirements:* For master's, thesis or alternative, comprehensive written and/or oral exams; for Ed S, thesis. *Entrance requirements:* For master's and Ed S, GRE General Test or MAT. Additional exam requirements/recommendations for international students: Required—TOEFL (minimum score 523 paper-based; 193 computer-based). Electronic applications accepted. *Faculty research:* Using Bender-Gestalt to predict graphomotor dimensions of the draw-a-person test, neurobehavioral hemispheric dominance.

Valparaiso University, Graduate School, Department of Psychology, Valparaiso, IN 46383. Offers business management (for counseling students) (Certificate); clinical mental health counseling (MA); community counseling (MA); JD/MA. Part-time and evening/weekend programs available. *Faculty:* 9 part-time/adjunct (4 women). *Students:* 38 full-time (34 women), 9 part-time (3 women); includes 7 minority (3 African Americans, 4 Hispanic Americans), 2 international. Average age 29. In 2009, 18 master's awarded. *Degree requirements:* For master's, thesis or alternative, internship. *Entrance requirements:* For master's, minimum GPA of 3.0; 15 credits in the social/behavioral sciences (psychology, sociology, human development, etc.) with a minimum GPA of 3.0; course in introductory psychology; recent statistics course with minimum B average. Additional exam requirements/recommendations for international students: Required—TOEFL (minimum score 550 paper-based; 213 computer-based; 80 iBT). *Application deadline:* For fall admission, 3/1 priority date for domestic students. Applications are processed on a rolling basis. Application fee: $30 ($50 for international students). Electronic applications accepted. *Financial support:* Career-related internships or fieldwork, scholarships/grants, traineeships, and unspecified assistantships available. Support available to part-time students. Financial award applicants required to submit FAFSA. *Faculty research:* Environmental psychology, human sexuality, racial identity development models, social psychology. *Unit head:* Dr. James Nelson, Director of Graduate Programs, 219-464-5443, Fax: 219-464-6878, E-mail: jim.nelson@valpo.edu. *Application contact:* Jamie Haney, Coordinator of Graduate Admission, 219-464-5313, Fax: 219-464-5381, E-mail: jamie.haney@valpo.edu.

Vanderbilt University, Graduate School, Program in Psychological Sciences, Nashville, TN 37240-1001. Offers MA, MS, PhD. *Accreditation:* APA (one or more programs are accredited). *Faculty:* 55 full-time (22 women). *Students:* 93 full-time (65 women), 2 part-time (1 woman); includes 17 minority (6 African Americans, 6 Asian Americans or Pacific Islanders, 5 Hispanic Americans), 19 international. Average age 28. 441 applicants, 7% accepted, 19 enrolled. In 2009, 4 master's, 4 doctorates awarded. *Degree requirements:* For doctorate, comprehensive exam, thesis/dissertation, final and qualifying exams. *Entrance requirements:* For doctorate, GRE General Test, GRE Subject Test. Additional exam requirements/recommendations for international students: Required—TOEFL (minimum score 570 paper-based; 230 computer-based; 88 iBT). *Application deadline:* For fall admission, 12/15 for domestic and international students. Application fee: $0. Electronic applications accepted. *Financial support:* Fellowships with full and partial tuition reimbursements, research assistantships with full and partial tuition reimbursements, teaching assistantships with full and partial tuition reimbursements, career-related internships or fieldwork, Federal Work-Study, institutionally sponsored loans, scholarships/grants, traineeships, and health care benefits available. Financial award application deadline: 1/15; financial award applicants required to submit CSS PROFILE or FAFSA. *Faculty research:* Clinical, cognitive, developmental, and social psychology; neuroscience; vision; behavior. *Unit head:* Andrew J. Tomarken, Co-Chair, 615-322-2874, Fax: 615-343-8449, E-mail: andrew.j.tomarken@vanderbilt.edu. *Application contact:* Thomas J. Palmeri, Co-Director of Graduate Studies, 615-322-2874, Fax: 615-343-8449, E-mail: thomas.j.palmeri@vanderbilt.edu.

Vanderbilt University, Peabody College, Department of Psychology and Human Development, Nashville, TN 37240-1001. Offers child studies (M Ed). *Accreditation:* APA. Part-time programs available. *Faculty:* 28 full-time (15 women), 3 part-time/adjunct (1 woman). *Students:* 15 full-time (all women), 3 part-time (2 women); includes 5 minority (4 African Americans, 1 Hispanic American). Average age 25. 38 applicants, 50% accepted, 12 enrolled. In 2009, 13 master's awarded. *Degree requirements:* For master's, comprehensive exam, thesis optional. *Entrance requirements:* For master's, GRE General Test. Additional exam requirements/recommendations for international students: Required—TOEFL (minimum score 550 paper-based; 213 computer-based). *Application deadline:* For fall admission, 12/31 for domestic and international students; for spring admission, 11/1 for domestic and international students. Applications are processed on a rolling basis. Application fee: $0. Electronic applications accepted. *Financial support:* In 2009–10, 17 students received support, including 11 research assistantships with full and partial tuition reimbursements available, 1 teaching assistantship with full and partial tuition reimbursement available; fellowships with full and partial tuition reimbursements available, Federal Work-Study, institutionally sponsored loans, scholarships/grants, tuition waivers (partial), and unspecified assistantships also available. Financial award application deadline: 2/1; financial award applicants required to submit FAFSA. *Faculty research:* Cognitive, language and social development; stress, coping and emotion; quantitative methods and evaluation; clinical intervention and prevention; individual differences, disabilities and developmental psychopathology. *Unit head:* Dr. David Cole, Acting Chair, 615-322-8141, Fax: 615-343-9494, E-mail: david.cole@vanderbilt.edu. *Application contact:* Sharone Hall, Educational Coordinator, 615-343-4963, Fax: 615-343-9494, E-mail: sharone.k.hall@vanderbilt.edu.

Villanova University, Graduate School of Liberal Arts and Sciences, Department of Psychology, Villanova, PA 19085-1699. Offers MS. Part-time and evening/weekend programs available. *Faculty:* 8 full-time (4 women), 1 (woman) part-time/adjunct. *Students:* 36 full-time (22 women), 8 part-time (7 women). Average age 24. 108 applicants, 44% accepted, 21 enrolled. In 2009, 17 master's awarded. *Degree requirements:* For master's, thesis. *Entrance requirements:* For master's, GRE General Test, minimum GPA of 3.0. Additional exam requirements/recommendations for international students: Required—TOEFL. *Application deadline:* For fall admission, 3/1 priority date for domestic and international students; for spring admission, 11/15 priority date for domestic and international students. Applications are processed on a rolling basis. Application fee: $50. Electronic applications accepted. *Expenses:* Tuition: Part-time $630 per credit. Required fees: $60 per credit. Part-time tuition and fees vary according to degree level and program. *Financial support:* Research assistantships, Federal Work-Study and scholarships/grants available. Financial award applicants required to submit FAFSA. *Unit head:* Dr. Thomas Toppino, Chair, 610-519-4720. *Application contact:* Dr. Adele Lindenmeyr, Dean, Graduate School of Liberal Arts and Sciences, 610-519-7093, Fax: 610-519-7096.

See Close-Up on page 1107.

Virginia Commonwealth University, Graduate School, College of Humanities and Sciences, Department of Psychology, Program in General Psychology, Richmond, VA 23284-9005. Offers PhD. *Degree requirements:* For doctorate, thesis/dissertation. *Entrance requirements:* For doctorate, GRE General Test.

Virginia Polytechnic Institute and State University, Graduate School, College of Science, Department of Psychology, Blacksburg, VA 24061. Offers bio-behavioral sciences (PhD); clinical psychology (PhD); developmental psychology (PhD); industrial/organizational psychology (PhD); psychology (MS). *Accreditation:* APA (one or more programs are accredited). *Faculty:* 23 full-time (7 women). *Students:* 71 full-time (45 women), 6 part-time (3 women); includes 18 minority (6 American Indian/Alaska Native, 8 Asian Americans or Pacific Islanders, 4 Hispanic Americans), 1 international. Average age 27. 201 applicants, 7% accepted, 14 enrolled. In 2009, 20 master's, 14 doctorates awarded. *Entrance requirements:* For master's and doctorate, GRE, GMAT. Additional exam requirements/recommendations for international students: Required—TOEFL (minimum score 550 paper-based; 213 computer-based). *Application deadline:* For fall admission, 5/15 for international students; for spring admission, 10/15 for international students. Applications are processed on a rolling basis. Application fee: $65. Electronic applications accepted. *Expenses:* Tuition, area resident: Full-time $10,228; part-time $459 per credit hour. Tuition, nonresident: full-time $17,892; part-time $865 per credit hour. Required fees: $1966; $451 per semester. *Financial support:* In 2009–10, 18 research assistantships with full tuition reimbursements (averaging $16,153 per year), 41 teaching assistantships with full tuition reimbursements (averaging $16,053 per year) were awarded; career-related internships or fieldwork, Federal Work-Study, scholarships/grants, and unspecified assistantships also available. Financial award application deadline: 1/15. *Faculty research:* Infant development from electrophysical point of view, work motivation and personnel selection, EEG, ERP and hypnosis with reference to chronic pain, intimate violence. Total annual research expenditures: $2.1 million. *Unit head:* Dr. Robert S. Stephens, Dean, 540-231-6304, Fax: 540-231-3652, E-mail: stephens@vt.edu. *Application contact:* Kirby Deater-Deckard, Information Contact, 540-231-6581, Fax: 540-231-3652, E-mail: kirbydd@vt.edu.

Virginia State University, School of Graduate Studies, Research, and Outreach, School of Engineering, Science and Technology, Department of Psychology, Petersburg, VA 23806-0001. Offers behavioral and community health sciences (PhD); clinical health psychology (PhD); clinical psychology (MS); general psychology (MS). *Degree requirements:* For master's, one foreign language, thesis. *Entrance requirements:* For master's, GRE General Test.

Wake Forest University, Graduate School of Arts and Sciences, Department of Psychology, Winston-Salem, NC 27109. Offers MA. *Degree requirements:* For master's, one foreign language, comprehensive exam, thesis. *Entrance requirements:* For master's, GRE General Test. Additional exam requirements/recommendations for international students: Required—TOEFL (minimum score 213 computer-based; 79 iBT). Electronic applications accepted. *Faculty research:* Developmental, social, personality, experimental, and physiological psychology.

Walden University, Graduate Programs, School of Psychology, Minneapolis, MN 55401. Offers clinical child psychology (Post-Doctoral Certificate); clinical psychology (Post-Doctoral Certificate); counseling psychology (Post-Doctoral Certificate); forensic psychology (MS), including forensic psychology in the community, general program, mental health applications, program planning and evaluation in forensic settings, psychology and legal systems; general psychology (Post-Doctoral Certificate); health psychology (Post-Doctoral Certificate); organizational psychology (Post-Doctoral Certificate); organizational psychology and development (Postbaccalaureate Certificate); psychology (MS, PhD), including clinical psychology (PhD), counseling psychology (PhD), crisis management and response (MS), general program (MS), general psychology (PhD), health psychology, leadership development and coaching (MS), media psychology (MS), organizational psychology (PhD), organizational psychology and development (MS), organizational psychology and nonprofit management (MS), program evaluation and research (MS), psychology of culture (MS), psychology, public administration, and social change (MS), social psychology (MS), terrorism and security (MS); teaching online (Post-Master's Certificate). Part-time and evening/weekend programs available. Postbaccalaureate distance learning degree programs offered (minimal on-campus study). *Faculty:* 33 full-time, 222 part-time/adjunct. *Students:* 3,546 full-time (2,761 women), 1,133 part-time (908 women); includes 1,723 minority (1,319 African Americans, 56 American Indian/Alaska Native, 101 Asian Americans or Pacific Islanders, 247 Hispanic Americans), 80 international. Average age 41. In 2009, 495 master's, 70 doctorates, 2 other advanced degrees awarded. Terminal master's awarded for partial completion of doctoral program. *Degree requirements:* For master's, thesis optional; for doctorate, thesis/dissertation, residency. *Entrance requirements:* For master's, bachelor's degree or equivalent in related field; minimum GPA of 2.5; official transcripts; goal statement; access to computer and Internet; for doctorate, master's degree or equivalent in related field; minimum GPA of 3.0;3 years of related professional/academic experience (preferred). Additional exam requirements/recommendations for international students: Required—TOEFL (minimum score 550 paper-based; 213 computer-based), IELTS (minimum score 6.5), or Michigan English Language Assessment Battery (minimum score 82). *Application deadline:* Applications are processed on a rolling basis. Application fee: $50. Electronic applications accepted. *Expenses:* Tuition: Full-time $13,665; part-time $560 per credit. Required fees: $1375. Tuition and fees vary according to course load, degree level and program. *Financial support:* In 2009–10, 290 students received support; fellowships, Federal Work-Study, scholarships/grants, unspecified assistantships, and family tuition reduction, active duty/veteran tuition reduction, group tuition reduction, interest-free payment plans available. Support available to part-time students. Financial award applicants required to submit FAFSA. *Unit head:* Dr. Melanie Storms, Associate Dean, 800-925-3368. *Application contact:* Jennifer Hall, Director of Enrollment, 866-4-WALDEN, E-mail: info@waldenu.edu.

Washburn University, College of Arts and Sciences, Department of Psychology, Topeka, KS 66621. Offers clinical psychology (MA). Part-time programs available. *Degree requirements:* For master's, thesis. *Entrance requirements:* For master's, GRE General Test, 15 hours of course work in psychology. Electronic applications accepted. *Faculty research:* Animal behavior, correctional psychology, children's social development, metacognition and metamemory, psychology of exercise, Gibsonian Ecological Psychology, treatment of anxiety disorders.

Washington College, Graduate Programs, Department of Psychology, Chestertown, MD 21620-1197. Offers MA. Part-time and evening/weekend programs available. *Entrance requirements:* For master's, GRE General Test.

Washington State University, Graduate School, College of Liberal Arts, Department of Psychology, Pullman, WA 99164. Offers clinical psychology (PhD); experimental psychology (PhD); psychology (MS). *Accreditation:* APA (one or more programs are accredited). *Faculty:* 22. *Students:* 49 full-time (34 women), 4 part-time (2 women); includes 7 minority (2 Asian Americans or Pacific Islanders, 5 Hispanic Americans), 7 international. Average age 29. 262 applicants, 6% accepted, 12 enrolled. In 2009, 7 master's, 8 doctorates awarded. *Degree requirements:* For master's, comprehensive exam (for some programs), thesis (for some programs), oral exam; for doctorate, comprehensive exam, thesis/dissertation, oral exam, written exam. *Entrance requirements:* For master's, minimum undergraduate GPA of 3.0; research experiences; clinical experiences; at least 18 hours of psychology, including a class in statistics; three letters of recommendation, official transcripts; for doctorate, three letters of reference; summary data form; at least 18 credits of study in psychology; at least one course in statistics and research methodology; official transcripts; minimum cumulative undergraduate GPA of 3.0 or master's degree in psychology. *Application deadline:* For fall admission, 12/15 priority date for domestic and international students. Applications are processed on a rolling basis. Application fee: $50. *Financial support:* In 2009–10, 5 research assistantships with full and partial tuition reimbursements (averaging $13,917 per year), 39 teaching assistantships with full and partial tuition reimbursements (averaging $13,056 per year) were awarded; fellowships, career-related internships or fieldwork, Federal Work-Study, institutionally sponsored loans, and unspecified assistantships also available. Financial award application deadline: 2/15; financial award applicants required to submit FAFSA. *Faculty research:* Childhood conduct disorders, etiology of depression, treatment of reading disorders, applied behavior analysis, selective attention. *Unit head:* Dr. John Hinson, Chair, 509-335-1089, Fax: 509-335-5043, E-mail: hinson@mail.wsu.edu. *Application contact:* Graduate School Admissions, 800-GRADWSU, Fax: 509-335-16949, E-mail: gradsch@wsu.edu.

Washington University in St. Louis, Graduate School of Arts and Sciences, Department of Philosophy, Program in Philosophy/Neuroscience/Psychology, St. Louis, MO 63130-4899. Offers PhD. *Degree requirements:* For doctorate, thesis/dissertation. *Entrance requirements:* For doctorate, GRE General Test, sample of written work. Electronic applications accepted.

Washington University in St. Louis, Graduate School of Arts and Sciences, Department of Psychology, St. Louis, MO 63130-4899. Offers clinical psychology (PhD); general experimental psychology (PhD); social psychology (PhD). *Accreditation:* APA. Terminal master's awarded for partial completion of doctoral program. *Degree requirements:* For doctorate, thesis/dissertation. *Entrance requirements:* For doctorate, GRE General Test. Electronic applications accepted.

Wayne State University, College of Liberal Arts and Sciences, Department of Psychology, Detroit, MI 48202. Offers human development (MA); psychology (MA, MS, PhD), including behavioral and cognitive neuroscience (PhD), clinical psychology (PhD), cognitive and social psychology (PhD), industrial/organizational psychology (PhD), psychology (MA, MS). *Accreditation:* APA (one or more programs are accredited). *Degree requirements:* For doctorate, thesis/dissertation. *Entrance requirements:* For doctorate, GRE General Test, GRE Subject Test, letters of recommendation. Additional exam requirements/recommendations for international students: Required—TOEFL (minimum score 550 paper-based; 213 computer-based); Recommended—TWE (minimum score 6). Electronic applications accepted. *Faculty research:* Clinical neuropsychology; high risk factors in development; human aging and neuroscience; industrial/organizational psychology; health psychology.

West Chester University of Pennsylvania, Office of Graduate Studies, College of Arts and Sciences, Department of Psychology, West Chester, PA 19383. Offers clinical mental health (Certificate); clinical psychology (MA); general psychology (MA); industrial psychology (MA). Part-time and evening/weekend programs available. *Students:* 36 full-time (30 women), 77 part-time (55 women); includes 12 minority (5 African Americans, 4 Asian Americans or Pacific Islanders, 3 Hispanic Americans), 2 international. Average age 26. 175 applicants, 76% accepted, 58 enrolled. In 2009, 38 master's, 2 other advanced degrees awarded. *Degree requirements:* For master's, comprehensive exam, thesis (for some programs). *Entrance requirements:* For master's, GRE General Test or MAT, minimum GPA of 3.0, 3.25 in psychology; three letters of reference. Additional exam requirements/recommendations for international students: Required—TOEFL (minimum score 550 paper-based; 213 computer-based; 80 iBT). *Application deadline:* For fall admission, 4/15 priority date for domestic students, 3/15 for international students; for spring admission, 10/15 for domestic students, 9/1 for international students. Applications are processed on a rolling basis. Application fee: $35. Electronic applications accepted. *Expenses:* Tuition, state resident: full-time $6666; part-time $370 per credit. Tuition, nonresident: full-time $10,666; part-time $593 per credit. Required fees: $122.56 per credit. *Financial support:* In 2009–10, 19 research assistantships with full and partial tuition reimbursements (averaging $5,000 per year) were awarded; unspecified assistantships also available. Support available to part-time students. Financial award application deadline: 2/15; financial award applicants required to submit FAFSA. *Faculty research:* Animal learning and cognition. *Unit head:* Dr. Loretta Rieser-Danner, Chairperson, 610-436-3106, E-mail: lrieser-danner@wcupa.edu. *Application contact:* Dr. Stefani Yorges, Graduate Coordinator, 610-436-3154, E-mail: syorges@wcupa.edu.

Western Carolina University, Graduate School, College of Education and Allied Professions, Department of Psychology, Cullowhee, NC 28723. Offers general psychology (MA); school psychology (MA). Part-time programs available. *Students:* 47 full-time (33 women), 4 part-time (3 women). Average age 25. 73 applicants, 42% accepted, 24 enrolled. In 2009, 10 master's awarded. *Degree requirements:* For master's, comprehensive exam, thesis. *Entrance requirements:* For master's, GRE General Test, appropriate undergraduate degree, interview, 3 letters of recommendation. Additional exam requirements/recommendations for international students: Required—TOEFL (minimum score 550 paper-based; 270 computer-based; 79 iBT). *Application deadline:* For fall admission, 2/1 for domestic students. Application fee: $40. *Financial support:* In 2009–10, 32 students received support, including 32 teaching assistantships with full and partial tuition reimbursements available (averaging $7,000 per year); fellowships, research assistantships with full and partial tuition reimbursements available, career-related internships or fieldwork, institutionally sponsored loans, scholarships/grants, and unspecified assistantships also available. Financial award application deadline: 3/31; financial award applicants required to submit FAFSA. *Faculty research:* Five-factor model of personality, evolutionary psychology, stress and worry, body image and physical attractiveness, moral decision-making, memory, learning styles. *Unit head:* Dr. David McCord, Head, 828-227-7361, Fax: 828-227-7005, E-mail: mccord@email.wcu.edu. *Application contact:* Admissions Specialist for Psychology, 828-227-7398, Fax: 828-227-7480, E-mail: gradsch@email.wcu.edu.

Western Illinois University, School of Graduate Studies, College of Arts and Sciences, Department of Psychology, Macomb, IL 61455-1390. Offers clinical/community mental health (MS); general psychology (MS); psychology (MS, SSP); school psychology (SSP). Part-time programs available. *Students:* 42 full-time (21 women), 14 part-time (11 women); includes 2 minority (both Asian Americans or Pacific Islanders), 2 international. Average age 25. 75 applicants, 37% accepted. In 2009, 11 master's, 10 other advanced degrees awarded. *Degree requirements:* For master's, comprehensive exam (for some programs), thesis or alternative. *Entrance requirements:* For master's and SSP, GRE General Test. Additional exam requirements/recommendations for international students: Required—TOEFL (minimum score 550 paper-based; 213 computer-based; 80 iBT). *Application deadline:* Applications are processed on a rolling basis. Application fee: $30. Electronic applications accepted. *Expenses:* Tuition, state resident: full-time $4486; part-time $249.21 per credit hour. Tuition, nonresident: full-time $8972; part-time $498.42 per credit hour. Required fees: $72.62 per credit hour. *Financial support:* In 2009–10, 38 students received support, including 38 research assistantships with full tuition reimbursements available (averaging $7,280 per year). Financial award applicants required to submit FAFSA. *Unit head:* Dr. Steven Dworkin, Chairperson, 309-298-1593. *Application contact:* Evelyn Hoing, Assistant Director of Graduate Studies, 309-298-1806, Fax: 309-298-2345, E-mail: grad-office@wiu.edu.

Western Kentucky University, Graduate Studies, College of Education and Behavioral Sciences, Department of Psychology, Bowling Green, KY 42101. Offers psychology (MA); school psychology (Ed S). *Degree requirements:* For master's, comprehensive exam, thesis (for some programs); for Ed S, thesis, oral exam. *Entrance requirements:* For master's, GRE General Test; for Ed S, GRE General Test, minimum GPA of 3.5. Additional exam requirements/recommendations for international students: Required—TOEFL (minimum score 555 paper-based; 213 computer-based; 79 iBT). *Expenses:* Tuition, state resident: full-time $4160; part-time $416 per credit hour. Tuition, nonresident: full-time $9550; part-time $506 per credit hour. Tuition and fees vary according to campus/location and reciprocity agreements. *Faculty research:* Neural regeneration, enhancing mobility in the elderly, improvement in visual processing in older adults, lifespan development.

Western Michigan University, Graduate College, College of Arts and Sciences, Department of Psychology, Kalamazoo, MI 49008. Offers behavior analysis (MA, PhD); clinical psychology (PhD); industrial/organizational psychology (MA). *Accreditation:* APA (one or more programs are accredited). *Degree requirements:* For master's, variable foreign language requirement, thesis, oral exams; for doctorate, 2 foreign languages, comprehensive exam, thesis/dissertation, oral exams. *Entrance requirements:* For master's and doctorate, GRE General Test.

Western New England College, School of Arts and Sciences, Program in Behavior Analysis, Springfield, MA 01119. Offers applied behavior analysis (Postbaccalaureate Certificate); behavior analysis (PhD). Part-time programs available. *Students:* 22 part-time (18 women); includes 1 Asian American or Pacific Islander, 3 Hispanic Americans. *Entrance requirements:* For doctorate, GRE, master's degree in behavior analysis with minimum GPA of 3.6. *Application deadline:* For fall admission, 1/15 for domestic and international students. Application fee: $30. *Expenses:* Tuition: Part-time $552 per credit hour. Part-time tuition and fees vary according to program. *Financial support:* Available to part-time students. Applicants required to submit FAFSA. *Unit head:* Gregory Hanley, Director, 413-796-2367, E-mail: ghanley@wnec.edu. *Application contact:* Assistant Vice President, Graduate Studies and Continuing Education, 413-782-1517, Fax: 413-782-1777, E-mail: study@wnec.edu.

Western Washington University, Graduate School, College of Humanities and Social Sciences, Department of Psychology, Bellingham, WA 98225-5996. Offers experimental psychology (MS); mental health counseling (MS); school counseling (M Ed). *Accreditation:* ACA (one or more programs are accredited). *Degree requirements:* For master's, comprehensive exam, thesis (for some programs). *Entrance requirements:* For master's, GRE General Test, minimum GPA of 3.0 in last 60 semester hours or last 90 quarter hours. Additional exam requirements/recommendations for international students: Required—TOEFL (minimum score 567 paper-based; 227 computer-based). *Faculty research:* Social, cognitive, behavioral neuroscience, counseling/clinical, developmental.

Westfield State College, Division of Graduate and Continuing Education, Department of Psychology, Westfield, MA 01086. Offers applied behavior analysis (MA); mental health counseling (MA); school guidance (MA). Part-time and evening/weekend programs available. *Degree requirements:* For master's, comprehensive exam. *Entrance requirements:* For master's, GRE General Test, MAT, minimum undergraduate GPA of 2.7.

West Texas A&M University, College of Education and Social Sciences, Department of Behavioral Sciences, Canyon, TX 79016-0001. Offers psychology (MA). Part-time and evening/weekend programs available. *Degree requirements:* For master's, comprehensive exam, thesis optional. *Entrance requirements:* For master's, GRE General Test, 3 letters of recommendation; interview; minimum GPA of 3.25 in psychology, 3.0 overall. Additional exam requirements/recommendations for international students: Required—TOEFL (minimum score 550 paper-based). Electronic applications accepted. *Faculty research:* Application of sociological principles to historical and contemporary analyses of social systems.

West Virginia University, Eberly College of Arts and Sciences, Department of Psychology, Morgantown, WV 26506. Offers behavior analysis (PhD); clinical psychology (MA, PhD); development psychology (PhD); psychology (MS). *Accreditation:* APA (one or more programs are accredited). Part-time programs available. Terminal master's awarded for partial completion of doctoral program. *Degree requirements:* For master's, thesis optional; for doctorate, comprehensive exam, thesis/dissertation. *Entrance requirements:* For master's and doctorate, GRE General Test, minimum GPA of 3.0. Additional exam requirements/recommendations for international students: Required—TOEFL. *Faculty research:* Adult and child clinical psychology, behavioral assessment and therapy, child and adolescent behavior, life span development, experimental and applied behavior analysis.

Wheaton College, Graduate School, Department of Psychology, Wheaton, IL 60187-5593. Offers clinical psychology (MA, Psy D); counseling ministries (MA). *Accreditation:* APA (one or more programs are accredited). Terminal master's awarded for partial completion of doctoral program. *Degree requirements:* For master's, thesis or alternative; for doctorate, thesis/dissertation, internship. *Entrance requirements:* For master's, GRE General Test, 18 hours of course work in psychology; for doctorate, GRE General Test.

Psychology—General

Wichita State University, Graduate School, Fairmount College of Liberal Arts and Sciences, Department of Psychology, Wichita, KS 67260. Offers clinical (PhD); community (PhD); human factors (PhD). *Accreditation:* APA. Part-time programs available. *Expenses:* Tuition, state resident: full-time $4247; part-time $235.95 per credit hour. Tuition, nonresident: full-time $11,171; part-time $620.60 per credit hour. Required fees: $34; $3.60 per credit hour. $17 per term. Tuition and fees vary according to campus/location and program. *Unit head:* Dr. Charles Burdsal, Chair, 316-978-3170, Fax: 316-978-3006, E-mail: charles.burdsal@wichita.edu. *Application contact:* Dr. Charles Burdsal, Chair, 316-978-3170, Fax: 316-978-3006, E-mail: charles.burdsal@wichita.edu.

Widener University, School of Human Service Professions, Institute for Graduate Clinical Psychology, Law-Psychology Program, Chester, PA 19013-5792. Offers JD/Psy D. *Faculty:* 15 full-time (6 women), 18 part-time/adjunct (10 women). *Students:* 13 full-time (9 women); includes 2 minority (1 American Indian/Alaska Native, 1 Asian American or Pacific Islander). Average age 23. 21 applicants, 19% accepted. *Application deadline:* For fall admission, 2/1 for domestic students. Applications are processed on a rolling basis. Application fee: $60. Electronic applications accepted. *Financial support:* In 2009–10, 12 students received support; research assistantships, career-related internships or fieldwork, Federal Work-Study, institutionally sponsored loans, and scholarships/grants available. Financial award application deadline: 5/31. *Unit head:* Dr. Amiram Elwork, Director, 610-499-1206, Fax: 610-499-4625, E-mail: amiram.elwork@widener.edu. *Application contact:* Maureen A. Brennan, Admissions Coordinator, 610-499-1206, Fax: 610-499-4625, E-mail: maureen.a.brennan@widener.edu.

Wilfrid Laurier University, Faculty of Graduate Studies, Faculty of Science, Department of Psychology, Waterloo, ON N2L 3C5, Canada. Offers brain and cognition (M Sc, PhD); community psychology (MA, PhD); social and developmental psychology (MA, PhD). *Degree requirements:* For master's, thesis; for doctorate, thesis/dissertation. *Entrance requirements:* For master's, GRE General Test, honors BA or the equivalent in psychology, minimum B average in undergraduate course work; for doctorate, GRE General Test, master's degree, minimum A- average. Additional exam requirements/recommendations for international students: Required—TOEFL (minimum score 230 computer-based; 89 iBT). Electronic applications accepted. *Faculty research:* Brain and cognition, community psychology, social and developmental psychology.

William Carey University, School of Psychology and Counseling, Hattiesburg, MS 39401-5499. Offers counseling psychology (MS). Part-time programs available. *Entrance requirements:* For master's, GRE, PRAXIS, MAT, minimum GPA of 2.5. Additional exam requirements/recommendations for international students: Required—TOEFL (minimum score 550 paper-based; 213 computer-based). *Expenses:* Contact institution. *Faculty research:* Addiction prevention, psychometric measurement, crisis counseling, gerontology.

Winthrop University, College of Arts and Sciences, Department of Psychology, Rock Hill, SC 29733. Offers MS, SSP. *Degree requirements:* For master's and SSP, comprehensive exam. *Entrance requirements:* For master's, GRE General Test, interview, minimum GPA of 3.0, 3 letters of recommendation, 15 hours of psychology courses in specified subject areas. Electronic applications accepted.

Wisconsin School of Professional Psychology, Program in Clinical Psychology, Milwaukee, WI 53225-4960. Offers MA, Psy D. *Accreditation:* APA. Part-time and evening/weekend programs available. Terminal master's awarded for partial completion of doctoral program. *Degree requirements:* For master's, candidacy exam, 500 hours of supervised clinical practica; for doctorate, thesis/dissertation, 1 year clinical intern and practicum experience (2000 hrs), candidacy and clinical exams. *Entrance requirements:* For master's, GRE General Test, GRE Subject Test, bachelor's degree in psychology, writing sample; for doctorate, GRE General Test, GRE Subject Test, master's degree in clinical psychology or equivalent, writing sample. *Faculty research:* Violence prevention, psychology of women, forensic psychology, custody evaluation, aging, harm reduction in AODA.

Wright Institute, Program in Clinical Psychology, Berkeley, CA 94704-1796. Offers clinical psychology (Psy D); counseling psychology (MA). *Accreditation:* APA (one or more programs are accredited). Evening/weekend programs available. *Faculty:* 11 full-time (10 women), 58 part-time/adjunct (29 women). *Students:* 338 full-time (239 women); includes 74 minority (16 African Americans, 1 American Indian/Alaska Native, 23 Asian Americans or Pacific Islanders, 34 Hispanic Americans), 6 international. Average age 34. 333 applicants, 38% accepted, 59 enrolled. In 2009, 20 master's, 38 doctorates awarded. *Degree requirements:* For doctorate, comprehensive exam, thesis/dissertation. *Entrance requirements:* Additional exam requirements/recommendations for international students: Required—TOEFL (minimum score 600 paper-based). *Application deadline:* For fall admission, 1/15 priority date for domestic students, 1/15 for international students. Application fee: $50. Electronic applications accepted. *Expenses:* Tuition: Full-time $25,550. Full-time tuition and fees vary according to degree level and program. *Financial support:* In 2009–10, 78 students received support, including 42 teaching assistantships (averaging $1,600 per year); fellowships, research assistantships, career-related internships or fieldwork and Federal Work-Study also available. Financial award application deadline: 7/1. *Faculty research:* Time-limited dynamic psychotherapy; mindfulness/ACT; psychotherapy integration; empathy, altruism and survivor guilt; culturally informed practice. *Unit head:* Dr. Charles Alexander, Dean, 510-841-9230 Ext. 101, E-mail: calexander@wi.edu. *Application contact:* Liz Hertz, Director of Admissions, 510-841-9230 Ext. 111, Fax: 510-841-0167, E-mail: lhertz@wrightinst.edu.

Wright State University, School of Graduate Studies, College of Liberal Arts, Program in Applied Behavioral Science, Dayton, OH 45435. Offers criminal justice and social problems (MA); international and comparative politics (MA). *Degree requirements:* For master's, thesis optional. *Entrance requirements:* Additional exam requirements/recommendations for international students: Required—TOEFL. *Faculty research:* Training and development, criminal justice and social problems, community systems, human factors, industrial/organizational psychology.

Wright State University, School of Graduate Studies, College of Science and Mathematics, Department of Psychology, Dayton, OH 45435. Offers human factors and industrial/organizational psychology (MS, PhD). *Degree requirements:* For master's, thesis; for doctorate, thesis/dissertation. *Entrance requirements:* For master's, GRE General Test. Additional exam requirements/recommendations for international students: Required—TOEFL.

Wright State University, School of Professional Psychology, Dayton, OH 45435. Offers clinical psychology (Psy D). *Accreditation:* APA. *Degree requirements:* For doctorate, thesis/dissertation. *Entrance requirements:* For doctorate, GRE General Test, GRE Subject Test. Additional exam requirements/recommendations for international students: Required—TOEFL. *Expenses:* Contact institution.

Xavier University, College of Social Sciences, Health and Education, Department of Psychology, Cincinnati, OH 45207. Offers clinical psychology (Psy D); psychology (MA), including general experimental, industrial-organizational. *Accreditation:* APA (one or more programs are accredited). *Faculty:* 19 full-time (9 women), 3 part-time/adjunct (2 women). *Students:* 111 full-time (87 women), 6 part-time (4 women); includes 13 minority (5 African Americans, 1 American Indian/Alaska Native, 4 Asian Americans or Pacific Islanders, 3 Hispanic Americans), 2 international. Average age 27. 272 applicants, 23% accepted, 37 enrolled. In 2009, 27 master's, 16 doctorates awarded. *Degree requirements:* For master's, one foreign language, comprehensive exam, thesis, internship; for doctorate, one foreign language, comprehensive exam, thesis/dissertation, internship. *Entrance requirements:* For master's and doctorate, GRE. Additional exam requirements/recommendations for international students: Required—TOEFL. *Application deadline:* For fall admission, 12/15 for domestic and international students. Application fee: $35. Electronic applications accepted. *Expenses:* Contact institution. *Financial support:* In 2009–10, 61 students received support, including 41 research assistantships with partial tuition reimbursements available, 20 teaching assistantships with partial tuition reimbursements available; scholarships/grants and unspecified assistantships also available. Financial award application deadline: 3/1; financial award applicants required to submit FAFSA. *Unit head:* Dr. Christine M. Dacey, Chair, 513-745-3533, Fax: 513-745-3327, E-mail: dacey@xavier.edu. *Application contact:* Margaret Maybury, Assistant Director, Enrollment and Student Services, 513-745-1053, Fax: 513-745-3347, E-mail: maybury@xavier.edu.

Yale University, Graduate School of Arts and Sciences, Department of Psychology, New Haven, CT 06520. Offers behavioral neuroscience (PhD); clinical psychology (PhD); cognitive psychology (PhD); developmental psychology (PhD); social/personality psychology (PhD). *Accreditation:* APA. *Degree requirements:* For doctorate, thesis/dissertation. *Entrance requirements:* For doctorate, GRE General Test.

Yeshiva University, Ferkauf Graduate School of Psychology, New York, NY 10033-3201. Offers MA, PhD, Psy D. *Accreditation:* APA (one or more programs are accredited). Part-time programs available. *Degree requirements:* For doctorate, comprehensive exam, thesis/dissertation. *Entrance requirements:* For master's and doctorate, GRE General Test. *Expenses:* Tuition: Full-time $24,918; part-time $1022 per credit. Required fees: $175.

York University, Faculty of Graduate Studies, Faculty of Health, Program in Psychology, Toronto, ON M3J 1P3, Canada. Offers MA, PhD. *Accreditation:* APA (one or more programs are accredited). Part-time programs available. *Degree requirements:* For master's, thesis, practicum; for doctorate, thesis/dissertation, practicum. *Entrance requirements:* For master's, GRE. Electronic applications accepted.

Youngstown State University, Graduate School, College of Liberal Arts and Social Sciences, Department of Psychology, Youngstown, OH 44555-0001. Offers applied behavior analysis (MS).

Addictions/Substance Abuse Counseling

Adler School of Professional Psychology, Programs in Psychology, Chicago, IL 60601-7203. Offers art therapy (MA, Certificate); clinical hypnosis (Certificate); clinical psychology (Psy D); counseling (MA); counseling and organizational psychology (MA); forensic psychology (MA); gerontological counseling (MA); marriage and family counseling (MA); marriage and family therapy (Certificate); organizational psychology (MA); police psychology (MA); rehabilitation counseling (MA); sport and health psychology (MA); substance abuse counseling (Certificate); Psy D/Certificate; Psy D/MACAT; Psy D/MACP; Psy D/MAMFC; Psy D/MASAC. *Accreditation:* APA. Part-time and evening/weekend programs available. Postbaccalaureate distance learning degree programs offered (minimal on-campus study). *Faculty:* 41 full-time (21 women), 44 part-time/adjunct (19 women). *Students:* 551 full-time (441 women), 161 part-time (137 women). Average age 27.Terminal master's awarded for partial completion of doctoral program. *Degree requirements:* For master's, thesis or alternative, oral exam, practicum; for doctorate, thesis/dissertation, clinical exam, internship, oral exam, practicum, written qualifying exam. *Entrance requirements:* For master's, 12 semester hours in psychology, minimum GPA of 3.0; for doctorate, 18 semester hours in psychology, minimum GPA of 3.25; for Certificate, appropriate master's or doctoral degree. Additional exam requirements/recommendations for international students: Required—TOEFL (minimum score 550 paper-based; 213 computer-based; 79 iBT). *Application deadline:* For fall admission, 2/15 priority date for domestic students, 12/1 priority date for international students. Applications are processed on a rolling basis. Application fee: $50. Electronic applications accepted. *Expenses:* Tuition: Part-time $930 per credit. Required fees: $220 per term. *Financial support:* Career-related internships or fieldwork, Federal Work-Study, scholarships/grants, and tuition waivers (full and partial) available. Support available to part-time students. Financial award application deadline: 5/15; financial award applicants required to submit FAFSA. *Unit head:* Dr. Frank Gruba-McAllister, Vice President of Academic Affairs, 312-201-5900 Ext. 209, Fax: 312-201-5917. *Application contact:* Craig A. Hines, Associate Vice President of Admissions, 312-201-5900 Ext. 226, Fax: 312-201-5917, E-mail: chines@adler.edu.

See Close-Up on page 1047.

Alliant International University–Los Angeles, California School of Professional Psychology, Program in Marital and Family Therapy, Alhambra, CA 91803-1360. Offers biofeedback (MA); chemical dependency (MA); gerontology (MA); Latin American family therapy (MA). *Accreditation:* AAMFT/COAMFTE.

Argosy University, Hawai'i, College of Psychology and Behavioral Sciences, Program in Substance Abuse Counseling, Honolulu, HI 96813. Offers Certificate.

See Close-Up on page 1057.

Cambridge College, School of Psychology and Counseling, Cambridge, MA 02138-5304. Offers addiction counseling (M Ed); alcohol & drug counseling (Certificate); counseling psychology (M Ed, CAGS); counseling psychology: forensic counseling (M Ed); marriage and family therapy (M Ed); mental health and addiction counseling (M Ed); mental health counseling (M Ed); mental health counseling for school guidance counselors (Post Master's Certificate); psychological studies (M Ed); school adjustment and mental health counseling (M Ed); school adjustment, mental health and addiction counseling (M Ed); school guidance counselor (M Ed); trauma studies (Certificate). Part-time and evening/weekend programs available. *Faculty:* 5 full-time (2 women), 87 part-time/adjunct (50 women). *Students:* 501 full-time (395 women), 307 part-time (245 women); includes 382 minority (295 African Americans, 2 American Indian/Alaska Native, 6 Asian Americans or Pacific Islanders, 79 Hispanic Americans), 4 international. Average age 38. In 2009, 237 master's, 15 other advanced degrees awarded. *Degree requirements:* For master's, thesis, practicum/internship; for other advanced degree, thesis, practicum/Internship. *Entrance requirements:* For master's, resume, 2 professional references; for other advanced degree, official transcripts, documents for transfer credit evaluation, resume, written personal statement/essay, 2 professional references, health insurance, immunizations form. Additional exam requirements/recommendations for international students: Required—TOEFL (minimum score 550 paper-based; 213 computer-based; 79 iBT); Recommended—IELTS (minimum score 6). *Application deadline:* Applications are processed on a rolling basis. Application fee: $30. Electronic applications accepted. *Expenses:* Contact institution. *Financial support:* In 2009–10, 686 students received support. Career-related internships or fieldwork, Federal Work-Study, and scholarships/grants available. Financial award applicants required to submit FAFSA. *Unit head:* Dr. Niti Seth, Dean, 617-873-0208, Fax: 617-349-3561, E-mail: nseth@cambridgecollege.edu. *Application contact:* Stephen Lyons, Director of Enrollment, Graduate and N.I.T.E. Programs, 617-868-1000, Fax: 617-349-3561, E-mail: stephen.lyons@cambridgecollege.edu.

Capella University, School of Human Services, Minneapolis, MN 55402. Offers addictions counseling (Certificate); counseling studies (MS, PhD); criminal justice (MS, PhD, Certificate); diversity studies (Certificate); general human services (MS, PhD); health care administration (MS, PhD, Certificate); management of nonprofit agencies (MS, PhD, Certificate); marital, couple and family counseling/therapy (MS); marriage and family services (Certificate); mental health counseling (MS); professional counseling (Certificate); social and community services (MS, PhD, Certificate). Part-time and evening/weekend programs available. Postbaccalaureate distance learning degree programs offered (minimal on-campus study). Terminal master's awarded for partial completion of doctoral program. *Degree requirements:* For master's, thesis optional, integrative project; for doctorate, comprehensive exam, thesis/dissertation. *Entrance requirements:* Additional exam requirements/recommendations for international students: Required—TOEFL (minimum score 550 paper-based; 213 computer-based), TWE (minimum score 4). Electronic applications accepted. *Faculty research:* Compulsive and addictive behaviors, substance abuse, assessment of psychopathology and neuropsychology.

Cleveland State University, College of Graduate Studies, College of Education and Human Services, Department of Counseling, Administration, Supervision and Adult Learning (CASAL), Cleveland, OH 44115. Offers accelerated degree in adult learning and development (M Ed); adult learning and development (M Ed); chemical dependency counseling (Certificate); community agency counseling (M Ed); counseling and pupil personnel administration (Ed S); early childhood mental health counseling (Certificate); educational administration and supervision (M Ed); school administration (Ed S); school counseling (M Ed). *Accreditation:* ACA (one or more programs are accredited). Part-time and evening/weekend programs available. *Degree requirements:* For master's, comprehensive exam (for some programs), thesis optional; for other advanced degree, comprehensive exam, thesis optional, internship. *Entrance requirements:* For master's, GRE General Test or MAT, letter of recommendation, minimum GPA of 2.75. Additional exam requirements/recommendations for international students: Required—TOEFL (minimum score 525 paper-based; 197 computer-based), IELTS (minimum score 6). Electronic applications accepted. *Faculty research:* Education law, career development, women in school administration, psychopharmacology, counseling and spirituality.

The College of New Jersey, Graduate Division, School of Education, Department of Counselor Education, Program in Community Counseling: Substance Abuse and Addiction Specialization, Ewing, NJ 08628. Offers MA, Certificate. Part-time programs available. *Students:* 3 full-time (all women), 4 part-time (all women); includes 4 minority (2 African Americans, 2 Hispanic Americans). 13 applicants, 62% accepted. In 2009, 2 master's, 2 other advanced degrees awarded. *Degree requirements:* For master's, comprehensive exam. *Entrance requirements:* For master's, GRE, minimum GPA of 3.0 in field or 2.75 overall; for Certificate, previous master's degree or higher. Additional exam requirements/recommendations for international students: Required—TOEFL. *Application deadline:* For fall admission, 2/1 for domestic students; for spring admission, 10/1 for domestic students. Application fee: $70. Electronic applications accepted. *Expenses:* Tuition, state resident: part-time $573.70 per credit. Tuition, nonresident: part-time $887.75 per credit. Required fees: $140.85 per credit. One-time fee: $10 part-time. *Financial support:* Tuition waivers (partial) and unspecified assistantships available. Financial award application deadline: 5/1; financial award applicants required to submit FAFSA. *Unit head:* Dr. Mark Woodford, Coordinator, 609-771-3018, Fax: 609-637-5166, E-mail: woodford@tcnj.edu. *Application contact:* Susan L. Hydro, Assistant Dean, Office of Graduate Studies, 609-771-2300, Fax: 609-637-5105, E-mail: graduate@tcnj.edu.

College of St. Joseph, Graduate Programs, Division of Psychology and Human Services, Program in Alcohol and Substance Abuse Counseling, Rutland, VT 05701-3899. Offers MS. Part-time programs available. *Entrance requirements:* For master's, 2 letters of reference, interview. Electronic applications accepted. *Expenses:* Tuition: Full-time $13,500; part-time $350 per credit. Required fees: $45 per term. One-time fee: $445. Tuition and fees vary according to program.

The College of William and Mary, School of Education, Program in Counselor Education, Williamsburg, VA 23187-8795. Offers community and addictions counseling (M Ed); community counseling (M Ed); counselor education (PhD); family counseling (M Ed); school counseling (M Ed). *Accreditation:* ACA; NCATE. Part-time and evening/weekend programs available. *Faculty:* 6 full-time (3 women), 6 part-time/adjunct (all women). *Students:* 60 full-time (48 women), 7 part-time (5 women); includes 14 minority (11 African Americans, 1 American Indian/Alaska Native, 2 Asian Americans or Pacific Islanders), 1 international. Average age 30. 126 applicants, 52% accepted, 36 enrolled. In 2009, 28 master's, 6 doctorates awarded. *Degree requirements:* For doctorate, comprehensive exam, thesis/dissertation. *Entrance requirements:* For master's, GRE, minimum GPA of 2.5; for doctorate, GRE, minimum GPA of 3.5. Additional exam requirements/recommendations for international students: Required—TOEFL. *Application deadline:* For fall admission, 1/15 for domestic and international students. Application fee: $45. Electronic applications accepted. *Expenses:* Tuition, state resident: full-time $6400; part-time $315 per credit hour. Tuition, nonresident: full-time $19,720; part-time $840 per credit hour. Required fees: $4114. *Financial support:* In 2009–10, 45 students received support, including 1 fellowship with full tuition reimbursement available (averaging $20,000 per year), 36 research assistantships with full tuition reimbursements available (averaging $11,000 per year); career-related internships or fieldwork, Federal Work-Study, institutionally sponsored loans, scholarships/grants, and unspecified assistantships also available. Financial award application deadline: 1/15; financial award applicants required to submit FAFSA. *Faculty research:* Sexuality, multicultural education, substance abuse, transpersonal psychology. *Unit head:* Dr. Charles McAdams, Area Coordinator, 757-221-2338, E-mail: crmcad@wm.edu. *Application contact:* Dorothy Smith Osborne, Director of Admissions, 757-221-2317, Fax: 757-221-2293, E-mail: dsosbo@wm.edu.

Coppin State University, Division of Graduate Studies, Division of Arts and Sciences, Department of Applied Psychology and Rehabilitation Counseling, Program in Alcohol and Substance Abuse Counseling, Baltimore, MD 21216-3698. Offers MS. Part-time programs available. *Degree requirements:* For master's, comprehensive exam (for some programs), thesis optional, internship, clinical requirement. *Entrance requirements:* For master's, GRE General Test, interview, minimum GPA of 3.0.

East Carolina University, Graduate School, School of Allied Health Sciences, Program in Rehabilitation Studies, Greenville, NC 27858-4353. Offers rehabilitation counseling (MS); substance abuse and clinical counseling (MS); vocational evaluation (MS). *Accreditation:* CORE. Part-time and evening/weekend programs available. *Degree requirements:* For master's, comprehensive exam, thesis or alternative, internship. *Entrance requirements:* For master's, GRE General Test or MAT. Additional exam requirements/recommendations for international students: Required—TOEFL.

Eastern Michigan University, Graduate School, College of Health and Human Services, School of Social Work, Ypsilanti, MI 48197. Offers family and children's services (MSW); mental health and chemical dependency (MSW); services to the aging (MSW). *Accreditation:* CSWE. Part-time and evening/weekend programs available. *Faculty:* 20 full-time (16 women). *Students:* 34 full-time (30 women), 179 part-time (159 women); includes 69 minority (63 African Americans, 2 American Indian/Alaska Native, 2 Asian Americans or Pacific Islanders, 2 Hispanic Americans), 1 international. Average age 35. 220 applicants, 54% accepted, 99 enrolled. In 2009, 56 master's awarded. *Entrance requirements:* Additional exam requirements/recommendations for international students: Required—TOEFL. *Application deadline:* For fall admission, 1/15 priority date for domestic students. Applications are processed on a rolling basis. Application fee: $35. Tuition and fees vary according to course level. *Financial support:* Fellowships, research assistantships with full tuition reimbursements, teaching assistantships with full tuition reimbursements, career-related internships or fieldwork, Federal Work-Study, institutionally sponsored loans, scholarships/grants, tuition waivers (partial), and unspecified assistantships available. Support available to part-time students. Financial award applicants required to submit FAFSA. *Unit head:* Dr. Ann Alvarez, Director, 734-487-0393, Fax: 734-487-6832, E-mail: aalvare4@emich.edu. *Application contact:* Julie Harkema, Admissions Director, 734-487-4206, Fax: 734-487-6832, E-mail: jharkema@emich.edu.

Governors State University, College of Health Professions, Program in Addictions Studies, University Park, IL 60466-0975. Offers MHS. Part-time and evening/weekend programs available. *Degree requirements:* For master's, comprehensive exam, thesis or alternative, internship. *Entrance requirements:* For master's, minimum undergraduate GPA of 2.5; 9 hours of course work in behavioral sciences; 6 hours of course work in biological sciences or chemistry, statistics or research methods.

Grand Canyon University, College of Nursing and Health Sciences, Phoenix, AZ 85017-1097. Offers addiction counseling (MS); nursing (MS), including adult clinical nurse specialist, family nurse practitioner, nursing education, nursing leadership in health care system; professional counseling (MS). Part-time and evening/weekend programs available. Postbaccalaureate distance learning degree programs offered (no on-campus study). *Entrance requirements:* Additional exam requirements/recommendations for international students: Required—TOEFL (minimum score 575 paper-based; 233 computer-based; 90 iBT), IELTS (minimum score 7).

Hazelden Graduate School of Addiction Studies, Graduate Programs, Center City, MN 55012. Offers addiction counseling (MA, Certificate). Part-time programs available. *Entrance requirements:* Additional exam requirements/recommendations for international students: Required—TOEFL.

Indiana University–Purdue University Indianapolis, School of Science, Department of Psychology, Psychobiology of Addictions Program, Indianapolis, IN 46202-2896. Offers MS, PhD. *Faculty:* 7 full-time (3 women). *Students:* 12 full-time (10 women), 5 part-time (3 women); includes 3 minority (all African Americans). Average age 28. *Entrance requirements:* For master's, GRE General Test, minimum undergraduate GPA of 3.2. *Application deadline:* For fall admission, 1/1 for domestic students. Application fee: $50 ($60 for international students). *Financial support:* Fellowships with partial tuition reimbursements, research assistantships with partial tuition reimbursements, teaching assistantships with partial tuition reimbursements, career-related internships or fieldwork and Federal Work-Study available. Financial award application deadline: 3/1; financial award applicants required to submit FAFSA. *Faculty research:* Behavioral genetics, behavior pharmacology, animal models, developmental psychology, neurobehavioral toxicology, neuropsychology of learning and memory, animal models of fetal alcohol syndrome. *Unit head:* Dr. J. Gregor Fetterman, Chairman, 317-274-6945, Fax: 317-274-6756, E-mail: gfetter@iupui.edu. *Application contact:* Dr. J. Gregor Fetterman, Chairman, 317-274-6945, Fax: 317-274-6756, E-mail: gfetter@iupui.edu.

Indiana Wesleyan University, College of Graduate Studies, Graduate Studies in Counseling, Marion, IN 46953. Offers addictions counseling (MS); community counseling (MS); marriage and family counseling (MS); school counseling (MS). *Accreditation:* ACA. Part-time programs available. *Degree requirements:* For master's, thesis or alternative. *Entrance requirements:* For master's, GRE General Test. Additional exam requirements/recommendations for international students: Required—TOEFL. Electronic applications accepted. *Expenses:* Contact institution. *Faculty research:* Community counseling, multicultural counseling, addictions.

The Johns Hopkins University, Bloomberg School of Public Health, Department of Mental Health, Baltimore, MD 21218-2699. Offers children's mental health services (PhD); drug dependence epidemiology (PhD); mental health (MHS, Dr PH); psychiatric epidemiology (PhD). *Faculty:* 26 full-time (14 women), 46 part-time/adjunct (18 women). *Students:* 44 full-time (36 women), 13 part-time (9 women); includes 20 minority (7 African Americans, 9 Asian Americans or Pacific Islanders, 4 Hispanic Americans), 9 international. Average age 28. 73 applicants, 67% accepted, 27 enrolled. In 2009, 17 master's, 6 doctorates awarded. *Degree requirements:* For master's, thesis (for some programs); for doctorate, thesis/dissertation, 1 year full-time residency, oral and written exams. *Entrance requirements:* For master's, GRE General Test, MCAT, 3 letters of recommendation, curriculum vitae; for doctorate, GRE General Test, MCAT or GMAT, 3 letters of recommendation, curriculum vitae. Additional exam requirements/recommendations for international students: Required—TOEFL (minimum score 600 paper-based; 250 computer-based; 100 iBT). *Application deadline:* For fall admission, 12/1 priority date for domestic and international students. Applications are processed on a rolling basis. Application fee: $45. Electronic applications accepted. *Financial support:* In 2009–10, 1 fellowship (averaging $32,000 per year) was awarded; Federal Work-Study, institutionally sponsored loans, scholarships/grants, traineeships, and stipends also available. Support available to part-time students. Financial award application deadline: 3/15; financial award applicants required to submit FAFSA. *Faculty research:* Etiology, development and prevention of aggressive and antisocial behavior; epidemiology of mental disorders; genetic epidemiology of mental disorders; brain and behavior. Total annual research expenditures: $12 million. *Unit head:* Dr. William W. Eaton, Chair, 410-955-3910, Fax: 410-614-7469, E-mail: weaton@jhsph.edu. *Application contact:* Patricia E. Scott, Senior Academic Program Coordinator, 410-955-1906, Fax: 410-955-9088, E-mail: mhdept@jhsph.edu.

Kean University, College of Education, Program in Counselor Education, Union, NJ 07083. Offers alcohol and drug abuse counseling (MA); business and industry counseling (MA); community/agency counseling (MA); school counseling (MA). *Accreditation:* ACA; NCATE. Part-time programs available. *Faculty:* 5 full-time (3 women). *Students:* 61 full-time (56 women), 184 part-time (162 women); includes 74 minority (41 African Americans, 3 Asian Americans or Pacific Islanders, 30 Hispanic Americans). Average age 32. 153 applicants, 89% accepted, 73 enrolled. In 2009, 64 master's awarded. *Degree requirements:* For master's, comprehensive exam, thesis, practicum, internship. *Entrance requirements:* For master's, GRE General Test or MAT, minimum GPA of 3.0, 2 letters of recommendation, interview, initial teacher certification (school counseling). *Application deadline:* For fall admission, 5/1 for domestic students; for spring admission, 11/1 for domestic students. Application fee: $60 ($150 for international students). Electronic applications accepted. *Expenses:* Tuition, state resident: full-time $10,440; part-time $435 per credit. Tuition, nonresident: full-time $14,160; part-time $590 per credit. Required fees: $2642; $110 per credit. Part-time tuition and fees vary according to course load and degree level. *Financial support:* In 2009–10, 2 research assistantships with full tuition reimbursements (averaging $3,263 per year) were awarded; unspecified assistantships also available. *Unit head:* Dr. J. Barry Mascari, Program Coordinator, 908-737-3863, E-mail: jmascari@kean.edu. *Application contact:* Steven Koch, Pre-Admissions Coordinator, 908-737-5924, Fax: 908-737-5965, E-mail: skoch@kean.edu.

Lewis & Clark College, Graduate School of Education and Counseling, Department of Counseling Psychology, Program in Addictions Treatment, Portland, OR 97219-7899. Offers MA, MS. Part-time and evening/weekend programs available. *Faculty:* 1 full-time (0 women), 1 (woman) part-time/adjunct. *Students:* 24 full-time (17 women), 8 part-time (6 women); includes 2 minority (1 Asian American or Pacific Islander, 1 Hispanic American). Average age 32. 13 applicants, 92% accepted, 7 enrolled. In 2009, 16 master's awarded. *Degree requirements:* For master's, thesis (MS). *Entrance requirements:* For master's, GRE General Test, minimum undergraduate GPA of 2.75. Additional exam requirements/recommendations for international students: Required—TOEFL (minimum score 575 paper-based; 233 computer-based). *Application deadline:* For fall admission, 2/1 priority date for domestic and international students; for spring admission, 10/1 priority date for domestic and international students. Application fee: $50. Electronic applications accepted. *Expenses:* Tuition: Part-time $713 per semester hour. Tuition and fees vary according to course level and campus/location. *Financial support:* In 2009–10, 32 students received support. Career-related internships or fieldwork, Federal Work-Study, institutionally sponsored loans, scholarships/grants, health care benefits, and tuition waivers (partial) available. Support available to part-time students. Financial award applicants required to submit FAFSA. *Unit head:* Dr. Boyd Pidcock, Program Coordinator, 503-768-6060,

Addictions/Substance Abuse Counseling

Lewis & Clark College (continued)
Fax: 503-768-6065, E-mail: cpsy@lclark.edu. *Application contact:* Becky Haas, Director of Admissions, 503-768-6200, Fax: 503-768-6205, E-mail: gseadmit@lclark.edu.

Maryville University of Saint Louis, School of Health Professions, Program in Rehabilitation Counseling, St. Louis, MO 63141-7299. Offers marriage and family therapy (MARC); music therapy (MARC); rehabilitation counseling (CAGS); substance abuse (MARC). *Accreditation:* CORE. Part-time and evening/weekend programs available. *Students:* 16 full-time (12 women), 31 part-time (21 women); includes 7 African Americans, 1 Asian American or Pacific Islander, 2 Hispanic Americans. Average age 31. In 2009, 6 master's awarded. *Degree requirements:* For master's, internship, seminar. *Entrance requirements:* For master's, minimum cumulative GPA of 3.0, 2 letters of recommendation, interview. Additional exam requirements/recommendations for international students: Required—TOEFL (minimum score 550 paper-based). *Application deadline:* For fall admission, 1/15 for domestic students; for spring admission, 10/1 for domestic students. Application fee: $40 ($60 for international students). Electronic applications accepted. *Expenses:* Tuition: Full-time $20,384; part-time $627.50 per credit hour. Required fees: $100 per semester. *Financial support:* Career-related internships or fieldwork, Federal Work-Study, and campus employment available. Financial award application deadline: 3/1; financial award applicants required to submit FAFSA. *Unit head:* Barbara Parker, Director, 314-529-9437, Fax: 314-529-9495, E-mail: bparker@maryville.edu. *Application contact:* Barbara Parker, Director, 314-529-9437, Fax: 314-529-9495, E-mail: bparker@maryville.edu.

McNeese State University, Doré School of Graduate Studies, Burton College of Education, Department of Psychology, Lake Charles, LA 70609. Offers addiction treatment (MA); applied behavior analysis (MA); counseling psychology (MA); general/experimental psychology (MA). Evening/weekend programs available. *Faculty:* 6 full-time (3 women). *Students:* 34 full-time (24 women), 30 part-time (22 women); includes 10 minority (7 African Americans, 1 Asian American or Pacific Islander, 2 Hispanic Americans), 2 international. In 2009, 18 master's awarded. *Entrance requirements:* For master's, GRE. *Application deadline:* For fall admission, 5/15 priority date for domestic and international students; for spring admission, 10/15 priority date for domestic and international students. Applications are processed on a rolling basis. Application fee: $20 ($30 for international students). *Expenses:* Tuition, area resident: Full-time $2556. Tuition, state resident: full-time $2556. Required fees: $1031. Tuition and fees vary according to course load. *Financial support:* Application deadline: 5/1. *Unit head:* Dr. Dena L. Matzenbacher, Head, 337-475-5457, Fax: 337-562-4115, E-mail: dena@mcneese.edu. *Application contact:* Dr. George F. Mead, Interim Dean of Dore' School of Graduate Studies, 337-475-5396, Fax: 337-475-5397, E-mail: admissions@mcneese.edu.

Mercy College, School of Social and Behavioral Sciences, Program in Counseling, Dobbs Ferry, NY 10522-1189. Offers alcohol and substance abuse counseling (Certificate); counseling (MS); family counseling (Certificate). Part-time and evening/weekend programs available. Postbaccalaureate distance learning degree programs offered (no on-campus study). *Students:* 137 full-time (121 women), 213 part-time (185 women); includes 223 minority (89 African Americans, 3 American Indian/Alaska Native, 4 Asian Americans or Pacific Islanders, 127 Hispanic Americans), 1 international. Average age 35. 226 applicants, 53% accepted, 87 enrolled. In 2009, 92 master's, 14 other advanced degrees awarded. *Degree requirements:* For master's, comprehensive exam. *Entrance requirements:* For master's, interview, two professional letters of recommendation, minimum undergraduate GPA of 3.0, resume. Additional exam requirements/recommendations for international students: Required—TOEFL (minimum score 600 paper-based; 250 computer-based; 100 iBT). *Application deadline:* For fall admission, 8/1 for international students. Applications are processed on a rolling basis. Application fee: $40. Electronic applications accepted. *Expenses:* Tuition: Full-time $13,158; part-time $731 per credit. Required fees: $500. Tuition and fees vary according to degree level and program. *Financial support:* Career-related internships or fieldwork, Federal Work-Study, scholarships/grants, and unspecified assistantships available. Support available to part-time students. Financial award applicants required to submit FAFSA. *Faculty research;* Ethics, drug abuse problems, human development, domestic violence. *Unit head:* Dr. Arthur Mc Cann, Assistant Professor, Psychology and Behavioral Science, 914-674-7670, E-mail: amccann@mercy.edu. *Application contact:* Dr. Arthur Mc Cann, Assistant Professor, Psychology and Behavioral Science, 914-674-7670, E-mail: amccann@mercy.edu.

Montclair State University, The Graduate School, College of Education and Human Services, Department of Counseling, Human Development, and Educational Leadership, Montclair, NJ 07043-1624. Offers administration and supervision (MA), including administration and supervision, educator/trainer; advanced counseling (Certificate); counseling and guidance (MA), including addictions counseling, community counseling, student affairs; counselor education (PhD); principal (Certificate); school administrator (Certificate); school business administrator (Certificate); school counselor (Certificate); substance awareness coordinator (Certificate). *Accreditation:* NCATE. Part-time and evening/weekend programs available. *Faculty:* 17 full-time (12 women), 13 part-time/adjunct (7 women). *Students:* 161 full-time (126 women), 425 part-time (325 women). Average age 33. 269 applicants, 55% accepted, 125 enrolled. In 2009, 91 master's awarded. *Degree requirements:* For master's, comprehensive exam, thesis or alternative; for doctorate, comprehensive exam, thesis/dissertation. *Entrance requirements:* For master's, GRE General Test, interview, 2 letters of recommendation; for doctorate, GRE General Test, interview, 3 letters of recommendation. Additional exam requirements/recommendations for international students: Required—TOEFL (minimum score 83 computer-based), or IELTS. *Application deadline:* For fall admission, 6/1 for international students; for spring admission, 10/1 for international students. Applications are processed on a rolling basis. Application fee: $60. Electronic applications accepted. *Expenses:* Tuition, area resident: Part-time $486.74 per credit. Tuition, state resident: part-time $486.74 per credit. Tuition, nonresident: part-time $751.34 per credit. Tuition and fees vary according to degree level and program. *Financial support:* In 2009–10, 28 research assistantships with full tuition reimbursements (averaging $7,000 per year), 2 teaching assistantships (averaging $15,000 per year) were awarded; Federal Work-Study, scholarships/grants, and unspecified assistantships also available. Support available to part-time students. Financial award application deadline: 3/1; financial award applicants required to submit FAFSA. *Faculty research:* K-12 education, data collection. *Unit head:* Dr. Larry Burlew, Chairperson, 973-655-7611. *Application contact:* Amy Aiello, Director of Graduate Admissions and Operations, 973-655-5147, Fax: 973-655-7869, E-mail: graduate.school@montclair.edu.

Pace University, Dyson College of Arts and Sciences, Department of Psychology, Program in Counseling-Substance Abuse, New York, NY 10038. Offers loss and grief (MS); mental health (MS); substance abuse (MS). Offered at Pleasantville, NY location only. Part-time and evening/weekend programs available. *Students:* 64 full-time (52 women), 49 part-time (42 women); includes 21 African Americans, 1 Asian American or Pacific Islander, 8 Hispanic Americans, 2 international. Average age 32. 95 applicants, 91% accepted, 38 enrolled. In 2009, 50 master's awarded. *Degree requirements:* For master's, comprehensive exam, qualifying exams, internship. *Entrance requirements:* For master's, GRE, interview. Additional exam requirements/recommendations for international students: Required—TOEFL. *Application deadline:* For fall admission, 8/1 priority date for domestic students; for spring admission, 12/1 priority date for domestic students. Applications are processed on a rolling basis. Application fee: $70. Electronic applications accepted. *Expenses:* Tuition: Part-time $954 per credit. Tuition and fees vary according to course load, degree level and program. *Financial support:* Research assistantships, teaching assistantships, career-related internships or fieldwork, Federal Work-Study, and tuition waivers (partial) available. Financial award applicants required to submit FAFSA. *Unit head:* Dr. Ross Robak, Head, 914-773-3673. *Application contact:* Joanna Broda, Director of Admissions, 914-422-4283, Fax: 914-422-4287, E-mail: gradwp@pace.edu.

Palm Beach Atlantic University, School of Education and Behavioral Studies, West Palm Beach, FL 33416-4708. Offers counseling psychology (MSCP), including addictions/mental health, marriage and family therapy, mental health counseling, school guidance counseling. Part-time and evening/weekend programs available. *Faculty:* 16 full-time (8 women), 2 part-time/adjunct (0 women). *Students:* 230 full-time (193 women), 74 part-time (63 women); includes 109 minority (70 African Americans, 1 Asian American or Pacific Islander, 38 Hispanic Americans), 8 international. Average age 35. 136 applicants, 70% accepted, 88 enrolled. In 2009, 86 master's awarded. *Entrance requirements:* For master's, GRE, minimum GPA of 3.0. Additional exam requirements/recommendations for international students: Required—TOEFL (minimum score 550 paper-based; 213 computer-based). *Application deadline:* For fall admission, 7/15 priority date for domestic students; for spring admission, 11/15 priority date for domestic students. Applications are processed on a rolling basis. Application fee: $45. Electronic applications accepted. *Expenses:* Tuition: Full-time $8010; part-time $445 per credit hour. Required fees: $99 per semester. Tuition and fees vary according to course load and degree level. *Financial support:* Applicants required to submit FAFSA. *Unit head:* Dr. Lisa Stubbs, Program Director, 561-803-2286. *Application contact:* Graduate Admissions, 888-468-6722, Fax: 561-803-2115, E-mail: grad@pba.edu.

St. Mary's University, Graduate School, Department of Counseling and Human Services, San Antonio, TX 78228-8507. Offers community counseling (MA); counseling (Sp C); counseling education and supervision (PhD); marriage and family relations (Certificate); marriage and family therapy (MA, PhD); mental health (MA); mental health and substance abuse counseling (Certificate); substance abuse (MA). *Accreditation:* AAMFT/COAMFTE (one or more programs are accredited); ACA (one or more programs are accredited). Postbaccalaureate distance learning degree programs offered (minimal on-campus study). *Degree requirements:* For master's, comprehensive exam, internship; for doctorate, comprehensive exam, thesis/dissertation, internship. *Entrance requirements:* For master's, GRE General Test, MAT; for doctorate, GRE General Test, recommendation from employers, admissions committee and department faculty. Additional exam requirements/recommendations for international students: Required—TOEFL (minimum score 550 paper-based; 213 computer-based; 80 iBT). Electronic applications accepted. *Expenses:* Contact institution.

Shippensburg University of Pennsylvania, School of Graduate Studies, College of Education and Human Services, Department of Counseling, Shippensburg, PA 17257-2299. Offers Adlerian studies (Certificate); advanced study in counseling (Certificate); alcohol and drug counseling (Certificate); counseling (M Ed, MS), including college counseling (MS), community counseling (MS), elementary school counseling, mental health counseling (MS), secondary school counseling (MS), student personnel services (MS); couple and family counseling (Certificate). *Accreditation:* ACA (one or more programs are accredited); NCATE. Part-time and evening/weekend programs available. *Degree requirements:* For master's, fieldwork, research project, internship, candidacy. *Entrance requirements:* For master's, GRE or MAT (community, mental health, student personnel, and college counseling applicants if GPA is less than 2.75), minimum GPA of 2.75 (3.0 for M Ed), interview, resume, 3 letters of recommendation, supplemental data forms, one year of relevant work experience, on-campus interview. Additional exam requirements/recommendations for international students: Required—TOEFL (minimum score 560 paper-based; 220 computer-based); Recommended—IELTS (minimum score 6). Electronic applications accepted.

Southeastern Louisiana University, College of Education and Human Development, Department of Counseling and Human Development, Hammond, LA 70402. Offers counselor education (M Ed), including community counseling, marriage and family therapy, school counseling, substance abuse counseling. *Accreditation:* ACA; NCATE. Part-time programs available. *Faculty:* 7 full-time (5 women), 1 part-time/adjunct (0 women). *Students:* 58 full-time (54 women), 45 part-time (41 women); includes 16 minority (15 African Americans, 1 Hispanic American). Average age 29. 38 applicants, 100% accepted, 23 enrolled. In 2009, 23 master's awarded. *Degree requirements:* For master's, comprehensive exam, thesis optional. *Entrance requirements:* For master's, GRE (verbal and quantitative). Additional exam requirements/recommendations for international students: Required—TOEFL (minimum score 500 paper-based; 173 computer-based; 61 iBT). *Application deadline:* For fall admission, 7/15 priority date for domestic students, 6/1 priority date for international students; for spring admission, 12/1 priority date for domestic students, 10/1 priority date for international students. Applications are processed on a rolling basis. Application fee: $20 ($30 for international students). Electronic applications accepted. *Expenses:* Tuition, state resident: full-time $3086; part-time $225 per credit hour. Tuition, nonresident: part-time $529 per credit hour. Required fees: $1195. Tuition and fees vary according to course level and course load. *Financial support:* In 2009–10, 6 students received support. Career-related internships or fieldwork, Federal Work-Study, institutionally sponsored loans, and administrative assistantships available. Support available to part-time students. Financial award application deadline: 5/1; financial award applicants required to submit FAFSA. *Faculty research:* Marriage counseling, family of origin, counselor training, substance abuse counseling, childhood and adolescent obesity. *Unit head:* Dr. June Williams, Interim Department Head, 985-549-2309, Fax: 985-549-3758, E-mail: jwilliams@selu.edu. *Application contact:* Sandra Meyers, Graduate Admissions Analyst, 985-549-2066, Fax: 985-549-5632, E-mail: admissions@selu.edu.

Southern New Hampshire University, School of Liberal Arts, Manchester, NH 03106-1045. Offers clinical services for adults psychiatric disabilities (Certificate); clinical services for children and adolescents with psychiatric disabilities (Certificate); clinical services for persons with co-occurring substance abuse and psychiatric disabilities (Certificate); community mental health (MS); fiction writing (MFA); non-fiction writing (MFA); teaching English as a foreign language (MS). Part-time and evening/weekend programs available. *Degree requirements:* For master's, one foreign language, thesis. *Entrance requirements:* For master's, minimum GPA of 2.75: MS-TEFL, 3.0: MFA. Additional exam requirements/recommendations for international students: Required—TOEFL (minimum score 550 paper-based; 213 computer-based; 79 iBT), IELTS (minimum score 6.5), TWE (minimum score 5). Electronic applications accepted. *Expenses:* Contact institution. *Faculty research:* Action research, state of the art practice in behavioral health services, wraparound approaches to working with youth, learning styles.

Springfield College, Graduate Programs, Programs in Rehabilitation Counseling and Services, Springfield, MA 01109-3797. Offers alcohol rehabilitation/substance abuse counseling (M Ed, MS); deaf counseling (M Ed, MS); developmental disabilities (M Ed, MS); general counseling and casework (M Ed, MS); psychiatric rehabilitation/mental health counseling (M Ed, MS); special services (M Ed, MS). *Accreditation:* CORE (one or more programs are accredited). Part-time programs available. *Degree requirements:* For master's, comprehensive exam. *Entrance requirements:* Additional exam requirements/recommendations for international students: Required—TOEFL (minimum score 550 paper-based; 213 computer-based). Electronic applications accepted. *Expenses:* Tuition: Full-time $19,800; part-time $825 per credit hour. Required fees: $150.

Stony Brook University, State University of New York, Stony Brook University Medical Center, School of Medicine, Program in Public Health, Stony Brook, NY 11794. Offers community health (MPH); evaluation sciences (MPH); family violence (MPH); health economics (MPH); population health (MPH); substance abuse (MPH). *Accreditation:* CEPH. *Students:* 16 full-time (8 women), 29 part-time (24 women); includes 14 minority (6 African Americans, 6 Asian Americans or Pacific Islanders, 2 Hispanic Americans), 5 international. Average age 39. 77 applicants, 64% accepted. In 2009, 10 master's awarded. *Entrance requirements:* For master's, GRE, 3 references. Additional exam requirements/recommendations for international students: Required—TOEFL. *Application deadline:* For fall admission, 1/15 for domestic and international students. Application fee: $60. Electronic applications accepted. *Expenses:* Tuition, state resident: full-time $8370; part-time $349 per credit. Tuition, nonresident: full-time $13,250; part-time $552 per credit. Required fees: $933. *Faculty research:* Population health, health service research, health economics. *Unit head:* Dr. Raymond L. Goldsteen, Director, 631-444-2074, Fax: 631-444-3480, E-mail: raymond.goldsteen@stonybrook.edu. *Application contact:*

Dr. Raymond L. Goldsteen, Director, 631-444-2074, Fax: 631-444-3480, E-mail: raymond.goldsteen@stonybrook.edu.

Syracuse University, College of Human Ecology, Program in Addiction Studies, Syracuse, NY 13244. Offers CAS. Part-time programs available. *Entrance requirements:* Additional exam requirements/recommendations for international students: Required—TOEFL (minimum score 100 iBT). *Application deadline:* For fall admission, 3/15 priority date for domestic and international students. Application fee: $75. Electronic applications accepted. *Expenses:* Tuition: Full-time $26,808; part-time $1117 per credit. Required fees: $1024. *Financial support:* Application deadline: 1/1. *Unit head:* Dr. Maureen Thompson, Program Contact, 315-443-9815, Fax: 315-443-2562, E-mail: mlthomps@syr.edu. *Application contact:* Felecia Otero, Director, College Relations, 315-443-5555, Fax: 315-443-2562, E-mail: inquire@hshp.syr.edu.

Troy University, Graduate School, College of Education, Program in Counseling and Psychology, Troy, AL 36082. Offers agency counsleing (Ed S); clinical mental health (MS); community counseling (MS, Ed S); corrections counseling (MS); rehabilitation counseling (MS); school psychology (MS, Ed S); school psychometry (MS); social service counseling (MS); student affairs counseling (MS); substance abuse counseling (MS). *Accreditation:* ACA; CORE; NCATE. Part-time and evening/weekend programs available. *Students:* 375 full-time (302 women), 753 part-time (642 women); includes 664 minority (610 African Americans, 8 American Indian/Alaska Native, 9 Asian Americans or Pacific Islanders, 37 Hispanic Americans). Average age 33. 493 applicants, 92% accepted. In 2009, 102 master's, 191 other advanced degrees awarded. *Degree requirements:* For master's, comprehensive exam, thesis. *Entrance requirements:* For master's, MAT, minimum GPA of 2.5. Additional exam requirements/recommendations for international students: Required—TOEFL (minimum score 523 paper-based; 193 computer-based; 70 iBT), IELTS (minimum score 6). *Application deadline:* Applications are processed on a rolling basis. Application fee: $50. Electronic applications accepted. *Unit head:* Dr. Andrew Creamer, Chair, 334-670-3350, Fax: 334-670-32961, E-mail: drcreamer@troy.edu. *Application contact:* Brenda K. Campbell, Director of Graduate Admissions, 334-670-3178, Fax: 334-670-3733, E-mail: bcamp@troy.edu.

Universidad Central del Caribe, Program in Substance Abuse Counseling, Bayamón, PR 00960-6032. Offers MHS.

University of Arkansas at Pine Bluff, School of Arts and Sciences, Pine Bluff, AR 71601-2799. Offers MS.

University of California, Berkeley, UC Berkeley Extension, Certificate Programs in Behavioral and Health Sciences, Berkeley, CA 94720-1500. Offers alcohol and drug abuse studies (Certificate). *Unit head:* Diana Wu, Dean, 510-642-4181. *Application contact:* Behavioral and Health Sciences, 510-643-3883, E-mail: counspsych@unex.berkeley.edu.

University of Central Oklahoma, College of Graduate Studies and Research, College of Liberal Arts, Department of Sociology, Criminal Justice and Substance Abuse Studies, Edmond, OK 73034-5209. Offers criminal justice management and administration (MA). Part-time programs available. *Entrance requirements:* Additional exam requirements/recommendations for international students: Required—TOEFL (minimum score 550 paper-based; 213 computer-based). Electronic applications accepted. *Expenses:* Tuition, state resident: full-time $4128; part-time $172 per credit hour. Tuition, nonresident: full-time $10,373; part-time $432.20 per credit hour. Required fees: $433.20; $18.05 per credit hour. *Faculty research:* Gender issues, violent offenders.

University of Detroit Mercy, College of Liberal Arts and Education, Department of Counseling and Addiction Studies, Program in Addiction Studies, Detroit, MI 48221. Offers Certificate. Part-time programs available.

University of Detroit Mercy, College of Liberal Arts and Education, Department of Counseling and Addiction Studies, Program in Counseling, Detroit, MI 48221. Offers addiction counseling (MA); community counseling (MA); school counseling (MA). *Accreditation:* ACA. Part-time and evening/weekend programs available. *Degree requirements:* For master's, thesis or alternative. *Entrance requirements:* For master's, minimum GPA of 2.75.

University of Illinois at Springfield, Graduate Programs, College of Education and Human Services, Program in Human Services, Springfield, IL 62703-5407. Offers alcoholism and substance abuse (MA); child and family services (MA); gerontology (MA); social services administration (MA). Part-time and evening/weekend programs available. Postbaccalaureate distance learning degree programs offered (no on-campus study). *Faculty:* 4 full-time (3 women), 1 (woman) part-time/adjunct. *Students:* 34 full-time (32 women), 91 part-time (76 women); includes 34 minority (31 African Americans, 1 American Indian/Alaska Native, 1 Asian American or Pacific Islander, 1 Hispanic American), 1 international. Average age 36. 76 applicants, 54% accepted, 33 enrolled. In 2009, 20 master's awarded. *Degree requirements:* For master's, internship; project or thesis. *Entrance requirements:* For master's, minimum undergraduate GPA of 3.0, 2 letters of recommendation. Additional exam requirements/recommendations for international students: Required—TOEFL (minimum score 500 paper-based; 176 computer-based; 61 iBT). Application fee: $50 ($60 for international students). Electronic applications accepted. *Expenses:* Tuition, state resident: full-time $6390; part-time $266.25 per credit hour. Tuition, nonresident: full-time $14,226; part-time $592.75 per credit hour. Required fees: $2044; $14.36 per credit hour. $722.50 per term. *Financial support:* In 2009–10, research assistantships with full tuition reimbursements (averaging $8,109 per year), teaching assistantships with full tuition reimbursements (averaging $8,109 per year) were awarded; career-related internships or fieldwork, scholarships/grants, health care benefits, and unspecified assistantships also available. Support available to part-time students. Financial award application deadline: 11/15. *Unit head:* Dr. Carolyn Peck, Program Administrator, 217-206-7577, Fax: 217-206-6775, E-mail: peck.carolyn@uis.edu. *Application contact:* Dr. Lynn Pardie, Office of Graduate Studies, 800-252-8533, Fax: 217-206-7623, E-mail: pardie.lynn@uis.edu.

University of Lethbridge, School of Graduate Studies, Lethbridge, AB T1K 3M4, Canada. Offers accounting (MScM); addictions counseling (M Sc); agricultural biotechnology (M Sc); agricultural studies (M Sc, MA); anthropology (MA); archaeology (MA); art (MA, MFA); biochemistry (M Sc); biological sciences (M Sc); biomolecular science (PhD); biosystems and biodiversity (PhD); Canadian studies (MA); chemistry (M Sc); computer science (M Sc); computer science and geographical information science (M Sc); counseling psychology (M Ed); dramatic arts (MA); earth, space, and physical science (PhD); economics (MA); educational leadership (M Ed); English (MA); environmental science (M Sc); evolution and behavior (PhD); exercise science (M Sc); finance (MScM); French (MA); French/German (MA); French/Spanish (MA); general education (M Ed); general management (MScM); geography (M Sc, MA); German (MA); health science (M Sc); health sciences (MA); history (MA); human resource management and labour relations (MScM); individualized multidisciplinary (M Sc, MA); information systems (MScM); international management (MScM); kinesiology (M Sc, MA); management (M Sc, MA); marketing (MScM); mathematics (M Sc); music (M Mus, MA); Native American studies (MA); neuroscience (M Sc, PhD); new media (MA); nursing (M Sc); philosophy (MA); physics (M Sc); policy and strategy (MScM); political science (MA); psychology (M Sc, MA); religious studies (MA); social sciences (MA); sociology (MA); theatre and dramatic arts (MFA); theoretical and computational science (PhD); urban and regional studies (MA); women's studies (MA). Part-time and evening/weekend programs available. *Degree requirements:* For doctorate, comprehensive exam, thesis/dissertation. *Entrance requirements:* For master's, GMAT (M Sc in management), bachelor's degree in related field, minimum GPA of 3.0 during previous 20 graded semester courses, 2 years teaching or related experience (M Ed); for doctorate, master's degree, minimum graduate GPA of 3.5. Additional exam requirements/recommendations for international students: Required—TOEFL. *Faculty research:* Movement and brain plasticity, gibberellin physiology, photosynthesis, carbon cycling, molecular properties of main-group ring components.

University of Louisiana at Monroe, Graduate School, College of Education and Human Development, Department of Educational Leadership and Counseling, Program in Substance Abuse Counseling, Monroe, LA 71209-0001. Offers MA. Part-time and evening/weekend programs available. *Students:* 6 full-time (4 women), 1 part-time (0 women); includes 3 minority (2 African Americans, 1 Asian American or Pacific Islander). Average age 36. In 2009, 6 master's awarded. *Degree requirements:* For master's, thesis optional, 600 hours clinical internship. *Entrance requirements:* For master's, GRE General Test, minimum GPA of 2.8 in last 60 hours. Additional exam requirements/recommendations for international students: Required—TOEFL (minimum score 500 paper-based; 173 computer-based; 61 iBT). *Application deadline:* For fall admission, 8/24 priority date for domestic students, 7/1 for international students; for winter admission, 12/14 for domestic students; for spring admission, 1/19 for domestic students, 11/1 for international students. Applications are processed on a rolling basis. Application fee: $20 ($30 for international students). Electronic applications accepted. *Expenses:* Tuition, state resident: part-time $159 per credit hour. Tuition, nonresident: part-time $159 per credit hour. Required fees: $1300 per year. Tuition and fees vary according to course load. *Financial support:* Career-related internships or fieldwork, Federal Work-Study, and unspecified assistantships available. Financial award application deadline: 4/1; financial award applicants required to submit FAFSA. *Faculty research:* Addictionology. *Unit head:* Dr. Mitchell Young, Coordinator, 318-342-1255, Fax: 318-342-3131, E-mail: myoung@ulm.edu. *Application contact:* Dr. Mitchell Young, Coordinator, 318-342-1255, Fax: 318-342-3131, E-mail: myoung@ulm.edu.

University of Louisville, Graduate School, Raymond A. Kent School of Social Work, Louisville, KY 40292-0001. Offers marriage and family therapy (PMC); social work (MSSW, PhD), including alcohol and drug counseling (MSSW), gerontology (MSSW), school social work (MSSW). *Accreditation:* AAMFT/COAMFTE; CSWE (one or more programs are accredited). Part-time and evening/weekend programs available. *Faculty:* 23 full-time (15 women), 38 part-time/adjunct (21 women). *Students:* 279 full-time (221 women), 64 part-time (52 women); includes 79 minority (70 African Americans, 2 American Indian/Alaska Native, 2 Asian Americans or Pacific Islanders, 5 Hispanic Americans), 5 international. Average age 32. 288 applicants, 74% accepted, 145 enrolled. In 2009, 137 master's, 4 doctorates awarded. *Degree requirements:* For doctorate, comprehensive exam, thesis/dissertation. *Entrance requirements:* For master's, GRE or minimum GPA of 2.75; for doctorate, GRE General Test, interview, writing sample. Additional exam requirements/recommendations for international students: Required—TOEFL (minimum score 550 paper-based; 213 computer-based; 79 iBT). *Application deadline:* For fall admission, 7/31 for domestic and international students. Applications are processed on a rolling basis. Application fee: $50. Electronic applications accepted. *Financial support:* In 2009–10, 70 students received support, including 9 research assistantships with full tuition reimbursements available (averaging $19,000 per year), 1 teaching assistantship (averaging $19,000 per year); Federal Work-Study, institutionally sponsored loans, scholarships/grants, health care benefits, and unspecified assistantships also available. Support available to part-time students. Financial award application deadline: 5/15; financial award applicants required to submit FAFSA. *Faculty research:* Child welfare, substance abuse, gerontology, family functioning, health behavior. Total annual research expenditures: $2.8 million. *Unit head:* Dr. Terry Singer, Dean, 502-852-6402, Fax: 502-852-0422, E-mail: terry.singer@louisville.edu. *Application contact:* Libby Leggett, Director, Graduate Admissions, 502-852-3101, Fax: 502-852-6536, E-mail: gradadm@louisville.edu.

University of Mary, Division of Social and Behavioral Sciences, Bismarck, ND 58504-9652. Offers addiction counseling (MSC); community counseling (MSC); school counseling (MSC). Part-time programs available. Postbaccalaureate distance learning degree programs offered (minimal on-campus study). *Degree requirements:* For master's, thesis, internship. *Entrance requirements:* For master's, coursework/experience in psychology, statistics. Additional exam requirements/recommendations for international students: Required—TOEFL. *Expenses:* Tuition: Full-time $10,062; part-time $430 per credit. Tuition and fees vary according to course load, degree level, program and student level.

University of Nevada, Las Vegas, Graduate College, College of Education, Department of Counselor Education, Las Vegas, NV 89154-3066. Offers addiction studies (Advanced Certificate); community mental health (MS); rehabilitation counseling (Advanced Certificate); school counseling (M Ed). *Faculty:* 7 full-time (2 women), 10 part-time/adjunct (7 women). *Students:* 47 full-time (39 women), 37 part-time (31 women); includes 14 minority (3 African Americans, 1 Asian American or Pacific Islander, 10 Hispanic Americans). Average age 32. 97 applicants, 95% accepted, 57 enrolled. In 2009, 19 master's awarded. *Degree requirements:* For master's, comprehensive exam (for some programs), thesis (for some programs); for Advanced Certificate, thesis (for some programs). *Entrance requirements:* Additional exam requirements/recommendations for international students: Required—TOEFL (minimum score 550 paper-based; 213 computer-based; 80 iBT), IELTS (minimum score 7). *Application deadline:* For fall admission, 2/1 priority date for domestic and international students. Applications are processed on a rolling basis. Application fee: $60 ($95 for international students). Electronic applications accepted. *Financial support:* In 2009–10, 10 students received support, including 6 research assistantships with partial tuition reimbursements available (averaging $10,000 per year), 4 teaching assistantships with partial tuition reimbursements available (averaging $10,000 per year); institutionally sponsored loans, scholarships/grants, health care benefits, and unspecified assistantships also available. Financial award application deadline: 3/1. *Faculty research:* Social justice and multicultural competencies for counselors, therapeutic storytelling and bibliotherapy, school counselor education pedagogy, counseling program evaluation, addictions prevention and related trauma. *Unit head:* Dr. Dale Pehrsson, Chair/ Associate Professor, 702-895-5994, Fax: 702-895-5550, E-mail: dale.pehrsson@unlv.edu. *Application contact:* Graduate College Admissions Evaluator, 702-895-3320, Fax: 702-895-4180, E-mail: gradcollege@unlv.edu.

University of New England, Westbrook College of Health Professions, School of Social Work, Biddeford, ME 04005-9526. Offers addictions counseling (Certificate); gerontology (Certificate); social work (MSW). *Accreditation:* CSWE. Part-time programs available. *Faculty:* 12 full-time (8 women), 4 part-time/adjunct (all women). *Students:* 159 full-time (134 women), 2 part-time (both women); includes 6 minority (5 African Americans, 1 American Indian/Alaska Native), 3 international. In 2009, 44 master's awarded. *Degree requirements:* For master's, field internships. *Entrance requirements:* Additional exam requirements/recommendations for international students: Required—TOEFL (minimum score 550 paper-based; 213 computer-based). *Application deadline:* For fall admission, 1/15 priority date for domestic students; for spring admission, 3/31 priority date for domestic students, 3/31 for international students. Applications are processed on a rolling basis. Application fee: $40. Electronic applications accepted. *Financial support:* In 2009–10, 40 students received support. Scholarships/grants and tuition waivers (partial) available. Financial award application deadline: 5/1; financial award applicants required to submit FAFSA. *Faculty research:* Domestic violence, solution-focused practice, empowerment models, adverse childhood experiences. *Unit head:* Martha Wilson, Director, 207-221-4513, E-mail: mwilson@une.edu. *Application contact:* Stacy Gato, Assistant Director of Graduate Admissions, 207-221-4225, Fax: 207-221-4898, E-mail: gradadmissions@une.edu.

Waynesburg University, Graduate and Professional Studies, Waynesburg, PA 15370-1222. Offers business (MBA), including finance, health systems, human resources, leadership, market development; counseling (MA), including addictions counseling, clinical mental health; education (MAT); nursing (MSN), including administration, education, informatics, palliative care; nursing practice (DNP); special education (M Ed); technology (M Ed); MSN/MBA. *Accreditation:* AACN. Part-time and evening/weekend programs available. *Faculty:* 11 full-time

Waynesburg University (continued)
(5 women), 136 part-time/adjunct (80 women). *Students:* 116 full-time (85 women), 984 part-time (682 women). 711 applicants, 80% accepted, 485 enrolled. In 2009, 320 master's, 41 doctorates awarded. *Degree requirements:* For doctorate, thesis/dissertation. *Entrance requirements:* Additional exam requirements/recommendations for international students: Required—TOEFL. *Application deadline:* For fall admission, 8/1 priority date for domestic students. Applications are processed on a rolling basis. Electronic applications accepted. *Expenses:* Tuition: Part-time $520 per credit. *Financial support:* Available to part-time students. Application deadline: 5/1. *Unit head:* David Mariner, Dean, 724-743-4420, Fax: 724-743-4425, E-mail: dmariner@waynesburg.edu. *Application contact:* Michael Bednarski, Director of Admissions, 724-743-4420, Fax: 724-743-4425, E-mail: mbednars@waynesburg.edu.

Wayne State University, Graduate School, Interdisciplinary Program in Alcohol and Drug Abuse Studies, Detroit, MI 48202. Offers Certificate. *Entrance requirements:* For degree, graduate degree or enrolled in graduate program; letter of reference. Additional exam requirements/recommendations for international students: Required—TOEFL (minimum score 550 paper-based; 213 computer-based); Recommended—TWE (minimum score 6). Electronic applications accepted. *Faculty research:* Epidemiology and etiology of substance use, substance abuse prevention and treatment; treatment for substance abuse and co-occurring disorders; faculty and professional development in substance abuse.

Clinical Psychology

Abilene Christian University, Graduate School, College of Arts and Sciences, Department of Psychology, Program in Clinical Psychology, Abilene, TX 79699-9100. Offers MS. Part-time programs available. *Students:* 14 full-time (10 women), 1 (woman) part-time; includes 4 minority (1 African American, 1 Asian American or Pacific Islander, 2 Hispanic Americans), 1 international. 17 applicants, 71% accepted, 8 enrolled. In 2009, 5 master's awarded. *Degree requirements:* For master's, comprehensive exam, thesis. *Entrance requirements:* For master's, GRE General Test. *Application deadline:* For fall admission, 4/1 priority date for domestic students; for spring admission, 11/1 for domestic students. Applications are processed on a rolling basis. Application fee: $40. Electronic applications accepted. *Expenses:* Tuition: Full-time $11,520; part-time $640 per hour. Required fees: $1090; $53.50 per hour. $10 per term. Tuition and fees vary according to program. *Financial support:* In 2009–10, 15 students received support. Career-related internships or fieldwork and Federal Work-Study available. Support available to part-time students. Financial award application deadline: 4/1; financial award applicants required to submit FAFSA. *Unit head:* Dr. Robert McKelvain, Graduate Advisor, 325-674-2286, Fax: 325-674-6968, E-mail: mckelvainr@acu.edu. *Application contact:* William Horn, Graduate Admissions Counselor, 325-674-2656, Fax: 325-674-6717, E-mail: gradinfo@acu.edu.

Acadia University, Faculty of Pure and Applied Science, Department of Psychology, Wolfville, NS B4P 2R6, Canada. Offers clinical psychology (M Sc). *Faculty:* 12 full-time (6 women), 11 part-time/adjunct (5 women). *Students:* 8 full-time (7 women). Average age 26. 44 applicants, 20% accepted, 5 enrolled. In 2009, 4 master's awarded. *Degree requirements:* For master's, thesis. *Entrance requirements:* For master's, GRE General Test, GRE Subject Test, honors degree or equivalent. Additional exam requirements/recommendations for international students: Required—TOEFL (minimum score 580 paper-based; 237 computer-based; 93 iBT), IELTS (minimum score 6.5). *Application deadline:* For fall admission, 2/1 priority date for domestic students, 2/1 for international students. Applications are processed on a rolling basis. Application fee: $50. *Financial support:* Teaching assistantships, career-related internships or fieldwork, scholarships/grants, and unspecified assistantships available. Financial award application deadline: 2/1. *Faculty research:* Social psychology, job stress, psychotherapy, cognition perception, development. *Unit head:* Dr. Peter McLeod, Head, 902-585-1301, Fax: 902-585-1078, E-mail: peter.mcleod@acadiau.ca. *Application contact:* Dr. Peter Horvath, Information Contact, 902-585-1200, Fax: 902-585-1078, E-mail: peter.horvath@acadiau.ca.

Adelphi University, Derner Institute of Advanced Psychological Studies, Program in Clinical Psychology, Garden City, NY 11530-0701. Offers PhD. *Students:* 80 full-time (58 women), 34 part-time (28 women); includes 16 minority (6 African Americans, 8 Asian Americans or Pacific Islanders, 2 Hispanic Americans), 12 international. Average age 32. In 2009, 12 doctorates awarded. *Degree requirements:* For doctorate, thesis/dissertation, research (second year), 1 year internship. *Entrance requirements:* For doctorate, GRE General Test, GRE Subject Test, interview; resume, undergraduate courses in psychology, experimental psychology, statistics, developmental psychology, and abnormal psychology. Additional exam requirements/recommendations for international students: Required—TOEFL (minimum score 550 paper-based; 213 computer-based; 80 iBT). *Application deadline:* For fall admission, 1/15 priority date for domestic and international students. Application fee: $50. Electronic applications accepted. *Expenses:* Tuition: Full-time $28,340; part-time $830 per credit. Required fees: $600; $250 per credit. Full-time tuition and fees vary according to course load and program. *Financial support:* Research assistantships with full and partial tuition reimbursements, teaching assistantships, career-related internships or fieldwork, Federal Work-Study, institutionally sponsored loans, and unspecified assistantships available. Financial award application deadline: 2/15; financial award applicants required to submit FAFSA. *Unit head:* Dr. Christopher J. Muran, Associate Dean, 516-877-4803, E-mail: jcmuran@adelphi.edu. *Application contact:* Christine Murphy, Director of Admissions, 516-877-3050, Fax: 516-877-3039, E-mail: graduateadmissions@adelphi.edu.

Adler School of Professional Psychology, Programs in Psychology, Chicago, IL 60601-7203. Offers art therapy (MA, Certificate); clinical hypnosis (Certificate); clinical psychology (Psy D); counseling (MA); counseling and organizational psychology (MA); forensic psychology (MA); gerontological counseling (MA); marriage and family counseling (MA); marriage and family therapy (Certificate); organizational psychology (MA); police psychology (MA); rehabilitation counseling (MA); sport and health psychology (MA); substance abuse counseling (Certificate); Psy D/Certificate; Psy D/MACAT; Psy D/MACP; Psy D/MAMFC; Psy D/MASAC. *Accreditation:* APA. Part-time and evening/weekend programs available. Postbaccalaureate distance learning degree programs offered (minimal on-campus study). *Faculty:* 41 full-time (21 women), 44 part-time/adjunct (19 women). *Students:* 551 full-time (441 women), 161 part-time (137 women). Average age 27.Terminal master's awarded for partial completion of doctoral program. *Degree requirements:* For master's, thesis or alternative, oral exam, practicum; for doctorate, thesis/dissertation, clinical exam, internship, oral exam, practicum, written qualifying exam. *Entrance requirements:* For master's, 12 semester hours in psychology, minimum GPA of 3.0; for doctorate, 18 semester hours in psychology, minimum GPA of 3.25; for Certificate, appropriate master's or doctoral degree. Additional exam requirements/recommendations for international students: Required—TOEFL (minimum score 550 paper-based; 213 computer-based; 79 iBT). *Application deadline:* For fall admission, 2/15 priority date for domestic students, 12/1 priority date for international students. Applications are processed on a rolling basis. Application fee: $50. Electronic applications accepted. *Expenses:* Tuition: Part-time $930 per credit. Required fees: $220 per term. *Financial support:* Career-related internships or fieldwork, Federal Work-Study, scholarships/grants, and tuition waivers (full and partial) available. Support available to part-time students. Financial award application deadline: 5/15; financial award applicants required to submit FAFSA. *Unit head:* Dr. Frank Gruba-McAllister, Vice President of Academic Affairs, 312-201-5900 Ext. 209, Fax: 312-201-5917. *Application contact:* Craig A. Hines, Associate Vice President of Admissions, 312-201-5900 Ext. 226, Fax: 312-201-5917, E-mail: chines@adler.edu.

See Close-Up on page 1047.

Alabama Agricultural and Mechanical University, School of Graduate Studies, School of Education, Department of Counseling and Special Education, Huntsville, AL 35811. Offers communicative disorders (M Ed, MS); psychology and counseling (MS, Ed S), including clinical psychology (MS), counseling and guidance, counseling psychology (MS), personnel management (MS), psychometry (MS), school psychology (MS); special education (M Ed, MS). *Accreditation:* CORE; NCATE. Part-time and evening/weekend programs available. *Degree requirements:* For master's, comprehensive exam. *Entrance requirements:* For master's, GRE General Test. Additional exam requirements/recommendations for international students: Required—TOEFL (minimum score 500 paper-based; 173 computer-based; 61 iBT). *Faculty research:* Increasing numbers of minorities in special education and speech-language pathology.

Alliant International University–Fresno, California School of Professional Psychology, PhD Program in Clinical Psychology, Fresno, CA 93727. Offers PhD. *Degree requirements:* For doctorate, thesis/dissertation. *Entrance requirements:* For doctorate, interview, minimum GPA of 3.0 in both psychology and overall, letters of recommendation. Additional exam requirements/recommendations for international students: Required—TOEFL (minimum score 600 paper-based; 250 computer-based), TWE (minimum score 5). *Faculty research:* Teaching, ecosystemic child psychology, health psychology, clinical forensic psychology.

Alliant International University–Fresno, California School of Professional Psychology, Psy D Program in Clinical Psychology, Fresno, CA 93727. Offers Psy D. *Accreditation:* APA. *Degree requirements:* For doctorate, comprehensive exam, thesis/dissertation. *Entrance requirements:* For doctorate, interview, minimum GPA of 3.0 in both psychology and overall, letters of recommendation. Additional exam requirements/recommendations for international students: Required—TOEFL (minimum score 600 paper-based; 250 computer-based), TWE (minimum score 5). Electronic applications accepted. *Faculty research:* Ecosystemic child clinical health psychology, eating disorders.

Alliant International University–Los Angeles, California School of Professional Psychology, PhD Program in Clinical Psychology, Alhambra, CA 91803-1360. Offers PhD. *Accreditation:* APA. *Degree requirements:* For doctorate, comprehensive exam, thesis/dissertation. *Entrance requirements:* For doctorate, interview, minimum GPA of 3.0 in both psychology and overall. Additional exam requirements/recommendations for international students: Required—TOEFL (minimum score 600 paper-based; 250 computer-based), TWE (minimum score 5). Electronic applications accepted. *Faculty research:* Multicultural and community clinical psychology, health psychology, individual and family psychology.

Alliant International University–Los Angeles, California School of Professional Psychology, Psy D Program in Clinical Psychology, Alhambra, CA 91803-1360. Offers Psy D. *Accreditation:* APA. *Degree requirements:* For doctorate, thesis/dissertation. *Entrance requirements:* For doctorate, interview, minimum GPA of 3.0 in both psychology and overall. Additional exam requirements/recommendations for international students: Required—TOEFL (minimum score 600 paper-based; 250 computer-based), TWE. Electronic applications accepted. *Faculty research:* Child and family psychology, multicultural and community psychology, acculturation, lesbian and gay issues, women's health.

Alliant International University–Sacramento, California School of Professional Psychology, Program in Clinical Psychology, Sacramento, CA 95825. Offers Psy D. *Entrance requirements:* For doctorate, minimum GPA of 3.0, letters of recommendation, interview. Electronic applications accepted. *Faculty research:* Health psychology, infant-preschool mental health, community mental, health trauma, aging.

Alliant International University–San Diego, California School of Professional Psychology, PhD Program in Clinical Psychology, San Diego, CA 92131-1799. Offers PhD. *Accreditation:* APA. *Degree requirements:* For doctorate, thesis/dissertation. *Entrance requirements:* For doctorate, interview, minimum GPA of 3.0 in both psychology and overall. Additional exam requirements/recommendations for international students: Required—TOEFL (minimum score 600 paper-based; 250 computer-based), TWE (minimum score 5). Electronic applications accepted. *Faculty research:* Family conflict in adolescence, anxiety disorders, PTSD, childhood psychopathology, regressed memory.

Alliant International University–San Diego, California School of Professional Psychology, Psy D Program in Clinical Psychology, San Diego, CA 92131-1799. Offers Psy D. *Accreditation:* APA. *Degree requirements:* For doctorate, thesis/dissertation. *Entrance requirements:* For doctorate, interview, minimum GPA of 3.0 in both psychology and overall. Additional exam requirements/recommendations for international students: Required—TOEFL (minimum score 600 paper-based; 250 computer-based), TWE (minimum score 5). Electronic applications accepted. *Faculty research:* Forensic psychology, health psychology, integrative psychology, family and child psychology.

Alliant International University–San Diego, Marshall Goldsmith School of Management, Organizational Psychology Division, San Diego, CA 92131-1799. Offers clinical/industrial organizational psychology (PhD); consulting psychology (PhD); industrial/organizational psychology (MA, MS, PhD); organizational behavior (MA). Part-time and evening/weekend programs available. Terminal master's awarded for partial completion of doctoral program. *Degree requirements:* For doctorate, thesis/dissertation. *Entrance requirements:* For master's and doctorate, interview, minimum GPA of 3.0 in both psychology and overall. Additional exam requirements/recommendations for international students: Required—TOEFL (minimum score 600 paper-based; 250 computer-based), TWE (minimum score 5). Electronic applications accepted. *Faculty research:* Cultural diversity in the workplace, work motivation, personnel, performance management.

Alliant International University–San Francisco, California School of Professional Psychology, PhD Program in Clinical Psychology, San Francisco, CA 94133-1221. Offers PhD. *Degree requirements:* For doctorate, thesis/dissertation. *Entrance requirements:* For doctorate, interview, minimum GPA of 3.0 in both psychology and overall. Additional exam requirements/recommendations for international students: Required—TOEFL (minimum score 600 paper-based; 250 computer-based), TWE (minimum score 5). Electronic applications accepted. *Faculty research:* Social model of disability, feminist models of clinical training, post-traumatic stress disorder, HIV, psychology of women.

Alliant International University–San Francisco, California School of Professional Psychology, Psy D Program in Clinical Psychology, San Francisco, CA 94133-1221. Offers Psy D, Certificate. *Accreditation:* APA (one or more programs are accredited). *Degree requirements:* For doctorate, thesis/dissertation. *Entrance requirements:* For doctorate, interview, minimum GPA of 3.0 in both psychology and overall. Additional exam requirements/recommendations for international students: Required—TOEFL (minimum score 600 paper-based; 250 computer-based), TWE (minimum score 5). Electronic applications accepted. *Faculty research:* Health psychology, family and child psychology, psychodynamic psychology, multicultural and community psychology, gender issues.

American International College, School of Arts, Education and Sciences, Department of Psychology, Program in Clinical Psychology, Springfield, MA 01109-3189. Offers MA. *Degree requirements:* For master's, practicum. *Entrance requirements:* For master's, minimum B average in undergraduate course work. Additional exam requirements/recommendations for international students: Required—TOEFL. Electronic applications accepted. *Expenses:* Tuition: Full-time $12,510; part-time $695 per credit hour. Required fees: $35 per term.

American University, College of Arts and Sciences, Department of Psychology, Program in Clinical Psychology, Washington, DC 22016-8062. Offers psychology (PhD), including clinical psychology. *Accreditation:* APA. *Students:* 23 full-time (19 women), 20 part-time (17 women); includes 9 minority (3 African Americans, 1 Asian American or Pacific Islander, 5 Hispanic Americans). Average age 29. 215 applicants, 5% accepted, 7 enrolled. In 2009, 7 doctorates awarded. *Degree requirements:* For doctorate, comprehensive exam, thesis/dissertation, internship. *Entrance requirements:* For doctorate, GRE General Test, GRE Subject Test, recommendations. Additional exam requirements/recommendations for international students: Required—TOEFL. *Application deadline:* For fall admission, 1/1 for domestic students. Application fee: $80. *Expenses:* Tuition: Full-time $22,266; part-time $1237 per credit hour. Required fees: $430. Tuition and fees vary according to program. *Financial support:* Fellowships, research assistantships, teaching assistantships, career-related internships or fieldwork, Federal Work-Study, institutionally sponsored loans, tuition waivers (full and partial), and unspecified assistantships available. Support available to part-time students. Financial award application deadline: 2/1. *Faculty research:* Depression, eating disorders, anxiety disorders, addictions, behavior therapy. *Application contact:* Sara Holland, Senior Administrative Assistant, 202-885-1717, Fax: 202-885-1023.

Antioch University Los Angeles, Graduate Programs, Program in Psychology, Culver City, CA 90230. Offers clinical psychology (MA); psychology (MA). Part-time programs available. *Degree requirements:* For master's, thesis (for some programs), internship. *Entrance requirements:* For master's, interview. Additional exam requirements/recommendations for international students: Required—TOEFL. *Faculty research:* Creativity and humor, ethnic humor, adult development, Jungian theory, psychoanalytic theory.

Antioch University New England, Graduate School, Department of Applied Psychology, Program in Clinical Mental Health Counseling, Keene, NH 03431-3552. Offers MA. *Accreditation:* ACA. *Degree requirements:* For master's, internship, practicum. *Entrance requirements:* For master's, previous course work and work experience in psychology. Additional exam requirements/recommendations for international students: Required—TOEFL (minimum score 600 paper-based; 250 computer-based). Electronic applications accepted. *Expenses:* Contact institution. *Faculty research:* Multicultural issues in field supervision.

Antioch University New England, Graduate School, Department of Clinical Psychology, Keene, NH 03431-3552. Offers Psy D. *Accreditation:* APA. *Degree requirements:* For doctorate, thesis/dissertation, internship, practicum. *Entrance requirements:* For doctorate, GRE General Test, GRE Subject Test, previous course work in psychology. Additional exam requirements/recommendations for international students: Required—TOEFL (minimum score 600 paper-based; 250 computer-based). *Expenses:* Contact institution. *Faculty research:* Psychotherapy outcome and process in private practice, neuropsychiatric evaluations, effects of trauma on adults, supervision, clinical training evaluation.

Antioch University Santa Barbara, Program in Clinical Psychology, Santa Barbara, CA 93101-1581. Offers Psy D. *Entrance requirements:* Additional exam requirements/recommendations for international students: Required—TOEFL (minimum score 550 paper-based; 213 computer-based). Electronic applications accepted.

Appalachian State University, Cratis D. Williams Graduate School, Department of Psychology, Boone, NC 28608. Offers clinical health psychology (MA); general experimental psychology (MA); industrial and organizational psychology (MA). Part-time programs available. *Faculty:* 31 full-time (11 women). *Students:* 51 full-time (37 women), 13 part-time (10 women); includes 4 minority (2 African Americans, 2 Asian Americans or Pacific Islanders), 2 international. 181 applicants, 25% accepted, 26 enrolled. In 2009, 22 master's, 7 other advanced degrees awarded. *Degree requirements:* For master's and MS/Specialist, comprehensive exam, thesis optional, GRE Subject Test exit exam. *Entrance requirements:* For master's and MS/Specialist, GRE General Test, 3 letters of recommendation. Additional exam requirements/recommendations for international students: Required—TOEFL (minimum score 550 paper-based; 230 computer-based; 79 iBT), or IELTS (minimum score 6.5). *Application deadline:* For fall admission, 3/1 for domestic students, 2/1 for international students. Applications are processed on a rolling basis. Application fee: $50. Electronic applications accepted. *Expenses:* Tuition, state resident: full-time $2960. Tuition, nonresident: full-time $14,051. Required fees: $2320. *Financial support:* In 2009–10, 34 research assistantships (averaging $4,000 per year), 25 teaching assistantships (averaging $4,000 per year) were awarded; fellowships, career-related internships or fieldwork, Federal Work-Study, scholarships/grants, and unspecified assistantships also available. Financial award application deadline: 4/1; financial award applicants required to submit FAFSA. *Faculty research:* Eating disorders, school-based consultations, organizational behavior management, brain mechanisms of sound localization, parenting styles. Total annual research expenditures: $114,200. *Unit head:* Dr. James Denniston, Chair, 828-262-2272, Fax: 828-262-2272, E-mail: dennistonjc@appstate.edu. *Application contact:* Dr. Denise Martz, Graduate Coordinator, 828-262-2715, E-mail: martzdm@appstate.edu.

Argosy University, Atlanta, College of Psychology and Behavioral Sciences, Atlanta, GA 30328. Offers clinical psychology (MA, Psy D, Postdoctoral Respecialization Certificate), including child and family psychology (Psy D), general adult clinical (Psy D), health psychology (Psy D), neuropsychology/geropsychology (Psy D); community counseling (MA), including marriage and family therapy; counselor education and supervision (Ed D); forensic psychology (MA); industrial organizational psychology (MA); marriage and family therapy (Certificate); sport-exercise psychology (MA). *Accreditation:* APA.

See Close-Up on page 1049.

Argosy University, Chicago, College of Psychology and Behavioral Sciences, Doctoral Program in Clinical Psychology, Chicago, IL 60601. Offers child and adolescent psychology (Psy D); client-centered and experiential psychotherapies (Psy D); diversity and multicultural psychology (Psy D); family psychology (Psy D); forensic psychology (Psy D); health psychology (Psy D); neuropsychology (Psy D); organizational consulting (Psy D); psychoanalytic psychology (Psy D); psychology and spirituality (Psy D). *Accreditation:* APA.

See Close-Up on page 1051.

Argosy University, Chicago, College of Psychology and Behavioral Sciences, Master's Program in Clinical Psychology, Chicago, IL 60601. Offers MA.

See Close-Up on page 1051.

Argosy University, Dallas, College of Psychology and Behavioral Sciences, Program in Clinical Psychology, Farmers Branch, TX 75244. Offers MA, Psy D.

See Close-Up on page 1053.

Argosy University, Denver, College of Psychology and Behavioral Sciences, Denver, CO 80231. Offers clinical mental health counseling (MA); clinical psychology (MA, Psy D); counseling psychology (Ed D); counselor education and supervision (Ed D); forensic psychology (MA); industrial organizational psychology (MA); marriage and family therapy (MA, DMFT).

See Close-Up on page 1055.

Argosy University, Hawai'i, College of Psychology and Behavioral Sciences, Program in Clinical Psychology, Honolulu, HI 96813. Offers clinical psychology (MA, Psy D, Postdoctoral Respecialization Certificate), including child and family clinical practice (Psy D), diversity in clinical practice (Psy D). *Accreditation:* APA.

See Close-Up on page 1057.

Argosy University, Inland Empire, College of Psychology and Behavioral Sciences, San Bernardino, CA 92408. Offers clinical psychology/marriage and family therapy (MA); counseling psychology (Ed D); counseling psychology/marriage and family therapy (MA); forensic psychology (MA); industrial organizational psychology (MA); sport-exercise psychology (MA).

See Close-Up on page 1059.

Argosy University, Los Angeles, College of Psychology and Behavioral Sciences, Santa Monica, CA 90045. Offers clinical psychology/marriage and family therapy (MA); counseling psychology (Ed D); counseling psychology/marriage and family therapy (MA); forensic psychology (MA).

See Close-Up on page 1061.

Argosy University, Orange County, College of Psychology and Behavioral Sciences, Program in Clinical Psychology, Orange, CA 92868. Offers child and adolescent psychology (Psy D); forensic psychology (Psy D); marriage and family therapy (MA).

See Close-Up on page 1065.

Argosy University, Phoenix, College of Psychology and Behavioral Sciences, Program in Clinical Psychology, Phoenix, AZ 85021. Offers clinical psychology (MA); neuropsychology (Psy D); sports-exercise psychology (Psy D). *Accreditation:* APA (one or more programs are accredited).

See Close-Up on page 1067.

Argosy University, San Diego, College of Psychology and Behavioral Sciences, San Diego, CA 92108. Offers clinical psychology/marriage and family therapy (MA); counseling psychology (Ed D); counseling psychology/marriage and family therapy (MA); forensic psychology (MA).

See Close-Up on page 1071.

Argosy University, San Francisco Bay Area, College of Psychology and Behavioral Sciences, Alameda, CA 94501. Offers clinical psychology (MA, Psy D); counseling psychology (MA, Ed D); forensic psychology (MA); sport-exercise psychology (MA). *Accreditation:* APA (one or more programs are accredited).

See Close-Up on page 1073.

Argosy University, Schaumburg, College of Psychology and Behavioral Sciences, Schaumburg, IL 60173-5403. Offers clinical health psychology (Post-Graduate Certificate); clinical psychology (MA, Psy D), including child and family psychology (Psy D), clinical health psychology (Psy D), diversity and multicultural psychology (Psy D), forensic psychology (Psy D), neuropsychology (Psy D); community counseling (MA); counseling psychology (Ed D), including counselor education and supervision; counselor education and supervision (Ed D); forensic psychology (Post-Graduate Certificate); industrial organizational psychology (MA). *Accreditation:* ACA; APA.

See Close-Up on page 1077.

Argosy University, Seattle, College of Psychology and Behavioral Sciences, Program in Clinical Psychology, Seattle, WA 98121. Offers MA, Psy D, Postdoctoral Respecialization Certificate.

See Close-Up on page 1079.

Argosy University, Tampa, College of Psychology and Behavioral Sciences, Program in Clinical Psychology, Tampa, FL 33607. Offers clinical psychology (MA, Psy D), including child and adolescent psychology (Psy D), geropsychology (Psy D), marriage/couples and family therapy (Psy D), neuropsychology (Psy D). *Accreditation:* APA.

See Close-Up on page 1081.

Argosy University, Twin Cities, College of Psychology and Behavioral Sciences, Eagan, MN 55121. Offers clinical psychology (MA, Psy D), including child and family psychology (Psy D), forensic psychology (Psy D), health and neuropsychology (Psy D), trauma (Psy D); forensic counseling (Post-Graduate Certificate); forensic psychology (MA); industrial organizational psychology (MA); marriage and family therapy (MA, DMFT), including forensic counseling (MA). *Accreditation:* APA.

See Close-Up on page 1083.

Argosy University, Washington DC, College of Psychology and Behavioral Sciences, Arlington, VA 22209. Offers clinical psychology (MA, Psy D), including child and family psychology (Psy D), diversity and multicultural psychology (Psy D), forensic psychology (Psy D), health and neuropsychology (Psy D); community counseling (MA); counseling psychology (Ed D), including counselor education and supervision; counselor education and supervision (Ed D); forensic psychology (MA). *Accreditation:* APA.

See Close-Up on page 1085.

Arizona State University, Graduate College, College of Liberal Arts and Sciences, Division of Natural Sciences, Department of Psychology, Tempe, AZ 85287. Offers behavioral neuroscience (PhD); clinical psychology (PhD); cognition, action and perception (PhD); developmental psychology (PhD); quantitative psychology (PhD); social psychology (PhD). *Accreditation:* APA. *Degree requirements:* For doctorate, thesis/dissertation. *Entrance requirements:* For doctorate, GRE General Test, GRE Subject Test.

Azusa Pacific University, School of Behavioral and Applied Sciences, Department of Graduate Psychology, Azusa, CA 91702-7000. Offers clinical psychology (MA, Psy D), including family therapy (MA). *Accreditation:* APA (one or more programs are accredited). Part-time and evening/weekend programs available. *Degree requirements:* For master's, comprehensive exam, 250 hours of clinical experience, individual and group therapy. *Entrance requirements:* For master's, interview, minimum GPA of 3.0, Minnesota Multiphasic Personality Inventory. Additional exam requirements/recommendations for international students: Required—TOEFL (minimum score 600 paper-based).

Ball State University, Graduate School, College of Sciences and Humanities, Department of Psychological Science, Program in Clinical Psychology, Muncie, IN 47306-1099. Offers MA. *Entrance requirements:* For master's, GRE General Test, interview.

Clinical Psychology

Barry University, School of Arts and Sciences, Department of Psychology, Miami Shores, FL 33161-6695. Offers clinical psychology (MS); school psychology (MS, SSP). Part-time and evening/weekend programs available. *Degree requirements:* For master's, thesis, practicum. *Entrance requirements:* For master's, GRE General Test, minimum GPA of 3.0, course work in psychology. Electronic applications accepted. *Faculty research:* Closed head injury, memory and aging, infant/mother interaction, evolutionary aspects of behavior, gender roles.

Baylor University, Graduate School, College of Arts and Sciences, Department of Psychology and Neuroscience, Program in Clinical Psychology, Waco, TX 76798. Offers MSCP, Psy D. *Accreditation:* APA. *Students:* 30 full-time (22 women), 3 part-time (2 women); includes 9 minority (7 Asian Americans or Pacific Islanders, 2 Hispanic Americans). In 2009, 10 master's, 3 doctorates awarded. *Degree requirements:* For doctorate, comprehensive exam. *Entrance requirements:* For master's, GRE General Test; for doctorate, GRE General Test, interview. *Application deadline:* For fall admission, 2/1 for domestic students. Applications are processed on a rolling basis. Application fee: $25. *Financial support:* Research assistantships, teaching assistantships, career-related internships or fieldwork, institutionally sponsored loans, tuition waivers (partial), and practicum stipends available. Financial award applicants required to submit FAFSA. *Faculty research:* Professional training in clinical psychology, human systems and dynamics, social skills validation, child therapy and assessment. *Unit head:* Dr. Gary Elkins, Graduate Program Director, 254-710-2961, Fax: 254-710-3033, E-mail: gary_elkins@baylor.edu. *Application contact:* Barbara Prisco, Graduate Coordinator, 254-757-0535, Fax: 254-710-2470, E-mail: barbara_prisco@baylor.edu.

Benedictine University, Graduate Programs, Program in Clinical Psychology, Lisle, IL 60532-0900. Offers MS. Part-time programs available. *Faculty:* 1 full-time (0 women), 7 part-time/adjunct (4 women). *Students:* 30 full-time (28 women), 36 part-time (26 women); includes 12 minority (6 African Americans, 3 Asian Americans or Pacific Islanders, 3 Hispanic Americans). Average age 33. 41 applicants, 49% accepted, 19 enrolled. In 2009, 31 master's awarded. *Degree requirements:* For master's, comprehensive exam, internship. *Entrance requirements:* For master's, MAT. Additional exam requirements/recommendations for international students: Required—TOEFL (minimum score 550 paper-based; 213 computer-based). *Application deadline:* For fall admission, 9/1 for domestic students; for winter admission, 12/1 for domestic students; for spring admission, 2/15 for domestic students. Applications are processed on a rolling basis. Application fee: $40. Electronic applications accepted. *Expenses:* Tuition: Part-time $750 per credit hour. Tuition and fees vary according to campus/location and program. *Financial support:* Career-related internships or fieldwork and health care benefits available. Support available to part-time students. *Unit head:* Dr. James Crissmon, Director, 630-829-6490, E-mail: jcrissmon@ben.edu. *Application contact:* Kari Gibbons, Director, Admissions, 630-829-6200, Fax: 630-829-6584, E-mail: kgibbons@ben.edu.

Bethany University, Program in Clinical Psychology, Scotts Valley, CA 95066-2820. Offers MS. Part-time and evening/weekend programs available.

Bowling Green State University, Graduate College, College of Arts and Sciences, Department of Psychology, Bowling Green, OH 43403. Offers clinical psychology (MA, PhD); developmental psychology (MA, PhD); experimental psychology (MA, PhD); industrial/organizational psychology (MA, PhD); quantitative psychology (MA, PhD). *Accreditation:* APA (one or more programs are accredited). *Degree requirements:* For doctorate, thesis/dissertation. *Entrance requirements:* For doctorate, GRE General Test, GRE Subject Test. Additional exam requirements/recommendations for international students: Required—TOEFL. Electronic applications accepted. *Faculty research:* Personnel psychology, developmental-mathematical models, behavioral medication, brain process, child/adolescent social cognition.

Brigham Young University, Graduate Studies, College of Family, Home, and Social Sciences, Department of Psychology, Provo, UT 84602. Offers clinical psychology (PhD); general psychology (MS); psychology (PhD), including applied social psychology, behavioral neurobiology. *Accreditation:* APA (one or more programs are accredited). *Faculty:* 27 full-time (5 women). *Students:* 90 full-time (30 women); includes 7 minority (3 African Americans, 4 Hispanic Americans), 8 international. Average age 24. 91 applicants, 20% accepted, 18 enrolled. In 2009, 9 master's, 14 doctorates awarded. *Degree requirements:* For master's, thesis; for doctorate, comprehensive exam, thesis/dissertation, publishable paper. *Entrance requirements:* For master's and doctorate, GRE General Test, minimum GPA of 3.0 in last 60 hours of upper division course work. Additional exam requirements/recommendations for international students: Required—TOEFL. *Application deadline:* For fall admission, 1/5 for domestic students. Application fee: $50. Electronic applications accepted. *Expenses:* Tuition: Full-time $5580; part-time $301 per credit hour. Tuition and fees vary according to student's religious affiliation. *Financial support:* In 2009–10, 85 students received support, including 20 research assistantships with partial tuition reimbursements available (averaging $10,000 per year), 30 teaching assistantships with partial tuition reimbursements available (averaging $10,000 per year); fellowships, career-related internships or fieldwork, scholarships/grants, tuition waivers (partial), and unspecified assistantships also available. Financial award application deadline: 5/31. *Faculty research:* Psychotherapy process, Alzheimer's disease/dementia, psychology and law, health, psychology, developmental. Total annual research expenditures: $1 million. *Unit head:* Dr. Ramona Hopkins, Chair, 801-422-1170, Fax: 801-422-0602, E-mail: ramona_hopkins@byu.edu. *Application contact:* Karen A. Christensen, Coordinator of Student Programs, 801-422-4560, Fax: 801-422-0602, E-mail: karen_christensen@byu.edu.

Bryn Mawr College, Graduate School of Arts and Sciences, Department of Psychology, Bryn Mawr, PA 19010-2899. Offers clinical developmental psychology (PhD). Part-time programs available. *Degree requirements:* For doctorate, one foreign language, comprehensive exam, thesis/dissertation. *Entrance requirements:* For doctorate, GRE General Test. Additional exam requirements/recommendations for international students: Required—TOEFL (minimum score 600 paper-based; 250 computer-based). *Expenses:* Tuition: Full-time $31,340. Required fees: $430.

California Institute of Integral Studies, School of Professional Psychology, San Francisco, CA 94103. Offers clinical psychology (Psy D); community mental health (MA); drama therapy (MA); expressive arts therapy (MA); integral counseling psychology (MA); integral counseling psychology–weekend (MA); somatic psychology (MA). *Accreditation:* APA. Part-time programs available. *Students:* 639 full-time (483 women), 53 part-time (43 women); includes 148 minority (32 African Americans, 2 American Indian/Alaska Native, 62 Asian Americans or Pacific Islanders, 52 Hispanic Americans). Average age 38. 476 applicants, 71% accepted, 202 enrolled. In 2009, 136 master's, 21 doctorates awarded. *Degree requirements:* For master's, comprehensive exam; for doctorate, comprehensive exam, thesis/dissertation. *Entrance requirements:* For master's, minimum GPA of 3.0, letters of recommendation, writing sample; for doctorate, GRE, MA in psychology or social work with appropriate practical experience for advanced standing, or BA with a minimum GPA of 3.1; letters of recommendation; writing sample. Additional exam requirements/recommendations for international students: Required—TOEFL. *Application deadline:* For fall admission, 2/1 priority date for domestic and international students; for spring admission, 10/15 priority date for domestic and international students. Applications are processed on a rolling basis. Application fee: $65. Electronic applications accepted. *Expenses:* Tuition: Full-time $15,300; part-time $850 per credit hour. Required fees: $110 per semester. Tuition and fees vary according to degree level. *Financial support:* In 2009–10, 677 students received support; research assistantships with tuition reimbursements available, teaching assistantships with tuition reimbursements available, career-related internships or fieldwork, Federal Work-Study, scholarships/grants, and tuition waivers (partial) available. Support available to part-time students. Financial award application deadline: 4/15; financial award applicants required to submit FAFSA. *Faculty research:* Somatic psychology, comparative psychology, art therapy, transpersonal psychology, eco-psychology. *Application contact:* David Townes, Senior Admissions Counselor, 415-575-6152, Fax: 415-575-1268, E-mail: dtownes@ciis.edu.

California Lutheran University, Graduate Studies, Department of Psychology, Thousand Oaks, CA 91360-2787. Offers clinical psychology (MS, Psy D); marital and family therapy (MS). Part-time programs available. *Degree requirements:* For master's, thesis or comprehensive exams; for doctorate, internship. *Entrance requirements:* For master's, GRE General Test, interview, minimum GPA of 3.0.

California State University, Dominguez Hills, College of Natural and Behavioral Sciences, Program in Psychology, Carson, CA 90747-0001. Offers clinical psychology (MA). Part-time and evening/weekend programs available. *Faculty:* 7 full-time (5 women), 1 (woman) part-time/adjunct. *Students:* 35 full-time (30 women), 15 part-time (13 women); includes 32 minority (10 African Americans, 1 Asian American or Pacific Islander, 21 Hispanic Americans), 1 international. Average age 32. 46 applicants, 74% accepted, 22 enrolled. In 2009, 5 master's awarded. Terminal master's awarded for partial completion of doctoral program. *Degree requirements:* For master's, comprehensive exam, thesis optional. *Entrance requirements:* For master's, GRE General Test or MAT, interview, minimum GPA of 3.0, prerequisite psychology courses. Additional exam requirements/recommendations for international students: Required—TOEFL (minimum score 550 paper-based). *Application deadline:* For fall admission, 3/1 for domestic and international students. Application fee: $55. Electronic applications accepted. *Expenses:* Tuition, nonresident: full-time $6696; part-time $372 per unit. Required fees: $5946; $1752 per semester. *Faculty research:* Culture and health, neuropsychology and HIV, psychohistory of the Holocaust, community and adolescents, malingering. *Unit head:* Dr. Ramona Davis, Chair, 310-243-3474, E-mail: rdavis@csudh.edu. *Application contact:* Dr. Karen I. Mason, Coordinator, 310-243-3642, Fax: 310-516-3642, E-mail: kmason@csudh.edu.

California State University, Fullerton, Graduate Studies, College of Humanities and Social Sciences, Department of Psychology, Fullerton, CA 92834-9480. Offers clinical/community psychology (MS); psychology (MA). Part-time programs available. *Students:* 17 full-time (9 women), 29 part-time (18 women); includes 20 minority (2 African Americans, 13 Asian Americans or Pacific Islanders, 5 Hispanic Americans), 3 international. Average age 26. 140 applicants, 31% accepted, 36 enrolled. In 2009, 19 master's awarded. *Degree requirements:* For master's, thesis. *Entrance requirements:* For master's, GRE General Test, GRE Subject Test, undergraduate major in psychology or related field. Application fee: $55. *Expenses:* Tuition, nonresident: full-time $11,160; part-time $373 per credit. Required fees: $1440 per term. Tuition and fees vary according to course load, degree level and program. *Financial support:* Career-related internships or fieldwork, Federal Work-Study, institutionally sponsored loans, and scholarships/grants available. Support available to part-time students. Financial award application deadline: 3/1; financial award applicants required to submit FAFSA. *Unit head:* Dr. Daniel Kee, Chair, 657-278-3514. *Application contact:* Admissions/Applications, 657-278-2371.

California State University, Northridge, Graduate Studies, College of Social and Behavioral Sciences, Department of Psychology, Northridge, CA 91330. Offers clinical psychology (MA); general-experimental psychology (MA); human factors and applied experimental psychology (MA). *Faculty:* 27 full-time (16 women), 19 part-time/adjunct (8 women). *Students:* 67 full-time (42 women), 25 part-time (19 women); includes 33 minority (2 African Americans, 9 Asian Americans or Pacific Islanders, 22 Hispanic Americans), 4 international. Average age 27. 173 applicants, 19% accepted, 29 enrolled. In 2009, 18 master's awarded. *Degree requirements:* For master's, thesis. *Entrance requirements:* For master's, GRE General Test, GRE Subject Test, minimum GPA of 3.0, letters of recommendation. Additional exam requirements/recommendations for international students: Required—TOEFL. *Application deadline:* For fall admission, 11/30 for domestic students. Application fee: $55. *Financial support:* Application deadline: 3/1. *Unit head:* Dr. Carrie Saetermoe, Chair, 818-677-3506. *Application contact:* Dr. Carrie Saetermoe, Chair, 818-677-3506.

California State University, San Bernardino, Graduate Studies, College of Social and Behavioral Sciences, Department of Psychology, Program in Clinical/Counseling Psychology, San Bernardino, CA 92407-2397. Offers clinical psychology (MS). *Students:* 24 full-time (23 women), 1 (woman) part-time; includes 12 minority (2 African Americans, 2 Asian Americans or Pacific Islanders, 8 Hispanic Americans). Average age 28. 96 applicants, 40% accepted, 14 enrolled. In 2009, 14 master's awarded. *Degree requirements:* For master's, comprehensive exam or thesis. *Entrance requirements:* For master's, minimum GPA of 3.0 in major. *Application deadline:* For fall admission, 8/31 priority date for domestic students. Application fee: $55. *Financial support:* Fellowships, research assistantships, teaching assistantships, career-related internships or fieldwork, Federal Work-Study, and unspecified assistantships available. Financial award application deadline: 3/1. *Faculty research:* Psychology of women, fathering, depression, families, cross-cultural counseling. *Unit head:* Dr. Robert Cramer, Chair, 909-537-5576, Fax: 909-537-7003, E-mail: rcramer@csusb.edu. *Application contact:* Stacy Brooks, Graduate Secretary, 909-880-5570, Fax: 909-880-7003, E-mail: sbrooks@csusb.edu.

Capella University, Harold Abel School of Psychology, Minneapolis, MN 55402. Offers child and adolescent development (MS); clinical psychology (MS, Psy D); counseling psychology (MS); educational psychology (MS, PhD); evaluation, research, and measurement (MS); general psychology (MS, PhD); industrial/organizational psychology (MS, PhD); leadership coaching psychology (MS); organizational leader development (MS); school psychology (MS); sport psychology (MS). Part-time and evening/weekend programs available. Postbaccalaureate distance learning degree programs offered (minimal on-campus study). Terminal master's awarded for partial completion of doctoral program. *Degree requirements:* For master's, thesis optional, project; for doctorate, thesis/dissertation. *Entrance requirements:* For degree, master's degree in school psychology. Additional exam requirements/recommendations for international students: Required—TOEFL (minimum score 550 paper-based; 213 computer-based), TWE (minimum score 4); Recommended—IELTS. Electronic applications accepted.

Cardinal Stritch University, College of Arts and Sciences, Department of Psychology, Milwaukee, WI 53217-3985. Offers clinical psychology (MA). Part-time and evening/weekend programs available. *Degree requirements:* For master's, thesis, portfolio, clinical practicum. *Entrance requirements:* For master's, GRE General Test, GRE Subject Test (psychology), interview, minimum GPA of 3.0, 3 letters of recommendation.

Carlos Albizu University, Graduate Programs, San Juan, PR 00901. Offers clinical psychology (MS, PhD, Psy D); general psychology (PhD); industrial/organizational psychology (MS, PhD); speech and language pathology (MS). *Accreditation:* APA (one or more programs are accredited). Part-time and evening/weekend programs available. Terminal master's awarded for partial completion of doctoral program. *Degree requirements:* For master's, one foreign language, comprehensive exam, thesis; for doctorate, one foreign language, comprehensive exam, thesis/dissertation, written qualifying exams. *Entrance requirements:* For master's, GRE General Test or EXADEP, interview; minimum GPA of 3.0 (industrial/organizational psychology), 3.25 (speech and language pathology); for doctorate, GRE General Test or EXADEP, interview; minimum GPA of 3.0 (industrial/organizational psychology), 3.25 (PhD and Psy D in clinical psychology). *Faculty research:* Psychotherapeutic techniques for Hispanics, psychology of the aged, school dropouts, stress, violence.

Carlos Albizu University, Miami Campus, Graduate Programs, Miami, FL 33172-2209. Offers clinical psychology (Psy D); entrepreneurship (MBA); exceptional student education (MS); industrial/organizational psychology (MS); marriage and family therapy (MS); mental health counseling (MS); nonprofit management (MBA); organizational management (MBA); psychology (MS); school counseling (MS); teaching English as a second language (MS). *Accreditation:* APA. Part-time and evening/weekend programs available. *Faculty:* 23 full-time (13 women), 41 part-time/adjunct (21 women). *Students:* 529 full-time (420 women), 171 part-time (139 women); includes 551 minority (55 African Americans, 1 American Indian/Alaska Native, 5 Asian Americans or Pacific Islanders, 490 Hispanic Americans). Average age 37. 278 applicants, 57% accepted, 142 enrolled. In 2009, 139 master's, 26 doctorates awarded.

Terminal master's awarded for partial completion of doctoral program. *Degree requirements:* For master's, one foreign language, comprehensive exam, integrative project (MBA), research project (exceptional student education, teaching English as a second language); for doctorate, one foreign language, comprehensive exam, internship, project. *Entrance requirements:* For master's, 3 letters of recommendation, interview, minimum GPA of 3.0, resume; for doctorate, 3 letters of recommendation, minimum GPA of 3.0, resume, interview. *Application deadline:* For fall admission, 8/1 priority date for domestic students; for spring admission, 11/30 priority date for domestic students. Applications are processed on a rolling basis. Application fee: $50. Electronic applications accepted. *Expenses:* Tuition: Full-time $9090; part-time $505 per credit hour. Required fees: $298 per term. Tuition and fees vary according to course load, degree level and program. *Financial support:* In 2009–10, 127 students received support. Federal Work-Study, scholarships/grants, and tuition discounts available. Financial award application deadline: 6/1; financial award applicants required to submit FAFSA. *Faculty research:* Psychotherapy, forensic psychology, neuropsychology, marketing strategy, entrepreneurship, special education. *Unit head:* Dr. Carmen S. Roca, Chancellor, 305-593-1223 Ext. 120, Fax: 305-629-8052, E-mail: croca@albizu.edu. *Application contact:* Annalye Alonso, Secretary, 305-593-1223 Ext. 137, Fax: 305-593-1854, E-mail: aalonso@albizu.edu.

Case Western Reserve University, School of Graduate Studies, Department of Psychology, Program in Clinical Psychology, Cleveland, OH 44106. Offers PhD. *Accreditation:* APA. Part-time programs available. *Faculty:* 7 full-time (5 women), 12 part-time/adjunct (6 women). *Students:* 30 full-time (29 women); includes 4 minority (1 African American, 3 Hispanic Americans). Average age 26. 140 applicants, 6% accepted, 5 enrolled. *Degree requirements:* For doctorate, thesis/dissertation, internship. *Entrance requirements:* For doctorate, GRE General Test, GRE Subject Test. Additional exam requirements/recommendations for international students: Required—TOEFL (minimum score 550 paper-based; 213 computer-based; 79 iBT). *Application deadline:* For fall admission, 1/5 for domestic students. Application fee: $50. Electronic applications accepted. *Financial support:* Fellowships, research assistantships, teaching assistantships available. Financial award application deadline: 2/15; financial award applicants required to submit FAFSA. *Faculty research:* Pediatric psychology, family functioning, depression, geriatric psychopathology, creativity and play. *Unit head:* Director of Clinical Training. *Application contact:* Dr. James C. Overholser, Director of Clinical Training, 216-368-2686, Fax: 216-368-4891, E-mail: overholser@case.edu.

The Catholic University of America, School of Arts and Sciences, Department of Psychology, Washington, DC 20064. Offers applied experimental psychology (PhD); clinical psychology (PhD); general psychology (MA); human factors (MA); MA/JD. *Accreditation:* APA (one or more programs are accredited). Part-time programs available. *Faculty:* 12 full-time (6 women), 3 part-time/adjunct (0 women). *Students:* 40 full-time (25 women), 38 part-time (33 women); includes 14 minority (5 African Americans, 4 Asian Americans or Pacific Islanders, 5 Hispanic Americans), 1 international. Average age 29. 200 applicants, 36% accepted, 25 enrolled. In 2009, 16 master's, 6 doctorates awarded. *Degree requirements:* For master's, comprehensive exam, thesis (for some programs); for doctorate, comprehensive exam, thesis/dissertation. *Entrance requirements:* For master's, GRE General Test, 3 letters of recommendation; for doctorate, GRE General Test, GRE Subject Test, statement of purpose, official copies of academic transcripts, three letters of recommendation. Additional exam requirements/recommendations for international students: Required—TOEFL (minimum score 580 paper-based; 237 computer-based). *Application deadline:* For fall admission, 8/1 priority date for domestic students, 7/15 for international students; for spring admission, 12/1 priority date for domestic students, 10/15 for international students. Applications are processed on a rolling basis. Application fee: $55. Electronic applications accepted. *Expenses:* Tuition: Full-time $31,740; part-time $1245 per credit hour. Required fees: $50; $25 per semester hour. One-time fee: $425. *Financial support:* Fellowships, research assistantships, teaching assistantships, Federal Work-Study, scholarships/grants, tuition waivers (full and partial), and unspecified assistantships available. Financial award application deadline: 2/1; financial award applicants required to submit FAFSA. *Faculty research:* Clinical psychology, applied cognitive science, psychopathology, cognitive neuroscience, psychotherapy. Total annual research expenditures: $409,988. *Unit head:* Dr. Marc M. Sebrechts, Chair, 202-319-5757, Fax: 202-319-6263, E-mail: sebrechts@cua.edu. *Application contact:* Julie Schwing, Director of Graduate Admissions, 202-319-5057, Fax: 202-319-6533, E-mail: cua-admissions@cua.edu.

Central Michigan University, College of Graduate Studies, College of Humanities and Social and Behavioral Sciences, Department of Psychology, Program in Clinical Psychology, Mount Pleasant, MI 48859. Offers MA, PhD. *Accreditation:* APA. Terminal master's awarded for partial completion of doctoral program. *Degree requirements:* For master's, thesis, completion of first 2 years of the PhD program in clinical psychology; for doctorate, thesis/dissertation. *Entrance requirements:* For master's and doctorate, GRE. Electronic applications accepted. *Faculty research:* Applied youth development; emotional processes, personality disorders, and assessment; influence of affective variables on cognitive performance; post-traumatic stress disorder and panic disorder; validation of clinical inferences from psychological tests.

Chestnut Hill College, School of Graduate Studies, Division of Psychology, Program in Clinical and Counseling Psychology, Philadelphia, PA 19118-2693. Offers MA, MS, CAS. Part-time and evening/weekend programs available. *Degree requirements:* For master's, thesis optional, practica. *Entrance requirements:* For master's, GRE, writing sample, letters of recommendation; for CAS, GRE, master's degree in counseling or related discipline, transcripts, letters of recommendation, statement of professional goals, writing sample. Additional exam requirements/recommendations for international students: Required—TOEFL (minimum score 550 paper-based; 213 computer-based). *Faculty research:* Play therapy, eating disorders, addictions, group psychology and group therapy, health psychology.

Chestnut Hill College, School of Graduate Studies, Division of Psychology, Program in Clinical Psychology, Philadelphia, PA 19118-2693. Offers Psy D. *Accreditation:* APA. Part-time and evening/weekend programs available. *Degree requirements:* For doctorate, comprehensive exam, thesis/dissertation, internships, practica. *Entrance requirements:* For doctorate, GRE, letters of recommendation, writing sample, master's degree in clinical/counseling psychology or closely related field. Additional exam requirements/recommendations for international students: Required—TOEFL (minimum score 500 paper-based; 213 computer-based). *Faculty research:* Psychological testing and assessment, GLBT issues, autism and developmental disorders, stepfamilies, gender issues.

The Chicago School of Professional Psychology, Program in Applied Behavior Analysis, Chicago, IL 60610. Offers applied behavior analysis (Psy D); clinical psychology (applied behavior analysis specialization) (MA). *Students:* 104 full-time (88 women), 26 part-time (22 women); includes 17 African Americans, 9 Asian Americans or Pacific Islanders, 10 Hispanic Americans, 4 international. 105 applicants, 94% accepted, 59 enrolled. In 2009, 10 master's awarded. *Degree requirements:* For master's, thesis, practicum; for doctorate, thesis/dissertation, practicum. *Entrance requirements:* For doctorate, GRE. Additional exam requirements/recommendations for international students: Required—TOEFL. *Financial support:* In 2009–10, research assistantships (averaging $6,000 per year), teaching assistantships (averaging $6,000 per year) were awarded; Federal Work-Study, institutionally sponsored loans, and scholarships/grants also available. Financial award application deadline: 3/1; financial award applicants required to submit FAFSA. *Unit head:* Dr. Charles Merbitz, Department Chair, 312-329-6628, E-mail: cmerbitz@thechicagoschool.edu. *Application contact:* Andrea Schmoyer, Director of Admission, 312-329-6666, Fax: 312-644-3333, E-mail: admissions@thechicagoschool.edu.

The Chicago School of Professional Psychology, Program in Clinical Forensic Psychology, Chicago, IL 60610. Offers Psy D. *Students:* 30 full-time (25 women); includes 5 minority (2 African Americans, 3 Hispanic Americans). 52 applicants, 67% accepted, 30 enrolled. In 2009, 71 doctorates awarded. *Degree requirements:* For doctorate, thesis/dissertation. *Entrance requirements:* For doctorate, GRE. Additional exam requirements/recommendations for international students: Required—TOEFL, IELTS. *Financial support:* In 2009–10, fellowships (averaging $10,000 per year), research assistantships (averaging $6,000 per year), teaching assistantships (averaging $6,000 per year) were awarded; Federal Work-Study, institutionally sponsored loans, and scholarships/grants also available. Financial award application deadline: 3/1; financial award applicants required to submit FAFSA. *Unit head:* Dr. James Galezewski, Department Chair, 312-467-2169, E-mail: jgalezewski@thechicagoschool.edu. *Application contact:* Andrea Schmoyer, Director of Admission, 312-329-6666, Fax: 312-644-3333, E-mail: admissions@thechicagoschool.edu.

The Chicago School of Professional Psychology, Program in Clinical Psychology, Chicago, IL 60610. Offers applied behavior analysis (MA); clinical psychology (Psy D); counseling (MA). *Students:* 341 full-time (268 women), 10 part-time (7 women); includes 52 minority (22 African Americans, 2 American Indian/Alaska Native, 15 Asian Americans or Pacific Islanders, 13 Hispanic Americans), 16 international. 452 applicants, 54% accepted, 106 enrolled. In 2009, 71 doctorates awarded. *Degree requirements:* For master's, thesis (for some programs); for doctorate, comprehensive exam, thesis/dissertation. *Entrance requirements:* For master's, minimum undergraduate GPA of 3.0, 1 course in psychology, 1 course in either statistics or research methods; for doctorate, GRE, 18 hours of psychology credit (including courses in statistics, normal psychology and human development); minimum GPA of 3.2. Additional exam requirements/recommendations for international students: Required—TOEFL. Electronic applications accepted. *Financial support:* In 2009–10, fellowships with partial tuition reimbursements (averaging $10,000 per year), research assistantships (averaging $6,000 per year), teaching assistantships (averaging $6,000 per year) were awarded; Federal Work-Study, institutionally sponsored loans, and scholarships/grants also available. Financial award application deadline: 3/1; financial award applicants required to submit FAFSA. *Unit head:* Dr. James Galezewski, Department Chair, 312-467-2169, E-mail: jgalezewski@thechicagoschool.edu. *Application contact:* Andrea Schmoyer, Director of Admission, 312-329-6666, Fax: 312-644-3333, E-mail: admissions@thechicagoschool.edu.

The Chicago School of Professional Psychology at Downtown Los Angeles, Clinical Forensic Psychology, Los Angeles, CA 90017. Offers Psy D. *Students:* 38 full-time (34 women), 4 part-time (3 women); includes 20 minority (9 African Americans, 2 Asian Americans or Pacific Islanders, 9 Hispanic Americans). 44 applicants, 89% accepted, 30 enrolled. *Unit head:* Dr. Debra Warner, Lead Faculty, 213-615-7203, E-mail: dwarner@thechicagoschool.edu. *Application contact:* Heather LaBelle, Director of Admissions, 213-615-7200, Fax: 213-627-1985, E-mail: admissions@thechicagoschool.edu.

The Chicago School of Professional Psychology at Downtown Los Angeles, Clinical Psychology, Los Angeles, CA 90017. Offers applied behavior analysis (MA); clinical psychology (Psy D); marital and family therapy (MA). *Students:* 196 full-time (168 women), 8 part-time (6 women); includes 75 minority (23 African Americans, 1 American Indian/Alaska Native, 23 Asian Americans or Pacific Islanders, 28 Hispanic Americans), 1 international. 152 applicants, 94% accepted, 57 enrolled. *Application contact:* Heather LaBelle, Director of Admissions, 213-615-7200, Fax: 213-627-1985, E-mail: admissions@thechicagoschool.edu.

The Chicago School of Professional Psychology at Grayslake, Program in Clinical Counseling Psychology, Chicago, IL 60610. Offers counseling (MA), including child and adolescent treatment, generalist, health psychology, Latino mental health, supervision and leadership in mental health, treatment of addiction disorders. *Unit head:* Dr. Virginia Quinonez, Department Chair, 312-329-6623, E-mail: vquinonez@thechicagoschool.edu. *Application contact:* Andrea Schmoyer, Director of Admissions, 312-329-6666, Fax: 312-644-3333, E-mail: admissions@thechicagoschool.edu.

The Chicago School of Professional Psychology at Irvine, Program in Clinical Forensic Psychology, Irvine, CA 92612. Offers Psy D. *Unit head:* Dr. Debra Warner, Lead Faculty, 213-615-7203, E-mail: dwarner@thechicagoschool.edu. *Application contact:* Betty Vu, Director of Admissions, 949-737-5460, Fax: 949-737-5467, E-mail: admissions@thechicagoschool.edu.

The Chicago School of Professional Psychology at Westwood, Clinical Psychology MFT, Los Angeles, CA 90024. Offers marital and family therapy (MA). *Students:* 24 full-time (19 women), 2 part-time (both women); includes 7 minority (1 African American, 3 Asian Americans or Pacific Islanders, 3 Hispanic Americans), 1 international. 43 applicants, 86% accepted. *Application contact:* Heather LaBelle, Director of Admissions, 310-208-4240, Fax: 310-208-0684, E-mail: admissions@thechicagoschool.edu.

City College of the City University of New York, Graduate School, College of Liberal Arts and Science, Division of Social Science, Department of Psychology, New York, NY 10031-9198. Offers clinical psychology (PhD); experimental cognition (PhD); general psychology (MA); mental health counseling (MA). *Accreditation:* APA (one or more programs are accredited). Part-time programs available. *Degree requirements:* For master's, one foreign language, comprehensive exam, thesis. *Entrance requirements:* For master's, GRE. Additional exam requirements/recommendations for international students: Required—TOEFL (minimum score 550 paper-based; 79 iBT). Electronic applications accepted. *Faculty research:* Social/personality psychology, physiological psychology, cognition and development.

Clark University, Graduate School, Department of Psychology, Program in Clinical Psychology, Worcester, MA 01610-1477. Offers PhD. *Accreditation:* APA. *Degree requirements:* For doctorate, thesis/dissertation. *Entrance requirements:* For doctorate, GRE General Test. Additional exam requirements/recommendations for international students: Required—TOEFL. *Application deadline:* For fall admission, 12/28 priority date for domestic students. Applications are processed on a rolling basis. Application fee: $50. *Expenses:* Tuition: Full-time $34,900; part-time $4362.50 per course. *Financial support:* In 2009–10, fellowships with full tuition reimbursements (averaging $15,700 per year), research assistantships with full tuition reimbursements (averaging $15,700 per year), teaching assistantships with full tuition reimbursements (averaging $15,700 per year) were awarded; tuition waivers (full) also available. *Faculty research:* Development of psychological processes in sociocultural context, conceptualizing and reasoning, symbolization, psychotherapy, metaphor, emotions and personalities. *Unit head:* Dr. James Cordova, Chair, 508-793-7268. *Application contact:* Peggy Moskowitz, Graduate School Secretary, 508-793-7274, Fax: 508-793-7265, E-mail: psychology@clarku.edu.

Cleveland State University, College of Graduate Studies, College of Science, Department of Psychology, Cleveland, OH 44115. Offers adult development and aging (PhD); clinical psychology (MA); consumer/industrial research (MA); diversity management (MA); experimental research psychology (MA); school psychology (Psy S). *Degree requirements:* For master's, comprehensive exam (for some programs), thesis (for some programs); for doctorate, comprehensive exam, thesis/dissertation; for Psy S, internship. *Entrance requirements:* For master's and doctorate, GRE General Test. Additional exam requirements/recommendations for international students: Required—TOEFL (minimum score 525 paper-based; 197 computer-based). Electronic applications accepted. *Faculty research:* Cognitive and social psychology, consumer psychology, clinical psychology, school psychology, aging.

College of St. Joseph, Graduate Programs, Division of Psychology and Human Services, Program in Clinical Mental Health Counseling, Rutland, VT 05701-3899. Offers MS. Part-time programs available. *Degree requirements:* For master's, comprehensive exam. *Entrance requirements:* For master's, 2 letters of reference, interview. Electronic applications accepted. *Expenses:* Tuition: Full-time $13,500; part-time $350 per credit. Required fees: $45 per term. One-time fee: $445. Tuition and fees vary according to program.

College of St. Joseph, Graduate Programs, Division of Psychology and Human Services, Program in Clinical Psychology, Rutland, VT 05701-3899. Offers MS. Part-time and evening/weekend programs available. *Degree requirements:* For master's, comprehensive exam, thesis

Clinical Psychology

College of St. Joseph (continued)
optional. *Entrance requirements:* For master's, 2 letters of reference, interview. Electronic applications accepted. *Expenses:* Tuition: Full-time $13,500; part-time $350 per credit. Required fees: $45 per term. One-time fee: $445. Tuition and fees vary according to program.

Concordia University, School of Graduate Studies, Faculty of Arts and Science, Department of Psychology, Program in Psychology (Clinical), Montréal, QC H3G 1M8, Canada. Offers MA, PhD, Certificate. *Accreditation:* APA (one or more programs are accredited). *Degree requirements:* For master's, comprehensive exam, thesis; for doctorate, comprehensive exam, thesis/dissertation. *Entrance requirements:* For master's, GRE General Test, GRE Subject Test, honors degree in psychology or equivalent; for doctorate, master's degree in psychology. *Faculty research:* Developmental-clinical psychology, sensory deficits, sexual dysfunction.

Dalhousie University, Faculty of Science, Department of Psychology, Halifax, NS B3H 4R2, Canada. Offers clinical psychology (PhD); psychology (M Sc, PhD); psychology/neuroscience (M Sc, PhD). *Accreditation:* APA (one or more programs are accredited). *Faculty:* 30 full-time (8 women), 34 part-time/adjunct (14 women). *Students:* 56 full-time (35 women); includes 2 minority (both Asian Americans or Pacific Islanders). 200 applicants, 8% accepted. In 2009, 8 master's, 7 doctorates awarded. *Degree requirements:* For master's, thesis; for doctorate, thesis/dissertation. *Entrance requirements:* For doctorate, GRE General Test. Additional exam requirements/recommendations for international students: Required—TOEFL, IELTS, CANTEST, CAEL, or Michigan English Language Assessment Battery. Application fee: $70. Electronic applications accepted. *Financial support:* In 2009–10, 19 fellowships, 26 teaching assistantships (averaging $1,853 per year) were awarded; career-related internships or fieldwork, scholarships/grants, and health care benefits also available. Financial award application deadline: 2/1. *Faculty research:* Physiological psychology, psychology of learning, learning and behavior, forensic clinical health psychology, development perception and cognition. Total annual research expenditures: $1.9 million. *Unit head:* Dr. Tracy Taylor-Helmick, Graduate Coordinator, 902-494-3001, Fax: 902-494-6585, E-mail: tracy.taylor.helmick@dal.ca. *Application contact:* Mary Macconnachie, Graduate Secretary, 902-494-3839, Fax: 902-494-6585, E-mail: mary.macconnachie@dal.ca.

DePaul University, College of Liberal Arts and Sciences, Department of Psychology, Chicago, IL 60604-2287. Offers clinical psychology (MA, PhD), including child clinical psychology, community clinical psychology; experimental psychology (MA, PhD); general psychology (MS); industrial/organizational psychology (MA, PhD); MA/PhD. *Accreditation:* APA (one or more programs are accredited). *Faculty:* 31 full-time (19 women), 6 part-time/adjunct (4 women). *Students:* 59 full-time (36 women), 54 part-time (35 women); includes 26 minority (10 African Americans, 5 Asian Americans or Pacific Islanders, 11 Hispanic Americans), 2 international. Average age 28. 332 applicants, 14% accepted, 23 enrolled. In 2009, 14 master's, 17 doctorates awarded. *Degree requirements:* For master's, thesis, oral exam; for doctorate, comprehensive exam, thesis/dissertation, oral and written exams. *Entrance requirements:* For master's and doctorate, GRE General Test, GRE Subject Test, 32 quarter hours of course work in psychology, 3 letters of recommendation. Additional exam requirements/recommendations for international students: Required—TOEFL. Application fee: $40. Electronic applications accepted. *Expenses:* Tuition: Full-time $37,525; part-time $620 per credit hour. *Financial support:* In 2009–10, 48 students received support, including 35 research assistantships with full tuition reimbursements available (averaging $11,800 per year), 13 teaching assistantships with full tuition reimbursements available (averaging $11,800 per year); career-related internships or fieldwork, scholarships/grants, traineeships, tuition waivers (full and partial), and unspecified assistantships also available. Financial award application deadline: 1/10. *Faculty research:* Adolescent stress and depression, minority adolescents sexuality, public policy, community influences in child adjustment. *Unit head:* Dr. Christopher B. Keys, Chairman, 773-325-7887, Fax: 773-325-7888. *Application contact:* Alison Pereida Knapp, Graduate Admissions Assistant, 773-325-7887, Fax: 773-325-7888.

Drexel University, College of Arts and Sciences, Department of Psychology, Clinical Psychology Program, Philadelphia, PA 19104-2875. Offers clinical psychology (PhD); forensic psychology (PhD); health psychology (PhD); neuropsychology (PhD). *Accreditation:* APA. Terminal master's awarded for partial completion of doctoral program. *Degree requirements:* For doctorate, thesis/dissertation, qualifying exam. *Entrance requirements:* For doctorate, GRE General Test, GRE Subject Test, minimum GPA of 3.0. Electronic applications accepted. *Expenses:* Contact institution. *Faculty research:* Cognitive behavioral therapy, stress and coping, eating disorders, substance abuse, developmental disabilities.

Drexel University, College of Arts and Sciences, Department of Psychology, Program in Law-Psychology, Philadelphia, PA 19104-2875. Offers JD/PhD. Electronic applications accepted. *Expenses:* Contact institution. *Faculty research:* Mental health law issues, professional ethics, social science applications to law.

Duke University, Graduate School, Department of Psychology, Durham, NC 27708-0586. Offers biological psychology (PhD); clinical psychology (PhD); cognitive psychology (PhD); developmental psychology (PhD); experimental psychology (PhD); health psychology (PhD); human social development (PhD); JD/MA. *Accreditation:* APA (one or more programs are accredited). *Faculty:* 40 full-time. *Students:* 92 full-time (70 women); includes 13 minority (5 African Americans, 2 Asian Americans or Pacific Islanders, 6 Hispanic Americans), 14 international. 478 applicants, 8% accepted, 21 enrolled. In 2009, 10 doctorates awarded. *Degree requirements:* For doctorate, thesis/dissertation. *Entrance requirements:* For doctorate, GRE General Test. Additional exam requirements/recommendations for international students: Required—TOEFL (minimum score 550 paper-based; 213 computer-based; 83 iBT), IELTS (minimum score 7). *Application deadline:* For fall admission, 12/8 priority date for domestic and international students. Application fee: $75. Electronic applications accepted. *Financial support:* Fellowships, research assistantships, teaching assistantships, career-related internships or fieldwork and Federal Work-Study available. Financial award application deadline: 12/31. *Unit head:* Melanie Bonner, Director of Graduate Studies, Fax: 919-660-5715, E-mail: morrell@duke.edu. *Application contact:* Cynthia Robertson, Associate Dean for Enrollment Services, 919-684-3913, E-mail: grad-admissions@duke.edu.

Duquesne University, Graduate School of Liberal Arts, Department of Psychology, Pittsburgh, PA 15282-0001. Offers clinical psychology (PhD). *Accreditation:* APA. *Faculty:* 14 full-time (5 women). *Students:* 49 full-time (24 women); includes 1 minority (Hispanic American), 8 international. Average age 25. 111 applicants, 6% accepted, 5 enrolled. In 2009, 9 doctorates awarded. *Degree requirements:* For doctorate, comprehensive exam, thesis/dissertation. *Entrance requirements:* For doctorate, GRE General Test, MA in psychology. Additional exam requirements/recommendations for international students: Required—TOEFL. *Application deadline:* For fall admission, 12/15 for domestic and international students. Electronic applications accepted. *Expenses:* Tuition: Part-time $851 per credit. Required fees: $81 per credit. *Financial support:* In 2009–10, 1 research assistantship with full tuition reimbursement (averaging $13,000 per year), 14 teaching assistantships with full tuition reimbursements (averaging $13,000 per year) were awarded; fellowships with full tuition reimbursements, career-related internships or fieldwork, scholarships/grants, tuition waivers (partial), and unspecified assistantships also available. Financial award application deadline: 5/1. *Faculty research:* Emotion, language motivation, imagination, development. *Unit head:* Dr. Daniel Burston, Chair, 412-396-5067. *Application contact:* Dr. Daniel Buston, Chair, 412-396-5067.

East Carolina University, Graduate School, Thomas Harriot College of Arts and Sciences, Department of Psychology, Program in Clinical Psychology, Greenville, NC 27858-4353. Offers MA. *Degree requirements:* For master's, one foreign language, comprehensive exam, thesis. *Entrance requirements:* For master's, GRE General Test, GRE Subject Test. Additional exam requirements/recommendations for international students: Required—TOEFL.

Eastern Illinois University, Graduate School, College of Sciences, Charleston, IL 61920-3099. Offers biological sciences (MS); chemistry (MS); communication disorders and sciences (MS); economics (MA); mathematics and computer science (MA), including mathematics, mathematics education; natural sciences (MS); political science (MA); psychology (MA, SSP), including clinical psychology (MA), school psychology (SSP). Part-time programs available. *Faculty:* 193 full-time (40 women). In 2009, 83 master's, 11 other advanced degrees awarded. *Degree requirements:* For SSP, thesis. *Entrance requirements:* For degree, GRE General Test. *Application deadline:* For fall admission, 3/31 priority date for domestic students. Applications are processed on a rolling basis. Application fee: $30. *Expenses:* Tuition, state resident: full-time $9434; part-time $239 per credit hour. Tuition, nonresident: full-time $23,774; part-time $717 per credit hour. Required fees: $802.63. *Financial support:* In 2009–10, research assistantships with tuition reimbursements (averaging $8,100 per year), teaching assistantships with tuition reimbursements (averaging $8,100 per year) were awarded; career-related internships or fieldwork and Federal Work-Study also available. Support available to part-time students. *Unit head:* Dr. Mary Ann Hanner, Dean, 217-581-3328, Fax: 217-581-7110, E-mail: mahanner@eiu.edu. *Application contact:* Bill Elliott, Director of Graduate Admissions, 217-581-7489, Fax: 217-581-6020, E-mail: wjelliott@eiu.edu.

Eastern Illinois University, Graduate School, College of Sciences, Department of Psychology, Program in Clinical Psychology, Charleston, IL 61920-3099. Offers MA. In 2009, 10 master's awarded. *Degree requirements:* For master's, comprehensive exam. *Entrance requirements:* For master's, GRE General Test. *Application deadline:* For fall admission, 3/31 priority date for domestic students. Applications are processed on a rolling basis. Application fee: $30. *Expenses:* Tuition, state resident: full-time $9434; part-time $239 per credit hour. Tuition, nonresident: full-time $23,774; part-time $717 per credit hour. Required fees: $802.63. *Financial support:* In 2009–10, research assistantships with tuition reimbursements (averaging $8,100 per year), 5 teaching assistantships with tuition reimbursements (averaging $8,100 per year) were awarded. *Unit head:* Dr. Anu Sharma, Coordinator, 217-581-2127, Fax: 217-581-6764, E-mail: asharma@eiu.edu. *Application contact:* Dr. Anu Sharma, Coordinator, 217-581-2127, Fax: 217-581-6764, E-mail: asharma@eiu.edu.

Eastern Kentucky University, The Graduate School, College of Arts and Sciences, Department of Psychology, Richmond, KY 40475-3102. Offers clinical psychology (MS); industrial/organizational psychology (MS); school psychology (Psy S). Part-time programs available. *Entrance requirements:* For master's and Psy S, GRE General Test, minimum GPA of 2.5. *Faculty research:* Autism, social psychology, parenting, assessment of depression/anxiety, reading.

Eastern Michigan University, Graduate School, College of Arts and Sciences, Department of Psychology, Ypsilanti, MI 48197. Offers clinical behavioral psychology (MS); clinical psychology (MS, PhD); experimental psychology (MS). *Accreditation:* APA. *Faculty:* 24 full-time (14 women). *Students:* 44 full-time (34 women), 46 part-time (34 women); includes 9 minority (2 African Americans, 4 Asian Americans or Pacific Islanders, 3 Hispanic Americans), 4 international. Average age 27. 181 applicants, 19% accepted, 33 enrolled. In 2009, 17 master's, 12 doctorates awarded. *Degree requirements:* For master's, 600 hour practicum; for doctorate, 1500-hour practicum; 2000 hour internship. *Entrance requirements:* For master's and doctorate, GRE. *Application deadline:* For fall admission, 2/15 for domestic students. Application fee: $35. Tuition and fees vary according to course level. *Financial support:* In 2009–10, 33 fellowships (averaging $15,000 per year) were awarded. *Unit head:* Dr. Carol Freedman-Doan, Interim Department Head, 734-487-1155, Fax: 734-487-6553, E-mail: cfreedman@emich.edu. *Application contact:* Dawn Stentzel, Graduate Secretary, 734-487-1155, Fax: 734-487-6553.

Eastern Virginia Medical School, The Virginia Consortium Program in Clinical Psychology, Norfolk, VA 23501-1980. Offers Psy D. *Faculty:* 33. *Students:* 55 full-time (41 women); includes 5 African Americans, 6 Asian Americans or Pacific Islanders, 3 Hispanic Americans. 214 applicants, 7% accepted, 6 enrolled. In 2009, 4 doctorates awarded. *Entrance requirements:* For doctorate, GRE, BS in behavioral sciences or equivalent. Additional exam requirements/recommendations for international students: Required—TOEFL. *Application deadline:* For fall admission, 1/15 for domestic students. Application fee: $40. *Expenses:* Contact institution. *Unit head:* Dr. Michael L. Stutts, Director, 757-446-8400, Fax: 757-446-8401, E-mail: stuttsml@evms.edu. *Application contact:* Eileen O'Neill, Administrative Coordinator, 757-368-1820, Fax: 757-446-8401, E-mail: exoneill@odu.edu.

Eastern Washington University, Graduate Studies, College of Social and Behavioral Sciences, Department of Psychology, Cheney, WA 99004-2431. Offers clinical psychology (MS); experimental psychology (MS); psychology (MS); school psychology (MS). *Degree requirements:* For master's, comprehensive exam, thesis or alternative. *Entrance requirements:* For master's, GRE General Test, minimum GPA of 3.0. *Expenses:* Tuition, state resident: full-time $7476; part-time $249 per quarter hour. Tuition, nonresident: full-time $18,030; part-time $601 per quarter hour. Required fees: $3.50 per quarter hour. $142 per quarter.

East Tennessee State University, School of Graduate Studies, College of Arts and Sciences, Department of Psychology, Johnson City, TN 37614. Offers clinical psychology (MA); general psychology (MA). *Degree requirements:* For master's, thesis, oral exams. *Entrance requirements:* For master's, GRE General Test, GRE Subject Test, minimum GPA of 3.0. Additional exam requirements/recommendations for international students: Required—TOEFL (minimum score 550 paper-based; 213 computer-based). *Faculty research:* Language acquisition, recovery of brain function after injury or damage, violence in domestic relationships and road rage, reasons for living, unhealthy tanning behaviors.

Edinboro University of Pennsylvania, School of Graduate Studies and Research, School of Liberal Arts, Department of Psychology, Edinboro, PA 16444. Offers clinical psychology (MA). Part-time and evening/weekend programs available. *Faculty:* 3 full-time (all women). *Students:* 14 full-time (13 women), 2 part-time (both women). Average age 26. In 2009, 4 master's awarded. *Degree requirements:* For master's, comprehensive exam, thesis or alternative, project. *Entrance requirements:* For master's, GRE or MAT, minimum QPA of 2.5. *Application deadline:* For fall admission, 3/15 priority date for domestic students. Applications are processed on a rolling basis. Application fee: $30. Electronic applications accepted. *Expenses:* Tuition, state resident: full-time $6666; part-time $370 per credit. Tuition, nonresident: full-time $10,666; part-time $593 per credit. Required fees: $2206.28. One-time fee: $204 part-time. *Financial support:* In 2009–10, 3 research assistantships with full and partial tuition reimbursements (averaging $4,050 per year) were awarded; career-related internships or fieldwork, Federal Work-Study, scholarships/grants, and unspecified assistantships also available. Support available to part-time students. Financial award application deadline: 2/15; financial award applicants required to submit FAFSA.

Emory University, Graduate School of Arts and Sciences, Department of Psychology, Atlanta, GA 30322-1100. Offers clinical psychology (PhD); cognition and development (PhD); neuroscience and animal behavior (PhD). *Accreditation:* APA. *Degree requirements:* For doctorate, comprehensive exam, thesis/dissertation. *Entrance requirements:* For doctorate, GRE General Test, minimum GPA of 3.25. Additional exam requirements/recommendations for international students: Required—TOEFL. Electronic applications accepted. *Faculty research:* Neuroscience and animal behavior; adult and child psychopathology, cognition development assessment.

Emporia State University, School of Graduate Studies, The Teachers College, Department of Psychology, Art Therapy, Rehabilitation and Mental Health Counseling, Program in Clinical Psychology, Emporia, KS 66801-5087. Offers MS. Part-time programs available. *Students:* 20 full-time (14 women), 6 part-time (3 women); includes 2 minority (1 African American, 1 Asian American or Pacific Islander), 1 international. 16 applicants, 81% accepted, 10 enrolled. In 2009, 6 master's awarded. *Degree requirements:* For master's, comprehensive exam, clinical internship. *Entrance requirements:* For master's, GRE or MAT, 24 hours of course work in undergraduate psychology, 3 letters of recommendation. Additional exam requirements/recommendations for international students: Required—TOEFL (minimum score 520 paper-based; 133 computer-based; 68 iBT). *Application deadline:* For fall admission, 8/15 for domestic students. Applications are processed on a rolling basis. Application fee: $30 ($75 for international students). Electronic applications accepted. *Expenses:* Tuition, state resident: full-time $4154; part-time $173 per credit hour. Tuition, nonresident: full-time $12,864; part-time $536 per credit hour. Required fees: $948; $58 per credit hour. Tuition and fees vary according to campus/location. *Financial support:* Career-related internships or fieldwork, Federal Work-Study, institutionally sponsored loans, health care benefits, and unspecified assistantships available. Support available to part-time students. Financial award application deadline: 3/15; financial award applicants required to submit FAFSA. *Unit head:* Dr. Brian W. Schrader, Chair, 620-341-5317, E-mail: schrade@emporia.edu. *Application contact:* Mary Sewell, Admissions Coordinator, 800-950-GRAD, Fax: 620-341-5909, E-mail: msewell@emporia.edu.

Evangel University, Department of Psychology, Springfield, MO 65802. Offers clinical psychology (MS); counseling psychology (MS). Part-time programs available. *Faculty:* 3 full-time (2 women), 2 part-time/adjunct (1 woman). *Students:* 19 full-time (13 women), 14 part-time (12 women). Average age 27. 17 applicants, 100% accepted, 15 enrolled. In 2009, 6 master's awarded. *Degree requirements:* For master's, comprehensive exam, thesis optional. *Entrance requirements:* For master's, GRE General Test or MAT, minimum undergraduate GPA of 3.0, undergraduate major or minor in psychology. Additional exam requirements/recommendations for international students: Required—TOEFL (minimum score 550 paper-based; 213 computer-based). *Application deadline:* For fall admission, 2/1 priority date for domestic students; for spring admission, 10/15 priority date for domestic students. Applications are processed on a rolling basis. Application fee: $25. Electronic applications accepted. *Financial support:* In 2009–10, 6 students received support. Career-related internships or fieldwork, scholarships/grants, and unspecified assistantships available. Support available to part-time students. Financial award application deadline: 3/1; financial award applicants required to submit FAFSA. *Unit head:* Dr. Grant Jones, Chair, 417-865-2815 Ext. 8619, E-mail: jonesg@evangel.edu. *Application contact:* Charity H. Fahlstrom, Admissions Representative, Graduate and Professional Studies, 417-865-2815 Ext. 7227, Fax: 417-575-5484, E-mail: fahlstromc@evangel.edu.

Fairleigh Dickinson University, Metropolitan Campus, University College: Arts, Sciences, and Professional Studies, School of Psychology, Program in Clinical Psychology, Teaneck, NJ 07666-1914. Offers MA, PhD. *Accreditation:* APA. *Students:* 77 full-time (54 women). Average age 30. 25 applicants, 56% accepted, 14 enrolled. In 2009, 23 doctorates awarded. *Application deadline:* Applications are processed on a rolling basis. Application fee: $40. *Application contact:* Susan Brooman, University Director of Graduate Admissions, 201-692-2554, Fax: 201-692-2560, E-mail: globaleducation@fdu.edu.

Fairleigh Dickinson University, Metropolitan Campus, University College: Arts, Sciences, and Professional Studies, School of Psychology, Program in Clinical Psychopharmacology, Teaneck, NJ 07666-1914. Offers MA. *Students:* 30 part-time (21 women), 2 international. Average age 48. 25 applicants, 100% accepted, 16 enrolled. In 2009, 27 master's awarded. *Application contact:* Susan Brooman, University Director of Graduate Admissions, 201-692-2554, Fax: 201-692-2560, E-mail: globaleducation@fdu.edu.

Fielding Graduate University, Graduate Programs, School of Psychology, Santa Barbara, CA 93105-3538. Offers clinical psychology (PhD); clinical psychology respecialization (Post-Doctoral Certificate); media psychology (PhD); media psychology and social change (MA); neuropsychology (Post-Doctoral Certificate). *Accreditation:* APA. Postbaccalaureate distance learning degree programs offered (minimal on-campus study). *Faculty:* 31 full-time (17 women), 10 part-time/adjunct (6 women). *Students:* 509 full-time (380 women), 104 part-time (71 women); includes 126 minority (34 African Americans, 8 American Indian/Alaska Native, 28 Asian Americans or Pacific Islanders, 56 Hispanic Americans), 20 international. Average age 43. 337 applicants, 47% accepted, 96 enrolled. In 2009, 2 master's, 43 doctorates, 18 other advanced degrees awarded. Terminal master's awarded for partial completion of doctoral program. *Degree requirements:* For master's, thesis or alternative, capstone project; for doctorate, comprehensive exam, thesis/dissertation. *Entrance requirements:* For doctorate, writing sample, minimum GPA of 3.0, 3 letters of recommendation, resume. *Application deadline:* For fall admission, 2/23 for domestic and international students; for spring admission, 8/25 for domestic and international students. Application fee: $75. Electronic applications accepted. *Expenses:* Contact institution. *Financial support:* In 2009–10, 403 students received support. Scholarships/grants and health care benefits available. Support available to part-time students. Financial award application deadline: 5/15; financial award applicants required to submit FAFSA. *Unit head:* Dr. Raymond Trybus, Dean, 805-898-2909, E-mail: rtrybus@fielding.edu. *Application contact:* Kathryn Romero, Admission Counselor, 800-340-1099, Fax: 805-687-9793, E-mail: kromero@fielding.edu.

Fisk University, Division of Graduate Studies, Department of Psychology, Nashville, TN 37208-3051. Offers clinical psychology (MA); psychology (MA). *Faculty:* 4 full-time (2 women), 1 (woman) part-time/adjunct. *Students:* 6 full-time (2 women), 9 part-time (8 women); all minorities (14 African Americans, 1 Hispanic American). Average age 26. 9 applicants, 44% accepted, 4 enrolled. In 2009, 1 master's awarded. *Degree requirements:* For master's, thesis. *Entrance requirements:* For master's, GRE General Test, GRE Subject Test, minimum GPA of 3.0. *Application deadline:* For fall admission, 6/1 priority date for domestic students. Applications are processed on a rolling basis. Application fee: $50. Electronic applications accepted. *Expenses:* Tuition: Full-time $16,848; part-time $936 per credit hour. Required fees: $1510; $465 per semester. *Financial support:* In 2009–10, 5 students received support, including 3 fellowships (averaging $17,060 per year); research assistantships, teaching assistantships with partial tuition reimbursements available, traineeships, tuition waivers (full and partial), and unspecified assistantships also available. *Faculty research:* Ethnic and gender identity, development, female adolescent development, juvenile delinquency prevention. *Unit head:* Dr. Sheila Peters, Chair, 615-329-8617, E-mail: speters@fisk.edu. *Application contact:* Keith Chandler, Dean of Admission, 615-329-8819, Fax: 615-329-8774, E-mail: kchandler@fisk.edu.

Florida Institute of Technology, Graduate Programs, College of Psychology and Liberal Arts, School of Psychology, Melbourne, FL 32901-6975. Offers applied behavior analysis (MS); applied behavior analysis and organizational behavior management (MS, PhD); clinical psychology (Psy D); industrial/organizational psychology (MS, PhD); organizational behavior management (MS). *Accreditation:* APA (one or more programs are accredited). Part-time programs available. *Faculty:* 24 full-time (11 women), 6 part-time/adjunct (1 woman). *Students:* 210 full-time (169 women), 4 part-time (2 women); includes 31 minority (8 African Americans, 6 Asian Americans or Pacific Islanders, 17 Hispanic Americans), 21 international. Average age 27. 195 applicants, 59% accepted, 55 enrolled. In 2009, 30 master's, 3 doctorates awarded. Terminal master's awarded for partial completion of doctoral program. *Degree requirements:* For master's, comprehensive exam (for some programs), thesis (for some programs), BCBA certification, final exam; for doctorate, comprehensive exam, thesis/dissertation, internship, full time resident of school for 4 years (8 semesters, 3 summers). *Entrance requirements:* For master's, GRE General Test, 3 letters of recommendation, minimum GPA of 3.0, resume; for doctorate, GRE General Test, GRE Subject Test (psychology), 3 letters of recommendation, minimum GPA of 3.2, resume, statement of objectives. Additional exam requirements/recommendations for international students: Required—TOEFL (minimum score 550 paper-based; 213 computer-based; 79 iBT). *Application deadline:* For fall admission, 1/15 for domestic and international students. Applications are processed on a rolling basis. Application fee: $50. Electronic applications accepted. *Expenses:* Tuition: Part-time $1015 per credit. Tuition and fees vary according to campus/location and program. *Financial support:* In 2009–10, 19 students received support, including 14 research assistantships with full and partial tuition reimbursements available (averaging $4,079 per year), 5 teaching assistantships with full and partial tuition reimbursements available (averaging $7,002 per year); fellowships with full and partial tuition reimbursements available, career-related internships or fieldwork, institutionally sponsored loans, tuition waivers (partial), unspecified assistantships, and tuition remissions also available. Support available to part-time students. Financial award application deadline: 3/1; financial award applicants required to submit FAFSA. *Faculty research:* Addictions, neuropsychology, child abuse, assessment, psychological trauma. Total annual research expenditures: $836,475. *Unit head:* Dr. Mary Beth Kenkel, Dean, 321-674-8142, Fax: 321-674-7105, E-mail: mkenkel@fit.edu. *Application contact:* Thomas M. Shea, Director of Graduate Admissions, 321-674-7577, Fax: 321-723-9468, E-mail: tshea@fit.edu.

See Close-Up on page 1089.

Florida State University, The Graduate School, College of Arts and Sciences, Department of Psychology, Program in Clinical Psychology, Tallahassee, FL 32306. Offers PhD. *Accreditation:* APA. *Faculty:* 15 full-time (7 women). *Students:* 58 full-time (45 women), 6 part-time (4 women); includes 9 minority (3 African Americans, 1 American Indian/Alaska Native, 5 Hispanic Americans), 1 international. Average age 25. 175 applicants, 11% accepted, 15 enrolled. In 2009, 8 doctorates awarded. Terminal master's awarded for partial completion of doctoral program. *Degree requirements:* For doctorate, thesis/dissertation, preliminary exam, independent project. *Entrance requirements:* For doctorate, GRE General Test, minimum GPA of 3.2, research experience, letters of recommendation. Additional exam requirements/recommendations for international students: Required—TOEFL (minimum score 550 paper-based; 213 computer-based; 80 iBT). *Application deadline:* For fall admission, 12/1 for domestic and international students. Application fee: $30. Electronic applications accepted. *Expenses:* Tuition, state resident: full-time $7413. Tuition, nonresident: full-time $22,567. *Financial support:* In 2009–10, 50 students received support, including 17 fellowships with full tuition reimbursements available (averaging $18,000 per year), 20 research assistantships with full tuition reimbursements available (averaging $16,000 per year), 13 teaching assistantships with full tuition reimbursements available (averaging $15,000 per year); career-related internships or fieldwork, Federal Work-Study, institutionally sponsored loans, scholarships/grants, traineeships, health care benefits, and unspecified assistantships also available. Financial award applicants required to submit FAFSA. *Faculty research:* Antisocial behavior, depression, addictive behavior, developmental psychopathology, anxiety. Total annual research expenditures: $2.6 million. *Unit head:* Dr. Norman Bradley Schmidt, Director, 850-644-1707, Fax: 850-644-7739, E-mail: schmidt@psy.fsu.edu. *Application contact:* Cherie P. Miller, Graduate Program Assistant, 850-644-2499, Fax: 850-644-7739, E-mail: grad-info@psy.fsu.edu.

Fordham University, Graduate School of Arts and Sciences, Department of Psychology, Program in Clinical Psychology, New York, NY 10458. Offers PhD. *Students:* 39 full-time (26 women), 35 part-time (24 women); includes 25 minority (9 African Americans, 1 American Indian/Alaska Native, 7 Asian Americans or Pacific Islanders, 8 Hispanic Americans), 3 international. Average age 28. 496 applicants, 4% accepted, 11 enrolled. In 2009, 13 doctorates awarded. Terminal master's awarded for partial completion of doctoral program. *Degree requirements:* For doctorate, comprehensive exam, thesis/dissertation, clinical internship. *Entrance requirements:* For doctorate, GRE General Test, GRE Subject Test. Additional exam requirements/recommendations for international students: Required—TOEFL (minimum score 600 paper-based; 250 computer-based). *Application deadline:* For fall admission, 12/14 for domestic students. Application fee: $70. Electronic applications accepted. *Financial support:* In 2009–10, 32 students received support, including 3 fellowships with tuition reimbursements available (averaging $21,133 per year), 22 research assistantships with tuition reimbursements available (averaging $18,688 per year), 7 teaching assistantships with tuition reimbursements available (averaging $17,216 per year); career-related internships or fieldwork, institutionally sponsored loans, tuition waivers (full and partial), and unspecified assistantships also available. Financial award application deadline: 12/14. Total annual research expenditures: $2 million. *Unit head:* Dr. Barry Rosenfeld, Director, 718-817-3782, Fax: 718-817-3785. *Application contact:* Charlene Dundie, Director of Graduate Admissions, 718-817-4420, Fax: 718-817-3566, E-mail: dundie@fordham.edu.

Francis Marion University, Graduate Programs, Department of Psychology, Florence, SC 29502-0547. Offers applied psychology (MS), including clinical/counseling, school psychology; school psychology (MS). Part-time and evening/weekend programs available. *Faculty:* 10 full-time (4 women), 5 part-time/adjunct (4 women). *Students:* 16 full-time (15 women), 19 part-time (18 women); includes 6 minority (all African Americans). Average age 35. 44 applicants, 55% accepted, 8 enrolled. In 2009, 19 degrees awarded. *Degree requirements:* For master's, internship. *Entrance requirements:* For master's, GRE General Test. *Application deadline:* For fall admission, 3/15 for domestic students; for spring admission, 10/15 for domestic students. Applications are processed on a rolling basis. Application fee: $30. *Expenses:* Tuition, state resident: full-time $8345; part-time $417.25 per semester hour. Tuition, nonresident: full-time $16,690; part-time $814.50 per semester hour. Required fees: $335; $12.25 per semester hour. $30 per semester. *Financial support:* In 2009–10, 13 students received support, including 1 research assistantship (averaging $7,000 per year), 3 teaching assistantships (averaging $8,000 per year); career-related internships or fieldwork, unspecified assistantships, and scholarships with out-of-state waivers also available. Support available to part-time students. Financial award application deadline: 3/1; financial award applicants required to submit FAFSA. *Faculty research:* Parenting and family relationships, child development, applied behavioral analysis, posttraumatic stress disorder, clinical psychology in adults. *Unit head:* Dr. John R. Hester, Chair, 843-661-1635, Fax: 843-661-1628. *Application contact:* Jennifer Taylor, Administrative Assistant, 843-661-1378, Fax: 843-661-1628.

Fuller Theological Seminary, Graduate School of Psychology, Department of Clinical Psychology, Pasadena, CA 91182. Offers PhD, Psy D. *Accreditation:* APA (one or more programs are accredited). *Degree requirements:* For doctorate, thesis/dissertation, internships. *Entrance requirements:* For doctorate, GRE General Test, GRE Subject Test, interview. Additional exam requirements/recommendations for international students: Required—TOEFL. *Expenses:* Contact institution. *Faculty research:* Psychoneuroimmunology, psychology of religion, coping, shame, depression.

Gallaudet University, The Graduate School, College of Arts and Sciences, Department of Psychology, Program in Clinical Psychology, Washington, DC 20002-3625. Offers PhD. MA in psychology given as part of PhD program. *Accreditation:* APA. *Degree requirements:* For doctorate, thesis/dissertation. *Entrance requirements:* For doctorate, GRE General Test or MAT, interview. Electronic applications accepted.

George Fox University, Graduate Department of Clinical Psychology, Newberg, OR 97132-2697. Offers MA, Psy D. *Accreditation:* APA. *Faculty:* 7 full-time (3 women), 4 part-time/adjunct (1 woman). *Students:* 86 full-time (60 women), 14 part-time (7 women); includes 9 minority (1 American Indian/Alaska Native, 5 Asian Americans or Pacific Islanders, 3 Hispanic Americans). Average age 29. 70 applicants, 56% accepted, 21 enrolled. In 2009, 18 master's, 19 doctorates awarded. *Degree requirements:* For master's, comprehensive exam, 60 semester hours of required and elective courses; for doctorate, thesis/dissertation, internship. *Entrance requirements:* For master's and doctorate, GRE General Test, bachelor's degree from regionally-accredited university or college, minimum undergraduate GPA of 3.0 during previous 2 years, interview. Additional exam requirements/recommendations for international students: Required—TOEFL (minimum score 577 paper-based; 233 computer-based; 90 iBT). *Application deadline:* For fall admission, 1/15 priority date for domestic and international students. Application fee: $40. Electronic applications accepted. *Expenses:* Contact institution. *Financial support:* Scholarships/grants available. Financial award application deadline: 5/15; financial award applicants required to submit FAFSA. *Faculty research:* Psychological assessment, impact of psychological services on medical outcome, spirituality and wellness, effectiveness of clinical training and supervision, shame. *Unit head:* Dr. Wayne Adams, Professor/Chairperson, 800-765-4369 Ext. 2372, E-mail: wadams@georgefox.edu. *Application contact:* Adina McConaughey, Admission Counselor, 800-631-0921 Ext. 2263, Fax: 503-554-2263, E-mail: psyd@georgefox.edu.

Clinical Psychology

The George Washington University, Columbian College of Arts and Sciences, Department of Psychology, Washington, DC 20052. Offers applied social psychology (PhD); clinical psychology (PhD); cognitive neuroscience (PhD). *Accreditation:* APA. Part-time and evening/weekend programs available. *Faculty:* 27 full-time (15 women), 25 part-time/adjunct (14 women). *Students:* 117 full-time (94 women), 89 part-time (73 women); includes 56 minority (16 African Americans, 2 American Indian/Alaska Native, 23 Asian Americans or Pacific Islanders, 15 Hispanic Americans), 4 international. Average age 28. 787 applicants, 6% accepted, 43 enrolled. In 2009, 49 doctorates awarded. *Degree requirements:* For doctorate, thesis/dissertation or alternative, general exam. *Entrance requirements:* For doctorate, GRE General Test, minimum GPA of 3.0. Additional exam requirements/recommendations for international students: Required—TOEFL (minimum score 550 paper-based; 213 computer-based; 80 iBT). *Application deadline:* For fall admission, 1/15 for domestic and international students. Application fee: $60. *Financial support:* In 2009–10, 62 students received support; fellowships with tuition reimbursements available, teaching assistantships with tuition reimbursements available, career-related internships or fieldwork, Federal Work-Study, and tuition waivers available. *Unit head:* Dr. Paul Poppen, Chair, 202-994-6324, E-mail: pjp@gwu.edu. *Application contact:* Information Contact, 202-994-6320, Fax: 202-994-1602, E-mail: psydept@gwu.edu.

Graduate School and University Center of the City University of New York, Graduate Studies, Program in Psychology, New York, NY 10016-4039. Offers basic applied neurocognition (PhD); biopsychology (PhD); clinical psychology (PhD); developmental psychology (PhD); environmental psychology (PhD); experimental psychology (PhD); industrial psychology (PhD); learning processes (PhD); neuropsychology (PhD); psychology (PhD); social personality (PhD). *Faculty:* 119 full-time (40 women). *Students:* 559 full-time (414 women), 1 part-time (0 women); includes 101 minority (34 African Americans, 25 Asian Americans or Pacific Islanders, 42 Hispanic Americans), 57 international. Average age 33. 750 applicants, 16% accepted, 84 enrolled. In 2009, 54 doctorates awarded. *Degree requirements:* For doctorate, one foreign language, thesis/dissertation. *Entrance requirements:* For doctorate, GRE General Test. Additional exam requirements/recommendations for international students: Required—TOEFL. *Application deadline:* For fall admission, 12/15 priority date for domestic students. Application fee: $125. Electronic applications accepted. *Financial support:* In 2009–10, 371 students received support, including 340 fellowships, 34 research assistantships, 33 teaching assistantships; career-related internships or fieldwork, Federal Work-Study, institutionally sponsored loans, and tuition waivers (full and partial) also available. Financial award application deadline: 2/1; financial award applicants required to submit FAFSA. *Unit head:* Dr. Joseph Glick, Executive Officer, 212-817-8706, Fax: 212-817-1533, E-mail: jglick@gc.cuny.edu. *Application contact:* Les Gribben, Director of Admissions, 212-817-7470, Fax: 212-817-1624, E-mail: lgribben@gc.cuny.edu.

Hofstra University, College of Liberal Arts and Sciences, Department of Psychology, Program in Clinical Psychology, Hempstead, NY 11549. Offers PhD. *Accreditation:* APA; NCATE. *Faculty:* 32 full-time (10 women), 11 part-time/adjunct (3 women). *Students:* 73 full-time (48 women), 6 part-time (5 women); includes 9 minority (3 African Americans, 5 Asian Americans or Pacific Islanders, 1 Hispanic American), 1 international. Average age 27. 182 applicants, 8% accepted, 14 enrolled. In 2009, 20 doctorates awarded. Terminal master's awarded for partial completion of doctoral program. *Degree requirements:* For doctorate, comprehensive exam, thesis/dissertation, 1st year qualifying examination, 2nd year research project, successful practicum/externship placements, written presentation and successful oral defense of dissertation, completion of full-time internship. *Entrance requirements:* For doctorate, GRE General Test, GRE Subject Test (psychology), 3 letters of recommendation, interview, curriculum vitae. Additional exam requirements/recommendations for international students: Required—TOEFL (minimum score 550 paper-based; 213 computer-based; 80 iBT). *Application deadline:* For fall admission, 1/15 for domestic and international students. Application fee: $60. Electronic applications accepted. *Expenses:* Tuition: Full-time $16,200; part-time $900 per credit hour. Required fees: $970; $145 per term. Tuition and fees vary according to program. *Financial support:* In 2009–10, 52 students received support, including 46 fellowships with full and partial tuition reimbursements available (averaging $7,987 per year), 7 research assistantships with full and partial tuition reimbursements available (averaging $2,658 per year); career-related internships or fieldwork, Federal Work-Study, institutionally sponsored loans, scholarships/grants, tuition waivers (full and partial), unspecified assistantships, and some externship placements offer support stipends also available. Support available to part-time students. Financial award applicants required to submit FAFSA. *Faculty research:* Parent child interaction training; treatment of anger; cognitions of cocaine-addicted schizophrenics; applications of mindfulness in treatment of psychopathology, virtual reality treatment for phobia and trauma treatment. *Unit head:* Dr. Mitchell L. Schare, Program Director, 516-463-5009, Fax: 516-463-6052, E-mail: psymls@hofstra.edu. *Application contact:* Carol Drummer, Dean of Graduate Admissions, 516-463-4876, Fax: 516-463-4664, E-mail: gradstudent@hofstra.edu.

Howard University, Graduate School, Department of Psychology, Washington, DC 20059-0002. Offers clinical psychology (PhD); developmental psychology (PhD); experimental psychology (PhD); neuropsychology (PhD); personality psychology (PhD); psychology (MS); social psychology (PhD). *Accreditation:* APA (one or more programs are accredited). Part-time programs available. *Degree requirements:* For master's, thesis; for doctorate, comprehensive exam, thesis/dissertation, qualifying exam. *Entrance requirements:* For master's, GRE General Test, minimum GPA of 2.5, bachelor's degree in psychology or related field; for doctorate, GRE General Test, minimum GPA of 3.0. *Faculty research:* Personality and psychophysiology, educational and social development of African-American children, child and adult psychopathology.

Idaho State University, Office of Graduate Studies, College of Arts and Sciences, Department of Psychology, Program in Clinical Psychology, Pocatello, ID 83209-8112. Offers PhD. *Students:* 22 full-time (13 women), 10 part-time (9 women); includes 2 minority (1 Asian American or Pacific Islander, 1 Hispanic American), 1 international. Average age 30. In 2009, 4 doctorates awarded. *Degree requirements:* For doctorate, comprehensive exam, thesis/dissertation, 1 year full-time clinical internship. *Entrance requirements:* For doctorate, GRE General Test, GRE Subject Test, MS in psychology. Additional exam requirements/recommendations for international students: Required—TOEFL (minimum score 550 paper-based; 213 computer-based; 80 iBT). *Application deadline:* For fall admission, 7/1 for domestic students, 6/1 for international students; for spring admission, 12/1 for domestic students, 11/1 for international students. Applications are processed on a rolling basis. Application fee: $55. Electronic applications accepted. *Expenses:* Tuition, state resident: full-time $3318; part-time $297 per credit hour. Tuition, nonresident: full-time $13,120; part-time $437 per credit hour. Required fees: $2530. Tuition and fees vary according to program. *Financial support:* In 2009–10, 7 teaching assistantships with full and partial tuition reimbursements (averaging $10,841 per year) were awarded; career-related internships or fieldwork, Federal Work-Study, institutionally sponsored loans, scholarships/grants, traineeships, health care benefits, tuition waivers (full and partial), and unspecified assistantships also available. Support available to part-time students. Financial award application deadline: 1/1; financial award applicants required to submit FAFSA. *Faculty research:* Pre-adolescent behavior, substance abuse training, trauma related problems. *Unit head:* Dr. Shannon Lynch, Chairman, 208-282-2462, Fax: 208-282-4832, E-mail: lyncshan@isu.edu. *Application contact:* Tami Carson, Graduate School Technical Records Specialist, 208-282-2150, Fax: 208-282-4847, E-mail: carstami@isu.edu.

Illinois Institute of Technology, Graduate College, Institute of Psychology, Chicago, IL 60616-3793. Offers clinical psychology (PhD); industrial/organizational psychology (PhD); personnel/human resource development (MS); psychology (MS); rehabilitation counseling (MS); rehabilitation counselor education (PhD). *Accreditation:* APA (one or more programs are accredited); CORE. Part-time and evening/weekend programs available. *Faculty:* 19 full-time (8 women), 5 part-time/adjunct (all women). *Students:* 118 full-time (88 women), 82 part-time (62 women); includes 33 minority (10 African Americans, 1 American Indian/Alaska Native, 14 Asian Americans or Pacific Islanders, 8 Hispanic Americans), 24 international. Average age 29. 281 applicants, 33% accepted, 28 enrolled. In 2009, 37 master's, 13 doctorates awarded. Terminal master's awarded for partial completion of doctoral program. *Degree requirements:* For master's, thesis (for some programs); for doctorate, comprehensive exam, thesis/dissertation, 96-108 credit hours, internship for Clinical and I/O specializations. *Entrance requirements:* For master's, GRE General Test, minimum high school GPA of 3.0, official transcripts, 3 letters of recommendation, personal statement; for doctorate, GRE General Test, minimum high school GPA of 3.0, official transcriptions, 3 letters of recommendation, personal statement. Additional exam requirements/recommendations for international students: Required—TOEFL (minimum score 550 paper-based; 80 iBT). *Application deadline:* For fall admission, 2/15 for domestic and international students. Application fee: $40. Electronic applications accepted. *Expenses:* Tuition: Full-time $17,550; part-time $888 per credit hour. Required fees: $850; $7.50 per credit hour. One-time fee: $50 full-time. Full-time tuition and fees vary according to program. *Financial support:* In 2009–10, 39 fellowships with partial tuition reimbursements (averaging $2,798 per year), 1 research assistantship with partial tuition reimbursement, 24 teaching assistantships with partial tuition reimbursements (averaging $4,405 per year) were awarded; career-related internships or fieldwork, Federal Work-Study, institutionally sponsored loans, scholarships/grants, traineeships, health care benefits, tuition waivers (partial), and unspecified assistantships also available. Support available to part-time students. Financial award application deadline: 1/15; financial award applicants required to submit FAFSA. *Faculty research:* Stigma and mental illness, depression, couples communication, leadership, psychometric theory. Total annual research expenditures: $426,090. *Unit head:* Dr. M. Ellen Mitchell, Dean, 312-567-3362, Fax: 312-567-3493, E-mail: mitchelle@iit.edu. *Application contact:* Institute of Psychology Graduate Admissions, 312-567-3500, Fax: 312-567-3493, E-mail: psychology@iit.edu.

Illinois State University, Graduate School, College of Arts and Sciences, Department of Psychology, Normal, IL 61790-2200. Offers psychology (MA, MS), including clinical psychology, counseling psychology, developmental psychology, educational psychology, experimental psychology, measurement-evaluation, organizational-industrial psychology; school psychology (PhD, SSP). *Accreditation:* APA. *Degree requirements:* For master's, thesis or alternative; for doctorate, variable foreign language requirement, thesis/dissertation, 2 terms of residency, internship, practicum. *Entrance requirements:* For master's, GRE General Test, GRE Subject Test, minimum GPA of 3.0 in last 60 hours of course work; for doctorate, GRE General Test. *Faculty research:* Comprehensive evaluation system for the central region professional development grant, Illinois school psychology internship consortium, for children's sake.

Immaculata University, College of Graduate Studies, Department of Psychology, Immaculata, PA 19345. Offers clinical psychology (Psy D); counseling psychology (MA, Certificate), including school guidance counselor (Certificate), school psychologist (Certificate). *Accreditation:* APA. Part-time and evening/weekend programs available. *Degree requirements:* For master's, comprehensive exam, thesis optional; for doctorate, comprehensive exam, thesis/dissertation. *Entrance requirements:* For master's, GRE General Test or MAT, minimum GPA of 3.0; for doctorate, GRE General Test, minimum GPA of 3.5. Additional exam requirements/recommendations for international students: Required—TOEFL, IELTS. *Faculty research:* Supervision ethics, psychology of teaching, gender.

Indiana State University, School of Graduate Studies, College of Arts and Sciences, Department of Psychology, Terre Haute, IN 47809. Offers clinical psychology (Psy D); general psychology (MA, MS). *Accreditation:* APA (one or more programs are accredited). Terminal master's awarded for partial completion of doctoral program. *Degree requirements:* For master's, thesis (for some programs); for doctorate, comprehensive exam, thesis/dissertation, internship, professional research project. *Entrance requirements:* For master's, GRE General Test, 12 semester hours of course work in psychology, minimum GPA of 2.75; for doctorate, GRE General Test, minimum GPA of 3.0. Additional exam requirements/recommendations for international students: Required—TOEFL (minimum score 550 paper-based). Electronic applications accepted.

Indiana University of Pennsylvania, School of Graduate Studies and Research, College of Natural Sciences and Mathematics, Department of Psychology, Program in Clinical Psychology, Indiana, PA 15705-1087. Offers Psy D. *Accreditation:* APA. Part-time programs available. *Faculty:* 14 full-time (8 women). *Students:* 41 full-time (33 women), 17 part-time (16 women); includes 2 minority (both Hispanic Americans). Average age 28. 109 applicants, 8% accepted, 9 enrolled. In 2009, 15 doctorates awarded. *Degree requirements:* For doctorate, comprehensive exam, thesis/dissertation, internship, practicum. *Entrance requirements:* For doctorate, GRE General Test, minimum GPA of 3.0, 3 letters of recommendation, interview. Additional exam requirements/recommendations for international students: Required—TOEFL. *Application deadline:* For fall admission, 1/10 for domestic students. Application fee: $40. *Expenses:* Tuition, state resident: full-time $6666; part-time $370 per credit hour. Tuition, nonresident: full-time $10,666; part-time $593 per credit hour. Required fees: $813 per semester. *Financial support:* In 2009–10, 3 fellowships (averaging $2,667 per year), 39 research assistantships with full and partial tuition reimbursements (averaging $4,018 per year), 1 teaching assistantship (averaging $21,536 per year) were awarded; Federal Work-Study and scholarships/grants also available. Financial award application deadline: 3/15; financial award applicants required to submit FAFSA. *Unit head:* Dr. Beverly Goodwin, Graduate Coordinator, 724-357-4522, E-mail: beverly.goodwin@iup.edu. *Application contact:* Dr. Donald Robertson, Graduate Coordinator, 724-357-4522, E-mail: durobert@iup.edu.

Indiana University–Purdue University Indianapolis, School of Science, Department of Psychology, Indianapolis, IN 46202-3275. Offers clinical rehabilitation psychology (MS); industrial/organizational psychology (MS); psychobiology of addictions (MS, PhD). *Accreditation:* APA (one or more programs are accredited). *Faculty:* 10 full-time (2 women). *Students:* 50 full-time (45 women), 11 part-time (9 women); includes 7 minority (4 African Americans, 2 Asian Americans or Pacific Islanders, 1 Hispanic American), 3 international. Average age 28. 132 applicants, 17% accepted, 22 enrolled. In 2009, 7 master's awarded. Terminal master's awarded for partial completion of doctoral program. *Degree requirements:* For master's, thesis; for doctorate, thesis/dissertation. *Entrance requirements:* For master's, GRE General Test, minimum undergraduate GPA of 3.0; for doctorate, GRE General Test, GRE Subject Test (clinical rehabilitation psychology), minimum undergraduate GPA of 3.2. *Application deadline:* For fall admission, 1/1 priority date for domestic students. Application fee: $55 ($65 for international students). *Financial support:* In 2009–10, 5 fellowships with partial tuition reimbursements (averaging $12,218 per year), 23 teaching assistantships with partial tuition reimbursements (averaging $7,553 per year) were awarded; research assistantships with partial tuition reimbursements, career-related internships or fieldwork, Federal Work-Study, and institutionally sponsored loans also available. Financial award application deadline: 3/1; financial award applicants required to submit FAFSA. *Faculty research:* Psychiatric rehabilitation, chronic stress, neurological research, language and cognitive development in infants, alcoholism and psychopathology. *Unit head:* Dr. J. Gregor Fetterman, Chairman, 317-274-6945, Fax: 317-274-6756, E-mail: gfetter@iupui.edu. *Application contact:* Dr. J. Gregor Fetterman, Chairman, 317-274-6945, Fax: 317-274-6756, E-mail: gfetter@iupui.edu.

Institute of Transpersonal Psychology, Residential Programs, Palo Alto, CA 94303. Offers counseling psychology (MA); spiritually oriented clinical psychology (Psy D); transpersonal psychology (MA, PhD). Part-time and evening/weekend programs available. Terminal master's awarded for partial completion of doctoral program. *Degree requirements:* For doctorate, thesis/dissertation. *Entrance requirements:* For master's and doctorate, bachelor's degree.

Jackson State University, Graduate School, School of Liberal Arts, Department of Psychology, Jackson, MS 39217. Offers clinical psychology (PhD). *Accreditation:* APA. *Degree requirements:* For doctorate, comprehensive exam, thesis/dissertation. *Entrance requirements:* For doctorate, MAT, GRE.

James Madison University, The Graduate School, College of Integrated Science and Technology, Department of Graduate Psychology, Clinical Mental Health Counseling Program, Harrisonburg, VA 22807. Offers M Ed, MA, Ed S. *Accreditation:* ACA (one or more programs are accredited); APA (one or more programs are accredited). Part-time and evening/weekend programs available. *Students:* 50 full-time (39 women), 31 part-time (24 women); includes 9 minority (7 African Americans, 1 Asian American or Pacific Islander, 1 Hispanic American), 1 international. Average age 27. In 2009, 35 master's, 17 other advanced degrees awarded. *Degree requirements:* For Ed S, comprehensive exam, thesis, internship. *Entrance requirements:* For master's, GRE General Test, 3 reference forms, interview, criminal history check. Additional exam requirements/recommendations for international students: Required—TOEFL. *Application deadline:* For fall admission, 2/1 priority date for domestic students. Applications are processed on a rolling basis. Application fee: $55. Electronic applications accepted. *Expenses:* Tuition, area resident: Part-time $305 per credit hour. Tuition, state resident: part-time $305 per credit hour. Tuition, nonresident: part-time $890 per credit hour. *Financial support:* In 2009–10, 44 students received support; teaching assistantships with full tuition reimbursements available, career-related internships or fieldwork and Federal Work-Study available. Financial award application deadline: 3/1; financial award applicants required to submit FAFSA. *Unit head:* Dr. Lennis G. Echerling, Program Director, 540-568-6552. *Application contact:* Dr. Lennis G. Echerling, Program Director, 540-568-6552.

James Madison University, The Graduate School, College of Integrated Science and Technology, Department of Graduate Psychology, Program in Combined-Integrated Clinical and School Psychology, Harrisonburg, VA 22807. Offers Psy D. Part-time and evening/weekend programs available. *Students:* 20 full-time (16 women), 1 (woman) part-time; includes 3 minority (2 African Americans, 1 Asian American or Pacific Islander), 3 international. Average age 27. In 2009, 6 doctorates awarded. *Degree requirements:* For doctorate, thesis/dissertation, 12-month internship. *Entrance requirements:* For doctorate, GRE General Test, GRE Subject Test (advanced psychology), 3 letters of recommendation. Additional exam requirements/recommendations for international students: Required—TOEFL. *Application deadline:* For fall admission, 2/1 for domestic students. Applications are processed on a rolling basis. Application fee: $55. Electronic applications accepted. *Expenses:* Tuition, area resident: Part-time $305 per credit hour. Tuition, state resident: part-time $305 per credit hour. Tuition, nonresident: part-time $890 per credit hour. *Financial support:* In 2009–10, 12 students received support, including 3 teaching assistantships with full tuition reimbursements available (averaging $8,664 per year). Financial award application deadline: 3/1; financial award applicants required to submit FAFSA. *Unit head:* Dr. Gregg R. Henriques, Program Director, 540-568-7857. *Application contact:* Dr. Gregg R. Henriques, Program Director, 540-568-7857.

The Johns Hopkins University, Bloomberg School of Public Health, Department of Mental Health, Baltimore, MD 21218-2699. Offers children's mental health services (PhD); drug dependence epidemiology (PhD); mental health (MHS, Dr PH); psychiatric epidemiology (PhD). *Faculty:* 26 full-time (14 women), 46 part-time/adjunct (18 women). *Students:* 44 full-time (36 women), 13 part-time (9 women); includes 20 minority (7 African Americans, 9 Asian Americans or Pacific Islanders, 4 Hispanic Americans), 9 international. Average age 28. 73 applicants, 67% accepted, 27 enrolled. In 2009, 17 master's, 6 doctorates awarded. *Degree requirements:* For master's, thesis (for some programs); for doctorate, thesis/dissertation, 1 year full-time residency, oral and written exams. *Entrance requirements:* For master's, GRE General Test, MCAT, 3 letters of recommendation, curriculum vitae; for doctorate, GRE General Test, MCAT or GMAT, 3 letters of recommendation, curriculum vitae. Additional exam requirements/recommendations for international students: Required—TOEFL (minimum score 600 paper-based; 250 computer-based; 100 iBT). *Application deadline:* For fall admission, 12/1 priority date for domestic and international students. Applications are processed on a rolling basis. Application fee: $45. Electronic applications accepted. *Financial support:* In 2009–10, 1 fellowship (averaging $32,000 per year) was awarded; Federal Work-Study, institutionally sponsored loans, scholarships/grants, traineeships, and stipends also available. Support available to part-time students. Financial award application deadline: 3/15; financial award applicants required to submit FAFSA. *Faculty research:* Etiology, development and prevention of aggressive and antisocial behavior; epidemiology of mental disorders; genetic epidemiology of mental disorders; brain and behavior. Total annual research expenditures: $12 million. *Unit head:* Dr. William W. Eaton, Chair, 410-955-3910, Fax: 410-614-7469, E-mail: weaton@jhsph.edu. *Application contact:* Patricia E. Scott, Senior Academic Program Coordinator, 410-955-1906, Fax: 410-955-9088, E-mail: mhdept@jhsph.edu.

Kean University, Nathan Weiss Graduate College, Program in School and Clinical Psychology, Union, NJ 07083. Offers Psy D. Evening/weekend programs available. *Faculty:* 2 full-time (0 women). *Students:* 10 full-time (9 women); includes 1 minority (Hispanic American). Average age 25. 26 applicants, 54% accepted, 10 enrolled. *Degree requirements:* For doctorate, comprehensive exam, thesis/dissertation, externship. *Entrance requirements:* For doctorate, GRE General Test (minimum score 500 verbal, 500 quantitative, 4.0 writing), GRE Subject Test in psychology taken within the last 5 years (minimum score 550), minimum undergraduate GPA of 3.3, graduate 3.5; 3 letters of recommendation (at least one from a professor); personal interview; prerequisite coursework in theories of personality, abnormal psychology, tests and measurements, statistics, and experimental psychology. *Application deadline:* For fall admission, 1/30 for domestic students. Application fee: $60 ($150 for international students). Electronic applications accepted. *Expenses:* Contact institution. *Financial support:* In 2009–10, 7 research assistantships (averaging $3,263 per year) were awarded; unspecified assistantships also available. *Unit head:* Dr. Frank Gardner, Program Coordinator, 908-737-5862, E-mail: fgardner@kean.edu. *Application contact:* Steven Koch, Pre-Admissions Coordinator, 908-737-5924, Fax: 908-737-5965, E-mail: skoch@kean.edu.

Kent State University, College of Arts and Sciences, Department of Psychology, Kent, OH 44242-0001. Offers clinical psychology (MA, PhD); experimental psychology (MA, PhD). *Accreditation:* APA (one or more programs are accredited). *Degree requirements:* For master's, thesis; for doctorate, thesis/dissertation. *Entrance requirements:* For master's, GRE, minimum GPA of 3.0, minimum 18 semester hours in psychology with one course in statistics and one experimental course with a lab component; for doctorate, GRE, minimum GPA of 3.0. Additional exam requirements/recommendations for international students: Required—TOEFL (minimum score 525 paper-based), Michigan English Language Assessment Battery (minimum score: 77).

Lakehead University, Graduate Studies, Department of Psychology, Thunder Bay, ON P7B 5E1, Canada. Offers clinical psychology (PhD); experimental psychology (MA). Part-time and evening/weekend programs available. *Degree requirements:* For master's, thesis optional; for doctorate, thesis/dissertation, 2 comprehensive exams, internship. *Entrance requirements:* For master's, GRE, honors degree in psychology, advanced course work in statistics, minimum B average; for doctorate, GRE, minimum B average. Additional exam requirements/recommendations for international students: Required—TOEFL. *Faculty research:* Chaos theory, health psychology, counseling psychology, gerontology, women's studies.

Lamar University, College of Graduate Studies, College of Arts and Sciences, Department of Psychology, Beaumont, TX 77710. Offers community/clinical psychology (MS); industrial/organizational psychology (MS). Part-time programs available. *Faculty:* 6 full-time (3 women). *Students:* 14 full-time (10 women), 11 part-time (5 women); includes 4 minority (2 African Americans, 2 Hispanic Americans), 1 international. Average age 25. 34 applicants, 18% accepted, 4 enrolled. In 2009, 1 master's awarded. *Degree requirements:* For master's, thesis, practicum. *Entrance requirements:* For master's, GRE General Test, minimum GPA of 2.75 in last 60 hours of undergraduate course work. Additional exam requirements/recommendations for international students: Required—TOEFL. *Application deadline:* For fall admission, 8/1 for domestic students; for spring admission, 12/1 for domestic students. Application fee: $25 ($50 for international students). *Financial support:* In 2009–10, 12 students received support, including 3 teaching assistantships (averaging $4,500 per year); fellowships, research assistantships, career-related internships or fieldwork, Federal Work-Study, scholarships/grants, and tuition waivers (partial) also available. Support available to part-time students. Financial award application deadline: 4/1. *Faculty research:* Groupthink, health psychology, school psychology, behavioral neuroscience. *Application contact:* Assistant Dean, 409-880-7978, E-mail: westgate@hal.lamar.edu.

La Salle University, School of Arts and Sciences, Program in Clinical-Counseling Psychology, Philadelphia, PA 19141-1199. Offers MA. *Accreditation:* APA. Part-time and evening/weekend programs available. *Degree requirements:* For master's, comprehensive exam. *Entrance requirements:* For master's, GRE or MAT, 15 undergraduate credits in psychology. *Expenses:* Contact institution. *Faculty research:* Cognitive therapy, attribution theory, work habits, single parent families, treatment of addictions.

La Salle University, School of Arts and Sciences, Program in Psychology, Philadelphia, PA 19141-1199. Offers clinical psychology (Psy D); family psychology (Psy D); rehabilitation psychology (Psy D). Part-time and evening/weekend programs available. *Entrance requirements:* For doctorate, GRE, minimum GPA of 3.0. *Expenses:* Contact institution. *Faculty research:* Cognitive therapy, attribution theory, treatment of addiction.

Lesley University, Graduate School of Arts and Social Sciences, Cambridge, MA 02138-2790. Offers clinical mental health counseling (MA), including expressive therapies counseling, holistic counseling, school and community counseling; counseling psychology (MA, CAGS), including professional counseling (MA), school counseling (MA); creative arts in learning (CAGS); creative writing (MFA); ecological teaching and learning (MS); environmental education (MS); expressive therapies (MA, PhD, CAGS), including art (MA), dance (MA), expressive therapies, music (MA); independent studies (CAGS); independent study (MA); intercultural relations (MA, CAGS); interdisciplinary studies (MA), including individualized studies, integrative holistic health, women's studies; urban environmental leadership (MA); visual arts (MFA). Part-time and evening/weekend programs available. Postbaccalaureate distance learning degree programs offered (minimal on-campus study). *Degree requirements:* For master's, internship, practicum, thesis (expressive therapies); for doctorate, thesis/dissertation, arts apprenticeship, field placement; for CAGS, thesis, internship (counseling psychology, expressive therapies). *Entrance requirements:* For master's, MAT (counseling psychology), interview, writing samples, art portfolio; for doctorate, GRE or MAT; for CAGS, interview, master's degree. Additional exam requirements/recommendations for international students: Required—TOEFL (minimum score 550 paper-based; 213 computer-based; 80 iBT). Electronic applications accepted. *Faculty research:* Psychotherapy and culture; psychotherapy and psychological trauma; women's issues in art, teaching and psychotherapy; community based art, psycho-spiritual inquiry.

Long Island University, Brooklyn Campus, Richard L. Conolly College of Liberal Arts and Sciences, Department of Psychology, Program in Clinical Psychology, Brooklyn, NY 11201-8423. Offers PhD. *Accreditation:* APA. *Degree requirements:* For doctorate, thesis/dissertation. *Entrance requirements:* For doctorate, GRE Subject Test, GRE General Test. Additional exam requirements/recommendations for international students: Required—TOEFL (minimum score 500 paper-based; 173 computer-based). Electronic applications accepted. *Faculty research:* Ethnicity and human development.

Long Island University, C.W. Post Campus, College of Liberal Arts and Sciences, Department of Psychology, Program in Clinical Psychology, Brookville, NY 11548-1300. Offers Psy D. *Accreditation:* APA. *Degree requirements:* For doctorate, thesis/dissertation, internship. *Entrance requirements:* For doctorate, GRE General Test, GRE Subject Test, GRE Analytical Writing, bachelor's degree in psychology, minimum GPA of 3.25, 18 credit hours of undergraduate psychology, 3 letters of recommendation. *Expenses:* Contact institution. *Faculty research:* Family violence, schizophrenia, developmental disabilities, psychotherapy, terror and trauma.

Louisiana State University and Agricultural and Mechanical College, Graduate School, College of Arts and Sciences, Department of Psychology, Baton Rouge, LA 70803. Offers biological psychology (MA, PhD); clinical psychology (MA, PhD); cognitive psychology (MA, PhD); developmental psychology (MA, PhD); industrial/organizational psychology (MA, PhD); school psychology (MA, PhD). *Accreditation:* APA (one or more programs are accredited). *Faculty:* 27 full-time (10 women). *Students:* 94 full-time (68 women), 17 part-time (12 women); includes 14 minority (6 African Americans, 2 American Indian/Alaska Native, 2 Asian Americans or Pacific Islanders, 4 Hispanic Americans), 3 international. Average age 27. 232 applicants, 18% accepted, 29 enrolled. In 2009, 13 master's, 14 doctorates awarded. Terminal master's awarded for partial completion of doctoral program. *Degree requirements:* For master's, thesis; for doctorate, thesis/dissertation, 1 year internship. *Entrance requirements:* For master's and doctorate, GRE General Test, minimum GPA of 3.0. Additional exam requirements/recommendations for international students: Required—TOEFL (minimum score 550 paper-based; 213 computer-based; 79 iBT) or IELTS (minimum score 6.5). *Application deadline:* For fall admission, 1/15 for domestic and international students. Applications are processed on a rolling basis. Application fee: $50 ($70 for international students). Electronic applications accepted. *Financial support:* In 2009–10, 108 students received support, including 5 fellowships (averaging $26,974 per year), 2 research assistantships with partial tuition reimbursements available (averaging $18,000 per year), 74 teaching assistantships with partial tuition reimbursements available (averaging $14,751 per year); career-related internships or fieldwork, Federal Work-Study, institutionally sponsored loans, scholarships/grants, health care benefits, and tuition waivers (full and partial) also available. Financial award applicants required to submit FAFSA. *Faculty research:* Clinical psychology, autism, anxiety, addition, neuropsychology, school psychology, cognitive psychology, experimental psychology. Total annual research expenditures: $1 million. *Unit head:* Dr. Robert Matthews, Chair, 225-578-8745, Fax: 225-578-4125, E-mail: psmath@lsu.edu. *Application contact:* Dr. Jason Hicks, Coordinator of Graduate Studies, 225-578-4109, Fax: 225-578-4125, E-mail: jhicks@lsu.edu.

Loyola University Chicago, Graduate School, Department of Psychology, Program in Clinical Psychology, Chicago, IL 60660. Offers MA, PhD. *Accreditation:* APA. *Faculty:* 10 full-time (5 women). *Students:* 35 full-time (30 women); includes 6 minority (3 African Americans, 1 Asian American or Pacific Islander, 2 Hispanic Americans). Average age 27. 304 applicants, 3% accepted, 6 enrolled. In 2009, 7 master's, 9 doctorates awarded. Terminal master's awarded for partial completion of doctoral program. *Degree requirements:* For master's, thesis; for doctorate, comprehensive exam, thesis/dissertation. *Entrance requirements:* For doctorate, GRE General Test, GRE Subject Test, letters of recommendation. *Application deadline:* For fall admission, 12/1 for domestic students. Application fee: $50. Electronic applications accepted. *Expenses:* Tuition: Full-time $14,220; part-time $790 per credit hour. Required fees: $60 per semester hour. Tuition and fees vary according to program. *Financial support:* In 2009–10, 2 fellowships with full tuition reimbursements (averaging $15,000 per year), 17 research assistantships with full tuition reimbursements (averaging $15,000 per year), 7 teaching assistantships with full tuition reimbursements (averaging $15,000 per year) were awarded; career-related internships or fieldwork, Federal Work-Study, scholarships/grants, traineeships, and unspecified assistantships also available. Financial award application deadline: 12/1; financial award applicants required to submit FAFSA. *Faculty research:* Child and family, AIDS, ethics and professional practice, psychotherapy, stress and coping, positive youth development, pediatric psychology, adolescence, inner city youth. *Unit head:* Dr. Grayson Holmbeck, Director, 773-508-2967, Fax: 773-508-8713, E-mail: gholmbe@luc.edu. *Application contact:* Jacquie Hamilton, Senior Secretary, 773-508-2974, Fax: 773-508-8713, E-mail: jhamilt@luc.edu.

Loyola University Maryland, Graduate Programs, College of Arts and Sciences, Department of Psychology, Program in Clinical Psychology, Baltimore, MD 21210-2699. Offers MS, Psy D, CAS. *Accreditation:* APA. Part-time and evening/weekend programs available. *Entrance requirements:* For master's, doctorate, and CAS, GRE General Test, GRE Subject Test (recommended). Additional exam requirements/recommendations for international students: Required—TOEFL (minimum score 550 paper-based; 213 computer-based).

Clinical Psychology

Madonna University, Department of Psychology, Livonia, MI 48150-1173. Offers clinical psychology (MSCP). Part-time and evening/weekend programs available. *Degree requirements:* For master's, thesis or alternative. *Entrance requirements:* Additional exam requirements/recommendations for international students: Required—TOEFL. Electronic applications accepted.

Marquette University, Graduate School, College of Arts and Sciences, Department of Psychology, Milwaukee, WI 53201-1881. Offers clinical psychology (MS); psychology (PhD). *Accreditation:* APA. Part-time programs available. *Faculty:* 17 full-time (8 women), 3 part-time/adjunct (1 woman). *Students:* 34 full-time (25 women), 14 part-time (7 women); includes 4 minority (2 African Americans, 1 American Indian/Alaska Native, 1 Hispanic American), 2 international. Average age 27. 107 applicants, 10% accepted, 8 enrolled. In 2009, 6 master's, 5 doctorates awarded. *Degree requirements:* For master's, comprehensive exam, thesis or alternative; for doctorate, thesis/dissertation, internship, qualifying exam. *Entrance requirements:* For master's, GRE General Test, GRE Subject Test, MAT; for doctorate, GRE General Test, GRE Subject Test, sample of scholarly writing. Additional exam requirements/recommendations for international students: Required—TOEFL. *Application deadline:* For fall admission, 2/15 for domestic students. Application fee: $40. *Financial support:* In 2009–10, 3 research assistantships, 16 teaching assistantships were awarded; career-related internships or fieldwork, Federal Work-Study, institutionally sponsored loans, scholarships/grants, and tuition waivers (full and partial) also available. Support available to part-time students. Financial award application deadline: 2/15. *Faculty research:* Mental imagery, moral development, organizational behavior, depression, psychotherapy outcomes. *Unit head:* Dr. Mike Wierzbicki, Chair, 414-288-7218, Fax: 414-288-5333. *Application contact:* Dr. Steve Saunders, Information Contact, 414-288-7459.

Marshall University, Academic Affairs Division, College of Liberal Arts, Department of Psychology, Huntington, WV 25755. Offers clinical psychology (MA); general psychology (MA); industrial and organizational psychology (MA); psychology (Psy D). *Accreditation:* APA. *Faculty:* 13 full-time (4 women), 1 part-time/adjunct (0 women). *Students:* 101 full-time (71 women), 19 part-time (14 women); includes 6 minority (4 African Americans, 2 Hispanic Americans), 4 international. Average age 29. In 2009, 33 master's, 3 doctorates awarded. *Degree requirements:* For master's, thesis optional. *Entrance requirements:* For master's, GRE General Test or MAT. *Application deadline:* For fall admission, 3/1 for domestic students; for spring admission, 11/1 for domestic students. Application fee: $40. *Financial support:* Teaching assistantships with tuition reimbursements available. *Unit head:* Dr. Steven Mewaldt, Chairperson, 304-696-27tt, E-mail: mewaldt@marshall.edu. *Application contact:* Graduate Admissions, 304-746-1900, Fax: 304-746-1902, E-mail: services@marshall.edu.

Marywood University, Academic Affairs, Reap College of Education and Human Development, Department of Psychology and Counseling, Program in Clinical Psychology, Scranton, PA 18509-1598. Offers Psy D. *Accreditation:* APA. *Faculty:* 13. *Students:* 24 full-time (20 women), 14 part-time (11 women); includes 1 minority (African American). Average age 28. In 2009, 7 doctorates awarded. *Entrance requirements:* Additional exam requirements/recommendations for international students: Required—TOEFL (minimum score 550 paper-based; 213 computer-based; 79 iBT). *Application deadline:* For fall admission, 1/8 priority date for domestic and international students. Application fee: $35. Electronic applications accepted. *Expenses:* Contact institution. *Financial support:* Career-related internships or fieldwork, scholarships/grants, and unspecified assistantships available. Support available to part-time students. Financial award application deadline: 6/30; financial award applicants required to submit FAFSA. *Unit head:* Dr. Brooke Cannon, Director, 570-348-6211 Ext. 2324. *Application contact:* Tammy Manka, Assistant Director of Graduate Admissions, 866-279-9663, E-mail: tmanka@marywood.edu.

Marywood University, Academic Affairs, Reap College of Education and Human Development, Department of Psychology and Counseling, Program in Psychology, Scranton, PA 18509-1598. Offers clinical services (MA); general theoretical (MA). *Students:* 23 full-time (16 women), 20 part-time (16 women); includes 2 minority (both Hispanic Americans). Average age 26. 62 applicants, 66% accepted. In 2009, 30 master's awarded. *Entrance requirements:* Additional exam requirements/recommendations for international students: Required—TOEFL (minimum score 550 paper-based; 213 computer-based; 79 iBT). *Application deadline:* For fall admission, 4/1 priority date for domestic students, 3/30 priority date for international students; for spring admission, 11/1 priority date for domestic students, 8/31 priority date for international students. Applications are processed on a rolling basis. Application fee: $35. Electronic applications accepted. *Expenses:* Tuition: Part-time $715 per credit. Required fees: $270 per semester. Tuition and fees vary according to degree level, campus/location and program. *Financial support:* Career-related internships or fieldwork, scholarships/grants, and unspecified assistantships available. Support available to part-time students. Financial award application deadline: 6/30; financial award applicants required to submit FAFSA. *Faculty research:* Personality disorders, counselor training, preschool development, self-esteem measurement, family dynamics. *Unit head:* Dr. Edward Crawley, Chairperson, 570-348-6211 Ext. 2325, E-mail: crawley@marywood.edu. *Application contact:* Tammy Manka, Assistant Director of Graduate Admissions, 866-279-9663, E-mail: tmanka@marywood.edu.

Massachusetts School of Professional Psychology, Graduate Programs, Boston, MA 02132. Offers clinical psychology (Psy D); clinical psychopharmacology (Post-Doctoral MS); counseling psychology (MA); executive coaching (Graduate Certificate); forensic psychology (MA); organizational psychology (MA); respecialization in clinical psychology (Certificate); MA/CAGS. *Accreditation:* APA. *Degree requirements:* For master's, comprehensive exam; for doctorate, thesis/dissertation. *Entrance requirements:* For doctorate, GRE General Test. Additional exam requirements/recommendations for international students: Required—TOEFL (minimum score 550 paper-based; 213 computer-based). Electronic applications accepted.

McGill University, Faculty of Graduate and Postdoctoral Studies, Faculty of Science, Department of Psychology, Montréal, QC H3A 2T5, Canada. Offers clinical psychology (PhD); experimental psychology (M Sc, MA, PhD). *Accreditation:* APA (one or more programs are accredited).

Michigan School of Professional Psychology, Programs in Humanistic and Clinical Psychology, Farmington Hills, MI 48334. Offers MA, Psy D. *Students:* 111 full-time (92 women), 3 part-time (all women); includes 20 minority (13 African Americans, 7 Asian Americans or Pacific Islanders). Average age 38. *Degree requirements:* For master's, thesis, practicum; for doctorate, thesis/dissertation, internship, practicum. *Entrance requirements:* For master's, 1 year of work experience, interview, minimum GPA of 3.0, curriculum vitae, personal essay, bachelor's degree, 3 letters of recommendation; for doctorate, 3 years of work experience, 2 interviews, minimum graduate GPA of 3.0, scholarly writing sample, curriculum vitae, personal essay, MA, 3 letters of recommendation. Additional exam requirements/recommendations for international students: Required—TOEFL. *Application deadline:* For fall admission, 1/15 priority date for domestic students. Applications are processed on a rolling basis. Application fee: $75. Electronic applications accepted. *Financial support:* Application deadline: 6/30. *Faculty research:* Qualitative research, existential-phenomenological psychology, applications to clinical practice. *Unit head:* Dr. Kerry Moustakas, President, 248-476-1122, Fax: 248-476-1125, E-mail: kmoustakas@mispp.edu. *Application contact:* Linda Potter-Gallant, Admissions Advisor, 248-476-1122 Ext. 117, Fax: 248-476-1125, E-mail: lpgallant@mispp.edu.

Middle Tennessee State University, College of Graduate Studies, College of Education and Behavioral Science, Department of Psychology, Murfreesboro, TN 37132. Offers clinical psychology (MA); experimental psychology (MA); industrial/organizational psychology (MA); professional counseling (M Ed, Ed S), including curriculum and instruction (Ed S), mental health counseling (M Ed), school counseling (M Ed); psychology (MA); quantitative psychology (MA); school psychology (MA, Ed S). Part-time and evening/weekend programs available. Postbaccalaureate distance learning degree programs offered. *Faculty:* 36 full-time (16 women), 2 part-time/adjunct (0 women). *Students:* 23 full-time (19 women), 161 part-time (131 women); includes 21 minority (11 African Americans, 8 Asian Americans or Pacific Islanders, 2 Hispanic Americans). Average age 26. 251 applicants, 55% accepted, 138 enrolled. In 2009, 60 master's, 7 other advanced degrees awarded. *Degree requirements:* For master's, variable foreign language requirement, comprehensive exam, thesis (for some programs). *Entrance requirements:* Additional exam requirements/recommendations for international students: Required—TOEFL (minimum score 525 paper-based; 195 computer-based; 71 iBT) or IELTS (minimum score 6). *Application deadline:* For fall admission, 6/1 for domestic and international students. Applications are processed on a rolling basis. Application fee: $25 ($30 for international students). Electronic applications accepted. *Expenses:* Tuition, state resident: full-time $4404. Tuition, nonresident: full-time $10,956. *Financial support:* In 2009–10, 16 students received support. Career-related internships or fieldwork and institutionally sponsored loans available. Support available to part-time students. Financial award application deadline: 5/1; financial award applicants required to submit FAFSA. *Faculty research:* Industrial/organizational, social/personality/sports, counseling/clinical/school, cognitive/language/learning/perception, developmental/aging. *Unit head:* Dr. Dennis Papini, Chair, 615-898-2706, Fax: 615-898-5027. *Application contact:* Dr. Michael Allen, Dean and Vice Provost for Research, 615-898-2840, Fax: 615-904-8020, E-mail: mallen@mtsu.edu.

Midwestern University, Downers Grove Campus, College of Health Sciences, Illinois Campus, Program in Clinical Psychology, Downers Grove, IL 60515-1235. Offers MA, Psy D. *Faculty:* 10 full-time (7 women). *Students:* 86 full-time (71 women), 3 part-time (all women); includes 11 minority (6 African Americans, 2 Asian Americans or Pacific Islanders, 3 Hispanic Americans), 2 international. Average age 27. 77 applicants, 61% accepted, 26 enrolled. In 2009, 16 master's awarded. *Degree requirements:* For doctorate, thesis/dissertation, qualifying examination. *Entrance requirements:* For master's and doctorate, GRE, minimum overall GPA of 2.75, 3 letters of recommendation. Additional exam requirements/recommendations for international students: Required—TOEFL. *Application deadline:* Applications are processed on a rolling basis. Application fee: $50. *Unit head:* Dr. Frank J. Prerost, Director, 630-515-7405, Fax: 630-971-6402, E-mail: fprero@midwestern.edu. *Application contact:* Michael Laken, Director of Admissions, 630-515-6171, Fax: 630-971-6086, E-mail: admissil@midwestern.edu.

Midwestern University, Glendale Campus, College of Health Sciences, Arizona Campus, Program in Clinical Psychology, Glendale, AZ 85308. Offers Psy D. *Faculty:* 5 full-time (3 women). *Students:* 23 full-time (17 women); includes 2 minority (1 African American, 1 Hispanic American), 1 international. Average age 27. 31 applicants, 55% accepted, 11 enrolled. *Unit head:* Dr. Philinda Hutchings, Program Director and Professor, 623-572-3861, Fax: 623-572-3449. *Application contact:* James Walter, Director of Admissions, 888-247-9277, Fax: 623-572-3229, E-mail: admissaz@midwestern.edu.

Millersville University of Pennsylvania, College of Graduate and Professional Studies, School of Education, Department of Psychology, Program in Psychology, Millersville, PA 17551-0302. Offers clinical psychology (MS); school psychology (MS). Part-time programs available. *Faculty:* 18 full-time (12 women), 9 part-time/adjunct (5 women). *Students:* 48 full-time (39 women), 46 part-time (42 women); includes 4 minority (3 African Americans, 1 Hispanic American), 1 international. Average age 29. 68 applicants, 54% accepted, 24 enrolled. In 2009, 29 master's awarded. *Degree requirements:* For master's, comprehensive exam, thesis optional. *Entrance requirements:* For master's, GRE, 3 letters of recommendation; interview (in-person). Additional exam requirements/recommendations for international students: Required—TOEFL (minimum score 500 paper-based; 183 computer-based; 65 iBT) or IELTS (minimum score 6). *Application deadline:* For fall admission, 1/15 for domestic and international students; for winter admission, 10/1 for domestic and international students; for spring admission, 10/1 for domestic and international students. Application fee: $40 ($50 for international students). Electronic applications accepted. *Expenses:* Tuition, state resident: full-time $6666; part-time $370 per credit. Tuition, nonresident: full-time $10,666; part-time $593 per credit. Required fees: $1578.50; $76.25 per credit. One-time fee: $60 part-time. Tuition and fees vary according to course load. *Financial support:* In 2009–10, 43 students received support, including 43 research assistantships with full and partial tuition reimbursements available (averaging $4,059 per year); institutionally sponsored loans and unspecified assistantships also available. Support available to part-time students. Financial award application deadline: 3/15; financial award applicants required to submit FAFSA. *Faculty research:* Parenting and alcohol risk, time perceptions, time management, stress and coping, autism and behavioral disorders. *Unit head:* Dr. Claudia Haferkamp, Director of Clinical Psychology Program, 717-872-3826, Fax: 717-871-2480, E-mail: claudia.haferkamp@millersville.edu. *Application contact:* Dr. Victor S. DeSantis, Dean of Graduate and Professional Studies, 717-872-3099, Fax: 717-872-3453, E-mail: victor.desantis@millersville.edu.

Minnesota State University Mankato, College of Graduate Studies, College of Social and Behavioral Sciences, Department of Psychology, Mankato, MN 56001. Offers clinical psychology (MA); industrial/organizational psychology (MA); school psychology (Psy D). Part-time programs available. *Students:* 51 full-time (32 women), 3 part-time (1 woman). *Degree requirements:* For master's, one foreign language, comprehensive exam, thesis (for some programs). *Entrance requirements:* For master's, GRE General Test, GRE Subject Test (clinical psychology), minimum GPA of 3.0 during previous 2 years, 3 letters of reference. Additional exam requirements/recommendations for international students: Required—TOEFL. *Application deadline:* For fall admission, 1/1 priority date for domestic students. Applications are processed on a rolling basis. Application fee: $40. Electronic applications accepted. *Expenses:* Tuition, state resident: full-time $5364. Tuition, nonresident: full-time $8314. *Financial support:* Research assistantships, teaching assistantships with full tuition reimbursements, career-related internships or fieldwork, Federal Work-Study, institutionally sponsored loans, and unspecified assistantships available. Support available to part-time students. Financial award application deadline: 3/15; financial award applicants required to submit FAFSA. *Faculty research:* Professional competency in hospitals, mood disturbance, 360-degree feedback, employee selection, planning fallacy. *Unit head:* Dr. Barry Ries, Chairperson, 507-389-2724. *Application contact:* 507-389-2321, E-mail: grad@mnsu.edu.

Mississippi State University, College of Arts and Sciences, Department of Psychology, Mississippi State, MS 39762. Offers cognitive science (PhD); psychology (MS), including clinical psychology, experimental psychology. *Faculty:* 13 full-time (5 women). *Students:* 40 full-time (26 women), 4 part-time (3 women); includes 3 minority (2 African Americans, 1 Asian American or Pacific Islander), 3 international. Average age 26. 69 applicants, 46% accepted, 20 enrolled. In 2009, 11 master's awarded. Terminal master's awarded for partial completion of doctoral program. *Degree requirements:* For master's, comprehensive exam, thesis; for doctorate, thesis/dissertation, qualifying exam, comprehensive written and oral exam. *Entrance requirements:* For master's, GRE General Test, minimum GPA of 2.75 on last two years of undergraduate courses; for doctorate, GRE General Test, proficiency in at least 1 computer language. Additional exam requirements/recommendations for international students: Required—TOEFL (minimum score 475 paper-based; 153 computer-based; 53 iBT); Recommended—IELTS (minimum score 4.5). *Application deadline:* For fall admission, 1/15 priority date for domestic students, 5/1 for international students; for spring admission, 11/1 priority date for domestic students, 9/1 for international students. Applications are processed on a rolling basis. Application fee: $40. Electronic applications accepted. *Expenses:* Tuition, state resident: full-time $2575.50; part-time $286.25 per credit hour. Tuition, nonresident: full-time $6510; part-time $723.50 per credit hour. Tuition and fees vary according to course load. *Financial support:* In 2009–10, 7 research assistantships with full tuition reimbursements (averaging $11,132 per year), 15 teaching assistantships with full tuition reimbursements (averaging $9,023 per year) were awarded; career-related internships or fieldwork, Federal Work-Study, institutionally sponsored loans, scholarships/grants, and unspecified assistantships also available. Financial award application deadline: 4/1; financial award applicants required to submit FAFSA. *Faculty research:* Personality type, alcoholism, blindness and low vision, mental retardation, language comprehension. Total annual research expenditures: $2.2 million. *Unit head:* Dr. Stephen B. Klein, Department Head, 662-325-3202, Fax: 662-325-7212, E-mail: sbkl@ra.

msstate.edu. *Application contact:* Dr. Keven J. Armstrong, Graduate Coordinator, 662-325-3202, Fax: 662-325-7212, E-mail: grad@psychology.msstate.edu.

Missouri State University, Graduate College, College of Health and Human Services, Department of Psychology, Springfield, MO 65897. Offers psychology (MS), including clinical, experimental, industrial/organizational. *Faculty:* 26 full-time (11 women), 1 part-time/adjunct (0 women). *Students:* 44 full-time (28 women), 5 part-time (3 women); includes 2 minority (1 African American, 1 Hispanic American). Average age 26. 63 applicants, 56% accepted, 22 enrolled. In 2009, 21 master's awarded. *Degree requirements:* For master's, comprehensive exam, thesis. *Entrance requirements:* For master's, GRE General Test, GRE Subject Test, minimum GPA of 3.25 in major, 3.0 overall; 20 hours of course work in psychology (experimental and statistics). Additional exam requirements/recommendations for international students: Required—TOEFL (minimum score 550 paper-based; 213 computer-based; 79 iBT). *Application deadline:* For fall admission, 3/1 priority date for domestic and international students. Application fee: $35 ($50 for international students). Electronic applications accepted. *Expenses:* Tuition, state resident: full-time $3852; part-time $214 per credit hour. Tuition, nonresident: full-time $7524; part-time $418 per credit hour. Required fees: $696; $172 per semester. Tuition and fees vary according to course level, course load, degree level and program. *Financial support:* In 2009–10, 7 research assistantships with full tuition reimbursements (averaging $8,023 per year), 3 teaching assistantships with full tuition reimbursements (averaging $9,730 per year) were awarded; career-related internships or fieldwork, Federal Work-Study, institutionally sponsored loans, scholarships/grants, and unspecified assistantships also available. Financial award application deadline: 3/31; financial award applicants required to submit FAFSA. *Faculty research:* Work-family conflict, child forensic psychology, sports psychology, body image assessment, visual learning. *Unit head:* Dr. Robert G. Jones, Head, 417-836-5797, Fax: 417-836-8330, E-mail: psychology@missouristate.edu. *Application contact:* Eric Eckert, Coordinator of Admissions and Recruitment, 417-836-5331, Fax: 417-836-6200, E-mail: ericeckert@missouristate.edu.

Montclair State University, The Graduate School, College of Humanities and Social Sciences, Department of Psychology, Montclair, NJ 07043-1624. Offers educational psychology (MA), including child/adolescent clinical psychology, clinical psychology for Spanish/English bilinguals; psychology (MA, Certificate), including industrial and organizational psychology (MA); school psychologist (Certificate). Part-time and evening/weekend programs available. *Faculty:* 29 full-time (14 women), 26 part-time/adjunct (14 women). *Students:* 37 full-time (27 women), 33 part-time (23 women). Average age 27. 72 applicants, 47% accepted, 20 enrolled. In 2009, 7 master's awarded. *Degree requirements:* For master's, comprehensive exam, thesis or alternative. *Entrance requirements:* For master's, GRE General Test, 2 letters of recommendation. Additional exam requirements/recommendations for international students: Required—TOEFL (minimum score 83 computer-based), or IELTS. *Application deadline:* For fall admission, 2/1 for domestic and international students; for spring admission, 10/1 for domestic and international students. Applications are processed on a rolling basis. Application fee: $60. Electronic applications accepted. *Expenses:* Tuition, area resident: Part-time $486.74 per credit. Tuition, state resident: part-time $486.74 per credit. Tuition, nonresident: part-time $751.34 per credit. Tuition and fees vary according to degree level and program. *Financial support:* In 2009–10, 17 research assistantships with full tuition reimbursements (averaging $7,000 per year) were awarded; Federal Work-Study, scholarships/grants, and unspecified assistantships also available. Support available to part-time students. Financial award application deadline: 3/1; financial award applicants required to submit FAFSA. *Faculty research:* Engaged learning, academic and civic development. Total annual research expenditures: $10,000. *Unit head:* Dr. Peter Vietze, Chairperson, 973-655-5201. *Application contact:* Amy Aiello, Director of Admissions and Operations, 973-655-5147, Fax: 973-655-7869, E-mail: graduate.school@montclair.edu.

Morehead State University, Graduate Programs, College of Science and Technology, Department of Psychology, Morehead, KY 40351. Offers clinical/counseling psychology (MS); general/experimental psychology (MS). Part-time and evening/weekend programs available. *Faculty:* 7 full-time (2 women). *Students:* 32 full-time (23 women), 2 part-time (1 woman), 1 international. Average age 25. 39 applicants, 51% accepted, 19 enrolled. In 2009, 12 master's awarded. *Degree requirements:* For master's, comprehensive exam, thesis optional. *Entrance requirements:* For master's, GRE General Test, 18 undergraduate hours in psychology, minimum GPA of 3.0, 3 letters of recommendation. Additional exam requirements/recommendations for international students: Required—TOEFL (minimum score 500 paper-based; 173 computer-based). *Application deadline:* For fall admission, 8/1 priority date for domestic and international students; for spring admission, 12/1 for domestic students, 12/1 priority date for international students. Applications are processed on a rolling basis. Application fee: $30. Electronic applications accepted. *Expenses:* Tuition, state resident: full-time $6318; part-time $351 per credit hour. Tuition, nonresident: full-time $15,804; part-time $878 per credit hour. *Financial support:* In 2009–10, 26 research assistantships (averaging $10,000 per year) were awarded; career-related internships or fieldwork, Federal Work-Study, and unspecified assistantships also available. Financial award application deadline: 3/15; financial award applicants required to submit FAFSA. *Faculty research:* Mood induction effects, serotonin receptor activity, stress, perceptual processes. *Unit head:* Dr. Laurie Couch, Interim Department Chair, 606-783-2950. *Application contact:* Michelle Barber, Graduate Recruitment and Retention Assistant Director, 606-783-5127, Fax: 606-783-5061, E-mail: m.barber@moreheadstate.edu.

Murray State University, College of Humanities and Fine Arts, Program in Psychology, Murray, KY 42071. Offers clinical psychology (MA, MS); psychology (MA, MS). Part-time programs available. *Degree requirements:* For master's, one foreign language, comprehensive exam (for some programs), thesis. *Entrance requirements:* For master's, GRE General Test. Additional exam requirements/recommendations for international students: Required—TOEFL.

Naropa University, Graduate Programs, Program in Transpersonal Psychology, Boulder, CO 80302-6697. Offers ecopsychology (MA); transpersonal psychology (MA). Part-time and evening/weekend programs available. Postbaccalaureate distance learning degree programs offered (minimal on-campus study). *Degree requirements:* For master's, thesis, service learning. *Entrance requirements:* For master's, interview (by phone or in-person), technology form, resume, letter of interest, 3 letters of recommendation. Additional exam requirements/recommendations for international students: Required—TOEFL (minimum score 600 paper-based; 250 computer-based). Electronic applications accepted.

New Mexico Highlands University, Graduate Studies, College of Arts and Sciences, Department of Behavioral Sciences, Las Vegas, NM 87701. Offers psychology (MS), including clinical psychology, general psychology. Part-time programs available. *Degree requirements:* For master's, comprehensive exam, thesis or alternative. *Entrance requirements:* For master's, minimum undergraduate GPA of 3.0. Additional exam requirements/recommendations for international students: Required—TOEFL (minimum score 540 paper-based; 207 computer-based). *Faculty research:* Southwest Native American resettlement development, community-level interventions, neurochemistry of personality, comparative criminal justice, social theory and activism.

The New School: A University, The New School for Social Research, Department of Psychology, New York, NY 10011. Offers clinical psychology (PhD); cognitive, social and developmental psychology (PhD); general psychology (MA). *Accreditation:* APA (one or more programs are accredited). Part-time programs available. *Faculty:* 13 full-time (5 women). *Students:* 172 full-time (130 women), 105 part-time (87 women); includes 49 minority (13 African Americans, 1 American Indian/Alaska Native, 15 Asian Americans or Pacific Islanders, 20 Hispanic Americans), 41 international. Average age 30. 299 applicants, 80% accepted, 76 enrolled. In 2009, 74 master's, 17 doctorates awarded. Terminal master's awarded for partial completion of doctoral program. *Degree requirements:* For master's, comprehensive exam (for some programs), thesis (for some programs); for doctorate, thesis/dissertation, qualifying exam. *Entrance requirements:* For master's, GRE General Test; for doctorate, GRE General Test, MA. Additional exam requirements/recommendations for international students: Required—TOEFL (minimum score 600 paper-based; 250 computer-based; 100 iBT). *Application deadline:* For fall admission, 1/17 priority date for domestic and international students; for spring admission, 10/15 priority date for domestic and international students. Applications are processed on a rolling basis. Application fee: $50. Electronic applications accepted. *Financial support:* Fellowships, research assistantships, teaching assistantships, Federal Work-Study, scholarships/grants, tuition waivers (full and partial), and unspecified assistantships available. Support available to part-time students. Financial award application deadline: 3/1; financial award applicants required to submit FAFSA. *Faculty research:* Consciousness, memory, language, perceptions, psychopathology. *Unit head:* Dr. McWelling Todman, Chair, 212-229-5727 Ext. 3258, E-mail: todmanm@newschool.edu. *Application contact:* Robert MacDonald, Director of Admissions, 212-229-5727 Ext. 3007, Fax: 212-989-7102, E-mail: macdonar@newschool.edu.

Norfolk State University, School of Graduate Studies, School of Liberal Arts, Department of Psychology, Program in Community/Clinical Psychology, Norfolk, VA 23504. Offers MA. *Degree requirements:* For master's, comprehensive exam, thesis or alternative. *Entrance requirements:* For master's, minimum GPA of 2.7.

North Dakota State University, College of Graduate and Interdisciplinary Studies, College of Science and Mathematics, Department of Psychology, Fargo, ND 58108. Offers clinical psychology (MS); cognitive and visual neuroscience (PhD); health and social psychology (PhD); psychology (MS). *Faculty:* 18 full-time (4 women), 2 part-time/adjunct (1 woman). *Students:* 36 full-time (27 women); includes 4 minority (1 African American, 2 Asian Americans or Pacific Islanders, 1 Hispanic American), 1 international. Average age 24. 46 applicants, 33% accepted, 10 enrolled. In 2009, 3 master's, 1 doctorate awarded. *Degree requirements:* For master's, thesis; for doctorate, thesis/dissertation. *Entrance requirements:* For master's and doctorate, GRE General Test, GRE Subject Test. Additional exam requirements/recommendations for international students: Required—TOEFL (minimum score 525 paper-based; 197 computer-based; 71 iBT). *Application deadline:* For fall admission, 3/1 for domestic and international students. Application fee: $45 ($60 for international students). Electronic applications accepted. *Financial support:* In 2009–10, 36 students received support, including 2 fellowships with full tuition reimbursements available (averaging $16,000 per year), 23 research assistantships with full tuition reimbursements available (averaging $16,000 per year), 11 teaching assistantships with full tuition reimbursements available (averaging $6,000 per year); career-related internships or fieldwork, Federal Work-Study, institutionally sponsored loans, tuition waivers (full and partial), and unspecified assistantships also available. Support available to part-time students. Financial award application deadline: 3/1. *Faculty research:* Cognition science, neuropsychology, group behavior, applied behavior analysis, behavior therapy. Total annual research expenditures: $2 million. *Unit head:* Dr. Paul D. Rokke, Chair, 701-231-8622, Fax: 701-231-8426, E-mail: paul.rokke@ndsu.edu. *Application contact:* Dr. Paul D. Rokke, Chair, 701-231-8622, Fax: 701-231-8426, E-mail: paul.rokke@ndsu.edu.

Northern Arizona University, Graduate College, College of Social and Behavioral Sciences, Department of Psychology, Flagstaff, AZ 86011. Offers applied health psychology (MA); clinical psychology (MA); general psychology (MA); teaching of psychology (MA). Part-time programs available. *Faculty:* 20 full-time (10 women). *Students:* 26 full-time (15 women), 6 part-time (all women); includes 4 minority (1 American Indian/Alaska Native, 3 Hispanic Americans), 2 international. Average age 30. 58 applicants, 41% accepted, 16 enrolled. In 2009, 4 master's awarded. *Degree requirements:* For master's, comprehensive exam (for some programs), thesis (for some programs), oral defense. *Entrance requirements:* For master's, GRE General Test. Additional exam requirements/recommendations for international students: Required—TOEFL (minimum score 550 paper-based; 213 computer-based; 80 iBT), IELTS (minimum score 7), or a bachelor's degree from an English-speaking university and demonstrated proficiency. *Application deadline:* For fall admission, 2/15 priority date for domestic students, 9/1 priority date for international students. Applications are processed on a rolling basis. Application fee: $65. Electronic applications accepted. *Financial support:* In 2009–10, 12 teaching assistantships with partial tuition reimbursements (averaging $10,439 per year) were awarded; career-related internships or fieldwork, Federal Work-Study, institutionally sponsored loans, scholarships/grants, health care benefits, tuition waivers (full and partial), and unspecified assistantships also available. Support available to part-time students. Financial award application deadline: 3/30; financial award applicants required to submit FAFSA. *Unit head:* Dr. Laurie Dickson, Chair, 928-523-0575, Fax: 928-523-6777, E-mail: laurie.dickson@nau.edu. *Application contact:* Dr. Steven Barger, Graduate Coordinator, 928-523-1829, Fax: 928-523-6777, E-mail: steven.barger@nau.edu.

Northwestern State University of Louisiana, Graduate Studies and Research, Department of Psychology, Natchitoches, LA 71497. Offers clinical psychology (MS). *Degree requirements:* For master's, comprehensive exam, thesis or alternative. *Entrance requirements:* For master's, GRE General Test, GRE Subject Test, minimum undergraduate GPA of 2.5.

Northwestern University, The Graduate School, Judd A. and Marjorie Weinberg College of Arts and Sciences, Department of Psychology, Evanston, IL 60208. Offers brain, behavior and cognition (PhD); clinical psychology (PhD); cognitive psychology (PhD); personality (PhD); social psychology (PhD); JD/PhD. Admissions and degrees offered through The Graduate School. *Accreditation:* APA (one or more programs are accredited). Part-time programs available. *Degree requirements:* For doctorate, thesis/dissertation. *Entrance requirements:* For doctorate, GRE General Test, GRE Subject Test. Additional exam requirements/recommendations for international students: Required—TOEFL. Electronic applications accepted. *Faculty research:* Memory and higher order cognition, anxiety and depression, effectiveness of psychotherapy, social cognition, molecular basis of memory.

Northwestern University, The Graduate School and Northwestern University Feinberg School of Medicine, Program in Clinical Psychology, Evanston, IL 60208. Offers clinical psychology (PhD), including clinical neuropsychology, general clinical. PhD admissions and degree offered through The Graduate School. *Accreditation:* APA. *Degree requirements:* For doctorate, thesis/dissertation, clinical internship. *Entrance requirements:* For doctorate, GRE General Test, GRE Subject Test, minimum GPA of 3.2, course work in psychology. Additional exam requirements/recommendations for international students: Required—TOEFL. *Faculty research:* Cancer and cardiovascular risk reduction, evaluation of mental health services and policy, neuropsychological assessment, outcome of psychotherapy, cognitive therapy, pediatric and clinical child psychology.

Notre Dame de Namur University, Division of Academic Affairs, College of Arts and Sciences, Department of Clinical Psychology and Gerontology, Program in Clinical Psychology, Belmont, CA 94002-1908. Offers MS. Part-time programs available. *Students:* 25 full-time (21 women), 45 part-time (38 women); includes 24 minority (3 African Americans, 9 Asian Americans or Pacific Islanders, 12 Hispanic Americans), 2 international. Average age 34. In 2009, 24 master's awarded. *Entrance requirements:* Additional exam requirements/recommendations for international students: Required—TOEFL (minimum score 550 paper-based; 213 computer-based; 79 iBT). Application fee: $60. *Expenses:* Tuition: Part-time $720 per credit. Required fees: $35 per semester hour. *Financial support:* Available to part-time students. Applicants required to submit FAFSA. *Unit head:* Dr. Nusha Askari, 650-508-3728, E-mail: naskari@ndnu.edu. *Application contact:* Candace Hallmark, Associate Director of Admissions, 650-508-3592, Fax: 650-508-3426, E-mail: grad.admit@ndnu.edu.

Nova Southeastern University, Center for Psychological Studies, Program in Clinical Psychology, Fort Lauderdale, FL 33314-7796. Offers PhD, Psy D, SPS. *Accreditation:* APA. *Faculty:* 31 full-time (9 women), 12 part-time/adjunct (6 women). *Students:* 515 full-time (417 women); includes 141 minority (32 African Americans, 2 American Indian/Alaska Native, 19 Asian Americans or Pacific Islanders, 88 Hispanic Americans), 15 international. 474 applicants,

Clinical Psychology

Nova Southeastern University (continued)
30% accepted, 95 enrolled. In 2009, 82 doctorates awarded. *Degree requirements:* For doctorate, thesis/dissertation, clinical internship, competency exam; for SPS, comprehensive exam, internship. *Entrance requirements:* For doctorate, GRE General Test, GRE Subject Test (recommended), 18 credits of course work in psychology including 1 hour of experimental psychology and 3 hours of statistics, minimum undergraduate GPA of 3.0; for SPS, GRE General Test. Additional exam requirements/recommendations for international students: Required—TOEFL (minimum score 550 paper-based; 213 computer-based). *Application deadline:* For fall admission, 1/8 for domestic students. Application fee: $50. Electronic applications accepted. *Expenses:* Contact institution. *Financial support:* In 2009–10, 5 research assistantships, 33 teaching assistantships (averaging $1,000 per year) were awarded; career-related internships or fieldwork, Federal Work-Study, scholarships/grants, and unspecified assistantships also available. Financial award application deadline: 4/1. *Faculty research:* Eating disorders, neuropsychology, family violence, sports psychology, child-pediatric psychology. *Unit head:* Karen Grosby, Dean, 954-262-5701, Fax: 954-262-3859, E-mail: grosby@nova.edu. *Application contact:* Carlos Perez, Enrollment Management, 954-262-5790, Fax: 954-262-3893, E-mail: cpsinfo@cps.nova.edu.

The Ohio State University, Graduate School, College of Social and Behavioral Sciences, School of Social and Behavioral Science, Department of Psychology, Columbus, OH 43210. Offers behavioral neuroscience (PhD); clinical psychology (PhD); cognitive psychology (PhD); developmental psychology (PhD); mental retardation and developmental disabilities (PhD); psychology (MA); quantitative psychology (PhD); social psychology (PhD). *Accreditation:* APA (one or more programs are accredited). *Faculty:* 60. *Students:* 88 full-time (59 women), 47 part-time (31 women); includes 20 minority (7 African Americans, 1 American Indian/Alaska Native, 5 Asian Americans or Pacific Islanders, 7 Hispanic Americans), 20 international. Average age 27. In 2009, 15 master's, 20 doctorates awarded. *Degree requirements:* For doctorate, thesis/dissertation. *Entrance requirements:* For master's and doctorate, GRE General Test. Additional exam requirements/recommendations for international students: Required—TOEFL (minimum score 600 paper-based; 250 computer-based). *Application deadline:* For fall admission, 12/31 for domestic students, 11/30 for international students. Applications are processed on a rolling basis. Application fee: $40 ($50 for international students). Electronic applications accepted. *Expenses:* Tuition, state resident: full-time $10,683. Tuition, nonresident: full-time $25,923. Tuition and fees vary according to course load and program. *Financial support:* Fellowships, research assistantships, teaching assistantships available. *Unit head:* Michael Vasey, Graduate Studies Committee Chair, E-mail: vasey.1@osu.edu. *Application contact:* 614-292-9444, Fax: 614-292-3895, E-mail: domestic.grad@osu.edu.

Ohio University, Graduate College, College of Arts and Sciences, Department of Psychology, Program in Clinical Psychology, Athens, OH 45701-2979. Offers PhD. *Accreditation:* APA. *Faculty:* 11 full-time (6 women). *Students:* 43 full-time (32 women), 9 part-time (5 women); includes 5 minority (1 American Indian/Alaska Native, 1 Asian American or Pacific Islander, 3 Hispanic Americans), 7 international. Average age 28. 176 applicants, 10% accepted, 11 enrolled. In 2009, 11 doctorates awarded. *Degree requirements:* For doctorate, one foreign language, comprehensive exam, thesis/dissertation. *Entrance requirements:* For doctorate, GRE General Test, GRE Subject Test, minimum graduate GPA of 3.4. Additional exam requirements/recommendations for international students: Required—TOEFL. *Application deadline:* For fall admission, 1/1 for domestic students. Application fee: $50 ($55 for international students). *Expenses:* Tuition, state resident: full-time $7839; part-time $323 per quarter hour. Tuition, nonresident: full-time $15,831; part-time $654 per quarter hour. Required fees: $2931. *Financial support:* In 2009–10, 41 students received support, including 6 fellowships with full tuition reimbursements available (averaging $16,400 per year), 1 research assistantship with full tuition reimbursement available (averaging $13,200 per year), 9 teaching assistantships with full tuition reimbursements available (averaging $13,200 per year); career-related internships or fieldwork, Federal Work-Study, institutionally sponsored loans, traineeships, tuition waivers (full), and unspecified assistantships also available. Financial award application deadline: 1/15. *Faculty research:* Health psychology, child clinical psychology, psychotherapy outcome. Total annual research expenditures: $7.3 million. *Unit head:* Christine Gidycz, Director of Clinical Studies, 740-593-1092, Fax: 740-593-0579, E-mail: gidycz@ohio.edu. *Application contact:* Karyl Jones, Administrative Secretary, 740-593-1090, Fax: 740-593-0579, E-mail: psychology@ohio.edu.

Oklahoma State University, College of Arts and Sciences, Department of Psychology, Stillwater, OK 74078. Offers clinical psychology (PhD); general psychology (MS); lifespan development psychology (PhD). *Accreditation:* APA (one or more programs are accredited). *Faculty:* 26 full-time (12 women). *Students:* 36 full-time (23 women), 15 part-time (8 women); includes 8 minority (2 African Americans, 3 American Indian/Alaska Native, 3 Hispanic Americans), 2 international. Average age 28. 120 applicants, 9% accepted, 7 enrolled. In 2009, 10 master's, 9 doctorates awarded. *Degree requirements:* For master's, thesis or alternative; for doctorate, comprehensive exam, thesis/dissertation. *Entrance requirements:* For master's and doctorate, GRE General Test. Additional exam requirements/recommendations for international students: Required—TOEFL (minimum score 550 paper-based; 79 iBT). *Application deadline:* For fall admission, 3/1 priority date for international students; for spring admission, 8/1 priority date for international students. Applications are processed on a rolling basis. Application fee: $40 ($75 for international students). Electronic applications accepted. *Expenses:* Tuition, state resident: full-time $3716; part-time $154.85 per credit hour. Tuition, nonresident: full-time $14,448; part-time $602 per credit hour. Required fees: $1772; $73.85 per credit hour. One-time fee: $50. Tuition and fees vary according to course load and campus/location. *Financial support:* In 2009–10, 16 research assistantships (averaging $13,215 per year), 29 teaching assistantships (averaging $13,370 per year) were awarded; career-related internships or fieldwork, Federal Work-Study, scholarships/grants, health care benefits, tuition waivers (partial), and unspecified assistantships also available. Support available to part-time students. Financial award application deadline: 3/1; financial award applicants required to submit FAFSA. *Unit head:* Dr. Larry Mullins, Head, 405-744-6028, Fax: 405-744-8067. *Application contact:* Dr. Gordon Emslie, Dean, 405-744-6368, Fax: 405-744-0355, E-mail: grad-i@okstate.edu.

Old Dominion University, College of Sciences, Virginia Consortium Program in Clinical Psychology, Norfolk, VA 23529. Offers Psy D. *Faculty:* 10 full-time (5 women). *Students:* 46 full-time (34 women); includes 15 minority (4 African Americans, 8 Asian Americans or Pacific Islanders, 3 Hispanic Americans). Average age 29. 207 applicants, 8% accepted, 6 enrolled. In 2009, 11 doctorates awarded. *Degree requirements:* For doctorate, comprehensive exam, thesis/dissertation, internship. *Entrance requirements:* For doctorate, GRE General Test. Additional exam requirements/recommendations for international students: Required—TOEFL. *Application deadline:* For fall admission, 1/2 for domestic and international students. Application fee: $40. *Expenses:* Contact institution. *Financial support:* In 2009–10, 29 students received support, including 26 research assistantships with partial tuition reimbursements available (averaging $7,550 per year), 3 teaching assistantships with partial tuition reimbursements available (averaging $8,000 per year); career-related internships or fieldwork, scholarships/grants, and unspecified assistantships also available. Financial award application deadline: 1/2; financial award applicants required to submit FAFSA. *Faculty research:* Depression, coping with stress, minority and women's issues, family therapy, neuropsychology, assessment, alcohol abuse. *Unit head:* Dr. Louis Janda, Graduate Program Director, 757-683-4211, Fax: 757-368-1823, E-mail: ljanda@odu.edu. *Application contact:* Eileen O'Neill, Coordinator, 757-368-1820, Fax: 757-368-1823, E-mail: exoneill@odu.edu.

Pace University, Dyson College of Arts and Sciences, Department of Psychology, Program in School-Clinical Child Psychology, New York, NY 10038. Offers school psychology (MS Ed); school-clinical psychology (Psy D). *Accreditation:* APA (one or more programs are accredited). *Students:* 83 full-time (74 women), 35 part-time (31 women); includes 20 minority (4 African Americans, 10 Asian Americans or Pacific Islanders, 6 Hispanic Americans), 7 international. Average age 27. 234 applicants, 34% accepted, 27 enrolled. In 2009, 5 master's, 26 doctorates awarded. Terminal master's awarded for partial completion of doctoral program. *Degree requirements:* For master's, comprehensive exam, qualifying exams, internship; for doctorate, comprehensive exam, qualifying exams, externship, internship, project. *Entrance requirements:* For master's, GRE General Test, GRE Subject Test, interview; for doctorate, GRE General Test, GRE Subject Test (psychology), interview, transcripts, 3 letters of reference. Additional exam requirements/recommendations for international students: Required—TOEFL. *Application deadline:* For fall admission, 2/1 priority date for domestic students. Applications are processed on a rolling basis. Application fee: $70. Electronic applications accepted. *Expenses:* Tuition: Part-time $954 per credit. Tuition and fees vary according to course load, degree level and program. *Financial support:* Research assistantships, teaching assistantships, career-related internships or fieldwork, Federal Work-Study, and tuition waivers (partial) available. Support available to part-time students. Financial award applicants required to submit FAFSA. *Unit head:* Dr. Barbara Mowder, Director, 212-346-1506. *Application contact:* Susan Ford-Goldschein, Director of Admissions, 212-346-1652, Fax: 212-346-1585, E-mail: gradnyc@pace.edu.

Pacifica Graduate Institute, Graduate Programs, Carpinteria, CA 93013. Offers clinical psychology (PhD); counseling psychology (MA); depth psychology (MA, PhD); mythological studies (MA, PhD). Terminal master's awarded for partial completion of doctoral program. *Degree requirements:* For master's, thesis (for some programs), practicum; for doctorate, comprehensive exam, thesis/dissertation, internship. *Entrance requirements:* For master's, resume, 3 letters of recommendation, writing sample, interview; for doctorate, resumé, 4 letters of recommendation, writing sample, interview. Additional exam requirements/recommendations for international students: Required—TOEFL. *Faculty research:* Imaginal and archetypal theory; post-Colonial psychoanalytic and Jungian theory; myth literature as it applies to the theory and practice of psychology.

Palo Alto University, PGSP-Stanford Psy D Consortium Program, Palo Alto, CA 94303-4232. Offers Psy D. *Degree requirements:* For doctorate, thesis/dissertation. *Entrance requirements:* For doctorate, GRE, BA or MA in psychology or related area, minimum undergraduate GPA of 3.0, minimum graduate GPA of 3.3. Additional exam requirements/recommendations for international students: Required—TOEFL. Electronic applications accepted. *Expenses:* Tuition: Full-time $33,009; part-time $916 per credit hour. Required fees: $1243 per quarter. *Faculty research:* Biopsychosocial research, neurobiology, psychopharmacology.

Palo Alto University, Program in Clinical Psychology, Palo Alto, CA 94303-4232. Offers PhD, JD/PhD, MBA/PhD. *Degree requirements:* For doctorate, comprehensive exam, thesis/dissertation, 2000 hour clinical internship, oral clinical competency exam. *Entrance requirements:* For doctorate, GRE General Test, BA or MA in psychology or related area, minimum undergraduate GPA of 3.0, 3.3 graduate. Additional exam requirements/recommendations for international students: Required—TOEFL. Electronic applications accepted. *Expenses:* Tuition: Full-time $33,009; part-time $916 per credit hour. Required fees: $1243 per quarter. *Faculty research:* Child/family studies, health psychology, neuropsychology, personality development, assessment.

Pepperdine University, Graduate School of Education and Psychology, Division of Psychology, Program in Clinical Psychology, Malibu, CA 90263. Offers clinical psychology (Psy D); clinical psychology (daytime) (MA), including marriage and family therapy; clinical psychology (evening) (MA), including marriage and family therapy. *Accreditation:* APA. Part-time and evening/weekend programs available. *Entrance requirements:* For master's, GRE General Test, bachelor's degree in psychology or related field. Additional exam requirements/recommendations for international students: Required—TOEFL. *Expenses:* Tuition: Full-time $37,516; part-time $1310 per unit. Required fees: $80.

Philadelphia College of Osteopathic Medicine, Graduate and Professional Programs, Department of Psychology, Philadelphia, PA 19131-1694. Offers clinical psychology (Psy D); counseling and clinical health psychology (MS); organizational leadership and development (MS); psychology (Certificate, Post-Doctoral Certificate); school psychology (MS, Psy D, Ed S). *Accreditation:* APA. *Degree requirements:* For master's, thesis; for doctorate, comprehensive exam, thesis/dissertation, final project, fieldwork. *Entrance requirements:* For master's, GRE or MAT, minimum GPA of 3.0; course work in biology, chemistry, English, physics; for other advanced degree, PRAXIS. *Faculty research:* Depression in primary care, integrated primary care, geriatric mental health.

See Close-Up on page 1091.

Phillips Graduate Institute, Program in Clinical Family Psychology and Organizational Consulting, Encino, CA 91316-1509. Offers clinical psychology (Psy D); organizational consulting (Psy D). Evening/weekend programs available. *Degree requirements:* For doctorate, thesis/dissertation. *Entrance requirements:* For doctorate, minimum GPA of 3.0, interview.

Ponce School of Medicine, Program in Clinical Psychology, Ponce, PR 00732-7004. Offers PhD, Psy D. *Accreditation:* APA. *Faculty:* 24 full-time (16 women), 5 part-time/adjunct (4 women). *Students:* 197 full-time (173 women); includes 174 minority (all Hispanic Americans). Average age 27. 122 applicants, 44% accepted, 48 enrolled. In 2009, 34 doctorates awarded. *Degree requirements:* For doctorate, one foreign language, comprehensive exam, thesis/dissertation, internship. *Entrance requirements:* For doctorate, GRE General Test or EXADEP, proficiency in Spanish and English, 2 letters of recommendation, minimum undergraduate GPA of 2.7, PhD GPA 3.00, criminal background check. *Application deadline:* For fall admission, 3/15 for domestic and international students. Application fee: $100. *Financial support:* In 2009–10, 153 students received support; fellowships, scholarships/grants available. Financial award application deadline: 4/30; financial award applicants required to submit FAFSA. *Unit head:* Dr. Jose Pons, Head, 787-840-2575, E-mail: jpons@psm.edu. *Application contact:* Maria Colon, Admissions Officer, 787-840-2575 Ext. 2143, E-mail: mcolon@psm.edu.

Pontifical Catholic University of Puerto Rico, Institute of Graduate Studies in Behavioral Science and Community Affairs, Program in Clinical Psychology (Doctorate), Ponce, PR 00717-0777. Offers PhD, Psy D. Part-time and evening/weekend programs available. *Degree requirements:* For doctorate, comprehensive exam, thesis/dissertation. *Entrance requirements:* For doctorate, EXADEP, minimum GPA of 2.75.

Pontifical Catholic University of Puerto Rico, Institute of Graduate Studies in Behavioral Science and Community Affairs, Program in Clinical Psychology (Master's), Ponce, PR 00717-0777. Offers MA, MS. Part-time and evening/weekend programs available. *Degree requirements:* For master's, thesis. *Entrance requirements:* For master's, EXADEP, 3 letters of recommendation, interview, minimum GPA of 2.75.

Prairie View A&M University, College of Arts and Sciences, Department of Biology, Prairie View, TX 77446-0519. Offers bio- environmental toxicology (MS); biology (MS). Part-time and evening/weekend programs available. *Faculty:* 5 full-time (2 women). *Students:* 4 full-time (all women), 4 part-time (2 women); all minorities (7 African Americans, 1 Hispanic American). Average age 24. 14 applicants, 86% accepted. In 2009, 8 master's awarded. *Degree requirements:* For master's, comprehensive exam, thesis optional. *Entrance requirements:* For master's, GRE General Test. Additional exam requirements/recommendations for international students: Required—TOEFL. *Application deadline:* For fall admission, 7/1 for domestic and international students; for spring admission, 11/1 for domestic and international students. Applications are processed on a rolling basis. *Expenses:* Tuition, state resident: full-time $2200. Tuition, nonresident: full-time $5600. Required fees: $1720. Tuition and fees vary according to course load. *Financial support:* Federal Work-Study and unspecified assistantships available. Financial award application deadline: 4/1; financial award applicants required to submit FAFSA. *Faculty research:* Geonomics, hypertension, control of gene express, proteins, kigands that interact with hormone receptors, prostate cancer, renin-angiotensin yeast metabolism. *Unit head:* Dr. Harriette Howard-Lee-Block, Head, 936-261-3160, Fax: 936-261-3179, E-mail: hlblock@pvamu.edu. *Application contact:* Dr. Seab A. Smith, Associate Professor, 936-261-3169, Fax: 936-261-3179, E-mail: sasmith@pvamu.edu.

Prairie View A&M University, College of Juvenile Justice and Psychology, Prairie View, TX 77446-0519. Offers clinical adolescent psychology (PhD); juvenile forensic psychology (MSJFP); juvenile justice (MSJJ, PhD). Part-time and evening/weekend programs available. *Faculty:* 12 full-time (7 women). *Students:* 25 full-time (18 women), 50 part-time (41 women); includes 64 minority (61 African Americans, 1 Asian American or Pacific Islander, 2 Hispanic Americans), 2 international. Average age 26. 55 applicants, 60% accepted, 33 enrolled. In 2009, 5 master's, 5 doctorates awarded. *Degree requirements:* For master's, comprehensive exam (for some programs), thesis (for some programs); for doctorate, comprehensive exam, thesis/dissertation. *Entrance requirements:* For master's, GRE, minimum GPA of 2.75; for doctorate, GRE, previous course work in clinical adolescent psychology, minimum GPA of 3.5. Additional exam requirements/recommendations for international students: Required—TOEFL. *Application deadline:* For fall admission, 3/1 for domestic and international students; for spring admission, 10/1 for domestic and international students. Applications are processed on a rolling basis. Application fee: $50. *Expenses:* Tuition, state resident: full-time $2200. Tuition, nonresident: full-time $5600. Required fees: $1720. Tuition and fees vary according to course load. *Financial support:* In 2009–10, 18 students received support; research assistantships, teaching assistantships, career-related internships or fieldwork, Federal Work-Study, institutionally sponsored loans, tuition waivers (full and partial), and unspecified assistantships available. Support available to part-time students. Financial award application deadline: 3/1; financial award applicants required to submit FAFSA. *Faculty research:* Juvenile justice, juvenile forensic psychology, teen court, graduate education, capital punishment. Total annual research expenditures: $2,888. *Unit head:* Dr. Elaine Rodney, Dean, 936-261-5200, Fax: 936-261-5252, E-mail: ehrodney@pvamu.edu. *Application contact:* Sandy Siegmund, Executive Secretary, Graduate Program, 936-261-5234, Fax: 936-261-5249, E-mail: sisiegmund@pvamu.edu.

Queens College of the City University of New York, Division of Graduate Studies, Mathematics and Natural Sciences Division, Department of Psychology, Flushing, NY 11367-1597. Offers clinical behavioral applications in mental health settings (MA); psychology (MA). Part-time programs available. *Faculty:* 27 full-time (13 women). *Students:* 16 full-time (12 women), 84 part-time (74 women). 134 applicants, 47% accepted, 48 enrolled. In 2009, 17 master's awarded. *Degree requirements:* For master's, comprehensive exam, thesis or alternative. *Entrance requirements:* For master's, GRE, minimum GPA of 3.0. Additional exam requirements/recommendations for international students: Required—TOEFL. *Application deadline:* For fall admission, 4/1 for domestic students; for spring admission, 11/1 for domestic students. Applications are processed on a rolling basis. Application fee: $125. *Expenses:* Tuition, state resident: full-time $7360; part-time $310 per credit. Tuition, nonresident: part-time $575 per credit. One-time fee: $195.25 full-time; $145.25 part-time. *Financial support:* Career-related internships or fieldwork, Federal Work-Study, institutionally sponsored loans, and tuition waivers (partial) available. Support available to part-time students. Financial award application deadline: 4/1; financial award applicants required to submit FAFSA. *Unit head:* Dr. Richard Bodnar, Chairperson, 718-997-3200. *Application contact:* Dr. Philip Ramsey, Graduate Adviser, 718-997-3200, E-mail: philip_ramsey@qc.edu.

Queen's University at Kingston, School of Graduate Studies and Research, Faculty of Arts and Sciences, Department of Psychology, Kingston, ON K7L 3N6, Canada. Offers brain behavior and cognitive science (MA, PhD); clinical psychology (MA, PhD); developmental psychology (MA, PhD); social personality psychology (MA, PhD). *Accreditation:* APA (one or more programs are accredited). *Degree requirements:* For master's, thesis; for doctorate, comprehensive exam, thesis/dissertation. *Entrance requirements:* For master's and doctorate, GRE General Test. Additional exam requirements/recommendations for international students: Required—TOEFL. *Faculty research:* Human development, social, personality, behavioral neuroscience, forensic.

Radford University, College of Graduate and Professional Studies, College of Humanities and Behavioral Sciences, Program in Psychology, Radford, VA 24142. Offers clinical psychology (MA, MS); experimental psychology (MA); general psychology (MS); industrial/organizational psychology (MA, MS). Part-time programs available. *Faculty:* 21 full-time (9 women), 6 part-time/adjunct (2 women). *Students:* 44 full-time (25 women), 1 (woman) part-time; includes 5 minority (3 African Americans, 2 Asian Americans or Pacific Islanders), 1 international. Average age 25. 110 applicants, 65% accepted, 22 enrolled. In 2009, 31 master's awarded. *Degree requirements:* For master's, comprehensive exam, thesis (for some programs). *Entrance requirements:* For master's, GRE, minimum GPA of 3.0; 3 letters of reference; essay. Additional exam requirements/recommendations for international students: Required—TOEFL (minimum score 550 paper-based; 213 computer-based; 79 iBT). *Application deadline:* For fall admission, 2/15 priority date for domestic students, 12/1 for international students. Applications are processed on a rolling basis. Application fee: $50. Electronic applications accepted. *Expenses:* Tuition, state resident: full-time $5086; part-time $211 per credit hour. Tuition, nonresident: full-time $12,608; part-time $525 per credit hour. Required fees: $2508; $105 per credit hour. *Financial support:* In 2009–10, 34 students received support, including 20 research assistantships with partial tuition reimbursements available (averaging $8,000 per year), 14 teaching assistantships with partial tuition reimbursements available (averaging $8,700 per year); career-related internships or fieldwork, institutionally sponsored loans, scholarships/grants, and unspecified assistantships also available. Financial award application deadline: 3/1; financial award applicants required to submit FAFSA. *Unit head:* Dr. Hilary M. Lips, Chair, 540-831-5387, Fax: 540-831-6113, E-mail: hlips@radford.edu. *Application contact:* Graduate Admissions Office, 540-831-5431, Fax: 540-831-6061, E-mail: gradcollege@radford.edu.

Regent University, Graduate School, School of Psychology and Counseling, Virginia Beach, VA 23464-9800. Offers clinical psychology (MA, Psy D); counseling (MA), including community counseling, human services counseling, school counseling; counseling studies (CAGS); counselor education and supervision (PhD); M Div/MA; M Ed/MA; MBA/MA. PhD program offered online only. *Accreditation:* ACA; APA (one or more programs are accredited). Part-time and evening/weekend programs available. Postbaccalaureate distance learning degree programs offered (minimal on-campus study). *Faculty:* 24 full-time (12 women), 19 part-time/adjunct (12 women). *Students:* 209 full-time (171 women), 189 part-time (137 women); includes 107 minority (92 African Americans, 4 Asian Americans or Pacific Islanders, 11 Hispanic Americans), 14 international. Average age 34. 417 applicants, 50% accepted, 104 enrolled. In 2009, 108 master's, 40 doctorates awarded. *Degree requirements:* For master's, thesis or alternative, internship, practicum, written competency exam; for doctorate, thesis/dissertation or alternative. *Entrance requirements:* For master's, GRE General Test including writing exam, minimum undergraduate GPA of 2.75, 3 recommendations, resume, transcripts, writing sample; for doctorate, GRE General Test including writing exam, GRE Subject Test, minimum undergraduate GPA of 3.0, 3.5 (PhD), 10-15 minute VHS tape demonstrating counseling skills, writing sample, 3 recommendations, resume. Additional exam requirements/recommendations for international students: Required—TOEFL (minimum score 577 paper-based; 233 computer-based). *Application deadline:* For fall admission, 4/1 priority date for domestic students; for spring admission, 11/1 priority date for domestic students. Applications are processed on a rolling basis. Application fee: $50. Electronic applications accepted. *Expenses:* Contact institution. *Financial support:* In 2009–10, 368 students received support; research assistantships with full and partial tuition reimbursements available, teaching assistantships with full and partial tuition reimbursements available, career-related internships or fieldwork, scholarships/grants, and tuition waivers (full and partial) available. Support available to part-time students. Financial award application deadline: 9/1; financial award applicants required to submit FAFSA. *Faculty research:* Marriage enrichment, AIDS counseling, troubled youth, faith and learning, trauma. *Unit head:* Dr. William Hathaway, Acting Dean, 757-352-4294, Fax: 757-352-4282, E-mail: willhat@regent.edu. *Application contact:* Matthew Chadwick, Director of Admissions, 800-373-5504, Fax: 757-352-4381, E-mail: admissions@regent.edu.

Roosevelt University, Graduate Division, College of Arts and Sciences, Department of Psychology, Program in Clinical Professional Psychology, Chicago, IL 60605. Offers MA, Psy D. *Accreditation:* APA.

Rowan University, Graduate School, College of Liberal Arts and Sciences, Department of Psychology, Program in Clinical Mental Health Counseling, Glassboro, NJ 08028-1701. Offers MA. Part-time and evening/weekend programs available. *Students:* 14 full-time (10 women), 5 part-time (all women); includes 4 minority (all African Americans). Average age 26. 34 applicants, 26% accepted, 9 enrolled. *Entrance requirements:* For master's, GRE General Test. Additional exam requirements/recommendations for international students: Required—TOEFL. *Application deadline:* Applications are processed on a rolling basis. Application fee: $50. Electronic applications accepted. *Expenses:* Tuition, state resident: full-time $10,624; part-time $590 per semester hour. Tuition, nonresident: full-time $10,624; part-time $590 per semester hour. Required fees: $2320; $125 per semester hour. *Financial support:* Career-related internships or fieldwork, Federal Work-Study, and unspecified assistantships available. Support available to part-time students. *Unit head:* Dr. Mira Lalovic-Hand, Interim Associate Provost/Director of Graduate School, 856-256-5120, E-mail: lalovic-hand@rowan.edu. *Application contact:* Karen Haynes, Graduate Coordinator, 856-256-4052, Fax: 856-256-4436, E-mail: haynes@rowan.edu.

Rutgers, The State University of New Jersey, New Brunswick, Graduate School-New Brunswick, Program in Psychology, Piscataway, NJ 08854-8097. Offers behavioral neuroscience (PhD); clinical psychology (PhD); cognitive psychology (PhD); interdisciplinary health psychology (PhD); social psychology (PhD). *Accreditation:* APA. *Degree requirements:* For doctorate, comprehensive exam, thesis/dissertation. *Entrance requirements:* For doctorate, GRE General Test, 3 letters of recommendation. Additional exam requirements/recommendations for international students: Required—TOEFL (minimum score 577 paper-based; 233 computer-based). Electronic applications accepted. *Faculty research:* Learning and memory, behavioral ecology, hormones and behavior, psychopharmacology, anxiety disorders.

Rutgers, The State University of New Jersey, New Brunswick, Graduate School of Applied and Professional Psychology, Department of Clinical Psychology, Piscataway, NJ 08854-8097. Offers Psy M, Psy D. *Accreditation:* APA (one or more programs are accredited). *Degree requirements:* For doctorate, comprehensive exam, thesis/dissertation, 1 year internship. *Entrance requirements:* For doctorate, GRE General Test, GRE Subject Test, bachelor's degree in psychology or equivalent. Additional exam requirements/recommendations for international students: Required—TOEFL. Electronic applications accepted. *Expenses:* Contact institution. *Faculty research:* Long- and short-term dynamic therapy, community psychology, cognitive-behavioral therapy: anxiety and depressive disorders, addictive behaviors: eating disorders and alcoholism.

St. John's University, St. John's College of Liberal Arts and Sciences, Department of Psychology, Program in Clinical Psychology, Queens, NY 11439. Offers clinical psychology-child (PhD); clinical psychology-general (PhD). *Accreditation:* APA. *Students:* 45 full-time (34 women), 22 part-time (20 women); includes 15 minority (5 African Americans, 6 Asian Americans or Pacific Islanders, 4 Hispanic Americans), 5 international. Average age 27. 272 applicants, 9% accepted, 12 enrolled. In 2009, 10 doctorates awarded. *Degree requirements:* For doctorate, comprehensive exam, thesis/dissertation, internship, externship. *Entrance requirements:* For doctorate, GRE General Test, GRE Subject Test, 24 credits of undergraduate course work in psychology, 2 writing samples. Additional exam requirements/recommendations for international students: Required—TOEFL (minimum score 500 paper-based; 173 computer-based; 61 iBT), IELTS (minimum score 5.5). *Application deadline:* For fall admission, 1/15 priority date for domestic and international students; for spring admission, 11/1 priority date for domestic and international students. Applications are processed on a rolling basis. Application fee: $70. Electronic applications accepted. *Expenses:* Contact institution. *Financial support:* Fellowships, research assistantships, career-related internships or fieldwork and scholarships/grants available. Support available to part-time students. Financial award application deadline: 3/1; financial award applicants required to submit FAFSA. *Faculty research:* Cognitive-behavioral therapy, sucking cessation pedagogical research and implicit attitudes. *Unit head:* Dr. Jeffrey S. Nevid, Director, 718-990-1548, E-mail: nevidj@stjohns.edu. *Application contact:* Kathleen Davis, Director of Graduate Admission, 718-990-2790, Fax: 718-990-5686, E-mail: gradhelp@stjohns.edu.

Saint Louis University, Graduate School, College of Arts and Sciences and Graduate School, Department of Psychology, St. Louis, MO 63103-2097. Offers clinical psychology (MS-R, PhD); experimental psychology (MS-R, PhD); industrial-organizational psychology (PhD); psychology (PhD). *Accreditation:* APA (one or more programs are accredited). Part-time programs available. *Degree requirements:* For master's, comprehensive exam, thesis; for doctorate, thesis/dissertation, clinical internship (for clinical psychology PhD). *Entrance requirements:* For master's, GRE General Test, interview, letters of recommendation, resume; for doctorate, GRE General Test, interview, letters of recommendation, resumé, transcripts, goal statement. Additional exam requirements/recommendations for international students: Required—TOEFL (minimum score 550 paper-based; 213 computer-based). Electronic applications accepted. *Faculty research:* Violence and trauma; neural basis of learning and memory function; eating disorders; body image and health behavior; prejudice, stereotyping, and victimization; memory, cognitive aging and language processing.

St. Mary's University, Graduate School, Department of Psychology, Program in Clinical Psychology, San Antonio, TX 78228-8507. Offers MA, MS. Part-time programs available. *Degree requirements:* For master's, comprehensive exam, practica. *Entrance requirements:* For master's, GRE General Test. Additional exam requirements/recommendations for international students: Required—TOEFL (minimum score 550 paper-based; 213 computer-based; 80 iBT). Electronic applications accepted. *Expenses:* Tuition: Full-time $8004. Required fees: $536. One-time fee: $5 full-time. Full-time tuition and fees vary according to program.

Saint Michael's College, Graduate Programs, Program in Clinical Psychology, Colchester, VT 05439. Offers MA. Part-time and evening/weekend programs available. *Degree requirements:* For master's, thesis or alternative, internship, practicum, research seminar. *Entrance requirements:* For master's, GRE General Test, GRE Subject Test, undergraduate major in psychology or related area, minimum 12 credits in psychology, minimum GPA of 3.0. Electronic applications accepted. *Faculty research:* Psychodynamic psychotherapy, family therapy, philosophical foundations of clinical psychology.

Sam Houston State University, College of Humanities and Social Sciences, Department of Psychology and Philosophy, Huntsville, TX 77341. Offers clinical psychology (PhD); psychology (MA). *Accreditation:* APA. Part-time programs available. *Faculty:* 13 full-time (5 women), 1 part-time/adjunct (0 women). *Students:* 61 full-time (46 women), 27 part-time (21 women); includes 21 minority (8 African Americans, 3 Asian Americans or Pacific Islanders, 10 Hispanic Americans), 3 international. Average age 26. 113 applicants, 29% accepted, 24 enrolled. In 2009, 20 master's, 4 doctorates awarded. *Degree requirements:* For master's, thesis. *Entrance requirements:* For master's, GRE General Test or MAT, minimum GPA of 3.0. Additional exam requirements/recommendations for international students: Required—TOEFL (minimum score 550 paper-based; 213 computer-based; 79 iBT). *Application deadline:* For fall admission, 8/1 for domestic students; for spring admission, 12/1 for domestic students. Applications are processed on a rolling basis. Application fee: $20. *Expenses:* Tuition, state resident: full-time $3690; part-time $205 per credit hour. Tuition, nonresident: full-time $8676; part-time $482 per credit hour. Required fees: $1474. Tuition and fees vary according to course load and campus/location. *Financial support:* Research assistantships, teaching assistantships, career-related internships or fieldwork and institutionally sponsored loans available. Support available to

Clinical Psychology

Sam Houston State University (continued)
part-time students. Financial award application deadline: 5/31; financial award applicants required to submit FAFSA. *Unit head:* Dr. Christopher Wilson, Chair, 936-294-3052, Fax: 936-294-3798, E-mail: psy_dcw@shsu.edu. *Application contact:* Dr. Jeffrey Anastasi, Coordinator, 936-294-3049, Fax: 936-294-3798, E-mail: jsa001@shsu.edu.

San Diego State University, Graduate and Research Affairs, College of Sciences, Department of Psychology, San Diego, CA 92182. Offers clinical psychology (MS, PhD); industrial and organizational psychology (MS); program evaluation (MS); psychology (MA). *Accreditation:* APA (one or more programs are accredited). Terminal master's awarded for partial completion of doctoral program. *Degree requirements:* For master's, thesis, oral exam; for doctorate, thesis/dissertation. *Entrance requirements:* For master's, GRE General Test, GRE Subject Test, 3 letters of recommendation; for doctorate, GRE General Test, GRE Subject Test, minimum GPA of 3.0, 3 letters of recommendation. Additional exam requirements/recommendations for international students: Required—TOEFL. Electronic applications accepted.

San Jose State University, Graduate Studies and Research, College of Social Sciences, Department of Psychology, San Jose, CA 95192-0001. Offers clinical psychology (MS); experimental psychology (MA); industrial/organizational psychology (MS); psychology (MA). *Students:* 51 full-time (37 women), 20 part-time (14 women); includes 18 minority (1 African American, 1 American Indian/Alaska Native, 12 Asian Americans or Pacific Islanders, 4 Hispanic Americans), 6 international. Average age 28. 153 applicants, 20% accepted, 26 enrolled. In 2009, 17 master's awarded. *Degree requirements:* For master's, comprehensive exam, thesis (for some programs). *Entrance requirements:* For master's, GRE General Test, minimum GPA of 3.0. *Application deadline:* For fall admission, 6/29 for domestic students; for spring admission, 11/30 for domestic students. Applications are processed on a rolling basis. Application fee: $59. Electronic applications accepted. *Financial support:* Teaching assistantships, career-related internships or fieldwork and institutionally sponsored loans available. Financial award application deadline: 3/1; financial award applicants required to submit FAFSA. *Faculty research:* Drug and alcohol abuse, neurohormonal mechanisms in motion sickness, behavior modification, sleep research, genetics. *Unit head:* Dr. Sheila Bienenfeld, Chair, 408-924-5642, Fax: 408-924-5605. *Application contact:* Dr. Sheila Bienenfeld, Chair, 408-924-5642, Fax: 408-924-5605.

Saybrook University, Graduate College of Psychology and Humanistic Studies, San Francisco, CA 94111-1920. Offers clinical psychology (Psy D); human science (MA, PhD), including consciousness and spirituality, humanistic and transpersonal psychology, integrative health studies, organizational systems, social transformation, transformative social change (MA); organizational systems (MA, PhD), including consciousness and spirituality, humanistic and transpersonal psychology, integrative health studies, leadership of sustainable systems (MA), organizational systems, social transformation; psychology (MA, PhD), including clinical psychology (PhD), consciousness and spirituality, creativity studies (MA), humanistic and transpersonal psychology, integrative health studies, Jungian studies, marriage and family therapy (MA), organizational systems, social transformation. Postbaccalaureate distance learning degree programs offered (minimal on-campus study). Terminal master's awarded for partial completion of doctoral program. *Degree requirements:* For master's, thesis or alternative; for doctorate, thesis/dissertation. Electronic applications accepted. *Faculty research:* Humanistic theory, health studies, organizational systems, consciousness and spirituality, social transformation.

The School of Professional Psychology at Forest Institute, Graduate Programs, Springfield, MO 65807. Offers clinical psychology (MA, Psy D); counseling psychology (MA); marriage and family therapy (MA, PGC). *Accreditation:* AAMFT/COAMFTE; APA (one or more programs are accredited). *Faculty:* 18 full-time (9 women), 18 part-time/adjunct (10 women). *Students:* 214 full-time (144 women), 46 part-time (35 women); includes 35 minority (11 African Americans, 9 American Indian/Alaska Native, 5 Asian Americans or Pacific Islanders, 10 Hispanic Americans), 3 international. Average age 28. 176 applicants, 69% accepted, 45 enrolled. In 2009, 35 master's, 31 doctorates awarded. Terminal master's awarded for partial completion of doctoral program. *Degree requirements:* For master's, thesis, practicum; for doctorate, comprehensive exam, thesis/dissertation, internship, practicum. *Entrance requirements:* For master's, GRE General Test, interview, minimum GPA of 3.0, 12 hours in psychology; for doctorate, GRE General Test, interview, minimum GPA of 3.0, 18 hours in psychology. Additional exam requirements/recommendations for international students: Required—TOEFL (minimum score 550 paper-based; 213 computer-based). *Application deadline:* For fall admission, 1/15 priority date for domestic and international students; for spring admission, 8/1 priority date for domestic and international students. Applications are processed on a rolling basis. Application fee: $50. Electronic applications accepted. *Expenses:* Tuition: Full-time $23,625; part-time $675 per credit hour. Required fees: $275 per semester. Tuition and fees vary according to course load and program. *Financial support:* In 2009–10, 59 students received support, including 5 fellowships with partial tuition reimbursements available (averaging $7,200 per year), 11 teaching assistantships (averaging $100 per year); career-related internships or fieldwork, Federal Work-Study, scholarships/grants, tuition waivers (partial), and unspecified assistantships also available. Financial award applicants required to submit FAFSA. *Faculty research:* Forensics/corrections, marriage and family therapy, child and adolescent, integrated health care, neuropsychology. *Unit head:* Dr. Mark E. Skrade, President, 417-823-3477, Fax: 417-823-3442, E-mail: mskrade@forest.edu. *Application contact:* Bethany Ritter, Admissions Counselor, 417-823-3477, Fax: 417-823-3442, E-mail: britter@forest.edu.

Seattle Pacific University, PhD in Clinical Psychology Program, Seattle, WA 98119-1997. Offers PhD. *Accreditation:* APA. *Faculty:* 9 full-time (5 women), 3 part-time/adjunct (0 women). *Students:* 47 full-time (39 women), 29 part-time (23 women); includes 10 minority (1 African American, 1 American Indian/Alaska Native, 5 Asian Americans or Pacific Islanders, 3 Hispanic Americans). Average age 29. 114 applicants, 13% accepted, 15 enrolled. In 2009, 16 doctorates awarded. *Degree requirements:* For doctorate, thesis/dissertation, clinical internship, practicum. *Entrance requirements:* For doctorate, GRE (preferred minimum score 1100 verbal and quantitative, taken within the last five years). Additional exam requirements/recommendations for international students: Required—TOEFL (minimum score 600 paper-based; 250 computer-based). *Application deadline:* For fall admission, 12/15 for domestic and international students. Electronic applications accepted. *Expenses:* Contact institution. *Financial support:* In 2009–10, 65 students received support; fellowships, scholarships/grants available. Financial award applicants required to submit FAFSA. *Faculty research:* Social network support, attachment, integration of faith and family psychology, developmental psychology. *Unit head:* Dr. Jay Skidmore, Chair, 206-281-2916. *Application contact:* The Grad Center, 206-281-2091.

Southern Illinois University Carbondale, Graduate School, College of Liberal Arts, Department of Psychology, Carbondale, IL 62901-4701. Offers clinical psychology (MA, MS, PhD); counseling psychology (MA, MS, PhD); experimental psychology (MA, MS, PhD). *Accreditation:* APA (one or more programs are accredited). *Degree requirements:* For master's, thesis; for doctorate, thesis/dissertation. *Entrance requirements:* For master's, GRE General Test, GRE Subject Test, minimum GPA of 2.7; for doctorate, GRE General Test, GRE Subject Test, minimum GPA of 3.25. Additional exam requirements/recommendations for international students: Required—TOEFL. *Faculty research:* Developmental neuropsychology; smoking, affect, and cognition; personality measurement; vocational psychology; program evaluation.

Southern Illinois University Edwardsville, Graduate Studies and Research, School of Education, Department of Psychology, Program in Clinical-Adult Psychology, Edwardsville, IL 62026-0001. Offers MA. Part-time programs available. *Students:* 12 full-time (9 women), 19 part-time (13 women); includes 1 minority (Asian American or Pacific Islander). Average age 26. In 2009, 6 master's awarded. *Degree requirements:* For master's, thesis. *Entrance requirements:* For master's, GRE. Additional exam requirements/recommendations for international students: Required—TOEFL (minimum score 550 paper-based; 213 computer-based; 79 iBT), IELTS (minimum score 6.5). *Application deadline:* For fall admission, 2/1 for domestic and international students. Application fee: $30. Electronic applications accepted. *Expenses:* Tuition, state resident: part-time $1252.50 per semester. Tuition, nonresident: part-time $3131.25 per semester. Required fees: $586.85 per semester. Tuition and fees vary according to course load. *Financial support:* Career-related internships or fieldwork, Federal Work-Study, institutionally sponsored loans, scholarships/grants, traineeships, and unspecified assistantships available. Support available to part-time students. Financial award application deadline: 3/1; financial award applicants required to submit FAFSA. *Unit head:* Dr. Andrew Pomerantz, Director, 618-650-2202, E-mail: apomera@siue.edu. *Application contact:* Dr. Andrew Pomerantz, Director, 618-650-2202, E-mail: apomera@siue.edu.

Southern Illinois University Edwardsville, Graduate Studies and Research, School of Education, Department of Psychology, Program in Clinical Child and School Psychology, Edwardsville, IL 62026-0001. Offers MS. Part-time programs available. *Students:* 20 full-time (19 women); includes 1 minority (Asian American or Pacific Islander), 1 international. Average age 26. In 2009, 9 master's awarded. *Degree requirements:* For master's, thesis (for some programs), research project. *Entrance requirements:* For master's, GRE. Additional exam requirements/recommendations for international students: Required—TOEFL (minimum score 550 paper-based; 213 computer-based; 79 iBT), IELTS (minimum score 6.5). *Application deadline:* For fall admission, 2/1 for domestic and international students. Application fee: $30. Electronic applications accepted. *Expenses:* Tuition, state resident: part-time $1252.50 per semester. Tuition, nonresident: part-time $3131.25 per semester. Required fees: $586.85 per semester. Tuition and fees vary according to course load. *Financial support:* Career-related internships or fieldwork, Federal Work-Study, institutionally sponsored loans, scholarships/grants, traineeships, and unspecified assistantships available. Support available to part-time students. Financial award application deadline: 3/1; financial award applicants required to submit FAFSA. *Unit head:* Dr. Emily Krohn, Director, 618-650-2202, E-mail: ekrohn@siue.edu. *Application contact:* Dr. Emily Krohn, Director, 618-650-2202, E-mail: ekrohn@siue.edu.

Southern Methodist University, Dedman College, Department of Psychology, Program in Clinical Psychology, Dallas, TX 75275. Offers PhD. *Faculty:* 16 full-time (6 women), 7 part-time/adjunct (all women). *Students:* 16 full-time (14 women); includes 4 minority (1 American Indian/Alaska Native, 1 Asian American or Pacific Islander, 2 Hispanic Americans). Average age 32. 84 applicants, 8% accepted, 4 enrolled. In 2009, 1 doctorate awarded. *Degree requirements:* For doctorate, comprehensive exam, thesis/dissertation, research presentation and publication. *Entrance requirements:* For doctorate, GRE General Test, minimum GPA of 3.0, 3 letters of recommendation. Additional exam requirements/recommendations for international students: Required—TOEFL (minimum score 550 paper-based). *Application deadline:* For fall admission, 1/1 priority date for domestic and international students. Application fee: $60. Electronic applications accepted. *Financial support:* In 2009–10, 9 students received support, including 8 research assistantships with full tuition reimbursements available (averaging $14,000 per year); career-related internships or fieldwork also available. Financial award application deadline: 1/1; financial award applicants required to submit FAFSA. *Faculty research:* Family violence, family assessment, anxiety disorders, personality disorders. Total annual research expenditures: $500,000. *Unit head:* Dr. Robert B. Hampson, Director, 214-768-2734, Fax: 214-768-3910, E-mail: rhampson@smu.edu. *Application contact:* Ann Conner, Assistant to Director of Graduate Studies, 214-768-4924, Fax: 214-768-3910, E-mail: aconner@smu.edu.

Southern New Hampshire University, School of Liberal Arts, Manchester, NH 03106-1045. Offers clinical services for adults psychiatric disabilities (Certificate); clinical services for children and adolescents with psychiatric disabilities (Certificate); clinical services for persons with co-occurring substance abuse and psychiatric disabilities (Certificate); community mental health (MS); fiction writing (MFA); non-fiction writing (MFA); teaching English as a foreign language (MS). Part-time and evening/weekend programs available. *Degree requirements:* For master's, one foreign language, thesis. *Entrance requirements:* For master's, minimum GPA of 2.75: MS-TEFL, 3.0: MFA. Additional exam requirements/recommendations for international students: Required—TOEFL (minimum score 550 paper-based; 213 computer-based; 79 iBT), IELTS (minimum score 6.5), TWE (minimum score 5). Electronic applications accepted. *Expenses:* Contact institution. *Faculty research:* Action research, state of the art practice in behavioral health services, wraparound approaches to working with youth, learning styles.

Spalding University, Graduate Studies, College of Social Sciences and Humanities, School of Professional Psychology, Louisville, KY 40203-2188. Offers clinical psychology (MA, Psy D). *Accreditation:* APA (one or more programs are accredited). Part-time programs available. *Faculty:* 9 full-time (5 women), 12 part-time/adjunct (3 women). *Students:* 100 full-time (76 women), 47 part-time (35 women); includes 16 minority (3 African Americans, 2 American Indian/Alaska Native, 7 Asian Americans or Pacific Islanders, 4 Hispanic Americans), 1 international. Average age 30. 122 applicants, 46% accepted, 34 enrolled. In 2009, 14 master's, 16 doctorates awarded. Terminal master's awarded for partial completion of doctoral program. *Degree requirements:* For master's, comprehensive exam; for doctorate, thesis/dissertation. *Entrance requirements:* For master's, GRE General Test, 18 hours of undergraduate course work in psychology, interview; for doctorate, GRE General Test, interview, 18 hours of coursework in psychology. Additional exam requirements/recommendations for international students: Required—TOEFL (minimum score 535 paper-based; 203 computer-based). *Application deadline:* For fall admission, 1/15 for domestic students, 2/15 for international students. Application fee: $30. *Expenses:* Tuition: Full-time $11,340; part-time $630 per credit hour. Tuition and fees vary according to program. *Financial support:* In 2009–10, 112 students received support, including 41 research assistantships with partial tuition reimbursements available (averaging $4,831 per year); career-related internships or fieldwork, Federal Work-Study, scholarships/grants, and unspecified assistantships also available. Financial award application deadline: 3/15; financial award applicants required to submit FAFSA. *Faculty research:* Substance abuse, prayer research, end-of-life issues, complementary and alternative medicine, research methodology and statistical inference. *Unit head:* Dr. Steven Katsikas, Chair, 502-585-9911 Ext. 2700, E-mail: skatsikas@spalding.edu. *Application contact:* Elizabeth A. Simpson, Administrative Assistant, 502-585-7127, Fax: 502-585-7159, E-mail: esimpson@spalding.edu.

State University of New York at Binghamton, Graduate School, School of Arts and Sciences, Department of Psychology, Specialization in Clinical Psychology, Binghamton, NY 13902-6000. Offers MA, PhD. *Accreditation:* APA (one or more programs are accredited). *Students:* 20 full-time (16 women), 18 part-time (14 women); includes 5 minority (2 African Americans, 3 Hispanic Americans), 1 international. Average age 28. 211 applicants, 2% accepted, 4 enrolled. In 2009, 9 master's, 10 doctorates awarded. *Degree requirements:* For master's, thesis; for doctorate, thesis/dissertation, departmental qualifying exam. *Entrance requirements:* For master's and doctorate, GRE General Test, GRE Subject Test. Additional exam requirements/recommendations for international students: Required—TOEFL (minimum score 550 paper-based; 213 computer-based; 80 iBT). *Application deadline:* For fall admission, 12/15 priority date for domestic and international students. Applications are processed on a rolling basis. Application fee: $60. Electronic applications accepted. *Financial support:* Fellowships, research assistantships, teaching assistantships, career-related internships or fieldwork, Federal Work-Study, institutionally sponsored loans, scholarships/grants, traineeships, health care benefits, and unspecified assistantships available. Financial award application deadline: 2/15; financial award applicants required to submit FAFSA. *Unit head:* Dr. Stephen Lisman, Graduate Coordinator, 607-777-4929, E-mail: slisman@binghamton.edu. *Application contact:* Victoria Williams, Recruiting and Admissions Coordinator, 607-777-2151, Fax: 607-777-2501, E-mail: vwilliam@binghamton.edu.

Stony Brook University, State University of New York, Graduate School, College of Arts and Sciences, Department of Psychology, Program in Clinical Psychology, Stony Brook, NY 11794. Offers PhD. *Accreditation:* APA. *Students:* 38 full-time (35 women); includes 5 minority

(2 Asian Americans or Pacific Islanders, 3 Hispanic Americans). Average age 27. 322 applicants, 3% accepted. In 2009, 7 doctorates awarded. *Degree requirements:* For doctorate, thesis/dissertation. *Entrance requirements:* For doctorate, GRE General Test, GRE Subject Test. Additional exam requirements/recommendations for international students: Required—TOEFL. *Application deadline:* For fall admission, 1/15 for domestic students. Application fee: $60. *Expenses:* Tuition, state resident: full-time $8370; part-time $349 per credit. Tuition, nonresident: full-time $13,250; part-time $552 per credit. Required fees: $933. *Unit head:* Dr. Daniel O'Leary, Head, 631-632-7850, E-mail: k.d.oleary@stonybrook.edu. *Application contact:* Graduate Director, 631-632-7792, Fax: 631-632-7876.

Suffolk University, College of Arts and Sciences, Department of Psychology, Boston, MA 02108-2770. Offers clinical psychology (PhD). *Accreditation:* APA. *Faculty:* 19 full-time (11 women). *Students:* 37 full-time (33 women), 2 part-time (both women); includes 1 Asian American or Pacific Islander, 3 Hispanic Americans, 2 international. Average age 26. 252 applicants, 10% accepted, 13 enrolled. In 2009, 14 doctorates awarded. *Degree requirements:* For doctorate, thesis/dissertation, practicum. *Entrance requirements:* For doctorate, GRE General Test or MAT, 2 letters of recommendation, resume. Additional exam requirements/recommendations for international students: Required—TOEFL (minimum score 550 paper-based; 213 computer-based; 80 iBT). *Application deadline:* For fall admission, 12/15 for domestic and international students. Applications are processed on a rolling basis. Application fee: $50. Electronic applications accepted. *Expenses:* Contact institution. *Financial support:* In 2009–10, 39 students received support, including 38 fellowships with full and partial tuition reimbursements available (averaging $19,539 per year); career-related internships or fieldwork, Federal Work-Study, and institutionally sponsored loans also available. Support available to part-time students. Financial award application deadline: 4/1; financial award applicants required to submit FAFSA. *Faculty research:* Olfaction decision-making in substance-dependent individuals, ego development, experiential avoidance in generalized anxiety disorder. *Unit head:* Dr. Krisanne Bursik, Chairperson, 617-573-8293, Fax: 617-367-2924, E-mail: kbursik@suffolk.edu. *Application contact:* Judith Reynolds, Director of Graduate Admissions, 617-573-8302, Fax: 617-305-1733, E-mail: grad.admission@suffolk.edu.

Syracuse University, College of Arts and Sciences, Program in Clinical Psychology, Syracuse, NY 13244. Offers PhD. *Accreditation:* APA. *Students:* 25 full-time (18 women), 3 part-time (all women); includes 2 minority (both Asian Americans or Pacific Islanders), 2 international. Average age 28. 117 applicants, 6% accepted, 3 enrolled. In 2009, 4 doctorates awarded. *Degree requirements:* For doctorate, thesis/dissertation. *Entrance requirements:* For doctorate, GRE General Test, GRE Subject Test. Additional exam requirements/recommendations for international students: Required—TOEFL (minimum score 100 iBT). *Application deadline:* For fall admission, 1/1 priority date for domestic and international students. Application fee: $75. Electronic applications accepted. *Expenses:* Tuition: Full-time $26,808; part-time $1117 per credit. Required fees: $1024. *Financial support:* Fellowships with full tuition reimbursements, research assistantships with full and partial tuition reimbursements, teaching assistantships with full and partial tuition reimbursements available. Financial award application deadline: 1/1; financial award applicants required to submit FAFSA. *Unit head:* Dr. Kevin S. Masters, Graduate Director, 315-443-3666, Fax: 315-443-4085, E-mail: kemaster@syr.edu. *Application contact:* Sue Bova, Information Contact, 315-443-1050, E-mail: skbova@syr.edu.

Syracuse University, School of Education, Program in Clinical Mental Health Counseling, Syracuse, NY 13244. Offers MS. *Entrance requirements:* For master's, GRE General Test or MAT, interview. Additional exam requirements/recommendations for international students: Required—TOEFL (minimum score 100 iBT). *Application deadline:* For fall admission, 2/1 priority date for domestic students; for spring admission, 10/15 priority date for domestic and international students. Electronic applications accepted. *Expenses:* Tuition: Full-time $26,808; part-time $1117 per credit. Required fees: $1024. *Financial support:* Application deadline: 1/1. *Unit head:* Dr. Dennis Gilbride, Department Chair, 315-443-2266, E-mail: ddgilbri@syr.edu. *Application contact:* Liza Rochelson, Graduate Recruiter, School of Education, 315-443-2505, E-mail: e-gradrcrt@syr.edu.

Teachers College, Columbia University, Graduate Faculty of Education, Department of Counseling and Clinical Psychology, Program in Clinical Psychology, New York, NY 10027-6696. Offers PhD. *Accreditation:* APA. *Faculty:* 4 full-time (2 women). *Students:* 16 full-time (10 women), 28 part-time (20 women); includes 10 minority (2 African Americans, 7 Asian Americans or Pacific Islanders, 1 Hispanic American), 5 international. Average age 30. 93 applicants, 6% accepted, 5 enrolled. In 2009, 8 doctorates awarded. *Application deadline:* For fall admission, 12/15 for domestic students. Application fee: $65. *Financial support:* Career-related internships or fieldwork, Federal Work-Study, institutionally sponsored loans, and tuition waivers (partial) available. Support available to part-time students. Financial award application deadline: 2/1. *Faculty research:* Psychotherapy education, trauma, stress, psychopathology, life span and aging issues. *Unit head:* Maria Miville, Head, 212-678-3257. *Application contact:* Melba Remice, Assistant Director of Admission, 212-678-4035, Fax: 212-678-4171, E-mail: ms2545@columbia.edu.

Temple University, Graduate School, College of Liberal Arts, Department of Psychology, Program in Clinical Psychology, Philadelphia, PA 19122-6096. Offers PhD. *Accreditation:* APA. *Degree requirements:* For doctorate, thesis/dissertation. *Entrance requirements:* For doctorate, GRE General Test, minimum GPA of 3.0. Additional exam requirements/recommendations for international students: Required—TOEFL (minimum score 550 paper-based; 213 computer-based; 79 iBT). Electronic applications accepted. *Faculty research:* Depression, addictive disorders, parenting and families, social phobia, child and adolescent treatment research.

Texas A&M University, College of Liberal Arts, Department of Psychology, College Station, TX 77843. Offers behavioral and cellular neuroscience (MS, PhD); clinical psychology (MS, PhD); cognitive psychology (MS, PhD); developmental psychology (MS, PhD); industrial/organizational psychology (MS, PhD); social psychology (MS, PhD). *Accreditation:* APA (one or more programs are accredited). *Faculty:* 36. *Students:* 84 full-time (58 women), 6 part-time (5 women); includes 26 minority (6 African Americans, 3 Asian Americans or Pacific Islanders, 17 Hispanic Americans), 6 international. In 2009, 12 master's, 8 doctorates awarded. *Degree requirements:* For master's, thesis; for doctorate, comprehensive exam (for some programs), thesis/dissertation. *Entrance requirements:* For master's and doctorate, GRE General Test. Additional exam requirements/recommendations for international students: Required—TOEFL. *Application deadline:* For fall admission, 1/5 for domestic and international students. Application fee: $50 ($75 for international students). Electronic applications accepted. *Expenses:* Tuition, state resident: full-time $3991; part-time $221.74 per credit hour. Tuition, nonresident: full-time $9049; part-time $502.74 per credit hour. *Financial support:* Fellowships with partial tuition reimbursements, research assistantships with partial tuition reimbursements, teaching assistantships with partial tuition reimbursements, career-related internships or fieldwork, institutionally sponsored loans, health care benefits, and unspecified assistantships available. Financial award application deadline: 1/5; financial award applicants required to submit FAFSA. *Unit head:* Dr. Les Morey, Head, 979-845-2581, Fax: 979-845-4727, E-mail: lmorey@psych.tamu.edu. *Application contact:* Sharon Starr, Graduate Admissions Supervisor, 979-458-1710, Fax: 979-845-4727, E-mail: gradadv@psyc.tamu.edu.

Texas Tech University, Graduate School, College of Arts and Sciences, Department of Psychology, Lubbock, TX 79409. Offers clinical psychology (PhD); counseling psychology (MA, PhD); experimental psychology (MA, PhD); psychology (MA, PhD). *Accreditation:* APA (one or more programs are accredited). Part-time programs available. *Faculty:* 25 full-time (11 women). *Students:* 96 full-time (69 women), 16 part-time (10 women); includes 13 minority (5 African Americans, 8 Hispanic Americans), 7 international. Average age 28. 248 applicants, 13% accepted, 18 enrolled. In 2009, 11 master's, 12 doctorates awarded. *Degree requirements:* For doctorate, thesis/dissertation. *Entrance requirements:* For master's and doctorate, GRE General Test, GRE Subject Test. Additional exam requirements/recommendations for international students: Required—TOEFL (minimum score 550 paper-based; 213 computer-based). *Application deadline:* For fall admission, 3/1 priority date for international students; for spring admission, 11/1 priority date for international students. Applications are processed on a rolling basis. Application fee: $50 ($75 for international students). Electronic applications accepted. *Expenses:* Tuition, state resident: full-time $5100; part-time $213 per credit hour. Tuition, nonresident: full-time $11,748; part-time $490 per credit hour. Required fees: $2298; $50 per credit hour. $555 per semester. *Financial support:* In 2009–10, 1 research assistantship with partial tuition reimbursement (averaging $11,742 per year), 69 teaching assistantships with partial tuition reimbursements (averaging $20,157 per year) were awarded; career-related internships or fieldwork, Federal Work-Study, and institutionally sponsored loans also available. Support available to part-time students. Financial award application deadline: 4/15; financial award applicants required to submit FAFSA. *Faculty research:* Failure/success in relationships, peer rejection in school, stress and coping, group processes, clinical and health psychology. Total annual research expenditures: $144,070. *Unit head:* Dr. Susan S. Hendrick, Chair, 806-742-3711 Ext. 224, Fax: 806-742-0818, E-mail: s.hendrick@ttu.edu. *Application contact:* Dr. Lee M. Cohen, Director of Clinical Program, 806-742-3711 Ext. 254, Fax: 806-742-0818, E-mail: lee.cohen@ttu.edu.

Towson University, College of Graduate Studies and Research, Program in Clinical Psychology, Towson, MD 21252-0001. Offers MA. Part-time and evening/weekend programs available. *Degree requirements:* For master's, thesis (for some programs), exams. *Entrance requirements:* For master's, GRE, minimum GPA of 3.0, 15 credits in related course work. Additional exam requirements/recommendations for international students: Required—TOEFL. Electronic applications accepted. *Faculty research:* Cognitive behavior, issues affecting the aging, relaxation hypnosis and imagery, medicalization of male sexuality.

Troy University, Graduate School, College of Education, Program in Counseling and Psychology, Troy, AL 36082. Offers agency counsleing (Ed S); clinical mental health (MS); community counseling (MS, Ed S); corrections counseling (MS); rehabilitation counseling (MS); school psychology (MS, Ed S); school psychometry (MS); social service counseling (MS); student affairs counseling (MS); substance abuse counseling (MS). *Accreditation:* ACA; CORE; NCATE. Part-time and evening/weekend programs available. *Students:* 375 full-time (302 women), 753 part-time (642 women); includes 664 minority (610 African Americans, 8 American Indian/Alaska Native, 9 Asian Americans or Pacific Islanders, 37 Hispanic Americans). Average age 33. 493 applicants, 92% accepted. In 2009, 102 master's, 191 other advanced degrees awarded. *Degree requirements:* For master's, comprehensive exam, thesis. *Entrance requirements:* For master's, MAT, minimum GPA of 2.5. Additional exam requirements/recommendations for international students: Required—TOEFL (minimum score 523 paper-based; 193 computer-based; 70 iBT), IELTS (minimum score 6). *Application deadline:* Applications are processed on a rolling basis. Application fee: $50. Electronic applications accepted. *Unit head:* Dr. Andrew Creamer, Chair, 334-670-3350, Fax: 334-670-32961, E-mail: drcreamer@troy.edu. *Application contact:* Brenda K. Campbell, Director of Graduate Admissions, 334-670-3178, Fax: 334-670-3733, E-mail: bcamp@troy.edu.

Uniformed Services University of the Health Sciences, School of Medicine, Graduate Programs in the Biomedical Sciences and Public Health, Department of Medical and Clinical Psychology, Bethesda, MD 20814. Offers clinical psychology (PhD); medical and clinical psychology (clinical/dual track) (PhD); medical and clinical psychology (research track) (PhD). Clinical psychology available to active duty military only. *Accreditation:* APA. *Faculty:* 8 full-time (3 women), 42 part-time/adjunct (13 women). *Students:* 24 full-time (14 women); includes 2 minority (1 African American, 1 Hispanic American). Average age 27. 69 applicants, 16% accepted, 8 enrolled. In 2009, 3 doctorates awarded. Terminal master's awarded for partial completion of doctoral program. *Degree requirements:* For doctorate, comprehensive exam, thesis/dissertation, qualifying exam. *Entrance requirements:* For doctorate, GRE General Test, minimum GPA of 3.0, U.S. citizenship. Additional exam requirements/recommendations for international students: Required—TOEFL. *Application deadline:* For fall admission, 1/15 priority date for domestic and international students. Applications are processed on a rolling basis. Application fee: $0. Electronic applications accepted. *Financial support:* In 2009–10, fellowships with full tuition reimbursements (averaging $26,000 per year); career-related internships or fieldwork, scholarships/grants, health care benefits, and tuition waivers (full) also available. *Faculty research:* Addictive and appetitive behavior, psychopharmacology, stress and eating, obesity, health. *Unit head:* Dr. Andrew M. Waters, Graduate Program Director, 301-295-9675, Fax: 301-295-3034, E-mail: andrew.waters@usuhs.mil. *Application contact:* Elena Marina Sherman, Graduate Program Coordinator, 301-295-3913, Fax: 301-295-6772, E-mail: elena.sherman@usuhs.mil.

Union College, Graduate Programs, Department of Psychology, Barbourville, KY 40906-1499. Offers clinical psychology (MA); counseling psychology (MA); school psychology (MA).

Union Institute & University, MA Program in Psychology and Counseling, Brattleboro, VT 05301. Offers clinical mental health counseling (MA); clinical psychology (MA); counseling psychology (MA); developmental psychology (MA); educational psychology (MA); organizational psychology (MA). Postbaccalaureate distance learning degree programs offered (minimal on-campus study). *Faculty:* 2 full-time (1 woman), 8 part-time/adjunct (2 women). *Students:* 57 full-time (50 women), 20 part-time (16 women); includes 4 minority (1 African American, 3 Hispanic Americans). Average age 41. In 2009, 23 master's awarded. *Degree requirements:* For master's, thesis, internship (depending on concentration). *Application deadline:* Applications are processed on a rolling basis. Electronic applications accepted. Tuition and fees vary according to course load, degree level, campus/location and program. *Unit head:* Dr. Nicholas Young, Director, 802-257-8911, E-mail: nick.young@myunion.edu. *Application contact:* Diane Robinson, Director of Admissions, Brattleboro, 800-336-6794, E-mail: diane.robinson@myunion.edu.

Union Institute & University, PsyD Program in Clinical Psychology, Brattleboro, VT 05301. Offers family therapy (Psy D). Postbaccalaureate distance learning degree programs offered (minimal on-campus study). *Faculty:* 5 full-time (3 women), 5 part-time/adjunct (2 women). *Students:* 40 full-time (29 women), 2 part-time (both women); includes 6 minority (3 African Americans, 1 Asian American or Pacific Islander, 2 Hispanic Americans). Average age 43. *Degree requirements:* For doctorate, comprehensive exam, thesis/dissertation, internship, practicum. *Entrance requirements:* For doctorate, master's degree, letters of recommendation, interview. *Application deadline:* Applications are processed on a rolling basis. Application fee: $50. Tuition and fees vary according to course load, degree level, campus/location and program. *Financial support:* Federal Work-Study, scholarships/grants, and tuition waivers (partial) available. Financial award application deadline: 5/1; financial award applicants required to submit FAFSA. *Unit head:* Dr. William Lax, Dean, 802-254-0152, E-mail: william.lax@myunion.edu. *Application contact:* Diane Robinson, Director of Admissions-Brattleboro, 800-336-6794, E-mail: diane.robinson@myunion.edu.

Universidad de Iberoamerica, Graduate School, San Jose, Costa Rica. Offers clinical neuropsychology (PhD); clinical psychology (M Psych); educational psychology (M Psych); forensic psychology (M Psych); hospital management (MHA); intensive care nursing (MN); medicine (MD). *Entrance requirements:* For master's, 2 letters of recommendation, interview.

Université Laval, Faculty of Social Sciences, School of Psychology, Programs in Psychology, Québec, QC G1K 7P4, Canada. Offers clinical psychology (PhD); community psychology (PhD); psychology (PhD, Psy D). *Degree requirements:* For doctorate, comprehensive exam, thesis/dissertation. *Entrance requirements:* For doctorate, comprehension of written English, knowledge of French, interview. Electronic applications accepted.

University at Albany, State University of New York, College of Arts and Sciences, Department of Psychology, Albany, NY 12222-0001. Offers autism (Certificate); biopsychology (PhD);

Clinical Psychology

University at Albany, State University of New York (continued)
clinical psychology (PhD); general/experimental psychology (PhD); industrial/organizational psychology (PhD); psychology (MA); social/personality psychology (PhD). *Accreditation:* APA (one or more programs are accredited). *Degree requirements:* For doctorate, thesis/dissertation. *Entrance requirements:* For doctorate, GRE General Test, GRE Subject Test. Additional exam requirements/recommendations for international students: Required—TOEFL (minimum score 550 paper-based; 213 computer-based). Electronic applications accepted.

University at Buffalo, the State University of New York, Graduate School, College of Arts and Sciences, Department of Psychology, Buffalo, NY 14260. Offers behavioral neuroscience (PhD); clinical psychology (PhD); cognitive psychology (PhD); general psychology (MA); social-personality psychology (PhD). *Accreditation:* APA (one or more programs are accredited). *Faculty:* 32 full-time (12 women), 8 part-time/adjunct (6 women). *Students:* 94 full-time (64 women), 7 part-time (2 women); includes 5 minority (2 African Americans, 3 Hispanic Americans), 12 international. Average age 27. 353 applicants, 11% accepted. In 2009, 18 master's, 7 doctorates awarded. Terminal master's awarded for partial completion of doctoral program. *Degree requirements:* For master's, project; for doctorate, thesis/dissertation. *Entrance requirements:* For master's and doctorate, GRE General Test. Additional exam requirements/recommendations for international students: Required—TOEFL (minimum score 550 paper-based; 213 computer-based; 79 iBT). *Application deadline:* For fall admission, 1/5 for domestic and international students. Application fee: $50. Electronic applications accepted. *Financial support:* In 2009–10, 81 students received support, including 20 fellowships with full tuition reimbursements available (averaging $14,400 per year), 1 research assistantship with full tuition reimbursement available (averaging $10,400 per year), 38 teaching assistantships with full tuition reimbursements available (averaging $10,400 per year); career-related internships or fieldwork, Federal Work-Study, institutionally sponsored loans, scholarships/grants, and tuition waivers (partial) also available. Financial award application deadline: 1/5; financial award applicants required to submit FAFSA. *Faculty research:* Neural, endocrine, and molecular bases of behavior; adult mood and anxiety disorders; relationship dysfunction; attention deficit/hyperactivity disorder; psycho-linguistics. Total annual research expenditures: $7.9 million. *Unit head:* Dr. Paul A. Luce, Chair, 716-645-3650 Ext. 203, Fax: 716-645-3801, E-mail: psychair@acsu.buffalo.edu. *Application contact:* Michele Nowacki, Coordinator of Admissions, 716-645-3650 Ext. 209, Fax: 716-645-3801, E-mail: psych@acsu.buffalo.edu.

The University of Alabama, Graduate School, College of Arts and Sciences, Department of Psychology, Tuscaloosa, AL 35487. Offers clinical psychology (PhD); experimental psychology (PhD). *Accreditation:* APA. *Faculty:* 22 full-time (9 women), 2 part-time/adjunct (both women). *Students:* 77 full-time (60 women), 19 part-time (11 women); includes 13 minority (6 African Americans, 3 Asian Americans or Pacific Islanders, 4 Hispanic Americans), 4 international. Average age 27. 266 applicants, 10% accepted, 16 enrolled. In 2009, 14 doctorates awarded. *Median time to degree:* Of those who began their doctoral program in fall 2001, 78% received their degree in 8 years or less. *Degree requirements:* For doctorate, thesis/dissertation, internship for clinical students. *Entrance requirements:* For doctorate, GRE. Additional exam requirements/recommendations for international students: Required—TOEFL (minimum score 550 paper-based). *Application deadline:* For fall admission, 12/1 for domestic and international students. Application fee: $50 ($60 for international students). Electronic applications accepted. *Expenses:* Tuition, state resident: full-time $7000. Tuition, nonresident: full-time $19,200. *Financial support:* In 2009–10, 73 students received support, including 12 fellowships with full tuition reimbursements available (averaging $15,000 per year), 34 research assistantships with full and partial tuition reimbursements available (averaging $11,142 per year), 26 teaching assistantships with tuition reimbursements available (averaging $11,142 per year); career-related internships or fieldwork, institutionally sponsored loans, scholarships/grants, health care benefits, and unspecified assistantships also available. Financial award application deadline: 12/1. *Faculty research:* Cognitive development/disability, child clinical, psychology and law, health/aging, social psychology. Total annual research expenditures: $2.1 million. *Unit head:* Dr. Beverly E. Thorn, Chair, 205-348-1919, Fax: 205-348-8648, E-mail: bthorn@bama.ua.edu. *Application contact:* Colett Thomas, Information Contact, 205-348-1913, Fax: 205-348-8648, E-mail: cthomas@as.ua.edu.

University of Alaska Anchorage, College of Arts and Sciences, Department of Psychology, Anchorage, AK 99508. Offers clinical psychology (MS); clinical-community psychology with rural-indigenous emphasis (PhD). Part-time programs available. *Degree requirements:* For master's, thesis. *Entrance requirements:* For master's, GRE General Test, GRE Subject Test, interview, references; for doctorate, interview, bachelor's or master's degree in psychology. Additional exam requirements/recommendations for international students: Required—TOEFL (minimum score 550 paper-based; 213 computer-based). *Faculty research:* Substance abuse, childhood autism, biofeedback, psychological assessment, mental health in Native Alaskans.

University of Alaska Fairbanks, College of Liberal Arts, Department of Psychology, Fairbanks, AK 99775-6480. Offers clinical-community psychology (PhD), including rural cross-cultural emphasis. *Faculty:* 10 full-time (5 women), 3 part-time/adjunct (1 woman). *Students:* 4 full-time (1 woman), 20 part-time (17 women); includes 8 minority (1 African American, 5 American Indian/Alaska Native, 2 Hispanic Americans), 1 international. Average age 35. 34 applicants, 32% accepted, 9 enrolled. In 2009, 1 doctorate awarded. *Degree requirements:* For doctorate, comprehensive exam, thesis/dissertation, oral exam, oral defense. *Entrance requirements:* For doctorate, disclosure statement. Additional exam requirements/recommendations for international students: Required—TOEFL (minimum score 550 paper-based; 213 computer-based; 80 iBT). *Application deadline:* For fall admission, 12/15 for domestic and international students. Application fee: $60. *Expenses:* Tuition, state resident: full-time $7584; part-time $316 per credit. Tuition, nonresident: full-time $15,504; part-time $646 per credit. Required fees: $23 per credit. $135 per semester. Tuition and fees vary according to course level, course load and reciprocity agreements. *Financial support:* In 2009–10, 2 fellowships (averaging $15,270 per year), 7 research assistantships (averaging $16,089 per year), 8 teaching assistantships (averaging $15,611 per year) were awarded; career-related internships or fieldwork, Federal Work-Study, scholarships/grants, health care benefits, and unspecified assistantships also available. Support available to part-time students. Financial award application deadline: 7/1; financial award applicants required to submit FAFSA. *Faculty research:* Clinical and community psychology; rural, indigenous, and cultural psychology. *Unit head:* Dr. Dani Sheppard, Department Chair, 907-474-7007, Fax: 907-474-5781, E-mail: fypsych@uaf.edu. *Application contact:* Dr. Dani Sheppard, Department Chair, 907-474-7007, Fax: 907-474-5781, E-mail: fypsych@uaf.edu.

The University of British Columbia, Faculty of Arts and Faculty of Graduate Studies, Department of Psychology, Vancouver, BC V6T 1Z4, Canada. Offers behavioral neuroscience (MA, PhD); clinical psychology (MA, PhD); cognitive science (MA, PhD); developmental psychology (MA, PhD); health psychology (MA, PhD); quantitative methods (MA, PhD); social/personality psychology (MA, PhD). *Accreditation:* APA (one or more programs are accredited). Terminal master's awarded for partial completion of doctoral program. *Degree requirements:* For master's, thesis; for doctorate, comprehensive exam, thesis/dissertation. *Entrance requirements:* For master's and doctorate, GRE General Test. Additional exam requirements/recommendations for international students: Required—TOEFL (minimum score 550 paper-based; 230 computer-based; 80 iBT). Electronic applications accepted. *Faculty research:* Clinical, developmental, social/personality, cognition, behavioral neuroscience.

University of Calgary, Faculty of Graduate Studies, Faculty of Social Sciences, Department of Psychology, Program in Clinical Psychology, Calgary, AB T2N 1N4, Canada. Offers M Sc, PhD. *Degree requirements:* For master's, thesis, practical training; for doctorate, thesis/dissertation, practical training. *Entrance requirements:* For master's, GRE General Test, bachelor's degree in psychology or equivalent, minimum GPA of 3.6; for doctorate, GRE General Test, bachelor's degree in psychology, master's degree. Additional exam requirements/recommendations for international students: Required—TOEFL (minimum score 600 paper-based; 250 computer-based). Electronic applications accepted. *Faculty research:* Depression, schizophrenia, aging, neuropsychology, cognitive and linguistic development in infancy.

University of California, San Diego, Office of Graduate Studies, Group in Clinical Psychology, La Jolla, CA 92093. Offers PhD. Electronic applications accepted.

University of California, Santa Barbara, Graduate Division, Gevirtz Graduate School of Education, Santa Barbara, CA 93106-9490. Offers counseling, clinical and school psychology (PhD), including clinical psychology, counseling psychology, school psychology; education (M Ed, MA, PhD), including child and adolescent development (MA, PhD), cultural perspectives and comparative education (MA, PhD), educational leadership and organizations (MA, PhD), research methodology (MA, PhD), special education disabilities and risk studies (MA), special education, disabilities and risk studies (PhD), teaching (M Ed), teaching and learning (MA, PhD); educational leadership (Ed D); school psychology (M Ed); MA/PhD. *Accreditation:* APA (one or more programs are accredited). Postbaccalaureate distance learning degree programs offered (minimal on-campus study). *Faculty:* 42 full-time (20 women), 10 part-time/adjunct (4 women). *Students:* 390 full-time (303 women); includes 149 minority (14 African Americans, 3 American Indian/Alaska Native, 57 Asian Americans or Pacific Islanders, 75 Hispanic Americans), 16 international. Average age 31. 717 applicants, 40% accepted, 170 enrolled. In 2009, 140 master's, 46 doctorates awarded. Terminal master's awarded for partial completion of doctoral program. *Degree requirements:* For master's, comprehensive exam (for some programs), thesis (for some programs); for doctorate, comprehensive exam (for some programs), thesis/dissertation, qualifying exam. *Entrance requirements:* For master's, GRE, 3 letters of recommendation, resume/curriculum vitae; for doctorate, GRE, 3 letters of recommendation, statement of purpose, personal achievements/contributions statement, resume/curriculum vitae, transcripts for post-secondary institutions attended. Additional exam requirements/recommendations for international students: Required—TOEFL (minimum score 550 paper-based; 213 computer-based; 80 iBT) or IELTS (minimum score 7). Application fee: $70 ($90 for international students). Electronic applications accepted. *Financial support:* In 2009–10, 253 students received support, including 206 fellowships with full and partial tuition reimbursements available (averaging $5,000 per year), 62 research assistantships with full and partial tuition reimbursements available (averaging $6,200 per year), 87 teaching assistantships with partial tuition reimbursements available (averaging $6,500 per year); career-related internships or fieldwork, Federal Work-Study, institutionally sponsored loans, scholarships/grants, traineeships, health care benefits, and unspecified assistantships also available. Financial award applicants required to submit FAFSA. *Faculty research:* Professional development, early childhood development, school violence, literacy, science/math initiative. Total annual research expenditures: $4.4 million. *Unit head:* Dr. Jane Conoley, Chair, 805-893-2185, E-mail: jane-conoley@education.ucsb.edu. *Application contact:* Kathryn Marie Tucciarone, Student Affairs Officer, 805-893-2137, E-mail: katiet@education.ucsb.edu.

University of Central Florida, College of Sciences, Department of Psychology, Program in Clinical Psychology, Orlando, FL 32816. Offers MA, MS, PhD. *Accreditation:* APA. Part-time and evening/weekend programs available. *Students:* 66 full-time (53 women), 4 part-time (3 women); includes 12 minority (1 African American, 2 Asian Americans or Pacific Islanders, 9 Hispanic Americans), 2 international. Average age 26. 97 applicants, 30% accepted, 21 enrolled. In 2009, 14 master's, 7 doctorates awarded. *Degree requirements:* For master's, thesis or alternative, clinical internship; for doctorate, thesis/dissertation, candidacy exam, internship. *Entrance requirements:* For master's and doctorate, GRE General Test, minimum GPA of 3.0 in last 60 hours, resume. Additional exam requirements/recommendations for international students: Required—TOEFL. *Application deadline:* For fall admission, 2/15 for domestic students. Application fee: $30. Electronic applications accepted. *Expenses:* Tuition, state resident: part-time $306.31 per credit hour. Tuition, nonresident: part-time $1099.01 per credit hour. Part-time tuition and fees vary according to degree level and program. *Financial support:* In 2009–10, 36 students received support, including 17 fellowships with partial tuition reimbursements available (averaging $4,500 per year), 4 research assistantships with partial tuition reimbursements available (averaging $7,500 per year), 22 teaching assistantships with partial tuition reimbursements available (averaging $5,200 per year); career-related internships or fieldwork, Federal Work-Study, institutionally sponsored loans, tuition waivers (partial), and unspecified assistantships also available. Financial award application deadline: 3/1; financial award applicants required to submit FAFSA. *Faculty research:* Professional ethical decision making, computer experience and anxiety, effects of expert testimony on decision making in a rape trial, religiosity, relationship beliefs and marital adjustment. *Unit head:* Dr. Deborah Beidel, Director, 407-254-3908, E-mail: dbeidel@mail.ucf.edu. *Application contact:* Dr. Deborah Beidel, Director, 407-254-3908, E-mail: dbeidel@mail.ucf.edu.

University of Cincinnati, Graduate School, McMicken College of Arts and Sciences, Department of Psychology, Cincinnati, OH 45221. Offers clinical psychology (PhD); experimental psychology (PhD). *Accreditation:* APA. *Degree requirements:* For doctorate, comprehensive exam, thesis/dissertation. *Entrance requirements:* For doctorate, GRE General Test. Additional exam requirements/recommendations for international students: Required—TOEFL. *Faculty research:* Neuropsychology, human factors, health.

University of Colorado Denver, College of Liberal Arts and Sciences, Program in Clinical Health Psychology, Denver, CO 80217-3364. Offers PhD. *Students:* 9 full-time (7 women), 1 international. 28 applicants, 18% accepted, 4 enrolled. *Unit head:* Dr. Allison Bashe, Program Director, 303-556-2669, E-mail: allison.bashe@cudenver.edu. *Application contact:* Dr. Brenda Allen, Associate Dean of Student Affairs, 303-556-6713, E-mail: brenda.j.allen@ucdenver.edu.

University of Connecticut, Graduate School, College of Liberal Arts and Sciences, Department of Psychology, Storrs, CT 06269. Offers behavioral neuroscience (PhD); biopsychology (PhD); clinical psychology (MA, PhD); cognition and instruction (PhD); developmental psychology (MA, PhD); ecological psychology (PhD); experimental psychology (PhD); general psychology (MA, PhD); health psychology (Graduate Certificate); industrial/organizational psychology (PhD); language and cognition (PhD); neuroscience (PhD); occupational health psychology (Graduate Certificate); social psychology (MA, PhD). *Accreditation:* APA. *Faculty:* 59 full-time (26 women). *Students:* 194 full-time (133 women), 24 part-time (12 women); includes 48 minority (12 African Americans, 21 Asian Americans or Pacific Islanders, 15 Hispanic Americans), 25 international. Average age 28. 585 applicants, 4% accepted, 14 enrolled. In 2009, 22 master's, 24 doctorates awarded. Terminal master's awarded for partial completion of doctoral program. *Degree requirements:* For master's, comprehensive exam; for doctorate, thesis/dissertation. *Entrance requirements:* For master's and doctorate, GRE General Test, GRE Subject Test. Additional exam requirements/recommendations for international students: Required—TOEFL (minimum score 550 paper-based; 213 computer-based). *Application deadline:* For fall admission, 2/1 priority date for domestic and international students; for spring admission, 11/1 for domestic students, 10/1 for international students. Applications are processed on a rolling basis. Application fee: $55. Electronic applications accepted. *Expenses:* Tuition, state resident: full-time $4725; part-time $525 per credit. Tuition, nonresident: full-time $12,267; part-time $1363 per credit. Required fees: $346 per semester. Tuition and fees vary according to course load. *Financial support:* In 2009–10, 109 research assistantships with full tuition reimbursements, 72 teaching assistantships with full tuition reimbursements were awarded; fellowships, career-related internships or fieldwork, Federal Work-Study, scholarships/grants, health care benefits, and unspecified assistantships also available. Financial award application deadline: 2/1; financial award applicants required to submit FAFSA. *Unit head:* Charles A. Lowe, Head, 860-486-3517, Fax: 860-486-2760, E-mail: charles.lowe@uconn.edu. *Application contact:* Charles A. Lowe, Head, 860-486-3517, Fax: 860-486-2760, E-mail: charles.lowe@uconn.edu.

University of Dayton, Graduate School, College of Arts and Sciences, Department of Psychology, Program in Clinical Psychology, Dayton, OH 45469-1300. Offers MA. Part-time programs available. *Faculty:* 8 full-time (3 women), 2 part-time/adjunct (1 woman). *Students:*

20 full-time (16 women); includes 5 minority (3 African Americans, 2 Hispanic Americans), 1 international. Average age 25. 99 applicants, 8% accepted, 8 enrolled. In 2009, 13 master's awarded. *Degree requirements:* For master's, thesis. *Entrance requirements:* For master's, GRE General Test, GRE Subject Test (recommended), minimum undergraduate GPA of 3.0, 3.3 during final 2 years of course work. Additional exam requirements/recommendations for international students: Required—TOEFL (minimum score 550 paper-based; 213 computer-based; 80 iBT). *Application deadline:* For fall admission, 3/1 priority date for domestic and international students; for winter admission, 7/1 priority date for international students; for spring admission, 1/1 priority date for international students. Application fee: $0 ($50 for international students). Electronic applications accepted. *Expenses:* Tuition: Full-time $8412; part-time $701 per credit hour. Required fees: $325; $65 per course. $25 per semester. Tuition and fees vary according to course load, degree level and program. *Financial support:* In 2009–10, 18 students received support, including 3 research assistantships with full tuition reimbursements available (averaging $10,096 per year); institutionally sponsored loans, traineeships, and tuition waivers (partial) also available. Financial award application deadline: 3/1. *Faculty research:* Family issues, modes and mechanisms of therapy, gender issues, personality disorders, stress and coping. *Unit head:* Dr. Roger N. Reeb, Director, 937-229-2395, Fax: 937-229-3900, E-mail: roger.reeb@notes.udayton.edu. *Application contact:* Graduate Admissions, 937-229-4411, Fax: 937-229-4729, E-mail: gradadmission@udayton.edu.

University of Delaware, College of Arts and Sciences, Department of Psychology, Newark, DE 19716. Offers behavioral neuroscience (PhD); clinical psychology (PhD); cognitive psychology (PhD); social psychology (PhD). *Accreditation:* APA. *Degree requirements:* For doctorate, thesis/dissertation. *Entrance requirements:* For doctorate, GRE General Test. Additional exam requirements/recommendations for international students: Required—TOEFL (minimum score 600 paper-based; 250 computer-based). Electronic applications accepted. *Faculty research:* Emotion development, neural and cognitive aspects of memory, neural control of feeding, intergroup relations, social cognition and communication.

University of Denver, Graduate School of Professional Psychology, Denver, CO 80208. Offers clinical psychology (Psy D); psychology (MA). *Accreditation:* APA. *Faculty:* 14 full-time (7 women), 32 part-time/adjunct (15 women). *Students:* 203 full-time (161 women), 26 part-time (22 women); includes 24 minority (6 African Americans, 2 American Indian/Alaska Native, 7 Asian Americans or Pacific Islanders, 9 Hispanic Americans), 4 international. Average age 26. 524 applicants, 38% accepted, 114 enrolled. In 2009, 74 master's, 36 doctorates awarded. *Degree requirements:* For doctorate, paper, internship. *Entrance requirements:* For master's and doctorate, GRE General Test. Additional exam requirements/recommendations for international students: Required—TOEFL. *Application deadline:* For fall admission, 1/5 for domestic students. Application fee: $50. Electronic applications accepted. *Expenses:* Tuition: Full-time $34,596; part-time $961 per quarter hour. Required fees: $4 per quarter hour. Tuition and fees vary according to course load, campus/location and program. *Financial support:* In 2009–10, 36 teaching assistantships with full and partial tuition reimbursements (averaging $3,500 per year) were awarded; career-related internships or fieldwork, Federal Work-Study, institutionally sponsored loans, scholarships/grants, and clinical assistantships also available. Support available to part-time students. Financial award application deadline: 3/1; financial award applicants required to submit FAFSA. *Unit head:* Dr. Peter Buirski, Dean, 303-871-2382. *Application contact:* Admissions, 303-871-3873, Fax: 303-871-4220, E-mail: gsppinfo@du.edu.

University of Detroit Mercy, College of Liberal Arts and Education, Department of Psychology, Program in Clinical Psychology, Detroit, MI 48221. Offers MA, PhD. *Accreditation:* APA. *Degree requirements:* For doctorate, departmental qualifying exam.

University of Florida, Graduate School, College of Public Health and Health Professions, Department of Clinical and Health Psychology, Gainesville, FL 32611. Offers PhD. *Accreditation:* APA. *Degree requirements:* For doctorate, thesis/dissertation. *Entrance requirements:* For doctorate, GRE General Test, minimum GPA of 3.0. Additional exam requirements/recommendations for international students: Required—TOEFL (minimum score 550 paper-based; 213 computer-based). Electronic applications accepted. *Faculty research:* Child psychology, pediatric psychology, health/medical psychology, neuropsychology.

University of Guelph, Graduate Program Services, College of Social and Applied Human Sciences, Department of Psychology, Guelph, ON N1G 2W1, Canada. Offers applied social psychology (MA, PhD); clinical psychology applied development emphasis (PhD); clinical psychology applied developmental emphasis (MA); industrial/organizational psychology (MA, PhD); neuroscience and applied cognitive science (MA, PhD). *Degree requirements:* For master's, thesis; for doctorate, comprehensive exam, thesis/dissertation. *Entrance requirements:* For master's, GRE General Test, GRE Subject Test, minimum B+ average during previous 2 years of course work; for doctorate, GRE General Test, GRE Subject Test, minimum A- average. Additional exam requirements/recommendations for international students: Required—TOEFL (minimum score 89 iBT). Electronic applications accepted. *Faculty research:* Organizational psychology, reading comprehension and mathematical ability, drug addiction and relapse, gender issues and culture, memory, clinical psychology.

University of Hartford, College of Arts and Sciences, Department of Psychology, Program in Clinical Practices, West Hartford, CT 06117-1599. Offers clinical practices (Psy D); psychology (MA). *Accreditation:* APA. *Degree requirements:* For master's, comprehensive exam, thesis optional. *Entrance requirements:* For master's, GRE General Test, GRE Subject Test, minimum GPA of 3.0, 3 letters of recommendation. Additional exam requirements/recommendations for international students: Required—TOEFL (minimum score 550 paper-based; 213 computer-based). Electronic applications accepted. *Faculty research:* Attachment issues, child abuse prevention, master's psychologist issues, neuropsychology.

University of Hawaii at Manoa, Graduate Division, College of Social Sciences, Department of Psychology, Honolulu, HI 96822. Offers clinical psychology (PhD); community and cultural psychology (PhD); community and culture (MA); psychology (MA, PhD, Graduate Certificate). *Accreditation:* APA (one or more programs are accredited). Part-time programs available. *Faculty:* 27 full-time (10 women), 17 part-time/adjunct (1 woman). *Students:* 70 full-time (52 women), 18 part-time (13 women); includes 27 minority (2 African Americans, 1 American Indian/Alaska Native, 21 Asian Americans or Pacific Islanders, 3 Hispanic Americans), 14 international. Average age 28. 202 applicants, 10% accepted, 16 enrolled. In 2009, 5 master's, 9 doctorates, 1 other advanced degree awarded. Terminal master's awarded for partial completion of doctoral program. *Degree requirements:* For master's, comprehensive exam, thesis; for doctorate, comprehensive exam, thesis/dissertation. *Entrance requirements:* For master's and doctorate, GRE General Test, GRE Subject Test. Additional exam requirements/recommendations for international students: Required—TOEFL (minimum score 600 paper-based; 250 computer-based; 100 iBT), IELTS (minimum score 7). *Application deadline:* For fall admission, 1/1 for domestic and international students. Application fee: $60. *Expenses:* Tuition, state resident: full-time $8900; part-time $372 per credit. Tuition, nonresident: full-time $21,400; part-time $898 per credit. Required fees: $207 per semester. *Financial support:* In 2009–10, 6 students received support, including 6 fellowships (averaging $3,969 per year), 41 research assistantships (averaging $17,740 per year), 14 teaching assistantships (averaging $14,802 per year); career-related internships or fieldwork, institutionally sponsored loans, and tuition waivers (full and partial) also available. Financial award application deadline: 1/1. *Faculty research:* Cross-cultural psychology, health psychology, marine mammals, child/adult psychopathology. Total annual research expenditures: $1.3 million. *Application contact:* Catherine Sophian, Graduate Chair, 808-956-8414, Fax: 808-956-4700, E-mail: csophian@hawaii.edu.

University of Houston–Clear Lake, School of Human Sciences and Humanities, Programs in Human Sciences, Houston, TX 77058-1098. Offers behavioral sciences (MA), including criminology, cross cultural studies, general psychology, sociology; clinical psychology (MA); criminology (MA); cross cultural studies (MA); family therapy (MA); fitness and human performance (MA); school psychology (MA). *Accreditation:* AAMFT/COAMFTE. Part-time and evening/weekend programs available. Postbaccalaureate distance learning degree programs offered (minimal on-campus study). *Degree requirements:* For master's, thesis or alternative. *Entrance requirements:* For master's, GRE General Test. Additional exam requirements/recommendations for international students: Required—TOEFL (minimum score 550 paper-based; 213 computer-based). Electronic applications accepted. *Faculty research:* Smoking cessation, adolescent sexuality, white collar crime, serial murder, human factors/human computer interaction.

University of Indianapolis, Graduate Programs, School of Psychological Sciences, Indianapolis, IN 46227-3697. Offers clinical psychology (Psy D); clinical psychology/mental health counseling (MA). *Accreditation:* APA. *Faculty:* 6 full-time (1 woman), 1 (woman) part-time/adjunct. *Students:* 107 full-time (96 women), 63 part-time (51 women); includes 8 minority (6 African Americans, 1 Asian American or Pacific Islander, 1 Hispanic American), 7 international. Average age 27. *Degree requirements:* For master's, practicum; for doctorate, comprehensive exam, thesis/dissertation, 1200 hours of clinical practicum, 2000 hour internship. *Entrance requirements:* For master's, GRE, 3 letters of recommendation; for doctorate, GRE, minimum GPA of 3.0, 18 hours of course work in psychology, 3 letters of recommendation. Additional exam requirements/recommendations for international students: Required—TOEFL (minimum score 550 paper-based; 213 computer-based). *Application deadline:* For fall admission, 2/25 for domestic students. Application fee: $50. *Financial support:* Federal Work-Study available. *Unit head:* Dr. E. John McIlvried, Dean, 317-788-3274, Fax: 317-788-3480, E-mail: jmcilvried@uindy.edu. *Application contact:* Dr. E. John McIlvried, Associate Provost for Graduate and International Programs, 317-788-3274, E-mail: jmcilvried@uindy.edu.

The University of Kansas, Graduate Studies, College of Liberal Arts and Sciences, Department of Psychology and Department of Psychology, Program in Clinical Child Psychology, Lawrence, KS 66045. Offers MA, PhD. *Accreditation:* APA. *Faculty:* 4 full-time (1 woman). *Students:* 22 full-time (14 women), 3 part-time (2 women); includes 6 minority (2 African Americans, 3 Asian Americans or Pacific Islanders, 1 Hispanic American). Average age 27. 106 applicants, 7% accepted, 4 enrolled. In 2009, 3 master's, 6 doctorates awarded. *Degree requirements:* For master's, thesis; for doctorate, comprehensive exam, thesis/dissertation, clinical internship. *Entrance requirements:* For master's, GRE General Test, GRE Subject Test; for doctorate, GRE General Test, GRE Subject Test, minimum GPA of 3.5. Additional exam requirements/recommendations for international students: Required—TOEFL. *Application deadline:* For fall admission, 12/1 for domestic and international students. Application fee: $45 ($55 for international students). Electronic applications accepted. *Expenses:* Tuition, state resident: full-time $6492; part-time $270.50 per credit hour. Tuition, nonresident: full-time $15,510; part-time $646.25 per credit hour. Required fees: $847; $70.56 per credit hour. Tuition and fees vary according to course load and program. *Financial support:* Fellowships with tuition reimbursements, research assistantships with full tuition reimbursements, teaching assistantships with full tuition reimbursements, career-related internships or fieldwork, scholarships/grants, traineeships, health care benefits, and unspecified assistantships available. Financial award application deadline: 12/1. *Faculty research:* Pediatric psychology; serious emotional disorders; responses to disasters and terrorism; anxiety, stress, and coping; psychotherapy with children; childhood obesity; child maltreatment; classification issues. *Unit head:* Dr. Michael Roberts, Director, 785-864-4226, Fax: 785-864-5024, E-mail: mroberts@ku.edu. *Application contact:* Tammie Zordel, Graduate Admissions, 785-864-4226, Fax: 785-864-5024, E-mail: ccpp@ku.edu.

University of Kentucky, Graduate School, College of Arts and Sciences, Program in Psychology, Lexington, KY 40506-0032. Offers clinical psychology (MA); experimental psychology (MA). *Accreditation:* APA (one or more programs are accredited). *Degree requirements:* For master's, comprehensive exam, thesis; for doctorate, comprehensive exam, thesis/dissertation. *Entrance requirements:* For master's, GRE General Test, minimum undergraduate GPA of 2.75; for doctorate, GRE General Test, minimum graduate GPA of 3.0. Additional exam requirements/recommendations for international students: Required—TOEFL (minimum score 550 paper-based; 213 computer-based). Electronic applications accepted. *Faculty research:* Psychopharmacology and teratology, behavioral neuroscience, social psychology, cognitive psychology, development and developmental psychobiology.

University of La Verne, College of Arts and Sciences, Department of Psychology, Program in Clinical-Community Psychology, La Verne, CA 91750-4443. Offers Psy D. Part-time programs available. *Faculty:* 12 full-time (5 women), 22 part-time/adjunct (14 women). *Students:* 54 full-time (48 women), 35 part-time (28 women); includes 46 minority (11 African Americans, 8 Asian Americans or Pacific Islanders, 27 Hispanic Americans). Average age 28. In 2009, 15 doctorates awarded. *Degree requirements:* For doctorate, thesis/dissertation, clinical internship, competency exams, practicum, personal psychotherapy. *Entrance requirements:* For doctorate, minimum GPA of 3.0 undergraduate, 3.5 graduate; 3 letters of recommendation; curriculum vitae. Additional exam requirements/recommendations for international students: Required—TOEFL (minimum score 600 paper-based; 250 computer-based). *Application deadline:* For fall admission, 1/15 for domestic and international students. Application fee: $75. *Expenses:* Contact institution. *Financial support:* Career-related internships or fieldwork, institutionally sponsored loans, scholarships/grants, and unspecified assistantships available. Financial award application deadline: 3/2; financial award applicants required to submit FAFSA. *Unit head:* Dr. Valerie Jordan, Chairperson, 909-593-3511 Ext. 4174, E-mail: vjordan@laverne.edu. *Application contact:* Connie Hamlow, Admissions Information Specialist, 909-593-3511 Ext. 4519, Fax: 909-392-2761, E-mail: gradadmission@laverne.edu.

University of Louisville, Graduate School, College of Arts and Sciences, Department of Psychological and Brain Sciences, Louisville, KY 40292-0001. Offers clinical psychology (PhD); experimental psychology (PhD). *Accreditation:* APA. *Faculty:* 22 full-time (9 women), 4 part-time/adjunct (1 woman). *Students:* 68 full-time (49 women); includes 6 minority (3 African Americans, 2 Asian Americans or Pacific Islanders, 1 Hispanic American), 7 international. Average age 30. 194 applicants, 8% accepted, 4 enrolled. In 2009, 11 doctorates awarded. *Degree requirements:* For doctorate, thesis/dissertation, preliminary exam, research, internship. *Entrance requirements:* For doctorate, GRE General Test. Additional exam requirements/recommendations for international students: Required—TOEFL. *Application deadline:* For fall admission, 12/1 for domestic students, 11/1 for international students. Application fee: $50. Electronic applications accepted. *Financial support:* In 2009–10, 36 students received support, including 7 fellowships (averaging $22,000 per year), 29 teaching assistantships (averaging $22,000 per year); career-related internships or fieldwork also available. *Faculty research:* Health psychology, geropsychology, psychopathology, cognitive and development science, neuroscience and neuropsychology, vision and hearing. *Unit head:* Dr. Suzanne Meeks, Chair, 502-852-6068, Fax: 502-852-8904, E-mail: smeeks@louisville.edu. *Application contact:* Mary E. Leggett, Director, Graduate Admissions, 502-852-3101, Fax: 502-852-6536, E-mail: gradadm@louisville.edu.

University of Maine, Graduate School, College of Liberal Arts and Sciences, Department of Psychology, Orono, ME 04469. Offers clinical psychology (PhD); developmental psychology (MA); experimental psychology (MA, PhD); social psychology (MA). *Accreditation:* APA (one or more programs are accredited). *Faculty:* 17 full-time (8 women), 7 part-time/adjunct (3 women). *Students:* 27 full-time (16 women), 9 part-time (7 women); includes 2 minority (1 Asian American or Pacific Islander, 1 Hispanic American), 1 international. Average age 28. 134 applicants, 8% accepted, 7 enrolled. In 2009, 3 master's, 3 doctorates awarded. *Degree requirements:* For master's, thesis; for doctorate, thesis/dissertation. *Entrance requirements:* For master's and doctorate, GRE General Test, GRE Subject Test. Additional exam requirements/recommendations for international students: Required—TOEFL. *Application deadline:* For fall admission, 2/1 priority date for domestic students. Applications are processed on a rolling basis. Application fee: $65. Electronic applications accepted. *Financial support:* In 2009–10, 3 research assistantships with tuition reimbursements (averaging $14,063 per year), 21 teaching assistantships with tuition reimbursements (averaging $12,790 per year) were awarded; Federal

Clinical Psychology

University of Maine (continued)

Work-Study, institutionally sponsored loans, and tuition waivers (full and partial) also available. Financial award application deadline: 3/1. *Faculty research:* Social development, hypertension and aging, attitude change, self-confidence in achievement situations, health psychology. *Unit head:* Dr. Michael Robbins, Chair, 207-581-2051, Fax: 207-581-6128. *Application contact:* Scott G. Delcourt, Associate Dean of the Graduate School, 207-581-3291, Fax: 207-581-3232, E-mail: graduate@maine.edu.

University of Manitoba, Faculty of Graduate Studies, Faculty of Arts, Department of Psychology, Winnipeg, MB R3T 2N2, Canada. Offers clinical psychology (PhD); psychology (MA, PhD); school psychology (MA). *Accreditation:* APA (one or more programs are accredited). *Degree requirements:* For master's, thesis; for doctorate, one foreign language, thesis/dissertation. *Entrance requirements:* For master's and doctorate, GRE General Test.

University of Maryland, College Park, Academic Affairs, College of Behavioral and Social Sciences, Department of Psychology, College Park, MD 20742. Offers clinical psychology (PhD); developmental psychology (PhD); experimental psychology (PhD); industrial psychology (MA, MS, PhD); social psychology (PhD). *Accreditation:* APA (one or more programs are accredited). *Faculty:* 71 full-time (35 women), 8 part-time/adjunct (4 women). *Students:* 82 full-time (67 women); includes 13 minority (2 African Americans, 4 Asian Americans or Pacific Islanders, 7 Hispanic Americans), 12 international. 568 applicants, 4% accepted, 8 enrolled. In 2009, 13 master's, 10 doctorates awarded. *Degree requirements:* For master's, thesis; for doctorate, variable foreign language requirement, comprehensive exam, thesis/dissertation. *Entrance requirements:* For master's and doctorate, GRE General Test, GRE Subject Test, minimum GPA of 3.5, research and/or work experience, 3 letters of recommendation. *Application deadline:* For fall admission, 12/1 for domestic and international students. Applications are processed on a rolling basis. Application fee: $60. Electronic applications accepted. *Expenses:* Tuition, area resident: Part-time $471 per credit hour. Tuition, state resident: part-time $471 per credit hour. Tuition, nonresident: part-time $1016 per credit hour. Required fees: $337.04 per term. *Financial support:* In 2009–10, 11 fellowships with full and partial tuition reimbursements (averaging $19,195 per year), 5 research assistantships (averaging $17,734 per year), 45 teaching assistantships with tuition reimbursements (averaging $17,116 per year) were awarded; career-related internships or fieldwork, Federal Work-Study, and scholarships/grants also available. Support available to part-time students. Financial award applicants required to submit FAFSA. *Faculty research:* Social stereotyping and prejudice, anxiety disorders, auditory neuroethology, counseling and social psychology. Total annual research expenditures: $3.8 million. *Unit head:* Thomas S. Wallsten, Chair, 301-405-3562, Fax: 301-314-9566, E-mail: twallst@umd.edu. *Application contact:* Dean of Graduate School, 301-405-0358, Fax: 301-314-9305.

University of Massachusetts Amherst, Graduate School, College of Natural Sciences, Department of Psychology, Amherst, MA 01003. Offers clinical psychology (MS, PhD); cognitive psychology (MS, PhD); developmental science (MS, PhD); psychology of peace and violence (MS, PhD); social psychology (MS, PhD). *Accreditation:* APA (one or more programs are accredited). *Faculty:* 48 full-time (22 women). *Students:* 57 full-time (42 women), 13 part-time (10 women); includes 15 minority (6 African Americans, 6 Asian Americans or Pacific Islanders, 3 Hispanic Americans), 8 international. Average age 28. 381 applicants, 4% accepted, 11 enrolled. In 2009, 11 master's, 8 doctorates awarded. Terminal master's awarded for partial completion of doctoral program. *Degree requirements:* For master's, thesis; for doctorate, comprehensive exam, thesis/dissertation. *Entrance requirements:* For master's and doctorate, GRE General Test, 3 letters of recommendation. Additional exam requirements/recommendations for international students: Required—TOEFL (minimum score 550 paper-based; 213 computer-based; 80 iBT), IELTS (minimum score 6.5). *Application deadline:* For fall admission, 12/1 for domestic and international students. Applications are processed on a rolling basis. Application fee: $50 ($65 for international students). Electronic applications accepted. *Expenses:* Tuition, state resident: full-time $2640; part-time $110 per credit. Tuition, nonresident: full-time $9936; part-time $414 per credit. Tuition and fees vary according to course load. *Financial support:* In 2009–10, 8 fellowships with full tuition reimbursements (averaging $12,620 per year), 52 research assistantships with full tuition reimbursements (averaging $9,491 per year), 55 teaching assistantships with full tuition reimbursements (averaging $10,829 per year) were awarded; career-related internships or fieldwork, Federal Work-Study, scholarships/grants, traineeships, health care benefits, tuition waivers (full), and unspecified assistantships also available. Support available to part-time students. Financial award application deadline: 12/1. *Unit head:* Dr. Linda M. Isbell, Graduate Program Director, 413-545-2503, Fax: 413-545-0996. *Application contact:* Jean M. Ames, Supervisor of Admissions, 413-545-0722, Fax: 413-577-0010, E-mail: gradadm@grad.umass.edu.

University of Massachusetts Boston, Office of Graduate Studies, College of Liberal Arts, Program in Clinical Psychology, Boston, MA 02125-3393. Offers PhD. *Accreditation:* APA. *Degree requirements:* For doctorate, thesis/dissertation, practicum, qualifying exam, internship, dissertation. *Entrance requirements:* For doctorate, GRE General Test, GRE Subject Test, minimum GPA of 2.75. *Faculty research:* Community psychology, psychology, racism and mental health, gender and culture, posttraumatic stress disorder.

University of Massachusetts Dartmouth, Graduate School, College of Arts and Sciences, Department of Psychology, North Dartmouth, MA 02747-2300. Offers behavior analyst (Post-baccalaureate Certificate); clinical psychology (MA); general psychology (MA). Part-time programs available. *Faculty:* 18 full-time (9 women), 8 part-time/adjunct (4 women). *Students:* 19 full-time (15 women), 39 part-time (30 women); includes 5 minority (3 African Americans, 2 Hispanic Americans), 1 international. Average age 29. 91 applicants, 51% accepted, 30 enrolled. In 2009, 7 master's awarded. *Degree requirements:* For master's, thesis (for some programs). *Entrance requirements:* For master's, GRE General Test, minimum GPA of 2.75, 3 letters of recommendation. Additional exam requirements/recommendations for international students: Required—TOEFL (minimum score 500 paper-based). *Application deadline:* For fall admission, 3/31 for domestic students, 1/31 for international students. Application fee: $40 ($60 for international students). Electronic applications accepted. *Expenses:* Tuition, state resident: full-time $2071; part-time $86.29 per credit. Tuition, nonresident: full-time $8099; part-time $337.46 per credit. Required fees: $9446. Tuition and fees vary according to class time, course load and reciprocity agreements. *Financial support:* In 2009–10, 1 research assistantship with full tuition reimbursement (averaging $10,000 per year), 9 teaching assistantships with full tuition reimbursements (averaging $3,500 per year) were awarded; career-related internships or fieldwork, Federal Work-Study, and unspecified assistantships also available. Support available to part-time students. Financial award application deadline: 3/1; financial award applicants required to submit FAFSA. *Faculty research:* Nonverbal communication, behavioral medicine, psychotherapy, intimate relationships, learning. Total annual research expenditures: $62,000. *Unit head:* Dr. Paul Donnelly, Director, Clinical Psychology, 508-999-8334, E-mail: pdonnelly@umassd.edu. *Application contact:* Elan Turcotte-Shamski, Graduate Admissions Officer, 508-999-8604, Fax: 508-999-8183, E-mail: graduate@umassd.edu.

University of Memphis, Graduate School, College of Arts and Sciences, Department of Psychology, Memphis, TN 38152-3230. Offers psychology (MS, PhD), including clinical (PhD), experimental (PhD), general psychology (MS), school (PhD); school psychology (MA, Ed S); MS/PhD. *Faculty:* 28 full-time (9 women), 4 part-time/adjunct (0 women). *Students:* 115 full-time (81 women), 22 part-time (15 women); includes 23 minority (15 African Americans, 1 American Indian/Alaska Native, 4 Asian Americans or Pacific Islanders, 3 Hispanic Americans), 7 international. Average age 27. 220 applicants, 15% accepted, 29 enrolled. In 2009, 31 master's, 9 doctorates awarded. *Degree requirements:* For master's, comprehensive exam (for some programs), thesis (for some programs), 37 credit hours (MA); 33 credit hours with thesis or 36 with exam (MS); for doctorate, comprehensive exam (for some programs), thesis/dissertation, 80 semester hours, major area paper; clinical: 1 year placement and 1 year internship; internship (school psychology). *Entrance requirements:* For master's, GRE; for doctorate, GRE (minimum combined score of 1100), minimum GPA of 2.75, 18 hours of undergraduate psychology courses, transcripts, personal statement, letters of recommendation; for Ed S, GRE (minimum combined score of 1100), minimum GPA of 2.75, 18 hours of undergraduate psychology courses, letters of recommendation. Additional exam requirements/recommendations for international students: Required—TOEFL. *Application deadline:* For fall admission, 12/5 for domestic students. Applications are processed on a rolling basis. Application fee: $35 ($60 for international students). Electronic applications accepted. *Expenses:* Tuition, state resident: full-time $6246; part-time $347 per credit hour. Tuition, nonresident: full-time $15,894; part-time $883 per credit hour. Required fees: $1160. Full-time tuition and fees vary according to course load, degree level and program. *Financial support:* In 2009–10, 66 students received support; fellowships with full tuition reimbursements available, research assistantships with full tuition reimbursements available, teaching assistantships with full tuition reimbursements available, Federal Work-Study, scholarships/grants, tuition waivers (partial), and unspecified assistantships available. Financial award application deadline: 2/15; financial award applicants required to submit FAFSA. *Faculty research:* Clinical health; school, child and family research; psychotherapy research; cognitive and behavioral neuroscience research; industrial-organizational research. *Unit head:* Dr. Robert Cohen, Coordinator of Graduate Programs, 901-678-4679, Fax: 901-678-2579, E-mail: rcohen@memphis.edu. *Application contact:* Lynell Connable, Graduate Secretary, 901-678-4340, Fax: 901-678-2579, E-mail: dconnabl@memphis.edu.

University of Miami, Graduate School, College of Arts and Sciences, Department of Psychology, Coral Gables, FL 33124. Offers adult clinical (PhD); behavioral neuroscience (PhD); child clinical (PhD); developmental psychology (PhD); health clinical (PhD); psychology (MS). *Accreditation:* APA (one or more programs are accredited). *Degree requirements:* For doctorate, comprehensive exam, thesis/dissertation. *Entrance requirements:* For doctorate, GRE General Test, minimum GPA of 3.5. Additional exam requirements/recommendations for international students: Required—TOEFL. Electronic applications accepted. *Faculty research:* Behavioral factors in cardiovascular disease and cancer adult psychopathology, developmental disabilities, social and emotional development, mechanisms of coping.

University of Michigan, Horace H. Rackham School of Graduate Studies, College of Literature, Science, and the Arts, Department of Psychology, Ann Arbor, MI 48451. Offers biopsychology (PhD); clinical psychology (PhD); cognition and perception (PhD); developmental psychology (PhD); personality and social contexts (PhD); social psychology (PhD). *Accreditation:* APA. *Faculty:* 87 full-time (40 women), 28 part-time/adjunct (16 women). *Students:* 147 full-time (101 women); includes 40 minority (15 African Americans, 2 American Indian/Alaska Native, 18 Asian Americans or Pacific Islanders, 5 Hispanic Americans), 25 international. Average age 27. 621 applicants, 10% accepted, 37 enrolled. In 2009, 25 doctorates awarded. *Degree requirements:* For doctorate, comprehensive exam, thesis/dissertation, oral defense of dissertation, preliminary exam. *Entrance requirements:* For doctorate, GRE General Test. Additional exam requirements/recommendations for international students: Required—TOEFL. *Application deadline:* For fall admission, 12/1 for domestic and international students. Application fee: $60 ($75 for international students). Electronic applications accepted. *Expenses:* Tuition, state resident: full-time $17,286; part-time $1099 per credit hour. Tuition, nonresident: full-time $34,944; part-time $2080 per credit hour. Required fees: $95 per semester. Tuition and fees vary according to course load, degree level and program. *Financial support:* In 2009–10, 133 students received support, including 52 fellowships with full tuition reimbursements available (averaging $20,900 per year), 16 research assistantships with full tuition reimbursements available (averaging $20,900 per year), 79 teaching assistantships with full tuition reimbursements available (averaging $16,694 per year); career-related internships or fieldwork also available. Financial award application deadline: 4/15. *Unit head:* Prof. Theresa Lee, Chair, 734-764-7429. *Application contact:* Laurie Brannan, Psychology Student Academic Affairs, 731-764-2580, Fax: 734-615-7584, E-mail: psych.saa@umich.edu.

University of Michigan–Dearborn, College of Arts, Sciences, and Letters, Master of Science in Psychology Program, Dearborn, MI 48128. Offers clinical health psychology (MS); health psychology (MS). Part-time programs available. *Faculty:* 8 full-time (4 women), 1 part-time/adjunct (0 women). *Students:* 23 full-time (19 women), 11 part-time (10 women); includes 6 minority (2 African Americans, 3 Asian Americans or Pacific Islanders, 1 Hispanic American). Average age 34. 40 applicants, 40% accepted, 13 enrolled. In 2009, 15 master's awarded. *Degree requirements:* For master's, oral defense of thesis. *Entrance requirements:* For master's, GRE, 3 letters of recommendation. Additional exam requirements/recommendations for international students: Required—TOEFL (minimum score 560 paper-based; 220 computer-based). *Application deadline:* For fall admission, 3/15 for domestic and international students. Application fee: $60 ($75 for international students). *Expenses:* Tuition, area resident: Part-time $504.10 per credit hour. Tuition, state resident: part-time $504.10 per credit hour. Tuition, nonresident: part-time $957.90 per credit hour. *Financial support:* In 2009–10, 4 students received support. Scholarships/grants available. *Faculty research:* Cardiovascular reactivity, coping, addiction, psychoneuroimmunology. *Unit head:* Dr. Pam McAuslan, Program Director, 313-593-5376, E-mail: pmcausla@umd.umich.edu. *Application contact:* Carol Ligienza, Graduate Program Coordinator, CASL Graduate Programs, 313-593-1183, Fax: 313-583-6700, E-mail: caslgrad@umd.umich.edu.

University of Minnesota, Twin Cities Campus, Graduate School, College of Liberal Arts, Department of Psychology, Program in Clinical Psychology, Minneapolis, MN 55455-0213. Offers PhD. *Accreditation:* APA. *Degree requirements:* For doctorate, comprehensive exam, thesis/dissertation, internship. *Entrance requirements:* For doctorate, GRE General Test, minimum GPA of 3.5; 12 credits of upper-level psychology courses, including statistics or psychological measurement; previous course work in abnormal psychology. Additional exam requirements/recommendations for international students: Required—TOEFL (minimum score 550 paper-based; 213 computer-based; 79 iBT).

University of Mississippi, Graduate School, College of Liberal Arts, Department of Psychology, Oxford, University, MS 38677. Offers clinical psychology (PhD); experimental psychology (PhD); psychology (MA). *Accreditation:* APA (one or more programs are accredited). *Faculty:* 18 full-time (8 women), 2 part-time/adjunct (both women). *Students:* 52 full-time (38 women), 6 part-time (4 women); includes 10 minority (7 African Americans, 1 American Indian/Alaska Native, 1 Asian American or Pacific Islander, 1 Hispanic American), 1 international. In 2009, 3 master's, 6 doctorates awarded. *Degree requirements:* For master's, thesis; for doctorate, thesis/dissertation. *Entrance requirements:* For master's, GRE General Test, minimum GPA of 3.0; for doctorate, GRE General Test. Additional exam requirements/recommendations for international students: Required—TOEFL. *Application deadline:* For fall admission, 1/15 for domestic students; for spring admission, 10/1 for domestic students. Applications are processed on a rolling basis. Application fee: $25. Electronic applications accepted. *Financial support:* Scholarships/grants available. Financial award application deadline: 3/1; financial award applicants required to submit FAFSA. *Unit head:* Dr. Michael T. Allen, Chairman, 662-915-5190, Fax: 662-915-5398, E-mail: mta1@olemiss.edu. *Application contact:* Dr. Christy M. Wyandt, Associate Dean, 662-915-7474, Fax: 662-915-7577, E-mail: cwyandt@olemiss.edu.

University of Missouri–Kansas City, College of Arts and Sciences, Department of Psychology, Kansas City, MO 64110-2499. Offers clinical psychology (PhD); community psychology (PhD); health psychology (PhD); psychology (MA). PhD (interdisciplinary) offered through the School of Graduate Studies. *Accreditation:* APA. *Faculty:* 12 full-time (9 women), 3 part-time/adjunct (2 women). *Students:* 15 full-time (12 women), 7 part-time (6 women); includes 2 minority (1 African American, 1 Hispanic American). Average age 31. 86 applicants, 3% accepted, 3 enrolled. In 2009, 4 master's, 4 doctorates awarded. Terminal master's awarded for partial completion of doctoral program. *Degree requirements:* For master's, thesis; for doctorate, comprehensive exam, thesis/dissertation, residency. *Entrance requirements:* For master's, GRE, minimum GPA of 3.5, letter of recommendation; for doctorate, GRE, minimum GPA of

3.25. Additional exam requirements/recommendations for international students: Required—TOEFL (minimum score 550 paper-based; 213 computer-based; 80 iBT). *Application deadline:* For fall admission, 1/15 for domestic and international students. Applications are processed on a rolling basis. Application fee: $45 ($50 for international students). Electronic applications accepted. *Expenses:* Tuition, state resident: full-time $5378; part-time $299 per credit hour. Tuition, nonresident: full-time $13,881; part-time $771 per credit hour. Required fees: $641; $71 per credit hour. Tuition and fees vary according to course load and program. *Financial support:* In 2009–10, 18 research assistantships (averaging $11,500 per year), 3 teaching assistantships (averaging $8,000 per year) were awarded; career-related internships or fieldwork, Federal Work-Study, and institutionally sponsored loans also available. Support available to part-time students. Financial award application deadline: 3/1; financial award applicants required to submit FAFSA. *Faculty research:* HIV/AIDS research group, psycho-oncology, sensory and cognitive neuroscience, cognitive psychophysiology, obesity and related metabolic disorders. Total annual research expenditures: $673,228. *Unit head:* Dr. Tamera Murdock, Chairperson/Professor, 816-235-1318, Fax: 816-235-1062, E-mail: murdockt@umkc.edu. *Application contact:* Dr. Lisa Terre, Director, Graduate Programs, 816-235-1318, Fax: 816-235-1062, E-mail: terrel@umkc.edu.

University of Missouri–St. Louis, College of Arts and Sciences, Department of Psychology, St. Louis, MO 63121. Offers behavioral neuroscience (PhD); clinical psychology respecialization (Certificate); community psychology (PhD); general psychology (MA); industrial/organizational psychology (PhD). *Accreditation:* APA (one or more programs are accredited). Evening/weekend programs available. *Faculty:* 21 full-time (10 women), 5 part-time/adjunct (3 women). *Students:* 35 full-time (29 women), 39 part-time (30 women); includes 4 minority (1 American Indian/Alaska Native, 1 Asian American or Pacific Islander, 2 Hispanic Americans). Average age 28. 208 applicants, 9% accepted, 13 enrolled. In 2009, 16 master's, 6 doctorates awarded. Terminal master's awarded for partial completion of doctoral program. *Degree requirements:* For master's, thesis; for doctorate, thesis/dissertation. *Entrance requirements:* For master's and doctorate, GRE General Test, GRE Subject Test, 3 letters of recommendation. Additional exam requirements/recommendations for international students: Required—TOEFL (minimum score 550 paper-based; 213 computer-based). *Application deadline:* For fall admission, 1/15 for domestic and international students. Application fee: $35 ($40 for international students). Electronic applications accepted. *Expenses:* Tuition, state resident: full-time $5377; part-time $297.70 per credit hour. Tuition, nonresident: full-time $13,882; part-time $771.20 per credit hour. Required fees: $220; $12.20 per credit hour. One-time fee: $12. Tuition and fees vary according to course level, campus/location and program. *Financial support:* In 2009–10, 7 research assistantships with full and partial tuition reimbursements (averaging $10,600 per year), 20 teaching assistantships with full and partial tuition reimbursements (averaging $9,788 per year) were awarded; fellowships with full tuition reimbursements also available. Financial award applicants required to submit FAFSA. *Faculty research:* Bereavement and loss, neuroscience, post-traumatic stress disorder, conflict and negotiation, social psychology. *Unit head:* Dr. George Taylor, Chair, 314-516-5391, Fax: 314-516-5392, E-mail: umslpsychology@msx.umsl.edu. *Application contact:* 314-516-5458, Fax: 314-516-6996, E-mail: gradadm@umsl.edu.

The University of Montana, Graduate School, College of Arts and Sciences, Department of Psychology, Missoula, MT 59812-0002. Offers clinical psychology (PhD); experimental psychology (PhD), including animal behavior psychology, developmental psychology; school psychology (MA, PhD, Ed S). *Accreditation:* APA (one or more programs are accredited). Terminal master's awarded for partial completion of doctoral program. *Degree requirements:* For master's, thesis; for doctorate, thesis/dissertation. *Entrance requirements:* For master's, doctorate, and Ed S, GRE General Test. Additional exam requirements/recommendations for international students: Required—TOEFL.

University of Nebraska–Lincoln, Graduate College, College of Arts and Sciences, Department of Psychology, Lincoln, NE 68588. Offers biopsychology (PhD); clinical psychology (PhD); cognitive psychology (PhD); developmental psychology (PhD); psychology (MA); social/personality psychology (PhD); JD/MA; JD/PhD. *Accreditation:* APA (one or more programs are accredited). *Degree requirements:* For master's, thesis optional; for doctorate, comprehensive exam, thesis/dissertation. *Entrance requirements:* For master's and doctorate, GRE General Test. Additional exam requirements/recommendations for international students: Required—TOEFL (minimum score 550 paper-based; 213 computer-based). Electronic applications accepted. *Faculty research:* Law and psychology, rural mental health, chronic mental illness, neuropsychology, child clinical psychology.

University of Nevada, Reno, Graduate School, College of Liberal Arts, Department of Psychology, Program in Clinical Psychology, Reno, NV 89557. Offers PhD. Terminal master's awarded for partial completion of doctoral program. *Degree requirements:* For doctorate, comprehensive exam, thesis/dissertation. *Entrance requirements:* For doctorate, GRE Subject Test (psychology), minimum GPA of 3.0. Additional exam requirements/recommendations for international students: Required—TOEFL (minimum score 500 paper-based; 173 computer-based; 61 iBT), IELTS (minimum score 6). Electronic applications accepted. *Faculty research:* Health behavior, domestic violence, verbal relations, anxiety.

University of New Brunswick Fredericton, School of Graduate Studies, Faculty of Arts, Department of Psychology, Fredericton, NB E3B 5A3, Canada. Offers clinical (PhD); experimental (MA). Part-time programs available. *Faculty:* 14 full-time (9 women). *Students:* 25 full-time (20 women), 2 part-time (both women). In 2009, 4 doctorates awarded. *Degree requirements:* For doctorate, comprehensive exam, thesis/dissertation. *Entrance requirements:* For doctorate, GRE General Test, GRE Subject Test, minimum GPA of 3.7. Additional exam requirements/recommendations for international students: Required—TOEFL (minimum score 600 paper-based). *Application deadline:* For fall admission, 1/15 priority date for domestic and international students. Application fee: $50 Canadian dollars. Tuition and fees charges are reported in Canadian dollars. *Expenses:* Tuition, area resident: Full-time $5562 Canadian dollars; part-time $2781 Canadian dollars per year. Required fees: $49.75 Canadian dollars per term. *Financial support:* In 2009–10, 8 fellowships (averaging $35,000 per year), 15 research assistantships (averaging $11,000 per year), 15 teaching assistantships (averaging $4,000 per year) were awarded. Financial award application deadline: 1/15. *Faculty research:* Depression, adolescence, human sexuality, family violence, autism. *Unit head:* Dr. Daniel Voyer, Director of Graduate Studies, 506-453-7974, Fax: 506-447-3063, E-mail: psycdogs@unb.ca. *Application contact:* Theresa Mills, Graduate Secretary, 506-453-4707, Fax: 506-447-3063, E-mail: tmills@unb.ca.

University of New Brunswick Saint John, Department of Psychology, Saint John, NB E2L 4L5, Canada. Offers applied and experimental psychology (PhD); clinical psychology (PhD); experimental psychology (MA). Part-time programs available. *Faculty:* 9 full-time (4 women). *Students:* 4 full-time (2 women), 1 (woman) part-time. In 2009, 3 master's, 1 doctorate awarded. *Degree requirements:* For master's, thesis. *Entrance requirements:* For master's, GRE General and Subject Tests, honours thesis. Additional exam requirements/recommendations for international students: Required—TOEFL (minimum score 550 paper-based), TWE. *Application deadline:* For fall admission, 2/1 for domestic students. Application fee: $50. *Financial support:* In 2009–10, 4 research assistantships (averaging $9,000 per year), 4 teaching assistantships (averaging $4,500 per year) were awarded; unspecified assistantships also available. Support available to part-time students. Financial award application deadline: 2/1. *Faculty research:* Psychopharmacology and addictions, forensic psychology and criminal justice, interpersonal relations, perception and graphical perception, lie detection. *Unit head:* Dr. Lily Both, Director of Graduate Studies, 506-648-5769, Fax: 506-648-5780, E-mail: lboth@unbsj.ca. *Application contact:* Frances Stevens, Secretary, 506-648-5640, Fax: 506-648-5780, E-mail: fstevens@unb.ca.

University of New Mexico, Graduate School, College of Arts and Sciences, Department of Psychology, Program in Clinical Psychology, Albuquerque, NM 87131-2039. Offers MS, PhD. *Accreditation:* APA (one or more programs are accredited). *Students:* 7 full-time (5 women); includes 2 minority (both Hispanic Americans). Average age 34. In 2009, 1 doctorate awarded. *Degree requirements:* For master's, thesis; for doctorate, comprehensive exam, thesis/dissertation, pre-doctoral internship. *Entrance requirements:* For doctorate, GRE General Test, GRE Subject Test (psychology), minimum GPA of 3.0. Additional exam requirements/recommendations for international students: Required—TOEFL. *Application deadline:* For fall admission, 1/15 priority date for domestic and international students. Applications are processed on a rolling basis. Application fee: $50. Electronic applications accepted. *Expenses:* Tuition, state resident: full-time $2099; part-time $233.20 per credit hour. Tuition, nonresident: full-time $6650. Required fees: $25 per semester. Tuition and fees vary according to course load, program and reciprocity agreements. *Financial support:* In 2009–10, research assistantships with full and partial tuition reimbursements (averaging $13,445 per year), teaching assistantships with full and partial tuition reimbursements (averaging $13,445 per year) were awarded; fellowships, career-related internships or fieldwork, Federal Work-Study, scholarships/grants, health care benefits, tuition waivers (full and partial), and unspecified assistantships also available. Financial award application deadline: 3/1; financial award applicants required to submit FAFSA. *Faculty research:* Addictive behaviors; cognitive, behavioral, community psychology; cross-cultural issues; eating disorders; empirically-supported treatment; health psychology; neurobiological, psychological trauma and sexual victimization. *Unit head:* Dr. Sarah Erickson, Director of Clinical Training, 505-277-4121, Fax: 505-277-1394, E-mail: erickson@unm.edu. *Application contact:* Tonya Bryant, Coordinator, Program Advisement, 505-277-5009, Fax: 505-277-1394, E-mail: advising@unm.edu.

The University of North Carolina at Chapel Hill, Graduate School, College of Arts and Sciences, Department of Psychology, Chapel Hill, NC 27599. Offers biological psychology (PhD); clinical psychology (PhD); cognitive psychology (PhD); developmental psychology (PhD); quantitative psychology (PhD); social psychology (PhD). *Accreditation:* APA. *Degree requirements:* For doctorate, comprehensive exam, thesis/dissertation. *Entrance requirements:* For doctorate, GRE General Test, minimum GPA of 3.0. Electronic applications accepted. *Faculty research:* Expressed emotion, cognitive development, social cognitive neuroscience, human memory personality.

The University of North Carolina at Charlotte, Graduate School, College of Arts and Sciences, Department of Psychology, Program in Community/Clinical Psychology, Charlotte, NC 28223-0001. Offers MA. Part-time programs available. *Faculty:* 10 full-time (3 women), 5 part-time/adjunct (2 women). *Students:* 8 full-time (all women), 8 part-time (7 women); includes 4 minority (3 African Americans, 1 Hispanic American). Average age 26. 143 applicants, 4% accepted, 5 enrolled. In 2009, 10 master's awarded. Terminal master's awarded for partial completion of doctoral program. *Degree requirements:* For master's, comprehensive exam, thesis. *Entrance requirements:* For master's, GRE General Test, GRE Subject Test, minimum GPA of 3.0 in undergraduate major, 2.8 overall. Additional exam requirements/recommendations for international students: Required—TOEFL (minimum score 557 paper-based; 220 computer-based; 83 iBT). *Application deadline:* For fall admission, 3/1 for domestic and international students. Application fee: $55. Electronic applications accepted. *Financial support:* In 2009–10, 6 students received support, including 5 teaching assistantships (averaging $10,755 per year); career-related internships or fieldwork, Federal Work-Study, institutionally sponsored loans, scholarships/grants, and administrative assistantship also available. Support available to part-time students. Financial award application deadline: 4/1; financial award applicants required to submit FAFSA. *Faculty research:* Identifying biopsychosocial risk and resilience factors, development of community based support for youth, pain and emotion, posttraumatic disorders, relationships in online groups. Total annual research expenditures: $476,892. *Unit head:* Dr. David Gilmore, Interim Chair, 704-687-4731, Fax: 704-687-3096, E-mail: dcgilmor@uncc.edu. *Application contact:* Kathy B. Giddings, Director of Graduate Admissions, 704-687-5503, Fax: 704-687-3279, E-mail: gradadm@uncc.edu.

The University of North Carolina at Greensboro, Graduate School, College of Arts and Sciences, Department of Psychology, Greensboro, NC 27412-5001. Offers clinical psychology (MA, PhD); cognitive psychology (MA, PhD); developmental psychology (MA, PhD); social psychology (MA, PhD). *Accreditation:* APA (one or more programs are accredited). Terminal master's awarded for partial completion of doctoral program. *Degree requirements:* For master's, comprehensive exam, thesis; for doctorate, one foreign language, thesis/dissertation, preliminary exam. *Entrance requirements:* For master's and doctorate, GRE General Test. Additional exam requirements/recommendations for international students: Required—TOEFL. Electronic applications accepted. *Faculty research:* Sensory and perceptual determinants; evoked potential: disorders, deafness, and development.

University of North Dakota, Graduate School, College of Arts and Sciences, Department of Psychology, Grand Forks, ND 58202. Offers clinical psychology (PhD); counseling psychology (PhD); experimental psychology (PhD); forensic psychology (MA, MS); psychology (MA). *Accreditation:* APA (one or more programs are accredited). *Degree requirements:* For master's, thesis, final exam; for doctorate, comprehensive exam, thesis/dissertation, internship, final exam. *Entrance requirements:* For master's, GRE General Test, GRE Subject Test, minimum GPA of 3.0; for doctorate, GRE General Test, GRE Subject Test, minimum GPA of 3.5. Additional exam requirements/recommendations for international students: Required—TOEFL (minimum score 550 paper-based; 213 computer-based; 79 iBT), IELTS (minimum score 6.5). Electronic applications accepted. *Faculty research:* Developmental psychology, clinical social psychology, educational psychology, personality disorders.

University of North Texas, Robert B. Toulouse School of Graduate Studies, College of Arts and Sciences, Department of Psychology, Denton, TX 76203-5017. Offers clinical psychology (PhD); counseling psychology (MA, MS, PhD); experimental psychology (MA, MS, PhD); health psychology and behavioral medicine (PhD). *Accreditation:* APA (one or more programs are accredited). Terminal master's awarded for partial completion of doctoral program. *Degree requirements:* For master's, comprehensive exam, thesis or alternative; for doctorate, one foreign language, comprehensive exam, thesis/dissertation. *Entrance requirements:* For master's and doctorate, GRE General Test, interview. Additional exam requirements/recommendations for international students: Required—proof of English language proficiency required for non-native English speakers; Recommended—TOEFL (minimum score 550 paper-based; 213 computer-based; 79 iBT). *Application deadline:* Applications are processed on a rolling basis. Application fee: $50 ($75 for international students). Electronic applications accepted. *Expenses:* Tuition, state resident: full-time $4298; part-time $239 per contact hour. Tuition, nonresident: full-time $9878; part-time $549 per contact hour. Required fees: $265 per contact hour. *Financial support:* Fellowships, research assistantships, teaching assistantships, career-related internships or fieldwork, Federal Work-Study, and institutionally sponsored loans available. Financial award applicants required to submit FAFSA. *Application contact:* Graduate Coordinator, 940-565-2671, Fax: 940-565-4682, E-mail: amym@unt.edu.

University of Oregon, Graduate School, College of Arts and Sciences, Department of Psychology, Program in Clinical Psychology, Eugene, OR 97403. Offers PhD. *Accreditation:* APA. *Degree requirements:* For doctorate, thesis/dissertation. *Entrance requirements:* For doctorate, GRE General Test. Additional exam requirements/recommendations for international students: Required—TOEFL.

University of Puerto Rico, Río Piedras, College of Social Sciences, Department of Psychology, San Juan, PR 00931-3300. Offers clinical psychology (MA); industrial organizational psychology (MA); investigative academic psychology (MA); psychology (PhD); social-community psychology (MA). Part-time programs available. *Degree requirements:* For master's, comprehensive exam, thesis; for doctorate, comprehensive exam, thesis/dissertation, internship. *Entrance requirements:* For master's, GRE or PAEG, interview, minimum GPA of 3.0; for doctorate, GRE or PAEG, interview, master's degree, minimum GPA of 3.0. *Faculty research:* Intervention on Depressed Latino Youth, biosychosocial training.

University of Regina, Faculty of Graduate Studies and Research, Faculty of Arts, Department of Psychology, Regina, SK S4S 0A2, Canada. Offers clinical psychology (MA, PhD); experimental and applied psychology (MA, PhD). *Faculty:* 18 full-time (10 women). *Students:* 57 full-time (40

Clinical Psychology

University of Regina (continued)

women), 5 part-time (all women). 54 applicants, 30% accepted. In 2009, 6 master's, 5 doctorates awarded. *Degree requirements:* For master's, thesis; for doctorate, comprehensive exam, thesis/dissertation. *Entrance requirements:* For master's, GRE General Test, GRE Subject Test; for doctorate, GRE General Test, GRE Subject Test (optional for students who hold a master's degree from a Canadian university). Additional exam requirements/recommendations for international students: Required—TOEFL (minimum score 580 paper-based; 237 computer-based; 80 iBT). *Application deadline:* For fall admission, 2/15 for domestic students. Application fee: $90 ($100 for international students). Electronic applications accepted. *Financial support:* In 2009–10, 23 fellowships (averaging $19,000 per year), 3 research assistantships (averaging $16,910 per year), 10 teaching assistantships (averaging $6,650 per year) were awarded; career-related internships or fieldwork and scholarships/grants also available. Financial award application deadline: 6/15. *Faculty research:* Clinical, experimental and applied psychology. *Unit head:* Dr. William E. Smythe, Head, 306-585-4157, Fax: 306-585-5429, E-mail: william.smythe@uregina.ca. *Application contact:* Dr. Dongyan Blachford, Associate Dean, 306-585-5186, Fax: 306-337-2444, E-mail: dongyan.blachford@uregina.ca.

University of Rhode Island, Graduate School, College of Arts and Sciences, Department of Psychology, Kingston, RI 02881. Offers behavioral science (PhD); clinical psychology (MA, PhD); school psychology (MS, PhD). *Accreditation:* APA (one or more programs are accredited). Part-time programs available. *Faculty:* 25 full-time (10 women), 5 part-time/adjunct (1 woman). *Students:* 72 full-time (56 women), 33 part-time (27 women); includes 20 minority (7 African Americans, 6 Asian Americans or Pacific Islanders, 7 Hispanic Americans), 4 international. In 2009, 12 master's, 11 doctorates awarded. *Degree requirements:* For master's, comprehensive exam, thesis optional; for doctorate, thesis/dissertation. *Entrance requirements:* For master's and doctorate, GRE, 3 letters of recommendation. Additional exam requirements/recommendations for international students: Required—TOEFL (minimum score 550 paper-based; 213 computer-based). Application fee: $65. Electronic applications accepted. *Expenses:* Tuition, state resident: full-time $8828; part-time $490 per credit hour. Tuition, nonresident: full-time $22,100; part-time $1228 per credit hour. Required fees: $1118; $57 per semester. Tuition and fees vary according to program. *Financial support:* In 2009–10, 3 research assistantships with full and partial tuition reimbursements (averaging $8,519 per year), 20 teaching assistantships with full and partial tuition reimbursements (averaging $12,364 per year) were awarded. Financial award applicants required to submit FAFSA. Total annual research expenditures: $4.6 million. *Unit head:* Dr. Patricia Morokoff, Chairperson, 401-874-4239, Fax: 401-874-2157, E-mail: morokoff@uri.edu. *Application contact:* Dr. Patricia Morokoff, Chairperson, 401-874-4239, Fax: 401-874-2157, E-mail: morokoff@uri.edu.

University of Rochester, The College, Arts and Sciences, Department of Clinical and Social Sciences in Psychology, Rochester, NY 14627. Offers clinical psychology (PhD); developmental psychology (PhD); psychology (MA); social-personality psychology (PhD). *Accreditation:* APA (one or more programs are accredited). Terminal master's awarded for partial completion of doctoral program. *Degree requirements:* For doctorate, thesis/dissertation, qualifying exam. *Entrance requirements:* For doctorate, GRE General Test. Additional exam requirements/recommendations for international students: Required—TOEFL.

University of South Africa, College of Human Sciences, Pretoria, South Africa. Offers adult education (M Ed); African languages (MA, PhD); African politics (MA, PhD); Afrikaans (MA, PhD); ancient history (MA, PhD); ancient Near Eastern studies (MA, PhD); anthropology (MA, PhD); applied linguistics (MA); Arabic (MA, PhD); archaeology (MA); art history (MA); Biblical archaeology (MA); Biblical studies (M Th, D Th, PhD); Christian spirituality (M Th, D Th); church history (M Th, D Th); classical studies (MA, PhD); clinical psychology (MA); communication (MA, PhD); comparative education (M Ed, Ed D); consulting psychology (D Admin, D Com, PhD); curriculum studies (M Ed, Ed D); development studies (M Admin, MA, D Admin, PhD); didactics (M Ed, Ed D); education (M Tech); education management (M Ed, Ed D); educational psychology (M Ed); English (MA); environmental education (M Ed); French (MA, PhD); German (MA, PhD); Greek (MA); guidance and counseling (M Ed); health studies (MA, PhD), including health sciences education (MA), health services management (MA), medical and surgical nursing science (critical care general) (MA), midwifery and neonatal nursing science (MA), trauma and emergency care (MA); history (MA, PhD); history of education (Ed D); inclusive education (M Ed, Ed D); information and communications technology policy and regulation (MA); information science (MA, MIS, PhD); international politics (MA, PhD); Islamic studies (MA, PhD); Italian (MA, PhD); Judaica (MA, PhD); linguistics (MA, PhD); mathematical education (M Ed); mathematics education (MA); missiology (M Th, D Th); modern Hebrew (MA, PhD); musicology (MA, MMus, D Mus, PhD); natural science education (M Ed); New Testament (M Th, D Th); Old Testament (D Th); pastoral therapy (M Th, D Th); philosophy (MA); philosophy of education (M Ed, Ed D); politics (MA, PhD); Portuguese (MA, PhD); practical theology (M Th, D Th); psychology (MA, MS, PhD); psychology of education (M Ed, Ed D); public health (MA); religious studies (MA, D Th, PhD); Romance languages (MA); Russian (MA, PhD); Semitic languages (MA, PhD); social behavior studies in HIV/AIDS (MA); social science (mental health) (MA); social science in development studies (MA); social science in psychology (MA); social science in social work (MA); social science in sociology (MA); social work (MSW, DSW, PhD); socio-education (M Ed, Ed D); sociolinguistics (MA); sociology (MA, PhD); Spanish (MA, PhD); systematic theology (M Th, D Th); TESOL (teaching English to speakers of other languages) (MA); theological ethics (M Th, D Th); theory of literature (MA, PhD); urban ministries (D Th); urban ministry (M Th).

University of South Carolina, The Graduate School, College of Arts and Sciences, Department of Psychology, Program in Clinical/Community Psychology, Columbia, SC 29208. Offers clinical/community psychology (PhD); general psychology (MA). *Accreditation:* APA. *Degree requirements:* For master's, comprehensive exam, thesis; for doctorate, comprehensive exam, thesis/dissertation. *Entrance requirements:* For doctorate, GRE General Test, minimum GPA of 3.2. Additional exam requirements/recommendations for international students: Required—TOEFL. Electronic applications accepted. *Faculty research:* Developmental psychopathology, health disparities, community-level interventions for psychological well being.

University of South Carolina Aiken, Program in Applied Clinical Psychology, Aiken, SC 29801-6309. Offers MS. Part-time and evening/weekend programs available. *Degree requirements:* For master's, thesis. *Entrance requirements:* For master's, GRE General Test, GRE Subject Test (psychology). Electronic applications accepted.

The University of South Dakota, Graduate School, College of Arts and Sciences, Department of Psychology, Vermillion, SD 57069-2390. Offers clinical psychology (MA, PhD); human factors (MA, PhD). *Accreditation:* APA (one or more programs are accredited). *Degree requirements:* For master's, comprehensive exam, thesis; for doctorate, comprehensive exam, thesis/dissertation. *Entrance requirements:* For master's, GRE, minimum GPA of 2.7; for doctorate, GRE General Test, GRE Subject Test, minimum GPA of 2.7. Additional exam requirements/recommendations for international students: Required—TOEFL (minimum score 550 paper-based; 213 computer-based; 79 iBT). Electronic applications accepted. *Faculty research:* Human-computer interactions, perceptual-cognitive processing, medical psychology, depression, moral psychology.

University of Southern California, Graduate School, College of Letters, Arts and Sciences, Department of Psychology, Los Angeles, CA 90089. Offers brain and cognitive science (PhD); clinical science (PhD); developmental psychology (PhD); human behavior (MHB); psychology (MA); quantitative methods (PhD); social psychology (PhD); PhD/MPH. *Accreditation:* APA. *Faculty:* 34 full-time (10 women), 17 part-time/adjunct (7 women). *Students:* 107 full-time (73 women); includes 38 minority (6 African Americans, 21 Asian Americans or Pacific Islanders, 11 Hispanic Americans), 19 international. 430 applicants, 6% accepted, 13 enrolled. In 2009, 17 master's, 12 doctorates awarded. *Degree requirements:* For doctorate, comprehensive exam, thesis/dissertation, one-year internship (for clinical science students). *Entrance requirements:* For doctorate, GRE. Additional exam requirements/recommendations for international students: Recommended—TOEFL (minimum score 600 paper-based; 250 computer-based; 100 iBT). *Application deadline:* For fall admission, 12/1 for domestic and international students. Application fee: $95. Electronic applications accepted. *Expenses:* Tuition: Full-time $25,980; part-time $1315 per unit. Required fees: $554. One-time fee: $35 full-time. Full-time tuition and fees vary according to degree level and program. *Financial support:* In 2009–10, 80 students received support, including 16 fellowships with full tuition reimbursements available (averaging $22,500 per year), 22 research assistantships with full tuition reimbursements available (averaging $19,000 per year), 38 teaching assistantships with full tuition reimbursements available (averaging $19,000 per year); career-related internships or fieldwork, scholarships/grants, traineeships, and health care benefits also available. *Faculty research:* Affective neuroscience; children and families; vision, culture and ethnicity; intergroup relations; aggression and violence; language and reading development; substance abuse. *Unit head:* Dr. Margaret Gatz, Chair and Professor, 213-740-2203, Fax: 213-746-9028, E-mail: gatz@usc.edu. *Application contact:* Irene Takaragawa, Graduate Advisor, 213-740-2205, E-mail: itakarag@usc.edu.

University of Southern Mississippi, Graduate School, College of Education and Psychology, Department of Psychology, Hattiesburg, MS 39406-0001. Offers clinical psychology (MA, PhD); counseling psychology (PhD); experimental psychology (MA, PhD); psychology (MS); school psychology (MA, PhD). *Accreditation:* APA (one or more programs are accredited). *Faculty:* 32 full-time (9 women). *Students:* 104 full-time (80 women), 29 part-time (19 women); includes 14 minority (7 African Americans, 2 Asian Americans or Pacific Islanders, 5 Hispanic Americans), 7 international. Average age 29. 225 applicants, 16% accepted, 30 enrolled. In 2009, 23 master's, 13 doctorates awarded. Terminal master's awarded for partial completion of doctoral program. *Degree requirements:* For master's, comprehensive exam, thesis; for doctorate, comprehensive exam, thesis/dissertation. *Entrance requirements:* For master's, GRE General Test, minimum GPA of 3.0; for doctorate, GRE General Test, interview, minimum GPA of 3.0. Additional exam requirements/recommendations for international students: Required—TOEFL. *Application deadline:* For fall admission, 3/1 priority date for domestic students, 3/1 for international students. Applications are processed on a rolling basis. Application fee: $35. *Expenses:* Tuition, state resident: full-time $5096; part-time $284 per hour. Tuition, nonresident: full-time $13,052; part-time $726 per hour. Required fees: $402. Tuition and fees vary according to course level and course load. *Financial support:* In 2009–10, 48 research assistantships with full tuition reimbursements (averaging $8,802 per year), 48 teaching assistantships with full tuition reimbursements (averaging $6,500 per year) were awarded; career-related internships or fieldwork, Federal Work-Study, and institutionally sponsored loans also available. Financial award application deadline: 3/15; financial award applicants required to submit FAFSA. *Faculty research:* Dolphin cognition, sleep, neuropsychology, health-related behaviors, psychopathology. Total annual research expenditures: $101,200. *Unit head:* Dr. Joesph Olmi, Chair, 601-266-4177, Fax: 601-266-5580. *Application contact:* Dr. Heather Sterling-Turner, Graduate Coordinator, 601-266-4177, Fax: 601-266-5580.

University of South Florida, Graduate School, College of Arts and Sciences, Department of Psychology, Tampa, FL 33620-9951. Offers clinical psychology (PhD); cognitive and neural sciences (PhD); industrial-organizational psychology (PhD). *Accreditation:* APA. *Faculty:* 32 full-time (9 women). *Students:* 98 full-time (55 women), 21 part-time (13 women); includes 16 minority (3 African Americans, 7 Asian Americans or Pacific Islanders, 6 Hispanic Americans), 11 international. Average age 32. 437 applicants, 8% accepted, 24 enrolled. In 2009, 24 doctorates awarded. *Degree requirements:* For doctorate, comprehensive exam, thesis/dissertation, internship. *Entrance requirements:* For doctorate, GRE General Test, minimum GPA of 3.0 in last 60 hours of course work. Additional exam requirements/recommendations for international students: Required—TOEFL (minimum score 550 paper-based; 213 computer-based). *Application deadline:* For fall admission, 12/1 for domestic and international students. Application fee: $30. Electronic applications accepted. *Expenses:* Contact institution. *Financial support:* In 2009–10, teaching assistantships with tuition reimbursements (averaging $27,086 per year); tuition waivers (partial) and unspecified assistantships also available. Financial award applicants required to submit FAFSA. *Faculty research:* Clinical, cognitive, neuroscience, social, industrial/organizational. Total annual research expenditures: $4.7 million. *Unit head:* Michael Brannick, Chairperson, 813-974-0478, Fax: 813-974-4617, E-mail: mbrannick@usf.edu. *Application contact:* William Sacco, Program Director, 813-974-0375, Fax: 813-974-4617, E-mail: sacco@cas.usf.edu.

The University of Tennessee, Graduate School, College of Arts and Sciences, Department of Psychology, Knoxville, TN 37996. Offers clinical psychology (PhD); experimental psychology (MA, PhD); psychology (MA). *Accreditation:* APA (one or more programs are accredited). Terminal master's awarded for partial completion of doctoral program. *Degree requirements:* For master's, thesis; for doctorate, thesis/dissertation. *Entrance requirements:* For master's and doctorate, GRE General Test, GRE Subject Test, minimum GPA of 2.7. Additional exam requirements/recommendations for international students: Required—TOEFL. Electronic applications accepted. *Expenses:* Tuition, state resident: full-time $6826; part-time $380 per semester hour. Tuition, nonresident: full-time $21,844; part-time $1147 per semester hour. Tuition and fees vary according to program.

The University of Texas at El Paso, Graduate School, College of Liberal Arts, Department of Psychology, El Paso, TX 79968-0001. Offers clinical psychology (MA); experimental psychology (MA); psychology (PhD). Part-time and evening/weekend programs available. *Students:* 47 (28 women); includes 20 minority (1 Asian American or Pacific Islander, 19 Hispanic Americans), 6 international. Average age 34. In 2009, 11 master's, 5 doctorates awarded. *Degree requirements:* For master's, thesis; for doctorate, thesis/dissertation. *Entrance requirements:* For master's, GRE, letters of recommendation; for doctorate, GRE, Statement of Purpose, Letters of Recommendation. Additional exam requirements/recommendations for international students: Required—TOEFL; Recommended—IELTS. *Application deadline:* For fall admission, 8/1 for domestic students, 3/1 for international students; for spring admission, 11/1 for domestic students, 9/1 for international students. Applications are processed on a rolling basis. Application fee: $45 ($80 for international students). Electronic applications accepted. *Financial support:* In 2009–10, research assistantships with partial tuition reimbursements (averaging $18,625 per year), teaching assistantships with partial tuition reimbursements (averaging $14,900 per year) were awarded; fellowships with partial tuition reimbursements, institutionally sponsored loans, scholarships/grants, health care benefits, tuition waivers (partial), and unspecified assistantships also available. Support available to part-time students. Financial award application deadline: 3/15; financial award applicants required to submit FAFSA. *Unit head:* Dr. Edward Casta?eda, Chair, 915-747-5551, Fax: 915-747-6553, E-mail: ecastaneda9@utep.edu. *Application contact:* Dr. Patricia D. Witherspoon, Dean of the Graduate School, 915-747-5491, Fax: 915-747-5788, E-mail: withersp@utep.edu.

The University of Texas at Tyler, College of Education and Psychology, Department of Psychology and Counseling, Tyler, TX 75799-0001. Offers clinical psychology (MS), including neuropsychology, school psychology; counseling psychology (MA), including general, marriage and family; interdisciplinary studies (MSIS); school counseling (MA). Part-time and evening/weekend programs available. *Faculty:* 11 full-time (3 women). *Students:* 80 full-time (63 women), 46 part-time (38 women); includes 5 minority (3 African Americans, 1 American Indian/Alaska Native, 1 Hispanic American). Average age 29. 64 applicants, 77% accepted, 28 enrolled. In 2009, 36 master's awarded. *Degree requirements:* For master's, comprehensive exam, thesis optional. *Entrance requirements:* For master's, GRE General Test, minimum GPA of 3.0. Additional exam requirements/recommendations for international students: Required—TOEFL (minimum score 79 computer-based). *Application deadline:* For fall admission, 8/17 priority date for domestic students, 7/1 priority date for international students; for spring admission, 12/21 priority date for domestic students, 11/1 priority date for international students. Application fee: $25 ($50 for international students). Electronic applications accepted. *Expenses:* Tuition, state resident: part-time $665 per semester hour. Tuition, nonresident: part-time $942 per semester hour. Part-time tuition and fees vary according to degree level and program. *Financial support:* In 2009–10, fellowships with partial tuition reimbursements (averaging $3,000 per year), research assistantships (averaging $5,000 per year), teaching assistantships (averaging $1,500 per year) were awarded; career-related internships or fieldwork,

Federal Work-Study, and institutionally sponsored loans also available. Support available to part-time students. Financial award application deadline: 7/1. *Faculty research:* Neuropsychology, child abuse, psychometric properties of psychological instruments, maternal behavior, clinical practice issues, victimization of women, post-traumatic stress disorder. *Unit head:* Dr. Charles B. Barke, Chair/Professor, 903-565-5875, Fax: 903-565-5560, E-mail: cbarke@uttyler.edu. *Application contact:* Dr. Charles Barke.

The University of Texas of the Permian Basin, Office of Graduate Studies, College of Arts and Sciences, Department of Psychology, Odessa, TX 79762-0001. Offers applied research psychology (MA); clinical psychology (MA). Part-time and evening/weekend programs available. *Degree requirements:* For master's, comprehensive exam, thesis, practicum. *Entrance requirements:* For master's, GRE General Test, 3 letters of recommendation. Additional exam requirements/recommendations for international students: Required—TOEFL (minimum score 550 paper-based; 213 computer-based).

The University of Texas–Pan American, College of Social and Behavioral Sciences, Department of Psychology and Anthropology, Edinburg, TX 78539. Offers psychology (MA), including clinical psychology, experimental psychology. Part-time and evening/weekend programs available. *Degree requirements:* For master's, comprehensive exam, thesis optional, internship. *Entrance requirements:* For master's, GRE, letters of recommendation. Additional exam requirements/recommendations for international students: Required—TOEFL. Electronic applications accepted. *Expenses:* Tuition, state resident: full-time $3630.60; part-time $201.70 per credit hour. Tuition, nonresident: full-time $8617; part-time $478.70 per credit hour. Required fees: $806.50. *Faculty research:* Biofeedback, acculturation, health, stress/trauma, neuropsychological assessment, false memories, children's theory of mind.

The University of Texas Southwestern Medical Center at Dallas, Southwestern Graduate School of Biomedical Sciences, Division of Clinical Science, Clinical Psychology Program, Dallas, TX 75390. Offers PhD. *Accreditation:* APA. *Faculty:* 41 full-time (20 women), 30 part-time/adjunct (11 women). *Students:* 44 full-time (31 women); includes 11 minority (2 African Americans, 5 Asian Americans or Pacific Islanders, 4 Hispanic Americans), 1 international. Average age 28. 146 applicants, 5% accepted, 7 enrolled. In 2009, 9 doctorates awarded. *Degree requirements:* For doctorate, thesis/dissertation, clinical and qualifying exams. *Entrance requirements:* For doctorate, GRE General Test, minimum undergraduate GPA of 3.0. *Application deadline:* For fall admission, 1/1 for domestic students. Application fee: $0. Electronic applications accepted. *Financial support:* Research assistantships, career-related internships or fieldwork and institutionally sponsored loans available. Financial award application deadline: 3/1; financial award applicants required to submit FAFSA. *Faculty research:* Health psychology, depression, cross-cultural research, neuropsychology, sequelae children's illness. *Unit head:* Dr. C. Munro Cullum, Chair, 214-648-4640, Fax: 214-648-5250, E-mail: munro.cullum@utsouthwestern.edu. *Application contact:* Kimberly Jones, Education Coordinator, 214-648-5267, Fax: 214-648-5297, E-mail: kelsey.stutzman@utsouthwestern.edu.

University of the District of Columbia, College of Arts and Sciences, Department of Psychology and Counseling, Program in Clinical Psychology, Washington, DC 20008-1175. Offers MS. *Students:* 5 part-time (4 women); includes 4 minority (all African Americans). Average age 33. *Expenses:* Tuition, state resident: full-time $7580. Tuition, nonresident: full-time $14,580. Required fees: $620. *Unit head:* Dr. Doris Johnson, Chairperson, 202-274-5701, E-mail: djohnson@udc.edu. *Application contact:* Ann Marie Waterman, Associate Vice President for Admission, Recruitment and Financial Aid, 202-274-6069.

The University of Toledo, College of Graduate Studies, College of Arts and Sciences, Department of Psychology, Toledo, OH 43606-3390. Offers behavioral (PhD), including cognitive, psychobiology and learning, social; clinical psychology (PhD); experimental psychology (MA). *Accreditation:* APA. *Degree requirements:* For master's, thesis; for doctorate, one foreign language, thesis/dissertation. *Entrance requirements:* For master's and doctorate, GRE General Test, GRE Subject Test. *Faculty research:* Neural taste response.

University of Tulsa, Graduate School, College of Arts and Sciences, Department of Psychology, Program in Clinical Psychology, Tulsa, OK 74104-3189. Offers MA, PhD, JD/MA. *Accreditation:* APA (one or more programs are accredited). Part-time programs available. *Faculty:* 13 full-time (5 women), 1 (woman) part-time/adjunct. *Students:* 24 full-time (19 women), 20 part-time (18 women); includes 3 minority (1 African American, 2 Hispanic Americans), 1 international. Average age 29. 64 applicants, 23% accepted, 6 enrolled. In 2009, 4 master's, 8 doctorates awarded. Terminal master's awarded for partial completion of doctoral program. *Degree requirements:* For master's, thesis (for some programs), 6 credit hours of practicum training; for doctorate, comprehensive exam, thesis/dissertation, 1 year pre-doctoral internship. *Entrance requirements:* For master's and doctorate, GRE General Test, interview, resume. Additional exam requirements/recommendations for international students: Required—TOEFL (minimum score 575 paper-based; 231 computer-based; 91 iBT), IELTS (minimum score 6.5). *Application deadline:* For fall admission, 12/1 for domestic and international students. Application fee: $40. Electronic applications accepted. *Expenses:* Tuition: Full-time $16,182; part-time $899 per credit hour. Required fees: $4 per credit hour. Tuition and fees vary according to course load. *Financial support:* In 2009–10, 26 students received support, including 8 fellowships with full and partial tuition reimbursements available (averaging $4,187 per year), 8 research assistantships with full and partial tuition reimbursements available (averaging $13,416 per year), 15 teaching assistantships with full and partial tuition reimbursements available (averaging $11,472 per year); career-related internships or fieldwork, Federal Work-Study, health care benefits, tuition waivers (full and partial), and unspecified assistantships also available. Support available to part-time students. Financial award application deadline: 2/1; financial award applicants required to submit FAFSA. *Faculty research:* Traumatic stress studies, randomized control trials of exposure treatments, pain modulation, neuropsychological assessment of health/mental health, psychological assessment, psychometrics, ethics, longitudinal assessment of child development, trauma and journalism, MMPI studies. Total annual research expenditures: $2.9 million. *Unit head:* Dr. Elana Newman, Director, 918-631-3151, Fax: 918-631-2836, E-mail: elana-newman@utulsa.edu. *Application contact:* Information Contact, E-mail: grad@utulsa.edu.

University of Utah, The Graduate School, College of Social and Behavioral Science, Department of Psychology, Salt Lake City, UT 84112. Offers clinical psychology (PhD); psychology (PhD). *Accreditation:* APA. *Faculty:* 32 full-time (15 women), 1 part-time/adjunct (0 women). *Students:* 48 full-time (33 women), 12 part-time (8 women); includes 5 minority (4 Asian Americans or Pacific Islanders, 1 Hispanic American), 4 international. Average age 30. 249 applicants, 6% accepted, 15 enrolled. In 2009, 12 doctorates awarded. *Degree requirements:* For doctorate, thesis/dissertation. *Entrance requirements:* For doctorate, GRE General Test. Additional exam requirements/recommendations for international students: Required—TOEFL (minimum score 500 paper-based; 173 computer-based). *Application deadline:* For fall admission, 12/15 for domestic and international students. Applications are processed on a rolling basis. Application fee: $55 ($65 for international students). Electronic applications accepted. *Expenses:* Tuition, state resident: full-time $4004; part-time $1674 per semester. Tuition, nonresident: full-time $14,134; part-time $5915 per semester. Required fees: $324 per semester. Tuition and fees vary according to course load, degree level and program. *Financial support:* In 2009–10, 46 students received support, including 4 fellowships with full tuition reimbursements available (averaging $11,000 per year), 21 research assistantships with full tuition reimbursements available (averaging $11,000 per year), 26 teaching assistantships with full tuition reimbursements available (averaging $11,000 per year); career-related internships or fieldwork also available. Financial award applicants required to submit FAFSA. *Faculty research:* Cognitive neuroscience, health, social cognition, psychopathology, cognitive and social development. Total annual research expenditures: $1.7 million. *Unit head:* Dr. Cynthia A. Berg, Chair, 801-581-8925, Fax: 801-581-5841, E-mail: cynthia.berg@psych.utah.edu. *Application contact:* Nancy Seegmiller, Administrative Assistant, 801-581-8925, Fax: 801-581-5841, E-mail: nancy.seegmiller@psych.utah.edu.

University of Vermont, Graduate College, College of Arts and Sciences, Department of Psychology, Burlington, VT 05405. Offers clinical psychology (PhD); psychology (PhD). *Accreditation:* APA. *Students:* 54 (44 women); includes 6 minority (1 African American, 1 Asian American or Pacific Islander, 4 Hispanic Americans), 3 international. 231 applicants, 5% accepted, 7 enrolled. In 2009, 5 doctorates awarded. *Degree requirements:* For doctorate, thesis/dissertation. *Entrance requirements:* For doctorate, GRE General Test. Additional exam requirements/recommendations for international students: Required—TOEFL (minimum score 550 paper-based; 213 computer-based; 80 iBT). *Application deadline:* For fall admission, 12/1 for domestic students. Application fee: $40. Electronic applications accepted. *Expenses:* Tuition, state resident: part-time $508 per credit hour. Tuition, nonresident: part-time $1281 per credit hour. *Financial support:* Fellowships, research assistantships, teaching assistantships available. Financial award application deadline: 2/1. *Unit head:* Dr. William Falls, Chairperson, 802-656-2670. *Application contact:* Dr. Rex Forehand, Coordinator, 802-656-2670.

University of Victoria, Faculty of Graduate Studies, Faculty of Social Sciences, Department of Psychology, Victoria, BC V8W 2Y2, Canada. Offers clinical psychology (PhD); clinical psychology (neuropsychology) (M Sc); cognition and brain science (M Sc, PhD); experimental neuropsychology (M Sc, PhD); individualized study (M Sc, PhD); life span development psychology (PhD); life span developmental psychology (M Sc); social psychology (M Sc, PhD). *Accreditation:* APA (one or more programs are accredited). *Degree requirements:* For master's, thesis; for doctorate, thesis/dissertation, candidacy exam. *Entrance requirements:* For master's and doctorate, GRE General Test. Additional exam requirements/recommendations for international students: Required—TOEFL (minimum score 600 paper-based; 250 computer-based). Electronic applications accepted. *Faculty research:* Life span development psychology and aging, behavioral neuroscience, cognitive psychology, behavioral psychology, environmental psychology.

University of Virginia, Curry School of Education, Department of Human Services, Program in Clinical and School Psychology, Charlottesville, VA 22903. Offers PhD. *Students:* 26 full-time (22 women), 1 (woman) part-time; includes 6 minority (3 African Americans, 2 Asian Americans or Pacific Islanders, 1 Hispanic American). Average age 27. 48 applicants, 10% accepted, 2 enrolled. In 2009, 6 doctorates awarded. *Unit head:* Dr. Peter L. Sheras, Director, 434-924-0795, E-mail: pls@virginia.edu. *Application contact:* Lynn Renfroe, Information Contact, 434-924-6254, E-mail: ldr9t@virginia.edu.

University of Washington, Graduate School, College of Arts and Sciences, Department of Psychology, Seattle, WA 98195. Offers animal behavior (PhD); child psychology (PhD); clinical psychology (PhD); cognition and perception (PhD); developmental psychology (PhD); quantitative psychology (PhD); social psychology and personality (PhD). *Accreditation:* APA. *Degree requirements:* For doctorate, thesis/dissertation. *Entrance requirements:* For doctorate, GRE General Test, minimum GPA of 3.0. Electronic applications accepted. *Faculty research:* Addictive behaviors, artificial intelligence, child psychopathology, mechanisms and development of vision, physiology of ingestive behaviors.

University of Windsor, Faculty of Graduate Studies, Faculty of Arts and Social Sciences, Department of Psychology, Windsor, ON N9B 3P4, Canada. Offers adult clinical (MA, PhD); applied social psychology (MA, PhD); child clinical (MA, PhD); clinical neuropsychology (MA, PhD). *Accreditation:* APA (one or more programs are accredited). *Degree requirements:* For master's, thesis; for doctorate, comprehensive exam, thesis/dissertation. *Entrance requirements:* For master's, GRE General Test, GRE Subject Test in psychology, minimum B average; for doctorate, GRE General Test, GRE Subject Test in psychology, master's degree. Additional exam requirements/recommendations for international students: Required—TOEFL (minimum score 600 paper-based; 250 computer-based). Electronic applications accepted. *Faculty research:* Gambling, suicidology, emotional competence, psychotherapy and trauma.

University of Wisconsin–Madison, Graduate School, College of Letters and Science, Department of Psychology, Program in Clinical Psychology, Madison, WI 53706-1380. Offers PhD. *Accreditation:* APA. *Degree requirements:* For doctorate, comprehensive exam, thesis/dissertation. *Entrance requirements:* For doctorate, GRE General Test, minimum undergraduate GPA of 3.0. Additional exam requirements/recommendations for international students: Required—TOEFL. Electronic applications accepted. *Expenses:* Tuition, state resident: part-time $594 per credit. Tuition, nonresident: part-time $1504 per credit. Required fees: $65 per credit. Tuition and fees vary according to course load, program and reciprocity agreements.

University of Wisconsin–Milwaukee, Graduate School, College of Letters and Sciences, Department of Psychology, Milwaukee, WI 53201-0413. Offers clinical psychology (MS, PhD); psychology (MS, PhD). *Accreditation:* APA (one or more programs are accredited). *Faculty:* 23 full-time (6 women). *Students:* 54 full-time (32 women), 17 part-time (11 women); includes 12 minority (3 African Americans, 2 Asian Americans or Pacific Islanders, 7 Hispanic Americans), 4 international. Average age 28. 162 applicants, 14% accepted, 11 enrolled. In 2009, 14 master's, 11 doctorates awarded. *Degree requirements:* For master's, thesis; for doctorate, variable foreign language requirement, thesis/dissertation. *Entrance requirements:* For master's and doctorate, GRE General Test, GRE Subject Test. Additional exam requirements/recommendations for international students: Required—TOEFL (minimum score 550 paper-based; 79 iBT), IELTS (minimum score 6.5). *Application deadline:* For fall admission, 1/1 priority date for domestic students; for spring admission, 9/1 for domestic students. Applications are processed on a rolling basis. Application fee: $45 ($75 for international students). *Expenses:* Tuition, state resident: full-time $8800. Tuition, nonresident: full-time $20,760. Tuition and fees vary according to program and reciprocity agreements. *Financial support:* In 2009–10, 2 research assistantships, 42 teaching assistantships were awarded; career-related internships or fieldwork and unspecified assistantships also available. Support available to part-time students. Financial award application deadline: 4/15. Total annual research expenditures: $1.4 million. *Unit head:* Hobart Davies, Representative, 414-229-6594, Fax: 414-229-5219, E-mail: hobart@uwm.edu. *Application contact:* Susan Lima, General Information Contact, 414-229-4359, Fax: 414-229-6967, E-mail: suelima@uwm.edu.

Utah State University, School of Graduate Studies, College of Education and Human Services, Department of Psychology, Logan, UT 84322. Offers clinical/counseling/school psychology (PhD); research and evaluation methodology (PhD); school counseling (MS); school psychology (MS). *Accreditation:* APA (one or more programs are accredited). Part-time and evening/weekend programs available. Postbaccalaureate distance learning degree programs offered (no on-campus study). Terminal master's awarded for partial completion of doctoral program. *Degree requirements:* For master's, thesis (for some programs); for doctorate, thesis/dissertation. *Entrance requirements:* For master's, GRE General Test (school psychology), MAT (school counseling), minimum GPA of 3.5; for doctorate, GRE General Test, minimum GPA of 3.5. Additional exam requirements/recommendations for international students: Required—TOEFL. *Faculty research:* Hearing loss detection in infancy, ADHD, eating disorders, domestic violence, neuropsychology, bilingual/Spanish speaking students/parents.

Valdosta State University, Graduate School, Department of Psychology and Counseling, Valdosta, GA 31698. Offers clinical/counseling psychology (MS); industrial/organizational psychology (MS); school counseling (M Ed, Ed S); school psychology (Ed S). Part-time and evening/weekend programs available. *Degree requirements:* For master's, thesis or alternative, comprehensive written and/or oral exams; for Ed S, thesis. *Entrance requirements:* For master's and Ed S, GRE General Test or MAT. Additional exam requirements/recommendations for international students: Required—TOEFL (minimum score 523 paper-based; 193 computer-based). Electronic applications accepted. *Faculty research:* Using Bender-Gestalt to predict graphomotor dimensions of the draw-a-person test, neurobehavioral hemispheric dominance.

Valparaiso University, Graduate School, Department of Psychology, Valparaiso, IN 46383. Offers business management (for counseling students) (Certificate); clinical mental health counseling (MA); community counseling (MA); JD/MA. Part-time and evening/weekend programs available. *Faculty:* 9 part-time/adjunct (4 women). *Students:* 38 full-time (34 women), 9 part-time (3 women); includes 7 minority (3 African Americans, 4 Hispanic Americans), 2 international.

Clinical Psychology

Valparaiso University (continued)

Average age 29. In 2009, 18 master's awarded. *Degree requirements:* For master's, thesis or alternative, internship. *Entrance requirements:* For master's, minimum GPA of 3.0; 15 credits in the social/behavioral sciences (psychology, sociology, human development, etc.) with a minimum GPA of 3.0; course in introductory psychology; recent statistics course with minimum B average. Additional exam requirements/recommendations for international students: Required—TOEFL (minimum score 550 paper-based; 213 computer-based; 80 iBT). *Application deadline:* For fall admission, 3/1 priority date for domestic students. Applications are processed on a rolling basis. Application fee: $30 ($50 for international students). Electronic applications accepted. *Financial support:* Career-related internships or fieldwork, scholarships/grants, traineeships, and unspecified assistantships available. Support available to part-time students. Financial award applicants required to submit FAFSA. *Faculty research:* Environmental psychology, human sexuality, racial identity development models, social psychology. *Unit head:* Dr. James Nelson, Director of Graduate Programs, 219-464-5443, Fax: 219-464-6878, E-mail: jim.nelson@valpo.edu. *Application contact:* Jamie Haney, Coordinator of Graduate Admission, 219-464-5313, Fax: 219-464-5381, E-mail: jamie.haney@valpo.edu.

Vanguard University of Southern California, Graduate Program in Clinical Psychology, Costa Mesa, CA 92626-9601. Offers clinical psychology (MS). Part-time and evening/weekend programs available. *Faculty:* 2 full-time (both women), 8 part-time/adjunct (4 women). *Students:* 49 full-time (39 women), 22 part-time (19 women); includes 20 minority (3 African Americans, 1 American Indian/Alaska Native, 4 Asian Americans or Pacific Islanders, 12 Hispanic Americans). Average age 31. 65 applicants, 65% accepted, 25 enrolled. In 2009, 22 master's awarded. *Degree requirements:* For master's, thesis or alternative, completion of personal therapy. *Entrance requirements:* For master's, minimum GPA of 3.0. Additional exam requirements/recommendations for international students: Required—TOEFL (minimum score 550 paper-based; 213 computer-based; 79 iBT). *Application deadline:* For fall admission, 4/1 priority date for domestic and international students; for spring admission, 10/1 priority date for domestic and international students. Applications are processed on a rolling basis. Application fee: $45. Electronic applications accepted. *Expenses:* Contact institution. *Financial support:* Scholarships/grants and unspecified assistantships available. Support available to part-time students. Financial award application deadline: 3/2; financial award applicants required to submit FAFSA. *Faculty research:* Children, play therapy, death and dying, trauma, marital and family counseling. *Unit head:* Dr. Jerre White, Director, 714-556-3610 Ext. 3550, Fax: 714-662-5226, E-mail: jwhite@vanguard.edu. *Application contact:* Asha Harrington, Graduate Psychology Coordinator, 714-556-3610 Ext. 3550, Fax: 714-662-5226, E-mail: gradpsych@vanguard.edu.

Virginia Commonwealth University, Graduate School, College of Humanities and Sciences, Department of Psychology, Program in Clinical Psychology, Richmond, VA 23284-9005. Offers PhD. *Accreditation:* APA. *Degree requirements:* For doctorate, thesis/dissertation. *Entrance requirements:* For doctorate, GRE General Test.

Virginia Polytechnic Institute and State University, Graduate School, College of Science, Department of Psychology, Blacksburg, VA 24061. Offers bio-behavioral sciences (PhD); clinical psychology (PhD); developmental psychology (PhD); industrial/organizational psychology (PhD); psychology (MS). *Accreditation:* APA (one or more programs are accredited). *Faculty:* 23 full-time (7 women). *Students:* 71 full-time (45 women), 6 part-time (3 women); includes 18 minority (6 American Indian/Alaska Native, 8 Asian Americans or Pacific Islanders, 4 Hispanic Americans), 1 international. Average age 27. 201 applicants, 7% accepted, 14 enrolled. In 2009, 20 master's, 14 doctorates awarded. *Entrance requirements:* For master's and doctorate, GRE, GMAT. Additional exam requirements/recommendations for international students: Required—TOEFL (minimum score 550 paper-based; 213 computer-based). *Application deadline:* For fall admission, 5/15 for international students; for spring admission, 10/15 for international students. Applications are processed on a rolling basis. Application fee: $65. Electronic applications accepted. *Expenses:* Tuition, area resident: Full-time $10,228; part-time $459 per credit hour. Tuition, nonresident: full-time $17,892; part-time $865 per credit hour. Required fees: $1966; $451 per semester. *Financial support:* In 2009–10, 18 research assistantships with full tuition reimbursements (averaging $16,153 per year), 41 teaching assistantships with full tuition reimbursements (averaging $16,053 per year) were awarded; career-related internships or fieldwork, Federal Work-Study, scholarships/grants, and unspecified assistantships also available. Financial award application deadline: 1/15. *Faculty research:* Infant development from electrophysical point of view, work motivation and personnel selection, EEG, ERP and hypnosis with reference to chronic pain, intimate violence. Total annual research expenditures: $2.1 million. *Unit head:* Dr. Robert S. Stephens, Dean, 540-231-6304, Fax: 540-231-3652, E-mail: stephens@vt.edu. *Application contact:* Kirby Deater-Deckard, Information Contact, 540-231-6581, Fax: 540-231-3652, E-mail: kirbydd@vt.edu.

Virginia State University, School of Graduate Studies, Research, and Outreach, School of Engineering, Science and Technology, Department of Psychology, Petersburg, VA 23806-0001. Offers behavioral and community health sciences (PhD); clinical health psychology (PhD); clinical psychology (MS); general psychology (MS). *Degree requirements:* For master's, one foreign language, thesis. *Entrance requirements:* For master's, GRE General Test.

Walden University, Graduate Programs, School of Psychology, Minneapolis, MN 55401. Offers clinical child psychology (Post-Doctoral Certificate); clinical psychology (Post-Doctoral Certificate); counseling psychology (Post-Doctoral Certificate); forensic psychology (MS), including forensic psychology in the community, general program, mental health applications, program planning and evaluation in forensic settings, psychology and legal systems; general psychology (Post-Doctoral Certificate); health psychology (Post-Doctoral Certificate); organizational psychology (Post-Doctoral Certificate); organizational psychology and development (Postbaccalaureate Certificate); psychology (MS, PhD), including clinical psychology (PhD), counseling psychology (PhD), crisis management and response (MS), general program (MS), general psychology (PhD), health psychology, leadership development and coaching (MS), media psychology (MS), organizational psychology (PhD), organizational psychology and development (MS), organizational psychology and nonprofit management (MS), program evaluation and research (MS), psychology of culture (MS), psychology, public administration, and social change (MS), social psychology (MS), terrorism and security (MS); teaching online (Post-Master's Certificate). Part-time and evening/weekend programs available. Postbaccalaureate distance learning degree programs offered (minimal on-campus study). *Faculty:* 33 full-time, 222 part-time/adjunct. *Students:* 3,546 full-time (2,761 women), 1,133 part-time (908 women); includes 1,723 minority (1,319 African Americans, 56 American Indian/Alaska Native, 101 Asian Americans or Pacific Islanders, 247 Hispanic Americans), 80 international. Average age 41. In 2009, 495 master's, 70 doctorates, 2 other advanced degrees awarded. Terminal master's awarded for partial completion of doctoral program. *Degree requirements:* For master's, thesis optional; for doctorate, thesis/dissertation, residency. *Entrance requirements:* For master's, bachelor's degree or equivalent in related field; minimum GPA of 2.5; official transcripts; goal statement; access to computer and Internet; for doctorate, master's degree or equivalent in related field; minimum GPA of 3.0;3 years of related professional/academic experience (preferred). Additional exam requirements/recommendations for international students: Required—TOEFL (minimum score 550 paper-based; 213 computer-based), IELTS (minimum score 6.5), or Michigan English Language Assessment Battery (minimum score 82). *Application deadline:* Applications are processed on a rolling basis. Application fee: $50. Electronic applications accepted. *Expenses:* Tuition: Full-time $13,665; part-time $560 per credit. Required fees: $1375. Tuition and fees vary according to course load, degree level and program. *Financial support:* In 2009–10, 290 students received support; fellowships, Federal Work-Study, scholarships/grants, unspecified assistantships, and family tuition reduction, active duty/veteran tuition reduction, group tuition reduction, interest-free payment plans available. Support available to part-time students. Financial award applicants required to submit FAFSA. *Unit head:* Dr. Melanie Storms, Associate Dean, 800-925-3368. *Application contact:* Jennifer Hall, Director of Enrollment, 866-4-WALDEN, E-mail: info@waldenu.edu.

Washburn University, College of Arts and Sciences, Department of Psychology, Topeka, KS 66621. Offers clinical psychology (MA). Part-time programs available. *Degree requirements:* For master's, thesis. *Entrance requirements:* For master's, GRE General Test, 15 hours of course work in psychology. Electronic applications accepted. *Faculty research:* Animal behavior, correctional psychology, children's social development, metacognition and metamemory, psychology of exercise, Gibsonian Ecological Psychology, treatment of anxiety disorders.

Washington State University, Graduate School, College of Liberal Arts, Department of Psychology, Pullman, WA 99164. Offers clinical psychology (PhD); experimental psychology (PhD); psychology (MS). *Accreditation:* APA (one or more programs are accredited). *Faculty:* 22. *Students:* 49 full-time (34 women), 4 part-time (2 women); includes 7 minority (2 Asian Americans or Pacific Islanders, 5 Hispanic Americans), 7 international. Average age 29. 262 applicants, 6% accepted, 12 enrolled. In 2009, 7 master's, 8 doctorates awarded. *Degree requirements:* For master's, comprehensive exam (for some programs), thesis (for some programs), oral exam; for doctorate, comprehensive exam, thesis/dissertation, oral exam, written exam. *Entrance requirements:* For master's, minimum undergraduate GPA of 3.0; research experiences; clinical experiences; at least 18 hours of psychology, including a class in statistics; three letters of recommendation, official transcripts; for doctorate, three letters of reference; summary data form; at least 18 credits of study in psychology; at least one course in statistics and research methodology; official transcripts; minimum cumulative undergraduate GPA of 3.0 or master's degree in psychology. *Application deadline:* For fall admission, 12/15 priority date for domestic and international students. Applications are processed on a rolling basis. Application fee: $50. *Financial support:* In 2009–10, 5 research assistantships with full and partial tuition reimbursements (averaging $13,917 per year), 39 teaching assistantships with full and partial tuition reimbursements (averaging $13,056 per year) were awarded; fellowships, career-related internships or fieldwork, Federal Work-Study, institutionally sponsored loans, and unspecified assistantships also available. Financial award application deadline: 2/15; financial award applicants required to submit FAFSA. *Faculty research:* Childhood conduct disorders, etiology of depression, treatment of reading disorders, applied behavior analysis, selective attention. *Unit head:* Dr. John Hinson, Chair, 509-335-1089, Fax: 509-335-5043, E-mail: hinson@mail.wsu.edu. *Application contact:* Graduate School Admissions, 800-GRADWSU, Fax: 509-335-16949, E-mail: gradsch@wsu.edu.

Washington University in St. Louis, Graduate School of Arts and Sciences, Department of Psychology, St. Louis, MO 63130-4899. Offers clinical psychology (PhD); general experimental psychology (PhD); social psychology (PhD). *Accreditation:* APA. Terminal master's awarded for partial completion of doctoral program. *Degree requirements:* For doctorate, thesis/dissertation. *Entrance requirements:* For doctorate, GRE General Test. Electronic applications accepted.

Waynesburg University, Graduate and Professional Studies, Waynesburg, PA 15370-1222. Offers business (MBA), including finance, health systems, human resources, leadership, market development; counseling (MA), including addictions counseling, clinical mental health; education (MAT); nursing (MSN), including administration, education, informatics, palliative care; nursing practice (DNP); special education (M Ed); technology (M Ed); MSN/MBA. *Accreditation:* AACN. Part-time and evening/weekend programs available. *Faculty:* 11 full-time (5 women), 136 part-time/adjunct (80 women). *Students:* 116 full-time (85 women), 984 part-time (682 women). 711 applicants, 80% accepted, 485 enrolled. In 2009, 320 master's, 41 doctorates awarded. *Degree requirements:* For doctorate, thesis/dissertation. *Entrance requirements:* Additional exam requirements/recommendations for international students: Required—TOEFL. *Application deadline:* For fall admission, 8/1 priority date for domestic students. Applications are processed on a rolling basis. Electronic applications accepted. *Expenses:* Tuition: Part-time $520 per credit. *Financial support:* Available to part-time students. Application deadline: 5/1. *Unit head:* David Mariner, Dean, 724-743-4420, Fax: 724-743-4425, E-mail: dmariner@waynesburg.edu. *Application contact:* Michael Bednarski, Director of Admissions, 724-743-4420, Fax: 724-743-4425, E-mail: mbednars@waynesburg.edu.

Wayne State University, College of Education, Division of Theoretical and Behavioral Foundations, Detroit, MI 48202. Offers counseling (M Ed, MA, Ed D, PhD, Ed S); education evaluation and research (M Ed, Ed D, PhD); educational psychology (M Ed, Ed D, PhD, Ed S); educational sociology (M Ed, Ed D, PhD, Ed S); history and philosophy of education (M Ed, Ed D, PhD); rehabilitation counseling and community inclusion (MA, Ed S); school and community psychology (MA, Ed S); school clinical psychology (Ed S). *Accreditation:* ACA (one or more programs are accredited); CORE (one or more programs are accredited). Evening/weekend programs available. *Degree requirements:* For doctorate, thesis/dissertation. *Entrance requirements:* For master's, GRE; for doctorate, GRE, interview, minimum GPA of 3.0, curriculum vitae, references. Additional exam requirements/recommendations for international students: Required—TOEFL (minimum score 550 paper-based; 213 computer-based), TWE (minimum score 6). Electronic applications accepted. *Faculty research:* Adolescents at risk, supervision of counseling.

Wayne State University, College of Liberal Arts and Sciences, Department of Psychology, Program in Psychology, Detroit, MI 48202. Offers behavioral and cognitive neuroscience (PhD); clinical psychology (PhD); cognitive and social psychology (PhD); industrial/organizational psychology (PhD); psychology (MA, MS). *Accreditation:* APA (one or more programs are accredited). *Degree requirements:* For doctorate, thesis/dissertation. *Entrance requirements:* For doctorate, GRE General Test, GRE Subject Test. Additional exam requirements/recommendations for international students: Required—TOEFL (minimum score 550 paper-based; 213 computer-based); Recommended—TWE (minimum score 6). Electronic applications accepted.

West Chester University of Pennsylvania, Office of Graduate Studies, College of Arts and Sciences, Department of Psychology, West Chester, PA 19383. Offers clinical mental health (Certificate); clinical psychology (MA); general psychology (MA); industrial psychology (MA). Part-time and evening/weekend programs available. *Students:* 36 full-time (30 women), 77 part-time (55 women); includes 12 minority (5 African Americans, 4 Asian Americans or Pacific Islanders, 3 Hispanic Americans), 2 international. Average age 26. 175 applicants, 76% accepted, 58 enrolled. In 2009, 38 master's, 2 other advanced degrees awarded. *Degree requirements:* For master's, comprehensive exam, thesis (for some programs). *Entrance requirements:* For master's, GRE General Test or MAT, minimum GPA of 3.0, 3.25 in psychology; three letters of reference. Additional exam requirements/recommendations for international students: Required—TOEFL (minimum score 550 paper-based; 213 computer-based; 80 iBT). *Application deadline:* For fall admission, 4/15 priority date for domestic students, 3/15 for international students; for spring admission, 10/15 for domestic students, 9/1 for international students. Applications are processed on a rolling basis. Application fee: $35. Electronic applications accepted. *Expenses:* Tuition, state resident: full-time $6666; part-time $370 per credit. Tuition, nonresident: full-time $10,666; part-time $593 per credit. Required fees: $122.56 per credit. *Financial support:* In 2009–10, 19 research assistantships with full and partial tuition reimbursements (averaging $5,000 per year) were awarded; unspecified assistantships also available. Support available to part-time students. Financial award application deadline: 2/15; financial award applicants required to submit FAFSA. *Faculty research:* Animal learning and cognition. *Unit head:* Dr. Loretta Rieser-Danner, Chairperson, 610-436-3106, E-mail: lrieser-danner@wcupa.edu. *Application contact:* Dr. Stefani Yorges, Graduate Coordinator, 610-436-3154, E-mail: syorges@wcupa.edu.

Western Illinois University, School of Graduate Studies, College of Arts and Sciences, Department of Psychology, Macomb, IL 61455-1390. Offers clinical/community mental health (MS); general psychology (MS); psychology (MS, SSP); school psychology (SSP). Part-time programs available. *Students:* 42 full-time (21 women), 14 part-time (11 women); includes 2 minority (both Asian Americans or Pacific Islanders), 2 international. Average age 25. 75 applicants, 37% accepted. In 2009, 11 master's, 10 other advanced degrees awarded. *Degree requirements:* For master's, comprehensive exam (for some programs), thesis or alternative. *Entrance requirements:* For master's and SSP, GRE General Test. Additional exam requirements/recommendations for international students: Required—TOEFL (minimum score 550 paper-based; 213 computer-based; 80 iBT). *Application deadline:* Applications are processed on a rolling basis. Application fee: $30. Electronic applications accepted. *Expenses:* Tuition, state resident: full-time $4486; part-time $249.21 per credit hour. Tuition, nonresident: full-time $8972; part-time $498.42 per credit hour. Required fees: $72.62 per credit hour. *Financial support:* In 2009–10, 38 students received support, including 38 research assistantships with full tuition reimbursements available (averaging $7,280 per year). Financial award applicants required to submit FAFSA. *Unit head:* Dr. Steven Dworkin, Chairperson, 309-298-1593. *Application contact:* Evelyn Hoing, Assistant Director of Graduate Studies, 309-298-1806, Fax: 309-298-2345, E-mail: grad-office@wiu.edu.

Western Michigan University, Graduate College, College of Arts and Sciences, Department of Psychology, Kalamazoo, MI 49008. Offers behavior analysis (MA, PhD); clinical psychology (PhD); industrial/organizational psychology (MA). *Accreditation:* APA (one or more programs are accredited). *Degree requirements:* For master's, variable foreign language requirement, thesis, oral exams; for doctorate, 2 foreign languages, comprehensive exam, thesis/dissertation, oral exams. *Entrance requirements:* For master's and doctorate, GRE General Test.

West Virginia University, Eberly College of Arts and Sciences, Department of Psychology, Morgantown, WV 26506. Offers behavior analysis (PhD); clinical psychology (MA, PhD); development psychology (PhD); psychology (MS). *Accreditation:* APA (one or more programs are accredited). Part-time programs available. Terminal master's awarded for partial completion of doctoral program. *Degree requirements:* For master's, thesis optional; for doctorate, comprehensive exam, thesis/dissertation. *Entrance requirements:* For master's and doctorate, GRE General Test, minimum GPA of 3.0. Additional exam requirements/recommendations for international students: Required—TOEFL. *Faculty research:* Adult and child clinical psychology, behavioral assessment and therapy, child and adolescent behavior, life span development, experimental and applied behavior analysis.

Wheaton College, Graduate School, Department of Psychology, Wheaton, IL 60187-5593. Offers clinical psychology (MA, Psy D); counseling ministries (MA). *Accreditation:* APA (one or more programs are accredited). Terminal master's awarded for partial completion of doctoral program. *Degree requirements:* For master's, thesis or alternative; for doctorate, thesis/dissertation, internship. *Entrance requirements:* For master's, GRE General Test, 18 hours of course work in psychology; for doctorate, GRE General Test.

Wichita State University, Graduate School, Fairmount College of Liberal Arts and Sciences, Department of Psychology, Wichita, KS 67260. Offers clinical (PhD); community (PhD); human factors (PhD). *Accreditation:* APA. Part-time programs available. *Expenses:* Tuition, state resident: full-time $4247; part-time $235.95 per credit hour. Tuition, nonresident: full-time $11,171; part-time $620.60 per credit hour. Required fees: $34; $3.60 per credit hour. $17 per term. Tuition and fees vary according to campus/location and program. *Unit head:* Dr. Charles Burdsal, Chair, 316-978-3170, Fax: 316-978-3006, E-mail: charles.burdsal@wichita.edu. *Application contact:* Dr. Charles Burdsal, Chair, 316-978-3170, Fax: 316-978-3006, E-mail: charles.burdsal@wichita.edu.

Widener University, School of Human Service Professions, Institute for Graduate Clinical Psychology, Program in Clinical Psychology, Chester, PA 19013-5792. Offers Psy D, Psy D/M Ed, Psy D/MA, Psy D/MBA, Psy D/MHA, Psy D/MPA, Psy D/MSHR. *Accreditation:* APA. *Students:* Average age 24. In 2009, 26 doctorates awarded. *Degree requirements:* For doctorate, thesis/dissertation, final oral and written qualifying exams. *Entrance requirements:* For doctorate, GRE General Test or MAT. *Application deadline:* For fall admission, 12/31 for domestic students. Application fee: $75. Electronic applications accepted. *Expenses:* Contact institution. *Financial support:* Career-related internships or fieldwork, Federal Work-Study, institutionally sponsored loans, scholarships/grants, and stipends available. Financial award application deadline: 4/15. *Faculty research:* Cognitive and personality diagnostic testing, depression, child and adolescent competencies, learning disabilities, family therapy. *Unit head:* Dr. Virginia Brabender, Associate Dean/Director, 610-499-1208, Fax: 610-499-4625, E-mail: graduate.psychology@widener.edu. *Application contact:* Ellen Madison, Admissions Coordinator, 611-499-1206, Fax: 610-499-4625, E-mail: ellen.t.madison@widener.edu.

Widener University, School of Human Service Professions, Institute for Graduate Clinical Psychology, Program in Clinical Psychology and Health and Medical Services Administration, Chester, PA 19013-5792. Offers Psy D/MBA, Psy D/MHA. *Accreditation:* APA (one or more programs are accredited); CAHME. *Faculty:* 15 full-time (6 women), 18 part-time/adjunct (10 women). *Students:* 6 full-time (4 women), 1 part-time (0 women); includes 1 minority (African American). Average age 28. *Application deadline:* For fall admission, 12/31 for domestic students. Application fee: $75. Electronic applications accepted. *Financial support:* Career-related internships or fieldwork, Federal Work-Study, and institutionally sponsored loans available. Financial award application deadline: 5/31. *Faculty research:* Psychosocial competence, family systems, medical care systems and financing. *Unit head:* Dr. Hal Shorey, Director, 610-499-4598, Fax: 610-499-4625. *Application contact:* Admissions Coordinator.

William Paterson University of New Jersey, College of the Humanities and Social Sciences, Wayne, NJ 07470-8420. Offers clinical and counseling psychology (MA); English (MA); history (MA); public policy and international affairs (MA); sociology (MA). Part-time and evening/weekend programs available. *Students:* 39 full-time (22 women), 123 part-time (90 women); includes 42 minority (11 African Americans, 5 Asian Americans or Pacific Islanders, 26 Hispanic Americans), 2 international. *Application deadline:* Applications are processed on a rolling basis. Application fee: $50. Electronic applications accepted. *Financial support:* In 2009–10, 13 students received support; research assistantships with full tuition reimbursements available, teaching assistantships with full tuition reimbursements available, unspecified assistantships available. Support available to part-time students. Financial award application deadline: 4/1; financial award applicants required to submit FAFSA. *Unit head:* Dr. Kara Rabbitt, Dean. College of Humanities and Social Sciences, 973-720-2180, Fax: 973-720-2955, E-mail: rabbittk@wpunj.edu. *Application contact:* Tinu Adeniran, Assistant Director, Graduate Admissions, 973-720-2764, Fax: 973-720-2035, E-mail: adenirant@wpunj.edu.

Wisconsin School of Professional Psychology, Program in Clinical Psychology, Milwaukee, WI 53225-4960. Offers MA, Psy D. *Accreditation:* APA. Part-time and evening/weekend programs available. Terminal master's awarded for partial completion of doctoral program. *Degree requirements:* For master's, candidacy exam, 500 hours of supervised clinical practica; for doctorate, thesis/dissertation, 1 year clinical intern and practicum experience (2000 hrs), candidacy and clinical exams. *Entrance requirements:* For master's, GRE General Test, GRE Subject Test, bachelor's degree in psychology, writing sample; for doctorate, GRE General Test, GRE Subject Test, master's degree in clinical psychology or equivalent, writing sample. *Faculty research:* Violence prevention, psychology of women, forensic psychology, custody evaluation, aging, harm reduction in AODA.

Wright Institute, Program in Clinical Psychology, Berkeley, CA 94704-1796. Offers clinical psychology (Psy D); counseling psychology (MA). *Accreditation:* APA (one or more programs are accredited). Evening/weekend programs available. *Faculty:* 11 full-time (10 women), 58 part-time/adjunct (29 women). *Students:* 338 full-time (239 women); includes 74 minority (16 African Americans, 1 American Indian/Alaska Native, 23 Asian Americans or Pacific Islanders, 34 Hispanic Americans), 6 international. Average age 34. 333 applicants, 38% accepted, 59 enrolled. In 2009, 20 master's, 38 doctorates awarded. *Degree requirements:* For doctorate, comprehensive exam, thesis/dissertation. *Entrance requirements:* Additional exam requirements/recommendations for international students: Required—TOEFL (minimum score 600 paper-based). *Application deadline:* For fall admission, 1/15 priority date for domestic students, 1/15 for international students. Application fee: $50. Electronic applications accepted. *Expenses:* Tuition: Full-time $25,550. Full-time tuition and fees vary according to degree level and program. *Financial support:* In 2009–10, 78 students received support, including 42 teaching assistantships (averaging $1,600 per year); fellowships, research assistantships, career-related internships or fieldwork and Federal Work-Study also available. Financial award application deadline: 7/1. *Faculty research:* Time-limited dynamic psychotherapy; mindfulness/ACT; psychotherapy integration; empathy, altruism and survivor guilt; culturally informed practice. *Unit head:* Dr. Charles Alexander, Dean, 510-841-9230 Ext. 101, E-mail: calexander@wi.edu. *Application contact:* Liz Hertz, Director of Admissions, 510-841-9230 Ext. 111, Fax: 510-841-0167, E-mail: lhertz@wrightinst.edu.

Wright State University, School of Professional Psychology, Dayton, OH 45435. Offers clinical psychology (Psy D). *Accreditation:* APA. *Degree requirements:* For doctorate, thesis/dissertation. *Entrance requirements:* For doctorate, GRE General Test, GRE Subject Test. Additional exam requirements/recommendations for international students: Required—TOEFL. *Expenses:* Contact institution.

Xavier University, College of Social Sciences, Health and Education, Department of Psychology, Cincinnati, OH 45207. Offers clinical psychology (Psy D); psychology (MA), including general experimental, industrial-organizational. *Accreditation:* APA (one or more programs are accredited). *Faculty:* 19 full-time (9 women), 3 part-time/adjunct (2 women). *Students:* 111 full-time (87 women), 6 part-time (4 women); includes 13 minority (5 African Americans, 1 American Indian/Alaska Native, 4 Asian Americans or Pacific Islanders, 3 Hispanic Americans), 2 international. Average age 27. 272 applicants, 23% accepted, 37 enrolled. In 2009, 27 master's, 16 doctorates awarded. *Degree requirements:* For master's, one foreign language, comprehensive exam, thesis, internship; for doctorate, one foreign language, comprehensive exam, thesis/dissertation, internship. *Entrance requirements:* For master's and doctorate, GRE. Additional exam requirements/recommendations for international students: Required—TOEFL. *Application deadline:* For fall admission, 12/15 for domestic and international students. Application fee: $35. Electronic applications accepted. *Expenses:* Contact institution. *Financial support:* In 2009–10, 61 students received support, including 41 research assistantships with partial tuition reimbursements available, 20 teaching assistantships with partial tuition reimbursements available; scholarships/grants and unspecified assistantships also available. Financial award application deadline: 3/1; financial award applicants required to submit FAFSA. *Unit head:* Dr. Christine M. Dacey, Chair, 513-745-3533, Fax: 513-745-3327, E-mail: dacey@xavier.edu. *Application contact:* Margaret Maybury, Assistant Director, Enrollment and Student Services, 513-745-1053, Fax: 513-745-3347, E-mail: maybury@xavier.edu.

Yale University, Graduate School of Arts and Sciences, Department of Psychology, New Haven, CT 06520. Offers behavioral neuroscience (PhD); clinical psychology (PhD); cognitive psychology (PhD); developmental psychology (PhD); social/personality psychology (PhD). *Accreditation:* APA. *Degree requirements:* For doctorate, thesis/dissertation. *Entrance requirements:* For doctorate, GRE General Test.

Yeshiva University, Ferkauf Graduate School of Psychology, Program in Clinical Psychology, New York, NY 10033-3201. Offers Psy D. *Accreditation:* APA. Part-time programs available. *Degree requirements:* For doctorate, comprehensive exam, thesis/dissertation. *Entrance requirements:* For doctorate, GRE General Test. *Expenses:* Tuition: Full-time $24,918; part-time $1022 per credit. Required fees: $175. *Faculty research:* Psychotherapy, family therapy, psychoanalysis, cognitive behavior therapy.

Yeshiva University, Ferkauf Graduate School of Psychology, Program in School/Clinical-Child Psychology, New York, NY 10033-3201. Offers Psy D. *Accreditation:* APA. Part-time programs available. *Degree requirements:* For doctorate, comprehensive exam, thesis/dissertation. *Entrance requirements:* For doctorate, GRE General Test. *Expenses:* Tuition: Full-time $24,918; part-time $1022 per credit. Required fees: $175. *Faculty research:* Testing, early childhood intervention, child and adolescent psychotherapy, clinical child psychology.

Cognitive Sciences

Arizona State University, Graduate College, College of Liberal Arts and Sciences, Division of Natural Sciences, Department of Psychology, Tempe, AZ 85287. Offers behavioral neuroscience (PhD); clinical psychology (PhD); cognition, action and perception (PhD); developmental psychology (PhD); quantitative psychology (PhD); social psychology (PhD). *Accreditation:* APA. *Degree requirements:* For doctorate, thesis/dissertation. *Entrance requirements:* For doctorate, GRE General Test, GRE Subject Test.

Ball State University, Graduate School, College of Sciences and Humanities, Department of Psychological Science, Program in Cognitive and Social Processes, Muncie, IN 47306-1099. Offers MA.

Boston University, Graduate School of Arts and Sciences, Department of Cognitive and Neural Systems, Boston, MA 02215. Offers MA, PhD. *Students:* 47 full-time (10 women), 6 part-time (2 women); includes 5 minority (4 Asian Americans or Pacific Islanders, 1 Hispanic American), 18 international. Average age 30. 61 applicants, 31% accepted, 8 enrolled. Terminal master's awarded for partial completion of doctoral program. *Degree requirements:* For master's, one foreign language, comprehensive exam; for doctorate, one foreign language, comprehensive exam, thesis/dissertation. *Entrance requirements:* For master's and doctorate, GRE General Test, GRE Subject Test (recommended), 3 letters of recommendation. Additional exam requirements/recommendations for international students: Required—TOEFL (minimum score 550 paper-based; 213 computer-based). *Application deadline:* For fall admission, 1/15 for domestic and international students; for spring admission, 10/15 for domestic and international students. Application fee: $70. Electronic applications accepted. *Expenses:* Tuition: Full-time $37,910; part-time $1184 per credit hour. Required fees: $386; $40 per semester. Part-time tuition and fees vary according to class time, course level, degree level and program. *Financial support:* In 2009–10, 3 fellowships with full tuition reimbursements (averaging $18,900 per year), 35 research assistantships with full tuition reimbursements (averaging $18,400 per year), 2 teaching assistantships with full tuition reimbursements were awarded; Federal Work-Study and unspecified assistantships also available. Support available to part-time students. Financial award application deadline: 1/15; financial award applicants required to submit FAFSA. *Unit head:* Ennio Mingolla, Chairman, 617-353-9485, Fax: 617-353-7755, E-mail: ennio@bu.edu. *Application contact:* Carol Y. Jefferson, Administrative Assistant, 617-353-7676, Fax: 617-353-7755, E-mail: caroly@bu.edu.

Brandeis University, Graduate School of Arts and Sciences, Department of Psychology, Waltham, MA 02454-9110. Offers brain, body and behavior (PhD); cognitive neuroscience (PhD); general psychology (MA); social/developmental psychology (PhD). Part-time programs available. *Faculty:* 16 full-time (4 women), 3 part-time/adjunct (2 women). *Students:* 35 full-time (27 women), 1 (woman) part-time; includes 2 minority (both Asian Americans or Pacific Islanders), 7 international. Average age 26. 121 applicants, 31% accepted, 13 enrolled. In 2009, 9 master's, 3 doctorates awarded. *Degree requirements:* For doctorate, comprehensive exam, thesis/dissertation. *Entrance requirements:* For master's, GRE General Test, GRE Subject Test (recommended), 3 letters of recommendation, statement of purpose; for doctorate,

Cognitive Sciences

Brandeis University (continued)
GRE General Test, GRE Subject Test (recommended), 3 letters of recommendation. Additional exam requirements/recommendations for international students: Required—TOEFL (minimum score 600 paper-based; 250 computer-based; 100 iBT); Recommended—IELTS (minimum score 7). *Application deadline:* For fall admission, 1/15 for domestic and international students. Applications are processed on a rolling basis. Application fee: $75. Electronic applications accepted. *Financial support:* In 2009–10, 16 fellowships with full tuition reimbursements (averaging $20,000 per year), 3 research assistantships with full tuition reimbursements (averaging $20,000 per year), 9 teaching assistantships with partial tuition reimbursements (averaging $3,200 per year) were awarded; institutionally sponsored loans, scholarships/grants, traineeships, health care benefits, tuition waivers (full), and unspecified assistantships also available. Support available to part-time students. Financial award applicants required to submit FAFSA. *Faculty research:* Development, cognition, social aging, perception, social/developmental psychology, cognitive neuroscience, brain, body and behavior, motor control, visual perception, taste physiology and psychophysics, memory, learning, aggression, emotion, personality and cognition in adulthood and old age, social relations and health, stereotypes and nonverbal communication. *Unit head:* Prof. Paul DiZio, Director of Graduate Studies, 781-736-3300, Fax: 781-736-3291, E-mail: dizio@brandeis.edu. *Application contact:* Donna J. Coletti, Graduate Admissions Coordinator, 781-736-3303, Fax: 781-736-3291, E-mail: coletti@brandeis.edu.

Brown University, Graduate School, Department of Cognitive and Linguistic Sciences, Providence, RI 02912. Offers cognitive science (Sc M, PhD); linguistics (AM, PhD). *Degree requirements:* For master's, one foreign language, thesis or alternative; for doctorate, 2 foreign languages, thesis/dissertation.

Brown University, Graduate School, Department of Psychology, Providence, RI 02912. Offers behavioral neuroscience (PhD); cognitive processes (PhD); sensation and perception (PhD); social/developmental (PhD); MS/PhD. *Degree requirements:* For doctorate, thesis/dissertation. *Entrance requirements:* For doctorate, GRE General Test, GRE Subject Test.

Carleton University, Faculty of Graduate Studies, Faculty of Arts and Social Sciences, Program in Cognitive Science, Ottawa, ON K1S 5B6, Canada. Offers PhD. *Degree requirements:* For doctorate, thesis/dissertation. *Entrance requirements:* For doctorate, master's degree. *Faculty research:* Language, attention, artificial intelligence, symbol recognition, consciousness.

Carnegie Mellon University, College of Humanities and Social Sciences, Department of Psychology, Area of Cognitive Neuroscience, Pittsburgh, PA 15213-3891. Offers PhD. *Degree requirements:* For doctorate, comprehensive exam, thesis/dissertation. *Entrance requirements:* For doctorate, GRE General Test. Additional exam requirements/recommendations for international students: Required—TOEFL.

Carnegie Mellon University, College of Humanities and Social Sciences, Department of Psychology, Area of Cognitive Psychology, Pittsburgh, PA 15213-3891. Offers PhD. *Degree requirements:* For doctorate, comprehensive exam, thesis/dissertation. *Entrance requirements:* For doctorate, GRE General Test. Additional exam requirements/recommendations for international students: Required—TOEFL.

Case Western Reserve University, School of Graduate Studies, Department of Cognitive Science, Cleveland, OH 44106. Offers cognitive linguistics (MA). Part-time programs available. *Faculty:* 6 full-time (2 women), 2 part-time/adjunct (1 woman). *Students:* 2 full-time (1 woman), 4 part-time (2 women). Average age 32. 6 applicants, 100% accepted, 1 enrolled. *Degree requirements:* For master's, thesis. *Entrance requirements:* For master's, GRE, recommendations. Additional exam requirements/recommendations for international students: Required—TOEFL (minimum score 550 paper-based; 213 computer-based; 79 iBT). *Application deadline:* For fall admission, 5/1 priority date for domestic students. Application fee: $50. Electronic applications accepted. *Faculty research:* Integrated, trans-disciplinary research into human higher-order cognition with emphases including the workings of the human mind in design, art, and technology, the interaction of brain and culture in development and evolution, the origins of human higher-order cognition. *Unit head:* Dr. Todd Oakley, Chair, 216-368-4753, E-mail: cogsci@case.edu. *Application contact:* Dr. Todd Oakley, Co-Director of Admission, 216-368-4753, E-mail: coglingadmission@case.edu.

Claremont Graduate University, Graduate Programs, School of Behavioral and Organizational Sciences, Department of Psychology, Claremont, CA 91711-6160. Offers advanced study in evaluation (Certificate); cognitive psychology (MA, PhD); developmental psychology (MA, PhD); evaluation and applied research methods (MA, PhD); health behavior research and evaluation (MA, PhD); human resource development and evaluation (MA); industrial/organizational psychology (MA, PhD); organizational behavior (MA, PhD); organizational psychology (MA, PhD); social psychology (MA, PhD); MBA/PhD. Part-time programs available. *Faculty:* 17 full-time (7 women), 1 part-time/adjunct (0 women). *Students:* 231 full-time (155 women), 25 part-time (18 women); includes 62 minority (13 African Americans, 1 American Indian/Alaska Native, 31 Asian Americans or Pacific Islanders, 17 Hispanic Americans), 21 international. Average age 30. In 2009, 37 master's, 12 doctorates, 8 other advanced degrees awarded. Terminal master's awarded for partial completion of doctoral program. *Entrance requirements:* For master's and doctorate, GRE General Test. Additional exam requirements/recommendations for international students: Required—TOEFL (minimum score 550 paper-based; 213 computer-based; 80 iBT). *Application deadline:* For fall admission, 1/15 priority date for domestic students. Applications are processed on a rolling basis. Application fee: $60. Electronic applications accepted. *Expenses:* Tuition: Full-time $35,046; part-time $1524 per credit. Required fees: $161 per semester. *Financial support:* Fellowships, research assistantships, teaching assistantships, Federal Work-Study, institutionally sponsored loans, scholarships/grants, and tuition waivers (full and partial) available. Support available to part-time students. Financial award application deadline: 2/15; financial award applicants required to submit FAFSA. *Faculty research:* Social intervention, diversity in organizations, eyewitness memory, aging and cognition, drug policy. *Unit head:* Stewart Donaldson, Dean, 909-607-9001, Fax: 909-621-8905, E-mail: stewart.donaldson@cgu.edu. *Application contact:* Paul Thomas, Director, External Affairs, 909-607-9016, Fax: 909-621-8905, E-mail: paul.thomas@cgu.edu.

Cornell University, Graduate School, Graduate Fields of Arts and Sciences, Field of Information Science, Ithaca, NY 14853-0001. Offers cognition (PhD); human computer interaction (PhD); information systems (PhD); social aspects of information (PhD). *Faculty:* 35 full-time (10 women). *Students:* 14 full-time (4 women); includes 1 minority (Asian American or Pacific Islander), 6 international. Average age 31. 53 applicants, 9% accepted, 5 enrolled. In 2009, 3 doctorates awarded. *Degree requirements:* For doctorate, comprehensive exam, thesis/dissertation. *Entrance requirements:* For doctorate, GRE General Test, 3 letters of recommendation. Additional exam requirements/recommendations for international students: Required—TOEFL (minimum score 550 paper-based; 213 computer-based; 77 iBT). *Application deadline:* For fall admission, 1/1 for domestic students. Application fee: $70. Electronic applications accepted. *Expenses:* Tuition: Full-time $29,500. Required fees: $70. Full-time tuition and fees vary according to degree level, program and student level. *Financial support:* In 2009–10, 10 students received support, including 1 fellowship with full tuition reimbursement available, 2 research assistantships with full tuition reimbursements available, 2 teaching assistantships with full tuition reimbursements available; institutionally sponsored loans, scholarships/grants, tuition waivers (full and partial), and unspecified assistantships also available. Financial award applicants required to submit FAFSA. *Faculty research:* Digital libraries, game theory, data mining, human-computer interaction, computational linguistics. *Unit head:* Director of Graduate Studies, 607-255-5925. *Application contact:* Graduate Field Assistant, 607-255-5925, E-mail: info@infosci.cornell.edu.

Dartmouth College, Arts and Sciences Graduate Programs, Department of Psychological and Brain Sciences, Program in Cognitive Neuroscience, Hanover, NH 03755. Offers PhD. *Faculty:* 20 full-time (6 women). *Students:* 1 full-time (0 women). Average age 23. 88 applicants, 15% accepted. In 2009, 1 doctorate awarded. *Entrance requirements:* Additional exam requirements/recommendations for international students: Required—TOEFL. *Application deadline:* For fall admission, 1/6 for domestic students. *Unit head:* Dr. Howard C. Hughes, Chair, 603-646-3181, Fax: 603-646-1419, E-mail: howard.hughes@dartmouth.edu. *Application contact:* Nancy Tenney, Department Administration, 603-646-3181, E-mail: nancy.tenney@dartmouth.edu.

Duke University, Graduate School, Department of Psychology, Durham, NC 27708-0586. Offers biological psychology (PhD); clinical psychology (PhD); cognitive psychology (PhD); developmental psychology (PhD); experimental psychology (PhD); health psychology (PhD); human social development (PhD); JD/MA. *Accreditation:* APA (one or more programs are accredited). *Faculty:* 40 full-time. *Students:* 92 full-time (70 women); includes 13 minority (5 African Americans, 2 Asian Americans or Pacific Islanders, 6 Hispanic Americans), 14 international. 478 applicants, 8% accepted, 21 enrolled. In 2009, 10 doctorates awarded. *Degree requirements:* For doctorate, thesis/dissertation. *Entrance requirements:* For doctorate, GRE General Test. Additional exam requirements/recommendations for international students: Required—TOEFL (minimum score 550 paper-based; 213 computer-based; 83 iBT), IELTS (minimum score 7). *Application deadline:* For fall admission, 12/8 priority date for domestic and international students. Application fee: $75. Electronic applications accepted. *Financial support:* Fellowships, research assistantships, teaching assistantships, career-related internships or fieldwork and Federal Work-Study available. Financial award application deadline: 12/31. *Unit head:* Melanie Bonner, Director of Graduate Studies, Fax: 919-660-5715, E-mail: morrell@duke.edu. *Application contact:* Cynthia Robertson, Associate Dean for Enrollment Services, 919-684-3913, E-mail: grad-admissions@duke.edu.

Emory University, Graduate School of Arts and Sciences, Department of Psychology, Atlanta, GA 30322-1100. Offers clinical psychology (PhD); cognition and development (PhD); neuroscience and animal behavior (PhD). *Accreditation:* APA. *Degree requirements:* For doctorate, comprehensive exam, thesis/dissertation. *Entrance requirements:* For doctorate, GRE General Test, minimum GPA of 3.25. Additional exam requirements/recommendations for international students: Required—TOEFL. Electronic applications accepted. *Faculty research:* Neuroscience and animal behavior; adult and child psychopathology, cognition development assessment.

Florida State University, The Graduate School, College of Arts and Sciences, Department of Psychology, Program in Cognitive Psychology, Tallahassee, FL 32306. Offers PhD. *Faculty:* 9 full-time (1 woman). *Students:* 22 full-time (7 women), 1 international. Average age 28. 47 applicants, 17% accepted, 6 enrolled.Terminal master's awarded for partial completion of doctoral program. *Degree requirements:* For doctorate, thesis/dissertation, preliminary exam. *Entrance requirements:* For doctorate, GRE General Test, minimum GPA of 3.0, research experience, letters of recommendation. Additional exam requirements/recommendations for international students: Required—TOEFL (minimum score 550 paper-based; 213 computer-based; 80 iBT). *Application deadline:* For fall admission, 1/11 for domestic and international students. Application fee: $30. Electronic applications accepted. *Expenses:* Tuition, state resident: full-time $7413. Tuition, nonresident: full-time $22,567. *Financial support:* In 2009–10, 21 students received support, including 3 fellowships with full tuition reimbursements available (averaging $18,000 per year), 6 research assistantships with full tuition reimbursements available (averaging $15,000 per year), 12 teaching assistantships with full tuition reimbursements available (averaging $15,000 per year); Federal Work-Study, institutionally sponsored loans, scholarships/grants, traineeships, health care benefits, and unspecified assistantships also available. *Faculty research:* Memory, learning and reading disabilities; expert performance; aging. Total annual research expenditures: $434,342. *Unit head:* Dr. Michael Kaschak, Director, 850-644-9363, Fax: 850-644-7739, E-mail: kaschak@psy.fsu.edu. *Application contact:* Cherie P. Miller, Graduate Program Assistant, 850-644-2499, Fax: 850-644-7739, E-mail: grad-info@psy.fsu.edu.

George Mason University, College of Humanities and Social Sciences, Department of Psychology, Fairfax, VA 22030. Offers aviation psychology (Certificate); cognitive neuroscience (Certificate); psychology (MA, PhD); school psychology (Certificate); usability (Certificate). *Accreditation:* APA. *Faculty:* 48 full-time (20 women), 14 part-time/adjunct (8 women). *Students:* 98 full-time (64 women), 133 part-time (94 women); includes 27 minority (8 African Americans, 13 Asian Americans or Pacific Islanders, 6 Hispanic Americans), 8 international. Average age 28. 598 applicants, 23% accepted, 70 enrolled. In 2009, 60 master's, 24 doctorates, 11 other advanced degrees awarded. Terminal master's awarded for partial completion of doctoral program. *Degree requirements:* For master's, comprehensive exam, thesis (for biopsychology); for doctorate, comprehensive exam, thesis/dissertation, 2nd year project. *Entrance requirements:* For master's, GRE General Test, minimum GPA of 3.25 in last 60 hours of course work, undergraduate course work in psychology, 3 letters of recommendation, resume; for doctorate, GRE General Test, minimum undergraduate GPA of 3.5, 3 letters of recommendation, resume, expanded goals statement. Additional exam requirements/recommendations for international students: Required—TOEFL (minimum score 575 paper-based; 230 computer-based; 88 iBT). *Application deadline:* For fall admission, 3/1 priority date for domestic students; for spring admission, 10/15 for domestic students. Application fee: $75. Electronic applications accepted. *Expenses:* Tuition, state resident: full-time $7568; part-time $315.33 per credit hour. Tuition, nonresident: full-time $21,704; part-time $904.33 per credit hour. Required fees: $2184; $91 per credit hour. *Financial support:* In 2009–10, 105 students received support, including 3 fellowships with full tuition reimbursements available (averaging $18,000 per year), 67 research assistantships with full and partial tuition reimbursements available (averaging $7,530 per year), 59 teaching assistantships with full and partial tuition reimbursements available (averaging $3,699 per year); career-related internships or fieldwork, scholarships/grants, traineeships, tuition waivers (partial), unspecified assistantships, and health care benefits (full-time research or teaching assistantship recipients) also available. Financial award application deadline: 3/1; financial award applicants required to submit FAFSA. *Faculty research:* Applied developmental psychology, biopsychology, clinical psychology, human factors/applied cognition psychology, industrial/organizational psychology, school psychology. Total annual research expenditures: $4.1 million. *Unit head:* Dr. Deborah Boehm-Davis, Chairperson, 703-993-1398, Fax: 703-993-1359, E-mail: dbdavis@gmu.edu. *Application contact:* Darby Wiggins, Graduate Program Assistant, 703-993-1548, E-mail: dwiggin3@gmu.edu.

The George Washington University, Columbian College of Arts and Sciences, Department of Psychology, Washington, DC 20052. Offers applied social psychology (PhD); clinical psychology (PhD); cognitive neuroscience (PhD). *Accreditation:* APA. Part-time and evening/weekend programs available. *Faculty:* 27 full-time (15 women), 25 part-time/adjunct (14 women). *Students:* 117 full-time (94 women), 89 part-time (73 women); includes 56 minority (16 African Americans, 2 American Indian/Alaska Native, 23 Asian Americans or Pacific Islanders, 15 Hispanic Americans), 4 international. Average age 28. 787 applicants, 6% accepted, 43 enrolled. In 2009, 49 doctorates awarded. *Degree requirements:* For doctorate, thesis/dissertation or alternative, general exam. *Entrance requirements:* For doctorate, GRE General Test, minimum GPA of 3.0. Additional exam requirements/recommendations for international students: Required—TOEFL (minimum score 550 paper-based; 213 computer-based; 80 iBT). *Application deadline:* For fall admission, 1/15 for domestic and international students. Application fee: $60. *Financial support:* In 2009–10, 62 students received support; fellowships with tuition reimbursements available, teaching assistantships with tuition reimbursements available, career-related internships or fieldwork, Federal Work-Study, and tuition waivers available. *Unit head:* Dr. Paul Poppen, Chair, 202-994-6324, E-mail: pjp@gwu.edu. *Application contact:* Information Contact, 202-994-6320, Fax: 202-994-1602, E-mail: psydept@gwu.edu.

Graduate School and University Center of the City University of New York, Graduate Studies, Program in Psychology, New York, NY 10016-4039. Offers basic applied neurocognition (PhD); biopsychology (PhD); clinical psychology (PhD); developmental psychology (PhD); environmental psychology (PhD); experimental psychology (PhD); industrial psychology (PhD); learning processes (PhD); neuropsychology (PhD); psychology (PhD); social personality (PhD). *Faculty:* 119 full-time (40 women). *Students:* 559 full-time (414 women), 1 part-time (0 women);

includes 101 minority (34 African Americans, 25 Asian Americans or Pacific Islanders, 42 Hispanic Americans), 57 international. Average age 33. 750 applicants, 16% accepted, 84 enrolled. In 2009, 54 doctorates awarded. *Degree requirements:* For doctorate, one foreign language, thesis/dissertation. *Entrance requirements:* For doctorate, GRE General Test. Additional exam requirements/recommendations for international students: Required—TOEFL. *Application deadline:* For fall admission, 12/15 priority date for domestic students. Application fee: $125. Electronic applications accepted. *Financial support:* In 2009–10, 371 students received support, including 340 fellowships, 34 research assistantships, 33 teaching assistantships; career-related internships or fieldwork, Federal Work-Study, institutionally sponsored loans, and tuition waivers (full and partial) also available. Financial award application deadline: 2/1; financial award applicants required to submit FAFSA. *Unit head:* Dr. Joseph Glick, Executive Officer, 212-817-8706, Fax: 212-817-1533, E-mail: jglick@gc.cuny.edu. *Application contact:* Les Gribben, Director of Admissions, 212-817-7470, Fax: 212-817-1624, E-mail: lgribben@gc.cuny.edu.

Harvard University, Graduate School of Arts and Sciences, Department of Psychology, Cambridge, MA 02138. Offers psychology (PhD), including behavior and decision analysis, cognition, developmental psychology, experimental psychology, personality, psychobiology, psychopathology; social psychology (PhD). *Accreditation:* APA. *Degree requirements:* For doctorate, thesis/dissertation, general exams. *Entrance requirements:* For doctorate, GRE General Test. Additional exam requirements/recommendations for international students: Required—TOEFL. *Expenses:* Tuition: Full-time $33,696. Required fees: $1126. Full-time tuition and fees vary according to program.

Harvard University, Graduate School of Education, Master's Programs in Education, Cambridge, MA 02138. Offers arts in education (Ed M); education policy and management (Ed M); higher education (Ed M); human development and psychology (Ed M); international education policy (Ed M); language and literacy (Ed M); learning and teaching (Ed M); mid-career mathematics and science (teaching certificate) (Ed M); mind brain and education (Ed M); risk and prevention (Ed M); school leadership (Ed M); special studies (Ed M); teaching and curriculum (teaching certificate) (Ed M); technology innovation and education (Ed M). Part-time programs available. *Faculty:* 70 full-time (33 women), 36 part-time/adjunct (20 women). *Students:* 598 full-time (448 women), 76 part-time (60 women); includes 132 minority (40 African Americans, 2 American Indian/Alaska Native, 58 Asian Americans or Pacific Islanders, 32 Hispanic Americans), 103 international. Average age 28. 1,574 applicants, 58% accepted, 640 enrolled. In 2009, 556 master's awarded. *Entrance requirements:* For master's, GRE General Test, 3 letters of recommendation. Additional exam requirements/recommendations for international students: Required—TOEFL (minimum score 600 paper-based; 250 computer-based; 100 iBT), TWE (minimum score 5). *Application deadline:* For fall admission, 1/4 for domestic and international students. Application fee: $85. Electronic applications accepted. *Expenses:* Contact institution. *Financial support:* In 2009–10, 424 students received support, including 25 fellowships with full and partial tuition reimbursements available (averaging $15,890 per year); career-related internships or fieldwork, Federal Work-Study, institutionally sponsored loans, scholarships/grants, health care benefits, tuition waivers (full and partial), and unspecified assistantships also available. Support available to part-time students. Financial award application deadline: 2/1; financial award applicants required to submit FAFSA. *Faculty research:* Learning and development, educational leadership and organizations, educational policy analysis. Total annual research expenditures: $18.1 million. *Unit head:* Jennifer L. Petrallia, Assistant Dean for Master's Studies, 617-495-8445. *Application contact:* Information Contact, 617-495-3414, Fax: 617-496-3577, E-mail: gseadmissions@harvard.edu.

Hunter College of the City University of New York, Graduate School, School of Arts and Sciences, Department of Psychology, New York, NY 10021-5085. Offers applied and evaluative psychology (MA); biopsychology and comparative psychology (MA); social, cognitive, and developmental psychology (MA). Part-time and evening/weekend programs available. *Faculty:* 18 full-time (9 women), 2 part-time/adjunct (0 women). *Students:* 12 full-time (10 women), 68 part-time (56 women); includes 13 minority (2 African Americans, 3 Asian Americans or Pacific Islanders, 8 Hispanic Americans). Average age 28. 122 applicants, 37% accepted, 24 enrolled. In 2009, 15 master's awarded. *Degree requirements:* For master's, comprehensive exam, thesis. *Entrance requirements:* For master's, GRE General Test, minimum 12 credits of course work in psychology, including statistics and experimental psychology; 2 letters of recommendation. Additional exam requirements/recommendations for international students: Required—TOEFL. *Application deadline:* For fall admission, 4/1 for domestic students, 2/1 for international students; for spring admission, 11/1 for domestic students, 9/1 for international students. Applications are processed on a rolling basis. Application fee: $125. *Expenses:* Tuition, state resident: full-time $7360; part-time $310 per credit. Required fees: $250 per semester. *Financial support:* Federal Work-Study, scholarships/grants, and tuition waivers (partial) available. Support available to part-time students. *Faculty research:* Personality, cognitive and linguistic development, hormonal and neural control of behavior, gender and culture, social cognition of health and attitudes. *Unit head:* Dr. Jeffrey Parsons, Chairperson, 212-772-5550, Fax: 212-772-5620, E-mail: jeffrey.parsons@hunter.cuny.edu. *Application contact:* Martin Braun, Acting Program Director, 212-772-4482, Fax: 212-650-3336, E-mail: cbraun@hunter.cuny.edu.

Indiana University Bloomington, University Graduate School, College of Arts and Sciences, Cognitive Science Program, Bloomington, IN 47406-7512. Offers PhD. *Faculty:* 76 full-time (17 women). *Students:* 17 full-time (4 women); includes 1 minority (Hispanic American), 5 international. Average age 30. 53 applicants, 6% accepted, 3 enrolled. In 2009, 9 doctorates awarded. *Degree requirements:* For doctorate, comprehensive exam, thesis/dissertation. *Entrance requirements:* For doctorate, GRE, 3 letters of reference, departmental questions form. Additional exam requirements/recommendations for international students: Required—TOEFL (minimum score 600 paper-based; 94 iBT). *Application deadline:* For fall admission, 1/15 for domestic students, 12/1 for international students. Application fee: $55 ($65 for international students). Electronic applications accepted. *Financial support:* In 2009–10, 17 students received support, including 6 fellowships (averaging $16,000 per year), 5 research assistantships (averaging $17,850 per year), 5 teaching assistantships (averaging $17,850 per year). *Faculty research:* Learning concepts, neural network models, language, animal cognition, dynamic and robotics systems approaches to behavior and cognition. *Unit head:* Robert Goldstone, Director, 812-856-3889, E-mail: rgoldsto@indiana.edu. *Application contact:* Susan Towle, Information Contact, 812-855-0031, E-mail: stowle@indiana.edu.

Indiana University Bloomington, University Graduate School, College of Arts and Sciences, Department of Psychological and Brain Sciences, Bloomington, IN 47405-7000. Offers biology and behavior (PhD); clinical science (PhD); cognitive psychology (PhD); developmental psychology (PhD); psychological and brain sciences (MA); social psychology (PhD). *Accreditation:* APA (one or more programs are accredited). *Faculty:* 53 full-time (16 women). *Students:* 92 full-time (51 women); includes 12 minority (4 African Americans, 4 Asian Americans or Pacific Islanders, 4 Hispanic Americans), 19 international. Average age 28. 239 applicants, 10% accepted, 15 enrolled. In 2009, 3 master's, 13 doctorates awarded. *Degree requirements:* For doctorate, comprehensive exam, thesis/dissertation, 1st and 2nd year projects, 1 year as associate instructor, qualifying exam, student teaching. *Entrance requirements:* For doctorate, GRE. Additional exam requirements/recommendations for international students: Required—TOEFL (minimum score 550 paper-based; 213 computer-based). *Application deadline:* For fall admission, 12/15 for domestic students, 12/1 for international students. Application fee: $55 ($65 for international students). Electronic applications accepted. *Financial support:* In 2009–10, 25 fellowships with full tuition reimbursements (averaging $23,000 per year), 11 research assistantships with full tuition reimbursements (averaging $17,850 per year), 7 teaching assistantships with full tuition reimbursements (averaging $17,850 per year) were awarded; scholarships/grants, health care benefits, and unspecified assistantships also available. *Unit head:* Dr. Linda B. Smith, Chair, 812-855-3991, Fax: 812-855-4691, E-mail: smith4@indiana.edu. *Application contact:* Patricia G. Crouch, Academic Services Coordinator, 812-855-4528, Fax: 812-855-4691, E-mail: pcrouch@indiana.edu.

Iowa State University of Science and Technology, Graduate College, College of Liberal Arts and Sciences, Department of Psychology, Ames, IA 50011. Offers cognitive psychology (PhD); counseling psychology (PhD); social psychology (PhD). *Accreditation:* APA. *Faculty:* 25 full-time (8 women), 8 part-time/adjunct (4 women). *Degree requirements:* For doctorate, comprehensive exam, thesis/dissertation. *Entrance requirements:* For doctorate, GRE General Test, GRE Subject Test (psychology), 3 letters of recommendation. Additional exam requirements/recommendations for international students: Required—TOEFL (minimum score 560 paper-based; 220 computer-based). *Application deadline:* For fall admission, 1/2 priority date for domestic and international students. Application fee: $30 ($70 for international students). Electronic applications accepted. *Expenses:* Tuition, state resident: full-time $6716. Tuition, nonresident: full-time $8908. Tuition and fees vary according to course level, course load, program and student level. *Financial support:* In 2009–10, fellowships with full tuition reimbursements (averaging $14,055 per year), research assistantships with full tuition reimbursements (averaging $12,200 per year), teaching assistantships with full tuition reimbursements (averaging $12,200 per year) were awarded; scholarships/grants, health care benefits, and unspecified assistantships also available. *Faculty research:* Counseling psychology, cognitive psychology, social psychology, health psychology, psychology and public policy. *Unit head:* Carolyn Cutrona, Chair, 515-294-0283, Fax: 515-294-6424, E-mail: ccutrona@iastate.edu. *Application contact:* Ann Schmidt, Graduate Admissions Secretary, 515-294-1743, Fax: 515-294-6424, E-mail: psychadm@iastate.edu.

The Johns Hopkins University, Zanvyl Krieger School of Arts and Sciences, Department of Cognitive Science, Baltimore, MD 21218-2699. Offers PhD. *Faculty:* 8 full-time (3 women). *Students:* 19 full-time (12 women); includes 3 minority (1 African American, 2 Hispanic Americans), 3 international. Average age 26. 56 applicants, 11% accepted, 6 enrolled. In 2009, 3 doctorates awarded. Terminal master's awarded for partial completion of doctoral program. *Degree requirements:* For doctorate, thesis/dissertation, 2 research papers. *Entrance requirements:* For doctorate, GRE General Test, letters of recommendation, sample of work. Additional exam requirements/recommendations for international students: Required—TOEFL (minimum score 600 paper-based; 250 computer-based; 100 iBT), IELTS. *Application deadline:* For fall admission, 1/17 for domestic and international students. Application fee: $75. Electronic applications accepted. *Financial support:* In 2009–10, 1 fellowship with full tuition reimbursement (averaging $30,000 per year), research assistantships with full tuition reimbursements (averaging $20,000 per year), 19 teaching assistantships with full tuition reimbursements (averaging $30,000 per year) were awarded; scholarships/grants, health care benefits, and fellowship award, 19 teaching assistantships ($30,000 average) also available. Financial award application deadline: 1/17; financial award applicants required to submit FAFSA. *Faculty research:* Acquisition and development, cognitive neuropsychology and neuroscience, computational studies, psycholinguistics and cognitive psychology, theoretical linguistics. Total annual research expenditures: $1.8 million. *Unit head:* Dr. Barbara Landau, Dick & Lydia Todd Professor, Department Chair, 410-516-5255, Fax: 410-516-8020, E-mail: landau@cogsci.jhu.edu. *Application contact:* Barbara Ann Fisher, Academic Program Coordinator, 410-516-5250, Fax: 410-516-8020, E-mail: fisher@cogsci.jhu.edu.

Louisiana State University and Agricultural and Mechanical College, Graduate School, College of Arts and Sciences, Department of Psychology, Baton Rouge, LA 70803. Offers biological psychology (MA, PhD); clinical psychology (MA, PhD); cognitive psychology (MA, PhD); developmental psychology (MA, PhD); industrial/organizational psychology (MA, PhD); school psychology (MA, PhD). *Accreditation:* APA (one or more programs are accredited). *Faculty:* 27 full-time (10 women). *Students:* 94 full-time (68 women), 17 part-time (12 women); includes 14 minority (6 African Americans, 2 American Indian/Alaska Native, 2 Asian Americans or Pacific Islanders, 4 Hispanic Americans), 3 international. Average age 27. 232 applicants, 18% accepted, 29 enrolled. In 2009, 13 master's, 14 doctorates awarded. Terminal master's awarded for partial completion of doctoral program. *Degree requirements:* For master's, thesis; for doctorate, thesis/dissertation, 1 year internship. *Entrance requirements:* For master's and doctorate, GRE General Test, minimum GPA of 3.0. Additional exam requirements/recommendations for international students: Required—TOEFL (minimum score 550 paper-based; 213 computer-based; 79 iBT) or IELTS (minimum score 6.5). *Application deadline:* For fall admission, 1/15 for domestic and international students. Applications are processed on a rolling basis. Application fee: $50 ($70 for international students). Electronic applications accepted. *Financial support:* In 2009–10, 108 students received support, including 5 fellowships (averaging $26,974 per year), 2 research assistantships with partial tuition reimbursements available (averaging $18,000 per year), 74 teaching assistantships with partial tuition reimbursements available (averaging $14,751 per year); career-related internships or fieldwork, Federal Work-Study, institutionally sponsored loans, scholarships/grants, health care benefits, and tuition waivers (full and partial) also available. Financial award applicants required to submit FAFSA. *Faculty research:* Clinical psychology, autism, anxiety, addition, neuropsychology, school psychology, cognitive psychology, experimental psychology. Total annual research expenditures: $1 million. *Unit head:* Dr. Robert Matthews, Chair, 225-578-8745, Fax: 225-578-4125, E-mail: psmath@lsu.edu. *Application contact:* Dr. Jason Hicks, Coordinator of Graduate Studies, 225-578-4109, Fax: 225-578-4125, E-mail: jhicks@lsu.edu.

Loyola University Chicago, Graduate School, Department of Psychology, Program in Human Perception, Chicago, IL 60660. Offers MS. *Entrance requirements:* For master's, two letters of recommendation, minimum GPA of 3.5. Application fee: $50. *Expenses:* Tuition: Full-time $14,220; part-time $790 per credit hour. Required fees: $60 per semester hour. Tuition and fees vary according to program. *Faculty research:* Auditory information processing, visual information processing, attention, sensory memory, decision theory. *Unit head:* Dr. Raymond Dye, Program Director, 773-508-3018, Fax: 773-508-8713, E-mail: rdye@luc.edu. *Application contact:* Ron Martin, Assistant Director of Enrollment Management, 312-915-8950, Fax: 312-915-8905, E-mail: gradapp@luc.edu.

Massachusetts Institute of Technology, School of Science, Department of Brain and Cognitive Sciences, Cambridge, MA 02139-4307. Offers cognitive science (PhD); neuroscience (PhD). *Faculty:* 38 full-time (14 women). *Students:* 93 full-time (32 women); includes 21 minority (3 African Americans, 1 American Indian/Alaska Native, 9 Asian Americans or Pacific Islanders, 8 Hispanic Americans), 16 international. Average age 27. 371 applicants, 6% accepted, 10 enrolled. In 2009, 13 doctorates awarded. *Degree requirements:* For doctorate, comprehensive exam, thesis/dissertation. *Entrance requirements:* For doctorate, GRE General Test. Additional exam requirements/recommendations for international students: Required—TOEFL (minimum score 577 paper-based; 233 computer-based; 90 iBT), IELTS (minimum score 7). *Application deadline:* For fall admission, 12/10 for domestic and international students. Application fee: $75. Electronic applications accepted. *Expenses:* Tuition: Full-time $37,510; part-time $585 per unit. Required fees: $272. *Financial support:* In 2009–10, 91 students received support, including 61 fellowships with tuition reimbursements available (averaging $27,103 per year), 18 research assistantships with tuition reimbursements available (averaging $29,154 per year), 9 teaching assistantships with tuition reimbursements available (averaging $30,040 per year); Federal Work-Study, institutionally sponsored loans, scholarships/grants, traineeships, health care benefits, and unspecified assistantships also available. *Faculty research:* Vision—perception and physiology, learning, memory, and executive control—molecular and systems approaches, sensorimotor systems—physiology and computation, neural and cognitive development and plasticity, language and high-level cognition—learning, acquisition, and computation. Total annual research expenditures: $19.7 million. *Unit head:* Prof. Mriganka Sur, Head, 617-253-9344, E-mail: bcs-info@mit.edu. *Application contact:* Academic Office, 617-253-7403, Fax: 617-253-9216, E-mail: bcs-admissions@mit.edu.

Mississippi State University, College of Arts and Sciences, Department of Psychology, Mississippi State, MS 39762. Offers cognitive science (PhD); psychology (MS), including clinical psychology, experimental psychology. *Faculty:* 13 full-time (5 women). *Students:* 40 full-time (26 women), 4 part-time (3 women); includes 3 minority (2 African Americans, 1 Asian American or Pacific Islander), 3 international. Average age 26. 69 applicants, 46% accepted, 20 enrolled. In 2009, 11 master's awarded. Terminal master's awarded for partial completion of doctoral program. *Degree requirements:* For master's, comprehensive exam, thesis; for

Cognitive Sciences

Mississippi State University (continued)
doctorate, thesis/dissertation, qualifying exam, comprehensive written and oral exam. *Entrance requirements:* For master's, GRE General Test, minimum GPA of 2.75 on last two years of undergraduate courses; for doctorate, GRE General Test, proficiency in at least 1 computer language. Additional exam requirements/recommendations for international students: Required—TOEFL (minimum score 475 paper-based; 153 computer-based; 53 iBT); Recommended—IELTS (minimum score 4.5). *Application deadline:* For fall admission, 1/15 priority date for domestic students, 5/1 for international students; for spring admission, 11/1 priority date for domestic students, 9/1 for international students. Applications are processed on a rolling basis. Application fee: $40. Electronic applications accepted. *Expenses:* Tuition, state resident: full-time $2575.50; part-time $286.25 per credit hour. Tuition, nonresident: full-time $6510; part-time $723.50 per credit hour. Tuition and fees vary according to course load. *Financial support:* In 2009–10, 7 research assistantships with full tuition reimbursements (averaging $11,132 per year), 15 teaching assistantships with full tuition reimbursements (averaging $9,023 per year) were awarded; career-related internships or fieldwork, Federal Work-Study, institutionally sponsored loans, scholarships/grants, and unspecified assistantships also available. Financial award application deadline: 4/1; financial award applicants required to submit FAFSA. *Faculty research:* Personality type, alcoholism, blindness and low vision, mental retardation, language comprehension. Total annual research expenditures: $2.2 million. *Unit head:* Dr. Stephen B. Klein, Department Head, 662-325-3202, Fax: 662-325-7212, E-mail: sbkl@ra.msstate.edu. *Application contact:* Dr. Keven J. Armstrong, Graduate Coordinator, 662-325-3202, Fax: 662-325-7212, E-mail: grad@psychology.msstate.edu.

The New School: A University, The New School for Social Research, Department of Psychology, New York, NY 10011. Offers clinical psychology (PhD); cognitive, social and developmental psychology (PhD); general psychology (MA). *Accreditation:* APA (one or more programs are accredited). Part-time programs available. *Faculty:* 13 full-time (5 women). *Students:* 172 full-time (130 women), 105 part-time (87 women); includes 49 minority (13 African Americans, 1 American Indian/Alaska Native, 15 Asian Americans or Pacific Islanders, 20 Hispanic Americans), 41 international. Average age 30. 299 applicants, 80% accepted, 76 enrolled. In 2009, 74 master's, 17 doctorates awarded. Terminal master's awarded for partial completion of doctoral program. *Degree requirements:* For master's, comprehensive exam (for some programs), thesis (for some programs); for doctorate, thesis/dissertation, qualifying exam. *Entrance requirements:* For master's, GRE General Test; for doctorate, GRE General Test, MA. Additional exam requirements/recommendations for international students: Required—TOEFL (minimum score 600 paper-based; 250 computer-based; 100 iBT). *Application deadline:* For fall admission, 1/17 priority date for domestic and international students; for spring admission, 10/15 priority date for domestic and international students. Applications are processed on a rolling basis. Application fee: $50. Electronic applications accepted. *Financial support:* Fellowships, research assistantships, teaching assistantships, Federal Work-Study, scholarships/grants, tuition waivers (full and partial), and unspecified assistantships available. Support available to part-time students. Financial award application deadline: 3/1; financial award applicants required to submit FAFSA. *Faculty research:* Consciousness, memory, language, perceptions, psychopathology. *Unit head:* Dr. McWelling Todman, Chair, 212-229-5727 Ext. 3258, E-mail: todmanm@newschool.edu. *Application contact:* Robert MacDonald, Director of Admissions, 212-229-5727 Ext. 3007, Fax: 212-989-7102, E-mail: macdonar@newschool.edu.

New York University, Graduate School of Arts and Science, Department of Psychology, New York, NY 10012-1019. Offers cognition and perception (PhD); community psychology (PhD); general psychology (MA); industrial/organizational psychology (MA); psychotherapy and psychoanalysis (Advanced Certificate); social/personality psychology (PhD). Part-time programs available. *Students:* 151 full-time (94 women), 273 part-time (192 women); includes 59 minority (13 African Americans, 1 American Indian/Alaska Native, 27 Asian Americans or Pacific Islanders, 18 Hispanic Americans), 62 international. Average age 32. 748 applicants, 46% accepted, 122 enrolled. In 2009, 100 master's, 11 doctorates, 8 other advanced degrees awarded. Terminal master's awarded for partial completion of doctoral program. *Degree requirements:* For master's, comprehensive exam, thesis or alternative; for doctorate, thesis/dissertation. *Entrance requirements:* For master's, GRE General Test, minimum GPA of 3.0; for doctorate, GRE General Test, GRE Subject Test; for Advanced Certificate, doctoral degree, minimum GPA of 3.0. Additional exam requirements/recommendations for international students: Required—TOEFL. *Application deadline:* For fall admission, 12/18 for domestic students. Application fee: $90. *Expenses:* Tuition: Full-time $30,528; part-time $1272 per credit. Required fees: $2177. *Financial support:* Fellowships with tuition reimbursements, research assistantships with tuition reimbursements, teaching assistantships with tuition reimbursements, career-related internships or fieldwork, Federal Work-Study, institutionally sponsored loans, scholarships/grants, traineeships, health care benefits, and unspecified assistantships available. Financial award application deadline: 12/18; financial award applicants required to submit FAFSA. *Faculty research:* Vision, memory, social cognition, social and cognitive development, relationships. *Unit head:* Madeline Heilman, Director of Ph.D. Program, 212-998-7900, Fax: 212-995-4018, E-mail: psychq@psych.nyu.edu. *Application contact:* Barry Cohen, Director of M.A. Program, 212-998-7900, Fax: 212-995-4018, E-mail: psychq@psych.nyu.edu.

North Dakota State University, College of Graduate and Interdisciplinary Studies, College of Science and Mathematics, Department of Psychology, Fargo, ND 58108. Offers clinical psychology (MS); cognitive and visual neuroscience (PhD); health and social psychology (PhD); psychology (MS). *Faculty:* 18 full-time (4 women), 2 part-time/adjunct (1 woman). *Students:* 36 full-time (27 women); includes 4 minority (1 African American, 2 Asian Americans or Pacific Islanders, 1 Hispanic American), 1 international. Average age 24. 48 applicants, 33% accepted, 10 enrolled. In 2009, 3 master's, 1 doctorate awarded. *Degree requirements:* For master's, thesis; for doctorate, thesis/dissertation. *Entrance requirements:* For master's and doctorate, GRE General Test, GRE Subject Test. Additional exam requirements/recommendations for international students: Required—TOEFL (minimum score 525 paper-based; 197 computer-based; 71 iBT). *Application deadline:* For fall admission, 3/1 for domestic and international students. Application fee: $45 ($60 for international students). Electronic applications accepted. *Financial support:* In 2009–10, 36 students received support, including 2 fellowships with full tuition reimbursements available (averaging $16,000 per year), 23 research assistantships with full tuition reimbursements available (averaging $16,000 per year), 11 teaching assistantships with full tuition reimbursements available (averaging $6,000 per year); career-related internships or fieldwork, Federal Work-Study, institutionally sponsored loans, tuition waivers (full and partial), and unspecified assistantships also available. Support available to part-time students. Financial award application deadline: 3/1. *Faculty research:* Cognition science, neuropsychology, group behavior, applied behavior analysis, behavior therapy. Total annual research expenditures: $2 million. *Unit head:* Dr. Paul D. Rokke, Chair, 701-231-8622, Fax: 701-231-8426, E-mail: paul.rokke@ndsu.edu. *Application contact:* Dr. Paul D. Rokke, Chair, 701-231-8622, Fax: 701-231-8426, E-mail: paul.rokke@ndsu.edu.

Northwestern University, The Graduate School, Judd A. and Marjorie Weinberg College of Arts and Sciences, Department of Psychology, Evanston, IL 60208. Offers brain, behavior and cognition (PhD); clinical psychology (PhD); cognitive psychology (PhD); personality (PhD); social psychology (PhD); JD/PhD. Admissions and degrees offered through The Graduate School. *Accreditation:* APA (one or more programs are accredited). Part-time programs available. *Degree requirements:* For doctorate, thesis/dissertation. *Entrance requirements:* For doctorate, GRE General Test, GRE Subject Test. Additional exam requirements/recommendations for international students: Required—TOEFL. Electronic applications accepted. *Faculty research:* Memory and higher order cognition, anxiety and depression, effectiveness of psychotherapy, social cognition, molecular basis of memory.

The Ohio State University, Graduate School, College of Social and Behavioral Sciences, School of Social and Behavioral Science, Department of Psychology, Columbus, OH 43210. Offers behavioral neuroscience (PhD); clinical psychology (PhD); cognitive psychology (PhD); developmental psychology (PhD); mental retardation and developmental disabilities (PhD); psychology (MA); quantitative psychology (PhD); social psychology (PhD). *Accreditation:* APA (one or more programs are accredited). *Faculty:* 60. *Students:* 88 full-time (59 women), 47 part-time (31 women); includes 20 minority (7 African Americans, 1 American Indian/Alaska Native, 5 Asian Americans or Pacific Islanders, 7 Hispanic Americans), 20 international. Average age 27. In 2009, 15 master's, 20 doctorates awarded. *Degree requirements:* For doctorate, thesis/dissertation. *Entrance requirements:* For master's and doctorate, GRE General Test. Additional exam requirements/recommendations for international students: Required—TOEFL (minimum score 600 paper-based; 250 computer-based). *Application deadline:* For fall admission, 12/31 for domestic students, 11/30 for international students. Applications are processed on a rolling basis. Application fee: $40 ($50 for international students). Electronic applications accepted. *Expenses:* Tuition, state resident: full-time $10,683. Tuition, nonresident: full-time $25,923. Tuition and fees vary according to course load and program. *Financial support:* Fellowships, research assistantships, teaching assistantships available. *Unit head:* Michael Vasey, Graduate Studies Committee Chair, E-mail: vasey.1@osu.edu. *Application contact:* 614-292-9444, Fax: 614-292-3895, E-mail: domestic.grad@osu.edu.

Queen's University at Kingston, School of Graduate Studies and Research, Faculty of Arts and Sciences, Department of Psychology, Kingston, ON K7L 3N6, Canada. Offers brain behavior and cognitive science (MA, PhD); clinical psychology (MA, PhD); developmental psychology (MA, PhD); social personality psychology (MA, PhD). *Accreditation:* APA (one or more programs are accredited). *Degree requirements:* For master's, thesis; for doctorate, comprehensive exam, thesis/dissertation. *Entrance requirements:* For master's and doctorate, GRE General Test. Additional exam requirements/recommendations for international students: Required—TOEFL. *Faculty research:* Human development, social, personality, behavioral neuroscience, forensic.

Rensselaer Polytechnic Institute, Graduate School, School of Humanities and Social Sciences, Department of Cognitive Science, Troy, NY 12180-3590. Offers PhD. *Faculty:* 13 full-time (1 woman). *Students:* 18 full-time (4 women), 4 part-time (3 women); includes 4 Asian Americans or Pacific Islanders, 1 Hispanic American. Average age 23. 30 applicants, 27% accepted, 5 enrolled. In 2009, 5 doctorates awarded. *Degree requirements:* For doctorate, thesis/dissertation. *Entrance requirements:* For doctorate, GRE General Test. Additional exam requirements/recommendations for international students: Required—TOEFL (minimum score 600 paper-based; 250 computer-based; 88 iBT), IELTS (minimum score 7.5). *Application deadline:* For fall admission, 1/15 priority date for domestic and international students. Applications are processed on a rolling basis. Application fee: $75. Electronic applications accepted. *Expenses:* Tuition: Full-time $38,100. *Financial support:* In 2009–10, 10 students received support, including 1 fellowship with full tuition reimbursement available (averaging $22,000 per year), 8 research assistantships with full tuition reimbursements available (averaging $23,500 per year), 5 teaching assistantships with full tuition reimbursements available (averaging $16,500 per year); institutionally sponsored loans, scholarships/grants, and unspecified assistantships also available. Financial award application deadline: 2/1. *Faculty research:* Perception and action, logic, artificial intelligence, cognitive engineering, computational cognitive modeling. Total annual research expenditures: $1.6 million. *Unit head:* Dr. Selmer Bringsjord, Professor and Chair, 518-276-8105, Fax: 518-276-8268, E-mail: brings@rpi.edu. *Application contact:* Betty Osganian, Student Services Administrator, 518-276-6473, Fax: 518-276-8268, E-mail: osgane@rpi.edu.

Rice University, Graduate Programs, School of Social Sciences, Department of Psychology, Houston, TX 77251-1892. Offers cognitive sciences (MA, PhD); industrial-organizational/social psychology (MA, PhD); psychology (MA, PhD). *Faculty:* 16 full-time (6 women), 26 part-time/adjunct (13 women). *Students:* 44 full-time (29 women); includes 12 minority (3 African Americans, 3 Asian Americans or Pacific Islanders, 6 Hispanic Americans), 9 international. Average age 29. 146 applicants, 7% accepted, 7 enrolled. In 2009, 6 master's, 7 doctorates awarded. Terminal master's awarded for partial completion of doctoral program. *Degree requirements:* For master's, thesis; for doctorate, thesis/dissertation. *Entrance requirements:* For doctorate, GRE General Test, minimum GPA of 3.0. Additional exam requirements/recommendations for international students: Required—TOEFL. *Application deadline:* For fall admission, 1/15 priority date for domestic and international students. Applications are processed on a rolling basis. Application fee: $35. Electronic applications accepted. *Financial support:* In 2009–10, 29 students received support, including 25 fellowships with full tuition reimbursements available (averaging $18,500 per year), 5 research assistantships with full tuition reimbursements available (averaging $18,500 per year); career-related internships or fieldwork, Federal Work-Study, institutionally sponsored loans, scholarships/grants, health care benefits, tuition waivers (full), and unspecified assistantships also available. Financial award application deadline: 1/15; financial award applicants required to submit FAFSA. *Faculty research:* Cognitive, cognitive neuropsychology, human factors, human-computer interaction, industrial-organizational psychology. Total annual research expenditures: $754,120. *Unit head:* Dr. James L. Dannemiller, Chairman, 713-348-4850, Fax: 713-348-5221, E-mail: psyc@rice.edu. *Application contact:* Lanita K. Martin, Coordinator, 713-348-4850, Fax: 713-348-5221, E-mail: psyc@rice.edu.

Rutgers, The State University of New Jersey, Newark, Graduate School, Program in Psychology, Newark, NJ 07102. Offers cognitive neuroscience (PhD); cognitive science (PhD); perception (PhD); psychobiology (PhD); social cognition (PhD). *Degree requirements:* For doctorate, comprehensive exam, thesis/dissertation. *Entrance requirements:* For doctorate, GRE General Test, GRE Subject Test, minimum undergraduate B average. Electronic applications accepted. *Faculty research:* Visual perception (luminance, motion), neuroendocrine mechanisms in behavior (reproduction, pain), attachment theory, connectionist modeling of cognition.

See Close-Up on page 1093.

Rutgers, The State University of New Jersey, New Brunswick, Graduate School-New Brunswick, Program in Psychology, Piscataway, NJ 08854-8097. Offers behavioral neuroscience (PhD); clinical psychology (PhD); cognitive psychology (PhD); interdisciplinary health psychology (PhD); social psychology (PhD). *Accreditation:* APA. *Degree requirements:* For doctorate, comprehensive exam, thesis/dissertation. *Entrance requirements:* For doctorate, GRE General Test, 3 letters of recommendation. Additional exam requirements/recommendations for international students: Required—TOEFL (minimum score 577 paper-based; 233 computer-based). Electronic applications accepted. *Faculty research:* Learning and memory, behavioral ecology, hormones and behavior, psychopharmacology, anxiety disorders.

State University of New York at Binghamton, Graduate School, School of Arts and Sciences, Department of Psychology, Specialization in Cognitive and Behavioral Science, Binghamton, NY 13902-6000. Offers MA, PhD. *Students:* 11 full-time (4 women), 7 part-time (4 women); includes 2 minority (1 Asian American or Pacific Islander, 1 Hispanic American), 2 international. Average age 27. 17 applicants, 18% accepted, 2 enrolled. In 2009, 4 master's, 2 doctorates awarded. *Degree requirements:* For master's, thesis; for doctorate, thesis/dissertation, departmental qualifying exam. *Entrance requirements:* For master's and doctorate, GRE General Test, GRE Subject Test. Additional exam requirements/recommendations for international students: Required—TOEFL (minimum score 550 paper-based; 213 computer-based; 80 iBT). *Application deadline:* For fall admission, 1/15 priority date for domestic and international students. Applications are processed on a rolling basis. Application fee: $60. Electronic applications accepted. *Financial support:* Fellowships, research assistantships, teaching assistantships, career-related internships or fieldwork, Federal Work-Study, institutionally sponsored loans, scholarships/grants, traineeships, health care benefits, and unspecified assistantships available. Financial award application deadline: 2/15; financial award applicants required to submit FAFSA. *Unit head:* Dr. Albrecht Inhoff, Graduate Coordinator, 607-777-3958, E-mail: inhoff@binghamton.edu. *Application contact:* Victoria Williams, Recruiting and Admissions Coordinator, 607-777-2151, Fax: 607-777-2501, E-mail: vwilliam@binghamton.edu.

Temple University, Graduate School, College of Liberal Arts, Department of Psychology, Program in Cognitive Psychology, Philadelphia, PA 19122-6096. Offers PhD. *Degree requirements:* For doctorate, thesis/dissertation. *Entrance requirements:* For doctorate, GRE General Test, minimum GPA of 3.0. Additional exam requirements/recommendations for international students: Required—TOEFL (minimum score 550 paper-based; 213 computer-based; 79 iBT). Electronic applications accepted. *Faculty research:* Language development, creativity, childhood memory, visual perception, aging.

Texas A&M University, College of Liberal Arts, Department of Psychology, College Station, TX 77843. Offers behavioral and cellular neuroscience (MS, PhD); clinical psychology (MS, PhD); cognitive psychology (MS, PhD); developmental psychology (MS, PhD); industrial/organizational psychology (MS, PhD); social psychology (MS, PhD). *Accreditation:* APA (one or more programs are accredited). *Faculty:* 36. *Students:* 84 full-time (58 women), 6 part-time (5 women); includes 26 minority (6 African Americans, 3 Asian Americans or Pacific Islanders, 17 Hispanic Americans), 6 international. In 2009, 12 master's, 8 doctorates awarded. *Degree requirements:* For master's, thesis; for doctorate, comprehensive exam (for some programs), thesis/dissertation. *Entrance requirements:* For master's and doctorate, GRE General Test. Additional exam requirements/recommendations for international students: Required—TOEFL. *Application deadline:* For fall admission, 1/5 for domestic and international students. Application fee: $50 ($75 for international students). Electronic applications accepted. *Expenses:* Tuition, state resident: full-time $3991; part-time $221.74 per credit hour. Tuition, nonresident: full-time $9049; part-time $502.74 per credit hour. *Financial support:* Fellowships with partial tuition reimbursements, research assistantships with partial tuition reimbursements, teaching assistantships with partial tuition reimbursements, career-related internships or fieldwork, institutionally sponsored loans, health care benefits, and unspecified assistantships available. Financial award application deadline: 1/5; financial award applicants required to submit FAFSA. *Unit head:* Dr. Les Morey, Head, 979-845-2581, Fax: 979-845-4727, E-mail: lmorey@psych.tamu.edu. *Application contact:* Sharon Starr, Graduate Admissions Supervisor, 979-458-1710, Fax: 979-845-4727, E-mail: gradadv@psyc.tamu.edu.

Texas A&M University–Commerce, Graduate School, College of Education and Human Services, Department of Psychology and Special Education, Commerce, TX 75429-3011. Offers cognition and instruction (PhD); psychology (MA, MS); special education (M Ed, MA, MS). Part-time programs available. Terminal master's awarded for partial completion of doctoral program. *Degree requirements:* For master's, comprehensive exam, thesis (for some programs); for doctorate, thesis/dissertation, departmental qualifying exam. *Entrance requirements:* For master's, GRE General Test; for doctorate, GRE General Test, 3 letters of recommendation. Electronic applications accepted. *Faculty research:* Human learning, study skills, multicultural bilingual, diversity and special education, educationally handicapped.

Texas Christian University, College of Science and Engineering, Department of Psychology, Fort Worth, TX 76129-0002. Offers experimental psychology (PhD), including cognitive psychology, learning, neuropsychology, social psychology; psychology (MA, MS). *Degree requirements:* For master's, thesis; for doctorate, thesis/dissertation. *Entrance requirements:* For master's and doctorate, GRE General Test. Additional exam requirements/recommendations for international students: Required—TOEFL. *Application deadline:* For fall admission, 3/1 for domestic and international students; for spring admission, 12/1 for domestic students. Applications are processed on a rolling basis. Application fee: $50. *Expenses:* Tuition: Full-time $17,640; part-time $980 per credit hour. Tuition and fees vary according to program. *Financial support:* In 2009–10, 20 students received support; teaching assistantships with full tuition reimbursements available, unspecified assistantships available. Financial award application deadline: 3/1. *Unit head:* Dr. Charles Lord, Graduate Director, 817-257-7410, E-mail: c.lord@tcu.edu. *Application contact:* Marilyn Eudaly, Department Manager, 817-257-6437.

University at Buffalo, the State University of New York, Graduate School, College of Arts and Sciences, Department of Psychology, Buffalo, NY 14260. Offers behavioral neuroscience (PhD); clinical psychology (PhD); cognitive psychology (PhD); general psychology (MA); social-personality psychology (PhD). *Accreditation:* APA (one or more programs are accredited). *Faculty:* 32 full-time (12 women), 8 part-time/adjunct (6 women). *Students:* 94 full-time (64 women), 7 part-time (2 women); includes 5 minority (2 African Americans, 3 Hispanic Americans), 12 international. Average age 27. 353 applicants, 11% accepted. In 2009, 18 master's, 7 doctorates awarded. Terminal master's awarded for partial completion of doctoral program. *Degree requirements:* For master's, project; for doctorate, thesis/dissertation. *Entrance requirements:* For master's and doctorate, GRE General Test. Additional exam requirements/recommendations for international students: Required—TOEFL (minimum score 550 paper-based; 213 computer-based; 79 iBT). *Application deadline:* For fall admission, 1/5 for domestic and international students. Application fee: $50. Electronic applications accepted. *Financial support:* In 2009–10, 81 students received support, including 20 fellowships with full tuition reimbursements available (averaging $14,400 per year), 1 research assistantship with full tuition reimbursement available (averaging $10,400 per year), 38 teaching assistantships with full tuition reimbursements available (averaging $10,400 per year); career-related internships or fieldwork, Federal Work-Study, institutionally sponsored loans, scholarships/grants, and tuition waivers (partial) also available. Financial award application deadline: 1/5; financial award applicants required to submit FAFSA. *Faculty research:* Neural, endocrine, and molecular bases of behavior; adult mood and anxiety disorders; relationship dysfunction; attention deficit/hyperactivity disorder; psycho-linguistics. Total annual research expenditures: $7.9 million. *Unit head:* Dr. Paul A. Luce, Chair, 716-645-3650 Ext. 203, Fax: 716-645-3801, E-mail: psychair@acsu.buffalo.edu. *Application contact:* Michele Nowacki, Coordinator of Admissions, 716-645-3650 Ext. 209, Fax: 716-645-3801, E-mail: psych@acsu.buffalo.edu.

The University of British Columbia, Faculty of Arts and Faculty of Graduate Studies, Department of Psychology, Vancouver, BC V6T 1Z4, Canada. Offers behavioral neuroscience (MA, PhD); clinical psychology (MA, PhD); cognitive science (MA, PhD); developmental psychology (MA, PhD); health psychology (MA, PhD); quantitative methods (MA, PhD); social/personality psychology (MA, PhD). *Accreditation:* APA (one or more programs are accredited). Terminal master's awarded for partial completion of doctoral program. *Degree requirements:* For master's, thesis; for doctorate, comprehensive exam, thesis/dissertation. *Entrance requirements:* For master's and doctorate, GRE General Test. Additional exam requirements/recommendations for international students: Required—TOEFL (minimum score 550 paper-based; 230 computer-based; 80 iBT). Electronic applications accepted. *Faculty research:* Clinical, developmental, social/personality, cognition, behavioral neuroscience.

University of California, Merced, Division of Graduate Studies, School of Social Sciences, Humanities and Arts, Merced, CA 95343. Offers social and cognitive sciences (MA, PhD); world cultures (MA, PhD). *Expenses:* Tuition, nonresident: full-time $15,102. Required fees: $10,919.

University of California, San Diego, Office of Graduate Studies, Department of Cognitive Science, La Jolla, CA 92093. Offers PhD. *Degree requirements:* For doctorate, one foreign language, thesis/dissertation. *Entrance requirements:* For doctorate, GRE General Test. Additional exam requirements/recommendations for international students: Required—TOEFL (minimum score 550 paper-based; 213 computer-based; 79 iBT). Electronic applications accepted. *Faculty research:* Neural networks, neurobiology of cognition, cognitive modeling, distributed cognition, psycholinguistics.

University of California, San Diego, Office of Graduate Studies, Interdisciplinary Program in Cognitive Science, La Jolla, CA 92093. Offers cognitive science/anthropology (PhD); cognitive science/communication (PhD); cognitive science/computer science and engineering (PhD); cognitive science/linguistics (PhD); cognitive science/neuroscience (PhD); cognitive science/philosophy (PhD); cognitive science/psychology (PhD); cognitive science/sociology (PhD). Admissions offered through affiliated departments. *Degree requirements:* For doctorate, thesis/dissertation. *Entrance requirements:* For doctorate, GRE General Test, acceptance into one of the eight participating departments. *Faculty research:* Language and cognition, philosophy of mind, visual perception, biological anthropology, sociolinguistics.

University of California, Santa Barbara, Graduate Division, College of Letters and Sciences, Division of Humanities and Fine Arts, Department of Linguistics, Santa Barbara, CA 93106-3100. Offers applied linguistics (PhD); cognitive science (PhD); human development (PhD); language, interaction, and social organizations (PhD); MA/PhD. *Faculty:* 23 full-time (12 women). *Students:* 25 full-time (14 women). Average age 32. 63 applicants, 17% accepted, 5 enrolled. In 2009, 5 doctorates awarded. *Degree requirements:* For doctorate, one foreign language, comprehensive exam, thesis/dissertation. *Entrance requirements:* For doctorate, GRE, 3 letters of recommendation, resume/curriculum vitae. Additional exam requirements/recommendations for international students: Required—TOEFL (minimum score 550 paper-based; 213 computer-based; 80 iBT), or IELTS (minimum score 7). *Application deadline:* For fall admission, 12/1 priority date for domestic and international students. Application fee: $70 ($90 for international students). Electronic applications accepted. *Financial support:* In 2009–10, 24 students received support, including 19 fellowships with full and partial tuition reimbursements available (averaging $12,400 per year), 1 research assistantship with full and partial tuition reimbursement available (averaging $3,000 per year), 13 teaching assistantships with partial tuition reimbursements available (averaging $5,600 per year); Federal Work-Study, institutionally sponsored loans, scholarships/grants, health care benefits, and unspecified assistantships also available. Financial award application deadline: 12/1; financial award applicants required to submit FAFSA. *Faculty research:* Language, race and subcultural identities among California teenagers; language acquisition, psycholinguistics; language documentation, fieldwork; syntax of nominalization in 5 Tibeto-Burman languages; perceptual correlates of syllable weight. *Unit head:* Prof. Patricia M. Clancy, Chair, 805-893-8658, Fax: 805-893-7769, E-mail: pclancy@linguistics.ucsb.edu. *Application contact:* Mary Rae Staton, Graduate Program Assistant, 805-893-3776, Fax: 805-893-7769, E-mail: staton@linguistics.ucsb.edu.

University of California, Santa Barbara, Graduate Division, College of Letters and Sciences, Division of Mathematics, Life, and Physical Sciences, Department of Geography, Santa Barbara, CA 93106-4060. Offers cognitive science (PhD); geography (MA); quantitative methods in the social sciences (PhD); transportation (PhD); MA/PhD. *Students:* 67 full-time (33 women). Average age 30. 92 applicants, 28% accepted, 15 enrolled. In 2009, 3 master's, 13 doctorates awarded. *Degree requirements:* For master's, comprehensive exam (for some programs), thesis; for doctorate, comprehensive exam, thesis/dissertation. *Entrance requirements:* For master's, GRE General Test, 3 letters of recommendation, resume/curriculum vitae; for doctorate, GRE General Test, 3 letters of recommendation, statement of purpose, personal achievements/contributions statement, resume/curriculum vitae, transcripts for post-secondary institutions attended. Additional exam requirements/recommendations for international students: Required—TOEFL (minimum score 550 paper-based; 213 computer-based; 80 iBT) or IELTS (minimum score 7). *Application deadline:* For fall admission, 2/1 for domestic and international students. Application fee: $70 ($90 for international students). Electronic applications accepted. *Financial support:* In 2009–10, 59 students received support, including 36 fellowships with full and partial tuition reimbursements available (averaging $10,700 per year), 29 research assistantships with full and partial tuition reimbursements available (averaging $8,600 per year), 31 teaching assistantships with partial tuition reimbursements available (averaging $8,000 per year); Federal Work-Study, institutionally sponsored loans, scholarships/grants, health care benefits, and unspecified assistantships also available. Financial award applicants required to submit FAFSA. *Faculty research:* Earth system science, human environment relations, modeling, measurement and computation, quantitative methods in social sciences. *Unit head:* Dr. Oliver Chadwick, Chair, 805-893-4223, E-mail: oac@geog.ucsb.edu. *Application contact:* Graduate Program Assistant, 805-893-3663, Fax: 805-893-3146, E-mail: grad_assistant@geog.ucsb.edu.

University of Connecticut, Graduate School, College of Liberal Arts and Sciences, Department of Psychology, Storrs, CT 06269. Offers behavioral neuroscience (PhD); biopsychology (PhD); clinical psychology (MA, PhD); cognition and instruction (PhD); developmental psychology (MA, PhD); ecological psychology (PhD); experimental psychology (PhD); general psychology (MA, PhD); health psychology (Graduate Certificate); industrial/organizational psychology (PhD); language and cognition (PhD); neuroscience (PhD); occupational health psychology (Graduate Certificate); social psychology (MA, PhD). *Accreditation:* APA. *Faculty:* 59 full-time (26 women). *Students:* 194 full-time (133 women), 24 part-time (12 women); includes 48 minority (12 African Americans, 21 Asian Americans or Pacific Islanders, 15 Hispanic Americans), 25 international. Average age 28. 585 applicants, 4% accepted, 14 enrolled. In 2009, 22 master's, 24 doctorates awarded. Terminal master's awarded for partial completion of doctoral program. *Degree requirements:* For master's, comprehensive exam; for doctorate, thesis/dissertation. *Entrance requirements:* For master's and doctorate, GRE General Test, GRE Subject Test. Additional exam requirements/recommendations for international students: Required—TOEFL (minimum score 550 paper-based; 213 computer-based). *Application deadline:* For fall admission, 2/1 priority date for domestic and international students; for spring admission, 11/1 for domestic students, 10/1 for international students. Applications are processed on a rolling basis. Application fee: $55. Electronic applications accepted. *Expenses:* Tuition, state resident: full-time $4725; part-time $525 per credit. Tuition, nonresident: full-time $12,267; part-time $1363 per credit. Required fees: $346 per semester. Tuition and fees vary according to course load. *Financial support:* In 2009–10, 109 research assistantships with full tuition reimbursements, 72 teaching assistantships with full tuition reimbursements were awarded; fellowships, career-related internships or fieldwork, Federal Work-Study, scholarships/grants, health care benefits, and unspecified assistantships also available. Financial award application deadline: 2/1; financial award applicants required to submit FAFSA. *Unit head:* Charles A. Lowe, Head, 860-486-3517, Fax: 860-486-2760, E-mail: charles.lowe@uconn.edu. *Application contact:* Charles A. Lowe, Head, 860-486-3517, Fax: 860-486-2760, E-mail: charles.lowe@uconn.edu.

University of Connecticut, Graduate School, Neag School of Education, Department of Educational Psychology, Program in Cognition and Instruction, Storrs, CT 06269. Offers MA, PhD, Post-Master's Certificate. *Faculty:* 16 full-time (6 women). *Students:* 14 full-time (7 women), 6 part-time (3 women); includes 3 minority (1 African American, 2 Hispanic Americans), 5 international. Average age 35. 13 applicants, 31% accepted, 2 enrolled. In 2009, 3 master's, 1 other advanced degree awarded. *Degree requirements:* For master's, comprehensive exam; for doctorate, thesis/dissertation. *Entrance requirements:* For doctorate, GRE General Test. Additional exam requirements/recommendations for international students: Required—TOEFL (minimum score 550 paper-based; 213 computer-based). *Application deadline:* For fall admission, 2/1 priority date for domestic and international students; for spring admission, 11/1 for domestic students, 10/1 for international students. Applications are processed on a rolling basis. Application fee: $55. Electronic applications accepted. *Expenses:* Tuition, state resident: full-time $4725; part-time $525 per credit. Tuition, nonresident: full-time $12,267; part-time $1363 per credit. Required fees: $346 per semester. Tuition and fees vary according to course load. *Financial support:* In 2009–10, 11 research assistantships with full tuition reimbursements were awarded; fellowships, teaching assistantships with full tuition reimbursements, Federal Work-Study, scholarships/grants, health care benefits, and unspecified assistantships also available. Financial award application deadline: 2/1; financial award applicants required to submit FAFSA. *Unit head:* Hariharan Swaminathan, Head, 860-486-4031, Fax: 860-486-0210, E-mail: hariharan.swaminathan@uconn.edu. *Application contact:* Cheryl Lowe, Program Assistant, 860-486-4031, Fax: 860-486-0180, E-mail: cheryl.lowe@uconn.edu.

University of Delaware, College of Arts and Sciences, Department of Psychology, Newark, DE 19716. Offers behavioral neuroscience (PhD); clinical psychology (PhD); cognitive psychology (PhD); social psychology (PhD). *Accreditation:* APA. *Degree requirements:* For doctorate, thesis/dissertation. *Entrance requirements:* For doctorate, GRE General Test. Additional exam requirements/recommendations for international students: Required—TOEFL (minimum score 600 paper-based; 250 computer-based). Electronic applications accepted. *Faculty research:* Emotion development, neural and cognitive aspects of memory, neural control of feeding, intergroup relations, social cognition and communication.

University of Florida, Graduate School, College of Liberal Arts and Sciences, Department of Psychology, Gainesville, FL 32611. Offers behavior analysis (PhD); behavioral neuroscience (MS, PhD); cognitive and sensory processes (PhD); counseling psychology (PhD); developmental psychology (PhD); social psychology (MS, PhD); JD/PhD. *Degree requirements:* For master's, thesis or alternative; for doctorate, thesis/dissertation. *Entrance requirements:* For master's and doctorate, GRE General Test, minimum GPA of 3.0. Additional exam requirements/

University of Florida (continued)
recommendations for international students: Required—TOEFL (minimum score 550 paper-based; 213 computer-based). Electronic applications accepted. *Faculty research:* Experimental analysis of behavior, psychobiology, cognition and sensory processes, counseling psychology, social psychology, developmental psychology.

University of Guelph, Graduate Program Services, College of Social and Applied Human Sciences, Department of Psychology, Guelph, ON N1G 2W1, Canada. Offers applied social psychology (MA, PhD); clinical psychology applied development emphasis (PhD); clinical psychology applied developmental emphasis (MA); industrial/organizational psychology (MA, PhD); neuroscience and applied cognitive science (MA, PhD). *Degree requirements:* For master's, thesis; for doctorate, comprehensive exam, thesis/dissertation. *Entrance requirements:* For master's, GRE General Test, GRE Subject Test, minimum B+ average during previous 2 years of course work; for doctorate, GRE General Test, GRE Subject Test, minimum A-average. Additional exam requirements/recommendations for international students: Required—TOEFL (minimum score 89 iBT). Electronic applications accepted. *Faculty research:* Organizational psychology, reading comprehension and mathematical ability, drug addiction and relapse, gender issues and culture, memory, clinical psychology.

The University of Kansas, Graduate Studies, College of Liberal Arts and Sciences, Department of Psychology, Lawrence, KS 66045. Offers clinical child psychology (MA, PhD); clinical health and rehabilitation (PhD); cognitive (PhD); developmental (PhD); quantitative (PhD); social (MA). *Accreditation:* APA (one or more programs are accredited). *Faculty:* 27 full-time (8 women), 9 part-time/adjunct (4 women). *Students:* 85 full-time (62 women), 11 part-time (9 women); includes 13 minority (4 African Americans, 1 American Indian/Alaska Native, 6 Asian Americans or Pacific Islanders, 2 Hispanic Americans), 7 international. Average age 27. 185 applicants, 15% accepted, 17 enrolled. In 2009, 13 master's, 10 doctorates awarded. *Degree requirements:* For master's, thesis; for doctorate, variable foreign language requirement, comprehensive exam, thesis/dissertation. *Entrance requirements:* For doctorate, GRE General Test, minimum GPA of 3.0; undergraduate degree with 15 hours of course work in psychology, vita, writing sample (Clinical Program Only). Additional exam requirements/recommendations for international students: Required—TOEFL. *Application deadline:* For fall admission, 12/1 for domestic and international students. Application fee: $45 ($55 for international students). Electronic applications accepted. *Expenses:* Tuition, state resident: full-time $6492; part-time $270.50 per credit hour. Tuition, nonresident: full-time $15,510; part-time $646.25 per credit hour. Required fees: $847; $70.56 per credit hour. Tuition and fees vary according to course load and program. *Financial support:* Fellowships with full tuition reimbursements, research assistantships with partial tuition reimbursements, teaching assistantships with full and partial tuition reimbursements, career-related internships or fieldwork and unspecified assistantships available. Financial award application deadline: 12/1; financial award applicants required to submit FAFSA. *Faculty research:* Information processing in depression, rape and other forms of sexual coerciom, motions on physical function, processes of memory and understanding text, social stigmas and hostile group environments. *Unit head:* Dr. Ruth Ann Atchley, Chair, 785-864-9821, Fax: 785-864-5696, E-mail: ratchley@ku.edu. *Application contact:* Cathy L. O'Keefe, Graduate Admissions Officer, 785-864-4195, Fax: 785-864-5696, E-mail: psycgrad@ku.edu.

University of Louisiana at Lafayette, College of Sciences, Institute of Cognitive Science, Lafayette, LA 70504. Offers PhD. *Degree requirements:* For doctorate, comprehensive exam, thesis/dissertation. *Entrance requirements:* For doctorate, GRE General Test, minimum GPA of 3.25. Additional exam requirements/recommendations for international students: Required—TOEFL (minimum score 550 paper-based; 213 computer-based). Electronic applications accepted. *Faculty research:* Computational models of cognition, comparative cognition, cognitive development, computational cognitive neuroscience, memory.

University of Maryland, Baltimore County, Graduate School, College of Natural and Mathematical Sciences, Department of Biological Sciences and Department of Psychology, Program in Neurosciences and Cognitive Sciences, Baltimore, MD 21250. Offers PhD. *Faculty:* 18 full-time (8 women). *Students:* 5 full-time (4 women); includes 3 minority (2 Asian Americans or Pacific Islanders, 1 Hispanic American). 13 applicants, 23% accepted, 0 enrolled. In 2009, 1 doctorate awarded. *Degree requirements:* For doctorate, comprehensive exam (for some programs), thesis/dissertation. *Entrance requirements:* For doctorate, GRE General Test, minimum GPA of 3.0. Additional exam requirements/recommendations for international students: Required—TOEFL. *Application deadline:* For fall admission, 1/15 for domestic students, 12/15 for international students. Applications are processed on a rolling basis. Application fee: $50. Electronic applications accepted. *Financial support:* In 2009–10, 5 students received support, including 3 research assistantships with full tuition reimbursements available (averaging $22,300 per year), 2 teaching assistantships with full tuition reimbursements available (averaging $21,300 per year). *Unit head:* Dr. Phyllis Robinson, Director, 410-455-3669, Fax: 410-455-3875, E-mail: biograd@umbc.edu. *Application contact:* Dr. Phyllis Robinson, Director, 410-455-3669, Fax: 410-455-3875, E-mail: biograd@umbc.edu.

University of Maryland, College Park, Academic Affairs, College of Behavioral and Social Sciences, Program in Neurosciences and Cognitive Sciences, College Park, MD 20742. Offers PhD. *Faculty:* 1 (woman) full-time. *Students:* 52 full-time (32 women); includes 5 minority (3 African Americans, 2 Asian Americans or Pacific Islanders), 14 international. 68 applicants, 25% accepted, 11 enrolled. In 2009, 4 doctorates awarded. *Degree requirements:* For doctorate, comprehensive exam, thesis/dissertation. *Entrance requirements:* For doctorate, GRE General Test, 3 letters of recommendation. Additional exam requirements/recommendations for international students: Required—TOEFL. *Application deadline:* For fall admission, 12/15 for domestic and international students. Applications are processed on a rolling basis. Application fee: $60. Electronic applications accepted. *Expenses:* Tuition, area resident: Part-time $471 per credit hour. Tuition, state resident: part-time $471 per credit hour. Tuition, nonresident: part-time $1016 per credit hour. Required fees: $337.04 per term. *Financial support:* In 2009–10, 7 fellowships with full and partial tuition reimbursements (averaging $17,343 per year), 15 research assistantships with tuition reimbursements (averaging $19,143 per year), 26 teaching assistantships (averaging $17,254 per year) were awarded; Federal Work-Study and scholarships/grants also available. Support available to part-time students. Financial award applicants required to submit FAFSA. *Faculty research:* Molecular neurobiology, cognition, neural and behavioral systems language, memory, human development. *Unit head:* Dr. Cynthia F. Moss, Director, 301-405-0353, Fax: 301-405-7104, E-mail: moss@umd.edu. *Application contact:* Dean of Graduate School, 301-405-0358, Fax: 301-314-9305.

University of Massachusetts Amherst, Graduate School, College of Natural Sciences, Department of Psychology, Amherst, MA 01003. Offers clinical psychology (MS, PhD); cognitive psychology (MS, PhD); developmental science (MS, PhD); psychology of peace and violence (MS, PhD); social psychology (MS, PhD). *Accreditation:* APA (one or more programs are accredited). *Faculty:* 48 full-time (22 women). *Students:* 57 full-time (42 women), 13 part-time (10 women); includes 15 minority (6 African Americans, 6 Asian Americans or Pacific Islanders, 3 Hispanic Americans), 8 international. Average age 28. 381 applicants, 4% accepted, 11 enrolled. In 2009, 11 master's, 8 doctorates awarded. Terminal master's awarded for partial completion of doctoral program. *Degree requirements:* For master's, thesis; for doctorate, comprehensive exam, thesis/dissertation. *Entrance requirements:* For master's and doctorate, GRE General Test, 3 letters of recommendation. Additional exam requirements/recommendations for international students: Required—TOEFL (minimum score 550 paper-based; 213 computer-based; 80 iBT), IELTS (minimum score 6.5). *Application deadline:* For fall admission, 12/1 for domestic and international students. Applications are processed on a rolling basis. Application fee: $50 ($65 for international students). Electronic applications accepted. *Expenses:* Tuition, state resident: full-time $2640; part-time $110 per credit. Tuition, nonresident: full-time $9936; part-time $414 per credit. Tuition and fees vary according to course load. *Financial support:* In 2009–10, 8 fellowships with full tuition reimbursements (averaging $12,620 per year), 52 research assistantships with full tuition reimbursements (averaging $9,491 per year), 55 teaching assistantships with full tuition reimbursements (averaging $10,829 per year) were awarded; career-related internships or fieldwork, Federal Work-Study, scholarships/grants, traineeships, health care benefits, tuition waivers (full), and unspecified assistantships also available. Support available to part-time students. Financial award application deadline: 12/1. *Unit head:* Dr. Linda M. Isbell, Graduate Program Director, 413-545-2503, Fax: 413-545-0996. *Application contact:* Jean M. Ames, Supervisor of Admissions, 413-545-0722, Fax: 413-577-0010, E-mail: gradadm@grad.umass.edu.

University of Massachusetts Amherst, Graduate School, Interdisciplinary Programs, Program in Neuroscience and Behavior, Amherst, MA 01003. Offers animal behavior and learning (PhD); molecular and cellular neuroscience (PhD); neural and behavioral development (PhD); neuroendocrinology (PhD); neuroscience and behavior (MS); sensorimotor, cognitive, and computational neuroscience (PhD). *Students:* 28 full-time (19 women); includes 4 minority (1 African American, 2 Asian Americans or Pacific Islanders, 1 Hispanic American), 3 international. Average age 26. 70 applicants, 26% accepted, 5 enrolled. In 2009, 4 master's, 5 doctorates awarded. Terminal master's awarded for partial completion of doctoral program. *Degree requirements:* For master's, thesis or alternative; for doctorate, comprehensive exam, thesis/dissertation. *Entrance requirements:* For master's and doctorate, GRE General Test. Additional exam requirements/recommendations for international students: Required—TOEFL (minimum score 550 paper-based; 213 computer-based; 80 iBT), IELTS (minimum score 6.5). *Application deadline:* For fall admission, 1/2 for domestic and international students. Applications are processed on a rolling basis. Application fee: $50 ($65 for international students). Electronic applications accepted. *Expenses:* Tuition, state resident: full-time $2640; part-time $110 per credit. Tuition, nonresident: full-time $9936; part-time $414 per credit. Tuition and fees vary according to course load. *Financial support:* In 2009–10, 1 fellowship with full tuition reimbursement (averaging $11,144 per year), 3 research assistantships with full tuition reimbursements (averaging $1,477 per year) were awarded; teaching assistantships, career-related internships or fieldwork, Federal Work-Study, scholarships/grants, traineeships, health care benefits, tuition waivers (full), and unspecified assistantships also available. Support available to part-time students. Financial award application deadline: 1/2. *Unit head:* Dr. Elizabeth A. Connor, Graduate Program Director, 413-545-2046, Fax: 413-545-3243. *Application contact:* Jean M. Ames, Supervisor of Admissions, 413-545-0722, Fax: 413-577-0010, E-mail: gradadm@grad.umass.edu.

University of Minnesota, Twin Cities Campus, Graduate School, College of Liberal Arts, Department of Psychology, Program in Cognitive and Biological Psychology, Minneapolis, MN 55455-0213. Offers PhD. *Degree requirements:* For doctorate, comprehensive exam, thesis/dissertation. *Entrance requirements:* For doctorate, GRE General Test, GRE Subject Test (recommended), 12 credits of upper-level psychology courses, including a course in statistics or psychological measurement. Additional exam requirements/recommendations for international students: Required—TOEFL (minimum score 550 paper-based; 213 computer-based; 79 iBT).

University of Nebraska–Lincoln, Graduate College, College of Arts and Sciences, Department of Psychology, Lincoln, NE 68588. Offers biopsychology (PhD); clinical psychology (PhD); cognitive psychology (PhD); developmental psychology (PhD); psychology (MA); social/personality psychology (PhD); JD/MA; JD/PhD. *Accreditation:* APA (one or more programs are accredited). *Degree requirements:* For master's, thesis optional; for doctorate, comprehensive exam, thesis/dissertation. *Entrance requirements:* For master's and doctorate, GRE General Test. Additional exam requirements/recommendations for international students: Required—TOEFL (minimum score 550 paper-based; 213 computer-based). Electronic applications accepted. *Faculty research:* Law and psychology, rural mental health, chronic mental illness, neuropsychology, child clinical psychology.

University of Nebraska–Lincoln, Graduate College, College of Education and Human Sciences, Department of Educational Psychology, Lincoln, NE 68588. Offers cognition, learning and development (MA); counseling psychology (MA); educational psychology (MA, Ed S); psychological studies in education (PhD), including cognition, learning and development, counseling psychology, quantitative, qualitative, and psychometric methods, school psychology; quantitative, qualitative, and psychometric methods (MA); school psychology (MA, Ed S). *Accreditation:* APA (one or more programs are accredited); NCATE. *Degree requirements:* For master's, thesis optional. *Entrance requirements:* For master's, GRE General Test. Additional exam requirements/recommendations for international students: Required—TOEFL (minimum score 500 paper-based; 173 computer-based). Electronic applications accepted. *Faculty research:* Measurement and assessment, metacognition, academic skills, child development, multicultural education and counseling.

University of Nevada, Reno, Graduate School, College of Liberal Arts, Department of Psychology, Program in Cognitive Brain Science, Reno, NV 89557. Offers MA, PhD. Terminal master's awarded for partial completion of doctoral program. *Degree requirements:* For master's, thesis optional; for doctorate, comprehensive exam, thesis/dissertation. *Entrance requirements:* For master's, GRE General Test, minimum GPA of 2.75; for doctorate, GRE General Test, minimum GPA of 3.0. Additional exam requirements/recommendations for international students: Required—TOEFL (minimum score 500 paper-based; 173 computer-based; 61 iBT), IELTS (minimum score 6). Electronic applications accepted. *Faculty research:* Comparative psychology, cognition, perception.

The University of North Carolina at Chapel Hill, Graduate School, College of Arts and Sciences, Department of Psychology, Chapel Hill, NC 27599. Offers biological psychology (PhD); clinical psychology (PhD); cognitive psychology (PhD); developmental psychology (PhD); quantitative psychology (PhD); social psychology (PhD). *Accreditation:* APA. *Degree requirements:* For doctorate, comprehensive exam, thesis/dissertation. *Entrance requirements:* For doctorate, GRE General Test, minimum GPA of 3.0. Electronic applications accepted. *Faculty research:* Expressed emotion, cognitive development, social cognitive neuroscience, human memory personality.

The University of North Carolina at Greensboro, Graduate School, College of Arts and Sciences, Department of Psychology, Greensboro, NC 27412-5001. Offers clinical psychology (MA, PhD); cognitive psychology (MA, PhD); developmental psychology (MA, PhD); social psychology (MA, PhD). *Accreditation:* APA (one or more programs are accredited). Terminal master's awarded for partial completion of doctoral program. *Degree requirements:* For master's, comprehensive exam, thesis; for doctorate, one foreign language, thesis/dissertation, preliminary exam. *Entrance requirements:* For master's and doctorate, GRE General Test. Additional exam requirements/recommendations for international students: Required—TOEFL. Electronic applications accepted. *Faculty research:* Sensory and perceptual determinants; evoked potential: disorders, deafness, and development.

University of Notre Dame, Graduate School, College of Arts and Letters, Division of Social Science, Department of Psychology, Notre Dame, IN 46556. Offers cognitive psychology (PhD); counseling psychology (PhD); developmental psychology (PhD); quantitative psychology (PhD). *Accreditation:* APA. *Degree requirements:* For doctorate, comprehensive exam, thesis/dissertation, candidacy exam. *Entrance requirements:* For doctorate, GRE General Test, GRE Subject Test (strongly recommended). Additional exam requirements/recommendations for international students: Required—TOEFL (minimum score 600 paper-based; 250 computer-based; 80 iBT). Electronic applications accepted. *Faculty research:* Cognitive and socio-emotional development, statistical methods and quantitative models applicable to psychology, interpersonal relations, life span development and developmental delay, childhood depression, structural equation and dynamical systems.

University of Oregon, Graduate School, College of Arts and Sciences, Department of Psychology, Eugene, OR 97403. Offers clinical psychology (PhD); cognitive psychology (MA, MS, PhD); developmental psychology (MA, MS, PhD); physiological psychology (MA, MS, PhD); psychology (MA, MS, PhD); social/personality psychology (MA, MS, PhD). *Accreditation:* APA (one or more programs are accredited). Terminal master's awarded for partial completion of doctoral program. *Degree requirements:* For doctorate, thesis/dissertation. *Entrance requirements:* For master's, GRE General Test, minimum GPA of 3.0; for doctorate, GRE General Test. Additional exam requirements/recommendations for international students: Required—TOEFL.

University of Pittsburgh, School of Education, Department of Instruction and Learning, Program in Cognitive Studies, Pittsburgh, PA 15260. Offers PhD. *Students:* 2 full-time (1 woman). Average age 29. 5 applicants, 60% accepted, 1 enrolled. In 2009, 1 doctorate awarded. *Degree requirements:* For doctorate, thesis/dissertation. *Entrance requirements:* For doctorate, GRE General Test. Additional exam requirements/recommendations for international students: Required—TOEFL. *Application deadline:* For fall admission, 2/1 for domestic and international students. Application fee: $50. Electronic applications accepted. *Expenses:* Tuition, state resident: full-time $16,402; part-time $665 per credit. Tuition, nonresident: full-time $28,694; part-time $1175 per credit. Required fees: $690; $175 per term. Tuition and fees vary according to program. *Financial support:* Research assistantships available. Financial award application deadline: 3/15; financial award applicants required to submit FAFSA. *Unit head:* Dr. Richard Donato, Chairman, 412-624-7248, Fax: 412-648-7081, E-mail: donato@pitt.edu. *Application contact:* Information Contact, 412-648-2230, Fax: 412-648-1899, E-mail: soeinfo@pitt.edu.

University of Rochester, The College, Arts and Sciences, Department of Brain and Cognitive Sciences, Rochester, NY 14627. Offers MS, PhD. Terminal master's awarded for partial completion of doctoral program. *Degree requirements:* For doctorate, thesis/dissertation, qualifying exam. *Entrance requirements:* For master's and doctorate, GRE General Test. Additional exam requirements/recommendations for international students: Required—TOEFL. Electronic applications accepted.

University of Southern California, Graduate School, College of Letters, Arts and Sciences, Department of Psychology, Los Angeles, CA 90089. Offers brain and cognitive science (PhD); clinical science (PhD); developmental psychology (PhD); human behavior (MHB); psychology (MA); quantitative methods (PhD); social psychology (PhD); PhD/MPH. *Accreditation:* APA. *Faculty:* 34 full-time (10 women), 17 part-time/adjunct (7 women). *Students:* 107 full-time (73 women); includes 38 minority (6 African Americans, 21 Asian Americans or Pacific Islanders, 11 Hispanic Americans), 19 international. 430 applicants, 6% accepted, 13 enrolled. In 2009, 17 master's, 12 doctorates awarded. *Degree requirements:* For doctorate, comprehensive exam, thesis/dissertation, one-year internship (for clinical science students). *Entrance requirements:* For doctorate, GRE. Additional exam requirements/recommendations for international students: Recommended—TOEFL (minimum score 600 paper-based; 250 computer-based; 100 iBT). *Application deadline:* For fall admission, 12/1 for domestic and international students. Application fee: $95. Electronic applications accepted. *Expenses:* Tuition: Full-time $25,980; part-time $1315 per unit. Required fees: $554. One-time fee: $35 full-time. Full-time tuition and fees vary according to degree level and program. *Financial support:* In 2009–10, 80 students received support, including 16 fellowships with full tuition reimbursements available (averaging $22,500 per year), 22 research assistantships with full tuition reimbursements available (averaging $19,000 per year), 38 teaching assistantships with full tuition reimbursements available (averaging $19,000 per year); career-related internships or fieldwork, scholarships/grants, traineeships, and health care benefits also available. *Faculty research:* Affective neuroscience; children and families; vision, culture and ethnicity; intergroup relations; aggression and violence; language and reading development; substance abuse. *Unit head:* Dr. Margaret Gatz, Chair and Professor, 213-740-2203, Fax: 213-746-9028, E-mail: gatz@usc.edu. *Application contact:* Irene Takaragawa, Graduate Advisor, 213-740-2205, E-mail: itakarag@usc.edu.

University of South Florida, Graduate School, College of Arts and Sciences, Department of Psychology, Tampa, FL 33620-9951. Offers clinical psychology (PhD); cognitive and neural sciences (PhD); industrial-organizational psychology (PhD). *Accreditation:* APA. *Faculty:* 32 full-time (9 women). *Students:* 98 full-time (55 women), 21 part-time (13 women); includes 16 minority (3 African Americans, 7 Asian Americans or Pacific Islanders, 6 Hispanic Americans), 11 international. Average age 32. 437 applicants, 8% accepted, 24 enrolled. In 2009, 24 doctorates awarded. *Degree requirements:* For doctorate, comprehensive exam, thesis/dissertation, internship. *Entrance requirements:* For doctorate, GRE General Test, minimum GPA of 3.0 in last 60 hours of course work. Additional exam requirements/recommendations for international students: Required—TOEFL (minimum score 550 paper-based; 213 computer-based). *Application deadline:* For fall admission, 12/1 for domestic and international students. Application fee: $30. Electronic applications accepted. *Expenses:* Contact institution. *Financial support:* In 2009–10, teaching assistantships with tuition reimbursements (averaging $27,086 per year); tuition waivers (partial) and unspecified assistantships also available. Financial award applicants required to submit FAFSA. *Faculty research:* Clinical, cognitive, neuroscience, social, industrial/organizational. Total annual research expenditures: $4.7 million. *Unit head:* Michael Brannick, Chairperson, 813-974-0478, Fax: 813-974-4617, E-mail: mbrannick@usf.edu. *Application contact:* William Sacco, Program Director, 813-974-0375, Fax: 813-974-4617, E-mail: sacco@cas.usf.edu.

The University of Texas at Austin, Graduate School, College of Education, Department of Educational Psychology, Austin, TX 78712-1111. Offers academic educational psychology (M Ed, MA); counseling psychology (PhD); counselor education (M Ed); human development and culture (PhD); learning, cognition and instruction (PhD); quantitative methods (PhD); school psychology (PhD). *Accreditation:* APA (one or more programs are accredited). *Degree requirements:* For master's, thesis optional; for doctorate, thesis/dissertation. *Entrance requirements:* For master's and doctorate, GRE General Test, 3 letters of recommendation. Additional exam requirements/recommendations for international students: Required—TOEFL.

The University of Texas at Dallas, School of Behavioral and Brain Sciences, Program in Cognition and Neuroscience, Richardson, TX 75080. Offers applied cognition and neuroscience (MS); cognition and neuroscience (PhD). Part-time and evening/weekend programs available. *Faculty:* 21 full-time (6 women). *Students:* 79 full-time (35 women), 27 part-time (12 women); includes 25 minority (3 African Americans, 17 Asian Americans or Pacific Islanders, 5 Hispanic Americans), 20 international. Average age 30. 71 applicants, 54% accepted, 31 enrolled. In 2009, 28 master's, 4 doctorates awarded. *Degree requirements:* For master's, internship; for doctorate, thesis/dissertation. *Entrance requirements:* For master's and doctorate, GRE General Test, minimum GPA of 3.0 in upper-level coursework in field. Additional exam requirements/recommendations for international students: Required—TOEFL (minimum score 550 paper-based; 213 computer-based). *Application deadline:* For fall admission, 7/15 for domestic students, 5/1 priority date for international students; for spring admission, 11/15 for domestic students, 9/1 priority date for international students. Applications are processed on a rolling basis. Application fee: $50 ($100 for international students). Electronic applications accepted. *Expenses:* Tuition, state resident: full-time $11,068; part-time $461 per credit hour. Tuition, nonresident: full-time $21,178; part-time $882 per credit hour. Tuition and fees vary according to course load. *Financial support:* In 2009–10, 10 research assistantships with full tuition reimbursements (averaging $13,526 per year), 28 teaching assistantships with full tuition reimbursements (averaging $10,792 per year) were awarded; fellowships, career-related internships or fieldwork, Federal Work-Study, institutionally sponsored loans, scholarships/grants, and unspecified assistantships also available. Support available to part-time students. Financial award application deadline: 4/30; financial award applicants required to submit FAFSA. *Faculty research:* Combination of biological, behavioral, and computational approaches for evaluating biological and artificial information processing systems. *Unit head:* Dr. James C. Bartlett, Head, PhD Program, 972-883-2079, Fax: 972-883-2491, E-mail: jbartlet@utdallas.edu. *Application contact:* Dr. Robert D. Stillman, Head, 972-883-3106, Fax: 972-883-3022, E-mail: stillman@utdallas.edu.

The University of Toledo, College of Graduate Studies, College of Arts and Sciences, Department of Psychology, Toledo, OH 43606-3390. Offers behavioral (PhD), including cognitive, psychobiology and learning, social; clinical psychology (PhD); experimental psychology (MA). *Accreditation:* APA. *Degree requirements:* For master's, thesis; for doctorate, one foreign language, thesis/dissertation. *Entrance requirements:* For master's and doctorate, GRE General Test, GRE Subject Test. *Faculty research:* Neural taste response.

University of Washington, Graduate School, College of Arts and Sciences, Department of Psychology, Seattle, WA 98195. Offers animal behavior (PhD); child psychology (PhD); clinical psychology (PhD); cognition and perception (PhD); developmental psychology (PhD); quantitative psychology (PhD); social psychology and personality (PhD). *Accreditation:* APA. *Degree requirements:* For doctorate, thesis/dissertation. *Entrance requirements:* For doctorate, GRE General Test, minimum GPA of 3.0. Electronic applications accepted. *Faculty research:* Addictive behaviors, artificial intelligence, child psychopathology, mechanisms and development of vision, physiology of ingestive behaviors.

University of Wisconsin–Madison, Graduate School, College of Letters and Science, Department of Psychology, Program in Cognitive Neurosciences, Madison, WI 53706-1380. Offers PhD. *Degree requirements:* For doctorate, comprehensive exam, thesis/dissertation. *Entrance requirements:* For doctorate, GRE General Test, minimum undergraduate GPA of 3.0. Additional exam requirements/recommendations for international students: Required—TOEFL. Electronic applications accepted. *Expenses:* Tuition, state resident: part-time $594 per credit. Tuition, nonresident: part-time $1504 per credit. Required fees: $65 per credit. Tuition and fees vary according to course load, program and reciprocity agreements.

University of Wisconsin–Madison, Graduate School, College of Letters and Science, Department of Psychology, Program in Perception, Madison, WI 53706-1380. Offers PhD. *Degree requirements:* For doctorate, comprehensive exam, thesis/dissertation. *Entrance requirements:* For doctorate, GRE General Test, minimum GPA of 3.0. Electronic applications accepted. *Expenses:* Tuition, state resident: part-time $594 per credit. Tuition, nonresident: part-time $1504 per credit. Required fees: $65 per credit. Tuition and fees vary according to course load, program and reciprocity agreements.

Wayne State University, College of Liberal Arts and Sciences, Department of Psychology, Program in Psychology, Detroit, MI 48202. Offers behavioral and cognitive neuroscience (PhD); clinical psychology (PhD); cognitive and social psychology (PhD); industrial/organizational psychology (PhD); psychology (MA, MS). *Accreditation:* APA (one or more programs are accredited). *Degree requirements:* For doctorate, thesis/dissertation. *Entrance requirements:* For doctorate, GRE General Test, GRE Subject Test. Additional exam requirements/recommendations for international students: Required—TOEFL (minimum score 550 paper-based; 213 computer-based); Recommended—TWE (minimum score 6). Electronic applications accepted.

Wilfrid Laurier University, Faculty of Graduate Studies, Faculty of Science, Department of Psychology, Waterloo, ON N2L 3C5, Canada. Offers brain and cognition (M Sc, PhD); community psychology (MA, PhD); social and developmental psychology (MA, PhD). *Degree requirements:* For master's, thesis; for doctorate, thesis/dissertation. *Entrance requirements:* For master's, GRE General Test, honors BA or the equivalent in psychology, minimum B average in undergraduate course work; for doctorate, GRE General Test, master's degree, minimum A- average. Additional exam requirements/recommendations for international students: Required—TOEFL (minimum score 230 computer-based; 89 iBT). Electronic applications accepted. *Faculty research:* Brain and cognition, community psychology, social and developmental psychology.

Yale University, Graduate School of Arts and Sciences, Department of Psychology, New Haven, CT 06520. Offers behavioral neuroscience (PhD); clinical psychology (PhD); cognitive psychology (PhD); developmental psychology (PhD); social/personality psychology (PhD). *Accreditation:* APA. *Degree requirements:* For doctorate, thesis/dissertation. *Entrance requirements:* For doctorate, GRE General Test.

Counseling Psychology

Abilene Christian University, Graduate School, College of Arts and Sciences, Department of Psychology, Program in Counseling Psychology, Abilene, TX 79699-9100. Offers MS. *Students:* 13 full-time (8 women), 3 part-time (2 women); includes 1 minority (African American), 1 international. 13 applicants, 54% accepted, 5 enrolled. In 2009, 6 master's awarded. *Degree requirements:* For master's, comprehensive exam, thesis optional. *Entrance requirements:* For master's, GRE General Test. *Application deadline:* For fall admission, 4/1 priority date for domestic students; for spring admission, 11/1 for domestic students. Applications are processed on a rolling basis. Application fee: $40. Electronic applications accepted. *Expenses:* Tuition: Full-time $11,520; part-time $640 per hour. Required fees: $1090; $53.50 per hour. $10 per term. Tuition and fees vary according to program. *Financial support:* In 2009–10, 15 students received support. Applicants required to submit FAFSA. *Unit head:* Dr. Robert McKelvain, Graduate Advisor, 325-674-2286, Fax: 325-674-6968, E-mail: mckevainr@acu.edu. *Application contact:* William Horn, Graduate Admissions Counselor, 325-674-2656, Fax: 325-674-6717, E-mail: gradinfo@acu.edu.

Adelphi University, Derner Institute of Advanced Psychological Studies, Program in Mental Health Counseling, Garden City, NY 11530-0701. Offers MA. *Students:* 32 full-time (27 women), 5 part-time (4 women); includes 7 minority (2 African Americans, 3 Asian Americans or Pacific Islanders, 2 Hispanic Americans), 2 international. Average age 27. In 2009, 14 master's awarded. *Degree requirements:* For master's, comprehensive exam. *Entrance requirements:* For master's, GRE General Test, GRE Subject Test, minimum cumulative GPA of 3.1; interview; course work in developmental psychology, research methods, and psycho-pathology; 2 letters of recommendation. Additional exam requirements/recommendations for international students: Required—TOEFL (minimum score 550 paper-based; 213 computer-based; 80 iBT). *Application deadline:* For fall admission, 4/1 priority date for domestic students, 5/1 priority date for international students. Application fee: $50. Electronic applications accepted. *Expenses:* Tuition: Full-time $28,340; part-time $830 per credit. Required fees: $600; $250 per credit. Full-time tuition and fees vary according to course load and program. *Financial support:* Research assistantships with full and partial tuition reimbursements, career-related internships or fieldwork, Federal Work-Study, institutionally sponsored loans, and unspecified assistantships available. *Unit head:* Dr. Errol Rodriguez, Assistant Dean, 516-237-8572, E-mail: erodriguez@adelphi.edu. *Application contact:* Christine Murphy, Director of Admissions, 516-877-3050, Fax: 516-877-3039, E-mail: graduateadmissions@adelphi.edu.

Adler Graduate School, Program in Adlerian Studies, Richfield, MN 55423. Offers art therapy specialization (MA); clinical counseling track (MA); coaching and consulting in organizations

Counseling Psychology

Adler Graduate School (continued)
(Certificate); management consulting and organizational leadership (MA); marriage and family track (MA); non-clinical Adlerian studies track (MA); personal and professional life coaching (Certificate); school counseling (MA). Part-time and evening/weekend programs available. *Degree requirements:* For master's, thesis or alternative, 500-700 hour internship (depending on license choice). *Entrance requirements:* For master's, minimum undergraduate GPA of 3.0, 12 credits of course work in psychology or related field.

Adler School of Professional Psychology, Programs in Psychology, Chicago, IL 60601-7203. Offers art therapy (MA, Certificate); clinical hypnosis (Certificate); clinical psychology (Psy D); counseling (MA); counseling and organizational psychology (MA); forensic psychology (MA); gerontological counseling (MA); marriage and family counseling (MA); marriage and family therapy (Certificate); organizational psychology (MA); police psychology (MA); rehabilitation counseling (MA); sport and health psychology (MA); substance abuse counseling (Certificate); Psy D/Certificate; Psy D/MACAT; Psy D/MACP; Psy D/MAMFC; Psy D/MASAC. *Accreditation:* APA. Part-time and evening/weekend programs available. Postbaccalaureate distance learning degree programs offered (minimal on-campus study). *Faculty:* 41 full-time (21 women), 44 part-time/adjunct (19 women). *Students:* 551 full-time (441 women), 161 part-time (137 women). Average age 27.Terminal master's awarded for partial completion of doctoral program. *Degree requirements:* For master's, thesis or alternative, oral exam, practicum; for doctorate, thesis/dissertation, clinical exam, internship, oral exam, practicum, written qualifying exam. *Entrance requirements:* For master's, 12 semester hours in psychology, minimum GPA of 3.0; for doctorate, 18 semester hours in psychology, minimum GPA of 3.25; for Certificate, appropriate master's or doctoral degree. Additional exam requirements/recommendations for international students: Required—TOEFL (minimum score 550 paper-based; 213 computer-based; 79 iBT). *Application deadline:* For fall admission, 2/15 priority date for domestic students, 12/1 priority date for international students. Applications are processed on a rolling basis. Application fee: $50. Electronic applications accepted. *Expenses:* Tuition: Part-time $930 per credit. Required fees: $220 per term. *Financial support:* Career-related internships or fieldwork, Federal Work-Study, scholarships/grants, and tuition waivers (full and partial) available. Support available to part-time students. Financial award application deadline: 5/15; financial award applicants required to submit FAFSA. *Unit head:* Dr. Frank Gruba-McAllister, Vice President of Academic Affairs, 312-201-5900 Ext. 209, Fax: 312-201-5917. *Application contact:* Craig A. Hines, Associate Vice President of Admissions, 312-201-5900 Ext. 226, Fax: 312-201-5917, E-mail: chines@adler.edu.

See Close-Up on page 1047.

Alabama Agricultural and Mechanical University, School of Graduate Studies, School of Education, Department of Counseling and Special Education, Huntsville, AL 35811. Offers communicative disorders (M Ed, MS); psychology and counseling (MS, Ed S), including clinical psychology (MS), counseling and guidance, counseling psychology (MS), personnel management (MS), psychometry (MS), school psychology (MS); special education (M Ed, MS). *Accreditation:* CORE; NCATE. Part-time and evening/weekend programs available. *Degree requirements:* For master's, comprehensive exam. *Entrance requirements:* For master's, GRE General Test. Additional exam requirements/recommendations for international students: Required—TOEFL (minimum score 500 paper-based; 173 computer-based; 61 iBT). *Faculty research:* Increasing numbers of minorities in special education and speech-language pathology.

Alaska Pacific University, Graduate Programs, Department of Counseling, Psychological Studies, and Human Services, Program in Counseling Psychology, Anchorage, AK 99508-4672. Offers MSCP.

Alliant International University–México City, Programs in Arts and Science, Mexico City, Mexico. Offers counseling psychology (MA); international relations (MA). Part-time programs available. *Degree requirements:* For master's, thesis optional. *Entrance requirements:* For master's, GRE General Test, letters of recommendation. Additional exam requirements/recommendations for international students: Required—TOEFL. Electronic applications accepted.

Amberton University, Graduate School, Program in Counseling, Garland, TX 75041-5595. Offers MA. *Entrance requirements:* For master's, minimum GPA of 3.0.

Amridge University, Graduate and Professional Programs, Montgomery, AL 36117. Offers behavioral leadership and management (MA); biblical studies (MA, PhD); family therapy (D Min); leadership and management (MS); marriage and family therapy (M Div, MA, PhD); ministerial leadership (M Div, MS); pastoral counseling (M Div, MS); practical theology (MA); professional counseling (M Div, MA); theology (M Div, D Min). *Accreditation:* ATS. Part-time and evening/weekend programs available. Postbaccalaureate distance learning degree programs offered (no on-campus study). *Faculty:* 44 full-time (9 women), 18 part-time/adjunct (7 women). *Students:* 175 full-time (95 women), 192 part-time (93 women); includes 182 minority (172 African Americans, 1 American Indian/Alaska Native, 1 Asian American or Pacific Islander, 8 Hispanic Americans). Average age 35. *Degree requirements:* For master's, one foreign language, comprehensive exam (for some programs), thesis (for some programs); for doctorate, comprehensive exam (for some programs), thesis/dissertation; for M Div, comprehensive exam (for some programs). *Entrance requirements:* For M Div, master's, and doctorate, GRE General Test or MAT. Additional exam requirements/recommendations for international students: Required—TOEFL. *Application deadline:* For fall admission, 9/1 priority date for domestic students; for spring admission, 1/1 priority date for domestic students. Applications are processed on a rolling basis. Application fee: $75. Electronic applications accepted. *Expenses:* Tuition: Full-time $10,080; part-time $560 per semester hour. Required fees: $600 per term. *Financial support:* Federal Work-Study and scholarships/grants available. Support available to part-time students. Financial award applicants required to submit FAFSA. *Faculty research:* Homiletics, hermeneutics, ancient Near Eastern history. *Unit head:* Director of Enrollment Management, 800-351-4040 Ext. 7513, Fax: 334-387-3878. *Application contact:* Ora Davis, Admissions Officer, 334-387-3877 Ext. 7524, Fax: 334-387-3878, E-mail: admissions@amridgeuniversity.edu.

Andrews University, School of Graduate Studies, School of Education, Department of Educational and Counseling Psychology, Program in Counseling Psychology, Berrien Springs, MI 49104. Offers PhD. *Students:* 4 full-time (2 women), 17 part-time (9 women); includes 3 minority (2 African Americans, 1 Hispanic American), 3 international. Average age 39. 10 applicants, 20% accepted, 1 enrolled. In 2009, 2 doctorates awarded. *Degree requirements:* For doctorate, thesis/dissertation. *Entrance requirements:* Additional exam requirements/recommendations for international students: Required—TOEFL (minimum score 550 paper-based). Application fee: $40. *Unit head:* Dr. Carole Woolford, Coordinator, 269-471-6074. *Application contact:* Carolyn Hurst, Supervisor of Graduate Admission, 800-253-2874, Fax: 269-471-6321, E-mail: graduate@andrews.edu.

Angelo State University, College of Graduate Studies, College of Liberal and Fine Arts, Department of Psychology, Sociology and Social Work, San Angelo, TX 76909. Offers psychology (MS), including counseling psychology, general psychology, industrial and organizational psychology. Part-time and evening/weekend programs available. *Faculty:* 8 full-time (2 women). *Students:* 33 full-time (22 women), 14 part-time (11 women); includes 10 minority (2 African Americans, 1 Asian American or Pacific Islander, 7 Hispanic Americans). Average age 29. 46 applicants, 78% accepted, 26 enrolled. In 2009, 23 master's awarded. *Degree requirements:* For master's, comprehensive exam, thesis optional. *Entrance requirements:* For master's, GRE General Test. Additional exam requirements/recommendations for international students: Required—TOEFL or IELTS. *Application deadline:* For fall admission, 7/15 priority date for domestic students, 6/10 for international students; for spring admission, 12/1 priority date for domestic students, 11/1 for international students. Applications are processed on a rolling basis. Application fee: $40 ($50 for international students). Electronic applications accepted. *Expenses:* Tuition, state resident: full-time $3396; part-time $142 per credit hour. Tuition, nonresident: full-time $10,152; part-time $423 per credit hour. Required fees: $1786; $36.25 per credit hour. $494 per semester. Full-time tuition and fees vary according to course load, degree level and program. *Financial support:* In 2009–10, 44 students received support, including 3 teaching assistantships (averaging $10,251 per year); career-related internships or fieldwork, Federal Work-Study, scholarships/grants, and unspecified assistantships also available. Support available to part-time students. Financial award application deadline: 3/1; financial award applicants required to submit FAFSA. *Faculty research:* Toddlers use of actors' intentions to learn verbs. Total annual research expenditures: $116,915. *Unit head:* Dr. William B. Davidson, Department Head, 325-942-2068 Ext. 248, Fax: 325-942-2290, E-mail: bill.davidson@angelo.edu. *Application contact:* Theresa Fortin, Graduate Admissions Assistant, 325-942-2169, Fax: 325-942-2194, E-mail: theresa.fortin@angelo.edu.

Anna Maria College, Graduate Division, Program in Counseling Psychology, Paxton, MA 01612. Offers counseling psychology (MA). Part-time and evening/weekend programs available. *Degree requirements:* For master's, comprehensive exam, practicum. *Entrance requirements:* Additional exam requirements/recommendations for international students: Required—TOEFL (minimum score 500 paper-based). Electronic applications accepted.

Antioch University Midwest, Graduate Programs, Individualized Liberal and Professional Studies Program, Yellow Springs, OH 45387-1609. Offers liberal and professional studies (MA), including counseling, creative writing, education, film studies, liberal studies, management, modern literature, psychology, theatre, visual arts. Part-time and evening/weekend programs available. Postbaccalaureate distance learning degree programs offered (minimal on-campus study). *Faculty:* 1 full-time (0 women), 2 part-time/adjunct (1 woman). *Students:* 23 full-time (13 women), 41 part-time (30 women); includes 13 minority (11 African Americans, 2 Hispanic Americans). Average age 40. 21 applicants, 76% accepted, 15 enrolled. In 2009, 24 master's awarded. *Degree requirements:* For master's, thesis or alternative. *Entrance requirements:* For master's, resume, 2 letters of reference. *Application deadline:* For fall admission, 8/1 for domestic students; for winter admission, 12/1 for domestic students; for spring admission, 3/10 for domestic students. Applications are processed on a rolling basis. Application fee: $50. Electronic applications accepted. *Expenses:* Contact institution. *Financial support:* Federal Work-Study available. Financial award applicants required to submit FAFSA. *Unit head:* Dr. Jon Saari, Chair, 937-769-1879, Fax: 937-769-1807, E-mail: jsaari@antioch.edu. *Application contact:* Seth Gordon, Assistant Director of Admissions, 937-769-1800 Ext. 1825, Fax: 937-769-1804, E-mail: sgordon@antioch.edu.

Antioch University New England, Graduate School, Department of Applied Psychology, Program in Clinical Mental Health Counseling, Keene, NH 03431-3552. Offers MA. *Accreditation:* ACA. *Degree requirements:* For master's, internship, practicum. *Entrance requirements:* For master's, previous course work and work experience in psychology. Additional exam requirements/recommendations for international students: Required—TOEFL (minimum score 600 paper-based; 250 computer-based). Electronic applications accepted. *Expenses:* Contact institution. *Faculty research:* Multicultural issues in field supervision.

Argosy University, Chicago, College of Psychology and Behavioral Sciences, Doctoral Program in Clinical Psychology, Chicago, IL 60601. Offers child and adolescent psychology (Psy D); client-centered and experiential psychotherapies (Psy D); diversity and multicultural psychology (Psy D); family psychology (Psy D); forensic psychology (Psy D); health psychology (Psy D); neuropsychology (Psy D); organizational consulting (Psy D); psychoanalytic psychology (Psy D); psychology and spirituality (Psy D). *Accreditation:* APA.

See Close-Up on page 1051.

Argosy University, Chicago, College of Psychology and Behavioral Sciences, Program in Counseling Psychology, Chicago, IL 60601. Offers counselor education and supervision (Ed D). Postbaccalaureate distance learning degree programs offered (minimal on-campus study).

See Close-Up on page 1051.

Argosy University, Denver, College of Psychology and Behavioral Sciences, Denver, CO 80231. Offers clinical mental health counseling (MA); clinical psychology (MA, Psy D); counseling psychology (Ed D); counselor education and supervision (Ed D); forensic psychology (MA); industrial organizational psychology (MA); marriage and family therapy (MA, DMFT).

See Close-Up on page 1055.

Argosy University, Hawai'i, College of Psychology and Behavioral Sciences, Program in Counseling Psychology, Honolulu, HI 96813. Offers Ed D.

See Close-Up on page 1057.

Argosy University, Inland Empire, College of Psychology and Behavioral Sciences, San Bernardino, CA 92408. Offers clinical psychology/marriage and family therapy (MA); counseling psychology (Ed D); counseling psychology/marriage and family therapy (MA); forensic psychology (MA); industrial organizational psychology (MA); sport-exercise psychology (MA).

See Close-Up on page 1059.

Argosy University, Los Angeles, College of Psychology and Behavioral Sciences, Santa Monica, CA 90045. Offers clinical psychology/marriage and family therapy (MA); counseling psychology (Ed D); counseling psychology/marriage and family therapy (MA); forensic psychology (MA).

See Close-Up on page 1061.

Argosy University, Nashville, College of Psychology and Behavioral Sciences, Nashville, TN 37214. Offers counselor education and supervision (Ed D); mental health counseling (MA).

See Close-Up on page 1063.

Argosy University, Orange County, College of Psychology and Behavioral Sciences, Program in Counseling Psychology, Orange, CA 92868. Offers counseling psychology (Ed D); marriage and family therapy (MA).

See Close-Up on page 1065.

Argosy University, Phoenix, College of Psychology and Behavioral Sciences, Program in Mental Health Counseling, Phoenix, AZ 85021. Offers MA.

See Close-Up on page 1067.

Argosy University, Salt Lake City, College of Psychology and Behavioral Sciences, Draper, UT 84020. Offers counseling psychology (Ed D); counselor education and supervision (Ed D); forensic psychology (MA); marriage and family therapy (MA, DMFT); mental health counseling (MA).

See Close-Up on page 1069.

Argosy University, San Diego, College of Psychology and Behavioral Sciences, San Diego, CA 92108. Offers clinical psychology/marriage and family therapy (MA); counseling psychology (Ed D); counseling psychology/marriage and family therapy (MA); forensic psychology (MA).

See Close-Up on page 1071.

Argosy University, San Francisco Bay Area, College of Psychology and Behavioral Sciences, Program in Counseling Psychology, Alameda, CA 94501. Offers MA, Ed D.

See Close-Up on page 1073.

Argosy University, Sarasota, College of Psychology and Behavioral Sciences, Sarasota, FL 34235. Offers community counseling (MA); counseling psychology (Ed D); counselor education and supervision (Ed D); forensic psychology (MA); marriage and family therapy (MA); mental health counseling (MA); pastoral community counseling (Ed D).

See Close-Up on page 1075.

Argosy University, Schaumburg, College of Psychology and Behavioral Sciences, Schaumburg, IL 60173-5403. Offers clinical health psychology (Post-Graduate Certificate); clinical psychology (MA, Psy D), including child and family psychology (Psy D), clinical health psychology (Psy D), diversity and multicultural psychology (Psy D), forensic psychology (Psy D), neuropsychology (Psy D); community counseling (MA); counseling psychology (Ed D), including counselor education and supervision; counselor education and supervision (Ed D); forensic psychology (Post-Graduate Certificate); industrial organizational psychology (MA). *Accreditation:* ACA; APA.

See Close-Up on page 1077.

Argosy University, Seattle, College of Psychology and Behavioral Sciences, Program in Counseling Psychology, Seattle, WA 98121. Offers MA, Ed D.

See Close-Up on page 1079.

Argosy University, Tampa, College of Psychology and Behavioral Sciences, Tampa, FL 33607. Offers clinical psychology (MA, Psy D), including clinical psychology; counselor education and supervision (Ed D); industrial organizational psychology (MA); marriage and family therapy (MA); mental health counseling (MA).

See Close-Up on page 1081.

Argosy University, Washington DC, College of Psychology and Behavioral Sciences, Arlington, VA 22209. Offers clinical psychology (MA, Psy D), including child and family psychology (Psy D), diversity and multicultural psychology (Psy D), forensic psychology (Psy D), health and neuropsychology (Psy D); community counseling (MA); counseling psychology (Ed D), including counselor education and supervision; counselor education and supervision (Ed D); forensic psychology (MA). *Accreditation:* APA.

See Close-Up on page 1085.

Arizona State University, Graduate College, Mary Lou Fulton College of Education, Division of Psychology in Education, Program in Counseling Psychology, Tempe, AZ 85287. Offers PhD. *Accreditation:* APA. *Degree requirements:* For doctorate, thesis/dissertation. *Entrance requirements:* For doctorate, GRE General Test or MAT.

Assumption College, Graduate School, Counseling Psychology Program, Worcester, MA 01609-1296. Offers child and family interventions (MA); cognitive and behavioral therapies (MA); counseling psychology (CAGS); general psychology (MA). Part-time and evening/weekend programs available. *Faculty:* 4 full-time (1 woman), 6 part-time/adjunct (2 women). *Students:* 50 full-time (42 women), 38 part-time (33 women); includes 9 minority (3 African Americans, 6 Hispanic Americans). Average age 24. 121 applicants, 86% accepted. In 2009, 20 master's, 2 other advanced degrees awarded. *Degree requirements:* For master's, comprehensive exam, internship, practicum, oral exam; for CAGS, comprehensive exam, oral exam. *Entrance requirements:* For master's, 3 letters of recommendation, resume; for CAGS, 3 letters of recommendation, resume, interview, essay. Additional exam requirements/recommendations for international students: Required—TOEFL (minimum score 540 paper-based; 200 computer-based; 76 iBT), IELTS (minimum score 6). *Application deadline:* For fall admission, 6/1 priority date for domestic students, 5/1 priority date for international students; for spring admission, 11/1 priority date for domestic students, 9/1 priority date for international students. Applications are processed on a rolling basis. Application fee: $30. Electronic applications accepted. *Expenses:* Tuition: Part-time $503 per credit. Required fees: $20 per semester. One-time fee: $100 part-time. Part-time tuition and fees vary according to campus/location. *Financial support:* In 2009–10, 19 fellowships with partial tuition reimbursements (averaging $6,808 per year), 2 teaching assistantships with full tuition reimbursements (averaging $9,940 per year) were awarded. Financial award application deadline: 3/1; financial award applicants required to submit FAFSA. *Faculty research:* Mood disorders, adjustment to life-threatening illness, perception of movement, socioemotional development of young children, discovery versus disclosure. *Unit head:* Dr. Leonard A. Doerfler, Director, 508-767-7549, Fax: 508-767-7263, E-mail: doerfler@assumption.edu. *Application contact:* Adrian O. Dumas, Director of Graduate Enrollment Management and Services, 508-767-7365, Fax: 508-767-7030, E-mail: adumas@assumption.edu.

Athabasca University, Graduate Centre for Applied Psychology, Athabasca, AB T9S 3A3, Canada. Offers art therapy (MC); career counseling (MC); counseling (Advanced Certificate); counseling psychology (MC); school counseling (MC). *Faculty:* 5 full-time (2 women). *Students:* 210 part-time. Average age 35. 117 applicants, 15 enrolled. In 2009, 36 master's, 1 Advanced Certificate awarded. *Application deadline:* For fall admission, 3/1 for domestic and international students. Application fee: $80. *Expenses:* Tuition: Part-time $16,500 per degree program. Required fees: $200 per year. One-time fee: $80 part-time. *Unit head:* Dr. Trevor Gilbert, Chair, 866-242-8768, Fax: 780-675-6186, E-mail: trevorg@athabascau.ca. *Application contact:* Information Contact, 800-788-9041, Fax: 780-675-6437.

Avila University, Department of Psychology, Kansas City, MO 64145-1698. Offers counseling psychology (MS); general psychology (MS). Part-time and evening/weekend programs available. *Faculty:* 6 full-time (5 women), 12 part-time/adjunct (7 women). *Students:* 125 full-time (101 women), 30 part-time (23 women); includes 32 minority (24 African Americans, 4 Asian Americans or Pacific Islanders, 4 Hispanic Americans), 8 international. Average age 32. 76 applicants, 79% accepted, 48 enrolled. In 2009, 36 master's awarded. *Degree requirements:* For master's, capstone project. *Entrance requirements:* For master's, minimum GPA of 3.0 in last 60 hours, 2 letters of recommendation. Additional exam requirements/recommendations for international students: Required—TOEFL. *Application deadline:* Applications are processed on a rolling basis. Application fee: $0. *Expenses:* Tuition: Full-time $8622; part-time $479 per credit hour. Required fees: $432; $24 per credit hour. Tuition and fees vary according to program. *Financial support:* In 2009–10, 132 students received support. Career-related internships or fieldwork, scholarships/grants, and unspecified assistantships available. Support available to part-time students. Financial award applicants required to submit FAFSA. *Faculty research:* Neuro/biofeedback, emotional regulation, perception, mindful wellness, trauma and restorative justice. *Unit head:* Shirlene Hess, Director of Graduate Psychology, 816-501-2969, Fax: 816-501-2455, E-mail: shirlene.hess@avila.edu. *Application contact:* Beth Brown, Administrative Assistant, 816-501-3698, Fax: 816-501-2455, E-mail: gradpsych@avila.edu.

Ball State University, Graduate School, Teachers College, Department of Counseling Psychology and Guidance Services, Program in Counseling Psychology, Muncie, IN 47306-1099. Offers MA, PhD. *Accreditation:* ACA. *Degree requirements:* For doctorate, thesis/dissertation. *Entrance requirements:* For doctorate, GRE General Test, interview, minimum graduate GPA of 3.2, resume.

Bemidji State University, School of Graduate Studies, College of Social and Natural Sciences, Field of Counseling Psychology, Bemidji, MN 56601-2699. Offers psychology (MS). Part-time programs available. *Entrance requirements:* For master's, GRE General Test, letters of recommendation, letter of intent, curriculum vitae/resume. Additional exam requirements/recommendations for international students: Required—TOEFL. Electronic applications accepted. *Faculty research:* Exercise and working memory; age and stability of self-esteem in rural women; traumatic stress; Post-Traumatic Stress Disorder treatment for vets; learning outcomes assessment.

Bethel University, Graduate School, Program in Counseling Psychology, St. Paul, MN 55112-6999. Offers child and adolescent and community counseling (MA). Part-time and evening/weekend programs available. *Faculty:* 6 full-time (2 women), 9 part-time/adjunct (5 women). *Students:* 71 full-time (56 women), 7 part-time (6 women); includes 5 minority (2 African Americans, 2 Asian Americans or Pacific Islanders, 1 Hispanic American). Average age 32. 60 applicants, 75% accepted, 35 enrolled. In 2009, 32 master's awarded. *Degree requirements:* For master's, comprehensive exam, thesis optional, practicum. *Entrance requirements:* For master's, MAT, minimum GPA of 3.0, course work in psychology and statistics, letters of reference. Additional exam requirements/recommendations for international students: Required—TOEFL (minimum score 550 paper-based; 213 computer-based; 80 iBT). *Application deadline:* For fall admission, 5/1 priority date for domestic students. Applications are processed on a rolling basis. Application fee: $25. Electronic applications accepted. *Expenses:* Tuition: Full-time $7920; part-time $440 per credit. One-time fee: $25. Tuition and fees vary according to course load, degree level and program. *Financial support:* Applicants required to submit FAFSA. *Unit head:* Dr. Diane Dahl, Assistant Dean, 651-635-8000, Fax: 651-635-8004, E-mail: diane-dahl@bethel.edu. *Application contact:* Michael Price, Director of Admissions, 651-635-8000, Fax: 651-635-8004, E-mail: m-price@bethel.edu.

Boston College, Lynch Graduate School of Education, Department of Counseling Psychology, Developmental, and Educational Psychology, Program in Counseling Psychology, Chestnut Hill, MA 02467-3800. Offers MA, PhD, MA/MA. *Accreditation:* APA (one or more programs are accredited). *Students:* 200 full-time (155 women), 6 part-time (4 women); includes 37 minority (13 African Americans, 1 American Indian/Alaska Native, 13 Asian Americans or Pacific Islanders, 10 Hispanic Americans), 24 international. 566 applicants, 48% accepted, 87 enrolled. In 2009, 65 master's, 7 doctorates awarded. Terminal master's awarded for partial completion of doctoral program. *Degree requirements:* For master's, comprehensive exam; for doctorate, comprehensive exam, thesis/dissertation. *Entrance requirements:* For master's and doctorate, GRE General Test. Additional exam requirements/recommendations for international students: Required—TOEFL (minimum score 550 paper-based; 213 computer-based; 81 iBT). Application fee: $60. Electronic applications accepted. *Financial support:* Fellowships with full and partial tuition reimbursements, research assistantships with full and partial tuition reimbursements, teaching assistantships with full and partial tuition reimbursements, career-related internships or fieldwork, Federal Work-Study, scholarships/grants, traineeships, health care benefits, tuition waivers (full and partial), and unspecified assistantships available. Support available to part-time students. Financial award applicants required to submit FAFSA. *Faculty research:* Reducing non-academic barriers to learning; race, gender, culture and social class issues in mental health; domestic violence; career development; community intervention and prevention. *Unit head:* Dr. M. Brinton Lykes, Chairperson, 617-552-4214, Fax: 617-552-0812. *Application contact:* Adam Poluzzi, Director, Graduate Admission and Financial Aid, 617-552-4214, Fax: 617-552-0398, E-mail: poluzzi@bc.edu.

Boston Graduate School of Psychoanalysis, Program in Psychoanalytic Counseling, Brookline, MA 02446-4602. Offers MA. *Degree requirements:* For master's, 100-hour practicum, 600-hour internship. *Entrance requirements:* For master's, interview, writing sample. Electronic applications accepted. *Faculty research:* Emotional learning in the classroom, addictions, the effect of extra-analytic contact with analysis, the geriatric setting, siblings.

Boston University, School of Education, Department of Literacy and Language, Counseling and Development, Program in Counseling Psychology, Boston, MA 02215. Offers Ed D. *Degree requirements:* For doctorate, comprehensive exam, thesis/dissertation. *Entrance requirements:* For doctorate, GRE General Test or MAT. Additional exam requirements/recommendations for international students: Required—TOEFL. Electronic applications accepted. *Expenses:* Tuition: Full-time $37,910; part-time $1184 per credit hour. Required fees: $386; $40 per semester. Part-time tuition and fees vary according to class time, course level, degree level and program. *Faculty research:* Cross-cultural counseling, parenting, women's development, mental health.

Bowie State University, Graduate Programs, Program in Counseling Psychology, Bowie, MD 20715-9465. Offers MA. Part-time and evening/weekend programs available. *Degree requirements:* For master's, comprehensive exam, thesis optional, research paper, practicum. *Entrance requirements:* For master's, minimum GPA of 2.5, 3 recommendations. Electronic applications accepted.

Bowie State University, Graduate Programs, Program in Mental Health Counseling, Bowie, MD 20715-9465. Offers MA. Part-time and evening/weekend programs available. *Degree requirements:* For master's, comprehensive exam. *Entrance requirements:* For master's, 3 letters of recommendation, 3.0 GPA, 12 undergraduate credit hours in couseling or psycology. Electronic applications accepted.

Bowling Green State University, Graduate College, College of Education and Human Development, School of Education and Intervention Services, Intervention Services Division, Program in Counseling, Bowling Green, OH 43403. Offers mental health counseling (MA); school counseling (M Ed). *Accreditation:* NCATE. Part-time programs available. *Degree requirements:* For master's, thesis or alternative. *Entrance requirements:* For master's, GRE General Test. Additional exam requirements/recommendations for international students: Required—TOEFL. Electronic applications accepted. *Faculty research:* Perfectionism, multicultural counseling, suicide, ethics and legal issues related to counseling, play therapy.

Brigham Young University, Graduate Studies, David O. McKay School of Education, Department of Counseling Psychology and Special Education, Provo, UT 84602-1001. Offers counseling psychology (PhD); school psychology (Ed S); special education (MS). *Accreditation:* NCATE. Part-time programs available. *Faculty:* 12 full-time (7 women), 13 part-time/adjunct (5 women). *Students:* 74 full-time (54 women), 15 part-time (14 women); includes 11 minority (2 African Americans, 2 American Indian/Alaska Native, 4 Asian Americans or Pacific Islanders, 3 Hispanic Americans), 10 international. Average age 31. 85 applicants, 41% accepted, 28 enrolled. In 2009, 2 master's, 4 doctorates, 10 other advanced degrees awarded. *Degree requirements:* For master's, comprehensive exam, thesis; for doctorate, comprehensive exam, thesis/dissertation. *Entrance requirements:* For master's and doctorate, GRE General Test, minimum GPA of 3.0 in last 60 hours of undergraduate coursework. Additional exam requirements/recommendations for international students: Required—TOEFL (minimum score 580 paper-based; 237 computer-based), IELTS (minimum score 7). *Application deadline:* For fall admission, 1/15 for domestic and international students. Application fee: $50. Electronic applications accepted. *Expenses:* Tuition: Full-time $5580; part-time $301 per credit hour. Tuition and fees vary according to student's religious affiliation. *Financial support:* In 2009–10, 53 students received support, including 36 research assistantships with partial tuition reimbursements available (averaging $6,706 per year), 3 teaching assistantships with partial tuition reimbursements available (averaging $7,457 per year); career-related internships or fieldwork, institutionally sponsored loans, and tuition waivers (partial) also available. Financial award application deadline: 3/30. *Faculty research:* Gender issues in education, psychotherapy progress and outcome, behavior disorders and ABA. *Unit head:* Dr. Mary Anne Prater, Chair, 801-422-3857, Fax: 801-422-0198, E-mail: prater@byu.edu. *Application contact:* Diane E. Hancock, Department Secretary, 801-422-3859, Fax: 801-422-0198, E-mail: diane_hancock@byu.edu.

Brooklyn College of the City University of New York, Division of Graduate Studies, Department of Health and Nutrition Science, Brooklyn, NY 11210-2889. Offers community health (MA, MPH, MS), including community health education (MA), computer science and health science (MS), health care management (MPH), health care policy and administration (MPH), thanatology (MA); grief counseling (CAS); nutrition (MS); public health (MPH), including community-public health. Part-time and evening/weekend programs available. *Students:* 24 full-time (16 women), 161 part-time (136 women); includes 89 minority (57 African Americans, 19 Asian Americans or Pacific Islanders, 13 Hispanic Americans), 16 international. Average age 34. 116 applicants, 78% accepted, 42 enrolled. In 2009, 44 master's, 1 other advanced degree awarded. *Degree requirements:* For master's, thesis or alternative. *Entrance requirements:* For master's, GRE, 18 credits, essay, 2 letters of recommendation. Additional exam requirements/recommendations for international students: Required—TOEFL. *Application deadline:* For fall admission, 3/1 priority date for domestic students, 2/1 priority date for international students; for spring admission, 11/1 priority date for domestic students, 10/1 priority date for international students. Applications are processed on a rolling basis. Application fee: $125. Electronic applications accepted. *Expenses:* Tuition, area resident: Full-time $7360; part-time $310 per credit hour. Tuition, state resident: full-time $7360; part-time $310 per credit hour. Tuition, nonresident: full-time $13,800; part-time $575 per credit hour. International

Counseling Psychology

Brooklyn College of the City University of New York (continued)
tuition: $13,800 full-time. Required fees: $140.10 per semester. *Financial support:* Career-related internships or fieldwork, Federal Work-Study, institutionally sponsored loans, and scholarships/grants available. Support available to part-time students. Financial award application deadline: 5/1; financial award applicants required to submit FAFSA. *Faculty research:* Medical ethics, relocation stress, risk reduction, disease prevention, history of public health, computer applications. *Unit head:* Dr. Janet Kolmer Grommet, Chairperson, 718-951-5026, Fax: 718-951-4670, E-mail: jgrommet@brooklyn.cuny.edu. *Application contact:* Hernan Sierra, Graduate Admissions Coordinator, 718-951-4536, Fax: 718-951-4506, E-mail: grads@brooklyn.cuny.edu.

Brooklyn College of the City University of New York, Division of Graduate Studies, Department of Psychology, Brooklyn, NY 11210-2889. Offers experimental psychology (MA); industrial and organizational psychology (MA), including human relations, organizational behavior; mental health counseling (MA); psychology (PhD). Part-time programs available. *Students:* 89 full-time (74 women), 131 part-time (97 women); includes 83 minority (52 African Americans, 11 Asian Americans or Pacific Islanders, 20 Hispanic Americans), 17 international. Average age 30. 322 applicants, 55% accepted, 98 enrolled. In 2009, 62 master's awarded. *Degree requirements:* For master's, comprehensive exam, thesis (for some programs). *Entrance requirements:* For master's, minimum GPA of 3.0, 2 letters of recommendation, essay; for doctorate, GRE. Additional exam requirements/recommendations for international students: Required—TOEFL (minimum score 520 paper-based; 190 computer-based; 69 iBT). *Application deadline:* For fall admission, 3/1 for domestic students, 2/1 for international students; for spring admission, 11/1 for domestic students, 10/1 for international students. Applications are processed on a rolling basis. Application fee: $125. Electronic applications accepted. *Expenses:* Tuition, area resident: Full-time $7360; part-time $310 per credit hour. Tuition, state resident: full-time $7360; part-time $310 per credit hour. Tuition, nonresident: full-time $13,800; part-time $575 per credit hour. International tuition: $13,800 full-time. Required fees: $140.10 per semester. *Financial support:* Career-related internships or fieldwork, Federal Work-Study, institutionally sponsored loans, scholarships/grants, and tuition waivers (partial) available. Support available to part-time students. Financial award application deadline: 5/1; financial award applicants required to submit FAFSA. *Unit head:* Dr. Margaret-Ellen Pipe, Chairperson, 718-951-5601, Fax: 718-951-4814, E-mail: mepipe@brooklyn.cuny.edu. *Application contact:* Hernan Sierra, Graduate Admissions Coordinator, 718-951-4536, Fax: 718-951-4506, E-mail: grads@brooklyn.cuny.edu.

Caldwell College, Graduate Studies, Program in Counseling Psychology, Caldwell, NJ 07006-6195. Offers art therapy (MA); counseling psychology (MA); school counseling (MA). Part-time and evening/weekend programs available. *Degree requirements:* For master's, comprehensive exam, practicum. *Entrance requirements:* For master's, GRE General Test, minimum GPA of 3.0. Additional exam requirements/recommendations for international students: Required—TOEFL (minimum score 580 paper-based; 237 computer-based). Electronic applications accepted.

California Baptist University, Program in Counseling Psychology, Riverside, CA 92504-3206. Offers professional counseling (MS); professional ministry (MS). Part-time programs available. *Faculty:* 10 full-time (6 women), 4 part-time/adjunct (1 woman). *Students:* 112 full-time (88 women), 43 part-time (39 women); includes 70 minority (20 African Americans, 1 American Indian/Alaska Native, 9 Asian Americans or Pacific Islanders, 40 Hispanic Americans), 2 international. 97 applicants, 55% accepted, 51 enrolled. In 2009, 49 master's awarded. *Degree requirements:* For master's, comprehensive exam, 24 hours (individual) or 50 hours (group) psychotherapy, 300 hours of field work. *Entrance requirements:* For master's, Minnesota Multiphasic Personality Inventory, Myers-Briggs Type Indicator, course work in developmental psychology, theories of personality, and statistics; minimum undergraduate GPA of 2.75. Additional exam requirements/recommendations for international students: Required—TOEFL (minimum score 575 paper-based; 230 computer-based; 89 iBT). *Application deadline:* For fall admission, 9/1 for domestic students, 7/1 for international students; for spring admission, 1/3 for domestic students, 10/15 for international students. Applications are processed on a rolling basis. Application fee: $45. Electronic applications accepted. *Expenses:* Contact institution. *Financial support:* Career-related internships or fieldwork, Federal Work-Study, and scholarships/grants available. Support available to part-time students. Financial award applicants required to submit FAFSA. *Unit head:* Dr. Mischa Routon, Director, 951-343-4206, Fax: 951-343-4569, E-mail: mrouton@calbaptist.edu. *Application contact:* Gail Ronveaux, Dean of Graduate Enrollment, 951-343-5045, Fax: 951-343-5095, E-mail: graduateadmissions@calbaptist.edu.

California Institute of Integral Studies, School of Professional Psychology, San Francisco, CA 94103. Offers clinical psychology (Psy D); community mental health (MA); drama therapy (MA); expressive arts therapy (MA); integral counseling psychology (MA); integral counseling psychology–weekend (MA); somatic psychology (MA). *Accreditation:* APA. Part-time programs available. *Students:* 639 full-time (483 women), 53 part-time (43 women); includes 148 minority (32 African Americans, 2 American Indian/Alaska Native, 62 Asian Americans or Pacific Islanders, 52 Hispanic Americans). Average age 38. 476 applicants, 71% accepted, 202 enrolled. In 2009, 136 master's, 21 doctorates awarded. *Degree requirements:* For master's, comprehensive exam; for doctorate, comprehensive exam, thesis/dissertation. *Entrance requirements:* For master's, minimum GPA of 3.0, letters of recommendation, writing sample; for doctorate, GRE, MA in psychology or social work with appropriate practical experience for advanced standing, or BA with a minimum GPA of 3.1; letters of recommendation; writing sample. Additional exam requirements/recommendations for international students: Required—TOEFL. *Application deadline:* For fall admission, 2/1 priority date for domestic and international students; for spring admission, 10/15 priority date for domestic and international students. Applications are processed on a rolling basis. Application fee: $65. Electronic applications accepted. *Expenses:* Tuition: Full-time $15,300; part-time $850 per credit hour. Required fees: $110 per semester. Tuition and fees vary according to degree level. *Financial support:* In 2009–10, 677 students received support; research assistantships with tuition reimbursements available, teaching assistantships with tuition reimbursements available, career-related internships or fieldwork, Federal Work-Study, scholarships/grants, and tuition waivers (partial) available. Support available to part-time students. Financial award application deadline: 4/15; financial award applicants required to submit FAFSA. *Faculty research:* Somatic psychology, comparative psychology, art therapy, transpersonal psychology, eco-psychology. *Application contact:* David Townes, Senior Admissions Counselor, 415-575-6152, Fax: 415-575-1268, E-mail: dtownes@ciis.edu.

California State University, Bakersfield, Division of Graduate Studies, School of Humanities and Social Sciences, Program in Counseling Psychology, Bakersfield, CA 93311. Offers MS.

California State University, Sacramento, Graduate Studies, College of Social Sciences and Interdisciplinary Studies, Department of Psychology, Sacramento, CA 95819. Offers counseling psychology (MA). Part-time programs available. *Degree requirements:* For master's, thesis, writing proficiency exam. *Entrance requirements:* For master's, GRE Subject Test, minimum GPA of 3.0 during previous 2 years. Additional exam requirements/recommendations for international students: Required—TOEFL. Electronic applications accepted.

California State University, San Bernardino, Graduate Studies, College of Social and Behavioral Sciences, Department of Psychology, Program in Clinical/Counseling Psychology, San Bernardino, CA 92407-2397. Offers clinical psychology (MS). *Students:* 24 full-time (23 women), 1 (woman) part-time; includes 12 minority (2 African Americans, 2 Asian Americans or Pacific Islanders, 8 Hispanic Americans). Average age 28. 96 applicants, 40% accepted, 14 enrolled. In 2009, 14 master's awarded. *Degree requirements:* For master's, comprehensive exam or thesis. *Entrance requirements:* For master's, minimum GPA of 3.0 in major. *Application deadline:* For fall admission, 8/31 priority date for domestic students. Application fee: $55. *Financial support:* Fellowships, research assistantships, teaching assistantships, career-related internships or fieldwork, Federal Work-Study, and unspecified assistantships available. Financial award application deadline: 3/1. *Faculty research:* Psychology of women, fathering, depression, families, cross-cultural counseling. *Unit head:* Dr. Robert Cramer, Chair, 909-537-5576, Fax: 909-537-7003, E-mail: rcramer@csusb.edu. *Application contact:* Stacy Brooks, Graduate Secretary, 909-880-5570, Fax: 909-880-7003, E-mail: sbrooks@csusb.edu.

Cambridge College, School of Psychology and Counseling, Cambridge, MA 02138-5304. Offers addiction counseling (M Ed); alcohol & drug counseling (Certificate); counseling psychology (M Ed, CAGS); counseling psychology: forensic counseling (M Ed); marriage and family therapy (M Ed); mental health and addiction counseling (M Ed); mental health counseling (M Ed); mental health counseling for school guidance counselors (Post Master's Certificate); psychological studies (M Ed); school adjustment and mental health counseling (M Ed); school adjustment, mental health and addiction counseling (M Ed); school guidance counselor (M Ed); trauma studies (Certificate). Part-time and evening/weekend programs available. *Faculty:* 5 full-time (2 women), 87 part-time/adjunct (50 women). *Students:* 501 full-time (395 women), 307 part-time (245 women); includes 382 minority (295 African Americans, 2 American Indian/Alaska Native, 6 Asian Americans or Pacific Islanders, 79 Hispanic Americans), 4 international. Average age 38. In 2009, 237 master's, 15 other advanced degrees awarded. *Degree requirements:* For master's, thesis, practicum/internship; for other advanced degree, thesis, practicum/Internship. *Entrance requirements:* For master's, resume, 2 professional references; for other advanced degree, official transcripts, documents for transfer credit evaluation, resume, written personal statement/essay, 2 professional references, health insurance, immunizations form. Additional exam requirements/recommendations for international students: Required—TOEFL (minimum score 550 paper-based; 213 computer-based; 79 iBT); Recommended—IELTS (minimum score 6). *Application deadline:* Applications are processed on a rolling basis. Application fee: $30. Electronic applications accepted. *Expenses:* Contact institution. *Financial support:* In 2009–10, 686 students received support. Career-related internships or fieldwork, Federal Work-Study, and scholarships/grants available. Financial award applicants required to submit FAFSA. *Unit head:* Dr. Niti Seth, Dean, 617-873-0208, Fax: 617-349-3561, E-mail: nseth@cambridgecollege.edu. *Application contact:* Stephen Lyons, Director of Enrollment, Graduate and N.I.T.E. Programs, 617-868-1000, Fax: 617-349-3561, E-mail: stephen.lyons@cambridgecollege.edu.

Capella University, Harold Abel School of Psychology, Minneapolis, MN 55402. Offers child and adolescent development (MS); clinical psychology (MS, Psy D); counseling psychology (MS); educational psychology (MS, PhD); evaluation, research, and measurement (MS); general psychology (MS, PhD); industrial/organizational psychology (MS, PhD); leadership coaching psychology (MS); organizational leader development (MS); school psychology (MS); sport psychology (MS). Part-time and evening/weekend programs available. Postbaccalaureate distance learning degree programs offered (minimal on-campus study). Terminal master's awarded for partial completion of doctoral program. *Degree requirements:* For master's, thesis optional, project; for doctorate, thesis/dissertation. *Entrance requirements:* For degree, master's degree in school psychology. Additional exam requirements/recommendations for international students: Required—TOEFL (minimum score 550 paper-based; 213 computer-based), TWE (minimum score 4); Recommended—IELTS. Electronic applications accepted.

Capella University, School of Human Services, Minneapolis, MN 55402. Offers addictions counseling (Certificate); counseling studies (MS, PhD); criminal justice (MS, PhD, Certificate); diversity studies (Certificate); general human services (MS, PhD); health care administration (MS, PhD, Certificate); management of nonprofit agencies (MS, PhD, Certificate); marital, couple and family counseling/therapy (MS); marriage and family services (Certificate); mental health counseling (MS); professional counseling (Certificate); social and community services (MS, PhD, Certificate). Part-time and evening/weekend programs available. Postbaccalaureate distance learning degree programs offered (minimal on-campus study). Terminal master's awarded for partial completion of doctoral program. *Degree requirements:* For master's, thesis optional, integrative project; for doctorate, comprehensive exam, thesis/dissertation. *Entrance requirements:* Additional exam requirements/recommendations for international students: Required—TOEFL (minimum score 550 paper-based; 213 computer-based), TWE (minimum score 4). Electronic applications accepted. *Faculty research:* Compulsive and addictive behaviors, substance abuse, assessment of psychopathology and neuropsychology.

Carlos Albizu University, Miami Campus, Graduate Programs, Miami, FL 33172-2209. Offers clinical psychology (Psy D); entrepreneurship (MBA); exceptional student education (MS); industrial/organizational psychology (MS); marriage and family therapy (MS); mental health counseling (MS); nonprofit management (MBA); organizational management (MBA); psychology (MS); school counseling (MS); teaching English as a second language (MS). *Accreditation:* APA. Part-time and evening/weekend programs available. *Faculty:* 23 full-time (13 women), 41 part-time/adjunct (21 women). *Students:* 529 full-time (420 women), 171 part-time (139 women); includes 551 minority (55 African Americans, 1 American Indian/Alaska Native, 5 Asian Americans or Pacific Islanders, 490 Hispanic Americans). Average age 37. 278 applicants, 57% accepted, 142 enrolled. In 2009, 139 master's, 26 doctorates awarded. Terminal master's awarded for partial completion of doctoral program. *Degree requirements:* For master's, one foreign language, comprehensive exam, integrative project (MBA), research project (exceptional student education, teaching English as a second language); for doctorate, one foreign language, comprehensive exam, internship, project. *Entrance requirements:* For master's, 3 letters of recommendation, interview, minimum GPA of 3.0, resume; for doctorate, 3 letters of recommendation, minimum GPA of 3.0, resume, interview. *Application deadline:* For fall admission, 8/1 priority date for domestic students; for spring admission, 11/30 priority date for domestic students. Applications are processed on a rolling basis. Application fee: $50. Electronic applications accepted. *Expenses:* Tuition: Full-time $9090; part-time $505 per credit hour. Required fees: $298 per term. Tuition and fees vary according to course load, degree level and program. *Financial support:* In 2009–10, 127 students received support. Federal Work-Study, scholarships/grants, and tuition discounts available. Financial award application deadline: 6/1; financial award applicants required to submit FAFSA. *Faculty research:* Psychotherapy, forensic psychology, neuropsychology, marketing strategy, entrepreneurship, special education. *Unit head:* Dr. Carmen S. Roca, Chancellor, 305-593-1223 Ext. 120, Fax: 305-629-8052, E-mail: croca@albizu.edu. *Application contact:* Annalye Alonso, Secretary, 305-593-1223 Ext. 137, Fax: 305-593-1864, E-mail: aalonso@albizu.edu.

Carlow University, School for Social Change, Pittsburgh, PA 15213-3165. Offers professional counseling (MS); professional counseling: school counseling (MS); professional leadership: management for nonprofit organizations (MS); professional leadership: organizational influence and policy (MS); professional leadership: training and development (MS). Part-time and evening/weekend programs available. *Entrance requirements:* Additional exam requirements/recommendations for international students: Required—TOEFL (minimum score 550 paper-based; 213 computer-based). Electronic applications accepted. *Expenses:* Tuition: Full-time $11,250; part-time $625 per credit. Tuition and fees vary according to course load, degree level and program. *Faculty research:* Gender and leadership, cross cultural communications and leadership, organizational culture.

Centenary College, Program in Counseling Psychology, Hackettstown, NJ 07840-2100. Offers counseling (MA); counseling psychology (MA). Part-time and evening/weekend programs available. Postbaccalaureate distance learning degree programs offered (minimal on-campus study). *Degree requirements:* For master's, thesis, fieldwork.

Central Michigan University, Central Michigan University Off-Campus Programs, Program in Counseling, Mount Pleasant, MI 48859. Offers professional counseling (MA); school counseling (MA). Part-time and evening/weekend programs available. *Entrance requirements:* For master's, MAT, minimum GPA of 2.7. Additional exam requirements/recommendations for international students: Required—TOEFL. Electronic applications accepted. *Financial support:* Scholarships/grants available. Support available to part-time students. *Unit head:* Dr. Suzanne Shellady, Chair, 989-774-3507, E-mail: shell1sm@cmich.edu. *Application contact:* 877-268-4636, E-mail: cmuoffcampus@cmich.edu.

Central Michigan University, College of Graduate Studies, College of Humanities and Social and Behavioral Sciences, Department of Psychology, Program in School Psychology, Mount

Pleasant, MI 48859. Offers psychological services (S Psy S); school psychology (PhD). *Accreditation:* APA; NCATE. *Degree requirements:* For doctorate, thesis/dissertation; for S Psy S, thesis. *Entrance requirements:* For doctorate, GRE. Electronic applications accepted. *Faculty research:* Psychology and education foundations, psychology and education assessment, intervention strategies.

Central Washington University, Graduate Studies and Research, College of the Sciences, Department of Psychology, Program in Mental Health Counseling, Ellensburg, WA 98926. Offers MS. *Accreditation:* ACA. *Faculty:* 32 full-time (16 women). *Students:* 24 full-time (15 women), 2 part-time (both women); includes 2 minority (both Hispanic Americans). *Degree requirements:* For master's, thesis, internship. *Entrance requirements:* For master's, GRE General Test, minimum GPA of 3.0. Additional exam requirements/recommendations for international students: Required—TOEFL (minimum score 550 paper-based; 213 computer-based; 79 iBT). *Application deadline:* For fall admission, 2/1 for domestic students. Application fee: $50. *Expenses:* Tuition, state resident: full-time $7353; part-time $245 per credit. Tuition, nonresident: full-time $16,383; part-time $546 per credit. Required fees: $882. Tuition and fees vary according to degree level. *Financial support:* Research assistantships with full and partial tuition reimbursements, teaching assistantships with full and partial tuition reimbursements, career-related internships or fieldwork, Federal Work-Study, health care benefits, and unspecified assistantships available. Financial award application deadline: 3/1; financial award applicants required to submit FAFSA. *Unit head:* Dr. Robyn Brammer, Program Coordinator, 509-963-2501, E-mail: brammerr@cwu.edu. *Application contact:* Justine Eason, Admissions Program Coordinator, 509-963-3103, Fax: 509-963-1799, E-mail: masters@cwu.edu.

Chaminade University of Honolulu, Graduate Services, Program in Counseling Psychology, Honolulu, HI 96816-1578. Offers MSCP. Part-time and evening/weekend programs available. *Degree requirements:* For master's, comprehensive exam. *Entrance requirements:* For master's, minimum undergraduate GPA of 3.0, 3 letters of recommendation. Additional exam requirements/recommendations for international students: Required—TOEFL (minimum score 550 paper-based). *Faculty research:* Taoist/Buddhist psychology, psychology of T'ai Chi Ch'uan, sleep disorders, drug/alcohol prevention with adolescent girls, anger/aggression with kids.

Chatham University, Program in Counseling Psychology, Pittsburgh, PA 15232-2826. Offers child, adolescent and family (MSCP); counseling psychology (Psy D); health and holistic (MSCP); infant mental health (MSCP); organization and supervision (MSCP); sport and exercise (MSCP). Part-time and evening/weekend programs available. *Students:* 107 full-time (93 women), 77 part-time (67 women). Average age 29. 141 applicants, 76% accepted, 75 enrolled. In 2009, 63 master's awarded. *Degree requirements:* For master's, thesis optional, supervised internship; for doctorate, thesis/dissertation, internship. *Entrance requirements:* For master's, minimum GPA of 3.0; 2 letters of recommendation; resume; prerequisite coursework in statistics, biology, and psychology; for doctorate, GRE. Additional exam requirements/recommendations for international students: Required—TOEFL (minimum score 600 paper-based; 250 computer-based; 100 iBT), IELTS (minimum score 6.5), TWE. *Application deadline:* For fall admission, 5/1 priority date for domestic students, 6/1 priority date for international students; for spring admission, 12/1 for domestic students, 11/1 for international students. Applications are processed on a rolling basis. Application fee: $45. Electronic applications accepted. *Financial support:* Career-related internships or fieldwork available. Financial award applicants required to submit FAFSA. *Faculty research:* Trauma and recovery, hypnosis, psychospiritual dimensions of healing, psychotherapy of schizophrenia. *Unit head:* Dr. Mary Beth Mannarino, Director, 412-365-1196, Fax: 412-365-1505, E-mail: mmannarino@chatham.edu. *Application contact:* Dory Perry, Associate Director of Graduate Admissions, 412-365-2758, Fax: 412-365-1609, E-mail: gradadmissions@chatham.edu.

Chestnut Hill College, School of Graduate Studies, Division of Psychology, Program in Clinical and Counseling Psychology, Philadelphia, PA 19118-2693. Offers MA, MS, CAS. Part-time and evening/weekend programs available. *Degree requirements:* For master's, thesis optional, practica. *Entrance requirements:* For master's, GRE, writing sample, letters of recommendation; for CAS, GRE, master's degree in counseling or related discipline, transcripts, letters of recommendation, statement of professional goals, writing sample. Additional exam requirements/recommendations for international students: Required—TOEFL (minimum score 550 paper-based; 213 computer-based). *Faculty research:* Play therapy, eating disorders, addictions, group psychology and group therapy, health psychology.

The Chicago School of Professional Psychology at Grayslake, Program in Clinical Counseling Psychology, Chicago, IL 60610. Offers counseling (MA), including child and adolescent treatment, generalist, health psychology, Latino mental health, supervision and leadership in mental health, treatment of addiction disorders. *Unit head:* Dr. Virginia Quinonez, Department Chair, 312-329-6623, E-mail: vquinonez@thechicagoschool.edu. *Application contact:* Andrea Schmoyer, Director of Admissions, 312-329-6666, Fax: 312-644-3333, E-mail: admissions@thechicagoschool.edu.

City College of the City University of New York, Graduate School, College of Liberal Arts and Science, Program in Mental Health Counseling, New York, NY 10031-9198. Offers MA.

City University of Seattle, Graduate Division, Division of Arts and Sciences, Bellevue, WA 98005. Offers counseling psychology (MA). Part-time and evening/weekend programs available. *Degree requirements:* For master's, comprehensive exam (for some programs), thesis (for some programs). *Entrance requirements:* Additional exam requirements/recommendations for international students: Recommended—TOEFL (minimum score 567 paper-based; 227 computer-based; 87 iBT), IELTS, TWE. Electronic applications accepted. *Expenses:* Contact institution.

Clemson University, Graduate School, College of Health, Education, and Human Development, School of Education, Program in Counselor Education, Clemson, SC 29634. Offers clinical mental health counseling (M Ed); community counseling (M Ed); school counseling (M Ed); student affairs (M Ed). *Accreditation:* ACA; NCATE. *Students:* 118 full-time (92 women), 55 part-time (45 women); includes 16 minority (11 African Americans, 2 Asian Americans or Pacific Islanders, 3 Hispanic Americans), 1 international. Average age 28. 194 applicants, 59% accepted, 50 enrolled. In 2009, 65 master's awarded. *Entrance requirements:* For master's, GRE General Test. Additional exam requirements/recommendations for international students: Required—TOEFL. *Application deadline:* For fall admission, 2/1 for domestic students; for spring admission, 10/1 for domestic students. Applications are processed on a rolling basis. Application fee: $70 ($80 for international students). Electronic applications accepted. *Expenses:* Contact institution. *Financial support:* In 2009–10, 63 students received support, including 9 research assistantships with partial tuition reimbursements available (averaging $10,221 per year), 4 teaching assistantships with partial tuition reimbursements available (averaging $11,750 per year); career-related internships or fieldwork, institutionally sponsored loans, scholarships/grants, health care benefits, and unspecified assistantships also available. Support available to part-time students. Financial award application deadline: 6/1; financial award applicants required to submit FAFSA. *Unit head:* Dr. Michael J. Padilla, Director/Associate Dean, 864-656-4444, Fax: 864-656-0311, E-mail: padilla@clemson.edu. *Application contact:* Dr. David Fleming, Graduate Coordinator, 864-656-1881, Fax: 864-656-0311, E-mail: dflemin@clemson.edu.

Cleveland State University, College of Graduate Studies, College of Education and Human Services, Department of Counseling, Administration, Supervision and Adult Learning (CASAL), Cleveland, OH 44115. Offers accelerated degree in adult learning and development (M Ed); adult learning and development (M Ed); chemical dependency counseling (Certificate); community agency counseling (M Ed); counseling and pupil personnel administration (Ed S); early childhood mental health counseling (Certificate); educational administration and supervision (M Ed); school administration (Ed S); school counseling (M Ed). *Accreditation:* ACA (one or more programs are accredited). Part-time and evening/weekend programs available. *Degree requirements:* For master's, comprehensive exam (for some programs), thesis optional; for other advanced degree, comprehensive exam, thesis optional, internship. *Entrance requirements:* For master's, GRE General Test or MAT, letter of recommendation, minimum GPA of 2.75. Additional exam requirements/recommendations for international students: Required—TOEFL (minimum score 525 paper-based; 197 computer-based), IELTS (minimum score 6). Electronic applications accepted. *Faculty research:* Education law, career development, women in school administration, psychopharmacology, counseling and spirituality.

Cleveland State University, College of Graduate Studies, College of Education and Human Services, Program in Urban Education, Cleveland, OH 44115. Offers counseling (PhD); counseling psychology (PhD); leadership and lifelong learning (PhD); learning and development (PhD); policy studies (PhD); school administration (PhD). Part-time programs available. *Degree requirements:* For doctorate, one foreign language, comprehensive exam, thesis/dissertation. *Entrance requirements:* For doctorate, GRE General Test, minimum graduate GPA of 3.25. Additional exam requirements/recommendations for international students: Required—TOEFL (minimum score 525 paper-based; 197 computer-based), IELTS (minimum score 6). *Faculty research:* Equity issues (race, ethnicity, and gender), education development consequences for special needs of urban populations, urban education programming, counseling the violent or aggressive adolescent.

The College at Brockport, State University of New York, School of Education and Human Services, Department of Counselor Education, Brockport, NY 14420-2997. Offers college counseling (MS Ed); mental health counseling (MS); school counseling (MS Ed, CAS). *Accreditation:* ACA (one or more programs are accredited). Part-time programs available. *Students:* 29 full-time (18 women), 53 part-time (35 women); includes 19 minority (14 African Americans, 1 Asian American or Pacific Islander, 4 Hispanic Americans). 73 applicants, 25% accepted, 18 enrolled. In 2009, 14 master's, 4 other advanced degrees awarded. *Degree requirements:* For master's, thesis, internship, project. *Entrance requirements:* For master's, group interview, letters of recommendation, facilitation score, written objectives and focused answers; for CAS, master's degree, New York state school counselor certificate. Additional exam requirements/recommendations for international students: Required—TOEFL (minimum score 550 paper-based; 213 computer-based; 79 iBT). *Application deadline:* For fall admission, 2/1 priority date for domestic and international students; for spring admission, 9/1 priority date for domestic and international students. Application fee: $80. Electronic applications accepted. *Expenses:* Tuition, state resident: full-time $8370; part-time $349 per credit. Tuition, nonresident: full-time $13,250; part-time $522 per credit. *Financial support:* In 2009–10, 1 teaching assistantship with full tuition reimbursement (averaging $6,000 per year) was awarded; Federal Work-Study, scholarships/grants, and unspecified assistantships also available. Support available to part-time students. Financial award application deadline: 3/15; financial award applicants required to submit FAFSA. *Faculty research:* Gender and diversity issues; counseling outcomes; spirituality; school, college and mental health counseling; obesity. *Unit head:* Dr. Thomas J. Hernandez, Chairperson, 585-395-2258, Fax: 585-395-2366, E-mail: thernandez@brockport.edu. *Application contact:* Dr. Thomas J. Hernandez, Chairperson, 585-395-2258, Fax: 585-395-2366, E-mail: thernandez@brockport.edu.

The College of New Rochelle, Graduate School, Division of Human Services, Program in Guidance and Counseling, New Rochelle, NY 10805-2308. Offers MS. Part-time programs available. *Degree requirements:* For master's, internship. *Entrance requirements:* For master's, interview, minimum GPA of 3.0.

The College of New Rochelle, Graduate School, Division of Human Services, Program in Mental Health Counseling, New Rochelle, NY 10805-2308. Offers Certificate. *Degree requirements:* For Certificate, internship.

College of Saint Elizabeth, Department of Psychology, Morristown, NJ 07960-6989. Offers counseling psychology (MA); forensic psychology (MA); student affairs in higher education (Certificate). Part-time and evening/weekend programs available. *Faculty:* 5 full-time (2 women), 10 part-time/adjunct (9 women). *Students:* 23 full-time (19 women), 73 part-time (67 women); includes 25 minority (12 African Americans, 2 Asian Americans or Pacific Islanders, 11 Hispanic Americans), 2 international. Average age 32. 104 applicants, 58% accepted, 47 enrolled. In 2009, 10 master's awarded. *Degree requirements:* For master's, thesis or alternative, portfolio. *Entrance requirements:* For master's, minimum GPA of 3.0, BA in psychology (preferred), 12 credits of course work in psychology. *Application deadline:* For fall admission, 4/14 priority date for domestic students; for spring admission, 11/15 for domestic students. Applications are processed on a rolling basis. Application fee: $35. Electronic applications accepted. *Expenses:* Tuition: Part-time $797 per credit hour. Required fees: $65 per credit hour. *Financial support:* Career-related internships or fieldwork, tuition waivers (partial), and unspecified assistantships available. Support available to part-time students. Financial award application deadline: 3/15; financial award applicants required to submit FAFSA. *Faculty research:* Family systems, dissociative identity disorder, multicultural counseling, outcomes assessment. *Unit head:* Dr. Valerie Scott, Director of the Graduate Program in Counseling Psychology, 973-290-4102, Fax: 973-290-4676, E-mail: vscott@cse.edu. *Application contact:* Donna Tatarka, Dean of Admission, 973-290-4705, Fax: 973-290-4710, E-mail: dtatarka@cse.edu.

College of St. Joseph, Graduate Programs, Division of Psychology and Human Services, Program in Clinical Mental Health Counseling, Rutland, VT 05701-3899. Offers MS. Part-time programs available. *Degree requirements:* For master's, comprehensive exam. *Entrance requirements:* For master's, 2 letters of reference, interview. Electronic applications accepted. *Expenses:* Tuition: Full-time $13,500; part-time $350 per credit. Required fees: $45 per term. One-time fee: $445. Tuition and fees vary according to program.

College of Staten Island of the City University of New York, Graduate Programs, Program in Mental Health Counseling, Staten Island, NY 10314-6600. Offers MA. *Faculty:* 4 full-time (all women). *Students:* 16 full-time (14 women); includes 5 minority (2 African Americans, 3 Hispanic Americans). Average age 33. 41 applicants, 49% accepted, 16 enrolled. *Degree requirements:* For master's, comprehensive exam. *Entrance requirements:* For master's, BA/BS with five undergraduate courses in psychology, minimum GPA of 3.0, 2 letters of recommendation. Additional exam requirements/recommendations for international students: Required—TOEFL (minimum score 600 paper-based; 250 computer-based; 100 iBT). *Application deadline:* For fall admission, 3/10 priority date for domestic and international students. Applications are processed on a rolling basis. Application fee: $125. Electronic applications accepted. *Expenses:* Tuition, state resident: full-time $7360; part-time $310 per credit. Tuition, nonresident: part-time $575 per credit. Required fees: $378; $113 per semester. *Financial support:* In 2009–10, 1 student received support. Federal Work-Study available. Support available to part-time students. *Unit head:* Dr. Judith Kuppersmith, Director, 718-982-4185, E-mail: judith.kuppersmith@csi.cuny.edu. *Application contact:* Sasha Spence, Assistant Director of Graduate Recruitment and Admissions, 718-982-2699, Fax: 718-982-2500, E-mail: sasha.spence@csi.cuny.edu.

Colorado Christian University, Program in Counseling, Lakewood, CO 80226. Offers MA. Part-time and evening/weekend programs available. *Degree requirements:* For master's, thesis optional. *Entrance requirements:* For master's, GRE General Test, 3 letters of recommendation. Additional exam requirements/recommendations for international students: Required—TOEFL. Electronic applications accepted. *Expenses:* Contact institution.

Columbus State University, Graduate Studies, College of Education and Health Professions, Department of Counseling, Foundations, and Leadership, Columbus, GA 31907-5645. Offers community counseling (MS); curriculum and leadership (Ed D); educational leadership (M Ed, Ed S); school counseling (M Ed). *Accreditation:* ACA; NCATE. Part-time and evening/weekend programs available. Postbaccalaureate distance learning degree programs offered (minimal on-campus study). *Faculty:* 11 full-time (3 women), 7 part-time/adjunct (3 women). *Students:* 92 full-time (65 women), 110 part-time (88 women); includes 68 minority (62 African Americans, 1 American Indian/Alaska Native, 1 Asian American or Pacific Islander, 4 Hispanic Americans), 1 international. Average age 35. 134 applicants, 65% accepted, 61 enrolled. In 2009, 32 master's, 34 other advanced degrees awarded. *Degree requirements:* For master's, thesis, exit exam; for Ed S, thesis or alternative. *Entrance requirements:* For master's, GRE General Test, minimum GPA of 2.75; for doctorate, minimum graduate GPA of 3.5, four years of

Counseling Psychology

Columbus State University (continued)
professional service; for Ed S, GRE General Test. Additional exam requirements/recommendations for international students: Required—TOEFL (minimum score 550 paper-based; 213 computer-based; 79 iBT). *Application deadline:* For fall admission, 5/1 priority date for domestic students, 5/1 for international students; for spring admission, 11/1 for domestic and international students. Applications are processed on a rolling basis. Application fee: $30. Electronic applications accepted. *Financial support:* In 2009–10, 110 students received support, including 7 research assistantships with partial tuition reimbursements available (averaging $3,000 per year); career-related internships or fieldwork, Federal Work-Study, institutionally sponsored loans, scholarships/grants, tuition waivers (partial), and unspecified assistantships also available. Support available to part-time students. Financial award application deadline: 5/1; financial award applicants required to submit FAFSA. *Unit head:* Dr. Paul Tom Hackett, Chair, 706-568-5061, Fax: 706-569-3134, E-mail: hackett_paul@colstate.edu. *Application contact:* Katie Thornton, Graduate Admissions Specialist, 706-568-2035, Fax: 706-568-2462, E-mail: thornton_katie@colstate.edu.

Concordia University Chicago, College of Graduate and Innovative Programs, Program in Community Counseling, River Forest, IL 60305-1499. Offers MA. *Accreditation:* ACA. *Degree requirements:* For master's, final project. *Entrance requirements:* For master's, minimum GPA of 2.9. Additional exam requirements/recommendations for international students: Required—TOEFL (minimum score 550 paper-based; 195 computer-based). Electronic applications accepted.

Concordia University Wisconsin, Graduate Programs, Department of Psychology, Program in Professional Counseling, Mequon, WI 53097-2402. Offers MPC. Postbaccalaureate distance learning degree programs offered (minimal on-campus study). *Degree requirements:* For master's, comprehensive exam, thesis or alternative. *Entrance requirements:* For master's, minimum GPA of 3.0. Additional exam requirements/recommendations for international students: Required—TOEFL.

Dallas Baptist University, College of Humanities and Social Sciences, Counseling Program (Main Campus), Dallas, TX 75211-9299. Offers MA. Part-time and evening/weekend programs available. *Entrance requirements:* For master's, GRE General Test, minimum GPA of 3.0. Additional exam requirements/recommendations for international students: Required—TOEFL. Electronic applications accepted. *Expenses:* Tuition: Full-time $10,674; part-time $593 per credit hour. *Faculty research:* Therapy effectiveness.

Dallas Baptist University, College of Humanities and Social Sciences, Counseling Program (North Campus), Dallas, TX 75211-9299. Offers). Part-time and evening/weekend programs available. *Expenses:* Tuition: Full-time $10,674; part-time $593 per credit hour.

Dominican University of California, Graduate Programs, School of Education and Counseling Psychology, Program in Counseling Psychology, San Rafael, CA 94901-2298. Offers MFT, MS. Part-time programs available. *Degree requirements:* For master's, comprehensive exam (for some programs), thesis (for some programs). *Entrance requirements:* For master's, minimum GPA of 3.0 for last 60 units. Additional exam requirements/recommendations for international students: Required—TOEFL (minimum score 550 paper-based; 213 computer-based). Electronic applications accepted. *Expenses:* Contact institution.

Eastern Nazarene College, Adult and Graduate Studies, Program in Family Counseling, Quincy, MA 02170. Offers marriage and family therapy (MS). Part-time and evening/weekend programs available. *Entrance requirements:* For master's, 3 letters of recommendation, resume. Additional exam requirements/recommendations for international students: Required—TOEFL (minimum score 550 paper-based).

Eastern University, Department of Counseling Psychology, St. Davids, PA 19087-3696. Offers community/clinical counseling (MA); school counseling (MA, Certificate); school psychology (MS, Certificate). *Degree requirements:* For master's, internship. *Entrance requirements:* For master's, minimum GPA of 2.5. Additional exam requirements/recommendations for international students: Required—TOEFL.

Eastern Washington University, Graduate Studies, College of Education and Human Development, Program in Mental Health Counseling, Cheney, WA 99004-2431. Offers applied psychology (MS); mental health counseling (MS). *Expenses:* Tuition, state resident: full-time $7476; part-time $249 per quarter hour. Tuition, nonresident: full-time $18,030; part-time $601 per quarter hour. Required fees: $3.50 per quarter hour. $142 per quarter.

Eastern Washington University, Graduate Studies, College of Education and Human Development, Program in School Counseling, Cheney, WA 99004-2431. Offers applied psychology (MS); school counseling (MS). *Accreditation:* ACA; NCATE. *Degree requirements:* For master's, comprehensive exam, thesis or alternative. *Entrance requirements:* For master's, GRE General Test, minimum GPA of 3.0. *Expenses:* Tuition, state resident: full-time $7476; part-time $249 per quarter hour. Tuition, nonresident: full-time $18,030; part-time $601 per quarter hour. Required fees: $3.50 per quarter hour. $142 per quarter.

Emporia State University, School of Graduate Studies, The Teachers College, Department of Psychology, Art Therapy, Rehabilitation and Mental Health Counseling, Program in Mental Health Counseling, Emporia, KS 66801-5087. Offers MS. *Accreditation:* ACA. Part-time programs available. *Students:* 24 full-time (21 women), 3 part-time (all women); includes 1 minority (African American), 4 international. 12 applicants, 92% accepted, 9 enrolled. In 2009, 14 master's awarded. *Degree requirements:* For master's, comprehensive exam, internship. *Entrance requirements:* For master's, GRE or MAT. Additional exam requirements/recommendations for international students: Required—TOEFL (minimum score 520 paper-based; 133 computer-based; 68 iBT). *Application deadline:* For fall admission, 8/15 for domestic students. Applications are processed on a rolling basis. Application fee: $30 ($75 for international students). Electronic applications accepted. *Expenses:* Tuition, state resident: full-time $4154; part-time $173 per credit hour. Tuition, nonresident: full-time $12,864; part-time $536 per credit hour. Required fees: $948; $58 per credit hour. Tuition and fees vary according to campus/location. *Financial support:* Federal Work-Study, institutionally sponsored loans, health care benefits, and unspecified assistantships available. Financial award application deadline: 3/15; financial award applicants required to submit FAFSA. *Unit head:* Dr. Brian A. Schrader, Chair, 620-341-5317, E-mail: bschrade@emporia.edu. *Application contact:* Mary Sewell, Admissions Coordinator, 800-950-GRAD, Fax: 620-341-5909, E-mail: msewell@emporia.edu.

Evangel University, Department of Psychology, Springfield, MO 65802. Offers clinical psychology (MS); counseling psychology (MS). Part-time programs available. *Faculty:* 3 full-time (2 women), 2 part-time/adjunct (1 woman). *Students:* 19 full-time (13 women), 14 part-time (12 women). Average age 27. 17 applicants, 100% accepted, 15 enrolled. In 2009, 6 master's awarded. *Degree requirements:* For master's, comprehensive exam, thesis optional. *Entrance requirements:* For master's, GRE General Test or MAT, minimum undergraduate GPA of 3.0, undergraduate major or minor in psychology. Additional exam requirements/recommendations for international students: Required—TOEFL (minimum score 550 paper-based; 213 computer-based). *Application deadline:* For fall admission, 2/1 priority date for domestic students; for spring admission, 10/15 priority date for domestic students. Applications are processed on a rolling basis. Application fee: $25. Electronic applications accepted. *Financial support:* In 2009–10, 6 students received support. Career-related internships or fieldwork, scholarships/grants, and unspecified assistantships available. Support available to part-time students. Financial award application deadline: 3/1; financial award applicants required to submit FAFSA. *Unit head:* Dr. Grant Jones, Chair, 417-865-2815 Ext. 8619, E-mail: jonesg@evangel.edu. *Application contact:* Charity H. Fahlstrom, Admissions Representative, Graduate and Professional Studies, 417-865-2815 Ext. 7227, Fax: 417-575-5484, E-mail: fahlstromc@evangel.edu.

Fairleigh Dickinson University, College at Florham, Maxwell Becton College of Arts and Sciences, Department of Psychology, Program in Counseling, Madison, NJ 07940-1099. Offers MA. *Students:* 56 full-time (41 women), 72 part-time (55 women). Average age 31. 84 applicants, 70% accepted, 29 enrolled. In 2009, 39 master's awarded. *Unit head:* Dr. Diane Wentworth, Chairperson, 973-443-8548. *Application contact:* Susan Brooman, University Director, Graduate Admissions, 973-443-8905, Fax: 973-443-8088, E-mail: grad@fdu.edu.

Felician College, Program in Counseling Psychology, Lodi, NJ 07644-2117. Offers MA. *Students:* 10 part-time (all women); includes 4 minority (2 African Americans, 2 Hispanic Americans). *Application contact:* Dr. Wendy Lin-Cook, Director of Adult and Graduate Admission, 201-559-6077, Fax: 201-559-6138, E-mail: adultandgraduate@felician.edu.

See Close-Up on page 1087.

Fitchburg State University, Division of Graduate and Continuing Education, Programs in Counseling, Fitchburg, MA 01420-2697. Offers elementary school guidance counseling (MS); mental health counseling (MS); secondary school guidance counseling (MS). *Accreditation:* NCATE. Part-time and evening/weekend programs available. *Students:* 15 full-time (all women), 57 part-time (50 women); includes 6 minority (1 African American, 1 American Indian/Alaska Native, 1 Asian American or Pacific Islander, 3 Hispanic Americans). Average age 32. 16 applicants, 88% accepted, 11 enrolled. In 2009, 23 master's awarded. *Entrance requirements:* For master's, GRE General Test or MAT, letters of recommendation, resume. Additional exam requirements/recommendations for international students: Required—TOEFL (minimum score 550 paper-based; 213 computer-based; 79 iBT). *Application deadline:* Applications are processed on a rolling basis. Application fee: $25 ($50 for international students). *Expenses:* Tuition, area resident: Part-time $150 per credit. Tuition, state resident: part-time $150 per credit. Tuition, nonresident: part-time $150 per credit. Required fees: $120 per credit. *Financial support:* In 2009–10, research assistantships with partial tuition reimbursements (averaging $5,500 per year); Federal Work-Study, scholarships/grants, and unspecified assistantships also available. Support available to part-time students. Financial award application deadline: 3/1; financial award applicants required to submit FAFSA. *Unit head:* Dr. John Hancock, Chair, 978-665-3604, Fax: 978-665-3658, E-mail: gce@fsc.edu. *Application contact:* Director of Admissions, 978-665-3144, Fax: 978-665-4540, E-mail: admissions@fsc.edu.

Florida Atlantic University, College of Education, Department of Counselor Education, Boca Raton, FL 33431-0991. Offers counselor education (M Ed, PhD, Ed S); marriage and family therapy (Ed S); mental health counseling (M Ed, Ed S); rehabilitation counseling (M Ed); school counseling (M Ed, Ed S). *Accreditation:* ACA; NCATE. Part-time and evening/weekend programs available. *Faculty:* 7 full-time (2 women), 6 part-time/adjunct (5 women). *Students:* 65 full-time (52 women), 95 part-time (83 women); includes 59 minority (19 African Americans, 5 Asian Americans or Pacific Islanders, 35 Hispanic Americans), 2 international. Average age 33. 109 applicants, 40% accepted, 27 enrolled. In 2009, 54 master's, 2 doctorates awarded. *Degree requirements:* For Ed S, departmental qualifying exam. *Entrance requirements:* For master's, GRE General Test, minimum GPA of 3.0 during previous 2 years; for Ed S, GRE General Test, minimum graduate GPA of 3.25. Additional exam requirements/recommendations for international students: Required—TOEFL. *Application deadline:* For fall admission, 3/1 for domestic students, 2/1 for international students; for spring admission, 9/15 for domestic students, 7/1 for international students. Applications are processed on a rolling basis. Application fee: $30. *Expenses:* Tuition, state resident: full-time $7055; part-time $293.94 per credit hour. Tuition, nonresident: full-time $22,096; part-time $920.66 per credit hour. *Financial support:* Research assistantships with partial tuition reimbursements, teaching assistantships, career-related internships or fieldwork, scholarships/grants, and unspecified assistantships available. *Faculty research:* Brief therapy, psychological type, marriage and family counseling, international programs, integrated services. *Unit head:* Dr. Irene Johnson, Chair, 561-297-2136, Fax: 561-297-2309. *Application contact:* Susan Foley, Senior Secretary, 561-297-3602, Fax: 561-297-2309, E-mail: cnslred@fau.edu.

Florida International University, College of Education, Department of Educational and Psychological Studies, Program in Counselor Education, Miami, FL 33199. Offers mental health counseling (MS); rehabilitation counseling (MS); school counseling (MS). *Accreditation:* ACA; NCATE. Part-time and evening/weekend programs available. *Entrance requirements:* For master's, General Knowledge test, College Level Academic Skills Test, GRE General Test or PRAXIS (school counseling track), minimum GPA of 3.0, interview. Additional exam requirements/recommendations for international students: Required—TOEFL (minimum score 550 paper-based; 213 computer-based; 80 iBT), IELTS (minimum score 6.3). Electronic applications accepted. *Expenses:* Tuition, state resident: full-time $8008; part-time $4004 per year. Tuition, nonresident: full-time $20,104; part-time $10,052 per year. Required fees: $298; $149 per term.

Florida State University, The Graduate School, College of Education, Department of Educational Psychology and Learning Systems, Program in Psychological Services, Tallahassee, FL 32306. Offers MS, PhD, Ed S. *Accreditation:* ACA (one or more programs are accredited). *Faculty:* 5 full-time (3 women), 5 part-time/adjunct (2 women). *Students:* 43 full-time (30 women), 9 part-time (7 women); includes 17 minority (12 African Americans, 1 Asian American or Pacific Islander, 4 Hispanic Americans). 64 applicants, 61% accepted, 27 enrolled. In 2009, 18 master's, 6 doctorates, 19 other advanced degrees awarded. *Degree requirements:* For master's and Ed S, comprehensive exam, thesis optional. *Entrance requirements:* For master's and Ed S, GRE General Test, minimum GPA of 3.0. Additional exam requirements/recommendations for international students: Required—TOEFL (minimum score 550 paper-based; 213 computer-based; 80 iBT). *Application deadline:* For fall admission, 6/1 priority date for domestic students, 6/1 for international students; for spring admission, 10/1 for domestic and international students. Applications are processed on a rolling basis. Application fee: $30. *Expenses:* Tuition, state resident: full-time $7413. Tuition, nonresident: full-time $22,567. *Financial support:* In 2009–10, 2 fellowships with full and partial tuition reimbursements, 11 research assistantships with full and partial tuition reimbursements, 14 teaching assistantships with full and partial tuition reimbursements were awarded; career-related internships or fieldwork also available. Financial award applicants required to submit FAFSA. *Faculty research:* Social, emotional, and vocational capabilities of learners; rehabilitation counseling; technology and learners; talent identification. *Unit head:* Dr. Frances Prevatt, Program Leader, 850-644-9445, Fax: 850-644-8776, E-mail: fprevatt@coe.fsu.edu. *Application contact:* Sally Gadson, Program Assistant, 850-644-8046, Fax: 850-644-5067, E-mail: gadson@coe.fsu.edu.

Fordham University, Graduate School of Education, Division of Psychological and Educational Services, New York, NY 10023. Offers counseling and personnel services (MSE, Adv C); counseling psychology (PhD); educational psychology (MSE, PhD); school psychology (PhD); urban and urban bilingual school psychology (Adv C). *Accreditation:* APA (one or more programs are accredited); NCATE. *Degree requirements:* For doctorate, thesis/dissertation. *Entrance requirements:* For doctorate, GRE General Test.

Fort Valley State University, College of Graduate Studies and Extended Education, Department of Counseling Psychology, Program in Mental Health Counseling, Fort Valley, GA 31030. Offers MS. Part-time programs available. *Degree requirements:* For master's, comprehensive exam (for some programs), thesis optional. *Entrance requirements:* For master's, GRE General Test or MAT.

Franciscan University of Steubenville, Graduate Programs, Department of Counseling, Steubenville, OH 43952-1763. Offers MA. Part-time programs available. *Degree requirements:* For master's, case presentation, integrative paper. *Entrance requirements:* For master's, GRE General Test or MAT, minimum undergraduate GPA of 3.0.

Francis Marion University, Graduate Programs, Department of Psychology, Florence, SC 29502-0547. Offers applied psychology (MS), including clinical/counseling, school psychology; school psychology (MS). Part-time and evening/weekend programs available. *Faculty:* 10 full-time (4 women), 5 part-time/adjunct (4 women). *Students:* 16 full-time (15 women), 19 part-time (18 women); includes 6 minority (all African Americans). Average age 35. 44 applicants,

55% accepted, 8 enrolled. In 2009, 19 degrees awarded. *Degree requirements:* For master's, internship. *Entrance requirements:* For master's, GRE General Test. *Application deadline:* For fall admission, 3/15 for domestic students; for spring admission, 10/15 for domestic students. Applications are processed on a rolling basis. Application fee: $30. *Expenses:* Tuition, state resident: full-time $8345; part-time $417.25 per semester hour. Tuition, nonresident: full-time $16,690; part-time $814.50 per semester hour. Required fees: $335; $12.25 per semester hour. $30 per semester. *Financial support:* In 2009–10, 13 students received support, including 1 research assistantship (averaging $7,000 per year), 3 teaching assistantships (averaging $8,000 per year); career-related internships or fieldwork, unspecified assistantships, and scholarships with out-of-state waivers also available. Support available to part-time students. Financial award application deadline: 3/1; financial award applicants required to submit FAFSA. *Faculty research:* Parenting and family relationships, child development, applied behavioral analysis, posttraumatic stress disorder, clinical psychology in adults. *Unit head:* Dr. John R. Hester, Chair, 843-661-1635, Fax: 843-661-1628. *Application contact:* Jennifer Taylor, Administrative Assistant, 843-661-1378, Fax: 843-661-1628.

Frostburg State University, Graduate School, College of Liberal Arts and Sciences, Department of Psychology, Program in Counseling Psychology, Frostburg, MD 21532-1099. Offers MS. Part-time and evening/weekend programs available. *Faculty:* 6 full-time (3 women), 2 part-time/adjunct (both women). *Students:* 33 full-time (31 women), 4 part-time (all women); includes 1 minority (African American), 3 international. Average age 26. 38 applicants, 29% accepted, 9 enrolled. In 2009, 10 master's awarded. *Degree requirements:* For master's, internship. *Entrance requirements:* For master's, GRE General Test or MAT, interview, minimum GPA of 3.0, resume. Additional exam requirements/recommendations for international students: Required—TOEFL. *Application deadline:* For fall admission, 2/1 for domestic students. Applications are processed on a rolling basis. Application fee: $30. Electronic applications accepted. *Expenses:* Tuition, state resident: full-time $5706; part-time $317 per credit hour. Tuition, nonresident: full-time $6948; part-time $386 per credit hour. Required fees: $1476; $82 per credit hour. $11 per term. One-time fee: $30 full-time. *Financial support:* In 2009–10, 7 research assistantships with full tuition reimbursements (averaging $5,000 per year) were awarded; career-related internships or fieldwork and Federal Work-Study also available. Financial award application deadline: 4/1; financial award applicants required to submit FAFSA. *Unit head:* Dr. Mike Murtagh, Coordinator, 301-687-4193, E-mail: mpmurtagh@frostburg.edu. *Application contact:* Vickie Mazer, Director, Graduate Services, 301-687-7053, Fax: 301-687-4597, E-mail: vmmazer@frostburg.edu.

Gallaudet University, The Graduate School, Department of Counseling, Washington, DC 20002-3625. Offers mental health counseling (MA); school counseling (MA). *Accreditation:* ACA; NCATE. *Degree requirements:* For master's, thesis optional. *Entrance requirements:* For master's, GRE General Test or MAT. Electronic applications accepted.

Gannon University, School of Graduate Studies, College of Humanities, Education, and Social Sciences, School of Humanities, Program in Counseling Psychology, Erie, PA 16541-0001. Offers PhD. *Accreditation:* ACA. Part-time and evening/weekend programs available. *Students:* 14 part-time (10 women); includes 1 minority (Asian American or Pacific Islander), 2 international. Average age 41. In 2009, 8 doctorates awarded. *Degree requirements:* For doctorate, thesis/dissertation, internship. *Entrance requirements:* For doctorate, GRE General Test, master's degree, minimum QPA of 3.5. Additional exam requirements/recommendations for international students: Required—TOEFL (minimum score 79 iBT). *Application deadline:* Applications are processed on a rolling basis. Application fee: $50. Electronic applications accepted. *Expenses:* Contact institution. *Financial support:* Career-related internships or fieldwork, Federal Work-Study, scholarships/grants, and unspecified assistantships available. Financial award application deadline: 7/1; financial award applicants required to submit FAFSA. *Unit head:* Dr. Linda Fleming, Director, 814-871-7262, Fax: 814-871-5511, E-mail: fleming006@gannon.edu. *Application contact:* Kara Morgan, Assistant Director of Graduate Admissions, 814-871-5831, Fax: 814-871-5827, E-mail: graduate@gannon.edu.

Gardner-Webb University, Graduate School, School of Psychology, Program in Mental Health Counseling, Boiling Springs, NC 28017. Offers MA. *Accreditation:* ACA. Part-time and evening/weekend programs available. *Faculty:* 7 full-time (4 women), 1 part-time/adjunct (0 women). *Students:* 36 part-time (33 women); includes 8 minority (5 African Americans, 3 Hispanic Americans). Average age 32. In 2009, 15 master's awarded. *Degree requirements:* For master's, comprehensive exam. *Entrance requirements:* For master's, GRE General Test, MAT, minimum GPA of 2.7. *Application deadline:* For fall admission, 7/1 priority date for domestic students. Applications are processed on a rolling basis. Application fee: $25. Electronic applications accepted. *Expenses:* Tuition: Part-time $305 per credit hour. *Financial support:* Unspecified assistantships available. *Unit head:* Dr. Frieda Brown, Coordinator, 704-406-4436, Fax: 704-406-4329, E-mail: fbrown@gardner-webb.edu. *Application contact:* Dr. Franki Burch, Dean, Graduate School, 704-406-4422, Fax: 704-406-4329, E-mail: gradschool@gardner-webb.edu.

Geneva College, Program in Counseling, Beaver Falls, PA 15010-3599. Offers marriage and family (MA); mental health (MA); school counseling (MA). *Accreditation:* ACA. Part-time and evening/weekend programs available. *Faculty:* 5 full-time (2 women), 2 part-time/adjunct (1 woman). *Students:* 28 full-time (21 women), 21 part-time (17 women); includes 6 minority (5 African Americans, 1 Asian American or Pacific Islander). Average age 26. 32 applicants, 97% accepted, 18 enrolled. In 2009, 11 master's awarded. *Degree requirements:* For master's, comprehensive exam, internship. *Entrance requirements:* For master's, GRE General Test or MAT, minimum GPA of 3.0 (preferred), letters of recommendation, faith statement. Additional exam requirements/recommendations for international students: Required—TOEFL. *Application deadline:* For fall admission, 7/1 priority date for domestic students; for spring admission, 11/1 priority date for domestic students. Applications are processed on a rolling basis. Application fee: $50 ($100 for international students). Electronic applications accepted. *Expenses:* Tuition: Full-time $11,250; part-time $625 per credit. Tuition and fees vary according to program. *Financial support:* In 2009–10, 8 teaching assistantships (averaging $3,500 per year) were awarded; career-related internships or fieldwork and unspecified assistantships also available. Financial award applicants required to submit FAFSA. *Unit head:* Dr. Carol Luce, Director, 724-847-6622, Fax: 724-847-6101, E-mail: cbluce@geneva.edu. *Application contact:* JoAnn Westover, Graduate Program Manager, 724-847-6697, E-mail: counseling@geneva.edu.

George Fox University, School of Education, Graduate Department of Counseling, Newberg, OR 97132-2697. Offers counseling (MA); marriage and family therapy (MA, Certificate); mental health trauma (Certificate); school counseling (MA, Certificate); school psychology (Certificate, Ed S). Part-time programs available. *Faculty:* 9 full-time (3 women), 7 part-time/adjunct (5 women). *Students:* 100 full-time (77 women), 122 part-time (103 women); includes 24 minority (7 African Americans, 4 American Indian/Alaska Native, 9 Asian Americans or Pacific Islanders, 4 Hispanic Americans). Average age 36. 102 applicants, 75% accepted, 59 enrolled. In 2009, 61 master's, 2 other advanced degrees awarded. *Degree requirements:* For master's, clinical project. *Entrance requirements:* For master's, MAT or GRE, bachelor's degree from regionally-accredited college or university, minimum cumulative GPA of 3.0, 1 professional and 1 academic reference, resume, on-campus interview. Additional exam requirements/recommendations for international students: Required—TOEFL (minimum score 577 paper-based; 233 computer-based; 90 iBT). *Application deadline:* For fall admission, 5/30 for domestic and international students; for winter admission, 11/1 for domestic and international students; for spring admission, 2/28 for domestic and international students. Applications are processed on a rolling basis. Application fee: $40. Electronic applications accepted. *Expenses:* Contact institution. *Financial support:* Career-related internships or fieldwork available. *Unit head:* Dr. Richard Shaw, Associate Professor of Marriage and Family Therapy/Chair, 503-554-6142, E-mail: rshaw@georgefox.edu. *Application contact:* Kathy Grant, Admissions Counselor, 800-493-4937, Fax: 503-554-6111, E-mail: counseling@georgefox.edu.

Georgian Court University, School of Sciences and Mathematics, Lakewood, NJ 08701-2697. Offers biology (MS); counseling psychology (MA); holistic health (Certificate); holistic health studies (MA); mathematics (MA); professional counselor (Certificate); school psychology (Certificate). Part-time and evening/weekend programs available. *Faculty:* 18 full-time (11 women), 9 part-time/adjunct (6 women). *Students:* 74 full-time (67 women), 79 part-time (67 women); includes 19 minority (8 African Americans, 1 American Indian/Alaska Native, 2 Asian Americans or Pacific Islanders, 8 Hispanic Americans), 2 international. Average age 32. 137 applicants, 50% accepted, 54 enrolled. In 2009, 27 master's, 2 other advanced degrees awarded. *Degree requirements:* For master's, comprehensive exam (for some programs), thesis (for some programs). *Entrance requirements:* For master's, GRE General Test, GRE Subject Test in biology (MS), 3 letters of recommendation. Additional exam requirements/recommendations for international students: Required—TOEFL (minimum score 550 paper-based; 213 computer-based). *Application deadline:* For fall admission, 8/1 priority date for domestic students, 4/1 for international students; for spring admission, 1/1 priority date for domestic students, 7/1 for international students. Applications are processed on a rolling basis. Application fee: $40. Electronic applications accepted. *Expenses:* Tuition: Full-time $12,510; part-time $695 per credit. Required fees: $416 per year. Tuition and fees vary according to campus/location. *Financial support:* Scholarships/grants, health care benefits, and unspecified assistantships available. Financial award application deadline: 4/15; financial award applicants required to submit FAFSA. *Unit head:* Dr. Linda James, Dean, 732-987-2617, Fax: 732-987-2007. *Application contact:* Eugene Soltys, Director of Graduate Admissions, 732-987-2770, Fax: 732-987-2084, E-mail: graduateadmissions@georgian.edu.

Georgia State University, College of Education, Department of Counseling and Psychological Services, Program in Professional Counseling, Atlanta, GA 30302-3083. Offers counseling psychology (PhD); counselor education and practice (PhD); professional counseling (MS, Ed S). *Accreditation:* ACA (one or more programs are accredited); APA (one or more programs are accredited). *Degree requirements:* For master's, comprehensive exam; for doctorate, comprehensive exam, thesis/dissertation. *Entrance requirements:* For master's, GRE General Test, minimum GPA of 2.5; for doctorate, GRE General Test, minimum GPA of 3.3; for Ed S, GRE General Test, minimum graduate GPA of 3.25. *Faculty research:* Dropout prevention, school reform, school violence, lifestyle correlates, stress management.

Goddard College, Graduate Division, Master of Arts in Psychology and Counseling Program, Plainfield, VT 05667-9432. Offers organizational development (MA); psychology and counseling (MA); sexual orientation (MA). Part-time programs available. Postbaccalaureate distance learning degree programs offered (minimal on-campus study). *Faculty:* 7 part-time/adjunct (5 women). *Students:* 57 full-time. Average age 40. 34 applicants, 76% accepted, 18 enrolled. *Degree requirements:* For master's, thesis. *Entrance requirements:* For master's, recent undergraduate degree in psychology or closely related field (preparatory semester at Goddard can substitute), 3 letters of recommendation, interview. *Application deadline:* Applications are processed on a rolling basis. Application fee: $40. Electronic applications accepted. *Expenses:* Tuition: Part-time $7223 per semester. Part-time tuition and fees vary according to program. *Financial support:* In 2009–10, 48 students received support. Applicants required to submit FAFSA. *Unit head:* Dr. Steve James, Director, 802-454-8311, Fax: 802-454-7835, E-mail: steven.james@goddard.edu. *Application contact:* David DeLucca, Senior Admissions Counselor, 800-906-8312 Ext. 248, Fax: 802-454-1029, E-mail: david.delucca@goddard.edu.

Gonzaga University, School of Education, Program in Counseling Psychology, Spokane, WA 99258. Offers MAC, MAP. *Accreditation:* ACA. *Faculty:* 3 full-time (0 women), 5 part-time/adjunct (3 women). *Students:* 34 full-time (27 women), 80 part-time (64 women); includes 6 minority (3 American Indian/Alaska Native, 2 Asian Americans or Pacific Islanders, 1 Hispanic American), 1 international. Average age 33. In 2009, 49 master's awarded. *Degree requirements:* For master's, comprehensive exam. *Entrance requirements:* For master's, GRE General Test or MAT, minimum B average in undergraduate course work. Additional exam requirements/recommendations for international students: Required—TOEFL. *Application deadline:* For fall admission, 3/1 for domestic students. Application fee: $50. Tuition and fees vary according to course level, course load, degree level, campus/location and program. *Financial support:* Teaching assistantships available. Support available to part-time students. Financial award application deadline: 3/1. *Unit head:* Dr. Lisa Bennett, Director, 509-328-4220 Ext. 3512. *Application contact:* Julie McCulloh, Dean of Admissions, 509-313-6592, Fax: 509-313-5780, E-mail: mcculloh@gu.gonzaga.edu.

Governors State University, College of Education, Program in Counseling, University Park, IL 60466-0975. Offers MA. *Accreditation:* ACA. Part-time and evening/weekend programs available. *Degree requirements:* For master's, practicum. *Entrance requirements:* For master's, minimum GPA of 2.5 in last 60 hours of course work or minimum GPA of 2.25 and GRE General Test.

Grace College, Graduate School in Counseling and Interpersonal Relations, Program in Counseling, Winona Lake, IN 46590-1294. Offers counseling (MA); interpersonal relations (MA). *Accreditation:* ACA. Part-time and evening/weekend programs available. *Degree requirements:* For master's, comprehensive exam, portfolio. *Entrance requirements:* For master's, GRE (counseling). Additional exam requirements/recommendations for international students: Required—TOEFL. Electronic applications accepted.

Grace University, College of Graduate Studies, Counseling Program, Omaha, NE 68108. Offers MA. *Entrance requirements:* For master's, minimum undergraduate GPA of 3.0.

Harding University, College of Bible and Religion, Program in Marriage and Family Therapy, Searcy, AR 72149-0001. Offers marriage and family therapy (MS); mental health counseling (MS). Part-time programs available. *Faculty:* 4 full-time (0 women), 5 part-time/adjunct (1 woman). *Students:* 24 full-time (14 women), 3 part-time (2 women); includes 2 minority (both African Americans). Average age 28. 23 applicants, 70% accepted, 13 enrolled. In 2009, 11 master's awarded. *Degree requirements:* For master's, comprehensive exam, 15-month practicum. *Entrance requirements:* For master's, GRE General Test, minimum undergraduate GPA of 2.75, graduate 3.0. *Application deadline:* For fall admission, 4/1 priority date for domestic students. Applications are processed on a rolling basis. Application fee: $40. *Expenses:* Tuition: Full-time $9720; part-time $540 per credit hour. Required fees: $22 per credit hour. Tuition and fees vary according to course load and program. *Financial support:* In 2009–10, 6 students received support. Scholarships/grants available. *Faculty research:* Forgiveness, substance abuse, post traumatic stress disorder. *Unit head:* Dr. Lewis L. Moore, Chairman, 501-279-4347, Fax: 501-279-4417, E-mail: lmoore@harding.edu. *Application contact:* Ruth Ann Dawson, Office Manager, 501-279-4347, Fax: 501-279-4417, E-mail: radawson@harding.edu.

Heidelberg University, Program in Counseling, Tiffin, OH 44883-2462. Offers MA. Part-time and evening/weekend programs available. *Faculty:* 3 full-time (2 women), 7 part-time/adjunct (4 women). *Students:* 91 part-time (71 women); includes 9 minority (6 African Americans, 2 American Indian/Alaska Native, 1 Hispanic American). Average age 30. 47 applicants, 85% accepted, 31 enrolled. In 2009, 14 master's awarded. *Degree requirements:* For master's, thesis or alternative, counseling practicum, internship. *Entrance requirements:* For master's, GRE General Test, 12 hours course work in behavioral sciences, minimum GPA of 2.9, 3 letters of reference. Additional exam requirements/recommendations for international students: Required—TOEFL. *Application deadline:* Applications are processed on a rolling basis. Application fee: $25. *Expenses:* Tuition: Part-time $415 per credit hour. *Financial support:* In 2009–10, 51 students received support, including 1 teaching assistantship; Federal Work-Study also available. Support available to part-time students. Financial award applicants required to submit FAFSA. *Unit head:* Dr. Jo-Ann Lipford Sanders, Director of Graduate Studies, 419-448-2312, Fax: 419-448-2072, E-mail: jsanders@heidelberg.edu. *Application contact:* Melissa Nye, Administrative Assistant, Graduate Studies Office, 419-448-2288, Fax: 419-448-2072, E-mail: mnye@heidelberg.edu.

Henderson State University, Graduate Studies, School of Education, Department of Counselor Education, Arkadelphia, AR 71999-0001. Offers clinical mental health counseling (MSE); elementary school counseling (MSE); secondary school counseling (MSE). *Accreditation:*

Counseling Psychology

Henderson State University (continued)
ACA; NCATE. Part-time programs available. *Entrance requirements:* For master's, GRE General Test or MAT, letters of recommendation, minimum GPA of 2.7, teacher certification. Additional exam requirements/recommendations for international students: Required—TOEFL (minimum score 550 paper-based; 213 computer-based); Recommended—IELTS (minimum score 6). *Application deadline:* For fall admission, 8/1 priority date for domestic students, 6/30 priority date for international students; for spring admission, 1/1 priority date for domestic students, 11/30 priority date for international students. Application fee: $25 ($75 for international students). Electronic applications accepted. *Expenses:* Tuition, state resident: full-time $3798; part-time $211 per credit hour. Tuition, nonresident: full-time $7596; part-time $422 per credit hour. Required fees: $903. *Financial support:* Teaching assistantships with tuition reimbursements available. *Unit head:* Dr. Blair Olson, Chairperson, 870-230-5395, Fax: 870-230-5459, E-mail: olsonb@hsu.edu. *Application contact:* Dr. Marck L. Beggs, Graduate Dean, 870-230-5126, Fax: 870-230-5479, E-mail: beggsm@hsu.edu.

Hofstra University, School of Education, Health, and Human Services, Department of Counseling, Research, Special Education and Rehabilitation, Program in Rehabilitation Counseling, Hempstead, NY 11549. Offers rehabilitation administration (PD); rehabilitation counseling (MS Ed); rehabilitation counseling in mental health (MS Ed). *Accreditation:* CORE. Part-time and evening/weekend programs available. *Students:* 23 full-time (19 women), 6 part-time (all women); includes 12 minority (9 African Americans, 1 Asian American or Pacific Islander, 2 Hispanic Americans). Average age 32. 18 applicants, 89% accepted, 12 enrolled. In 2009, 12 master's awarded. *Degree requirements:* For master's, comprehensive exam, 600-hour internship, 100-hour practicum. *Entrance requirements:* For master's, 4 letters of recommendation, interview, professional experience; for PD, 3 letters of recommendation, master's degree in related field, professional experience. Additional exam requirements/recommendations for international students: Required—TOEFL (minimum score 550 paper-based; 213 computer-based; 80 iBT). *Application deadline:* Applications are processed on a rolling basis. Application fee: $60. Electronic applications accepted. *Expenses:* Tuition: Full-time $16,200; part-time $900 per credit hour. Required fees: $970; $145 per term. Tuition and fees vary according to program. *Financial support:* In 2009–10, 14 students received support, including 1 fellowship with full and partial tuition reimbursement available (averaging $3,000 per year), 2 research assistantships with full and partial tuition reimbursements available (averaging $15,575 per year); career-related internships or fieldwork, Federal Work-Study, institutionally sponsored loans, scholarships/grants, traineeships, tuition waivers (full and partial), and unspecified assistantships also available. Support available to part-time students. Financial award applicants required to submit FAFSA. *Faculty research:* Workplace socialization and individuals with disabilities; collaboration among rehabilitation agencies and consumer outcomes; job retention among rehabilitation counseling professionals; transition services for youth with disabilities. Total annual research expenditures: $210,000. *Unit head:* Dr. Jamie Mitus, Director, 516-463-7453, Fax: 516-463-6184, E-mail: cprjsm@hofstra.edu. *Application contact:* Carol Drummer, Dean of Graduate Admissions, 516-463-4876, Fax: 516-463-4664, E-mail: gradstudent@hofstra.edu.

Holy Family University, Graduate School, School of Arts and Sciences, Philadelphia, PA 19114. Offers counseling psychology (MS); criminal justice (MA). Part-time and evening/weekend programs available. *Faculty:* 1 full-time (0 women), 4 part-time/adjunct (2 women). *Students:* 39 full-time (31 women), 137 part-time (108 women); includes 34 minority (18 African Americans, 2 Asian Americans or Pacific Islanders, 14 Hispanic Americans), 1 international. Average age 31. 111 applicants, 61% accepted, 45 enrolled. In 2009, 20 master's awarded. *Degree requirements:* For master's, comprehensive exam, thesis optional. *Entrance requirements:* For master's, MAT, interview, minimum GPA of 3.0. *Application deadline:* For fall admission, 7/1 priority date for domestic students; for winter admission, 11/1 for domestic students. Applications are processed on a rolling basis. Application fee: $25. *Expenses:* Tuition: Part-time $600 per credit. Required fees: $58 per semester. *Financial support:* Research assistantships with full and partial tuition reimbursements, Federal Work-Study available. Support available to part-time students. Financial award application deadline: 2/15; financial award applicants required to submit FAFSA. *Unit head:* Dr. Michael Markowitz, Dean, 267-341-3286, Fax: 215-827-0492, E-mail: mmarkowitz@holyfamily.edu. *Application contact:* Gidget Marie Montelibans, Graduate Admissions Counselor, 267-341-3558, Fax: 215-637-1478, E-mail: gmontelibano@holyfamily.edu.

Holy Names University, Graduate Division, Department of Counseling Psychology, Oakland, CA 94619-1699. Offers counseling psychology (MA); forensic psychology (MA, Certificate); pastoral counseling (MA, Certificate). Part-time and evening/weekend programs available. *Degree requirements:* For master's, comprehensive paper, seminars. *Entrance requirements:* For master's, minimum undergraduate GPA of 2.6 overall, 3.0 in major. Additional exam requirements/recommendations for international students: Required—TOEFL (minimum score 550 paper-based; 213 computer-based; 80 iBT). *Faculty research:* Cognitive psychology, anger management, grief and grief counseling, post-modernism and psychotherapy, spirituality and psychology.

Houston Baptist University, College of Education and Behavioral Sciences, Program in Christian Counseling, Houston, TX 77074-3298. Offers MACC. *Degree requirements:* For master's, comprehensive exam. *Entrance requirements:* For master's, GRE General Test, minimum GPA of 3.0. Additional exam requirements/recommendations for international students: Required—TOEFL (minimum score 550 paper-based; 213 computer-based).

Howard University, School of Education, Department of Human Development and Psychoeducational Studies, Program in Counseling Psychology, Washington, DC 20059-0002. Offers M Ed, MA, PhD, CAGS. *Accreditation:* APA. Part-time programs available. *Faculty:* 3 full-time (2 women), 2 part-time/adjunct (both women). *Students:* 30 full-time (23 women), 12 part-time (11 women); includes 32 minority (31 African Americans, 1 Asian American or Pacific Islander), 2 international. Average age 29. 36 applicants, 61% accepted, 12 enrolled. In 2009, 11 master's, 2 doctorates awarded. Terminal master's awarded for partial completion of doctoral program. *Degree requirements:* For master's, comprehensive exam, thesis (for some programs), expository writing exam; for doctorate, one foreign language, comprehensive exam, thesis/dissertation, expository writing exam, internship. *Entrance requirements:* For master's, GRE General Test (MA), minimum GPA of 2.7; for doctorate, GRE General Test, minimum GPA of 3.4; for CAGS, GRE General Test, minimum graduate GPA of 3.0. *Application deadline:* For fall admission, 12/15 priority date for domestic students; for spring admission, 11/1 for domestic students. Application fee: $45. Electronic applications accepted. *Financial support:* In 2009–10, 8 students received support, including 3 fellowships with full and partial tuition reimbursements available (averaging $15,000 per year), 5 research assistantships with full and partial tuition reimbursements available (averaging $4,583 per year); career-related internships or fieldwork, institutionally sponsored loans, scholarships/grants, and unspecified assistantships also available. Financial award application deadline: 12/15. *Faculty research:* Cultural issues in counseling and psychotherapy, counseling theory construction, self-actualization black psychology. *Unit head:* Dr. Angela D. Ferguson, Associate Professor/Coordinator, Doctoral Program, 202-806-6412, Fax: 202-806-5205, E-mail: adferguson@howard.edu. *Application contact:* Dr. Mercedes Ebanks, Assistant Professor/Coordinator, Master's Program, 202-806-5780, Fax: 202-806-5205, E-mail: mebanks@howard.edu.

Humboldt State University, Graduate Studies, College of Professional Studies, Department of Psychology, Arcata, CA 95521-8299. Offers psychology (MA), including academic research, counseling, school psychology. *Students:* 60 full-time (45 women), 10 part-time (6 women); includes 13 minority (2 African Americans, 1 American Indian/Alaska Native, 3 Asian Americans or Pacific Islanders, 7 Hispanic Americans), 1 international. Average age 29. 64 applicants, 38% accepted, 21 enrolled. In 2009, 16 master's awarded. *Degree requirements:* For master's, thesis. *Entrance requirements:* For master's, appropriate bachelor's degree, minimum GPA of 2.5. Additional exam requirements/recommendations for international students: Required—TOEFL (minimum score 500 paper-based; 173 computer-based). *Application deadline:* For fall admission, 2/15 for domestic and international students. Applications are processed on a rolling basis. Application fee: $55. *Expenses:* Tuition, nonresident: full-time $8928. Required fees: $6102. Tuition and fees vary according to program. *Financial support:* Career-related internships or fieldwork available. Financial award application deadline: 3/1; financial award applicants required to submit FAFSA. *Faculty research:* School psychology, counseling, eating disorders, mood induction, depression. *Unit head:* Dr. Brent Duncan, Chair, 707-826-3755, Fax: 707-826-4993, E-mail: bbd1@humboldt.edu. *Application contact:* Dr. Chris Aberson, Coordinator, 707-826-3670, Fax: 707-826-4993, E-mail: cla18@humboldt.edu.

Husson University, School of Graduate and Professional Studies, Program in Counseling Psychology, Bangor, ME 04401-2999. Offers MS.

Idaho State University, Office of Graduate Studies, Kasiska College of Health Professions, Department of Counseling, Pocatello, ID 83209-8120. Offers counseling (M Coun, Ed S), including marriage and family counseling (M Coun), mental health counseling (M Coun), school counseling (M Coun), student affairs and college counseling (M Coun); counselor education and counseling (PhD). *Accreditation:* ACA (one or more programs are accredited). Part-time programs available. *Faculty:* 7 full-time (4 women). *Students:* 72 full-time (52 women), 29 part-time (18 women); includes 11 minority (2 African Americans, 1 American Indian/Alaska Native, 2 Asian Americans or Pacific Islanders, 6 Hispanic Americans). Average age 32. In 2009, 25 master's, 5 doctorates, 1 other advanced degree awarded. *Degree requirements:* For master's, comprehensive exam, thesis, 4 semesters resident graduate study, practicum/internship; for doctorate, comprehensive exam, thesis/dissertation, 3 semesters internship, 4 consecutive semesters doctoral-level study on campus; for Ed S, comprehensive exam, thesis, case studies, oral exam. *Entrance requirements:* For master's, GRE General Test, MAT, minimum GPA of 3.0, bachelors degree, interview, 3 letters of recommendation; for doctorate, GRE General Test, MAT, minimum graduate GPA of 3.0, resume, interview, counseling license, master's degree; for Ed S, GRE General Test, minimum graduate GPA of 3.0, master's degree in counseling, 3 letters of recommendation, 2 years work experience. Additional exam requirements/recommendations for international students: Required—TOEFL (minimum score 600 paper-based; 213 computer-based; 80 iBT). *Application deadline:* For fall admission, 7/1 for domestic students, 6/1 for international students; for spring admission, 12/1 for domestic students, 11/1 for international students. Applications are processed on a rolling basis. Application fee: $55. Electronic applications accepted. *Expenses:* Tuition, state resident: full-time $3318; part-time $297 per credit hour. Tuition, nonresident: full-time $13,120; part-time $437 per credit hour. Required fees: $2530. Tuition and fees vary according to program. *Financial support:* In 2009–10, 12 teaching assistantships with full and partial tuition reimbursements (averaging $10,841 per year) were awarded; career-related internships or fieldwork, Federal Work-Study, institutionally sponsored loans, scholarships/grants, traineeships, health care benefits, tuition waivers (full and partial), and unspecified assistantships also available. Support available to part-time students. Financial award application deadline: 1/1; financial award applicants required to submit FAFSA. *Faculty research:* Group counseling, multicultural counseling, family counseling, child therapy, supervision. *Unit head:* Dr. Nicole Hill, Interim Chair, 208-282-3663, Fax: 208-282-2583, E-mail: hillnico@isu.edu. *Application contact:* Tami Carson, Graduate School Technical Records Specialist, 208-282-2150, Fax: 208-282-4847, E-mail: carstami@isu.edu.

Illinois State University, Graduate School, College of Arts and Sciences, Department of Psychology, Normal, IL 61790-2200. Offers psychology (MA, MS), including clinical psychology, counseling psychology, developmental psychology, educational psychology, experimental psychology, measurement-evaluation, organizational-industrial psychology; school psychology (PhD, SSP). *Accreditation:* APA. *Degree requirements:* For master's, thesis or alternative; for doctorate, variable foreign language requirement, thesis/dissertation, 2 terms of residency, internship, practicum. *Entrance requirements:* For master's, GRE General Test, GRE Subject Test, minimum GPA of 3.0 in last 60 hours of course work; for doctorate, GRE General Test. *Faculty research:* Comprehensive evaluation system for the central region professional development grant, Illinois school psychology internship consortium, for children's sake.

Immaculata University, College of Graduate Studies, Department of Psychology, Immaculata, PA 19345. Offers clinical psychology (Psy D); counseling psychology (MA, Certificate), including school guidance counselor (Certificate), school psychologist (Certificate). *Accreditation:* APA. Part-time and evening/weekend programs available. *Degree requirements:* For master's, comprehensive exam, thesis optional; for doctorate, comprehensive exam, thesis/dissertation. *Entrance requirements:* For master's, GRE General Test or MAT, minimum GPA of 3.0; for doctorate, GRE General Test, minimum GPA of 3.5. Additional exam requirements/recommendations for international students: Required—TOEFL, IELTS. *Faculty research:* Supervision ethics, psychology of teaching, gender.

Indiana State University, School of Graduate Studies, College of Education, Department of Communication Disorders, Counseling and School and Educational Psychology, Terre Haute, IN 47809. Offers counseling psychology (MS, PhD); counselor education (PhD); mental health counseling (MS); school counseling (M Ed); school psychology (PhD, Ed S); MA/MS. *Accreditation:* ACA; NCATE. Part-time and evening/weekend programs available. *Degree requirements:* For master's, thesis optional; for doctorate, thesis/dissertation, research tools proficiency tests. *Entrance requirements:* For master's, GRE General Test or MAT, minimum undergraduate GPA of 2.75; for doctorate, GRE General Test, master's degree, minimum undergraduate GPA of 3.5. Electronic applications accepted. *Faculty research:* Vocational development supervision.

Indiana University Bloomington, School of Education, Department of Counseling and Educational Psychology, Bloomington, IN 47405-1006. Offers counseling (MS, PhD, Ed S); counseling psychology (PhD); counselor education (MS, Ed S); educational psychology (MS, PhD); inquiry methodology (PhD); learning and developmental sciences (MS, PhD); school psychology (PhD, Ed S). *Accreditation:* ACA (one or more programs are accredited); APA (one or more programs are accredited); NCATE. *Faculty:* 32 full-time (13 women), 20 part-time/adjunct (10 women). *Students:* 218 full-time (165 women), 34 part-time (29 women); includes 45 minority (19 African Americans, 2 American Indian/Alaska Native, 12 Asian Americans or Pacific Islanders, 12 Hispanic Americans), 42 international. Average age 30. 348 applicants, 41% accepted, 53 enrolled. In 2009, 57 master's, 21 doctorates, 22 other advanced degrees awarded. Terminal master's awarded for partial completion of doctoral program. *Degree requirements:* For master's, thesis optional; for doctorate, thesis/dissertation; for Ed S, comprehensive exam or project. *Entrance requirements:* For master's, doctorate, and Ed S, GRE General Test. Additional exam requirements/recommendations for international students: Required—TOEFL. *Application deadline:* Applications are processed on a rolling basis. Application fee: $55 ($65 for international students). Electronic applications accepted. *Financial support:* In 2009–10, 58 students received support, including 7 fellowships with partial tuition reimbursements available (averaging $15,000 per year), 15 research assistantships with partial tuition reimbursements available (averaging $12,000 per year), 36 teaching assistantships with partial tuition reimbursements available (averaging $14,280 per year); career-related internships or fieldwork, Federal Work-Study, institutionally sponsored loans, scholarships/grants, and unspecified assistantships also available. Support available to part-time students. Financial award application deadline: 1/1; financial award applicants required to submit FAFSA. *Faculty research:* Counseling psychology, inquiry methodology, school psychology, learning sciences, human development, educational psychology. *Unit head:* Dr. Joyce Alexander, Chairperson, 812-856-8300, Fax: 812-856-8333, E-mail: cep@indiana.edu. *Application contact:* Jessica Durnal, Student Services Specialist, 812-856-8300, Fax: 812-856-8333, E-mail: cep@indiana.edu.

Indiana Wesleyan University, College of Graduate Studies, Graduate Studies in Counseling, Marion, IN 46953. Offers addictions counseling (MS); community counseling (MS); marriage and family counseling (MS); school counseling (MS). *Accreditation:* ACA. Part-time programs available. *Degree requirements:* For master's, thesis or alternative. *Entrance requirements:* For master's, GRE General Test. Additional exam requirements/recommendations for international students: Required—TOEFL. Electronic applications accepted. *Expenses:* Contact institution. *Faculty research:* Community counseling, multicultural counseling, addictions.

Institute of Transpersonal Psychology, Low-Residency Programs, Palo Alto, CA 94303. Offers counseling psychology (online) (MA); spiritual guidance (MA); women's spirituality (MA). Postbaccalaureate distance learning degree programs offered (minimal on-campus study).

Institute of Transpersonal Psychology, Residential Programs, Palo Alto, CA 94303. Offers counseling psychology (MA); spiritually oriented clinical psychology (Psy D); transpersonal psychology (MA, PhD). Part-time and evening/weekend programs available. Terminal master's awarded for partial completion of doctoral program. *Degree requirements:* For doctorate, thesis/dissertation. *Entrance requirements:* For master's and doctorate, bachelor's degree.

Inter American University of Puerto Rico, Aguadilla Campus, Graduate School, Aguadilla, PR 00605. Offers accounting (MBA); business information systems (MBA); counseling psychology with an emphasis in family (MS); criminal justice (MA); educative management and leadership (MA); elementary education (MA); finance (MBA); human resources (MBA); industrial management (MBA); marketing (MBA). Part-time and evening/weekend programs available. *Degree requirements:* For master's, comprehensive exam. *Entrance requirements:* For master's, EXADEP, 2 letters of recommendation, minimum GPA of 2.5. Electronic applications accepted.

Inter American University of Puerto Rico, Metropolitan Campus, Graduate Programs, Program in Psychology, San Juan, PR 00919-1293. Offers counseling psychology (MA, PhD); industrial/organizational psychology (MA, PhD); labor relations (MA); school psychology (MA, PhD). *Degree requirements:* For master's, comprehensive exam. *Entrance requirements:* For master's, GRE or EXADEP, interview. Electronic applications accepted.

Inter American University of Puerto Rico, San Germán Campus, Graduate Studies Center, Program in Psychology, San Germán, PR 00683-5008. Offers counseling psychology (MA, PhD); school psychology (MA, PhD). Part-time and evening/weekend programs available. *Degree requirements:* For master's, comprehensive exam, thesis; for doctorate, comprehensive exam, thesis/dissertation. *Entrance requirements:* For master's, GRE General Test or EXADEP, minimum GPA of 3.0; for doctorate, GRE, EXADEP or MAT, minimum GPA of 3.0.

Iona College, School of Arts and Science, Department of Psychology, New Rochelle, NY 10801-1890. Offers experimental psychology (MA); industrial-organizational psychology (MA); mental health counseling (MA); psychology (MA); school psychology (MA). Part-time and evening/weekend programs available. *Faculty:* 14 full-time (8 women), 10 part-time/adjunct (8 women). *Students:* 74 full-time (58 women), 46 part-time (34 women); includes 28 minority (13 African Americans, 1 American Indian/Alaska Native, 3 Asian Americans or Pacific Islanders, 11 Hispanic Americans), 1 international. Average age 25. 186 applicants, 61% accepted, 44 enrolled. In 2009, 35 master's awarded. *Degree requirements:* For master's, thesis. *Entrance requirements:* For master's, GRE or minimum GPA of 3.0. Additional exam requirements/recommendations for international students: Required—TOEFL (minimum score 550 paper-based; 213 computer-based). *Application deadline:* Applications are processed on a rolling basis. Application fee: $50. Electronic applications accepted. *Expenses:* Tuition: Part-time $830 per credit. *Financial support:* Career-related internships or fieldwork, tuition waivers (partial), and unspecified assistantships available. Support available to part-time students. Financial award application deadline: 4/15; financial award applicants required to submit FAFSA. *Unit head:* Dr. Paul Greene, Chair, 914-633-2048, E-mail: pgreene@iona.edu. *Application contact:* Veronica Jarek-Prinz, Director of Graduate Admissions, 914-633-2420, Fax: 914-633-2277, E-mail: vjarekprinz@iona.edu.

Iowa State University of Science and Technology, Graduate College, College of Liberal Arts and Sciences, Department of Psychology, Ames, IA 50011. Offers cognitive psychology (PhD); counseling psychology (PhD); social psychology (PhD). *Accreditation:* APA. *Faculty:* 25 full-time (8 women), 8 part-time/adjunct (4 women). *Degree requirements:* For doctorate, comprehensive exam, thesis/dissertation. *Entrance requirements:* For doctorate, GRE General Test, GRE Subject Test (psychology), 3 letters of recommendation. Additional exam requirements/recommendations for international students: Required—TOEFL (minimum score 560 paper-based; 220 computer-based). *Application deadline:* For fall admission, 1/2 priority date for domestic and international students. Application fee: $30 ($70 for international students). Electronic applications accepted. *Expenses:* Tuition, state resident: full-time $6716. Tuition, nonresident: full-time $8908. Tuition and fees vary according to course level, course load, program and student level. *Financial support:* In 2009–10, fellowships with full tuition reimbursements (averaging $14,055 per year), research assistantships with full tuition reimbursements (averaging $12,200 per year), teaching assistantships with full tuition reimbursements (averaging $12,200 per year) were awarded; scholarships/grants, health care benefits, and unspecified assistantships also available. *Faculty research:* Counseling psychology, cognitive psychology, social psychology, health psychology, psychology and public policy. *Unit head:* Carolyn Cutrona, Chair, 515-294-0283, Fax: 515-294-6424, E-mail: ccutrona@iastate.edu. *Application contact:* Ann Schmidt, Graduate Admissions Secretary, 515-294-1743, Fax: 515-294-6424, E-mail: psychadm@iastate.edu.

James Madison University, The Graduate School, College of Integrated Science and Technology, Department of Graduate Psychology, Clinical Mental Health Counseling Program, Harrisonburg, VA 22807. Offers M Ed, MA, Ed S. *Accreditation:* ACA (one or more programs are accredited); APA (one or more programs are accredited). Part-time and evening/weekend programs available. *Students:* 50 full-time (39 women), 31 part-time (24 women); includes 9 minority (7 African Americans, 1 Asian American or Pacific Islander, 1 Hispanic American), 1 international. Average age 27. In 2009, 35 master's, 17 other advanced degrees awarded. *Degree requirements:* For Ed S, comprehensive exam, thesis, internship. *Entrance requirements:* For master's, GRE General Test, 3 reference forms, interview, criminal history check. Additional exam requirements/recommendations for international students: Required—TOEFL. *Application deadline:* For fall admission, 2/1 priority date for domestic students. Applications are processed on a rolling basis. Application fee: $55. Electronic applications accepted. *Expenses:* Tuition, area resident: Part-time $305 per credit hour. Tuition, state resident: part-time $305 per credit hour. Tuition, nonresident: part-time $890 per credit hour. *Financial support:* In 2009–10, 44 students received support; teaching assistantships with full tuition reimbursements available, career-related internships or fieldwork and Federal Work-Study available. Financial award application deadline: 3/1; financial award applicants required to submit FAFSA. *Unit head:* Dr. Lennis G. Echerling, Program Director, 540-568-6552. *Application contact:* Dr. Lennis G. Echerling, Program Director, 540-568-6552.

John Carroll University, Graduate School, Program in Community Counseling, University Heights, OH 44118-4581. Offers clinical counseling (Certificate); community counseling (MA). *Accreditation:* ACA. Part-time and evening/weekend programs available. *Degree requirements:* For master's, comprehensive exam, internship, practicum. *Entrance requirements:* For master's, MAT or GRE, minimum GPA of 2.75, statement of volunteer experience, interview, 12-18 hours social science course work, survey. Additional exam requirements/recommendations for international students: Required—TOEFL. Electronic applications accepted. *Faculty research:* Child and adolescent development, HIV, hypnosis, wellness, women's issues.

John F. Kennedy University, Graduate School of Holistic Studies, Department of Counseling Psychology, Program in Counseling Psychology, Pleasant Hill, CA 94523-4817. Offers holistic studies (MA); somatic psychology (MA); transpersonal psychology (MA). Part-time and evening/weekend programs available. *Degree requirements:* For master's, thesis or alternative. *Entrance requirements:* For master's, interview. Additional exam requirements/recommendations for international students: Required—TOEFL.

John F. Kennedy University, Graduate School of Professional Psychology, Program in Counseling Psychology, Pleasant Hill, CA 94523-4817. Offers MA. *Accreditation:* APA. Part-time and evening/weekend programs available. *Degree requirements:* For master's, thesis or alternative. *Entrance requirements:* For master's, interview. Additional exam requirements/recommendations for international students: Required—TOEFL.

Kean University, College of Humanities and Social Sciences, Program in Psychology, Union, NJ 07083. Offers human behavior and organizational psychology (MA); psychological services (MA). Part-time and evening/weekend programs available. *Faculty:* 15 full-time (13 women). *Students:* 14 full-time (10 women), 35 part-time (30 women); includes 20 minority (11 African Americans, 2 Asian Americans or Pacific Islanders, 7 Hispanic Americans), 2 international. Average age 30. 28 applicants, 82% accepted, 15 enrolled. In 2009, 15 master's awarded. *Degree requirements:* For master's, comprehensive exam, thesis, research. *Entrance requirements:* For master's, GRE General Test, minimum GPA of 3.0, 2 letters of recommendation, interview, 12 credits in psychology. *Application deadline:* For fall admission, 5/1 for domestic students; for spring admission, 11/1 for domestic students. Application fee: $60 ($150 for international students). Electronic applications accepted. *Expenses:* Tuition, state resident: full-time $10,440; part-time $435 per credit. Tuition, nonresident: full-time $14,160; part-time $590 per credit. Required fees: $2642; $110 per credit. Part-time tuition and fees vary according to course load and degree level. *Financial support:* In 2009–10, 1 research assistantship with full tuition reimbursement (averaging $3,263 per year) was awarded; unspecified assistantships also available. *Unit head:* Dr. Joanne Walsh, Program Coordinator, 908-737-5870, E-mail: jwalsh@kean.edu. *Application contact:* Reenat Hasan, Pre-Admissions Coordinator, 908-737-5923, Fax: 908-737-5965, E-mail: rhasan@exchange.kean.edu.

Kutztown University of Pennsylvania, College of Education, Program in Counseling Psychology, Kutztown, PA 19530-0730. Offers agency counseling (MA); marital and family therapy (MA). Part-time and evening/weekend programs available. *Faculty:* 8 full-time (1 woman). *Students:* 33 full-time (29 women), 24 part-time (17 women); includes 3 minority (all African Americans). Average age 28. 41 applicants, 68% accepted, 10 enrolled. In 2009, 9 master's awarded. *Degree requirements:* For master's, comprehensive exam, thesis optional. *Entrance requirements:* For master's, GRE General Test, interview. Additional exam requirements/recommendations for international students: Required—TOEFL. *Application deadline:* For fall admission, 2/1 for domestic and international students; for spring admission, 8/1 for domestic and international students. Application fee: $35. Electronic applications accepted. *Expenses:* Tuition, state resident: full-time $6666; part-time $370 per credit. Tuition, nonresident: full-time $10,666; part-time $593 per credit. Required fees: $62 per credit. $60 per semester. *Financial support:* Career-related internships or fieldwork, Federal Work-Study, scholarships/grants, and unspecified assistantships available. Financial award application deadline: 3/1; financial award applicants required to submit FAFSA. *Faculty research:* Family addictions. *Unit head:* Dr. Deborah Barlieb, Chairperson, 610-683-4204, Fax: 610-683-1585, E-mail: barlieb@kutztown.edu. *Application contact:* Kelly D. Burr, Associate Director, Graduate Admissions, 610-683-4200, Fax: 610-683-1393, E-mail: graduate@kutztown.edu.

La Salle University, School of Arts and Sciences, Program in Clinical-Counseling Psychology, Philadelphia, PA 19141-1199. Offers MA. *Accreditation:* APA. Part-time and evening/weekend programs available. *Degree requirements:* For master's, comprehensive exam. *Entrance requirements:* For master's, GRE or MAT, 15 undergraduate credits in psychology. *Expenses:* Contact institution. *Faculty research:* Cognitive therapy, attribution theory, work habits, single parent families, treatment of addictions.

Lee University, Graduate Studies in Counseling, Cleveland, TN 37320-3450. Offers mental health counseling (MS); school counseling (MS). Part-time programs available. *Faculty:* 6 full-time (2 women), 7 part-time/adjunct (4 women). *Students:* 64 full-time (55 women), 28 part-time (26 women); includes 10 minority (1 African American, 4 American Indian/Alaska Native, 3 Asian Americans or Pacific Islanders, 2 Hispanic Americans), 1 international. Average age 26. 66 applicants, 95% accepted, 52 enrolled. In 2009, 24 master's awarded. *Degree requirements:* For master's, variable foreign language requirement, comprehensive exam, thesis, internship. *Entrance requirements:* For master's, GRE General Test or MAT, minimum undergraduate GPA of 3.0, 3 letters of recommendation, interview. Additional exam requirements/recommendations for international students: Required—TOEFL (minimum score 450 paper-based; 45 computer-based). *Application deadline:* For fall admission, 4/1 priority date for domestic and international students; for spring admission, 10/1 priority date for domestic and international students. Applications are processed on a rolling basis. Application fee: $25. *Expenses:* Tuition: Full-time $11,100; part-time $463 per credit. Required fees: $305. *Financial support:* Teaching assistantships, career-related internships or fieldwork, Federal Work-Study, institutionally sponsored loans, scholarships/grants, and unspecified assistantships available. Financial award application deadline: 3/1; financial award applicants required to submit FAFSA. *Unit head:* Dr. Trevor Milliron, Director, 423-614-8126, Fax: 423-614-8129, E-mail: tmilliron@leeuniversity.edu. *Application contact:* Vicki Glasscock, Graduate Admissions Director, 423-614-8059, E-mail: vglasscock@leeuniversity.edu.

Lehigh University, College of Education, Program in Counseling Psychology, Bethlehem, PA 18015. Offers counseling and human services (M Ed); counseling psychology (PhD); elementary counseling with certification (M Ed); international counseling (Certificate); international counseling with certification (M Ed); secondary school counseling (M Ed). *Accreditation:* APA (one or more programs are accredited). Part-time and evening/weekend programs available. Postbaccalaureate distance learning degree programs offered (minimal on-campus study). *Faculty:* 6 full-time (4 women), 10 part-time/adjunct (5 women). *Students:* 40 full-time (33 women), 37 part-time (32 women); includes 13 minority (7 African Americans, 1 American Indian/Alaska Native, 3 Asian Americans or Pacific Islanders, 2 Hispanic Americans), 4 international. Average age 29. 194 applicants, 24% accepted, 17 enrolled. In 2009, 34 master's, 3 doctorates awarded. *Degree requirements:* For doctorate, comprehensive exam, thesis/dissertation. *Entrance requirements:* For master's, minimum GPA of 3.0, 2 letters of recommendation, essay, transcript; for doctorate, GRE General Test (Verbal and Quantitative), 2 letters of recommendation, supplemental application, transcript, essay; for Certificate, minimum GPA of 3.0. Additional exam requirements/recommendations for international students: Required—TOEFL (minimum score 600 paper-based; 250 computer-based; 93 iBT). *Application deadline:* For fall admission, 11/15 for domestic and international students; for winter admission, 2/1 for international students. Application fee: $65. Electronic applications accepted. *Financial support:* In 2009–10, 11 students received support, including 2 fellowships with full and partial tuition reimbursements available (averaging $24,000 per year), 2 research assistantships with full and partial tuition reimbursements available (averaging $13,000 per year); career-related internships or fieldwork, Federal Work-Study, institutionally sponsored loans, scholarships/grants, and tuition waivers (full and partial) also available. Financial award application deadline: 1/31; financial award applicants required to submit FAFSA. *Faculty research:* Supervision, violence prevention, multicultural training and counseling, career development and health interventions. *Unit head:* Dr. Arpana Inman, Coordinator, 610-758-4443, Fax: 610-758-3227, E-mail: agi2@lehigh.edu. *Application contact:* Donna M. Johnson, Coordinator, 610-758-3231, Fax: 610-758-6223, E-mail: dmj4@lehigh.edu.

Lesley University, Graduate School of Arts and Social Sciences, Program in Counseling Psychology, Cambridge, MA 02138-2790. Offers professional counseling (MA); school counseling (MA). Part-time and evening/weekend programs available. Postbaccalaureate distance learning degree programs offered (no on-campus study). Terminal master's awarded for partial completion of doctoral program. *Degree requirements:* For master's, internship, practicum. *Entrance requirements:* For master's, MAT. Additional exam requirements/recommendations for international students: Required—TOEFL (minimum score 550 paper-based; 213 computer-based; 80 iBT).

Lewis & Clark College, Graduate School of Education and Counseling, Department of Counseling Psychology, Portland, OR 97219-7899. Offers addictions treatment (MA, MS); community counseling (MA, MS); marriage, couple and family therapy (MA, MS); psychological and cultural studies (MA, MS); school psychology (Ed S). Part-time and evening/weekend programs available. *Faculty:* 11 full-time (7 women), 22 part-time/adjunct (15 women). *Students:* 103 full-time (87 women), 146 part-time (115 women); includes 22 minority (3 African Americans,

Counseling Psychology

Lewis & Clark College (continued)
9 Asian Americans or Pacific Islanders, 10 Hispanic Americans), 3 international. Average age 31. 157 applicants, 78% accepted, 75 enrolled. In 2009, 69 master's, 13 other advanced degrees awarded. *Degree requirements:* For master's, thesis proposal (MS). *Entrance requirements:* For master's, GRE General Test, minimum undergraduate GPA of 2.75. Additional exam requirements/recommendations for international students: Required—TOEFL (minimum score 575 paper-based; 233 computer-based). *Application deadline:* For fall admission, 2/1 priority date for domestic and international students; for spring admission, 10/1 priority date for domestic and international students. Application fee: $50. Electronic applications accepted. *Expenses:* Tuition: Part-time $713 per semester hour. Tuition and fees vary according to course level and campus/location. *Financial support:* In 2009–10, 230 students received support. Career-related internships or fieldwork, Federal Work-Study, institutionally sponsored loans, scholarships/grants, health care benefits, and tuition waivers (partial) available. Support available to part-time students. Financial award application deadline: 3/1; financial award applicants required to submit FAFSA. *Unit head:* Dr. Tod Sloan, Chair, 503-768-6060, Fax: 503-768-6065, E-mail: cpsy@lclark.edu. *Application contact:* Becky Haas, Director of Admissions, 503-768-6200, Fax: 503-768-6205, E-mail: gseadmit@lclark.edu.

Lewis University, College of Arts and Sciences, Program in Counseling Psychology, Romeoville, IL 60446. Offers child and adolescent counseling (MA); mental health counseling (MA). Part-time and evening/weekend programs available. *Faculty:* 9 full-time (6 women), 5 part-time/adjunct (2 women). *Students:* 32 full-time (28 women), 65 part-time (60 women); includes 23 minority (15 African Americans, 8 Hispanic Americans). Average age 28. In 2009, 21 master's awarded. *Degree requirements:* For master's, comprehensive exam (for some programs), thesis optional, practicum, internship. *Entrance requirements:* For master's, 15 hours of psychology, including statistics or research; 2 letters of recommendation; writing assessment; minimum GPA of 3.0 in last 60 hours, interview. Additional exam requirements/recommendations for international students: Required—TOEFL (minimum score 550 paper-based; 213 computer-based). *Application deadline:* For fall admission, 5/1 priority date for international students; for spring admission, 11/15 priority date for international students. Applications are processed on a rolling basis. Application fee: $40. Electronic applications accepted. *Expenses:* Tuition: Full-time $6480; part-time $720 per credit. One-time fee: $40. Tuition and fees vary according to course load, degree level and program. *Financial support:* Federal Work-Study, scholarships/grants, tuition waivers, and unspecified assistantships available. Financial award application deadline: 5/1; financial award applicants required to submit FAFSA. *Faculty research:* Cognitive development, attitude formation, juvenile delinquency, gender issues, work-family conflict. *Unit head:* Dr. Katherine Helm, Director, 815-838-0500 Ext. 5604, Fax: 815-836-5032, E-mail: helmka@lewisu.edu. *Application contact:* Nancy Hanley, Information Contact, 815-838-0500 Ext. 5604, E-mail: hanleyna@lewisu.edu.

Liberty University, College of Arts and Sciences, Lynchburg, VA 24502. Offers counseling (MA); nursing (MSN); pastoral care and counseling (PhD); professional counseling (PhD). *Accreditation:* AACN. Part-time programs available. Postbaccalaureate distance learning degree programs offered (minimal on-campus study). *Degree requirements:* For master's, comprehensive exam (for some programs); for doctorate, comprehensive exam, thesis/dissertation. *Entrance requirements:* For master's, GRE General Test (MSN), minimum undergraduate GPA of 3.0; for doctorate, GRE General Test, minimum master's GPA of 3.25. Additional exam requirements/recommendations for international students: Required—TOEFL (minimum score 600 paper-based; 250 computer-based). Electronic applications accepted. *Expenses:* Tuition: Full-time $7110; part-time $415 per credit hour. Required fees: $150 per semester. Tuition and fees vary according to course load, degree level, campus/location and program. *Faculty research:* God concept and adult attachment, building marital strength, image of God and gender, breastfeeding behavior among adolescent mothers, osteoporosis.

Lindenwood University, Graduate Programs, School of Education, St. Charles, MO 63301-1695. Offers education (MA); educational administration (MA, Ed D, Ed S); instructional leadership (Ed D, Ed S); library media (MA); professional and school counseling (MA); professional counseling (MA); school administration (Ed S); school counseling (MA); teaching (MA). Part-time and evening/weekend programs available. *Faculty:* 33 full-time (13 women), 176 part-time/adjunct (83 women). *Students:* 558 full-time (415 women), 1,957 part-time (1,516 women); includes 580 minority (549 African Americans, 6 American Indian/Alaska Native, 16 Asian Americans or Pacific Islanders, 9 Hispanic Americans), 13 international. Average age 35. 248 applicants, 120 enrolled. In 2009, 730 master's, 62 doctorates, 67 other advanced degrees awarded. *Degree requirements:* For master's, thesis (for some programs); for doctorate, thesis/dissertation, minimum GPA of 3.0; for Ed S, comprehensive exam, specialist project, minimum GPA of 3.0. *Entrance requirements:* For master's, interview, minimum GPA of 3.0, writing sample, letter of recommendation; for doctorate, GRE, minimum graduate GPA of 3.4, resume, interview, writing sample, 4 letters of recommendation; for Ed S, master's degree in education, relevant work experience. Additional exam requirements/recommendations for international students: Required—TOEFL (minimum score 550 paper-based; 213 computer-based; 80 iBT). *Application deadline:* For fall admission, 8/27 priority date for domestic and international students; for spring admission, 1/28 priority date for domestic and international students. Applications are processed on a rolling basis. Application fee: $30 ($100 for international students). Electronic applications accepted. *Expenses:* Tuition: Full-time $12,960; part-time $370 per credit hour. Required fees: $340. One-time fee: $30 full-time. Tuition and fees vary according to course level and course load. *Financial support:* In 2009–10, 1,591 students received support. Career-related internships or fieldwork, institutionally sponsored loans, tuition waivers (partial), and unspecified assistantships available. Financial award application deadline: 6/30; financial award applicants required to submit FAFSA. *Unit head:* Dr. Cynthia Bice, Dean, 636-949-4618, Fax: 636-949-4197, E-mail: cbice@lindenwood.edu. *Application contact:* Brett Barger, Dean of Evening Admissions and Extension Campuses, 636-949-4934, Fax: 636-949-4109, E-mail: adultadmissions@lindenwood.edu.

Lindsey Wilson College, School of Professional Counseling, Columbia, KY 42728. Offers counseling and human development (M Ed). *Accreditation:* ACA. Part-time and evening/weekend programs available.

Lipscomb University, Program in Counseling, Nashville, TN 37204-3951. Offers counseling psychology (Certificate); professional counseling (MS); psychology (MS). Part-time and evening/weekend programs available. Postbaccalaureate distance learning degree programs offered (minimal on-campus study). *Faculty:* 4 full-time (0 women), 13 part-time/adjunct (6 women). *Students:* 67 full-time (48 women), 39 part-time (26 women); includes 16 minority (9 African Americans, 1 American Indian/Alaska Native, 2 Asian Americans or Pacific Islanders, 4 Hispanic Americans), 1 international. Average age 30. 72 applicants, 82% accepted, 42 enrolled. *Entrance requirements:* For master's, GRE, resume, 3 reference letters, minimum GPA of 3.0. Application fee: $50. Electronic applications accepted. *Expenses:* Tuition: Full-time $16,002; part-time $889 per credit hour. Tuition and fees vary according to program. *Faculty research:* Cognitive psychology, neuroscience, health psychology, grief issues. *Unit head:* Dr. Jake Morris, Graduate Program Director and Professor of Psychology, E-mail: jake.morris@lipscomb.edu. *Application contact:* Elena Zemmel, Administrative Assistant, 615-966-5906, E-mail: elena.zemmel@lipscomb.edu.

Long Island University, Brentwood Campus, School of Education, Brentwood, NY 11717. Offers childhood education (MS); early childhood education (MS); literacy (MS); mental health counseling (MS); school counseling (MS); special education (MS). Part-time and evening/weekend programs available.

Long Island University, Rockland Graduate Campus, Graduate School, Program in Counseling and Development, Orangeburg, NY 10962. Offers mental health counseling (MS); school counselor (MS). *Faculty:* 2 full-time (both women), 7 part-time/adjunct (3 women). *Students:* 18 full-time (12 women), 60 part-time (51 women). In 2009, 25 master's awarded. *Application deadline:* Applications are processed on a rolling basis. Application fee: $30. *Expenses:* Tuition: Part-time $930 per credit. Required fees: $200 per semester. *Financial support:* Applicants required to submit FAFSA. *Unit head:* Dr. Linda Rosen, Program Director, 845-359-7200 Ext. 5406, Fax: 845-359-7248, E-mail: kathleen.keefe-cooperman@liu.edu. *Application contact:* Peter S. Reiner, Director of Admissions and Marketing, 845-359-7200, Fax: 845-359-7248, E-mail: peter.reiner@liu.edu.

Long Island University, Westchester Graduate Campus, Program in Mental Health Counseling, Purchase, NY 10577. Offers MS.

Louisiana State University in Shreveport, College of Education and Human Development, Program in Counseling Psychology, Shreveport, LA 71115-2399. Offers MS. *Students:* 28 full-time (24 women), 16 part-time (13 women); includes 9 minority (6 African Americans, 1 American Indian/Alaska Native, 2 Hispanic Americans), 2 international. Average age 30. 33 applicants, 100% accepted, 14 enrolled. In 2009, 15 master's awarded. *Degree requirements:* For master's, comprehensive exam, internship (600 clock hours). *Entrance requirements:* For master's, GRE, references. Additional exam requirements/recommendations for international students: Required—TOEFL (minimum score 500 paper-based; 173 computer-based; 61 iBT). *Application deadline:* For fall admission, 6/30 for domestic and international students; for spring admission, 11/30 for domestic and international students. Applications are processed on a rolling basis. Application fee: $10 ($20 for international students). *Financial support:* In 2009–10, 3 research assistantships with partial tuition reimbursements (averaging $30,000 per year) were awarded. *Unit head:* Dr. Meredith G. Nelson, Program Director, 318-797-5199, E-mail: mnelson@pilot.lsus.edu. *Application contact:* Dr. Meredith G. Nelson, Program Director, 318-797-5199, E-mail: mnelson@pilot.lsus.edu.

Louisiana Tech University, Graduate School, College of Education, Department of Behavioral Sciences and Psychology, Ruston, LA 71272. Offers counseling (MA); counseling psychology (PhD); industrial/organizational psychology (MA); special education (MA). *Accreditation:* APA (one or more programs are accredited). Part-time programs available. *Degree requirements:* For master's, thesis or alternative; for doctorate, thesis/dissertation. *Entrance requirements:* For master's and doctorate, GRE General Test.

Loyola University Chicago, School of Education, Program in Counseling Psychology, Chicago, IL 60660. Offers PhD. Offered through the Graduate School. *Accreditation:* APA. *Faculty:* 5 full-time (4 women), 4 part-time/adjunct (2 women). *Students:* 25. Average age 26. 48 applicants, 10% accepted, 4 enrolled. In 2009, 6 doctorates awarded. *Degree requirements:* For doctorate, comprehensive exam, thesis/dissertation. *Entrance requirements:* For doctorate, GRE General Test, GRE Subject Test, interview; minimum graduate GPA of 3.5, undergraduate 3.0; letters of recommendation. Additional exam requirements/recommendations for international students: Required—TOEFL (minimum score 550 paper-based; 213 computer-based; 79 iBT). *Application deadline:* For fall admission, 12/1 for domestic and international students. Application fee: $50. Electronic applications accepted. *Expenses:* Tuition: Full-time $14,220; part-time $790 per credit hour. Required fees: $60 per semester hour. Tuition and fees vary according to program. *Financial support:* In 2009–10, 4 fellowships with full tuition reimbursements (averaging $14,000 per year), 10 research assistantships with full tuition reimbursements (averaging $12,500 per year) were awarded; teaching assistantships with full tuition reimbursements, career-related internships or fieldwork, Federal Work-Study, traineeships, and unspecified assistantships also available. Financial award application deadline: 2/15; financial award applicants required to submit FAFSA. *Faculty research:* Career choice and development, multicultural counseling, psychological measurement, prevention and intervention, family therapy. *Unit head:* Dr. Steve Brown, Director, 312-915-6311, E-mail: sbrown@luc.edu. *Application contact:* Marie Rosin-Dittmar, Information Contact, 312-915-6800, E-mail: schleduc@luc.edu.

Loyola University Maryland, Graduate Programs, College of Arts and Sciences, Department of Psychology, Program in Counseling Psychology, Baltimore, MD 21210-2699. Offers MS, CAS. Part-time and evening/weekend programs available. *Entrance requirements:* For master's and CAS, GRE General Test, GRE Subject Test (recommended). Additional exam requirements/recommendations for international students: Required—TOEFL (minimum score 550 paper-based; 213 computer-based).

Marist College, Graduate Programs, School of Social and Behavioral Sciences, Poughkeepsie, NY 12601-1387. Offers counseling psychology (MA); education (M Ed); education psychology (MA); school psychology (MA, Adv C). Part-time and evening/weekend programs available. *Degree requirements:* For master's, thesis optional. *Entrance requirements:* For master's, GRE General Test, letters of recommendation, minimum undergraduate GPA of 3.0, interview. Additional exam requirements/recommendations for international students: Required—TOEFL (minimum score 550 paper-based; 213 computer-based; 80 iBT); Recommended—IELTS (minimum score 6.5). Electronic applications accepted. *Expenses:* Tuition: Full-time $12,510; part-time $695 per credit hour. *Faculty research:* AIDS prevention, educational intervention, humanistic counseling research, aging and development, neuroimaging.

Mars Hill Graduate School, Graduate Programs, Seattle, WA 98121. Offers Christian studies (MA); counseling psychology (MA); divinity (MS). Part-time programs available. *Entrance requirements:* For master's, MAT.

Marylhurst University, Department of Art Therapy Counseling, Marylhurst, OR 97036-0261. Offers art therapy (PGC); art therapy counseling (MA); counseling (PGC). Part-time programs available. *Faculty:* 3 full-time (all women), 4 part-time/adjunct (all women). *Students:* 45 full-time (43 women), 3 part-time (all women); includes 2 minority (1 African American, 1 Asian American or Pacific Islander). Average age 32. 27 applicants, 67% accepted, 18 enrolled. In 2009, 21 master's awarded. *Degree requirements:* For master's, comprehensive exam, practicums. *Entrance requirements:* For master's, Miller Analogy Test, minimum GPA of 3.0, course work in psychology and art, slide portfolio, letters of reference, resume, autobiography, portfolio. Additional exam requirements/recommendations for international students: Required—TOEFL (minimum score 550 paper-based; 213 computer-based; 80 iBT). *Application deadline:* For fall admission, 1/31 priority date for domestic and international students. Applications are processed on a rolling basis. Application fee: $40 ($50 for international students). *Expenses:* Contact institution. *Financial support:* Scholarships/grants available. Support available to part-time students. Financial award applicants required to submit FAFSA. *Faculty research:* Scientific approaches to art therapy research, child and adolescent psychotherapy, multicultural counseling. *Unit head:* Christine Turner, Chair, 503-636-8141, Fax: 503-636-9526, E-mail: cturner@marylhurst.edu. *Application contact:* Kathleen Schneff, Admissions Specialist, 800-634-9982 Ext. 3322, Fax: 503-635-6585, E-mail: admissions@marylhurst.edu.

Marymount University, School of Education and Human Services, Program in Community Counseling, Arlington, VA 22207-4299. Offers MA, Certificate. *Accreditation:* ACA (one or more programs are accredited). Part-time and evening/weekend programs available. *Faculty:* 7 full-time (4 women), 5 part-time/adjunct (3 women). *Students:* 39 full-time (34 women), 49 part-time (47 women); includes 17 minority (10 African Americans, 4 Asian Americans or Pacific Islanders, 3 Hispanic Americans). Average age 30. 73 applicants, 70% accepted, 34 enrolled. In 2009, 29 master's awarded. *Entrance requirements:* For master's, GRE, 2 letters of recommendation, interview, resume, personal statement; for Certificate, master's degree in counseling. Additional exam requirements/recommendations for international students: Required—TOEFL (minimum score 600 paper-based; 250 computer-based; 96 iBT), IELTS (minimum score 6.5). *Application deadline:* For fall admission, 1/15 for domestic students, 7/1 for international students; for spring admission, 10/5 for domestic students, 10/15 for international students. Applications are processed on a rolling basis. Application fee: $40. Electronic applications accepted. *Expenses:* Tuition: Full-time $13,050; part-time $725 per credit hour. Required fees: $135; $7.50 per credit hour. *Financial support:* In 2009–10, 3 students received support; research assistantships with full tuition reimbursements available, career-related internships or fieldwork, Federal Work-Study, scholarships/grants, and unspecified assistantships available. Support available to part-time students. Financial award applicants required to submit FAFSA. *Unit head:* Dr. Lisa Jackson-Cherry, Director, 703-284-1633, Fax: 703-284-

5708, E-mail: lisa.jackson-cherry@marymount.edu. *Application contact:* Francesca Reed, Director, Graduate Admissions, 703-284-5901, Fax: 703-527-3815, E-mail: grad.admissions@marymount.edu.

Marywood University, Academic Affairs, Reap College of Education and Human Development, Department of Psychology and Counseling, Program in Mental Health Counseling, Scranton, PA 18509-1598. Offers MA. *Accreditation:* ACA. *Students:* 12 full-time (10 women), 8 part-time (7 women); includes 2 minority (1 African American, 1 American Indian/Alaska Native). Average age 30. In 2009, 2 master's awarded. *Entrance requirements:* Additional exam requirements/recommendations for international students: Required—TOEFL (minimum score 550 paper-based; 213 computer-based; 79 iBT). *Application deadline:* For fall admission, 4/1 for domestic students, 3/31 for international students; for spring admission, 11/1 for domestic students, 8/31 for international students. Applications are processed on a rolling basis. Application fee: $35. Electronic applications accepted. *Expenses:* Tuition: Part-time $715 per credit. Required fees: $270 per semester. Tuition and fees vary according to degree level, campus/location and program. *Financial support:* Career-related internships or fieldwork, scholarships/grants, and unspecified assistantships available. Support available to part-time students. Financial award application deadline: 6/30. *Unit head:* Dr. John Lemoncelli, Director, 570-348-6211 Ext. 2317, E-mail: lemoncelli@marywood.edu. *Application contact:* Tammy Manka, Assistant Director of Graduate Admissions, 866-279-9663, E-mail: tmanka@marywood.edu.

Massachusetts School of Professional Psychology, Graduate Programs, Boston, MA 02132. Offers clinical psychology (Psy D); clinical psychopharmacology (Post-Doctoral MS); counseling psychology (MA); executive coaching (Graduate Certificate); forensic psychology (MA); organizational psychology (MA); respecialization in clinical psychology (Certificate); MA/CAGS. *Accreditation:* APA. *Degree requirements:* For master's, comprehensive exam; for doctorate, thesis/dissertation. *Entrance requirements:* For doctorate, GRE General Test. Additional exam requirements/recommendations for international students: Required—TOEFL (minimum score 550 paper-based; 213 computer-based). Electronic applications accepted.

McGill University, Faculty of Graduate and Postdoctoral Studies, Faculty of Education, Department of Educational and Counseling Psychology, Montréal, QC H3A 2T5, Canada. Offers counseling psychology (MA, PhD); educational psychology (M Ed, MA, PhD); school/applied child psychology and applied developmental psychology (M Ed, MA, PhD, Diploma), including school psychology. *Accreditation:* APA.

McKendree University, Graduate Programs, Master of Arts in Professional Counseling Program, Lebanon, IL 62254-1299. Offers MA. Part-time and evening/weekend programs available. *Faculty:* 1 full-time (0 women), 7 part-time/adjunct (4 women). *Students:* 26 full-time (22 women), 35 part-time (30 women); includes 8 minority (6 African Americans, 1 American Indian/Alaska Native, 1 Hispanic American). Average age 31. 43 applicants, 37% accepted, 8 enrolled. In 2009, 16 master's awarded. *Degree requirements:* For master's, comprehensive exam, internship. *Entrance requirements:* For master's, official transcripts from institutions attended, minimum GPA of 3.0, three letters of recommendation, personal statement, interview, completion of six hours in behavior science. *Application deadline:* Applications are processed on a rolling basis. Application fee: $0. Electronic applications accepted. *Expenses:* Tuition: Full-time $6300; part-time $350 per credit hour. One-time fee: $125. *Financial support:* Applicants required to submit FAFSA. *Unit head:* Dr. Jim Cook, Director, 618-537-6875, E-mail: jhcook@mckendree.edu. *Application contact:* Brie Knaus, Graduate Admission Counselor, 618-537-6574, Fax: 618-537-6410, E-mail: blknaus@mckendree.edu.

McNeese State University, Doré School of Graduate Studies, Burton College of Education, Department of Psychology, Lake Charles, LA 70609. Offers addiction treatment (MA); applied behavior analysis (MA); counseling psychology (MA); general/experimental psychology (MA). Evening/weekend programs available. *Faculty:* 6 full-time (3 women). *Students:* 34 full-time (24 women), 30 part-time (22 women); includes 10 minority (7 African Americans, 1 Asian American or Pacific Islander, 2 Hispanic Americans), 2 international. In 2009, 18 master's awarded. *Entrance requirements:* For master's, GRE. *Application deadline:* For fall admission, 5/15 priority date for domestic and international students; for spring admission, 10/15 priority date for domestic and international students. Applications are processed on a rolling basis. Application fee: $20 ($30 for international students). *Expenses:* Tuition, area resident: Full-time $2556. Tuition, state resident: full-time $2556. Required fees: $1031. Tuition and fees vary according to course load. *Financial support:* Application deadline: 5/1. *Unit head:* Dr. Dena L. Matzenbacher, Head, 337-475-5457, Fax: 337-562-4115, E-mail: dena@mcneese.edu. *Application contact:* Dr. George F. Mead, Interim Dean of Dore' School of Graduate Studies, 337-475-5396, Fax: 337-475-5397, E-mail: admissions@mcneese.edu.

Medaille College, Programs in Psychology, Buffalo, NY 14214-2695. Offers mental health counseling (MA); psychology (MA). Part-time and evening/weekend programs available. *Faculty:* 4 full-time (2 women), 9 part-time/adjunct (6 women). *Students:* 223 full-time (188 women); includes 45 minority (42 African Americans, 1 Asian American or Pacific Islander, 2 Hispanic Americans). Average age 31. 51 applicants, 45% accepted, 22 enrolled. In 2009, 74 master's awarded. *Degree requirements:* For master's, comprehensive exam (for some programs), thesis (for some programs). *Entrance requirements:* For master's, GRE General Test (psychology), minimum GPA of 2.75 (psychology). Additional exam requirements/recommendations for international students: Required—TOEFL (minimum score 550 paper-based; 213 computer-based). *Application deadline:* Applications are processed on a rolling basis. Application fee: $35. Electronic applications accepted. *Financial support:* In 2009–10, 90 students received support. Federal Work-Study available. Financial award applicants required to submit FAFSA. *Faculty research:* Schizophrenia, Parkinson's Disease, eyewitness testimony, methodology. *Unit head:* Dr. Judith Horowitz, Dean of Adult and Graduate Studies, 716-880-2229, Fax: 716-884-0291, E-mail: jhorowitz@medaille.edu. *Application contact:* Jacqueline Matheny, Executive Director of Marketing and Enrollment, 716-932-2541, Fax: 716-632-1811, E-mail: jmatheny@medaille.edu.

Mercy College, School of Social and Behavioral Sciences, Program in Counseling, Dobbs Ferry, NY 10522-1189. Offers alcohol and substance abuse counseling (Certificate); counseling (MS); family counseling (Certificate). Part-time and evening/weekend programs available. Postbaccalaureate distance learning degree programs offered (no on-campus study). *Students:* 137 full-time (121 women), 213 part-time (185 women); includes 223 minority (89 African Americans, 3 American Indian/Alaska Native, 4 Asian Americans or Pacific Islanders, 127 Hispanic Americans), 1 international. Average age 35. 226 applicants, 53% accepted, 87 enrolled. In 2009, 92 master's, 14 other advanced degrees awarded. *Degree requirements:* For master's, comprehensive exam. *Entrance requirements:* For master's, interview, two professional letters of recommendation, minimum undergraduate GPA of 3.0, resume. Additional exam requirements/recommendations for international students: Required—TOEFL (minimum score 600 paper-based; 250 computer-based; 100 iBT). *Application deadline:* For fall admission, 8/1 for international students. Applications are processed on a rolling basis. Application fee: $40. Electronic applications accepted. *Expenses:* Tuition: Full-time $13,158; part-time $731 per credit. Required fees: $500. Tuition and fees vary according to degree level and program. *Financial support:* Career-related internships or fieldwork, Federal Work-Study, scholarships/grants, and unspecified assistantships available. Support available to part-time students. Financial award applicants required to submit FAFSA. *Faculty research:* Ethics, drug abuse problems, human development, domestic violence. *Unit head:* Dr. Arthur Mc Cann, Assistant Professor, Psychology and Behavioral Science, 914-674-7670, E-mail: amccann@mercy.edu. *Application contact:* Dr. Arthur Mc Cann, Assistant Professor, Psychology and Behavioral Science, 914-674-7670, E-mail: amccann@mercy.edu.

Mercy College, School of Social and Behavioral Sciences, Program in Mental Health Counseling, Dobbs Ferry, NY 10522-1189. Offers MS. Part-time and evening/weekend programs available. *Students:* 42 full-time (36 women), 31 part-time (28 women); includes 26 African Americans, 2 Asian Americans or Pacific Islanders, 14 Hispanic Americans, 2 international. Average age 37. 74 applicants, 39% accepted, 22 enrolled. In 2009, 27 master's awarded. *Entrance requirements:* For master's, resume, interview, two professional letters of recommendation, 2- to 3-page essay on reason(s) for pursuing counseling degree. Additional exam requirements/recommendations for international students: Required—TOEFL (minimum score 600 paper-based; 250 computer-based; 100 iBT). *Application deadline:* For fall admission, 8/1 for international students. Application fee: $40. *Expenses:* Tuition: Full-time $13,158; part-time $731 per credit. Required fees: $500. Tuition and fees vary according to degree level and program. *Financial support:* In 2009–10, 1 student received support. Career-related internships or fieldwork, Federal Work-Study, scholarships/grants, and unspecified assistantships available. Support available to part-time students. Financial award applicants required to submit FAFSA. *Unit head:* Dr. Diana Trevouledes, Program Director, 914-674-7401, E-mail: dtrevouledes@mercy.edu. *Application contact:* Dr. Diana Trevouledes, Program Director, 914-674-7401, E-mail: dtrevouledes@mercy.edu.

Messiah College, Program in Counseling, Grantham, PA 17027. Offers counseling (CAGS); marriage, couple, and family counseling (MAC); mental health counseling (MAC); school counseling (MAC). Part-time programs available. *Entrance requirements:* For master's, minimum undergraduate cumulative GPA of 3.0, 2 recommendations, resume or curriculum vitae, interview; for CAGS, bachelor's degree, minimum undergraduate cumulative GPA of 3.0, essay, two recommendations, resume or curriculum vitae, interview. *Application deadline:* Applications are processed on a rolling basis. Application fee: $30. Electronic applications accepted. *Expenses:* Tuition: Part-time $518 per credit hour. *Financial support:* Applicants required to submit FAFSA. *Unit head:* Dr. John Addleman, Director, 717-796-1800 Ext. 2980, Fax: 717-691-2386, E-mail: jaddlemn@messiah.edu. *Application contact:* Dr. John Addleman, Director, 717-796-1800 Ext. 2980, Fax: 717-691-2386, E-mail: jaddlemn@messiah.edu.

Michigan Theological Seminary, Graduate Programs, Plymouth, MI 48170. Offers Bible (Graduate Certificate); Christian education (MA); counseling psychology (MA); divinity (M Div); theological studies (MA). *Accreditation:* ATS. Part-time and evening/weekend programs available. *Degree requirements:* For master's, one foreign language, thesis; for M Div, 2 foreign languages. *Faculty research:* Judaism, cults, world religions.

Mid-America Christian University, Program in Counseling, Oklahoma City, OK 73170-4504. Offers marital and family therapy (MS); pastoral/spiritual direction (MS); professional counselor (MS). *Entrance requirements:* For master's, MAT, bachelor's degree from a regionally accredited college or university, minimum overall cumulative GPA of 2.75 of bachelor course work. Additional exam requirements/recommendations for international students: Required—TOEFL (minimum score 550 paper-based; 213 computer-based).

MidAmerica Nazarene University, Graduate Studies in Counseling, Olathe, KS 66062-1899. Offers counseling (MAC); play therapy (PMC). Evening/weekend programs available. *Faculty:* 6 full-time (2 women), 7 part-time/adjunct (4 women). *Students:* 80 full-time (57 women), 3 part-time (all women); includes 13 minority (7 African Americans, 4 American Indian/Alaska Native, 2 Hispanic Americans). Average age 36. In 2009, 19 master's awarded. *Entrance requirements:* For master's, Minnesota Multiphasic Personality Inventory, minimum GPA of 3.0. *Application deadline:* For fall admission, 6/15 for domestic students. Application fee: $75. *Expenses:* Contact institution. *Unit head:* Dr. Todd Frye, Director, 913-971-3449, Fax: 913-971-3402, E-mail: tmfrye@mnu.edu. *Application contact:* Aileen Douglas, Secretary, 913-791-3449, Fax: 913-791-3402, E-mail: adouglas@mnu.edu.

Middle Tennessee State University, College of Graduate Studies, College of Education and Behavioral Science, Department of Psychology, Program in Professional Counseling, Murfreesboro, TN 37132. Offers curriculum and instruction (Ed S), including school psychology; mental health counseling (M Ed); school counseling (M Ed). *Accreditation:* ACA; NCATE. Part-time and evening/weekend programs available. Postbaccalaureate distance learning degree programs offered. *Students:* 66 part-time (57 women); includes 6 minority (5 African Americans, 1 Asian American or Pacific Islander). 35 applicants, 69% accepted, 24 enrolled. In 2009, 27 master's, 7 other advanced degrees awarded. *Degree requirements:* For master's, comprehensive exam. *Entrance requirements:* For master's, GRE or MAT. Additional exam requirements/recommendations for international students: Required—TOEFL (minimum score 525 paper-based; 195 computer-based; 71 iBT) or IELTS (minimum score 6). *Application deadline:* For fall admission, 6/1 for domestic and international students. Applications are processed on a rolling basis. Application fee: $25 ($30 for international students). Electronic applications accepted. *Expenses:* Tuition, state resident: full-time $4404. Tuition, nonresident: full-time $10,956. *Financial support:* Application deadline: 5/1. *Application contact:* Dr. Michael Allen, Dean and Vice Provost for Research, 615-898-2840, Fax: 615-904-8020, E-mail: mallen@mtsu.edu.

Mississippi College, Graduate School, School of Education, Department of Psychology and Counseling, Clinton, MS 39058. Offers counseling (Ed S); marriage and family counseling (MS); mental health counseling (MS); school counseling (M Ed). Part-time programs available. *Faculty:* 8 full-time (3 women), 5 part-time/adjunct (2 women). *Students:* 60 full-time (54 women), 70 part-time (63 women); includes 64 minority (63 African Americans, 1 American Indian/Alaska Native), 3 international. Average age 31. In 2009, 38 master's awarded. *Degree requirements:* For master's and Ed S, comprehensive exam, thesis optional. *Entrance requirements:* For master's, GRE or NTE. Additional exam requirements/recommendations for international students: Recommended—IELTS. *Application deadline:* For fall admission, 6/1 for domestic students; for spring admission, 9/1 for domestic students. Application fee: $30. Electronic applications accepted. *Expenses:* Tuition: Part-time $452 per credit hour. Required fees: $101 per semester. Tuition and fees vary according to degree level, campus/location, program and student level. *Financial support:* Career-related internships or fieldwork, Federal Work-Study, and unspecified assistantships available. Support available to part-time students. Financial award applicants required to submit FAFSA. *Unit head:* Dr. Buddy Wagner, Interim Chair, 601-925-3354, E-mail: bwagner@mc.edu. *Application contact:* Elnora Lewis, Secretary, 601-925-3225, Fax: 601-925-3889, E-mail: lewis09@mc.edu.

Monmouth University, Graduate School, Department of Psychology, West Long Branch, NJ 07764-1898. Offers mental health counseling (MS); psychological counseling (MA, PMC). *Accreditation:* ACA. Part-time and evening/weekend programs available. *Faculty:* 6 full-time (2 women), 6 part-time/adjunct (all women). *Students:* 126 full-time (110 women), 124 part-time (103 women); includes 45 minority (20 African Americans, 2 American Indian/Alaska Native, 10 Asian Americans or Pacific Islanders, 13 Hispanic Americans), 1 international. Average age 30. 169 applicants, 95% accepted, 98 enrolled. In 2009, 54 master's awarded. *Degree requirements:* For master's, thesis optional, fieldwork. *Entrance requirements:* For master's, GRE General Test, minimum GPA of 3.0 in major, 24 credits in psychology. Additional exam requirements/recommendations for international students: Required—TOEFL (minimum score 550 paper-based; 213 computer-based; 79 iBT), IELTS (minimum score 5), Michigan English Language Assessment Battery (minimum score 77), Cambridge A, B, C. *Application deadline:* For fall admission, 7/15 priority date for domestic students, 6/1 for international students; for spring admission, 11/15 priority date for domestic students, 11/1 for international students. Applications are processed on a rolling basis. Application fee: $50. Electronic applications accepted. *Expenses:* Tuition: Part-time $773 per credit. Required fees: $157 per semester. *Financial support:* In 2009–10, 159 students received support, including 149 fellowships (averaging $1,946 per year), 12 research assistantships (averaging $10,848 per year); career-related internships or fieldwork, scholarships/grants, and unspecified assistantships also available. Support available to part-time students. Financial award applicants required to submit FAFSA. *Faculty research:* Violent crime, single parenting, the African-American male, counseling older women, successful behavior for under-achieving youth. *Unit head:* Dr. George Kapalka, Director, 732-263-5583, Fax: 732-263-5159, E-mail: gkapalka@monmouth.edu. *Application contact:* Kevin Roane, Director, Office of Graduate Admission, 732-571-3452, Fax: 732-263-5123, E-mail: gradadm@monmouth.edu.

Montclair State University, The Graduate School, College of Education and Human Services, Department of Counseling, Human Development, and Educational Leadership, Montclair, NJ 07043-1624. Offers administration and supervision (MA), including administration and supervision, educator/trainer; advanced counseling (Certificate); counseling and guidance

Counseling Psychology

Montclair State University (continued)
(MA), including addictions counseling, community counseling, student affairs; counselor education (PhD); principal (Certificate); school administrator (Certificate); school business administrator (Certificate); school counselor (Certificate); substance awareness coordinator (Certificate). *Accreditation:* NCATE. Part-time and evening/weekend programs available. *Faculty:* 17 full-time (12 women), 13 part-time/adjunct (7 women). *Students:* 161 full-time (126 women), 425 part-time (325 women). Average age 33. 269 applicants, 55% accepted, 125 enrolled. In 2009, 91 master's awarded. *Degree requirements:* For master's, comprehensive exam, thesis or alternative; for doctorate, comprehensive exam, thesis/dissertation. *Entrance requirements:* For master's, GRE General Test, interview, 2 letters of recommendation; for doctorate, GRE General Test, interview; 3 letters of recommendation. Additional exam requirements/recommendations for international students: Required—TOEFL (minimum score 83 computer-based), or IELTS. *Application deadline:* For fall admission, 6/1 for international students; for spring admission, 10/1 for international students. Applications are processed on a rolling basis. Application fee: $60. Electronic applications accepted. *Expenses:* Tuition, area resident: Part-time $486.74 per credit. Tuition, state resident: part-time $486.74 per credit. Tuition, nonresident: part-time $751.34 per credit. Tuition and fees vary according to degree level and program. *Financial support:* In 2009–10, 28 research assistantships with full tuition reimbursements (averaging $7,000 per year), 2 teaching assistantships (averaging $15,000 per year) were awarded; Federal Work-Study, scholarships/grants, and unspecified assistantships also available. Support available to part-time students. Financial award application deadline: 3/1; financial award applicants required to submit FAFSA. *Faculty research:* K-12 education, data collection. *Unit head:* Dr. Larry Burlew, Chairperson, 973-655-7611. *Application contact:* Amy Aiello, Director of Graduate Admissions and Operations, 973-655-5147, Fax: 973-655-7869, E-mail: graduate.school@montclair.edu.

Morehead State University, Graduate Programs, College of Science and Technology, Department of Psychology, Morehead, KY 40351. Offers clinical/counseling psychology (MS); general/experimental psychology (MS). Part-time and evening/weekend programs available. *Faculty:* 7 full-time (2 women). *Students:* 32 full-time (23 women), 2 part-time (1 woman), 1 international. Average age 25. 39 applicants, 51% accepted, 19 enrolled. In 2009, 12 master's awarded. *Degree requirements:* For master's, comprehensive exam, thesis optional. *Entrance requirements:* For master's, GRE General Test, 18 undergraduate hours in psychology, minimum GPA of 3.0, 3 letters of recommendation. Additional exam requirements/recommendations for international students: Required—TOEFL (minimum score 500 paper-based; 173 computer-based). *Application deadline:* For fall admission, 8/1 priority date for domestic and international students; for spring admission, 12/1 for domestic students, 12/1 priority date for international students. Applications are processed on a rolling basis. Application fee: $30. Electronic applications accepted. *Expenses:* Tuition, state resident: full-time $6318; part-time $351 per credit hour. Tuition, nonresident: full-time $15,804; part-time $878 per credit hour. *Financial support:* In 2009–10, 26 research assistantships (averaging $10,000 per year) were awarded; career-related internships or fieldwork, Federal Work-Study, and unspecified assistantships also available. Financial award application deadline: 3/15; financial award applicants required to submit FAFSA. *Faculty research:* Mood induction effects, serotonin receptor activity, stress, perceptual processes. *Unit head:* Dr. Laurie Couch, Interim Department Chair, 606-783-2950. *Application contact:* Michelle Barber, Graduate Recruitment and Retention Assistant Director, 606-783-5127, Fax: 606-783-5061, E-mail: m.barber@moreheadstate.edu.

Mount St. Mary's College, Graduate Division, Program in Counseling Psychology, Los Angeles, CA 90049-1599. Offers counseling psychology (MS); marriage and family therapy (MS); psychology (MS). Part-time and evening/weekend programs available. *Faculty:* 3 full-time (2 women), 6 part-time/adjunct (5 women). *Students:* 43 full-time (38 women), 4 part-time (3 women); includes 10 minority (1 African American, 2 Asian Americans or Pacific Islanders, 7 Hispanic Americans). Average age 31. In 2009, 12 master's awarded. *Degree requirements:* For master's, research project. *Entrance requirements:* For master's, minimum GPA of 3.0. *Application deadline:* For fall admission, 7/15 for domestic students; for spring admission, 11/15 for domestic students. *Expenses:* Tuition: Part-time $730 per unit. Part-time tuition and fees vary according to degree level and program. *Financial support:* Institutionally sponsored loans and tuition waivers (partial) available. Support available to part-time students. Financial award application deadline: 3/15; financial award applicants required to submit FAFSA. *Unit head:* Dr. Gregory Travis, Director, Graduate Psychology, 213-477-2654, E-mail: gtravis@msmc.la.edu. *Application contact:* Director of Graduate Admission.

Naropa University, Graduate Programs, Program in Transpersonal Counseling Psychology, Boulder, CO 80302-6697. Offers art therapy (MA); counseling psychology (MA); wilderness therapy (MA). *Degree requirements:* For master's, internships. *Entrance requirements:* For master's, in-person interview, course work in psychology, 3 letters of recommendation, resume. Additional exam requirements/recommendations for international students: Required—TOEFL (minimum score 600 paper-based; 250 computer-based). Electronic applications accepted.

National University, Academic Affairs, College of Letters and Sciences, Department of Psychology, La Jolla, CA 92037-1011. Offers counseling psychology (MA); human behavior (MA). Part-time and evening/weekend programs available. Postbaccalaureate distance learning degree programs offered (no on-campus study). *Faculty:* 15 full-time (8 women), 66 part-time/adjunct (40 women). *Students:* 421 full-time (340 women), 443 part-time (356 women); includes 343 minority (118 African Americans, 4 American Indian/Alaska Native, 47 Asian Americans or Pacific Islanders, 174 Hispanic Americans), 6 international. Average age 36. 585 applicants, 100% accepted, 320 enrolled. In 2009, 226 master's awarded. *Degree requirements:* For master's, thesis (for some programs). *Entrance requirements:* For master's, interview, minimum GPA of 2.5. Additional exam requirements/recommendations for international students: Required—TOEFL (minimum score 550 paper-based; 213 computer-based; 79 iBT), IELTS (minimum score 6). *Application deadline:* Applications are processed on a rolling basis. Application fee: $60 ($65 for international students). Electronic applications accepted. *Expenses:* Tuition: Part-time $338 per quarter hour. *Financial support:* Career-related internships or fieldwork, institutionally sponsored loans, scholarships/grants, and tuition waivers (partial) available. Support available to part-time students. Financial award application deadline: 6/30; financial award applicants required to submit FAFSA. *Unit head:* Dr. Maureen O'Hara, Chair and Professor, 858-642-8464, Fax: 858-642-8715, E-mail: mohara@nu.edu. *Application contact:* Dominick Giovanniello, Associate Regional Dean—San Diego, 800-NAT-UNIV, Fax: 858-541-7792, E-mail: dgiovann@nu.edu.

New England College, Program in Community Mental Health Counseling, Henniker, NH 03242-3293. Offers human services (MS); mental health counseling (MS). Part-time and evening/weekend programs available. *Degree requirements:* For master's, internship.

New Jersey City University, Graduate Studies and Continuing Education, Debra Cannon Partridge Wolfe College of Education, Program in Counseling, Jersey City, NJ 07305-1597. Offers MA. Part-time and evening/weekend programs available. *Faculty:* 9. *Students:* 41 full-time (32 women), 40 part-time (31 women); includes 27 minority (6 African Americans, 1 American Indian/Alaska Native, 3 Asian Americans or Pacific Islanders, 17 Hispanic Americans), 2 international. Average age 30. In 2009, 27 master's awarded. *Expenses:* Tuition, area resident: Part-time $456.75 per credit. Tuition, nonresident: part-time $842.55 per credit. Required fees: $65 per term. *Unit head:* Dr. Jane Webber, Coordinator, 201-200-3124, E-mail: jwebber@njcu.edu. *Application contact:* Dr. Jane Webber, Coordinator, 201-200-3124, E-mail: jwebber@njcu.edu.

New Mexico State University, Graduate School, College of Education, Department of Counseling and Educational Psychology, Las Cruces, NM 88003-8001. Offers counseling and guidance (MA); counseling psychology (PhD); school psychology (Ed S). *Accreditation:* ACA; APA (one or more programs are accredited); NCATE. Part-time programs available. *Faculty:* 12 full-time (8 women), 4 part-time/adjunct (2 women). *Students:* 70 full-time (52 women), 34 part-time (27 women); includes 52 minority (3 African Americans, 2 American Indian/Alaska Native, 1 Asian American or Pacific Islander, 46 Hispanic Americans), 2 international. Average age 32. 111 applicants, 88% accepted, 35 enrolled. In 2009, 13 master's, 3 doctorates, 5 other advanced degrees awarded. *Degree requirements:* For master's, comprehensive exam, thesis optional, internship; for doctorate, comprehensive exam, thesis/dissertation, internship; for Ed S, thesis or alternative, internship. *Entrance requirements:* For master's, doctorate, and Ed S, GRE General Test, minimum GPA of 3.0. *Application deadline:* For fall admission, 12/15 for domestic students; for spring admission, 4/1 priority date for domestic students. Application fee: $30 ($50 for international students). Electronic applications accepted. *Expenses:* Tuition, state resident: full-time $4080; part-time $223 per credit. Tuition, nonresident: full-time $14,256; part-time $647 per credit. Required fees: $1278; $639 per semester. *Financial support:* In 2009–10, 13 research assistantships with partial tuition reimbursements (averaging $8,108 per year), 32 teaching assistantships with partial tuition reimbursements (averaging $8,239 per year) were awarded; fellowships with partial tuition reimbursements, career-related internships or fieldwork, Federal Work-Study, institutionally sponsored loans, scholarships/grants, traineeships, health care benefits, and unspecified assistantships also available. Support available to part-time students. Financial award application deadline: 4/1. *Faculty research:* Multicultural counseling, integrative health psychology group, career development school counseling. *Unit head:* Dr. Michael Waldo, Head, 575-646-2121, Fax: 575-646-8035, E-mail: miwaldo@nmsu.edu. *Application contact:* Elena Luna, Coordinator, 575-646-3498, Fax: 575-646-7721, E-mail: rosluna@nmsu.edu.

New York Institute of Technology, Graduate Division, School of Education, Program in Mental Health Counseling, Old Westbury, NY 11568-8000. Offers MS. *Students:* 8 full-time (7 women), 12 part-time (8 women); includes 8 minority (6 African Americans, 1 Asian American or Pacific Islander, 1 Hispanic American). Average age 33. In 2009, 4 master's awarded. *Degree requirements:* For master's, thesis, internship. *Entrance requirements:* For master's, minimum GPA of 3.0, interview, 3 letters of reference. Additional exam requirements/recommendations for international students: Required—TOEFL (minimum score 550 paper-based; 213 computer-based). *Application deadline:* For fall admission, 7/1 priority date for domestic students; for spring admission, 12/1 priority date for domestic students. Application fee: $50. *Expenses:* Tuition: Part-time $825 per credit. *Financial support:* Research assistantships with partial tuition reimbursements, career-related internships or fieldwork, institutionally sponsored loans, and unspecified assistantships available. Support available to part-time students. Financial award applicants required to submit FAFSA. *Unit head:* Dr. Carol Dahir, Coordinator, 516-686-7616, Fax: 516-686-7655, E-mail: cdahir@nyit.edu. *Application contact:* Jacquelyn Nealon, Dean of Admissions and Financial Aid, 516-686-7925, Fax: 516-686-7613, E-mail: jnealon@nyit.edu.

New York University, Steinhardt School of Culture, Education, and Human Development, Department of Applied Psychology, Program in Counselor Education, New York, NY 10012-1019. Offers counseling and guidance (MA, Advanced Certificate), including bilingual school counseling (MA), school counseling (MA); counseling for mental health and wellness (MA); counseling psychology (PhD). *Accreditation:* APA (one or more programs are accredited). Part-time programs available. *Students:* 123 full-time (89 women), 77 part-time (60 women); includes 72 minority (24 African Americans, 1 American Indian/Alaska Native, 24 Asian Americans or Pacific Islanders, 23 Hispanic Americans), 20 international. Average age 30. 769 applicants, 27% accepted, 80 enrolled. In 2009, 80 master's, 6 doctorates awarded. *Degree requirements:* For master's, thesis (for some programs); for doctorate, thesis/dissertation. *Entrance requirements:* For doctorate, GRE General Test, interview. Additional exam requirements/recommendations for international students: Required—TOEFL. *Application deadline:* For fall admission, 12/15 priority date for domestic and international students. Applications are processed on a rolling basis. Application fee: $75. Electronic applications accepted. *Expenses:* Tuition: Full-time $30,528; part-time $1272 per credit. Required fees: $2177. *Financial support:* Fellowships with full and partial tuition reimbursements, research assistantships, teaching assistantships with partial tuition reimbursements, career-related internships or fieldwork, Federal Work-Study, institutionally sponsored loans, scholarships/grants, tuition waivers (partial), and unspecified assistantships available. Support available to part-time students. Financial award application deadline: 2/1; financial award applicants required to submit FAFSA. *Faculty research:* Cross-cultural counseling; group dynamics; culture, race and ethnicity; religiosity and psychological development; well-being and mental health. *Application contact:* 212-998-5030, Fax: 212-995-4328, E-mail: steinhardt.gradadmissions@nyu.edu.

Nicholls State University, Graduate Studies, College of Education, Department of Psychology and Counselor Education, Thibodaux, LA 70310. Offers psychological counseling (MA); school psychology (SSP). *Accreditation:* NCATE. Part-time and evening/weekend programs available. *Degree requirements:* For master's, comprehensive exam; for SSP, comprehensive exam, internship. *Entrance requirements:* For master's, GRE General Test. Electronic applications accepted.

Northeastern State University, Graduate College, College of Education, Department of Psychology and Counseling, Program in Counseling Psychology, Tahlequah, OK 74464-2399. Offers MS. Part-time and evening/weekend programs available. *Degree requirements:* For master's, thesis, internship, practicum. *Entrance requirements:* For master's, GRE, minimum GPA of 2.5. Additional exam requirements/recommendations for international students: Required—TOEFL (minimum score 213 computer-based). Electronic applications accepted.

Northeastern University, Bouvé College of Health Sciences Graduate School, Department of Counseling and Applied Educational Psychology, Program in Counseling Psychology, Boston, MA 02115-5096. Offers MS, PhD, CAGS. *Accreditation:* APA (one or more programs are accredited). Part-time programs available. *Students:* 52 full-time (45 women), 4 part-time (3 women); includes 7 African Americans, 2 Asian Americans or Pacific Islanders, 5 Hispanic Americans, 6 international. 194 applicants, 33% accepted, 27 enrolled. In 2009, 15 master's, 7 doctorates awarded. *Degree requirements:* For doctorate, comprehensive exam, thesis/dissertation, qualifying exams; for CAGS, comprehensive exam. *Entrance requirements:* For master's and CAGS, GRE General Test or MAT; for doctorate, GRE General Test. Additional exam requirements/recommendations for international students: Required—TOEFL (minimum score 100 iBT). *Application deadline:* For fall admission, 6/1 for domestic and international students; for winter admission, 1/5 for domestic and international students. Applications are processed on a rolling basis. Application fee: $50. Electronic applications accepted. *Financial support:* In 2009–10, 2 teaching assistantships with full tuition reimbursements (averaging $13,832 per year) were awarded; career-related internships or fieldwork, Federal Work-Study, tuition waivers (partial), and unspecified assistantships also available. Support available to part-time students. Financial award application deadline: 3/1; financial award applicants required to submit FAFSA. *Faculty research:* Culture, gender and political psychology; child and adolescent counseling; health psychology forensic counseling; early intervention. *Unit head:* Dr. Mary B. Ballou, Director, 617-373-5937, Fax: 617-373-8892, E-mail: m.ballou@neu.edu. *Application contact:* Margaret Schnabel, Director of Graduate Admissions, 617-373-2708, E-mail: bouvegrad@neu.edu.

Northern Arizona University, Graduate College, College of Education, Program in Educational Psychology, Flagstaff, AZ 86011. Offers counseling psychology (PhD); learning and instruction (PhD); school psychology (PhD). *Faculty:* 20 full-time (10 women). *Students:* 13 full-time (9 women), 14 part-time (8 women); includes 5 minority (3 American Indian/Alaska Native, 1 Asian American or Pacific Islander, 1 Hispanic American). Average age 35. 14 applicants, 29% accepted, 4 enrolled. In 2009, 7 doctorates awarded. *Degree requirements:* For doctorate, comprehensive exam, thesis/dissertation, internship. *Entrance requirements:* For doctorate, GRE (verbal and quantitative). Additional exam requirements/recommendations for international students: Required—TOEFL (minimum score 550 paper-based; 213 computer-based; 80 iBT), IELTS (minimum score 7), or a bachelor's degree from an English-speaking university and demonstrated proficiency. *Application deadline:* For fall admission, 1/15 priority date for domestic students, 9/1 priority date for international students; for spring admission, 9/15 priority date for domestic students. Application fee: $65. Electronic applications accepted. *Financial support:* In 2009–10, 2 research assistantships with partial tuition reimbursements (averaging $10,000 per year), 8 teaching assistantships with partial tuition reimbursements (averaging $10,000 per year) were awarded; career-related internships or fieldwork, Federal Work-Study, health care benefits, tuition waivers, and unspecified assistantships also available. Support available to part-time students. Financial award application deadline: 3/30; financial award applicants required to submit FAFSA. *Unit head:* Dr. Kathy Bohan, Chair, 928-523-0362, Fax: 928-523-9284, E-mail: kathy.bohan@nau.edu. *Application contact:* Dr. Kathy Bohan, Chair, 928-523-0362, Fax: 928-523-9284, E-mail: kathy.bohan@nau.edu.

Northwestern Oklahoma State University, School of Professional Studies, Program in Counseling Psychology, Alva, OK 73717-2799. Offers MCP. Part-time programs available. *Faculty:* 5 full-time (2 women), 2 part-time/adjunct (1 woman). *Students:* 33 full-time (23 women), 33 part-time (26 women); includes 2 minority (1 African American, 1 American Indian/Alaska Native). Average age 31. 10 applicants, 90% accepted. In 2009, 9 master's awarded. *Degree requirements:* For master's, comprehensive exam. *Entrance requirements:* For master's, GRE General Test or MAT, minimum GPA of 2.75. *Application deadline:* Applications are processed on a rolling basis. Application fee: $15. *Financial support:* Fellowships, Federal Work-Study available. Support available to part-time students. Financial award application deadline: 5/1; financial award applicants required to submit FAFSA. *Unit head:* Dr. Nancy Knous, Coordinator, 580-327-8443. *Application contact:* Leah Haines, Coordinator of Graduate Studies, 580-327-8410, E-mail: ldhaines@nwosu.edu.

Northwestern University, The Graduate School, Interdepartmental Programs, Program in Counseling Psychology, Evanston, IL 60201. Offers MA. Admissions and degrees offered through The Graduate School. Part-time programs available. *Degree requirements:* For master's, comprehensive exam. *Entrance requirements:* For master's, GRE General Test. Electronic applications accepted. *Faculty research:* Family psychology, adult development and pathology, minority counseling, groups and systems, clinical training, stress and coping, health psychology.

Northwest University, College of Social and Behavioral Sciences, Kirkland, WA 98033. Offers counseling psychology (MA, Psy D); international care and community development (MA). Evening/weekend programs available. *Faculty:* 5 full-time (2 women), 11 part-time/adjunct (5 women). *Students:* 87 full-time (68 women), 30 part-time (26 women); includes 17 minority (5 African Americans, 6 Asian Americans or Pacific Islanders, 6 Hispanic Americans), 2 international. 156 applicants, 86% accepted, 77 enrolled. In 2009, 39 master's awarded. *Entrance requirements:* For master's, 3 character references. Additional exam requirements/recommendations for international students: Required—TOEFL (minimum score 580 paper-based; 237 computer-based). *Application deadline:* For fall admission, 12/1 priority date for domestic and international students; for spring admission, 4/1 priority date for domestic and international students. Applications are processed on a rolling basis. Application fee: $75. *Expenses:* Contact institution. *Financial support:* Career-related internships or fieldwork, health care benefits, and international student scholarships available. Financial award application deadline: 6/30. *Unit head:* Dr. William Herkelrath, Dean, 425-889-5328, Fax: 425-739-4602, E-mail: william.herkelrath@northwestu.edu. *Application contact:* Jon Troll, Director of Student Services, 425-889-5249, Fax: 425-739-4602, E-mail: jon.troll@northwestu.edu.

Nova Southeastern University, Center for Psychological Studies, Master's Programs in Counseling, Mental Health, School Guidance, and Clinical Pharmacology, Fort Lauderdale, FL 33314-7796. Offers clinical pharmacology (MS); mental health counseling (MS); school guidance and counseling (MS). Part-time and evening/weekend programs available. *Faculty:* 7 full-time (2 women), 27 part-time/adjunct (8 women). *Students:* 270 full-time (238 women), 586 part-time (521 women); includes 417 minority (186 African Americans, 14 Asian Americans or Pacific Islanders, 217 Hispanic Americans), 23 international. 562 applicants, 65% accepted, 262 enrolled. In 2009, 232 master's awarded. *Degree requirements:* For master's, comprehensive exam, 3 practica. *Entrance requirements:* Additional exam requirements/recommendations for international students: Required—TOEFL (minimum score 550 paper-based; 213 computer-based). *Application deadline:* For fall admission, 7/29 for domestic students; for winter admission, 11/29 for domestic students; for spring admission, 3/29 for domestic students. Applications are processed on a rolling basis. Application fee: $50. Electronic applications accepted. *Financial support:* Career-related internships or fieldwork, Federal Work-Study, and institutionally sponsored loans available. Financial award application deadline: 4/1. *Faculty research:* Clinical and child clinical psychology, geriatrics, interpersonal violence. *Unit head:* Karen S. Grosby, Dean, 954-262-5701, Fax: 954-262-3859. *Application contact:* Carlos Perez, Enrollment Management, 954-262-5790, Fax: 954-262-3893, E-mail: cpsinfo@cps.nova.edu.

Oakland University, Graduate Study and Lifelong Learning, School of Education and Human Services, Department of Counseling, Rochester, MI 48309-4401. Offers MA, PhD, Certificate. *Accreditation:* ACA (one or more programs are accredited). Part-time and evening/weekend programs available. *Degree requirements:* For doctorate, thesis/dissertation. *Entrance requirements:* Additional exam requirements/recommendations for international students: Required—TOEFL (minimum score 550 paper-based; 213 computer-based). Electronic applications accepted.

Ottawa University, Graduate Studies-Arizona, Program in Professional Counseling, Ottawa, KS 66067-3399. Offers Christian counseling (MA); expressive arts therapy (MA); marriage and family therapy (MA); treatment of trauma, abuse and deprivation (MA). Programs offered in Mesa, Phoenix, Tempe and West Valley, AZ. Part-time and evening/weekend programs available. Postbaccalaureate distance learning degree programs offered. *Degree requirements:* For master's, comprehensive exam, thesis or alternative, field experience, practicum. *Entrance requirements:* For master's, minimum undergraduate GPA of 3.0; course work in theories of personality, abnormal psychology, and human growth and development. Additional exam requirements/recommendations for international students: Required—TOEFL (minimum score 550 paper-based; 213 computer-based).

Our Lady of the Lake University of San Antonio, School of Professional Studies, Program in Psychology, San Antonio, TX 78207-4689. Offers counseling psychology (MS, Psy D); marriage and family therapy (MS); school psychology (MS). *Accreditation:* APA (one or more programs are accredited). Part-time and evening/weekend programs available. *Students:* 111 full-time (90 women), 84 part-time (75 women); includes 118 minority (19 African Americans, 1 American Indian/Alaska Native, 4 Asian Americans or Pacific Islanders, 94 Hispanic Americans), 5 international. Average age 30. In 2009, 42 master's, 3 doctorates awarded. *Degree requirements:* For master's, comprehensive exam, thesis optional, practicum; for doctorate, thesis/dissertation, internship, qualifying exam. *Entrance requirements:* For master's and doctorate, GRE General Test or MAT, interview. Additional exam requirements/recommendations for international students: Required—TOEFL. *Application deadline:* For fall admission, 3/1 priority date for domestic and international students. Applications are processed on a rolling basis. Application fee: $25 ($50 for international students). Electronic applications accepted. *Expenses:* Tuition: Full-time $12,330; part-time $685 per contact hour. Required fees: $139; $12 per contact hour. $57 per semester. Tuition and fees vary according to campus/location. *Financial support:* Research assistantships, teaching assistantships, career-related internships or fieldwork available. Support available to part-time students. Financial award application deadline: 4/15. *Faculty research:* Marriage and family therapy, supervision, cross-cultural counseling, violence. *Unit head:* Dr. Joan Biever, Chair, 210-434-6711, E-mail: jbiever@lake.ollusa.edu. *Application contact:* 210-434-6711, Fax: 210-431-4036, E-mail: gradadm@lake.ollusa.edu.

Pace University, Dyson College of Arts and Sciences, Department of Psychology, Program in Counseling-Substance Abuse, New York, NY 10038. Offers loss and grief (MS); mental health (MS); substance abuse (MS). Offered at Pleasantville, NY location only. Part-time and evening/weekend programs available. *Students:* 64 full-time (52 women), 49 part-time (42 women); includes 21 African Americans, 1 Asian American or Pacific Islander, 8 Hispanic Americans, 2 international. Average age 32. 95 applicants, 91% accepted, 38 enrolled. In 2009, 50 master's awarded. *Degree requirements:* For master's, comprehensive exam, qualifying exams, internship. *Entrance requirements:* For master's, GRE, interview. Additional exam requirements/recommendations for international students: Required—TOEFL. *Application deadline:* For fall admission, 8/1 priority date for domestic students; for spring admission, 12/1 priority date for domestic students. Applications are processed on a rolling basis. Application fee: $70. Electronic applications accepted. *Expenses:* Tuition: Part-time $954 per credit. Tuition and fees vary according to course load, degree level and program. *Financial support:* Research assistantships, teaching assistantships, career-related internships or fieldwork, Federal Work-Study, and tuition waivers (partial) available. Financial award applicants required to submit FAFSA. *Unit head:* Dr. Ross Robak, Head, 914-773-3673. *Application contact:* Joanna Broda, Director of Admissions, 914-422-4283, Fax: 914-422-4287, E-mail: gradwp@pace.edu.

Pacifica Graduate Institute, Graduate Programs, Carpinteria, CA 93013. Offers clinical psychology (PhD); counseling psychology (MA); depth psychology (MA, PhD); mythological studies (MA, PhD). Terminal master's awarded for partial completion of doctoral program. *Degree requirements:* For master's, thesis (for some programs), practicum; for doctorate, comprehensive exam, thesis/dissertation, internship. *Entrance requirements:* For master's, resume, 3 letters of recommendation, writing sample, interview; for doctorate, resumé, 4 letters of recommendation, writing sample, interview. Additional exam requirements/recommendations for international students: Required—TOEFL. *Faculty research:* Imaginal and archetypal theory; post-Colonial psychoanalytic and Jungian theory; myth literature as it applies to the theory and practice of psychology.

Palm Beach Atlantic University, School of Education and Behavioral Studies, West Palm Beach, FL 33416-4708. Offers counseling psychology (MSCP), including addictions/mental health, marriage and family therapy, mental health counseling, school guidance counseling. Part-time and evening/weekend programs available. *Faculty:* 16 full-time (8 women), 2 part-time/adjunct (0 women). *Students:* 230 full-time (193 women), 74 part-time (63 women); includes 109 minority (70 African Americans, 1 Asian American or Pacific Islander, 38 Hispanic Americans), 8 international. Average age 35. 136 applicants, 70% accepted, 88 enrolled. In 2009, 86 master's awarded. *Entrance requirements:* For master's, GRE, minimum GPA of 3.0. Additional exam requirements/recommendations for international students: Required—TOEFL (minimum score 550 paper-based; 213 computer-based). *Application deadline:* For fall admission, 7/15 priority date for domestic students; for spring admission, 11/15 priority date for domestic students. Applications are processed on a rolling basis. Application fee: $45. Electronic applications accepted. *Expenses:* Tuition: Full-time $8010; part-time $445 per credit hour. Required fees: $99 per semester. Tuition and fees vary according to course load and degree level. *Financial support:* Applicants required to submit FAFSA. *Unit head:* Dr. Lisa Stubbs, Program Director, 561-803-2286. *Application contact:* Graduate Admissions, 888-468-6722, Fax: 561-803-2115, E-mail: grad@pba.edu.

Penn State University Park, Graduate School, College of Education, Department of Counselor Education, Counseling Psychology and Rehabilitation Services, State College, University Park, PA 16802-1503. Offers M Ed, MS, D Ed, PhD. *Accreditation:* ACA (one or more programs are accredited); APA (one or more programs are accredited); NCATE.

Philadelphia College of Osteopathic Medicine, Graduate and Professional Programs, Department of Psychology, Philadelphia, PA 19131-1694. Offers clinical psychology (Psy D); counseling and clinical health psychology (MS); organizational leadership and development (MS); psychology (Certificate, Post-Doctoral Certificate); school psychology (MS, Psy D, Ed S). *Accreditation:* APA. *Degree requirements:* For master's, thesis; for doctorate, comprehensive exam, thesis/dissertation, final project, fieldwork. *Entrance requirements:* For master's, GRE or MAT, minimum GPA of 3.0; course work in biology, chemistry, English, physics; for other advanced degree, PRAXIS. *Faculty research:* Depression in primary care, integrated primary care, geriatric mental health.

See Close-Up on page 1091.

Phoenix Seminary, Graduate Programs, Scottsdale, AZ 85254. Offers biblical communication (M Div); biblical leadership (MA); biblical studies (Graduate Diploma); Christian counseling (Graduate Diploma); counseling and family (M Div); intercultural studies (Graduate Diploma); leadership development (M Div, Graduate Diploma); ministry (D Min); professional counseling (MA); women's studies (Graduate Diploma). *Accreditation:* ATS (one or more programs are accredited). Part-time and evening/weekend programs available. *Faculty:* 5 full-time (0 women), 5 part-time/adjunct (0 women). *Students:* 26 full-time (8 women), 151 part-time (39 women); includes 34 minority (18 African Americans, 2 American Indian/Alaska Native, 5 Asian Americans or Pacific Islanders, 9 Hispanic Americans), 1 international. 41 applicants, 90% accepted, 30 enrolled. In 2009, 21 master's, 2 doctorates, 12 other advanced degrees awarded. *Degree requirements:* For master's, 2 foreign languages, comprehensive exam; for doctorate, 2 foreign languages, thesis/dissertation. *Entrance requirements:* For master's, undergraduate degree with minimum GPA of 2.5; for doctorate, M Div (94 hours) with minimum GPA of 3.0. Additional exam requirements/recommendations for international students: Required—TOEFL (minimum score 587 paper-based; 240 computer-based; 92 iBT), TWE (minimum score 4.5). *Application deadline:* For fall admission, 7/1 for domestic students; for spring admission, 11/1 for domestic students. Applications are processed on a rolling basis. Application fee: $90. *Expenses:* Tuition: Full-time $9420; part-time $410 per credit hour. Required fees: $60 per semester. Tuition and fees vary according to course load and degree level. *Financial support:* Institutionally sponsored loans and scholarships/grants available. Support available to part-time students. Financial award application deadline: 6/1; financial award applicants required to submit FAFSA. *Application contact:* Roma Royer, Director of Admissions and Academic Services, 602-850-8000 Ext. 111, Fax: 602-850-8080, E-mail: rroyer@ps.edu.

Prescott College, Graduate Programs, Program in Counseling and Psychology, Prescott, AZ 86301. Offers adventure based psychotherapy (MA); counseling psychology (MA); ecopsychology (MA); ecotherapy (MA); equine-assisted mental health (MA); expressive arts therapy (MA); somatic psychology (MA); student-directed independent study (MA). Part-time programs available. Postbaccalaureate distance learning degree programs offered (minimal on-campus study). *Faculty:* 3 full-time (all women), 35 part-time/adjunct (25 women). *Students:* 65 full-time (47 women), 44 part-time (39 women); includes 8 minority (2 African Americans, 2 American Indian/Alaska Native, 4 Hispanic Americans), 9 international. Average age 38. 77 applicants, 77% accepted, 40 enrolled. In 2009, 34 master's awarded. *Degree requirements:* For master's, thesis, fieldwork or internship, practicum. *Entrance requirements:* For master's, 2 letters of recommendation, resume. Additional exam requirements/recommendations for international students: Required—TOEFL (minimum score 500 paper-based; 173 computer-based). *Application deadline:* For fall admission, 4/15 priority date for domestic and international students; for spring admission, 9/15 priority date for domestic and international students. Applications are processed on a rolling basis. Application fee: $40. Electronic applications accepted. *Expenses:* Tuition: Full-time $14,712; part-time $613 per credit. Required fees: $50 per term. One-time fee: $150. Tuition and fees vary according to course load and degree level. *Financial support:* Career-related internships or fieldwork, Federal Work-Study, and scholarships/grants available. Financial award applicants required to submit FAFSA. *Unit head:* Dr. Christine Frydenborg, Chair, Fax: 928-776-5151, E-mail: csmith@prescott.edu. *Application contact:* Kerstin Alicki, Admissions Counselor, 877-412-8705, Fax: 928-277-4695, E-mail: admissions@prescott.edu.

Providence College and Theological Seminary, Theological Seminary, Otterburne, MB R0A 1G0, Canada. Offers children's ministry (Certificate); Christian studies (MA, Certificate); counseling (MA); cross-cultural discipleship (Certificate); divinity (M Div); educational studies (MA), including counseling psychology, educational ministries, student development, teaching English to speakers of other languages, training teachers of English to speakers of other languages; global studies (MA); lay counseling (Diploma); ministry (D Min); teaching English to speakers of other languages (Certificate); theological studies (MA); training teacher of English to speakers of other languages (Certificate); youth ministry (Certificate). *Accreditation:* ATS. Part-time programs available. *Degree requirements:* For master's, variable foreign language requirement, thesis (for some programs); for doctorate, thesis/dissertation; for M Div, 2 foreign languages, comprehensive exam, thesis/dissertation (for some programs). *Entrance requirements:* Additional exam requirements/recommendations for international students: Recommended—

Counseling Psychology

Providence College and Theological Seminary (continued)
TOEFL (minimum score 550 paper-based; 213 computer-based). *Faculty research:* Studies in Isaiah, theology of sin.

Purdue University Calumet, Graduate School, School of Education, Program in Counseling, Hammond, IN 46323-2094. Offers human services (MS Ed); mental health counseling (MS Ed); school counseling (MS Ed). *Entrance requirements:* Additional exam requirements/recommendations for international students: Required—TOEFL.

Quincy University, Program in Counseling, Quincy, IL 62301-2699. Offers clinical mental health counseling (MS Ed); school counseling (MS Ed). Part-time and evening/weekend programs available. *Faculty:* 2 full-time (0 women), 1 part-time/adjunct (0 women). *Students:* 10 full-time (8 women), 21 part-time (16 women); includes 2 African Americans. In 2009, 12 master's awarded. *Degree requirements:* For master's, comprehensive exam, practicum, internship. *Entrance requirements:* For master's, MAT or GRE. Additional exam requirements/recommendations for international students: Required—TOEFL. *Application deadline:* Applications are processed on a rolling basis. Application fee: $25. Electronic applications accepted. *Expenses:* Tuition: Full-time $8400; part-time $350 per credit hour. Required fees: $360; $15 per credit hour. Tuition and fees vary according to course load, campus/location and program. *Financial support:* Available to part-time students. Applicants required to submit FAFSA. *Unit head:* Dr. Kenneth Oliver, Director, 217-228-5432 Ext. 3113, E-mail: oliveke@quincy.edu. *Application contact:* Jennifer O'Donnell, Coordinator of Adult Studies, 217-228-5404, Fax: 217-228-5479, E-mail: admissions@quincy.edu.

Radford University, College of Graduate and Professional Studies, College of Education and Human Development, Department of Counselor Education, Radford, VA 24142. Offers community counseling (MS); school counseling (MS); student affairs—administration (MS); student affairs—counseling (MS). *Accreditation:* ACA; NCATE. Part-time and evening/weekend programs available. *Faculty:* 7 full-time (4 women), 20 part-time/adjunct (13 women). *Students:* 62 full-time (50 women), 60 part-time (50 women); includes 11 minority (8 African Americans, 1 American Indian/Alaska Native, 1 Asian American or Pacific Islander, 1 Hispanic American). Average age 29. 85 applicants, 88% accepted, 38 enrolled. In 2009, 53 master's awarded. *Degree requirements:* For master's, comprehensive exam, thesis optional. *Entrance requirements:* For master's, GRE or MAT, minimum GPA of 2.75, 3 letters of reference. Additional exam requirements/recommendations for international students: Required—TOEFL (minimum score 550 paper-based; 213 computer-based; 79 iBT). *Application deadline:* For fall admission, 4/15 priority date for domestic students, 12/1 for international students. Applications are processed on a rolling basis. Application fee: $50. Electronic applications accepted. *Expenses:* Tuition, state resident: full-time $5086; part-time $211 per credit hour. Tuition, nonresident: full-time $12,608; part-time $525 per credit hour. Required fees: $2508; $105 per credit hour. *Financial support:* In 2009–10, 27 students received support, including 11 research assistantships with partial tuition reimbursements available (averaging $8,000 per year), 9 teaching assistantships with partial tuition reimbursements available (averaging $8,700 per year); career-related internships or fieldwork, Federal Work-Study, institutionally sponsored loans, scholarships/grants, and unspecified assistantships also available. Financial award application deadline: 3/1; financial award applicants required to submit FAFSA. *Unit head:* Dr. Alan Forrest, Chair, 540-831-5487, Fax: 540-831-6755, E-mail: aforrest@radford.edu. *Application contact:* Graduate Admissions, 540-831-5431, Fax: 540-831-6061, E-mail: gradcollege@radford.edu.

Radford University, College of Graduate and Professional Studies, College of Humanities and Behavioral Sciences, Program in Counseling Psychology, Radford, VA 24142. Offers Psy D. *Faculty:* 5 full-time (3 women). *Students:* 7 full-time (5 women). Average age 28. 7 applicants, 86% accepted, 2 enrolled. *Degree requirements:* For doctorate, thesis/dissertation. *Entrance requirements:* For doctorate, GRE General Test, master's degree; minimum GPA of 3.5; letter of interest; curriculum vitae; writing sample; 3 letters of recommendation. Additional exam requirements/recommendations for international students: Required—TOEFL (minimum score 550 paper-based; 213 computer-based; 79 iBT). *Application deadline:* For fall admission, 1/15 priority date for domestic students, 12/1 for international students. Applications are processed on a rolling basis. Application fee: $50. Electronic applications accepted. *Expenses:* Tuition, state resident: full-time $5086; part-time $211 per credit hour. Tuition, nonresident: full-time $12,608; part-time $525 per credit hour. Required fees: $2508; $105 per credit hour. *Financial support:* In 2009–10, 7 students received support, including 7 research assistantships with full tuition reimbursements available (averaging $13,800 per year); career-related internships or fieldwork, Federal Work-Study, institutionally sponsored loans, and scholarships/grants also available. Financial award application deadline: 3/1; financial award applicants required to submit FAFSA. *Unit head:* Dr. James L. Werth, Program Director, 540-831-6817, Fax: 540-831-6113, E-mail: jwerth@radford.edu. *Application contact:* Graduate Admissions, 540-831-5431, Fax: 540-831-6061, E-mail: gradcollege@radford.edu.

Regent University, Graduate School, School of Psychology and Counseling, Virginia Beach, VA 23464-9800. Offers clinical psychology (MA, Psy D); counseling (MA), including community counseling, human services counseling, school counseling; counseling studies (CAGS); counselor education and supervision (PhD); M Div/MA; M Ed/MA; MBA/MA. PhD program offered online only. *Accreditation:* ACA; APA (one or more programs are accredited). Part-time and evening/weekend programs available. Postbaccalaureate distance learning degree programs offered (minimal on-campus study). *Faculty:* 24 full-time (12 women), 19 part-time/adjunct (12 women). *Students:* 209 full-time (171 women), 189 part-time (137 women); includes 107 minority (92 African Americans, 4 Asian Americans or Pacific Islanders, 11 Hispanic Americans), 14 international. Average age 34. 417 applicants, 50% accepted, 104 enrolled. In 2009, 108 master's, 40 doctorates awarded. *Degree requirements:* For master's, thesis or alternative, internship, practicum, written competency exam; for doctorate, thesis/dissertation or alternative. *Entrance requirements:* For master's, GRE General Test including writing exam, minimum undergraduate GPA of 2.75, 3 recommendations, resume, transcripts, writing sample; for doctorate, GRE General Test including writing exam, GRE Subject Test, minimum undergraduate GPA of 3.0, 3.5 (PhD), 10-15 minute VHS tape demonstrating counseling skills, writing sample, 3 recommendations, resume. Additional exam requirements/recommendations for international students: Required—TOEFL (minimum score 577 paper-based; 233 computer-based). *Application deadline:* For fall admission, 4/1 priority date for domestic students; for spring admission, 11/1 priority date for domestic students. Applications are processed on a rolling basis. Application fee: $50. Electronic applications accepted. *Expenses:* Contact institution. *Financial support:* In 2009–10, 368 students received support; research assistantships with full and partial tuition reimbursements available, teaching assistantships with full and partial tuition reimbursements available, career-related internships or fieldwork, scholarships/grants, and tuition waivers (full and partial) available. Support available to part-time students. Financial award application deadline: 9/1; financial award applicants required to submit FAFSA. *Faculty research:* Marriage enrichment, AIDS counseling, troubled youth, faith and learning, trauma. *Unit head:* Dr. William Hathaway, Acting Dean, 757-352-4294, Fax: 757-352-4282, E-mail: willhat@regent.edu. *Application contact:* Matthew Chadwick, Director of Admissions, 800-373-5504, Fax: 757-352-4381, E-mail: admissions@regent.edu.

Regis University, College for Professional Studies, Graduate Counseling Program, Denver, CO 80221-1099. Offers community counseling (MAC); counseling children and adolescents (Post-Graduate Certificate); marriage and family therapy (Post-Graduate Certificate). Program offered in Henderson and Las Vegas (Summerlin), NV. *Accreditation:* ACA. Part-time and evening/weekend programs available. *Degree requirements:* For master's, internships, practicum. *Entrance requirements:* For master's, interview, 2 recommendations, resume, criminal background check. Additional exam requirements/recommendations for international students: Required—TOEFL (minimum score 213 computer-based), TWE (minimum score 5). *Expenses:* Contact institution. *Faculty research:* Group Development, Counselor Education, Counsel and Therapy, Influence of Technology on Psychology, Dream finding groups, Adult Development, Depression.

Richmont Graduate University, Graduate Programs, Atlanta, GA 30327. Offers Christian psychological studies (MS); marriage and family therapy (MA); professional counseling (MA).

Rivier College, School of Graduate Studies, Department of Education, Nashua, NH 03060. Offers curriculum and instruction (M Ed); early childhood education (M Ed); educational administration (M Ed); educational studies (M Ed); elementary education (M Ed); elementary education and general special education (M Ed); emotional and behavioral disorders (M Ed); general social education (M Ed); leadership and learning (Ed D, CAGS); learning disabilities (M Ed); learning disabilities and reading (M Ed); mental health counseling (MA); reading (M Ed); school counseling (M Ed). Part-time and evening/weekend programs available. *Faculty:* 13 full-time (9 women), 38 part-time/adjunct (25 women). *Students:* 87 full-time (78 women), 293 part-time (246 women); includes 10 minority (3 African Americans, 4 Asian Americans or Pacific Islanders, 3 Hispanic Americans). Average age 38. 182 applicants, 82% accepted, 72 enrolled. In 2009, 110 master's, 18 other advanced degrees awarded. *Degree requirements:* For master's, comprehensive exam (for some programs), internships. *Entrance requirements:* For master's, GRE General Test or MAT. *Application deadline:* Applications are processed on a rolling basis. Application fee: $25. *Expenses:* Tuition: Part-time $447 per credit. *Financial support:* Available to part-time students. Application deadline: 2/1. *Unit head:* Dr. Patricia Howson, Chairman, 603-897-8562, E-mail: phowson@rivier.edu. *Application contact:* Mathew Kittredge, Director of Graduate Admissions, 603-897-8129, Fax: 603-897-8810, E-mail: mkittredge@rivier.edu.

Rosemont College, Schools of Graduate and Professional Studies, Program in Counseling Psychology, Rosemont, PA 19010-1699. Offers human services (MA); school counseling (MA). Part-time and evening/weekend programs available. *Degree requirements:* For master's, thesis or alternative, practicum. *Entrance requirements:* For master's, minimum undergraduate GPA of 3.0, 3 letters of recommendation. Additional exam requirements/recommendations for international students: Required—TOEFL. Electronic applications accepted. *Expenses:* Contact institution. *Faculty research:* Addictions counseling.

Rowan University, Graduate School, College of Liberal Arts and Sciences, Department of Psychology, Program in Mental Health Counseling, Glassboro, NJ 08028-1701. Offers MA. Part-time and evening/weekend programs available. *Students:* 1 (woman) full-time, 15 part-time (13 women); includes 2 minority (1 African American, 1 Asian American or Pacific Islander). Average age 31. In 2009, 8 master's awarded. *Degree requirements:* For master's, thesis. *Entrance requirements:* For master's, GRE General Test. Additional exam requirements/recommendations for international students: Required—TOEFL. *Application deadline:* For spring admission, 2/15 for domestic students. Applications are processed on a rolling basis. Application fee: $50. Electronic applications accepted. *Expenses:* Tuition, state resident: full-time $10,624; part-time $590 per semester hour. Tuition, nonresident: full-time $10,624; part-time $590 per semester hour. Required fees: $2320; $125 per semester hour. *Financial support:* Career-related internships or fieldwork, scholarships/grants, health care benefits, and unspecified assistantships available. *Unit head:* Dr. Mira Lalovic-Hand, Interim Associate Provost/Director of Graduate School, 856-256-5120, E-mail: lalovic-hand@rowan.edu. *Application contact:* Karen Haynes, Graduate Coordinator, 856-256-4052, Fax: 856-256-4436, E-mail: haynes@rowan.edu.

Rowan University, Graduate School, College of Liberal Arts and Sciences, Program in Mental Health Counseling and Applied Psychology, Glassboro, NJ 08028-1701. Offers MA. Part-time and evening/weekend programs available. *Students:* 8 full-time (all women), 21 part-time (18 women); includes 4 minority (3 African Americans, 1 Asian American or Pacific Islander). Average age 31. 32 applicants, 72% accepted, 22 enrolled. In 2009, 31 master's awarded. *Degree requirements:* For master's, thesis. *Entrance requirements:* For master's, GRE General Test. Additional exam requirements/recommendations for international students: Required—TOEFL. *Application deadline:* Applications are processed on a rolling basis. Application fee: $50. Electronic applications accepted. *Expenses:* Tuition, state resident: full-time $10,624; part-time $590 per semester hour. Tuition, nonresident: full-time $10,624; part-time $590 per semester hour. Required fees: $2320; $125 per semester hour. *Financial support:* Career-related internships or fieldwork, scholarships/grants, health care benefits, and unspecified assistantships available. *Unit head:* Dr. Mira Lalovic-Hand, Interim Associate Provost/Director of Graduate School, 856-256-5120, E-mail: lalovic-hand@rowan.edu. *Application contact:* Karen Haynes, Graduate Coordinator, 856-256-4052, Fax: 856-256-4436, E-mail: haynes@rowan.edu.

Rutgers, The State University of New Jersey, New Brunswick, Graduate School of Education, Department of Educational Psychology, Program in Counseling Psychology, Piscataway, NJ 08854-8097. Offers Ed M. Part-time and evening/weekend programs available. *Entrance requirements:* For master's, GRE General Test, 3 letters of recommendation. Additional exam requirements/recommendations for international students: Required—TOEFL (minimum score 550 paper-based; 233 computer-based; 83 iBT). Electronic applications accepted. *Faculty research:* Children and family in a cross-cultural context, attachment theory, multicultural counseling, therapy relationship.

Sage Graduate School, Graduate School, School of Health Sciences, Department of Psychology, Program in Counseling and Community Psychology, Troy, NY 12180-4115. Offers MA. *Faculty:* 3 full-time (all women), 5 part-time/adjunct (3 women). *Students:* 27 full-time (26 women), 41 part-time (37 women); includes 10 minority (6 African Americans, 1 American Indian/Alaska Native, 3 Hispanic Americans). Average age 27. 64 applicants, 41% accepted, 11 enrolled. In 2009, 16 master's awarded. *Degree requirements:* For master's, externship, internship, thesis or research seminar. *Entrance requirements:* For master's, minimum undergraduate GPA of 3.0, interview. *Application deadline:* Applications are processed on a rolling basis. Application fee: $40. *Expenses:* Tuition: Full-time $10,620; part-time $590 per credit hour. *Unit head:* Dr. Jean Poppei, Chair, 518-244-2076, Fax: 518-244-4545, E-mail: poppei@sage.edu. *Application contact:* Wendy D. Diefendorf, Director of Graduate and Adult Admission, 518-244-2443, Fax: 518-244-6880, E-mail: diefew@sage.edu.

St. Bonaventure University, School of Graduate Studies, School of Education, Program in Counselor Education, St. Bonaventure, NY 14778-2284. Offers community mental health counseling (MS Ed); school counseling (MS Ed); school counselor (Adv C). *Accreditation:* ACA. Part-time and evening/weekend programs available. *Faculty:* 7 full-time (2 women), 6 part-time/adjunct (2 women). *Students:* 80 full-time (65 women), 31 part-time (20 women); includes 7 minority (3 African Americans, 1 American Indian/Alaska Native, 3 Hispanic Americans), 1 international. Average age 30. 116 applicants, 65% accepted, 51 enrolled. In 2009, 36 master's, 5 Adv Cs awarded. *Degree requirements:* For master's, comprehensive exam, thesis optional. *Entrance requirements:* For master's, interview, writing sample, minimum undergraduate GPA of 3.0. Additional exam requirements/recommendations for international students: Required—TOEFL (minimum score 550 paper-based; 240 computer-based; 95 iBT). *Application deadline:* For fall admission, 8/1 priority date for domestic students, 12/15 for international students; for spring admission, 10/15 priority date for domestic students, 3/15 for international students. Applications are processed on a rolling basis. Application fee: $30. *Expenses:* Tuition: Full-time $11,700; part-time $650 per credit. *Financial support:* In 2009–10, 7 students received support, including 9 research assistantships with full and partial tuition reimbursements available; career-related internships or fieldwork and scholarships/grants also available. Support available to part-time students. Financial award application deadline: 4/15; financial award applicants required to submit FAFSA. *Faculty research:* Parent education, learning disabilities, stress management, cyber bullying. *Unit head:* Dr. Craig Zuckerman, Director, 716-375-2374, Fax: 716-375-2360, E-mail: czuck@sbu.edu. *Application contact:* Bruce Campbell, Director of Graduate Admissions, 716-375-2429, E-mail: gradsch@sbu.edu.

St. Edward's University, New College, Program in Counseling, Austin, TX 78704. Offers MA. Part-time and evening/weekend programs available. *Students:* 68 full-time (55 women), 162 part-time (135 women); includes 40 minority (12 African Americans, 4 American Indian/Alaska Native, 3 Asian Americans or Pacific Islanders, 21 Hispanic Americans). Average age 34. 99 applicants, 70% accepted, 58 enrolled. In 2009, 72 master's awarded. *Degree requirements:*

For master's, minimum of 24 resident hours. *Entrance requirements:* For master's, GRE General Test, minimum GPA of 3.0 in last 60 hours or 2.75 overall. Additional exam requirements/recommendations for international students: Required—TOEFL (minimum score 550 paper-based; 213 computer-based; 79 iBT) or IELTS (minimum score 6). *Application deadline:* For fall admission, 7/1 for domestic and international students; for spring admission, 11/1 for domestic and international students. Applications are processed on a rolling basis. Application fee: $45 ($50 for international students). Electronic applications accepted. *Expenses:* Tuition: Full-time $14,922; part-time $829 per credit hour. Required fees: $50 per trimester. Full-time tuition and fees vary according to course load and program. *Financial support:* In 2009–10, 6 students received support. Scholarships/grants available. *Unit head:* Dr. Elizabeth Katz, Director, 512-464-8833, Fax: 512-448-8492, E-mail: elizk@stedwards.edu. *Application contact:* Anna Alkin, Graduate Admissions Coordinator, 512-448-8745, Fax: 512-428-1032, E-mail: annaa@stedwards.edu.

St. Edward's University, School of Management and Business, Program in Human Services, Austin, TX 78704. Offers administration (Certificate); conflict resolution (Certificate); family mediation (Certificate); human services (MA), including administration, conflict resolution, human resource management, organization development and training, social and psychological services; mediation (Certificate); organization development and training (Certificate). Part-time and evening/weekend programs available. *Students:* 4 full-time (3 women), 51 part-time (43 women); includes 24 minority (9 African Americans, 2 Asian Americans or Pacific Islanders, 13 Hispanic Americans). Average age 34. 23 applicants, 96% accepted, 18 enrolled. In 2009, 19 master's awarded. *Degree requirements:* For master's, minimum of 24 resident hours. *Entrance requirements:* For master's, GRE General Test, GMAT, minimum GPA of 2.75 in last 60 hours of course work. Additional exam requirements/recommendations for international students: Required—TOEFL (minimum score 550 paper-based; 213 computer-based; 79 iBT) or IELTS (minimum score 6). *Application deadline:* For fall admission, 7/1 for domestic and international students; for spring admission, 11/1 for domestic and international students. Applications are processed on a rolling basis. Application fee: $45 ($50 for international students). Electronic applications accepted. *Expenses:* Tuition: Full-time $14,922; part-time $829 per credit hour. Required fees: $50 per trimester. Full-time tuition and fees vary according to course load and program. *Financial support:* In 2009–10, 2 students received support. Scholarships/grants available. *Faculty research:* Leadership development, organizational management, public policy. *Unit head:* Dr. Constance D. Porter, Director, 512-416-5827, Fax: 512-448-8492, E-mail: constanp@stedwards.edu. *Application contact:* Kay L. Arnold, Assistant Director of Admissions, 512-233-1636, Fax: 512-428-1032, E-mail: kayla@stedwards.edu.

St. John Fisher College, Wegmans School of Nursing, Program in Mental Health Counseling, Rochester, NY 14618-3597. Offers MS. *Accreditation:* ACA. Part-time programs available. *Faculty:* 4 full-time (2 women), 2 part-time/adjunct (0 women). *Students:* 32 full-time (28 women), 28 part-time (25 women); includes 9 minority (5 African Americans, 4 Hispanic Americans). Average age 31. 75 applicants, 51% accepted, 27 enrolled. In 2009, 14 master's awarded. *Degree requirements:* For master's, practicum experience, internship. *Entrance requirements:* For master's, GRE (if GPA below 3.0), 2 letters of recommendation, personal statement, current resume, undergraduate course work in abnormal psychology, interview. Additional exam requirements/recommendations for international students: Required—TOEFL (minimum score 575 paper-based; 233 computer-based; 80 iBT). *Application deadline:* Applications are processed on a rolling basis. Application fee: $30. Electronic applications accepted. *Expenses:* Tuition: Part-time $680 per credit hour. Required fees: $25 per semester. Tuition and fees vary according to degree level and program. *Financial support:* In 2009–10, 47 students received support. Federal Work-Study and scholarships/grants available. Financial award applicants required to submit FAFSA. *Faculty research:* Social class issues, clinical supervision, counselor education, play therapy. *Unit head:* Dr. Signe M. Kastberg, Director, 585-385-7222, E-mail: skastberg@sjfc.edu. *Application contact:* Jose Perales, Director of Graduate Admissions, 585-385-8067, E-mail: jperales@sjfc.edu.

Saint Joseph College, Department of Counselor Education, West Hartford, CT 06117-2700. Offers community counseling (MA); school counseling (MA). Part-time and evening/weekend programs available. *Students:* 42 full-time (37 women), 94 part-time (83 women); includes 20 minority (16 African Americans, 4 Hispanic Americans). *Degree requirements:* For master's, comprehensive exam, thesis optional. *Entrance requirements:* For master's, 2 letters of recommendation. *Application deadline:* Applications are processed on a rolling basis. Application fee: $50. Electronic applications accepted. *Expenses:* Tuition: Part-time $595 per credit. Required fees: $30 per credit. Tuition and fees vary according to program. *Financial support:* Career-related internships or fieldwork and unspecified assistantships available. Support available to part-time students. Financial award applicants required to submit FAFSA. *Application contact:* Graduate Admissions Office, 860-231-5261, E-mail: graduate@sjc.edu.

Saint Martin's University, Graduate Programs, Program in Counseling Psychology, Lacey, WA 98503. Offers MAC. Part-time and evening/weekend programs available. *Faculty:* 3 full-time (2 women), 3 part-time/adjunct (all women). *Students:* 40 full-time (29 women), 58 part-time (52 women); includes 14 minority (3 African Americans, 1 American Indian/Alaska Native, 6 Asian Americans or Pacific Islanders, 4 Hispanic Americans), 1 international. Average age 36. 24 applicants, 79% accepted, 18 enrolled. In 2009, 17 master's awarded. *Degree requirements:* For master's, clinical experience, interview. *Entrance requirements:* For master's, BA in psychology or related field, clinical experience. Additional exam requirements/recommendations for international students: Required—TOEFL. *Application deadline:* For fall admission, 7/1 for domestic students, 2/15 for international students; for spring admission, 11/1 priority date for domestic students, 7/1 for international students. Applications are processed on a rolling basis. Application fee: $35. *Expenses:* Tuition: Full-time $12,440; part-time $827 per credit hour. *Financial support:* In 2009–10, 97 students received support. Career-related internships or fieldwork, Federal Work-Study, and institutionally sponsored loans available. Support available to part-time students. Financial award application deadline: 3/1. *Faculty research:* Alcohol studies, clinical effectiveness, social justice, parent adolescent interaction. *Unit head:* Dr. Godfrey J. Ellis, Director, 360-438-4560, E-mail: gellis@stmartin.edu. *Application contact:* Sandy Brandt, Administrative Assistant, 360-438-4560, E-mail: sbrandt@stmartin.edu.

St. Mary's University, Graduate School, Department of Counseling and Human Services, Program in Mental Health, San Antonio, TX 78228-8507. Offers MA. Part-time programs available. *Degree requirements:* For master's, comprehensive exam, internship. *Entrance requirements:* For master's, GRE, MAT. Additional exam requirements/recommendations for international students: Required—TOEFL (minimum score 550 paper-based; 213 computer-based; 80 iBT). Electronic applications accepted. *Expenses:* Tuition: Full-time $8004. Required fees: $536. One-time fee: $5 full-time. Full-time tuition and fees vary according to program.

Saint Mary's University of Minnesota, Schools of Graduate and Professional Programs, Graduate School of Health and Human Services, Counseling and Psychological Services Program, Winona, MN 55987-1399. Offers MA. *Unit head:* Dr. Christina Huck, Director, 612-728-5113, Fax: 612-728-5121, E-mail: chuck@smumn.edu. *Application contact:* Yasin Alsaidi, Director of Admissions for Graduate and Professional Programs, 612-728-5207, Fax: 612-728-5121, E-mail: yalsaidi@smumn.edu.

Saint Paul University, Faculty of Human Sciences, Program in Counseling and Spirituality, Ottawa, ON K1S 1C4, Canada. Offers individual or marital/couple counseling (MA); spiritual care (MA). Part-time programs available. *Degree requirements:* For master's, research project or thesis. *Entrance requirements:* For master's, honors BA in human sciences, minimum B average, 12 theology credits.

St. Thomas University, Biscayne College, Department of Social Sciences and Counseling, Program in Mental Health Counseling, Miami Gardens, FL 33054-6459. Offers MS. Part-time and evening/weekend programs available. *Degree requirements:* For master's, comprehensive exam. *Entrance requirements:* For master's, interview, minimum GPA of 3.0 or GRE. Additional exam requirements/recommendations for international students: Required—TOEFL (minimum score 550 paper-based; 213 computer-based; 79 iBT). Electronic applications accepted.

Saint Xavier University, Graduate Studies, School of Arts and Sciences, Department of Psychology, Chicago, IL 60655-3105. Offers adult counseling (Certificate); child/adolescent counseling (Certificate); core counseling (Certificate); counseling psychology (MA). Part-time and evening/weekend programs available. *Entrance requirements:* For master's, GRE General Test, minimum GPA of 3.0, interview. *Expenses:* Tuition: Part-time $743 per credit hour. Required fees: $135 per semester.

Salem State College, School of Graduate Studies, Program in Counseling and Psychological Services, Salem, MA 01970-5353. Offers MS. Part-time and evening/weekend programs available. *Students:* 41 full-time (32 women), 41 part-time (31 women); includes 7 minority (1 African American, 6 Hispanic Americans), 2 international. Average age 33. 22 applicants, 95% accepted, 21 enrolled. In 2009, 19 master's awarded. *Entrance requirements:* For master's, GRE or MAT. Additional exam requirements/recommendations for international students: Required—TOEFL (minimum score 550 paper-based; 80 iBT), or IELTS (minimum score 5.5). *Application deadline:* For fall admission, 5/1 for domestic students; for spring admission, 10/1 for domestic students. Applications are processed on a rolling basis. Application fee: $50. *Expenses:* Tuition, state resident: full-time $2520; part-time $275 per credit hour. Tuition, nonresident: full-time $4140; part-time $365 per credit hour. Required fees: $2430. *Financial support:* In 2009–10, 6 students received support. Career-related internships or fieldwork, Federal Work-Study, scholarships/grants, and unspecified assistantships available. Support available to part-time students. Financial award application deadline: 5/1; financial award applicants required to submit FAFSA. *Unit head:* Dr. Patrice Miller, Coordinator, 978-542-6075, Fax: 978-542-6596, E-mail: pmiller@salemstate.edu. *Application contact:* Dr. Lee A. Brossoit, Assistant Dean of Graduate Admissions, 978-542-6673, Fax: 978-542-7215, E-mail: lbrossoit@salemstate.edu.

Salem State College, School of Graduate Studies, Program of Advanced Professional Studies in Counseling, Salem, MA 01970-5353. Offers Graduate Certificate. Part-time and evening/weekend programs available. *Students:* 7 part-time (5 women), 1 international. Average age 32. 4 applicants, 50% accepted, 2 enrolled. *Entrance requirements:* Additional exam requirements/recommendations for international students: Required—TOEFL (minimum score 550 paper-based; 80 iBT), or IELTS (minimum score 5.5). *Application deadline:* For fall admission, 5/1 for domestic students; for spring admission, 10/1 for domestic students. Applications are processed on a rolling basis. Application fee: $50. *Expenses:* Tuition, state resident: full-time $2520; part-time $275 per credit hour. Tuition, nonresident: full-time $4140; part-time $365 per credit hour. Required fees: $2430. *Financial support:* Career-related internships or fieldwork, Federal Work-Study, scholarships/grants, and unspecified assistantships available. Support available to part-time students. Financial award application deadline: 5/1; financial award applicants required to submit FAFSA. *Unit head:* Dr. Patrice Miller, Program Coordinator, 978-542-6075, Fax: 978-542-7215, E-mail: pmiller@salemstate.edu. *Application contact:* Dr. Lee A. Brossoit, Assistant Dean of Graduate Admissions, 978-542-6675, Fax: 978-542-7215, E-mail: lbrossoit@salemstate.edu.

Salve Regina University, Graduate Studies, Holistic Graduate Programs, Newport, RI 02840-4192. Offers expressive and creative arts (CAGS); holistic counseling (MA); holistic leadership (MA, CAGS); mental health (CAGS). Part-time and evening/weekend programs available. *Faculty:* 4 full-time (2 women), 9 part-time/adjunct (6 women). *Students:* 17 full-time (15 women), 73 part-time (64 women). Average age 42. 32 applicants, 81% accepted, 20 enrolled. In 2009, 7 master's, 18 other advanced degrees awarded. *Degree requirements:* For master's, internship, project. *Entrance requirements:* For master's, GMAT, GRE General Test, or MAT. Additional exam requirements/recommendations for international students: Required—TOEFL (minimum score 600 paper-based; 250 computer-based; 100 iBT), or IELTS. *Application deadline:* For fall admission, 3/15 priority date for domestic and international students; for spring admission, 9/15 priority date for domestic and international students. Applications are processed on a rolling basis. Application fee: $60. Electronic applications accepted. *Expenses:* Tuition: Part-time $395 per credit. Part-time tuition and fees vary according to degree level. *Financial support:* Career-related internships or fieldwork and Federal Work-Study available. Support available to part-time students. Financial award application deadline: 3/1; financial award applicants required to submit FAFSA. *Unit head:* Dr. Peter F. Mullen, Director, 401-341-3278, Fax: 401-341-2977, E-mail: mullenp@salve.edu. *Application contact:* Kelly Alverson, Graduate Admissions Counselor, 401-341-2153, Fax: 401-341-2973, E-mail: kelly.alverson@salve.edu.

Salve Regina University, Graduate Studies, Program in Rehabilitation Counseling, Newport, RI 02840-4192. Offers mental health counseling (CAGS); rehabilitation counseling (MA). Part-time and evening/weekend programs available. *Faculty:* 1 (woman) full-time, 4 part-time/adjunct (all women). *Students:* 16 full-time (14 women), 28 part-time (22 women); includes 2 minority (both Hispanic Americans). Average age 35. 23 applicants, 83% accepted, 16 enrolled. In 2009, 4 master's, 6 other advanced degrees awarded. *Entrance requirements:* For master's, GMAT, GRE General Test or MAT. Additional exam requirements/recommendations for international students: Required—TOEFL (minimum score 600 paper-based; 250 computer-based; 100 iBT), IELTS. *Application deadline:* For fall admission, 3/15 priority date for domestic and international students; for spring admission, 9/15 priority date for domestic and international students. Applications are processed on a rolling basis. Application fee: $60. Electronic applications accepted. *Expenses:* Tuition: Part-time $395 per credit. Part-time tuition and fees vary according to degree level. *Financial support:* Career-related internships or fieldwork and Federal Work-Study available. Support available to part-time students. Financial award application deadline: 3/1; financial award applicants required to submit FAFSA. *Unit head:* Dr. Dimity Peter, Director, 401-341-3189, Fax: 401-341-2993, E-mail: dimity.peter@salve.edu. *Application contact:* Kelly Alverson, Graduate Admissions Counselor, 401-341-2153, Fax: 401-341-2973, E-mail: kelly.alverson@salve.edu.

San Francisco State University, Division of Graduate Studies, College of Health and Human Services, Department of Counseling, San Francisco, CA 94132-1722. Offers counseling (MS); marriage, family, and child counseling (MSC); rehabilitation counseling (MS). *Accreditation:* ACA (one or more programs are accredited). Part-time programs available.

Santa Clara University, School of Education and Counseling Psychology, Department of Counseling Psychology, Program in Counseling Psychology, Santa Clara, CA 95053. Offers counseling psychology (MA), including career development, correctional psychology, health psychology, Latino counseling. Part-time and evening/weekend programs available. *Students:* 89 full-time (82 women), 113 part-time (90 women); includes 55 minority (1 African American, 21 Asian Americans or Pacific Islanders, 33 Hispanic Americans), 6 international. Average age 32. 88 applicants, 72% accepted, 40 enrolled. In 2009, 59 master's awarded. *Degree requirements:* For master's, comprehensive exam, thesis optional. *Entrance requirements:* For master's, GRE or MAT, minimum GPA of 3.0, 1 year of related experience. Additional exam requirements/recommendations for international students: Required—TOEFL. *Application deadline:* Applications are processed on a rolling basis. *Expenses:* Contact institution. *Financial support:* Fellowships, Federal Work-Study, institutionally sponsored loans, and scholarships/grants available. Support available to part-time students. Financial award application deadline: 5/15; financial award applicants required to submit FAFSA.

Saybrook University, LIOS Graduate College, Systems Counseling Track, San Francisco, CA 94111-1920. Offers MA. *Degree requirements:* For master's, thesis (for some programs), oral exams. *Entrance requirements:* For master's, bachelor's degree from an accredited university or college. *Faculty research:* Family systems theory, marriage and family therapy, systems consultation, family and culture of origin, personal authority.

The School of Professional Psychology at Forest Institute, Graduate Programs, Springfield, MO 65807. Offers clinical psychology (MA, Psy D); counseling psychology (MA); marriage and family therapy (MA, PGC). *Accreditation:* AAMFT/COAMFTE; APA (one or more programs are accredited). *Faculty:* 18 full-time (9 women), 18 part-time/adjunct (10 women). *Students:* 214 full-time (144 women), 46 part-time (35 women); includes 35 minority (11 African Americans, 9 American Indian/Alaska Native, 5 Asian Americans or Pacific Islanders, 10 Hispanic Americans),

Counseling Psychology

The School of Professional Psychology at Forest Institute (continued)

3 international. Average age 28. 176 applicants, 69% accepted, 45 enrolled. In 2009, 35 master's, 31 doctorates awarded. Terminal master's awarded for partial completion of doctoral program. *Degree requirements:* For master's, thesis, practicum; for doctorate, comprehensive exam, thesis/dissertation, internship, practicum. *Entrance requirements:* For master's, GRE General Test, interview, minimum GPA of 3.0, 12 hours in psychology; for doctorate, GRE General Test, interview, minimum GPA of 3.0, 18 hours in psychology. Additional exam requirements/recommendations for international students: Required—TOEFL (minimum score 550 paper-based; 213 computer-based). *Application deadline:* For fall admission, 1/15 priority date for domestic and international students; for spring admission, 8/1 priority date for domestic and international students. Applications are processed on a rolling basis. Application fee: $50. Electronic applications accepted. *Expenses:* Tuition: Full-time $23,625; part-time $675 per credit hour. Required fees: $275 per semester. Tuition and fees vary according to course load and program. *Financial support:* In 2009–10, 59 students received support, including 5 fellowships with partial tuition reimbursements available (averaging $7,200 per year), 11 teaching assistantships (averaging $100 per year); career-related internships or fieldwork, Federal Work-Study, scholarships/grants, tuition waivers (partial), and unspecified assistantships also available. Financial award applicants required to submit FAFSA. *Faculty research:* Forensics/corrections, marriage and family therapy, child and adolescent, integrated health care, neuropsychology. *Unit head:* Dr. Mark E. Skrade, President, 417-823-3477, Fax: 417-823-3442, E-mail: mskrade@forest.edu. *Application contact:* Bethany Ritter, Admissions Counselor, 417-823-3477, Fax: 417-823-3442, E-mail: britter@forest.edu.

Seton Hall University, College of Education and Human Services, Department of Professional Psychology and Family Therapy, Program in Counseling Psychology, South Orange, NJ 07079-2697. Offers MA, PhD. *Accreditation:* APA. *Faculty:* 5 full-time (1 woman). *Students:* 32 full-time (22 women), 118 part-time (94 women); includes 35 minority (19 African Americans, 5 Asian Americans or Pacific Islanders, 11 Hispanic Americans), 2 international. Average age 35. 133 applicants, 39% accepted, 28 enrolled. In 2009, 75 master's, 4 doctorates awarded. *Degree requirements:* For doctorate, comprehensive exam, thesis/dissertation, internship. *Entrance requirements:* For doctorate, GRE, interview. *Application deadline:* For fall admission, 1/15 for domestic students. Application fee: $50. *Financial support:* In 2009–10, 1 research assistantship with full tuition reimbursement (averaging $4,500 per year) was awarded; career-related internships or fieldwork also available. Financial award application deadline: 2/1. *Faculty research:* Vocational indecision, coping skills, cognitive behavioral interventions, vocational development. *Application contact:* Information Contact, 973-761-9451.

Shippensburg University of Pennsylvania, School of Graduate Studies, College of Education and Human Services, Department of Counseling, Shippensburg, PA 17257-2299. Offers Adlerian studies (Certificate); advanced study in counseling (Certificate); alcohol and drug counseling (Certificate); counseling (M Ed, MS), including college counseling (MS), community counseling (MS), elementary school counseling, mental health counseling (MS), secondary school counseling (MS), student personnel services (MS); couple and family counseling (Certificate). *Accreditation:* ACA (one or more programs are accredited); NCATE. Part-time and evening/weekend programs available. *Degree requirements:* For master's, fieldwork, research project, internship, candidacy. *Entrance requirements:* For master's, GRE or MAT (community, mental health, student personnel, and college counseling applicants if GPA is less than 2.75), minimum GPA of 2.75 (3.0 for M Ed), interview, resume, 3 letters of recommendation, supplemental data forms, one year of relevant work experience, on-campus interview. Additional exam requirements/recommendations for international students: Required—TOEFL (minimum score 560 paper-based; 220 computer-based); Recommended—IELTS (minimum score 6). Electronic applications accepted.

Simpson University, MA in Counseling Psychology Program, Redding, CA 96003-8606. Offers MA. Evening/weekend programs available. *Faculty:* 2 full-time (1 woman), 5 part-time/adjunct (4 women). *Students:* 15 full-time (10 women); includes 1 Asian American or Pacific Islander, 1 Hispanic American, 1 international. 21 applicants, 86% accepted, 15 enrolled. *Degree requirements:* For master's, completed portfolio, clinical evaluation project. *Entrance requirements:* For master's, BA, minimum GPA of 3.0, resume, 3 letters of recommendation, personal statement, official transcripts. Additional exam requirements/recommendations for international students: Required—TOEFL (minimum score 550 paper-based; 213 computer-based; 79 iBT). *Application deadline:* For fall admission, 4/15 for domestic and international students; for winter admission, 9/15 for domestic and international students. Application fee: $50. Electronic applications accepted. *Financial support:* Applicants required to submit FAFSA. *Faculty research:* Development of executive functioning in young children, cognitive neuropsychology, historical issues in the neurosciences, neurotheology. *Unit head:* Adeline Jackson, Director, 530-226-4788, E-mail: ajackson@simpsonu.edu. *Application contact:* Kim Snow, Enrollment Counselor, Graduate Studies, 530-226-4633, Fax: 530-226-4861, E-mail: ksnow@simpsonu.edu.

Sonoma State University, School of Social Sciences, Department of Counseling, Rohnert Park, CA 94928. Offers counseling (MA); marriage, family, and child counseling (MA); pupil personnel services (MA). *Accreditation:* ACA. Part-time programs available. *Faculty:* 2 full-time (1 woman), 8 part-time/adjunct (5 women). *Students:* 58 full-time (42 women), 26 part-time (22 women); includes 8 minority (1 American Indian/Alaska Native, 1 Asian American or Pacific Islander, 6 Hispanic Americans), 1 international. Average age 33. 148 applicants, 28% accepted, 13 enrolled. In 2009, 40 master's awarded. *Degree requirements:* For master's, internship. *Entrance requirements:* For master's, minimum GPA of 3.0. Additional exam requirements/recommendations for international students: Required—TOEFL (minimum score 500 paper-based; 173 computer-based). *Application deadline:* For fall admission, 11/30 for domestic students. Application fee: $55. *Expenses:* Tuition, nonresident: full-time $11,160. Required fees: $6226. Full-time tuition and fees vary according to course load. *Financial support:* Career-related internships or fieldwork available. Financial award application deadline: 3/2; financial award applicants required to submit FAFSA. *Unit head:* Jaymala Madathil, Program Coordinator, 707-664-4067, E-mail: jaymala.madathil@sonoma.edu. *Application contact:* Stephanie Wilkinson, Administrative Analyst, 707-664-2544, Fax: 707-664-2038, E-mail: stephanie.wilkinson@sonoma.edu.

Southeastern University, Department of Behavioral and Social Sciences, Lakeland, FL 33801-6099. Offers human services (MA); professional counseling (MS); school counseling (MS). Evening/weekend programs available.

Southeast Missouri State University, School of Graduate Studies, Department of Educational Leadership and Counseling, Counseling Program, Cape Girardeau, MO 63701-4799. Offers counseling education (Ed S); mental health counseling (MA); school counseling (MA), including elementary counseling, secondary counseling. *Accreditation:* ACA; NCATE. Part-time and evening/weekend programs available. *Degree requirements:* For master's, comprehensive exam, thesis optional, portfolio, oral exam; for Ed S, oral exam. *Entrance requirements:* For master's, GRE General Test, MAT, minimum undergraduate GPA of 3.0; for Ed S, GRE General Test or MAT, minimum graduate GPA of 3.5. Additional exam requirements/recommendations for international students: Required—TOEFL (minimum score 550 paper-based; 213 computer-based); Recommended—IELTS (minimum score 6). Electronic applications accepted. *Expenses:* Tuition, state resident: full-time $4266; part-time $237 per credit hour. Tuition, nonresident: full-time $7506; part-time $417 per credit hour. Required fees: $427; $427. *Faculty research:* Counselor development, cognitive development of counselors, counselor supervision, issues in school counseling, issues in mental health counseling.

Southern Adventist University, School of Education and Psychology, Collegedale, TN 37315-0370. Offers clinical mental health counseling (MS); inclusive education (MS Ed); instructional leadership (MS Ed); literacy education (MS Ed); outdoor teacher education (MS Ed); school counseling (MS). *Accreditation:* NCATE. Part-time and evening/weekend programs available. *Faculty:* 4 full-time (2 women), 8 part-time/adjunct (5 women). *Students:* 33 full-time (15 women), 17 part-time (13 women); includes 16 minority (7 African Americans, 9 Hispanic Americans). Average age 30. In 2009, 23 master's awarded. *Degree requirements:* For master's, comprehensive exam (for some programs), thesis optional, position paper (MS), portfolio (MS Ed in outdoor teacher education). *Entrance requirements:* For master's, interview (MS); 9 semester hours of upper division course work in psychology or related field, including 1 course in psychology research or statistics; 9 semester hours of education (MS Ed). Additional exam requirements/recommendations for international students: Required—TOEFL (minimum score 600 paper-based; 250 computer-based; 100 iBT). *Application deadline:* For fall admission, 7/1 priority date for domestic students, 6/1 priority date for international students; for winter admission, 11/1 priority date for domestic students, 10/1 priority date for international students; for spring admission, 4/1 priority date for domestic students, 3/1 priority date for international students. Applications are processed on a rolling basis. Application fee: $25. Electronic applications accepted. *Expenses:* Tuition: Full-time $13,149; part-time $487 per credit hour. *Financial support:* In 2009–10, 7 students received support, including 1 research assistantship with full tuition reimbursement available (averaging $15,000 per year), 5 teaching assistantships with full tuition reimbursements available (averaging $15,000 per year); career-related internships or fieldwork, scholarships/grants, tuition waivers (partial), and unspecified assistantships also available. Support available to part-time students. Financial award application deadline: 4/1; financial award applicants required to submit FAFSA. *Unit head:* Dr. Wesley Taylor, Dean, 423-236-2444, Fax: 423-236-1765, E-mail: jwtv@southern.edu. *Application contact:* Mikhaile Spence, Information Contact, 423-236-2496, Fax: 423-236-1765, E-mail: maspence@southern.edu.

Southern Arkansas University–Magnolia, Graduate Programs, Magnolia, AR 71753. Offers agriculture (MS); business administration (MBA); computer and information sciences (MS); counseling (MS); education (M Ed), including counseling and development, curriculum and instruction emphasis, educational administration and supervision, elementary education, middle level emphasis, reading emphasis, secondary education, TESOL emphasis; kinesiology (MS); library media and information specialist (M Ed); mental health and clinical counseling (MS); public administration (EMPA); school counseling (M Ed); teaching (MAT). *Accreditation:* NCATE. Part-time and evening/weekend programs available. *Faculty:* 43 full-time (24 women), 12 part-time/adjunct (7 women). *Students:* 116 full-time (78 women), 333 part-time (255 women); includes 105 minority (98 African Americans, 3 American Indian/Alaska Native, 3 Asian Americans or Pacific Islanders, 1 Hispanic American), 11 international. Average age 33. In 2009, 88 master's awarded. *Degree requirements:* For master's, comprehensive exam, thesis optional. *Entrance requirements:* For master's, GRE, MAT or GMAT, minimum GPA of 2.75. *Application deadline:* For fall admission, 8/15 for domestic students; for winter admission, 1/8 for domestic students; for spring admission, 1/8 for domestic students. Applications are processed on a rolling basis. Application fee: $0. *Expenses:* Tuition, state resident: full-time $3798; part-time $211 per hour. Tuition, nonresident: full-time $5580; part-time $310 per hour. Required fees: $584. *Financial support:* Career-related internships or fieldwork, Federal Work-Study, scholarships/grants, tuition waivers (full), and unspecified assistantships available. Financial award applicants required to submit FAFSA. *Faculty research:* Alternative certification for teachers, supervision of instruction, instructional leadership, counseling. *Unit head:* Dr. Kim Bloss, Dean, Graduate Studies, 870-235-4150, Fax: 870-235-5227, E-mail: kkbloss@saumag.edu. *Application contact:* Dr. Kim Bloss, Dean, Graduate Studies, 870-235-4150, Fax: 870-235-5227, E-mail: kkbloss@saumag.edu.

Southern California Seminary, Graduate and Professional Programs, El Cajon, CA 92019. Offers biblical studies (MA); counseling psychology (MACP); psychology (Psy D); religious studies (MRS); theology (M Div). Part-time and evening/weekend programs available. Postbaccalaureate distance learning degree programs offered (minimal on-campus study). *Degree requirements:* For master's, thesis (for some programs); for doctorate, thesis/dissertation; for M Div, 2 foreign languages. *Entrance requirements:* For doctorate, master's degree in psychology. Additional exam requirements/recommendations for international students: Required—TOEFL (minimum score 550 paper-based). Electronic applications accepted.

Southern Illinois University Carbondale, Graduate School, College of Liberal Arts, Department of Psychology, Carbondale, IL 62901-4701. Offers clinical psychology (MA, MS, PhD); counseling psychology (MA, MS, PhD); experimental psychology (MA, MS, PhD). *Accreditation:* APA (one or more programs are accredited). *Degree requirements:* For master's, thesis; for doctorate, thesis/dissertation. *Entrance requirements:* For master's, GRE General Test, GRE Subject Test, minimum GPA of 2.7; for doctorate, GRE General Test, GRE Subject Test, minimum GPA of 3.25. Additional exam requirements/recommendations for international students: Required—TOEFL. *Faculty research:* Developmental neuropsychology; smoking, affect, and cognition; personality measurement; vocational psychology; program evaluation.

Southern Nazarene University, Graduate College, School of Psychology, Bethany, OK 73008. Offers counseling psychology (MSCP); marriage and family therapy (MA). *Degree requirements:* For master's, thesis optional. *Entrance requirements:* For master's, English proficiency exam, minimum GPA of 3.0 in last 60 hours/major, 2.7 overall.

Southern Oregon University, Graduate Studies, College of Arts and Sciences, Department of Psychology, Ashland, OR 97520. Offers mental health counseling (MAP). Part-time programs available. *Degree requirements:* For master's, thesis, portfolio and oral defense. *Entrance requirements:* For master's, GRE General Test, minimum GPA of 3.0. Electronic applications accepted.

South University, Graduate Programs, College of Arts and Sciences, Program in Professional Counseling, Savannah, GA 31406. Offers MA.

See Close-Up on page 1101.

South University, Program in Professional Counseling, Montgomery, AL 36116-1120. Offers MA.

See Close-Up on page 1097.

South University, Program in Professional Counseling, Columbia, SC 29203. Offers MA.

See Close-Up on page 1095.

South University, Program in Professional Counseling, Royal Palm Beach, FL 33411. Offers MA.

See Close-Up on page 1105.

South University, Program in Professional Counseling, Glen Allen, VA 23060. Offers MA.

See Close-Up on page 1099.

South University, Program in Professional Counseling, Virginia Beach, VA 23452. Offers MA.

See Close-Up on page 1103.

Southwestern Assemblies of God University, Thomas F. Harrison School of Graduate Studies, Program in Counseling Psychology, Waxahachie, TX 75165-5735. Offers counseling psychology (clinical) (MCP); human services counseling (MS). Part-time programs available. *Degree requirements:* For master's, comprehensive written and oral exams. *Entrance requirements:* For master's, GRE General Test, minimum GPA of 2.5. Electronic applications accepted.

Southwestern College, Program in Art Therapy/Counseling, Santa Fe, NM 87502-4788. Offers MA. Part-time and evening/weekend programs available. *Faculty:* 3 full-time (2 women), 8 part-time/adjunct (all women). *Students:* 22 full-time (20 women), 24 part-time (all women); includes 1 American Indian/Alaska Native, 1 Asian American or Pacific Islander, 4 Hispanic Americans. Average age 33. 40 applicants, 88% accepted, 31 enrolled. In 2009, 22 master's awarded. *Degree requirements:* For master's, internship. *Entrance requirements:* For master's, resume, slide portfolio, interview, 3 letters of reference. Additional exam requirements/

recommendations for international students: Required—TOEFL. *Application deadline:* For fall admission, 6/1 priority date for domestic students; for winter admission, 10/15 priority date for domestic students; for spring admission, 1/30 priority date for domestic students. Applications are processed on a rolling basis. Application fee: $50. *Financial support:* In 2009–10, 35 students received support. Career-related internships or fieldwork, institutionally sponsored loans, and scholarships/grants available. Support available to part-time students. Financial award application deadline: 6/15; financial award applicants required to submit FAFSA. *Unit head:* Debbie Schroder, Chair, 505-471-5756. *Application contact:* Dru Phoenix, Director of Admissions, 505-471-5756 Ext. 26, Fax: 505-471-4071, E-mail: admissions@swc.edu.

Southwestern College, Program in Counseling, Santa Fe, NM 87502-4788. Offers MA. Part-time and evening/weekend programs available. *Faculty:* 5 full-time (4 women), 20 part-time/adjunct (13 women). *Students:* 31 full-time (25 women), 36 part-time (31 women); includes 7 Hispanic Americans, 1 international. Average age 37. 44 applicants, 39% accepted, 17 enrolled. In 2009, 20 master's awarded. *Degree requirements:* For master's, internship. *Entrance requirements:* For master's, resume, 3 letters of reference, interview. Additional exam requirements/recommendations for international students: Required—TOEFL. *Application deadline:* For fall admission, 6/1 priority date for domestic students; for winter admission, 10/15 priority date for domestic students; for spring admission, 1/15 priority date for domestic students. Applications are processed on a rolling basis. Application fee: $50. *Financial support:* In 2009–10, 52 students received support. Career-related internships or fieldwork, institutionally sponsored loans, and scholarships/grants available. Support available to part-time students. Financial award application deadline: 6/15; financial award applicants required to submit FAFSA. *Unit head:* Dr. Carol Parker, Chair, 877-471-5756 Ext. 13. *Application contact:* Dru Phoenix, Director of Admissions, 505-471-5756 Ext. 26, Fax: 505-471-4071, E-mail: admissions@swc.edu.

Southwestern College, Program in Grief, Loss and Trauma Counseling, Santa Fe, NM 87502-4788. Offers MA, Certificate. Part-time and evening/weekend programs available. Postbaccalaureate distance learning degree programs offered (minimal on-campus study). *Students:* Average age 37. In 2009, 11 other advanced degrees awarded. *Entrance requirements:* For master's, interview, references, resume; for Certificate, 3 letters of reference, interview. *Application deadline:* Applications are processed on a rolling basis. *Unit head:* Dr. Janet Schreiber, Director, Fax: 877-471-4071. *Application contact:* Dru Phoenix, Director of Admissions, 505-471-5756 Ext. 26, Fax: 505-471-4071, E-mail: admissions@swc.edu.

Spring Arbor University, School of Graduate and Professional Studies, Spring Arbor, MI 49283-9799. Offers counseling (MAC); family studies (MAFS); nursing (MSN); organizational management (MAOM). Part-time and evening/weekend programs available. Postbaccalaureate distance learning degree programs offered (no on-campus study). *Faculty:* 8 full-time (3 women), 99 part-time/adjunct (45 women). *Students:* 412 full-time (327 women), 420 part-time (351 women); includes 215 minority (182 African Americans, 2 American Indian/Alaska Native, 10 Asian Americans or Pacific Islanders, 21 Hispanic Americans), 3 international. Average age 40. In 2009, 257 master's awarded. *Entrance requirements:* For master's, minimum GPA of 3.0, interview, writing sample, 2 professional references. Additional exam requirements/recommendations for international students: Required—TOEFL (minimum score 550 paper-based; 220 computer-based). *Application deadline:* Applications are processed on a rolling basis. Application fee: $40. Electronic applications accepted. *Expenses:* Tuition: Full-time $5400; part-time $450 per credit hour. Required fees: $240; $150 per year. Tuition and fees vary according to course load and program. *Financial support:* Scholarships/grants available. Support available to part-time students. Financial award applicants required to submit FAFSA. *Unit head:* Dr. Robert Hamill, Dean of Graduate and Professional Studies, 517-750-1200 Ext. 1343, Fax: 517-750-6602, E-mail: rhamill@arbor.edu. *Application contact:* Greg Bentle, Coordinator of Graduate Recruitment, 517-750-6763, Fax: 517-750-6624, E-mail: gbentle@arbor.edu.

Springfield College, Graduate Programs, Program in Human Services, Springfield, MA 01109-3797. Offers human services (MS), including community counseling psychology, mental health counseling, organizational management and leadership. Part-time programs available. *Degree requirements:* For master's, comprehensive exam, thesis (for some programs), research project. *Entrance requirements:* For master's, GRE. Additional exam requirements/recommendations for international students: Required—TOEFL (minimum score 550 paper-based; 213 computer-based). Electronic applications accepted. *Expenses:* Contact institution.

Springfield College, Graduate Programs, Programs in Psychology and Counseling, Springfield, MA 01109-3797. Offers athletic counseling (M Ed, MS, CAGS); industrial/organizational psychology (M Ed, MS, CAGS); marriage and family therapy (M Ed, MS, CAGS); mental health counseling (M Ed, MS, CAGS); school guidance and counseling (M Ed, MS, CAGS); student personnel in higher education (M Ed, MS, CAGS). Part-time programs available. *Degree requirements:* For master's, research project, portfolio. *Entrance requirements:* Additional exam requirements/recommendations for international students: Required—TOEFL (minimum score 550 paper-based; 213 computer-based). Electronic applications accepted. *Expenses:* Tuition: Full-time $19,800; part-time $825 per credit hour. Required fees: $150.

Stanford University, School of Education, Program in Psychological Studies in Education, Stanford, CA 94305-9991. Offers child and adolescent development (PhD); counseling psychology (PhD); educational psychology (PhD). *Degree requirements:* For doctorate, thesis/dissertation. *Entrance requirements:* For doctorate, GRE General Test. Electronic applications accepted. *Expenses:* Tuition: Full-time $37,380; part-time $2760 per quarter. Required fees: $501.

State University of New York at New Paltz, Graduate School, School of Liberal Arts and Sciences, Department of Psychology, New Paltz, NY 12561. Offers mental health counseling (MS); psychology (MA); school counseling (MS). Part-time and evening/weekend programs available. *Faculty:* 11 full-time (8 women), 1 (woman) part-time/adjunct. *Students:* 40 full-time (33 women), 11 part-time (7 women); includes 3 minority (1 African American, 1 Asian American or Pacific Islander, 1 Hispanic American), 3 international. Average age 26. 113 applicants, 44% accepted, 33 enrolled. In 2009, 24 master's awarded. *Degree requirements:* For master's, comprehensive exam, thesis. *Entrance requirements:* For master's, GRE General Test, minimum GPA of 3.0. Additional exam requirements/recommendations for international students: Required—TOEFL (minimum score 550 paper-based; 213 computer-based; 80 iBT), IELTS (minimum score 6.5). *Application deadline:* For fall admission, 1/20 priority date for domestic and international students; for spring admission, 11/15 for domestic and international students. Application fee: $50. Electronic applications accepted. *Financial support:* In 2009–10, 7 students received support, including 6 teaching assistantships with partial tuition reimbursements available (averaging $5,000 per year); career-related internships or fieldwork, Federal Work-Study, institutionally sponsored loans, traineeships, tuition waivers (full), and unspecified assistantships also available. Financial award application deadline: 8/1; financial award applicants required to submit FAFSA. *Faculty research:* Disaster mental health, women's objectification, mate selection, cultural psychology, achievement motivation. *Unit head:* Dr. Glenn Geher, Chair, 845-257-3091, E-mail: geherg@newpaltz.edu. *Application contact:* Dr. Jonathan Raskin, Coordinator, 845-257-3471, E-mail: raskinj@newpaltz.edu.

State University of New York at Oswego, Graduate Studies, School of Education, Department of Counseling and Psychological Services, Program in Counseling Services, Oswego, NY 13126. Offers MS, CAS, MS/CAS. *Degree requirements:* For master's, comprehensive exam, fieldwork; for CAS, thesis, fieldwork. *Entrance requirements:* For master's, GRE General Test, interview, minimum GPA of 3.0; for CAS, GRE General Test, GRE Subject Test, 18 hours of course work in behavioral science or education, interview, minimum GPA of 3.0. Additional exam requirements/recommendations for international students: Required—TOEFL (minimum score 560 paper-based; 220 computer-based). *Faculty research:* Psychological applications in education and human services, evaluation of standard tests for admissions criteria.

State University of New York at Oswego, Graduate Studies, School of Education, Department of Counseling and Psychological Services, Program in Human Services/Counseling, Oswego, NY 13126. Offers MS. Part-time programs available. *Degree requirements:* For master's, comprehensive exam. *Entrance requirements:* For master's, GRE General Test, interview, minimum GPA of 3.0. Additional exam requirements/recommendations for international students: Required—TOEFL (minimum score 560 paper-based; 220 computer-based).

Stephens College, Division of Graduate and Continuing Studies, Programs in Counseling, Columbia, MO 65215-0002. Offers counseling (M Ed), including marriage and family therapy, professional counseling, school counseling. Part-time and evening/weekend programs available. *Faculty:* 1 (woman) full-time, 11 part-time/adjunct (10 women). *Students:* 130 full-time (116 women), 32 part-time (28 women); includes 16 minority (13 African Americans, 2 Asian Americans or Pacific Islanders, 1 Hispanic American). Average age 33. 47 applicants, 68% accepted, 28 enrolled. In 2009, 35 master's awarded. *Degree requirements:* For master's, thesis. *Entrance requirements:* For master's, minimum GPA of 3.0 in last 60 hours. Additional exam requirements/recommendations for international students: Required—TOEFL (minimum score 213 computer-based). *Application deadline:* For fall admission, 7/25 priority date for domestic and international students; for winter admission, 12/1 priority date for domestic and international students; for spring admission, 4/25 priority date for domestic and international students. Applications are processed on a rolling basis. Application fee: $40. Electronic applications accepted. *Expenses:* Tuition: Part-time $350 per credit. Required fees: $25 per credit. *Financial support:* In 2009–10, 70 students received support. Scholarships/grants and unspecified assistantships available. Financial award application deadline: 12/5; financial award applicants required to submit FAFSA. *Unit head:* Dr. Linda Thompson, Program Chair, 800-388-7579. *Application contact:* Meredith Julian, Assistant Director of Marketing and Recruitment, 800-388-7579, E-mail: online@stephens.edu.

Suffolk University, College of Arts and Sciences, Department of Education and Human Services, Program in Mental Health Counseling, Boston, MA 02108-2770. Offers MS, CAGS, MPA/MSMHC. Part-time programs available. *Entrance requirements:* For master's, GRE General Test or MAT, statement of professional goals, official transcripts, 2 letters of recommendation, resume. Application fee: $50. *Expenses:* Tuition: Full-time $33,000; part-time $1100 per credit. Required fees: $20. Tuition and fees vary according to program. *Unit head:* Dr. David Medoff, Director, 617-573-8540, Fax: 617-305-1743. *Application contact:* Judith Reynolds, Director of Graduate Admissions, 617-573-8302, Fax: 617-305-1733, E-mail: grad.admission@suffolk.edu.

Tarleton State University, College of Graduate Studies, College of Education, Department of Psychology and Counseling, Stephenville, TX 76402. Offers counseling and psychology (M Ed), including counseling, counseling psychology, educational psychology; educational administration (M Ed); secondary education (Certificate); special education (Certificate). Part-time and evening/weekend programs available. Postbaccalaureate distance learning degree programs offered (minimal on-campus study). *Degree requirements:* For master's, comprehensive exam, thesis optional. *Entrance requirements:* For master's, GRE General Test, minimum GPA of 3.0. Additional exam requirements/recommendations for international students: Required—TOEFL (minimum score 550 paper-based; 213 computer-based; 80 iBT). Electronic applications accepted.

Teachers College, Columbia University, Graduate Faculty of Education, Department of Counseling and Clinical Psychology, Program in Counseling Psychology, New York, NY 10027-6696. Offers Ed M, Ed D, PhD. *Accreditation:* APA (one or more programs are accredited). Part-time programs available. *Faculty:* 7 full-time (4 women). *Students:* 180 full-time (155 women), 96 part-time (89 women); includes 91 minority (42 African Americans, 25 Asian Americans or Pacific Islanders, 24 Hispanic Americans), 31 international. Average age 27. 512 applicants, 45% accepted, 99 enrolled. In 2009, 168 master's, 6 doctorates awarded. *Degree requirements:* For doctorate, thesis/dissertation. *Entrance requirements:* For doctorate, GRE General Test. *Application deadline:* For fall admission, 5/15 for domestic students. Application fee: $65. *Financial support:* Fellowships, research assistantships, teaching assistantships, career-related internships or fieldwork, Federal Work-Study, institutionally sponsored loans, and tuition waivers (full and partial) available. Support available to part-time students. Financial award application deadline: 2/1. *Faculty research:* Career development, mentoring racial identity, adult development, gender issues. *Unit head:* Maria Miville, Head, 212-678-3257. *Application contact:* Melba Remice, Assistant Director of Admission, 212-678-4035, Fax: 212-678-4171, E-mail: ms2545@columbia.edu.

Teachers College, Columbia University, Graduate Faculty of Education, Department of Counseling and Clinical Psychology, Program in Psychological Counseling, New York, NY 10027-6696. Offers Ed M.

Temple University, Graduate School, College of Education, Department of Psychological Studies in Education, Counseling Psychology Program, Philadelphia, PA 19122-6096. Offers Ed M, PhD. *Accreditation:* APA (one or more programs are accredited). Part-time programs available. Terminal master's awarded for partial completion of doctoral program. *Degree requirements:* For master's, thesis or alternative; for doctorate, thesis/dissertation. *Entrance requirements:* For master's, GRE General Test or MAT, minimum GPA of 2.8; for doctorate, GRE General Test, GRE Subject Test in psychology. *Faculty research:* Multi-cultural and diversity training, health psychology/supervision/addictions.

Tennessee State University, The School of Graduate Studies and Research, College of Education, Department of Psychology, Nashville, TN 37209-1561. Offers counseling and guidance (MS), including counseling, elementary school counseling, organizational counseling, secondary school counseling; counseling psychology (PhD); psychology (MS, PhD); school psychology (MS, PhD). *Accreditation:* APA. *Degree requirements:* For doctorate, thesis/dissertation (for some programs). *Entrance requirements:* For master's, GRE General Test or MAT; for doctorate, GRE General Test or MAT, minimum GPA of 3.25, work experience. Electronic applications accepted.

Texas A&M International University, Office of Graduate Studies and Research, College of Arts and Sciences, Department of Behavioral, Applied Sciences, and Criminal Justice, Laredo, TX 78041-1900. Offers counseling psychology (MACP); criminal justice (MS); psychology (MS); sociology (MA). *Faculty:* 8 full-time (3 women), 1 part-time/adjunct (0 women). *Students:* 13 full-time (8 women), 88 part-time (63 women); includes 94 minority (1 African American, 93 Hispanic Americans). Average age 30. 68 applicants, 69% accepted, 47 enrolled. In 2009, 14 master's awarded. *Degree requirements:* For master's, thesis (for some programs). *Entrance requirements:* For master's, GRE General Test. Additional exam requirements/recommendations for international students: Required—TOEFL (minimum score 550 paper-based; 213 computer-based). *Application deadline:* For fall admission, 4/30 priority date for domestic students; for spring admission, 11/30 for domestic students. Applications are processed on a rolling basis. Application fee: $25. *Financial support:* In 2009–10, 17 students received support, including 3 research assistantships, 1 teaching assistantship. Financial award application deadline: 11/1. *Unit head:* Dr. Roberto Heredia, Chair, 956-326-2637, Fax: 956-326-2459, E-mail: rheredia@tamiu.edu. *Application contact:* Rosie Espinoza-Dickinson, Director of Admissions, 956-326-2200, Fax: 956-326-2199, E-mail: enroll@tamiu.edu.

Texas A&M University, College of Education and Human Development, Department of Educational Psychology, College Station, TX 77843. Offers counseling psychology (PhD); educational psychology (PhD); educational technology (M Ed); gifted and talented education (M Ed, MS); Hispanic bilingual education (M Ed, PhD); human learning and development (MS); intelligence, creativity, and giftedness (PhD); learning, development, and instruction (PhD); research, measurement and statistics (MS); research, measurement, and statistics (PhD); school counseling (M Ed); school psychology (PhD); special education (M Ed, PhD). *Accreditation:* APA (one or more programs are accredited); NCATE. Part-time and evening/weekend programs available. Postbaccalaureate distance learning degree programs offered (no on-campus study). *Faculty:* 45. *Students:* 160 full-time (126 women), 144 part-time (118 women); includes 99 minority (25 African Americans, 13 Asian Americans or Pacific Islanders,

Counseling Psychology

Texas A&M University (continued)
61 Hispanic Americans), 41 international. In 2009, 53 master's, 30 doctorates awarded. *Degree requirements:* For master's, thesis optional; for doctorate, thesis/dissertation. *Entrance requirements:* For master's and doctorate, GRE General Test. Additional exam requirements/recommendations for international students: Required—TOEFL. Application fee: $50 ($75 for international students). Electronic applications accepted. *Expenses:* Tuition, state resident: full-time $3991; part-time $221.74 per credit hour. Tuition, nonresident: full-time $9049; part-time $502.74 per credit hour. *Financial support:* In 2009–10, fellowships (averaging $12,000 per year), research assistantships (averaging $9,000 per year), teaching assistantships (averaging $9,000 per year) were awarded; career-related internships or fieldwork, institutionally sponsored loans, scholarships/grants, and unspecified assistantships also available. Financial award applicants required to submit FAFSA. *Unit head:* Dr. Victor Willson, Head, 979-845-1800. *Application contact:* Carol A. Wagner, Director of Advising, 979-845-1833, Fax: 979-862-1256, E-mail: epsyadvisor@tamu.edu.

Texas A&M University–Commerce, Graduate School, College of Education and Human Services, Department of Counseling, Commerce, TX 75429-3011. Offers M Ed, MS, PhD. *Accreditation:* ACA (one or more programs are accredited). Part-time programs available. Terminal master's awarded for partial completion of doctoral program. *Degree requirements:* For master's, comprehensive exam, thesis (for some programs); for doctorate, thesis/dissertation, departmental qualifying exam. *Entrance requirements:* For master's and doctorate, GRE General Test. *Faculty research:* Emergency responders, efficacy and effect of web-based instruction, family violence, play therapy.

Texas A&M University–Texarkana, Graduate Studies and Research, College of Health and Behavioral Sciences, Texarkana, TX 75505-5518. Offers counseling psychology (MS). Part-time and evening/weekend programs available. *Degree requirements:* For master's, comprehensive exam (for some programs), thesis or alternative. *Entrance requirements:* For master's, minimum GPA of 3.0 in last 60 hours of bachelor's degree. Additional exam requirements/recommendations for international students: Required—TOEFL. Electronic applications accepted.

Texas Tech University, Graduate School, College of Arts and Sciences, Department of Psychology, Lubbock, TX 79409. Offers clinical psychology (PhD); counseling psychology (MA, PhD); experimental psychology (MA, PhD); psychology (MA, PhD). *Accreditation:* APA (one or more programs are accredited). Part-time programs available. *Faculty:* 25 full-time (11 women). *Students:* 96 full-time (69 women), 16 part-time (10 women); includes 13 minority (5 African Americans, 8 Hispanic Americans), 7 international. Average age 28. 248 applicants, 13% accepted, 18 enrolled. In 2009, 11 master's, 12 doctorates awarded. *Degree requirements:* For doctorate, thesis/dissertation. *Entrance requirements:* For master's and doctorate, GRE General Test, GRE Subject Test. Additional exam requirements/recommendations for international students: Required—TOEFL (minimum score 550 paper-based; 213 computer-based). *Application deadline:* For fall admission, 3/1 priority date for international students; for spring admission, 11/1 priority date for international students. Applications are processed on a rolling basis. Application fee: $50 ($75 for international students). Electronic applications accepted. *Expenses:* Tuition, state resident: full-time $5100; part-time $213 per credit hour. Tuition, nonresident: full-time $11,748; part-time $490 per credit hour. Required fees: $2298; $50 per credit hour. $555 per semester. *Financial support:* In 2009–10, 1 research assistantship with partial tuition reimbursement (averaging $11,742 per year), 69 teaching assistantships with partial tuition reimbursements (averaging $20,157 per year) were awarded; career-related internships or fieldwork, Federal Work-Study, and institutionally sponsored loans also available. Support available to part-time students. Financial award application deadline: 4/15; financial award applicants required to submit FAFSA. *Faculty research:* Failure/success in relationships, peer rejection in school, stress and coping, group processes, clinical and health psychology. Total annual research expenditures: $144,070. *Unit head:* Dr. Susan S. Hendrick, Chair, 806-742-3711 Ext. 224, Fax: 806-742-0818, E-mail: s.hendrick@ttu.edu. *Application contact:* Dr. Lee M. Cohen, Director of Clinical Program, 806-742-3711 Ext. 254, Fax: 806-742-0818, E-mail: lee.cohen@ttu.edu.

Texas Wesleyan University, Graduate Programs, Programs in Education, Fort Worth, TX 76105-1536. Offers education (M Ed, Ed D); marriage and family therapy (MSMFT); professional counseling (MA); school counseling (MS). Part-time and evening/weekend programs available. Postbaccalaureate distance learning degree programs offered (no on-campus study). *Faculty:* 11 full-time (7 women), 3 part-time/adjunct (2 women). *Students:* 56 full-time (47 women), 208 part-time (174 women); includes 102 minority (54 African Americans, 2 American Indian/Alaska Native, 3 Asian Americans or Pacific Islanders, 43 Hispanic Americans), 4 international. Average age 36. 102 applicants, 77% accepted, 66 enrolled. In 2009, 179 master's awarded. *Entrance requirements:* For master's, GRE General Test, minimum GPA of 3.0 in final 60 hours of undergraduate course work, interview. *Application deadline:* For fall admission, 6/15 priority date for domestic students; for spring admission, 10/15 priority date for domestic students. Applications are processed on a rolling basis. Application fee: $40 ($50 for international students). Tuition and fees vary according to degree level. *Financial support:* Career-related internships or fieldwork, Federal Work-Study, scholarships/grants, and tuition waivers (full and partial) available. Support available to part-time students. Financial award application deadline: 3/15; financial award applicants required to submit FAFSA. *Faculty research:* Teacher effectiveness, bilingual education, analytic teaching. *Unit head:* Dr. Carlos Martinez, Dean, School of Education, 817-531-4940, Fax: 817-531-4943. *Application contact:* DeTrae Warren, Graduate Admission Recruiter, 817-531-4931, Fax: 817-531-4935, E-mail: dwarren@txwes.edu.

Texas Woman's University, Graduate School, College of Arts and Sciences, Department of Psychology and Philosophy, Denton, TX 76201. Offers counseling psychology (MA, PhD); school psychology (PhD, SSP). *Accreditation:* APA (one or more programs are accredited). *Faculty:* 15 full-time (9 women). *Students:* 66 full-time (55 women), 53 part-time (48 women); includes 24 minority (9 African Americans, 1 American Indian/Alaska Native, 7 Asian Americans or Pacific Islanders, 7 Hispanic Americans), 2 international. Average age 30. 105 applicants, 100% accepted, 11 enrolled. In 2009, 18 master's, 12 doctorates awarded. Terminal master's awarded for partial completion of doctoral program. *Degree requirements:* For master's, thesis; for doctorate, comprehensive exam, thesis/dissertation, internship, residency. *Entrance requirements:* For master's, GRE (minimum score 500 verbal, 500 quantitative), BA/BS or 18 hours in psychology, minimum GPA of 3.5 in undergraduate psychology classes, 3 letters of reference; for doctorate, GRE (Verbal 500, Quantitative 500, Analytical 4), 3 letters of reference; minimum overall and psychology undergraduate GPA of 3.0; BS/BA in psychology or 18 hours of required psychology classes, essay. Additional exam requirements/recommendations for international students: Required—TOEFL (minimum score 550 paper-based; 213 computer-based; 79 iBT). *Application deadline:* For fall admission, 12/15 priority date for domestic and international students. Applications are processed on a rolling basis. Application fee: $50. Electronic applications accepted. *Expenses:* Tuition, state resident: full-time $3564; part-time $198 per credit hour. Tuition, nonresident: full-time $8550; part-time $475 per credit hour. Required fees: $69.26 per credit hour. Tuition and fees vary according to course load. *Financial support:* In 2009–10, 49 students received support, including 14 research assistantships (averaging $10,746 per year), 10 teaching assistantships (averaging $10,746 per year); career-related internships or fieldwork, Federal Work-Study, institutionally sponsored loans, scholarships/grants, traineeships, health care benefits, and unspecified assistantships also available. Support available to part-time students. Financial award application deadline: 3/1; financial award applicants required to submit FAFSA. *Faculty research:* Women's anger, pre-school assessments, body image dysfunction, traumatic stress, classical ethics, mental health and behavioral needs of adolescents in alternative education. *Unit head:* Dr. Dan Miller, Chair, 940-898-2303, Fax: 940-898-2301, E-mail: dmiller@twu.edu. *Application contact:* Samuel Wheeler, Assistant Director of Admissions, 940-898-3188, Fax: 940-898-3081, E-mail: wheelersr@twu.edu.

Towson University, College of Graduate Studies and Research, Program in Counseling Psychology, Towson, MD 21252-0001. Offers CAS. Part-time and evening/weekend programs available.

Trevecca Nazarene University, Graduate Division, Graduate Psychology Programs, Major in Counseling Psychology, Nashville, TN 37210-2877. Offers MA. Part-time and evening/weekend programs available. *Students:* 40 full-time (27 women), 5 part-time (4 women); includes 9 minority (8 African Americans, 1 Asian American or Pacific Islander). In 2009, 2 master's awarded. *Degree requirements:* For master's, comprehensive exam, thesis (for some programs), practicum. *Entrance requirements:* For master's, GRE General Test or MAT, minimum GPA of 2.7, 2 reference assessment forms. Additional exam requirements/recommendations for international students: Required—TOEFL (minimum score 550 paper-based; 213 computer-based). *Application deadline:* Applications are processed on a rolling basis. Application fee: $25. *Expenses:* Contact institution. *Financial support:* Applicants required to submit FAFSA. *Unit head:* Dr. Peter Wilson, Director of Graduate Psychology Program, 615-248-1384, Fax: 615-248-1662, E-mail: admissions_psy@trevecca.edu. *Application contact:* Heather Ambrefe, Department Secretary, 615-248-1384, Fax: 615-248-1662, E-mail: admissions_psy@trevecca.edu.

Trinity International University, Trinity Evangelical Divinity School, Deerfield, IL 60015-1284. Offers Biblical and Near Eastern archaeology and languages (MA); Christian studies (MA, Certificate); Christian thought (MA); church history (MA, Th M); congregational ministry: pastor-teacher (M Div); congregational ministry: team ministry (M Div); counseling ministries (MA); counseling psychology (MA); cross-cultural ministry (M Div); educational studies (PhD); evangelism (MA); history of Christianity in America (MA); intercultural studies (MA, PhD); leadership and ministry management (D Min); military chaplaincy (D Min); ministry (MA); mission and evangelism (Th M); missions and evangelism (D Min); New Testament (MA, Th M); Old Testament (Th M); Old Testament and Semitic languages (MA); pastoral care (M Div); pastoral care and counseling (D Min); pastoral counseling and psychology (Th M); pastoral theology (Th M); philosophy of religion (MA); preaching (D Min); religion (MA); research ministry (M Div); systematic theology (Th M); theological studies (PhD); urban ministry (MA). *Accreditation:* ATS (one or more programs are accredited). Part-time programs available. Postbaccalaureate distance learning degree programs offered (minimal on-campus study). *Degree requirements:* For master's, comprehensive exam, thesis, fieldwork; for doctorate, comprehensive exam (for some programs), thesis/dissertation; for M Div, 2 foreign languages, fieldwork; for Certificate, comprehensive exam, integrative papers. *Entrance requirements:* For M Div, GRE, MAT; for master's, GRE, MAT, minimum cumulative undergraduate GPA of 3.0; for doctorate, GRE, minimum cumulative graduate GPA of 3.2; for Certificate, GRE, MAT, minimum undergraduate GPA of 2.5. Additional exam requirements/recommendations for international students: Required—TOEFL (minimum score 580 paper-based; 237 computer-based), TWE (minimum score 4). Electronic applications accepted.

Trinity International University, Trinity Graduate School, Deerfield, IL 60015-1284. Offers bioethics (MA); communication and culture (MA); counseling psychology (MA); instructional leadership (M Ed); teaching (MA). Part-time and evening/weekend programs available. Postbaccalaureate distance learning degree programs offered (minimal on-campus study). *Degree requirements:* For master's, comprehensive exam. *Entrance requirements:* For master's, GRE General Test or MAT, minimum undergraduate GPA of 3.0. Additional exam requirements/recommendations for international students: Required—TOEFL (minimum score 580 paper-based; 237 computer-based), TWE (minimum score 4). Electronic applications accepted.

Trinity International University, South Florida Campus, Graduate School, Miami, FL 33132-1996. Offers MA.

Trinity Western University, Faculty of Graduate Studies, Program in Counseling Psychology, Langley, BC V2Y 1Y1, Canada. Offers MA. *Accreditation:* ACA. Part-time programs available. *Degree requirements:* For master's, comprehensive exam, thesis. *Entrance requirements:* For master's, GRE (if out of school for 5 years prior to applying), BA in honors psychology, minimum GPA of 3.0 for 3rd and 4th year of BA. Additional exam requirements/recommendations for international students: Required—TOEFL (minimum score 600 paper-based; 250 computer-based). *Faculty research:* Meaning, group counseling, trauma, counseling supervision.

Union College, Graduate Programs, Department of Psychology, Barbourville, KY 40906-1499. Offers clinical psychology (MA); counseling psychology (MA); school psychology (MA).

Union Institute & University, MA Program in Psychology and Counseling, Brattleboro, VT 05301. Offers clinical mental health counseling (MA); clinical psychology (MA); counseling psychology (MA); developmental psychology (MA); educational psychology (MA); organizational psychology (MA). Postbaccalaureate distance learning degree programs offered (minimal on-campus study). *Faculty:* 2 full-time (1 woman), 8 part-time/adjunct (2 women). *Students:* 57 full-time (50 women), 20 part-time (16 women); includes 4 minority (1 African American, 3 Hispanic Americans). Average age 41. In 2009, 23 master's awarded. *Degree requirements:* For master's, thesis, internship (depending on concentration). *Application deadline:* Applications are processed on a rolling basis. Electronic applications accepted. Tuition and fees vary according to course load, degree level, campus/location and program. *Unit head:* Dr. Nicholas Young, Director, 802-257-8911, E-mail: nick.young@myunion.edu. *Application contact:* Diane Robinson, Director of Admissions, Brattleboro, 800-336-6794, E-mail: diane.robinson@myunion.edu.

United States International University, School of Arts and Sciences, Nairobi, Kenya. Offers counseling psychology (MA); international relations (MA). Part-time and evening/weekend programs available. *Degree requirements:* For master's, thesis, practicum. *Entrance requirements:* For master's, GRE General Test, 2 letters of recommendation, resume. Additional exam requirements/recommendations for international students: Required—TOEFL (minimum score 550 paper-based; 213 computer-based). *Faculty research:* Trauma in children, African intellectualism, psychological assessment tools.

Universidad del Turabo, Graduate Programs, School of Social Sciences and Humanities, Programs in Psychology, Program in Counseling Psychology, Gurabo, PR 00778-3030. Offers M Psych, Psy D, Certificate. *Students:* 127 full-time (96 women), 109 part-time (83 women); includes 223 Hispanic Americans. Average age 33. 98 applicants, 77% accepted, 58 enrolled. In 2009, 45 master's, 2 doctorates awarded. *Unit head:* David Mendez, Head, 787-743-7979. *Application contact:* Virginia Gonzalez, Admissions Officer, 787-746-3009.

University at Albany, State University of New York, School of Education, Department of Educational and Counseling Psychology, Albany, NY 12222-0001. Offers counseling psychology (MS, PhD, CAS); educational psychology (Ed D); educational psychology and statistics (MS); measurements and evaluation (Ed D); rehabilitation counseling (MS), including counseling psychology; school counselor (CAS); school psychology (Psy D, CAS); special education (MS); statistics and research design (Ed D). *Accreditation:* APA (one or more programs are accredited). Evening/weekend programs available. *Degree requirements:* For doctorate, thesis/dissertation. *Entrance requirements:* For doctorate, GRE General Test. Additional exam requirements/recommendations for international students: Required—TOEFL (minimum score 550 paper-based; 213 computer-based). Electronic applications accepted.

University at Buffalo, the State University of New York, Graduate School, Graduate School of Education, Department of Counseling, School, and Educational Psychology, Buffalo, NY 14260. Offers counseling/school psychology (PhD); counselor education (PhD); educational psychology (MA, PhD); general education (Ed M); mental health counseling (MS); rehabilitation counseling (MS); school counseling (Ed M, Certificate); Singapore school counseling (Ed M). *Accreditation:* CORE (one or more programs are accredited). Postbaccalaureate distance learning degree programs offered (no on-campus study). *Faculty:* 17 full-time (8 women), 36 part-time/adjunct (28 women). *Students:* 152 full-time (125 women), 127 part-time (97 women); includes 33 minority (22 African Americans, 2 American Indian/Alaska Native, 3 Asian Americans or Pacific Islanders, 6 Hispanic Americans), 27 international. Average age 30. 396 applicants, 41% accepted, 119 enrolled. In 2009, 60 master's, 12 doctorates, 24 other advanced degrees awarded. *Degree requirements:* For master's, comprehensive exam (for some programs), thesis (for some programs); for doctorate, comprehensive exam, thesis/dissertation. *Entrance* *requirements:* For master's and doctorate, GRE General Test, interview, letters of reference. Additional exam requirements/recommendations for international students: Required—TOEFL (minimum score 79 iBT). *Application deadline:* For fall admission, 2/1 priority date for domestic and international students. Application fee: $50. Electronic applications accepted. *Financial support:* In 2009–10, 14 fellowships with full tuition reimbursements (averaging $9,000 per year), 28 research assistantships with full tuition reimbursements (averaging $9,000 per year) were awarded; teaching assistantships with tuition reimbursements, career-related internships or fieldwork, Federal Work-Study, institutionally sponsored loans, and unspecified assistantships also available. Financial award application deadline: 2/1; financial award applicants required to submit FAFSA. *Faculty research:* Multicultural counseling, class size effects, good work in counseling, eating disorders, outcome assessment, change agents and therapeutic factors in group counseling. Total annual research expenditures: $3.7 million. *Unit head:* Dr. Timothy Janikowski, Chair, 716-645-2484, Fax: 716-645-6616, E-mail: tjanikow@buffalo.edu. *Application contact:* Rochelle Cohen, Admissions Assistant, 716-645-2110, Fax: 716-645-7937, E-mail: recohen@buffalo.edu.

The University of Akron, Graduate School, Buchtel College of Arts and Sciences, Department of Psychology, Program in Counseling Psychology, Akron, OH 44325. Offers MA, PhD. *Accreditation:* APA (one or more programs are accredited). *Students:* 18 full-time (16 women), 13 part-time (12 women); includes 3 minority (2 African Americans, 1 Hispanic American), 2 international. Average age 29. 46 applicants, 7% accepted, 1 enrolled. In 2009, 4 doctorates awarded. *Degree requirements:* For master's, thesis or specialty exam; for doctorate, comprehensive exam, thesis/dissertation. *Entrance requirements:* For master's, GRE General Test, GRE Subject Test, minimum GPA of 2.75, letters of recommendation, curriculum vitae; for doctorate, GRE General Test, GRE Subject Test, minimum GPA of 3.25, letters of recommendation, personal statement, curriculum vitae. Additional exam requirements/recommendations for international students: Required—TOEFL (minimum score 550 paper-based; 213 computer-based; 79 iBT). *Application deadline:* For fall admission, 1/15 for domestic and international students. Application fee: $30 ($40 for international students). Electronic applications accepted. *Expenses:* Tuition, state resident: full-time $6570; part-time $365 per credit hour. Tuition, nonresident: full-time $11,250; part-time $625 per credit hour. *Financial support:* Fellowships with full tuition reimbursements, research assistantships with full tuition reimbursements, teaching assistantships with full tuition reimbursements, career-related internships or fieldwork, Federal Work-Study, and institutionally sponsored loans available. *Faculty research:* Counseling process and outcome, suicide, diversity issues and counseling psychology (e.g., gender, race, ethnicity, sexual orientation) vocational psychology, assessment. *Unit head:* Dr. Linda Subich, Coordinator, 330-972-8379, E-mail: lsubich@uakron.edu. *Application contact:* Dr. Linda Subich, Coordinator, 330-972-8379, E-mail: lsubich@uakron.edu.

The University of Akron, Graduate School, College of Education, Department of Counseling, Program in Counseling Psychology, Akron, OH 44325. Offers PhD. *Accreditation:* APA. *Students:* 13 full-time (8 women), 14 part-time (all women). Average age 32. 41 applicants, 20% accepted, 5 enrolled. In 2009, 4 doctorates awarded. *Degree requirements:* For doctorate, one foreign language, comprehensive exam, thesis/dissertation, written and oral exams. *Entrance requirements:* For doctorate, GRE, interview, minimum GPA of 3.25, letters of recommendation. Additional exam requirements/recommendations for international students: Required—TOEFL (minimum score 550 paper-based; 213 computer-based). *Application deadline:* For fall admission, 1/15 for domestic and international students. Application fee: $30 ($40 for international students). Electronic applications accepted. *Expenses:* Tuition, state resident: full-time $6570; part-time $365 per credit hour. Tuition, nonresident: full-time $11,250; part-time $625 per credit hour. *Financial support:* In 2009–10, 8 research assistantships with full tuition reimbursements, 8 teaching assistantships with full tuition reimbursements were awarded. *Unit head:* Dr. James Rogers, Coordinator, 330-972-8635, E-mail: jrrogers@uakron.edu. *Application contact:* Dr. James Rogers, Coordinator, 330-972-8635, E-mail: jrrogers@uakron.edu.

University of Alberta, Faculty of Graduate Studies and Research, Department of Educational Psychology, Edmonton, AB T6G 2E1, Canada. Offers counseling psychology (M Ed, PhD); educational psychology (M Ed, PhD); instructional technology (M Ed); school counseling (M Ed); school psychology (M Ed, PhD); special education (M Ed, PhD); special education-deafness studies (M Ed); teaching English as a second language (M Ed). Part-time programs available. *Faculty:* 34 full-time (14 women), 12 part-time/adjunct (6 women). *Students:* 117 full-time (93 women), 173 part-time (121 women). Average age 36. 252 applicants, 34% accepted. In 2009, 30 master's, 10 doctorates awarded. *Degree requirements:* For master's, thesis optional; for doctorate, comprehensive exam, thesis/dissertation. *Entrance requirements:* For master's and doctorate, minimum GPA of 3.0. Additional exam requirements/recommendations for international students: Required—TOEFL. *Application deadline:* For fall admission, 2/1 priority date for domestic and international students. Applications are processed on a rolling basis. Tuition and fees charges are reported in Canadian dollars. *Expenses:* Tuition, area resident: Full-time $4626 Canadian dollars; part-time $99.72 Canadian dollars per unit. International tuition: $8216 Canadian dollars full-time. Required fees: $3590 Canadian dollars; $99.72 Canadian dollars per unit. $215 Canadian dollars per term. *Financial support:* In 2009–10, 10 fellowships with full tuition reimbursements (averaging $16,120 per year), 36 research assistantships with full tuition reimbursements (averaging $12,614 per year), 46 teaching assistantships with full tuition reimbursements (averaging $5,462 per year) were awarded; career-related internships or fieldwork and scholarships/grants also available. *Faculty research:* Human learning, development and assessment. *Unit head:* Dr. Linda M. McDonald, Chair, 780-492-1149, Fax: 780-492-1318, E-mail: linda.mcdonald@ualberta.ca. *Application contact:* Judy Maynes, Information Contact, 780-492-1149, Fax: 780-492-1318, E-mail: edpygrad@ualberta.ca.

University of Baltimore, Graduate School, The Yale Gordon College of Liberal Arts, Program in Applied Psychology, Baltimore, MD 21201-5779. Offers applied psychology (MS), including counseling, industrial and organizational psychology, psychological applications. Part-time and evening/weekend programs available. *Degree requirements:* For master's, thesis optional. *Entrance requirements:* For master's, GRE, minimum GPA of 3.0. Additional exam requirements/recommendations for international students: Required—TOEFL (minimum score 550 paper-based; 213 computer-based). Electronic applications accepted. *Expenses:* Contact institution. *Faculty research:* Participatory decision making, counter productive workplace behavior, organizational consulting, substance abuse treatment, cognitive functioning in head injured.

The University of British Columbia, Faculty of Education, Department of Educational and Counseling Psychology, and Special Education, Vancouver, BC V6T 1Z1, Canada. Offers counseling psychology (M Ed, MA, PhD); development, learning and culture (PhD); guidance studies (Diploma); human development, learning and culture (M Ed, MA); measurement and evaluation and research methodology (M Ed); measurement, evaluation and research methodology (MA); measurement, evaluation, and research methodology (PhD); school psychology (M Ed, MA, PhD); special education (M Ed, MA, PhD, Diploma). Part-time programs available. *Degree requirements:* For master's, thesis (for some programs); for doctorate, comprehensive exam, thesis/dissertation. *Entrance requirements:* For master's, GRE General Test (counseling psychology MA); for doctorate, GRE General Test. Additional exam requirements/recommendations for international students: Required—TOEFL. Electronic applications accepted. *Faculty research:* Women, family, social problems, career transition, stress and coping problems.

University of Calgary, Faculty of Graduate Studies, Faculty of Education, Division of Applied Psychology, Calgary, AB T2N 1N4, Canada. Offers counseling psychology (M Ed, M Sc, PhD); human development and learning (M Ed, M Sc, PhD); school psychology (M Ed, M Sc, PhD); special education (M Ed, M Sc, PhD). Part-time programs available. *Degree requirements:* For master's, thesis (for some programs), final oral exam; for doctorate, thesis/dissertation, candidacy exam, final oral exam. *Entrance requirements:* For master's, minimum GPA of 3.0, 3 letters of reference; for doctorate, minimum GPA of 3.5, 3 letters of reference. *Faculty research:* Counselor education, family life studies, learning and cognition.

University of California, Berkeley, UC Berkeley Extension, Certificate Programs in Behavioral and Health Sciences, Berkeley, CA 94720-1500. Offers alcohol and drug abuse studies (Certificate). *Unit head:* Diana Wu, Dean, 510-642-4181. *Application contact:* Behavioral and Health Sciences, 510-643-3883, E-mail: counspsych@unex.berkeley.edu.

University of California, Santa Barbara, Graduate Division, Gevirtz Graduate School of Education, Santa Barbara, CA 93106-9490. Offers counseling, clinical and school psychology (PhD), including clinical psychology, counseling psychology, school psychology; education (M Ed, MA, PhD), including child and adolescent development (MA, PhD), cultural perspectives and comparative education (MA, PhD), educational leadership and organizations (MA, PhD), research methodology (MA, PhD), special education disabilities and risk studies (MA), special education, disabilities and risk studies (PhD), teaching (M Ed), teaching and learning (MA, PhD); educational leadership (Ed D); school psychology (M Ed); MA/PhD. *Accreditation:* APA (one or more programs are accredited). Postbaccalaureate distance learning degree programs offered (minimal on-campus study). *Faculty:* 42 full-time (20 women), 10 part-time/adjunct (4 women). *Students:* 390 full-time (303 women); includes 149 minority (14 African Americans, 3 American Indian/Alaska Native, 57 Asian Americans or Pacific Islanders, 75 Hispanic Americans), 16 international. Average age 31. 717 applicants, 40% accepted, 170 enrolled. In 2009, 140 master's, 46 doctorates awarded. Terminal master's awarded for partial completion of doctoral program. *Degree requirements:* For master's, comprehensive exam (for some programs), thesis (for some programs); for doctorate, comprehensive exam (for some programs), thesis/dissertation, qualifying exam. *Entrance requirements:* For master's, GRE, 3 letters of recommendation, resume/curriculum vitae; for doctorate, GRE, 3 letters of recommendation, statement of purpose, personal achievements/contributions statement, resume/curriculum vitae, transcripts for post-secondary institutions attended. Additional exam requirements/recommendations for international students: Required—TOEFL (minimum score 550 paper-based; 213 computer-based; 80 iBT) or IELTS (minimum score 7). Application fee: $70 ($90 for international students). Electronic applications accepted. *Financial support:* In 2009–10, 253 students received support, including 206 fellowships with full and partial tuition reimbursements available (averaging $5,000 per year), 62 research assistantships with full and partial tuition reimbursements available (averaging $6,200 per year), 87 teaching assistantships with partial tuition reimbursements available (averaging $6,500 per year); career-related internships or fieldwork, Federal Work-Study, institutionally sponsored loans, scholarships/grants, traineeships, health care benefits, and unspecified assistantships also available. Financial award applicants required to submit FAFSA. *Faculty research:* Professional development, early childhood development, school violence, literacy, science/math initiative. Total annual research expenditures: $4.4 million. *Unit head:* Dr. Jane Conoley, Chair, 805-893-2185, E-mail: jane-conoley@education.ucsb.edu. *Application contact:* Kathryn Marie Tucciarone, Student Affairs Officer, 805-893-2137, E-mail: katiet@education.ucsb.edu.

University of Central Arkansas, Graduate School, College of Health and Behavioral Sciences, Department of Counseling and Psychology, Program in Counseling Psychology, Conway, AR 72035-0001. Offers MS. *Students:* 19 full-time (18 women), 15 part-time (13 women); includes 4 minority (3 African Americans, 1 Asian American or Pacific Islander). Average age 27. 16 applicants, 81% accepted, 9 enrolled. In 2009, 17 master's awarded. *Degree requirements:* For master's, comprehensive exam, thesis optional. *Entrance requirements:* For master's, GRE General Test, minimum GPA of 2.7. Additional exam requirements/recommendations for international students: Required—TOEFL (minimum score 550 paper-based; 213 computer-based). *Application deadline:* For fall admission, 3/1 priority date for domestic and international students; for spring admission, 10/1 priority date for domestic and international students. Applications are processed on a rolling basis. Application fee: $25 ($40 for international students). *Expenses:* Tuition, state resident: full-time $5136; part-time $214 per credit hour. Required fees: $379.50; $127 per term. Tuition and fees vary according to course level, course load and campus/location. *Financial support:* Federal Work-Study, scholarships/grants, and unspecified assistantships available. Financial award applicants required to submit FAFSA. *Unit head:* Dr. Elson Bihm, Head, 501-450-3193, Fax: 501-450-5424, E-mail: elsonb@uca.edu. *Application contact:* Patti Hornor, Administrative Assistant, 501-450-5063, Fax: 501-450-5678, E-mail: pattih@uca.edu.

University of Central Missouri, The Graduate School, College of Education, Warrensburg, MO 64093. Offers career and technical education administration (MS); career and technical education industry training (MS); career and technical education leadership/teaching (MS); college student personnel administration (MS); counseling (MS); curriculum and instruction (Ed S); educational leadership (Ed D); educational technology (MS); elementary education/educational foundations and literacy (MSE); elementary school administration (MSE); elementary school principalship (Ed S); human services/learning resources (Ed S); human services/professional counseling (Ed S); human services/special education (Ed S); human services/technology and occupational education (Ed S); K-12 education/educational foundations and literacy (MSE); K-12 special education (MSE); library science and information services (MS); literacy education (MSE); secondary education/educational foundations & literacy (MSE); secondary school administration (MSE); secondary school principalship (Ed S); superintendency (Ed S); teaching (MAT). Part-time programs available. Postbaccalaureate distance learning degree programs offered. *Faculty:* 42. *Students:* 123 full-time (82 women), 721 part-time (552 women); includes 58 minority (38 African Americans, 3 American Indian/Alaska Native, 6 Asian Americans or Pacific Islanders, 11 Hispanic Americans), 6 international. Average age 34. 229 applicants, 88% accepted, 190 enrolled. In 2009, 212 master's, 47 other advanced degrees awarded. *Entrance requirements:* Additional exam requirements/recommendations for international students: Required—TOEFL (minimum score 550 paper-based; 79 computer-based). *Application deadline:* For fall admission, 6/1 priority date for domestic students, 5/1 for international students; for spring admission, 10/1 priority date for domestic students, 10/1 for international students. Applications are processed on a rolling basis. Application fee: $30 ($75 for international students). Electronic applications accepted. *Expenses:* Tuition, area resident: Part-time $245.80 per credit hour. Tuition, nonresident: part-time $491.60 per credit hour. Required fees: $24.20 per credit hour. Full-time tuition and fees vary according to course load, degree level, campus/location and reciprocity agreements. *Financial support:* Research assistantships with full and partial tuition reimbursements, teaching assistantships with full and partial tuition reimbursements, career-related internships or fieldwork, Federal Work-Study, scholarships/grants, and administrative and laboratory assistantships available. Support available to part-time students. Financial award application deadline: 3/1; financial award applicants required to submit FAFSA. *Unit head:* Dr. Michael Wright, Dean, 660-543-4272, Fax: 660-543-8753, E-mail: mwright@ucmo.edu. *Application contact:* Laurie Delap, Admissions Coordinator, 660-543-4621, Fax: 660-543-4778, E-mail: gradinfo@ucmo.edu.

University of Central Oklahoma, College of Graduate Studies and Research, College of Education, Department of Psychology, Program in Counseling Psychology, Edmond, OK 73034-5209. Offers MS. *Entrance requirements:* For master's, GRE General Test. Additional exam requirements/recommendations for international students: Required—TOEFL (minimum score 550 paper-based; 213 computer-based). Electronic applications accepted. *Expenses:* Tuition, state resident: full-time $4128; part-time $172 per credit hour. Tuition, nonresident: full-time $10,373; part-time $432.20 per credit hour. Required fees: $433.20; $18.05 per credit hour.

University of Colorado Denver, School of Education and Human Development, Program in Counseling Psychology and Counselor Education, Denver, CO 80217-3364. Offers MA, Ed S. *Accreditation:* ACA (one or more programs are accredited); NCATE. Part-time and evening/weekend programs available. *Students:* 110 full-time (97 women), 198 part-time (175 women); includes 35 minority (6 African Americans, 3 American Indian/Alaska Native, 9 Asian Americans or Pacific Islanders, 17 Hispanic Americans), 6 international. 86 applicants, 40% accepted, 17 enrolled. In 2009, 122 master's, 7 other advanced degrees awarded. *Degree requirements:* For master's, comprehensive exam, thesis optional. *Entrance requirements:* For master's, GRE or MAT, minimum GPA of 2.75, 4 letters of recommendation, interview, resume. Additional exam requirements/recommendations for international students: Required—TOEFL (minimum score 525 paper-based; 197 computer-based). *Application deadline:* For fall admission, 2/15 for domestic students; for spring admission, 9/15 for domestic students. Applications are processed on a rolling basis. Application fee: $50 ($75 for international students). Electronic

Counseling Psychology

University of Colorado Denver (continued)

applications accepted. *Financial support:* Research assistantships, teaching assistantships, Federal Work-Study available. Financial award application deadline: 4/1; financial award applicants required to submit FAFSA. *Faculty research:* Spiritual issues in counseling, multicultural and diversity issues in counseling, adolescent suicide, career development. *Unit head:* Dr. Marsha Wiggins-Frame, Division Coordinator, 303-315-6332, E-mail: marsha.wiggins@ucdenver.edu. *Application contact:* Lori Sisneros, Student Services Coordinator, 303-315-4979, Fax: 303-315-6311, E-mail: lori.sisneros@ucdenver.edu.

University of Connecticut, Graduate School, Neag School of Education, Department of Educational Psychology, Program in Counseling Psychology, Storrs, CT 06269. Offers counseling psychology (PhD); school counseling (MA, Post-Master's Certificate). *Accreditation:* ACA. *Faculty:* 15 full-time (6 women). *Students:* 38 full-time (31 women), 14 part-time (9 women); includes 9 minority (6 African Americans, 3 Hispanic Americans), 4 international. Average age 29. 63 applicants, 35% accepted, 9 enrolled. In 2009, 13 master's, 2 doctorates, 1 other advanced degree awarded. Terminal master's awarded for partial completion of doctoral program. *Degree requirements:* For master's, comprehensive exam, thesis or alternative; for doctorate, thesis/dissertation. *Entrance requirements:* For doctorate, GRE General Test. Additional exam requirements/recommendations for international students: Required—TOEFL (minimum score 550 paper-based; 213 computer-based). *Application deadline:* For fall admission, 2/1 priority date for domestic and international students; for spring admission, 11/1 for domestic students, 10/1 for international students. Applications are processed on a rolling basis. Application fee: $55. Electronic applications accepted. *Expenses:* Tuition, state resident: full-time $4725; part-time $525 per credit. Tuition, nonresident: full-time $12,267; part-time $1363 per credit. Required fees: $346 per semester. Tuition and fees vary according to course load. *Financial support:* In 2009–10, 15 research assistantships with full tuition reimbursements, 2 teaching assistantships with full tuition reimbursements were awarded; fellowships, Federal Work-Study, scholarships/grants, health care benefits, and unspecified assistantships also available. Financial award application deadline: 2/1; financial award applicants required to submit FAFSA. *Unit head:* Hariharan Swaminathan, Head, 860-486-4031, Fax: 860-486-0210, E-mail: hariharan.swaminathan@uconn.edu. *Application contact:* Cheryl Lowe, Program Assistant, 860-486-4031, Fax: 860-486-0180, E-mail: cheryl.lowe@uconn.edu.

University of Denver, College of Education, Denver, CO 80208. Offers counseling psychology (MA, PhD); curriculum and instruction (MA, PhD, Certificate), including curriculum leadership (MA, PhD); educational administration and policy studies (Certificate); educational psychology (MA, PhD, Ed S), including child and family studies (MA, PhD), quantitative research methods (MA, PhD), school psychology (PhD, Ed S); higher education and adult studies (MA, PhD); library and information science (MLIS); library and information sciences (Certificate); school administration (PhD). *Accreditation:* ALA; APA (one or more programs are accredited). Part-time and evening/weekend programs available. Postbaccalaureate distance learning degree programs offered (no on-campus study). *Faculty:* 33 full-time (24 women), 62 part-time/adjunct (41 women). *Students:* 384 full-time (305 women), 453 part-time (336 women); includes 164 minority (47 African Americans, 8 American Indian/Alaska Native, 14 Asian Americans or Pacific Islanders, 95 Hispanic Americans), 20 international. Average age 34. 1,065 applicants, 59% accepted, 433 enrolled. In 2009, 206 master's, 38 doctorates, 117 other advanced degrees awarded. Terminal master's awarded for partial completion of doctoral program. *Degree requirements:* For master's, comprehensive exam; for doctorate, 2 foreign languages, comprehensive exam, thesis/dissertation. *Entrance requirements:* For master's and doctorate, GRE General Test or MAT. *Application deadline:* Applications are processed on a rolling basis. Application fee: $50. Electronic applications accepted. *Expenses:* Tuition: Full-time $34,596; part-time $961 per quarter hour. Required fees: $4 per quarter hour. Tuition and fees vary according to course load, campus/location and program. *Financial support:* In 2009–10, 78 teaching assistantships with full and partial tuition reimbursements (averaging $11,700 per year) were awarded; career-related internships or fieldwork, Federal Work-Study, institutionally sponsored loans, and scholarships/grants also available. Support available to part-time students. Financial award application deadline: 3/1; financial award applicants required to submit FAFSA. *Faculty research:* Parkinson's disease, personnel training, development and assessments, gifted education, service-learning, transportation, public schools. Total annual research expenditures: $340,000. *Unit head:* Dr. Gregory M. Anderson, Dean, 303-871-3665. *Application contact:* Janet Erickson, Director of Graduate Admission, 303-871-2485, E-mail: edinfo@du.edu.

University of Florida, Graduate School, College of Liberal Arts and Sciences, Department of Psychology, Gainesville, FL 32611. Offers behavior analysis (PhD); behavioral neuroscience (MS, PhD); cognitive and sensory processes (PhD); counseling psychology (PhD); developmental psychology (PhD); social psychology (MS, PhD); JD/PhD. *Degree requirements:* For master's, thesis or alternative; for doctorate, thesis/dissertation. *Entrance requirements:* For master's and doctorate, GRE General Test, minimum GPA of 3.0. Additional exam requirements/recommendations for international students: Required—TOEFL (minimum score 550 paper-based; 213 computer-based). Electronic applications accepted. *Faculty research:* Experimental analysis of behavior, psychobiology, cognition and sensory processes, counseling psychology, social psychology, developmental psychology.

University of Great Falls, Graduate Studies, Program in Counseling, Great Falls, MT 59405. Offers counseling psychology (MSC). Part-time and evening/weekend programs available. *Degree requirements:* For master's, thesis optional, internship. *Entrance requirements:* For master's, GRE General Test, 3 letters of recommendation. Additional exam requirements/recommendations for international students: Required—TOEFL (minimum score 500 paper-based; 205 computer-based). Electronic applications accepted. *Faculty research:* Self concept and adolescent offenders, juvenile delinquency, community mental health counseling.

University of Hawaii at Hilo, Program in Counseling Psychology, Hilo, HI 96720-4091. Offers MA. *Degree requirements:* For master's, project or thesis.

University of Houston, College of Education, Department of Educational Psychology, Houston, TX 77204. Offers counseling (M Ed); counseling psychology (PhD); educational psychology (M Ed); school psychology (PhD); school psychology and individual differences (PhD); special education (M Ed, Ed D). *Accreditation:* NCATE. Part-time and evening/weekend programs available. *Faculty:* 21 full-time (11 women), 12 part-time/adjunct (8 women). *Students:* 121 full-time (103 women), 123 part-time (106 women); includes 86 minority (23 African Americans, 3 American Indian/Alaska Native, 24 Asian Americans or Pacific Islanders, 36 Hispanic Americans), 11 international. Average age 30. 139 applicants, 52% accepted, 38 enrolled. In 2009, 32 master's, 16 doctorates awarded. *Degree requirements:* For master's, comprehensive exam or thesis; for doctorate, comprehensive exam, thesis/dissertation. *Entrance requirements:* For master's, GRE, recommendations, vitae/resume; for doctorate, GRE, GPA, recommendations, VITA/Resume, Goal statement, writing sample. Additional exam requirements/recommendations for international students: Required—TOEFL. *Application deadline:* For fall admission, 12/1 for domestic and international students; for spring admission, 9/15 for domestic and international students. Application fee: $45 ($75 for international students). *Expenses:* Tuition, state resident: full-time $7676; part-time $320 per credit hour. Tuition, nonresident: full-time $14,324; part-time $597 per credit hour. Required fees: $3034. *Financial support:* In 2009–10, 2 fellowships with full tuition reimbursements (averaging $9,500 per year), 2 research assistantships with full tuition reimbursements (averaging $10,225 per year), 46 teaching assistantships with full tuition reimbursements (averaging $10,225 per year) were awarded; career-related internships or fieldwork, Federal Work-Study, institutionally sponsored loans, scholarships/grants, health care benefits, and unspecified assistantships also available. Support available to part-time students. Financial award application deadline: 2/1. *Faculty research:* Evidence-based assessment and intervention, multicultural issues in psychology, social and cultural context of learning, systemic barriers to college, motivational aspects of self-regulated learning. *Unit head:* Dr. Tom Kubiszyn, Chairperson, 713-743-9865, Fax: 713-743-4996, E-mail: tkubiszyn@uh.edu. *Application contact:* Kimberly A. Zainfeld, Academic Advisor, 713-743-9830, Fax: 713-743-4996, E-mail: kzainfeld@uh.edu.

University of Houston–Victoria, School of Arts and Sciences, Program in Psychology, Victoria, TX 77901-4450. Offers counseling psychology (MA); school psychology (MA). Part-time and evening/weekend programs available. Postbaccalaureate distance learning degree programs offered. *Degree requirements:* For master's, project or thesis. *Entrance requirements:* For master's, GRE General Test. Additional exam requirements/recommendations for international students: Required—TOEFL (minimum score 550 paper-based; 213 computer-based). Electronic applications accepted.

University of Indianapolis, Graduate Programs, School of Psychological Sciences, Indianapolis, IN 46227-3697. Offers clinical psychology (Psy D); clinical psychology/mental health counseling (MA). *Accreditation:* APA. *Faculty:* 6 full-time (1 woman), 1 (woman) part-time/adjunct. *Students:* 107 full-time (96 women), 63 part-time (51 women); includes 8 minority (6 African Americans, 1 Asian American or Pacific Islander, 1 Hispanic American), 7 international. Average age 27. *Degree requirements:* For master's, practicum; for doctorate, comprehensive exam, thesis/dissertation, 1200 hours of clinical practicum, 2000 hour internship. *Entrance requirements:* For master's, GRE, 3 letters of recommendation; for doctorate, GRE, minimum GPA of 3.0, 18 hours of course work in psychology, 3 letters of recommendation. Additional exam requirements/recommendations for international students: Required—TOEFL (minimum score 550 paper-based; 213 computer-based). *Application deadline:* For fall admission, 2/25 for domestic students. Application fee: $50. *Financial support:* Federal Work-Study available. *Unit head:* Dr. E. John McIlvried, Dean, 317-788-3274, Fax: 317-788-3480, E-mail: jmcilvried@uindy.edu. *Application contact:* Dr. E. John McIlvried, Associate Provost for Graduate and International Programs, 317-788-3274, E-mail: jmcilvried@uindy.edu.

The University of Iowa, Graduate College, College of Education, Department of Psychological and Quantitative Foundations, Iowa City, IA 52242-1316. Offers counseling psychology (PhD); educational measurement and statistics (MA, PhD); educational psychology (MA, PhD); school psychology (PhD, Ed S); JD/PhD. *Accreditation:* APA. *Degree requirements:* For master's, thesis optional, exam; for doctorate, comprehensive exam, thesis/dissertation; for Ed S, exam. *Entrance requirements:* For master's, doctorate, and Ed S, GRE General Test, minimum GPA of 3.0. Additional exam requirements/recommendations for international students: Required—TOEFL (minimum score 550 paper-based; 213 computer-based; 81 iBT). Electronic applications accepted.

The University of Kansas, Graduate Studies, School of Education, Department of Psychology and Research in Education, Program in Counseling Psychology, Lawrence, KS 66045. Offers MS, PhD. *Accreditation:* APA (one or more programs are accredited). Part-time programs available. *Students:* 67 full-time (48 women), 12 part-time (11 women); includes 13 minority (5 African Americans, 1 American Indian/Alaska Native, 2 Asian Americans or Pacific Islanders, 5 Hispanic Americans), 2 international. Average age 29. 112 applicants, 40% accepted, 18 enrolled. In 2009, 19 master's, 5 doctorates awarded. Terminal master's awarded for partial completion of doctoral program. *Degree requirements:* For master's, thesis or alternative; for doctorate, comprehensive exam, thesis/dissertation. *Entrance requirements:* For master's and doctorate, GRE General Test, minimum GPA of 3.0. Additional exam requirements/recommendations for international students: Required—TOEFL. *Application deadline:* For fall admission, 12/15 for domestic and international students. Application fee: $45 ($55 for international students). Electronic applications accepted. *Expenses:* Tuition, state resident: full-time $6492; part-time $270.50 per credit hour. Tuition, nonresident: full-time $15,510; part-time $646.25 per credit hour. Required fees: $847; $70.56 per credit hour. Tuition and fees vary according to course load and program. *Financial support:* Fellowships, research assistantships with full and partial tuition reimbursements, teaching assistantships with full and partial tuition reimbursements, career-related internships or fieldwork, scholarships/grants, and unspecified assistantships available. Financial award application deadline: 1/15. *Faculty research:* Career development, assessment and intervention, multi-cultural counseling, counselor training, positive psychology. *Unit head:* James Litchenberg, Professor and Director of Training, 785-864-3931, Fax: 785-864-3820, E-mail: jlicht@ku.edu. *Application contact:* Admissions Coordinator, 785-864-3931, Fax: 785-864-3820, E-mail: preadmit@ku.edu.

University of Kentucky, Graduate School, College of Education, Program in Educational and Counseling Psychology, Lexington, KY 40506-0032. Offers counseling psychology (MS Ed, PhD, Ed S); educational and counseling psychology (MS Ed); educational psychology (Ed D, PhD, Ed S); school psychometrist and school psychology (MA Ed). *Accreditation:* APA (one or more programs are accredited); NCATE. *Degree requirements:* For master's, comprehensive exam, thesis optional; for doctorate, comprehensive exam, thesis/dissertation; for Ed S, comprehensive exam. *Entrance requirements:* For master's, GRE General Test, minimum undergraduate GPA of 2.75; for doctorate, GRE General Test, minimum graduate GPA of 3.0; for Ed S, GRE General Test. Additional exam requirements/recommendations for international students: Required—TOEFL (minimum score 550 paper-based; 213 computer-based). Electronic applications accepted.

University of La Verne, College of Arts and Sciences, Department of Psychology, Programs in Counseling, La Verne, CA 91750-4443. Offers counseling (MS), including student services; marriage and family therapy (MS). Part-time programs available. *Faculty:* 12 full-time (5 women), 22 part-time/adjunct (14 women). *Students:* 29 full-time (25 women), 73 part-time (68 women); includes 69 minority (17 African Americans, 5 Asian Americans or Pacific Islanders, 47 Hispanic Americans). Average age 29. In 2009, 36 master's awarded. *Degree requirements:* For master's, thesis, competency exam, personal psychotherapy. *Entrance requirements:* For master's, minimum undergraduate GPA of 3.0; 3 letters of recommendations; interview. Additional exam requirements/recommendations for international students: Required—TOEFL (minimum score 600 paper-based; 250 computer-based). *Application deadline:* Applications are processed on a rolling basis. Application fee: $50. *Expenses:* Contact institution. *Financial support:* Career-related internships or fieldwork, institutionally sponsored loans, and scholarships/grants available. Financial award application deadline: 3/2; financial award applicants required to submit FAFSA. *Unit head:* Patricia Long, 909-593-3511 Ext. 4091, E-mail: plong@laverne.edu. *Application contact:* Connie Hamlow, Admissions Information Specialist, 909-593-3511 Ext. 4519, Fax: 909-392-2761, E-mail: gradadmission@laverne.edu.

University of Lethbridge, School of Graduate Studies, Lethbridge, AB T1K 3M4, Canada. Offers accounting (MScM); addictions counseling (M Sc); agricultural biotechnology (M Sc); agricultural studies (M Sc, MA); anthropology (MA); archaeology (MA); art (MA, MFA); biochemistry (M Sc); biological sciences (M Sc); biomolecular science (PhD); biosystems and biodiversity (PhD); Canadian studies (MA); chemistry (M Sc); computer science (M Sc); computer science and geographical information science (M Sc); counseling psychology (M Ed); dramatic arts (MA); earth, space, and physical science (PhD); economics (MA); educational leadership (M Ed); English (MA); environmental science (M Sc); evolution and behavior (PhD); exercise science (M Sc); finance (MScM); French (MA); French/German (MA); French/Spanish (MA); general education (M Ed); general management (MScM); geography (M Sc, MA); German (MA); health science (M Sc); health sciences (MA); history (MA); human resource management and labour relations (MScM); individualized multidisciplinary (M Sc, MA); information systems (MScM); international management (MScM); kinesiology (M Sc, MA); management (M Sc, MA); marketing (MScM); mathematics (M Sc); music (M Mus, MA); Native American studies (MA); neuroscience (M Sc, PhD); new media (MA); nursing (M Sc); philosophy (MA); physics (M Sc); policy and strategy (MScM); political science (MA); psychology (M Sc, MA); religious studies (MA); social sciences (MA); sociology (MA); theatre and dramatic arts (MFA); theoretical and computational science (PhD); urban and regional studies (MA); women's studies (MA). Part-time and evening/weekend programs available. *Degree requirements:* For doctorate, comprehensive exam, thesis/dissertation. *Entrance requirements:* For master's, GMAT (M Sc in management), bachelor's degree in related field, minimum GPA of 3.0 during previous 20 graded semester courses, 2 years teaching or related experience (M Ed); for doctorate, master's degree, minimum graduate GPA of 3.5. Additional exam requirements/recommendations for international students: Required—TOEFL. *Faculty research:* Movement and brain plasticity, gibberellin physiology, photosynthesis, carbon cycling, molecular properties of main-group ring components.

University of Mary Hardin-Baylor, Graduate Studies in Counseling and Psychology, Belton, TX 76513. Offers community counseling (MA); marriage and family Christian counseling (MA); psychology and counseling (MA); school counseling and psychology (MA). Part-time and evening/weekend programs available. *Degree requirements:* For master's, comprehensive exam. *Entrance requirements:* For master's, GRE General Test, minimum GPA of 3.0 in last 60 hours or 2.75 overall. Electronic applications accepted.

University of Maryland, College Park, Academic Affairs, College of Education, Department of Counseling and Personnel Services, College Park, MD 20742. Offers college student personnel (M Ed, MA); college student personnel administration (PhD); community counseling (CAGS); community/career counseling (M Ed, MA); counseling and personnel services (M Ed, MA, PhD), including art therapy (M Ed), college student personnel (M Ed), counseling and personnel services (PhD), counseling psychology (M Ed), mental health counseling (M Ed), school counseling (M Ed); counseling psychology (PhD); counselor education (PhD); rehabilitation counseling (M Ed, MA, AGSC); school counseling (M Ed, MA); school psychology (M Ed, MA, PhD). *Accreditation:* ACA (one or more programs are accredited); APA (one or more programs are accredited); CORE (one or more programs are accredited); NCATE. Part-time and evening/weekend programs available. Postbaccalaureate distance learning degree programs offered (no on-campus study). *Faculty:* 34 full-time (21 women), 8 part-time/adjunct (6 women). *Students:* 152 full-time (117 women), 25 part-time (18 women); includes 67 minority (32 African Americans, 2 American Indian/Alaska Native, 20 Asian Americans or Pacific Islanders, 13 Hispanic Americans), 16 international. 319 applicants, 15% accepted, 32 enrolled. In 2009, 24 master's, 15 doctorates, 4 other advanced degrees awarded. *Degree requirements:* For master's, thesis (for some programs); for doctorate, thesis/dissertation. *Entrance requirements:* For master's, GRE General Test or MAT, minimum GPA of 3.0, 3 letters of recommendation; for doctorate, GRE General Test or MAT, minimum GPA of 3.5, 3 letters of recommendation. Additional exam requirements/recommendations for international students: Required—TOEFL. *Application deadline:* For fall admission, 12/15 for domestic and international students; for spring admission, 10/1 for domestic students, 6/1 for international students. Applications are processed on a rolling basis. Application fee: $60. Electronic applications accepted. *Expenses:* Tuition, area resident: Part-time $471 per credit hour. Tuition, state resident: part-time $471 per credit hour. Tuition, nonresident: part-time $1016 per credit hour. Required fees: $337.04 per term. *Financial support:* In 2009–10, 4 fellowships with partial tuition reimbursements (averaging $10,402 per year), 8 research assistantships (averaging $16,454 per year), 93 teaching assistantships with tuition reimbursements (averaging $16,109 per year) were awarded; career-related internships or fieldwork, Federal Work-Study, and scholarships/grants also available. Support available to part-time students. Financial award applicants required to submit FAFSA. *Faculty research:* Educational psychology, counseling, health. Total annual research expenditures: $1.5 million. *Unit head:* Dr. Dennis Kivlighan, Chair, 301-405-2858, E-mail: dennisk@umd.edu. *Application contact:* Dean of Graduate School, 301-405-0358.

University of Massachusetts Boston, Office of Graduate Studies, Graduate College of Education, Counseling and School Psychology Department, Boston, MA 02125-3393. Offers family therapy (M Ed, CAGS); forensic counseling (M Ed, CAGS); mental health counseling (M Ed, CAGS); rehabilitation counseling (M Ed, CAGS); school guidance counseling (M Ed, CAGS); school psychology (M Ed, CAGS). *Degree requirements:* For master's and CAGS, comprehensive exam. *Entrance requirements:* For master's, GRE General Test or MAT; for CAGS, minimum GPA of 2.75.

University of Medicine and Dentistry of New Jersey, School of Health Related Professions, Department of Psychiatric Rehabilitation and Counseling Professions, Newark, NJ 07107-1709. Offers professional counseling (Certificate); psychiatric rehabilitation (MS, PhD); rehabilitation counseling (MS), including psychiatric rehabilitation, vocational rehabilitation. *Accreditation:* CORE. *Degree requirements:* For master's, internship, practicum. *Entrance requirements:* For master's, minimum 2 years of psychiatric rehabilitation or related professional experience or GRE General Test, interview; for doctorate, GRE General Test. Additional exam requirements/recommendations for international students: Required—TOEFL. Electronic applications accepted.

University of Memphis, Graduate School, College of Education, Department of Counseling, Educational Psychology and Research, Memphis, TN 38152. Offers counseling (MS, Ed D), including community counseling (MS), rehabilitation counseling (MS), school counseling (MS); counseling psychology (PhD); educational psychology and research (MS, PhD), including educational psychology, educational research. *Accreditation:* ACA (one or more programs are accredited); APA (one or more programs are accredited); CORE (one or more programs are accredited); NCATE. *Faculty:* 26 full-time (13 women), 9 part-time/adjunct (5 women). *Students:* 95 full-time (73 women), 104 part-time (81 women); includes 62 minority (56 African Americans, 3 American Indian/Alaska Native, 1 Asian American or Pacific Islander, 2 Hispanic Americans), 5 international. Average age 33. 118 applicants, 63% accepted, 36 enrolled. In 2009, 46 master's, 14 doctorates awarded. *Degree requirements:* For master's, comprehensive exam, thesis or alternative; for doctorate, comprehensive exam, thesis/dissertation. *Entrance requirements:* For master's, GRE General Test or MAT, minimum GPA of 2.5; for doctorate, GRE General Test. *Application deadline:* For fall admission, 10/1 for domestic students; for spring admission, 4/1 for domestic students. Application fee: $35 ($60 for international students). *Expenses:* Tuition, state resident: full-time $6246; part-time $347 per credit hour. Tuition, nonresident: full-time $15,894; part-time $883 per credit hour. Required fees: $1160. Full-time tuition and fees vary according to course load, degree level and program. *Financial support:* In 2009–10, 130 students received support; fellowships with full tuition reimbursements available, research assistantships with full tuition reimbursements available, teaching assistantships with full tuition reimbursements available, career-related internships or fieldwork, Federal Work-Study, scholarships/grants, and unspecified assistantships available. Financial award application deadline: 2/15; financial award applicants required to submit FAFSA. *Faculty research:* Anger management, aging and disability, supervision, multicultural counseling. *Unit head:* Dr. Douglas C. Strohmer, Chair, 901-678-2841, Fax: 901-678-5114. *Application contact:* Dr. Ernest A. Rakow, Associate Dean of Administration and Graduate Programs, 901-678-2399, Fax: 901-678-4778.

University of Miami, Graduate School, School of Education, Department of Educational and Psychological Studies, Program in Counseling Psychology, Coral Gables, FL 33124. Offers PhD. *Accreditation:* APA. *Students:* 34 full-time (27 women); includes 13 minority (5 African Americans, 8 Hispanic Americans), 2 international. Average age 30. 86 applicants, 8% accepted, 7 enrolled. In 2009, 5 doctorates awarded. *Degree requirements:* For doctorate, thesis/dissertation, qualifying exam. *Entrance requirements:* For doctorate, GRE General Test. Additional exam requirements/recommendations for international students: Required—TOEFL (minimum score 550 paper-based; 80 iBT); Recommended—IELTS (minimum score 6.5). *Application deadline:* For fall admission, 12/15 for domestic students, 10/15 for international students. Application fee: $65. Electronic applications accepted. *Financial support:* In 2009–10, 25 students received support. Career-related internships or fieldwork, institutionally sponsored loans, health care benefits, and unspecified assistantships available. Financial award application deadline: 3/1; financial award applicants required to submit FAFSA. *Faculty research:* Cocaine recidivism, family systems, behavior and health, nontraditional families, stress and coping. *Unit head:* Dr. Brian Lewis, Clinical Assistant Professor and Director of Training, 305-284-2260, Fax: 305-284-3003, E-mail: blewis@miami.edu. *Application contact:* Marissa Stevenson-Jacobs, Graduate Admissions Coordinator, 305-284-2167, Fax: 305-284-3003, E-mail: mstevenson@miami.edu.

University of Minnesota, Twin Cities Campus, Graduate School, College of Liberal Arts, Department of Psychology, Program in Counseling Psychology, Minneapolis, MN 55455-0213. Offers PhD. *Accreditation:* APA. *Degree requirements:* For doctorate, comprehensive exam, thesis/dissertation, internship. *Entrance requirements:* For doctorate, GRE General Test, GRE Subject Test (recommended), 12 credits of upper-level psychology courses, including a course in statistics or psychological measurement. Additional exam requirements/recommendations for international students: Required—TOEFL (minimum score 550 paper-based; 213 computer-based; 79 iBT).

University of Missouri, Graduate School, College of Education, Department of Educational, School, and Counseling Psychology, Columbia, MO 65211. Offers counseling psychology (M Ed, MA, PhD, Ed S); educational psychology (M Ed, MA, PhD, Ed S); learning and instruction (M Ed); school psychology (M Ed, MA, PhD, Ed S). *Accreditation:* APA (one or more programs are accredited). Part-time programs available. *Degree requirements:* For doctorate, thesis/dissertation. *Entrance requirements:* For master's, doctorate, and Ed S, GRE General Test, minimum GPA of 3.0. Additional exam requirements/recommendations for international students: Required—TOEFL (minimum score 580 paper-based; 237 computer-based; 92 iBT).

University of Missouri–Kansas City, School of Education, Kansas City, MO 64110-2499. Offers administration (Ed D); counseling and guidance (MA, Ed S); counseling psychology (PhD); curriculum and instruction (MA, Ed S); education (PhD); educational administration (Ed S); reading education (MA, Ed S); special education (MA). PhD with concentration in education (interdisciplinary) is offered through the School of Graduate Studies. *Accreditation:* NCATE. Part-time and evening/weekend programs available. *Faculty:* 62 full-time (52 women), 45 part-time/adjunct (34 women). *Students:* 207 full-time (154 women), 401 part-time (290 women); includes 142 minority (107 African Americans, 14 Asian Americans or Pacific Islanders, 21 Hispanic Americans), 18 international. Average age 34. 294 applicants, 61% accepted, 150 enrolled. In 2009, 184 master's, 9 doctorates, 49 other advanced degrees awarded. *Degree requirements:* For doctorate, thesis/dissertation, internship, practicum. *Entrance requirements:* For master's, GRE, minimum GPA of 2.75, 2 letters of reference, written statement of purpose; for doctorate, GRE, minimum GPA of 3.0; for Ed S, minimum GPA of 3.0. Additional exam requirements/recommendations for international students: Required—TOEFL (minimum score 550 paper-based; 213 computer-based; 80 iBT). *Application deadline:* For fall admission, 4/1 priority date for domestic and international students; for spring admission, 11/1 priority date for domestic and international students. Applications are processed on a rolling basis. Application fee: $45 ($50 for international students). *Expenses:* Tuition, state resident: full-time $5378; part-time $299 per credit hour. Tuition, nonresident: full-time $13,881; part-time $771 per credit hour. Required fees: $641; $71 per credit hour. Tuition and fees vary according to course load and program. *Financial support:* In 2009–10, 19 research assistantships with partial tuition reimbursements (averaging $9,821 per year) were awarded; career-related internships or fieldwork, Federal Work-Study, institutionally sponsored loans, and tuition waivers (full and partial) also available. Support available to part-time students. Financial award application deadline: 3/1; financial award applicants required to submit FAFSA. *Faculty research:* Urban education, inquiry-based field study, theories of counseling and psychotherapy, school literacy, educational technology. Total annual research expenditures: $2.9 million. *Unit head:* Dr. Wanda Blanchett, Dean, 816-235-2234, Fax: 816-235-5270, E-mail: education@umkc.edu. *Application contact:* Erica Hernandez-Scott, Student Recruiter, 816-235-1295, Fax: 816-235-5270, E-mail: hernandeze@umkc.edu.

The University of Montana, Graduate School, School of Education, Department of Educational Leadership and Counseling, Program in Counselor Education, Missoula, MT 59812-0002. Offers counselor education (Ed S); counselor education and supervision (Ed D); mental health counseling (MA); school counseling (MA). *Accreditation:* ACA. *Degree requirements:* For doctorate, thesis/dissertation. *Entrance requirements:* For master's, doctorate, and Ed S, GRE General Test. Additional exam requirements/recommendations for international students: Required—TOEFL.

University of Nebraska–Lincoln, Graduate College, College of Education and Human Sciences, Department of Educational Psychology, Lincoln, NE 68588. Offers cognition, learning and development (MA); counseling psychology (MA); educational psychology (MA, Ed S); psychological studies in education (PhD), including cognition, learning and development, counseling psychology, quantitative, qualitative, and psychometric methods, school psychology; quantitative, qualitative, and psychometric methods (MA); school psychology (MA, Ed S). *Accreditation:* APA (one or more programs are accredited); NCATE. *Degree requirements:* For master's, thesis optional. *Entrance requirements:* For master's, GRE General Test. Additional exam requirements/recommendations for international students: Required—TOEFL (minimum score 500 paper-based; 173 computer-based). Electronic applications accepted. *Faculty research:* Measurement and assessment, metacognition, academic skills, child development, multicultural education and counseling.

The University of North Carolina at Greensboro, Graduate School, School of Education, Department of Counseling and Educational Development, Greensboro, NC 27412-5001. Offers advanced school counseling (PMC); counseling and counselor education (PhD); counseling and educational development (MS); couple and family counseling (PMC); school counseling (PMC); MS/Ed S. *Accreditation:* ACA (one or more programs are accredited); NCATE. *Degree requirements:* For master's, comprehensive exam, practicum, internship; for doctorate, comprehensive exam, thesis/dissertation. *Entrance requirements:* For master's, doctorate, and PMC, GRE General Test. Additional exam requirements/recommendations for international students: Required—TOEFL. Electronic applications accepted. *Faculty research:* Gerontology, invitational theory, career development, marriage and family therapy, drug and alcohol abuse prevention.

University of North Dakota, Graduate School, College of Education and Human Development, Department of Counseling, Grand Forks, ND 58202. Offers MA. *Degree requirements:* For master's, comprehensive exam, thesis or alternative. *Entrance requirements:* For master's, GRE General Test or MAT, minimum GPA of 3.0. Additional exam requirements/recommendations for international students: Required—TOEFL (minimum score 550 paper-based; 213 computer-based; 79 iBT), IELTS (minimum score 6.5). Electronic applications accepted. *Faculty research:* Group dynamics, addictive behavior, item response theory, geopsychology, women's health.

University of Northern Colorado, Graduate School, College of Education and Behavioral Sciences, School of Applied Psychology and Counselor Education, Program in Counseling Psychology, Greeley, CO 80639. Offers Psy D. *Accreditation:* ACA; APA; NCATE. Part-time and evening/weekend programs available. *Faculty:* 5 full-time (3 women). *Students:* 3 full-time (2 women), 1 (woman) part-time. Average age 38. 54 applicants, 4% accepted, 2 enrolled. In 2009, 3 doctorates awarded. *Degree requirements:* For doctorate, comprehensive exam, thesis/dissertation. *Entrance requirements:* For doctorate, GRE General Test, 3 letters of reference. *Application deadline:* Applications are processed on a rolling basis. Application fee: $50 ($60 for international students). *Expenses:* Tuition, state resident: full-time $5770; part-time $320.55 per credit hour. Tuition, nonresident: full-time $13,847; part-time $769.27 per credit hour. Required fees: $948.78; $52.72 per credit. *Financial support:* Fellowships, research assistantships, teaching assistantships, unspecified assistantships available. Financial award application deadline: 3/1; financial award applicants required to submit FAFSA. *Unit head:* Dr. Brian Johnson, Program Coordinator, 970-351-2731. *Application contact:* Linda Sisson, Graduate Student Admission Coordinator, 970-351-1807, Fax: 970-351-2371, E-mail: linda.sisson@unco.edu.

University of North Florida, College of Arts and Sciences, Department of Psychology, Jacksonville, FL 32224. Offers counseling psychology (MAC); general psychology (MA). Part-time and evening/weekend programs available. *Faculty:* 14 full-time (5 women). *Students:* 61 full-time (37 women), 7 part-time (5 women); includes 10 minority (4 African Americans, 1 American Indian/Alaska Native, 5 Hispanic Americans). Average age 27. 110 applicants, 25% accepted, 15 enrolled. In 2009, 15 master's awarded. *Degree requirements:* For master's, comprehensive exam, thesis optional, practicum. *Entrance requirements:* For master's, GRE General Test, 2 letters of recommendation, minimum GPA of 3.0 in last 60 hours of course work. Additional exam requirements/recommendations for international students: Required—

Counseling Psychology

University of North Florida (continued)
TOEFL (minimum score 500 paper-based; 173 computer-based). *Application deadline:* For fall admission, 6/1 priority date for domestic students, 4/1 for international students. Applications are processed on a rolling basis. Application fee: $30. Electronic applications accepted. *Expenses:* Tuition, state resident: full-time $6649.20; part-time $277.05 per credit hour. Tuition, nonresident: full-time $22,970; part-time $957.08 per credit hour. Required fees: $985; $41.03 per credit hour. *Financial support:* In 2009–10, 45 students received support, including 3 research assistantships (averaging $2,476 per year), 4 teaching assistantships (averaging $3,499 per year); Federal Work-Study and tuition waivers (partial) also available. Support available to part-time students. Financial award application deadline: 4/1; financial award applicants required to submit FAFSA. *Faculty research:* Sensory perception, social cognition, sexual behavior, evolutionary psychology, psychology and law. Total annual research expenditures: $89,642. *Unit head:* Dr. Michael Toglia, Chair, 904-620-1624, E-mail: m.toglia@unf.edu. *Application contact:* Dr. Randy Russac, Graduate Coordinator for General Psychology, 904-620-2807, Fax: 904-620-3814, E-mail: rrussac@unf.edu.

University of North Florida, College of Education and Human Services, Department of Leadership, Counseling and Instructional Technology, Program in Counselor Education, Jacksonville, FL 32224. Offers mental health counseling (M Ed); school counseling (M Ed). *Accreditation:* ACA; NCATE. Part-time and evening/weekend programs available. *Faculty:* 18 full-time (11 women). *Students:* 19 full-time (15 women), 22 part-time (19 women); includes 11 minority (8 African Americans, 2 Asian Americans or Pacific Islanders, 1 Hispanic American). Average age 29. 6 applicants, 33% accepted, 0 enrolled. In 2009, 30 master's awarded. *Entrance requirements:* For master's, GRE General Test, minimum GPA of 3.0 in last 60 hours, 3 letters of recommendation, portfolio, interview, writing sample. Additional exam requirements/recommendations for international students: Required—TOEFL (minimum score 500 paper-based; 173 computer-based). *Application deadline:* For fall admission, 5/15 for domestic students, 4/23 for international students; for spring admission, 9/26 for domestic students. Application fee: $30. Electronic applications accepted. *Expenses:* Tuition, state resident: full-time $6649.20; part-time $277.05 per credit hour. Tuition, nonresident: full-time $22,970; part-time $957.08 per credit hour. Required fees: $985; $41.03 per credit hour. *Financial support:* In 2009–10, 30 students received support, including 3 research assistantships (averaging $3,600 per year); career-related internships or fieldwork, Federal Work-Study, and tuition waivers (partial) also available. Support available to part-time students. Financial award application deadline: 4/1; financial award applicants required to submit FAFSA. *Unit head:* Dr. Edgar N. Jackson, Chair, 904-620-2990, Fax: 904-620-2982, E-mail: newton.jackson@unf.edu. *Application contact:* Kiersten Jarvis, Graduate Admissions Coordinator, 904-620-1360, Fax: 904-620-1362, E-mail: kiersten.jarvis@unf.edu.

University of North Texas, Robert B. Toulouse School of Graduate Studies, College of Arts and Sciences, Department of Psychology, Denton, TX 76203-5017. Offers clinical psychology (PhD); counseling psychology (MA, MS, PhD); experimental psychology (MA, MS, PhD); health psychology and behavioral medicine (PhD). *Accreditation:* APA (one or more programs are accredited). Terminal master's awarded for partial completion of doctoral program. *Degree requirements:* For master's, comprehensive exam, thesis or alternative; for doctorate, one foreign language, comprehensive exam, thesis/dissertation. *Entrance requirements:* For master's and doctorate, GRE General Test, interview. Additional exam requirements/recommendations for international students: Required—proof of English language proficiency required for non-native English speakers; Recommended—TOEFL (minimum score 550 paper-based; 213 computer-based; 79 iBT). *Application deadline:* Applications are processed on a rolling basis. Application fee: $50 ($75 for international students). Electronic applications accepted. *Expenses:* Tuition, state resident: full-time $4298; part-time $239 per contact hour. Tuition, nonresident: full-time $9878; part-time $549 per contact hour. Required fees: $265 per contact hour. *Financial support:* Fellowships, research assistantships, teaching assistantships, career-related internships or fieldwork, Federal Work-Study, and institutionally sponsored loans available. Financial award applicants required to submit FAFSA. *Application contact:* Graduate Coordinator, 940-565-2671, Fax: 940-565-4682, E-mail: amym@unt.edu.

University of Notre Dame, Graduate School, College of Arts and Letters, Division of Social Science, Department of Psychology, Notre Dame, IN 46556. Offers cognitive psychology (PhD); counseling psychology (PhD); developmental psychology (PhD); quantitative psychology (PhD). *Accreditation:* APA. *Degree requirements:* For doctorate, comprehensive exam, thesis/dissertation, candidacy exam. *Entrance requirements:* For doctorate, GRE General Test, GRE Subject Test (strongly recommended). Additional exam requirements/recommendations for international students: Required—TOEFL (minimum score 600 paper-based; 250 computer-based; 80 iBT). Electronic applications accepted. *Faculty research:* Cognitive and socio-emotional development, statistical methods and quantitative models applicable to psychology, interpersonal relations, life span development and developmental delay, childhood depression, structural equation and dynamical systems.

University of Oklahoma, Graduate College, College of Education, Department of Educational Psychology, Program in Counseling Psychology, Norman, OK 73019. Offers PhD. *Accreditation:* APA. *Students:* 25 full-time (14 women), 18 part-time (12 women); includes 11 minority (2 African Americans, 6 American Indian/Alaska Native, 1 Asian American or Pacific Islander, 2 Hispanic Americans), 1 international. 39 applicants, 8% accepted, 3 enrolled. In 2009, 6 doctorates awarded. *Degree requirements:* For doctorate, thesis/dissertation, general exam. *Entrance requirements:* For doctorate, GRE General Test, master's degree, 3 letters of recommendation, interview, curriculum vitae. Additional exam requirements/recommendations for international students: Required—TOEFL (minimum score 550 paper-based; 213 computer-based). *Application deadline:* For fall admission, 1/10 for domestic and international students; for spring admission, 11/1 for domestic students, 9/1 for international students. Applications are processed on a rolling basis. Application fee: $40 ($90 for international students). Electronic applications accepted. *Expenses:* Tuition, state resident: full-time $3744; part-time $156 per credit hour. Tuition, nonresident: full-time $13,577; part-time $565.70 per credit hour. Required fees: $2415; $90.10 per credit hour. *Financial support:* In 2009–10, 20 students received support. Career-related internships or fieldwork, Federal Work-Study, institutionally sponsored loans, scholarships/grants, health care benefits, and unspecified assistantships available. Support available to part-time students. Financial award application deadline: 3/1; financial award applicants required to submit FAFSA. *Faculty research:* Counseling assessment; process and outcome; diversity issues; health psychology; marriage and family; education, training and supervision. *Unit head:* Dr. Terri K. Debacker, Chair, 405-325-1068, Fax: 405-325-6655, E-mail: debacker@ou.edu. *Application contact:* Rashida Y. Douglas, Graduate Programs Officer, 405-325-4525, Fax: 405-325-6655, E-mail: ryd618@ou.edu.

University of Pennsylvania, Graduate School of Education, Division of Applied Psychology and Human Development, Program in Counseling and Psychological Services, Philadelphia, PA 19104. Offers PhD. *Students:* 14 full-time (13 women), 5 part-time (all women); includes 3 minority (1 Asian American or Pacific Islander, 2 Hispanic Americans). 152 applicants, 64% accepted. *Degree requirements:* For doctorate, thesis/dissertation, exams. *Entrance requirements:* For doctorate, GRE General Test, GRE Subject Test. *Application deadline:* For fall admission, 12/15 priority date for domestic students. Applications are processed on a rolling basis. Application fee: $70. Electronic applications accepted. *Expenses:* Contact institution. *Financial support:* Fellowships, institutionally sponsored loans, scholarships/grants, traineeships, health care benefits, and unspecified assistantships available. *Faculty research:* Therapeutic interventions at a preschool level, childhood stress, college psychology, school and community psychology.

University of Pennsylvania, Graduate School of Education, Division of Applied Psychology and Human Development, Program in Professional Counseling and Mental Health Services, Philadelphia, PA 19104. Offers counseling and mental health services (MS Ed); professional counseling (M Phil); school counseling (MS Ed). *Students:* 77 full-time (62 women), 11 part-time (9 women); includes 21 minority (12 African Americans, 1 American Indian/Alaska Native, 2 Asian Americans or Pacific Islanders, 6 Hispanic Americans), 1 international. 22 applicants, 100% accepted, 22 enrolled. *Degree requirements:* For master's, exam. *Entrance requirements:* For master's, GRE General Test. *Application deadline:* For fall admission, 12/15 priority date for domestic students. Applications are processed on a rolling basis. Application fee: $70. Electronic applications accepted. *Expenses:* Contact institution. *Financial support:* Applicants required to submit FAFSA. *Faculty research:* Counseling in school, college, or agency.

University of Phoenix–Las Vegas Campus, The Artemis School, College of Health and Human Services, Las Vegas, NV 89128. Offers administration of justice and security (MS); health administration (MHA); health care management (MBA); marriage, family, and child therapy (MSC); mental health counseling (MSC); nursing (MSN); nursing/health care education (MSN); psychology (MS); MSN/MBA; MSN/MHA. Postbaccalaureate distance learning degree programs offered. *Entrance requirements:* For master's, minimum undergraduate GPA of 2.5, 3 years of work experience. Additional exam requirements/recommendations for international students: Required—TOEFL (minimum score 550 paper-based; 213 computer-based; 79 iBT). Electronic applications accepted.

University of Phoenix–Puerto Rico Campus, The Artemis School, College of Health and Human Services, Guaynabo, PR 00968. Offers marriage and family counseling (MSC); mental health counseling (MSC). Evening/weekend programs available. *Degree requirements:* For master's, thesis (for some programs). *Entrance requirements:* For master's, Counselor Preparation Comprehensive Examination, minimum undergraduate GPA of 2.5, 3 years work experience. Additional exam requirements/recommendations for international students: Required—TOEFL (minimum score 550 paper-based; 213 computer-based; 79 iBT). Electronic applications accepted.

University of Phoenix–Sacramento Valley Campus, The Artemis School, College of Health and Human Services, Sacramento, CA 95833-3632. Offers administration of justice and security (MS); community counseling (MSC); family nurse practitioner (MSN); health administration (MHA); health care education (MSN); health care management (MBA); marriage, family and child counseling (MSC); nursing (MSN); psychology (MS); MSN/MBA. Evening/weekend programs available. *Degree requirements:* For master's, thesis (for some programs). *Entrance requirements:* For master's, RN license, minimum undergraduate GPA of 2.5, 3 years work experience. Additional exam requirements/recommendations for international students: Required—TOEFL (minimum score 550 paper-based; 213 computer-based; 79 iBT). Electronic applications accepted.

University of Phoenix–Utah Campus, The Artemis School, College of Health and Human Services, Salt Lake City, UT 84123-4617. Offers health care management (MBA); healthcare education (MSN); mental health counseling (MSC); nursing (MSN); MSN/MBA. Evening/weekend programs available. *Degree requirements:* For master's, thesis (for some programs). *Entrance requirements:* For master's, minimum undergraduate GPA of 2.5, 3 years work experience, RN license. Additional exam requirements/recommendations for international students: Required—TOEFL (minimum score 550 paper-based; 213 computer-based; 79 iBT). Electronic applications accepted.

University of Puget Sound, Graduate Studies, School of Education, Program in Counseling, Tacoma, WA 98416. Offers mental health counseling (M Ed); pastoral counseling (M Ed); school counseling (M Ed). *Accreditation:* NCATE. Part-time programs available. *Faculty:* 2 full-time (both women). *Students:* 1 (woman) full-time, 26 part-time (20 women); includes 4 minority (1 African American, 3 Hispanic Americans). Average age 32. 25 applicants, 56% accepted, 11 enrolled. In 2009, 10 master's awarded. *Entrance requirements:* For master's, GRE General Test, minimum GPA of 3.0. Additional exam requirements/recommendations for international students: Required—TOEFL (minimum score 550 paper-based; 213 computer-based; 80 iBT). *Application deadline:* For fall admission, 3/1 priority date for domestic and international students. Applications are processed on a rolling basis. Application fee: $60. Electronic applications accepted. *Expenses:* Contact institution. *Financial support:* Teaching assistantships, career-related internships or fieldwork available. Financial award application deadline: 3/31; financial award applicants required to submit FAFSA. *Faculty research:* Cross-role professional preparation, suicide prevention. *Unit head:* Dr. John Woodward, Dean, 253-879-3375, E-mail: woodward@pugetsound.edu. *Application contact:* Dr. George H. Mills, Vice President for Enrollment, 253-879-3211, Fax: 253-879-3993, E-mail: admission@pugetsound.edu.

University of Rhode Island, Graduate School, College of Human Science and Services, Department of Human Development and Family Studies, Kingston, RI 02881. Offers college student personnel (MS); human development and family studies (MS); marriage and family therapy (MS). *Accreditation:* AAMFT/COAMFTE. Part-time programs available. *Faculty:* 14 full-time (11 women), 4 part-time/adjunct (2 women). *Students:* 36 full-time (31 women), 18 part-time (16 women); includes 11 minority (6 African Americans, 2 Asian Americans or Pacific Islanders, 3 Hispanic Americans). In 2009, 27 master's awarded. *Degree requirements:* For master's, comprehensive exam (for some programs), thesis optional. *Entrance requirements:* For master's, GRE or MAT, 2 letters of recommendation. Additional exam requirements/recommendations for international students: Required—TOEFL (minimum score 550 paper-based; 213 computer-based). Application fee: $65. Electronic applications accepted. *Expenses:* Tuition, state resident: full-time $8828; part-time $490 per credit hour. Tuition, nonresident: full-time $22,100; part-time $1228 per credit hour. Required fees: $1118; $57 per semester. Tuition and fees vary according to program. *Financial support:* In 2009–10, 3 research assistantships with full and partial tuition reimbursements (averaging $10,421 per year), 4 teaching assistantships with full and partial tuition reimbursements (averaging $7,443 per year) were awarded. Financial award applicants required to submit FAFSA. Total annual research expenditures: $833,866. *Unit head:* Dr. Jerome Adams, Chair, 401-874-5962, Fax: 401-874-4020, E-mail: jadams@uri.edu. *Application contact:* Dr. Jerome Adams, Chair, 401-874-5962, Fax: 401-874-4020, E-mail: jadams@uri.edu.

University of Saint Francis, Graduate School, Department of Psychology and Counseling, Fort Wayne, IN 46808-3994. Offers general psychology (MS); mental health counseling (MS); pastoral counseling (MS); school counseling (MS Ed). Part-time and evening/weekend programs available. *Entrance requirements:* For master's, interview, minimum undergraduate GPA of 3.0.

University of St. Thomas, Graduate Studies, Graduate School of Professional Psychology, St. Paul, MN 55105-1096. Offers counseling psychology (MA, Psy D); marriage and family psychology (MA, Certificate). *Accreditation:* APA. Part-time and evening/weekend programs available. *Faculty:* 11 full-time (5 women), 13 part-time/adjunct (6 women). *Students:* 68 full-time (54 women), 141 part-time (113 women); includes 21 minority (5 African Americans, 13 Asian Americans or Pacific Islanders, 3 Hispanic Americans), 4 international. Average age 29. 578 applicants, 42% accepted. In 2009, 22 master's, 11 doctorates awarded. *Degree requirements:* For master's, comprehensive exam, practicum; for doctorate, comprehensive exam, thesis/dissertation, qualifying exam, practicum, internship. *Entrance requirements:* For master's, GRE, minimum GPA of 2.75, letters of recommendation, personal statement; for doctorate, GRE, minimum GPA of 3.2, letters of recommendation, personal statement. Additional exam requirements/recommendations for international students: Required—TOEFL (minimum score 550 paper-based; 213 computer-based; 80 iBT). *Application deadline:* For fall admission, 3/1 priority date for domestic students; for winter admission, 2/1 priority date for domestic students; for spring admission, 9/15 priority date for domestic students, 3/1 for international students. Application fee: $50. *Expenses:* Contact institution. *Financial support:* In 2009–10, 2 fellowships (averaging $5,000 per year) were awarded; research assistantships, institutionally sponsored loans and scholarships/grants also available. Support available to part-time students. Financial award application deadline: 8/1; financial award applicants required to submit FAFSA. *Faculty research:* Elderly, eating disorders, anxiety, family. *Unit head:* Dr. Christopher S. Vye, Associate Dean, 651-962-4666, Fax: 651-962-4666, E-mail: bnolan@stthomas.edu. *Application contact:* Laurie Dupont, Administrative Assistant, 651-962-4669, Fax: 651-962-4651, E-mail: ldupont@stthomas.edu.

University of San Diego, School of Leadership and Education Sciences, Program in Counseling, San Diego, CA 92110-2492. Offers clinical mental health counseling (MA); school counseling (MA). Part-time and evening/weekend programs available. *Faculty:* 6 full-time (2 women), 7 part-time/adjunct (6 women). *Students:* 84 full-time (74 women), 25 part-time (20 women); includes 45 minority (4 African Americans, 16 Asian Americans or Pacific Islanders, 25 Hispanic Americans), 1 international. Average age 27. 132 applicants, 70% accepted, 54 enrolled. In 2009, 36 master's awarded. *Degree requirements:* For master's, comprehensive exam. *Entrance requirements:* For master's, minimum GPA of 3.0, interview with faculty member. Additional exam requirements/recommendations for international students: Required—TOEFL (minimum score 580 paper-based; 237 computer-based; 83 iBT), TWE. *Application deadline:* For fall admission, 3/1 priority date for domestic students, 3/1 for international students. Application fee: $45. Electronic applications accepted. *Expenses:* Tuition: Full-time $21,042; part-time $1169 per unit. Required fees: $224. Full-time tuition and fees vary according to course load and degree level. *Financial support:* In 2009–10, 102 students received support. Career-related internships or fieldwork, Federal Work-Study, institutionally sponsored loans, unspecified assistantships, and stipends available. Support available to part-time students. Financial award application deadline: 4/1; financial award applicants required to submit FAFSA. *Faculty research:* Action research, forensic psychology, lifespan and career development, multicultural counseling, school counseling. *Unit head:* Dr. Lonnie Rowell, Graduate Program Co-Director, 619-260-4212, Fax: 619-260-8095. *Application contact:* Dr. John Mosby, Associate Director of Graduate Admissions, 619-260-4524, Fax: 619-260-4158, E-mail: grads@sandiego.edu.

University of San Francisco, School of Education, Department of Counseling Psychology, San Francisco, CA 94117-1080. Offers counseling (MA), including educational counseling, life transitions counseling, marital and family therapy; counseling psychology (Ed D). *Faculty:* 7 full-time (3 women), 37 part-time/adjunct (26 women). *Students:* 277 full-time (228 women), 9 part-time (7 women); includes 97 minority (16 African Americans, 1 American Indian/Alaska Native, 35 Asian Americans or Pacific Islanders, 45 Hispanic Americans), 8 international. Average age 31. 354 applicants, 66% accepted, 132 enrolled. In 2009, 150 master's awarded. *Degree requirements:* For doctorate, thesis/dissertation. *Entrance requirements:* For doctorate, GRE General Test. Application fee: $55 ($65 for international students). *Expenses:* Tuition: Full-time $19,710; part-time $1095 per unit. Part-time tuition and fees vary according to degree level, campus/location and program. *Financial support:* In 2009–10, 227 students received support; fellowships, research assistantships, teaching assistantships available. Financial award application deadline: 3/2; financial award applicants required to submit FAFSA. *Unit head:* Dr. Brian Gerrard, Chair, 415-422-6868. *Application contact:* Beth Teague, Associate Director of Graduate Outreach, 415-422-5467, E-mail: schoolofeducation@usfca.edu.

The University of Scranton, College of Graduate and Continuing Education, Department of Counseling and Human Services, Scranton, PA 18510. Offers community counseling (MS); professional counseling (CAGS); rehabilitation counseling (MS); school counseling (MS). *Accreditation:* ACA (one or more programs are accredited). Part-time and evening/weekend programs available. *Faculty:* 9 full-time (6 women), 10 part-time/adjunct (5 women). *Students:* 136 full-time (103 women), 25 part-time (17 women); includes 16 minority (9 African Americans, 2 Asian Americans or Pacific Islanders, 5 Hispanic Americans), 1 international. Average age 29. 117 applicants, 62% accepted. In 2009, 46 master's awarded. *Degree requirements:* For master's, comprehensive exam, capstone experience. *Entrance requirements:* For master's, minimum GPA of 2.75. Additional exam requirements/recommendations for international students: Required—TOEFL (minimum score 500 paper-based; 173 computer-based), IELTS (minimum score 5.5). *Application deadline:* For fall admission, 3/1 for domestic students. Application fee: $0. *Financial support:* In 2009–10, 20 students received support, including 20 teaching assistantships with full and partial tuition reimbursements available (averaging $5,115 per year); fellowships, career-related internships or fieldwork, Federal Work-Study, and unspecified assistantships also available. Support available to part-time students. Financial award application deadline: 3/1. *Unit head:* Dr. Lee Ann Eschbach, Chair, 570-941-6299, Fax: 570-941-4201, E-mail: eschbach@scranton.edu. *Application contact:* Joseph M. Robach, Director of Admissions, 570-941-4385, Fax: 570-941-5928, E-mail: robachj2@scranton.edu.

University of South Africa, College of Human Sciences, Pretoria, South Africa. Offers adult education (M Ed); African languages (MA, PhD); African politics (MA, PhD); Afrikaans (MA, PhD); ancient history (MA, PhD); ancient Near Eastern studies (MA, PhD); anthropology (MA, PhD); applied linguistics (MA); Arabic (MA, PhD); archaeology (MA); art history (MA); Biblical archaeology (MA); Biblical studies (M Th, D Th, PhD); Christian spirituality (M Th, D Th); church history (M Th, D Th); classical studies (MA, PhD); clinical psychology (MA); communication (MA, PhD); comparative education (M Ed, Ed D); consulting psychology (D Admin, D Com, PhD); curriculum studies (M Ed, Ed D); development studies (M Admin, MA, D Admin, PhD); didactics (M Ed, Ed D); education (M Tech); education management (M Ed, Ed D); educational psychology (M Ed); English (MA); environmental education (M Ed); French (MA, PhD); German (MA, PhD); Greek (MA); guidance and counseling (M Ed); health studies (MA, PhD), including health sciences education (MA), health services management (MA), medical and surgical nursing science (critical care general) (MA), midwifery and neonatal nursing science (MA), trauma and emergency care (MA); history (MA, PhD); history of education (Ed D); inclusive education (M Ed, Ed D); information and communications technology policy and regulation (MA); information science (MA, MIS, PhD); international politics (MA, PhD); Islamic studies (MA, PhD); Italian (MA, PhD); Judaica (MA, PhD); linguistics (MA, PhD); mathematical education (M Ed); mathematics education (MA); missiology (M Th, D Th); modern Hebrew (MA, PhD); musicology (MA, MMus, D Mus, PhD); natural science education (M Ed); New Testament (M Th, D Th); Old Testament (D Th); pastoral therapy (M Th, D Th); philosophy (MA); philosophy of education (M Ed, Ed D); politics (MA, PhD); Portuguese (MA, PhD); practical theology (M Th, D Th); psychology (MA, MS, PhD); psychology of education (M Ed, Ed D); public health (MA); religious studies (MA, D Th, PhD); Romance languages (MA); Russian (MA, PhD); Semitic languages (MA, PhD); social behavior studies in HIV/AIDS (MA); social science (mental health) (MA); social science in development studies (MA); social science in psychology (MA); social science in social work (MA); social science in sociology (MA); social work (MSW, DSW, PhD); socio-education (M Ed, Ed D); sociolinguistics (MA); sociology (MA, PhD); Spanish (MA, PhD); systematic theology (M Th, D Th); TESOL (teaching English to speakers of other languages) (MA); theological ethics (M Th, D Th); theory of literature (MA, PhD); urban ministries (D Th); urban ministry (M Th).

University of Southern Maine, College of Education and Human Development, Program in Counselor Education, Portland, ME 04104-9300. Offers clinical mental health (MS); counseling (CAS); mental health rehabilitation technician/community (Certificate); rehabilitation counseling (MS); school counseling (MS). *Accreditation:* ACA (one or more programs are accredited); CORE; NCATE; Teacher Education Accreditation Council. Part-time and evening/weekend programs available. *Faculty:* 8 full-time (4 women); 2 part-time/adjunct (1 woman). *Students:* 110 full-time (83 women), 33 part-time (23 women); includes 5 minority (1 African American, 1 American Indian/Alaska Native, 3 Hispanic Americans). 79 applicants, 72% accepted, 44 enrolled. In 2009, 37 master's, 2 other advanced degrees awarded. *Degree requirements:* For master's, comprehensive exam, thesis or alternative; for other advanced degree, thesis or alternative. *Entrance requirements:* For master's, GRE General Test or MAT, interview; for other advanced degree, master's degree. Additional exam requirements/recommendations for international students: Required—TOEFL (minimum score 550 paper-based; 213 computer-based; 79 iBT). *Application deadline:* For fall admission, 11/15 for domestic students. Application fee: $50. Electronic applications accepted. *Financial support:* In 2009–10, 12 students received support, including 3 research assistantships with partial tuition reimbursements available (averaging $4,500 per year); career-related internships or fieldwork, Federal Work-Study, institutionally sponsored loans, scholarships/grants, and unspecified assistantships also available. Support available to part-time students. Financial award application deadline: 3/1; financial award applicants required to submit FAFSA. *Faculty research:* Counselor licensure. *Unit head:* Dr. E. Michael Brady, Chair, Human Resource Development Department, 207-780-5316, Fax: 207-780-5043, E-mail: mbrady@usm.maine.edu. *Application contact:* Mary Sloan, Director of Graduate Admissions, 207-780-4386, Fax: 207-780-4969, E-mail: msloan@usm.maine.edu.

University of Southern Mississippi, Graduate School, College of Education and Psychology, Department of Psychology, Hattiesburg, MS 39406-0001. Offers clinical psychology (MA, PhD); counseling psychology (PhD); experimental psychology (MA, PhD); psychology (MS); school psychology (MA, PhD). *Accreditation:* APA (one or more programs are accredited). *Faculty:* 32 full-time (9 women). *Students:* 104 full-time (80 women), 29 part-time (19 women); includes 14 minority (7 African Americans, 2 Asian Americans or Pacific Islanders, 5 Hispanic Americans), 7 international. Average age 29. 225 applicants, 16% accepted, 30 enrolled. In 2009, 23 master's, 13 doctorates awarded. Terminal master's awarded for partial completion of doctoral program. *Degree requirements:* For master's, comprehensive exam, thesis; for doctorate, comprehensive exam, thesis/dissertation. *Entrance requirements:* For master's, GRE General Test, minimum GPA of 3.0; for doctorate, GRE General Test, interview, minimum GPA of 3.0. Additional exam requirements/recommendations for international students: Required—TOEFL. *Application deadline:* For fall admission, 3/1 priority date for domestic students, 3/1 for international students. Applications are processed on a rolling basis. Application fee: $35. *Expenses:* Tuition, state resident: full-time $5096; part-time $284 per hour. Tuition, nonresident: full-time $13,052; part-time $726 per hour. Required fees: $402. Tuition and fees vary according to course level and course load. *Financial support:* In 2009–10, 48 research assistantships with full tuition reimbursements (averaging $8,802 per year), 48 teaching assistantships with full tuition reimbursements (averaging $6,500 per year) were awarded; career-related internships or fieldwork, Federal Work-Study, and institutionally sponsored loans also available. Financial award application deadline: 3/15; financial award applicants required to submit FAFSA. *Faculty research:* Dolphin cognition, sleep, neuropsychology, health-related behaviors, psychopathology. Total annual research expenditures: $101,200. *Unit head:* Dr. Joesph Olmi, Chair, 601-266-4177, Fax: 601-266-5580. *Application contact:* Dr. Heather Sterling-Turner, Graduate Coordinator, 601-266-4177, Fax: 601-266-5580.

The University of Tennessee, Graduate School, College of Education, Health and Human Sciences, Department of Educational Psychology and Counseling, Knoxville, TN 37996. Offers adult education (MS); applied educational psychology (MS); collaborative learning (Ed D); college student personnel (MS); mental health counseling (MS); rehabilitation counseling (MS); school counseling (MS). *Accreditation:* ACA (one or more programs are accredited); CORE (one or more programs are accredited); NCATE. Part-time and evening/weekend programs available. *Degree requirements:* For master's, thesis optional. *Entrance requirements:* For master's, GRE General Test, minimum GPA of 2.7. Additional exam requirements/recommendations for international students: Required—TOEFL. Electronic applications accepted. *Expenses:* Tuition, state resident: full-time $6826; part-time $380 per semester hour. Tuition, nonresident: full-time $21,844; part-time $1147 per semester hour. Tuition and fees vary according to program.

The University of Texas at Austin, Graduate School, College of Education, Department of Educational Psychology, Austin, TX 78712-1111. Offers academic educational psychology (M Ed, MA); counseling psychology (PhD); counselor education (M Ed); human development and culture (PhD); learning, cognition and instruction (PhD); quantitative methods (PhD); school psychology (PhD). *Accreditation:* APA (one or more programs are accredited). *Degree requirements:* For master's, thesis optional; for doctorate, thesis/dissertation. *Entrance requirements:* For master's and doctorate, GRE General Test, 3 letters of recommendation. Additional exam requirements/recommendations for international students: Required—TOEFL.

The University of Texas at Tyler, College of Education and Psychology, Department of Psychology and Counseling, Tyler, TX 75799-0001. Offers clinical psychology (MS), including neuropsychology, school psychology; counseling psychology (MA), including general, marriage and family; interdisciplinary studies (MSIS); school counseling (MA). Part-time and evening/weekend programs available. *Faculty:* 11 full-time (3 women). *Students:* 80 full-time (63 women), 46 part-time (38 women); includes 5 minority (3 African Americans, 1 American Indian/Alaska Native, 1 Hispanic American). Average age 29. 64 applicants, 77% accepted, 28 enrolled. In 2009, 36 master's awarded. *Degree requirements:* For master's, comprehensive exam, thesis optional. *Entrance requirements:* For master's, GRE General Test, minimum GPA of 3.0. Additional exam requirements/recommendations for international students: Required—TOEFL (minimum score 79 computer-based). *Application deadline:* For fall admission, 8/17 priority date for domestic students, 7/1 priority date for international students; for spring admission, 12/21 priority date for domestic students, 11/1 priority date for international students. Application fee: $25 ($50 for international students). Electronic applications accepted. *Expenses:* Tuition, state resident: part-time $665 per semester hour. Tuition, nonresident: part-time $942 per semester hour. Part-time tuition and fees vary according to degree level and program. *Financial support:* In 2009–10, fellowships with partial tuition reimbursements (averaging $3,000 per year), research assistantships (averaging $5,000 per year), teaching assistantships (averaging $1,500 per year) were awarded; career-related internships or fieldwork, Federal Work-Study, and institutionally sponsored loans also available. Support available to part-time students. Financial award application deadline: 7/1. *Faculty research:* Neuropsychology, child abuse, psychometric properties of psychological instruments, maternal behavior, clinical practice issues, victimization of women, post-traumatic stress disorder. *Unit head:* Dr. Charles B. Barke, Chair/Professor, 903-565-5875, Fax: 903-565-5560, E-mail: cbarke@uttyler.edu. *Application contact:* Dr. Charles Barke.

University of the District of Columbia, College of Arts and Sciences, Department of Psychology and Counseling, Program in Counseling, Washington, DC 20008-1175. Offers MS. *Students:* 7 full-time (5 women), 10 part-time (8 women); includes 12 minority (all African Americans). Average age 34. *Application deadline:* For fall admission, 5/15 for domestic and international students; for winter admission, 9/15 for domestic students; for spring admission, 9/15 for domestic and international students. Applications are processed on a rolling basis. Application fee: $75. *Expenses:* Tuition, state resident: full-time $7580. Tuition, nonresident: full-time $14,580. Required fees: $620. *Unit head:* Dr. Eugene Johnson, Chairperson, 202-274-7406. *Application contact:* Ann Marie Waterman, Associate Vice President for Admission, Recruitment and Financial Aid, 202-274-6069.

University of the Southwest, Graduate Programs, Hobbs, NM 88240-9129. Offers business administration (MBA); curriculum and instruction (MSE); curriculum and instruction: bilingual (MSE); curriculum and instruction: reading (MSE); curriculum and instruction: TESOL (MSE); early childhood education (MSE); educational diagnostician (MSE); mental health counseling (MSE); school business administration (MSE); school counseling (MSE); special education (MSE). Part-time and evening/weekend programs available. Postbaccalaureate distance learning degree programs offered (no on-campus study). *Faculty:* 10 full-time (6 women), 10 part-time/adjunct (4 women). *Students:* 112 full-time (93 women), 99 part-time (72 women). Average age 35. 94 applicants, 47% accepted, 39 enrolled. In 2009, 32 master's awarded. *Degree requirements:* For master's, comprehensive exam. *Application deadline:* For fall admission, 3/1 priority date for domestic students; for spring admission, 10/1 for domestic students. Applications are processed on a rolling basis. Application fee: $25. Electronic applications accepted. *Expenses:* Tuition: Part-time $512 per hour. Tuition and fees vary according to course load. *Financial support:* In 2009–10, 196 students received support; research assistantships with partial tuition reimbursements available, Federal Work-Study, scholarships/grants, and tuition waivers (partial) available. Support available to part-time students. Financial award application deadline: 4/1; financial award applicants required to submit FAFSA. *Unit head:* Dr. Mary Harris, Dean of Education, 575-392-6561 Ext. 1056, Fax: 575-392-6006, E-mail: mharris@usw.edu. *Application contact:* Ryanne Evans, Assistant Registrar, 575-392-6561 Ext. 1031, Fax: 575-392-6006, E-mail: revans@usw.edu.

University of Utah, The Graduate School, College of Education, Department of Educational Psychology, Salt Lake City, UT 84112. Offers counseling psychology (PhD); educational psychology (MA); instructional design and educational technology (M Ed); learning and cognition (MS, PhD); professional counseling (MS); professional psychology (M Ed); reading and literacy (M Ed, PhD); school counseling (M Ed, MS); school psychology (MS, PhD); statistics (M Stat). *Accreditation:* APA (one or more programs are accredited). Evening/weekend programs available. Postbaccalaureate distance learning degree programs offered (minimal on-campus study).

Counseling Psychology

University of Utah (continued)

Faculty: 21 full-time (11 women), 8 part-time/adjunct (5 women). *Students:* 92 full-time (67 women), 74 part-time (43 women); includes 16 minority (4 Asian Americans or Pacific Islanders, 12 Hispanic Americans), 2 international. Average age 33. 177 applicants, 34% accepted, 50 enrolled. In 2009, 44 master's, 9 doctorates awarded. *Degree requirements:* For master's, variable foreign language requirement, comprehensive exam, thesis (for some programs); for doctorate, variable foreign language requirement, thesis/dissertation, oral exam. *Entrance requirements:* For master's and doctorate, GRE General Test, minimum GPA of 3.0. Additional exam requirements/recommendations for international students: Required—TOEFL (minimum score 500 paper-based; 173 computer-based). *Application deadline:* For fall admission, 4/1 for domestic and international students; for spring admission, 11/1 for domestic and international students. Application fee: $55 ($65 for international students). *Expenses:* Tuition, state resident: full-time $4004; part-time $1674 per semester. Tuition, nonresident: full-time $14,134; part-time $5915 per semester. Required fees: $324 per semester. Tuition and fees vary according to course load, degree level and program. *Financial support:* In 2009–10, 55 students received support, including 20 fellowships with full tuition reimbursements available (averaging $11,000 per year), 5 research assistantships with full tuition reimbursements available (averaging $11,000 per year), 32 teaching assistantships with full and partial tuition reimbursements available (averaging $11,000 per year); career-related internships or fieldwork, Federal Work-Study, institutionally sponsored loans, scholarships/grants, and unspecified assistantships also available. Financial award application deadline: 2/1; financial award applicants required to submit FAFSA. *Faculty research:* Autism, computer technology and instruction, cognitive behavior, aging, group counseling. Total annual research expenditures: $151,911. *Unit head:* Dr. Elaine Clark, Chair, 801-581-7148, Fax: 801-581-5566, E-mail: clark@ed.utah.edu. *Application contact:* Jenna Atkinson, Academic Program Specialist, 801-581-7148, Fax: 801-581-5566, E-mail: jenna.atkinson@utah.edu.

University of Vermont, Graduate College, College of Education and Social Services, Department of Integrated Professional Studies, Counseling Program, Burlington, VT 05405. Offers MS. *Accreditation:* ACA; NCATE. *Faculty:* 3 full-time (2 women), 6 part-time/adjunct (2 women). *Students:* 42 (36 women); includes 3 minority (2 American Indian/Alaska Native, 1 Asian American or Pacific Islander), 2 international. 46 applicants, 67% accepted, 13 enrolled. In 2009, 14 master's awarded. *Entrance requirements:* For master's, GRE General Test, resume. Additional exam requirements/recommendations for international students: Required—TOEFL (minimum score 550 paper-based; 213 computer-based; 80 iBT). *Application deadline:* For fall admission, 2/1 priority date for domestic students. Applications are processed on a rolling basis. Application fee: $40. Electronic applications accepted. *Expenses:* Tuition, state resident: part-time $508 per credit hour. Tuition, nonresident: part-time $1281 per credit hour. *Financial support:* Fellowships, research assistantships, teaching assistantships available. Financial award application deadline: 2/1. *Faculty research:* Women and tenure, counseling children and adolescents. *Unit head:* Anne Geroski, Coordinator, 802-656-3888, Fax: 802-656-3173. *Application contact:* Anne Geroski, Coordinator, 802-656-3888, Fax: 802-656-3173.

University of Victoria, Faculty of Graduate Studies, Faculty of Education, Department of Educational Psychology and Leadership Studies, Victoria, BC V8W 2Y2, Canada. Offers aboriginal communities counseling (M Ed); counseling (M Ed, MA); educational psychology (M Ed, MA, PhD), including counseling psychology (M Ed, MA), leadership studies (PhD), learning and development (MA, PhD), measurement and evaluation, special education (M Ed, MA); leadership studies (M Ed, MA). Part-time programs available. *Degree requirements:* For master's, thesis (for some programs), comprehensive exam (M Ed); for doctorate, comprehensive exam, thesis/dissertation, candidacy exam. *Entrance requirements:* For master's, 2 years of work experience in a relevant field; for doctorate, GRE, 2 years of work experience in a relevant field, minimum B average. Additional exam requirements/recommendations for international students: Required—TOEFL (minimum score 575 paper-based; 233 computer-based), IELTS (minimum score 7). *Faculty research:* Learning and development (child, adolescent and adult), special education and exceptional children.

The University of Western Ontario, Faculty of Graduate Studies, Social Sciences Division, Faculty of Education, Program in Counseling Psychology, London, ON N6A 5B8, Canada. Offers M Ed. Part-time programs available. *Entrance requirements:* For master's, minimum B average, 3 yr experience in helping profession. *Faculty research:* Women's issues in counseling, causes for sexual harassment in the workplace, counselor memory and confidence in clinical judgements.

University of West Florida, College of Arts and Sciences: Arts, Department of Psychology, Pensacola, FL 32514-5750. Offers counseling (MA); counseling-licensed mental health counselor (MA); general (MA); industrial-organizational (MA). Part-time programs available. *Faculty:* 10 full-time (3 women), 2 part-time/adjunct (1 woman). *Students:* 69 full-time (50 women), 45 part-time (35 women); includes 14 minority (11 African Americans, 1 Asian American or Pacific Islander, 2 Hispanic Americans), 5 international. Average age 27. 124 applicants, 60% accepted, 34 enrolled. In 2009, 16 master's awarded. *Degree requirements:* For master's, thesis (for some programs). *Entrance requirements:* For master's, GRE General Test, GRE Subject Test, minimum GPA of 3.0. Additional exam requirements/recommendations for international students: Required—TOEFL (minimum score 550 paper-based; 213 computer-based). *Application deadline:* For fall admission, 6/1 for domestic students, 5/15 for international students; for spring admission, 11/1 for domestic students, 10/1 for international students. Applications are processed on a rolling basis. Application fee: $30. *Expenses:* Tuition, state resident: full-time $4982; part-time $260 per credit hour. Tuition, nonresident: full-time $20,059; part-time $919 per credit hour. Required fees: $1247; $52 per credit hour. *Financial support:* In 2009–10, 3 research assistantships with partial tuition reimbursements (averaging $3,760 per year), 3 teaching assistantships with partial tuition reimbursements (averaging $5,000 per year) were awarded; career-related internships or fieldwork and unspecified assistantships also available. Financial award application deadline: 4/15; financial award applicants required to submit FAFSA. *Faculty research:* Prose recall, brain imaging, peak performance, biofeedback and pain control, comparable worth. Total annual research expenditures: $15,000. *Unit head:* Dr. Laura Koppes, Chairperson, 850-474-3493. *Application contact:* Terry McCray, Assistant Director of Graduate Admissions, 850-473-7718, Fax: 850-473-7714, E-mail: gradadmissions@uwf.edu.

University of West Georgia, Graduate School, College of Education, Department of Counseling and Educational Psychology, Carrollton, GA 30118. Offers professional counseling (M Ed, Certificate, Ed S); professional counseling and supervision (Ed D). *Accreditation:* ACA; NCATE. Part-time programs available. *Faculty:* 10 full-time (7 women). *Students:* 52 full-time (44 women), 97 part-time (82 women); includes 38 minority (32 African Americans, 1 American Indian/Alaska Native, 5 Hispanic Americans), 1 international. Average age 33. 78 applicants, 55% accepted, 19 enrolled. In 2009, 44 master's, 14 other advanced degrees awarded. *Degree requirements:* For master's, comprehensive exam; for doctorate, thesis/dissertation; for other advanced degree, comprehensive exam, research project. *Entrance requirements:* For master's, GRE General Test, minimum GPA of 2.7, interview, letter of reference; for doctorate, GRE General Test, Ed S, interview, letters of reference; for other advanced degree, GRE General Test, master's degree, minimum graduate GPA of 3.25, letter of reference. Additional exam requirements/recommendations for international students: Required—TOEFL. *Application deadline:* For fall admission, 7/17 for domestic students; for spring admission, 11/20 for domestic students. Applications are processed on a rolling basis. Application fee: $30. Electronic applications accepted. *Expenses:* Tuition, state resident: full-time $2952; part-time $164 per semester hour. Tuition, nonresident: full-time $11,808; part-time $656 per semester hour. Required fees: $42.90 per semester hour. $307 per semester. Tuition and fees vary according to course load. *Financial support:* In 2009–10, 4 students received support, including 3 research assistantships with full tuition reimbursements available (averaging $4,000 per year); career-related internships or fieldwork, scholarships/grants, and unspecified assistantships also available. Support available to part-time students. Financial award application deadline: 7/1; financial award applicants required to submit FAFSA. *Faculty research:* Academic and career development counseling, professional and ethical issues, transforming school counseling. *Unit head:* Dr. Rebecca Stanard, Interim Chair, 678-839-6554, Fax: 678-839-6098, E-mail: rstanard@westga.edu. *Application contact:* Dr. Charles W. Clark, Dean, 678-839-6508, E-mail: cclark@westga.edu.

University of Wisconsin–Madison, Graduate School, School of Education, Department of Counseling Psychology, Program in Counseling Psychology, Madison, WI 53706-1380. Offers PhD. *Accreditation:* APA. *Degree requirements:* For doctorate, thesis/dissertation. Application fee: $56. *Expenses:* Tuition, state resident: part-time $594 per credit. Tuition, nonresident: part-time $1504 per credit. Required fees: $65 per credit. Tuition and fees vary according to course load, program and reciprocity agreements. *Unit head:* Dr. Bruce Wampold, Chair, 608-262-0461. *Application contact:* Dr. Bruce Wampold, Chair, 608-262-0461.

University of Wisconsin–Milwaukee, Graduate School, School of Education, Department of Educational Psychology, Milwaukee, WI 53201-0413. Offers counseling (school, community) (MS); counseling psychology (PhD); learning and development (MS); research methodology (MS, PhD); school psychology (PhD). *Accreditation:* APA. Part-time programs available. *Faculty:* 22 full-time (14 women). *Students:* 124 full-time (107 women), 47 part-time (35 women); includes 20 minority (10 African Americans, 4 Asian Americans or Pacific Islanders, 6 Hispanic Americans), 2 international. Average age 30. 263 applicants, 52% accepted, 51 enrolled. In 2009, 55 master's, 13 doctorates awarded. *Degree requirements:* For master's, comprehensive exam, thesis; for doctorate, thesis/dissertation. *Entrance requirements:* For master's, minimum GPA of 3.0; for doctorate, GRE General Test, minimum GPA of 3.0. Additional exam requirements/recommendations for international students: Required—TOEFL (minimum score 550 paper-based; 79 iBT), IELTS (minimum score 6.5). *Application deadline:* For fall admission, 1/1 priority date for domestic students; for spring admission, 9/1 for domestic students. Applications are processed on a rolling basis. Application fee: $45 ($75 for international students). *Expenses:* Tuition, state resident: full-time $8800. Tuition, nonresident: full-time $20,760. Tuition and fees vary according to program and reciprocity agreements. *Financial support:* In 2009–10, 9 teaching assistantships were awarded; career-related internships or fieldwork and unspecified assistantships also available. Support available to part-time students. Financial award application deadline: 4/15. Total annual research expenditures: $1.3 million. *Unit head:* Bo Zhang, Graduate Program Representative, 414-229-5742, Fax: 414-229-4939, E-mail: boz@uwm.edu. *Application contact:* General Information Contact, 414-229-4982, Fax: 414-229-6967, E-mail: gradschool@uwm.edu.

University of Wisconsin–Stout, Graduate School, College of Human Development, Program in Mental Health Counseling, Menomonie, WI 54751. Offers MS. Part-time programs available. *Degree requirements:* For master's, comprehensive exam or thesis. *Entrance requirements:* For master's, minimum GPA of 2.75. Additional exam requirements/recommendations for international students: Required—TOEFL (minimum score 500 paper-based; 173 computer-based; 61 iBT). Electronic applications accepted. *Faculty research:* Body image, gender issues, eating disorders, cognitive behavioral therapy.

University of Wisconsin–Stout, Graduate School, School of Education, Program in School Counseling, Menomonie, WI 54751. Offers MS. Part-time programs available. *Degree requirements:* For master's, thesis. *Entrance requirements:* For master's, minimum GPA of 2.75. Additional exam requirements/recommendations for international students: Required—TOEFL (minimum score 500 paper-based; 173 computer-based; 61 iBT). Electronic applications accepted. *Faculty research:* Adventure-based learning, body image, domestic violence, resilience, school climate.

Utah State University, School of Graduate Studies, College of Education and Human Services, Department of Psychology, Logan, UT 84322. Offers clinical/counseling/school psychology (PhD); research and evaluation methodology (PhD); school counseling (MS); school psychology (MS). *Accreditation:* APA (one or more programs are accredited). Part-time and evening/weekend programs available. Postbaccalaureate distance learning degree programs offered (no on-campus study). Terminal master's awarded for partial completion of doctoral program. *Degree requirements:* For master's, thesis (for some programs); for doctorate, thesis/dissertation. *Entrance requirements:* For master's, GRE General Test (school psychology), MAT (school counseling), minimum GPA of 3.5; for doctorate, GRE General Test, minimum GPA of 3.5. Additional exam requirements/recommendations for international students: Required—TOEFL. *Faculty research:* Hearing loss detection in infancy, ADHD, eating disorders, domestic violence, neuropsychology, bilingual/Spanish speaking students/parents.

Valdosta State University, Graduate School, Department of Psychology and Counseling, Valdosta, GA 31698. Offers clinical/counseling psychology (MS); industrial/organizational psychology (MS); school counseling (M Ed, Ed S); school psychology (Ed S). Part-time and evening/weekend programs available. *Degree requirements:* For master's, thesis or alternative, comprehensive written and/or oral exams; for Ed S, thesis. *Entrance requirements:* For master's and Ed S, GRE General Test or MAT. Additional exam requirements/recommendations for international students: Required—TOEFL (minimum score 523 paper-based; 193 computer-based). Electronic applications accepted. *Faculty research:* Using Bender-Gestalt to predict graphomotor dimensions of the draw-a-person test, neurobehavioral hemispheric dominance.

Valparaiso University, Graduate School, Department of Psychology, Valparaiso, IN 46383. Offers business management (for counseling students) (Certificate); clinical mental health counseling (MA); community counseling (MA); JD/MA. Part-time and evening/weekend programs available. *Faculty:* 9 part-time/adjunct (4 women). *Students:* 38 full-time (34 women), 9 part-time (3 women); includes 7 minority (3 African Americans, 4 Hispanic Americans), 2 international. Average age 29. In 2009, 18 master's awarded. *Degree requirements:* For master's, thesis or alternative, internship. *Entrance requirements:* For master's, minimum GPA of 3.0; 15 credits in the social/behavioral sciences (psychology, sociology, human development, etc.) with a minimum GPA of 3.0; course in introductory psychology; recent statistics course with minimum B average. Additional exam requirements/recommendations for international students: Required—TOEFL (minimum score 550 paper-based; 213 computer-based; 80 iBT). *Application deadline:* For fall admission, 3/1 priority date for domestic students. Applications are processed on a rolling basis. Application fee: $30 ($50 for international students). Electronic applications accepted. *Financial support:* Career-related internships or fieldwork, scholarships/grants, traineeships, and unspecified assistantships available. Support available to part-time students. Financial award applicants required to submit FAFSA. *Faculty research:* Environmental psychology, human sexuality, racial identity development models, social psychology. *Unit head:* Dr. James Nelson, Director of Graduate Programs, 219-464-5443, Fax: 219-464-6878, E-mail: jim.nelson@valpo.edu. *Application contact:* Jamie Haney, Coordinator of Graduate Admission, 219-464-5313, Fax: 219-464-5381, E-mail: jamie.haney@valpo.edu.

Virginia Commonwealth University, Graduate School, College of Humanities and Sciences, Department of Psychology, Program in Counseling Psychology, Richmond, VA 23284-9005. Offers PhD. *Accreditation:* ACA; APA. *Degree requirements:* For doctorate, thesis/dissertation. *Entrance requirements:* For doctorate, GRE General Test, GRE Subject Test. *Faculty research:* Life span development counseling, couple/family therapy, health psychology, psychotherapy.

Virginia Commonwealth University, Graduate School, School of Allied Health Professions, Program in Patient Counseling, Richmond, VA 23284-9005. Offers MS, CPC. *Accreditation:* ACA. *Entrance requirements:* For master's, GRE General Test.

Walden University, Graduate Programs, School of Counseling and Social Service, Minneapolis, MN 55401. Offers counselor education and supervision (PhD), including consultation, counseling and social change, forensic mental health counseling, general program, nonprofit management and leadership, trauma and crisis; human services (PhD), including clinical social work, counseling, criminal justice, family studies and intervention strategies, general program, human services administration, self-designed, social policy analysis and planning; marriage, couple, and family counseling (MS), including forensic counseling, trauma and crisis counseling; mental health counseling (MS), including forensic counseling. Part-time and evening/

weekend programs available. Postbaccalaureate distance learning degree programs offered (minimal on-campus study). *Faculty:* 13 full-time, 78 part-time/adjunct. *Students:* 1,932 full-time (1,624 women), 210 part-time (181 women); includes 945 minority (817 African Americans, 24 American Indian/Alaska Native, 24 Asian Americans or Pacific Islanders, 80 Hispanic Americans), 34 international. Average age 39. In 2009, 55 master's, 5 doctorates awarded. *Degree requirements:* For master's, residency (for some programs); for doctorate, thesis/dissertation, residency. *Entrance requirements:* For master's, bachelor's degree or equivalent in related field, minimum GPA of 2.5; for doctorate, master's degree or equivalent in related field; minimum GPA of 3.0; official transcripts; three years' related professional/academic experience (preferred); access to computer and Internet. Additional exam requirements/recommendations for international students: Required—TOEFL (minimum score 550 paper-based; 213 computer-based), IELTS (minimum score 6.5), or Michigan English Language Assessment Battery (minimum score 82). *Application deadline:* Applications are processed on a rolling basis. Application fee: $50. Electronic applications accepted. *Expenses:* Tuition: Full-time $13,665; part-time $560 per credit. Required fees: $1375. Tuition and fees vary according to course load, degree level and program. *Financial support:* In 2009–10, 200 students received support; fellowships, Federal Work-Study, scholarships/grants, unspecified assistantships, and family tuition reduction, active duty/veteran tuition reduction, group tuition reduction, interest-free payment plans available. Support available to part-time students. Financial award applicants required to submit FAFSA. *Unit head:* Dr. Savitri Dixon-Saxon, Associate Dean, 800-925-3368. *Application contact:* Jennifer Hall, Director of Enrollment, 866-4-WALDEN, E-mail: info@waldenu.edu.

Walden University, Graduate Programs, School of Psychology, Minneapolis, MN 55401. Offers clinical child psychology (Post-Doctoral Certificate); clinical psychology (Post-Doctoral Certificate); counseling psychology (Post-Doctoral Certificate); forensic psychology (MS), including forensic psychology in the community, general program, mental health applications, program planning and evaluation in forensic settings, psychology and legal systems; general psychology (Post-Doctoral Certificate); health psychology (Post-Doctoral Certificate); organizational psychology (Post-Doctoral Certificate); organizational psychology and development (Postbaccalaureate Certificate); psychology (MS, PhD), including clinical psychology (PhD), counseling psychology (PhD), crisis management and response (MS), general program (MS), general psychology (PhD), health psychology, leadership development and coaching (MS), media psychology (MS), organizational psychology (PhD), organizational psychology and development (MS), organizational psychology and nonprofit management (MS), program evaluation and research (MS), psychology of culture (MS), psychology, public administration, and social change (MS), social psychology (MS), terrorism and security (MS); teaching online (Post-Master's Certificate). Part-time and evening/weekend programs available. Postbaccalaureate distance learning degree programs offered (minimal on-campus study). *Faculty:* 33 full-time, 222 part-time/adjunct. *Students:* 3,546 full-time (2,761 women), 1,133 part-time (908 women); includes 1,723 minority (1,319 African Americans, 56 American Indian/Alaska Native, 101 Asian Americans or Pacific Islanders, 247 Hispanic Americans), 80 international. Average age 41. In 2009, 495 master's, 70 doctorates, 2 other advanced degrees awarded. Terminal master's awarded for partial completion of doctoral program. *Degree requirements:* For master's, thesis optional; for doctorate, thesis/dissertation, residency. *Entrance requirements:* For master's, bachelor's degree or equivalent in related field; minimum GPA of 2.5; official transcripts; goal statement; access to computer and Internet; for doctorate, master's degree or equivalent in related field; minimum GPA of 3.0;3 years of related professional/academic experience (preferred). Additional exam requirements/recommendations for international students: Required—TOEFL (minimum score 550 paper-based; 213 computer-based), IELTS (minimum score 6.5), or Michigan English Language Assessment Battery (minimum score 82). *Application deadline:* Applications are processed on a rolling basis. Application fee: $50. Electronic applications accepted. *Expenses:* Tuition: Full-time $13,665; part-time $560 per credit. Required fees: $1375. Tuition and fees vary according to course load, degree level and program. *Financial support:* In 2009–10, 290 students received support; fellowships, Federal Work-Study, scholarships/grants, unspecified assistantships, and family tuition reduction, active duty/veteran tuition reduction, group tuition reduction, interest-free payment plans available. Support available to part-time students. Financial award applicants required to submit FAFSA. *Unit head:* Dr. Melanie Storms, Associate Dean, 800-925-3368. *Application contact:* Jennifer Hall, Director of Enrollment, 866-4-WALDEN, E-mail: info@waldenu.edu.

Walla Walla University, Graduate School, School of Education and Psychology, Specialization in Counseling Psychology, College Place, WA 99324-1198. Offers MA. Part-time programs available. *Faculty:* 6 full-time (2 women). *Students:* 16 full-time (8 women), 8 part-time (4 women); includes 1 American Indian/Alaska Native, 1 Hispanic American. Average age 34. 17 applicants, 65% accepted, 10 enrolled. *Degree requirements:* For master's, thesis (for some programs). *Entrance requirements:* For master's, GRE General Test, minimum GPA of 2.75, course work in education and psychology. Additional exam requirements/recommendations for international students: Required—TOEFL (minimum score 550 paper-based; 213 computer-based; 79 iBT). *Application deadline:* For fall admission, 4/1 priority date for domestic students. Applications are processed on a rolling basis. Application fee: $50. Electronic applications accepted. *Expenses:* Tuition: Full-time $19,929. *Financial support:* Teaching assistantships with partial tuition reimbursements available. Financial award application deadline: 4/1; financial award applicants required to submit FAFSA. *Faculty research:* Instructional psychology, moral development. *Unit head:* Dr. Lee Stough, Program Director, 509-527-2943, Fax: 509-527-2248, E-mail: lee.stough@wallawalla.edu. *Application contact:* Dr. Joe G. Galusha, Dean of Graduate Studies, 509-527-2421, Fax: 509-527-2237, E-mail: joe.galusha@wallawalla.edu.

Walsh University, Graduate Studies, Program in Counseling and Human Development, North Canton, OH 44720-3396. Offers mental health counseling (MA); school counseling (MA). *Accreditation:* ACA. Part-time and evening/weekend programs available. *Faculty:* 5 full-time (4 women), 3 part-time/adjunct (all women). *Students:* 32 full-time (23 women), 50 part-time (42 women); includes 5 minority (3 African Americans, 1 American Indian/Alaska Native, 1 Hispanic American), 3 international. Average age 31. 36 applicants, 61% accepted, 19 enrolled. In 2009, 30 master's awarded. *Degree requirements:* For master's, comprehensive exam, internship, practicum. *Entrance requirements:* For master's, GRE General Test, MAT, interview, minimum GPA of 3.0, writing sample, reference forms, moral affidavit. Additional exam requirements/recommendations for international students: Required—TOEFL (minimum score 500 paper-based; 173 computer-based; 61 iBT). *Application deadline:* For fall admission, 7/15 priority date for domestic students. Applications are processed on a rolling basis. Application fee: $25. Electronic applications accepted. *Expenses:* Tuition: Full-time $9630; part-time $535 per credit hour. Tuition and fees vary according to course load and program. *Financial support:* In 2009–10, 79 students received support, including 12 research assistantships with tuition reimbursements available (averaging $6,020 per year); tuition waivers (partial) and tuition discounts also available. Financial award application deadline: 12/31. *Faculty research:* Mind-body connections in trauma and trauma counseling, grief/loss issues regarding counselor training, supervision, family counseling and counselor education, refugee mental health, grief counseling and grief counseling training. *Unit head:* Dr. Linda Barclay, Program Director, 330-490-7264, Fax: 330-490-7323, E-mail: lbarclay@walsh.edu. *Application contact:* Stephanie Wheeler, Director of Graduate and Transfer Admissions, 330-490-7181, Fax: 330-490-7165, E-mail: swheeler@walsh.edu.

Washington Adventist University, Program in Counseling Psychology, Takoma Park, MD 20912. Offers MA. Part-time programs available. *Students:* 11 part-time (all women); includes 4 minority (2 African Americans, 2 Asian Americans or Pacific Islanders), 1 international. *Application deadline:* Applications are processed on a rolling basis. *Financial support:* Applicants required to submit FAFSA. *Unit head:* Dr. Davenia Lea, Dean, School of Graduate and Professional Studies, 301-891-4464, E-mail: dlea@wau.edu. *Application contact:* Dr. Davenia Lea, Dean, School of Graduate and Professional Studies, 301-891-4464, E-mail: dlea@wau.edu.

Washington Adventist University, Program in Professional Counseling Psychology, Takoma Park, MD 20912. Offers MA. Part-time programs available. *Students:* 1 (woman) full-time, 7 part-time (5 women); includes 5 minority (4 African Americans, 1 Hispanic American). *Application deadline:* Applications are processed on a rolling basis. *Financial support:* Applicants required to submit FAFSA. *Unit head:* Dr. Davenia Lea, Dean, School of Graduate and Professional Studies, 301-891-4464, E-mail: dlea@wau.edu. *Application contact:* Dr. Davenia Lea, Dean, School of Graduate and Professional Studies, 301-891-4464, E-mail: dlea@wau.edu.

Washington State University, Graduate School, College of Education, Department of Educational Leadership and Counseling Psychology, Program in Counseling Psychology, Pullman, WA 99164. Offers counseling psychology (Ed M, MA, PhD); school psychologist (Certificate). *Accreditation:* APA (one or more programs are accredited). Terminal master's awarded for partial completion of doctoral program. *Degree requirements:* For master's, comprehensive exam (for some programs), thesis (for some programs), oral or written exam; for doctorate, comprehensive exam, thesis/dissertation, oral and written exam. *Entrance requirements:* For master's and doctorate, GRE General Test, minimum GPA of 3.0, 3 letters of recommendation. Additional exam requirements/recommendations for international students: Required—TOEFL (minimum score 550 paper-based; 213 computer-based). Electronic applications accepted. *Faculty research:* Hypnosis supervision, multicultural counseling, American Indian mental health, eating disorders.

Wayland Baptist University, Graduate Programs, Program in Counseling, Plainview, TX 79072-6998. Offers counseling (MA); government administration (MPA); homeland security (MPA); justice administration (MPA). Part-time and evening/weekend programs available. Postbaccalaureate distance learning degree programs offered. *Faculty:* 9 full-time (2 women). *Students:* 71 part-time (58 women); includes 16 minority (5 African Americans, 1 American Indian/Alaska Native, 10 Hispanic Americans). Average age 34. 21 applicants, 90% accepted, 11 enrolled. In 2009, 16 master's awarded. *Degree requirements:* For master's, comprehensive exam. *Entrance requirements:* For master's, GRE, MAT. Additional exam requirements/recommendations for international students: Required—TOEFL (minimum score 500 paper-based; 173 computer-based; 61 iBT). *Application deadline:* Applications are processed on a rolling basis. Application fee: $50. Electronic applications accepted. *Expenses:* Tuition: Full-time $5796; part-time $322 per credit hour. Required fees: $782; $9 per credit hour. $60 per semester. Tuition and fees vary according to course load and campus/location. *Financial support:* Federal Work-Study, institutionally sponsored loans, and scholarships/grants available. Support available to part-time students. Financial award application deadline: 5/1; financial award applicants required to submit FAFSA. *Unit head:* Dr. Estelle Owens, Chairman, 806-291-1171, Fax: 806-291-1972, E-mail: owensest@wbu.edu. *Application contact:* Amanda Stanton, Graduate Studies, 806-291-3423, Fax: 806-291-1950, E-mail: stanton@wbu.edu.

Waynesburg University, Graduate and Professional Studies, Waynesburg, PA 15370-1222. Offers business (MBA), including finance, health systems, human resources, leadership, market development; counseling (MA), including addictions counseling, clinical mental health; education (MAT); nursing (MSN), including administration, education, informatics, palliative care; nursing practice (DNP); special education (M Ed); technology (M Ed); MSN/MBA. *Accreditation:* AACN. Part-time and evening/weekend programs available. *Faculty:* 11 full-time (5 women), 136 part-time/adjunct (80 women). *Students:* 116 full-time (85 women), 984 part-time (682 women). 711 applicants, 80% accepted, 485 enrolled. In 2009, 320 master's, 41 doctorates awarded. *Degree requirements:* For doctorate, thesis/dissertation. *Entrance requirements:* Additional exam requirements/recommendations for international students: Required—TOEFL. *Application deadline:* For fall admission, 8/1 priority date for domestic students. Applications are processed on a rolling basis. Electronic applications accepted. *Expenses:* Tuition: Part-time $520 per credit. *Financial support:* Available to part-time students. Application deadline: 5/1. *Unit head:* David Mariner, Dean, 724-743-4420, Fax: 724-743-4425, E-mail: dmariner@waynesburg.edu. *Application contact:* Michael Bednarski, Director of Admissions, 724-743-4420, Fax: 724-743-4425, E-mail: mbednars@waynesburg.edu.

Webster University, College of Arts and Sciences, Department of Behavioral and Social Sciences, Program in Counseling, St. Louis, MO 63119-3194. Offers MA. Part-time programs available. *Entrance requirements:* Additional exam requirements/recommendations for international students: Required—TOEFL. *Expenses:* Tuition: Part-time $565 per credit hour. Tuition and fees vary according to degree level, campus/location and program.

Western Michigan University, Graduate College, College of Education, Department of Counselor Education and Counseling Psychology, Kalamazoo, MI 49008. Offers counseling psychology (MA, PhD); counselor education (MA, PhD); human resources development (MA). *Accreditation:* ACA (one or more programs are accredited); APA (one or more programs are accredited); CORE; NCATE. *Degree requirements:* For doctorate, thesis/dissertation, oral exams. *Entrance requirements:* For doctorate, GRE General Test.

Western Washington University, Graduate School, College of Humanities and Social Sciences, Department of Psychology, Program in Mental Health Counseling, Bellingham, WA 98225-5996. Offers MS. *Accreditation:* ACA. *Degree requirements:* For master's, thesis optional. *Entrance requirements:* For master's, GRE General Test, minimum GPA of 3.0 in last 60 semester hours or last 90 quarter hours. Additional exam requirements/recommendations for international students: Required—TOEFL (minimum score 567 paper-based; 227 computer-based). Electronic applications accepted.

Westfield State College, Division of Graduate and Continuing Education, Department of Psychology, Westfield, MA 01086. Offers applied behavior analysis (MA); mental health counseling (MA); school guidance (MA). Part-time and evening/weekend programs available. *Degree requirements:* For master's, comprehensive exam. *Entrance requirements:* For master's, GRE General Test, MAT, minimum undergraduate GPA of 2.7.

Westminster College, Program in Counseling Psychology, Salt Lake City, UT 84105-3697. Offers MSPC. Part-time and evening/weekend programs available. *Faculty:* 7 full-time (all women), 6 part-time/adjunct (5 women). *Students:* 27 full-time (18 women), 8 part-time (7 women); includes 5 minority (2 Asian Americans or Pacific Islanders, 3 Hispanic Americans). Average age 30. 35 applicants, 49% accepted, 13 enrolled. *Degree requirements:* For master's, comprehensive exam, thesis, internship. *Entrance requirements:* For master's, GRE, 3 professional or academic recommendations, background check. Additional exam requirements/recommendations for international students: Required—TOEFL (minimum score 600 paper-based; 214 computer-based; 100 iBT). *Application deadline:* For fall admission, 4/16 for domestic and international students. Applications are processed on a rolling basis. Application fee: $40. Electronic applications accepted. *Expenses:* Contact institution. *Financial support:* In 2009–10, 20 students received support. Career-related internships or fieldwork and tuition reimbursement, tuition remission available. Support available to part-time students. Financial award applicants required to submit FAFSA. *Faculty research:* Trauma, substance abuse treatment, object relations, refugee populations, attachment theory. *Unit head:* Janine Wanlass, Director, 801-832-2428, E-mail: jwanlass@westminstercollege.edu. *Application contact:* Joel Bauman, Vice President of Enrollment Services, 801-832-2200, Fax: 801-832-3101, E-mail: admission@westminstercollege.edu.

West Virginia University, College of Human Resources and Education, Department of Counseling, Rehabilitation Counseling, and Counseling Psychology, Program in Counseling Psychology, Morgantown, WV 26506. Offers PhD. *Accreditation:* ACA; APA. *Degree requirements:* For doctorate, comprehensive exam, thesis/dissertation, APA-approved 1 year internship. *Entrance requirements:* For doctorate, GRE General Test, interview. Additional exam requirements/recommendations for international students: Required—TOEFL (minimum score 550 paper-based; 213 computer-based; 65 iBT). Electronic applications accepted.

William Carey University, School of Psychology and Counseling, Hattiesburg, MS 39401-5499. Offers counseling psychology (MS). Part-time programs available. *Entrance requirements:* For master's, GRE, PRAXIS, MAT, minimum GPA of 2.5. Additional exam requirements/recommendations for international students: Required—TOEFL (minimum score 550 paper-

Counseling Psychology

William Carey University (continued)

based; 213 computer-based). *Expenses:* Contact institution. *Faculty research:* Addiction prevention, psychometric measurement, crisis counseling, gerontology.

William Paterson University of New Jersey, College of the Humanities and Social Sciences, Wayne, NJ 07470-8420. Offers clinical and counseling psychology (MA); English (MA); history (MA); public policy and international affairs (MA); sociology (MA). Part-time and evening/weekend programs available. *Students:* 39 full-time (22 women), 123 part-time (90 women); includes 42 minority (11 African Americans, 5 Asian Americans or Pacific Islanders, 26 Hispanic Americans), 2 international. *Application deadline:* Applications are processed on a rolling basis. Application fee: $50. Electronic applications accepted. *Financial support:* In 2009–10, 13 students received support; research assistantships with full tuition reimbursements available, teaching assistantships with full tuition reimbursements available, unspecified assistantships available. Support available to part-time students. Financial award application deadline: 4/1; financial award applicants required to submit FAFSA. *Unit head:* Dr. Kara Rabbitt, Dean, College of Humanities and Social Sciences, 973-720-2180, Fax: 973-720-2955, E-mail: rabbittk@wpunj.edu. *Application contact:* Tinu Adeniran, Assistant Director, Graduate Admissions, 973-720-2764, Fax: 973-720-2035, E-mail: adenirant@wpunj.edu.

Wright Institute, Program in Clinical Psychology, Berkeley, CA 94704-1796. Offers clinical psychology (Psy D); counseling psychology (MA). *Accreditation:* APA (one or more programs are accredited). Evening/weekend programs available. *Faculty:* 11 full-time (10 women), 58 part-time/adjunct (29 women). *Students:* 338 full-time (239 women); includes 74 minority (16 African Americans, 1 American Indian/Alaska Native, 23 Asian Americans or Pacific Islanders, 34 Hispanic Americans), 6 international. Average age 34. 333 applicants, 38% accepted, 59 enrolled. In 2009, 20 master's, 38 doctorates awarded. *Degree requirements:* For doctorate, comprehensive exam, thesis/dissertation. *Entrance requirements:* Additional exam requirements/recommendations for international students: Required—TOEFL (minimum score 600 paper-based). *Application deadline:* For fall admission, 1/15 priority date for domestic students, 1/15 for international students. Application fee: $50. Electronic applications accepted. *Expenses:* Tuition: Full-time $25,550. Full-time tuition and fees vary according to degree level and program. *Financial support:* In 2009–10, 78 students received support, including 42 teaching assistantships (averaging $1,600 per year); fellowships, research assistantships, career-related internships or fieldwork and Federal Work-Study also available. Financial award application deadline: 7/1. *Faculty research:* Time-limited dynamic psychotherapy; mindfulness/ACT; psychotherapy integration; empathy, altruism and survivor guilt; culturally informed practice. *Unit head:* Dr. Charles Alexander, Dean, 510-841-9230 Ext. 101, E-mail: calexander@wi.edu. *Application contact:* Liz Hertz, Director of Admissions, 510-841-9230 Ext. 111, Fax: 510-841-0167, E-mail: lhertz@wrightinst.edu.

Wright Institute, Program in Counseling Psychology, Berkeley, CA 94704-1796. Offers MA. *Faculty:* 6 full-time (5 women). *Students:* Average age 38. *Application deadline:* Applications are processed on a rolling basis. Electronic applications accepted. *Expenses:* Tuition: Full-time $25,550. Full-time tuition and fees vary according to degree level and program. *Unit head:* Dr. Milena Esherick, Program Director, 510-841-9230. *Application contact:* Liz Hertz, Director of Admissions, 510-841-9230 Ext. 111, Fax: 510-841-0167, E-mail: lhertz@wrightinst.edu.

Yeshiva University, Ferkauf Graduate School of Psychology, Program in Mental Health Counseling Psychology, New York, NY 10033-3201. Offers MA. Part-time programs available. *Entrance requirements:* For master's, GRE General Test. *Expenses:* Tuition: Full-time $24,918; part-time $1022 per credit. Required fees: $175. *Faculty research:* Substance abuse treatment, group therapy.

Youngstown State University, Graduate School, Beeghly College of Education, Department of Counseling, Youngstown, OH 44555-0001. Offers community counseling (MS Ed); school counseling (MS Ed). *Accreditation:* ACA; NCATE. Part-time and evening/weekend programs available. *Degree requirements:* For master's, comprehensive exam. *Entrance requirements:* For master's, MAT, interview, minimum GPA of 2.7. Additional exam requirements/recommendations for international students: Required—TOEFL. *Faculty research:* Suicide, euthanasia, ethical issues, marriage and family.

Developmental Psychology

Andrews University, School of Graduate Studies, School of Education, Department of Educational and Counseling Psychology, Program in Educational and Developmental Psychology, Berrien Springs, MI 49104. Offers educational and developmental psychology (MA); educational psychology (Ed D, PhD). *Students:* 9 full-time (7 women), 10 part-time (7 women); includes 9 minority (5 African Americans, 1 Asian American or Pacific Islander, 3 Hispanic Americans), 4 international. Average age 34. 16 applicants, 75% accepted, 8 enrolled. In 2009, 2 master's awarded. *Degree requirements:* For master's, thesis optional. *Entrance requirements:* For master's, GRE. Additional exam requirements/recommendations for international students: Required—TOEFL (minimum score 550 paper-based). *Application deadline:* Applications are processed on a rolling basis. Application fee: $40. *Unit head:* Dr. Jimmy Kijai, Coordinator, 269-471-6240. *Application contact:* Carolyn Hurst, Supervisor of Graduate Admission, 800-253-2874, Fax: 269-471-6321, E-mail: graduate@andrews.edu.

Arizona State University, Graduate College, College of Liberal Arts and Sciences, Division of Natural Sciences, Department of Psychology, Tempe, AZ 85287. Offers behavioral neuroscience (PhD); clinical psychology (PhD); cognition, action and perception (PhD); developmental psychology (PhD); quantitative psychology (PhD); social psychology (PhD). *Accreditation:* APA. *Degree requirements:* For doctorate, thesis/dissertation. *Entrance requirements:* For doctorate, GRE General Test, GRE Subject Test.

Bethel University, Graduate School, Program in Counseling Psychology, St. Paul, MN 55112-6999. Offers child and adolescent and community counseling (MA). Part-time and evening/weekend programs available. *Faculty:* 6 full-time (2 women), 9 part-time/adjunct (5 women). *Students:* 71 full-time (56 women), 7 part-time (6 women); includes 5 minority (2 African Americans, 2 Asian Americans or Pacific Islanders, 1 Hispanic American). Average age 32. 60 applicants, 75% accepted, 35 enrolled. In 2009, 32 master's awarded. *Degree requirements:* For master's, comprehensive exam, thesis optional, practicum. *Entrance requirements:* For master's, MAT, minimum GPA of 3.0, course work in psychology and statistics, letters of reference. Additional exam requirements/recommendations for international students: Required—TOEFL (minimum score 550 paper-based; 213 computer-based; 80 iBT). *Application deadline:* For fall admission, 5/1 priority date for domestic students. Applications are processed on a rolling basis. Application fee: $25. Electronic applications accepted. *Expenses:* Tuition: Full-time $7920; part-time $440 per credit. One-time fee: $25. Tuition and fees vary according to course load, degree level and program. *Financial support:* Applicants required to submit FAFSA. *Unit head:* Dr. Diane Dahl, Assistant Dean, 651-635-8000, Fax: 651-635-8004, E-mail: diane-dahl@bethel.edu. *Application contact:* Michael Price, Director of Admissions, 651-635-8000, Fax: 651-635-8004, E-mail: m-price@bethel.edu.

Boston College, Lynch Graduate School of Education, Department of Counseling Psychology, Developmental, and Educational Psychology, Program in Developmental and Educational Psychology, Chestnut Hill, MA 02467-3800. Offers MA, PhD. Part-time and evening/weekend programs available. *Students:* 15 full-time (13 women), 30 part-time (all women); includes 7 minority (1 African American, 3 Asian Americans or Pacific Islanders, 3 Hispanic Americans), 9 international. 122 applicants, 48% accepted, 26 enrolled. In 2009, 19 master's, 3 doctorates awarded. Terminal master's awarded for partial completion of doctoral program. *Degree requirements:* For master's, comprehensive exam; for doctorate, comprehensive exam, thesis/dissertation. *Entrance requirements:* For master's and doctorate, GRE General Test. Additional exam requirements/recommendations for international students: Required—TOEFL (minimum score 550 paper-based; 213 computer-based; 81 iBT). Application fee: $60. Electronic applications accepted. *Financial support:* Fellowships with full and partial tuition reimbursements, research assistantships with full and partial tuition reimbursements, teaching assistantships with full and partial tuition reimbursements, career-related internships or fieldwork, Federal Work-Study, scholarships/grants, traineeships, health care benefits, tuition waivers (full and partial), and unspecified assistantships available. Support available to part-time students. Financial award applicants required to submit FAFSA. *Faculty research:* Cognitive learning and culture, effects of social policy reform on children and families, psychosocial trauma, human rights and international justice; positive youth development; children and adolescents living in poverty. *Unit head:* Dr. M. Brinton Lykes, Chairperson, 617-552-4214, Fax: 617-552-0812. *Application contact:* Adam Poluzzi, Director, Graduate Admission and Financial Aid, 617-552-4214, Fax: 617-552-0398, E-mail: poluzzi@bc.edu.

Bowling Green State University, Graduate College, College of Arts and Sciences, Department of Psychology, Bowling Green, OH 43403. Offers clinical psychology (MA, PhD); developmental psychology (MA, PhD); experimental psychology (MA, PhD); industrial/organizational psychology (MA, PhD); quantitative psychology (MA, PhD). *Accreditation:* APA (one or more programs are accredited). *Degree requirements:* For doctorate, thesis/dissertation. *Entrance requirements:* For doctorate, GRE General Test, GRE Subject Test. Additional exam requirements/recommendations for international students: Required—TOEFL. Electronic applications accepted. *Faculty research:* Personnel psychology, developmental-mathematical models, behavioral medication, brain process, child/adolescent social cognition.

Brandeis University, Graduate School of Arts and Sciences, Department of Psychology, Waltham, MA 02454-9110. Offers brain, body and behavior (PhD); cognitive neuroscience (PhD); general psychology (MA); social/developmental psychology (PhD). Part-time programs available. *Faculty:* 16 full-time (4 women), 3 part-time/adjunct (2 women). *Students:* 35 full-time (27 women), 1 (woman) part-time; includes 2 minority (both Asian Americans or Pacific Islanders), 7 international. Average age 26. 121 applicants, 31% accepted, 13 enrolled. In 2009, 9 master's, 3 doctorates awarded. *Degree requirements:* For doctorate, comprehensive exam, thesis/dissertation. *Entrance requirements:* For master's, GRE General Test, GRE Subject Test (recommended), 3 letters of recommendation, statement of purpose; for doctorate, GRE General Test, GRE Subject Test (recommended), 3 letters of recommendation. Additional exam requirements/recommendations for international students: Required—TOEFL (minimum score 600 paper-based; 250 computer-based; 100 iBT); Recommended—IELTS (minimum score 7). *Application deadline:* For fall admission, 1/15 for domestic and international students. Applications are processed on a rolling basis. Application fee: $75. Electronic applications accepted. *Financial support:* In 2009–10, 16 fellowships with full tuition reimbursements (averaging $20,000 per year), 3 research assistantships with full tuition reimbursements (averaging $20,000 per year), 9 teaching assistantships with partial tuition reimbursements (averaging $3,200 per year) were awarded; institutionally sponsored loans, scholarships/grants, traineeships, health care benefits, tuition waivers (full), and unspecified assistantships also available. Support available to part-time students. Financial award applicants required to submit FAFSA. *Faculty research:* Development, cognition, social aging, perception, social/developmental psychology, cognitive neuroscience, brain, body and behavior, motor control, visual perception, taste physiology and psychophysics, memory, learning, aggression, emotion, personality and cognition in adulthood and old age, social relations and health, stereotypes and nonverbal communication. *Unit head:* Prof. Paul DiZio, Director of Graduate Studies, 781-736-3300, Fax: 781-736-3291, E-mail: dizio@brandeis.edu. *Application contact:* Donna J. Coletti, Graduate Admissions Coordinator, 781-736-3303, Fax: 781-736-3291, E-mail: coletti@brandeis.edu.

Brown University, Graduate School, Department of Psychology, Providence, RI 02912. Offers behavioral neuroscience (PhD); cognitive processes (PhD); sensation and perception (PhD); social/developmental (PhD); MS/PhD. *Degree requirements:* For doctorate, thesis/dissertation. *Entrance requirements:* For doctorate, GRE General Test, GRE Subject Test.

Bryn Mawr College, Graduate School of Arts and Sciences, Department of Psychology, Bryn Mawr, PA 19010-2899. Offers clinical developmental psychology (PhD). Part-time programs available. *Degree requirements:* For doctorate, one foreign language, comprehensive exam, thesis/dissertation. *Entrance requirements:* For doctorate, GRE General Test. Additional exam requirements/recommendations for international students: Required—TOEFL (minimum score 600 paper-based; 250 computer-based). *Expenses:* Tuition: Full-time $31,340. Required fees: $430.

Capella University, Harold Abel School of Psychology, Minneapolis, MN 55402. Offers child and adolescent development (MS); clinical psychology (MS, Psy D); counseling psychology (MS); educational psychology (MS, PhD); evaluation, research, and measurement (MS); general psychology (MS, PhD); industrial/organizational psychology (MS, PhD); leadership coaching psychology (MS); organizational leader development (MS); school psychology (MS); sport psychology (MS). Part-time and evening/weekend programs available. Postbaccalaureate distance learning degree programs offered (minimal on-campus study). Terminal master's awarded for partial completion of doctoral program. *Degree requirements:* For master's, thesis optional, project; for doctorate, thesis/dissertation. *Entrance requirements:* For degree, master's degree in school psychology. Additional exam requirements/recommendations for international students: Required—TOEFL (minimum score 550 paper-based; 213 computer-based), TWE (minimum score 4); Recommended—IELTS. Electronic applications accepted.

Carnegie Mellon University, College of Humanities and Social Sciences, Department of Psychology, Area of Developmental Psychology, Pittsburgh, PA 15213-3891. Offers PhD. *Degree requirements:* For doctorate, comprehensive exam, thesis/dissertation. *Entrance requirements:* For doctorate, GRE General Test. Additional exam requirements/recommendations for international students: Required—TOEFL. *Faculty research:* Cognitive development, language acquisition.

Chatham University, Program in Counseling Psychology, Pittsburgh, PA 15232-2826. Offers child, adolescent and family (MSCP); counseling psychology (Psy D); health and holistic (MSCP); infant mental health (MSCP); organization and supervision (MSCP); sport and exercise (MSCP). Part-time and evening/weekend programs available. *Students:* 107 full-time (93 women), 77 part-time (67 women). Average age 29. 141 applicants, 76% accepted, 75 enrolled. In 2009, 63 master's awarded. *Degree requirements:* For master's, thesis optional, supervised internship; for doctorate, thesis/dissertation, internship. *Entrance requirements:* For master's, minimum GPA of 3.0; 2 letters of recommendation; resume; prerequisite coursework in statistics, biology, and psychology; for doctorate, GRE. Additional exam requirements/recommendations for international students: Required—TOEFL (minimum score 600 paper-based; 250 computer-based; 100 iBT), IELTS (minimum score 6.5), TWE. *Application deadline:* For fall admission, 5/1 priority date for domestic students, 6/1 priority date for international students; for spring admission, 12/1 for domestic students, 11/1 for international students. Applications are processed on a rolling basis. Application fee: $45. Electronic applications accepted. *Financial support:* Career-related internships or fieldwork available. Financial award applicants required to submit FAFSA. *Faculty research:* Trauma and recovery, hypnosis, psychospiritual dimensions of healing, psychotherapy of schizophrenia. *Unit head:* Dr. Mary Beth Mannarino, Director, 412-365-1196, Fax: 412-365-1505, E-mail: mmannarino@chatham.edu. *Application contact:* Dory Perry, Associate Director of Graduate Admissions, 412-365-2758, Fax: 412-365-1609, E-mail: gradadmissions@chatham.edu.

Claremont Graduate University, Graduate Programs, School of Behavioral and Organizational Sciences, Department of Psychology, Claremont, CA 91711-6160. Offers advanced study in evaluation (Certificate); cognitive psychology (MA, PhD); developmental psychology (MA, PhD); evaluation and applied research methods (MA, PhD); health behavior research and evaluation (MA, PhD); human resource development and evaluation (MA); industrial/organizational psychology (MA, PhD); organizational behavior (MA, PhD); organizational psychology (MA, PhD); social psychology (MA, PhD); MBA/PhD. Part-time programs available. *Faculty:* 17 full-time (7 women), 1 part-time/adjunct (0 women). *Students:* 231 full-time (155 women), 25 part-time (18 women); includes 62 minority (13 African Americans, 1 American Indian/Alaska Native, 31 Asian Americans or Pacific Islanders, 17 Hispanic Americans), 21 international. Average age 30. In 2009, 37 master's, 12 doctorates, 8 other advanced degrees awarded. Terminal master's awarded for partial completion of doctoral program. *Entrance requirements:* For master's and doctorate, GRE General Test. Additional exam requirements/recommendations for international students: Required—TOEFL (minimum score 550 paper-based; 213 computer-based; 80 iBT). *Application deadline:* For fall admission, 1/15 priority date for domestic students. Applications are processed on a rolling basis. Application fee: $60. Electronic applications accepted. *Expenses:* Tuition: Full-time $35,046; part-time $1524 per credit. Required fees: $161 per semester. *Financial support:* Fellowships, research assistantships, teaching assistantships, Federal Work-Study, institutionally sponsored loans, scholarships/grants, and tuition waivers (full and partial) available. Support available to part-time students. Financial award application deadline: 2/15; financial award applicants required to submit FAFSA. *Faculty research:* Social intervention, diversity in organizations, eyewitness memory, aging and cognition, drug policy. *Unit head:* Stewart Donaldson, Dean, 909-607-9001, Fax: 909-621-8905, E-mail: stewart.donaldson@cgu.edu. *Application contact:* Paul Thomas, Director, External Affairs, 909-607-9016, Fax: 909-621-8905, E-mail: paul.thomas@cgu.edu.

Clark University, Graduate School, Department of Psychology, Program in Developmental Psychology, Worcester, MA 01610-1477. Offers PhD. *Degree requirements:* For doctorate, thesis/dissertation. *Entrance requirements:* For doctorate, GRE General Test. Additional exam requirements/recommendations for international students: Required—TOEFL. *Application deadline:* For fall admission, 12/28 priority date for domestic students. Applications are processed on a rolling basis. Application fee: $50. *Expenses:* Tuition: Full-time $34,900; part-time $4362.50 per course. *Financial support:* In 2009–10, fellowships with full tuition reimbursements (averaging $15,700 per year), research assistantships with full tuition reimbursements (averaging $15,700 per year), teaching assistantships with full tuition reimbursements (averaging $15,700 per year) were awarded; tuition waivers (full) also available. *Faculty research:* Development of psychological processes in sociocultural context, conceptualizing and reasoning, symbolization, psychotherapy, metaphor, emotions and personalities. *Unit head:* Dr. Michael Bambert, Chair, 508-793-7274. *Application contact:* Peggy Moskowitz, Graduate School Secretary, 508-793-7274, Fax: 508-793-7265, E-mail: psychology@clarku.edu.

Cornell University, Graduate School, Graduate Fields of Human Ecology, Field of Human Development, Ithaca, NY 14853-0001. Offers developmental psychology (PhD), including cognitive development, developmental psychopathology, ecology of human development, social and personality development; human development and family studies (PhD), including ecology of human development, family studies and the life course. *Faculty:* 42 full-time (18 women). *Students:* 38 full-time (27 women); includes 3 minority (all Asian Americans or Pacific Islanders), 13 international. Average age 28. 81 applicants, 25% accepted, 12 enrolled. In 2009, 2 doctorates awarded. *Degree requirements:* For doctorate, comprehensive exam, thesis/dissertation, pre-doctoral research project, teaching experience. *Entrance requirements:* For doctorate, GRE General Test, 2 letters of recommendation. Additional exam requirements/recommendations for international students: Required—TOEFL (minimum score 550 paper-based; 213 computer-based; 77 iBT). *Application deadline:* For fall admission, 1/15 for domestic students. Application fee: $70. Electronic applications accepted. *Expenses:* Tuition: Full-time $29,500. Required fees: $70. Full-time tuition and fees vary according to degree level, program and student level. *Financial support:* In 2009–10, 26 students received support, including 2 fellowships with full tuition reimbursements available, 4 teaching assistantships with full tuition reimbursements available; research assistantships with full tuition reimbursements available, institutionally sponsored loans, scholarships/grants, health care benefits, tuition waivers (full and partial), and unspecified assistantships also available. Financial award applicants required to submit FAFSA. *Faculty research:* Cognitive development, developmental psychopathology, ecology of human development, family studies and the life course, social and personality development. *Unit head:* Director of Graduate Studies, 607-255-3181, Fax: 607-255-9856. *Application contact:* Graduate Field Assistant, 607-255-3181, Fax: 607-255-9856, E-mail: hdfs@cornell.edu.

Duke University, Graduate School, Department of Psychology, Durham, NC 27708-0586. Offers biological psychology (PhD); clinical psychology (PhD); cognitive psychology (PhD); developmental psychology (PhD); experimental psychology (PhD); health psychology (PhD); human social development (PhD); JD/MA. *Accreditation:* APA (one or more programs are accredited). *Faculty:* 40 full-time. *Students:* 92 full-time (70 women); includes 13 minority (5 African Americans, 2 Asian Americans or Pacific Islanders, 6 Hispanic Americans), 14 international. 478 applicants, 8% accepted, 21 enrolled. In 2009, 10 doctorates awarded. *Degree requirements:* For doctorate, thesis/dissertation. *Entrance requirements:* For doctorate, GRE General Test. Additional exam requirements/recommendations for international students: Required—TOEFL (minimum score 550 paper-based; 213 computer-based; 83 iBT), IELTS (minimum score 7). *Application deadline:* For fall admission, 12/8 priority date for domestic and international students. Application fee: $75. Electronic applications accepted. *Financial support:* Fellowships, research assistantships, teaching assistantships, career-related internships or fieldwork and Federal Work-Study available. Financial award application deadline: 12/31. *Unit head:* Melanie Bonner, Director of Graduate Studies, Fax: 919-660-5715, E-mail: morrell@duke.edu. *Application contact:* Cynthia Robertson, Associate Dean for Enrollment Services, 919-684-3913, E-mail: grad-admissions@duke.edu.

Emory University, Graduate School of Arts and Sciences, Department of Psychology, Atlanta, GA 30322-1100. Offers clinical psychology (PhD); cognition and development (PhD); neuroscience and animal behavior (PhD). *Accreditation:* APA. *Degree requirements:* For doctorate, comprehensive exam, thesis/dissertation. *Entrance requirements:* For doctorate, GRE General Test, minimum GPA of 3.25. Additional exam requirements/recommendations for international students: Required—TOEFL. Electronic applications accepted. *Faculty research:* Neuroscience and animal behavior; adult and child psychopathology, cognition development assessment.

Erikson Institute, Academic Programs, Chicago, IL 60654. Offers administration (Certificate); bilingual/ESL (Certificate); child development (MS); early childhood education (MS); infant mental health (Certificate); infant studies (Certificate); MS/MSW. Part-time and evening/weekend programs available. *Degree requirements:* For master's, comprehensive exam, internship; for Certificate, internship. *Entrance requirements:* For master's and Certificate, minimum GPA of 2.75. Additional exam requirements/recommendations for international students: Required—TOEFL. *Faculty research:* Assessment strategies from early childhood through elementary years; language, literacy, and the arts in children's development; inclusive special education; parent-child relationships; cognitive development.

Florida State University, The Graduate School, College of Arts and Sciences, Department of Psychology, Program in Developmental Psychology, Tallahassee, FL 32306. Offers PhD. *Faculty:* 12 full-time (3 women). *Students:* 10 full-time (7 women); includes 3 minority (1 African American, 1 Asian American or Pacific Islander, 1 Hispanic American). Average age 26. 19 applicants, 11% accepted, 2 enrolled. In 2009, 2 doctorates awarded. Terminal master's awarded for partial completion of doctoral program. *Degree requirements:* For doctorate, thesis/dissertation, preliminary exam. *Entrance requirements:* For doctorate, GRE General Test, minimum GPA of 3.0, research experience, letters of recommendation. Additional exam requirements/recommendations for international students: Required—TOEFL (minimum score 550 paper-based; 213 computer-based; 80 iBT). *Application deadline:* For fall admission, 1/15 for domestic and international students. Application fee: $30. Electronic applications accepted. *Expenses:* Tuition, state resident: full-time $7413. Tuition, nonresident: full-time $22,567. *Financial support:* In 2009–10, 7 students received support, including 5 fellowships with full tuition reimbursements available (averaging $18,000 per year), 2 research assistantships with full tuition reimbursements available (averaging $18,000 per year), teaching assistantships with full tuition reimbursements available (averaging $15,000 per year); Federal Work-Study, institutionally sponsored loans, scholarships/grants, health care benefits, and unspecified assistantships also available. *Faculty research:* Learning disabilities, phonological processing, psychology of reading, emergent literacy, aging. *Unit head:* Dr. Christopher Schatschneider, Director, 850-644-4323, Fax: 850-644-7739, E-mail: schatschneider@psy.fsu.edu. *Application contact:* Cherie P. Miller, Graduate Program Assistant, 850-644-2499, Fax: 850-644-7739, E-mail: grad-info@psy.fsu.edu.

Fordham University, Graduate School of Arts and Sciences, Department of Psychology, Program in Applied Developmental Psychology, New York, NY 10458. Offers PhD. *Students:* 16 full-time (13 women), 19 part-time (14 women); includes 9 minority (5 African Americans, 3 Asian Americans or Pacific Islanders, 1 Hispanic American), 3 international. Average age 29. 23 applicants, 52% accepted, 6 enrolled. In 2009, 4 doctorates awarded. *Degree requirements:* For doctorate, comprehensive exam, thesis/dissertation. *Entrance requirements:* For doctorate, GRE General Test, GRE Subject Test. Additional exam requirements/recommendations for international students: Required—TOEFL (minimum score 600 paper-based; 250 computer-based). *Application deadline:* For fall admission, 12/14 for domestic students. Application fee: $70. Electronic applications accepted. *Financial support:* In 2009–10, 15 students received support, including 4 fellowships with tuition reimbursements available (averaging $21,300 per year), 11 research assistantships with tuition reimbursements available (averaging $18,836 per year), 1 teaching assistantship with tuition reimbursement available (averaging $20,600 per year); career-related internships or fieldwork, institutionally sponsored loans, tuition waivers (full and partial), and unspecified assistantships also available. Financial award application deadline: 12/14. *Faculty research:* Development of citizenship, impact of participation in community service, impact of poverty on children, development of moral reasoning and behavior. Total annual research expenditures: $1.4 million. *Unit head:* Dr. Ann D'Allesandro, Director, 718-817-3789, Fax: 718-817-3785, E-mail: sherrod@fordham.edu. *Application contact:* Charlene Dundie, Director of Graduate Admissions, 718-817-4420, Fax: 718-817-3566, E-mail: dundie@fordham.edu.

Gallaudet University, The Graduate School, College of Arts and Sciences, Department of Psychology, Program in School Psychology, Washington, DC 20002-3625. Offers developmental psychology (MA); school psychology (Psy S). *Accreditation:* NCATE. *Degree requirements:* For master's, thesis optional. *Entrance requirements:* For master's, GRE General Test or MAT. Electronic applications accepted.

Graduate School and University Center of the City University of New York, Graduate Studies, Program in Psychology, New York, NY 10016-4039. Offers basic applied neurocognition (PhD); biopsychology (PhD); clinical psychology (PhD); developmental psychology (PhD); environmental psychology (PhD); experimental psychology (PhD); industrial psychology (PhD); learning processes (PhD); neuropsychology (PhD); psychology (PhD); social personality (PhD). *Faculty:* 119 full-time (40 women). *Students:* 559 full-time (414 women), 1 part-time (0 women); includes 101 minority (34 African Americans, 25 Asian Americans or Pacific Islanders, 42 Hispanic Americans), 57 international. Average age 33. 750 applicants, 16% accepted, 84 enrolled. In 2009, 54 doctorates awarded. *Degree requirements:* For doctorate, one foreign language, thesis/dissertation. *Entrance requirements:* For doctorate, GRE General Test. Additional exam requirements/recommendations for international students: Required—TOEFL. *Application deadline:* For fall admission, 12/15 priority date for domestic students. Application fee: $125. Electronic applications accepted. *Financial support:* In 2009–10, 371 students received support, including 340 fellowships, 34 research assistantships, 33 teaching assistantships; career-related internships or fieldwork, Federal Work-Study, institutionally sponsored loans, and tuition waivers (full and partial) also available. Financial award application deadline: 2/1; financial award applicants required to submit FAFSA. *Unit head:* Dr. Joseph Glick, Executive Officer, 212-817-8706, Fax: 212-817-1533, E-mail: jglick@gc.cuny.edu. *Application contact:* Les Gribben, Director of Admissions, 212-817-7470, Fax: 212-817-1624, E-mail: lgribben@gc.cuny.edu.

Harvard University, Graduate School of Arts and Sciences, Department of Psychology, Cambridge, MA 02138. Offers psychology (PhD), including behavior and decision analysis, cognition, developmental psychology, experimental psychology, personality, psychobiology, psychopathology; social psychology (PhD). *Accreditation:* APA. *Degree requirements:* For doctorate, thesis/dissertation, general exams. *Entrance requirements:* For doctorate, GRE General Test. Additional exam requirements/recommendations for international students: Required—TOEFL. *Expenses:* Tuition: Full-time $33,696. Required fees: $1126. Full-time tuition and fees vary according to program.

Howard University, Graduate School, Department of Psychology, Washington, DC 20059-0002. Offers clinical psychology (PhD); developmental psychology (PhD); experimental psychology (PhD); neuropsychology (PhD); personality psychology (PhD); psychology (MS); social psychology (PhD). *Accreditation:* APA (one or more programs are accredited). Part-time programs available. *Degree requirements:* For master's, thesis; for doctorate, comprehensive exam, thesis/dissertation, qualifying exam. *Entrance requirements:* For master's, GRE General Test, minimum GPA of 2.5, bachelor's degree in psychology or related field; for doctorate, GRE General Test, minimum GPA of 3.0. *Faculty research:* Personality and psychophysiology, educational and social development of African-American children, child and adult psychopathology.

Illinois State University, Graduate School, College of Arts and Sciences, Department of Psychology, Normal, IL 61790-2200. Offers psychology (MA, MS), including clinical psychology, counseling psychology, developmental psychology, educational psychology, experimental psychology, measurement-evaluation, organizational-industrial psychology; school psychology (PhD, SSP). *Accreditation:* APA. *Degree requirements:* For master's, thesis or alternative; for doctorate, variable foreign language requirement, thesis/dissertation, 2 terms of residency, internship, practicum. *Entrance requirements:* For master's, GRE General Test, GRE Subject Test, minimum GPA of 3.0 in last 60 hours of course work; for doctorate, GRE General Test. *Faculty research:* Comprehensive evaluation system for the central region professional development grant, Illinois school psychology internship consortium, for children's sake.

Indiana University Bloomington, University Graduate School, College of Arts and Sciences, Department of Psychological and Brain Sciences, Bloomington, IN 47405-7000. Offers biology and behavior (PhD); clinical science (PhD); cognitive psychology (PhD); developmental psychology (PhD); psychological and brain sciences (MA); social psychology (PhD). *Accreditation:* APA (one or more programs are accredited). *Faculty:* 53 full-time (16 women). *Students:* 92 full-time (51 women); includes 12 minority (4 African Americans, 4 Asian Americans or Pacific Islanders, 4 Hispanic Americans), 19 international. Average age 28. 239 applicants, 10% accepted, 15 enrolled. In 2009, 3 master's, 13 doctorates awarded. *Degree requirements:* For doctorate, comprehensive exam, thesis/dissertation, 1st and 2nd year projects, 1 year as associate instructor, qualifying exam, student teaching. *Entrance requirements:* For doctorate, GRE. Additional exam requirements/recommendations for international students: Required—TOEFL (minimum score 550 paper-based; 213 computer-based). *Application deadline:* For fall admission, 12/15 for domestic students, 12/1 for international students. Application fee: $55

Developmental Psychology

Indiana University Bloomington (continued)

($65 for international students). Electronic applications accepted. *Financial support:* In 2009–10, 25 fellowships with full tuition reimbursements (averaging $23,000 per year), 11 research assistantships with full tuition reimbursements (averaging $17,850 per year), 7 teaching assistantships with full tuition reimbursements (averaging $17,850 per year) were awarded; scholarships/grants, health care benefits, and unspecified assistantships also available. *Unit head:* Dr. Linda B. Smith, Chair, 812-855-3991, Fax: 812-855-4691, E-mail: smith4@indiana.edu. *Application contact:* Patricia G. Crouch, Academic Services Coordinator, 812-855-4528, Fax: 812-855-4691, E-mail: pcrouch@indiana.edu.

Louisiana State University and Agricultural and Mechanical College, Graduate School, College of Arts and Sciences, Department of Psychology, Baton Rouge, LA 70803. Offers biological psychology (MA, PhD); clinical psychology (MA, PhD); cognitive psychology (MA, PhD); developmental psychology (MA, PhD); industrial/organizational psychology (MA, PhD); school psychology (MA, PhD). *Accreditation:* APA (one or more programs are accredited). *Faculty:* 27 full-time (10 women). *Students:* 94 full-time (68 women), 17 part-time (12 women); includes 14 minority (6 African Americans, 2 American Indian/Alaska Native, 2 Asian Americans or Pacific Islanders, 4 Hispanic Americans), 3 international. Average age 27. 232 applicants, 18% accepted, 29 enrolled. In 2009, 13 master's, 14 doctorates awarded. Terminal master's awarded for partial completion of doctoral program. *Degree requirements:* For master's, thesis; for doctorate, thesis/dissertation, 1 year internship. *Entrance requirements:* For master's and doctorate, GRE General Test, minimum GPA of 3.0. Additional exam requirements/recommendations for international students: Required—TOEFL (minimum score 550 paper-based; 213 computer-based; 79 iBT) or IELTS (minimum score 6.5). *Application deadline:* For fall admission, 1/15 for domestic and international students. Applications are processed on a rolling basis. Application fee: $50 ($70 for international students). Electronic applications accepted. *Financial support:* In 2009–10, 108 students received support, including 5 fellowships (averaging $26,974 per year), 2 research assistantships with partial tuition reimbursements available (averaging $18,000 per year), 74 teaching assistantships with partial tuition reimbursements available (averaging $14,751 per year); career-related internships or fieldwork, Federal Work-Study, institutionally sponsored loans, scholarships/grants, health care benefits, and tuition waivers (full and partial) also available. Financial award applicants required to submit FAFSA. *Faculty research:* Clinical psychology, autism, anxiety, addition, neuropsychology, school psychology, cognitive psychology, experimental psychology. Total annual research expenditures: $1 million. *Unit head:* Dr. Robert Matthews, Chair, 225-578-8745, Fax: 225-578-4125, E-mail: psmath@lsu.edu. *Application contact:* Dr. Jason Hicks, Coordinator of Graduate Studies, 225-578-4109, Fax: 225-578-4125, E-mail: jhicks@lsu.edu.

Loyola University Chicago, Graduate School, Department of Psychology, Program in Developmental Psychology, Chicago, IL 60660. Offers MA, PhD. *Faculty:* 6 full-time (4 women), 1 (woman) part-time/adjunct. *Students:* 24 full-time (22 women), 6 part-time (all women); includes 7 minority (4 African Americans, 1 American Indian/Alaska Native, 2 Hispanic Americans), 2 international. Average age 32. 31 applicants, 23% accepted, 7 enrolled. In 2009, 1 master's awarded. *Degree requirements:* For doctorate, comprehensive exam, thesis/dissertation, internship or student teaching. *Entrance requirements:* For doctorate, GRE General Test, GRE Subject Test. Additional exam requirements/recommendations for international students: Required—TOEFL (minimum score 500 paper-based). *Application deadline:* For fall admission, 1/15 for domestic students. Application fee: $50. Electronic applications accepted. *Expenses:* Tuition: Full-time $14,220; part-time $790 per credit hour. Required fees: $60 per semester hour. Tuition and fees vary according to program. *Financial support:* In 2009–10, 5 students received support, including fellowships with full tuition reimbursements available (averaging $14,000 per year), research assistantships with full tuition reimbursements available (averaging $14,000 per year), teaching assistantships with full tuition reimbursements available (averaging $14,000 per year); career-related internships or fieldwork, scholarships/grants, and unspecified assistantships also available. Financial award application deadline: 2/1; financial award applicants required to submit FAFSA. *Faculty research:* Cognitive development, parenting, bilingualism, memory development, emotion development, aggression and violence, racism stereotyping. Total annual research expenditures: $10,000. *Unit head:* Dr. Denise Davidson, Director, 773-508-3008, Fax: 773-508-2813, E-mail: ddavids@luc.edu. *Application contact:* Ron Martin, Assistant Director of Enrollment Management, 312-915-8950, Fax: 312-915-8905, E-mail: gradapp@luc.edu.

McGill University, Faculty of Graduate and Postdoctoral Studies, Faculty of Education, Department of Educational and Counseling Psychology, Montréal, QC H3A 2T5, Canada. Offers counseling psychology (MA, PhD); educational psychology (M Ed, MA, PhD); school/applied child psychology and applied developmental psychology (M Ed, MA, PhD, Diploma), including school psychology. *Accreditation:* APA.

The New School: A University, The New School for Social Research, Department of Psychology, New York, NY 10011. Offers clinical psychology (PhD); cognitive, social and developmental psychology (PhD); general psychology (MA). *Accreditation:* APA (one or more programs are accredited). Part-time programs available. *Faculty:* 13 full-time (5 women). *Students:* 172 full-time (130 women), 105 part-time (87 women); includes 49 minority (13 African Americans, 1 American Indian/Alaska Native, 15 Asian Americans or Pacific Islanders, 20 Hispanic Americans), 41 international. Average age 30. 299 applicants, 80% accepted, 76 enrolled. In 2009, 74 master's, 17 doctorates awarded. Terminal master's awarded for partial completion of doctoral program. *Degree requirements:* For master's, comprehensive exam (for some programs), thesis (for some programs); for doctorate, thesis/dissertation, qualifying exam. *Entrance requirements:* For master's, GRE General Test; for doctorate, GRE General Test, MA. Additional exam requirements/recommendations for international students: Required—TOEFL (minimum score 600 paper-based; 250 computer-based; 100 iBT). *Application deadline:* For fall admission, 1/17 priority date for domestic and international students; for spring admission, 10/15 priority date for domestic and international students. Applications are processed on a rolling basis. Application fee: $50. Electronic applications accepted. *Financial support:* Fellowships, research assistantships, teaching assistantships, Federal Work-Study, scholarships/grants, tuition waivers (full and partial), and unspecified assistantships available. Support available to part-time students. Financial award application deadline: 3/1; financial award applicants required to submit FAFSA. *Faculty research:* Consciousness, memory, language, perceptions, psychopathology. *Unit head:* Dr. McWelling Todman, Chair, 212-229-5727 Ext. 3258, E-mail: todmanm@newschool.edu. *Application contact:* Robert MacDonald, Director of Admissions, 212-229-5727 Ext. 3007, Fax: 212-989-7102, E-mail: macdonar@newschool.edu.

New York University, Steinhardt School of Culture, Education, and Human Development, Department of Applied Psychology, Programs in Educational and Developmental Psychology, New York, NY 10012-1019. Offers educational psychology (MA); human development and social intervention (MA); psychological development (PhD); psychology and social intervention (PhD). *Accreditation:* APA (one or more programs are accredited). Part-time programs available. *Students:* 48 full-time (42 women), 36 part-time (30 women); includes 24 minority (9 African Americans, 4 Asian Americans or Pacific Islanders, 11 Hispanic Americans), 11 international. Average age 29. 233 applicants, 30% accepted, 26 enrolled. In 2009, 29 master's, 9 doctorates awarded. *Degree requirements:* For master's, thesis (for some programs); for doctorate, thesis/dissertation. *Entrance requirements:* For doctorate, GRE General Test, interview. Additional exam requirements/recommendations for international students: Required—TOEFL. *Application deadline:* For fall admission, 12/15 priority date for domestic and international students. Applications are processed on a rolling basis. Application fee: $75. Electronic applications accepted. *Expenses:* Tuition: Full-time $30,528; part-time $1272 per credit. Required fees: $2177. *Financial support:* Teaching assistantships with partial tuition reimbursements, career-related internships or fieldwork, Federal Work-Study, institutionally sponsored loans, and tuition waivers (partial) available. Support available to part-time students. Financial award application deadline: 2/1; financial award applicants required to submit FAFSA. *Faculty research:* High risk children and youth; child and adolescent developments; families and schooling; infant cognition; exploration, language, and symbolic play in toddlerhood. *Unit head:* Dr. LaRue Allen, Director, 212-998-5555, Fax: 212-995-4358. *Application contact:* 212-998-5030, Fax: 212-995-4328, E-mail: steinhardt.gradadmissions@nyu.edu.

North Carolina State University, Graduate School, College of Humanities and Social Sciences, Department of Psychology, Raleigh, NC 27695. Offers developmental psychology (PhD); ergonomics and experimental psychology (PhD); industrial/organizational psychology (PhD); psychology in the public interest (PhD); school psychology (PhD). *Accreditation:* APA. *Degree requirements:* For doctorate, comprehensive exam, thesis/dissertation. *Entrance requirements:* For doctorate, GRE General Test, GRE Subject Test (industrial/organizational psychology), MAT (recommended), minimum GPA of 3.0 in major. Electronic applications accepted. *Faculty research:* Cognitive and social development (human factors, families, the workplace, community issues and health, aging).

The Ohio State University, Graduate School, College of Social and Behavioral Sciences, School of Social and Behavioral Science, Department of Psychology, Columbus, OH 43210. Offers behavioral neuroscience (PhD); clinical psychology (PhD); cognitive psychology (PhD); developmental psychology (PhD); mental retardation and developmental disabilities (PhD); psychology (MA); quantitative psychology (PhD); social psychology (PhD). *Accreditation:* APA (one or more programs are accredited). *Faculty:* 60. *Students:* 88 full-time (59 women), 47 part-time (31 women); includes 20 minority (7 African Americans, 1 American Indian/Alaska Native, 5 Asian Americans or Pacific Islanders, 7 Hispanic Americans), 20 international. Average age 27. In 2009, 15 master's, 20 doctorates awarded. *Degree requirements:* For doctorate, thesis/dissertation. *Entrance requirements:* For master's and doctorate, GRE General Test. Additional exam requirements/recommendations for international students: Required—TOEFL (minimum score 600 paper-based; 250 computer-based). *Application deadline:* For fall admission, 12/31 for domestic students, 11/30 for international students. Applications are processed on a rolling basis. Application fee: $40 ($50 for international students). Electronic applications accepted. *Expenses:* Tuition, state resident: full-time $10,683. Tuition, nonresident: full-time $25,923. Tuition and fees vary according to course load and program. *Financial support:* Fellowships, research assistantships, teaching assistantships available. *Unit head:* Michael Vasey, Graduate Studies Committee Chair, E-mail: vasey.1@osu.edu. *Application contact:* 614-292-9444, Fax: 614-292-3895, E-mail: domestic.grad@osu.edu.

Queen's University at Kingston, School of Graduate Studies and Research, Faculty of Arts and Sciences, Department of Psychology, Kingston, ON K7L 3N6, Canada. Offers brain behavior and cognitive science (MA, PhD); clinical psychology (MA, PhD); developmental psychology (MA, PhD); social personality psychology (MA, PhD). *Accreditation:* APA (one or more programs are accredited). *Degree requirements:* For master's, thesis; for doctorate, comprehensive exam, thesis/dissertation. *Entrance requirements:* For master's and doctorate, GRE General Test. Additional exam requirements/recommendations for international students: Required—TOEFL. *Faculty research:* Human development, social, personality, behavioral neuroscience, forensic.

Stanford University, School of Education, Program in Psychological Studies in Education, Stanford, CA 94305-9991. Offers child and adolescent development (PhD); counseling psychology (PhD); educational psychology (PhD). *Degree requirements:* For doctorate, thesis/dissertation. *Entrance requirements:* For doctorate, GRE General Test. Electronic applications accepted. *Expenses:* Tuition: Full-time $37,380; part-time $2760 per quarter. Required fees: $501.

Teachers College, Columbia University, Graduate Faculty of Education, Department of Human Development, Program in Cognitive Studies in Education, New York, NY 10027-6696. Offers MA, Ed D, PhD.

Teachers College, Columbia University, Graduate Faculty of Education, Department of Human Development, Program in Developmental Psychology, New York, NY 10027-6696. Offers MA, Ed D, PhD. *Faculty:* 6 full-time (5 women). *Students:* 39 full-time (33 women), 61 part-time (47 women); includes 37 minority (8 African Americans, 16 Asian Americans or Pacific Islanders, 13 Hispanic Americans), 8 international. Average age 28. 115 applicants, 72% accepted, 35 enrolled. In 2009, 36 master's awarded. *Degree requirements:* For doctorate, thesis/dissertation, integrative project. *Entrance requirements:* For doctorate, GRE General Test. *Application deadline:* For fall admission, 5/15 for domestic students. Application fee: $65. *Financial support:* Research assistantships, teaching assistantships, career-related internships or fieldwork, Federal Work-Study, institutionally sponsored loans, and tuition waivers (full and partial) available. Support available to part-time students. Financial award application deadline: 2/1. *Faculty research:* Language development in infants, psychology of mathematics education, intellectual development, testing and assessment, cognitive development. *Unit head:* Office of Admissions, 212-678-3710, Fax: 212-678-4171. *Application contact:* Melba Remice, Assistant Director of Admission, 212-678-4035, Fax: 212-678-4171, E-mail: ms2545@columbia.edu.

Temple University, Graduate School, College of Liberal Arts, Department of Psychology, Program in Developmental Psychology, Philadelphia, PA 19122-6096. Offers PhD. *Degree requirements:* For doctorate, thesis/dissertation. *Entrance requirements:* For doctorate, GRE General Test, minimum GPA of 3.0. Additional exam requirements/recommendations for international students: Required—TOEFL (minimum score 550 paper-based; 213 computer-based; 79 iBT). Electronic applications accepted. *Faculty research:* Social development, cognitive development, emotional development, research methodology.

Texas A&M University, College of Liberal Arts, Department of Psychology, College Station, TX 77843. Offers behavioral and cellular neuroscience (MS, PhD); clinical psychology (MS, PhD); cognitive psychology (MS, PhD); developmental psychology (MS, PhD); industrial/organizational psychology (MS, PhD); social psychology (MS, PhD). *Accreditation:* APA (one or more programs are accredited). *Faculty:* 36. *Students:* 84 full-time (58 women), 6 part-time (5 women); includes 26 minority (6 African Americans, 3 Asian Americans or Pacific Islanders, 17 Hispanic Americans), 6 international. In 2009, 12 master's, 8 doctorates awarded. *Degree requirements:* For master's, thesis; for doctorate, comprehensive exam (for some programs), thesis/dissertation. *Entrance requirements:* For master's and doctorate, GRE General Test. Additional exam requirements/recommendations for international students: Required—TOEFL. *Application deadline:* For fall admission, 1/5 for domestic and international students. Application fee: $50 ($75 for international students). Electronic applications accepted. *Expenses:* Tuition, state resident: full-time $3991; part-time $221.74 per credit hour. Tuition, nonresident: full-time $9049; part-time $502.74 per credit hour. *Financial support:* Fellowships with partial tuition reimbursements, research assistantships with partial tuition reimbursements, teaching assistantships with partial tuition reimbursements, career-related internships or fieldwork, institutionally sponsored loans, health care benefits, and unspecified assistantships available. Financial award application deadline: 1/5; financial award applicants required to submit FAFSA. *Unit head:* Dr. Les Morey, Head, 979-845-2581, Fax: 979-845-4727, E-mail: lmorey@psych.tamu.edu. *Application contact:* Sharon Starr, Graduate Admissions Supervisor, 979-458-1710, Fax: 979-845-4727, E-mail: gradadv@psyc.tamu.edu.

Union Institute & University, MA Program in Psychology and Counseling, Brattleboro, VT 05301. Offers clinical mental health counseling (MA); clinical psychology (MA); counseling psychology (MA); developmental psychology (MA); educational psychology (MA); organizational psychology (MA). Postbaccalaureate distance learning degree programs offered (minimal on-campus study). *Faculty:* 2 full-time (1 woman), 8 part-time/adjunct (2 women). *Students:* 57 full-time (50 women), 20 part-time (16 women); includes 4 minority (1 African American, 3 Hispanic Americans). Average age 41. In 2009, 23 master's awarded. *Degree requirements:* For master's, thesis, internship (depending on concentration). *Application deadline:* Applications are processed on a rolling basis. Electronic applications accepted. Tuition and fees vary according to course load, degree level, campus/location and program. *Unit head:* Dr. Nicholas Young, Director, 802-257-8911, E-mail: nick.young@myunion.edu. *Application contact:* Diane Robinson, Director of Admissions, Brattleboro, 800-336-6794, E-mail: diane.robinson@myunion.edu.

Université de Montréal, Faculty of Arts and Sciences, School of Psychoeducation, Montréal, QC H3C 3J7, Canada. Offers M Sc, PhD, Certificate. Part-time programs available. *Degree requirements:* For master's, one foreign language, thesis. Electronic applications accepted. *Faculty research:* Child maladjustment, family, prevention, treatment, antisocial behavior.

The University of British Columbia, Faculty of Arts and Faculty of Graduate Studies, Department of Psychology, Vancouver, BC V6T 1Z4, Canada. Offers behavioral neuroscience (MA, PhD); clinical psychology (MA, PhD); cognitive science (MA, PhD); developmental psychology (MA, PhD); health psychology (MA, PhD); quantitative methods (MA, PhD); social/personality psychology (MA, PhD). *Accreditation:* APA (one or more programs are accredited). Terminal master's awarded for partial completion of doctoral program. *Degree requirements:* For master's, thesis; for doctorate, comprehensive exam, thesis/dissertation. *Entrance requirements:* For master's and doctorate, GRE General Test. Additional exam requirements/recommendations for international students: Required—TOEFL (minimum score 550 paper-based; 230 computer-based; 80 iBT). Electronic applications accepted. *Faculty research:* Clinical, developmental, social/personality, cognition, behavioral neuroscience.

University of California, Santa Barbara, Graduate Division, Gevirtz Graduate School of Education, Santa Barbara, CA 93106-9490. Offers counseling, clinical and school psychology (PhD), including clinical psychology, counseling psychology, school psychology; education (M Ed, MA, PhD), including child and adolescent development (MA, PhD), cultural perspectives and comparative education (MA, PhD), educational leadership and organizations (MA, PhD), research methodology (MA, PhD), special education disabilities and risk studies (MA), special education, disabilities and risk studies (PhD), teaching (M Ed), teaching and learning (MA, PhD); educational leadership (Ed D); school psychology (M Ed); MA/PhD. *Accreditation:* APA (one or more programs are accredited). Postbaccalaureate distance learning degree programs offered (minimal on-campus study). *Faculty:* 42 full-time (20 women), 10 part-time/adjunct (4 women). *Students:* 390 full-time (303 women); includes 149 minority (14 African Americans, 3 American Indian/Alaska Native, 57 Asian Americans or Pacific Islanders, 75 Hispanic Americans), 16 international. Average age 31. 717 applicants, 40% accepted, 170 enrolled. In 2009, 140 master's, 46 doctorates awarded. Terminal master's awarded for partial completion of doctoral program. *Degree requirements:* For master's, comprehensive exam (for some programs), thesis (for some programs); for doctorate, comprehensive exam (for some programs), thesis/dissertation, qualifying exam. *Entrance requirements:* For master's, GRE, 3 letters of recommendation, resume/curriculum vitae; for doctorate, GRE, 3 letters of recommendation, statement of purpose, personal achievements/contributions statement, resume/curriculum vitae, transcripts for post-secondary institutions attended. Additional exam requirements/recommendations for international students: Required—TOEFL (minimum score 550 paper-based; 213 computer-based; 80 iBT) or IELTS (minimum score 7). Application fee: $70 ($90 for international students). Electronic applications accepted. *Financial support:* In 2009–10, 253 students received support, including 206 fellowships with full and partial tuition reimbursements available (averaging $5,000 per year), 62 research assistantships with full and partial tuition reimbursements available (averaging $6,200 per year), 87 teaching assistantships with partial tuition reimbursements available (averaging $6,500 per year); career-related internships or fieldwork, Federal Work-Study, institutionally sponsored loans, scholarships/grants, traineeships, health care benefits, and unspecified assistantships also available. Financial award applicants required to submit FAFSA. *Faculty research:* Professional development, early childhood development, school violence, literacy, science/math initiative. Total annual research expenditures: $4.4 million. *Unit head:* Dr. Jane Conoley, Chair, 805-893-2185, E-mail: jane-conoley@education.ucsb.edu. *Application contact:* Kathryn Marie Tucciarone, Student Affairs Officer, 805-893-2137, E-mail: katiet@education.ucsb.edu.

University of Connecticut, Graduate School, College of Liberal Arts and Sciences, Department of Psychology, Storrs, CT 06269. Offers behavioral neuroscience (PhD); biopsychology (PhD); clinical psychology (MA, PhD); cognition and instruction (PhD); developmental psychology (MA, PhD); ecological psychology (PhD); experimental psychology (PhD); general psychology (MA, PhD); health psychology (Graduate Certificate); industrial/organizational psychology (PhD); language and cognition (PhD); neuroscience (PhD); occupational health psychology (Graduate Certificate); social psychology (MA, PhD). *Accreditation:* APA. *Faculty:* 59 full-time (26 women). *Students:* 194 full-time (133 women), 24 part-time (12 women); includes 48 minority (12 African Americans, 21 Asian Americans or Pacific Islanders, 15 Hispanic Americans), 25 international. Average age 28. 585 applicants, 4% accepted, 14 enrolled. In 2009, 22 master's, 24 doctorates awarded. Terminal master's awarded for partial completion of doctoral program. *Degree requirements:* For master's, comprehensive exam; for doctorate, thesis/dissertation. *Entrance requirements:* For master's and doctorate, GRE General Test, GRE Subject Test. Additional exam requirements/recommendations for international students: Required—TOEFL (minimum score 550 paper-based; 213 computer-based). *Application deadline:* For fall admission, 2/1 priority date for domestic and international students; for spring admission, 11/1 for domestic students, 10/1 for international students. Applications are processed on a rolling basis. Application fee: $55. Electronic applications accepted. *Expenses:* Tuition, state resident: full-time $4725; part-time $525 per credit. Tuition, nonresident: full-time $12,267; part-time $1363 per credit. Required fees: $346 per semester. Tuition and fees vary according to course load. *Financial support:* In 2009–10, 109 research assistantships with full tuition reimbursements, 72 teaching assistantships with full tuition reimbursements were awarded; fellowships, career-related internships or fieldwork, Federal Work-Study, scholarships/grants, health care benefits, and unspecified assistantships also available. Financial award application deadline: 2/1; financial award applicants required to submit FAFSA. *Unit head:* Charles A. Lowe, Head, 860-486-3517, Fax: 860-486-2760, E-mail: charles.lowe@uconn.edu. *Application contact:* Charles A. Lowe, Head, 860-486-3517, Fax: 860-486-2760, E-mail: charles.lowe@uconn.edu.

University of Florida, Graduate School, College of Liberal Arts and Sciences, Department of Psychology, Gainesville, FL 32611. Offers behavior analysis (PhD); behavioral neuroscience (MS, PhD); cognitive and sensory processes (PhD); counseling psychology (PhD); developmental psychology (PhD); social psychology (MS, PhD); JD/PhD. *Degree requirements:* For master's, thesis or alternative; for doctorate, thesis/dissertation. *Entrance requirements:* For master's and doctorate, GRE General Test, minimum GPA of 3.0. Additional exam requirements/recommendations for international students: Required—TOEFL (minimum score 550 paper-based; 213 computer-based). Electronic applications accepted. *Faculty research:* Experimental analysis of behavior, psychobiology, cognition and sensory processes, counseling psychology, social psychology, developmental psychology.

The University of Kansas, Graduate Studies, College of Liberal Arts and Sciences, Department of Psychology, Lawrence, KS 66045. Offers clinical child psychology (MA, PhD); clinical health and rehabilitation (PhD); cognitive (PhD); developmental (PhD); quantitative (PhD); social (MA). *Accreditation:* APA (one or more programs are accredited). *Faculty:* 27 full-time (8 women), 9 part-time/adjunct (4 women). *Students:* 85 full-time (62 women), 11 part-time (9 women); includes 13 minority (4 African Americans, 1 American Indian/Alaska Native, 6 Asian Americans or Pacific Islanders, 2 Hispanic Americans), 7 international. Average age 27. 185 applicants, 15% accepted, 17 enrolled. In 2009, 13 master's, 10 doctorates awarded. *Degree requirements:* For master's, thesis; for doctorate, variable foreign language requirement, comprehensive exam, thesis/dissertation. *Entrance requirements:* For doctorate, GRE General Test, minimum GPA of 3.0; undergraduate degree with 15 hours of course work in psychology, vita, writing sample (Clinical Program Only). Additional exam requirements/recommendations for international students: Required—TOEFL. *Application deadline:* For fall admission, 12/1 for domestic and international students. Application fee: $45 ($55 for international students). Electronic applications accepted. *Expenses:* Tuition, state resident: full-time $6492; part-time $270.50 per credit hour. Tuition, nonresident: full-time $15,510; part-time $646.25 per credit hour. Required fees: $847; $70.56 per credit hour. Tuition and fees vary according to course load and program. *Financial support:* Fellowships with full tuition reimbursements, research assistantships with partial tuition reimbursements, teaching assistantships with full and partial tuition reimbursements, career-related internships or fieldwork and unspecified assistantships available. Financial award application deadline: 12/1; financial award applicants required to submit FAFSA. *Faculty research:* Information processing in depression, rape and other forms of sexual coerciom, motions on physical function, processes of memory and understanding text, social stigmas and hostile group environments. *Unit head:* Dr. Ruth Ann Atchley, Chair, 785-864-9821, Fax: 785-864-5696, E-mail: ratchley@ku.edu. *Application contact:* Cathy L. O'Keefe, Graduate Admissions Officer, 785-864-4195, Fax: 785-864-5696, E-mail: psycgrad@ku.edu.

The University of Kansas, Graduate Studies, College of Liberal Arts and Sciences, Program in Child Language, Lawrence, KS 66045. Offers MA, PhD. *Students:* 8 full-time (6 women); includes 1 minority (African American), 1 international. Average age 29. 3 applicants, 67% accepted, 2 enrolled. *Degree requirements:* For master's, thesis; for doctorate, comprehensive exam, thesis/dissertation, written preliminary exam. *Entrance requirements:* For master's and doctorate, GRE, minimum GPA of 3.5, 3 letters of reference. Additional exam requirements/recommendations for international students: Required—TOEFL. *Application deadline:* For fall admission, 2/1 priority date for domestic and international students; for spring admission, 11/1 for domestic and international students. Applications are processed on a rolling basis. Application fee: $45 ($55 for international students). Electronic applications accepted. *Expenses:* Tuition, state resident: full-time $6492; part-time $270.50 per credit hour. Tuition, nonresident: full-time $15,510; part-time $646.25 per credit hour. Required fees: $847; $70.56 per credit hour. Tuition and fees vary according to course load and program. *Financial support:* Fellowships with full tuition reimbursements, research assistantships with full tuition reimbursements, career-related internships or fieldwork, traineeships, and unspecified assistantships available. Financial award application deadline: 2/1. *Faculty research:* Etiology of language impairments, word recognition processes, cultural context and linguistic patterns, language acquisition. *Unit head:* Mabel Rice, Director, 785-864-4570, E-mail: mabel@ku.edu. *Application contact:* Susan Kemper, Graduate Adviser, 785-864-0748, E-mail: skemper@ku.edu.

University of Maine, Graduate School, College of Liberal Arts and Sciences, Department of Psychology, Orono, ME 04469. Offers clinical psychology (PhD); developmental psychology (MA); experimental psychology (MA, PhD); social psychology (MA). *Accreditation:* APA (one or more programs are accredited). *Faculty:* 17 full-time (8 women), 7 part-time/adjunct (3 women). *Students:* 27 full-time (16 women), 9 part-time (7 women); includes 2 minority (1 Asian American or Pacific Islander, 1 Hispanic American), 1 international. Average age 28. 134 applicants, 8% accepted, 7 enrolled. In 2009, 3 master's, 3 doctorates awarded. *Degree requirements:* For master's, thesis; for doctorate, thesis/dissertation. *Entrance requirements:* For master's and doctorate, GRE General Test, GRE Subject Test. Additional exam requirements/recommendations for international students: Required—TOEFL. *Application deadline:* For fall admission, 2/1 priority date for domestic students. Applications are processed on a rolling basis. Application fee: $65. Electronic applications accepted. *Financial support:* In 2009–10, 3 research assistantships with tuition reimbursements (averaging $14,063 per year), 21 teaching assistantships with tuition reimbursements (averaging $12,790 per year) were awarded; Federal Work-Study, institutionally sponsored loans, and tuition waivers (full and partial) also available. Financial award application deadline: 3/1. *Faculty research:* Social development, hypertension and aging, attitude change, self-confidence in achievement situations, health psychology. *Unit head:* Dr. Michael Robbins, Chair, 207-581-2051, Fax: 207-581-6128. *Application contact:* Scott G. Delcourt, Associate Dean of the Graduate School, 207-581-3291, Fax: 207-581-3232, E-mail: graduate@maine.edu.

University of Maryland, Baltimore County, Graduate School, College of Arts, Humanities and Social Sciences, Department of Psychology, Program in Applied Developmental Psychology, Baltimore, MD 21250. Offers PhD. *Faculty:* 7 full-time (4 women), 11 part-time/adjunct (4 women). *Students:* 22 full-time (20 women), 10 part-time (9 women); includes 6 minority (1 African American, 4 Asian Americans or Pacific Islanders, 1 Hispanic American). Average age 29. 18 applicants, 28% accepted, 1 enrolled. In 2009, 1 doctorate awarded. *Degree requirements:* For doctorate, comprehensive exam, thesis/dissertation. *Entrance requirements:* For doctorate, GRE General Test, GRE Subject Test, minimum GPA of 3.0. Additional exam requirements/recommendations for international students: Required—TOEFL. *Application deadline:* For fall admission, 1/9 for domestic and international students. Application fee: $70. Electronic applications accepted. *Financial support:* In 2009–10, fellowships with partial tuition reimbursements (averaging $2,200 per year), 3 research assistantships with full and partial tuition reimbursements (averaging $14,857 per year), 10 teaching assistantships with full and partial tuition reimbursements (averaging $14,857 per year) were awarded; career-related internships or fieldwork, Federal Work-Study, health care benefits, and unspecified assistantships also available. Financial award application deadline: 3/1; financial award applicants required to submit FAFSA. *Faculty research:* Early intervention and development, schooling and development, cultural aspects of development, development in high risk children, social-emotional development. Total annual research expenditures: $2.3 million. *Unit head:* Dr. Susan Sonnenschein, Director, 410-455-2361, Fax: 410-455-1055, E-mail: sonnenschein@umbc.edu. *Application contact:* Nicole Mooney, Program Management Specialist, 410-455-2567, Fax: 410-455-1055, E-mail: psycdept@umbc.edu.

University of Maryland, College Park, Academic Affairs, College of Behavioral and Social Sciences, Department of Psychology, College Park, MD 20742. Offers clinical psychology (PhD); developmental psychology (PhD); experimental psychology (PhD); industrial psychology (MA, MS, PhD); social psychology (PhD). *Accreditation:* APA (one or more programs are accredited). *Faculty:* 71 full-time (35 women), 8 part-time/adjunct (4 women). *Students:* 82 full-time (67 women); includes 13 minority (2 African Americans, 4 Asian Americans or Pacific Islanders, 7 Hispanic Americans), 12 international. 568 applicants, 4% accepted, 8 enrolled. In 2009, 13 master's, 10 doctorates awarded. *Degree requirements:* For master's, thesis; for doctorate, variable foreign language requirement, comprehensive exam, thesis/dissertation. *Entrance requirements:* For master's and doctorate, GRE General Test, GRE Subject Test, minimum GPA of 3.5, research and/or work experience, 3 letters of recommendation. *Application deadline:* For fall admission, 12/1 for domestic and international students. Applications are processed on a rolling basis. Application fee: $60. Electronic applications accepted. *Expenses:* Tuition, area resident: Part-time $471 per credit hour. Tuition, state resident: part-time $471 per credit hour. Tuition, nonresident: part-time $1016 per credit hour. Required fees: $337.04 per term. *Financial support:* In 2009–10, 11 fellowships with full and partial tuition reimbursements (averaging $19,195 per year), 5 research assistantships (averaging $17,734 per year), 45 teaching assistantships with tuition reimbursements (averaging $17,116 per year) were awarded; career-related internships or fieldwork, Federal Work-Study, and scholarships/grants also available. Support available to part-time students. Financial award applicants required to submit FAFSA. *Faculty research:* Social stereotyping and prejudice, anxiety disorders, auditory neuroethology, counseling and social psychology. Total annual research expenditures: $3.8 million. *Unit head:* Thomas S. Wallsten, Chair, 301-405-3562, Fax: 301-314-9566, E-mail: twallst@umd.edu. *Application contact:* Dean of Graduate School, 301-405-0358, Fax: 301-314-9305.

University of Massachusetts Amherst, Graduate School, College of Natural Sciences, Department of Psychology, Amherst, MA 01003. Offers clinical psychology (MS, PhD); cognitive psychology (MS, PhD); developmental science (MS, PhD); psychology of peace and violence (MS, PhD); social psychology (MS, PhD). *Accreditation:* APA (one or more programs are accredited). *Faculty:* 48 full-time (22 women). *Students:* 57 full-time (42 women), 13 part-time (10 women); includes 15 minority (6 Asian Americans, 6 Asian Americans or Pacific Islanders, 3 Hispanic Americans), 8 international. Average age 28. 381 applicants, 4% accepted, 11 enrolled. In 2009, 11 master's, 8 doctorates awarded. Terminal master's awarded for partial completion of doctoral program. *Degree requirements:* For master's, thesis; for doctorate, comprehensive exam, thesis/dissertation. *Entrance requirements:* For master's and doctorate, GRE General Test, 3 letters of recommendation. Additional exam requirements/recommendations for international students: Required—TOEFL (minimum score 550 paper-based; 213 computer-based; 80 iBT), IELTS (minimum score 6.5). *Application deadline:* For fall admission, 12/1 for domestic and international students. Applications are processed on a rolling basis. Application fee: $50 ($65 for international students). Electronic applications accepted. *Expenses:* Tuition, state resident: full-time $2640; part-time $110 per credit. Tuition, nonresident: full-time $9936; part-time $414 per credit. Tuition and fees vary according to course load. *Financial support:* In

Developmental Psychology

University of Massachusetts Amherst (continued)
2009–10, 8 fellowships with full tuition reimbursements (averaging $12,620 per year), 52 research assistantships with full tuition reimbursements (averaging $9,491 per year), 55 teaching assistantships with full tuition reimbursements (averaging $10,829 per year) were awarded; career-related internships or fieldwork, Federal Work-Study, scholarships/grants, traineeships, health care benefits, tuition waivers (full), and unspecified assistantships also available. Support available to part-time students. Financial award application deadline: 12/1. *Unit head:* Dr. Linda M. Isbell, Graduate Program Director, 413-545-2503, Fax: 413-545-0996. *Application contact:* Jean M. Ames, Supervisor of Admissions, 413-545-0722, Fax: 413-577-0010, E-mail: gradadm@grad.umass.edu.

University of Miami, Graduate School, College of Arts and Sciences, Department of Psychology, Coral Gables, FL 33124. Offers adult clinical (PhD); behavioral neuroscience (PhD); child clinical (PhD); developmental psychology (PhD); health clinical (PhD); psychology (MS). *Accreditation:* APA (one or more programs are accredited). *Degree requirements:* For doctorate, comprehensive exam, thesis/dissertation. *Entrance requirements:* For doctorate, GRE General Test, minimum GPA of 3.5. Additional exam requirements/recommendations for international students: Required—TOEFL. Electronic applications accepted. *Faculty research:* Behavioral factors in cardiovascular disease and cancer adult psychopathology, developmental disabilities, social and emotional development, mechanisms of coping.

University of Michigan, Horace H. Rackham School of Graduate Studies, College of Literature, Science, and the Arts, Department of Psychology, Ann Arbor, MI 48451. Offers biopsychology (PhD); clinical psychology (PhD); cognition and perception (PhD); developmental psychology (PhD); personality and social contexts (PhD); social psychology (PhD). *Accreditation:* APA. *Faculty:* 87 full-time (40 women), 28 part-time/adjunct (16 women). *Students:* 147 full-time (101 women); includes 40 minority (15 African Americans, 2 American Indian/Alaska Native, 18 Asian Americans or Pacific Islanders, 5 Hispanic Americans), 25 international. Average age 27. 621 applicants, 10% accepted, 37 enrolled. In 2009, 25 doctorates awarded. *Degree requirements:* For doctorate, comprehensive exam, thesis/dissertation, oral defense of dissertation, preliminary exam. *Entrance requirements:* For doctorate, GRE General Test. Additional exam requirements/recommendations for international students: Required—TOEFL. *Application deadline:* For fall admission, 12/1 for domestic and international students. Application fee: $60 ($75 for international students). Electronic applications accepted. *Expenses:* Tuition, state resident: full-time $17,286; part-time $1099 per credit hour. Tuition, nonresident: full-time $34,944; part-time $2080 per credit hour. Required fees: $95 per semester. Tuition and fees vary according to course load, degree level and program. *Financial support:* In 2009–10, 133 students received support, including 52 fellowships with full tuition reimbursements available (averaging $20,900 per year), 16 research assistantships with full tuition reimbursements available (averaging $20,900 per year), 79 teaching assistantships with full tuition reimbursements available (averaging $16,694 per year); career-related internships or fieldwork also available. Financial award application deadline: 4/15. *Unit head:* Prof. Theresa Lee, Chair, 734-764-7429. *Application contact:* Laurie Brannan, Psychology Student Academic Affairs, 731-764-2580, Fax: 734-615-7584, E-mail: psych.saa@umich.edu.

The University of Montana, Graduate School, College of Arts and Sciences, Department of Psychology, Missoula, MT 59812-0002. Offers clinical psychology (PhD); experimental psychology (PhD), including animal behavior psychology, developmental psychology; school psychology (MA, PhD, Ed S). *Accreditation:* APA (one or more programs are accredited). Terminal master's awarded for partial completion of doctoral program. *Degree requirements:* For master's, thesis; for doctorate, thesis/dissertation. *Entrance requirements:* For master's, doctorate, and Ed S, GRE General Test. Additional exam requirements/recommendations for international students: Required—TOEFL.

University of Nebraska at Omaha, Graduate Studies, College of Arts and Sciences, Department of Psychology, Omaha, NE 68182. Offers developmental psychology (PhD); industrial/organizational psychology (MS, PhD); psychobiology (PhD); psychology (MA); school psychology (MS, Ed S). Part-time programs available. *Faculty:* 18 full-time (8 women). *Students:* 44 full-time (36 women), 23 part-time (18 women); includes 3 minority (1 African American, 1 Asian American or Pacific Islander, 1 Hispanic American), 2 international. Average age 26. 116 applicants, 34% accepted, 28 enrolled. In 2009, 30 master's, 5 other advanced degrees awarded. *Degree requirements:* For master's, comprehensive exam, thesis (for some programs). *Entrance requirements:* For master's, GRE General Test, GRE Subject Test, previous course work in psychology, including statistics and a laboratory course; minimum GPA of 3.0, 3 letters of recommendation; for doctorate, GRE General Test. Additional exam requirements/recommendations for international students: Required—TOEFL (minimum score 500 paper-based; 173 computer-based; 61 iBT). *Application deadline:* For fall admission, 1/5 for domestic students. Application fee: $45. Electronic applications accepted. *Financial support:* In 2009–10, 44 students received support; fellowships, research assistantships with tuition reimbursements available, teaching assistantships with tuition reimbursements available, career-related internships or fieldwork, Federal Work-Study, institutionally sponsored loans, scholarships/grants, tuition waivers (partial), and unspecified assistantships available. Support available to part-time students. Financial award application deadline: 3/1; financial award applicants required to submit FAFSA. *Unit head:* Dr. Kenneth Deffenbacher, Chairperson, 402-554-2592. *Application contact:* Dr. Joseph Brown, Student Contact, 402-554-2592.

University of Nebraska–Lincoln, Graduate College, College of Arts and Sciences, Department of Psychology, Lincoln, NE 68588. Offers biopsychology (PhD); clinical psychology (PhD); cognitive psychology (PhD); developmental psychology (PhD); psychology (MA); social/personality psychology (PhD); JD/MA; JD/PhD. *Accreditation:* APA (one or more programs are accredited). *Degree requirements:* For master's, thesis optional; for doctorate, comprehensive exam, thesis/dissertation. *Entrance requirements:* For master's and doctorate, GRE General Test. Additional exam requirements/recommendations for international students: Required—TOEFL (minimum score 550 paper-based; 213 computer-based). Electronic applications accepted. *Faculty research:* Law and psychology, rural mental health, chronic mental illness, neuropsychology, child clinical psychology.

University of Nebraska–Lincoln, Graduate College, College of Education and Human Sciences, Department of Educational Psychology, Lincoln, NE 68588. Offers cognition, learning and development (MA); counseling psychology (MA); educational psychology (MA, Ed S); psychological studies in education (PhD), including cognition, learning and development, counseling psychology, quantitative, qualitative, and psychometric methods, school psychology; quantitative, qualitative, and psychometric methods (MA); school psychology (MA, Ed S). *Accreditation:* APA (one or more programs are accredited); NCATE. *Degree requirements:* For master's, thesis optional. *Entrance requirements:* For master's, GRE General Test. Additional exam requirements/recommendations for international students: Required—TOEFL (minimum score 500 paper-based; 173 computer-based). Electronic applications accepted. *Faculty research:* Measurement and assessment, metacognition, academic skills, child development, multicultural education and counseling.

The University of North Carolina at Chapel Hill, Graduate School, College of Arts and Sciences, Department of Psychology, Chapel Hill, NC 27599. Offers biological psychology (PhD); clinical psychology (PhD); cognitive psychology (PhD); developmental psychology (PhD); quantitative psychology (PhD); social psychology (PhD). *Accreditation:* APA. *Degree requirements:* For doctorate, comprehensive exam, thesis/dissertation. *Entrance requirements:* For doctorate, GRE General Test, minimum GPA of 3.0. Electronic applications accepted. *Faculty research:* Expressed emotion, cognitive development, social cognitive neuroscience, human memory personality.

The University of North Carolina at Greensboro, Graduate School, College of Arts and Sciences, Department of Psychology, Greensboro, NC 27412-5001. Offers clinical psychology (MA, PhD); cognitive psychology (MA, PhD); developmental psychology (MA, PhD); social psychology (MA, PhD). *Accreditation:* APA (one or more programs are accredited). Terminal master's awarded for partial completion of doctoral program. *Degree requirements:* For master's, comprehensive exam, thesis; for doctorate, one foreign language, thesis/dissertation, preliminary exam. *Entrance requirements:* For master's and doctorate, GRE General Test. Additional exam requirements/recommendations for international students: Required—TOEFL. Electronic applications accepted. *Faculty research:* Sensory and perceptual determinants; evoked potential: disorders, deafness, and development.

University of Notre Dame, Graduate School, College of Arts and Letters, Division of Social Science, Department of Psychology, Notre Dame, IN 46556. Offers cognitive psychology (PhD); counseling psychology (PhD); developmental psychology (PhD); quantitative psychology (PhD). *Accreditation:* APA. *Degree requirements:* For doctorate, comprehensive exam, thesis/dissertation, candidacy exam. *Entrance requirements:* For doctorate, GRE General Test, GRE Subject Test (strongly recommended). Additional exam requirements/recommendations for international students: Required—TOEFL (minimum score 600 paper-based; 250 computer-based; 80 iBT). Electronic applications accepted. *Faculty research:* Cognitive and socio-emotional development, statistical methods and quantitative models applicable to psychology, interpersonal relations, life span development and developmental delay, childhood depression, structural equation and dynamical systems.

University of Oregon, Graduate School, College of Arts and Sciences, Department of Psychology, Eugene, OR 97403. Offers clinical psychology (PhD); cognitive psychology (MA, MS, PhD); developmental psychology (MA, MS, PhD); physiological psychology (MA, MS, PhD); psychology (MA, MS, PhD); social/personality psychology (MA, MS, PhD). *Accreditation:* APA (one or more programs are accredited). Terminal master's awarded for partial completion of doctoral program. *Degree requirements:* For doctorate, thesis/dissertation. *Entrance requirements:* For master's, GRE General Test, minimum GPA of 3.0; for doctorate, GRE General Test. Additional exam requirements/recommendations for international students: Required—TOEFL.

University of Pittsburgh, School of Education, Department of Psychology in Education, Program in Applied Developmental Psychology, Pittsburgh, PA 15260. Offers M Ed, MS, PhD. Part-time and evening/weekend programs available. *Students:* 54 full-time (50 women), 54 part-time (45 women); includes 23 minority (20 African Americans, 3 Asian Americans or Pacific Islanders), 9 international. Average age 30. 96 applicants, 70% accepted, 41 enrolled. In 2009, 34 master's, 5 doctorates awarded. *Degree requirements:* For master's, thesis. *Entrance requirements:* For doctorate, GRE. Additional exam requirements/recommendations for international students: Required—TOEFL. *Application deadline:* For fall admission, 2/1 for domestic students, 2/1 priority date for international students; for spring admission, 7/1 priority date for international students. Applications are processed on a rolling basis. Application fee: $50. Electronic applications accepted. *Expenses:* Tuition, state resident: full-time $16,402; part-time $665 per credit. Tuition, nonresident: full-time $28,694; part-time $1175 per credit. Required fees: $690; $175 per term. Tuition and fees vary according to program. *Financial support:* Tuition waivers (partial) available. Support available to part-time students. Financial award applicants required to submit FAFSA. *Unit head:* Dr. Carl N. Johnson, Chairman, 412-624-6942, Fax: 412-624-7231, E-mail: johnson@pitt.edu. *Application contact:* Dr. Marjorie K. Schermer, Enrollment Manager, 412-648-2230, Fax: 412-648-1899, E-mail: soeinfo@pitt.edu.

University of Rochester, The College, Arts and Sciences, Department of Clinical and Social Sciences in Psychology, Rochester, NY 14627. Offers clinical psychology (PhD); developmental psychology (PhD); psychology (MA); social-personality psychology (PhD). *Accreditation:* APA (one or more programs are accredited). Terminal master's awarded for partial completion of doctoral program. *Degree requirements:* For doctorate, thesis/dissertation, qualifying exam. *Entrance requirements:* For doctorate, GRE General Test. Additional exam requirements/recommendations for international students: Required—TOEFL.

University of Southern California, Graduate School, College of Letters, Arts and Sciences, Department of Psychology, Los Angeles, CA 90089. Offers brain and cognitive science (PhD); clinical science (PhD); developmental psychology (PhD); human behavior (MHB); psychology (MA); quantitative methods (PhD); social psychology (PhD); PhD/MPH. *Accreditation:* APA. *Faculty:* 34 full-time (10 women), 17 part-time/adjunct (7 women). *Students:* 107 full-time (73 women); includes 38 minority (6 African Americans, 21 Asian Americans or Pacific Islanders, 11 Hispanic Americans), 19 international. 430 applicants, 6% accepted, 13 enrolled. In 2009, 17 master's, 12 doctorates awarded. *Degree requirements:* For doctorate, comprehensive exam, thesis/dissertation, one-year internship (for clinical science students). *Entrance requirements:* For doctorate, GRE. Additional exam requirements/recommendations for international students: Recommended—TOEFL (minimum score 600 paper-based; 250 computer-based; 100 iBT). *Application deadline:* For fall admission, 12/1 for domestic and international students. Application fee: $95. Electronic applications accepted. *Expenses:* Tuition: Full-time $25,980; part-time $1315 per unit. Required fees: $554. One-time fee: $35 full-time. Full-time tuition and fees vary according to degree level and program. *Financial support:* In 2009–10, 80 students received support, including 16 fellowships with full tuition reimbursements available (averaging $22,500 per year), 22 research assistantships with full tuition reimbursements available (averaging $19,000 per year), 38 teaching assistantships with full tuition reimbursements available (averaging $19,000 per year); career-related internships or fieldwork, scholarships/grants, traineeships, and health care benefits also available. *Faculty research:* Affective neuroscience; children and families; vision, culture and ethnicity; intergroup relations; aggression and violence; language and reading development; substance abuse. *Unit head:* Dr. Margaret Gatz, Chair and Professor, 213-740-2203, Fax: 213-746-9028, E-mail: gatz@usc.edu. *Application contact:* Irene Takaragawa, Graduate Advisor, 213-740-2205, E-mail: itakarag@usc.edu.

University of Victoria, Faculty of Graduate Studies, Faculty of Social Sciences, Department of Psychology, Victoria, BC V8W 2Y2, Canada. Offers clinical psychology (PhD); clinical psychology (neuropsychology) (M Sc); cognition and brain science (M Sc, PhD); experimental neuropsychology (M Sc, PhD); individualized study (M Sc, PhD); life span development psychology (PhD); life span developmental psychology (M Sc); social psychology (M Sc, PhD). *Accreditation:* APA (one or more programs are accredited). *Degree requirements:* For master's, thesis; for doctorate, thesis/dissertation, candidacy exam. *Entrance requirements:* For master's and doctorate, GRE General Test. Additional exam requirements/recommendations for international students: Required—TOEFL (minimum score 600 paper-based; 250 computer-based). Electronic applications accepted. *Faculty research:* Life span development psychology and aging, behavioral neuroscience, cognitive psychology, behavioral psychology, environmental psychology.

University of Washington, Graduate School, College of Arts and Sciences, Department of Psychology, Seattle, WA 98195. Offers animal behavior (PhD); child psychology (PhD); clinical psychology (PhD); cognition and perception (PhD); developmental psychology (PhD); quantitative psychology (PhD); social psychology and personality (PhD). *Accreditation:* APA. *Degree requirements:* For doctorate, thesis/dissertation. *Entrance requirements:* For doctorate, GRE General Test, minimum GPA of 3.0. Electronic applications accepted. *Faculty research:* Addictive behaviors, artificial intelligence, child psychopathology, mechanisms and development of vision, physiology of ingestive behaviors.

University of Wisconsin–Madison, Graduate School, College of Letters and Science, Department of Psychology, Program in Developmental Psychology, Madison, WI 53706-1380. Offers PhD. *Degree requirements:* For doctorate, comprehensive exam, thesis/dissertation. *Entrance requirements:* For doctorate, GRE General Test, minimum undergraduate GPA of 3.0. Additional exam requirements/recommendations for international students: Required—TOEFL. Electronic applications accepted. *Expenses:* Tuition, state resident: part-time $594 per credit. Tuition, nonresident: part-time $1504 per credit. Required fees: $65 per credit. Tuition and fees vary according to course load, program and reciprocity agreements.

University of Wisconsin–Milwaukee, Graduate School, School of Education, Department of Educational Psychology, Milwaukee, WI 53201-0413. Offers counseling (school, community) (MS); counseling psychology (PhD); learning and development (MS); research methodology (MS, PhD); school psychology (PhD). *Accreditation:* APA. Part-time programs available. *Faculty:* 22 full-time (14 women). *Students:* 124 full-time (107 women), 47 part-time (35 women); includes 20 minority (10 African Americans, 4 Asian Americans or Pacific Islanders, 6 Hispanic Americans), 2 international. Average age 30. 263 applicants, 52% accepted, 51 enrolled. In 2009, 55 master's, 13 doctorates awarded. *Degree requirements:* For master's, comprehensive exam, thesis; for doctorate, thesis/dissertation. *Entrance requirements:* For master's, minimum GPA of 3.0; for doctorate, GRE General Test, minimum GPA of 3.0. Additional exam requirements/recommendations for international students: Required—TOEFL (minimum score 550 paper-based; 79 iBT), IELTS (minimum score 6.5). *Application deadline:* For fall admission, 1/1 priority date for domestic students; for spring admission, 9/1 for domestic students. Applications are processed on a rolling basis. Application fee: $45 ($75 for international students). *Expenses:* Tuition, state resident: full-time $8800. Tuition, nonresident: full-time $20,760. Tuition and fees vary according to program and reciprocity agreements. *Financial support:* In 2009–10, 9 teaching assistantships were awarded; career-related internships or fieldwork and unspecified assistantships also available. Support available to part-time students. Financial award application deadline: 4/15. Total annual research expenditures: $1.3 million. *Unit head:* Bo Zhang, Graduate Program Representative, 414-229-5742, Fax: 414-229-4939, E-mail: boz@uwm.edu. *Application contact:* General Information Contact, 414-229-4982, Fax: 414-229-6967, E-mail: gradschool@uwm.edu.

Virginia Polytechnic Institute and State University, Graduate School, College of Science, Department of Psychology, Blacksburg, VA 24061. Offers bio-behavioral sciences (PhD); clinical psychology (PhD); developmental psychology (PhD); industrial/organizational psychology (PhD); psychology (MS). *Accreditation:* APA (one or more programs are accredited). *Faculty:* 23 full-time (7 women). *Students:* 71 full-time (45 women), 6 part-time (3 women); includes 18 minority (6 American Indian/Alaska Native, 8 Asian Americans or Pacific Islanders, 4 Hispanic Americans), 1 international. Average age 27. 201 applicants, 7% accepted, 14 enrolled. In 2009, 20 master's, 14 doctorates awarded. *Entrance requirements:* For master's and doctorate, GRE, GMAT. Additional exam requirements/recommendations for international students: Required—TOEFL (minimum score 550 paper-based; 213 computer-based). *Application deadline:* For fall admission, 5/15 for international students; for spring admission, 10/15 for international students. Applications are processed on a rolling basis. Application fee: $65. Electronic applications accepted. *Expenses:* Tuition, area resident: Full-time $10,228; part-time $459 per credit hour. Tuition, nonresident: full-time $17,892; part-time $865 per credit hour. Required fees: $1966; $451 per semester. *Financial support:* In 2009–10, 18 research assistantships with full tuition reimbursements (averaging $16,153 per year), 41 teaching assistantships with full tuition reimbursements (averaging $16,053 per year) were awarded; career-related internships or fieldwork, Federal Work-Study, scholarships/grants, and unspecified assistantships also available. Financial award application deadline: 1/15. *Faculty research:* Infant development from electrophysical point of view, work motivation and personnel selection, EEG, ERP and hypnosis with reference to chronic pain, intimate violence. Total annual research expenditures: $2.1 million. *Unit head:* Dr. Robert S. Stephens, Dean, 540-231-6304, Fax: 540-231-3652, E-mail: stephens@vt.edu. *Application contact:* Kirby Deater-Deckard, Information Contact, 540-231-6581, Fax: 540-231-3652, E-mail: kirbydd@vt.edu.

Walden University, Graduate Programs, School of Psychology, Minneapolis, MN 55401. Offers clinical child psychology (Post-Doctoral Certificate); clinical psychology (Post-Doctoral Certificate); counseling psychology (Post-Doctoral Certificate); forensic psychology (MS), including forensic psychology in the community, general program, mental health applications, program planning and evaluation in forensic settings, psychology and legal systems; general psychology (Post-Doctoral Certificate); health psychology (Post-Doctoral Certificate); organizational psychology (Post-Doctoral Certificate); organizational psychology and development (Postbaccalaureate Certificate); psychology (MS, PhD), including clinical psychology (PhD), counseling psychology (PhD), crisis management and response (MS), general program (MS), general psychology (PhD), health psychology, leadership development and coaching (MS), media psychology (MS), organizational psychology (PhD), organizational psychology and development (MS), organizational psychology and nonprofit management (MS), program evaluation and research (MS), psychology of culture (MS), psychology, public administration, and social change (MS), social psychology (MS), terrorism and security (MS); teaching online (Post-Master's Certificate). Part-time and evening/weekend programs available. Post-baccalaureate distance learning degree programs offered (minimal on-campus study). *Faculty:* 33 full-time, 222 part-time/adjunct. *Students:* 3,546 full-time (2,761 women), 1,133 part-time (908 women); includes 1,723 minority (1,319 African Americans, 56 American Indian/Alaska Native, 101 Asian Americans or Pacific Islanders, 247 Hispanic Americans), 80 international. Average age 41. In 2009, 495 master's, 70 doctorates, 2 other advanced degrees awarded. Terminal master's awarded for partial completion of doctoral program. *Degree requirements:* For master's, thesis optional; for doctorate, thesis/dissertation, residency. *Entrance requirements:* For master's, bachelor's degree or equivalent in related field; minimum GPA of 2.5; official transcripts; goal statement; access to computer and Internet; for doctorate, master's degree or equivalent in related field; minimum GPA of 3.0;3 years of related professional/academic experience (preferred). Additional exam requirements/recommendations for international students: Required—TOEFL (minimum score 550 paper-based; 213 computer-based), IELTS (minimum score 6.5), or Michigan English Language Assessment Battery (minimum score 82). *Application deadline:* Applications are processed on a rolling basis. Application fee: $50. Electronic applications accepted. *Expenses:* Tuition: Full-time $13,665; part-time $560 per credit. Required fees: $1375. Tuition and fees vary according to course load, degree level and program. *Financial support:* In 2009–10, 290 students received support; fellowships, Federal Work-Study, scholarships/grants, unspecified assistantships, and family tuition reduction, active duty/veteran tuition reduction, group tuition reduction, interest-free payment plans available. Support available to part-time students. Financial award applicants required to submit FAFSA. *Unit head:* Dr. Melanie Storms, Associate Dean, 800-925-3368. *Application contact:* Jennifer Hall, Director of Enrollment, 866-4-WALDEN, E-mail: info@waldenu.edu.

Wayne State University, College of Liberal Arts and Sciences, Department of Psychology, Program in Psychology, Detroit, MI 48202. Offers behavioral and cognitive neuroscience (PhD); clinical psychology (PhD); cognitive and social psychology (PhD); industrial/organizational psychology (PhD); psychology (MA, MS). *Accreditation:* APA (one or more programs are accredited). *Degree requirements:* For doctorate, thesis/dissertation. *Entrance requirements:* For doctorate, GRE General Test, GRE Subject Test. Additional exam requirements/recommendations for international students: Required—TOEFL (minimum score 550 paper-based; 213 computer-based); Recommended—TWE (minimum score 6). Electronic applications accepted.

West Virginia University, Eberly College of Arts and Sciences, Department of Psychology, Morgantown, WV 26506. Offers behavior analysis (PhD); clinical psychology (MA, PhD); development psychology (PhD); psychology (MS). *Accreditation:* APA (one or more programs are accredited). Part-time programs available. Terminal master's awarded for partial completion of doctoral program. *Degree requirements:* For master's, thesis optional; for doctorate, comprehensive exam, thesis/dissertation. *Entrance requirements:* For master's and doctorate, GRE General Test, minimum GPA of 3.0. Additional exam requirements/recommendations for international students: Required—TOEFL. *Faculty research:* Adult and child clinical psychology, behavioral assessment and therapy, child and adolescent behavior, life span development, experimental and applied behavior analysis.

Wilfrid Laurier University, Faculty of Graduate Studies, Faculty of Science, Department of Psychology, Waterloo, ON N2L 3C5, Canada. Offers brain and cognition (M Sc, PhD); community psychology (MA, PhD); social and developmental psychology (MA, PhD). *Degree requirements:* For master's, thesis; for doctorate, thesis/dissertation. *Entrance requirements:* For master's, GRE General Test, honors BA or the equivalent in psychology, minimum B average in undergraduate course work; for doctorate, GRE General Test, master's degree, minimum A- average. Additional exam requirements/recommendations for international students: Required—TOEFL (minimum score 230 computer-based; 89 iBT). Electronic applications accepted. *Faculty research:* Brain and cognition, community psychology, social and developmental psychology.

Yale University, Graduate School of Arts and Sciences, Department of Psychology, New Haven, CT 06520. Offers behavioral neuroscience (PhD); clinical psychology (PhD); cognitive psychology (PhD); developmental psychology (PhD); social/personality psychology (PhD). *Accreditation:* APA. *Degree requirements:* For doctorate, thesis/dissertation. *Entrance requirements:* For doctorate, GRE General Test.

Experimental Psychology

American University, College of Arts and Sciences, Department of Psychology, Program in Psychology, Washington, DC 22016-8062. Offers experimental/biological psychology (MA); general psychology (MA); personality/social psychology (MA). Part-time programs available. *Students:* 30 full-time (27 women), 17 part-time (14 women); includes 9 minority (3 African Americans, 3 Asian Americans or Pacific Islanders, 3 Hispanic Americans), 1 international. Average age 27. 190 applicants, 36% accepted, 17 enrolled. In 2009, 35 master's awarded. *Degree requirements:* For master's, comprehensive exam, thesis or alternative. *Entrance requirements:* For master's, GRE General Test, GRE Subject Test. Additional exam requirements/recommendations for international students: Required—TOEFL. *Application deadline:* For fall admission, 3/1 for domestic students. Applications are processed on a rolling basis. Application fee: $80. *Expenses:* Tuition: Full-time $22,266; part-time $1237 per credit hour. Required fees: $430. Tuition and fees vary according to program. *Financial support:* Research assistantships, teaching assistantships available. Financial award application deadline: 2/1. *Faculty research:* Behavior therapy, cognitive behavior modification, pro-social behavior, conditioning and learning, olfaction. *Application contact:* Sara Holland, Senior Administrative Assistant, 202-885-1717, Fax: 202-885-1023.

Appalachian State University, Cratis D. Williams Graduate School, Department of Psychology, Boone, NC 28608. Offers clinical health psychology (MA); general experimental psychology (MA); industrial and organizational psychology (MA). Part-time programs available. *Faculty:* 31 full-time (11 women). *Students:* 51 full-time (37 women), 13 part-time (10 women); includes 4 minority (2 African Americans, 2 Asian Americans or Pacific Islanders), 2 international. 181 applicants, 25% accepted, 26 enrolled. In 2009, 22 master's, 7 other advanced degrees awarded. *Degree requirements:* For master's and MS/Specialist, comprehensive exam, thesis optional, GRE Subject Test exit exam. *Entrance requirements:* For master's and MS/Specialist, GRE General Test, 3 letters of recommendation. Additional exam requirements/recommendations for international students: Required—TOEFL (minimum score 550 paper-based; 230 computer-based; 79 iBT), or IELTS (minimum score 6.5). *Application deadline:* For fall admission, 3/1 for domestic students, 2/1 for international students. Applications are processed on a rolling basis. Application fee: $50. Electronic applications accepted. *Expenses:* Tuition, state resident: full-time $2960. Tuition, nonresident: full-time $14,051. Required fees: $2320. *Financial support:* In 2009–10, 34 research assistantships (averaging $4,000 per year), 25 teaching assistantships (averaging $4,000 per year) were awarded; fellowships, career-related internships or fieldwork, Federal Work-Study, scholarships/grants, and unspecified assistantships also available. Financial award application deadline: 4/1; financial award applicants required to submit FAFSA. *Faculty research:* Eating disorders, school-based consultations, organizational behavior management, brain mechanisms of sound localization, parenting styles. Total annual research expenditures: $114,200. *Unit head:* Dr. James Denniston, Chair, 828-262-2272, Fax: 828-262-2272, E-mail: dennistonjc@appstate.edu. *Application contact:* Dr. Denise Martz, Graduate Coordinator, 828-262-2715, E-mail: martzdm@appstate.edu.

Auburn University, Graduate School, College of Liberal Arts, Department of Psychology, Auburn University, AL 36849. Offers applied behavior analysis in developmental disabilities (MS); clinical psychology (PhD); experimental psychology (PhD); industrial/organizational psychology (PhD). *Accreditation:* APA (one or more programs are accredited). Part-time programs available. *Faculty:* 24 full-time (7 women), 4 part-time/adjunct (3 women). *Students:* 36 full-time (28 women), 57 part-time (33 women); includes 15 minority (6 African Americans, 4 Asian Americans or Pacific Islanders, 5 Hispanic Americans). Average age 26. 293 applicants, 9% accepted, 19 enrolled. In 2009, 20 master's, 11 doctorates awarded. *Degree requirements:* For doctorate, thesis/dissertation. *Entrance requirements:* For master's, GRE General Test, GRE Subject Test, minimum GPA of 3.25 in psychology, 3.0 overall; for doctorate, GRE General Test, GRE Subject Test. *Application deadline:* For fall admission, 7/7 for domestic students; for spring admission, 11/24 for domestic students. Applications are processed on a rolling basis. Application fee: $50 ($60 for international students). Electronic applications accepted. *Expenses:* Tuition, state resident: full-time $6240. Tuition, nonresident: full-time $18,720. International tuition: $18,938 full-time. Required fees: $492. Tuition and fees vary according to course load, program and reciprocity agreements. *Financial support:* Research assistantships, teaching assistantships, Federal Work-Study available. Support available to part-time students. Financial award application deadline: 3/15; financial award applicants required to submit FAFSA. *Faculty research:* Clinical psychology, learning, industrial psychology, organizational psychology. Total annual research expenditures: $200,000. *Unit head:* Dr. Barry Burkhart, Chair, 334-844-4412. *Application contact:* Dr. George Flowers, Dean of the Graduate School, 334-844-2125.

Bowling Green State University, Graduate College, College of Arts and Sciences, Department of Psychology, Bowling Green, OH 43403. Offers clinical psychology (MA, PhD); developmental psychology (MA, PhD); experimental psychology (MA, PhD); industrial/organizational psychology (MA, PhD); quantitative psychology (MA, PhD). *Accreditation:* APA (one or more programs are accredited). *Degree requirements:* For doctorate, thesis/dissertation. *Entrance requirements:* For doctorate, GRE General Test, GRE Subject Test. Additional exam requirements/recommendations for international students: Required—TOEFL. Electronic applications accepted. *Faculty research:* Personnel psychology, developmental-mathematical models, behavioral medication, brain process, child/adolescent social cognition.

Brooklyn College of the City University of New York, Division of Graduate Studies, Department of Psychology, Brooklyn, NY 11210-2889. Offers experimental psychology (MA); industrial and organizational psychology (MA), including human relations, organizational behavior; mental health counseling (MA); psychology (PhD). Part-time programs available. *Students:* 89 full-time (74 women), 131 part-time (97 women); includes 83 minority (52 African Americans, 11 Asian Americans or Pacific Islanders, 20 Hispanic Americans), 17 international. Average age 30. 322 applicants, 55% accepted, 98 enrolled. In 2009, 62 master's awarded. *Degree*

Experimental Psychology

Brooklyn College of the City University of New York (continued)
requirements: For master's, comprehensive exam, thesis (for some programs). *Entrance requirements:* For master's, minimum GPA of 3.0, 2 letters of recommendation, essay; for doctorate, GRE. Additional exam requirements/recommendations for international students: Required—TOEFL (minimum score 520 paper-based; 190 computer-based; 69 iBT). *Application deadline:* For fall admission, 3/1 for domestic students, 2/1 for international students; for spring admission, 11/1 for domestic students, 10/1 for international students. Applications are processed on a rolling basis. Application fee: $125. Electronic applications accepted. *Expenses:* Tuition, area resident: Full-time $7360; part-time $310 per credit hour. Tuition, state resident: full-time $7360; part-time $310 per credit hour. Tuition, nonresident: full-time $13,800; part-time $575 per credit hour. International tuition: $13,800 full-time. Required fees: $140.10 per semester. *Financial support:* Career-related internships or fieldwork, Federal Work-Study, institutionally sponsored loans, scholarships/grants, and tuition waivers (partial) available. Support available to part-time students. Financial award application deadline: 5/1; financial award applicants required to submit FAFSA. *Unit head:* Dr. Margaret-Ellen Pipe, Chairperson, 718-951-5601, Fax: 718-951-4814, E-mail: mepipe@brooklyn.cuny.edu. *Application contact:* Hernan Sierra, Graduate Admissions Coordinator, 718-951-4536, Fax: 718-951-4506, E-mail: grads@brooklyn.cuny.edu.

California State University, Northridge, Graduate Studies, College of Social and Behavioral Sciences, Department of Psychology, Northridge, CA 91330. Offers clinical psychology (MA); general-experimental psychology (MA); human factors and applied experimental psychology (MA). *Faculty:* 27 full-time (16 women), 19 part-time/adjunct (8 women). *Students:* 67 full-time (42 women), 25 part-time (19 women); includes 33 minority (2 African Americans, 9 Asian Americans or Pacific Islanders, 22 Hispanic Americans), 4 international. Average age 27. 173 applicants, 19% accepted, 29 enrolled. In 2009, 18 master's awarded. *Degree requirements:* For master's, thesis. *Entrance requirements:* For master's, GRE General Test, GRE Subject Test, minimum GPA of 3.0, letters of recommendation. Additional exam requirements/recommendations for international students: Required—TOEFL. *Application deadline:* For fall admission, 11/30 for domestic students. Application fee: $55. *Financial support:* Application deadline: 3/1. *Unit head:* Dr. Carrie Saetermoe, Chair, 818-677-3506. *Application contact:* Dr. Carrie Saetermoe, Chair, 818-677-3506.

California State University, San Bernardino, Graduate Studies, College of Social and Behavioral Sciences, Department of Psychology, Program in General/Experimental Psychology, San Bernardino, CA 92407-2397. Offers psychology (MA). *Students:* 29 full-time (21 women), 17 part-time (11 women); includes 18 minority (1 African American, 5 Asian Americans or Pacific Islanders, 12 Hispanic Americans), 2 international. Average age 28. 44 applicants, 59% accepted, 17 enrolled. In 2009, 8 master's awarded. *Degree requirements:* For master's, thesis. *Entrance requirements:* For master's, minimum GPA of 3.0 in major. *Application deadline:* For fall admission, 4/1 for domestic students; for spring admission, 3/1 for domestic students. Application fee: $55. *Financial support:* Unspecified assistantships available. *Unit head:* Dr. Robert Ricco, Director, 909-537-5485, Fax: 909-537-7003, E-mail: rricco@csusb.edu. *Application contact:* Stacy Brooks, Graduate Secretary, 909-537-5570, Fax: 909-537-7003, E-mail: sbrooks@csusb.edu.

Case Western Reserve University, School of Graduate Studies, Department of Psychology, Program in Experimental Psychology, Cleveland, OH 44106. Offers PhD. *Faculty:* 9 full-time (4 women), 3 part-time/adjunct (0 women). *Students:* 10 full-time (4 women); includes 1 minority (Asian American or Pacific Islander), 1 international. Average age 31. 140 applicants, 6% accepted, 3 enrolled. *Degree requirements:* For doctorate, thesis/dissertation, internship. *Entrance requirements:* For doctorate, GRE General Test, GRE Subject Test. Additional exam requirements/recommendations for international students: Required—TOEFL (minimum score 550 paper-based; 213 computer-based; 79 iBT). *Application deadline:* For fall admission, 2/15 priority date for domestic students. Application fee: $50. Electronic applications accepted. *Financial support:* Research assistantships, teaching assistantships available. *Faculty research:* Memory and intelligence, brain function in rats. *Application contact:* Dr. James C. Overholser, Director of Clinical Training, 216-368-2686, Fax: 216-368-4891, E-mail: overholser@case.edu.

The Catholic University of America, School of Arts and Sciences, Department of Psychology, Washington, DC 20064. Offers applied experimental psychology (PhD); clinical psychology (PhD); general psychology (MA); human factors (MA); MA/JD. *Accreditation:* APA (one or more programs are accredited). Part-time programs available. *Faculty:* 12 full-time (6 women), 3 part-time/adjunct (0 women). *Students:* 40 full-time (25 women), 38 part-time (33 women); includes 14 minority (5 African Americans, 4 Asian Americans or Pacific Islanders, 5 Hispanic Americans), 1 international. Average age 29. 200 applicants, 36% accepted, 25 enrolled. In 2009, 16 master's, 6 doctorates awarded. *Degree requirements:* For master's, comprehensive exam, thesis (for some programs); for doctorate, comprehensive exam, thesis/dissertation. *Entrance requirements:* For master's, GRE General Test, 3 letters of recommendation; for doctorate, GRE General Test, GRE Subject Test, statement of purpose, official copies of academic transcripts, three letters of recommendation. Additional exam requirements/recommendations for international students: Required—TOEFL (minimum score 580 paper-based; 237 computer-based). *Application deadline:* For fall admission, 8/1 priority date for domestic students, 7/15 for international students; for spring admission, 12/1 priority date for domestic students, 10/15 for international students. Applications are processed on a rolling basis. Application fee: $55. Electronic applications accepted. *Expenses:* Tuition: Full-time $31,740; part-time $1245 per credit hour. Required fees: $50; $25 per semester hour. One-time fee: $425. *Financial support:* Fellowships, research assistantships, teaching assistantships, Federal Work-Study, scholarships/grants, tuition waivers (full and partial), and unspecified assistantships available. Financial award application deadline: 2/1; financial award applicants required to submit FAFSA. *Faculty research:* Clinical psychology, applied cognitive science, psychopathology, cognitive neuroscience, psychotherapy. Total annual research expenditures: $409,988. *Unit head:* Dr. Marc M. Sebrechts, Chair, 202-319-5757, Fax: 202-319-6263, E-mail: sebrechts@cua.edu. *Application contact:* Julie Schwing, Director of Graduate Admissions, 202-319-5057, Fax: 202-319-6533, E-mail: cua-admissions@cua.edu.

Central Michigan University, College of Graduate Studies, College of Humanities and Social and Behavioral Sciences, Department of Psychology, Program in Experimental Psychology, Mount Pleasant, MI 48859. Offers applied experimental psychology (PhD); experimental psychology (MS). Part-time programs available. *Degree requirements:* For master's, thesis or alternative; for doctorate, thesis/dissertation. Electronic applications accepted. *Faculty research:* Behavioral neuroscience; human development; perception and cognition; social/personal problem solving; psychophysiology.

Central Washington University, Graduate Studies and Research, College of the Sciences, Department of Psychology, Program in Experimental Psychology, Ellensburg, WA 98926. Offers MS. *Faculty:* 32 full-time (16 women). *Students:* 21 full-time (8 women), 5 part-time (all women); includes 4 minority (2 American Indian/Alaska Native, 1 Asian American or Pacific Islander, 1 Hispanic American). 9 applicants, 44% accepted, 4 enrolled. In 2009, 5 master's awarded. *Degree requirements:* For master's, thesis. *Entrance requirements:* For master's, GRE General Test, minimum GPA of 3.0. Additional exam requirements/recommendations for international students: Required—TOEFL (minimum score 550 paper-based; 213 computer-based; 79 iBT). *Application deadline:* For fall admission, 2/1 priority date for domestic students. Applications are processed on a rolling basis. Application fee: $50. *Expenses:* Tuition, state resident: full-time $7353; part-time $245 per credit. Tuition, nonresident: full-time $16,383; part-time $546 per credit. Required fees: $882. Tuition and fees vary according to degree level. *Financial support:* In 2009–10, research assistantships with full and partial tuition reimbursements (averaging $9,145 per year), teaching assistantships with full and partial tuition reimbursements (averaging $9,145 per year) were awarded; career-related internships or fieldwork, Federal Work-Study, health care benefits, and unspecified assistantships also available. Financial award application deadline: 3/1. *Unit head:* Dr. Wendy Williams, Chair, 509-963-3679, E-mail: williamw@cwu.edu. *Application contact:* Justine Eason, Admissions Program Coordinator, 509-963-3103, Fax: 509-963-1799, E-mail: masters@cwu.edu.

City College of the City University of New York, Graduate School, College of Liberal Arts and Science, Division of Social Science, Department of Psychology, New York, NY 10031-9198. Offers clinical psychology (PhD); experimental cognition (PhD); general psychology (MA); mental health counseling (MA). *Accreditation:* APA (one or more programs are accredited). Part-time programs available. *Degree requirements:* For master's, one foreign language, comprehensive exam, thesis. *Entrance requirements:* For master's, GRE. Additional exam requirements/recommendations for international students: Required—TOEFL (minimum score 550 paper-based; 79 iBT). Electronic applications accepted. *Faculty research:* Social/personality psychology, physiological psychology, cognition and development.

Cleveland State University, College of Graduate Studies, College of Science, Department of Psychology, Cleveland, OH 44115. Offers adult development and aging (PhD); clinical psychology (MA); consumer/industrial research (MA); diversity management (MA); experimental research psychology (MA); school psychology (Psy S). *Degree requirements:* For master's, comprehensive exam (for some programs), thesis (for some programs); for doctorate, comprehensive exam, thesis/dissertation; for Psy S, internship. *Entrance requirements:* For master's and doctorate, GRE General Test. Additional exam requirements/recommendations for international students: Required—TOEFL (minimum score 525 paper-based; 197 computer-based). Electronic applications accepted. *Faculty research:* Cognitive and social psychology, consumer psychology, clinical psychology, school psychology, aging.

The College of William and Mary, Faculty of Arts and Sciences, Department of Psychology, Williamsburg, VA 23187-8795. Offers MA. *Faculty:* 20 full-time (7 women). *Students:* 14 full-time (7 women), 1 international. Average age 23. 65 applicants, 22% accepted, 7 enrolled. In 2009, 7 master's awarded. *Degree requirements:* For master's, thesis. *Entrance requirements:* For master's, GRE. Additional exam requirements/recommendations for international students: Required—TOEFL. *Application deadline:* For fall admission, 2/15 for domestic and international students. Application fee: $45. *Expenses:* Tuition, state resident: full-time $6400; part-time $315 per credit hour. Tuition, nonresident: full-time $19,720; part-time $840 per credit hour. Required fees: $4114. *Faculty research:* Personality, developmental, cognition, applied decision theory, social psychology. Total annual research expenditures: $412,149. *Unit head:* Dr. Constance Pilkington, Chair, 757-221-3875, E-mail: cjpilk@wm.edu. *Application contact:* Tracy Coates, Administrator of Graduate Student Services, 757-221-3870, Fax: 757-221-3896, E-mail: tlcoates@wm.edu.

Columbia University, Graduate School of Arts and Sciences, Division of Natural Sciences, Department of Psychology, New York, NY 10027. Offers experimental psychology (M Phil, MA, PhD); psychobiology (M Phil, MA, PhD); social psychology (M Phil, MA, PhD); JD/MA; JD/PhD; MD/PhD. *Degree requirements:* For master's, thesis; for doctorate, thesis/dissertation. *Entrance requirements:* For master's and doctorate, GRE General Test. Additional exam requirements/recommendations for international students: Required—TOEFL.

Cornell University, Graduate School, Graduate Fields of Arts and Sciences, Field of Psychology, Ithaca, NY 14853-0001. Offers biopsychology (PhD); human experimental psychology (PhD); personality and social psychology (PhD). *Faculty:* 49 full-time (17 women). *Students:* 37 full-time (24 women); includes 5 minority (1 African American, 2 Asian Americans or Pacific Islanders, 2 Hispanic Americans), 10 international. Average age 29. 221 applicants, 4% accepted, 8 enrolled. In 2009, 3 doctorates awarded. *Degree requirements:* For doctorate, comprehensive exam, thesis/dissertation, 2 semesters of teaching experience. *Entrance requirements:* For doctorate, GRE General Test, 3 letters of recommendation. Additional exam requirements/recommendations for international students: Required—TOEFL (minimum score 550 paper-based; 213 computer-based; 77 iBT). *Application deadline:* For fall admission, 12/15 for domestic students. Application fee: $70. Electronic applications accepted. *Expenses:* Tuition: Full-time $29,500. Required fees: $70. Full-time tuition and fees vary according to degree level, program and student level. *Financial support:* In 2009–10, 36 students received support, including 6 fellowships with full tuition reimbursements available, 2 teaching assistantships with full tuition reimbursements available; research assistantships with full tuition reimbursements available, institutionally sponsored loans, scholarships/grants, health care benefits, tuition waivers (full and partial), and unspecified assistantships also available. Financial award applicants required to submit FAFSA. *Faculty research:* Sensory and perceptual systems, social cognition, cognitive development, quantitative and computational modeling, behavioral neuroscience. *Unit head:* Director of Graduate Studies, 607-255-6364, Fax: 607-255-8433. *Application contact:* Graduate Field Assistant, 607-255-3834, Fax: 607-255-8433, E-mail: psychapp@cornell.edu.

Dallas Baptist University, Gary Cook School of Leadership, Program in Christian Education, Dallas, TX 75211-9299. Offers adult ministry (MA); business ministry (MA); childhood ministry (MA); collegiate ministry (MA); communication ministry (MA); counseling ministry (MA); education ministry (MA); general ministry (MA); missions ministry (MA); student ministry (MA); worship ministry (MA). Part-time and evening/weekend programs available. *Entrance requirements:* For master's, minimum GPA of 3.0. Additional exam requirements/recommendations for international students: Required—TOEFL. Electronic applications accepted. *Expenses:* Tuition: Full-time $10,674; part-time $593 per credit hour.

DePaul University, College of Liberal Arts and Sciences, Department of Psychology, Chicago, IL 60604-2287. Offers clinical psychology (MA, PhD), including child clinical psychology, community clinical psychology; experimental psychology (MA, PhD); general psychology (MS); industrial/organizational psychology (MA, PhD); MA/PhD. *Accreditation:* APA (one or more programs are accredited). *Faculty:* 31 full-time (19 women), 6 part-time/adjunct (4 women). *Students:* 59 full-time (36 women), 54 part-time (35 women); includes 26 minority (10 African Americans, 5 Asian Americans or Pacific Islanders, 11 Hispanic Americans), 2 international. Average age 28. 332 applicants, 14% accepted, 23 enrolled. In 2009, 14 master's, 17 doctorates awarded. *Degree requirements:* For master's, thesis, oral exam; for doctorate, comprehensive exam, thesis/dissertation, oral and written exams. *Entrance requirements:* For master's and doctorate, GRE General Test, GRE Subject Test, 32 quarter hours of course work in psychology, 3 letters of recommendation. Additional exam requirements/recommendations for international students: Required—TOEFL. Application fee: $40. Electronic applications accepted. *Expenses:* Tuition: Full-time $37,525; part-time $620 per credit hour. *Financial support:* In 2009–10, 48 students received support, including 35 research assistantships with full tuition reimbursements available (averaging $11,800 per year), 13 teaching assistantships with full tuition reimbursements available (averaging $11,800 per year); career-related internships or fieldwork, scholarships/grants, traineeships, tuition waivers (full and partial), and unspecified assistantships also available. Financial award application deadline: 1/10. *Faculty research:* Adolescent stress and depression, minority adolescents sexuality, public policy, community influences in child adjustment. *Unit head:* Dr. Christopher B. Keys, Chairman, 773-325-7887, Fax: 773-325-7888. *Application contact:* Alison Pereida Knapp, Graduate Admissions Assistant, 773-325-7887, Fax: 773-325-7888.

Duke University, Graduate School, Department of Psychology, Durham, NC 27708-0586. Offers biological psychology (PhD); clinical psychology (PhD); cognitive psychology (PhD); developmental psychology (PhD); experimental psychology (PhD); health psychology (PhD); human social development (PhD); JD/MA. *Accreditation:* APA (one or more programs are accredited). *Faculty:* 40 full-time. *Students:* 92 full-time (70 women); includes 13 minority (5 African Americans, 2 Asian Americans or Pacific Islanders, 6 Hispanic Americans), 14 international. 478 applicants, 8% accepted, 21 enrolled. In 2009, 10 doctorates awarded. *Degree requirements:* For doctorate, thesis/dissertation. *Entrance requirements:* For doctorate, GRE General Test. Additional exam requirements/recommendations for international students: Required—TOEFL (minimum score 550 paper-based; 213 computer-based; 83 iBT), IELTS (minimum score 7). *Application deadline:* For fall admission, 12/8 priority date for domestic and international students. Application fee: $75. Electronic applications accepted. *Financial support:* Fellowships, research assistantships, teaching assistantships, career-related internships or fieldwork and Federal Work-Study available. Financial award application deadline: 12/31. *Unit head:* Melanie Bonner, Director of Graduate Studies, Fax: 919-660-5715, E-mail: morrell@duke.edu. *Application contact:* Cynthia Robertson, Associate Dean for Enrollment Services, 919-684-3913, E-mail: grad-admissions@duke.edu.

Eastern Washington University, Graduate Studies, College of Social and Behavioral Sciences, Department of Psychology, Cheney, WA 99004-2431. Offers clinical psychology (MS); experimental psychology (MS); psychology (MS); school psychology (MS). *Degree requirements:* For master's, comprehensive exam, thesis or alternative. *Entrance requirements:* For master's, GRE General Test, minimum GPA of 3.0. *Expenses:* Tuition, state resident: full-time $7476; part-time $249 per quarter hour. Tuition, nonresident: full-time $18,030; part-time $601 per quarter hour. Required fees: $3.50 per quarter hour. $142 per quarter.

Fairleigh Dickinson University, Metropolitan Campus, University College: Arts, Sciences, and Professional Studies, School of Psychology, Program in General-Theoretical Psychology, Teaneck, NJ 07666-1914. Offers MA, Certificate. *Students:* 13 full-time (12 women), 10 part-time (8 women), 3 international. Average age 31. 28 applicants, 93% accepted, 10 enrolled. In 2009, 22 master's awarded. *Application deadline:* Applications are processed on a rolling basis. Application fee: $40. *Application contact:* Susan Brooman, University Director of Graduate Admissions, 201-692-2554, Fax: 201-692-2560, E-mail: globaleducation@fdu.edu.

Georgia Institute of Technology, Graduate Studies and Research, College of Sciences, School of Psychology, Atlanta, GA 30332-0001. Offers human computer interaction (MSHCI); psychology (MS, MS Psy, PhD), including engineering psychology (PhD), experimental psychology (PhD), industrial/organizational psychology (PhD). Terminal master's awarded for partial completion of doctoral program. *Degree requirements:* For master's, thesis; for doctorate, thesis/dissertation. *Entrance requirements:* For master's and doctorate, GRE General Test, GRE Subject Test, minimum GPA of 3.0. Additional exam requirements/recommendations for international students: Required—TOEFL. Electronic applications accepted. *Faculty research:* Experimental, industrial-organizational, and engineering psychology; cognitive aging and processes; leadership; human factors.

Graduate School and University Center of the City University of New York, Graduate Studies, Program in Psychology, New York, NY 10016-4039. Offers basic applied neurocognition (PhD); biopsychology (PhD); clinical psychology (PhD); developmental psychology (PhD); environmental psychology (PhD); experimental psychology (PhD); industrial psychology (PhD); learning processes (PhD); neuropsychology (PhD); psychology (PhD); social personality (PhD). *Faculty:* 119 full-time (40 women). *Students:* 559 full-time (414 women), 1 part-time (0 women); includes 101 minority (34 African Americans, 25 Asian Americans or Pacific Islanders, 42 Hispanic Americans), 57 international. Average age 33. 750 applicants, 16% accepted, 84 enrolled. In 2009, 54 doctorates awarded. *Degree requirements:* For doctorate, one foreign language, thesis/dissertation. *Entrance requirements:* For doctorate, GRE General Test. Additional exam requirements/recommendations for international students: Required—TOEFL. *Application deadline:* For fall admission, 12/15 priority date for domestic students. Application fee: $125. Electronic applications accepted. *Financial support:* In 2009–10, 371 students received support, including 340 fellowships, 34 research assistantships, 33 teaching assistantships; career-related internships or fieldwork, Federal Work-Study, institutionally sponsored loans, and tuition waivers (full and partial) also available. Financial award application deadline: 2/1; financial award applicants required to submit FAFSA. *Unit head:* Dr. Joseph Glick, Executive Officer, 212-817-8706, Fax: 212-817-1533, E-mail: jglick@gc.cuny.edu. *Application contact:* Les Gribben, Director of Admissions, 212-817-7470, Fax: 212-817-1624, E-mail: lgribben@gc.cuny.edu.

Harvard University, Graduate School of Arts and Sciences, Department of Psychology, Cambridge, MA 02138. Offers psychology (PhD), including behavior and decision analysis, cognition, developmental psychology, experimental psychology, personality, psychobiology, psychopathology; social psychology (PhD). *Accreditation:* APA. *Degree requirements:* For doctorate, thesis/dissertation, general exams. *Entrance requirements:* For doctorate, GRE General Test. Additional exam requirements/recommendations for international students: Required—TOEFL. *Expenses:* Tuition: Full-time $33,696. Required fees: $1126. Full-time tuition and fees vary according to program.

Howard University, Graduate School, Department of Psychology, Washington, DC 20059-0002. Offers clinical psychology (PhD); developmental psychology (PhD); experimental psychology (PhD); neuropsychology (PhD); personality psychology (PhD); psychology (MS); social psychology (PhD). *Accreditation:* APA (one or more programs are accredited). Part-time programs available. *Degree requirements:* For master's, thesis; for doctorate, comprehensive exam, thesis/dissertation, qualifying exam. *Entrance requirements:* For master's, GRE General Test, minimum GPA of 2.5, bachelor's degree in psychology or related field; for doctorate, GRE General Test, minimum GPA of 3.0. *Faculty research:* Personality and psychophysiology, educational and social development of African-American children, child and adult psychopathology.

Illinois State University, Graduate School, College of Arts and Sciences, Department of Psychology, Normal, IL 61790-2200. Offers psychology (MA, MS), including clinical psychology, counseling psychology, developmental psychology, educational psychology, experimental psychology, measurement-evaluation, organizational-industrial psychology; school psychology (PhD, SSP). *Accreditation:* APA. *Degree requirements:* For master's, thesis or alternative; for doctorate, variable foreign language requirement, thesis/dissertation, 2 terms of residency, internship, practicum. *Entrance requirements:* For master's, GRE General Test, GRE Subject Test, minimum GPA of 3.0 in last 60 hours of course work; for doctorate, GRE General Test. *Faculty research:* Comprehensive evaluation system for the central region professional development grant, Illinois school psychology internship consortium, for children's sake.

Iona College, School of Arts and Science, Department of Psychology, New Rochelle, NY 10801-1890. Offers experimental psychology (MA); industrial-organizational psychology (MA); mental health counseling (MA); psychology (MA); school psychology (MA). Part-time and evening/weekend programs available. *Faculty:* 14 full-time (8 women), 10 part-time/adjunct (8 women). *Students:* 74 full-time (58 women), 46 part-time (34 women); includes 28 minority (13 African Americans, 1 American Indian/Alaska Native, 3 Asian Americans or Pacific Islanders, 11 Hispanic Americans), 1 international. Average age 25. 186 applicants, 61% accepted, 44 enrolled. In 2009, 35 master's awarded. *Degree requirements:* For master's, thesis. *Entrance requirements:* For master's, GRE or minimum GPA of 3.0. Additional exam requirements/recommendations for international students: Required—TOEFL (minimum score 550 paper-based; 213 computer-based). *Application deadline:* Applications are processed on a rolling basis. Application fee: $50. Electronic applications accepted. *Expenses:* Tuition: Part-time $830 per credit. *Financial support:* Career-related internships or fieldwork, tuition waivers (partial), and unspecified assistantships available. Support available to part-time students. Financial award application deadline: 4/15; financial award applicants required to submit FAFSA. *Unit head:* Dr. Paul Greene, Chair, 914-633-2048, E-mail: pgreene@iona.edu. *Application contact:* Veronica Jarek-Prinz, Director of Graduate Admissions, 914-633-2420, Fax: 914-633-2277, E-mail: vjarekprinz@iona.edu.

Kent State University, College of Arts and Sciences, Department of Psychology, Kent, OH 44242-0001. Offers clinical psychology (MA, PhD); experimental psychology (MA, PhD). *Accreditation:* APA (one or more programs are accredited). *Degree requirements:* For master's, thesis; for doctorate, thesis/dissertation. *Entrance requirements:* For master's, GRE, minimum GPA of 3.0, minimum 18 semester hours in psychology with one course in statistics and one experimental course with a lab component; for doctorate, GRE, minimum GPA of 3.0. Additional exam requirements/recommendations for international students: Required—TOEFL (minimum score 525 paper-based), Michigan English Language Assessment Battery (minimum score: 77).

Lakehead University, Graduate Studies, Department of Psychology, Thunder Bay, ON P7B 5E1, Canada. Offers clinical psychology (PhD); experimental psychology (MA). Part-time and evening/weekend programs available. *Degree requirements:* For master's, thesis optional; for doctorate, thesis/dissertation, 2 comprehensive exams, internship. *Entrance requirements:* For master's, GRE, honors degree in psychology, advanced course work in statistics, minimum B average; for doctorate, GRE, minimum B average. Additional exam requirements/recommendations for international students: Required—TOEFL. *Faculty research:* Chaos theory, health psychology, counseling psychology, gerontology, women's studies.

Laurentian University, School of Graduate Studies and Research, Programme in Psychology, Sudbury, ON P3E 2C6, Canada. Offers applied psychology (MA); experimental psychology (MA).

McGill University, Faculty of Graduate and Postdoctoral Studies, Faculty of Science, Department of Psychology, Montréal, QC H3A 2T5, Canada. Offers clinical psychology (PhD); experimental psychology (M Sc, MA, PhD). *Accreditation:* APA (one or more programs are accredited).

McNeese State University, Doré School of Graduate Studies, Burton College of Education, Department of Psychology, Lake Charles, LA 70609. Offers addiction treatment (MA); applied behavior analysis (MA); counseling psychology (MA); general/experimental psychology (MA). Evening/weekend programs available. *Faculty:* 6 full-time (3 women). *Students:* 34 full-time (24 women), 30 part-time (22 women); includes 10 minority (7 African Americans, 1 Asian American or Pacific Islander, 2 Hispanic Americans), 2 international. In 2009, 18 master's awarded. *Entrance requirements:* For master's, GRE. *Application deadline:* For fall admission, 5/15 priority date for domestic and international students; for spring admission, 10/15 priority date for domestic and international students. Applications are processed on a rolling basis. Application fee: $20 ($30 for international students). *Expenses:* Tuition, area resident: Full-time $2556. Tuition, state resident: full-time $2556. Required fees: $1031. Tuition and fees vary according to course load. *Financial support:* Application deadline: 5/1. *Unit head:* Dr. Dena L. Matzenbacher, Head, 337-475-5457, Fax: 337-562-4115, E-mail: dena@mcneese.edu. *Application contact:* Dr. George F. Mead, Interim Dean of Dore' School of Graduate Studies, 337-475-5396, Fax: 337-475-5397, E-mail: admissions@mcneese.edu.

Memorial University of Newfoundland, School of Graduate Studies, Department of Psychology, St. John's, NL A1C 5S7, Canada. Offers applied social psychology (MASP); experimental psychology (M Sc, PhD). Part-time programs available. *Degree requirements:* For master's, workterms (MASP), thesis (M Sc); for doctorate, comprehensive exam, thesis/dissertation, oral thesis defense. *Entrance requirements:* For master's, GRE, honors bachelor's degree of high second class standing or equivalent; for doctorate, GRE, master's or honors degree. Electronic applications accepted. *Faculty research:* Behavioral neuroscience, cognition, theory and research on abnormal behavior.

Middle Tennessee State University, College of Graduate Studies, College of Education and Behavioral Science, Department of Psychology, Murfreesboro, TN 37132. Offers clinical psychology (MA); experimental psychology (MA); industrial/organizational psychology (MA); professional counseling (M Ed, Ed S), including curriculum and instruction (Ed S), mental health counseling (M Ed), school counseling (M Ed); psychology (MA); quantitative psychology (MA); school psychology (MA, Ed S). Part-time and evening/weekend programs available. Postbaccalaureate distance learning degree programs offered. *Faculty:* 36 full-time (16 women), 2 part-time/adjunct (0 women). *Students:* 23 full-time (19 women), 161 part-time (131 women); includes 21 minority (11 African Americans, 8 Asian Americans or Pacific Islanders, 2 Hispanic Americans). Average age 26. 251 applicants, 55% accepted, 138 enrolled. In 2009, 60 master's, 7 other advanced degrees awarded. *Degree requirements:* For master's, variable foreign language requirement, comprehensive exam, thesis (for some programs). *Entrance requirements:* Additional exam requirements/recommendations for international students: Required—TOEFL (minimum score 525 paper-based; 195 computer-based; 71 iBT) or IELTS (minimum score 6). *Application deadline:* For fall admission, 6/1 for domestic and international students. Applications are processed on a rolling basis. Application fee: $25 ($30 for international students). Electronic applications accepted. *Expenses:* Tuition, state resident: full-time $4404. Tuition, nonresident: full-time $10,956. *Financial support:* In 2009–10, 16 students received support. Career-related internships or fieldwork and institutionally sponsored loans available. Support available to part-time students. Financial award application deadline: 5/1; financial award applicants required to submit FAFSA. *Faculty research:* Industrial/organizational, social/personality/sports, counseling/clinical/school, cognitive/language/learning/perception, developmental/aging. *Unit head:* Dr. Dennis Papini, Chair, 615-898-2706, Fax: 615-898-5027. *Application contact:* Dr. Michael Allen, Dean and Vice Provost for Research, 615-898-2840, Fax: 615-904-8020, E-mail: mallen@mtsu.edu.

Mississippi State University, College of Arts and Sciences, Department of Psychology, Mississippi State, MS 39762. Offers cognitive science (PhD); psychology (MS), including clinical psychology, experimental psychology. *Faculty:* 13 full-time (5 women). *Students:* 40 full-time (26 women), 4 part-time (3 women); includes 3 minority (2 African Americans, 1 Asian American or Pacific Islander), 3 international. Average age 26. 69 applicants, 46% accepted, 20 enrolled. In 2009, 11 master's awarded. Terminal master's awarded for partial completion of doctoral program. *Degree requirements:* For master's, comprehensive exam, thesis; for doctorate, thesis/dissertation, qualifying exam, comprehensive written and oral exam. *Entrance requirements:* For master's, GRE General Test, minimum GPA of 2.75 on last two years of undergraduate courses; for doctorate, GRE General Test, proficiency in at least 1 computer language. Additional exam requirements/recommendations for international students: Required—TOEFL (minimum score 475 paper-based; 153 computer-based; 53 iBT); Recommended—IELTS (minimum score 4.5). *Application deadline:* For fall admission, 1/15 priority date for domestic students, 5/1 for international students; for spring admission, 11/1 priority date for domestic students, 9/1 for international students. Applications are processed on a rolling basis. Application fee: $40. Electronic applications accepted. *Expenses:* Tuition, state resident: full-time $2575.50; part-time $286.25 per credit hour. Tuition, nonresident: full-time $6510; part-time $723.50 per credit hour. Tuition and fees vary according to course load. *Financial support:* In 2009–10, 7 research assistantships with full tuition reimbursements (averaging $11,132 per year), 15 teaching assistantships with full tuition reimbursements (averaging $9,023 per year) were awarded; career-related internships or fieldwork, Federal Work-Study, institutionally sponsored loans, scholarships/grants, and unspecified assistantships also available. Financial award application deadline: 4/1; financial award applicants required to submit FAFSA. *Faculty research:* Personality type, alcoholism, blindness and low vision, mental retardation, language comprehension. Total annual research expenditures: $2.2 million. *Unit head:* Dr. Stephen B. Klein, Department Head, 662-325-3202, Fax: 662-325-7212, E-mail: sbkl@ra.msstate.edu. *Application contact:* Dr. Keven J. Armstrong, Graduate Coordinator, 662-325-3202, Fax: 662-325-7212, E-mail: grad@psychology.msstate.edu.

Missouri State University, Graduate College, College of Health and Human Services, Department of Psychology, Springfield, MO 65897. Offers psychology (MS), including clinical, experimental, industrial/organizational. *Faculty:* 26 full-time (11 women), 1 part-time/adjunct (0 women). *Students:* 44 full-time (28 women), 5 part-time (3 women); includes 2 minority (1 African American, 1 Hispanic American). Average age 26. 63 applicants, 56% accepted, 22 enrolled. In 2009, 21 master's awarded. *Degree requirements:* For master's, comprehensive exam, thesis. *Entrance requirements:* For master's, GRE General Test, GRE Subject Test, minimum GPA of 3.25 in major, 3.0 overall; 20 hours of course work in psychology (experimental and statistics). Additional exam requirements/recommendations for international students: Required—TOEFL (minimum score 550 paper-based; 213 computer-based; 79 iBT). *Application deadline:* For fall admission, 3/1 priority date for domestic and international students. Application fee: $35 ($50 for international students). Electronic applications accepted. *Expenses:* Tuition, state resident: full-time $3852; part-time $214 per credit hour. Tuition, nonresident: full-time $7524; part-time $418 per credit hour. Required fees: $696; $172 per semester. Tuition and fees vary according to course level, course load, degree level and program. *Financial support:* In 2009–10, 7 research assistantships with full tuition reimbursements (averaging $8,023 per year), 3 teaching assistantships with full tuition reimbursements (averaging $9,730 per year)

Experimental Psychology

Missouri State University (continued)
were awarded; career-related internships or fieldwork, Federal Work-Study, institutionally sponsored loans, scholarships/grants, and unspecified assistantships also available. Financial award application deadline: 3/31; financial award applicants required to submit FAFSA. *Faculty research:* Work-family conflict, child forensic psychology, sports psychology, body image assessment, visual learning. *Unit head:* Dr. Robert G. Jones, Head, 417-836-5797, Fax: 417-836-8330, E-mail: psychology@missouristate.edu. *Application contact:* Eric Eckert, Coordinator of Admissions and Recruitment, 417-836-5331, Fax: 417-836-6200, E-mail: ericeckert@missouristate.edu.

Morehead State University, Graduate Programs, College of Science and Technology, Department of Psychology, Morehead, KY 40351. Offers clinical/counseling psychology (MS); general/experimental psychology (MS). Part-time and evening/weekend programs available. *Faculty:* 7 full-time (2 women). *Students:* 32 full-time (23 women), 2 part-time (1 woman), 1 international. Average age 25. 39 applicants, 51% accepted, 19 enrolled. In 2009, 12 master's awarded. *Degree requirements:* For master's, comprehensive exam, thesis optional. *Entrance requirements:* For master's, GRE General Test, 18 undergraduate hours in psychology, minimum GPA of 3.0, 3 letters of recommendation. Additional exam requirements/recommendations for international students: Required—TOEFL (minimum score 500 paper-based; 173 computer-based). *Application deadline:* For fall admission, 8/1 priority date for domestic and international students; for spring admission, 12/1 for domestic students, 12/1 priority date for international students. Applications are processed on a rolling basis. Application fee: $30. Electronic applications accepted. *Expenses:* Tuition, state resident: full-time $6318; part-time $351 per credit hour. Tuition, nonresident: full-time $15,804; part-time $878 per credit hour. *Financial support:* In 2009–10, 26 research assistantships (averaging $10,000 per year) were awarded; career-related internships or fieldwork, Federal Work-Study, and unspecified assistantships also available. Financial award application deadline: 3/15; financial award applicants required to submit FAFSA. *Faculty research:* Mood induction effects, serotonin receptor activity, stress, perceptual processes. *Unit head:* Dr. Laurie Couch, Interim Department Chair, 606-783-2950. *Application contact:* Michelle Barber, Graduate Recruitment and Retention Assistant Director, 606-783-5127, Fax: 606-783-5061, E-mail: m.barber@moreheadstate.edu.

North Carolina State University, Graduate School, College of Humanities and Social Sciences, Department of Psychology, Raleigh, NC 27695. Offers developmental psychology (PhD); ergonomics and experimental psychology (PhD); industrial/organizational psychology (PhD); psychology in the public interest (PhD); school psychology (PhD). *Accreditation:* APA. *Degree requirements:* For doctorate, comprehensive exam, thesis/dissertation. *Entrance requirements:* For doctorate, GRE General Test, GRE Subject Test (industrial/organizational psychology), MAT (recommended), minimum GPA of 3.0 in major. Electronic applications accepted. *Faculty research:* Cognitive and social development (human factors, families, the workplace, community issues and health, aging).

Northeastern University, College of Science, Department of Psychology, Boston, MA 02115-5096. Offers experimental psychology (MA, PhD). *Faculty:* 24 full-time (8 women), 8 part-time/adjunct (6 women). *Students:* 167 full-time (138 women), 44 part-time (39 women); includes 28 minority (11 African Americans, 3 Asian Americans or Pacific Islanders, 14 Hispanic Americans), 15 international. 104 applicants, 9% accepted, 6 enrolled. In 2009, 6 master's, 7 doctorates awarded. *Degree requirements:* For doctorate, thesis/dissertation. *Entrance requirements:* For master's and doctorate, GRE General Test. Additional exam requirements/recommendations for international students: Required—TOEFL. *Application deadline:* For fall admission, 1/1 for domestic and international students. Applications are processed on a rolling basis. Application fee: $50. Electronic applications accepted. *Financial support:* In 2009–10, 1 fellowship with full tuition reimbursement, 22 teaching assistantships with full tuition reimbursements (averaging $16,760 per year) were awarded; research assistantships with full tuition reimbursements, career-related internships or fieldwork and traineeships also available. Financial award application deadline: 1/15; financial award applicants required to submit FAFSA. *Faculty research:* Behavioral, neuroscience language and cognition, perception, personality and social. *Unit head:* Dr. Rhea Eskew, Chair, 617-373-3076, Fax: 617-373-8714, E-mail: psychology@neu.edu. *Application contact:* Rhonda Johnson, Graduate Coordinator, 617-373-3076, Fax: 617-373-8714, E-mail: psychology@neu.edu.

Ohio University, Graduate College, College of Arts and Sciences, Department of Psychology, Program in Experimental Psychology, Athens, OH 45701-2979. Offers PhD. *Faculty:* 12 full-time (4 women). *Students:* 19 full-time (11 women), 4 part-time (0 women); includes 1 minority (Asian American or Pacific Islander), 6 international. Average age 28. 32 applicants, 44% accepted, 6 enrolled. In 2009, 2 doctorates awarded. *Degree requirements:* For doctorate, one foreign language, comprehensive exam, thesis/dissertation. *Entrance requirements:* For doctorate, GRE General Test, GRE Subject Test, minimum graduate GPA of 3.4. Additional exam requirements/recommendations for international students: Required—TOEFL. *Application deadline:* For fall admission, 1/1 for domestic students. Application fee: $50 ($55 for international students). *Expenses:* Tuition, state resident: full-time $7839; part-time $323 per quarter hour. Tuition, nonresident: full-time $15,831; part-time $654 per quarter hour. Required fees: $2931. *Financial support:* In 2009–10, 14 students received support, including 5 fellowships with full tuition reimbursements available (averaging $16,400 per year), research assistantships with full tuition reimbursements available (averaging $13,200 per year), 8 teaching assistantships with full tuition reimbursements available (averaging $13,200 per year); Federal Work-Study, institutionally sponsored loans, tuition waivers (full), and unspecified assistantships also available. Financial award application deadline: 1/15. *Faculty research:* Cognitive psychology, quantitative psychology, social psychology, judgment and decision making, health psychology. Total annual research expenditures: $3.8 million. *Unit head:* Jeffrey Vancouver, Director of Experimental Studies, 740-593-1071, Fax: 740-593-0579. *Application contact:* Karyl Jones, Administrative Secretary, 740-593-1090, Fax: 740-593-0579, E-mail: psychology@ohio.edu.

Old Dominion University, College of Sciences, Doctoral Program in Psychology, Norfolk, VA 23529. Offers applied experimental psychology (PhD); human factors psychology (PhD); industrial/organizational psychology (PhD). *Faculty:* 21 full-time (9 women). *Students:* 24 full-time (17 women), 12 part-time (8 women); includes 2 minority (both Hispanic Americans), 1 international. Average age 29. 60 applicants, 15% accepted, 9 enrolled. In 2009, 4 doctorates awarded. *Degree requirements:* For doctorate, thesis/dissertation, candidacy exam. *Entrance requirements:* For doctorate, GRE General Test, GRE Subject Test, 3 recommendation letters. Additional exam requirements/recommendations for international students: Required—TOEFL (minimum score 550 paper-based). *Application deadline:* For winter admission, 1/5 for domestic and international students. Application fee: $40. Electronic applications accepted. *Expenses:* Tuition, state resident: full-time $8112; part-time $338 per credit. Tuition, nonresident: full-time $20,256; part-time $844 per credit. Required fees: $119 per semester. One-time fee: $50. *Financial support:* In 2009–10, 13 students received support, including 2 fellowships with full tuition reimbursements available (averaging $18,000 per year), research assistantships with full tuition reimbursements available (averaging $12,000 per year), 11 teaching assistantships with full tuition reimbursements available (averaging $12,000 per year). Financial award application deadline: 1/15. *Faculty research:* Human factors, industrial psychology, organizational psychology, applied experimental (health, developmental, quantitative). Total annual research expenditures: $493,384. *Unit head:* Dr. Brian Porter, Graduate Program Director, 757-683-4458, Fax: 757-683-5087, E-mail: bporter@odu.edu. *Application contact:* Dr. Brian Porter, Graduate Program Director, 757-683-4458, Fax: 757-683-5087, E-mail: bporter@odu.edu.

Radford University, College of Graduate and Professional Studies, College of Humanities and Behavioral Sciences, Program in Psychology, Radford, VA 24142. Offers clinical psychology (MA, MS); experimental psychology (MA); general psychology (MS); industrial/organizational psychology (MA, MS). Part-time programs available. *Faculty:* 21 full-time (9 women), 6 part-time/adjunct (2 women). *Students:* 44 full-time (25 women), 1 (woman) part-time; includes 5 minority (3 African Americans, 2 Asian Americans or Pacific Islanders), 1 international. Average age 25. 110 applicants, 65% accepted, 22 enrolled. In 2009, 31 master's awarded. *Degree requirements:* For master's, comprehensive exam, thesis (for some programs). *Entrance requirements:* For master's, GRE, minimum GPA of 3.0; 3 letters of reference; essay. Additional exam requirements/recommendations for international students: Required—TOEFL (minimum score 550 paper-based; 213 computer-based; 79 iBT). *Application deadline:* For fall admission, 2/15 priority date for domestic students, 12/1 for international students. Applications are processed on a rolling basis. Application fee: $50. Electronic applications accepted. *Expenses:* Tuition, state resident: full-time $5086; part-time $211 per credit hour. Tuition, nonresident: full-time $12,608; part-time $525 per credit hour. Required fees: $2508; $105 per credit hour. *Financial support:* In 2009–10, 34 students received support, including 20 research assistantships with partial tuition reimbursements available (averaging $8,000 per year), 14 teaching assistantships with partial tuition reimbursements available (averaging $8,700 per year); career-related internships or fieldwork, institutionally sponsored loans, scholarships/grants, and unspecified assistantships also available. Financial award application deadline: 3/1; financial award applicants required to submit FAFSA. *Unit head:* Dr. Hilary M. Lips, Chair, 540-831-5387, Fax: 540-831-6113, E-mail: hlips@radford.edu. *Application contact:* Graduate Admissions Office, 540-831-5431, Fax: 540-831-6061, E-mail: gradcollege@radford.edu.

St. John's University, St. John's College of Liberal Arts and Sciences, Department of Psychology, Program in General Experimental Psychology, Queens, NY 11439. Offers MA. Part-time and evening/weekend programs available. *Students:* 12 full-time (8 women), 7 part-time (all women); includes 7 minority (2 African Americans, 2 Asian Americans or Pacific Islanders, 3 Hispanic Americans), 2 international. Average age 28. 39 applicants, 51% accepted, 8 enrolled. In 2009, 1 master's awarded. *Degree requirements:* For master's, comprehensive exam, thesis optional. *Entrance requirements:* For master's, minimum GPA of 3.0, 2 writing samples. Additional exam requirements/recommendations for international students: Required—TOEFL (minimum score 500 paper-based; 173 computer-based; 61 iBT), IELTS (minimum score 5.5). *Application deadline:* For fall admission, 5/1 priority date for domestic and international students; for spring admission, 11/1 priority date for domestic and international students. Applications are processed on a rolling basis. Application fee: $70. Electronic applications accepted. *Expenses:* Tuition: Full-time $16,290; part-time $905 per credit. Required fees: $300; $150 per semester. Tuition and fees vary according to program. *Financial support:* Research assistantships, career-related internships or fieldwork, scholarships/grants, and unspecified assistantships available. Support available to part-time students. Financial award application deadline: 3/1; financial award applicants required to submit FAFSA. *Faculty research:* Learning and memory neuropsychology, perception, social psychology, developmental psychology. *Unit head:* Dr. Leonard Brosgole, Coordinator, 718-990-1552, E-mail: brosgoll@stjohns.edu. *Application contact:* Kathleen Davis, Director of Graduate Admission, 718-990-2790, Fax: 718-990-5686, E-mail: gradhelp@stjohns.edu.

Saint Louis University, Graduate School, College of Arts and Sciences and Graduate School, Department of Psychology, St. Louis, MO 63103-2097. Offers clinical psychology (MS-R, PhD); experimental psychology (MS-R, PhD); industrial-organizational psychology (PhD); psychology (PhD). *Accreditation:* APA (one or more programs are accredited). Part-time programs available. *Degree requirements:* For master's, comprehensive exam, thesis; for doctorate, thesis/dissertation, clinical internship (for clinical psychology PhD). *Entrance requirements:* For master's, GRE General Test, interview, letters of recommendation, resume; for doctorate, GRE General Test, interview, letters of recommendation, resumé, transcripts, goal statement. Additional exam requirements/recommendations for international students: Required—TOEFL (minimum score 550 paper-based; 213 computer-based). Electronic applications accepted. *Faculty research:* Violence and trauma; neural basis of learning and memory function; eating disorders; body image and health behavior; prejudice, stereotyping, and victimization; memory, cognitive aging and language processing.

San Jose State University, Graduate Studies and Research, College of Social Sciences, Department of Psychology, San Jose, CA 95192-0001. Offers clinical psychology (MS); experimental psychology (MA); industrial/organizational psychology (MS); psychology (MA). *Students:* 51 full-time (37 women), 20 part-time (14 women); includes 18 minority (1 African American, 1 American Indian/Alaska Native, 12 Asian Americans or Pacific Islanders, 4 Hispanic Americans), 6 international. Average age 28. 153 applicants, 20% accepted, 26 enrolled. In 2009, 17 master's awarded. *Degree requirements:* For master's, comprehensive exam, thesis (for some programs). *Entrance requirements:* For master's, GRE General Test, minimum GPA of 3.0. *Application deadline:* For fall admission, 6/29 for domestic students; for spring admission, 11/30 for domestic students. Applications are processed on a rolling basis. Application fee: $59. Electronic applications accepted. *Financial support:* Teaching assistantships, career-related internships or fieldwork and institutionally sponsored loans available. Financial award application deadline: 3/1; financial award applicants required to submit FAFSA. *Faculty research:* Drug and alcohol abuse, neurohormonal mechanisms in motion sickness, behavior modification, sleep research, genetics. *Unit head:* Dr. Sheila Bienenfeld, Chair, 408-924-5642, Fax: 408-924-5605. *Application contact:* Dr. Sheila Bienenfeld, Chair, 408-924-5642, Fax: 408-924-5605.

Seton Hall University, College of Arts and Sciences, Department of Psychology, South Orange, NJ 07079-2697. Offers experimental psychology (MS), including behavioral neuroscience. Part-time and evening/weekend programs available. *Faculty:* 12 full-time (7 women). *Students:* 14 full-time (7 women); includes 3 minority (2 Asian Americans or Pacific Islanders, 1 Hispanic American). Average age 25. 28 applicants, 71% accepted, 10 enrolled. In 2009, 5 master's awarded. *Entrance requirements:* For master's, GRE. Additional exam requirements/recommendations for international students: Required—TOEFL. *Application deadline:* For fall admission, 7/1 priority date for domestic and international students. Applications are processed on a rolling basis. Application fee: $50. Electronic applications accepted. *Financial support:* Research assistantships, teaching assistantships with full tuition reimbursements, career-related internships or fieldwork, Federal Work-Study, scholarships/grants, and unspecified assistantships available. Financial award applicants required to submit FAFSA. *Faculty research:* Behavioral neuroscience, cognitive psychology, social psychology, perception/motor skills, memory, depression, anxiety. *Unit head:* Dr. Susan A. Nolan, Chair, 973-761-9484, Fax: 973-275-5829, E-mail: nolansus@shu.edu. *Application contact:* Dr. Janine P. Buckner, Director of Graduate Studies, 973-761-9484, Fax: 973-275-5829, E-mail: buckneja@shu.edu.

Southern Illinois University Carbondale, Graduate School, College of Liberal Arts, Department of Psychology, Carbondale, IL 62901-4701. Offers clinical psychology (MA, MS, PhD); counseling psychology (MA, MS, PhD); experimental psychology (MA, MS, PhD). *Accreditation:* APA (one or more programs are accredited). *Degree requirements:* For master's, thesis; for doctorate, thesis/dissertation. *Entrance requirements:* For master's, GRE General Test, GRE Subject Test, minimum GPA of 2.7; for doctorate, GRE General Test, GRE Subject Test, minimum GPA of 3.25. Additional exam requirements/recommendations for international students: Required—TOEFL. *Faculty research:* Developmental neuropsychology; smoking, affect, and cognition; personality measurement; vocational psychology; program evaluation.

Stony Brook University, State University of New York, Graduate School, College of Arts and Sciences, Department of Psychology, Program in Cognitive/Experimental Psychology, Stony Brook, NY 11794. Offers PhD. *Students:* 16 full-time (7 women); includes 1 minority (Hispanic American), 2 international. Average age 28. 36 applicants, 28% accepted. In 2009, 4 doctorates awarded. *Degree requirements:* For doctorate, thesis/dissertation. *Entrance requirements:* For doctorate, GRE General Test, GRE Subject Test. Additional exam requirements/recommendations for international students: Required—TOEFL. *Application deadline:* For fall admission, 1/15 for domestic students. Application fee: $60. *Expenses:* Tuition, state resident: full-time $8370; part-time $349 per credit. Tuition, nonresident: full-time $13,250; part-time $552 per credit. Required fees: $933. *Unit head:* Dr. Nancy Franklin, Head, 631-632-7840, E-mail: nancy.franklin@stonybrook.edu. *Application contact:* Graduate Director, 631-632-7792, Fax: 631-632-7876.

Syracuse University, College of Arts and Sciences, Program in Experimental Psychology, Syracuse, NY 13244. Offers PhD. Part-time programs available. *Students:* 9 full-time (7 women), 2 part-time (1 woman); includes 1 minority (Asian American or Pacific Islander), 2 international. Average age 28. 13 applicants, 46% accepted, 3 enrolled. In 2009, 1 doctorate awarded. *Degree requirements:* For doctorate, thesis/dissertation. *Entrance requirements:* For doctorate, GRE General Test. Additional exam requirements/recommendations for international students: Required—TOEFL (minimum score 100 iBT). *Application deadline:* For fall admission, 1/10 priority date for domestic and international students. Application fee: $75. Electronic applications accepted. *Expenses:* Tuition: Full-time $26,808; part-time $1117 per credit. Required fees: $1024. *Financial support:* Fellowships with full tuition reimbursements, research assistantships with full tuition reimbursements, teaching assistantships with full tuition reimbursements, tuition waivers available. Financial award application deadline: 1/1. *Unit head:* Dr. William Hoyer, Graduate Director, 315-443-3663, E-mail: wjhoyer@syr.edu. *Application contact:* Sue Bova, Information Contact, 315-443-1050, E-mail: skbova@syr.edu.

Texas Christian University, College of Science and Engineering, Department of Psychology, Fort Worth, TX 76129-0002. Offers experimental psychology (PhD), including cognitive psychology, learning, neuropsychology, social psychology; psychology (MA, MS). *Degree requirements:* For master's, thesis; for doctorate, thesis/dissertation. *Entrance requirements:* For master's and doctorate, GRE General Test. Additional exam requirements/recommendations for international students: Required—TOEFL. *Application deadline:* For fall admission, 3/1 for domestic and international students; for spring admission, 12/1 for domestic students. Applications are processed on a rolling basis. Application fee: $50. *Expenses:* Tuition: Full-time $17,640; part-time $980 per credit hour. Tuition and fees vary according to program. *Financial support:* In 2009–10, 20 students received support; teaching assistantships with full tuition reimbursements available, unspecified assistantships available. Financial award application deadline: 3/1. *Unit head:* Dr. Charles Lord, Graduate Director, 817-257-7410, E-mail: c.lord@tcu.edu. *Application contact:* Marilyn Eudaly, Department Manager, 817-257-6437.

Texas Tech University, Graduate School, College of Arts and Sciences, Department of Psychology, Lubbock, TX 79409. Offers clinical psychology (PhD); counseling psychology (MA, PhD); experimental psychology (MA, PhD); psychology (MA, PhD). *Accreditation:* APA (one or more programs are accredited). Part-time programs available. *Faculty:* 25 full-time (11 women). *Students:* 96 full-time (69 women), 16 part-time (10 women); includes 13 minority (5 African Americans, 8 Hispanic Americans), 7 international. Average age 28. 248 applicants, 13% accepted, 18 enrolled. In 2009, 11 master's, 12 doctorates awarded. *Degree requirements:* For doctorate, thesis/dissertation. *Entrance requirements:* For master's and doctorate, GRE General Test, GRE Subject Test. Additional exam requirements/recommendations for international students: Required—TOEFL (minimum score 550 paper-based; 213 computer-based). *Application deadline:* For fall admission, 3/1 priority date for international students; for spring admission, 11/1 priority date for international students. Applications are processed on a rolling basis. Application fee: $50 ($75 for international students). Electronic applications accepted. *Expenses:* Tuition, state resident: full-time $5100; part-time $213 per credit hour. Tuition, nonresident: full-time $11,748; part-time $490 per credit hour. Required fees: $2298; $50 per credit hour. $555 per semester. *Financial support:* In 2009–10, 1 research assistantship with partial tuition reimbursement (averaging $11,742 per year), 69 teaching assistantships with partial tuition reimbursements (averaging $20,157 per year) were awarded; career-related internships or fieldwork, Federal Work-Study, and institutionally sponsored loans also available. Support available to part-time students. Financial award application deadline: 4/15; financial award applicants required to submit FAFSA. *Faculty research:* Failure/success in relationships, peer rejection in school, stress and coping, group processes, clinical and health psychology. Total annual research expenditures: $144,070. *Unit head:* Dr. Susan S. Hendrick, Chair, 806-742-3711 Ext. 224, Fax: 806-742-0818, E-mail: s.hendrick@ttu.edu. *Application contact:* Dr. Lee M. Cohen, Director of Clinical Program, 806-742-3711 Ext. 254, Fax: 806-742-0818, E-mail: lee.cohen@ttu.edu.

University at Albany, State University of New York, College of Arts and Sciences, Department of Psychology, Albany, NY 12222-0001. Offers autism (Certificate); biopsychology (PhD); clinical psychology (PhD); general/experimental psychology (PhD); industrial/organizational psychology (PhD); psychology (MA); social/personality psychology (PhD). *Accreditation:* APA (one or more programs are accredited). *Degree requirements:* For doctorate, thesis/dissertation. *Entrance requirements:* For doctorate, GRE General Test, GRE Subject Test. Additional exam requirements/recommendations for international students: Required—TOEFL (minimum score 550 paper-based; 213 computer-based). Electronic applications accepted.

The University of Alabama, Graduate School, College of Arts and Sciences, Department of Psychology, Tuscaloosa, AL 35487. Offers clinical psychology (PhD); experimental psychology (PhD). *Accreditation:* APA. *Faculty:* 22 full-time (9 women), 2 part-time/adjunct (both women). *Students:* 77 full-time (60 women), 19 part-time (11 women); includes 13 minority (6 African Americans, 3 Asian Americans or Pacific Islanders, 4 Hispanic Americans), 4 international. Average age 27. 266 applicants, 10% accepted, 16 enrolled. In 2009, 14 doctorates awarded. *Median time to degree:* Of those who began their doctoral program in fall 2001, 78% received their degree in 8 years or less. *Degree requirements:* For doctorate, thesis/dissertation, internship for clinical students. *Entrance requirements:* For doctorate, GRE. Additional exam requirements/recommendations for international students: Required—TOEFL (minimum score 550 paper-based). *Application deadline:* For fall admission, 12/1 for domestic and international students. Application fee: $50 ($60 for international students). Electronic applications accepted. *Expenses:* Tuition, state resident: full-time $7000. Tuition, nonresident: full-time $19,200. *Financial support:* In 2009–10, 73 students received support, including 12 fellowships with full tuition reimbursements available (averaging $15,000 per year), 34 research assistantships with full and partial tuition reimbursements available (averaging $11,142 per year), 26 teaching assistantships with tuition reimbursements available (averaging $11,142 per year); career-related internships or fieldwork, institutionally sponsored loans, scholarships/grants, health care benefits, and unspecified assistantships also available. Financial award application deadline: 12/1. *Faculty research:* Cognitive development/disability, child clinical, psychology and law, health/aging, social psychology. Total annual research expenditures: $2.1 million. *Unit head:* Dr. Beverly E. Thorn, Chair, 205-348-1919, Fax: 205-348-8648, E-mail: bthorn@bama.ua.edu. *Application contact:* Colett Thomas, Information Contact, 205-348-1913, Fax: 205-348-8648, E-mail: cthomas@as.ua.edu.

University of Central Florida, College of Sciences, Department of Psychology, Program in Applied Experimental and Human Factors Psychology, Orlando, FL 32816. Offers MA, PhD. *Accreditation:* APA. *Students:* 40 full-time (21 women), 3 part-time (2 women); includes 4 minority (2 Asian Americans or Pacific Islanders, 2 Hispanic Americans), 1 international. Average age 29. In 2009, 3 master's, 4 doctorates awarded. *Degree requirements:* For doctorate, thesis/dissertation, departmental candidacy exam. *Entrance requirements:* For doctorate, GRE General Test, minimum GPA of 3.2 in last 60 hours or master's qualifying exam. Additional exam requirements/recommendations for international students: Required—TOEFL. *Application deadline:* For fall admission, 2/1 for domestic students. Application fee: $30. Electronic applications accepted. *Expenses:* Tuition, state resident: part-time $306.31 per credit hour. Tuition, nonresident: part-time $1099.01 per credit hour. Part-time tuition and fees vary according to degree level and program. *Financial support:* In 2009–10, 32 students received support, including 22 research assistantships with partial tuition reimbursements available (averaging $10,700 per year), 19 teaching assistantships with partial tuition reimbursements available (averaging $6,230 per year); career-related internships or fieldwork, Federal Work-Study, institutionally sponsored loans, tuition waivers (partial), and unspecified assistantships also available. Financial award application deadline: 3/1; financial award applicants required to submit FAFSA. *Faculty research:* Visual performance, team training, controls/displays, synthetic speech, alarms/warning. *Unit head:* Dr. Richard Gilson, Program Director, 407-823-2755, E-mail: gilson@mail.ucf.edu. *Application contact:* Dr. Richard Gilson, Program Director, 407-823-2755, E-mail: gilson@mail.ucf.edu.

University of Cincinnati, Graduate School, McMicken College of Arts and Sciences, Department of Psychology, Cincinnati, OH 45221. Offers clinical psychology (PhD); experimental psychology (PhD). *Accreditation:* APA. *Degree requirements:* For doctorate, comprehensive exam, thesis/dissertation. *Entrance requirements:* For doctorate, GRE General Test. Additional exam requirements/recommendations for international students: Required—TOEFL. *Faculty research:* Neuropsychology, human factors, health.

University of Connecticut, Graduate School, College of Liberal Arts and Sciences, Department of Psychology, Storrs, CT 06269. Offers behavioral neuroscience (PhD); biopsychology (PhD); clinical psychology (MA, PhD); cognition and instruction (PhD); developmental psychology (MA, PhD); ecological psychology (PhD); experimental psychology (PhD); general psychology (MA, PhD); health psychology (Graduate Certificate); industrial/organizational psychology (PhD); language and cognition (PhD); neuroscience (PhD); occupational health psychology (Graduate Certificate); social psychology (MA, PhD). *Accreditation:* APA. *Faculty:* 59 full-time (26 women). *Students:* 194 full-time (133 women), 24 part-time (12 women); includes 48 minority (12 African Americans, 21 Asian Americans or Pacific Islanders, 15 Hispanic Americans), 25 international. Average age 28. 585 applicants, 4% accepted, 14 enrolled. In 2009, 22 master's, 24 doctorates awarded. Terminal master's awarded for partial completion of doctoral program. *Degree requirements:* For master's, comprehensive exam; for doctorate, thesis/dissertation. *Entrance requirements:* For master's and doctorate, GRE General Test, GRE Subject Test. Additional exam requirements/recommendations for international students: Required—TOEFL (minimum score 550 paper-based; 213 computer-based). *Application deadline:* For fall admission, 2/1 priority date for domestic and international students; for spring admission, 11/1 for domestic students, 10/1 for international students. Applications are processed on a rolling basis. Application fee: $55. Electronic applications accepted. *Expenses:* Tuition, state resident: full-time $4725; part-time $525 per credit. Tuition, nonresident: full-time $12,267; part-time $1363 per credit. Required fees: $346 per semester. Tuition and fees vary according to course load. *Financial support:* In 2009–10, 109 research assistantships with full tuition reimbursements, 72 teaching assistantships with full tuition reimbursements were awarded; fellowships, career-related internships or fieldwork, Federal Work-Study, scholarships/grants, health care benefits, and unspecified assistantships also available. Financial award application deadline: 2/1; financial award applicants required to submit FAFSA. *Unit head:* Charles A. Lowe, Head, 860-486-3517, Fax: 860-486-2760, E-mail: charles.lowe@uconn.edu. *Application contact:* Charles A. Lowe, Head, 860-486-3517, Fax: 860-486-2760, E-mail: charles.lowe@uconn.edu.

University of Hartford, College of Arts and Sciences, Department of Psychology, Program in General Experimental Psychology, West Hartford, CT 06117-1599. Offers MA. Part-time programs available. *Degree requirements:* For master's, comprehensive exam, thesis or alternative. *Entrance requirements:* For master's, GRE General Test, GRE Subject Test, minimum GPA of 3.0, 3 letters of recommendation. Additional exam requirements/recommendations for international students: Required—TOEFL (minimum score 550 paper-based; 213 computer-based). Electronic applications accepted. *Faculty research:* Decision making, social judgment and stereotyping, stress and health.

University of Kentucky, Graduate School, College of Arts and Sciences, Program in Psychology, Lexington, KY 40506-0032. Offers clinical psychology (MA); experimental psychology (MA). *Accreditation:* APA (one or more programs are accredited). *Degree requirements:* For master's, comprehensive exam, thesis; for doctorate, comprehensive exam, thesis/dissertation. *Entrance requirements:* For master's, GRE General Test, minimum undergraduate GPA of 2.75; for doctorate, GRE General Test, minimum graduate GPA of 3.0. Additional exam requirements/recommendations for international students: Required—TOEFL (minimum score 550 paper-based; 213 computer-based). Electronic applications accepted. *Faculty research:* Psychopharmacology and teratology, behavioral neuroscience, social psychology, cognitive psychology, development and developmental psychobiology.

University of Louisiana at Monroe, Graduate School, College of Education and Human Development, Department of Psychology, Program in General Psychology, Monroe, LA 71209-0001. Offers MS. Part-time and evening/weekend programs available. *Faculty:* 7 full-time (0 women), 1 part-time/adjunct (0 women). *Students:* 12 full-time (7 women), 8 part-time (4 women); includes 3 minority (2 African Americans, 1 Asian American or Pacific Islander). Average age 28. In 2009, 5 master's awarded. *Degree requirements:* For master's, comprehensive exam, thesis. *Entrance requirements:* For master's, minimum GPA of 2.5 or GRE General Test. Additional exam requirements/recommendations for international students: Required—TOEFL (minimum score 500 paper-based; 173 computer-based; 61 iBT). *Application deadline:* For fall admission, 8/24 priority date for domestic students, 7/1 for international students; for winter admission, 12/14 priority date for domestic students; for spring admission, 1/19 for domestic students, 11/1 for international students. Applications are processed on a rolling basis. Application fee: $20 ($30 for international students). Electronic applications accepted. *Expenses:* Tuition, state resident: part-time $159 per credit hour. Tuition, nonresident: part-time $159 per credit hour. Required fees: $1300 per year. Tuition and fees vary according to course load. *Financial support:* In 2009–10, 9 research assistantships (averaging $2,500 per year) were awarded; career-related internships or fieldwork, Federal Work-Study, and unspecified assistantships also available. Financial award application deadline: 4/1; financial award applicants required to submit FAFSA. *Unit head:* Dr. Joe McGahan, Coordinator, 818-342-1338, Fax: 318-342-1352, E-mail: mcgahan@ulm.edu. *Application contact:* Dr. Joe McGahan, Coordinator, 818-342-1338, Fax: 318-342-1352, E-mail: mcgahan@ulm.edu.

University of Louisville, Graduate School, College of Arts and Sciences, Department of Psychological and Brain Sciences, Louisville, KY 40292-0001. Offers clinical psychology (PhD); experimental psychology (PhD). *Accreditation:* APA. *Faculty:* 22 full-time (9 women), 4 part-time/adjunct (1 woman). *Students:* 68 full-time (49 women); includes 6 minority (3 African Americans, 2 Asian Americans or Pacific Islanders, 1 Hispanic American), 7 international. Average age 30. 194 applicants, 8% accepted, 4 enrolled. In 2009, 11 doctorates awarded. *Degree requirements:* For doctorate, thesis/dissertation, preliminary exam, research, internship. *Entrance requirements:* For doctorate, GRE General Test. Additional exam requirements/recommendations for international students: Required—TOEFL. *Application deadline:* For fall admission, 12/1 for domestic students, 11/1 for international students. Application fee: $50. Electronic applications accepted. *Financial support:* In 2009–10, 36 students received support, including 7 fellowships (averaging $22,000 per year), 29 teaching assistantships (averaging $22,000 per year); career-related internships or fieldwork also available. *Faculty research:* Health psychology, geropsychology, psychopathology, cognitive and development science, neuroscience and neuropsychology, vision and hearing. *Unit head:* Dr. Suzanne Meeks, Chair, 502-852-6068, Fax: 502-852-8904, E-mail: smeeks@louisville.edu. *Application contact:* Mary E. Leggett, Director, Graduate Admissions, 502-852-3101, Fax: 502-852-6536, E-mail: gradadm@louisville.edu.

University of Maine, Graduate School, College of Liberal Arts and Sciences, Department of Psychology, Orono, ME 04469. Offers clinical psychology (PhD); developmental psychology (MA); experimental psychology (MA, PhD); social psychology (MA). *Accreditation:* APA (one or more programs are accredited). *Faculty:* 17 full-time (8 women), 7 part-time/adjunct (3 women). *Students:* 27 full-time (16 women), 9 part-time (7 women); includes 2 minority (1 Asian American or Pacific Islander, 1 Hispanic American), 1 international. Average age 28. 134 applicants, 8% accepted, 7 enrolled. In 2009, 3 master's, 3 doctorates awarded. *Degree requirements:* For master's, thesis; for doctorate, thesis/dissertation. *Entrance requirements:* For master's and doctorate, GRE General Test, GRE Subject Test. Additional exam requirements/recommendations for international students: Required—TOEFL. *Application deadline:* For fall admission, 2/1 priority date for domestic students. Applications are processed on a rolling basis. Application fee: $65. Electronic applications accepted. *Financial support:* In 2009–10, 3 research assistantships with tuition reimbursements (averaging $14,063 per year); 21 teaching assistantships with tuition reimbursements (averaging $12,790 per year) were awarded; Federal Work-Study, institutionally sponsored loans, and tuition waivers (full and partial) also available. Financial award application deadline: 3/1. *Faculty research:* Social development, hypertension and aging, attitude change, self-confidence in achievement situations, health psychology. *Unit head:* Dr. Michael Robbins, Chair, 207-581-2051, Fax: 207-581-6128. *Application contact:*

Experimental Psychology

University of Maine (continued)
Scott G. Delcourt, Associate Dean of the Graduate School, 207-581-3291, Fax: 207-581-3232, E-mail: graduate@maine.edu.

University of Maryland, College Park, Academic Affairs, College of Behavioral and Social Sciences, Department of Psychology, College Park, MD 20742. Offers clinical psychology (PhD); developmental psychology (PhD); experimental psychology (PhD); industrial psychology (MA, MS, PhD); social psychology (PhD). *Accreditation:* APA (one or more programs are accredited). *Faculty:* 71 full-time (35 women), 8 part-time/adjunct (4 women). *Students:* 82 full-time (67 women); includes 13 minority (2 African Americans, 4 Asian Americans or Pacific Islanders, 7 Hispanic Americans), 12 international. 568 applicants, 4% accepted, 8 enrolled. In 2009, 13 master's, 10 doctorates awarded. *Degree requirements:* For master's, thesis; for doctorate, variable foreign language requirement, comprehensive exam, thesis/dissertation. *Entrance requirements:* For master's and doctorate, GRE General Test, GRE Subject Test, minimum GPA of 3.5, research and/or work experience, 3 letters of recommendation. *Application deadline:* For fall admission, 12/1 for domestic and international students. Applications are processed on a rolling basis. Application fee: $60. Electronic applications accepted. *Expenses:* Tuition, area resident: Part-time $471 per credit hour. Tuition, state resident: part-time $471 per credit hour. Tuition, nonresident: part-time $1016 per credit hour. Required fees: $337.04 per term. *Financial support:* In 2009–10, 11 fellowships with full and partial tuition reimbursements (averaging $19,195 per year), 5 research assistantships (averaging $17,734 per year), 45 teaching assistantships with tuition reimbursements (averaging $17,116 per year) were awarded; career-related internships or fieldwork, Federal Work-Study, and scholarships/grants also available. Support available to part-time students. Financial award applicants required to submit FAFSA. *Faculty research:* Social stereotyping and prejudice, anxiety disorders, auditory neuroethology, counseling and social psychology. Total annual research expenditures: $3.8 million. *Unit head:* Thomas S. Wallsten, Chair, 301-405-3562, Fax: 301-314-9566, E-mail: twallst@umd.edu. *Application contact:* Dean of Graduate School, 301-405-0358, Fax: 301-314-9305.

University of Memphis, Graduate School, College of Arts and Sciences, Department of Psychology, Memphis, TN 38152-3230. Offers psychology (MS, PhD), including clinical (PhD), experimental (PhD), general psychology (MS), school (PhD); school psychology (MA, Ed S); MS/PhD. *Faculty:* 28 full-time (9 women), 4 part-time/adjunct (0 women). *Students:* 115 full-time (81 women), 22 part-time (15 women); includes 23 minority (15 African Americans, 1 American Indian/Alaska Native, 4 Asian Americans or Pacific Islanders, 3 Hispanic Americans), 7 international. Average age 27. 220 applicants, 15% accepted, 29 enrolled. In 2009, 31 master's, 9 doctorates awarded. *Degree requirements:* For master's, comprehensive exam (for some programs), thesis (for some programs), 37 credit hours (MA); 33 credit hours with thesis or 36 with exam (MS); for doctorate, comprehensive exam (for some programs), thesis/dissertation, 80 semester hours, major area paper; clinical: 1 year placement and 1 year internship; internship (school psychology). *Entrance requirements:* For master's, GRE; for doctorate, GRE (minimum combined score of 1100), minimum GPA of 2.75, 18 hours of undergraduate psychology courses, transcripts, personal statement, letters of recommendation; for Ed S, GRE (minimum combined score of 1100), minimum GPA of 2.75, 18 hours of undergraduate psychology courses, letters of recommendation. Additional exam requirements/recommendations for international students: Required—TOEFL. *Application deadline:* For fall admission, 12/5 for domestic students. Applications are processed on a rolling basis. Application fee: $35 ($60 for international students). Electronic applications accepted. *Expenses:* Tuition, state resident: full-time $6246; part-time $347 per credit hour. Tuition, nonresident: full-time $15,894; part-time $883 per credit hour. Required fees: $1160. Full-time tuition and fees vary according to course load, degree level and program. *Financial support:* In 2009–10, 66 students received support; fellowships with full tuition reimbursements available, research assistantships with full tuition reimbursements available, teaching assistantships with full tuition reimbursements available, Federal Work-Study, scholarships/grants, tuition waivers (partial), and unspecified assistantships available. Financial award application deadline: 2/15; financial award applicants required to submit FAFSA. *Faculty research:* Clinical health; school, child and family research; psychotherapy research; cognitive and behavioral neuroscience research; industrial-organizational research. *Unit head:* Dr. Robert Cohen, Coordinator of Graduate Programs, 901-678-4679, Fax: 901-678-2579, E-mail: rcohen@memphis.edu. *Application contact:* Lynell Connable, Graduate Secretary, 901-678-4340, Fax: 901-678-2579, E-mail: dconnabl@memphis.edu.

University of Michigan, Horace H. Rackham School of Graduate Studies, College of Literature, Science, and the Arts, Department of Psychology, Ann Arbor, MI 48451. Offers biopsychology (PhD); clinical psychology (PhD); cognition and perception (PhD); developmental psychology (PhD); personality and social contexts (PhD); social psychology (PhD). *Accreditation:* APA. *Faculty:* 87 full-time (40 women), 28 part-time/adjunct (16 women). *Students:* 147 full-time (101 women); includes 40 minority (15 African Americans, 2 American Indian/Alaska Native, 18 Asian Americans or Pacific Islanders, 5 Hispanic Americans), 25 international. Average age 27. 621 applicants, 10% accepted, 37 enrolled. In 2009, 25 doctorates awarded. *Degree requirements:* For doctorate, comprehensive exam, thesis/dissertation, oral defense of dissertation, preliminary exam. *Entrance requirements:* For doctorate, GRE General Test. Additional exam requirements/recommendations for international students: Required—TOEFL. *Application deadline:* For fall admission, 12/1 for domestic and international students. Application fee: $60 ($75 for international students). Electronic applications accepted. *Expenses:* Tuition, state resident: full-time $17,286; part-time $1099 per credit hour. Tuition, nonresident: full-time $34,944; part-time $2080 per credit hour. Required fees: $95 per semester. Tuition and fees vary according to course load, degree level and program. *Financial support:* In 2009–10, 133 students received support, including 52 fellowships with full tuition reimbursements available (averaging $20,900 per year), 16 research assistantships with full tuition reimbursements available (averaging $20,900 per year), 79 teaching assistantships with full tuition reimbursements available (averaging $16,694 per year); career-related internships or fieldwork also available. Financial award application deadline: 4/15. *Unit head:* Prof. Theresa Lee, Chair, 734-764-7429. *Application contact:* Laurie Brannan, Psychology Student Academic Affairs, 731-764-2580, Fax: 734-615-7584, E-mail: psych.saa@umich.edu.

University of Mississippi, Graduate School, College of Liberal Arts, Department of Psychology, Oxford, University, MS 38677. Offers clinical psychology (PhD); experimental psychology (PhD); psychology (MA). *Accreditation:* APA (one or more programs are accredited). *Faculty:* 18 full-time (8 women), 2 part-time/adjunct (both women). *Students:* 52 full-time (38 women), 6 part-time (4 women); includes 10 minority (7 African Americans, 1 American Indian/Alaska Native, 1 Asian American or Pacific Islander, 1 Hispanic American), 1 international. In 2009, 3 master's, 6 doctorates awarded. *Degree requirements:* For master's, thesis; for doctorate, thesis/dissertation. *Entrance requirements:* For master's, GRE General Test, minimum GPA of 3.0; for doctorate, GRE General Test. Additional exam requirements/recommendations for international students: Required—TOEFL. *Application deadline:* For fall admission, 1/15 for domestic students; for spring admission, 10/1 for domestic students. Applications are processed on a rolling basis. Application fee: $25. Electronic applications accepted. *Financial support:* Scholarships/grants available. Financial award application deadline: 3/1; financial award applicants required to submit FAFSA. *Unit head:* Dr. Michael T. Allen, Chairman, 662-915-5190, Fax: 662-915-5398, E-mail: mta1@olemiss.edu. *Application contact:* Dr. Christy M. Wyandt, Associate Dean, 662-915-7474, Fax: 662-915-7577, E-mail: cwyandt@olemiss.edu.

The University of Montana, Graduate School, College of Arts and Sciences, Department of Psychology, Missoula, MT 59812-0002. Offers clinical psychology (PhD); experimental psychology (PhD), including animal behavior psychology, developmental psychology; school psychology (MA, PhD, Ed S). *Accreditation:* APA (one or more programs are accredited). Terminal master's awarded for partial completion of doctoral program. *Degree requirements:* For master's, thesis; for doctorate, thesis/dissertation. *Entrance requirements:* For master's, doctorate, and Ed S, GRE General Test. Additional exam requirements/recommendations for international students: Required—TOEFL.

University of New Brunswick Fredericton, School of Graduate Studies, Faculty of Arts, Department of Psychology, Fredericton, NB E3B 5A3, Canada. Offers clinical (PhD); experimental (MA). Part-time programs available. *Faculty:* 14 full-time (9 women). *Students:* 25 full-time (20 women), 2 part-time (both women). In 2009, 4 doctorates awarded. *Degree requirements:* For doctorate, comprehensive exam, thesis/dissertation. *Entrance requirements:* For doctorate, GRE General Test, GRE Subject Test, minimum GPA of 3.7. Additional exam requirements/recommendations for international students: Required—TOEFL (minimum score 600 paper-based). *Application deadline:* For fall admission, 1/15 priority date for domestic and international students. Application fee: $50 Canadian dollars. Tuition and fees charges are reported in Canadian dollars. *Expenses:* Tuition, area resident: Full-time $5562 Canadian dollars; part-time $2781 Canadian dollars per year. Required fees: $49.75 Canadian dollars per term. *Financial support:* In 2009–10, 8 fellowships (averaging $35,000 per year), 15 research assistantships (averaging $11,000 per year), 15 teaching assistantships (averaging $4,000 per year) were awarded. Financial award application deadline: 1/15. *Faculty research:* Depression, adolescence, human sexuality, family violence, autism. *Unit head:* Dr. Daniel Voyer, Director of Graduate Studies, 506-453-7974, Fax: 506-447-3063, E-mail: psycdogs@unb.ca. *Application contact:* Theresa Mills, Graduate Secretary, 506-453-4707, Fax: 506-447-3063, E-mail: tmills@unb.ca.

University of New Brunswick Saint John, Department of Psychology, Saint John, NB E2L 4L5, Canada. Offers applied and experimental psychology (PhD); clinical psychology (PhD); experimental psychology (MA). Part-time programs available. *Faculty:* 9 full-time (4 women). *Students:* 4 full-time (2 women), 1 (woman) part-time. In 2009, 3 master's, 1 doctorate awarded. *Degree requirements:* For master's, thesis. *Entrance requirements:* For master's, GRE General and Subject Tests, honours thesis. Additional exam requirements/recommendations for international students: Required—TOEFL (minimum score 550 paper-based), TWE. *Application deadline:* For fall admission, 2/1 for domestic students. Application fee: $50. *Financial support:* In 2009–10, 4 research assistantships (averaging $9,000 per year), 4 teaching assistantships (averaging $4,500 per year) were awarded; unspecified assistantships also available. Support available to part-time students. Financial award application deadline: 2/1. *Faculty research:* Psychopharmacology and addictions, forensic psychology and criminal justice, interpersonal relations, perception and graphical perception, lie detection. *Unit head:* Dr. Lily Both, Director of Graduate Studies, 506-648-5769, Fax: 506-648-5780, E-mail: lboth@unbsj.ca. *Application contact:* Frances Stevens, Secretary, 506-648-5640, Fax: 506-648-5780, E-mail: fstevens@unb.ca.

The University of North Carolina at Chapel Hill, Graduate School, College of Arts and Sciences, Department of Psychology, Chapel Hill, NC 27599. Offers biological psychology (PhD); clinical psychology (PhD); cognitive psychology (PhD); developmental psychology (PhD); quantitative psychology (PhD); social psychology (PhD). *Accreditation:* APA. *Degree requirements:* For doctorate, comprehensive exam, thesis/dissertation. *Entrance requirements:* For doctorate, GRE General Test, minimum GPA of 3.0. Electronic applications accepted. *Faculty research:* Expressed emotion, cognitive development, social cognitive neuroscience, human memory personality.

University of North Dakota, Graduate School, College of Arts and Sciences, Department of Psychology, Grand Forks, ND 58202. Offers clinical psychology (PhD); counseling psychology (PhD); experimental psychology (PhD); forensic psychology (MA, MS); psychology (MA). *Accreditation:* APA (one or more programs are accredited). *Degree requirements:* For master's, thesis, final exam; for doctorate, comprehensive exam, thesis/dissertation, internship, final exam. *Entrance requirements:* For master's, GRE General Test, GRE Subject Test, minimum GPA of 3.0; for doctorate, GRE General Test, GRE Subject Test, minimum GPA of 3.5. Additional exam requirements/recommendations for international students: Required—TOEFL (minimum score 550 paper-based; 213 computer-based; 79 iBT), IELTS (minimum score 6.5). Electronic applications accepted. *Faculty research:* Developmental psychology, clinical social psychology, educational psychology, personality disorders.

University of North Texas, Robert B. Toulouse School of Graduate Studies, College of Arts and Sciences, Department of Psychology, Denton, TX 76203-5017. Offers clinical psychology (PhD); counseling psychology (MA, MS, PhD); experimental psychology (MA, MS, PhD); health psychology and behavioral medicine (PhD). *Accreditation:* APA (one or more programs are accredited). Terminal master's awarded for partial completion of doctoral program. *Degree requirements:* For master's, comprehensive exam, thesis or alternative; for doctorate, one foreign language, comprehensive exam, thesis/dissertation. *Entrance requirements:* For master's and doctorate, GRE General Test, interview. Additional exam requirements/recommendations for international students: Required—proof of English language proficiency required for non-native English speakers; Recommended—TOEFL (minimum score 550 paper-based; 213 computer-based; 79 iBT). *Application deadline:* Applications are processed on a rolling basis. Application fee: $50 ($75 for international students). Electronic applications accepted. *Expenses:* Tuition, state resident: full-time $4298; part-time $239 per contact hour. Tuition, nonresident: full-time $9878; part-time $549 per contact hour. Required fees: $265 per contact hour. *Financial support:* Fellowships, research assistantships, teaching assistantships, career-related internships or fieldwork, Federal Work-Study, and institutionally sponsored loans available. Financial award applicants required to submit FAFSA. *Application contact:* Graduate Coordinator, 940-565-2671, Fax: 940-565-4682, E-mail: amym@unt.edu.

University of Regina, Faculty of Graduate Studies and Research, Faculty of Arts, Department of Psychology, Regina, SK S4S 0A2, Canada. Offers clinical psychology (MA, PhD); experimental and applied psychology (MA, PhD). *Faculty:* 18 full-time (10 women). *Students:* 57 full-time (40 women), 5 part-time (all women). 54 applicants, 30% accepted. In 2009, 6 master's, 5 doctorates awarded. *Degree requirements:* For master's, thesis; for doctorate, comprehensive exam, thesis/dissertation. *Entrance requirements:* For master's, GRE General Test, GRE Subject Test; for doctorate, GRE General Test, GRE Subject Test (optional for students who hold a master's degree from a Canadian university). Additional exam requirements/recommendations for international students: Required—TOEFL (minimum score 580 paper-based; 237 computer-based; 80 iBT). *Application deadline:* For fall admission, 2/15 for domestic students. Application fee: $90 ($100 for international students). Electronic applications accepted. *Financial support:* In 2009–10, 23 fellowships (averaging $19,000 per year), 3 research assistantships (averaging $16,910 per year), 10 teaching assistantships (averaging $6,650 per year) were awarded; career-related internships or fieldwork and scholarships/grants also available. Financial award application deadline: 6/15. *Faculty research:* Clinical, experimental and applied psychology. *Unit head:* Dr. William E. Smythe, Head, 306-585-4157, Fax: 306-585-5429, E-mail: william.smythe@uregina.ca. *Application contact:* Dr. Dongyan Blachford, Associate Dean, 306-585-5186, Fax: 306-337-2444, E-mail: dongyan.blachford@uregina.ca.

University of South Carolina, The Graduate School, College of Arts and Sciences, Department of Psychology, Program in Experimental Psychology, Columbia, SC 29208. Offers MA, PhD. Terminal master's awarded for partial completion of doctoral program. *Degree requirements:* For master's, comprehensive exam, thesis; for doctorate, comprehensive exam, thesis/dissertation. *Entrance requirements:* For master's and doctorate, GRE General Test. Additional exam requirements/recommendations for international students: Required—TOEFL. Electronic applications accepted. *Faculty research:* Cognition, development, neuroscience.

University of Southern Mississippi, Graduate School, College of Education and Psychology, Department of Psychology, Hattiesburg, MS 39406-0001. Offers clinical psychology (MA, PhD); counseling psychology (PhD); experimental psychology (MA, PhD); psychology (MS); school psychology (MA, PhD). *Accreditation:* APA (one or more programs are accredited). *Faculty:* 32 full-time (9 women). *Students:* 104 full-time (80 women), 29 part-time (19 women); includes 14 minority (7 African Americans, 2 Asian Americans or Pacific Islanders, 5 Hispanic Americans), 7 international. Average age 29. 225 applicants, 16% accepted, 30 enrolled. In 2009, 23 master's, 13 doctorates awarded. Terminal master's awarded for partial completion of doctoral program. *Degree requirements:* For master's, comprehensive exam, thesis; for doctorate, comprehensive exam, thesis/dissertation. *Entrance requirements:* For master's, GRE General Test, minimum GPA of 3.0; for doctorate, GRE General Test, interview, minimum

GPA of 3.0. Additional exam requirements/recommendations for international students: Required—TOEFL. *Application deadline:* For fall admission, 3/1 priority date for domestic students, 3/1 for international students. Applications are processed on a rolling basis. Application fee: $35. *Expenses:* Tuition, state resident: full-time $5096; part-time $284 per hour. Tuition, nonresident: full-time $13,052; part-time $726 per hour. Required fees: $402. Tuition and fees vary according to course level and course load. *Financial support:* In 2009–10, 48 research assistantships with full tuition reimbursements (averaging $8,802 per year), 48 teaching assistantships with full tuition reimbursements (averaging $6,500 per year) were awarded; career-related internships or fieldwork, Federal Work-Study, and institutionally sponsored loans also available. Financial award application deadline: 3/15; financial award applicants required to submit FAFSA. *Faculty research:* Dolphin cognition, sleep, neuropsychology, health-related behaviors, psychopathology. Total annual research expenditures: $101,200. *Unit head:* Dr. Joesph Olmi, Chair, 601-266-4177, Fax: 601-266-5580. *Application contact:* Dr. Heather Sterling-Turner, Graduate Coordinator, 601-266-4177, Fax: 601-266-5580.

The University of Tennessee, Graduate School, College of Arts and Sciences, Department of Psychology, Knoxville, TN 37996. Offers clinical psychology (PhD); experimental psychology (MA, PhD); psychology (MA). *Accreditation:* APA (one or more programs are accredited). Terminal master's awarded for partial completion of doctoral program. *Degree requirements:* For master's, thesis; for doctorate, thesis/dissertation. *Entrance requirements:* For master's and doctorate, GRE General Test, GRE Subject Test, minimum GPA of 2.7. Additional exam requirements/recommendations for international students: Required—TOEFL. Electronic applications accepted. *Expenses:* Tuition, state resident: full-time $6826; part-time $380 per semester hour. Tuition, nonresident: full-time $21,844; part-time $1147 per semester hour. Tuition and fees vary according to program.

The University of Tennessee at Chattanooga, Graduate School, College of Arts and Sciences, Department of Psychology, Chattanooga, TN 37403. Offers industrial/organizational psychology (MS); research psychology (MS). Part-time and evening/weekend programs available. *Faculty:* 6 full-time (1 woman). *Students:* 39 full-time (24 women), 5 part-time (3 women); includes 7 minority (4 African Americans, 2 Asian Americans or Pacific Islanders, 1 Hispanic American), 1 international. Average age 29. 75 applicants, 85% accepted, 16 enrolled. In 2009, 21 master's awarded. *Degree requirements:* For master's, thesis (for some programs), practicum (industrial/organizational psychology). *Entrance requirements:* For master's, GRE General Test, minimum GPA of 2.5 on all undergraduate coursework or 3.0 in senior year. Additional exam requirements/recommendations for international students: Required—TOEFL (minimum score 550 paper-based; 213 computer-based; 79 iBT), IELTS (minimum score 6). *Application deadline:* For fall admission, 8/1 priority date for domestic students, 6/1 for international students; for spring admission, 12/1 priority date for domestic students, 10/1 for international students. Applications are processed on a rolling basis. Application fee: $35. Electronic applications accepted. *Expenses:* Tuition, state resident: full-time $5404; part-time $300 per credit hour. Tuition, nonresident: full-time $16,702; part-time $928 per credit hour. Required fees: $1150; $130 per credit hour. *Financial support:* In 2009–10, 20 research assistantships with full and partial tuition reimbursements (averaging $5,500 per year) were awarded; career-related internships or fieldwork, scholarships/grants, and unspecified assistantships also available. Support available to part-time students. *Faculty research:* Decision processes, philosophical psychology, memory, social cognition, employee selection. Total annual research expenditures: $35,031. *Unit head:* Dr. Paul J. Watson, Department Head, 423-425-4262, Fax: 423-425-4284, E-mail: paul-watson@utc.edu. *Application contact:* Dr. Stephanie Bellar, Dean of Graduate Studies, 423-425-4666, Fax: 423-425-5223, E-mail: stephanie-bellar@utc.edu.

The University of Texas at Arlington, Graduate School, College of Science, Department of Psychology, Arlington, TX 76019. Offers experimental psychology (PhD); health psychology (PhD); industrial organizational psychology (MS); psychology (MS). Part-time programs available. *Faculty:* 16 full-time (5 women), 1 part-time/adjunct (0 women). *Students:* 62 full-time (41 women), 10 part-time (7 women); includes 13 minority (5 African Americans, 2 Asian Americans or Pacific Islanders, 6 Hispanic Americans), 7 international. 72 applicants, 90% accepted, 22 enrolled. In 2009, 16 master's, 6 doctorates awarded. Terminal master's awarded for partial completion of doctoral program. *Degree requirements:* For master's, comprehensive exam or thesis; for doctorate, thesis/dissertation (for some programs). *Entrance requirements:* For master's and doctorate, GRE General Test, minimum GPA of 3.0 in last 60 hours of course work. Additional exam requirements/recommendations for international students: Required—TOEFL (minimum score 550 paper-based; 213 computer-based). *Application deadline:* For fall admission, 6/16 for domestic students. Applications are processed on a rolling basis. Application fee: $35 ($50 for international students). *Financial support:* In 2009–10, 4 fellowships (averaging $1,000 per year), 2 research assistantships with tuition reimbursements (averaging $15,000 per year), 28 teaching assistantships with tuition reimbursements (averaging $15,000 per year) were awarded; career-related internships or fieldwork, Federal Work-Study, institutionally sponsored loans, scholarships/grants, traineeships, tuition waivers (partial), and unspecified assistantships also available. Financial award application deadline: 6/1; financial award applicants required to submit FAFSA. *Unit head:* Dr. Robert Gatchel, Chair, 817-272-2281, Fax: 817-272-2364, E-mail: gatchel@uta.edu. *Application contact:* Dr. Jared Kenworthy, Graduate Advisor, 817-272-2281, Fax: 817-272-2364, E-mail: kenworthy@uta.edu.

The University of Texas at El Paso, Graduate School, College of Liberal Arts, Department of Psychology, El Paso, TX 79968-0001. Offers clinical psychology (MA); experimental psychology (MA); psychology (PhD). Part-time and evening/weekend programs available. *Students:* 47 (28 women); includes 20 minority (1 Asian American or Pacific Islander, 19 Hispanic Americans), 6 international. Average age 34. In 2009, 11 master's, 5 doctorates awarded. *Degree requirements:* For master's, thesis; for doctorate, thesis/dissertation. *Entrance requirements:* For master's, GRE, letters of recommendation; for doctorate, GRE, Statement of Purpose, Letters of Recommendation. Additional exam requirements/recommendations for international students: Required—TOEFL; Recommended—IELTS. *Application deadline:* For fall admission, 8/1 for domestic students, 3/1 for international students; for spring admission, 11/1 for domestic students, 9/1 for international students. Applications are processed on a rolling basis. Application fee: $45 ($80 for international students). Electronic applications accepted. *Financial support:* In 2009–10, research assistantships with partial tuition reimbursements (averaging $18,625 per year), teaching assistantships with partial tuition reimbursements (averaging $14,900 per year) were awarded; fellowships with partial tuition reimbursements, institutionally sponsored loans, scholarships/grants, health care benefits, tuition waivers (partial), and unspecified assistantships also available. Support available to part-time students. Financial award application deadline: 3/15; financial award applicants required to submit FAFSA. *Unit head:* Dr. Edward Casta?eda, Chair, 915-747-5551, Fax: 915-747-6553, E-mail: ecastaneda9@utep.edu. *Application contact:* Dr. Patricia D. Witherspoon, Dean of the Graduate School, 915-747-5491, Fax: 915-747-5788, E-mail: withersp@utep.edu.

The University of Texas of the Permian Basin, Office of Graduate Studies, College of Arts and Sciences, Department of Psychology, Odessa, TX 79762-0001. Offers applied research psychology (MA); clinical psychology (MA). Part-time and evening/weekend programs available. *Degree requirements:* For master's, comprehensive exam, thesis, practicum. *Entrance requirements:* For master's, GRE General Test, 3 letters of recommendation. Additional exam requirements/recommendations for international students: Required—TOEFL (minimum score 550 paper-based; 213 computer-based).

The University of Texas–Pan American, College of Social and Behavioral Sciences, Department of Psychology and Anthropology, Edinburg, TX 78539. Offers psychology (MA), including clinical psychology, experimental psychology. Part-time and evening/weekend programs available. *Degree requirements:* For master's, comprehensive exam, thesis optional, internship. *Entrance requirements:* For master's, GRE, letters of recommendation. Additional exam requirements/recommendations for international students: Required—TOEFL. Electronic applications accepted. *Expenses:* Tuition, state resident: full-time $3630.60; part-time $201.70 per credit hour. Tuition, nonresident: full-time $8617; part-time $478.70 per credit hour. Required fees: $806.50. *Faculty research:* Biofeedback, acculturation, health, stress/trauma, neuropsychological assessment, false memories, children's theory of mind.

The University of Toledo, College of Graduate Studies, College of Arts and Sciences, Department of Psychology, Toledo, OH 43606-3390. Offers behavioral (PhD), including cognitive, psychobiology and learning, social; clinical psychology (PhD); experimental psychology (MA). *Accreditation:* APA. *Degree requirements:* For master's, thesis; for doctorate, one foreign language, thesis/dissertation. *Entrance requirements:* For master's and doctorate, GRE General Test, GRE Subject Test. *Faculty research:* Neural taste response.

University of Victoria, Faculty of Graduate Studies, Faculty of Social Sciences, Department of Psychology, Victoria, BC V8W 2Y2, Canada. Offers clinical psychology (PhD); clinical psychology (neuropsychology) (M Sc); cognition and brain science (M Sc, PhD); experimental neuropsychology (M Sc, PhD); individualized study (M Sc, PhD); life span development psychology (PhD); life span developmental psychology (M Sc); social psychology (M Sc, PhD). *Accreditation:* APA (one or more programs are accredited). *Degree requirements:* For master's, thesis; for doctorate, thesis/dissertation, candidacy exam. *Entrance requirements:* For master's and doctorate, GRE General Test. Additional exam requirements/recommendations for international students: Required—TOEFL (minimum score 600 paper-based; 250 computer-based). Electronic applications accepted. *Faculty research:* Life span development psychology and aging, behavioral neuroscience, cognitive psychology, behavioral psychology, environmental psychology.

University of Wisconsin–Oshkosh, The Office of Graduate Studies, College of Letters and Science, Department of Psychology, Oshkosh, WI 54901. Offers experimental psychology (MS); industrial/organizational psychology (MS). *Degree requirements:* For master's, thesis. *Entrance requirements:* For master's, GRE, 10 semester hours of undergraduate course work in psychology. Additional exam requirements/recommendations for international students: Required—TOEFL (minimum score 550 paper-based; 213 computer-based; 79 iBT). Electronic applications accepted. *Faculty research:* Performance evaluation, training, biological bases of behavior, tactile perception, aging.

Washington State University, Graduate School, College of Liberal Arts, Department of Psychology, Pullman, WA 99164. Offers clinical psychology (PhD); experimental psychology (PhD); psychology (MS). *Accreditation:* APA (one or more programs are accredited). *Faculty:* 22. *Students:* 49 full-time (34 women), 4 part-time (2 women); includes 7 minority (2 Asian Americans or Pacific Islanders, 5 Hispanic Americans), 7 international. Average age 29. 262 applicants, 6% accepted, 12 enrolled. In 2009, 7 master's, 8 doctorates awarded. *Degree requirements:* For master's, comprehensive exam (for some programs), thesis (for some programs), oral exam; for doctorate, comprehensive exam, thesis/dissertation, oral exam, written exam. *Entrance requirements:* For master's, minimum undergraduate GPA of 3.0; research experiences; clinical experiences; at least 18 hours of psychology, including a class in statistics; three letters of recommendation, official transcripts; for doctorate, three letters of reference; summary data form; at least 18 credits of study in psychology; at least one course in statistics and research methodology; official transcripts; minimum cumulative undergraduate GPA of 3.0 or master's degree in psychology. *Application deadline:* For fall admission, 12/15 priority date for domestic and international students. Applications are processed on a rolling basis. Application fee: $50. *Financial support:* In 2009–10, 5 research assistantships with full and partial tuition reimbursements (averaging $13,917 per year), 39 teaching assistantships with full and partial tuition reimbursements (averaging $13,056 per year) were awarded; fellowships, career-related internships or fieldwork, Federal Work-Study, institutionally sponsored loans, and unspecified assistantships also available. Financial award application deadline: 2/15; financial award applicants required to submit FAFSA. *Faculty research:* Childhood conduct disorders, etiology of depression, treatment of reading disorders, applied behavior analysis, selective attention. *Unit head:* Dr. John Hinson, Chair, 509-335-1089, Fax: 509-335-5043, E-mail: hinson@mail.wsu.edu. *Application contact:* Graduate School Admissions, 800-GRADWSU, Fax: 509-335-16949, E-mail: gradsch@wsu.edu.

Washington University in St. Louis, Graduate School of Arts and Sciences, Department of Psychology, St. Louis, MO 63130-4899. Offers clinical psychology (PhD); general experimental psychology (PhD); social psychology (PhD). *Accreditation:* APA. Terminal master's awarded for partial completion of doctoral program. *Degree requirements:* For doctorate, thesis/dissertation. *Entrance requirements:* For doctorate, GRE General Test. Electronic applications accepted.

Western Michigan University, Graduate College, College of Arts and Sciences, Department of Psychology, Kalamazoo, MI 49008. Offers behavior analysis (MA, PhD); clinical psychology (PhD); industrial/organizational psychology (MA). *Accreditation:* APA (one or more programs are accredited). *Degree requirements:* For master's, variable foreign language requirement, thesis, oral exams; for doctorate, 2 foreign languages, comprehensive exam, thesis/dissertation, oral exams. *Entrance requirements:* For master's and doctorate, GRE General Test.

Western Washington University, Graduate School, College of Humanities and Social Sciences, Department of Psychology, Program in Experimental Psychology, Bellingham, WA 98225-5996. Offers MS. *Degree requirements:* For master's, thesis. *Entrance requirements:* For master's, GRE General Test, minimum GPA of 3.0 in last 60 semester hours or last 90 quarter hours. Additional exam requirements/recommendations for international students: Required—TOEFL (minimum score 567 paper-based; 227 computer-based). Electronic applications accepted.

Xavier University, College of Social Sciences, Health and Education, Department of Psychology, Cincinnati, OH 45207. Offers clinical psychology (Psy D); psychology (MA), including general experimental, industrial-organizational. *Accreditation:* APA (one or more programs are accredited). *Faculty:* 19 full-time (9 women), 3 part-time/adjunct (2 women). *Students:* 111 full-time (87 women), 6 part-time (4 women); includes 13 minority (5 African Americans, 1 American Indian/Alaska Native, 4 Asian Americans or Pacific Islanders, 3 Hispanic Americans), 2 international. Average age 27. 272 applicants, 23% accepted, 37 enrolled. In 2009, 27 master's, 16 doctorates awarded. *Degree requirements:* For master's, one foreign language, comprehensive exam, thesis, internship; for doctorate, one foreign language, comprehensive exam, thesis/dissertation, internship. *Entrance requirements:* For master's and doctorate, GRE. Additional exam requirements/recommendations for international students: Required—TOEFL. *Application deadline:* For fall admission, 12/15 for domestic and international students. Application fee: $35. Electronic applications accepted. *Expenses:* Contact institution. *Financial support:* In 2009–10, 61 students received support, including 41 research assistantships with partial tuition reimbursements available, 20 teaching assistantships with partial tuition reimbursements available; scholarships/grants and unspecified assistantships also available. Financial award application deadline: 3/1; financial award applicants required to submit FAFSA. *Unit head:* Dr. Christine M. Dacey, Chair, 513-745-3533, Fax: 513-745-3327, E-mail: dacey@xavier.edu. *Application contact:* Margaret Maybury, Assistant Director, Enrollment and Student Services, 513-745-1053, Fax: 513-745-3347, E-mail: maybury@xavier.edu.

Forensic Psychology

Adler School of Professional Psychology, Programs in Psychology, Chicago, IL 60601-7203. Offers art therapy (MA, Certificate); clinical hypnosis (Certificate); clinical psychology (Psy D); counseling (MA); counseling and organizational psychology (MA); forensic psychology (MA); gerontological counseling (MA); marriage and family counseling (MA); marriage and family therapy (Certificate); organizational psychology (MA); police psychology (MA); rehabilitation counseling (MA); sport and health psychology (MA); substance abuse counseling (Certificate); Psy D/Certificate; Psy D/MACAT; Psy D/MACP; Psy D/MAMFC; Psy D/MASAC. *Accreditation:* APA. Part-time and evening/weekend programs available. Postbaccalaureate distance learning degree programs offered (minimal on-campus study). *Faculty:* 41 full-time (21 women), 44 part-time/adjunct (19 women). *Students:* 551 full-time (441 women), 161 part-time (137 women). Average age 27.Terminal master's awarded for partial completion of doctoral program. *Degree requirements:* For master's, thesis or alternative, oral exam, practicum; for doctorate, thesis/dissertation, clinical exam, internship, oral exam, practicum, written qualifying exam. *Entrance requirements:* For master's, 12 semester hours in psychology, minimum GPA of 3.0; for doctorate, 18 semester hours in psychology, minimum GPA of 3.25; for Certificate, appropriate master's or doctoral degree. Additional exam requirements/recommendations for international students: Required—TOEFL (minimum score 550 paper-based; 213 computer-based; 79 iBT). *Application deadline:* For fall admission, 2/15 priority date for domestic students, 12/1 priority date for international students. Applications are processed on a rolling basis. Application fee: $50. Electronic applications accepted. *Expenses:* Tuition: Part-time $930 per credit. Required fees: $220 per term. *Financial support:* Career-related internships or fieldwork, Federal Work-Study, scholarships/grants, and tuition waivers (full and partial) available. Support available to part-time students. Financial award application deadline: 5/15; financial award applicants required to submit FAFSA. *Unit head:* Dr. Frank Gruba-McAllister, Vice President of Academic Affairs, 312-201-5900 Ext. 209, Fax: 312-201-5917. *Application contact:* Craig A. Hines, Associate Vice President of Admissions, 312-201-5900 Ext. 226, Fax: 312-201-5917, E-mail: chines@adler.edu.

See Close-Up on page 1047.

Alliant International University–Fresno, Center for Forensic Studies, Fresno, CA 93727. Offers forensic psychology (PhD, Psy D). *Degree requirements:* For doctorate, thesis/dissertation. *Entrance requirements:* For doctorate, interview; master's degree in psychology, forensic psychology, criminology, criminal justice, social work or law; minimum GPA of 3.0 in psychology and overall. Additional exam requirements/recommendations for international students: Required—TOEFL (minimum score 600 paper-based; 250 computer-based), TWE (minimum score 5). Electronic applications accepted. *Faculty research:* Domestic violence, serial killers, court evaluations, drug and alcohol abuse.

Alliant International University–Irvine, Center for Forensic Studies, Irvine, CA 92612. Offers Psy D.

Alliant International University–Los Angeles, Center for Forensic Studies, Alhambra, CA 91803-1360. Offers forensic psychology (Psy D). *Degree requirements:* For doctorate, thesis/dissertation. *Entrance requirements:* For doctorate, interview; master's degree in psychology, forensic psychology, criminology, criminal justice, social work or law; minimum GPA of 3.0 in psychology and overall. Additional exam requirements/recommendations for international students: Required—TOEFL (minimum score 600 paper-based; 250 computer-based), TWE (minimum score 5). *Faculty research:* Court testimony.

American International College, School of Arts, Education and Sciences, Department of Psychology, Program in Forensic Psychology, Springfield, MA 01109-3189. Offers MS. Part-time and evening/weekend programs available. *Degree requirements:* For master's, comprehensive exam (for some programs), thesis optional. *Entrance requirements:* For master's, minimum B-average in undergraduate course work, BS or BA. Additional exam requirements/recommendations for international students: Required—TOEFL. Electronic applications accepted. *Expenses:* Tuition: Full-time $12,510; part-time $695 per credit hour. Required fees: $35 per term.

Argosy University, Atlanta, College of Psychology and Behavioral Sciences, Atlanta, GA 30328. Offers clinical psychology (MA, Psy D, Postdoctoral Respecialization Certificate), including child and family psychology (Psy D), general adult clinical (Psy D), health psychology (Psy D), neuropsychology/geropsychology (Psy D); community counseling (MA), including marriage and family therapy; counselor education and supervision (Ed D); forensic psychology (MA); industrial organizational psychology (MA); marriage and family therapy (Certificate); sport-exercise psychology (MA). *Accreditation:* APA.

See Close-Up on page 1049.

Argosy University, Chicago, College of Psychology and Behavioral Sciences, Doctoral Program in Clinical Psychology, Chicago, IL 60601. Offers child and adolescent psychology (Psy D); client-centered and experiential psychotherapies (Psy D); diversity and multicultural psychology (Psy D); family psychology (Psy D); forensic psychology (Psy D); health psychology (Psy D); neuropsychology (Psy D); organizational consulting (Psy D); psychoanalytic psychology (Psy D); psychology and spirituality (Psy D). *Accreditation:* APA.

See Close-Up on page 1051.

Argosy University, Dallas, College of Psychology and Behavioral Sciences, Program in Forensic Psychology, Farmers Branch, TX 75244. Offers MA.

See Close-Up on page 1053.

Argosy University, Denver, College of Psychology and Behavioral Sciences, Denver, CO 80231. Offers clinical mental health counseling (MA); clinical psychology (MA, Psy D); counseling psychology (Ed D); counselor education and supervision (Ed D); forensic psychology (MA); industrial organizational psychology (MA); marriage and family therapy (MA, DMFT).

See Close-Up on page 1055.

Argosy University, Hawai'i, College of Psychology and Behavioral Sciences, Program in Forensic Psychology, Honolulu, HI 96813. Offers MA.

See Close-Up on page 1057.

Argosy University, Inland Empire, College of Psychology and Behavioral Sciences, San Bernardino, CA 92408. Offers clinical psychology/marriage and family therapy (MA); counseling psychology (Ed D); counseling psychology/marriage and family therapy (MA); forensic psychology (MA); industrial organizational psychology (MA); sport-exercise psychology (MA).

See Close-Up on page 1059.

Argosy University, Los Angeles, College of Psychology and Behavioral Sciences, Santa Monica, CA 90045. Offers clinical psychology/marriage and family therapy (MA); counseling psychology (Ed D); counseling psychology/marriage and family therapy (MA); forensic psychology (MA).

See Close-Up on page 1061.

Argosy University, Orange County, College of Psychology and Behavioral Sciences, Program in Forensic Psychology, Orange, CA 92868. Offers MA. *Unit head:* Dr. Gary Bruss, Dean, 800-716-9598, Fax: 714-437-1284, E-mail: gbruss@argosy.edu. *Application contact:* Mark Betz, Director of Admissions, 800-716-9598, Fax: 714-437-1697, E-mail: mbetz@argosy.edu.

See Close-Up on page 1065.

Argosy University, Phoenix, College of Psychology and Behavioral Sciences, Program in Forensic Psychology, Phoenix, AZ 85021. Offers MA.

See Close-Up on page 1067.

Argosy University, Salt Lake City, College of Psychology and Behavioral Sciences, Draper, UT 84020. Offers counseling psychology (Ed D); counselor education and supervision (Ed D); forensic psychology (MA); marriage and family therapy (MA, DMFT); mental health counseling (MA).

See Close-Up on page 1069.

Argosy University, San Diego, College of Psychology and Behavioral Sciences, San Diego, CA 92108. Offers clinical psychology/marriage and family therapy (MA); counseling psychology (Ed D); counseling psychology/marriage and family therapy (MA); forensic psychology (MA).

See Close-Up on page 1071.

Argosy University, San Francisco Bay Area, College of Psychology and Behavioral Sciences, Program in Forensic Psychology, Alameda, CA 94501. Offers MA.

See Close-Up on page 1073.

Argosy University, Sarasota, College of Psychology and Behavioral Sciences, Sarasota, FL 34235. Offers community counseling (MA); counseling psychology (Ed D); counselor education and supervision (Ed D); forensic psychology (MA); marriage and family therapy (MA); mental health counseling (MA); pastoral community counseling (Ed D).

See Close-Up on page 1075.

Argosy University, Schaumburg, College of Psychology and Behavioral Sciences, Schaumburg, IL 60173-5403. Offers clinical health psychology (Post-Graduate Certificate); clinical psychology (MA, Psy D), including child and family psychology (Psy D), clinical health psychology (Psy D), diversity and multicultural psychology (Psy D), forensic psychology (Psy D), neuropsychology (Psy D); community counseling (MA); counseling psychology (Ed D), including counselor education and supervision; counselor education and supervision (Ed D); forensic psychology (Post-Graduate Certificate); industrial organizational psychology (MA). *Accreditation:* ACA; APA.

See Close-Up on page 1077.

Argosy University, Twin Cities, College of Psychology and Behavioral Sciences, Eagan, MN 55121. Offers clinical psychology (MA, Psy D), including child and family psychology (Psy D), forensic psychology (Psy D), health and neuropsychology (Psy D), trauma (Psy D); forensic counseling (Post-Graduate Certificate); forensic psychology (MA); industrial organizational psychology (MA); marriage and family therapy (MA, DMFT), including forensic counseling (MA). *Accreditation:* APA.

See Close-Up on page 1083.

Argosy University, Washington DC, College of Psychology and Behavioral Sciences, Arlington, VA 22209. Offers clinical psychology (MA, Psy D), including child and family psychology (Psy D), diversity and multicultural psychology (Psy D), forensic psychology (Psy D), health and neuropsychology (Psy D); community counseling (MA); counseling psychology (Ed D), including counselor education and supervision; counselor education and supervision (Ed D); forensic psychology (MA). *Accreditation:* APA.

See Close-Up on page 1085.

California Baptist University, Program in Forensic Psychology, Riverside, CA 92504-3206. Offers MA. Part-time programs available. *Faculty:* 1 (woman) full-time. *Students:* 16 full-time (14 women), 4 part-time (3 women); includes 8 minority (1 American Indian/Alaska Native, 1 Asian American or Pacific Islander, 6 Hispanic Americans). 19 applicants, 53% accepted, 10 enrolled. In 2009, 3 master's awarded. *Entrance requirements:* For master's, Minnesota Multiphasic Personality Inventory-2, minimum GPA of 2.75; 15 units of pre-requisite coursework. Additional exam requirements/recommendations for international students: Required—TOEFL (minimum score 575 paper-based; 230 computer-based; 89 iBT). *Application deadline:* For fall admission, 8/1 priority date for domestic students, 7/1 for international students; for spring admission, 12/1 priority date for domestic students, 10/15 for international students. Applications are processed on a rolling basis. Application fee: $45. Electronic applications accepted. *Expenses:* Tuition: Full-time $8352; part-time $464 per semester hour. Required fees: $125 per semester. Tuition and fees vary according to course load, campus/location and program. *Financial support:* Federal Work-Study and scholarships/grants available. Support available to part-time students. Financial award applicants required to submit FAFSA. *Unit head:* Dr. Anne-Marie Larsen, Director, 951-343-4761, E-mail: alarsen@calbaptist.edu. *Application contact:* Gail Ronveaux, Dean of Graduate Enrollment, 951-343-5045, Fax: 951-343-5095, E-mail: graduateadmissions@calbaptist.edu.

Cambridge College, School of Psychology and Counseling, Cambridge, MA 02138-5304. Offers addiction counseling (M Ed); alcohol & drug counseling (Certificate); counseling psychology (M Ed, CAGS); counseling psychology: forensic counseling (M Ed); marriage and family therapy (M Ed); mental health and addiction counseling (M Ed); mental health counseling (M Ed); mental health counseling for school guidance counselors (Post Master's Certificate); psychological studies (M Ed); school adjustment and mental health counseling (M Ed); school adjustment, mental health and addiction counseling (M Ed); school guidance counselor (M Ed); trauma studies (Certificate). Part-time and evening/weekend programs available. *Faculty:* 5 full-time (2 women), 87 part-time/adjunct (50 women). *Students:* 501 full-time (395 women), 307 part-time (245 women); includes 382 minority (295 African Americans, 2 American Indian/Alaska Native, 6 Asian Americans or Pacific Islanders, 79 Hispanic Americans), 4 international. Average age 38. In 2009, 237 master's, 15 other advanced degrees awarded. *Degree requirements:* For master's, thesis, practicum/internship; for other advanced degree, thesis, practicum/Internship. *Entrance requirements:* For master's, resume, 2 professional references; for other advanced degree, official transcripts, documents for transfer credit evaluation, resume, written personal statement/essay, 2 professional references, health insurance, immunizations form. Additional exam requirements/recommendations for international students: Required—TOEFL (minimum score 550 paper-based; 213 computer-based; 79 iBT); Recommended—IELTS (minimum score 6). *Application deadline:* Applications are processed on a rolling basis. Application fee: $30. Electronic applications accepted. *Expenses:* Contact institution. *Financial support:* In 2009–10, 686 students received support. Career-related internships or fieldwork, Federal Work-Study, and scholarships/grants available. Financial award applicants required to submit FAFSA. *Unit head:* Dr. Niti Seth, Dean, 617-873-0208, Fax: 617-349-3561, E-mail: nseth@cambridgecollege.edu. *Application contact:* Stephen Lyons, Director of Enrollment, Graduate and N.I.T.E. Programs, 617-868-1000, Fax: 617-349-3561, E-mail: stephen.lyons@cambridgecollege.edu.

Castleton State College, Division of Graduate Studies, Department of Psychology, Castleton, VT 05735. Offers forensic psychology (MA). *Degree requirements:* For master's, thesis. *Entrance requirements:* For master's, GRE General Test, minimum undergraduate GPA of 3.5, previous course work in research methodology and statistics. Additional exam requirements/recommendations for international students: Required—TOEFL. *Expenses:* Tuition, state resident: full-time $10,290; part-time $429 per credit. Tuition, nonresident: full-time $15,420; part-time $643 per credit. One-time fee: $200 full-time. *Faculty research:* Psychology and law, juvenile delinquency, criminal psychology, correctional psychology, police psychology.

The Chicago School of Professional Psychology, Program in Clinical Forensic Psychology, Chicago, IL 60610. Offers Psy D. *Students:* 30 full-time (25 women); includes 5 minority (2

African Americans, 3 Hispanic Americans). 52 applicants, 67% accepted, 30 enrolled. In 2009, 71 doctorates awarded. *Degree requirements:* For doctorate, thesis/dissertation. *Entrance requirements:* For doctorate, GRE. Additional exam requirements/recommendations for international students: Required—TOEFL, IELTS. *Financial support:* In 2009–10, fellowships (averaging $10,000 per year), research assistantships (averaging $6,000 per year), teaching assistantships (averaging $6,000 per year) were awarded; Federal Work-Study, institutionally sponsored loans, and scholarships/grants also available. Financial award application deadline: 3/1; financial award applicants required to submit FAFSA. *Unit head:* Dr. James Galezewski, Department Chair, 312-467-2169, E-mail: jgalezewski@thechicagoschool.edu. *Application contact:* Andrea Schmoyer, Director of Admission, 312-329-6666, Fax: 312-644-3333, E-mail: admissions@thechicagoschool.edu.

The Chicago School of Professional Psychology, Program in Forensic Psychology, Chicago, IL 60610. Offers MA. *Students:* 157 full-time (140 women), 46 part-time (39 women); includes 43 minority (24 African Americans, 8 Asian Americans or Pacific Islanders, 11 Hispanic Americans), 1 international. 169 applicants, 85% accepted, 87 enrolled. *Degree requirements:* For master's, thesis optional. *Entrance requirements:* For master's, GRE (highly recommended), 1 course in research methods, statistics, 1 course in psychology. Additional exam requirements/recommendations for international students: Required—TOEFL (minimum score 550 paper-based; 213 computer-based; 79 iBT). Application fee: $50. *Financial support:* Federal Work-Study and scholarships/grants available. Financial award application deadline: 3/1; financial award applicants required to submit FAFSA. *Unit head:* Dr. Michael Fogel, Department Chair, 312-410-8959, E-mail: mfogel@thechicagoschool.edu. *Application contact:* Andrea Schmoyer, Director of Admission, 312-329-6666, Fax: 312-644-3333, E-mail: admissions@thechicagoschool.edu.

The Chicago School of Professional Psychology at Downtown Los Angeles, Clinical Forensic Psychology, Los Angeles, CA 90017. Offers Psy D. *Students:* 38 full-time (34 women), 4 part-time (3 women); includes 20 minority (9 African Americans, 2 Asian Americans or Pacific Islanders, 9 Hispanic Americans). 44 applicants, 89% accepted, 30 enrolled. *Unit head:* Dr. Debra Warner, Lead Faculty, 213-615-7203, E-mail: dwarner@thechicagoschool.edu. *Application contact:* Heather LaBelle, Director of Admissions, 213-615-7200, Fax: 213-627-1985, E-mail: admissions@thechicagoschool.edu.

The Chicago School of Professional Psychology at Irvine, Program in Clinical Forensic Psychology, Irvine, CA 92612. Offers Psy D. *Unit head:* Dr. Debra Warner, Lead Faculty, 213-615-7203, E-mail: dwarner@thechicagoschool.edu. *Application contact:* Betty Vu, Director of Admissions, 949-737-5460, Fax: 949-737-5467, E-mail: admissions@thechicagoschool.edu.

The Chicago School of Professional Psychology: Online, Applied Forensic Psychology Services, Chicago, IL 60654. Offers MA, Certificate. *Students:* 251 part-time (217 women). *Unit head:* Dr. Ilianna Kwaske, Dean of Academic Affairs, 312-467-8601, E-mail: ikwaske@thechicagoschool.edu. *Application contact:* Pari Pinyo, Director of Online Admission, 312-329-6666, Fax: 312-644-3333, E-mail: admissions@thechicagoschool.edu.

College of Saint Elizabeth, Department of Psychology, Morristown, NJ 07960-6989. Offers counseling psychology (MA); forensic psychology (MA); student affairs in higher education (Certificate). Part-time and evening/weekend programs available. *Faculty:* 5 full-time (2 women), 10 part-time/adjunct (9 women). *Students:* 23 full-time (19 women), 73 part-time (67 women); includes 25 minority (12 African Americans, 2 Asian Americans or Pacific Islanders, 11 Hispanic Americans), 2 international. Average age 32. 104 applicants, 58% accepted, 47 enrolled. In 2009, 10 master's awarded. *Degree requirements:* For master's, thesis or alternative, portfolio. *Entrance requirements:* For master's, minimum GPA of 3.0, BA in psychology (preferred), 12 credits of course work in psychology. *Application deadline:* For fall admission, 4/14 priority date for domestic students; for spring admission, 11/15 for domestic students. Applications are processed on a rolling basis. Application fee: $35. Electronic applications accepted. *Expenses:* Tuition: Part-time $797 per credit hour. Required fees: $65 per credit hour. *Financial support:* Career-related internships or fieldwork, tuition waivers (partial), and unspecified assistantships available. Support available to part-time students. Financial award application deadline: 3/15; financial award applicants required to submit FAFSA. *Faculty research:* Family systems, dissociative identity disorder, multicultural counseling, outcomes assessment. *Unit head:* Dr. Valerie Scott, Director of the Graduate Program in Counseling Psychology, 973-290-4102, Fax: 973-290-4676, E-mail: vscott@cse.edu. *Application contact:* Donna Tatarka, Dean of Admission, 973-290-4705, Fax: 973-290-4710, E-mail: dtatarka@cse.edu.

Drexel University, College of Arts and Sciences, Department of Psychology, Clinical Psychology Program, Philadelphia, PA 19104-2875. Offers clinical psychology (PhD); forensic psychology (PhD); health psychology (PhD); neuropsychology (PhD). *Accreditation:* APA. Terminal master's awarded for partial completion of doctoral program. *Degree requirements:* For doctorate, thesis/dissertation, qualifying exam. *Entrance requirements:* For doctorate, GRE General Test, GRE Subject Test, minimum GPA of 3.0. Electronic applications accepted. *Expenses:* Contact institution. *Faculty research:* Cognitive behavioral therapy, stress and coping, eating disorders, substance abuse, developmental disabilities.

Fairleigh Dickinson University, Metropolitan Campus, University College: Arts, Sciences, and Professional Studies, School of Psychology, Program in Forensic Psychology, Teaneck, NJ 07666-1914. Offers MA. *Students:* 16 full-time (14 women), 1 (woman) part-time. Average age 24. 43 applicants, 56% accepted, 7 enrolled. *Application contact:* Susan Brooman, University Director of Graduate Admissions, 201-692-2554, Fax: 201-692-2560, E-mail: globaleducation@fdu.edu.

Holy Names University, Graduate Division, Department of Counseling Psychology, Oakland, CA 94619-1699. Offers counseling psychology (MA); forensic psychology (MA, Certificate); pastoral counseling (MA, Certificate). Part-time and evening/weekend programs available. *Degree requirements:* For master's, comprehensive paper, seminars. *Entrance requirements:* For master's, minimum undergraduate GPA of 2.6 overall, 3.0 in major. Additional exam requirements/recommendations for international students: Required—TOEFL (minimum score 550 paper-based; 213 computer-based; 80 iBT). *Faculty research:* Cognitive psychology, anger management, grief and grief counseling, post-modernism and psychotherapy, spirituality and psychology.

John Jay College of Criminal Justice of the City University of New York, Graduate Studies, Program in Forensic Psychology, New York, NY 10019-1093. Offers MA, PhD. Part-time and evening/weekend programs available. *Degree requirements:* For master's, thesis or alternative, externship. *Entrance requirements:* For master's, GRE General Test, minimum B average in major. Additional exam requirements/recommendations for international students: Required—TOEFL (minimum score 500 paper-based; 173 computer-based).

John Jay College of Criminal Justice of the City University of New York, Graduate Studies, Programs in Criminal Justice, New York, NY 10019-1093. Offers criminal justice (MA, PhD); criminology and deviance (PhD); forensic psychology (PhD); forensic science (PhD); law and philosophy (PhD); organizational behavior (PhD); public policy (PhD). Part-time and evening/weekend programs available. Terminal master's awarded for partial completion of doctoral program. *Degree requirements:* For master's, thesis or alternative; for doctorate, one foreign language, thesis/dissertation. *Entrance requirements:* For master's, GRE General Test, minimum B average; for doctorate, GRE General Test. Additional exam requirements/recommendations for international students: Required—TOEFL (minimum score 500 paper-based; 173 computer-based).

Marymount University, School of Education and Human Services, Program in Forensic Psychology, Arlington, VA 22207-4299. Offers MA. Part-time and evening/weekend programs available. *Faculty:* 3 full-time (2 women), 8 part-time/adjunct (7 women). *Students:* 117 full-time (95 women), 50 part-time (38 women); includes 28 minority (15 African Americans, 5 Asian Americans or Pacific Islanders, 8 Hispanic Americans), 3 international. Average age 25. 160 applicants, 87% accepted, 78 enrolled. In 2009, 74 master's awarded. *Entrance requirements:* For master's, GRE, 2 letters of recommendation, resume. Additional exam requirements/recommendations for international students: Required—TOEFL (minimum score 600 paper-based; 250 computer-based; 96 iBT), IELTS (minimum score 6.5). *Application deadline:* For fall admission, 2/16 for domestic and international students. Applications are processed on a rolling basis. Application fee: $40. Electronic applications accepted. *Expenses:* Tuition: Full-time $13,050; part-time $725 per credit hour. Required fees: $135; $7.50 per credit hour. *Financial support:* In 2009–10, 13 students received support; research assistantships with full tuition reimbursements available, career-related internships or fieldwork, Federal Work-Study, scholarships/grants, and unspecified assistantships available. Support available to part-time students. Financial award applicants required to submit FAFSA. *Unit head:* Dr. Jason Doll, Chair, 703-526-6821, Fax: 703-284-5708, E-mail: jason.doll@marymount.edu. *Application contact:* Francesca Reed, Director, Graduate Admissions, 703-284-5901, Fax: 703-527-3815, E-mail: grad.admissions@marymount.edu.

Massachusetts School of Professional Psychology, Graduate Programs, Boston, MA 02132. Offers clinical psychology (Psy D); clinical psychopharmacology (Post-Doctoral MS); counseling psychology (MA); executive coaching (Graduate Certificate); forensic psychology (MA); organizational psychology (MA); respecialization in clinical psychology (Certificate); MA/CAGS. *Accreditation:* APA. *Degree requirements:* For master's, comprehensive exam; for doctorate, thesis/dissertation. *Entrance requirements:* For doctorate, GRE General Test. Additional exam requirements/recommendations for international students: Required—TOEFL (minimum score 550 paper-based; 213 computer-based). Electronic applications accepted.

Oklahoma State University Center for Health Sciences, Graduate Program in Forensic Sciences, Tulsa, OK 74107-1898. Offers forensic DNA/molecular biology (MS); forensic examination of questioned documents (MFSA, Certificate); forensic pathology (MS); forensic psychology (MS); forensic sciences (MFSA); forensic toxicology (MS). Part-time and evening/weekend programs available. Postbaccalaureate distance learning degree programs offered (no on-campus study). *Degree requirements:* For master's, comprehensive exam (for some programs), thesis (for some programs). *Entrance requirements:* For master's, MAT (MFSA) or GRE General Test, professional experience (MFSA). Additional exam requirements/recommendations for international students: Required—TOEFL (minimum score 600 paper-based; 250 computer-based), TWE (minimum score 5). *Faculty research:* DNA typing, DNA polymorphism, identification through DNA, disease transmission, forensic dentistry, neurotoxicity of HIV, forensic toxicology method development, toxin detection and characterization.

Prairie View A&M University, College of Juvenile Justice and Psychology, Prairie View, TX 77446-0519. Offers clinical adolescent psychology (PhD); juvenile forensic psychology (MSJFP); juvenile justice (MSJJ, PhD). Part-time and evening/weekend programs available. *Faculty:* 12 full-time (7 women). *Students:* 25 full-time (18 women), 50 part-time (41 women); includes 64 minority (61 African Americans, 1 Asian American or Pacific Islander, 2 Hispanic Americans), 2 international. Average age 26. 55 applicants, 60% accepted, 33 enrolled. In 2009, 5 master's, 5 doctorates awarded. *Degree requirements:* For master's, comprehensive exam (for some programs), thesis (for some programs); for doctorate, comprehensive exam, thesis/dissertation. *Entrance requirements:* For master's, GRE, minimum GPA of 2.75; for doctorate, GRE, previous course work in clinical adolescent psychology, minimum GPA of 3.5. Additional exam requirements/recommendations for international students: Required—TOEFL. *Application deadline:* For fall admission, 3/1 for domestic and international students; for spring admission, 10/1 for domestic and international students. Applications are processed on a rolling basis. Application fee: $50. *Expenses:* Tuition, state resident: full-time $2200. Tuition, nonresident: full-time $5600. Required fees: $1720. Tuition and fees vary according to course load. *Financial support:* In 2009–10, 18 students received support; research assistantships, teaching assistantships, career-related internships or fieldwork, Federal Work-Study, institutionally sponsored loans, tuition waivers (full and partial), and unspecified assistantships available. Support available to part-time students. Financial award application deadline: 3/1; financial award applicants required to submit FAFSA. *Faculty research:* Juvenile justice, juvenile forensic psychology, teen court, graduate education, capital punishment. Total annual research expenditures: $2,888. *Unit head:* Dr. Elaine Rodney, Dean, 936-261-5200, Fax: 936-261-5252, E-mail: ehrodney@pvamu.edu. *Application contact:* Sandy Siegmund, Executive Secretary, Graduate Program, 936-261-5234, Fax: 936-261-5249, E-mail: sisiegmund@pvamu.edu.

Roger Williams University, Feinstein College of Arts and Sciences, Program in Forensic Psychology, Bristol, RI 02809. Offers MA. Part-time programs available. *Degree requirements:* For master's, thesis optional. *Entrance requirements:* For master's, GRE, 3 letters of recommendation. Additional exam requirements/recommendations for international students: Recommended—IELTS. Electronic applications accepted. *Expenses:* Contact institution.

Sage Graduate School, Graduate School, Program in Forensic Mental Health, Troy, NY 12180-4115. Offers MS, Certificate. Part-time and evening/weekend programs available. *Faculty:* 3 part-time/adjunct (1 woman). *Students:* 25 full-time (20 women), 17 part-time (16 women); includes 6 minority (all African Americans). Average age 28. 42 applicants, 64% accepted, 20 enrolled. In 2009, 2 master's, 1 other advanced degree awarded. *Entrance requirements:* Additional exam requirements/recommendations for international students: Required—TOEFL (minimum score 550 paper-based; 213 computer-based). *Application deadline:* Applications are processed on a rolling basis. Application fee: $40. *Expenses:* Tuition: Full-time $10,620; part-time $590 per credit hour. *Financial support:* Fellowships, research assistantships, Federal Work-Study, scholarships/grants, and unspecified assistantships available. Support available to part-time students. *Unit head:* Dr. Maureen McLeod, Chair, 518-244-2245, E-mail: mcleom@sage.edu. *Application contact:* Wendy D. Diefendorf, Director of Graduate and Adult Admission, 518-244-2443, Fax: 518-244-6880, E-mail: diefew@sage.edu.

Tiffin University, Program in Criminal Justice, Tiffin, OH 44883-2161. Offers crime analysis (MSCJ); criminal behavior (MSCJ); forensic psychology (MSCJ); homeland security administration (MSCJ); justice administration (MSCJ). Part-time and evening/weekend programs available. Postbaccalaureate distance learning degree programs offered (no on-campus study). *Degree requirements:* For master's, thesis optional. *Entrance requirements:* For master's, minimum undergraduate GPA of 2.5, work experience. Additional exam requirements/recommendations for international students: Required—TOEFL (minimum score 550 paper-based; 213 computer-based). Electronic applications accepted. *Faculty research:* Terrorism, intelligence, homeland security, guns and crime.

Universidad de Iberoamerica, Graduate School, San Jose, Costa Rica. Offers clinical neuropsychology (PhD); clinical psychology (M Psych); educational psychology (M Psych); forensic psychology (M Psych); hospital management (MHA); intensive care nursing (MN); medicine (MD). *Entrance requirements:* For master's, 2 letters of recommendation, interview.

University of Massachusetts Boston, Office of Graduate Studies, Graduate College of Education, Counseling and School Psychology Department, Program in Mental Health Counseling, Boston, MA 02125-3393. Offers forensic counseling (M Ed, CAGS).

University of New Haven, Graduate School, College of Arts and Sciences, Program in Community Psychology, West Haven, CT 06516-1916. Offers applications of psychology (Certificate); community clinical services (MA); forensic psychology (Certificate). Part-time and evening/weekend programs available. *Faculty:* 9 full-time (3 women), 12 part-time/adjunct (6 women). *Students:* 33 full-time (29 women), 15 part-time (11 women); includes 10 minority (8 African Americans, 2 Hispanic Americans), 4 international. Average age 27. 54 applicants, 72% accepted, 17 enrolled. In 2009, 9 master's, 2 other advanced degrees awarded. *Degree requirements:* For master's, thesis or alternative. *Entrance requirements:* Additional exam requirements/recommendations for international students: Required—TOEFL (minimum score 520 paper-based; 190 computer-based; 70 iBT); Recommended—IELTS (minimum score 5.5). *Application deadline:* For fall admission, 5/31 for international students; for winter admission, 10/15 for international students; for spring admission, 1/15 for international students. Applications are processed on a rolling basis. Application fee: $50. Electronic applications accepted. *Expenses:* Tuition: Part-time $700 per credit. Required fees: $45 per term. One-time fee: $390

Forensic Psychology

University of New Haven (continued)
part-time. *Financial support:* Research assistantships with partial tuition reimbursements, teaching assistantships with partial tuition reimbursements, career-related internships or fieldwork, Federal Work-Study, scholarships/grants, tuition waivers, and unspecified assistantships available. Support available to part-time students. Financial award application deadline: 5/1; financial award applicants required to submit FAFSA. *Unit head:* Dr. Michael A. Morris, Coordinator, 203-932-7281. *Application contact:* Eloise Gormley, Director of Graduate Admissions, 203-932-7449, Fax: 203-932-7137, E-mail: gradinfo@newhaven.edu.

University of New Haven, Graduate School, Henry C. Lee College of Criminal Justice and Forensic Sciences, Program in Criminal Justice, West Haven, CT 06516-1916. Offers crime analysis (MS); criminal justice management (MS); forensic computer investigation (MS, Certificate); forensic psychology (MS); victim advocacy and services management (Certificate); victimology (MS). Part-time and evening/weekend programs available. *Faculty:* 8 full-time (2 women), 10 part-time/adjunct (4 women). *Students:* 25 full-time (17 women), 37 part-time (26 women); includes 20 minority (12 African Americans, 1 Asian American or Pacific Islander, 7 Hispanic Americans), 1 international. Average age 25. 62 applicants, 85% accepted, 28 enrolled. In 2009, 30 master's awarded. *Degree requirements:* For master's, thesis or alternative. *Entrance requirements:* Additional exam requirements/recommendations for international students: Required—TOEFL (minimum score 520 paper-based; 190 computer-based; 70 iBT), IELTS (minimum score 5.5). *Application deadline:* For fall admission, 5/31 for international students; for winter admission, 10/15 for international students; for spring admission, 1/15 for international students. Applications are processed on a rolling basis. Application fee: $50. Electronic applications accepted. *Expenses:* Tuition: Part-time $700 per credit. Required fees: $45 per term. One-time fee: $390 part-time. *Financial support:* Research assistantships with partial tuition reimbursements, teaching assistantships with partial tuition reimbursements, career-related internships or fieldwork, Federal Work-Study, scholarships/grants, tuition waivers, and unspecified assistantships available. Support available to part-time students. Financial award applicants required to submit FAFSA. *Unit head:* Dr. James J. Cassidy, Coordinator, 203-932-7374. *Application contact:* Eloise Gormley, Director of Graduate Admissions, 203-932-7449, Fax: 203-932-7137, E-mail: gradinfo@newhaven.edu.

University of North Dakota, Graduate School, College of Arts and Sciences, Department of Psychology, Grand Forks, ND 58202. Offers clinical psychology (PhD); counseling psychology (PhD); experimental psychology (PhD); forensic psychology (MA, MS); psychology (MA). *Accreditation:* APA (one or more programs are accredited). *Degree requirements:* For master's, thesis, final exam; for doctorate, comprehensive exam, thesis/dissertation, internship, final exam. *Entrance requirements:* For master's, GRE General Test, GRE Subject Test, minimum GPA of 3.0; for doctorate, GRE General Test, GRE Subject Test, minimum GPA of 3.5. Additional exam requirements/recommendations for international students: Required—TOEFL (minimum score 550 paper-based; 213 computer-based; 79 iBT), IELTS (minimum score 6.5). Electronic applications accepted. *Faculty research:* Developmental psychology, clinical social psychology, educational psychology, personality disorders.

Walden University, Graduate Programs, School of Counseling and Social Service, Minneapolis, MN 55401. Offers counselor education and supervision (PhD), including consultation, counseling and social change, forensic mental health counseling, general program, nonprofit management and leadership, trauma and crisis; human services (PhD), including clinical social work, counseling, criminal justice, family studies and intervention strategies, general program, human services administration, self-designed, social policy analysis and planning; marriage, couple, and family counseling (MS), including forensic counseling, trauma and crisis counseling; mental health counseling (MS), including forensic counseling. Part-time and evening/weekend programs available. Postbaccalaureate distance learning degree programs offered (minimal on-campus study). *Faculty:* 13 full-time, 78 part-time/adjunct. *Students:* 1,932 full-time (1,624 women), 210 part-time (181 women); includes 945 minority (817 African Americans, 24 American Indian/Alaska Native, 24 Asian Americans or Pacific Islanders, 80 Hispanic Americans), 34 international. Average age 39. In 2009, 55 master's, 5 doctorates awarded. *Degree requirements:* For master's, residency (for some programs); for doctorate, thesis/dissertation, residency. *Entrance requirements:* For master's, bachelor's degree or equivalent in related field, minimum GPA of 2.5; for doctorate, master's degree or equivalent in related field; minimum GPA of 3.0; official transcripts; three years' related professional/academic experience (preferred); access to computer and Internet. Additional exam requirements/recommendations for international students: Required—TOEFL (minimum score 550 paper-based; 213 computer-based), IELTS (minimum score 6.5), or Michigan English Language Assessment Battery (minimum score 82). *Application deadline:* Applications are processed on a rolling basis. Application fee: $50. Electronic applications accepted. *Expenses:* Tuition: Full-time $13,665; part-time $560 per credit. Required fees: $1375. Tuition and fees vary according to course load, degree level and program. *Financial support:* In 2009–10, 200 students received support; fellowships, Federal Work-Study, scholarships/grants, unspecified assistantships, and family tuition reduction, active duty/veteran tuition reduction, group tuition reduction, interest-free payment plans available. Support available to part-time students. Financial award applicants required to submit FAFSA. *Unit head:* Dr. Savitri Dixon-Saxon, Associate Dean, 800-925-3368. *Application contact:* Jennifer Hall, Director of Enrollment, 866-4-WALDEN, E-mail: info@waldenu.edu.

Walden University, Graduate Programs, School of Psychology, Minneapolis, MN 55401. Offers clinical child psychology (Post-Doctoral Certificate); clinical psychology (Post-Doctoral Certificate); counseling psychology (Post-Doctoral Certificate); forensic psychology (MS), including forensic psychology in the community, general program, mental health applications, program planning and evaluation in forensic settings, psychology and legal systems; general psychology (Post-Doctoral Certificate); health psychology (Post-Doctoral Certificate); organizational psychology (Post-Doctoral Certificate); organizational psychology and development (Postbaccalaureate Certificate); psychology (MS, PhD), including clinical psychology (PhD), counseling psychology (PhD), crisis management and response (MS), general program (MS), general psychology (PhD), health psychology, leadership development and coaching (MS), media psychology (MS), organizational psychology (PhD), organizational psychology and development (MS), organizational psychology and nonprofit management (MS), program evaluation and research (MS), psychology of culture (MS), psychology, public administration, and social change (MS), social psychology (MS), terrorism and security (MS); teaching online (Post-Master's Certificate). Part-time and evening/weekend programs available. Postbaccalaureate distance learning degree programs offered (minimal on-campus study). *Faculty:* 33 full-time, 222 part-time/adjunct. *Students:* 3,546 full-time (2,761 women), 1,133 part-time (908 women); includes 1,723 minority (1,319 African Americans, 56 American Indian/Alaska Native, 101 Asian Americans or Pacific Islanders, 247 Hispanic Americans), 80 international. Average age 41. In 2009, 495 master's, 70 doctorates, 2 other advanced degrees awarded. Terminal master's awarded for partial completion of doctoral program. *Degree requirements:* For master's, thesis optional; for doctorate, thesis/dissertation, residency. *Entrance requirements:* For master's, bachelor's degree or equivalent in related field; minimum GPA of 2.5; official transcripts; goal statement; access to computer and Internet; for doctorate, master's degree or equivalent in related field; minimum GPA of 3.0;3 years of related professional/academic experience (preferred). Additional exam requirements/recommendations for international students: Required—TOEFL (minimum score 550 paper-based; 213 computer-based), IELTS (minimum score 6.5), or Michigan English Language Assessment Battery (minimum score 82). *Application deadline:* Applications are processed on a rolling basis. Application fee: $50. Electronic applications accepted. *Expenses:* Tuition: Full-time $13,665; part-time $560 per credit. Required fees: $1375. Tuition and fees vary according to course load, degree level and program. *Financial support:* In 2009–10, 290 students received support; fellowships, Federal Work-Study, scholarships/grants, unspecified assistantships, and family tuition reduction, active duty/veteran tuition reduction, group tuition reduction, interest-free payment plans available. Support available to part-time students. Financial award applicants required to submit FAFSA. *Unit head:* Dr. Melanie Storms, Associate Dean, 800-925-3368. *Application contact:* Jennifer Hall, Director of Enrollment, 866-4-WALDEN, E-mail: info@waldenu.edu.

Genetic Counseling

Arcadia University, Graduate Studies, Program in Genetic Counseling, Glenside, PA 19038-3295. Offers MSGC. *Students:* 27 full-time (26 women), 1 international. Average age 24. In 2009, 12 master's awarded. *Degree requirements:* For master's, thesis. *Entrance requirements:* For master's, GRE. Additional exam requirements/recommendations for international students: Required—TOEFL. *Application deadline:* For fall admission, 3/1 for domestic students. Application fee: $50. *Expenses:* Contact institution. *Financial support:* In 2009–10, 9 students received support. Tuition waivers (partial) and unspecified assistantships available. *Unit head:* Kathleen Valverde, Director, 215-572-4058. *Application contact:* 215-572-2910, Fax: 215-572-4049, E-mail: admiss@arcadia.edu.

Brandeis University, Graduate School of Arts and Sciences, Program in Genetic Counseling, Waltham, MA 02454-9110. Offers MS. *Faculty:* 1 (woman) full-time, 7 part-time/adjunct (6 women). *Students:* 23 full-time (all women), 2 international. Average age 28. 104 applicants, 22% accepted, 11 enrolled. In 2009, 10 master's awarded. *Degree requirements:* For master's, thesis. *Entrance requirements:* For master's, GRE General Test, resume, 3 letters of recommendation. Additional exam requirements/recommendations for international students: Required—TOEFL (minimum score 600 paper-based; 250 computer-based; 100 iBT); Recommended—IELTS (minimum score 7). *Application deadline:* For fall admission, 2/1 for domestic and international students. Application fee: $75. Electronic applications accepted. *Expenses:* Contact institution. *Financial support:* In 2009–10, 20 students received support. Career-related internships or fieldwork, scholarships/grants, and tuition waivers (partial) available. Financial award application deadline: 4/15; financial award applicants required to submit FAFSA. *Faculty research:* Molecular biology, human genetics, medical genetics, human reproductive biology, counseling skills, research methodology, biomedical law and ethics, genetic counseling, medical sociology, psychology, health policy. *Unit head:* Dr. Judith Tsipis, Director, 781-736-3179, Fax: 781-736-3107, E-mail: tsipis@brandeis.edu. *Application contact:* Missy Goldberg, Department Administrator, 781-736-3179, Fax: 781-736-3107, E-mail: goldberg@brandeis.edu.

California State University, Stanislaus, College of Natural Sciences, Department of Biological Sciences, Turlock, CA 95382. Offers ecology and sustainability (MS); genetic counseling (MS); marine sciences (MS). Part-time programs available. *Degree requirements:* For master's, thesis. *Entrance requirements:* For master's, GRE General Test, GRE Subject Test, minimum GPA of 3.0, 3 letters of reference. Additional exam requirements/recommendations for international students: Required—TOEFL (minimum score 550 paper-based; 213 computer-based). Electronic applications accepted. *Faculty research:* Long-term smoking and pregnancy rate, vertebrate paleobiology, terrestrial animals, benthic invertebrates of central California coastline.

Case Western Reserve University, School of Medicine and School of Graduate Studies, Graduate Programs in Medicine, Department of Genetics, Program in Genetic Counseling, Cleveland, OH 44106. Offers MS. *Degree requirements:* For master's, thesis. *Entrance requirements:* For master's, GRE General Test. Additional exam requirements/recommendations for international students: Required—TOEFL. *Faculty research:* Genetic testing, ethical issues in genetics, cancer genetics, reproductive genetics, prenatal diagnosis.

The Johns Hopkins University, Bloomberg School of Public Health, Department of Health, Behavior and Society, Baltimore, MD 21218-2699. Offers genetic counseling (Sc M); health education and health communication (MHS); social and behavioral sciences (Dr PH, PhD, Sc D); social factors in health (MHS). *Faculty:* 43 full-time (30 women), 59 part-time/adjunct (40 women). *Students:* 100 full-time (89 women), 4 part-time (3 women); includes 28 minority (13 African Americans, 12 Asian Americans or Pacific Islanders, 3 Hispanic Americans), 13 international. Average age 29. 227 applicants, 31% accepted, 26 enrolled. In 2009, 25 master's, 8 doctorates awarded. *Degree requirements:* For master's, comprehensive exam (for some programs), thesis (for some programs); for doctorate, comprehensive exam, thesis/dissertation. *Entrance requirements:* For master's, GRE, curriculum vitae, 3 letters of recommendation; for doctorate, GRE, transcripts, curriculum vitae, statement, 3 recommendation letters. Additional exam requirements/recommendations for international students: Required—TOEFL (minimum score 600 paper-based; 250 computer-based; 100 iBT). *Application deadline:* For fall admission, 12/1 for domestic and international students. Applications are processed on a rolling basis. Application fee: $45. Electronic applications accepted. *Financial support:* In 2009–10, 96 students received support, including 17 fellowships with tuition reimbursements available (averaging $23,634 per year), 30 research assistantships (averaging $7,800 per year), 25 teaching assistantships (averaging $2,759 per year); career-related internships or fieldwork, Federal Work-Study, scholarships/grants, traineeships, health care benefits, unspecified assistantships, and stipends also available. Financial award application deadline: 3/15. *Faculty research:* Social determinants of health, and structural- and community-level inventions to improve health; communication and health education; behavioral and social aspects of genetic counseling. Total annual research expenditures: $6.3 million. *Unit head:* Georgean Smith, Administrator, 410-502-3715, Fax: 410-502-4333, E-mail: gcsmith@jhsph.edu. *Application contact:* Barbara W. Diehl, Senior Academic Program Coordinator, 410-502-4415, Fax: 410-502-4333, E-mail: bdiehl@jhsph.edu.

McGill University, Faculty of Graduate and Postdoctoral Studies, Faculty of Medicine, Department of Human Genetics, Montréal, QC H3A 2T5, Canada. Offers genetic counseling (M Sc); human genetics (M Sc, PhD).

Mount Sinai School of Medicine of New York University, Graduate School of Biological Sciences, New York, NY 10029-6504. Offers bioethics (MS); biological sciences (PhD); clinical research (MS); community medicine (MPH); genetic counseling (MS); neurosciences (PhD); MD/PhD. Terminal master's awarded for partial completion of doctoral program. *Degree requirements:* For master's, thesis; for doctorate, comprehensive exam, thesis/dissertation. *Entrance requirements:* For master's, GRE General Test; for doctorate, GRE General Test, GRE Subject Test, 3 years of college pre-med course work. Additional exam requirements/recommendations for international students: Required—TOEFL. Electronic applications accepted. *Faculty research:* Cancer, genetics and genomics, immunology, neuroscience, developmental and stem cell biology, translational research.

Northwestern University, The Graduate School, Program in Genetic Counseling, Evanston, IL 60208. Offers MS. *Degree requirements:* For master's, thesis. *Entrance requirements:* For master's, GRE General Test, interview. Additional exam requirements/recommendations for international students: Required—TOEFL. *Faculty research:* Preimplantation genetic diagnosis, gene expression in preimplantation embryos, fetal cells in maternal blood: first trimester prenatal screening for Down's Syndrome, genetic counseling efficacy and counseling issues in prenatal diagnosis.

Sarah Lawrence College, Graduate Studies, Joan H. Marks Graduate Program in Human Genetics, Bronxville, NY 10708-5999. Offers MS. Part-time programs available. *Faculty:* 21 part-time/adjunct (16 women). *Students:* 41 full-time (40 women), 5 part-time (all women); includes 5 minority (3 Asian Americans or Pacific Islanders, 2 Hispanic Americans), 13 international. 137 applicants, 30% accepted, 24 enrolled. In 2009, 16 master's awarded. *Degree requirements:* For master's, thesis, fieldwork. *Entrance requirements:* For master's, previous course work in biology, chemistry, developmental biology, genetics, probability and statistics. *Application deadline:* For fall admission, 1/15 for domestic students. Application fee: $60. *Expenses:* Contact institution. *Financial support:* In 2009–10, 26 students received support, including 38 fellowships; career-related internships or fieldwork, Federal Work-Study, scholarships/grants, and unspecified assistantships also available. Support available to part-time students. Financial award application deadline: 3/1; financial award applicants required to submit CSS PROFILE or FAFSA. *Unit head:* Caroline Lieber, Director, 914-395-2371. *Application contact:* Susan Guma, Dean of Graduate Studies, 914-395-2373, E-mail: sguma@mail.slc.edu.

Université de Montréal, Faculty of Medicine, Programs in Genetic Counseling, Montréal, QC H3C 3J7, Canada.

University of Arkansas for Medical Sciences, Graduate School, Program in Genetic Counseling, Little Rock, AR 72205-7199. Offers MS. *Faculty:* 8 full-time (5 women), 4 part-time/adjunct (3 women). *Students:* 11 full-time. In 2009, 3 master's awarded. *Degree requirements:* For master's, thesis. *Entrance requirements:* For master's, GRE. Additional exam requirements/recommendations for international students: Required—TOEFL. *Application deadline:* For fall admission, 2/15 for domestic and international students. *Unit head:* Bruce Haas, Chair and Program Director, 501-526-7701, E-mail: brhaas@uams.edu. *Application contact:* Bruce Haas, Chair and Program Director, 501-526-7701, E-mail: brhaas@uams.edu.

The University of British Columbia, Faculty of Medicine, Department of Medical Genetics, M Sc Program in Genetic Counselling, Vancouver, BC V6H 3N1, Canada. Offers M Sc. Electronic applications accepted.

University of California, Irvine, School of Medicine, Department of Pediatrics, Program in Genetic Counseling, Irvine, CA 92697. Offers MS. *Students:* 11 full-time (6 women); includes 3 minority (2 Asian Americans or Pacific Islanders, 1 Hispanic American), 3 international. Average age 30. In 2009, 4 master's awarded. *Degree requirements:* For master's, thesis. *Entrance requirements:* For master's, GRE General Test, minimum GPA of 3.0. Additional exam requirements/recommendations for international students: Required—TOEFL (minimum score 550 paper-based; 213 computer-based). *Application deadline:* For fall admission, 1/15 priority date for domestic students, 1/15 for international students. Applications are processed on a rolling basis. Application fee: $70 ($90 for international students). Electronic applications accepted. *Financial support:* In 2009–10, 3 students received support; research assistantships with full tuition reimbursements available, teaching assistantships, career-related internships or fieldwork, institutionally sponsored loans, traineeships, health care benefits, and unspecified assistantships available. Financial award application deadline: 3/1; financial award applicants required to submit FAFSA. *Faculty research:* Gene mapping and linkage analysis, delineation of new malformation and chromosomal syndromes, ethical and counseling issues in genetics. *Unit head:* Dr. Ann P. Walker, Director, 714-456-5789, Fax: 714-456-5330, E-mail: awalker@uci.edu. *Application contact:* Evelyn Hohlfeld, Administrative Assistant, 714-456-8520, Fax: 714-456-5330, E-mail: eahohlfe@uci.edu.

University of Cincinnati, Graduate School, College of Allied Health Sciences, Program in Genetic Counseling, Cincinnati, OH 45221. Offers medical genetics (MS). Part-time programs available. *Degree requirements:* For master's, thesis. *Entrance requirements:* For master's, GRE General Test. Additional exam requirements/recommendations for international students: Required—TOEFL. Electronic applications accepted. *Faculty research:* Lysosomal disease, Tourette's syndrome, epidemiology of Down syndrome, genetic counseling, genetic disease treatment.

University of Colorado Denver, School of Medicine, Program in Medical Genetics and Genetic Counseling, Denver, CO 80217-3364. Offers genetic counseling (MS); human medical genetics (PhD). *Students:* 22 full-time (17 women). In 2009, 6 master's, 14 doctorates awarded. *Degree requirements:* For doctorate, thesis/dissertation, 3 laboratory rotations. *Entrance requirements:* For doctorate, GRE General Test, minimum GPA of 3.0, 4 letters of recommendation. Additional exam requirements/recommendations for international students: Required—TOEFL (minimum score 550 paper-based; 213 computer-based). *Application deadline:* For fall admission, 1/1 for domestic students. Application fee: $50. *Financial support:* Fellowships, research assistantships, teaching assistantships, Federal Work-Study and institutionally sponsored loans available. Support available to part-time students. Financial award application deadline: 3/15; financial award applicants required to submit FAFSA. *Faculty research:* Genetics of colon cancer, cancer cytogenetics, tumor suppressor genes and cancer, molecular basis of inherited human disease, neurodevelopmental genetics. *Unit head:* Dr. Richard A. Spritz, Director, 303-724-3107, E-mail: richard.spritz@ucdenver.edu. *Application contact:* M. J. Stewart, Administrator, 303-724-3102, Fax: 303-724-3100, E-mail: mj.stewart@ucdenver.edu.

University of Michigan, Horace H. Rackham School of Graduate Studies, Program in Biomedical Sciences (PIBS), Department of Human Genetics, Ann Arbor, MI 48109. Offers human genetics (MS, PhD), including genetic counseling (PhD). Part-time programs available. Terminal master's awarded for partial completion of doctoral program. *Degree requirements:* For master's, research project; for doctorate, thesis/dissertation, oral defense of dissertation, oral preliminary exam. *Entrance requirements:* For master's, GRE General Test, 3 letters of recommendation; for doctorate, GRE General Test, GRE Subject Test (biology, biochemistry recommended), 3 letters of recommendation. Additional exam requirements/recommendations for international students: Required—TOEFL (minimum score 84 iBT). Electronic applications accepted. *Expenses:* Tuition, state resident: full-time $17,286; part-time $1099 per credit hour. Tuition, nonresident: full-time $34,944; part-time $2080 per credit hour. Required fees: $95 per semester. Tuition and fees vary according to course load, degree level and program. *Faculty research:* Molecular, developmental, statistical, and population genetics.

University of Minnesota, Twin Cities Campus, Graduate School, Program in Molecular, Cellular, Developmental Biology and Genetics, Minneapolis, MN 55455-0213. Offers genetic counseling (MS); molecular, cellular, developmental biology and genetics (PhD). *Faculty:* 89 full-time (31 women), 19 part-time/adjunct (17 women). *Students:* 86 full-time (49 women); includes 6 minority (1 American Indian/Alaska Native, 4 Asian Americans or Pacific Islanders, 1 Hispanic American), 23 international. Average age 24. 179 applicants, 11% accepted, 19 enrolled. In 2009, 12 master's, 6 doctorates awarded. Terminal master's awarded for partial completion of doctoral program. *Degree requirements:* For master's, thesis optional; for doctorate, thesis/dissertation. *Entrance requirements:* For master's and doctorate, GRE General Test. Additional exam requirements/recommendations for international students: Required—TOEFL (minimum score 625 paper-based; 263 computer-based; 80 iBT). *Application deadline:* For fall admission, 12/15 priority date for domestic and international students. Applications are processed on a rolling basis. Application fee: $55 ($75 for international students). Electronic applications accepted. *Financial support:* In 2009–10, 10 fellowships with full tuition reimbursements (averaging $23,000 per year), 79 research assistantships with full tuition reimbursements (averaging $24,500 per year), 11 teaching assistantships with partial tuition reimbursements (averaging $9,236 per year) were awarded; scholarships/grants, traineeships, and health care benefits also available. Financial award application deadline: 12/15. *Faculty research:* Membrane receptors and membrane transport, cell interactions, cytoskeleton and cell mobility, regulation of gene expression, plant cell and molecular biology. Total annual research expenditures: $9.1 million. *Unit head:* Kathleen Conklin, Director of Graduate Studies, 612-626-0445, Fax: 612-626-6140, E-mail: conkl001@umn.edu. *Application contact:* Sue Knoblauch, Student Support Coordinator, 612-624-7470, Fax: 612-626-6140, E-mail: mcdbg@umn.edu.

The University of North Carolina at Greensboro, Graduate School, Program in Genetic Counseling, Greensboro, NC 27412-5001. Offers MS. Electronic applications accepted.

University of Oklahoma Health Sciences Center, College of Medicine and Graduate College, Department of Genetic Counseling, Oklahoma City, OK 73190. Offers MS. *Entrance requirements:* For master's, GRE General Test, 3 letters of recommendation. *Expenses:* Tuition, state resident: full-time $3120; part-time $156 per credit hour. Tuition, nonresident: full-time $11,314; part-time $409.70 per credit hour. Required fees: $1471; $51.20 per credit hour. $223.25 per term.

University of Pittsburgh, Graduate School of Public Health, Department of Human Genetics, Program in Genetic Counseling, Pittsburgh, PA 15260. Offers MS. *Students:* 10 full-time (9 women), 10 part-time (all women); includes 1 minority (African American), 1 international. Average age 26. 66 applicants, 17% accepted, 10 enrolled. In 2009, 9 master's awarded. *Degree requirements:* For master's, comprehensive exam, thesis, clinical internship. *Entrance requirements:* For master's, GRE General Test, previous course work in biochemistry, calculus, and genetics. Additional exam requirements/recommendations for international students: Required—TOEFL (minimum score 550 paper-based; 213 computer-based; 80 iBT). *Application deadline:* For fall admission, 2/1 for domestic students, 4/1 for international students; for winter admission, 9/1 for international students; for spring admission, 2/1 for international students. Application fee: $95. Electronic applications accepted. *Expenses:* Tuition, state resident: full-time $16,402; part-time $665 per credit. Tuition, nonresident: full-time $28,694; part-time $1175 per credit. Required fees: $690; $175 per term. Tuition and fees vary according to program. *Financial support:* In 2009–10, 18 students received support, including 18 research assistantships with full tuition reimbursements available (averaging $31,140 per year). *Faculty research:* Statistical genetics, molecular genetics, cytogenetics, gene therapy. *Unit head:* Elizabeth A. Gettig, Director, 412-624-3018, Fax: 412-624-3020, E-mail: bgettig@pitt.edu. *Application contact:* Jeanette Norbut, Administrative Secretary, 412-624-3018, Fax: 412-624-3020, E-mail: jeanette.norbut@hgen.pitt.edu.

University of South Carolina, School of Medicine and The Graduate School, Graduate Programs in Medicine, Program in Genetic Counseling, Columbia, SC 29203. Offers MS. *Degree requirements:* For master's, comprehensive exam, internship, practicum. *Entrance requirements:* For master's, GRE General Test. Electronic applications accepted. *Expenses:* Contact institution. *Faculty research:* Genetic counseling, international, transition, prenatal diagnosis.

The University of Texas Health Science Center at Houston, Graduate School of Biomedical Sciences, Program in Genetic Counseling, Houston, TX 77225-0036. Offers MS. *Degree requirements:* For master's, thesis. *Entrance requirements:* For master's, GRE General Test. Additional exam requirements/recommendations for international students: Required—TOEFL. Electronic applications accepted. *Faculty research:* Psychosocial aspects of genetic counseling, risk assessment, cancer genetic counseling, multicultural genetic counseling, prenatal counseling.

University of Toronto, School of Graduate Studies, Life Sciences Division, Department of Molecular and Medical Genetics, Toronto, ON M5S 1A1, Canada. Offers genetic counseling (M Sc); molecular and medical genetics (M Sc, PhD). *Degree requirements:* For master's, thesis; for doctorate, thesis/dissertation. *Entrance requirements:* For master's, B Sc or equivalent; for doctorate, M Sc or equivalent, minimum B+ average. Additional exam requirements/recommendations for international students: Required—TOEFL, IELTS (minimum score: 7), Michigan English Language Assessment Battery (minimum score: 85) or COPE (minimum score: 4). *Faculty research:* Structural biology, developmental genetics, molecular medicine, genetic counseling.

University of Wisconsin–Madison, Graduate School, College of Agricultural and Life Sciences and Graduate Programs in Medicine, Department of Genetics, Program in Genetic Counseling, Madison, WI 53706-1380. Offers MS. *Expenses:* Tuition, state resident: part-time $594 per credit. Tuition, nonresident: part-time $1504 per credit. Required fees: $65 per credit. Tuition and fees vary according to course load, program and reciprocity agreements.

Health Psychology

Adler School of Professional Psychology, Programs in Psychology, Chicago, IL 60601-7203. Offers art therapy (MA, Certificate); clinical hypnosis (Certificate); clinical psychology (Psy D); counseling (MA); counseling and organizational psychology (MA); forensic psychology (MA); gerontological counseling (MA); marriage and family counseling (MA); marriage and family therapy (Certificate); organizational psychology (MA); police psychology (MA); rehabilitation counseling (MA); sport and health psychology (MA); substance abuse counseling (Certificate); Psy D/Certificate; Psy D/MACAT; Psy D/MACP; Psy D/MAMFC; Psy D/MASAC. *Accreditation:* APA. Part-time and evening/weekend programs available. Postbaccalaureate distance learning degree programs offered (minimal on-campus study). *Faculty:* 41 full-time (21 women), 44 part-time/adjunct (19 women). *Students:* 551 full-time (441 women), 161 part-time (137 women). Average age 27.Terminal master's awarded for partial completion of doctoral program. *Degree requirements:* For master's, thesis or alternative, oral exam, practicum; for doctorate, thesis/dissertation, clinical exam, internship, oral exam, practicum, written qualifying exam. *Entrance requirements:* For master's, 12 semester hours in psychology, minimum GPA of 3.0; for doctorate, 18 semester hours in psychology, minimum GPA of 3.25; for Certificate, appropriate master's or doctoral degree. Additional exam requirements/recommendations for international students: Required—TOEFL (minimum score 550 paper-based; 213 computer-based; 79 iBT). *Application deadline:* For fall admission, 2/15 priority date for domestic students, 12/1 priority date for international students. Applications are processed on a rolling basis. Application fee: $50. Electronic applications accepted. *Expenses:* Tuition: Part-time $930 per credit. Required fees: $220 per term. *Financial support:* Career-related internships or fieldwork, Federal Work-Study, scholarships/grants, and tuition waivers (full and partial) available. Support available to part-time students. Financial award application deadline: 5/15; financial award applicants required to submit FAFSA. *Unit head:* Dr. Frank Gruba-McAllister, Vice President of Academic Affairs, 312-201-5900 Ext. 209, Fax: 312-201-

Health Psychology

Adler School of Professional Psychology (continued)
5917. *Application contact:* Craig A. Hines, Associate Vice President of Admissions, 312-201-5900 Ext. 226, Fax: 312-201-5917, E-mail: chines@adler.edu.

See Close-Up on page 1047.

American University of Beirut, Graduate Programs, Faculty of Health Sciences, Beirut, Lebanon. Offers environmental sciences (MSES), including environmental health; epidemiology (MS); epidemiology and biostatistics (MPH); health behavior and education (MPH); population health (MS); public health (MPH). Part-time programs available. *Degree requirements:* For master's, one foreign language, comprehensive exam, thesis (for some programs). *Entrance requirements:* For master's, 2 letters of recommendation. Additional exam requirements/recommendations for international students: Required—TOEFL (minimum score 573 paper-based; 230 computer-based; 98 iBT), IELTS (minimum score 7.5). Electronic applications accepted. *Faculty research:* Urban health, childbirth, tobacco control, HIV/AIDS surveillance, health finance and policies.

Appalachian State University, Cratis D. Williams Graduate School, Department of Psychology, Boone, NC 28608. Offers clinical health psychology (MA); general experimental psychology (MA); industrial and organizational psychology (MA). Part-time programs available. *Faculty:* 31 full-time (11 women). *Students:* 51 full-time (37 women), 13 part-time (10 women); includes 4 minority (2 African Americans, 2 Asian Americans or Pacific Islanders), 2 international. 181 applicants, 25% accepted, 26 enrolled. In 2009, 22 master's, 7 other advanced degrees awarded. *Degree requirements:* For master's and MS/Specialist, comprehensive exam, thesis optional, GRE Subject Test exit exam. *Entrance requirements:* For master's and MS/Specialist, GRE General Test, 3 letters of recommendation. Additional exam requirements/recommendations for international students: Required—TOEFL (minimum score 550 paper-based; 230 computer-based; 79 iBT), or IELTS (minimum score 6.5). *Application deadline:* For fall admission, 3/1 for domestic students, 2/1 for international students. Applications are processed on a rolling basis. Application fee: $50. Electronic applications accepted. *Expenses:* Tuition, state resident: full-time $2960. Tuition, nonresident: full-time $14,051. Required fees: $2320. *Financial support:* In 2009–10, 34 research assistantships (averaging $4,000 per year), 25 teaching assistantships (averaging $4,000 per year) were awarded; fellowships, career-related internships or fieldwork, Federal Work-Study, scholarships/grants, and unspecified assistantships also available. Financial award application deadline: 4/1; financial award applicants required to submit FAFSA. *Faculty research:* Eating disorders, school-based consultations, organizational behavior management, brain mechanisms of sound localization, parenting styles. Total annual research expenditures: $114,200. *Unit head:* Dr. James Denniston, Chair, 828-262-2272, Fax: 828-262-2272, E-mail: dennistonjc@appstate.edu. *Application contact:* Dr. Denise Martz, Graduate Coordinator, 828-262-2715, E-mail: martzdm@appstate.edu.

Argosy University, Atlanta, College of Psychology and Behavioral Sciences, Atlanta, GA 30328. Offers clinical psychology (MA, Psy D, Postdoctoral Respecialization Certificate), including child and family psychology (Psy D), general adult clinical (Psy D), health psychology (Psy D), neuropsychology/geropsychology (Psy D); community counseling (MA), including marriage and family therapy; counselor education and supervision (Ed D); forensic psychology (MA); industrial organizational psychology (MA); marriage and family therapy (Certificate); sport-exercise psychology (MA). *Accreditation:* APA.

See Close-Up on page 1049.

Argosy University, Chicago, College of Psychology and Behavioral Sciences, Doctoral Program in Clinical Psychology, Chicago, IL 60601. Offers child and adolescent psychology (Psy D); client-centered and experiential psychotherapies (Psy D); diversity and multicultural psychology (Psy D); family psychology (Psy D); forensic psychology (Psy D); health psychology (Psy D); neuropsychology (Psy D); organizational consulting (Psy D); psychoanalytic psychology (Psy D); psychology and spirituality (Psy D). *Accreditation:* APA.

See Close-Up on page 1051.

Argosy University, Schaumburg, College of Psychology and Behavioral Sciences, Schaumburg, IL 60173-5403. Offers clinical health psychology (Post-Graduate Certificate); clinical psychology (MA, Psy D), including child and family psychology (Psy D), clinical health psychology (Psy D), diversity and multicultural psychology (Psy D), forensic psychology (Psy D), neuropsychology (Psy D); community counseling (MA); counseling psychology (Ed D), including counselor education and supervision; counselor education and supervision (Ed D); forensic psychology (Post-Graduate Certificate); industrial organizational psychology (MA). *Accreditation:* ACA; APA.

See Close-Up on page 1077.

Argosy University, Twin Cities, College of Psychology and Behavioral Sciences, Eagan, MN 55121. Offers clinical psychology (MA, Psy D), including child and family psychology (Psy D), forensic psychology (Psy D), health and neuropsychology (Psy D), trauma (Psy D); forensic counseling (Post-Graduate Certificate); forensic psychology (MA); industrial organizational psychology (MA); marriage and family therapy (MA, DMFT), including forensic counseling (MA). *Accreditation:* APA.

See Close-Up on page 1083.

Argosy University, Washington DC, College of Psychology and Behavioral Sciences, Arlington, VA 22209. Offers clinical psychology (MA, Psy D), including child and family psychology (Psy D), diversity and multicultural psychology (Psy D), forensic psychology (Psy D), health and neuropsychology (Psy D); community counseling (MA); counseling psychology (Ed D), including counselor education and supervision; counselor education and supervision (Ed D); forensic psychology (MA). *Accreditation:* APA.

See Close-Up on page 1085.

Bastyr University, School of Nutrition and Exercise Science, Kenmore, WA 98028-4966. Offers nutrition (MS); nutrition and clinical health psychology (MS). Part-time programs available. *Students:* 86 full-time (84 women), 20 part-time (18 women). Average age 32. In 2009, 43 master's awarded. *Degree requirements:* For master's, thesis optional. *Entrance requirements:* For master's, 1 year of course work in chemistry, biochemistry, physiology and nutrition. Additional exam requirements/recommendations for international students: Required—TOEFL (minimum score 550 paper-based; 213 computer-based; 79 iBT). *Application deadline:* For fall admission, 3/15 priority date for domestic and international students. Applications are processed on a rolling basis. Application fee: $75. *Expenses:* Tuition: Full-time $23,478. Tuition and fees vary according to course level, course load and program. *Financial support:* Career-related internships or fieldwork, Federal Work-Study, and scholarships/grants available. Support available to part-time students. Financial award application deadline: 4/15; financial award applicants required to submit FAFSA. *Unit head:* Debra Boutin, Chair, 425-823-1300, Fax: 425-823-6222. *Application contact:* Admissions Office, 425-602-3330, Fax: 425-602-3090, E-mail: admissions@bastyr.edu.

California Institute of Integral Studies, School of Consciousness and Transformation, San Francisco, CA 94103. Offers creative inquiry (MFA); cultural anthropology and social transformation (MA); East-West psychology (MA, PhD); integrative health studies (MA); philosophy and religion (MA, PhD), including Asian and comparative studies, philosophy, cosmology, and consciousness, women's spirituality; social and cultural anthropology (PhD); transformative leadership (MA); transformative studies (PhD); writing and consciousness (MFA). Part-time and evening/weekend programs available. Postbaccalaureate distance learning degree programs offered (minimal on-campus study). *Students:* 334 full-time (218 women), 126 part-time (77 women); includes 116 minority (40 African Americans, 4 American Indian/Alaska Native, 42 Asian Americans or Pacific Islanders, 30 Hispanic Americans). Average age 38. 265 applicants, 90% accepted, 149 enrolled. In 2009, 64 master's, 22 doctorates awarded. Terminal master's awarded for partial completion of doctoral program. *Degree requirements:* For master's, comprehensive exam (for some programs), thesis optional; for doctorate, comprehensive exam, thesis/dissertation, 1 foreign language (Asian comparative studies). *Entrance requirements:* For master's, minimum GPA of 3.0, letters of recommendation, writing sample; for doctorate, master's degree, minimum GPA of 3.0, letters of recommendation, writing sample. Additional exam requirements/recommendations for international students: Required—TOEFL. *Application deadline:* For fall admission, 2/1 priority date for domestic and international students; for spring admission, 10/15 priority date for domestic and international students. Applications are processed on a rolling basis. Application fee: $65. Electronic applications accepted. *Expenses:* Tuition: Full-time $15,300; part-time $850 per credit hour. Required fees: $110 per semester. Tuition and fees vary according to degree level. *Financial support:* In 2009–10, 330 students received support; research assistantships, teaching assistantships, career-related internships or fieldwork, Federal Work-Study, scholarships/grants, and tuition waivers (partial) available. Support available to part-time students. Financial award application deadline: 4/15; financial award applicants required to submit FAFSA. *Faculty research:* Altered states of consciousness, dreams, cosmology, postcolonial studies, integrative health studies. *Application contact:* Allyson Werner, Associate Director of Admissions, 415-575-6155, Fax: 415-575-1268.

California Institute of Integral Studies, School of Professional Psychology, San Francisco, CA 94103. Offers clinical psychology (Psy D); community mental health (MA); drama therapy (MA); expressive arts therapy (MA); integral counseling psychology (MA); integral counseling psychology–weekend (MA); somatic psychology (MA). *Accreditation:* APA. Part-time programs available. *Students:* 639 full-time (483 women), 53 part-time (43 women); includes 148 minority (32 African Americans, 2 American Indian/Alaska Native, 62 Asian Americans or Pacific Islanders, 52 Hispanic Americans). Average age 38. 476 applicants, 71% accepted, 202 enrolled. In 2009, 136 master's, 21 doctorates awarded. *Degree requirements:* For master's, comprehensive exam; for doctorate, comprehensive exam, thesis/dissertation. *Entrance requirements:* For master's, minimum GPA of 3.0, letters of recommendation, writing sample; for doctorate, GRE, MA in psychology or social work with appropriate practical experience for advanced standing, or BA with a minimum GPA of 3.1; letters of recommendation; writing sample. Additional exam requirements/recommendations for international students: Required—TOEFL. *Application deadline:* For fall admission, 2/1 priority date for domestic and international students; for spring admission, 10/15 priority date for domestic and international students. Applications are processed on a rolling basis. Application fee: $65. Electronic applications accepted. *Expenses:* Tuition: Full-time $15,300; part-time $850 per credit hour. Required fees: $110 per semester. Tuition and fees vary according to degree level. *Financial support:* In 2009–10, 677 students received support; research assistantships with tuition reimbursements available, teaching assistantships with tuition reimbursements available, career-related internships or fieldwork, Federal Work-Study, scholarships/grants, and tuition waivers (partial) available. Support available to part-time students. Financial award application deadline: 4/15; financial award applicants required to submit FAFSA. *Faculty research:* Somatic psychology, comparative psychology, art therapy, transpersonal psychology, eco-psychology. *Application contact:* David Townes, Senior Admissions Counselor, 415-575-6152, Fax: 415-575-1268, E-mail: dtownes@ciis.edu.

Central Connecticut State University, School of Graduate Studies, School of Arts and Sciences, Department of Psychology, New Britain, CT 06050-4010. Offers community psychology (MA); general psychology (MA); health psychology (MA). Part-time and evening/weekend programs available. *Faculty:* 20 full-time (13 women), 22 part-time/adjunct (7 women). *Students:* 21 full-time (19 women), 31 part-time (27 women); includes 9 minority (4 African Americans, 5 Hispanic Americans). Average age 27. 49 applicants, 43% accepted, 17 enrolled. In 2009, 8 master's awarded. *Degree requirements:* For master's, comprehensive exam, thesis or alternative. *Entrance requirements:* For master's, minimum undergraduate GPA of 2.7, essay. Additional exam requirements/recommendations for international students: Required—TOEFL. *Application deadline:* For fall admission, 4/25 for domestic students; for spring admission, 12/1 for domestic students. Applications are processed on a rolling basis. Application fee: $50. Electronic applications accepted. *Expenses:* Tuition, area resident: Full-time $4662; part-time $440 per credit. Tuition, state resident: full-time $6994; part-time $440 per credit. Tuition, nonresident: full-time $12,988; part-time $440 per credit. Required fees: $3606. One-time fee: $62 part-time. *Financial support:* In 2009–10, 8 students received support, including 6 research assistantships; career-related internships or fieldwork, Federal Work-Study, scholarships/grants, and unspecified assistantships also available. Support available to part-time students. Financial award application deadline: 3/1; financial award applicants required to submit FAFSA. *Faculty research:* Clinical psychology, general psychology, child development, cognitive development, drugs/behavior. *Unit head:* Dr. Laura Bowman, Chair, 860-832-3100. *Application contact:* Dr. Laura Bowman, Chair, 860-832-3100.

Chatham University, Program in Counseling Psychology, Pittsburgh, PA 15232-2826. Offers child, adolescent and family (MSCP); counseling psychology (Psy D); health and holistic (MSCP); infant mental health (MSCP); organization and supervision (MSCP); sport and exercise (MSCP). Part-time and evening/weekend programs available. *Students:* 107 full-time (93 women), 77 part-time (67 women). Average age 29. 141 applicants, 76% accepted, 75 enrolled. In 2009, 63 master's awarded. *Degree requirements:* For master's, thesis optional, supervised internship; for doctorate, thesis/dissertation, internship. *Entrance requirements:* For master's, minimum GPA of 3.0; 2 letters of recommendation; resume; prerequisite coursework in statistics, biology, and psychology; for doctorate, GRE. Additional exam requirements/recommendations for international students: Required—TOEFL (minimum score 600 paper-based; 250 computer-based; 100 iBT), IELTS (minimum score 6.5), TWE. *Application deadline:* For fall admission, 5/1 priority date for domestic students, 6/1 priority date for international students; for spring admission, 12/1 for domestic students, 11/1 for international students. Applications are processed on a rolling basis. Application fee: $45. Electronic applications accepted. *Financial support:* Career-related internships or fieldwork available. Financial award applicants required to submit FAFSA. *Faculty research:* Trauma and recovery, hypnosis, psychospiritual dimensions of healing, psychotherapy of schizophrenia. *Unit head:* Dr. Mary Beth Mannarino, Director, 412-365-1196, Fax: 412-365-1505, E-mail: mmannarino@chatham.edu. *Application contact:* Dory Perry, Associate Director of Graduate Admissions, 412-365-2758, Fax: 412-365-1609, E-mail: gradadmissions@chatham.edu.

Claremont Graduate University, Graduate Programs, School of Behavioral and Organizational Sciences, Department of Psychology, Claremont, CA 91711-6160. Offers advanced study in evaluation (Certificate); cognitive psychology (MA, PhD); developmental psychology (MA, PhD); evaluation and applied research methods (MA, PhD); health behavior research and evaluation (MA, PhD); human resource development and evaluation (MA); industrial/organizational psychology (MA, PhD); organizational behavior (MA, PhD); organizational psychology (MA, PhD); social psychology (MA, PhD); MBA/PhD. Part-time programs available. *Faculty:* 17 full-time (7 women), 1 part-time/adjunct (0 women). *Students:* 231 full-time (155 women), 25 part-time (18 women); includes 62 minority (13 African Americans, 1 American Indian/Alaska Native, 31 Asian Americans or Pacific Islanders, 17 Hispanic Americans), 21 international. Average age 30. In 2009, 37 master's, 12 doctorates, 8 other advanced degrees awarded. Terminal master's awarded for partial completion of doctoral program. *Entrance requirements:* For master's and doctorate, GRE General Test. Additional exam requirements/recommendations for international students: Required—TOEFL (minimum score 550 paper-based; 213 computer-based; 80 iBT). *Application deadline:* For fall admission, 1/15 priority date for domestic students. Applications are processed on a rolling basis. Application fee: $60. Electronic applications accepted. *Expenses:* Tuition: Full-time $35,046; part-time $1524 per credit. Required fees: $161 per semester. *Financial support:* Fellowships, research assistantships, teaching assistantships, Federal Work-Study, institutionally sponsored loans, scholarships/grants, and tuition waivers (full and partial) available. Support available to part-time students. Financial award application deadline: 2/15; financial award applicants required to submit FAFSA. *Faculty research:* Social intervention, diversity in organizations, eyewitness memory, aging and cognition, drug policy. *Unit head:* Stewart Donaldson, Dean, 909-607-9001, Fax: 909-621-8905, E-mail: stewart.donaldson@cgu.edu. *Application contact:* Paul Thomas, Director, External Affairs, 909-607-9016, Fax: 909-621-8905, E-mail: paul.thomas@cgu.edu.

Drexel University, College of Arts and Sciences, Department of Psychology, Clinical Psychology Program, Philadelphia, PA 19104-2875. Offers clinical psychology (PhD); forensic psychology (PhD); health psychology (PhD); neuropsychology (PhD). *Accreditation:* APA. Terminal master's awarded for partial completion of doctoral program. *Degree requirements:* For doctorate, thesis/dissertation, qualifying exam. *Entrance requirements:* For doctorate, GRE General Test, GRE Subject Test, minimum GPA of 3.0. Electronic applications accepted. *Expenses:* Contact institution. *Faculty research:* Cognitive behavioral therapy, stress and coping, eating disorders, substance abuse, developmental disabilities.

Drexel University, College of Arts and Sciences, Department of Psychology, Program in Law-Psychology, Philadelphia, PA 19104-2875. Offers JD/PhD. Electronic applications accepted. *Expenses:* Contact institution. *Faculty research:* Mental health law issues, professional ethics, social science applications to law.

Duke University, Graduate School, Department of Psychology, Durham, NC 27708-0586. Offers biological psychology (PhD); clinical psychology (PhD); cognitive psychology (PhD); developmental psychology (PhD); experimental psychology (PhD); health psychology (PhD); human social development (PhD); JD/MA. *Accreditation:* APA (one or more programs are accredited). *Faculty:* 40 full-time. *Students:* 92 full-time (70 women); includes 13 minority (5 African Americans, 2 Asian Americans or Pacific Islanders, 6 Hispanic Americans), 14 international. 478 applicants, 8% accepted, 21 enrolled. In 2009, 10 doctorates awarded. *Degree requirements:* For doctorate, thesis/dissertation. *Entrance requirements:* For doctorate, GRE General Test. Additional exam requirements/recommendations for international students: Required—TOEFL (minimum score 550 paper-based; 213 computer-based; 83 iBT), IELTS (minimum score 7). *Application deadline:* For fall admission, 12/8 priority date for domestic and international students. Application fee: $75. Electronic applications accepted. *Financial support:* Fellowships, research assistantships, teaching assistantships, career-related internships or fieldwork and Federal Work-Study available. Financial award application deadline: 12/31. *Unit head:* Melanie Bonner, Director of Graduate Studies, Fax: 919-660-5715, E-mail: morrell@duke.edu. *Application contact:* Cynthia Robertson, Associate Dean for Enrollment Services, 919-684-3913, E-mail: grad-admissions@duke.edu.

East Carolina University, Graduate School, Thomas Harriot College of Arts and Sciences, Department of Psychology, Program in Health Psychology, Greenville, NC 27858-4353. Offers PhD. *Entrance requirements:* For doctorate, GRE.

John F. Kennedy University, Graduate School of Holistic Studies, Department of Counseling Psychology, Program in Counseling Psychology, Pleasant Hill, CA 94523-4817. Offers holistic studies (MA); somatic psychology (MA); transpersonal psychology (MA). Part-time and evening/weekend programs available. *Degree requirements:* For master's, thesis or alternative. *Entrance requirements:* For master's, interview. Additional exam requirements/recommendations for international students: Required—TOEFL.

Lesley University, Graduate School of Arts and Social Sciences, Self-Designed Master's Program in Interdisciplinary Studies, Cambridge, MA 02138-2790. Offers individualized studies (MA); integrative holistic health (MA); women's studies (MA). Part-time and evening/weekend programs available. Postbaccalaureate distance learning degree programs offered (no on-campus study). *Entrance requirements:* For master's, 3 letters of recommendation. Additional exam requirements/recommendations for international students: Required—TOEFL (minimum score 550 paper-based; 213 computer-based; 80 iBT).

National-Louis University, College of Arts and Sciences, Program in Psychology, Chicago, IL 60603. Offers community psychology (PhD); cultural psychology (MA); health psychology (MA); human development (MA); organizational psychology (MA); psychology (Certificate), including general, health, human development, organizational, psychological assessment. Part-time and evening/weekend programs available. *Degree requirements:* For master's, thesis, internship (health psychology). *Entrance requirements:* For master's, GRE General Test, MAT, or Watson-Glaser Critical Thinking Appraisal, interview, minimum GPA of 3.0; for Certificate, GRE, MAT, or Watson-Glaser Critical Thinking Appraisal, interview, minimum GPA of 3.0, undergraduate course work in psychology. *Expenses:* Tuition: Full-time $17,160; part-time $715 per semester hour. Tuition and fees vary according to course load, degree level, campus/location and program. *Faculty research:* Human development, personality theory, abnormal psychology.

North Dakota State University, College of Graduate and Interdisciplinary Studies, College of Science and Mathematics, Department of Psychology, Fargo, ND 58108. Offers clinical psychology (MS); cognitive and visual neuroscience (PhD); health and social psychology (PhD); psychology (MS). *Faculty:* 18 full-time (4 women), 2 part-time/adjunct (1 woman). *Students:* 36 full-time (27 women); includes 4 minority (1 African American, 2 Asian Americans or Pacific Islanders, 1 Hispanic American), 1 international. Average age 24. 48 applicants, 33% accepted, 10 enrolled. In 2009, 3 master's, 1 doctorate awarded. *Degree requirements:* For master's, thesis; for doctorate, thesis/dissertation. *Entrance requirements:* For master's and doctorate, GRE General Test, GRE Subject Test. Additional exam requirements/recommendations for international students: Required—TOEFL (minimum score 525 paper-based; 197 computer-based; 71 iBT). *Application deadline:* For fall admission, 3/1 for domestic and international students. Application fee: $45 ($60 for international students). Electronic applications accepted. *Financial support:* In 2009–10, 36 students received support, including 2 fellowships with full tuition reimbursements available (averaging $16,000 per year), 23 research assistantships with full tuition reimbursements available (averaging $16,000 per year), 11 teaching assistantships with full tuition reimbursements available (averaging $6,000 per year); career-related internships or fieldwork, Federal Work-Study, institutionally sponsored loans, tuition waivers (full and partial), and unspecified assistantships also available. Support available to part-time students. Financial award application deadline: 3/1. *Faculty research:* Cognition science, neuropsychology, group behavior, applied behavior analysis, behavior therapy. Total annual research expenditures: $2 million. *Unit head:* Dr. Paul D. Rokke, Chair, 701-231-8622, Fax: 701-231-8426, E-mail: paul.rokke@ndsu.edu. *Application contact:* Dr. Paul D. Rokke, Chair, 701-231-8622, Fax: 701-231-8426, E-mail: paul.rokke@ndsu.edu.

Northern Arizona University, Graduate College, College of Social and Behavioral Sciences, Department of Psychology, Flagstaff, AZ 86011. Offers applied health psychology (MA); clinical psychology (MA); general psychology (MA); teaching of psychology (MA). Part-time programs available. *Faculty:* 20 full-time (10 women). *Students:* 26 full-time (15 women), 6 part-time (all women); includes 4 minority (1 American Indian/Alaska Native, 3 Hispanic Americans), 2 international. Average age 30. 58 applicants, 41% accepted, 16 enrolled. In 2009, 4 master's awarded. *Degree requirements:* For master's, comprehensive exam (for some programs), thesis (for some programs), oral defense. *Entrance requirements:* For master's, GRE General Test. Additional exam requirements/recommendations for international students: Required—TOEFL (minimum score 550 paper-based; 213 computer-based; 80 iBT), IELTS (minimum score 7), or a bachelor's degree from an English-speaking university and demonstrated proficiency. *Application deadline:* For fall admission, 2/15 priority date for domestic students, 9/1 priority date for international students. Applications are processed on a rolling basis. Application fee: $65. Electronic applications accepted. *Financial support:* In 2009–10, 12 teaching assistantships with partial tuition reimbursements (averaging $10,439 per year) were awarded; career-related internships or fieldwork, Federal Work-Study, institutionally sponsored loans, scholarships/grants, health care benefits, tuition waivers (full and partial), and unspecified assistantships also available. Support available to part-time students. Financial award application deadline: 3/30; financial award applicants required to submit FAFSA. *Unit head:* Dr. Laurie Dickson, Chair, 928-523-0575, Fax: 928-523-6777, E-mail: laurie.dickson@nau.edu. *Application contact:* Dr. Steven Barger, Graduate Coordinator, 928-523-1829, Fax: 928-523-6777, E-mail: steven.barger@nau.edu.

Northern Kentucky University, Office of Graduate Programs, College of Arts and Sciences, Program in Industrial-Organizational Psychology, Highland Heights, KY 41099. Offers industrial psychology (Certificate); industrial-organizational psychology (MS); occupational health psychology (Certificate); organizational psychology (Certificate). Part-time and evening/weekend programs available. *Students:* 8 full-time (6 women), 34 part-time (24 women); includes 2 minority (both African Americans), 2 international. Average age 29. 31 applicants, 74% accepted, 15 enrolled. In 2009, 14 master's, 4 other advanced degrees awarded. *Degree requirements:* For master's, thesis optional, capstone. *Entrance requirements:* For master's, GRE (minimum score 450 verbal, 450 quantitative, 3.5 writing), minimum GPA of 3.0, at least 9 semester hours of undergraduate psychology, 1 course in statistics. Additional exam requirements/recommendations for international students: Required—TOEFL (minimum score 550 paper-based; 213 computer-based; 79 iBT); Recommended—IELTS (minimum score 6.5). *Application deadline:* For fall admission, 6/1 priority date for domestic students, 6/1 for international students; for spring admission, 11/1 priority date for domestic students, 10/1 for international students. Applications are processed on a rolling basis. Application fee: $40. Electronic applications accepted. *Expenses:* Tuition, state resident: full-time $6912; part-time $384 per credit hour. Tuition, nonresident: full-time $12,150; part-time $675 per credit hour. Tuition and fees vary according to course load, program and reciprocity agreements. *Financial support:* Unspecified assistantships available. Financial award applicants required to submit FAFSA. *Faculty research:* Attitude development, employee surveys, factor analysis, the effect of gender and racial stereotypes on employment decisions, social conflict and human factors in the workplace, workplace abuse and bullying, psychological testing/measurement, leader social-cognitive skills. *Unit head:* Dr. Jeffrey Smith, Director, 859-572-5317, Fax: 859-572-6085, E-mail: smithj@nku.edu. *Application contact:* Dr. Peg Griffin, Director of Graduate Programs, 859-572-6934, Fax: 859-572-6670, E-mail: griffinp@nku.edu.

Philadelphia College of Osteopathic Medicine, Graduate and Professional Programs, Department of Psychology, Philadelphia, PA 19131-1694. Offers clinical psychology (Psy D); counseling and clinical health psychology (MS); organizational leadership and development (MS); psychology (Certificate, Post-Doctoral Certificate); school psychology (MS, Psy D, Ed S). *Accreditation:* APA. *Degree requirements:* For master's, thesis; for doctorate, comprehensive exam, thesis/dissertation, final project, fieldwork. *Entrance requirements:* For master's, GRE or MAT, minimum GPA of 3.0; course work in biology, chemistry, English, physics; for other advanced degree, PRAXIS. *Faculty research:* Depression in primary care, integrated primary care, geriatric mental health.

See Close-Up on page 1091.

Prescott College, Graduate Programs, Program in Counseling and Psychology, Prescott, AZ 86301. Offers adventure-based psychotherapy (MA); counseling psychology (MA); ecopsychology (MA); ecotherapy (MA); equine-assisted mental health (MA); expressive arts therapy (MA); somatic psychology (MA); student-directed independent study (MA). Part-time programs available. Postbaccalaureate distance learning degree programs offered (minimal on-campus study). *Faculty:* 3 full-time (all women), 35 part-time/adjunct (25 women). *Students:* 65 full-time (47 women), 44 part-time (39 women); includes 8 minority (2 African Americans, 2 American Indian/Alaska Native, 4 Hispanic Americans), 9 international. Average age 38. 77 applicants, 77% accepted, 40 enrolled. In 2009, 34 master's awarded. *Degree requirements:* For master's, thesis, fieldwork or internship, practicum. *Entrance requirements:* For master's, 2 letters of recommendation, resume. Additional exam requirements/recommendations for international students: Required—TOEFL (minimum score 500 paper-based; 173 computer-based). *Application deadline:* For fall admission, 4/15 priority date for domestic and international students; for spring admission, 9/15 priority date for domestic and international students. Applications are processed on a rolling basis. Application fee: $40. Electronic applications accepted. *Expenses:* Tuition: Full-time $14,712; part-time $613 per credit. Required fees: $50 per term. One-time fee: $150. Tuition and fees vary according to course load and degree level. *Financial support:* Career-related internships or fieldwork, Federal Work-Study, and scholarships/grants available. Financial award applicants required to submit FAFSA. *Unit head:* Dr. Christine Frydenborg, Chair, Fax: 928-776-5151, E-mail: csmith@prescott.edu. *Application contact:* Kerstin Alicki, Admissions Counselor, 877-412-8705, Fax: 928-277-4695, E-mail: admissions@prescott.edu.

Rutgers, The State University of New Jersey, New Brunswick, Graduate School-New Brunswick, Program in Psychology, Piscataway, NJ 08854-8097. Offers behavioral neuroscience (PhD); clinical psychology (PhD); cognitive psychology (PhD); interdisciplinary health psychology (PhD); social psychology (PhD). *Accreditation:* APA. *Degree requirements:* For doctorate, comprehensive exam, thesis/dissertation. *Entrance requirements:* For doctorate, GRE General Test, 3 letters of recommendation. Additional exam requirements/recommendations for international students: Required—TOEFL (minimum score 577 paper-based; 233 computer-based). Electronic applications accepted. *Faculty research:* Learning and memory, behavioral ecology, hormones and behavior, psychopharmacology, anxiety disorders.

San Diego State University, Graduate and Research Affairs, College of Health and Human Services, Graduate School of Public Health, San Diego, CA 92182. Offers environmental health (MPH); epidemiology (MPH, PhD), including biostatistics (MPH); global emergency preparedness and response (MS); global health (PhD); health behavior (PhD); health promotion (MPH); health services administration (MPH); toxicology (MS); MPH/MA; MSW/MPH. *Accreditation:* ABET (one or more programs are accredited); CAHME (one or more programs are accredited); CEPH (one or more programs are accredited). Part-time programs available. *Degree requirements:* For master's, comprehensive exam (for some programs), thesis (for some programs); for doctorate, thesis/dissertation. *Entrance requirements:* For master's, GMAT (MPH in health services administration), GRE General Test; for doctorate, GRE General Test. Additional exam requirements/recommendations for international students: Required—TOEFL. *Faculty research:* Evaluation of tobacco, AIDS prevalence and prevention, mammography, infant death project, Alzheimer's in elderly Chinese.

Santa Clara University, School of Education and Counseling Psychology, Department of Counseling Psychology, Program in Counseling, Santa Clara, CA 95053. Offers counseling (MA), including career development, correctional psychology, health psychology, Latino counseling. Part-time and evening/weekend programs available. *Students:* 2 full-time (both women), 17 part-time (14 women); includes 4 minority (1 African American, 2 Asian Americans or Pacific Islanders, 1 Hispanic American), 2 international. Average age 33. 6 applicants, 50% accepted, 0 enrolled. In 2009, 10 master's awarded. *Degree requirements:* For master's, comprehensive exam, thesis optional. *Entrance requirements:* For master's, GRE or MAT, minimum GPA of 3.0, 1 year of related experience. Additional exam requirements/recommendations for international students: Required—TOEFL. *Application deadline:* Applications are processed on a rolling basis. *Expenses:* Contact institution. *Financial support:* Fellowships, career-related internships or fieldwork, Federal Work-Study, institutionally sponsored loans, and scholarships/grants available. Support available to part-time students. Financial award application deadline: 5/15; financial award applicants required to submit FAFSA.

Santa Clara University, School of Education and Counseling Psychology, Department of Counseling Psychology, Program in Counseling Psychology, Santa Clara, CA 95053. Offers counseling psychology (MA), including career development, correctional psychology, health psychology, Latino counseling. Part-time and evening/weekend programs available. *Students:* 89 full-time (82 women), 113 part-time (90 women); includes 55 minority (1 African American, 21 Asian Americans or Pacific Islanders, 33 Hispanic Americans), 6 international. Average age 32. 88 applicants, 72% accepted, 40 enrolled. In 2009, 59 master's awarded. *Degree requirements:* For master's, comprehensive exam, thesis optional. *Entrance requirements:* For master's, GRE or MAT, minimum GPA of 3.0, 1 year of related experience. Additional exam requirements/recommendations for international students: Required—TOEFL. *Application deadline:* Applications are processed on a rolling basis. *Expenses:* Contact institution. *Financial support:* Fellowships, Federal Work-Study, institutionally sponsored loans, and scholarships/grants available. Support available to part-time students. Financial award application deadline: 5/15; financial award applicants required to submit FAFSA.

Saybrook University, Graduate College of Psychology and Humanistic Studies, San Francisco, CA 94111-1920. Offers clinical psychology (Psy D); human science (MA, PhD), including

Health Psychology

Saybrook University (continued)
consciousness and spirituality, humanistic and transpersonal psychology, integrative health studies, organizational systems, social transformation, transformative social change (MA); organizational systems (MA, PhD), including consciousness and spirituality, humanistic and transpersonal psychology, integrative health studies, leadership of sustainable systems (MA), organizational systems, social transformation; psychology (MA, PhD), including clinical psychology (PhD), consciousness and spirituality, creativity studies (MA), humanistic and transpersonal psychology, integrative health studies, Jungian studies, marriage and family therapy (MA), organizational systems, social transformation. Postbaccalaureate distance learning degree programs offered (minimal on-campus study). Terminal master's awarded for partial completion of doctoral program. *Degree requirements:* For master's, thesis or alternative; for doctorate, thesis/dissertation. Electronic applications accepted. *Faculty research:* Humanistic theory, health studies, organizational systems, consciousness and spirituality, social transformation.

Southwestern College, Program in Integral Somatic Psychology, Santa Fe, NM 87502-4788. Offers Certificate. *Faculty:* 1 (woman) full-time. *Students:* 9 part-time (6 women); includes 1 Hispanic American. 9 applicants, 100% accepted, 9 enrolled.Application fee: $25. *Application contact:* Dru Phoenix, Director of Admissions, 505-471-5756 Ext. 26, Fax: 505-471-4071, E-mail: admissions@swc.edu.

Stony Brook University, State University of New York, Graduate School, College of Arts and Sciences, Department of Psychology, Program in Social and Health Psychology, Stony Brook, NY 11794. Offers PhD. *Students:* 23 full-time (18 women); includes 6 minority (3 Asian Americans or Pacific Islanders, 3 Hispanic Americans), 3 international. Average age 28. 95 applicants, 12% accepted. In 2009, 9 doctorates awarded. *Degree requirements:* For doctorate, thesis/dissertation. *Entrance requirements:* For doctorate, GRE General Test, GRE Subject Test. Additional exam requirements/recommendations for international students: Required—TOEFL. *Application deadline:* For fall admission, 1/15 for domestic students. Application fee: $60. *Expenses:* Tuition, state resident: full-time $8370; part-time $349 per credit. Tuition, nonresident: full-time $13,250; part-time $552 per credit. Required fees: $933. *Unit head:* Dr. Marci Lobel, Head, 631-632-7651, E-mail: marci.lobel@stonybrook.edu. *Application contact:* Dr. Marci Lobel, Head, 631-632-7651, E-mail: marci.lobel@stonybrook.edu.

Texas State University–San Marcos, Graduate School, College of Liberal Arts, Department of Psychology, San Marcos, TX 78666. Offers health psychology (MA). *Faculty:* 13 full-time (6 women), 1 part-time/adjunct (0 women). *Students:* 32 full-time (26 women), 11 part-time (9 women); includes 14 minority (2 Asian Americans or Pacific Islanders, 12 Hispanic Americans). Average age 27. 38 applicants, 68% accepted, 15 enrolled. In 2009, 16 master's awarded. *Degree requirements:* For master's, comprehensive exam, thesis (for some programs). *Entrance requirements:* For master's, GRE General Test, minimum GPA of 3.0 in last 60 hours, in psychology, and in psychology core courses; 3 letters of recommendation; statement of purpose. Additional exam requirements/recommendations for international students: Required—TOEFL (minimum score 550 paper-based; 213 computer-based). *Application deadline:* For fall admission, 3/15 for domestic and international students. Applications are processed on a rolling basis. Application fee: $40 ($90 for international students). Electronic applications accepted. *Expenses:* Tuition, state resident: full-time $5784; part-time $241 per credit hour. Tuition, nonresident: part-time $551 per credit hour. Required fees: $1728; $48 per credit hour. $306. Tuition and fees vary according to course load. *Financial support:* In 2009–10, 26 students received support, including 2 research assistantships (averaging $5,467 per year), 14 teaching assistantships (averaging $2,946 per year). Financial award application deadline: 4/1. *Faculty research:* Gaze interaction, stress and alcohol. Total annual research expenditures: $67,834. *Unit head:* Dr. Maria Czyzewska, Graduate Advisor, 512-245-2526, Fax: 512-245-3153, E-mail: mc07@txstate.edu. *Application contact:* Dr. Michael Willoughby, Dean of Graduate College, 512-245-2581, Fax: 512-245-8365, E-mail: gradcollege@txstate.edu.

The University of British Columbia, Faculty of Arts and Faculty of Graduate Studies, Department of Psychology, Vancouver, BC V6T 1Z4, Canada. Offers behavioral neuroscience (MA, PhD); clinical psychology (MA, PhD); cognitive science (MA, PhD); developmental psychology (MA, PhD); health psychology (MA, PhD); quantitative methods (MA, PhD); social/personality psychology (MA, PhD). *Accreditation:* APA (one or more programs are accredited). Terminal master's awarded for partial completion of doctoral program. *Degree requirements:* For master's, thesis; for doctorate, comprehensive exam, thesis/dissertation. *Entrance requirements:* For master's and doctorate, GRE General Test. Additional exam requirements/recommendations for international students: Required—TOEFL (minimum score 550 paper-based; 230 computer-based; 80 iBT). Electronic applications accepted. *Faculty research:* Clinical, developmental, social/personality, cognition, behavioral neuroscience.

University of Colorado Denver, College of Liberal Arts and Sciences, Program in Clinical Health Psychology, Denver, CO 80217-3364. Offers PhD. *Students:* 9 full-time (7 women), 1 international. 28 applicants, 18% accepted, 4 enrolled.*Unit head:* Dr. Allison Bashe, Program Director, 303-556-2669, E-mail: allison.bashe@cudenver.edu. *Application contact:* Dr. Brenda Allen, Associate Dean of Student Affairs, 303-556-6713, E-mail: brenda.j.allen@ucdenver.edu.

University of Connecticut, Graduate School, College of Liberal Arts and Sciences, Department of Psychology, Storrs, CT 06269. Offers behavioral neuroscience (PhD); biopsychology (PhD); clinical psychology (MA, PhD); cognition and instruction (PhD); developmental psychology (MA, PhD); ecological psychology (PhD); experimental psychology (PhD); general psychology (MA, PhD); health psychology (Graduate Certificate); industrial/organizational psychology (PhD); language and cognition (PhD); neuroscience (PhD); occupational health psychology (Graduate Certificate); social psychology (MA, PhD). *Accreditation:* APA. *Faculty:* 59 full-time (26 women). *Students:* 194 full-time (133 women), 24 part-time (12 women); includes 48 minority (12 African Americans, 21 Asian Americans or Pacific Islanders, 15 Hispanic Americans), 25 international. Average age 28. 585 applicants, 4% accepted, 14 enrolled. In 2009, 22 master's, 24 doctorates awarded. Terminal master's awarded for partial completion of doctoral program. *Degree requirements:* For master's, comprehensive exam; for doctorate, thesis/dissertation. *Entrance requirements:* For master's and doctorate, GRE General Test, GRE Subject Test. Additional exam requirements/recommendations for international students: Required—TOEFL (minimum score 550 paper-based; 213 computer-based). *Application deadline:* For fall admission, 2/1 priority date for domestic and international students; for spring admission, 11/1 for domestic students, 10/1 for international students. Applications are processed on a rolling basis. Application fee: $55. Electronic applications accepted. *Expenses:* Tuition, state resident: full-time $4725; part-time $525 per credit. Tuition, nonresident: full-time $12,267; part-time $1363 per credit. Required fees: $346 per semester. Tuition and fees vary according to course load. *Financial support:* In 2009–10, 109 research assistantships with full tuition reimbursements, 72 teaching assistantships with full tuition reimbursements were awarded; fellowships, career-related internships or fieldwork, Federal Work-Study, scholarships/grants, health care benefits, and unspecified assistantships also available. Financial award application deadline: 2/1; financial award applicants required to submit FAFSA. *Unit head:* Charles A. Lowe, Head, 860-486-3517, Fax: 860-486-2760, E-mail: charles.lowe@uconn.edu. *Application contact:* Charles A. Lowe, Head, 860-486-3517, Fax: 860-486-2760, E-mail: charles.lowe@uconn.edu.

University of Florida, Graduate School, College of Public Health and Health Professions, Department of Clinical and Health Psychology, Gainesville, FL 32611. Offers PhD. *Accreditation:* APA. *Degree requirements:* For doctorate, thesis/dissertation. *Entrance requirements:* For doctorate, GRE General Test, minimum GPA of 3.0. Additional exam requirements/recommendations for international students: Required—TOEFL (minimum score 550 paper-based; 213 computer-based). Electronic applications accepted. *Faculty research:* Child psychology, pediatric psychology, health/medical psychology, neuropsychology.

University of Michigan–Dearborn, College of Arts, Sciences, and Letters, Master of Science in Psychology Program, Dearborn, MI 48128. Offers clinical health psychology (MS); health psychology (MS). Part-time programs available. *Faculty:* 8 full-time (4 women), 1 part-time/adjunct (0 women). *Students:* 23 full-time (19 women), 11 part-time (10 women); includes 6 minority (2 African Americans, 3 Asian Americans or Pacific Islanders, 1 Hispanic American). Average age 34. 40 applicants, 40% accepted, 13 enrolled. In 2009, 15 master's awarded. *Degree requirements:* For master's, oral defense of thesis. *Entrance requirements:* For master's, GRE, 3 letters of recommendation. Additional exam requirements/recommendations for international students: Required—TOEFL (minimum score 560 paper-based; 220 computer-based). *Application deadline:* For fall admission, 3/15 for domestic and international students. Application fee: $60 ($75 for international students). *Expenses:* Tuition, area resident: Part-time $504.10 per credit hour. Tuition, state resident: part-time $504.10 per credit hour. Tuition, nonresident: part-time $957.90 per credit hour. *Financial support:* In 2009–10, 4 students received support. Scholarships/grants available. *Faculty research:* Cardiovascular reactivity, coping, addiction, psychoneuroimmunology. *Unit head:* Dr. Pam McAuslan, Program Director, 313-593-5376, E-mail: pmcausla@umd.umich.edu. *Application contact:* Carol Ligienza, Graduate Program Coordinator, CASL Graduate Programs, 313-593-1183, Fax: 313-583-6700, E-mail: caslgrad@umd.umich.edu.

University of Missouri–Kansas City, College of Arts and Sciences, Department of Psychology, Kansas City, MO 64110-2499. Offers clinical psychology (PhD); community psychology (PhD); health psychology (PhD); psychology (MA). PhD (interdisciplinary) offered through the School of Graduate Studies. *Accreditation:* APA. *Faculty:* 12 full-time (9 women), 3 part-time/adjunct (2 women). *Students:* 15 full-time (12 women), 7 part-time (6 women); includes 2 minority (1 African American, 1 Hispanic American). Average age 31. 86 applicants, 3% accepted, 3 enrolled. In 2009, 4 master's, 4 doctorates awarded. Terminal master's awarded for partial completion of doctoral program. *Degree requirements:* For master's, thesis; for doctorate, comprehensive exam, thesis/dissertation, residency. *Entrance requirements:* For master's, GRE, minimum GPA of 3.5, letter of recommendation; for doctorate, GRE, minimum GPA of 3.25. Additional exam requirements/recommendations for international students: Required—TOEFL (minimum score 550 paper-based; 213 computer-based; 80 iBT). *Application deadline:* For fall admission, 1/15 for domestic and international students. Applications are processed on a rolling basis. Application fee: $45 ($50 for international students). Electronic applications accepted. *Expenses:* Tuition, state resident: full-time $5378; part-time $299 per credit hour. Tuition, nonresident: full-time $13,881; part-time $771 per credit hour. Required fees: $641; $71 per credit hour. Tuition and fees vary according to course load and program. *Financial support:* In 2009–10, 18 research assistantships (averaging $11,500 per year), 3 teaching assistantships (averaging $8,000 per year) were awarded; career-related internships or fieldwork, Federal Work-Study, and institutionally sponsored loans also available. Support available to part-time students. Financial award application deadline: 3/1; financial award applicants required to submit FAFSA. *Faculty research:* HIV/AIDS research group, psycho-oncology, sensory and cognitive neuroscience, cognitive psychophysiology, obesity and related metabolic disorders. Total annual research expenditures: $673,228. *Unit head:* Dr. Tamera Murdock, Chairperson/Professor, 816-235-1318, Fax: 816-235-1062, E-mail: murdockt@umkc.edu. *Application contact:* Dr. Lisa Terre, Director, Graduate Programs, 816-235-1318, Fax: 816-235-1062, E-mail: terrel@umkc.edu.

The University of North Carolina at Charlotte, Graduate School, College of Arts and Sciences, Department of Psychology, Program in Health Psychology, Charlotte, NC 28223-0001. Offers PhD. *Faculty:* 21 full-time (8 women), 7 part-time/adjunct (5 women). *Students:* 21 full-time (17 women), 7 part-time (all women); includes 2 African Americans, 3 Hispanic Americans. Average age 30. 41 applicants, 24% accepted, 3 enrolled.Terminal master's awarded for partial completion of doctoral program. *Entrance requirements:* For doctorate, GRE, minimum GPA of 3.0 in undergraduate major. Additional exam requirements/recommendations for international students: Required—TOEFL (minimum score 557 paper-based; 220 computer-based; 83 iBT). *Application deadline:* For fall admission, 12/1 for domestic and international students. Application fee: $55. *Financial support:* In 2009–10, 15 students received support, including 4 research assistantships (averaging $17,750 per year), 10 teaching assistantships (averaging $10,755 per year); fellowships, career-related internships or fieldwork, institutionally sponsored loans, scholarships/grants, traineeships, and administrative assistantship also available. Support available to part-time students. Financial award application deadline: 4/1; financial award applicants required to submit FAFSA. Total annual research expenditures: $476,892. *Unit head:* Dr. David Gilmore, Director, 704-687-4731, Fax: 704-687-3096, E-mail: dcgilmor@uncc.edu. *Application contact:* Kathy B. Giddings, Director of Graduate Admissions, 704-687-5503, Fax: 704-687-3279, E-mail: gradadm@uncc.edu.

University of North Texas, Robert B. Toulouse School of Graduate Studies, College of Arts and Sciences, Department of Psychology, Denton, TX 76203-5017. Offers clinical psychology (PhD); counseling psychology (MA, MS, PhD); experimental psychology (MA, MS, PhD); health psychology and behavioral medicine (PhD). *Accreditation:* APA (one or more programs are accredited). Terminal master's awarded for partial completion of doctoral program. *Degree requirements:* For master's, comprehensive exam, thesis or alternative; for doctorate, one foreign language, comprehensive exam, thesis/dissertation. *Entrance requirements:* For master's and doctorate, GRE General Test, interview. Additional exam requirements/recommendations for international students: Required—proof of English language proficiency required for non-native English speakers; Recommended—TOEFL (minimum score 550 paper-based; 213 computer-based; 79 iBT). *Application deadline:* Applications are processed on a rolling basis. Application fee: $50 ($75 for international students). Electronic applications accepted. *Expenses:* Tuition, state resident: full-time $4298; part-time $239 per contact hour. Tuition, nonresident: full-time $9878; part-time $549 per contact hour. Required fees: $265 per contact hour. *Financial support:* Fellowships, research assistantships, teaching assistantships, career-related internships or fieldwork, Federal Work-Study, and institutionally sponsored loans available. Financial award applicants required to submit FAFSA. *Application contact:* Graduate Coordinator, 940-565-2671, Fax: 940-565-4682, E-mail: amym@unt.edu.

The University of Texas at Arlington, Graduate School, College of Science, Department of Psychology, Arlington, TX 76019. Offers experimental psychology (PhD); health psychology (PhD); industrial organizational psychology (MS); psychology (MS). Part-time programs available. *Faculty:* 16 full-time (5 women), 1 part-time/adjunct (0 women). *Students:* 62 full-time (41 women), 10 part-time (7 women); includes 13 minority (5 African Americans, 2 Asian Americans or Pacific Islanders, 6 Hispanic Americans), 7 international. 72 applicants, 90% accepted, 22 enrolled. In 2009, 16 master's, 6 doctorates awarded. Terminal master's awarded for partial completion of doctoral program. *Degree requirements:* For master's, comprehensive exam or thesis; for doctorate, thesis/dissertation (for some programs). *Entrance requirements:* For master's and doctorate, GRE General Test, minimum GPA of 3.0 in last 60 hours of course work. Additional exam requirements/recommendations for international students: Required—TOEFL (minimum score 550 paper-based; 213 computer-based). *Application deadline:* For fall admission, 6/16 for domestic students. Applications are processed on a rolling basis. Application fee: $35 ($50 for international students). *Financial support:* In 2009–10, 4 fellowships (averaging $1,000 per year), 2 research assistantships with tuition reimbursements (averaging $15,000 per year), 28 teaching assistantships with tuition reimbursements (averaging $15,000 per year) were awarded; career-related internships or fieldwork, Federal Work-Study, institutionally sponsored loans, scholarships/grants, traineeships, tuition waivers (partial), and unspecified assistantships also available. Financial award application deadline: 6/1; financial award applicants required to submit FAFSA. *Unit head:* Dr. Robert Gatchel, Chair, 817-272-2281, Fax: 817-272-2364, E-mail: gatchel@uta.edu. *Application contact:* Dr. Jared Kenworthy, Graduate Advisor, 817-272-2281, Fax: 817-272-2364, E-mail: kenworthy@uta.edu.

University of the Sciences in Philadelphia, College of Graduate Studies, Program in Health Psychology, Philadelphia, PA 19104-4495. Offers MS. *Entrance requirements:* For master's, bachelor's degree in related field, minimum GPA of 3.0 in major. Additional exam requirements/recommendations for international students: Required—TOEFL, TWE. *Expenses:* Contact institution. *Faculty research:* Stress and immune system, women's health and breast cancer, memory, health care policy.

Virginia State University, School of Graduate Studies, Research, and Outreach, School of Engineering, Science and Technology, Department of Psychology, Petersburg, VA 23806-

0001. Offers behavioral and community health sciences (PhD); clinical health psychology (PhD); clinical psychology (MS); general psychology (MS). *Degree requirements:* For master's, one foreign language, thesis. *Entrance requirements:* For master's, GRE General Test.

Walden University, Graduate Programs, School of Psychology, Minneapolis, MN 55401. Offers clinical child psychology (Post-Doctoral Certificate); clinical psychology (Post-Doctoral Certificate); counseling psychology (Post-Doctoral Certificate); forensic psychology (MS), including forensic psychology in the community, general program, mental health applications, program planning and evaluation in forensic settings, psychology and legal systems; general psychology (Post-Doctoral Certificate); health psychology (Post-Doctoral Certificate); organizational psychology (Post-Doctoral Certificate); organizational psychology and development (Postbaccalaureate Certificate); psychology (MS, PhD), including clinical psychology (PhD), counseling psychology (PhD), crisis management and response (MS), general program (MS), general psychology (PhD), health psychology, leadership development and coaching (MS), media psychology (MS), organizational psychology (PhD), organizational psychology and development (MS), organizational psychology and nonprofit management (MS), program evaluation and research (MS), psychology of culture (MS), psychology, public administration, and social change (MS), social psychology (MS), terrorism and security (MS); teaching online (Post-Master's Certificate). Part-time and evening/weekend programs available. Postbaccalaureate distance learning degree programs offered (minimal on-campus study). *Faculty:* 33 full-time, 222 part-time/adjunct. *Students:* 3,546 full-time (2,761 women), 1,133 part-time (908 women); includes 1,723 minority (1,319 African Americans, 56 American Indian/Alaska Native, 101 Asian Americans or Pacific Islanders, 247 Hispanic Americans), 80 international. Average age 41. In 2009, 495 master's, 70 doctorates, 2 other advanced degrees awarded. Terminal master's awarded for partial completion of doctoral program. *Degree requirements:* For master's, thesis optional; for doctorate, thesis/dissertation, residency. *Entrance requirements:* For master's, bachelor's degree or equivalent in related field; minimum GPA of 2.5; official transcripts; goal statement; access to computer and Internet; for doctorate, master's degree or equivalent in related field; minimum GPA of 3.0;3 years of related professional/academic experience (preferred). Additional exam requirements/recommendations for international students: Required—TOEFL (minimum score 550 paper-based; 213 computer-based), IELTS (minimum score 6.5), or Michigan English Language Assessment Battery (minimum score 82). *Application deadline:* Applications are processed on a rolling basis. Application fee: $50. Electronic applications accepted. *Expenses:* Tuition: Full-time $13,665; part-time $560 per credit. Required fees: $1375. Tuition and fees vary according to course load, degree level and program. *Financial support:* In 2009–10, 290 students received support; fellowships, Federal Work-Study, scholarships/grants, unspecified assistantships, and family tuition reduction, active duty/veteran tuition reduction, group tuition reduction, interest-free payment plans available. Support available to part-time students. Financial award applicants required to submit FAFSA. *Unit head:* Dr. Melanie Storms, Associate Dean, 800-925-3368. *Application contact:* Jennifer Hall, Director of Enrollment, 866-4-WALDEN, E-mail: info@waldenu.edu.

West Chester University of Pennsylvania, Office of Graduate Studies, College of Health Sciences, Department of Health, West Chester, PA 19383. Offers emergency preparedness (Certificate); health care administration (Certificate); integrative health (Certificate); public health (MPH), including administration, community, environment, integrative, nutrition; school health (M Ed). *Accreditation:* CEPH. Part-time and evening/weekend programs available. *Students:* 15 full-time (9 women), 128 part-time (91 women); includes 41 minority (34 African Americans, 2 American Indian/Alaska Native, 5 Asian Americans or Pacific Islanders), 22 international. Average age 30. 83 applicants, 88% accepted, 41 enrolled. In 2009, 45 master's, 8 other advanced degrees awarded. *Degree requirements:* For master's, thesis (for some programs). *Entrance requirements:* For master's, one-page statement of career objectives, two letters of reference. Additional exam requirements/recommendations for international students: Required—TOEFL (minimum score 550 paper-based; 213 computer-based; 80 iBT). *Application deadline:* For fall admission, 4/15 priority date for domestic students, 3/15 for international students; for spring admission, 10/15 for domestic students, 9/1 for international students. Applications are processed on a rolling basis. Application fee: $35. Electronic applications accepted. *Expenses:* Tuition, state resident: full-time $6666; part-time $370 per credit. Tuition, nonresident: full-time $10,666; part-time $593 per credit. Required fees: $122.56 per credit. *Financial support:* In 2009–10, 11 research assistantships with full and partial tuition reimbursements (averaging $5,000 per year) were awarded; unspecified assistantships also available. Support available to part-time students. Financial award application deadline: 2/15; financial award applicants required to submit FAFSA. *Faculty research:* HIV/AIDS education, teacher preparation, water quality. *Unit head:* Dr. Roger Mustalish, Chair, 610-436-2931, E-mail: rmustalish@wcupa.edu. *Application contact:* Dr. Bethann Cinelli, Graduate Coordinator, 610-436-2267, E-mail: bcinelli@wcupa.edu.

Yeshiva University, Ferkauf Graduate School of Psychology, Program in Clinical Health Psychology, New York, NY 10033-3201. Offers PhD. *Accreditation:* APA. Part-time programs available. *Degree requirements:* For doctorate, comprehensive exam, thesis/dissertation. *Entrance requirements:* For doctorate, GRE General Test. *Expenses:* Tuition: Full-time $24,918; part-time $1022 per credit. Required fees: $175. *Faculty research:* Dieting, substance abuse, adolescent depression and suicide, cancer research, MS research.

Human Development

Argosy University, Chicago, College of Psychology and Behavioral Sciences, Doctoral Program in Clinical Psychology, Chicago, IL 60601. Offers child and adolescent psychology (Psy D); client-centered and experiential psychotherapies (Psy D); diversity and multicultural psychology (Psy D); family psychology (Psy D); forensic psychology (Psy D); health psychology (Psy D); neuropsychology (Psy D); organizational consulting (Psy D); psychoanalytic psychology (Psy D); psychology and spirituality (Psy D). *Accreditation:* APA.

See Close-Up on page 1051.

Arizona State University, Graduate College, College of Liberal Arts and Sciences, Division of Social Sciences, School of Social and Family Dynamics, Tempe, AZ 85287. Offers family and human development (MS, PhD); infant-family practice (MAS); marriage and family therapy (MAS); sociology (MA, PhD). *Degree requirements:* For master's, thesis or alternative; for doctorate, thesis/dissertation. *Entrance requirements:* For master's and doctorate, GRE.

Auburn University, Graduate School, College of Human Sciences, Department of Human Development and Family Studies, Auburn University, AL 36849. Offers MS, PhD. *Accreditation:* AAMFT/COAMFTE (one or more programs are accredited). Part-time programs available. *Faculty:* 20 full-time (12 women), 1 (woman) part-time/adjunct. *Students:* 28 full-time (24 women), 26 part-time (22 women); includes 18 minority (10 African Americans, 6 Asian Americans or Pacific Islanders, 2 Hispanic Americans), 6 international. Average age 28. 56 applicants, 55% accepted, 18 enrolled. In 2009, 15 master's, 2 doctorates awarded. *Degree requirements:* For master's, thesis, oral exam; for doctorate, thesis/dissertation. *Entrance requirements:* For master's, GRE General Test; for doctorate, GRE General Test, master's degree. *Application deadline:* For fall admission, 7/7 for domestic students; for spring admission, 11/24 for domestic students. Applications are processed on a rolling basis. Application fee: $50 ($60 for international students). *Expenses:* Tuition, state resident: full-time $6240. Tuition, nonresident: full-time $18,720. International tuition: $18,938 full-time. Required fees: $492. Tuition and fees vary according to course load, program and reciprocity agreements. *Financial support:* Research assistantships, teaching assistantships, Federal Work-Study available. Support available to part-time students. Financial award application deadline: 3/15; financial award applicants required to submit FAFSA. *Faculty research:* Family influences on personality and social development, parent-child relations, infancy, day care, parent education. *Unit head:* Dr. Leanne K. Lamke, Head, 334-844-4151, E-mail: mbradbar@humsci.auburn.edu. *Application contact:* Dr. George Flowers, Dean of the Graduate School, 334-844-2125.

Boston University, School of Education, Department of Literacy and Language, Counseling and Development, Program in Developmental Studies, Boston, MA 02215. Offers Ed M, Ed D, CAGS. *Degree requirements:* For doctorate, comprehensive exam, thesis/dissertation; for CAGS, comprehensive exam. *Entrance requirements:* For master's, doctorate, and CAGS, GRE General Test or MAT. Additional exam requirements/recommendations for international students: Required—TOEFL. Electronic applications accepted. *Expenses:* Tuition: Full-time $37,910; part-time $1184 per credit hour. Required fees: $386; $40 per semester. Part-time tuition and fees vary according to class time, course level, degree level and program. *Faculty research:* Moral development, social and cognitive development, language and literacy development, cross-cultural development.

Bowling Green State University, Graduate College, College of Education and Human Development, School of Family and Consumer Sciences, Bowling Green, OH 43403. Offers food and nutrition (MFCS); human development and family studies (MFCS). Part-time programs available. *Degree requirements:* For master's, thesis. *Entrance requirements:* For master's, GRE General Test, minimum GPA of 3.0. Additional exam requirements/recommendations for international students: Required—TOEFL. Electronic applications accepted. *Faculty research:* Public health, wellness, social issues and policies, ethnic foods, nutrition and aging.

Bradley University, Graduate School, College of Education and Health Sciences, Department of Educational Leadership and Human Development, Peoria, IL 61625-0002. Offers human development counseling (MA), including community and agency counseling, school counseling; leadership in educational administration (MA); leadership in human service administration (MA). *Accreditation:* ACA; NCATE. Part-time and evening/weekend programs available. *Degree requirements:* For master's, comprehensive exam, thesis optional. *Entrance requirements:* For master's, GRE General Test or MAT, interview, 3 letters of recommendation. Additional exam requirements/recommendations for international students: Required—TOEFL (minimum score 550 paper-based; 213 computer-based; 79 iBT).

Brigham Young University, Graduate Studies, College of Family, Home, and Social Sciences, Program in Marriage, Family and Human Development, Provo, UT 84602. Offers MS, PhD. *Accreditation:* AAMFT/COAMFTE. *Faculty:* 24 full-time (5 women). *Students:* 22 full-time (15 women); includes 1 minority (Asian American or Pacific Islander), 2 international. Average age 33. 27 applicants, 41% accepted, 8 enrolled. In 2009, 3 master's, 1 doctorate awarded. *Degree requirements:* For master's, thesis; for doctorate, comprehensive exam, thesis/dissertation, 2 publishable papers. *Entrance requirements:* For master's and doctorate, GRE General Test, minimum GPA of 3.0 in last 60 semester hours, letters of recommendation. Additional exam requirements/recommendations for international students: Required—TOEFL (minimum score 580 paper-based; 237 computer-based; 85 iBT), IELTS (minimum score 7). *Application deadline:* For fall admission, 1/10 for domestic and international students. Application fee: $50. Electronic applications accepted. *Expenses:* Tuition: Full-time $5580; part-time $301 per credit hour. Tuition and fees vary according to student's religious affiliation. *Financial support:* In 2009–10, 9 students received support, including 20 research assistantships with full and partial tuition reimbursements available (averaging $5,096 per year), 5 teaching assistantships with full and partial tuition reimbursements available (averaging $5,096 per year); scholarships/grants and unspecified assistantships also available. Financial award application deadline: 3/27. *Faculty research:* Family studies and family process; marriage; adolescence and emerging adulthood; adult development and aging; child development. *Unit head:* Dr. Richard Miller, Director, School of Life, 801-422-2069, Fax: 801-422-0230, E-mail: rick_miller@byu.edu. *Application contact:* Graduate Secretary, 801-422-2060, E-mail: mfhdgrad@byu.edu.

Brock University, Faculty of Graduate Studies, Faculty of Social Sciences, Program in Psychology, St. Catharines, ON L2S 3A1, Canada. Offers behavioral neuroscience (MA, PhD); life span development (MA, PhD); social personality (MA, PhD). Part-time programs available. *Degree requirements:* For master's, thesis; for doctorate, thesis/dissertation. *Entrance requirements:* For master's, GRE, honors degree; for doctorate, GRE, master's degree. Additional exam requirements/recommendations for international students: Required—TOEFL (minimum score 550 paper-based; 213 computer-based; 80 iBT), IELTS (minimum score 6.5), TWE (minimum score 4). Electronic applications accepted. *Faculty research:* Social personality, behavioral neuroscience, life-span development.

California State University, San Bernardino, Graduate Studies, College of Social and Behavioral Sciences, Department of Psychology, Program in Child Development, San Bernardino, CA 92407-2397. Offers psychology-life span (MA). *Students:* 13 full-time (all women), 9 part-time (8 women); includes 10 minority (2 African Americans, 8 Hispanic Americans). Average age 29. 29 applicants, 48% accepted, 12 enrolled. In 2009, 7 master's awarded. *Degree requirements:* For master's, comprehensive exam. *Entrance requirements:* For master's, minimum GPA of 3.0 in major. *Application deadline:* For fall admission, 8/31 priority date for domestic students. Application fee: $55. *Unit head:* Dr. Cherie Ward, Director, 909-537-7304, E-mail: sward@csusb.edu. *Application contact:* Stacy Brooks, Graduate Secretary, 909-537-5570, Fax: 909-537-7003, E-mail: sbrooks@csusb.edu.

Central Michigan University, College of Graduate Studies, College of Education and Human Services, Department of Human Environmental Studies, Mount Pleasant, MI 48859. Offers apparel product development and merchandising technology (MS); human development and family studies (MA); nutrition and dietetics (MS). Part-time and evening/weekend programs available. *Degree requirements:* For master's, thesis or alternative. Electronic applications accepted. *Faculty research:* Human growth and development, family studies and human sexuality, human nutrition and dietetics, apparel and textile retailing, computer-aided design for apparel.

Claremont Graduate University, Graduate Programs, School of Educational Studies, Claremont, CA 91711-6160. Offers Africana education (Certificate); education and policy (MA, PhD); higher education/student affairs (MA, PhD); human development (MA, PhD); public school administration (MA, PhD); quantitative evaluation (MA, PhD); special education (MA, PhD); teacher education (MA); teaching and learning (MA, PhD); urban leadership (PhD); MBA/PhD. Part-time programs available. *Faculty:* 18 full-time (12 women), 1 part-time/adjunct (0 women). *Students:* 279 full-time (190 women), 174 part-time (122 women); includes 196 minority (50 African Americans, 1 American Indian/Alaska Native, 37 Asian Americans or Pacific Islanders, 108 Hispanic Americans), 10 international. Average age 37. In 2009, 84 master's, 23 doctorates awarded. Terminal master's awarded for partial completion of doctoral program. *Entrance requirements:* For master's and doctorate, GRE General Test. Additional exam requirements/recommendations for international students: Required—TOEFL (minimum score 550 paper-based; 213 computer-based; 80 iBT). *Application deadline:* For fall admission, 2/1 priority date for domestic students. Applications are processed on a rolling basis. Application

Human Development

Claremont Graduate University (continued)

fee: $60. Electronic applications accepted. *Expenses:* Tuition: Full-time $35,046; part-time $1524 per credit. Required fees: $161 per semester. *Financial support:* Fellowships, research assistantships, Federal Work-Study, institutionally sponsored loans, and scholarships/grants available. Support available to part-time students. Financial award application deadline: 2/15; financial award applicants required to submit FAFSA. *Faculty research:* Education administration, K-12 and higher education, multicultural education, education policy, diversity in higher education, faculty issues. *Unit head:* Margaret Grogan, Dean, 909-621-8075, Fax: 909-621-8734, E-mail: margaret.grogan@cgu.edu. *Application contact:* Nicole Kouyoumdjian, Director of External Affairs, 909-607-8493, Fax: 909-621-8734, E-mail: nicole.kouyoumdjian@cgu.edu.

Clemson University, Graduate School, College of Health, Education, and Human Development, Program in Youth Development, Clemson, SC 29634. Offers MS. *Faculty:* 12 full-time (6 women). *Students:* 1 full-time (0 women), 39 part-time (27 women); includes 14 minority (13 African Americans, 1 Hispanic American). Average age 29. 12 applicants, 67% accepted, 5 enrolled. In 2009, 11 master's awarded. *Entrance requirements:* For master's, GRE General Test. Additional exam requirements/recommendations for international students: Required—TOEFL. *Application deadline:* Applications are processed on a rolling basis. Application fee: $70 ($80 for international students). Electronic applications accepted. *Expenses:* Contact institution. Total annual research expenditures: $22,010. *Unit head:* Dr. Kathy Headley, Associate Dean for Research and Graduate Programs, 864-656-2181, Fax: 864-656-5488, E-mail: ksn1177@clemson.edu. *Application contact:* Dr. William Quinn, Graduate Program Coordinator, 864-656-1501, Fax: 864-656-5488, E-mail: wquinn@clemson.edu.

Colorado State University, Graduate School, College of Applied Human Sciences, Department of Human Development and Family Studies, Fort Collins, CO 80523-1570. Offers MS, PhD. *Accreditation:* AAMFT/COAMFTE. Part-time programs available. *Faculty:* 15 full-time (10 women). *Students:* 24 full-time (23 women), 12 part-time (10 women); includes 2 minority (1 African American, 1 Hispanic American), 3 international. Average age 29. 84 applicants, 33% accepted, 5 enrolled. In 2009, 6 master's awarded. Terminal master's awarded for partial completion of doctoral program. *Degree requirements:* For master's, thesis or alternative; for doctorate, comprehensive exam (for some programs), thesis/dissertation, competency exams. *Entrance requirements:* For master's, GRE General Test, minimum GPA of 3.0; course work in human development, family studies, and statistics; letters of recommendation; interview; BS/BA in human development and family studies or related field; for doctorate, GRE General Test (50th percentile on Verbal and Quantitative sections and 4.5 on Analytical Writing section), minimum GPA of 3.0; coursework in human development, family studies, and statistics; letters of recommendation; departmental application; interview; BS/BA or master's degree in related field. Additional exam requirements/recommendations for international students: Required—TOEFL (minimum score 550 paper-based; 213 computer-based; 80 iBT). *Application deadline:* For fall admission, 1/2 for domestic and international students. Applications are processed on a rolling basis. Application fee: $50. Electronic applications accepted. *Expenses:* Tuition, state resident: full-time $6434; part-time $359.10 per credit. Tuition, nonresident: full-time $18,116; part-time $1006.45 per credit. Required fees: $1496; $83 per credit. *Financial support:* In 2009–10, 23 students received support, including 1 fellowship (averaging $31,140 per year), 9 research assistantships with full and partial tuition reimbursements available (averaging $8,905 per year), 13 teaching assistantships with full and partial tuition reimbursements available (averaging $7,006 per year); career-related internships or fieldwork, Federal Work-Study, institutionally sponsored loans, scholarships/grants, health care benefits, and unspecified assistantships also available. Financial award application deadline: 3/1; financial award applicants required to submit FAFSA. *Faculty research:* Promoting resiliency and optimal development; gender, culture and diversity; gerontology/aging; child and adolescent health; disabilities. Total annual research expenditures: $898,742. *Unit head:* Dr. Lise Youngblade, Department Head, 970-491-5558, Fax: 970-491-7975, E-mail: lise.youngblade@colostate.edu. *Application contact:* Dr. Karen C. Barrett, Graduate Chair, 970-491-7382, Fax: 970-491-7975, E-mail: karen.barrett@colostate.edu.

Cornell University, Graduate School, Graduate Fields of Human Ecology, Field of Human Development, Ithaca, NY 14853-0001. Offers developmental psychology (PhD), including cognitive development, developmental psychopathology, ecology of human development, social and personality development; human development and family studies (PhD), including ecology of human development, family studies and the life course. *Faculty:* 42 full-time (18 women). *Students:* 38 full-time (27 women); includes 3 minority (all Asian Americans or Pacific Islanders), 13 international. Average age 28. 81 applicants, 25% accepted, 12 enrolled. In 2009, 2 doctorates awarded. *Degree requirements:* For doctorate, comprehensive exam, thesis/dissertation, pre-doctoral research project, teaching experience. *Entrance requirements:* For doctorate, GRE General Test, 2 letters of recommendation. Additional exam requirements/recommendations for international students: Required—TOEFL (minimum score 550 paper-based; 213 computer-based; 77 iBT). *Application deadline:* For fall admission, 1/15 for domestic students. Application fee: $70. Electronic applications accepted. *Expenses:* Tuition: Full-time $29,500. Required fees: $70. Full-time tuition and fees vary according to degree level, program and student level. *Financial support:* In 2009–10, 26 students received support, including 2 fellowships with full tuition reimbursements available, 4 teaching assistantships with full tuition reimbursements available; research assistantships with full tuition reimbursements available, institutionally sponsored loans, scholarships/grants, health care benefits, tuition waivers (full and partial), and unspecified assistantships also available. Financial award applicants required to submit FAFSA. *Faculty research:* Cognitive development, developmental psychopathology, ecology of human development, family studies and the life course, social and personality development. *Unit head:* Director of Graduate Studies, 607-255-3181, Fax: 607-255-9856. *Application contact:* Graduate Field Assistant, 607-255-3181, Fax: 607-255-9856, E-mail: hdfs@cornell.edu.

DePaul University, School of Education, Chicago, IL 60106. Offers bilingual and bicultural education (M Ed, MA); curriculum studies (M Ed, MA, Ed D); educational leadership (M Ed, MA, Ed D), including administration and supervision (M Ed, MA), Catholic school leadership (M Ed, MA), physical education (M Ed, MA); human development and learning (MA); human services and counseling (M Ed, MA), including agencies, family concerns, and higher education, elementary schools, human services management, secondary schools; reading and learning disabilities (M Ed, MA); social culture studies in education and development (M Ed, MA), including curriculum studies/development; teaching and learning (early childhood, elementary and secondary) (M Ed), including elementary education (M Ed, MA), secondary education (M Ed, MA); teaching and learning (early childhood, elementary, and secondary) (MA), including elementary education (M Ed, MA), secondary education (M Ed, MA). *Accreditation:* NCATE. Part-time and evening/weekend programs available. *Faculty:* 61 full-time (40 women), 66 part-time/adjunct (41 women). *Students:* 799 full-time (779 women), 470 part-time (365 women); includes 319 minority (153 African Americans, 3 American Indian/Alaska Native, 48 Asian Americans or Pacific Islanders, 115 Hispanic Americans), 15 international. Average age 30. 635 applicants, 74% accepted, 318 enrolled. In 2009, 604 master's, 5 doctorates awarded. *Degree requirements:* For doctorate, thesis/dissertation. *Entrance requirements:* For master's, interview, minimum GPA of 2.75, 2 letters of recommendation; for doctorate, interview, master's degree, writing sample, 3 letters of recommendation. Additional exam requirements/recommendations for international students: Required—TOEFL (minimum score 550 paper-based; 213 computer-based; 80 iBT). *Application deadline:* Applications are processed on a rolling basis. Application fee: $40. Electronic applications accepted. *Expenses:* Tuition: Full-time $37,525; part-time $620 per credit hour. *Financial support:* In 2009–10, 14 research assistantships with tuition reimbursements (averaging $5,800 per year) were awarded; career-related internships or fieldwork also available. *Faculty research:* Reflective teaching, children at risk, loss, ethnicity, urban education. Total annual research expenditures: $1.6 million. *Unit head:* Dr. Marie Donovan, Dean, 773-325-7581, Fax: 773-325-7713, E-mail: mdonovan@depaul.edu. *Application contact:* Brandon Washington, Data Project Manager, 773-325-1152, Fax: 773-325-2270, E-mail: bwashin3@depaul.edu.

Duke University, Graduate School, Department of Psychology, Durham, NC 27708-0586. Offers biological psychology (PhD); clinical psychology (PhD); cognitive psychology (PhD); developmental psychology (PhD); experimental psychology (PhD); health psychology (PhD); human social development (PhD); JD/MA. *Accreditation:* APA (one or more programs are accredited). *Faculty:* 40 full-time. *Students:* 92 full-time (70 women); includes 13 minority (5 African Americans, 2 Asian Americans or Pacific Islanders, 6 Hispanic Americans), 14 international. 478 applicants, 8% accepted, 21 enrolled. In 2009, 10 doctorates awarded. *Degree requirements:* For doctorate, thesis/dissertation. *Entrance requirements:* For doctorate, GRE General Test. Additional exam requirements/recommendations for international students: Required—TOEFL (minimum score 550 paper-based; 213 computer-based; 83 iBT), IELTS (minimum score 7). *Application deadline:* For fall admission, 12/8 priority date for domestic and international students. Application fee: $75. Electronic applications accepted. *Financial support:* Fellowships, research assistantships, teaching assistantships, career-related internships or fieldwork and Federal Work-Study available. Financial award application deadline: 12/31. *Unit head:* Melanie Bonner, Director of Graduate Studies, Fax: 919-660-5715, E-mail: morrell@duke.edu. *Application contact:* Cynthia Robertson, Associate Dean for Enrollment Services, 919-684-3913, E-mail: grad-admissions@duke.edu.

East Tennessee State University, School of Graduate Studies, College of Education, Department of Human Development and Learning, Johnson City, TN 37614. Offers advanced practitioner (M Ed); community agency counseling (M Ed, MA); comprehensive concentration (M Ed); counseling (M Ed, MA); early childhood education (M Ed, MA); early childhood general (M Ed); early childhood special education (M Ed); early childhood teaching (M Ed); elementary and secondary (school counseling) (M Ed, MA); marriage and family therapy (M Ed, MA); modified concentration (M Ed). *Accreditation:* ACA; NCATE. Part-time programs available. *Degree requirements:* For master's, comprehensive exam, thesis (for some programs). *Entrance requirements:* For master's, GRE General Test, minimum GPA of 3.0. Additional exam requirements/recommendations for international students: Required—TOEFL (minimum score 550 paper-based; 213 computer-based). *Faculty research:* Drug and alcohol abuse, marriage and family counseling, severe mental retardation, parenting of children with disabilities.

Erikson Institute, Academic Programs, Chicago, IL 60654. Offers administration (Certificate); bilingual/ESL (Certificate); child development (MS); early childhood education (MS); infant mental health (Certificate); infant studies (Certificate); MS/MSW. Part-time and evening/weekend programs available. *Degree requirements:* For master's, comprehensive exam, internship; for Certificate, internship. *Entrance requirements:* For master's and Certificate, minimum GPA of 2.75. Additional exam requirements/recommendations for international students: Required—TOEFL. *Faculty research:* Assessment strategies from early childhood through elementary years; language, literacy, and the arts in children's development; inclusive special education; parent-child relationships; cognitive development.

Fielding Graduate University, Graduate Programs, School of Human and Organization Development, Santa Barbara, CA 93105-3538. Offers evidence-based coaching (Certificate); human and organizational systems (PhD); human development (PhD); integral studies (Certificate); organization management and development (MA, Certificate). Postbaccalaureate distance learning degree programs offered (minimal on-campus study). *Faculty:* 29 full-time (15 women), 20 part-time/adjunct (7 women). *Students:* 453 full-time (317 women), 161 part-time (111 women); includes 119 minority (63 African Americans, 5 American Indian/Alaska Native, 23 Asian Americans or Pacific Islanders, 28 Hispanic Americans), 46 international. Average age 48. 198 applicants, 95% accepted, 126 enrolled. In 2009, 42 master's, 45 doctorates, 90 other advanced degrees awarded. Terminal master's awarded for partial completion of doctoral program. *Degree requirements:* For master's, thesis or alternative; for doctorate, comprehensive exam, thesis/dissertation. *Entrance requirements:* For master's, minimum GPA of 2.5, letter of recommendation; for doctorate, 2 letters of recommendation, writing sample, resume, self-assessment statement. *Application deadline:* For fall admission, 3/1 for domestic and international students; for spring admission, 9/1 for domestic and international students. Application fee: $75. Electronic applications accepted. *Expenses:* Contact institution. *Financial support:* In 2009–10, 267 students received support. Scholarships/grants and health care benefits available. Support available to part-time students. Financial award application deadline: 5/15; financial award applicants required to submit FAFSA. *Unit head:* Dr. Charles McClintock, Dean, 805-898-2930, Fax: 805-687-4590, E-mail: cmcclintock@fielding.edu. *Application contact:* Carmen Kuchera, Admission Counselor, 800-340-1099, Fax: 805-687-9793, E-mail: ckuchera@fielding.edu.

The George Washington University, Graduate School of Education and Human Development, Individualized Master's Program, Washington, DC 20052. Offers MA Ed. *Students:* 1 (woman) part-time. 4 applicants, 100% accepted, 0 enrolled. In 2009, 8 master's awarded. *Degree requirements:* For master's, comprehensive exam. *Entrance requirements:* For master's, GRE General Test or MAT, minimum GPA of 2.75. *Application deadline:* For fall admission, 3/1 priority date for domestic students; for spring admission, 10/1 for domestic students. Applications are processed on a rolling basis. Application fee: $60. *Financial support:* Application deadline: 1/15. *Application contact:* Sarah Lang, Director of Graduate Admissions, 202-994-1447, Fax: 202-994-7207, E-mail: slang@gwu.edu.

Harvard University, Graduate School of Education, Doctoral Program in Education, Cambridge, MA 02138. Offers culture, communities and education (Ed D); education policy, leadership and instructional practice (Ed D); higher education (Ed D); human development and education (Ed D); quantitative policy analysis in education (Ed D); urban superintendency (Ed D). Part-time programs available. *Faculty:* 70 full-time (33 women), 36 part-time/adjunct (20 women). *Students:* 295 full-time (198 women), 23 part-time (11 women); includes 103 minority (40 African Americans, 4 American Indian/Alaska Native, 34 Asian Americans or Pacific Islanders, 25 Hispanic Americans), 33 international. Average age 32. 551 applicants, 9% accepted, 39 enrolled. In 2009, 41 doctorates awarded. Terminal master's awarded for partial completion of doctoral program. *Degree requirements:* For doctorate, thesis/dissertation. *Entrance requirements:* For doctorate, GRE General Test, 3 letters of recommendation. Additional exam requirements/recommendations for international students: Required—TOEFL (minimum score 600 paper-based; 250 computer-based; 100 iBT), TWE (minimum score 5). *Application deadline:* For fall admission, 12/14 for domestic and international students. Application fee: $85. Electronic applications accepted. *Expenses:* Contact institution. *Financial support:* In 2009–10, 265 students received support, including 129 fellowships with full and partial tuition reimbursements available (averaging $11,142 per year), 41 research assistantships (averaging $11,990 per year), 173 teaching assistantships (averaging $9,174 per year); career-related internships or fieldwork, Federal Work-Study, institutionally sponsored loans, scholarships/grants, health care benefits, tuition waivers (full and partial), and unspecified assistantships also available. Support available to part-time students. Financial award application deadline: 2/1; financial award applicants required to submit FAFSA. *Faculty research:* Learning and development, educational leadership and organizations, education policy analysis. Total annual research expenditures: $18.1 million. *Unit head:* Dr. Shu-Ling Chen, Assistant Dean for Doctoral Studies, 617-496-4406. *Application contact:* Information Contact, 617-495-3414, Fax: 617-496-3577, E-mail: gseadmissions@harvard.edu.

Harvard University, Graduate School of Education, Master's Programs in Education, Cambridge, MA 02138. Offers arts in education (Ed M); education policy and management (Ed M); higher education (Ed M); human development and psychology (Ed M); international education policy (Ed M); language and literacy (Ed M); learning and teaching (Ed M); mid-career mathematics and science (teaching certificate) (Ed M); mind brain and education (Ed M); risk and prevention (Ed M); school leadership (Ed M); special studies (Ed M); teaching and curriculum (teaching certificate) (Ed M); technology innovation and education (Ed M). Part-time programs available. *Faculty:* 70 full-time (33 women), 36 part-time/adjunct (20 women). *Students:* 598 full-time (448 women), 76 part-time (60 women); includes 132 minority (40 African Americans, 2 American Indian/Alaska Native, 58 Asian Americans or Pacific Islanders, 32 Hispanic Americans), 103 international. Average age 28. 1,574 applicants, 58% accepted, 640 enrolled. In 2009, 556 master's awarded. *Entrance requirements:* For master's,

GRE General Test, 3 letters of recommendation. Additional exam requirements/recommendations for international students: Required—TOEFL (minimum score 600 paper-based; 250 computer-based; 100 iBT), TWE (minimum score 5). *Application deadline:* For fall admission, 1/4 for domestic and international students. Application fee: $85. Electronic applications accepted. *Expenses:* Contact institution. *Financial support:* In 2009–10, 424 students received support, including 25 fellowships with full and partial tuition reimbursements available (averaging $15,890 per year); career-related internships or fieldwork, Federal Work-Study, institutionally sponsored loans, scholarships/grants, health care benefits, tuition waivers (full and partial), and unspecified assistantships also available. Support available to part-time students. Financial award application deadline: 2/1; financial award applicants required to submit FAFSA. *Faculty research:* Learning and development, educational leadership and organizations, educational policy analysis. Total annual research expenditures: $18.1 million. *Unit head:* Jennifer L. Petrallia, Assistant Dean for Master's Studies, 617-495-8445. *Application contact:* Information Contact, 617-495-3414, Fax: 617-496-3577, E-mail: gseadmissions@harvard.edu.

Hofstra University, School of Education, Health, and Human Services, Department of Curriculum and Teaching, Program in Learning and Teaching, Hempstead, NY 11549. Offers learning and teaching (Ed D), including applied linguistics, art education, arts and humanities, early childhood education, English education, human development, math education, math, science, and technology, multicultural education, physical education, science education, social studies education, special education. Part-time and evening/weekend programs available. *Students:* 5 full-time (all women), 21 part-time (17 women); includes 2 minority (1 African American, 1 Hispanic American), 1 international. Average age 38. 22 applicants, 68% accepted, 11 enrolled. *Degree requirements:* For doctorate, comprehensive exam, thesis/dissertation. *Entrance requirements:* For doctorate, GRE, 3 letters of recommendation, interview, 2 years full-time teaching experience. Additional exam requirements/recommendations for international students: Required—TOEFL (minimum score 550 paper-based; 213 computer-based; 80 iBT). *Application deadline:* Applications are processed on a rolling basis. Application fee: $60. Electronic applications accepted. *Expenses:* Tuition: Full-time $16,200; part-time $900 per credit hour. Required fees: $970; $145 per term. Tuition and fees vary according to program. *Financial support:* In 2009–10, 24 students received support, including 20 fellowships with full and partial tuition reimbursements available (averaging $4,906 per year); research assistantships with full and partial tuition reimbursements available, Federal Work-Study, institutionally sponsored loans, scholarships/grants, and tuition waivers (full and partial) also available. Support available to part-time students. Financial award applicants required to submit FAFSA. *Faculty research:* Critical thinking, professional development, teacher quality, quantitative research. *Unit head:* Dr. Bruce A. Torff, Director, 516-463-5803, Fax: 516-463-6196, E-mail: catajs@hofstra.edu. *Application contact:* Carol Drummer, Dean of Graduate Admissions, 516-463-4876, Fax: 516-463-4664, E-mail: gradstudent@hofstra.edu.

Hood College, Graduate School, Programs in Human Sciences, Frederick, MD 21701-8575. Offers human sciences (MA), including psychology; thanatology (MA, Certificate). Part-time and evening/weekend programs available. *Faculty:* 6 full-time (3 women), 6 part-time/adjunct (3 women). *Students:* 13 full-time (11 women), 86 part-time (77 women); includes 16 minority (11 African Americans, 2 American Indian/Alaska Native, 2 Asian Americans or Pacific Islanders, 1 Hispanic American), 2 international. Average age 35. 54 applicants, 89% accepted, 26 enrolled. In 2009, 42 master's, 31 other advanced degrees awarded. *Degree requirements:* For master's, comprehensive exam, capstone/research project. *Entrance requirements:* For master's, minimum GPA of 2.75. Additional exam requirements/recommendations for international students: Required—TOEFL (minimum score 575 paper-based; 231 computer-based; 89 iBT). *Application deadline:* For fall admission, 7/15 for domestic and international students; for spring admission, 12/15 for domestic and international students. Applications are processed on a rolling basis. Application fee: $35. Electronic applications accepted. *Expenses:* Tuition: Full-time $6480; part-time $360 per credit. Required fees: $100; $50 per term. *Financial support:* Applicants required to submit FAFSA. *Faculty research:* Mind-body medicine and multicultural healing, the New Orleans jazz funeral, death practices in African-American culture, bereavement theories and gender differences, Piaget's theory of cognitive development as a formal mathematical model. *Unit head:* Dr. Dana G. Cable, Director, 301-696-3758, Fax: 301-696-3597, E-mail: cable@hood.edu. *Application contact:* Dr. Allen P. Flora, Dean of Graduate School, 301-696-3811, Fax: 301-696-3597, E-mail: gofurther@hood.edu.

Howard University, School of Education, Department of Human Development and Psychoeducational Studies, Program in Human Development, Washington, DC 20059-0002. Offers MS. Offered through the Graduate School of Arts and Sciences. Part-time programs available. *Faculty:* 5 full-time (4 women), 2 part-time/adjunct (both women). *Students:* 1 (woman) full-time, 2 part-time (1 woman); all minorities (2 African Americans, 1 Hispanic American). Average age 28. 1 applicant, 100% accepted, 0 enrolled. In 2009, 2 master's awarded. *Degree requirements:* For master's, comprehensive exam, thesis, expository writing exam. *Entrance requirements:* For master's, GRE General Test, minimum GPA of 2.7. *Application deadline:* For fall admission, 2/15 priority date for domestic students; for spring admission, 11/1 for domestic students. Applications are processed on a rolling basis. Application fee: $45. Electronic applications accepted. *Financial support:* In 2009–10, fellowships with full and partial tuition reimbursements (averaging $15,000 per year), research assistantships with full and partial tuition reimbursements (averaging $4,583 per year) were awarded; career-related internships or fieldwork, Federal Work-Study, institutionally sponsored loans, scholarships/grants, tuition waivers (full and partial), and unspecified assistantships also available. Financial award application deadline: 2/15. *Faculty research:* Excess weight and obesity in black youth, diabetes, sickle–cell anemia. *Unit head:* Dr. Sylvan Alleyne, Professor/Coordinator, 202-806-7522, Fax: 202-806-5205, E-mail: salleyne@howard.edu. *Application contact:* Frazier Tate-Jackson, Administration Assistant, Department of HDPES, 202-806-7350, Fax: 202-806-5205, E-mail: fjackson@howard.edu.

Indiana University Bloomington, School of Health, Physical Education and Recreation, Department of Applied Health Science, Bloomington, IN 47405-7000. Offers health behavior (PhD); health promotion (MS); human development/family studies (MS); nutrition science (MS); public health (MPH); safety management (MS); school and college health programs (MS). *Accreditation:* CEPH (one or more programs are accredited). *Faculty:* 24 full-time (12 women). *Students:* 131 full-time (92 women), 22 part-time (20 women); includes 35 minority (22 African Americans, 1 American Indian/Alaska Native, 5 Asian Americans or Pacific Islanders, 7 Hispanic Americans), 29 international. Average age 31. 118 applicants, 71% accepted, 52 enrolled. In 2009, 43 master's, 6 doctorates awarded. *Degree requirements:* For master's, thesis optional; for doctorate, thesis/dissertation. *Entrance requirements:* For master's, GRE (MS in nutrition science), 3 recommendations; for doctorate, GRE, 3 recommendations. Additional exam requirements/recommendations for international students: Required—TOEFL (minimum score 550 paper-based; 213 computer-based; 79 iBT). *Application deadline:* For fall admission, 4/30 priority date for domestic students, 12/1 priority date for international students; for spring admission, 11/15 priority date for domestic students, 9/1 priority date for international students. Application fee: $55 ($65 for international students). *Financial support:* In 2009–10, 80 students received support, including 12 fellowships (averaging $2,316 per year), 50 research assistantships with full and partial tuition reimbursements available (averaging $6,973 per year), 27 teaching assistantships with full and partial tuition reimbursements available (averaging $11,067 per year); career-related internships or fieldwork, Federal Work-Study, institutionally sponsored loans, scholarships/grants, tuition waivers (partial), and fee remissions also available. Financial award application deadline: 3/1. *Faculty research:* Cancer education, HIV/AIDS and drug education, public health, parent-child interactions, safety education. Total annual research expenditures: $2.8 million. *Unit head:* Dr. Mohammad R. Torabi, Chair, 812-855-4808, Fax: 812-855-3936, E-mail: torabi@indiana.edu. *Application contact:* Dr. Mohammad R. Torabi, Chair, 812-855-4808, Fax: 812-855-3936, E-mail: torabi@indiana.edu.

Instituto Tecnologico de Santo Domingo, Graduate School, Santo Domingo, Dominican Republic. Offers applied linguistics (MA); construction administration (M Mgmt); corporate finance (M Mgmt); education (M Ed); engineering (M Eng), including data telecommunications, industrial engineering, logistics and supply chain, maintenance engineering, sanitary and environmental engineering, structural engineering; environmental science (M En S), including environmental education, environmental management, marine and coastal ecosystems, natural resources management; family therapy (MA); food science and technology (MS); human development (MA); human resources administration (M Mgmt); international business (M Mgmt); labor risks (M Mgmt); management (M Mgmt); marketing (M Mgmt); mathematics (MS); organizational development (M Mgmt); planning and taxation (M Mgmt); psychology (MA); social science (M Ed); upper management (M Mgmt). *Entrance requirements:* For master's, birth certificate, minimum GPA of 2.0.

Iowa State University of Science and Technology, Graduate College, College of Human Sciences, Department of Human Development and Family Studies, Ames, IA 50011. Offers human development and family studies (MFCS, MS, PhD). *Accreditation:* AAMFT/COAMFTE. *Faculty:* 23 full-time (18 women), 7 part-time/adjunct (5 women). *Students:* 62 full-time (54 women), 13 part-time (11 women); includes 6 minority (2 African Americans, 1 American Indian/Alaska Native, 3 Hispanic Americans), 12 international. 44 applicants, 82% accepted, 23 enrolled. In 2009, 11 master's, 3 doctorates awarded. *Degree requirements:* For master's, thesis; for doctorate, thesis/dissertation. *Entrance requirements:* For master's and doctorate, GRE General Test. Additional exam requirements/recommendations for international students: Required—TOEFL (minimum score 550 paper-based; 79 iBT) or IELTS (minimum score 6.5). *Application deadline:* For fall admission, 12/1 priority date for domestic and international students. Application fee: $40 ($90 for international students). Electronic applications accepted. *Expenses:* Tuition, state resident: full-time $6716. Tuition, nonresident: full-time $8908. Tuition and fees vary according to course level, course load, program and student level. *Financial support:* In 2009–10, 45 research assistantships with full and partial tuition reimbursements (averaging $14,880 per year), 11 teaching assistantships with full and partial tuition reimbursements (averaging $14,880 per year) were awarded; fellowships, scholarships/grants also available. *Faculty research:* Child development, early childhood education, family resource management and housing, life span studies. *Unit head:* Dr. Dianne Draper, Interim Chair, 515-294-6316, Fax: 515-294-2502, E-mail: hdfs-grad-adm@iastate.edu. *Application contact:* Dr. Dianne Draper, Interim Chair, 515-294-6316, Fax: 515-294-2502, E-mail: hdfs-grad-adm@iastate.edu.

Kansas State University, Graduate School, College of Human Ecology, Program in Human Ecology, Manhattan, KS 66506. Offers apparel and textiles (PhD); family life education and consultation (PhD); food service and hospitality management (PhD); lifespan and human development (PhD); marriage and family therapy (PhD); personal financial planning (PhD). *Faculty:* 3 full-time (all women). *Students:* 29 full-time (19 women), 43 part-time (23 women); includes 15 minority (13 African Americans, 1 American Indian/Alaska Native, 1 Asian American or Pacific Islander), 16 international. Average age 37. 29 applicants, 66% accepted, 16 enrolled. In 2009, 10 doctorates awarded. *Degree requirements:* For doctorate, thesis/dissertation. *Application deadline:* For fall admission, 2/1 priority date for domestic and international students; for spring admission, 8/1 priority date for domestic and international students. Applications are processed on a rolling basis. Application fee: $40 ($55 for international students). Electronic applications accepted. *Financial support:* Application deadline: 3/1. *Application contact:* Connie Fechter, Application Contact, 785-532-1473, Fax: 785-532-3796, E-mail: fechter@ksu.edu.

Kansas State University, Graduate School, College of Human Ecology, School of Family Studies and Human Services, Manhattan, KS 66506. Offers communication sciences and disorders (MS); early childhood education (MS); family studies (MS); life span human development (MS); marriage and family therapy (MS). *Accreditation:* AAMFT/COAMFTE; ASHA. Part-time programs available. *Faculty:* 25 full-time (15 women), 3 part-time/adjunct (2 women). *Students:* 76 full-time (67 women), 101 part-time (61 women); includes 17 minority (7 African Americans, 1 American Indian/Alaska Native, 2 Asian Americans or Pacific Islanders, 7 Hispanic Americans), 1 international. Average age 32. 117 applicants, 68% accepted, 47 enrolled. In 2009, 63 master's awarded. *Degree requirements:* For master's, thesis or alternative, oral exam, residency. *Entrance requirements:* For master's, GRE, minimum GPA of 3.0 in last 2 years of undergraduate study. Additional exam requirements/recommendations for international students: Required—TOEFL (minimum score 600 paper-based; 250 computer-based). *Application deadline:* For fall admission, 2/1 priority date for domestic and international students; for spring admission, 8/1 priority date for domestic and international students. Applications are processed on a rolling basis. Application fee: $40 ($55 for international students). Electronic applications accepted. *Financial support:* In 2009–10, 26 research assistantships (averaging $10,867 per year), 17 teaching assistantships with full and partial tuition reimbursements (averaging $11,635 per year) were awarded; Federal Work-Study, institutionally sponsored loans, scholarships/grants, and unspecified assistantships also available. Support available to part-time students. Financial award application deadline: 3/1; financial award applicants required to submit FAFSA. *Faculty research:* Health and security of military families, personal and family risk assessment and evaluation, disorders of communication and swallowing, families and health. Total annual research expenditures: $10.1 million. *Unit head:* Dr. Maurice McDonald, Head, 785-532-1472, E-mail: morey@ksu.edu. *Application contact:* Connie Fechter, Administrative Specialist, 785-532-1473, Fax: 785-532-5505, E-mail: fechter@ksu.edu.

Kent State University, Graduate School of Education, Health, and Human Services, School of Lifespan Development and Educational Sciences, Program in Counseling and Human Development Services, Kent, OH 44242-0001. Offers PhD. *Accreditation:* ACA; NCATE. *Faculty:* 8 full-time (4 women), 16 part-time/adjunct (11 women). *Students:* 49 full-time (39 women), 12 part-time (9 women); includes 12 minority (9 African Americans, 2 Asian Americans or Pacific Islanders, 1 Hispanic American). 23 applicants, 57% accepted. In 2009, 6 doctorates awarded. *Degree requirements:* For doctorate, comprehensive exam, thesis/dissertation. *Entrance requirements:* For doctorate, GRE General Test. Additional exam requirements/recommendations for international students: Required—TOEFL. *Application deadline:* For fall admission, 2/15 for domestic students. Application fee: $30. Electronic applications accepted. *Financial support:* In 2009–10, 12 fellowships with full tuition reimbursements (averaging $11,000 per year), research assistantships with full tuition reimbursements (averaging $11,000 per year), teaching assistantships with full tuition reimbursements (averaging $11,000 per year) were awarded; career-related internships or fieldwork, Federal Work-Study, institutionally sponsored loans, scholarships/grants, health care benefits, and unspecified assistantships also available. Support available to part-time students. Financial award application deadline: 4/1; financial award applicants required to submit FAFSA. *Faculty research:* Family/child therapy, clinical supervision, group work, experiential training methods. *Unit head:* Dr. John L. West, Coordinator, 330-672-0713, Fax: 330-672-5396, E-mail: jwest@kent.edu. *Application contact:* Nancy Miller, Academic Program Coordinator, Office of Graduate Student Services, 330-672-2576, Fax: 330-672-9162, E-mail: ogs@kent.edu.

Kent State University, Graduate School of Education, Health, and Human Services, School of Lifespan Development and Educational Sciences, Program in Family Studies, Kent, OH 44242-0001. Offers gerontology (MA); human development and family studies (MA). *Faculty:* 14 full-time (10 women), 9 part-time/adjunct (8 women). *Students:* 5 full-time (all women), 7 part-time (6 women); includes 1 minority (African American). 3 applicants, 100% accepted. In 2009, 2 master's awarded. Application fee: $30. *Financial support:* In 2009–10, 2 research assistantships (averaging $8,313 per year) were awarded. *Unit head:* Dr. Rhonda Richardson, Coordinator, 330-672-2026, E-mail: rrichard@kent.edu. *Application contact:* Nancy Miller, Academic Program Coordinator, 330-672-2576, Fax: 330-672-9162, E-mail: ogs@kent.edu.

Laurentian University, School of Graduate Studies and Research, Programme in Human Development, Sudbury, ON P3E 2C6, Canada. Offers M Sc, MA. Interdisciplinary program consisting of the Departments of Psychology, Sociology, and Human Movement. Part-time programs available. *Degree requirements:* For master's, thesis or alternative. *Entrance requirements:* For master's, honors degree with second class or better. *Faculty research:* Aging and well-being, physical, social and cognitive development of children, social cognition and social relationships including peers and family, education and schooling.

Human Development

Lehigh University, College of Arts and Sciences, Department of Psychology, Bethlehem, PA 18015. Offers human cognition and development (MS, PhD). *Faculty:* 13 full-time (7 women). *Students:* 14 full-time (11 women), 1 (woman) part-time, 4 international. Average age 27. 56 applicants, 14% accepted, 3 enrolled. In 2009, 5 master's awarded. *Degree requirements:* For master's, thesis; for doctorate, comprehensive exam, thesis/dissertation. *Entrance requirements:* For doctorate, GRE General Test. Additional exam requirements/recommendations for international students: Required—TOEFL. *Application deadline:* For fall admission, 1/15 for domestic and international students. Application fee: $75. Electronic applications accepted. *Expenses:* Contact institution. *Financial support:* In 2009–10, 15 students received support, including 1 fellowship with full tuition reimbursement available (averaging $22,000 per year), 3 research assistantships with full tuition reimbursements available (averaging $17,400 per year), 11 teaching assistantships with full tuition reimbursements available (averaging $17,400 per year); scholarships/grants, tuition waivers (full and partial), and unspecified assistantships also available. Financial award application deadline: 1/15. *Faculty research:* Cognition, memory, language, and their development; prosocial cognition, emotion, and action; conflict and cooperation between and within groups; self-control of cognition and emotion; optimizing developmental and relational outcomes. Total annual research expenditures: $142,283. *Unit head:* Diane Hyland, Chairperson, 610-758-3631, Fax: 610-758-6277, E-mail: dthl@lehigh.edu. *Application contact:* Dr. Michael Gill, Program Director, 610-758-3630, Fax: 610-758-6277, E-mail: inpsy@lehigh.edu.

Lindsey Wilson College, School of Professional Counseling, Columbia, KY 42728. Offers counseling and human development (M Ed). *Accreditation:* ACA. Part-time and evening/weekend programs available.

Marywood University, Academic Affairs, Reap College of Education and Human Development, Department of Human Development, Doctoral Program in Human Development, Scranton, PA 18509-1598. Offers PhD. *Students:* 5 full-time (4 women), 94 part-time (70 women); includes 4 minority (2 African Americans, 2 Hispanic Americans), 1 international. Average age 40. In 2009, 10 doctorates awarded. *Entrance requirements:* Additional exam requirements/recommendations for international students: Required—TOEFL (minimum score 550 paper-based; 213 computer-based; 79 iBT). *Application deadline:* For fall admission, 1/30 priority date for domestic and international students. Applications are processed on a rolling basis. Application fee: $35. Electronic applications accepted. *Expenses:* Contact institution. *Financial support:* Career-related internships or fieldwork, scholarships/grants, and unspecified assistantships available. Support available to part-time students. Financial award application deadline: 6/30; financial award applicants required to submit FAFSA. *Unit head:* Dr. Brook Cannon, Director, 570-348-6211 Ext. 2324, E-mail: cannon@marywood.edu. *Application contact:* Tammy Manka, Assistant Director of Graduate Admissions, 866-279-9663, E-mail: tmanka@marywood.edu.

Montana State University, College of Graduate Studies, College of Education, Health, and Human Development, Department of Health and Human Development, Bozeman, MT 59717. Offers health and human development (MS), including counseling, exercise and nutrition sciences, family and consumer sciences, family financial planning, health promotion and education. *Accreditation:* ACA. Part-time programs available. Postbaccalaureate distance learning degree programs offered (no on-campus study). *Faculty:* 27 full-time (18 women), 7 part-time/adjunct (6 women). *Students:* 54 full-time (47 women), 18 part-time (15 women); includes 1 minority (Hispanic American). Average age 30. 32 applicants, 34% accepted, 10 enrolled. In 2009, 26 master's awarded. *Degree requirements:* For master's, comprehensive exam. *Entrance requirements:* For master's, GRE General Test. Additional exam requirements/recommendations for international students: Required—TOEFL (minimum score 550 paper-based; 213 computer-based). *Application deadline:* For fall admission, 7/15 priority date for domestic students, 5/15 priority date for international students; for spring admission, 12/1 priority date for domestic students, 10/1 priority date for international students. Applications are processed on a rolling basis. Application fee: $30. Electronic applications accepted. *Expenses:* Tuition, state resident: full-time $5635; part-time $3492 per year. Tuition, nonresident: full-time $17,212; part-time $7865.10 per year. Required fees: $1441; $153.15 per credit. Tuition and fees vary according to course load and program. *Financial support:* In 2009–10, 24 students received support, including 7 research assistantships (averaging $1,000 per year), 17 teaching assistantships with full tuition reimbursements available (averaging $8,000 per year). Financial award application deadline: 3/1; financial award applicants required to submit FAFSA. *Faculty research:* Gait analysis, cancer prevention, obesity prevention, energy expenditure, decision making. Total annual research expenditures: $2.8 million. *Unit head:* Dr. Tim Dunnagan, Head, 404-994-3242, Fax: 404-994-2013, E-mail: dunnagan@montana.edu. *Application contact:* Dr. Carl Fox.

National-Louis University, College of Arts and Sciences, Program in Psychology, Chicago, IL 60603. Offers community psychology (PhD); cultural psychology (MA); health psychology (MA); human development (MA); organizational psychology (MA); psychology (Certificate), including general, health, human development, organizational, psychological assessment. Part-time and evening/weekend programs available. *Degree requirements:* For master's, thesis, internship (health psychology). *Entrance requirements:* For master's, GRE General Test, MAT, or Watson-Glaser Critical Thinking Appraisal, interview, minimum GPA of 3.0; for Certificate, GRE, MAT, or Watson-Glaser Critical Thinking Appraisal, interview, minimum GPA of 3.0, undergraduate course work in psychology. *Expenses:* Tuition: Full-time $17,160; part-time $715 per semester hour. Tuition and fees vary according to course load, degree level, campus/location and program. *Faculty research:* Human development, personality theory, abnormal psychology.

National-Louis University, National College of Education, Doctoral Programs in Education, Program in Human Learning and Development, Chicago, IL 60603. Offers Ed D. Part-time and evening/weekend programs available. *Degree requirements:* For doctorate, comprehensive exam, thesis/dissertation, internship. *Entrance requirements:* For doctorate, GRE General Test, minimum GPA of 3.25, interview, resume, writing sample. *Expenses:* Tuition: Full-time $17,160; part-time $715 per semester hour. Tuition and fees vary according to course load, degree level, campus/location and program.

National-Louis University, National College of Education, Program in Educational Psychology/Human Learning and Development, Chicago, IL 60603. Offers educational psychology (CAS, Ed S); educational psychology/human learning and development (M Ed, MS Ed). Part-time and evening/weekend programs available. *Degree requirements:* For master's, thesis (for some programs). *Entrance requirements:* For master's, MAT or GRE, minimum GPA of 3.0, teaching certificate; for other advanced degree, master's degree, teaching certificate. Electronic applications accepted. *Expenses:* Tuition: Full-time $17,160; part-time $715 per semester hour. Tuition and fees vary according to course load, degree level, campus/location and program.

New York University, Steinhardt School of Culture, Education, and Human Development, New York, NY 10003. Offers MA, MFA, MM, MPH, MS, DPS, DPT, Ed D, PhD, Advanced Certificate, MM/Advanced Certificate, MPA/MA. *Accreditation:* Teacher Education Accreditation Council. Part-time programs available. *Faculty:* 259 full-time (151 women), 898 part-time/adjunct (488 women). *Students:* 2,357 full-time (1,841 women), 1,414 part-time (1,098 women); includes 820 minority (242 African Americans, 7 American Indian/Alaska Native, 289 Asian Americans or Pacific Islanders, 282 Hispanic Americans), 552 international. Average age 30. 6,436 applicants, 47% accepted, 1308 enrolled. In 2009, 1,286 master's, 122 doctorates, 18 other advanced degrees awarded. *Degree requirements:* For master's, thesis (for some programs); for doctorate, comprehensive exam (for some programs), thesis/dissertation. *Entrance requirements:* For doctorate, GRE General Test, interview. Additional exam requirements/recommendations for international students: Required—TOEFL. *Application deadline:* For fall admission, 12/15 priority date for domestic students, 12/15 for international students; for spring admission, 1/1 for domestic and international students. Applications are processed on a rolling basis. Application fee: $75. Electronic applications accepted. *Expenses:* Contact institution. *Financial support:* Fellowships with full and partial tuition reimbursements, research assistantships with full and partial tuition reimbursements, teaching assistantships with full and partial tuition reimbursements, career-related internships or fieldwork, Federal Work-Study, institutionally sponsored loans, scholarships/grants, traineeships, tuition waivers (partial), and unspecified assistantships available. Support available to part-time students. Financial award application deadline: 2/1; financial award applicants required to submit FAFSA. *Faculty research:* Equity, urban adolescents, arts in education, globalization, community and public health. Total annual research expenditures: $22.8 million. *Unit head:* Dr. Mary Brabeck, Dean, 212-998-5000. *Application contact:* John Myers, Director of Enrollment Management, 212-998-5030, Fax: 212-995-4328, E-mail: steinhardt.gradadmissions@nyu.edu.

New York University, Steinhardt School of Culture, Education, and Human Development, Department of Applied Psychology, Programs in Educational and Developmental Psychology, New York, NY 10012-1019. Offers educational psychology (MA); human development and social intervention (MA); psychological development (PhD); psychology and social intervention (PhD). *Accreditation:* APA (one or more programs are accredited). Part-time programs available. *Students:* 48 full-time (42 women), 36 part-time (30 women); includes 24 minority (9 African Americans, 4 Asian Americans or Pacific Islanders, 11 Hispanic Americans), 11 international. Average age 29. 233 applicants, 30% accepted, 26 enrolled. In 2009, 29 master's, 9 doctorates awarded. *Degree requirements:* For master's, thesis (for some programs); for doctorate, thesis/dissertation. *Entrance requirements:* For doctorate, GRE General Test, interview. Additional exam requirements/recommendations for international students: Required—TOEFL. *Application deadline:* For fall admission, 12/15 priority date for domestic and international students. Applications are processed on a rolling basis. Application fee: $75. Electronic applications accepted. *Expenses:* Tuition: Full-time $30,528; part-time $1272 per credit. Required fees: $2177. *Financial support:* Teaching assistantships with partial tuition reimbursements, career-related internships or fieldwork, Federal Work-Study, institutionally sponsored loans, and tuition waivers (partial) available. Support available to part-time students. Financial award application deadline: 2/1; financial award applicants required to submit FAFSA. *Faculty research:* High risk children and youth; child and adolescent developments; families and schooling; infant cognition; exploration, language, and symbolic play in toddlerhood. *Unit head:* Dr. LaRue Allen, Director, 212-998-5555, Fax: 212-995-4358. *Application contact:* 212-998-5030, Fax: 212-995-4328, E-mail: steinhardt.gradadmissions@nyu.edu.

New York University, Steinhardt School of Culture, Education, and Human Development, Department of Humanities and Social Sciences in the Professions, Program in International Education, New York, NY 10012-1019. Offers human development and social intervention (MA); international education (MA, PhD, Advanced Certificate), including cross cultural exchange and training (PhD), global education (PhD), international development education (PhD). Part-time programs available. *Students:* 68 full-time (61 women), 63 part-time (55 women); includes 32 minority (5 African Americans, 13 Asian Americans or Pacific Islanders, 14 Hispanic Americans), 21 international. Average age 27. 217 applicants, 70% accepted, 40 enrolled. In 2009, 46 master's, 3 doctorates awarded. *Degree requirements:* For master's, thesis (for some programs); for doctorate, thesis/dissertation. *Entrance requirements:* For doctorate, GRE General Test, interview; for Advanced Certificate, master's degree. Additional exam requirements/recommendations for international students: Required—TOEFL. *Application deadline:* For fall admission, 12/15 priority date for domestic and international students; for spring admission, 11/1 for domestic and international students. Applications are processed on a rolling basis. Application fee: $75. Electronic applications accepted. *Expenses:* Tuition: Full-time $30,528; part-time $1272 per credit. Required fees: $2177. *Financial support:* Fellowships with full and partial tuition reimbursements, career-related internships or fieldwork, Federal Work-Study, institutionally sponsored loans, and scholarships/grants available. Support available to part-time students. Financial award application deadline: 2/1; financial award applicants required to submit FAFSA. *Faculty research:* Civic education; ethnic identity among students and teachers; comparative education; education during emergencies; cross-cultural exchange. *Unit head:* Dr. Philip Hosay, Director, 212-998-5496, Fax: 212-995-4832, E-mail: pmh2@nyu.edu. *Application contact:* 212-998-5030, Fax: 212-995-4328, E-mail: steinhardt.gradadmissions@nyu.edu.

North Dakota State University, College of Graduate and Interdisciplinary Studies, College of Human Development and Education, Program in Human Development, Fargo, ND 58108. Offers PhD. *Students:* 22 full-time (14 women), 16 part-time (12 women); includes 8 minority (1 African American, 5 American Indian/Alaska Native, 1 Asian American or Pacific Islander, 1 Hispanic American), 1 international. In 2009, 9 doctorates awarded. *Degree requirements:* For doctorate, comprehensive exam, thesis/dissertation. *Entrance requirements:* Additional exam requirements/recommendations for international students: Required—TOEFL (minimum score 525 paper-based; 197 computer-based; 71 iBT). *Application deadline:* For fall admission, 2/1 priority date for domestic and international students. Applications are processed on a rolling basis. Application fee: $45 ($60 for international students). *Financial support:* In 2009–10, 12 students received support; research assistantships with full tuition reimbursements available, teaching assistantships with full tuition reimbursements available, scholarships/grants, tuition waivers (partial), and unspecified assistantships available. *Faculty research:* Gerontology, wellness, counselor education. Total annual research expenditures: $1.3 million. *Unit head:* Dr. Greg Sanders, Coordinator, 701-231-8211, E-mail: greg.sanders@ndsu.edu. *Application contact:* Dr. Greg Sanders, Coordinator, 701-231-8211, E-mail: greg.sanders@ndsu.edu.

Northern Arizona University, Graduate College, College of Social and Behavioral Sciences, Institute for Human Development, Flagstaff, AZ 86011. Offers assistive technology (Certificate); disability policy and practice (Certificate); positive behavior support (Certificate). *Faculty:* 1 (woman) full-time. *Students:* 28 full-time (all women), 9 part-time (4 women); includes 1 African American, 1 American Indian/Alaska Native, 5 Hispanic Americans. Average age 25. 55 applicants, 58% accepted, 26 enrolled. *Entrance requirements:* Additional exam requirements/recommendations for international students: Required—TOEFL (minimum score 550 paper-based; 213 computer-based; 80 iBT), IELTS (minimum score 7), or a bachelor's degree from an English-speaking university and demonstrated proficiency. *Application deadline:* Applications are processed on a rolling basis. Application fee: $65. Electronic applications accepted. *Unit head:* Richard Carroll, Chair, 928-523-4791, Fax: 928-523-9127, E-mail: richard.carroll@nau.edu. *Application contact:* Karen Applequist, Graduate Coordinator, 928-523-9276, E-mail: karen.applequist@nau.edu.

Northwestern University, The Graduate School, School of Education and Social Policy, Program in Human Development and Social Policy, Evanston, IL 60208. Offers PhD. Admissions and degrees offered through The Graduate School. *Faculty:* 12 full-time (5 women), 7 part-time/adjunct (2 women). *Students:* 30 full-time (28 women); includes 8 minority (4 African Americans, 4 Asian Americans or Pacific Islanders), 1 international. Average age 30. 70 applicants, 13% accepted, 5 enrolled. In 2009, 4 doctorates awarded. *Degree requirements:* For doctorate, comprehensive exam, thesis/dissertation. *Entrance requirements:* For doctorate, GRE General Test. Additional exam requirements/recommendations for international students: Required—TOEFL (minimum score 600 paper-based; 250 computer-based; 100 iBT). *Application deadline:* For fall admission, 12/31 priority date for domestic and international students. Application fee: $75. Electronic applications accepted. *Financial support:* In 2009–10, 26 students received support, including 8 fellowships with full tuition reimbursements available, 15 research assistantships with full tuition reimbursements available, 3 teaching assistantships with full tuition reimbursements available; institutionally sponsored loans, scholarships/grants, health care benefits, and unspecified assistantships also available. Financial award application deadline: 12/31; financial award applicants required to submit FAFSA. *Faculty research:* Individual development and the personal narrative; the life course and culture; development, intervention and culture; the life course and policy; analysis of policy effects on lives. *Unit head:* Prof. Barton J. Hirsch, Coordinator, Program in Human Development and Social Policy, 847-491-4418, Fax: 847-491-8999, E-mail: bhirsch@northwestern.edu. *Application contact:* Erika Arlene Chavez, Program Assistant, 847-491-4329, Fax: 847-491-8999, E-mail: e-chavez@northwestern.edu.

The Ohio State University, Graduate School, College of Education and Human Ecology, Department of Human Development and Family Science, Columbus, OH 43210. Offers M Ed, MS, PhD. *Faculty:* 24. *Students:* 20 full-time (18 women), 21 part-time (14 women); includes 5 minority (3 African Americans, 1 American Indian/Alaska Native, 1 Asian American or Pacific Islander), 11 international. Average age 27. In 2009, 3 master's, 5 doctorates awarded. *Degree requirements:* For master's, thesis optional; for doctorate, thesis/dissertation. *Entrance requirements:* For master's and doctorate, GRE General Test. Additional exam requirements/recommendations for international students: Required—TOEFL (minimum score 577 paper-based; 233 computer-based). *Application deadline:* For fall admission, 8/15 priority date for domestic students, 7/1 priority date for international students; for winter admission, 12/1 priority date for domestic students, 11/1 priority date for international students; for spring admission, 3/1 priority date for domestic students, 2/1 priority date for international students. Applications are processed on a rolling basis. Application fee: $40 ($50 for international students). Electronic applications accepted. *Expenses:* Tuition, state resident: full-time $10,683. Tuition, nonresident: full-time $25,923. Tuition and fees vary according to course load and program. *Financial support:* Fellowships, research assistantships, teaching assistantships, Federal Work-Study and institutionally sponsored loans available. Support available to part-time students. *Unit head:* Julianne Serovich, Chair, 614-292-5685, Fax: 614-292-4365, E-mail: jserovich@ehe.osu.edu. *Application contact:* 614-292-9444, Fax: 614-292-3895, E-mail: domestic.grad@osu.edu.

Oklahoma State University, College of Arts and Sciences, Department of Psychology, Stillwater, OK 74078. Offers clinical psychology (PhD); general psychology (MS); lifespan development psychology (PhD). *Accreditation:* APA (one or more programs are accredited). *Faculty:* 26 full-time (12 women). *Students:* 36 full-time (23 women), 15 part-time (8 women); includes 8 minority (2 African Americans, 3 American Indian/Alaska Native, 3 Hispanic Americans), 2 international. Average age 28. 120 applicants, 9% accepted, 7 enrolled. In 2009, 10 master's, 9 doctorates awarded. *Degree requirements:* For master's, thesis or alternative; for doctorate, comprehensive exam, thesis/dissertation. *Entrance requirements:* For master's and doctorate, GRE General Test. Additional exam requirements/recommendations for international students: Required—TOEFL (minimum score 550 paper-based; 79 iBT). *Application deadline:* For fall admission, 3/1 priority date for international students; for spring admission, 8/1 priority date for international students. Applications are processed on a rolling basis. Application fee: $40 ($75 for international students). Electronic applications accepted. *Expenses:* Tuition, state resident: full-time $3716; part-time $154.85 per credit hour. Tuition, nonresident: full-time $14,448; part-time $602 per credit hour. Required fees: $1772; $73.85 per credit hour. One-time fee: $50. Tuition and fees vary according to course load and campus/location. *Financial support:* In 2009–10, 16 research assistantships (averaging $13,215 per year), 29 teaching assistantships (averaging $13,370 per year) were awarded; career-related internships or fieldwork, Federal Work-Study, scholarships/grants, health care benefits, tuition waivers (partial), and unspecified assistantships also available. Support available to part-time students. Financial award application deadline: 3/1; financial award applicants required to submit FAFSA. *Unit head:* Dr. Larry Mullins, Head, 405-744-6028, Fax: 405-744-8067. *Application contact:* Dr. Gordon Emslie, Dean, 405-744-6368, Fax: 405-744-0355, E-mail: grad-i@okstate.edu.

Oregon State University, Graduate School, College of Health and Human Sciences, Department of Human Development and Family Sciences, Corvallis, OR 97331. Offers gerontology (MAIS); human development and family studies (MS, PhD). *Faculty:* 11 full-time (7 women), 6 part-time/adjunct (2 women). *Students:* 28 full-time (20 women), 3 part-time (all women); includes 5 minority (3 Asian Americans or Pacific Islanders, 2 Hispanic Americans), 4 international. Average age 35. In 2009, 3 master's, 4 doctorates awarded. *Degree requirements:* For doctorate, thesis/dissertation. *Entrance requirements:* For master's and doctorate, GRE, minimum GPA of 3.0 in last 90 hours. Additional exam requirements/recommendations for international students: Required—TOEFL. *Application deadline:* Applications are processed on a rolling basis. Application fee: $50. *Expenses:* Tuition, state resident: full-time $9774; part-time $362 per credit. Tuition, nonresident: full-time $15,849; part-time $587 per credit. Required fees: $1639. Full-time tuition and fees vary according to course load and program. *Financial support:* Research assistantships, teaching assistantships, career-related internships or fieldwork, Federal Work-Study, and institutionally sponsored loans available. Support available to part-time students. Financial award application deadline: 2/1. *Unit head:* Dr. Carolyn Aldwin, Chair, 541-737-2024, Fax: 541-737-1076, E-mail: carolyn.aldwin@oregonstate.edu. *Application contact:* Dr. Carolyn Aldwin, Chair, 541-737-2024, Fax: 541-737-1076, E-mail: carolyn.aldwin@oregonstate.edu.

Our Lady of the Lake University of San Antonio, School of Professional Studies, Program in Human Sciences, San Antonio, TX 78207-4689. Offers MA. Part-time and evening/weekend programs available. *Students:* 8 full-time (7 women), 27 part-time (24 women); includes 26 minority (11 African Americans, 15 Hispanic Americans). Average age 40. In 2009, 9 master's awarded. *Entrance requirements:* For master's, GRE General Test or MAT, interview. Additional exam requirements/recommendations for international students: Required—TOEFL. *Application deadline:* Applications are processed on a rolling basis. Application fee: $25 ($50 for international students). Electronic applications accepted. *Expenses:* Tuition: Full-time $12,330; part-time $685 per contact hour. Required fees: $139; $12 per contact hour. $57 per semester. Tuition and fees vary according to campus/location. *Financial support:* Application deadline: 4/15. *Unit head:* Dr. Steve Blanchard, Chair, 210-434-6711 Ext. 2273, E-mail: blank@lake.ollusa.com. *Application contact:* 210-434-6711 Ext. 2314, Fax: 210-431-4036, E-mail: gradadm@lake.ollusa.edu.

Pacific Oaks College, Graduate School, Program in Human Development, Pasadena, CA 91103. Offers MA. Part-time and evening/weekend programs available. Postbaccalaureate distance learning degree programs offered (minimal on-campus study). *Degree requirements:* For master's, thesis. *Entrance requirements:* Additional exam requirements/recommendations for international students: Required—TOEFL (minimum score 550 paper-based; 213 computer-based). *Faculty research:* Bicultural development, teaching adults, art education, literacy development, adolescent development.

Penn State University Park, Graduate School, College of Health and Human Development, Department of Human Development and Family Studies, State College, University Park, PA 16802-1503. Offers MS, PhD. *Unit head:* Dr. Steven H. Zarit, Head, 814-865-5260, Fax: 814-863-7963, E-mail: z67@psu.edu. *Application contact:* Dr. Douglas M. Teti, Professor in Charge of Graduate Program, 814-865-2644, E-mail: dmt16@psu.edu.

Purdue University, Graduate School, College of Consumer and Family Sciences, Department of Child Development and Family Studies, West Lafayette, IN 47907. Offers developmental studies (MS, PhD); family studies (MS, PhD); marriage and family therapy (MS, PhD). *Accreditation:* AAMFT/COAMFTE (one or more programs are accredited). Part-time programs available. Terminal master's awarded for partial completion of doctoral program. *Degree requirements:* For master's, thesis; for doctorate, thesis/dissertation. *Entrance requirements:* For master's and doctorate, GRE General Test. Additional exam requirements/recommendations for international students: Required—TWE. Electronic applications accepted. *Faculty research:* Inclusion of children with special needs, families as learning environments, relationships in child care, work-family relations, AIDS prevention.

Saint Joseph College, Department of Gerontology, West Hartford, CT 06117-2700. Offers human development/gerontology (MA, Certificate). Part-time and evening/weekend programs available. *Students:* 3 full-time (all women), 22 part-time (20 women); includes 7 minority (4 African Americans, 1 Asian American or Pacific Islander, 2 Hispanic Americans). *Entrance requirements:* For master's, 2 letters of recommendation. *Application deadline:* Applications are processed on a rolling basis. Application fee: $50. Electronic applications accepted. *Expenses:* Tuition: Part-time $595 per credit. Required fees: $30 per credit. Tuition and fees vary according to program. *Financial support:* Career-related internships or fieldwork and unspecified assistantships available. Support available to part-time students. Financial award applicants required to submit FAFSA. *Application contact:* Graduate Admissions Office, 860-231-5261, E-mail: graduate@sjc.edu.

St. Lawrence University, Department of Education, Program in Counseling and Human Development, Canton, NY 13617-1455. Offers mental health counseling (MS); school counseling (M Ed, CAS). Part-time and evening/weekend programs available. *Entrance requirements:* For master's, GRE General Test. *Faculty research:* Defense mechanisms and mediation.

Saint Louis University, Graduate School, College of Education and Public Service and Graduate School, Department of Counseling and Family Therapy, St. Louis, MO 63103-2097. Offers counseling and family therapy (PhD); human development counseling (MA); marriage and family therapy (Certificate); school counseling (MA, MA-R). *Accreditation:* AAMFT; NCATE. Part-time programs available. *Degree requirements:* For master's, comprehensive exam, thesis (for some programs); for doctorate, comprehensive exam, thesis/dissertation, preliminary oral and written exams. *Entrance requirements:* For master's, GRE General Test, letters of recommendation, resume; for doctorate, GRE General Test, letters of recommendation, resumé, transcripts, goal statement. Additional exam requirements/recommendations for international students: Required—TOEFL (minimum score 550 paper-based; 213 computer-based). Electronic applications accepted. *Faculty research:* Medical family therapy/collaborative health care multicultural counseling, mental health needs of diverse, minority, or Immigrant/refugee populations, divorce, aging families.

Saint Mary's University of Minnesota, Schools of Graduate and Professional Programs, Graduate School of Business and Technology, Human Development Program, Winona, MN 55987-1399. Offers MA. *Unit head:* Dr. Priscilla Herbison, Director, 612-728-5103, Fax: 612-728-5121, E-mail: pherbiso@smumn.edu. *Application contact:* Yasin Alsaidi, Director of Admissions for Graduate and Professional Programs, 612-728-5207, Fax: 612-728-5121, E-mail: yalsaidi@smumn.edu.

South Dakota State University, Graduate School, College of Education and Human Sciences, Department of Human Development, Consumer and Family Sciences, Brookings, SD 57007. Offers MFCS. *Entrance requirements:* For master's, resume. Additional exam requirements/recommendations for international students: Required—TOEFL (minimum score 525 paper-based).

Southern Illinois University Carbondale, Graduate School, College of Education, Department of Educational Psychology and Special Education, Program in Educational Psychology, Carbondale, IL 62901-4701. Offers counselor education (MS Ed, PhD); educational psychology (PhD); human learning and development (MS Ed); measurement and statistics (PhD). *Accreditation:* NCATE. *Degree requirements:* For master's, thesis; for doctorate, thesis/dissertation. *Entrance requirements:* For master's, GRE General Test, minimum GPA of 2.7; for doctorate, minimum GPA of 3.25. Additional exam requirements/recommendations for international students: Required—TOEFL. *Faculty research:* Career development, problem solving, learning and instruction, cognitive development, family assessment.

Texas A&M University, College of Education and Human Development, Department of Educational Psychology, College Station, TX 77843. Offers counseling psychology (PhD); educational psychology (PhD); educational technology (M Ed); gifted and talented education (M Ed, MS); Hispanic bilingual education (M Ed, PhD); human learning and development (MS); intelligence, creativity, and giftedness (PhD); learning, development, and instruction (PhD); research, measurement and statistics (MS); research, measurement, and statistics (PhD); school counseling (M Ed); school psychology (PhD); special education (M Ed, PhD). *Accreditation:* APA (one or more programs are accredited); NCATE. Part-time and evening/weekend programs available. Postbaccalaureate distance learning degree programs offered (no on-campus study). *Faculty:* 45. *Students:* 160 full-time (126 women), 144 part-time (118 women); includes 99 minority (25 African Americans, 13 Asian Americans or Pacific Islanders, 61 Hispanic Americans), 41 international. In 2009, 53 master's, 30 doctorates awarded. *Degree requirements:* For master's, thesis optional; for doctorate, thesis/dissertation. *Entrance requirements:* For master's and doctorate, GRE General Test. Additional exam requirements/recommendations for international students: Required—TOEFL. Application fee: $50 ($75 for international students). Electronic applications accepted. *Expenses:* Tuition, state resident: full-time $3991; part-time $221.74 per credit hour. Tuition, nonresident: full-time $9049; part-time $502.74 per credit hour. *Financial support:* In 2009–10, fellowships (averaging $12,000 per year), research assistantships (averaging $9,000 per year), teaching assistantships (averaging $9,000 per year) were awarded; career-related internships or fieldwork, institutionally sponsored loans, scholarships/grants, and unspecified assistantships also available. Financial award applicants required to submit FAFSA. *Unit head:* Dr. Victor Willson, Head, 979-845-1800. *Application contact:* Carol A. Wagner, Director of Advising, 979-845-1833, Fax: 979-862-1256, E-mail: epsyadvisor@tamu.edu.

Texas Tech University, Graduate School, College of Human Sciences, Department of Human Development and Family Studies, Lubbock, TX 79409. Offers gerontology (MS); human development and family studies (MS, PhD). *Accreditation:* AAMFT/COAMFTE (one or more programs are accredited). Part-time programs available. *Faculty:* 19 full-time (15 women). *Students:* 42 full-time (35 women), 11 part-time (5 women); includes 6 minority (1 American Indian/Alaska Native, 1 Asian American or Pacific Islander, 4 Hispanic Americans), 14 international. Average age 33. 47 applicants, 62% accepted, 9 enrolled. In 2009, 7 master's, 5 doctorates awarded. *Degree requirements:* For master's, thesis; for doctorate, thesis/dissertation. *Entrance requirements:* For master's and doctorate, GRE General Test. Additional exam requirements/recommendations for international students: Required—TOEFL (minimum score 550 paper-based; 213 computer-based). *Application deadline:* For fall admission, 3/1 priority date for international students; for spring admission, 11/1 priority date for international students. Applications are processed on a rolling basis. Application fee: $50 ($75 for international students). Electronic applications accepted. *Expenses:* Tuition, state resident: full-time $5100; part-time $213 per credit hour. Tuition, nonresident: full-time $11,748; part-time $490 per credit hour. Required fees: $2298; $50 per credit hour. $555 per semester. *Financial support:* In 2009–10, 4 research assistantships with partial tuition reimbursements (averaging $25,450 per year), 21 teaching assistantships with partial tuition reimbursements (averaging $21,163 per year) were awarded; career-related internships or fieldwork, Federal Work-Study, institutionally sponsored loans, and scholarships/grants also available. Support available to part-time students. Financial award application deadline: 4/15; financial award applicants required to submit FAFSA. *Faculty research:* Parenting, marital and premarital relationships, adolescent risky behaviors, life span; child development. Total annual research expenditures: $60,398. *Unit head:* Malinda Colwell, Chair, 806-742-3000 Ext. 279, Fax: 806-742-0285, E-mail: malinda.colwell@ttu.edu. *Application contact:* Monya Castle, Graduate Secretary, 806-742-3000 Ext. 250, Fax: 806-742-0285, E-mail: monya.castle@ttu.edu.

The University of Alabama, Graduate School, College of Human Environmental Sciences, Department of Human Development and Family Studies, Tuscaloosa, AL 35487. Offers MSHES. *Faculty:* 7 full-time (5 women). *Students:* 28 full-time (27 women), 8 part-time (all women); includes 11 minority (9 African Americans, 1 Asian American or Pacific Islander, 1 Hispanic American). Average age 27. 30 applicants, 57% accepted, 13 enrolled. In 2009, 13 degrees awarded. *Degree requirements:* For master's, thesis (for some programs). *Entrance requirements:* For master's, GRE General Test or MAT, minimum GPA of 3.0. Additional exam requirements/recommendations for international students: Required—TOEFL. *Application deadline:* For fall admission, 2/1 priority date for domestic and international students. Applications are processed on a rolling basis. Application fee: $50 ($60 for international students). Electronic applications accepted. *Expenses:* Tuition, state resident: full-time $7000. Tuition, nonresident: full-time $19,200. *Financial support:* In 2009–10, 10 students received support, including 1 fellowship with full tuition reimbursement available (averaging $15,000 per year), 4 research assistantships with full tuition reimbursements available (averaging $10,908 per year), 5 teaching assistantships (averaging $10,000 per year); career-related internships or fieldwork, Federal Work-Study, scholarships/grants, health care benefits, and unspecified assistantships also available. Financial award application deadline: 2/15. *Faculty research:*

Human Development

The University of Alabama (continued)

Parent/child relationships, preschool curricula and quality measures for child care programs, family strengths and adolescent behaviors, depression in mothers and infants, word association and word learning in young children. *Unit head:* Dr. Carroll M. Tingle, Chair, 205-348-6158, Fax: 205-348-8153, E-mail: ctingle@ches.ua.edu. *Application contact:* Dr. Maria Hernandez-Reif, Associate Professor, 205-348-5894, Fax: 205-348-8153, E-mail: mhernandez-reif@ches.ua.edu.

The University of Arizona, Graduate College, College of Education, Department of Disability and Psychoeducational Studies, Division of Family Studies and Human Development, Tucson, AZ 85721. Offers M Ed. *Faculty:* 17 full-time (9 women). *Students:* 23 full-time (20 women), 4 part-time (all women); includes 3 minority (1 American Indian/Alaska Native, 2 Hispanic Americans), 1 international. Average age 28. 30 applicants, 70% accepted, 14 enrolled. In 2009, 25 master's awarded. Terminal master's awarded for partial completion of doctoral program. *Entrance requirements:* Additional exam requirements/recommendations for international students: Required—TOEFL (minimum score 600 paper-based). *Application deadline:* For fall admission, 2/1 for domestic students. Applications are processed on a rolling basis. Application fee: $65. *Expenses:* Tuition, state resident: full-time $9028. Tuition, nonresident: full-time $24,890. *Financial support:* In 2009–10, 4 research assistantships with full tuition reimbursements (averaging $12,828 per year), 4 teaching assistantships with full tuition reimbursements (averaging $12,378 per year) were awarded. *Unit head:* Dr. Ron Marx, Dean, 520-621-1081, E-mail: ronmarx@email.arizona.edu. *Application contact:* Cecilia Carlon, Administrative Assistant, 520-626-1248, E-mail: ccarlon@email.arizona.edu.

The University of British Columbia, Faculty of Education, Department of Educational and Counseling Psychology, and Special Education, Vancouver, BC V6T 1Z1, Canada. Offers counseling psychology (M Ed, MA, PhD); development, learning and culture (PhD); guidance studies (Diploma); human development, learning and culture (M Ed, MA); measurement and evaluation and research methodology (M Ed); measurement, evaluation and research methodology (MA); measurement, evaluation, and research methodology (PhD); school psychology (M Ed, MA, PhD); special education (M Ed, MA, PhD, Diploma). Part-time programs available. *Degree requirements:* For master's, thesis (for some programs); for doctorate, comprehensive exam, thesis/dissertation. *Entrance requirements:* For master's, GRE General Test (counseling psychology MA); for doctorate, GRE General Test. Additional exam requirements/recommendations for international students: Required—TOEFL. Electronic applications accepted. *Faculty research:* Women, family, social problems, career transition, stress and coping problems.

University of Calgary, Faculty of Graduate Studies, Faculty of Education, Division of Applied Psychology, Calgary, AB T2N 1N4, Canada. Offers counseling psychology (M Ed, M Sc, PhD); human development and learning (M Ed, M Sc, PhD); school psychology (M Ed, M Sc, PhD); special education (M Ed, M Sc, PhD). Part-time programs available. *Degree requirements:* For master's, thesis (for some programs), final oral exam; for doctorate, thesis/dissertation, candidacy exam, final oral exam. *Entrance requirements:* For master's, minimum GPA of 3.0, 3 letters of reference; for doctorate, minimum GPA of 3.5, 3 letters of reference. *Faculty research:* Counselor education, family life studies, learning and cognition.

University of California, Berkeley, Graduate Division, School of Education, Programs in Education, Berkeley, CA 94720-1500. Offers development in mathematics and science (MA); education in mathematics, science, and technology (MA, PhD); human development and education (MA, PhD); special education (PhD); MA/Credential; Ph D/Credential; PhD/MA. *Students:* 374 full-time (270 women). Average age 33. 674 applicants, 111 enrolled. In 2009, 120 master's, 25 doctorates awarded. Terminal master's awarded for partial completion of doctoral program. *Degree requirements:* For master's, exam or thesis; for doctorate, thesis/dissertation, oral qualifying exam. *Entrance requirements:* For master's and doctorate, GRE General Test, minimum GPA of 3.0 during last 2 years of undergraduate course work. *Application deadline:* For fall admission, 12/1 for domestic students. Application fee: $70 ($90 for international students). Electronic applications accepted. *Financial support:* Fellowships, research assistantships, teaching assistantships, unspecified assistantships available. *Faculty research:* Human development, social and moral educational psychology, developmental teacher preparation. *Unit head:* Prof. P. David Pearson, Dean, 510-642-3726, E-mail: gsedeansoffice@lists.berkeley.edu. *Application contact:* Admissions Office, 510-642-0841, Fax: 510-642-4808, E-mail: gse_info@uclink.berkeley.edu.

University of California, Davis, Graduate Studies, Graduate Group in Human Development, Davis, CA 95616. Offers PhD. *Degree requirements:* For doctorate, thesis/dissertation. *Entrance requirements:* For doctorate, GRE General Test, GRE Subject Test, minimum GPA of 3.0. Additional exam requirements/recommendations for international students: Required—TOEFL (minimum score 550 paper-based; 213 computer-based). Electronic applications accepted. *Faculty research:* Life span socioemotional and cognitive development, individual differences, relationship between biological and behavioral development, cross-cultural and cross-generational development.

University of California, Santa Barbara, Graduate Division, College of Letters and Sciences, Division of Humanities and Fine Arts, Department of Linguistics, Santa Barbara, CA 93106-3100. Offers applied linguistics (PhD); cognitive science (PhD); human development (PhD); language, interaction, and social organizations (PhD); MA/PhD. *Faculty:* 23 full-time (12 women). *Students:* 25 full-time (14 women). Average age 32. 63 applicants, 17% accepted, 5 enrolled. In 2009, 5 doctorates awarded. *Degree requirements:* For doctorate, one foreign language, comprehensive exam, thesis/dissertation. *Entrance requirements:* For doctorate, GRE, 3 letters of recommendation, resume/curriculum vitae. Additional exam requirements/recommendations for international students: Required—TOEFL (minimum score 550 paper-based; 213 computer-based; 80 iBT), or IELTS (minimum score 7). *Application deadline:* For fall admission, 12/1 priority date for domestic and international students. Application fee: $70 ($90 for international students). Electronic applications accepted. *Financial support:* In 2009–10, 24 students received support, including 19 fellowships with full and partial tuition reimbursements available (averaging $12,400 per year), 1 research assistantship with full and partial tuition reimbursement available (averaging $3,000 per year), 13 teaching assistantships with partial tuition reimbursements available (averaging $5,600 per year); Federal Work-Study, institutionally sponsored loans, scholarships/grants, health care benefits, and unspecified assistantships also available. Financial award application deadline: 12/1; financial award applicants required to submit FAFSA. *Faculty research:* Language, race and subcultural identities among California teenagers; language acquisition, psycholinguistics; language documentation, fieldwork; syntax of nominalization in 5 Tibeto-Burman languages; perceptual correlates of syllable weight. *Unit head:* Prof. Patricia M. Clancy, Chair, 805-893-8658, Fax: 805-893-7769, E-mail: pclancy@linguistics.ucsb.edu. *Application contact:* Mary Rae Staton, Graduate Program Assistant, 805-893-3776, Fax: 805-893-7769, E-mail: staton@linguistics.ucsb.edu.

University of California, Santa Barbara, Graduate Division, College of Letters and Sciences, Division of Social Sciences, Department of Communication, Santa Barbara, CA 93106-4020. Offers human development (PhD); MA/PhD. *Faculty:* 20 full-time (8 women), 1 part-time/adjunct (0 women). *Students:* 38 full-time (26 women). Average age 28. 155 applicants, 12% accepted, 10 enrolled. In 2009, 2 doctorates awarded. *Degree requirements:* For doctorate, comprehensive exam, thesis/dissertation. *Entrance requirements:* For doctorate, GRE General Test, 3 letters of recommendation, resume/curriculum vitae. Additional exam requirements/recommendations for international students: Required—TOEFL (minimum score 600 paper-based; 213 computer-based; 80 iBT), or IELTS. *Application deadline:* For fall admission, 1/1 for domestic and international students. Application fee: $70 ($90 for international students). Electronic applications accepted. *Financial support:* In 2009–10, 38 students received support, including 38 fellowships with full and partial tuition reimbursements available (averaging $5,500 per year), 5 research assistantships with full and partial tuition reimbursements available (averaging $7,800 per year), 34 teaching assistantships with partial tuition reimbursements available (averaging $11,000 per year); Federal Work-Study, institutionally sponsored loans, scholarships/grants, health care benefits, tuition waivers (full and partial), and unspecified assistantships also available. Financial award application deadline: 1/1; financial award applicants required to submit FAFSA. *Faculty research:* Interpersonal communication, organizational communication, media communication, political communication, intrapersonal communication. Total annual research expenditures: $100,000. *Unit head:* Prof. Michael Stohl, Chair, 805-893-7935, Fax: 805-893-7102, E-mail: mstohl@comm.ucsb.edu. *Application contact:* Nancy Siris-Rawls, Graduate Program Assistant, 805-893-3046, Fax: 805-893-7102, E-mail: nsiris@comm.ucsb.edu.

University of California, Santa Barbara, Graduate Division, College of Letters and Sciences, Division of Social Sciences, Department of Sociology, Santa Barbara, CA 93106-9430. Offers global studies (PhD); human development (PhD); language, interaction and social organization (PhD); technology and society (PhD); women's studies (PhD); MA/PhD. *Faculty:* 35 full-time (14 women). *Students:* 77 full-time (50 women). Average age 30. 155 applicants, 9% accepted, 8 enrolled. In 2009, 10 doctorates awarded. Terminal master's awarded for partial completion of doctoral program. *Degree requirements:* For doctorate, comprehensive exam, thesis/dissertation. *Entrance requirements:* For doctorate, GRE General Test, sample of written work, 3 letters of recommendation, resume/curriculum vitae. Additional exam requirements/recommendations for international students: Required—TOEFL (minimum score 550 paper-based; 213 computer-based; 80 iBT), or IELTS. *Application deadline:* For fall admission, 12/10 for domestic students. Application fee: $70 ($90 for international students). Electronic applications accepted. *Financial support:* In 2009–10, 69 students received support, including 50 fellowships with full tuition reimbursements available (averaging $7,900 per year), 6 research assistantships with full and partial tuition reimbursements available (averaging $2,600 per year), 53 teaching assistantships with partial tuition reimbursements available (averaging $9,200 per year); career-related internships or fieldwork, Federal Work-Study, institutionally sponsored loans, scholarships/grants, health care benefits, and unspecified assistantships also available. Financial award applicants required to submit FAFSA. *Faculty research:* Conversation analysis, social movements, human sexuality, urban sociology, race and ethnic relations. *Unit head:* Prof. Verta Taylor, Chair, 805-893-3118, Fax: 805-893-3324, E-mail: grad-soc@soc.ucsb.edu. *Application contact:* Ra Thea, Graduate Staff Advisor, 805-893-3328, Fax: 805-893-3324, E-mail: grad-soc@soc.ucsb.edu.

University of Central Oklahoma, College of Graduate Studies and Research, College of Education, Department of Human Environmental Sciences, Edmond, OK 73034-5209. Offers family and child studies (MS); family and consumer science education (MS); interior design (MS); nutrition-food management (MS). Part-time programs available. *Entrance requirements:* Additional exam requirements/recommendations for international students: Required—TOEFL (minimum score 550 paper-based; 213 computer-based). Electronic applications accepted. *Expenses:* Tuition, state resident: full-time $4128; part-time $172 per credit hour. Tuition, nonresident: full-time $10,373; part-time $432.20 per credit hour. Required fees: $433.20; $18.05 per credit hour. *Faculty research:* Dietetics and food science.

University of Chicago, Division of Social Sciences, Department of Comparative Human Development, Chicago, IL 60637-1513. Offers PhD. *Students:* 64. In 2009, 5 doctorates awarded. *Degree requirements:* For doctorate, one foreign language, thesis/dissertation, pre-doctoral written exams. *Entrance requirements:* For doctorate, GRE General Test, GRE Subject Test. Additional exam requirements/recommendations for international students: Required—TOEFL, IELTS (minimum score 7). *Application deadline:* For fall admission, 12/10 for domestic and international students. Application fee: $55. Electronic applications accepted. *Financial support:* Fellowships, research assistantships, teaching assistantships, Federal Work-Study, institutionally sponsored loans, scholarships/grants, traineeships, health care benefits, and unspecified assistantships available. Financial award application deadline: 12/10; financial award applicants required to submit FAFSA. *Unit head:* Prof. John A. Lucy, Chair, 773-702-3971. *Application contact:* Office of the Dean of Students, 773-702-8415.

University of Connecticut, Graduate School, College of Liberal Arts and Sciences, Department of Human Development and Family Studies, Storrs, CT 06269. Offers culture, health and human development (Graduate Certificate); human development and family studies (MA, PhD). *Accreditation:* AAMFT/COAMFTE (one or more programs are accredited). *Faculty:* 28 full-time (18 women). *Students:* 41 full-time (35 women), 11 part-time (10 women); includes 11 minority (2 African Americans, 5 Asian Americans or Pacific Islanders, 4 Hispanic Americans), 7 international. Average age 30. 61 applicants, 20% accepted, 5 enrolled. In 2009, 13 master's, 3 doctorates awarded. Terminal master's awarded for partial completion of doctoral program. *Degree requirements:* For master's, comprehensive exam; for doctorate, thesis/dissertation. *Entrance requirements:* For doctorate, GRE General Test. Additional exam requirements/recommendations for international students: Required—TOEFL (minimum score 550 paper-based; 213 computer-based). *Application deadline:* For fall admission, 2/1 priority date for domestic and international students; for spring admission, 11/1 for domestic students, 10/1 for international students. Applications are processed on a rolling basis. Application fee: $55. Electronic applications accepted. *Expenses:* Tuition, state resident: full-time $4725; part-time $525 per credit. Tuition, nonresident: full-time $12,267; part-time $1363 per credit. Required fees: $346 per semester. Tuition and fees vary according to course load. *Financial support:* In 2009–10, 16 research assistantships with full tuition reimbursements, 18 teaching assistantships with full tuition reimbursements were awarded; fellowships, career-related internships or fieldwork, Federal Work-Study, scholarships/grants, health care benefits, and unspecified assistantships also available. Financial award application deadline: 2/1; financial award applicants required to submit FAFSA. *Unit head:* Ronald M. Sabatelli, Head, 860-486-4726, Fax: 860-486-3452, E-mail: ronald.sabatelli@uconn.edu. *Application contact:* Nancy W. Sheehan, Chairperson, 860-486-4043, Fax: 860-486-3452, E-mail: nancy.w.sheehan@uconn.edu.

University of Dayton, Graduate School, School of Education and Allied Professions, Department of Counselor Education and Human Services, Dayton, OH 45469-1300. Offers college student personnel (MS Ed); community counseling (MS Ed); higher education administration (MS Ed); human services (MS Ed); school counseling (MS Ed); school psychology (MS Ed, Ed S); teacher as child/youth development specialist (MS Ed). *Accreditation:* NCATE. Part-time and evening/weekend programs available. *Faculty:* 11 full-time (8 women), 33 part-time/adjunct (22 women). *Students:* 254 full-time (207 women), 207 part-time (180 women); includes 76 minority (69 African Americans, 3 Asian Americans or Pacific Islanders, 4 Hispanic Americans), 2 international. Average age 32. 359 applicants, 47% accepted, 114 enrolled. In 2009, 163 master's, 11 Ed Ss awarded. *Degree requirements:* For master's, comprehensive exam (for some programs), thesis (for some programs), exit exam. *Entrance requirements:* For master's, MAT or GRE (if GPA less than 2.75), interview, writing sample. Additional exam requirements/recommendations for international students: Required—TOEFL (minimum score 550 paper-based; 213 computer-based; 80 iBT). *Application deadline:* For fall admission, 4/10 for domestic students, 3/1 priority date for international students; for winter admission, 9/10 for domestic students, 7/1 priority date for international students; for spring admission, 1/10 for domestic students, 1/1 priority date for international students. Applications are processed on a rolling basis. Application fee: $0 ($50 for international students). Electronic applications accepted. *Expenses:* Tuition: Full-time $8412; part-time $701 per credit hour. Required fees: $325; $65 per course. $25 per semester. Tuition and fees vary according to course load, degree level and program. *Financial support:* In 2009–10, 7 research assistantships with full tuition reimbursements (averaging $8,000 per year), 1 teaching assistantship with full tuition reimbursement (averaging $8,000 per year) were awarded; career-related internships or fieldwork, institutionally sponsored loans, health care benefits, and unspecified assistantships also available. Financial award applicants required to submit FAFSA. *Faculty research:* Anger as part of the grief process, inclusion of children with severe disabilities, comparisons of school counselors in Bosnia and the U. S., graduate and professional student socialization, use of cohort groups in doctoral programs, bullying in schools, impact of space on learning, sophomore experience. *Unit head:* Dr. Alan Demmitt, Chairperson, 937-229-3644, Fax: 937-229-1055. *Application contact:* Graduate Admissions, 937-229-4411, Fax: 937-229-4729, E-mail: gradadmission@udayton.edu.

University of Delaware, College of Human Services, Education and Public Policy, Department of Individual and Family Studies, Newark, DE 19716. Offers human development and family studies (MS, PhD). Part-time programs available. Terminal master's awarded for partial completion of doctoral program. *Degree requirements:* For master's, thesis or alternative; for doctorate, comprehensive exam, thesis/dissertation. *Entrance requirements:* For master's and doctorate, GRE General Test, 3 letters of recommendation. Additional exam requirements/recommendations for international students: Required—TOEFL. Electronic applications accepted. *Faculty research:* Early childhood inclusive education, relationships, family risk and resilience, disability issues, program development and evaluation.

University of Guelph, Graduate Program Services, College of Social and Applied Human Sciences, Department of Family Relations and Applied Nutrition, Guelph, ON N1G 2W1, Canada. Offers applied nutrition (MAN); family relations and human development (M Sc, PhD), including applied human nutrition, couple and family therapy (M Sc), family relations and human development. *Accreditation:* AAMFT/COAMFTE (one or more programs are accredited). Part-time programs available. *Degree requirements:* For master's, thesis (for some programs); for doctorate, comprehensive exam, thesis/dissertation. *Entrance requirements:* For master's, minimum B+ average; for doctorate, master's degree in family relations and human development or related field with a minimum B+ average or master's degree in applied human nutrition. Additional exam requirements/recommendations for international students: Required—TOEFL (minimum score 600 paper-based; 250 computer-based). Electronic applications accepted. *Faculty research:* Child and adolescent development, social gerontology, family roles and relations, couple and family therapy, applied human nutrition.

University of Houston, College of Technology, Department of Human Development and Consumer Science, Houston, TX 77204. Offers M Tech, MS. Part-time and evening/weekend programs available. *Faculty:* 3 full-time (2 women), 3 part-time/adjunct (1 woman). *Students:* 35 full-time (23 women), 56 part-time (36 women); includes 35 minority (22 African Americans, 4 Asian Americans or Pacific Islanders, 9 Hispanic Americans), 18 international. Average age 32. 41 applicants, 90% accepted, 30 enrolled. In 2009, 17 master's awarded. *Degree requirements:* For master's, project or thesis. *Entrance requirements:* For master's, GMAT, MAT. Additional exam requirements/recommendations for international students: Required—TOEFL (minimum score 550 paper-based; 79 iBT). *Application deadline:* For fall admission, 7/1 for domestic students, 4/1 for international students; for spring admission, 12/1 for domestic students, 10/1 for international students. Applications are processed on a rolling basis. Application fee: $75 ($150 for international students). Electronic applications accepted. *Expenses:* Tuition, state resident: full-time $7676; part-time $320 per credit hour. Tuition, nonresident: full-time $14,324; part-time $597 per credit hour. Required fees: $3034. *Financial support:* In 2009–10, 5 teaching assistantships with full tuition reimbursements (averaging $10,500 per year) were awarded. *Unit head:* Carole Goodson, Chairperson, 713-743-4046, Fax: 713-743-4033. *Application contact:* Tiffany Roosa, Academic Advisor, 713-743-2987, Fax: 713-743-4151, E-mail: troosa@uh.edu.

University of Illinois at Chicago, Graduate College, College of Applied Health Sciences, Department of Disability and Human Development, Chicago, IL 60607-7128. Offers disability and human development (MS); disability studies (PhD). *Accreditation:* AOTA. Part-time programs available. *Degree requirements:* For master's, thesis optional; for doctorate, thesis/dissertation. *Entrance requirements:* For master's and doctorate, GRE General Test. Additional exam requirements/recommendations for international students: Required—TOEFL. Electronic applications accepted. *Faculty research:* Emerging trends in disability, demography and financial structure of disability services, aging and disability, empowerment of people with disabilities, health promotion in disabilities.

University of Illinois at Springfield, Graduate Programs, College of Education and Human Services, Program in Human Development Counseling, Springfield, IL 62703-5407. Offers MA. *Accreditation:* ACA. Part-time and evening/weekend programs available. *Faculty:* 4 full-time (2 women), 1 part-time/adjunct (0 women). *Students:* 28 full-time (20 women), 42 part-time (34 women); includes 4 minority (2 African Americans, 1 Asian American or Pacific Islander, 1 Hispanic American). Average age 32. 68 applicants, 54% accepted, 16 enrolled. In 2009, 19 master's awarded. *Degree requirements:* For master's, project, thesis, or comprehensive exam. *Entrance requirements:* For master's, minimum undergraduate GPA of 3.0 in last 60 hours of coursework, personal references, interview. Additional exam requirements/recommendations for international students: Required—TOEFL (minimum score 500 paper-based; 176 computer-based; 61 iBT). Application fee: $50 ($60 for international students). Electronic applications accepted. *Expenses:* Tuition, state resident: full-time $6390; part-time $266.25 per credit hour. Tuition, nonresident: full-time $14,226; part-time $592.75 per credit hour. Required fees: $2044; $14.36 per credit hour. $722.50 per term. *Financial support:* In 2009–10, research assistantships with full tuition reimbursements (averaging $8,109 per year), teaching assistantships with full tuition reimbursements (averaging $8,109 per year) were awarded; career-related internships or fieldwork, Federal Work-Study, scholarships/grants, health care benefits, and unspecified assistantships also available. Support available to part-time students. Financial award application deadline: 11/15; financial award applicants required to submit FAFSA. *Unit head:* Dr. William Abler, Program Administrator, 217-206-7567, Fax: 217-206-6775, E-mail: abler.william@uis.edu. *Application contact:* Dr. Lynn Pardie, Office of Graduate Studies, 800-252-8533, Fax: 217-206-7623, E-mail: pardie.lynn@uis.edu.

University of Illinois at Urbana–Champaign, Graduate College, College of Agricultural, Consumer and Environmental Sciences, Department of Human and Community Development, Champaign, IL 61820. Offers agricultural education (MS); human and community development (MS, PhD); MS/MSW. *Faculty:* 16 full-time (10 women), 1 part-time/adjunct (0 women). *Students:* 31 full-time (26 women), 3 part-time (2 women); includes 9 minority (4 African Americans, 5 Asian Americans or Pacific Islanders), 3 international. 30 applicants, 37% accepted, 10 enrolled. In 2009, 18 master's, 1 doctorate awarded. *Entrance requirements:* For master's and doctorate, GRE, minimum GPA of 3.0. Additional exam requirements/recommendations for international students: Required—TOEFL (minimum score 550 paper-based; 213 computer-based; 79 iBT). *Application deadline:* Applications are processed on a rolling basis. Application fee: $60 ($75 for international students). Electronic applications accepted. *Financial support:* In 2009–10, 12 fellowships, 18 research assistantships, 19 teaching assistantships were awarded; tuition waivers (full and partial) also available. *Unit head:* Robert Hughes, Head, 217-333-3790, Fax: 217-244-7877, E-mail: hughesro@illinois.edu. *Application contact:* Leann Topol, Clerk, 217-333-3869, Fax: 217-244-7877, E-mail: ltopol@illinois.edu.

University of Maine, Graduate School, College of Education and Human Development, Department of Human Development and Family Relations, Orono, ME 04469. Offers human development (MS). Part-time programs available. *Students:* 10 full-time (8 women), 3 part-time (all women); includes 5 minority (2 African Americans, 2 American Indian/Alaska Native, 1 Asian American or Pacific Islander), 1 international. Average age 30. 8 applicants, 63% accepted, 5 enrolled. In 2009, 3 master's awarded. *Degree requirements:* For master's, thesis. *Entrance requirements:* For master's, GRE General Test. Additional exam requirements/recommendations for international students: Required—TOEFL. *Application deadline:* For fall admission, 2/1 priority date for domestic students. Applications are processed on a rolling basis. Application fee: $65. Electronic applications accepted. *Financial support:* Career-related internships or fieldwork, Federal Work-Study, institutionally sponsored loans, tuition waivers (full and partial), and unspecified assistantships available. Financial award application deadline: 3/1. *Faculty research:* Methods to assess nutrient intake and risk, carnitine-supplemented diets for protein-calorie malnutrition, nutrition education, grandfathers' perceptions of relations to grandchildren, social participation of spouses in distressed and nondistressed marriages. *Unit head:* Dr. Janet Spector, Coordinator, 207-581-3162, Fax: 207-581-3120. *Application contact:* Scott G. Delcourt, Associate Dean of the Graduate School, 207-581-3291, Fax: 207-581-3232, E-mail: graduate@maine.edu.

University of Maryland, College Park, Academic Affairs, College of Arts and Humanities, School of Languages, Literature, and Cultures, Program in Second Language Acquisition and Application, College Park, MD 20742. Offers French (MA); German (MA); Japanese (MA); Russian (MA); second language instruction (PhD); second language learning (PhD); second language measurement and assessment (PhD); second language use (PhD); Spanish (MA). *Students:* 12 full-time (10 women), 5 part-time (3 women); includes 2 minority (both Asian Americans or Pacific Islanders), 5 international. 47 applicants, 15% accepted, 3 enrolled. In 2009, 7 master's awarded. *Entrance requirements:* For master's, BA or BS in related field, demonstrated language competency, 3 letters of reference. *Application deadline:* For fall admission, 1/15 for domestic and international students; for spring admission, 6/1 for domestic and international students. Applications are processed on a rolling basis. Application fee: $60. Electronic applications accepted. *Expenses:* Tuition, area resident: Part-time $471 per credit hour. Tuition, state resident: part-time $471 per credit hour. Tuition, nonresident: part-time $1016 per credit hour. Required fees: $337.04 per term. *Financial support:* In 2009–10, 2 fellowships with full and partial tuition reimbursements (averaging $13,928 per year), 4 research assistantships (averaging $21,457 per year), 6 teaching assistantships (averaging $20,933 per year) were awarded. *Faculty research:* Second language acquisition, pedagogical perspectives, technological applications, language use in professional contexts. *Unit head:* Carol Mossman, Director, School of Languages, Literatures, and Cultures, 301-405-4025, E-mail: cmossman@umd.edu. *Application contact:* Dean of Graduate School, 301-405-0376, Fax: 301-314-9305.

University of Maryland, College Park, Academic Affairs, College of Education, Department of Human Development, College Park, MD 20742. Offers early childhood/elementary education (M Ed, MA, Ed D, PhD); human development (M Ed, MA, Ed D, PhD). *Accreditation:* NCATE. Part-time and evening/weekend programs available. Postbaccalaureate distance learning degree programs offered. *Faculty:* 52 full-time (45 women), 18 part-time/adjunct (14 women). *Students:* 54 full-time (48 women), 35 part-time (24 women); includes 18 minority (8 African Americans, 7 Asian Americans or Pacific Islanders, 3 Hispanic Americans), 8 international. 86 applicants, 35% accepted, 21 enrolled. In 2009, 24 master's, 7 doctorates awarded. *Degree requirements:* For master's, comprehensive exam, thesis optional; for doctorate, comprehensive exam, thesis/dissertation, essay, exam, research paper. *Entrance requirements:* For master's, GRE General Test, minimum GPA of 3.0, 3 letters of recommendation; for doctorate, GRE General Test or MAT, minimum undergraduate GPA of 3.0, graduate 3.5; 3 letters of recommendation. Additional exam requirements/recommendations for international students: Required—TOEFL. *Application deadline:* For fall admission, 3/15 for domestic students, 12/15 for international students; for spring admission, 10/1 priority date for domestic students, 6/1 for international students. Applications are processed on a rolling basis. Application fee: $60. Electronic applications accepted. *Expenses:* Tuition, area resident: Part-time $471 per credit hour. Tuition, state resident: part-time $471 per credit hour. Tuition, nonresident: part-time $1016 per credit hour. Required fees: $337.04 per term. *Financial support:* In 2009–10, 12 fellowships with full and partial tuition reimbursements (averaging $14,577 per year), 3 research assistantships with tuition reimbursements (averaging $17,558 per year), 29 teaching assistantships with tuition reimbursements (averaging $17,113 per year) were awarded; Federal Work-Study and scholarships/grants also available. Support available to part-time students. Financial award applicants required to submit FAFSA. *Faculty research:* Developmental science, educational psychology, cognitive development, language development. Total annual research expenditures: $2.4 million. *Unit head:* Dr. Allan L. Wigfield, Chair, 301-405-1659, Fax: 301-405-2891, E-mail: awigfield@umd.edu. *Application contact:* Dean of Graduate School, 301-405-0358, Fax: 301-314-9305.

University of Missouri, Graduate School, College of Human Environmental Science, Department of Human Development and Family Studies, Columbia, MO 65211. Offers MA, MS, PhD. *Entrance requirements:* For master's, GRE General Test, minimum GPA of 3.0. Additional exam requirements/recommendations for international students: Required—TOEFL (minimum score 550 paper-based; 213 computer-based; 80 iBT).

University of Nebraska–Lincoln, Graduate College, College of Education and Human Sciences, Department of Child, Youth and Family Studies, Lincoln, NE 68588. Offers child development/early childhood education (MS, PhD); child, youth and family studies (MS); family and consumer sciences education (MS, PhD); family financial planning (MS); family science (MS, PhD); gerontology (PhD); human sciences (PhD), including child, youth and family studies, gerontology, medical family therapy; marriage and family therapy (MS); medical family therapy (PhD); youth development (MS). *Accreditation:* AAMFT/COAMFTE (one or more programs are accredited). Postbaccalaureate distance learning degree programs offered. *Degree requirements:* For master's, thesis optional. *Entrance requirements:* For master's, GRE. Additional exam requirements/recommendations for international students: Required—TOEFL (minimum score 550 paper-based; 213 computer-based). Electronic applications accepted. *Faculty research:* Marriage and family therapy, child development/early childhood education, family financial management.

University of Nebraska–Lincoln, Graduate College, College of Education and Human Sciences, Department of Special Education and Communication Disorders, Lincoln, NE 68588. Offers audiology research (PhD); clinical audiology (Au D); educational studies (PhD); human sciences (PhD), including communication disorders; special education (M Ed, MA, Ed S), including special education (M Ed, MA), special education and communication disorders (Ed S); speech-language pathology and audiology (MS, Au D), including audiology and hearing science (Au D), speech-language pathology (Au D), speech-language pathology and audiology (MS). *Accreditation:* ASHA (one or more programs are accredited); NCATE. *Degree requirements:* For master's, thesis optional. *Entrance requirements:* For master's, GRE General Test. Additional exam requirements/recommendations for international students: Required—TOEFL. Electronic applications accepted. *Faculty research:* Curriculum-based assessment, paraprofessional and parent training, behavior management for special needs individuals, augmentative communication, speech/language disorders.

University of Nebraska–Lincoln, Graduate College, College of Education and Human Sciences, Department of Textiles, Clothing and Design, Lincoln, NE 68588. Offers human sciences (PhD), including textiles, clothing and design (MS, PhD); merchandising (MS); textile history/quilt studies (MA); textile science (MS); textile-apparel (MA); textiles, clothing and design (MA, MS), including textiles, clothing and design (MS, PhD). Part-time programs available. Postbaccalaureate distance learning degree programs offered (minimal on-campus study). *Degree requirements:* For master's, thesis optional. *Entrance requirements:* For master's, GRE General Test. Additional exam requirements/recommendations for international students: Required—TOEFL (minimum score 550 paper-based; 213 computer-based). Electronic applications accepted. *Faculty research:* Merchandising, textile science, fiber arts, textile history, quilt studies.

University of Nevada, Reno, Graduate School, College of Education, Department of Human Development and Family Studies, Reno, NV 89557. Offers MS. *Degree requirements:* For master's, thesis optional. *Entrance requirements:* For master's, GRE General Test, minimum GPA of 2.75. Additional exam requirements/recommendations for international students: Required—TOEFL (minimum score 500 paper-based; 173 computer-based; 61 iBT), IELTS (minimum score 6). Electronic applications accepted. *Faculty research:* Early childhood/adolescent development, family studies.

The University of North Carolina at Greensboro, Graduate School, School of Human Environmental Sciences, Department of Human Development and Family Studies, Greensboro, NC 27412-5001. Offers M Ed, MS, PhD. *Degree requirements:* For master's, one foreign language; for doctorate, one foreign language, thesis/dissertation. *Entrance requirements:* For master's and doctorate, GRE General Test. Additional exam requirements/recommendations for international students: Required—TOEFL. Electronic applications accepted. *Expenses:* Contact institution. *Faculty research:* Adolescent mothers, multi-handicapped, older adults.

University of North Texas, Robert B. Toulouse School of Graduate Studies, College of Education, Department of Educational Psychology, Program in Development and Family Studies, Denton, TX 76203. Offers MS, Certificate. Evening/weekend programs available.

Human Development

University of North Texas (continued)

Degree requirements: For master's, comprehensive exam, thesis optional. *Entrance requirements:* For master's, GRE General Test, resume, references. Additional exam requirements/recommendations for international students: Required—proof of English language proficiency required for non-native English speakers; Recommended—TOEFL (minimum score 550 paper-based; 213 computer-based). *Application deadline:* Applications are processed on a rolling basis. Application fee: $50 ($75 for international students). Electronic applications accepted. *Expenses:* Tuition, state resident: full-time $4298; part-time $239 per contact hour. Tuition, nonresident: full-time $9878; part-time $549 per contact hour. Required fees: $265 per contact hour. *Financial support:* Teaching assistantships, career-related internships or fieldwork, Federal Work-Study, and institutionally sponsored loans available. Financial award applicants required to submit FAFSA. *Faculty research:* Parent-child issues, cognitive development, social development. *Application contact:* Becky Glover, Graduate Advisor, 940-565-4876, E-mail: becky.glover@unt.edu.

University of Pennsylvania, Graduate School of Education, Division of Applied Psychology and Human Development, Interdisciplinary Studies in Human Development, Philadelphia, PA 19104. Offers MS Ed, PhD. Part-time programs available. *Students:* 36 full-time (28 women), 6 part-time (5 women); includes 16 minority (14 African Americans, 1 Asian American or Pacific Islander, 1 Hispanic American), 10 international. 84 applicants, 45% accepted, 19 enrolled. In 2009, 6 master's, 4 doctorates awarded. Terminal master's awarded for partial completion of doctoral program. *Degree requirements:* For master's, exam; for doctorate, thesis/dissertation, exam. *Entrance requirements:* For master's, GRE General Test; for doctorate, GRE General Test, GRE Subject Test. *Application deadline:* For fall admission, 12/15 priority date for domestic students. Applications are processed on a rolling basis. Application fee: $70. Electronic applications accepted. *Expenses:* Contact institution. *Financial support:* Fellowships, research assistantships, institutionally sponsored loans, scholarships/grants, traineeships, health care benefits, and unspecified assistantships available. *Faculty research:* Child development, risk and resilience among vulnerable youth in high-risk environments.

University of St. Thomas, Graduate Studies, School of Education, Program in Organization Learning and Development, St. Paul, MN 55105-1096. Offers career development (Certificate); e-learning (Certificate); human resource management (Certificate); human resources and change leadership (MA); learning technology (Certificate); learning technology for learning development and change (MA); organization development (Ed D, Certificate). Part-time and evening/weekend programs available. Postbaccalaureate distance learning degree programs offered (minimal on-campus study). *Faculty:* 5 full-time (4 women), 6 part-time/adjunct (2 women). *Students:* 6 full-time (5 women), 161 part-time (130 women); includes 24 minority (13 African Americans, 7 Asian Americans or Pacific Islanders, 4 Hispanic Americans), 1 international. Average age 37. 115 applicants, 75% accepted, 85 enrolled. In 2009, 29 master's, 7 doctorates, 18 other advanced degrees awarded. *Degree requirements:* For doctorate, comprehensive exam, thesis/dissertation. *Entrance requirements:* For master's, minimum GPA of 3.0, 2 letters of reference, personal statement; for doctorate, minimum GPA of 3.5, interview; for Certificate, minimum graduate GPA of 3.25. Additional exam requirements/recommendations for international students: Required—TOEFL (minimum score 550 paper-based; 213 computer-based). *Application deadline:* For fall admission, 8/1 priority date for domestic and international students; for winter admission, 12/1 priority date for domestic students, 12/1 for international students; for spring admission, 12/1 priority date for domestic and international students. Applications are processed on a rolling basis. Application fee: $50. *Expenses:* Contact institution. *Financial support:* Fellowships, research assistantships, institutionally sponsored loans and scholarships/grants available. Support available to part-time students. Financial award applicants required to submit FAFSA. *Faculty research:* Workplace conflict, physician leaders, entrepreneurship education, mentoring. *Unit head:* Dr. Christopher S. Vye, Acting Department Chair, 651-962-4666, Fax: 651-962-4169, E-mail: csvye@stthomas.edu. *Application contact:* Liz G. Knight, Department Coordinator, 651-962-4459, Fax: 651-962-4169, E-mail: egknight@stthomas.edu.

University of South Africa, College of Human Sciences, Pretoria, South Africa. Offers adult education (M Ed); African languages (MA, PhD); African politics (MA, PhD); Afrikaans (MA, PhD); ancient history (MA, PhD); ancient Near Eastern studies (MA, PhD); anthropology (MA, PhD); applied linguistics (MA); Arabic (MA, PhD); archaeology (MA); art history (MA); Biblical archaeology (MA); Biblical studies (M Th, D Th, PhD); Christian spirituality (M Th, D Th); church history (M Th, D Th); classical studies (MA, PhD); clinical psychology (MA); communication (MA, PhD); comparative education (M Ed, Ed D); consulting psychology (D Admin, D Com, PhD); curriculum studies (M Ed, Ed D); development studies (M Admin, MA, D Admin, PhD); didactics (M Ed, Ed D); education (M Tech); education management (M Ed, Ed D); educational psychology (M Ed); English (MA); environmental education (M Ed); French (MA, PhD); German (MA, PhD); Greek (MA); guidance and counseling (M Ed); health studies (MA, PhD), including health sciences education (MA), health services management (MA), medical and surgical nursing science (critical care general) (MA), midwifery and neonatal nursing science (MA), trauma and emergency care (MA); history (MA, PhD); history of education (Ed D); inclusive education (M Ed, Ed D); information and communications technology policy and regulation (MA); information science (MA, MIS, PhD); international politics (MA, PhD); Islamic studies (MA, PhD); Italian (MA, PhD); Judaica (MA, PhD); linguistics (MA, PhD); mathematical education (M Ed); mathematics education (MA); missiology (M Th, D Th); modern Hebrew (MA, PhD); musicology (MA, MMus, D Mus, PhD); natural science education (M Ed); New Testament (M Th, D Th); Old Testament (D Th); pastoral therapy (M Th, D Th); philosophy (MA); philosophy of education (M Ed, Ed D); politics (MA, PhD); Portuguese (MA, PhD); practical theology (M Th, D Th); psychology (MA, MS, PhD); psychology of education (M Ed, Ed D); public health (MA); religious studies (MA, D Th, PhD); Romance languages (MA); Russian (MA, PhD); Semitic languages (MA, PhD); social behavior studies in HIV/AIDS (MA); social science (mental health) (MA); social science in development studies (MA); social science in psychology (MA); social science in social work (MA); social science in sociology (MA); social work (MSW, DSW, PhD); socio-education (M Ed, Ed D); sociolinguistics (MA); sociology (MA, PhD); Spanish (MA, PhD); systematic theology (M Th, D Th); TESOL (teaching English to speakers of other languages) (MA); theological ethics (M Th, D Th); theory of literature (MA, PhD); urban ministry (D Th); urban ministry (M Th).

The University of Texas at Austin, Graduate School, College of Education, Department of Educational Psychology, Austin, TX 78712-1111. Offers academic educational psychology (M Ed, MA); counseling psychology (PhD); counselor education (M Ed); human development and culture (PhD); learning, cognition and instruction (PhD); quantitative methods (PhD); school psychology (PhD). *Accreditation:* APA (one or more programs are accredited). *Degree requirements:* For master's, thesis optional; for doctorate, thesis/dissertation. *Entrance requirements:* For master's and doctorate, GRE General Test, 3 letters of recommendation. Additional exam requirements/recommendations for international students: Required—TOEFL.

University of Utah, The Graduate School, College of Social and Behavioral Science, Department of Family and Consumer Studies, Salt Lake City, UT 84112-0080. Offers human development and social policy (MS). Part-time and evening/weekend programs available. *Faculty:* 16 full-time (7 women), 1 (woman) part-time/adjunct. *Students:* 9 full-time (7 women), 5 part-time (all women), 1 international. Average age 36. 16 applicants, 38% accepted, 6 enrolled. In 2009, 2 master's awarded. *Degree requirements:* For master's, thesis optional. *Entrance requirements:* For master's, GRE General Test, minimum undergraduate GPA of 3.0, courses in research methods and statistics. Additional exam requirements/recommendations for international students: Required—TOEFL (minimum score 500 paper-based; 173 computer-based). *Application deadline:* For fall admission, 3/1 priority date for domestic and international students. Application fee: $55 ($65 for international students). Electronic applications accepted. *Expenses:* Tuition, state resident: full-time $4004; part-time $1674 per semester. Tuition, nonresident: full-time $14,134; part-time $5915 per semester. Required fees: $324 per semester. Tuition and fees vary according to course load, degree level and program. *Financial support:* In 2009–10, 10 students received support, including 1 research assistantship with partial tuition reimbursement available (averaging $5,500 per year), 9 teaching assistantships with partial tuition reimbursements available (averaging $5,500 per year). Financial award application deadline: 2/1. *Faculty research:* Social, physical and economic contexts of families and communities. Total annual research expenditures: $350,000. *Unit head:* Dr. Cheryl Wright, Chair, 801-581-7712, Fax: 801-581-5156, E-mail: cheryl.wright@fcs.utah.edu. *Application contact:* Dr. Marissa Diener, Graduate Director, 801-581-6521, E-mail: marissa.diener@fcs.utah.edu.

University of Victoria, Faculty of Graduate Studies, Faculty of Education, Department of Educational Psychology and Leadership Studies, Victoria, BC V8W 2Y2, Canada. Offers aboriginal communities counseling (M Ed); counseling (M Ed, MA); educational psychology (M Ed, MA, PhD), including counseling psychology (M Ed, MA), leadership studies (PhD), learning and development (MA, PhD), measurement and evaluation, special education (M Ed, MA); leadership studies (M Ed, MA). Part-time programs available. *Degree requirements:* For master's, thesis (for some programs), comprehensive exam (M Ed); for doctorate, comprehensive exam, thesis/dissertation, candidacy exam. *Entrance requirements:* For master's, 2 years of work experience in a relevant field; for doctorate, GRE, 2 years of work experience in a relevant field, minimum B average. Additional exam requirements/recommendations for international students: Required—TOEFL (minimum score 575 paper-based; 233 computer-based), IELTS (minimum score 7). *Faculty research:* Learning and development (child, adolescent and adult), special education and exceptional children.

University of Victoria, Faculty of Graduate Studies, Faculty of Human and Social Development, Studies in Policy and Practice Program, Victoria, BC V8W 2Y2, Canada. Offers MA. Part-time programs available. *Degree requirements:* For master's, thesis. *Entrance requirements:* For master's, resume. Additional exam requirements/recommendations for international students: Required—TOEFL (minimum score 575 paper-based; 233 computer-based), IELTS (minimum score 7). Electronic applications accepted. *Faculty research:* Women's issues, public policy formation and implementation, health promotion and education, children, youth and families.

University of Washington, Graduate School, College of Education, Program in Educational Psychology, Seattle, WA 98195. Offers educational psychology (PhD); human development and cognition (M Ed); learning sciences (M Ed, PhD); measurement, statistics and research design (M Ed); school psychology (M Ed). *Accreditation:* APA. *Degree requirements:* For master's, thesis optional; for doctorate, thesis/dissertation. *Entrance requirements:* For master's and doctorate, GRE General Test, minimum GPA of 3.0. Additional exam requirements/recommendations for international students: Required—TOEFL.

University of Wisconsin–Madison, Graduate School, School of Human Ecology, Program in Human Development and Family Studies, Madison, WI 53706-1380. Offers MS, PhD. Part-time programs available. Terminal master's awarded for partial completion of doctoral program. *Degree requirements:* For master's, thesis; for doctorate, comprehensive exam, thesis/dissertation. *Entrance requirements:* For master's, GRE General Test, 3 letters of recommendation; for doctorate, GRE General Test, MS or MA, 3 letters of recommendation. Additional exam requirements/recommendations for international students: Required—TOEFL. Electronic applications accepted. *Expenses:* Tuition, state resident: part-time $594 per credit. Tuition, nonresident: part-time $1504 per credit. Required fees: $65 per credit. Tuition and fees vary according to course load, program and reciprocity agreements. *Faculty research:* Human development, adolescence, adulthood, prevention, intervention.

University of Wisconsin–Stevens Point, College of Professional Studies, School of Health Promotion and Human Development, Stevens Point, WI 54481-3897. Offers human and community resources (MS); nutritional sciences (MS). Part-time programs available. *Students:* 4 full-time (all women), 2 part-time (both women); includes 2 African Americans. *Degree requirements:* For master's, thesis or alternative. *Entrance requirements:* For master's, minimum GPA of 2.75. *Application deadline:* For fall admission, 5/1 priority date for domestic students. Applications are processed on a rolling basis. Application fee: $45. *Expenses:* Tuition, state resident: full-time $7740; part-time $430 per credit hour. Tuition, nonresident: full-time $17,804; part-time $989 per credit hour. Tuition and fees vary according to course load and reciprocity agreements. *Financial support:* Research assistantships, teaching assistantships, career-related internships or fieldwork, Federal Work-Study, and unspecified assistantships available. Support available to part-time students. Financial award application deadline: 5/1; financial award applicants required to submit FAFSA. *Unit head:* Dr. Marty Loy, Head, 715-346-2830, Fax: 715-346-2720. *Application contact:* Dr. Jasia Steinmetz, Information Contact, 715-346-2830, Fax: 715-346-2720, E-mail: jsteinme@uwsp.edu.

University of Wisconsin–Stout, Graduate School, College of Human Development, Program in Family Studies and Human Development, Menomonie, WI 54751. Offers MS. Part-time programs available. *Degree requirements:* For master's, thesis. *Entrance requirements:* For master's, minimum GPA of 2.75. Additional exam requirements/recommendations for international students: Required—TOEFL (minimum score 500 paper-based; 173 computer-based; 61 iBT). Electronic applications accepted. *Faculty research:* Diversity, work and family medical ethics, family policy, dementia and families.

Utah State University, School of Graduate Studies, College of Education and Human Services, Department of Family, Consumer, and Human Development, Logan, UT 84322. Offers family and human development (MFHD); family, consumer, and human development (MS, PhD), including adolescence/youth (MS), adult development/aging (MS), consumer science (MS), infancy/childhood (MS), marriage and family relations (MS), marriage and family therapy (MS). *Accreditation:* AAMFT/COAMFTE (one or more programs are accredited). Part-time and evening/weekend programs available. Postbaccalaureate distance learning degree programs offered (minimal on-campus study). *Degree requirements:* For master's, thesis; for doctorate, comprehensive exam, thesis/dissertation, competencies. *Entrance requirements:* For master's, GRE General Test or MAT, minimum GPA of 3.0, 3 letters of recommendation; for doctorate, GRE, minimum GPA of 3.0, 3 letters of recommendation. Additional exam requirements/recommendations for international students: Required—TOEFL. Electronic applications accepted. *Faculty research:* Marriage and family relations, adolescent problem behavior, family financial management, early literacy, mental health in the elderly, parent child attachment.

Vanderbilt University, Peabody College, Department of Human and Organizational Development, Nashville, TN 37240-1001. Offers community development and action (M Ed); human development counseling (M Ed). *Accreditation:* ACA; NCATE. Part-time programs available. *Faculty:* 29 full-time (14 women), 27 part-time/adjunct (19 women). *Students:* 88 full-time (82 women), 7 part-time (all women); includes 16 minority (11 African Americans, 1 Asian American or Pacific Islander, 4 Hispanic Americans), 1 international. Average age 27. 141 applicants, 57% accepted, 56 enrolled. In 2009, 31 master's awarded. *Degree requirements:* For master's, comprehensive exam, thesis optional. *Entrance requirements:* For master's, GRE General Test, MAT. Additional exam requirements/recommendations for international students: Required—TOEFL (minimum score 550 paper-based; 213 computer-based). *Application deadline:* For fall admission, 12/31 priority date for domestic and international students; for spring admission, 11/1 priority date for domestic and international students. Applications are processed on a rolling basis. Application fee: $0. Electronic applications accepted. *Financial support:* In 2009–10, 86 students received support, including 31 research assistantships with full and partial tuition reimbursements available, 20 teaching assistantships with full and partial tuition reimbursements available, fellowships with full and partial tuition reimbursements available, Federal Work-Study, institutionally sponsored loans, scholarships/grants, tuition waivers (partial), and unspecified assistantships also available. Support available to part-time students. Financial award application deadline: 2/1; financial award applicants required to submit FAFSA. *Faculty research:* Community psychology, community development and urban policy, counseling and mental health services, organizational development and institutional change; youth physical and behavioral health in schools and communities. *Unit head:* Dr. Marybeth Shinn, Chair, 615-322-6881, Fax: 615-322-1141, E-mail: marybeth.shinn@vanderbilt.edu. *Application contact:* Sherrie Lane, Office Assistant, 615-322-8484, Fax: 615-322-1141, E-mail: sherrie.a.lane@vanderbilt.edu.

Virginia Polytechnic Institute and State University, Graduate School, College of Liberal Arts and Human Sciences, Department of Human Development, Blacksburg, VA 24061. Offers adult development and aging (MS, PhD); adult learning and human resource development (MS, PhD); child development (MS, PhD); family studies (MS, PhD); marriage and family therapy (MS, PhD). *Accreditation:* AAMFT/COAMFTE (one or more programs are accredited). *Faculty:* 22 full-time (18 women). *Students:* 49 full-time (38 women), 64 part-time (44 women); includes 30 minority (1 African American, 7 American Indian/Alaska Native, 16 Asian Americans or Pacific Islanders, 6 Hispanic Americans), 2 international. Average age 34. 64 applicants, 34% accepted, 16 enrolled. In 2009, 10 master's, 14 doctorates awarded. *Entrance requirements:* For master's and doctorate, GRE, GMAT. Additional exam requirements/recommendations for international students: Required—TOEFL (minimum score 550 paper-based; 213 computer-based). *Application deadline:* For fall admission, 5/15 for international students; for spring admission, 10/15 for international students. Applications are processed on a rolling basis. Application fee: $65. Electronic applications accepted. *Expenses:* Tuition, area resident: Full-time $10,228; part-time $459 per credit hour. Tuition, nonresident: full-time $17,892; part-time $865 per credit hour. Required fees: $1966; $451 per semester. *Financial support:* In 2009–10, 7 research assistantships with full tuition reimbursements (averaging $10,933 per year), 25 teaching assistantships with full tuition reimbursements (averaging $9,387 per year) were awarded; career-related internships or fieldwork, Federal Work-Study, scholarships/grants, and unspecified assistantships also available. Financial award application deadline: 1/15. *Faculty research:* Stress management, children's play, dual-career families, social cognition, relationships of elderly. Total annual research expenditures: $823,581. *Unit head:* Dr. Shannon E. Jarrott, Head, 540-231-4794, Fax: 540-231-7012, E-mail: sjarrott@vt.edu. *Application contact:* Mark Benson, Information Contact, 540-231-5720, Fax: 540-231-7012, E-mail: mbenson@vt.edu.

Washington State University, Graduate School, College of Agricultural, Human, and Natural Resource Sciences, Department of Human Development, Pullman, WA 99164. Offers MA. Part-time programs available. *Faculty:* 13 full-time. *Students:* 13 full-time (11 women), 3 international. Average age 25. 21 applicants, 43% accepted, 6 enrolled. In 2009, 6 master's awarded. *Degree requirements:* For master's, comprehensive exam (for some programs), thesis (for some programs), oral exam. *Entrance requirements:* For master's, GRE General Test, bachelor's degree in human development or related field; written statement specifying qualifications, educational goals, and career objectives; official copies of all college transcripts; three letters of reference. Additional exam requirements/recommendations for international students: Required—TOEFL. *Application deadline:* For fall admission, 1/10 priority date for domestic students, 1/10 for international students. Application fee: $50. Electronic applications accepted. *Financial support:* In 2009–10, 12 students received support, including 1 research assistantship with partial tuition reimbursement available (averaging $13,917 per year), 11 teaching assistantships with partial tuition reimbursements available (averaging $13,056 per year); Federal Work-Study, institutionally sponsored loans, tuition waivers (partial), and teaching associateships also available. Financial award application deadline: 2/15; financial award applicants required to submit FAFSA. *Faculty research:* Family processes, social development of children, quality child care, community collaborations, parent-child relationships. Total annual research expenditures: $450,000. *Unit head:* Dr. Thomas G. Power, Chair, 509-355-9540, Fax: 509-335-2456, E-mail: tompower@wsu.edu. *Application contact:* Graduate School Admissions, 800-GRADWSU, Fax: 509-335-1949, E-mail: gradsch@wsu.edu.

Wayne State University, College of Liberal Arts and Sciences, Department of Psychology, Program in Human Development, Detroit, MI 48202. Offers MA. *Entrance requirements:* For master's, GRE General Test. Additional exam requirements/recommendations for international students: Required—TOEFL (minimum score 550 paper-based; 213 computer-based); Recommended—TWE (minimum score 6). Electronic applications accepted. *Faculty research:* Emotional expression, peer influence in adolescence, preschool concept formation and memory, mother-infant interaction.

West Virginia University, Davis College of Agriculture, Forestry and Consumer Sciences, Division of Resource Management and Sustainable Development, Morgantown, WV 26506. Offers agricultural and extension education (MS, PhD), including agricultural and extension education, teaching vocational-agriculture (MS); agricultural and resource economics (MS); human and community development (PhD); natural resource economics (PhD); resource management (PhD); resource management and sustainable development (PhD). Part-time programs available. *Degree requirements:* For master's, thesis; for doctorate, comprehensive exam, thesis/dissertation. *Entrance requirements:* For master's, GRE General Test. Additional exam requirements/recommendations for international students: Required—TOEFL. *Faculty research:* Environmental economics, energy economics, agriculture.

Wheelock College, Graduate Programs, Division of Arts and Sciences, Boston, MA 02215-4176. Offers human development (MS). *Entrance requirements:* Additional exam requirements/recommendations for international students: Required—TOEFL. Electronic applications accepted.

Industrial and Organizational Psychology

Adler Graduate School, Program in Adlerian Studies, Richfield, MN 55423. Offers art therapy specialization (MA); clinical counseling track (MA); coaching and consulting in organizations (Certificate); management consulting and organizational leadership (MA); marriage and family track (MA); non-clinical Adlerian studies track (MA); personal and professional life coaching (Certificate); school counseling (MA). Part-time and evening/weekend programs available. *Degree requirements:* For master's, thesis or alternative, 500-700 hour internship (depending on license choice). *Entrance requirements:* For master's, minimum undergraduate GPA of 3.0, 12 credits of course work in psychology or related field.

Adler School of Professional Psychology, Programs in Psychology, Chicago, IL 60601-7203. Offers art therapy (MA, Certificate); clinical hypnosis (Certificate); clinical psychology (Psy D); counseling (MA); counseling and organizational psychology (MA); forensic psychology (MA); gerontological counseling (MA); marriage and family counseling (MA); marriage and family therapy (Certificate); organizational psychology (MA); police psychology (MA); rehabilitation counseling (MA); sport and health psychology (MA); substance abuse counseling (Certificate); Psy D/Certificate; Psy D/MACAT; Psy D/MACP; Psy D/MAMFC; Psy D/MASAC. *Accreditation:* APA. Part-time and evening/weekend programs available. Postbaccalaureate distance learning degree programs offered (minimal on-campus study). *Faculty:* 41 full-time (21 women), 44 part-time/adjunct (19 women). *Students:* 551 full-time (441 women), 161 part-time (137 women). Average age 27.Terminal master's awarded for partial completion of doctoral program. *Degree requirements:* For master's, thesis or alternative, oral exam, practicum; for doctorate, thesis/dissertation, clinical exam, internship, oral exam, practicum, written qualifying exam. *Entrance requirements:* For master's, 12 semester hours in psychology, minimum GPA of 3.0; for doctorate, 18 semester hours in psychology, minimum GPA of 3.25; for Certificate, appropriate master's or doctoral degree. Additional exam requirements/recommendations for international students: Required—TOEFL (minimum score 550 paper-based; 213 computer-based; 79 iBT). *Application deadline:* For fall admission, 2/15 priority date for domestic students, 12/1 priority date for international students. Applications are processed on a rolling basis. Application fee: $50. Electronic applications accepted. *Expenses:* Tuition: Part-time $930 per credit. Required fees: $220 per term. *Financial support:* Career-related internships or fieldwork, Federal Work-Study, scholarships/grants, and tuition waivers (full and partial) available. Support available to part-time students. Financial award application deadline: 5/15; financial award applicants required to submit FAFSA. *Unit head:* Dr. Frank Gruba-McAllister, Vice President of Academic Affairs, 312-201-5900 Ext. 209, Fax: 312-201-5917. *Application contact:* Craig A. Hines, Associate Vice President of Admissions, 312-201-5900 Ext. 226, Fax: 312-201-5917, E-mail: chines@adler.edu.

See Close-Up on page 1047.

Alliant International University–Fresno, Marshall Goldsmith School of Management, Organizational Psychology Division, Fresno, CA 93727. Offers organizational behavior (MA); organizational development (Psy D); MA/PhD; Psy D/MA. Part-time and evening/weekend programs available. *Degree requirements:* For doctorate, thesis/dissertation. *Entrance requirements:* For doctorate, interview, minimum GPA of 3.0. Additional exam requirements/recommendations for international students: Required—TOEFL (minimum score 600 paper-based; 250 computer-based), TWE (minimum score 5). Electronic applications accepted. *Faculty research:* Leadership, ethics and management, career development, human resources management.

Alliant International University–Los Angeles, Marshall Goldsmith School of Management, Organizational Psychology Division, Alhambra, CA 91803-1360. Offers industrial/organizational psychology (MA, PhD). Part-time programs available. Terminal master's awarded for partial completion of doctoral program. *Degree requirements:* For doctorate, thesis/dissertation. *Entrance requirements:* For master's and doctorate, interview, minimum GPA of 3.0 in both psychology and overall. Additional exam requirements/recommendations for international students: Required—TOEFL (minimum score 600 paper-based; 250 computer-based), TWE (minimum score 5). Electronic applications accepted. *Faculty research:* Organizational transitions, productivity, work force demographics, management technology, comparative and international research.

Alliant International University–Sacramento, Marshall Goldsmith School of Management, Program in Organizational Development, Sacramento, CA 95825. Offers Psy D. *Entrance requirements:* For doctorate, minimum GPA of 3.0, interview, letters of recommendation.

Alliant International University–San Diego, Marshall Goldsmith School of Management, Organizational Psychology Division, San Diego, CA 92131-1799. Offers clinical/industrial organizational psychology (PhD); consulting psychology (PhD); industrial/organizational psychology (MA, MS, PhD); organizational behavior (MA). Part-time and evening/weekend programs available. Terminal master's awarded for partial completion of doctoral program. *Degree requirements:* For doctorate, thesis/dissertation. *Entrance requirements:* For master's and doctorate, interview, minimum GPA of 3.0 in both psychology and overall. Additional exam requirements/recommendations for international students: Required—TOEFL (minimum score 600 paper-based; 250 computer-based), TWE (minimum score 5). Electronic applications accepted. *Faculty research:* Cultural diversity in the workplace, work motivation, personnel, performance management.

Alliant International University–San Francisco, Marshall Goldsmith School of Management, Organizational Psychology Division, San Francisco, CA 94133-1221. Offers organization development (MA); organizational psychology (MA, PhD). Part-time and evening/weekend programs available. Terminal master's awarded for partial completion of doctoral program. *Degree requirements:* For doctorate, thesis/dissertation. *Entrance requirements:* For master's and doctorate, interview, minimum GPA of 3.0. Additional exam requirements/recommendations for international students: Required—TOEFL (minimum score 650 paper-based; 250 computer-based), TWE (minimum score 5). Electronic applications accepted. *Faculty research:* Leadership, ethics and management, career development, organizational behavior, strategic change.

American InterContinental University Online, Program in Business Administration, Hoffman Estates, IL 60192. Offers accounting and finance (MBA); finance (MBA); healthcare management (MBA); human resource management (MBA); international business (MBA); management (MBA); marketing (MBA); operations management (MBA); organizational psychology and development (MBA); project management (MBA). Evening/weekend programs available. Postbaccalaureate distance learning degree programs offered (no on-campus study). *Entrance requirements:* Additional exam requirements/recommendations for international students: Required—TOEFL (minimum score 550 paper-based; 213 computer-based). Electronic applications accepted.

Angelo State University, College of Graduate Studies, College of Liberal and Fine Arts, Department of Psychology, Sociology and Social Work, San Angelo, TX 76909. Offers psychology (MS), including counseling psychology, general psychology, industrial and organizational psychology. Part-time and evening/weekend programs available. *Faculty:* 8 full-time (2 women). *Students:* 33 full-time (22 women), 14 part-time (11 women); includes 10 minority (2 African Americans, 1 Asian American or Pacific Islander, 7 Hispanic Americans). Average age 29. 46 applicants, 78% accepted, 26 enrolled. In 2009, 23 master's awarded. *Degree requirements:* For master's, comprehensive exam, thesis optional. *Entrance requirements:* For master's, GRE General Test. Additional exam requirements/recommendations for international students: Required—TOEFL or IELTS. *Application deadline:* For fall admission, 7/15 priority date for domestic students, 6/10 for international students; for spring admission, 12/1 priority date for domestic students, 11/1 for international students. Applications are processed on a rolling basis. Application fee: $40 ($50 for international students). Electronic applications accepted. *Expenses:* Tuition, state resident: full-time $3396; part-time $142 per credit hour. Tuition, nonresident: full-time $10,152; part-time $423 per credit hour. Required fees: $1786; $36.25 per credit hour. $494 per semester. Full-time tuition and fees vary according to course load, degree level and program. *Financial support:* In 2009–10, 44 students received support, including 3 teaching assistantships (averaging $10,251 per year); career-related internships or fieldwork, Federal Work-Study, scholarships/grants, and unspecified assistantships also available. Support available to part-time students. Financial award application deadline: 3/1; financial award applicants required to submit FAFSA. *Faculty research:* Toddlers use of actors' intentions to learn verbs. Total annual research expenditures: $116,915. *Unit head:* Dr. William B. Davidson, Department Head, 325-942-2068 Ext. 248, Fax: 325-942-2290, E-mail: bill.davidson@angelo.edu. *Application contact:* Theresa Fortin, Graduate Admissions Assistant, 325-942-2169, Fax: 325-942-2194, E-mail: theresa.fortin@angelo.edu.

Antioch University Seattle, Graduate Programs, Center for Creative Change, Seattle, WA 98121-1814. Offers environment and community (MA); management (MS); organizational psychology (MA); strategic communications (MA); whole system design (MA). Evening/weekend programs available. Electronic applications accepted. *Expenses:* Contact institution.

Appalachian State University, Cratis D. Williams Graduate School, Department of Psychology, Boone, NC 28608. Offers clinical health psychology (MA); general experimental psychology (MA); industrial and organizational psychology (MA). Part-time programs available. *Faculty:* 31 full-time (11 women). *Students:* 51 full-time (37 women), 13 part-time (10 women); includes 4 minority (2 African Americans, 2 Asian Americans or Pacific Islanders), 2 international. 181 applicants, 25% accepted, 26 enrolled. In 2009, 22 master's, 7 other advanced degrees awarded. *Degree requirements:* For master's and MS/Specialist, comprehensive exam, thesis optional, GRE Subject Test exit exam. *Entrance requirements:* For master's and MS/Specialist, GRE General Test, 3 letters of recommendation. Additional exam requirements/recommendations

Industrial and Organizational Psychology

Appalachian State University (continued)
for international students: Required—TOEFL (minimum score 550 paper-based; 230 computer-based; 79 iBT), or IELTS (minimum score 6.5). *Application deadline:* For fall admission, 3/1 for domestic students, 2/1 for international students. Applications are processed on a rolling basis. Application fee: $50. Electronic applications accepted. *Expenses:* Tuition, state resident: full-time $2960. Tuition, nonresident: full-time $14,051. Required fees: $2320. *Financial support:* In 2009–10, 34 research assistantships (averaging $4,000 per year), 25 teaching assistantships (averaging $4,000 per year) were awarded; fellowships, career-related internships or fieldwork, Federal Work-Study, scholarships/grants, and unspecified assistantships also available. Financial award application deadline: 4/1; financial award applicants required to submit FAFSA. *Faculty research:* Eating disorders, school-based consultations, organizational behavior management, brain mechanisms of sound localization, parenting styles. Total annual research expenditures: $114,200. *Unit head:* Dr. James Denniston, Chair, 828-262-2272, Fax: 828-262-2272, E-mail: dennistonjc@appstate.edu. *Application contact:* Dr. Denise Martz, Graduate Coordinator, 828-262-2715, E-mail: martzdm@appstate.edu.

Argosy University, Atlanta, College of Psychology and Behavioral Sciences, Atlanta, GA 30328. Offers clinical psychology (MA, Psy D, Postdoctoral Respecialization Certificate), including child and family psychology (Psy D), general adult clinical (Psy D), health psychology (Psy D), neuropsychology/geropsychology (Psy D); community counseling (MA), including marriage and family therapy; counselor education and supervision (Ed D); forensic psychology (MA); industrial organizational psychology (MA); marriage and family therapy (Certificate); sport-exercise psychology (MA). *Accreditation:* APA.

See Close-Up on page 1049.

Argosy University, Chicago, College of Psychology and Behavioral Sciences, Chicago, IL 60601. Offers clinical psychology (MA, Psy D), including child and adolescent psychology (Psy D), client-centered and experiential psychotherapies (Psy D), diversity and multicultural psychology (Psy D), family psychology (Psy D), forensic psychology (Psy D), health psychology (Psy D), neuropsychology (Psy D), organizational consulting (Psy D), psychoanalytic psychology (Psy D), psychology and spirituality (Psy D); community counseling (MA); counseling psychology (Ed D), including counselor education and supervision; counselor education and supervision (Ed D); industrial organizational psychology (MA). *Accreditation:* APA (one or more programs are accredited). Postbaccalaureate distance learning degree programs offered (minimal on-campus study).

See Close-Up on page 1051.

Argosy University, Dallas, College of Psychology and Behavioral Sciences, Program in Industrial Organizational Psychology, Farmers Branch, TX 75244. Offers MA.

See Close-Up on page 1053.

Argosy University, Denver, College of Psychology and Behavioral Sciences, Denver, CO 80231. Offers clinical mental health counseling (MA); clinical psychology (MA, Psy D); counseling psychology (Ed D); counselor education and supervision (Ed D); forensic psychology (MA); industrial organizational psychology (MA); marriage and family therapy (MA, DMFT).

See Close-Up on page 1055.

Argosy University, Inland Empire, College of Psychology and Behavioral Sciences, San Bernardino, CA 92408. Offers clinical psychology/marriage and family therapy (MA); counseling psychology (Ed D); counseling psychology/marriage and family therapy (MA); forensic psychology (MA); industrial organizational psychology (MA); sport-exercise psychology (MA).

See Close-Up on page 1059.

Argosy University, Phoenix, College of Psychology and Behavioral Sciences, Program in Industrial Organizational Psychology, Phoenix, AZ 85021. Offers MA.

See Close-Up on page 1067.

Argosy University, Schaumburg, College of Psychology and Behavioral Sciences, Schaumburg, IL 60173-5403. Offers clinical health psychology (Post-Graduate Certificate); clinical psychology (MA, Psy D), including child and family psychology (Psy D), clinical health psychology (Psy D), diversity and multicultural psychology (Psy D), forensic psychology (Psy D), neuropsychology (Psy D); community counseling (MA); counseling psychology (Ed D), including counselor education and supervision; counselor education and supervision (Ed D); forensic psychology (Post-Graduate Certificate); industrial organizational psychology (MA). *Accreditation:* ACA; APA.

See Close-Up on page 1077.

Argosy University, Tampa, College of Psychology and Behavioral Sciences, Tampa, FL 33607. Offers clinical psychology (MA, Psy D), including clinical psychology; counselor education and supervision (Ed D); industrial organizational psychology (MA); marriage and family therapy (MA); mental health counseling (MA).

See Close-Up on page 1081.

Argosy University, Twin Cities, College of Psychology and Behavioral Sciences, Eagan, MN 55121. Offers clinical psychology (MA, Psy D), including child and family psychology (Psy D), forensic psychology (Psy D), health and neuropsychology (Psy D), trauma (Psy D); forensic counseling (Post-Graduate Certificate); forensic psychology (MA); industrial organizational psychology (MA); marriage and family therapy (MA, DMFT), including forensic counseling (MA). *Accreditation:* APA.

See Close-Up on page 1083.

Auburn University, Graduate School, College of Liberal Arts, Department of Psychology, Auburn University, AL 36849. Offers applied behavior analysis in developmental disabilities (MS); clinical psychology (PhD); experimental psychology (PhD); industrial/organizational psychology (PhD). *Accreditation:* APA (one or more programs are accredited). Part-time programs available. *Faculty:* 24 full-time (7 women), 4 part-time/adjunct (3 women). *Students:* 36 full-time (28 women), 57 part-time (33 women); includes 15 minority (6 African Americans, 4 Asian Americans or Pacific Islanders, 5 Hispanic Americans). Average age 26. 293 applicants, 9% accepted, 19 enrolled. In 2009, 20 master's, 11 doctorates awarded. *Degree requirements:* For doctorate, thesis/dissertation. *Entrance requirements:* For master's, GRE General Test, GRE Subject Test, minimum GPA of 3.25 in psychology, 3.0 overall; for doctorate, GRE General Test, GRE Subject Test. *Application deadline:* For fall admission, 7/7 for domestic students; for spring admission, 11/24 for domestic students. Applications are processed on a rolling basis. Application fee: $50 ($60 for international students). Electronic applications accepted. *Expenses:* Tuition, state resident: full-time $6240. Tuition, nonresident: full-time $18,720. International tuition: $18,938 full-time. Required fees: $492. Tuition and fees vary according to course load, program and reciprocity agreements. *Financial support:* Research assistantships, teaching assistantships, Federal Work-Study available. Support available to part-time students. Financial award application deadline: 3/15; financial award applicants required to submit FAFSA. *Faculty research:* Clinical psychology, learning, industrial psychology, organizational psychology. Total annual research expenditures: $200,000. *Unit head:* Dr. Barry Burkhart, Chair, 334-844-4412. *Application contact:* Dr. George Flowers, Dean of the Graduate School, 334-844-2125.

Bayamón Central University, Graduate Programs, Program in Education, Bayamón, PR 00960-1725. Offers administration and supervision (MA Ed); commercial education (MA Ed); education of the autistic (MA Ed); elementary education (K–3) (MA Ed); elementary education (K–6) (MA Ed); guidance and counseling (MA Ed); organizational psychology (MA); pre-elementary teacher (MA Ed); rehabilitation counseling (MA Ed); special education (MA Ed), including attention deficit disorder, learning disabilities. Part-time and evening/weekend programs available. *Degree requirements:* For master's, comprehensive exam. *Entrance requirements:* For master's, EXADEP, bachelor's degree in education or related field.

Bernard M. Baruch College of the City University of New York, Weissman School of Arts and Sciences, Program in Industrial Organizational Psychology, New York, NY 10010-5585. Offers MS.

Bernard M. Baruch College of the City University of New York, Zicklin School of Business, Program in Industrial and Organizational Psychology, New York, NY 10010-5585. Offers MBA, MS, PhD, Certificate. Part-time and evening/weekend programs available. *Degree requirements:* For master's, thesis or alternative; for doctorate, comprehensive exam, thesis/dissertation. *Entrance requirements:* For master's, GMAT or GRE General Test, 2 letters of recommendation, resumé, 2 years of work experience; for doctorate, GMAT or GRE General Test. Additional exam requirements/recommendations for international students: Required—TOEFL (minimum score 590 paper-based; 243 computer-based), TWE. *Faculty research:* Job attitudes, power and leadership in organizations, measurement issues in organizational behavior, work motivation, fair employment practices.

Bowling Green State University, Graduate College, College of Arts and Sciences, Department of Psychology, Bowling Green, OH 43403. Offers clinical psychology (MA, PhD); developmental psychology (MA, PhD); experimental psychology (MA, PhD); industrial/organizational psychology (MA, PhD); quantitative psychology (MA, PhD). *Accreditation:* APA (one or more programs are accredited). *Degree requirements:* For doctorate, thesis/dissertation. *Entrance requirements:* For doctorate, GRE General Test, GRE Subject Test. Additional exam requirements/recommendations for international students: Required—TOEFL. Electronic applications accepted. *Faculty research:* Personnel psychology, developmental-mathematical models, behavioral medication, brain process, child/adolescent social cognition.

Brooklyn College of the City University of New York, Division of Graduate Studies, Department of Psychology, Program in Industrial and Organizational Psychology, Brooklyn, NY 11210-2889. Offers human relations (MA); organizational behavior (MA). *Students:* 9 full-time (8 women), 96 part-time (73 women); includes 50 minority (33 African Americans, 7 Asian Americans or Pacific Islanders, 10 Hispanic Americans), 10 international. Average age 31. 123 applicants, 63% accepted, 44 enrolled. In 2009, 20 master's awarded. *Degree requirements:* For master's, comprehensive exam, thesis. *Entrance requirements:* For master's, 2 letters of recommendation. Additional exam requirements/recommendations for international students: Required—TOEFL (minimum score 520 paper-based; 190 computer-based; 69 iBT). *Application deadline:* For fall admission, 3/1 priority date for domestic students, 2/1 for international students. Applications are processed on a rolling basis. Electronic applications accepted. *Expenses:* Tuition, area resident: Full-time $7360; part-time $310 per credit hour. Tuition, state resident: full-time $7360; part-time $310 per credit hour. Tuition, nonresident: full-time $13,800; part-time $575 per credit hour. International tuition: $13,800 full-time. Required fees: $140.10 per semester. *Unit head:* Benzion Chanowitz, Graduate Advisor, 718-951-5601, E-mail: bchanowitz@brooklyn.cuny.edu. *Application contact:* Hernan Sierra, Graduate Admissions Coordinator, 718-951-4536, Fax: 718-951-4506, E-mail: grads@brooklyn.cuny.edu.

California State University, Long Beach, Graduate Studies, College of Liberal Arts, Department of Psychology, Long Beach, CA 90840. Offers human factors (MS); industrial/organizational psychology (MS); psychology (MA). Part-time and evening/weekend programs available. *Faculty:* 14 full-time (3 women), 4 part-time/adjunct (2 women). *Students:* 41 full-time (30 women), 19 part-time (12 women); includes 23 minority (5 African Americans, 8 Asian Americans or Pacific Islanders, 10 Hispanic Americans). Average age 26. 161 applicants, 25% accepted, 34 enrolled. *Degree requirements:* For master's, comprehensive exam, thesis. *Entrance requirements:* For master's, GRE General Test, GRE Subject Test. *Application deadline:* For fall admission, 3/1 for domestic students. Applications are processed on a rolling basis. Application fee: $55. Electronic applications accepted. *Expenses:* Required fees: $1802 per semester. Part-time tuition and fees vary according to course load. *Financial support:* Federal Work-Study, institutionally sponsored loans, and scholarships/grants available. Financial award application deadline: 3/2. *Faculty research:* Physiological psychology, social and personality psychology, community-clinical psychology, industrial-organizational psychology, developmental psychology. *Unit head:* Dr. Kenneth Green, Chair, 562-985-5049, Fax: 562-985-8004, E-mail: kgreen@csulb.edu. *Application contact:* Dr. Kenneth Green, Chair, 562-985-5049, Fax: 562-985-8004, E-mail: kgreen@csulb.edu.

California State University, San Bernardino, Graduate Studies, College of Social and Behavioral Sciences, Department of Psychology, Program in Industrial/Organizational Psychology, San Bernardino, CA 92407-2397. Offers organizational psychology (MS). *Students:* 19 full-time (10 women), 9 part-time (5 women); includes 7 minority (1 African American, 2 Asian Americans or Pacific Islanders, 4 Hispanic Americans), 6 international. Average age 27. 47 applicants, 74% accepted, 22 enrolled. In 2009, 7 master's awarded. *Degree requirements:* For master's, thesis. *Entrance requirements:* For master's, minimum GPA of 3.0 in major. *Application deadline:* For fall admission, 8/31 priority date for domestic students. Application fee: $55. *Unit head:* Dr. Robert Cramer, Head, 909-537-5576, Fax: 909-537-7003, E-mail: rcramer@csusb.edu. *Application contact:* Stacy Brooks, Graduate Secretary, 909-537-5570, Fax: 909-537-7003, E-mail: sbrooks@csusb.edu.

Capella University, Harold Abel School of Psychology, Minneapolis, MN 55402. Offers child and adolescent development (MS); clinical psychology (MS, Psy D); counseling psychology (MS); educational psychology (MS, PhD); evaluation, research, and measurement (MS); general psychology (MS, PhD); industrial/organizational psychology (MS, PhD); leadership coaching psychology (MS); organizational leader development (MS); school psychology (MS); sport psychology (MS). Part-time and evening/weekend programs available. Postbaccalaureate distance learning degree programs offered (minimal on-campus study). Terminal master's awarded for partial completion of doctoral program. *Degree requirements:* For master's, thesis optional, project; for doctorate, thesis/dissertation. *Entrance requirements:* For degree, master's degree in school psychology. Additional exam requirements/recommendations for international students: Required—TOEFL (minimum score 550 paper-based; 213 computer-based), TWE (minimum score 4); Recommended—IELTS. Electronic applications accepted.

Carlos Albizu University, Graduate Programs, San Juan, PR 00901. Offers clinical psychology (MS, PhD, Psy D); general psychology (PhD); industrial/organizational psychology (MS, PhD); speech and language pathology (MS). *Accreditation:* APA (one or more programs are accredited). Part-time and evening/weekend programs available. Terminal master's awarded for partial completion of doctoral program. *Degree requirements:* For master's, one foreign language, comprehensive exam, thesis; for doctorate, one foreign language, comprehensive exam, thesis/dissertation, written qualifying exams. *Entrance requirements:* For master's, GRE General Test or EXADEP, interview; minimum GPA of 3.0 (industrial/organizational psychology), 3.25 (speech and language pathology); for doctorate, GRE General Test or EXADEP, interview; minimum GPA of 3.0 (industrial/organizational psychology), 3.25 (PhD and Psy D in clinical psychology). *Faculty research:* Psychotherapeutic techniques for Hispanics, psychology of the aged, school dropouts, stress, violence.

Carlos Albizu University, Miami Campus, Graduate Programs, Miami, FL 33172-2209. Offers clinical psychology (Psy D); entrepreneurship (MBA); exceptional student education (MS); industrial/organizational psychology (MS); marriage and family therapy (MS); mental health counseling (MS); nonprofit management (MBA); organizational management (MBA); psychology (MS); school counseling (MS); teaching English as a second language (MS). *Accreditation:* APA. Part-time and evening/weekend programs available. *Faculty:* 23 full-time (13 women), 41 part-time/adjunct (21 women). *Students:* 529 full-time (420 women), 171 part-time (139 women); includes 551 minority (55 African Americans, 1 American Indian/Alaska Native, 5 Asian Americans or Pacific Islanders, 490 Hispanic Americans). Average age 37. 278 applicants, 57% accepted, 142 enrolled. In 2009, 139 master's, 26 doctorates awarded. Terminal master's awarded for partial completion of doctoral program. *Degree requirements:* For master's, one foreign language, comprehensive exam, integrative project (MBA), research project (exceptional student education, teaching English as a second language); for doctorate, one foreign language, comprehensive exam, internship, project. *Entrance requirements:* For master's, 3 letters of recommendation, interview, minimum GPA of 3.0, resume; for doctorate, 3 letters of recommendation, minimum GPA of 3.0, resume, interview. *Application deadline:* For fall admission, 8/1 priority date for domestic students; for spring admission, 11/30 priority date for domestic students. Applications are processed on a rolling basis. Application fee: $50. Electronic applications accepted. *Expenses:* Tuition: Full-time $9090; part-time $505 per credit hour. Required fees: $298 per term. Tuition and fees vary according to course load, degree level and program. *Financial support:* In 2009–10, 127 students received support. Federal Work-Study, scholarships/grants, and tuition discounts available. Financial award application deadline: 6/1; financial award applicants required to submit FAFSA. *Faculty research:* Psychotherapy, forensic psychology, neuropsychology, marketing strategy, entrepreneurship, special education. *Unit head:* Dr. Carmen S. Roca, Chancellor, 305-593-1223 Ext. 120, Fax: 305-629-8052, E-mail: croca@albizu.edu. *Application contact:* Annalye Alonso, Secretary, 305-593-1223 Ext. 137, Fax: 305-593-1854, E-mail: aalonso@albizu.edu.

Central Michigan University, College of Graduate Studies, College of Humanities and Social and Behavioral Sciences, Department of Psychology, Program in Industrial and Organizational Psychology, Mount Pleasant, MI 48859. Offers MA, PhD. *Degree requirements:* For master's, thesis; for doctorate, comprehensive exam, thesis/dissertation. *Entrance requirements:* For master's and doctorate, GRE. Electronic applications accepted. *Faculty research:* Job stress, retirement, leadership, and careers; personality in the workplace, personnel selection, and structural equation modeling in I/O psychology; personnel psychology, evolutionary psychology, and influences on HRM utilization; occupational health psychology and job stress; work attitudes, psychological ownership in work, and performance appraisal.

Chatham University, Program in Counseling Psychology, Pittsburgh, PA 15232-2826. Offers child, adolescent and family (MSCP); counseling psychology (Psy D); health and holistic (MSCP); infant mental health (MSCP); organization and supervision (MSCP); sport and exercise (MSCP). Part-time and evening/weekend programs available. *Students:* 107 full-time (93 women), 77 part-time (67 women). Average age 29. 141 applicants, 76% accepted, 75 enrolled. In 2009, 63 master's awarded. *Degree requirements:* For master's, thesis optional, supervised internship; for doctorate, thesis/dissertation, internship. *Entrance requirements:* For master's, minimum GPA of 3.0; 2 letters of recommendation; resume; prerequisite coursework in statistics, biology, and psychology; for doctorate, GRE. Additional exam requirements/recommendations for international students: Required—TOEFL (minimum score 600 paper-based; 250 computer-based; 100 iBT), IELTS (minimum score 6.5), TWE. *Application deadline:* For fall admission, 5/1 priority date for domestic students, 6/1 priority date for international students; for spring admission, 12/1 for domestic students, 11/1 for international students. Applications are processed on a rolling basis. Application fee: $45. Electronic applications accepted. *Financial support:* Career-related internships or fieldwork available. Financial award applicants required to submit FAFSA. *Faculty research:* Trauma and recovery, hypnosis, psychospiritual dimensions of healing, psychotherapy of schizophrenia. *Unit head:* Dr. Mary Beth Mannarino, Director, 412-365-1196, Fax: 412-365-1505, E-mail: mmannarino@chatham.edu. *Application contact:* Dory Perry, Associate Director of Graduate Admissions, 412-365-2758, Fax: 412-365-1609, E-mail: gradadmissions@chatham.edu.

The Chicago School of Professional Psychology, Program in Industrial and Organizational Psychology, Chicago, IL 60610. Offers business psychology (Psy D); industrial and organizational psychology (MA). Part-time and evening/weekend programs available. *Students:* 125 full-time (108 women), 21 part-time (17 women); includes 43 minority (20 African Americans, 7 Asian Americans or Pacific Islanders, 16 Hispanic Americans), 9 international. 148 applicants, 93% accepted, 55 enrolled. *Degree requirements:* For master's, internship; for doctorate, thesis/dissertation, internship. *Entrance requirements:* For master's, 1 course in psychology and statistics and research methods; for doctorate, GRE, writing test, 12 hours of psychology credit including a course in statistics and research methods. Additional exam requirements/recommendations for international students: Required—TOEFL (minimum score 550 paper-based; 213 computer-based; 79 iBT). *Financial support:* Federal Work-Study and scholarships/grants available. Financial award application deadline: 3/1; financial award applicants required to submit FAFSA. *Unit head:* Dr. Keith Carroll, Department Chair, 312-467-2533. *Application contact:* Andrea Schmoyer, Director of Admissions, 312-329-6666, Fax: 312-644-3333, E-mail: admissions@thechicagoschool.edu.

The Chicago School of Professional Psychology at Downtown Los Angeles, Program in Industrial and Organizational Psychology, Los Angeles, CA 90017. Offers MA. *Students:* 27 full-time (21 women); includes 14 minority (3 African Americans, 5 Asian Americans or Pacific Islanders, 6 Hispanic Americans). 25 applicants, 92% accepted, 15 enrolled. *Unit head:* Dr. Albert Edwards, Lead Faculty, E-mail: aedwards@thechicagoschool.edu. *Application contact:* Heather LaBelle, Director of Admission, 213-615-7200, Fax: 213-627-1985, E-mail: admissions@thechicagoschool.edu.

The Chicago School of Professional Psychology: Online, Applied Industrial and Organizational Psychology, Chicago, IL 60654. Offers MA, Certificate. *Students:* 23 part-time (20 women). *Unit head:* Dr. Ilianna Kwaske, Dean of Academic Affairs, 312-467-8601, E-mail: ikwaske@thechicagoschool.edu. *Application contact:* Pari Pinyo, Director of Online Admissions, 312-329-6666, Fax: 312-644-3333, E-mail: admissions@thechicagoschool.edu.

The Chicago School of Professional Psychology: Online, PhD Program in Organizational Leadership, Chicago, IL 60654. Offers PhD. *Students:* 23 part-time (10 women); includes 5 minority (1 Asian American or Pacific Islander, 4 Hispanic Americans). *Unit head:* Dr. Ilianna Kwaske, Dean of Academic Affairs, 312-467-8601, E-mail: ikwaske@thechicagoschool.edu. *Application contact:* Pari Pinyo, Director of Online Admission, 312-329-6666, Fax: 312-644-3333, E-mail: admissions@thechicagoschool.edu.

Claremont Graduate University, Graduate Programs, School of Behavioral and Organizational Sciences, Department of Psychology, Claremont, CA 91711-6160. Offers advanced study in evaluation (Certificate); cognitive psychology (MA, PhD); developmental psychology (MA, PhD); evaluation and applied research methods (MA, PhD); health behavior research and evaluation (MA, PhD); human resource development and evaluation (MA); industrial/organizational psychology (MA, PhD); organizational behavior (MA, PhD); organizational psychology (MA, PhD); social psychology (MA, PhD); MBA/PhD. Part-time programs available. *Faculty:* 17 full-time (7 women), 1 part-time/adjunct (0 women). *Students:* 231 full-time (155 women), 25 part-time (18 women); includes 62 minority (13 African Americans, 1 American Indian/Alaska Native, 31 Asian Americans or Pacific Islanders, 17 Hispanic Americans), 21 international. Average age 30. In 2009, 37 master's, 12 doctorates, 8 other advanced degrees awarded. Terminal master's awarded for partial completion of doctoral program. *Entrance requirements:* For master's and doctorate, GRE General Test. Additional exam requirements/recommendations for international students: Required—TOEFL (minimum score 550 paper-based; 213 computer-based; 80 iBT). *Application deadline:* For fall admission, 1/15 priority date for domestic students. Applications are processed on a rolling basis. Application fee: $60. Electronic applications accepted. *Expenses:* Tuition: Full-time $35,046; part-time $1524 per credit. Required fees: $161 per semester. *Financial support:* Fellowships, research assistantships, teaching assistantships, Federal Work-Study, institutionally sponsored loans, scholarships/grants, and tuition waivers (full and partial) available. Support available to part-time students. Financial award application deadline: 2/15; financial award applicants required to submit FAFSA. *Faculty research:* Social intervention, diversity in organizations, eyewitness memory, aging and cognition, drug policy. *Unit head:* Stewart Donaldson, Dean, 909-607-9001, Fax: 909-621-8905, E-mail: stewart.donaldson@cgu.edu. *Application contact:* Paul Thomas, Director, External Affairs, 909-607-9016, Fax: 909-621-8905, E-mail: paul.thomas@cgu.edu.

Clemson University, Graduate School, College of Business and Behavioral Science, Department of Psychology, Program in Industrial/Organizational Psychology, Clemson, SC 29634. Offers PhD. *Students:* 14 full-time (8 women), 5 part-time (2 women); includes 1 minority (African American), 1 international. Average age 28. 85 applicants, 6% accepted, 3 enrolled. In 2009, 2 doctorates awarded. *Degree requirements:* For doctorate, thesis/dissertation. *Entrance requirements:* For doctorate, GRE General Test. Additional exam requirements/recommendations for international students: Required—TOEFL. *Application deadline:* For fall admission, 12/15 for domestic students. Application fee: $70 ($80 for international students). Electronic applications accepted. *Expenses:* Contact institution. *Financial support:* In 2009–10, 16 students received support, including 2 fellowships with full and partial tuition reimbursements available (averaging $10,000 per year), 4 research assistantships with partial tuition reimbursements available (averaging $15,125 per year), 12 teaching assistantships with partial tuition reimbursements available (averaging $12,083 per year); career-related internships or fieldwork, institutionally sponsored loans, scholarships/grants, health care benefits, and unspecified assistantships also available. Support available to part-time students. Financial award application deadline: 3/15; financial award applicants required to submit FAFSA. *Unit head:* Dr. Patrick Raymark, Chair, 864-656-4715, Fax: 864-656-0358, E-mail: praymar@clemson.edu. *Application contact:* Dr. Robert Sinclair, Graduate Program Coordinator, 864-656-3931, Fax: 864-656-0358.

Cleveland State University, College of Graduate Studies, College of Science, Department of Psychology, Cleveland, OH 44115. Offers adult development and aging (PhD); clinical psychology (MA); consumer/industrial research (MA); diversity management (MA); experimental research psychology (MA); school psychology (Psy S). *Degree requirements:* For master's, comprehensive exam (for some programs), thesis (for some programs); for doctorate, comprehensive exam, thesis/dissertation; for Psy S, internship. *Entrance requirements:* For master's and doctorate, GRE General Test. Additional exam requirements/recommendations for international students: Required—TOEFL (minimum score 525 paper-based; 197 computer-based). Electronic applications accepted. *Faculty research:* Cognitive and social psychology, consumer psychology, clinical psychology, school psychology, aging.

DePaul University, College of Liberal Arts and Sciences, Department of Psychology, Chicago, IL 60604-2287. Offers clinical psychology (MA, PhD), including child clinical psychology, community clinical psychology; experimental psychology (MA, PhD); general psychology (MS); industrial/organizational psychology (MA, PhD); MA/PhD. *Accreditation:* APA (one or more programs are accredited). *Faculty:* 31 full-time (19 women), 6 part-time/adjunct (4 women). *Students:* 59 full-time (36 women), 54 part-time (35 women); includes 26 minority (10 African Americans, 5 Asian Americans or Pacific Islanders, 11 Hispanic Americans), 2 international. Average age 28. 332 applicants, 14% accepted, 23 enrolled. In 2009, 14 master's, 17 doctorates awarded. *Degree requirements:* For master's, thesis, oral exam; for doctorate, comprehensive exam, thesis/dissertation, oral and written exams. *Entrance requirements:* For master's and doctorate, GRE General Test, GRE Subject Test, 32 quarter hours of course work in psychology, 3 letters of recommendation. Additional exam requirements/recommendations for international students: Required—TOEFL. Application fee: $40. Electronic applications accepted. *Expenses:* Tuition: Full-time $37,525; part-time $620 per credit hour. *Financial support:* In 2009–10, 48 students received support, including 35 research assistantships with full tuition reimbursements available (averaging $11,800 per year), 13 teaching assistantships with full tuition reimbursements available (averaging $11,800 per year); career-related internships or fieldwork, scholarships/grants, traineeships, tuition waivers (full and partial), and unspecified assistantships also available. Financial award application deadline: 1/10. *Faculty research:* Adolescent stress and depression, minority adolescents sexuality, public policy, community influences in child adjustment. *Unit head:* Dr. Christopher B. Keys, Chairman, 773-325-7887, Fax: 773-325-7888. *Application contact:* Alison Pereida Knapp, Graduate Admissions Assistant, 773-325-7887, Fax: 773-325-7888.

Eastern Kentucky University, The Graduate School, College of Arts and Sciences, Department of Psychology, Richmond, KY 40475-3102. Offers clinical psychology (MS); industrial/organizational psychology (MS); school psychology (Psy S). Part-time programs available. *Entrance requirements:* For master's and Psy S, GRE General Test, minimum GPA of 2.5. *Faculty research:* Autism, social psychology, parenting, assessment of depression/anxiety, reading.

Elmhurst College, Graduate Programs, Program in Industrial/Organizational Psychology, Elmhurst, IL 60126-3296. Offers MA. Part-time and evening/weekend programs available. *Faculty:* 2 full-time (1 woman), 3 part-time/adjunct (1 woman). *Students:* 33 part-time (23 women); includes 2 minority (1 Asian American or Pacific Islander, 1 Hispanic American). Average age 23. 51 applicants, 63% accepted, 17 enrolled. In 2009, 5 master's awarded. *Degree requirements:* For master's, thesis optional. *Entrance requirements:* For master's, GRE General Test, 3 recommendations. Additional exam requirements/recommendations for international students: Required—TOEFL (minimum score 550 paper-based; 213 computer-based). *Application deadline:* Applications are processed on a rolling basis. Application fee: $25. Electronic applications accepted. *Expenses:* Tuition: Part-time $700 per credit hour. Required fees: $60 per semester. Tuition and fees vary according to program. *Financial support:* In 2009–10, 21 students received support. Federal Work-Study and scholarships/grants available. Support available to part-time students. Financial award application deadline: 6/1; financial award applicants required to submit FAFSA. *Unit head:* Dr. Ted Lerud, Associate Dean of the Faculty, 630-617-3661, Fax: 630-617-6415, E-mail: gradadm@elmhurst.edu. *Application contact:* Elizabeth D. Kuebler, Director of Adult and Graduate Admission, 630-617-3069, Fax: 630-617-5501, E-mail: betsyk@elmhurst.edu.

Emporia State University, School of Graduate Studies, The Teachers College, Department of Psychology, Art Therapy, Rehabilitation and Mental Health Counseling, Program in Psychology, Emporia, KS 66801-5087. Offers general psychology (MS); industrial/organizational psychology (MS). Part-time programs available. *Students:* 10 full-time (6 women), 12 part-time (7 women); includes 1 minority (Hispanic American), 5 international. 4 applicants, 100% accepted, 4 enrolled. In 2009, 2 master's awarded. *Degree requirements:* For master's, comprehensive exam or thesis, internship. *Entrance requirements:* For master's, GRE General Test or MAT, graduate essay exam, appropriate bachelor's degree, letters of recommendation. Additional exam requirements/recommendations for international students: Required—TOEFL (minimum score 520 paper-based; 133 computer-based; 68 iBT). *Application deadline:* For fall admission, 6/1 priority date for domestic students; for spring admission, 10/1 for domestic students. Applications are processed on a rolling basis. Application fee: $30 ($75 for international students). Electronic applications accepted. *Expenses:* Tuition, state resident: full-time $4154; part-time $173 per credit hour. Tuition, nonresident: full-time $12,864; part-time $536 per credit hour. Required fees: $948; $58 per credit hour. Tuition and fees vary according to campus/location. *Financial support:* Career-related internships or fieldwork, Federal Work-Study, institutionally sponsored loans, health care benefits, and unspecified assistantships available. Financial award application deadline: 3/15; financial award applicants required to submit FAFSA. *Faculty research:* Driving under the influence (DUI) personality, lifestyles and imposter phenomenon. *Unit head:* Dr. Brian W. Schrader, Chair, 620-341-5317, E-mail: bschrade@emporia.edu. *Application contact:* Mary Sewell, Admissions Coordinator, 800-950-GRAD, Fax: 620-341-5909, E-mail: msewell@emporia.edu.

Fairfield University, Graduate School of Education and Allied Professions, Department of Psychological and Educational Consultation, Fairfield, CT 06824-5195. Offers applied psychology (MA), including foundations of advanced psychology, human services, industrial/organizational/personnel; media/educational technology (MA); school media specialist (MA); school psychology (MA, CAS); special education (MA, CAS). Part-time and evening/weekend programs available. *Degree requirements:* For master's, comprehensive exam, thesis optional. *Entrance requirements:* For master's, PRAXIS I (PPST), minimum QPA of 3.0, 2 recommendations, resume. Additional exam requirements/recommendations for international students: Required—TOEFL (minimum score 550 paper-based; 213 computer-based; 80 iBT). Electronic applications accepted. *Faculty research:* Child neuropsychology, disabilities, effect of pre-treatment orientation on treatment, autism, technology in business and classroom, collaboration with schools, communities and industry.

Fairleigh Dickinson University, College at Florham, Maxwell Becton College of Arts and Sciences, Department of Psychology, Program in Industrial/Organizational Psychology, Madison,

Industrial and Organizational Psychology

Fairleigh Dickinson University, College at Florham (continued)
NJ 07940-1099. Offers MA, MA/MBA. *Students:* 8 full-time (4 women), 1 (woman) part-time, 1 international. Average age 26. 23 applicants, 61% accepted, 3 enrolled. In 2009, 12 master's awarded. *Entrance requirements:* For master's, GRE General Test. *Application deadline:* Applications are processed on a rolling basis. Application fee: $40. *Application contact:* Susan Brooman, University Director, Graduate Admissions, 973-443-8905, Fax: 973-443-8088, E-mail: grad@fdu.edu.

Florida Institute of Technology, Graduate Programs, College of Psychology and Liberal Arts, School of Psychology, Melbourne, FL 32901-6975. Offers applied behavior analysis (MS); applied behavior analysis and organizational behavior management (MS, PhD); clinical psychology (Psy D); industrial/organizational psychology (MS, PhD); organizational behavior management (MS). *Accreditation:* APA (one or more programs are accredited). Part-time programs available. *Faculty:* 24 full-time (11 women), 6 part-time/adjunct (1 woman). *Students:* 210 full-time (169 women), 4 part-time (2 women); includes 31 minority (8 African Americans, 6 Asian Americans or Pacific Islanders, 17 Hispanic Americans), 21 international. Average age 27. 195 applicants, 59% accepted, 55 enrolled. In 2009, 30 master's, 3 doctorates awarded. Terminal master's awarded for partial completion of doctoral program. *Degree requirements:* For master's, comprehensive exam (for some programs), thesis (for some programs), BCBA certification, final exam; for doctorate, comprehensive exam, thesis/dissertation, internship, full time resident of school for 4 years (8 semesters, 3 summers). *Entrance requirements:* For master's, GRE General Test, 3 letters of recommendation, minimum GPA of 3.0, resume; for doctorate, GRE General Test, GRE Subject Test (psychology), 3 letters of recommendation, minimum GPA of 3.2, resume, statement of objectives. Additional exam requirements/recommendations for international students: Required—TOEFL (minimum score 550 paper-based; 213 computer-based; 79 iBT). *Application deadline:* For fall admission, 1/15 for domestic and international students. Applications are processed on a rolling basis. Application fee: $50. Electronic applications accepted. *Expenses:* Tuition: Part-time $1015 per credit. Tuition and fees vary according to campus/location and program. *Financial support:* In 2009–10, 19 students received support, including 14 research assistantships with full and partial tuition reimbursements available (averaging $4,079 per year), 5 teaching assistantships with full and partial tuition reimbursements available (averaging $7,002 per year); fellowships with full and partial tuition reimbursements available, career-related internships or fieldwork, institutionally sponsored loans, tuition waivers (partial), unspecified assistantships, and tuition remissions also available. Support available to part-time students. Financial award application deadline: 3/1; financial award applicants required to submit FAFSA. *Faculty research:* Addictions, neuropsychology, child abuse, assessment, psychological trauma. Total annual research expenditures: $836,475. *Unit head:* Dr. Mary Beth Kenkel, Dean, 321-674-8142, Fax: 321-674-7105, E-mail: mkenkel@fit.edu. *Application contact:* Thomas M. Shea, Director of Graduate Admissions, 321-674-7577, Fax: 321-723-9468, E-mail: tshea@fit.edu.

See Close-Up on page 1089.

The George Washington University, Columbian College of Arts and Sciences, Department of Organizational Sciences and Communication, Washington, DC 20052. Offers human resources management (MA); industrial/organizational psychology (PhD); organizational management (MA). Part-time and evening/weekend programs available. *Faculty:* 10 full-time (6 women), 18 part-time/adjunct (15 women). *Students:* 23 full-time (13 women), 41 part-time (34 women); includes 15 minority (7 African Americans, 2 Asian Americans or Pacific Islanders, 6 Hispanic Americans), 8 international. Average age 29. 74 applicants, 84% accepted, 32 enrolled. In 2009, 28 master's awarded. *Degree requirements:* For master's, comprehensive exam. *Entrance requirements:* For master's, GRE General Test, minimum GPA of 3.0. Additional exam requirements/recommendations for international students: Required—TOEFL (minimum score 500 paper-based; 213 computer-based; 80 iBT). *Application deadline:* For fall admission, 1/15 priority date for domestic and international students; for spring admission, 10/1 priority date for domestic students, 9/1 priority date for international students. Applications are processed on a rolling basis. Application fee: $60. Electronic applications accepted. *Financial support:* Federal Work-Study and institutionally sponsored loans available. *Unit head:* Dr. David Costanza, Acting Director, 202-994-1875, Fax: 202-994-1881, E-mail: dconstanz@gwu.edu. *Application contact:* Information Contact, 202-994-1880, Fax: 202-994-1881.

Georgia Institute of Technology, Graduate Studies and Research, College of Sciences, School of Psychology, Atlanta, GA 30332-0001. Offers human computer interaction (MSHCI); psychology (MS, MS Psy, PhD), including engineering psychology (PhD), experimental psychology (PhD), industrial/organizational psychology (PhD). Terminal master's awarded for partial completion of doctoral program. *Degree requirements:* For master's, thesis; for doctorate, thesis/dissertation. *Entrance requirements:* For master's and doctorate, GRE General Test, GRE Subject Test, minimum GPA of 3.0. Additional exam requirements/recommendations for international students: Required—TOEFL. Electronic applications accepted. *Faculty research:* Experimental, industrial-organizational, and engineering psychology; cognitive aging and processes; leadership; human factors.

Goddard College, Graduate Division, Master of Arts in Psychology and Counseling Program, Plainfield, VT 05667-9432. Offers organizational development (MA); psychology and counseling (MA); sexual orientation (MA). Part-time programs available. Postbaccalaureate distance learning degree programs offered (minimal on-campus study). *Faculty:* 7 part-time/adjunct (5 women). *Students:* 57 full-time. Average age 40. 34 applicants, 76% accepted, 18 enrolled. *Degree requirements:* For master's, thesis. *Entrance requirements:* For master's, recent undergraduate degree in psychology or closely related field (preparatory semester at Goddard can substitute), 3 letters of recommendation, interview. *Application deadline:* Applications are processed on a rolling basis. Application fee: $40. Electronic applications accepted. *Expenses:* Tuition: Part-time $7223 per semester. Part-time tuition and fees vary according to program. *Financial support:* In 2009–10, 48 students received support. Applicants required to submit FAFSA. *Unit head:* Dr. Steve James, Director, 802-454-8311, Fax: 802-454-7835, E-mail: steven.james@goddard.edu. *Application contact:* David DeLucca, Senior Admissions Counselor, 800-906-8312 Ext. 248, Fax: 802-454-1029, E-mail: david.delucca@goddard.edu.

Graduate School and University Center of the City University of New York, Graduate Studies, Program in Psychology, New York, NY 10016-4039. Offers basic applied neurocognition (PhD); biopsychology (PhD); clinical psychology (PhD); developmental psychology (PhD); environmental psychology (PhD); experimental psychology (PhD); industrial psychology (PhD); learning processes (PhD); neuropsychology (PhD); psychology (PhD); social personality (PhD). *Faculty:* 119 full-time (40 women). *Students:* 559 full-time (414 women), 1 part-time (0 women); includes 101 minority (34 African Americans, 25 Asian Americans or Pacific Islanders, 42 Hispanic Americans), 57 international. Average age 33. 750 applicants, 16% accepted, 84 enrolled. In 2009, 54 doctorates awarded. *Degree requirements:* For doctorate, one foreign language, thesis/dissertation. *Entrance requirements:* For doctorate, GRE General Test. Additional exam requirements/recommendations for international students: Required—TOEFL. *Application deadline:* For fall admission, 12/15 priority date for domestic students. Application fee: $125. Electronic applications accepted. *Financial support:* In 2009–10, 371 students received support, including 340 fellowships, 34 research assistantships, 33 teaching assistantships; career-related internships or fieldwork, Federal Work-Study, institutionally sponsored loans, and tuition waivers (full and partial) also available. Financial award application deadline: 2/1; financial award applicants required to submit FAFSA. *Unit head:* Dr. Joseph Glick, Executive Officer, 212-817-8706, Fax: 212-817-1533, E-mail: jglick@gc.cuny.edu. *Application contact:* Les Gribben, Director of Admissions, 212-817-7470, Fax: 212-817-1624, E-mail: lgribben@gc.cuny.edu.

Hofstra University, College of Liberal Arts and Sciences, Department of Psychology, Program in Applied Organizational Psychology, Hempstead, NY 11549. Offers PhD. *Students:* 17 full-time (10 women), 13 part-time (8 women); includes 8 minority (2 African Americans, 6 Asian Americans or Pacific Islanders). Average age 32. 19 applicants, 68% accepted, 10 enrolled. In 2009, 7 doctorates awarded. *Degree requirements:* For doctorate, comprehensive exam, thesis/dissertation. *Entrance requirements:* For doctorate, GRE, 2 letters of recommendation, interview. Additional exam requirements/recommendations for international students: Required—TOEFL (minimum score 550 paper-based; 213 computer-based; 80 iBT). *Application deadline:* For fall admission, 4/1 for domestic and international students. Application fee: $60. Electronic applications accepted. *Expenses:* Tuition: Full-time $16,200; part-time $900 per credit hour. Required fees: $970; $145 per term. Tuition and fees vary according to program. *Financial support:* In 2009–10, 19 students received support, including 19 fellowships with full and partial tuition reimbursements available (averaging $7,763 per year); research assistantships with full and partial tuition reimbursements available, career-related internships or fieldwork, Federal Work-Study, institutionally sponsored loans, scholarships/grants, tuition waivers (full and partial), and unspecified assistantships also available. Support available to part-time students. Financial award applicants required to submit FAFSA. *Faculty research:* Customer satisfaction, personnel selection, performance management, organizational health, team effectiveness. Total annual research expenditures: $130,000. *Unit head:* Dr. William Metlay, Program Director, 516-463-6344, Fax: 516-463-7306, E-mail: psywzm@hofstra.edu. *Application contact:* Carol Drummer, Dean of Graduate Admissions, 516-463-4876, Fax: 516-463-4664, E-mail: gradstudent@hofstra.edu.

Hofstra University, College of Liberal Arts and Sciences, Department of Psychology, Program in Industrial/Organizational Psychology, Hempstead, NY 11549. Offers MA. Part-time and evening/weekend programs available. *Students:* 43 full-time (30 women), 11 part-time (5 women); includes 11 minority (5 African Americans, 6 Asian Americans or Pacific Islanders), 2 international. Average age 24. 71 applicants, 77% accepted, 28 enrolled. In 2009, 26 master's awarded. *Degree requirements:* For master's, comprehensive exam, thesis optional, internship. *Entrance requirements:* For master's, GRE General Test, minimum GPA of 3.0, interview. Additional exam requirements/recommendations for international students: Required—TOEFL (minimum score 550 paper-based; 213 computer-based; 80 iBT). Application fee: $60. Electronic applications accepted. *Expenses:* Tuition: Full-time $16,200; part-time $900 per credit hour. Required fees: $970; $145 per term. Tuition and fees vary according to program. *Financial support:* In 2009–10, 15 students received support, including 13 fellowships with full and partial tuition reimbursements available (averaging $5,223 per year), 1 research assistantship with full and partial tuition reimbursement available (averaging $15,300 per year); Federal Work-Study, institutionally sponsored loans, scholarships/grants, tuition waivers (full and partial), and unspecified assistantships also available. Support available to part-time students. Financial award applicants required to submit FAFSA. *Faculty research:* Selection interviews; selection bias; occupational health; multi-source feedback; customer service. *Unit head:* Dr. Comila Shahani-Denning, Director, 516-463-6343, Fax: 516-463-6354, E-mail: psyczs@hofstra.edu. *Application contact:* Carol Drummer, Dean of Graduate Admissions, 516-463-4876, Fax: 516-463-4664, E-mail: gradstudent@hofstra.edu.

Illinois Institute of Technology, Graduate College, Institute of Psychology, Chicago, IL 60616-3793. Offers clinical psychology (PhD); industrial/organizational psychology (PhD); personnel/human resource development (MS); psychology (MS); rehabilitation counseling (MS); rehabilitation counselor education (PhD). *Accreditation:* APA (one or more programs are accredited); CORE. Part-time and evening/weekend programs available. *Faculty:* 19 full-time (8 women), 5 part-time/adjunct (all women). *Students:* 118 full-time (88 women), 82 part-time (62 women); includes 33 minority (10 African Americans, 1 American Indian/Alaska Native, 14 Asian Americans or Pacific Islanders, 8 Hispanic Americans), 24 international. Average age 29. 281 applicants, 33% accepted, 28 enrolled. In 2009, 37 master's, 13 doctorates awarded. Terminal master's awarded for partial completion of doctoral program. *Degree requirements:* For master's, thesis (for some programs); for doctorate, comprehensive exam, thesis/dissertation, 96-108 credit hours, internship for Clinical and I/O specializations. *Entrance requirements:* For master's, GRE General Test, minimum high school GPA of 3.0, official transcripts, 3 letters of recommendation, personal statement; for doctorate, GRE General Test, minimum high school GPA of 3.0, official transcriptions, 3 letters of recommendation, personal statement. Additional exam requirements/recommendations for international students: Required—TOEFL (minimum score 550 paper-based; 80 iBT). *Application deadline:* For fall admission, 2/15 for domestic and international students. Application fee: $40. Electronic applications accepted. *Expenses:* Tuition: Full-time $17,550; part-time $888 per credit hour. Required fees: $850; $7.50 per credit hour. One-time fee: $50 full-time. Full-time tuition and fees vary according to program. *Financial support:* In 2009–10, 39 fellowships with partial tuition reimbursements (averaging $2,798 per year), 1 research assistantship with partial tuition reimbursement, 24 teaching assistantships with partial tuition reimbursements (averaging $4,405 per year) were awarded; career-related internships or fieldwork, Federal Work-Study, institutionally sponsored loans, scholarships/grants, traineeships, health care benefits, tuition waivers (partial), and unspecified assistantships also available. Support available to part-time students. Financial award application deadline: 1/15; financial award applicants required to submit FAFSA. *Faculty research:* Stigma and mental illness, depression, couples communication, leadership, psychometric theory. Total annual research expenditures: $426,090. *Unit head:* Dr. M. Ellen Mitchell, Dean, 312-567-3362, Fax: 312-567-3493, E-mail: mitchelle@iit.edu. *Application contact:* Institute of Psychology Graduate Admissions, 312-567-3500, Fax: 312-567-3493, E-mail: psychology@iit.edu.

Illinois State University, Graduate School, College of Arts and Sciences, Department of Psychology, Normal, IL 61790-2200. Offers psychology (MA, MS), including clinical psychology, counseling psychology, developmental psychology, educational psychology, experimental psychology, measurement-evaluation, organizational-industrial psychology; school psychology (PhD, SSP). *Accreditation:* APA. *Degree requirements:* For master's, thesis or alternative; for doctorate, variable foreign language requirement, thesis/dissertation, 2 terms of residency, internship, practicum. *Entrance requirements:* For master's, GRE General Test, GRE Subject Test, minimum GPA of 3.0 in last 60 hours of course work; for doctorate, GRE General Test. *Faculty research:* Comprehensive evaluation system for the central region professional development grant, Illinois school psychology internship consortium, for children's sake.

Indiana University–Purdue University Indianapolis, School of Science, Department of Psychology, Program in Industrial/Organizational Psychology, Indianapolis, IN 46202-2896. Offers MS. *Faculty:* 5 full-time (3 women). *Students:* 9 full-time (7 women), 6 part-time (all women); includes 1 minority (African American), 2 international. Average age 25. *Entrance requirements:* For master's, GRE General Test (minimum score 1100 verbal and quantitative, quantitative 550), minimum undergraduate GPA of 3.0. Application fee: $50 ($60 for international students). *Financial support:* In 2009–10, 12 students received support; fellowships with partial tuition reimbursements available, research assistantships with partial tuition reimbursements available, teaching assistantships with partial tuition reimbursements available, career-related internships or fieldwork, Federal Work-Study, and institutionally sponsored loans available. Financial award application deadline: 3/1; financial award applicants required to submit FAFSA. *Faculty research:* Stereotyping and prejudice biases, performance feedback, personnel psychology, organizational decision making, counterproductive behaviors. *Unit head:* Dr. J. Gregor Fetterman, Chairman, 317-274-6945, Fax: 317-274-6756, E-mail: gfetter@iupui.edu. *Application contact:* Dr. J. Gregor Fetterman, Chairman, 317-274-6945, Fax: 317-274-6756, E-mail: gfetter@iupui.edu.

Inter American University of Puerto Rico, Metropolitan Campus, Graduate Programs, Program in Psychology, San Juan, PR 00919-1293. Offers counseling psychology (MA, PhD); industrial/organizational psychology (MA, PhD); labor relations (MA); school psychology (MA, PhD). *Degree requirements:* For master's, comprehensive exam. *Entrance requirements:* For master's, GRE or EXADEP, interview. Electronic applications accepted.

Iona College, School of Arts and Science, Department of Psychology, New Rochelle, NY 10801-1890. Offers experimental psychology (MA); industrial-organizational psychology (MA); mental health counseling (MA); psychology (MA); school psychology (MA). Part-time and evening/weekend programs available. *Faculty:* 14 full-time (8 women), 10 part-time/adjunct (8 women). *Students:* 74 full-time (58 women), 46 part-time (34 women); includes 28 minority (13 African Americans, 1 American Indian/Alaska Native, 3 Asian Americans or Pacific Islanders,

11 Hispanic Americans), 1 international. Average age 25. 186 applicants, 61% accepted, 44 enrolled. In 2009, 35 master's awarded. *Degree requirements:* For master's, thesis. *Entrance requirements:* For master's, GRE or minimum GPA of 3.0. Additional exam requirements/recommendations for international students: Required—TOEFL (minimum score 550 paper-based; 213 computer-based). *Application deadline:* Applications are processed on a rolling basis. Application fee: $50. Electronic applications accepted. *Expenses:* Tuition: Part-time $830 per credit. *Financial support:* Career-related internships or fieldwork, tuition waivers (partial), and unspecified assistantships available. Support available to part-time students. Financial award application deadline: 4/15; financial award applicants required to submit FAFSA. *Unit head:* Dr. Paul Greene, Chair, 914-633-2048, E-mail: pgreene@iona.edu. *Application contact:* Veronica Jarek-Prinz, Director of Graduate Admissions, 914-633-2420, Fax: 914-633-2277, E-mail: vjarekprinz@iona.edu.

John F. Kennedy University, Graduate School of Professional Psychology, Program in Organizational Psychology, Pleasant Hill, CA 94523-4817. Offers MA, Certificate. *Accreditation:* APA. Part-time and evening/weekend programs available. *Degree requirements:* For master's, thesis or alternative. *Entrance requirements:* For master's, interview. Additional exam requirements/recommendations for international students: Required—TOEFL.

Kean University, College of Humanities and Social Sciences, Program in Psychology, Union, NJ 07083. Offers human behavior and organizational psychology (MA); psychological services (MA). Part-time and evening/weekend programs available. *Faculty:* 15 full-time (13 women). *Students:* 14 full-time (10 women), 35 part-time (30 women); includes 20 minority (11 African Americans, 2 Asian Americans or Pacific Islanders, 7 Hispanic Americans), 2 international. Average age 30. 28 applicants, 82% accepted, 15 enrolled. In 2009, 15 master's awarded. *Degree requirements:* For master's, comprehensive exam, thesis, research. *Entrance requirements:* For master's, GRE General Test, minimum GPA of 3.0, 2 letters of recommendation, interview, 12 credits in psychology. *Application deadline:* For fall admission, 5/1 for domestic students; for spring admission, 11/1 for domestic students. Application fee: $60 ($150 for international students). Electronic applications accepted. *Expenses:* Tuition, state resident: full-time $10,440; part-time $435 per credit. Tuition, nonresident: full-time $14,160; part-time $590 per credit. Required fees: $2642; $110 per credit. Part-time tuition and fees vary according to course load and degree level. *Financial support:* In 2009–10, 1 research assistantship with full tuition reimbursement (averaging $3,263 per year) was awarded; unspecified assistantships also available. *Unit head:* Dr. Joanne Walsh, Program Coordinator, 908-737-5870, E-mail: jwalsh@kean.edu. *Application contact:* Reenat Hasan, Pre-Admissions Coordinator, 908-737-5923, Fax: 908-737-5965, E-mail: rhasan@exchange.kean.edu.

Lamar University, College of Graduate Studies, College of Arts and Sciences, Department of Psychology, Beaumont, TX 77710. Offers community/clinical psychology (MS); industrial/organizational psychology (MS). Part-time programs available. *Faculty:* 6 full-time (3 women). *Students:* 14 full-time (10 women), 11 part-time (5 women); includes 4 minority (2 African Americans, 2 Hispanic Americans), 1 international. Average age 25. 34 applicants, 18% accepted, 4 enrolled. In 2009, 1 master's awarded. *Degree requirements:* For master's, thesis, practicum. *Entrance requirements:* For master's, GRE General Test, minimum GPA of 2.75 in last 60 hours of undergraduate course work. Additional exam requirements/recommendations for international students: Required—TOEFL. *Application deadline:* For fall admission, 8/1 for domestic students; for spring admission, 12/1 for domestic students. Application fee: $25 ($50 for international students). *Financial support:* In 2009–10, 12 students received support, including 3 teaching assistantships (averaging $4,500 per year); fellowships, research assistantships, career-related internships or fieldwork, Federal Work-Study, scholarships/grants, and tuition waivers (partial) also available. Support available to part-time students. Financial award application deadline: 4/1. *Faculty research:* Groupthink, health psychology, school psychology, behavioral neuroscience. *Application contact:* Assistant Dean, 409-880-7978, E-mail: westgate@hal.lamar.edu.

Louisiana State University and Agricultural and Mechanical College, Graduate School, College of Arts and Sciences, Department of Psychology, Baton Rouge, LA 70803. Offers biological psychology (MA, PhD); clinical psychology (MA, PhD); cognitive psychology (MA, PhD); developmental psychology (MA, PhD); industrial/organizational psychology (MA, PhD); school psychology (MA, PhD). *Accreditation:* APA (one or more programs are accredited). *Faculty:* 27 full-time (10 women). *Students:* 94 full-time (68 women), 17 part-time (12 women); includes 14 minority (6 African Americans, 2 American Indian/Alaska Native, 2 Asian Americans or Pacific Islanders, 4 Hispanic Americans), 3 international. Average age 27. 232 applicants, 18% accepted, 29 enrolled. In 2009, 13 master's, 14 doctorates awarded. Terminal master's awarded for partial completion of doctoral program. *Degree requirements:* For master's, thesis; for doctorate, thesis/dissertation, 1 year internship. *Entrance requirements:* For master's and doctorate, GRE General Test, minimum GPA of 3.0. Additional exam requirements/recommendations for international students: Required—TOEFL (minimum score 550 paper-based; 213 computer-based; 79 iBT) or IELTS (minimum score 6.5). *Application deadline:* For fall admission, 1/15 for domestic and international students. Applications are processed on a rolling basis. Application fee: $50 ($70 for international students). Electronic applications accepted. *Financial support:* In 2009–10, 108 students received support, including 5 fellowships (averaging $26,974 per year), 2 research assistantships with partial tuition reimbursements available (averaging $18,000 per year), 74 teaching assistantships with partial tuition reimbursements available (averaging $14,751 per year); career-related internships or fieldwork, Federal Work-Study, institutionally sponsored loans, scholarships/grants, health care benefits, and tuition waivers (full and partial) also available. Financial award applicants required to submit FAFSA. *Faculty research:* Clinical psychology, autism, anxiety, addition, neuropsychology, school psychology, cognitive psychology, experimental psychology. Total annual research expenditures: $1 million. *Unit head:* Dr. Robert Matthews, Chair, 225-578-8745, Fax: 225-578-4125, E-mail: psmath@lsu.edu. *Application contact:* Dr. Jason Hicks, Coordinator of Graduate Studies, 225-578-4109, Fax: 225-578-4125, E-mail: jhicks@lsu.edu.

Louisiana Tech University, Graduate School, College of Education, Department of Behavioral Sciences and Psychology, Ruston, LA 71272. Offers counseling (MA); counseling psychology (PhD); industrial/organizational psychology (MA); special education (MA). *Accreditation:* APA (one or more programs are accredited). Part-time programs available. *Degree requirements:* For master's, thesis or alternative; for doctorate, thesis/dissertation. *Entrance requirements:* For master's and doctorate, GRE General Test.

Marshall University, Academic Affairs Division, College of Liberal Arts, Department of Psychology, Huntington, WV 25755. Offers clinical psychology (MA); general psychology (MA); industrial and organizational psychology (MA); psychology (Psy D). *Accreditation:* APA. *Faculty:* 13 full-time (4 women), 1 part-time/adjunct (0 women). *Students:* 101 full-time (71 women), 19 part-time (14 women); includes 6 minority (4 African Americans, 2 Hispanic Americans), 4 international. Average age 29. In 2009, 33 master's, 3 doctorates awarded. *Degree requirements:* For master's, thesis optional. *Entrance requirements:* For master's, GRE General Test or MAT. *Application deadline:* For fall admission, 3/1 for domestic students; for spring admission, 11/1 for domestic students. Application fee: $40. *Financial support:* Teaching assistantships with tuition reimbursements available. *Unit head:* Dr. Steven Mewaldt, Chairperson, 304-696-27tt, E-mail: mewaldt@marshall.edu. *Application contact:* Graduate Admissions, 304-746-1900, Fax: 304-746-1902, E-mail: services@marshall.edu.

Massachusetts School of Professional Psychology, Graduate Programs, Boston, MA 02132. Offers clinical psychology (Psy D); clinical psychopharmacology (Post-Doctoral MS); counseling psychology (MA); executive coaching (Graduate Certificate); forensic psychology (MA); organizational psychology (MA); respecialization in clinical psychology (Certificate); MA/CAGS. *Accreditation:* APA. *Degree requirements:* For master's, comprehensive exam; for doctorate, thesis/dissertation. *Entrance requirements:* For doctorate, GRE General Test. Additional exam requirements/recommendations for international students: Required—TOEFL (minimum score 550 paper-based; 213 computer-based). Electronic applications accepted.

Middle Tennessee State University, College of Graduate Studies, College of Education and Behavioral Science, Department of Psychology, Murfreesboro, TN 37132. Offers clinical psychology (MA); experimental psychology (MA); industrial/organizational psychology (MA); professional counseling (M Ed, Ed S), including curriculum and instruction (Ed S), mental health counseling (M Ed), school counseling (M Ed); psychology (MA); quantitative psychology (MA); school psychology (MA, Ed S). Part-time and evening/weekend programs available. Postbaccalaureate distance learning degree programs offered. *Faculty:* 36 full-time (16 women), 2 part-time/adjunct (0 women). *Students:* 23 full-time (19 women), 161 part-time (131 women); includes 21 minority (11 African Americans, 8 Asian Americans or Pacific Islanders, 2 Hispanic Americans). Average age 26. 251 applicants, 55% accepted, 138 enrolled. In 2009, 60 master's, 7 other advanced degrees awarded. *Degree requirements:* For master's, variable foreign language requirement, comprehensive exam, thesis (for some programs). *Entrance requirements:* Additional exam requirements/recommendations for international students: Required—TOEFL (minimum score 525 paper-based; 195 computer-based; 71 iBT) or IELTS (minimum score 6). *Application deadline:* For fall admission, 6/1 for domestic and international students. Applications are processed on a rolling basis. Application fee: $25 ($30 for international students). Electronic applications accepted. *Expenses:* Tuition, state resident: full-time $4404. Tuition, nonresident: full-time $10,956. *Financial support:* In 2009–10, 16 students received support. Career-related internships or fieldwork and institutionally sponsored loans available. Support available to part-time students. Financial award application deadline: 5/1; financial award applicants required to submit FAFSA. *Faculty research:* Industrial/organizational, social/personality/sports, counseling/clinical/school, cognitive/language/learning/perception, developmental/aging. *Unit head:* Dr. Dennis Papini, Chair, 615-898-2706, Fax: 615-898-5027. *Application contact:* Dr. Michael Allen, Dean and Vice Provost for Research, 615-898-2840, Fax: 615-904-8020, E-mail: mallen@mtsu.edu.

Minnesota State University Mankato, College of Graduate Studies, College of Social and Behavioral Sciences, Department of Psychology, Mankato, MN 56001. Offers clinical psychology (MA); industrial/organizational psychology (MA); school psychology (Psy D). Part-time programs available. *Students:* 51 full-time (32 women), 3 part-time (1 woman). *Degree requirements:* For master's, one foreign language, comprehensive exam, thesis (for some programs). *Entrance requirements:* For master's, GRE General Test, GRE Subject Test (clinical psychology), minimum GPA of 3.0 during previous 2 years, 3 letters of reference. Additional exam requirements/recommendations for international students: Required—TOEFL. *Application deadline:* For fall admission, 1/1 priority date for domestic students. Applications are processed on a rolling basis. Application fee: $40. Electronic applications accepted. *Expenses:* Tuition, state resident: full-time $5364. Tuition, nonresident: full-time $8314. *Financial support:* Research assistantships, teaching assistantships with full tuition reimbursements, career-related internships or fieldwork, Federal Work-Study, institutionally sponsored loans, and unspecified assistantships available. Support available to part-time students. Financial award application deadline: 3/15; financial award applicants required to submit FAFSA. *Faculty research:* Professional competency in hospitals, mood disturbance, 360-degree feedback, employee selection, planning fallacy. *Unit head:* Dr. Barry Ries, Chairperson, 507-389-2724. *Application contact:* 507-389-2321, E-mail: grad@mnsu.edu.

Missouri State University, Graduate College, College of Health and Human Services, Department of Psychology, Springfield, MO 65897. Offers psychology (MS), including clinical, experimental, industrial/organizational. *Faculty:* 26 full-time (11 women), 1 part-time/adjunct (0 women). *Students:* 44 full-time (28 women), 5 part-time (3 women); includes 2 minority (1 African American, 1 Hispanic American). Average age 26. 63 applicants, 56% accepted, 22 enrolled. In 2009, 21 master's awarded. *Degree requirements:* For master's, comprehensive exam, thesis. *Entrance requirements:* For master's, GRE General Test, GRE Subject Test, minimum GPA of 3.25 in major, 3.0 overall; 20 hours of course work in psychology (experimental and statistics). Additional exam requirements/recommendations for international students: Required—TOEFL (minimum score 550 paper-based; 213 computer-based; 79 iBT). *Application deadline:* For fall admission, 3/1 priority date for domestic and international students. Application fee: $35 ($50 for international students). Electronic applications accepted. *Expenses:* Tuition, state resident: full-time $3852; part-time $214 per credit hour. Tuition, nonresident: full-time $7524; part-time $418 per credit hour. Required fees: $696; $172 per semester. Tuition and fees vary according to course level, course load, degree level and program. *Financial support:* In 2009–10, 7 research assistantships with full tuition reimbursements (averaging $8,023 per year), 3 teaching assistantships with full tuition reimbursements (averaging $9,730 per year) were awarded; career-related internships or fieldwork, Federal Work-Study, institutionally sponsored loans, scholarships/grants, and unspecified assistantships also available. Financial award application deadline: 3/31; financial award applicants required to submit FAFSA. *Faculty research:* Work-family conflict, child forensic psychology, sports psychology, body image assessment, visual learning. *Unit head:* Dr. Robert G. Jones, Head, 417-836-5797, Fax: 417-836-8330, E-mail: psychology@missouristate.edu. *Application contact:* Eric Eckert, Coordinator of Admissions and Recruitment, 417-836-5331, Fax: 417-836-6200, E-mail: ericeckert@missouristate.edu.

Montclair State University, The Graduate School, College of Humanities and Social Sciences, Department of Psychology, Montclair, NJ 07043-1624. Offers educational psychology (MA), including child/adolescent clinical psychology, clinical psychology for Spanish/English bilinguals; psychology (MA, Certificate), including industrial and organizational psychology (MA); school psychologist (Certificate). Part-time and evening/weekend programs available. *Faculty:* 29 full-time (14 women), 26 part-time/adjunct (14 women). *Students:* 37 full-time (27 women), 33 part-time (23 women). Average age 27. 72 applicants, 47% accepted, 20 enrolled. In 2009, 7 master's awarded. *Degree requirements:* For master's, comprehensive exam, thesis or alternative. *Entrance requirements:* For master's, GRE General Test, 2 letters of recommendation. Additional exam requirements/recommendations for international students: Required—TOEFL (minimum score 83 computer-based), or IELTS. *Application deadline:* For fall admission, 2/1 for domestic and international students; for spring admission, 10/1 for domestic and international students. Applications are processed on a rolling basis. Application fee: $60. Electronic applications accepted. *Expenses:* Tuition, area resident: Part-time $486.74 per credit. Tuition, state resident: part-time $486.74 per credit. Tuition, nonresident: part-time $751.34 per credit. Tuition and fees vary according to degree level and program. *Financial support:* In 2009–10, 17 research assistantships with full tuition reimbursements (averaging $7,000 per year) were awarded; Federal Work-Study, scholarships/grants, and unspecified assistantships also available. Support available to part-time students. Financial award application deadline: 3/1; financial award applicants required to submit FAFSA. *Faculty research:* Engaged learning, academic and civic development. Total annual research expenditures: $10,000. *Unit head:* Dr. Peter Vietze, Chairperson, 973-655-5201. *Application contact:* Amy Aiello, Director of Admissions and Operations, 973-655-5147, Fax: 973-655-7869, E-mail: graduate.school@montclair.edu.

National-Louis University, College of Arts and Sciences, Program in Psychology, Chicago, IL 60603. Offers community psychology (PhD); cultural psychology (MA); health psychology (MA); human development (MA); organizational psychology (MA); psychology (Certificate), including general, health, human development, organizational, psychological assessment. Part-time and evening/weekend programs available. *Degree requirements:* For master's, thesis, internship (health psychology). *Entrance requirements:* For master's, GRE General Test, MAT, or Watson-Glaser Critical Thinking Appraisal, interview, minimum GPA of 3.0; for Certificate, GRE, MAT, or Watson-Glaser Critical Thinking Appraisal, interview, minimum GPA of 3.0, undergraduate course work in psychology. *Expenses:* Tuition: Full-time $17,160; part-time $715 per semester hour. Tuition and fees vary according to course load, degree level, campus/location and program. *Faculty research:* Human development, personality theory, abnormal psychology.

New York University, Graduate School of Arts and Science, Department of Psychology, New York, NY 10012-1019. Offers cognition and perception (PhD); community psychology (PhD); general psychology (MA); industrial/organizational psychology (MA); psychotherapy and psychoanalysis (Advanced Certificate); social/personality psychology (PhD). Part-time programs

Industrial and Organizational Psychology

New York University (continued)

available. *Students:* 151 full-time (94 women), 273 part-time (192 women); includes 59 minority (13 African Americans, 1 American Indian/Alaska Native, 27 Asian Americans or Pacific Islanders, 18 Hispanic Americans), 62 international. Average age 32. 748 applicants, 46% accepted, 122 enrolled. In 2009, 100 master's, 11 doctorates, 8 other advanced degrees awarded. Terminal master's awarded for partial completion of doctoral program. *Degree requirements:* For master's, comprehensive exam, thesis or alternative; for doctorate, thesis/dissertation. *Entrance requirements:* For master's, GRE General Test, minimum GPA of 3.0; for doctorate, GRE General Test, GRE Subject Test; for Advanced Certificate, doctoral degree, minimum GPA of 3.0. Additional exam requirements/recommendations for international students: Required—TOEFL. *Application deadline:* For fall admission, 12/18 for domestic students. Application fee: $90. *Expenses:* Tuition: Full-time $30,528; part-time $1272 per credit. Required fees: $2177. *Financial support:* Fellowships with tuition reimbursements, research assistantships with tuition reimbursements, teaching assistantships with tuition reimbursements, career-related internships or fieldwork, Federal Work-Study, institutionally sponsored loans, scholarships/grants, traineeships, health care benefits, and unspecified assistantships available. Financial award application deadline: 12/18; financial award applicants required to submit FAFSA. *Faculty research:* Vision, memory, social cognition, social and cognitive development, relationships. *Unit head:* Madeline Heilman, Director of Ph.D. Program, 212-998-7900, Fax: 212-995-4018, E-mail: psychq@psych.nyu.edu. *Application contact:* Barry Cohen, Director of M.A. Program, 212-998-7900, Fax: 212-995-4018, E-mail: psychq@psych.nyu.edu.

North Carolina State University, Graduate School, College of Humanities and Social Sciences, Department of Psychology, Raleigh, NC 27695. Offers developmental psychology (PhD); ergonomics and experimental psychology (PhD); industrial/organizational psychology (PhD); psychology in the public interest (PhD); school psychology (PhD). *Accreditation:* APA. *Degree requirements:* For doctorate, comprehensive exam, thesis/dissertation. *Entrance requirements:* For doctorate, GRE General Test, GRE Subject Test (industrial/organizational psychology), MAT (recommended), minimum GPA of 3.0 in major. Electronic applications accepted. *Faculty research:* Cognitive and social development (human factors, families, the workplace, community issues and health, aging).

Northern Kentucky University, Office of Graduate Programs, College of Arts and Sciences, Program in Industrial-Organizational Psychology, Highland Heights, KY 41099. Offers industrial psychology (Certificate); industrial-organizational psychology (MS); occupational health psychology (Certificate); organizational psychology (Certificate). Part-time and evening/weekend programs available. *Students:* 8 full-time (6 women), 34 part-time (24 women); includes 2 minority (both African Americans), 2 international. Average age 29. 31 applicants, 74% accepted, 15 enrolled. In 2009, 14 master's, 4 other advanced degrees awarded. *Degree requirements:* For master's, thesis optional, capstone. *Entrance requirements:* For master's, GRE (minimum score 450 verbal, 450 quantitative, 3.5 writing), minimum GPA of 3.0, at least 9 semester hours of undergraduate psychology, 1 course in statistics. Additional exam requirements/recommendations for international students: Required—TOEFL (minimum score 550 paper-based; 213 computer-based; 79 iBT); Recommended—IELTS (minimum score 6.5). *Application deadline:* For fall admission, 6/1 priority date for domestic students, 6/1 for international students; for spring admission, 11/1 priority date for domestic students, 10/1 for international students. Applications are processed on a rolling basis. Application fee: $40. Electronic applications accepted. *Expenses:* Tuition, state resident: full-time $6912; part-time $384 per credit hour. Tuition, nonresident: full-time $12,150; part-time $675 per credit hour. Tuition and fees vary according to course load, program and reciprocity agreements. *Financial support:* Unspecified assistantships available. Financial award applicants required to submit FAFSA. *Faculty research:* Attitude development, employee surveys, factor analysis, the effect of gender and racial stereotypes on employment decisions, social conflict and human factors in the workplace, workplace abuse and bullying, psychological testing/measurement, leader social-cognitive skills. *Unit head:* Dr. Jeffrey Smith, Director, 859-572-5317, Fax: 859-572-6085, E-mail: smithj@nku.edu. *Application contact:* Dr. Peg Griffin, Director of Graduate Programs, 859-572-6934, Fax: 859-572-6670, E-mail: griffinp@nku.edu.

Ohio University, Graduate College, College of Arts and Sciences, Department of Psychology, Program in Organizational Psychology, Athens, OH 45701-2979. Offers PhD. *Faculty:* 3 full-time (1 woman). *Students:* 3 full-time (1 woman), 2 part-time (0 women). 18 applicants, 17% accepted, 3 enrolled. In 2009, 2 doctorates awarded. *Degree requirements:* For doctorate, one foreign language, comprehensive exam, thesis/dissertation. *Entrance requirements:* For doctorate, GRE General Test, GRE Subject Test. Additional exam requirements/recommendations for international students: Required—TOEFL. *Application deadline:* For fall admission, 1/1 for domestic students. Application fee: $50 ($55 for international students). *Expenses:* Tuition, state resident: full-time $7839; part-time $323 per quarter hour. Tuition, nonresident: full-time $15,831; part-time $654 per quarter hour. Required fees: $2931. *Financial support:* In 2009–10, 1 fellowship with full tuition reimbursement (averaging $16,400 per year), 2 teaching assistantships with full tuition reimbursements (averaging $12,000 per year) were awarded; research assistantships with full tuition reimbursements, career-related internships or fieldwork, Federal Work-Study, institutionally sponsored loans, tuition waivers (full), and unspecified assistantships also available. Financial award application deadline: 1/15. *Faculty research:* Performance appraisal, job satisfaction, organizational entry, sexual harassment. *Unit head:* Rodger Griffeth, Coordinator of Organizational Studies, 740-593-1069, Fax: 740-593-0579. *Application contact:* Karyl Jones, Administrative Secretary, 740-593-1090, Fax: 740-593-0579, E-mail: psychology@ohio.edu.

Old Dominion University, College of Sciences, Doctoral Program in Psychology, Norfolk, VA 23529. Offers applied experimental psychology (PhD); human factors psychology (PhD); industrial/organizational psychology (PhD). *Faculty:* 21 full-time (9 women). *Students:* 24 full-time (17 women), 12 part-time (8 women); includes 2 minority (both Hispanic Americans), 1 international. Average age 29. 60 applicants, 15% accepted, 9 enrolled. In 2009, 4 doctorates awarded. *Degree requirements:* For doctorate, thesis/dissertation, candidacy exam. *Entrance requirements:* For doctorate, GRE General Test, GRE Subject Test, 3 recommendation letters. Additional exam requirements/recommendations for international students: Required—TOEFL (minimum score 550 paper-based). *Application deadline:* For winter admission, 1/5 for domestic and international students. Application fee: $40. Electronic applications accepted. *Expenses:* Tuition, state resident: full-time $8112; part-time $338 per credit. Tuition, nonresident: full-time $20,256; part-time $844 per credit. Required fees: $119 per semester. One-time fee: $50. *Financial support:* In 2009–10, 13 students received support, including 2 fellowships with full tuition reimbursements available (averaging $18,000 per year), research assistantships with full tuition reimbursements available (averaging $12,000 per year), 11 teaching assistantships with full tuition reimbursements available (averaging $12,000 per year). Financial award application deadline: 1/15. *Faculty research:* Human factors, industrial psychology, organizational psychology, applied experimental (health, developmental, quantitative). Total annual research expenditures: $493,384. *Unit head:* Dr. Brian Porter, Graduate Program Director, 757-683-4458, Fax: 757-683-5087, E-mail: bporter@odu.edu. *Application contact:* Dr. Brian Porter, Graduate Program Director, 757-683-4458, Fax: 757-683-5087, E-mail: bporter@odu.edu.

Philadelphia College of Osteopathic Medicine, Graduate and Professional Programs, Department of Psychology, Philadelphia, PA 19131-1694. Offers clinical psychology (Psy D); counseling and clinical health psychology (MS); organizational leadership and development (MS); psychology (Certificate, Post-Doctoral Certificate); school psychology (MS, Psy D, Ed S). *Accreditation:* APA. *Degree requirements:* For master's, thesis; for doctorate, comprehensive exam, thesis/dissertation, final project, fieldwork. *Entrance requirements:* For master's, GRE or MAT, minimum GPA of 3.0; course work in biology, chemistry, English, physics; for other advanced degree, PRAXIS. *Faculty research:* Depression in primary care, integrated primary care, geriatric mental health.

See Close-Up on page 1091.

Pontifical Catholic University of Puerto Rico, Institute of Graduate Studies in Behavioral Science and Community Affairs, Program in Industrial Psychology (Doctorate), Ponce, PR 00717-0777. Offers PhD. Part-time and evening/weekend programs available. *Entrance requirements:* For doctorate, EXADEP, minimum GPA of 2.75.

Pontifical Catholic University of Puerto Rico, Institute of Graduate Studies in Behavioral Science and Community Affairs, Program in Industrial Psychology (Master's), Ponce, PR 00717-0777. Offers MS. Part-time and evening/weekend programs available. *Degree requirements:* For master's, thesis. *Entrance requirements:* For master's, EXADEP, 3 letters of recommendation, interview, minimum GPA of 2.75.

Radford University, College of Graduate and Professional Studies, College of Humanities and Behavioral Sciences, Program in Psychology, Radford, VA 24142. Offers clinical psychology (MA, MS); experimental psychology (MA); general psychology (MS); industrial/organizational psychology (MA, MS). Part-time programs available. *Faculty:* 21 full-time (9 women), 6 part-time/adjunct (2 women). *Students:* 44 full-time (25 women), 1 (woman) part-time; includes 5 minority (3 African Americans, 2 Asian Americans or Pacific Islanders), 1 international. Average age 25. 110 applicants, 65% accepted, 22 enrolled. In 2009, 31 master's awarded. *Degree requirements:* For master's, comprehensive exam, thesis (for some programs). *Entrance requirements:* For master's, GRE, minimum GPA of 3.0; 3 letters of reference; essay. Additional exam requirements/recommendations for international students: Required—TOEFL (minimum score 550 paper-based; 213 computer-based; 79 iBT). *Application deadline:* For fall admission, 2/15 priority date for domestic students, 12/1 for international students. Applications are processed on a rolling basis. Application fee: $50. Electronic applications accepted. *Expenses:* Tuition, state resident: full-time $5086; part-time $211 per credit hour. Tuition, nonresident: full-time $12,608; part-time $525 per credit hour. Required fees: $2508; $105 per credit hour. *Financial support:* In 2009–10, 34 students received support, including 20 research assistantships with partial tuition reimbursements available (averaging $8,000 per year), 14 teaching assistantships with partial tuition reimbursements available (averaging $8,700 per year); career-related internships or fieldwork, institutionally sponsored loans, scholarships/grants, and unspecified assistantships also available. Financial award application deadline: 3/1; financial award applicants required to submit FAFSA. *Unit head:* Dr. Hilary M. Lips, Chair, 540-831-5387, Fax: 540-831-6113, E-mail: hlips@radford.edu. *Application contact:* Graduate Admissions Office, 540-831-5431, Fax: 540-831-6061, E-mail: gradcollege@radford.edu.

Rice University, Graduate Programs, School of Social Sciences, Department of Psychology, Houston, TX 77251-1892. Offers cognitive sciences (MA, PhD); industrial-organizational/social psychology (MA, PhD); psychology (MA, PhD). *Faculty:* 16 full-time (6 women), 26 part-time/adjunct (13 women). *Students:* 44 full-time (29 women); includes 12 minority (3 African Americans, 3 Asian Americans or Pacific Islanders, 6 Hispanic Americans), 9 international. Average age 29. 146 applicants, 7% accepted, 7 enrolled. In 2009, 6 master's, 7 doctorates awarded. Terminal master's awarded for partial completion of doctoral program. *Degree requirements:* For master's, thesis; for doctorate, thesis/dissertation. *Entrance requirements:* For doctorate, GRE General Test, minimum GPA of 3.0. Additional exam requirements/recommendations for international students: Required—TOEFL. *Application deadline:* For fall admission, 1/15 priority date for domestic and international students. Applications are processed on a rolling basis. Application fee: $35. Electronic applications accepted. *Financial support:* In 2009–10, 29 students received support, including 25 fellowships with full tuition reimbursements available (averaging $18,500 per year), 5 research assistantships with full tuition reimbursements available (averaging $18,500 per year); career-related internships or fieldwork, Federal Work-Study, institutionally sponsored loans, scholarships/grants, health care benefits, tuition waivers (full), and unspecified assistantships also available. Financial award application deadline: 1/15; financial award applicants required to submit FAFSA. *Faculty research:* Cognitive, cognitive neuropsychology, human factors, human-computer interaction, industrial-organizational psychology. Total annual research expenditures: $754,120. *Unit head:* Dr. James L. Dannemiller, Chairman, 713-348-4850, Fax: 713-348-5221, E-mail: psyc@rice.edu. *Application contact:* Lanita K. Martin, Coordinator, 713-348-4850, Fax: 713-348-5221, E-mail: psyc@rice.edu.

Roosevelt University, Graduate Division, College of Arts and Sciences, Department of Psychology, Program in Industrial/Organizational Psychology, Chicago, IL 60605. Offers MA.

Rutgers, The State University of New Jersey, New Brunswick, Graduate School of Applied and Professional Psychology, Program in Organizational Psychology, Piscataway, NJ 08854-8097. Offers Psy M, Psy D. *Degree requirements:* For doctorate, comprehensive exam, thesis/dissertation, 1 year internship. *Entrance requirements:* For doctorate, GRE General Test, GRE Subject Test (psychology), BA in psychology or equivalent. Additional exam requirements/recommendations for international students: Required—TOEFL. Electronic applications accepted. *Expenses:* Contact institution. *Faculty research:* Organizational assessment, managerial and organizational practice, consultation, organizational development, decision making.

St. Cloud State University, School of Graduate Studies, College of Social Sciences, Program in Industrial-Organizational Psychology, St. Cloud, MN 56301-4498. Offers MS. *Faculty:* 11 full-time (6 women). *Students:* 16 full-time (12 women), 2 part-time (1 woman), 4 international. 23 applicants, 39% accepted. In 2009, 10 master's awarded. *Degree requirements:* For master's, thesis or alternative. *Entrance requirements:* For master's, GRE General Test, minimum GPA of 2.75. Additional exam requirements/recommendations for international students: Required—Michigan English Language Assessment Battery; Recommended—TOEFL (minimum score 550 paper-based; 213 computer-based), IELTS (minimum score 6.5). *Application deadline:* For fall admission, 3/1 for domestic and international students. Electronic applications accepted. *Financial support:* Federal Work-Study, scholarships/grants, and unspecified assistantships available. *Unit head:* Dr. Daren Protolipac, Coordinator, 320-308-4157, E-mail: dsprotolipac@stcloudstate.edu. *Application contact:* Linda Lou Krueger, School of Graduate Studies, 320-308-2113, Fax: 320-308-5371, E-mail: lekrueger@stcloudstate.edu.

Saint Joseph's University, College of Arts and Sciences, Organization Development and Leadership Programs, Philadelphia, PA 19131-1395. Offers adult learning and training (MS, Certificate); organization dynamics and leadership (MS, Certificate); organizational psychology and development (MS, Certificate). Part-time and evening/weekend programs available. Post-baccalaureate distance learning degree programs offered (no on-campus study). *Students:* 9 full-time (6 women), 75 part-time (50 women); includes 23 minority (20 African Americans, 1 Asian American or Pacific Islander, 2 Hispanic Americans), 10 international. Average age 37. In 2009, 29 master's awarded. *Entrance requirements:* For master's, GRE (if GPA less than 2.7), minimum GPA of 2.7, 2 letters of recommendation, resume. Additional exam requirements/recommendations for international students: Required—TOEFL (minimum score 550 paper-based; 213 computer-based; 79 iBT). *Application deadline:* For fall admission, 7/15 priority date for domestic students, 4/15 for international students; for winter admission, 1/15 for international students; for spring admission, 11/15 priority date for domestic students, 10/15 for international students. Applications are processed on a rolling basis. Application fee: $35. Electronic applications accepted. *Expenses:* Tuition: Part-time $729 per credit hour. Tuition and fees vary according to degree level and program. *Financial support:* Applicants required to submit FAFSA. *Unit head:* Dr. Felice Tilin, Director, 610-660-1575, E-mail: ftilin@sju.edu. *Application contact:* Kate McConnell, Director, Graduate College of Arts and Sciences Admissions and Retention, 610-660-3184, Fax: 610-660-3230, E-mail: kate.mcconnell@sju.edu.

Saint Louis University, Graduate School, College of Arts and Sciences and Graduate School, Department of Psychology, St. Louis, MO 63103-2097. Offers clinical psychology (MS-R, PhD); experimental psychology (MS-R, PhD); industrial-organizational psychology (PhD); psychology (PhD). *Accreditation:* APA (one or more programs are accredited). Part-time programs available. *Degree requirements:* For master's, comprehensive exam, thesis; for doctorate, thesis/dissertation, clinical internship (for clinical psychology PhD). *Entrance requirements:* For master's, GRE General Test, interview, letters of recommendation, resume; for doctorate, GRE General Test, interview, letters of recommendation, resumé, transcripts, goal statement. Additional exam requirements/recommendations for international students: Required—TOEFL (minimum score 550 paper-based; 213 computer-based). Electronic applications accepted. *Faculty research:* Violence and trauma; neural basis of learning and memory function; eating disorders; body image and health behavior; prejudice, stereotyping, and victimization; memory, cognitive aging and language processing.

Saint Mary's University, Faculty of Science, Department of Psychology, Halifax, NS B3H 3C3, Canada. Offers applied psychology (M Sc, PhD), including industrial/organizational psychology (M Sc). Part-time programs available. *Degree requirements:* For master's, thesis, 500-hour internship; for doctorate, comprehensive exam, thesis/dissertation, research project. *Entrance requirements:* For master's and doctorate, GRE General Test. *Application deadline:* For fall admission, 2/1 for domestic students. Application fee: $35. *Financial support:* Fellowships, research assistantships, teaching assistantships, career-related internships or fieldwork and scholarships/grants available. Support available to part-time students. *Faculty research:* Assessment, health psychology, social psychology, cognition. *Unit head:* Dr. Victor Catano, Chairperson, 902-420-5845. *Application contact:* Dr. Mark Fleming, Graduate Program Coordinator, 902-420-5273, E-mail: mark.fleming@smu.ca.

St. Mary's University, Graduate School, Department of Psychology, Program in Industrial/Organizational Psychology, San Antonio, TX 78228-8507. Offers MA, MS. Part-time programs available. *Degree requirements:* For master's, comprehensive exam, thesis optional. *Entrance requirements:* For master's, GRE General Test. Additional exam requirements/recommendations for international students: Required—TOEFL (minimum score 550 paper-based; 213 computer-based; 80 iBT). Electronic applications accepted. *Expenses:* Tuition: Full-time $8004. Required fees: $536. One-time fee: $5 full-time. Full-time tuition and fees vary according to program.

San Diego State University, Graduate and Research Affairs, College of Sciences, Department of Psychology, San Diego, CA 92182. Offers clinical psychology (MS, PhD); industrial and organizational psychology (MS); program evaluation (MS); psychology (MA). *Accreditation:* APA (one or more programs are accredited). Terminal master's awarded for partial completion of doctoral program. *Degree requirements:* For master's, thesis, oral exam; for doctorate, thesis/dissertation. *Entrance requirements:* For master's, GRE General Test, GRE Subject Test, 3 letters of recommendation; for doctorate, GRE General Test, GRE Subject Test, minimum GPA of 3.0, 3 letters of recommendation. Additional exam requirements/recommendations for international students: Required—TOEFL. Electronic applications accepted.

San Jose State University, Graduate Studies and Research, College of Social Sciences, Department of Psychology, San Jose, CA 95192-0001. Offers clinical psychology (MS); experimental psychology (MA); industrial/organizational psychology (MS); psychology (MA). *Students:* 51 full-time (37 women), 20 part-time (14 women); includes 18 minority (1 African American, 1 American Indian/Alaska Native, 12 Asian Americans or Pacific Islanders, 4 Hispanic Americans), 6 international. Average age 28. 153 applicants, 20% accepted, 26 enrolled. In 2009, 17 master's awarded. *Degree requirements:* For master's, comprehensive exam, thesis (for some programs). *Entrance requirements:* For master's, GRE General Test, minimum GPA of 3.0. *Application deadline:* For fall admission, 6/29 for domestic students; for spring admission, 11/30 for domestic students. Applications are processed on a rolling basis. Application fee: $59. Electronic applications accepted. *Financial support:* Teaching assistantships, career-related internships or fieldwork and institutionally sponsored loans available. Financial award application deadline: 3/1; financial award applicants required to submit FAFSA. *Faculty research:* Drug and alcohol abuse, neurohormonal mechanisms in motion sickness, behavior modification, sleep research, genetics. *Unit head:* Dr. Sheila Bienenfeld, Chair, 408-924-5642, Fax: 408-924-5605. *Application contact:* Dr. Sheila Bienenfeld, Chair, 408-924-5642, Fax: 408-924-5605.

Seattle Pacific University, Industrial Organizational Psychology Program, Seattle, WA 98119-1997. Offers MA, PhD. *Faculty:* 4 full-time (1 woman), 1 part-time/adjunct (0 women). *Students:* 29 full-time (20 women), 32 part-time (27 women); includes 11 minority (3 African Americans, 8 Asian Americans or Pacific Islanders), 2 international. Average age 28. 72 applicants, 35% accepted, 25 enrolled. In 2009, 16 master's awarded. *Degree requirements:* For master's, research project; for doctorate, thesis/dissertation, field placement. *Entrance requirements:* Additional exam requirements/recommendations for international students: Required—TOEFL (minimum score 550 paper-based; 213 computer-based). *Application deadline:* For fall admission, 2/15 for domestic and international students. Application fee: $50. Electronic applications accepted. *Expenses:* Tuition: Part-time $485 per credit. Part-time tuition and fees vary according to course level, degree level and program. *Financial support:* In 2009–10, 44 students received support. Applicants required to submit FAFSA. *Unit head:* Dr. Robert B. McKenna, Chair, 206-281-2629, E-mail: rmckenna@spu.edu. *Application contact:* The Grad Center, 206-281-2091.

Southern Illinois University Edwardsville, Graduate Studies and Research, School of Education, Department of Psychology, Program in Industrial-Organizational Psychology, Edwardsville, IL 62026-0001. Offers MA. Part-time programs available. *Students:* 19 full-time (16 women), 9 part-time (5 women); includes 2 minority (1 African American, 1 Hispanic American), 1 international. Average age 26. In 2009, 8 master's awarded. *Degree requirements:* For master's, thesis. *Entrance requirements:* For master's, GRE. Additional exam requirements/recommendations for international students: Required—TOEFL (minimum score 550 paper-based; 213 computer-based; 79 iBT), IELTS (minimum score 6.5). *Application deadline:* For fall admission, 2/1 for domestic and international students. Application fee: $30. Electronic applications accepted. *Expenses:* Tuition, state resident: part-time $1252.50 per semester. Tuition, nonresident: part-time $3131.25 per semester. Required fees: $586.85 per semester. Tuition and fees vary according to course load. *Financial support:* Career-related internships or fieldwork, Federal Work-Study, institutionally sponsored loans, scholarships/grants, traineeships, and unspecified assistantships available. Support available to part-time students. Financial award application deadline: 3/1; financial award applicants required to submit FAFSA. *Unit head:* Dr. Cynthia Nordstrom, Director, 618-650-2202, E-mail: cnordst@siue.edu. *Application contact:* Dr. Cynthia Nordstrom, Director, 618-650-2202, E-mail: cnordst@siue.edu.

Springfield College, Graduate Programs, Programs in Psychology and Counseling, Springfield, MA 01109-3797. Offers athletic counseling (M Ed, MS, CAGS); industrial/organizational psychology (M Ed, MS, CAGS); marriage and family therapy (M Ed, MS, CAGS); mental health counseling (M Ed, MS, CAGS); school guidance and counseling (M Ed, MS, CAGS); student personnel in higher education (M Ed, MS, CAGS). Part-time programs available. *Degree requirements:* For master's, research project, portfolio. *Entrance requirements:* Additional exam requirements/recommendations for international students: Required—TOEFL (minimum score 550 paper-based; 213 computer-based). Electronic applications accepted. *Expenses:* Tuition: Full-time $19,800; part-time $825 per credit hour. Required fees: $150.

Teachers College, Columbia University, Graduate Faculty of Education, Department of Organization and Leadership, Program in Social and Organizational Psychology, New York, NY 10027-6696. Offers organizational psychology (MA, Ed D, PhD); social psychology (Ed D, PhD). *Faculty:* 8 full-time (5 women), 5 part-time/adjunct (0 women). *Students:* 133 full-time (87 women), 111 part-time (82 women); includes 67 minority (17 African Americans, 33 Asian Americans or Pacific Islanders, 17 Hispanic Americans), 26 international. Average age 28. 238 applicants, 61% accepted, 69 enrolled. In 2009, 136 master's, 3 doctorates awarded. Terminal master's awarded for partial completion of doctoral program. *Degree requirements:* For master's, comprehensive exam; for doctorate, thesis/dissertation. *Entrance requirements:* For master's, minimum GPA of 3.0; for doctorate, GRE General Test. *Application deadline:* For fall admission, 5/15 for domestic students; for spring admission, 12/1 for domestic students. Application fee: $65. *Financial support:* Fellowships, research assistantships, career-related internships or fieldwork, Federal Work-Study, institutionally sponsored loans, and tuition waivers (full and partial) available. Support available to part-time students. Financial award application deadline: 2/1. *Faculty research:* Conflict resolution, human resource and organization development, management competence, organizational culture, leadership. *Unit head:* Warner Burke, Chair, 212-678-3258. *Application contact:* Debbie Lesperance, Assistant Director of Admission, 212-678-3710, Fax: 212-678-4171.

Temple University, Graduate School, College of Education, Department of Psychological Studies in Education, Program in Adult and Organizational Development, Philadelphia, PA 19122-6096. Offers Ed M. Part-time and evening/weekend programs available. *Degree requirements:* For master's, thesis or alternative. *Entrance requirements:* For master's, GRE General Test or MAT, minimum GPA of 3.0. Additional exam requirements/recommendations for international students: Required—TOEFL (minimum score 550 paper-based; 213 computer-based; 79 iBT). Electronic applications accepted.

Texas A&M University, College of Liberal Arts, Department of Psychology, College Station, TX 77843. Offers behavioral and cellular neuroscience (MS, PhD); clinical psychology (MS, PhD); cognitive psychology (MS, PhD); developmental psychology (MS, PhD); industrial/organizational psychology (MS, PhD); social psychology (MS, PhD). *Accreditation:* APA (one or more programs are accredited). *Faculty:* 36. *Students:* 84 full-time (58 women), 6 part-time (5 women); includes 26 minority (6 African Americans, 3 Asian Americans or Pacific Islanders, 17 Hispanic Americans), 6 international. In 2009, 12 master's, 8 doctorates awarded. *Degree requirements:* For master's, thesis; for doctorate, comprehensive exam (for some programs), thesis/dissertation. *Entrance requirements:* For master's and doctorate, GRE General Test. Additional exam requirements/recommendations for international students: Required—TOEFL. *Application deadline:* For fall admission, 1/5 for domestic and international students. Application fee: $50 ($75 for international students). Electronic applications accepted. *Expenses:* Tuition, state resident: full-time $3991; part-time $221.74 per credit hour. Tuition, nonresident: full-time $9049; part-time $502.74 per credit hour. *Financial support:* Fellowships with partial tuition reimbursements, research assistantships with partial tuition reimbursements, teaching assistantships with partial tuition reimbursements, career-related internships or fieldwork, institutionally sponsored loans, health care benefits, and unspecified assistantships available. Financial award application deadline: 1/5; financial award applicants required to submit FAFSA. *Unit head:* Dr. Les Morey, Head, 979-845-2581, Fax: 979-845-4727, E-mail: lmorey@psych.tamu.edu. *Application contact:* Sharon Starr, Graduate Admissions Supervisor, 979-458-1710, Fax: 979-845-4727, E-mail: gradadv@psyc.tamu.edu.

Union Institute & University, MA Program in Psychology and Counseling, Brattleboro, VT 05301. Offers clinical mental health counseling (MA); clinical psychology (MA); counseling psychology (MA); developmental psychology (MA); educational psychology (MA); organizational psychology (MA). Postbaccalaureate distance learning degree programs offered (minimal on-campus study). *Faculty:* 2 full-time (1 woman), 8 part-time/adjunct (2 women). *Students:* 57 full-time (50 women), 20 part-time (16 women); includes 4 minority (1 African American, 3 Hispanic Americans). Average age 41. In 2009, 23 master's awarded. *Degree requirements:* For master's, thesis, internship (depending on concentration). *Application deadline:* Applications are processed on a rolling basis. Electronic applications accepted. Tuition and fees vary according to course load, degree level, campus/location and program. *Unit head:* Dr. Nicholas Young, Director, 802-257-8911, E-mail: nick.young@myunion.edu. *Application contact:* Diane Robinson, Director of Admissions, Brattleboro, 800-336-6794, E-mail: diane.robinson@myunion.edu.

University at Albany, State University of New York, College of Arts and Sciences, Department of Psychology, Albany, NY 12222-0001. Offers autism (Certificate); biopsychology (PhD); clinical psychology (PhD); general/experimental psychology (PhD); industrial/organizational psychology (PhD); psychology (MA); social/personality psychology (PhD). *Accreditation:* APA (one or more programs are accredited). *Degree requirements:* For doctorate, thesis/dissertation. *Entrance requirements:* For doctorate, GRE General Test, GRE Subject Test. Additional exam requirements/recommendations for international students: Required—TOEFL (minimum score 550 paper-based; 213 computer-based). Electronic applications accepted.

The University of Akron, Graduate School, Buchtel College of Arts and Sciences, Department of Psychology, Program in Industrial/Organizational Psychology, Akron, OH 44325. Offers MA, PhD. *Students:* 29 full-time (24 women), 10 part-time (5 women); includes 5 minority (2 African Americans, 3 Asian Americans or Pacific Islanders), 3 international. Average age 28. 54 applicants, 22% accepted, 0 enrolled. In 2009, 8 doctorates awarded. Terminal master's awarded for partial completion of doctoral program. *Degree requirements:* For master's, thesis optional, thesis or specialty exam; for doctorate, one foreign language, comprehensive exam, thesis/dissertation. *Entrance requirements:* For master's, GRE General Test, GRE Subject Test, minimum GPA of 2.75, letters of recommendation; for doctorate, GRE General Test, GRE Subject Test, minimum graduate GPA of 3.25, letters of recommendation, personal statement, curriculum vitae. Additional exam requirements/recommendations for international students: Required—TOEFL (minimum score 550 paper-based; 213 computer-based; 79 iBT). *Application deadline:* For fall admission, 1/15 for domestic and international students. Application fee: $30 ($40 for international students). Electronic applications accepted. *Expenses:* Tuition, state resident: full-time $6570; part-time $365 per credit hour. Tuition, nonresident: full-time $11,250; part-time $625 per credit hour. *Financial support:* Fellowships with full tuition reimbursements, research assistantships with full tuition reimbursements, teaching assistantships with full tuition reimbursements available. *Faculty research:* Personnel selection, performance management, leadership, self-regulation, affect. *Unit head:* Dr. Rosalie Hall, Coordinator, 330-972-8375, E-mail: rhall@uakron.edu. *Application contact:* Dr. Rosalie Hall, Coordinator, 330-972-8375, E-mail: rhall@uakron.edu.

University of Baltimore, Graduate School, The Yale Gordon College of Liberal Arts, Program in Applied Psychology, Baltimore, MD 21201-5779. Offers applied psychology (MS), including counseling, industrial and organizational psychology, psychological applications. Part-time and evening/weekend programs available. *Degree requirements:* For master's, thesis optional. *Entrance requirements:* For master's, GRE, minimum GPA of 3.0. Additional exam requirements/recommendations for international students: Required—TOEFL (minimum score 550 paper-based; 213 computer-based). Electronic applications accepted. *Expenses:* Contact institution. *Faculty research:* Participatory decision making, counter productive workplace behavior, organizational consulting, substance abuse treatment, cognitive functioning in head injured.

University of Central Florida, College of Sciences, Department of Psychology, Program in Industrial/Organizational Psychology, Orlando, FL 32816. Offers MS, PhD. *Accreditation:* APA. Part-time and evening/weekend programs available. *Students:* 33 full-time (21 women), 5 part-time (3 women); includes 13 minority (3 African Americans, 3 Asian Americans or Pacific Islanders, 7 Hispanic Americans). Average age 26. 78 applicants, 47% accepted, 18 enrolled. In 2009, 11 master's, 7 doctorates awarded. *Degree requirements:* For master's, comprehensive exam, thesis, practicum. *Entrance requirements:* For master's, GRE General Test, minimum GPA of 3.0 in last 60 hours, resume. Additional exam requirements/recommendations for international students: Required—TOEFL. *Application deadline:* For fall admission, 2/1 for domestic students. Application fee: $30. Electronic applications accepted. *Expenses:* Tuition, state resident: part-time $306.31 per credit hour. Tuition, nonresident: part-time $1099.01 per credit hour. Part-time tuition and fees vary according to degree level and program. *Financial support:* In 2009–10, 3 students received support, including 3 research assistantships with partial tuition reimbursements available (averaging $9,620 per year); career-related internships or fieldwork, Federal Work-Study, institutionally sponsored loans, tuition waivers (partial), and unspecified assistantships also available. Financial award application deadline: 3/1; financial award applicants required to submit FAFSA. *Faculty research:* Sports psychology, electronic selection systems, team training, stress effects, psychometrics. *Unit head:* Dr. Robert Pritchard, Program Director, 407-823-2560, E-mail: rpritcha@ucf.edu. *Application contact:* Dr. Robert Pritchard, Program Director, 407-823-2560, E-mail: rpritcha@ucf.edu.

University of Connecticut, Graduate School, College of Liberal Arts and Sciences, Department of Psychology, Storrs, CT 06269. Offers behavioral neuroscience (PhD); biopsychology (PhD); clinical psychology (MA, PhD); cognition and instruction (PhD); developmental psychology (MA, PhD); ecological psychology (PhD); experimental psychology (PhD); general psychology (MA, PhD); health psychology (Graduate Certificate); industrial/organizational psychology (PhD); language and cognition (PhD); neuroscience (PhD); occupational health psychology (Graduate Certificate); social psychology (MA, PhD). *Accreditation:* APA. *Faculty:* 59 full-time (26 women).

Industrial and Organizational Psychology

University of Connecticut (continued)
Students: 194 full-time (133 women), 24 part-time (12 women); includes 48 minority (12 African Americans, 21 Asian Americans or Pacific Islanders, 15 Hispanic Americans), 25 international. Average age 28. 585 applicants, 4% accepted, 14 enrolled. In 2009, 22 master's, 24 doctorates awarded. Terminal master's awarded for partial completion of doctoral program. *Degree requirements:* For master's, comprehensive exam; for doctorate, thesis/dissertation. *Entrance requirements:* For master's and doctorate, GRE General Test, GRE Subject Test. Additional exam requirements/recommendations for international students: Required—TOEFL (minimum score 550 paper-based; 213 computer-based). *Application deadline:* For fall admission, 2/1 priority date for domestic and international students; for spring admission, 11/1 for domestic students, 10/1 for international students. Applications are processed on a rolling basis. Application fee: $55. Electronic applications accepted. *Expenses:* Tuition, state resident: full-time $4725; part-time $525 per credit. Tuition, nonresident: full-time $12,267; part-time $1363 per credit. Required fees: $346 per semester. Tuition and fees vary according to course load. *Financial support:* In 2009–10, 109 research assistantships with full tuition reimbursements, 72 teaching assistantships with full tuition reimbursements were awarded; fellowships, career-related internships or fieldwork, Federal Work-Study, scholarships/grants, health care benefits, and unspecified assistantships also available. Financial award application deadline: 2/1; financial award applicants required to submit FAFSA. *Unit head:* Charles A. Lowe, Head, 860-486-3517, Fax: 860-486-2760, E-mail: charles.lowe@uconn.edu. *Application contact:* Charles A. Lowe, Head, 860-486-3517, Fax: 860-486-2760, E-mail: charles.lowe@uconn.edu.

University of Detroit Mercy, College of Liberal Arts and Education, Department of Psychology, Program in Industrial/Organizational Psychology, Detroit, MI 48221. Offers MA. *Entrance requirements:* For master's, GRE General Test, minimum GPA of 3.0.

University of Guelph, Graduate Program Services, College of Social and Applied Human Sciences, Department of Psychology, Guelph, ON N1G 2W1, Canada. Offers applied social psychology (MA, PhD); clinical psychology applied development emphasis (PhD); clinical psychology applied developmental emphasis (MA); industrial/organizational psychology (MA, PhD); neuroscience and applied cognitive science (MA, PhD). *Degree requirements:* For master's, thesis; for doctorate, comprehensive exam, thesis/dissertation. *Entrance requirements:* For master's, GRE General Test, GRE Subject Test, minimum B+ average during previous 2 years of course work; for doctorate, GRE General Test, GRE Subject Test, minimum A- average. Additional exam requirements/recommendations for international students: Required—TOEFL (minimum score 89 iBT). Electronic applications accepted. *Faculty research:* Organizational psychology, reading comprehension and mathematical ability, drug addiction and relapse, gender issues and culture, memory, clinical psychology.

University of Maryland, Baltimore County, Graduate School, College of Arts, Humanities and Social Sciences, Department of Psychology, Program in Industrial Organizational Psychology, Rockville, MD 20850. Offers MPS. Part-time and evening/weekend programs available. *Faculty:* 2 full-time (1 woman), 5 part-time/adjunct (2 women). *Students:* 20 full-time (17 women), 31 part-time (28 women); includes 19 minority (8 African Americans, 1 American Indian/Alaska Native, 3 Asian Americans or Pacific Islanders, 7 Hispanic Americans), 4 international. Average age 28. 51 applicants, 51% accepted, 24 enrolled. *Entrance requirements:* Additional exam requirements/recommendations for international students: Required—TOEFL. *Application deadline:* For fall admission, 3/1 for domestic students, 1/1 for international students. Application fee: $50. Electronic applications accepted. *Unit head:* Dr. Diane Alonso, Program Director, 301-738-6318, E-mail: dalonso@umbc.edu. *Application contact:* Sonya Crosby, Assistant Director, 301-738-6184, E-mail: scrosby@umbc.edu.

University of Maryland, College Park, Academic Affairs, College of Behavioral and Social Sciences, Department of Psychology, College Park, MD 20742. Offers clinical psychology (PhD); developmental psychology (PhD); experimental psychology (PhD); industrial psychology (MA, MS, PhD); social psychology (PhD). *Accreditation:* APA (one or more programs are accredited). *Faculty:* 71 full-time (35 women), 8 part-time/adjunct (4 women). *Students:* 82 full-time (67 women); includes 13 minority (2 African Americans, 4 Asian Americans or Pacific Islanders, 7 Hispanic Americans), 12 international. 568 applicants, 4% accepted, 8 enrolled. In 2009, 13 master's, 10 doctorates awarded. *Degree requirements:* For master's, thesis; for doctorate, variable foreign language requirement, comprehensive exam, thesis/dissertation. *Entrance requirements:* For master's and doctorate, GRE General Test, GRE Subject Test, minimum GPA of 3.5, research and/or work experience, 3 letters of recommendation. *Application deadline:* For fall admission, 12/1 for domestic and international students. Applications are processed on a rolling basis. Application fee: $60. Electronic applications accepted. *Expenses:* Tuition, area resident: Part-time $471 per credit hour. Tuition, state resident: part-time $471 per credit hour. Tuition, nonresident: part-time $1016 per credit hour. Required fees: $337.04 per term. *Financial support:* In 2009–10, 11 fellowships with full and partial tuition reimbursements (averaging $19,195 per year), 5 research assistantships (averaging $17,734 per year), 45 teaching assistantships with tuition reimbursements (averaging $17,116 per year) were awarded; career-related internships or fieldwork, Federal Work-Study, and scholarships/grants also available. Support available to part-time students. Financial award applicants required to submit FAFSA. *Faculty research:* Social stereotyping and prejudice, anxiety disorders, auditory neuroethology, counseling and social psychology. Total annual research expenditures: $3.8 million. *Unit head:* Thomas S. Wallsten, Chair, 301-405-3562, Fax: 301-314-9566, E-mail: twallst@umd.edu. *Application contact:* Dean of Graduate School, 301-405-0358, Fax: 301-314-9305.

University of Minnesota, Twin Cities Campus, Graduate School, College of Liberal Arts, Department of Psychology, Program in Industrial/Organizational Psychology, Minneapolis, MN 55455-0213. Offers PhD. *Degree requirements:* For doctorate, comprehensive exam, thesis/dissertation. *Entrance requirements:* For doctorate, GRE General Test, GRE Subject Test (recommended), 12 credits of upper-level psychology courses, including a course in statistics or psychological measurement. Additional exam requirements/recommendations for international students: Required—TOEFL (minimum score 550 paper-based; 213 computer-based; 79 iBT).

University of Missouri–St. Louis, College of Arts and Sciences, Department of Psychology, St. Louis, MO 63121. Offers behavioral neuroscience (PhD); clinical psychology respecialization (Certificate); community psychology (PhD); general psychology (MA); industrial/organizational psychology (PhD). *Accreditation:* APA (one or more programs are accredited). Evening/weekend programs available. *Faculty:* 21 full-time (10 women), 5 part-time/adjunct (3 women). *Students:* 35 full-time (29 women), 39 part-time (30 women); includes 4 minority (1 American Indian/Alaska Native, 1 Asian American or Pacific Islander, 2 Hispanic Americans). Average age 28. 208 applicants, 9% accepted, 13 enrolled. In 2009, 16 master's, 6 doctorates awarded. Terminal master's awarded for partial completion of doctoral program. *Degree requirements:* For master's, thesis; for doctorate, thesis/dissertation. *Entrance requirements:* For master's and doctorate, GRE General Test, GRE Subject Test, 3 letters of recommendation. Additional exam requirements/recommendations for international students: Required—TOEFL (minimum score 550 paper-based; 213 computer-based). *Application deadline:* For fall admission, 1/15 for domestic and international students. Application fee: $35 ($40 for international students). Electronic applications accepted. *Expenses:* Tuition, state resident: full-time $5377; part-time $297.70 per credit hour. Tuition, nonresident: full-time $13,882; part-time $771.20 per credit hour. Required fees: $220; $12.20 per credit hour. One-time fee: $12. Tuition and fees vary according to course level, campus/location and program. *Financial support:* In 2009–10, 7 research assistantships with full and partial tuition reimbursements (averaging $10,600 per year), 20 teaching assistantships with full and partial tuition reimbursements (averaging $9,788 per year) were awarded; fellowships with full tuition reimbursements also available. Financial award applicants required to submit FAFSA. *Faculty research:* Bereavement and loss, neuroscience, post-traumatic stress disorder, conflict and negotiation, social psychology. *Unit head:* Dr. George Taylor, Chair, 314-516-5391, Fax: 314-516-5392, E-mail: umslpsychology@msx.umsl.edu. *Application contact:* 314-516-5458, Fax: 314-516-6996, E-mail: gradadm@umsl.edu.

University of Nebraska at Omaha, Graduate Studies, College of Arts and Sciences, Department of Psychology, Omaha, NE 68182. Offers developmental psychology (PhD); industrial/organizational psychology (MS, PhD); psychobiology (PhD); psychology (MA); school psychology (MS, Ed S). Part-time programs available. *Faculty:* 18 full-time (8 women). *Students:* 44 full-time (36 women), 23 part-time (18 women); includes 3 minority (1 African American, 1 Asian American or Pacific Islander, 1 Hispanic American), 2 international. Average age 26. 116 applicants, 34% accepted, 28 enrolled. In 2009, 30 master's, 5 other advanced degrees awarded. *Degree requirements:* For master's, comprehensive exam, thesis (for some programs). *Entrance requirements:* For master's, GRE General Test, GRE Subject Test, previous course work in psychology, including statistics and a laboratory course; minimum GPA of 3.0, 3 letters of recommendation; for doctorate, GRE General Test. Additional exam requirements/recommendations for international students: Required—TOEFL (minimum score 500 paper-based; 173 computer-based; 61 iBT). *Application deadline:* For fall admission, 1/5 for domestic students. Application fee: $45. Electronic applications accepted. *Financial support:* In 2009–10, 44 students received support; fellowships, research assistantships with tuition reimbursements available, teaching assistantships with tuition reimbursements available, career-related internships or fieldwork, Federal Work-Study, institutionally sponsored loans, scholarships/grants, tuition waivers (partial), and unspecified assistantships available. Support available to part-time students. Financial award application deadline: 3/1; financial award applicants required to submit FAFSA. *Unit head:* Dr. Kenneth Deffenbacher, Chairperson, 402-554-2592. *Application contact:* Dr. Joseph Brown, Student Contact, 402-554-2592.

University of New Haven, Graduate School, College of Arts and Sciences, Program in Industrial and Organizational Psychology, West Haven, CT 06516-1916. Offers conflict management (MA); human resource management (MA); industrial organizational psychology (MA); organizational development (MA); psychology of conflict management (Certificate). Part-time and evening/weekend programs available. *Faculty:* 5 full-time (3 women), 10 part-time/adjunct (5 women). *Students:* 97 full-time (59 women), 34 part-time (26 women); includes 20 minority (9 African Americans, 2 American Indian/Alaska Native, 2 Asian Americans or Pacific Islanders, 7 Hispanic Americans), 11 international. Average age 28. 85 applicants, 98% accepted, 48 enrolled. In 2009, 71 master's awarded. *Degree requirements:* For master's, thesis or alternative. *Entrance requirements:* Additional exam requirements/recommendations for international students: Required—TOEFL (minimum score 520 paper-based; 190 computer-based; 70 iBT); Recommended—IELTS (minimum score 5.5). *Application deadline:* For fall admission, 5/31 for international students; for winter admission, 10/15 for international students; for spring admission, 1/15 for international students. Applications are processed on a rolling basis. Application fee: $50. Electronic applications accepted. *Expenses:* Contact institution. *Financial support:* Research assistantships with partial tuition reimbursements, teaching assistantships with partial tuition reimbursements, career-related internships or fieldwork, Federal Work-Study, scholarships/grants, tuition waivers, and unspecified assistantships available. Support available to part-time students. Financial award applicants required to submit FAFSA. *Unit head:* Dr. Stuart D. Sidle, Coordinator, 203-932-7341. *Application contact:* Eloise Gormley, Information Contact, 203-932-7449.

The University of North Carolina at Charlotte, Graduate School, College of Arts and Sciences, Department of Psychology, Program in Industrial/Organizational Psychology, Charlotte, NC 28223-0001. Offers MA. *Faculty:* 8 full-time (4 women), 2 part-time/adjunct (0 women). *Students:* 11 full-time (8 women), 4 part-time (3 women); includes 4 minority (1 African American, 1 Asian American or Pacific Islander, 2 Hispanic Americans). Average age 24. 95 applicants, 12% accepted, 7 enrolled. In 2009, 13 master's awarded. *Degree requirements:* For master's, comprehensive exam, thesis. *Entrance requirements:* For master's, GRE General Test, GRE Subject Test, minimum undergraduate GPA of 3.0 in major, 2.8 overall. Additional exam requirements/recommendations for international students: Required—TOEFL (minimum score 557 paper-based; 220 computer-based; 83 iBT). *Application deadline:* For fall admission, 2/1 for domestic and international students. Application fee: $55. Electronic applications accepted. *Financial support:* In 2009–10, 10 students received support, including 4 research assistantships (averaging $17,750 per year), 5 teaching assistantships (averaging $10,755 per year); fellowships, career-related internships or fieldwork, Federal Work-Study, institutionally sponsored loans, scholarships/grants, and unspecified assistantships also available. Support available to part-time students. Financial award application deadline: 4/1; financial award applicants required to submit FAFSA. Total annual research expenditures: $476,892. *Unit head:* Dr. Steven G. Rogelberg, Coordinator, 704-687-4742, Fax: 704-687-3096, E-mail: sgrogelb@uncc.edu. *Application contact:* Kathy B. Giddings, Director of Graduate Admissions, 704-687-5503, Fax: 704-687-3279, E-mail: gradadm@uncc.edu.

The University of North Carolina at Charlotte, Graduate School, College of Arts and Sciences, Department of Psychology, Program in Organizational Science, Charlotte, NC 28223-0001. Offers PhD. *Faculty:* 14 full-time (6 women), 12 part-time/adjunct (6 women). *Students:* 21 full-time (14 women); includes 2 minority (1 African American, 1 Hispanic American), 2 international. Average age 27. 54 applicants, 17% accepted, 7 enrolled. *Degree requirements:* For doctorate, thesis/dissertation, 77 semester hours; minimum GPA of 3.0. *Entrance requirements:* For doctorate, GRE (minimum score 1100), GMAT (minimum score 600). *Financial support:* In 2009–10, 10 students received support, including 4 research assistantships (averaging $17,750 per year), 5 teaching assistantships (averaging $10,755 per year); administrative assistantships also available. *Faculty research:* Computer mediated communication, personality differences in the interview process, individual differences in the workplace, employment practices of large international corporations, diversity communication. Total annual research expenditures: $476,892. *Unit head:* Dr. Steven G. Rogelberg, Coordinator, 704-687-4520, Fax: 704-687-3096, E-mail: sgrogelb@uncc.edu. *Application contact:* Kathy Giddings, Director of Graduate Admissions, 704-687-5503, Fax: 704-687-3279, E-mail: gradadm@uncc.edu.

University of Puerto Rico, Río Piedras, College of Social Sciences, Department of Psychology, San Juan, PR 00931-3300. Offers clinical psychology (MA); industrial organizational psychology (MA); investigative academic psychology (MA); psychology (PhD); social-community psychology (MA). Part-time programs available. *Degree requirements:* For master's, comprehensive exam, thesis; for doctorate, comprehensive exam, thesis/dissertation, internship. *Entrance requirements:* For master's, GRE or PAEG, interview, minimum GPA of 3.0; for doctorate, GRE or PAEG, interview, master's degree, minimum GPA of 3.0. *Faculty research:* Intervention on Depressed Latino Youth, biosychosocial training.

University of South Africa, College of Economic and Management Sciences, Pretoria, South Africa. Offers accounting (D Admin, D Com); accounting science (DA); auditing (D Admin, D Com); business administration (M Tech); business economics (D Admin); business leadership (DBL); business management (D Admin, D Com); economic management analysis (M Tech); economics (D Admin, D Com, PhD); human resource development (M Tech); industrial psychology (D Admin, D Com, PhD); logistics (D Com); marketing (M Tech); public administration (D Admin, D Com, DPA, PhD); public management (M Tech); quantitative management (D Admin, D Com); real estate (M Tech); statistics (D Admin, PhD); tourism management (D Admin, D Com); transport economics (D Admin, D Com).

University of South Africa, College of Human Sciences, Pretoria, South Africa. Offers adult education (M Ed); African languages (MA, PhD); African politics (MA, PhD); Afrikaans (MA, PhD); ancient history (MA, PhD); ancient Near Eastern studies (MA, PhD); anthropology (MA, PhD); applied linguistics (MA); Arabic (MA, PhD); archaeology (MA); art history (MA); Biblical archaeology (MA); Biblical studies (M Th, D Th, PhD); Christian spirituality (M Th, D Th); church history (M Th, D Th); classical studies (MA, PhD); clinical psychology (MA); communication (MA, PhD); comparative education (M Ed, Ed D); consulting psychology (D Admin, D Com, PhD); curriculum studies (M Ed, Ed D); development studies (M Admin, MA, D Admin, PhD); didactics (M Ed, Ed D); education (M Tech); education management (M Ed, Ed D); educational psychology (M Ed); English (MA); environmental education (M Ed); French (MA, PhD); German (MA, PhD); Greek (MA); guidance and counseling (M Ed); health studies (MA, PhD), including health sciences education (MA), health services management (MA), medical and surgical nursing science (critical care general) (MA), midwifery and neonatal nursing science (MA), trauma and emergency care (MA); history (MA, PhD); history of education (Ed D); inclusive education (M Ed, Ed D); information and communications technology policy and regulation (MA); information science (MA, MIS, PhD); international politics (MA, PhD); Islamic studies (MA, PhD); Italian (MA, PhD); Judaica (MA, PhD); linguistics (MA, PhD); mathematical education (M Ed); mathematics education (MA); missiology (M Th, D Th); modern Hebrew (MA, PhD); musicology (MA, MMus, D Mus, PhD); natural science education (M Ed); New Testament (M Th, D Th); Old Testament (D Th); pastoral therapy (M Th, D Th); philosophy (MA); philosophy of education (M Ed, Ed D); politics (MA, PhD); Portuguese (MA, PhD); practical theology (M Th, D Th); psychology (MA, MS, PhD); psychology of education (M Ed, Ed D); public health (MA); religious studies (MA, D Th, PhD); Romance languages (MA); Russian (MA, PhD); Semitic languages (MA, PhD); social behavior studies in HIV/AIDS (MA); social science (mental health) (MA); social science in development studies (MA); social science in psychology (MA); social science in social work (MA); social science in sociology (MA); social work (MSW, DSW, PhD); socio-education (M Ed, Ed D); sociolinguistics (MA); sociology (MA, PhD); Spanish (MA, PhD); systematic theology (M Th, D Th); TESOL (teaching English to speakers of other languages) (MA); theological ethics (M Th, D Th); theory of literature (MA, PhD); urban ministries (D Th); urban ministry (M Th).

University of South Florida, Graduate School, College of Arts and Sciences, Department of Psychology, Tampa, FL 33620-9951. Offers clinical psychology (PhD); cognitive and neural sciences (PhD); industrial-organizational psychology (PhD). *Accreditation:* APA. *Faculty:* 32 full-time (9 women). *Students:* 98 full-time (55 women), 21 part-time (13 women); includes 16 minority (3 African Americans, 7 Asian Americans or Pacific Islanders, 6 Hispanic Americans), 11 international. Average age 32. 437 applicants, 8% accepted, 24 enrolled. In 2009, 24 doctorates awarded. *Degree requirements:* For doctorate, comprehensive exam, thesis/dissertation, internship. *Entrance requirements:* For doctorate, GRE General Test, minimum GPA of 3.0 in last 60 hours of course work. Additional exam requirements/recommendations for international students: Required—TOEFL (minimum score 550 paper-based; 213 computer-based). *Application deadline:* For fall admission, 12/1 for domestic and international students. Application fee: $30. Electronic applications accepted. *Expenses:* Contact institution. *Financial support:* In 2009–10, teaching assistantships with tuition reimbursements (averaging $27,086 per year); tuition waivers (partial) and unspecified assistantships also available. Financial award applicants required to submit FAFSA. *Faculty research:* Clinical, cognitive, neuroscience, social, industrial/organizational. Total annual research expenditures: $4.7 million. *Unit head:* Michael Brannick, Chairperson, 813-974-0478, Fax: 813-974-4617, E-mail: mbrannick@usf.edu. *Application contact:* William Sacco, Program Director, 813-974-0375, Fax: 813-974-4617, E-mail: sacco@cas.usf.edu.

The University of Tennessee, Graduate School, College of Business Administration, Program in Industrial and Organizational Psychology, Knoxville, TN 37996. Offers PhD. *Degree requirements:* For doctorate, thesis/dissertation. *Entrance requirements:* For doctorate, GRE General Test, minimum GPA of 2.7. Additional exam requirements/recommendations for international students: Required—TOEFL. Electronic applications accepted. *Expenses:* Tuition, state resident: full-time $6826; part-time $380 per semester hour. Tuition, nonresident: full-time $21,844; part-time $1147 per semester hour. Tuition and fees vary according to program.

The University of Tennessee at Chattanooga, Graduate School, College of Arts and Sciences, Department of Psychology, Chattanooga, TN 37403. Offers industrial/organizational psychology (MS); research psychology (MS). Part-time and evening/weekend programs available. *Faculty:* 6 full-time (1 woman). *Students:* 39 full-time (24 women), 5 part-time (3 women); includes 7 minority (4 African Americans, 2 Asian Americans or Pacific Islanders, 1 Hispanic American), 1 international. Average age 29. 75 applicants, 85% accepted, 16 enrolled. In 2009, 21 master's awarded. *Degree requirements:* For master's, thesis (for some programs), practicum (industrial/organizational psychology). *Entrance requirements:* For master's, GRE General Test, minimum GPA of 2.5 on all undergraduate coursework or 3.0 in senior year. Additional exam requirements/recommendations for international students: Required—TOEFL (minimum score 550 paper-based; 213 computer-based; 79 iBT), IELTS (minimum score 6). *Application deadline:* For fall admission, 8/1 priority date for domestic students, 6/1 for international students; for spring admission, 12/1 priority date for domestic students, 10/1 for international students. Applications are processed on a rolling basis. Application fee: $35. Electronic applications accepted. *Expenses:* Tuition, state resident: full-time $5404; part-time $300 per credit hour. Tuition, nonresident: full-time $16,702; part-time $928 per credit hour. Required fees: $1150; $130 per credit hour. *Financial support:* In 2009–10, 20 research assistantships with full and partial tuition reimbursements (averaging $5,500 per year) were awarded; career-related internships or fieldwork, scholarships/grants, and unspecified assistantships also available. Support available to part-time students. *Faculty research:* Decision processes, philosophical psychology, memory, social cognition, employee selection. Total annual research expenditures: $35,031. *Unit head:* Dr. Paul J. Watson, Department Head, 423-425-4262, Fax: 423-425-4284, E-mail: paul-watson@utc.edu. *Application contact:* Dr. Stephanie Bellar, Dean of Graduate Studies, 423-425-4666, Fax: 423-425-5223, E-mail: stephanie-bellar@utc.edu.

The University of Texas at Arlington, Graduate School, College of Science, Department of Psychology, Arlington, TX 76019. Offers experimental psychology (PhD); health psychology (PhD); industrial organizational psychology (MS); psychology (MS). Part-time programs available. *Faculty:* 16 full-time (5 women), 1 part-time/adjunct (0 women). *Students:* 62 full-time (41 women), 10 part-time (7 women); includes 13 minority (5 African Americans, 2 Asian Americans or Pacific Islanders, 6 Hispanic Americans), 7 international. 72 applicants, 90% accepted, 22 enrolled. In 2009, 16 master's, 6 doctorates awarded. Terminal master's awarded for partial completion of doctoral program. *Degree requirements:* For master's, comprehensive exam or thesis; for doctorate, thesis/dissertation (for some programs). *Entrance requirements:* For master's and doctorate, GRE General Test, minimum GPA of 3.0 in last 60 hours of course work. Additional exam requirements/recommendations for international students: Required—TOEFL (minimum score 550 paper-based; 213 computer-based). *Application deadline:* For fall admission, 6/16 for domestic students. Applications are processed on a rolling basis. Application fee: $35 ($50 for international students). *Financial support:* In 2009–10, 4 fellowships (averaging $1,000 per year), 2 research assistantships with tuition reimbursements (averaging $15,000 per year), 28 teaching assistantships with tuition reimbursements (averaging $15,000 per year) were awarded; career-related internships or fieldwork, Federal Work-Study, institutionally sponsored loans, scholarships/grants, traineeships, tuition waivers (partial), and unspecified assistantships also available. Financial award application deadline: 6/1; financial award applicants required to submit FAFSA. *Unit head:* Dr. Robert Gatchel, Chair, 817-272-2281, Fax: 817-272-2364, E-mail: gatchel@uta.edu. *Application contact:* Dr. Jared Kenworthy, Graduate Advisor, 817-272-2281, Fax: 817-272-2364, E-mail: kenworthy@uta.edu.

University of Tulsa, Graduate School, College of Arts and Sciences, Department of Psychology, Program in Industrial/Organizational Psychology, Tulsa, OK 74104-3189. Offers MA, PhD, JD/MA. Part-time programs available. *Faculty:* 6 full-time (2 women). *Students:* 19 full-time (14 women), 5 part-time (2 women); includes 4 minority (1 African American, 1 American Indian/Alaska Native, 1 Asian American or Pacific Islander, 1 Hispanic American), 1 international. Average age 26. 58 applicants, 43% accepted, 9 enrolled. In 2009, 2 master's, 1 doctorate awarded. Terminal master's awarded for partial completion of doctoral program. *Degree requirements:* For master's, comprehensive exam, thesis (for some programs), 200 hour internship; for doctorate, comprehensive exam, thesis/dissertation. *Entrance requirements:* For master's and doctorate, GRE General Test. Additional exam requirements/recommendations for international students: Required—TOEFL (minimum score 575 paper-based; 231 computer-based; 91 iBT), IELTS (minimum score 6.5). *Application deadline:* For fall admission, 1/15 for domestic and international students. Application fee: $40. Electronic applications accepted. *Expenses:* Tuition: Full-time $16,182; part-time $899 per credit hour. Required fees: $4 per credit hour. Tuition and fees vary according to course load. *Financial support:* In 2009–10, 19 students received support, including 4 fellowships with full and partial tuition reimbursements available (averaging $1,499 per year), 3 research assistantships with full and partial tuition reimbursements available (averaging $4,532 per year), 17 teaching assistantships with full and partial tuition reimbursements available (averaging $11,319 per year); career-related internships or fieldwork, Federal Work-Study, scholarships/grants, health care benefits, tuition waivers (full and partial), and unspecified assistantships also available. Support available to part-time students. Financial award application deadline: 2/1; financial award applicants required to submit FAFSA. *Faculty research:* Personnel testing and selection, training, performance appraisal, organizational development, job attitudes and motivation, leadership. Total annual research expenditures: $1 million. *Unit head:* Dr. John McNulty, Director, 918-631-2835, Fax: 918-631-2833, E-mail: john-mcnulty@utulsa.edu. *Application contact:* Information Contact, E-mail: grad@utulsa.edu.

University of West Florida, College of Arts and Sciences: Arts, Department of Psychology, Pensacola, FL 32514-5750. Offers counseling (MA); counseling-licensed mental health counselor (MA); general (MA); industrial-organizational (MA). Part-time programs available. *Faculty:* 10 full-time (3 women), 2 part-time/adjunct (1 woman). *Students:* 69 full-time (50 women), 45 part-time (35 women); includes 14 minority (11 African Americans, 1 Asian American or Pacific Islander, 2 Hispanic Americans), 5 international. Average age 27. 124 applicants, 60% accepted, 34 enrolled. In 2009, 16 master's awarded. *Degree requirements:* For master's, thesis (for some programs). *Entrance requirements:* For master's, GRE General Test, GRE Subject Test, minimum GPA of 3.0. Additional exam requirements/recommendations for international students: Required—TOEFL (minimum score 550 paper-based; 213 computer-based). *Application deadline:* For fall admission, 6/1 for domestic students, 5/15 for international students; for spring admission, 11/1 for domestic students, 10/1 for international students. Applications are processed on a rolling basis. Application fee: $30. *Expenses:* Tuition, state resident: full-time $4982; part-time $260 per credit hour. Tuition, nonresident: full-time $20,059; part-time $919 per credit hour. Required fees: $1247; $52 per credit hour. *Financial support:* In 2009–10, 3 research assistantships with partial tuition reimbursements (averaging $3,760 per year), 3 teaching assistantships with partial tuition reimbursements (averaging $5,000 per year) were awarded; career-related internships or fieldwork and unspecified assistantships also available. Financial award application deadline: 4/15; financial award applicants required to submit FAFSA. *Faculty research:* Prose recall, brain imaging, peak performance, biofeedback and pain control, comparable worth. Total annual research expenditures: $15,000. *Unit head:* Dr. Laura Koppes, Chairperson, 850-474-3493. *Application contact:* Terry McCray, Assistant Director of Graduate Admissions, 850-473-7718, Fax: 850-473-7714, E-mail: gradadmissions@uwf.edu.

University of Wisconsin–Oshkosh, The Office of Graduate Studies, College of Letters and Science, Department of Psychology, Oshkosh, WI 54901. Offers experimental psychology (MS); industrial/organizational psychology (MS). *Degree requirements:* For master's, thesis. *Entrance requirements:* For master's, GRE, 10 semester hours of undergraduate course work in psychology. Additional exam requirements/recommendations for international students: Required—TOEFL (minimum score 550 paper-based; 213 computer-based; 79 iBT). Electronic applications accepted. *Faculty research:* Performance evaluation, training, biological bases of behavior, tactile perception, aging.

Valdosta State University, Graduate School, Department of Psychology and Counseling, Valdosta, GA 31698. Offers clinical/counseling psychology (MS); industrial/organizational psychology (MS); school counseling (M Ed, Ed S); school psychology (Ed S). Part-time and evening/weekend programs available. *Degree requirements:* For master's, thesis or alternative, comprehensive written and/or oral exams; for Ed S, thesis. *Entrance requirements:* For master's and Ed S, GRE General Test or MAT. Additional exam requirements/recommendations for international students: Required—TOEFL (minimum score 523 paper-based; 193 computer-based). Electronic applications accepted. *Faculty research:* Using Bender-Gestalt to predict graphomotor dimensions of the draw-a-person test, neurobehavioral hemispheric dominance.

Virginia Polytechnic Institute and State University, Graduate School, College of Science, Department of Psychology, Blacksburg, VA 24061. Offers bio-behavioral sciences (PhD); clinical psychology (PhD); developmental psychology (PhD); industrial/organizational psychology (PhD); psychology (MS). *Accreditation:* APA (one or more programs are accredited). *Faculty:* 23 full-time (7 women). *Students:* 71 full-time (45 women), 6 part-time (3 women); includes 18 minority (6 American Indian/Alaska Native, 8 Asian Americans or Pacific Islanders, 4 Hispanic Americans), 1 international. Average age 27. 201 applicants, 7% accepted, 14 enrolled. In 2009, 20 master's, 14 doctorates awarded. *Entrance requirements:* For master's and doctorate, GRE, GMAT. Additional exam requirements/recommendations for international students: Required—TOEFL (minimum score 550 paper-based; 213 computer-based). *Application deadline:* For fall admission, 5/15 for international students; for spring admission, 10/15 for international students. Applications are processed on a rolling basis. Application fee: $65. Electronic applications accepted. *Expenses:* Tuition, area resident: Full-time $10,228; part-time $459 per credit hour. Tuition, nonresident: full-time $17,892; part-time $865 per credit hour. Required fees: $1966; $451 per semester. *Financial support:* In 2009–10, 18 research assistantships with full tuition reimbursements (averaging $16,153 per year), 41 teaching assistantships with full tuition reimbursements (averaging $16,053 per year) were awarded; career-related internships or fieldwork, Federal Work-Study, scholarships/grants, and unspecified assistantships also available. Financial award application deadline: 1/15. *Faculty research:* Infant development from electrophysical point of view, work motivation and personnel selection, EEG, ERP and hypnosis with reference to chronic pain, intimate violence. Total annual research expenditures: $2.1 million. *Unit head:* Dr. Robert S. Stephens, Dean, 540-231-6304, Fax: 540-231-3652, E-mail: stephens@vt.edu. *Application contact:* Kirby Deater-Deckard, Information Contact, 540-231-6581, Fax: 540-231-3652, E-mail: kirbydd@vt.edu.

Walden University, Graduate Programs, School of Psychology, Minneapolis, MN 55401. Offers clinical child psychology (Post-Doctoral Certificate); clinical psychology (Post-Doctoral Certificate); counseling psychology (Post-Doctoral Certificate); forensic psychology (MS), including forensic psychology in the community, general program, mental health applications, program planning and evaluation in forensic settings, psychology and legal systems; general psychology (Post-Doctoral Certificate); health psychology (Post-Doctoral Certificate); organizational psychology (Post-Doctoral Certificate); organizational psychology and development (Postbaccalaureate Certificate); psychology (MS, PhD), including clinical psychology (PhD), counseling psychology (PhD), crisis management and response (MS), general program (MS), general psychology (PhD), health psychology, leadership development and coaching (MS), media psychology (MS), organizational psychology (PhD), organizational psychology and development (MS), organizational psychology and nonprofit management (MS), program evaluation and research (MS), psychology of culture (MS), psychology, public administration, and social change (MS), social psychology (MS), terrorism and security (MS); teaching online (Post-Master's Certificate). Part-time and evening/weekend programs available. Postbaccalaureate distance learning degree programs offered (minimal on-campus study). *Faculty:* 33 full-time, 222 part-time/adjunct. *Students:* 3,546 full-time (2,761 women), 1,133 part-time (908 women); includes 1,723 minority (1,319 African Americans, 56 American Indian/Alaska Native, 101 Asian Americans or Pacific Islanders, 247 Hispanic Americans), 80 international. Average age 41. In 2009, 495 master's, 70 doctorates, 2 other advanced degrees awarded. Terminal master's awarded for partial completion of doctoral program. *Degree requirements:* For master's, thesis optional; for doctorate, thesis/dissertation, residency. *Entrance requirements:* For master's, bachelor's degree or equivalent in related field; minimum GPA of 2.5; official transcripts; goal statement; access to computer and Internet; for doctorate, master's degree or equivalent in related field; minimum GPA of 3.0;3 years of related professional/academic experience (preferred). Additional exam requirements/recommendations for international students: Required—TOEFL (minimum score 550 paper-based; 213 computer-based), IELTS (minimum score 6.5), or Michigan English Language Assessment Battery (minimum score 82). *Application deadline:* Applications are processed on a rolling basis. Application fee: $50. Electronic applications accepted. *Expenses:* Tuition: Full-time $13,665; part-time $560 per credit. Required fees: $1375. Tuition and fees vary according to course load, degree level and program. *Financial support:* In 2009–10, 290 students received support; fellowships, Federal Work-Study, scholarships/grants, unspecified assistantships, and family tuition reduction, active

Industrial and Organizational Psychology

Walden University (continued)
duty/veteran tuition reduction, group tuition reduction, interest-free payment plans available. Support available to part-time students. Financial award applicants required to submit FAFSA. *Unit head:* Dr. Melanie Storms, Associate Dean, 800-925-3368. *Application contact:* Jennifer Hall, Director of Enrollment, 866-4-WALDEN, E-mail: info@waldenu.edu.

Wayne State University, College of Liberal Arts and Sciences, Department of Psychology, Program in Psychology, Detroit, MI 48202. Offers behavioral and cognitive neuroscience (PhD); clinical psychology (PhD); cognitive and social psychology (PhD); industrial/organizational psychology (PhD); psychology (MA, MS). *Accreditation:* APA (one or more programs are accredited). *Degree requirements:* For doctorate, thesis/dissertation. *Entrance requirements:* For doctorate, GRE General Test, GRE Subject Test. Additional exam requirements/recommendations for international students: Required—TOEFL (minimum score 550 paper-based; 213 computer-based); Recommended—TWE (minimum score 6). Electronic applications accepted.

West Chester University of Pennsylvania, Office of Graduate Studies, College of Arts and Sciences, Department of Psychology, West Chester, PA 19383. Offers clinical mental health (Certificate); clinical psychology (MA); general psychology (MA); industrial psychology (MA). Part-time and evening/weekend programs available. *Students:* 36 full-time (30 women), 77 part-time (55 women); includes 12 minority (5 African Americans, 4 Asian Americans or Pacific Islanders, 3 Hispanic Americans), 2 international. Average age 26. 175 applicants, 76% accepted, 58 enrolled. In 2009, 38 master's, 2 other advanced degrees awarded. *Degree requirements:* For master's, comprehensive exam, thesis (for some programs). *Entrance requirements:* For master's, GRE General Test or MAT, minimum GPA of 3.0, 3.25 in psychology; three letters of reference. Additional exam requirements/recommendations for international students: Required—TOEFL (minimum score 550 paper-based; 213 computer-based; 80 iBT). *Application deadline:* For fall admission, 4/15 priority date for domestic students, 3/15 for international students; for spring admission, 10/15 for domestic students, 9/1 for international students. Applications are processed on a rolling basis. Application fee: $35. Electronic applications accepted. *Expenses:* Tuition, state resident: full-time $6666; part-time $370 per credit. Tuition, nonresident: full-time $10,666; part-time $593 per credit. Required fees: $122.56 per credit. *Financial support:* In 2009–10, 19 research assistantships with full and partial tuition reimbursements (averaging $5,000 per year) were awarded; unspecified assistantships also available. Support available to part-time students. Financial award application deadline: 2/15; financial award applicants required to submit FAFSA. *Faculty research:* Animal learning and cognition. *Unit head:* Dr. Loretta Rieser-Danner, Chairperson, 610-436-3106, E-mail: lrieser-danner@wcupa.edu. *Application contact:* Dr. Stefani Yorges, Graduate Coordinator, 610-436-3154, E-mail: syorges@wcupa.edu.

Western Michigan University, Graduate College, College of Arts and Sciences, Department of Psychology, Kalamazoo, MI 49008. Offers behavior analysis (MA, PhD); clinical psychology (PhD); industrial/organizational psychology (MA). *Accreditation:* APA (one or more programs are accredited). *Degree requirements:* For master's, variable foreign language requirement, thesis, oral exams; for doctorate, 2 foreign languages, comprehensive exam, thesis/dissertation, oral exams. *Entrance requirements:* For master's and doctorate, GRE General Test.

Wright State University, School of Graduate Studies, College of Science and Mathematics, Department of Psychology, Program in Human Factors and Industrial/Organizational Psychology, Dayton, OH 45435. Offers MS, PhD. *Degree requirements:* For master's, thesis; for doctorate, thesis/dissertation.

Xavier University, College of Social Sciences, Health and Education, Department of Psychology, Cincinnati, OH 45207. Offers clinical psychology (Psy D); psychology (MA), including general experimental, industrial-organizational. *Accreditation:* APA (one or more programs are accredited). *Faculty:* 19 full-time (9 women), 3 part-time/adjunct (2 women). *Students:* 111 full-time (87 women), 6 part-time (4 women); includes 13 minority (5 African Americans, 1 American Indian/Alaska Native, 4 Asian Americans or Pacific Islanders, 3 Hispanic Americans), 2 international. Average age 27. 272 applicants, 23% accepted, 37 enrolled. In 2009, 27 master's, 16 doctorates awarded. *Degree requirements:* For master's, one foreign language, comprehensive exam, thesis, internship; for doctorate, one foreign language, comprehensive exam, thesis/dissertation, internship. *Entrance requirements:* For master's and doctorate, GRE. Additional exam requirements/recommendations for international students: Required—TOEFL. *Application deadline:* For fall admission, 12/15 for domestic and international students. Application fee: $35. Electronic applications accepted. *Expenses:* Contact institution. *Financial support:* In 2009–10, 61 students received support, including 41 research assistantships with partial tuition reimbursements available, 20 teaching assistantships with partial tuition reimbursements available; scholarships/grants and unspecified assistantships also available. Financial award application deadline: 3/1; financial award applicants required to submit FAFSA. *Unit head:* Dr. Christine M. Dacey, Chair, 513-745-3533, Fax: 513-745-3327, E-mail: dacey@xavier.edu. *Application contact:* Margaret Maybury, Assistant Director, Enrollment and Student Services, 513-745-1053, Fax: 513-745-3347, E-mail: maybury@xavier.edu.

Marriage and Family Therapy

Abilene Christian University, Graduate School, College of Biblical Studies, Program in Marriage and Family Therapy, Abilene, TX 79699-9100. Offers MMFT. *Accreditation:* AAMFT/COAMFTE. *Faculty:* 2 full-time (both women), 6 part-time/adjunct (2 women). *Students:* 34 full-time (19 women); includes 2 minority (1 Asian American or Pacific Islander, 1 Hispanic American). 41 applicants, 59% accepted, 18 enrolled. In 2009, 18 master's awarded. *Degree requirements:* For master's, comprehensive exam. *Entrance requirements:* For master's, GRE General Test, interview. *Application deadline:* For fall admission, 4/1 priority date for domestic students; for spring admission, 11/1 for domestic students. Applications are processed on a rolling basis. Application fee: $40. Electronic applications accepted. *Expenses:* Tuition: Full-time $11,520; part-time $640 per hour. Required fees: $1090; $53.50 per hour. $10 per term. Tuition and fees vary according to program. *Financial support:* In 2009–10, 34 students received support; teaching assistantships, career-related internships or fieldwork available. Support available to part-time students. Financial award application deadline: 4/1; financial award applicants required to submit FAFSA. *Faculty research:* Overeating variables, family systems, intervention strategies. *Unit head:* Dr. Jaime Goff, Chairperson, 325-674-3778, Fax: 325-674-3749, E-mail: jaime.goff@acu.edu. *Application contact:* William Horn, Graduate Admissions Counselor, 325-674-2656, Fax: 325-674-6717, E-mail: gradinfo@acu.edu.

Adler Graduate School, Program in Adlerian Studies, Richfield, MN 55423. Offers art therapy specialization (MA); clinical counseling track (MA); coaching and consulting in organizations (Certificate); management consulting and organizational leadership (MA); marriage and family track (MA); non-clinical Adlerian studies track (MA); personal and professional life coaching (Certificate); school counseling (MA). Part-time and evening/weekend programs available. *Degree requirements:* For master's, thesis or alternative, 500-700 hour internship (depending on license choice). *Entrance requirements:* For master's, minimum undergraduate GPA of 3.0, 12 credits of course work in psychology or related field.

Adler School of Professional Psychology, Programs in Psychology, Chicago, IL 60601-7203. Offers art therapy (MA, Certificate); clinical hypnosis (Certificate); clinical psychology (Psy D); counseling (MA); counseling and organizational psychology (MA); forensic psychology (MA); gerontological counseling (MA); marriage and family counseling (MA); marriage and family therapy (Certificate); organizational psychology (MA); police psychology (MA); rehabilitation counseling (MA); sport and health psychology (MA); substance abuse counseling (Certificate); Psy D/Certificate; Psy D/MACAT; Psy D/MACP; Psy D/MAMFC; Psy D/MASAC. *Accreditation:* APA. Part-time and evening/weekend programs available. Postbaccalaureate distance learning degree programs offered (minimal on-campus study). *Faculty:* 41 full-time (21 women), 44 part-time/adjunct (19 women). *Students:* 551 full-time (441 women), 161 part-time (137 women). Average age 27. Terminal master's awarded for partial completion of doctoral program. *Degree requirements:* For master's, thesis or alternative, oral exam, practicum; for doctorate, thesis/dissertation, clinical exam, internship, oral exam, practicum, written qualifying exam. *Entrance requirements:* For master's, 12 semester hours in psychology, minimum GPA of 3.0; for doctorate, 18 semester hours in psychology, minimum GPA of 3.25; for Certificate, appropriate master's or doctoral degree. Additional exam requirements/recommendations for international students: Required—TOEFL (minimum score 550 paper-based; 213 computer-based; 79 iBT). *Application deadline:* For fall admission, 2/15 priority date for domestic students, 12/1 priority date for international students. Applications are processed on a rolling basis. Application fee: $50. Electronic applications accepted. *Expenses:* Tuition: Part-time $930 per credit. Required fees: $220 per term. *Financial support:* Career-related internships or fieldwork, Federal Work-Study, scholarships/grants, and tuition waivers (full and partial) available. Support available to part-time students. Financial award application deadline: 5/15; financial award applicants required to submit FAFSA. *Unit head:* Dr. Frank Gruba-McAllister, Vice President of Academic Affairs, 312-201-5900 Ext. 209, Fax: 312-201-5917. *Application contact:* Craig A. Hines, Associate Vice President of Admissions, 312-201-5900 Ext. 226, Fax: 312-201-5917, E-mail: chines@adler.edu.

See Close-Up on page 1047.

Alliant International University–Irvine, California School of Professional Psychology, Program in Marital and Family Therapy, Irvine, CA 92612. Offers MA, Psy D. *Accreditation:* AAMFT/COAMFTE. Part-time programs available. *Degree requirements:* For doctorate, thesis/dissertation. *Entrance requirements:* For master's, minimum GPA of 3.0, letters of recommendation, interview; for doctorate, letters of recommendation, minimum GPA of 3.0, interview. Additional exam requirements/recommendations for international students: Required—TOEFL (minimum score 600 paper-based; 250 computer-based), TWE (minimum score 5). Electronic applications accepted. *Faculty research:* Chemical dependency, observational research.

Alliant International University–Los Angeles, California School of Professional Psychology, Program in Marital and Family Therapy, Alhambra, CA 91803-1360. Offers biofeedback (MA); chemical dependency (MA); gerontology (MA); Latin American family therapy (MA). *Accreditation:* AAMFT/COAMFTE.

Alliant International University–Sacramento, California School of Professional Psychology, Program in Marital and Family Therapy, Sacramento, CA 95825. Offers MA. *Accreditation:* AAMFT/COAMFTE. *Entrance requirements:* For master's, minimum GPA of 3.0, letters of recommendation, interview. Additional exam requirements/recommendations for international students: Required—TOEFL (minimum score 600 paper-based; 250 computer-based), TWE (minimum score 5). Electronic applications accepted. *Faculty research:* Couples therapy, marital myths, cross-cultural issues.

Alliant International University–San Diego, California School of Professional Psychology, Program in Marital and Family Therapy, San Diego, CA 92131-1799. Offers MA, Psy D. *Accreditation:* AAMFT/COAMFTE. Part-time programs available. *Degree requirements:* For doctorate, thesis/dissertation. *Entrance requirements:* For master's and doctorate, minimum GPA of 3.0, letters of recommendation, interview. Additional exam requirements/recommendations for international students: Required—TOEFL (minimum score 600 paper-based; 250 computer-based), TWE (minimum score 5). Electronic applications accepted. *Faculty research:* Chemical dependency, women's issues, emotionally focused therapy, couple relationships, work/family/parenting.

Amridge University, Graduate and Professional Programs, Montgomery, AL 36117. Offers behavioral leadership and management (MA); biblical studies (MA, PhD); family therapy (D Min); leadership and management (MS); marriage and family therapy (M Div, MA, PhD); ministerial leadership (M Div, MS); pastoral counseling (M Div, MS); practical theology (MA); professional counseling (M Div, MA); theology (M Div, D Min). *Accreditation:* ATS. Part-time and evening/weekend programs available. Postbaccalaureate distance learning degree programs offered (no on-campus study). *Faculty:* 44 full-time (9 women), 18 part-time/adjunct (7 women). *Students:* 175 full-time (95 women), 192 part-time (93 women); includes 182 minority (172 African Americans, 1 American Indian/Alaska Native, 1 Asian American or Pacific Islander, 8 Hispanic Americans). Average age 35. *Degree requirements:* For master's, one foreign language, comprehensive exam (for some programs), thesis (for some programs); for doctorate, comprehensive exam (for some programs), thesis/dissertation; for M Div, comprehensive exam (for some programs). *Entrance requirements:* For M Div, master's, and doctorate, GRE General Test or MAT. Additional exam requirements/recommendations for international students: Required—TOEFL. *Application deadline:* For fall admission, 9/1 priority date for domestic students; for spring admission, 1/1 priority date for domestic students. Applications are processed on a rolling basis. Application fee: $75. Electronic applications accepted. *Expenses:* Tuition: Full-time $10,080; part-time $560 per semester hour. Required fees: $600 per term. *Financial support:* Federal Work-Study and scholarships/grants available. Support available to part-time students. Financial award applicants required to submit FAFSA. *Faculty research:* Homiletics, hermeneutics, ancient Near Eastern history. *Unit head:* Director of Enrollment Management, 800-351-4040 Ext. 7513, Fax: 334-387-3878. *Application contact:* Ora Davis, Admissions Officer, 334-387-3877 Ext. 7524, Fax: 334-387-3878, E-mail: admissions@amridgeuniversity.edu.

Antioch University New England, Graduate School, Department of Applied Psychology, Program in Marriage and Family Therapy, Keene, NH 03431-3552. Offers MA, PhD. *Accreditation:* AAMFT/COAMFTE. *Degree requirements:* For master's, internship, practicum. *Entrance requirements:* For master's, previous course work and work experience in psychology; resume; 3 letters of recommendation. Additional exam requirements/recommendations for international students: Required—TOEFL (minimum score 600 paper-based; 250 computer-based). Electronic applications accepted. *Expenses:* Contact institution. *Faculty research:* Use of reflective team model in case teaching and in organizational consulting, executive mentoring and coaching.

Appalachian State University, Cratis D. Williams Graduate School, Department of Human Development and Psychological Counseling, Boone, NC 28608. Offers college student development (MA); community counseling (MA); marriage and family therapy (MA); school counseling (MA). *Accreditation:* AAMFT/COAMFTE; ACA; NCATE. Part-time programs available. *Faculty:* 15 full-time (5 women), 21 part-time/adjunct (14 women). *Students:* 98 full-time (95 women), 32 part-time (25 women); includes 8 minority (5 African Americans, 2 Asian Americans or Pacific Islanders, 1 Hispanic American), 1 international. 149 applicants, 54% accepted, 59 enrolled. In 2009, 78 master's awarded. *Degree requirements:* For master's, comprehensive exam (for some programs), thesis optional, internships. *Entrance requirements:* For master's,

GRE General Test, 3 letters of recommendation. Additional exam requirements/recommendations for international students: Required—TOEFL (minimum score 570 paper-based; 230 computer-based; 79 iBT), IELTS (minimum score 6.5). *Application deadline:* For fall admission, 2/1 priority date for domestic students, 2/1 for international students; for spring admission, 2/1 for international students. Applications are processed on a rolling basis. Application fee: $50. Electronic applications accepted. *Expenses:* Tuition, state resident: full-time $2960. Tuition, nonresident: full-time $14,051. Required fees: $2320. *Financial support:* In 2009–10, 20 research assistantships (averaging $8,000 per year), 7 teaching assistantships (averaging $8,000 per year) were awarded; fellowships, career-related internships or fieldwork, Federal Work-Study, scholarships/grants, and unspecified assistantships also available. Financial award application deadline: 4/1; financial award applicants required to submit FAFSA. *Faculty research:* Multicultural counseling, addictions counseling, play therapy, expressive arts, child and adolescent therapy, sexual abuse counseling. *Unit head:* Dr. Lee Baruth, Chairman, 828-262-2055, E-mail: baruthlg@appstate.edu. *Application contact:* Sandy Krause, Director of Admissions and Recruiting, 828-262-2130, Fax: 828-262-2709, E-mail: krausesl@appstate.edu.

Argosy University, Atlanta, College of Psychology and Behavioral Sciences, Atlanta, GA 30328. Offers clinical psychology (MA, Psy D, Postdoctoral Respecialization Certificate), including child and family psychology (Psy D), general adult clinical (Psy D), health psychology (Psy D), neuropsychology/geropsychology (Psy D); community counseling (MA), including marriage and family therapy; counselor education and supervision (Ed D); forensic psychology (MA); industrial organizational psychology (MA); marriage and family therapy (Certificate); sport-exercise psychology (MA). *Accreditation:* APA.

See Close-Up on page 1049.

Argosy University, Chicago, College of Psychology and Behavioral Sciences, Doctoral Program in Clinical Psychology, Chicago, IL 60601. Offers child and adolescent psychology (Psy D); client-centered and experiential psychotherapies (Psy D); diversity and multicultural psychology (Psy D); family psychology (Psy D); forensic psychology (Psy D); health psychology (Psy D); neuropsychology (Psy D); organizational consulting (Psy D); psychoanalytic psychology (Psy D); psychology and spirituality (Psy D). *Accreditation:* APA.

See Close-Up on page 1051.

Argosy University, Denver, College of Psychology and Behavioral Sciences, Denver, CO 80231. Offers clinical mental health counseling (MA); clinical psychology (MA, Psy D); counseling psychology (Ed D); counselor education and supervision (Ed D); forensic psychology (MA); industrial organizational psychology (MA); marriage and family therapy (MA, DMFT).

See Close-Up on page 1055.

Argosy University, Hawai'i, College of Psychology and Behavioral Sciences, Program in Marriage and Family Therapy, Honolulu, HI 96813. Offers MA.

See Close-Up on page 1057.

Argosy University, Inland Empire, College of Psychology and Behavioral Sciences, San Bernardino, CA 92408. Offers clinical psychology/marriage and family therapy (MA); counseling psychology (Ed D); counseling psychology/marriage and family therapy (MA); forensic psychology (MA); industrial organizational psychology (MA); sport-exercise psychology (MA).

See Close-Up on page 1059.

Argosy University, Los Angeles, College of Psychology and Behavioral Sciences, Santa Monica, CA 90045. Offers clinical psychology/marriage and family therapy (MA); counseling psychology (Ed D); counseling psychology/marriage and family therapy (MA); forensic psychology (MA).

See Close-Up on page 1061.

Argosy University, Orange County, College of Psychology and Behavioral Sciences, Program in Clinical Psychology, Orange, CA 92868. Offers child and adolescent psychology (Psy D); forensic psychology (Psy D); marriage and family therapy (MA).

See Close-Up on page 1065.

Argosy University, Orange County, College of Psychology and Behavioral Sciences, Program in Counseling Psychology, Orange, CA 92868. Offers counseling psychology (Ed D); marriage and family therapy (MA).

See Close-Up on page 1065.

Argosy University, Salt Lake City, College of Psychology and Behavioral Sciences, Draper, UT 84020. Offers counseling psychology (Ed D); counselor education and supervision (Ed D); forensic psychology (MA); marriage and family therapy (MA, DMFT); mental health counseling (MA).

See Close-Up on page 1069.

Argosy University, San Diego, College of Psychology and Behavioral Sciences, San Diego, CA 92108. Offers clinical psychology/marriage and family therapy (MA); counseling psychology (Ed D); counseling psychology/marriage and family therapy (MA); forensic psychology (MA).

See Close-Up on page 1071.

Argosy University, Sarasota, College of Psychology and Behavioral Sciences, Sarasota, FL 34235. Offers community counseling (MA); counseling psychology (Ed D); counselor education and supervision (Ed D); forensic psychology (MA); marriage and family therapy (MA); mental health counseling (MA); pastoral community counseling (Ed D).

See Close-Up on page 1075.

Argosy University, Schaumburg, College of Psychology and Behavioral Sciences, Schaumburg, IL 60173-5403. Offers clinical health psychology (Post-Graduate Certificate); clinical psychology (MA, Psy D), including child and family psychology (Psy D), clinical health psychology (Psy D), diversity and multicultural psychology (Psy D), forensic psychology (Psy D), neuropsychology (Psy D); community counseling (MA); counseling psychology (Ed D), including counselor education and supervision; counselor education and supervision (Ed D); forensic psychology (Post-Graduate Certificate); industrial organizational psychology (MA). *Accreditation:* ACA; APA.

See Close-Up on page 1077.

Argosy University, Tampa, College of Psychology and Behavioral Sciences, Program in Clinical Psychology, Tampa, FL 33607. Offers clinical psychology (MA, Psy D), including child and adolescent psychology (Psy D), geropsychology (Psy D), marriage/couples and family therapy (Psy D), neuropsychology (Psy D). *Accreditation:* APA.

See Close-Up on page 1081.

Argosy University, Twin Cities, College of Psychology and Behavioral Sciences, Eagan, MN 55121. Offers clinical psychology (MA, Psy D), including child and family psychology (Psy D), forensic psychology (Psy D), health and neuropsychology (Psy D), trauma (Psy D); forensic counseling (Post-Graduate Certificate); forensic psychology (MA); industrial organizational psychology (MA); marriage and family therapy (MA, DMFT), including forensic counseling (MA). *Accreditation:* APA.

See Close-Up on page 1083.

Argosy University, Washington DC, College of Psychology and Behavioral Sciences, Arlington, VA 22209. Offers clinical psychology (MA, Psy D), including child and family psychology (Psy D), diversity and multicultural psychology (Psy D), forensic psychology (Psy D), health and neuropsychology (Psy D); community counseling (MA); counseling psychology (Ed D), including counselor education and supervision; counselor education and supervision (Ed D); forensic psychology (MA). *Accreditation:* APA.

See Close-Up on page 1085.

Arizona State University, Graduate College, College of Liberal Arts and Sciences, Division of Social Sciences, School of Social and Family Dynamics, Tempe, AZ 85287. Offers family and human development (MS, PhD); infant-family practice (MAS); marriage and family therapy (MAS); sociology (MA, PhD). *Degree requirements:* For master's, thesis or alternative; for doctorate, thesis/dissertation. *Entrance requirements:* For master's and doctorate, GRE.

Azusa Pacific University, School of Behavioral and Applied Sciences, Department of Graduate Psychology, Azusa, CA 91702-7000. Offers clinical psychology (MA, Psy D), including family therapy (MA). *Accreditation:* APA (one or more programs are accredited). Part-time and evening/weekend programs available. *Degree requirements:* For master's, comprehensive exam, 250 hours of clinical experience, individual and group therapy. *Entrance requirements:* For master's, interview, minimum GPA of 3.0, Minnesota Multiphasic Personality Inventory. Additional exam requirements/recommendations for international students: Required—TOEFL (minimum score 600 paper-based).

Barry University, School of Education, Program in Marital, Couple and Family Counseling/Therapy, Miami Shores, FL 33161-6695. Offers MS, Ed S. Part-time and evening/weekend programs available. *Degree requirements:* For master's, comprehensive exam, scholarly paper; for Ed S, comprehensive exam. *Entrance requirements:* For master's, GRE General Test or MAT, minimum GPA of 3.0; for Ed S, GRE General Test, minimum GPA of 3.0. Electronic applications accepted.

Bethel Seminary, Graduate and Professional Programs, St. Paul, MN 55112-6998. Offers applied ministry (MA); biblical studies (MATS, Certificate); children's and family ministry (MACFM); Christian education (MACE); Christian thought (M Div, MACT); church leadership (D Min); community ministry leadership (MA, Certificate); congregation and family care (D Min); global and contextual studies (MA, MATS); historical studies (MATS); lay ministry (Certificate); marriage and family studies (M Div, MATS); marriage and family therapy (MAMFT, Certificate); ministry leadership (Certificate); pastoral care and counseling (MATS); pastoral ministries (M Div); spiritual formation (Certificate); theological studies (MATS, Certificate); transformational leadership (MATL, Certificate); youth ministries (MACE). *Accreditation:* ACIPE; ATS (one or more programs are accredited). Part-time and evening/weekend programs available. Postbaccalaureate distance learning degree programs offered (minimal on-campus study). *Faculty:* 26 full-time (3 women), 76 part-time/adjunct (30 women). *Students:* 725 full-time (269 women), 300 part-time (104 women); includes 204 minority (115 African Americans, 1 American Indian/Alaska Native, 65 Asian Americans or Pacific Islanders, 23 Hispanic Americans), 13 international. Average age 37. 516 applicants, 78% accepted, 261 enrolled. In 2009, 50 first professional degrees, 100 master's, 6 doctorates awarded. *Degree requirements:* For master's, variable foreign language requirement, thesis (for some programs); for doctorate, thesis/dissertation; for M Div, one foreign language. *Entrance requirements:* For M Div and master's, letters of reference, transcripts, personal statement; for doctorate, M Div, letters of reference, organizational support. Additional exam requirements/recommendations for international students: Required—TOEFL (minimum score 550 paper-based; 213 computer-based; 87 iBT). *Application deadline:* For fall admission, 8/1 priority date for domestic students, 3/1 for international students; for winter admission, 12/1 priority date for domestic students; for spring admission, 3/1 priority date for domestic students. Applications are processed on a rolling basis. Application fee: $20. Electronic applications accepted. *Financial support:* In 2009–10, 847 students received support, including 18 teaching assistantships; career-related internships or fieldwork, Federal Work-Study, scholarships/grants, and tuition waivers (full) also available. Financial award application deadline: 7/15; financial award applicants required to submit FAFSA. *Faculty research:* Nature of theology, ethics, Biblical commentaries, nature of God, science and theology. *Unit head:* Dr. David Ridder, Vice President and Dean, 651-638-6553. *Application contact:* Joseph V. Dworak, Director of Admissions, 651-638-6288, Fax: 651-638-6002, E-mail: j-dworak@bethel.edu.

Briercrest Seminary, Graduate Programs, Program in Christian Ministries, Caronport, SK S0H 0S0, Canada. Offers leadership (MA); marriage and family counseling (MA); missions (MA); pastoral counseling (MA); worship (MA); youth and family ministry (MA). Part-time programs available. *Degree requirements:* For master's, comprehensive exam, thesis optional. *Entrance requirements:* Additional exam requirements/recommendations for international students: Required—TOEFL (minimum score 550 paper-based; 213 computer-based).

Brigham Young University, Graduate Studies, College of Family, Home, and Social Sciences, Marriage and Family Therapy Program, Provo, UT 84602. Offers MS, PhD. *Faculty:* 8 full-time (1 woman), 4 part-time/adjunct (2 women). *Students:* 39 full-time (22 women); includes 8 minority (2 African Americans, 2 American Indian/Alaska Native, 1 Asian American or Pacific Islander, 3 Hispanic Americans), 2 international. Average age 28. 91 applicants, 23% accepted, 19 enrolled. In 2009, 8 master's awarded. *Degree requirements:* For master's, comprehensive exam, thesis; for doctorate, comprehensive exam, thesis/dissertation. *Entrance requirements:* For master's and doctorate, GRE General Test, GRE Writing Test, minimum GPA of 3.0 in last 60 hours of course work. Additional exam requirements/recommendations for international students: Required—TOEFL. *Application deadline:* For fall admission, 12/15 for domestic and international students. Application fee: $50. Electronic applications accepted. *Expenses:* Tuition: Full-time $5580; part-time $301 per credit hour. Tuition and fees vary according to student's religious affiliation. *Financial support:* In 2009–10, 38 students received support, including 26 research assistantships with full and partial tuition reimbursements available (averaging $12,900 per year); fellowships, teaching assistantships, career-related internships or fieldwork, scholarships/grants, and tuition waivers (partial) also available. Financial award application deadline: 1/10. *Faculty research:* Therapy processes and outcome, preparation for marriage, family relationships across the life cycle, adjustment to medical illnesses, healthcare costs. Total annual research expenditures: $10,000. *Unit head:* Dr. Leslie L. Feinauer, Program Director, 801-422-7750, Fax: 801-422-0163, E-mail: leslie_feinauer@byu.edu. *Application contact:* Linda Kader, Program Secretary, 801-422-5680, Fax: 801-422-0163, E-mail: linda_kader@byu.edu.

California Lutheran University, Graduate Studies, Department of Psychology, Thousand Oaks, CA 91360-2787. Offers clinical psychology (MS, Psy D); marital and family therapy (MS). Part-time programs available. *Degree requirements:* For master's, thesis or comprehensive exams; for doctorate, internship. *Entrance requirements:* For master's, GRE General Test, interview, minimum GPA of 3.0.

California State University, Chico, Graduate School, College of Behavioral and Social Sciences, Department of Psychology, Program in Marriage and Family Therapy, Chico, CA 95929-0722. Offers MS. *Degree requirements:* For master's, thesis or alternative. *Entrance requirements:* For master's, GRE General Test or MAT, 3 letters of recommendation on departmental form. Additional exam requirements/recommendations for international students: Required—TOEFL (minimum score 550 paper-based; 213 computer-based; 80 iBT), IELTS (minimum score 6.5).

California State University, Dominguez Hills, College of Professional Studies, School of Health and Human Services, Program in Marital and Family Therapy, Carson, CA 90747-0001. Offers MS. Part-time and evening/weekend programs available. *Faculty:* 2 full-time (both women), 3 part-time/adjunct (all women). *Students:* 128 full-time (103 women), 30 part-time (25 women); includes 97 minority (52 African Americans, 4 Asian Americans or Pacific Islanders, 41 Hispanic Americans), 2 international. Average age 37. 80 applicants, 90% accepted, 52 enrolled. In 2009, 24 master's awarded. *Degree requirements:* For master's, comprehensive exam. *Entrance requirements:* For master's, minimum GPA of 3.0. *Application deadline:* For fall admission, 8/1 for domestic students; for spring admission, 12/15 for domestic students.

Marriage and Family Therapy

California State University, Dominguez Hills (continued)
Applications are processed on a rolling basis. Application fee: $55. Electronic applications accepted. *Expenses:* Tuition, nonresident: full-time $6696; part-time $372 per unit. Required fees: $5946; $1752 per semester. *Faculty research:* Sociology of the family, clinical psychology theory, employee assistance programs, race and sport, secondary trauma. *Unit head:* Dr. Michele Shaw, Coordinator, 310-243-2693, E-mail: mlinden@csudh.edu. *Application contact:* Dr. Gayle Ball-Parker, Director of Admissions, 310-243-3645, E-mail: gball@csudh.edu.

California State University, Fresno, Division of Graduate Studies, School of Education and Human Development, Department of Counseling and Special Education, Program in Marriage and Family Therapy, Fresno, CA 93740-8027. Offers MS. *Accreditation:* ACA. Part-time and evening/weekend programs available. *Degree requirements:* For master's, thesis or alternative. *Entrance requirements:* For master's, GRE General Test, MAT, minimum GPA of 3.0. Additional exam requirements/recommendations for international students: Required—TOEFL. Electronic applications accepted. *Faculty research:* Child abuse prevention, early childhood education.

California State University, Long Beach, Graduate Studies, College of Education, Department of Advanced Studies in Education and Counseling, Master of Science in Counseling Program, Long Beach, CA 90840. Offers marriage and family therapy (MS); school counseling (MS); student development in higher education (MS). *Accreditation:* NCATE. *Students:* 139 full-time (103 women), 73 part-time (54 women); includes 137 minority (27 African Americans, 35 Asian Americans or Pacific Islanders, 75 Hispanic Americans), 5 international. Average age 30. *Degree requirements:* For master's, comprehensive exam or thesis. *Application deadline:* For fall admission, 3/1 for domestic students. Applications are processed on a rolling basis. Application fee: $55. Electronic applications accepted. *Expenses:* Required fees: $1802 per semester. Part-time tuition and fees vary according to course load. *Financial support:* Federal Work-Study, institutionally sponsored loans, and scholarships/grants available. Financial award application deadline: 3/2. *Unit head:* Dr. Jennifer Coots, Chair, 562-985-4517, Fax: 562-985-4534, E-mail: jcoots@csulb.edu. *Application contact:* Dr. Bita Ghafoori, Assistant Chair, 562-985-7864, Fax: 562-985-4534, E-mail: bghafoor@csulb.edu.

California State University, Northridge, Graduate Studies, College of Education, Department of Educational Psychology and Counseling, Northridge, CA 91330. Offers counseling (MS), including career counseling, college counseling and student services, marriage and family therapy, school counseling, school psychology; educational psychology (MA Ed), including development, learning, and instruction, early childhood education. *Accreditation:* ACA (one or more programs are accredited); NCATE. Part-time and evening/weekend programs available. *Faculty:* 19 full-time (11 women), 42 part-time/adjunct (26 women). *Students:* 341 full-time (301 women), 135 part-time (121 women); includes 21 African Americans, 31 Asian Americans or Pacific Islanders, 149 Hispanic Americans, 11 international. Average age 31. 498 applicants, 39% accepted, 167 enrolled. In 2009, 119 master's awarded. *Entrance requirements:* For master's, GRE General Test or minimum GPA of 3.0. Additional exam requirements/recommendations for international students: Required—TOEFL. *Application deadline:* For fall admission, 11/30 for domestic students. Application fee: $55. *Financial support:* Scholarships/grants available. Support available to part-time students. Financial award application deadline: 3/1. *Unit head:* Dr. Shari Tarver-Behring, Chair, 818-677-2599. *Application contact:* Dr. Shari Tarver-Behring, Chair, 818-677-2599.

Cambridge College, School of Psychology and Counseling, Cambridge, MA 02138-5304. Offers addiction counseling (M Ed); alcohol & drug counseling (Certificate); counseling psychology (M Ed, CAGS); counseling psychology: forensic counseling (M Ed); marriage and family therapy (M Ed); mental health and addiction counseling (M Ed); mental health counseling (M Ed); mental health counseling for school guidance counselors (Post Master's Certificate); psychological studies (M Ed); school adjustment and mental health counseling (M Ed); school adjustment, mental health and addiction counseling (M Ed); school guidance counselor (M Ed); trauma studies (Certificate). Part-time and evening/weekend programs available. *Faculty:* 5 full-time (2 women), 87 part-time/adjunct (50 women). *Students:* 501 full-time (395 women), 307 part-time (245 women); includes 382 minority (295 African Americans, 2 American Indian/Alaska Native, 6 Asian Americans or Pacific Islanders, 79 Hispanic Americans), 4 international. Average age 38. In 2009, 237 master's, 15 other advanced degrees awarded. *Degree requirements:* For master's, thesis, practicum/internship; for other advanced degree, thesis, practicum/Internship. *Entrance requirements:* For master's, resume, 2 professional references; for other advanced degree, official transcripts, documents for transfer credit evaluation, resume, written personal statement/essay, 2 professional references, health insurance, immunizations form. Additional exam requirements/recommendations for international students: Required—TOEFL (minimum score 550 paper-based; 213 computer-based; 79 iBT); Recommended—IELTS (minimum score 6). *Application deadline:* Applications are processed on a rolling basis. Application fee: $30. Electronic applications accepted. *Expenses:* Contact institution. *Financial support:* In 2009–10, 686 students received support. Career-related internships or fieldwork, Federal Work-Study, and scholarships/grants available. Financial award applicants required to submit FAFSA. *Unit head:* Dr. Niti Seth, Dean, 617-873-0208, Fax: 617-349-3561, E-mail: nseth@cambridgecollege.edu. *Application contact:* Stephen Lyons, Director of Enrollment, Graduate and N.I.T.E. Programs, 617-868-1000, Fax: 617-349-3561, E-mail: stephen.lyons@cambridgecollege.edu.

Capella University, School of Human Services, Minneapolis, MN 55402. Offers addictions counseling (Certificate); counseling studies (MS, PhD); criminal justice (MS, PhD, Certificate); diversity studies (Certificate); general human services (MS, PhD); health care administration (MS, PhD, Certificate); management of nonprofit agencies (MS, PhD, Certificate); marital, couple and family counseling/therapy (MS); marriage and family services (Certificate); mental health counseling (MS); professional counseling (Certificate); social and community services (MS, PhD, Certificate). Part-time and evening/weekend programs available. Postbaccalaureate distance learning degree programs offered (minimal on-campus study). Terminal master's awarded for partial completion of doctoral program. *Degree requirements:* For master's, thesis optional, integrative project; for doctorate, comprehensive exam, thesis/dissertation. *Entrance requirements:* Additional exam requirements/recommendations for international students: Required—TOEFL (minimum score 550 paper-based; 213 computer-based), TWE (minimum score 4). Electronic applications accepted. *Faculty research:* Compulsive and addictive behaviors, substance abuse, assessment of psychopathology and neuropsychology.

Carlos Albizu University, Miami Campus, Graduate Programs, Miami, FL 33172-2209. Offers clinical psychology (Psy D); entrepreneurship (MBA); exceptional student education (MS); industrial/organizational psychology (MS); marriage and family therapy (MS); mental health counseling (MS); nonprofit management (MBA); organizational management (MBA); psychology (MS); school counseling (MS); teaching English as a second language (MS). *Accreditation:* APA. Part-time and evening/weekend programs available. *Faculty:* 23 full-time (13 women), 41 part-time/adjunct (21 women). *Students:* 529 full-time (420 women), 171 part-time (139 women); includes 551 minority (55 African Americans, 1 American Indian/Alaska Native, 5 Asian Americans or Pacific Islanders, 490 Hispanic Americans). Average age 37. 278 applicants, 57% accepted, 142 enrolled. In 2009, 139 master's, 26 doctorates awarded. Terminal master's awarded for partial completion of doctoral program. *Degree requirements:* For master's, one foreign language, comprehensive exam, integrative project (MBA), research project (exceptional student education, teaching English as a second language); for doctorate, one foreign language, comprehensive exam, internship, project. *Entrance requirements:* For master's, 3 letters of recommendation, interview, minimum GPA of 3.0, resume; for doctorate, 3 letters of recommendation, minimum GPA of 3.0, resume, interview. *Application deadline:* For fall admission, 8/1 priority date for domestic students; for spring admission, 11/30 priority date for domestic students. Applications are processed on a rolling basis. Application fee: $50. Electronic applications accepted. *Expenses:* Tuition: Full-time $9090; part-time $505 per credit hour. Required fees: $298 per term. Tuition and fees vary according to course load, degree level and program. *Financial support:* In 2009–10, 127 students received support. Federal Work-Study, scholarships/grants, and tuition discounts available. Financial award application deadline: 6/1; financial award applicants required to submit FAFSA. *Faculty research:* Psychotherapy, forensic psychology, neuropsychology, marketing strategy, entrepreneurship, special education. *Unit head:* Dr. Carmen S. Roca, Chancellor, 305-593-1223 Ext. 120, Fax: 305-629-8052, E-mail: croca@albizu.edu. *Application contact:* Annalye Alonso, Secretary, 305-593-1223 Ext. 137, Fax: 305-593-1854, E-mail: aalonso@albizu.edu.

Central Connecticut State University, School of Graduate Studies, School of Education and Professional Studies, Department of Counseling and Family Therapy, New Britain, CT 06050-4010. Offers marriage and family therapy (MS); professional counseling (MS, Certificate); school counseling (MS); student development in higher education (MS). *Accreditation:* AAMFT/COAMFTE. Part-time and evening/weekend programs available. *Faculty:* 8 full-time (5 women), 14 part-time/adjunct (9 women). *Students:* 117 full-time (97 women), 189 part-time (159 women); includes 52 minority (27 African Americans, 3 American Indian/Alaska Native, 3 Asian Americans or Pacific Islanders, 19 Hispanic Americans), 4 international. Average age 33. 249 applicants, 39% accepted, 84 enrolled. In 2009, 78 master's awarded. *Degree requirements:* For master's, comprehensive exam, thesis or alternative; for Certificate, qualifying exam. *Entrance requirements:* For master's, minimum undergraduate GPA of 2.7. Additional exam requirements/recommendations for international students: Required—TOEFL. *Application deadline:* For fall admission, 5/1 for domestic students. Applications are processed on a rolling basis. Application fee: $50. Electronic applications accepted. *Expenses:* Tuition, area resident: Full-time $4662; part-time $440 per credit. Tuition, state resident: full-time $6994; part-time $440 per credit. Tuition, nonresident: full-time $12,988; part-time $440 per credit. Required fees: $3606. One-time fee: $62 part-time. *Financial support:* In 2009–10, 29 students received support, including 22 research assistantships; career-related internships or fieldwork, Federal Work-Study, scholarships/grants, and unspecified assistantships also available. Support available to part-time students. Financial award application deadline: 3/1; financial award applicants required to submit FAFSA. *Faculty research:* Elementary/secondary school counseling, marriage/family therapy, rehabilitation counseling, counseling in higher educational settings. *Unit head:* Dr. Connie Tait, Chair, 860-832-2154. *Application contact:* Dr. Connie Tait, Chair, 860-832-2154.

Chapman University, Graduate Studies, Schmid College of Science, Department of Psychology, Orange, CA 92866. Offers marriage and family therapy (MA). Part-time and evening/weekend programs available. *Faculty:* 12 full-time (5 women), 6 part-time/adjunct (3 women). *Students:* 39 full-time (36 women), 25 part-time (20 women); includes 16 minority (2 African Americans, 7 Asian Americans or Pacific Islanders, 7 Hispanic Americans), 1 international. Average age 28. 100 applicants, 47% accepted, 20 enrolled. In 2009, 26 master's awarded. *Degree requirements:* For master's, comprehensive exam, thesis optional. *Entrance requirements:* For master's, GRE, minimum undergraduate GPA of 2.5. Additional exam requirements/recommendations for international students: Required—TOEFL (minimum score 550 paper-based; 213 computer-based; 80 iBT). *Application deadline:* For fall admission, 3/1 for domestic students; for spring admission, 11/1 for domestic students. Application fee: $50. Electronic applications accepted. *Expenses:* Contact institution. *Financial support:* Fellowships, Federal Work-Study and scholarships/grants available. Financial award application deadline: 6/30; financial award applicants required to submit FAFSA. *Unit head:* Dr. Georg Eifert, Chair, 714-997-6776, E-mail: eifert@chapman.edu. *Application contact:* Susan Read-Weil, Coordinator, 714-744-7837, E-mail: sreadwei@chapman.edu.

Chatham University, Program in Counseling Psychology, Pittsburgh, PA 15232-2826. Offers child, adolescent and family (MSCP); counseling psychology (Psy D); health and holistic (MSCP); infant mental health (MSCP); organization and supervision (MSCP); sport and exercise (MSCP). Part-time and evening/weekend programs available. *Students:* 107 full-time (93 women), 77 part-time (67 women). Average age 29. 141 applicants, 76% accepted, 75 enrolled. In 2009, 63 master's awarded. *Degree requirements:* For master's, thesis optional, supervised internship; for doctorate, thesis/dissertation, internship. *Entrance requirements:* For master's, minimum GPA of 3.0; 2 letters of recommendation; resume; prerequisite coursework in statistics, biology, and psychology; for doctorate, GRE. Additional exam requirements/recommendations for international students: Required—TOEFL (minimum score 600 paper-based; 250 computer-based; 100 iBT), IELTS (minimum score 6.5), TWE. *Application deadline:* For fall admission, 5/1 priority date for domestic students, 6/1 priority date for international students; for spring admission, 12/1 for domestic students, 11/1 for international students. Applications are processed on a rolling basis. Application fee: $45. Electronic applications accepted. *Financial support:* Career-related internships or fieldwork available. Financial award applicants required to submit FAFSA. *Faculty research:* Trauma and recovery, hypnosis, psychospiritual dimensions of healing, psychotherapy of schizophrenia. *Unit head:* Dr. Mary Beth Mannarino, Director, 412-365-1196, Fax: 412-365-1505, E-mail: mmannarino@chatham.edu. *Application contact:* Dory Perry, Associate Director of Graduate Admissions, 412-365-2758, Fax: 412-365-1609, E-mail: gradadmissions@chatham.edu.

The Chicago School of Professional Psychology at Downtown Los Angeles, Clinical Psychology, Los Angeles, CA 90017. Offers applied behavior analysis (MA); clinical psychology (Psy D); marital and family therapy (MA). *Students:* 196 full-time (168 women), 8 part-time (6 women); includes 75 minority (23 African Americans, 1 American Indian/Alaska Native, 23 Asian Americans or Pacific Islanders, 28 Hispanic Americans), 1 international. 152 applicants, 94% accepted, 57 enrolled. *Application contact:* Heather LaBelle, Director of Admissions, 213-615-7200, Fax: 213-627-1985, E-mail: admissions@thechicagoschool.edu.

The Chicago School of Professional Psychology at Irvine, Marital and Family Therapy, Irvine, CA 92612. Offers clinical psychology (MA), including marital and family therapy; management practice (Psy D); psychodynamic psychotherapy (Psy D). *Students:* 19 full-time (17 women); includes 8 minority (1 African American, 2 Asian Americans or Pacific Islanders, 5 Hispanic Americans). *Unit head:* Dr. Richard Sinacola, Lead Faculty, 949-737-5460, Fax: 949-737-5467, E-mail: admissions@thechicagoschool.edu. *Application contact:* Betty Vu, Director of Admissions, 949-737-5460, Fax: 949-737-5467, E-mail: admissions@thechicagoschool.edu.

The Chicago School of Professional Psychology at Westwood, Clinical Psychology MFT, Los Angeles, CA 90024. Offers marital and family therapy (MA). *Students:* 24 full-time (19 women), 2 part-time (both women); includes 7 minority (1 African American, 3 Asian Americans or Pacific Islanders, 3 Hispanic Americans), 1 international. 43 applicants, 86% accepted. *Application contact:* Heather LaBelle, Director of Admissions, 310-208-4240, Fax: 310-208-0684, E-mail: admissions@thechicagoschool.edu.

The Chicago School of Professional Psychology at Westwood, Marital and Family Therapy, Los Angeles, CA 90024. Offers management practice (Psy D); psychodynamic psychotherapy (Psy D).

Christian Theological Seminary, Graduate and Professional Programs, Indianapolis, IN 46208-3301. Offers educational and arts ministries (MA); marriage and family therapy (MA); pastoral care and counseling (D Min); psychotherapy and faith (MA); theological studies (MTS); theology (M Div). *Accreditation:* AAMFT/COAMFTE (one or more programs are accredited); ACIPE; ATS. Part-time programs available. *Faculty:* 18 full-time (8 women), 18 part-time/adjunct (4 women). *Students:* 152 full-time (98 women), 53 part-time (28 women); includes 73 minority (53 African Americans, 1 American Indian/Alaska Native, 4 Asian Americans or Pacific Islanders, 15 Hispanic Americans), 2 international. Average age 41. 120 applicants, 86% accepted, 71 enrolled. In 2009, 31 first professional degrees, 22 master's, 3 doctorates awarded. Terminal master's awarded for partial completion of doctoral program. *Degree requirements:* For master's, comprehensive exam (for some programs), thesis (for some programs); for doctorate, comprehensive exam, thesis/dissertation; for M Div, comprehensive exam, thesis/dissertation (for some programs), missionary and cross-cultural experience. *Entrance requirements:* For master's, GRE General Test, MAT; for doctorate, M Div or BD. *Application deadline:* For fall admission, 7/15 for domestic and international students; for spring admission, 11/15 for domestic and international students. Applications are processed on a rolling basis. Application fee: $30. Electronic applications accepted. *Expenses:* Tuition:

Full-time $9310; part-time $490 per credit hour. Required fees: $180; $160 per semester. Tuition and fees vary according to course load. *Financial support:* In 2009–10, 187 students received support, including 12 teaching assistantships (averaging $350 per year); career-related internships or fieldwork, Federal Work-Study, scholarships/grants, and tuition waivers (full and partial) also available. Support available to part-time students. Financial award application deadline: 4/1; financial award applicants required to submit FAFSA. *Faculty research:* Faith formation, peer learning post graduation. *Unit head:* Dr. Edward L. Wheeler, President, 317-931-2304, Fax: 317-923-1961, E-mail: wheeler@cts.edu. *Application contact:* Rev. Mary Harris, Associate Dean for Student Services, 317-931-2300, Fax: 317-923-1961, E-mail: mharris@cts.edu.

The College of New Jersey, Graduate Division, School of Education, Department of Counselor Education, Program in Marriage and Family Therapy, Ewing, NJ 08628. Offers Ed S. Part-time programs available. *Students:* 1 (woman) full-time, 14 part-time (13 women); includes 2 minority (both African Americans). 22 applicants, 45% accepted. In 2009, 10 Ed Ss awarded. *Entrance requirements:* For degree, previous master's degree or higher. Additional exam requirements/recommendations for international students: Required—TOEFL. *Application deadline:* For fall admission, 2/1 priority date for domestic students; for spring admission, 10/1 priority date for domestic students. Applications are processed on a rolling basis. Application fee: $70. *Expenses:* Tuition, state resident: part-time $573.70 per credit. Tuition, nonresident: part-time $887.75 per credit. Required fees: $140.85 per credit. One-time fee: $10 part-time. *Financial support:* Tuition waivers (partial) and unspecified assistantships available. Financial award application deadline: 5/1; financial award applicants required to submit FAFSA. *Unit head:* Dr. Charlene Alderfer, Coordinator, 609-771-2136, Fax: 609-637-5116, E-mail: alderfer@tcnj.edu. *Application contact:* Susan L. Hydro, Assistant Dean, Office of Graduate Studies, 609-771-2300, Fax: 609-637-5105, E-mail: graduate@tcnj.edu.

The College of William and Mary, School of Education, Program in Counselor Education, Williamsburg, VA 23187-8795. Offers community and addictions counseling (M Ed); community counseling (M Ed); counselor education (PhD); family counseling (M Ed); school counseling (M Ed). *Accreditation:* ACA; NCATE. Part-time and evening/weekend programs available. *Faculty:* 6 full-time (3 women), 6 part-time/adjunct (all women). *Students:* 60 full-time (48 women), 7 part-time (5 women); includes 14 minority (11 African Americans, 1 American Indian/Alaska Native, 2 Asian Americans or Pacific Islanders), 1 international. Average age 30. 126 applicants, 52% accepted, 36 enrolled. In 2009, 28 master's, 6 doctorates awarded. *Degree requirements:* For doctorate, comprehensive exam, thesis/dissertation. *Entrance requirements:* For master's, GRE, minimum GPA of 2.5; for doctorate, GRE, minimum GPA of 3.5. Additional exam requirements/recommendations for international students: Required—TOEFL. *Application deadline:* For fall admission, 1/15 for domestic and international students. Application fee: $45. Electronic applications accepted. *Expenses:* Tuition, state resident: full-time $6400; part-time $315 per credit hour. Tuition, nonresident: full-time $19,720; part-time $840 per credit hour. Required fees: $4114. *Financial support:* In 2009–10, 45 students received support, including 1 fellowship with full tuition reimbursement available (averaging $20,000 per year), 36 research assistantships with full tuition reimbursements available (averaging $11,000 per year); career-related internships or fieldwork, Federal Work-Study, institutionally sponsored loans, scholarships/grants, and unspecified assistantships also available. Financial award application deadline: 1/15; financial award applicants required to submit FAFSA. *Faculty research:* Sexuality, multicultural education, substance abuse, transpersonal psychology. *Unit head:* Dr. Charles McAdams, Area Coordinator, 757-221-2338, E-mail: crmcad@wm.edu. *Application contact:* Dorothy Smith Osborne, Director of Admissions, 757-221-2317, Fax: 757-221-2293, E-mail: dsosbo@wm.edu.

Converse College, School of Education and Graduate Studies, Education Specialist Program, Spartanburg, SC 29302-0006. Offers administration and supervision (Ed S); curriculum and instruction (Ed S); marriage and family therapy (Ed S). *Accreditation:* AAMFT/COAMFTE. Part-time programs available. *Entrance requirements:* For degree, GRE or MAT (marriage and family therapy), minimum GPA of 3.0. Electronic applications accepted.

Denver Seminary, Graduate and Professional Programs, Littleton, CO 80120. Offers apologetics (Certificate); biblical studies (MA); Christian formation and soul care (MA, Certificate); Christian studies (MA, Certificate); church and parachurch leadership (D Min); counseling licensure (MA); counseling ministry (MA); intercultural ministry (Certificate); leadership (MA, Certificate); marriage and family counseling (D Min); pastoral ministry (D Min); philosophy of religion (MA); spiritual guidance (Certificate); theology (M Div, Certificate); worship (Certificate); youth and family ministry (MA). *Accreditation:* ACA; ACIPE; ATS (one or more programs are accredited). Part-time and evening/weekend programs available. Postbaccalaureate distance learning degree programs offered. *Degree requirements:* For master's, 2 foreign languages, thesis (for some programs); for doctorate, 2 foreign languages, thesis/dissertation; for M Div, 2 foreign languages. *Entrance requirements:* For M Div, minimum undergraduate GPA of 2.5; for master's, minimum undergraduate GPA of 3.0; for doctorate, M Div, 3 years of ministry experience. Additional exam requirements/recommendations for international students: Required—TOEFL (minimum score 575 paper-based; 233 computer-based; 90 iBT). Electronic applications accepted.

Dominican University of California, Graduate Programs, School of Education and Counseling Psychology, Program in Counseling Psychology, San Rafael, CA 94901-2298. Offers MFT, MS. Part-time programs available. *Degree requirements:* For master's, comprehensive exam (for some programs), thesis (for some programs). *Entrance requirements:* For master's, minimum GPA of 3.0 for last 60 units. Additional exam requirements/recommendations for international students: Required—TOEFL (minimum score 550 paper-based; 213 computer-based). Electronic applications accepted. *Expenses:* Contact institution.

Drexel University, College of Nursing and Health Professions, Program in Couples and Family Therapy, Philadelphia, PA 19104-2875. Offers couples and family therapy (PhD); family therapy (MFT). *Accreditation:* AAMFT/COAMFTE (one or more programs are accredited). Part-time programs available. Terminal master's awarded for partial completion of doctoral program. *Degree requirements:* For master's, comprehensive exam, thesis; for doctorate, thesis/dissertation, qualifying exam. *Entrance requirements:* For master's, GRE General Test or MAT, minimum GPA of 2.75; for doctorate, GRE General Test, minimum GPA of 3.0. Electronic applications accepted. *Faculty research:* Family assessment, gender issues, chronic illness, early intervention.

East Carolina University, Graduate School, College of Human Ecology, Department of Child Development and Family Relations, Greenville, NC 27858-4353. Offers child development and family relations (MS); marriage and family therapy (MS). *Accreditation:* AAMFT/COAMFTE. Part-time programs available. *Degree requirements:* For master's, comprehensive exam, thesis optional. *Faculty research:* Child care quality, mental health delivery systems for children, family violence.

Eastern Nazarene College, Adult and Graduate Studies, Program in Family Counseling, Quincy, MA 02170. Offers marriage and family therapy (MS). Part-time and evening/weekend programs available. *Entrance requirements:* For master's, 3 letters of recommendation, resume. Additional exam requirements/recommendations for international students: Required—TOEFL (minimum score 550 paper-based).

Eastern University, Palmer Theological Seminary, Program in Ministry, St. Davids, PA 19087-3696. Offers marriage and family (D Min). Part-time programs available. *Degree requirements:* For doctorate, thesis/dissertation. *Entrance requirements:* For doctorate, 3 years of experience, involvement in ministry, church endorsement. *Expenses:* Contact institution.

East Tennessee State University, School of Graduate Studies, College of Education, Department of Human Development and Learning, Johnson City, TN 37614. Offers advanced practitioner (M Ed); community agency counseling (M Ed, MA); comprehensive concentration (M Ed); counseling (M Ed, MA); early childhood education (M Ed, MA); early childhood general (M Ed); early childhood special education (M Ed); early childhood teaching (M Ed); elementary and secondary (school counseling) (M Ed, MA); marriage and family therapy (M Ed, MA); modified concentration (M Ed). *Accreditation:* ACA; NCATE. Part-time programs available. *Degree requirements:* For master's, comprehensive exam, thesis (for some programs). *Entrance requirements:* For master's, GRE General Test, minimum GPA of 3.0. Additional exam requirements/recommendations for international students: Required—TOEFL (minimum score 550 paper-based; 213 computer-based). *Faculty research:* Drug and alcohol abuse, marriage and family counseling, severe mental retardation, parenting of children with disabilities.

Edgewood College, Program in Marriage and Family Therapy, Madison, WI 53711-1997. Offers MS. *Accreditation:* AAMFT. Part-time and evening/weekend programs available. *Students:* 22 full-time (18 women), 11 part-time (9 women); includes 5 minority (2 African Americans, 1 Asian American or Pacific Islander, 2 Hispanic Americans). Average age 30. In 2009, 10 master's awarded. *Degree requirements:* For master's, research project. *Entrance requirements:* For master's, minimum GPA of 2.75, 2 letters of reference, interviews. Additional exam requirements/recommendations for international students: Required—TOEFL (minimum score 213 computer-based). *Application deadline:* For fall admission, 3/1 for domestic students. Application fee: $25. Electronic applications accepted. *Expenses:* Tuition: Part-time $688 per credit hour. *Unit head:* Dr. Peter Fabian, Chair, 608-663-2233, Fax: 608-663-3291, E-mail: fabian@edgewood.edu. *Application contact:* Joann Eastman, Admissions Counselor, 608-663-3250, Fax: 608-663-2214, E-mail: gps@edgewood.edu.

Evangelical Theological Seminary, Graduate and Professional Programs, Myerstown, PA 17067-1212. Offers Biblical studies (MAR); congregational ministry (M Div); global and contextual studies (M Div, MAR); historical and theological studies (MAR); interdisciplinary studies (MAR); marriage and family counseling (M Div); marriage and family therapy (MA); New Testament (MAR); Old Testament (MAR); spiritual formation (MAR); teaching ministry (M Div); youth ministry (M Div). *Accreditation:* ATS (one or more programs are accredited). Part-time programs available. Postbaccalaureate distance learning degree programs offered (minimal on-campus study). *Degree requirements:* For master's, 2 foreign languages; for M Div, 2 foreign languages, ministry internship. *Entrance requirements:* For M Div and master's, minimum GPA of 2.5. Additional exam requirements/recommendations for international students: Required—TOEFL (minimum score 550 paper-based; 213 computer-based). *Faculty research:* Literary form and structure within the Hebrew and Greek scriptures, Wesley studies, esoteric biblical languages, the Mosaic law and the Christian, ethics.

Fairfield University, Graduate School of Education and Allied Professions, Department of Marriage and Family Therapy, Fairfield, CT 06824-5195. Offers MA. *Accreditation:* AAMFT/COAMFTE. Part-time and evening/weekend programs available. *Degree requirements:* For master's, comprehensive exam. *Entrance requirements:* For master's, minimum QPA of 3.0, 2 recommendations, resume. Additional exam requirements/recommendations for international students: Required—TOEFL (minimum score 550 paper-based; 213 computer-based; 80 iBT). Electronic applications accepted. *Faculty research:* Diversity and multiculturalism, accreditation, professional ethics, program development and alumni engagement, international family therapy.

Florida Atlantic University, College of Education, Department of Counselor Education, Boca Raton, FL 33431-0991. Offers counselor education (M Ed, PhD, Ed S); marriage and family therapy (Ed S); mental health counseling (M Ed, Ed S); rehabilitation counseling (M Ed); school counseling (M Ed, Ed S). *Accreditation:* ACA; NCATE. Part-time and evening/weekend programs available. *Faculty:* 7 full-time (2 women), 6 part-time/adjunct (5 women). *Students:* 65 full-time (52 women), 95 part-time (83 women); includes 59 minority (19 African Americans, 5 Asian Americans or Pacific Islanders, 35 Hispanic Americans), 2 international. Average age 33. 109 applicants, 40% accepted, 27 enrolled. In 2009, 54 master's, 2 doctorates awarded. *Degree requirements:* For Ed S, departmental qualifying exam. *Entrance requirements:* For master's, GRE General Test, minimum GPA of 3.0 during previous 2 years; for Ed S, GRE General Test, minimum graduate GPA of 3.25. Additional exam requirements/recommendations for international students: Required—TOEFL. *Application deadline:* For fall admission, 3/1 for domestic students, 2/1 for international students; for spring admission, 9/15 for domestic students, 7/1 for international students. Applications are processed on a rolling basis. Application fee: $30. *Expenses:* Tuition, state resident: full-time $7055; part-time $293.94 per credit hour. Tuition, nonresident: full-time $22,096; part-time $920.66 per credit hour. *Financial support:* Research assistantships with partial tuition reimbursements, teaching assistantships, career-related internships or fieldwork, scholarships/grants, and unspecified assistantships available. *Faculty research:* Brief therapy, psychological type, marriage and family counseling, international programs, integrated services. *Unit head:* Dr. Irene Johnson, Chair, 561-297-2136, Fax: 561-297-2309. *Application contact:* Susan Foley, Senior Secretary, 561-297-3602, Fax: 561-297-2309, E-mail: cnslred@fau.edu.

Florida State University, The Graduate School, College of Human Sciences, Department of Family and Child Sciences, Tallahassee, FL 32306. Offers family and child sciences (MS); family relations (PhD); marriage and family therapy (PhD). *Accreditation:* AAMFT/COAMFTE. Part-time programs available. *Faculty:* 12 full-time (8 women), 2 part-time/adjunct (both women). *Students:* 34 full-time (28 women), 22 part-time (19 women); includes 20 minority (18 African Americans, 2 Asian Americans or Pacific Islanders), 2 international. 48 applicants, 31% accepted, 14 enrolled. In 2009, 2 master's, 6 doctorates awarded. *Degree requirements:* For master's, comprehensive exam, thesis optional; for doctorate, thesis/dissertation, preliminary examination; clinical examination (for marriage and family therapy). *Entrance requirements:* For master's and doctorate, GRE General Test, minimum GPA of 3.0. Additional exam requirements/recommendations for international students: Required—TOEFL (minimum score 80 iBT). *Application deadline:* For fall admission, 7/1 for domestic students, 5/1 for international students; for spring admission, 11/1 priority date for domestic students, 10/1 priority date for international students. Application fee: $30. Electronic applications accepted. *Expenses:* Tuition, state resident: full-time $7413. Tuition, nonresident: full-time $22,567. *Financial support:* In 2009–10, 25 students received support, including 1 fellowship with full tuition reimbursement available (averaging $15,000 per year), 6 research assistantships with full tuition reimbursements available (averaging $15,000 per year), 19 teaching assistantships with full tuition reimbursements available (averaging $15,000 per year); career-related internships or fieldwork, Federal Work-Study, institutionally sponsored loans, scholarships/grants, and unspecified assistantships also available. Financial award application deadline: 1/5; financial award applicants required to submit FAFSA. *Faculty research:* Family therapy, parent-child relations, distressed families and foster care, marital processes, relational interventions. *Unit head:* Dr. Kay Pasley, Chair, 850-644-3217, Fax: 850-644-3439, E-mail: kpasley@admin.fsu.edu. *Application contact:* Candy Tookes, Academic Support Assistant, 850-644-3217, Fax: 850-644-3439, E-mail: ctookes@admin.fsu.edu.

Friends University, Graduate School, Division of Science, Arts, and Education, Program in Family Therapy, Wichita, KS 67213. Offers MSFT. *Accreditation:* AAMFT/COAMFTE. Evening/weekend programs available. *Entrance requirements:* Additional exam requirements/recommendations for international students: Required—TOEFL (minimum score 560 paper-based; 220 computer-based). Electronic applications accepted.

Fuller Theological Seminary, Graduate School of Psychology, Department of Marriage and Family Therapy, Pasadena, CA 91182. Offers family studies (MA); marital and family therapy (MS); marriage and family enrichment (Certificate). *Degree requirements:* For master's, practicum. *Entrance requirements:* For master's, GRE General Test. Additional exam requirements/recommendations for international students: Required—TOEFL. *Expenses:* Contact institution. *Faculty research:* Marital intimacy, sex-roles, psychoanalytical theory, men's issues.

Geneva College, Program in Counseling, Beaver Falls, PA 15010-3599. Offers marriage and family (MA); mental health (MA); school counseling (MA). *Accreditation:* ACA. Part-time and evening/weekend programs available. *Faculty:* 5 full-time (2 women), 2 part-time/adjunct (1 woman). *Students:* 28 full-time (21 women), 21 part-time (17 women); includes 6 minority (5 African Americans, 1 Asian American or Pacific Islander). Average age 26. 32 applicants, 97% accepted, 18 enrolled. In 2009, 11 master's awarded. *Degree requirements:* For master's, comprehensive exam, internship. *Entrance requirements:* For master's, GRE General Test or

Marriage and Family Therapy

Geneva College (continued)
MAT, minimum GPA of 3.0 (preferred), letters of recommendation, faith statement. Additional exam requirements/recommendations for international students: Required—TOEFL. *Application deadline:* For fall admission, 7/1 priority date for domestic students; for spring admission, 11/1 priority date for domestic students. Applications are processed on a rolling basis. Application fee: $50 ($100 for international students). Electronic applications accepted. *Expenses:* Tuition: Full-time $11,250; part-time $625 per credit. Tuition and fees vary according to program. *Financial support:* In 2009–10, 8 teaching assistantships (averaging $3,500 per year) were awarded; career-related internships or fieldwork and unspecified assistantships also available. Financial award applicants required to submit FAFSA. *Unit head:* Dr. Carol Luce, Director, 724-847-6622, Fax: 724-847-6101, E-mail: cbluce@geneva.edu. *Application contact:* JoAnn Westover, Graduate Program Manager, 724-847-6697, E-mail: counseling@geneva.edu.

George Fox University, School of Education, Graduate Department of Counseling, Newberg, OR 97132-2697. Offers counseling (MA); marriage and family therapy (MA, Certificate); mental health trauma (Certificate); school counseling (MA, Certificate); school psychology (Certificate, Ed S). Part-time programs available. *Faculty:* 9 full-time (3 women), 7 part-time/adjunct (5 women). *Students:* 100 full-time (77 women), 122 part-time (103 women); includes 24 minority (7 African Americans, 4 American Indian/Alaska Native, 9 Asian Americans or Pacific Islanders, 4 Hispanic Americans). Average age 36. 102 applicants, 75% accepted, 59 enrolled. In 2009, 61 master's, 2 other advanced degrees awarded. *Degree requirements:* For master's, clinical project. *Entrance requirements:* For master's, MAT or GRE, bachelor's degree from regionally-accredited college or university, minimum cumulative GPA of 3.0, 1 professional and 1 academic reference, resume, on-campus interview. Additional exam requirements/recommendations for international students: Required—TOEFL (minimum score 577 paper-based; 233 computer-based; 90 iBT). *Application deadline:* For fall admission, 5/30 for domestic and international students; for winter admission, 11/1 for domestic and international students; for spring admission, 2/28 for domestic and international students. Applications are processed on a rolling basis. Application fee: $40. Electronic applications accepted. *Expenses:* Contact institution. *Financial support:* Career-related internships or fieldwork available. *Unit head:* Dr. Richard Shaw, Associate Professor of Marriage and Family Therapy/Chair, 503-554-6142, E-mail: rshaw@georgefox.edu. *Application contact:* Kathy Grant, Admissions Counselor, 800-493-4937, Fax: 503-554-6111, E-mail: counseling@georgefox.edu.

Harding University, College of Bible and Religion, Program in Marriage and Family Therapy, Searcy, AR 72149-0001. Offers marriage and family therapy (MS); mental health counseling (MS). Part-time programs available. *Faculty:* 4 full-time (0 women), 5 part-time/adjunct (1 woman). *Students:* 24 full-time (14 women), 3 part-time (2 women); includes 2 minority (both African Americans). Average age 28. 23 applicants, 70% accepted, 13 enrolled. In 2009, 11 master's awarded. *Degree requirements:* For master's, comprehensive exam, 15-month practicum. *Entrance requirements:* For master's, GRE General Test, minimum undergraduate GPA of 2.75, graduate 3.0. *Application deadline:* For fall admission, 4/1 priority date for domestic students. Applications are processed on a rolling basis. Application fee: $40. *Expenses:* Tuition: Full-time $9720; part-time $540 per credit hour. Required fees: $22 per credit hour. Tuition and fees vary according to course load and program. *Financial support:* In 2009–10, 6 students received support. Scholarships/grants available. *Faculty research:* Forgiveness, substance abuse, post traumatic stress disorder. *Unit head:* Dr. Lewis L. Moore, Chairman, 501-279-4347, Fax: 501-279-4417, E-mail: lmoore@harding.edu. *Application contact:* Ruth Ann Dawson, Office Manager, 501-279-4347, Fax: 501-279-4417, E-mail: radawson@harding.edu.

Hardin-Simmons University, Graduate School, Cynthia Ann Parker College of Liberal Arts, Department of Psychology, Program in Family Psychology, Abilene, TX 79698-0001. Offers MA. Part-time programs available. *Faculty:* 6 full-time (2 women). *Students:* 12 full-time (8 women), 6 part-time (5 women); includes 2 minority (both Hispanic Americans). Average age 25. 10 applicants, 90% accepted, 9 enrolled. In 2009, 7 master's awarded. *Degree requirements:* For master's, comprehensive exam, clinical experience, project. *Entrance requirements:* For master's, minimum undergraduate GPA of 3.0 in major, 2.7 overall; 21 semester hours of course work in psychology, 18 of those in upper division classes; writing sample; letters of recommendation. Additional exam requirements/recommendations for international students: Required—TOEFL (minimum score 550 paper-based; 213 computer-based; 75 iBT). *Application deadline:* For fall admission, 8/15 priority date for domestic students, 4/1 for international students; for spring admission, 1/5 priority date for domestic students, 9/1 for international students. Applications are processed on a rolling basis. Application fee: $50. *Expenses:* Tuition: Full-time $11,430; part-time $635 per credit hour. Required fees: $650; $110 per semester. Tuition and fees vary according to degree level. *Financial support:* In 2009–10, 14 students received support, including 16 fellowships (averaging $900 per year); career-related internships or fieldwork and scholarships/grants also available. Support available to part-time students. Financial award application deadline: 6/30; financial award applicants required to submit FAFSA. *Faculty research:* Family stress management, spirituality in marriage, intimacy and sexuality in marriage, sex education in the church, role of faith in marital satisfaction. *Unit head:* Dr. Sue Lucas, Director, 325-670-1538, Fax: 325-670-1458, E-mail: slucas@hsutx.edu. *Application contact:* Dr. Gary Stanlake, Dean of Graduate Studies, 325-670-1298, Fax: 325-670-1564, E-mail: gradoff@hsutx.edu.

Hofstra University, School of Education, Health, and Human Services, Department of Health Professions and Family Studies, Program in Marriage and Family Therapy, Hempstead, NY 11549. Offers MA. Part-time programs available. *Students:* 41 full-time (37 women), 15 part-time (13 women); includes 9 minority (4 African Americans, 5 Hispanic Americans), 1 international. Average age 26. 35 applicants, 71% accepted, 15 enrolled. In 2009, 19 master's awarded. *Degree requirements:* For master's, comprehensive exam, 300 client-contact hours during practicum and internship. *Entrance requirements:* For master's, GRE General Test, interview, letters of recommendation. Additional exam requirements/recommendations for international students: Required—TOEFL (minimum score 550 paper-based; 213 computer-based; 80 iBT). *Application deadline:* Applications are processed on a rolling basis. Application fee: $60. Electronic applications accepted. *Expenses:* Tuition: Full-time $16,200; part-time $900 per credit hour. Required fees: $970; $145 per term. Tuition and fees vary according to program. *Financial support:* In 2009–10, 17 students received support, including 7 fellowships with full and partial tuition reimbursements available (averaging $2,679 per year), 2 research assistantships with full and partial tuition reimbursements available (averaging $19,057 per year); Federal Work-Study, institutionally sponsored loans, tuition waivers (full and partial), unspecified assistantships, and partial scholarships also available. Support available to part-time students. Financial award applicants required to submit FAFSA. *Faculty research:* Marriage and family therapy; interplay between common factors and model-specific factors in marriage and family therapy.; divorce mediation; human sexuality; post hysterectomy experiences and sexuality. *Unit head:* Prof. George M. Simon, Program Director, 516-463-4622, Fax: 516-463-4810, E-mail: hprgms@hofstra.edu. *Application contact:* Carol Drummer, Dean of Graduate Admissions, 516-463-4876, Fax: 516-463-4664, E-mail: gradstudent@hofstra.edu.

Hope International University, School of Graduate and Professional Studies, Program in Marriage and Family Therapy, Fullerton, CA 92831-3138. Offers MA, MFT. *Accreditation:* AAMFT. *Degree requirements:* For master's, comprehensive exam, thesis (for some programs), final exam, practicum. *Entrance requirements:* For master's, minimum GPA of 3.0, interview, bachelor's degree, 2 references. Additional exam requirements/recommendations for international students: Required—TOEFL (minimum score 550 paper-based; 213 computer-based; 86 iBT); Recommended—IELTS (minimum score 6.5). Electronic applications accepted. *Expenses:* Contact institution.

Idaho State University, Office of Graduate Studies, Kasiska College of Health Professions, Department of Counseling, Pocatello, ID 83209-8120. Offers counseling (M Coun, Ed S), including marriage and family counseling (M Coun), mental health counseling (M Coun), school counseling (M Coun), student affairs and college counseling (M Coun); counselor education and counseling (PhD). *Accreditation:* ACA (one or more programs are accredited). Part-time programs available. *Faculty:* 7 full-time (4 women). *Students:* 72 full-time (52 women), 29 part-time (18 women); includes 11 minority (2 African Americans, 1 American Indian/Alaska Native, 2 Asian Americans or Pacific Islanders, 6 Hispanic Americans). Average age 32. In 2009, 25 master's, 5 doctorates, 1 other advanced degree awarded. *Degree requirements:* For master's, comprehensive exam, thesis, 4 semesters resident graduate study, practicum/internship; for doctorate, comprehensive exam, thesis/dissertation, 3 semesters internship, 4 consecutive semesters doctoral-level study on campus; for Ed S, comprehensive exam, thesis, case studies, oral exam. *Entrance requirements:* For master's, GRE General Test, MAT, minimum GPA of 3.0, bachelors degree, interview, 3 letters of recommendation; for doctorate, GRE General Test, MAT, minimum graduate GPA of 3.0, resume, interview, counseling license, master's degree; for Ed S, GRE General Test, minimum graduate GPA of 3.0, master's degree in counseling, 3 letters of recommendation, 2 years work experience. Additional exam requirements/recommendations for international students: Required—TOEFL (minimum score 600 paper-based; 213 computer-based; 80 iBT). *Application deadline:* For fall admission, 7/1 for domestic students, 6/1 for international students; for spring admission, 12/1 for domestic students, 11/1 for international students. Applications are processed on a rolling basis. Application fee: $55. Electronic applications accepted. *Expenses:* Tuition, state resident: full-time $3318; part-time $297 per credit hour. Tuition, nonresident: full-time $13,120; part-time $437 per credit hour. Required fees: $2530. Tuition and fees vary according to program. *Financial support:* In 2009–10, 12 teaching assistantships with full and partial tuition reimbursements (averaging $10,841 per year) were awarded; career-related internships or fieldwork, Federal Work-Study, institutionally sponsored loans, scholarships/grants, traineeships, health care benefits, tuition waivers (full and partial), and unspecified assistantships also available. Support available to part-time students. Financial award application deadline: 1/1; financial award applicants required to submit FAFSA. *Faculty research:* Group counseling, multicultural counseling, family counseling, child therapy, supervision. *Unit head:* Dr. Nicole Hill, Interim Chair, 208-282-3663, Fax: 208-282-2583, E-mail: hillnico@isu.edu. *Application contact:* Tami Carson, Graduate School Technical Records Specialist, 208-282-2150, Fax: 208-282-4847, E-mail: carstami@isu.edu.

Indiana University–Purdue University Fort Wayne, School of Education, Department of Professional Studies, Fort Wayne, IN 46805-1499. Offers counseling education (MS Ed); educational leadership (MS Ed); marriage and family therapy (MS Ed); school counseling (MS Ed); special education (MS Ed, Certificate). Part-time programs available. *Faculty:* 10 full-time (5 women). *Students:* 2 full-time (both women), 159 part-time (120 women); includes 19 minority (12 African Americans, 1 Asian American or Pacific Islander, 6 Hispanic Americans). Average age 35. 47 applicants, 98% accepted, 38 enrolled. In 2009, 64 master's awarded. *Degree requirements:* For master's, comprehensive exam, practicum, internship, portfolio. *Entrance requirements:* For master's, minimum GPA of 2.5. Additional exam requirements/recommendations for international students: Required—TOEFL (minimum score 550 paper-based; 213 computer-based; 77 iBT). *Application deadline:* For fall admission, 4/1 priority date for domestic and international students. Applications are processed on a rolling basis. Application fee: $55. *Expenses:* Tuition, state resident: full-time $4595; part-time $255 per credit. Tuition, nonresident: full-time $10,963; part-time $609 per credit. Required fees: $528; $29.35 per credit. Tuition and fees vary according to course load. *Financial support:* In 2009–10, 1 teaching assistantship with partial tuition reimbursement (averaging $12,740 per year) was awarded; research assistantships with partial tuition reimbursements, scholarships/grants also available. Support available to part-time students. Financial award application deadline: 3/1; financial award applicants required to submit FAFSA. *Unit head:* Dr. James Burg, Interim Chair, 260-481-5406, Fax: 260-481-5408, E-mail: burgj@ipfw.edu. *Application contact:* Vicky L. Schmidt, Graduate Recorder, 260-481-6450, Fax: 260-481-5408, E-mail: schmidt@ipfw.edu.

Indiana Wesleyan University, College of Graduate Studies, Graduate Studies in Counseling, Marion, IN 46953. Offers addictions counseling (MS); community counseling (MS); marriage and family counseling (MS); school counseling (MS). *Accreditation:* ACA. Part-time programs available. *Degree requirements:* For master's, thesis or alternative. *Entrance requirements:* For master's, GRE General Test. Additional exam requirements/recommendations for international students: Required—TOEFL. Electronic applications accepted. *Expenses:* Contact institution. *Faculty research:* Community counseling, multicultural counseling, addictions.

Instituto Tecnologico de Santo Domingo, Graduate School, Santo Domingo, Dominican Republic. Offers applied linguistics (MA); construction administration (M Mgmt); corporate finance (M Mgmt); education (M Ed); engineering (M Eng), including data telecommunications, industrial engineering, logistics and supply chain, maintenance engineering, sanitary and environmental engineering, structural engineering; environmental science (M En S), including environmental education, environmental management, marine and coastal ecosystems, natural resources management; family therapy (MA); food science and technology (MS); human development (MA); human resources administration (M Mgmt); international business (M Mgmt); labor risks (M Mgmt); management (M Mgmt); marketing (M Mgmt); mathematics (MS); organizational development (M Mgmt); planning and taxation (M Mgmt); psychology (MA); social science (M Ed); upper management (M Mgmt). *Entrance requirements:* For master's, birth certificate, minimum GPA of 2.0.

Iona College, School of Arts and Science, Department of Family and Pastoral Counseling, New Rochelle, NY 10801-1890. Offers family counseling (MS, Certificate); pastoral counseling (MS). Part-time and evening/weekend programs available. *Faculty:* 4 full-time (0 women), 3 part-time/adjunct (all women). *Students:* 29 full-time (23 women), 12 part-time (11 women); includes 14 minority (7 African Americans, 7 Hispanic Americans). Average age 33. 38 applicants, 58% accepted, 14 enrolled. In 2009, 15 master's awarded. *Degree requirements:* For master's, thesis, project. *Entrance requirements:* For master's, draw-a-person test, sentence completion test, interview, minimum GPA of 3.0. *Application deadline:* Applications are processed on a rolling basis. Application fee: $50. Electronic applications accepted. *Expenses:* Contact institution. *Financial support:* Career-related internships or fieldwork, tuition waivers (partial), and unspecified assistantships available. Support available to part-time students. Financial award application deadline: 4/15; financial award applicants required to submit FAFSA. *Faculty research:* Marriage counseling. *Unit head:* Dr. Robert Burns, Chair, 914-633-2418, E-mail: rburns@iona.edu. *Application contact:* Veronica Jarek-Prinz, Director of Graduate Admissions, 914-633-2420, Fax: 914-633-2277, E-mail: vjarekprinz@iona.edu.

John Brown University, Graduate Counseling Division, Siloam Springs, AR 72761-2121. Offers community counseling (MS); marriage and family therapy (MS); school counseling (MS). *Accreditation:* NCATE. Part-time and evening/weekend programs available. *Faculty:* 7 full-time (1 woman), 4 part-time/adjunct (0 women). *Students:* 72 full-time (55 women), 65 part-time (47 women); includes 10 minority (5 African Americans, 3 American Indian/Alaska Native, 1 Asian American or Pacific Islander, 1 Hispanic American), 1 international. Average age 33. 64 applicants, 86% accepted, 38 enrolled. In 2009, 55 master's awarded. *Degree requirements:* For master's, practica or internships. *Entrance requirements:* For master's, GRE General Test, MAT, minimum GPA of 3.0. Additional exam requirements/recommendations for international students: Required—TOEFL (minimum score 550 paper-based; 173 computer-based). *Application deadline:* For fall admission, 8/11 priority date for domestic students; for spring admission, 1/12 for domestic students. Applications are processed on a rolling basis. Application fee: $35 ($100 for international students). Electronic applications accepted. *Expenses:* Tuition: Full-time $8100; part-time $450 per credit. *Financial support:* In 2009–10, 3 students received support, including 3 research assistantships (averaging $6,210 per year); scholarships/grants, tuition waivers (full), and unspecified assistantships also available. Financial award application deadline: 3/1; financial award applicants required to submit FAFSA. *Unit head:* Dr. John V. Carmack, Program Director, 479-524-7460, Fax: 479-524-9548, E-mail: jcarmack@jbu.edu. *Application contact:* Lynne Jackson, Graduate Admissions Representative—Counseling, 479-524-7425, E-mail: ljackson@jbu.edu.

Johnson Bible College, Department of Marriage and Family Therapy, Knoxville, TN 37998-1001. Offers marriage and family therapy/professional counseling (MA). *Degree requirements:*

For master's, variable foreign language requirement, comprehensive exam, thesis (for some programs), internship (500 client contact hours). *Entrance requirements:* For master's, interview, minimum GPA of 3.0, 20 credits of course work in psychology, 15 credits of course work in Bible. Additional exam requirements/recommendations for international students: Required—TOEFL.

Kansas State University, Graduate School, College of Human Ecology, Program in Human Ecology, Manhattan, KS 66506. Offers apparel and textiles (PhD); family life education and consultation (PhD); food service and hospitality management (PhD); lifespan and human development (PhD); marriage and family therapy (PhD); personal financial planning (PhD). *Faculty:* 3 full-time (all women). *Students:* 29 full-time (19 women), 43 part-time (23 women); includes 15 minority (13 African Americans, 1 American Indian/Alaska Native, 1 Asian American or Pacific Islander), 16 international. Average age 37. 29 applicants, 66% accepted, 16 enrolled. In 2009, 10 doctorates awarded. *Degree requirements:* For doctorate, thesis/dissertation. *Application deadline:* For fall admission, 2/1 priority date for domestic and international students; for spring admission, 8/1 priority date for domestic and international students. Applications are processed on a rolling basis. Application fee: $40 ($55 for international students). Electronic applications accepted. *Financial support:* Application deadline: 3/1. *Application contact:* Connie Fechter, Application Contact, 785-532-1473, Fax: 785-532-3796, E-mail: fechter@ksu.edu.

Kansas State University, Graduate School, College of Human Ecology, School of Family Studies and Human Services, Manhattan, KS 66506. Offers communication sciences and disorders (MS); early childhood education (MS); family studies (MS); life span human development (MS); marriage and family therapy (MS). *Accreditation:* AAMFT/COAMFTE; ASHA. Part-time programs available. *Faculty:* 25 full-time (15 women), 3 part-time/adjunct (2 women). *Students:* 76 full-time (67 women), 101 part-time (61 women); includes 17 minority (7 African Americans, 1 American Indian/Alaska Native, 2 Asian Americans or Pacific Islanders, 7 Hispanic Americans), 1 international. Average age 32. 117 applicants, 68% accepted, 47 enrolled. In 2009, 63 master's awarded. *Degree requirements:* For master's, thesis or alternative, oral exam, residency. *Entrance requirements:* For master's, GRE, minimum GPA of 3.0 in last 2 years of undergraduate study. Additional exam requirements/recommendations for international students: Required—TOEFL (minimum score 600 paper-based; 250 computer-based). *Application deadline:* For fall admission, 2/1 priority date for domestic and international students; for spring admission, 8/1 priority date for domestic and international students. Applications are processed on a rolling basis. Application fee: $40 ($55 for international students). Electronic applications accepted. *Financial support:* In 2009–10, 26 research assistantships (averaging $10,867 per year), 17 teaching assistantships with full and partial tuition reimbursements (averaging $11,635 per year) were awarded; Federal Work-Study, institutionally sponsored loans, scholarships/grants, and unspecified assistantships also available. Support available to part-time students. Financial award application deadline: 3/1; financial award applicants required to submit FAFSA. *Faculty research:* Health and security of military families, personal and family risk assessment and evaluation, disorders of communication and swallowing, families and health. Total annual research expenditures: $10.1 million. *Unit head:* Dr. Maurice McDonald, Head, 785-532-1472, E-mail: morey@ksu.edu. *Application contact:* Connie Fechter, Administrative Specialist, 785-532-1473, Fax: 785-532-5505, E-mail: fechter@ksu.edu.

Kean University, College of Humanities and Social Sciences, Program in Marriage and Family Therapy, Union, NJ 07083. Offers Diploma. Part-time and evening/weekend programs available. *Faculty:* 15 full-time (13 women). *Students:* 10 full-time (8 women), 8 part-time (6 women); includes 8 minority (4 African Americans, 1 Asian American or Pacific Islander, 3 Hispanic Americans). Average age 30. 8 applicants, 100% accepted, 5 enrolled. In 2009, 7 Diplomas awarded. *Degree requirements:* For Diploma, comprehensive exam, thesis, internship, practicum. *Entrance requirements:* For degree, GRE General Test, minimum GPA of 3.0, 3 letters of recommendation, 12 credits in psychology, interview. *Application deadline:* For fall admission, 5/1 for domestic students; for spring admission, 11/1 for domestic students. Application fee: $60 ($150 for international students). Electronic applications accepted. *Expenses:* Tuition, state resident: full-time $10,440; part-time $435 per credit. Tuition, nonresident: full-time $14,160; part-time $590 per credit. Required fees: $2642; $110 per credit. Part-time tuition and fees vary according to course load and degree level. *Financial support:* In 2009–10, 2 research assistantships with full tuition reimbursements (averaging $3,263 per year) were awarded; unspecified assistantships also available. *Unit head:* Dr. Muriel B. Singer, Program Coordinator, 908-737-5886, E-mail: msinger@kean.edu. *Application contact:* Dorothy Rowe, Pre-Admissions Coordinator, 908-737-5928, Fax: 908-737-5965, E-mail: drowe@kean.edu.

Kutztown University of Pennsylvania, College of Education, Program in Counseling Psychology, Kutztown, PA 19530-0730. Offers agency counseling (MA); marital and family therapy (MA). Part-time and evening/weekend programs available. *Faculty:* 8 full-time (1 woman). *Students:* 33 full-time (29 women), 24 part-time (17 women); includes 3 minority (all African Americans). Average age 28. 41 applicants, 68% accepted, 10 enrolled. In 2009, 9 master's awarded. *Degree requirements:* For master's, comprehensive exam, thesis optional. *Entrance requirements:* For master's, GRE General Test, interview. Additional exam requirements/recommendations for international students: Required—TOEFL. *Application deadline:* For fall admission, 2/1 for domestic and international students; for spring admission, 8/1 for domestic and international students. Application fee: $35. Electronic applications accepted. *Expenses:* Tuition, state resident: full-time $6666; part-time $370 per credit. Tuition, nonresident: full-time $10,666; part-time $593 per credit. Required fees: $62 per credit. $60 per semester. *Financial support:* Career-related internships or fieldwork, Federal Work-Study, scholarships/grants, and unspecified assistantships available. Financial award application deadline: 3/1; financial award applicants required to submit FAFSA. *Faculty research:* Family addictions. *Unit head:* Dr. Deborah Barlieb, Chairperson, 610-683-4204, Fax: 610-683-1585, E-mail: barlieb@kutztown.edu. *Application contact:* Kelly D. Burr, Associate Director, Graduate Admissions, 610-683-4200, Fax: 610-683-1393, E-mail: graduate@kutztown.edu.

La Salle University, School of Arts and Sciences, Program in Psychology, Philadelphia, PA 19141-1199. Offers clinical psychology (Psy D); family psychology (Psy D); rehabilitation psychology (Psy D). Part-time and evening/weekend programs available. *Entrance requirements:* For doctorate, GRE, minimum GPA of 3.0. *Expenses:* Contact institution. *Faculty research:* Cognitive therapy, attribution theory, treatment of addiction.

Lewis & Clark College, Graduate School of Education and Counseling, Department of Counseling Psychology, Program in Marriage, Couple and Family Therapy, Portland, OR 97219-7899. Offers MA, MS. Part-time and evening/weekend programs available. *Faculty:* 2 full-time (1 woman), 3 part-time/adjunct (1 woman). *Students:* 30 full-time (28 women), 21 part-time (17 women); includes 5 minority (2 African Americans, 1 Asian American or Pacific Islander, 2 Hispanic Americans), 1 international. Average age 28. 43 applicants, 63% accepted, 16 enrolled. In 2009, 4 master's awarded. *Degree requirements:* For master's, thesis (MS). *Entrance requirements:* For master's, GRE General Test, minimum undergraduate GPA of 2.75. Additional exam requirements/recommendations for international students: Required—TOEFL (minimum score 575 paper-based; 233 computer-based). *Application deadline:* For fall admission, 2/1 priority date for domestic and international students. Application fee: $50. Electronic applications accepted. *Expenses:* Tuition: Part-time $713 per semester hour. Tuition and fees vary according to course level and campus/location. *Financial support:* In 2009–10, 47 students received support. Career-related internships or fieldwork, Federal Work-Study, institutionally sponsored loans, scholarships/grants, health care benefits, and tuition waivers (partial) available. Support available to part-time students. Financial award application deadline: 3/1; financial award applicants required to submit FAFSA. *Unit head:* Dr. Teresa McDowell, Program Coordinator, 503-768-6060, Fax: 503-768-6005, E-mail: teresamc@lclark.edu. *Application contact:* Becky Haas, Director of Admissions, 503-768-6200, Fax: 503-768-6205, E-mail: gseadmit@lclark.edu.

Loyola Marymount University, College of Fine Arts, Department of Marital and Family Therapy, Program in Marital and Family Therapy, Los Angeles, CA 90045-. Offers MA. *Faculty:* 3 full-time (all women), 5 part-time/adjunct (4 women). *Students:* 43 full-time (42 women), 1 (woman) part-time; includes 17 minority (3 African Americans, 1 American Indian/Alaska Native, 8 Asian Americans or Pacific Islanders, 5 Hispanic Americans). Average age 32. 60 applicants, 47% accepted, 23 enrolled. In 2009, 23 master's awarded. *Degree requirements:* For master's, thesis, 840-hour internship. *Entrance requirements:* For master's, MAT, art portfolio, interview. Additional exam requirements/recommendations for international students: Required—TOEFL (minimum score 600 paper-based; 250 computer-based; 100 iBT). *Application deadline:* For fall admission, 1/4 priority date for domestic students. Application fee: $50. Electronic applications accepted. *Expenses:* Contact institution. *Financial support:* In 2009–10, 38 students received support, including 2 research assistantships (averaging $1,020 per year); career-related internships or fieldwork, institutionally sponsored loans, scholarships/grants, and unspecified assistantships also available. Financial award application deadline: 2/8; financial award applicants required to submit FAFSA. *Unit head:* Dr. Debra B. Linesch, Chair, 310-338-7674, Fax: 310-338-4518, E-mail: dlinesch@lmu.edu. *Application contact:* Chake H. Kouyoumjian, Associate Dean of the Graduate Division, 310-338-2721, Fax: 310-338-6086, E-mail: ckouyoum@lmu.edu.

Maryville University of Saint Louis, School of Health Professions, Program in Rehabilitation Counseling, St. Louis, MO 63141-7299. Offers marriage and family therapy (MARC); music therapy (MARC); rehabilitation counseling (CAGS); substance abuse (MARC). *Accreditation:* CORE. Part-time and evening/weekend programs available. *Students:* 16 full-time (12 women), 31 part-time (21 women); includes 7 African Americans, 1 Asian American or Pacific Islander, 2 Hispanic Americans. Average age 31. In 2009, 6 master's awarded. *Degree requirements:* For master's, internship, seminar. *Entrance requirements:* For master's, minimum cumulative GPA of 3.0, 2 letters of recommendation, interview. Additional exam requirements/recommendations for international students: Required—TOEFL (minimum score 550 paper-based). *Application deadline:* For fall admission, 1/15 for domestic students; for spring admission, 10/1 for domestic students. Application fee: $40 ($60 for international students). Electronic applications accepted. *Expenses:* Tuition: Full-time $20,384; part-time $627.50 per credit hour. Required fees: $100 per semester. *Financial support:* Career-related internships or fieldwork, Federal Work-Study, and campus employment available. Financial award application deadline: 3/1; financial award applicants required to submit FAFSA. *Unit head:* Barbara Parker, Director, 314-529-9437, Fax: 314-529-9495, E-mail: bparker@maryville.edu. *Application contact:* Barbara Parker, Director, 314-529-9437, Fax: 314-529-9495, E-mail: bparker@maryville.edu.

Mennonite Brethren Biblical Seminary, School of Theology, Program in Marriage, Family, and Child Counseling, Fresno, CA 93727-5097. Offers MAMFCC, Diploma. *Degree requirements:* For master's, thesis or alternative. *Entrance requirements:* For master's, GRE General Test, MAT. Additional exam requirements/recommendations for international students: Required—TOEFL (minimum score 550 paper-based; 213 computer-based).

Mercy College, School of Social and Behavioral Sciences, Program in Counseling, Dobbs Ferry, NY 10522-1189. Offers alcohol and substance abuse counseling (Certificate); counseling (MS); family counseling (Certificate). Part-time and evening/weekend programs available. Postbaccalaureate distance learning degree programs offered (no on-campus study). *Students:* 137 full-time (121 women), 213 part-time (185 women); includes 223 minority (89 African Americans, 3 American Indian/Alaska Native, 4 Asian Americans or Pacific Islanders, 127 Hispanic Americans), 1 international. Average age 35. 226 applicants, 53% accepted, 87 enrolled. In 2009, 92 master's, 14 other advanced degrees awarded. *Degree requirements:* For master's, comprehensive exam. *Entrance requirements:* For master's, interview, two professional letters of recommendation, minimum undergraduate GPA of 3.0, resume. Additional exam requirements/recommendations for international students: Required—TOEFL (minimum score 600 paper-based; 250 computer-based; 100 iBT). *Application deadline:* For fall admission, 8/1 for international students. Applications are processed on a rolling basis. Application fee: $40. Electronic applications accepted. *Expenses:* Tuition: Full-time $13,158; part-time $731 per credit. Required fees: $500. Tuition and fees vary according to degree level and program. *Financial support:* Career-related internships or fieldwork, Federal Work-Study, scholarships/grants, and unspecified assistantships available. Support available to part-time students. Financial award applicants required to submit FAFSA. *Faculty research:* Ethics, drug abuse problems, human development, domestic violence. *Unit head:* Dr. Arthur Mc Cann, Assistant Professor, Psychology and Behavioral Science, 914-674-7670, E-mail: amccann@mercy.edu. *Application contact:* Dr. Arthur Mc Cann, Assistant Professor, Psychology and Behavioral Science, 914-674-7670, E-mail: amccann@mercy.edu.

Mercy College, School of Social and Behavioral Sciences, Program in Marriage and Family Therapy, Dobbs Ferry, NY 10522-1189. Offers MS. Part-time and evening/weekend programs available. *Students:* 29 full-time (27 women), 42 part-time (35 women); includes 21 African Americans, 3 Asian Americans or Pacific Islanders, 8 Hispanic Americans, 2 international. Average age 34. 65 applicants, 25% accepted, 13 enrolled. In 2009, 15 master's awarded. *Entrance requirements:* For master's, current resume, interview with program director, written recommendations from 2 instructors. Additional exam requirements/recommendations for international students: Required—TOEFL (minimum score 600 paper-based; 250 computer-based; 100 iBT). *Application deadline:* For fall admission, 8/1 for international students. Applications are processed on a rolling basis. Application fee: $40. Electronic applications accepted. *Expenses:* Tuition: Full-time $13,158; part-time $731 per credit. Required fees: $500. Tuition and fees vary according to degree level and program. *Financial support:* Career-related internships or fieldwork, Federal Work-Study, scholarships/grants, and unspecified assistantships available. Support available to part-time students. Financial award applicants required to submit FAFSA. *Unit head:* Evan Imber-Black, Program Director, 914-674-7800, E-mail: eimberblack@mercy.edu. *Application contact:* Evan Imber-Black, Program Director, 914-674-7800, E-mail: eimberblack@mercy.edu.

Messiah College, Program in Counseling, Grantham, PA 17027. Offers counseling (CAGS); marriage, couple, and family counseling (MAC); mental health counseling (MAC); school counseling (MAC). Part-time programs available. *Entrance requirements:* For master's, minimum undergraduate cumulative GPA of 3.0, 2 recommendations, resume or curriculum vitae, interview; for CAGS, bachelor's degree, minimum undergraduate cumulative GPA of 3.0, essay, two recommendations, resume or curriculum vitae, interview. *Application deadline:* Applications are processed on a rolling basis. Application fee: $30. Electronic applications accepted. *Expenses:* Tuition: Part-time $518 per credit hour. *Financial support:* Applicants required to submit FAFSA. *Unit head:* Dr. John Addleman, Director, 717-796-1800 Ext. 2980, Fax: 717-691-2386, E-mail: jaddlemn@messiah.edu. *Application contact:* Dr. John Addleman, Director, 717-796-1800 Ext. 2980, Fax: 717-691-2386, E-mail: jaddlemn@messiah.edu.

Michigan State University, The Graduate School, College of Social Science, Department of Family and Child Ecology, East Lansing, MI 48824. Offers child development (MA); community services (MS); family and child ecology (PhD); family studies (MA); marriage and family therapy (MA); youth development (MA). *Accreditation:* AAMFT/COAMFTE (one or more programs are accredited). *Faculty:* 19 full-time (14 women). *Students:* 64 full-time (54 women), 56 part-time (49 women); includes 18 minority (9 African Americans, 1 American Indian/Alaska Native, 5 Asian Americans or Pacific Islanders, 3 Hispanic Americans), 16 international. Average age 33. 52 applicants, 50% accepted. In 2009, 28 master's, 11 doctorates awarded. *Entrance requirements:* For master's, GRE General Test, minimum GPA of 3.0 in last 2 years of undergraduate course work, 3 letters of recommendation; for doctorate, GRE General Test, minimum GPA of 3.0, 3 letters of recommendation, background in behavioral sciences. Additional exam requirements/recommendations for international students: Required—TOEFL. Electronic applications accepted. *Expenses:* Tuition, state resident: part-time $478.25 per credit hour. Tuition, nonresident: part-time $966.50 per credit hour. Part-time tuition and fees vary according to program. *Financial support:* In 2009–10, 18 research assistantships with tuition reimbursements (averaging $6,363 per year), 10 teaching assistantships with tuition reimbursements (averaging $6,308 per year) were awarded. Total annual research expenditures: $216,042. *Unit head:* Dr. Karen Wampler, Chairperson, 517-355-7680, Fax: 517-432-2953, E-mail:

Marriage and Family Therapy

Michigan State University (continued)
kwampler@msu.edu. *Application contact:* Ruth Sedelmaier, Graduate Program Secretary, 517-353-5248, Fax: 517-432-3320, E-mail: sedelmai@msu.edu.

Mid-America Christian University, Program in Counseling, Oklahoma City, OK 73170-4504. Offers marital and family therapy (MS); pastoral/spiritual direction (MS); professional counselor (MS). *Entrance requirements:* For master's, MAT, bachelor's degree from a regionally accredited college or university, minimum overall cumulative GPA of 2.75 of bachelor course work. Additional exam requirements/recommendations for international students: Required—TOEFL (minimum score 550 paper-based; 213 computer-based).

Minnesota State University Mankato, College of Graduate Studies, College of Education, Department of Counseling and Student Personnel, Mankato, MN 56001. Offers college student affairs (MS); counselor education and supervision (Ed D); marriage and family counseling (Certificate); professional community counseling (MS); professional school counseling (MS). *Accreditation:* ACA (one or more programs are accredited); NCATE. *Students:* 67 full-time (57 women), 41 part-time (32 women). *Degree requirements:* For master's, comprehensive exam, thesis or alternative. *Entrance requirements:* For master's, GRE General Test or MAT (if GPA less than 3.0 for last 2 years), minimum GPA of 3.0 during previous 2 years, 3 letters of reference. Additional exam requirements/recommendations for international students: Required—TOEFL. *Application deadline:* For fall admission, 1/15 priority date for domestic students. Applications are processed on a rolling basis. Application fee: $40. Electronic applications accepted. *Expenses:* Tuition, state resident: full-time $5364. Tuition, nonresident: full-time $8314. *Financial support:* Research assistantships with full tuition reimbursements, teaching assistantships with full tuition reimbursements, career-related internships or fieldwork, Federal Work-Study, institutionally sponsored loans, and unspecified assistantships available. Support available to part-time students. Financial award application deadline: 3/15; financial award applicants required to submit FAFSA. *Unit head:* Dr. Jacqueline Lewis, Chairperson, 507-389-5658. *Application contact:* 507-389-2321, E-mail: grad@mnsu.edu.

Mississippi College, Graduate School, School of Education, Department of Psychology and Counseling, Clinton, MS 39058. Offers counseling (Ed S); marriage and family counseling (MS); mental health counseling (MS); school counseling (M Ed). Part-time programs available. *Faculty:* 8 full-time (3 women), 5 part-time/adjunct (2 women). *Students:* 60 full-time (54 women), 70 part-time (63 women); includes 64 minority (63 African Americans, 1 American Indian/Alaska Native), 3 international. Average age 31. In 2009, 38 master's awarded. *Degree requirements:* For master's and Ed S, comprehensive exam, thesis optional. *Entrance requirements:* For master's, GRE or NTE. Additional exam requirements/recommendations for international students: Recommended—IELTS. *Application deadline:* For fall admission, 6/1 for domestic students; for spring admission, 9/1 for domestic students. Application fee: $30. Electronic applications accepted. *Expenses:* Tuition: Part-time $452 per credit hour. Required fees: $101 per semester. Tuition and fees vary according to degree level, campus/location, program and student level. *Financial support:* Career-related internships or fieldwork, Federal Work-Study, and unspecified assistantships available. Support available to part-time students. Financial award applicants required to submit FAFSA. *Unit head:* Dr. Buddy Wagner, Interim Chair, 601-925-3354, E-mail: bwagner@mc.edu. *Application contact:* Elnora Lewis, Secretary, 601-925-3225, Fax: 601-925-3889, E-mail: lewis09@mc.edu.

Montclair State University, The Graduate School, College of Humanities and Social Sciences, Center for Child Advocacy, Montclair, NJ 07043-1624. Offers child advocacy (MA, Certificate); public child welfare (MA). Part-time and evening/weekend programs available. Postbaccalaureate distance learning degree programs offered. *Faculty:* 3 full-time (all women). *Students:* 6 full-time (all women), 121 part-time (108 women). Average age 33. 47 applicants, 85% accepted, 37 enrolled. In 2009, 14 master's, 26 other advanced degrees awarded. *Degree requirements:* For master's, comprehensive exam (for some programs), thesis (for some programs). *Entrance requirements:* For master's, GRE, 2 letters of recommendation. Additional exam requirements/recommendations for international students: Required—TOEFL (minimum score 83 computer-based), or IELTS. Application fee: $60. *Expenses:* Tuition, area resident: Part-time $486.74 per credit. Tuition, state resident: part-time $486.74 per credit. Tuition, nonresident: part-time $751.34 per credit. Tuition and fees vary according to degree level and program. *Financial support:* In 2009–10, 3 research assistantships with full tuition reimbursements (averaging $7,000 per year) were awarded; Federal Work-Study, scholarships/grants, and unspecified assistantships also available. Support available to part-time students. Financial award application deadline: 3/1; financial award applicants required to submit FAFSA. *Unit head:* Dr. Robert McCormick, Head, 973-655-4188. *Application contact:* Amy Aiello, Director of Graduate Admissions and Operations, 973-655-5147, Fax: 973-655-7869, E-mail: graduate.school@montclair.edu.

Montclair State University, The Graduate School, College of Humanities and Social Sciences, Department of Psychology, Montclair, NJ 07043-1624. Offers educational psychology (MA), including child/adolescent clinical psychology, clinical psychology for Spanish/English bilinguals; psychology (MA, Certificate), including industrial and organizational psychology (MA); school psychologist (Certificate). Part-time and evening/weekend programs available. *Faculty:* 29 full-time (14 women), 26 part-time/adjunct (14 women). *Students:* 37 full-time (27 women), 33 part-time (23 women). Average age 27. 72 applicants, 47% accepted, 20 enrolled. In 2009, 7 master's awarded. *Degree requirements:* For master's, comprehensive exam, thesis or alternative. *Entrance requirements:* For master's, GRE General Test, 2 letters of recommendation. Additional exam requirements/recommendations for international students: Required—TOEFL (minimum score 83 computer-based), or IELTS. *Application deadline:* For fall admission, 2/1 for domestic and international students; for spring admission, 10/1 for domestic and international students. Applications are processed on a rolling basis. Application fee: $60. Electronic applications accepted. *Expenses:* Tuition, area resident: Part-time $486.74 per credit. Tuition, state resident: part-time $486.74 per credit. Tuition, nonresident: part-time $751.34 per credit. Tuition and fees vary according to degree level and program. *Financial support:* In 2009–10, 17 research assistantships with full tuition reimbursements (averaging $7,000 per year) were awarded; Federal Work-Study, scholarships/grants, and unspecified assistantships also available. Support available to part-time students. Financial award application deadline: 3/1; financial award applicants required to submit FAFSA. *Faculty research:* Engaged learning, academic and civic development. Total annual research expenditures: $10,000. *Unit head:* Dr. Peter Vietze, Chairperson, 973-655-5201. *Application contact:* Amy Aiello, Director of Admissions and Operations, 973-655-5147, Fax: 973-655-7869, E-mail: graduate.school@montclair.edu.

Mount St. Mary's College, Graduate Division, Program in Counseling Psychology, Los Angeles, CA 90049-1599. Offers counseling psychology (MS); marriage and family therapy (MS); psychology (MS). Part-time and evening/weekend programs available. *Faculty:* 3 full-time (2 women), 6 part-time/adjunct (5 women). *Students:* 43 full-time (38 women), 4 part-time (3 women); includes 10 minority (1 African American, 2 Asian Americans or Pacific Islanders, 7 Hispanic Americans). Average age 31. In 2009, 12 master's awarded. *Degree requirements:* For master's, research project. *Entrance requirements:* For master's, minimum GPA of 3.0. *Application deadline:* For fall admission, 7/15 for domestic students; for spring admission, 11/15 for domestic students. *Expenses:* Tuition: Part-time $730 per unit. Part-time tuition and fees vary according to degree level and program. *Financial support:* Institutionally sponsored loans and tuition waivers (partial) available. Support available to part-time students. Financial award application deadline: 3/15; financial award applicants required to submit FAFSA. *Unit head:* Dr. Gregory Travis, Director, Graduate Psychology, 213-477-2654, E-mail: gtravis@msmc.la.edu. *Application contact:* Director of Graduate Admission.

Northcentral University, Graduate Studies, Prescott Valley, AZ 86314. Offers business (MBA, DBA, PhD, CAGS); education (M Ed, Ed D, PhD, CAGS); marriage and family therapy (MA, PhD); psychology (MA, PhD, CAGS). Evening/weekend programs available. Postbaccalaureate distance learning degree programs offered (no on-campus study). *Students:* 8,148 full-time (4,063 women); includes 984 minority (646 African Americans, 54 American Indian/Alaska Native, 125 Asian Americans or Pacific Islanders, 159 Hispanic Americans). Average age 43. In 2009, 271 master's, 189 doctorates, 13 other advanced degrees awarded. *Entrance requirements:* For master's, Bachelor's degree from regionally accredited institution & current resume; for doctorate and CAGS, A conferred master's from a regionally accredited university. Additional exam requirements/recommendations for international students: Required—TOEFL (minimum score 95 computer-based), IELTS (minimum score 7), Pearson Test of English (minimum score 65). *Application deadline:* Applications are processed on a rolling basis. Application fee: $75. *Expenses:* Tuition: Part-time $560 per credit. Part-time tuition and fees vary according to degree level and program. *Financial support:* Scholarships/grants available. *Unit head:* Dr. Barnaby Barratt, Provost and Professor of Psychology, 888-327-2877, Fax: 928-759-6381, E-mail: bbarratt@ncu.edu. *Application contact:* Kevin Lustig, Director of Admissions, 480-478-7490, Fax: 928-759-6285, E-mail: klustig@ncu.edu.

North Dakota State University, College of Graduate and Interdisciplinary Studies, College of Human Development and Education, Department of Child Development and Family Science, Fargo, ND 58108. Offers child development and family science (MS); couple and family therapy (MS); family financial planning (MS); gerontology (MS, PhD). *Accreditation:* AAMFT/COAMFTE. Part-time and evening/weekend programs available. Postbaccalaureate distance learning degree programs offered (no on-campus study). *Faculty:* 12 full-time (7 women). *Students:* 26 full-time (25 women), 21 part-time (18 women); includes 1 African American, 2 international. 22 applicants, 64% accepted, 12 enrolled. In 2009, 12 master's awarded. *Degree requirements:* For master's, thesis or alternative; for doctorate, thesis/dissertation. *Entrance requirements:* Additional exam requirements/recommendations for international students: Required—TOEFL (minimum score 525 paper-based; 197 computer-based; 71 iBT). *Application deadline:* For fall admission, 2/1 for domestic and international students; for spring admission, 10/1 for domestic and international students. Application fee: $45 ($60 for international students). *Financial support:* In 2009–10, 17 students received support, including research assistantships with full tuition reimbursements available (averaging $3,000 per year), 17 teaching assistantships with full tuition reimbursements available (averaging $3,000 per year); career-related internships or fieldwork, Federal Work-Study, institutionally sponsored loans, and tuition waivers (full) also available. Financial award application deadline: 4/1. *Faculty research:* Family therapy, resilience, parenting, adolescent development, mental health. Total annual research expenditures: $333,582. *Unit head:* Dr. James Deal, Head, 701-231-7568, Fax: 701-231-9645, E-mail: jim_deal@ndsu.edu. *Application contact:* Theresa Anderson, Administrative Assistant, 701-231-8628, Fax: 701-231-9645, E-mail: theresa.anderson@ndsu.edu.

Northern Kentucky University, Office of Graduate Programs, College of Informatics, Program in Communication, Highland Heights, KY 41099. Offers communication (MA); communication teaching (Certificate); documentary studies (Certificate); public relations (Certificate); relationships (Certificate). Part-time and evening/weekend programs available. *Students:* 9 full-time (8 women), 42 part-time (32 women); includes 5 minority (4 African Americans, 1 Asian American or Pacific Islander), 1 international. Average age 31. 48 applicants, 63% accepted, 23 enrolled. In 2009, 20 master's awarded. *Degree requirements:* For master's, thesis (for some programs), capstone experience, internship. *Entrance requirements:* For master's, GRE, minimum GPA of 3.0, 3 letters of recommendation. Additional exam requirements/recommendations for international students: Required—TOEFL (minimum score 550 paper-based; 213 computer-based; 79 iBT); Recommended—IELTS (minimum score 6.5). *Application deadline:* For fall admission, 2/1 priority date for domestic students, 6/1 for international students; for spring admission, 7/1 priority date for domestic students, 10/1 for international students. Applications are processed on a rolling basis. Application fee: $40. Electronic applications accepted. *Expenses:* Tuition, state resident: full-time $6912; part-time $384 per credit hour. Tuition, nonresident: full-time $12,150; part-time $675 per credit hour. Tuition and fees vary according to course load, program and reciprocity agreements. *Financial support:* Unspecified assistantships available. Financial award applicants required to submit FAFSA. *Faculty research:* Business/organizational communication, interpersonal/relational communication, public relations, communication teaching/pedagogy, media (production, criticism, popular culture). Total annual research expenditures: $29,000. *Unit head:* Dr. Jimmy Manning, Graduate Program Director, 859-572-1329, E-mail: manningj1@nku.edu. *Application contact:* Dr. Peg Griffin, Director of Graduate Programs, 859-572-6934, Fax: 859-572-6670, E-mail: griffinp@nku.edu.

Northwestern University, The Graduate School, Program in Marital and Family Therapy, Evanston, IL 60208. Offers MS. *Accreditation:* AAMFT/COAMFTE. *Entrance requirements:* For master's, GRE General Test. *Faculty research:* Marital and family therapy training, gender, psychotherapy outcome, adolescents and pre-school children at risk, families.

Northwest Nazarene University, Graduate Studies, Program in Counselor Education, Nampa, ID 83686-5897. Offers community counseling (MS); marriage and family counseling (MS); school counseling (MS).

Notre Dame de Namur University, Division of Academic Affairs, College of Arts and Sciences, Department of Art Therapy Psychology, Belmont, CA 94002-1908. Offers art therapy (MA); marriage and family therapy (MA). Part-time programs available. *Faculty:* 2 full-time (1 woman), 8 part-time/adjunct (7 women). *Students:* 38 full-time (all women), 56 part-time (54 women); includes 17 minority (1 African American, 11 Asian Americans or Pacific Islanders, 5 Hispanic Americans). Average age 34. 33 applicants, 94% accepted, 22 enrolled. In 2009, 26 master's awarded. *Degree requirements:* For master's, thesis, oral presentation, portfolio. *Entrance requirements:* For master's, interview, minimum GPA of 2.5. Additional exam requirements/recommendations for international students: Required—TOEFL (minimum score 550 paper-based; 213 computer-based; 79 iBT). *Application deadline:* For fall admission, 8/1 priority date for domestic students; for spring admission, 12/1 priority date for domestic students. Applications are processed on a rolling basis. Application fee: $60. Electronic applications accepted. *Expenses:* Tuition: Part-time $720 per credit. Required fees: $35 per semester hour. *Financial support:* Career-related internships or fieldwork available. Support available to part-time students. Financial award applicants required to submit FAFSA. *Unit head:* Dr. Richard Carolan, Chair, 650-508-3556, Fax: 650-508-3736. *Application contact:* Candace Hallmark, Associate Director of Admissions, 650-508-3592, Fax: 650-508-3426, E-mail: grad.admit@ndnu.edu.

Notre Dame de Namur University, Division of Academic Affairs, College of Arts and Sciences, Department of Clinical Psychology and Gerontology, Program in Clinical Psychology: Marital and Family Therapy, Belmont, CA 94002-1908. Offers MS. *Entrance requirements:* Additional exam requirements/recommendations for international students: Required—TOEFL (minimum score 550 paper-based; 213 computer-based; 79 iBT). Application fee: $60. *Expenses:* Tuition: Part-time $720 per credit. Required fees: $35 per semester hour. *Unit head:* Dr. Nusha Askari, 650-508-3728, E-mail: naskari@ndnu.edu. *Application contact:* Candace Hallmark, Associate Director of Admissions, 650-508-3592, Fax: 650-508-3426, E-mail: grad.admit@ndnu.edu.

Nova Southeastern University, Graduate School of Humanities and Social Sciences, Department of Family Therapy, Doctor of Marriage and Family Therapy Program, Fort Lauderdale, FL 33314-7796. Offers DMFT. Part-time programs available. *Faculty:* 10 full-time (5 women), 16 part-time/adjunct (13 women). *Students:* 6 full-time (all women), 7 part-time (6 women); includes 5 minority (3 African Americans, 2 Hispanic Americans), 1 international. 12 applicants, 58% accepted, 5 enrolled. In 2009, 1 doctorate awarded. *Degree requirements:* For doctorate, thesis/dissertation or alternative, qualifying exams, portfolio. *Entrance requirements:* For doctorate, minimum GPA of 3.0, interview, master's degree in related field, samples of written work. Additional exam requirements/recommendations for international students: Required—TOEFL. *Application deadline:* For fall admission, 7/1 priority date for domestic and international students; for winter admission, 11/1 priority date for domestic and international students; for spring admission, 3/1 priority date for domestic and international students. Applications are processed on a rolling basis. Application fee: $50. Electronic applications accepted. *Financial support:* In 2009–10, 1 research assistantship (averaging $15,000 per year) was awarded; career-related internships or fieldwork, Federal Work-Study, scholarships/

grants, and unspecified assistantships also available. Financial award applicants required to submit CSS PROFILE. *Faculty research:* Diversity, family business, brief therapy, medical family therapy, human sexuality, family therapy in schools. *Unit head:* Tommie Boyd, Chair, 954-262-3027, Fax: 954-262-3968, E-mail: tommie@nova.edu. *Application contact:* Marcia Arango, Student Recruitment Coordinator, 954-262-3006, Fax: 954-262-3968, E-mail: marango@nsu.nova.edu.

Nova Southeastern University, Graduate School of Humanities and Social Sciences, Department of Family Therapy, Master's Program in Family Therapy, Fort Lauderdale, FL 33314-7796. Offers family studies (Certificate); family systems healthcare (Certificate); family therapy (MS). *Accreditation:* AAMFT/COAMFTE (one or more programs are accredited). Part-time programs available. *Faculty:* 11 full-time (6 women), 16 part-time/adjunct (13 women). *Students:* 80 full-time (68 women), 59 part-time (53 women); includes 60 minority (30 African Americans, 3 Asian Americans or Pacific Islanders, 27 Hispanic Americans), 9 international. 142 applicants, 42% accepted, 51 enrolled. In 2009, 57 master's awarded. *Degree requirements:* For master's, comprehensive exam. *Entrance requirements:* For master's, minimum GPA of 3.0, interview, writing sample. Additional exam requirements/recommendations for international students: Required—TOEFL. *Application deadline:* For fall admission, 6/1 priority date for domestic students; for winter admission, 11/1 priority date for domestic students; for spring admission, 3/1 priority date for domestic students. Applications are processed on a rolling basis. Application fee: $50. Electronic applications accepted. *Financial support:* Career-related internships or fieldwork, Federal Work-Study, and scholarships/grants available. Financial award application deadline: 4/1; financial award applicants required to submit CSS PROFILE. *Faculty research:* Cross-cultural counseling, family business, medical family therapy, brief therapy, diversity, family therapy in schools. *Unit head:* Tommie Boyd, Chair, 954-262-3027, Fax: 954-262-3968, E-mail: tommie@nova.edu. *Application contact:* Marcia Arango, Student Recruitment Coordinator, 954-262-3006, Fax: 954-262-3968, E-mail: marango@nsu.nova.edu.

Nova Southeastern University, Graduate School of Humanities and Social Sciences, Department of Family Therapy, PhD Program in Family Therapy, Fort Lauderdale, FL 33314-7796. Offers PhD. *Accreditation:* AAMFT/COAMFTE. Part-time programs available. *Faculty:* 10 full-time (5 women), 16 part-time/adjunct (13 women). *Students:* 71 full-time (60 women), 30 part-time (28 women); includes 41 minority (32 African Americans, 1 Asian American or Pacific Islander, 8 Hispanic Americans), 9 international. 32 applicants, 63% accepted, 17 enrolled. In 2009, 7 doctorates awarded. *Degree requirements:* For doctorate, thesis/dissertation, qualifying exams. *Entrance requirements:* For doctorate, master's degree in related field, minimum GPA of 3.0, interview, writing sample. Additional exam requirements/recommendations for international students: Required—TOEFL. *Application deadline:* For fall admission, 7/1 priority date for domestic and international students; for winter admission, 11/1 priority date for domestic and international students; for spring admission, 3/1 priority date for domestic and international students. Applications are processed on a rolling basis. Application fee: $50. Electronic applications accepted. *Financial support:* In 2009–10, 63 students received support, including 3 research assistantships (averaging $10,000 per year); career-related internships or fieldwork, Federal Work-Study, scholarships/grants, and unspecified assistantships also available. Financial award application deadline: 4/1. *Faculty research:* Medical family therapy, brief therapy, family business, diversity, human sexuality and therapy, family therapy in schools. *Unit head:* Tommie Boyd, Chair, 954-262-3027, Fax: 954-262-3968, E-mail: tommie@nova.edu. *Application contact:* Marcia Arango, Student Recruitment Coordinator, 954-262-3006, Fax: 954-262-3968, E-mail: marango@nsu.nova.edu.

Oral Roberts University, School of Theology and Missions, Tulsa, OK 74171. Offers biblical literature (MA), including advanced languages, Judaic-Christian studies; Christian counseling (MA), including marriage and family therapy; divinity (M Div); missions (MA); practical theology (MA); theological/historical studies (MA); theology (D Min). *Accreditation:* ATS; NASM. Part-time programs available. Postbaccalaureate distance learning degree programs offered (minimal on-campus study). *Degree requirements:* For master's, thesis (for some programs), practicum/internship; for doctorate, thesis/dissertation, applied research project; for M Div, one foreign language, field experience. *Entrance requirements:* For M Div and master's, GRE General Test or MAT, minimum GPA of 2.5; for doctorate, M Div, minimum GPA of 3.0, 3 years of full-time ministry experience. Additional exam requirements/recommendations for international students: Required—TOEFL (minimum score 550 paper-based; 213 computer-based; 79 iBT). Electronic applications accepted.

Ottawa University, Graduate Studies-Arizona, Program in Professional Counseling, Ottawa, KS 66067-3399. Offers Christian counseling (MA); expressive arts therapy (MA); marriage and family therapy (MA); treatment of trauma, abuse and deprivation (MA). Programs offered in Mesa, Phoenix, Tempe and West Valley, AZ. Part-time and evening/weekend programs available. Postbaccalaureate distance learning degree programs offered. *Degree requirements:* For master's, comprehensive exam, thesis or alternative, field experience, practicum. *Entrance requirements:* For master's, minimum undergraduate GPA of 3.0; course work in theories of personality, abnormal psychology, and human growth and development. Additional exam requirements/recommendations for international students: Required—TOEFL (minimum score 550 paper-based; 213 computer-based).

Our Lady of Holy Cross College, Program in Education and Counseling, New Orleans, LA 70131-7399. Offers administration and supervision (M Ed); curriculum and instruction (M Ed); marriage and family counseling (MA); school counseling (M Ed, MA). *Accreditation:* ACA; NCATE. Part-time and evening/weekend programs available. *Degree requirements:* For master's, thesis. *Entrance requirements:* For master's, GRE General Test, minimum GPA of 2.7.

Our Lady of the Lake University of San Antonio, School of Professional Studies, Program in Psychology, San Antonio, TX 78207-4689. Offers counseling psychology (MS, Psy D); marriage and family therapy (MS); school psychology (MS). *Accreditation:* APA (one or more programs are accredited). Part-time and evening/weekend programs available. *Students:* 111 full-time (90 women), 84 part-time (75 women); includes 118 minority (19 African Americans, 1 American Indian/Alaska Native, 4 Asian Americans or Pacific Islanders, 94 Hispanic Americans), 5 international. Average age 30. In 2009, 42 master's, 3 doctorates awarded. *Degree requirements:* For master's, comprehensive exam, thesis optional, practicum; for doctorate, thesis/dissertation, internship, qualifying exam. *Entrance requirements:* For master's and doctorate, GRE General Test or MAT, interview. Additional exam requirements/recommendations for international students: Required—TOEFL. *Application deadline:* For fall admission, 3/1 priority date for domestic and international students. Applications are processed on a rolling basis. Application fee: $25 ($50 for international students). Electronic applications accepted. *Expenses:* Tuition: Full-time $12,330; part-time $685 per contact hour. Required fees: $139; $12 per contact hour. $57 per semester. Tuition and fees vary according to campus/location. *Financial support:* Research assistantships, teaching assistantships, career-related internships or fieldwork available. Support available to part-time students. Financial award application deadline: 4/15. *Faculty research:* Marriage and family therapy, supervision, cross-cultural counseling, violence. *Unit head:* Dr. Joan Biever, Chair, 210-434-6711, E-mail: jbiever@lake.ollusa.edu. *Application contact:* 210-434-6711, Fax: 210-431-4036, E-mail: gradadm@lake.ollusa.edu.

Pacific Lutheran University, Division of Graduate Studies, Division of Social Sciences, Program in Marriage and Family Therapy, Tacoma, WA 98447. Offers MA. *Accreditation:* AAMFT/COAMFTE. *Faculty:* 3 full-time (2 women), 5 part-time/adjunct (3 women). *Students:* 39 full-time (36 women), 9 part-time (6 women); includes 7 minority (1 African American, 3 Asian Americans or Pacific Islanders, 3 Hispanic Americans). Average age 28. In 2009, 20 master's awarded. *Degree requirements:* For master's, thesis optional, clinical competency. *Entrance requirements:* For master's, GRE, interview (selected applicants). Additional exam requirements/recommendations for international students: Required—TOEFL (minimum score 550 paper-based; 213 computer-based). *Application deadline:* For fall admission, 1/31 priority date for domestic and international students; for spring admission, 3/1 priority date for domestic students. Application fee: $40. Electronic applications accepted. *Financial support:* Fellowships, Federal Work-Study, scholarships/grants, and unspecified assistantships available. Financial award application deadline: 3/1; financial award applicants required to submit FAFSA. *Unit head:* Dr. Charles York, Chair, 253-535-7747, Fax: 253-536-5139, E-mail: yorkcd@plu.edu. *Application contact:* Linda DuBay, Senior Office Assistant, 253-535-7151, Fax: 253-536-5136, E-mail: admissions@plu.edu.

Pacific Oaks College, Graduate School, Program in Marriage and Family Therapy, Pasadena, CA 91103. Offers marriage, family and child counseling (MA). Part-time and evening/weekend programs available. *Degree requirements:* For master's, thesis. *Entrance requirements:* For master's, interview. Additional exam requirements/recommendations for international students: Required—TOEFL (minimum score 550 paper-based; 213 computer-based). *Faculty research:* Family systems, cross-cultural development, therapeutic intervention and Latino families, battered women.

Palm Beach Atlantic University, School of Education and Behavioral Studies, West Palm Beach, FL 33416-4708. Offers counseling psychology (MSCP), including addictions/mental health, marriage and family therapy, mental health counseling, school guidance counseling. Part-time and evening/weekend programs available. *Faculty:* 16 full-time (8 women), 2 part-time/adjunct (0 women). *Students:* 230 full-time (193 women), 74 part-time (63 women); includes 109 minority (70 African Americans, 1 Asian American or Pacific Islander, 38 Hispanic Americans), 8 international. Average age 35. 136 applicants, 70% accepted, 88 enrolled. In 2009, 86 master's awarded. *Entrance requirements:* For master's, GRE, minimum GPA of 3.0. Additional exam requirements/recommendations for international students: Required—TOEFL (minimum score 550 paper-based; 213 computer-based). *Application deadline:* For fall admission, 7/15 priority date for domestic students; for spring admission, 11/15 priority date for domestic students. Applications are processed on a rolling basis. Application fee: $45. Electronic applications accepted. *Expenses:* Tuition: Full-time $8010; part-time $445 per credit hour. Required fees: $99 per semester. Tuition and fees vary according to course load and degree level. *Financial support:* Applicants required to submit FAFSA. *Unit head:* Dr. Lisa Stubbs, Program Director, 561-803-2286. *Application contact:* Graduate Admissions, 888-468-6722, Fax: 561-803-2115, E-mail: grad@pba.edu.

Pepperdine University, Graduate School of Education and Psychology, Division of Psychology, Program in Clinical Psychology, Malibu, CA 90263. Offers clinical psychology (Psy D); clinical psychology (daytime) (MA), including marriage and family therapy; clinical psychology (evening) (MA), including marriage and family therapy. *Accreditation:* APA. Part-time and evening/weekend programs available. *Entrance requirements:* For master's, GRE General Test, bachelor's degree in psychology or related field. Additional exam requirements/recommendations for international students: Required—TOEFL. *Expenses:* Tuition: Full-time $37,516; part-time $1310 per unit. Required fees: $80.

Phillips Graduate Institute, Program in Clinical Family Psychology and Organizational Consulting, Encino, CA 91316-1509. Offers clinical psychology (Psy D); organizational consulting (Psy D). Evening/weekend programs available. *Degree requirements:* For doctorate, thesis/dissertation. *Entrance requirements:* For doctorate, minimum GPA of 3.0, interview.

Phillips Graduate Institute, Programs in Marriage and Family Therapy, School Counseling and School Psychology, Encino, CA 91316-1509. Offers marital and family therapy (MA); organizational consulting (MA); school counseling (MA). Evening/weekend programs available. *Degree requirements:* For master's, comprehensive exam, thesis. *Entrance requirements:* For master's, minimum GPA of 2.5. *Faculty research:* Integration of interpersonal psychological theory, systems approach, firsthand experiential learning.

Purdue University, Graduate School, College of Consumer and Family Sciences, Department of Child Development and Family Studies, West Lafayette, IN 47907. Offers developmental studies (MS, PhD); family studies (MS, PhD); marriage and family therapy (MS, PhD). *Accreditation:* AAMFT/COAMFTE (one or more programs are accredited). Part-time programs available. Terminal master's awarded for partial completion of doctoral program. *Degree requirements:* For master's, thesis; for doctorate, thesis/dissertation. *Entrance requirements:* For master's and doctorate, GRE General Test. Additional exam requirements/recommendations for international students: Required—TWE. Electronic applications accepted. *Faculty research:* Inclusion of children with special needs, families as learning environments, relationships in child care, work-family relations, AIDS prevention.

Purdue University Calumet, Graduate School, School of Liberal Arts and Social Sciences, Department of Behavioral Sciences, Hammond, IN 46323-2094. Offers marriage and family therapy (MS). *Accreditation:* AAMFT/COAMFTE. Part-time programs available. *Degree requirements:* For master's, thesis. *Entrance requirements:* For master's, GRE, interview. Additional exam requirements/recommendations for international students: Required—TOEFL. *Faculty research:* Substance abuse, sexual abuse, couple therapy, professional issues, adolescent therapy.

Reformed Theological Seminary–Jackson Campus, Graduate and Professional Programs, Jackson, MS 39209-3099. Offers Bible, theology, and missions (Certificate); biblical studies (MA); Christian education (M Div, MA); counseling (M Div); divinity (M Div, Diploma); marriage and family therapy (MA); ministry (D Min); missions (M Div, MA, D Min); New Testament (Th M); Old Testament (Th M); theological studies (MA); theology (Th M); M Div/MA. *Accreditation:* AAMFT/COAMFTE (one or more programs are accredited); ATS (one or more programs are accredited). *Degree requirements:* For master's, thesis (for some programs), fieldwork; for doctorate, 2 foreign languages, thesis/dissertation; for M Div, 2 foreign languages, thesis/dissertation (for some programs). *Entrance requirements:* For M Div and master's, minimum GPA of 2.6; for doctorate, minimum GPA of 3.0. Additional exam requirements/recommendations for international students: Required—TOEFL.

Regis University, College for Professional Studies, Graduate Counseling Program, Denver, CO 80221-1099. Offers community counseling (MAC); counseling children and adolescents (Post-Graduate Certificate); marriage and family therapy (Post-Graduate Certificate). Program offered in Henderson and Las Vegas (Summerlin), NV. *Accreditation:* ACA. Part-time and evening/weekend programs available. *Degree requirements:* For master's, internships, practicum. *Entrance requirements:* For master's, interview, 2 recommendations, resume, criminal background check. Additional exam requirements/recommendations for international students: Required—TOEFL (minimum score 213 computer-based), TWE (minimum score 5). *Expenses:* Contact institution. *Faculty research:* Group Development, Counselor Education, Counsel and Therapy, Influence of Technology on Psychology, Dream finding groups, Adult Development, Depression.

Richmont Graduate University, Graduate Programs, Atlanta, GA 30327. Offers Christian psychological studies (MS); marriage and family therapy (MA); professional counseling (MA).

St. Cloud State University, School of Graduate Studies, College of Education, Department of Educational Leadership and Community Psychology, Program in Marriage and Family Therapy, St. Cloud, MN 56301-4498. Offers MS. *Faculty:* 2 full-time (1 woman). *Students:* 35 full-time (30 women), 6 part-time (all women); includes 5 minority (1 American Indian/Alaska Native, 2 Asian Americans or Pacific Islanders, 2 Hispanic Americans), 1 international. 38 applicants, 45% accepted. In 2009, 10 master's awarded. *Entrance requirements:* Additional exam requirements/recommendations for international students: Required—Michigan English Language Assessment Battery; Recommended—TOEFL (minimum score 550 paper-based; 213 computer-based), IELTS (minimum score 6.5). Electronic applications accepted. *Financial support:* Federal Work-Study, scholarships/grants, and unspecified assistantships available. *Unit head:* Dr. Manijeh Daneshpour, Coordinator, 320-308-0121. *Application contact:* Linda Lou Krueger, School of Graduate Studies, 320-308-2113, Fax: 320-308-5371, E-mail: lekrueger@stcloudstate.edu.

Saint Joseph College, Department of Marriage and Family Therapy, West Hartford, CT 06117-2700. Offers marriage and family therapy (MA). *Accreditation:* AAMFT/COAMFTE.

Marriage and Family Therapy

Saint Joseph College (continued)
Part-time and evening/weekend programs available. *Students:* 12 full-time (11 women), 36 part-time (32 women); includes 13 minority (8 African Americans, 1 Asian American or Pacific Islander, 4 Hispanic Americans). *Degree requirements:* For master's, comprehensive exam, thesis or alternative. *Entrance requirements:* For master's, 2 letters of recommendation. *Application deadline:* Applications are processed on a rolling basis. Application fee: $50. Electronic applications accepted. *Expenses:* Tuition: Part-time $595 per credit. Required fees: $30 per credit. Tuition and fees vary according to program. *Financial support:* Career-related internships or fieldwork and unspecified assistantships available. Support available to part-time students. Financial award applicants required to submit FAFSA. *Application contact:* Graduate Admissions Office, 860-231-5261, E-mail: graduate@sjc.edu.

Saint Louis University, Graduate School, College of Education and Public Service and Graduate School, Department of Counseling and Family Therapy, St. Louis, MO 63103-2097. Offers counseling and family therapy (PhD); human development counseling (MA); marriage and family therapy (Certificate); school counseling (MA, MA-R). *Accreditation:* AAMFT; NCATE. Part-time programs available. *Degree requirements:* For master's, comprehensive exam, thesis (for some programs); for doctorate, comprehensive exam, thesis/dissertation, preliminary oral and written exams. *Entrance requirements:* For master's, GRE General Test, letters of recommendation, resume; for doctorate, GRE General Test, letters of recommendation, resumé, transcripts, goal statement. Additional exam requirements/recommendations for international students: Required—TOEFL (minimum score 550 paper-based; 213 computer-based). Electronic applications accepted. *Faculty research:* Medical family therapy/collaborative health care multicultural counseling, mental health needs of diverse, minority, or Immigrant/refugee populations, divorce, aging families.

Saint Mary's College of California, Kalmanovitz School of Education, Program in Counseling, Moraga, CA 94556. Offers general counseling (MA); marital and family therapy (MA); school counseling (MA). Part-time and evening/weekend programs available. *Faculty:* 6 full-time (5 women), 16 part-time/adjunct (13 women). *Students:* 68 full-time (55 women), 133 part-time (106 women); includes 42 minority (13 African Americans, 1 American Indian/Alaska Native, 10 Asian Americans or Pacific Islanders, 18 Hispanic Americans), 7 international. Average age 35. In 2009, 48 master's awarded. *Degree requirements:* For master's, thesis or alternative. *Entrance requirements:* For master's, interview, minimum GPA of 3.0. *Application deadline:* Applications are processed on a rolling basis. Application fee: $50. *Expenses:* Tuition: Full-time $35,087; part-time $956 per credit hour. One-time fee: $50 full-time. Part-time tuition and fees vary according to course level, course load, degree level, campus/location and program. *Financial support:* In 2009–10, 5 students received support. Career-related internships or fieldwork and Federal Work-Study available. Support available to part-time students. Financial award application deadline: 2/15; financial award applicants required to submit FAFSA. *Faculty research:* Counselor training effectiveness, multicultural development, empathy, the interface of spirituality and psychotherapy, gender issues. *Unit head:* Dr. Laura Heid, Director, 925-631-4293, Fax: 925-376-8379, E-mail: lheid@stmarys.ca.edu. *Application contact:* Jane Joyce, Coordinator, Recruitment and Admissions, 925-631-4700, Fax: 925-376-8379, E-mail: soereq@stmarys-ca.edu.

St. Mary's University, Graduate School, Department of Counseling and Human Services, Program in Marriage and Family Therapy, San Antonio, TX 78228-8507. Offers MA, PhD. Part-time programs available. *Degree requirements:* For master's, comprehensive exam, thesis optional, internship; for doctorate, comprehensive exam, thesis/dissertation, internship. *Entrance requirements:* For master's, GRE, MAT; for doctorate, GRE, master's degree, work experience, letters of recommendation. Additional exam requirements/recommendations for international students: Required—TOEFL (minimum score 550 paper-based; 213 computer-based; 80 iBT). Electronic applications accepted. *Expenses:* Tuition: Full-time $8004. Required fees: $536. One-time fee: $5 full-time. Full-time tuition and fees vary according to program.

Saint Mary's University of Minnesota, Schools of Graduate and Professional Programs, Graduate School of Health and Human Services, Marriage and Family Therapy Program, Winona, MN 55987-1399. Offers marriage and family therapy (MA, Certificate); play therapy (Certificate). *Unit head:* Dr. Steve W. Peltier, Director, 612-728-5140, Fax: 612-728-5121, E-mail: speltier@smumn.edu. *Application contact:* Yasin Alsaidi, Director of Admissions for Graduate and Professional Programs, 612-728-5207, Fax: 612-728-5121, E-mail: yalsaidi@smumn.edu.

Saint Paul University, Faculty of Human Sciences, Program in Counseling and Spirituality, Ottawa, ON K1S 1C4, Canada. Offers individual or marital/couple counseling (MA); spiritual care (MA). Part-time programs available. *Degree requirements:* For master's, research project or thesis. *Entrance requirements:* For master's, honors BA in human sciences, minimum B average, 12 theology credits.

St. Thomas University, Biscayne College, Department of Social Sciences and Counseling, Program in Marriage and Family Therapy, Miami Gardens, FL 33054-6459. Offers MS, Post-Master's Certificate. Part-time and evening/weekend programs available. *Degree requirements:* For master's, comprehensive exam. *Entrance requirements:* For master's, interview, minimum GPA of 3.0 or GRE. Additional exam requirements/recommendations for international students: Required—TOEFL. Electronic applications accepted.

San Francisco State University, Division of Graduate Studies, College of Health and Human Services, Department of Counseling, San Francisco, CA 94132-1722. Offers counseling (MS); marriage, family, and child counseling (MSC); rehabilitation counseling (MS). *Accreditation:* ACA (one or more programs are accredited). Part-time programs available.

Saybrook University, Graduate College of Psychology and Humanistic Studies, San Francisco, CA 94111-1920. Offers clinical psychology (Psy D); human science (MA, PhD), including consciousness and spirituality, humanistic and transpersonal psychology, integrative health studies, organizational systems, social transformation, transformative social change (MA); organizational systems (MA, PhD), including consciousness and spirituality, humanistic and transpersonal psychology, integrative health studies, leadership of sustainable systems (MA), organizational systems, social transformation; psychology (MA, PhD), including clinical psychology (PhD), consciousness and spirituality, creativity studies (MA), humanistic and transpersonal psychology, integrative health studies, Jungian studies, marriage and family therapy (MA), organizational systems, social transformation. Postbaccalaureate distance learning degree programs offered (minimal on-campus study). Terminal master's awarded for partial completion of doctoral program. *Degree requirements:* For master's, thesis or alternative; for doctorate, thesis/dissertation. Electronic applications accepted. *Faculty research:* Humanistic theory, health studies, organizational systems, consciousness and spirituality, social transformation.

The School of Professional Psychology at Forest Institute, Graduate Programs, Springfield, MO 65807. Offers clinical psychology (MA, Psy D); counseling psychology (MA); marriage and family therapy (MA, PGC). *Accreditation:* AAMFT/COAMFTE; APA (one or more programs are accredited). *Faculty:* 18 full-time (9 women), 18 part-time/adjunct (10 women). *Students:* 214 full-time (144 women), 46 part-time (35 women); includes 35 minority (11 African Americans, 9 American Indian/Alaska Native, 5 Asian Americans or Pacific Islanders, 10 Hispanic Americans), 3 international. Average age 28. 176 applicants, 69% accepted, 45 enrolled. In 2009, 35 master's, 31 doctorates awarded. Terminal master's awarded for partial completion of doctoral program. *Degree requirements:* For master's, thesis, practicum; for doctorate, comprehensive exam, thesis/dissertation, internship, practicum. *Entrance requirements:* For master's, GRE General Test, interview, minimum GPA of 3.0, 12 hours in psychology; for doctorate, GRE General Test, interview, minimum GPA of 3.0, 18 hours in psychology. Additional exam requirements/recommendations for international students: Required—TOEFL (minimum score 550 paper-based; 213 computer-based). *Application deadline:* For fall admission, 1/15 priority date for domestic and international students; for spring admission, 8/1 priority date for domestic and international students. Applications are processed on a rolling basis. Application fee: $50. Electronic applications accepted. *Expenses:* Tuition: Full-time $23,625; part-time $675 per credit hour. Required fees: $275 per semester. Tuition and fees vary according to course load and program. *Financial support:* In 2009–10, 59 students received support, including 5 fellowships with partial tuition reimbursements available (averaging $7,200 per year), 11 teaching assistantships (averaging $100 per year); career-related internships or fieldwork, Federal Work-Study, scholarships/grants, tuition waivers (partial), and unspecified assistantships also available. Financial award applicants required to submit FAFSA. *Faculty research:* Forensics/corrections, marriage and family therapy, child and adolescent, integrated health care, neuropsychology. *Unit head:* Dr. Mark E. Skrade, President, 417-823-3477, Fax: 417-823-3442, E-mail: mskrade@forest.edu. *Application contact:* Bethany Ritter, Admissions Counselor, 417-823-3477, Fax: 417-823-3442, E-mail: britter@forest.edu.

Seattle Pacific University, MS in Marriage and Family Therapy Program, Seattle, WA 98119-1997. Offers marriage and family therapy (MS); medical family therapy (Certificate). *Accreditation:* AAMFT/COAMFTE. Part-time programs available. *Faculty:* 4 full-time (2 women), 3 part-time/adjunct (1 woman). *Students:* 52 full-time (41 women), 18 part-time (14 women); includes 6 minority (all Asian Americans or Pacific Islanders), 3 international. Average age 31. 96 applicants. In 2009, 20 master's awarded. *Degree requirements:* For master's, thesis optional, internship, clinical portfolio. *Entrance requirements:* For master's, GRE General Test or MAT. Additional exam requirements/recommendations for international students: Required—TOEFL (minimum score 550 paper-based; 213 computer-based). *Application deadline:* For fall admission, 2/1 for domestic and international students. Applications are processed on a rolling basis. Application fee: $50. Electronic applications accepted. *Expenses:* Contact institution. *Financial support:* In 2009–10, 51 students received support; fellowships, Federal Work-Study available. Financial award applicants required to submit FAFSA. *Faculty research:* Roles of therapists, models of collaboration, medical and mental health theories of marriage and family therapy. *Unit head:* Dr. Claudia Grauf-Grounds, Chair, 206-281-2632, Fax: 206-281-2695, E-mail: claudiagg@spu.edu. *Application contact:* The Grad Center, 206-281-2091.

Seton Hall University, College of Education and Human Services, Department of Professional Psychology and Family Therapy, Program in Marriage and Family Therapy, South Orange, NJ 07079-2697. Offers MS, PhD, Ed S. *Accreditation:* AAMFT/COAMFTE. *Faculty:* 5 full-time (3 women). *Students:* 18 full-time (16 women), 9 part-time (all women). Average age 35. 20 applicants, 85% accepted, 12 enrolled. In 2009, 2 doctorates, 12 other advanced degrees awarded. *Degree requirements:* For master's, comprehensive exam, case study; for Ed S, comprehensive exam, internship. *Entrance requirements:* For master's, GRE; for Ed S, GRE or MAT, interview. *Application deadline:* For fall admission, 2/15 for domestic students. Application fee: $50. *Financial support:* In 2009–10, 1 research assistantship with full tuition reimbursement (averaging $4,500 per year), 1 teaching assistantship with full tuition reimbursement (averaging $4,500 per year) were awarded. Financial award application deadline: 2/1. *Faculty research:* Family systems. *Unit head:* Dr. Robert Massey, Director, 973-761-9591, E-mail: masseyro@shu.edu. *Application contact:* Information Contact, 973-761-9451.

Seton Hill University, Program in Marriage and Family Therapy, Greensburg, PA 15601. Offers MA. *Accreditation:* AAMFT/COAMFTE. Part-time and evening/weekend programs available. *Faculty:* 3 full-time (2 women), 5 part-time/adjunct (3 women). *Students:* 20 full-time (17 women), 21 part-time (17 women); includes 2 minority (1 African American, 1 Asian American or Pacific Islander). Average age 31. 31 applicants, 65% accepted, 16 enrolled. In 2009, 6 master's awarded. *Entrance requirements:* For master's, minimum GPA of 3.0, 12 credits of course work in psychology. Additional exam requirements/recommendations for international students: Required—TOEFL (minimum score 650 paper-based; 280 computer-based), IELTS (minimum score 7). *Application deadline:* For fall admission, 8/15 priority date for domestic students; for spring admission, 12/15 for domestic students. Applications are processed on a rolling basis. Application fee: $35. Electronic applications accepted. *Expenses:* Tuition: Full-time $12,780; part-time $710 per credit. Required fees: $300; $150 per semester. Tuition and fees vary according to course load and program. *Financial support:* Scholarships/grants, tuition waivers (partial), and unspecified assistantships available. Support available to part-time students. Financial award application deadline: 8/15; financial award applicants required to submit FAFSA. *Faculty research:* Social cognition, feminist psychology, psychology of gender, developmental psychology, systemic theory. *Unit head:* Dr. Rebecca Harvey, Director, 724-552-0339, E-mail: harvey@setonhill.edu. *Application contact:* Laurel Pellis, Advisor, 724-838-4209, Fax: 724-830-1891, E-mail: lpellis@setonhill.edu.

Shippensburg University of Pennsylvania, School of Graduate Studies, College of Education and Human Services, Department of Counseling, Shippensburg, PA 17257-2299. Offers Adlerian studies (Certificate); advanced study in counseling (Certificate); alcohol and drug counseling (Certificate); counseling (M Ed, MS), including college counseling (MS), community counseling (MS), elementary school counseling, mental health counseling (MS), secondary school counseling (MS), student personnel services (MS); couple and family counseling (Certificate). *Accreditation:* ACA (one or more programs are accredited); NCATE. Part-time and evening/weekend programs available. *Degree requirements:* For master's, fieldwork, research project, internship, candidacy. *Entrance requirements:* For master's, GRE or MAT (community, mental health, student personnel, and college counseling applicants if GPA is less than 2.75), minimum GPA of 2.75 (3.0 for M Ed), interview, resume, 3 letters of recommendation, supplemental data forms, one year of relevant work experience, on-campus interview. Additional exam requirements/recommendations for international students: Required—TOEFL (minimum score 560 paper-based; 220 computer-based); Recommended—IELTS (minimum score 6). Electronic applications accepted.

Sioux Falls Seminary, Graduate and Professional Programs, Program in Marriage and Family Therapy, Sioux Falls, SD 57105-1599. Offers MA. *Entrance requirements:* For master's, minimum GPA of 3.0.

Sonoma State University, School of Social Sciences, Department of Counseling, Rohnert Park, CA 94928. Offers counseling (MA); marriage, family, and child counseling (MA); pupil personnel services (MA). *Accreditation:* ACA. Part-time programs available. *Faculty:* 2 full-time (1 woman), 8 part-time/adjunct (5 women). *Students:* 58 full-time (42 women), 26 part-time (22 women); includes 8 minority (1 American Indian/Alaska Native, 1 Asian American or Pacific Islander, 6 Hispanic Americans), 1 international. Average age 33. 148 applicants, 28% accepted, 13 enrolled. In 2009, 40 master's awarded. *Degree requirements:* For master's, internship. *Entrance requirements:* For master's, minimum GPA of 3.0. Additional exam requirements/recommendations for international students: Required—TOEFL (minimum score 500 paper-based; 173 computer-based). *Application deadline:* For fall admission, 11/30 for domestic students. Application fee: $55. *Expenses:* Tuition, nonresident: full-time $11,160. Required fees: $6226. Full-time tuition and fees vary according to course load. *Financial support:* Career-related internships or fieldwork available. Financial award application deadline: 3/2; financial award applicants required to submit FAFSA. *Unit head:* Jaymala Madathil, Program Coordinator, 707-664-4067, E-mail: jaymala.madathil@sonoma.edu. *Application contact:* Stephanie Wilkinson, Administrative Analyst, 707-664-2544, Fax: 707-664-2038, E-mail: stephanie.wilkinson@sonoma.edu.

Southeastern Louisiana University, College of Education and Human Development, Department of Counseling and Human Development, Hammond, LA 70402. Offers counselor education (M Ed), including community counseling, marriage and family therapy, school counseling, substance abuse counseling. *Accreditation:* ACA; NCATE. Part-time programs available. *Faculty:* 7 full-time (5 women), 1 part-time/adjunct (0 women). *Students:* 58 full-time (54 women), 45 part-time (41 women); includes 16 minority (15 African Americans, 1 Hispanic American). Average age 29. 38 applicants, 100% accepted, 23 enrolled. In 2009, 23 master's awarded. *Degree requirements:* For master's, comprehensive exam, thesis optional. *Entrance requirements:* For master's, GRE (verbal and quantitative). Additional exam requirements/recommendations for international students: Required—TOEFL (minimum score 500 paper-based; 173 computer-based; 61 iBT). *Application deadline:* For fall admission, 7/15 priority date for domestic students, 6/1 priority date for international students; for spring admission,

12/1 priority date for domestic students, 10/1 priority date for international students. Applications are processed on a rolling basis. Application fee: $20 ($30 for international students). Electronic applications accepted. *Expenses:* Tuition, state resident: full-time $3086; part-time $225 per credit hour. Tuition, nonresident: part-time $529 per credit hour. Required fees: $1195. Tuition and fees vary according to course level and course load. *Financial support:* In 2009–10, 6 students received support. Career-related internships or fieldwork, Federal Work-Study, institutionally sponsored loans, and administrative assistantships available. Support available to part-time students. Financial award application deadline: 5/1; financial award applicants required to submit FAFSA. *Faculty research:* Marriage counseling, family of origin, counselor training, substance abuse counseling, childhood and adolescent obesity. *Unit head:* Dr. June Williams, Interim Department Head, 985-549-2309, Fax: 985-549-3758, E-mail: jwilliams@selu.edu. *Application contact:* Sandra Meyers, Graduate Admissions Analyst, 985-549-2066, Fax: 985-549-5632, E-mail: admissions@selu.edu.

Southern Nazarene University, Graduate College, School of Psychology, Bethany, OK 73008. Offers counseling psychology (MSCP); marriage and family therapy (MA). *Degree requirements:* For master's, thesis optional. *Entrance requirements:* For master's, English proficiency exam, minimum GPA of 3.0 in last 60 hours/major, 2.7 overall.

Springfield College, Graduate Programs, Programs in Psychology and Counseling, Springfield, MA 01109-3797. Offers athletic counseling (M Ed, MS, CAGS); industrial/organizational psychology (M Ed, MS, CAGS); marriage and family therapy (M Ed, MS, CAGS); mental health counseling (M Ed, MS, CAGS); school guidance and counseling (M Ed, MS, CAGS); student personnel in higher education (M Ed, MS, CAGS). Part-time programs available. *Degree requirements:* For master's, research project, portfolio. *Entrance requirements:* Additional exam requirements/recommendations for international students: Required—TOEFL (minimum score 550 paper-based; 213 computer-based). Electronic applications accepted. *Expenses:* Tuition: Full-time $19,800; part-time $825 per credit hour. Required fees: $150.

Stephens College, Division of Graduate and Continuing Studies, Programs in Counseling, Columbia, MO 65215-0002. Offers counseling (M Ed), including marriage and family therapy, professional counseling, school counseling. Part-time and evening/weekend programs available. *Faculty:* 1 (woman) full-time, 11 part-time/adjunct (10 women). *Students:* 130 full-time (116 women), 32 part-time (28 women); includes 16 minority (13 African Americans, 2 Asian Americans or Pacific Islanders, 1 Hispanic American). Average age 33. 47 applicants, 68% accepted, 28 enrolled. In 2009, 35 master's awarded. *Degree requirements:* For master's, thesis. *Entrance requirements:* For master's, minimum GPA of 3.0 in last 60 hours. Additional exam requirements/recommendations for international students: Required—TOEFL (minimum score 213 computer-based). *Application deadline:* For fall admission, 7/25 priority date for domestic and international students; for winter admission, 12/1 priority date for domestic and international students; for spring admission, 4/25 priority date for domestic and international students. Applications are processed on a rolling basis. Application fee: $40. Electronic applications accepted. *Expenses:* Tuition: Part-time $350 per credit. Required fees: $25 per credit. *Financial support:* In 2009–10, 70 students received support. Scholarships/grants and unspecified assistantships available. Financial award application deadline: 12/5; financial award applicants required to submit FAFSA. *Unit head:* Dr. Linda Thompson, Program Chair, 800-388-7579. *Application contact:* Meredith Julian, Assistant Director of Marketing and Recruitment, 800-388-7579, E-mail: online@stephens.edu.

Stetson University, College of Arts and Sciences, Division of Education, Department of Counselor Education, DeLand, FL 32723. Offers marriage and family therapy (MS); mental health counseling (MS); school guidance and family consultation (MS). *Accreditation:* ACA. Evening/weekend programs available. *Students:* 66 full-time (59 women), 12 part-time (11 women); includes 19 minority (9 African Americans, 2 American Indian/Alaska Native, 8 Hispanic Americans), 2 international. Average age 32. In 2009, 28 master's awarded. *Entrance requirements:* For master's, GRE General Test. *Application deadline:* For fall admission, 3/1 priority date for domestic students; for spring admission, 11/1 for domestic students. Applications are processed on a rolling basis. Application fee: $25. Tuition and fees vary according to course load, campus/location and program. *Unit head:* Dr. Brigid Noonan-Klima, Chair, 386-822-8992. *Application contact:* Diana Belian, Office of Graduate Studies, 386-822-7075, Fax: 386-822-7388, E-mail: dbelian@stetson.edu.

Syracuse University, College of Human Ecology, Program in Marriage and Family Therapy, Syracuse, NY 13244. Offers MA. *Accreditation:* AAMFT/COAMFTE. Part-time programs available. *Students:* 31 full-time (29 women), 19 part-time (17 women); includes 14 minority (10 African Americans, 1 American Indian/Alaska Native, 1 Asian American or Pacific Islander, 2 Hispanic Americans), 7 international. Average age 29. 57 applicants, 91% accepted, 21 enrolled. In 2009, 9 master's awarded. *Entrance requirements:* For master's, GRE General Test. Additional exam requirements/recommendations for international students: Required—TOEFL (minimum score 100 iBT). *Application deadline:* For fall admission, 3/15 priority date for domestic students, 2/15 priority date for international students. Application fee: $75. Electronic applications accepted. *Expenses:* Tuition: Full-time $26,808; part-time $1117 per credit. Required fees: $1024. *Financial support:* Fellowships with tuition reimbursements, research assistantships with full and partial tuition reimbursements, teaching assistantships with full and partial tuition reimbursements, tuition waivers (partial) available. Financial award application deadline: 1/1; financial award applicants required to submit FAFSA. *Unit head:* Thomas DeLara, Chair, 315-443-9403, E-mail: inquire@hshp.syr.edu. *Application contact:* Amy Pangborn, Information Contact, 315-443-5555, E-mail: inquire@hshp.syr.edu.

Texas Tech University, Graduate School, College of Human Sciences, Department of Applied and Professional Studies, Lubbock, TX 79409. Offers family and consumer sciences education (MS, PhD); marriage and family therapy (MS, PhD); personal financial planning (MS, PhD); JD/MS; MS/MBA; MS/MS. Part-time programs available. *Faculty:* 17 full-time (11 women), 1 part-time/adjunct (0 women). *Students:* 111 full-time (44 women), 45 part-time (28 women); includes 24 minority (8 African Americans, 1 American Indian/Alaska Native, 1 Asian American or Pacific Islander, 14 Hispanic Americans), 16 international. Average age 31. 169 applicants, 63% accepted, 36 enrolled. In 2009, 31 master's, 13 doctorates awarded. Terminal master's awarded for partial completion of doctoral program. *Degree requirements:* For master's, thesis or alternative; for doctorate, thesis/dissertation. *Entrance requirements:* For master's and doctorate, GRE General Test. Additional exam requirements/recommendations for international students: Required—TOEFL (minimum score 550 paper-based; 213 computer-based). *Application deadline:* For fall admission, 3/1 priority date for international students; for spring admission, 11/1 priority date for international students. Applications are processed on a rolling basis. Application fee: $50 ($75 for international students). *Expenses:* Tuition, state resident: full-time $5100; part-time $213 per credit hour. Tuition, nonresident: full-time $11,748; part-time $490 per credit hour. Required fees: $2298; $50 per credit hour. $555 per semester. *Financial support:* In 2009–10, 13 research assistantships with partial tuition reimbursements (averaging $27,402 per year), 5 teaching assistantships with partial tuition reimbursements (averaging $19,601 per year) were awarded; career-related internships or fieldwork, Federal Work-Study, institutionally sponsored loans, and tuition waivers (partial) also available. Support available to part-time students. Financial award application deadline: 4/15; financial award applicants required to submit FAFSA. *Faculty research:* Functional interior design applications for special needs populations; retirement planning and income/expenditure patterns for teachers; surface design, purchase, and consumption of leather products; financial counseling outcome and assessment of college students; multicultural housing environments and behavior correlations. Total annual research expenditures: $1 million. *Unit head:* Dr. Sterling Shumway, Chair, 806-742-5050, Fax: 806-742-5033, E-mail: sterling.shumway@ttu.edu. *Application contact:* Dr. Sterling Shumway, Chair, 806-742-5050, Fax: 806-742-5033, E-mail: sterling.shumway@ttu.edu.

Texas Wesleyan University, Graduate Programs, Programs in Education, Fort Worth, TX 76105-1536. Offers education (M Ed, Ed D); marraige and family therapy (MSMFT); professional counseling (MA); school counseling (MS). Part-time and evening/weekend programs available. Postbaccalaureate distance learning degree programs offered (no on-campus study). *Faculty:* 11 full-time (7 women), 3 part-time/adjunct (2 women). *Students:* 56 full-time (47 women), 208 part-time (174 women); includes 102 minority (54 African Americans, 2 American Indian/Alaska Native, 3 Asian Americans or Pacific Islanders, 43 Hispanic Americans), 4 international. Average age 36. 102 applicants, 77% accepted, 66 enrolled. In 2009, 179 master's awarded. *Entrance requirements:* For master's, GRE General Test, minimum GPA of 3.0 in final 60 hours of undergraduate course work, interview. *Application deadline:* For fall admission, 6/15 priority date for domestic students; for spring admission, 10/15 priority date for domestic students. Applications are processed on a rolling basis. Application fee: $40 ($50 for international students). Tuition and fees vary according to degree level. *Financial support:* Career-related internships or fieldwork, Federal Work-Study, scholarships/grants, and tuition waivers (full and partial) available. Support available to part-time students. Financial award application deadline: 3/15; financial award applicants required to submit FAFSA. *Faculty research:* Teacher effectiveness, bilingual education, analytic teaching. *Unit head:* Dr. Carlos Martinez, Dean, School of Education, 817-531-4940, Fax: 817-531-4943. *Application contact:* DeTrae Warren, Graduate Admission Recruiter, 817-531-4931, Fax: 817-531-4935, E-mail: dwarren@txwes.edu.

Texas Woman's University, Graduate School, College of Professional Education, Department of Family Sciences, Denton, TX 76201. Offers child development (MS, PhD); counseling and development (MS); early childhood education (M Ed, MA, MS, Ed D); family studies (MS, PhD); family therapy (MS, PhD). *Accreditation:* ACA (one or more programs are accredited). Part-time and evening/weekend programs available. *Faculty:* 25 full-time (21 women), 4 part-time/adjunct (all women). *Students:* 111 full-time (105 women), 294 part-time (269 women); includes 149 minority (99 African Americans, 3 American Indian/Alaska Native, 7 Asian Americans or Pacific Islanders, 40 Hispanic Americans), 22 international. Average age 36. 179 applicants, 86% accepted, 72 enrolled. In 2009, 86 master's, 22 doctorates awarded. Terminal master's awarded for partial completion of doctoral program. *Degree requirements:* For master's, portfolio; for doctorate, comprehensive exam, thesis/dissertation. *Entrance requirements:* For master's, interview, letter of intent, curriculum vitae; for doctorate, interview, minimum GPA of 3.5 in last 60 hours of course work. Additional exam requirements/recommendations for international students: Required—TOEFL (minimum score 550 paper-based; 213 computer-based; 79 iBT). *Application deadline:* For fall admission, 2/15 priority date for domestic students, 3/1 for international students; for spring admission, 9/15 priority date for domestic students, 8/1 for international students. Applications are processed on a rolling basis. Application fee: $50. Electronic applications accepted. *Expenses:* Tuition, state resident: full-time $3564; part-time $198 per credit hour. Tuition, nonresident: full-time $8550; part-time $475 per credit hour. Required fees: $69.26 per credit hour. Tuition and fees vary according to course load. *Financial support:* In 2009–10, 96 students received support, including 13 research assistantships (averaging $10,746 per year), 7 teaching assistantships (averaging $10,746 per year); career-related internships or fieldwork, Federal Work-Study, institutionally sponsored loans, scholarships/grants, traineeships, health care benefits, and unspecified assistantships also available. Support available to part-time students. Financial award application deadline: 3/1; financial award applicants required to submit FAFSA. *Faculty research:* Parenting/parent education, distance education, play therapy, family sexuality, diversity, ANTHEM healthy marriages initiative. *Unit head:* Dr. Larry LeFlore, Chair, 940-898-2685, Fax: 940-898-2676, E-mail: famsci@twu.edu. *Application contact:* Samuel Wheeler, Assistant Director of Admissions, 940-898-3188, Fax: 940-898-3081, E-mail: wheelersr@twu.edu.

Thomas Jefferson University, Jefferson College of Health Professions, Couple and Family Therapy Department, Philadelphia, PA 19107. Offers family therapy (MS). *Expenses:* Tuition: Full-time $26,858; part-time $879 per credit. Required fees: $525.

Trevecca Nazarene University, Graduate Division, Graduate Psychology Programs, Major in Marriage and Family Therapy, Nashville, TN 37210-2877. Offers MMFT. Part-time and evening/weekend programs available. *Students:* 70 full-time (59 women), 10 part-time (7 women); includes 21 minority (19 African Americans, 1 American Indian/Alaska Native, 1 Hispanic American). In 2009, 32 master's awarded. *Degree requirements:* For master's, comprehensive exam, practicum. *Entrance requirements:* For master's, GRE General Test or MAT, minimum GPA of 2.7, letters of reference. Additional exam requirements/recommendations for international students: Required—TOEFL (minimum score 550 paper-based; 213 computer-based). *Application deadline:* Applications are processed on a rolling basis. Application fee: $25. *Expenses:* Contact institution. *Financial support:* Applicants required to submit FAFSA. *Unit head:* Dr. Peter Wilson, Director of Graduate Psychology Program, 615-248-1384, Fax: 615-248-1662, E-mail: admissions_psy@trevecca.edu. *Application contact:* Heather Ambrefe, Department Secretary, 615-248-1384, Fax: 615-248-1662, E-mail: admissions_psy@trevecca.edu.

Union Institute & University, PsyD Program in Clinical Psychology, Brattleboro, VT 05301. Offers family therapy (Psy D). Postbaccalaureate distance learning degree programs offered (minimal on-campus study). *Faculty:* 5 full-time (3 women), 5 part-time/adjunct (2 women). *Students:* 40 full-time (29 women), 2 part-time (both women); includes 6 minority (3 African Americans, 1 Asian American or Pacific Islander, 2 Hispanic Americans). Average age 43. *Degree requirements:* For doctorate, comprehensive exam, thesis/dissertation, internship, practicum. *Entrance requirements:* For doctorate, master's degree, letters of recommendation, interview. *Application deadline:* Applications are processed on a rolling basis. Application fee: $50. Tuition and fees vary according to course load, degree level, campus/location and program. *Financial support:* Federal Work-Study, scholarships/grants, and tuition waivers (partial) available. Financial award application deadline: 5/1; financial award applicants required to submit FAFSA. *Unit head:* Dr. William Lax, Dean, 802-254-0152, E-mail: william.lax@myunion.edu. *Application contact:* Diane Robinson, Director of Admissions-Brattleboro, 800-336-6794, E-mail: diane.robinson@myunion.edu.

Universidad de las Americas, A.C., Program in Psychology, Mexico City, Mexico. Offers family therapy (MA).

The University of Akron, Graduate School, College of Education, Department of Counseling, Program in Marriage and Family Therapy, Akron, OH 44325. Offers MA, MS. *Accreditation:* AAMFT/COAMFTE; ACA. *Students:* 43 full-time (37 women), 24 part-time (23 women); includes 10 minority (8 African Americans, 1 Asian American or Pacific Islander, 1 Hispanic American), 2 international. Average age 32. 8 applicants, 75% accepted, 5 enrolled. In 2009, 16 master's awarded. *Degree requirements:* For master's, comprehensive exam. *Entrance requirements:* For master's, minimum GPA of 2.75, interview, letters of recommendation, supplemental form. Additional exam requirements/recommendations for international students: Required—TOEFL (minimum score 550 paper-based; 213 computer-based; 79 iBT). *Application deadline:* For fall admission, 3/15 for domestic and international students; for spring admission, 10/1 for domestic and international students. Application fee: $30 ($40 for international students). Electronic applications accepted. *Expenses:* Tuition, state resident: full-time $6570; part-time $365 per credit hour. Tuition, nonresident: full-time $11,250; part-time $625 per credit hour. *Unit head:* Dr. Patricia Parr, Coordinator, 330-972-8151, E-mail: pparr@uakron.edu. *Application contact:* Dr. Patricia Parr, Coordinator, 330-972-8151, E-mail: pparr@uakron.edu.

University of Arkansas at Little Rock, Graduate School, College of Professional Studies, School of Social Work, Program in Marriage and Family Therapy, Little Rock, AR 72204-1099. Offers Graduate Certificate.

University of Central Florida, College of Education, Department of Child, Family and Community Sciences, Program in Marriage and Family Therapy, Orlando, FL 32816. Offers MA, Certificate. *Students:* 46 full-time (37 women), 11 part-time (all women); includes 20 minority (4 African Americans, 3 Asian Americans or Pacific Islanders, 13 Hispanic Americans). Average age 25. 51 applicants, 51% accepted, 19 enrolled. In 2009, 8 master's, 10 other advanced degrees awarded. *Expenses:* Tuition, state resident: part-time $306.31 per credit hour. Tuition, nonresident: part-time $1099.01 per credit hour. Part-time tuition and fees vary according to

Marriage and Family Therapy

University of Central Florida (continued)

degree level and program. *Financial support:* In 2009–10, 9 students received support, including 3 fellowships (averaging $1,300 per year), 7 research assistantships (averaging $6,000 per year).

University of Florida, Graduate School, College of Education, Department of Counselor Education, Gainesville, FL 32611. Offers marriage and family counseling (M Ed, MAE, Ed D, PhD, Ed S); mental health counseling (M Ed, MAE, Ed D, PhD, Ed S); school counseling and guidance (M Ed, MAE, Ed D, PhD, Ed S). *Accreditation:* ACA (one or more programs are accredited); NCATE. Part-time programs available. Terminal master's awarded for partial completion of doctoral program. *Degree requirements:* For master's, thesis optional; for doctorate, thesis/dissertation. *Entrance requirements:* For master's and doctorate, GRE General Test, minimum GPA of 3.0 (undergraduate), 3.5 (graduate); for Ed S, GRE General Test. Additional exam requirements/recommendations for international students: Required—TOEFL (minimum score 550 paper-based; 213 computer-based). Electronic applications accepted.

University of Guelph, Graduate Program Services, College of Social and Applied Human Sciences, Department of Family Relations and Applied Nutrition, Guelph, ON N1G 2W1, Canada. Offers applied nutrition (MAN); family relations and human development (M Sc, PhD), including applied human nutrition, couple and family therapy (M Sc), family relations and human development. *Accreditation:* AAMFT/COAMFTE (one or more programs are accredited). Part-time programs available. *Degree requirements:* For master's, thesis (for some programs); for doctorate, comprehensive exam, thesis/dissertation. *Entrance requirements:* For master's, minimum B+ average; for doctorate, master's degree in family relations and human development or related field with a minimum B+ average or master's degree in applied human nutrition. Additional exam requirements/recommendations for international students: Required—TOEFL (minimum score 600 paper-based; 250 computer-based). Electronic applications accepted. *Faculty research:* Child and adolescent development, social gerontology, family roles and relations, couple and family therapy, applied human nutrition.

University of Houston–Clear Lake, School of Human Sciences and Humanities, Programs in Human Sciences, Houston, TX 77058-1098. Offers behavioral sciences (MA), including criminology, cross cultural studies, general psychology, sociology; clinical psychology (MA); criminology (MA); cross cultural studies (MA); family therapy (MA); fitness and human performance (MA); school psychology (MA). *Accreditation:* AAMFT/COAMFTE. Part-time and evening/weekend programs available. Postbaccalaureate distance learning degree programs offered (minimal on-campus study). *Degree requirements:* For master's, thesis or alternative. *Entrance requirements:* For master's, GRE General Test. Additional exam requirements/recommendations for international students: Required—TOEFL (minimum score 550 paper-based; 213 computer-based). Electronic applications accepted. *Faculty research:* Smoking cessation, adolescent sexuality, white collar crime, serial murder, human factors/human computer interaction.

University of La Verne, College of Arts and Sciences, Department of Psychology, Programs in Counseling, La Verne, CA 91750-4443. Offers counseling (MS), including student services; marriage and family therapy (MS). Part-time programs available. *Faculty:* 12 full-time (5 women), 22 part-time/adjunct (14 women). *Students:* 29 full-time (25 women), 73 part-time (68 women); includes 69 minority (17 African Americans, 5 Asian Americans or Pacific Islanders, 47 Hispanic Americans). Average age 29. In 2009, 36 master's awarded. *Degree requirements:* For master's, thesis, competency exam, personal psychotherapy. *Entrance requirements:* For master's, minimum undergraduate GPA of 3.0; 3 letters of recommendations; interview. Additional exam requirements/recommendations for international students: Required—TOEFL (minimum score 600 paper-based; 250 computer-based). *Application deadline:* Applications are processed on a rolling basis. Application fee: $50. *Expenses:* Contact institution. *Financial support:* Career-related internships or fieldwork, institutionally sponsored loans, and scholarships/grants available. Financial award application deadline: 3/2; financial award applicants required to submit FAFSA. *Unit head:* Patricia Long, 909-593-3511 Ext. 4091, E-mail: plong@laverne.edu. *Application contact:* Connie Hamlow, Admissions Information Specialist, 909-593-3511 Ext. 4519, Fax: 909-392-2761, E-mail: gradadmission@laverne.edu.

University of Louisiana at Monroe, Graduate School, College of Education and Human Development, Department of Educational Leadership and Counseling, Program in Marriage and Family Therapy, Monroe, LA 71209-0001. Offers MA, PhD. *Accreditation:* AAMFT/COAMFTE (one or more programs are accredited); ACA. Part-time and evening/weekend programs available. *Faculty:* 10 full-time (2 women). *Students:* 47 full-time (39 women), 17 part-time (12 women); includes 10 minority (all African Americans), 2 international. Average age 29. In 2009, 17 master's, 4 doctorates awarded. *Degree requirements:* For master's, thesis optional; for doctorate, comprehensive exam, thesis/dissertation, clinical experience. *Entrance requirements:* For master's, GRE General Test, minimum GPA of 2.8; for doctorate, GRE General Test, minimum GPA of 3.5. Additional exam requirements/recommendations for international students: Required—TOEFL (minimum score 500 paper-based; 173 computer-based; 61 iBT). *Application deadline:* For fall admission, 8/24 priority date for domestic students, 7/1 for international students; for winter admission, 12/14 priority date for domestic students; for spring admission, 1/19 for domestic students, 11/1 for international students. Applications are processed on a rolling basis. Application fee: $20 ($30 for international students). Electronic applications accepted. *Expenses:* Tuition, state resident: part-time $159 per credit hour. Tuition, nonresident: part-time $159 per credit hour. Required fees: $1300 per year. Tuition and fees vary according to course load. *Financial support:* Career-related internships or fieldwork, Federal Work-Study, and unspecified assistantships available. Financial award application deadline: 4/1; financial award applicants required to submit FAFSA. *Faculty research:* Family systems, substance abuse. Total annual research expenditures: $20,000. *Unit head:* Dr. Lamar Woodham, Program Director, 318-362-3008, Fax: 318-342-3131, E-mail: woodham@ulm.edu. *Application contact:* Dr. Harper Gaushell, Admissions Coordinator, 318-343-8441, Fax: 318-342-3131, E-mail: gaushell@ulm.edu.

University of Louisville, Graduate School, Raymond A. Kent School of Social Work, Louisville, KY 40292-0001. Offers marriage and family therapy (PMC); social work (MSSW, PhD), including alcohol and drug counseling (MSSW), gerontology (MSSW), school social work (MSSW). *Accreditation:* AAMFT/COAMFTE; CSWE (one or more programs are accredited). Part-time and evening/weekend programs available. *Faculty:* 23 full-time (15 women), 38 part-time/adjunct (21 women). *Students:* 279 full-time (221 women), 64 part-time (52 women); includes 79 minority (70 African Americans, 2 American Indian/Alaska Native, 2 Asian Americans or Pacific Islanders, 5 Hispanic Americans), 5 international. Average age 32. 288 applicants, 74% accepted, 145 enrolled. In 2009, 137 master's, 4 doctorates awarded. *Degree requirements:* For doctorate, comprehensive exam, thesis/dissertation. *Entrance requirements:* For master's, GRE or minimum GPA of 2.75; for doctorate, GRE General Test, interview, writing sample. Additional exam requirements/recommendations for international students: Required—TOEFL (minimum score 550 paper-based; 213 computer-based; 79 iBT). *Application deadline:* For fall admission, 7/31 for domestic and international students. Applications are processed on a rolling basis. Application fee: $50. Electronic applications accepted. *Financial support:* In 2009–10, 70 students received support, including 9 research assistantships with full tuition reimbursements available (averaging $19,000 per year), 1 teaching assistantship (averaging $19,000 per year); Federal Work-Study, institutionally sponsored loans, scholarships/grants, health care benefits, and unspecified assistantships also available. Support available to part-time students. Financial award application deadline: 5/15; financial award applicants required to submit FAFSA. *Faculty research:* Child welfare, substance abuse, gerontology, family functioning, health behavior. Total annual research expenditures: $2.8 million. *Unit head:* Dr. Terry Singer, Dean, 502-852-6402, Fax: 502-852-0422, E-mail: terry.singer@louisville.edu. *Application contact:* Libby Leggett, Director, Graduate Admissions, 502-852-3101, Fax: 502-852-6536, E-mail: gradadm@louisville.edu.

University of Mary Hardin-Baylor, Graduate Studies in Counseling and Psychology, Belton, TX 76513. Offers community counseling (MA); marriage and family Christian counseling (MA); psychology and counseling (MA); school counseling and psychology (MA). Part-time and evening/weekend programs available. *Degree requirements:* For master's, comprehensive exam. *Entrance requirements:* For master's, GRE General Test, minimum GPA of 3.0 in last 60 hours or 2.75 overall. Electronic applications accepted.

University of Maryland, College Park, Academic Affairs, School of Public Health, Department of Family Science, College Park, MD 20742. Offers family studies (PhD); marriage and family therapy (MS); maternal and child health (PhD). *Accreditation:* AAMFT/COAMFTE. Part-time and evening/weekend programs available. *Faculty:* 13 full-time (9 women), 14 part-time/adjunct (12 women). *Students:* 46 full-time (43 women), 2 part-time (both women); includes 13 minority (9 African Americans, 2 Asian Americans or Pacific Islanders, 2 Hispanic Americans), 3 international. 99 applicants, 15% accepted, 14 enrolled. In 2009, 7 master's, 4 doctorates awarded. *Degree requirements:* For master's, thesis or alternative; for doctorate, comprehensive exam, thesis/dissertation, oral defense. *Entrance requirements:* For master's, GRE General Test, minimum GPA of 3.0, 3 letters of recommendation; for doctorate, GRE General Test, minimum GPA of 3.0, 3 letters of recommendation, research sample. *Application deadline:* For fall admission, 12/1 for domestic and international students; for spring admission, 6/1 for international students. Applications are processed on a rolling basis. Application fee: $60. Electronic applications accepted. *Expenses:* Tuition, area resident: Part-time $471 per credit hour. Tuition, state resident: part-time $471 per credit hour. Tuition, nonresident: part-time $1016 per credit hour. Required fees: $337.04 per term. *Financial support:* In 2009–10, 6 fellowships with full and partial tuition reimbursements (averaging $10,021 per year), 40 teaching assistantships with tuition reimbursements (averaging $16,096 per year) were awarded; research assistantships with tuition reimbursements, career-related internships or fieldwork, Federal Work-Study, and scholarships/grants also available. Support available to part-time students. Financial award applicants required to submit FAFSA. *Faculty research:* Family life quality, interracial couples, child support, homeless families, family and child well-being. Total annual research expenditures: $346,806. *Unit head:* Elaine Anderson, Chairman, 301-405-4009, Fax: 301-314-9161, E-mail: eanders@umd.edu. *Application contact:* Dean of Graduate School, 301-405-0358.

University of Massachusetts Boston, Office of Graduate Studies, Graduate College of Education, Counseling and School Psychology Department, Program in Family Therapy, Boston, MA 02125-3393. Offers M Ed, CAGS. *Accreditation:* AAMFT/COAMFTE.

University of Miami, Graduate School, School of Education, Department of Educational and Psychological Studies, Program in Counseling, Coral Gables, FL 33124. Offers bilingual and bicultural counseling (Certificate); counseling and research (MS Ed); marriage and family therapy (MS Ed); mental health counseling (MS Ed). Part-time and evening/weekend programs available. *Students:* 49 full-time (44 women), 15 part-time (13 women); includes 26 minority (2 African Americans, 1 American Indian/Alaska Native, 1 Asian American or Pacific Islander, 22 Hispanic Americans), 5 international. Average age 26. 82 applicants, 61% accepted, 24 enrolled. In 2009, 15 master's awarded. *Degree requirements:* For master's, comprehensive exam, personal growth experience. *Entrance requirements:* For master's, GRE General Test. Additional exam requirements/recommendations for international students: Required—TOEFL (minimum score 550 paper-based; 80 iBT); Recommended—IELTS (minimum score 6.5). *Application deadline:* Applications are processed on a rolling basis. Application fee: $65. Electronic applications accepted. *Financial support:* In 2009–10, 38 students received support. Career-related internships or fieldwork, institutionally sponsored loans, scholarships/grants, and unspecified assistantships available. Support available to part-time students. Financial award application deadline: 3/1; financial award applicants required to submit FAFSA. *Faculty research:* Cocaine recidivism, HIV, non-traditional families, health psychology, diversity. *Unit head:* Dr. Stephanie Schmitz, Assistant Clinical Professor and Program Director, 305-284-4829, Fax: 305-284-3003, E-mail: sschmitz@miami.edu. *Application contact:* Marissa Stevenson-Jacobs, Graduate Admissions Coordinator, 305-284-2167, Fax: 305-284-3003, E-mail: mstevenson@miami.edu.

University of Minnesota, Twin Cities Campus, Graduate School, College of Education and Human Development, Department of Family Social Science, Minneapolis, MN 55455-0213. Offers marriage and family therapy (MA, PhD). *Accreditation:* AAMFT/COAMFTE (one or more programs are accredited). *Faculty:* 16 full-time (12 women). *Students:* 52 full-time (42 women), 13 part-time (10 women); includes 12 minority (3 African Americans, 2 American Indian/Alaska Native, 5 Asian Americans or Pacific Islanders, 2 Hispanic Americans), 14 international. Average age 34. 22 applicants, 50% accepted, 9 enrolled. In 2009, 5 master's, 5 doctorates awarded. *Degree requirements:* For master's, thesis; for doctorate, thesis/dissertation. *Entrance requirements:* For master's and doctorate, GRE General Test, minimum undergraduate GPA of 3.0 (preferred). Additional exam requirements/recommendations for international students: Required—TOEFL. *Application deadline:* For fall admission, 12/15 for domestic students. Application fee: $55 ($75 for international students). *Financial support:* In 2009–10, 1 fellowship (averaging $22,500 per year), 69 research assistantships (averaging $25,877 per year), 15 teaching assistantships (averaging $26,130 per year) were awarded; career-related internships or fieldwork, Federal Work-Study, institutionally sponsored loans, and tuition waivers (partial) also available. Financial award application deadline: 6/30; financial award applicants required to submit FAFSA. *Faculty research:* Families and diversity, families and health, families and economic well-being, individuals and relationships across the lifespan. Total annual research expenditures: $1.2 million. *Unit head:* Dr. Jan McCulloch, Head, 612-624-1208, Fax: 612-625-4227, E-mail: jmcculloch@che.umn.edu. *Application contact:* Roberta Daigle, Information Contact, 612-625-3116, E-mail: rdaigle@che.umn.edu.

University of Mobile, Graduate Programs, Program in Religious Studies, Mobile, AL 36613. Offers biblical/theological studies (MA); marriage and family counseling (MA). Part-time and evening/weekend programs available. *Faculty:* 4 full-time (0 women), 1 (woman) part-time/adjunct. *Students:* 12 full-time (11 women), 34 part-time (22 women); includes 24 minority (23 African Americans, 1 American Indian/Alaska Native). Average age 32. 20 applicants, 100% accepted, 16 enrolled. In 2009, 12 master's awarded. *Degree requirements:* For master's, 2 foreign languages, comprehensive exam, thesis optional. *Entrance requirements:* For master's, GRE General Test. Additional exam requirements/recommendations for international students: Required—TOEFL (minimum score 550 paper-based; 213 computer-based; 80 iBT). *Application deadline:* For fall admission, 8/3 priority date for domestic students; for spring admission, 12/23 for domestic students. Applications are processed on a rolling basis. Application fee: $40 ($50 for international students). *Financial support:* Federal Work-Study available. Support available to part-time students. Financial award application deadline: 8/1. *Unit head:* Dr. Cecil Taylor, Dean, School of Christian Studies, 251-442-2255, Fax: 251-442-2523, E-mail: ctaylor@mail.umobile.edu. *Application contact:* Tammy C. Eubanks, Administrative Assistant to Dean of Graduate Programs, 251-442-2270, Fax: 251-442-2523, E-mail: teubanks@umobile.edu.

University of Montevallo, College of Education, Program in Counseling, Montevallo, AL 35115. Offers community counseling (M Ed); marriage and family (M Ed); school counseling (M Ed). *Accreditation:* ACA; NCATE. Part-time and evening/weekend programs available. *Students:* 36 full-time (32 women), 46 part-time (41 women); includes 14 minority (12 African Americans, 1 Asian American or Pacific Islander, 1 Hispanic American), 2 international. In 2009, 14 master's awarded. *Entrance requirements:* For master's, GRE General Test or MAT, minimum undergraduate GPA of 2.75 in last 60 hours or 2.5 overall, interview. Additional exam requirements/recommendations for international students: Required—TOEFL (minimum score 550 paper-based). *Application deadline:* For fall admission, 7/15 for domestic students; for spring admission, 11/15 for domestic students. Application fee: $25. *Expenses:* Tuition, state resident: full-time $5592; part-time $233 per credit. Tuition, nonresident: full-time $11,184; part-time $466 per credit hour. Required fees: $482; $241 per semester. One-time fee: $25 part-time. *Financial support:* Federal Work-Study, scholarships/grants, and unspecified assistantships available. *Unit head:* Dr. Leland Doebler, Chair, 205-665-6380. *Application contact:* Dr. Leland Doebler, Chair, 205-665-6380.

University of Nebraska–Lincoln, Graduate College, College of Education and Human Sciences, Department of Child, Youth and Family Studies, Lincoln, NE 68588. Offers child development/early childhood education (MS, PhD); child, youth and family studies (MS); family and consumer sciences education (MS, PhD); family financial planning (MS); family science (MS, PhD); gerontology (PhD); human sciences (PhD), including child, youth and family studies, gerontology, medical family therapy; marriage and family therapy (MS); medical family therapy (PhD); youth development (MS). *Accreditation:* AAMFT/COAMFTE (one or more programs are accredited). Postbaccalaureate distance learning degree programs offered. *Degree requirements:* For master's, thesis optional. *Entrance requirements:* For master's, GRE. Additional exam requirements/recommendations for international students: Required—TOEFL (minimum score 550 paper-based; 213 computer-based). Electronic applications accepted. *Faculty research:* Marriage and family therapy, child development/early childhood education, family financial management.

University of Nevada, Las Vegas, Graduate College, Greenspun College of Urban Affairs, Department of Marriage and Family Therapy, Las Vegas, NV 89154-3045. Offers MS, Advanced Certificate. *Accreditation:* ACA. Part-time programs available. *Faculty:* 4 full-time (2 women). *Students:* 15 full-time (all women), 16 part-time (14 women); includes 3 minority (1 African American, 1 Asian American or Pacific Islander, 1 Hispanic American). Average age 37. 56 applicants, 32% accepted, 14 enrolled. In 2009, 6 master's awarded. *Degree requirements:* For master's, comprehensive exam (for some programs), thesis (for some programs). *Entrance requirements:* For master's and Advanced Certificate, GRE General Test. Additional exam requirements/recommendations for international students: Required—TOEFL (minimum score 550 paper-based; 213 computer-based; 80 iBT), IELTS (minimum score 7). *Application deadline:* For fall admission, 1/15 priority date for domestic and international students. Applications are processed on a rolling basis. Application fee: $60 ($95 for international students). Electronic applications accepted. *Financial support:* In 2009–10, 4 students received support, including 4 research assistantships with partial tuition reimbursements available (averaging $10,000 per year); institutionally sponsored loans, scholarships/grants, health care benefits, and unspecified assistantships also available. Financial award application deadline: 3/1. *Faculty research:* Marriage and family therapy. *Unit head:* Dr. Gerald Weeks, Chair/Professor, 702-895-1392, Fax: 702-895-1869, E-mail: gerald.weeks@unlv.edu. *Application contact:* Graduate College Admissions Evaluator, 702-895-3320, Fax: 702-895-4180, E-mail: gradcollege@unlv.edu.

University of New Hampshire, Graduate School, School of Health and Human Services, Department of Family Studies, Durham, NH 03824. Offers family studies (MS); marriage and family therapy (MS). Program offered in fall only. *Accreditation:* AAMFT/COAMFTE. Part-time programs available. *Faculty:* 9 full-time (6 women). *Students:* 17 full-time (15 women), 8 part-time (all women); includes 3 minority (1 African American, 2 Asian Americans or Pacific Islanders). Average age 33. 18 applicants, 72% accepted, 7 enrolled. In 2009, 6 master's awarded. *Degree requirements:* For master's, thesis or alternative. *Entrance requirements:* For master's, GRE General Test. Additional exam requirements/recommendations for international students: Required—TOEFL (minimum score 550 paper-based; 213 computer-based; 80 iBT). *Application deadline:* For fall admission, 5/15 priority date for domestic students, 4/1 for international students. Applications are processed on a rolling basis. Application fee: $65. Electronic applications accepted. *Expenses:* Tuition, state resident: full-time $10,380; part-time $577 per credit hour. Tuition, nonresident: full-time $24,350; part-time $1002 per credit hour. Required fees: $1550; $387.50 per semester. Tuition and fees vary according to course load and program. *Financial support:* In 2009–10, 13 students received support, including 5 teaching assistantships; fellowships, research assistantships, career-related internships or fieldwork, Federal Work-Study, scholarships/grants, and tuition waivers (full and partial) also available. Support available to part-time students. Financial award application deadline: 2/15. *Unit head:* Dr. Kerry Kazura, Chairperson, 603-862-2135. *Application contact:* Matty Leighton, Administrative Assistant, 603-862-5021, E-mail: family.studies@unh.edu.

The University of North Carolina at Greensboro, Graduate School, School of Education, Department of Counseling and Educational Development, Greensboro, NC 27412-5001. Offers advanced school counseling (PMC); counseling and counselor education (PhD); counseling and educational development (MS); couple and family counseling (PMC); school counseling (PMC); MS/Ed S. *Accreditation:* ACA (one or more programs are accredited); NCATE. *Degree requirements:* For master's, comprehensive exam, practicum, internship; for doctorate, comprehensive exam, thesis/dissertation. *Entrance requirements:* For master's, doctorate, and PMC, GRE General Test. Additional exam requirements/recommendations for international students: Required—TOEFL. Electronic applications accepted. *Faculty research:* Gerontology, invitational theory, career development, marriage and family therapy, drug and alcohol abuse prevention.

University of Phoenix, The Artemis School, College of Health and Human Services, Phoenix, AZ 85034-7209. Offers administration of justice and security (MS); community counseling (MSC); education (MHA); family nurse practitioner (MSN); gerontology (MHA); health administration (MHA); health care education (MSN); health care management (MBA, MSN); informatics (MHA); marriage, family, and child therapy (MSC); nursing (MSN); nursing for nurse practitioners (MSN); psychology (MS); MSN/MBA; MSN/MHA. *Accreditation:* AACN. Evening/weekend programs available. Postbaccalaureate distance learning degree programs offered. *Degree requirements:* For master's, thesis (for some programs). *Entrance requirements:* For master's, 3 years of work experience, minimum undergraduate GPA of 2.5, RN license. Additional exam requirements/recommendations for international students: Required—TOEFL (minimum score 550 paper-based; 213 computer-based; 79 iBT). Electronic applications accepted.

University of Phoenix–Bay Area Campus, The Artemis School, College of Health and Human Services, Pleasanton, CA 94588-3677. Offers administration of justice and security (MS); family nurse practitioner (MSN); health care management (MBA); marriage, family and child therapy (MSC); nursing (MSN); nursing/health care education (MSN); MSN/MBA. Evening/weekend programs available. Postbaccalaureate distance learning degree programs offered (no on-campus study). *Degree requirements:* For master's, thesis (for some programs). *Entrance requirements:* For master's, minimum undergraduate GPA of 2.5, 3 years of work experience, RN license. Additional exam requirements/recommendations for international students: Required—TOEFL (minimum score 550 paper-based; 213 computer-based; 79 iBT). Electronic applications accepted.

University of Phoenix–Central Valley Campus, College of Social and Behavioral Science, Fresno, CA 93720-1562. Offers marriage, family and child therapy (MSC).

University of Phoenix–Denver Campus, The Artemis School, College of Health and Human Services, Lone Tree, CO 80124-5453. Offers administration of justice and security (MS); community counseling (MSC); health administration (MHA); health care management (MBA); marriage, family and child therapy (MSC); nursing (MSN); psychology (MS); MSN/MBA; MSN/MHA. Evening/weekend programs available. Postbaccalaureate distance learning degree programs offered. *Degree requirements:* For master's, thesis (for some programs). *Entrance requirements:* For master's, minimum undergraduate GPA of 2.5, 3 years work experience, RN license. Additional exam requirements/recommendations for international students: Required—TOEFL (minimum score 550 paper-based; 213 computer-based; 79 iBT). Electronic applications accepted.

University of Phoenix–Hawaii Campus, The Artemis School, College of Health and Human Services, Honolulu, HI 96813-4317. Offers administration of justice and security (MS); community counseling (MSC); education (MHA); family nurse practitioner (MSN); gerontology (MHA); health administration (MHA); health care management (MBA); marriage, family and child therapy (MSC); nursing (MSN); nursing/health care education (MSN); psychology (MS); MSN/MBA. Evening/weekend programs available. *Degree requirements:* For master's, thesis (for some programs). *Entrance requirements:* For master's, minimum undergraduate GPA of 2.5, 3 years of work experience, RN license. Additional exam requirements/recommendations for international students: Required—TOEFL (minimum score 550 paper-based; 213 computer-based; 79 iBT). Electronic applications accepted.

University of Phoenix–Las Vegas Campus, The Artemis School, College of Health and Human Services, Las Vegas, NV 89128. Offers administration of justice and security (MS); health administration (MHA); health care management (MBA); marriage, family, and child therapy (MSC); mental health counseling (MSC); nursing (MSN); nursing/health care education (MSN); psychology (MS); MSN/MBA; MSN/MHA. Postbaccalaureate distance learning degree programs offered. *Entrance requirements:* For master's, minimum undergraduate GPA of 2.5, 3 years of work experience. Additional exam requirements/recommendations for international students: Required—TOEFL (minimum score 550 paper-based; 213 computer-based; 79 iBT). Electronic applications accepted.

University of Phoenix–New Mexico Campus, The Artemis School, College of Health and Human Services, Albuquerque, NM 87113-1570. Offers administration of justice and security (MS); health administration (MHA); health care education (MSN); health care management (MBA); marriage and family therapy (MSC); nursing (MSN); psychology (MS); MSN/MBA. Evening/weekend programs available. *Degree requirements:* For master's, thesis (for some programs). *Entrance requirements:* For master's, minimum undergraduate GPA of 2.5, 3 years of work experience, RN license. Additional exam requirements/recommendations for international students: Required—TOEFL (minimum score 550 paper-based; 213 computer-based; 79 iBT). Electronic applications accepted.

University of Phoenix–Northern Nevada Campus, College of Social and Behavioral Science, Reno, NV 89521-5862. Offers administration of justice and security (MS); marriage, family and child therapy (MSC); psychology (MS); school counseling (MSC).

University of Phoenix–Phoenix Campus, The Artemis School, College of Health and Human Services, Phoenix, AZ 85040-1958. Offers community counseling (MSC); education (MHA); family nurse practitioner (MSN); gerontology (MHA); health administration (MHA); health care education (MSN); health care management (MBA); informatics (MHA); marriage, family, and child therapy (MSC); nurse practitioner (Certificate); nursing (MSN); nursing health care education (Certificate); psychology (MS); MSN/MBA; MSN/MHA. Evening/weekend programs available. *Degree requirements:* For master's, thesis (for some programs). *Entrance requirements:* For master's, 3 years of work experience in field, minimum undergraduate GPA of 2.5, RN license. Additional exam requirements/recommendations for international students: Required—TOEFL (minimum score 550 paper-based; 213 computer-based; 79 iBT). Electronic applications accepted.

University of Phoenix–Puerto Rico Campus, The Artemis School, College of Health and Human Services, Guaynabo, PR 00968. Offers marriage and family counseling (MSC); mental health counseling (MSC). Evening/weekend programs available. *Degree requirements:* For master's, thesis (for some programs). *Entrance requirements:* For master's, Counselor Preparation Comprehensive Examination, minimum undergraduate GPA of 2.5, 3 years work experience. Additional exam requirements/recommendations for international students: Required—TOEFL (minimum score 550 paper-based; 213 computer-based; 79 iBT). Electronic applications accepted.

University of Phoenix–Sacramento Valley Campus, The Artemis School, College of Health and Human Services, Sacramento, CA 95833-3632. Offers administration of justice and security (MS); community counseling (MSC); family nurse practitioner (MSN); health administration (MHA); health care education (MSN); health care management (MBA); marriage, family and child counseling (MSC); nursing (MSN); psychology (MS); MSN/MBA. Evening/weekend programs available. *Degree requirements:* For master's, thesis (for some programs). *Entrance requirements:* For master's, RN license, minimum undergraduate GPA of 2.5, 3 years work experience. Additional exam requirements/recommendations for international students: Required—TOEFL (minimum score 550 paper-based; 213 computer-based; 79 iBT). Electronic applications accepted.

University of Phoenix–San Diego Campus, The Artemis School, College of Health and Human Services, San Diego, CA 92123. Offers administration of justice and security (MS); health care education (MSN); health care management (MBA); marriage, family and child counseling (MSC); marriage, family and child therapy (MSC); nursing (MSN); MSN/MBA. Evening/weekend programs available. *Degree requirements:* For master's, thesis (for some programs). *Entrance requirements:* For master's, minimum undergraduate GPA of 2.5, 3 years work experience, RN license. Additional exam requirements/recommendations for international students: Required—TOEFL (minimum score 550 paper-based; 213 computer-based; 79 iBT). Electronic applications accepted.

University of Phoenix–Southern Arizona Campus, The Artemis School, College of Health and Human Services, Tucson, AZ 85711. Offers administration of justice and security (MS); family nurse practitioner (MSN, Certificate); health administration (MHA); health care management (MBA); marriage, family and child therapy (MSC); nursing (MSN); psychology (MS). Evening/weekend programs available. *Degree requirements:* For master's, thesis (for some programs). *Entrance requirements:* For master's, minimum undergraduate GPA of 2.5, 3 years of work experience, RN license. Additional exam requirements/recommendations for international students: Required—TOEFL (minimum score 550 paper-based; 213 computer-based; 79 iBT). Electronic applications accepted.

University of Phoenix–Southern California Campus, The Artemis School, College of Health and Human Services, Costa Mesa, CA 92626. Offers administration of justice and security (MS); family nurse practitioner (MSN, Certificate); health administration (MHA); health care education (MSN); health care management (MBA); marriage, family and child therapy (MSC); nursing (MSN); psychology (MS); MSN/MBA; MSN/MHA. Evening/weekend programs available. *Degree requirements:* For master's, thesis (for some programs). *Entrance requirements:* For master's, minimum undergraduate GPA of 2.5, 3 years work experience, RN license. Additional exam requirements/recommendations for international students: Required—TOEFL (minimum score 550 paper-based; 213 computer-based; 79 iBT). Electronic applications accepted.

University of Phoenix–Southern Colorado Campus, The Artemis School, College of Health and Human Services, Colorado Springs, CO 80919-2335. Offers administration of justice and security (MS); community counseling (MSC); education (MHA); gerontology (MHA); health administration (MHA); health care management (MBA); marriage, family and child therapy (MSC); nursing (MSN); psychology (MS); MSN/MBA. Evening/weekend programs available. *Degree requirements:* For master's, thesis (for some programs). *Entrance requirements:* For master's, minimum undergraduate GPA of 2.5, 3 years of work experience, RN license. Additional exam requirements/recommendations for international students: Required—TOEFL (minimum score 550 paper-based; 213 computer-based; 79 iBT). Electronic applications accepted.

University of Rochester, School of Medicine and Dentistry, Graduate Programs in Medicine and Dentistry, Department of Psychiatry, Rochester, NY 14627. Offers marriage and family therapy (MS). *Accreditation:* AAMFT/COAMFTE. Part-time programs available. *Degree requirements:* For master's, projects. *Entrance requirements:* For master's, GRE General Test.

University of St. Thomas, Graduate Studies, Graduate School of Professional Psychology, St. Paul, MN 55105-1096. Offers counseling psychology (MA, Psy D); marriage and family psychology (MA, Certificate). *Accreditation:* APA. Part-time and evening/weekend programs available. *Faculty:* 11 full-time (5 women), 13 part-time/adjunct (6 women). *Students:* 68 full-time (54 women), 141 part-time (113 women); includes 21 minority (5 African Americans, 13 Asian Americans or Pacific Islanders, 3 Hispanic Americans), 4 international. Average age 29. 578 applicants, 42% accepted. In 2009, 22 master's, 11 doctorates awarded. *Degree requirements:* For master's, comprehensive exam, practicum; for doctorate, comprehensive exam, thesis/dissertation, qualifying exam, practicum, internship. *Entrance requirements:* For master's, GRE, minimum GPA of 2.75, letters of recommendation, personal statement; for doctorate, GRE, minimum GPA of 3.2, letters of recommendation, personal statement. Additional exam requirements/recommendations for international students: Required—TOEFL (minimum score 550 paper-based; 213 computer-based; 80 iBT). *Application deadline:* For fall admission,

Marriage and Family Therapy

University of St. Thomas (continued)
3/1 priority date for domestic students; for winter admission, 2/1 priority date for domestic students; for spring admission, 9/15 priority date for domestic students, 3/1 for international students. Application fee: $50. *Expenses:* Contact institution. *Financial support:* In 2009–10, 2 fellowships (averaging $5,000 per year) were awarded; research assistantships, institutionally sponsored loans and scholarships/grants also available. Support available to part-time students. Financial award application deadline: 8/1; financial award applicants required to submit FAFSA. *Faculty research:* Elderly, eating disorders, anxiety, family. *Unit head:* Dr. Christopher S. Vye, Associate Dean, 651-962-4666, Fax: 651-962-4666, E-mail: bnolan@stthomas.edu. *Application contact:* Laurie Dupont, Administrative Assistant, 651-962-4669, Fax: 651-962-4651, E-mail: ldupont@stthomas.edu.

University of San Diego, School of Leadership and Education Sciences, Program in Marital and Family Therapy, San Diego, CA 92110-2492. Offers MA. *Accreditation:* AAMFT/COAMFTE. *Faculty:* 4 full-time (2 women), 9 part-time/adjunct (5 women). *Students:* 54 full-time (50 women), 2 part-time (both women); includes 13 minority (1 American Indian/Alaska Native, 2 Asian Americans or Pacific Islanders, 10 Hispanic Americans), 2 international. Average age 25. 114 applicants, 50% accepted, 27 enrolled. In 2009, 33 master's awarded. *Degree requirements:* For master's, comprehensive exam. *Entrance requirements:* For master's, GRE General Test or MAT, minimum GPA of 3.0, 3 letters of recommendation, resume. Additional exam requirements/recommendations for international students: Required—TOEFL (minimum score 580 paper-based; 237 computer-based; 83 iBT), TWE. *Application deadline:* For fall admission, 3/1 for domestic and international students; for spring admission, 10/15 for domestic and international students. Application fee: $45. *Expenses:* Tuition: Full-time $21,042; part-time $1169 per unit. Required fees: $224. Full-time tuition and fees vary according to course load and degree level. *Financial support:* In 2009–10, 49 students received support. Career-related internships or fieldwork, Federal Work-Study, institutionally sponsored loans, scholarships/grants, unspecified assistantships, and stipends available. Support available to part-time students. Financial award application deadline: 4/1; financial award applicants required to submit FAFSA. *Faculty research:* Child and family interventions and assessment strategies, collaboration between family therapists and medical professionals, family therapy training and supervision, health care reform, premarital counseling. *Unit head:* Dr. Todd M. Edwards, Director, 619-260-5963, Fax: 619-260-6835, E-mail: tedwards@sandiego.edu. *Application contact:* Dr. John Mosby, Associate Director of Graduate Admissions, 619-260-4524, Fax: 619-260-4158, E-mail: grads@sandiego.edu.

University of San Francisco, School of Education, Department of Counseling Psychology, San Francisco, CA 94117-1080. Offers counseling (MA), including educational counseling, life transitions counseling, marital and family therapy; counseling psychology (Ed D). *Faculty:* 7 full-time (3 women), 37 part-time/adjunct (26 women). *Students:* 277 full-time (228 women), 9 part-time (7 women); includes 97 minority (16 African Americans, 1 American Indian/Alaska Native, 35 Asian Americans or Pacific Islanders, 45 Hispanic Americans), 8 international. Average age 31. 354 applicants, 66% accepted, 132 enrolled. In 2009, 150 master's awarded. *Degree requirements:* For doctorate, thesis/dissertation. *Entrance requirements:* For doctorate, GRE General Test. Application fee: $55 ($65 for international students). *Expenses:* Tuition: Full-time $19,710; part-time $1095 per unit. Part-time tuition and fees vary according to degree level, campus/location and program. *Financial support:* In 2009–10, 227 students received support; fellowships, research assistantships, teaching assistantships available. Financial award application deadline: 3/2; financial award applicants required to submit FAFSA. *Unit head:* Dr. Brian Gerrard, Chair, 415-422-6868. *Application contact:* Beth Teague, Associate Director of Graduate Outreach, 415-422-5467, E-mail: schoolofeducation@usfca.edu.

University of Southern California, Graduate School, Rossier School of Education, Master's Programs in Education, Los Angeles, CA 90089-4038. Offers marriage, family and child counseling (MMFT); postsecondary administration and student affairs [PASA] (ME); school counseling (ME); teaching (MA); teaching and teaching credential (MAT); teaching English to speakers of other languages (MAT, MS). Part-time and evening/weekend programs available. Postbaccalaureate distance learning degree programs offered (no on-campus study). *Faculty:* 26 full-time (17 women), 24 part-time/adjunct (14 women). *Students:* 579 full-time (455 women), 85 part-time (56 women); includes 302 minority (50 African Americans, 4 American Indian/Alaska Native, 110 Asian Americans or Pacific Islanders, 138 Hispanic Americans), 62 international. 1,282 applicants, 67% accepted, 484 enrolled. In 2009, 228 master's awarded. *Degree requirements:* For master's, thesis optional. *Entrance requirements:* For master's, GRE (for all programs except MAT). Additional exam requirements/recommendations for international students: Required—TOEFL (minimum score 250 computer-based; 100 iBT). Application fee: $85. Electronic applications accepted. *Expenses:* Tuition: Full-time $25,980; part-time $1315 per unit. Required fees: $554. One-time fee: $35 full-time. Full-time tuition and fees vary according to degree level and program. *Financial support:* Career-related internships or fieldwork, Federal Work-Study, scholarships/grants, traineeships, and unspecified assistantships available. Support available to part-time students. Financial award application deadline: 4/10; financial award applicants required to submit FAFSA. *Faculty research:* College access and equity; preparing teachers for culturally diverse populations; sociocultural basis of learning as mediated by instruction with focus on reading and literacy in English learners; social and political aspects of teaching and learning English; school counselor development and training. *Unit head:* Dr. Kristan Venegas, Director/Assistant Professor of Clinical Education, 213-740-3255, E-mail: rsoemast@usc.edu. *Application contact:* Michael Jackson, 213-740-0224, E-mail: soeinfo@usc.edu.

University of Southern Mississippi, Graduate School, College of Education and Psychology, Department of Child and Family Studies, Hattiesburg, MS 39406-0001. Offers child and family studies (MS); early intervention (MS); marriage and family therapy (MS). *Accreditation:* AAMFT/COAMFTE. Part-time programs available. *Faculty:* 7 full-time (3 women). *Students:* 28 full-time (all women), 37 part-time (all women); includes 18 minority (17 African Americans, 1 Asian American or Pacific Islander), 1 international. Average age 29. 57 applicants, 61% accepted, 34 enrolled. In 2009, 15 master's awarded. *Degree requirements:* For master's, comprehensive exam, thesis optional. *Entrance requirements:* For master's, GRE General Test, minimum GPA of 2.75 in last 60 hours. Additional exam requirements/recommendations for international students: Required—TOEFL. *Application deadline:* For fall admission, 3/1 priority date for domestic students, 3/1 for international students. Applications are processed on a rolling basis. Application fee: $35. Electronic applications accepted. *Expenses:* Tuition, state resident: full-time $5096; part-time $284 per hour. Tuition, nonresident: full-time $13,052; part-time $726 per hour. Required fees: $402. Tuition and fees vary according to course level and course load. *Financial support:* In 2009–10, 21 students received support, including 3 research assistantships with full tuition reimbursements available (averaging $7,300 per year); fellowships, career-related internships or fieldwork, Federal Work-Study, institutionally sponsored loans, scholarships/grants, and unspecified assistantships also available. Financial award application deadline: 3/15; financial award applicants required to submit FAFSA. *Faculty research:* School food service, teen pregnancy, diet and cholesterol metabolism. *Unit head:* Dr. Ann Blackwell, Chair, 601-266-5661, Fax: 601-266-4680. *Application contact:* Dr. Ann Blackwell, Chair, 601-266-5661, Fax: 601-266-4680.

The University of Texas at Tyler, College of Education and Psychology, Department of Psychology and Counseling, Tyler, TX 75799-0001. Offers clinical psychology (MS), including neuropsychology, school psychology; counseling psychology (MA), including general, marriage and family; interdisciplinary studies (MSIS); school counseling (MA). Part-time and evening/weekend programs available. *Faculty:* 11 full-time (3 women). *Students:* 80 full-time (63 women), 46 part-time (38 women); includes 5 minority (3 African Americans, 1 American Indian/Alaska Native, 1 Hispanic American). Average age 29. 64 applicants, 77% accepted, 28 enrolled. In 2009, 36 master's awarded. *Degree requirements:* For master's, comprehensive exam, thesis optional. *Entrance requirements:* For master's, GRE General Test, minimum GPA of 3.0. Additional exam requirements/recommendations for international students: Required—TOEFL (minimum score 79 computer-based). *Application deadline:* For fall admission, 8/17 priority date for domestic students, 7/1 priority date for international students; for spring admission, 12/21 priority date for domestic students, 11/1 priority date for international students. Application fee: $25 ($50 for international students). Electronic applications accepted. *Expenses:* Tuition, state resident: part-time $665 per semester hour. Tuition, nonresident: part-time $942 per semester hour. Part-time tuition and fees vary according to degree level and program. *Financial support:* In 2009–10, fellowships with partial tuition reimbursements (averaging $3,000 per year), research assistantships (averaging $5,000 per year), teaching assistantships (averaging $1,500 per year) were awarded; career-related internships or fieldwork, Federal Work-Study, and institutionally sponsored loans also available. Support available to part-time students. Financial award application deadline: 7/1. *Faculty research:* Neuropsychology, child abuse, psychometric properties of psychological instruments, maternal behavior, clinical practice issues, victimization of women, post-traumatic stress disorder. *Unit head:* Dr. Charles B. Barke, Chair/Professor, 903-565-5875, Fax: 903-565-5560, E-mail: cbarke@uttyler.edu. *Application contact:* Dr. Charles Barke.

The University of Winnipeg, Faculty of Theology, Winnipeg, MB R3B 2E9, Canada. Offers marriage and family therapy (MMFT, Certificate); sacred theology (STM); theology (M Div). *Accreditation:* AAMFT/COAMFTE; ATS. Part-time programs available. *Degree requirements:* For M Div, thesis/dissertation optional.

University of Wisconsin–Milwaukee, Graduate School, School of Social Welfare, Department of Social Work, Milwaukee, WI 53201-0413. Offers applied gerontology (Certificate); marriage and family therapy (Certificate); non-profit management (Certificate); social work (MSW, PhD). *Accreditation:* CSWE. Part-time programs available. *Faculty:* 18 full-time (11 women). *Students:* 173 full-time (157 women), 101 part-time (92 women); includes 55 minority (38 African Americans, 2 American Indian/Alaska Native, 7 Asian Americans or Pacific Islanders, 8 Hispanic Americans). Average age 31. 303 applicants, 62% accepted, 93 enrolled. In 2009, 105 master's awarded. *Degree requirements:* For master's, thesis or alternative. *Entrance requirements:* For doctorate, GRE, bachelor's degree. Additional exam requirements/recommendations for international students: Required—TOEFL (minimum score 550 paper-based; 79 iBT), IELTS (minimum score 6.5). *Application deadline:* For fall admission, 1/1 priority date for domestic students; for spring admission, 9/1 for domestic students. Applications are processed on a rolling basis. Application fee: $45 ($75 for international students). *Expenses:* Tuition, state resident: full-time $8800. Tuition, nonresident: full-time $20,760. Tuition and fees vary according to program and reciprocity agreements. *Financial support:* In 2009–10, 3 fellowships, 4 teaching assistantships were awarded; research assistantships, career-related internships or fieldwork and unspecified assistantships also available. Support available to part-time students. Financial award application deadline: 4/15. Total annual research expenditures: $806,977. *Unit head:* Deborah Padgett, Representative, 414-229-4851, Fax: 414-229-5311, E-mail: dpadgett@uwm.edu. *Application contact:* Steve McMurtry, General Information Contact, 414-229-2249, Fax: 414-229-6967, E-mail: mcmurtry@uwm.edu.

University of Wisconsin–Stout, Graduate School, College of Human Development, Program in Marriage and Family Therapy, Menomonie, WI 54751. Offers MS. *Accreditation:* AAMFT/COAMFTE. Part-time programs available. *Degree requirements:* For master's, thesis or alternative. *Entrance requirements:* For master's, minimum GPA of 2.75. Additional exam requirements/recommendations for international students: Required—TOEFL (minimum score 500 paper-based; 173 computer-based; 61 iBT). Electronic applications accepted. *Faculty research:* Abuse, addiction, resilience, diversity, narrative therapy.

Utah State University, School of Graduate Studies, College of Education and Human Services, Department of Family, Consumer, and Human Development, Logan, UT 84322. Offers family and human development (MFHD); family, consumer, and human development (MS, PhD), including adolescence/youth (MS), adult development/aging (MS), consumer science (MS), infancy/childhood (MS), marriage and family relations (MS), marriage and family therapy (MS). *Accreditation:* AAMFT/COAMFTE (one or more programs are accredited). Part-time and evening/weekend programs available. Postbaccalaureate distance learning degree programs offered (minimal on-campus study). *Degree requirements:* For master's, thesis; for doctorate, comprehensive exam, thesis/dissertation, competencies. *Entrance requirements:* For master's, GRE General Test or MAT, minimum GPA of 3.0, 3 letters of recommendation; for doctorate, GRE, minimum GPA of 3.0, 3 letters of recommendation. Additional exam requirements/recommendations for international students: Required—TOEFL. Electronic applications accepted. *Faculty research:* Marriage and family relations, adolescent problem behavior, family financial management, early literacy, mental health in the elderly, parent child attachment.

Valdosta State University, Graduate School, Department of Sociology, Anthropology, and Criminal Justice, Valdosta, GA 31698. Offers criminal justice (MS); marriage and family therapy (MS); sociology (MS). *Accreditation:* AAMFT/COAMFTE. Part-time and evening/weekend programs available. *Degree requirements:* For master's, thesis or alternative, comprehensive written and/or oral exams. *Entrance requirements:* For master's, GRE General Test or MAT (sociology, marriage and family therapy), minimum GPA of 2.5. Additional exam requirements/recommendations for international students: Required—TOEFL (minimum score 523 paper-based; 193 computer-based). Electronic applications accepted. *Faculty research:* Police-civilian ride-along project.

Virginia Polytechnic Institute and State University, Graduate School, College of Liberal Arts and Human Sciences, Department of Human Development, Blacksburg, VA 24061. Offers adult development and aging (MS, PhD); adult learning and human resource development (MS, PhD); child development (MS, PhD); family studies (MS, PhD); marriage and family therapy (MS, PhD). *Accreditation:* AAMFT/COAMFTE (one or more programs are accredited). *Faculty:* 22 full-time (18 women). *Students:* 49 full-time (38 women), 64 part-time (44 women); includes 30 minority (1 African American, 7 American Indian/Alaska Native, 16 Asian Americans or Pacific Islanders, 6 Hispanic Americans), 2 international. Average age 34. 64 applicants, 34% accepted, 16 enrolled. In 2009, 10 master's, 14 doctorates awarded. *Entrance requirements:* For master's and doctorate, GRE, GMAT. Additional exam requirements/recommendations for international students: Required—TOEFL (minimum score 550 paper-based; 213 computer-based). *Application deadline:* For fall admission, 5/15 for international students; for spring admission, 10/15 for international students. Applications are processed on a rolling basis. Application fee: $65. Electronic applications accepted. *Expenses:* Tuition, area resident: Full-time $10,228; part-time $459 per credit hour. Tuition, nonresident: full-time $17,892; part-time $865 per credit hour. Required fees: $1966; $451 per semester. *Financial support:* In 2009–10, 7 research assistantships with full tuition reimbursements (averaging $10,933 per year), 25 teaching assistantships with full tuition reimbursements (averaging $9,387 per year) were awarded; career-related internships or fieldwork, Federal Work-Study, scholarships/grants, and unspecified assistantships also available. Financial award application deadline: 1/15. *Faculty research:* Stress management, children's play, dual-career families, social cognition, relationships of elderly. Total annual research expenditures: $823,581. *Unit head:* Dr. Shannon E. Jarrott, Head, 540-231-4794, Fax: 540-231-7012, E-mail: sjarrott@vt.edu. *Application contact:* Mark Benson, Information Contact, 540-231-5720, Fax: 540-231-7012, E-mail: mbenson@vt.edu.

Walden University, Graduate Programs, School of Counseling and Social Service, Minneapolis, MN 55401. Offers counselor education and supervision (PhD), including consultation, counseling and social change, forensic mental health counseling, general program, nonprofit management and leadership, trauma and crisis; human services (PhD), including clinical social work, counseling, criminal justice, family studies and intervention strategies, general program, human services administration, self-designed, social policy analysis and planning; marriage, couple, and family counseling (MS), including forensic counseling, trauma and crisis counseling; mental health counseling (MS), including forensic counseling. Part-time and evening/weekend programs available. Postbaccalaureate distance learning degree programs offered (minimal on-campus study). *Faculty:* 13 full-time, 78 part-time/adjunct. *Students:* 1,932 full-time (1,624 women), 210 part-time (181 women); includes 945 minority (817 African Americans, 24 American Indian/Alaska Native, 24 Asian Americans or Pacific Islanders, 80 Hispanic Americans),

34 international. Average age 39. In 2009, 55 master's, 5 doctorates awarded. *Degree requirements:* For master's, residency (for some programs); for doctorate, thesis/dissertation, residency. *Entrance requirements:* For master's, bachelor's degree or equivalent in related field, minimum GPA of 2.5; for doctorate, master's degree or equivalent in related field; minimum GPA of 3.0; official transcripts; three years' related professional/academic experience (preferred); access to computer and Internet. Additional exam requirements/recommendations for international students: Required—TOEFL (minimum score 550 paper-based; 213 computer-based), IELTS (minimum score 6.5), or Michigan English Language Assessment Battery (minimum score 82). *Application deadline:* Applications are processed on a rolling basis. Application fee: $50. Electronic applications accepted. *Expenses:* Tuition: Full-time $13,665; part-time $560 per credit. Required fees: $1375. Tuition and fees vary according to course load, degree level and program. *Financial support:* In 2009–10, 200 students received support; fellowships, Federal Work-Study, scholarships/grants, unspecified assistantships, and family tuition reduction, active duty/veteran tuition reduction, group tuition reduction, interest-free payment plans available. Support available to part-time students. Financial award applicants required to submit FAFSA. *Unit head:* Dr. Savitri Dixon-Saxon, Associate Dean, 800-925-3368. *Application contact:* Jennifer Hall, Director of Enrollment, 866-4-WALDEN, E-mail: info@waldenu.edu.

Wesley Biblical Seminary, Graduate Programs, Jackson, MS 39206. Offers apologetics (MA); Biblical studies (MA); Christian studies (MA); evangelism (M Div); family life ministry (M Div); honors research (M Div); missions (M Div); pastoral ministry (M Div); teaching (M Div); theological studies (MA). *Accreditation:* ATS. Part-time programs available. *Faculty:* 11 full-time (2 women), 5 part-time/adjunct (0 women). *Students:* 43 full-time (5 women), 89 part-time (33 women). *Degree requirements:* For master's, thesis. *Entrance requirements:* Additional exam requirements/recommendations for international students: Required—TOEFL. *Application deadline:* For fall admission, 7/1 priority date for domestic students; for spring admission, 12/1 priority date for domestic students. Applications are processed on a rolling basis. Application fee: $40. Electronic applications accepted. *Expenses:* Tuition: Full-time $8000; part-time $320 per credit hour. Required fees: $310; $160 per semester. Tuition and fees vary according to course load, campus/location and program. *Financial support:* Scholarships/grants available. Support available to part-time students. *Faculty research:* Patristics, missiology, culture, hermeneutics. *Unit head:* Dr. Ray R. Easley, Vice President for Academic Affairs, 601-366-8880 Ext. 112, Fax: 601-366-8832. *Application contact:* Laura McMillan, Assistant to the Vice President for Business and Student Development, 601-366-8880 Ext. 110, Fax: 601-366-8832, E-mail: admissions@wbs.edu.

Western Michigan University, Graduate College, College of Education, Department of Counselor Education and Counseling Psychology, Kalamazoo, MI 49008. Offers counseling psychology (MA, PhD); counselor education (MA, PhD); human resources development (MA). *Accreditation:* ACA (one or more programs are accredited); APA (one or more programs are accredited); CORE; NCATE. *Degree requirements:* For doctorate, thesis/dissertation, oral exams. *Entrance requirements:* For doctorate, GRE General Test.

Western Seminary–Sacramento Campus, Graduate Programs, Sacramento, CA 95821. Offers exegetical theology (MA); marital and family therapy (MA); ministry (M Div); specialized ministry (MA). Postbaccalaureate distance learning degree programs offered. *Entrance requirements:* For M Div, minimum GPA of 2.5; for master's, minimum GPA of 3.0.

Western Seminary–San Jose Campus, Graduate Programs, Los Gatos, CA 95032-4520. Offers exegetical theology (MA); expositional ministry (M Div); marital and family therapy (MA); ministry (M Div); pastoral ministry (M Div); specialized ministry (MA). Postbaccalaureate distance learning degree programs offered. *Degree requirements:* For master's, 2 foreign languages; for M Div, 3 foreign languages. *Entrance requirements:* For M Div, minimum GPA of 2.5; for master's, minimum GPA of 3.0.

Psychoanalysis and Psychotherapy

Adler Graduate School, Program in Adlerian Studies, Richfield, MN 55423. Offers art therapy specialization (MA); clinical counseling track (MA); coaching and consulting in organizations (Certificate); management consulting and organizational leadership (MA); marriage and family track (MA); non-clinical Adlerian studies track (MA); personal and professional life coaching (Certificate); school counseling (MA). Part-time and evening/weekend programs available. *Degree requirements:* For master's, thesis or alternative, 500-700 hour internship (depending on license choice). *Entrance requirements:* For master's, minimum undergraduate GPA of 3.0, 12 credits of course work in psychology or related field.

Argosy University, Chicago, College of Psychology and Behavioral Sciences, Doctoral Program in Clinical Psychology, Chicago, IL 60601. Offers child and adolescent psychology (Psy D); client-centered and experiential psychotherapies (Psy D); diversity and multicultural psychology (Psy D); family psychology (Psy D); forensic psychology (Psy D); health psychology (Psy D); neuropsychology (Psy D); organizational consulting (Psy D); psychoanalytic psychology (Psy D); psychology and spirituality (Psy D). *Accreditation:* APA.

See Close-Up on page 1051.

Boston Graduate School of Psychoanalysis, Master's, Certificate, and Doctoral Programs, Brookline, MA 02446-4602. Offers MA, Psya D, Certificate. Part-time programs available. Terminal master's awarded for partial completion of doctoral program. *Degree requirements:* For master's and Certificate, thesis. *Entrance requirements:* For master's and doctorate, interview, writing sample; for Certificate, interview, MA. Electronic applications accepted. *Faculty research:* The effect of extra-analytic contact on the analysis, psychoanalytic intervention with schizophrenia, emotional learning in the classroom, psychoanalytic techniques in the geriatric setting, addictions research.

Boston Graduate School of Psychoanalysis, Master's Program—New York, New York, NY 10011. Offers MA. Part-time programs available. *Entrance requirements:* For master's, interview, writing sample.

Boston Graduate School of Psychoanalysis, Programs in Psychoanalysis and Culture, Brookline, MA 02446-4602. Offers MA, Psya D. Evening/weekend programs available. *Degree requirements:* For doctorate, thesis/dissertation. *Entrance requirements:* For master's, interview, writing sample, letters of reference, transcripts; for doctorate, interview, writing sample, letters of reference. Electronic applications accepted. *Faculty research:* Institutional violence, developmental impulse control, psychodynamics of murderers, community violence, psychodynamics in the Salem Witch Trials.

Naropa University, Graduate Programs, Program in Contemplative Psychotherapy, Boulder, CO 80302-6697. Offers MA. *Degree requirements:* For master's, thesis, internship. *Entrance requirements:* For master's, in-person interview, resume, 3 letters of recommendation. Additional exam requirements/recommendations for international students: Required—TOEFL (minimum score 600 paper-based; 250 computer-based). Electronic applications accepted.

Naropa University, Graduate Programs, Program in Somatic Counseling Psychotherapy, Concentration in Body Psychotherapy, Boulder, CO 80302-6697. Offers MA. Part-time programs available. *Degree requirements:* For master's, comprehensive exam, thesis, internship, fieldwork, portfolio. *Entrance requirements:* For master's, interview; body-mind discipline; course work in psychology, anatomy; resume, 3 letters of recommendation. Additional exam requirements/recommendations for international students: Required—TOEFL (minimum score 600 paper-based; 250 computer-based). Electronic applications accepted.

New York University, Graduate School of Arts and Science, Department of Psychology, New York, NY 10012-1019. Offers cognition and perception (PhD); community psychology (PhD); general psychology (MA); industrial/organizational psychology (MA); psychotherapy and psychoanalysis (Advanced Certificate); social/personality psychology (PhD). Part-time programs available. *Students:* 151 full-time (94 women), 273 part-time (192 women); includes 59 minority (13 African Americans, 1 American Indian/Alaska Native, 27 Asian Americans or Pacific Islanders, 18 Hispanic Americans), 62 international. Average age 32. 748 applicants, 46% accepted, 122 enrolled. In 2009, 100 master's, 11 doctorates, 8 other advanced degrees awarded. Terminal master's awarded for partial completion of doctoral program. *Degree requirements:* For master's, comprehensive exam, thesis or alternative; for doctorate, thesis/dissertation. *Entrance requirements:* For master's, GRE General Test, minimum GPA of 3.0; for doctorate, GRE General Test, GRE Subject Test; for Advanced Certificate, doctoral degree, minimum GPA of 3.0. Additional exam requirements/recommendations for international students: Required—TOEFL. *Application deadline:* For fall admission, 12/18 for domestic students. Application fee: $90. *Expenses:* Tuition: Full-time $30,528; part-time $1272 per credit. Required fees: $2177. *Financial support:* Fellowships with tuition reimbursements, research assistantships with tuition reimbursements, teaching assistantships with tuition reimbursements, career-related internships or fieldwork, Federal Work-Study, institutionally sponsored loans, scholarships/grants, traineeships, health care benefits, and unspecified assistantships available. Financial award application deadline: 12/18; financial award applicants required to submit FAFSA. *Faculty research:* Vision, memory, social cognition, social and cognitive development, relationships. *Unit head:* Madeline Heilman, Director of Ph.D. Program, 212-998-7900, Fax: 212-995-4018, E-mail: psychq@psych.nyu.edu. *Application contact:* Barry Cohen, Director of M.A. Program, 212-998-7900, Fax: 212-995-4018, E-mail: psychq@psych.nyu.edu.

Prescott College, Graduate Programs, Program in Counseling and Psychology, Prescott, AZ 86301. Offers adventure-based psychotherapy (MA); counseling psychology (MA); ecopsychology (MA); ecotherapy (MA); equine-assisted mental health (MA); expressive arts therapy (MA); somatic psychology (MA); student-directed independent study (MA). Part-time programs available. Postbaccalaureate distance learning degree programs offered (minimal on-campus study). *Faculty:* 3 full-time (all women), 35 part-time/adjunct (25 women). *Students:* 65 full-time (47 women), 44 part-time (39 women); includes 8 minority (2 African Americans, 2 American Indian/Alaska Native, 4 Hispanic Americans), 9 international. Average age 38. 77 applicants, 77% accepted, 40 enrolled. In 2009, 34 master's awarded. *Degree requirements:* For master's, thesis, fieldwork or internship, practicum. *Entrance requirements:* For master's, 2 letters of recommendation, resume. Additional exam requirements/recommendations for international students: Required—TOEFL (minimum score 500 paper-based; 173 computer-based). *Application deadline:* For fall admission, 4/15 priority date for domestic and international students; for spring admission, 9/15 priority date for domestic and international students. Applications are processed on a rolling basis. Application fee: $40. Electronic applications accepted. *Expenses:* Tuition: Full-time $14,712; part-time $613 per credit. Required fees: $50 per term. One-time fee: $150. Tuition and fees vary according to course load and degree level. *Financial support:* Career-related internships or fieldwork, Federal Work-Study, and scholarships/grants available. Financial award applicants required to submit FAFSA. *Unit head:* Dr. Christine Frydenborg, Chair, Fax: 928-776-5151, E-mail: csmith@prescott.edu. *Application contact:* Kerstin Alicki, Admissions Counselor, 877-412-8705, Fax: 928-277-4695, E-mail: admissions@prescott.edu.

Rehabilitation Counseling

Adler School of Professional Psychology, Programs in Psychology, Chicago, IL 60601-7203. Offers art therapy (MA, Certificate); clinical hypnosis (Certificate); clinical psychology (Psy D); counseling (MA); counseling and organizational psychology (MA); forensic psychology (MA); gerontological counseling (MA); marriage and family counseling (MA); marriage and family therapy (Certificate); organizational psychology (MA); police psychology (MA); rehabilitation counseling (MA); sport and health psychology (MA); substance abuse counseling (Certificate); Psy D/Certificate; Psy D/MACAT; Psy D/MACP; Psy D/MAMFC; Psy D/MASAC. *Accreditation:* APA. Part-time and evening/weekend programs available. Postbaccalaureate distance learning degree programs offered (minimal on-campus study). *Faculty:* 41 full-time (21 women), 44 part-time/adjunct (19 women). *Students:* 551 full-time (441 women), 161 part-time (137 women). Average age 27.Terminal master's awarded for partial completion of doctoral program. *Degree requirements:* For master's, thesis or alternative, oral exam, practicum; for doctorate, thesis/dissertation, clinical exam, internship, oral exam, practicum, written qualifying exam. *Entrance requirements:* For master's, 12 semester hours in psychology, minimum GPA of 3.0; for doctorate, 18 semester hours in psychology, minimum GPA of 3.25; for Certificate, appropriate master's or doctoral degree. Additional exam requirements/recommendations for international students: Required—TOEFL (minimum score 550 paper-based; 213 computer-based; 79 iBT). *Application deadline:* For fall admission, 2/15 priority date for domestic students, 12/1 priority date for international students. Applications are processed on a rolling basis. Application fee: $50. Electronic applications accepted. *Expenses:* Tuition: Part-time $930 per credit. Required fees: $220 per term. *Financial support:* Career-related internships or fieldwork, Federal Work-Study, scholarships/grants, and tuition waivers (full and partial) available. Support available to part-time students. Financial award application deadline: 5/15; financial award applicants required to submit FAFSA. *Unit head:* Dr. Frank Gruba-McAllister, Vice President of Academic Affairs, 312-201-5900 Ext. 209, Fax: 312-201-

Rehabilitation Counseling

Adler School of Professional Psychology (continued)
5917. *Application contact:* Craig A. Hines, Associate Vice President of Admissions, 312-201-5900 Ext. 226, Fax: 312-201-5917, E-mail: chines@adler.edu.

See Close-Up on page 1047.

Arkansas State University—Jonesboro, Graduate School, College of Education, Department of Psychology and Counseling, Jonesboro, State University, AR 72467. Offers college student personnel services (MS); counselor education (Ed S), including college student personnel services, psychoeducational diagnosis, school counseling; rehabilitation counseling (MRC); school counseling (MSE); student affairs (Certificate). *Accreditation:* ACA (one or more programs are accredited); CORE (one or more programs are accredited); NCATE. Part-time programs available. *Faculty:* 11 full-time (6 women), 6 part-time/adjunct (2 women). *Students:* 49 full-time (37 women), 100 part-time (81 women); includes 32 minority (31 African Americans, 1 American Indian/Alaska Native), 1 international. Average age 32. 70 applicants, 46% accepted, 30 enrolled. In 2009, 23 master's, 11 other advanced degrees awarded. *Degree requirements:* For master's and other advanced degree, comprehensive exam, thesis or alternative. *Entrance requirements:* For master's, GRE General Test or MAT (MSE), appropriate bachelor's degree, interview, letters of reference; for other advanced degree, GRE General Test, interview, master's degree, letters of reference, official transcript, personal statement, immunization records. Additional exam requirements/recommendations for international students: Required—TOEFL (minimum score 550 paper-based; 213 computer-based; 79 iBT), IELTS (minimum score 6). *Application deadline:* For fall admission, 7/15 for domestic students, 7/1 for international students; for spring admission, 12/1 for domestic students, 11/13 for international students. Applications are processed on a rolling basis. Application fee: $30 ($40 for international students). Electronic applications accepted. *Expenses:* Tuition, state resident: full-time $3744; part-time $208 per credit hour. Tuition, nonresident: full-time $9540; part-time $530 per credit hour. Required fees: $896; $47 per credit hour. $25 per term. One-time fee: $50. Tuition and fees vary according to course load and program. *Financial support:* In 2009–10, 24 students received support; teaching assistantships, career-related internships or fieldwork, scholarships/grants, and unspecified assistantships available. Financial award application deadline: 7/1; financial award applicants required to submit FAFSA. *Unit head:* Dr. Loretta McGregor, Chair, 870-972-3064, Fax: 870-972-3962, E-mail: lmcgregor@astate.edu. *Application contact:* Dr. Andrew Sustich, Dean of the Graduate School, 870-972-3029, Fax: 870-972-3857, E-mail: sustich@astate.edu.

Assumption College, Graduate School, Rehabilitation Counseling Program, Worcester, MA 01609-1296. Offers MA, CAGS. *Accreditation:* CORE. Part-time and evening/weekend programs available. Postbaccalaureate distance learning degree programs offered (minimal on-campus study). *Faculty:* 2 full-time (0 women), 16 part-time/adjunct (10 women). *Students:* 32 full-time (25 women), 67 part-time (53 women); includes 17 minority (6 African Americans, 3 American Indian/Alaska Native, 2 Asian Americans or Pacific Islanders, 6 Hispanic Americans). Average age 28. 54 applicants, 91% accepted. In 2009, 38 master's, 12 other advanced degrees awarded. *Degree requirements:* For master's, comprehensive exam, internship, practicum. *Entrance requirements:* For master's, 3 letters of recommendation, resume, interview; for CAGS, 3 letters of recommendation, resume, interview, essay. Additional exam requirements/recommendations for international students: Required—TOEFL (minimum score 540 paper-based; 200 computer-based; 76 iBT), IELTS (minimum score 6). *Application deadline:* For fall admission, 6/1 priority date for domestic students, 5/1 priority date for international students; for spring admission, 11/1 priority date for domestic students, 9/1 priority date for international students. Applications are processed on a rolling basis. Application fee: $30. Electronic applications accepted. *Expenses:* Tuition: Part-time $503 per credit. Required fees: $20 per semester. One-time fee: $100 part-time. Part-time tuition and fees vary according to campus/location. *Financial support:* In 2009–10, 81 students received support, including 45 fellowships with full and partial tuition reimbursements available (averaging $5,124 per year), 1 teaching assistantship (averaging $19,860 per year); scholarships/grants and traineeships also available. Financial award application deadline: 6/1; financial award applicants required to submit FAFSA. *Faculty research:* Job placement for severe disabilities, vocational counseling, conflict resolution, health issues in mental illness. *Unit head:* A. Lee Pearson, Director, 508-767-7063, Fax: 508-767-7030, E-mail: lpearson@assumption.edu. *Application contact:* Adrian O. Dumas, Director of Graduate Enrollment Management and Services, 508-767-7365, Fax: 508-767-7030, E-mail: adumas@assumption.edu.

Auburn University, Graduate School, College of Education, Department of Special Education, Rehabilitation, Counseling and School Psychology, Auburn University, AL 36849. Offers collaborative teacher special education (M Ed, MS); early childhood special education (M Ed, MS); rehabilitation counseling (M Ed, MS, PhD). *Accreditation:* CORE; NCATE. Part-time programs available. *Faculty:* 20 full-time (13 women), 8 part-time/adjunct (6 women). *Students:* 149 full-time (117 women), 94 part-time (78 women); includes 63 minority (56 African Americans, 1 American Indian/Alaska Native, 2 Asian Americans or Pacific Islanders, 4 Hispanic Americans), 4 international. Average age 31. 226 applicants, 51% accepted, 87 enrolled. In 2009, 48 master's, 20 doctorates awarded. *Degree requirements:* For master's, thesis (for some programs); for doctorate, thesis/dissertation. *Entrance requirements:* For master's, GRE General Test; for doctorate, GRE General Test, interview. *Application deadline:* For fall admission, 7/17 for domestic students; for spring admission, 11/24 for domestic students. Applications are processed on a rolling basis. Application fee: $50 ($60 for international students). Electronic applications accepted. *Expenses:* Tuition, state resident: full-time $6240. Tuition, nonresident: full-time $18,720. International tuition: $18,938 full-time. Required fees: $492. Tuition and fees vary according to course load, program and reciprocity agreements. *Financial support:* Research assistantships, teaching assistantships, Federal Work-Study available. Support available to part-time students. Financial award application deadline: 3/15; financial award applicants required to submit FAFSA. *Faculty research:* Emotional conflict/behavior disorders, gifted and talented, learning disabilities, mental retardation, multi-handicapped. *Unit head:* Dr. Philip L. Browning, Head, 334-844-5943. *Application contact:* Dr. George Flowers, Dean of the Graduate School, 334-844-2125.

Barry University, School of Education, Program in Rehabilitation Counseling, Miami Shores, FL 33161-6695. Offers MS, Ed S. Part-time and evening/weekend programs available. *Degree requirements:* For master's, comprehensive exam, scholarly paper; for Ed S, comprehensive exam. *Entrance requirements:* For master's, GRE General Test or MAT, minimum GPA of 3.0; for Ed S, GRE General Test, minimum GPA of 3.0. Electronic applications accepted.

Bayamón Central University, Graduate Programs, Program in Education, Bayamón, PR 00960-1725. Offers administration and supervision (MA Ed); commercial education (MA Ed); education of the autistic (MA Ed); elementary education (K–3) (MA Ed); elementary education (K–6) (MA Ed); guidance and counseling (MA Ed); organizational psychology (MA); pre-elementary teacher (MA Ed); rehabilitation counseling (MA Ed); special education (MA Ed), including attention deficit disorder, learning disabilities. Part-time and evening/weekend programs available. *Degree requirements:* For master's, comprehensive exam. *Entrance requirements:* For master's, EXADEP, bachelor's degree in education or related field.

Bowling Green State University, Graduate College, College of Education and Human Development, School of Education and Intervention Services, Intervention Services Division, Program in Rehabilitation Counseling, Bowling Green, OH 43403. Offers MRC. *Accreditation:* CORE. Part-time programs available. *Degree requirements:* For master's, thesis or alternative. *Entrance requirements:* For master's, GRE General Test, interview. Additional exam requirements/recommendations for international students: Required—TOEFL. Electronic applications accepted. *Faculty research:* Depression, disability management, schizophrenia, job analysis, rehabilitation counseling curriculum.

California State University, Fresno, Division of Graduate Studies, School of Education and Human Development, Department of Counseling and Special Education, Rehabilitation Counseling Program, Fresno, CA 93740-8027. Offers MS. *Accreditation:* CORE. Part-time and evening/weekend programs available. *Degree requirements:* For master's, thesis optional. *Entrance requirements:* For master's, GRE General Test, MAT, minimum GPA of 2.75. Additional exam requirements/recommendations for international students: Required—TOEFL. Electronic applications accepted. *Faculty research:* Aging, career development, job retention, rehabilitation administration.

California State University, Los Angeles, Graduate Studies, Charter College of Education, Division of Special Education and Counseling, Los Angeles, CA 90032-8530. Offers counseling (MS), including applied behavior analysis, community college counseling, rehabilitation counseling, school counseling and school psychology; special education (MA, PhD). *Accreditation:* ACA. Part-time and evening/weekend programs available. *Faculty:* 20 full-time (15 women), 18 part-time/adjunct (10 women). *Students:* 361 full-time (288 women), 366 part-time (284 women); includes 450 minority (43 African Americans, 65 Asian Americans or Pacific Islanders, 342 Hispanic Americans), 40 international. Average age 34. 181 applicants, 99% accepted, 108 enrolled. In 2009, 143 master's awarded. *Entrance requirements:* For master's, minimum GPA of 2.75 in last 90 units of course work, teaching certificate. Additional exam requirements/recommendations for international students: Required—TOEFL (minimum score 500 paper-based; 173 computer-based). *Application deadline:* For fall admission, 5/1 for domestic and international students. Applications are processed on a rolling basis. Application fee: $55. Electronic applications accepted. *Financial support:* Career-related internships or fieldwork and Federal Work-Study available. Support available to part-time students. Financial award application deadline: 3/1. *Unit head:* Dr. Randy Campbell, Chair, 323-343-4400, Fax: 323-343-5605, E-mail: rcampbe@calstatela.edu. *Application contact:* Dr. Cheryl L. Ney, Associate Vice President for Academic Affairs and Dean of Graduate Studies, 323-343-3820, Fax: 323-343-5653, E-mail: cney@cslanet.calstatela.edu.

California State University, San Bernardino, Graduate Studies, College of Education, Program in Educational Psychology and Counseling, San Bernardino, CA 92407-2397. Offers correctional and alternative education (MA); counseling and guidance (MS); rehabilitation counseling (MA). *Accreditation:* NCATE. Part-time and evening/weekend programs available. *Faculty:* 7 full-time (3 women), 4 part-time/adjunct (1 woman). *Students:* 110 full-time (95 women), 5 part-time (all women); includes 73 minority (12 African Americans, 4 Asian Americans or Pacific Islanders, 57 Hispanic Americans). Average age 32. 25 applicants, 80% accepted, 9 enrolled. In 2009, 34 master's awarded. *Degree requirements:* For master's, comprehensive exam, thesis or alternative, counselor preparation comprehensive examination. *Entrance requirements:* For master's, minimum GPA of 3.0 in education. *Application deadline:* For fall admission, 8/31 priority date for domestic students. Application fee: $55. *Financial support:* Career-related internships or fieldwork and Federal Work-Study available. Support available to part-time students. *Unit head:* Dr. Ruth Ann Sandlin, Chair, 909-537-5641, Fax: 909-537-7040, E-mail: rsandlin@csusb.edu. *Application contact:* Olivia Rosas, Director of Admissions, 909-537-7577, Fax: 909-537-7034, E-mail: orosas@csusb.edu.

California State University, San Bernardino, Graduate Studies, College of Education, Programs in Special Education and Rehabilitation Counseling, San Bernardino, CA 92407-2397. Offers rehabilitation counseling (MA); special education (MA). *Accreditation:* CORE; NCATE. Part-time and evening/weekend programs available. *Faculty:* 11 full-time (8 women), 9 part-time/adjunct (6 women). *Students:* 225 full-time (170 women), 67 part-time (53 women); includes 131 minority (44 African Americans, 3 American Indian/Alaska Native, 12 Asian Americans or Pacific Islanders, 72 Hispanic Americans), 2 international. Average age 39. 158 applicants, 90% accepted, 85 enrolled. In 2009, 81 master's awarded. *Degree requirements:* For master's, thesis or alternative, advancement to candidacy. *Entrance requirements:* For master's, minimum GPA of 3.0 in education. *Application deadline:* For fall admission, 8/31 priority date for domestic students. Application fee: $55. *Financial support:* Career-related internships or fieldwork and Federal Work-Study available. Support available to part-time students. *Unit head:* Dr. Ruth Ann Sandlin, Chair, 909-537-5641, Fax: 909-537-7040, E-mail: rsandlin@csusb.edu. *Application contact:* Olivia Rosas, Director of Admissions, 909-537-7577, Fax: 909-537-7034, E-mail: orosas@csusb.edu.

Central Connecticut State University, School of Graduate Studies, School of Education and Professional Studies, Department of Counseling and Family Therapy, New Britain, CT 06050-4010. Offers marriage and family therapy (MS); professional counseling (MS, Certificate); school counseling (MS); student development in higher education (MS). *Accreditation:* AAMFT/COAMFTE. Part-time and evening/weekend programs available. *Faculty:* 8 full-time (5 women), 14 part-time/adjunct (9 women). *Students:* 117 full-time (97 women), 189 part-time (159 women); includes 52 minority (27 African Americans, 3 American Indian/Alaska Native, 3 Asian Americans or Pacific Islanders, 19 Hispanic Americans), 4 international. Average age 33. 249 applicants, 39% accepted, 84 enrolled. In 2009, 78 master's awarded. *Degree requirements:* For master's, comprehensive exam, thesis or alternative; for Certificate, qualifying exam. *Entrance requirements:* For master's, minimum undergraduate GPA of 2.7. Additional exam requirements/recommendations for international students: Required—TOEFL. *Application deadline:* For fall admission, 5/1 for domestic students. Applications are processed on a rolling basis. Application fee: $50. Electronic applications accepted. *Expenses:* Tuition, area resident: Full-time $4662; part-time $440 per credit. Tuition, state resident: full-time $6994; part-time $440 per credit. Tuition, nonresident: full-time $12,988; part-time $440 per credit. Required fees: $3606. One-time fee: $62 part-time. *Financial support:* In 2009–10, 29 students received support, including 22 research assistantships; career-related internships or fieldwork, Federal Work-Study, scholarships/grants, and unspecified assistantships also available. Support available to part-time students. Financial award application deadline: 3/1; financial award applicants required to submit FAFSA. *Faculty research:* Elementary/secondary school counseling, marriage/family therapy, rehabilitation counseling, counseling in higher educational settings. *Unit head:* Dr. Connie Tait, Chair, 860-832-2154. *Application contact:* Dr. Connie Tait, Chair, 860-832-2154.

Coppin State University, Division of Graduate Studies, Division of Arts and Sciences, Department of Applied Psychology and Rehabilitation Counseling, Program in Rehabilitation Counseling, Baltimore, MD 21216-3698. Offers M Ed. *Accreditation:* CORE. Part-time programs available. *Degree requirements:* For master's, comprehensive exam (for some programs), thesis optional, internship, clinical requirements. *Entrance requirements:* For master's, GRE General Test, interview, minimum GPA of 3.0.

East Carolina University, Graduate School, School of Allied Health Sciences, Program in Rehabilitation Studies, Greenville, NC 27858-4353. Offers rehabilitation counseling (MS); substance abuse and clinical counseling (MS); vocational evaluation (MS). *Accreditation:* CORE. Part-time and evening/weekend programs available. *Degree requirements:* For master's, comprehensive exam, thesis or alternative, internship. *Entrance requirements:* For master's, GRE General Test or MAT. Additional exam requirements/recommendations for international students: Required—TOEFL.

East Central University, School of Graduate Studies, Department of Human Resources, Ada, OK 74820-6899. Offers administration (MSHR); counseling (MSHR); criminal justice (MSHR); rehabilitation counseling (MSHR). *Accreditation:* CORE. Part-time and evening/weekend programs available. *Degree requirements:* For master's, thesis optional. *Entrance requirements:* For master's, GRE General Test, MAT, minimum GPA of 2.5. Electronic applications accepted.

Edinboro University of Pennsylvania, School of Graduate Studies and Research, School of Education, Department of Professional Studies, Edinboro, PA 16444. Offers counseling (MA), including community counseling, elementary guidance, rehabilitation counseling, secondary guidance, student personnel services; educational leadership (M Ed), including elementary school administration, secondary school administration; letter of eligibility (Certificate). Part-time and evening/weekend programs available. *Faculty:* 21 full-time (15 women), 12 part-time/adjunct (7 women). *Students:* 153 full-time (113 women), 785 part-time (598 women); includes 28 minority (19 African Americans, 3 American Indian/Alaska Native, 2 Asian Americans or Pacific Islanders, 4 Hispanic Americans). Average age 32. In 2009, 124 master's, 60 other advanced degrees awarded. *Degree requirements:* For master's, thesis or alternative, competency exam; for Certificate, thesis or alternative. *Entrance requirements:* For master's and Certificate, GRE or MAT, minimum QPA of 2.5. *Application deadline:* Applications are processed on a rolling basis. Application fee: $30. Electronic applications accepted. *Expenses:* Tuition, state resident: full-time $6666; part-time $370 per credit. Tuition, nonresident: full-time $10,666; part-time $593 per credit. Required fees: $2206.28. One-time fee: $204 part-time. *Financial support:* In 2009–10, 60 research assistantships with full and partial tuition reimbursements (averaging $4,050 per year) were awarded; career-related internships or fieldwork, Federal Work-Study, scholarships/grants, and unspecified assistantships also available. Support available to part-time students. Financial award application deadline: 2/15; financial award applicants required to submit FAFSA. *Unit head:* Dr. Susan Norton, Program Head, Counseling, 814-732-2260, E-mail: scnorton@edinboro.edu. *Application contact:* Dr. Andrew Pushchack, Program Head, Educational Leadership, 814-732-1548, E-mail: apushchack@edinboro.edu.

Emporia State University, School of Graduate Studies, The Teachers College, Department of Psychology, Art Therapy, Rehabilitation and Mental Health Counseling, Program in Rehabilitation Counseling, Emporia, KS 66801-5087. Offers MS. *Accreditation:* CORE. Part-time programs available. *Students:* 16 full-time (13 women), 10 part-time (9 women); includes 3 minority (2 African Americans, 1 Hispanic American). 8 applicants, 100% accepted, 6 enrolled. In 2009, 6 master's awarded. *Degree requirements:* For master's, comprehensive exam or thesis, practicum. *Entrance requirements:* For master's, GRE or MAT, graduate essay exam, appropriate bachelor's degree, interview, letters of recommendation. *Application deadline:* For fall admission, 8/15 priority date for domestic students. Applications are processed on a rolling basis. Application fee: $30 ($75 for international students). Electronic applications accepted. *Expenses:* Tuition, state resident: full-time $4154; part-time $173 per credit hour. Tuition, nonresident: full-time $12,864; part-time $536 per credit hour. Required fees: $948; $58 per credit hour. Tuition and fees vary according to campus/location. *Financial support:* Career-related internships or fieldwork, Federal Work-Study, institutionally sponsored loans, health care benefits, and unspecified assistantships available. Financial award application deadline: 3/15; financial award applicants required to submit FAFSA. *Unit head:* Dr. James Costello, Graduate Co-Coordinator, 620-341-5791, E-mail: jcostell@emporia.edu. *Application contact:* Dr. James Costello, Graduate Co-Coordinator, 620-341-5791, E-mail: jcostell@emporia.edu.

Florida Atlantic University, College of Education, Department of Counselor Education, Boca Raton, FL 33431-0991. Offers counselor education (M Ed, PhD, Ed S); marriage and family therapy (Ed S); mental health counseling (M Ed, Ed S); rehabilitation counseling (M Ed); school counseling (M Ed, Ed S). *Accreditation:* ACA; NCATE. Part-time and evening/weekend programs available. *Faculty:* 7 full-time (2 women), 6 part-time/adjunct (5 women). *Students:* 65 full-time (52 women), 95 part-time (83 women); includes 59 minority (19 African Americans, 5 Asian Americans or Pacific Islanders, 35 Hispanic Americans), 2 international. Average age 33. 109 applicants, 40% accepted, 27 enrolled. In 2009, 54 master's, 2 doctorates awarded. *Degree requirements:* For Ed S, departmental qualifying exam. *Entrance requirements:* For master's, GRE General Test, minimum GPA of 3.0 during previous 2 years; for Ed S, GRE General Test, minimum graduate GPA of 3.25. Additional exam requirements/recommendations for international students: Required—TOEFL. *Application deadline:* For fall admission, 3/1 for domestic students, 2/1 for international students; for spring admission, 9/15 for domestic students, 7/1 for international students. Applications are processed on a rolling basis. Application fee: $30. *Expenses:* Tuition, state resident: full-time $7055; part-time $293.94 per credit hour. Tuition, nonresident: full-time $22,096; part-time $920.66 per credit hour. *Financial support:* Research assistantships with partial tuition reimbursements, teaching assistantships, career-related internships or fieldwork, scholarships/grants, and unspecified assistantships available. *Faculty research:* Brief therapy, psychological type, marriage and family counseling, international programs, integrated services. *Unit head:* Dr. Irene Johnson, Chair, 561-297-2136, Fax: 561-297-2309. *Application contact:* Susan Foley, Senior Secretary, 561-297-3602, Fax: 561-297-2309, E-mail: cnslred@fau.edu.

Florida International University, College of Education, Department of Educational and Psychological Studies, Program in Counselor Education, Miami, FL 33199. Offers mental health counseling (MS); rehabilitation counseling (MS); school counseling (MS). *Accreditation:* ACA; NCATE. Part-time and evening/weekend programs available. *Entrance requirements:* For master's, General Knowledge test, College Level Academic Skills Test, GRE General Test or PRAXIS (school counseling track), minimum GPA of 3.0, interview. Additional exam requirements/recommendations for international students: Required—TOEFL (minimum score 550 paper-based; 213 computer-based; 80 iBT), IELTS (minimum score 6.3). Electronic applications accepted. *Expenses:* Tuition, state resident: full-time $8008; part-time $4004 per year. Tuition, nonresident: full-time $20,104; part-time $10,052 per year. Required fees: $298; $149 per term.

Florida State University, The Graduate School, College of Education, School of Teacher Education, Program in Special Education, Tallahassee, FL 32306. Offers emotional disturbance/learning disabilities (MS); mental retardation (MS); rehabilitation counseling (MS, PhD, Ed S); special education (PhD, Ed S); visual disabilities (MS). *Accreditation:* CORE. *Faculty:* 5 full-time (4 women), 1 (woman) part-time/adjunct. *Students:* 45 full-time (39 women), 108 part-time (103 women); includes 38 minority (27 African Americans, 6 Asian Americans or Pacific Islanders, 5 Hispanic Americans). 111 applicants, 67% accepted, 44 enrolled. In 2009, 37 master's, 3 doctorates, 1 other advanced degree awarded. *Degree requirements:* For master's, comprehensive exam, thesis optional; for doctorate, comprehensive exam, thesis/dissertation; for Ed S, comprehensive exam. *Entrance requirements:* For master's, doctorate, and Ed S, GRE General Test, minimum GPA of 3.0. Additional exam requirements/recommendations for international students: Required—TOEFL (minimum score 550 paper-based; 213 computer-based; 80 iBT); Recommended—TWE. *Application deadline:* For fall admission, 7/1 for domestic students; for spring admission, 11/1 for domestic students. Applications are processed on a rolling basis. Application fee: $20. *Expenses:* Tuition, state resident: full-time $7413. Tuition, nonresident: full-time $22,567. *Financial support:* In 2009–10, 5 research assistantships with full and partial tuition reimbursements, 7 teaching assistantships with full and partial tuition reimbursements were awarded; fellowships with full and partial tuition reimbursements, career-related internships or fieldwork and traineeships also available. Financial award applicants required to submit FAFSA. *Unit head:* Dr. Mary Frances Hanline, Chair, 850-644-4880, Fax: 850-644-8715, E-mail: hanline@mail.coe.fsu.edu. *Application contact:* Timolin Lynette Bodison-Baker, Program Assistant, 850-644-5458, Fax: 850-644-7736, E-mail: bodison@coe.fsu.edu.

Fort Valley State University, College of Graduate Studies and Extended Education, Department of Counseling Psychology, Program in Rehabilitation Counseling, Fort Valley, GA 31030. Offers MS. *Accreditation:* CORE. Part-time programs available. *Degree requirements:* For master's, comprehensive exam (for some programs), thesis optional. *Entrance requirements:* For master's, GRE General Test or MAT.

The George Washington University, Graduate School of Education and Human Development, Department of Counseling/Human and Organizational Studies, Programs in Counseling: School, Community and Rehabilitation, Washington, DC 20052. Offers community counseling (MA Ed); rehabilitation counseling (MA Ed); school counseling (MA Ed). School counseling program also offered in Alexandria, VA. *Accreditation:* ACA; CORE; NCATE. *Students:* 72 full-time (63 women), 67 part-time (53 women); includes 33 minority (22 African Americans, 2 American Indian/Alaska Native, 5 Asian Americans or Pacific Islanders, 4 Hispanic Americans), 4 international. Average age 33. 104 applicants, 94% accepted, 51 enrolled. In 2009, 93 master's awarded. *Degree requirements:* For master's, comprehensive exam. *Entrance requirements:* For master's, GRE General Test or MAT, minimum GPA of 2.75. *Application deadline:* For fall admission, 1/15 priority date for domestic students; for spring admission, 10/1 for domestic students. Applications are processed on a rolling basis. Application fee: $60. *Financial support:* In 2009–10, 27 students received support; fellowships, research assistantships, teaching assistantships, career-related internships or fieldwork, Federal Work-Study, and tuition waivers (full and partial) available. *Faculty research:* Adjustment to disability, head injury rehabilitation, cross-cultural counseling. *Application contact:* Sarah Lang, Director of Graduate Admissions, 202-994-1447, Fax: 202-994-7207, E-mail: slang@gwu.edu.

Georgia State University, College of Education, Department of Counseling and Psychological Services, Program in Rehabilitation Counseling, Atlanta, GA 30302-3083. Offers MS. *Accreditation:* CORE. Part-time and evening/weekend programs available. *Degree requirements:* For master's, comprehensive exam. *Entrance requirements:* For master's, GRE General Test, minimum GPA of 2.5. *Faculty research:* Catastrophic injuries, private sector rehabilitation, closed head injuries, persons with multiple handicaps.

Hofstra University, School of Education, Health, and Human Services, Department of Counseling, Research, Special Education and Rehabilitation, Program in Rehabilitation Counseling, Hempstead, NY 11549. Offers rehabilitation administration (PD); rehabilitation counseling (MS Ed); rehabilitation counseling in mental health (MS Ed). *Accreditation:* CORE. Part-time and evening/weekend programs available. *Students:* 23 full-time (19 women), 6 part-time (all women); includes 12 minority (9 African Americans, 1 Asian American or Pacific Islander, 2 Hispanic Americans). Average age 32. 18 applicants, 89% accepted, 12 enrolled. In 2009, 12 master's awarded. *Degree requirements:* For master's, comprehensive exam, 600-hour internship, 100-hour practicum. *Entrance requirements:* For master's, 4 letters of recommendation, interview, professional experience; for PD, 3 letters of recommendation, master's degree in related field, professional experience. Additional exam requirements/recommendations for international students: Required—TOEFL (minimum score 550 paper-based; 213 computer-based; 80 iBT). *Application deadline:* Applications are processed on a rolling basis. Application fee: $60. Electronic applications accepted. *Expenses:* Tuition: Full-time $16,200; part-time $900 per credit hour. Required fees: $970; $145 per term. Tuition and fees vary according to program. *Financial support:* In 2009–10, 14 students received support, including 1 fellowship with full and partial tuition reimbursement available (averaging $3,000 per year), 2 research assistantships with full and partial tuition reimbursements available (averaging $15,575 per year); career-related internships or fieldwork, Federal Work-Study, institutionally sponsored loans, scholarships/grants, traineeships, tuition waivers (full and partial), and unspecified assistantships also available. Support available to part-time students. Financial award applicants required to submit FAFSA. *Faculty research:* Workplace socialization and individuals with disabilities; collaboration among rehabilitation agencies and consumer outcomes; job retention among rehabilitation counseling professionals; transition services for youth with disabilities. Total annual research expenditures: $210,000. *Unit head:* Dr. Jamie Mitus, Director, 516-463-7453, Fax: 516-463-6184, E-mail: cprjsm@hofstra.edu. *Application contact:* Carol Drummer, Dean of Graduate Admissions, 516-463-4876, Fax: 516-463-4664, E-mail: gradstudent@hofstra.edu.

Hunter College of the City University of New York, Graduate School, School of Education, Department of Educational Foundations and Counseling Programs, Program in Rehabilitation Counseling, New York, NY 10021-5085. Offers MS Ed. *Accreditation:* CORE. *Faculty:* 48 full-time (42 women), 21 part-time/adjunct (6 women). *Students:* 18 full-time (10 women), 48 part-time (37 women); includes 42 minority (14 African Americans, 22 Asian Americans or Pacific Islanders, 6 Hispanic Americans). Average age 37. 37 applicants, 41% accepted, 13 enrolled. In 2009, 27 master's awarded. *Degree requirements:* For master's, thesis, seminar. *Entrance requirements:* For master's, interview, minimum GPA of 2.7, recommendations. Additional exam requirements/recommendations for international students: Required—TOEFL, TWE. *Application deadline:* For fall admission, 4/1 for domestic students, 2/1 for international students; for spring admission, 11/1 for domestic students, 9/1 for international students. Applications are processed on a rolling basis. Application fee: $125. *Expenses:* Tuition, state resident: full-time $7360; part-time $310 per credit. Required fees: $250 per semester. *Financial support:* Federal Work-Study and tuition waivers (partial) available. Support available to part-time students. *Unit head:* Dr. Arnold Wolf, Adviser, 212-772-4616, E-mail: awo@hunter.cuny.edu. *Application contact:* William Zlata, Director for Graduate Admissions, 212-772-4482, Fax: 212-650-3336, E-mail: admissions@hunter.cuny.edu.

Illinois Institute of Technology, Graduate College, Institute of Psychology, Chicago, IL 60616-3793. Offers clinical psychology (PhD); industrial/organizational psychology (PhD); personnel/human resource development (MS); psychology (MS); rehabilitation counseling (MS); rehabilitation counselor education (PhD). *Accreditation:* APA (one or more programs are accredited); CORE. Part-time and evening/weekend programs available. *Faculty:* 19 full-time (8 women), 5 part-time/adjunct (all women). *Students:* 118 full-time (88 women), 82 part-time (62 women); includes 33 minority (10 African Americans, 1 American Indian/Alaska Native, 14 Asian Americans or Pacific Islanders, 8 Hispanic Americans), 24 international. Average age 29. 281 applicants, 33% accepted, 28 enrolled. In 2009, 37 master's, 13 doctorates awarded. Terminal master's awarded for partial completion of doctoral program. *Degree requirements:* For master's, thesis (for some programs); for doctorate, comprehensive exam, thesis/dissertation, 96-108 credit hours, internship for Clinical and I/O specializations. *Entrance requirements:* For master's, GRE General Test, minimum high school GPA of 3.0, official transcripts, 3 letters of recommendation, personal statement; for doctorate, GRE General Test, minimum high school GPA of 3.0, official transcriptions, 3 letters of recommendation, personal statement. Additional exam requirements/recommendations for international students: Required—TOEFL (minimum score 550 paper-based; 80 iBT). *Application deadline:* For fall admission, 2/15 for domestic and international students. Application fee: $40. Electronic applications accepted. *Expenses:* Tuition: Full-time $17,550; part-time $888 per credit hour. Required fees: $850; $7.50 per credit hour. One-time fee: $50 full-time. Full-time tuition and fees vary according to program. *Financial support:* In 2009–10, 39 fellowships with partial tuition reimbursements (averaging $2,798 per year), 1 research assistantship with partial tuition reimbursement, 24 teaching assistantships with partial tuition reimbursements (averaging $4,405 per year) were awarded; career-related internships or fieldwork, Federal Work-Study, institutionally sponsored loans, scholarships/grants, traineeships, health care benefits, tuition waivers (partial), and unspecified assistantships also available. Support available to part-time students. Financial award application deadline: 1/15; financial award applicants required to submit FAFSA. *Faculty research:* Stigma and mental illness, depression, couples communication, leadership, psychometric theory. Total annual research expenditures: $426,090. *Unit head:* Dr. M. Ellen Mitchell, Dean, 312-567-3362, Fax: 312-567-3493, E-mail: mitchelle@iit.edu. *Application contact:* Institute of Psychology Graduate Admissions, 312-567-3500, Fax: 312-567-3493, E-mail: psychology@iit.edu.

Indiana University–Purdue University Indianapolis, School of Science, Department of Psychology, Indianapolis, IN 46202-3275. Offers clinical rehabilitation psychology (MS); industrial/organizational psychology (MS); psychobiology of addictions (MS, PhD). *Accreditation:* APA (one or more programs are accredited). *Faculty:* 10 full-time (2 women). *Students:* 50 full-time (45 women), 11 part-time (9 women); includes 7 minority (4 African Americans, 2 Asian Americans or Pacific Islanders, 1 Hispanic American), 3 international. Average age 28. 132 applicants, 17% accepted, 22 enrolled. In 2009, 7 master's awarded. Terminal master's awarded for partial completion of doctoral program. *Degree requirements:* For master's, thesis; for doctorate, thesis/dissertation. *Entrance requirements:* For master's, GRE General Test, minimum undergraduate GPA of 3.0; for doctorate, GRE General Test, GRE Subject Test (clinical rehabilitation psychology), minimum undergraduate GPA of 3.2. *Application deadline:* For fall admission, 1/1 priority date for domestic students. Application fee: $55 ($65 for international students). *Financial support:* In 2009–10, 5 fellowships with partial tuition reimbursements (averaging $12,218 per year), 23 teaching assistantships with partial tuition reimbursements (averaging $7,553 per year) were awarded; research assistantships with partial tuition reimbursements, career-related internships or fieldwork, Federal Work-Study, and institutionally sponsored loans also available. Financial award application deadline: 3/1; financial award applicants required to submit FAFSA. *Faculty research:* Psychiatric rehabilitation, chronic stress, neurological research, language and cognitive development in infants, alcoholism and psychopathology. *Unit head:* Dr. J. Gregor Fetterman, Chairman, 317-274-6945, Fax: 317-274-6756, E-mail: gfetter@iupui.edu. *Application contact:* Dr. J. Gregor Fetterman, Chairman, 317-274-6945, Fax: 317-274-6756, E-mail: gfetter@iupui.edu.

Jackson State University, Graduate School, School of Education, Department of Counseling and Human Resource Education, Jackson, MS 39217. Offers community and agency counseling (MS); guidance and counseling (MS, MS Ed, Ed S); rehabilitative counseling (MS Ed).

Rehabilitation Counseling

Jackson State University (continued)
Accreditation: ACA; CORE (one or more programs are accredited); NCATE. Part-time and evening/weekend programs available. *Degree requirements:* For master's, comprehensive exam, thesis. *Entrance requirements:* For master's, GRE General Test. Additional exam requirements/recommendations for international students: Required—TOEFL.

Jackson State University, Graduate School, School of Education, Department of Special Education and Rehabilitative Services, Jackson, MS 39217. Offers rehabilitative counseling service (MS Ed); special education (MS Ed, Ed S). *Accreditation:* NCATE. Evening/weekend programs available. *Degree requirements:* For master's, comprehensive exam, thesis or alternative. *Entrance requirements:* For master's, GRE General Test. Additional exam requirements/recommendations for international students: Required—TOEFL.

Kent State University, Graduate School of Education, Health, and Human Services, School of Lifespan Development and Educational Sciences, Program in Rehabilitation Counseling, Kent, OH 44242-0001. Offers M Ed, MA, Ed S. *Accreditation:* CORE (one or more programs are accredited). *Faculty:* 2 full-time (1 woman), 5 part-time/adjunct (3 women). *Students:* 21 full-time (19 women), 20 part-time (14 women); includes 5 minority (4 African Americans, 1 Asian American or Pacific Islander), 2 international. 25 applicants, 80% accepted. In 2009, 8 master's awarded. *Degree requirements:* For master's, thesis (for some programs). *Entrance requirements:* For degree, GRE General Test. Additional exam requirements/recommendations for international students: Required—TOEFL. *Application deadline:* Applications are processed on a rolling basis. Application fee: $30. Electronic applications accepted. *Financial support:* In 2009–10, 3 research assistantships with full tuition reimbursements (averaging $8,313 per year) were awarded; Federal Work-Study, scholarships/grants, and unspecified assistantships also available. Financial award application deadline: 4/1; financial award applicants required to submit FAFSA. *Unit head:* Dr. Phillip Rumrill, Coordinator, 330-672-0600, E-mail: prumrill@kent.edu. *Application contact:* Nancy Miller, Academic Program Coordinator, Office of Graduate Student Services, 330-672-2576, Fax: 330-672-9162, E-mail: ogs@kent.edu.

Langston University, School of Education and Behavioral Sciences, Langston, OK 73050. Offers bilingual/multicultural (M Ed); elementary education (M Ed); English as a second language (M Ed); rehabilitation counseling (M Sc); urban education (M Ed). *Accreditation:* CORE; NCATE (one or more programs are accredited). Part-time programs available. *Degree requirements:* For master's, comprehensive exam, thesis optional. *Entrance requirements:* For master's, GRE, writing skills test, minimum GPA of 2.5, 3 letters of recommendation. Additional exam requirements/recommendations for international students: Required—TOEFL, TWE. *Faculty research:* Bilingual/multicultural education, financing post-secondary education.

La Salle University, School of Arts and Sciences, Program in Psychology, Philadelphia, PA 19141-1199. Offers clinical psychology (Psy D); family psychology (Psy D); rehabilitation psychology (Psy D). Part-time and evening/weekend programs available. *Entrance requirements:* For doctorate, GRE, minimum GPA of 3.0. *Expenses:* Contact institution. *Faculty research:* Cognitive therapy, attribution theory, treatment of addiction.

Louisiana State University Health Sciences Center, School of Allied Health Professions, Department of Rehabilitation Counseling, New Orleans, LA 70112-2262. Offers MHS. *Accreditation:* CORE. Part-time programs available. *Degree requirements:* For master's, clinical internship. *Entrance requirements:* For master's, GRE General Test, minimum GPA of 2.5, 2 letters recommendation. *Faculty research:* Job placement, clinical judgement, counseling process, consumer satisfaction, vocational assessment.

Maryville University of Saint Louis, School of Health Professions, Program in Rehabilitation Counseling, St. Louis, MO 63141-7299. Offers marriage and family therapy (MARC); music therapy (MARC); rehabilitation counseling (CAGS); substance abuse (MARC). *Accreditation:* CORE. Part-time and evening/weekend programs available. *Students:* 16 full-time (12 women), 31 part-time (21 women); includes 7 African Americans, 1 Asian American or Pacific Islander, 2 Hispanic Americans. Average age 31. In 2009, 6 master's awarded. *Degree requirements:* For master's, internship, seminar. *Entrance requirements:* For master's, minimum cumulative GPA of 3.0, 2 letters of recommendation, interview. Additional exam requirements/recommendations for international students: Required—TOEFL (minimum score 550 paper-based). *Application deadline:* For fall admission, 1/15 for domestic students; for spring admission, 10/1 for domestic students. Application fee: $40 ($60 for international students). Electronic applications accepted. *Expenses:* Tuition: Full-time $20,384; part-time $627.50 per credit hour. Required fees: $100 per semester. *Financial support:* Career-related internships or fieldwork, Federal Work-Study, and campus employment available. Financial award application deadline: 3/1; financial award applicants required to submit FAFSA. *Unit head:* Barbara Parker, Director, 314-529-9437, Fax: 314-529-9495, E-mail: bparker@maryville.edu. *Application contact:* Barbara Parker, Director, 314-529-9437, Fax: 314-529-9495, E-mail: bparker@maryville.edu.

Michigan State University, The Graduate School, College of Education, Department of Counseling, Educational Psychology and Special Education, East Lansing, MI 48824. Offers counseling (MA); educational psychology and educational technology (PhD); educational technology (MA); measurement and quantitative methods (PhD); rehabilitation counseling (MA); rehabilitation counselor education (PhD); school psychology (MA, PhD, Ed S); special education (MA, PhD). *Accreditation:* APA (one or more programs are accredited); CORE (one or more programs are accredited). Part-time programs available. *Faculty:* 35 full-time (13 women). *Students:* 217 full-time (154 women), 144 part-time (107 women); includes 48 minority (25 African Americans, 13 Asian Americans or Pacific Islanders, 10 Hispanic Americans), 71 international. Average age 32. 238 applicants, 46% accepted. In 2009, 117 master's, 36 doctorates awarded. *Entrance requirements:* Additional exam requirements/recommendations for international students: Required—TOEFL. Electronic applications accepted. *Expenses:* Tuition, state resident: part-time $478.25 per credit hour. Tuition, nonresident: part-time $966.50 per credit hour. Part-time tuition and fees vary according to program. *Financial support:* In 2009–10, 71 research assistantships with tuition reimbursements (averaging $6,836 per year), 74 teaching assistantships with tuition reimbursements (averaging $6,858 per year) were awarded. Total annual research expenditures: $2.3 million. *Unit head:* Dr. Richard S. Prawat, Chairperson, 517-353-6417, Fax: 517-353-6393, E-mail: rsprawat@msu.edu. *Application contact:* Kathy Dimoff, Graduate Admissions Coordinator, 517-355-6683, Fax: 517-353-6393, E-mail: dimoff@msu.edu.

Minnesota State University Mankato, College of Graduate Studies, College of Allied Health and Nursing, Program in Rehabilitation Counseling, Mankato, MN 56001. Offers MS. *Accreditation:* CORE. *Students:* 7 full-time (6 women), 13 part-time (8 women). *Degree requirements:* For master's, comprehensive exam. *Entrance requirements:* For master's, GRE General Test, minimum GPA of 3.0 during previous 2 years, references. *Application deadline:* For fall admission, 3/1 priority date for domestic students. Applications are processed on a rolling basis. Application fee: $40. *Expenses:* Tuition, state resident: full-time $5364. Tuition, nonresident: full-time $8314. *Financial support:* Research assistantships with full tuition reimbursements, teaching assistantships with full tuition reimbursements available. Financial award application deadline: 3/15; financial award applicants required to submit FAFSA. *Unit head:* Dr. Bruce Poburka, Graduate Coordinator, 507-389-5843. *Application contact:* 507-389-2321, E-mail: grad@mnsu.edu.

Montana State University Billings, College of Allied Health Professions, Department of Rehabilitation and Human Services, Billings, MT 59101-0298. Offers MSRC. *Accreditation:* CORE. Part-time programs available. *Degree requirements:* For master's, thesis or professional paper and/or field experience. *Entrance requirements:* For master's, GRE General Test or MAT, minimum GPA of 3.0.

North Carolina Agricultural and Technical State University, Graduate School, School of Education, Department of Human Development and Services, Greensboro, NC 27411. Offers adult education (MS); counselor education (MS); human resources-agency counseling (MS); human resources-rehabilitation counseling (MS); leadership studies (PhD); school administration (MS). *Accreditation:* ACA. Part-time and evening/weekend programs available. *Degree requirements:* For master's, comprehensive exam, thesis, qualifying exam. *Entrance requirements:* For master's, GRE General Test, minimum GPA of 3.0.

Northeastern University, Bouvé College of Health Sciences Graduate School, Department of Counseling and Applied Educational Psychology, Program in Applied Behavior Analysis, Boston, MA 02115-5096. Offers MS. Part-time programs available. *Faculty:* 10 part-time/adjunct (5 women). *Students:* 74 full-time (58 women), 37 part-time (33 women); includes 3 African Americans, 1 Asian American or Pacific Islander, 7 Hispanic Americans, 4 international. Average age 29. 65 applicants, 86% accepted, 40 enrolled. In 2009, 31 master's awarded. *Degree requirements:* For master's, thesis. *Entrance requirements:* For master's, GRE General Test or MAT. Additional exam requirements/recommendations for international students: Required—TOEFL (minimum score 100 iBT). *Application deadline:* For fall admission, 8/1 for domestic students; for spring admission, 12/1 for domestic students. Applications are processed on a rolling basis. Application fee: $50. Electronic applications accepted. *Financial support:* Career-related internships or fieldwork available. Support available to part-time students. Financial award application deadline: 3/1; financial award applicants required to submit FAFSA. *Faculty research:* Stimulus control, failure-to-thrive children, severe behavior disorders, autism. *Unit head:* Karen Gould, Director, 781-440-0400 Ext. 215, E-mail: kgould@mayinstitute.org. *Application contact:* Margaret Schnabel, Director of Graduate Admissions, 617-373-2708, E-mail: bouvegrad@neu.edu.

Ohio University, Graduate College, College of Education, Department of Counseling and Higher Education, Athens, OH 45701-2979. Offers college student personnel (M Ed); community/agency counseling (M Ed); counselor education (PhD); higher education (PhD); rehabilitation counseling (M Ed); school counseling (M Ed). *Accreditation:* ACA; CORE. Part-time and evening/weekend programs available. *Faculty:* 12 full-time (6 women), 7 part-time/adjunct (1 woman). *Students:* 164 full-time (120 women), 51 part-time (30 women); includes 36 minority (27 African Americans, 3 American Indian/Alaska Native, 3 Asian Americans or Pacific Islanders, 3 Hispanic Americans), 9 international. 129 applicants, 58% accepted, 57 enrolled. In 2009, 60 master's, 16 doctorates awarded. *Degree requirements:* For master's, comprehensive exam (for some programs), thesis or alternative; for doctorate, comprehensive exam, thesis/dissertation. *Entrance requirements:* For master's, GRE General Test or MAT (if GPA less than 2.9), 3 letters of reference; for doctorate, GRE General Test, work experience, minimum GPA of 3.4. Additional exam requirements/recommendations for international students: Required—TOEFL (minimum score 550 paper-based; 80 iBT) or IELTS Academic (minimum score 6.5). *Application deadline:* For fall admission, 1/15 for domestic and international students. Application fee: $50 ($55 for international students). Electronic applications accepted. *Expenses:* Tuition, state resident: full-time $7839; part-time $323 per quarter hour. Tuition, nonresident: full-time $15,831; part-time $654 per quarter hour. Required fees: $2931. *Financial support:* Research assistantships with full tuition reimbursements, teaching assistantships with full tuition reimbursements, Federal Work-Study, institutionally sponsored loans, tuition waivers (partial), and unspecified assistantships available. Financial award application deadline: 1/15. *Faculty research:* Youth violence, gender studies, student affairs, chemical dependency, disabilities issues. Total annual research expenditures: $527,983. *Unit head:* Dr. Tracy Leinbaugh, Chair, 740-593-0846, Fax: 740-593-0477, E-mail: leinbaug@ohio.edu. *Application contact:* Floyd J. Doney, Director of Student Affairs, 740-593-4400, Fax: 740-593-9310, E-mail: doney@ohio.edu.

Pontifical Catholic University of Puerto Rico, Institute of Graduate Studies in Behavioral Science and Community Affairs, Program in Vocational Rehabilitation Counseling, Ponce, PR 00717-0777. Offers MSS. Part-time programs available. *Degree requirements:* For master's, thesis. *Entrance requirements:* For master's, EXADEP, GRE General Test, 3 letters of recommendation, interview, minimum GPA of 2.75.

St. Cloud State University, School of Graduate Studies, College of Education, Department of Counselor Education, Higher Education, and Educational Psychology, Program in Rehabilitation Counseling, St. Cloud, MN 56301-4498. Offers MS. *Accreditation:* CORE. *Faculty:* 12 full-time (5 women). *Students:* 17 full-time (9 women), 6 part-time (4 women); includes 2 minority (1 American Indian/Alaska Native, 1 Asian American or Pacific Islander). 6 applicants, 100% accepted. *Degree requirements:* For master's, comprehensive exam (for some programs), thesis or alternative. *Entrance requirements:* For master's, GRE General Test, minimum GPA of 2.75. Additional exam requirements/recommendations for international students: Required—Michigan English Language Assessment Battery; Recommended—TOEFL (minimum score 550 paper-based; 213 computer-based), IELTS (minimum score 6.5). *Application deadline:* For fall admission, 3/1 for domestic and international students. Application fee: $35. Electronic applications accepted. *Financial support:* Career-related internships or fieldwork, Federal Work-Study, scholarships/grants, and unspecified assistantships available. Financial award application deadline: 3/1. *Unit head:* Dr. Bradley Kuhlman, Coordinator, 320-308-2240, E-mail: bkuhlman@stcloudstate.edu. *Application contact:* Linda Lou Krueger, School of Graduate Studies, 320-308-2113, Fax: 320-308-5371, E-mail: lekrueger@stcloudstate.edu.

St. John's University, The School of Education, Department of Human Services and Counseling, Queens, NY 11439. Offers bilingual school counseling (MS Ed, PD); bilingual/multicultural education/teaching English to speakers of other languages (MS Ed); literacy (MS Ed, PhD), including teaching literacy 5-12 (MS Ed), teaching literacy B-12 (MS Ed), teaching literacy B-6 (MS Ed); mental health counseling (MS Ed); school counseling (MS Ed, PD); teaching children with disabilities in childhood education (MS Ed). Part-time and evening/weekend programs available. *Students:* 158 full-time (142 women), 301 part-time (265 women); includes 131 minority (27 African Americans, 22 Asian Americans or Pacific Islanders, 82 Hispanic Americans), 11 international. Average age 29. 342 applicants, 78% accepted, 153 enrolled. In 2009, 121 master's, 1 other advanced degree awarded. *Degree requirements:* For master's, comprehensive exam, thesis, residency. *Entrance requirements:* For doctorate, MAT, GRE General Test (analytical), official transcript showing conferral of degree with minimum GPA of 3.2, 2 letters of recommendation, statement of goals, resume, evidence of teaching experience; for PD, statement of goals, official transcript showing conferral of degree with minimum GPA of 3.0, 2 letters of recommendation, interview. Additional exam requirements/recommendations for international students: Required—TOEFL (minimum score 500 paper-based; 173 computer-based; 61 iBT), IELTS (minimum score 5.5). *Application deadline:* For fall admission, 4/1 priority date for domestic students, 6/1 priority date for international students; for spring admission, 11/1 priority date for domestic and international students. Applications are processed on a rolling basis. Application fee: $70. Electronic applications accepted. *Expenses:* Tuition: Full-time $16,290; part-time $905 per credit. Required fees: $300; $150 per semester. Tuition and fees vary according to program. *Financial support:* Research assistantships, career-related internships or fieldwork and scholarships/grants available. Support available to part-time students. Financial award application deadline: 3/1; financial award applicants required to submit FAFSA. *Faculty research:* Assisting troubled children and teens with substance abuse, truancy, and coping skills; literacy development for ESL learners; investigating Caribbean and Creole language and culture. *Unit head:* Dr. Francine Guastello, Acting Chair, 718-990-1475, Fax: 718-990-1614, E-mail: guastelf@stjohns.edu. *Application contact:* Dr. Kelly K. Ronayne, Associate Dean for Graduate Admissions, 718-990-2303, Fax: 718-990-2343, E-mail: graded@stjohns.edu.

Salve Regina University, Graduate Studies, Program in Rehabilitation Counseling, Newport, RI 02840-4192. Offers mental health counseling (CAGS); rehabilitation counseling (MA). Part-time and evening/weekend programs available. *Faculty:* 1 (woman) full-time, 4 part-time/adjunct (all women). *Students:* 16 full-time (14 women), 28 part-time (22 women); includes 2 minority (both Hispanic Americans). Average age 35. 23 applicants, 83% accepted, 16 enrolled. In 2009, 4 master's, 6 other advanced degrees awarded. *Entrance requirements:* For master's, GMAT, GRE General Test or MAT. Additional exam requirements/recommendations for international students: Required—TOEFL (minimum score 600 paper-based; 250 computer-based; 100 iBT), IELTS. *Application deadline:* For fall admission, 3/15 priority date for domestic and international students; for spring admission, 9/15 priority date for domestic and international students. Applications are processed on a rolling basis. Application fee: $60. Electronic applications accepted. *Expenses:* Tuition: Part-time $395 per credit. Part-time tuition and fees vary according to degree level. *Financial support:* Career-related internships or fieldwork and Federal Work-Study available. Support available to part-time students. Financial award application deadline: 3/1; financial award applicants required to submit FAFSA. *Unit head:* Dr. Dimity Peter, Director, 401-341-3189, Fax: 401-341-2993, E-mail: dimity.peter@salve.edu. *Application contact:* Kelly Alverson, Graduate Admissions Counselor, 401-341-2153, Fax: 401-341-2973, E-mail: kelly.alverson@salve.edu.

San Diego State University, Graduate and Research Affairs, College of Education, Department of Administration, Rehabilitation and Post-Secondary Education, San Diego, CA 92182. Offers educational leadership in post-secondary education (MA); rehabilitation counseling (MS), including deafness. Evening/weekend programs available. Postbaccalaureate distance learning degree programs offered. *Degree requirements:* For master's, comprehensive exam (for some programs), thesis (for some programs). *Entrance requirements:* For master's, GRE General Test, letters of reference. Additional exam requirements/recommendations for international students: Required—TOEFL. Electronic applications accepted. *Faculty research:* Rehabilitation in cultural diversity, distance learning technology.

San Francisco State University, Division of Graduate Studies, College of Health and Human Services, Department of Counseling, San Francisco, CA 94132-1722. Offers counseling (MS); marriage, family, and child counseling (MSC); rehabilitation counseling (MS). *Accreditation:* ACA (one or more programs are accredited). Part-time programs available.

South Carolina State University, School of Graduate Studies, Department of Human Services, Orangeburg, SC 29117-0001. Offers elementary counselor education (M Ed); rehabilitation counseling (MA); secondary counselor education (M Ed). *Accreditation:* CORE. Part-time and evening/weekend programs available. *Degree requirements:* For master's, comprehensive exam (for some programs), departmental qualifying exam, internship. *Entrance requirements:* For master's, GRE, MAT, minimum GPA of 2.7. Electronic applications accepted. *Expenses:* Tuition, state resident: part-time $470 per credit hour. Tuition, nonresident: part-time $924 per credit hour. *Faculty research:* Handicap, disability, rehabilitation evaluation, vocation.

Southern Illinois University Carbondale, Graduate School, College of Education, Rehabilitation Institute, Carbondale, IL 62901-4701. Offers behavioral analysis and therapy (MS); communication disorders and sciences (MS); rehabilitation (Rh D); rehabilitation administration and services (MS); rehabilitation counseling (MS). *Accreditation:* CORE. Part-time programs available. *Degree requirements:* For master's, thesis; for doctorate, thesis/dissertation. *Entrance requirements:* For master's, GRE; for doctorate, GRE or MAT, minimum GPA of 3.25. Additional exam requirements/recommendations for international students: Required—TOEFL. *Faculty research:* Professional ethics.

Southern University and Agricultural and Mechanical College, Graduate School, College of Sciences, Department of Psychology, Program in Rehabilitation Counseling, Baton Rouge, LA 70813. Offers MS. *Accreditation:* CORE. *Degree requirements:* For master's, comprehensive exam, thesis optional. *Entrance requirements:* For master's, GMAT or GRE General Test. Additional exam requirements/recommendations for international students: Required—TOEFL. *Faculty research:* Cultural diversity, professional preparation and participation of minorities, needs and satisfaction of students with disabilities, prediction model for rehabilitation outcome, diabetes.

Springfield College, Graduate Programs, Programs in Rehabilitation Counseling and Services, Springfield, MA 01109-3797. Offers alcohol rehabilitation/substance abuse counseling (M Ed, MS); deaf counseling (M Ed, MS); developmental disabilities (M Ed, MS); general counseling and casework (M Ed, MS); psychiatric rehabilitation/mental health counseling (M Ed, MS); special services (M Ed, MS). *Accreditation:* CORE (one or more programs are accredited). Part-time programs available. *Degree requirements:* For master's, comprehensive exam. *Entrance requirements:* Additional exam requirements/recommendations for international students: Required—TOEFL (minimum score 550 paper-based; 213 computer-based). Electronic applications accepted. *Expenses:* Tuition: Full-time $19,800; part-time $825 per credit hour. Required fees: $150.

Teachers College, Columbia University, Graduate Faculty of Education, Department of Health and Behavioral Studies, Program in Guidance and Rehabilitation, New York, NY 10027-6696. Offers MA.

Texas Tech University Health Sciences Center, School of Allied Health Sciences, Program in Rehabilitation Counseling, Lubbock, TX 79430. Offers MRC. *Accreditation:* CORE. Part-time programs available. *Faculty:* 4 full-time (3 women). *Students:* 78 full-time (60 women), 7 part-time (5 women); includes 34 minority (19 African Americans, 1 American Indian/Alaska Native, 1 Asian American or Pacific Islander, 13 Hispanic Americans). Average age 40. 57 applicants, 86% accepted, 49 enrolled. In 2009, 23 master's awarded. *Entrance requirements:* Additional exam requirements/recommendations for international students: Required—TOEFL. *Application deadline:* For fall admission, 6/1 for domestic students; for spring admission, 10/1 for domestic students. Application fee: $35. Electronic applications accepted. *Financial support:* Career-related internships or fieldwork and institutionally sponsored loans available. *Unit head:* Dr. Robin Satterwhite, Chair, 806-743-2263, Fax: 806-743-3249, E-mail: robin.satterwhite@ttuhsc.edu. *Application contact:* Jeri Moravcik, Assistant Director of Admissions and Student Affairs, 806-743-3220, Fax: 806-743-2994, E-mail: jeri.moravcik@ttuhsc.edu.

Thomas University, Department of Human Services, Thomasville, GA 31792-7499. Offers community counseling (MSCC); rehabilitation counseling (MRC). *Accreditation:* CORE. Part-time programs available. *Entrance requirements:* For master's, resume, 3 academic/professional references. Additional exam requirements/recommendations for international students: Required—TOEFL (minimum score 600 paper-based; 250 computer-based). Electronic applications accepted.

Troy University, Graduate School, College of Education, Program in Counseling and Psychology, Troy, AL 36082. Offers agency counsleing (Ed S); clinical mental health (MS); community counseling (MS, Ed S); corrections counseling (MS); rehabilitation counseling (MS); school psychology (MS, Ed S); school psychometry (MS); social service counseling (MS); student affairs counseling (MS); substance abuse counseling (MS). *Accreditation:* ACA; CORE; NCATE. Part-time and evening/weekend programs available. *Students:* 375 full-time (302 women), 753 part-time (642 women); includes 664 minority (610 African Americans, 8 American Indian/Alaska Native, 9 Asian Americans or Pacific Islanders, 37 Hispanic Americans). Average age 33. 493 applicants, 92% accepted. In 2009, 102 master's, 191 other advanced degrees awarded. *Degree requirements:* For master's, comprehensive exam, thesis. *Entrance requirements:* For master's, MAT, minimum GPA of 2.5. Additional exam requirements/recommendations for international students: Required—TOEFL (minimum score 523 paper-based; 193 computer-based; 70 iBT), IELTS (minimum score 6). *Application deadline:* Applications are processed on a rolling basis. Application fee: $50. Electronic applications accepted. *Unit head:* Dr. Andrew Creamer, Chair, 334-670-3350, Fax: 334-670-32961, E-mail: drcreamer@troy.edu. *Application contact:* Brenda K. Campbell, Director of Graduate Admissions, 334-670-3178, Fax: 334-670-3733, E-mail: bcamp@troy.edu.

Université de Montréal, Faculty of Medicine, Program in Specialized Studies, Montréal, QC H3C 3J7, Canada. Offers anesthesia (DESS); diagnostic radiology (DESS); family medicine (DESS); gastroenterology (DESS); geriatry (DESS); intensive care (DESS); medical biochemistry (DESS); medical genetics (DESS); medicine (DESS); microbiology and infectious diseases (DESS); nuclear medicine (DESS); obstetrics and gynecology (DESS); ophthalmology (DESS); pediatrics (DESS); pneumology (DESS); psychiatry (DESS); radiology-oncology (DESS); rheumatology (DESS); surgery (DESS). *Entrance requirements:* For degree, proficiency in French. Electronic applications accepted.

University at Albany, State University of New York, School of Education, Department of Educational and Counseling Psychology, Program in Rehabilitation Counseling, Albany, NY 12222-0001. Offers counseling psychology (MS). Evening/weekend programs available. *Entrance requirements:* For master's, GRE General Test. Additional exam requirements/recommendations for international students: Required—TOEFL (minimum score 550 paper-based; 213 computer-based). Electronic applications accepted.

University at Buffalo, the State University of New York, Graduate School, Graduate School of Education, Department of Counseling, School, and Educational Psychology, Buffalo, NY 14260. Offers counseling/school psychology (PhD); counselor education (PhD); educational psychology (MA, PhD); general education (Ed M); mental health counseling (MS); rehabilitation counseling (MS); school counseling (Ed M, Certificate); Singapore school counseling (Ed M). *Accreditation:* CORE (one or more programs are accredited). Postbaccalaureate distance learning degree programs offered (no on-campus study). *Faculty:* 17 full-time (8 women), 36 part-time/adjunct (28 women). *Students:* 152 full-time (125 women), 127 part-time (97 women); includes 33 minority (22 African Americans, 2 American Indian/Alaska Native, 3 Asian Americans or Pacific Islanders, 6 Hispanic Americans), 27 international. Average age 30. 396 applicants, 41% accepted, 119 enrolled. In 2009, 60 master's, 12 doctorates, 24 other advanced degrees awarded. *Degree requirements:* For master's, comprehensive exam (for some programs), thesis (for some programs); for doctorate, comprehensive exam, thesis/dissertation. *Entrance requirements:* For master's and doctorate, GRE General Test, interview, letters of reference. Additional exam requirements/recommendations for international students: Required—TOEFL (minimum score 79 iBT). *Application deadline:* For fall admission, 2/1 priority date for domestic and international students. Application fee: $50. Electronic applications accepted. *Financial support:* In 2009–10, 14 fellowships with full tuition reimbursements (averaging $9,000 per year), 28 research assistantships with full tuition reimbursements (averaging $9,000 per year) were awarded; teaching assistantships with tuition reimbursements, career-related internships or fieldwork, Federal Work-Study, institutionally sponsored loans, and unspecified assistantships also available. Financial award application deadline: 2/1; financial award applicants required to submit FAFSA. *Faculty research:* Multicultural counseling, class size effects, good work in counseling, eating disorders, outcome assessment, change agents and therapeutic factors in group counseling. Total annual research expenditures: $3.7 million. *Unit head:* Dr. Timothy Janikowski, Chair, 716-645-2484, Fax: 716-645-6616, E-mail: tjanikow@buffalo.edu. *Application contact:* Rochelle Cohen, Admissions Assistant, 716-645-2110, Fax: 716-645-7937, E-mail: recohen@buffalo.edu.

The University of Arizona, Graduate College, College of Education, Department of Disability and Psychoeducational Studies, Program in Rehabilitation, Tucson, AZ 85721. Offers MA, PhD. *Faculty:* 17 full-time (9 women). *Students:* 21 full-time (16 women), 22 part-time (17 women); includes 1 minority (American Indian/Alaska Native), 2 international. Average age 41. 35 applicants, 60% accepted, 11 enrolled. In 2009, 19 master's, 4 doctorates awarded. *Entrance requirements:* For master's, GMAT, 3 letters of recommendation, statement of purpose; for doctorate, GMAT, 3 letters of recommendation. Additional exam requirements/recommendations for international students: Required—TOEFL (minimum score 550 paper-based; 213 computer-based; 79 iBT). *Application deadline:* For fall admission, 2/15 for domestic students, 12/1 for international students. Application fee: $65. Electronic applications accepted. *Expenses:* Tuition, state resident: full-time $9028. Tuition, nonresident: full-time $24,890. *Financial support:* In 2009–10, 4 research assistantships with full tuition reimbursements (averaging $12,828 per year), 4 teaching assistantships with full tuition reimbursements (averaging $12,378 per year) were awarded. *Unit head:* Dr. Linda R. Shaw, Department Head, 520-621-7822, Fax: 520-621-3821, E-mail: lshaw@email.arizona.edu. *Application contact:* Cecilia Carlon, Coordinator, 520-621-7822, Fax: 520-621-3821, E-mail: ccarlon@email.arizona.edu.

University of Arkansas, Graduate School, College of Education and Health Professions, Department of Rehabilitation, Human Resources and Communication Disorders, Program in Rehabilitation, Fayetteville, AR 72701-1201. Offers MS, PhD. *Accreditation:* CORE (one or more programs are accredited). Part-time programs available. *Students:* 29 full-time (21 women), 27 part-time (16 women); includes 9 minority (5 African Americans, 2 American Indian/Alaska Native, 1 Asian American or Pacific Islander, 1 Hispanic American), 2 international. In 2009, 9 master's, 2 doctorates awarded. *Degree requirements:* For doctorate, thesis/dissertation. *Entrance requirements:* For doctorate, GRE General Test. Application fee: $40 ($50 for international students). *Expenses:* Tuition, state resident: full-time $7355; part-time $356.58 per hour. Tuition, nonresident: full-time $17,401; part-time $775.17 per hour. Required fees: $1203. *Financial support:* In 2009–10, 5 fellowships with tuition reimbursements, 9 research assistantships, 1 teaching assistantship were awarded; career-related internships or fieldwork and Federal Work-Study also available. Support available to part-time students. Financial award application deadline: 4/1; financial award applicants required to submit FAFSA. *Unit head:* Dr. Fran Hagstrom, Department Chairperson, 479-575-4758, Fax: 479-575-2492, E-mail: fhagstr@uark.edu. *Application contact:* Dr. Brent Williams, Graduate Coordinator, 479-575-4758, E-mail: btwilli@uark.edu.

University of Arkansas at Little Rock, Graduate School, College of Education, Department of Counseling and Rehabilitation Education, Little Rock, AR 72204-1099. Offers adult education (M Ed); counselor education (M Ed), including school counseling; orientation and mobility of the blind (Graduate Certificate); rehabilitation counseling (MA, Graduate Certificate); rehabilitation of the blind (MA). *Accreditation:* CORE; NCATE. Part-time programs available. *Entrance requirements:* For master's, interview, minimum GPA of 2.75. *Faculty research:* Low vision, orientation and mobility instruction.

University of Florida, Graduate School, College of Public Health and Health Professions, Department of Behavioral Science and Community Health, Gainesville, FL 32611. Offers rehabilitation counseling (MHS). Part-time programs available. *Entrance requirements:* For master's, GRE General Test, minimum GPA of 3.0. Electronic applications accepted. *Faculty research:* Overcoming mental, physical, or emotional handicaps toward personal/vocational independence.

The University of Iowa, Graduate College, College of Education, Department of Counseling, Rehabilitation, and Student Development, Iowa City, IA 52242-1316. Offers administration and research (PhD); community/rehabilitation counseling (MA); counselor education and supervision (PhD); rehabilitation counselor education (PhD); school counseling (MA); student development (MA, PhD). *Accreditation:* ACA (one or more programs are accredited); CORE (one or more programs are accredited). *Degree requirements:* For master's, thesis optional, exam; for doctorate, comprehensive exam, thesis/dissertation. *Entrance requirements:* For master's and doctorate, GRE General Test, minimum GPA of 3.0. Additional exam requirements/recommendations for international students: Required—TOEFL (minimum score 550 paper-based; 213 computer-based; 81 iBT). Electronic applications accepted.

The University of Kansas, Graduate Studies, College of Liberal Arts and Sciences, Department of Psychology, Lawrence, KS 66045. Offers clinical child psychology (MA, PhD); clinical health and rehabilitation (PhD); cognitive (PhD); developmental (PhD); quantitative (PhD); social (MA). *Accreditation:* APA (one or more programs are accredited). *Faculty:* 27 full-time (8 women), 9 part-time/adjunct (4 women). *Students:* 85 full-time (62 women), 11 part-time (9 women); includes 13 minority (4 African Americans, 1 American Indian/Alaska Native, 6 Asian Americans or Pacific Islanders, 2 Hispanic Americans), 7 international. Average age 27. 185 applicants, 15% accepted, 17 enrolled. In 2009, 13 master's, 10 doctorates awarded. *Degree requirements:* For master's, thesis; for doctorate, variable foreign language requirement, comprehensive exam, thesis/dissertation. *Entrance requirements:* For doctorate, GRE General Test, minimum GPA of 3.0; undergraduate degree with 15 hours of course work in psychology, vita, writing sample (Clinical Program Only). Additional exam requirements/recommendations for international students: Required—TOEFL. *Application deadline:* For fall admission, 12/1 for domestic and international students. Application fee: $45 ($55 for international students). Electronic applications accepted. *Expenses:* Tuition, state resident: full-time $6492; part-time $270.50 per credit hour. Tuition, nonresident: full-time $15,510; part-time $646.25 per credit hour. Required fees: $847; $70.56 per credit hour. Tuition and fees vary according to course

Rehabilitation Counseling

The University of Kansas (continued)
load and program. *Financial support:* Fellowships with full tuition reimbursements, research assistantships with partial tuition reimbursements, teaching assistantships with full and partial tuition reimbursements, career-related internships or fieldwork and unspecified assistantships available. Financial award application deadline: 12/1; financial award applicants required to submit FAFSA. *Faculty research:* Information processing in depression, rape and other forms of sexual coerciom, motions on physical function, processes of memory and understanding text, social stigmas and hostile group environments. *Unit head:* Dr. Ruth Ann Atchley, Chair, 785-864-9821, Fax: 785-864-5696, E-mail: ratchley@ku.edu. *Application contact:* Cathy L. O'Keefe, Graduate Admissions Officer, 785-864-4195, Fax: 785-864-5696, E-mail: psycgrad@ku.edu.

University of Kentucky, Graduate School, College of Education, Program in Special Education, Lexington, KY 40506-0032. Offers early childhood special education (MS Ed); rehabilitation counseling (MRC); special education (MS Ed); special education leadership personnel preparation (Ed D). *Accreditation:* CORE; NCATE. Terminal master's awarded for partial completion of doctoral program. *Degree requirements:* For master's, comprehensive exam, thesis optional; for doctorate, comprehensive exam, thesis/dissertation. *Entrance requirements:* For master's, GRE General Test, minimum undergraduate GPA of 2.75; for doctorate, GRE General Test, minimum graduate GPA of 3.0. Additional exam requirements/recommendations for international students: Required—TOEFL (minimum score 550 paper-based; 213 computer-based). Electronic applications accepted. *Faculty research:* Applied behavior analysis applications in special education, single subject research design in classroom settings, transition research across life span, rural special education personnel.

University of Louisiana at Lafayette, College of Liberal Arts, Department of Psychology, Program in Rehabilitation Counseling, Lafayette, LA 70504. Offers MS. *Entrance requirements:* For master's, GRE General Test, minimum GPA of 3.0. Additional exam requirements/recommendations for international students: Required—TOEFL (minimum score 550 paper-based; 213 computer-based). Electronic applications accepted. *Faculty research:* Vocational assessment, psychology.

University of Maryland, College Park, Academic Affairs, College of Education, Department of Counseling and Personnel Services, College Park, MD 20742. Offers college student personnel (M Ed, MA); college student personnel administration (PhD); community counseling (CAGS); community/career counseling (M Ed, MA); counseling and personnel services (M Ed, MA, PhD), including art therapy (M Ed), college student personnel (M Ed), counseling and personnel services (PhD), counseling psychology (M Ed), mental health counseling (M Ed), school counseling (M Ed); counseling psychology (PhD); counselor education (PhD); rehabilitation counseling (M Ed, MA, AGSC); school counseling (M Ed, MA); school psychology (M Ed, MA, PhD). *Accreditation:* ACA (one or more programs are accredited); APA (one or more programs are accredited); CORE (one or more programs are accredited); NCATE. Part-time and evening/weekend programs available. Postbaccalaureate distance learning degree programs offered (no on-campus study). *Faculty:* 34 full-time (21 women), 8 part-time/adjunct (6 women). *Students:* 152 full-time (117 women), 25 part-time (18 women); includes 67 minority (32 African Americans, 2 American Indian/Alaska Native, 20 Asian Americans or Pacific Islanders, 13 Hispanic Americans), 16 international. 319 applicants, 15% accepted, 32 enrolled. In 2009, 24 master's, 15 doctorates, 4 other advanced degrees awarded. *Degree requirements:* For master's, thesis (for some programs); for doctorate, thesis/dissertation. *Entrance requirements:* For master's, GRE General Test or MAT, minimum GPA of 3.0, 3 letters of recommendation; for doctorate, GRE General Test or MAT, minimum GPA of 3.5, 3 letters of recommendation. Additional exam requirements/recommendations for international students: Required—TOEFL. *Application deadline:* For fall admission, 12/15 for domestic and international students; for spring admission, 10/1 for domestic students, 6/1 for international students. Applications are processed on a rolling basis. Application fee: $60. Electronic applications accepted. *Expenses:* Tuition, area resident: Part-time $471 per credit hour. Tuition, state resident: part-time $471 per credit hour. Tuition, nonresident: part-time $1016 per credit hour. Required fees: $337.04 per term. *Financial support:* In 2009–10, 4 fellowships with partial tuition reimbursements (averaging $10,402 per year), 8 research assistantships (averaging $16,454 per year), 93 teaching assistantships with tuition reimbursements (averaging $16,109 per year) were awarded; career-related internships or fieldwork, Federal Work-Study, and scholarships/grants also available. Support available to part-time students. Financial award applicants required to submit FAFSA. *Faculty research:* Educational psychology, counseling, health. Total annual research expenditures: $1.5 million. *Unit head:* Dr. Dennis Kivlighan, Chair, 301-405-2858, E-mail: dennisk@umd.edu. *Application contact:* Dean of Graduate School, 301-405-0358.

University of Maryland Eastern Shore, Graduate Programs, Department of Rehabilitation Services, Princess Anne, MD 21853-1299. Offers rehabilitation counseling (MS). *Accreditation:* CORE. Part-time and evening/weekend programs available. *Degree requirements:* For master's, internship. *Entrance requirements:* For master's, interview. Additional exam requirements/recommendations for international students: Required—TOEFL (minimum score 213 computer-based; 80 iBT). Electronic applications accepted. *Faculty research:* Long-term rehabilitation training.

University of Massachusetts Boston, Office of Graduate Studies, Graduate College of Education, Counseling and School Psychology Department, Program in Rehabilitation Counseling, Boston, MA 02125-3393. Offers M Ed, CAGS. *Accreditation:* CORE.

University of Medicine and Dentistry of New Jersey, School of Health Related Professions, Department of Psychiatric Rehabilitation and Counseling Professions, Program in Psychiatric Rehabilitation, Newark, NJ 07107-1709. Offers MS, PhD. *Accreditation:* CORE. *Entrance requirements:* For doctorate, GRE General Test. Additional exam requirements/recommendations for international students: Required—TOEFL. Electronic applications accepted.

University of Medicine and Dentistry of New Jersey, School of Health Related Professions, Department of Psychiatric Rehabilitation and Counseling Professions, Program in Rehabilitation Counseling, Newark, NJ 07107-1709. Offers psychiatric rehabilitation (MS); vocational rehabilitation (MS). Programs offered at Scotch Plains and Stratford campuses. *Accreditation:* CORE. *Degree requirements:* For master's, internship, practicum. *Entrance requirements:* For master's, minimum 2 years of psychiatric rehabilitation or related professional experience or GRE General Test, interview. Additional exam requirements/recommendations for international students: Required—TOEFL. Electronic applications accepted.

University of Memphis, Graduate School, College of Education, Department of Counseling, Educational Psychology and Research, Memphis, TN 38152. Offers counseling (MS, Ed D), including community counseling (MS), rehabilitation counseling (MS), school counseling (MS); counseling psychology (PhD); educational psychology and research (MS, PhD), including educational psychology, educational research. *Accreditation:* ACA (one or more programs are accredited); APA (one or more programs are accredited); CORE (one or more programs are accredited); NCATE. *Faculty:* 26 full-time (13 women), 9 part-time/adjunct (5 women). *Students:* 95 full-time (73 women), 104 part-time (81 women); includes 62 minority (56 African Americans, 3 American Indian/Alaska Native, 1 Asian American or Pacific Islander, 2 Hispanic Americans), 5 international. Average age 33. 118 applicants, 63% accepted, 36 enrolled. In 2009, 46 master's, 14 doctorates awarded. *Degree requirements:* For master's, comprehensive exam, thesis or alternative; for doctorate, comprehensive exam, thesis/dissertation. *Entrance requirements:* For master's, GRE General Test or MAT, minimum GPA of 2.5; for doctorate, GRE General Test. *Application deadline:* For fall admission, 10/1 for domestic students; for spring admission, 4/1 for domestic students. Application fee: $35 ($60 for international students). *Expenses:* Tuition, state resident: full-time $6246; part-time $347 per credit hour. Tuition, nonresident: full-time $15,894; part-time $883 per credit hour. Required fees: $1160. Full-time tuition and fees vary according to course load, degree level and program. *Financial support:* In 2009–10, 130 students received support; fellowships with full tuition reimbursements available, research assistantships with full tuition reimbursements available, teaching assistantships with full tuition reimbursements available, career-related internships or fieldwork, Federal Work-Study, scholarships/grants, and unspecified assistantships available. Financial award application deadline: 2/15; financial award applicants required to submit FAFSA. *Faculty research:* Anger management, aging and disability, supervision, multicultural counseling. *Unit head:* Dr. Douglas C. Strohmer, Chair, 901-678-2841, Fax: 901-678-5114. *Application contact:* Dr. Ernest A. Rakow, Associate Dean of Administration and Graduate Programs, 901-678-2399, Fax: 901-678-4778.

University of Nevada, Las Vegas, Graduate College, College of Education, Department of Counselor Education, Las Vegas, NV 89154-3066. Offers addiction studies (Advanced Certificate); community mental health (MS); rehabilitation counseling (Advanced Certificate); school counseling (M Ed). *Faculty:* 7 full-time (2 women), 10 part-time/adjunct (7 women). *Students:* 47 full-time (39 women), 37 part-time (31 women); includes 14 minority (3 African Americans, 1 Asian American or Pacific Islander, 10 Hispanic Americans). Average age 32. 97 applicants, 95% accepted, 57 enrolled. In 2009, 19 master's awarded. *Degree requirements:* For master's, comprehensive exam (for some programs), thesis (for some programs); for Advanced Certificate, thesis (for some programs). *Entrance requirements:* Additional exam requirements/recommendations for international students: Required—TOEFL (minimum score 550 paper-based; 213 computer-based; 80 iBT), IELTS (minimum score 7). *Application deadline:* For fall admission, 2/1 priority date for domestic and international students. Applications are processed on a rolling basis. Application fee: $60 ($95 for international students). Electronic applications accepted. *Financial support:* In 2009–10, 10 students received support, including 6 research assistantships with partial tuition reimbursements available (averaging $10,000 per year), 4 teaching assistantships with partial tuition reimbursements available (averaging $10,000 per year); institutionally sponsored loans, scholarships/grants, health care benefits, and unspecified assistantships also available. Financial award application deadline: 3/1. *Faculty research:* Social justice and multicultural competencies for counselors, therapeutic storytelling and bibliotherapy, school counselor education pedagogy, counseling program evaluation, addictions prevention and related trauma. *Unit head:* Dr. Dale Pehrsson, Chair/ Associate Professor, 702-895-5994, Fax: 702-895-5550, E-mail: dale.pehrsson@unlv.edu. *Application contact:* Graduate College Admissions Evaluator, 702-895-3320, Fax: 702-895-4180, E-mail: gradcollege@unlv.edu.

The University of North Carolina at Chapel Hill, School of Medicine and Graduate School, Graduate Programs in Medicine, Chapel Hill, NC 27599. Offers allied health sciences (MPT, MS, Au D, DPT, PhD), including human movement science (MS, PhD), occupational science (MS, PhD), physical therapy (MPT, MS, DPT), rehabilitation counseling and psychology (MS), speech and hearing sciences (MS, Au D, PhD); biochemistry and biophysics (MS, PhD); biomedical engineering (MS, PhD); cell and developmental biology (PhD); cell and molecular physiology (PhD); genetics and molecular biology (PhD); microbiology and immunology (MS, PhD), including immunology, microbiology; neurobiology (PhD); pathology and laboratory medicine (PhD), including experimental pathology; pharmacology (PhD); MD/PhD. Post-baccalaureate distance learning degree programs offered. Terminal master's awarded for partial completion of doctoral program. *Degree requirements:* For master's, comprehensive exam; for doctorate, thesis/dissertation. Electronic applications accepted. *Expenses:* Contact institution.

The University of North Carolina at Chapel Hill, School of Medicine and Graduate School, Graduate Programs in Medicine, Department of Allied Health Sciences, Division of Rehabilitation Counseling and Psychology, Chapel Hill, NC 27599. Offers MS. *Accreditation:* CORE. *Faculty:* 4 full-time (3 women), 1 (woman) part-time/adjunct. *Students:* 29 full-time (27 women), 4 part-time (all women); includes 5 minority (all African Americans). Average age 27. 34 applicants, 71% accepted, 19 enrolled. In 2009, 5 master's awarded. *Degree requirements:* For master's, comprehensive exam, thesis or alternative, internship. *Entrance requirements:* For master's, GRE. Additional exam requirements/recommendations for international students: Required—TOEFL (minimum score 550 paper-based; 79 computer-based). *Application deadline:* For fall admission, 4/1 for domestic students, 1/1 for international students. Application fee: $75. *Financial support:* In 2009–10, 2 research assistantships (averaging $4,300 per year) were awarded; teaching assistantships, Federal Work-Study, institutionally sponsored loans, traineeships, and unspecified assistantships also available. Financial award application deadline: 1/1. *Faculty research:* Motor development, motor control; treatment of sports/orthopedic patient problems; movement in older adults; postural control across the lifespan; research in clinical practice; fetal, preterm, and infant movement; functional assessment across the lifespan. *Unit head:* Charles Bernacchio, Director, 919-843-4730, Fax: 919-966-9007, E-mail: cbernacchio@med.unc.edu. *Application contact:* Holly Kathryn Maguire, Program Assistant, 919-966-8788, Fax: 919-966-9007, E-mail: holly_maguire@med.unc.edu.

University of Northern Colorado, Graduate School, College of Natural and Health Sciences, School of Human Sciences, Program in Rehabilitation, Greeley, CO 80639. Offers human rehabilitation (PhD); rehabilitation counseling (MA). *Accreditation:* CORE (one or more programs are accredited). Part-time programs available. *Faculty:* 3 full-time (1 woman). *Students:* 12 full-time (10 women), 8 part-time (4 women); includes 2 minority (1 African American, 1 Hispanic American), 3 international. Average age 35. 7 applicants, 86% accepted, 5 enrolled. In 2009, 6 master's awarded. *Degree requirements:* For master's, comprehensive exam, thesis or alternative; for doctorate, comprehensive exam, thesis/dissertation. *Entrance requirements:* For master's, GRE General Test or MAT, 2 letters of recommendation; for doctorate, GRE General Test, 2 letters of recommendation. *Application deadline:* Applications are processed on a rolling basis. Application fee: $50 ($60 for international students). Electronic applications accepted. *Expenses:* Tuition, state resident: full-time $5770; part-time $320.55 per credit hour. Tuition, nonresident: full-time $13,847; part-time $769.27 per credit hour. Required fees: $948.78; $52.72 per credit. *Financial support:* Fellowships, research assistantships, teaching assistantships, unspecified assistantships available. Financial award application deadline: 3/1; financial award applicants required to submit FAFSA. *Unit head:* Dr. Joe Ososkie, Program Coordinator, 970-351-2403. *Application contact:* Linda Sisson, Graduate Student Admission Coordinator, 970-351-1807, Fax: 970-351-2371, E-mail: linda.sisson@unco.edu.

University of North Florida, Brooks College of Health, Department of Public Health, Jacksonville, FL 32224. Offers community health (MPH); geriatric management (MSH); health administration (MHA); health behavior research and evaluation (Certificate); nutrition (MSH); rehabilitation counseling (MS). *Accreditation:* CEPH; CORE. Part-time and evening/weekend programs available. *Faculty:* 23 full-time (17 women). *Students:* 118 full-time (91 women), 82 part-time (61 women); includes 42 minority (23 African Americans, 8 Asian Americans or Pacific Islanders, 11 Hispanic Americans), 9 international. Average age 31. 192 applicants, 26% accepted, 23 enrolled. In 2009, 69 master's awarded. *Degree requirements:* For master's, thesis optional. *Entrance requirements:* For master's, GRE General Test (MSH, MS, MPH); GMAT or GRE General Test (MHA), minimum GPA of 3.0 in last 60 hours. Additional exam requirements/recommendations for international students: Required—TOEFL (minimum score 500 paper-based; 173 computer-based). *Application deadline:* For fall admission, 7/1 priority date for domestic students, 5/1 for international students; for spring admission, 11/1 priority date for domestic students, 10/1 for international students. Applications are processed on a rolling basis. Application fee: $30. Electronic applications accepted. *Expenses:* Tuition, state resident: full-time $6649.20; part-time $277.05 per credit hour. Tuition, nonresident: full-time $22,970; part-time $957.08 per credit hour. Required fees: $985; $41.03 per credit hour. *Financial support:* In 2009–10, 99 students received support, including 1 teaching assistantship (averaging $1,004 per year); research assistantships, career-related internships or fieldwork, Federal Work-Study, scholarships/grants, and tuition waivers (partial) also available. Support available to part-time students. Financial award application deadline: 4/1; financial award applicants required to submit FAFSA. *Faculty research:* Dietary supplements; alcohol, tobacco, and other drug use prevention; turnover among health professionals; aging; psychosocial aspects of disabilities. Total annual research expenditures: $335,106. *Unit head:* Dr. JoAnn Nolin, Chair, 904-620-2840, Fax: 904-620-2848, E-mail: jnolin@unf.edu. *Application contact:*

Heather Kenney, Director of Advising, 904-620-2810, Fax: 904-620-1030, E-mail: heather.kenney@unf.edu.

University of North Texas, Robert B. Toulouse School of Graduate Studies, College of Public Affairs and Community Service, Department of Rehabilitation, Social Work, and Addictions, Denton, TX 76203. Offers rehabilitation counseling (MS). *Accreditation:* CORE. Part-time and evening/weekend programs available. Postbaccalaureate distance learning degree programs offered (no on-campus study). *Degree requirements:* For master's, comprehensive exam, thesis optional, 100 hour practicum, 600 hour internship. *Entrance requirements:* For master's, GRE General Test or 2 years experience, minimum overall GPA of 2.8, 3.0 in last 60 hours. Additional exam requirements/recommendations for international students: Required—proof of English language proficiency required for non-native English speakers; Recommended—TOEFL (minimum score 550 paper-based; 213 computer-based; 79 iBT). *Application deadline:* Applications are processed on a rolling basis. Application fee: $50 ($75 for international students). Electronic applications accepted. *Expenses:* Tuition, state resident: full-time $4298; part-time $239 per contact hour. Tuition, nonresident: full-time $9878; part-time $549 per contact hour. Required fees: $265 per contact hour. *Financial support:* Career-related internships or fieldwork, Federal Work-Study, institutionally sponsored loans, and scholarships/grants available. Financial award application deadline: 4/15; financial award applicants required to submit FAFSA. *Faculty research:* Resiliency, multiculturalism, substance abuse and co-existing disabilities, social work pedagogy, spiritual aspects of disability and aging. *Application contact:* Program Coordinator, 940-565-4054, Fax: 940-369-8649.

University of Pittsburgh, School of Health and Rehabilitation Sciences, Master's Programs in Health and Rehabilitation Sciences, Pittsburgh, PA 15260. Offers health and rehabilitation sciences (MS), including clinical dietetics and nutrition, health care supervision and management, health information systems, occupational therapy, physical therapy, rehabilitation counseling, rehabilitation science and technology, sports medicine, wellness and human performance. *Accreditation:* APTA. Part-time and evening/weekend programs available. *Faculty:* 30 full-time (14 women), 4 part-time/adjunct (3 women). *Students:* 81 full-time (47 women), 54 part-time (27 women); includes 10 minority (6 African Americans, 4 Asian Americans or Pacific Islanders), 44 international. Average age 29. 326 applicants, 65% accepted, 130 enrolled. In 2009, 93 master's awarded. *Degree requirements:* For master's, comprehensive exam (for some programs), thesis optional. *Entrance requirements:* For master's, minimum GPA of 3.0. Additional exam requirements/recommendations for international students: Required—TOEFL, IELTS. *Application deadline:* For fall admission, 1/31 for international students; for spring admission, 7/31 for international students. Applications are processed on a rolling basis. Application fee: $50. Electronic applications accepted. *Expenses:* Contact institution. *Financial support:* In 2009–10, 3 research assistantships with full tuition reimbursements (averaging $18,450 per year) were awarded; teaching assistantships, Federal Work-Study, institutionally sponsored loans, traineeships, and unspecified assistantships also available. Financial award applicants required to submit FAFSA. *Faculty research:* Assistive technology, seating and wheeled mobility, cellular neurophysiology, low back syndrome, augmentative communication. Total annual research expenditures: $6.5 million. *Unit head:* Dr. Clifford E. Brubaker, Dean, 412-383-6560, Fax: 412-383-6535, E-mail: cliffb@pitt.edu. *Application contact:* Shameem Gangjee, Director of Admissions, 412-383-6558, Fax: 412-383-6535, E-mail: admissions@shrs.pitt.edu.

University of Puerto Rico, Río Piedras, College of Social Sciences, Graduate School of Rehabilitation Counseling, San Juan, PR 00931-3300. Offers MRC. *Accreditation:* CORE. Part-time programs available. *Degree requirements:* For master's, comprehensive exam, thesis, internship. *Entrance requirements:* For master's, GRE or PAEG, interview, minimum GPA of 3.0, letter of recommendation.

The University of Scranton, College of Graduate and Continuing Education, Department of Counseling and Human Services, Program in Rehabilitation Counseling, Scranton, PA 18510. Offers MS. *Accreditation:* CORE. Part-time and evening/weekend programs available. *Students:* 38 full-time (27 women), 6 part-time (2 women); includes 7 minority (5 African Americans, 1 Asian American or Pacific Islander, 1 Hispanic American). Average age 28. 17 applicants, 76% accepted. In 2009, 9 master's awarded. *Degree requirements:* For master's, comprehensive exam, capstone experience. *Entrance requirements:* For master's, minimum GPA of 2.75. Additional exam requirements/recommendations for international students: Required—TOEFL (minimum score 500 paper-based; 173 computer-based), IELTS (minimum score 5.5). *Application deadline:* For fall admission, 3/1 for domestic students. Application fee: $0. *Financial support:* Teaching assistantships, career-related internships or fieldwork and Federal Work-Study available. Support available to part-time students. Financial award application deadline: 3/1. *Unit head:* Dr. Lori Bruch, Program Director, 570-941-4308, Fax: 570-941-5882, E-mail: bruchl1@scranton.edu. *Application contact:* Joseph M. Roback, Director of Admissions, 570-941-4385, Fax: 570-941-5928, E-mail: robackj2@scranton.edu.

University of South Alabama, Graduate School, College of Education, Department of Professional Studies, Mobile, AL 36688-0002. Offers community counseling (MS); educational media (M Ed, MS); instructional design and development (MS, PhD); rehabilitation counseling (MS); school counseling (M Ed); school psychometry (M Ed). *Accreditation:* NCATE. Part-time programs available. *Degree requirements:* For master's, comprehensive exam. *Entrance requirements:* For master's, GRE General Test or MAT, minimum GPA of 3.0. *Expenses:* Tuition, state resident: part-time $218 per contact hour. Required fees: $1102 per year. *Faculty research:* Agency counseling, rehabilitation counseling, school psychometry.

University of South Carolina, School of Medicine and The Graduate School, Graduate Programs in Medicine, Program in Rehabilitation Counseling, Columbia, SC 29208. Offers psychiatric rehabilitation (Certificate); rehabilitation counseling (MRC). *Accreditation:* CORE. Part-time and evening/weekend programs available. *Degree requirements:* For master's, comprehensive exam, internship, practicum. *Entrance requirements:* For master's and Certificate, GRE General Test or GMAT. Electronic applications accepted. *Expenses:* Contact institution. *Faculty research:* Quality of life, alcohol dependency, technology for disabled, psychiatric rehabilitation, women with disabilities.

University of Southern Maine, College of Education and Human Development, Program in Counselor Education, Portland, ME 04104-9300. Offers clinical mental health (MS); counseling (CAS); mental health rehabilitation technician/community (Certificate); rehabilitation counseling (MS); school counseling (MS). *Accreditation:* ACA (one or more programs are accredited); CORE; NCATE; Teacher Education Accreditation Council. Part-time and evening/weekend programs available. *Faculty:* 8 full-time (4 women), 2 part-time/adjunct (1 woman). *Students:* 110 full-time (83 women), 33 part-time (23 women); includes 5 minority (1 African American, 1 American Indian/Alaska Native, 3 Hispanic Americans). 79 applicants, 72% accepted, 44 enrolled. In 2009, 37 master's, 2 other advanced degrees awarded. *Degree requirements:* For master's, comprehensive exam, thesis or alternative; for other advanced degree, thesis or alternative. *Entrance requirements:* For master's, GRE General Test or MAT, interview; for other advanced degree, master's degree. Additional exam requirements/recommendations for international students: Required—TOEFL (minimum score 550 paper-based; 213 computer-based; 79 iBT). *Application deadline:* For fall admission, 11/15 for domestic students. Application fee: $50. Electronic applications accepted. *Financial support:* In 2009–10, 12 students received support, including 3 research assistantships with partial tuition reimbursements available (averaging $4,500 per year); career-related internships or fieldwork, Federal Work-Study, institutionally sponsored loans, scholarships/grants, and unspecified assistantships also available. Support available to part-time students. Financial award application deadline: 3/1; financial award applicants required to submit FAFSA. *Faculty research:* Counselor licensure. *Unit head:* Dr. E. Michael Brady, Chair, Human Resource Development Department, 207-780-5316, Fax: 207-780-5043, E-mail: mbrady@usm.maine.edu. *Application contact:* Mary Sloan, Director of Graduate Admissions, 207-780-4386, Fax: 207-780-4969, E-mail: msloan@usm.maine.edu.

University of South Florida, Graduate School, College of Behavioral and Community Sciences, Department of Rehabilitation and Mental Health Counseling, Tampa, FL 33620-9951. Offers MA. *Accreditation:* CORE. Part-time and evening/weekend programs available. *Faculty:* 8 full-time (2 women), 5 part-time/adjunct (3 women). *Students:* 97 full-time (80 women), 58 part-time (45 women); includes 41 minority (12 African Americans, 1 American Indian/Alaska Native, 5 Asian Americans or Pacific Islanders, 23 Hispanic Americans), 1 international. Average age 32. 109 applicants, 43% accepted, 35 enrolled. In 2009, 21 master's awarded. *Degree requirements:* For master's, comprehensive exam, thesis. *Entrance requirements:* For master's, GRE General Test, minimum GPA of 3.0 in last 60 hours. Additional exam requirements/recommendations for international students: Required—TOEFL (minimum score 550 paper-based; 213 computer-based), TWE. *Application deadline:* For fall admission, 2/15 for domestic students, 1/2 for international students; for spring admission, 10/15 for domestic students, 6/1 for international students. Application fee: $30. Electronic applications accepted. *Financial support:* Application deadline: 6/30. *Faculty research:* Allied health, multiculturalism, couples therapy, addictions. *Unit head:* Charotte G. Dixon, Director, 813-974-2855, Fax: 813-974-8080, E-mail: dixon@chuma1.cas.usf.edu. *Application contact:* Gary DuDell, Director, 813-974-1257, Fax: 813-974-8080, E-mail: gdudell@cas.usf.edu.

The University of Tennessee, Graduate School, College of Education, Health and Human Sciences, Department of Educational Psychology and Counseling, Knoxville, TN 37996. Offers adult education (MS); applied educational psychology (MS); collaborative learning (Ed D); college student personnel (MS); mental health counseling (MS); rehabilitation counseling (MS); school counseling (MS). *Accreditation:* ACA (one or more programs are accredited); CORE (one or more programs are accredited); NCATE. Part-time and evening/weekend programs available. *Degree requirements:* For master's, thesis optional. *Entrance requirements:* For master's, GRE General Test, minimum GPA of 2.7. Additional exam requirements/recommendations for international students: Required—TOEFL. Electronic applications accepted. *Expenses:* Tuition, state resident: full-time $6826; part-time $380 per semester hour. Tuition, nonresident: full-time $21,844; part-time $1147 per semester hour. Tuition and fees vary according to program.

The University of Texas at El Paso, Graduate School, College of Health Sciences, Rehabilitation Counseling Program, El Paso, TX 79968-0001. Offers MRC. *Degree requirements:* For master's, thesis optional. *Entrance requirements:* For master's, GRE, Minimum GPA of 3.0, Brief statement summarizing professional goals, Letters of recommendation. Additional exam requirements/recommendations for international students: Required—TOEFL; Recommended—IELTS. *Application deadline:* For fall admission, 8/1 for domestic students, 3/1 for international students; for spring admission, 11/1 for domestic students, 9/1 for international students. Applications are processed on a rolling basis. Application fee: $45 ($80 for international students). Electronic applications accepted. *Financial support:* Fellowships with partial tuition reimbursements, research assistantships with partial tuition reimbursements, teaching assistantships with partial tuition reimbursements, institutionally sponsored loans, scholarships/grants, health care benefits, tuition waivers (partial), and unspecified assistantships available. Support available to part-time students. Financial award application deadline: 3/15; financial award applicants required to submit FAFSA. *Unit head:* Dr. Timothy Tansey, Program Director, 915-747-7233, E-mail: tntansey@utep.edu. *Application contact:* Dr. Patricia D. Witherspoon, Dean of the Graduate School, 915-747-5491, Fax: 915-747-5788, E-mail: withersp@utep.edu.

The University of Texas–Pan American, College of Health Sciences and Human Services, Department of Rehabilitation, Edinburg, TX 78539. Offers rehabilitation counseling (MS). *Accreditation:* CORE. Part-time and evening/weekend programs available. *Degree requirements:* For master's, comprehensive exam, thesis optional. *Entrance requirements:* For master's, minimum GPA of 3.0. *Expenses:* Tuition, state resident: full-time $3630.60; part-time $201.70 per credit hour. Tuition, nonresident: full-time $8617; part-time $478.70 per credit hour. Required fees: $806.50. *Faculty research:* Attitudes and disability, substance abuse, multicultural counseling, Hispanics and disability, Social Security beneficiary characteristics.

The University of Texas Southwestern Medical Center at Dallas, Southwestern School of Health Professions, Rehabilitation Counseling Psychology Program, Dallas, TX 75390. Offers MRC. *Accreditation:* CORE. *Faculty:* 19 full-time (14 women), 10 part-time/adjunct (3 women). *Students:* 20 full-time (15 women); includes 4 minority (1 Asian American or Pacific Islander, 3 Hispanic Americans). Average age 26. In 2009, 4 master's awarded. *Degree requirements:* For master's, thesis. *Entrance requirements:* For master's, GRE General Test, minimum GPA of 3.0. *Application deadline:* For fall admission, 5/1 for domestic students. Applications are processed on a rolling basis. Application fee: $0. Electronic applications accepted. *Financial support:* Career-related internships or fieldwork and institutionally sponsored loans available. Financial award application deadline: 3/1; financial award applicants required to submit FAFSA. *Faculty research:* Psychophysiology of stress and emotion, psychosocial rehabilitation, assessment of learning disabilities. *Unit head:* Dr. Cheryl Silver, Chair, 214-648-1750, Fax: 214-648-1076, E-mail: cheryl.silver@utsouthwestern.edu. *Application contact:* Lisa Halliburton, Administrative Assistant, 214-648-1544, Fax: 214-648-1076, E-mail: wanda.madyun@utsouthwestern.edu.

University of Wisconsin–Madison, Graduate School, School of Education, Department of Rehabilitation Psychology and Special Education, Program in Rehabilitation Psychology, Madison, WI 53706-1380. Offers MA, MS, PhD. *Accreditation:* CORE (one or more programs are accredited). *Degree requirements:* For doctorate, thesis/dissertation. *Application deadline:* For fall admission, 2/15 for domestic and international students; for spring admission, 10/15 for domestic and international students. Application fee: $56. *Expenses:* Tuition, state resident: part-time $594 per credit. Tuition, nonresident: part-time $1504 per credit. Required fees: $65 per credit. Tuition and fees vary according to course load, program and reciprocity agreements. *Financial support:* Fellowships with full tuition reimbursements, research assistantships with full tuition reimbursements, teaching assistantships with full tuition reimbursements, project assistantships available. *Unit head:* Dr. David Rosenthal, Chair, 608-262-5860. *Application contact:* Dr. David Rosenthal, Chair, 608-262-5860.

University of Wisconsin–Stout, Graduate School, College of Human Development, Program in Vocational Rehabilitation, Menomonie, WI 54751. Offers MS. *Accreditation:* CORE. Part-time programs available. Postbaccalaureate distance learning degree programs offered (no on-campus study). *Degree requirements:* For master's, comprehensive exam or thesis. *Entrance requirements:* For master's, minimum GPA of 2.75. Additional exam requirements/recommendations for international students: Required—TOEFL (minimum score 500 paper-based; 173 computer-based; 61 iBT). Electronic applications accepted. *Faculty research:* Aging/gerontology, athletics, neuropsychology, recreation, transition to work.

Utah State University, School of Graduate Studies, College of Education and Human Services, Department of Special Education and Rehabilitation, Program in Rehabilitation Counselor Education, Logan, UT 84322. Offers MRC. *Accreditation:* CORE. Part-time programs available. Postbaccalaureate distance learning degree programs offered (minimal on-campus study). *Degree requirements:* For master's, internship. *Entrance requirements:* For master's, GRE General Test, minimum GPA of 3.0. Additional exam requirements/recommendations for international students: Required—TOEFL (minimum score 550 paper-based; 213 computer-based). Electronic applications accepted. *Expenses:* Contact institution. *Faculty research:* Distance education, Hispanic rehabilitation, transition from school to work.

Virginia Commonwealth University, Graduate School, School of Allied Health Professions, Department of Rehabilitation Counseling, Richmond, VA 23284-9005. Offers MS, CPC. *Accreditation:* CORE (one or more programs are accredited). *Entrance requirements:* For master's, GRE General Test or MAT. *Faculty research:* Substance abuse/addictions, lifelong disabilities, consumer empowerment, counseling models, adjustment to disability.

Wayne State University, College of Education, Division of Theoretical and Behavioral Foundations, Detroit, MI 48202. Offers counseling (M Ed, MA, Ed D, PhD, Ed S); education evaluation and research (M Ed, Ed D, PhD); educational psychology (M Ed, Ed D, PhD, Ed S); educational sociology (M Ed, Ed D, PhD, Ed S); history and philosophy of education (M Ed, Ed D, PhD); rehabilitation counseling and community inclusion (MA, Ed S); school and community psychology

Rehabilitation Counseling

Wayne State University (continued)
(MA, Ed S); school clinical psychology (Ed S). *Accreditation:* ACA (one or more programs are accredited); CORE (one or more programs are accredited). Evening/weekend programs available. *Degree requirements:* For doctorate, thesis/dissertation. *Entrance requirements:* For master's, GRE; for doctorate, GRE, interview, minimum GPA of 3.0, curriculum vitae, references. Additional exam requirements/recommendations for international students: Required—TOEFL (minimum score 550 paper-based; 213 computer-based), TWE (minimum score 6). Electronic applications accepted. *Faculty research:* Adolescents at risk, supervision of counseling.

Wayne State University, Graduate School, Interdisciplinary Program in Developmental Disabilities, Detroit, MI 48202. Offers Certificate. *Entrance requirements:* Additional exam requirements/recommendations for international students: Required—TOEFL (minimum score 550 paper-based; 213 computer-based); Recommended—TWE (minimum score 6). Electronic applications accepted.

Western Michigan University, Graduate College, College of Health and Human Services, Department of Blindness and Low Vision Studies, Kalamazoo, MI 49008. Offers orientation and mobility (MA); orientation and mobility of children (MA); vision rehabilitation teaching (MA). *Accreditation:* CORE.

Western Oregon University, Graduate Programs, College of Education, Division of Special Education, Program in Rehabilitation Counseling, Monmouth, OR 97361-1394. Offers MS. *Accreditation:* CORE. *Degree requirements:* For master's, thesis optional, oral exam, portfolio. *Entrance requirements:* For master's, interview, minimum GPA of 3.0. Additional exam requirements/recommendations for international students: Required—TOEFL (minimum score 550 paper-based; 213 computer-based; 79 iBT), IELTS (minimum score 6.5). *Faculty research:* Deafness, rehabilitation counseling.

Western Washington University, Graduate School, Woodring College of Education, Program in Rehabilitation Counseling, Bellingham, WA 98225-5996. Offers MA. *Accreditation:* CORE. Part-time and evening/weekend programs available. Postbaccalaureate distance learning degree programs offered (minimal on-campus study). *Degree requirements:* For master's, research project. *Entrance requirements:* For master's, GRE General Test or MAT, minimum GPA of 3.0 in last 60 semester hours or last 90 quarter hours of course work. Additional exam requirements/recommendations for international students: Required—TOEFL (minimum score 567 paper-based; 227 computer-based). Electronic applications accepted. *Faculty research:* Employment issues for individuals with significant disabilities, research and statistics techniques, rehabilitation counselor education.

West Virginia University, College of Human Resources and Education, Department of Counseling, Rehabilitation Counseling, and Counseling Psychology, Program in Rehabilitation Counseling, Morgantown, WV 26506. Offers MS. *Accreditation:* CORE. Part-time programs available. Postbaccalaureate distance learning degree programs offered (minimal on-campus study). *Degree requirements:* For master's, content exams. *Entrance requirements:* For master's, GRE General Test, minimum GPA of 2.5, interview. Additional exam requirements/recommendations for international students: Required—TOEFL (minimum score 550 paper-based; 213 computer-based; 65 iBT). Electronic applications accepted. *Faculty research:* Work adjustment, job modification for the handicapped, computer resource networks, vocational evaluation.

Wilberforce University, Program in Rehabilitation Counseling, Wilberforce, OH 45384. Offers MS. *Entrance requirements:* For master's, bachelor's degree, 3 letters of recommendation, interview. Additional exam requirements/recommendations for international students: Required—TOEFL.

Winston-Salem State University, Program in Rehabilitation Counseling, Winston-Salem, NC 27110-0003. Offers MRC. Part-time programs available. Postbaccalaureate distance learning degree programs offered (minimal on-campus study). *Degree requirements:* For master's, thesis optional. *Entrance requirements:* For master's, GRE, 3 letters of recommendation. Electronic applications accepted. *Faculty research:* Drug addiction, recovery, HIV/AIDS interventions.

Wright State University, School of Graduate Studies, College of Education and Human Services, Department of Human Services, Program in Rehabilitation Counseling, Dayton, OH 45435. Offers chemical dependency (MRC); severe disabilities (MRC). *Accreditation:* CORE. *Degree requirements:* For master's, comprehensive exam. *Entrance requirements:* For master's, GRE General Test, MAT, interview. Additional exam requirements/recommendations for international students: Required—TOEFL.

School Psychology

Abilene Christian University, Graduate School, College of Arts and Sciences, Department of Psychology, Program in School Psychology, Abilene, TX 79699-9100. Offers Specialist. *Students:* 18 full-time (15 women), 7 part-time (all women); includes 2 minority (both African Americans), 1 international. 18 applicants, 89% accepted, 12 enrolled. *Application deadline:* For fall admission, 4/1 priority date for domestic students; for spring admission, 11/1 for domestic students. Applications are processed on a rolling basis. Application fee: $40. Electronic applications accepted. *Expenses:* Tuition: Full-time $11,520; part-time $640 per hour. Required fees: $1090; $53.50 per hour. $10 per term. Tuition and fees vary according to program. *Financial support:* In 2009–10, 19 students received support. Federal Work-Study available. Support available to part-time students. Financial award application deadline: 4/1; financial award applicants required to submit FAFSA. *Unit head:* Dr. Jennifer Shewmaker, Graduate Advisor, 325-674-2381, Fax: 325-674-6968, E-mail: jennifer.shewmaker@acu.edu. *Application contact:* William Horn, Graduate Admissions Counselor, 325-674-2656, Fax: 325-674-6717, E-mail: gradinfo@acu.edu.

Adelphi University, Derner Institute of Advanced Psychological Studies, Program in School Psychology, Garden City, NY 11530-0701. Offers MA. Part-time programs available. *Students:* 39 full-time (33 women), 31 part-time (28 women); includes 13 minority (6 African Americans, 2 Asian Americans or Pacific Islanders, 5 Hispanic Americans). Average age 25. In 2009, 27 master's awarded. *Degree requirements:* For master's, comprehensive exam. *Entrance requirements:* For master's, minimum GPA of 3.0; 15 credits of course work in psychology including general psychology, developmental child or adolescent psychology, abnormal personality in school psychology, tests and measurements, statistics; 3 letters of recommendation. Additional exam requirements/recommendations for international students: Required—TOEFL (minimum score 550 paper-based; 213 computer-based; 80 iBT). *Application deadline:* For fall admission, 5/1 for domestic students, 4/1 for international students. Application fee: $50. Electronic applications accepted. *Expenses:* Tuition: Full-time $28,340; part-time $830 per credit. Required fees: $600; $250 per credit. Full-time tuition and fees vary according to course load and program. *Financial support:* Research assistantships with full and partial tuition reimbursements, career-related internships or fieldwork, Federal Work-Study, institutionally sponsored loans, and unspecified assistantships available. *Unit head:* Dr. Ionas Sapountzis, 516-877-4743, E-mail: isapountzis@adelphi.edu. *Application contact:* Christine Murphy, Director of Admissions, 516-877-3050, Fax: 516-877-3039, E-mail: graduateadmissions@adelphi.edu.

Alabama Agricultural and Mechanical University, School of Graduate Studies, School of Education, Department of Counseling and Special Education, Huntsville, AL 35811. Offers communicative disorders (M Ed, MS); psychology and counseling (MS, Ed S), including clinical psychology (MS), counseling and guidance, counseling psychology (MS), personnel management (MS), psychometry (MS), school psychology (MS); special education (M Ed, MS). *Accreditation:* CORE; NCATE. Part-time and evening/weekend programs available. *Degree requirements:* For master's, comprehensive exam. *Entrance requirements:* For master's, GRE General Test. Additional exam requirements/recommendations for international students: Required—TOEFL (minimum score 500 paper-based; 173 computer-based; 61 iBT). *Faculty research:* Increasing numbers of minorities in special education and speech-language pathology.

Alfred University, Graduate School, Program in School Psychology, Alfred, NY 14802-1205. Offers school counseling (MS Ed, CAS); school psychology (MA, Psy D, CAS). *Accreditation:* APA. *Degree requirements:* For master's, internship; for doctorate, thesis/dissertation, internship. *Entrance requirements:* For master's and doctorate, GRE General Test. Additional exam requirements/recommendations for international students: Required—TOEFL (minimum score 590 paper-based; 243 computer-based; 90 iBT); Recommended—IELTS (minimum score 6.5). Electronic applications accepted. *Expenses:* Tuition: Full-time $33,296; part-time $708 per credit hour. Required fees: $880; $144 per year. Full-time tuition and fees vary according to program. *Faculty research:* Family processes, alternative assessment approaches, behavior disorders in children, parent involvement, school psychology training issues.

Alliant International University–Irvine, Graduate School of Education, Educational Psychology Programs, Irvine, CA 92612. Offers educational psychology (Psy D); pupil personnel services (Credential); school psychology (MA). Part-time programs available. *Degree requirements:* For doctorate, thesis/dissertation. *Entrance requirements:* For master's, minimum GPA of 3.0, letters of recommendation; for doctorate, interview, minimum GPA of 3.0, letters of recommendation. Additional exam requirements/recommendations for international students: Required—TOEFL (minimum score 550 paper-based; 213 computer-based), TWE (minimum score 5). *Faculty research:* School based mental health.

Alliant International University–Los Angeles, Graduate School of Education, Educational Psychology Programs, Alhambra, CA 91803-1360. Offers educational psychology (Psy D); pupil personnel services (Credential); school psychology (MA). Part-time programs available. *Degree requirements:* For doctorate, thesis/dissertation. *Entrance requirements:* For master's, minimum GPA of 3.0, letters of recommendation; for doctorate, interview, minimum GPA of 3.0, letters of recommendation. Additional exam requirements/recommendations for international students: Required—TOEFL (minimum score 550 paper-based; 213 computer-based), TWE (minimum score 5). Electronic applications accepted. *Faculty research:* Early identification and intervention with high-risk preschoolers, pediatric neuropsychology, interpersonal violence, ADHD, learning theories.

Alliant International University–San Diego, Graduate School of Education, Educational Psychology Programs, San Diego, CA 92131-1799. Offers educational psychology (Psy D); pupil personnel services (Credential); school psychology (MA); student personnel services (Certificate). Part-time programs available. *Degree requirements:* For doctorate, thesis/dissertation. *Entrance requirements:* For master's, minimum GPA of 3.0, letters of recommendation; for doctorate, interview, letters of recommendation. Additional exam requirements/recommendations for international students: Required—TOEFL (minimum score 550 paper-based; 213 computer-based), TWE (minimum score 5). Electronic applications accepted.

Alliant International University–San Francisco, Graduate School of Education, Educational Psychology Programs, San Francisco, CA 94133-1221. Offers educational psychology (Psy D); pupil personnel services (Credential); school psychology (MA). Part-time programs available. *Degree requirements:* For doctorate, thesis/dissertation. *Entrance requirements:* For master's, minimum GPA of 3.0, letters of recommendation; for doctorate, interview, minimum GPA of 3.0, letters of recommendation. Additional exam requirements/recommendations for international students: Required—TOEFL (minimum score 550 paper-based; 213 computer-based), TWE (minimum score 5). Electronic applications accepted. *Faculty research:* Social skills, ADHD, effects of sightedness on areas of knowledge.

Andrews University, School of Graduate Studies, School of Education, Department of Educational and Counseling Psychology, Program in School Counseling, Berrien Springs, MI 49104. Offers MA. *Students:* 6 full-time (5 women), 1 (woman) part-time; includes 3 minority (all African Americans). Average age 26. 9 applicants, 67% accepted, 4 enrolled. In 2009, 2 master's awarded. *Degree requirements:* For master's, thesis optional. *Entrance requirements:* For master's, GRE. Additional exam requirements/recommendations for international students: Required—TOEFL (minimum score 550 paper-based). Application fee: $40. *Unit head:* Dr. Frederick A. Kosinski, Coordinator, 269-471-3466. *Application contact:* Carolyn Hurst, Supervisor of Graduate Admission, 800-253-2874, Fax: 269-471-6321, E-mail: graduate@andrews.edu.

Andrews University, School of Graduate Studies, School of Education, Department of Educational and Counseling Psychology, Program in School Psychology, Berrien Springs, MI 49104. Offers Ed S. Part-time programs available. *Students:* 17 full-time (11 women), 6 part-time (4 women); includes 7 minority (4 African Americans, 1 Asian American or Pacific Islander, 2 Hispanic Americans), 2 international. Average age 30. 18 applicants, 28% accepted, 4 enrolled. In 2009, 6 Ed Ss awarded. *Entrance requirements:* Additional exam requirements/recommendations for international students: Required—TOEFL (minimum score 550 paper-based). *Application deadline:* Applications are processed on a rolling basis. Application fee: $40. *Unit head:* Dr. Elizabeth Lundy, Coordinator, 269-471-6251. *Application contact:* Carolyn Hurst, Supervisor of Graduate Admission, 800-253-2874, Fax: 269-471-6321, E-mail: graduate@andrews.edu.

Appalachian State University, Cratis D. Williams Graduate School, Department of Human Development and Psychological Counseling, Boone, NC 28608. Offers college student development (MA); community counseling (MA); marriage and family therapy (MA); school counseling (MA). *Accreditation:* AAMFT/COAMFTE; ACA; NCATE. Part-time programs available. *Faculty:* 15 full-time (5 women), 21 part-time/adjunct (14 women). *Students:* 98 full-time (95 women), 32 part-time (25 women); includes 8 minority (5 African Americans, 2 Asian Americans or Pacific Islanders, 1 Hispanic American), 1 international. 149 applicants, 54% accepted, 59 enrolled. In 2009, 78 master's awarded. *Degree requirements:* For master's, comprehensive exam (for some programs), thesis optional, internships. *Entrance requirements:* For master's, GRE General Test, 3 letters of recommendation. Additional exam requirements/recommendations for international students: Required—TOEFL (minimum score 570 paper-based; 230 computer-based; 79 iBT), IELTS (minimum score 6.5). *Application deadline:* For fall admission, 2/1 priority date for domestic students, 2/1 for international students; for spring admission, 2/1 for international students. Applications are processed on a rolling basis. Application fee: $50. Electronic applications accepted. *Expenses:* Tuition, state resident: full-time $2960. Tuition, nonresident: full-time $14,051. Required fees: $2320. *Financial support:* In 2009–10, 20 research assistantships (averaging $8,000 per year), 7 teaching assistantships (averaging $8,000 per year) were awarded; fellowships, career-related internships or fieldwork, Federal Work-Study, scholarships/grants, and unspecified assistantships also available. Financial award application deadline: 4/1; financial award applicants required to submit FAFSA. *Faculty research:* Multicultural counseling, addictions counseling, play therapy, expressive arts, child and adolescent therapy, sexual abuse counseling. *Unit head:* Dr. Lee Baruth, Chairman, 828-262-2055, E-mail: baruthlg@appstate.edu. *Application contact:* Sandy Krause, Director of Admissions and Recruiting, 828-262-2130, Fax: 828-262-2709, E-mail: krausesl@appstate.edu.

Arcadia University, Graduate Studies, Department of Psychology, Glenside, PA 19038-3295. Offers community counseling (MACP); school counseling (MACP). Part-time programs available. *Faculty:* 4 full-time (2 women), 6 part-time/adjunct (4 women). *Students:* 30 full-time (26 women), 30 part-time (23 women); includes 6 minority (5 African Americans, 1 Asian American or Pacific Islander), 1 international. Average age 27. In 2009, 3 master's awarded. *Degree requirements:* For master's, practicum. *Entrance requirements:* For master's, GRE General Test or MAT. *Application deadline:* Applications are processed on a rolling basis. Application fee: $50. *Expenses:* Tuition: Full-time $30,450; part-time $620 per credit hour. Required fees: $165. Tuition and fees vary according to program. *Financial support:* Research assistantships, career-related internships or fieldwork and unspecified assistantships available. Support available to part-time students. Financial award application deadline: 8/15. *Unit head:* Dr. Eleonora Bartoli, Director, 215-572-4693. *Application contact:* 215-572-2925, Fax: 215-572-2126, E-mail: grad@arcadia.edu.

Argosy University, Dallas, College of Education, Farmers Branch, TX 75244. Offers educational administration (MA Ed); educational leadership (Ed D); higher and postsecondary education (MA Ed); instructional leadership (MA Ed); school psychology (MA).

Argosy University, Hawai'i, College of Education, Program in School Psychology, Honolulu, HI 96813. Offers MA.

See Close-Up on page 1057.

Argosy University, Phoenix, College of Education, Program in School Psychology, Phoenix, AZ 85021. Offers MA, Psy D.

See Close-Up on page 1067.

Argosy University, Sarasota, College of Education, Sarasota, FL 34235. Offers community college executive leadership (Ed D); educational leadership (MA Ed, Ed D, Ed S), including higher education administration (Ed D), K-12 education (Ed D); school counseling (MA, Ed S); school psychology (MA); teaching and learning (MA Ed, Ed D, Ed S), including education technology (Ed D), higher education (Ed D), K-12 education (Ed D).

Arkansas State University—Jonesboro, Graduate School, College of Education, Department of Psychology and Counseling, Jonesboro, State University, AR 72467. Offers college student personnel services (MS); counselor education (Ed S), including college student personnel services, psychoeducational diagnosis, school counseling; rehabilitation counseling (MRC); school counseling (MSE); student affairs (Certificate). *Accreditation:* ACA (one or more programs are accredited); CORE (one or more programs are accredited); NCATE. Part-time programs available. *Faculty:* 11 full-time (6 women), 6 part-time/adjunct (2 women). *Students:* 49 full-time (37 women), 100 part-time (81 women); includes 32 minority (31 African Americans, 1 American Indian/Alaska Native), 1 international. Average age 32. 70 applicants, 46% accepted, 30 enrolled. In 2009, 23 master's, 11 other advanced degrees awarded. *Degree requirements:* For master's and other advanced degree, comprehensive exam, thesis or alternative. *Entrance requirements:* For master's, GRE General Test or MAT (MSE), appropriate bachelor's degree, interview, letters of reference; for other advanced degree, GRE General Test, interview, master's degree, letters of reference, official transcript, personal statement, immunization records. Additional exam requirements/recommendations for international students: Required—TOEFL (minimum score 550 paper-based; 213 computer-based; 79 iBT), IELTS (minimum score 6). *Application deadline:* For fall admission, 7/15 for domestic students, 7/1 for international students; for spring admission, 12/1 for domestic students, 11/13 for international students. Applications are processed on a rolling basis. Application fee: $30 ($40 for international students). Electronic applications accepted. *Expenses:* Tuition, state resident: full-time $3744; part-time $208 per credit hour. Tuition, nonresident: full-time $9540; part-time $530 per credit hour. Required fees: $896; $47 per credit hour. $25 per term. One-time fee: $50. Tuition and fees vary according to course load and program. *Financial support:* In 2009–10, 24 students received support; teaching assistantships, career-related internships or fieldwork, scholarships/grants, and unspecified assistantships available. Financial award application deadline: 7/1; financial award applicants required to submit FAFSA. *Unit head:* Dr. Loretta McGregor, Chair, 870-972-3064, Fax: 870-972-3962, E-mail: lmcgregor@astate.edu. *Application contact:* Dr. Andrew Sustich, Dean of the Graduate School, 870-972-3029, Fax: 870-972-3857, E-mail: sustich@astate.edu.

Assumption College, Graduate School, School Counseling Program, Worcester, MA 01609-1296. Offers MA, CAGS. Part-time and evening/weekend programs available. *Faculty:* 4 full-time (1 woman), 6 part-time/adjunct (3 women). *Students:* 48 full-time (41 women), 14 part-time (13 women); includes 3 minority (1 African American, 2 Hispanic Americans). Average age 24. 56 applicants, 93% accepted. In 2009, 27 master's, 2 other advanced degrees awarded. *Degree requirements:* For master's, comprehensive exam, internship; for CAGS, comprehensive exam. *Entrance requirements:* For master's, 3 letters of recommendation, resume, interview, essay; for CAGS, 3 letters of recommendation, resume, essay, interview. Additional exam requirements/recommendations for international students: Required—TOEFL (minimum score 540 paper-based; 200 computer-based; 76 iBT), IELTS (minimum score 6). *Application deadline:* For fall admission, 6/1 priority date for domestic students, 5/1 priority date for international students; for spring admission, 11/1 priority date for domestic students, 9/1 priority date for international students. Applications are processed on a rolling basis. Application fee: $30. Electronic applications accepted. *Expenses:* Tuition: Part-time $503 per credit. Required fees: $20 per semester. One-time fee: $100 part-time. Part-time tuition and fees vary according to campus/location. *Financial support:* In 2009–10, 47 students received support. Tuition waivers (partial) available. Financial award application deadline: 6/1; financial award applicants required to submit FAFSA. *Unit head:* Dr. Mary Ann Mariani, Director, 508-767-7087, Fax: 508-767-7263, E-mail: mmariani@assumption.edu. *Application contact:* Adrian O. Dumas, Director of Graduate Enrollment Management and Services, 508-767-7365, Fax: 508-767-7030, E-mail: adumas@assumption.edu.

Azusa Pacific University, School of Education, Department of School Counseling and School Psychology, Program in Educational Psychology, Azusa, CA 91702-7000. Offers MA.

Ball State University, Graduate School, Teachers College, Department of Educational Psychology, Program in School Psychology, Muncie, IN 47306-1099. Offers MA, PhD, Ed S. *Accreditation:* APA (one or more programs are accredited); NCATE. *Degree requirements:* For doctorate, thesis/dissertation; for Ed S, thesis. *Entrance requirements:* For master's and Ed S, GRE General Test; for doctorate, GRE General Test, interview, minimum graduate GPA of 3.2.

Barry University, School of Arts and Sciences, Department of Psychology, Miami Shores, FL 33161-6695. Offers clinical psychology (MS); school psychology (MS, SSP). Part-time and evening/weekend programs available. *Degree requirements:* For master's, thesis, practicum. *Entrance requirements:* For master's, GRE General Test, minimum GPA of 3.0, course work in psychology. Electronic applications accepted. *Faculty research:* Closed head injury, memory and aging, infant/mother interaction, evolutionary aspects of behavior, gender roles.

Bowling Green State University, Graduate College, College of Education and Human Development, School of Education and Intervention Services, Intervention Services Division, Program in School Psychology, Bowling Green, OH 43403. Offers M Ed, Sp Ed. *Accreditation:* NCATE. Part-time programs available. *Degree requirements:* For master's, thesis or alternative, internship. *Entrance requirements:* For master's, GRE General Test. Additional exam requirements/recommendations for international students: Required—TOEFL. Electronic applications accepted. *Faculty research:* Family therapists/multicultural issues, pre-school readiness skills, family relations, multifaceted evaluation, multidisciplinary decision-making.

Brigham Young University, Graduate Studies, David O. McKay School of Education, Department of Counseling Psychology and Special Education, Provo, UT 84602-1001. Offers counseling psychology (PhD); school psychology (Ed S); special education (MS). *Accreditation:* NCATE. Part-time programs available. *Faculty:* 12 full-time (7 women), 13 part-time/adjunct (5 women). *Students:* 74 full-time (54 women), 15 part-time (14 women); includes 11 minority (2 African Americans, 2 American Indian/Alaska Native, 4 Asian Americans or Pacific Islanders, 3 Hispanic Americans), 10 international. Average age 31. 85 applicants, 41% accepted, 28 enrolled. In 2009, 2 master's, 4 doctorates, 10 other advanced degrees awarded. *Degree requirements:* For master's, comprehensive exam, thesis; for doctorate, comprehensive exam, thesis/dissertation. *Entrance requirements:* For master's and doctorate, GRE General Test, minimum GPA of 3.0 in last 60 hours of undergraduate coursework. Additional exam requirements/recommendations for international students: Required—TOEFL (minimum score 580 paper-based; 237 computer-based), IELTS (minimum score 7). *Application deadline:* For fall admission, 1/15 for domestic and international students. Application fee: $50. Electronic applications accepted. *Expenses:* Tuition: Full-time $5580; part-time $301 per credit hour. Tuition and fees vary according to student's religious affiliation. *Financial support:* In 2009–10, 53 students received support, including 36 research assistantships with partial tuition reimbursements available (averaging $6,706 per year), 3 teaching assistantships with partial tuition reimbursements available (averaging $7,457 per year); career-related internships or fieldwork, institutionally sponsored loans, and tuition waivers (partial) also available. Financial award application deadline: 3/30. *Faculty research:* Gender issues in education, psychotherapy progress and outcome, behavior disorders and ABA. *Unit head:* Dr. Mary Anne Prater, Chair, 801-422-3857, Fax: 801-422-0198, E-mail: prater@byu.edu. *Application contact:* Diane E. Hancock, Department Secretary, 801-422-3859, Fax: 801-422-0198, E-mail: diane_hancock@byu.edu.

Brooklyn College of the City University of New York, Division of Graduate Studies, School of Education, Program in School Psychologist, Brooklyn, NY 11210-2889. Offers school psychologist (MS Ed, CAS); school psychologist-bilingual (CAS). Part-time and evening/weekend programs available. *Students:* 33 full-time (28 women), 50 part-time (48 women); includes 29 minority (14 African Americans, 1 American Indian/Alaska Native, 3 Asian Americans or Pacific Islanders, 11 Hispanic Americans), 1 international. Average age 27. 128 applicants, 45% accepted, 33 enrolled. In 2009, 28 master's, 19 CASs awarded. *Degree requirements:* For master's, internship. *Entrance requirements:* For master's, interview, previous course work in education and psychology, teaching certificate, resume, 2 letters of recommendation; for CAS, master's degree, teaching experience. Additional exam requirements/recommendations for international students: Required—TOEFL (minimum score 500 paper-based; 173 computer-based; 61 iBT). *Application deadline:* For fall admission, 3/1 priority date for domestic students, 2/1 priority date for international students. Applications are processed on a rolling basis. Application fee: $125. Electronic applications accepted. *Expenses:* Tuition, area resident: Full-time $7360; part-time $310 per credit hour. Tuition, state resident: full-time $7360; part-time $310 per credit hour. Tuition, nonresident: full-time $13,800; part-time $575 per credit hour. International tuition: $13,800 full-time. Required fees: $140.10 per semester. *Financial support:* Career-related internships or fieldwork, Federal Work-Study, institutionally sponsored loans, and scholarships/grants available. Support available to part-time students. Financial award application deadline: 5/1; financial award applicants required to submit FAFSA. *Unit head:* Prof. Florence Rubinson, Program Head, E-mail: rubinson@brooklyn.cuny.edu. *Application contact:* Hernan Sierra, Graduate Admissions Coordinator, 718-951-4536, Fax: 718-951-4506, E-mail: grads@brooklyn.cuny.edu.

Bucknell University, Graduate Studies, College of Arts and Sciences, Department of Education, Specialization in School Psychology, Lewisburg, PA 17837. Offers MS Ed. *Degree requirements:* For master's, thesis or alternative. *Entrance requirements:* For master's, GRE General Test, minimum GPA of 2.8. Additional exam requirements/recommendations for international students: Required—TOEFL.

California Baptist University, Program in Education, Riverside, CA 92504-3206. Offers cross-cultural language and academic development (MA); educational leadership (MS); educational leadership and faith-based instruction (MS); educational technology (MS); instructional computer applications (MS); reading (MS); school counseling (MS); school psychology (MS); special education (MS); special education in mild/moderate disabilities (MS); special education in moderate/severe disabilities (MS); teaching (MS); teaching and learning (MS Ed). Part-time programs available. *Faculty:* 16 full-time (9 women), 10 part-time/adjunct (all women). *Students:* 73 full-time (60 women), 368 part-time (298 women); includes 170 minority (34 African Americans, 4 American Indian/Alaska Native, 18 Asian Americans or Pacific Islanders, 114 Hispanic Americans). 266 applicants, 72% accepted, 169 enrolled. In 2009, 120 master's awarded. *Degree requirements:* For master's, comprehensive exam (for some programs), thesis optional. *Entrance requirements:* For master's, minimum undergraduate GPA of 2.75, 12 semester hours of pre-requisite course work in education. Additional exam requirements/recommendations for international students: Required—TOEFL (minimum score 575 paper-based; 230 computer-based; 89 iBT). *Application deadline:* For fall admission, 8/1 priority date for domestic students, 7/1 for international students; for spring admission, 12/1 priority date for domestic students, 10/15 priority date for international students. Applications are processed on a rolling basis. Application fee: $45. Electronic applications accepted. *Expenses:* Tuition: Full-time $8352; part-time $464 per semester hour. Required fees: $125 per semester. Tuition and fees vary according to course load, campus/location and program. *Financial support:* Career-related internships or fieldwork, Federal Work-Study, and scholarships/grants available. Support available to part-time students. Financial award applicants required to submit FAFSA. *Unit head:* Dr. Mary Crist, Dean, School of Education, 951-343-4313, Fax: 951-343-4516, E-mail: mcrist@calbaptist.edu. *Application contact:* Gail Ronveaux, Dean of Graduate Enrollment, 951-343-5045, Fax: 951-343-5095, E-mail: graduateadmissions@calbaptist.edu.

California State University, Los Angeles, Graduate Studies, Charter College of Education, Division of Special Education and Counseling, Los Angeles, CA 90032-8530. Offers counseling (MS), including applied behavior analysis, community college counseling, rehabilitation counseling, school counseling and school psychology; special education (MA, PhD). *Accreditation:* ACA. Part-time and evening/weekend programs available. *Faculty:* 20 full-time (15 women), 18 part-time/adjunct (10 women). *Students:* 361 full-time (288 women), 366 part-time (284 women); includes 450 minority (43 African Americans, 65 Asian Americans or Pacific Islanders, 342 Hispanic Americans), 40 international. Average age 34. 181 applicants, 99% accepted, 108 enrolled. In 2009, 143 master's awarded. *Entrance requirements:* For master's, minimum GPA of 2.75 in last 90 units of course work, teaching certificate. Additional exam requirements/recommendations for international students: Required—TOEFL (minimum score 500 paper-based; 173 computer-based). *Application deadline:* For fall admission, 5/1 for domestic and international students. Applications are processed on a rolling basis. Application fee: $55. Electronic applications accepted. *Financial support:* Career-related internships or fieldwork and Federal Work-Study available. Support available to part-time students. Financial award application deadline: 3/1. *Unit head:* Dr. Randy Campbell, Chair, 323-343-4400, Fax: 323-343-5605, E-mail: rcampbe@calstatela.edu. *Application contact:* Dr. Cheryl L. Ney, Associate Vice President for Academic Affairs and Dean of Graduate Studies, 323-343-3820, Fax: 323-343-5653, E-mail: cney@cslanet.calstatela.edu.

California State University, Northridge, Graduate Studies, College of Education, Department of Educational Psychology and Counseling, Northridge, CA 91330. Offers counseling (MS), including career counseling, college counseling and student services, marriage and family therapy, school counseling, school psychology; educational psychology (MA Ed), including development, learning, and instruction, early childhood education. *Accreditation:* ACA (one or more programs are accredited); NCATE. Part-time and evening/weekend programs available. *Faculty:* 19 full-time (11 women), 42 part-time/adjunct (26 women). *Students:* 341 full-time (301 women), 135 part-time (121 women); includes 21 African Americans, 31 Asian Americans or Pacific Islanders, 149 Hispanic Americans, 11 international. Average age 31. 498 applicants, 39% accepted, 167 enrolled. In 2009, 119 master's awarded. *Entrance requirements:* For

School Psychology

California State University, Northridge (continued)
master's, GRE General Test or minimum GPA of 3.0. Additional exam requirements/recommendations for international students: Required—TOEFL. *Application deadline:* For fall admission, 11/30 for domestic students. Application fee: $55. *Financial support:* Scholarships/grants available. Support available to part-time students. Financial award application deadline: 3/1. *Unit head:* Dr. Shari Tarver-Behring, Chair, 818-677-2599. *Application contact:* Dr. Shari Tarver-Behring, Chair, 818-677-2599.

California State University, Sacramento, Graduate Studies, College of Education, Department of Special Education, Rehabilitation, and School Psychology, Sacramento, CA 95819. Offers school psychology (MS); special education (MA); vocational rehabilitation (MS). *Accreditation:* CORE. Part-time programs available. *Degree requirements:* For master's, thesis or alternative, writing proficiency exam. *Entrance requirements:* For master's, minimum GPA of 2.5. Additional exam requirements/recommendations for international students: Required—TOEFL. Electronic applications accepted.

California University of Pennsylvania, School of Graduate Studies and Research, School of Education, Program in School Psychology, California, PA 15419-1394. Offers MS. *Accreditation:* NCATE. Part-time and evening/weekend programs available. *Degree requirements:* For master's, comprehensive exam, thesis optional, internship. *Entrance requirements:* For master's, MAT or GRE, minimum GPA of 3.0, work experience in psychology, letters of reference. Additional exam requirements/recommendations for international students: Required—TOEFL (minimum score 550 paper-based; 213 computer-based; 80 iBT). Electronic applications accepted.

Cambridge College, School of Education, Cambridge, MA 02138-5304. Offers autism specialist (M Ed); autism/behavior analyst (M Ed); behavior analyst (Post-Master's Certificate); behavioral management (M Ed); early childhood teacher (M Ed); education specialist in curriculum and instruction (CAGS); educational leadership (Ed D); elementary teacher (M Ed); English as a second language (M Ed, Certificate); general science (M Ed); health education, health promotion (Post-Master's Certificate); health/family and consumer sciences (M Ed); history (M Ed); individualized degree (M Ed); information technology literacy (M Ed); instructional technology (M Ed); interdisciplinary studies (M Ed); library teacher (M Ed); literacy education (M Ed); mathematics (M Ed); mathematics specialist (Certificate); middle school mathematics and science (M Ed); school administration (M Ed, CAGS); school guidance counselor (M Ed); school nurse education (M Ed); school social worker/school adjustment counselor (M Ed); special education administrator (CAGS); special education/moderate disabilities (M Ed); teaching skills and methodologies (M Ed). Part-time and evening/weekend programs available. Postbaccalaureate distance learning degree programs offered (minimal on-campus study). *Faculty:* 10 full-time (3 women), 283 part-time/adjunct (187 women). *Students:* 974 full-time (755 women), 1,071 part-time (835 women); includes 940 minority (762 African Americans, 4 American Indian/Alaska Native, 22 Asian Americans or Pacific Islanders, 152 Hispanic Americans), 28 international. Average age 39. In 2009, 866 master's, 4 doctorates, 209 other advanced degrees awarded. *Degree requirements:* For master's, thesis, internship/practicum (licensure program only); for doctorate, thesis/dissertation; for other advanced degree, thesis. *Entrance requirements:* For master's, interview, resume, documentation of licensure, 2 professional references; for doctorate, official transcripts, interview, resume, documentation of licensure (if any), written personal statement/essay, portfolio of scholarly and professional work, qualifying assessment, 2 professional references, health insurance, immunizations form; for other advanced degree, official transcripts, interview, resume, documentation of licensure (if any), written personal statement/essay, 2 professional references, health insurance, immunizations form. Additional exam requirements/recommendations for international students: Required—TOEFL (minimum score 550 paper-based; 213 computer-based; 79 iBT); Recommended—IELTS (minimum score 6). *Application deadline:* Applications are processed on a rolling basis. Application fee: $30. Electronic applications accepted. *Expenses:* Contact institution. *Financial support:* In 2009–10, 1,373 students received support. Career-related internships or fieldwork, Federal Work-Study, and scholarships/grants available. Financial award applicants required to submit FAFSA. *Faculty research:* Adult education, accelerated learning, mathematics education, brain compatible learning, special education and law. *Unit head:* Dr. N. Alan Sheppard, Interim Associate Dean, 617-873-0619, E-mail: alan.sheppard@cambridgecollege.edu. *Application contact:* Stephen Lyons, Director of Enrollment, Graduate and N.I.T.E. Programs, 617-868-1000, Fax: 617-349-3561, E-mail: stephen.lyons@cambridgecollege.edu.

Cambridge College, School of Psychology and Counseling, Cambridge, MA 02138-5304. Offers addiction counseling (M Ed); alcohol & drug counseling (Certificate); counseling psychology (M Ed, CAGS); counseling psychology: forensic counseling (M Ed); marriage and family therapy (M Ed); mental health and addiction counseling (M Ed); mental health counseling (M Ed); mental health counseling for school guidance counselors (Post Master's Certificate); psychological studies (M Ed); school adjustment and mental health counseling (M Ed); school adjustment, mental health and addiction counseling (M Ed); school guidance counselor (M Ed); trauma studies (Certificate). Part-time and evening/weekend programs available. *Faculty:* 5 full-time (2 women), 87 part-time/adjunct (50 women). *Students:* 501 full-time (395 women), 307 part-time (245 women); includes 382 minority (295 African Americans, 2 American Indian/Alaska Native, 6 Asian Americans or Pacific Islanders, 79 Hispanic Americans), 4 international. Average age 38. In 2009, 237 master's, 15 other advanced degrees awarded. *Degree requirements:* For master's, thesis, practicum/internship; for other advanced degree, thesis, practicum/Internship. *Entrance requirements:* For master's, resume, 2 professional references; for other advanced degree, official transcripts, documents for transfer credit evaluation, resume, written personal statement/essay, 2 professional references, health insurance, immunizations form. Additional exam requirements/recommendations for international students: Required—TOEFL (minimum score 550 paper-based; 213 computer-based; 79 iBT); Recommended—IELTS (minimum score 6). *Application deadline:* Applications are processed on a rolling basis. Application fee: $30. Electronic applications accepted. *Expenses:* Contact institution. *Financial support:* In 2009–10, 686 students received support. Career-related internships or fieldwork, Federal Work-Study, and scholarships/grants available. Financial award applicants required to submit FAFSA. *Unit head:* Dr. Niti Seth, Dean, 617-873-0208, Fax: 617-349-3561, E-mail: nseth@cambridgecollege.edu. *Application contact:* Stephen Lyons, Director of Enrollment, Graduate and N.I.T.E. Programs, 617-868-1000, Fax: 617-349-3561, E-mail: stephen.lyons@cambridgecollege.edu.

Canisius College, Graduate Division, School of Education and Human Services, Department of Counseling and Human Services, Buffalo, NY 14208-1098. Offers community mental health counseling (MS); general counseling (MS); school counseling (MS). *Accreditation:* ACA. Part-time and evening/weekend programs available. *Faculty:* 5 full-time (3 women), 6 part-time/adjunct (2 women). *Students:* 110 full-time (89 women), 62 part-time (56 women); includes 23 minority (18 African Americans, 2 Asian Americans or Pacific Islanders, 3 Hispanic Americans), 3 international. Average age 30. 106 applicants, 84% accepted, 43 enrolled. In 2009, 51 master's awarded. *Degree requirements:* For master's, thesis, research project. *Entrance requirements:* For master's, interview, minimum GPA of 2.5. *Application deadline:* Applications are processed on a rolling basis. Application fee: $25. Electronic applications accepted. *Financial support:* In 2009–10, 2 research assistantships with partial tuition reimbursements (averaging $8,500 per year) were awarded; career-related internships or fieldwork, Federal Work-Study, institutionally sponsored loans, health care benefits, and unspecified assistantships also available. Support available to part-time students. Financial award applicants required to submit FAFSA. *Faculty research:* Positive psychology, wellness, school violence prevention, chronic pain. *Unit head:* Dr. David L. Farrugia, Chairman, 716-888-2393, Fax: 716-888-3290, E-mail: farrugia@canisius.edu. *Application contact:* James D. Bagwell, Director of Graduate Recruitment and Admissions, 716-888-2544, Fax: 716-888-3290, E-mail: bagwellj@canisius.edu.

Capella University, Harold Abel School of Psychology, Minneapolis, MN 55402. Offers child and adolescent development (MS); clinical psychology (MS, Psy D); counseling psychology (MS); educational psychology (MS, PhD); evaluation, research, and measurement (MS); general psychology (MS, PhD); industrial/organizational psychology (MS, PhD); leadership coaching psychology (MS); organizational leader development (MS); school psychology (MS); sport psychology (MS). Part-time and evening/weekend programs available. Postbaccalaureate distance learning degree programs offered (minimal on-campus study). Terminal master's awarded for partial completion of doctoral program. *Degree requirements:* For master's, thesis optional, project; for doctorate, thesis/dissertation. *Entrance requirements:* For degree, master's degree in school psychology. Additional exam requirements/recommendations for international students: Required—TOEFL (minimum score 550 paper-based; 213 computer-based), TWE (minimum score 4); Recommended—IELTS. Electronic applications accepted.

Carlos Albizu University, Miami Campus, Graduate Programs, Miami, FL 33172-2209. Offers clinical psychology (Psy D); entrepreneurship (MBA); exceptional student education (MS); industrial/organizational psychology (MS); marriage and family therapy (MS); mental health counseling (MS); nonprofit management (MBA); organizational management (MBA); psychology (MS); school counseling (MS); teaching English as a second language (MS). *Accreditation:* APA. Part-time and evening/weekend programs available. *Faculty:* 23 full-time (13 women), 41 part-time/adjunct (21 women). *Students:* 529 full-time (420 women), 171 part-time (139 women); includes 551 minority (55 African Americans, 1 American Indian/Alaska Native, 5 Asian Americans or Pacific Islanders, 490 Hispanic Americans). Average age 37. 278 applicants, 57% accepted, 142 enrolled. In 2009, 139 master's, 26 doctorates awarded. Terminal master's awarded for partial completion of doctoral program. *Degree requirements:* For master's, one foreign language, comprehensive exam, integrative project (MBA), research project (exceptional student education, teaching English as a second language); for doctorate, one foreign language, comprehensive exam, internship, project. *Entrance requirements:* For master's, 3 letters of recommendation, interview, minimum GPA of 3.0, resume; for doctorate, 3 letters of recommendation, minimum GPA of 3.0, resume, interview. *Application deadline:* For fall admission, 8/1 priority date for domestic students; for spring admission, 11/30 priority date for domestic students. Applications are processed on a rolling basis. Application fee: $50. Electronic applications accepted. *Expenses:* Tuition: Full-time $9090; part-time $505 per credit hour. Required fees: $298 per term. Tuition and fees vary according to course load, degree level and program. *Financial support:* In 2009–10, 127 students received support. Federal Work-Study, scholarships/grants, and tuition discounts available. Financial award application deadline: 6/1; financial award applicants required to submit FAFSA. *Faculty research:* Psychotherapy, forensic psychology, neuropsychology, marketing strategy, entrepreneurship, special education. *Unit head:* Dr. Carmen S. Roca, Chancellor, 305-593-1223 Ext. 120, Fax: 305-629-8052, E-mail: croca@albizu.edu. *Application contact:* Annalye Alonso, Secretary, 305-593-1223 Ext. 137, Fax: 305-593-1854, E-mail: aalonso@albizu.edu.

Central Connecticut State University, School of Graduate Studies, School of Education and Professional Studies, Department of Counseling and Family Therapy, New Britain, CT 06050-4010. Offers marriage and family therapy (MS); professional counseling (MS, Certificate); school counseling (MS); student development in higher education (MS). *Accreditation:* AAMFT/COAMFTE. Part-time and evening/weekend programs available. *Faculty:* 8 full-time (5 women), 14 part-time/adjunct (9 women). *Students:* 117 full-time (97 women), 189 part-time (159 women); includes 52 minority (27 African Americans, 3 American Indian/Alaska Native, 3 Asian Americans or Pacific Islanders, 19 Hispanic Americans), 4 international. Average age 33. 249 applicants, 39% accepted, 84 enrolled. In 2009, 78 master's awarded. *Degree requirements:* For master's, comprehensive exam, thesis or alternative; for Certificate, qualifying exam. *Entrance requirements:* For master's, minimum undergraduate GPA of 2.7. Additional exam requirements/recommendations for international students: Required—TOEFL. *Application deadline:* For fall admission, 5/1 for domestic students. Applications are processed on a rolling basis. Application fee: $50. Electronic applications accepted. *Expenses:* Tuition, area resident: Full-time $4662; part-time $440 per credit. Tuition, state resident: full-time $6994; part-time $440 per credit. Tuition, nonresident: full-time $12,988; part-time $440 per credit. Required fees: $3606. One-time fee: $62 part-time. *Financial support:* In 2009–10, 29 students received support, including 22 research assistantships; career-related internships or fieldwork, Federal Work-Study, scholarships/grants, and unspecified assistantships also available. Support available to part-time students. Financial award application deadline: 3/1; financial award applicants required to submit FAFSA. *Faculty research:* Elementary/secondary school counseling, marriage/family therapy, rehabilitation counseling, counseling in higher educational settings. *Unit head:* Dr. Connie Tait, Chair, 860-832-2154. *Application contact:* Dr. Connie Tait, Chair, 860-832-2154.

Central Michigan University, College of Graduate Studies, College of Humanities and Social and Behavioral Sciences, Department of Psychology, Program in School Psychology, Mount Pleasant, MI 48859. Offers psychological services (S Psy S); school psychology (PhD). *Accreditation:* APA; NCATE. *Degree requirements:* For doctorate, thesis/dissertation; for S Psy S, thesis. *Entrance requirements:* For doctorate, GRE. Electronic applications accepted. *Faculty research:* Psychology and education foundations, psychology and education assessment, intervention strategies.

Central Washington University, Graduate Studies and Research, College of the Sciences, Department of Psychology, Program in School Psychology, Ellensburg, WA 98926. Offers M Ed. *Faculty:* 32 full-time (16 women). *Students:* 16 full-time (9 women); includes 2 minority (1 African American, 1 Hispanic American). In 2009, 8 master's awarded. *Degree requirements:* For master's, thesis, internship. *Entrance requirements:* For master's, GRE General Test, minimum GPA of 3.0. Additional exam requirements/recommendations for international students: Required—TOEFL (minimum score 550 paper-based; 213 computer-based; 79 iBT). *Application deadline:* For fall admission, 2/1 priority date for domestic students. Applications are processed on a rolling basis. Application fee: $50. Electronic applications accepted. *Expenses:* Tuition, state resident: full-time $7353; part-time $245 per credit. Tuition, nonresident: full-time $16,383; part-time $546 per credit. Required fees: $882. Tuition and fees vary according to degree level. *Financial support:* Research assistantships with full and partial tuition reimbursements, career-related internships or fieldwork, Federal Work-Study, health care benefits, and unspecified assistantships available. Financial award application deadline: 3/1; financial award applicants required to submit FAFSA. *Unit head:* Dr. Gene Johnson, Chair, 509-963-2501, E-mail: johnsong@cwu.edu. *Application contact:* Justine Eason, Admissions Program Coordinator, 509-963-3103, Fax: 509-963-1799, E-mail: masters@cwu.edu.

Chapman University, Graduate Studies, College of Educational Studies, Program in Education: School Psychology, Orange, CA 92866. Offers PhD. Part-time and evening/weekend programs available. *Faculty:* 24 full-time (15 women), 25 part-time/adjunct (16 women). *Students:* 1 (woman) full-time, 9 part-time (6 women); includes 3 minority (all Asian Americans or Pacific Islanders). Average age 39. 2 applicants, 100% accepted, 2 enrolled. *Degree requirements:* For doctorate, thesis/dissertation. *Entrance requirements:* Additional exam requirements/recommendations for international students: Required—TOEFL. Application fee: $55. Tuition and fees vary according to course load, degree level and program. *Financial support:* Fellowships, Federal Work-Study and scholarships/grants available. *Unit head:* Dr. Joel Colbert, Director, 714-744-7076. *Application contact:* Rika Judd, Graduate Admission Counselor, 714-997-6786, Fax: 714-997-6713, E-mail: rjudd@chapman.edu.

Chapman University, Graduate Studies, College of Educational Studies, Program in School Psychology, Orange, CA 92866. Offers educational psychology (MA); school psychology (Ed S). Part-time and evening/weekend programs available. *Faculty:* 24 full-time (15 women), 25 part-time/adjunct (16 women). *Students:* 41 full-time (38 women), 16 part-time (15 women); includes 26 minority (9 Asian Americans or Pacific Islanders, 17 Hispanic Americans). Average age 27. 52 applicants, 38% accepted, 11 enrolled. In 2009, 40 master's awarded. *Degree requirements:* For master's, comprehensive exam. *Entrance requirements:* For master's, GRE General Test, MAT, or California Subject Examinations for Teachers, minimum undergraduate GPA of 2.75. Additional exam requirements/recommendations for international students: Required—TOEFL (minimum score 550 paper-based). *Application deadline:* Applications are processed on a rolling basis. Application fee: $55. Electronic applications accepted. *Expenses:* Contact institution. *Financial support:* Fellowships, Federal Work-Study and scholarships/grants available. Financial award application deadline: 6/30; financial award applicants required to submit FAFSA. *Unit head:* Dr. Michael Hass, Coordinator, 714-997-6781, E-mail: hass@chapman.edu. *Application contact:* Rika Judd, Information Contact, 714-997-6786, Fax: 714-997-6713, E-mail: rjudd@chapman.edu.

The Chicago School of Professional Psychology, Program in School Psychology, Chicago, IL 60610. Offers Ed S. *Accreditation:* APA. Part-time programs available. *Students:* 125 full-time (108 women), 22 part-time (18 women); includes 34 minority (13 African Americans, 6 Asian Americans or Pacific Islanders, 15 Hispanic Americans). 160 applicants, 68% accepted, 53 enrolled. *Entrance requirements:* For degree, GRE (recommended), minimum GPA of 3.2 (recommended); completion of one course in statistics or research methods and one course in psychology. Additional exam requirements/recommendations for international students: Required—TOEFL (minimum score 550 paper-based; 213 computer-based; 79 iBT). *Financial support:* Federal Work-Study and scholarships/grants available. Financial award application deadline: 4/1; financial award applicants required to submit FAFSA. *Unit head:* Dr. James Walsh, Department Chair, 312-410-8996, E-mail: jwalsh@thechicagoschool.edu. *Application contact:* Andrea Schmoyer, Director of Admission, 312-329-6666, Fax: 312-644-3333, E-mail: admissions@thechicagoschool.edu.

The Chicago School of Professional Psychology at Grayslake, School Psychology, Grayslake, IL 60030. Offers Ed S. *Unit head:* Dr. James Walsh, Department Chair, 312-410-8996, E-mail: jwalsh@thechicagoschool.edu. *Application contact:* Andrea Schmoyer, Director of Admissions, 312-329-6666, Fax: 312-644-3333, E-mail: admissions@thechicagoschool.edu.

The Citadel, The Military College of South Carolina, Citadel Graduate College, Department of Psychology, Program in School Psychology, Charleston, SC 29409. Offers Ed S. *Accreditation:* NCATE. Part-time and evening/weekend programs available. *Faculty:* 10 full-time (3 women), 2 part-time/adjunct (1 woman). *Students:* 39 full-time (37 women), 19 part-time (17 women); includes 5 minority (3 African Americans, 1 Asian American or Pacific Islander, 1 Hispanic American). Average age 27. In 2009, 2 Ed Ss awarded. *Degree requirements:* For Ed S, comprehensive exam, thesis, internship. *Entrance requirements:* For degree, GRE (minimum score 1000) or MAT with prior permission (minimum score 410), minimum undergraduate GPA of 3.0, 2 letters of reference. Additional exam requirements/recommendations for international students: Required—TOEFL (minimum score 550 paper-based; 213 computer-based). *Application deadline:* For fall admission, 3/15 for domestic students. Application fee: $30. Electronic applications accepted. *Expenses:* Tuition, state resident: part-time $400 per credit hour. Tuition, nonresident: part-time $657 per credit hour. Required fees: $40 per term. *Financial support:* Research assistantships, career-related internships or fieldwork, health care benefits, and unspecified assistantships available. Support available to part-time students. Financial award application deadline: 7/1; financial award applicants required to submit FAFSA. *Faculty research:* Childhood depression, violence against women, developmental disorders, eyewitness testimony. *Unit head:* Dr. Kerry S. Lassiter, Coordinator, 843-953-6740, Fax: 843-953-6769, E-mail: kerry.lassiter@citadel.edu. *Application contact:* Dr. Steve A. Nida, Associate Provost, The Citadel Graduate College, 843-953-5089, Fax: 843-953-7630, E-mail: cgc@citadel.edu.

City University of Seattle, Graduate Division, Gordon Albright School of Education, Bellevue, WA 98005. Offers curriculum and instruction (M Ed); educational leadership (M Ed); educational leadership: administrator certification (Certificate); executive leadership: superintendent certification (Certificate); guidance and counseling (M Ed); leadership (M Ed); leadership and school counseling (M Ed); professional certification for teachers (Certificate); reading and literacy (M Ed); reading and literacy in education (M Ed); teacher certification (elementary K-8) (MIT); teacher certification (special education K-12) (MIT); technology, curriculum, and instruction (M Ed). Part-time and evening/weekend programs available. Postbaccalaureate distance learning degree programs offered (no on-campus study). *Entrance requirements:* Additional exam requirements/recommendations for international students: Required—TOEFL (minimum score 540 paper-based; 207 computer-based); Recommended—IELTS. Electronic applications accepted. *Expenses:* Contact institution.

Cleveland State University, College of Graduate Studies, College of Science, Department of Psychology, Cleveland, OH 44115. Offers adult development and aging (PhD); clinical psychology (MA); consumer/industrial research (MA); diversity management (MA); experimental research psychology (MA); school psychology (Psy S). *Degree requirements:* For master's, comprehensive exam (for some programs), thesis (for some programs); for doctorate, comprehensive exam, thesis/dissertation; for Psy S, internship. *Entrance requirements:* For master's and doctorate, GRE General Test. Additional exam requirements/recommendations for international students: Required—TOEFL (minimum score 525 paper-based; 197 computer-based). Electronic applications accepted. *Faculty research:* Cognitive and social psychology, consumer psychology, clinical psychology, school psychology, aging.

The College of New Rochelle, Graduate School, Division of Human Services, Program in Community-School Psychology, New Rochelle, NY 10805-2308. Offers MS. *Degree requirements:* For master's, comprehensive exam, clinical fieldwork, journal. *Entrance requirements:* For master's, interview, minimum GPA of 3.0, course work in psychology, sample of written work.

College of St. Joseph, Graduate Programs, Division of Psychology and Human Services, Program in School Guidance Counseling, Rutland, VT 05701-3899. Offers MS. Part-time and evening/weekend programs available. *Degree requirements:* For master's, comprehensive exam, thesis optional. *Entrance requirements:* For master's, PRAXIS I, 2 letters of reference, interview. Electronic applications accepted. *Expenses:* Tuition: Full-time $13,500; part-time $350 per credit. Required fees: $45 per term. One-time fee: $445. Tuition and fees vary according to program.

The College of Saint Rose, Graduate Studies, School of Education, Educational and School Psychology Department, Albany, NY 12203-1419. Offers applied technology education (MS Ed); educational psychology (MS Ed); school psychology (MS, Certificate). Part-time and evening/weekend programs available. *Entrance requirements:* For master's, minimum undergraduate GPA of 3.0. Additional exam requirements/recommendations for international students: Required—TOEFL (minimum score 550 paper-based; 213 computer-based). Electronic applications accepted.

The College of William and Mary, School of Education, Program in School Psychology, Williamsburg, VA 23187-8795. Offers M Ed, Ed S. *Accreditation:* NCATE. *Faculty:* 4 full-time (2 women), 1 (woman) part-time/adjunct. *Students:* 23 full-time (20 women), 11 part-time (10 women); includes 5 minority (all African Americans). Average age 27. 85 applicants, 45% accepted, 24 enrolled. In 2009, 11 master's, 12 other advanced degrees awarded. *Degree requirements:* For Ed S, internship. *Entrance requirements:* For master's, GRE, minimum GPA of 3.0; for Ed S, GRE, minimum GPA of 3.5. Additional exam requirements/recommendations for international students: Required—TOEFL. *Application deadline:* For fall admission, 1/15 for domestic and international students. Application fee: $45. Electronic applications accepted. *Expenses:* Tuition, state resident: full-time $6400; part-time $315 per credit hour. Tuition, nonresident: full-time $19,720; part-time $840 per credit hour. Required fees: $4114. *Financial support:* In 2009–10, 22 students received support, including 22 research assistantships (averaging $8,000 per year); career-related internships or fieldwork, Federal Work-Study, institutionally sponsored loans, scholarships/grants, and unspecified assistantships also available. Financial award application deadline: 1/15; financial award applicants required to submit FAFSA. *Faculty research:* Home schooling, gifted preschoolers, inclusive schools, ability testing. *Unit head:* Dr. Thomas J. Ward, Associate Dean, 757-221-2358, E-mail: tjward@wm.edu. *Application contact:* Dorothy Smith Osborne, Director of Admissions, 757-221-2317, Fax: 757-221-2293, E-mail: dsosbo@wm.edu.

Duquesne University, School of Education, Department of Counseling, Psychology, and Special Education, Program in School Psychology, Pittsburgh, PA 15282-0001. Offers child psychology (MS Ed); school psychology (PhD, CAGS). Part-time and evening/weekend programs available. *Faculty:* 6 full-time (4 women), 2 part-time/adjunct (0 women). *Students:* 69 full-time (60 women), 25 part-time (23 women); includes 6 minority (4 African Americans, 1 Asian American or Pacific Islander, 1 Hispanic American), 2 international. Average age 31. 134 applicants, 36% accepted, 22 enrolled. In 2009, 17 master's, 14 doctorates awarded. *Degree requirements:* For master's, thesis optional; for doctorate, thesis/dissertation. *Entrance requirements:* For master's, MAT, minimum GPA of 3.0; for doctorate, GRE, 3 letters of reference, letter of intent; for CAGS, MAT, interview. Additional exam requirements/recommendations for international students: Required—TOEFL (minimum score 550 paper-based; 80 computer-based). *Application deadline:* For fall admission, 1/15 priority date for domestic students. Applications are processed on a rolling basis. Application fee: $0. Electronic applications accepted. *Expenses:* Tuition: Part-time $851 per credit. Required fees: $81 per credit. *Financial support:* Research assistantships, Federal Work-Study available. Support available to part-time students. *Unit head:* Dr. Laura Crothers, Associate Professor, 412-396-1409, Fax: 412-396-1340, E-mail: crothersl@duq.edu. *Application contact:* Michael Dolinger, Director of Student and Academic Services, 412-396-6647, Fax: 412-396-5585, E-mail: dolingerm@duq.edu.

East Carolina University, Graduate School, Thomas Harriot College of Arts and Sciences, Department of Psychology, Program in School Psychology, Greenville, NC 27858-4353. Offers MA/CAS. *Accreditation:* NCATE. Part-time and evening/weekend programs available.

Eastern Illinois University, Graduate School, College of Sciences, Charleston, IL 61920-3099. Offers biological sciences (MS); chemistry (MS); communication disorders and sciences (MS); economics (MA); mathematics and computer science (MA), including mathematics, mathematics education; natural sciences (MS); political science (MA); psychology (MA, SSP), including clinical psychology (MA), school psychology (SSP). Part-time programs available. *Faculty:* 193 full-time (40 women). In 2009, 83 master's, 11 other advanced degrees awarded. *Degree requirements:* For SSP, thesis. *Entrance requirements:* For degree, GRE General Test. *Application deadline:* For fall admission, 3/31 priority date for domestic students. Applications are processed on a rolling basis. Application fee: $30. *Expenses:* Tuition, state resident: full-time $9434; part-time $239 per credit hour. Tuition, nonresident: full-time $23,774; part-time $717 per credit hour. Required fees: $802.63. *Financial support:* In 2009–10, research assistantships with tuition reimbursements (averaging $8,100 per year), teaching assistantships with tuition reimbursements (averaging $8,100 per year) were awarded; career-related internships or fieldwork and Federal Work-Study also available. Support available to part-time students. *Unit head:* Dr. Mary Ann Hanner, Dean, 217-581-3328, Fax: 217-581-7110, E-mail: mahanner@eiu.edu. *Application contact:* Bill Elliott, Director of Graduate Admissions, 217-581-7489, Fax: 217-581-6020, E-mail: wjelliott@eiu.edu.

Eastern Illinois University, Graduate School, College of Sciences, Department of Psychology, Program in School Psychology, Charleston, IL 61920-3099. Offers SSP. *Accreditation:* NCATE. In 2009, 11 SSPs awarded. *Degree requirements:* For SSP, thesis. *Entrance requirements:* For degree, GRE General Test. *Application deadline:* For fall admission, 3/31 priority date for domestic students. Applications are processed on a rolling basis. Application fee: $30. *Expenses:* Tuition, state resident: full-time $9434; part-time $239 per credit hour. Tuition, nonresident: full-time $23,774; part-time $717 per credit hour. Required fees: $802.63. *Financial support:* In 2009–10, research assistantships with tuition reimbursements (averaging $8,100 per year), 4 teaching assistantships with tuition reimbursements (averaging $8,100 per year) were awarded; career-related internships or fieldwork also available. *Unit head:* Dr. Assege Michael Haile Mariam, Coordinator, 217-581-2127, Fax: 217-581-6764, E-mail: ahailemariam@eiu.edu. *Application contact:* Dr. Assege Michael Haile Mariam, Coordinator, 217-581-2127, Fax: 217-581-6764, E-mail: ahailemariam@eiu.edu.

Eastern Kentucky University, The Graduate School, College of Arts and Sciences, Department of Psychology, Richmond, KY 40475-3102. Offers clinical psychology (MS); industrial/organizational psychology (MS); school psychology (Psy S). Part-time programs available. *Entrance requirements:* For master's and Psy S, GRE General Test, minimum GPA of 2.5. *Faculty research:* Autism, social psychology, parenting, assessment of depression/anxiety, reading.

Eastern University, Department of Counseling Psychology, St. Davids, PA 19087-3696. Offers community/clinical counseling (MA); school counseling (MA, Certificate); school psychology (MS, Certificate). *Degree requirements:* For master's, internship. *Entrance requirements:* For master's, minimum GPA of 2.5. Additional exam requirements/recommendations for international students: Required—TOEFL.

Eastern Washington University, Graduate Studies, College of Education and Human Development, Program in School Psychology, Cheney, WA 99004-2431. Offers MS. *Degree requirements:* For master's, comprehensive exam, thesis or alternative. *Entrance requirements:* For master's, GRE General Test, minimum GPA of 3.0. *Expenses:* Tuition, state resident: full-time $7476; part-time $249 per quarter hour. Tuition, nonresident: full-time $18,030; part-time $601 per quarter hour. Required fees: $3.50 per quarter hour. $142 per quarter.

Eastern Washington University, Graduate Studies, College of Social and Behavioral Sciences, Department of Psychology, Cheney, WA 99004-2431. Offers clinical psychology (MS); experimental psychology (MS); psychology (MS); school psychology (MS). *Degree requirements:* For master's, comprehensive exam, thesis or alternative. *Entrance requirements:* For master's, GRE General Test, minimum GPA of 3.0. *Expenses:* Tuition, state resident: full-time $7476; part-time $249 per quarter hour. Tuition, nonresident: full-time $18,030; part-time $601 per quarter hour. Required fees: $3.50 per quarter hour. $142 per quarter.

Emporia State University, School of Graduate Studies, The Teachers College, Department of Psychology, Art Therapy, Rehabilitation and Mental Health Counseling, Program in School Psychology, Emporia, KS 66801-5087. Offers MS, Ed S. *Accreditation:* NCATE. Part-time programs available. *Students:* 16 full-time (14 women), 6 part-time (5 women); includes 1 minority (African American). 5 applicants, 100% accepted, 5 enrolled. In 2009, 12 master's, 10 other advanced degrees awarded. *Degree requirements:* For master's, comprehensive exam or thesis, internship; for Ed S, comprehensive exam, thesis or alternative, internship. *Entrance requirements:* For master's, GRE General Test or MAT, graduate essay exam, appropriate bachelor's degree, teacher certification, letters of recommendation; for Ed S, GRE, graduate essay exam, letters of recommendation, teacher certification. Additional exam requirements/recommendations for international students: Required—TOEFL (minimum score 520 paper-based; 133 computer-based; 68 iBT). *Application deadline:* For fall admission, 8/15 priority date for domestic students. Applications are processed on a rolling basis. Application fee: $30 ($75 for international students). Electronic applications accepted. *Expenses:* Tuition, state resident: full-time $4154; part-time $173 per credit hour. Tuition, nonresident: full-time $12,864; part-time $536 per credit hour. Required fees: $948; $58 per credit hour. Tuition and fees vary according to campus/location. *Financial support:* Career-related internships or fieldwork, Federal Work-Study, institutionally sponsored loans, health care benefits, and unspecified assistantships available. Financial award application deadline: 3/15; financial award applicants required to submit FAFSA. *Unit head:* Dr. Brian W. Schrader, Chair, 620-341-5317, E-mail: bschrade@emporia.edu. *Application contact:* Mary Sewell, Admissions Coordinator, 800-950-GRAD, Fax: 620-341-5909, E-mail: msewell@emporia.edu.

Evangel University, School Counseling Program, Springfield, MO 65802. Offers MS. Part-time programs available. *Faculty:* 2 full-time (both women), 3 part-time/adjunct (2 women). *Students:* 10 full-time (9 women), 61 part-time (48 women). Average age 32. 17 applicants, 94% accepted, 14 enrolled. In 2009, 9 master's awarded. *Degree requirements:* For master's, comprehensive exam (for some programs), thesis or alternative. *Entrance requirements:* For master's, MAT (preferred) or GRE, teaching certificate. Additional exam requirements/recommendations for international students: Required—TOEFL (minimum score 550 paper-based; 213 computer-based). *Application deadline:* For fall admission, 7/15 priority date for domestic and international students; for spring admission, 11/15 priority date for domestic and international students. Applications are processed on a rolling basis. Application fee: $25. Electronic applications accepted. *Financial support:* In 2009–10, 2 students received support.

School Psychology

Evangel University (continued)
Career-related internships or fieldwork, scholarships/grants, and unspecified assistantships available. Support available to part-time students. Financial award application deadline: 3/1; financial award applicants required to submit FAFSA. *Unit head:* Debbie Bicket, Chair, 417-865-2815 Ext. 8567, Fax: 417-575-5484, E-mail: bicketd@evangel.edu. *Application contact:* Charity H. Fahlstrom, Admissions Representative, Graduate and Professional Studies, 417-865-2815 Ext. 7227, Fax: 417-575-5484, E-mail: fahlstromc@evangel.edu.

Fairfield University, Graduate School of Education and Allied Professions, Department of Psychological and Educational Consultation, Fairfield, CT 06824-5195. Offers applied psychology (MA), including foundations of advanced psychology, human services, industrial/organizational/personnel; media/educational technology (MA); school media specialist (MA); school psychology (MA, CAS); special education (MA, CAS). Part-time and evening/weekend programs available. *Degree requirements:* For master's, comprehensive exam, thesis optional. *Entrance requirements:* For master's, PRAXIS I (PPST), minimum QPA of 3.0, 2 recommendations, resume. Additional exam requirements/recommendations for international students: Required—TOEFL (minimum score 550 paper-based; 213 computer-based; 80 iBT). Electronic applications accepted. *Faculty research:* Child neuropsychology, disabilities, effect of pre-treatment orientation on treatment, autism, technology in business and classroom, collaboration with schools, communities and industry.

Fairleigh Dickinson University, Metropolitan Campus, University College: Arts, Sciences, and Professional Studies, School of Psychology, Program in School Psychology, Teaneck, NJ 07666-1914. Offers MA, Psy D. *Students:* 98 full-time (71 women), 3 part-time (2 women), 1 international. Average age 31. 68 applicants, 71% accepted, 27 enrolled. In 2009, 8 master's, 4 doctorates awarded. *Application deadline:* Applications are processed on a rolling basis. Application fee: $40. *Application contact:* Susan Brooman, University Director of Graduate Admissions, 201-692-2554, Fax: 201-692-2560, E-mail: globaleducation@fdu.edu.

Florida Agricultural and Mechanical University, Division of Graduate Studies, Research, and Continuing Education, College of Arts and Sciences, Department of Psychology, Program in School Psychology, Tallahassee, FL 32307-3200. Offers MS. *Accreditation:* NCATE. *Students:* 19 full-time (15 women), 22 part-time (15 women); includes 39 minority (all African Americans), 1 international. In 2009, 13 master's awarded. *Degree requirements:* For master's, thesis. *Entrance requirements:* For master's, GRE General Test, minimum GPA of 3.0, letters of recommendation (3). Additional exam requirements/recommendations for international students: Required—TOEFL. *Application deadline:* For fall admission, 5/18 for domestic students, 12/18 for international students; for spring admission, 11/12 for domestic students, 5/12 for international students. Application fee: $30. *Unit head:* Dr. Yvonne Bell, Chairperson, 850-599-3468, Fax: 850-561-2540, E-mail: yvonne.bell@famu.edu. *Application contact:* Dr. Chanta M. Haywood, Dean of Graduate Studies, Research, and Continuing Education, 850-599-3315, Fax: 850-599-3727.

Florida International University, College of Education, Department of Educational and Psychological Studies, Program in Counselor Education, Miami, FL 33199. Offers mental health counseling (MS); rehabilitation counseling (MS); school counseling (MS). *Accreditation:* ACA; NCATE. Part-time and evening/weekend programs available. *Entrance requirements:* For master's, General Knowledge test, College Level Academic Skills Test, GRE General Test or PRAXIS (school counseling track), minimum GPA of 3.0, interview. Additional exam requirements/recommendations for international students: Required—TOEFL (minimum score 550 paper-based; 213 computer-based; 80 iBT), IELTS (minimum score 6.3). Electronic applications accepted. *Expenses:* Tuition, state resident: full-time $8008; part-time $4004 per year. Tuition, nonresident: full-time $20,104; part-time $10,052 per year. Required fees: $298; $149 per term.

Florida International University, College of Education, Department of Educational and Psychological Studies, Program in School Psychology, Miami, FL 33199. Offers Ed S. *Accreditation:* NCATE. Part-time and evening/weekend programs available. *Degree requirements:* For Ed S, internship. *Entrance requirements:* For degree, General Knowledge test, College Level Academic Skills Test, GRE General Test or PRAXIS I, minimum GPA of 3.0 in last 60 undergraduate credits. Additional exam requirements/recommendations for international students: Required—TOEFL (minimum score 550 paper-based; 213 computer-based; 80 iBT), IELTS (minimum score 6.3). Electronic applications accepted. *Expenses:* Tuition, state resident: full-time $8008; part-time $4004 per year. Tuition, nonresident: full-time $20,104; part-time $10,052 per year. Required fees: $298; $149 per term. *Faculty research:* Incidence assessment, personality evaluation, psychopathology in children and adolescents, school psychology licensure, biased assessment.

Florida State University, The Graduate School, College of Education, Department of Educational Psychology and Learning Systems, Program in School Psychology, Tallahassee, FL 32306. Offers MS, Ed S. *Faculty:* 2 full-time (both women), 1 (woman) part-time/adjunct. *Students:* 56 full-time (46 women), 23 part-time (21 women); includes 22 minority (9 African Americans, 4 Asian Americans or Pacific Islanders, 9 Hispanic Americans), 2 international. In 2009, 32 master's, 32 other advanced degrees awarded. *Degree requirements:* For master's, comprehensive exam; for Ed S, comprehensive exam, thesis. *Entrance requirements:* For master's and Ed S, GRE General Test, minimum GPA of 3.0. Additional exam requirements/recommendations for international students: Required—TOEFL (minimum score 550 paper-based; 213 computer-based; 80 iBT); Recommended—TWE. *Application deadline:* For fall admission, 6/1 priority date for domestic and international students; for spring admission, 10/1 for domestic students, 10/1 priority date for international students. Applications are processed on a rolling basis. Application fee: $30. *Expenses:* Tuition, state resident: full-time $7413. Tuition, nonresident: full-time $22,567. *Financial support:* In 2009–10, 12 teaching assistantships with full and partial tuition reimbursements were awarded; fellowships with full and partial tuition reimbursements, research assistantships with full and partial tuition reimbursements, career-related internships or fieldwork also available. Financial award applicants required to submit FAFSA. *Faculty research:* Practitioner-scholar models, cultural diversity in populations. *Unit head:* Dr. Briley Proctor, Program Leader, 850-644-3742, Fax: 850-644-8776, E-mail: proctor@coe.fsu.edu. *Application contact:* Sally Gadson, Program Assistant, 850-644-8046, Fax: 850-644-5067, E-mail: gadson@coe.fsu.edu.

Fordham University, Graduate School of Education, Division of Psychological and Educational Services, New York, NY 10023. Offers counseling and personnel services (MSE, Adv C); counseling psychology (PhD); educational psychology (MSE, PhD); school psychology (PhD); urban and urban bilingual school psychology (Adv C). *Accreditation:* APA (one or more programs are accredited); NCATE. *Degree requirements:* For doctorate, thesis/dissertation. *Entrance requirements:* For doctorate, GRE General Test.

Fort Hays State University, Graduate School, College of Arts and Sciences, Department of Psychology, Program in School Psychology, Hays, KS 67601-4099. Offers Ed S. *Accreditation:* NCATE. *Degree requirements:* For Ed S, comprehensive exam, thesis. *Entrance requirements:* Additional exam requirements/recommendations for international students: Required—TOEFL (minimum score 550 paper-based; 213 computer-based). Electronic applications accepted.

Francis Marion University, Graduate Programs, Department of Psychology, Florence, SC 29502-0547. Offers applied psychology (MS), including clinical/counseling, school psychology; school psychology (MS). Part-time and evening/weekend programs available. *Faculty:* 10 full-time (4 women), 5 part-time/adjunct (4 women). *Students:* 16 full-time (15 women), 19 part-time (18 women); includes 6 minority (all African Americans). Average age 35. 44 applicants, 55% accepted, 8 enrolled. In 2009, 19 degrees awarded. *Degree requirements:* For master's, internship. *Entrance requirements:* For master's, GRE General Test. *Application deadline:* For fall admission, 3/15 for domestic students; for spring admission, 10/15 for domestic students. Applications are processed on a rolling basis. Application fee: $30. *Expenses:* Tuition, state resident: full-time $8345; part-time $417.25 per semester hour. Tuition, nonresident: full-time $16,690; part-time $814.50 per semester hour. Required fees: $335; $12.25 per semester hour. $30 per semester. *Financial support:* In 2009–10, 13 students received support, including 1 research assistantship (averaging $7,000 per year), 3 teaching assistantships (averaging $8,000 per year); career-related internships or fieldwork, unspecified assistantships, and scholarships with out-of-state waivers also available. Support available to part-time students. Financial award application deadline: 3/1; financial award applicants required to submit FAFSA. *Faculty research:* Parenting and family relationships, child development, applied behavioral analysis, posttraumatic stress disorder, clinical psychology in adults. *Unit head:* Dr. John R. Hester, Chair, 843-661-1635, Fax: 843-661-1628. *Application contact:* Jennifer Taylor, Administrative Assistant, 843-661-1378, Fax: 843-661-1628.

Fresno Pacific University, Graduate Programs, School of Education, Fresno, CA 93702-4709. Offers administration (MA Ed), including administrative services; foundations, curriculum and teaching (MA Ed), including curriculum and teaching, school library and information technology; language, literacy, and culture (MA Ed), including bilingual/cross-cultural education, language development, multilingual contexts, reading; mathematics/science/computer education (MA Ed), including educational technology, integrated mathematics/science education, mathematics education; pupil personnel services (MA Ed), including school counseling, school psychology; special education (MA Ed), including mild/moderate, moderate/severe, physical and health impairments. Part-time and evening/weekend programs available. *Degree requirements:* For master's, thesis (for some programs). *Entrance requirements:* For master's, interview; GMAT, GRE, MAT, or 6 units of course work with a faculty recommendation. Additional exam requirements/recommendations for international students: Required—TOEFL (minimum score 550 paper-based; 213 computer-based). Electronic applications accepted.

Fresno Pacific University, Graduate Programs, School of Education, Division of Pupil Personnel Services, Program in School Psychology, Fresno, CA 93702-4709. Offers MA Ed. Part-time and evening/weekend programs available. *Degree requirements:* For master's, thesis or alternative. *Entrance requirements:* Additional exam requirements/recommendations for international students: Required—TOEFL (minimum score 550 paper-based; 213 computer-based).

Gallaudet University, The Graduate School, College of Arts and Sciences, Department of Psychology, Program in School Psychology, Washington, DC 20002-3625. Offers developmental psychology (MA); school psychology (Psy S). *Accreditation:* NCATE. *Degree requirements:* For master's, thesis optional. *Entrance requirements:* For master's, GRE General Test or MAT. Electronic applications accepted.

Gardner-Webb University, Graduate School, School of Psychology, Program in School Counseling, Boiling Springs, NC 28017. Offers MA. *Accreditation:* NCATE. Part-time and evening/weekend programs available. *Faculty:* 7 full-time (4 women), 1 part-time/adjunct (0 women). *Students:* 35 part-time (27 women); includes 8 minority (all African Americans). Average age 32. In 2009, 12 master's awarded. *Degree requirements:* For master's, comprehensive exam. *Entrance requirements:* For master's, GRE General Test, MAT, minimum GPA of 2.7. *Application deadline:* For fall admission, 7/1 priority date for domestic students. Applications are processed on a rolling basis. Application fee: $25. Electronic applications accepted. *Expenses:* Tuition: Part-time $305 per credit hour. *Financial support:* Unspecified assistantships available. *Unit head:* Dr. David Carscaddon, Coordinator, 704-406-4437, Fax: 704-406-4329, E-mail: ppartin@gardner-webb.edu. *Application contact:* Dr. Franki Burch, Dean, Graduate School, 704-406-4422, Fax: 704-406-4329, E-mail: gradschool@gardner-webb.edu.

George Fox University, School of Education, Graduate Department of Counseling, Newberg, OR 97132-2697. Offers counseling (MA); marriage and family therapy (MA, Certificate); mental health trauma (Certificate); school counseling (MA, Certificate); school psychology (Certificate, Ed S). Part-time programs available. *Faculty:* 9 full-time (3 women), 7 part-time/adjunct (5 women). *Students:* 100 full-time (77 women), 122 part-time (103 women); includes 24 minority (7 African Americans, 4 American Indian/Alaska Native, 9 Asian Americans or Pacific Islanders, 4 Hispanic Americans). Average age 36. 102 applicants, 75% accepted, 59 enrolled. In 2009, 61 master's, 2 other advanced degrees awarded. *Degree requirements:* For master's, clinical project. *Entrance requirements:* For master's, MAT or GRE, bachelor's degree from regionally-accredited college or university, minimum cumulative GPA of 3.0, 1 professional and 1 academic reference, resume, on-campus interview. Additional exam requirements/recommendations for international students: Required—TOEFL (minimum score 577 paper-based; 233 computer-based; 90 iBT). *Application deadline:* For fall admission, 5/30 for domestic and international students; for winter admission, 11/1 for domestic and international students; for spring admission, 2/28 for domestic and international students. Applications are processed on a rolling basis. Application fee: $40. Electronic applications accepted. *Expenses:* Contact institution. *Financial support:* Career-related internships or fieldwork available. *Unit head:* Dr. Richard Shaw, Associate Professor of Marriage and Family Therapy/Chair, 503-554-6142, E-mail: rshaw@georgefox.edu. *Application contact:* Kathy Grant, Admissions Counselor, 800-493-4937, Fax: 503-554-6111, E-mail: counseling@georgefox.edu.

George Mason University, College of Humanities and Social Sciences, Department of Psychology, Program in School Psychology, Fairfax, VA 22030. Offers Certificate. *Accreditation:* NCATE. *Faculty:* 48 full-time (20 women), 14 part-time/adjunct (8 women). *Students:* 6 part-time (all women); includes 2 minority (1 African American, 1 Asian American or Pacific Islander). Average age 30. 16 applicants. In 2009, 8 Certificates awarded. *Entrance requirements:* Additional exam requirements/recommendations for international students: Required—TOEFL. *Application deadline:* For fall admission, 1/15 for domestic students. Application fee: $75. Electronic applications accepted. *Expenses:* Tuition, state resident: full-time $7568; part-time $315.33 per credit hour. Tuition, nonresident: full-time $21,704; part-time $904.33 per credit hour. Required fees: $2184; $91 per credit hour. *Financial support:* Unspecified assistantships and health care benefits (full-time research or teaching assistantship recipients) available. Support available to part-time students. Financial award application deadline: 3/1; financial award applicants required to submit FAFSA. *Faculty research:* Psychological and educational assessment of children and adults, cognitive processing based academic instruction, theories of measurement of intelligence, fair assessment of culturally and linguistically diverse population. *Unit head:* Darby Wiggins, Coordinator, 703-993-1548, E-mail: dwiggin3@gmu.edu. *Application contact:* Darby Wiggins, Information Contact, 703-993-1548, E-mail: dwiggin3@gmu.edu.

Georgia Southern University, Jack N. Averitt College of Graduate Studies, College of Education, Department of Leadership, Technology, and Human Development, Program in School Psychology, Statesboro, GA 30460. Offers M Ed, Ed S. *Accreditation:* NCATE. Part-time and evening/weekend programs available. *Students:* 42 full-time (39 women), 32 part-time (26 women); includes 22 minority (19 African Americans, 3 Hispanic Americans). Average age 30. 24 applicants, 83% accepted, 5 enrolled. In 2009, 17 master's, 7 other advanced degrees awarded. *Degree requirements:* For Ed S, comprehensive exam. *Entrance requirements:* For degree, GRE General Test or MAT, minimum graduate GPA of 3.25, letters of reference, interview. Additional exam requirements/recommendations for international students: Required—TOEFL (minimum score 550 paper-based; 213 computer-based; 80 iBT). *Application deadline:* For fall admission, 3/1 priority date for domestic and international students; for spring admission, 10/1 priority date for domestic students, 10/1 for international students. Applications are processed on a rolling basis. Application fee: $50. Electronic applications accepted. *Expenses:* Tuition, state resident: full-time $5040; part-time $210 per credit hour. Tuition, nonresident: full-time $20,136; part-time $839 per credit hour. Required fees: $1644. *Financial support:* In 2009–10, 56 students received support, including research assistantships with partial tuition reimbursements available (averaging $7,200 per year), teaching assistantships with partial tuition reimbursements available (averaging $7,200 per year); career-related internships or fieldwork, Federal Work-Study, scholarships/grants, tuition waivers (partial), and unspecified assistantships also available. Support available to part-time students. Financial award application deadline: 4/15; financial award applicants required to submit FAFSA. *Unit head:* Dr. Terry Diamanduros, Coordinator, 912-478-1548, Fax: 912-478-7104, E-mail: tdiamanduros@

georgiasouthern.edu. *Application contact:* Dr. Charles Ziglar, Coordinator for Graduate Student Recruitment, 912-478-5635, Fax: 912-478-0740, E-mail: gradadmissions@georgiasouthern.edu.

Georgia State University, College of Education, Department of Counseling and Psychological Services, Program in School Psychology, Atlanta, GA 30302-3083. Offers M Ed, PhD, Ed S. *Accreditation:* APA (one or more programs are accredited); NCATE. *Degree requirements:* For master's, comprehensive exam; for doctorate, comprehensive exam, thesis/dissertation. *Entrance requirements:* For master's, GRE General Test, minimum GPA of 2.5; for doctorate, GRE General Test, minimum GPA of 3.3; for Ed S, GRE General Test, minimum graduate GPA of 3.25. *Faculty research:* School reform, reading (early intervention), school violence.

Grand Valley State University, College of Education, Program in School Counseling, Allendale, MI 49401-9403. Offers M Ed. Part-time programs available. *Faculty:* 3 full-time (2 women). *Students:* 20 full-time (16 women), 68 part-time (54 women); includes 10 minority (7 African Americans, 1 American Indian/Alaska Native, 1 Asian American or Pacific Islander, 1 Hispanic American). Average age 32. 25 applicants, 96% accepted, 8 enrolled. In 2009, 30 master's awarded. *Degree requirements:* For master's, thesis or project. *Entrance requirements:* For master's, GRE General Test or minimum GPA of 3.0. Additional exam requirements/recommendations for international students: Required—TOEFL. *Application deadline:* Applications are processed on a rolling basis. Application fee: $30. Electronic applications accepted. *Expenses:* Tuition, state resident: part-time $471 per credit hour. Tuition, nonresident: part-time $646 per credit hour. Tuition and fees vary according to course level. *Financial support:* In 2009–10, 4 students received support, including 2 fellowships (averaging $13,691 per year), 2 research assistantships with full and partial tuition reimbursements available (averaging $8,000 per year); career-related internships or fieldwork also available. *Faculty research:* Multicultural issues in counselor education, use of technology in counseling programs. *Unit head:* Dr. Claudia Sowa-Wojciakowski, Chair of Community Outreach, 616-331-6706, E-mail: sowac@gvsu.edu. *Application contact:* Stephen Worst, Student Information and Services Center, 616-331-6650, Fax: 616-331-2000, E-mail: worsts@gvsu.edu.

Hofstra University, College of Liberal Arts and Sciences, Department of Psychology, Program in School-Community Psychology, Hempstead, NY 11549. Offers Psy D. *Accreditation:* NCATE. *Students:* 40 full-time (34 women), 9 part-time (8 women); includes 8 minority (1 African American, 4 Asian Americans or Pacific Islanders, 3 Hispanic Americans). Average age 26. 69 applicants, 35% accepted, 11 enrolled. In 2009, 17 doctorates awarded. Terminal master's awarded for partial completion of doctoral program. *Degree requirements:* For doctorate, comprehensive exam, thesis/dissertation. *Entrance requirements:* For doctorate, GRE General Test, GRE Subject Test (psychology), interview, 3 letters of recommendation. Additional exam requirements/recommendations for international students: Required—TOEFL (minimum score 550 paper-based; 213 computer-based; 80 iBT). *Application deadline:* For fall admission, 1/15 for domestic and international students. Application fee: $60. Electronic applications accepted. *Expenses:* Tuition: Full-time $16,200; part-time $900 per credit hour. Required fees: $970; $145 per term. Tuition and fees vary according to program. *Financial support:* In 2009–10, 22 students received support, including 21 fellowships with full and partial tuition reimbursements available (averaging $5,697 per year), 1 research assistantship with full and partial tuition reimbursement available (averaging $9,000 per year); Federal Work-Study, institutionally sponsored loans, scholarships/grants, and tuition waivers (full and partial) also available. Support available to part-time students. Financial award applicants required to submit FAFSA. *Faculty research:* Cross-cultural psychology, school psychology, childhood and adult trauma, positive psychology, autism spectrum disorders. *Unit head:* Dr. Robert Motta, Program Director, 516-463-5029, Fax: 516-463-6052, E-mail: psyrwm@hofstra.edu. *Application contact:* Carol Drummer, Dean of Graduate Admissions, 516-463-4876, Fax: 516-463-4664, E-mail: gradstudent@hofstra.edu.

Howard University, School of Education, Department of Human Development and Psychoeducational Studies, Program in School Psychology, Washington, DC 20059-0002. Offers M Ed, MA, Ed D, PhD, CAGS. MA and PhD offered through the Graduate School of Arts and Sciences. *Accreditation:* NCATE. *Faculty:* 2 full-time (0 women), 1 part-time/adjunct (0 women). *Students:* 21 full-time (16 women), 12 part-time (6 women); includes 27 minority (25 African Americans, 2 Hispanic Americans), 1 international. Average age 33. 26 applicants, 81% accepted, 17 enrolled. In 2009, 5 master's, 2 doctorates, 1 other advanced degree awarded. *Degree requirements:* For master's, comprehensive exam, thesis (MA), expository writing exam, practicum; for doctorate, one foreign language, comprehensive exam, thesis/dissertation, expository writing exam, internship. *Entrance requirements:* For master's, GRE General Test, minimum GPA of 2.7; for doctorate, GRE General Test, minimum GPA of 3.4; for CAGS, GRE General Test, minimum graduate GPA of 3.0, master's degree. *Application deadline:* For fall admission, 2/15 priority date for domestic students; for spring admission, 11/1 for domestic students. Applications are processed on a rolling basis. Application fee: $45. Electronic applications accepted. *Financial support:* In 2009–10, 3 students received support, including 2 fellowships with full and partial tuition reimbursements available (averaging $15,000 per year), 1 research assistantship (averaging $4,583 per year); career-related internships or fieldwork, Federal Work-Study, institutionally sponsored loans, scholarships/grants, and unspecified assistantships also available. Financial award application deadline: 2/15. *Faculty research:* Psychopathology, maltreatment abuse and neglect, children exposed to political unrest, family conflict and community violence. *Unit head:* Dr. Salman M. Elbedour, Professor/Coordinator, 202-806-6412, Fax: 202-806-5205, E-mail: selbedour@howard.edu. *Application contact:* Frazier Tate-Jackson, Administration Assistant, Department of HDPES, 202-806-7350, Fax: 202-806-5205, E-mail: fjackson@howard.edu.

Humboldt State University, Graduate Studies, College of Professional Studies, Department of Psychology, Arcata, CA 95521-8299. Offers psychology (MA), including academic research, counseling, school psychology. *Students:* 60 full-time (45 women), 10 part-time (6 women); includes 13 minority (2 African Americans, 1 American Indian/Alaska Native, 3 Asian Americans or Pacific Islanders, 7 Hispanic Americans), 1 international. Average age 29. 64 applicants, 38% accepted, 21 enrolled. In 2009, 16 master's awarded. *Degree requirements:* For master's, thesis. *Entrance requirements:* For master's, appropriate bachelor's degree, minimum GPA of 2.5. Additional exam requirements/recommendations for international students: Required—TOEFL (minimum score 500 paper-based; 173 computer-based). *Application deadline:* For fall admission, 2/15 for domestic and international students. Applications are processed on a rolling basis. Application fee: $55. *Expenses:* Tuition, nonresident: full-time $8928. Required fees: $6102. Tuition and fees vary according to program. *Financial support:* Career-related internships or fieldwork available. Financial award application deadline: 3/1; financial award applicants required to submit FAFSA. *Faculty research:* School psychology, counseling, eating disorders, mood induction, depression. *Unit head:* Dr. Brent Duncan, Chair, 707-826-3755, Fax: 707-826-4993, E-mail: bbd1@humboldt.edu. *Application contact:* Dr. Chris Aberson, Coordinator, 707-826-3670, Fax: 707-826-4993, E-mail: cla18@humboldt.edu.

Idaho State University, Office of Graduate Studies, College of Education, Department of Educational Learning and Development, Pocatello, ID 83209-8059. Offers human exceptionality (M Ed); school psychology (Ed S); special education (Ed S). Part-time programs available. *Faculty:* 3 full-time (1 woman). *Students:* 18 full-time (13 women), 7 part-time (6 women); includes 1 minority (American Indian/Alaska Native), 1 international. Average age 34. In 2009, 6 master's, 11 other advanced degrees awarded. *Degree requirements:* For master's, comprehensive exam, thesis (for some programs), oral thesis defense or written comprehensive exam and oral exam; for Ed S, comprehensive exam, thesis (for some programs), oral exam, specialist paper or portfolio. *Entrance requirements:* For master's, GRE or MAT, minimum undergraduate GPA of 3.0, bachelor's degree, professional experience in an educational context; for Ed S, GRE or MAT, master's degree in related field. Additional exam requirements/recommendations for international students: Required—TOEFL (minimum score 550 paper-based; 213 computer-based; 80 iBT). *Application deadline:* For fall admission, 7/1 for domestic students, 6/1 for international students; for spring admission, 12/1 for domestic students, 11/1 for international students. Applications are processed on a rolling basis. Application fee: $55. Electronic applications accepted. *Expenses:* Tuition, state resident: full-time $3318; part-time $297 per credit hour. Tuition, nonresident: full-time $13,120; part-time $437 per credit hour. Required fees: $2530. Tuition and fees vary according to program. *Financial support:* Teaching assistantships with full and partial tuition reimbursements, career-related internships or fieldwork, Federal Work-Study, institutionally sponsored loans, scholarships/grants, health care benefits, and unspecified assistantships available. Support available to part-time students. Financial award application deadline: 1/1; financial award applicants required to submit FAFSA. *Faculty research:* Literacy, school psychology, special education. *Unit head:* Dr. David Mercaldo, Interim Chairman, 208-282-5188, Fax: 208-282-4697, E-mail: mercdavi@isu.edu. *Application contact:* Dr. Peter Denner, Assistant Dean, 208-282-3807, Fax: 208-282-4697, E-mail: dennpete@isu.edu.

Idaho State University, Office of Graduate Studies, Kasiska College of Health Professions, Department of Counseling, Pocatello, ID 83209-8120. Offers counseling (M Coun, Ed S), including marriage and family counseling (M Coun), mental health counseling (M Coun), school counseling (M Coun), student affairs and college counseling (M Coun); counselor education and counseling (PhD). *Accreditation:* ACA (one or more programs are accredited). Part-time programs available. *Faculty:* 7 full-time (4 women). *Students:* 72 full-time (52 women), 29 part-time (18 women); includes 11 minority (2 African Americans, 1 American Indian/Alaska Native, 2 Asian Americans or Pacific Islanders, 6 Hispanic Americans). Average age 32. In 2009, 25 master's, 5 doctorates, 1 other advanced degree awarded. *Degree requirements:* For master's, comprehensive exam, thesis, 4 semesters resident graduate study, practicum/internship; for doctorate, comprehensive exam, thesis/dissertation, 3 semesters internship, 4 consecutive semesters doctoral-level study on campus; for Ed S, comprehensive exam, thesis, case studies, oral exam. *Entrance requirements:* For master's, GRE General Test, MAT, minimum GPA of 3.0, bachelors degree, interview, 3 letters of recommendation; for doctorate, GRE General Test, MAT, minimum graduate GPA of 3.0, resume, interview, counseling license, master's degree; for Ed S, GRE General Test, minimum graduate GPA of 3.0, master's degree in counseling, 3 letters of recommendation, 2 years work experience. Additional exam requirements/recommendations for international students: Required—TOEFL (minimum score 600 paper-based; 213 computer-based; 80 iBT). *Application deadline:* For fall admission, 7/1 for domestic students, 6/1 for international students; for spring admission, 12/1 for domestic students, 11/1 for international students. Applications are processed on a rolling basis. Application fee: $55. Electronic applications accepted. *Expenses:* Tuition, state resident: full-time $3318; part-time $297 per credit hour. Tuition, nonresident: full-time $13,120; part-time $437 per credit hour. Required fees: $2530. Tuition and fees vary according to program. *Financial support:* In 2009–10, 12 teaching assistantships with full and partial tuition reimbursements (averaging $10,841 per year) were awarded; career-related internships or fieldwork, Federal Work-Study, institutionally sponsored loans, scholarships/grants, traineeships, health care benefits, tuition waivers (full and partial), and unspecified assistantships also available. Support available to part-time students. Financial award application deadline: 1/1; financial award applicants required to submit FAFSA. *Faculty research:* Group counseling, multicultural counseling, family counseling, child therapy, supervision. *Unit head:* Dr. Nicole Hill, Interim Chair, 208-282-3663, Fax: 208-282-2583, E-mail: hillnico@isu.edu. *Application contact:* Tami Carson, Graduate School Technical Records Specialist, 208-282-2150, Fax: 208-282-4847, E-mail: carstami@isu.edu.

Illinois State University, Graduate School, College of Arts and Sciences, Department of Psychology, Program in School Psychology, Normal, IL 61790-2200. Offers PhD, SSP. *Accreditation:* APA (one or more programs are accredited); NCATE (one or more programs are accredited). *Degree requirements:* For doctorate, variable foreign language requirement, thesis/dissertation, 2 terms of residency, internship, practicum. *Entrance requirements:* For doctorate, GRE General Test.

Immaculata University, College of Graduate Studies, Department of Psychology, Immaculata, PA 19345. Offers clinical psychology (Psy D); counseling psychology (MA, Certificate), including school guidance counselor (Certificate), school psychologist (Certificate). *Accreditation:* APA. Part-time and evening/weekend programs available. *Degree requirements:* For master's, comprehensive exam, thesis optional; for doctorate, comprehensive exam, thesis/dissertation. *Entrance requirements:* For master's, GRE General Test or MAT, minimum GPA of 3.0; for doctorate, GRE General Test, minimum GPA of 3.5. Additional exam requirements/recommendations for international students: Required—TOEFL, IELTS. *Faculty research:* Supervision ethics, psychology of teaching, gender.

Indiana State University, School of Graduate Studies, College of Education, Department of Communication Disorders, Counseling and School and Educational Psychology, Terre Haute, IN 47809. Offers counseling psychology (MS, PhD); counselor education (PhD); mental health counseling (MS); school counseling (M Ed); school psychology (PhD, Ed S); MA/MS. *Accreditation:* ACA; NCATE. Part-time and evening/weekend programs available. *Degree requirements:* For master's, thesis optional; for doctorate, thesis/dissertation, research tools proficiency tests. *Entrance requirements:* For master's, GRE General Test or MAT, minimum undergraduate GPA of 2.75; for doctorate, GRE General Test, master's degree, minimum undergraduate GPA of 3.5. Electronic applications accepted. *Faculty research:* Vocational development supervision.

Indiana University Bloomington, School of Education, Department of Counseling and Educational Psychology, Bloomington, IN 47405-1006. Offers counseling (MS, PhD, Ed S); counseling psychology (PhD); counselor education (MS, Ed S); educational psychology (MS, PhD); inquiry methodology (PhD); learning and developmental sciences (MS, PhD); school psychology (PhD, Ed S). *Accreditation:* ACA (one or more programs are accredited); APA (one or more programs are accredited); NCATE. *Faculty:* 32 full-time (13 women), 20 part-time/adjunct (10 women). *Students:* 218 full-time (165 women), 34 part-time (29 women); includes 45 minority (19 African Americans, 2 American Indian/Alaska Native, 12 Asian Americans or Pacific Islanders, 12 Hispanic Americans), 42 international. Average age 30. 348 applicants, 41% accepted, 53 enrolled. In 2009, 57 master's, 21 doctorates, 22 other advanced degrees awarded. Terminal master's awarded for partial completion of doctoral program. *Degree requirements:* For master's, thesis optional; for doctorate, thesis/dissertation; for Ed S, comprehensive exam or project. *Entrance requirements:* For master's, doctorate, and Ed S, GRE General Test. Additional exam requirements/recommendations for international students: Required—TOEFL. *Application deadline:* Applications are processed on a rolling basis. Application fee: $55 ($65 for international students). Electronic applications accepted. *Financial support:* In 2009–10, 58 students received support, including 7 fellowships with partial tuition reimbursements available (averaging $15,000 per year), 15 research assistantships with partial tuition reimbursements available (averaging $12,000 per year), 36 teaching assistantships with partial tuition reimbursements available (averaging $14,280 per year); career-related internships or fieldwork, Federal Work-Study, institutionally sponsored loans, scholarships/grants, and unspecified assistantships also available. Support available to part-time students. Financial award application deadline: 1/1; financial award applicants required to submit FAFSA. *Faculty research:* Counseling psychology, inquiry methodology, school psychology, learning sciences, human development, educational psychology. *Unit head:* Dr. Joyce Alexander, Chairperson, 812-856-8300, Fax: 812-856-8333, E-mail: cep@indiana.edu. *Application contact:* Jessica Durnal, Student Services Specialist, 812-856-8300, Fax: 812-856-8333, E-mail: cep@indiana.edu.

Indiana University of Pennsylvania, School of Graduate Studies and Research, College of Education and Educational Technology, Department of Educational and School Psychology, Program in School Psychology, Indiana, PA 15705-1087. Offers D Ed, Certificate. *Accreditation:* NCATE. Part-time programs available. *Faculty:* 14 full-time (8 women). *Students:* 13 full-time (11 women), 53 part-time (37 women); includes 3 minority (2 African Americans, 1 Hispanic American). Average age 31. 38 applicants, 58% accepted, 15 enrolled. In 2009, 12 doctorates, 17 other advanced degrees awarded. *Degree requirements:* For doctorate, comprehensive exam, thesis/dissertation. *Entrance requirements:* For doctorate, GRE General Test, GRE Subject Test, 2 letters of recommendation. Additional exam requirements/recommendations for international students: Required—TOEFL. *Application deadline:* For fall admission, 1/10 for

School Psychology

Indiana University of Pennsylvania (continued)

domestic students. Applications are processed on a rolling basis. Application fee: $40. *Expenses:* Tuition, state resident: full-time $6666; part-time $370 per credit hour. Tuition, nonresident: full-time $10,666; part-time $593 per credit hour. Required fees: $813 per semester. *Financial support:* In 2009–10, 3 fellowships (averaging $2,333 per year), 12 research assistantships with full and partial tuition reimbursements (averaging $4,385 per year), 3 teaching assistantships with partial tuition reimbursements (averaging $10,768 per year) were awarded; career-related internships or fieldwork and Federal Work-Study also available. Support available to part-time students. Financial award application deadline: 3/15; financial award applicants required to submit FAFSA. *Unit head:* Dr. John Quirk, Graduate Coordinator, 724-357-3785. *Application contact:* Dr. Edward Nardi, Interim Associate Dean, 724-357-2480, Fax: 724-357-5595, E-mail: ewnardi@iup.edu.

Inter American University of Puerto Rico, Metropolitan Campus, Graduate Programs, Program in Psychology, San Juan, PR 00919-1293. Offers counseling psychology (MA, PhD); industrial/organizational psychology (MA, PhD); labor relations (MA); school psychology (MA, PhD). *Degree requirements:* For master's, comprehensive exam. *Entrance requirements:* For master's, GRE or EXADEP, interview. Electronic applications accepted.

Inter American University of Puerto Rico, San Germán Campus, Graduate Studies Center, Program in Psychology, San Germán, PR 00683-5008. Offers counseling psychology (MA, PhD); school psychology (MA, PhD). Part-time and evening/weekend programs available. *Degree requirements:* For master's, comprehensive exam, thesis; for doctorate, comprehensive exam, thesis/dissertation. *Entrance requirements:* For master's, GRE General Test or EXADEP, minimum GPA of 3.0; for doctorate, GRE, EXADEP or MAT, minimum GPA of 3.0.

Iona College, School of Arts and Science, Department of Psychology, New Rochelle, NY 10801-1890. Offers experimental psychology (MA); industrial-organizational psychology (MA); mental health counseling (MA); psychology (MA); school psychology (MA). Part-time and evening/weekend programs available. *Faculty:* 14 full-time (8 women), 10 part-time/adjunct (8 women). *Students:* 74 full-time (58 women), 46 part-time (34 women); includes 28 minority (13 African Americans, 1 American Indian/Alaska Native, 3 Asian Americans or Pacific Islanders, 11 Hispanic Americans), 1 international. Average age 25. 186 applicants, 61% accepted, 44 enrolled. In 2009, 35 master's awarded. *Degree requirements:* For master's, thesis. *Entrance requirements:* For master's, GRE or minimum GPA of 3.0. Additional exam requirements/recommendations for international students: Required—TOEFL (minimum score 550 paper-based; 213 computer-based). *Application deadline:* Applications are processed on a rolling basis. Application fee: $50. Electronic applications accepted. *Expenses:* Tuition: Part-time $830 per credit. *Financial support:* Career-related internships or fieldwork, tuition waivers (partial), and unspecified assistantships available. Support available to part-time students. Financial award application deadline: 4/15; financial award applicants required to submit FAFSA. *Unit head:* Dr. Paul Greene, Chair, 914-633-2048, E-mail: pgreene@iona.edu. *Application contact:* Veronica Jarek-Prinz, Director of Graduate Admissions, 914-633-2420, Fax: 914-633-2277, E-mail: vjarekprinz@iona.edu.

James Madison University, The Graduate School, College of Integrated Science and Technology, Department of Graduate Psychology, Program in Combined-Integrated Clinical and School Psychology, Harrisonburg, VA 22807. Offers Psy D. Part-time and evening/weekend programs available. *Students:* 20 full-time (16 women), 1 (woman) part-time; includes 3 minority (2 African Americans, 1 Asian American or Pacific Islander), 3 international. Average age 27. In 2009, 6 doctorates awarded. *Degree requirements:* For doctorate, thesis/dissertation, 12-month internship. *Entrance requirements:* For doctorate, GRE General Test, GRE Subject Test (advanced psychology), 3 letters of recommendation. Additional exam requirements/recommendations for international students: Required—TOEFL. *Application deadline:* For fall admission, 2/1 for domestic students. Applications are processed on a rolling basis. Application fee: $55. Electronic applications accepted. *Expenses:* Tuition, area resident: Part-time $305 per credit hour. Tuition, state resident: part-time $305 per credit hour. Tuition, nonresident: part-time $890 per credit hour. *Financial support:* In 2009–10, 12 students received support, including 3 teaching assistantships with full tuition reimbursements available (averaging $8,664 per year). Financial award application deadline: 3/1; financial award applicants required to submit FAFSA. *Unit head:* Dr. Gregg R. Henriques, Program Director, 540-568-7857. *Application contact:* Dr. Gregg R. Henriques, Program Director, 540-568-7857.

James Madison University, The Graduate School, College of Integrated Science and Technology, Department of Graduate Psychology, Program in School Psychology, Harrisonburg, VA 22807. Offers school counseling (Ed S); school psychology (MA). *Accreditation:* APA (one or more programs are accredited); NCATE (one or more programs are accredited). Part-time and evening/weekend programs available. *Students:* 16 full-time (13 women), 6 part-time (5 women); includes 4 minority (1 African American, 1 Asian American or Pacific Islander, 2 Hispanic Americans). Average age 27. In 2009, 5 master's, 10 other advanced degrees awarded. *Degree requirements:* For master's, comprehensive exam; for Ed S, thesis, research project, 10-month internship. *Entrance requirements:* For master's, GRE General Test, interview, 3 letters of recommendation. Additional exam requirements/recommendations for international students: Required—TOEFL. *Application deadline:* For fall admission, 2/1 priority date for domestic students. Applications are processed on a rolling basis. Application fee: $55. Electronic applications accepted. *Expenses:* Tuition, area resident: Part-time $305 per credit hour. Tuition, state resident: part-time $305 per credit hour. Tuition, nonresident: part-time $890 per credit hour. *Financial support:* In 2009–10, 14 students received support, including teaching assistantships with full tuition reimbursements available (averaging $8,664 per year); career-related internships or fieldwork and Federal Work-Study also available. Financial award application deadline: 3/1; financial award applicants required to submit FAFSA. *Unit head:* Dr. Patricia J. Warner, Program Director, 540-568-3358. *Application contact:* Dr. Patricia J. Warner, Program Director, 540-568-3358.

The Johns Hopkins University, School of Education, Department of Counseling and Human Services, Baltimore, MD 21218. Offers clinical community counseling (Certificate); clinical supervision (Certificate); counseling (MS, CAGS), including clinical community counseling (MS), school counseling (MS); play therapy (Certificate). Part-time and evening/weekend programs available. *Faculty:* 4 full-time (2 women), 36 part-time/adjunct (20 women). *Students:* 69 full-time (64 women), 316 part-time (275 women); includes 104 minority (75 African Americans, 12 Asian Americans or Pacific Islanders, 17 Hispanic Americans), 8 international. Average age 32. 186 applicants, 57% accepted, 72 enrolled. In 2009, 115 master's, 28 other advanced degrees awarded. *Degree requirements:* For master's, comprehensive exam. *Entrance requirements:* For master's, bachelor's degree, minimum undergraduate GPA of 3.0, 3 letters of recommendation, curriculum vitae/resume, group interview; for other advanced degree, master's degree, minimum undergraduate GPA of 3.0, 3 letters of recommendation, curriculum vitae/resume, interview. Additional exam requirements/recommendations for international students: Required—TOEFL (minimum score 600 paper-based; 250 computer-based; 100 iBT). *Application deadline:* For fall admission, 3/1 for domestic students, 5/1 for international students; for spring admission, 10/1 for domestic students, 10/15 for international students. Applications are processed on a rolling basis. Application fee: $80. Electronic applications accepted. *Financial support:* Scholarships/grants available. Support available to part-time students. Financial award application deadline: 6/1; financial award applicants required to submit FAFSA. *Faculty research:* College access of low-income students and students-of-color; multicultural counseling training; domestic violence, resilience, and traumatic stress; application of behaviorally-based and ethical practices to criminal justice setting and systems. *Unit head:* Dr. Cheryl Holcomb-McCoy, Chair, 410-516-7928, Fax: 410-516-3939, E-mail: counseling@jhu.edu. *Application contact:* Jennifer Shaffer, Director of Admissions, 410-516-9797 Ext. 410, Fax: 410-516-9799, E-mail: educationinfo@jhu.edu.

Kean University, College of Humanities and Social Sciences, Program in School Psychology, Union, NJ 07083. Offers Diploma. Part-time and evening/weekend programs available. *Faculty:* 15 full-time (13 women). *Students:* 19 full-time (17 women), 5 part-time (all women). Average age 26. 30 applicants, 47% accepted, 10 enrolled. In 2009, 10 Diplomas awarded. *Degree requirements:* For Diploma, comprehensive exam, practicum, externship. *Entrance requirements:* For degree, GRE General Test, minimum GPA of 3.0, interview, 3 letters of recommendation, prerequisites in psychology, official transcripts from all institutions attended. *Application deadline:* For fall admission, 3/15 for domestic students. Application fee: $60 ($150 for international students). Electronic applications accepted. *Expenses:* Tuition, state resident: full-time $10,440; part-time $435 per credit. Tuition, nonresident: full-time $14,160; part-time $590 per credit. Required fees: $2642; $110 per credit. Part-time tuition and fees vary according to course load and degree level. *Financial support:* In 2009–10, 10 research assistantships with full tuition reimbursements (averaging $3,263 per year) were awarded; unspecified assistantships also available. *Unit head:* Dr. Dennis Finger, Program Coordinator, 908-737-5870, E-mail: dfinger@kean.edu. *Application contact:* Ann-Marie Kay, Assistant Director of Graduate Admissions, 908-737-5922, Fax: 908-737-5965, E-mail: akay@kean.edu.

Kean University, Nathan Weiss Graduate College, Program in School and Clinical Psychology, Union, NJ 07083. Offers Psy D. Evening/weekend programs available. *Faculty:* 2 full-time (0 women). *Students:* 10 full-time (9 women); includes 1 minority (Hispanic American). Average age 25. 26 applicants, 54% accepted, 10 enrolled. *Degree requirements:* For doctorate, comprehensive exam, thesis/dissertation, externship. *Entrance requirements:* For doctorate, GRE General Test (minimum score 500 verbal, 500 quantitative, 4.0 writing), GRE Subject Test in psychology taken within the last 5 years (minimum score 550), minimum undergraduate GPA of 3.3, graduate 3.5; 3 letters of recommendation (at least one from a professor); personal interview; prerequisite coursework in theories of personality, abnormal psychology, tests and measurements, statistics, and experimental psychology. *Application deadline:* For fall admission, 1/30 for domestic students. Application fee: $60 ($150 for international students). Electronic applications accepted. *Expenses:* Contact institution. *Financial support:* In 2009–10, 7 research assistantships (averaging $3,263 per year) were awarded; unspecified assistantships also available. *Unit head:* Dr. Frank Gardner, Program Coordinator, 908-737-5862, E-mail: fgardner@kean.edu. *Application contact:* Steven Koch, Pre-Admissions Coordinator, 908-737-5924, Fax: 908-737-5965, E-mail: skoch@kean.edu.

Keene State College, School of Professional and Graduate Studies, Keene, NH 03435. Offers curriculum and instruction (M Ed); education leadership (PMC); educational leadership (M Ed); school counselor (M Ed, PMC); special education (M Ed); teacher certification (Post-baccalaureate Certificate). *Accreditation:* NCATE. Part-time and evening/weekend programs available. *Faculty:* 21 full-time (13 women), 14 part-time/adjunct (13 women). *Students:* 8 full-time (5 women), 80 part-time (56 women); includes 1 Asian American or Pacific Islander, 1 Hispanic American, 1 international. Average age 34. 94 applicants, 80% accepted, 62 enrolled. In 2009, 55 master's, 10 other advanced degrees awarded. *Entrance requirements:* For master's, PRAXIS I, resume; minimum GPA of 2.5. Additional exam requirements/recommendations for international students: Required—TOEFL (minimum score 550 paper-based; 173 computer-based; 61 iBT). *Application deadline:* For fall admission, 4/1 for domestic students; for spring admission, 12/1 for domestic students. Application fee: $40. *Expenses:* Tuition, state resident: part-time $320 per credit. Tuition, nonresident: part-time $350 per credit. Required fees: $92 per credit. $10 per term. Tuition and fees vary according to course load. *Financial support:* Research assistantships, career-related internships or fieldwork, Federal Work-Study, institutionally sponsored loans, and unspecified assistantships available. Support available to part-time students. Financial award application deadline: 3/1; financial award applicants required to submit FAFSA. *Unit head:* Dr. Melinda Treadwell, Dean, 603-358-2220. *Application contact:* Peggy Richmond, Director of Admissions, 603-358-2276, Fax: 603-358-2767, E-mail: admissions@keene.edu.

Kent State University, Graduate School of Education, Health, and Human Services, School of Lifespan Development and Educational Sciences, Program in School Psychology, Kent, OH 44242-0001. Offers M Ed, PhD, Ed S. *Accreditation:* APA; NCATE. *Faculty:* 4 full-time (1 woman), 2 part-time/adjunct (both women). *Students:* 61 full-time (52 women), 2 part-time (1 woman); includes 8 minority (5 African Americans, 3 Hispanic Americans), 1 international. 40 applicants, 50% accepted. In 2009, 14 master's, 2 doctorates, 13 other advanced degrees awarded. *Degree requirements:* For doctorate, comprehensive exam, thesis/dissertation. *Entrance requirements:* For master's and doctorate, GRE General Test; for Ed S, GRE General Test, MAT or minimum graduate GPA of 3.5. Additional exam requirements/recommendations for international students: Required—TOEFL. *Application deadline:* For fall admission, 6/15 for domestic students; for spring admission, 10/15 for domestic students. Application fee: $30. Electronic applications accepted. *Financial support:* In 2009–10, fellowships with full tuition reimbursements (averaging $10,952 per year), 12 research assistantships with full tuition reimbursements (averaging $8,313 per year) were awarded; teaching assistantships with full tuition reimbursements, Federal Work-Study, scholarships/grants, and unspecified assistantships also available. Financial award application deadline: 4/1; financial award applicants required to submit FAFSA. *Faculty research:* Special education policy and practice, treatment fidelity, school-based consultation. *Unit head:* Dr. Richard Cowan, Coordinator, 330-672-4450, E-mail: rcowan1@kent.edu. *Application contact:* Nancy Miller, Academic Program Coordinator, Office of Graduate Student Services, 330-672-2576, Fax: 330-672-9162, E-mail: ogs@kent.edu.

La Sierra University, School of Education, Department of School Psychology and Counseling, Riverside, CA 92515. Offers counseling (MA); educational psychology (Ed S); school psychology (Ed S). Part-time and evening/weekend programs available. *Degree requirements:* For master's, thesis optional; for Ed S, practicum (educational psychology). *Entrance requirements:* For master's, California Basic Educational Skills Test, NTE, minimum GPA of 3.0; for Ed S, minimum GPA of 3.3. *Faculty research:* Equivalent score scales, self perception.

Lehigh University, College of Education, Program in School Psychology, Bethlehem, PA 18015. Offers PhD, Ed S. *Accreditation:* APA (one or more programs are accredited). Part-time and evening/weekend programs available. *Faculty:* 6 full-time (4 women). *Students:* 38 full-time (32 women), 11 part-time (all women); includes 5 minority (3 African Americans, 2 Asian Americans or Pacific Islanders). Average age 26. 102 applicants, 21% accepted, 12 enrolled. In 2009, 6 doctorates, 3 other advanced degrees awarded. *Degree requirements:* For doctorate, comprehensive exam, internship, research qualifying exam; for Ed S, internship. *Entrance requirements:* For doctorate, GRE General Test, minimum GPA of 3.0, 2 letters of recommendation; for Ed S, GRE General Test, minimum GPA of 3.0. Additional exam requirements/recommendations for international students: Required—TOEFL (minimum score 600 paper-based; 250 computer-based; 85 iBT). *Application deadline:* For fall admission, 1/1 for domestic and international students. Application fee: $65. Electronic applications accepted. *Financial support:* In 2009–10, 15 students received support, including 11 research assistantships (averaging $15,000 per year); fellowships, career-related internships or fieldwork, Federal Work-Study, institutionally sponsored loans, tuition waivers (full and partial), and unspecified assistantships also available. Financial award application deadline: 1/31. *Faculty research:* Applied behavior analysis, developmental disabilities, at-risk students, learning and behavior problems, pediatric psychology. *Unit head:* Dr. Christine L. Cole, Coordinator, 610-758-3256, Fax: 610-758-6223, E-mail: clc2@lehigh.edu. *Application contact:* Sharon Y. Warden, Coordinator, 610-758-3256, Fax: 610-758-6223, E-mail: sy00@lehigh.edu.

Lenoir-Rhyne University, Graduate Programs, School of Counseling and Human Services, Program in School Counseling, Hickory, NC 28601. Offers MA. Part-time and evening/weekend programs available. *Degree requirements:* For master's, comprehensive exam, thesis optional. *Entrance requirements:* For master's, GRE General Test, minimum undergraduate GPA of 2.7, graduate 3.0; writing sample. Additional exam requirements/recommendations for international students: Required—TOEFL (minimum score 600 paper-based). Electronic applications accepted.

Lesley University, Graduate School of Arts and Social Sciences, Program in Counseling Psychology, Cambridge, MA 02138-2790. Offers professional counseling (MA); school counseling (MA). Part-time and evening/weekend programs available. Postbaccalaureate distance learning degree programs offered (no on-campus study). Terminal master's awarded for partial completion of doctoral program. *Degree requirements:* For master's, internship, practicum. *Entrance requirements:* For master's, MAT. Additional exam requirements/recommendations for international students: Required—TOEFL (minimum score 550 paper-based; 213 computer-based; 80 iBT).

Lewis & Clark College, Graduate School of Education and Counseling, Department of Counseling Psychology, Program in School Psychology, Portland, OR 97219-7899. Offers Ed S. Part-time and evening/weekend programs available. *Faculty:* 2 full-time (1 woman), 7 part-time/adjunct (4 women). *Students:* 16 full-time (15 women), 33 part-time (28 women); includes 5 minority (1 African American, 3 Asian Americans or Pacific Islanders, 1 Hispanic American). Average age 30. 42 applicants, 57% accepted, 15 enrolled. In 2009, 12 Ed Ss awarded. *Entrance requirements:* Additional exam requirements/recommendations for international students: Required—TOEFL (minimum score 575 paper-based; 233 computer-based). *Application deadline:* For fall admission, 2/1 for domestic and international students. Application fee: $50. Electronic applications accepted. *Expenses:* Tuition: Part-time $713 per semester hour. Tuition and fees vary according to course level and campus/location. *Financial support:* In 2009–10, 47 students received support. Career-related internships or fieldwork, Federal Work-Study, institutionally sponsored loans, scholarships/grants, health care benefits, and tuition waivers (partial) available. Support available to part-time students. Financial award application deadline: 3/1; financial award applicants required to submit FAFSA. *Unit head:* Dr. Peter Mortola, Program Coordinator, 503-768-6060, Fax: 503-768-6065, E-mail: cpsy@lclark.edu. *Application contact:* Becky Haas, Director of Admissions, 503-768-6200, Fax: 503-768-6205, E-mail: gseadmit@lclark.edu.

Lewis & Clark College, Graduate School of Education and Counseling, Department of Educational Leadership, Program in School Counseling, Portland, OR 97219-7899. Offers M Ed. Part-time and evening/weekend programs available. *Faculty:* 2 full-time (1 woman), 7 part-time/adjunct (5 women). *Students:* 34 full-time (24 women), 31 part-time (24 women); includes 19 minority (4 African Americans, 3 American Indian/Alaska Native, 3 Asian Americans or Pacific Islanders, 9 Hispanic Americans), 1 international. Average age 32. 68 applicants, 51% accepted, 24 enrolled. In 2009, 19 master's awarded. *Entrance requirements:* For master's, minimum undergraduate GPA of 2.75. Additional exam requirements/recommendations for international students: Required—TOEFL (minimum score 575 paper-based; 233 computer-based). *Application deadline:* For fall admission, 2/1 for domestic and international students. Application fee: $50. Electronic applications accepted. *Expenses:* Tuition: Part-time $713 per semester hour. Tuition and fees vary according to course level and campus/location. *Financial support:* In 2009–10, 58 students received support. Career-related internships or fieldwork, Federal Work-Study, institutionally sponsored loans, scholarships/grants, health care benefits, and tuition waivers (partial) available. Support available to part-time students. Financial award application deadline: 3/1; financial award applicants required to submit FAFSA. *Unit head:* Dr. Laura Pedersen, Coordinator, 503-768-6140, Fax: 503-768-6085, E-mail: schcoun@lclark.edu. *Application contact:* Becky Haas, Director of Admissions, 503-768-6200, Fax: 503-768-6205, E-mail: gseadmit@lclark.edu.

Lindenwood University, Graduate Programs, School of Education, St. Charles, MO 63301-1695. Offers education (MA); educational administration (MA, Ed D, Ed S); instructional leadership (Ed D, Ed S); library media (MA); professional and school counseling (MA); professional counseling (MA); school administration (Ed S); school counseling (MA); teaching (MA). Part-time and evening/weekend programs available. *Faculty:* 33 full-time (13 women), 176 part-time/adjunct (83 women). *Students:* 558 full-time (415 women), 1,957 part-time (1,516 women); includes 580 minority (549 African Americans, 6 American Indian/Alaska Native, 16 Asian Americans or Pacific Islanders, 9 Hispanic Americans), 13 international. Average age 35. 248 applicants, 120 enrolled. In 2009, 730 master's, 62 doctorates, 67 other advanced degrees awarded. *Degree requirements:* For master's, thesis (for some programs); for doctorate, thesis/dissertation, minimum GPA of 3.0; for Ed S, comprehensive exam, specialist project, minimum GPA of 3.0. *Entrance requirements:* For master's, interview, minimum GPA of 3.0, writing sample, letter of recommendation; for doctorate, GRE, minimum graduate GPA of 3.4, resume, interview, writing sample, 4 letters of recommendation; for Ed S, master's degree in education, relevant work experience. Additional exam requirements/recommendations for international students: Required—TOEFL (minimum score 550 paper-based; 213 computer-based; 80 iBT). *Application deadline:* For fall admission, 8/27 priority date for domestic and international students; for spring admission, 1/28 priority date for domestic and international students. Applications are processed on a rolling basis. Application fee: $30 ($100 for international students). Electronic applications accepted. *Expenses:* Tuition: Full-time $12,960; part-time $370 per credit hour. Required fees: $340. One-time fee: $30 full-time. Tuition and fees vary according to course level and course load. *Financial support:* In 2009–10, 1,591 students received support. Career-related internships or fieldwork, institutionally sponsored loans, tuition waivers (partial), and unspecified assistantships available. Financial award application deadline: 6/30; financial award applicants required to submit FAFSA. *Unit head:* Dr. Cynthia Bice, Dean, 636-949-4618, Fax: 636-949-4197, E-mail: cbice@lindenwood.edu. *Application contact:* Brett Barger, Dean of Evening Admissions and Extension Campuses, 636-949-4934, Fax: 636-949-4109, E-mail: adultadmissions@lindenwood.edu.

Long Island University, Brooklyn Campus, School of Education, Department of Human Development and Leadership, Program in School Psychology, Brooklyn, NY 11201-8423. Offers MS Ed. Part-time and evening/weekend programs available. *Degree requirements:* For master's, thesis optional. *Entrance requirements:* For master's, 2 letters of recommendation. Additional exam requirements/recommendations for international students: Required—TOEFL (minimum score 500 paper-based; 173 computer-based). Electronic applications accepted.

Long Island University, Westchester Graduate Campus, Programs in Education-School Counselor and School Psychology, Purchase, NY 10577. Offers school counselor (MS Ed); school psychologist (MS Ed). Part-time and evening/weekend programs available.

Louisiana State University and Agricultural and Mechanical College, Graduate School, College of Arts and Sciences, Department of Psychology, Baton Rouge, LA 70803. Offers biological psychology (MA, PhD); clinical psychology (MA, PhD); cognitive psychology (MA, PhD); developmental psychology (MA, PhD); industrial/organizational psychology (MA, PhD); school psychology (MA, PhD). *Accreditation:* APA (one or more programs are accredited). *Faculty:* 27 full-time (10 women). *Students:* 94 full-time (68 women), 17 part-time (12 women); includes 14 minority (6 African Americans, 2 American Indian/Alaska Native, 2 Asian Americans or Pacific Islanders, 4 Hispanic Americans), 3 international. Average age 27. 232 applicants, 18% accepted, 29 enrolled. In 2009, 13 master's, 14 doctorates awarded. Terminal master's awarded for partial completion of doctoral program. *Degree requirements:* For master's, thesis; for doctorate, thesis/dissertation, 1 year internship. *Entrance requirements:* For master's and doctorate, GRE General Test, minimum GPA of 3.0. Additional exam requirements/recommendations for international students: Required—TOEFL (minimum score 550 paper-based; 213 computer-based; 79 iBT) or IELTS (minimum score 6.5). *Application deadline:* For fall admission, 1/15 for domestic and international students. Applications are processed on a rolling basis. Application fee: $50 ($70 for international students). Electronic applications accepted. *Financial support:* In 2009–10, 108 students received support, including 5 fellowships (averaging $26,974 per year), 2 research assistantships with partial tuition reimbursements available (averaging $18,000 per year), 74 teaching assistantships with partial tuition reimbursements available (averaging $14,751 per year); career-related internships or fieldwork, Federal Work-Study, institutionally sponsored loans, scholarships/grants, health care benefits, and tuition waivers (full and partial) also available. Financial award applicants required to submit FAFSA. *Faculty research:* Clinical psychology, autism, anxiety, addition, neuropsychology, school psychology, cognitive psychology, experimental psychology. Total annual research expenditures: $1 million. *Unit head:* Dr. Robert Matthews, Chair, 225-578-8745, Fax: 225-578-4125, E-mail: psmath@lsu.edu. *Application contact:* Dr. Jason Hicks, Coordinator of Graduate Studies, 225-578-4109, Fax: 225-578-4125, E-mail: jhicks@lsu.edu.

Louisiana State University in Shreveport, College of Education and Human Development, Program in School Psychology, Shreveport, LA 71115-2399. Offers SSP. *Students:* 17 full-time (13 women), 11 part-time (9 women); includes 5 minority (all African Americans), 1 international. Average age 28. 15 applicants, 100% accepted, 10 enrolled. In 2009, 6 SSPs awarded. *Entrance requirements:* For degree, GRE General Test, minimum GPA of 2.75. Additional exam requirements/recommendations for international students: Required—TOEFL (minimum score 500 paper-based; 173 computer-based; 61 iBT). *Application deadline:* For fall admission, 6/30 for domestic and international students; for spring admission, 11/30 for domestic and international students. Applications are processed on a rolling basis. Application fee: $10 ($20 for international students). *Financial support:* In 2009–10, 2 research assistantships with partial tuition reimbursements (averaging $10,000 per year) were awarded. Financial award applicants required to submit FAFSA. *Unit head:* Dr. Rebecca Nolan, Program Director, 318-797-5050, E-mail: rnolan@lsus.edu. *Application contact:* Dr. Rebecca Nolan, Program Director, 318-797-5050, E-mail: rnolan@lsus.edu.

Loyola Marymount University, School of Education, Department of Educational Support Services, Program in School Psychology, Los Angeles, CA 90045. Offers MA. Part-time and evening/weekend programs available. *Faculty:* 9 full-time (6 women), 22 part-time/adjunct (19 women). *Students:* 47 full-time (41 women), 1 (woman) part-time; includes 23 minority (5 African Americans, 5 Asian Americans or Pacific Islanders, 13 Hispanic Americans). Average age 25. 59 applicants, 58% accepted, 16 enrolled. In 2009, 11 master's awarded. *Degree requirements:* For master's, comprehensive exam. *Entrance requirements:* For master's, GRE, CBEST, 3 letters of recommendation. Additional exam requirements/recommendations for international students: Required—TOEFL (minimum score 600 paper-based; 250 computer-based; 100 iBT). *Application deadline:* For fall admission, 2/8 for domestic students. Application fee: $50. Electronic applications accepted. *Financial support:* In 2009–10, 41 students received support, including 3 research assistantships (averaging $1,120 per year); scholarships/grants and unspecified assistantships also available. Support available to part-time students. Financial award application deadline: 2/8; financial award applicants required to submit FAFSA. Total annual research expenditures: $5,922. *Unit head:* Dr. Tom Batsis, 310-338-7303, E-mail: tbatsis@lmu.edu. *Application contact:* Chake H. Kouyoumjian, Director, Graduate Admissions, 310-338-2721, Fax: 310-338-6086, E-mail: ckouyoum@lmu.edu.

Loyola University Chicago, School of Education, Program in School Psychology, Chicago, IL 60660. Offers PhD, Ed S. PhD offered through the Graduate School. Part-time and evening/weekend programs available. *Faculty:* 7 full-time (5 women), 6 part-time/adjunct (3 women). *Students:* 63. Average age 28. 147 applicants, 32% accepted, 18 enrolled. In 2009, 3 doctorates, 19 other advanced degrees awarded. Terminal master's awarded for partial completion of doctoral program. *Degree requirements:* For doctorate, comprehensive exam, thesis/dissertation. *Entrance requirements:* For doctorate, GRE, interview, letters of recommendation, minimum GPA of 3.0. Additional exam requirements/recommendations for international students: Required—TOEFL (minimum score 550 paper-based; 213 computer-based; 79 iBT). *Application deadline:* For fall admission, 12/15 for domestic and international students. Application fee: $50. Electronic applications accepted. *Expenses:* Tuition: Full-time $14,220; part-time $790 per credit hour. Required fees: $60 per semester hour. Tuition and fees vary according to program. *Financial support:* In 2009–10, 2 fellowships (averaging $14,000 per year), 9 research assistantships with full tuition reimbursements (averaging $11,000 per year) were awarded; institutionally sponsored loans, scholarships/grants, and tuition waivers (full and partial) also available. Financial award application deadline: 2/15. *Faculty research:* Learning theory and teaching, school reform, instructional intervention, violence prevention, mental health programming in schools and communities. *Unit head:* Dr. Pamela Fenning, Director, 312-915-6803, E-mail: pfennin@luc.edu. *Application contact:* Marie Rosin-Dittmar, Information Contact, 312-915-6800, E-mail: schleduc@luc.edu.

Marist College, Graduate Programs, School of Social and Behavioral Sciences, Poughkeepsie, NY 12601-1387. Offers counseling psychology (MA); education (M Ed); education psychology (MA); school psychology (MA, Adv C). Part-time and evening/weekend programs available. *Degree requirements:* For master's, thesis optional. *Entrance requirements:* For master's, GRE General Test, letters of recommendation, minimum undergraduate GPA of 3.0, interview. Additional exam requirements/recommendations for international students: Required—TOEFL (minimum score 550 paper-based; 213 computer-based; 80 iBT); Recommended—IELTS (minimum score 6.5). Electronic applications accepted. *Expenses:* Tuition: Full-time $12,510; part-time $695 per credit hour. *Faculty research:* AIDS prevention, educational intervention, humanistic counseling research, aging and development, neuroimaging.

Marshall University, Academic Affairs Division, Graduate School of Education and Professional Development, Program in School Psychology, Huntington, WV 25755. Offers Ed S. *Accreditation:* NCATE. Part-time and evening/weekend programs available. *Faculty:* 3 full-time (1 woman), 4 part-time/adjunct (1 woman). *Students:* 28 full-time (24 women), 16 part-time (12 women); includes 1 minority (African American). Average age 28. In 2009, 3 Ed Ss awarded. *Entrance requirements:* For degree, master's degree in psychology. Application fee: $40. *Financial support:* Career-related internships or fieldwork and tuition waivers (full) available. Support available to part-time students. Financial award applicants required to submit FAFSA. *Unit head:* Dr. Fred Kreig, Program Director, 304-746-2067, E-mail: fkreig@marshall.edu. *Application contact:* Information Contact, 304-746-1900, Fax: 304-746-1902, E-mail: services@marshall.edu.

Marywood University, Academic Affairs, Reap College of Education and Human Development, Department of Psychology and Counseling, Program in School Psychology, Scranton, PA 18509-1598. Offers Ed S. *Students:* 15 full-time (14 women), 11 part-time (9 women); includes 2 minority (1 American Indian/Alaska Native, 1 Hispanic American). Average age 27. In 2009, 9 Ed Ss awarded. *Entrance requirements:* Additional exam requirements/recommendations for international students: Required—TOEFL (minimum score 550 paper-based; 213 computer-based; 79 iBT). *Application deadline:* For fall admission, 1/16 priority date for domestic and international students. Application fee: $35. Electronic applications accepted. *Expenses:* Tuition: Part-time $715 per credit. Required fees: $270 per semester. Tuition and fees vary according to degree level, campus/location and program. *Financial support:* Career-related internships or fieldwork, scholarships/grants, and unspecified assistantships available. Support available to part-time students. Financial award application deadline: 6/30; financial award applicants required to submit FAFSA. *Unit head:* Dr. Edward Crawley, Chairperson, 570-348-6211 Ext. 2325, E-mail: crawley@marywood.edu. *Application contact:* Tammy Manka, Assistant Director of Graduate Admissions, 866-279-9663, E-mail: tmanka@marywood.edu.

Massachusetts School of Professional Psychology, Graduate Programs, Boston, MA 02132. Offers clinical psychology (Psy D); clinical psychopharmacology (Post-Doctoral MS); counseling psychology (MA); executive coaching (Graduate Certificate); forensic psychology (MA); organizational psychology (MA); respecialization in clinical psychology (Certificate); MA/CAGS. *Accreditation:* APA. *Degree requirements:* For master's, comprehensive exam; for doctorate, thesis/dissertation. *Entrance requirements:* For doctorate, GRE General Test. Additional exam requirements/recommendations for international students: Required—TOEFL (minimum score 550 paper-based; 213 computer-based). Electronic applications accepted.

McGill University, Faculty of Graduate and Postdoctoral Studies, Faculty of Education, Department of Educational and Counseling Psychology, Montréal, QC H3A 2T5, Canada. Offers counseling psychology (MA, PhD); educational psychology (M Ed, MA, PhD); school/applied child psychology and applied developmental psychology (M Ed, MA, PhD, Diploma), including school psychology. *Accreditation:* APA.

McNeese State University, Doré School of Graduate Studies, Burton College of Education, Department of Teacher Education, Program in School Counseling, Lake Charles, LA 70609. Offers M Ed. *Accreditation:* NCATE. Evening/weekend programs available. *Faculty:* 2 full-time (both women). *Students:* 7 full-time (all women), 20 part-time (18 women); includes 7 minority (all African Americans). In 2009, 6 master's awarded. *Entrance requirements:* For master's, GRE, 18 hours in professional education. *Application deadline:* For fall admission, 5/15 priority

School Psychology

McNeese State University (continued)
date for domestic and international students; for spring admission, 10/15 priority date for domestic and international students. Applications are processed on a rolling basis. Application fee: $20 ($30 for international students). *Expenses:* Tuition, area resident: Full-time $2556. Tuition, state resident: full-time $2556. Required fees: $1031. Tuition and fees vary according to course load. *Financial support:* Application deadline: 5/1. *Unit head:* Dr. Royce Zant, Head, 337-475-5404, Fax: 337-475-5398, E-mail: rzant@mcneese.edu. *Application contact:* Dr. George F. Mead, Interim Dean of Dore' School of Graduate Studies, 337-475-5396, Fax: 337-475-5397, E-mail: admissions@mcneese.edu.

Mercy College, School of Social and Behavioral Sciences, Program in School Psychology, Dobbs Ferry, NY 10522-1189. Offers MS. Part-time and evening/weekend programs available. *Students:* 30 full-time (27 women), 30 part-time (29 women); includes 34 minority (8 African Americans, 1 American Indian/Alaska Native, 2 Asian Americans or Pacific Islanders, 23 Hispanic Americans), 3 international. Average age 30. 64 applicants, 39% accepted, 14 enrolled. In 2009, 6 master's awarded. *Degree requirements:* For master's, practica, fieldwork, internship, integrative project. *Entrance requirements:* For master's, current resume; interview; written recommendation from 3 instructors; bachelor's degree with a major in psychology, sociology, behavioral science, or education. Additional exam requirements/recommendations for international students: Required—TOEFL (minimum score 600 paper-based; 250 computer-based; 100 iBT). *Application deadline:* For fall admission, 8/1 for international students. Applications are processed on a rolling basis. Application fee: $40. Electronic applications accepted. *Expenses:* Tuition: Full-time $13,158; part-time $731 per credit. Required fees: $500. Tuition and fees vary according to degree level and program. *Financial support:* In 2009–10, 1 student received support. Career-related internships or fieldwork, Federal Work-Study, scholarships/grants, and unspecified assistantships available. Support available to part-time students. Financial award applicants required to submit FAFSA. *Faculty research:* Consultation, effective intervention and prevention practices, psychology. *Unit head:* Dr. Jeffrey Cohen, Program Director, 914-674-7503, E-mail: jcohen@mercy.edu. *Application contact:* Dr. Jeffrey Cohen, Program Director, 914-674-7503, E-mail: jcohen@mercy.edu.

Miami University, Graduate School, School of Education and Allied Professions, Department of Educational Psychology, Oxford, OH 45056. Offers educational psychology (M Ed); instructional design and technology (M Ed, MA); school psychology (MS, Ed S); special education (M Ed). *Accreditation:* NCATE. *Students:* 39 full-time (34 women), 42 part-time (39 women); includes 5 minority (2 African Americans, 2 Asian Americans or Pacific Islanders, 1 Hispanic American), 9 international. *Entrance requirements:* For master's, GRE General Test or MAT, minimum undergraduate GPA of 3.0 during previous 2 years or 2.75 overall; for Ed S, GRE General Test or MAT. Additional exam requirements/recommendations for international students: Required—TOEFL. Application fee: $50. *Expenses:* Tuition, state resident: full-time $11,280. Tuition, nonresident: full-time $24,912. Required fees: $516. *Financial support:* Fellowships with full tuition reimbursements, research assistantships with full tuition reimbursements, teaching assistantships with full tuition reimbursements, career-related internships or fieldwork, Federal Work-Study, health care benefits, tuition waivers (full), and unspecified assistantships available. Financial award application deadline: 3/1. *Unit head:* Dr. Nelda Cambron-McCabe, Chair, 513-529-6836, Fax: 513-529-6621, E-mail: edp@muohio.edu. *Application contact:* Dr. Nelda Cambron-McCabe, Chair, 513-529-6836, Fax: 513-529-6621, E-mail: edp@muohio.edu.

Michigan State University, The Graduate School, College of Education, Department of Counseling, Educational Psychology and Special Education, East Lansing, MI 48824. Offers counseling (MA); educational psychology and educational technology (PhD); educational technology (MA); measurement and quantitative methods (PhD); rehabilitation counseling (MA); rehabilitation counselor education (PhD); school psychology (MA, PhD, Ed S); special education (MA, PhD). *Accreditation:* APA (one or more programs are accredited); CORE (one or more programs are accredited). Part-time programs available. *Faculty:* 35 full-time (13 women). *Students:* 217 full-time (154 women), 144 part-time (107 women); includes 48 minority (25 African Americans, 13 Asian Americans or Pacific Islanders, 10 Hispanic Americans), 71 international. Average age 32. 238 applicants, 46% accepted. In 2009, 117 master's, 36 doctorates awarded. *Entrance requirements:* Additional exam requirements/recommendations for international students: Required—TOEFL. Electronic applications accepted. *Expenses:* Tuition, state resident: part-time $478.25 per credit hour. Tuition, nonresident: part-time $966.50 per credit hour. Part-time tuition and fees vary according to program. *Financial support:* In 2009–10, 71 research assistantships with tuition reimbursements (averaging $6,836 per year), 74 teaching assistantships with tuition reimbursements (averaging $6,858 per year) were awarded. Total annual research expenditures: $2.3 million. *Unit head:* Dr. Richard S. Prawat, Chairperson, 517-353-6417, Fax: 517-353-6393, E-mail: rsprawat@msu.edu. *Application contact:* Kathy Dimoff, Graduate Admissions Coordinator, 517-355-6683, Fax: 517-353-6393, E-mail: dimoff@msu.edu.

Middle Tennessee State University, College of Graduate Studies, College of Education and Behavioral Science, Department of Psychology, Program in Professional Counseling, Murfreesboro, TN 37132. Offers curriculum and instruction (Ed S), including school psychology; mental health counseling (M Ed); school counseling (M Ed). *Accreditation:* ACA; NCATE. Part-time and evening/weekend programs available. Postbaccalaureate distance learning degree programs offered. *Students:* 66 part-time (57 women); includes 6 minority (5 African Americans, 1 Asian American or Pacific Islander). 35 applicants, 69% accepted, 24 enrolled. In 2009, 27 master's, 7 other advanced degrees awarded. *Degree requirements:* For master's, comprehensive exam. *Entrance requirements:* For master's, GRE or MAT. Additional exam requirements/recommendations for international students: Required—TOEFL (minimum score 525 paper-based; 195 computer-based; 71 iBT) or IELTS (minimum score 6). *Application deadline:* For fall admission, 6/1 for domestic and international students. Applications are processed on a rolling basis. Application fee: $25 ($30 for international students). Electronic applications accepted. *Expenses:* Tuition, state resident: full-time $4404. Tuition, nonresident: full-time $10,956. *Financial support:* Application deadline: 5/1. *Application contact:* Dr. Michael Allen, Dean and Vice Provost for Research, 615-898-2840, Fax: 615-904-8020, E-mail: mallen@mtsu.edu.

Millersville University of Pennsylvania, College of Graduate and Professional Studies, School of Education, Department of Psychology, Program in Psychology, Millersville, PA 17551-0302. Offers clinical psychology (MS); school psychology (MS). Part-time programs available. *Faculty:* 18 full-time (12 women), 9 part-time/adjunct (5 women). *Students:* 48 full-time (39 women), 46 part-time (42 women); includes 4 minority (3 African Americans, 1 Hispanic American), 1 international. Average age 29. 68 applicants, 54% accepted, 24 enrolled. In 2009, 29 master's awarded. *Degree requirements:* For master's, comprehensive exam, thesis optional. *Entrance requirements:* For master's, GRE, 3 letters of recommendation; interview (in-person). Additional exam requirements/recommendations for international students: Required—TOEFL (minimum score 500 paper-based; 183 computer-based; 65 iBT) or IELTS (minimum score 6). *Application deadline:* For fall admission, 1/15 for domestic and international students; for winter admission, 10/1 for domestic and international students; for spring admission, 10/1 for domestic and international students. Application fee: $40 ($50 for international students). Electronic applications accepted. *Expenses:* Tuition, state resident: full-time $6666; part-time $370 per credit. Tuition, nonresident: full-time $10,666; part-time $593 per credit. Required fees: $1578.50; $76.25 per credit. One-time fee: $60 part-time. Tuition and fees vary according to course load. *Financial support:* In 2009–10, 43 students received support, including 43 research assistantships with full and partial tuition reimbursements available (averaging $4,059 per year); institutionally sponsored loans and unspecified assistantships also available. Support available to part-time students. Financial award application deadline: 3/15; financial award applicants required to submit FAFSA. *Faculty research:* Parenting and alcohol risk, time perceptions, time management, stress and coping, autism and behavioral disorders. *Unit head:* Dr. Claudia Haferkamp, Director of Clinical Psychology Program, 717-872-3826, Fax: 717-871-2480, E-mail: claudia.haferkamp@millersville.edu. *Application contact:* Dr. Victor S. DeSantis, Dean of Graduate and Professional Studies, 717-872-3099, Fax: 717-872-3453, E-mail: victor.desantis@millersville.edu.

Millersville University of Pennsylvania, College of Graduate and Professional Studies, School of Education, Department of Psychology, Program in School Counseling, Millersville, PA 17551-0302. Offers M Ed. *Accreditation:* NCATE. Part-time programs available. *Faculty:* 18 full-time (12 women), 9 part-time/adjunct (5 women). *Students:* 6 full-time (5 women), 33 part-time (27 women); includes 3 minority (1 Asian American or Pacific Islander, 2 Hispanic Americans). Average age 30. 13 applicants, 23% accepted, 3 enrolled. In 2009, 17 master's awarded. *Degree requirements:* For master's, comprehensive exam, thesis optional. *Entrance requirements:* For master's, GRE, 3 letters of recommendation, interview (in-person). Additional exam requirements/recommendations for international students: Required—TOEFL (minimum score 500 paper-based; 183 computer-based; 65 iBT) or IELTS (minimum score 6). *Application deadline:* For fall admission, 1/15 for domestic and international students; for winter admission, 10/1 for domestic and international students; for spring admission, 10/1 for domestic and international students. Application fee: $40 ($50 for international students). Electronic applications accepted. *Expenses:* Tuition, state resident: full-time $6666; part-time $370 per credit. Tuition, nonresident: full-time $10,666; part-time $593 per credit. Required fees: $1578.50; $76.25 per credit. One-time fee: $60 part-time. Tuition and fees vary according to course load. *Financial support:* In 2009–10, 11 students received support, including 11 research assistantships with full and partial tuition reimbursements available (averaging $3,811 per year); institutionally sponsored loans and unspecified assistantships also available. Support available to part-time students. Financial award application deadline: 3/15; financial award applicants required to submit FAFSA. *Faculty research:* Solution-focused counseling, sustainability, technology in counseling. *Unit head:* Dr. Nadine E. Garner, Coordinator, 717-872-3097, Fax: 717-871-2480, E-mail: nadine.garner@millersville.edu. *Application contact:* Dr. Victor S. DeSantis, Dean of Graduate and Professional Studies, 717-872-3099, Fax: 717-872-3453, E-mail: victor.desantis@millersville.edu.

Minnesota State University Mankato, College of Graduate Studies, College of Social and Behavioral Sciences, Department of Psychology, Mankato, MN 56001. Offers clinical psychology (MA); industrial/organizational psychology (MA); school psychology (Psy D). Part-time programs available. *Students:* 51 full-time (32 women), 3 part-time (1 woman). *Degree requirements:* For master's, one foreign language, comprehensive exam, thesis (for some programs). *Entrance requirements:* For master's, GRE General Test, GRE Subject Test (clinical psychology), minimum GPA of 3.0 during previous 2 years, 3 letters of reference. Additional exam requirements/recommendations for international students: Required—TOEFL. *Application deadline:* For fall admission, 1/1 priority date for domestic students. Applications are processed on a rolling basis. Application fee: $40. Electronic applications accepted. *Expenses:* Tuition, state resident: full-time $5364. Tuition, nonresident: full-time $8314. *Financial support:* Research assistantships, teaching assistantships with full tuition reimbursements, career-related internships or fieldwork, Federal Work-Study, institutionally sponsored loans, and unspecified assistantships available. Support available to part-time students. Financial award application deadline: 3/15; financial award applicants required to submit FAFSA. *Faculty research:* Professional competency in hospitals, mood disturbance, 360-degree feedback, employee selection, planning fallacy. *Unit head:* Dr. Barry Ries, Chairperson, 507-389-2724. *Application contact:* 507-389-2321, E-mail: grad@mnsu.edu.

Minnesota State University Moorhead, Graduate Studies, College of Social and Natural Sciences, Program in School Psychology, Moorhead, MN 56563-0002. Offers MS, Psy S. *Accreditation:* NCATE (one or more programs are accredited). *Degree requirements:* For master's, thesis, final oral and written comprehensive exams. *Entrance requirements:* For master's, GRE General Test, interview, minimum GPA of 3.0, 3 letters of recommendation; for Psy S, MS in school psychology. Additional exam requirements/recommendations for international students: Required—TOEFL (minimum score 550 paper-based; 213 computer-based). Electronic applications accepted.

Minot State University, Graduate School, Program in School Psychology, Minot, ND 58707-0002. Offers Ed Sp. *Entrance requirements:* For degree, GRE General Test, minimum GPA of 3.0. Additional exam requirements/recommendations for international students: Required—TOEFL. *Expenses:* Tuition, state resident: full-time $5720; part-time $283 per credit hour. Tuition, nonresident: full-time $5720; part-time $283 per credit hour. Required fees: $1034; $1034 per year. Tuition and fees vary according to course load, degree level and program. *Faculty research:* Oppositional defiance disorder and autism, experimental psychology, statistical genetics, adults with developmental disabilities, psychopharmacology.

Mississippi State University, College of Education, Department of Counseling and Educational Psychology, Mississippi State, MS 39762. Offers college/postsecondary student counseling and personnel services (PhD); counselor education (MS); counselor education/student counseling and guidance services (PhD); education (Ed S), including counselor education, school psychology; educational psychology (MS, PhD). *Accreditation:* ACA (one or more programs are accredited); APA; CORE (one or more programs are accredited); NCATE. Part-time programs available. Postbaccalaureate distance learning degree programs offered (minimal on-campus study). *Faculty:* 14 full-time (10 women), 1 (woman) part-time/adjunct. *Students:* 116 full-time (95 women), 99 part-time (84 women); includes 63 minority (57 African Americans, 2 American Indian/Alaska Native, 2 Asian Americans or Pacific Islanders, 2 Hispanic Americans), 3 international. Average age 32. 154 applicants, 62% accepted, 69 enrolled. In 2009, 56 master's, 9 doctorates, 17 other advanced degrees awarded. Terminal master's awarded for partial completion of doctoral program. *Degree requirements:* For master's, comprehensive exam, thesis optional; for doctorate, thesis/dissertation, comprehensive oral and written exam. *Entrance requirements:* For master's, GRE, minimum QPA of 3.0; for doctorate, GRE, interview, minimum GPA of 3.4; for Ed S, GRE, MS in counseling or related field. Additional exam requirements/recommendations for international students: Required—TOEFL (minimum score 475 paper-based; 153 computer-based; 53 iBT); Recommended—IELTS (minimum score 4.5). *Application deadline:* For fall admission, 2/1 priority date for domestic and international students. Applications are processed on a rolling basis. Application fee: $40. Electronic applications accepted. *Expenses:* Tuition, state resident: full-time $2575.50; part-time $286.25 per credit hour. Tuition, nonresident: full-time $6510; part-time $723.50 per credit hour. Tuition and fees vary according to course load. *Financial support:* In 2009–10, 4 teaching assistantships with full tuition reimbursements (averaging $8,603 per year) were awarded; career-related internships or fieldwork, Federal Work-Study, institutionally sponsored loans, and unspecified assistantships also available. Financial award application deadline: 2/1; financial award applicants required to submit FAFSA. *Faculty research:* HIV-AIDS in college population, substance abuse in youth and college students, ADHD and conduct disorders in youth, assessment and identification of early childhood disabilities, assessment and vocational transition of the disabled. *Unit head:* Dr. Daniel Wong, Professor/Head, 662-325-7928, Fax: 662-325-3263, E-mail: dwong@colled.msstate.edu. *Application contact:* Dr. Tony Doggett, Associate Professor and Graduate Coordinator, 662-325-3312, Fax: 662-325-3263, E-mail: tdoggett@colled.msstate.edu.

Montana State University, College of Graduate Studies, College of Education, Health, and Human Development, Department of Education, Bozeman, MT 59717. Offers adult and higher education (Ed D); curriculum and instruction (Ed D, Ed S); education (M Ed), including adult and higher education, curriculum and instruction, educational leadership, school counseling; educational leadership (Ed D, Ed S). Part-time programs available. Postbaccalaureate distance learning degree programs offered (minimal on-campus study). *Faculty:* 22 full-time (13 women), 18 part-time/adjunct (14 women). *Students:* 15 full-time (8 women), 210 part-time (126 women); includes 29 minority (27 American Indian/Alaska Native, 1 Asian American or Pacific Islander, 1 Hispanic American), 2 international. Average age 37. 52 applicants. In 2009, 62 master's, 9 doctorates awarded. *Degree requirements:* For master's, comprehensive exam; for doctorate, comprehensive exam, thesis/dissertation. *Entrance requirements:* For master's and doctorate, GRE General Test. Additional exam requirements/recommendations for international students: Required—TOEFL (minimum score 550 paper-based; 213 computer-based). *Application* *deadline:* For fall admission, 7/15 priority date for domestic students, 5/15 priority date for international students; for spring admission, 12/1 priority date for domestic students, 10/1 priority date for international students. Applications are processed on a rolling basis. Application fee: $30. Electronic applications accepted. *Expenses:* Tuition, state resident: full-time $5635; part-time $3492 per year. Tuition, nonresident: full-time $17,212; part-time $7865.10 per year. Required fees: $1441; $153.15 per credit. Tuition and fees vary according to course load and program. *Financial support:* In 2009–10, 45 students received support, including 5 teaching assistantships with tuition reimbursements available (averaging $9,000 per year); traineeships, tuition waivers (full and partial), and unspecified assistantships also available. Financial award application deadline: 3/1; financial award applicants required to submit FAFSA. *Faculty research:* Online teaching and learning, statistical strategies to course and student assessment, environmental education, copyright issues/web-based resources, multicultural education, curriculum design, preparation for North American teachers to be administrators, NCES data sets, relational trust in public school administration. Total annual research expenditures: $1.2 million. *Unit head:* Dr. Joanne Erickson, Interim Department Head, 406-994-6670, Fax: 406-994-3261, E-mail: jle@montana.edu. *Application contact:* Dr. Carl A. Fox, Vice Provost for Graduate Education, 406-994-4145, Fax: 406-994-7433, E-mail: gradstudy@montana.edu.

Montclair State University, The Graduate School, College of Humanities and Social Sciences, Department of Psychology, Montclair, NJ 07043-1624. Offers educational psychology (MA), including child/adolescent clinical psychology, clinical psychology for Spanish/English bilinguals; psychology (MA, Certificate), including industrial and organizational psychology (MA); school psychologist (Certificate). Part-time and evening/weekend programs available. *Faculty:* 29 full-time (14 women), 26 part-time/adjunct (14 women). *Students:* 37 full-time (27 women), 33 part-time (23 women). Average age 27. 72 applicants, 47% accepted, 20 enrolled. In 2009, 7 master's awarded. *Degree requirements:* For master's, comprehensive exam, thesis or alternative. *Entrance requirements:* For master's, GRE General Test, 2 letters of recommendation. Additional exam requirements/recommendations for international students: Required—TOEFL (minimum score 83 computer-based), or IELTS. *Application deadline:* For fall admission, 2/1 for domestic and international students; for spring admission, 10/1 for domestic and international students. Applications are processed on a rolling basis. Application fee: $60. Electronic applications accepted. *Expenses:* Tuition, area resident: Part-time $486.74 per credit. Tuition, state resident: part-time $486.74 per credit. Tuition, nonresident: part-time $751.34 per credit. Tuition and fees vary according to degree level and program. *Financial support:* In 2009–10, 17 research assistantships with full tuition reimbursements (averaging $7,000 per year) were awarded; Federal Work-Study, scholarships/grants, and unspecified assistantships also available. Support available to part-time students. Financial award application deadline: 3/1; financial award applicants required to submit FAFSA. *Faculty research:* Engaged learning, academic and civic development. Total annual research expenditures: $10,000. *Unit head:* Dr. Peter Vietze, Chairperson, 973-655-5201. *Application contact:* Amy Aiello, Director of Admissions and Operations, 973-655-5147, Fax: 973-655-7869, E-mail: graduate.school@montclair.edu.

Mount Saint Vincent University, Graduate Programs, Faculty of Education, Program in School Psychology, Halifax, NS B3M 2J6, Canada. Offers MASP. *Degree requirements:* For master's, thesis, 500 hour practicum. *Entrance requirements:* For master's, bachelor's degree in psychology or equivalent, related work experience. Electronic applications accepted. *Faculty research:* Relationship between cognitive and emotional development, expression of emotions, cognitive-behavioral constituents of racism.

National-Louis University, National College of Education, Doctoral Programs in Education, Program in Educational Psychology/School Psychology, Chicago, IL 60603. Offers Ed D. Part-time and evening/weekend programs available. *Degree requirements:* For doctorate, comprehensive exam, thesis/dissertation, internship. *Entrance requirements:* For doctorate, GRE General Test, minimum GPA of 3.25, interview, resume, writing sample. *Expenses:* Tuition: Full-time $17,160; part-time $715 per semester hour. Tuition and fees vary according to course load, degree level, campus/location and program.

National-Louis University, National College of Education, Programs in School Psychology, Chicago, IL 60603. Offers M Ed, Ed S. *Degree requirements:* For master's and Ed S, internship. *Entrance requirements:* For master's, GRE or MAT, minimum GPA of 3.0; for Ed S, GRE, interview, master's degree, writing sample. *Expenses:* Tuition: Full-time $17,160; part-time $715 per semester hour. Tuition and fees vary according to course load, degree level, campus/location and program.

National University, Academic Affairs, School of Education, Department of School Counseling and Psychology, La Jolla, CA 92037-1011. Offers educational counseling (MS); school psychology (MS). Part-time and evening/weekend programs available. Postbaccalaureate distance learning degree programs offered (no on-campus study). *Faculty:* 12 full-time (5 women), 82 part-time/adjunct (49 women). *Students:* 657 full-time (529 women), 565 part-time (451 women); includes 556 minority (131 African Americans, 6 American Indian/Alaska Native, 89 Asian Americans or Pacific Islanders, 330 Hispanic Americans), 1 international. Average age 34. 566 applicants, 100% accepted, 366 enrolled. In 2009, 121 master's awarded. *Degree requirements:* For master's, thesis (for some programs). *Entrance requirements:* For master's, interview, minimum GPA of 2.5. Additional exam requirements/recommendations for international students: Required—TOEFL (minimum score 550 paper-based; 213 computer-based; 79 iBT), IELTS (minimum score 6). *Application deadline:* Applications are processed on a rolling basis. Application fee: $60 ($65 for international students). Electronic applications accepted. *Expenses:* Tuition: Part-time $338 per quarter hour. *Financial support:* Career-related internships or fieldwork, institutionally sponsored loans, scholarships/grants, and tuition waivers (partial) available. Support available to part-time students. Financial award application deadline: 6/30; financial award applicants required to submit FAFSA. *Unit head:* Dr. Susan Eldred, Chair, 858-642-8372, Fax: 858-642-8724, E-mail: seldred@nu.edu. *Application contact:* Dominick Giovanniello, Associate Regional Dean—San Diego, 800-NAT-UNIV, Fax: 858-541-7792, E-mail: dgiovann@nu.edu.

New Jersey City University, Graduate Studies and Continuing Education, William J. Maxwell College of Arts and Sciences, Program in Educational Psychology, Jersey City, NJ 07305-1597. Offers educational psychology (MA); school psychology (PD). Part-time and evening/weekend programs available. *Faculty:* 9. *Students:* 12 full-time (11 women), 13 part-time (11 women); includes 14 minority (2 African Americans, 3 Asian Americans or Pacific Islanders, 9 Hispanic Americans), 1 international. Average age 30. In 2009, 12 master's, 5 other advanced degrees awarded. *Degree requirements:* For PD, summer internship or externship. *Entrance requirements:* For master's, GRE General Test or MAT; for PD, GRE General Test. Additional exam requirements/recommendations for international students: Required—TOEFL. *Application deadline:* For fall admission, 8/1 priority date for domestic students; for spring admission, 12/1 for domestic students. Applications are processed on a rolling basis. Application fee: $0. *Expenses:* Tuition, area resident: Part-time $456.75 per credit. Tuition, nonresident: part-time $842.55 per credit. Required fees: $65 per term. *Financial support:* Unspecified assistantships available. *Unit head:* Dr. James Lennon, Director, 201-200-3309, E-mail: jlennon@njcu.edu. *Application contact:* Dr. James Lennon, Director, 201-200-3309, E-mail: jlennon@njcu.edu.

New Jersey City University, Graduate Studies and Continuing Education, William J. Maxwell College of Arts and Sciences, Program in School Psychology, Jersey City, NJ 07305-1597. Offers PD. Part-time and evening/weekend programs available. *Students:* 22 full-time (19 women), 14 part-time (11 women); includes 5 minority (2 African Americans, 3 Hispanic Americans). *Entrance requirements:* Additional exam requirements/recommendations for international students: Required—TOEFL. *Expenses:* Tuition, area resident: Part-time $456.75 per credit. Tuition, nonresident: part-time $842.55 per credit. Required fees: $65 per term. *Unit head:* Dr. James Lennon, Director, 201-200-3309, E-mail: jlennon@njcu.edu. *Application contact:* Dr. James Lennon, Director, 201-200-3309, E-mail: jlennon@njcu.edu.

New Mexico Highlands University, Graduate Studies, School of Education, Las Vegas, NM 87701. Offers curriculum and instruction (MA); education (MA), including counseling, school counseling; educational leadership (MA); exercise and sport sciences (MA), including human performance and sport, sports administration, teacher education; guidance and counseling (MA), including professional counseling, rehabilitation counseling, school counseling; special education (MA), including). Part-time programs available. *Degree requirements:* For master's, comprehensive exam, thesis or alternative. *Entrance requirements:* For master's, minimum undergraduate GPA of 3.0. Additional exam requirements/recommendations for international students: Required—TOEFL (minimum score 540 paper-based; 207 computer-based). *Faculty research:* Teaching the United States Constitution, middle school curriculum, integrated computer applications for pre-service classroom teachers, adolescent literacy, narrative cognitive modes in NM multicultural setting.

New Mexico State University, Graduate School, College of Education, Department of Counseling and Educational Psychology, Las Cruces, NM 88003-8001. Offers counseling and guidance (MA); counseling psychology (PhD); school psychology (Ed S). *Accreditation:* ACA; APA (one or more programs are accredited); NCATE. Part-time programs available. *Faculty:* 12 full-time (8 women), 4 part-time/adjunct (2 women). *Students:* 70 full-time (52 women), 34 part-time (27 women); includes 52 minority (3 African Americans, 2 American Indian/Alaska Native, 1 Asian American or Pacific Islander, 46 Hispanic Americans), 2 international. Average age 32. 111 applicants, 88% accepted, 35 enrolled. In 2009, 13 master's, 3 doctorates, 5 other advanced degrees awarded. *Degree requirements:* For master's, comprehensive exam, thesis optional, internship; for doctorate, comprehensive exam, thesis/dissertation, internship; for Ed S, thesis or alternative, internship. *Entrance requirements:* For master's, doctorate, and Ed S, GRE General Test, minimum GPA of 3.0. *Application deadline:* For fall admission, 12/15 for domestic students; for spring admission, 4/1 priority date for domestic students. Application fee: $30 ($50 for international students). Electronic applications accepted. *Expenses:* Tuition, state resident: full-time $4080; part-time $223 per credit. Tuition, nonresident: full-time $14,256; part-time $647 per credit. Required fees: $1278; $639 per semester. *Financial support:* In 2009–10, 13 research assistantships with partial tuition reimbursements (averagihg $8,108 per year), 32 teaching assistantships with partial tuition reimbursements (averaging $8,239 per year) were awarded; fellowships with partial tuition reimbursements, career-related internships or fieldwork, Federal Work-Study, institutionally sponsored loans, scholarships/grants, traineeships, health care benefits, and unspecified assistantships also available. Support available to part-time students. Financial award application deadline: 4/1. *Faculty research:* Multicultural counseling, integrative health psychology group, career development school counseling. *Unit head:* Dr. Michael Waldo, Head, 575-646-2121, Fax: 575-646-8035, E-mail: miwaldo@nmsu.edu. *Application contact:* Elena Luna, Coordinator, 575-646-3498, Fax: 575-646-7721, E-mail: rosluna@nmsu.edu.

Niagara University, Graduate Division of Education, Concentration in School Psychology, Niagara Falls, Niagara University, NY 14109. Offers MS, Certificate.

Nicholls State University, Graduate Studies, College of Education, Department of Psychology and Counselor Education, Thibodaux, LA 70310. Offers psychological counseling (MA); school psychology (SSP). *Accreditation:* NCATE. Part-time and evening/weekend programs available. *Degree requirements:* For master's, comprehensive exam; for SSP, comprehensive exam, internship. *Entrance requirements:* For master's, GRE General Test. Electronic applications accepted.

North Carolina State University, Graduate School, College of Humanities and Social Sciences, Department of Psychology, Raleigh, NC 27695. Offers developmental psychology (PhD); ergonomics and experimental psychology (PhD); industrial/organizational psychology (PhD); psychology in the public interest (PhD); school psychology (PhD). *Accreditation:* APA. *Degree requirements:* For doctorate, comprehensive exam, thesis/dissertation. *Entrance requirements:* For doctorate, GRE General Test, GRE Subject Test (industrial/organizational psychology), MAT (recommended), minimum GPA of 3.0 in major. Electronic applications accepted. *Faculty research:* Cognitive and social development (human factors, families, the workplace, community issues and health, aging).

Northeastern University, Bouvé College of Health Sciences Graduate School, Department of Counseling and Applied Educational Psychology, Program in School Psychology, Boston, MA 02115-5096. Offers PhD, CAGS. *Accreditation:* APA (one or more programs are accredited). Part-time programs available. *Faculty:* 4 full-time (2 women), 3 part-time/adjunct (all women). *Students:* 45 full-time (40 women); includes 1 Asian American or Pacific Islander. Average age 29. 153 applicants, 41% accepted, 22 enrolled. *Degree requirements:* For doctorate, comprehensive exam, thesis/dissertation, qualifying exams; for CAGS, comprehensive exam. *Entrance requirements:* For doctorate, GRE General Test, school psychologist certificate; for CAGS, GRE General Test or MAT, MS in school psychology or related field. Additional exam requirements/recommendations for international students: Required—TOEFL (minimum score 100 iBT). *Application deadline:* For fall admission, 5/1 for domestic students. Application fee: $50. Electronic applications accepted. *Financial support:* Research assistantships, teaching assistantships, career-related internships or fieldwork, Federal Work-Study, tuition waivers (partial), and unspecified assistantships available. Financial award application deadline: 3/1; financial award applicants required to submit FAFSA. *Faculty research:* Multicultural education, early intervention. *Unit head:* Louis J. Kruger, Director, 617-373-5897, E-mail: l.kruger@neu.edu. *Application contact:* Margaret Schnabel, Director of Graduate Admissions, 617-373-2708, E-mail: bouvegrad@neu.edu.

Northern Arizona University, Graduate College, College of Education, Program in Educational Psychology, Flagstaff, AZ 86011. Offers counseling psychology (PhD); learning and instruction (PhD); school psychology (PhD). *Faculty:* 20 full-time (10 women). *Students:* 13 full-time (9 women), 14 part-time (8 women); includes 5 minority (3 American Indian/Alaska Native, 1 Asian American or Pacific Islander, 1 Hispanic American). Average age 35. 14 applicants, 29% accepted, 4 enrolled. In 2009, 7 doctorates awarded. *Degree requirements:* For doctorate, comprehensive exam, thesis/dissertation, internship. *Entrance requirements:* For doctorate, GRE (verbal and quantitative). Additional exam requirements/recommendations for international students: Required—TOEFL (minimum score 550 paper-based; 213 computer-based; 80 iBT), IELTS (minimum score 7), or a bachelor's degree from an English-speaking university and demonstrated proficiency. *Application deadline:* For fall admission, 1/15 priority date for domestic students, 9/1 priority date for international students; for spring admission, 9/15 priority date for domestic students. Application fee: $65. Electronic applications accepted. *Financial support:* In 2009–10, 2 research assistantships with partial tuition reimbursements (averaging $10,000 per year), 8 teaching assistantships with partial tuition reimbursements (averaging $10,000 per year) were awarded; career-related internships or fieldwork, Federal Work-Study, health care benefits, tuition waivers, and unspecified assistantships also available. Support available to part-time students. Financial award application deadline: 3/30; financial award applicants required to submit FAFSA. *Unit head:* Dr. Kathy Bohan, Chair, 928-523-0362, Fax: 928-523-9284, E-mail: kathy.bohan@nau.edu. *Application contact:* Dr. Kathy Bohan, Chair, 928-523-0362, Fax: 928-523-9284, E-mail: kathy.bohan@nau.edu.

Northern Arizona University, Graduate College, College of Education, Program in School Psychology, Flagstaff, AZ 86011. Offers MA. *Faculty:* 20 full-time (10 women). *Students:* 12 full-time (8 women), 4 part-time (3 women); includes 3 minority (1 African American, 1 American Indian/Alaska Native, 1 Hispanic American), 1 international. Average age 32. 30 applicants, 67% accepted, 5 enrolled. In 2009, 11 master's awarded. *Degree requirements:* For master's, internship. *Entrance requirements:* For master's, GRE (verbal and quantitative). Additional exam requirements/recommendations for international students: Required—TOEFL (minimum score 550 paper-based; 213 computer-based; 80 iBT), IELTS (minimum score 7), or a bachelor's degree from an English-speaking university and demonstrated proficiency. *Application deadline:* For fall admission, 2/15 for domestic students, 9/1 for international students; for spring admission, 9/15 for domestic students. Application fee: $65. Electronic applications accepted. *Financial support:* Research assistantships with partial tuition reimbursements, teaching assistantships with partial tuition reimbursements, scholarships/grants, tuition waivers, and unspecified assistantships available. Financial award application deadline: 3/30. *Unit head:* Dr. Kathy

School Psychology

Northern Arizona University (continued)
Bohan, Chair, 928-523-0362, Fax: 928-523-9284, E-mail: kathy.bohan@nau.edu. *Application contact:* Dr. Kathy Bohan, Chair, 928-523-0362, Fax: 928-523-9284, E-mail: kathy.bohan@nau.edu.

Northwest Nazarene University, Graduate Studies, Program in Counselor Education, Nampa, ID 83686-5897. Offers community counseling (MS); marriage and family counseling (MS); school counseling (MS).

Nova Southeastern University, Center for Psychological Studies, Specialist Program in School Psychology, Fort Lauderdale, FL 33314-7796. Offers Psy S. Evening/weekend programs available. Postbaccalaureate distance learning degree programs offered. *Faculty:* 6 full-time (3 women), 16 part-time/adjunct (10 women). *Students:* 68 full-time (61 women), 48 part-time (41 women); includes 55 minority (27 African Americans, 5 Asian Americans or Pacific Islanders, 23 Hispanic Americans), 3 international. 110 applicants, 50% accepted, 37 enrolled. In 2009, 33 Psy Ss awarded. *Degree requirements:* For Psy S, comprehensive exam, internship. *Entrance requirements:* Additional exam requirements/recommendations for international students: Required—TOEFL (minimum score 530 paper-based; 213 computer-based). *Application deadline:* For fall admission, 2/22 priority date for domestic and international students; for winter admission, 6/30 priority date for domestic and international students. Applications are processed on a rolling basis. Application fee: $50. Electronic applications accepted. *Financial support:* In 2009–10, 1 teaching assistantship was awarded; research assistantships, career-related internships or fieldwork, Federal Work-Study, scholarships/grants, and unspecified assistantships also available. *Unit head:* Karen S. Grosby, Dean, 954-262-5701, Fax: 954-262-3859. *Application contact:* Carlos Perez, Enrollment Management, 954-262-5790, Fax: 954-262-3893, E-mail: cpsinfo@cps.nova.edu.

Oregon State University–Cascades, Program in Counseling, Bend, OR 97701. Offers community counseling (MS); school counseling (MS).

Ottawa University, Graduate Studies-Arizona, Program in Education, Ottawa, KS 66067-3399. Offers community college counseling (MA); curriculum and instruction (MA); early childhood (MA); education intervention (MA); education leadership (MA); education technology (MA); Montessori early childhood education (MA); Montessori elementary education (MA); professional development (MA); school guidance counseling (MA); special education—cross categorical (MA). Programs offered in Mesa, Phoenix, Tempe and West Valley, AZ. *Accreditation:* NCATE. Part-time programs available. *Degree requirements:* For master's, thesis or alternative. *Entrance requirements:* For master's, minimum undergraduate GPA of 3.0, copy of current state certification or teaching license. Additional exam requirements/recommendations for international students: Required—TOEFL (minimum score 550 paper-based; 213 computer-based). Electronic applications accepted. *Expenses:* Contact institution.

Our Lady of the Lake University of San Antonio, School of Professional Studies, Program in Psychology, San Antonio, TX 78207-4689. Offers counseling psychology (MS, Psy D); marriage and family therapy (MS); school psychology (MS). *Accreditation:* APA (one or more programs are accredited). Part-time and evening/weekend programs available. *Students:* 111 full-time (90 women), 84 part-time (75 women); includes 118 minority (19 African Americans, 1 American Indian/Alaska Native, 4 Asian Americans or Pacific Islanders, 94 Hispanic Americans), 5 international. Average age 30. In 2009, 42 master's, 3 doctorates awarded. *Degree requirements:* For master's, comprehensive exam, thesis optional, practicum; for doctorate, thesis/dissertation, internship, qualifying exam. *Entrance requirements:* For master's and doctorate, GRE General Test or MAT, interview. Additional exam requirements/recommendations for international students: Required—TOEFL. *Application deadline:* For fall admission, 3/1 priority date for domestic and international students. Applications are processed on a rolling basis. Application fee: $25 ($50 for international students). Electronic applications accepted. *Expenses:* Tuition: Full-time $12,330; part-time $685 per contact hour. Required fees: $139; $12 per contact hour. $57 per semester. Tuition and fees vary according to campus/location. *Financial support:* Research assistantships, teaching assistantships, career-related internships or fieldwork available. Support available to part-time students. Financial award application deadline: 4/15. *Faculty research:* Marriage and family therapy, supervision, cross-cultural counseling, violence. *Unit head:* Dr. Joan Biever, Chair, 210-434-6711, E-mail: jbiever@lake.ollusa.edu. *Application contact:* 210-434-6711, Fax: 210-431-4036, E-mail: gradadm@lake.ollusa.edu.

Pace University, Dyson College of Arts and Sciences, Department of Psychology, Program in School-Clinical Child Psychology, New York, NY 10038. Offers school psychology (MS Ed); school-clinical psychology (Psy D). *Accreditation:* APA (one or more programs are accredited). *Students:* 83 full-time (74 women), 35 part-time (31 women); includes 20 minority (4 African Americans, 10 Asian Americans or Pacific Islanders, 6 Hispanic Americans), 7 international. Average age 27. 234 applicants, 34% accepted, 27 enrolled. In 2009, 5 master's, 26 doctorates awarded. Terminal master's awarded for partial completion of doctoral program. *Degree requirements:* For master's, comprehensive exam, qualifying exams, internship; for doctorate, comprehensive exam, qualifying exams, externship, internship, project. *Entrance requirements:* For master's, GRE General Test, GRE Subject Test, interview; for doctorate, GRE General Test, GRE Subject Test (psychology), interview, transcripts, 3 letters of reference. Additional exam requirements/recommendations for international students: Required—TOEFL. *Application deadline:* For fall admission, 2/1 priority date for domestic students. Applications are processed on a rolling basis. Application fee: $70. Electronic applications accepted. *Expenses:* Tuition: Part-time $954 per credit. Tuition and fees vary according to course load, degree level and program. *Financial support:* Research assistantships, teaching assistantships, career-related internships or fieldwork, Federal Work-Study, and tuition waivers (partial) available. Support available to part-time students. Financial award applicants required to submit FAFSA. *Unit head:* Dr. Barbara Mowder, Director, 212-346-1506. *Application contact:* Susan Ford-Goldschein, Director of Admissions, 212-346-1652, Fax: 212-346-1585, E-mail: gradnyc@pace.edu.

Penn State University Park, Graduate School, College of Education, Department of Educational and School Psychology and Special Education, State College, University Park, PA 16802-1503. Offers M Ed, MS, PhD.

Philadelphia College of Osteopathic Medicine, Graduate and Professional Programs, Department of Psychology, Philadelphia, PA 19131-1694. Offers clinical psychology (Psy D); counseling and clinical health psychology (MS); organizational leadership and development (MS); psychology (Certificate, Post-Doctoral Certificate); school psychology (MS, Psy D, Ed S). *Accreditation:* APA. *Degree requirements:* For master's, thesis; for doctorate, comprehensive exam, thesis/dissertation, final project, fieldwork. *Entrance requirements:* For master's, GRE or MAT, minimum GPA of 3.0; course work in biology, chemistry, English, physics; for other advanced degree, PRAXIS. *Faculty research:* Depression in primary care, integrated primary care, geriatric mental health.

See Close-Up on page 1091.

Pittsburg State University, Graduate School, College of Education, Department of Psychology and Counseling, Program in School Psychology, Pittsburg, KS 66762. Offers Ed S. *Accreditation:* NCATE. *Degree requirements:* For Ed S, thesis or alternative. *Entrance requirements:* For degree, GRE General Test, minimum GPA of 3.0. *Expenses:* Tuition, state resident: full-time $4212; part-time $176 per credit. Tuition, nonresident: full-time $11,530; part-time $480 per credit. Required fees: $940; $43 per credit. Tuition and fees vary according to course level, course load, degree level, campus/location, reciprocity agreements and student level.

Purdue University Calumet, Graduate School, School of Education, Program in Counseling, Hammond, IN 46323-2094. Offers human services (MS Ed); mental health counseling (MS Ed); school counseling (MS Ed). *Entrance requirements:* Additional exam requirements/recommendations for international students: Required—TOEFL.

Queens College of the City University of New York, Division of Graduate Studies, Division of Education, Department of Educational and Community Programs, Program in School Psychology, Flushing, NY 11367-1597. Offers MS Ed, AC. Part-time programs available. *Faculty:* 4 full-time (3 women). *Students:* 31 full-time (28 women), 61 part-time (59 women). 156 applicants, 31% accepted, 34 enrolled. In 2009, 34 master's awarded. *Degree requirements:* For master's, internship, research project; for AC, thesis optional, internship. *Entrance requirements:* For master's, minimum GPA of 3.0; for AC, master's degree or equivalent. Additional exam requirements/recommendations for international students: Required—TOEFL. *Application deadline:* For fall admission, 4/1 for domestic students; for spring admission, 11/1 for domestic students. Applications are processed on a rolling basis. Application fee: $125. *Expenses:* Tuition, state resident: full-time $7360; part-time $310 per credit. Tuition, nonresident: part-time $575 per credit. One-time fee: $195.25 full-time; $145.25 part-time. *Financial support:* Career-related internships or fieldwork, Federal Work-Study, institutionally sponsored loans, and tuition waivers (partial) available. Support available to part-time students. Financial award application deadline: 4/1; financial award applicants required to submit FAFSA. *Unit head:* Dr. Marion Fish, Coordinator/Graduate Adviser, 718-997-5230. *Application contact:* Mario Caruso, Director of Graduate Admissions, 718-997-5200, Fax: 718-997-5193, E-mail: graduate_admissions@qc.edu.

Quincy University, Program in Counseling, Quincy, IL 62301-2699. Offers clinical mental health counseling (MS Ed); school counseling (MS Ed). Part-time and evening/weekend programs available. *Faculty:* 2 full-time (0 women), 1 part-time/adjunct (0 women). *Students:* 10 full-time (8 women), 21 part-time (16 women); includes 2 African Americans. In 2009, 12 master's awarded. *Degree requirements:* For master's, comprehensive exam, practicum, internship. *Entrance requirements:* For master's, MAT or GRE. Additional exam requirements/recommendations for international students: Required—TOEFL. *Application deadline:* Applications are processed on a rolling basis. Application fee: $25. Electronic applications accepted. *Expenses:* Tuition: Full-time $8400; part-time $350 per credit hour. Required fees: $360; $15 per credit hour. Tuition and fees vary according to course load, campus/location and program. *Financial support:* Available to part-time students. Applicants required to submit FAFSA. *Unit head:* Dr. Kenneth Oliver, Director, 217-228-5432 Ext. 3113, E-mail: oliveke@quincy.edu. *Application contact:* Jennifer O'Donnell, Coordinator of Adult Studies, 217-228-5404, Fax: 217-228-5479, E-mail: admissions@quincy.edu.

Radford University, College of Graduate and Professional Studies, College of Education and Human Development, Department of Counselor Education, Radford, VA 24142. Offers community counseling (MS); school counseling (MS); student affairs—administration (MS); student affairs—counseling (MS). *Accreditation:* ACA; NCATE. Part-time and evening/weekend programs available. *Faculty:* 7 full-time (4 women), 20 part-time/adjunct (13 women). *Students:* 62 full-time (50 women), 60 part-time (50 women); includes 11 minority (8 African Americans, 1 American Indian/Alaska Native, 1 Asian American or Pacific Islander, 1 Hispanic American). Average age 29. 85 applicants, 88% accepted, 38 enrolled. In 2009, 53 master's awarded. *Degree requirements:* For master's, comprehensive exam, thesis optional. *Entrance requirements:* For master's, GRE or MAT, minimum GPA of 2.75, 3 letters of reference. Additional exam requirements/recommendations for international students: Required—TOEFL (minimum score 550 paper-based; 213 computer-based; 79 iBT). *Application deadline:* For fall admission, 4/15 priority date for domestic students, 12/1 for international students. Applications are processed on a rolling basis. Application fee: $50. Electronic applications accepted. *Expenses:* Tuition, state resident: full-time $5086; part-time $211 per credit hour. Tuition, nonresident: full-time $12,608; part-time $525 per credit hour. Required fees: $2508; $105 per credit hour. *Financial support:* In 2009–10, 27 students received support, including 11 research assistantships with partial tuition reimbursements available (averaging $8,000 per year), 9 teaching assistantships with partial tuition reimbursements available (averaging $8,700 per year); career-related internships or fieldwork, Federal Work-Study, institutionally sponsored loans, scholarships/grants, and unspecified assistantships also available. Financial award application deadline: 3/1; financial award applicants required to submit FAFSA. *Unit head:* Dr. Alan Forrest, Chair, 540-831-5487, Fax: 540-831-6755, E-mail: aforrest@radford.edu. *Application contact:* Graduate Admissions, 540-831-5431, Fax: 540-831-6061, E-mail: gradcollege@radford.edu.

Radford University, College of Graduate and Professional Studies, College of Humanities and Behavioral Sciences, Program in School Psychology, Radford, VA 24142. Offers Ed S. *Accreditation:* NCATE. *Faculty:* 16 full-time (6 women), 6 part-time/adjunct (2 women). *Students:* 23 full-time (20 women), 5 part-time (all women); includes 3 minority (2 African Americans, 1 Asian American or Pacific Islander). Average age 25. 29 applicants, 72% accepted, 13 enrolled. In 2009, 9 Ed Ss awarded. *Degree requirements:* For Ed S, comprehensive exam. *Entrance requirements:* For degree, GRE, minimum GPA of 3.0; 2 letters of reference; essay. Additional exam requirements/recommendations for international students: Required—TOEFL (minimum score 550 paper-based; 213 computer-based; 79 iBT). *Application deadline:* For fall admission, 2/15 priority date for domestic students, 12/1 for international students. Applications are processed on a rolling basis. Application fee: $50. Electronic applications accepted. *Expenses:* Tuition, state resident: full-time $5086; part-time $211 per credit hour. Tuition, nonresident: full-time $12,608; part-time $525 per credit hour. Required fees: $2508; $105 per credit hour. *Financial support:* In 2009–10, 12 students received support, including 10 research assistantships with partial tuition reimbursements available (averaging $8,000 per year); career-related internships or fieldwork, Federal Work-Study, institutionally sponsored loans, scholarships/grants, and unspecified assistantships also available. Financial award application deadline: 3/1; financial award applicants required to submit FAFSA. *Unit head:* Dr. Jayne Bucy, Coordinator, 540-831-5341, Fax: 540-831-6113, E-mail: jebucy@radford.edu. *Application contact:* Graduate Admissions, 540-831-5431, Fax: 540-831-6061, E-mail: gradcollege@radford.edu.

Rider University, Department of Graduate Education, Leadership and Counseling, Program in School Psychology, Lawrenceville, NJ 08648-3001. Offers Certificate, Ed S. *Entrance requirements:* For degree, GRE or MAT, resume, 2 professional references, interview, 1 year of counseling experience. Additional exam requirements/recommendations for international students: Required—TOEFL (minimum score 550 paper-based; 213 computer-based). *Faculty research:* Prenatal factors on child development, child abuse developmental assessments.

Roberts Wesleyan College, Division of Social Sciences, Rochester, NY 14624-1997. Offers counseling in ministry (MA); school counseling (MS); school psychology (MS).

Rowan University, Graduate School, College of Education, Department of Special Educational Services/Instruction, Program in School Psychology, Glassboro, NJ 08028-1701. Offers MA, Ed S. *Accreditation:* NCATE. Part-time and evening/weekend programs available. *Students:* 51 full-time (46 women), 34 part-time (25 women); includes 9 minority (3 African Americans, 3 Asian Americans or Pacific Islanders, 3 Hispanic Americans). Average age 27. 36 applicants, 97% accepted, 26 enrolled. In 2009, 43 master's awarded. *Degree requirements:* For master's, comprehensive exam, thesis; for Ed S, thesis or alternative. *Entrance requirements:* For master's and Ed S, GRE General Test, GRE Subject Test, interview, minimum GPA of 3.0. Additional exam requirements/recommendations for international students: Required—TOEFL. *Application deadline:* For fall admission, 10/15 for domestic students; for winter admission, 12/1 priority date for domestic students; for spring admission, 4/1 priority date for domestic students. Applications are processed on a rolling basis. Application fee: $50. Electronic applications accepted. *Expenses:* Tuition, state resident: full-time $10,624; part-time $590 per semester hour. Tuition, nonresident: full-time $10,624; part-time $590 per semester hour. Required fees: $2320; $125 per semester hour. *Financial support:* Career-related internships or fieldwork, scholarships/grants, and unspecified assistantships available. Support available to part-time students. *Unit head:* Dr. Mira Lalovic-Hand, Interim Associate Provost/Director of Graduate

School, 856-256-5120, E-mail: lalovic-hand@rowan.edu. *Application contact:* Karen Haynes, Graduate Coordinator, 856-256-4052, Fax: 856-256-4436, E-mail: haynes@rowan.edu.

Rutgers, The State University of New Jersey, New Brunswick, Graduate School of Applied and Professional Psychology, Program in School Psychology, Piscataway, NJ 08854-8097. Offers Psy M, Psy D. *Accreditation:* APA (one or more programs are accredited). *Degree requirements:* For doctorate, comprehensive exam, thesis/dissertation, 1 year internship. *Entrance requirements:* For doctorate, GRE General Test, GRE Subject Test, bachelor's degree in psychology or equivalent. Additional exam requirements/recommendations for international students: Required—TOEFL. Electronic applications accepted. *Expenses:* Contact institution. *Faculty research:* Consultation, program evaluation, applied educational psychology, exceptional children, crisis intervention.

St. John's University, St. John's College of Liberal Arts and Sciences, Department of Psychology, Program in School Psychology, Queens, NY 11439. Offers MS, Psy D. Part-time programs available. *Students:* 151 full-time (134 women), 32 part-time (27 women); includes 24 minority (5 African Americans, 4 Asian Americans or Pacific Islanders, 15 Hispanic Americans), 5 international. Average age 26. 191 applicants, 44% accepted, 44 enrolled. In 2009, 28 master's, 25 doctorates awarded. *Degree requirements:* For master's, comprehensive exam, thesis optional; for doctorate, comprehensive exam, thesis/dissertation, internship. *Entrance requirements:* For master's, GRE General Test, GRE Subject Test, minimum GPA of 3.0, 2 writing samples; for doctorate, GRE General Test, GRE Subject Test, interview, minimum GPA of 3.0. Additional exam requirements/recommendations for international students: Required—TOEFL (minimum score 500 paper-based; 173 computer-based; 61 iBT), IELTS (minimum score 5.5). *Application deadline:* For fall admission, 1/15 for domestic students, 1/15 priority date for international students; for spring admission, 11/1 for domestic students, 11/1 priority date for international students. Applications are processed on a rolling basis. Application fee: $70. Electronic applications accepted. *Expenses:* Contact institution. *Financial support:* Fellowships, research assistantships, career-related internships or fieldwork, scholarships/grants, and unspecified assistantships available. Support available to part-time students. Financial award application deadline: 3/1; financial award applicants required to submit FAFSA. *Faculty research:* Therapeutic alliance, intelligence testing, multicultural assessment, neuropsychological assessment, adolescent suicide. *Unit head:* Dr. Dawn Flanagan, Director, 718-990-1551, E-mail: flanagad@stjohns.edu. *Application contact:* Kathleen Davis, Director of Graduate Admission, 718-990-2790, Fax: 718-990-5686, E-mail: gradhelp@stjohns.edu.

San Diego State University, Graduate and Research Affairs, College of Education, Department of Counseling and School Psychology, San Diego, CA 92182. Offers MS. *Accreditation:* NCATE. Evening/weekend programs available. *Degree requirements:* For master's, comprehensive exam (for some programs), thesis (for some programs). *Entrance requirements:* For master's, GRE General Test, interview, letters of reference. Additional exam requirements/recommendations for international students: Required—TOEFL. Electronic applications accepted. *Faculty research:* Multicultural and cross-cultural counseling and training, AIDS counseling.

Seattle University, College of Education, Program in Counseling and School Psychology, Seattle, WA 98122-1090. Offers MA, Certificate, Ed S. *Accreditation:* NCATE. Part-time and evening/weekend programs available. *Degree requirements:* For master's, comprehensive exam. *Entrance requirements:* For master's, interview; GRE, MAT, or minimum GPA of 3.0; related work experience. Additional exam requirements/recommendations for international students: Required—TOEFL.

Seton Hall University, College of Education and Human Services, Department of Professional Psychology and Family Therapy, Program in School Psychology, South Orange, NJ 07079-2697. Offers Ed S. *Faculty:* 2 full-time (1 woman). *Students:* 3 full-time (all women), 27 part-time (23 women); includes 4 minority (1 African American, 3 Hispanic Americans). Average age 27. 15 applicants, 27% accepted, 1 enrolled. In 2009, 10 Ed Ss awarded. *Degree requirements:* For Ed S, comprehensive exam, thesis, internship. *Entrance requirements:* For degree, GRE or MAT, interview. *Application deadline:* Applications are processed on a rolling basis. Application fee: $50. *Financial support:* In 2009–10, 1 research assistantship with full tuition reimbursement (averaging $4,500 per year) was awarded. Financial award application deadline: 2/1. *Faculty research:* Family systems, ethical behavior, childhood depression. *Unit head:* Dr. Thomas Masserelli, Director, 973-313-6129, Fax: 973-275-2188, E-mail: massarth@shu.edu. *Application contact:* Information Contact, 973-761-9451.

Southeast Missouri State University, School of Graduate Studies, Department of Educational Leadership and Counseling, Counseling Program, Cape Girardeau, MO 63701-4799. Offers counseling education (Ed S); mental health counseling (MA); school counseling (MA), including elementary counseling, secondary counseling. *Accreditation:* ACA; NCATE. Part-time and evening/weekend programs available. *Degree requirements:* For master's, comprehensive exam, thesis optional, portfolio, oral exam; for Ed S, oral exam. *Entrance requirements:* For master's, GRE General Test, MAT, minimum undergraduate GPA of 3.0; for Ed S, GRE General Test or MAT, minimum graduate GPA of 3.5. Additional exam requirements/recommendations for international students: Required—TOEFL (minimum score 550 paper-based; 213 computer-based); Recommended—IELTS (minimum score 6). Electronic applications accepted. *Expenses:* Tuition, state resident: full-time $4266; part-time $237 per credit hour. Tuition, nonresident: full-time $7506; part-time $417 per credit hour. Required fees: $427; $427. *Faculty research:* Counselor development, cognitive development of counselors, counselor supervision, issues in school counseling, issues in mental health counseling.

Southern Connecticut State University, School of Graduate Studies, School of Education, Department of Counseling and School Psychology, New Haven, CT 06515-1355. Offers community counseling (MS); counseling (Diploma); school counseling (MS); school psychology (MS, Diploma). *Accreditation:* ACA (one or more programs are accredited); NCATE. *Faculty:* 8 full-time, 10 part-time/adjunct. *Students:* 87 full-time (74 women), 77 part-time (67 women); includes 24 minority (18 African Americans, 6 Hispanic Americans), 3 international. 179 applicants, 27% accepted, 45 enrolled. In 2009, 44 master's, 12 other advanced degrees awarded. *Degree requirements:* For master's, comprehensive exam. *Entrance requirements:* For master's, interview, previous course work in behavioral sciences, minimum QPA of 2.7. *Application deadline:* For fall admission, 1/15 for domestic students; for spring admission, 10/15 for domestic students. Application fee: $50. Electronic applications accepted. Tuition and fees vary according to program. *Financial support:* Teaching assistantships, career-related internships or fieldwork available. Financial award application deadline: 4/15; financial award applicants required to submit FAFSA. *Unit head:* Dr. Patricia DeBarbieri, Chairperson, 203-392-5483, E-mail: debarbierip1@southernct.edu. *Application contact:* Dr. Louisa Foss, Graduate Coordinator, Clinical Mental Health Counseling, 203-392-5154, E-mail: fossl1@southernct.edu.

Southern Illinois University Edwardsville, Graduate Studies and Research, School of Education, Department of Psychology, Program in School Psychology, Edwardsville, IL 62026-0001. Offers SD. *Accreditation:* NCATE. Part-time programs available. *Students:* 10 part-time (all women). Average age 26. 15 applicants, 0% accepted. In 2009, 7 SDs awarded. *Degree requirements:* For SD, thesis. *Entrance requirements:* For degree, GRE. Additional exam requirements/recommendations for international students: Required—TOEFL (minimum score 550 paper-based; 213 computer-based; 79 iBT), IELTS (minimum score 6.5). *Application deadline:* For spring admission, 2/1 for domestic and international students. Application fee: $30. Electronic applications accepted. *Expenses:* Tuition, state resident: part-time $1252.50 per semester. Tuition, nonresident: part-time $3131.25 per semester. Required fees: $586.85 per semester. Tuition and fees vary according to course load. *Financial support:* Fellowships, research assistantships, teaching assistantships, career-related internships or fieldwork, Federal Work-Study, institutionally sponsored loans, scholarships/grants, traineeships, and unspecified assistantships available. Support available to part-time students. Financial award application deadline: 3/1; financial award applicants required to submit FAFSA. *Unit head:* Dr. Emily Krohn, Director, 618-650-2202, E-mail: ekrohn@siue.edu. *Application contact:* Dr. Emily Krohn, Director, 618-650-2202, E-mail: ekrohn@siue.edu.

Southwestern Oklahoma State University, College of Professional and Graduate Studies, School of Behavioral Sciences and Education, Specialization in School Psychology, Weatherford, OK 73096-3098. Offers MS.

State University of New York at Oswego, Graduate Studies, School of Education, Department of Counseling and Psychological Services, Program in School Psychology, Oswego, NY 13126. Offers MS, CAS, MS/CAS. *Degree requirements:* For master's, comprehensive exam, fieldwork; for CAS, thesis, fieldwork. *Entrance requirements:* For master's, GRE General Test, interview, minimum GPA of 3.0; for CAS, GRE General Test, interview, MA or MS, minimum GPA of 3.0. Additional exam requirements/recommendations for international students: Required—TOEFL (minimum score 560 paper-based; 220 computer-based). *Faculty research:* Psychological applications in education and human services, evaluation of standard tests for admissions criteria.

State University of New York at Plattsburgh, Faculty of Arts and Science, Department of Psychology, Plattsburgh, NY 12901-2681. Offers school psychology (MA, CAS). Part-time programs available. *Faculty:* 4 full-time (1 woman), 2 part-time/adjunct (both women). *Students:* 20 full-time (19 women), 10 part-time (7 women); includes 5 minority (2 Asian Americans or Pacific Islanders, 3 Hispanic Americans), 2 international. Average age 26. 24 applicants, 88% accepted, 11 enrolled. In 2009, 15 master's, 8 other advanced degrees awarded. *Degree requirements:* For master's, thesis, internship. *Entrance requirements:* For master's, GRE General Test, minimum GPA of 3.0. Additional exam requirements/recommendations for international students: Required—TOEFL (minimum score 550 paper-based; 213 computer-based; 79 iBT). *Application deadline:* For fall admission, 2/15 priority date for domestic students. Applications are processed on a rolling basis. Application fee: $75. *Expenses:* Tuition, state resident: full-time $8370; part-time $349 per credit hour. Tuition, nonresident: full-time $13,250; part-time $552 per credit hour. Required fees: $1130. *Financial support:* Federal Work-Study available. Support available to part-time students. Financial award application deadline: 4/15; financial award applicants required to submit FAFSA. *Faculty research:* Alzheimer's disease, adolescent behavior, intellectual assessment, learning disabilities, reading skill acquisition. *Unit head:* Dr. Wendy Braje, Chair, 518-564-3383, E-mail: brajewl@plattsburgh.edu. *Application contact:* Marguerite Adelman, Assistant Director, Graduate Admissions, 518-564-4723, Fax: 518-564-4722, E-mail: adelmaml@plattsburgh.edu.

Stephen F. Austin State University, Graduate School, College of Education, Department of Human Services, Nacogdoches, TX 75962. Offers counseling (MA); school psychology (MA); special education (M Ed); speech pathology (MS). *Accreditation:* ACA (one or more programs are accredited); ASHA (one or more programs are accredited); CORE; NCATE. *Degree requirements:* For master's, comprehensive exam, thesis (for some programs). *Entrance requirements:* For master's, GRE General Test, minimum GPA of 2.8. Additional exam requirements/recommendations for international students: Required—TOEFL.

Syracuse University, College of Arts and Sciences, Program in School Psychology, Syracuse, NY 13244. Offers PhD. *Accreditation:* APA. *Students:* 13 full-time (12 women), 1 (woman) part-time, 1 international. Average age 26. 39 applicants, 10% accepted, 2 enrolled. In 2009, 5 doctorates awarded. *Degree requirements:* For doctorate, comprehensive exam, thesis/dissertation. *Entrance requirements:* For doctorate, GRE General Test, GRE Subject Test. Additional exam requirements/recommendations for international students: Required—TOEFL (minimum score 100 iBT). *Application deadline:* For fall admission, 1/1 priority date for domestic and international students. Application fee: $75. Electronic applications accepted. *Expenses:* Tuition: Full-time $26,808; part-time $1117 per credit. Required fees: $1024. *Financial support:* Fellowships with full tuition reimbursements, research assistantships with full tuition reimbursements, teaching assistantships with full tuition reimbursements available. Financial award application deadline: 1/1; financial award applicants required to submit FAFSA. *Unit head:* Dr. Tanya Eckert, Graduate Director, 315-443-2354, Fax: 315-443-4085, E-mail: taeckert@syr.edu. *Application contact:* Sue Bova, Information Contact, 315-443-1050, E-mail: skbova@syr.edu.

Syracuse University, School of Education, Program in School Counseling, Syracuse, NY 13244. Offers MS, CAS. *Students:* 20 full-time (18 women), 8 part-time (all women); includes 3 minority (2 African Americans, 1 Asian American or Pacific Islander), 1 international. Average age 26. 35 applicants, 69% accepted, 12 enrolled. In 2009, 6 master's, 2 other advanced degrees awarded. *Entrance requirements:* For master's, GRE General Test or MAT, interview; for CAS, There are two different CAS tracks:one requiring M.S. in School Counseling and the other not requiring an M.S. in School. counseling. Additional exam requirements/recommendations for international students: Required—TOEFL (minimum score 100 iBT). *Application deadline:* For fall admission, 2/1 priority date for domestic and international students; for spring admission, 10/15 priority date for domestic and international students. Applications are processed on a rolling basis. Application fee: $75. Electronic applications accepted. *Expenses:* Tuition: Full-time $26,808; part-time $1117 per credit. Required fees: $1024. *Financial support:* Fellowships with tuition reimbursements, research assistantships with tuition reimbursements, teaching assistantships with tuition reimbursements, tuition waivers (partial) available. Financial award application deadline: 1/1; financial award applicants required to submit FAFSA. *Unit head:* Dr. Dennis Gilbride, Chair, 315-443-2266, Fax: 315-443-5732, E-mail: ddgilbr@syr.edu. *Application contact:* Liza Rochelson, Graduate Recruiter, School of Education, 315-443-2505, E-mail: e-gradrcrt@syr.edu.

Tarleton State University, College of Graduate Studies, College of Education, Department of Psychology and Counseling, Stephenville, TX 76402. Offers counseling and psychology (M Ed), including counseling, counseling psychology, educational psychology; educational administration (M Ed); secondary education (Certificate); special education (Certificate). Part-time and evening/weekend programs available. Postbaccalaureate distance learning degree programs offered (minimal on-campus study). *Degree requirements:* For master's, comprehensive exam, thesis optional. *Entrance requirements:* For master's, GRE General Test, minimum GPA of 3.0. Additional exam requirements/recommendations for international students: Required—TOEFL (minimum score 550 paper-based; 213 computer-based; 80 iBT). Electronic applications accepted.

Teachers College, Columbia University, Graduate Faculty of Education, Department of Health and Behavioral Studies, Program in Applied Educational Psychology–School Psychology, New York, NY 10027-6696. Offers Ed M, MA, Ed D, PhD. *Accreditation:* APA (one or more programs are accredited). *Students:* 37 full-time (31 women), 56 part-time (52 women); includes 20 minority (5 African Americans, 12 Asian Americans or Pacific Islanders, 3 Hispanic Americans), 2 international. Average age 26. 166 applicants, 35% accepted, 23 enrolled. In 2009, 22 master's, 5 doctorates awarded. *Degree requirements:* For master's, integrative paper; for doctorate, thesis/dissertation, integrative project. *Entrance requirements:* For doctorate, GRE General Test. *Application deadline:* For fall admission, 5/15 for domestic students. Application fee: $65. *Financial support:* Fellowships, research assistantships, career-related internships or fieldwork, Federal Work-Study, institutionally sponsored loans, and tuition waivers (full and partial) available. Support available to part-time students. Financial award application deadline: 2/1. *Faculty research:* Psychoeducational assessment, observation and concept acquisition in young children, reading, mathematical thinking, memory. *Unit head:* Dr. Chuck Basch, Chair, 212-678-3964, E-mail: ceb35@columbia.edu. *Application contact:* Peter Shon, Assistant Director of Admission, 212-678-3305, Fax: 212-678-4171, E-mail: shon@exchange.tc.columbia.edu.

Temple University, Graduate School, College of Education, Department of Psychological Studies in Education, Program in School Psychology, Philadelphia, PA 19122-6096. Offers

School Psychology

Temple University (continued)
Ed M, PhD. *Accreditation:* APA (one or more programs are accredited). Part-time and evening/weekend programs available. Terminal master's awarded for partial completion of doctoral program. *Degree requirements:* For master's, thesis or alternative; for doctorate, thesis/dissertation. *Entrance requirements:* For master's and doctorate, GRE General Test, GRE Subject Test, minimum GPA of 3.0. Additional exam requirements/recommendations for international students: Required—TOEFL (minimum score 550 paper-based; 213 computer-based; 79 iBT). Electronic applications accepted.

Tennessee State University, The School of Graduate Studies and Research, College of Education, Department of Psychology, Nashville, TN 37209-1561. Offers counseling and guidance (MS), including counseling, elementary school counseling, organizational counseling, secondary school counseling; counseling psychology (PhD); psychology (MS, PhD); school psychology (MS, PhD). *Accreditation:* APA. *Degree requirements:* For doctorate, thesis/dissertation (for some programs). *Entrance requirements:* For master's, GRE General Test or MAT; for doctorate, GRE General Test or MAT, minimum GPA of 3.25, work experience. Electronic applications accepted.

Texas A&M University, College of Education and Human Development, Department of Educational Psychology, College Station, TX 77843. Offers counseling psychology (PhD); educational psychology (PhD); educational technology (M Ed); gifted and talented education (M Ed, MS); Hispanic bilingual education (M Ed, PhD); human learning and development (MS); intelligence, creativity, and giftedness (PhD); learning, development, and instruction (PhD); research, measurement and statistics (MS); research, measurement, and statistics (PhD); school counseling (M Ed); school psychology (PhD); special education (M Ed, PhD). *Accreditation:* APA (one or more programs are accredited); NCATE. Part-time and evening/weekend programs available. Postbaccalaureate distance learning degree programs offered (no on-campus study). *Faculty:* 45. *Students:* 160 full-time (126 women), 144 part-time (118 women); includes 99 minority (25 African Americans, 13 Asian Americans or Pacific Islanders, 61 Hispanic Americans), 41 international. In 2009, 53 master's, 30 doctorates awarded. *Degree requirements:* For master's, thesis optional; for doctorate, thesis/dissertation. *Entrance requirements:* For master's and doctorate, GRE General Test. Additional exam requirements/recommendations for international students: Required—TOEFL. Application fee: $50 ($75 for international students). Electronic applications accepted. *Expenses:* Tuition, state resident: full-time $3991; part-time $221.74 per credit hour. Tuition, nonresident: full-time $9049; part-time $502.74 per credit hour. *Financial support:* In 2009–10, fellowships (averaging $12,000 per year), research assistantships (averaging $9,000 per year), teaching assistantships (averaging $9,000 per year) were awarded; career-related internships or fieldwork, institutionally sponsored loans, scholarships/grants, and unspecified assistantships also available. Financial award applicants required to submit FAFSA. *Unit head:* Dr. Victor Willson, Head, 979-845-1800. *Application contact:* Carol A. Wagner, Director of Advising, 979-845-1833, Fax: 979-862-1256, E-mail: epsyadvisor@tamu.edu.

Texas State University–San Marcos, Graduate School, College of Education, Department of Counseling, Leadership, Adult Education, and School Psychology, Program in School Psychology, San Marcos, TX 78666. Offers MA. Part-time programs available. *Faculty:* 3 full-time (all women), 2 part-time/adjunct (1 woman). *Students:* 41 full-time (33 women), 16 part-time (12 women); includes 16 minority (3 African Americans, 1 American Indian/Alaska Native, 1 Asian American or Pacific Islander, 11 Hispanic Americans). Average age 27. 41 applicants, 63% accepted, 13 enrolled. In 2009, 20 master's awarded. *Degree requirements:* For master's, comprehensive exam. *Entrance requirements:* For master's, GRE General Test, interview, minimum GPA of 2.75 in last 60 hours of course work. Additional exam requirements/recommendations for international students: Required—TOEFL (minimum score 550 paper-based; 213 computer-based). *Application deadline:* For fall admission, 2/15 for domestic and international students; for spring admission, 10/15 for domestic students, 10/1 for international students. Applications are processed on a rolling basis. Application fee: $40 ($90 for international students). Electronic applications accepted. *Expenses:* Tuition, state resident: full-time $5784; part-time $241 per credit hour. Tuition, nonresident: part-time $551 per credit hour. Required fees: $1728; $48 per credit hour. $306. Tuition and fees vary according to course load. *Financial support:* In 2009–10, 46 students received support, including 2 research assistantships (averaging $5,393 per year), 5 teaching assistantships (averaging $1,288 per year); career-related internships or fieldwork, Federal Work-Study, and institutionally sponsored loans also available. Support available to part-time students. Financial award application deadline: 4/1; financial award applicants required to submit FAFSA. *Unit head:* Dr. Cynthia Plotts, Graduate Advisor, 512-245-3083, Fax: 512-245-8872, E-mail: cp11@txstate.edu. *Application contact:* Dr. J. Michael Willoughby, Dean of Graduate School, 512-245-2581, Fax: 512-245-8365, E-mail: gradcollege@txstate.edu.

Texas Woman's University, Graduate School, College of Arts and Sciences, Department of Psychology and Philosophy, Denton, TX 76201. Offers counseling psychology (MA, PhD); school psychology (PhD, SSP). *Accreditation:* APA (one or more programs are accredited). *Faculty:* 15 full-time (9 women). *Students:* 66 full-time (55 women), 53 part-time (48 women); includes 24 minority (9 African Americans, 1 American Indian/Alaska Native, 7 Asian Americans or Pacific Islanders, 7 Hispanic Americans), 2 international. Average age 30. 105 applicants, 100% accepted, 11 enrolled. In 2009, 18 master's, 12 doctorates awarded. Terminal master's awarded for partial completion of doctoral program. *Degree requirements:* For master's, thesis; for doctorate, comprehensive exam, thesis/dissertation, internship, residency. *Entrance requirements:* For master's, GRE (minimum score 500 verbal, 500 quantitative), BA/BS or 18 hours in psychology, minimum GPA of 3.5 in undergraduate psychology classes, 3 letters of reference; for doctorate, GRE (Verbal 500, Quantitative 500, Analytical 4), 3 letters of reference; minimum overall and psychology undergraduate GPA of 3.0; BS/BA in psychology or 18 hours of required psychology classes, essay. Additional exam requirements/recommendations for international students: Required—TOEFL (minimum score 550 paper-based; 213 computer-based; 79 iBT). *Application deadline:* For fall admission, 12/15 priority date for domestic and international students. Applications are processed on a rolling basis. Application fee: $50. Electronic applications accepted. *Expenses:* Tuition, state resident: full-time $3564; part-time $198 per credit hour. Tuition, nonresident: full-time $8550; part-time $475 per credit hour. Required fees: $69.26 per credit hour. Tuition and fees vary according to course load. *Financial support:* In 2009–10, 49 students received support, including 14 research assistantships (averaging $10,746 per year), 10 teaching assistantships (averaging $10,746 per year); career-related internships or fieldwork, Federal Work-Study, institutionally sponsored loans, scholarships/grants, traineeships, health care benefits, and unspecified assistantships also available. Support available to part-time students. Financial award application deadline: 3/1; financial award applicants required to submit FAFSA. *Faculty research:* Women's anger, pre-school assessments, body image dysfunction, traumatic stress, classical ethics, mental health and behavioral needs of adolescents in alternative education. *Unit head:* Dr. Dan Miller, Chair, 940-898-2303, Fax: 940-898-2301, E-mail: dmiller@twu.edu. *Application contact:* Samuel Wheeler, Assistant Director of Admissions, 940-898-3188, Fax: 940-898-3081, E-mail: wheelersr@twu.edu.

Towson University, College of Graduate Studies and Research, Program in School Psychology, Towson, MD 21252-0001. Offers CAS. Part-time and evening/weekend programs available. Electronic applications accepted. *Faculty research:* Cognitive behavior, issues affecting the aging, relaxation hypnosis and imagery, lesbian and gay issues.

Trinity University, Department of Education, Program in School Psychology, San Antonio, TX 78212-7200. Offers MA. *Accreditation:* NCATE. *Entrance requirements:* For master's, GRE General Test, minimum GPA of 3.0, interview.

Troy University, Graduate School, College of Education, Program in Counseling and Psychology, Troy, AL 36082. Offers agency counsleing (Ed S); clinical mental health (MS); community counseling (MS, Ed S); corrections counseling (MS); rehabilitation counseling (MS); school psychology (MS, Ed S); school psychometry (MS); social service counseling (MS); student affairs counseling (MS); substance abuse counseling (MS). *Accreditation:* ACA; CORE; NCATE. Part-time and evening/weekend programs available. *Students:* 375 full-time (302 women), 753 part-time (642 women); includes 664 minority (610 African Americans, 8 American Indian/Alaska Native, 9 Asian Americans or Pacific Islanders, 37 Hispanic Americans). Average age 33. 493 applicants, 92% accepted. In 2009, 102 master's, 191 other advanced degrees awarded. *Degree requirements:* For master's, comprehensive exam, thesis. *Entrance requirements:* For master's, MAT, minimum GPA of 2.5. Additional exam requirements/recommendations for international students: Required—TOEFL (minimum score 523 paper-based; 193 computer-based; 70 iBT), IELTS (minimum score 6). *Application deadline:* Applications are processed on a rolling basis. Application fee: $50. Electronic applications accepted. *Unit head:* Dr. Andrew Creamer, Chair, 334-670-3350, Fax: 334-670-32961, E-mail: drcreamer@troy.edu. *Application contact:* Brenda K. Campbell, Director of Graduate Admissions, 334-670-3178, Fax: 334-670-3733, E-mail: bcamp@troy.edu.

Tufts University, Graduate School of Arts and Sciences, Department of Education, Program in School Psychology, Medford, MA 02155. Offers MA, Ed S. *Faculty:* 13 full-time, 9 part-time/adjunct. *Students:* 47 full-time (38 women); includes 9 minority (2 African Americans, 1 American Indian/Alaska Native, 3 Asian Americans or Pacific Islanders, 3 Hispanic Americans). Average age 27. 69 applicants, 52% accepted, 17 enrolled. In 2009, 16 master's, 16 other advanced degrees awarded. *Entrance requirements:* For master's, GRE General Test. Additional exam requirements/recommendations for international students: Required—TOEFL (minimum score 550 paper-based; 213 computer-based; 80 iBT). *Application deadline:* For fall admission, 2/1 for domestic students, 12/15 for international students. Applications are processed on a rolling basis. Application fee: $75. Electronic applications accepted. *Expenses:* Tuition: Full-time $38,096; part-time $3962 per credit. Required fees: $686; $40 per year. Tuition and fees vary according to course level, course load, degree level, program and student level. *Financial support:* Federal Work-Study, scholarships/grants, and tuition waivers (full and partial) available. Financial award application deadline: 2/1. *Unit head:* Steve Luz-Alterman, Program Director, 617-627-3244. *Application contact:* Patricia Romeo, Information Contact, 617-627-3244.

Union College, Graduate Programs, Department of Psychology, Barbourville, KY 40906-1499. Offers clinical psychology (MA); counseling psychology (MA); school psychology (MA).

University at Albany, State University of New York, School of Education, Department of Educational and Counseling Psychology, Albany, NY 12222-0001. Offers counseling psychology (MS, PhD, CAS); educational psychology (Ed D); educational psychology and statistics (MS); measurements and evaluation (Ed D); rehabilitation counseling (MS), including counseling psychology; school counselor (CAS); school psychology (Psy D, CAS); special education (MS); statistics and research design (Ed D). *Accreditation:* APA (one or more programs are accredited). Evening/weekend programs available. *Degree requirements:* For doctorate, thesis/dissertation. *Entrance requirements:* For doctorate, GRE General Test. Additional exam requirements/recommendations for international students: Required—TOEFL (minimum score 550 paper-based; 213 computer-based). Electronic applications accepted.

The University of Akron, Graduate School, College of Education, Department of Counseling, Program in Classroom Guidance for Teachers, Akron, OH 44325. Offers MA, MS. *Accreditation:* NCATE. *Students:* 2 part-time (1 woman). Average age 38. 2 applicants, 50% accepted. In 2009, 1 master's awarded. *Degree requirements:* For master's, comprehensive exam. *Entrance requirements:* For master's, minimum GPA of 2.75, interview, letters of recommendation, criminal background check, resume, supplemental forms. Additional exam requirements/recommendations for international students: Required—TOEFL (minimum score 550 paper-based; 213 computer-based; 79 iBT). *Application deadline:* For fall admission, 3/15 for domestic and international students; for spring admission, 10/1 for domestic and international students. Application fee: $30 ($40 for international students). Electronic applications accepted. *Expenses:* Tuition, state resident: full-time $6570; part-time $365 per credit hour. Tuition, nonresident: full-time $11,250; part-time $625 per credit hour. *Unit head:* Dr. Cynthia Reynolds, Coordinator, 330-972-6748, E-mail: creynol@uakron.edu. *Application contact:* Dr. Cynthia Reynolds, Coordinator, 330-972-6748, E-mail: creynol@uakron.edu.

University of Alberta, Faculty of Graduate Studies and Research, Department of Educational Psychology, Edmonton, AB T6G 2E1, Canada. Offers counseling psychology (M Ed, PhD); educational psychology (M Ed, PhD); instructional technology (M Ed); school counseling (M Ed); school psychology (M Ed, PhD); special education (M Ed, PhD); special education-deafness studies (M Ed); teaching English as a second language (M Ed). Part-time programs available. *Faculty:* 34 full-time (14 women), 12 part-time/adjunct (6 women). *Students:* 117 full-time (93 women), 173 part-time (121 women). Average age 36. 252 applicants, 34% accepted. In 2009, 30 master's, 10 doctorates awarded. *Degree requirements:* For master's, thesis optional; for doctorate, comprehensive exam, thesis/dissertation. *Entrance requirements:* For master's and doctorate, minimum GPA of 3.0. Additional exam requirements/recommendations for international students: Required—TOEFL. *Application deadline:* For fall admission, 2/1 priority date for domestic and international students. Applications are processed on a rolling basis. Tuition and fees charges are reported in Canadian dollars. *Expenses:* Tuition, area resident: Full-time $4626 Canadian dollars; part-time $99.72 Canadian dollars per unit. International tuition: $8216 Canadian dollars full-time. Required fees: $3590 Canadian dollars; $99.72 Canadian dollars per unit. $215 Canadian dollars per term. *Financial support:* In 2009–10, 10 fellowships with full tuition reimbursements (averaging $16,120 per year), 36 research assistantships with full tuition reimbursements (averaging $12,614 per year), 46 teaching assistantships with full tuition reimbursements (averaging $5,462 per year) were awarded; career-related internships or fieldwork and scholarships/grants also available. *Faculty research:* Human learning, development and assessment. *Unit head:* Dr. Linda M. McDonald, Chair, 780-492-1149, Fax: 780-492-1318, E-mail: linda.mcdonald@ualberta.ca. *Application contact:* Judy Maynes, Information Contact, 780-492-1149, Fax: 780-492-1318, E-mail: edpygrad@ualberta.ca.

The University of British Columbia, Faculty of Education, Department of Educational and Counseling Psychology, and Special Education, Vancouver, BC V6T 1Z1, Canada. Offers counseling psychology (M Ed, MA, PhD); development, learning and culture (PhD); guidance studies (Diploma); human development, learning and culture (M Ed, MA); measurement and evaluation and research methodology (M Ed); measurement, evaluation and research methodology (MA); measurement, evaluation, and research methodology (PhD); school psychology (M Ed, MA, PhD); special education (M Ed, MA, PhD, Diploma). Part-time programs available. *Degree requirements:* For master's, thesis (for some programs); for doctorate, comprehensive exam, thesis/dissertation. *Entrance requirements:* For master's, GRE General Test (counseling psychology MA); for doctorate, GRE General Test. Additional exam requirements/recommendations for international students: Required—TOEFL. Electronic applications accepted. *Faculty research:* Women, family, social problems, career transition, stress and coping problems.

University of Calgary, Faculty of Graduate Studies, Faculty of Education, Division of Applied Psychology, Calgary, AB T2N 1N4, Canada. Offers counseling psychology (M Ed, M Sc, PhD); human development and learning (M Ed, M Sc, PhD); school psychology (M Ed, M Sc, PhD); special education (M Ed, M Sc, PhD). Part-time programs available. *Degree requirements:* For master's, thesis (for some programs), final oral exam; for doctorate, thesis/dissertation, candidacy exam, final oral exam. *Entrance requirements:* For master's, minimum GPA of 3.0, 3 letters of reference; for doctorate, minimum GPA of 3.5, 3 letters of reference. *Faculty research:* Counselor education, family life studies, learning and cognition.

University of California, Riverside, Graduate Division, Graduate School of Education, Riverside, CA 92521-0102. Offers autism (M Ed); curriculum and instruction (MA, PhD); diversity and equity (M Ed); educational leadership and policy (MA, PhD); educational psychology (MA,

PhD); general education (M Ed); higher education administration and policy (M Ed, PhD); leadership (M Ed); reading (M Ed); school psychology (PhD); special education (M Ed, MA, PhD). *Faculty:* 23 full-time (12 women), 12 part-time/adjunct (8 women). *Students:* 230 full-time (183 women), 6 part-time (3 women); includes 75 minority (12 African Americans, 1 American Indian/Alaska Native, 21 Asian Americans or Pacific Islanders, 41 Hispanic Americans), 6 international. Average age 32. 288 applicants, 60% accepted, 118 enrolled. In 2009, 68 master's, 13 doctorates awarded. Terminal master's awarded for partial completion of doctoral program. *Degree requirements:* For master's, comprehensive exam (for some programs), comprehensive exams or thesis (MA), case study or analytical report (M Ed); for doctorate, thesis/dissertation, written and oral qualifying exams, college teaching practicum. *Entrance requirements:* For master's, GRE General Test, GRE Subject Test, CBEST, CSET, minimum GPA of 3.2; for doctorate, GRE General Test, GRE Subject Test, master's degree (desirable), minimum GPA of 3.2. Additional exam requirements/recommendations for international students: Required—TOEFL (minimum score 550 paper-based; 213 computer-based; 80 iBT). *Application deadline:* For fall admission, 9/1 for domestic students, 4/1 for international students; for winter admission, 12/1 for domestic students, 9/1 for international students; for spring admission, 3/1 for domestic students, 10/1 for international students. Applications are processed on a rolling basis. Application fee: $70 ($85 for international students). Electronic applications accepted. *Financial support:* In 2009–10, 55 students received support, including 13 fellowships with full and partial tuition reimbursements available (averaging $26,809 per year), 21 research assistantships with full and partial tuition reimbursements available (averaging $14,238 per year), 1 teaching assistantship with full and partial tuition reimbursement available (averaging $16,638 per year); career-related internships or fieldwork, Federal Work-Study, institutionally sponsored loans, scholarships/grants, and unspecified assistantships also available. Financial award application deadline: 1/5; financial award applicants required to submit FAFSA. *Faculty research:* Responsiveness to intervention, faculty core, response to intervention of English language learners, advanced modeling techniques, study on social capital, trust, and motivation. Total annual research expenditures: $5.6 million. *Unit head:* Dr. Steven T. Bossert, Dean, 951-827-5802, Fax: 951-827-3942, E-mail: steven.bossert@ucr.edu. *Application contact:* Dr. John Wills, Graduate Advisor for Admission, 951-827-6362, Fax: 951-827-3942, E-mail: edgrad@ucr.edu.

University of California, Santa Barbara, Graduate Division, Gevirtz Graduate School of Education, Santa Barbara, CA 93106-9490. Offers counseling, clinical and school psychology (PhD), including clinical psychology, counseling psychology, school psychology; education (M Ed, MA, PhD), including child and adolescent development (MA, PhD), cultural perspectives and comparative education (MA, PhD), educational leadership and organizations (MA, PhD), research methodology (MA, PhD), special education disabilities and risk studies (MA), special education, disabilities and risk studies (PhD), teaching (M Ed), teaching and learning (MA, PhD); educational leadership (Ed D); school psychology (M Ed); MA/PhD. *Accreditation:* APA (one or more programs are accredited). Postbaccalaureate distance learning degree programs offered (minimal on-campus study). *Faculty:* 42 full-time (20 women), 10 part-time/adjunct (4 women). *Students:* 390 full-time (303 women); includes 149 minority (14 African Americans, 3 American Indian/Alaska Native, 57 Asian Americans or Pacific Islanders, 75 Hispanic Americans), 16 international. Average age 31. 717 applicants, 40% accepted, 170 enrolled. In 2009, 140 master's, 46 doctorates awarded. Terminal master's awarded for partial completion of doctoral program. *Degree requirements:* For master's, comprehensive exam (for some programs), thesis (for some programs); for doctorate, comprehensive exam (for some programs), thesis/dissertation, qualifying exam. *Entrance requirements:* For master's, GRE, 3 letters of recommendation, resume/curriculum vitae; for doctorate, GRE, 3 letters of recommendation, statement of purpose, personal achievements/contributions statement, resume/curriculum vitae, transcripts for post-secondary institutions attended. Additional exam requirements/recommendations for international students: Required—TOEFL (minimum score 550 paper-based; 213 computer-based; 80 iBT) or IELTS (minimum score 7). Application fee: $70 ($90 for international students). Electronic applications accepted. *Financial support:* In 2009–10, 253 students received support, including 206 fellowships with full and partial tuition reimbursements available (averaging $5,000 per year), 62 research assistantships with full and partial tuition reimbursements available (averaging $6,200 per year), 87 teaching assistantships with partial tuition reimbursements available (averaging $6,500 per year); career-related internships or fieldwork, Federal Work-Study, institutionally sponsored loans, scholarships/grants, traineeships, health care benefits, and unspecified assistantships also available. Financial award applicants required to submit FAFSA. *Faculty research:* Professional development, early childhood development, school violence, literacy, science/math initiative. Total annual research expenditures: $4.4 million. *Unit head:* Dr. Jane Conoley, Chair, 805-893-2185, E-mail: jane-conoley@education.ucsb.edu. *Application contact:* Kathryn Marie Tucciarone, Student Affairs Officer, 805-893-2137, E-mail: katiet@education.ucsb.edu.

University of Central Arkansas, Graduate School, College of Health and Behavioral Sciences, Department of Counseling and Psychology, Program in School Psychology, Conway, AR 72035-0001. Offers MS, PhD. *Accreditation:* APA; NCATE. *Students:* 27 full-time (22 women), 16 part-time (15 women); includes 3 minority (2 African Americans, 1 Hispanic American), 1 international. Average age 25. 13 applicants, 77% accepted, 8 enrolled. In 2009, 7 master's awarded. Terminal master's awarded for partial completion of doctoral program. *Degree requirements:* For master's, comprehensive exam, thesis optional; for doctorate, comprehensive exam, thesis/dissertation. *Entrance requirements:* For master's, GRE General Test, minimum GPA of 2.7; for doctorate, GRE General Test. Additional exam requirements/recommendations for international students: Required—TOEFL (minimum score 550 paper-based; 213 computer-based). *Application deadline:* For fall admission, 3/1 priority date for domestic and international students; for spring admission, 10/1 for domestic and international students. Applications are processed on a rolling basis. Application fee: $25 ($50 for international students). *Expenses:* Tuition, state resident: full-time $5136; part-time $214 per credit hour. Required fees: $379.50; $127 per term. Tuition and fees vary according to course level, course load and campus/location. *Financial support:* Career-related internships or fieldwork, Federal Work-Study, scholarships/grants, tuition waivers (partial), and unspecified assistantships available. Financial award application deadline: 2/15; financial award applicants required to submit FAFSA. *Unit head:* Dr. Ron Bramlett, Coordinator, 501-450-5405. *Application contact:* Patti Hornor, Administrative Assistant, 501-450-5063, Fax: 501-450-5678, E-mail: pattih@uca.edu.

University of Central Florida, College of Education, Department of Child, Family and Community Sciences, Program in School Psychology, Orlando, FL 32816. Offers Ed S. Part-time and evening/weekend programs available. *Students:* 41 full-time (36 women); includes 11 minority (3 African Americans, 1 Asian American or Pacific Islander, 7 Hispanic Americans), 1 international. Average age 26. 36 applicants, 47% accepted, 15 enrolled. In 2009, 13 Ed Ss awarded. *Degree requirements:* For Ed S, thesis or alternative, practicum, internship. *Entrance requirements:* For degree, GRE General Test, minimum GPA of 3.0, resume, interview. Additional exam requirements/recommendations for international students: Required—TOEFL. *Application deadline:* For fall admission, 3/1 for domestic students. Application fee: $30. Electronic applications accepted. *Expenses:* Tuition, state resident: part-time $306.31 per credit hour. Tuition, nonresident: part-time $1099.01 per credit hour. Part-time tuition and fees vary according to degree level and program. *Financial support:* In 2009–10, 6 students received support, including 3 research assistantships with partial tuition reimbursements available (averaging $7,600 per year), 3 teaching assistantships with partial tuition reimbursements available (averaging $7,400 per year); career-related internships or fieldwork, Federal Work-Study, institutionally sponsored loans, tuition waivers (partial), and unspecified assistantships also available. Financial award application deadline: 3/1; financial award applicants required to submit FAFSA.

University of Cincinnati, Graduate School, College of Education, Criminal Justice, and Human Services, Division of Human Services, Program in School Psychology, Cincinnati, OH 45221. Offers PhD, Ed S. *Accreditation:* NCATE. Part-time programs available. *Degree requirements:* For doctorate, comprehensive exam, thesis/dissertation. *Entrance requirements:* For doctorate, GRE General Test, GRE Subject Test. Additional exam requirements/recommendations for international students: Required—TOEFL (minimum score 520 paper-based; 190 computer-based; 68 iBT), OEPT. Electronic applications accepted. *Faculty research:* School psychology services delivery, direct assessment and intervention.

University of Connecticut, Graduate School, Neag School of Education, Department of Educational Psychology, Program in School Psychology, Storrs, CT 06269. Offers MA, PhD, Post-Master's Certificate. *Accreditation:* APA; NCATE. *Faculty:* 17 full-time (8 women). *Students:* 27 full-time (22 women), 10 part-time (7 women); includes 2 minority (both Asian Americans or Pacific Islanders), 1 international. Average age 28. 78 applicants, 29% accepted, 12 enrolled. In 2009, 10 master's, 6 doctorates, 6 other advanced degrees awarded. Terminal master's awarded for partial completion of doctoral program. *Degree requirements:* For master's, comprehensive exam, thesis or alternative; for doctorate, thesis/dissertation. *Entrance requirements:* For doctorate, GRE General Test. Additional exam requirements/recommendations for international students: Required—TOEFL (minimum score 550 paper-based; 213 computer-based). *Application deadline:* For fall admission, 2/1 priority date for domestic and international students; for spring admission, 11/1 for domestic students, 10/1 for international students. Applications are processed on a rolling basis. Application fee: $55. Electronic applications accepted. *Expenses:* Tuition, state resident: full-time $4725; part-time $525 per credit. Tuition, nonresident: full-time $12,267; part-time $1363 per credit. Required fees: $346 per semester. Tuition and fees vary according to course load. *Financial support:* In 2009–10, 13 research assistantships with full tuition reimbursements, 2 teaching assistantships with full tuition reimbursements were awarded; fellowships, Federal Work-Study, scholarships/grants, health care benefits, and unspecified assistantships also available. Financial award application deadline: 2/1; financial award applicants required to submit FAFSA. *Unit head:* Hariharan Swaminathan, Head, 860-486-4031, Fax: 860-486-0210, E-mail: hariharan.swaminathan@uconn.edu. *Application contact:* Cheryl Lowe, Program Assistant, 860-486-4031, Fax: 860-486-0180, E-mail: cheryl.lowe@uconn.edu.

University of Dayton, Graduate School, School of Education and Allied Professions, Department of Counselor Education and Human Services, Dayton, OH 45469-1300. Offers college student personnel (MS Ed); community counseling (MS Ed); higher education administration (MS Ed); human services (MS Ed); school counseling (MS Ed); school psychology (MS Ed, Ed S); teacher as child/youth development specialist (MS Ed). *Accreditation:* NCATE. Part-time and evening/weekend programs available. *Faculty:* 11 full-time (8 women), 33 part-time/adjunct (22 women). *Students:* 254 full-time (207 women), 207 part-time (180 women); includes 76 minority (69 African Americans, 3 Asian Americans or Pacific Islanders, 4 Hispanic Americans), 2 international. Average age 32. 359 applicants, 47% accepted, 114 enrolled. In 2009, 163 master's, 11 Ed Ss awarded. *Degree requirements:* For master's, comprehensive exam (for some programs), thesis (for some programs), exit exam. *Entrance requirements:* For master's, MAT or GRE (if GPA less than 2.75), interview, writing sample. Additional exam requirements/recommendations for international students: Required—TOEFL (minimum score 550 paper-based; 213 computer-based; 80 iBT). *Application deadline:* For fall admission, 4/10 for domestic students, 3/1 priority date for international students; for winter admission, 9/10 for domestic students, 7/1 priority date for international students; for spring admission, 1/10 for domestic students, 1/1 priority date for international students. Applications are processed on a rolling basis. Application fee: $0 ($50 for international students). Electronic applications accepted. *Expenses:* Tuition: Full-time $8412; part-time $701 per credit hour. Required fees: $325; $65 per course. $25 per semester. Tuition and fees vary according to course load, degree level and program. *Financial support:* In 2009–10, 7 research assistantships with full tuition reimbursements (averaging $8,000 per year), 1 teaching assistantship with full tuition reimbursement (averaging $8,000 per year) were awarded; career-related internships or fieldwork, institutionally sponsored loans, health care benefits, and unspecified assistantships also available. Financial award applicants required to submit FAFSA. *Faculty research:* Anger as part of the grief process, inclusion of children with severe disabilities, comparisons of school counselors in Bosnia and the U. S., graduate and professional student socialization, use of cohort groups in doctoral programs, bullying in schools, impact of space on learning, sophomore experience. *Unit head:* Dr. Alan Demmitt, Chairperson, 937-229-3644, Fax: 937-229-1055. *Application contact:* Graduate Admissions, 937-229-4411, Fax: 937-229-4729, E-mail: gradadmission@udayton.edu.

University of Delaware, College of Human Services, Education and Public Policy and Department of Individual and Family Studies, Program in Counseling in Higher Education, Newark, DE 19716. Offers M Ed, MA. *Accreditation:* NCATE. *Degree requirements:* For master's, comprehensive exam. *Entrance requirements:* For master's, GRE (quantitative and verbal), on-campus interview, letters of recommendation. Additional exam requirements/recommendations for international students: Required—TOEFL (minimum score 600 paper-based). Electronic applications accepted. *Faculty research:* Counseling outcomes, student culture, group counseling.

University of Delaware, College of Human Services, Education and Public Policy, School of Education, Newark, DE 19716. Offers education (PhD); educational leadership (Ed D); higher education (M Ed); instruction (MI); reading (M Ed); school leadership (M Ed); school psychology (MA, Ed S); teaching English as a second language (TESL) (MA). *Accreditation:* NCATE. Part-time and evening/weekend programs available. Terminal master's awarded for partial completion of doctoral program. *Degree requirements:* For master's, comprehensive exam (for some programs), thesis (for some programs); for doctorate, comprehensive exam (for some programs), thesis/dissertation. *Entrance requirements:* For master's and doctorate, GRE, 3 letters of recommendation. Additional exam requirements/recommendations for international students: Required—TOEFL (minimum score 600 paper-based; 250 computer-based). Electronic applications accepted. *Faculty research:* Teacher education; curriculum theory and development; community based education models, educational leadership.

University of Denver, College of Education, Denver, CO 80208. Offers counseling psychology (MA, PhD); curriculum and instruction (MA, PhD, Certificate), including curriculum leadership (MA, PhD); educational administration and policy studies (Certificate); educational psychology (MA, PhD, Ed S), including child and family studies (MA, PhD), quantitative research methods (MA, PhD), school psychology (PhD, Ed S); higher education and adult studies (MA, PhD); library and information science (MLIS); library and information sciences (Certificate); school administration (PhD). *Accreditation:* ALA; APA (one or more programs are accredited). Part-time and evening/weekend programs available. Postbaccalaureate distance learning degree programs offered (no on-campus study). *Faculty:* 33 full-time (24 women), 62 part-time/adjunct (41 women). *Students:* 384 full-time (305 women), 453 part-time (336 women); includes 164 minority (47 African Americans, 8 American Indian/Alaska Native, 14 Asian Americans or Pacific Islanders, 95 Hispanic Americans), 20 international. Average age 34. 1,065 applicants, 59% accepted, 433 enrolled. In 2009, 206 master's, 38 doctorates, 117 other advanced degrees awarded. Terminal master's awarded for partial completion of doctoral program. *Degree requirements:* For master's, comprehensive exam; for doctorate, 2 foreign languages, comprehensive exam, thesis/dissertation. *Entrance requirements:* For master's and doctorate, GRE General Test or MAT. *Application deadline:* Applications are processed on a rolling basis. Application fee: $50. Electronic applications accepted. *Expenses:* Tuition: Full-time $34,596; part-time $961 per quarter hour. Required fees: $4 per quarter hour. Tuition and fees vary according to course load, campus/location and program. *Financial support:* In 2009–10, 78 teaching assistantships with full and partial tuition reimbursements (averaging $11,700 per year) were awarded; career-related internships or fieldwork, Federal Work-Study, institutionally sponsored loans, and scholarships/grants also available. Support available to part-time students. Financial award application deadline: 3/1; financial award applicants required to submit FAFSA. *Faculty research:* Parkinson's disease, personnel training, development and assessments, gifted education, service-learning, transportation, public schools. Total annual research expenditures: $340,000. *Unit head:* Dr. Gregory M. Anderson, Dean, 303-871-3665. *Application contact:* Janet Erickson, Director of Graduate Admission, 303-871-2485, E-mail: edinfo@du.edu.

School Psychology

University of Detroit Mercy, College of Liberal Arts and Education, Department of Psychology, Program in School Psychology, Detroit, MI 48221. Offers Spec.

University of Florida, Graduate School, College of Education, Department of Educational Psychology, Gainesville, FL 32611. Offers educational psychology (M Ed, MAE, Ed D, PhD, Ed S); research and evaluation methodology (M Ed, MAE, Ed D, PhD, Ed S); school psychology (M Ed, MAE, Ed D, PhD, Ed S). *Accreditation:* NCATE. Terminal master's awarded for partial completion of doctoral program. *Degree requirements:* For master's, thesis (MAE); for doctorate, variable foreign language requirement, thesis/dissertation. *Entrance requirements:* For master's and doctorate, GRE General Test, minimum GPA of 3.0; for Ed S, GRE General Test. Additional exam requirements/recommendations for international students: Required—TOEFL (minimum score 550 paper-based; 213 computer-based). Electronic applications accepted. *Faculty research:* School improvement, teaching and learning, item response theory.

University of Hartford, College of Arts and Sciences, Department of Psychology, Program in School Psychology, West Hartford, CT 06117-1599. Offers MS. *Accreditation:* NCATE. Part-time programs available. *Degree requirements:* For master's, comprehensive exam. *Entrance requirements:* For master's, GRE General Test, GRE Subject Test, minimum GPA of 3.0, 3 letters of recommendation. Additional exam requirements/recommendations for international students: Required—TOEFL (minimum score 550 paper-based; 213 computer-based). Electronic applications accepted. *Faculty research:* Family therapy, child developments, clinical supervision.

University of Houston–Clear Lake, School of Human Sciences and Humanities, Programs in Human Sciences, Houston, TX 77058-1098. Offers behavioral sciences (MA), including criminology, cross cultural studies, general psychology, sociology; clinical psychology (MA); criminology (MA); cross cultural studies (MA); family therapy (MA); fitness and human performance (MA); school psychology (MA). *Accreditation:* AAMFT/COAMFTE. Part-time and evening/weekend programs available. Postbaccalaureate distance learning degree programs offered (minimal on-campus study). *Degree requirements:* For master's, thesis or alternative. *Entrance requirements:* For master's, GRE General Test. Additional exam requirements/recommendations for international students: Required—TOEFL (minimum score 550 paper-based; 213 computer-based). Electronic applications accepted. *Faculty research:* Smoking cessation, adolescent sexuality, white collar crime, serial murder, human factors/human computer interaction.

University of Houston–Victoria, School of Arts and Sciences, Program in Psychology, Victoria, TX 77901-4450. Offers counseling psychology (MA); school psychology (MA). Part-time and evening/weekend programs available. Postbaccalaureate distance learning degree programs offered. *Degree requirements:* For master's, project or thesis. *Entrance requirements:* For master's, GRE General Test. Additional exam requirements/recommendations for international students: Required—TOEFL (minimum score 550 paper-based; 213 computer-based). Electronic applications accepted.

University of Idaho, College of Graduate Studies, College of Education, Department of Counseling and School Psychology, Special Education, and Educational Leadership, Program in School Psychology, Moscow, ID 83844-2282. Offers Ed S. *Accreditation:* NCATE. *Students:* 15 full-time, 4 part-time. In 2009, 15 Ed Ss awarded. *Application deadline:* For fall admission, 8/1 for domestic students; for spring admission, 12/15 for domestic students. Application fee: $55 ($60 for international students). *Expenses:* Tuition, state resident: full-time $6120. Tuition, nonresident: full-time $17,712. *Financial support:* Application deadline: 2/15. *Unit head:* Dr. Russell A. Joki, Chair, 208-364-4099, E-mail: rjoki@uidaho.edu. *Application contact:* Dr. Russell A. Joki, Chair, 208-364-4099, E-mail: rjoki@uidaho.edu.

The University of Iowa, Graduate College, College of Education, Department of Psychological and Quantitative Foundations, Iowa City, IA 52242-1316. Offers counseling psychology (PhD); educational measurement and statistics (MA, PhD); educational psychology (MA, PhD); school psychology (PhD, Ed S); JD/PhD. *Accreditation:* APA. *Degree requirements:* For master's, thesis optional, exam; for doctorate, comprehensive exam, thesis/dissertation; for Ed S, exam. *Entrance requirements:* For master's, doctorate, and Ed S, GRE General Test, minimum GPA of 3.0. Additional exam requirements/recommendations for international students: Required—TOEFL (minimum score 550 paper-based; 213 computer-based; 81 iBT). Electronic applications accepted.

The University of Kansas, Graduate Studies, School of Education, Department of Psychology and Research in Education, Program in School Psychology, Lawrence, KS 66045. Offers PhD, Ed S. *Accreditation:* APA (one or more programs are accredited); NCATE. *Students:* 31 full-time (21 women); includes 2 minority (both Hispanic Americans), 2 international. Average age 26. 40 applicants, 53% accepted, 11 enrolled. In 2009, 1 doctorate, 10 other advanced degrees awarded. *Degree requirements:* For doctorate, comprehensive exam, thesis/dissertation; for Ed S, comprehensive exam. *Entrance requirements:* For doctorate, GRE General Test; for Ed S, GRE General Test, minimum GPA of 3.0. Additional exam requirements/recommendations for international students: Required—TOEFL. *Application deadline:* For fall admission, 12/15 for domestic and international students. Application fee: $45 ($50 for international students). Electronic applications accepted. *Expenses:* Tuition, state resident: full-time $6492; part-time $270.50 per credit hour. Tuition, nonresident: full-time $15,510; part-time $646.25 per credit hour. Required fees: $847; $70.56 per credit hour. Tuition and fees vary according to course load and program. *Financial support:* Fellowships, research assistantships with full and partial tuition reimbursements, teaching assistantships with full and partial tuition reimbursements available. Financial award application deadline: 2/1. *Faculty research:* Classroom management, anxiety in children and youth, child behavior and learning problems, behavioral and personality assessment, home/school/community partnerships. *Unit head:* Patricia A. Lowe, Director of Training, 785-864-9710, Fax: 785-864-3820, E-mail: tlowe@ku.edu. *Application contact:* Admissions Coordinator, 785-864-3931, Fax: 785-864-3820, E-mail: preadmit@ku.edu.

University of Kentucky, Graduate School, College of Education, Program in Educational and Counseling Psychology, Lexington, KY 40506-0032. Offers counseling psychology (MS Ed, PhD, Ed S); educational and counseling psychology (MS Ed); educational psychology (Ed D, PhD, Ed S); school psychometrist and school psychology (MA Ed). *Accreditation:* APA (one or more programs are accredited); NCATE. *Degree requirements:* For master's, comprehensive exam, thesis optional; for doctorate, comprehensive exam, thesis/dissertation; for Ed S, comprehensive exam. *Entrance requirements:* For master's, GRE General Test, minimum undergraduate GPA of 2.75; for doctorate, GRE General Test, minimum graduate GPA of 3.0; for Ed S, GRE General Test. Additional exam requirements/recommendations for international students: Required—TOEFL (minimum score 550 paper-based; 213 computer-based). Electronic applications accepted.

University of Louisiana at Monroe, Graduate School, College of Education and Human Development, Department of Psychology, Program in School Psychology, Monroe, LA 71209-0001. Offers MS, SSP. *Accreditation:* NCATE. *Faculty:* 2 full-time (both women), 2 part-time/adjunct (1 woman). *Students:* 6 full-time (5 women), 2 part-time (1 woman); includes 2 minority (both African Americans). Average age 29. In 2009, 2 other advanced degrees awarded. *Degree requirements:* For SSP, comprehensive exam, thesis, field and practicum experience (400 hours), internship (1250 hours). *Entrance requirements:* For master's, GRE, minimum cumulative GPA of 2.75; for SSP, GRE General Test, minimum GPA of 3.25. Additional exam requirements/recommendations for international students: Required—TOEFL (minimum score 500 paper-based; 173 computer-based; 61 iBT). *Application deadline:* For fall admission, 8/24 priority date for domestic students, 7/1 for international students; for winter admission, 12/14 priority date for domestic students; for spring admission, 1/19 for domestic students, 11/1 for international students. Applications are processed on a rolling basis. Application fee: $20 ($30 for international students). Electronic applications accepted. *Expenses:* Tuition, state resident: part-time $159 per credit hour. Tuition, nonresident: part-time $159 per credit hour. Required fees: $1300 per year. Tuition and fees vary according to course load. *Financial support:* Career-related internships or fieldwork, Federal Work-Study, and unspecified assistantships available. Financial award application deadline: 4/1; financial award applicants required to submit FAFSA. *Unit head:* Dr. Veronica Lewis, Coordinator, 818-342-1332, E-mail: vlewis@ulm.edu. *Application contact:* Dr. Veronica Lewis, Coordinator, 818-342-1332, E-mail: vlewis@ulm.edu.

University of Manitoba, Faculty of Graduate Studies, Faculty of Arts, Department of Psychology, Winnipeg, MB R3T 2N2, Canada. Offers clinical psychology (PhD); psychology (MA, PhD); school psychology (MA). *Accreditation:* APA (one or more programs are accredited). *Degree requirements:* For master's, thesis; for doctorate, one foreign language, thesis/dissertation. *Entrance requirements:* For master's and doctorate, GRE General Test.

University of Mary, Division of Social and Behavioral Sciences, Bismarck, ND 58504-9652. Offers addiction counseling (MSC); community counseling (MSC); school counseling (MSC). Part-time programs available. Postbaccalaureate distance learning degree programs offered (minimal on-campus study). *Degree requirements:* For master's, thesis, internship. *Entrance requirements:* For master's, coursework/experience in psychology, statistics. Additional exam requirements/recommendations for international students: Required—TOEFL. *Expenses:* Tuition: Full-time $10,062; part-time $430 per credit. Tuition and fees vary according to course load, degree level, program and student level.

University of Mary Hardin-Baylor, Graduate Studies in Counseling and Psychology, Belton, TX 76513. Offers community counseling (MA); marriage and family Christian counseling (MA); psychology and counseling (MA); school counseling and psychology (MA). Part-time and evening/weekend programs available. *Degree requirements:* For master's, comprehensive exam. *Entrance requirements:* For master's, GRE General Test, minimum GPA of 3.0 in last 60 hours or 2.75 overall. Electronic applications accepted.

University of Maryland, College Park, Academic Affairs, College of Education, Department of Counseling and Personnel Services, College Park, MD 20742. Offers college student personnel (M Ed, MA); college student personnel administration (PhD); community counseling (CAGS); community/career counseling (M Ed, MA); counseling and personnel services (M Ed, MA, PhD), including art therapy (M Ed), college student personnel (M Ed), counseling and personnel services (PhD), counseling psychology (M Ed), mental health counseling (M Ed), school counseling (M Ed); counseling psychology (PhD); counselor education (PhD); rehabilitation counseling (M Ed, MA, AGSC); school counseling (M Ed, MA); school psychology (M Ed, MA, PhD). *Accreditation:* ACA (one or more programs are accredited); APA (one or more programs are accredited); CORE (one or more programs are accredited); NCATE. Part-time and evening/weekend programs available. Postbaccalaureate distance learning degree programs offered (no on-campus study). *Faculty:* 34 full-time (21 women), 8 part-time/adjunct (6 women). *Students:* 152 full-time (117 women), 25 part-time (18 women); includes 67 minority (32 African Americans, 2 American Indian/Alaska Native, 20 Asian Americans or Pacific Islanders, 13 Hispanic Americans), 16 international. 319 applicants, 15% accepted, 32 enrolled. In 2009, 24 master's, 15 doctorates, 4 other advanced degrees awarded. *Degree requirements:* For master's, thesis (for some programs); for doctorate, thesis/dissertation. *Entrance requirements:* For master's, GRE General Test or MAT, minimum GPA of 3.0, 3 letters of recommendation; for doctorate, GRE General Test or MAT, minimum GPA of 3.5, 3 letters of recommendation. Additional exam requirements/recommendations for international students: Required—TOEFL. *Application deadline:* For fall admission, 12/15 for domestic and international students; for spring admission, 10/1 for domestic students, 6/1 for international students. Applications are processed on a rolling basis. Application fee: $60. Electronic applications accepted. *Expenses:* Tuition, area resident: Part-time $471 per credit hour. Tuition, state resident: part-time $471 per credit hour. Tuition, nonresident: part-time $1016 per credit hour. Required fees: $337.04 per term. *Financial support:* In 2009–10, 4 fellowships with partial tuition reimbursements (averaging $10,402 per year), 8 research assistantships (averaging $16,454 per year), 93 teaching assistantships with tuition reimbursements (averaging $16,109 per year) were awarded; career-related internships or fieldwork, Federal Work-Study, and scholarships/grants also available. Support available to part-time students. Financial award applicants required to submit FAFSA. *Faculty research:* Educational psychology, counseling, health. Total annual research expenditures: $1.5 million. *Unit head:* Dr. Dennis Kivlighan, Chair, 301-405-2858, E-mail: dennisk@umd.edu. *Application contact:* Dean of Graduate School, 301-405-0358.

University of Massachusetts Amherst, Graduate School, School of Education, Program in Education, Amherst, MA 01003. Offers bilingual, English as a second language, and multicultural education (M Ed, CAGS); child study and early education (M Ed); children, families and schools (Ed D, CAGS); early childhood and elementary teacher education (M Ed); education policy and leadership (CAGS); educational administration (M Ed, CAGS); educational policy and leadership (Ed D); higher education (M Ed, CAGS); international education (M Ed); language, literacy and culture (Ed D); learning, media and technology (M Ed, CAGS); mathematics, science, and learning technologies (Ed D); policy studies (M Ed); policy studies in education (CAGS); reading and writing (M Ed); research and evaluation methods (Ed D); school counselor education (M Ed, CAGS); school psychology (CAGS); science education (CAGS); secondary teacher education (M Ed); social justice education (M Ed, Ed D, CAGS); special education (M Ed, Ed D, CAGS). *Accreditation:* NCATE. Part-time programs available. Postbaccalaureate distance learning degree programs offered (minimal on-campus study). *Faculty:* 74 full-time (41 women). *Students:* 377 full-time (268 women), 347 part-time (232 women); includes 115 minority (59 African Americans, 2 American Indian/Alaska Native, 16 Asian Americans or Pacific Islanders, 38 Hispanic Americans), 108 international. Average age 35. 708 applicants, 68% accepted, 266 enrolled. In 2009, 183 master's, 17 doctorates awarded. Terminal master's awarded for partial completion of doctoral program. *Degree requirements:* For master's, thesis or alternative; for doctorate, comprehensive exam, thesis/dissertation. *Entrance requirements:* Additional exam requirements/recommendations for international students: Required—TOEFL (minimum score 550 paper-based; 213 computer-based; 80 iBT), IELTS (minimum score 6.5). *Application deadline:* For fall admission, 1/15 for domestic and international students. Applications are processed on a rolling basis. Application fee: $50 ($65 for international students). Electronic applications accepted. *Expenses:* Tuition, state resident: full-time $2640; part-time $110 per credit. Tuition, nonresident: full-time $9936; part-time $414 per credit. Tuition and fees vary according to course load. *Financial support:* In 2009–10, 1 fellowship with full tuition reimbursement (averaging $8,036 per year), 92 research assistantships with full tuition reimbursements (averaging $8,555 per year), 83 teaching assistantships with full tuition reimbursements (averaging $4,661 per year) were awarded; career-related internships or fieldwork, Federal Work-Study, scholarships/grants, traineeships, health care benefits, tuition waivers (full), and unspecified assistantships also available. Support available to part-time students. Financial award application deadline: 1/15. *Unit head:* Dr. Linda L. Griffin, Graduate Program Director, 413-545-6984, Fax: 413-545-2873. *Application contact:* Jean M. Ames, Supervisor of Admissions, 413-545-0722, Fax: 413-577-0010, E-mail: gradadm@grad.umass.edu.

University of Massachusetts Amherst, Graduate School, School of Education, Program in School Psychology, Amherst, MA 01003. Offers PhD. *Accreditation:* APA; NCATE. Part-time programs available. *Students:* 19 full-time (16 women), 4 part-time (all women); includes 2 minority (1 African American, 1 Asian American or Pacific Islander), 1 international. Average age 27. 52 applicants, 17% accepted, 3 enrolled. In 2009, 5 doctorates awarded. Terminal master's awarded for partial completion of doctoral program. *Degree requirements:* For doctorate, comprehensive exam, thesis/dissertation. *Entrance requirements:* For doctorate, 3 letters of recommendation. Additional exam requirements/recommendations for international students: Required—TOEFL (minimum score 550 paper-based; 213 computer-based; 80 iBT), IELTS (minimum score 6.5). *Application deadline:* For fall admission, 1/15 for domestic and international students. Applications are processed on a rolling basis. Application fee: $50 ($65 for international students). Electronic applications accepted. *Expenses:* Tuition, state resident: full-time $2640; part-time $110 per credit. Tuition, nonresident: full-time $9936; part-time $414 per credit. Tuition and fees vary according to course load. *Financial support:* Fellowships, research assistantships, teaching assistantships, career-related internships or fieldwork, Federal Work-Study, scholarships/grants, traineeships, health care benefits, tuition waivers (full), and unspecified assistantships available. Support available to part-time students. Financial award application deadline: 1/15. *Unit head:* Dr. Linda L. Griffin, Graduate Program Director, 413-545-6984, Fax: 413-545-1523. *Application contact:* Jean M. Ames, Supervisor of Admissions, 413-545-0722, Fax: 413-577-0010, E-mail: gradadm@grad.umass.edu.

University of Massachusetts Boston, Office of Graduate Studies, Graduate College of Education, Counseling and School Psychology Department, Program in School Guidance Counseling, Boston, MA 02125-3393. Offers M Ed, CAGS.

University of Massachusetts Boston, Office of Graduate Studies, Graduate College of Education, Counseling and School Psychology Department, Program in School Psychology, Boston, MA 02125-3393. Offers M Ed, CAGS. Part-time and evening/weekend programs available. *Degree requirements:* For master's, comprehensive exam, practicum, final project; for CAGS, comprehensive exam. *Entrance requirements:* For master's, GRE General Test or MAT, minimum GPA of 3.0; for CAGS, minimum GPA of 2.75. *Faculty research:* School psychology services, assessment of children, cultural and gender differences on psychological adjustment to disabilities.

University of Memphis, Graduate School, College of Arts and Sciences, Department of Psychology, Memphis, TN 38152-3230. Offers psychology (MS, PhD), including clinical (PhD), experimental (PhD), general psychology (MS), school (PhD); school psychology (MA, Ed S); MS/PhD. *Faculty:* 28 full-time (9 women), 4 part-time/adjunct (0 women). *Students:* 115 full-time (81 women), 22 part-time (15 women); includes 23 minority (15 African Americans, 1 American Indian/Alaska Native, 4 Asian Americans or Pacific Islanders, 3 Hispanic Americans), 7 international. Average age 27. 220 applicants, 15% accepted, 29 enrolled. In 2009, 31 master's, 9 doctorates awarded. *Degree requirements:* For master's, comprehensive exam (for some programs), thesis (for some programs), 37 credit hours (MA); 33 credit hours with thesis or 36 with exam (MS); for doctorate, comprehensive exam (for some programs), thesis/dissertation, 80 semester hours, major area paper; clinical: 1 year placement and 1 year internship; internship (school psychology). *Entrance requirements:* For master's, GRE; for doctorate, GRE (minimum combined score of 1100), minimum GPA of 2.75, 18 hours of undergraduate psychology courses, transcripts, personal statement, letters of recommendation; for Ed S, GRE (minimum combined score of 1100), minimum GPA of 2.75, 18 hours of undergraduate psychology courses, letters of recommendation. Additional exam requirements/recommendations for international students: Required—TOEFL. *Application deadline:* For fall admission, 12/5 for domestic students. Applications are processed on a rolling basis. Application fee: $35 ($60 for international students). Electronic applications accepted. *Expenses:* Tuition, state resident: full-time $6246; part-time $347 per credit hour. Tuition, nonresident: full-time $15,894; part-time $883 per credit hour. Required fees: $1160. Full-time tuition and fees vary according to course load, degree level and program. *Financial support:* In 2009–10, 66 students received support; fellowships with full tuition reimbursements available, research assistantships with full tuition reimbursements available, teaching assistantships with full tuition reimbursements available, Federal Work-Study, scholarships/grants, tuition waivers (partial), and unspecified assistantships available. Financial award application deadline: 2/15; financial award applicants required to submit FAFSA. *Faculty research:* Clinical health; school, child and family research; psychotherapy research; cognitive and behavioral neuroscience research; industrial-organizational research. *Unit head:* Dr. Robert Cohen, Coordinator of Graduate Programs, 901-678-4679, Fax: 901-678-2579, E-mail: rcohen@memphis.edu. *Application contact:* Lynell Connable, Graduate Secretary, 901-678-4340, Fax: 901-678-2579, E-mail: dconnabl@memphis.edu.

University of Minnesota, Twin Cities Campus, Graduate School, College of Education and Human Development, Department of Educational Psychology, Program in School Psychology, Minneapolis, MN 55455-0213. Offers MA, PhD, Ed S. *Accreditation:* APA. *Students:* 49 full-time (42 women), 19 part-time (16 women); includes 7 minority (1 African American, 1 American Indian/Alaska Native, 3 Asian Americans or Pacific Islanders, 2 Hispanic Americans), 2 international. Average age 28. 67 applicants, 28% accepted, 13 enrolled. In 2009, 7 master's, 6 doctorates, 1 other advanced degree awarded. *Unit head:* Dr. Susan Hupp, Chair, 612-624-1003, Fax: 612-624-8241, E-mail: shupp@umn.edu. *Application contact:* Dr. Mary Trettin, Associate Dean, 612-625-6501, Fax: 612-626-1580, E-mail: mtrettin@umn.edu.

University of Minnesota, Twin Cities Campus, Graduate School, College of Education and Human Development, Institute of Child Development, Minneapolis, MN 55455-0213. Offers child psychology (MA, PhD); early childhood education (M Ed, MA, PhD); school psychology (MA, PhD). *Faculty:* 17 full-time (7 women). *Students:* 108 full-time (99 women), 34 part-time (32 women); includes 13 minority (2 African Americans, 3 American Indian/Alaska Native, 5 Asian Americans or Pacific Islanders, 3 Hispanic Americans), 11 international. Average age 31. 149 applicants, 29% accepted, 37 enrolled. In 2009, 45 master's, 7 doctorates awarded. *Financial support:* In 2009–10, 26 fellowships (averaging $24,044 per year), 23 research assistantships with full tuition reimbursements (averaging $26,058 per year), 39 teaching assistantships with full tuition reimbursements (averaging $27,413 per year) were awarded. *Faculty research:* Developmental affective and cognitive neuroscience; developmental psychopathology; intervention and prevention science; social and emotional development; cognitive, language, and perceptual development. Total annual research expenditures: $3.8 million. *Unit head:* Dr. Nicki Crick, Director, 612-625-8879, Fax: 612-624-6373, E-mail: crick001@umn.edu. *Application contact:* Claudia Johnston, Information Contact, 612-624-2576, Fax: 612-624-6373, E-mail: johnstc@staff.tc.umn.edu.

University of Minnesota, Twin Cities Campus, Graduate School, College of Liberal Arts, Department of Psychology, Minneapolis, MN 55455-0213. Offers biological psychopathology (PhD); clinical psychology (PhD); cognitive and biological psychology (PhD); counseling psychology (PhD); industrial/organizational psychology (PhD); personality, individual differences, and behavior genetics (PhD); quantitative/psychometric methods (PhD); school psychology (PhD); social psychology (PhD). *Accreditation:* APA. *Degree requirements:* For doctorate, comprehensive exam, thesis/dissertation. *Entrance requirements:* For doctorate, GRE General Test, GRE Subject Test (recommended), 12 credits of upper-level psychology courses, including a course in statistics or psychological measurement. Additional exam requirements/recommendations for international students: Required—TOEFL (minimum score 550 paper-based; 213 computer-based; 79 iBT).

University of Missouri, Graduate School, College of Education, Department of Educational, School, and Counseling Psychology, Columbia, MO 65211. Offers counseling psychology (M Ed, MA, PhD, Ed S); educational psychology (M Ed, MA, PhD, Ed S); learning and instruction (M Ed); school psychology (M Ed, MA, PhD, Ed S). *Accreditation:* APA (one or more programs are accredited). Part-time programs available. *Degree requirements:* For doctorate, thesis/dissertation. *Entrance requirements:* For master's, doctorate, and Ed S, GRE General Test, minimum GPA of 3.0. Additional exam requirements/recommendations for international students: Required—TOEFL (minimum score 580 paper-based; 237 computer-based; 92 iBT).

University of Missouri–St. Louis, College of Education, Division of Educational Psychology, Research, and Evaluation, St. Louis, MO 63121. Offers education (Ed D); educational psychology (PhD); program evaluation and assessment (Certificate); school psychology (Ed S). *Faculty:* 13 full-time (4 women), 8 part-time/adjunct (4 women). *Students:* 27 full-time (24 women), 27 part-time (20 women); includes 12 minority (all African Americans), 2 international. Average age 36. In 2009, 39 doctorates awarded. *Degree requirements:* For other advanced degree, internship. *Entrance requirements:* For degree, GRE General Test, 2-4 letters of recommendation, personal interview. Additional exam requirements/recommendations for international students: Recommended—TOEFL (minimum score 550 paper-based; 213 computer-based). *Application deadline:* For fall admission, 3/1 for domestic and international students. Application fee: $35 ($40 for international students). Electronic applications accepted. *Expenses:* Tuition, state resident: full-time $5377; part-time $297.70 per credit hour. Tuition, nonresident: full-time $13,882; part-time $771.20 per credit hour. Required fees: $220; $12.20 per credit hour. One-time fee: $12. Tuition and fees vary according to course level, campus/location and program. *Financial support:* In 2009–10, 1 research assistantship (averaging $12,240 per year), 2 teaching assistantships (averaging $8,306 per year) were awarded. Financial award application deadline: 4/1; financial award applicants required to submit FAFSA. *Faculty research:* Child/adolescent psychology, quantitative and qualitative methodology, evaluation processes, measurement and assessment. *Unit head:* Dr. Matthew Keefer, Chairperson, 314-516-5783, Fax: 314-516-5784, E-mail: keefer@umsl.edu. *Application contact:* 314-516-5458, Fax: 314-516-6996, E-mail: gradadm@umsl.edu.

The University of Montana, Graduate School, College of Arts and Sciences, Department of Psychology, Program in School Psychology, Missoula, MT 59812-0002. Offers MA, PhD, Ed S. *Degree requirements:* For master's, oral exam, professional paper; for Ed S, thesis. *Entrance requirements:* For master's, GRE General Test, GRE Subject Test, minimum GPA of 3.25 during previous 2 years; for Ed S, GRE General Test. Additional exam requirements/recommendations for international students: Required—TOEFL. *Faculty research:* Child development and creativity, psychological measurement.

University of Nebraska at Kearney, College of Graduate Study, College of Education, Department of Counseling and School Psychology, Kearney, NE 68849-0001. Offers counseling (MS Ed, Ed S); school psychology (Ed S). *Accreditation:* ACA; NCATE. Part-time and evening/weekend programs available. *Degree requirements:* For master's, thesis optional; for Ed S, thesis. *Entrance requirements:* For master's and Ed S, interview. Additional exam requirements/recommendations for international students: Required—TOEFL (minimum score 550 paper-based; 213 computer-based). Electronic applications accepted. *Faculty research:* Multicultural counseling and diversity issues, team decision making, adult development, women's issues, brief therapy.

University of Nebraska at Omaha, Graduate Studies, College of Arts and Sciences, Department of Psychology, Omaha, NE 68182. Offers developmental psychology (PhD); industrial/organizational psychology (MS, PhD); psychobiology (PhD); psychology (MA); school psychology (MS, Ed S). Part-time programs available. *Faculty:* 18 full-time (8 women). *Students:* 44 full-time (36 women), 23 part-time (18 women); includes 3 minority (1 African American, 1 Asian American or Pacific Islander, 1 Hispanic American), 2 international. Average age 26. 116 applicants, 34% accepted, 28 enrolled. In 2009, 30 master's, 5 other advanced degrees awarded. *Degree requirements:* For master's, comprehensive exam, thesis (for some programs). *Entrance requirements:* For master's, GRE General Test, GRE Subject Test, previous course work in psychology, including statistics and a laboratory course; minimum GPA of 3.0, 3 letters of recommendation; for doctorate, GRE General Test. Additional exam requirements/recommendations for international students: Required—TOEFL (minimum score 500 paper-based; 173 computer-based; 61 iBT). *Application deadline:* For fall admission, 1/5 for domestic students. Application fee: $45. Electronic applications accepted. *Financial support:* In 2009–10, 44 students received support; fellowships, research assistantships with tuition reimbursements available, teaching assistantships with tuition reimbursements available, career-related internships or fieldwork, Federal Work-Study, institutionally sponsored loans, scholarships/grants, tuition waivers (partial), and unspecified assistantships available. Support available to part-time students. Financial award application deadline: 3/1; financial award applicants required to submit FAFSA. *Unit head:* Dr. Kenneth Deffenbacher, Chairperson, 402-554-2592. *Application contact:* Dr. Joseph Brown, Student Contact, 402-554-2592.

University of Nebraska–Lincoln, Graduate College, College of Education and Human Sciences, Department of Educational Psychology, Lincoln, NE 68588. Offers cognition, learning and development (MA); counseling psychology (MA); educational psychology (MA, Ed S); psychological studies in education (PhD), including cognition, learning and development, counseling psychology, quantitative, qualitative, and psychometric methods, school psychology; quantitative, qualitative, and psychometric methods (MA); school psychology (MA, Ed S). *Accreditation:* APA (one or more programs are accredited); NCATE. *Degree requirements:* For master's, thesis optional. *Entrance requirements:* For master's, GRE General Test. Additional exam requirements/recommendations for international students: Required—TOEFL (minimum score 500 paper-based; 173 computer-based). Electronic applications accepted. *Faculty research:* Measurement and assessment, metacognition, academic skills, child development, multicultural education and counseling.

The University of North Carolina at Chapel Hill, Graduate School, School of Education, Program in School Psychology, Chapel Hill, NC 27599. Offers M Ed, MA, PhD. *Accreditation:* APA (one or more programs are accredited); NCATE. *Students:* 46 full-time (45 women), 12 part-time (all women); includes 9 minority (5 African Americans, 2 Asian Americans or Pacific Islanders, 2 Hispanic Americans), 4 international. Average age 27. 114 applicants, 26% accepted, 13 enrolled. In 2009, 4 master's, 3 doctorates awarded. *Degree requirements:* For master's, comprehensive exam, thesis (for some programs); for doctorate, comprehensive exam, thesis/dissertation. *Entrance requirements:* For master's and doctorate, GRE General Test, minimum GPA of 3.0 during last 2 years of undergraduate course work. Additional exam requirements/recommendations for international students: Required—TOEFL (minimum score 550 paper-based; 79 computer-based). *Application deadline:* For fall admission, 1/1 priority date for domestic and international students. Applications are processed on a rolling basis. Application fee: $77. Electronic applications accepted. *Financial support:* Application deadline: 3/1. *Unit head:* Dr. Barbara H. Wasik, Coordinator, 919-962-9197, E-mail: wasik@unc.edu. *Application contact:* Amy Butler, Student Services Assistant, 919-966-1346, Fax: 919-962-1533, E-mail: abutler@email.unc.edu.

The University of North Carolina at Greensboro, Graduate School, School of Education, Department of Counseling and Educational Development, Greensboro, NC 27412-5001. Offers advanced school counseling (PMC); counseling and counselor education (PhD); counseling and educational development (MS); couple and family counseling (PMC); school counseling (PMC); MS/Ed S. *Accreditation:* ACA (one or more programs are accredited); NCATE. *Degree requirements:* For master's, comprehensive exam, practicum, internship; for doctorate, comprehensive exam, thesis/dissertation. *Entrance requirements:* For master's, doctorate, and PMC, GRE General Test. Additional exam requirements/recommendations for international students: Required—TOEFL. Electronic applications accepted. *Faculty research:* Gerontology, invitational theory, career development, marriage and family therapy, drug and alcohol abuse prevention.

University of Northern Colorado, Graduate School, College of Education and Behavioral Sciences, School of Applied Psychology and Counselor Education, Program in School Psychology, Greeley, CO 80639. Offers PhD, Ed S. *Accreditation:* APA (one or more programs are accredited); NCATE. Part-time and evening/weekend programs available. *Faculty:* 5 full-time (3 women). *Students:* 32 full-time (27 women), 27 part-time (18 women); includes 6 minority (3 Asian Americans or Pacific Islanders, 3 Hispanic Americans). Average age 29. 56 applicants, 68% accepted, 13 enrolled. In 2009, 11 doctorates, 10 other advanced degrees awarded. *Degree requirements:* For doctorate, comprehensive exam, thesis/dissertation; for Ed S, comprehensive exam. *Entrance requirements:* For doctorate, GRE General Test, curriculum vitae, 3 letters of recommendation. *Application deadline:* For fall admission, 1/1 for domestic and international students. Applications are processed on a rolling basis. Application fee: $50 ($60 for international students). Electronic applications accepted. *Expenses:* Tuition, state resident: full-time $5770; part-time $320.55 per credit hour. Tuition, nonresident: full-time $13,847; part-time $769.27 per credit hour. Required fees: $948.78; $52.72 per credit. *Financial*

School Psychology

University of Northern Colorado (continued)

support: Fellowships, research assistantships, teaching assistantships, unspecified assistantships available. Financial award application deadline: 3/1; financial award applicants required to submit FAFSA. *Unit head:* Diane Greenshields, Program Coordinator, 970-351-2731, Fax: 970-351-2625. *Application contact:* Linda Sisson, Graduate Student Admission Coordinator, 970-351-1807, Fax: 970-351-2371, E-mail: linda.sisson@unco.edu.

University of Northern Iowa, Graduate College, College of Education, Department of Educational Psychology and Foundations, Cedar Falls, IA 50614. Offers educational psychology (MAE); professional development for teachers (MAE); school psychology (Ed S). Part-time and evening/weekend programs available. *Students:* 19 full-time (14 women), 16 part-time (11 women); includes 1 minority (Hispanic American), 2 international. 40 applicants, 48% accepted, 17 enrolled. In 2009, 20 master's, 6 other advanced degrees awarded. *Degree requirements:* For master's, comprehensive exam (for some programs), thesis or alternative; for Ed S, thesis or alternative. *Entrance requirements:* For master's, GRE General Test, minimum GPA of 3.0; for Ed S, GRE General Test. Additional exam requirements/recommendations for international students: Required—TOEFL (minimum score 500 paper-based; 180 computer-based; 61 iBT). *Application deadline:* For fall admission, 8/1 priority date for domestic students. Applications are processed on a rolling basis. Application fee: $30 ($50 for international students). Electronic applications accepted. *Financial support:* Career-related internships or fieldwork, Federal Work-Study, scholarships/grants, and tuition waivers (full and partial) available. Support available to part-time students. Financial award application deadline: 2/1. *Unit head:* Dr. Radhi Al-Mabuk, Interim Head, 319-273-2609, Fax: 319-273-5175, E-mail: radhi.al-mabuk@uni.edu. *Application contact:* Laurie S. Russell, Record Analyst, 319-273-2623, Fax: 319-273-6792, E-mail: laurie.russell@uni.edu.

University of North Texas, Robert B. Toulouse School of Graduate Studies, College of Education, Department of Educational Psychology, Program in School Psychology, Denton, TX 76203. Offers MS. *Degree requirements:* For master's, comprehensive exam, thesis optional, school psychology licensure. *Entrance requirements:* For master's, GRE General Test, undergraduate major in psychology; minimum GPA of 2.8, 3.0 in psychology. Additional exam requirements/recommendations for international students: Required—proof of English language proficiency required for non-native English speakers; Recommended—TOEFL (minimum score 550 paper-based; 213 computer-based; 79 iBT). Application fee: $50 ($75 for international students). *Expenses:* Tuition, state resident: full-time $4298; part-time $239 per contact hour. Tuition, nonresident: full-time $9878; part-time $549 per contact hour. Required fees: $265 per contact hour. *Financial support:* Application deadline: 4/15. *Faculty research:* Minority families, behavioral assessment in natural settings. *Application contact:* Administrative Assistant, 940-565-3486.

University of Oklahoma, Graduate College, College of Education, Department of Educational Psychology, Norman, OK 73019. Offers community counseling (M Ed); counseling psychology (PhD); instructional psychology (M Ed, PhD); school counseling (M Ed); special education (M Ed, PhD). *Accreditation:* NCATE. Part-time programs available. *Faculty:* 24 full-time (16 women), 1 part-time/adjunct (0 women). *Students:* 91 full-time (64 women), 80 part-time (63 women); includes 40 minority (15 African Americans, 12 American Indian/Alaska Native, 5 Asian Americans or Pacific Islanders, 8 Hispanic Americans), 17 international. 69 applicants, 29% accepted, 17 enrolled. In 2009, 15 master's, 9 doctorates awarded. Terminal master's awarded for partial completion of doctoral program. *Degree requirements:* For doctorate, thesis/dissertation. *Entrance requirements:* For master's, minimum GPA of 3.0, 12 hours of course work in education; for doctorate, GRE General Test, master's degree, minimum graduate GPA of 3.25. Additional exam requirements/recommendations for international students: Required—TOEFL (minimum score 550 paper-based; 213 computer-based). *Application deadline:* For fall admission, 6/1 for domestic students, 4/1 for international students; for spring admission, 11/1 for domestic students, 9/1 for international students. Applications are processed on a rolling basis. Application fee: $40 ($90 for international students). Electronic applications accepted. *Expenses:* Tuition, state resident: full-time $3744; part-time $156 per credit hour. Tuition, nonresident: full-time $13,577; part-time $565.70 per credit hour. Required fees: $2415; $90.10 per credit hour. *Financial support:* In 2009–10, 75 students received support, including 8 fellowships with full tuition reimbursements available (averaging $5,000 per year), 17 research assistantships with partial tuition reimbursements available (averaging $10,828 per year), 13 teaching assistantships with partial tuition reimbursements available (averaging $11,055 per year); career-related internships or fieldwork, Federal Work-Study, institutionally sponsored loans, health care benefits, and unspecified assistantships also available. Financial award applicants required to submit FAFSA. *Faculty research:* Counseling assessment, process and outcome, diversity issues, health psychology, marriage and family, education, training and supervision. Total annual research expenditures: $587,160. *Unit head:* Dr. Terri K. Debacker, Chair, 405-325-1068, Fax: 405-325-6655, E-mail: debacker@ou.edu. *Application contact:* Applications Officer, 405-325-4525, Fax: 405-325-6655, E-mail: gpoedpsych@ou.edu.

University of Phoenix–Denver Campus, The Artemis School, College of Education, Lone Tree, CO 80124-5453. Offers administration and supervision (MAEd); curriculum instruction (MAEd); elementary teacher education (MAEd); school counseling (MSC); secondary teacher education (MAEd). Evening/weekend programs available. *Degree requirements:* For master's, thesis (for some programs). *Entrance requirements:* For master's, minimum undergraduate GPA of 2.5, 3 years work experience. Additional exam requirements/recommendations for international students: Required—TOEFL (minimum score 550 paper-based; 213 computer-based; 79 iBT). Electronic applications accepted.

University of Phoenix–Las Vegas Campus, The Artemis School, College of Education, Las Vegas, NV 89128. Offers administration and supervision (MA Ed); curriculum and instruction (MA Ed); school counseling (MSC); teacher education-elementary licensure (MA Ed). Evening/weekend programs available. *Degree requirements:* For master's, thesis (for some programs). *Entrance requirements:* For master's, minimum undergraduate GPA of 2.5, 3 years of work experience. Additional exam requirements/recommendations for international students: Required—TOEFL (minimum score 550 paper-based; 213 computer-based; 79 iBT). Electronic applications accepted.

University of Phoenix–Northern Nevada Campus, College of Social and Behavioral Science, Reno, NV 89521-5862. Offers administration of justice and security (MS); marriage, family and child therapy (MSC); psychology (MS); school counseling (MSC).

University of Phoenix–Puerto Rico Campus, The Artemis School, College of Education, Guaynabo, PR 00968. Offers administration and supervision (MA Ed); early childhood education (MA Ed); school counselor (MSC). Evening/weekend programs available. *Degree requirements:* For master's, thesis (for some programs). *Entrance requirements:* For master's, minimum undergraduate GPA of 2.5, 3 years work experience. Additional exam requirements/recommendations for international students: Required—TOEFL (minimum score 550 paper-based; 213 computer-based; 79 iBT). Electronic applications accepted.

University of Phoenix–Southern Colorado Campus, The Artemis School, College of Education, Colorado Springs, CO 80919-2335. Offers administration and supervision (MA Ed); curriculum and instruction (MA Ed); elementary teacher education (MA Ed); principal licensure certification (Certificate); school counseling (MSC); secondary teacher education (MA Ed). Evening/weekend programs available. *Degree requirements:* For master's, thesis (for some programs). *Entrance requirements:* For master's, minimum undergraduate GPA of 2.5, 3 years of work experience. Additional exam requirements/recommendations for international students: Required—TOEFL (minimum score 550 paper-based; 213 computer-based; 79 iBT). Electronic applications accepted.

University of Phoenix–Utah Campus, The Artemis School, College of Education, Salt Lake City, UT 84123-4617. Offers administration and supervision (MA Ed); curriculum and instruction (MA Ed); elementary teacher education (MA Ed); school counseling (MSC); secondary teacher education (MA Ed); special education (MA Ed). Evening/weekend programs available. *Degree requirements:* For master's, thesis (for some programs). *Entrance requirements:* For master's, minimum undergraduate GPA of 2.5, 3 years work experience. Additional exam requirements/recommendations for international students: Required—TOEFL (minimum score 550 paper-based; 213 computer-based; 79 iBT). Electronic applications accepted.

University of Rhode Island, Graduate School, College of Arts and Sciences, Department of Psychology, Kingston, RI 02881. Offers behavioral science (PhD); clinical psychology (MA, PhD); school psychology (MS, PhD). *Accreditation:* APA (one or more programs are accredited). Part-time programs available. *Faculty:* 25 full-time (10 women), 5 part-time/adjunct (1 woman). *Students:* 72 full-time (56 women), 33 part-time (27 women); includes 20 minority (7 African Americans, 6 Asian Americans or Pacific Islanders, 7 Hispanic Americans), 4 international. In 2009, 12 master's, 11 doctorates awarded. *Degree requirements:* For master's, comprehensive exam, thesis optional; for doctorate, thesis/dissertation. *Entrance requirements:* For master's and doctorate, GRE, 3 letters of recommendation. Additional exam requirements/recommendations for international students: Required—TOEFL (minimum score 550 paper-based; 213 computer-based). Application fee: $65. Electronic applications accepted. *Expenses:* Tuition, state resident: full-time $8828; part-time $490 per credit hour. Tuition, nonresident: full-time $22,100; part-time $1228 per credit hour. Required fees: $1118; $57 per semester. Tuition and fees vary according to program. *Financial support:* In 2009–10, 3 research assistantships with full and partial tuition reimbursements (averaging $8,519 per year), 20 teaching assistantships with full and partial tuition reimbursements (averaging $12,364 per year) were awarded. Financial award applicants required to submit FAFSA. Total annual research expenditures: $4.6 million. *Unit head:* Dr. Patricia Morokoff, Chairperson, 401-874-4239, Fax: 401-874-2157, E-mail: morokoff@uri.edu. *Application contact:* Dr. Patricia Morokoff, Chairperson, 401-874-4239, Fax: 401-874-2157, E-mail: morokoff@uri.edu.

University of South Alabama, Graduate School, College of Education, Department of Professional Studies, Mobile, AL 36688-0002. Offers community counseling (MS); educational media (M Ed, MS); instructional design and development (MS, PhD); rehabilitation counseling (MS); school counseling (M Ed); school psychometry (M Ed). *Accreditation:* NCATE. Part-time programs available. *Degree requirements:* For master's, comprehensive exam. *Entrance requirements:* For master's, GRE General Test or MAT, minimum GPA of 3.0. *Expenses:* Tuition, state resident: part-time $218 per contact hour. Required fees: $1102 per year. *Faculty research:* Agency counseling, rehabilitation counseling, school psychometry.

University of South Carolina, The Graduate School, College of Arts and Sciences, Department of Psychology, Program in School Psychology, Columbia, SC 29208. Offers PhD. *Accreditation:* APA; NCATE. *Degree requirements:* For doctorate, thesis/dissertation. *Entrance requirements:* For doctorate, GRE General Test, minimum GPA of 3.0. Additional exam requirements/recommendations for international students: Required—TOEFL. Electronic applications accepted. *Faculty research:* Preschool services, families and diversity life satisfaction, ADHD intervention, attachment.

University of Southern Maine, College of Education and Human Development, Program in School Psychology, Portland, ME 04104-9300. Offers school psychology (MS, Psy D). *Accreditation:* NCATE. Part-time and evening/weekend programs available. *Faculty:* 4 full-time (1 woman). *Students:* 20 full-time (16 women), 6 part-time (all women). 17 applicants, 65% accepted, 9 enrolled. In 2009, 8 master's, 3 doctorates awarded. Terminal master's awarded for partial completion of doctoral program. *Degree requirements:* For master's, comprehensive exam, thesis or alternative, portfolio; for doctorate, comprehensive exam, thesis/dissertation, dissertation defense. *Entrance requirements:* For master's, GRE General Test or MAT, interview; for doctorate, GRE General Test, interview. Additional exam requirements/recommendations for international students: Required—TOEFL (minimum score 550 paper-based; 213 computer-based; 79 iBT). *Application deadline:* For fall admission, 12/1 for domestic students. Application fee: $50. Electronic applications accepted. *Financial support:* In 2009–10, 2 students received support, including 10 research assistantships with partial tuition reimbursements available (averaging $4,500 per year); teaching assistantships with partial tuition reimbursements available, career-related internships or fieldwork, Federal Work-Study, institutionally sponsored loans, scholarships/grants, and unspecified assistantships also available. Support available to part-time students. Financial award application deadline: 3/1; financial award applicants required to submit FAFSA. *Unit head:* Dr. E. Michael Brady, Chair, Human Resource Development Department, 207-780-5316, Fax: 207-780-5043, E-mail: mbrady@usm.maine.edu. *Application contact:* Mary Sloan, Director of Graduate Admissions, 207-780-4386, Fax: 207-780-4969, E-mail: msloan@usm.maine.edu.

University of Southern Mississippi, Graduate School, College of Education and Psychology, Department of Psychology, Hattiesburg, MS 39406-0001. Offers clinical psychology (MA, PhD); counseling psychology (PhD); experimental psychology (MA, PhD); psychology (MS); school psychology (MA, PhD). *Accreditation:* APA (one or more programs are accredited). *Faculty:* 32 full-time (9 women). *Students:* 104 full-time (80 women), 29 part-time (19 women); includes 14 minority (7 African Americans, 2 Asian Americans or Pacific Islanders, 5 Hispanic Americans), 7 international. Average age 29. 225 applicants, 16% accepted, 30 enrolled. In 2009, 23 master's, 13 doctorates awarded. Terminal master's awarded for partial completion of doctoral program. *Degree requirements:* For master's, comprehensive exam, thesis; for doctorate, comprehensive exam, thesis/dissertation. *Entrance requirements:* For master's, GRE General Test, minimum GPA of 3.0; for doctorate, GRE General Test, interview, minimum GPA of 3.0. Additional exam requirements/recommendations for international students: Required—TOEFL. *Application deadline:* For fall admission, 3/1 priority date for domestic students, 3/1 for international students. Applications are processed on a rolling basis. Application fee: $35. *Expenses:* Tuition, state resident: full-time $5096; part-time $284 per hour. Tuition, nonresident: full-time $13,052; part-time $726 per hour. Required fees: $402. Tuition and fees vary according to course level and course load. *Financial support:* In 2009–10, 48 research assistantships with full tuition reimbursements (averaging $8,802 per year), 48 teaching assistantships with full tuition reimbursements (averaging $6,500 per year) were awarded; career-related internships or fieldwork, Federal Work-Study, and institutionally sponsored loans also available. Financial award application deadline: 3/15; financial award applicants required to submit FAFSA. *Faculty research:* Dolphin cognition, sleep, neuropsychology, health-related behaviors, psychopathology. Total annual research expenditures: $101,200. *Unit head:* Dr. Joesph Olmi, Chair, 601-266-4177, Fax: 601-266-5580. *Application contact:* Dr. Heather Sterling-Turner, Graduate Coordinator, 601-266-4177, Fax: 601-266-5580.

University of South Florida, Graduate School, College of Education–Main Campus, Department of Psychological and Social Foundations of Education, Tampa, FL 33620-9951. Offers college student affairs (M Ed); counselor education (MA, PhD, Ed S); interdisciplinary (PhD, Ed S); school psychology (PhD, Ed S). Part-time and evening/weekend programs available. *Faculty:* 22 full-time (13 women), 6 part-time/adjunct (4 women). *Students:* 154 full-time (123 women), 88 part-time (69 women); includes 62 minority (28 African Americans, 8 Asian Americans or Pacific Islanders, 26 Hispanic Americans), 7 international. Average age 30. 260 applicants, 43% accepted, 97 enrolled. In 2009, 41 master's, 7 doctorates, 5 other advanced degrees awarded. *Degree requirements:* For master's, comprehensive exam, thesis (for some programs); for doctorate, comprehensive exam, thesis/dissertation. *Entrance requirements:* For master's, GRE General Test, minimum GPA of 3.5 in last 60 hours of course work; for doctorate, GRE General Test, MAT, minimum GPA of 3.5 in last 60 hours of course work; for Ed S, GRE General Test. Additional exam requirements/recommendations for international students: Required—TOEFL (minimum score 550 paper-based; 213 computer-based; 79 iBT). *Application deadline:* For fall admission, 1/1 for domestic and international students. Application fee: $30. Electronic applications accepted. *Financial support:* In 2009–10, 47 students received support, including 6 fellowships with full tuition reimbursements available (averaging $10,000 per year), 21 teaching assistantships with full tuition reimbursements available (averaging $10,200 per year); career-related internships or fieldwork, scholarships/grants, and unspecified assistantships also available. Financial award application deadline: 1/1; financial award applicants required to submit CSS PROFILE. *Faculty research:* College student affairs, counselor education, educational psychology, school psychology, social foundations. Total annual research expenditures: $4.2 million. *Unit head:* Dr. Herbert Exum, Chairperson, 813-974-8395, Fax: 813-974-5814, E-mail: exum@tempest.coedu.usf.edu. *Application contact:* Dr. Kathy Bradley, Program Director, School Psychology, 813-974-9486, Fax: 813-974-5814, E-mail: kbradley@usf.edu.

The University of Tennessee, Graduate School, College of Education, Health and Human Sciences, Program in Education, Knoxville, TN 37996. Offers art education (MS); counseling education (PhD); cultural studies in education (PhD); curriculum (MS, Ed S); curriculum, educational research and evaluation (Ed D, PhD); early childhood education (PhD); early childhood special education (MS); education of deaf and hard of hearing (MS); educational administration and policy studies (Ed D, PhD); educational administration and supervision (Ed S); educational psychology (Ed D, PhD); elementary education (MS, Ed S); elementary teaching (MS); English education (MS, Ed S); exercise science (PhD); foreign language/ESL education (MS, Ed S); instructional technology (MS, Ed D, PhD, Ed S); literacy, language and ESL education (PhD); literacy, language education, and ESL education (Ed D); mathematics education (MS, Ed S); modified and comprehensive special education (MS); reading education (MS, Ed S); school counseling (Ed S); school psychology (PhD, Ed S); science education (MS, Ed S); secondary teaching (MS); social foundations (MS); social science education (MS, Ed S); socio-cultural foundations of sports and education (PhD); special education (Ed S); teacher education (Ed D, PhD). *Accreditation:* NCATE. Part-time and evening/weekend programs available. *Degree requirements:* For master's and Ed S, thesis optional; for doctorate, variable foreign language requirement, thesis/dissertation. *Entrance requirements:* For master's, minimum GPA of 2.7; for doctorate and Ed S, GRE General Test, minimum GPA of 2.7. Additional exam requirements/recommendations for international students: Required—TOEFL. Electronic applications accepted. *Expenses:* Tuition, state resident: full-time $6826; part-time $380 per semester hour. Tuition, nonresident: full-time $21,844; part-time $1147 per semester hour. Tuition and fees vary according to program.

The University of Tennessee at Chattanooga, Graduate School, College of Health, Education and Professional Studies, Graduate Studies Division of Education, Program for Educational Specialist, Chattanooga, TN 37403-2598. Offers educational technology (Ed S); school psychology (Ed S). Part-time and evening/weekend programs available. *Faculty:* 4 full-time (0 women), 1 part-time/adjunct (0 women). *Students:* 27 full-time (23 women), 14 part-time (10 women); includes 6 minority (5 African Americans, 1 Hispanic American). Average age 39. 14 applicants, 86% accepted, 6 enrolled. In 2009, 27 Ed Ss awarded. *Degree requirements:* For Ed S, internship. *Entrance requirements:* For degree, GRE (minimum score 1350), letters of reference. Additional exam requirements/recommendations for international students: Required—TOEFL (minimum score 550 paper-based; 213 computer-based; 79 iBT), IELTS (minimum score 6). *Application deadline:* For fall admission, 8/1 priority date for domestic students, 6/1 for international students; for spring admission, 12/1 priority date for domestic students, 10/1 for international students. Applications are processed on a rolling basis. Application fee: $35. Electronic applications accepted. *Expenses:* Tuition, state resident: full-time $5404; part-time $300 per credit hour. Tuition, nonresident: full-time $16,702; part-time $928 per credit hour. Required fees: $1150; $130 per credit hour. *Financial support:* In 2009–10, 5 research assistantships with full and partial tuition reimbursements (averaging $5,500 per year) were awarded; career-related internships or fieldwork, scholarships/grants, and unspecified assistantships also available. Support available to part-time students. *Faculty research:* Educational technology, using technology in the classroom, interactive media, distance learning, instructional design technological implementation. *Unit head:* Dr. Lloyd D. Davis, Coordinator, 423-425-4161, Fax: 423-425-5380, E-mail: lloyd-davis@utc.edu. *Application contact:* Dr. Stephanie Bellar, Dean of Graduate Studies, 423-425-4666, Fax: 423-425-5223, E-mail: stephanie-bellar@utc.edu.

The University of Texas at Austin, Graduate School, College of Education, Department of Educational Psychology, Austin, TX 78712-1111. Offers academic educational psychology (M Ed, MA); counseling psychology (PhD); counselor education (M Ed); human development and culture (PhD); learning, cognition and instruction (PhD); quantitative methods (PhD); school psychology (PhD). *Accreditation:* APA (one or more programs are accredited). *Degree requirements:* For master's, thesis optional; for doctorate, thesis/dissertation. *Entrance requirements:* For master's and doctorate, GRE General Test, 3 letters of recommendation. Additional exam requirements/recommendations for international students: Required—TOEFL.

The University of Texas at Tyler, College of Education and Psychology, Department of Psychology and Counseling, Tyler, TX 75799-0001. Offers clinical psychology (MS), including neuropsychology, school psychology; counseling psychology (MA), including general, marriage and family; interdisciplinary studies (MSIS); school counseling (MA). Part-time and evening/weekend programs available. *Faculty:* 11 full-time (3 women). *Students:* 80 full-time (63 women), 46 part-time (38 women); includes 5 minority (3 African Americans, 1 American Indian/Alaska Native, 1 Hispanic American). Average age 29. 64 applicants, 77% accepted, 28 enrolled. In 2009, 36 master's awarded. *Degree requirements:* For master's, comprehensive exam, thesis optional. *Entrance requirements:* For master's, GRE General Test, minimum GPA of 3.0. Additional exam requirements/recommendations for international students: Required—TOEFL (minimum score 79 computer-based). *Application deadline:* For fall admission, 8/17 priority date for domestic students, 7/1 priority date for international students; for spring admission, 12/21 priority date for domestic students, 11/1 priority date for international students. Application fee: $25 ($50 for international students). Electronic applications accepted. *Expenses:* Tuition, state resident: part-time $665 per semester hour. Tuition, nonresident: part-time $942 per semester hour. Part-time tuition and fees vary according to degree level and program. *Financial support:* In 2009–10, fellowships with partial tuition reimbursements (averaging $3,000 per year), research assistantships (averaging $5,000 per year), teaching assistantships (averaging $1,500 per year) were awarded; career-related internships or fieldwork, Federal Work-Study, and institutionally sponsored loans also available. Support available to part-time students. Financial award application deadline: 7/1. *Faculty research:* Neuropsychology, child abuse, psychometric properties of psychological instruments, maternal behavior, clinical practice issues, victimization of women, post-traumatic stress disorder. *Unit head:* Dr. Charles B. Barke, Chair/Professor, 903-565-5875, Fax: 903-565-5560, E-mail: cbarke@uttyler.edu. *Application contact:* Dr. Charles Barke.

The University of Texas–Pan American, College of Education, Department of Educational Psychology, Edinburg, TX 78539. Offers counseling (M Ed); educational diagnostician (M Ed); gifted education (M Ed); school psychology (MA); special education (M Ed). Part-time and evening/weekend programs available. *Degree requirements:* For master's, comprehensive exam (for some programs), thesis (for some programs). *Entrance requirements:* For master's, GRE General Test, interview. *Expenses:* Tuition, state resident: full-time $3630.60; part-time $201.70 per credit hour. Tuition, nonresident: full-time $8617; part-time $478.70 per credit hour. Required fees: $806.50. *Faculty research:* Reading instruction, assessment practice, behavior interventions consultation, mental retardation.

University of the Pacific, School of Education, Department of Educational and School Psychology, Stockton, CA 95211-0197. Offers educational psychology (MA, Ed D); school psychology (Ed S). *Accreditation:* NCATE. *Faculty:* 4 full-time (3 women), 1 (woman) part-time/adjunct. *Students:* 18 full-time (12 women), 13 part-time (11 women); includes 14 minority (1 African American, 6 Asian Americans or Pacific Islanders, 7 Hispanic Americans). Average age 29. 14 applicants, 86% accepted, 9 enrolled. In 2009, 6 master's, 3 doctorates awarded. *Degree requirements:* For master's, thesis (for some programs); for doctorate, thesis/dissertation. *Entrance requirements:* For master's and doctorate, GRE General Test, GRE Subject Test. Additional exam requirements/recommendations for international students: Required—TOEFL (minimum score 475 paper-based; 150 computer-based). *Application deadline:* For fall admission, 3/1 priority date for domestic students; for spring admission, 10/1 priority date for domestic students. Applications are processed on a rolling basis. Application fee: $75. *Financial support:* In 2009–10, 6 teaching assistantships were awarded. Financial award application deadline: 3/1; financial award applicants required to submit FAFSA. *Unit head:* Dr. Linda Webster, Chairperson, 209-946-2559, E-mail: lwebster@pacific.edu. *Application contact:* Office of Graduate Admissions, 209-946-2344.

The University of Toledo, College of Graduate Studies, College of Health Science and Human Service, Division of Human Services, Toledo, OH 43606-3390. Offers counselor education and school psychology (MA, PhD, Ed S), including counselor education, guidance/counselor education (PhD), school psychology (MA, Ed S); criminal justice (MA, Certificate), including criminal justice (MA), juvenile justice (Certificate), severe behavioral spectrum (Certificate); health and rehabilitative services (MA), including speech language pathology; health education (PhD); kinesiology (MSX, PhD), including exercise science; recreation and leisure (MA); social work (MSW); speech-language pathology (MA).

The University of Toledo, College of Graduate Studies, College of Health Science and Human Service, Division of Human Services, Department of Counselor Education and School Psychology, Program in School Psychology, Toledo, OH 43606-3390. Offers school counseling (MA); school psychology (Ed S). *Entrance requirements:* For master's, GRE.

University of Utah, The Graduate School, College of Education, Department of Educational Psychology, Salt Lake City, UT 84112. Offers counseling psychology (PhD); educational psychology (MA); instructional design and educational technology (M Ed); learning and cognition (MS, PhD); professional counseling (MS); professional psychology (M Ed); reading and literacy (M Ed, PhD); school counseling (M Ed, MS); school psychology (MS, PhD); statistics (M Stat). *Accreditation:* APA (one or more programs are accredited). Evening/weekend programs available. Postbaccalaureate distance learning degree programs offered (minimal on-campus study). *Faculty:* 21 full-time (11 women), 8 part-time/adjunct (5 women). *Students:* 92 full-time (67 women), 74 part-time (43 women); includes 16 minority (4 Asian Americans or Pacific Islanders, 12 Hispanic Americans), 2 international. Average age 33. 177 applicants, 34% accepted, 50 enrolled. In 2009, 44 master's, 9 doctorates awarded. *Degree requirements:* For master's, variable foreign language requirement, comprehensive exam, thesis (for some programs); for doctorate, variable foreign language requirement, thesis/dissertation, oral exam. *Entrance requirements:* For master's and doctorate, GRE General Test, minimum GPA of 3.0. Additional exam requirements/recommendations for international students: Required—TOEFL (minimum score 500 paper-based; 173 computer-based). *Application deadline:* For fall admission, 4/1 for domestic and international students; for spring admission, 11/1 for domestic and international students. Application fee: $55 ($65 for international students). *Expenses:* Tuition, state resident: full-time $4004; part-time $1674 per semester. Tuition, nonresident: full-time $14,134; part-time $5915 per semester. Required fees: $324 per semester. Tuition and fees vary according to course load, degree level and program. *Financial support:* In 2009–10; 55 students received support, including 20 fellowships with full tuition reimbursements available (averaging $11,000 per year), 5 research assistantships with full tuition reimbursements available (averaging $11,000 per year), 32 teaching assistantships with full and partial tuition reimbursements available (averaging $11,000 per year); career-related internships or fieldwork, Federal Work-Study, institutionally sponsored loans, scholarships/grants, and unspecified assistantships also available. Financial award application deadline: 2/1; financial award applicants required to submit FAFSA. *Faculty research:* Autism, computer technology and instruction, cognitive behavior, aging, group counseling. Total annual research expenditures: $151,911. *Unit head:* Dr. Elaine Clark, Chair, 801-581-7148, Fax: 801-581-5566, E-mail: clark@ed.utah.edu. *Application contact:* Jenna Atkinson, Academic Program Specialist, 801-581-7148, Fax: 801-581-5566, E-mail: jenna.atkinson@utah.edu.

University of Virginia, Curry School of Education, Department of Human Services, Program in Clinical and School Psychology, Charlottesville, VA 22903. Offers PhD. *Students:* 26 full-time (22 women), 1 (woman) part-time; includes 6 minority (3 African Americans, 2 Asian Americans or Pacific Islanders, 1 Hispanic American). Average age 27. 48 applicants, 10% accepted, 2 enrolled. In 2009, 6 doctorates awarded. *Unit head:* Dr. Peter L. Sheras, Director, 434-924-0795, E-mail: pls@virginia.edu. *Application contact:* Lynn Renfroe, Information Contact, 434-924-6254, E-mail: ldr9t@virginia.edu.

University of Virginia, Curry School of Education, Program in Education, Charlottesville, VA 22903. Offers administration and supervision (PhD); applied developmental science (PhD); counselor education (PhD); curriculum and instruction (PhD); early childhood-developmental risk (MT); education evaluation (PhD); educational psychology (PhD); educational research (PhD); elementary (MT, PhD); English education (MT, PhD); foreign language education (MT); higher education (PhD); instructional technology (PhD); kinesiology (MT, PhD); math education (PhD); reading education (PhD); research statistics and evaluation (PhD); school psychology (PhD); science education (PhD); social studies education (MT, PhD); special education (PhD); world languages education (MT). *Students:* 336 full-time (239 women), 88 part-time (54 women); includes 43 minority (24 African Americans, 2 American Indian/Alaska Native, 11 Asian Americans or Pacific Islanders, 6 Hispanic Americans), 18 international. Average age 27. 199 applicants, 48% accepted, 55 enrolled. In 2009, 127 master's, 52 doctorates awarded. *Degree requirements:* For master's, comprehensive exam (for some programs), field project; for doctorate, comprehensive exam, thesis/dissertation. *Entrance requirements:* For doctorate, GRE General Test. Additional exam requirements/recommendations for international students: Required—TOEFL (minimum score 600 paper-based; 250 computer-based; 90 iBT), IELTS (minimum score 7). *Application deadline:* Applications are processed on a rolling basis. Application fee: $60. Electronic applications accepted. *Financial support:* Fellowships, research assistantships, teaching assistantships available. Financial award application deadline: 1/5; financial award applicants required to submit FAFSA.

University of Washington, Graduate School, College of Education, Program in Educational Psychology, Seattle, WA 98195. Offers educational psychology (PhD); human development and cognition (M Ed); learning sciences (M Ed, PhD); measurement, statistics and research design (M Ed); school psychology (M Ed). *Accreditation:* APA. *Degree requirements:* For master's, thesis optional; for doctorate, thesis/dissertation. *Entrance requirements:* For master's and doctorate, GRE General Test, minimum GPA of 3.0. Additional exam requirements/recommendations for international students: Required—TOEFL.

University of Wisconsin–Eau Claire, College of Arts and Sciences, Department of Psychology, Eau Claire, WI 54702-4004. Offers school psychology (MSE, Ed S). Part-time programs available. *Faculty:* 17 full-time (9 women). *Students:* 18 full-time (16 women), 10 part-time (7 women), 2 international. Average age 24. 46 applicants, 39% accepted, 16 enrolled. In 2009, 8 master's, 6 other advanced degrees awarded. *Degree requirements:* For master's, comprehensive exam, thesis, National Certified School Psychologist Professional Exam, written exam, externship. *Entrance requirements:* For master's, GRE, minimum undergraduate GPA of 3.0; courses in exceptional children and youth, statistics, psychopathology, and theories of counseling. Additional exam requirements/recommendations for international students: Required—TOEFL (minimum score 550 paper-based; 213 computer-based; 79 iBT). *Application deadline:* For fall admission, 3/1 priority date for domestic students, 6/1 priority date for international students; for spring admission, 11/1 priority date for international students. Applications are processed on a rolling basis. Application fee: $56. Electronic applications accepted. *Expenses:* Tuition, state resident: full-time $6705.90; part-time $372.55 per credit. Tuition, nonresident: full-time $16,771; part-time $931.74 per credit. Required fees: $925.50; $51.19 per credit. One-time fee: $56. *Financial support:* In 2009–10, 21 students received support, including 5 fellowships (averaging $1,100 per year); Federal Work-Study and unspecified assistantships also available. Financial award application deadline: 3/1; financial award applicants

School Psychology

University of Wisconsin–Eau Claire (continued)
required to submit FAFSA. *Unit head:* Dr. Lori Bica, Chair, 715-836-5733, Fax: 715-836-2214, E-mail: bicala@uwec.edu. *Application contact:* Kristina Anderson, Director of Admissions, 715-836-5415, Fax: 715-836-2409, E-mail: admissions@uwec.edu.

University of Wisconsin–La Crosse, Office of University Graduate Studies, College of Liberal Studies, Department of Psychology, Program in School Psychology, La Crosse, WI 54601-3742. Offers MS Ed, Ed S. *Students:* 24 full-time (all women), 30 part-time (25 women); includes 1 minority (Hispanic American). Average age 26. 60 applicants, 35% accepted, 12 enrolled. In 2009, 24 master's awarded. *Degree requirements:* For master's, comprehensive exam, thesis. *Entrance requirements:* For master's, GRE, 3 letters of recommendation, writing sample, resume. *Application deadline:* For fall admission, 1/15 priority date for domestic students. Application fee: $56. Electronic applications accepted. *Financial support:* Research assistantships available. *Unit head:* Dr. Rob Dixon, Program Director, 608-785-6893, Fax: 608-785-8443, E-mail: dixon.rob@uwlax.edu. *Application contact:* Kathryn Kiefer, Associate Director of Admissions, 608-785-8939, E-mail: admissions@uwlac.edu.

University of Wisconsin–Milwaukee, Graduate School, School of Education, Program in School Psychology, Milwaukee, WI 53201-0413. Offers PhD, Ed S. *Accreditation:* APA. *Students:* 8 full-time (6 women), 6 part-time (all women). Average age 25. 11 applicants, 82% accepted, 5 enrolled. In 2009, 10 doctorates awarded. *Expenses:* Tuition, state resident: full-time $8800. Tuition, nonresident: full-time $20,760. Tuition and fees vary according to program and reciprocity agreements. *Unit head:* Anthony A. Hains, Representative, 414-229-4590, E-mail: aahains@uwm.edu. *Application contact:* General Information Contact, 414-229-4982, Fax: 414-229-6967, E-mail: gradschool@uwm.edu.

University of Wisconsin–River Falls, Outreach and Graduate Studies, College of Education and Professional Studies, Department of Counseling and School Psychology, River Falls, WI 54022. Offers counseling (MSE); school psychology (MSE, Ed S). Part-time programs available. *Entrance requirements:* For master's, minimum GPA of 2.75, resume, 3 letters of reference, vita. Additional exam requirements/recommendations for international students: Required—TOEFL (minimum score 500 paper-based; 65 iBT), IELTS (minimum score 5.5). Electronic applications accepted.

University of Wisconsin–Stout, Graduate School, School of Education, Program in School Psychology, Menomonie, WI 54751. Offers MS Ed, Ed S. Part-time programs available. *Degree requirements:* For master's and Ed S, thesis. *Entrance requirements:* For master's, minimum GPA of 3.0; for Ed S, minimum GPA of 3.25. Additional exam requirements/recommendations for international students: Required—TOEFL (minimum score 500 paper-based; 173 computer-based; 61 iBT). Electronic applications accepted. *Faculty research:* Intelligence assessment, eating disorders, intervention models, resilience, school violence.

University of Wisconsin–Superior, Graduate Division, Department of Counseling and Psychological Professions, Superior, WI 54880-4500. Offers community counseling (MSE); human relations (MSE); school counseling (MSE). Part-time and evening/weekend programs available. *Faculty:* 3 full-time (1 woman), 4 part-time/adjunct (all women). *Students:* 34 full-time (23 women), 69 part-time (51 women); includes 10 minority (4 African Americans, 4 American Indian/Alaska Native, 2 Asian Americans or Pacific Islanders), 3 international. Average age 27. 19 applicants, 100% accepted. In 2009, 24 master's awarded. *Degree requirements:* For master's, position paper, practicum. *Entrance requirements:* For master's, GRE and/or MAT, minimum GPA of 2.75. *Application deadline:* For fall admission, 4/1 priority date for domestic students; for spring admission, 10/15 priority date for domestic students. Applications are processed on a rolling basis. Application fee: $45. Electronic applications accepted. *Financial support:* In 2009–10, 10 fellowships with partial tuition reimbursements (averaging $6,500 per year), 2 research assistantships with partial tuition reimbursements (averaging $5,000 per year) were awarded; career-related internships or fieldwork, Federal Work-Study, institutionally sponsored loans, scholarships/grants, traineeships, and tuition waivers (partial) also available. Support available to part-time students. Financial award application deadline: 4/15; financial award applicants required to submit FAFSA. *Faculty research:* Women and power, intrafamily dynamics. *Unit head:* Terri Kronzer, Chairperson, 715-394-8506. *Application contact:* Sandy Wallgren, Program Assistant/Status Examiner, 715-394-8295, Fax: 715-394-8146, E-mail: gradstudy@uwsuper.edu.

University of Wisconsin–Whitewater, School of Graduate Studies, College of Education, Department of Counselor Education, Whitewater, WI 53190-1790. Offers community counseling (MS Ed); higher education (MS Ed); school counseling (MS Ed). *Accreditation:* ACA; NCATE. Part-time and evening/weekend programs available. *Degree requirements:* For master's, thesis or alternative. *Entrance requirements:* For master's, resume, 2 letters of reference. Additional exam requirements/recommendations for international students: Required—TOEFL (minimum score 550 paper-based; 213 computer-based). Electronic applications accepted. *Faculty research:* Alcohol and other drugs, counseling effectiveness, teacher mentoring.

University of Wisconsin–Whitewater, School of Graduate Studies, College of Letters and Sciences, Department of Psychology, Program in School Psychology, Whitewater, WI 53190-1790. Offers Ed S. Part-time and evening/weekend programs available. Postbaccalaureate distance learning degree programs offered (no on-campus study). *Degree requirements:* For Ed S, specialist project. *Entrance requirements:* For degree, master's degree in school psychology from an accredited school. Additional exam requirements/recommendations for international students: Required—TOEFL (minimum score 550 paper-based; 213 computer-based). Electronic applications accepted.

Utah State University, School of Graduate Studies, College of Education and Human Services, Department of Psychology, Logan, UT 84322. Offers clinical/counseling/school psychology (PhD); research and evaluation methodology (PhD); school counseling (MS); school psychology (MS). *Accreditation:* APA (one or more programs are accredited). Part-time and evening/weekend programs available. Postbaccalaureate distance learning degree programs offered (no on-campus study). Terminal master's awarded for partial completion of doctoral program. *Degree requirements:* For master's, thesis (for some programs); for doctorate, thesis/dissertation. *Entrance requirements:* For master's, GRE General Test (school psychology), MAT (school counseling), minimum GPA of 3.5; for doctorate, GRE General Test, minimum GPA of 3.5. Additional exam requirements/recommendations for international students: Required—TOEFL. *Faculty research:* Hearing loss detection in infancy, ADHD, eating disorders, domestic violence, neuropsychology, bilingual/Spanish speaking students/parents.

Valdosta State University, Graduate School, Department of Psychology and Counseling, Valdosta, GA 31698. Offers clinical/counseling psychology (MS); industrial/organizational psychology (MS); school counseling (M Ed, Ed S); school psychology (Ed S). Part-time and evening/weekend programs available. *Degree requirements:* For master's, thesis or alternative, comprehensive written and/or oral exams; for Ed S, thesis. *Entrance requirements:* For master's and Ed S, GRE General Test or MAT. Additional exam requirements/recommendations for international students: Required—TOEFL (minimum score 523 paper-based; 193 computer-based). Electronic applications accepted. *Faculty research:* Using Bender-Gestalt to predict graphomotor dimensions of the draw-a-person test, neurobehavioral hemispheric dominance.

Valparaiso University, Graduate School, Department of Education, Program in School Psychology, Valparaiso, IN 46383. Offers M Ed/Ed S. Part-time and evening/weekend programs available. *Students:* 13 full-time (11 women), 15 part-time (13 women), 2 international. Average age 27. *Entrance requirements:* Additional exam requirements/recommendations for international students: Required—TOEFL (minimum score 550 paper-based; 213 computer-based; 80 iBT). *Application deadline:* Applications are processed on a rolling basis. Application fee: $30 ($50 for international students). Electronic applications accepted. *Financial support:* Scholarships/grants and unspecified assistantships available. Support available to part-time students. Financial award applicants required to submit FAFSA. *Unit head:* Dr. Jan Westrick, Chair, Department of Education, 219-464-5077, Fax: 219-464-6720, E-mail: jan.westrick@valpo.edu. *Application contact:* Jamie Haney, Coordinator of Graduate Admission, 219-464-5313, Fax: 219-464-5381, E-mail: jamie.haney@valpo.edu.

Washington State University, Graduate School, College of Education, Department of Educational Leadership and Counseling Psychology, Program in Counseling Psychology, Pullman, WA 99164. Offers counseling psychology (Ed M, MA, PhD); school psychologist (Certificate). *Accreditation:* APA (one or more programs are accredited). Terminal master's awarded for partial completion of doctoral program. *Degree requirements:* For master's, comprehensive exam (for some programs), thesis (for some programs), oral or written exam; for doctorate, comprehensive exam, thesis/dissertation, oral and written exam. *Entrance requirements:* For master's and doctorate, GRE General Test, minimum GPA of 3.0, 3 letters of recommendation. Additional exam requirements/recommendations for international students: Required—TOEFL (minimum score 550 paper-based; 213 computer-based). Electronic applications accepted. *Faculty research:* Hypnosis supervision, multicultural counseling, American Indian mental health, eating disorders.

Wayne State University, College of Education, Division of Theoretical and Behavioral Foundations, Detroit, MI 48202. Offers counseling (M Ed, MA, Ed D, PhD, Ed S); education evaluation and research (M Ed, Ed D, PhD); educational psychology (M Ed, Ed D, PhD, Ed S); educational sociology (M Ed, Ed D, PhD, Ed S); history and philosophy of education (M Ed, Ed D, PhD); rehabilitation counseling and community inclusion (MA, Ed S); school and community psychology (MA, Ed S); school clinical psychology (Ed S). *Accreditation:* ACA (one or more programs are accredited); CORE (one or more programs are accredited). Evening/weekend programs available. *Degree requirements:* For doctorate, thesis/dissertation. *Entrance requirements:* For master's, GRE; for doctorate, GRE, interview, minimum GPA of 3.0, curriculum vitae, references. Additional exam requirements/recommendations for international students: Required—TOEFL (minimum score 550 paper-based; 213 computer-based), TWE (minimum score 6). Electronic applications accepted. *Faculty research:* Adolescents at risk, supervision of counseling.

Western Carolina University, Graduate School, College of Education and Allied Professions, Department of Human Services, Program in Counseling, Cullowhee, NC 28723. Offers community counseling (M Ed, MS); school counseling (MA Ed). *Accreditation:* ACA. Part-time and evening/weekend programs available. *Students:* 63 full-time (48 women), 35 part-time (25 women). Average age 30. 87 applicants, 80% accepted, 52 enrolled. In 2009, 37 master's awarded. *Degree requirements:* For master's, comprehensive exam, thesis or alternative. *Entrance requirements:* For master's, GRE General Test, appropriate undergraduate degree with minimum GPA of 3.0, 3 recommendations, writing sample, resume. Additional exam requirements/recommendations for international students: Required—TOEFL (minimum score 550 paper-based; 270 computer-based; 79 iBT). *Application deadline:* For fall admission, 2/1 for domestic students. Application fee: $40. *Financial support:* In 2009–10, 33 students received support, including 25 research assistantships with full and partial tuition reimbursements available (averaging $6,880 per year), 8 teaching assistantships with full and partial tuition reimbursements available (averaging $7,000 per year); fellowships, career-related internships or fieldwork, institutionally sponsored loans, scholarships/grants, and unspecified assistantships also available. Financial award application deadline: 3/31; financial award applicants required to submit FAFSA. *Faculty research:* Marital and family development, spirituality in counseling, home school law, sexuality education, family functioning models. *Unit head:* Dr. Lisa Bloom, Head, 828-227-7310, E-mail: bloom@email.wcu.edu. *Application contact:* Admissions Specialist for Counseling, 828-227-7398, Fax: 828-227-6280, E-mail: gradsch@email.wcu.edu.

Western Carolina University, Graduate School, College of Education and Allied Professions, Department of Psychology, Cullowhee, NC 28723. Offers general psychology (MA); school psychology (MA). Part-time programs available. *Students:* 47 full-time (33 women), 4 part-time (3 women). Average age 25. 73 applicants, 42% accepted, 24 enrolled. In 2009, 10 master's awarded. *Degree requirements:* For master's, comprehensive exam, thesis. *Entrance requirements:* For master's, GRE General Test, appropriate undergraduate degree, interview, 3 letters of recommendation. Additional exam requirements/recommendations for international students: Required—TOEFL (minimum score 550 paper-based; 270 computer-based; 79 iBT). *Application deadline:* For fall admission, 2/1 for domestic students. Application fee: $40. *Financial support:* In 2009–10, 32 students received support, including 32 teaching assistantships with full and partial tuition reimbursements available (averaging $7,000 per year); fellowships, research assistantships with full and partial tuition reimbursements available, career-related internships or fieldwork, institutionally sponsored loans, scholarships/grants, and unspecified assistantships also available. Financial award application deadline: 3/31; financial award applicants required to submit FAFSA. *Faculty research:* Five-factor model of personality, evolutionary psychology, stress and worry, body image and physical attractiveness, moral decision-making, memory, learning styles. *Unit head:* Dr. David McCord, Head, 828-227-7361, Fax: 828-227-7005, E-mail: mccord@email.wcu.edu. *Application contact:* Admissions Specialist for Psychology, 828-227-7398, Fax: 828-227-7480, E-mail: gradsch@email.wcu.edu.

Western Illinois University, School of Graduate Studies, College of Arts and Sciences, Department of Psychology, Macomb, IL 61455-1390. Offers clinical/community mental health (MS); general psychology (MS); psychology (MS, SSP); school psychology (SSP). Part-time programs available. *Students:* 42 full-time (21 women), 14 part-time (11 women); includes 2 minority (both Asian Americans or Pacific Islanders), 2 international. Average age 25. 75 applicants, 37% accepted. In 2009, 11 master's, 10 other advanced degrees awarded. *Degree requirements:* For master's, comprehensive exam (for some programs), thesis or alternative. *Entrance requirements:* For master's and SSP, GRE General Test. Additional exam requirements/recommendations for international students: Required—TOEFL (minimum score 550 paper-based; 213 computer-based; 80 iBT). *Application deadline:* Applications are processed on a rolling basis. Application fee: $30. Electronic applications accepted. *Expenses:* Tuition, state resident: full-time $4486; part-time $249.21 per credit hour. Tuition, nonresident: full-time $8972; part-time $498.42 per credit hour. Required fees: $72.62 per credit hour. *Financial support:* In 2009–10, 38 students received support, including 38 research assistantships with full tuition reimbursements available (averaging $7,280 per year). Financial award applicants required to submit FAFSA. *Unit head:* Dr. Steven Dworkin, Chairperson, 309-298-1593. *Application contact:* Evelyn Hoing, Assistant Director of Graduate Studies, 309-298-1806, Fax: 309-298-2345, E-mail: grad-office@wiu.edu.

Western Kentucky University, Graduate Studies, College of Education and Behavioral Sciences, Department of Psychology, Bowling Green, KY 42101. Offers psychology (MA); school psychology (Ed S). *Degree requirements:* For master's, comprehensive exam, thesis (for some programs); for Ed S, thesis, oral exam. *Entrance requirements:* For master's, GRE General Test; for Ed S, GRE General Test, minimum GPA of 3.5. Additional exam requirements/recommendations for international students: Required—TOEFL (minimum score 555 paper-based; 213 computer-based; 79 iBT). *Expenses:* Tuition, state resident: full-time $4160; part-time $416 per credit hour. Tuition, nonresident: full-time $9550; part-time $506 per credit hour. Tuition and fees vary according to campus/location and reciprocity agreements. *Faculty research:* Neural regeneration, enhancing mobility in the elderly, improvement in visual processing in older adults, lifespan development.

Western New Mexico University, Graduate Division, School of Education, Silver City, NM 88062-0680. Offers bilingual education (MAT); counseling (MA); educational leadership (MA); elementary education (MAT); reading (MAT); school psychology (MA); secondary education (MAT); special education (MAT); TESOL (teaching English to speakers of other languages) (MAT). *Accreditation:* NCATE. *Degree requirements:* For master's, comprehensive exam.

Entrance requirements: For master's, GRE General Test, GRE Subject Test, minimum GPA of 3.2 in last 64 hours of undergraduate study. Additional exam requirements/recommendations for international students: Required—TOEFL (minimum score 550 paper-based; 213 computer-based). Electronic applications accepted.

Wichita State University, Graduate School, College of Education, Department of Counseling, Educational and School Psychology, Wichita, KS 67260. Offers counseling (M Ed); educational psychology (M Ed); school psychology (Ed S). *Accreditation:* NCATE. Part-time and evening/weekend programs available. *Expenses:* Tuition, state resident: full-time $4247; part-time $235.95 per credit hour. Tuition, nonresident: full-time $11,171; part-time $620.60 per credit hour. Required fees: $34; $3.60 per credit hour. $17 per term. Tuition and fees vary according to campus/location and program. *Unit head:* Dr. Marlene Schommer-Aikins, Chairperson, 316-978-3326, Fax: 316-978-3102, E-mail: marlene.schommer-aikins@wichita.edu. *Application contact:* Dr. Marlene Schommer-Aikins, Chairperson, 316-978-3326, Fax: 316-978-3102, E-mail: marlene.schommer-aikins@wichita.edu.

Worcester State College, Graduate Studies, Department of Education, Program in School Psychology, Worcester, MA 01602-2597. Offers M Ed, CAGS. *Faculty:* 9 full-time (7 women), 19 part-time/adjunct (7 women). *Students:* 16 full-time (15 women), 9 part-time (8 women); includes 1 minority (Hispanic American). Average age 28. 21 applicants, 90% accepted, 12 enrolled. In 2009, 3 master's, 3 other advanced degrees awarded. *Degree requirements:* For master's, comprehensive exam (for some programs), thesis optional. *Entrance requirements:* Additional exam requirements/recommendations for international students: Required—TOEFL (minimum score 550 paper-based; 213 computer-based; 79 iBT). *Application deadline:* For fall admission, 3/15 priority date for domestic and international students. Application fee: $30. *Expenses:* Tuition, area resident: Part-time $150 per credit. Tuition, state resident: part-time $150 per credit. Tuition, nonresident: part-time $150 per credit. Required fees: $85. *Financial support:* Career-related internships or fieldwork, scholarships/grants, and unspecified assistantships available. Financial award application deadline: 3/1; financial award applicants required to submit FAFSA. *Unit head:* Diane Tighe Cooke, Coordinator, 508-929-8673, Fax: 508-929-8164, E-mail: dcooke@worcester.edu. *Application contact:* Nicole Brown, Assistant Dean of Graduate and Continuing Education, 508-929-8787, Fax: 508-929-8100, E-mail: nbrown@worcester.edu.

Yeshiva University, Ferkauf Graduate School of Psychology, Program in School/Clinical-Child Psychology, New York, NY 10033-3201. Offers Psy D. *Accreditation:* APA. Part-time programs available. *Degree requirements:* For doctorate, comprehensive exam, thesis/dissertation. *Entrance requirements:* For doctorate, GRE General Test. *Expenses:* Tuition: Full-time $24,918; part-time $1022 per credit. Required fees: $175. *Faculty research:* Testing, early childhood intervention, child and adolescent psychotherapy, clinical child psychology.

Youngstown State University, Graduate School, Beeghly College of Education, Department of Counseling, Youngstown, OH 44555-0001. Offers community counseling (MS Ed); school counseling (MS Ed). *Accreditation:* ACA; NCATE. Part-time and evening/weekend programs available. *Degree requirements:* For master's, comprehensive exam. *Entrance requirements:* For master's, MAT, interview, minimum GPA of 2.7. Additional exam requirements/recommendations for international students: Required—TOEFL. *Faculty research:* Suicide, euthanasia, ethical issues, marriage and family.

Social Psychology

Alvernia University, Graduate Studies, Department of Psychology and Counseling, Reading, PA 19607-1799. Offers community counseling (MA). *Entrance requirements:* For master's, GRE or MAT.

American University, College of Arts and Sciences, Department of Psychology, Program in Psychology, Washington, DC 22016-8062. Offers experimental/biological psychology (MA); general psychology (MA); personality/social psychology (MA). Part-time programs available. *Students:* 30 full-time (27 women), 17 part-time (14 women); includes 9 minority (3 African Americans, 3 Asian Americans or Pacific Islanders, 3 Hispanic Americans), 1 international. Average age 27. 190 applicants, 36% accepted, 17 enrolled. In 2009, 35 master's awarded. *Degree requirements:* For master's, comprehensive exam, thesis or alternative. *Entrance requirements:* For master's, GRE General Test, GRE Subject Test. Additional exam requirements/recommendations for international students: Required—TOEFL. *Application deadline:* For fall admission, 3/1 for domestic students. Applications are processed on a rolling basis. Application fee: $80. *Expenses:* Tuition: Full-time $22,266; part-time $1237 per credit hour. Required fees: $430. Tuition and fees vary according to program. *Financial support:* Research assistantships, teaching assistantships available. Financial award application deadline: 2/1. *Faculty research:* Behavior therapy, cognitive behavior modification, pro-social behavior, conditioning and learning, olfaction. *Application contact:* Sara Holland, Senior Administrative Assistant, 202-885-1717, Fax: 202-885-1023.

Andrews University, School of Graduate Studies, School of Education, Department of Educational and Counseling Psychology, Program in Community Counseling, Berrien Springs, MI 49104. Offers MA. *Students:* 21 full-time (15 women), 6 part-time (2 women); includes 18 minority (8 African Americans, 10 Hispanic Americans), 3 international. Average age 33. 22 applicants, 59% accepted, 10 enrolled. In 2009, 10 master's awarded. *Degree requirements:* For master's, thesis optional. *Entrance requirements:* For master's, GRE. Additional exam requirements/recommendations for international students: Required—TOEFL (minimum score 550 paper-based). Application fee: $40. *Unit head:* Dr. Nancy Carbonell, Coordinator, 269-471-3472. *Application contact:* Carolyn Hurst, Supervisor of Graduate Admission, 800-253-2874, Fax: 269-471-6321, E-mail: graduate@andrews.edu.

Appalachian State University, Cratis D. Williams Graduate School, Department of Human Development and Psychological Counseling, Boone, NC 28608. Offers college student development (MA); community counseling (MA); marriage and family therapy (MA); school counseling (MA). *Accreditation:* AAMFT/COAMFTE; ACA; NCATE. Part-time programs available. *Faculty:* 15 full-time (5 women), 21 part-time/adjunct (14 women). *Students:* 98 full-time (95 women), 32 part-time (25 women); includes 8 minority (5 African Americans, 2 Asian Americans or Pacific Islanders, 1 Hispanic American), 1 international. 149 applicants, 54% accepted, 59 enrolled. In 2009, 78 master's awarded. *Degree requirements:* For master's, comprehensive exam (for some programs), thesis optional, internships. *Entrance requirements:* For master's, GRE General Test, 3 letters of recommendation. Additional exam requirements/recommendations for international students: Required—TOEFL (minimum score 570 paper-based; 230 computer-based; 79 iBT), IELTS (minimum score 6.5). *Application deadline:* For fall admission, 2/1 priority date for domestic students, 2/1 for international students; for spring admission, 2/1 for international students. Applications are processed on a rolling basis. Application fee: $50. Electronic applications accepted. *Expenses:* Tuition, state resident: full-time $2960. Tuition, nonresident: full-time $14,051. Required fees: $2320. *Financial support:* In 2009–10, 20 research assistantships (averaging $8,000 per year), 7 teaching assistantships (averaging $8,000 per year) were awarded; fellowships, career-related internships or fieldwork, Federal Work-Study, scholarships/grants, and unspecified assistantships also available. Financial award application deadline: 4/1; financial award applicants required to submit FAFSA. *Faculty research:* Multicultural counseling, addictions counseling, play therapy, expressive arts, child and adolescent therapy, sexual abuse counseling. *Unit head:* Dr. Lee Baruth, Chairman, 828-262-2055, E-mail: baruthlg@appstate.edu. *Application contact:* Sandy Krause, Director of Admissions and Recruiting, 828-262-2130, Fax: 828-262-2709, E-mail: krausesl@appstate.edu.

Arcadia University, Graduate Studies, Department of Psychology, Glenside, PA 19038-3295. Offers community counseling (MACP); school counseling (MACP). Part-time programs available. *Faculty:* 4 full-time (2 women), 6 part-time/adjunct (4 women). *Students:* 30 full-time (26 women), 30 part-time (23 women); includes 6 minority (5 African Americans, 1 Asian American or Pacific Islander), 1 international. Average age 27. In 2009, 3 master's awarded. *Degree requirements:* For master's, practicum. *Entrance requirements:* For master's, GRE General Test or MAT. *Application deadline:* Applications are processed on a rolling basis. Application fee: $50. *Expenses:* Tuition: Full-time $30,450; part-time $620 per credit hour. Required fees: $165. Tuition and fees vary according to program. *Financial support:* Research assistantships, career-related internships or fieldwork and unspecified assistantships available. Support available to part-time students. Financial award application deadline: 8/15. *Unit head:* Dr. Eleonora Bartoli, Director, 215-572-4693. *Application contact:* 215-572-2925, Fax: 215-572-2126, E-mail: grad@arcadia.edu.

Argosy University, Atlanta, College of Psychology and Behavioral Sciences, Atlanta, GA 30328. Offers clinical psychology (MA, Psy D, Postdoctoral Respecialization Certificate), including child and family psychology (Psy D), general adult clinical (Psy D), health psychology (Psy D), neuropsychology/geropsychology (Psy D); community counseling (MA), including marriage and family therapy; counselor education and supervision (Ed D); forensic psychology (MA); industrial organizational psychology (MA); marriage and family therapy (Certificate); sport-exercise psychology (MA). *Accreditation:* APA.

See Close-Up on page 1049.

Argosy University, Chicago, College of Psychology and Behavioral Sciences, Chicago, IL 60601. Offers clinical psychology (MA, Psy D), including child and adolescent psychology (Psy D), client-centered and experiential psychotherapies (Psy D), diversity and multicultural psychology (Psy D), family psychology (Psy D), forensic psychology (Psy D), health psychology (Psy D), neuropsychology (Psy D), organizational consulting (Psy D), psychoanalytic psychology (Psy D), psychology and spirituality (Psy D); community counseling (MA); counseling psychology (Ed D), including counselor education and supervision; counselor education and supervision (Ed D); industrial organizational psychology (MA). *Accreditation:* APA (one or more programs are accredited). Postbaccalaureate distance learning degree programs offered (minimal on-campus study).

See Close-Up on page 1051.

Argosy University, Dallas, College of Psychology and Behavioral Sciences, Program in Community Counseling, Farmers Branch, TX 75244. Offers MA.

See Close-Up on page 1053.

Argosy University, Sarasota, College of Psychology and Behavioral Sciences, Sarasota, FL 34235. Offers community counseling (MA); counseling psychology (Ed D); counselor education and supervision (Ed D); forensic psychology (MA); marriage and family therapy (MA); mental health counseling (MA); pastoral community counseling (Ed D).

See Close-Up on page 1075.

Argosy University, Schaumburg, College of Psychology and Behavioral Sciences, Schaumburg, IL 60173-5403. Offers clinical health psychology (Post-Graduate Certificate); clinical psychology (MA, Psy D), including child and family psychology (Psy D), clinical health psychology (Psy D), diversity and multicultural psychology (Psy D), forensic psychology (Psy D), neuropsychology (Psy D); community counseling (MA); counseling psychology (Ed D), including counselor education and supervision; counselor education and supervision (Ed D); forensic psychology (Post-Graduate Certificate); industrial organizational psychology (MA). *Accreditation:* ACA; APA.

See Close-Up on page 1077.

Argosy University, Washington DC, College of Psychology and Behavioral Sciences, Arlington, VA 22209. Offers clinical psychology (MA, Psy D), including child and family psychology (Psy D), diversity and multicultural psychology (Psy D), forensic psychology (Psy D), health and neuropsychology (Psy D); community counseling (MA); counseling psychology (Ed D), including counselor education and supervision; counselor education and supervision (Ed D); forensic psychology (MA). *Accreditation:* APA.

See Close-Up on page 1085.

Arizona State University, Graduate College, College of Liberal Arts and Sciences, Division of Natural Sciences, Department of Psychology, Tempe, AZ 85287. Offers behavioral neuroscience (PhD); clinical psychology (PhD); cognition, action and perception (PhD); developmental psychology (PhD); quantitative psychology (PhD); social psychology (PhD). *Accreditation:* APA. *Degree requirements:* For doctorate, thesis/dissertation. *Entrance requirements:* For doctorate, GRE General Test, GRE Subject Test.

Ball State University, Graduate School, Teachers College, Department of Counseling Psychology and Guidance Services, Program in Social Psychology, Muncie, IN 47306-1099. Offers MA. *Entrance requirements:* For master's, GRE General Test.

Bethel University, Graduate School, Program in Counseling Psychology, St. Paul, MN 55112-6999. Offers child and adolescent and community counseling (MA). Part-time and evening/weekend programs available. *Faculty:* 6 full-time (2 women), 9 part-time/adjunct (5 women). *Students:* 71 full-time (56 women), 7 part-time (6 women); includes 5 minority (2 African Americans, 2 Asian Americans or Pacific Islanders, 1 Hispanic American). Average age 32. 60 applicants, 75% accepted, 35 enrolled. In 2009, 32 master's awarded. *Degree requirements:* For master's, comprehensive exam, thesis optional, practicum. *Entrance requirements:* For master's, MAT, minimum GPA of 3.0, course work in psychology and statistics, letters of reference. Additional exam requirements/recommendations for international students: Required—TOEFL (minimum score 550 paper-based; 213 computer-based; 80 iBT). *Application deadline:* For fall admission, 5/1 priority date for domestic students. Applications are processed on a rolling basis. Application fee: $25. Electronic applications accepted. *Expenses:* Tuition: Full-time $7920; part-time $440 per credit. One-time fee: $25. Tuition and fees vary according to course load, degree level and program. *Financial support:* Applicants required to submit FAFSA. *Unit head:* Dr. Diane Dahl, Assistant Dean, 651-635-8000, Fax: 651-635-8004, E-mail: diane-dahl@bethel.edu. *Application contact:* Michael Price, Director of Admissions, 651-635-8000, Fax: 651-635-8004, E-mail: m-price@bethel.edu.

Social Psychology

Bowling Green State University, Graduate College, College of Arts and Sciences, Department of Sociology, Bowling Green, OH 43403. Offers demography and population studies (MA); social psychology (MA); sociology (PhD). Part-time programs available. *Degree requirements:* For master's, thesis or alternative; for doctorate, comprehensive exam, thesis/dissertation. *Entrance requirements:* For master's and doctorate, GRE General Test. Additional exam requirements/recommendations for international students: Required—TOEFL. Electronic applications accepted. *Faculty research:* Applied demography, criminology and deviance, family studies, population studies, social psychology.

Brandeis University, Graduate School of Arts and Sciences, Department of Psychology, Waltham, MA 02454-9110. Offers brain, body and behavior (PhD); cognitive neuroscience (PhD); general psychology (MA); social/developmental psychology (PhD). Part-time programs available. *Faculty:* 16 full-time (4 women), 3 part-time/adjunct (2 women). *Students:* 35 full-time (27 women), 1 (woman) part-time; includes 2 minority (both Asian Americans or Pacific Islanders), 7 international. Average age 26. 121 applicants, 31% accepted, 13 enrolled. In 2009, 9 master's, 3 doctorates awarded. *Degree requirements:* For doctorate, comprehensive exam, thesis/dissertation. *Entrance requirements:* For master's, GRE General Test, GRE Subject Test (recommended), 3 letters of recommendation, statement of purpose; for doctorate, GRE General Test, GRE Subject Test (recommended), 3 letters of recommendation. Additional exam requirements/recommendations for international students: Required—TOEFL (minimum score 600 paper-based; 250 computer-based; 100 iBT); Recommended—IELTS (minimum score 7). *Application deadline:* For fall admission, 1/15 for domestic and international students. Applications are processed on a rolling basis. Application fee: $75. Electronic applications accepted. *Financial support:* In 2009–10, 16 fellowships with full tuition reimbursements (averaging $20,000 per year), 3 research assistantships with full tuition reimbursements (averaging $20,000 per year), 9 teaching assistantships with partial tuition reimbursements (averaging $3,200 per year) were awarded; institutionally sponsored loans, scholarships/grants, traineeships, health care benefits, tuition waivers (full), and unspecified assistantships also available. Support available to part-time students. Financial award applicants required to submit FAFSA. *Faculty research:* Development, cognition, social aging, perception, social/developmental psychology, cognitive neuroscience, brain, body and behavior, motor control, visual perception, taste physiology and psychophysics, memory, learning, aggression, emotion, personality and cognition in adulthood and old age, social relations and health, stereotypes and nonverbal communication. *Unit head:* Prof. Paul DiZio, Director of Graduate Studies, 781-736-3300, Fax: 781-736-3291, E-mail: dizio@brandeis.edu. *Application contact:* Donna J. Coletti, Graduate Admissions Coordinator, 781-736-3303, Fax: 781-736-3291, E-mail: coletti@brandeis.edu.

Brigham Young University, Graduate Studies, College of Family, Home, and Social Sciences, Department of Psychology, Provo, UT 84602. Offers clinical psychology (PhD); general psychology (MS); psychology (PhD), including applied social psychology, behavioral neurobiology. *Accreditation:* APA (one or more programs are accredited). *Faculty:* 27 full-time (5 women). *Students:* 90 full-time (30 women); includes 7 minority (3 African Americans, 4 Hispanic Americans), 8 international. Average age 24. 91 applicants, 20% accepted, 18 enrolled. In 2009, 9 master's, 14 doctorates awarded. *Degree requirements:* For master's, thesis; for doctorate, comprehensive exam, thesis/dissertation, publishable paper. *Entrance requirements:* For master's and doctorate, GRE General Test, minimum GPA of 3.0 in last 60 hours of upper division course work. Additional exam requirements/recommendations for international students: Required—TOEFL. *Application deadline:* For fall admission, 1/5 for domestic students. Application fee: $50. Electronic applications accepted. *Expenses:* Tuition: Full-time $5580; part-time $301 per credit hour. Tuition and fees vary according to student's religious affiliation. *Financial support:* In 2009–10, 85 students received support, including 20 research assistantships with partial tuition reimbursements available (averaging $10,000 per year), 30 teaching assistantships with partial tuition reimbursements available (averaging $10,000 per year); fellowships, career-related internships or fieldwork, scholarships/grants, tuition waivers (partial), and unspecified assistantships also available. Financial award application deadline: 5/31. *Faculty research:* Psychotherapy process, Alzheimer's disease/dementia, psychology and law, health, psychology, developmental. Total annual research expenditures: $1 million. *Unit head:* Dr. Ramona Hopkins, Chair, 801-422-1170, Fax: 801-422-0602, E-mail: ramona_hopkins@byu.edu. *Application contact:* Karen A. Christensen, Coordinator of Student Programs, 801-422-4560, Fax: 801-422-0602, E-mail: karen_christensen@byu.edu.

Brock University, Faculty of Graduate Studies, Faculty of Social Sciences, Program in Psychology, St. Catharines, ON L2S 3A1, Canada. Offers behavioral neuroscience (MA, PhD); life span development (MA, PhD); social personality (MA, PhD). Part-time programs available. *Degree requirements:* For master's, thesis; for doctorate, thesis/dissertation. *Entrance requirements:* For master's, GRE, honors degree; for doctorate, GRE, master's degree. Additional exam requirements/recommendations for international students: Required—TOEFL (minimum score 550 paper-based; 213 computer-based; 80 iBT), IELTS (minimum score 6.5), TWE (minimum score 4). Electronic applications accepted. *Faculty research:* Social personality, behavioral neuroscience, life-span development.

Brooklyn College of the City University of New York, Division of Graduate Studies, Department of Psychology, Program in Industrial and Organizational Psychology, Brooklyn, NY 11210-2889. Offers human relations (MA); organizational behavior (MA). *Students:* 9 full-time (8 women), 96 part-time (73 women); includes 50 minority (33 African Americans, 7 Asian Americans or Pacific Islanders, 10 Hispanic Americans), 10 international. Average age 31. 123 applicants, 63% accepted, 44 enrolled. In 2009, 20 master's awarded. *Degree requirements:* For master's, comprehensive exam, thesis. *Entrance requirements:* For master's, 2 letters of recommendation. Additional exam requirements/recommendations for international students: Required—TOEFL (minimum score 520 paper-based; 190 computer-based; 69 iBT). *Application deadline:* For fall admission, 3/1 priority date for domestic students, 2/1 for international students. Applications are processed on a rolling basis. Electronic applications accepted. *Expenses:* Tuition, area resident: Full-time $7360; part-time $310 per credit hour. Tuition, state resident: full-time $7360; part-time $310 per credit hour. Tuition, nonresident: full-time $13,800; part-time $575 per credit hour. International tuition: $13,800 full-time. Required fees: $140.10 per semester. *Unit head:* Benzion Chanowitz, Graduate Advisor, 718-951-5601, E-mail: bchanowitz@brooklyn.cuny.edu. *Application contact:* Hernan Sierra, Graduate Admissions Coordinator, 718-951-4536, Fax: 718-951-4506, E-mail: grads@brooklyn.cuny.edu.

Brown University, Graduate School, Department of Psychology, Providence, RI 02912. Offers behavioral neuroscience (PhD); cognitive processes (PhD); sensation and perception (PhD); social/developmental (PhD); MS/PhD. *Degree requirements:* For doctorate, thesis/dissertation. *Entrance requirements:* For doctorate, GRE General Test, GRE Subject Test.

California Institute of Integral Studies, School of Professional Psychology, San Francisco, CA 94103. Offers clinical psychology (Psy D); community mental health (MA); drama therapy (MA); expressive arts therapy (MA); integral counseling psychology (MA); integral counseling psychology–weekend (MA); somatic psychology (MA). *Accreditation:* APA. Part-time programs available. *Students:* 639 full-time (483 women), 53 part-time (43 women); includes 148 minority (32 African Americans, 2 American Indian/Alaska Native, 62 Asian Americans or Pacific Islanders, 52 Hispanic Americans). Average age 38. 476 applicants, 71% accepted, 202 enrolled. In 2009, 136 master's, 21 doctorates awarded. *Degree requirements:* For master's, comprehensive exam; for doctorate, comprehensive exam, thesis/dissertation. *Entrance requirements:* For master's, minimum GPA of 3.0, letters of recommendation, writing sample; for doctorate, GRE, MA in psychology or social work with appropriate practical experience for advanced standing, or BA with a minimum GPA of 3.1; letters of recommendation; writing sample. Additional exam requirements/recommendations for international students: Required—TOEFL. *Application deadline:* For fall admission, 2/1 priority date for domestic and international students; for spring admission, 10/15 priority date for domestic and international students. Applications are processed on a rolling basis. Application fee: $65. Electronic applications accepted. *Expenses:* Tuition: Full-time $15,300; part-time $850 per credit hour. Required fees: $110 per semester. Tuition and fees vary according to degree level. *Financial support:* In 2009–10, 677 students received support; research assistantships with tuition reimbursements available, teaching assistantships with tuition reimbursements available, career-related internships or fieldwork, Federal Work-Study, scholarships/grants, and tuition waivers (partial) available. Support available to part-time students. Financial award application deadline: 4/15; financial award applicants required to submit FAFSA. *Faculty research:* Somatic psychology, comparative psychology, art therapy, transpersonal psychology, eco-psychology. *Application contact:* David Townes, Senior Admissions Counselor, 415-575-6152, Fax: 415-575-1268, E-mail: dtownes@ciis.edu.

California State University, Fullerton, Graduate Studies, College of Humanities and Social Sciences, Department of Psychology, Fullerton, CA 92834-9480. Offers clinical/community psychology (MS); psychology (MA). Part-time programs available. *Students:* 17 full-time (9 women), 29 part-time (18 women); includes 20 minority (2 African Americans, 13 Asian Americans or Pacific Islanders, 5 Hispanic Americans), 3 international. Average age 26. 140 applicants, 31% accepted, 36 enrolled. In 2009, 19 master's awarded. *Degree requirements:* For master's, thesis. *Entrance requirements:* For master's, GRE General Test, GRE Subject Test, undergraduate major in psychology or related field. Application fee: $55. *Expenses:* Tuition, nonresident: full-time $11,160; part-time $373 per credit. Required fees: $1440 per term. Tuition and fees vary according to course load, degree level and program. *Financial support:* Career-related internships or fieldwork, Federal Work-Study, institutionally sponsored loans, and scholarships/grants available. Support available to part-time students. Financial award application deadline: 3/1; financial award applicants required to submit FAFSA. *Unit head:* Dr. Daniel Kee, Chair, 657-278-3514. *Application contact:* Admissions/Applications, 657-278-2371.

Canisius College, Graduate Division, School of Education and Human Services, Department of Counseling and Human Services, Buffalo, NY 14208-1098. Offers community mental health counseling (MS); general counseling (MS); school counseling (MS). *Accreditation:* ACA. Part-time and evening/weekend programs available. *Faculty:* 5 full-time (3 women), 6 part-time/adjunct (2 women). *Students:* 110 full-time (89 women), 62 part-time (56 women); includes 23 minority (18 African Americans, 2 Asian Americans or Pacific Islanders, 3 Hispanic Americans), 3 international. Average age 30. 106 applicants, 84% accepted, 43 enrolled. In 2009, 51 master's awarded. *Degree requirements:* For master's, thesis, research project. *Entrance requirements:* For master's, interview, minimum GPA of 2.5. *Application deadline:* Applications are processed on a rolling basis. Application fee: $25. Electronic applications accepted. *Financial support:* In 2009–10, 2 research assistantships with partial tuition reimbursements (averaging $8,500 per year) were awarded; career-related internships or fieldwork, Federal Work-Study, institutionally sponsored loans, health care benefits, and unspecified assistantships also available. Support available to part-time students. Financial award applicants required to submit FAFSA. *Faculty research:* Positive psychology, wellness, school violence prevention, chronic pain. *Unit head:* Dr. David L. Farrugia, Chairman, 716-888-2393, Fax: 716-888-3290, E-mail: farrugia@canisius.edu. *Application contact:* James D. Bagwell, Director of Graduate Recruitment and Admissions, 716-888-2544, Fax: 716-888-3290, E-mail: bagwellj@canisius.edu.

Carnegie Mellon University, College of Humanities and Social Sciences, Department of Psychology, Program in Social/Personality/Health Psychology, Pittsburgh, PA 15213-3891. Offers PhD. *Degree requirements:* For doctorate, comprehensive exam, thesis/dissertation. *Entrance requirements:* For doctorate, GRE General Test. Additional exam requirements/recommendations for international students: Required—TOEFL.

Central Connecticut State University, School of Graduate Studies, School of Arts and Sciences, Department of Psychology, New Britain, CT 06050-4010. Offers community psychology (MA); general psychology (MA); health psychology (MA). Part-time and evening/weekend programs available. *Faculty:* 20 full-time (13 women), 22 part-time/adjunct (7 women). *Students:* 21 full-time (19 women), 31 part-time (27 women); includes 9 minority (4 African Americans, 5 Hispanic Americans). Average age 27. 49 applicants, 43% accepted, 17 enrolled. In 2009, 8 master's awarded. *Degree requirements:* For master's, comprehensive exam, thesis or alternative. *Entrance requirements:* For master's, minimum undergraduate GPA of 2.7, essay. Additional exam requirements/recommendations for international students: Required—TOEFL. *Application deadline:* For fall admission, 4/25 for domestic students; for spring admission, 12/1 for domestic students. Applications are processed on a rolling basis. Application fee: $50. Electronic applications accepted. *Expenses:* Tuition, area resident: Full-time $4662; part-time $440 per credit. Tuition, state resident: full-time $6994; part-time $440 per credit. Tuition, nonresident: full-time $12,988; part-time $440 per credit. Required fees: $3606. One-time fee: $62 part-time. *Financial support:* In 2009–10, 8 students received support, including 6 research assistantships; career-related internships or fieldwork, Federal Work-Study, scholarships/grants, and unspecified assistantships also available. Support available to part-time students. Financial award application deadline: 3/1; financial award applicants required to submit FAFSA. *Faculty research:* Clinical psychology, general psychology, child development, cognitive development, drugs/behavior. *Unit head:* Dr. Laura Bowman, Chair, 860-832-3100. *Application contact:* Dr. Laura Bowman, Chair, 860-832-3100.

Claremont Graduate University, Graduate Programs, School of Behavioral and Organizational Sciences, Department of Psychology, Claremont, CA 91711-6160. Offers advanced study in evaluation (Certificate); cognitive psychology (MA, PhD); developmental psychology (MA, PhD); evaluation and applied research methods (MA, PhD); health behavior research and evaluation (MA, PhD); human resource development and evaluation (MA); industrial/organizational psychology (MA, PhD); organizational behavior (MA, PhD); organizational psychology (MA, PhD); social psychology (MA, PhD); MBA/PhD. Part-time programs available. *Faculty:* 17 full-time (7 women), 1 part-time/adjunct (0 women). *Students:* 231 full-time (155 women), 25 part-time (18 women); includes 62 minority (13 African Americans, 1 American Indian/Alaska Native, 31 Asian Americans or Pacific Islanders, 17 Hispanic Americans), 21 international. Average age 30. In 2009, 37 master's, 12 doctorates, 8 other advanced degrees awarded. Terminal master's awarded for partial completion of doctoral program. *Entrance requirements:* For master's and doctorate, GRE General Test. Additional exam requirements/recommendations for international students: Required—TOEFL (minimum score 550 paper-based; 213 computer-based; 80 iBT). *Application deadline:* For fall admission, 1/15 priority date for domestic students. Applications are processed on a rolling basis. Application fee: $60. Electronic applications accepted. *Expenses:* Tuition: Full-time $35,046; part-time $1524 per credit. Required fees: $161 per semester. *Financial support:* Fellowships, research assistantships, teaching assistantships, Federal Work-Study, institutionally sponsored loans, scholarships/grants, and tuition waivers (full and partial) available. Support available to part-time students. Financial award application deadline: 2/15; financial award applicants required to submit FAFSA. *Faculty research:* Social intervention, diversity in organizations, eyewitness memory, aging and cognition, drug policy. *Unit head:* Stewart Donaldson, Dean, 909-607-9001, Fax: 909-621-8905, E-mail: stewart.donaldson@cgu.edu. *Application contact:* Paul Thomas, Director, External Affairs, 909-607-9016, Fax: 909-621-8905, E-mail: paul.thomas@cgu.edu.

Clark University, Graduate School, Department of Psychology, Program in Social-Personality Psychology, Worcester, MA 01610-1477. Offers PhD. *Degree requirements:* For doctorate, thesis/dissertation. *Entrance requirements:* For doctorate, GRE General Test. Additional exam requirements/recommendations for international students: Required—TOEFL. *Application deadline:* For fall admission, 12/28 priority date for domestic students. Applications are processed on a rolling basis. Application fee: $50. *Expenses:* Tuition: Full-time $34,900; part-time $4362.50 per course. *Financial support:* In 2009–10, fellowships with full tuition reimbursements (averaging $15,700 per year), research assistantships with full tuition reimbursements (averaging $15,700 per year), teaching assistantships with full tuition reimbursements (averaging $15,700 per year) were awarded; tuition waivers (full) also available. *Faculty research:* Development of psychological processes in sociocultural context, conceptualizing and reasoning, symbolization, psychotherapy, metaphor, emotions and personalities. *Unit head:* Dr. Joseph deRivera, Director, 508-793-7274. *Application contact:* Peggy Moskowitz, Graduate School Secretary, 508-793-7274, Fax: 508-793-7265, E-mail: psychology@clarku.edu.

The College of New Rochelle, Graduate School, Division of Human Services, Program in Community-School Psychology, New Rochelle, NY 10805-2308. Offers MS. *Degree requirements:* For master's, comprehensive exam, clinical fieldwork, journal. *Entrance requirements:* For master's, interview, minimum GPA of 3.0, course work in psychology, sample of written work.

College of St. Joseph, Graduate Programs, Division of Psychology and Human Services, Program in Community Counseling, Rutland, VT 05701-3899. Offers MS. Part-time and evening/weekend programs available. *Degree requirements:* For master's, comprehensive exam, thesis optional. *Entrance requirements:* For master's, 2 letters of reference, interview. Electronic applications accepted. *Expenses:* Tuition: Full-time $13,500; part-time $350 per credit. Required fees: $45 per term. One-time fee: $445. Tuition and fees vary according to program.

Columbia University, Graduate School of Arts and Sciences, Division of Natural Sciences, Department of Psychology, New York, NY 10027. Offers experimental psychology (M Phil, MA, PhD); psychobiology (M Phil, MA, PhD); social psychology (M Phil, MA, PhD); JD/MA; JD/PhD; MD/PhD. *Degree requirements:* For master's, thesis; for doctorate, thesis/dissertation. *Entrance requirements:* For master's and doctorate, GRE General Test. Additional exam requirements/recommendations for international students: Required—TOEFL.

Cornell University, Graduate School, Graduate Fields of Arts and Sciences, Field of Psychology, Ithaca, NY 14853-0001. Offers biopsychology (PhD); human experimental psychology (PhD); personality and social psychology (PhD). *Faculty:* 49 full-time (17 women). *Students:* 37 full-time (24 women); includes 5 minority (1 African American, 2 Asian Americans or Pacific Islanders, 2 Hispanic Americans), 10 international. Average age 29. 221 applicants, 4% accepted, 8 enrolled. In 2009, 3 doctorates awarded. *Degree requirements:* For doctorate, comprehensive exam, thesis/dissertation, 2 semesters of teaching experience. *Entrance requirements:* For doctorate, GRE General Test, 3 letters of recommendation. Additional exam requirements/recommendations for international students: Required—TOEFL (minimum score 550 paper-based; 213 computer-based; 77 iBT). *Application deadline:* For fall admission, 12/15 for domestic students. Application fee: $70. Electronic applications accepted. *Expenses:* Tuition: Full-time $29,500. Required fees: $70. Full-time tuition and fees vary according to degree level, program and student level. *Financial support:* In 2009–10, 36 students received support, including 6 fellowships with full tuition reimbursements available, 2 teaching assistantships with full tuition reimbursements available; research assistantships with full tuition reimbursements available, institutionally sponsored loans, scholarships/grants, health care benefits, tuition waivers (full and partial), and unspecified assistantships also available. Financial award applicants required to submit FAFSA. *Faculty research:* Sensory and perceptual systems, social cognition, cognitive development, quantitative and computational modeling, behavioral neuroscience. *Unit head:* Director of Graduate Studies, 607-255-6364, Fax: 607-255-8433. *Application contact:* Graduate Field Assistant, 607-255-3834, Fax: 607-255-8433, E-mail: psychapp@cornell.edu.

Cornell University, Graduate School, Graduate Fields of Arts and Sciences, Field of Sociology, Ithaca, NY 14853-0001. Offers economy and society (MA, PhD); gender and life course (MA, PhD); methodology (MA, PhD); organizations (MA, PhD); policy analysis (MA, PhD); political sociology/social movements (MA, PhD); racial and ethnic relations (MA, PhD); social networks (MA, PhD); social psychology (MA, PhD); social stratification (MA, PhD). *Faculty:* 41 full-time (17 women). *Students:* 39 full-time (19 women); includes 4 minority (all Asian Americans or Pacific Islanders), 10 international. Average age 31. 153 applicants, 8% accepted, 7 enrolled. In 2009, 2 master's, 2 doctorates awarded. Terminal master's awarded for partial completion of doctoral program. *Degree requirements:* For master's, thesis; for doctorate, thesis/dissertation, 1 year of teaching experience. *Entrance requirements:* For master's and doctorate, GRE General Test, 2 letters of recommendation, writing sample. Additional exam requirements/recommendations for international students: Required—TOEFL (minimum score 550 paper-based; 213 computer-based; 77 iBT). *Application deadline:* For fall admission, 1/15 for domestic students. Application fee: $70. Electronic applications accepted. *Expenses:* Tuition: Full-time $29,500. Required fees: $70. Full-time tuition and fees vary according to degree level, program and student level. *Financial support:* In 2009–10, 32 students received support, including 6 fellowships with full tuition reimbursements available; research assistantships with full tuition reimbursements available, teaching assistantships with full tuition reimbursements available, institutionally sponsored loans, scholarships/grants, health care benefits, tuition waivers (full and partial), and unspecified assistantships also available. Financial award applicants required to submit FAFSA. *Faculty research:* Comparative societal analysis, work and family, simulations, social class and mobility, racial segregation and inequality. *Unit head:* Director of Graduate Studies, 607-255-4266. *Application contact:* Graduate Field Assistant, 607-255-4266, E-mail: sociology@cornell.edu.

Creighton University, Graduate School, College of Arts and Sciences, Department of Education, Program in Counselor Education, Omaha, NE 68178-0001. Offers college student affairs (MS); community counseling (MS); elementary school guidance (MS); secondary school guidance (MS). Part-time and evening/weekend programs available. *Faculty:* 13 full-time (8 women). *Students:* 1 full-time (0 women), 42 part-time (33 women); includes 8 minority (3 African Americans, 1 American Indian/Alaska Native, 2 Asian Americans or Pacific Islanders, 2 Hispanic Americans), 4 international. Average age 32. 10 applicants, 60% accepted, 6 enrolled. In 2009, 18 master's awarded. *Entrance requirements:* For master's, GRE General Test, resume, 3 letters of recommendation. Additional exam requirements/recommendations for international students: Required—TOEFL (minimum score 550 paper-based; 213 computer-based; 80 iBT). *Application deadline:* For fall admission, 7/1 for domestic students, 3/1 for international students; for winter admission, 10/1 for domestic students, 7/1 for international students; for spring admission, 3/1 for domestic students, 9/1 for international students. Applications are processed on a rolling basis. Application fee: $50. Electronic applications accepted. *Expenses:* Tuition: Full-time $11,700; part-time $650 per credit hour. Required fees: $126 per semester. *Financial support:* Scholarships/grants available. Support available to part-time students. Financial award applicants required to submit FAFSA. *Unit head:* Dr. Debra L. Ponec, Associate Professor of Education, 402-280-2557, E-mail: dlponec@creighton.edu. *Application contact:* Taunya Plater, Senior Program Coordinator, 402-280-2870, Fax: 402-280-2899, E-mail: taunyaplater@creighton.edu.

DePaul University, College of Liberal Arts and Sciences, Department of Psychology, Chicago, IL 60604-2287. Offers clinical psychology (MA, PhD), including child clinical psychology, community clinical psychology; experimental psychology (MA, PhD); general psychology (MS); industrial/organizational psychology (MA, PhD); MA/PhD. *Accreditation:* APA (one or more programs are accredited). *Faculty:* 31 full-time (19 women), 6 part-time/adjunct (4 women). *Students:* 59 full-time (36 women), 54 part-time (35 women); includes 26 minority (10 African Americans, 5 Asian Americans or Pacific Islanders, 11 Hispanic Americans), 2 international. Average age 28. 332 applicants, 14% accepted, 23 enrolled. In 2009, 14 master's, 17 doctorates awarded. *Degree requirements:* For master's, thesis, oral exam; for doctorate, comprehensive exam, thesis/dissertation, oral and written exams. *Entrance requirements:* For master's and doctorate, GRE General Test, GRE Subject Test, 32 quarter hours of course work in psychology, 3 letters of recommendation. Additional exam requirements/recommendations for international students: Required—TOEFL. Application fee: $40. Electronic applications accepted. *Expenses:* Tuition: Full-time $37,525; part-time $620 per credit hour. *Financial support:* In 2009–10, 48 students received support, including 35 research assistantships with full tuition reimbursements available (averaging $11,800 per year), 13 teaching assistantships with full tuition reimbursements available (averaging $11,800 per year); career-related internships or fieldwork, scholarships/grants, traineeships, tuition waivers (full and partial), and unspecified assistantships also available. Financial award application deadline: 1/10. *Faculty research:* Adolescent stress and depression, minority adolescents sexuality, public policy, community influences in child adjustment. *Unit head:* Dr. Christopher B. Keys, Chairman, 773-325-7887, Fax: 773-325-7888. *Application contact:* Alison Pereida Knapp, Graduate Admissions Assistant, 773-325-7887, Fax: 773-325-7888.

Eastern Michigan University, Graduate School, College of Education, Department of Leadership and Counseling, Programs in Counseling, Ypsilanti, MI 48197. Offers college counseling (MA); community counseling (MA); helping interventions in a multicultural society (Graduate Certificate); school counseling (MA); school counselor (MA); school counselor licensure (Post Master's Certificate). Part-time and evening/weekend programs available. *Students:* 17 full-time (14 women), 108 part-time (93 women); includes 31 minority (25 African Americans, 2 American Indian/Alaska Native, 2 Asian Americans or Pacific Islanders, 2 Hispanic Americans), 2 international. Average age 33. In 2009, 28 master's, 1 other advanced degree awarded. *Degree requirements:* For master's, comprehensive exam, internship. *Entrance requirements:* Additional exam requirements/recommendations for international students: Required—TOEFL. *Application deadline:* For fall admission, 5/1 for domestic and international students; for winter admission, 9/15 for domestic and international students; for spring admission, 2/10 for domestic and international students. Applications are processed on a rolling basis. Application fee: $35. Tuition and fees vary according to course level. *Financial support:* Fellowships, research assistantships with full tuition reimbursements, teaching assistantships with full tuition reimbursements, career-related internships or fieldwork, Federal Work-Study, institutionally sponsored loans, scholarships/grants, tuition waivers (partial), and unspecified assistantships available. Support available to part-time students. Financial award applicants required to submit FAFSA. *Application contact:* Dr. Dibya Choudhuri, Advisor, 734-487-0255, Fax: 734-487-4608, E-mail: dibya.chouduri@emich.edu.

Eastern University, Department of Counseling Psychology, St. Davids, PA 19087-3696. Offers community/clinical counseling (MA); school counseling (MA, Certificate); school psychology (MS, Certificate). *Degree requirements:* For master's, internship. *Entrance requirements:* For master's, minimum GPA of 2.5. Additional exam requirements/recommendations for international students: Required—TOEFL.

Florida Agricultural and Mechanical University, Division of Graduate Studies, Research, and Continuing Education, College of Arts and Sciences, Department of Psychology, Program in Community Psychology, Tallahassee, FL 32307-3200. Offers MS. *Faculty:* 11 full-time (6 women). *Students:* 19 full-time (15 women), 22 part-time (15 women); includes 39 minority (all African Americans), 1 international. In 2009, 1 master's awarded. *Degree requirements:* For master's, thesis, internship. *Entrance requirements:* For master's, GRE General Test, minimum GPA of 3.0, letters of recommendation (3). Additional exam requirements/recommendations for international students: Required—TOEFL. *Application deadline:* For fall admission, 5/18 for domestic students, 12/18 for international students; for spring admission, 11/12 for domestic students, 5/12 for international students. Application fee: $30. *Financial support:* Fellowships, research assistantships, career-related internships or fieldwork, Federal Work-Study, institutionally sponsored loans, and tuition waivers (partial) available. *Faculty research:* African-American personality and mental health, racism in the socialization of black children. *Unit head:* Dr. Yvonne Bell, Chairperson, 850-599-3468, Fax: 850-561-2540, E-mail: yvonne.bell@famu.edu. *Application contact:* Dr. Chanta M. Haywood, Dean of Graduate Studies, Research, and Continuing Education, 850-599-3315, Fax: 850-599-3727.

Florida State University, The Graduate School, College of Arts and Sciences, Department of Psychology, Program in Social Psychology, Tallahassee, FL 32306. Offers PhD. *Faculty:* 6 full-time (4 women). *Students:* 21 full-time (10 women); includes 3 minority (2 Asian Americans or Pacific Islanders, 1 Hispanic American), 1 international. Average age 24. 102 applicants, 3% accepted, 3 enrolled. In 2009, 2 doctorates awarded. Terminal master's awarded for partial completion of doctoral program. *Degree requirements:* For doctorate, thesis/dissertation, preliminary exam. *Entrance requirements:* For doctorate, GRE General Test, minimum GPA of 3.0, research experience, letters of recommendation. Additional exam requirements/recommendations for international students: Required—TOEFL (minimum score 550 paper-based; 213 computer-based; 80 iBT). *Application deadline:* For fall admission, 12/15 for domestic and international students. Application fee: $30. *Expenses:* Tuition, state resident: full-time $7413. Tuition, nonresident: full-time $22,567. *Financial support:* In 2009–10, 20 students received support, including 1 fellowship with full tuition reimbursement available (averaging $18,000 per year), 6 research assistantships with full tuition reimbursements available (averaging $15,000 per year), 13 teaching assistantships with full tuition reimbursements available (averaging $15,000 per year); Federal Work-Study, institutionally sponsored loans, scholarships/grants, traineeships, and unspecified assistantships also available. *Faculty research:* The self, prejudice, stereotyping. Total annual research expenditures: $464,634. *Unit head:* Dr. Jon Maner, Director, 850-645-1409, Fax: 850-644-7739, E-mail: maner@psy.fsu.edu. *Application contact:* Cherie P. Miller, Graduate Program Assistant, 850-644-2499, Fax: 850-644-7739, E-mail: grad-info@psy.fsu.edu.

The George Washington University, Columbian College of Arts and Sciences, Department of Psychology, Washington, DC 20052. Offers applied social psychology (PhD); clinical psychology (PhD); cognitive neuroscience (PhD). *Accreditation:* APA. Part-time and evening/weekend programs available. *Faculty:* 27 full-time (15 women), 25 part-time/adjunct (14 women). *Students:* 117 full-time (94 women), 89 part-time (73 women); includes 56 minority (16 African Americans, 2 American Indian/Alaska Native, 23 Asian Americans or Pacific Islanders, 15 Hispanic Americans), 4 international. Average age 28. 787 applicants, 6% accepted, 43 enrolled. In 2009, 49 doctorates awarded. *Degree requirements:* For doctorate, thesis/dissertation or alternative, general exam. *Entrance requirements:* For doctorate, GRE General Test, minimum GPA of 3.0. Additional exam requirements/recommendations for international students: Required—TOEFL (minimum score 550 paper-based; 213 computer-based; 80 iBT). *Application deadline:* For fall admission, 1/15 for domestic and international students. Application fee: $60. *Financial support:* In 2009–10, 62 students received support; fellowships with tuition reimbursements available, teaching assistantships with tuition reimbursements available, career-related internships or fieldwork, Federal Work-Study, and tuition waivers available. *Unit head:* Dr. Paul Poppen, Chair, 202-994-6324, E-mail: pjp@gwu.edu. *Application contact:* Information Contact, 202-994-6320, Fax: 202-994-1602, E-mail: psydept@gwu.edu.

The George Washington University, Graduate School of Education and Human Development, Department of Counseling/Human and Organizational Studies, Programs in Counseling: School, Community and Rehabilitation, Washington, DC 20052. Offers community counseling (MA Ed); rehabilitation counseling (MA Ed); school counseling (MA Ed). School counseling program also offered in Alexandria, VA. *Accreditation:* ACA; CORE; NCATE. *Students:* 72 full-time (63 women), 67 part-time (53 women); includes 33 minority (22 African Americans, 2 American Indian/Alaska Native, 5 Asian Americans or Pacific Islanders, 4 Hispanic Americans), 4 international. Average age 33. 104 applicants, 94% accepted, 51 enrolled. In 2009, 93 master's awarded. *Degree requirements:* For master's, comprehensive exam. *Entrance requirements:* For master's, GRE General Test or MAT, minimum GPA of 2.75. *Application deadline:* For fall admission, 1/15 priority date for domestic students; for spring admission, 10/1 for domestic students. Applications are processed on a rolling basis. Application fee: $60. *Financial support:* In 2009–10, 27 students received support; fellowships, research assistantships, teaching assistantships, career-related internships or fieldwork, Federal Work-Study, and tuition waivers (full and partial) available. *Faculty research:* Adjustment to disability, head injury rehabilitation, cross-cultural counseling. *Application contact:* Sarah Lang, Director of Graduate Admissions, 202-994-1447, Fax: 202-994-7207, E-mail: slang@gwu.edu.

Graduate School and University Center of the City University of New York, Graduate Studies, Program in Psychology, New York, NY 10016-4039. Offers basic applied neurocognition (PhD); biopsychology (PhD); clinical psychology (PhD); developmental psychology (PhD); environmental psychology (PhD); experimental psychology (PhD); industrial psychology (PhD);

Social Psychology

Graduate School and University Center of the City University of New York (continued)
learning processes (PhD); neuropsychology (PhD); psychology (PhD); social personality (PhD). *Faculty:* 119 full-time (40 women). *Students:* 559 full-time (414 women), 1 part-time (0 women); includes 101 minority (34 African Americans, 25 Asian Americans or Pacific Islanders, 42 Hispanic Americans), 57 international. Average age 33. 750 applicants, 16% accepted, 84 enrolled. In 2009, 54 doctorates awarded. *Degree requirements:* For doctorate, one foreign language, thesis/dissertation. *Entrance requirements:* For doctorate, GRE General Test. Additional exam requirements/recommendations for international students: Required—TOEFL. *Application deadline:* For fall admission, 12/15 priority date for domestic students. Application fee: $125. Electronic applications accepted. *Financial support:* In 2009–10, 371 students received support, including 340 fellowships, 34 research assistantships, 33 teaching assistantships; career-related internships or fieldwork, Federal Work-Study, institutionally sponsored loans, and tuition waivers (full and partial) also available. Financial award application deadline: 2/1; financial award applicants required to submit FAFSA. *Unit head:* Dr. Joseph Glick, Executive Officer, 212-817-8706, Fax: 212-817-1533, E-mail: jglick@gc.cuny.edu. *Application contact:* Les Gribben, Director of Admissions, 212-817-7470, Fax: 212-817-1624, E-mail: lgribben@gc.cuny.edu.

Harvard University, Graduate School of Arts and Sciences, Department of Psychology, Cambridge, MA 02138. Offers psychology (PhD), including behavior and decision analysis, cognition, developmental psychology, experimental psychology, personality, psychobiology, psychopathology; social psychology (PhD). *Accreditation:* APA. *Degree requirements:* For doctorate, thesis/dissertation, general exams. *Entrance requirements:* For doctorate, GRE General Test. Additional exam requirements/recommendations for international students: Required—TOEFL. *Expenses:* Tuition: Full-time $33,696. Required fees: $1126. Full-time tuition and fees vary according to program.

Hofstra University, College of Liberal Arts and Sciences, Department of Psychology, Program in School-Community Psychology, Hempstead, NY 11549. Offers Psy D. *Accreditation:* NCATE. *Students:* 40 full-time (34 women), 9 part-time (8 women); includes 8 minority (1 African American, 4 Asian Americans or Pacific Islanders, 3 Hispanic Americans). Average age 26. 69 applicants, 35% accepted, 11 enrolled. In 2009, 17 doctorates awarded. Terminal master's awarded for partial completion of doctoral program. *Degree requirements:* For doctorate, comprehensive exam, thesis/dissertation. *Entrance requirements:* For doctorate, GRE General Test, GRE Subject Test (psychology), interview, 3 letters of recommendation. Additional exam requirements/recommendations for international students: Required—TOEFL (minimum score 550 paper-based; 213 computer-based; 80 iBT). *Application deadline:* For fall admission, 1/15 for domestic and international students. Application fee: $60. Electronic applications accepted. *Expenses:* Tuition: Full-time $16,200; part-time $900 per credit hour. Required fees: $970; $145 per term. Tuition and fees vary according to program. *Financial support:* In 2009–10, 22 students received support, including 21 fellowships with full and partial tuition reimbursements available (averaging $5,697 per year), 1 research assistantship with full and partial tuition reimbursement available (averaging $9,000 per year); Federal Work-Study, institutionally sponsored loans, scholarships/grants, and tuition waivers (full and partial) also available. Support available to part-time students. Financial award applicants required to submit FAFSA. *Faculty research:* Cross-cultural psychology, school psychology, childhood and adult trauma, positive psychology, autism spectrum disorders. *Unit head:* Dr. Robert Motta, Program Director, 516-463-5029, Fax: 516-463-6052, E-mail: psyrwm@hofstra.edu. *Application contact:* Carol Drummer, Dean of Graduate Admissions, 516-463-4876, Fax: 516-463-4664, E-mail: gradstudent@hofstra.edu.

Howard University, Graduate School, Department of Psychology, Washington, DC 20059-0002. Offers clinical psychology (PhD); developmental psychology (PhD); experimental psychology (PhD); neuropsychology (PhD); personality psychology (PhD); psychology (MS); social psychology (PhD). *Accreditation:* APA (one or more programs are accredited). Part-time programs available. *Degree requirements:* For master's, thesis; for doctorate, comprehensive exam, thesis/dissertation, qualifying exam. *Entrance requirements:* For master's, GRE General Test, minimum GPA of 2.5, bachelor's degree in psychology or related field; for doctorate, GRE General Test, minimum GPA of 3.0. *Faculty research:* Personality and psychophysiology, educational and social development of African-American children, child and adult psychopathology.

Hunter College of the City University of New York, Graduate School, School of Arts and Sciences, Department of Psychology, New York, NY 10021-5085. Offers applied and evaluative psychology (MA); biopsychology and comparative psychology (MA); social, cognitive, and developmental psychology (MA). Part-time and evening/weekend programs available. *Faculty:* 18 full-time (9 women), 2 part-time/adjunct (0 women). *Students:* 12 full-time (10 women), 68 part-time (56 women); includes 13 minority (2 African Americans, 3 Asian Americans or Pacific Islanders, 8 Hispanic Americans). Average age 28. 122 applicants, 37% accepted, 24 enrolled. In 2009, 15 master's awarded. *Degree requirements:* For master's, comprehensive exam, thesis. *Entrance requirements:* For master's, GRE General Test, minimum 12 credits of course work in psychology, including statistics and experimental psychology; 2 letters of recommendation. Additional exam requirements/recommendations for international students: Required—TOEFL. *Application deadline:* For fall admission, 4/1 for domestic students, 2/1 for international students; for spring admission, 11/1 for domestic students, 9/1 for international students. Applications are processed on a rolling basis. Application fee: $125. *Expenses:* Tuition, state resident: full-time $7360; part-time $310 per credit. Required fees: $250 per semester. *Financial support:* Federal Work-Study, scholarships/grants, and tuition waivers (partial) available. Support available to part-time students. *Faculty research:* Personality, cognitive and linguistic development, hormonal and neural control of behavior, gender and culture, social cognition of health and attitudes. *Unit head:* Dr. Jeffrey Parsons, Chairperson, 212-772-5550, Fax: 212-772-5620, E-mail: jeffrey.parsons@hunter.cuny.edu. *Application contact:* Martin Braun, Acting Program Director, 212-772-4482, Fax: 212-650-3336, E-mail: cbraun@hunter.cuny.edu.

Indiana University Bloomington, University Graduate School, College of Arts and Sciences, Department of Psychological and Brain Sciences, Bloomington, IN 47405-7000. Offers biology and behavior (PhD); clinical science (PhD); cognitive psychology (PhD); developmental psychology (PhD); psychological and brain sciences (MA); social psychology (PhD). *Accreditation:* APA (one or more programs are accredited). *Faculty:* 53 full-time (16 women). *Students:* 92 full-time (51 women); includes 12 minority (4 African Americans, 4 Asian Americans or Pacific Islanders, 4 Hispanic Americans), 19 international. Average age 28. 239 applicants, 10% accepted, 15 enrolled. In 2009, 3 master's, 13 doctorates awarded. *Degree requirements:* For doctorate, comprehensive exam, thesis/dissertation, 1st and 2nd year projects, 1 year as associate instructor, qualifying exam, student teaching. *Entrance requirements:* For doctorate, GRE. Additional exam requirements/recommendations for international students: Required—TOEFL (minimum score 550 paper-based; 213 computer-based). *Application deadline:* For fall admission, 12/15 for domestic students, 12/1 for international students. Application fee: $55 ($65 for international students). Electronic applications accepted. *Financial support:* In 2009–10, 25 fellowships with full tuition reimbursements (averaging $23,000 per year), 11 research assistantships with full tuition reimbursements (averaging $17,850 per year), 7 teaching assistantships with full tuition reimbursements (averaging $17,850 per year) were awarded; scholarships/grants, health care benefits, and unspecified assistantships also available. *Unit head:* Dr. Linda B. Smith, Chair, 812-855-3991, Fax: 812-855-4691, E-mail: smith4@indiana.edu. *Application contact:* Patricia G. Crouch, Academic Services Coordinator, 812-855-4528, Fax: 812-855-4691, E-mail: pcrouch@indiana.edu.

Indiana Wesleyan University, College of Graduate Studies, Graduate Studies in Counseling, Marion, IN 46953. Offers addictions counseling (MS); community counseling (MS); marriage and family counseling (MS); school counseling (MS). *Accreditation:* ACA. Part-time programs available. *Degree requirements:* For master's, thesis or alternative. *Entrance requirements:* For master's, GRE General Test. Additional exam requirements/recommendations for international students: Required—TOEFL. Electronic applications accepted. *Expenses:* Contact institution. *Faculty research:* Community counseling, multicultural counseling, addictions.

Iowa State University of Science and Technology, Graduate College, College of Liberal Arts and Sciences, Department of Psychology, Ames, IA 50011. Offers cognitive psychology (PhD); counseling psychology (PhD); social psychology (PhD). *Accreditation:* APA. *Faculty:* 25 full-time (8 women), 8 part-time/adjunct (4 women). *Degree requirements:* For doctorate, comprehensive exam, thesis/dissertation. *Entrance requirements:* For doctorate, GRE General Test, GRE Subject Test (psychology), 3 letters of recommendation. Additional exam requirements/recommendations for international students: Required—TOEFL (minimum score 560 paper-based; 220 computer-based). *Application deadline:* For fall admission, 1/2 priority date for domestic and international students. Application fee: $30 ($70 for international students). Electronic applications accepted. *Expenses:* Tuition, state resident: full-time $6716. Tuition, nonresident: full-time $8908. Tuition and fees vary according to course level, course load, program and student level. *Financial support:* In 2009–10, fellowships with full tuition reimbursements (averaging $14,055 per year), research assistantships with full tuition reimbursements (averaging $12,200 per year), teaching assistantships with full tuition reimbursements (averaging $12,200 per year) were awarded; scholarships/grants, health care benefits, and unspecified assistantships also available. *Faculty research:* Counseling psychology, cognitive psychology, social psychology, health psychology, psychology and public policy. *Unit head:* Carolyn Cutrona, Chair, 515-294-0283, Fax: 515-294-6424, E-mail: ccutrona@iastate.edu. *Application contact:* Ann Schmidt, Graduate Admissions Secretary, 515-294-1743, Fax: 515-294-6424, E-mail: psychadm@iastate.edu.

Kent State University, Graduate School of Education, Health, and Human Services, School of Lifespan Development and Educational Sciences, Program in Community Counseling, Kent, OH 44242-0001. Offers M Ed, MA. *Accreditation:* ACA; NCATE. *Faculty:* 8 full-time (4 women), 16 part-time/adjunct (11 women). *Students:* 75 full-time (63 women), 62 part-time (51 women); includes 19 minority (18 African Americans, 1 Asian American or Pacific Islander), 4 international. 74 applicants, 62% accepted. In 2009, 32 master's awarded. *Degree requirements:* For master's, thesis (for some programs). *Entrance requirements:* Additional exam requirements/recommendations for international students: Required—TOEFL. *Application deadline:* For fall admission, 6/1 for domestic students; for spring admission, 10/1 for domestic students. Application fee: $30. Electronic applications accepted. *Financial support:* In 2009–10, 2 research assistantships with full tuition reimbursements (averaging $8,313 per year) were awarded; career-related internships or fieldwork, Federal Work-Study, institutionally sponsored loans, scholarships/grants, health care benefits, and unspecified assistantships also available. Support available to part-time students. Financial award application deadline: 4/1; financial award applicants required to submit FAFSA. *Faculty research:* Group work, personality assessment, family/child therapy, substance abuse counseling, clinical supervision. *Unit head:* Dr. Jason McGlothlin, Coordinator, 330-672-0716, E-mail: jmcgloth@kent.edu. *Application contact:* Nancy Miller, Academic Program Coordinator, Office of Graduate Student Services, 330-672-2576, Fax: 330-672-9162, E-mail: ogs@kent.edu.

Lamar University, College of Graduate Studies, College of Arts and Sciences, Department of Psychology, Beaumont, TX 77710. Offers community/clinical psychology (MS); industrial/organizational psychology (MS). Part-time programs available. *Faculty:* 6 full-time (3 women). *Students:* 14 full-time (10 women), 11 part-time (5 women); includes 4 minority (2 African Americans, 2 Hispanic Americans), 1 international. Average age 25. 34 applicants, 18% accepted, 4 enrolled. In 2009, 1 master's awarded. *Degree requirements:* For master's, thesis, practicum. *Entrance requirements:* For master's, GRE General Test, minimum GPA of 2.75 in last 60 hours of undergraduate course work. Additional exam requirements/recommendations for international students: Required—TOEFL. *Application deadline:* For fall admission, 8/1 for domestic students; for spring admission, 12/1 for domestic students. Application fee: $25 ($50 for international students). *Financial support:* In 2009–10, 12 students received support, including 3 teaching assistantships (averaging $4,500 per year); fellowships, research assistantships, career-related internships or fieldwork, Federal Work-Study, scholarships/grants, and tuition waivers (partial) also available. Support available to part-time students. Financial award application deadline: 4/1. *Faculty research:* Groupthink, health psychology, school psychology, behavioral neuroscience. *Application contact:* Assistant Dean, 409-880-7978, E-mail: westgate@hal.lamar.edu.

Lenoir-Rhyne University, Graduate Programs, School of Counseling and Human Services, Programs in Counseling, Hickory, NC 28601. Offers agency counseling (MA); community counseling (MA). Part-time and evening/weekend programs available. *Degree requirements:* For master's, comprehensive exam, thesis optional. *Entrance requirements:* For master's, GRE General Test, writing sample, minimum undergraduate GPA of 2.7, minimum graduate GPA of 3.0. Additional exam requirements/recommendations for international students: Required—TOEFL (minimum score 600 paper-based). Electronic applications accepted.

Lesley University, Graduate School of Arts and Social Sciences, Cambridge, MA 02138-2790. Offers clinical mental health counseling (MA), including expressive therapies counseling, holistic counseling, school and community counseling; counseling psychology (MA, CAGS), including professional counseling (MA), school counseling (MA); creative arts in learning (CAGS); creative writing (MFA); ecological teaching and learning (MS); environmental education (MS); expressive therapies (MA, PhD, CAGS), including art (MA), dance (MA), expressive therapies, music (MA); independent studies (CAGS); independent study (MA); intercultural relations (MA, CAGS); interdisciplinary studies (MA), including individualized studies, integrative holistic health, women's studies; urban environmental leadership (MA); visual arts (MFA). Part-time and evening/weekend programs available. Postbaccalaureate distance learning degree programs offered (minimal on-campus study). *Degree requirements:* For master's, internship, practicum, thesis (expressive therapies); for doctorate, thesis/dissertation, arts apprenticeship, field placement; for CAGS, thesis, internship (counseling psychology, expressive therapies). *Entrance requirements:* For master's, MAT (counseling psychology), interview, writing samples, art portfolio; for doctorate, GRE or MAT; for CAGS, interview, master's degree. Additional exam requirements/recommendations for international students: Required—TOEFL (minimum score 550 paper-based; 213 computer-based; 80 iBT). Electronic applications accepted. *Faculty research:* Psychotherapy and culture; psychotherapy and psychological trauma; women's issues in art, teaching and psychotherapy; community based art, psycho-spiritual inquiry.

Lewis & Clark College, Graduate School of Education and Counseling, Department of Counseling Psychology, Program in Community Counseling, Portland, OR 97219-7899. Offers MA, MS. Part-time and evening/weekend programs available. *Faculty:* 6 full-time (5 women), 11 part-time/adjunct (9 women). *Students:* 45 full-time (35 women), 73 part-time (56 women); includes 10 minority (4 Asian Americans or Pacific Islanders, 6 Hispanic Americans), 2 international. Average age 32. 69 applicants, 96% accepted, 38 enrolled. In 2009, 37 master's awarded. *Degree requirements:* For master's, thesis (MS). *Entrance requirements:* For master's, GRE General Test, minimum undergraduate GPA of 2.75. Additional exam requirements/recommendations for international students: Required—TOEFL (minimum score 575 paper-based; 233 computer-based). *Application deadline:* For fall admission, 2/1 priority date for domestic and international students; for spring admission, 10/1 priority date for domestic and international students. Application fee: $50. Electronic applications accepted. *Expenses:* Tuition: Part-time $713 per semester hour. Tuition and fees vary according to course level and campus/location. *Financial support:* In 2009–10, 105 students received support. Career-related internships or fieldwork, Federal Work-Study, institutionally sponsored loans, scholarships/grants, and health care benefits available. Support available to part-time students. Financial award application deadline: 3/1; financial award applicants required to submit FAFSA. *Unit head:* Dr. Amy Rees-Turyn, Program Coordinator, 503-768-6060, Fax: 503-768-6065, E-mail:

cpsy@lclark.edu. *Application contact:* Becky Haas, Director of Admissions, 503-768-6200, Fax: 503-768-6205, E-mail: gseadmit@lclark.edu.

Loyola University Chicago, Graduate School, Department of Psychology, Program in Applied Social Psychology, Chicago, IL 60660. Offers MA, PhD. *Faculty:* 7 full-time (3 women), 2 part-time/adjunct (1 woman). *Students:* 38 full-time (27 women), 2 part-time (both women); includes 5 minority (2 African Americans, 2 Asian Americans or Pacific Islanders, 1 Hispanic American), 4 international. Average age 29. 88 applicants, 16% accepted, 9 enrolled. In 2009, 4 master's, 3 doctorates awarded. Terminal master's awarded for partial completion of doctoral program. *Degree requirements:* For master's, thesis; for doctorate, comprehensive exam, thesis/dissertation, internship. *Entrance requirements:* For master's and doctorate, GRE General Test, GRE Subject Test, sample of written work. *Application deadline:* For fall admission, 1/15 for domestic and international students. Applications are processed on a rolling basis. Application fee: $50. *Expenses:* Tuition: Full-time $14,220; part-time $790 per credit hour. Required fees: $60 per semester hour. Tuition and fees vary according to program. *Financial support:* In 2009–10, 1 fellowship with tuition reimbursement (averaging $14,000 per year), 5 research assistantships with tuition reimbursements (averaging $14,000 per year), 1 teaching assistantship (averaging $14,000 per year) were awarded; career-related internships or fieldwork, Federal Work-Study, and scholarships/grants also available. Financial award application deadline: 1/15; financial award applicants required to submit FAFSA. *Faculty research:* Program evaluation, attitudes and prejudice, psychological well-being, mass media, groups and organizations and communities. Total annual research expenditures: $200,000. *Unit head:* Dr. Scott Tindale, 773-508-3014. *Application contact:* Dr. Scott Tindale, 773-508-3014.

Lynchburg College, Graduate Studies, School of Education and Human Development, Lynchburg, VA 24501-3199. Offers community counseling (M Ed); counselor education (M Ed), including community counseling; curriculum and instruction (M Ed); educational leadership (M Ed); English education (M Ed); reading (M Ed); school counseling (M Ed); science education (M Ed); special education (M Ed), including autism spectrum disorder, early childhood special education, mental retardation, teaching children with learning disabilities, teaching the emotionally disturbed. Part-time and evening/weekend programs available. *Degree requirements:* For master's, comprehensive exam. *Entrance requirements:* For master's, GRE, minimum undergraduate GPA of 3.0. Additional exam requirements/recommendations for international students: Required—TOEFL. *Expenses:* Tuition: Full-time $7020; part-time $390 per credit hour.

Martin University, Division of Psychology, Indianapolis, IN 46218-3867. Offers community psychology (MS). Part-time and evening/weekend programs available. *Degree requirements:* For master's, thesis. *Entrance requirements:* For master's, GRE General Test, GRE Subject Test.

Memorial University of Newfoundland, School of Graduate Studies, Department of Psychology, St. John's, NL A1C 5S7, Canada. Offers applied social psychology (MASP); experimental psychology (M Sc, PhD). Part-time programs available. *Degree requirements:* For master's, workterms (MASP), thesis (M Sc); for doctorate, comprehensive exam, thesis/dissertation, oral thesis defense. *Entrance requirements:* For master's, GRE, honors bachelor's degree of high second class standing or equivalent; for doctorate, GRE, master's or honors degree. Electronic applications accepted. *Faculty research:* Behavioral neuroscience, cognition, theory and research on abnormal behavior.

Minnesota State University Mankato, College of Graduate Studies, College of Education, Department of Counseling and Student Personnel, Mankato, MN 56001. Offers college student affairs (MS); counselor education and supervision (Ed D); marriage and family counseling (Certificate); professional community counseling (MS); professional school counseling (MS). *Accreditation:* ACA (one or more programs are accredited); NCATE. *Students:* 67 full-time (57 women), 41 part-time (32 women). *Degree requirements:* For master's, comprehensive exam, thesis or alternative. *Entrance requirements:* For master's, GRE General Test or MAT (if GPA less than 3.0 for last 2 years), minimum GPA of 3.0 during previous 2 years, 3 letters of reference. Additional exam requirements/recommendations for international students: Required—TOEFL. *Application deadline:* For fall admission, 1/15 priority date for domestic students. Applications are processed on a rolling basis. Application fee: $40. Electronic applications accepted. *Expenses:* Tuition, state resident: full-time $5364. Tuition, nonresident: full-time $8314. *Financial support:* Research assistantships with full tuition reimbursements, teaching assistantships with full tuition reimbursements, career-related internships or fieldwork, Federal Work-Study, institutionally sponsored loans, and unspecified assistantships available. Support available to part-time students. Financial award application deadline: 3/15; financial award applicants required to submit FAFSA. *Unit head:* Dr. Jacqueline Lewis, Chairperson, 507-389-5658. *Application contact:* 507-389-2321, E-mail: grad@mnsu.edu.

Missouri State University, Graduate College, College of Education, Department of Counseling, Leadership, and Special Education, Program in Counseling, Springfield, MO 65897. Offers counseling (MS), including community agency counseling, elementary school counseling, secondary school counseling. Part-time and evening/weekend programs available. *Students:* 47 full-time (36 women), 87 part-time (71 women); includes 3 minority (2 African Americans, 1 Hispanic American), 2 international. Average age 33. 11 applicants, 100% accepted, 11 enrolled. In 2009, 42 master's awarded. *Degree requirements:* For master's, comprehensive exam, thesis or alternative. *Entrance requirements:* For master's, GRE or MAT, minimum GPA of 2.75. Additional exam requirements/recommendations for international students: Required—TOEFL (minimum score 550 paper-based; 213 computer-based; 79 iBT). *Application deadline:* For fall admission, 2/1 priority date for domestic students, 1/1 priority date for international students; for spring admission, 10/1 priority date for domestic students, 9/1 priority date for international students. Application fee: $35 ($50 for international students). Electronic applications accepted. *Expenses:* Tuition, state resident: full-time $3852; part-time $214 per credit hour. Tuition, nonresident: full-time $7524; part-time $418 per credit hour. Required fees: $696; $172 per semester. Tuition and fees vary according to course level, course load, degree level and program. *Financial support:* In 2009–10, 2 teaching assistantships with full tuition reimbursements (averaging $7,340 per year) were awarded; Federal Work-Study, institutionally sponsored loans, scholarships/grants, and unspecified assistantships also available. Financial award application deadline: 3/31; financial award applicants required to submit FAFSA. *Unit head:* Dr. Tamara Arthaud, Acting Department Head, 417-836-5449, Fax: 417-836-4918, E-mail: clse@missouristate.edu. *Application contact:* Eric Eckert, Coordinator of Admissions and Recruitment, 417-836-5331, Fax: 417-836-6888, E-mail: ericeckert@missouristate.edu.

Montclair State University, The Graduate School, College of Education and Human Services, Department of Counseling, Human Development, and Educational Leadership, Montclair, NJ 07043-1624. Offers administration and supervision (MA), including administration and supervision, educator/trainer; advanced counseling (Certificate); counseling and guidance (MA), including addictions counseling, community counseling, student affairs; counselor education (PhD); principal (Certificate); school administrator (Certificate); school business administrator (Certificate); school counselor (Certificate); substance awareness coordinator (Certificate). *Accreditation:* NCATE. Part-time and evening/weekend programs available. *Faculty:* 17 full-time (12 women), 13 part-time/adjunct (7 women). *Students:* 161 full-time (126 women), 425 part-time (325 women). Average age 33. 269 applicants, 55% accepted, 125 enrolled. In 2009, 91 master's awarded. *Degree requirements:* For master's, comprehensive exam, thesis or alternative; for doctorate, comprehensive exam, thesis/dissertation. *Entrance requirements:* For master's, GRE General Test, interview, 2 letters of recommendation; for doctorate, GRE General Test, interview, 3 letters of recommendation. Additional exam requirements/recommendations for international students: Required—TOEFL (minimum score 83 computer-based), or IELTS. *Application deadline:* For fall admission, 6/1 for international students; for spring admission, 10/1 for international students. Applications are processed on a rolling basis. Application fee: $60. Electronic applications accepted. *Expenses:* Tuition, area resident: Part-time $486.74 per credit. Tuition, state resident: part-time $486.74 per credit. Tuition, nonresident: part-time $751.34 per credit. Tuition and fees vary according to degree level and program. *Financial support:* In 2009–10, 28 research assistantships with full tuition reimbursements (averaging $7,000 per year), 2 teaching assistantships (averaging $15,000 per year) were awarded; Federal Work-Study, scholarships/grants, and unspecified assistantships also available. Support available to part-time students. Financial award application deadline: 3/1; financial award applicants required to submit FAFSA. *Faculty research:* K-12 education, data collection. *Unit head:* Dr. Larry Burlew, Chairperson, 973-655-7611. *Application contact:* Amy Aiello, Director of Graduate Admissions and Operations, 973-655-5147, Fax: 973-655-7869, E-mail: graduate.school@montclair.edu.

Montclair State University, The Graduate School, College of Humanities and Social Sciences, Department of Psychology, Montclair, NJ 07043-1624. Offers educational psychology (MA), including child/adolescent clinical psychology, clinical psychology for Spanish/English bilinguals; psychology (MA, Certificate), including industrial and organizational psychology (MA); school psychologist (Certificate). Part-time and evening/weekend programs available. *Faculty:* 29 full-time (14 women), 26 part-time/adjunct (14 women). *Students:* 37 full-time (27 women), 33 part-time (23 women). Average age 27. 72 applicants, 47% accepted, 20 enrolled. In 2009, 7 master's awarded. *Degree requirements:* For master's, comprehensive exam, thesis or alternative. *Entrance requirements:* For master's, GRE General Test, 2 letters of recommendation. Additional exam requirements/recommendations for international students: Required—TOEFL (minimum score 83 computer-based), or IELTS. *Application deadline:* For fall admission, 2/1 for domestic and international students; for spring admission, 10/1 for domestic and international students. Applications are processed on a rolling basis. Application fee: $60. Electronic applications accepted. *Expenses:* Tuition, area resident: Part-time $486.74 per credit. Tuition, state resident: part-time $486.74 per credit. Tuition, nonresident: part-time $751.34 per credit. Tuition and fees vary according to degree level and program. *Financial support:* In 2009–10, 17 research assistantships with full tuition reimbursements (averaging $7,000 per year) were awarded; Federal Work-Study, scholarships/grants, and unspecified assistantships also available. Support available to part-time students. Financial award application deadline: 3/1; financial award applicants required to submit FAFSA. *Faculty research:* Engaged learning, academic and civic development. Total annual research expenditures: $10,000. *Unit head:* Dr. Peter Vietze, Chairperson, 973-655-5201. *Application contact:* Amy Aiello, Director of Admissions and Operations, 973-655-5147, Fax: 973-655-7869, E-mail: graduate.school@montclair.edu.

Mount Aloysius College, Program in Community Counseling, Cresson, PA 16630-1999. Offers MS. Part-time programs available.

Mount Mary College, Graduate Programs, Program in Community Counseling, Milwaukee, WI 53222-4597. Offers community counseling (MS); pastoral counseling (MS); school counseling (MS). Part-time and evening/weekend programs available. *Faculty:* 2 full-time (both women), 8 part-time/adjunct (4 women). *Students:* 69 full-time (68 women), 23 part-time (all women); includes 25 minority (21 African Americans, 1 American Indian/Alaska Native, 3 Hispanic Americans). Average age 34. 68 applicants, 56% accepted, 28 enrolled. In 2009, 20 master's awarded. *Degree requirements:* For master's, comprehensive exam, thesis or alternative. *Entrance requirements:* For master's, minimum GPA of 3.0. Additional exam requirements/recommendations for international students: Required—TOEFL (minimum score 500 paper-based; 173 computer-based). *Application deadline:* For fall admission, 8/1 priority date for domestic and international students; for spring admission, 12/1 priority date for domestic and international students. Application fee: $35 ($100 for international students). *Expenses:* Tuition: Part-time $595 per credit. Tuition and fees vary according to program. *Financial support:* Career-related internships or fieldwork and Federal Work-Study available. Support available to part-time students. Financial award application deadline: 5/1; financial award applicants required to submit FAFSA. *Faculty research:* Cognitive behavioral interventions for depression, eating disorders and compliance. *Unit head:* Carrie King, Graduate Program Director, 414-258-4810 Ext. 318, E-mail: kingc@mtmary.edu. *Application contact:* Carrie King, Graduate Program Director, 414-258-4810 Ext. 318, E-mail: kingc@mtmary.edu.

Naropa University, Graduate Programs, Program in Transpersonal Psychology, Ecopsychology Concentration, Boulder, CO 80302-6697. Offers MA. Part-time and evening/weekend programs available. Postbaccalaureate distance learning degree programs offered (minimal on-campus study). *Degree requirements:* For master's, thesis, service learning. *Entrance requirements:* For master's, interview (by phone or in-person), technology form, resume, 3 letters of recommendation, letter of interest. Additional exam requirements/recommendations for international students: Required—TOEFL (minimum score 600 paper-based; 250 computer-based). Electronic applications accepted.

National-Louis University, College of Arts and Sciences, Department of Counseling and Human Services, Chicago, IL 60603. Offers community counseling (MS); school counseling (MS). Part-time programs available. *Degree requirements:* For master's, internship. *Entrance requirements:* For master's, GRE General Test, MAT, or Watson-Glaser Critical Thinking Appraisal, interview, minimum GPA of 3.0. *Expenses:* Tuition: Full-time $17,160; part-time $715 per semester hour. Tuition and fees vary according to course load, degree level, campus/location and program. *Faculty research:* Religion and aging, drug abuse prevention, hunger, homelessness, multicultural diversity.

National-Louis University, College of Arts and Sciences, Program in Psychology, Chicago, IL 60603. Offers community psychology (PhD); cultural psychology (MA); health psychology (MA); human development (MA); organizational psychology (MA); psychology (Certificate), including general, health, human development, organizational, psychological assessment. Part-time and evening/weekend programs available. *Degree requirements:* For master's, thesis, internship (health psychology). *Entrance requirements:* For master's, GRE General Test, MAT, or Watson-Glaser Critical Thinking Appraisal, interview, minimum GPA of 3.0; for Certificate, GRE, MAT, or Watson-Glaser Critical Thinking Appraisal, interview, minimum GPA of 3.0, undergraduate course work in psychology. *Expenses:* Tuition: Full-time $17,160; part-time $715 per semester hour. Tuition and fees vary according to course load, degree level, campus/location and program. *Faculty research:* Human development, personality theory, abnormal psychology.

New York University, Graduate School of Arts and Science, Department of Psychology, New York, NY 10012-1019. Offers cognition and perception (PhD); community psychology (PhD); general psychology (MA); industrial/organizational psychology (MA); psychotherapy and psychoanalysis (Advanced Certificate); social/personality psychology (PhD). Part-time programs available. *Students:* 151 full-time (94 women), 273 part-time (192 women); includes 59 minority (13 African Americans, 1 American Indian/Alaska Native, 27 Asian Americans or Pacific Islanders, 18 Hispanic Americans), 62 international. Average age 32. 748 applicants, 46% accepted, 122 enrolled. In 2009, 100 master's, 11 doctorates, 8 other advanced degrees awarded. Terminal master's awarded for partial completion of doctoral program. *Degree requirements:* For master's, comprehensive exam, thesis or alternative; for doctorate, thesis/dissertation. *Entrance requirements:* For master's, GRE General Test, minimum GPA of 3.0; for doctorate, GRE General Test, GRE Subject Test; for Advanced Certificate, doctoral degree, minimum GPA of 3.0. Additional exam requirements/recommendations for international students: Required—TOEFL. *Application deadline:* For fall admission, 12/18 for domestic students. Application fee: $90. *Expenses:* Tuition: Full-time $30,528; part-time $1272 per credit. Required fees: $2177. *Financial support:* Fellowships with tuition reimbursements, research assistantships with tuition reimbursements, teaching assistantships with tuition reimbursements, career-related internships or fieldwork, Federal Work-Study, institutionally sponsored loans, scholarships/grants, traineeships, health care benefits, and unspecified assistantships available. Financial award application deadline: 12/18; financial award applicants required to submit FAFSA. *Faculty research:* Vision, memory, social cognition, social and cognitive development,

Social Psychology

New York University (continued)

relationships. *Unit head:* Madeline Heilman, Director of Ph.D. Program, 212-998-7900, Fax: 212-995-4018, E-mail: psychq@psych.nyu.edu. *Application contact:* Barry Cohen, Director of M.A. Program, 212-998-7900, Fax: 212-995-4018, E-mail: psychq@psych.nyu.edu.

Norfolk State University, School of Graduate Studies, School of Liberal Arts, Department of Psychology, Program in Community/Clinical Psychology, Norfolk, VA 23504. Offers MA. *Degree requirements:* For master's, comprehensive exam, thesis or alternative. *Entrance requirements:* For master's, minimum GPA of 2.7.

North Carolina Central University, Division of Academic Affairs, School of Education, Department of Counselor Education, Durham, NC 27707-3129. Offers career counseling (MA); community agency counseling (MA); school counseling (MA). *Accreditation:* ACA; NCATE. Part-time and evening/weekend programs available. *Degree requirements:* For master's, comprehensive exam, thesis or alternative. *Entrance requirements:* For master's, GRE, minimum GPA of 3.0 in major, 2.5 overall. Additional exam requirements/recommendations for international students: Required—TOEFL. *Faculty research:* Becoming a leader, skill building in academia.

North Carolina State University, Graduate School, College of Education, Department of Curriculum and Instruction, Program in Agency Counseling, Raleigh, NC 27695. Offers M Ed, MS. *Degree requirements:* For master's, thesis optional. *Entrance requirements:* For master's, GRE General Test or MAT, minimum GPA of 3.0 in major. Electronic applications accepted. *Faculty research:* Cross-cultural issues, non-cognitive variables, achievement gaps, identity development, counseling supervision.

North Dakota State University, College of Graduate and Interdisciplinary Studies, College of Science and Mathematics, Department of Psychology, Fargo, ND 58108. Offers clinical psychology (MS); cognitive and visual neuroscience (PhD); health and social psychology (PhD); psychology (MS). *Faculty:* 18 full-time (4 women), 2 part-time/adjunct (1 woman). *Students:* 36 full-time (27 women); includes 4 minority (1 African American, 2 Asian Americans or Pacific Islanders, 1 Hispanic American), 1 international. Average age 24. 48 applicants, 33% accepted, 10 enrolled. In 2009, 3 master's, 1 doctorate awarded. *Degree requirements:* For master's, thesis; for doctorate, thesis/dissertation. *Entrance requirements:* For master's and doctorate, GRE General Test, GRE Subject Test. Additional exam requirements/recommendations for international students: Required—TOEFL (minimum score 525 paper-based; 197 computer-based; 71 iBT). *Application deadline:* For fall admission, 3/1 for domestic and international students. Application fee: $45 ($60 for international students). Electronic applications accepted. *Financial support:* In 2009–10, 36 students received support, including 2 fellowships with full tuition reimbursements available (averaging $16,000 per year), 23 research assistantships with full tuition reimbursements available (averaging $16,000 per year), 11 teaching assistantships with full tuition reimbursements available (averaging $6,000 per year); career-related internships or fieldwork, Federal Work-Study, institutionally sponsored loans, tuition waivers (full and partial), and unspecified assistantships also available. Support available to part-time students. Financial award application deadline: 3/1. *Faculty research:* Cognition science, neuropsychology, group behavior, applied behavior analysis, behavior therapy. Total annual research expenditures: $2 million. *Unit head:* Dr. Paul D. Rokke, Chair, 701-231-8622, Fax: 701-231-8426, E-mail: paul.rokke@ndsu.edu. *Application contact:* Dr. Paul D. Rokke, Chair, 701-231-8622, Fax: 701-231-8426, E-mail: paul.rokke@ndsu.edu.

Northern Arizona University, Graduate College, College of Education, Programs in Counseling, Flagstaff, AZ 86011. Offers community counseling (MA); school counseling (M Ed); student affairs (M Ed). *Accreditation:* ACA. Part-time programs available. *Faculty:* 20 full-time (10 women). *Students:* 101 full-time (73 women), 89 part-time (74 women); includes 68 minority (11 African Americans, 4 American Indian/Alaska Native, 4 Asian Americans or Pacific Islanders, 49 Hispanic Americans). Average age 45. 104 applicants, 65% accepted, 44 enrolled. In 2009, 35 master's awarded. *Degree requirements:* For master's, thesis optional. *Entrance requirements:* For master's, GRE (verbal and quantitative). Additional exam requirements/recommendations for international students: Required—TOEFL (minimum score 550 paper-based; 213 computer-based; 80 iBT), IELTS (minimum score 7), or a bachelor's degree from an English-speaking university and demonstrated proficiency. *Application deadline:* For fall admission, 2/15 priority date for domestic students, 9/15 for international students; for spring admission, 9/15 priority date for domestic students. Applications are processed on a rolling basis. Application fee: $65. Electronic applications accepted. *Financial support:* In 2009–10, 2 research assistantships with partial tuition reimbursements (averaging $10,000 per year), 12 teaching assistantships with partial tuition reimbursements (averaging $10,000 per year) were awarded; career-related internships or fieldwork, Federal Work-Study, health care benefits, tuition waivers (full and partial), and unspecified assistantships also available. Support available to part-time students. Financial award application deadline: 3/30; financial award applicants required to submit FAFSA. *Faculty research:* Early childhood assessment and development, cognitive psychology, multicultural issues, family functioning in abusive families, rehabilitation. *Unit head:* Dr. Kathy Bohan, Chair, 928-523-0362, Fax: 928-523-9284, E-mail: kathy.bohan@nau.edu. *Application contact:* Dr. Kathy Bohan, Chair, 928-523-0362, Fax: 928-523-9284, E-mail: kathy.bohan@nau.edu.

Northern Kentucky University, Office of Graduate Programs, College of Education and Human Services, Program in Community Counseling, Highland Heights, KY 41099. Offers college student development administration (Certificate); community counseling (MS). Part-time and evening/weekend programs available. *Students:* 13 full-time (12 women), 32 part-time (22 women); includes 3 minority (2 African Americans, 1 Asian American or Pacific Islander). Average age 29. 36 applicants, 47% accepted, 15 enrolled. In 2009, 9 master's, 2 other advanced degrees awarded. *Degree requirements:* For master's, comprehensive exam, internship. *Entrance requirements:* For master's, GRE, minimum GPA of 2.75, 3 letters of reference, criminal background check (state and federal), resume. Additional exam requirements/recommendations for international students: Required—TOEFL (minimum score 550 paper-based; 213 computer-based; 79 iBT); Recommended—IELTS (minimum score 6.5). *Application deadline:* For fall admission, 8/1 for domestic students, 6/1 priority date for international students; for spring admission, 10/1 priority date for international students. Applications are processed on a rolling basis. Application fee: $40. Electronic applications accepted. *Expenses:* Tuition, state resident: full-time $6912; part-time $384 per credit hour. Tuition, nonresident: full-time $12,150; part-time $675 per credit hour. Tuition and fees vary according to course load, program and reciprocity agreements. *Financial support:* Applicants required to submit FAFSA. *Faculty research:* Ethical decision making in counseling, clinical supervision in counseling, expectations about counseling inventory development. *Unit head:* Dr. Jacqueline Smith, Director, 859-572-6149, E-mail: smithjac@nku.edu. *Application contact:* Dr. Peg Griffin, Director, Graduate Programs, 859-572-6934, Fax: 859-572-6670, E-mail: griffinp@nku.edu.

North Georgia College & State University, Graduate Studies, Program in Community Counseling, Dahlonega, GA 30597. Offers MS. Part-time and evening/weekend programs available. *Degree requirements:* For master's, one foreign language, thesis optional. *Entrance requirements:* For master's, GRE General Test, minimum GPA of 3.0, 3 letters of recommendation, interview. Electronic applications accepted.

Northwestern University, The Graduate School, Judd A. and Marjorie Weinberg College of Arts and Sciences, Department of Psychology, Evanston, IL 60208. Offers brain, behavior and cognition (PhD); clinical psychology (PhD); cognitive psychology (PhD); personality (PhD); social psychology (PhD); JD/PhD. Admissions and degrees offered through The Graduate School. *Accreditation:* APA (one or more programs are accredited). Part-time programs available. *Degree requirements:* For doctorate, thesis/dissertation. *Entrance requirements:* For doctorate, GRE General Test, GRE Subject Test. Additional exam requirements/recommendations for international students: Required—TOEFL. Electronic applications accepted. *Faculty research:* Memory and higher order cognition, anxiety and depression, effectiveness of psychotherapy, social cognition, molecular basis of memory.

Northwest Nazarene University, Graduate Studies, Program in Counselor Education, Nampa, ID 83686-5897. Offers community counseling (MS); marriage and family counseling (MS); school counseling (MS).

The Ohio State University, Graduate School, College of Social and Behavioral Sciences, School of Social and Behavioral Science, Department of Psychology, Columbus, OH 43210. Offers behavioral neuroscience (PhD); clinical psychology (PhD); cognitive psychology (PhD); developmental psychology (PhD); mental retardation and developmental disabilities (PhD); psychology (MA); quantitative psychology (PhD); social psychology (PhD). *Accreditation:* APA (one or more programs are accredited). *Faculty:* 60. *Students:* 88 full-time (59 women), 47 part-time (31 women); includes 20 minority (7 African Americans, 1 American Indian/Alaska Native, 5 Asian Americans or Pacific Islanders, 7 Hispanic Americans), 20 international. Average age 27. In 2009, 15 master's, 20 doctorates awarded. *Degree requirements:* For doctorate, thesis/dissertation. *Entrance requirements:* For master's and doctorate, GRE General Test. Additional exam requirements/recommendations for international students: Required—TOEFL (minimum score 600 paper-based; 250 computer-based). *Application deadline:* For fall admission, 12/31 for domestic students, 11/30 for international students. Applications are processed on a rolling basis. Application fee: $40 ($50 for international students). Electronic applications accepted. *Expenses:* Tuition, state resident: full-time $10,683. Tuition, nonresident: full-time $25,923. Tuition and fees vary according to course load and program. *Financial support:* Fellowships, research assistantships, teaching assistantships available. *Unit head:* Michael Vasey, Graduate Studies Committee Chair, E-mail: vasey.1@osu.edu. *Application contact:* 614-292-9444, Fax: 614-292-3895, E-mail: domestic.grad@osu.edu.

Oregon State University–Cascades, Program in Counseling, Bend, OR 97701. Offers community counseling (MS); school counseling (MS).

Pittsburg State University, Graduate School, College of Education, Department of Psychology and Counseling, Program in Counselor Education, Pittsburg, KS 66762. Offers community counseling (MS); school counseling (MS). *Accreditation:* ACA; NCATE. *Degree requirements:* For master's, thesis or alternative. *Entrance requirements:* For master's, GRE General Test, minimum GPA of 2.8. *Expenses:* Tuition, state resident: full-time $4212; part-time $176 per credit. Tuition, nonresident: full-time $11,530; part-time $480 per credit. Required fees: $940; $43 per credit. Tuition and fees vary according to course level, course load, degree level, campus/location, reciprocity agreements and student level.

Queen's University at Kingston, School of Graduate Studies and Research, Faculty of Arts and Sciences, Department of Psychology, Kingston, ON K7L 3N6, Canada. Offers brain behavior and cognitive science (MA, PhD); clinical psychology (MA, PhD); developmental psychology (MA, PhD); social personality psychology (MA, PhD). *Accreditation:* APA (one or more programs are accredited). *Degree requirements:* For master's, thesis; for doctorate, comprehensive exam, thesis/dissertation. *Entrance requirements:* For master's and doctorate, GRE General Test. Additional exam requirements/recommendations for international students: Required—TOEFL. *Faculty research:* Human development, social, personality, behavioral neuroscience, forensic.

Regent University, Graduate School, School of Psychology and Counseling, Virginia Beach, VA 23464-9800. Offers clinical psychology (MA, Psy D); counseling (MA), including community counseling, human services counseling, school counseling; counseling studies (CAGS); counselor education and supervision (PhD); M Div/MA; M Ed/MA; MBA/MA. PhD program offered online only. *Accreditation:* ACA; APA (one or more programs are accredited). Part-time and evening/weekend programs available. Postbaccalaureate distance learning degree programs offered (minimal on-campus study). *Faculty:* 24 full-time (12 women), 19 part-time/adjunct (12 women). *Students:* 209 full-time (171 women), 189 part-time (137 women); includes 107 minority (92 African Americans, 4 Asian Americans or Pacific Islanders, 11 Hispanic Americans), 14 international. Average age 34. 417 applicants, 50% accepted, 104 enrolled. In 2009, 108 master's, 40 doctorates awarded. *Degree requirements:* For master's, thesis or alternative, internship, practicum, written competency exam; for doctorate, thesis/dissertation or alternative. *Entrance requirements:* For master's, GRE General Test including writing exam, minimum undergraduate GPA of 2.75, 3 recommendations, resume, transcripts, writing sample; for doctorate, GRE General Test including writing exam, GRE Subject Test, minimum undergraduate GPA of 3.0, 3.5 (PhD), 10-15 minute VHS tape demonstrating counseling skills, writing sample, 3 recommendations, resume. Additional exam requirements/recommendations for international students: Required—TOEFL (minimum score 577 paper-based; 233 computer-based). *Application deadline:* For fall admission, 4/1 priority date for domestic students; for spring admission, 11/1 priority date for domestic students. Applications are processed on a rolling basis. Application fee: $50. Electronic applications accepted. *Expenses:* Contact institution. *Financial support:* In 2009–10, 368 students received support; research assistantships with full and partial tuition reimbursements available, teaching assistantships with full and partial tuition reimbursements available, career-related internships or fieldwork, scholarships/grants, and tuition waivers (full and partial) available. Support available to part-time students. Financial award application deadline: 9/1; financial award applicants required to submit FAFSA. *Faculty research:* Marriage enrichment, AIDS counseling, troubled youth, faith and learning, trauma. *Unit head:* Dr. William Hathaway, Acting Dean, 757-352-4294, Fax: 757-352-4282, E-mail: willhat@regent.edu. *Application contact:* Matthew Chadwick, Director of Admissions, 800-373-5504, Fax: 757-352-4381, E-mail: admissions@regent.edu.

Regis University, College for Professional Studies, Graduate Counseling Program, Denver, CO 80221-1099. Offers community counseling (MAC); counseling children and adolescents (Post-Graduate Certificate); marriage and family therapy (Post-Graduate Certificate). Program offered in Henderson and Las Vegas (Summerlin), NV. *Accreditation:* ACA. Part-time and evening/weekend programs available. *Degree requirements:* For master's, internships, practicum. *Entrance requirements:* For master's, interview, 2 recommendations, resume, criminal background check. Additional exam requirements/recommendations for international students: Required—TOEFL (minimum score 213 computer-based), TWE (minimum score 5). *Expenses:* Contact institution. *Faculty research:* Group Development, Counselor Education, Counsel and Therapy, Influence of Technology on Psychology, Dream finding groups, Adult Development, Depression.

Rutgers, The State University of New Jersey, Newark, Graduate School, Program in Psychology, Newark, NJ 07102. Offers cognitive neuroscience (PhD); cognitive science (PhD); perception (PhD); psychobiology (PhD); social cognition (PhD). *Degree requirements:* For doctorate, comprehensive exam, thesis/dissertation. *Entrance requirements:* For doctorate, GRE General Test, GRE Subject Test, minimum undergraduate B average. Electronic applications accepted. *Faculty research:* Visual perception (luminance, motion), neuroendocrine mechanisms in behavior (reproduction, pain), attachment theory, connectionist modeling of cognition.

See Close-Up on page 1093.

Rutgers, The State University of New Jersey, New Brunswick, Graduate School-New Brunswick, Program in Psychology, Piscataway, NJ 08854-8097. Offers behavioral neuroscience (PhD); clinical psychology (PhD); cognitive psychology (PhD); interdisciplinary health psychology (PhD); social psychology (PhD). *Accreditation:* APA. *Degree requirements:* For doctorate, comprehensive exam, thesis/dissertation. *Entrance requirements:* For doctorate, GRE General Test, 3 letters of recommendation. Additional exam requirements/recommendations for international students: Required—TOEFL (minimum score 577 paper-based; 233 computer-based). Electronic applications accepted. *Faculty research:* Learning and memory, behavioral ecology, hormones and behavior, psychopharmacology, anxiety disorders.

Sage Graduate School, Graduate School, School of Health Sciences, Department of Psychology, Program in Counseling and Community Psychology, Troy, NY 12180-4115. Offers MA. *Faculty:* 3 full-time (all women), 5 part-time/adjunct (3 women). *Students:* 27 full-time (26 women), 41 part-time (37 women); includes 10 minority (6 African Americans, 1 American Indian/Alaska Native, 3 Hispanic Americans). Average age 27. 64 applicants, 41% accepted, 11 enrolled. In 2009, 16 master's awarded. *Degree requirements:* For master's, externship, internship, thesis or research seminar. *Entrance requirements:* For master's, minimum undergraduate GPA of 3.0, interview. *Application deadline:* Applications are processed on a rolling basis. Application fee: $40. *Expenses:* Tuition: Full-time $10,620; part-time $590 per credit hour. *Unit head:* Dr. Jean Poppei, Chair, 518-244-2076, Fax: 518-244-4545, E-mail: poppei@sage.edu. *Application contact:* Wendy D. Diefendorf, Director of Graduate and Adult Admission, 518-244-2443, Fax: 518-244-6880, E-mail: diefew@sage.edu.

St. Bonaventure University, School of Graduate Studies, School of Education, Program in Counselor Education, St. Bonaventure, NY 14778-2284. Offers community mental health counseling (MS Ed); school counseling (MS Ed); school counselor (Adv C). *Accreditation:* ACA. Part-time and evening/weekend programs available. *Faculty:* 7 full-time (2 women), 6 part-time/adjunct (2 women). *Students:* 80 full-time (65 women), 31 part-time (20 women); includes 7 minority (3 African Americans, 1 American Indian/Alaska Native, 3 Hispanic Americans), 1 international. Average age 30. 116 applicants, 65% accepted, 51 enrolled. In 2009, 36 master's, 5 Adv Cs awarded. *Degree requirements:* For master's, comprehensive exam, thesis optional. *Entrance requirements:* For master's, interview, writing sample, minimum undergraduate GPA of 3.0. Additional exam requirements/recommendations for international students: Required—TOEFL (minimum score 550 paper-based; 240 computer-based; 95 iBT). *Application deadline:* For fall admission, 8/1 priority date for domestic students, 12/15 for international students; for spring admission, 10/15 priority date for domestic students, 3/15 for international students. Applications are processed on a rolling basis. Application fee: $30. *Expenses:* Tuition: Full-time $11,700; part-time $650 per credit. *Financial support:* In 2009–10, 7 students received support, including 9 research assistantships with full and partial tuition reimbursements available; career-related internships or fieldwork and scholarships/grants also available. Support available to part-time students. Financial award application deadline: 4/15; financial award applicants required to submit FAFSA. *Faculty research:* Parent education, learning disabilities, stress management, cyber bullying. *Unit head:* Dr. Craig Zuckerman, Director, 716-375-2374, Fax: 716-375-2360, E-mail: czuck@sbu.edu. *Application contact:* Bruce Campbell, Director of Graduate Admissions, 716-375-2429, E-mail: gradsch@sbu.edu.

St. Cloud State University, School of Graduate Studies, College of Education, Department of Educational Leadership and Community Psychology, Program in Community Counseling, St. Cloud, MN 56301-4498. Offers MS. *Faculty:* 7 full-time (3 women), 3 part-time/adjunct (all women). *Students:* 31 full-time (27 women), 7 part-time (all women); includes 5 minority (2 African Americans, 1 American Indian/Alaska Native, 1 Asian American or Pacific Islander, 1 Hispanic American), 1 international. 16 applicants, 88% accepted. *Degree requirements:* For master's, comprehensive exam (for some programs), thesis or alternative. *Entrance requirements:* For master's, GRE General Test, minimum GPA of 2.75. Additional exam requirements/recommendations for international students: Required—Michigan English Language Assessment Battery; Recommended—TOEFL (minimum score 550 paper-based; 213 computer-based), IELTS (minimum score 6.5). *Application deadline:* For fall admission, 4/1 for domestic and international students. Applications are processed on a rolling basis. Application fee: $35. Electronic applications accepted. *Financial support:* Federal Work-Study, scholarships/grants, and unspecified assistantships available. *Unit head:* Dr. LeeAnn Jorgensen, Coordinator, 320-308-4915, E-mail: lsjorgensen@stcloudstate.edu. *Application contact:* Linda Lou Krueger, School of Graduate Studies, 320-308-2113, Fax: 320-308-5371, E-mail: lekrueger@stcloudstate.edu.

Saint Joseph College, Department of Counselor Education, West Hartford, CT 06117-2700. Offers community counseling (MA); school counseling (MA). Part-time and evening/weekend programs available. *Students:* 42 full-time (37 women), 94 part-time (83 women); includes 20 minority (16 African Americans, 4 Hispanic Americans). *Degree requirements:* For master's, comprehensive exam, thesis optional. *Entrance requirements:* For master's, 2 letters of recommendation. *Application deadline:* Applications are processed on a rolling basis. Application fee: $50. Electronic applications accepted. *Expenses:* Tuition: Part-time $595 per credit. Required fees: $30 per credit. Tuition and fees vary according to program. *Financial support:* Career-related internships or fieldwork and unspecified assistantships available. Support available to part-time students. Financial award applicants required to submit FAFSA. *Application contact:* Graduate Admissions Office, 860-231-5261, E-mail: graduate@sjc.edu.

Saint Martin's University, Graduate Programs, Program in Counseling Psychology, Lacey, WA 98503. Offers MAC. Part-time and evening/weekend programs available. *Faculty:* 3 full-time (2 women), 3 part-time/adjunct (all women). *Students:* 40 full-time (29 women), 58 part-time (52 women); includes 14 minority (3 African Americans, 1 American Indian/Alaska Native, 6 Asian Americans or Pacific Islanders, 4 Hispanic Americans), 1 international. Average age 36. 24 applicants, 79% accepted, 18 enrolled. In 2009, 17 master's awarded. *Degree requirements:* For master's, clinical experience, interview. *Entrance requirements:* For master's, BA in psychology or related field, clinical experience. Additional exam requirements/recommendations for international students: Required—TOEFL. *Application deadline:* For fall admission, 7/1 for domestic students, 2/15 for international students; for spring admission, 11/1 priority date for domestic students, 7/1 for international students. Applications are processed on a rolling basis. Application fee: $35. *Expenses:* Tuition: Full-time $12,440; part-time $827 per credit hour. *Financial support:* In 2009–10, 97 students received support. Career-related internships or fieldwork, Federal Work-Study, and institutionally sponsored loans available. Support available to part-time students. Financial award application deadline: 3/1. *Faculty research:* Alcohol studies, clinical effectiveness, social justice, parent adolescent interaction. *Unit head:* Dr. Godfrey J. Ellis, Director, 360-438-4560, E-mail: gellis@stmartin.edu. *Application contact:* Sandy Brandt, Administrative Assistant, 360-438-4560, E-mail: sbrandt@stmartin.edu.

St. Mary's University, Graduate School, Department of Counseling and Human Services, Program in Community Counseling, San Antonio, TX 78228-8507. Offers MA. Part-time programs available. *Degree requirements:* For master's, comprehensive exam, internship. *Entrance requirements:* For master's, GRE, GMAT. Additional exam requirements/recommendations for international students: Required—TOEFL (minimum score 550 paper-based; 213 computer-based; 80 iBT). Electronic applications accepted. *Expenses:* Tuition: Full-time $8004. Required fees: $536. One-time fee: $5 full-time. Full-time tuition and fees vary according to program.

Shippensburg University of Pennsylvania, School of Graduate Studies, College of Education and Human Services, Department of Counseling, Shippensburg, PA 17257-2299. Offers Adlerian studies (Certificate); advanced study in counseling (Certificate); alcohol and drug counseling (Certificate); counseling (M Ed, MS), including college counseling (MS), community counseling (MS), elementary school counseling, mental health counseling (MS), secondary school counseling (MS), student personnel services (MS); couple and family counseling (Certificate). *Accreditation:* ACA (one or more programs are accredited); NCATE. Part-time and evening/weekend programs available. *Degree requirements:* For master's, fieldwork, research project, internship, candidacy. *Entrance requirements:* For master's, GRE or MAT (community, mental health, student personnel, and college counseling applicants if GPA is less than 2.75), minimum GPA of 2.75 (3.0 for M Ed), interview, resume, 3 letters of recommendation, supplemental data forms, one year of relevant work experience, on-campus interview. Additional exam requirements/recommendations for international students: Required—TOEFL (minimum score 560 paper-based; 220 computer-based); Recommended—IELTS (minimum score 6). Electronic applications accepted.

Southeastern Louisiana University, College of Education and Human Development, Department of Counseling and Human Development, Hammond, LA 70402. Offers counselor education (M Ed), including community counseling, marriage and family therapy, school counseling, substance abuse counseling. *Accreditation:* ACA; NCATE. Part-time programs available. *Faculty:* 7 full-time (5 women), 1 part-time/adjunct (0 women). *Students:* 58 full-time (54 women), 45 part-time (41 women); includes 16 minority (15 African Americans, 1 Hispanic American). Average age 29. 38 applicants, 100% accepted, 23 enrolled. In 2009, 23 master's awarded. *Degree requirements:* For master's, comprehensive exam, thesis optional. *Entrance requirements:* For master's, GRE (verbal and quantitative). Additional exam requirements/recommendations for international students: Required—TOEFL (minimum score 500 paper-based; 173 computer-based; 61 iBT). *Application deadline:* For fall admission, 7/15 priority date for domestic students, 6/1 priority date for international students; for spring admission, 12/1 priority date for domestic students, 10/1 priority date for international students. Applications are processed on a rolling basis. Application fee: $20 ($30 for international students). Electronic applications accepted. *Expenses:* Tuition, state resident: full-time $3086; part-time $225 per credit hour. Tuition, nonresident: part-time $529 per credit hour. Required fees: $1195. Tuition and fees vary according to course level and course load. *Financial support:* In 2009–10, 6 students received support. Career-related internships or fieldwork, Federal Work-Study, institutionally sponsored loans, and administrative assistantships available. Support available to part-time students. Financial award application deadline: 5/1; financial award applicants required to submit FAFSA. *Faculty research:* Marriage counseling, family of origin, counselor training, substance abuse counseling, childhood and adolescent obesity. *Unit head:* Dr. June Williams, Interim Department Head, 985-549-2309, Fax: 985-549-3758, E-mail: jwilliams@selu.edu. *Application contact:* Sandra Meyers, Graduate Admissions Analyst, 985-549-2066, Fax: 985-549-5632, E-mail: admissions@selu.edu.

Southeastern Oklahoma State University, School of Behavioral Sciences, Durant, OK 74701-0609. Offers community counseling (MBS). Part-time and evening/weekend programs available. *Faculty:* 10 full-time (3 women). *Students:* 23 full-time (18 women), 18 part-time (14 women); includes 14 minority (2 African Americans, 10 American Indian/Alaska Native, 1 Asian American or Pacific Islander, 1 Hispanic American), 2 international. Average age 35. 11 applicants, 100% accepted, 11 enrolled. *Degree requirements:* For master's, thesis optional. *Entrance requirements:* For master's, GRE General Test, minimum GPA of 3.0 in last 60 hours or 2.75 overall. Additional exam requirements/recommendations for international students: Required—TOEFL (minimum score 550 paper-based; 213 computer-based). *Application deadline:* For fall admission, 8/1 for domestic students, 6/1 for international students; for spring admission, 1/5 for domestic students, 11/1 for international students. Application fee: $20 ($55 for international students). Electronic applications accepted. *Financial support:* Fellowships, research assistantships, teaching assistantships, Federal Work-Study available. Support available to part-time students. Financial award application deadline: 6/15. *Unit head:* Dr. Kimberly Donovan, Program Coordinator, 580-745-2312, E-mail: kdonovan@se.edu. *Application contact:* Carrie Williamson, Graduate Secretary, 580-745-2200, Fax: 580-745-7474, E-mail: cwilliamson@se.edu.

Southwestern College, Program in Transformational Ecopsychology, Santa Fe, NM 87502-4788. Offers Certificate. *Entrance requirements:* For degree, 3 letters of reference, interview. Application fee: $25. *Unit head:* Dr. Carol Parker, Program Director, 505-471-5756. *Application contact:* Dru Phoenix, Director of Admissions, 505-471-5756 Ext. 26, Fax: 505-471-4071, E-mail: admissions@swc.edu.

Springfield College, Graduate Programs, Program in Human Services, Springfield, MA 01109-3797. Offers human services (MS), including community counseling psychology, mental health counseling, organizational management and leadership. Part-time programs available. *Degree requirements:* For master's, comprehensive exam, thesis (for some programs), research project. *Entrance requirements:* For master's, GRE. Additional exam requirements/recommendations for international students: Required—TOEFL (minimum score 550 paper-based; 213 computer-based). Electronic applications accepted. *Expenses:* Contact institution.

Stony Brook University, State University of New York, Graduate School, College of Arts and Sciences, Department of Psychology, Program in Social and Health Psychology, Stony Brook, NY 11794. Offers PhD. *Students:* 23 full-time (18 women); includes 6 minority (3 Asian Americans or Pacific Islanders, 3 Hispanic Americans), 3 international. Average age 28. 95 applicants, 12% accepted. In 2009, 9 doctorates awarded. *Degree requirements:* For doctorate, thesis/dissertation. *Entrance requirements:* For doctorate, GRE General Test, GRE Subject Test. Additional exam requirements/recommendations for international students: Required—TOEFL. *Application deadline:* For fall admission, 1/15 for domestic students. Application fee: $60. *Expenses:* Tuition, state resident: full-time $8370; part-time $349 per credit. Tuition, nonresident: full-time $13,250; part-time $552 per credit. Required fees: $933. *Unit head:* Dr. Marci Lobel, Head, 631-632-7651, E-mail: marci.lobel@stonybrook.edu. *Application contact:* Dr. Marci Lobel, Head, 631-632-7651, E-mail: marci.lobel@stonybrook.edu.

Syracuse University, College of Arts and Sciences, Program in Social Psychology, Syracuse, NY 13244. Offers PhD. Part-time programs available. *Students:* 5 full-time (all women), 1 international. Average age 25. 52 applicants, 6% accepted, 1 enrolled. *Degree requirements:* For doctorate, thesis/dissertation. *Entrance requirements:* For doctorate, GRE General Test, GRE Subject Test (recommended). Additional exam requirements/recommendations for international students: Required—TOEFL (minimum score 100 iBT). *Application deadline:* For fall admission, 1/10 priority date for domestic and international students. Application fee: $75. Electronic applications accepted. *Expenses:* Tuition: Full-time $26,808; part-time $1117 per credit. Required fees: $1024. *Financial support:* Fellowships, research assistantships, teaching assistantships available. Financial award application deadline: 1/1. *Unit head:* Dr. Leonard Newman, Graduate Director, 315-443-2354, Fax: 315-443-4085, E-mail: lsnewman@syr.edu. *Application contact:* Sue Bova, Information Contact, 315-443-1050, E-mail: skbova@syr.edu.

Teachers College, Columbia University, Graduate Faculty of Education, Department of Organization and Leadership, Program in Social and Organizational Psychology, New York, NY 10027-6696. Offers organizational psychology (MA, Ed D, PhD); social psychology (Ed D, PhD). *Faculty:* 8 full-time (5 women), 5 part-time/adjunct (0 women). *Students:* 133 full-time (87 women), 111 part-time (82 women); includes 67 minority (17 African Americans, 33 Asian Americans or Pacific Islanders, 17 Hispanic Americans), 26 international. Average age 28. 238 applicants, 61% accepted, 69 enrolled. In 2009, 136 master's, 3 doctorates awarded. Terminal master's awarded for partial completion of doctoral program. *Degree requirements:* For master's, comprehensive exam; for doctorate, thesis/dissertation. *Entrance requirements:* For master's, minimum GPA of 3.0; for doctorate, GRE General Test. *Application deadline:* For fall admission, 5/15 for domestic students; for spring admission, 12/1 for domestic students. Application fee: $65. *Financial support:* Fellowships, research assistantships, career-related internships or fieldwork, Federal Work-Study, institutionally sponsored loans, and tuition waivers (full and partial) available. Support available to part-time students. Financial award application deadline: 2/1. *Faculty research:* Conflict resolution, human resource and organization development, management competence, organizational culture, leadership. *Unit head:* Warner Burke, Chair, 212-678-3258. *Application contact:* Debbie Lesperance, Assistant Director of Admission, 212-678-3710, Fax: 212-678-4171.

Temple University, Graduate School, College of Liberal Arts, Department of Psychology, Program in Social Psychology, Philadelphia, PA 19122-6096. Offers PhD. *Degree requirements:* For doctorate, thesis/dissertation, preliminary exam. *Entrance requirements:* For doctorate, GRE General Test, minimum GPA of 3.0. Additional exam requirements/recommendations for international students: Required—TOEFL (minimum score 550 paper-based; 213 computer-based; 79 iBT). Electronic applications accepted. *Faculty research:* Power and technology, organizational behavior, interpersonal dynamics, belief, consumer behavior.

Social Psychology

Texas A&M University, College of Liberal Arts, Department of Psychology, College Station, TX 77843. Offers behavioral and cellular neuroscience (MS, PhD); clinical psychology (MS, PhD); cognitive psychology (MS, PhD); developmental psychology (MS, PhD); industrial/organizational psychology (MS, PhD); social psychology (MS, PhD). *Accreditation:* APA (one or more programs are accredited). *Faculty:* 36. *Students:* 84 full-time (58 women), 6 part-time (5 women); includes 26 minority (6 African Americans, 3 Asian Americans or Pacific Islanders, 17 Hispanic Americans), 6 international. In 2009, 12 master's, 8 doctorates awarded. *Degree requirements:* For master's, thesis; for doctorate, comprehensive exam (for some programs), thesis/dissertation. *Entrance requirements:* For master's and doctorate, GRE General Test. Additional exam requirements/recommendations for international students: Required—TOEFL. *Application deadline:* For fall admission, 1/5 for domestic and international students. Application fee: $50 ($75 for international students). Electronic applications accepted. *Expenses:* Tuition, state resident: full-time $3991; part-time $221.74 per credit hour. Tuition, nonresident: full-time $9049; part-time $502.74 per credit hour. *Financial support:* Fellowships with partial tuition reimbursements, research assistantships with partial tuition reimbursements, teaching assistantships with partial tuition reimbursements, career-related internships or fieldwork, institutionally sponsored loans, health care benefits, and unspecified assistantships available. Financial award application deadline: 1/5; financial award applicants required to submit FAFSA. *Unit head:* Dr. Les Morey, Head, 979-845-2581, Fax: 979-845-4727, E-mail: lmorey@psych.tamu.edu. *Application contact:* Sharon Starr, Graduate Admissions Supervisor, 979-458-1710, Fax: 979-845-4727, E-mail: gradadv@psyc.tamu.edu.

Texas Christian University, College of Science and Engineering, Department of Psychology, Fort Worth, TX 76129-0002. Offers experimental psychology (PhD), including cognitive psychology, learning, neuropsychology, social psychology; psychology (MA, MS). *Degree requirements:* For master's, thesis; for doctorate, thesis/dissertation. *Entrance requirements:* For master's and doctorate, GRE General Test. Additional exam requirements/recommendations for international students: Required—TOEFL. *Application deadline:* For fall admission, 3/1 for domestic and international students; for spring admission, 12/1 for domestic students. Applications are processed on a rolling basis. Application fee: $50. *Expenses:* Tuition: Full-time $17,640; part-time $980 per credit hour. Tuition and fees vary according to program. *Financial support:* In 2009–10, 20 students received support; teaching assistantships with full tuition reimbursements available, unspecified assistantships available. Financial award application deadline: 3/1. *Unit head:* Dr. Charles Lord, Graduate Director, 817-257-7410, E-mail: c.lord@tcu.edu. *Application contact:* Marilyn Eudaly, Department Manager, 817-257-6437.

Thomas University, Department of Human Services, Thomasville, GA 31792-7499. Offers community counseling (MSCC); rehabilitation counseling (MRC). *Accreditation:* CORE. Part-time programs available. *Entrance requirements:* For master's, resume, 3 academic/professional references. Additional exam requirements/recommendations for international students: Required—TOEFL (minimum score 600 paper-based; 250 computer-based). Electronic applications accepted.

Troy University, Graduate School, College of Education, Program in Counseling and Psychology, Troy, AL 36082. Offers agency counsleing (Ed S); clinical mental health (MS); community counseling (MS, Ed S); corrections counseling (MS); rehabilitation counseling (MS); school psychology (MS, Ed S); school psychometry (MS); social service counseling (MS); student affairs counseling (MS); substance abuse counseling (MS). *Accreditation:* ACA; CORE; NCATE. Part-time and evening/weekend programs available. *Students:* 375 full-time (302 women), 753 part-time (642 women); includes 664 minority (610 African Americans, 8 American Indian/Alaska Native, 9 Asian Americans or Pacific Islanders, 37 Hispanic Americans). Average age 33. 493 applicants, 92% accepted. In 2009, 102 master's, 191 other advanced degrees awarded. *Degree requirements:* For master's, comprehensive exam, thesis. *Entrance requirements:* For master's, MAT, minimum GPA of 2.5. Additional exam requirements/recommendations for international students: Required—TOEFL (minimum score 523 paper-based; 193 computer-based; 70 iBT), IELTS (minimum score 6). *Application deadline:* Applications are processed on a rolling basis. Application fee: $50. Electronic applications accepted. *Unit head:* Dr. Andrew Creamer, Chair, 334-670-3350, Fax: 334-670-32961, E-mail: drcreamer@troy.edu. *Application contact:* Brenda K. Campbell, Director of Graduate Admissions, 334-670-3178, Fax: 334-670-3733, E-mail: bcamp@troy.edu.

Université du Québec à Rimouski, Graduate Programs, Program in Psychosocial Studies, Rimouski, QC G5L 3A1, Canada. Offers MA.

Université Laval, Faculty of Social Sciences, School of Psychology, Programs in Psychology, Québec, QC G1K 7P4, Canada. Offers clinical psychology (PhD); community psychology (PhD); psychology (PhD, Psy D). *Degree requirements:* For doctorate, comprehensive exam, thesis/dissertation. *Entrance requirements:* For doctorate, comprehension of written English, knowledge of French, interview. Electronic applications accepted.

University at Albany, State University of New York, College of Arts and Sciences, Department of Psychology, Albany, NY 12222-0001. Offers autism (Certificate); biopsychology (PhD); clinical psychology (PhD); general/experimental psychology (PhD); industrial/organizational psychology (PhD); psychology (MA); social/personality psychology (PhD). *Accreditation:* APA (one or more programs are accredited). *Degree requirements:* For doctorate, thesis/dissertation. *Entrance requirements:* For doctorate, GRE General Test, GRE Subject Test. Additional exam requirements/recommendations for international students: Required—TOEFL (minimum score 550 paper-based; 213 computer-based). Electronic applications accepted.

University at Buffalo, the State University of New York, Graduate School, College of Arts and Sciences, Department of Psychology, Buffalo, NY 14260. Offers behavioral neuroscience (PhD); clinical psychology (PhD); cognitive psychology (PhD); general psychology (MA); social-personality psychology (PhD). *Accreditation:* APA (one or more programs are accredited). *Faculty:* 32 full-time (12 women), 8 part-time/adjunct (6 women). *Students:* 94 full-time (64 women), 7 part-time (2 women); includes 5 minority (2 African Americans, 3 Hispanic Americans), 12 international. Average age 27. 353 applicants, 11% accepted. In 2009, 18 master's, 7 doctorates awarded. Terminal master's awarded for partial completion of doctoral program. *Degree requirements:* For master's, project; for doctorate, thesis/dissertation. *Entrance requirements:* For master's and doctorate, GRE General Test. Additional exam requirements/recommendations for international students: Required—TOEFL (minimum score 550 paper-based; 213 computer-based; 79 iBT). *Application deadline:* For fall admission, 1/5 for domestic and international students. Application fee: $50. Electronic applications accepted. *Financial support:* In 2009–10, 81 students received support, including 20 fellowships with full tuition reimbursements available (averaging $14,400 per year), 1 research assistantship with full tuition reimbursement available (averaging $10,400 per year), 38 teaching assistantships with full tuition reimbursements available (averaging $10,400 per year); career-related internships or fieldwork, Federal Work-Study, institutionally sponsored loans, scholarships/grants, and tuition waivers (partial) also available. Financial award application deadline: 1/5; financial award applicants required to submit FAFSA. *Faculty research:* Neural, endocrine, and molecular bases of behavior; adult mood and anxiety disorders; relationship dysfunction; attention deficit/hyperactivity disorder; psycho-linguistics. Total annual research expenditures: $7.9 million. *Unit head:* Dr. Paul A. Luce, Chair, 716-645-3650 Ext. 203, Fax: 716-645-3801, E-mail: psychair@acsu.buffalo.edu. *Application contact:* Michele Nowacki, Coordinator of Admissions, 716-645-3650 Ext. 209, Fax: 716-645-3801, E-mail: psych@acsu.buffalo.edu.

The University of Akron, Graduate School, College of Education, Department of Counseling, Program in Community Counseling, Akron, OH 44325. Offers MA, MS. *Accreditation:* ACA; NCATE. *Students:* 46 full-time (39 women), 25 part-time (20 women); includes 8 African Americans, 2 international. Average age 29. 40 applicants, 38% accepted, 11 enrolled. In 2009, 13 master's awarded. *Degree requirements:* For master's, comprehensive exam. *Entrance requirements:* For master's, minimum GPA of 2.75, interview, letters of recommendation, supplemental form. Additional exam requirements/recommendations for international students: Required—TOEFL (minimum score 550 paper-based; 213 computer-based; 79 iBT). *Application deadline:* Applications are processed on a rolling basis. Application fee: $30 ($40 for international students). Electronic applications accepted. *Expenses:* Tuition, state resident: full-time $6570; part-time $365 per credit hour. Tuition, nonresident: full-time $11,250; part-time $625 per credit hour. *Unit head:* Dr. Robert Schwartz, Coordinator, 330-972-8155, E-mail: rcs@uakron.edu. *Application contact:* Dr. Robert Schwartz, Coordinator, 330-972-8155, E-mail: rcs@uakron.edu.

University of Alaska Anchorage, College of Arts and Sciences, Department of Psychology, Anchorage, AK 99508. Offers clinical psychology (MS); clinical-community psychology with rural-indigenous emphasis (PhD). Part-time programs available. *Degree requirements:* For master's, thesis. *Entrance requirements:* For master's, GRE General Test, GRE Subject Test, interview, references; for doctorate, interview, bachelor's or master's degree in psychology. Additional exam requirements/recommendations for international students: Required—TOEFL (minimum score 550 paper-based; 213 computer-based). *Faculty research:* Substance abuse, childhood autism, biofeedback, psychological assessment, mental health in Native Alaskans.

University of Alaska Fairbanks, College of Liberal Arts, Department of Psychology, Fairbanks, AK 99775-6480. Offers clinical-community psychology (PhD), including rural cross-cultural emphasis. *Faculty:* 10 full-time (5 women), 3 part-time/adjunct (1 woman). *Students:* 4 full-time (1 woman), 20 part-time (17 women); includes 8 minority (1 African American, 5 American Indian/Alaska Native, 2 Hispanic Americans), 1 international. Average age 35. 34 applicants, 32% accepted, 9 enrolled. In 2009, 1 doctorate awarded. *Degree requirements:* For doctorate, comprehensive exam, thesis/dissertation, oral exam, oral defense. *Entrance requirements:* For doctorate, disclosure statement. Additional exam requirements/recommendations for international students: Required—TOEFL (minimum score 550 paper-based; 213 computer-based; 80 iBT). *Application deadline:* For fall admission, 12/15 for domestic and international students. Application fee: $60. *Expenses:* Tuition, state resident: full-time $7584; part-time $316 per credit. Tuition, nonresident: full-time $15,504; part-time $646 per credit. Required fees: $23 per credit. $135 per semester. Tuition and fees vary according to course level, course load and reciprocity agreements. *Financial support:* In 2009–10, 2 fellowships (averaging $15,270 per year), 7 research assistantships (averaging $16,089 per year), 8 teaching assistantships (averaging $15,611 per year) were awarded; career-related internships or fieldwork, Federal Work-Study, scholarships/grants, health care benefits, and unspecified assistantships also available. Support available to part-time students. Financial award application deadline: 7/1; financial award applicants required to submit FAFSA. *Faculty research:* Clinical and community psychology; rural, indigenous, and cultural psychology. *Unit head:* Dr. Dani Sheppard, Department Chair, 907-474-7007, Fax: 907-474-5781, E-mail: fypsych@uaf.edu. *Application contact:* Dr. Dani Sheppard, Department Chair, 907-474-7007, Fax: 907-474-5781, E-mail: fypsych@uaf.edu.

University of Alaska Fairbanks, School of Education, Program in Counseling, Fairbanks, AK 99775-7520. Offers counseling (M Ed), including community counseling, school counseling. *Students:* 17 full-time (12 women), 45 part-time (36 women); includes 6 minority (2 African Americans, 1 American Indian/Alaska Native, 1 Asian American or Pacific Islander, 2 Hispanic Americans). Average age 36. 52 applicants, 63% accepted, 29 enrolled. In 2009, 21 master's awarded. *Degree requirements:* For master's, comprehensive exam, thesis, oral defense. *Entrance requirements:* For master's, 1 year teaching or administrative experience. *Application deadline:* For fall admission, 6/1 for domestic students, 3/1 for international students; for spring admission, 10/15 for domestic students, 9/1 for international students. Applications are processed on a rolling basis. Application fee: $60. Electronic applications accepted. *Expenses:* Tuition, state resident: full-time $7584; part-time $316 per credit. Tuition, nonresident: full-time $15,504; part-time $646 per credit. Required fees: $23 per credit. $135 per semester. Tuition and fees vary according to course level, course load and reciprocity agreements. *Financial support:* In 2009–10, 4 teaching assistantships (averaging $13,067 per year) were awarded; fellowships, career-related internships or fieldwork, Federal Work-Study, scholarships/grants, health care benefits, and unspecified assistantships also available. Support available to part-time students. Financial award application deadline: 7/1; financial award applicants required to submit FAFSA. *Unit head:* Dr. Eric C. Madsen, Dean, 907-474-7341, Fax: 907-474-5451, E-mail: fysoed@uaf.edu. *Application contact:* Dr. Eric C. Madsen, Dean, 907-474-7341, Fax: 907-474-5451, E-mail: fysoed@uaf.edu.

The University of British Columbia, Faculty of Arts and Faculty of Graduate Studies, Department of Psychology, Vancouver, BC V6T 1Z4, Canada. Offers behavioral neuroscience (MA, PhD); clinical psychology (MA, PhD); cognitive science (MA, PhD); developmental psychology (MA, PhD); health psychology (MA, PhD); quantitative methods (MA, PhD); social/personality psychology (MA, PhD). *Accreditation:* APA (one or more programs are accredited). Terminal master's awarded for partial completion of doctoral program. *Degree requirements:* For master's, thesis; for doctorate, comprehensive exam, thesis/dissertation. *Entrance requirements:* For master's and doctorate, GRE General Test. Additional exam requirements/recommendations for international students: Required—TOEFL (minimum score 550 paper-based; 230 computer-based; 80 iBT). Electronic applications accepted. *Faculty research:* Clinical, developmental, social/personality, cognition, behavioral neuroscience.

University of Central Arkansas, Graduate School, College of Health and Behavioral Sciences, Department of Counseling and Psychology, Program in Community Service Counseling, Conway, AR 72035-0001. Offers MS. *Students:* 18 full-time (14 women), 14 part-time (11 women); includes 5 minority (4 African Americans, 1 American Indian/Alaska Native). 12 applicants, 83% accepted, 7 enrolled. In 2009, 11 master's awarded. *Degree requirements:* For master's, comprehensive exam, thesis optional. *Entrance requirements:* For master's, GRE General Test, minimum GPA of 2.7. Additional exam requirements/recommendations for international students: Required—TOEFL (minimum score 550 paper-based; 213 computer-based). *Application deadline:* For fall admission, 3/1 priority date for domestic students; for spring admission, 10/1 priority date for domestic students. Applications are processed on a rolling basis. Application fee: $25 ($50 for international students). *Expenses:* Tuition, state resident: full-time $5136; part-time $214 per credit hour. Required fees: $379.50; $127 per term. Tuition and fees vary according to course level, course load and campus/location. *Financial support:* Career-related internships or fieldwork, Federal Work-Study, scholarships/grants, tuition waivers (partial), and unspecified assistantships available. Support available to part-time students. Financial award application deadline: 2/15; financial award applicants required to submit FAFSA. *Unit head:* Dr. Art Gillaspy, Coordinator, 501-450-5410, Fax: 501-450-5424, E-mail: artg@uca.edu. *Application contact:* Patti Hornor, Administrative Assistant, 501-450-5063, Fax: 501-450-5678, E-mail: pattih@uca.edu.

University of Connecticut, Graduate School, College of Liberal Arts and Sciences, Department of Psychology, Storrs, CT 06269. Offers behavioral neuroscience (PhD); biopsychology (PhD); clinical psychology (MA, PhD); cognition and instruction (PhD); developmental psychology (MA, PhD); ecological psychology (PhD); experimental psychology (PhD); general psychology (MA, PhD); health psychology (Graduate Certificate); industrial/organizational psychology (PhD); language and cognition (PhD); neuroscience (PhD); occupational health psychology (Graduate Certificate); social psychology (MA, PhD). *Accreditation:* APA. *Faculty:* 59 full-time (26 women). *Students:* 194 full-time (133 women), 24 part-time (12 women); includes 48 minority (12 African Americans, 21 Asian Americans or Pacific Islanders, 15 Hispanic Americans), 25 international. Average age 28. 585 applicants, 4% accepted, 14 enrolled. In 2009, 22 master's, 24 doctorates awarded. Terminal master's awarded for partial completion of doctoral program. *Degree requirements:* For master's, comprehensive exam; for doctorate, thesis/dissertation. *Entrance requirements:* For master's and doctorate, GRE General Test, GRE Subject Test. Additional exam requirements/recommendations for international students: Required—TOEFL (minimum score 550 paper-based; 213 computer-based). *Application deadline:* For fall admission, 2/1 priority date for domestic and international students; for spring admission, 11/1 for domestic students, 10/1 for international students. Applications are processed on a rolling basis. Application fee: $55. Electronic applications accepted. *Expenses:* Tuition, state resident: full-time $4725; part-time $525 per credit. Tuition, nonresident: full-time $12,267; part-time $1363 per credit. Required fees: $346 per semester. Tuition and fees vary according to course load. *Financial support:* In 2009–10, 109 research assistantships with full tuition reimbursements, 72 teaching assistantships with full tuition reimbursements were awarded; fellowships, career-related internships or fieldwork, Federal Work-Study, scholarships/grants, health care benefits, and unspecified assistantships also available. Financial award application deadline: 2/1; financial award applicants required to submit FAFSA. *Unit head:* Charles A. Lowe, Head, 860-486-3517, Fax: 860-486-2760, E-mail: charles.lowe@uconn.edu. *Application contact:* Charles A. Lowe, Head, 860-486-3517, Fax: 860-486-2760, E-mail: charles.lowe@uconn.edu.

University of Dayton, Graduate School, School of Education and Allied Professions, Department of Counselor Education and Human Services, Dayton, OH 45469-1300. Offers college student personnel (MS Ed); community counseling (MS Ed); higher education administration (MS Ed); human services (MS Ed); school counseling (MS Ed); school psychology (MS Ed, Ed S); teacher as child/youth development specialist (MS Ed). *Accreditation:* NCATE. Part-time and evening/weekend programs available. *Faculty:* 11 full-time (8 women), 33 part-time/adjunct (22 women). *Students:* 254 full-time (207 women), 207 part-time (180 women); includes 76 minority (69 African Americans, 3 Asian Americans or Pacific Islanders, 4 Hispanic Americans), 2 international. Average age 32. 359 applicants, 47% accepted, 114 enrolled. In 2009, 163 master's, 11 Ed Ss awarded. *Degree requirements:* For master's, comprehensive exam (for some programs), thesis (for some programs), exit exam. *Entrance requirements:* For master's, MAT or GRE (if GPA less than 2.75), interview, writing sample. Additional exam requirements/recommendations for international students: Required—TOEFL (minimum score 550 paper-based; 213 computer-based; 80 iBT). *Application deadline:* For fall admission, 4/10 for domestic students, 3/1 priority date for international students; for winter admission, 9/10 for domestic students, 7/1 priority date for international students; for spring admission, 1/10 for domestic students, 1/1 priority date for international students. Applications are processed on a rolling basis. Application fee: $0 ($50 for international students). Electronic applications accepted. *Expenses:* Tuition: Full-time $8412; part-time $701 per credit hour. Required fees: $325; $65 per course. $25 per semester. Tuition and fees vary according to course load, degree level and program. *Financial support:* In 2009–10, 7 research assistantships with full tuition reimbursements (averaging $8,000 per year), 1 teaching assistantship with full tuition reimbursement (averaging $8,000 per year) were awarded; career-related internships or fieldwork, institutionally sponsored loans, health care benefits, and unspecified assistantships also available. Financial award applicants required to submit FAFSA. *Faculty research:* Anger as part of the grief process, inclusion of children with severe disabilities, comparisons of school counselors in Bosnia and the U. S., graduate and professional student socialization, use of cohort groups in doctoral programs, bullying in schools, impact of space on learning, sophomore experience. *Unit head:* Dr. Alan Demmitt, Chairperson, 937-229-3644, Fax: 937-229-1055. *Application contact:* Graduate Admissions, 937-229-4411, Fax: 937-229-4729, E-mail: gradadmission@udayton.edu.

University of Delaware, College of Arts and Sciences, Department of Psychology, Newark, DE 19716. Offers behavioral neuroscience (PhD); clinical psychology (PhD); cognitive psychology (PhD); social psychology (PhD). *Accreditation:* APA. *Degree requirements:* For doctorate, thesis/dissertation. *Entrance requirements:* For doctorate, GRE General Test. Additional exam requirements/recommendations for international students: Required—TOEFL (minimum score 600 paper-based; 250 computer-based). Electronic applications accepted. *Faculty research:* Emotion development, neural and cognitive aspects of memory, neural control of feeding, intergroup relations, social cognition and communication.

University of Florida, Graduate School, College of Liberal Arts and Sciences, Department of Psychology, Gainesville, FL 32611. Offers behavior analysis (PhD); behavioral neuroscience (MS, PhD); cognitive and sensory processes (PhD); counseling psychology (PhD); developmental psychology (PhD); social psychology (MS, PhD); JD/PhD. *Degree requirements:* For master's, thesis or alternative; for doctorate, thesis/dissertation. *Entrance requirements:* For master's and doctorate, GRE General Test, minimum GPA of 3.0. Additional exam requirements/recommendations for international students: Required—TOEFL (minimum score 550 paper-based; 213 computer-based). Electronic applications accepted. *Faculty research:* Experimental analysis of behavior, psychobiology, cognition and sensory processes, counseling psychology, social psychology, developmental psychology.

University of Guelph, Graduate Program Services, College of Social and Applied Human Sciences, Department of Psychology, Guelph, ON N1G 2W1, Canada. Offers applied social psychology (MA, PhD); clinical psychology applied development emphasis (PhD); clinical psychology applied developmental emphasis (MA); industrial/organizational psychology (MA, PhD); neuroscience and applied cognitive science (MA, PhD). *Degree requirements:* For master's, thesis; for doctorate, comprehensive exam, thesis/dissertation. *Entrance requirements:* For master's, GRE General Test, GRE Subject Test, minimum B+ average during previous 2 years of course work; for doctorate, GRE General Test, GRE Subject Test, minimum A-average. Additional exam requirements/recommendations for international students: Required—TOEFL (minimum score 89 iBT). Electronic applications accepted. *Faculty research:* Organizational psychology, reading comprehension and mathematical ability, drug addiction and relapse, gender issues and culture, memory, clinical psychology.

University of Hawaii at Manoa, Graduate Division, College of Social Sciences, Department of Psychology, Honolulu, HI 96822. Offers clinical psychology (PhD); community and cultural psychology (PhD); community and culture (MA); psychology (MA, PhD, Graduate Certificate). *Accreditation:* APA (one or more programs are accredited). Part-time programs available. *Faculty:* 27 full-time (10 women), 17 part-time/adjunct (1 woman). *Students:* 70 full-time (52 women), 18 part-time (13 women); includes 27 minority (2 African Americans, 1 American Indian/Alaska Native, 21 Asian Americans or Pacific Islanders, 3 Hispanic Americans), 14 international. Average age 28. 202 applicants, 10% accepted, 16 enrolled. In 2009, 5 master's, 9 doctorates, 1 other advanced degree awarded. Terminal master's awarded for partial completion of doctoral program. *Degree requirements:* For master's, comprehensive exam, thesis; for doctorate, comprehensive exam, thesis/dissertation. *Entrance requirements:* For master's and doctorate, GRE General Test, GRE Subject Test. Additional exam requirements/recommendations for international students: Required—TOEFL (minimum score 600 paper-based; 250 computer-based; 100 iBT), IELTS (minimum score 7). *Application deadline:* For fall admission, 1/1 for domestic and international students. Application fee: $60. *Expenses:* Tuition, state resident: full-time $8900; part-time $372 per credit. Tuition, nonresident: full-time $21,400; part-time $898 per credit. Required fees: $207 per semester. *Financial support:* In 2009–10, 6 students received support, including 6 fellowships (averaging $3,969 per year), 41 research assistantships (averaging $17,740 per year), 14 teaching assistantships (averaging $14,802 per year); career-related internships or fieldwork, institutionally sponsored loans, and tuition waivers (full and partial) also available. Financial award application deadline: 1/1. *Faculty research:* Cross-cultural psychology, health psychology, marine mammals, child/adult psychopathology. Total annual research expenditures: $1.3 million. *Application contact:* Catherine Sophian, Graduate Chair, 808-956-8414, Fax: 808-956-4700, E-mail: csophian@hawaii.edu.

The University of Iowa, Graduate College, College of Education, Department of Counseling, Rehabilitation, and Student Development, Iowa City, IA 52242-1316. Offers administration and research (PhD); community/rehabilitation counseling (MA); counselor education and supervision (PhD); rehabilitation counselor education (PhD); school counseling (MA); student development (MA, PhD). *Accreditation:* ACA (one or more programs are accredited); CORE (one or more programs are accredited). *Degree requirements:* For master's, thesis optional, exam; for doctorate, comprehensive exam, thesis/dissertation. *Entrance requirements:* For master's and doctorate, GRE General Test, minimum GPA of 3.0. Additional exam requirements/recommendations for international students: Required—TOEFL (minimum score 550 paper-based; 213 computer-based; 81 iBT). Electronic applications accepted.

The University of Kansas, Graduate Studies, College of Liberal Arts and Sciences, Department of Psychology, Lawrence, KS 66045. Offers clinical child psychology (MA, PhD); clinical health and rehabilitation (PhD); cognitive (PhD); developmental (PhD); quantitative (PhD); social (MA). *Accreditation:* APA (one or more programs are accredited). *Faculty:* 27 full-time (8 women), 9 part-time/adjunct (4 women). *Students:* 85 full-time (62 women), 11 part-time (9 women); includes 13 minority (4 African Americans, 1 American Indian/Alaska Native, 6 Asian Americans or Pacific Islanders, 2 Hispanic Americans), 7 international. Average age 27. 185 applicants, 15% accepted, 17 enrolled. In 2009, 13 master's, 10 doctorates awarded. *Degree requirements:* For master's, thesis; for doctorate, variable foreign language requirement, comprehensive exam, thesis/dissertation. *Entrance requirements:* For doctorate, GRE General Test, minimum GPA of 3.0; undergraduate degree with 15 hours of course work in psychology, vita, writing sample (Clinical Program Only). Additional exam requirements/recommendations for international students: Required—TOEFL. *Application deadline:* For fall admission, 12/1 for domestic and international students. Application fee: $45 ($55 for international students). Electronic applications accepted. *Expenses:* Tuition, state resident: full-time $6492; part-time $270.50 per credit hour. Tuition, nonresident: full-time $15,510; part-time $646.25 per credit hour. Required fees: $847; $70.56 per credit hour. Tuition and fees vary according to course load and program. *Financial support:* Fellowships with full tuition reimbursements, research assistantships with partial tuition reimbursements, teaching assistantships with full and partial tuition reimbursements, career-related internships or fieldwork and unspecified assistantships available. Financial award application deadline: 12/1; financial award applicants required to submit FAFSA. *Faculty research:* Information processing in depression, rape and other forms of sexual coerciom, motions on physical function, processes of memory and understanding text, social stigmas and hostile group environments. *Unit head:* Dr. Ruth Ann Atchley, Chair, 785-864-9821, Fax: 785-864-5696, E-mail: ratchley@ku.edu. *Application contact:* Cathy L. O'Keefe, Graduate Admissions Officer, 785-864-4195, Fax: 785-864-5696, E-mail: psycgrad@ku.edu.

University of La Verne, College of Arts and Sciences, Department of Psychology, Program in Clinical-Community Psychology, La Verne, CA 91750-4443. Offers Psy D. Part-time programs available. *Faculty:* 12 full-time (5 women), 22 part-time/adjunct (14 women). *Students:* 54 full-time (48 women), 35 part-time (28 women); includes 46 minority (11 African Americans, 8 Asian Americans or Pacific Islanders, 27 Hispanic Americans). Average age 28. In 2009, 15 doctorates awarded. *Degree requirements:* For doctorate, thesis/dissertation, clinical internship, competency exams, practicum, personal psychotherapy. *Entrance requirements:* For doctorate, minimum GPA of 3.0 undergraduate, 3.5 graduate; 3 letters of recommendation; curriculum vitae. Additional exam requirements/recommendations for international students: Required—TOEFL (minimum score 600 paper-based; 250 computer-based). *Application deadline:* For fall admission, 1/15 for domestic and international students. Application fee: $75. *Expenses:* Contact institution. *Financial support:* Career-related internships or fieldwork, institutionally sponsored loans, scholarships/grants, and unspecified assistantships available. Financial award application deadline: 3/2; financial award applicants required to submit FAFSA. *Unit head:* Dr. Valerie Jordan, Chairperson, 909-593-3511 Ext. 4174, E-mail: vjordan@laverne.edu. *Application contact:* Connie Hamlow, Admissions Information Specialist, 909-593-3511 Ext. 4519, Fax: 909-392-2761, E-mail: gradadmission@laverne.edu.

University of Maine, Graduate School, College of Liberal Arts and Sciences, Department of Psychology, Orono, ME 04469. Offers clinical psychology (PhD); developmental psychology (MA); experimental psychology (MA, PhD); social psychology (MA). *Accreditation:* APA (one or more programs are accredited). *Faculty:* 17 full-time (8 women), 7 part-time/adjunct (3 women). *Students:* 27 full-time (16 women), 9 part-time (7 women); includes 2 minority (1 Asian American or Pacific Islander, 1 Hispanic American), 1 international. Average age 28. 134 applicants, 8% accepted, 7 enrolled. In 2009, 3 master's, 3 doctorates awarded. *Degree requirements:* For master's, thesis; for doctorate, thesis/dissertation. *Entrance requirements:* For master's and doctorate, GRE General Test, GRE Subject Test. Additional exam requirements/recommendations for international students: Required—TOEFL. *Application deadline:* For fall admission, 2/1 priority date for domestic students. Applications are processed on a rolling basis. Application fee: $65. Electronic applications accepted. *Financial support:* In 2009–10, 3 research assistantships with tuition reimbursements (averaging $14,063 per year), 21 teaching assistantships with tuition reimbursements (averaging $12,790 per year) were awarded; Federal Work-Study, institutionally sponsored loans, and tuition waivers (full and partial) also available. Financial award application deadline: 3/1. *Faculty research:* Social development, hypertension and aging, attitude change, self-confidence in achievement situations, health psychology. *Unit head:* Dr. Michael Robbins, Chair, 207-581-2051, Fax: 207-581-6128. *Application contact:* Scott G. Delcourt, Associate Dean of the Graduate School, 207-581-3291, Fax: 207-581-3232, E-mail: graduate@maine.edu.

University of Mary, Division of Social and Behavioral Sciences, Bismarck, ND 58504-9652. Offers addiction counseling (MSC); community counseling (MSC); school counseling (MSC). Part-time programs available. Postbaccalaureate distance learning degree programs offered (minimal on-campus study). *Degree requirements:* For master's, thesis, internship. *Entrance requirements:* For master's, coursework/experience in psychology, statistics. Additional exam requirements/recommendations for international students: Required—TOEFL. *Expenses:* Tuition: Full-time $10,062; part-time $430 per credit. Tuition and fees vary according to course load, degree level, program and student level.

University of Mary Hardin-Baylor, Graduate Studies in Counseling and Psychology, Belton, TX 76513. Offers community counseling (MA); marriage and family Christian counseling (MA); psychology and counseling (MA); school counseling and psychology (MA). Part-time and evening/weekend programs available. *Degree requirements:* For master's, comprehensive exam. *Entrance requirements:* For master's, GRE General Test, minimum GPA of 3.0 in last 60 hours or 2.75 overall. Electronic applications accepted.

University of Maryland, College Park, Academic Affairs, College of Behavioral and Social Sciences, Department of Psychology, College Park, MD 20742. Offers clinical psychology (PhD); developmental psychology (PhD); experimental psychology (PhD); industrial psychology (MA, MS, PhD); social psychology (PhD). *Accreditation:* APA (one or more programs are accredited). *Faculty:* 71 full-time (35 women), 8 part-time/adjunct (4 women). *Students:* 82 full-time (67 women); includes 13 minority (2 African Americans, 4 Asian Americans or Pacific Islanders, 7 Hispanic Americans), 12 international. 568 applicants, 4% accepted, 8 enrolled. In 2009, 13 master's, 10 doctorates awarded. *Degree requirements:* For master's, thesis; for doctorate, variable foreign language requirement, comprehensive exam, thesis/dissertation. *Entrance requirements:* For master's and doctorate, GRE General Test, GRE Subject Test, minimum GPA of 3.5, research and/or work experience, 3 letters of recommendation. *Application deadline:* For fall admission, 12/1 for domestic and international students. Applications are processed on a rolling basis. Application fee: $60. Electronic applications accepted. *Expenses:* Tuition, area resident: Part-time $471 per credit hour. Tuition, state resident: part-time $471 per credit hour. Tuition, nonresident: part-time $1016 per credit hour. Required fees: $337.04 per term. *Financial support:* In 2009–10, 11 fellowships with full and partial tuition reimbursements (averaging $19,195 per year), 5 research assistantships (averaging $17,734 per year), 45 teaching assistantships with tuition reimbursements (averaging $17,116 per year) were awarded; career-related internships or fieldwork, Federal Work-Study, and scholarships/grants also available. Support available to part-time students. Financial award applicants required to submit FAFSA. *Faculty research:* Social stereotyping and prejudice, anxiety disorders, auditory neuroethology, counseling and social psychology. Total annual research expenditures: $3.8 million. *Unit head:* Thomas S. Wallsten, Chair, 301-405-3562, Fax: 301-314-9566, E-mail: twallst@umd.edu. *Application contact:* Dean of Graduate School, 301-405-0358, Fax: 301-314-9305.

Social Psychology

University of Massachusetts Amherst, Graduate School, College of Natural Sciences, Department of Psychology, Amherst, MA 01003. Offers clinical psychology (MS, PhD); cognitive psychology (MS, PhD); developmental science (MS, PhD); psychology of peace and violence (MS, PhD); social psychology (MS, PhD). *Accreditation:* APA (one or more programs are accredited). *Faculty:* 48 full-time (22 women). *Students:* 57 full-time (42 women), 13 part-time (10 women); includes 15 minority (6 African Americans, 6 Asian Americans or Pacific Islanders, 3 Hispanic Americans), 8 international. Average age 28. 381 applicants, 4% accepted, 11 enrolled. In 2009, 11 master's, 8 doctorates awarded. Terminal master's awarded for partial completion of doctoral program. *Degree requirements:* For master's, thesis; for doctorate, comprehensive exam, thesis/dissertation. *Entrance requirements:* For master's and doctorate, GRE General Test, 3 letters of recommendation. Additional exam requirements/recommendations for international students: Required—TOEFL (minimum score 550 paper-based; 213 computer-based; 80 iBT), IELTS (minimum score 6.5). *Application deadline:* For fall admission, 12/1 for domestic and international students. Applications are processed on a rolling basis. Application fee: $50 ($65 for international students). Electronic applications accepted. *Expenses:* Tuition, state resident: full-time $2640; part-time $110 per credit. Tuition, nonresident: full-time $9936; part-time $414 per credit. Tuition and fees vary according to course load. *Financial support:* In 2009–10, 8 fellowships with full tuition reimbursements (averaging $12,620 per year), 52 research assistantships with full tuition reimbursements (averaging $9,491 per year), 55 teaching assistantships with full tuition reimbursements (averaging $10,829 per year) were awarded; career-related internships or fieldwork, Federal Work-Study, scholarships/grants, traineeships, health care benefits, tuition waivers (full), and unspecified assistantships also available. Support available to part-time students. Financial award application deadline: 12/1. *Unit head:* Dr. Linda M. Isbell, Graduate Program Director, 413-545-2503, Fax: 413-545-0996. *Application contact:* Jean M. Ames, Supervisor of Admissions, 413-545-0722, Fax: 413-577-0010, E-mail: gradadm@grad.umass.edu.

University of Massachusetts Lowell, College of Arts and Sciences, Department of Psychology, Lowell, MA 01854-2881. Offers community social psychology (MA). Part-time programs available. *Degree requirements:* For master's, thesis optional. *Entrance requirements:* For master's, GRE General Test or MAT. Electronic applications accepted. *Faculty research:* Domestic violence, youth sports, teen pregnancy, substance abuse, family and work roles.

University of Michigan, Horace H. Rackham School of Graduate Studies, College of Literature, Science, and the Arts, Department of Psychology, Ann Arbor, MI 48451. Offers biopsychology (PhD); clinical psychology (PhD); cognition and perception (PhD); developmental psychology (PhD); personality and social contexts (PhD); social psychology (PhD). *Accreditation:* APA. *Faculty:* 87 full-time (40 women), 28 part-time/adjunct (16 women). *Students:* 147 full-time (101 women); includes 40 minority (15 African Americans, 2 American Indian/Alaska Native, 18 Asian Americans or Pacific Islanders, 5 Hispanic Americans), 25 international. Average age 27. 621 applicants, 10% accepted, 37 enrolled. In 2009, 25 doctorates awarded. *Degree requirements:* For doctorate, comprehensive exam, thesis/dissertation, oral defense of dissertation, preliminary exam. *Entrance requirements:* For doctorate, GRE General Test. Additional exam requirements/recommendations for international students: Required—TOEFL. *Application deadline:* For fall admission, 12/1 for domestic and international students. Application fee: $60 ($75 for international students). Electronic applications accepted. *Expenses:* Tuition, state resident: full-time $17,286; part-time $1099 per credit hour. Tuition, nonresident: full-time $34,944; part-time $2080 per credit hour. Required fees: $95 per semester. Tuition and fees vary according to course load, degree level and program. *Financial support:* In 2009–10, 133 students received support, including 52 fellowships with full tuition reimbursements available (averaging $20,900 per year), 16 research assistantships with full tuition reimbursements available (averaging $20,900 per year), 79 teaching assistantships with full tuition reimbursements available (averaging $16,694 per year); career-related internships or fieldwork also available. Financial award application deadline: 4/15. *Unit head:* Prof. Theresa Lee, Chair, 734-764-7429. *Application contact:* Laurie Brannan, Psychology Student Academic Affairs, 731-764-2580, Fax: 734-615-7584, E-mail: psych.saa@umich.edu.

University of Minnesota, Twin Cities Campus, Graduate School, College of Liberal Arts, Department of Psychology, Program in Social Psychology, Minneapolis, MN 55455-0213. Offers PhD. *Degree requirements:* For doctorate, comprehensive exam, thesis/dissertation. *Entrance requirements:* For doctorate, GRE General Test, GRE Subject Test (recommended), 12 credits of upper-level psychology courses, including a course in statistics or psychological measurement. Additional exam requirements/recommendations for international students: Required—TOEFL (minimum score 550 paper-based; 213 computer-based; 79 iBT).

University of Missouri–Kansas City, College of Arts and Sciences, Department of Psychology, Kansas City, MO 64110-2499. Offers clinical psychology (PhD); community psychology (PhD); health psychology (PhD); psychology (MA). PhD (interdisciplinary) offered through the School of Graduate Studies. *Accreditation:* APA. *Faculty:* 12 full-time (9 women), 3 part-time/adjunct (2 women). *Students:* 15 full-time (12 women), 7 part-time (6 women); includes 2 minority (1 African American, 1 Hispanic American). Average age 31. 86 applicants, 3% accepted, 3 enrolled. In 2009, 4 master's, 4 doctorates awarded. Terminal master's awarded for partial completion of doctoral program. *Degree requirements:* For master's, thesis; for doctorate, comprehensive exam, thesis/dissertation, residency. *Entrance requirements:* For master's, GRE, minimum GPA of 3.5, letter of recommendation; for doctorate, GRE, minimum GPA of 3.25. Additional exam requirements/recommendations for international students: Required—TOEFL (minimum score 550 paper-based; 213 computer-based; 80 iBT). *Application deadline:* For fall admission, 1/15 for domestic and international students. Applications are processed on a rolling basis. Application fee: $45 ($50 for international students). Electronic applications accepted. *Expenses:* Tuition, state resident: full-time $5378; part-time $299 per credit hour. Tuition, nonresident: full-time $13,881; part-time $771 per credit hour. Required fees: $641; $71 per credit hour. Tuition and fees vary according to course load and program. *Financial support:* In 2009–10, 18 research assistantships (averaging $11,500 per year), 3 teaching assistantships (averaging $8,000 per year) were awarded; career-related internships or fieldwork, Federal Work-Study, and institutionally sponsored loans also available. Support available to part-time students. Financial award application deadline: 3/1; financial award applicants required to submit FAFSA. *Faculty research:* HIV/AIDS research group, psycho-oncology, sensory and cognitive neuroscience, cognitive psychophysiology, obesity and related metabolic disorders. Total annual research expenditures: $673,228. *Unit head:* Dr. Tamera Murdock, Chairperson/Professor, 816-235-1318, Fax: 816-235-1062, E-mail: murdockt@umkc.edu. *Application contact:* Dr. Lisa Terre, Director, Graduate Programs, 816-235-1318, Fax: 816-235-1062, E-mail: terrel@umkc.edu.

University of Missouri–St. Louis, College of Arts and Sciences, Department of Psychology, St. Louis, MO 63121. Offers behavioral neuroscience (PhD); clinical psychology respecialization (Certificate); community psychology (PhD); general psychology (MA); industrial/organizational psychology (PhD). *Accreditation:* APA (one or more programs are accredited). Evening/weekend programs available. *Faculty:* 21 full-time (10 women), 5 part-time/adjunct (3 women). *Students:* 35 full-time (29 women), 39 part-time (30 women); includes 4 minority (1 American Indian/Alaska Native, 1 Asian American or Pacific Islander, 2 Hispanic Americans). Average age 28. 208 applicants, 9% accepted, 13 enrolled. In 2009, 16 master's, 6 doctorates awarded. Terminal master's awarded for partial completion of doctoral program. *Degree requirements:* For master's, thesis; for doctorate, thesis/dissertation. *Entrance requirements:* For master's and doctorate, GRE General Test, GRE Subject Test, 3 letters of recommendation. Additional exam requirements/recommendations for international students: Required—TOEFL (minimum score 550 paper-based; 213 computer-based). *Application deadline:* For fall admission, 1/15 for domestic and international students. Application fee: $35 ($40 for international students). Electronic applications accepted. *Expenses:* Tuition, state resident: full-time $5377; part-time $297.70 per credit hour. Tuition, nonresident: full-time $13,882; part-time $771.20 per credit hour. Required fees: $220; $12.20 per credit hour. One-time fee: $12. Tuition and fees vary according to course level, campus/location and program. *Financial support:* In 2009–10, 7 research assistantships with full and partial tuition reimbursements (averaging $10,600 per year), 20 teaching assistantships with full and partial tuition reimbursements (averaging $9,788 per year) were awarded; fellowships with full tuition reimbursements also available. Financial award applicants required to submit FAFSA. *Faculty research:* Bereavement and loss, neuroscience, post-traumatic stress disorder, conflict and negotiation, social psychology. *Unit head:* Dr. George Taylor, Chair, 314-516-5391, Fax: 314-516-5392, E-mail: umslpsychology@msx.umsl.edu. *Application contact:* 314-516-5458, Fax: 314-516-6996, E-mail: gradadm@umsl.edu.

University of Missouri–St. Louis, College of Education, Division of Counseling, St. Louis, MO 63121. Offers community counseling (M Ed); elementary school counseling (M Ed); secondary school counseling (M Ed). *Accreditation:* ACA; NCATE. Part-time and evening/weekend programs available. *Faculty:* 7 full-time (3 women), 11 part-time/adjunct (7 women). *Students:* 57 full-time (47 women), 152 part-time (128 women); includes 33 minority (27 African Americans, 1 American Indian/Alaska Native, 2 Asian Americans or Pacific Islanders, 3 Hispanic Americans), 8 international. Average age 31. 92 applicants, 59% accepted, 34 enrolled. In 2009, 63 master's awarded. *Degree requirements:* For master's, comprehensive exam. *Entrance requirements:* For master's, 3 letters of recommendation. Additional exam requirements/recommendations for international students: Required—TOEFL (minimum score 550 paper-based; 213 computer-based). *Application deadline:* For fall admission, 6/1 for domestic and international students; for spring admission, 10/1 for domestic and international students. Application fee: $35 ($40 for international students). Electronic applications accepted. *Expenses:* Tuition, state resident: full-time $5377; part-time $297.70 per credit hour. Tuition, nonresident: full-time $13,882; part-time $771.20 per credit hour. Required fees: $220; $12.20 per credit hour. One-time fee: $12. Tuition and fees vary according to course level, campus/location and program. *Financial support:* Application deadline: 4/1. *Faculty research:* Vocational interests, self-concept, decision-making factors, developmental differences. *Unit head:* Dr. Mark Pope, Chair, 314-516-5782. *Application contact:* 314-516-5458, Fax: 314-516-6996, E-mail: gradadm@umsl.edu.

University of Montevallo, College of Education, Program in Counseling, Montevallo, AL 35115. Offers community counseling (M Ed); marriage and family (M Ed); school counseling (M Ed). *Accreditation:* ACA; NCATE. Part-time and evening/weekend programs available. *Students:* 36 full-time (32 women), 46 part-time (41 women); includes 14 minority (12 African Americans, 1 Asian American or Pacific Islander, 1 Hispanic American), 2 international. In 2009, 14 master's awarded. *Entrance requirements:* For master's, GRE General Test or MAT, minimum undergraduate GPA of 2.75 in last 60 hours or 2.5 overall, interview. Additional exam requirements/recommendations for international students: Required—TOEFL (minimum score 550 paper-based). *Application deadline:* For fall admission, 7/15 for domestic students; for spring admission, 11/15 for domestic students. Application fee: $25. *Expenses:* Tuition, state resident: full-time $5592; part-time $233 per credit. Tuition, nonresident: full-time $11,184; part-time $466 per credit hour. Required fees: $482; $241 per semester. One-time fee: $25 part-time. *Financial support:* Federal Work-Study, scholarships/grants, and unspecified assistantships available. *Unit head:* Dr. Leland Doebler, Chair, 205-665-6380. *Application contact:* Dr. Leland Doebler, Chair, 205-665-6380.

University of Nebraska–Lincoln, Graduate College, College of Arts and Sciences, Department of Psychology, Lincoln, NE 68588. Offers biopsychology (PhD); clinical psychology (PhD); cognitive psychology (PhD); developmental psychology (PhD); psychology (MA); social/personality psychology (PhD); JD/MA; JD/PhD. *Accreditation:* APA (one or more programs are accredited). *Degree requirements:* For master's, thesis optional; for doctorate, comprehensive exam, thesis/dissertation. *Entrance requirements:* For master's and doctorate, GRE General Test. Additional exam requirements/recommendations for international students: Required—TOEFL (minimum score 550 paper-based; 213 computer-based). Electronic applications accepted. *Faculty research:* Law and psychology, rural mental health, chronic mental illness, neuropsychology, child clinical psychology.

University of Nevada, Reno, Graduate School, Interdisciplinary Program in Social Psychology, Reno, NV 89557. Offers PhD. *Degree requirements:* For doctorate, one foreign language, thesis/dissertation. *Entrance requirements:* For doctorate, GRE General Test, GRE Subject Test (psychology or sociology), minimum GPA of 3.0. Additional exam requirements/recommendations for international students: Required—TOEFL (minimum score 500 paper-based; 173 computer-based; 61 iBT), IELTS (minimum score 6). Electronic applications accepted. *Faculty research:* Social psychological theory, social psychology of law.

University of New Haven, Graduate School, College of Arts and Sciences, Program in Community Psychology, West Haven, CT 06516-1916. Offers applications of psychology (Certificate); community clinical services (MA); forensic psychology (Certificate). Part-time and evening/weekend programs available. *Faculty:* 9 full-time (3 women), 12 part-time/adjunct (6 women). *Students:* 33 full-time (29 women), 15 part-time (11 women); includes 10 minority (8 African Americans, 2 Hispanic Americans), 4 international. Average age 27. 54 applicants, 72% accepted, 17 enrolled. In 2009, 9 master's, 2 other advanced degrees awarded. *Degree requirements:* For master's, thesis or alternative. *Entrance requirements:* Additional exam requirements/recommendations for international students: Required—TOEFL (minimum score 520 paper-based; 190 computer-based; 70 iBT); Recommended—IELTS (minimum score 5.5). *Application deadline:* For fall admission, 5/31 for international students; for winter admission, 10/15 for international students; for spring admission, 1/15 for international students. Applications are processed on a rolling basis. Application fee: $50. Electronic applications accepted. *Expenses:* Tuition: Part-time $700 per credit. Required fees: $45 per term. One-time fee: $390 part-time. *Financial support:* Research assistantships with partial tuition reimbursements, teaching assistantships with partial tuition reimbursements, career-related internships or fieldwork, Federal Work-Study, scholarships/grants, tuition waivers, and unspecified assistantships available. Support available to part-time students. Financial award application deadline: 5/1; financial award applicants required to submit FAFSA. *Unit head:* Dr. Michael A. Morris, Coordinator, 203-932-7281. *Application contact:* Eloise Gormley, Director of Graduate Admissions, 203-932-7449, Fax: 203-932-7137, E-mail: gradinfo@newhaven.edu.

The University of North Carolina at Chapel Hill, Graduate School, College of Arts and Sciences, Department of Psychology, Chapel Hill, NC 27599. Offers biological psychology (PhD); clinical psychology (PhD); cognitive psychology (PhD); developmental psychology (PhD); quantitative psychology (PhD); social psychology (PhD). *Accreditation:* APA. *Degree requirements:* For doctorate, comprehensive exam, thesis/dissertation. *Entrance requirements:* For doctorate, GRE General Test, minimum GPA of 3.0. Electronic applications accepted. *Faculty research:* Expressed emotion, cognitive development, social cognitive neuroscience, human memory personality.

The University of North Carolina at Charlotte, Graduate School, College of Arts and Sciences, Department of Psychology, Program in Community/Clinical Psychology, Charlotte, NC 28223-0001. Offers MA. Part-time programs available. *Faculty:* 10 full-time (3 women), 5 part-time/adjunct (2 women). *Students:* 8 full-time (all women), 8 part-time (7 women); includes 4 minority (3 African Americans, 1 Hispanic American). Average age 26. 143 applicants, 4% accepted, 5 enrolled. In 2009, 10 master's awarded. Terminal master's awarded for partial completion of doctoral program. *Degree requirements:* For master's, comprehensive exam, thesis. *Entrance requirements:* For master's, GRE General Test, GRE Subject Test, minimum GPA of 3.0 in undergraduate major, 2.8 overall. Additional exam requirements/recommendations for international students: Required—TOEFL (minimum score 557 paper-based; 220 computer-based; 83 iBT). *Application deadline:* For fall admission, 3/1 for domestic and international students. Application fee: $55. Electronic applications accepted. *Financial support:* In 2009–10, 6 students received support, including 5 teaching assistantships (averaging $10,755 per year); career-related internships or fieldwork, Federal Work-Study, institutionally sponsored loans, scholarships/grants, and administrative assistantship also available. Support available to part-time students. Financial award application deadline: 4/1; financial award applicants required to submit FAFSA. *Faculty research:* Identifying biopsychosocial risk and resilience factors, development of community based support for youth, pain and emotion, posttraumatic disorders, relationships in online groups. Total annual research expenditures: $476,892. *Unit head:* Dr. David Gilmore, Interim Chair, 704-687-4731, Fax: 704-687-3096, E-mail: dcgilmor@uncc.edu. *Application contact:* Kathy B. Giddings, Director of Graduate Admissions, 704-687-5503, Fax: 704-687-3279, E-mail: gradadm@uncc.edu.

The University of North Carolina at Greensboro, Graduate School, College of Arts and Sciences, Department of Psychology, Greensboro, NC 27412-5001. Offers clinical psychology (MA, PhD); cognitive psychology (MA, PhD); developmental psychology (MA, PhD); social psychology (MA, PhD). *Accreditation:* APA (one or more programs are accredited). Terminal master's awarded for partial completion of doctoral program. *Degree requirements:* For master's, comprehensive exam, thesis; for doctorate, one foreign language, thesis/dissertation, preliminary exam. *Entrance requirements:* For master's and doctorate, GRE General Test. Additional exam requirements/recommendations for international students: Required—TOEFL. Electronic applications accepted. *Faculty research:* Sensory and perceptual determinants; evoked potential: disorders, deafness, and development.

University of Oklahoma, Graduate College, College of Education, Department of Educational Psychology, Program in Community Counseling, Norman, OK 73019. Offers M Ed. *Students:* 24 full-time (21 women), 2 part-time (1 woman); includes 6 minority (1 African American, 1 American Indian/Alaska Native, 2 Asian Americans or Pacific Islanders, 2 Hispanic Americans). 1 applicant, 0% accepted, 0 enrolled. In 2009, 22 master's awarded. Terminal master's awarded for partial completion of doctoral program. *Degree requirements:* For master's, comprehensive exam. *Entrance requirements:* For master's, GRE General Test, minimum GPA of 3.0. Additional exam requirements/recommendations for international students: Required—TOEFL (minimum score 550 paper-based; 213 computer-based). *Application deadline:* For fall admission, 1/31 for domestic students, 4/1 for international students; for spring admission, 11/1 for domestic students, 9/1 for international students. Applications are processed on a rolling basis. Application fee: $40 ($90 for international students). Electronic applications accepted. *Expenses:* Tuition, state resident: full-time $3744; part-time $156 per credit hour. Tuition, nonresident: full-time $13,577; part-time $565.70 per credit hour. Required fees: $2415; $90.10 per credit hour. *Financial support:* In 2009–10, 16 students received support. Career-related internships or fieldwork, Federal Work-Study, institutionally sponsored loans, scholarships/grants, health care benefits, and unspecified assistantships available. Support available to part-time students. Financial award application deadline: 3/1; financial award applicants required to submit FAFSA. *Faculty research:* Marriage and family; counseling assessment; process and outcome; diversity issues; health psychology; education, training and supervision. *Unit head:* Dr. Terri K. Debacker, Chair, 405-325-1068, Fax: 405-325-6655, E-mail: debacker@ou.edu. *Application contact:* Rashida Y. Douglas, Graduate Programs Officer, 405-325-4525, Fax: 405-325-6655, E-mail: ryd618@ou.edu.

University of Oregon, Graduate School, College of Arts and Sciences, Department of Psychology, Eugene, OR 97403. Offers clinical psychology (PhD); cognitive psychology (MA, MS, PhD); developmental psychology (MA, MS, PhD); physiological psychology (MA, MS, PhD); psychology (MA, MS, PhD); social/personality psychology (MA, MS, PhD). *Accreditation:* APA (one or more programs are accredited). Terminal master's awarded for partial completion of doctoral program. *Degree requirements:* For doctorate, thesis/dissertation. *Entrance requirements:* For master's, GRE General Test, minimum GPA of 3.0; for doctorate, GRE General Test. Additional exam requirements/recommendations for international students: Required—TOEFL.

University of Phoenix, The Artemis School, College of Health and Human Services, Phoenix, AZ 85034-7209. Offers administration of justice and security (MS); community counseling (MSC); education (MHA); family nurse practitioner (MSN); gerontology (MHA); health administration (MHA); health care education (MSN); health care management (MBA, MSN); informatics (MHA); marriage, family, and child therapy (MSC); nursing (MSN); nursing for nurse practitioners (MSN); psychology (MS); MSN/MBA; MSN/MHA. *Accreditation:* AACN. Evening/weekend programs available. Postbaccalaureate distance learning degree programs offered. *Degree requirements:* For master's, thesis (for some programs). *Entrance requirements:* For master's, 3 years of work experience, minimum undergraduate GPA of 2.5, RN license. Additional exam requirements/recommendations for international students: Required—TOEFL (minimum score 550 paper-based; 213 computer-based; 79 iBT). Electronic applications accepted.

University of Phoenix–Denver Campus, The Artemis School, College of Health and Human Services, Lone Tree, CO 80124-5453. Offers administration of justice and security (MS); community counseling (MSC); health administration (MHA); health care management (MBA); marriage, family and child therapy (MSC); nursing (MSN); psychology (MS); MSN/MBA; MSN/MHA. Evening/weekend programs available. Postbaccalaureate distance learning degree programs offered. *Degree requirements:* For master's, thesis (for some programs). *Entrance requirements:* For master's, minimum undergraduate GPA of 2.5, 3 years work experience, RN license. Additional exam requirements/recommendations for international students: Required—TOEFL (minimum score 550 paper-based; 213 computer-based; 79 iBT). Electronic applications accepted.

University of Phoenix–Hawaii Campus, The Artemis School, College of Health and Human Services, Honolulu, HI 96813-4317. Offers administration of justice and security (MS); community counseling (MSC); education (MHA); family nurse practitioner (MSN); gerontology (MHA); health administration (MHA); health care management (MBA); marriage, family and child therapy (MSC); nursing (MSN); nursing/health care education (MSN); psychology (MS); MSN/MBA. Evening/weekend programs available. *Degree requirements:* For master's, thesis (for some programs). *Entrance requirements:* For master's, minimum undergraduate GPA of 2.5, 3 years of work experience, RN license. Additional exam requirements/recommendations for international students: Required—TOEFL (minimum score 550 paper-based; 213 computer-based; 79 iBT). Electronic applications accepted.

University of Phoenix–Kansas City Campus, The Artemis School, College of Health and Human Services, Kansas City, MO 64131-4517. Offers administration of justice and security (MS); community counseling (MSC); health administration (MHA); health care management (MBA); nursing (MSN); MSN/MBA. Evening/weekend programs available. Postbaccalaureate distance learning degree programs offered. *Degree requirements:* For master's, thesis (for some programs). *Entrance requirements:* For master's, 3 years work experience, minimum undergraduate GPA of 2.5. Additional exam requirements/recommendations for international students: Required—TOEFL (minimum score 550 paper-based; 213 computer-based).

University of Phoenix–Minneapolis/St. Louis Park Campus, College of Health and Human Services, St. Louis Park, MN 55426. Offers community counseling (MSC); family nurse practitioner (MSN); health care education (MSN); health care management (MBA); nursing (MSN).

University of Phoenix–Phoenix Campus, The Artemis School, College of Health and Human Services, Phoenix, AZ 85040-1958. Offers community counseling (MSC); education (MHA); family nurse practitioner (MSN); gerontology (MHA); health administration (MHA); health care education (MSN); health care management (MBA); informatics (MHA); marriage, family, and child therapy (MSC); nurse practitioner (Certificate); nursing (MSN); nursing health care education (Certificate); psychology (MS); MSN/MBA; MSN/MHA. Evening/weekend programs available. *Degree requirements:* For master's, thesis (for some programs). *Entrance requirements:* For master's, 3 years of work experience in field, minimum undergraduate GPA of 2.5, RN license. Additional exam requirements/recommendations for international students: Required—TOEFL (minimum score 550 paper-based; 213 computer-based; 79 iBT). Electronic applications accepted.

University of Phoenix–Southern Colorado Campus, The Artemis School, College of Health and Human Services, Colorado Springs, CO 80919-2335. Offers administration of justice and security (MS); community counseling (MSC); education (MHA); gerontology (MHA); health administration (MHA); health care management (MBA); marriage, family and child therapy (MSC); nursing (MSN); psychology (MS); MSN/MBA. Evening/weekend programs available. *Degree requirements:* For master's, thesis (for some programs). *Entrance requirements:* For master's, minimum undergraduate GPA of 2.5, 3 years of work experience, RN license. Additional exam requirements/recommendations for international students: Required—TOEFL (minimum score 550 paper-based; 213 computer-based; 79 iBT). Electronic applications accepted.

University of Puerto Rico, Río Piedras, College of Social Sciences, Department of Psychology, San Juan, PR 00931-3300. Offers clinical psychology (MA); industrial organizational psychology (MA); investigative academic psychology (MA); psychology (PhD); social-community psychology (MA). Part-time programs available. *Degree requirements:* For master's, comprehensive exam, thesis; for doctorate, comprehensive exam, thesis/dissertation, internship. *Entrance requirements:* For master's, GRE or PAEG, interview, minimum GPA of 3.0; for doctorate, GRE or PAEG, interview, master's degree, minimum GPA of 3.0. *Faculty research:* Intervention on Depressed Latino Youth, biosychosocial training.

University of Rochester, The College, Arts and Sciences, Department of Clinical and Social Sciences in Psychology, Rochester, NY 14627. Offers clinical psychology (PhD); developmental psychology (PhD); psychology (MA); social-personality psychology (PhD). *Accreditation:* APA (one or more programs are accredited). Terminal master's awarded for partial completion of doctoral program. *Degree requirements:* For doctorate, thesis/dissertation, qualifying exam. *Entrance requirements:* For doctorate, GRE General Test. Additional exam requirements/recommendations for international students: Required—TOEFL.

The University of Scranton, College of Graduate and Continuing Education, Department of Counseling and Human Services, Program in Community Counseling, Scranton, PA 18510. Offers MS. *Accreditation:* ACA. Part-time and evening/weekend programs available. *Students:* 47 full-time (36 women), 6 part-time (all women); includes 5 minority (3 African Americans, 1 Asian American or Pacific Islander, 1 Hispanic American). Average age 31. 43 applicants, 67% accepted. In 2009, 8 master's awarded. *Degree requirements:* For master's, comprehensive exam, capstone experience. *Entrance requirements:* For master's, minimum GPA of 2.75. Additional exam requirements/recommendations for international students: Required—TOEFL (minimum score 500 paper-based; 173 computer-based), IELTS (minimum score 5.5). *Application deadline:* For fall admission, 3/1 for domestic students. Application fee: $0. *Financial support:* Teaching assistantships, career-related internships or fieldwork and Federal Work-Study available. Support available to part-time students. Financial award application deadline: 3/1. *Unit head:* Dr. Oliver J. Morgan, Program Director, 570-941-6171, Fax: 570-941-5882, E-mail: morgano1@scranton.edu. *Application contact:* Joseph M. Roback, Director of Admissions, 570-941-4385, Fax: 570-941-5928, E-mail: roback j2@scranton.edu.

University of South Carolina, The Graduate School, College of Arts and Sciences, Department of Psychology, Program in Clinical/Community Psychology, Columbia, SC 29208. Offers clinical/community psychology (PhD); general psychology (MA). *Accreditation:* APA. *Degree requirements:* For master's, comprehensive exam, thesis; for doctorate, comprehensive exam, thesis/dissertation. *Entrance requirements:* For doctorate, GRE General Test, minimum GPA of 3.2. Additional exam requirements/recommendations for international students: Required—TOEFL. Electronic applications accepted. *Faculty research:* Developmental psychopathology, health disparities, community-level interventions for psychological well being.

University of Southern California, Graduate School, College of Letters, Arts and Sciences, Department of Psychology, Los Angeles, CA 90089. Offers brain and cognitive science (PhD); clinical science (PhD); developmental psychology (PhD); human behavior (MHB); psychology (MA); quantitative methods (PhD); social psychology (PhD); PhD/MPH. *Accreditation:* APA. *Faculty:* 34 full-time (10 women), 17 part-time/adjunct (7 women). *Students:* 107 full-time (73 women); includes 38 minority (6 African Americans, 21 Asian Americans or Pacific Islanders, 11 Hispanic Americans), 19 international. 430 applicants, 6% accepted, 13 enrolled. In 2009, 17 master's, 12 doctorates awarded. *Degree requirements:* For doctorate, comprehensive exam, thesis/dissertation, one-year internship (for clinical science students). *Entrance requirements:* For doctorate, GRE. Additional exam requirements/recommendations for international students: Recommended—TOEFL (minimum score 600 paper-based; 250 computer-based; 100 iBT). *Application deadline:* For fall admission, 12/1 for domestic and international students. Application fee: $95. Electronic applications accepted. *Expenses:* Tuition: Full-time $25,980; part-time $1315 per unit. Required fees: $554. One-time fee: $35 full-time. Full-time tuition and fees vary according to degree level and program. *Financial support:* In 2009–10, 80 students received support, including 16 fellowships with full tuition reimbursements available (averaging $22,500 per year), 22 research assistantships with full tuition reimbursements available (averaging $19,000 per year), 38 teaching assistantships with full tuition reimbursements available (averaging $19,000 per year); career-related internships or fieldwork, scholarships/grants, traineeships, and health care benefits also available. *Faculty research:* Affective neuroscience; children and families; vision, culture and ethnicity; intergroup relations; aggression and violence; language and reading development; substance abuse. *Unit head:* Dr. Margaret Gatz, Chair and Professor, 213-740-2203, Fax: 213-746-9028, E-mail: gatz@usc.edu. *Application contact:* Irene Takaragawa, Graduate Advisor, 213-740-2205, E-mail: itakarag@usc.edu.

The University of Tennessee at Chattanooga, Graduate School, College of Health, Education and Professional Studies, Graduate Studies Division of Education, Program in Counseling, Chattanooga, TN 37403. Offers community counseling (M Ed); school counseling (M Ed). *Faculty:* 3 full-time (all women). *Students:* 26 full-time (24 women), 29 part-time (25 women); includes 13 minority (11 African Americans, 2 Hispanic Americans). Average age 29. 36 applicants, 69% accepted, 13 enrolled. In 2009, 10 master's awarded. *Degree requirements:* For master's, comprehensive exam. *Entrance requirements:* For master's, MAT or GRE. Additional exam requirements/recommendations for international students: Required—TOEFL (minimum score 550 paper-based; 213 computer-based; 79 iBT), IELTS (minimum score 6). *Application deadline:* For fall admission, 8/1 for domestic students, 6/1 for international students; for spring admission, 12/1 for domestic students, 10/1 for international students. Applications are processed on a rolling basis. Application fee: $35. Electronic applications accepted. *Expenses:* Tuition, state resident: full-time $5404; part-time $300 per credit hour. Tuition, nonresident: full-time $16,702; part-time $928 per credit hour. Required fees: $1150; $130 per credit hour. *Financial support:* In 2009–10, 4 research assistantships with full and partial tuition reimbursements (averaging $5,500 per year) were awarded; career-related internships or fieldwork, scholarships/grants, and unspecified assistantships also available. Support available to part-time students. *Faculty research:* Play therapy; clinical supervision; technology in marital infidelity; female inmates and recidivism; grief, loss and trauma in children. *Unit head:* Dr. John Freeman, Head, 423-425-4133, Fax: 423-425-5380, E-mail: john-freeman@utc.edu. *Application contact:* Dr. Stephanie Bellar, Dean of Graduate Studies, 423-425-4666, Fax: 423-425-5223, E-mail: stephanie-bellar@utc.edu.

The University of Tennessee at Martin, Graduate Programs, College of Education and Behavioral Sciences, Program in Counseling, Martin, TN 38238. Offers community counseling (MS Ed); school counseling (MS Ed). *Accreditation:* NCATE. Part-time programs available. Postbaccalaureate distance learning degree programs offered. *Students:* 53 (47 women). 57 applicants, 47% accepted, 20 enrolled. In 2009, 16 master's awarded. *Degree requirements:* For master's, comprehensive exam. *Entrance requirements:* For master's, GRE General Test, minimum GPA of 2.5, resume, letters of reference. Additional exam requirements/recommendations for international students: Required—TOEFL (minimum score 525 paper-based; 197 computer-based; 71 iBT). *Application deadline:* For fall admission, 8/1 priority date

Social Psychology

The University of Tennessee at Martin (continued)

for domestic students, 7/15 priority date for international students; for spring admission, 12/15 priority date for domestic students, 12/1 priority date for international students. Applications are processed on a rolling basis. Application fee: $30 ($130 for international students). Electronic applications accepted. *Expenses:* Tuition, state resident: full-time $6660; part-time $372 per hour. Tuition, nonresident: full-time $18,000; part-time $1005 per hour. *Financial support:* Scholarships/grants and unspecified assistantships available. Support available to part-time students. Financial award application deadline: 2/15; financial award applicants required to submit FAFSA. *Unit head:* Staci H. Fuqua, Staff Assistant, 731-881-7163, Fax: 731-881-7975, E-mail: sfuqua@utm.edu. *Application contact:* Linda S. Arant, Student Services Specialist, 731-881-7012, Fax: 731-881-7499, E-mail: larant@utm.edu.

The University of Toledo, College of Graduate Studies, College of Arts and Sciences, Department of Psychology, Toledo, OH 43606-3390. Offers behavioral (PhD), including cognitive, psychobiology and learning, social; clinical psychology (PhD); experimental psychology (MA). *Accreditation:* APA. *Degree requirements:* For master's, thesis; for doctorate, one foreign language, thesis/dissertation. *Entrance requirements:* For master's and doctorate, GRE General Test, GRE Subject Test. *Faculty research:* Neural taste response.

The University of Toledo, College of Graduate Studies, College of Health Science and Human Service, Division of Human Services, Department of Counselor Education and School Psychology, Program in Counselor Education, Toledo, OH 43606-3390. Offers community counseling (MA); counselor education (Ed S); counselor education and supervision (PhD).

University of Victoria, Faculty of Graduate Studies, Faculty of Education, Department of Educational Psychology and Leadership Studies, Victoria, BC V8W 2Y2, Canada. Offers aboriginal communities counseling (M Ed); counseling (M Ed, MA); educational psychology (M Ed, MA, PhD), including counseling psychology (M Ed, MA), leadership studies (PhD), learning and development (MA, PhD), measurement and evaluation, special education (M Ed, MA); leadership studies (M Ed, MA). Part-time programs available. *Degree requirements:* For master's, thesis (for some programs), comprehensive exam (M Ed); for doctorate, comprehensive exam, thesis/dissertation, candidacy exam. *Entrance requirements:* For master's, 2 years of work experience in a relevant field; for doctorate, GRE, 2 years of work experience in a relevant field, minimum B average. Additional exam requirements/recommendations for international students: Required—TOEFL (minimum score 575 paper-based; 233 computer-based), IELTS (minimum score 7). *Faculty research:* Learning and development (child, adolescent and adult), special education and exceptional children.

University of Victoria, Faculty of Graduate Studies, Faculty of Social Sciences, Department of Psychology, Victoria, BC V8W 2Y2, Canada. Offers clinical psychology (PhD); clinical psychology (neuropsychology) (M Sc); cognition and brain science (M Sc, PhD); experimental neuropsychology (M Sc, PhD); individualized study (M Sc, PhD); life span development psychology (PhD); life span developmental psychology (M Sc); social psychology (M Sc, PhD). *Accreditation:* APA (one or more programs are accredited). *Degree requirements:* For master's, thesis; for doctorate, thesis/dissertation, candidacy exam. *Entrance requirements:* For master's and doctorate, GRE General Test. Additional exam requirements/recommendations for international students: Required—TOEFL (minimum score 600 paper-based; 250 computer-based). Electronic applications accepted. *Faculty research:* Life span development psychology and aging, behavioral neuroscience, cognitive psychology, behavioral psychology, environmental psychology.

University of Washington, Graduate School, College of Arts and Sciences, Department of Psychology, Seattle, WA 98195. Offers animal behavior (PhD); child psychology (PhD); clinical psychology (PhD); cognition and perception (PhD); developmental psychology (PhD); quantitative psychology (PhD); social psychology and personality (PhD). *Accreditation:* APA. *Degree requirements:* For doctorate, thesis/dissertation. *Entrance requirements:* For doctorate, GRE General Test, minimum GPA of 3.0. Electronic applications accepted. *Faculty research:* Addictive behaviors, artificial intelligence, child psychopathology, mechanisms and development of vision, physiology of ingestive behaviors.

University of Windsor, Faculty of Graduate Studies, Faculty of Arts and Social Sciences, Department of Psychology, Windsor, ON N9B 3P4, Canada. Offers adult clinical (MA, PhD); applied social psychology (MA, PhD); child clinical (MA, PhD); clinical neuropsychology (MA, PhD). *Accreditation:* APA (one or more programs are accredited). *Degree requirements:* For master's, thesis; for doctorate, comprehensive exam, thesis/dissertation. *Entrance requirements:* For master's, GRE General Test, GRE Subject Test in psychology, minimum B average; for doctorate, GRE General Test, GRE Subject Test in psychology, master's degree. Additional exam requirements/recommendations for international students: Required—TOEFL (minimum score 600 paper-based; 250 computer-based). Electronic applications accepted. *Faculty research:* Gambling, suicidology, emotional competence, psychotherapy and trauma.

University of Wisconsin–Madison, Graduate School, College of Letters and Science, Department of Psychology, Program in Social and Personality Psychology, Madison, WI 53706-1380. Offers PhD. *Degree requirements:* For doctorate, comprehensive exam, thesis/dissertation. *Entrance requirements:* For doctorate, GRE General Test, minimum undergraduate GPA of 3.0. Additional exam requirements/recommendations for international students: Required—TOEFL. Electronic applications accepted. *Expenses:* Tuition, state resident: part-time $594 per credit. Tuition, nonresident: part-time $1504 per credit. Required fees: $65 per credit. Tuition and fees vary according to course load, program and reciprocity agreements.

University of Wisconsin–Milwaukee, Graduate School, School of Education, Department of Educational Psychology, Milwaukee, WI 53201-0413. Offers counseling (school, community) (MS); counseling psychology (PhD); learning and development (MS); research methodology (MS, PhD); school psychology (PhD). *Accreditation:* APA. Part-time programs available. *Faculty:* 22 full-time (14 women). *Students:* 124 full-time (107 women), 47 part-time (35 women); includes 20 minority (10 African Americans, 4 Asian Americans or Pacific Islanders, 6 Hispanic Americans), 2 international. Average age 30. 263 applicants, 52% accepted, 51 enrolled. In 2009, 55 master's, 13 doctorates awarded. *Degree requirements:* For master's, comprehensive exam, thesis; for doctorate, thesis/dissertation. *Entrance requirements:* For master's, minimum GPA of 3.0; for doctorate, GRE General Test, minimum GPA of 3.0. Additional exam requirements/recommendations for international students: Required—TOEFL (minimum score 550 paper-based; 79 iBT), IELTS (minimum score 6.5). *Application deadline:* For fall admission, 1/1 priority date for domestic students; for spring admission, 9/1 for domestic students. Applications are processed on a rolling basis. Application fee: $45 ($75 for international students). *Expenses:* Tuition, state resident: full-time $8800. Tuition, nonresident: full-time $20,760. Tuition and fees vary according to program and reciprocity agreements. *Financial support:* In 2009–10, 9 teaching assistantships were awarded; career-related internships or fieldwork and unspecified assistantships also available. Support available to part-time students. Financial award application deadline: 4/15. Total annual research expenditures: $1.3 million. *Unit head:* Bo Zhang, Graduate Program Representative, 414-229-5742, Fax: 414-229-4939, E-mail: boz@uwm.edu. *Application contact:* General Information Contact, 414-229-4982, Fax: 414-229-6967, E-mail: gradschool@uwm.edu.

University of Wisconsin–Superior, Graduate Division, Department of Counseling and Psychological Professions, Superior, WI 54880-4500. Offers community counseling (MSE); human relations (MSE); school counseling (MSE). Part-time and evening/weekend programs available. *Faculty:* 3 full-time (1 woman), 4 part-time/adjunct (all women). *Students:* 34 full-time (23 women), 69 part-time (51 women); includes 10 minority (4 African Americans, 4 American Indian/Alaska Native, 2 Asian Americans or Pacific Islanders), 3 international. Average age 27. 19 applicants, 100% accepted. In 2009, 24 master's awarded. *Degree requirements:* For master's, position paper, practicum. *Entrance requirements:* For master's, GRE and/or MAT, minimum GPA of 2.75. *Application deadline:* For fall admission, 4/1 priority date for domestic students; for spring admission, 10/15 priority date for domestic students. Applications are processed on a rolling basis. Application fee: $45. Electronic applications accepted. *Financial support:* In 2009–10, 10 fellowships with partial tuition reimbursements (averaging $6,500 per year), 2 research assistantships with partial tuition reimbursements (averaging $5,000 per year) were awarded; career-related internships or fieldwork, Federal Work-Study, institutionally sponsored loans, scholarships/grants, traineeships, and tuition waivers (partial) also available. Support available to part-time students. Financial award application deadline: 4/15; financial award applicants required to submit FAFSA. *Faculty research:* Women and power, intrafamily dynamics. *Unit head:* Terri Kronzer, Chairperson, 715-394-8506. *Application contact:* Sandy Wallgren, Program Assistant/Status Examiner, 715-394-8295, Fax: 715-394-8146, E-mail: gradstudy@uwsuper.edu.

University of Wisconsin–Whitewater, School of Graduate Studies, College of Education, Department of Counselor Education, Whitewater, WI 53190-1790. Offers community counseling (MS Ed); higher education (MS Ed); school counseling (MS Ed). *Accreditation:* ACA; NCATE. Part-time and evening/weekend programs available. *Degree requirements:* For master's, thesis or alternative. *Entrance requirements:* For master's, resume, 2 letters of reference. Additional exam requirements/recommendations for international students: Required—TOEFL (minimum score 550 paper-based; 213 computer-based). Electronic applications accepted. *Faculty research:* Alcohol and other drugs, counseling effectiveness, teacher mentoring.

Walden University, Graduate Programs, School of Psychology, Minneapolis, MN 55401. Offers clinical child psychology (Post-Doctoral Certificate); clinical psychology (Post-Doctoral Certificate); counseling psychology (Post-Doctoral Certificate); forensic psychology (MS), including forensic psychology in the community, general program, mental health applications, program planning and evaluation in forensic settings, psychology and legal systems; general psychology (Post-Doctoral Certificate); health psychology (Post-Doctoral Certificate); organizational psychology (Post-Doctoral Certificate); organizational psychology and development (Postbaccalaureate Certificate); psychology (MS, PhD), including clinical psychology (PhD), counseling psychology (PhD), crisis management and response (MS), general program (MS), general psychology (PhD), health psychology, leadership development and coaching (MS), media psychology (MS), organizational psychology (PhD), organizational psychology and development (MS), organizational psychology and nonprofit management (MS), program evaluation and research (MS), psychology of culture (MS), psychology, public administration, and social change (MS), social psychology (MS), terrorism and security (MS); teaching online (Post-Master's Certificate). Part-time and evening/weekend programs available. Postbaccalaureate distance learning degree programs offered (minimal on-campus study). *Faculty:* 33 full-time, 222 part-time/adjunct. *Students:* 3,546 full-time (2,761 women), 1,133 part-time (908 women); includes 1,723 minority (1,319 African Americans, 56 American Indian/Alaska Native, 101 Asian Americans or Pacific Islanders, 247 Hispanic Americans), 80 international. Average age 41. In 2009, 495 master's, 70 doctorates, 2 other advanced degrees awarded. Terminal master's awarded for partial completion of doctoral program. *Degree requirements:* For master's, thesis optional; for doctorate, thesis/dissertation, residency. *Entrance requirements:* For master's, bachelor's degree or equivalent in related field; minimum GPA of 2.5; official transcripts; goal statement; access to computer and Internet; for doctorate, master's degree or equivalent in related field; minimum GPA of 3.0;3 years of related professional/academic experience (preferred). Additional exam requirements/recommendations for international students: Required—TOEFL (minimum score 550 paper-based; 213 computer-based), IELTS (minimum score 6.5), or Michigan English Language Assessment Battery (minimum score 82). *Application deadline:* Applications are processed on a rolling basis. Application fee: $50. Electronic applications accepted. *Expenses:* Tuition: Full-time $13,665; part-time $560 per credit. Required fees: $1375. Tuition and fees vary according to course load, degree level and program. *Financial support:* In 2009–10, 290 students received support; fellowships, Federal Work-Study, scholarships/grants, unspecified assistantships, and family tuition reduction, active duty/veteran tuition reduction, group tuition reduction, interest-free payment plans available. Support available to part-time students. Financial award applicants required to submit FAFSA. *Unit head:* Dr. Melanie Storms, Associate Dean, 800-925-3368. *Application contact:* Jennifer Hall, Director of Enrollment, 866-4-WALDEN, E-mail: info@waldenu.edu.

Washington State University, Graduate School, College of Liberal Arts, Department of Sociology, Pullman, WA 99164. Offers crime and deviance (MA, PhD); environments, community and demographics (MA, PhD); institutions and social organizations (MA, PhD); political sociology (MA, PhD); social inequality (MA, PhD); social psychology and life course (MA, PhD). Terminal master's awarded for partial completion of doctoral program. *Degree requirements:* For master's, thesis; for doctorate, comprehensive exam, thesis/dissertation. *Entrance requirements:* For master's, GRE General Test, minimum GPA of 3.0; for doctorate, GRE General Test, MA in sociology, minimum GPA of 3.0. Additional exam requirements/recommendations for international students: Required—TOEFL (minimum score 550 paper-based). Electronic applications accepted. *Faculty research:* Crime/deviance, environmental sociology, social inequality, social psychology, gender.

Washington University in St. Louis, Graduate School of Arts and Sciences, Department of Psychology, St. Louis, MO 63130-4899. Offers clinical psychology (PhD); general experimental psychology (PhD); social psychology (PhD). *Accreditation:* APA. Terminal master's awarded for partial completion of doctoral program. *Degree requirements:* For doctorate, thesis/dissertation. *Entrance requirements:* For doctorate, GRE General Test. Electronic applications accepted.

Western Carolina University, Graduate School, College of Education and Allied Professions, Department of Human Services, Program in Counseling, Cullowhee, NC 28723. Offers community counseling (M Ed, MS); school counseling (MA Ed). *Accreditation:* ACA. Part-time and evening/weekend programs available. *Students:* 63 full-time (48 women), 35 part-time (25 women). Average age 30. 87 applicants, 80% accepted, 52 enrolled. In 2009, 37 master's awarded. *Degree requirements:* For master's, comprehensive exam, thesis or alternative. *Entrance requirements:* For master's, GRE General Test, appropriate undergraduate degree with minimum GPA of 3.0, 3 recommendations, writing sample, resume. Additional exam requirements/recommendations for international students: Required—TOEFL (minimum score 550 paper-based; 270 computer-based; 79 iBT). *Application deadline:* For fall admission, 2/1 for domestic students. Application fee: $40. *Financial support:* In 2009–10, 33 students received support, including 25 research assistantships with full and partial tuition reimbursements available (averaging $6,880 per year), 8 teaching assistantships with full and partial tuition reimbursements available (averaging $7,000 per year); fellowships, career-related internships or fieldwork, institutionally sponsored loans, scholarships/grants, and unspecified assistantships also available. Financial award application deadline: 3/31; financial award applicants required to submit FAFSA. *Faculty research:* Marital and family development, spirituality in counseling, home school law, sexuality education, family functioning models. *Unit head:* Dr. Lisa Bloom, Head, 828-227-7310, E-mail: bloom@email.wcu.edu. *Application contact:* Admissions Specialist for Counseling, 828-227-7398, Fax: 828-227-6280, E-mail: gradsch@email.wcu.edu.

Western Connecticut State University, Division of Graduate Studies, School of Professional Studies, Department of Education and Educational Psychology, Program in Community Counseling, Danbury, CT 06810-6885. Offers MS. *Accreditation:* ACA. Part-time programs available. *Students:* 17 full-time (14 women), 31 part-time (25 women); includes 1 minority (Hispanic American). Average age 38. 24 applicants, 71% accepted, 12 enrolled. In 2009, 12 master's awarded. *Degree requirements:* For master's, practicum, internship, completion of program in 6 years. *Entrance requirements:* For master's, minimum GPA of 2.8, 3 letters of reference, interview, 9 hours of psychology. Additional exam requirements/recommendations for international students: Recommended—TOEFL (minimum score 550 paper-based; 213

computer-based; 79 iBT), IELTS (minimum score 6). *Application deadline:* For fall admission, 8/5 priority date for domestic students; for spring admission, 1/5 for domestic students. Applications are processed on a rolling basis. Application fee: $50. *Expenses:* Tuition, state resident: full-time $5012; part-time $278 per credit hour. Tuition, nonresident: full-time $13,962; part-time $284 per credit hour. Required fees: $3886; $139 per credit hour. Full-time tuition and fees vary according to course load and program. Part-time tuition and fees vary according to course level, degree level and program. *Financial support:* In 2009–10, 1 student received support. Scholarships/grants available. Financial award application deadline: 5/1; financial award applicants required to submit FAFSA. *Unit head:* Dr. Mike Gilles, Assistant Professor, 203-837-8513, Fax: 203-837-8413, E-mail: gillesm@wcsu.edu. *Application contact:* Chris Shankle, Associate Director of Graduate Admissions, 203-837-9005, Fax: 203-837-8326, E-mail: shanklec@wcsu.edu.

Western Illinois University, School of Graduate Studies, College of Arts and Sciences, Department of Psychology, Macomb, IL 61455-1390. Offers clinical/community mental health (MS); general psychology (MS); psychology (MS, SSP); school psychology (SSP). Part-time programs available. *Students:* 42 full-time (21 women), 14 part-time (11 women); includes 2 minority (both Asian Americans or Pacific Islanders), 2 international. Average age 25. 75 applicants, 37% accepted. In 2009, 11 master's, 10 other advanced degrees awarded. *Degree requirements:* For master's, comprehensive exam (for some programs), thesis or alternative. *Entrance requirements:* For master's and SSP, GRE General Test. Additional exam requirements/recommendations for international students: Required—TOEFL (minimum score 550 paper-based; 213 computer-based; 80 iBT). *Application deadline:* Applications are processed on a rolling basis. Application fee: $30. Electronic applications accepted. *Expenses:* Tuition, state resident: full-time $4486; part-time $249.21 per credit hour. Tuition, nonresident: full-time $8972; part-time $498.42 per credit hour. Required fees: $72.62 per credit hour. *Financial support:* In 2009–10, 38 students received support, including 38 research assistantships with full tuition reimbursements available (averaging $7,280 per year). Financial award applicants required to submit FAFSA. *Unit head:* Dr. Steven Dworkin, Chairperson, 309-298-1593. *Application contact:* Evelyn Hoing, Assistant Director of Graduate Studies, 309-298-1806, Fax: 309-298-2345, E-mail: grad-office@wiu.edu.

Wichita State University, Graduate School, Fairmount College of Liberal Arts and Sciences, Department of Psychology, Wichita, KS 67260. Offers clinical (PhD); community (PhD); human factors (PhD). *Accreditation:* APA. Part-time programs available. *Expenses:* Tuition, state resident: full-time $4247; part-time $235.95 per credit hour. Tuition, nonresident: full-time $11,171; part-time $620.60 per credit hour. Required fees: $34; $3.60 per credit hour. $17 per term. Tuition and fees vary according to campus/location and program. *Unit head:* Dr. Charles Burdsal, Chair, 316-978-3170, Fax: 316-978-3006, E-mail: charles.burdsal@wichita.edu. *Application contact:* Dr. Charles Burdsal, Chair, 316-978-3170, Fax: 316-978-3006, E-mail: charles.burdsal@wichita.edu.

Wilfrid Laurier University, Faculty of Graduate Studies, Faculty of Science, Department of Psychology, Waterloo, ON N2L 3C5, Canada. Offers brain and cognition (M Sc, PhD); community psychology (MA, PhD); social and developmental psychology (MA, PhD). *Degree requirements:* For master's, thesis; for doctorate, thesis/dissertation. *Entrance requirements:* For master's, GRE General Test, honors BA or the equivalent in psychology, minimum B average in undergraduate course work; for doctorate, GRE General Test, master's degree, minimum A- average. Additional exam requirements/recommendations for international students: Required—TOEFL (minimum score 230 computer-based; 89 iBT). Electronic applications accepted. *Faculty research:* Brain and cognition, community psychology, social and developmental psychology.

Wilmington University, College of Social and Behavioral Sciences, New Castle, DE 19720-6491. Offers administration of human services (MS); administration of justice (MS); community counseling (MS). *Accreditation:* ACA. Part-time and evening/weekend programs available. *Entrance requirements:* Additional exam requirements/recommendations for international students: Required—TOEFL (minimum score 500 paper-based; 173 computer-based). Electronic applications accepted.

Yale University, Graduate School of Arts and Sciences, Department of Psychology, New Haven, CT 06520. Offers behavioral neuroscience (PhD); clinical psychology (PhD); cognitive psychology (PhD); developmental psychology (PhD); social/personality psychology (PhD). *Accreditation:* APA. *Degree requirements:* For doctorate, thesis/dissertation. *Entrance requirements:* For doctorate, GRE General Test.

Sport Psychology

Adler School of Professional Psychology, Programs in Psychology, Chicago, IL 60601-7203. Offers art therapy (MA, Certificate); clinical hypnosis (Certificate); clinical psychology (Psy D); counseling (MA); counseling and organizational psychology (MA); forensic psychology (MA); gerontological counseling (MA); marriage and family counseling (MA); marriage and family therapy (Certificate); organizational psychology (MA); police psychology (MA); rehabilitation counseling (MA); sport and health psychology (MA); substance abuse counseling (Certificate); Psy D/Certificate; Psy D/MACAT; Psy D/MACP; Psy D/MAMFC; Psy D/MASAC. *Accreditation:* APA. Part-time and evening/weekend programs available. Postbaccalaureate distance learning degree programs offered (minimal on-campus study). *Faculty:* 41 full-time (21 women), 44 part-time/adjunct (19 women). *Students:* 551 full-time (441 women), 161 part-time (137 women). Average age 27.Terminal master's awarded for partial completion of doctoral program. *Degree requirements:* For master's, thesis or alternative, oral exam, practicum; for doctorate, thesis/dissertation, clinical exam, internship, oral exam, practicum, written qualifying exam. *Entrance requirements:* For master's, 12 semester hours in psychology, minimum GPA of 3.0; for doctorate, 18 semester hours in psychology, minimum GPA of 3.25; for Certificate, appropriate master's or doctoral degree. Additional exam requirements/recommendations for international students: Required—TOEFL (minimum score 550 paper-based; 213 computer-based; 79 iBT). *Application deadline:* For fall admission, 2/15 priority date for domestic students, 12/1 priority date for international students. Applications are processed on a rolling basis. Application fee: $50. Electronic applications accepted. *Expenses:* Tuition: Part-time $930 per credit. Required fees: $220 per term. *Financial support:* Career-related internships or fieldwork, Federal Work-Study, scholarships/grants, and tuition waivers (full and partial) available. Support available to part-time students. Financial award application deadline: 5/15; financial award applicants required to submit FAFSA. *Unit head:* Dr. Frank Gruba-McAllister, Vice President of Academic Affairs, 312-201-5900 Ext. 209, Fax: 312-201-5917. *Application contact:* Craig A. Hines, Associate Vice President of Admissions, 312-201-5900 Ext. 226, Fax: 312-201-5917, E-mail: chines@adler.edu.

See Close-Up on page 1047.

Argosy University, Atlanta, College of Psychology and Behavioral Sciences, Atlanta, GA 30328. Offers clinical psychology (MA, Psy D, Postdoctoral Respecialization Certificate), including child and family psychology (Psy D), general adult clinical (Psy D), health psychology (Psy D), neuropsychology/geropsychology (Psy D); community counseling (MA), including marriage and family therapy; counselor education and supervision (Ed D); forensic psychology (MA); industrial organizational psychology (MA); marriage and family therapy (Certificate); sport-exercise psychology (MA). *Accreditation:* APA.

See Close-Up on page 1049.

Argosy University, Inland Empire, College of Psychology and Behavioral Sciences, San Bernardino, CA 92408. Offers clinical psychology/marriage and family therapy (MA); counseling psychology (Ed D); counseling psychology/marriage and family therapy (MA); forensic psychology (MA); industrial organizational psychology (MA); sport-exercise psychology (MA).

See Close-Up on page 1059.

Argosy University, Orange County, College of Psychology and Behavioral Sciences, Program in Sport-Exercise Psychology, Orange, CA 92868. Offers MA. *Unit head:* Dr. Gary Bruss, Dean, 800-716-9598, Fax: 714-437-1284, E-mail: gbruss@argosy.edu. *Application contact:* Mark Betz, Director of Admissions, 800-716-9598, Fax: 714-437-1697, E-mail: mbetz@argosy.edu.

See Close-Up on page 1065.

Argosy University, Phoenix, College of Psychology and Behavioral Sciences, Program in Clinical Psychology, Phoenix, AZ 85021. Offers clinical psychology (MA); neuropsychology (Psy D); sports-exercise psychology (Psy D). *Accreditation:* APA (one or more programs are accredited).

See Close-Up on page 1067.

Argosy University, Phoenix, College of Psychology and Behavioral Sciences, Program in Sport–Exercise Psychology, Phoenix, AZ 85021. Offers MA.

See Close-Up on page 1067.

Argosy University, San Francisco Bay Area, College of Psychology and Behavioral Sciences, Alameda, CA 94501. Offers clinical psychology (MA, Psy D); counseling psychology (MA, Ed D); forensic psychology (MA); sport-exercise psychology (MA). *Accreditation:* APA (one or more programs are accredited).

See Close-Up on page 1073.

Barry University, School of Human Performance and Leisure Sciences, Programs in Movement Science, Specialization in Sport and Exercise Psychology, Miami Shores, FL 33161-6695. Offers MS. *Entrance requirements:* For master's, GRE.

California State University, Fresno, Division of Graduate Studies, College of Health and Human Services, Department of Kinesiology, Fresno, CA 93740-8027. Offers exercise science (MA); sport psychology (MA). Part-time and evening/weekend programs available. *Degree requirements:* For master's, thesis or alternative. *Entrance requirements:* For master's, GRE General Test, minimum GPA of 2.7. Additional exam requirements/recommendations for international students: Required—TOEFL. Electronic applications accepted. *Faculty research:* Refugee education, homeless, geriatrics, fitness.

California State University, Long Beach, Graduate Studies, College of Health and Human Services, Department of Kinesiology, Long Beach, CA 90840. Offers adapted physical education (MA); coaching and student athlete development (MA); exercise physiology and nutrition (MS); exercise science (MS); individualized studies (MA); kinesiology (MA); pedagogical studies (MA); sport and exercise psychology (MS); sport management (MA); sports medicine and injury studies (MS). Part-time programs available. *Faculty:* 9 full-time (6 women), 1 part-time/adjunct (0 women). *Students:* 34 full-time (22 women), 23 part-time (14 women); includes 22 minority (4 African Americans, 2 American Indian/Alaska Native, 8 Asian Americans or Pacific Islanders, 8 Hispanic Americans), 9 international. Average age 27. 143 applicants, 59% accepted, 20 enrolled. *Degree requirements:* For master's, oral and written comprehensive exams or thesis. *Entrance requirements:* For master's, GRE General Test, minimum GPA of 2.75 during previous 2 years of course work. *Application deadline:* For fall admission, 6/1 for domestic students. Applications are processed on a rolling basis. Application fee: $55. Electronic applications accepted. *Expenses:* Required fees: $1802 per semester. Part-time tuition and fees vary according to course load. *Financial support:* Federal Work-Study, institutionally sponsored loans, and scholarships/grants available. Financial award application deadline: 3/2. *Faculty research:* Pulmonary functioning, feedback and practice structure, strength training, history and politics of sports, special population research issues. *Unit head:* Dr. Sharon R. Guthrie, Chair, 562-985-7487, Fax: 562-985-8067, E-mail: guthrie@csulb.edu. *Application contact:* Dr. Grant Hill, Graduate Advisor, 562-985-8856, Fax: 562-985-8067, E-mail: ghill@csulb.edu.

California University of Pennsylvania, School of Graduate Studies and Research, School of Education, Department of Athletic Training, Program in Exercise Science and Health Promotion, California, PA 15419-1394. Offers fitness and wellness (MS); performance enhancement and injury prevention (MS); rehabilitation sciences (MS); sport management (MS); sport psychology (MS). Part-time and evening/weekend programs available. Postbaccalaureate distance learning degree programs offered (no on-campus study). *Degree requirements:* For master's, comprehensive exam, thesis optional. *Entrance requirements:* For master's, minimum QPA of 3.0. Additional exam requirements/recommendations for international students: Required—TOEFL (minimum score 550 paper-based; 213 computer-based; 80 iBT). Electronic applications accepted. *Expenses:* Contact institution. *Faculty research:* Reducing obesity in children, sport performance, creating unique biomechanical assessment techniques, Web-based training for fitness professionals, Webcams.

Capella University, Harold Abel School of Psychology, Minneapolis, MN 55402. Offers child and adolescent development (MS); clinical psychology (MS, Psy D); counseling psychology (MS); educational psychology (MS, PhD); evaluation, research, and measurement (MS); general psychology (MS, PhD); industrial/organizational psychology (MS, PhD); leadership coaching psychology (MS); organizational leader development (MS); school psychology (MS); sport psychology (MS). Part-time and evening/weekend programs available. Postbaccalaureate distance learning degree programs offered (minimal on-campus study). Terminal master's awarded for partial completion of doctoral program. *Degree requirements:* For master's, thesis optional, project; for doctorate, thesis/dissertation. *Entrance requirements:* For degree, master's degree in school psychology. Additional exam requirements/recommendations for international students: Required—TOEFL (minimum score 550 paper-based; 213 computer-based), TWE (minimum score 4); Recommended—IELTS. Electronic applications accepted.

Chatham University, Program in Counseling Psychology, Pittsburgh, PA 15232-2826. Offers child, adolescent and family (MSCP); counseling psychology (Psy D); health and holistic (MSCP); infant mental health (MSCP); organization and supervision (MSCP); sport and exercise

Sport Psychology

Chatham University (continued)

(MSCP). Part-time and evening/weekend programs available. *Students:* 107 full-time (93 women), 77 part-time (67 women). Average age 29. 141 applicants, 76% accepted, 75 enrolled. In 2009, 63 master's awarded. *Degree requirements:* For master's, thesis optional, supervised internship; for doctorate, thesis/dissertation, internship. *Entrance requirements:* For master's, minimum GPA of 3.0; 2 letters of recommendation; resume; prerequisite coursework in statistics, biology, and psychology; for doctorate, GRE. Additional exam requirements/recommendations for international students: Required—TOEFL (minimum score 600 paper-based; 250 computer-based; 100 iBT), IELTS (minimum score 6.5), TWE. *Application deadline:* For fall admission, 5/1 priority date for domestic students, 6/1 priority date for international students; for spring admission, 12/1 for domestic students, 11/1 for international students. Applications are processed on a rolling basis. Application fee: $45. Electronic applications accepted. *Financial support:* Career-related internships or fieldwork available. Financial award applicants required to submit FAFSA. *Faculty research:* Trauma and recovery, hypnosis, psychospiritual dimensions of healing, psychotherapy of schizophrenia. *Unit head:* Dr. Mary Beth Mannarino, Director, 412-365-1196, Fax: 412-365-1505, E-mail: mmannarino@chatham.edu. *Application contact:* Dory Perry, Associate Director of Graduate Admissions, 412-365-2758, Fax: 412-365-1609, E-mail: gradadmissions@chatham.edu.

Cleveland State University, College of Graduate Studies, College of Education and Human Services, Department of Health, Physical Education, Recreation and Dance, Cleveland, OH 44115. Offers community health education (M Ed); exercise science (M Ed); human performance (M Ed); physical education pedagogy (M Ed); public health (MPH); school health education (M Ed); sport and exercise psychology (M Ed); sports management (M Ed). Part-time programs available. *Degree requirements:* For master's, comprehensive exam, thesis optional. *Entrance requirements:* For master's, GRE General Test or MAT (if undergraduate GPA less than 2.75), minimum undergraduate GPA of 2.75. Additional exam requirements/recommendations for international students: Required—TOEFL (minimum score 525 paper-based; 197 computer-based), IELTS (minimum score 6). Electronic applications accepted. *Faculty research:* Bone density, marketing fitness centers, motor development of disabled, online learning and survey research.

Eastern Washington University, Graduate Studies, College of Education and Human Development, Department of Physical Education, Health and Recreation, Cheney, WA 99004-2431. Offers exercise science (MS); sport and exercise psychology (MS); sports administration/pedagogy (MS). *Degree requirements:* For master's, comprehensive exam, thesis or alternative. *Entrance requirements:* For master's, minimum GPA of 3.0. *Expenses:* Tuition, state resident: full-time $7476; part-time $249 per quarter hour. Tuition, nonresident: full-time $18,030; part-time $601 per quarter hour. Required fees: $3.50 per quarter hour. $142 per quarter.

Florida State University, The Graduate School, College of Education, Department of Educational Psychology and Learning Systems, Program in Educational Psychology, Tallahassee, FL 32306. Offers learning and cognition (MS, PhD, Ed S); sports psychology (MS, PhD). *Faculty:* 5 full-time (3 women), 6 part-time/adjunct (2 women). *Students:* 58 full-time (32 women), 13 part-time (8 women); includes 16 minority (10 African Americans, 2 Asian Americans or Pacific Islanders, 4 Hispanic Americans), 12 international. 100 applicants, 39% accepted, 24 enrolled. In 2009, 10 master's, 8 doctorates awarded. *Degree requirements:* For master's, comprehensive exam, thesis optional; for doctorate, comprehensive exam, thesis/dissertation. *Entrance requirements:* For master's and doctorate, GRE General Test, minimum GPA of 3.0. Additional exam requirements/recommendations for international students: Required—TOEFL (minimum score 550 paper-based; 213 computer-based; 80 iBT). *Application deadline:* For fall admission, 7/1 priority date for domestic students; for spring admission, 11/1 for domestic students. Applications are processed on a rolling basis. Application fee: $30. *Expenses:* Tuition, state resident: full-time $7413. Tuition, nonresident: full-time $22,567. *Financial support:* In 2009–10, 1 fellowship with full and partial tuition reimbursement, 3 research assistantships with full and partial tuition reimbursements, 10 teaching assistantships with full and partial tuition reimbursements were awarded; career-related internships or fieldwork also available. Financial award applicants required to submit FAFSA. *Faculty research:* Learning and cognition, skill acquisition, self-perception, processes of motivation. *Unit head:* Dr. Susan Losh, Program Leader, 850-644-8776, Fax: 850-644-8776, E-mail: slosh@coe.fsu.edu. *Application contact:* Sally Gadson, Program Assistant, 850-644-8046, Fax: 850-644-5067, E-mail: gadson@coe.fsu.edu.

John F. Kennedy University, Graduate School of Professional Psychology, Program in Sport Psychology, Pleasant Hill, CA 94523-4817. Offers MA. *Accreditation:* APA. Part-time and evening/weekend programs available. *Degree requirements:* For master's, thesis or alternative. *Entrance requirements:* For master's, interview. Additional exam requirements/recommendations for international students: Required—TOEFL.

Memorial University of Newfoundland, School of Graduate Studies, School of Human Kinetics and Recreation, St. John's, NL A1C 5S7, Canada. Offers administration, curriculum and supervision (MPE); biomechanics/ergonomics (MS Kin); exercise and work physiology (MS Kin); sport psychology (MS Kin). Part-time programs available. *Degree requirements:* For master's, thesis optional, seminars, thesis presentations. *Entrance requirements:* For master's, bachelor's degree in a related field, minimum B average. Electronic applications accepted. *Faculty research:* Administration, sociology of sports, kinesiology, physiology/recreation.

Purdue University, Graduate School, College of Liberal Arts, Department of Health and Kinesiology, West Lafayette, IN 47907. Offers exercise, human physiology of movement and sport (PhD); health and fitness (MS); health promotion (MS); health promotion and disease prevention (PhD); movement and sport science (MS); pedagogy and administration (MS); pedagogy of physical activity and health (PhD); psychology of sport and exercise, and motor behavior (PhD). Part-time programs available. *Degree requirements:* For master's, thesis (for some programs); for doctorate, thesis/dissertation. *Entrance requirements:* For master's and doctorate, GRE General Test. Additional exam requirements/recommendations for international students: Required—TOEFL. Electronic applications accepted. *Faculty research:* Wellness, motivation, teaching effectiveness, learning and development.

Queen's University at Kingston, School of Graduate Studies and Research, School of Kinesiology and Health Studies, Kingston, ON K7L 3N6, Canada. Offers applied exercise science (PhD); biomechanics/ergonomics (M Sc); exercise physiology (M Sc); social psychology of sport and exercise rehabilitation (MA); sociology of sport (MA). Part-time programs available. *Degree requirements:* For master's, thesis (for some programs); for doctorate, comprehensive exam, thesis/dissertation. *Entrance requirements:* For master's and doctorate, minimum B+ average. Additional exam requirements/recommendations for international students: Required—TOEFL. Electronic applications accepted. *Faculty research:* Expert performance ergonomics, obesity research, pregnancy and exercise, gender and sport participation.

Southern Connecticut State University, School of Graduate Studies, School of Education, Department of Exercise Science, New Haven, CT 06515-1355. Offers human performance (MS); physical education (MS); school health education (MS); sport psychology (MS). Part-time and evening/weekend programs available. *Faculty:* 8 full-time. *Students:* 28 full-time (13 women), 54 part-time (28 women); includes 6 minority (2 African Americans, 4 Hispanic Americans), 1 international. 20 applicants, 55% accepted, 10 enrolled. In 2009, 18 master's awarded. *Degree requirements:* For master's, thesis or alternative. *Entrance requirements:* For master's, interview. *Application deadline:* For fall admission, 7/15 priority date for domestic students. Applications are processed on a rolling basis. Application fee: $50. Electronic applications accepted. Tuition and fees vary according to program. *Financial support:* In 2009–10, 8 teaching assistantships were awarded. Financial award application deadline: 4/15; financial award applicants required to submit FAFSA. *Unit head:* Dr. Daniel Swartz, Chairperson, 203-392-8721, Fax: 203-392-6911, E-mail: swartzd1@southernct.edu. *Application contact:* Dr. Robert Axtell, Coordinator, 203-392-6037, Fax: 203-392-6093, E-mail: axtell@southernct.edu.

Springfield College, Graduate Programs, Programs in Exercise Science and Sport Studies, Springfield, MA 01109-3797. Offers athletic training (MS); exercise physiology (MS), including clinical exercise physiology, science and research; exercise science and sport studies (PhD); health promotion and disease prevention (MS); sport psychology (MS). Part-time programs available. Terminal master's awarded for partial completion of doctoral program. *Degree requirements:* For master's, comprehensive exam, research project or thesis; for doctorate, comprehensive exam, thesis/dissertation. *Entrance requirements:* For master's and doctorate, GRE General Test. Additional exam requirements/recommendations for international students: Required—TOEFL (minimum score 550 paper-based; 213 computer-based). Electronic applications accepted. *Expenses:* Tuition: Full-time $19,800; part-time $825 per credit hour. Required fees: $150.

Springfield College, Graduate Programs, Programs in Psychology and Counseling, Springfield, MA 01109-3797. Offers athletic counseling (M Ed, MS, CAGS); industrial/organizational psychology (M Ed, MS, CAGS); marriage and family therapy (M Ed, MS, CAGS); mental health counseling (M Ed, MS, CAGS); school guidance and counseling (M Ed, MS, CAGS); student personnel in higher education (M Ed, MS, CAGS). Part-time programs available. *Degree requirements:* For master's, research project, portfolio. *Entrance requirements:* Additional exam requirements/recommendations for international students: Required—TOEFL (minimum score 550 paper-based; 213 computer-based). Electronic applications accepted. *Expenses:* Tuition: Full-time $19,800; part-time $825 per credit hour. Required fees: $150.

University of Florida, Graduate School, College of Health and Human Performance, Department of Applied Physiology and Kinesiology, Gainesville, FL 32611. Offers athletic training/sport medicine (MS, PhD); biomechanics (MS, PhD); clinical exercise physiology (MS); exercise physiology (MS, PhD); health and human performance (PhD); human performance (MS); motor learning/control (MS, PhD); sport and exercise psychology (MS). *Degree requirements:* For doctorate, thesis/dissertation. *Entrance requirements:* For doctorate, GRE General Test. Electronic applications accepted.

The University of Iowa, Graduate College, College of Liberal Arts and Sciences, Department of Health and Sport Studies, Iowa City, IA 52242-1316. Offers psychology of sport and physical activity (MA, PhD); sports studies (MA, PhD). *Degree requirements:* For master's, thesis optional, exam; for doctorate, comprehensive exam, thesis/dissertation. *Entrance requirements:* For master's and doctorate, GRE General Test, minimum GPA of 3.0. Additional exam requirements/recommendations for international students: Required—TOEFL (minimum score 600 paper-based; 250 computer-based; 100 iBT). Electronic applications accepted.

University of Rhode Island, Graduate School, College of Human Science and Services, Department of Kinesiology, Kingston, RI 02881. Offers cultural studies of sport and physical culture (MS); exercise science (MS); physical education pedagogy (MS); psychosocial/behavioral aspects of physical activity (MS). *Accreditation:* NCATE. Part-time programs available. *Faculty:* 13 full-time (7 women). *Students:* 16 full-time (8 women), 2 part-time (1 woman), 1 international. In 2009, 6 master's awarded. *Degree requirements:* For master's, thesis optional. *Entrance requirements:* For master's, GRE, 2 letters of recommendation. Additional exam requirements/recommendations for international students: Required—TOEFL (minimum score 550 paper-based; 213 computer-based). *Application deadline:* For fall admission, 4/15 for domestic students, 2/1 for international students; for spring admission, 11/15 for domestic students, 7/15 for international students. Application fee: $65. Electronic applications accepted. *Expenses:* Tuition, state resident: full-time $8828; part-time $490 per credit hour. Tuition, nonresident: full-time $22,100; part-time $1228 per credit hour. Required fees: $1118; $57 per semester. Tuition and fees vary according to program. *Financial support:* In 2009–10, 4 teaching assistantships with full and partial tuition reimbursements (averaging $7,939 per year) were awarded. Financial award application deadline: 4/15; financial award applicants required to submit FAFSA. *Faculty research:* Strength training and older adults, interventions to promote a healthy lifestyle as well as analysis of the psychosocial outcomes of those interventions, effects of exercise and nutrition on skeletal muscle of aging healthy adults with CVD and other metabolic related diseases, physical activity and fitness of deaf children and youth. Total annual research expenditures: $92,479. *Unit head:* Dr. Deborah Riebe, Chair, 401-874-5444, Fax: 401-874-4215, E-mail: debriebe@uri.edu. *Application contact:* Dr. Lori Ciccomascolo, Director of Graduate Studies, 401-874-5454, Fax: 401-874-4215, E-mail: lecicco@uri.edu.

The University of Texas at Austin, Graduate School, College of Education, Department of Kinesiology and Health Education, Austin, TX 78712-1111. Offers behavioral health (PhD); exercise and sport psychology (M Ed, MA); health education (M Ed, MA, Ed D, PhD); kinesiology (M Ed, MA). Part-time programs available. Terminal master's awarded for partial completion of doctoral program. *Degree requirements:* For master's, thesis (for some programs); for doctorate, thesis/dissertation. *Entrance requirements:* For master's and doctorate, GRE General Test. Additional exam requirements/recommendations for international students: Required—TOEFL. Electronic applications accepted. *Faculty research:* Health promotion, human performance and exercise biochemistry, motor behavior and biomechanics, sport management, aging and pediatric development.

West Virginia University, School of Physical Education, Morgantown, WV 26506. Offers athletic coaching education (MS); athletic training (MS); physical education/teacher education (MS, PhD), including curriculum and instruction (PhD), motor behavior (PhD), physical education supervision (PhD); sport and exercise psychology (PhD); sport management (MS). *Degree requirements:* For doctorate, comprehensive exam, thesis/dissertation, oral exam. *Entrance requirements:* For master's, GRE or MAT, minimum GPA of 3.0; for doctorate, GRE General Test or MAT, minimum GPA of 3.5. Additional exam requirements/recommendations for international students: Required—TOEFL (minimum score 550 paper-based; 213 computer-based). Electronic applications accepted. *Faculty research:* Sport psychosociology, teacher education, exercise psychology, counseling.

Thanatology

Brooklyn College of the City University of New York, Division of Graduate Studies, Department of Health and Nutrition Science, Program in Community Health, Brooklyn, NY 11210-2889. Offers community health education (MA); computer science and health science (MS); health care management (MPH); health care policy and administration (MPH); thanatology (MA). *Accreditation:* CEPH. *Students:* 5 full-time (3 women), 46 part-time (38 women); includes 39 minority (32 African Americans, 5 Asian Americans or Pacific Islanders, 2 Hispanic Americans), 2 international. Average age 36. 22 applicants, 95% accepted, 15 enrolled. In 2009, 9 master's awarded. *Degree requirements:* For master's, thesis or alternative. *Entrance requirements:* For master's, 18 credits, 2 letters of recommendation, essay. Additional exam requirements/recommendations for international students: Required—TOEFL. *Application deadline:* For fall admission, 3/1 priority date for domestic students, 2/1 priority date for international students; for spring admission, 11/1 priority date for domestic students, 10/1 priority date for international students. Applications are processed on a rolling basis. Application fee: $125. Electronic applications accepted. *Expenses:* Tuition, area resident: Full-time $7360; part-time $310 per credit hour. Tuition, state resident: full-time $7360; part-time $310 per credit hour. Tuition, nonresident: full-time $13,800; part-time $575 per credit hour. International tuition: $13,800 full-time. Required fees: $140.10 per semester. *Financial support:* Federal Work-Study, institutionally sponsored loans, and scholarships/grants available. Support available to part-time students. Financial award application deadline: 5/1; financial award applicants required to submit FAFSA. *Faculty research:* Diet restriction, religious practices in bereavement, diabetes, stress management, palliative care. *Unit head:* Dr. Elizabeth Eastwood, Graduate Deputy Chairperson, 718-951-5026, Fax: 718-951-4670, E-mail: eastwood@brooklyn.cuny.edu. *Application contact:* Hernan Sierra, Graduate Admissions Coordinator, 718-951-4536, Fax: 718-951-4506, E-mail: grads@brooklyn.cuny.edu.

Hood College, Graduate School, Programs in Human Sciences, Frederick, MD 21701-8575. Offers human sciences (MA), including psychology; thanatology (MA, Certificate). Part-time and evening/weekend programs available. *Faculty:* 6 full-time (3 women), 6 part-time/adjunct (3 women). *Students:* 13 full-time (11 women), 86 part-time (77 women); includes 16 minority (11 African Americans, 2 American Indian/Alaska Native, 2 Asian Americans or Pacific Islanders, 1 Hispanic American), 2 international. Average age 35. 54 applicants, 89% accepted, 26 enrolled. In 2009, 42 master's, 31 other advanced degrees awarded. *Degree requirements:* For master's, comprehensive exam, capstone/research project. *Entrance requirements:* For master's, minimum GPA of 2.75. Additional exam requirements/recommendations for international students: Required—TOEFL (minimum score 575 paper-based; 231 computer-based; 89 iBT). *Application deadline:* For fall admission, 7/15 for domestic and international students; for spring admission, 12/15 for domestic and international students. Applications are processed on a rolling basis. Application fee: $35. Electronic applications accepted. *Expenses:* Tuition: Full-time $6480; part-time $360 per credit. Required fees: $100; $50 per term. *Financial support:* Applicants required to submit FAFSA. *Faculty research:* Mind-body medicine and multicultural healing, the New Orleans jazz funeral, death practices in African-American culture, bereavement theories and gender differences, Piaget's theory of cognitive development as a formal mathematical model. *Unit head:* Dr. Dana G. Cable, Director, 301-696-3758, Fax: 301-696-3597, E-mail: cable@hood.edu. *Application contact:* Dr. Allen P. Flora, Dean of Graduate School, 301-696-3811, Fax: 301-696-3597, E-mail: gofurther@hood.edu.

Southwestern College, Program in Grief, Loss and Trauma Counseling, Santa Fe, NM 87502-4788. Offers MA, Certificate. Part-time and evening/weekend programs available. Postbaccalaureate distance learning degree programs offered (minimal on-campus study). *Students:* Average age 37. In 2009, 11 other advanced degrees awarded. *Entrance requirements:* For master's, interview, references, resume; for Certificate, 3 letters of reference, interview. *Application deadline:* Applications are processed on a rolling basis. *Unit head:* Dr. Janet Schreiber, Director, Fax: 877-471-4071. *Application contact:* Dru Phoenix, Director of Admissions, 505-471-5756 Ext. 26, Fax: 505-471-4071, E-mail: admissions@swc.edu.

Transpersonal and Humanistic Psychology

Atlantic University, Program in Transformative Theories and Practices, Virginia Beach, VA 23451-2061. Offers MA. Part-time and evening/weekend programs available. Postbaccalaureate distance learning degree programs offered (no on-campus study). *Faculty:* 24 part-time/adjunct (7 women). *Students:* 149 part-time (111 women); includes 8 minority (3 African Americans, 3 Asian Americans or Pacific Islanders, 2 Hispanic Americans), 5 international. Average age 46. 109 applicants, 33% accepted, 36 enrolled. In 2009, 15 master's awarded. *Degree requirements:* For master's, thesis. *Entrance requirements:* For master's, minimum undergraduate GPA of 2.5. Additional exam requirements/recommendations for international students: Required—TOEFL (minimum score 550 paper-based; 213 computer-based). *Application deadline:* Applications are processed on a rolling basis. Application fee: $50. Electronic applications accepted. *Expenses:* Tuition: Part-time $750 per course. *Unit head:* Kevin J. Todeschi, Chief Executive Officer, 757-631-8101, Fax: 757-631-8096, E-mail: info@atlanticuniv.edu. *Application contact:* Candis Collins, Director of Admissions, 757-631-8101, Fax: 757-631-8096, E-mail: candis.collins@atlanticuniv.edu.

Institute of Transpersonal Psychology, Global Online Programs, Palo Alto, CA 94303. Offers psychology (PhD); transpersonal psychology (MTP); transpersonal studies (Certificate). Postbaccalaureate distance learning degree programs offered (minimal on-campus study). Terminal master's awarded for partial completion of doctoral program. *Degree requirements:* For master's, thesis (for some programs); for doctorate, thesis/dissertation. *Entrance requirements:* For master's and doctorate, bachelor's degree. Additional exam requirements/recommendations for international students: Required—TOEFL. *Expenses:* Contact institution.

Institute of Transpersonal Psychology, Low-Residency Programs, Palo Alto, CA 94303. Offers counseling psychology (online) (MA); spiritual guidance (MA); women's spirituality (MA). Postbaccalaureate distance learning degree programs offered (minimal on-campus study).

Institute of Transpersonal Psychology, Residential Programs, Palo Alto, CA 94303. Offers counseling psychology (MA); spiritually oriented clinical psychology (Psy D); transpersonal psychology (MA, PhD). Part-time and evening/weekend programs available. Terminal master's awarded for partial completion of doctoral program. *Degree requirements:* For doctorate, thesis/dissertation. *Entrance requirements:* For master's and doctorate, bachelor's degree.

John F. Kennedy University, Graduate School of Holistic Studies, Department of Counseling Psychology, Program in Counseling Psychology, Pleasant Hill, CA 94523-4817. Offers holistic studies (MA); somatic psychology (MA); transpersonal psychology (MA). Part-time and evening/weekend programs available. *Degree requirements:* For master's, thesis or alternative. *Entrance requirements:* For master's, interview. Additional exam requirements/recommendations for international students: Required—TOEFL.

Michigan School of Professional Psychology, Programs in Humanistic and Clinical Psychology, Farmington Hills, MI 48334. Offers MA, Psy D. *Students:* 111 full-time (92 women), 3 part-time (all women); includes 20 minority (13 African Americans, 7 Asian Americans or Pacific Islanders). Average age 38. *Degree requirements:* For master's, thesis, practicum; for doctorate, thesis/dissertation, internship, practicum. *Entrance requirements:* For master's, 1 year of work experience, interview, minimum GPA of 3.0, curriculum vitae, personal essay, bachelor's degree, 3 letters of recommendation; for doctorate, 3 years of work experience, 2 interviews, minimum graduate GPA of 3.0, scholarly writing sample, curriculum vitae, personal essay, MA, 3 letters of recommendation. Additional exam requirements/recommendations for international students: Required—TOEFL. *Application deadline:* For fall admission, 1/15 priority date for domestic students. Applications are processed on a rolling basis. Application fee: $75. Electronic applications accepted. *Financial support:* Application deadline: 6/30. *Faculty research:* Qualitative research, existential-phenomenological psychology, applications to clinical practice. *Unit head:* Dr. Kerry Moustakas, President, 248-476-1122, Fax: 248-476-1125, E-mail: kmoustakas@mispp.edu. *Application contact:* Linda Potter-Gallant, Admissions Advisor, 248-476-1122 Ext. 117, Fax: 248-476-1125, E-mail: lpgallant@mispp.edu.

Naropa University, Graduate Programs, Program in Transpersonal Counseling Psychology, Boulder, CO 80302-6697. Offers art therapy (MA); counseling psychology (MA); wilderness therapy (MA). *Degree requirements:* For master's, internships. *Entrance requirements:* For master's, in-person interview, course work in psychology, 3 letters of recommendation, resume. Additional exam requirements/recommendations for international students: Required—TOEFL (minimum score 600 paper-based; 250 computer-based). Electronic applications accepted.

Naropa University, Graduate Programs, Program in Transpersonal Psychology, Boulder, CO 80302-6697. Offers ecopsychology (MA); transpersonal psychology (MA). Part-time and evening/weekend programs available. Postbaccalaureate distance learning degree programs offered (minimal on-campus study). *Degree requirements:* For master's, thesis, service learning. *Entrance requirements:* For master's, interview (by phone or in-person), technology form, resume, letter of interest, 3 letters of recommendation. Additional exam requirements/recommendations for international students: Required—TOEFL (minimum score 600 paper-based; 250 computer-based). Electronic applications accepted.

Saybrook University, Graduate College of Psychology and Humanistic Studies, San Francisco, CA 94111-1920. Offers clinical psychology (Psy D); human science (MA, PhD), including consciousness and spirituality, humanistic and transpersonal psychology, integrative health studies, organizational systems, social transformation, transformative social change (MA); organizational systems (MA, PhD), including consciousness and spirituality, humanistic and transpersonal psychology, integrative health studies, leadership of sustainable systems (MA), organizational systems, social transformation; psychology (MA, PhD), including clinical psychology (PhD), consciousness and spirituality, creativity studies (MA), humanistic and transpersonal psychology, integrative health studies, Jungian studies, marriage and family therapy (MA), organizational systems, social transformation. Postbaccalaureate distance learning degree programs offered (minimal on-campus study). Terminal master's awarded for partial completion of doctoral program. *Degree requirements:* For master's, thesis or alternative; for doctorate, thesis/dissertation. Electronic applications accepted. *Faculty research:* Humanistic theory, health studies, organizational systems, consciousness and spirituality, social transformation.

Seattle University, College of Arts and Sciences, Department of Psychology, Seattle, WA 98122-1090. Offers existential and phenomenological therapeutic psychology (MA Psych). *Degree requirements:* For master's, thesis. *Entrance requirements:* For master's, interview, minimum GPA of 3.0, previous undergraduate course work in psychology. *Faculty research:* Healing, transformations in relationships, therapy, dialogical research.

ADLER SCHOOL OF PROFESSIONAL PSYCHOLOGY

Graduate Programs

Programs of Study

Founded in 1952, Adler School of Professional Psychology is the oldest independent school of psychology in North America. The School is named after Alfred Adler (1870–1937), the first community psychologist, whose theories and teachings of psychology emphasize the uniqueness of every individual's relationship with society. Adler School is committed to continuing Adler's work by producing socially responsible graduates, providing holistic services to individuals and communities, and promoting social justice. Students come from all over the world to study in a collaborative atmosphere with accomplished clinical faculty. The School offers both campus-based and online classes to accommodate recent college graduates and working professionals.

The School was named a recipient of the 2007 American Psychological Association Board of Educational Affairs Award for Innovative Practices in Graduate Education in Psychology. The School takes pride in this recognition of its commitment to educate and train socially responsible psychologists through innovative programs that combine service learning and coursework that enables graduates to address a broad range of social issues that impact the clients they serve.

The Adler School of Professional Psychology offers the following degree programs:

The Doctor of Psychology (Psy.D.) in Clinical Psychology program prepares students for the general practice of professional clinical psychology. The program follows the practitioner model of training developed by the National Council of Schools and Programs of Professional Psychology. This model aims to develop the knowledge, skills, and values in six core competency areas: relationship, assessment, intervention, research and evaluation, consultation and education, and management and supervision. The Doctor of Psychology in Clinical Psychology program is accredited by the Committee on Accreditation of the American Psychological Association (APA), 750 First Street NE, Washington, D.C. 20002-4242; phone: 202-336-5510; Web site: http://www.apa.org/ed/accreditation.

The Master of Arts in Counseling Psychology program provides a foundation in the theories and methods of counseling psychology and hands-on, practical, supervised training with an emphasis on socially responsible practice. This broad-based program usually takes two years of full-time study and is offered part-time in an online/blended format. Graduates are prepared for entry-level professional work in a variety of public- and private-sector human services agencies and organizations.

The Master of Arts in Marriage and Family Counseling program prepares entry-level counselors to specialize in working with couples and families. Students complete course work and practicum experiences focused on the understanding and integration of individual lifestyle dynamics with marital and family systems. Graduates have a theoretical understanding of individual marital and family systems, including developmental issues and major variations, assessment skills in lifestyle and systemic diagnosis, and intervention skills based on major models of marital and family therapy, with the theory and methods of individual psychology as the foundation.

The Master of Arts in Counseling Psychology: Art Therapy program combines the theories and techniques of individual psychology with education and clinical training. The program approved by the American Art Therapy Association requires 65 credit hours of courses, including 700 hours of clinical practicum experience under at least partial supervision of a registered art therapist (ATR). The program provides students with the academic and predegree clinical experiences required to apply for registration as an art therapist as well as sit for the Licensed Professional Counselor (LPC) examination in the state of Illinois.

The Master of Arts in Counseling and Organizational Psychology program combines the theories and skills of counseling psychology with organizational theory, design, and development to prepare graduates for positions in business and industry, especially in organizational psychology and the related areas of talent management, team building, performance enhancement, executive coaching, organizational development, training, and employee assistance. This one-of-a-kind program prepares graduates to sit for state-level licensure as a master's-level counselor. Graduates are trained to assess and provide intervention in organizational settings at the individual level (personal selection, leadership development, executive coaching, career assessment, and counseling), work group level (team assessment, team issue resolution, and team building), and organizational level (talent audits, needs analysis, strategic planning, and organizational design and development).

The Master of Arts in Gerontological Counseling program is designed to provide students with the coursework and practical training to work with older adults. Students are exposed to the impact of biological, psychological, and sociocultural factors on the aging process in order to gain a holistic understanding of the needs and issues of older adults. With the increasing number of older adults, the U.S. Department of Labor projects faster than average growth in employment for individuals with a master's degree. Completion of foundational coursework, specialized studies, and supervised training ensures graduates are prepared to work in a variety of human services agencies and organizations with older adults who will have an appreciation for the value of psychology in promoting their quality of life.

The Master of Arts in Rehabilitation Counseling degree is designed to prepare students to become certified rehabilitation counselors (CRC). Rehabilitation counselors work with individuals who have mental, emotional, or physical handicaps, helping them to lead self-sufficient lives. Counselors determine the training and support their clients need to deal with the effects of their conditions. Rehabilitation counselors are employed by publicly funded agencies, schools, and medical facilities. Counselors evaluate clients and arrange for rehabilitation programs that may include medical care, psychological counseling, occupational therapy, and job placement.

The Master of Arts in Counseling Psychology with a specialization in forensic psychology program prepares graduates for a highly specialized career that integrates knowledge of human behavior with active participation in the criminal justice system. Specialized coursework exposes students to the predominant theories and techniques of forensic evaluation, including the determination of a defendant's competency to stand trial, sanity at the time of an offense, and qualification for the death penalty in the event of a conviction for a capital crime. Students also develop a comprehensive understanding of the techniques associated with the forensic practitioner's involvement in criminal investigations; activities such as forensic hypnosis, offender and geographic profiling, and the ongoing review of police interview and witness identification procedures. Students are introduced to such specialized topics as the psychological effects of incarceration, jury selection, the evaluation of sexually dangerous persons, and the psychosocial development of the criminal personality type.

The Master of Arts in Counseling Psychology with a specialization in sport and health psychology program prepares graduates to address individual and systemic issues that affect sport performance and health. These areas overlap in the types of interventions used to produce positive changes (goal-setting and self-monitoring to improve consistency of practice or to lose weight). Sport and health goals also share the influence of various social and community factors (coaches, family members, culture, access to facilities). This unique program provides training and understanding of assessment, intervention, and analysis of systems that will allow graduates to work within communities, schools, and professional organizations to address the diverse needs of people with varying ages, health issues, and athletic accomplishments.

The Master of Arts in Police Psychology program is designed for field officers, supervisory personnel, command members, and those interested in a career in law enforcement. The program blends numerous areas within the discipline of psychology with pragmatic applications to patrol, operational, and managerial concerns that arise daily in the field of law enforcement. This degree is not designed to teach students to conduct therapy or engage in psychological testing. There are no clinical hours required or practicum to complete. Rather, the program teaches students the practical applications of psychology to the field of law enforcement. Core professors and adjunct faculty members all have extensive experience in clinical psychology and/or law enforcement.

Research Facilities

The Sol and Elaine Mosak Library provides resources and services to foster the educational and intellectual inquiry of students and faculty members. In addition to its major holdings in Adlerian-oriented materials, the library contains a wide variety of materials in mental health and related disciplines. The library has a collection of more than 12,000 volumes, subscribes to more than 150 professional journals, and has an extensive collection of more than 1,000 audiotapes and videotapes.

The library's CD-ROM indexes facilitate research by extending its reach to the larger research community. Through interlibrary loans, cooperative agreements with local libraries, and membership in ILLINET, OCLC, and NLM-Docline, students have computer access to learning materials from all over the country.

Financial Aid

Adler School is approved by the U.S. Department of Education to participate in the Federal Family Education Loan Program and Federal Work-Study Program. The School offers a number of scholarships to students based on financial need, academic achievement, service to the community, and availability of funds.

Cost of Study

Tuition on the Chicago campus for 2010–11 is $925 per credit hour for M.A. programs and $1030 per credit hour for the doctorate program. Student activity and library fees are $215 per term. Tuition costs for each year vary depending on whether the student enrolls full-time or part-time. Full-time students enroll for 8 or more credit hours per term. Courses are offered during fall, spring, and summer semesters.

Living and Housing Costs

The School does not provide housing but assists students in securing off-campus housing. Students typically live in apartments in the Chicago area. Living expenses vary considerably according to standard of living, housing, and transportation.

Student Group

Adler School's commitment to social responsibility draws students from all over the world to study in a collaborative atmosphere with accomplished faculty members. The School attracts both recent college graduates and working professionals and offers significant cultural diversity by attracting the best students in the world. The Adler Student Association represents many different countries and encourages students to celebrate their heritage through on- and off-campus learning activities.

Location

Conveniently located in downtown Chicago, Illinois and Vancouver, British Columbia, both campuses are easily accessible by public transportation and provide students with a culturally diverse learning environment as well as hundreds of opportunities for clinical training across the United States and Canada.

The School

Founded in 1952 by Rudolf Dreikurs, M.D., the Adler School is committed to continuing the work of Alfred Adler, the first community psychologist. In addition to preparing individuals for the general practice of clinical psychology, Adler School also offers a community service practicum. Available in the first-year curriculum, this unique practicum allows students to get involved in community organizing, volunteer projects, political initiatives, advocacy, and public policy analysis.

The Adler Institutes for Social Change advance social justice for underserved and disadvantaged communities through applied research, community outreach, and public awareness initiatives. There are also two other institutes on campus: the Institute on Social Exclusion and the Institute on Public Safety and Social Justice.

Applying

All applicants must have at least a bachelor's degree from an accredited college or university. Applicants to the master's programs should ideally have a GPA of 3.0 or higher (on a 4.0 scale) and at least 12 credits of course work in psychology. Applicants to the doctoral program preferably have a GPA of 3.25 or higher (on a 4.0 scale) and at least 18 credits of course work in psychology. Applications are accepted for the fall and winter terms on a rolling basis. The priority deadline for the Psy.D. program is February 15. Applicants are strongly encouraged to begin the preliminary application process at least three months before they plan to begin taking classes.

Correspondence and Information

Adler School of Professional Psychology
Admissions Office
65 East Wacker Place, Suite 2100
Chicago, Illinois 60601-7203

Phone: 312-201-5900 Ext. 222
Fax: 312-201-5917
E-mail: admissions@adler.edu
Web site: http://www.adler.edu

Adler School of Professional Psychology

THE FACULTY

With an average class size of fewer than 12 students, faculty mentorship plays a very important role in the learning process at Adler School. Faculty members are licensed professionals who combine clinical practice with their instructional duties. Many hold or have held leadership positions in professional organizations, and most present workshops and seminars throughout the United States, Europe, Canada, and other countries. Adler School faculty members have a broad range of interest and specializations offering students a variety of expertise in the field of psychology.

ARGOSY UNIVERSITY

ARGOSY UNIVERSITY, ATLANTA

College of Psychology and Behavioral Sciences

Programs of Study

Argosy University, Atlanta, offers the Postdoctoral Respecialization Certificate in clinical psychology, the Master of Arts (M.A.) degree in clinical psychology, community counseling, forensic psychology, industrial organizational psychology, and sport-exercise psychology; the Doctor of Education (Ed.D.) degree in counselor education and supervision; and the Doctor of Psychology (Psy.D.) degree in clinical psychology. Students completing a program may wish to become licensed professionals. Argosy University, Atlanta does not guarantee third-party certification/licensure. Outside agencies control the requirements for taking and passing certification/licensing exams and are subject to change without notice to Argosy University, Atlanta.

The Postdoctoral Respecialization Certificate in Clinical Psychology is designed for qualified individuals with doctoral degrees in areas of psychology other than clinical psychology. It provides the opportunity to obtain clinical knowledge and skills through class work and through fieldwork experiences. Coursework and clinical training experiences are designed to enable program participants to seek licensure in clinical psychology.

The M.A. in clinical psychology program presents students with the opportunity for training as professionals in the mental health field. This program serves several purposes. First, it introduces students to basic clinical skills that can enable them to serve the mental health needs of populations with diverse backgrounds. Students who use the master's degree as a means of entering a professional career have the opportunity to receive theoretical background and professional training under the supervision of a qualified, practitioner-oriented faculty. The graduates of this program are then able to apply theoretical and clinical knowledge to individuals and groups in need of mental healthcare. Second, the Master of Arts degree often serves as a preliminary step to the doctorate degree. For these students, the program provides a foundation for work beyond the master's degree level and enables them to determine their interest in, and suitability for, the pursuit of more advanced study. In certain states, students holding an M.A. in clinical psychology are eligible to sit for licensure.

The M.A. in community counseling program is designed to provide students with a solid foundation for the practice of professional counseling. The program's curriculum integrates theoretical and conceptual foundations of professional counseling with training in appropriate client intervention and advocacy skills. The program emphasizes the development of attitudes, knowledge, and skills that are essential for professional counselors who are committed to the ethical provision of quality services. Students completing this program meet the academic requirements toward licensure as Licensed Professional Counselors (LPCs) in Georgia.

The M.A. in forensic psychology program is designed to educate and train individuals who are currently working, or wish to work, in fields that utilize the study and practice of forensic psychology. Curriculum provides for an understanding of theory, training, and practice of forensic psychology. It emphasizes the development of students who are committed to the ethical provision of quality services to diverse clients and organizations. The program maintains policies and delivery formats suitable for working adults. The M.A. in Forensic Psychology program provides coursework in forensic psychology for application to law enforcement, legal and organizational consultation, and program analysis.

The M.A. in industrial organizational psychology program is designed to apply the knowledge of industrial organizational psychology to issues involving individuals and groups in organizational and work settings. This program prepares students for careers in areas such as compensation, training, data analysis, consultation, statistical decision-making, organizational development, leadership, and human resource management positions. The curriculum is competency-based, focusing on the outcomes of training and on the knowledge, skills, and behavior necessary to function as a master's-level professional in industrial organizational psychology. This is an interdisciplinary program that combines the expertise of the faculty in the College of Psychology and Behavioral Sciences and the College of Business.

The M.A. in sport-exercise psychology program is designed to educate and train capable and ethical performance-enhancement specialists. This two-year degree is intended to meet the needs of students seeking employment in a variety of settings, including private practice, athletic departments, coaching, exercise/health, and education, as well as those planning to ultimately pursue their doctorate. The goals of the program include developing student competencies in the following areas: theoretical foundations, helping relationships, individual and group skills, normal and abnormal behavior, sport sciences, research and evaluation, diversity, and professional identity.

The Ed.D. in counselor education and supervision program aligns with the master's-level counselor education programs in order to encourage entry-level counseling students to work toward becoming doctoral-level advanced practitioners, educators, and supervisors. This program prepares counselors for a variety of settings by providing the advanced skills and knowledge necessary to provide leadership and advocacy, as well as serve in supervisory, training, and teaching positions in the counseling profession.

The Psy.D. in clinical psychology program has been designed to educate and train students so that they may eventually be able to function effectively as clinical psychologists. The curriculum provides for the meaningful integration of theory, training, and practice. The program emphasizes the development of attitudes, knowledge, and skills essential in the formation of professional psychologists who are committee do the ethical provision of quality services.

Research Facilities

Argosy University libraries provide curriculum support and educational resources, including current text materials, diagnostic training documents, reference materials and databases, journals and dissertations, and major and current titles in program areas. There is an online public-access catalog of library resources available throughout the Argosy University system. Students have remote access to the campus library database, enabling them to study and conduct research at home. Academic databases offer dissertation abstracts, academic journals, and professional periodicals. All library computers are Internet accessible. Software applications include Word, Excel, PowerPoint, SPSS, and various test-scoring programs.

Financial Aid

Financial aid is available to those who qualify. Argosy University, Atlanta, offers access to federal and state aid programs, merit-based awards, grants, loans, and a work-study program. As a first step, students should complete the Free Application for Federal Student Aid (FAFSA). Prospective students can apply electronically at http://www.fafsa.ed.gov or at the campus.

Cost of Study

Tuition varies by program. Students should contact Argosy University, Atlanta, for tuition information.

Living and Housing Costs

Students typically live in apartments in the metropolitan Atlanta area. Living expenses vary according to each student's preferred standard of living, housing, and transportation. The University does not offer or operate student housing. Most Argosy University students are full-time working professionals who live within driving distance of the campus. Several nearby hotels offer special rates for those who commute from long distances. The Admissions Department also maintains a list of housing options, including contact information for University students who wish to share housing. For more information, students should contact the Admissions Department.

Student Group

Admission to Argosy University, Atlanta, is selective to ensure a dynamic and engaged student body. The University encourages diversity in academic and employment backgrounds and promotes integration of the student body into professional life through established connections with local and national professional associations. Argosy University offers a professionally oriented education with rich opportunities to gain practical experience in class, field placements, and internships. Full-time students and working professionals can gain the extensive knowledge and range of skills necessary for effective performance in their chosen field.

Student Outcomes

Students can register with Argosy University's online career-services system and use select services from a distance, such as degree-specific career e-mail lists, national job posts, and virtual job fairs. Students should contact the University for more information.

Location

Argosy University, Atlanta, is housed in a modern building in Sandy Springs, a northern suburb of Atlanta. The campus features a café and outdoor lakeside terrace. Beyond the college, students will find a selection of housing options. This major metropolitan area offers many social and recreational opportunities, from clubs and concerts to galleries and museums, from a growing restaurant scene to Braves baseball games and rollerblading in Piedmont Park. The many hospitals, clinics, agencies, and educational institutions in the Atlanta area provide varied opportunities for student training. Atlanta's business environment includes technology companies such as EarthLink and Macquarium as well as corporate giants such as the Coca-Cola Company, CNN, Delta Air Lines, AT&T, and Georgia Pacific.

The University

Argosy University is a private institution with nineteen locations across the nation. Argosy University, Atlanta, provides a career resources office, an academic resources center, and extensive information access for research. It offers the resources of a large university plus the friendliness and personal attention of a small campus. The innovative programs feature dynamic, relevant, and practical curricula delivered in flexible class formats. Students enjoy scheduling options that make it easier to fit school into their busy lives, choosing from day and evening courses, on campus or online. Many students find a combination of class formats to be an ideal way of continuing their education while meeting family and professional demands.

Argosy University is accredited by the Higher Learning Commission and a member of the North Central Association (30 North LaSalle Street, Suite 2400, Chicago, Illinois 60602; 800-621-7440 (toll-free); http://www.ncahlc.org).

Applying

Argosy University, Atlanta, accepts students year-round on a rolling admissions basis, depending on availability of required courses. Applications for admission are available online or by contacting the campus.

Correspondence and Information

Argosy University, Atlanta
990 Hammond Drive, Suite 100
Atlanta, Georgia 30328
Phone: 770-671-1200
888-671-4777 (toll-free)
Fax: 770-671-0476
E-mail: auadmissions@argosy.edu
Web site: http://www.argosy.edu/atlanta

Argosy University, Atlanta

THE FACULTY

The Argosy University faculty is comprised of working professionals who are eager to help students succeed. Members bring real-world experience and the latest practice innovations to the academic setting. The diverse faculty members of the College of Psychology and Behavioral Sciences are widely recognized for contributions to the field. Many are published scholars, and most hold doctoral degrees. They are committed to providing a substantive education that combines comprehensive knowledge with critical skills and practical workplace relevance. Above all, faculty members are committed to their students' personal and professional development.

ARGOSY UNIVERSITY

ARGOSY UNIVERSITY, CHICAGO

College of Psychology and Behavioral Sciences

Programs of Study

Argosy University, Chicago, offers the Graduate Certificate in psychoanalytic psychology; the Master of Arts (M.A.) degree in clinical psychology, forensic psychology, industrial organizational psychology, and sport-exercise psychology; the Doctor of Education (Ed.D.) degree in counseling psychology, counselor education and supervision; and the Doctor of Psychology (Psy.D.) degree in clinical psychology. Students completing a program may wish to become licensed professionals. Argosy University, Chicago does not guarantee third-party certification/licensure. Outside agencies control the requirements for taking and passing certification/licensing exams and are subject to change without notice to Argosy University, Chicago.

The Graduate Certificate in psychoanalytic psychology provides specialized training in psychoanalytic psychology for post-master's and doctoral clinicians with relevant background and experience. The certificate is designed to meet the need for education and training in assessment, intervention, and supervision within a broad psychoanalytic model. The curriculum provides a firm grounding in major theoretical paradigms with special attention to those which are current and emerging. Graduates of the psychoanalytic psychology certificate will be prepared to work effectively within a psychoanalytic framework and begin additional training in psychoanalytic psychotherapy or psychoanalysis.

The M.A. in clinical psychology program has been designed to educate and train students to pursue a professional career as master's-level practitioners. The program is designed to provide students with an educational program with all the necessary theoretical and clinical elements that will allow them to be effective members of a mental health team. It introduces students to basic clinical skills that integrate individual and group theoretical foundations of applied psychology into appropriate client interaction and intervention skills. This program can be completed in as little as two years and must be completed in five years. In addition, the program offers preparation for those considering application to the Psy.D. in clinical psychology program.

The M.A. in forensic psychology program is designed to educate and train individuals who are currently working, or wish to work, in fields that utilize the study and practice of forensic psychology. Curriculum provides for an understanding of theory, training, and practice of forensic psychology. It emphasizes the development of students who are committed to the ethical provision of quality services to diverse clients and organizations. The program maintains policies and delivery formats suitable for working adults. The program provides course work in forensic psychology for application to law enforcement, legal and organizational consultation, and program analysis.

The M.A. in industrial organizational psychology is designed to apply the knowledge of industrial organizational psychology to issues involving individuals and groups in organizational and work settings. This program is designed to prepare students for careers in areas such as compensation, training, data analysis, consultation, statistical decision-making, organizational development, leadership, and human resource management positions. The curriculum is competency-based, focusing on the outcomes of training and on the knowledge, skills, and behavior necessary to function as a master's-level professional in industrial organizational psychology. This is an interdisciplinary program that combines the expertise of the faculty in the College of Psychology and Behavioral Sciences and the College of Business.

The M.A. in sport-exercise psychology program is designed to educate and train capable and ethical performance-enhancement specialists. This two-year degree is intended to meet the needs of students seeking employment in a variety of settings, including private practice, athletic departments, coaching, exercise/health, and education, as well as those planning to ultimately pursue their doctorate. The goals of the program include developing student competencies in the following areas: theoretical foundations, helping relationships, individual and group skills, normal and abnormal behavior, sport sciences, research and evaluation, diversity, and professional identity.

The Ed.D. in counseling psychology program is designed to meet the special requirements of working mental health professionals motivated to develop their knowledge and skills to handle the changing needs of modern organizations. The program is designed to provide working professionals with the opportunity to pursue their personal and professional goals through the completion of a graduate program. An optional concentration in counselor education and supervision is available.

The Ed.D. in counselor education and supervision program aligns with the master's-level counselor education programs in order to encourage entry-level counseling students to work toward becoming doctoral-level advanced practitioners, educators, and supervisors. The program prepares counselors for a variety of settings by providing the advanced skills and knowledge necessary to provide leadership and advocacy, as well as serve in supervisory, training, and teaching positions in the counseling profession. The program is designed to help current practitioners with existing master's-level preparation to advance their careers.

The Psy.D. in clinical psychology program has been designed to educate and train students so that they may be able to function effectively as clinical psychologists. To ensure that students are prepared adequately, the curriculum provides for the meaningful integration of theory, training, and practice. The program emphasizes the development of attitudes, knowledge, and skills essential in the formation of professional psychologists who are committed to the ethical provision of quality services.

Research Facilities

Argosy University libraries provide curriculum support and educational resources, including current text materials, diagnostic training documents, reference materials and databases, journals and dissertations, and major and current titles in program areas. There is an online public-access catalog of library resources available throughout the Argosy University system. Students have remote access to the campus library database, enabling them to study and conduct research at home. Academic databases offer dissertation abstracts, academic journals, and professional periodicals. All library computers are Internet accessible. Software applications include Word, Excel, PowerPoint, SPSS, and various test-scoring programs.

Financial Aid

Financial aid is available to those who qualify. Argosy University, Chicago, offers access to federal and state aid programs, merit-based awards, grants, loans, and a work-study program. As a first step, students should complete the Free Application for Federal Student Aid (FAFSA). Prospective students can apply electronically at http://www.fafsa.ed.gov or at the campus.

Cost of Study

Tuition varies by program. Students should contact Argosy University, Chicago, for tuition information.

Living and Housing Costs

Students typically live in apartments in the metropolitan Chicago area. Living expenses vary according to each student's preferred standard of living, housing, and transportation. The University does not offer or operate student housing. Most of the students are full-time working professionals who live within driving distance of the campus. Several nearby hotels offer special rates for those who commute from long distances. The Admissions Department also maintains a list of housing options, including contact information for university students who wish to share housing. For more information, students should contact the Admissions Department.

Student Group

Admission to Argosy University, Chicago, is selective to ensure a dynamic and engaged student body. The University encourages diversity in academic and employment backgrounds and promotes integration of the student body into professional life through established connections with local and national professional associations. Argosy University offers a professionally oriented education with rich opportunities to gain practical experience in class, field placements, and internships. Full-time students and working professionals gain the extensive knowledge and range of skills necessary for effective performance in their chosen fields.

Student Outcomes

Students can register with the University's online career-services system and use select services from a distance, such as degree-specific career e-mail lists, national job posts, and virtual job fairs. Students should contact the University for more information.

Location

Chicago is a city of world-class status and beauty, drawing visitors from around the globe. Argosy University, Chicago, sits in the heart of The Loop, the city's business and entertainment center. Located on the shores of Lake Michigan, Chicago is home to world-champion sports teams, an internationally acclaimed symphony orchestra, renowned architecture, and a variety of history and art museums. Recreational opportunities include hiking and cycling on miles of lakefront trails, golfing, and shopping. Chicago's business environment includes a broad array of companies including Boeing and Pepsi America. The commercial banking headquarters of JP Morgan Chase is also located in Chicago.

The University

Argosy University is a private institution with nineteen locations across the nation. Argosy University, Chicago, provides a career services office, an academic resources center, and extensive information access for research. It offers the resources of a large university plus the friendliness and personal attention of a small campus. Argosy University, Chicago, is closely associated with the Schaumburg, Illinois, campus, located 45 minutes from downtown Chicago.

The innovative programs feature dynamic, relevant, and practical curricula delivered in flexible class formats. Students enjoy scheduling options that make it easier to fit school into their busy lives, choosing from day and evening courses, on campus or online. Many students find a combination of class formats to be an ideal way of continuing their education while meeting family and professional demands.

Argosy University is accredited by the Higher Learning Commission and a member of the North Central Association (30 North LaSalle Street, Suite 2400, Chicago, Illinois 60602; 800-621-7440 (toll-free); http://www.ncahlc.org).

Applying

Argosy University, Chicago, accepts students year-round on a rolling admissions basis, depending on availability of required courses. Applications for admission are available online or by contacting the campus.

Correspondence and Information

Argosy University, Chicago
225 North Michigan Avenue, Suite 1300
Chicago, Illinois 60601
Phone: 312-777-7600
800-626-4123 (toll-free)
Fax: 312-777-7748
E-mail: auadmissions@argosy.edu
Web site: http://www.argosy.edu/chicago

Argosy University, Chicago

THE FACULTY

The Argosy University faculty is comprised of working professionals who are eager to help students succeed. Members bring real-world experience and the latest practice innovations to the academic setting. The diverse faculty members of the College of Psychology and Behavioral Sciences are widely recognized for contributions to the field. Many are published scholars, and most hold doctoral degrees. They are committed to providing a substantive education that combines comprehensive knowledge with critical skills and practical workplace relevance. Above all, faculty members are committed to their students' personal and professional development.

ARGOSY UNIVERSITY

ARGOSY UNIVERSITY, DALLAS

College of Psychology and Behavioral Sciences

Programs of Study

Argosy University, Dallas, offers the Master of Arts (M.A.) degree in clinical psychology, community counseling, forensic psychology, industrial organizational psychology, and school psychology; the Doctor of Education (Ed.D.) degree in counselor education and supervision; and the Doctor of Psychology (Psy.D.) degree in clinical psychology. Students completing a program may wish to become licensed professionals. Argosy University, Dallas does not guarantee third-party certification/licensure. Outside agencies control the requirements for taking and passing certification/licensing exams and are subject to change without notice to Argosy University, Dallas.

The M.A. in clinical psychology program is designed to educate and train students to enter professional careers as master's-level practitioners. Students are provided with an educational program that has all the necessary theoretical and clinical elements necessary for graduates to become effective members of a mental health team. The program introduces students to basic clinical skills that integrate individual and group theoretical foundations of applied psychology into appropriate client interaction and intervention skills. Additionally, it offers excellent preparation for those considering application to the Psy.D. in clinical psychology program.

The M.A. in community counseling program is designed to provide students with a sound foundation for the practice of community counseling, with a multifaceted focus on developmental and preventive mental health services. The program introduces students to the basic skills of counseling, integrating individual, group, family, and organizational interventions. The program emphasizes development of the attitudes, knowledge, and skills required for the ethical provision of quality professional counseling services. As such, the program is committed to educating and training students to enter the counseling profession as ethical, effective, skilled, and culturally competent practitioners, able to work in a variety of settings with diverse client populations. This goal is achieved through a curriculum designed to integrate foundational counseling skills, counseling theories, and clinical field experiences taught by experienced practitioners.

The M.A. in forensic psychology program is designed to educate and train individuals who are currently working, or wish to work, in fields that utilize the study and practice of forensic psychology. The curriculum is designed to provide for an understanding of theory, training, and practice of forensic psychology. It emphasizes the development of students who are committed to the ethical provision of quality services to diverse clients and organizations. The program maintains policies and delivery formats suitable for working adults. The program provides course work in forensic psychology for application to law enforcement, legal and organizational consultation, and program analysis.

The M.A. in industrial organizational psychology program is designed to apply the knowledge of industrial organizational psychology to issues involving individuals and groups in organizational and work settings. This program prepares students for careers in areas such as compensation, training, data analysis, consultation, statistical decision-making, organizational development, leadership, and human resource management positions. The curriculum is competency-based, focusing on the outcomes of training and on the knowledge, skills, and behavior necessary to function as a master's-level professional in industrial organizational psychology. This is an interdisciplinary program that combines the expertise of the faculty in the College of Psychology and Behavioral Sciences and the College of Business.

The M.A. in school psychology program is dedicated to producing ethical, responsible, and competent school psychologists who are able to serve effectively in a number of professional roles. During graduate training, students develop core competencies in psychological assessment, intervention, and consultation/education, as well as cultural and individual diversity. Graduates of the program may be eligible for department of education certification and will be prepared for employment as school psychologists. The program is designed to prepare students to become Nationally Certified School Psychologists (NCSPs) in accordance with criteria developed by the National Association of School Psychologists.

The Ed.D. in counselor education and supervision program aligns with the master's-level counselor education programs in order to encourage entry-level counseling students to work toward becoming doctoral-level advanced practitioners, educators, and supervisors. The program is designed to prepare counselors for a variety of settings by providing the advanced skills and knowledge necessary to provide leadership and advocacy, as well as serve in supervisory, training, and teaching positions in the counseling profession. The program is designed to help current practitioners with existing master's-level preparation to advance their careers. This doctorate provides expanded opportunities to compete in the marketplace, on par with the growing number of doctoral-level counseling practitioners.

The Psy.D. in clinical psychology program has been designed to educate and train students to function effectively for their eventual role as clinical psychologists. To enable students to be prepared adequately, the curriculum provides for the meaningful integration of theory and research as applied to practice. The program emphasizes the development of knowledge, skills, and attitudes essential in the formation of professional psychologists who are committed to the ethical provision of quality services.

Research Facilities

Argosy University libraries provide curriculum support and educational resources, including current text materials, diagnostic training documents, reference materials and databases, journals and dissertations, and major and current titles in program areas. There is an online public-access catalog of library resources available throughout the Argosy University system. Students have remote access to the campus library database, enabling them to study and conduct research at home. Academic databases offer dissertation abstracts, academic journals, and professional periodicals. All library computers are Internet accessible. Software applications include Word, Excel, PowerPoint, SPSS, and various test-scoring programs.

Financial Aid

Financial aid is available to those who qualify. Argosy University, Dallas, offers access to federal and state aid programs, merit-based awards, grants, loans, and a work-study program. As a first step, students should complete the Free Application for Federal Student Aid (FAFSA). Prospective students can apply electronically at http://www.fafsa.ed.gov or at the campus.

Cost of Study

Tuition varies by program. Students should contact Argosy University, Dallas, for tuition information.

Living and Housing Costs

Students typically live in apartments in the metropolitan Dallas area. Living expenses vary according to each student's preferred standard of living, housing, and transportation. The University does not offer or operate student housing. Most of the students are full-time working professionals who live within driving distance of the campus. Several nearby hotels offer special rates for those who commute from long distances. The Admissions Department also maintains a list of housing options, including contact information, for University students who wish to share housing. For more information, students should contact the Admissions Department.

Student Group

Admission to Argosy University, Dallas, is selective to ensure a dynamic and engaged student body. The University encourages diversity in academic and employment backgrounds and promotes integration of the student body into professional life through established connections with local and national professional associations. Argosy University offers a professionally oriented education with rich opportunities to gain practical experience in class, field placements, and internships. Full-time students and working professionals gain the extensive knowledge and range of skills necessary for effective performance in their chosen fields.

Student Outcomes

Students can register with the University's online career-services system and use select services from a distance, such as degree-specific career e-mail lists, national job posts, and virtual job fairs. Students should contact the University for more information.

Location

Argosy University, Dallas, offers a north-central location in Dallas, with easy access to freeways, neighboring colleges and universities, libraries, shops, restaurants, theaters, art museums, and other tourist attractions. The business environment in the Dallas–Fort Worth metropolitan area includes a broad array of companies, such as Lockheed Martin Corporation, Baylor University Medical System, and Southwest Airlines.

The University

Argosy University is a private institution with nineteen locations across the nation. Argosy University, Dallas, provides a career resources office, an academic resources center, and extensive information access for research. It offers the resources of a large university, plus the friendliness and personal attention of a small campus.

Argosy University, Dallas, offers the unique opportunity to take one class at a time, with each class lasting for one month. Students are never required to study for multiple exams at the same time. New classes start each month. This flexible format lets students begin working on a graduate degree without waiting for the traditional semester to start.

Argosy University is accredited by the Higher Learning Commission and a member of the North Central Association (30 North LaSalle Street, Suite 2400, Chicago, Illinois 60602; 800-621-7440 (toll-free); http://www.ncahlc.org).

Applying

Argosy University, Dallas, accepts students year-round on a rolling admissions basis, depending on availability of required courses. Applications for admission are available online or by contacting the campus.

Correspondence and Information

Argosy University, Dallas
5001 Lyndon B. Johnson Freeway
Heritage Square
Farmers Branch, Texas 75244
Phone: 214-890-9900
866-954-9900 (toll-free)
Fax: 214-378-8555
E-mail: http://auadmissions@argosy.edu
Web site: http://www.argosy.edu/dallas

Argosy University, Dallas

THE FACULTY

The Argosy University faculty is comprised of working professionals who are eager to help students succeed. Members bring real-world experience and the latest practice innovations to the academic setting. The diverse faculty members of the College of Psychology and Behavioral Sciences are widely recognized for contributions to the field. Many are published scholars, and most hold doctoral degrees. They are committed to providing a substantive education that combines comprehensive knowledge with critical skills and practical workplace relevance. Above all, faculty members are committed to their students' personal and professional development.

ARGOSY UNIVERSITY.

ARGOSY UNIVERSITY, DENVER

College of Psychology and Behavioral Sciences

Programs of Study

Argosy University, Denver, offers the Master of Arts (M.A.) degree in clinical psychology, community counseling, forensic psychology, industrial organizational psychology, and marriage and family therapy; the Doctor of Marriage and Family Therapy (D.M.F.T.) degree; the Doctor of Education (Ed.D.) degree in counseling psychology, counselor education and supervision, and organizational leadership; and the Doctor of Psychology (Psy.D.) degree in clinical psychology. Students completing a program may wish to become licensed professionals. Argosy University, Denver does not guarantee third-party certification/licensure. Outside agencies control the requirements for taking and passing certification/licensing exams and are subject to change without notice to Argosy University, Denver.

The M.A. in clinical psychology program prepares students with the clinical knowledge and skills required to serve the mental health needs of individuals and groups. Students develop proficiency in clinical observation, assessment, appropriate intervention, and evaluation. The program emphasizes a practitioner-oriented philosophy and integrates applied theory, research, and field experience. It is designed for students who are interested in a terminal degree and practice as a master's-level clinician or for students planning to transfer to the Psy.D. program.

The M.A. in community counseling program prepares students to enter the counseling profession as ethical, effective, skilled, and culturally competent practitioners. It provides a multifaceted focus on developmental and preventive mental health services. Students gain the knowledge and skills required for individual, group, family, and organizational interventions. The curriculum integrates foundational counseling skills and theories with clinical field experience.

The M.A. in forensic psychology program provides course work in forensic psychology for application to law enforcement, legal and organizational consultation, and program analysis. The program is designed to meet growing needs of the legal and criminal justice systems for professional counseling within victim assistance programs, probation and parole offices, court-mandated treatment programs, jails, and prisons. With the exception of the practicum component, courses are offered on weekends, allowing students to continue full-time employment while enrolled in this program.

The M.A. in industrial organizational psychology program is designed to apply the knowledge of industrial organizational psychology to issues involving individuals and groups in organizational and work settings. This program prepares students for careers in areas such as compensation, training, data analysis, consultation, statistical decision making, organizational development, leadership, and human resource management positions. The curriculum is competency based, focusing on the outcomes of training and on the knowledge, skills, and behavior necessary to function as a master's-level professional in industrial organizational psychology. This is an interdisciplinary program that combines the expertise of the faculty in the Colleges of Psychology and Behavioral Sciences and Business.

The M.A. in marriage and family therapy program is designed to develop the theoretical and clinical elements required to provide effective counseling to individuals, couples, families, and groups. The program introduces basic counseling skills that incorporate foundations of applied psychology and systems theory into the development of appropriate clinical relationships. Course work in addiction studies and substance-abuse counseling prepares students to work with families affected by this burgeoning problem. Marriage and family therapy is recognized by the Public Health Service Act as one of the five core mental health professions, and the National Institute of Mental Health accepts marriage and family therapists as qualified mental health professionals. The program is offered through weekend courses to allow concurrent employment.

The Doctor of Marriage and Family Therapy is a practice-oriented degree for licensed marriage and family therapists or professionals who can meet state requirements for licensure as a marriage and family therapist (meeting the Commission on Accreditation of Marriage and Family Therapy Education (COAMFTE) criteria for clinical practice prior to admission). The program seeks to build upon students' prior learning and professional experience by expanding and deepening their knowledge of human development, family dynamics, systemic thinking, interactional theories, traditional and contemporary marriage and family therapy theories and practices, and the cultural contexts within which these are embedded.

The Ed.D. in counseling psychology program is designed to prepare counselors with the skills and credentials necessary to pursue leadership, supervision, training, and teaching positions. Students have the opportunity to develop new interests and levels of competency through an applied research-practitioner approach to the role of professional counselor. An optional concentration in counselor education and supervision is available. The challenges of a changing society and the diversity of roles available to the mental health practitioner require a lifelong commitment to continuing education.

The Ed.D. in counselor education and supervision program is designed to develop the advanced skills and knowledge necessary for leadership and advocacy roles in a variety of settings. The field is dedicated to both the academic preparation and comprehensive supervision of counselors across multiple settings. This course of study aligns with the Master of Arts in professional counseling program to encourage entry-level counseling students to work toward becoming doctoral-level advanced practitioners, educators, and supervisors.

The Ed.D. in organizational leadership program is designed for working professionals who wish to develop the knowledge and skills required to hold leadership positions in complex organizations. The program focuses on transformational leadership skills in addition to managerial attributes. This approach prepares students for strategic challenges such as increasing globalization, changing economies, societal shifts, and individual-organizational relationships. Leaders prepared in this manner can become visionaries and innovators, leading viable organizations capable of meeting the challenges of the future.

The Psy.D. in clinical psychology program prepares students to deliver basic diagnostic and therapeutic services to diverse populations, including individuals, groups, and families. By integrating theory, training, research, and practice, students develop and apply the clinical skills of observation, assessment, intervention, and evaluation. Optional concentrations are available in child and family psychology, general adult clinical, health psychology, or neuropsychology/geropsychology. The program prepares graduates for positions in traditional settings, including, but not limited to, independent practice, mental health centers, hospitals, medical centers, and managed-care systems. Graduates are encouraged to utilize clinical skills in innovative ways to become more competitive. Eventual positions may include consulting in various corporate, governmental, academic, multimedia, law, scientific, marketing, and industrial settings.

Research Facilities

Argosy University libraries provide curriculum support and educational resources, including current text materials, diagnostic training documents, reference materials and databases, journals and dissertations, and major and current titles in program areas. There is an online public-access catalog of library resources available throughout the Argosy University system. Students have remote access to the campus library database, enabling them to study and conduct research at home. Academic databases offer dissertation abstracts, academic journals, and professional periodicals. All library computers are Internet accessible. Software applications include Word, Excel, PowerPoint, SPSS, and various test-scoring programs.

Financial Aid

Financial aid is available to those who qualify. Argosy University, Denver, offers access to federal and state aid programs, merit-based awards, grants, loans, and a work-study program. As a first step, students should complete the Free Application for Federal Student Aid (FAFSA). Prospective students can apply electronically at http://www.fafsa.ed.gov or at the campus.

Cost of Study

Tuition varies by program. Students should contact Argosy University, Denver, for tuition information.

Living and Housing Costs

Students typically live in apartments in the metropolitan Denver area. Living expenses vary according to each student's preferred standard of living, housing, and transportation. The University does not offer or operate student housing. Most of the students are full-time working professionals who live within driving distance of the campus. Several nearby hotels offer special rates for those who commute from long distances. The Admissions Department also maintains a list of housing options, including contact information for University students who wish to share housing. For more information, students should contact the Admissions Department.

Student Group

Admission to Argosy University, Denver, is selective to ensure a dynamic and engaged student body. The University encourages diversity in academic and employment backgrounds and promotes integration of the student body into professional life through established connections with local and national professional associations. Argosy University offers a professionally oriented education with rich opportunities to gain practical experience in class, field placements, and internships. Full-time students and working professionals gain the extensive knowledge and range of skills necessary for effective performance in their chosen fields.

Student Outcomes

Students can register with the University's online career-services system and use select services from a distance, such as degree-specific career e-mail lists, national job posts, and virtual job fairs. Students should contact the University for more information.

Location

Argosy University, Denver, is conveniently located at 7600 East Eastman Avenue in Denver, Colorado. The campus is close to a variety of local libraries, shops, restaurants, theaters, and art museums. Denver's thriving professional organizations, major corporations, high-tech companies, hospitals, schools, clinics, and social service agencies can also provide varied training opportunities for students.

The University

Argosy University is a private institution with nineteen locations across the nation. Argosy University, Denver, provides a career resources office, an academic resources center, and extensive information access for research. It offers the resources of a large university plus the friendliness and personal attention of a small campus.

The innovative programs feature dynamic, relevant, and practical curricula delivered in flexible class formats. Students enjoy scheduling options that make it easier to fit school into their busy lives, choosing from day and evening courses, on campus or online. Many students find a combination of class formats to be an ideal way of continuing their education while meeting family and professional demands.

Argosy University is accredited by the Higher Learning Commission and a member of the North Central Association (30 North LaSalle Street, Suite 2400, Chicago, Illinois 60602; 800-621-7440 (toll-free); http://www.ncahlc.org).

Applying

Argosy University, Denver, accepts students year-round on a rolling admissions basis, depending on availability of required courses. Applications for admission are available online or by contacting the campus.

Correspondence and Information

Argosy University, Denver
7600 East Eastman Avenue
Denver, Colorado 80213

Phone: 303-248-2700
866-431-5981 (toll-free)
Fax: 303-248-2600
E-mail: auadmissions@argosy.edu
Web site: http://www.argosy.edu/denver

Argosy University, Denver

THE FACULTY

The Argosy University faculty is comprised of working professionals who are eager to help students succeed. Members bring real-world experience and the latest practice innovations to the academic setting. The diverse faculty members of the College of Psychology and Behavioral Sciences are widely recognized for contributions to the field. Many are published scholars, and most hold doctoral degrees. They are committed to providing a substantive education that combines comprehensive knowledge with critical skills and practical workplace relevance. Above all, faculty members are committed to their students' personal and professional development.

ARGOSY UNIVERSITY.

ARGOSY UNIVERSITY, HAWAI'I

College of Psychology and Behavioral Sciences

Programs of Study

Argosy University, Hawai'i, offers the Master of Arts (M.A.) degree in clinical psychology, forensic psychology, and marriage and family therapy; the Master of Science (M.S.) in psychopharmacology; the Doctor of Education (Ed.D.) degree in counseling psychology, and counselor education and supervision; and the Doctor of Psychology (Psy.D.) degree in clinical psychology. Students completing a program may wish to become licensed professionals. Argosy University, Hawai'i does not guarantee third-party certification/licensure. Outside agencies control the requirements for taking and passing certification/ licensing exams and are subject to change without notice to Argosy University, Hawai'i.

The M.A. in clinical psychology program is designed as both a terminal degree and for those who plan to pursue doctoral study. The program is designed to provide a solid core of basic psychology, as well as a strong clinical orientation, with an emphasis in psychological assessment. The curriculum is designed to provide the theoretical and clinical elements to allow students to become effective members of mental health teams.

The M.A. in forensic psychology program is designed to educate and train individuals who are currently working, or wish to work, in fields that utilize the study and practice of forensic psychology. Curriculum provides for an understanding of theory, training, and practice of forensic psychology. It emphasizes the development of students who are committed to the ethical provision of quality services to diverse clients and organizations. The program maintains policies and delivery formats suitable for working adults. The program provides course work in forensic psychology for application to law enforcement, legal and organizational consultation, and program analysis.

The M.A. in marriage and family therapy program recognizes the need to provide marriage and family therapists with the knowledge and range of skills necessary to function effectively in their profession. The program introduces students to basic skills that integrate systemic theoretical foundations of marriage and family therapy into appropriate client interaction and intervention skills. The program emphasizes the development of attitudes, knowledge, and skills essential in the formation of marriage and family therapists who are committed to the ethical provision of quality services. The program has been developed by the school's faculty members to provide working students with the opportunity to pursue personal and professional goals through completion of a master's program.

The M.S. in psychopharmacology program incorporates course work and clinical practice to comprehensively train postdoctoral psychologists to prescribe medications independently, appropriately, effectively, and safely. It is a 32-credit-hour program with a practicum component requiring treatment of 100 patients. Upon successful completion of the program, students have the education and experience to prescribe psychopharmacological medications consistent with state and federal laws and work collaboratively with physicians, nurses, and other health-care providers to coordinate care. This program is intended to prepare students for the Psychopharmacology Exam for Psychologists (PEP).

The Ed.D. in counseling psychology program is designed to meet the special requirements of working mental health professionals who want to develop their knowledge and skills to handle the changing needs of modern organizations. The program is designed to provide working professionals with the opportunity to pursue their personal and professional goals through the completion of a graduate program.

The Ed.D. in counselor education and supervision program aligns with the master's-level counselor education programs in order to encourage entry-level counseling students to work toward becoming doctoral-level advanced practitioners, educators, and supervisors. This program prepares counselors for a variety of settings by providing the advanced skills and knowledge necessary to provide leadership and advocacy, as well as serve in supervisory, training, and teaching positions in the counseling profession.

The Psy.D. in clinical psychology program is designed to prepare students for both contemporary and emerging roles in the practice of professional psychology. Students are trained to be practitioner scholars who are skilled in local and contextual investigation and problem solving. The school offers a generalist program that supports the development of core competencies in psychological assessment, intervention, consultation/education, and management/ supervision. The curriculum provides for the meaningful integration of theory, research, and practice. The doctoral program emphasizes the acquisition of attitudes, knowledge bases, and skills essential for professional psychologists who are committed to the provision of ethical quality services.

Research Facilities

Argosy University libraries provide curriculum support and educational resources, including current text materials, diagnostic training documents, reference materials and databases, journals and dissertations, and major and current titles in program areas. There is an online public-access catalog of library resources available throughout the Argosy University system. Students have remote access to the campus library database, enabling them to study and conduct research at home. Academic databases offer dissertation abstracts, academic journals, and professional periodicals. All library computers are Internet accessible. Software applications include Word, Excel, PowerPoint, SPSS, and various test-scoring programs.

Financial Aid

Financial aid is available to those who qualify. Argosy University, Hawai'i, offers access to federal and state aid programs, merit-based awards, grants, loans, and a work-study program. As a first step, students should complete the Free Application for Federal Student Aid (FAFSA). Prospective students can apply electronically at http://www.fafsa.ed.gov or at the campus.

Cost of Study

Tuition varies by program. Students should contact Argosy University, Hawai'i, for tuition information.

Living and Housing Costs

Students typically live in apartments in the metropolitan Honolulu area. Living expenses vary according to each student's preferred standard of living, housing, and transportation. The University does not offer or operate student housing. Most of the students are full-time working professionals who live within driving distance of the campus. Several nearby hotels offer special rates for those who commute from long distances. The Admissions Department also maintains a list of housing options, including contact information for University students who wish to share housing. For more information, students should contact the Admissions Department.

Student Group

Admission to Argosy University, Hawai'i, is selective to ensure a dynamic and engaged student body. The University encourages diversity in academic and employment backgrounds and promotes integration of the student body into professional life through established connections with local and national professional associations. Argosy University offers a professionally oriented education with rich opportunities to gain practical experience in class, field placements, and internships. Full-time students and working professionals gain the extensive knowledge and range of skills necessary for effective performance in their chosen fields.

Student Outcomes

Students can register with the University's online career-services system and use select services from a distance, such as degree-specific career e-mail lists, national job posts, and virtual job fairs. Students should contact the University for more information.

Location

Argosy University, Hawai'i, is located in downtown Honolulu on Oahu. Additional satellite locations on Maui and in Hilo on the island of Hawaii offer programs to communities on the neighboring islands. These locations connect the campus to Hawaii and to the local and native communities of the Pacific Islands and the Pacific Rim. Students enjoy the cultural and recreational opportunities that these locations provide. University faculty and staff members often work in cooperation with the Hawaiian community to create an educational focus on social issues, human diversity, and programs that make a difference to underserved populations.

Honolulu's business environment includes a broad array of companies. The area's largest employers include Bank of Hawaii, Queens Medical Center, and the U.S. government. Many businesses in the metropolitan area provide varied opportunities for student training.

The University

Argosy University is a private institution with nineteen locations across the nation. Argosy University, Hawai'i, provides a career resources office, an academic resources center, and extensive information access for research. It offers the resources of a large university plus the friendliness and personal attention of a small campus.

The innovative programs feature dynamic, relevant, and practical curricula delivered in flexible class formats. Students enjoy scheduling options that make it easier to fit school into their busy lives, choosing from day and evening courses, on campus or online. Many students find a combination of class formats to be an ideal way of continuing their education while meeting family and professional demands.

Argosy University is accredited by the Higher Learning Commission and a member of the North Central Association (30 North LaSalle Street, Suite 2400, Chicago, Illinois 60602; 800-621-7440 (toll-free); http://www.ncahlc.org).

Applying

Argosy University, Hawai'i, accepts students year-round on a rolling admissions basis, depending on availability of required courses. Applications for admission are available online or by contacting the campus.

Correspondence and Information

Argosy University, Hawai'i
400 ASB Tower
1001 Bishop Street
Honolulu, Hawaii 96813

Phone: 808-536-5555
888-323-2777 (toll-free)
Fax: 808-536-5505
E-mail: auadmissions@argosy.edu
Web site: http://www.argosy.edu/hawaii

Argosy University, Hawai'i

THE FACULTY

The Argosy University faculty is comprised of working professionals who are eager to help students succeed. Members bring real-world experience and the latest practice innovations to the academic setting. The diverse faculty members of the College of Psychology and Behavioral Sciences are widely recognized for contributions to the field. Many are published scholars, and most hold doctoral degrees. They are committed to providing a substantive education that combines comprehensive knowledge with critical skills and practical workplace relevance. Above all, faculty members are committed to their students' personal and professional development.

ARGOSY UNIVERSITY.

ARGOSY UNIVERSITY, INLAND EMPIRE

College of Psychology and Behavioral Sciences

Programs of Study

Argosy University, Inland Empire, offers the Master of Arts (M.A.) degree in clinical psychology/marriage and family therapy, counseling psychology/marriage and family therapy, forensic psychology, industrial organizational psychology, and sport-exercise psychology; and the Doctor of Education (Ed.D.) degree in counseling psychology. Students completing a program may wish to become licensed professionals. Argosy University, Inland Empire does not guarantee third-party certification/licensure. Outside agencies control the requirements for taking and passing certification/licensing exams and are subject to change without notice to Argosy University, Inland Empire.

The M.A. in clinical psychology/marriage and family therapy program is designed for students who wish to pursue the clinical psychology track while receiving graduate-level training in the core curricular areas, including supervised clinical practice, required for licensure as a marriage and family therapist in California. Licensing requirements differ from state to state, so students should verify the current licensing requirements of the state in which they plan to become licensed. The program emphasizes a practitioner-oriented philosophy, and integrates applied theory and field experience.

The M.A. in counseling psychology/marriage and family therapy program prepares students to practice and pursue licensure in California as Marriage and Family Therapists (MFT). Students are provided with an educational program that has all the necessary theoretical and practical elements designed to allow them to be effective members of a mental health team. The program introduces students to skills that integrate individual and group theoretical foundations of counseling psychology into appropriate client interaction and intervention skills.

The M.A. in forensic psychology program is designed to educate and train individuals who are currently working, or wish to work, in fields that utilize the study and practice of forensic psychology. Curriculum provides for an understanding of theory, training, and practice of forensic psychology. It emphasizes the development of students who are committed to the ethical provision of quality services to diverse clients and organizations. The program maintains policies and delivery formats suitable for working adults. The program provides coursework in forensic psychology for application to law enforcement, legal and organizational consultation, and program analysis.

The M.A. in industrial organizational psychology program is designed to apply the knowledge of industrial organizational psychology to issues involving individuals and groups in organizational and work settings. This program prepares students for careers in areas such as compensation, training, data analysis, consultation, statistical decision-making, organizational development, leadership, and human resource management positions. The curriculum is competency-based, focusing on the outcomes of training and on the knowledge, skills, and behavior necessary to function as a master's-level professional in industrial organizational psychology. This is an interdisciplinary program that combines the expertise of the faculty in the College of Psychology and Behavioral Sciences and the College of Business.

The M.A. in sport-exercise psychology program is designed to educate and train capable and ethical performance-enhancement specialists. This two-year degree is intended to meet the needs of students seeking employment in a variety of settings, including private practice, athletic departments, coaching, exercise/health, and education, as well as those planning to ultimately pursue their doctorate. The goals of the program include developing student competencies in the following areas: theoretical foundations, helping relationships, individual and group skills, normal and abnormal behavior, sport sciences, research and evaluation, diversity, and professional identity.

The Ed.D. in counseling psychology program embraces a range of relevant theory and techniques applicable in the three major areas of counseling psychology: (a) the remedial (assisting in remedying problems in living); (b) the preventive (anticipating, circumventing, and forestalling difficulties that may arise in the future); and (c) the educative and developmental (discovering and developing potentialities). That is (a) the focus is on normal individuals, and developmental life stages challenges; (b) a focus on assets, strengths, and positive mental health; (c) an emphasis on relatively brief interventions; and (d) an emphasis on context, sociocultural/political influences, diversity, and person-environment interactions rather than exclusive emphasis on the individual.

Research Facilities

Argosy University libraries provide curriculum support and educational resources, including current text materials, diagnostic training documents, reference materials and databases, journals and dissertations, and major and current titles in program areas. There is an online public-access catalog of library resources available throughout the Argosy University system. Students have remote access to the campus library database, enabling them to study and conduct research at home. Academic databases offer dissertation abstracts, academic journals, and professional periodicals. All library computers are Internet accessible. Software applications include Word, Excel, PowerPoint, SPSS, and various test-scoring programs.

Financial Aid

Financial aid is available to those who qualify. Argosy University, Inland Empire, offers access to federal and state aid programs, merit-based awards, grants, loans, and a work-study program. As a first step, students should complete the Free Application for Federal Student Aid (FAFSA). Prospective students can apply electronically at http://www.fafsa.ed.gov or at the campus.

Cost of Study

Tuition varies by program. Students should contact Argosy University, Inland Empire, for tuition information.

Living and Housing Costs

Students typically live in apartments in the San Bernardino metropolitan area. Living expenses vary according to each student's preferred standard of living, housing, and transportation. The University does not offer or operate student housing. Most of the students are full-time working professionals who live within driving distance of the campus. Several nearby hotels offer special rates for those who commute from long distances. The Admissions Department also maintains a list of housing options, including contact information for University students who wish to share housing. For more information, students should contact the Admissions Department.

Student Group

Admission to Argosy University, Inland Empire, is selective to ensure a dynamic and engaged student body. The University encourages diversity in academic and employment backgrounds and promotes integration of the student body into professional life through established connections with local and national professional associations. Argosy University offers a professionally oriented education with rich opportunities to gain practical experience in class, field placements, and internships. Full-time students and working professionals gain the extensive knowledge and range of skills necessary for effective performance in their chosen field.

Student Outcomes

Students can register with the University's online career-services system and use select services from a distance, such as degree-specific career e-mail lists, national job posts, and virtual job fairs. Students should contact the University for more information.

Location

Argosy University, Inland Empire, is conveniently located in the Hospitality Lane section of San Bernardino, California. The facility features classrooms, computer labs, a resource center with Internet access, a student lounge, staff and faculty offices, and proximity to the region's many cultural and recreational attractions. The University provides a supportive educational environment with convenient class options that enable students to earn a degree while fulfilling other life responsibilities. All of the programs are thoroughly oriented to the real working world. Argosy University focuses on developing technical proficiency in each student's field as well as an overall professional career approach.

The University

Argosy University is a private institution with nineteen locations across the nation. Argosy University, Inland Empire, provides a career resources office, an academic resources center, and extensive information access for research. It offers the resources of a large university plus the friendliness and personal attention of a small campus.

The innovative programs feature dynamic, relevant, and practical curricula delivered in flexible class formats. Students enjoy scheduling options that make it easier to fit school into their busy lives, choosing from day and evening courses, on campus or online. Many students find a combination of class formats to be an ideal way of continuing their education while meeting family and professional demands.

Argosy University is accredited by the Higher Learning Commission and a member of the North Central Association (30 North LaSalle Street, Suite 2400, Chicago, Illinois 60602; 800-621-7440 (toll-free); http://www.ncahlc.org).

Applying

Argosy University, Inland Empire, accepts students year-round on a rolling admissions basis, depending on availability of required courses. Applications for admission are available online or by contacting the campus.

Correspondence and Information

Argosy University, Inland Empire
636 East Brier Drive, Suite 120
San Bernardino, California 92408
Phone: 909-915-3800
866-217-9075 (toll-free)
Fax: 909-915-3810
E-mail: auadmissions@argosy.edu
Web site: http://www.argosy.edu/inlandempire

Argosy University, Inland Empire

THE FACULTY

The Argosy University faculty is comprised of working professionals who are eager to help students succeed. Members bring real-world experience and the latest practice innovations to the academic setting. The diverse faculty members of the College of Psychology and Behavioral Sciences are widely recognized for contributions to the field. Many are published scholars, and most hold doctoral degrees. They are committed to providing a substantive education that combines comprehensive knowledge with critical skills and practical workplace relevance. Above all, faculty members are committed to their students' personal and professional development.

ARGOSY UNIVERSITY

ARGOSY UNIVERSITY, LOS ANGELES

College of Psychology and Behavioral Sciences

Programs of Study

Argosy University, Los Angeles, offers the Master of Arts (M.A.) degree in clinical psychology/marriage and family therapy, counseling psychology/marriage and family therapy, and forensic psychology; and the Doctor of Education (Ed.D.) degree in counseling psychology. Students completing a program may wish to become licensed professionals. Argosy University, Los Angeles does not guarantee third-party certification/licensure. Outside agencies control the requirements for taking and passing certification/licensing exams and are subject to change without notice to Argosy University, Los Angeles.

The M.A. in clinical psychology/marriage and family therapy program is designed for students who wish to pursue the clinical psychology track while receiving graduate-level training in the core curricular areas, including supervised clinical practice, required for licensure as a marriage and family therapist in California. Licensing requirements differ from state to state, so students should verify the current licensing requirements of the state in which they plan to become licensed. This program emphasizes a practitioner-oriented philosophy, and integrates applied theory and field experience.

The M.A. in counseling psychology/marriage and family therapy program is designed to prepare students to practice and pursue licensure in California as Marriage and Family Therapists (MFT). Students receive an educational program with all the necessary theoretical and practical elements designed to allow them to be effective members of a mental health team. The program introduces students to skills that integrate individual and group theoretical foundations of counseling psychology into appropriate client interaction and intervention skills.

The M.A. in forensic psychology program is designed to educate and train individuals who are currently working, or wish to work, in fields that utilize the study and practice of forensic psychology. Curriculum provides for an understanding of theory, training, and practice of forensic psychology. It emphasizes the development of students who are committed to the ethical provision of quality services to diverse clients and organizations. The program maintains policies and delivery formats suitable for working adults. The program provides course work in forensic psychology for application to law enforcement, legal and organizational consultation, and program analysis.

The Ed.D. in counseling psychology program embraces a range of relevant theory and techniques applicable in the three major areas of counseling psychology: (a) the remedial (assisting in remedying problems in living); (b) the preventive (anticipating, circumventing, and forestalling difficulties that may arise in the future); and (c) the educative and developmental (discovering and developing potentialities). That is (a) the focus is on normal individuals, and developmental life stages challenges; (b) a focus on assets, strengths, and positive mental health; (c) an emphasis on relatively brief interventions; and (d) an emphasis on context, sociocultural/political influences, diversity, and person-environment interactions rather than exclusive emphasis on the individual.

Research Facilities

Argosy University libraries provide curriculum support and educational resources, including current text materials, diagnostic training documents, reference materials and databases, journals and dissertations, and major and current titles in program areas. There is an online public-access catalog of library resources available throughout the Argosy University system. Students have remote access to the campus library database, enabling them to study and conduct research at home. Academic databases offer dissertation abstracts, academic journals, and professional periodicals. All library computers are Internet accessible. Software applications include Word, Excel, PowerPoint, SPSS, and various test-scoring programs.

Financial Aid

Financial aid is available to those who qualify. Argosy University, Los Angeles, offers access to federal and state aid programs, merit-based awards, grants, loans, and a work-study program. As a first step, students should complete the Free Application for Federal Student Aid (FAFSA). Prospective students can apply electronically at http://www.fafsa.ed.gov or at the campus.

Cost of Study

Tuition varies by program. Students should contact Argosy University, Los Angeles, for tuition information.

Living and Housing Costs

Students typically live in apartments in the metropolitan Santa Monica area. Living expenses vary according to each student's preferred standard of living, housing, and transportation. The University does not offer or operate student housing. Most Argosy University students are full-time working professionals who live within driving distance of the campus. Several nearby hotels offer special rates for those who commute from long distances. The Admissions Department also maintains a list of housing options, including contact information for University students who wish to share housing. For more information, students should contact the Admissions Department.

Student Group

Admission to Argosy University, Los Angeles, is selective to ensure a dynamic and engaged student body. The University encourages diversity in academic and employment backgrounds and promotes integration of the student body into professional life through established connections with local and national professional associations. Argosy University offers a professionally oriented education with rich opportunities to gain practical experience in class, field placements, and internships. Full-time students and working professionals gain the extensive knowledge and range of skills necessary for effective performance in their chosen fields.

Student Outcomes

Students can register with the University's online career-services system and use select services from a distance, such as degree-specific career e-mail lists, national job posts, and virtual job fairs. Students should contact the University for more information.

Location

Argosy University, Los Angeles, is conveniently located just minutes from Los Angeles International Airport and the Pacific coast, near the interchange between I-405 and I-105. The business environment in the Los Angeles metropolitan area offers a broad array of companies, including a proliferation of entertainment, technology, and software firms. Among the principal employers in the area are Yahoo!, MTV Networks, RAND Corporation, and Symantec Corporation. The many businesses in the area provide varied opportunities for student training.

The University

Argosy University is a private institution with nineteen locations across the nation. Argosy University, Los Angeles, provides students with a career resources office, an academic resources center, and extensive information access for research. It offers the resources of a large university plus the friendliness and personal attention of a small campus.

The innovative programs feature dynamic, relevant, and practical curricula delivered in flexible class formats. Students enjoy scheduling options that make it easier to fit school into their busy lives, choosing from day and evening courses, on campus or online. Many students find a combination of class formats to be an ideal way of continuing their education while meeting family and professional demands.

Argosy University is accredited by the Higher Learning Commission and a member of the North Central Association (30 North LaSalle Street, Suite 2400, Chicago, Illinois 60602; 800-621-7440 (toll-free); http://www.ncahlc.org).

Applying

Argosy University, Los Angeles, accepts students year-round on a rolling admissions basis, depending on availability of required courses. Applications for admission are available online or by contacting the campus.

Correspondence and Information

Argosy University, Los Angeles
5230 Pacific Concourse
Los Angeles, California 90045

Phone: 310-866-4000
866-505-0332 (toll-free)
Fax: 310-399-1804
E-mail: auadmissions@argosy.edu
Web site: http://www.argosy.edu/losangeles

Argosy University, Los Angeles

THE FACULTY

The Argosy University faculty is comprised of working professionals who are eager to help students succeed. Members bring real-world experience and the latest practice innovations to the academic setting. The diverse faculty members of the College of Psychology and Behavioral Sciences are is widely recognized for contributions to the field. Many are published scholars, and most hold doctoral degrees. They are committed to providing a substantive education that combines comprehensive knowledge with critical skills and practical workplace relevance. Above all, faculty members are committed to their students' personal and professional development.

ARGOSY UNIVERSITY

ARGOSY UNIVERSITY, NASHVILLE

College of Psychology and Behavioral Sciences

Programs of Study

Argosy University, Nashville, offers the Master of Arts (M.A.) degree in mental health counseling, the Doctor of Education (Ed.D.) degree in counselor education and supervision, and the Doctor of Psychology (Psy.D.) degree in clinical psychology. Students completing a program may wish to become licensed professionals. Argosy University, Nashville does not guarantee third-party certification/licensure. Outside agencies control the requirements for taking and passing certification/licensing exams and are subject to change without notice to Argosy University, Nashville.

The M.A. in mental health counseling is a 60-credit-hour program designed to provide students with a solid foundation for the practice of mental health counseling. The program's curriculum integrates the theoretical and conceptual foundations of mental health counseling with training in appropriate client intervention and therapy skills. The program emphasizes the development of attitudes, knowledge, and skills that are essential for mental health counselors who are committed to the ethical provision of quality services. Students completing this program meet the academic requirements toward licensure as Licensed Professional Counselors (LPCs) in Tennessee.

The Ed.D. in counselor education and supervision program aligns with the master's-level counselor education programs in order to encourage entry-level counseling students to work toward becoming doctoral-level advanced practitioners, educators, and supervisors. The program is designed to prepare counselors for a variety of settings by providing the advanced skills and knowledge necessary to provide leadership and advocacy, as well as serve in supervisory, training, and teaching positions in the counseling profession.

The Psy.D. in clinical psychology program has been designed to educate and train students so that they may be able to function effectively as clinical psychologists. To ensure that students are prepared adequately, the curriculum provides for the meaningful integration of theory, training, and practice. The program emphasizes the development of attitudes, knowledge, and skills essential in the formation of professional psychologists who are committed to the ethical provision of quality services.

Research Facilities

Argosy University libraries provide curriculum support and educational resources, including current text materials, diagnostic training documents, reference materials and databases, journals and dissertations, and major and current titles in program areas. There is an online public-access catalog of library resources available throughout the Argosy University system. Students have remote access to the campus library database, enabling them to study and conduct research at home. Academic databases offer dissertation abstracts, academic journals, and professional periodicals. All library computers are Internet accessible. Software applications include Word, Excel, PowerPoint, SPSS, and various test-scoring programs.

Financial Aid

Financial aid is available to those who qualify. Argosy University, Nashville, offers access to federal and state aid programs, merit-based awards, grants, loans, and a work-study program. As a first step, students should complete the Free Application for Federal Student Aid (FAFSA). Prospective students can apply electronically at http://www.fafsa.ed.gov or at the campus.

Cost of Study

Tuition varies by program. Students should contact Argosy University, Nashville, for tuition information.

Living and Housing Costs

Students typically live in apartments in the metropolitan Nashville area. Living expenses vary according to each student's preferred standard of living, housing, and transportation. The University does not offer or operate student housing. Most of the students are full-time working professionals who live within driving distance of the campus. Several nearby hotels offer special rates for those who commute from long distances. The Admissions Department also maintains a list of housing options, including contact information for University students who wish to share housing. For more information, students should contact the Admissions Department.

Student Group

Admission to Argosy University, Nashville, is selective to ensure a dynamic and engaged student body. The University encourages diversity in academic and employment backgrounds and promotes integration of the student body into professional life through established connections with local and national professional associations. Argosy University offers a professionally oriented education with rich opportunities to gain practical experience in class, field placements, and internships. Full-time students and working professionals gain the extensive knowledge and range of skills necessary for effective performance in their chosen field.

Student Outcomes

Students can register with the University's online career-services system and use select services from a distance, such as degree-specific career e-mail lists, national job posts, and virtual job fairs. Students should contact the University for more information.

Location

Argosy University, Nashville, is located at 100 Centerview Drive in Nashville, Tennessee. This city offers a variety of recreational activities, including the ballet and symphony, the newly established Frist Museum of Art, and professional sports. Nashville is known as Music City, USA, and is home to the Country Music Hall of Fame. The business environment includes companies such as Moses Cone Health Systems, Inc., and Novant Health, Inc.

The University

Argosy University is a private institution with nineteen locations across the nation. Argosy University, Nashville, provides a career resources office, an academic resources center, and extensive information access for research. It offers the resources of a large university plus the friendliness and personal attention of a small campus.

The innovative programs feature dynamic, relevant, and practical curricula delivered in flexible class formats. Students enjoy scheduling options that make it easier to fit school into their busy lives, choosing from day and evening courses, on campus or online. Many students find a combination of class formats to be an ideal way of continuing their education while meeting family and professional demands.

Argosy University, Nashville, is authorized by the Tennessee Higher Education Commission (Parkway Towers, Suite 1900, 404 James Robertson Parkway, Nashville, Tennessee 37243; 615-741-3605). This authorization must be renewed each year and is based on an evaluation against minimum standards concerning quality of education, ethical business practices, health and safety, and fiscal responsibility. Argosy University is accredited by the Higher Learning Commission and a member of the North Central Association (30 North LaSalle Street, Suite 2400, Chicago, Illinois 60602; 800-621-7440 (toll-free); http://www.ncahlc.org).

Applying

Argosy University, Nashville, accepts students year-round on a rolling admissions basis, depending on availability of required courses. Applications for admission are available online or by contacting the campus.

Correspondence and Information

Argosy University, Nashville
100 Centerview Drive, Suite 225
Nashville, Tennessee 37214
Phone: 615-525-2800
866-833-6598 (toll-free)
Fax: 615-525-2900
E-mail: auadmissions@argosy.edu
Web site: http://www.argosy.edu/nashville

Argosy University, Nashville

THE FACULTY

The Argosy University faculty is comprised of working professionals who are eager to help students succeed. Members bring real-world experience and the latest practice innovations to the academic setting. The diverse faculty members of the College of Psychology and Behavioral Sciences are widely recognized for contributions to the field. Many are published scholars, and most hold doctoral degrees. They are committed to providing a substantive education that combines comprehensive knowledge with critical skills and practical workplace relevance. Above all, faculty members are committed to their students' personal and professional development.

ARGOSY UNIVERSITY.

ARGOSY UNIVERSITY, ORANGE COUNTY

College of Psychology and Behavioral Sciences

Programs of Study

Argosy University, Orange County, offers the Master of Arts (M.A.) degree in clinical psychology/marriage and family therapy, counseling psychology/marriage and family therapy, forensic psychology, and sport-exercise psychology; the Doctor of Education (Ed.D.) degree in counseling psychology; and the Doctor of Psychology (Psy.D.) degree in clinical psychology. Students completing a program may wish to become licensed professionals. Argosy University, Orange County does not guarantee third-party certification/licensure. Outside agencies control the requirements for taking and passing certification/licensing exams and are subject to change without notice to Argosy University, Orange County.

The M.A. in clinical psychology/marriage and family therapy program is designed for students who wish to pursue the clinical psychology track while receiving graduate-level training in the core curricular areas, including supervised clinical practice, required for licensure as a marriage and family therapist in California. Licensing requirements differ from state to state, so students should verify the current licensing requirements of the state in which they plan to become licensed. The program emphasizes a practitioner-oriented philosophy, and integrates applied theory and field experience.

The M.A. in counseling psychology/marriage and family therapy program is designed to prepare students to practice and pursue licensure in California as Marriage and Family Therapists (MFT). Students receive an educational program with all the necessary theoretical and practical elements that will allow them to be effective members of a mental health team. The program introduces students to skills that integrate individual and group theoretical foundations of counseling psychology into appropriate client interaction and intervention skills.

The M.A. in forensic psychology program is designed to educate and train individuals who are currently working, or wish to work, in fields that utilize the study and practice of forensic psychology. Curriculum provides for an understanding of theory, training, and practice of forensic psychology. It emphasizes the development of students who are committed to the ethical provision of quality services to diverse clients and organizations. The program maintains policies and delivery formats suitable for working adults. The program provides course work in forensic psychology for application to law enforcement, legal and organizational consultation, and program analysis.

The M.A. in sport-exercise psychology program is designed to educate and train capable and ethical performance-enhancement specialists. This two-year degree is intended to meet the needs of students seeking employment in a variety of settings, including private practice, athletic departments, coaching, exercise/health, and education, as well as those planning to ultimately pursue their doctorate. The program provides a thorough grounding in both theory and practice. Based on the educational requirements outlined by the Association for the Advancement of Applied Sport Psychology (AAASP), the curriculum provides a foundation in applied sport psychology, an understanding of normal and abnormal psychological functioning, and a knowledge base in the physiological, motor, and psychosocial aspects of sport behavior. A supervised practicum provides experience in working directly with athletes or performers in applied settings.

The Ed.D. in counseling psychology program embraces a range of relevant theory and techniques applicable in the three major areas of counseling psychology: (a) the remedial (assisting in remedying problems in living); (b) the preventive (anticipating, circumventing, and forestalling difficulties that may arise in the future); and (c) the educative and developmental (discovering and developing potentialities). That is (a) the focus is on normal individuals, and developmental life stages challenges; (b) a focus on assets, strengths, and positive mental health; (c) an emphasis on relatively brief interventions; and (d) an emphasis on context, sociocultural/political influences, diversity, and person-environment interactions rather than exclusive emphasis on the individual.

The Psy.D. in clinical psychology program is designed to educate and train students so that they may eventually be able to function effectively as clinical psychologists. To ensure that students are prepared adequately, the curriculum provides for the meaningful integration of theory, training, and practice. This program emphasizes the development of attitudes, knowledge, and skills essential in the formation of professional psychologists who are committed to the ethical provision of quality services.

Research Facilities

Argosy University libraries provide curriculum support and educational resources, including current text materials, diagnostic training documents, reference materials and databases, journals and dissertations, and major and current titles in program areas. There is an online public-access catalog of library resources available throughout the Argosy University system. Students have remote access to the campus library database, enabling them to study and conduct research at home. Academic databases offer dissertation abstracts, academic journals, and professional periodicals. All library computers are Internet accessible. Software applications include Word, Excel, PowerPoint, SPSS, and various test-scoring programs.

Financial Aid

Financial aid is available to those who qualify. Argosy University, Orange County, offers access to federal and state aid programs, merit-based awards, grants, loans, and a work-study program. As a first step, students should complete the Free Application for Federal Student Aid (FAFSA). Prospective students can apply electronically at http://www.fafsa.ed.gov or at the campus.

Cost of Study

Tuition varies by program. Students should contact Argosy University, Orange County, for tuition information.

Living and Housing Costs

Students typically live in apartments in the Santa Ana metropolitan area. Living expenses vary according to each student's preferred standard of living, housing, and transportation. The University does not offer or operate student housing. Most Argosy University students are full-time working professionals who live within driving distance of the campus. Several nearby hotels offer special rates for those who commute from long distances. The Admissions Department also maintains a list of housing options, including contact information for University students who wish to share housing. For more information, students should contact the Admissions Department.

Student Group

Admission to Argosy University, Orange County, is selective to ensure a dynamic and engaged student body. The University encourages diversity in academic and employment backgrounds and promotes integration of the student body into professional life through established connections with local and national professional associations. Argosy University offers a professionally oriented education with rich opportunities to gain practical experience in class, field placements, and internships. Full-time students and working professionals gain the extensive knowledge and range of skills necessary for effective performance in their chosen field.

Student Outcomes

Students can register with Argosy University's online career-services system and use select services from a distance, such as degree-specific career e-mail lists, national job posts, and virtual job fairs. Students should contact the University for more information.

Location

Argosy University, Orange County, attracts students from Southern California as well as around the country and the world. Orange County features a temperate climate, sunny beaches, and a host of cultural and entertainment options. The campus is located approximately 30 miles south of downtown Los Angeles, 90 miles north of San Diego, and just minutes from one of the many freeways that connect the Southern California basin. Regional parks and preserved lands provide opportunities for hiking, biking, riding, and other recreational activities. Whether it's ultra-chic Newport Beach, artsy Laguna Beach, or unspoiled Catalina Island, Orange County's oceanside personalities are as varied as the people who visit the area.

Orange County's business environment includes a broad array of companies. The area's largest employers include Ingram Micro Inc., Orange County Register, ITT Industries, and OneSource.

The University

Argosy University is a private institution with nineteen locations across the nation. Argosy University, Orange County, provides a career resources office, an academic resources center, and extensive information access for research. It offers the resources of a large university plus the friendliness and personal attention of a small campus. The innovative programs feature dynamic, relevant, and practical curricula delivered in flexible class formats. Students enjoy scheduling options that make it easier to fit school into their busy lives, choosing from day and evening courses, on campus or online. Many students find a combination of class formats to be an ideal way of continuing their education while meeting family and professional demands.

Argosy University is accredited by the Higher Learning Commission and a member of the North Central Association (30 North LaSalle Street, Suite 2400, Chicago, Illinois 60602; 800-621-7440 (toll-free); http://www.ncahlc.org).

Applying

Argosy University, Orange County, accepts students year-round on a rolling admissions basis, depending on availability of required courses. Applications for admission are available online or by contacting the campus.

Correspondence and Information

Argosy University, Orange County
601 South Lewis Street
Orange, California 92868
Phone: 714-620-3700
800-716-9598 (toll-free)
Fax: 714-620-3800
E-mail: auadmissions@argosy.edu
Web site: http://www.argosy.edu/orangecounty/

Argosy University, Orange County

THE FACULTY

The Argosy University faculty is comprised of working professionals who are eager to help students succeed. Members bring real-world experience and the latest practice innovations to the academic setting. The diverse faculty members of the College of Psychology and Behavioral Sciences are widely recognized for contributions to the field. Many are published scholars, and most hold doctoral degrees. They are committed to providing a substantive education that combines comprehensive knowledge with critical skills and practical workplace relevance. Above all, faculty members are committed to their students' personal and professional development.

ARGOSY UNIVERSITY.

ARGOSY UNIVERSITY, PHOENIX

College of Psychology and Behavioral Sciences

Programs of Study

Argosy University, Phoenix, offers the Master of Arts (M.A.) degree in clinical psychology, forensic psychology, mental health counseling, sport-exercise psychology, and industrial organizational psychology; the Doctor of Education (Ed.D.) degree in counseling psychology; and the Doctor of Psychology (Psy.D.) degree in clinical psychology or school psychology. Students completing a program may wish to become licensed. Argosy University, Phoenix does not guarantee third-party certification/licensure. Outside agencies control the requirements for taking and passing certification/licensing exams and are subject to change without notice to Argosy University, Phoenix.

The M.A. in clinical psychology program is designed to educate and train students to enter professional careers as master's-level practitioners. Students receive an educational program with all the necessary theoretical and clinical elements designed to allow them to be effective members of a mental health team. The program introduces students to basic clinical skills that integrate individual and group theoretical foundations of applied psychology into appropriate client interaction and intervention skills. In addition, it offers comprehensive preparation for those considering application to the Doctor of Psychology in clinical psychology program.

The M.A. in forensic psychology program is designed to educate and train individuals who are currently working, or wish to work, in fields that utilize the study and practice of forensic psychology. Curriculum is designed to provide for an understanding of theory, training, and practice of forensic psychology. It emphasizes the development of students who are committed to the ethical provision of quality services to diverse clients and organizations. The program maintains policies and delivery formats suitable for working adults. The program provides course work in forensic psychology for application to law enforcement, legal and organizational consultation, and program analysis.

The M.A. in mental health counseling program is designed to provide students with a sound foundation for eventual practice of mental health counseling. The program introduces students to basic counseling skills that integrate individual and group theoretical foundations of professional counseling into appropriate client interaction and intervention skills. The program emphasizes the development of attitudes, knowledge, and skills essential in the formation of professional counselors who are committed to the ethical provision of quality services.

The M.A. in sport-exercise psychology program is designed to educate and train capable and ethical performance-enhancement specialists. This two-year degree is intended to meet the needs of students seeking employment in a variety of settings, including private practice, athletic departments, coaching, exercise/health, and education, as well as those planning to ultimately pursue their doctorate. The goals of the program include developing student competencies in the following areas: theoretical foundations, helping relationships, individual and group skills, normal and abnormal behavior, sport sciences, research and evaluation, diversity, and professional identity.

The M.A. in industrial organizational psychology program is designed to apply the knowledge of industrial organizational psychology to issues involving individuals and groups in organizational and work settings. This program prepares students for careers in areas such as compensation, training, data analysis, consultation, statistical decision-making, organizational development, leadership, and human resource management positions. The curriculum is competency-based, focusing on the outcomes of training and on the knowledge, skills, and behavior necessary to function as a master's-level professional in industrial organizational psychology. This is an interdisciplinary program that combines the expertise of the faculty in the College of Psychology and Behavioral Sciences and the College of Business.

The Ed.D. in counseling psychology program emphasizes the development of attitudes, knowledge, and skills essential in the formation of professionals committed to the ethical provision of quality services. To ensure that students are prepared adequately, the curriculum provides for the meaningful integration of theory, training, and practice. Specific objectives of the program include training practitioners capable of delivering effective treatment to diverse populations of clients in need of such treatment; developing counseling psychologists who understand the biological, psychological, and sociological bases of human functioning; training practitioners who are capable of exercising leadership both in the health care delivery system and in the training of mental health professionals; preparing counseling psychologists capable of expanding their role within society; and educating practitioners capable of working with other disciplines as part of a professional team.

The Psy.D. in clinical psychology program has been designed to educate and train students to function effectively as clinical psychologists. To ensure that students are adequately prepared, the curriculum provides for the meaningful integration of theory, training, and practice. The program emphasizes the development of attitudes, knowledge, and skills essential to the training of clinical psychologists committed to the ethical provision of quality services.

The Psy.D. in school psychology program is designed to prepare students to meet the criteria for state certification as school psychologists, and to prepare them to become nationally certified school psychologists in accordance with criteria developed by the National Association of School Psychologists (NASP). The program emphasizes the development of attitudes, knowledge, and skills essential to school psychologists who are committed to the ethical provision of quality services.

Research Facilities

Argosy University libraries provide curriculum support and educational resources, including current text materials, diagnostic training documents, reference materials and databases, journals and dissertations, and major and current titles in program areas. There is an online public-access catalog of library resources available throughout the Argosy University system. Students have remote access to the campus library database, enabling them to study and conduct research at home. Academic databases offer dissertation abstracts, academic journals, and professional periodicals. All library computers are Internet accessible. Software applications include Word, Excel, PowerPoint, SPSS, and various test-scoring programs.

Financial Aid

Financial aid is available to those who qualify. Argosy University, Phoenix, offers access to federal and state aid programs, merit-based awards, grants, loans, and a work-study program. As a first step, students should complete the Free Application for Federal Student Aid (FAFSA). Prospective students can apply electronically at http://www.fafsa.ed.gov or at the campus.

Cost of Study

Tuition varies by program. Students should contact Argosy University, Phoenix, for tuition information.

Living and Housing Costs

Students typically live in apartments in the metropolitan Phoenix area. Living expenses vary according to each student's preferred standard of living, housing, and transportation. The University does not offer or operate student housing. Most Argosy University students are full-time working professionals who live within driving distance of the campus. Several nearby hotels offer special rates for those who commute from long distances. The Admissions Department also maintains a list of housing options, including contact information for University students who wish to share housing. For more information, students should contact the Admissions Department.

Student Group

Admission to Argosy University, Phoenix, is selective to ensure a dynamic and engaged student body. The University encourages diversity in academic and employment backgrounds and promotes integration of the student body into professional life through established connections with local and national professional associations. Argosy University offers a professionally oriented education with rich opportunities to gain practical experience in class, field placements, and internships. Full-time students and working professionals gain the extensive knowledge and range of skills necessary for effective performance in their chosen field.

Student Outcomes

Students can register with Argosy University's online career-services system and use select services from a distance, such as degree-specific career e-mail lists, national job posts, and virtual job fairs. Students should contact the University for more information.

Location

Argosy University, Phoenix, offers a quality education in an intimate, small-group setting. The campus is located near I-17, close to shops, restaurants, and recreational areas. Phoenix is home to several major league sports teams, and the city offers an array of cultural activities ranging from opera and theatre to science museums. The multi-cultural environment of Arizona, coupled with Argosy University's professional training affiliations throughout the state, creates an exciting opportunity for students to work with urban, rural, and culturally diverse populations.

The business environment in Phoenix includes a wide variety of companies such as Intel and Go Daddy Group, an Internet company. Wells Fargo, Home Depot, Lowe's, and Wal-Mart also represent some of the area's largest employers.

The University

Argosy University is a private institution with nineteen locations across the nation. Argosy University, Phoenix, provides a career resources office, an academic resources center, and extensive information access for research. It offers the resources of a large university plus the friendliness and personal attention of a small campus. The innovative programs feature dynamic, relevant, and practical curricula delivered in flexible class formats. Students enjoy scheduling options that make it easier to fit school into their busy lives, choosing from day and evening courses, on campus or online. Many students find a combination of class formats to be an ideal way of continuing their education while meeting family and professional demands.

Argosy University is accredited by the Higher Learning Commission and a member of the North Central Association (30 North LaSalle Street, Suite 2400, Chicago, Illinois 60602; 800-621-7440 (toll-free); http://www.ncahlc.org).

Applying

Argosy University, Phoenix, accepts students year-round on a rolling admissions basis, depending on availability of required courses. Applications for admission are available online or by contacting the campus.

Correspondence and Information

Argosy University, Phoenix
2233 West Dunlap Avenue
Phoenix, Arizona 85021
Phone: 602-216-2600
866-216-2777 (toll-free)
Fax: 602-216-2601
E-mail: auadmissions@argosy.edu
Web site: http://www.argosy.edu/phoenix/

Argosy University, Phoenix

THE FACULTY

The Argosy University faculty is comprised of working professionals who are eager to help students succeed. Members bring real-world experience and the latest practice innovations to the academic setting. The diverse faculty members of the College of Psychology and Behavioral Sciences are widely recognized for contributions to the field. Many are published scholars, and most hold doctoral degrees. They are committed to providing a substantive education that combines comprehensive knowledge with critical skills and practical workplace relevance. Above all, faculty members are committed to their students' personal and professional development.

ARGOSY UNIVERSITY

ARGOSY UNIVERSITY, SALT LAKE CITY

College of Psychology and Behavioral Sciences

Programs of Study

Argosy University, Salt Lake City, offers the Master of Arts (M.A.) degree in clinical psychology, forensic psychology, marriage and family therapy, and mental health counseling; the Doctor of Education (Ed.D.) degree in counselor education and supervision; and the Doctor of Psychology (Psy.D.) degree in clinical psychology. Students completing a program may wish to become licensed professionals. Argosy University, Salt Lake City does not guarantee third-party certification/licensure. Outside agencies control the requirements for taking and passing certification/licensing exams and are subject to change without notice to Argosy University, Salt Lake City.

The M.A. in clinical psychology program has been designed to educate and train students to pursue a professional career as master's-level practitioners. The program is designed to provide students with an educational program with all the necessary theoretical and clinical elements that will allow them to be effective members of a mental health team. It introduces students to basic clinical skills that integrate individual and group theoretical foundations of applied psychology into appropriate client interaction and intervention skills. This program can be completed in as little as two years and must be completed in five years. In addition, the program offers preparation for those considering application to the Psy.D. in clinical psychology program.

The M.A. in forensic psychology program is designed to educate and train individuals who are currently working, or wish to work, in fields that utilize the study and practice of forensic psychology. Curriculum provides for an understanding of theory, training, and practice of forensic psychology. It emphasizes the development of students committed to the ethical provision of quality services to diverse clients and organizations. The program maintains policies and delivery formats suitable for working adults. The program provides course work in forensic psychology for application to law enforcement, legal and organizational consultation, and program analysis.

The M.A. in marriage and family therapy program recognizes the need to provide marriage and family therapists with the extensive knowledge and range of skills necessary to function effectively in their profession. The program introduces students to basic skills that integrate systemic theoretical foundations of marriage and family therapy into appropriate client interaction and intervention skills. It emphasizes the development of attitudes, knowledge, and skills essential in the formation of marriage and family therapists who are committed to the ethical provision of quality services. The program has been developed by the school faculty members to provide working students with the opportunity to pursue personal and professional goals through completion of a master's program.

The M.A. in mental health counseling program is designed to provide students with a sound foundation for eventual practice of mental health counseling. The program introduces students to basic counseling skills that integrate individual and group theoretical foundations of professional counseling into appropriate client interaction and intervention skills. It emphasizes the development of attitudes, knowledge, and skills essential in the formation of professional counselors who are committed to the ethical provision of quality services.

The Ed.D. in counselor education and supervision program aligns with the master's-level counselor education programs in order to encourage entry-level counseling students to work toward becoming doctoral-level advanced practitioners, educators, and supervisors. This program prepares counselors for a variety of settings by providing the advanced skills and knowledge necessary to provide leadership and advocacy, as well as serve in supervisory, training, and teaching positions in the counseling profession.

The Psy.D. in clinical psychology program has been designed to educate and train students so that they may be able to function effectively as clinical psychologists. To ensure that students are prepared adequately, the curriculum provides for the meaningful integration of theory, training, and practice. The program emphasizes the development of attitudes, knowledge, and skills essential in the formation of professional psychologists who are committed to the ethical provision of quality services.

Research Facilities

Argosy University libraries provide curriculum support and educational resources, including current text materials, diagnostic training documents, reference materials and databases, journals and dissertations, and major and current titles in program areas. There is an online public-access catalog of library resources available throughout the Argosy University system. Students have remote access to their campus library database, enabling them to study and conduct research at home. Academic databases offer dissertation abstracts, academic journals, and professional periodicals. All library computers are Internet accessible. Software applications include Word, Excel, PowerPoint, SPSS, and various test-scoring programs.

Financial Aid

Financial aid is available to those who qualify. Argosy University, Salt Lake City, offers access to federal and state aid programs, merit-based awards, grants, loans, and a work-study program. As a first step, students should complete the Free Application for Federal Student Aid (FAFSA). Prospective students can apply electronically at http://www.fafsa.ed.gov or at the campus.

Cost of Study

Tuition varies by program. Students should contact Argosy University, Salt Lake City, for tuition information.

Living and Housing Costs

Students typically live in apartments in the metropolitan Salt Lake City area. Living expenses vary according to each student's preferred standard of living, housing, and transportation. The University does not offer or operate student housing. Most of the students are full-time working professionals who live within driving distance of the campus. Several nearby hotels offer special rates for those who commute from long distances. The Admissions Department also maintains a list of housing options, including contact information for University students who wish to share housing. For more information, students should contact the Admissions Department.

Student Group

Admission to Argosy University, Salt Lake City, is selective to ensure a dynamic and engaged student body. The University encourages diversity in academic and employment backgrounds and promotes integration of the student body into professional life through established connections with local and national professional associations. Argosy University offers a professionally oriented education with rich opportunities to gain practical experience in class, field placements, and internships. Full-time students and working professionals gain the extensive knowledge and range of skills necessary for effective performance in their chosen field.

Student Outcomes

Students can register with Argosy University's online career-services system and use select services from a distance, such as degree-specific career e-mail lists, national job posts, and virtual job fairs. Students should contact the University for more information.

Location

Argosy University, Salt Lake City, offers a quality education in an intimate, small-group setting. Argosy University, Salt Lake City, is conveniently located in Draper, Utah, nestled in the Wasatch Mountains about 20 miles south of Salt Lake City. The area's business climate and numerous hospitals, schools, clinics, and social service agencies can provide many training opportunities for students.

The University

Argosy University is a private institution with nineteen locations across the nation. Argosy University, Salt Lake City, provides a career resources office, an academic resources center, and extensive information access for research. It offers the resources of a large university plus the friendliness and personal attention of a small campus. The innovative programs feature dynamic, relevant, and practical curricula delivered in flexible class formats. Students enjoy scheduling options that make it easier to fit school into their busy lives, choosing from day and evening courses, on campus or online. Many students find a combination of class formats to be an ideal way of continuing their education while meeting family and professional demands.

Argosy University is accredited by the Higher Learning Commission and a member of the North Central Association (30 North LaSalle Street, Suite 2400, Chicago, Illinois 60602; 800-621-7440 (toll-free); http://www.ncahlc.org).

Applying

Argosy University, Salt Lake City, accepts students on a rolling admissions basis year-round, depending on availability of required courses. Applications for admission may be obtained online or by contacting the campus.

Correspondence and Information

Argosy University, Salt Lake City
121 Election Road, Suite 300
Draper, Utah 84020

Phone: 801-601-5000
888-639-4756 (toll-free)
Fax: 801-601-4990
E-mail: auadmissions@argosy.edu
Web site: http://www.argosy.edu/saltlakecity

Argosy University, Salt Lake City

THE FACULTY

The Argosy University faculty is comprised of working professionals who are eager to help students succeed. Members bring real-world experience and the latest practice innovations to the academic setting. The diverse faculty members of the College of Psychology and Behavioral Sciences are widely recognized for contributions to the field. Many are published scholars, and most hold doctoral degrees. They are committed to providing a substantive education that combines comprehensive knowledge with critical skills and practical workplace relevance. Above all, faculty members are committed to their students' personal and professional development.

ARGOSY UNIVERSITY.

ARGOSY UNIVERSITY, SAN DIEGO

College of Psychology and Behavioral Sciences

Programs of Study

Argosy University, San Diego, offers the Master of Arts (M.A.) degree in clinical psychology/marriage and family therapy, counseling psychology/marriage and family therapy, and forensic psychology; and the Doctor of Education (Ed.D.) degree in counseling psychology. Students completing a program may wish to become licensed professionals. Argosy University, San Diego does not guarantee third-party certification/licensure. Outside agencies control the requirements for taking and passing certification/licensing exams and are subject to change without notice to Argosy University, San Diego.

The M.A. in clinical psychology/marriage and family therapy program is designed for students who wish to pursue the clinical psychology track while receiving graduate-level training in the core curricular areas, including supervised clinical practice, required for licensure as a marriage and family therapist in California. Licensing requirements differ from state to state, so students should verify the current licensing requirements of the state in which they plan to become licensed.

The M.A. in counseling psychology/marriage and family therapy program is designed to prepare students to practice and pursue licensure in California as a Marriage and Family Therapist (MFT). Students receive an educational program with all the necessary theoretical and practical elements designed to allow them to be effective members of a mental health team. The program introduces students to skills that integrate individual and group theoretical foundations of counseling psychology into appropriate client interaction and intervention skills.

The M.A. in forensic psychology program is designed to educate and train individuals who are currently working, or wish to work, in fields that utilize the study and practice of forensic psychology. Curriculum provides for an understanding of theory, training, and practice of forensic psychology. It emphasizes the development of students who are committed to the ethical provision of quality services to diverse clients and organizations. The program maintains policies and delivery formats suitable for working adults. The program provides course work in forensic psychology for application to law enforcement, legal and organizational consultation, and program analysis.

The Ed.D. in counseling psychology program embraces a range of relevant theory and techniques applicable in the three major areas of counseling psychology: (a) the remedial (assisting in remedying problems in living); (b) the preventive (anticipating, circumventing, and forestalling difficulties that may arise in the future); and (c) the educative and developmental (discovering and developing potentialities). That is (a) the focus is on normal individuals, and developmental life stages challenges; (b) a focus on assets, strengths, and positive mental health; (c) an emphasis on relatively brief interventions; and (d) an emphasis on context, sociocultural/political influences, diversity, and person-environment interactions rather than exclusive emphasis on the individual.

Research Facilities

Argosy University libraries provide curriculum support and educational resources, including current text materials, diagnostic training documents, reference materials and databases, journals and dissertations, and major and current titles in program areas. There is an online public-access catalog of library resources available throughout the Argosy University system. Students have remote access to the campus library database, enabling them to study and conduct research at home. Academic databases offer dissertation abstracts, academic journals, and professional periodicals. All library computers are Internet accessible. Software applications include Word, Excel, PowerPoint, SPSS, and various test-scoring programs.

Financial Aid

Financial aid is available to those who qualify. Argosy University, San Diego, offers access to federal and state aid programs, merit-based awards, grants, loans, and a work-study program. As a first step, students should complete the Free Application for Federal Student Aid (FAFSA). Prospective students can apply electronically at http://www.fafsa.ed.gov or at the campus.

Cost of Study

Tuition varies by program. Students should contact Argosy University, San Diego, for tuition information.

Living and Housing Costs

Students typically live in apartments in the San Diego metropolitan area. Living expenses vary according to each student's preferred standard of living, housing, and transportation. The University does not offer or operate student housing. Most of the students are full-time working professionals who live within driving distance of the campus. Several nearby hotels offer special rates for those who commute from long distances. The Admissions Department also maintains a list of housing options, including contact information for University students who wish to share housing. For more information, students should contact the Admissions Department.

Student Group

Admission to Argosy University, San Diego, is selective to ensure a dynamic and engaged student body. The University encourages diversity in academic and employment backgrounds and promotes integration of the student body into professional life through established connections with local and national professional associations. Argosy University offers a professionally oriented education with rich opportunities to gain practical experience in class, field placements, and internships. Full-time students and working professionals gain the extensive knowledge and range of skills necessary for effective performance in their chosen field.

Student Outcomes

Students can register with the University's online career-services system and use select services from a distance, such as degree-specific career e-mail lists, national job posts, and virtual job fairs. Students should contact the University for more information.

Location

San Diego, southern California's second-largest city, offers an ideal climate year-round, 70 miles of beautiful beaches, colorful neighborhoods, and a dynamic downtown district. Argosy University, San Diego, provides classrooms, a library resource center, a student lounge, staff and faculty offices, and other amenities. The area offers numerous attractions, including the famous San Diego Zoo, San Diego Wild Animal Park, and SeaWorld. San Diego's business environment includes several Fortune 500 companies such as QUALCOMM and Pfizer, Inc., and a concentration of technology companies.

The University

Argosy University is a private institution with nineteen locations across the nation. Argosy University, San Diego, provides a career resources office, an academic resources center, and extensive information access for research. It offers the resources of a large university plus the friendliness and personal attention of a small campus.

The innovative programs feature dynamic, relevant, and practical curricula delivered in flexible class formats. Students enjoy scheduling options that make it easier to fit school into their busy lives, choosing from day and evening courses, on campus or online. Many students find a combination of class formats to be an ideal way of continuing their education while meeting family and professional demands.

Argosy University is accredited by the Higher Learning Commission and a member of the North Central Association (30 North LaSalle Street, Suite 2400, Chicago, Illinois 60602; 800-621-7440 (toll-free); http://www.ncahlc.org).

Applying

Argosy University, San Diego, accepts students year-round on a rolling admissions basis, depending on availability of required courses. Applications for admission are available online or by contacting the campus.

Correspondence and Information

Argosy University, San Diego
1615 Murray Canyon Road
San Diego, California 92108
Phone: 619-321-3000
866-505-0333 (toll-free)
Fax: 619-321-3005
E-mail: auadmissions@argosy.edu
Web site: http://www.argosy.edu/sandiego/

Argosy University, San Diego

THE FACULTY

The Argosy University faculty is comprised of working professionals who are eager to help students succeed. Members bring real-world experience and the latest practice innovations to the academic setting. The diverse faculty members of the College of Psychology and Behavioral Sciences are widely recognized for contributions to the field. Many are published scholars, and most hold doctoral degrees. They are committed to providing a substantive education that combines comprehensive knowledge with critical skills and practical workplace relevance. Above all, faculty members are committed to their students' personal and professional development.

ARGOSY UNIVERSITY

ARGOSY UNIVERSITY, SAN FRANCISCO BAY AREA

College of Psychology and Behavioral Sciences

Programs of Study

Argosy University, San Francisco Bay Area, offers the Master of Arts (M.A.) degree in clinical psychology, clinical psychology/marriage and family therapy, counseling psychology, counseling psychology/marriage and family therapy, forensic psychology, and sport-exercise psychology; the Doctor of Education (Ed.D.) degree in counseling psychology; and the Doctor of Psychology (Psy.D.) degree in clinical psychology. Students completing a program may wish to become licensed professionals. Argosy University, San Francisco Bay Area does not guarantee third-party certification/licensure. Outside agencies control the requirements for taking and passing certification/licensing exams and are subject to change without notice to Argosy University, San Francisco Bay Area.

The M.A. in clinical psychology program has been designed to educate and train students to enter a professional career as master's-level practitioners. The program provides students an educational program with all the necessary theoretical and clinical elements designed to allow them to be effective members of a mental health team. It introduces students to basic clinical skills that integrate individual and group theoretical foundations of applied psychology into appropriate client interaction and intervention skills. In addition, the program offers excellent preparation for those considering application to the Psy.D. in clinical psychology program.

The M.A. in clinical psychology/marriage and family therapy program is designed for students who wish to pursue the clinical psychology track while receiving graduate-level training in the core curricular areas, including supervised clinical practice, required for licensure as a marriage and family therapist in California. Licensing requirements differ from state to state, so students should verify the current licensing requirements of the state in which they plan to become licensed. The program emphasizes a practitioner-oriented philosophy, and integrates applied theory and field experience.

The M.A. in counseling psychology program is designed to provide students with a sound foundation for the eventual practice of mental health counseling. The program emphasizes the development of attitudes, knowledge, and skills essential in the formation of professionals who are committed to the ethical provision of quality services. The program prepares students to enter a professional career as master's level counseling practitioners who can perform ethically and effectively as skilled professionals with demonstrated knowledge of social and cultural diversity.

The M.A. in counseling psychology/marriage and family therapy program is designed to prepare students to practice and pursue licensure in California as a Marriage and Family Therapist (MFT). Students receive an educational program with all the necessary theoretical and practical elements designed to allow them to be effective members of a mental health team. The program introduces students to skills that integrate individual and group theoretical foundations of counseling psychology into appropriate client interaction and intervention skills.

The M.A. in forensic psychology program is designed to educate and train individuals who are currently working, or wish to work, in fields that utilize the study and practice of forensic psychology. Curriculum provides for an understanding of theory, training, and practice of forensic psychology. It emphasizes the development of students who are committed to the ethical provision of quality services to diverse clients and organizations. The program maintains policies and delivery formats suitable for working adults. The program provides course work in forensic psychology for application to law enforcement, legal and organizational consultation, and program analysis.

The M.A. in sport-exercise psychology program is designed to educate and train capable and ethical performance-enhancement specialists. This two-year degree is intended to meet the needs of students seeking employment in a variety of settings, including private practice, athletic departments, coaching, exercise/health, and education, as well as those planning to ultimately pursue their doctorate. The goals of the program include developing student competencies in the following areas: theoretical foundations, helping relationships, individual and group skills, normal and abnormal behavior, sport sciences, research and evaluation, diversity, and professional identity.

The Ed.D. in counseling psychology program emphasizes the development of attitudes, knowledge, and skills essential in the formation of professionals who are committed to the ethical provision of quality services. To ensure that students are prepared adequately, the curriculum provides for the meaningful integration of theory, training, and practice.

The Psy.D. in clinical psychology program has been designed to educate and train students so that they may eventually be able to function effectively as clinical psychologists. The curriculum provides for the meaningful integration of theory, training, and practice. The program emphasizes the development of attitudes, knowledge, and skills essential in the formation of professional psychologists who are committed to the ethical provision of quality services.

Research Facilities

Argosy University libraries provide curriculum support and educational resources, including current text materials, diagnostic training documents, reference materials and databases, journals and dissertations, and major and current titles in program areas. There is an online public-access catalog of library resources available throughout the Argosy University system. Students have remote access to the campus library database, enabling them to study and conduct research at home. Academic databases offer dissertation abstracts, academic journals, and professional periodicals. All library computers are Internet accessible. Software applications include Word, Excel, PowerPoint, SPSS, and various test-scoring programs.

Financial Aid

Financial aid is available to those who qualify. Argosy University, San Francisco Bay Area, offers access to federal and state aid programs, merit-based awards, grants, loans, and a work-study program. As a first step, students should complete the Free Application for Federal Student Aid (FAFSA). Prospective students can apply electronically at http://www.fafsa.ed.gov or at the campus.

Cost of Study

Tuition varies by program. Students should contact Argosy University, San Francisco Bay Area for tuition information.

Living and Housing Costs

Students typically live in apartments in the San Francisco metropolitan area. Living expenses vary according to each student's preferred standard of living, housing, and transportation. The University does not offer or operate student housing. Most Argosy University students are full-time working professionals who live within driving distance of the campus. Several nearby hotels offer special rates for those who commute from long distances. The Admissions Department also maintains a list of housing options, including contact information for University students who wish to share housing. For more information, students should contact the Admissions Department.

Student Group

Admission to Argosy University, San Francisco Bay Area, is selective to ensure a dynamic and engaged student body. The University encourages diversity in academic and employment backgrounds and promotes integration of the student body into professional life through established connections with local and national professional associations. Argosy University offers a professionally oriented education with rich opportunities to gain practical experience in class, field placements, and internships. Full-time students and working professionals gain the extensive knowledge and range of skills necessary for effective performance in their chosen field.

Student Outcomes

Students can register with Argosy University's online career-services system and use select services from a distance, such as degree-specific career e-mail lists, national job posts, and virtual job fairs. Students should contact the University for more information.

Location

Located in northern California, Argosy University, San Francisco Bay Area, attracts students from the immediate area as well as from around the country and the world. In July 2007, the University moved to its new location at 1005 Atlantic Avenue, Alameda, California. The energy in San Francisco is contagious. Numerous surveys rank San Francisco as one of the most wired cities in the world, thanks to its high concentration of computer-savvy citizens and businesses.

Many educational institutions and agencies in the area provide varied opportunities for student training. The Bay Area and nearby Silicon Valley are home to leading new media companies such as Pixar, ILM, and Sega. A who's who of technology companies call the Bay Area home, including Apple, Cisco, Hewlett-Packard, Intel, Oracle, and Sun Microsystems. The Bay Area also is the home of traditional companies such as BankAmerica, Chevron, Levi-Strauss, Safeway, and Wells Fargo.

The University

Argosy University is a private institution with nineteen locations across the nation. Argosy University, San Francisco Bay Area, provides a career resources office, an academic resources center, and extensive information access for research. It offers the resources of a large university plus the friendliness and personal attention of a small campus. The innovative programs feature dynamic, relevant, and practical curricula delivered in flexible class formats. Students enjoy scheduling options that make it easier to fit school into their busy lives, choosing from day and evening courses, on campus or online. Many students find a combination of class formats to be an ideal way of continuing their education while meeting family and professional demands.

Argosy University is accredited by the Higher Learning Commission and a member of the North Central Association (30 North LaSalle Street, Suite 2400, Chicago, Illinois 60602; 800-621-7440 (toll-free); http://www.ncahlc.org).

Applying

Argosy University, San Francisco Bay Area, accepts students year-round on a rolling admissions basis, depending on availability of required courses. Applications for admission are available online or by contacting the campus.

Correspondence and Information

Argosy University, San Francisco Bay Area
1005 Atlantic Avenue
Alameda, California 94501
Phone: 510-215-0277
866-215-2777 (toll free)
Fax: 510-215-0299
E-mail: auadmissions@argosy.edu
Web site: http://www.argosy.edu/sanfrancisco

Argosy University, San Francisco Bay Area

THE FACULTY

The Argosy University faculty is comprised of working professionals who are eager to help students succeed. Members bring real-world experience and the latest practice innovations to the academic setting. The diverse faculty members of the College of Psychology and Behavioral Sciences are widely recognized for contributions to the field. Many are published scholars, and most hold doctoral degrees. They are committed to providing a substantive education that combines comprehensive knowledge with critical skills and practical workplace relevance. Above all, faculty members are committed to their students' personal and professional development.

ARGOSY UNIVERSITY

ARGOSY UNIVERSITY, SARASOTA

College of Psychology and Behavioral Sciences

Programs of Study

Argosy University, Sarasota, offers the Master of Arts (M.A.) degree in community counseling, forensic psychology, marriage and family therapy, mental health counseling, school counseling, and school psychology; the Education Specialist (Ed.S.) degree in school counseling; and the Doctor of Education (Ed.D.) degree in counseling psychology, counselor education and supervision, organizational leadership, and pastoral community counseling. Students completing a program may wish to become licensed professionals. Argosy University, Sarasota does not guarantee third-party certification/licensure. Outside agencies control the requirements for taking and passing certification/licensing exams and are subject to change without notice to Argosy University, Sarasota.

The M.A. in community counseling is a 48 credit-hour program designed to provide students with a solid foundation for the practice of professional counseling. The program's curriculum integrates theoretical and conceptual foundations of professional counseling with training in appropriate client intervention and advocacy skills. The program emphasizes the development of attitudes, knowledge, and skills that are essential for professional counselors committed to the ethical provision of quality services. Students completing this program meet the academic requirements toward licensure in Alabama, Georgia, and other states (because licensure requirements vary from state to state, students should verify the current licensing requirements for the state in which they plan to practice).

The M.A. in forensic psychology program is designed to educate and train individuals who are currently working, or wish to work, in fields that utilize the study and practice of forensic psychology. Curriculum provides for an understanding of theory, training, and practice of forensic psychology. It emphasizes the development of students who are committed to the ethical provision of quality services to diverse clients and organizations. The program maintains policies and delivery formats suitable for working adults. The program provides course work in forensic psychology for application to law enforcement, legal and organizational consultation, and program analysis.

The M.A. in marriage and family therapy program recognizes the need to provide marriage and family therapists with the extensive knowledge and range of skills necessary to function effectively in their profession. The program introduces students to basic skills that integrate systemic theoretical foundations of marriage and family therapy into appropriate client interaction and intervention skills. The program emphasizes the development of attitudes, knowledge, and skills essential in the formation of marriage and family therapists committed to the ethical provision of quality services. The program has been developed by the school faculty members to provide working students with the opportunity to pursue personal and professional goals through completion of a master's program.

The M.A. in mental health counseling program is designed to provide students with a sound foundation for the eventual practice of mental health counseling. The program introduces students to basic counseling skills that integrate individual and group theoretical foundations of mental health counseling into appropriate client interaction and intervention skills. The program emphasizes the development of attitudes, knowledge, and skills essential in the formation of mental health counselors who are committed to the ethical provision of quality services.

The M.A. in school counseling program serves adult students throughout the world. It provides a quality program in school counseling to meet the needs of students and the community. The focus on the program is student preparation and professional development while promoting teaching, learning, and service. The program remains faithful to its mission of preparing students to function at a high professional level in a rapidly changing world.

The M.A. in school psychology program is designed to produce ethical, responsible, and competent school psychologists who are able to serve effectively in a number of professional roles. During graduate training, students develop core competencies in psychological assessment, intervention, and consultation/education, as well as cultural and individual diversity. Graduates of the program may be eligible for department of education certification and will be prepared for employment as school psychologists. The program is designed to prepare students to become Nationally Certified School Psychologists (NCSPs) in accordance with criteria developed by the National Association of School Psychologists.

The Ed.S. in school counseling program is designed for experienced professionals who have master's degrees in other fields and wish to become school counselors. The program is a 30-semester-credit-hour program of study that incorporates course work designed to help students in meeting the specialization requirements for certification in guidance and counseling (grades K–12) in the state of Florida. Because of certification variations among states, students should check with regional authorities to confirm their requirements prior to entering the program.

The Ed.D. in counseling psychology program is designed to meet the special requirements of working professionals who want to develop their knowledge and skills to handle the changing needs of modern organizations. The program is designed to provide working professionals with the opportunity to pursue their personal and professional goals through the completion of a graduate program.

The Ed.D. in counselor education and supervision program aligns with the master's-level counselor education programs in order to encourage entry-level counseling students to work toward becoming doctoral-level advanced practitioners, educators, and supervisors. This program prepares counselors for a variety of settings by providing the advanced skills and knowledge necessary to provide leadership and advocacy, as well as serve in supervisory, training, and teaching positions in the counseling profession.

The Ed.D. in organizational leadership program is designed to meet the special requirements of working professionals who want to develop their knowledge and skills to handle the changing needs of modern organizations. The program is designed to enable working professionals to pursue their personal and professional goals through the completion of a graduate program.

The Ed.D. in pastoral community counseling program is based on the fundamental belief that religious and spiritual communities provide a unique opportunity for human growth and development. The program is designed to provide leaders in religious communities with an opportunity for personal and professional development, directed toward making a significant contribution to their community and to society. The program integrates the engagement of knowledge, the development of skills, reflective practice, and research in a manner that prepares the pastoral counselor to address individual and communal development in an ethically responsible fashion.

Research Facilities

Argosy University libraries provide curriculum support and educational resources, including current text materials, diagnostic training documents, reference materials and databases, journals and dissertations, and major and current titles in program areas. There is an online public-access catalog of library resources available throughout the Argosy University system. Students have remote access to the campus library database, enabling them to study and conduct research at home. Academic databases offer dissertation abstracts, academic journals, and professional periodicals. All library computers are Internet accessible. Software applications include Word, Excel, PowerPoint, SPSS, and various test-scoring programs.

Financial Aid

Financial aid is available to those who qualify. Argosy University, Sarasota, offers access to federal and state aid programs, merit-based awards, grants, loans, and a work-study program. As a first step, students should complete the Free Application for Federal Student Aid (FAFSA). Prospective students can apply electronically at http://www.fafsa.ed.gov or at the campus.

Cost of Study

Tuition varies by program. Students should contact Argosy University, Sarasota, for tuition information.

Living and Housing Costs

Students typically live in apartments in the metropolitan Sarasota area. Living expenses vary according to each student's preferred standard of living, housing, and transportation. The University does not offer or operate student housing. Most of the students are full-time working professionals who live within driving distance of the campus. Several nearby hotels offer special rates for those who commute from long distances to attend scheduled weeklong in-residence sessions. The Admissions Department also maintains a list of housing options, including contact information for University students who wish to share housing. For more information, students should contact the Admissions Department.

Student Group

Admission to Argosy University, Sarasota, is selective to ensure a dynamic and engaged student body. The University encourages diversity in academic and employment backgrounds and promotes integration of the student body into professional life through established connections with local and national professional associations. Argosy University offers a professionally oriented education with rich opportunities to gain practical experience in class, field placements, and internships. Full-time students and working professionals gain the extensive knowledge and range of skills necessary for effective performance in their chosen fields.

Student Outcomes

Students can register with the University's online career-services system and use select services from a distance, such as degree-specific career e-mail lists, national job posts, and virtual job fairs. Students should contact the University for more information.

Location

Located in northeast Sarasota, the campus is specifically designed for postsecondary and graduate-level instruction through a unique combination of in-residence course work, tutorials, and online study courses. Several programs are off-site tutorials and intensive one-week classroom sessions. Students may also complete up to 49 percent of the work in some degree programs via online courses that allow interaction with faculty members and classmates from any Internet connection.

Sarasota is recognized as Florida's cultural coast and is home to a professional symphony, ballet, and opera as well as dozens of theaters and art galleries. Well-known vacation attractions such as Disney World, Busch Gardens–Tampa, and the city of Miami are within a few hours' drive. The area enjoys mild winters and endless summer beauty.

The business sector in the Gulf Coast community helps make it one of the top 20 places to live and work. ASO Corporation, Nelson Publishing, and Select Technology Group are among the numerous companies headquartered in Sarasota County. The area's top employers include Sarasota Memorial Hospital and Publix Supermarkets.

The University

Argosy University is a private institution with nineteen locations across the nation. Argosy University, Sarasota, provides a career resources office, an academic resources center, and extensive information access for research. It offers the resources of a large university plus the friendliness and personal attention of a small campus.

The innovative programs feature dynamic, relevant, and practical curricula delivered in flexible class formats. Students enjoy scheduling options that make it easier to fit school into their busy lives, choosing from day and evening courses, on campus or online. Many students find a combination of class formats to be an ideal way of continuing their education while meeting family and professional demands.

Argosy University is accredited by the Higher Learning Commission and a member of the North Central Association (30 North LaSalle Street, Suite 2400, Chicago, Illinois 60602; 800-621-7440 (toll-free); http://www.ncahlc.org).

Applying

Argosy University, Sarasota, accepts students year-round on a rolling admissions basis, depending on availability of required courses. Applications for admission are available online or by contacting the campus.

Correspondence and Information

Argosy University, Sarasota
5250 17th Street
Sarasota, Florida 34235

Phone: 941-379-0404
800-331-5995 (toll-free)
Fax: 941-371-8910
E-mail: auadmissions@argosy.edu
Web site: http://www.argosy.edu/sarasota

Argosy University, Sarasota

THE FACULTY

The Argosy University faculty is comprised of working professionals who are eager to help students succeed. Members bring real-world experience and the latest practice innovations to the academic setting. The diverse faculty members of the College of Psychology and Behavioral Sciences are widely recognized for contributions to the field. Many are published scholars, and most hold doctoral degrees. They are committed to providing a substantive education that combines comprehensive knowledge with critical skills and practical workplace relevance. Above all, faculty members are committed to their students' personal and professional development.

ARGOSY UNIVERSITY

ARGOSY UNIVERSITY, SCHAUMBURG

College of Psychology and Behavioral Sciences

Programs of Study

Argosy University, Schaumburg, offers the Master of Arts (M.A.) degree in clinical psychology, community counseling, forensic psychology, industrial organizational psychology, and sport-exercise psychology; the Doctor of Education (Ed.D.) degree in counseling psychology, counselor education and supervision, and organizational leadership; and the Doctor of Psychology (Psy.D.) degree in clinical psychology. Students completing a program may wish to become licensed professionals. Argosy University, Schaumburg does not guarantee third-party certification/licensure. Outside agencies control the requirements for taking and passing certification/licensing exams and are subject to change without notice to Argosy University, Schaumburg.

The M.A. in clinical psychology program is designed to educate and train students to enter a professional career as master's-level practitioners. Students receive an educational program with all the necessary theoretical and clinical elements designed to allow them to be effective members of a mental health team. The program introduces students to basic clinical skills that integrate individual and group theoretical foundations of applied psychology into appropriate client interaction and intervention skills. In addition, the program offers comprehensive preparation for those considering application to the Psy.D. in clinical psychology program.

The M.A. in community counseling program is designed to provide students with a sound foundation for eventual practice of professional counseling. The program introduces students to basic counseling skills that integrate individual and group theoretical foundations of professional counseling into appropriate client interaction and intervention skills. The program emphasizes the development of attitudes, knowledge, and skills essential in the formation of professional counselors who are committed to the ethical provision of quality services. The program is committed to educating and training students to enter a professional career as master's-level counseling practitioners who can function ethically and effectively as skilled professionals with demonstrated knowledge of social and cultural diversity. Students are prepared for licensure as professional counselors in the state of Illinois; however, alumni serve clients throughout North America.

The M.A. in forensic psychology program is designed to educate and train individuals who are currently working, or wish to work, in fields that utilize the study and practice of forensic psychology. Curriculum provides for an understanding of theory, training, and practice of forensic psychology. It emphasizes the development of students who are committed to the ethical provision of quality services to diverse clients and organizations. The program maintains policies and delivery formats suitable for working adults. The program provides course work in forensic psychology for application to law enforcement, legal and organizational consultation, and program analysis.

The M.A. in industrial organizational psychology program is designed to apply the knowledge of industrial organizational psychology to issues involving individuals and groups in organizational and work settings. This program prepares students for careers in areas such as compensation, training, data analysis, consultation, statistical decision-making, organizational development, leadership, and human resource management positions. The curriculum is competency-based, focusing on the outcomes of training and on the knowledge, skills, and behavior necessary to function as a master's-level professional in industrial organizational psychology. This is an interdisciplinary program that combines the expertise of the faculty in the College of Psychology and Behavioral Sciences and the College of Business.

The M.A. in sport-exercise psychology program is designed to educate and train capable and ethical performance-enhancement specialists. This two-year degree is intended to meet the needs of students seeking employment in a variety of settings, including private practice, athletic departments, coaching, exercise/health, and education, as well as those planning to ultimately pursue their doctorate. The goals of the program include developing student competencies in the following areas: theoretical foundations, helping relationships, individual and group skills, normal and abnormal behavior, sport sciences, research and evaluation, diversity, and professional identity.

The Ed.D. in counseling psychology program is designed to meet the special requirements of working professionals who want to develop their knowledge and skills to handle the changing needs of modern organizations. The program is structured to provide working professionals with the opportunity to pursue their personal and professional goals through the completion of a graduate program.

The Ed.D. in counselor education and supervision program aligns with the master's-level counselor education programs in order to encourage entry-level counseling students to work toward becoming doctoral-level advanced practitioners, educators, and supervisors. The program prepares counselors for a variety of settings by providing the advanced skills and knowledge necessary to provide leadership and advocacy, as well as serve in supervisory, training, and teaching positions in the counseling profession.

The Ed.D. in organizational leadership program is designed to meet the special requirements of working professionals who want to develop their knowledge and skills to handle the changing needs of modern organizations. The program is designed to enable working professionals to pursue their personal and professional goals through the completion of a graduate program. It focuses on the qualities of transformational leadership, not just managerial attributes. This approach enables the faculty members to dedicate themselves to preparing students to lead complex organizations faced with an abundance of strategic challenges, such as increasing globalization, changing economies, societal shifts, and individual-organizational relationships. It is the premise of the program that leaders prepared in this manner can be visionaries and innovators, leading viable organizations capable of meeting the challenges of the future.

The Psy.D. in clinical psychology program has been designed to educate and train students to function effectively as clinical psychologists. To ensure that students are prepared adequately, the curriculum provides for the meaningful integration of theory, training, and practice. The program emphasizes the development of attitudes, knowledge, and skills essential in the formation of professional psychologists who are committed to the ethical provision of quality services.

Research Facilities

Argosy University libraries provide curriculum support and educational resources, including current text materials, diagnostic training documents, reference materials and databases, journals and dissertations, and major and current titles in program areas. There is an online public-access catalog of library resources available throughout the Argosy University system. Students have remote access to the campus library database, enabling them to study and conduct research at home. Academic databases offer dissertation abstracts, academic journals, and professional periodicals. All library computers are Internet accessible. Software applications include Word, Excel, PowerPoint, SPSS, and various test-scoring programs.

Financial Aid

Financial aid is available to those who qualify. Argosy University, Schaumburg, offers access to federal and state aid programs, merit-based awards, grants, loans, and a work-study program. As a first step, students should complete the Free Application for Federal Student Aid (FAFSA). Prospective students can apply electronically at http://www.fafsa.ed.gov or at the campus.

Cost of Study

Tuition varies by program. Students should contact Argosy University, Schaumburg, for tuition information.

Living and Housing Costs

Students typically live in apartments in the metropolitan Chicago area. Living expenses vary according to each student's preferred standard of living, housing, and transportation. The University does not offer or operate student housing. Most Argosy University students are full-time working professionals who live within driving distance of the campus. Several nearby hotels offer special rates for those who commute from long distances. The Admissions Department also maintains a list of housing options, including contact information for University students who wish to share housing. For more information, students should contact the Admissions Department.

Student Group

Admission to Argosy University, Schaumburg, is selective to ensure a dynamic and engaged student body. The University encourages diversity in academic and employment backgrounds and promotes integration of the student body into professional life through established connections with local and national professional associations. Argosy University offers a professionally oriented education with rich opportunities to gain practical experience in class, field placements, and internships. Full-time students and working professionals gain the extensive knowledge and range of skills necessary for effective performance in their chosen field.

Student Outcomes

Students can register with Argosy University's online career-services system and use select services from a distance, such as degree-specific career e-mail lists, national job posts, and virtual job fairs. Students should contact the University for more information.

Location

Argosy University, Schaumburg, is located in the northwest suburban area, approximately 45 minutes from downtown Chicago. The University's small size offers a highly personal atmosphere and flexible programs tailored to students' needs. Visitors to Chicago experience a range of attractions to stimulate both intellectual and recreational pursuits. Located on the shores of Lake Michigan in the Midwest, Chicago is home to world-champion sports teams, an internationally acclaimed symphony orchestra, renowned architecture, and nearly 3 million residents. Among the variety of history and art museums in the city, the Chicago Cultural Center offers more than 600 art programs and exhibits each year. Recreational opportunities include hiking and cycling on miles of lakefront trails, golfing, and shopping

Many facilities and agencies in the area provide opportunities for student training. Schaumburg's thriving business environment includes 5,000 businesses that employ 80,000 people. The area's largest employers are Motorola, Experian, Cingular, and IBM.

The University

Argosy University is a private institution with nineteen locations across the nation. Argosy University, Schaumburg, provides a career resources office, an academic resources center, and extensive information access for research. It offers the resources of a large university plus the friendliness and personal attention of a small campus. The innovative programs feature dynamic, relevant, and practical curricula delivered in flexible class formats. Students enjoy scheduling options that make it easier to fit school into their busy lives, choosing from day and evening courses, on campus or online. Many students find a combination of class formats to be an ideal way of continuing their education while meeting family and professional demands.

Argosy University is accredited by the Higher Learning Commission and a member of the North Central Association (30 North LaSalle Street, Suite 2400, Chicago, Illinois 60602; 800-621-7440 (toll-free); http://www.ncahlc.org).

Applying

Argosy University, Schaumburg, accepts students year-round on a rolling admissions basis, depending on availability of required courses. Applications for admission are available online or by contacting the campus.

Correspondence and Information

Argosy University, Schaumburg
999 North Plaza Drive, Suite 111
Schaumburg, Illinois 60173-5403
Phone: 847-969-7400
866-290-2777 (toll-free)
Fax: 847-969-4998
E-mail: auadmissions@argosy.edu
Web site: http://www.argosy.edu/schaumburg

Argosy University, Schaumburg

THE FACULTY

The Argosy University faculty is comprised of working professionals who are eager to help students succeed. Members bring real-world experience and the latest practice innovations to the academic setting. The diverse faculty members of the College of Psychology and Behavioral Sciences are widely recognized for contributions to the field. Many are published scholars, and most hold doctoral degrees. They are committed to providing a substantive education that combines comprehensive knowledge with critical skills and practical workplace relevance. Above all, faculty members are committed to their students' personal and professional development.

ARGOSY UNIVERSITY

ARGOSY UNIVERSITY, SEATTLE

College of Psychology and Behavioral Sciences

Programs of Study

Argosy University, Seattle, offers the Master of Arts (M.A.) degree in clinical psychology and counseling psychology, the Doctor of Education (Ed.D.) degree in counseling psychology, and the Doctor of Psychology (Psy.D.) degree in clinical psychology. Students completing a program may wish to become licensed professionals. Argosy University, Seattle does not guarantee third-party certification/licensure. Outside agencies control the requirements for taking and passing certification/licensing exams and are subject to change without notice to Argosy University, Seattle.

The M.A. in clinical psychology program has been designed to educate and train students to enter a professional career as master's-level practitioners. Students receive an educational program with all the necessary theoretical and clinical elements designed to allow them to be effective members of a mental health team. The program introduces students to basic clinical skills that integrate individual and group theoretical foundations of applied psychology into appropriate client interaction and intervention skills.

The M.A. in counseling psychology program is designed to provide students with a sound foundation for the eventual practice of mental health counseling. The program emphasizes the development of attitudes, knowledge, and skills essential in the formation of professionals committed to the ethical provision of quality services. The program prepares students to enter a professional career as master's level counseling practitioners who can perform ethically and effectively as skilled professionals with demonstrated knowledge of social and cultural diversity. Curriculum is designed to integrate basic counseling skills, theoretical foundations of professional counseling, and practicum field experience into appropriate client interaction and intervention skills for application in a wide variety of settings with diverse client populations. Since licensing may change and often varies from state to state, students should verify the current requirements of the state in which they plan to become licensed.

The Ed.D. in counseling psychology program emphasizes the development of attitudes, knowledge, and skills essential in the formation of professionals who are committed to the ethical provision of quality services. To ensure that students are prepared adequately, the curriculum is designed to provide for the meaningful integration of theory, training, and practice.

The Psy.D. in clinical psychology program utilizes a practitioner-scholar model of professional training and is designed to educate and train students to function effectively as clinical psychologists. The curriculum is designed to provide for the meaningful integration of theory, training, and practice. The program is competency-based and emphasizes the development of attitudes, knowledge, and skills essential to the training of clinical psychologists committed to the ethical provision of quality services to diverse populations. Students are prepared through the formal curriculum, which exposes them to the practice of professional psychology in both its breadth and depth. Concomitant professional development is supported through mentoring relationships with practitioner-scholar faculty who embody the integration of knowledge and skills with the ethical and professional attitudes required of clinical psychologists.

Research Facilities

Argosy University libraries provide curriculum support and educational resources, including current text materials, diagnostic training documents, reference materials and databases, journals and dissertations, and major and current titles in program areas. There is an online public-access catalog of library resources available throughout the Argosy University system. Students have full remote access to the campus library database, enabling them to study and conduct research at home. Academic databases offer dissertation abstracts, academic journals, and professional periodicals. All library computers are Internet accessible. Software applications include Word, Excel, PowerPoint, SPSS, and various test-scoring programs.

Financial Aid

Financial aid is available to those who qualify. Argosy University, Seattle, offers access to federal and state aid programs, merit-based awards, grants, loans, and a work-study program. As a first step, students should complete the Free Application for Federal Student Aid (FAFSA). Prospective students can apply electronically at http://www.fafsa.ed.gov or at the campus.

Cost of Study

Tuition varies by program. Students should contact Argosy University, Seattle, for tuition information.

Living and Housing Costs

Students typically live in apartments in the metropolitan Seattle area. Living expenses vary according to each student's preferred standard of living, housing, and transportation. The University does not offer or operate student housing. Most of the students are full-time working professionals who live within driving distance of the campus. Several nearby hotels offer special rates for those who commute from long distances. The Admissions Department also maintains a list of housing options, including contact information, for University students who wish to share housing. For more information, students should contact the Admissions Department.

Student Group

Admission to Argosy University, Seattle, is selective to ensure a dynamic and engaged student body. The University encourages diversity in academic and employment backgrounds and promotes integration of the student body into professional life through established connections with local and national professional associations. Argosy University offers a professionally oriented education with rich opportunities to gain practical experience in class, field placements, and internships. Full-time students and working professionals gain the extensive knowledge and range of skills necessary for effective performance in their chosen fields.

Student Outcomes

Students can register with the University's online career-services system and use select services from a distance, such as degree-specific career e-mail lists, national job posts, and virtual job fairs. Students should contact the University for more information.

Location

Argosy University, Seattle, aspires to provide a supportive, collaborative, and engaging yet challenging learning environment. Easily reached through the King County Public Transportation System, the campus sits in proximity to local libraries, shops, restaurants, theaters, and art museums. Seattle offers numerous historical and multicultural museums, a symphony, ballet, and many theater companies. The city is home to several major-league sports teams and offers a myriad of outdoor recreational opportunities, such as camping, hiking, fishing, skiing, and rock climbing. Seattle's business environment encompasses a wide range of industries and features such giants as Microsoft, Boeing, and Alaska Air Group. The Port of Seattle and the University of Washington are also among the area's largest employers.

The University

Argosy University is a private institution with nineteen locations across the nation. Argosy University, Seattle, provides a career resources office, an academic resources center, and extensive information access for research. It offers the resources of a large university, plus the friendliness and personal attention of a small campus.

The innovative programs feature dynamic, relevant, and practical curricula delivered in flexible class formats. Students enjoy scheduling options that make it easier to fit school into their busy lives, choosing from day and evening courses, on campus or online. Many students find a combination of class formats to be an ideal way of continuing their education while meeting family and professional demands.

Argosy University is accredited by the Higher Learning Commission and a member of the North Central Association (30 North LaSalle Street, Suite 2400, Chicago, Illinois 60602; 800-621-7440 (toll-free); http://www.ncahlc.org).

Applying

Argosy University, Seattle, accepts students year-round on a rolling admissions basis, depending on availability of required courses. Applications for admission are available online or by contacting the campus.

Correspondence and Information

Argosy University, Seattle
2601-A Elliott Avenue
Seattle, Washington 98121

Phone: 206-283-4500
866-283-2777 (toll-free)
Fax: 206-283-5777
E-mail: auadmissions@argosy.edu
Web site: http://www.argosy.edu/seattle

Argosy University, Seattle

THE FACULTY

The Argosy University faculty is comprised of working professionals who are eager to help students succeed. Members bring real-world experience and the latest practice innovations to the academic setting. The diverse faculty members of the College of Psychology and Behavioral Sciences are widely recognized for contributions to the field. Many are published scholars, and most hold doctoral degrees. They are committed to providing a substantive education that combines comprehensive knowledge with critical skills and practical workplace relevance. Above all, faculty members are committed to their students' personal and professional development.

ARGOSY UNIVERSITY.

ARGOSY UNIVERSITY, TAMPA

College of Psychology and Behavioral Sciences

Programs of Study

Argosy University, Tampa, offers the Master of Arts (M.A.) degree in clinical psychology, marriage and family therapy, mental health counseling, and school counseling; the Doctor of Education (Ed.D.) degree in counselor education and supervision and organizational leadership; and the Doctor of Psychology (Psy.D.) degree in clinical psychology. Students completing a program may wish to become licensed professionals. Argosy University, Tampa does not guarantee third-party certification/licensure. Outside agencies control the requirements for taking and passing certification/licensing exams and are subject to change without notice to Argosy University, Tampa.

The M.A. in clinical psychology program is designed to meet the needs of both those students seeking a terminal degree at the master's level and those who plan to pursue a doctoral degree. The terminal master's degree is not, however, license-eligible in the state of Florida. The master's degree provides students a strong clinical orientation with an emphasis in psychological assessment. The master's program offers several unique advantages to those individuals who hope to subsequently pursue a doctoral degree. Admission to the master's program or completion of the master's degree does not guarantee admission to the Psy.D. in clinical psychology program.

The M.A. in marriage and family therapy program recognizes the need to provide marriage and family therapists with the knowledge, skills, and attitudes essential in the formation of marriage and family therapists committed to the ethical provision of quality services. The program introduces students to basic skills that integrate systemic theoretical foundations of marriage and family therapy into appropriate client interaction and intervention skills. The program has been developed by the school faculty members to provide working students with the opportunity to pursue personal and professional goals through completion of a master's program.

The M.A. in mental health counseling program recognizes the need to provide counseling professionals with the extensive knowledge, range of skills, and attitudes necessary to function effectively in their professions. The program introduces students to basic counseling skills that integrate individual and group theoretical foundations of counseling into appropriate client interaction and intervention skills. The program emphasizes formation of professional counselors committed to the ethical provision of quality services. The program has been developed by the school faculty members to provide working professionals with the opportunity to pursue their personal and professional goals through completion of a master's program.

The M.A. in school counseling program serves adult students throughout the world. It provides a quality program in school counseling to meet the needs of students and the community. The focus of the program is student preparation and professional development while promoting teaching, learning, and service. The program remains faithful to its mission of preparing students to function at a high professional level in a rapidly changing world.

The Ed.D. in counselor education and supervision program aligns with the master's-level counselor education programs in order to encourage entry-level counseling students to work toward becoming doctoral-level advanced practitioners, educators, and supervisors. The program prepares counselors for a variety of settings by providing the advanced skills and knowledge necessary to provide leadership and advocacy, as well as serve in supervisory, training, and teaching positions in the counseling profession.

The Ed.D. in organizational leadership program is designed to meet the special requirements of working professionals who want to develop their knowledge and skills to handle the changing needs of modern organizations. The program can help working professionals pursue their personal and professional goals through completion of a graduate program. It focuses on the qualities of transformational leadership, not just managerial attributes. This approach enables the faculty members to dedicate themselves to preparing students to lead complex organizations faced with an abundance of strategic challenges, such as increasing globalization, changing economies, societal shifts, and individual-organizational relationships. It is the premise of the program that leaders prepared in this manner can be visionaries and innovators, leading viable organizations capable of meeting the challenges of the future.

The Psy.D. in clinical psychology program is designed to educate and train students so that they may eventually be able to function effectively as clinical psychologists. To ensure that students are prepared adequately, the curriculum is designed to provide for the meaningful integration of theory, training, and practice. The clinical psychology program emphasizes the development of attitudes, knowledge, and skills essential in the formation of professional psychologists who are committed to the ethical provision of quality services.

Research Facilities

Argosy University libraries provide curriculum support and educational resources, including current text materials, diagnostic training documents, reference materials and databases, journals and dissertations, and major and current titles in program areas. There is an online public-access catalog of library resources available throughout the Argosy University system. Students have remote access to the campus library database, enabling them to study and conduct research at home. Academic databases offer dissertation abstracts, academic journals, and professional periodicals. All library computers are Internet accessible. Software applications include Word, Excel, PowerPoint, SPSS, and various test-scoring programs.

Financial Aid

Financial aid is available to those who qualify. Argosy University, Tampa, offers access to federal and state aid programs, merit-based awards, grants, loans, and a work-study program. As a first step, students should complete the Free Application for Federal Student Aid (FAFSA). Prospective students can apply electronically at http://www.fafsa.ed.gov or at the campus.

Cost of Study

Tuition varies by program. Students should contact Argosy University, Tampa, for tuition information.

Living and Housing Costs

Students typically live in apartments in the metropolitan Tampa area. Living expenses vary according to each student's preferred standard of living, housing, and transportation. The University does not offer or operate student housing. Most of the students are full-time working professionals who live within driving distance of the campus. Several nearby hotels offer special rates for those who commute from long distances. The Admissions Department also maintains a list of housing options, including contact information, for University students who wish to share housing. For more information, students should contact the Admissions Department.

Student Group

Admission to Argosy University, Tampa, is selective to ensure a dynamic and engaged student body. The University encourages diversity in academic and employment backgrounds and promotes integration of the student body into professional life through established connections with local and national professional associations. Argosy University offers a professionally oriented education with rich opportunities to gain practical experience in class, field placements, and internships. Full-time students and working professionals gain the extensive knowledge and range of skills necessary for effective performance in their chosen fields.

Student Outcomes

Students can register with the University's online career-services system and use select services from a distance, such as degree-specific career e-mail lists, national job posts, and virtual job fairs. Students should contact the University for more information.

Location

Located in sunny Florida, Argosy University, Tampa, attracts a diverse student population from throughout the United States, the Caribbean, Europe, Africa, and Asia. Tampa's central location affords students the opportunity to work for major corporations and hear speakers of international acclaim. The school offers rigorous programs of study in a supportive, collaborative environment. The campus sits within an hour's drive of some of the most popular tourist destinations in the world, including the Disney theme parks, Busch Gardens, and the Florida Gulf Coast beaches. Major-league sporting events, concerts, theaters, and world-renowned restaurants are also within easy reach. Tampa combines the opportunities of a large city with the friendliness of a small town. The Tampa-St. Petersburg-Clearwater metropolitan area offers a diversified economic base fueled by a broad array of companies, including Verizon Communications and JP Morgan Chase. In addition, Tampa serves as headquarters for three Fortune 100 companies—OSI Restaurant Partners; TECO, an energy provider; and Raymond James Financial.

The University

Argosy University is a private institution with nineteen locations across the nation. Argosy University, Tampa, provides a network of resources, including a career resources office, an academic resources center, and extensive information access for research. It offers the resources of a large university, plus the friendliness and personal attention of a small campus.

The innovative programs feature dynamic, relevant, and practical curricula delivered in flexible class formats. Students enjoy scheduling options that make it easier to fit school into their busy lives, choosing from day and evening courses, on campus or online. Many students find a combination of class formats to be an ideal way of continuing their education while meeting family and professional demands.

Argosy University is accredited by the Higher Learning Commission and a member of the North Central Association (30 North LaSalle Street, Suite 2400, Chicago, Illinois 60602; 800-621-7440 (toll-free); http://www.ncahlc.org).

Applying

Argosy University, Tampa, accepts students year-round on a rolling admissions basis, depending on availability of required courses. Applications for admission are available online or by contacting the campus.

Correspondence and Information

Argosy University, Tampa
1403 North Howard Avenue
Tampa, Florida 33607
Phone: 813-393-5290
800-850-6488 (toll-free)
Fax: 813-874-1989
E-mail: auadmissions@argosy.edu
Web site: http://www.argosy.edu/tampa

Argosy University, Tampa

THE FACULTY

The Argosy University faculty is comprised of working professionals who are eager to help students succeed. Members bring real-world experience and the latest practice innovations to the academic setting. The diverse faculty members of the College of Psychology and Behavioral Sciences are widely recognized for contributions to the field. Many are published scholars, and most hold doctoral degrees. They are committed to providing a substantive education that combines comprehensive knowledge with critical skills and practical workplace relevance. Above all, faculty members are committed to their students' personal and professional development.

ARGOSY UNIVERSITY.

ARGOSY UNIVERSITY, TWIN CITIES

College of Psychology and Behavioral Sciences

Programs of Study

Argosy University, Twin Cities, offers the Master of Arts (M.A.) degree in clinical psychology, forensic psychology, and marriage and family therapy; the Doctor of Marriage and Family Therapy (D.M.F.T.); and the Doctor of Psychology (Psy.D.) degree in clinical psychology. Students completing a program may wish to become licensed professionals. Argosy University, Twin Cities does not guarantee third-party certification/licensure. Outside agencies control the requirements for taking and passing certification/licensing exams and are subject to change without notice to Argosy University, Twin Cities.

The M.A. in clinical psychology program is designed to prepare students with the clinical knowledge and skills required to serve the mental health needs of individuals and groups. Students develop proficiency in clinical observation, assessment, appropriate intervention, and evaluation. The program emphasizes a practitioner-oriented philosophy and integrates applied theory, research, and field experience. It is designed for students who are interested in a terminal degree and practice as a master's-level clinician, or for students planning to transfer to the Psy.D. program.

The M.A. in forensic psychology program is designed to provide course work in forensic psychology for application to law enforcement, legal and organizational consultation, and program analysis. The program is designed to meet growing needs of the legal and criminal justice systems for professional counseling within victim assistance programs, probation and parole offices, court-mandated treatment programs, jails, and prisons. With the exception of the practicum component, courses are offered on weekends, allowing students to continue full-time employment while enrolled in this program.

The M.A. in marriage and family therapy program is designed to develop the theoretical and clinical elements required to provide effective counseling to individuals, couples, families, and groups. The program introduces basic counseling skills that incorporate foundations of applied psychology and systems theory into the development of appropriate clinical relationships. Course work in addiction studies and substance-abuse counseling prepares students to work with families affected by this burgeoning problem. An optional concentration in forensic counseling is available. Marriage and family therapy is recognized by the Public Health Service Act as one of the five core mental health professions, and the National Institute of Mental Health accepts marriage and family therapists as qualified mental health professionals. The program is offered through weekend courses to allow concurrent employment.

The Doctor of Marriage and Family Therapy is a practice-oriented degree for licensed marriage and family therapists or professionals who can meet state requirements for licensure as a marriage and family therapist (meeting the Commission on Accreditation of Marriage and Family Therapy Education (COAMFTE) criteria for clinical practice prior to admission). The program seeks to build upon students' prior learning and professional experience by expanding and deepening their knowledge of human development, family dynamics, systemic thinking, interactional theories, traditional and contemporary marriage and family therapy theories and practices, and the cultural contexts within which these are embedded.

The Psy.D. in clinical psychology program is designed to prepare students to deliver basic diagnostic and therapeutic services to diverse populations, including individuals, groups, and families. By integrating theory, training, research, and practice, students develop and apply the clinical skills of observation, assessment, intervention, and evaluation. Optional concentrations are available in child and family psychology, forensic psychology, health psychology, marriage/couple and family therapy, or neuropsychology. The program prepares graduates for positions in traditional settings, including, but not limited to, independent practice, mental health centers, hospitals, medical centers, and managed-care systems. Graduates are encouraged to utilize clinical skills in innovative ways to become more competitive. Eventual positions may include consulting in various corporate, governmental, academic, multimedia, law, scientific, marketing, and industrial settings. The Doctor of Psychology in clinical psychology program at Argosy University, Twin Cities, is accredited by the Committee on Accreditation of the American Psychological Association (APA) (750 First Street NE, Washington, D.C. 20002-4242; 202-336-5510).

Research Facilities

Argosy University libraries provide curriculum support and educational resources, including current text materials, diagnostic training documents, reference materials and databases, journals and dissertations, and major and current titles in program areas. There is an online public-access catalog of library resources available throughout the Argosy University system. Students have remote access to the campus library database, enabling them to study and conduct research at home. Academic databases offer dissertation abstracts, academic journals, and professional periodicals. All library computers are Internet accessible. Software applications include Word, Excel, PowerPoint, SPSS, and various test-scoring programs.

Financial Aid

Financial aid is available to those who qualify. Argosy University, Twin Cities, offers access to federal and state aid programs, merit-based awards, grants, loans, and a work-study program. As a first step, students should complete the Free Application for Federal Student Aid (FAFSA). Prospective students can apply electronically at http://www.fafsa.ed.gov or at the campus.

Cost of Study

Tuition varies by program. Students should contact Argosy University, Twin Cities, for tuition information.

Living and Housing Costs

Students typically live in apartments in the metropolitan Twin Cities area. Living expenses vary according to each student's preferred standard of living, housing, and transportation. The University does not offer or operate student housing. Most Argosy University students are full-time working professionals who live within driving distance of the campus. Several nearby hotels offer special rates for those who commute from long distances. The Admissions Department also maintains a list of housing options, including contact information for University students who wish to share housing. For more information, students should contact the Admissions Department.

Student Group

Admission to Argosy University, Twin Cities, is selective to ensure a dynamic and engaged student body. The University encourages diversity in academic and employment backgrounds and promotes integration of the student body into professional life through established connections with local and national professional associations. Argosy University offers a professionally oriented education with rich opportunities to gain practical experience in class, field placements, and internships. Full-time students and working professionals gain the extensive knowledge and range of skills necessary for effective performance in their chosen field.

Student Outcomes

Students can register with Argosy University's online career-services system and use select services from a distance, such as degree-specific career e-mail lists, national job posts, and virtual job fairs. Students should contact the University for more information.

Location

Argosy University, Twin Cities, offers rigorous academics in a supportive environment. The campus is nestled in a parklike suburban setting within 10 miles of the airport and the Mall of America. Students enjoy the convenience of nearby shops, restaurants, and housing and easy freeway access. The neighboring Eagan Community Center offers many amenities, including walking paths, a fitness center, meeting rooms, and an outdoor amphitheater. The twin cities of Minneapolis and St. Paul have been rated by popular magazines as one of the most livable metropolitan areas in the country. With a population of 2.5 million, the area offers an abundance of recreational activities. Year-round outdoor activities and nationally acclaimed venues for theater, art, music, and professional sports teams attract residents and visitors alike. The Minneapolis-St. Paul metropolitan area offers a diversified economic base fueled by a broad array of companies. Among the numerous publicly traded companies headquartered in the area are Target, UnitedHealth Group, 3M, General Mills, and US Bancorp.

The University

Argosy University is a private institution with nineteen locations across the nation. Argosy University, Twin Cities, provides a career resources office, an academic resources center, and extensive information access for research. It offers the resources of a large university plus the friendliness and personal attention of a small campus. The innovative programs feature dynamic, relevant, and practical curricula delivered in flexible class formats. Students enjoy scheduling options that make it easier to fit school into their busy lives, choosing from day and evening courses, on campus or online. Many students find a combination of class formats to be an ideal way of continuing their education while meeting family and professional demands.

Argosy University is accredited by the Higher Learning Commission and a member of the North Central Association (30 North LaSalle Street, Suite 2400, Chicago, Illinois 60602; 800-621-7440 (toll-free); http://www.ncahlc.org).

Applying

Argosy University, Twin Cities, accepts students on a rolling admissions basis year-round, depending on availability of required courses. Applications for admission may be obtained online or by contacting the campus.

Correspondence and Information

Argosy University, Twin Cities
1515 Central Parkway
Eagan, Minnesota 55121

Phone: 651-846-2882
888-844-2004 (toll-free)
Fax: 651-994-7956
E-mail: auadmissions@argosy.edu
Web site: http://www.argosy.edu/twincities

Argosy University, Twin Cities

THE FACULTY

The Argosy University faculty is comprised of working professionals who are eager to help students succeed. Members bring real-world experience and the latest practice innovations to the academic setting. The diverse faculty members of the College of Psychology and Behavioral Sciences are widely recognized for contributions to the field. Many are published scholars, and most hold doctoral degrees. They are committed to providing a substantive education that combines comprehensive knowledge with critical skills and practical workplace relevance. Above all, faculty members are committed to their students' personal and professional development.

ARGOSY UNIVERSITY

ARGOSY UNIVERSITY, WASHINGTON D.C.

College of Psychology and Behavioral Sciences

Programs of Study

Argosy University, Washington D.C., offers the Master of Arts (M.A.) degree in clinical psychology, community counseling, and forensic psychology; the Doctor of Education (Ed.D.) degree in counselor education and supervision, and counseling psychology; and the Doctor of Psychology (Psy.D.) degree in clinical psychology. Students completing a program may wish to become licensed professionals. Argosy University, Washington D.C. does not guarantee third-party certification/licensure. Outside agencies control the requirements for taking and passing certification/licensing exams and are subject to change without notice to Argosy University, Washington D.C.

The M.A. in clinical psychology program is designed to meet the needs of both those students seeking a terminal degree at the master's level and those who eventually plan to pursue a doctoral degree. The master's degree provides students a strong clinical orientation as well as an emphasis in psychological assessment. The program has been structured to educate and train students so they might either be prepared to enter a doctoral program in clinical psychology or enter a professional career as master's-level practitioners. The program provides a strong background in assessment and introduces students to basic clinical interventions skills. Students also receive an introduction to scientific methodology and the bases of scientific psychology.

The M.A. in community counseling program is designed to provide students with a sound foundation for the practice of community counseling, with a multifaceted focus on developmental and preventive mental health services. The program introduces students to the basic skills of counseling, integrating individual, group, family, and organizational interventions. It emphasizes development of the attitudes, knowledge, and skills required for the ethical provision of quality professional counseling services. As such, the program is committed to educating and training students to enter the counseling profession as ethical, effective, skilled, and culturally competent practitioners, able to work in a variety of settings with diverse client populations. The curriculum integrates foundational counseling skills, counseling theories, and clinical field experiences taught by experienced practitioners.

The M.A. in forensic psychology program is designed to educate and train individuals who are currently working, or wish to work, in fields that utilize the study and practice of forensic psychology. Curriculum provides for an understanding of theory, training, and practice of forensic psychology. It emphasizes the development of students who are committed to the ethical provision of quality services to diverse clients and organizations. The program maintains policies and delivery formats suitable for working adults. The program provides course work in forensic psychology for application to law enforcement, legal and organizational consultation, and program analysis.

The Ed.D. in counselor education and supervision program aligns with the master's-level counselor education programs in order to encourage entry-level counseling students to work toward becoming doctoral-level advanced practitioners, educators, and supervisors. The program prepares counselors for a variety of settings by providing the advanced skills and knowledge necessary to provide leadership and advocacy, as well as serve in supervisory, training, and teaching positions in the counseling profession. The program is also designed to help current practitioners with existing master's-level preparation to advance their careers. This doctorate provides expanded opportunities to compete in the marketplace, on par with the growing number of doctoral-level counseling practitioners.

The Ed.D. in counseling psychology program is designed to meet the special requirements of working professionals who want to develop their knowledge and skills to handle the changing needs of modern organizations. The program provides working professionals with the opportunity to pursue their personal and professional goals through the completion of a graduate program. An optional concentration in counselor education and supervision is also available.

The Psy.D. in clinical psychology program is designed to educate and train students so they may eventually be able to function effectively as clinical psychologists. To enable students to prepare adequately, the curriculum provides for the meaningful integration of theory, training, and practice. The program emphasizes the development of attitudes, knowledge, and skills essential in the formation of professional psychologists who are committed to the ethical provision of quality services.

Research Facilities

Argosy University libraries provide curriculum support and educational resources, including current text materials, diagnostic training documents, reference materials and databases, journals and dissertations, and major and current titles in program areas. There is an online public-access catalog of library resources available throughout the Argosy University system. Students have remote access to the campus library database, enabling them to study and conduct research at home. Academic databases offer dissertation abstracts, academic journals, and professional periodicals. All library computers are Internet accessible. Software applications include Word, Excel, PowerPoint, SPSS, and various test-scoring programs.

Financial Aid

Financial aid is available to those who qualify. Argosy University, Washington D.C., offers access to federal and state aid programs, merit-based awards, grants, loans, and a work-study program. As a first step, students should complete the Free Application for Federal Student Aid (FAFSA). Prospective students can apply electronically at http://www.fafsa.ed.gov or at the campus.

Cost of Study

Tuition varies by program. Students should contact Argosy University, Washington D.C., for tuition information.

Living and Housing Costs

Students typically live in apartments in the metropolitan Washington, D.C., area. Living expenses vary according to each student's preferred standard of living, housing, and transportation. The University does not offer or operate student housing. Most Argosy University students are full-time working professionals who live within driving distance of the campus. Several nearby hotels offer special rates for those who commute from long distances. The Admissions Department also maintains a list of housing options, including contact information for University students who wish to share housing. For more information, students should contact the Admissions Department.

Student Group

Admission to Argosy University, Washington D.C., is selective to ensure a dynamic and engaged student body. The University encourages diversity in academic and employment backgrounds and promotes integration of the student body into professional life through established connections with local and national professional associations. Argosy University offers a professionally oriented education with rich opportunities to gain practical experience in class, field placements, and internships. Full-time students and working professionals gain the extensive knowledge and range of skills necessary for effective performance in their chosen field.

Student Outcomes

Students can register with Argosy University's online career-services system and use select services from a distance, such as degree-specific career e-mail lists, national job posts, and virtual job fairs. Students should contact the University for more information.

Location

Argosy University, Washington D.C., is located in suburban Arlington, Virginia. The school provides easy access to most major highways in area and is accessible by public transportation. With its proximity to Georgetown, students enjoy access to the many diverse attractions of the D.C. area. Additional campus space is located at the Art Institute of Washington Building (1820 Fort Myer Drive). The university houses administrative space and seven classrooms at this location. Perhaps best known as the home of the Pentagon and Arlington National Cemetery, Arlington, Virginia, is one of the most highly educated areas in the nation. It is also one of the most diverse. Major employers in the region include MCI Telecommunications Corporation; Bell Atlantic Network Services, Inc.; and Gannett/USA Today Company, Inc.

The University

Argosy University is a private institution with nineteen locations across the nation. Argosy University, Washington D.C., provides a career resources office, an academic resources center, and extensive information access for research. It offers the resources of a large university plus the friendliness and personal attention of a small campus. The innovative programs feature dynamic, relevant, and practical curricula delivered in flexible class formats. Students enjoy scheduling options that make it easier to fit school into their busy lives, choosing from day and evening courses, on campus or online. Many students find a combination of class formats to be an ideal way of continuing their education while meeting family and professional demands.

Argosy University is accredited by the Higher Learning Commission and a member of the North Central Association (30 North LaSalle Street, Suite 2400, Chicago, Illinois 60602; 800-621-7440 (toll-free); http://www.ncahlc.org).

Applying

Argosy University, Washington D.C., accepts students year-round on a rolling admissions basis, depending on availability of required courses. Applications for admission are available online or by contacting the campus.

Correspondence and Information

Argosy University, Washington D.C.
1550 Wilson Boulevard, Suite 600
Arlington, Virginia 22209
Phone: 703-526-5800
866-703-2777 (toll-free)
Fax: 703-243-8973
E-mail: auadmissions@argosy.edu
Web site: http://www.argosy.edu/washingtondc

Argosy University, Washington DC

THE FACULTY

The Argosy University faculty is comprised of working professionals who are eager to help students succeed. Members bring real-world experience and the latest practice innovations to the academic setting. The diverse faculty members of the College of Psychology and Behavioral Sciences are widely recognized for contributions to the field. Many are published scholars, and most hold doctoral degrees. They are committed to providing a substantive education that combines comprehensive knowledge with critical skills and practical workplace relevance. Above all, faculty members are committed to their students' personal and professional development.

FELICIAN COLLEGE

Program in Counseling Psychology

Program of Study

The Master of Arts in counseling psychology program is designed to train students to become knowledgeable, skillful, ethical counselors able to assist individuals in need of professional counseling services.

Graduates will be prepared to focus on psychological counseling for individuals, couples, families, and groups. In line with Franciscan mission and in keeping with the most current trends in psychology, Felician College has developed a unique approach to preparing professional counselors by placing an emphasis on mindfulness, spiritual development, and empowering the potential of others. Upon successful completion of the program, students will be qualified to seek employment as counselors in hospitals, schools, clinics, private group practices, and other settings in the community.

The Master of Arts in counseling psychology consists of 60 credits. The program conforms to the licensing expectations of the New Jersey Professional Counselor Licensing Law, and adheres to the accrediting guidelines of CACREP (Council for Accreditation of Counseling and Related Educational Programs), the professional accrediting body for counseling programs.

Research Facilities

The College Library is a two-story building that serves the needs of students, faculty and staff members, and alumni with more than 110,000 books and over 800 periodical subscriptions. This collection is enhanced by large holdings of materials in microform, which can be used on the library's reader/printer equipment. With its computers linked to information services such as Dialog and OCLC, and as a member of the New Jersey Library Network and VALE, the library locates and obtains information, journal articles, and books not available in its collection from sources all over the country. Computerized databases can also be accessed directly by users through the online FirstSearch workstation, where up-to-date information on 40 million books and an index of 15,000 periodicals is available. The library is also connected to the Internet and has several CD-ROM workstations. Through EBSCOhost, Bell & Howell's ProQuest, CINAHL, and other services, students and faculty and staff members have access to numerous online journal indexes—as well as articles from thousands of periodicals—from anywhere on the campus computer network or from their home computers. An experienced staff of professional librarians is available to assist users.

The College's computer facilities include an academic and administrative network, four computerized labs, a computerized learning center, and two computer centers that are available for students, with a total of about 200 computers available for student/faculty member use. All classrooms, offices, and facilities are wired for Internet and e-mail.

Financial Aid

To qualify for financial aid, a student must complete the Free Application for Federal Student Aid (FAFSA).

Cost of Study

In 2010–11, graduate tuition is $825 per credit. Fees are additional.

Living and Housing Costs

Students are housed in two dormitories on the Rutherford campus, Milton and Elliott Halls. Both buildings have housing organized around student suites containing semiprivate baths. On-campus room and board is approximately $10,150 per year. On-campus housing is not available to married students.

Student Group

Felician College enrolls approximately 2,300 students. In fall 2009, there were approximately 350 students enrolled in graduate programs.

Location

Felician College's Lodi campus is located on the banks of the Saddle River on a beautifully landscaped campus of 27 acres and offers a collegiate setting in suburban Bergen County, within easy driving distance of New York City. The Felician College Rutherford Campus is set on 10.5 beautifully landscaped acres in the heart of the historic community of Rutherford, New Jersey. Only 15 minutes from the Lodi campus, the Rutherford complex contains student residences, classroom buildings, a student center, and a gymnasium. The campus is a short distance from downtown Rutherford, where there are many shops and businesses of interest to students. Regular shuttle bus service between the two campuses is a quick 10-minute ride that turns two campuses into a one-campus home for the students.

The College

Felician College, a coeducational liberal arts college, is a Catholic, independent institution for students representing diverse religious, racial, and ethnic backgrounds. The College operates on two campuses in Lodi and Rutherford, New Jersey. The College is one of the institutions of higher learning conducted by the Felician Sisters in the United States. Its mission is to provide a values-oriented education based in the liberal arts while it prepares students for meaningful lives and careers in contemporary society. To meet the needs of students and to provide personal enrichment courses to matriculated and nonmatriculated students, Felician College offers day, evening, and weekend programs. The College is accredited by the Middle States Association of Colleges and Schools and carries program accreditation from the Commission on Collegiate Nursing Education, the International Assembly for Collegiate Business Education, and the Teacher Education Accreditation Council.

Applying

Applicants should complete the application for adult and graduate admission and submit it along with the $40 application fee; transcript(s) from all undergraduate and/or graduate institutions previously attended; scores from GRE or MAT; two letters of reference; and a personal statement. An interview and additional information may be required.

Correspondence and Information

Adult and Graduate Programs
Felician College
262 South Main Street
Lodi, New Jersey 07644-2117
Phone: 201-559-6077
Fax: 201-559-6138
E-mail: adultandgraduate@felician.edu
Web site: http://www.felician.edu/

Felician College

THE FACULTY

For specific information regarding the faculty of Felician College, please visit the College's Web site at http://www.felician.edu/.

FLORIDA INSTITUTE OF TECHNOLOGY

School of Psychology

Programs of Study

The School of Psychology offers Master of Science (M.S.) and Ph.D. degrees in the field of industrial/organizational psychology; three different M.S. degrees in behavior analysis: applied behavior analysis (ABA), organizational behavior management (OBM), and ABA+OBM; a Ph.D. in behavior analysis, and a Psy.D. degree in the field of clinical psychology.

The Clinical Doctor of Psychology, APA-accredited program is a practitioner-scientist model, emphasizing assessment, diagnosis, intervention, and evaluation skills, along with training in consultation, supervision, education, administration, and diversity. A strong generalist predoctoral focus is emphasized, with particular training opportunities in neuropsychology, child and family, forensic psychology, primary-care psychology, sexual abuse, and multiculturalism. Practicum placements occur across inpatient and outpatient sites, with a variety of populations and presenting issues. Students enter their internships possessing a wide variety of clinical skills and knowledge of the major treatment modalities. Program requirements include 121 semester hours for postbaccalaureate students, with a possible 18 semester hours of transfer credit for students with master's degrees in psychology or related disciplines; four years of residence; completion of a doctoral research project; completion of comprehensive and clinical qualification examinations; and completion of a one-year, 2,000-hour internship at an approved site.

The M.S. program in industrial/organizational psychology prepares graduate students to either continue their education in a doctoral program or to work in any of the broad human resource functions of business and industry. The program is based on the scientist-practitioner models in which students are encouraged to collect data while participating in organizational interventions. Scholarly works such as journal and conference submissions are encouraged and supported by the I/O faculty. Practical training is required as part of this 45-semester-hour program. Either the completion of a master's thesis or a nonthesis written summary of the student practicum is required. The Ph.D. program requires students to actively participate in academic research and provides students with opportunities to polish their consulting skills. Advanced statistical courses, electives, and research credits round out this 90-semester-hour program. Students can explore specific areas of concentration, including international I/O psychology. Comprehensive examinations take place at the end of the third year. Dissertation research is begun immediately after successful completion of the comprehensive exam. Ph.D. students are encouraged to finish the program in four years. Both programs prepare I/O psychology graduates for a wide variety of careers in academics, management, human resources, and consulting.

The behavior analysis M.S. degree programs at the School of Psychology are accredited by the Association for Behavior Analysis International (ABAI) and approved to meet all certification requirements for those seeking certification as a Board Certified Behavior Analyst (BCBA) by the Behavior Analyst Certification Board.

The M.S. degree in applied behavior analysis emphasizes clinical and educational applications. It requires a minimum of 48 credits, including core classes, ABA classes, foundations of bio-psychology, intensive practical training, and electives. The degree program is offered at both the Institute's main campus and the Orlando Graduate Center. The Orlando site program is offered on Friday afternoons and weekends. Most main campus students do their ABA practical training at the Institute's Scott Center, a state-of the art service/training/research facility. The M.S. degree program in organizational behavior management emphasizes applications of behavior analysis to business and industry. It requires a minimum of 42 credits, including core classes, ABA classes, foundations of I/O psychology, foundations of business administration and financial accounting, electives, and optional intensive practical training. The M.S. degree program in ABA+OBM combines the essentials of the other two M.S. degrees but eliminates electives. It requires a minimum of 57 credits. The OBM and ABA+OBM degree programs are offered only at the main campus, but a student may complete the first year at the Orlando site and transfer for their second year. All of the Institute's behavior analysis M.S. degree programs give students the option to complete either a thesis or a capstone project to fulfill graduation requirements. Passing a final program examination also is required prior to graduation. Only full-time students are accepted as the program integrates classroom-based training with hands-on practical training and research. The M.S. programs in behavior analysis prepare graduate students to either continue their education in a doctoral program or to work as a behavior analysis practitioner or consultant. These programs embrace the scientist-practitioner model; thus, students are required to systematically evaluate their interventions. Full-time students typically finish the degree in one summer short of two full academic years.

The School of Psychology also offers a Ph.D. degree in behavior analysis. Only persons who either already have completed an M.S. or M.A. degree in behavior analysis (or a related field with an emphasis in behavior analysis) are considered for admissions. The Institute's own M.S. degree students are encouraged to petition up. However, 3 to 5 students are accepted per academic year. The Ph.D. degree program prepares students for academic jobs and senior clinical and administrative positions. Degree requirements consist of a minimum of 83 postbaccalaureate graduate credits, of which a minimum of 36 credits must be post M.S./M.A. and 42 of which must be completed at the Institute. The four general competencies emphasized in the program are behavior analytic research, teaching, supervision, and consultation. The Ph.D. program requires a minimum residency of two years at the Institute's main campus.

Research Facilities

The School of Psychology includes the Psychology Building, the Scott Center for Autism Treatment and Psychological Services, the applied research lab, and the industrial-organizational psychology and the neuropsychology research labs. The East Central Florida Memory Clinic, the Family Learning Program, the Center for Organizational Effectiveness, and the Scott Center provide service, training, and research opportunities.

Financial Aid

A limited number of research and teaching assistantships are available to graduate students, providing yearly stipends and tuition remission packages ranging from $1800 to $7200. University Graduate Scholarships provide tuition remission for selected incoming students. A number of work-study positions, as well as various loan programs, are available to students who qualify. Advanced field placement sites usually provide student stipends.

Cost of Study

Graduate tuition for the 2010–11 academic year is $9555 per semester for the Psy.D. program and $1040 per credit hour for the M.S. and Ph.D. programs. Books and testing materials cost about $1800 for the first year of the clinical program.

Living and Housing Costs

Room and board on campus are approximately $5000 per semester in 2010–11. On-campus housing is available for full-time students. Many apartment complexes and rental houses are available near the campus.

Student Group

The School's graduate population averages 170 to 190 students. Approximately two thirds of the students are women, and about 12 percent are members of minority groups.

Twenty students are admitted into the clinical program each year, 8 to 12 into the industrial/organizational psychology master's program, 2 to 4 into the industrial/organizational Ph.D. program, 30 into the behavior analysis master's programs, and 3 to 4 into the behavioral analysis Ph.D. program.

Student Outcomes

Graduates from the Psy.D. program secure positions across a number of settings, including psychiatric hospitals, VA medical centers, community mental health centers, rehabilitation hospitals, and private practice. Graduates of the industrial/organizational program find positions in the following areas: employee selection and placement, performance appraisal, training and evaluation, career counseling, management development, organizational development, and employee relations. Graduates work in a variety of professional settings including consulting firms, for-profit organizations, the government, and academic institutions. Graduates of the applied behavioral analysis program find positions in schools, residential programs, group homes, foster- care programs, and consulting firms.

Location

Melbourne is located on the central east coast of Florida, a short drive from the John F. Kennedy Space Center and the city of Orlando.

The Institute

In response to a need for specialized and advanced educational opportunities, Florida Institute of Technology was founded in 1958 by a group of scientists and engineers pioneering America's space program at Cape Canaveral. Florida Tech has rapidly developed into a residential institution that is the second-largest private university in the state of Florida. The faculty and administration are committed to the pursuit of academic excellence in teaching and research in the sciences, engineering, aeronautics, management, and psychology.

Applying

All applicants must possess a bachelor's degree from an accredited institution. Although the degree need not be in psychology, no less than 18 hours of psychology course work must have been completed (including courses in statistics, personality, learning, social, abnormal, and physiological psychology for the clinical applicants). These prerequisite courses may be completed before admission outside of a degree program.

Master's applicants are expected to have a grade point average of 3.0 or higher on a scale where A = 4.0; doctoral program applicants are expected to have at least a 3.2 GPA. All applicants must submit three letters of recommendation, provide a statement of career objectives, and arrange for GRE General Test scores to be sent. The GRE Subject Test in psychology is recommended for application to the Psy.D. clinical program. Official transcripts of all undergraduate and graduate courses attempted must be submitted. Applications are accepted only for the fall term. Fall term application deadlines are January 15 for clinical Psy.D. and behavioral analysis Ph.D., and February 1 for industrial/organizational psychology and behavior analysis master's applicants.

Correspondence and Information

Office of Graduate Admissions
Florida Institute of Technology
150 West University Boulevard
Melbourne, Florida 32901-6988
Phone: 321-674-8027
Fax: 321-723-9468
E-mail: grad-admission@fit.edu
Web site: http://www.fit.edu

School of Psychology
Florida Institute of Technology
150 West University Boulevard
Melbourne, Florida 32901-6988
Phone: 321-674-8105
Fax: 321-674-7105
E-mail: lsorum@fit.edu
Web site: http://www.fit.edu

Florida Institute of Technology

THE FACULTY AND THEIR RESEARCH

G. Susanne Bahr, Associate Professor; Ph.D., Texas Christian. Mental model, information visualization in distributed team environments, usability methodology.

Elbert Q. Blakely, Jr., Assistant Professor; Ph.D., Western Michigan; BCBA. Developmental disabilities, behavioral pharmacology, experimental analysis of behavior, teaching, database development.

Guy S. Bruce, Assistant Professor; Ph.D., West Virginia; BCBA. Organizational behavior management, instructional design, performance management, human performance engineering, descriptive and functional analysis, philosophical and theoretical foundations of behavior analysis, behavioral medicine, measurement, evaluation, experimental design.

Alison Betz, Assistant Professor; Ph.D., Utah State; BCBA. Treatment of severe behavior in individuals with disabilities, interventions that produce positive behavior changes in young children with autism, staff and parent training methods.

Felipa T. Chavez, Assistant Professor; Ph.D., SUNY at Buffalo. Multiculturalism, parenting, child development, family dysfunction, impact of substance abuse on child maltreatment in different sociocultural contexts, social support networks as buffer to stress and family dysfunction, parent-child interaction therapy treatment effectiveness with minority populations and recovering families.

Ivy Chong, Assistant Professor and Director of Behavioral Service at the Scott Center; Ph.D., Western Michigan; BCBA. Behavior analysis, treatment of autism spectrum disorders.

Patrick D. Converse, Associate Professor; Ph.D., Michigan. Motivation, self-regulatory processes, personality measurement and cognitive ability, ability requirements of occupations.

Vanessa A. Edkins, Assistant Professor; Ph.D., Kansas. Juror decision-making, attitudes toward the legal system, legal entrapment.

Richard T. Elmore Jr., Associate Professor; Ph.D., Georgia State. Clinical hypnosis, marital and sex therapy, traumatology, occupational health psychology.

Philip D. Farber, Associate Professor; Ph.D., Wisconsin–Milwaukee. Psychological assessment, clinical training issues, competencies in professional psychology training, health psychology.

William K. Gabrenya, Professor; Ph.D., Missouri. Cross-cultural psychology, Chinese culture, social class and modernization, indigenous psychology, sex, work psychology.

Rich Griffith, Professor; Ph.D., Akron. International I/O psychology, response distortion on noncognitive selection procedures, advanced measurement issues, organizational innovation, cognitive process of work teams.

Julie Gross, Assistant Professor; Ph.D., NYU. Criminal aggression and treatment, psychopathology, sanity, deceit, psychoanalytic theory.

Arthur Gutman, Professor; Ph.D., Syracuse. Personnel law, applied statistics, program evaluation, personnel psychology, research design.

Thomas H. Harrell, Professor; Ph.D., Georgia. Psychometrics and computerized psychological assessment, use of the MMPI-2 in clinical evaluation, cognitive-behavioral approaches to assessment and therapy, adaptation to aging.

A. Celeste Harvey (Roberts), Assistant Professor; Ph.D., Vanderbilt; BCBA. Developmental disabilities, psychopathology, self-injurious behavior, intensive early intervention in autism.

Mark T. Harvey, Associate Professor; Ph.D., Oregon; BCBA. Applied behavior analysis, developmental disabilities, behavioral strategies in educational settings, sleep architecture, integration of biomedical and behavioral indices.

Marshall Jones, Instructor and Program Chair, Undergraduate Psychology; M.S., Alabama. Law enforcement leadership, law enforcement recruiting and retention, training technology, promotional assessment, racial profiling.

Maria Lavooy, Associate Professor; Ph.D., Miami (Ohio). Pedagogy in online teaching and learning, including confronting behavior and diversity, with primary focus on gender issues.

Mary Beth Kenkel, Professor and Dean; Ph.D., Miami (Ohio). Integrated behavioral health care, women and leadership, psychology and technology, prevention activities in psychology, future of professional psychology.

Radhika Krishnamurthy, Professor; Psy.D., Virginia Consortium for Professional Psychology. Personality assessment with MMPI-2/MMPI-A and Rorschach, child and adolescent development, interface between personality and neuropsychological functioning.

Jose Martinez-Diaz, Associate Professor and Chair, Behavioral Analysis Programs; Ph.D., West Virginia. Professional and conceptual issues, verbal behavior, antecedent events in treatment of problem behavior, treatment of persons with developmental disabilities and with schizophrenia.

Patrick McGreevy, Assistant Professor; Ph.D., Kansas; BCBA. Verbal behavior, developmental disabilities, teaching language to persons with developmental disabilities, treatment of severe problem behavior, educational applications of ABA, standard measurement and charting.

Kevin Mulligan, Professor and Chair, Clinical Psychology Program; Psy.D., Denver. Neuropsychological assessment and intervention, cognitive changes associated with normal aging and dementia, traumatic brain injury, prolonged exposure for combat-related posttraumatic stress disorder.

Barbara Paulillo, Associate Professor and Director of Psychological Services at the Scott Center; Psy.D., Florida Tech. Community mental health, psychological services delivery.

Todd Poch, Assistant Professor; Psy.D., Denver. Forensic psychology, diagnosis and treatment of stress disorders, men's issues, executive coaching.

Erin M. Richard, Assistant Professor; Ph.D., LSU. Emotional regulation in the workplace, individual differences related to work motivation.

Lisa Steelman, Associate Professor and Chair, Industrial Organizational Psychology Program; Ph.D., Akron. Feedback processes, multirater feedback, performance appraisal, work-related attitudes, employee commitment and engagement.

Kristi Sands Van Sickle, Assistant Professor; Psy.D., Florida Tech. Community health; integrated health care; clinical health psychology; health policy and legislative advocacy; self-care and professional competence.

Fran James-Warkomski, Associate Professor and Director of the Scott Center for Autism Treatment; Ed.D., Temple. School-based student improvement, special education, performance targets, autism spectrum disorders.

Frank M. Webbe, Professor; Ph.D., Florida. Aging and technology, sport neuropsychology.

David A. Wilder, Professor; Ph.D., Nevada, Reno. Functional analysis and function-based intervention in children with disruptive behavior, organizational behavior management (assessment in OBM, feedback), stimulus preference assessment methods.

Paula Wolfteich, Assistant Professor; Ph.D., Purdue. Child maltreatment investigation and treatment models, infant and preschool assessment and early intervention for behavior and developmental disorders, clinical training and supervision.

Adjunct Faculty

A complete directory of all faculty including adjunct faculty may be viewed at http://cpla.fit.edu/psych/faculty.php.

RECENT FACULTY PUBLICATIONS AND PRESENTATIONS

Adams, R., **G. S. Bahr,** and B. Moreno. Brain computer interfaces: Psychology and pragmatic perspectives for the future. Presented at AISB Convention on Communication, Interaction, and Social Intelligence, Aberdeen, Scotland, 2008.

Bahr, G. S., C. Balaban, M. Milanova, and H. Choe. Nonverbally smart user interfaces: Postural and facial expression data in human computer Interaction. In *Universal Access in Human-Computer Interaction, Part II,* pp. 740–9, ed. C. Stephanidis. Berlin: Springer-Verlag, 2007.

Betz, A., T. Higbee, K. N. Kelley, T. P. Sellers, and J. S Pollard. A comparison of the effects of scripts and script fading procedures, and extinction on the response variability of manding with children with autism. *J. Appl. Behav. Anal.,* in press.

Betz, A., T. S. Higbee, and J. S. Pollard. Promoting generalization of mands for information used by children with autism. *Research in Autism Spectral Disorders* 4(3):501–08, 2010.

Chavez, F. T., and D. Burrows. Racial differences in African-American and European-American families in treatment outcomes of child physical abuse and parental psychopathology using parent-child interaction therapy vs. traditional. Presented at International Family Violence and Child Victimization Research Conference, Portsmouth, N.H., 2007.

Chong, I. M., and J. E. Carr. Failure to demonstrate the differential outcomes effect in children with autism. *Behav. Interv.,* 2010. doi:10.1002/bin.318.

Chong, I. M. Behavioral assessment. In *Encyclopedia of Child Behavior and Development,* eds. S. Goldstein and J. A. Naglierei. New York: Springer, 2010.

Converse, P. D., E. Steinhauser, and J. Pathak. Individual differences in reactions to goal-performance discrepancies over time. *Person. Indiv. Differ.,* in press.

Converse, P. D., et al. Statement desirability ratings in forced-choice personality measure development: Implications for reducing score inflation and providing trait level information. *Hum. Perform.,* in press.

Adams, G., **V. Edkins,** D. Lacka, and K. Pickett. Teaching racism in psychology: Pernicious implications of the discipline's individualistic focus for students' perceptions of racism. (Presented at the Society for Personality and Social Psychology, Albuquerque, N.Mex., 2008.) *Basic Appl. Soc. Psychol.,* in press.

Cimino, A., and **R. Elmore.** Coping resources of ROTC cadets: PTSD risk factors for combat deployment. Also, Hurricanes Francis and Jeanne: Perceptions of stress among college students. Presented at the Southeastern Psychological Association, Atlanta, Ga., 2006.

Gabrenya, W. K. Jr. Are Taiwanese becoming (ever more) modern? A twenty-one-year longitudinal study. Presented at the International Association for Cross-Cultural Psychology, Melbourne, Australia, 2010.

Gabrenya, W. K. Jr., et al. The cultural intelligence scale: What does it measure? Presented at the International Congress of Applied Psychology, Melbourne, Australila, 2010.

Griffith, R. L., and **P. D. Converse.** The rules of evidence and the prevalence of applicant faking. In *New Perspectives on Faking in Personality Assessments,* eds. M. Ziegler, C. McCann, and R. Roberts. New York: Oxford University Press, in press.

Peterson, M. H., **R. L. Griffith,** and **P. D. Converse.** Examining the role of applicant faking in hiring decisions: Percentage of fakers hired and hiring discrepancies in single and multiple predictor selection. *J. Bus. Psychol.,* in press.

Juni, S., and **J. Gross.** Persuasive and emotional perception of fonts. *Percept. Mot. Skills,* 106:35–42, 2008.

Juni, S., **J. Gross,** and J. Sokolowska. Academic cheating as a function of defense mechanisms and object relations. *Psychological Reports,* 98:627–39, 2006.

Gutman, A. and E. Dunleavy. Legal update: Ricci, OFCCP enforcement, and implications for selection. Presented at the Society for Industrial and Organizational Psychology, Atlanta, Ga., 2010.

Harrel, T. H., and J. Owen. Psychological moderators of illness-related fatigue in rheumatoid arthritis. Presented at the American Psychological Association, San Francisco, Calif., 2007.

Harrel, T. H., and J. Owen. Effects and moderators of RA-related fatigue. Presented at the American College of Rheumatology/Association of Rheumatology Health Professionals, Washington, D.C., 2006.

Harvey, A. C., M. T. Harvey, M. B. Kenkel, and D. Russo. Funding of applied behavior analysis services: Current status and growing opportunities. *Psychol. Serv.,* in press.

Roberts **(Harvey),** C., et al. **(M. T. Harvey).** Varied effects of conventional antiepileptics on responding maintained by negative versus positive reinforcement. *Physiol. Behav.* 93(3):612–21, 2008.

Harvey, M. T., J. K. Luiselli, and S. E. Wong. Application of applied behavior analysis to mental health issues. *Psychol. Serv.* 6(3):212–22, 2009.

Kennedy, C. H., et al. **(M. T. Harvey).** Children with severe developmental disabilities and behavioral disorders have increased special health-care needs. *Dev. Med. Child Neurol.* 49(12):926–30, 2007.

Jones, M. Leadership's role in shaping organizational culture: The key to the future. In *Advancing Police Leadership: Considerations, Lessons Learned, and Preferable Futures,* vol. 6: *Proceedings of the Futures Working Group,* pp. 53–67, eds. J. A. Schafer and S. Boyd. Quantico, Va., 2010.

Jones, M., E. Moulton, and J. Reynolds. The "universality" of leadership and management in policing. In *Advancing Police Leadership: Considerations, Lessons Learned, and Preferable Futures,* vol. 6, *Proceedings of the Futures Working Group,* pp. 30–44, eds. J. A. Schafer and S. Boyd. Quantico, Va., 2010.

Kenkel, M. B. Adopting a competency model for professional psychology: Essential elements and resources. *Training and Education in Professional Psychology,* 3(4):S59–62, 2009.

DeLeon, P. H., **M. B. Kenkel,** J. Oliveira-Berry, and M. T. Sammons. Emerging policy issues for psychology: A key to the future of the profession. In *The Oxford Handbook of Clinical Psychology,* ed. D. Barlow. New York: Oxford University Press, in press.

Krishnamurthy, R. Assessment of adolescents using the PAI-A. In *Clinical Applications of the Personality Assessment Inventory,* pp. 55–76, eds. M. A. Blais, M. R. Baity, and C. J. Hopwood. New York: Routledge, 2010.

Krishnamurthy, R. Clinical psychology practice. In *Clinical Psychology: Assessment, Treatment, and Research,* pp. 477–93, eds. D. C. S. Richard and S. K. Huprich. San Diego, Calif.: Academic Press, 2008.

Lavooy, M. J. Beyond the classroom: Diversity and service learning. *Acad. Exchange Q.* 12(3):202–6, 2008.

Lavooy, M. J., and M. H. Newlin. Online chats and cyber-office hours: Everything but the office. *Int. J. e Learn.* 7(1):107–16, 2008.

Martinez-Diaz, J. A., T. R. Freeman, **M. P. Normand,** and T. E. Heron. The ethical practice of applied behavior analysis. In *Applied Behavior Analysis,* 2nd ed., eds. J. O. Cooper, T. E. Heron, and W. L. Heward. Upper Saddle River, N.J.: Prentice Hall, 2007.

Kelly, M., **K. Mulligan,** and M. Monahan. Fitness for duty. In *Military Neuropsychology,* pp. 57–80, eds. C. Kennedy and J. Moore. New York: Springer, 2010.

Diefendorff, J. M., **E. M. Richard,** and J. Yang. Emotion regulation at work: Linking strategies to affective events and discrete emotions. *J. Vocat. Behav.* 73:498–508, 2008.

Diefendorff, J. M., and **E. M. Richard.** Not all emotional display rules are created equal: Distinguishing between prescriptive and contextual display rules. In *Research Companion to Emotion in Organizations,* pp. 316–334, eds. N. M. Ashkanasy and C. L. Cooper. Northampton, Massachusetts: Edward Elgar, 2008.

Parks, K. M., and **L. A. Steelman.** Organizational wellness programs: A meta-analysis. *J. Occup. Health Psychol.* 13(1):58–68, 2008.

Domagalski, T., and **L. A. Steelman.** The impact of gender and organizational status on workplace anger expression. *Manag. Comm. Q.* 20(3):297–315, 2007.

Van Sickle, K. S., G. Curtiss, and R. Vanderploeg. Predictors of post-military onset of psychiatric disorders. Presented at the APA Convention, San Francisco, Calif., 2007.

Conner, C., **K. S. Van Sickle,** G. Hilley, J. Hook, and J. G. Shaw. Non-traditional students: Their obstacles, their strengths. Presented at the APA Convention, San Francisco, Calif., 2007.

Webbe, F. M. and C. Salinas. Pediatric sport neuropsychology. In *Handbook of Pediatric Neuropsychology,* ed. A. S. Davis. New York: Springer, 2010.

Webbe, F. M., C. Salinas, K. Quackenbush, and S. Tiedemann. Personality: Contributions to performance, injury risk, and rehabilitation. In *Praeger Handbook of Sports Medicine and Athlete Health* (three volumes), eds. C. T. Moorman, D. T. Kirkendall, and R. J. Echemendia. Santa Barbara, Calif.: Praeger Publishing Company, 2010.

Wilder, D. A., Noncompliance and oppositional behavior. In *Teaching and Behavior Support for Children and Adults with Autism Spectrum Disorders: A "How To" Practitioner's Guide,* ed. J. Luiselli. New York: Oxford University Press, in press.

Casella, S., et al. **(D. A. Wilder** and **I. Chong).** The effects of response effort on safe performance by therapists at an autism treatment facility. *J. Appl. Behav. Anal.* in press.

Flowers, L., J. Beebe, and **P. M. Wolfteich.** Difficulties in understanding teamwork in children's advocacy centers. Presented at the International Family Violence Research Conference, Portsmouth, N.H., 2005.

PHILADELPHIA COLLEGE OF OSTEOPATHIC MEDICINE

Graduate Programs in Clinical Psychology, Counseling and Clinical Health Psychology, and School Psychology

Programs of Study

Philadelphia College of Osteopathic Medicine (PCOM) offers eight graduate programs taught by an internationally renowned, highly credentialed faculty. All faculty members in PCOM's psychology department are teaching faculty members who work closely with students to help them achieve their professional goals. Students often have the opportunity to coauthor scholarly papers, books, and professional presentations with faculty members. PCOM has one of the only psychology departments in the country that provides a standardized patient program. The standardized patient program presents authentic clinical learning and skills situations in which "patients" simulate mental health conditions. Students conduct sessions with the patients, which are videotaped and reviewed by the faculty members to help train and assess students' skills. Students in the psychology program also have the opportunity for clinical experience at any of the College's urban health-care centers.

The 89-credit Psy.D. in clinical psychology program is designed to be completed in five years, including course work, practicum, internship, and dissertation. Graduates of this program are prepared to assume responsibilities in a broad range of clinical settings. Post-doctoral certificates in clinical health psychology and clinical neuropsychology will each provide one year (16 and 19 credits respectively) of post-doctoral specialty training to doctoral-level psychologists. The 61-credit Psy.D. in school psychology program takes three to five years to complete. The fourteen-month, 33-credit M.S. in school psychology program prepares paraprofessionals in community and school settings to provide mental health services to children, youth, and families. This program, taken in sequence with the Ed.S. degree program, leads to certification in school psychology. The three-year, 45-credit Ed.S. program provides students with the knowledge and skills to assume the role of a school psychologist in diverse settings. The two-year, 48-credit M.S. in counseling and clinical health psychology program trains graduates to provide evaluation, counseling, and therapy services to clients in a variety of clinical settings. There is also a 60-credit addictions and offenders counseling track for the M.S. degree. M.S. graduates may also take 12 additional credits offered by PCOM and earn a Certificate of Advanced Graduate Study to meet the education requirements of the licensed professional counseling (LPC) credential in Pennsylvania. Designed for the working professional, all classes for the M.S., Ed.S., and Psy.D. programs are held in the evening and on weekends.

Research Facilities

The academic facilities at PCOM include state-of-the-art amphitheaters and classroom facilities; computer laboratories with extensive software, including PsycLIT and SPSS; a comfortable, sophisticated library with online access to electronic textbooks, journals, databases, and Internet guides; and access to the digital library and statistical programs through the Internet.

Financial Aid

The Financial Aid Office at PCOM offers financial assistance to students through the Federal Direct Loan program, institutional grants, and various alternative private loan programs.

Cost of Study

In 2010–11, the direct tuition costs of attending PCOM (including tuition, fees, books, and supplies) for the year are approximately $20,830 for counseling and clinical health psychology M.S. students, $19,410 for school psychology M.S. students, $15,113 for Ed.S. students, $28,502 for clinical psychology Psy.D. students, and $26,437 for school psychology Psy.D. students.

Living and Housing Costs

Students live off-campus within the Philadelphia metropolitan and suburban areas, as there is no on-campus housing. Room and board costs vary by each student's individual preferences.

Student Group

The programs seek a diverse group of students who are committed to excellence. The Psy.D. in clinical psychology program recruits in-practice professionals who have earned master's degrees in psychology, social work, counseling, psychiatric nursing, or a related field and are working in human services. This population brings to their studies a high level of maturity, established skills, diverse backgrounds, and a strong motivation to succeed. The Psy.D. in school psychology program recruits working school psychologists who want to be leaders in psychoeducational and mental health services to children, youth, and families. For 2009, the clinical psychology Psy.D. class had 126 applicants. The average age of the 30 entering Psy.D. students was 27, with 63 percent women and 7 percent members of minority groups. For 2009, the Psy.D. in school psychology program had a class of 17 students, 88 percent women and 29 percent members of minority groups, with an average age of 36. The M.S. program in counseling and clinical health psychology totaled 39 students, 80 percent of whom were women and 10 percent of whom were members of minority groups, with an average age of 25. The M.S. program in school psychology had 20 students, 85 percent women and 25 percent members of minority groups, with an average age of 27. The Ed.S. program in school psychology numbered 24 students, 63 percent women and 21 percent members of minority groups, with an average age of 26.

Location

Located on City Avenue in Philadelphia, PCOM's 21-acre campus is minutes away from Fairmount Park, Philadelphia's historic district, art museums, theaters, restaurants, and professional sports complexes. Its renovated facilities include two large lecture halls, small classrooms, labs for teaching and research, and scenic landscaping, all in a suburban setting. PCOM also has four health-care centers in Philadelphia and one in LaPorte, Pennsylvania.

The College and The Programs

PCOM, which was chartered in 1899, enrolls approximately 2,200 students in its various programs across both the Philadelphia and Georgia campuses. The clinical and teaching facility in Philadelphia makes an ideal home for psychology graduate programs. The graduate psychology programs at PCOM are accredited by the Department of Education of the Commonwealth of Pennsylvania and the Middle States Association of Colleges and Schools. The clinical psychology Psy.D. program is accredited by the American Psychological Association and fulfills the requirements of the National Register for Healthcare Providers in Psychology. Clinical Psy.D. graduates qualify to take the Examination for Professional Practice of Psychology Licensure in Pennsylvania and New Jersey. The curriculum provides school psychology Psy.D. students with the knowledge and skills to assume the role of a school psychologist, practice in a variety of settings, and be prepared for eligibility for National Certification and for Pennsylvania licensure. The school psychology Psy.D. program has been approved by the National Association of School Psychologists. The M.S. program plus 12 credits has been designed to fulfill the Licensed Professional Counselor curriculum requirements in Pennsylvania.

Applying

Clinical psychology M.S. applicants need to have a baccalaureate degree from a regionally accredited institution, with basic psychology course work (introduction to psychology, abnormal psychology or psychopathology, and statistics). Psy.D. in clinical psychology applicants must have completed a master's degree in psychology or a related field at a regionally accredited institution and also completed developmental psychology, theories of personality, abnormal psychology or psychopathology, and statistics. Candidates for the post-doctoral certificate programs must have completed a doctoral degree in clinical psychology at a regionally accredited institution. Applicants to the M.S. in school psychology need to have a baccalaureate degree in psychology, education, or a related field from a regionally accredited institution and must have completed 6 credits each of English and math, abnormal psychology/psychopathology, or exceptional children and child psychology/adolescent psychology. Nine additional credits in psychology must also have been completed. Applicants to either M.S. program must have taken the GRE or MAT exam. Applicants to the Ed.S. program must have a master's degree in school psychology or a related field and must submit test scores from the GRE Psychology Subtest #81 and have successfully passed the Praxis I exam. Applicants to the Psy.D. in school psychology program must have a master's and specialist degree in school psychology and must be a licensed school psychologist. Candidates must also submit scores from the Praxis II School Psychology Specialty exam. All applicants must submit all college transcripts and three letters of recommendation with accompanying recommendation forms. The M.S., Ed.S., and Psy.D. programs utilize a rolling admissions policy. Finalists for all programs interview with the Admissions Committee and are then notified in writing of the committee's decision.

Correspondence and Information

Office of Admissions
Philadelphia College of Osteopathic Medicine
4170 City Avenue
Philadelphia, Pennsylvania 19131-1694
Phone: 215-871-6700
800-999-6998 (toll-free)
Fax: 215-871-6719
E-mail: gradadmissions@pcom.edu
Web site: http://www.pcom.edu

Philadelphia College of Osteopathic Medicine

THE FACULTY AND THEIR RESEARCH

Robert A. DiTomasso, Ph.D., ABPP, Professor; Chair, Department of Psychology; and Director, Institutional Outcomes Assessment. Dr. DiTomasso has extensive teaching experience and has published dozens of chapters, articles, reviews, and books. He specializes in behavioral medicine, the cognitive behavioral treatment of anxiety and stress-related medical disorders, research design, psychometrics, methodology, program evaluation, and primary-care consultation. He also specializes in patient nonadherence to medical advice and instrument development for cognitive distortions, anger, health risk behaviors, and patient satisfaction with medical services.

Stephanie Felgoise, Ph.D., ABPP, Professor; Vice Chair, Department of Psychology; and Director, Clinical Psy.D. Program. Dr. Felgoise has coauthored numerous national conference presentations and publications in psycho-oncology, sexual health and dysfunction, and coping and adjustment with chronic medical illness. Other interests include behavioral medicine, social problem solving, caregiver issues, and diversity issues in health care.

Michael Ascher, Ph.D., Clinical Professor. Dr. Ascher has done extensive research on the treatment of anxiety disorders (particularly agoraphobia, obsessive compulsive disorder, panic disorders, and phobias) within the context of behavior therapy. In addition, he has researched investor anxiety, including the emotional difficulties experienced by the average retail stock market investor, and the psychogenic disorders of sleep.

Virginia Burks Salzer, Ph.D., Clinical Associate Professor. Dr. Salzer's research interests include social information processing in the development of children's aggressive behavior, linkages between family and children's peer systems, comorbidity of children's externalizing and internalizing disorders, and impact of parental psychopathology and the development of childhood disorders.

Stacey C. Cahn, Ph.D., Assistant Professor. Dr. Cahn's area of expertise is broadly clinical health psychology, including eating disorders, as well as the areas of sleep, depression in heart disease, and aging.

William Clinton, M.A., Program Director, Organizational Development and Leadership Program. Mr. Clinton has extensive experience in organizational consultation and has held various leadership positions. His specialty is in training practitioners to become effective leaders who implement change in organizational settings.

Terri Erbacher, Ph.D., Clinical Assistant Professor. Dr. Erbacher is a certified school psychologist and licensed psychologist. Her specific population and program expertise includes nonpublic elementary and secondary schools, autistic support, learning support, early intervention, and supervision of school psychology interns.

Jessica Glass Kendorski, Ph.D., NCSP, Assistant Professor and Director, Clinical Training (School Psychology). Dr. Glass is a certified school psychologist. Her clinical experiences and research interests include data-based assessment and interventions in the residential and school settings, specifically, response to intervention, curriculum-based measurement, positive behavior support, and applied behavior analysis. She has extensive experience in supporting the emotional, social, and behavioral needs of children diagnosed with developmental disabilities.

Barbara Golden, Psy.D., ABPP, Associate Professor and Director, Clinical Services. Dr. Golden's experience includes clinical service, administration, supervision, consultation, and education. Her primary areas of interest and research are in behavioral medicine, including nonpharmacological pain management, stress management, and somatization disorder, as well as in psychology and primary-care medicine.

Elizabeth Gosch, Ph.D., ABPP, Professor and Director, M.S. Program in Counseling and Clinical Health Psychology. One of Dr. Gosch's primary areas of expertise is psychotherapy with children and adolescents. Her major research interest concerns the processes and effectiveness of psychotherapy with differing populations. She has published and lectured internationally on the cognitive behavioral treatment of anxiety in children.

Lisa Hain, Psy.D., NCSP, Assistant Professor. Dr. Hain's clinical experience and research interests include utilizing principles of neuropsychology in the practice of school psychology in identifying cognitively-based as well as emotionally-based disabilities affecting children and adolescents using a brain-behavior model in assessment, interpretation, and intervention.

Petra Kottsieper, Ph.D., Assistant Professor. Dr. Kottsieper's main research interests include forensic psychology, therapeutic process, mental health services research, professional development, ethics, and psychiatric rehabilitation for individuals with serious mental illnesses. Much of her clinical work has focused on the empirically-supported treatment and assessment of serious mental illnesses, co-occurring disorders (including developmental disabilities and substance misuse issues), and forensic issues.

Donald Masey, Psy.D., Clinical Assistant Professor. Dr. Masey's research interests include memory and aging, psychological assessment, hospital practice for psychologists, practice models and issues in professional psychology, medical psychology, adult learning disabilities, and adult ADHD.

George McCloskey, Ph.D., Associate Professor and Director of Research (School Psychology). Dr. McCloskey has accumulated a broad range of work experiences in the field of psychology over the last twenty-five years, including research, clinical work, administration, teaching, and business. His research and interests include neuropsychological process and learning, psychological and educational assessment and intervention, reading achievement, ADHD, executive dysfunction, memory problems, and expression disability.

Rosemary Mennuti, Ed.D., NCSP, Professor and Director, School Psychology Program. Dr. Mennuti has extensive experience as a school psychologist and in teaching. She has lectured and published in the areas of moral development, eating disorders, and therapist self-disclosure. Other areas of interest include female development, CBT in schools, and relational cultural theory in practice.

Susan Panichelli Mindel, Ph.D., Assistant Professor and Director of Research (Clinical Psychology). Dr. Mindel has extensive experience in the delivery of cognitive-behavioral empirically-supported treatments in children and adolescents. Her research interests include issues in clinical child psychology, with an emphasis on the prevention and treatment of anxiety disorders as well as diagnostic differences and treatment of subtypes of ADHD.

Stephen Poteau, Ph.D., Clinical Assistant Professor. Dr. Poteau's research interests include the implicit measurement of cognitive processes/implicit cognition, terror management theory, and social cognition/psychology.

Bradley Rosenfield, Psy.D., Assistant Professor. Dr. Rosenfield's research interests include cognitive behavioral therapy for adult ADHD, human-animal interactions, depressive disorders, somatic disorders, anxiety disorders, single session treatment for panic attacks, the social psychology of terrorism, multicultural counseling, communication skills, and treating difficult patients.

Matthew Schure, Ph.D., President and Chief Executive Officer. Dr. Schure's major areas of interest include personality correlates of learning, such as self-esteem, level of aspiration, and locus of control. In addition, he has done extensive research on community mental health interventions and family dynamics, including the outcome of dysfunctional parenting and parental rejection.

Marsha S. Singer, Ph.D., Clinical Assistant Professor and Associate Director, M.S. Program in Counseling and Clinical Health Psychology. Dr. Singer's main professional interest is clinical health psychology. She is very interested in the role of cultural, spiritual, and other psychosocial factors in health behavior and patient attitudes. She is also interested in the role of family members as social supports in medical and mental health settings.

Diane Smallwood, Psy.D., NCSP, Professor and Director, Ed.S. program. In addition to school-based work experience, for the past twenty years, Dr. Smallwood has been involved in leadership activities at both the state and national levels. Her professional interests include school crisis prevention, intervention, and response; social-emotional learning; classroom resiliency; bullying and violence in schools; and translating research to practice.

Takako Suzuki, Ph.D., Assistant Professor; Assistant Director of Clinical Services (Center for Brief Therapy); and Clinical Coordinator, Center for Academic Resources and Educational Services (CARES). Dr. Suzuki's major areas of interest include CBT of mood and anxiety disorders; multicultural issues such as development of cultural identity, acculturation process, and issues with expatriates; religion and spirituality; and emotional intelligence and development of empathy.

Shannon Sweitzer, Ph.D., NCSP, Clinical Assistant Professor. Dr. Sweitzer's research interests include cognitive deficits associated with childhood depression, childcare staff consultation, and training to develop environments that foster healthy social and emotional behaviors.

Yuma I. Tomes, Ph.D., Associate Professor and Director, M.S. Program in School Psychology. Dr. Tomes has accumulated a diverse range of work experiences in the field of psychology and education over the last ten years. He brings a unique perspective of clinical, teaching, research, and administrative experience to his position at PCOM. Dr. Tomes has worked as a psychologist in urban school districts. His major areas of interest are cross-cultural psychology, multicultural assessment, cognitive/learning styles, cognition and learning theories, psychological/educational assessments, consultation, and developmental issues.

Beverly White, Psy.D., Clinical Assistant Professor. Dr. White has worked extensively with traumatized children and adolescents. She has published and has research interests in the areas of psychological assessment, dreams in CBT-oriented treatment, and crisis/trauma, post-traumatic stress, and CBT interventions. Other research interests include right/left-hemisphere performance and malfunction and multicultural issues.

Bruce Zahn, Ed.D., ABPP, Professor and Director of Clinical Training (Clinical Psychology). Dr. Zahn has published on cognitive behavioral therapy, childhood sexual abuse, multimodal therapy programs for adolescents, and psychological functioning in survivors of traumatic brain injury. His areas of expertise include geropsychology, behavioral medicine, cognitive behavioral therapy, self-esteem, group therapy, and supervision. Dr. Zahn's mentoring and research interests are in the areas of psychological testing (including projective personality assessment), post-traumatic stress disorder, managed-care issues, and chronic mental illness.

RUTGERS, THE STATE UNIVERSITY OF NEW JERSEY, NEWARK

Graduate Program in Psychology

Concentrations in Cognitive Science, Cognitive Neuroscience, Perception, Biopsychology, and Social Psychology

Programs of Study

Students entering the graduate program in psychology can take courses of study leading to a Ph.D. in psychology with specializations in biopsychology, cognitive neuroscience, cognitive science, perception, and social psychology. Current research in the biopsychology of emotion and adaptive behavior focuses on the motivational, evolutionary, and developmental mechanisms underlying behavior. Research in cognitive neuroscience offers training in neuroimaging methods, concepts, and experimental paradigms. The neuroimaging research focus includes studies in motion and event perception, learning and memory, and how humans process rewards and punishments. Research in the area of cognitive science offers training in the computational and experimental study of cognitive processes. The curriculum provides basic instruction in computational and mathematical modeling methods, with a focus on connectionist systems, learning, memory, and categorization. The perception specialization offers training in the experimental study of motion and color perception as well as many advanced areas within vision science. The social psychology concentration focuses on attachment theory, the mediation of social and interpersonal conflict, aggression, violence and bullying, interracial feedback, social support, and the methods and techniques used most commonly in these areas.

Students are encouraged to take advantage of training opportunities in the adjacent Center for Molecular and Behavioral Neuroscience, the College of Business (Information Sciences), the College of Nursing, the Department of Biological Sciences, the University of Medicine and Dentistry of New Jersey (UMDNJ), and the New Jersey Institute of Technology as well as adjunct courses listed in related areas (such as linguistics, philosophy, or cognitive science) on the New Brunswick campus. A written qualifying examination is given after the completion of basic course work at the end of the second year. Upon satisfactory completion of these requirements, students advance to candidacy for the Ph.D. degree and must submit a thesis proposal, carry out their thesis research, and then defend their dissertation.

Research Facilities

The Department of Psychology occupies about 42,000 square feet on the first, third, fourth, and fifth floors of Smith Hall. The department has its own servers (http://psychology.rutgers.edu, http://www.psych.rutgers.edu), computing laboratory, and a series of individual laboratories for neurophysiological, neuroanatomical, and neuropharmacological research. There are more than 16,000 square feet for animal holding and testing. The Psychology Department with UMDNJ supports the Advanced Imaging Center with a state-of-the-art Siemens 3T Allegra head-only magnet (more information can be found at http://www.rutgers-newark.rutgers.edu/fmri) and 64-channel EEG (Neuroscan) and 32-channel EEG (Digital ANT) systems.

Additional equipment includes an optical motion capture system for the perception of biological movement, a variety of human observation and testing rooms, one-way observation rooms, video equipment, high-speed graphics computers, and access to a Hewlett Packard Itanium II Workstation linked to the department's 28-node Opteron computer cluster and storage system, which can hold one trillion bytes of data.

Financial Aid

Students accepted into the program receive a full stipend and tuition remission through one of the wide range of scholarships, fellowships, and assistantships offered by the Rutgers Graduate School to full-time Ph.D. students whose records demonstrate superior academic achievement and scholarly promise. Stipends range up to $18,000 plus tuition remission for fellowships and $21,400 for teaching or graduate assistantships. They may be renewed for one or more years depending on the availability of funds and the academic standing of the student. Students who are members of minority groups may also be eligible to receive additional support through the Minority Biomedical Research Support Program and other programs. Students also receive financial support from the Department of Psychology to attend conferences.

Cost of Study

Tuition for the 2008–09 academic year was about $14,500 (for New Jersey residents) and about $22,000 for out-of-state residents; graduate students receive tuition remission along with their source of support.

Living and Housing Costs

Graduate student housing is available in Talbott Apartments and University Square Apartments. Costs range from $7300 for an academic year lease to $10,500 for a calendar year lease. All options are single rooms in either a 3-person or 4-person shared apartment. A limited number of family apartment options are available for married/domestic partners and students with children in University-owned brownstones.

Student Group

There are currently 25 full-time graduate doctoral students carrying out research in the Department of Psychology. The faculty-student ratio of 1:2 affords ample opportunity for students to interact with faculty members. Students in the Department of Psychology are represented in policy decisions and are actively involved in the selection of new students.

Location

Rutgers' Newark campus is conveniently located in the center of a diverse and thriving educational, professional, and cultural community in the downtown area of New Jersey's largest city. Newark is also at the center of the nation's largest concentration of pharmaceutical industries. The campus is a modern complex serving more than 10,000 students and 500 faculty members. Rutgers-Newark is easily accessible by car or mass transit and is approximately 30 minutes by road or rail from midtown Manhattan. A free campus shuttle bus links the campus with the city's mass transit centers during the evening hours. The Department of Psychology is located one block from the University's jogging track, fully equipped gymnasium, and swimming pool.

The University

Rutgers, The State University of New Jersey, with more than 47,000 students on campuses in Camden, Newark, and New Brunswick, is one of the major state universities in the nation. The Newark campus is part of a complex of higher education institutions that includes the New Jersey Institute of Technology and the University of Medicine and Dentistry of New Jersey.

Applying

Students apply to enter the program on a full-time basis. Students should apply to the Department of Psychology and mention the area of study they are most interested in. Applications can be submitted at http://gradstudy.rutgers.edu/. The application deadline for the fall semester is January 15 and for the spring semester, November 1. Students should include scores for the General GRE and the Subject GRE in their area of interest.

Correspondence and Information

Kenneth Kressel, Ph.D., Director of Graduate Programs in Psychology
Department of Psychology
301 Smith Hall
Rutgers, The State University of New Jersey
101 Warren Street
Newark, New Jersey 07102
Phone: 973-353-5440 Ext. 232
Fax: 973-353-1171
E-mail: gradprogram@psychology.rutgers.edu
Web site: http://www.psych.rutgers.edu

Rutgers, The State University of New Jersey, Newark

THE FACULTY AND THEIR RESEARCH

Colin G. Beer, D.Phil., Oxford. Ethology, communication, and social development of birds; historical and philosophical aspects of ethology; comparative psychology.

Paul Boxer, Ph.D., Bowling Green. Aggression and violence, social development, contextual influences on behavior.

Mei-Fang Cheng, Ph.D., Bryn Mawr. Neuroethology; neurobiological study of vocal behavior and self-stimulation; mechanism and function of brain injury–induced neurogenesis in adult animals.

Mauricio Delgado, Ph.D., Pittsburgh. Behavioral and neural correlates of reward-related processing, with an emphasis on how the affective properties of outcomes or feedback influence choice behavior; using neuroimaging and behavioral and psychophysiological methods.

Alan Gilchrist, Ph.D., Rutgers. Visual cognition; surface-color perception.

Stephen José Hanson, Ph.D., Arizona State. Learning and memory, connectionist models, categorization, cognitive science.

Kent D. Harber, Ph.D., Stanford. Interracial feedback biases; social support and coping; emotion and social perception.

Barry R. Komisaruk, Ph.D., Rutgers. Neurophysiological, functional neuroanatomical, and neuropharmacological study of endogenous pain-blocking mechanisms related to sexual behavior and parturition in mammals, including humans; brain, spinal cord, autonomic, and peripheral nerve mechanisms, using functional magnetic resonance imaging (fMRI).

Ken Kressel, Ph.D., Columbia. Social and interpersonal conflict, mediation of conflict, conflict dynamics in organizational settings.

Maggie Shiffrar, Ph.D., Stanford. Visual motion perception; object recognition.

Harold I. Siegel, Ph.D., Rutgers. Attachment theory; adult attachment; attitudes toward mother and other adult relationships, attachment and sexual offenders.

Elizabeth Tricomi, Ph.D., Pittsburgh. Functional neuroimaging of learning and decision making, social and affective influences on reward processing and valuation, neural basis of goal-directed behavior.

Gretchen Van de Walle, Ph.D., Cornell. Conceptual understanding of physical objects and numbers and the interaction between conceptual development and linguistic abilities, particularly the relationship between children's ability to categorize and label classes of objects.

SouthUniversity℠

SOUTH UNIVERSITY

Columbia Campus
Professional Counseling Program

Program of Study

The Master of Arts in professional counseling degree program at South University is intended to meet the local and regional need for qualified professional counselors. The emphasis of the program is on community and agency counseling. The program is designed to enable program graduates to achieve all initial eligibility criteria to become certified as a National Certified Counselor (NCC) by the National Board for Certified Counselors (NBCC) and licensed in the state of South Carolina. The delivery structure of the program gives students the ability to balance the rigors of work and home while pursuing their master's degree. Students can complete one or two courses each term, with each quarter lasting ten weeks. Students select from the convenient Saturday sessions that meet once per week or attend two evenings during the week.

Students are taught via two primary modes of instruction. The majority of the program involves didactic and experiential classroom instruction, supplemented by computer-based assignments, including the use of Internet technology. The second mode of instruction focuses on supervised field experiences. Students are placed in community counseling settings (while on internship) and practice counseling under the supervision of an on-site supervisor. Students in field placements also receive weekly individual and group supervision from qualified faculty supervisors.

Research Facilities

Along with classrooms and offices, the campus includes a bookstore, student lounge, and career services center. Students may retrieve periodicals in paper or electronic form. The South University Library provides in-library and remote access to electronic databases. Both bibliographic and full-text databases are available via EBSCOhost (e.g., Academic Search Premier, SocINDEX, PsycINFO, PsycARTICLES, and Mental Measurements Yearbook), the search and retrieval system of EBSCO Information Services, and via the Library and Information Resources Network (e.g., Infotrac and ProQuest databases). Infotrac databases include counseling sources such as Expanded Academic ASAP, Academic OneFile, and InfotracOneFile, and ProQuest databases include counseling sources such as ProQuest Psychology Journals and ProQuest Research Library. Internet access is available on all computers throughout the campus.

Financial Aid

A wide range of financial aid options is available to students who qualify. The Columbia campus of South University offers access to federal and state programs, including grants, loans, and work-study programs. Eligible students may apply for veterans' educational benefits and are encouraged to investigate the availability of grants and scholarships through community resources. As a first step, students should complete the Free Application for Federal Student Aid (FAFSA) and add South University's campus code, 004922. Students may apply electronically at http://www.fafsa.ed.gov or through the campus Director of Student Financial Services. Applications should be submitted promptly to receive consideration for the maximum amount of aid.

Cost of Study

Tuition information for the professional counseling program may be obtained by contacting the Admissions Department at South University's Columbia campus.

Living and Housing Costs

South University does not offer or operate student housing. Professional counseling program students typically live in apartments in the Columbia area. Students who commute from long distances can arrange to stay at nearby hotels that offer long-term rates. More information is available by contacting the Admissions Department.

Student Group

The Columbia campus of South University has a diverse student body enrolled in both day and evening classes. Students are primarily commuters who live within 50 miles of the city.

Student Outcomes

The South University Career Services Department has been established to assist currently enrolled students in developing their career plans and reaching their employment goals. Career services include, but are not limited to, one-on-one career counseling, special career-related workshops and programs, coaching for resume and cover letter development, and resume referral to employers.

Location

South University recently relocated its Columbia campus to the growing east side of Columbia, just minutes from downtown. The new campus is conveniently located off of I-77 at Farrow Road and Parklane.

The campus surroundings are highlighted by a natural wooded landscape and vast greenspace featuring a tranquil campus courtyard. Convenient to malls, shopping, and the growing east side of Columbia, the new campus location provides easier access to students from throughout the greater Columbia area.

The University

South University is accredited by the Commission on Colleges of the Southern Association of Colleges and Schools (SACS) to award associate, bachelor's, master's, and doctoral degrees. Students should contact the Commission on Colleges at 1866 Southern Lane, Decatur, Georgia 30033-4097 or call 404-679-4500 for questions about the accreditation of South University.

Applying

Students are accepted into the Master of Arts in professional counseling degree program every academic quarter. Entrance into the program is gained through a formal application review and interview process. Acceptance is competitive and based on the admission committee's evaluation of the applicant's academic background and personal motivation. Application packets are available by contacting the South University Admissions Department (866-629-3031, toll-free) or visiting the University's Web site (http://www.southuniversity.edu).

Correspondence and Information

Applications for admission to the South University Master of Arts in professional counseling program are available by contacting:

Professional Counseling Program
South University
9 Science Court
Columbia, South Carolina 29203
Phone: 803-799-9082
866-629-3031 (toll-free)
Fax: 803-935-4382
E-mail: coladmis@southuniversity.edu
Web site: http://www.southuniversity.edu

South University

THE FACULTY

One of the most outstanding aspects of South University's professional counseling program is the dedication of the faculty members and their ability to cultivate a supportive learning environment. Faculty members are committed to their roles as mentors, teachers, and colearners. They are also dedicated to the training of students who can assume positions of leadership within the counseling field. A current list of program faculty members appears in the South University catalog, which is available on the South University Web site (http://www.southuniversity.edu).

SouthUniversity℠

SOUTH UNIVERSITY

Montgomery Campus
Professional Counseling Program

Program of Study

The Master of Arts in professional counseling degree program at South University is intended to meet the local and regional need for qualified professional counselors. The emphasis of the program is on community and agency counseling. The program is designed to enable program graduates to achieve all initial eligibility criteria to become certified as a National Certified Counselor (NCC) by the National Board for Certified Counselors (NBCC) and licensed in the state of Alabama. The delivery structure of the program gives students the ability to balance the rigors of work and home while pursuing their master's degree. Students can complete two courses each term, with each quarter lasting eleven weeks. Classes meet on Saturdays from 8:30 a.m. to 5 p.m.

Students are taught via two primary modes of instruction. The majority of the program involves didactic and experiential classroom instruction, supplemented by computer-based assignments, including the use of Internet technology. The second mode of instruction focuses on supervised field experiences. Students are placed in community counseling settings (during practicum and internship) and practice counseling under the supervision of an on-site supervisor. Students in field placements also receive weekly individual and group supervision from qualified faculty supervisors.

Research Facilities

South University in Montgomery is located in a modern 26,000-square-foot, two-story building on a 3¾-acre campus. This building houses computer and health professions labs, classrooms, a library, a student lounge, a bookstore, and faculty and administrative offices.

The South University library has wireless technology throughout, comfortable seating, and quiet study space. The South University library provides in-library and remote access to electronic databases. Both bibliographic and full-text databases are available via EBSCOhost (e.g., Academic Search Premier, SocINDEX, PsycINFO, PsycARTICLES, and Mental Measurements Yearbook), the search and retrieval system of EBSCO Information Services, and via the Library and Information Resources Network (e.g., Infotrac and ProQuest databases). Infotrac databases include counseling sources such as Expanded Academic ASAP, Academic OneFile, and InfotracOneFile, and ProQuest databases include counseling sources such as ProQuest Psychology Journals and ProQuest Research Library. Also for student use, the library has a modern computer lab with eleven workstations, each with Internet access, online database services, an office suite, tutorials, and class-support software.

Financial Aid

A wide range of financial aid options is available to students who qualify. South University offers access to federal and state programs, including grants, loans, and work-study programs. Eligible students may apply for veterans' educational benefits and are encouraged to investigate the availability of grants and scholarships through community resources. As a first step, students should complete the Free Application for Federal Student Aid (FAFSA). Students may apply electronically at http://www.fafsa.ed.gov or through the campus Director of Financial Aid. Applications should be submitted promptly to receive consideration for the maximum amount of aid.

Cost of Study

Tuition information for the professional counseling program may be obtained by contacting the admissions department at South University.

Living and Housing Costs

South University does not offer or operate student housing. Professional counseling program students typically live in private housing in the Montgomery area. Students who commute from long distances can arrange to stay at nearby hotels that offer long-term rates. More information is available by contacting the admissions department.

Student Group

South University in Montgomery has a diverse student body enrolled in both day and evening classes. Students are primarily commuters who live within 50 miles of the city.

Student Outcomes

The South University career services department has been established to assist currently enrolled students in developing their career plans and reaching their employment goals. Career services include, but are not limited to, one-on-one career counseling, special career-related workshops and programs, coaching for resume and cover letter development, and resume referral to employers.

Location

South University is located on the rapidly growing east side of Alabama's capital city. As the state capital, Montgomery is a hub of government, banking, and law as well as a state center for culture and entertainment. Montgomery is situated in the middle of the southeastern U.S. and is less than a 3-hour drive from Atlanta and the Gulf of Mexico.

The University

South University is accredited by the Commission on Colleges of the Southern Association of Colleges and Schools (SACS) to award associate, bachelor's, master's, and doctoral degrees. Students should contact the Commission on Colleges at 1866 Southern Lane, Decatur, Georgia 30033-4097 or call 404-679-4500 with questions about the accreditation of South University.

Applying

Students may be accepted into the Master of Arts in professional counseling degree program every academic quarter. Entrance into the program is gained through a formal application review and interview process. Acceptance is competitive and based on the admission committee's evaluation of the applicant's academic background (completed bachelor's degree with a cumulative minimum GPA of 2.7) and personal motivation. Application packets are available by contacting the South University admissions department or visiting the University's Web site.

Correspondence and Information

Applications for admission to the South University Master of Arts in professional counseling program are available by contacting:

Professional Counseling Program
South University
5355 Vaughn Road
Montgomery, Alabama 36116
Phone: 334-395-8800
866-629-2962 (toll-free)
Fax: 334-395-8859
E-mail: mtgadmis@southuniversity.edu
Web site: http://www.southuniversity.edu

South University

THE FACULTY

One of the most outstanding aspects of South University's professional counseling program is the dedication of the faculty members and their ability to cultivate a supportive learning environment. Faculty members are committed to their roles as mentors, teachers, and colearners. They are also dedicated to the education of students who can assume positions of leadership within the counseling field. A current list of program faculty members is available at the South University Web site (http://www.southuniversity.edu).

SouthUniversity℠

SOUTH UNIVERSITY

Richmond Campus
Professional Counseling Program

Program of Study

The Master of Arts in Professional Counseling degree program at South University is intended to meet the local and regional need for qualified professional counselors. The emphasis of the program is on community and agency counseling. The program is designed to enable program graduates to achieve all initial eligibility criteria to become certified as a National Certified Counselor (NCC) by the National Board for Certified Counselors (NBCC) and licensed in the state of South Carolina. The delivery structure of the program gives students the ability to balance the rigors of work and home while pursuing their master's degree. Students can complete two courses each term (or more with approval), with each quarter lasting ten weeks. Class meetings are held mostly on Saturdays between 8:30 a.m. and 12 noon and some weeknights.

Students are taught via two primary modes of instruction. The majority of the program involves didactic and experiential classroom instruction, supplemented by computer-based assignments, including the use of Internet technology. The second mode of instruction focuses on supervised field experiences. Students are placed in community counseling settings (while on internship) and practice counseling under the supervision of an on-site supervisor. Students in field placements also receive weekly individual and group supervision from qualified faculty supervisors.

Research Facilities

The South University Library provides in-library and remote access to electronic databases. Both bibliographic and full-text databases are available via EBSCOhost (e.g., Academic Search Premier, SocINDEX, PsycINFO, PsycARTICLES, and Mental Measurements Yearbook), the search and retrieval system of EBSCO Information Services, and via the Library and Information Resources Network (e.g., Infotrac and ProQuest databases). Infotrac databases include counseling sources such as Expanded Academic ASAP, Academic OneFile, and InfotracOneFile, and ProQuest databases include counseling sources such as ProQuest Psychology Journals and ProQuest Research Library.

Financial Aid

A wide range of financial aid options is available to students who qualify. The Richmond campus of South University offers access to federal and state programs, including grants, loans, and work-study programs. Eligible students may apply for veterans' educational benefits and are encouraged to investigate the availability of grants and scholarships through community resources. As a first step, students should complete the Free Application for Federal Student Aid (FAFSA). Students may apply electronically at http://www.fafsa.ed.gov or through the campus Director of Student Financial Services. Applications should be submitted promptly to receive consideration for the maximum amount of aid.

Cost of Study

Tuition information for the Professional Counseling Program may be obtained by contacting the Admissions Department at South University's Richmond campus.

Living and Housing Costs

South University–Richmond does not offer or operate student housing. Professional Counseling Program students typically live in apartments in the Richmond area. Students who commute from long distances can arrange to stay at nearby hotels that offer long-term rates. More information is available by contacting the Admissions Department.

Student Group

The Richmond campus of South University has a diverse student body enrolled in both day and evening classes. Students consist of commuters who live within 50 miles of the city.

Student Outcomes

The South University Career Services Department has been established to assist currently enrolled students in developing their career plans and reaching their employment goals. Career services include, but are not limited to, one-on-one career counseling, special career-related workshops and programs, coaching for resume and cover letter development, and resume referral to employers.

Location

South University–Richmond, one of South University's newest campus locations, occupies approximately 30,000 square feet of classroom, computer lab, library, and office space in Glen Allen, Virginia. The campus is located in the West Broad Village development in the Short Pump area.

The University

South University is accredited by the Commission on Colleges of the Southern Association of Colleges and Schools (SACS) to award associate, bachelor's, master's, and doctoral degrees. Students should contact the Commission on Colleges at 1866 Southern Lane, Decatur, Georgia 30033-4097 or call 404-679-4500 for questions about the accreditation of South University. South University–Richmond is certified by the State Council of Higher Education in Virginia.

Applying

Students are accepted into the Master of Arts in Professional Counseling degree program every academic quarter. Entrance into the program is gained through a formal application review and interview process. Acceptance is competitive and based on the admission committee's evaluation of the applicant's academic background (completed bachelor's degree with a cumulative minimum GPA of 2.7) and personal motivation. Application packets are available by contacting the South University Admissions Department or visiting the University's Web site.

Correspondence and Information

Applications for admission to the South University Master of Arts in Professional Counseling program are available by contacting:

Professional Counseling Program
South University
2151 Old Brick Road
Glen Allen, Virginia 23060
Phone: 804-727-6800
888-422-5076 (toll-free)
Fax: 804-727-6790
E-mail: suriadm@southuniversity.edu
Web site: http://www.southuniversity.edu

South University

THE FACULTY

One of the most outstanding aspects of South University's Professional Counseling Program is the dedication of the faculty members and their ability to cultivate a supportive learning environment. Faculty members are committed to their roles as mentors, teachers, and colearners. They are also dedicated to the training of students who can assume positions of leadership within the counseling field. A current list of program faculty members appears in the South University catalog, which is available on the South University Web site (http://www.southuniversity.edu).

South University–Richmond Campus.

South University℠

SOUTH UNIVERSITY

Savannah Campus
Professional Counseling Program

Program of Study

The Master of Arts in professional counseling degree program at South University is intended to meet the local and regional need for qualified professional counselors. The emphasis of the program is on community and agency counseling. The program is designed to enable program graduates to achieve all initial eligibility criteria to become certified as a National Certified Counselor (NCC) by the National Board for Certified Counselors (NBCC) and licensed in their state. The delivery structure of the program gives students the ability to balance the rigors of work and home while pursuing their master's degree. Students can complete two courses each term (or more with approval), with each quarter lasting ten weeks. Class meetings are held mostly on Saturdays between 8:30 a.m. and 12 noon and some weeknights.

Students are taught via two primary modes of instruction. The majority of the program involves didactic and experiential classroom instruction, supplemented by computer-based assignments, including the use of Internet technology. The second mode of instruction focuses on supervised field experiences. Students are placed in community counseling settings (during internship) and practice counseling under the supervision of an on-site supervisor. Students in field placements also receive weekly individual and group supervision from qualified faculty supervisors.

Research Facilities

In 2000, the 25,000-square-foot Health Professions building was opened on the Savannah campus to house classroom, computer, and lab facilities for graduate programs within the College of Health Professions Also in this building are the student lounge and administrative offices. In 2007, a new library facility was opened that provides comfortable study space for students, wireless capabilities for laptop network connectivity, and reference and interlibrary loan services. The South University Library also provides in-library and remote access to electronic databases. Both bibliographic and full-text databases are available via EBSCOhost (e.g., Academic Search Premier, SocINDEX, PsycINFO, PsycARTICLES, and Mental Measurements Yearbook), the search and retrieval system of EBSCO Information Services, and via the Library and Information Resources Network (e.g., Infotrac and ProQuest databases). Infotrac databases include counseling sources such as Expanded Academic ASAP, Academic OneFile, and InfotracOneFile, and ProQuest databases include counseling sources such as ProQuest Psychology Journals and ProQuest Research Library.

Financial Aid

A wide range of financial aid options is available to students who qualify. The Savannah campus of South University offers access to federal and state programs, including grants, loans, and work-study programs. Eligible students may apply for veterans' educational benefits and are encouraged to investigate the availability of grants and scholarships through community resources. As a first step, students should complete the Free Application for Federal Student Aid (FAFSA). Students may apply electronically at http://www.fafsa.ed.gov or through the campus Director of Financial Aid. Applications should be submitted promptly to receive consideration for the maximum amount of aid.

Cost of Study

Tuition information for the professional counseling program may be obtained by contacting the Admissions Department at South University's Savannah campus.

Living and Housing Costs

South University offers school-sponsored student housing at its Savannah, Georgia, campus in conjunction with a local apartment complex. Students who commute from long distances can arrange to stay at nearby hotels that offer long-term rates. More information is available by contacting the Director of Student Housing at 912-201-8000.

Student Group

The Savannah campus of South University has a diverse student body enrolled in both day and evening classes. Students consist of commuters who live within 50 miles of the city or students from other portions of the United States (e.g., California, Ohio, Pennsylvania, Connecticut) who have moved to Savannah to pursue the degree in professional counseling.

Student Outcomes

The South University Career Services Department has been established to assist currently enrolled students in developing their career plans and reaching their employment goals. Career services include, but are not limited to, one-on-one career counseling, special career-related workshops and programs, coaching for resume and cover letter development, and resume referral to employers.

Location

Located on the south side of the historic city of Savannah, the campus is situated on 9 acres of land. It is convenient to the city's bustling midtown section and a full range of educational and cultural activities. The Atlantic Ocean and recreational amenities of Tybee Island, including beaches and numerous outdoor activities, are just a short drive away. In addition, the campus is located just a short drive from Hilton Head Island and Charleston, South Carolina.

The University

South University is accredited by the Commission on Colleges of the Southern Association of Colleges and Schools (SACS) to award associate, bachelor's, master's, and doctoral degrees. Students should contact the Commission on Colleges at 1866 Southern Lane, Decatur, Georgia 30033-4097 or call 404-679-4500 with questions about the accreditation of South University.

Applying

Students are accepted into the Master of Arts in professional counseling degree program twice per year (fall and spring quarters). Entrance into the program is gained through a formal application review and interview process. Acceptance is competitive and based on the admission committee's evaluation of the applicant's academic background (completed bachelor's degree with a cumulative minimum GPA of 2.7) and personal motivation. Application packets are available by contacting the South University Admissions Department or visiting the University's Web site.

Correspondence and Information

Applications for admission to the South University Master of Arts in professional counseling program are available by contacting:

Professional Counseling Program
South University
709 Mall Boulevard
Savannah, Georgia 31406-4805
Phone: 912-201-8000
866-629-2901 (toll-free)
Fax: 912-201-8070
E-mail: savadmis@southuniversity.edu
Web site: http://www.southuniversity.edu

South University

THE FACULTY

One of the most outstanding aspects of South University's professional counseling program is the dedication of the faculty members and their ability to cultivate a supportive learning environment. Faculty members are committed to their roles as mentors, teachers, and colearners. They are also dedicated to the training of students who can assume positions of leadership within the counseling field. A current list of program faculty members is available at the South University Web site (http://www.southuniversity.edu).

SouthUniversity℠

SOUTH UNIVERSITY

Virginia Beach Campus
Professional Counseling Program

Program of Study

The Master of Arts in Professional Counseling degree program at South University is intended to meet the local and regional need for qualified professional counselors. The emphasis of the program is on community and agency counseling. The program is designed to enable program graduates to achieve all initial eligibility criteria to become certified as a National Certified Counselor (NCC) by the National Board for Certified Counselors (NBCC) and licensed in their state. The delivery structure of the program gives students the ability to balance the rigors of work and home while pursuing their master's degree. Students can complete two courses each term (or more with approval), with each quarter lasting ten weeks. Class meetings are held mostly on Saturdays between 8:30 a.m. and 12 noon and some weeknights from 6 to 9:30 p.m.

Students are taught via two primary modes of instruction. The majority of the program involves didactic and experiential classroom instruction, supplemented by computer-based assignments, including the use of Internet technology. The second mode of instruction focuses on supervised field experiences. Students are placed in community counseling settings (during internship) and practice counseling under the supervision of an on-site supervisor. Students in field placements also receive weekly individual and group supervision from qualified faculty supervisors.

Research Facilities

The South University Library provides in-library and remote access to electronic databases. Both bibliographic and full-text databases are available via EBSCOhost (e.g., Academic Search Premier, SocINDEX, PsycINFO, PsycARTICLES, and Mental Measurements Yearbook), the search and retrieval system of EBSCO Information Services, and via the Library and Information Resources Network (e.g., Infotrac and ProQuest databases). Infotrac databases include counseling sources such as Expanded Academic ASAP, Academic OneFile, and InfotracOneFile, and ProQuest databases include counseling sources such as ProQuest Psychology Journals and ProQuest Research Library.

Financial Aid

A wide range of financial aid options is available to students who qualify. The Savannah campus of South University offers access to federal and state programs, including grants, loans, and work-study programs. Eligible students may apply for veterans' educational benefits and are encouraged to investigate the availability of grants and scholarships through community resources. As a first step, students should complete the Free Application for Federal Student Aid (FAFSA). Students may apply electronically at http://www.fafsa.ed.gov or through the campus Director of Financial Aid. Applications should be submitted promptly to receive consideration for the maximum amount of aid.

Cost of Study

Tuition information for the Professional Counseling Program may be obtained by contacting the Admissions Department at South University's Virginia Beach campus.

Living and Housing Costs

South University does not offer or operate student housing. Professional Counseling Program students typically live in apartments in the Virginia Beach area. Students who commute from long distances can arrange to stay at nearby hotels that offer long-term rates. More information is available by contacting the Admissions Department.

Student Group

The Virginia Beach campus of South University has a diverse student body enrolled in both day and evening classes. Students consist of commuters who live within 50 miles of the city.

Student Outcomes

The South University Career Services Department has been established to assist currently enrolled students in developing their career plans and reaching their employment goals. Career services include, but are not limited to, one-on-one career counseling, special career-related workshops and programs, coaching for resume and cover letter development, and resume referral to employers.

Location

South University–Virginia Beach is located in 32,600 square feet of space in the attractive and convenient Convergence Center in Virginia Beach's popular Central Business District. The Virginia Beach campus features a distance learning center, a library, a bookstore, on-site security, student and faculty lounges, as well as health science labs.

The University

South University is accredited by the Commission on Colleges of the Southern Association of Colleges and Schools (SACS) to award associate, bachelor's, master's, and doctoral degrees. Students should contact the Commission on Colleges at 1866 Southern Lane, Decatur, Georgia 30033-4097 or call 404-679-4500 with questions about the accreditation of South University. South University–Virginia Beach is certified by the State Council of Higher Education in Virginia.

Applying

Students are accepted into the Master of Arts in Professional Counseling degree program twice per year (fall and spring quarters). Entrance into the program is gained through a formal application review and interview process. Acceptance is competitive and based on the admission committee's evaluation of the applicant's academic background (completed bachelor's degree with a cumulative minimum GPA of 2.7) and personal motivation. Application packets are available by contacting the South University Admissions Department or visiting the University's Web site.

Correspondence and Information

Applications for admission to the South University Master of Arts in Professional Counseling program are available by contacting:

Professional Counseling Program
South University
301 Bendix Road
Virginia Beach, Virginia 23452
Phone: 757-493-6900
877-206-1845(toll-free)
Fax: 757-493-6990
E-mail: suvbadm@southuniversity.edu
Web site: http://www.southuniversity.edu

South University

THE FACULTY

One of the most outstanding aspects of South University's Professional Counseling Program is the dedication of the faculty members and their ability to cultivate a supportive learning environment. Faculty members are committed to their roles as mentors, teachers, and colearners. They are also dedicated to the training of students who can assume positions of leadership within the counseling field. A current list of program faculty members is available at the South University Web site (http://www.southuniversity.edu).

South University–Virginia Beach.

SouthUniversity℠

SOUTH UNIVERSITY

West Palm Beach Campus
Professional Counseling Program

Program of Study

The Master of Arts in professional counseling degree program at South University is intended to meet the local and regional need for qualified professional counselors. The emphasis of the program is on community and agency counseling. The program is designed to enable program graduates to achieve all initial eligibility criteria to become certified as a National Certified Counselor (NCC) by the National Board for Certified Counselors (NBCC) and licensed in the state of Florida. The delivery structure of the program gives students the ability to balance the rigors of work and home while pursuing their master's degree. Students can complete two to three courses each term, with each quarter lasting ten weeks. Class meetings are held mostly on Saturdays between 8:30 a.m. and 5 p.m. and some weeknights from 6 to 9:30.

Students are taught via two primary modes of instruction. The majority of the program involves didactic and experiential classroom instruction, supplemented by computer-based assignments, including the use of Internet technology. The second mode of instruction focuses on supervised field experiences. Students are placed in community counseling settings (during practicum and internship) and practice counseling under the supervision of an on-site supervisor. Students in field placements also receive weekly individual and group supervision from qualified faculty supervisors.

Research Facilities

The South University library has wireless technology throughout, comfortable seating, and quiet study space. The South University library provides in-library and remote access to electronic databases. Both bibliographic and full-text databases are available via EBSCOhost (e.g., Academic Search Premier, SocINDEX, PsycINFO, PsycARTICLES, and Mental Measurements Yearbook), the search and retrieval system of EBSCO Information Services, and via the Library and Information Resources Network (e.g., Infotrac and ProQuest databases). Infotrac databases include counseling sources such as Expanded Academic ASAP, Academic OneFile, and InfotracOneFile, and ProQuest databases include counseling sources such as ProQuest Psychology Journals and ProQuest Research Library. Also for student use, the library has a modern computer lab with ten workstations, each with Internet access, online database services, an office suite, tutorials, and class-support software.

Financial Aid

A wide range of financial aid options is available to students who qualify. The West Palm Beach campus of South University offers access to federal and state programs, including grants, loans, and work-study programs. Eligible students may apply for veterans' educational benefits and are encouraged to investigate the availability of grants and scholarships through community resources. As a first step, students should complete the Free Application for Federal Student Aid (FAFSA). Students may apply electronically at http://www.fafsa.ed.gov or through the campus Director of Financial Aid. Applications should be submitted promptly to receive consideration for the maximum amount of aid.

Cost of Study

Tuition information for the professional counseling program may be obtained by contacting the Admissions Department at South University's West Palm Beach campus.

Living and Housing Costs

South University does not offer or operate student housing at its West Palm Beach campus. Professional counseling program students typically live in homes or apartments in or near the West Palm Beach area. Students who commute from long distances may arrange to stay at nearby hotels that offer long-term rates. More information is available by contacting the Admissions Department.

Student Group

The West Palm Beach campus of South University has a diverse student body enrolled in both day and evening classes. Students are primarily commuters who live within 50 miles of the city.

Student Outcomes

The South University Career Services Department has been established to assist currently enrolled students in developing their career plans and reaching their employment goals. Career services include, but are not limited to, one-on-one career counseling, special career-related workshops and programs, coaching for resume and cover letter development, and resume referral to employers.

Location

In 2010, South University–West Palm Beach moved into a new University Centre facility in Royal Palm Beach, Florida, to serve better students and the broader community in the Palm Beach County area. The facility features a hurricane-resistant infrastructure and includes several large labs, lecture halls, a library, and seminar rooms.

The University

South University is accredited by the Commission on Colleges of the Southern Association of Colleges and Schools (SACS) to award associate, bachelor's, master's, and doctoral degrees. Students should contact the Commission on Colleges at 1866 Southern Lane, Decatur, Georgia 30033-4097 or call 404-679-4500 with questions about the accreditation of South University.

Applying

Students are accepted into the Master of Arts in professional counseling degree program every academic quarter. Entrance into the program is gained through a formal application review and interview process. Acceptance is competitive and based on the admission committee's evaluation of the applicant's academic background (completed bachelor's degree with a cumulative minimum GPA of 2.7) and personal motivation. Application packets are available by contacting the South University Admissions Department or visiting the University's Web site.

Correspondence and Information

Applications for admission to the South University Master of Arts in professional counseling program are available by contacting:

Professional Counseling Program
South University
1760 North Congress Avenue
West Palm Beach, Florida 33409
Phone: 561-697-9200
866-629-2902 (toll-free)
Fax: 561-697-9944
Web site: http://www.southuniversity.edu

South University

THE FACULTY

One of the most outstanding aspects of South University's professional counseling program is the dedication of the faculty members and their ability to cultivate a supportive learning environment. Faculty members are committed to their roles as mentors, teachers, and colearners. They are also dedicated to the training of students who can assume positions of leadership within the counseling field. A current list of program faculty members appears in the South University catalog, which is available on the South University Web site (http://www.southuniversity.edu).

South University–West Palm Beach campus.

VILLANOVA UNIVERSITY

Department of Psychology

Program of Study

The Villanova Department of Psychology has offered a Master of Science (M.S.) degree in general psychology since 1961. This M.S. degree program is particularly well suited to provide a strong foundation for individuals seeking entry into Ph.D. programs in most subfields of psychology. In addition, the program serves the needs of students who are unsure of their future professional goals, of individuals who want a more gradual transition between undergraduate and Ph.D.-level work, and of those seeking a terminal master's degree.

The two-year curriculum is designed to provide excellent training in research skills. Students gain expertise in the formulation of research designs and in the acquisition, analysis, and interpretation of data. Laboratory courses in cognitive psychology, statistics, and physiological psychology are complemented by electives in many of the other subfields of psychology. In addition, students may elect to take a graduate course in a department other than psychology to round out their area of special interest. Biology, chemistry, computer science, human organization science, and statistics have been of particular interest in this regard. Students are required to complete a total of eight courses, including statistics and at least two laboratory courses, and to conduct an original piece of research under faculty supervision in the form of a thesis. The elective courses are designed to allow students the flexibility to tailor the program to their particular goals. The master's thesis is required, and additional independent research is strongly encouraged. There is no comprehensive examination or foreign language requirement.

The psychology faculty has maintained a consistently strong record for productivity and scholarly research. During a recent three-year period, seventy-seven journal articles, fourteen book chapters, three books, and fifty-eight convention presentations emerged from the Department of Psychology. Graduate students frequently coauthor the research published by their mentors, thereby enhancing their graduate education and preparation for a top-quality doctoral program. Villanova's master's program in psychology has been ranked among the top ten M.S.-only–granting departments (95th percentile) in the United States and Canada with regard to research productivity. Several of the Department's faculty members hold research grants from various government agencies.

Research Facilities

The University library contains more than 780,000 volumes and 5,600 current periodicals. Public computing facilities that consist of networked Windows-based microcomputers are available in a number of campus locations, including Tolentine Hall (the location of the Department of Psychology). All facilities are available to University students and faculty members. Computer facilities that are dedicated to the Department of Psychology and laboratories within the Department are also available.

Financial Aid

A limited number of University-funded assistantships and tuition scholarships are awarded to psychology graduate students on a competitive basis. These include research/teaching assistantships that carry a remission of tuition and fees and, in some instances, a monthly stipend. Students with assistantships and tuition scholarships are assigned to faculty members to help with their teaching and/or research efforts. Depending on the type of award, assistants and tuition scholars are expected to work from 7 to 20 hours per week under the supervision of their faculty mentor. Additional research assistantships, supported by extramural grants, are awarded by faculty members who hold the grants. Villanova University also has a number of additional scholarships and graduate assistantship, for which psychology program students may be eligible.

Cost of Study

Graduate tuition was $650 per credit hour in 2009–10.

Living and Housing Costs

The University does not maintain accommodations for graduate students, but second-year students are eligible for positions as resident counselors in the dormitories. The area has a wide selection of living quarters that are convenient to the campus.

Student Group

Approximately 20 students representing all geographical sections of the United States are selected for admission each year from approximately 150 applications. About 30 percent of the class comes from the Philadelphia area. The majority (58 percent) of students come from out of state, and a large proportion are from outside the Mid-Atlantic region (e.g., California, Arizona, Texas, Missouri, Kansas, Florida, Georgia, and Virginia).

Student Outcomes

While the program is not specifically designed to provide terminal training for mental health professionals, some graduates continue on to Ph.D. programs in clinical or counseling psychology. Others accept positions in the private sector as science writers, lab technicians, data analysts, and marketing researchers. The program enjoys a strong national reputation, thereby contributing to the success that a large proportion of graduates have in gaining admission to some of the top Ph.D. programs in psychology (e.g., Brown; Columbia; Cornell; Tufts University; University of California, Berkeley; University of California, San Diego; University of Colorado; University of Illinois; University of Michigan; University of Wisconsin; and Johns Hopkins). Additional information about graduates of the program can be found on the Web at the address given in this description.

Location

Located in the heart of the Philadelphia Region's Main Line suburbs, the University occupies more than 200 handsomely landscaped acres in the town of Villanova, 12 miles west of Philadelphia. The location combines the advantages of a tranquil suburban setting with proximity to a large metropolitan city known for its outstanding contributions in the areas of culture, education, history, recreation, religion, and sport.

The University

Villanova University is a private institution founded in 1842 by the Augustinian Fathers. Graduate programs were first administered separately in 1931. Currently, there are five academic units—the Colleges of Arts and Sciences, Engineering, and Nursing; the Villanova School of Business; and the School of Law.

Applying

Application forms and the *Graduate Studies Viewbook* may be obtained from the Graduate Studies Office. There is a $50 application fee. Additional information about the psychology program may be obtained by contacting the Department of Psychology. In addition to forwarding the completed application form, GRE scores, and official college transcripts, applicants must also arrange to have three letters of recommendation submitted on their behalf. Submission of a personal statement, describing the nature of the applicant's interest in psychology and in the Villanova program, is also suggested. Most successful applicants have an undergraduate GPA of at least 3.0 (with an average of 3.5) and above-average GRE scores (average verbal, 540; quantitative, 640; analytic writing, 5.0; Subject Test in psychology (optional), 620; statistics taken from the most recent three years).

Applications are accepted for fall admission only. Admissions are on a rolling basis, and applications are accepted for the following fall throughout the year. However, to receive full consideration for financial aid, completed applications should be received before March 1.

Correspondence and Information

For applications:
Graduate Studies Office
Kennedy Hall, 2nd Floor
Villanova University
800 Lancaster Avenue
Villanova, Pennsylvania 19085-1699
Phone: 610-519-7090
Fax: 610-519-7096

For further information about the M.S. program in psychology:
Graduate Admissions Committee
Department of Psychology
Villanova University
Villanova, Pennsylvania 19085-1699
Phone: 610-519-4720
Fax: 610-519-4269
E-mail: Visit Web site
Web site: http://www.villanova.edu/artsci/psychology

Villanova University

THE FACULTY AND THEIR RESEARCH

The Department of Psychology comprises 16 full-time faculty members, most of whom maintain active research laboratories in their specialties. Strong research specializations within the Department are provided in animal learning, clinical, cognition, developmental, human factors, organizational, perception, personality, physiological, and social psychology.

Cognitive Psychology/Cognitive Neuroscience/Human Factors

Dr. Diego Fernandez-Duque's research spans cognitive and social neuroscience. Within cognitive neuroscience, he studies how different aspects of attention change due to aging and pathology and why visual perception sometimes occurs in the absence of awareness. Within social neuroscience, he investigates impairments in social cognition brought about by brain insult, using frontotemporal dementia as a model disease in which to explore empathy and metacognition.

Dr. Charles Folk has been studying the nature of visual distractibility. What kinds of events capture attention, and to what degree is such capture under voluntary control? The outcome of his work has important implications for applied settings, such as aircraft cockpits, as well as for theoretical models of selective attention.

Dr. Irene Kan's general research interest is the cognitive architecture and neural bases of human memory. Combining cognitive neuroscientific, neuropsychological, and behavioral approaches, research in her laboratory is focused on understanding how semantic memory and episodic memory are organized and retrieved.

Dr. Thomas Toppino investigates human cognitive processes and the development of those processes in children. Most recently, he has studied fundamental factors underlying the effects of repetition and order of presentation in learning and memory. He also investigates the relationship between sensory and higher cognitive processes in visual perception, focusing especially on factors affecting the perception of ambiguous patterns.

Developmental Psychology

Dr. Pamela Blewitt studies both the cognitive and social/interactive processes involved in word learning. She examines how young children approach the word-learning task, traces changes in children's word meanings over time, and assesses the relationships between word learning and logical thinking. Her studies also examine parents' and teachers' contributions to children's vocabulary growth, including conversational, word defining, and book-reading strategies.

Dr. Rebecca Brand is interested in infants' knowledge acquisition across several domains. In the language domain, she has recently been investigating the development of inhibitory control and its role in early vocabulary development. In the action domain, she has been investigating the specialized action adults present toward infants ("motionese") and its role in infants' understanding of new action sequences.

Dr. Nicole Else-Quest studies psychological development across the lifespan, with special focus on gender roles and emotions. Her recent projects include an investigation of the roles of emotions, scaffolding and social relationships in mathematics learning, meta-analyses of gender differences in temperament and emotion, and a study of emotional adaptation to disease later in life.

Clinical/Social/Personality and Organizational Psychology

Dr. David Bush investigates gender differences in work-related issues such as gender stereotyping of jobs, performance appraisal, compensation, and negotiating strategies. He also conducts research on organizational changes related to downsizing and reorganization and their consequences for the organizational culture.

Dr. Deborah Kendzierski's social psychology research program focuses on the links between intentions and behavior in the context of adherence to health-behavior regimens. She is interested in the role of self-concept in linking intentions and such health behaviors as exercising and dieting.

Dr. Steven Krauss examines normal and disordered mood expression and personality across cultures. He also investigates the relationships between values, moral reasoning, relationship models, and individualism/collectivism from a cross-cultural perspective.

Dr. John Kurtz studies issues and techniques related to psychological assessment and the diagnosis of mental disorders. His recent research is concerned with factors related to change versus stability in personality traits during adulthood and the use of informants in personality assessment.

Dr. Patrick Markey's research program is focused on two broad issues: How people differ and if these differences are related to how they actually behave. Much of this research has related personality attributes to behaviors in diverse contexts, including Internet chat rooms, marital interactions, face-to-face communications among college students, and interactions between preadolescent children and their mothers.

Sensation/Perception

Dr. Gerald Long has focused on the validity and reliability of various visual assessment tasks that are often used to screen our visual abilities, including color vision, contrast sensitivity, and dynamic visual acuity. Another productive line of research has involved examination of the processes underlying certain classes of visual illusions. These illusions have proven to be useful research tools in identifying sensory and cognitive effects in perception.

Comparative/Physiological Psychology

Dr. Michael Brown's laboratory has been concerned with understanding basic cognitive processes by studying the behavior of nonhuman animals. Most recently, this research has centered on spatial abilities and decision processes in rats and spatial memory in honeybees.

Dr. Matthew Matell is interested in the cognitive and neural mechanisms underlying the perception of time and sequence. Primary techniques include ensemble electrophysiological recordings, pharmacology, and lesion techniques in rats, with a current focus on the role of cortical-striatal-thalamic interactions. Computational models of timing are also being developed.

Section 25
Public, Regional, and Industrial Affairs

This section contains a directory of institutions offering graduate work in public, regional, and industrial affairs, followed by in-depth entries submitted by institutions that chose to prepare detailed program descriptions. Additional information about programs listed in the directory but not augmented by an in-depth entry may be obtained by writing directly to the dean of a graduate school or chair of a department at the address given in the directory.

For programs offering related work, see also in this book *Architecture, Area and Cultural Studies, Criminology and Forensics, Economics, Humanities, Political Science and International Affairs,* and *Sociology, Anthropology, and Archaeology.* In the other guides in this series:

Graduate Programs in the Physical Sciences, Mathematics, Agricultural Sciences, the Environment & Natural Resources
See *Environmental Sciences and Management*
Graduate Programs in Engineering & Applied Sciences
See *Management of Engineering and Technology*
Graduate Programs in Business, Education, Health, Information Studies, Law & Social Work
See *Business Administration and Management, Law,* and *Public Health*

CONTENTS

Program Directories

Disability Studies 1110
Emergency Management 1110
Homeland Security 1113
Industrial and Labor Relations 1115
Philanthropic Studies 1118
Public Administration 1119
Public Affairs 1146
Public Policy 1151
Rural Planning and Studies 1163
Sustainable Development 1164
Urban and Regional Planning 1167
Urban Studies 1177

Close-Ups and Displays

Cornell University
Cornell Institute for Public Affairs 1181
ILR School 1183
George Mason University 1185
Hawai'i Pacific University 1187
Indiana University Bloomington 1189
The Johns Hopkins University 1191
Public Policy (Display) 1155
Rutgers, The State University of New Jersey, New Brunswick (Display) 1117
University of Delaware 1193
University of Maine (Display) 1138
University of Pennsylvania 1195

See also:

American University—Communication 673
American University—International Service 849
Monterey Institute of International Studies—International Policy Studies 853
Pratt Institute—Architecture 145
University of Pennsylvania—Design 147
The University of Texas at Dallas—Economic, Political, and Policy Sciences 759
Villanova University—Political Science 857

Disability Studies

Brandeis University, The Heller School for Social Policy and Management, Program in Social Policy, Waltham, MA 02454-9110. Offers assets and inequalities (PhD); children, youth and families (PhD); health and behavioral health (PhD). *Degree requirements:* For doctorate, thesis/dissertation, qualifying paper, 2-year residency. *Entrance requirements:* For doctorate, GRE General Test.

Brock University, Faculty of Graduate Studies, Faculty of Social Sciences, Program in Applied Disability Studies, St. Catharines, ON L2S 3A1, Canada. Offers MA, MADS, Diploma. Part-time programs available. *Degree requirements:* For master's, thesis (for some programs). *Entrance requirements:* For master's, honors degree. Additional exam requirements/recommendations for international students: Required—TOEFL (minimum score 550 paper-based; 213 computer-based; 80 iBT), IELTS (minimum score 6.5). Electronic applications accepted.

Chapman University, Graduate Studies, College of Educational Studies, Program in Education: Disability Studies, Orange, CA 92866. Offers PhD. *Faculty:* 24 full-time (15 women), 25 part-time/adjunct (16 women). *Students:* 20 part-time (16 women); includes 6 minority (1 African American, 1 American Indian/Alaska Native, 3 Asian Americans or Pacific Islanders, 1 Hispanic American). Average age 39. 12 applicants, 75% accepted, 6 enrolled. *Degree requirements:* For doctorate, thesis/dissertation. Tuition and fees vary according to course load, degree level and program. *Financial support:* Federal Work-Study and scholarships/grants available. *Unit head:* Dr. Joel Colbert, Director, 714-744-7076. *Application contact:* Rika Judd, Graduate Admission Counselor, 714-997-6786, Fax: 714-997-6713, E-mail: rjudd@chapman.edu.

Syracuse University, School of Education, Program in Disability Studies, Syracuse, NY 13244. Offers CAS. Part-time programs available. *Students:* 3 part-time (all women). Average age 44. 10 applicants, 90% accepted, 1 enrolled. In 2009, 7 CASs awarded. *Entrance requirements:* Additional exam requirements/recommendations for international students: Required—TOEFL (minimum score 100 iBT). *Application deadline:* For fall admission, 2/1 priority date for domestic and international students; for spring admission, 10/15 priority date for domestic and international students. Applications are processed on a rolling basis. Application fee: $75. Electronic applications accepted. *Expenses:* Tuition: Full-time $26,808; part-time $1117 per credit. Required fees: $1024. *Financial support:* Application deadline: 1/1. *Unit head:* Dr. Steve Taylor, Program Coordinator, 315-443-4484. *Application contact:* Liza Rochelson, Graduate Recruiter, School of Education, 315-443-2505, E-mail: e-gradrcrt@syr.edu.

University of Hawaii at Manoa, Graduate Division, College of Education, Program in Disability and Diversity Studies, Honolulu, HI 96822. Offers Graduate Certificate. Part-time programs available. *Faculty:* 2 full-time (0 women), 3 part-time/adjunct (2 women). *Students:* 6 full-time (all women), 3 part-time (0 women); includes 4 minority (1 African American, 2 Asian Americans or Pacific Islanders, 1 Hispanic American), 2 international. Average age 33. 6 applicants, 67% accepted, 3 enrolled. *Entrance requirements:* Additional exam requirements/recommendations for international students: Required—TOEFL (minimum score 500 paper-based; 173 computer-based; 61 iBT), IELTS (minimum score 5). *Application deadline:* For fall admission, 3/1 for domestic and international students; for spring admission, 10/1 for domestic and international students. Application fee: $60. *Expenses:* Tuition, state resident: full-time $8900; part-time $372 per credit. Tuition, nonresident: full-time $21,400; part-time $898 per credit. Required fees: $207 per semester. *Financial support:* In 2009–10, 5 fellowships (averaging $6,248 per year), 4 research assistantships (averaging $17,544 per year) were awarded. Total annual research expenditures: $12.4 million. *Application contact:* Norma Jean Stodden, Director, 808-956-4454, Fax: 808-956-3162, E-mail: nhemphil@hawaii.edu.

University of Illinois at Chicago, Graduate College, College of Applied Health Sciences, Department of Disability and Human Development, Chicago, IL 60607-7128. Offers disability and human development (MS); disability studies (PhD). *Accreditation:* AOTA. Part-time programs available. *Degree requirements:* For master's, thesis optional; for doctorate, thesis/dissertation. *Entrance requirements:* For master's and doctorate, GRE General Test. Additional exam requirements/recommendations for international students: Required—TOEFL. Electronic applications accepted. *Faculty research:* Emerging trends in disability, demography and financial structure of disability services, aging and disability, empowerment of people with disabilities, health promotion in disabilities.

University of Manitoba, Faculty of Graduate Studies, Interdisciplinary Programs, Program in Disability Studies, Winnipeg, MB R3T 2N2, Canada. Offers M Sc, MA.

University of Northern British Columbia, Office of Graduate Studies, Prince George, BC V2N 4Z9, Canada. Offers business administration (Diploma); community health science (M Sc); disability management (MA); education (M Ed); first nations studies (MA); gender studies (MA); history (MA); interdisciplinary studies (MA); international studies (MA); mathematical, computer and physical sciences (M Sc); natural resources and environmental studies (M Sc, MA, MNRES, PhD); political science (MA); psychology (M Sc, PhD); social work (MSW). Part-time and evening/weekend programs available. Postbaccalaureate distance learning degree programs offered (no on-campus study). *Degree requirements:* For master's, thesis; for doctorate, thesis/dissertation. *Entrance requirements:* For master's, GRE, minimum B average in undergraduate course work; for doctorate, candidacy exam, minimum A average in graduate course work.

University of Pittsburgh, School of Health and Rehabilitation Sciences, Disability Studies Program, Pittsburgh, PA 15260. Offers Certificate. *Faculty:* 1 (woman) full-time. *Students:* 1 (woman) part-time. *Expenses:* Tuition, state resident: full-time $16,402; part-time $665 per credit. Tuition, nonresident: full-time $28,694; part-time $1175 per credit. Required fees: $690; $175 per term. Tuition and fees vary according to program. *Unit head:* Dr. Rory Cooper, Chair and Distinguished Professor, 412-383-6596, E-mail: rcooper@pitt.edu. *Application contact:* Shameem Gangjee, Director of Admissions, 412-383-6558, Fax: 412-383-6535, E-mail: admissions@shrs.pitt.edu.

Utah State University, School of Graduate Studies, College of Education and Human Services, Department of Special Education and Rehabilitation, Logan, UT 84322. Offers disability disciplines (PhD); rehabilitation counselor education (MRC); special education (M Ed, MS, Ed S). *Accreditation:* NCATE (one or more programs are accredited). Part-time programs available. Postbaccalaureate distance learning degree programs offered (minimal on-campus study). *Degree requirements:* For master's, thesis (for some programs), internships (for some programs); for doctorate, comprehensive exam, thesis/dissertation. *Entrance requirements:* For master's and doctorate, GRE General Test, minimum GPA of 3.0. Additional exam requirements/recommendations for international students: Required—TOEFL (minimum score 550 paper-based; 213 computer-based). Electronic applications accepted. *Faculty research:* Applied behavior analysis, effective instructional practices, early childhood teacher training research, distance education, multicultural rehabilitation.

York University, Faculty of Graduate Studies, Faculty of Health, Program in Critical Disability Studies, Toronto, ON M3J 1P3, Canada. Offers MA, PhD. *Degree requirements:* For master's, thesis or alternative. *Entrance requirements:* Additional exam requirements/recommendations for international students: Required—TOEFL (minimum score 600 paper-based; 250 computer-based). Electronic applications accepted.

Emergency Management

Adelphi University, University College, Graduate Certificate in Emergency Management Program, Garden City, NY 11530-0701. Offers Certificate. Part-time and evening/weekend programs available. *Students:* 3 part-time (1 woman). Average age 27. 11 applicants, 55% accepted. *Application deadline:* For fall admission, 5/1 for international students; for spring admission, 12/1 for international students. Applications are processed on a rolling basis. Application fee: $50. Electronic applications accepted. *Expenses:* Tuition: Full-time $28,340; part-time $830 per credit. Required fees: $600; $250 per credit. Full-time tuition and fees vary according to course load and program. *Financial support:* Research assistantships with partial tuition reimbursements, Federal Work-Study and institutionally sponsored loans available. *Faculty research:* Emergency nursing, disaster management, disaster preparedness. *Unit head:* Shawn O'Riley, Executive Director, 516-877-3412, E-mail: ucinfo@adelphi.edu. *Application contact:* Christine Murphy, Director of Admissions, 516-877-3050, Fax: 516-877-3039, E-mail: graduateadmissions@adelphi.edu.

American Public University System, AMU/APU Graduate Programs, Charles Town, WV 25414. Offers air warfare (MA Military Studies); American Revolution (MA Military Studies); business administration (MBA); Civil War (MA Military Studies); criminal justice (MA); defense management (MA Military Studies); emergency and disaster management (MA); environmental policy and management (MS); fire science management (MA); global engagement (MA); history (MA); homeland security (MA); humanities (MA); intelligence (MA Military Studies, MA Strategic Intelligence); international peace and conflict resolution (MA); international relations and conflict resolution (MA); joint warfare (MA Military Studies); land warfare international perspective (MA Military Studies); management (MA); military history (MA); military leadership (MA Military Studies); national security studies (MA); naval warfare international (MA Military Studies); naval warfare US (MA Military Studies); political science (MA); public administration (MA); public health (MA); security management (MA); space studies (MS); special ops/LIC (MA Military Studies); sports management (MA); transportation and logistics management (MA); transportation management (MA); unconventional warfare (MA Military Studies); World War II (MA Military Studies). Programs offered via distance learning only. Part-time and evening/weekend programs available. Postbaccalaureate distance learning degree programs offered (no on-campus study). *Faculty:* 10 full-time (3 women), 188 part-time/adjunct (57 women). *Students:* 340 full-time (98 women), 3,567 part-time (790 women); includes 615 minority (317 African Americans, 28 American Indian/Alaska Native, 85 Asian Americans or Pacific Islanders, 185 Hispanic Americans), 20 international. Average age 36. 2,123 applicants, 100% accepted, 893 enrolled. In 2009, 829 degrees awarded. *Degree requirements:* For master's, comprehensive exam. *Entrance requirements:* For master's, bachelor's degree or equivalent, minimum GPA of 2.7 in last 60 hours of course work. *Application deadline:* Applications are processed on a rolling basis. Application fee: $0. Electronic applications accepted. *Financial support:* Applicants required to submit FAFSA. *Faculty research:* Military history, criminal justice, management performance, national security. *Unit head:* Dr. Frank McCluskey, Provost, 877-468-6268, Fax: 304-724-3780. *Application contact:* Terry Grant, Director of Enrollment Management, 877-468-6268, Fax: 304-724-3780, E-mail: info@apus.edu.

Anna Maria College, Graduate Division, Program in Emergency Management, Paxton, MA 01612. Offers MS, Graduate Certificate. Part-time and evening/weekend programs available. *Degree requirements:* For master's, thesis. *Entrance requirements:* For master's, minimum GPA of 2.7. Additional exam requirements/recommendations for international students: Required—TOEFL (minimum score 500 paper-based). Electronic applications accepted.

Arkansas Tech University, Graduate College, College of Applied Sciences, Russellville, AR 72801. Offers emergency management (MS); engineering (M Engr); information technology (MS). Part-time programs available. *Students:* 73 full-time (17 women), 50 part-time (22 women); includes 8 minority (4 African Americans, 1 American Indian/Alaska Native, 1 Asian American or Pacific Islander, 2 Hispanic Americans), 55 international. Average age 29. In 2009, 38 master's awarded. *Degree requirements:* For master's, comprehensive exam (for some programs), thesis (for some programs), internship. *Entrance requirements:* For master's, GRE General Test. Additional exam requirements/recommendations for international students: Required—TOEFL (minimum score 550 paper-based; 213 computer-based; 79 iBT), IELTS (minimum score 6). *Application deadline:* For fall admission, 3/1 priority date for domestic students, 5/1 priority date for international students; for spring admission, 10/1 priority date for domestic and international students. Applications are processed on a rolling basis. Application fee: $0 ($30 for international students). Electronic applications accepted. *Expenses:* Tuition, state resident: full-time $3438; part-time $191 per hour. Tuition, nonresident: full-time $6876; part-time $382 per hour. Required fees: $482; $9 per credit hour. $140 per semester. Tuition and fees vary according to course load. *Financial support:* In 2009–10, teaching assistantships with full tuition reimbursements (averaging $4,000 per year); research assistantships, career-related internships or fieldwork, Federal Work-Study, scholarships/grants, health care benefits, and unspecified assistantships also available. Support available to part-time students. Financial award application deadline: 4/15; financial award applicants required to submit FAFSA. *Unit head:* Dr. William Hoefler, Dean, 479-968-0353 Ext. 501, E-mail: whoeflerjr@atu.edu. *Application contact:* Dr. Mary B. Gunter, Dean of Graduate College, 479-968-0398, Fax: 479-964-0542, E-mail: graduate.school@atu.edu.

Benedictine University, Graduate Programs, Program in Public Health, Lisle, IL 60532-0900. Offers administration of health care institutions (MPH); dietetics (MPH); disaster management (MPH); health education (MPH); health information systems (MPH); MBA/MPH; MPH/MS. Part-time and evening/weekend programs available. Postbaccalaureate distance learning degree programs offered. *Faculty:* 2 full-time (0 women), 8 part-time/adjunct (3 women). *Students:* 28 full-time (23 women), 65 part-time (52 women); includes 35 minority (16 African Americans, 1 American Indian/Alaska Native, 14 Asian Americans or Pacific Islanders, 4 Hispanic Americans). Average age 33. 71 applicants, 61% accepted, 31 enrolled. In 2009, 39 degrees awarded. *Entrance requirements:* For master's, MAT, GRE, or GMAT. Additional exam requirements/recommendations for international students: Required—TOEFL (minimum score 550 paper-based; 213 computer-based). *Application deadline:* For fall admission, 9/1 for domestic students; for winter admission, 12/1 for domestic students; for spring admission, 2/15 for domestic students. Application fee: $40. *Financial support:* Career-related internships or fieldwork and health care benefits available. Support available to part-time students. *Unit head:* Dr. Alan Gorr, Director, 630-829-6566, Fax: 630-960-1126, E-mail: agorr@ben.edu. *Application contact:* Kari Gibbons, Director, Admissions, 630-829-6200, Fax: 630-829-6584, E-mail: kgibbons@ben.edu.

California State University, Long Beach, Graduate Studies, College of Health and Human Services, Department of Criminal Justice, Long Beach, CA 90840. Offers criminal justice (MS); emergency services administration (MS). Part-time programs available. *Faculty:* 8 full-time (5 women), 5 part-time/adjunct (1 woman). *Students:* 36 full-time (25 women), 16 part-time (11 women); includes 25 minority (5 African Americans, 8 Asian Americans or Pacific Islanders, 12

Hispanic Americans), 3 international. Average age 27. 118 applicants, 58% accepted, 22 enrolled. *Degree requirements:* For master's, comprehensive course or thesis. *Entrance requirements:* For master's, minimum GPA of 3.0. *Application deadline:* For fall admission, 5/1 for domestic students. Applications are processed on a rolling basis. Application fee: $55. Electronic applications accepted. *Expenses:* Required fees: $1802 per semester. Part-time tuition and fees vary according to course load. *Financial support:* Federal Work-Study, institutionally sponsored loans, and scholarships/grants available. Financial award application deadline: 3/2. *Unit head:* Dr. Henry F. Fradella, Chair, 562-985-2669, Fax: 562-985-8086, E-mail: hfradell@csulb.edu. *Application contact:* Dr. Connie Estrada Ireland, Graduate Advisor, 562-985-8711, Fax: 562-985-8086, E-mail: cireland@csulb.edu.

Capella University, School of Public Service Leadership, Minneapolis, MN 55402. Offers criminal justice (MS, PhD); emergency management (MS, PhD); general human services (MS, PhD); general public administration (MPA, DPA); gerontology (MS); health care administration (MS, PhD); health management and policy (MSPH); management of nonprofit agencies (MS, PhD); nurse educator (MS); public safety leadership (MS, PhD); social and community services (MS, PhD); social behavioral sciences (MSPH).

Drexel University, College of Nursing and Health Professions, Emergency and Public Safety Services Program, Philadelphia, PA 19104-2875. Offers MS. Part-time and evening/weekend programs available. *Degree requirements:* For master's, comprehensive exam. *Entrance requirements:* For master's, GRE General Test, minimum GPA of 2.75.

Florida Institute of Technology, Graduate Programs, College of Business, Extended Studies Division, Melbourne, FL 32901-6975. Offers acquisition and contract management (PMBA); business administration (PMBA); computer information systems (MS); e-business (PMBA); human resource management (PMBA); human resources management (MS); logistics management (MS), including humanitarian and disaster relief logistics; management (MS), including acquisition and contract management, e-business, human resource management, information systems, logistics management, management, transportation management; material acquisition management (MS); project management (MS), including information systems, operations research; public administration (MPA); quality management (MS); space management (MS); space systems (MS); systems management (MS), including information systems, operations research, systems management. Part-time and evening/weekend programs available. Postbaccalaureate distance learning degree programs offered (no on-campus study). *Faculty:* 12 full-time (3 women), 117 part-time/adjunct (20 women). *Students:* 74 full-time (32 women), 1,041 part-time (484 women); includes 343 minority (240 African Americans, 12 American Indian/Alaska Native, 44 Asian Americans or Pacific Islanders, 47 Hispanic Americans), 22 international. Average age 35. 520 applicants, 72% accepted, 279 enrolled. In 2009, 509 master's awarded. *Degree requirements:* For master's, capstone course. *Entrance requirements:* For master's, GMAT or resume showing 8 years of supervised experience, minimum GPA of 3.0, 2 letters of recommendation, resume. Additional exam requirements/recommendations for international students: Required—TOEFL (minimum score 550 paper-based; 213 computer-based; 79 iBT). *Application deadline:* For fall admission, 4/1 for international students; for spring admission, 9/30 for international students. Applications are processed on a rolling basis. Application fee: $50. Electronic applications accepted. *Expenses:* Tuition: Part-time $1015 per credit. Tuition and fees vary according to campus/location and program. *Financial support:* Application deadline: 3/1. *Unit head:* Dr. Clifford Bragdon, Dean, 321-674-8821, Fax: 321-674-7597, E-mail: cbragdon@fit.edu. *Application contact:* Carolyn Farrior, Director of Graduate Admissions Online Learning and Off Campus Programs, 321-674-7118, Fax: 321-674-8216, E-mail: cfarrior@fit.edu.

The George Washington University, School of Medicine and Health Sciences, Health Sciences Programs, Washington, DC 20052. Offers adult nurse practitioner (MSN, Post Master's Certificate); clinical practice management (MSHS); clinical research administration (MSHS); clinical research administration for nurses (MSN); emergency services management (MSHS); end-of-life care (MSHS, MSN); family nurse practitioner (MSN, Post Master's Certificate); immunohematology (MSHS); nursing (DNP); nursing leadership and management (MSN); physical therapy (DPT); physician assistant (MSHS); MSHS/MPH. Postbaccalaureate distance learning degree programs offered (no on-campus study). *Students:* 270 full-time (220 women), 491 part-time (406 women); includes 176 minority (83 African Americans, 5 American Indian/Alaska Native, 62 Asian Americans or Pacific Islanders, 26 Hispanic Americans), 26 international. Average age 35. 1,059 applicants, 47% accepted, 292 enrolled. In 2009, 155 master's, 22 doctorates, 75 other advanced degrees awarded. *Entrance requirements:* Additional exam requirements/recommendations for international students: Required—TOEFL (minimum score 550 paper-based; 213 computer-based). *Application deadline:* Applications are processed on a rolling basis. Application fee: $60. *Expenses:* Contact institution. *Unit head:* Jean E. Johnson, Senior Associate Dean, 202-994-3725, E-mail: jejohns@gwu.edu. *Application contact:* Joke Ogundiran, Director of Admission, 202-994-1668, Fax: 202-994-0870, E-mail: jokeogun@gwu.edu.

Georgia State University, Andrew Young School of Policy Studies, Department of Public Management and Policy, Atlanta, GA 30303. Offers disaster management (Certificate); nonprofit management (Certificate); planning and economic development (Certificate); public administration (MPA), including criminal justice, management and finance, nonprofit management, planning and economic development, policy analysis and evaluation, public health; public policy (MPP, PhD), including disaster policy (MPP), nonprofit policy (MPP), planning and economic development policy (MPP), public finance policy (MPP), social policy (MPP); JD/MPA. *Accreditation:* NASPAA (one or more programs are accredited). Part-time and evening/weekend programs available. Terminal master's awarded for partial completion of doctoral program. *Degree requirements:* For master's, thesis optional; for doctorate, comprehensive exam, thesis/dissertation. *Entrance requirements:* For master's and doctorate, GRE General Test. Additional exam requirements/recommendations for international students: Required—TOEFL. Electronic applications accepted. *Faculty research:* Public management, policy analysis, public finance, planning and economic development, nonprofit leadership and policy.

Indiana University of Pennsylvania, School of Graduate Studies and Research, College of Natural Sciences and Mathematics, Science for Disaster Response Program, Indiana, PA 15705-1087. Offers MS. *Faculty:* 5 full-time (3 women). *Students:* 4 full-time (0 women). Average age 33. 7 applicants, 71% accepted, 4 enrolled. In 2009, 4 master's awarded. Application fee: $40. *Expenses:* Tuition, state resident: full-time $6666; part-time $370 per credit hour. Tuition, nonresident: full-time $10,666; part-time $593 per credit hour. Required fees: $813 per semester. *Unit head:* Dr. Roberta Eddy, Director, 724-357-4482, E-mail: roberta.eddy@iup.edu. *Application contact:* Dr. Jacqueline Gorman, Dean's Associate, 724-357-2609, E-mail: jgorman@iup.edu.

Jacksonville State University, College of Graduate Studies and Continuing Education, College of Arts and Sciences, Department of Emergency Management, Jacksonville, AL 36265-1602. Offers MS. Part-time and evening/weekend programs available. *Faculty:* 4 full-time (1 woman). *Students:* 9 full-time (2 women), 108 part-time (44 women); includes 29 minority (23 African Americans, 1 American Indian/Alaska Native, 1 Asian American or Pacific Islander, 4 Hispanic Americans), 2 international. Average age 39. 55 applicants, 67% accepted, 25 enrolled. In 2009, 38 master's awarded. *Degree requirements:* For master's, comprehensive exam, thesis (for some programs). *Application deadline:* Applications are processed on a rolling basis. Application fee: $30. Electronic applications accepted. *Financial support:* In 2009–10, 41 students received support. Available to part-time students. Application deadline: 4/1. *Unit head:* Dr. Barry Cox, Head, 256-782-5926, E-mail: bcox@jsu.edu. *Application contact:* Dr. Jean Pugliese, Associate Dean, 256-782-8278, Fax: 256-782-5321, E-mail: pugliese@jsu.edu.

The Johns Hopkins University, School of Nursing, Nurse Practitioner Program, Baltimore, MD 21218-2699. Offers adult acute/critical care (MSN, Certificate); adult and pediatric primary care (MSN); adult or pediatric primary care (Certificate); emergency preparedness/disaster response (Certificate); family primary care (MSN, Certificate); women's health (Certificate). *Accreditation:* AACN; NLN (one or more programs are accredited). Part-time programs available. *Faculty:* 9 full-time (all women), 10 part-time/adjunct (all women). *Students:* 28 full-time (27 women), 75 part-time (73 women); includes 33 minority (14 African Americans, 16 Asian Americans or Pacific Islanders, 3 Hispanic Americans), 3 international. Average age 31. 223 applicants, 80% accepted, 29 enrolled. In 2009, 37 master's awarded. *Degree requirements:* For master's, thesis optional, scholarly project or portfolio. *Entrance requirements:* For master's, GRE, interview, minimum GPA of 3.0, BSN, Maryland RN license. Additional exam requirements/recommendations for international students: Required—TOEFL (minimum score 550 paper-based; 213 computer-based). *Application deadline:* For fall admission, 3/1 priority date for domestic and international students; for spring admission, 7/1 priority date for domestic and international students. Application fee: $75. Electronic applications accepted. *Expenses:* Contact institution. *Financial support:* In 2009–10, 25 students received support. Federal Work-Study, scholarships/grants, traineeships, and tuition waivers (partial) available. Support available to part-time students. Financial award application deadline: 3/1; financial award applicants required to submit FAFSA. *Faculty research:* Community outreach, primary care of underserved populations, substance abusing individuals, childhood violence, women's health. *Unit head:* Dr. Julie A. Stanik-Hutt, Director, Master's Programs, 410-502-0184, Fax: 410-955-7463, E-mail: jstanik1@son.jhmi.edu. *Application contact:* Mary O'Rourke, Director of Admissions/Student Services, 410-955-7548, Fax: 410-614-7086, E-mail: orourke@son.jhmi.edu.

Lynn University, College of Liberal Education, Boca Raton, FL 33431-5598. Offers applied psychology (MS); criminal justice administration (MS); emergency planning and administration (MS, Certificate). Part-time and evening/weekend programs available. Postbaccalaureate distance learning degree programs offered. *Entrance requirements:* For master's, GRE, resume, 2 letters of recommendation, minimum undergraduate GPA of 3.0. Additional exam requirements/recommendations for international students: Required—TOEFL (minimum score 550 paper-based; 213 computer-based). Application fee: $50. *Expenses:* Tuition: Part-time $580 per credit. One-time fee: $200 part-time. Part-time tuition and fees vary according to degree level. *Financial support:* Career-related internships or fieldwork, Federal Work-Study, institutionally sponsored loans, scholarships/grants, tuition waivers (full and partial), and unspecified assistantships available. Support available to part-time students. Financial award application deadline: 8/1; financial award applicants required to submit FAFSA. *Faculty research:* Terrorism, criminological theory, corrections, emergency planning. *Unit head:* Dr. Gregg Cox, Dean, 561-237-7210, E-mail: gcox@lynn.edu. *Application contact:* Dr. Larissa Baia, Assistant Director of Graduate Admissions, 561-237-7916, Fax: 561-237-7100, E-mail: admissionpm@lynn.edu.

Massachusetts Maritime Academy, Program in Emergency Management, Buzzards Bay, MA 02532-1803. Offers MS.

Millersville University of Pennsylvania, College of Graduate and Professional Studies, School of Humanities and Social Sciences, Center for Disaster Research and Education, Program in Emergency Management, Millersville, PA 17551-0302. Offers MS. Part-time and evening/weekend programs available. Postbaccalaureate distance learning degree programs offered (no on-campus study). *Faculty:* 6 full-time (4 women), 2 part-time/adjunct (1 woman). *Students:* 1 full-time (0 women), 24 part-time (12 women), 1 international. Average age 30. 13 applicants, 100% accepted, 12 enrolled. In 2009, 5 master's awarded. *Entrance requirements:* For master's, GRE or MAT (if GPA less than 2.75), 3 letters of recommendation, interview (by telephone), resume. Additional exam requirements/recommendations for international students: Required—TOEFL (minimum score 500 paper-based; 183 computer-based; 65 iBT) or IELTS (minimum score 6). *Application deadline:* For fall admission, 1/15 priority date for domestic and international students; for winter admission, 10/1 priority date for domestic and international students; for spring admission, 10/1 priority date for domestic and international students. Applications are processed on a rolling basis. Application fee: $40 ($50 for international students). Electronic applications accepted. *Expenses:* Tuition, state resident: full-time $6666; part-time $370 per credit. Tuition, nonresident: full-time $10,666; part-time $593 per credit. Required fees: $1578.50; $76.25 per credit. One-time fee: $60 part-time. Tuition and fees vary according to course load. *Financial support:* In 2009–10, 2 students received support, including 2 research assistantships with full tuition reimbursements available (averaging $5,200 per year); institutionally sponsored loans and unspecified assistantships also available. Support available to part-time students. Financial award application deadline: 3/15; financial award applicants required to submit FAFSA. *Unit head:* Dr. Sepidah Yalda, Coordinator, 717-872-3293, E-mail: sepi.yalda@millersville.edu. *Application contact:* Dr. Victor S. DeSantis, Dean of Graduate and Professional Studies, 717-872-3099, Fax: 717-872-3453, E-mail: victor.desantis@millersville.edu.

New Jersey Institute of Technology, Office of Graduate Studies, College of Computing Science, Program in Information Systems, Newark, NJ 07102. Offers business and information systems (MS); emergency management and business continuity (MS); information systems (MS, PhD). Part-time and evening/weekend programs available. Terminal master's awarded for partial completion of doctoral program. *Degree requirements:* For master's, thesis optional; for doctorate, thesis/dissertation. *Entrance requirements:* For master's, GRE General Test; for doctorate, GRE General Test, minimum graduate GPA of 3.5. Additional exam requirements/recommendations for international students: Required—TOEFL (minimum score 550 paper-based; 213 computer-based; 79 iBT). Electronic applications accepted.

New York Medical College, School of Health Sciences and Practice, Department of Health Policy and Management, Program in Emergency Preparedness, Valhalla, NY 10595-1691. Offers Graduate Certificate. Program offered in conjunction with NYMCs Center for Disaster Medicine. *Faculty:* 2 full-time, 5 part-time/adjunct. *Students:* 10 full-time, 25 part-time. Average age 32. 15 applicants, 67% accepted, 8 enrolled. *Application deadline:* For fall admission, 8/1 for domestic students, 5/15 for international students; for spring admission, 12/1 for domestic students, 10/15 for international students. Applications are processed on a rolling basis. Application fee: $50. Electronic applications accepted. *Expenses:* Tuition: Full-time $18,170; part-time $790 per credit. Required fees: $790 per credit. $20 per semester. One-time fee: $100. Tuition and fees vary according to class time, course level, course load, degree level, program, student level and student's religious affiliation. *Unit head:* Michael Reilly, Director, 914-594-4919, E-mail: michael_reilly@nymc.edu. *Application contact:* Pamela Suett, Director of Recruitment, 914-594-4510, Fax: 914-594-4292, E-mail: shsp_admissions@nymc.edu.

North Dakota State University, College of Graduate and Interdisciplinary Studies, College of Arts, Humanities and Social Sciences, Department of Sociology, Anthropology, and Emergency Management, Fargo, ND 58108. Offers emergency management (MS, PhD); social science (MA, MS); sociology (MS). Part-time programs available. *Faculty:* 8 full-time (3 women), 5 part-time/adjunct (2 women). *Students:* 35 full-time (17 women), 15 part-time (9 women); includes 5 minority (2 African Americans, 1 American Indian/Alaska Native, 1 Asian American or Pacific Islander, 1 Hispanic American), 2 international. Average age 27. 15 applicants, 60% accepted, 7 enrolled. In 2009, 9 master's awarded. *Degree requirements:* For master's, thesis; for doctorate, comprehensive exam, thesis/dissertation. *Entrance requirements:* For master's, GRE (emergency management), course work in sociology, minimum GPA of 3.2; for doctorate, GRE, minimum GPA of 3.2. Additional exam requirements/recommendations for international students: Required—TOEFL. *Application deadline:* For fall admission, 4/1 priority date for domestic students. Applications are processed on a rolling basis. Application fee: $45 ($60 for international students). *Financial support:* In 2009–10, 7 research assistantships with full tuition reimbursements (averaging $6,156 per year), 7 teaching assistantships with full tuition reimbursements (averaging $3,078 per year) were awarded; fellowships, career-related internships or fieldwork, Federal Work-Study, institutionally sponsored loans, and tuition waivers (full) also available. Support available to part-time students. Financial award application deadline: 4/15. *Faculty research:* Medical sociology, demography, ethnology, archaeology. Total annual research expenditures: $75,000. *Unit head:* Dr. Daniel J. Klenow, Chair, 701-231-8657, Fax: 701-231-1047, E-mail: daniel.klenow@ndsu.edu. *Application contact:* Dr. Daniel J. Klenow, Chair, 701-231-8657, Fax: 701-231-1047, E-mail: daniel.klenow@ndsu.edu.

Oklahoma State University, College of Arts and Sciences, Department of Political Science, Stillwater, OK 74078. Offers fire and emergency management administration (MS, PhD);

Emergency Management

Oklahoma State University (continued)
political science (MA). *Faculty:* 19 full-time (5 women), 5 part-time/adjunct (1 woman). *Students:* 27 full-time (4 women), 54 part-time (8 women); includes 10 minority (2 African Americans, 6 American Indian/Alaska Native, 1 Asian American or Pacific Islander, 1 Hispanic American), 20 international. Average age 35. 77 applicants, 45% accepted, 27 enrolled. In 2009, 22 master's awarded. *Degree requirements:* For master's, comprehensive exam, thesis or creative component; for doctorate, comprehensive exam, thesis/dissertation. *Entrance requirements:* For master's, GRE; for doctorate, GRE. Additional exam requirements/recommendations for international students: Required—TOEFL (minimum score 550 paper-based; 79 iBT). *Application deadline:* For fall admission, 3/1 priority date for international students; for spring admission, 8/1 priority date for international students. Applications are processed on a rolling basis. Application fee: $40 ($75 for international students). Electronic applications accepted. *Expenses:* Tuition, state resident: full-time $3716; part-time $154.85 per credit hour. Tuition, nonresident: full-time $14,448; part-time $602 per credit hour. Required fees: $1772; $73.85 per credit hour. One-time fee: $50. Tuition and fees vary according to course load and campus/location. *Financial support:* In 2009–10, 3 research assistantships (averaging $11,090 per year), 11 teaching assistantships (averaging $10,767 per year) were awarded; career-related internships or fieldwork, Federal Work-Study, scholarships/grants, health care benefits, tuition waivers (partial), and unspecified assistantships also available. Support available to part-time students. Financial award application deadline: 3/1; financial award applicants required to submit FAFSA. *Faculty research:* Fire and emergency management, environmental dispute resolution, voting and elections, women and politics, urban politics. *Unit head:* Dr. James Scott, Head, 405-744-5569, Fax: 405-744-6534. *Application contact:* Dr. Gordon Emslie, Dean, 405-744-6368, Fax: 405-744-0355, E-mail: grad-i@okstate.edu.

Park University, College of Graduate and Professional Studies, Kansas City, MO 54105. Offers adult education (M Ed); at-risk students (M Ed); disaster and emergency management (MPA); educational administration (M Ed); entrepreneurship (MBA); general business (MBA); general education (M Ed); government/business relations (MPA); healthcare/services management (MBA, MPA); international business (MBA); K-12 certification (MAT); management information systems (MBA); management of information systems (MPA); middle school certification (MAT); multi-cultural education (M Ed); nonprofit management (MPA); public management (MPA); school law (M Ed); secondary school certification (MAT); special education (M Ed). Part-time and evening/weekend programs available. Postbaccalaureate distance learning degree programs offered (no on-campus study). *Degree requirements:* For master's, comprehensive exam, thesis (for some programs). *Entrance requirements:* For master's, GRE, GMAT, teacher certification (M Ed). Additional exam requirements/recommendations for international students: Required—TOEFL (minimum score 550 paper-based). Electronic applications accepted. *Faculty research:* Literacy, leadership, brain based research, multicultural education, diversity.

Philadelphia University, School of Science and Health, Program in Disaster Medicine and Management, Philadelphia, PA 19144. Offers MS. Postbaccalaureate distance learning degree programs offered (minimal on-campus study).

Royal Roads University, Graduate Studies, Peace and Conflict Studies Program, Victoria, BC V9B 5Y2, Canada. Offers conflict analysis (G Dip); conflict analysis and management (MA); disaster and emergency management (MA); human security and peacebuilding (MA). Postbaccalaureate distance learning degree programs offered (minimal on-campus study). *Degree requirements:* For master's, thesis. *Entrance requirements:* For master's, 5-7 years of related work experience. Additional exam requirements/recommendations for international students: Required—TOEFL (paper-based 570; computer-based 233) or IELTS (paper-based 7) (recommended). Electronic applications accepted. *Faculty research:* Conflict analysis, ethno-political conflict reconciliation, international relations, displaced persons.

San Diego State University, Graduate and Research Affairs, College of Health and Human Services, Graduate School of Public Health, San Diego, CA 92182. Offers environmental health (MPH); epidemiology (MPH, PhD), including biostatistics (MPH); global emergency preparedness and response (MS); global health (PhD); health behavior (PhD); health promotion (MPH); health services administration (MPH); toxicology (MS); MPH/MA; MSW/MPH. *Accreditation:* ABET (one or more programs are accredited); CAHME (one or more programs are accredited); CEPH (one or more programs are accredited). Part-time programs available. *Degree requirements:* For master's, comprehensive exam (for some programs), thesis (for some programs); for doctorate, thesis/dissertation. *Entrance requirements:* For master's, GMAT (MPH in health services administration), GRE General Test; for doctorate, GRE General Test. Additional exam requirements/recommendations for international students: Required—TOEFL. *Faculty research:* Evaluation of tobacco, AIDS prevalence and prevention, mammography, infant death project, Alzheimer's in elderly Chinese.

TUI University, College of Health Sciences, Program in Health Sciences, Cypress, CA 90630. Offers clinical research administration (MS, Certificate); emergency and disaster management (MS, Certificate); environmental health science (Certificate); health care administration (PhD); health care management (MS), including health informatics; health education (MS, Certificate); health informatics (Certificate); health sciences (PhD); international health (MS); international health: educator or researcher option (PhD); international health: practitioner option (PhD); law and expert witness studies (MS, Certificate); public health (MS); quality assurance (Certificate). Part-time and evening/weekend programs available. Postbaccalaureate distance learning degree programs offered (no on-campus study). *Degree requirements:* For doctorate, comprehensive exam, thesis/dissertation, defense of dissertation. *Entrance requirements:* For master's, minimum GPA of 2.5 (students with GPA 3.0 or greater may transfer up to 30% of graduate level credits); for doctorate, minimum GPA of 3.4, curriculum vitae, course work in research methods or statistics. Additional exam requirements/recommendations for international students: Required—TOEFL. Electronic applications accepted.

Université de Montréal, Faculty of Medicine, Programs in Environment and Prevention, Montréal, QC H3C 3J7, Canada. Offers environment and prevention (DESS); environment, health and disaster management (DESS). Electronic applications accepted. *Faculty research:* Health, environment, pollutants, protection, waste.

University of Central Florida, College of Health and Public Affairs, Department of Public Administration, Orlando, FL 32816. Offers emergency management and homeland security (Certificate); non-profit management (MNM, Certificate); public administration (MPA, Certificate); urban and regional planning (Certificate). *Accreditation:* NASPAA. Part-time and evening/weekend programs available. *Faculty:* 11 full-time (2 women), 6 part-time/adjunct (1 woman). *Students:* 68 full-time (45 women), 235 part-time (166 women); includes 105 minority (64 African Americans, 10 Asian Americans or Pacific Islanders, 31 Hispanic Americans), 7 international. Average age 31. 184 applicants, 75% accepted, 95 enrolled. In 2009, 80 master's, 36 other advanced degrees awarded. *Degree requirements:* For master's, comprehensive exam, thesis or alternative, research report. *Entrance requirements:* For master's, GRE General Test. *Application deadline:* For fall admission, 7/1 for domestic students; for spring admission, 12/1 for domestic students. Application fee: $30. Electronic applications accepted. *Expenses:* Tuition, state resident: part-time $306.31 per credit hour. Tuition, nonresident: part-time $1099.01 per credit hour. Part-time tuition and fees vary according to degree level and program. *Financial support:* In 2009–10, 8 students received support, including 4 fellowships with partial tuition reimbursements available (averaging $10,000 per year), 2 research assistantships with partial tuition reimbursements available (averaging $3,100 per year), 3 teaching assistantships with partial tuition reimbursements available (averaging $5,200 per year); career-related internships or fieldwork, Federal Work-Study, institutionally sponsored loans, tuition waivers (partial), and unspecified assistantships also available. Financial award application deadline: 3/1; financial award applicants required to submit FAFSA. *Unit head:* Dr. MaryAnn Feldheim, Chair, 407-823-3693, Fax: 407-823-5651. *Application contact:* Dr. MaryAnn Feldheim, Chair, 407-823-3693, Fax: 407-823-5651.

University of Hawaii at Manoa, Graduate Division, College of Social Sciences, Department of Urban and Regional Planning, Program in Disaster Preparedness and Emergency Management, Honolulu, HI 96822. Offers Graduate Certificate. Part-time programs available. *Students:* 3 full-time (all women), 6 part-time (2 women); includes 3 minority (all Asian Americans or Pacific Islanders), 2 international. Average age 30. 7 applicants, 71% accepted, 3 enrolled. In 2009, 6 Graduate Certificates awarded. *Entrance requirements:* Additional exam requirements/recommendations for international students: Required—TOEFL (minimum score 500 paper-based; 173 computer-based; 61 iBT), IELTS (minimum score 5). *Application deadline:* For fall admission, 3/1 for domestic and international students; for spring admission, 9/1 for domestic and international students. Application fee: $60. *Expenses:* Tuition, state resident: full-time $8900; part-time $372 per credit. Tuition, nonresident: full-time $21,400; part-time $898 per credit. Required fees: $207 per semester. *Financial support:* In 2009–10, 1 fellowship (averaging $2,000 per year) was awarded. *Application contact:* Dolores Foley, Graduate Chair, 808-956-7280, Fax: 808-956-6870, E-mail: dolores@hawaii.edu.

University of Nevada, Las Vegas, Graduate College, Greenspun College of Urban Affairs, Department of Environmental Studies, Las Vegas, NV 89154-4030. Offers crisis and emergency management (MS); environmental science (MS, PhD); non-profit management (Certificate); public administration (MPA); public affairs (PhD). Part-time programs available. *Faculty:* 6 full-time (2 women). *Students:* 39 full-time (18 women), 145 part-time (79 women); includes 47 minority (22 African Americans, 4 American Indian/Alaska Native, 3 Asian Americans or Pacific Islanders, 18 Hispanic Americans), 7 international. Average age 39. 16 applicants, 31% accepted, 2 enrolled. In 2009, 50 master's, 3 doctorates, 27 other advanced degrees awarded. *Degree requirements:* For master's, comprehensive exam (for some programs), thesis; for doctorate, comprehensive exam (for some programs), thesis/dissertation. *Entrance requirements:* Additional exam requirements/recommendations for international students: Required—TOEFL (minimum score 550 paper-based; 213 computer-based; 80 iBT), IELTS (minimum score 7). *Application deadline:* For fall admission, 6/1 priority date for domestic students, 2/15 priority date for international students; for spring admission, 11/15 priority date for domestic students, 10/1 for international students. Applications are processed on a rolling basis. Application fee: $60 ($95 for international students). Electronic applications accepted. *Financial support:* In 2009–10, 9 students received support, including 6 research assistantships with partial tuition reimbursements available (averaging $13,850 per year), 3 teaching assistantships with partial tuition reimbursements available (averaging $10,666 per year); institutionally sponsored loans, scholarships/grants, health care benefits, and unspecified assistantships also available. Financial award application deadline: 3/1. *Faculty research:* Environmental chemistry, environmental policy and management. *Unit head:* Dr. Ed Weber, Chair/ Associate Professor, 702-895-4440, Fax: 702-895-4436, E-mail: edward.weber@unlv.edu. *Application contact:* Graduate College Admissions Evaluator, 702-895-3320, Fax: 702-895-4180, E-mail: gradcollege@unlv.edu.

University of Nevada, Las Vegas, Graduate College, Greenspun College of Urban Affairs, Department of Public Administration, Las Vegas, NV 89154-6026. Offers crisis and emergency management (MS); non-profit management (Certificate); public administration (MPA); public affairs (PhD); public management (Certificate). *Accreditation:* NASPAA. Part-time and evening/weekend programs available. *Faculty:* 5 full-time (3 women), 2 part-time/adjunct (1 woman). *Students:* 30 full-time (12 women), 129 part-time (70 women); includes 39 minority (21 African Americans, 4 Asian Americans or Pacific Islanders, 14 Hispanic Americans), 3 international. Average age 38. 95 applicants, 76% accepted, 53 enrolled. In 2009, 48 master's, 28 other advanced degrees awarded. *Degree requirements:* For master's, comprehensive exam, professional paper. *Entrance requirements:* For master's, GRE General Test, GMAT or LSAT. Additional exam requirements/recommendations for international students: Required—TOEFL (minimum score 550 paper-based; 213 computer-based; 80 iBT), IELTS (minimum score 7). *Application deadline:* For fall admission, 6/1 priority date for domestic students, 5/1 for international students; for spring admission, 11/1 priority date for domestic students, 10/1 for international students. Applications are processed on a rolling basis. Application fee: $60 ($95 for international students). Electronic applications accepted. *Financial support:* In 2009–10, 8 students received support, including 6 research assistantships with partial tuition reimbursements available (averaging $12,333 per year), 2 teaching assistantships with partial tuition reimbursements available (averaging $12,000 per year); institutionally sponsored loans, scholarships/grants, health care benefits, and unspecified assistantships also available. Financial award application deadline: 3/1. *Faculty research:* Emergency and crisis management, homeland security, public and non-profit management, public policy, policy analysis and evaluation. *Unit head:* Dr. Anna Lukemeyer, Chair/ Associate Professor, 702-895-4828, Fax: 702-895-1813, E-mail: anna.lukemeyer@unlv.edu. *Application contact:* Graduate College Admissions Evaluator, 702-895-3320, Fax: 702-895-4180, E-mail: gradcollege@unlv.edu.

University of New Haven, Graduate School, Henry C. Lee College of Criminal Justice and Forensic Sciences, Program in Fire Science, West Haven, CT 06516-1916. Offers emergency management (Certificate); fire administration (MS); fire science technology (Certificate); fire/arson investigation (MS, Certificate); forensic science/fire science (Certificate); public safety management (MS); public safety management (Certificate). Part-time and evening/weekend programs available. *Faculty:* 2 full-time (0 women). *Students:* 14 part-time (4 women); includes 1 minority (Hispanic American), 1 international. Average age 33. 6 applicants, 83% accepted, 3 enrolled. In 2009, 6 master's, 4 other advanced degrees awarded. *Degree requirements:* For master's, thesis or alternative. *Entrance requirements:* Additional exam requirements/recommendations for international students: Required—TOEFL (minimum score 520 paper-based; 190 computer-based; 70 iBT); Recommended—IELTS (minimum score 5.5). *Application deadline:* For fall admission, 5/31 for international students; for winter admission, 10/15 for international students; for spring admission, 1/15 for international students. Applications are processed on a rolling basis. Application fee: $50. Electronic applications accepted. *Expenses:* Tuition: Part-time $700 per credit. Required fees: $45 per term. One-time fee: $390 part-time. *Financial support:* Research assistantships with partial tuition reimbursements, teaching assistantships with partial tuition reimbursements, career-related internships or fieldwork, Federal Work-Study, scholarships/grants, tuition waivers, and unspecified assistantships available. Support available to part-time students. Financial award applicants required to submit FAFSA. *Unit head:* Robert E. Massicotte, Director, 203-932-7424. *Application contact:* Eloise Gormley, Director of Graduate Admissions, 203-932-7449, Fax: 203-932-7137, E-mail: gradinfo@newhaven.edu.

University of Oklahoma—Tulsa, College of Public Health, Tulsa, OK 74135-2512. Offers general public health (MPH); health administration and policy (MPH); public health preparedness and terrorism (MPH).

University of Pittsburgh, Graduate School of Public Health, Department of Environmental and Occupational Health, Pittsburgh, PA 15260. Offers environmental and occupational health (MPH, MS, PhD); environmental health risk assessment (Certificate); global health (Certificate); public health preparedness and disaster response (Certificate); MD/MPH. *Accreditation:* CEPH (one or more programs are accredited). Part-time programs available. *Faculty:* 28 full-time (8 women), 26 part-time/adjunct (6 women). *Students:* 23 full-time (11 women), 17 part-time (11 women); includes 3 minority (1 African American, 1 Asian American or Pacific Islander, 1 Hispanic American), 9 international. Average age 34. 69 applicants, 57% accepted, 16 enrolled. In 2009, 3 master's awarded. *Degree requirements:* For master's, comprehensive exam, thesis; for doctorate, comprehensive exam, thesis/dissertation, preliminary exams. *Entrance requirements:* For master's and Certificate, GRE General Test; for doctorate, GRE General Test, minimum GPA of 3.4; background in biology, physics, chemistry and calculus. Additional exam requirements/recommendations for international students: Required—TOEFL (minimum score 550 paper-based; 213 computer-based; 80 iBT). *Application deadline:* For fall admission, 2/15 priority date for domestic students, 2/15 for international students; for winter admission, 9/1 for international students; for spring admission, 2/1 for international students. Applications are processed on a rolling basis. Application fee: $95. Electronic applications accepted. *Expenses:* Tuition, state resident: full-time $16,402; part-time $665 per credit. Tuition, nonresident: full-time $28,694; part-time $1175 per credit. Required fees: $690; $175 per term. Tuition and fees vary according to program. *Financial support:* In 2009–10, 10 students received support, including 10 research assistantships with full tuition reimbursements available (averaging $24,000 per year); scholarships/grants and unspecified assistantships also available. *Faculty research:* Molecular toxicology, redox signaling, gene environment interaction, progenitor-progeny lineage, occupational and pulmonary medicine. Total annual research expenditures: $9.1 million. *Unit head:* Dr. Bruce R. Pitt, Chairman, 412-383-8400, Fax: 412-383-7658, E-mail: brucep@pitt.edu. *Application contact:* Eileen Penny Weiss, Student Affairs Administrator, 412-383-7297, Fax: 412-383-7658, E-mail: pweiss@pitt.edu.

University of Rochester, School of Nursing, Rochester, NY 14642. Offers acute care nurse practitioner (MS); adult nurse practitioner (MS); adult psychiatric mental health nurse practitioner (MS); adult/geriatric nurse practitioner (MS); care of children and families/pediatric nurse practitioner (MS); care of children and families/pediatric nurse practitioner with pediatric behavioral health (MS); care of children and families/pediatric nurse practitioner/neonatal nurse practitioner (MS); child and adolescent psychiatric mental health nurse practitioner (MS); clinical nurse leader (MS); disaster response and emergency preparedness (MS); family nurse practitioner (MS); health care organization management and leadership (MS); health practice research (PhD); health promotion, education and technology (MS); nursing (Certificate). *Accreditation:* AACN; NLN (one or more programs are accredited). Part-time programs available. Postbaccalaureate distance learning degree programs offered (minimal on-campus study). *Faculty:* 26 full-time (24 women), 20 part-time/adjunct (15 women). *Students:* 50 full-time (45 women), 178 part-time (165 women); includes 33 minority (17 African Americans, 2 American Indian/Alaska Native, 10 Asian Americans or Pacific Islanders, 4 Hispanic Americans), 11 international. Average age 35. 56 applicants, 80% accepted, 35 enrolled. In 2009, 53 master's, 5 doctorates awarded. Terminal master's awarded for partial completion of doctoral program. *Degree requirements:* For master's, comprehensive exam or thesis; for doctorate, thesis/dissertation. *Entrance requirements:* For master's, BS in nursing, minimum GPA of 3.0, course work in statistics; for doctorate, GRE General Test, MS in nursing, minimum GPA of 3.5; for Certificate, MS in nursing. Additional exam requirements/recommendations for international students: Recommended—TOEFL (minimum score 560 paper-based; 230 computer-based; 88 iBT). *Application deadline:* For fall admission, 11/1 priority date for domestic and international students. Application fee: $50. *Financial support:* In 2009–10, 53 students received support, including 14 fellowships with full and partial tuition reimbursements available (averaging $17,497 per year); scholarships/grants, traineeships, health care benefits, tuition waivers (partial), and unspecified assistantships also available. Support available to part-time students. Financial award application deadline: 6/30. *Faculty research:* Clinical research in aging, managing asthma in children, interventions to improve outcomes in critically ill children and their mothers, nurse home visitation studies, medical device evaluation, critical care clinical studies, high risk behavior and prevention, palliative care, pregnancy-related weight gain. Total annual research expenditures: $4.8 million. *Unit head:* Dr. Kathy P. Parker, Dean, 585-273-5639, Fax: 585-273-1268, E-mail: kathy_parker@urmc.rochester.edu. *Application contact:* Elaine Andolina, Director of Admissions, 585-275-2375, Fax: 585-756-8299, E-mail: elaine_andolina@urmc.rochester.edu.

Virginia Commonwealth University, Graduate School, College of Humanities and Sciences, Wilder School of Government and Public Affairs, Program in Homeland Security and Emergency Preparedness, Richmond, VA 23284-9005. Offers MA, Graduate Certificate. Postbaccalaureate distance learning degree programs offered.

West Chester University of Pennsylvania, Office of Graduate Studies, College of Health Sciences, Department of Health, West Chester, PA 19383. Offers emergency preparedness (Certificate); health care administration (Certificate); integrative health (Certificate); public health (MPH), including administration, community, environment, integrative, nutrition; school health (M Ed). *Accreditation:* CEPH. Part-time and evening/weekend programs available. *Students:* 15 full-time (9 women), 128 part-time (91 women); includes 41 minority (34 African Americans, 2 American Indian/Alaska Native, 5 Asian Americans or Pacific Islanders), 22 international. Average age 30. 83 applicants, 88% accepted, 41 enrolled. In 2009, 45 master's, 8 other advanced degrees awarded. *Degree requirements:* For master's, thesis (for some programs). *Entrance requirements:* For master's, one-page statement of career objectives, two letters of reference. Additional exam requirements/recommendations for international students: Required—TOEFL (minimum score 550 paper-based; 213 computer-based; 80 iBT). *Application deadline:* For fall admission, 4/15 priority date for domestic students, 3/15 for international students; for spring admission, 10/15 for domestic students, 9/1 for international students. Applications are processed on a rolling basis. Application fee: $35. Electronic applications accepted. *Expenses:* Tuition, state resident: full-time $6666; part-time $370 per credit. Tuition, nonresident: full-time $10,666; part-time $593 per credit. Required fees: $122.56 per credit. *Financial support:* In 2009–10, 11 research assistantships with full and partial tuition reimbursements (averaging $5,000 per year) were awarded; unspecified assistantships also available. Support available to part-time students. Financial award application deadline: 2/15; financial award applicants required to submit FAFSA. *Faculty research:* HIV/AIDS education, teacher preparation, water quality. *Unit head:* Dr. Roger Mustalish, Chair, 610-436-2931, E-mail: rmustalish@wcupa.edu. *Application contact:* Dr. Bethann Cinelli, Graduate Coordinator, 610-436-2267, E-mail: bcinelli@wcupa.edu.

York University, Faculty of Graduate Studies, Atkinson Faculty of Liberal and Professional Studies, Program in Disaster and Emergency Management, Toronto, ON M3J 1P3, Canada. Offers MA.

Homeland Security

American Public University System, AMU/APU Graduate Programs, Charles Town, WV 25414. Offers air warfare (MA Military Studies); American Revolution (MA Military Studies); business administration (MBA); Civil War (MA Military Studies); criminal justice (MA); defense management (MA Military Studies); emergency and disaster management (MA); environmental policy and management (MS); fire science management (MA); global engagement (MA); history (MA); homeland security (MA); humanities (MA); intelligence (MA Military Studies, MA Strategic Intelligence); international peace and conflict resolution (MA); international relations and conflict resolution (MA); joint warfare (MA Military Studies); land warfare international perspective (MA Military Studies); management (MA); military history (MA); military leadership (MA Military Studies); national security studies (MA); naval warfare international (MA Military Studies); naval warfare US (MA Military Studies); political science (MA); public administration (MA); public health (MA); security management (MA); space studies (MS); special ops/LIC (MA Military Studies); sports management (MA); transportation and logistics management (MA); transportation management (MA); unconventional warfare (MA Military Studies); World War II (MA Military Studies). Programs offered via distance learning only. Part-time and evening/weekend programs available. Postbaccalaureate distance learning degree programs offered (no on-campus study). *Faculty:* 10 full-time (3 women), 188 part-time/adjunct (57 women). *Students:* 340 full-time (98 women), 3,567 part-time (790 women); includes 615 minority (317 African Americans, 28 American Indian/Alaska Native, 85 Asian Americans or Pacific Islanders, 185 Hispanic Americans), 20 international. Average age 36. 2,123 applicants, 100% accepted, 893 enrolled. In 2009, 829 degrees awarded. *Degree requirements:* For master's, comprehensive exam. *Entrance requirements:* For master's, bachelor's degree or equivalent, minimum GPA of 2.7 in last 60 hours of course work. *Application deadline:* Applications are processed on a rolling basis. Application fee: $0. Electronic applications accepted. *Financial support:* Applicants required to submit FAFSA. *Faculty research:* Military history, criminal justice, management performance, national security. *Unit head:* Dr. Frank McCluskey, Provost, 877-468-6268, Fax: 304-724-3780. *Application contact:* Terry Grant, Director of Enrollment Management, 877-468-6268, Fax: 304-724-3780, E-mail: info@apus.edu.

Chaminade University of Honolulu, Graduate Services, Program in Criminal Justice Administration, Honolulu, HI 96816-1578. Offers criminal justice administration (MSCJA); homeland security (Certificate). Part-time and evening/weekend programs available. Postbaccalaureate distance learning degree programs offered (no on-campus study). *Degree requirements:* For master's, thesis optional. *Entrance requirements:* For master's, minimum undergraduate GPA of 3.0, 3 letters of recommendation. Additional exam requirements/recommendations for international students: Required—TOEFL (minimum score 550 paper-based). Electronic applications accepted. *Faculty research:* Penology, juvenile delinquency, multicultural and ethnic diversity in criminology, law enforcement administration and training, homeland security.

Drexel University, School of Technology and Professional Studies, Philadelphia, PA 19104-2875. Offers construction management (MS); engineering technology (MS); food science (MS); hospitality management (MS); professional studies: creativity studies (MS); professional studies: e-learning leadership (MS); professional studies: homeland security management (MS); project management (MS); property management (MS); sport management (MS). Postbaccalaureate distance learning degree programs offered.

Fairleigh Dickinson University, Metropolitan Campus, Anthony J. Petrocelli College of Continuing Studies, School of Administrative Science, Program in Homeland Security, Teaneck, NJ 07666-1914. Offers MSHS. *Students:* 5 full-time (1 woman), 28 part-time (5 women). Average age 35. 19 applicants, 84% accepted, 12 enrolled. In 2009, 3 master's awarded. *Application deadline:* Applications are processed on a rolling basis. Application fee: $40. *Unit head:* Dr. Paulette Laubsch, Head, 201-692-2000. *Application contact:* Susan Brooman, University Director of Graduate Admissions, 201-692-2554, Fax: 201-692-2560, E-mail: globaleducation@fdu.edu.

George Mason University, College of Humanities and Social Sciences, Department of Public and International Affairs, Fairfax, VA 22030. Offers association management (Certificate); biodefense (MS, PhD); critical analysis and strategic responses to terrorism (Certificate); nonprofit management (Certificate); political science (MA, PhD); public administration (MPA); public management (Certificate). *Accreditation:* NASPAA (one or more programs are accredited). *Faculty:* 37 full-time (14 women), 34 part-time/adjunct (7 women). *Students:* 115 full-time (62 women), 323 part-time (182 women); includes 60 minority (29 African Americans, 1 American Indian/Alaska Native, 18 Asian Americans or Pacific Islanders, 12 Hispanic Americans), 21 international. Average age 31. 458 applicants, 60% accepted, 129 enrolled. In 2009, 147 master's, 2 doctorates, 6 other advanced degrees awarded. *Entrance requirements:* For master's, GRE General Test, minimum GPA of 3.0 in last 60 hours of course work. Additional exam requirements/recommendations for international students: Required—TOEFL. *Application deadline:* For fall admission, 3/1 priority date for domestic students; for spring admission, 10/15 for domestic students. Application fee: $75. Electronic applications accepted. *Expenses:* Tuition, state resident: full-time $7568; part-time $315.33 per credit hour. Tuition, nonresident: full-time $21,704; part-time $904.33 per credit hour. Required fees: $2184; $91 per credit hour. *Financial support:* In 2009–10, 27 students received support, including 3 fellowships with full tuition reimbursements available (averaging $18,000 per year), 10 research assistantships with full and partial tuition reimbursements available (averaging $11,033 per year), 14 teaching assistantships with full and partial tuition reimbursements available (averaging $9,213 per year); Federal Work-Study, scholarships/grants, unspecified assistantships, and health care benefits (full-time research or teaching assistantship recipients) also available. Support available to part-time students. Financial award application deadline: 3/1; financial award applicants required to submit FAFSA. *Faculty research:* The Rehnquist Court and economic liberties; intersection of economic development with high-tech industry, telecommunications, and entrepreneurism; political economy of development; violence, terrorism and U.S. foreign policy; international security issues. Total annual research expenditures: $429,868. *Unit head:* Dr. Robert Dudley, Chair, 703-993-1400, Fax: 703-993-1399, E-mail: rdudley@gmu.edu. *Application contact:* Peg Koback, Information Contact, 703-993-9466, E-mail: mkoback@gmu.edu.

The Johns Hopkins University, Zanvyl Krieger School of Arts and Sciences, Advanced Academic Programs, Program in Government, Baltimore, MD 21218-2699. Offers government (MA); national securities study (Certificate); MA/MBA. Part-time and evening/weekend programs available. *Faculty:* 4 full-time (2 women), 35 part-time/adjunct (5 women). *Students:* 206 full-time (94 women), 240 part-time (103 women); includes 96 minority (39 African Americans, 3 American Indian/Alaska Native, 21 Asian Americans or Pacific Islanders, 33 Hispanic Americans), 13 international. Average age 29. 144 applicants, 73% accepted, 92 enrolled. In 2009, 85 master's awarded. *Degree requirements:* For master's, thesis. *Entrance requirements:* For master's, minimum GPA of 3.0. Additional exam requirements/recommendations for international students: Required—TOEFL (minimum score 250 computer-based; 100 iBT). *Application deadline:* For fall admission, 5/31 priority date for domestic students, 4/30 priority date for international students; for spring admission, 10/31 priority date for domestic and international students. Applications are processed on a rolling basis. Application fee: $75. Electronic applications accepted. *Financial support:* Applicants required to submit FAFSA. *Unit head:* Dr. Kathy Wagner, Associate Program Chair, 202-452-1953, E-mail: kwagner@jhu.edu. *Application contact:* Valana M. McMickens, Admissions Manager, 202-452-1941, Fax: 202-452-1970, E-mail: aapadmissions@jhu.edu.

Long Island University at Riverhead, Homeland Security Management Institute, Riverhead, NY 11901. Offers MS, Advanced Certificate. Part-time programs available. Postbaccalaureate distance learning degree programs offered (no on-campus study). *Faculty:* 2 full-time (0 women), 10 part-time/adjunct (1 woman). *Students:* 5 full-time (0 women), 107 part-time (17 women); includes 16 minority (8 African Americans, 1 American Indian/Alaska Native, 2 Asian Americans or Pacific Islanders, 5 Hispanic Americans). 48 applicants, 56% accepted, 23 enrolled. In 2009, 11 master's, 36 other advanced degrees awarded. *Degree requirements:* For master's, thesis. *Entrance requirements:* For master's, minimum GPA of 3.0, 2 letters of reference. *Application deadline:* Applications are processed on a rolling basis. Application fee: $0. Electronic applications accepted. *Financial support:* In 2009–10, 105 students received support. Career-related internships or fieldwork and scholarships/grants available. Support available to part-time students. Financial award applicants required to submit FAFSA. *Unit head:* Dr. Vincent E. Henry, Unit Head, 631-287-8010, Fax: 631-287-8130, E-mail: vincent.henry@liu.edu. *Application contact:* Andrea Borra, Admissions Counselor, 631-287-8010 Ext. 8326, Fax: 631-287-8253, E-mail: andrea.borra@liu.edu.

Monmouth University, Graduate School, Department of Criminal Justice, West Long Branch, NJ 07764-1898. Offers criminal justice administration (MA, Certificate); homeland security (Certificate). Part-time and evening/weekend programs available. *Faculty:* 3 full-time (0 women), 3 part-time/adjunct (2 women). *Students:* 21 full-time (11 women), 19 part-time (10 women); includes 7 minority (1 African American, 1 Asian American or Pacific Islander, 5 Hispanic Americans), 1 international. Average age 27. 36 applicants, 97% accepted, 23 enrolled. In 2009, 14 master's awarded. *Degree requirements:* For master's, comprehensive exam, thesis or alternative. *Entrance requirements:* For master's, minimum GPA of 3.0 in major, 2.5 overall.

Homeland Security

Monmouth University (continued)
Additional exam requirements/recommendations for international students: Required—TOEFL (minimum score 550 paper-based; 213 computer-based; 79 iBT), IELTS (minimum score 5), Michigan English Language Assessment Battery (minimum score 77), Cambridge A, B, C. *Application deadline:* For fall admission, 7/15 priority date for domestic students, 6/1 for international students; for spring admission, 11/15 priority date for domestic students, 11/1 for international students. Applications are processed on a rolling basis. Application fee: $50. Electronic applications accepted. *Expenses:* Tuition: Part-time $773 per credit. Required fees: $157 per semester. *Financial support:* In 2009–10, 25 students received support, including 20 fellowships (averaging $1,915 per year), 2 research assistantships (averaging $6,668 per year); career-related internships or fieldwork, scholarships/grants, and unspecified assistantships also available. Support available to part-time students. Financial award applicants required to submit FAFSA. *Faculty research:* Violent crimes, criminal pathology, terrorism, computer crime, comparative criminal justice systems. *Unit head:* Dr. Gregory Coram, Director, 732-571-3448, Fax: 732-263-5148, E-mail: coram@monmouth.edu. *Application contact:* Kevin Roane, Director, Office of Graduate Admission, 732-571-3452, Fax: 732-263-5123, E-mail: gradadm@monmouth.edu.

National Defense University, College of International Security Affairs, Washington, DC 20319-5066. Offers strategic security studies (MA), including conflict management, counterterrorism, homeland defense/ security, international security studies. Part-time and evening/weekend programs available. *Degree requirements:* For master's, thesis. *Entrance requirements:* Additional exam requirements/recommendations for international students: Required—TOEFL.

National University, Academic Affairs, School of Engineering and Technology, Department of Applied Engineering, La Jolla, CA 92037-1011. Offers database administration (MS); engineering management (MS); environmental engineering (MS); homeland security and safety engineering (MS); system engineering (MS); wireless communications (MS). Part-time and evening/weekend programs available. Postbaccalaureate distance learning degree programs offered (no on-campus study). *Faculty:* 6 full-time (1 woman), 7 part-time/adjunct (1 woman). *Students:* 61 full-time (16 women), 176 part-time (35 women); includes 54 minority (11 African Americans, 1 American Indian/Alaska Native, 23 Asian Americans or Pacific Islanders, 19 Hispanic Americans), 117 international. Average age 31. 133 applicants, 100% accepted, 83 enrolled. In 2009, 34 master's awarded. *Degree requirements:* For master's, thesis. *Entrance requirements:* For master's, interview, minimum GPA of 2.5. Additional exam requirements/recommendations for international students: Required—TOEFL (minimum score 550 paper-based; 213 computer-based; 79 iBT), IELTS (minimum score 6). *Application deadline:* Applications are processed on a rolling basis. Application fee: $60 ($65 for international students). Electronic applications accepted. *Expenses:* Tuition: Part-time $338 per quarter hour. *Financial support:* Career-related internships or fieldwork, institutionally sponsored loans, scholarships/grants, and tuition waivers (partial) available. Support available to part-time students. Financial award application deadline: 6/30; financial award applicants required to submit FAFSA. *Unit head:* Dr. Shekar Viswanathan, Chair and Associate Professor, 858-309-8416, Fax: 858-309-3420, E-mail: sviswana@nu.edu. *Application contact:* Dominick Giovanniello, Associate Regional Dean—San Diego, 800-NAT-UNIV, Fax: 858-541-7792, E-mail: dgiovann@nu.edu.

Pace University, Dyson College of Arts and Sciences, Department of Public Administration, New York, NY 10038. Offers environmental management (MPA); government management (MPA); health care administration (MPA); management for public safety and homeland security (MA); nonprofit management (MPA); JD/MPA. Offered at White Plains, NY location only. Part-time and evening/weekend programs available. *Faculty:* 4 full-time, 6 part-time/adjunct. *Students:* 52 full-time (31 women), 75 part-time (49 women); includes 47 minority (28 African Americans, 1 American Indian/Alaska Native, 1 Asian American or Pacific Islander, 17 Hispanic Americans), 8 international. Average age 30. 75 applicants, 100% accepted, 43 enrolled. In 2009, 38 master's awarded. *Degree requirements:* For master's, capstone project. *Entrance requirements:* For master's, GRE General Test. Additional exam requirements/recommendations for international students: Required—TOEFL. *Application deadline:* For fall admission, 8/1 priority date for domestic students; for spring admission, 12/1 priority date for domestic students. Applications are processed on a rolling basis. Application fee: $70. Electronic applications accepted. *Expenses:* Tuition: Part-time $954 per credit. Tuition and fees vary according to course load, degree level and program. *Financial support:* Research assistantships, career-related internships or fieldwork, Federal Work-Study, and tuition waivers (partial) available. Support available to part-time students. Financial award applicants required to submit FAFSA. *Unit head:* Dr. Farrokh Hormozi, Chairperson, 914-422-4285, E-mail: fhormozi@pace.edu. *Application contact:* Joanna Broda, Director of Admissions, 914-422-4283, Fax: 914-422-4287, E-mail: gradwp@pace.edu.

Regent University, Graduate School, Robertson School of Government, Virginia Beach, VA 23464. Offers american government (MA); global politics (MA); health care policy and administration (MA); international politics (MA); law and public policy (MA); Mid-East Politics (MA); political leadership and management (MA); political management (MA); political theory (MA); public administration (MA); public policy (MA); terrorism and homeland defense (MA); world economies and political development (MA); JD/MA; M Div/MA; M Ed/MA; MBA/MA. Part-time and evening/weekend programs available. Postbaccalaureate distance learning degree programs offered (minimal on-campus study). *Faculty:* 6 full-time (2 women), 11 part-time/adjunct (1 woman). *Students:* 77 full-time (55 women), 65 part-time (36 women); includes 47 minority (38 African Americans, 2 Asian Americans or Pacific Islanders, 7 Hispanic Americans), 4 international. Average age 30. 131 applicants, 65% accepted, 54 enrolled. In 2009, 51 master's awarded. *Degree requirements:* For master's, thesis optional, internship. *Entrance requirements:* For master's, GRE General Test or LSAT, minimum undergraduate GPA of 3.0, writing sample, resume, interview, references. Additional exam requirements/recommendations for international students: Required—TOEFL (minimum score 577 paper-based; 233 computer-based). *Application deadline:* For fall admission, 5/1 priority date for domestic students; for spring admission, 11/1 priority date for domestic students. Applications are processed on a rolling basis. Application fee: $50. Electronic applications accepted. *Expenses:* Contact institution. *Financial support:* In 2009–10, 130 students received support. Career-related internships or fieldwork, scholarships/grants, tuition waivers (full and partial), and unspecified assistantships available. Support available to part-time students. Financial award application deadline: 9/1; financial award applicants required to submit FAFSA. *Faculty research:* Education reform, political character issues, social capital concerns, administrative ethics, Biblical law and public policy. *Unit head:* Dr. Charles W. Dunn, Dean, 757-352-4322, Fax: 757-352-4643, E-mail: cwdunn@regent.edu. *Application contact:* Matthew Chadwick, Director of Admissions, 800-373-5504, Fax: 757-352-4381, E-mail: admissions@regent.edu.

Saint Joseph's University, College of Arts and Sciences, Programs in Public Safety and Management, Philadelphia, PA 19131-1395. Offers homeland security (MS, Certificate); public safety management (MS, Certificate). Part-time and evening/weekend programs available. *Students:* 64 part-time (3 women); includes 14 minority (10 African Americans, 2 Asian Americans or Pacific Islanders, 2 Hispanic Americans). Average age 40. In 2009, 18 master's awarded. *Entrance requirements:* For master's, GRE (if GPA less than 2.75), minimum GPA of 2.75, 2 letters of recommendation, resume. Additional exam requirements/recommendations for international students: Required—TOEFL (minimum score 550 paper-based; 213 computer-based; 79 iBT). *Application deadline:* For fall admission, 7/15 priority date for domestic students, 4/15 for international students; for winter admission, 1/15 for international students; for spring admission, 11/15 priority date for domestic students, 10/15 for international students. Applications are processed on a rolling basis. Application fee: $35. Electronic applications accepted. *Expenses:* Tuition: Part-time $729 per credit hour. Tuition and fees vary according to degree level and program. *Financial support:* Applicants required to submit FAFSA. *Unit head:* Patricia Griffin, Director, 610-660-1294, E-mail: pgriffin@sju.edu. *Application contact:* Kate McConnell, Assistant Director of Graduate Admissions, 610-660-3184, Fax: 610-660-3230, E-mail: kate.mcconnell@sju.edu.

Salve Regina University, Graduate Studies, Program in International Relations, Newport, RI 02840-4192. Offers homeland security (Certificate); international relations (MA, Certificate). Part-time and evening/weekend programs available. Postbaccalaureate distance learning degree programs offered (minimal on-campus study). *Faculty:* 3 full-time (0 women), 5 part-time/adjunct (2 women). *Students:* 11 full-time (6 women), 62 part-time (25 women); includes 3 minority (all Hispanic Americans), 1 international. Average age 34. 66 applicants, 56% accepted, 35 enrolled. In 2009, 35 master's awarded. *Entrance requirements:* For master's, GMAT, GRE General Test, MAT or LSAT. Additional exam requirements/recommendations for international students: Required—TOEFL (minimum score 600 paper-based; 250 computer-based; 100 iBT), IELTS. *Application deadline:* For fall admission, 3/15 priority date for domestic and international students; for spring admission, 9/15 priority date for domestic and international students. Applications are processed on a rolling basis. Application fee: $60. Electronic applications accepted. *Expenses:* Tuition: Part-time $395 per credit. Part-time tuition and fees vary according to degree level. *Financial support:* Career-related internships or fieldwork and Federal Work-Study available. Support available to part-time students. Financial award application deadline: 3/1; financial award applicants required to submit FAFSA. *Unit head:* Dr. Symeon Giannakos, Director, 401-341-3177, Fax: 401-341-2993, E-mail: symeon.giannakos@salve.edu. *Application contact:* Kelly Alverson, Graduate Admissions Counselor, 401-341-2153, Fax: 401-341-2973, E-mail: kelly.alverson@salve.edu.

Salve Regina University, Graduate Studies, Programs in Administration of Justice, Newport, RI 02840-4192. Offers justice and homeland security (MS); law enforcement leadership (MS). Part-time and evening/weekend programs available. *Faculty:* 2 full-time (0 women), 9 part-time/adjunct (1 woman). *Students:* 26 full-time (14 women), 39 part-time (6 women); includes 2 minority (1 African American, 1 Hispanic American). Average age 30. 13 applicants, 69% accepted, 9 enrolled. In 2009, 17 master's awarded. *Entrance requirements:* For master's, GMAT, GRE General Test, or MAT. Additional exam requirements/recommendations for international students: Required—TOEFL (minimum score 600 paper-based; 250 computer-based; 100 iBT). *Application deadline:* For fall admission, 3/5 priority date for domestic students, 3/15 priority date for international students; for spring admission, 9/15 priority date for domestic students, 9/5 priority date for international students. Applications are processed on a rolling basis. Application fee: $60. Electronic applications accepted. *Expenses:* Tuition: Part-time $395 per credit. Part-time tuition and fees vary according to degree level. *Financial support:* Career-related internships or fieldwork and Federal Work-Study available. Support available to part-time students. Financial award application deadline: 3/1; financial award applicants required to submit FAFSA. *Unit head:* Dr. Daniel Knight, Director, 401-341-3255, E-mail: knightd@salve.edu. *Application contact:* Kelly Alverson, Graduate Admissions Counselor, 401-341-2153, Fax: 401-341-2973, E-mail: kelly.alverson@salve.edu.

Texas A&M University, George Bush School of Government and Public Service, College Station, TX 77843. Offers advanced international affairs (Certificate); homeland security (Certificate); international affairs (MPIA), including international economics and development, national security affairs; nonprofit management (Certificate); public service and administration (MPSA), including public management, public policy analysis. *Accreditation:* NASPAA. *Faculty:* 51. *Students:* 209 full-time (97 women), 93 part-time (43 women); includes 48 minority (15 African Americans, 5 Asian Americans or Pacific Islanders, 28 Hispanic Americans), 19 international. Average age 24. In 2009, 87 master's awarded. *Degree requirements:* For master's, summer internship. *Entrance requirements:* For master's, GRE (preferred) or GMAT. *Application deadline:* For fall admission, 1/24 for domestic and international students. Application fee: $50 ($75 for international students). Electronic applications accepted. *Expenses:* Tuition, state resident: full-time $3991; part-time $221.74 per credit hour. Tuition, nonresident: full-time $9049; part-time $502.74 per credit hour. *Financial support:* In 2009–10, fellowships (averaging $11,000 per year), research assistantships (averaging $11,250 per year) were awarded; career-related internships or fieldwork, Federal Work-Study, and institutionally sponsored loans also available. Financial award application deadline: 2/1; financial award applicants required to submit FAFSA. *Faculty research:* Public policy, presidential studies, public leadership, economic policy, social policy. *Unit head:* A. Benton Cocanougher, Interim Dean, 979-862-8842, E-mail: bushschool@tamu.edu. *Application contact:* Kathryn Meyer, Recruitment and Placement Officer, 979-458-4767, Fax: 979-845-4155, E-mail: admissions@bushschool.tamu.edu.

Thomas Edison State College, Heavin School of Arts and Sciences, Program in Homeland Security, Trenton, NJ 08608-1176. Offers Graduate Certificate. Part-time programs available. Postbaccalaureate distance learning degree programs offered (no on-campus study). *Students:* 30 part-time (7 women); includes 6 minority (3 African Americans, 1 Asian American or Pacific Islander, 2 Hispanic Americans). Average age 39. In 2009, 5 Graduate Certificates awarded. *Entrance requirements:* Additional exam requirements/recommendations for international students: Required—TOEFL (minimum score 550 paper-based; 213 computer-based; 79 iBT). *Application deadline:* For fall admission, 8/15 priority date for domestic and international students; for winter admission, 11/15 priority date for domestic and international students; for spring admission, 2/15 priority date for domestic and international students. Applications are processed on a rolling basis. Application fee: $75. Electronic applications accepted. *Expenses:* Tuition, area resident: Part-time $479 per credit. Tuition, state resident: part-time $479 per credit. Tuition, nonresident: part-time $479 per credit. *Financial support:* Applicants required to submit FAFSA. *Unit head:* Dr. Susan Davenport, Dean, Heavin School of Arts and Sciences, 609-984-1130, Fax: 609-984-0740, E-mail: info@tesc.edu. *Application contact:* David Hoftiezer, Director of Admissions, 888-442-8372, Fax: 609-984-8447, E-mail: admissions@tesc.edu.

Tiffin University, Program in Criminal Justice, Tiffin, OH 44883-2161. Offers crime analysis (MSCJ); criminal behavior (MSCJ); forensic psychology (MSCJ); homeland security administration (MSCJ); justice administration (MSCJ). Part-time and evening/weekend programs available. Postbaccalaureate distance learning degree programs offered (no on-campus study). *Degree requirements:* For master's, thesis optional. *Entrance requirements:* For master's, minimum undergraduate GPA of 2.5, work experience. Additional exam requirements/recommendations for international students: Required—TOEFL (minimum score 550 paper-based; 213 computer-based). Electronic applications accepted. *Faculty research:* Terrorism, intelligence, homeland security, guns and crime.

Towson University, College of Graduate Studies and Research, Program in Integrated Homeland Security Management, Towson, MD 21252-0001. Offers integrated homeland security management (MS); security assessment and management (Certificate). Part-time and evening/weekend programs available. *Entrance requirements:* For master's, BA in related field, 3 years related work experience, resume.

University of Central Florida, College of Health and Public Affairs, Department of Public Administration, Orlando, FL 32816. Offers emergency management and homeland security (Certificate); non-profit management (MNM, Certificate); public administration (MPA, Certificate); urban and regional planning (Certificate). *Accreditation:* NASPAA. Part-time and evening/weekend programs available. *Faculty:* 11 full-time (2 women), 6 part-time/adjunct (1 woman). *Students:* 68 full-time (45 women), 235 part-time (166 women); includes 105 minority (64 African Americans, 10 Asian Americans or Pacific Islanders, 31 Hispanic Americans), 7 international. Average age 31. 184 applicants, 75% accepted, 95 enrolled. In 2009, 80 master's, 36 other advanced degrees awarded. *Degree requirements:* For master's, comprehensive exam, thesis or alternative, research report. *Entrance requirements:* For master's, GRE General Test. *Application deadline:* For fall admission, 7/1 for domestic students; for spring admission, 12/1 for domestic students. Application fee: $30. Electronic applications accepted. *Expenses:* Tuition, state resident: part-time $306.31 per credit hour. Tuition, nonresident: part-time $1099.01 per credit hour. Part-time tuition and fees vary according to degree level and program. *Financial support:* In 2009–10, 8 students received support, including 4 fellowships with partial tuition reimbursements available (averaging $10,000 per year), 2 research assistantships with partial tuition reimbursements available (averaging $3,100 per year), 3 teaching assistantships with partial tuition reimbursements available (averaging $5,200 per year); career-related internships or fieldwork, Federal Work-Study, institutionally sponsored loans, tuition waivers (partial), and unspecified assistantships also available. Financial award application deadline: 3/1; financial award applicants required to submit FAFSA. *Unit head:* Dr. MaryAnn Feldheim, Chair, 407-823-3693, Fax: 407-823-5651. *Application contact:* Dr. MaryAnn Feldheim, Chair, 407-823-3693, Fax: 407-823-5651.

University of Connecticut, Graduate School, Center for Continuing Studies, Program in Homeland Security Leadership, Storrs, CT 06269. Offers MPS. *Students:* 24 part-time (4 women); includes 3 minority (1 African American, 2 Hispanic Americans). Average age 37. 21 applicants, 67% accepted, 13 enrolled. In 2009, 3 master's awarded. *Expenses:* Tuition, state resident: full-time $4725; part-time $525 per credit. Tuition, nonresident: full-time $12,267; part-time $1363 per credit. Required fees: $346 per semester. Tuition and fees vary according to course load. *Application contact:* Peter Diplock, Information Contact, 860-486-2915, E-mail: peter.diplock@uconn.edu.

University of New Haven, Graduate School, Henry C. Lee College of Criminal Justice and Forensic Sciences, National Security and Public Safety Program, West Haven, CT 06516-1916. Offers information protection and security (MS); national security (Certificate); national security administration (Certificate). Part-time and evening/weekend programs available. *Faculty:* 8 full-time (2 women), 5 part-time/adjunct (0 women). *Students:* 34 full-time (10 women), 39 part-time (21 women); includes 19 minority (4 African Americans, 1 American Indian/Alaska Native, 4 Asian Americans or Pacific Islanders, 10 Hispanic Americans), 4 international. Average age 32. 39 applicants, 100% accepted, 33 enrolled. In 2009, 51 master's, 5 other advanced degrees awarded. *Entrance requirements:* Additional exam requirements/recommendations for international students: Required—TOEFL (minimum score 520 paper-based; 190 computer-based; 70 iBT); Recommended—IELTS (minimum score 5.5). *Application deadline:* For fall admission, 5/31 for international students; for winter admission, 10/15 for international students; for spring admission, 1/15 for international students. Applications are processed on a rolling basis. Application fee: $50. Electronic applications accepted. *Expenses:* Tuition: Part-time $700 per credit. Required fees: $45 per term. One-time fee: $390 part-time. *Financial support:* Research assistantships with partial tuition reimbursements, teaching assistantships with partial tuition reimbursements, career-related internships or fieldwork, Federal Work-Study, scholarships/grants, tuition waivers, and unspecified assistantships available. Support available to part-time students. Financial award applicants required to submit FAFSA. *Unit head:* Dr. William L. Tafoya, Dean, 203-932-7260. *Application contact:* Eloise Gormley, Director of Graduate Admissions, 203-932-7449, Fax: 203-932-7137, E-mail: gradinfo@newhaven.edu.

University of Oklahoma—Tulsa, College of Public Health, Tulsa, OK 74135-2512. Offers general public health (MPH); health administration and policy (MPH); public health preparedness and terrorism (MPH).

The University of Texas at El Paso, Graduate School, Institute for Policy and Economic Development, El Paso, TX 79968-0001. Offers border administration (Certificate); homeland security (Certificate); intelligence and national security (MS, Certificate); leadership studies (MA); public administration (MPA). *Accreditation:* NASPAA. Part-time and evening/weekend programs available. *Students:* 187 (57 women); includes 124 minority (19 African Americans, 1 American Indian/Alaska Native, 5 Asian Americans or Pacific Islanders, 99 Hispanic Americans), 5 international. 142 applicants, 77% accepted. In 2009, 76 master's awarded. *Degree requirements:* For master's, thesis optional. *Entrance requirements:* For master's, GRE, Statement of Purpose, Letters of Recommendation. Additional exam requirements/recommendations for international students: Required—TOEFL; Recommended—IELTS. *Application deadline:* For fall admission, 8/1 for domestic students, 3/1 for international students; for spring admission, 10/1 for domestic students, 9/1 for international students. Applications are processed on a rolling basis. Application fee: $45 ($80 for international students). Electronic applications accepted. *Financial support:* Fellowships with partial tuition reimbursements, research assistantships with partial tuition reimbursements, teaching assistantships with partial tuition reimbursements, institutionally sponsored loans, scholarships/grants, health care benefits, tuition waivers (partial), and unspecified assistantships available. Support available to part-time students. Financial award application deadline: 3/15; financial award applicants required to submit FAFSA. *Unit head:* Dr. Dennis Soden, Director, 915-747-7974, Fax: 915-747-7948, E-mail: desoden@utep.edu. *Application contact:* Dr. Patricia D. Witherspoon, Dean of the Graduate School, 915-747-5491, Fax: 915-747-5788, E-mail: withersp@utep.edu.

The University of Toledo, College of Graduate Studies, College of Medicine, Department of Public Health and Homeland Security, Toledo, OH 43606-3390. Offers occupational health (MSOH, Certificate); public health (MPH, Certificate), including biostatistics and epidemiology (Certificate), emergency response (Certificate), global health (Certificate), public health (MPH); MD/MPH. Part-time programs available. *Degree requirements:* For master's, thesis, qualifying exam. *Entrance requirements:* For master's, GRE. *Faculty research:* Hypertension, endocrinology, molecular biology.

Upper Iowa University, Online Master's Programs, Fayette, IA 52142-1857. Offers accounting (MBA); corporate financial management (MBA); global business (MBA); health and human services (MPA); higher education administration (MHEA); homeland security (MPA); human resources management (MBA); justice administration (MPA); organizational development (MBA); public personnel management (MPA); quality management (MBA). MBA also available at Madison, WI campus. Part-time programs available. Postbaccalaureate distance learning degree programs offered (no on-campus study). *Faculty:* 3 full-time (0 women), 66 part-time/adjunct (27 women). *Students:* 723 full-time (442 women). *Degree requirements:* For master's, research project. *Entrance requirements:* For master's, GMAT, GRE, or minimum GPA of 2.7 during last 60 hours. Additional exam requirements/recommendations for international students: Required—TOEFL (minimum score 570 paper-based; 230 computer-based). *Application deadline:* Applications are processed on a rolling basis. Application fee: $50. Electronic applications accepted. *Expenses:* Tuition: Full-time $6948; part-time $386 per credit hour. *Financial support:* Available to part-time students. Applicants required to submit FAFSA. *Faculty research:* Total quality management, CQI, teams, organization culture and climate, management. *Application contact:* David Hannum, Admissions Advisor, 800-603-3756, E-mail: hannumd@uiu.edu.

Virginia Commonwealth University, Graduate School, College of Humanities and Sciences, Wilder School of Government and Public Affairs, Program in Homeland Security and Emergency Preparedness, Richmond, VA 23284-9005. Offers MA, Graduate Certificate. Postbaccalaureate distance learning degree programs offered.

Walden University, Graduate Programs, School of Psychology, Minneapolis, MN 55401. Offers clinical child psychology (Post-Doctoral Certificate); clinical psychology (Post-Doctoral Certificate); counseling psychology (Post-Doctoral Certificate); forensic psychology (MS), including forensic psychology in the community, general program, mental health applications, program planning and evaluation in forensic settings, psychology and legal systems; general psychology (Post-Doctoral Certificate); health psychology (Post-Doctoral Certificate); organizational psychology (Post-Doctoral Certificate); organizational psychology and development (Postbaccalaureate Certificate); psychology (MS, PhD), including clinical psychology (PhD), counseling psychology (PhD), crisis management and response (MS), general program (MS), general psychology (PhD), health psychology, leadership development and coaching (MS), media psychology (MS), organizational psychology (PhD), organizational psychology and development (MS), organizational psychology and nonprofit management (MS), program evaluation and research (MS), psychology of culture (MS), psychology, public administration, and social change (MS), social psychology (MS), terrorism and security (MS); teaching online (Post-Master's Certificate). Part-time and evening/weekend programs available. Postbaccalaureate distance learning degree programs offered (minimal on-campus study). *Faculty:* 33 full-time, 222 part-time/adjunct. *Students:* 3,546 full-time (2,761 women), 1,133 part-time (908 women); includes 1,723 minority (1,319 African Americans, 56 American Indian/Alaska Native, 101 Asian Americans or Pacific Islanders, 247 Hispanic Americans), 80 international. Average age 41. In 2009, 495 master's, 70 doctorates, 2 other advanced degrees awarded. Terminal master's awarded for partial completion of doctoral program. *Degree requirements:* For master's, thesis optional; for doctorate, thesis/dissertation, residency. *Entrance requirements:* For master's, bachelor's degree or equivalent in related field; minimum GPA of 2.5; official transcripts; goal statement; access to computer and Internet; for doctorate, master's degree or equivalent in related field; minimum GPA of 3.0;3 years of related professional/academic experience (preferred). Additional exam requirements/recommendations for international students: Required—TOEFL (minimum score 550 paper-based; 213 computer-based), IELTS (minimum score 6.5), or Michigan English Language Assessment Battery (minimum score 82). *Application deadline:* Applications are processed on a rolling basis. Application fee: $50. Electronic applications accepted. *Expenses:* Tuition: Full-time $13,665; part-time $560 per credit. Required fees: $1375. Tuition and fees vary according to course load, degree level and program. *Financial support:* In 2009–10, 290 students received support; fellowships, Federal Work-Study, scholarships/grants, unspecified assistantships, and family tuition reduction, active duty/veteran tuition reduction, group tuition reduction, interest-free payment plans available. Support available to part-time students. Financial award applicants required to submit FAFSA. *Unit head:* Dr. Melanie Storms, Associate Dean, 800-925-3368. *Application contact:* Jennifer Hall, Director of Enrollment, 866-4-WALDEN, E-mail: info@waldenu.edu.

Walden University, Graduate Programs, School of Public Policy and Administration, Minneapolis, MN 55401. Offers general program (MPA); government management (Postbaccalaureate Certificate); health policy (MPA); homeland security policy (MPA); interdisciplinary policy studies (MPA); law and public policy (MPA); local government management for sustainable communities (MPA); nonprofit management (Postbaccalaureate Certificate); nonprofit management and leadership (MPA, MS); policy analysis (MPA); public management and leadership (MPA); public policy and administration (PhD), including criminal justice, health services, homeland security policy and coordination, international nongovernmental organizations, law and public policy, local government management for sustainable communities, nonprofit management and leadership, public management and leadership, public policy, public safety management, terrorism, mediation, and peace; terrorism, mediation, and peace (MPA). Part-time and evening/weekend programs available. Postbaccalaureate distance learning degree programs offered (minimal on-campus study). *Faculty:* 7 full-time, 62 part-time/adjunct. *Students:* 1,468 full-time (941 women), 233 part-time (162 women); includes 852 minority (761 African Americans, 9 American Indian/Alaska Native, 19 Asian Americans or Pacific Islanders, 63 Hispanic Americans), 53 international. Average age 40. In 2009, 173 master's, 13 doctorates awarded. *Degree requirements:* For doctorate, thesis/dissertation, residency. *Entrance requirements:* For master's, bachelor's degree or equivalent in related field, minimum GPA of 2.5; for doctorate, master's degree or equivalent in related field; minimum GPA of 3.0; official transcripts; three years of related professional/academic experience (preferred); access to computer and Internet. Additional exam requirements/recommendations for international students: Required—TOEFL (minimum score 550 paper-based; 213 computer-based), IELTS (minimum score 6.5), or Michigan English Language Assessment Battery (minimum score 82). *Application deadline:* Applications are processed on a rolling basis. Application fee: $50. Electronic applications accepted. *Expenses:* Tuition: Full-time $13,665; part-time $560 per credit. Required fees: $1375. Tuition and fees vary according to course load, degree level and program. *Financial support:* In 2009–10, 207 students received support; fellowships with tuition reimbursements available, Federal Work-Study, scholarships/grants, unspecified assistantships, and family tuition reduction, active duty/veteran tuition reduction, group tuition reduction, interest-free payment plans available. Support available to part-time students. Financial award applicants required to submit FAFSA. *Unit head:* Dr. Mark Gordon, Associate Dean, 800-925-3368. *Application contact:* Jennifer Hall, Director of Enrollment, 866-4-WALDEN, E-mail: info@waldenu.edu.

Wayland Baptist University, Graduate Programs, Program in Counseling, Plainview, TX 79072-6998. Offers counseling (MA); government administration (MPA); homeland security (MPA); justice administration (MPA). Part-time and evening/weekend programs available. Postbaccalaureate distance learning degree programs offered. *Faculty:* 9 full-time (2 women). *Students:* 71 part-time (58 women); includes 16 minority (5 African Americans, 1 American Indian/Alaska Native, 10 Hispanic Americans). Average age 34. 21 applicants, 90% accepted, 11 enrolled. In 2009, 16 master's awarded. *Degree requirements:* For master's, comprehensive exam. *Entrance requirements:* For master's, GRE, MAT. Additional exam requirements/recommendations for international students: Required—TOEFL (minimum score 500 paper-based; 173 computer-based; 61 iBT). *Application deadline:* Applications are processed on a rolling basis. Application fee: $50. Electronic applications accepted. *Expenses:* Tuition: Full-time $5796; part-time $322 per credit hour. Required fees: $782; $9 per credit hour. $60 per semester. Tuition and fees vary according to course load and campus/location. *Financial support:* Federal Work-Study, institutionally sponsored loans, and scholarships/grants available. Support available to part-time students. Financial award application deadline: 5/1; financial award applicants required to submit FAFSA. *Unit head:* Dr. Estelle Owens, Chairman, 806-291-1171, Fax: 806-291-1972, E-mail: owensest@wbu.edu. *Application contact:* Amanda Stanton, Graduate Studies, 806-291-3423, Fax: 806-291-1950, E-mail: stanton@wbu.edu.

Wilmington University, College of Business, New Castle, DE 19720-6491. Offers business administration (MBA); finance (MBA); health care administration (MBA, MS); homeland security (MBA, MS); human resource management (MS); management (MS); management information systems (MBA); organizational leadership (MS); public administration (MS); transportation and logistics (MBA, MS). Part-time and evening/weekend programs available. *Entrance requirements:* Additional exam requirements/recommendations for international students: Required—TOEFL (minimum score 500 paper-based; 173 computer-based). Electronic applications accepted.

Industrial and Labor Relations

Bernard M. Baruch College of the City University of New York, Zicklin School of Business, Zicklin Executive Programs, Baruch Executive Master of Science in Industrial and Labor Relations Program, New York, NY 10010-5585. Offers MS. Part-time and evening/weekend programs available. *Entrance requirements:* For master's, professional experience in HR or labor relations. Additional exam requirements/recommendations for international students: Required—TOEFL. *Expenses:* Contact institution.

Carnegie Mellon University, College of Humanities and Social Sciences, Department of History, Pittsburgh, PA 15213-3891. Offers African and African-American diaspora (PhD); culture and power (PhD); gender and the family (PhD); history (MA, MS); history and policy (MA); labor and politics (PhD); science, technology, medicine and environment (PhD). Part-time programs available. *Degree requirements:* For doctorate, oral and written comprehensive exams, dissertation defense. *Entrance requirements:* For doctorate, GRE General Test. Additional

Industrial and Labor Relations

Carnegie Mellon University (continued)
exam requirements/recommendations for international students: Required—TOEFL. Electronic applications accepted. *Faculty research:* Anthropology and history, African American history, technology/environment, cultural history analysis.

Case Western Reserve University, Weatherhead School of Management, Department of Marketing and Policy Studies, Division of Labor and Human Resource Policy, Cleveland, OH 44106. Offers MBA. Part-time and evening/weekend programs available. *Entrance requirements:* For master's, GMAT. *Application deadline:* Applications are processed on a rolling basis. Application fee: $100. *Financial support:* Career-related internships or fieldwork, Federal Work-Study, institutionally sponsored loans, and tuition waivers (full and partial) available. Financial award application deadline: 5/1. *Faculty research:* Strategic human resource management, negotiations and conflict management, human resources in high performance organizations, international human resources management, union management relations and collective bargaining. *Unit head:* Dr. Paul F. Gerhart, Head, 216-368-2045, E-mail: pfg2@po.cwru.edu. *Application contact:* Dr. Paul F. Gerhart, Head, 216-368-2045, E-mail: pfg2@po.cwru.edu.

Cleveland State University, Cleveland-Marshall College of Law, Cleveland, OH 44115. Offers business law (JD); civil litigation and dispute resolution (JD); criminal law (JD); employment labor law (JD); law (JD, LL M); JD/MAES; JD/MBA; JD/MPA; JD/MSES; JD/MUPDD. *Accreditation:* ABA. Part-time and evening/weekend programs available. *Degree requirements:* For master's, thesis (for graduates of U. S. law schools); for JD, 90 credits (42 in required courses). *Entrance requirements:* For JD, LSAT, bachelor's degree; for master's, JD or LL B. Additional exam requirements/recommendations for international students: Required—TOEFL (minimum score 600 paper-based; 250 computer-based; 100 iBT). Electronic applications accepted. *Expenses:* Contact institution. *Faculty research:* Health law, international law, constitutional law, commercial law, business organizations.

Cleveland State University, College of Graduate Studies, Nance College of Business Administration, Department of Management and Labor Relations, Cleveland, OH 44115. Offers labor relations and human resources (MLRHR). Part-time programs available. *Entrance requirements:* For master's, GMAT or GRE. Additional exam requirements/recommendations for international students: Required—TOEFL (minimum score 525 paper-based; 197 computer-based). Electronic applications accepted.

Cornell University, Graduate School, Graduate Fields of Industrial and Labor Relations, Ithaca, NY 14853-0001. Offers collective bargaining, labor law and labor history (MILR, MPS, MS, PhD); economic and social statistics (MILR); human resource studies (MILR, MPS, MS, PhD); industrial and labor relations problems (MILR, MPS, MS, PhD); international and comparative labor (MILR, MPS, MS, PhD); labor economics (MILR, MPS, MS, PhD); organizational behavior (MILR, MPS, MS, PhD). *Faculty:* 60 full-time (19 women). *Students:* 165 full-time (100 women); includes 35 minority (16 African Americans, 2 American Indian/Alaska Native, 11 Asian Americans or Pacific Islanders, 6 Hispanic Americans), 58 international. Average age 30. 271 applicants, 34% accepted, 69 enrolled. In 2009, 72 master's, 4 doctorates awarded. *Degree requirements:* For master's, thesis (MS); for doctorate, comprehensive exam, thesis/dissertation, teaching experience. *Entrance requirements:* For master's and doctorate, GMAT or GRE General Test, 2 academic recommendations. Additional exam requirements/recommendations for international students: Required—TOEFL (minimum score 550 paper-based; 213 computer-based; 77 iBT). Application fee: $70. Electronic applications accepted. *Expenses:* Contact institution. *Financial support:* In 2009–10, 73 students received support, including 7 fellowships with full tuition reimbursements available, 2 research assistantships with full tuition reimbursements available, 5 teaching assistantships with full tuition reimbursements available; institutionally sponsored loans, scholarships/grants, health care benefits, tuition waivers (full and partial), and unspecified assistantships also available. Financial award applicants required to submit FAFSA. *Unit head:* Director of Graduate Studies, 607-255-1522. *Application contact:* Graduate Field Assistant, 607-255-1522, E-mail: ilrgradapplicant@cornell.edu.

See Close-Up on page 1183.

Georgetown University, Graduate School of Arts and Sciences, Department of Economics, Washington, DC 20057. Offers econometrics (PhD); economic development (PhD); economic theory (PhD); industrial organization (PhD); international macro and finance (PhD); international trade (PhD); labor economics (PhD); macroeconomics (PhD); public economics and political economics (PhD); MA/PhD; MS/MA. *Degree requirements:* For doctorate, comprehensive exam, thesis/dissertation. *Entrance requirements:* For doctorate, GRE General Test. Additional exam requirements/recommendations for international students: Required—TOEFL. *Faculty research:* International economics, economic development.

Indiana University of Pennsylvania, School of Graduate Studies and Research, College of Health and Human Services, Department of Industrial and Labor Relations, Indiana, PA 15705-1087. Offers MA. Part-time and evening/weekend programs available. *Faculty:* 4 full-time (1 woman). *Students:* 39 full-time (21 women), 13 part-time (8 women); includes 7 minority (5 African Americans, 1 American Indian/Alaska Native, 1 Asian American or Pacific Islander). Average age 26. 62 applicants, 56% accepted, 32 enrolled. In 2009, 26 master's awarded. *Degree requirements:* For master's, thesis optional. *Entrance requirements:* For master's, 2 letters of recommendation. Additional exam requirements/recommendations for international students: Required—TOEFL. *Application deadline:* For fall admission, 7/1 priority date for domestic students; for spring admission, 11/1 for domestic students. Applications are processed on a rolling basis. Application fee: $40. *Expenses:* Tuition, state resident: full-time $6666; part-time $370 per credit hour. Tuition, nonresident: full-time $10,666; part-time $593 per credit hour. Required fees: $813 per semester. *Financial support:* In 2009–10, 1 fellowship (averaging $500 per year), 14 research assistantships with full and partial tuition reimbursements (averaging $4,089 per year) were awarded; career-related internships or fieldwork and Federal Work-Study also available. Support available to part-time students. Financial award application deadline: 3/15; financial award applicants required to submit FAFSA. *Faculty research:* Conflict resolution, labor-management cooperation, unemployment compensation, public sector labor relations, employee discipline. *Unit head:* Dr. Jennie K. Bullard, Chairperson and Graduate Coordinator, 724-357-4470, E-mail: jbullard@iup.edu. *Application contact:* Dr. Jacqueline Beck, Associate Dean, 724-357-2560, E-mail: jbeck@iup.edu.

Inter American University of Puerto Rico, Metropolitan Campus, Graduate Programs, Program in Labor Relations, San Juan, PR 00919-1293. Offers MA. *Degree requirements:* For master's, comprehensive exam. *Entrance requirements:* For master's, GRE or EXADEP, interview. Electronic applications accepted.

Inter American University of Puerto Rico, Metropolitan Campus, Graduate Programs, Program in Psychology, San Juan, PR 00919-1293. Offers counseling psychology (MA, PhD); industrial/organizational psychology (MA, PhD); labor relations (MA); school psychology (MA, PhD). *Degree requirements:* For master's, comprehensive exam. *Entrance requirements:* For master's, GRE or EXADEP, interview. Electronic applications accepted.

Loyola University Chicago, Graduate School of Business, Institute of Human Resources and Employee Relations, Chicago, IL 60660. Offers MSHR. Part-time programs available. *Entrance requirements:* For master's, GMAT or GRE General Test, letters of recommendation. Additional exam requirements/recommendations for international students: Required—TOEFL (minimum score 550 paper-based; 213 computer-based; 80 iBT). *Expenses:* Contact institution. *Faculty research:* Human resource management, labor relations, global human resource management, organizational development, compensation.

McMaster University, School of Graduate Studies, Faculty of Social Sciences, Program in Labour Studies, Hamilton, ON L8S 4M2, Canada. Offers work and society (MA).

Memorial University of Newfoundland, School of Graduate Studies, Interdisciplinary Program in Employment Relations, St. John's, NL A1C 5S7, Canada. Offers MER. Part-time programs available. *Degree requirements:* For master's, major supervised paper. *Entrance requirements:* For master's, undergraduate degree in related field, minimum B average. Electronic applications accepted.

Michigan State University, The Graduate School, College of Social Science, School of Labor and Industrial Relations, East Lansing, MI 48824. Offers human resources and labor relations (MLRHR); industrial relations and human resources (PhD). *Faculty:* 16 full-time (4 women). *Students:* 110 full-time (69 women), 37 part-time (25 women); includes 15 minority (8 African Americans, 1 American Indian/Alaska Native, 4 Asian Americans or Pacific Islanders, 2 Hispanic Americans), 37 international. Average age 26. 226 applicants, 44% accepted. In 2009, 67 master's, 1 doctorate awarded. *Entrance requirements:* Additional exam requirements/recommendations for international students: Required—TOEFL. *Application deadline:* For fall admission, 12/27 priority date for domestic students. *Expenses:* Tuition, state resident: part-time $478.25 per credit hour. Tuition, nonresident: part-time $966.50 per credit hour. Part-time tuition and fees vary according to program. *Financial support:* In 2009–10, 5 research assistantships with tuition reimbursements (averaging $6,879 per year), 1 teaching assistantship with tuition reimbursement (averaging $6,061 per year) were awarded. Total annual research expenditures: $257,815. *Unit head:* Dr. William N. Cooke, Director, 517-355-1801, Fax: 517-432-9443, E-mail: cookew@msu.edu. *Application contact:* Cheryl Mollitor, Graduate Program Administrator, 517-355-3285, Fax: 517-355-7656, E-mail: graduate@lir.msu.edu.

New York Institute of Technology, Graduate Division, School of Management, Program in Human Resources Management and Labor Relations, Old Westbury, NY 11568-8000. Offers human resources administration (Advanced Certificate); human resources management and labor relations (MS); labor relations (Advanced Certificate). Part-time and evening/weekend programs available. *Students:* 21 full-time (13 women), 71 part-time (54 women); includes 24 minority (13 African Americans, 6 Asian Americans or Pacific Islanders, 5 Hispanic Americans), 19 international. Average age 31. In 2009, 32 master's awarded. *Degree requirements:* For master's, comprehensive exam, thesis optional. *Entrance requirements:* For master's, GRE, minimum QPA of 2.85, interview, 2 letters of recommendation. *Application deadline:* For fall admission, 7/1 priority date for domestic students; for spring admission, 12/1 priority date for domestic students. Applications are processed on a rolling basis. Application fee: $50. Electronic applications accepted. *Expenses:* Tuition: Part-time $825 per credit. *Financial support:* Fellowships, research assistantships, career-related internships or fieldwork, institutionally sponsored loans, and tuition waivers (full and partial) available. Support available to part-time students. Financial award applicants required to submit FAFSA. *Faculty research:* Ethics in industrial relations, employee relations, public sector labor relations, benefits. *Unit head:* William Ninehan, Director, 646-273-6071, Fax: 516-686-7425, E-mail: wninehan@nyit.edu. *Application contact:* Dr. Jacquelyn Nealon, Vice President for Enrollment Services, 516-686-7925, Fax: 516-686-7597, E-mail: jnealon@nyit.edu.

The Ohio State University, Graduate School, Max M. Fisher College of Business, Program in Labor and Human Resources, Columbus, OH 43210. Offers MLHR, PhD. *Faculty:* 28. *Students:* 62 full-time (48 women), 39 part-time (34 women); includes 18 minority (6 African Americans, 1 American Indian/Alaska Native, 5 Asian Americans or Pacific Islanders, 6 Hispanic Americans), 14 international. Average age 28. In 2009, 44 master's, 1 doctorate awarded. *Degree requirements:* For master's, thesis optional; for doctorate, thesis/dissertation. *Entrance requirements:* For master's and doctorate, GRE General Test. Additional exam requirements/recommendations for international students: Recommended—TOEFL (minimum score 600 paper-based; 250 computer-based). *Application deadline:* For fall admission, 8/15 priority date for domestic students, 7/1 priority date for international students; for winter admission, 12/1 priority date for domestic students, 11/1 priority date for international students; for spring admission, 3/1 priority date for domestic students, 2/1 priority date for international students. Applications are processed on a rolling basis. Application fee: $40 ($50 for international students). Electronic applications accepted. *Expenses:* Tuition, state resident: full-time $10,683. Tuition, nonresident: full-time $25,923. Tuition and fees vary according to course load and program. *Financial support:* Fellowships, research assistantships, teaching assistantships, Federal Work-Study and institutionally sponsored loans available. Support available to part-time students. *Unit head:* Robert L. Heneman, Graduate Studies Committee Chair, 614-292-4587, Fax: 614-292-9006, E-mail: heneman.1@osu.edu. *Application contact:* 614-292-9444, Fax: 614-292-3895, E-mail: domestic.grad@osu.edu.

Penn State University Park, Graduate School, College of the Liberal Arts, Department of Labor Studies and Industrial Relations, State College, University Park, PA 16802-1503. Offers MPS, MS, Postbaccalaureate Certificate. Postbaccalaureate distance learning degree programs offered.

Pontificia Universidad Catolica Madre y Maestra, Graduate School, Santiago, Dominican Republic. Offers administration (M Adm); architecture of interiors (M Arch); architecture of tourist lodgings (M Arch); banking and financial management (M Mgmt); civil law (LL M); construction administration (ME); corporate business law (LL M); criminal procedure law (LL M); environmental engineering (ME, MEE); finance (M Mgmt); history applied to education (M Ed); human resources (EMBA); insurance (M Mgmt); international business (M Mgmt); labor law and Social Security (LL M); logistics management (ME); marketing (M Mgmt); renewable energy (ME); strategic cost management (M Mgmt). *Entrance requirements:* For master's, curriculum vitae, interview.

Queen's University at Kingston, School of Graduate Studies and Research, School of Industrial Relations, Kingston, ON K7L 3N6, Canada. Offers MIR. Part-time programs available. *Degree requirements:* For master's, research essay, skill seminars and modules. *Entrance requirements:* For master's, course work in micro-economics, macro-economics, and quantitative statistics. Additional exam requirements/recommendations for international students: Required—TOEFL (minimum score 600 paper-based; 250 computer-based). *Faculty research:* Collective bargaining and labor law, personnel and human relations, labor market analysis and policy, change management, teams.

Rutgers, The State University of New Jersey, New Brunswick, School of Management and Labor Relations, Program in Industrial Relations and Human Resources, Piscataway, NJ 08854-8097. Offers PhD. Part-time programs available. *Degree requirements:* For doctorate, comprehensive exam, thesis/dissertation. *Entrance requirements:* For doctorate, GRE. Additional exam requirements/recommendations for international students: Required—TOEFL (minimum score 575 paper-based; 233 computer-based; 91 iBT). Electronic applications accepted. *Faculty research:* Strategic human resources, labor relations, organizational change, worker representation.

See Display on page 1117.

Rutgers, The State University of New Jersey, New Brunswick, School of Management and Labor Relations, Program in Labor and Employment Relations, Piscataway, NJ 08854-8097. Offers MLER. Part-time and evening/weekend programs available. *Degree requirements:* For master's, thesis optional. *Entrance requirements:* For master's, GRE General Test. Additional exam requirements/recommendations for international students: Required—TOEFL. Electronic applications accepted. *Expenses:* Contact institution. *Faculty research:* Labor history, women and work, labor education, comparative labor movements, labor involvement and corporate decision making.

State University of New York Empire State College, Graduate Studies, Program in Labor and Policy Studies, Saratoga Springs, NY 12866-4391. Offers MA. Part-time and evening/weekend programs available. Postbaccalaureate distance learning degree programs offered (minimal on-campus study). *Degree requirements:* For master's, thesis, exam. *Entrance requirements:* Additional exam requirements/recommendations for international students: Required—TOEFL (minimum score 600 paper-based; 280 computer-based). Electronic applications accepted. *Faculty research:* Work and technology, collective bargaining, labor law, human resources management, trade union governance.

Université de Montréal, Faculty of Arts and Sciences, School of Industrial Relations, Montréal, QC H3C 3J7, Canada. Offers M Sc, PhD, DESS. Part-time programs available. *Degree requirements:* For master's, thesis; for doctorate, thesis/dissertation, general exam. *Entrance requirements:* For master's, BS in industrial relations. Electronic applications accepted. *Faculty research:* Labor law, health and safety at work, stress, job satisfaction, labor economics.

Université du Québec à Trois-Rivières, Graduate Programs, Program in Labor Relations, Trois-Rivières, QC G9A 5H7, Canada. Offers DESS.

Université du Québec à Trois-Rivières, Graduate Programs, Program in Labor Relations, Trois-Rivières, QC G9A 5H7, Canada. Offers DESS.

Université du Québec en Outaouais, Graduate Programs, Department of Industrial Relations, Gatineau, QC J8X 3X7, Canada. Offers M Sc, MA, PhD, Diploma. Part-time programs available. *Degree requirements:* For master's, thesis (for some programs); for doctorate, thesis/dissertation. *Entrance requirements:* For master's, appropriate bachelor's degree, proficiency in French; for doctorate, appropriate master's degree, proficiency in French.

Université Laval, Faculty of Social Sciences, Department of Industrial Relations, Programs in Industrial Relations, Québec, QC G1K 7P4, Canada. Offers MA, PhD. Terminal master's awarded for partial completion of doctoral program. *Degree requirements:* For master's, thesis (for some programs); for doctorate, comprehensive exam, thesis/dissertation. *Entrance requirements:* For master's and doctorate, knowledge of French, comprehension of written English. Electronic applications accepted.

University of Alberta, Faculty of Graduate Studies and Research, Doctoral Program in Business, Edmonton, AB T6G 2E1, Canada. Offers accounting (PhD); finance (PhD); human resources/industrial relations (PhD); management science (PhD); marketing (PhD); organizational analysis (PhD); MBA/PhD. *Accreditation:* AACSB. Part-time programs available. *Faculty:* 41 full-time (7 women), 1 part-time/adjunct (0 women). *Students:* 46 full-time (27 women), 5 part-time (3 women). Average age 34. 307 applicants, 7% accepted, 11 enrolled. In 2009, 2 doctorates awarded. *Degree requirements:* For doctorate, comprehensive exam, thesis/dissertation. *Entrance requirements:* For doctorate, GMAT. Additional exam requirements/recommendations for international students: Required—TOEFL (minimum score 550 paper-based; 213 computer-based). *Application deadline:* For fall admission, 6/1 priority date for domestic students; for winter admission, 5/1 for domestic students. Application fee: $0. Electronic applications accepted. Tuition and fees charges are reported in Canadian dollars. *Expenses:* Tuition, area resident: Full-time $4626 Canadian dollars; part-time $99.72 Canadian dollars per unit. International tuition: $8216 Canadian dollars full-time. Required fees: $3590 Canadian dollars; $99.72 Canadian dollars per unit. $215 Canadian dollars per term. *Financial support:* In 2009–10, 29 students received support, including 11 fellowships with full tuition reimbursements available (averaging $17,000 per year); scholarships/grants and tuition waivers (partial) also available. *Faculty research:* Accounting, capital markets and corporate finance, organizational change and human resource management, marketing, strategic management. Total annual research expenditures: $7.7 million. *Unit head:* Dr. Mike Percy, Director, 780-492-2361, Fax: 780-492-3325, E-mail: busphd@ualberta.ca. *Application contact:* Jeanette Gosine, Program Coordinator, 780-492-2361, Fax: 780-492-3325, E-mail: busphd@ualberta.ca.

University of California, Berkeley, Graduate Division, Haas School of Business, PhD in Business Administration Program, Berkeley, CA 94720-1500. Offers accounting (PhD); business and public policy (PhD); finance (PhD); management of organizations (PhD); marketing (PhD); operations management (PhD); real estate (PhD). *Accreditation:* AACSB. *Faculty:* 80 full-time (20 women), 130 part-time/adjunct (22 women). *Students:* 82 full-time (23 women); includes 22 minority (18 Asian Americans or Pacific Islanders, 4 Hispanic Americans), 29 international. Average age 30. 511 applicants, 5% accepted, 16 enrolled. In 2009, 8 doctorates awarded. *Degree requirements:* For doctorate, comprehensive exam, thesis/dissertation, oral exam, written preliminary exams. *Entrance requirements:* For doctorate, GMAT or GRE, minimum GPA of 3.0 in undergraduate and graduate coursework. Additional exam requirements/recommendations for international students: Required—TOEFL (minimum score 570 paper-based; 230 computer-based; 68 iBT), IELTS (minimum score 7). *Application deadline:* For fall admission, 12/10 for domestic and international students. Application fee: $70 ($90 for international students). Electronic applications accepted. *Financial support:* Fellowships with full and partial tuition reimbursements, research assistantships with full and partial tuition reimbursements, teaching assistantships with full and partial tuition reimbursements, career-related internships or fieldwork, Federal Work-Study, scholarships/grants, health care benefits, tuition waivers (full), unspecified assistantships, and transit pass, travel grants available. Financial award application deadline: 12/10; financial award applicants required to submit FAFSA. *Faculty research:* Accounting, business and public policy, finance, management of organizations, marketing, operations and information technology management, real estate. *Unit head:* Sunil Dutta, Director, 510-642-1229, Fax: 510-643-4255, E-mail: kimg@haas.berkeley.edu. *Application contact:* Kim Guilfoyle, Director, Student Affairs, 510-642-3944, Fax: 510-643-4255, E-mail: kimg@haas.berkeley.edu.

University of Cincinnati, Graduate School, McMicken College of Arts and Sciences, Center for Organizational Leadership, Program in Labor and Employment Relations, Cincinnati, OH 45221. Offers MALER. Part-time and evening/weekend programs available. *Degree requirements:* For master's, thesis or alternative, final experience project. *Entrance requirements:* For master's, minimum undergraduate GPA of 3.0. Additional exam requirements/recommendations for international students: Required—TOEFL (minimum score 560 paper-based). Electronic applications accepted. *Faculty research:* Human resource management, diversity, leadership.

University of Cincinnati, Graduate School, McMicken College of Arts and Sciences, Department of Economics, Cincinnati, OH 45221. Offers applied economics (MA); labor and employment relations (MALER). Part-time and evening/weekend programs available. Electronic applications accepted.

University of Illinois at Urbana–Champaign, Graduate College, School of Labor and Employment Relations, Champaign, IL 61820. Offers human resources and industrial relations (MHRIR, PhD); MHRIR/JD; MHRIR/MBA. Part-time programs available. *Faculty:* 14 full-time (5 women), 1 part-time/adjunct (0 women). *Students:* 180 full-time (126 women), 11 part-time (7 women); includes 39 minority (14 African Americans, 16 Asian Americans or Pacific Islanders, 9 Hispanic Americans), 55 international. 272 applicants, 44% accepted, 74 enrolled. In 2009, 95 master's, 6 doctorates awarded. Terminal master's awarded for partial completion of doctoral program. *Entrance requirements:* For master's and doctorate, GRE or GMAT, minimum GPA of 3.0. Additional exam requirements/recommendations for international students: Required—TOEFL (minimum score 590 paper-based; 243 computer-based; 96 iBT), or IELTS (minimum score 6.5). Application fee: $60 ($75 for international students). Electronic applications accepted. *Financial support:* In 2009–10, 23 fellowships, 12 research assistantships, 3 teaching assistantships were awarded; tuition waivers (full and partial) also available. *Unit head:* Dr. Joel E. Cutcher-Gershenfeld, Dean, 217-333-1482, Fax: 217-244-9290, E-mail: joelcg@illinois.edu. *Application contact:* Elizabeth Barker, Director of Student Services, 217-333-2381, Fax: 217-244-9290, E-mail: ebarker@illinois.edu.

University of Massachusetts Amherst, Graduate School, College of Social and Behavioral Sciences, The Labor Center, Amherst, MA 01003. Offers labor studies (MS); union leadership

Industrial and Labor Relations

University of Massachusetts Amherst (continued)
and administration (MS). Part-time programs available. Postbaccalaureate distance learning degree programs offered (minimal on-campus study). *Faculty:* 3 full-time (2 women). *Students:* 18 full-time (12 women), 58 part-time (20 women); includes 14 minority (5 African Americans, 3 Asian Americans or Pacific Islanders, 6 Hispanic Americans), 1 international. Average age 38. 25 applicants, 92% accepted, 15 enrolled. In 2009, 7 master's awarded. *Degree requirements:* For master's, thesis or alternative. *Entrance requirements:* Additional exam requirements/recommendations for international students: Required—TOEFL (minimum score 550 paper-based; 213 computer-based; 80 iBT), IELTS (minimum score 6.5). *Application deadline:* For fall admission, 2/1 for domestic and international students; for spring admission, 10/1 for domestic and international students. Applications are processed on a rolling basis. Application fee: $50 ($65 for international students). Electronic applications accepted. *Expenses:* Tuition, state resident: full-time $2640; part-time $110 per credit. Tuition, nonresident: full-time $9936; part-time $414 per credit. Tuition and fees vary according to course load. *Financial support:* In 2009–10, 10 teaching assistantships with full tuition reimbursements (averaging $5,722 per year) were awarded; fellowships, research assistantships, career-related internships or fieldwork, Federal Work-Study, scholarships/grants, traineeships, health care benefits, tuition waivers (full), and unspecified assistantships also available. Support available to part-time students. Financial award application deadline: 2/1. *Unit head:* Dr. Stephanie A. Luce, Graduate Program Director, 413-545-4875, Fax: 413-545-0110. *Application contact:* Jean M. Ames, Supervisor of Admissions, 413-545-0722, Fax: 413-577-0010, E-mail: gradadm@grad.umass.edu.

University of Minnesota, Twin Cities Campus, Carlson School of Management, Program in Human Resources and Industrial Relations, Minneapolis, MN 55455-0213. Offers MA, PhD. *Accreditation:* AACSB. Part-time and evening/weekend programs available. *Faculty:* 12 full-time (6 women), 6 part-time/adjunct (1 woman). *Students:* 196 full-time (138 women), 92 part-time (68 women); includes 36 minority (13 African Americans, 18 Asian Americans or Pacific Islanders, 5 Hispanic Americans), 62 international. Average age 26. 306 applicants, 44% accepted, 85 enrolled. In 2009, 96 master's, 5 doctorates awarded. Terminal master's awarded for partial completion of doctoral program. *Degree requirements:* For master's, thesis optional; for doctorate, thesis/dissertation. *Entrance requirements:* For master's, GMAT or GRE General Test; for doctorate, GRE General Test. Additional exam requirements/recommendations for international students: Required—TOEFL (minimum score 580 paper-based; 85 iBT). *Application deadline:* For fall admission, 6/15 for domestic and international students; for spring admission, 10/15 for domestic and international students. Applications are processed on a rolling basis. Application fee: $75 ($95 for international students). *Expenses:* Contact institution. *Financial support:* In 2009–10, 60 students received support, including 39 fellowships with partial tuition reimbursements available (averaging $6,500 per year), 14 research assistantships with full and partial tuition reimbursements available (averaging $12,500 per year), 7 teaching assistantships with full tuition reimbursements available (averaging $9,000 per year); career-related internships or fieldwork, Federal Work-Study, institutionally sponsored loans, and tuition waivers (full and partial) also available. Support available to part-time students. Financial award application deadline: 2/1; financial award applicants required to submit FAFSA. *Faculty research:* Staffing, training, and development; compensation and benefits; organization theory; collective bargaining. Total annual research expenditures: $200,000. *Unit head:* Theresa Glomb, Director of Graduate Studies, 612-624-4863, Fax: 612-624-8360, E-mail: tglomb@umn.edu. *Application contact:* Celeste Pape, Admissions Coordinator, 612-624-5704, Fax: 612-624-8360, E-mail: cpape@umn.edu.

University of New Haven, Graduate School; School of Business, Program in Industrial Relations, West Haven, CT 06516-1916. Offers industrial relations (MS); private sector track (MS); public sector track (MS). Part-time and evening/weekend programs available. *Faculty:* 5 full-time (2 women), 11 part-time/adjunct (4 women). *Students:* 8 full-time (4 women), 11 part-time (4 women); includes 7 minority (5 African Americans, 2 Hispanic Americans), 2 international. Average age 39. 21 applicants, 90% accepted, 8 enrolled. In 2009, 8 master's awarded. *Degree requirements:* For master's, thesis optional. *Entrance requirements:* For master's, two years of administrative, managerial, or professional work experience. Additional exam requirements/recommendations for international students: Required—TOEFL (minimum score 520 paper-based; 190 computer-based; 70 iBT); Recommended—IELTS (minimum score 5.5). *Application deadline:* For fall admission, 5/31 for international students; for winter admission, 10/15 for international students; for spring admission, 1/15 for international students. Applications are processed on a rolling basis. Application fee: $50. Electronic applications accepted. *Expenses:* Contact institution. *Financial support:* Research assistantships with partial tuition reimbursements, teaching assistantships with partial tuition reimbursements, career-related internships or fieldwork, Federal Work-Study, scholarships/grants, tuition waivers, and unspecified assistantships available. Support available to part-time students. Financial award applicants required to submit FAFSA. *Unit head:* Charles Coleman, Coordinator, 203-932-7375. *Application contact:* Eloise Gormley, Director of Graduate Admissions, 203-932-7449, Fax: 203-932-7137, E-mail: gradinfo@newhaven.edu.

University of New Haven, Graduate School, School of Business, Program in Public Administration, West Haven, CT 06516-1916. Offers personnel and labor relations (MPA); public administration (MPA, Certificate), including city management (MPA), community-clinical services (MPA), health care management (MPA), long-term health care (MPA), personnel and labor relations (MPA), public administration (Certificate), public management (Certificate), public personnel management (Certificate); MBA/MPA. Part-time and evening/weekend programs available. *Faculty:* 3 full-time (1 woman), 11 part-time/adjunct (5 women). *Students:* 17 full-time (9 women), 26 part-time (14 women); includes 11 minority (9 African Americans, 1 Asian American or Pacific Islander, 1 Hispanic American), 1 international. Average age 35. 35 applicants, 94% accepted, 8 enrolled. In 2009, 9 master's, 12 other advanced degrees awarded. *Degree requirements:* For master's, thesis or alternative. *Entrance requirements:* Additional exam requirements/recommendations for international students: Required—TOEFL (minimum score 520 paper-based; 190 computer-based; 70 iBT); Recommended—IELTS (minimum score 5.5). *Application deadline:* For fall admission, 5/31 for international students; for winter admission, 10/15 for international students; for spring admission, 1/15 for international students. Applications are processed on a rolling basis. Application fee: $50. Electronic applications accepted. *Expenses:* Contact institution. *Financial support:* Research assistantships with partial tuition reimbursements, teaching assistantships with partial tuition reimbursements, career-related internships or fieldwork, Federal Work-Study, scholarships/grants, tuition waivers, and unspecified assistantships available. Support available to part-time students. Financial award application deadline: 5/1; financial award applicants required to submit FAFSA. *Unit head:* Charles Coleman, Chairman, 203-932-7375. *Application contact:* Eloise Gormley, Director of Graduate Admissions, 203-932-7449, Fax: 203-932-7137, E-mail: gradinfo@newhaven.edu.

University of North Texas, Robert B. Toulouse School of Graduate Studies, College of Arts and Sciences, Department of Economics, Denton, TX 76203. Offers economic research (MS); economics (MA, MS); labor and industrial relations (MS). Part-time and evening/weekend programs available. *Degree requirements:* For master's, comprehensive exam, thesis (for some programs). *Entrance requirements:* For master's, GMAT, GRE General Test, minimum GPA of 3.0, 2 letters of recommendation, 500-word essay. Additional exam requirements/recommendations for international students: Required—proof of English language proficiency required for non-native English speakers; Recommended—TOEFL (minimum score 550 paper-based; 213 computer-based). Application fee: $50 ($75 for international students). *Expenses:* Tuition, state resident: full-time $4298; part-time $239 per contact hour. Tuition, nonresident: full-time $9878; part-time $549 per contact hour. Required fees: $265 per contact hour. *Financial support:* In 2009–10, 25 students received support; fellowships with partial tuition reimbursements available, research assistantships with partial tuition reimbursements available, teaching assistantships with partial tuition reimbursements available, career-related internships or fieldwork, Federal Work-Study, and institutionally sponsored loans available. Support available to part-time students. Financial award application deadline: 4/1. *Faculty research:* Econometrics, international trade and development, immigration, telecommunications, micro enterprise development. *Application contact:* Graduate Adviser, 940-565-3442, Fax: 940-565-4426, E-mail: tieslau@unt.edu.

University of Rhode Island, Graduate School, Labor Research Center, Kingston, RI 02881. Offers labor relations and human resources (MS); MS/JD. Part-time and evening/weekend programs available. *Faculty:* 2 full-time (0 women), 2 part-time/adjunct (1 woman). *Students:* 6 full-time (3 women), 25 part-time (21 women); includes 3 minority (2 African Americans, 1 Hispanic American), 2 international. In 2009, 4 master's awarded. *Entrance requirements:* For master's, GRE, MAT, GMAT, or LSAT, 2 letters of recommendation. Additional exam requirements/recommendations for international students: Required—TOEFL (minimum score 550 paper-based; 213 computer-based). *Application deadline:* For fall admission, 7/15 for domestic students, 2/1 for international students; for spring admission, 11/15 for domestic students, 7/15 for international students. Application fee: $65. Electronic applications accepted. *Expenses:* Tuition, state resident: full-time $8828; part-time $490 per credit hour. Tuition, nonresident: full-time $22,100; part-time $1228 per credit hour. Required fees: $1118; $57 per semester. Tuition and fees vary according to program. *Financial support:* In 2009–10, 1 teaching assistantship with full tuition reimbursement (averaging $13,894 per year) was awarded; institutionally sponsored loans also available. Financial award application deadline: 2/1; financial award applicants required to submit FAFSA. Total annual research expenditures: $11,637. *Unit head:* Dr. Richard W. Scholl, Director, 401-874-4347, Fax: 401-874-2954, E-mail: rscholl@uri.edu. *Application contact:* Dr. Richard W. Scholl, Director, 401-874-4347, Fax: 401-874-2954, E-mail: rscholl@uri.edu.

University of Saskatchewan, College of Graduate Studies and Research, Edwards School of Business, Department of Industrial Relations and Organizational Behavior, Saskatoon, SK S7N 5A2, Canada. Offers M Sc. Part-time programs available. *Degree requirements:* For master's, thesis. *Entrance requirements:* For master's, GMAT. Additional exam requirements/recommendations for international students: Required—TOEFL. Tuition and fees charges are reported in Canadian dollars. *Expenses:* Tuition, area resident: Full-time $3000 Canadian dollars; part-time $500 Canadian dollars per term. Required fees: $700 Canadian dollars; $100 Canadian dollars per term.

University of Toronto, School of Graduate Studies, Social Sciences Division, Centre for Industrial Relations and Human Resources, Toronto, ON M5S 1A1, Canada. Offers MHRIR, PhD. Part-time programs available. *Degree requirements:* For doctorate, thesis/dissertation. *Entrance requirements:* For master's, GRE or GMAT (for applicants who completed degree outside of Canada), minimum B+ in final 2 years of bachelor's degree completion, 2 letters of reference, resume; for doctorate, GRE or GMAT, MIR degree or equivalent, minimum B+ average, 3 letters of reference, resumé. Additional exam requirements/recommendations for international students: Required—TOEFL (minimum score 600 paper-based; 250 computer-based), TWE (minimum score 5), Michigan English Language Assessment Battery, IELTS, or COPE. *Expenses:* Contact institution.

University of Wisconsin–Milwaukee, Graduate School, College of Letters and Sciences, Interdepartmental Program in Human Resources and Labor Relations, Milwaukee, WI 53201-0413. Offers human resources and labor relations (MHRLR); international human resources and labor relations (Certificate); mediation and negotiation (Certificate). Part-time programs available. *Students:* 14 full-time (10 women), 44 part-time (34 women); includes 12 minority (5 African Americans, 2 Asian Americans or Pacific Islanders, 5 Hispanic Americans), 2 international. Average age 31. 37 applicants, 51% accepted, 5 enrolled. In 2009, 22 master's awarded. *Entrance requirements:* For master's, GMAT or GRE General Test. Additional exam requirements/recommendations for international students: Required—TOEFL (minimum score 550 paper-based; 79 iBT), IELTS (minimum score 6.5). *Application deadline:* For fall admission, 1/1 priority date for domestic students; for spring admission, 9/1 for domestic students. Applications are processed on a rolling basis. Application fee: $45 ($75 for international students). *Expenses:* Tuition, state resident: full-time $8800. Tuition, nonresident: full-time $20,760. Tuition and fees vary according to program and reciprocity agreements. *Financial support:* Career-related internships or fieldwork available. Support available to part-time students. Financial award application deadline: 4/15. *Unit head:* Susan M. Donohue-Davies, Representative, 414-299-4009, Fax: 414-229-5915, E-mail: suedono@uwm.edu. *Application contact:* General Information Contact, 414-229-4982, Fax: 414-229-6967, E-mail: gradschool@uwm.edu.

Wayne State University, College of Liberal Arts and Sciences, Interdisciplinary Program in Industrial Relations, Detroit, MI 48202. Offers MAIR. Part-time and evening/weekend programs available. *Degree requirements:* For master's, thesis optional. *Entrance requirements:* For master's, GMAT, GRE General Test. Additional exam requirements/recommendations for international students: Required—TOEFL (minimum score 550 paper-based; 213 computer-based); Recommended—TWE (minimum score 6). Electronic applications accepted. *Faculty research:* Two-tier wage system, affirmative action practices in higher education; employment relations in China.

West Virginia University, College of Business and Economics, Program in Industrial Relations, Morgantown, WV 26506. Offers MSIR. *Accreditation:* AACSB. *Entrance requirements:* For master's, GRE or GMAT, minimum GPA of 3.0. Additional exam requirements/recommendations for international students: Required—TOEFL. Electronic applications accepted. *Faculty research:* Labor relations, mediation, leadership, benefits.

Philanthropic Studies

Indiana University–Purdue University Indianapolis, School of Liberal Arts, Center on Philanthropy, Indianapolis, IN 46202. Offers philanthropic studies (MA, PhD); MA/MA; MPA/MA; MSN/MA. Part-time and evening/weekend programs available. Postbaccalaureate distance learning degree programs offered (minimal on-campus study). In 2009, 28 master's awarded. *Degree requirements:* For master's, thesis optional. *Entrance requirements:* For master's, GRE General Test or equivalent, minimum undergraduate GPA of 3.0. Application fee: $50 ($60 for international students). *Financial support:* Fellowships with full and partial tuition reimbursements, research assistantships with full and partial tuition reimbursements, career-related internships or fieldwork, Federal Work-Study, institutionally sponsored loans, and scholarships/grants available. Financial award applicants required to submit FAFSA. *Unit head:* Dr. Eugene Tempel, Executive Director, 317-274-4200. *Application contact:* Marsha Currin-McGriff, Director of Student Services, 317-278-8927, E-mail: mcurrin@iupui.edu.

Indiana University–Purdue University Indianapolis, School of Liberal Arts, Department of Philanthropic Studies, Indianapolis, IN 46202. Offers MA, XMA, PhD. *Faculty:* 52 full-time, 10 part-time/adjunct. *Students:* 36 full-time (23 women), 47 part-time (36 women); includes 12 minority (4 African Americans, 1 American Indian/Alaska Native, 4 Asian Americans or Pacific Islanders, 3 Hispanic Americans), 11 international. Average age 37. *Degree requirements:* For master's, thesis optional; for doctorate, thesis/dissertation. *Entrance requirements:* For master's, GRE General Test (minimum score 500 quantitative, 500 verbal, 4.5 analytical writing), minimum undergraduate GPA of 3.0; for doctorate, GRE General Test (minimum score: 500 quantitative, 500 verbal, 4.5 analytical writing), minimum GPA of 3.0, master's degree. *Application deadline:* For fall admission, 1/15 for domestic students, 1/1 for international students. Application fee: $50 ($60 for international students). *Financial support:* In 2009–10, 1 fellowship with partial tuition reimbursement (averaging $16,500 per year), 3 teaching assistantships (averaging $5,567 per year) were awarded; research assistantships with partial tuition reimbursements, career-related internships or fieldwork, Federal Work-Study, institutionally sponsored loans, and scholarships/grants also available. Financial award application deadline: 3/1; financial award applicants required to submit FAFSA. *Unit head:* Robert W. White, Dean, School of Liberal Arts, 317-274-8448. *Application contact:* Student Services, 317-274-4200, E-mail: maphil@iupui.edu.

Saint Mary's University of Minnesota, Schools of Graduate and Professional Programs, Graduate School of Business and Technology, Philanthropy and Development Program, Winona, MN 55987-1399. Offers MA. *Unit head:* Dr. Gary Kelsey, Director, 651-275-0206, E-mail: gkelsey@smumn.edu. *Application contact:* Jami Spitzer, Information Contact, 507-457-7500, E-mail: jspitzer@smumn.edu.

Public Administration

Adelphi University, University College, Graduate Certificate in Emergency Management Program, Garden City, NY 11530-0701. Offers Certificate. Part-time and evening/weekend programs available. *Students:* 3 part-time (1 woman). Average age 27. 11 applicants, 55% accepted. *Application deadline:* For fall admission, 5/1 for international students; for spring admission, 12/1 for international students. Applications are processed on a rolling basis. Application fee: $50. Electronic applications accepted. *Expenses:* Tuition: Full-time $28,340; part-time $830 per credit. Required fees: $600; $250 per credit. Full-time tuition and fees vary according to course load and program. *Financial support:* Research assistantships with partial tuition reimbursements, Federal Work-Study and institutionally sponsored loans available. *Faculty research:* Emergency nursing, disaster management, disaster preparedness. *Unit head:* Shawn O'Riley, Executive Director, 516-877-3412, E-mail: ucinfo@adelphi.edu. *Application contact:* Christine Murphy, Director of Admissions, 516-877-3050, Fax: 516-877-3039, E-mail: graduateadmissions@adelphi.edu.

Albany State University, College of Arts and Humanities, Department of History, Political Science and Public Administration, Albany, GA 31705-2717. Offers community and economic development administration (MPA); criminal justice administration (MPA); fiscal management (MPA); general management (MPA); health administration and policy (MPA); human resources management (MPA); public policy (MPA); water resource management and policy (MPA). *Accreditation:* NASPAA. *Students:* 17 full-time (11 women), 43 part-time (29 women); includes 57 minority (56 African Americans, 1 Asian American or Pacific Islander). Average age 34. 21 applicants, 100% accepted, 17 enrolled. In 2009, 17 master's awarded. *Entrance requirements:* For master's, Graduate Record Examination (GRE) or Miller Analogies Test (MAT). *Application deadline:* For fall admission, 11/16 for domestic students, 9/16 for international students; for spring admission, 4/19 for domestic students, 2/19 for international students. Applications are processed on a rolling basis. Application fee: $20. Electronic applications accepted. *Expenses:* Tuition, state resident: full-time $2970; part-time $162 per credit hour. Tuition, nonresident: full-time $12,168; part-time $676 per credit hour. Required fees: $962; $75 per credit hour. *Financial support:* Application deadline: 6/30. *Faculty research:* Public policy, strategic public human resources and human capital management, diversity management in the public sector and collective bargaining and labor relations in the public sector, e-government and public sector information systems, public administration pedagogy and business process modeling simulation, funded research- community development, non profit organizations, civic engagement and civic participation, health care disparities among minorities and poverty. Total annual research expenditures: $26,000. *Unit head:* Dr. Peter Ngwafu, Director, 229-430-4873, Fax: 229-430-7895, E-mail: peter.ngwafu@asurams.edu. *Application contact:* Nicole Lane, Interim Graduate Admissions Officer, 229-430-4862, Fax: 229-430-6398, E-mail: nicole.lane@asurams.edu.

Albany State University, College of Sciences and Health Professions, Department of Criminal Justice and Forensic Science, Albany, GA 31705-2717. Offers corrections (MS); forensic science (MS); law enforcement (MS); public administration (MS). Part-time programs available. *Students:* 11 full-time (10 women), 43 part-time (29 women); includes 51 minority (50 African Americans, 1 Asian American or Pacific Islander). Average age 35. 18 applicants, 94% accepted, 10 enrolled. In 2009, 8 master's awarded. *Degree requirements:* For master's, comprehensive exam, thesis optional. *Entrance requirements:* For master's, GRE General Test or MAT, minimum GPA of 2.5, ASU Medical and Immunization Forms. Additional exam requirements/recommendations for international students: Required—TOEFL. *Application deadline:* For fall admission, 11/16 for domestic students, 9/16 for international students; for spring admission, 4/19 for domestic students, 2/19 for international students. Applications are processed on a rolling basis. Application fee: $20. Electronic applications accepted. *Expenses:* Tuition, state resident: full-time $2970; part-time $162 per credit hour. Tuition, nonresident: full-time $12,168; part-time $676 per credit hour. Required fees: $962; $75 per credit hour. *Financial support:* Application deadline: 6/30. *Faculty research:* Criminal alcoholic program, prevention of juvenile delinquency, police selection, constitutional issues. *Unit head:* Dr. Charles Ochie, Chair, 229-430-4864, Fax: 229-430-1676, E-mail: charles.ochie@asurams.edu. *Application contact:* Nicole Lane, Interim Graduate Admissions Officer, 229-430-4862, Fax: 229-430-6398, E-mail: nicole.lane@asurams.edu.

American International College, School of Business Administration, Program in Public Administration, Springfield, MA 01109-3189. Offers MPA. Part-time and evening/weekend programs available. *Degree requirements:* For master's, comprehensive exam (for some programs), thesis (for some programs), oral exam, practicum. *Entrance requirements:* Additional exam requirements/recommendations for international students: Required—TOEFL. Electronic applications accepted. *Expenses:* Tuition: Full-time $12,510; part-time $695 per credit hour. Required fees: $35 per term.

American Public University System, AMU/APU Graduate Programs, Charles Town, WV 25414. Offers air warfare (MA Military Studies); American Revolution (MA Military Studies); business administration (MBA); Civil War (MA Military Studies); criminal justice (MA); defense management (MA Military Studies); emergency and disaster management (MA); environmental policy and management (MS); fire science management (MA); global engagement (MA); history (MA); homeland security (MA); humanities (MA); intelligence (MA Military Studies, MA Strategic Intelligence); international peace and conflict resolution (MA); international relations and conflict resolution (MA); joint warfare (MA Military Studies); land warfare international perspective (MA Military Studies); management (MA); military history (MA); military leadership (MA Military Studies); national security studies (MA); naval warfare international (MA Military Studies); naval warfare US (MA Military Studies); political science (MA); public administration (MA); public health (MA); security management (MA); space studies (MS); special ops/LIC (MA Military Studies); sports management (MA); transportation and logistics management (MA); transportation management (MA); unconventional warfare (MA Military Studies); World War II (MA Military Studies). Programs offered via distance learning only. Part-time and evening/weekend programs available. Postbaccalaureate distance learning degree programs offered (no on-campus study). *Faculty:* 10 full-time (3 women), 188 part-time/adjunct (57 women). *Students:* 340 full-time (98 women), 3,567 part-time (790 women); includes 615 minority (317 African Americans, 28 American Indian/Alaska Native, 85 Asian Americans or Pacific Islanders, 185 Hispanic Americans), 20 international. Average age 36. 2,123 applicants, 100% accepted, 893 enrolled. In 2009, 829 degrees awarded. *Degree requirements:* For master's, comprehensive exam. *Entrance requirements:* For master's, bachelor's degree or equivalent, minimum GPA of 2.7 in last 60 hours of course work. *Application deadline:* Applications are processed on a rolling basis. Application fee: $0. Electronic applications accepted. *Financial support:* Applicants required to submit FAFSA. *Faculty research:* Military history, criminal justice, management performance, national security. *Unit head:* Dr. Frank McCluskey, Provost, 877-468-6268, Fax: 304-724-3780. *Application contact:* Terry Grant, Director of Enrollment Management, 877-468-6268, Fax: 304-724-3780, E-mail: info@apus.edu.

American University, School of Public Affairs, Department of Public Administration, Program in Public Administration, Washington, DC 20016-8070. Offers MPA, PhD, Certificate. *Accreditation:* NASPAA (one or more programs are accredited). Part-time and evening/weekend programs available. *Students:* 86 full-time (55 women), 133 part-time (73 women); includes 53 minority (32 African Americans, 2 American Indian/Alaska Native, 12 Asian Americans or Pacific Islanders, 7 Hispanic Americans), 14 international. Average age 35. In 2009, 78 master's, 4 doctorates awarded. *Degree requirements:* For master's, comprehensive exam; for doctorate, comprehensive exam, thesis/dissertation. *Entrance requirements:* For master's, GRE, statement of purpose; 2 recommendations; for doctorate, GRE, 3 recommendations; for Certificate, bachelor's degree. Additional exam requirements/recommendations for international students: Required—TOEFL. *Application deadline:* For fall admission, 2/1 for domestic students; for spring admission, 11/1 for domestic students. Application fee: $55. *Expenses:* Tuition: Full-time $22,266; part-time $1237 per credit hour. Required fees: $430. Tuition and fees vary according to program. *Financial support:* Fellowships, teaching assistantships, career-related internships or fieldwork, Federal Work-Study, and institutionally sponsored loans available. Financial award application deadline: 2/1.

The American University in Cairo, Graduate Studies and Research, School of Humanities and Social Sciences, Program in Public Policy and Administration, Cairo, Egypt. Offers MA, Diploma.

American University of Beirut, Graduate Programs, Faculty of Arts and Sciences, Beirut, Lebanon. Offers anthropology (MA); Arabic language and literature (MA); archaeology (MA); biology (MS); chemistry (MS); computer science (MS); economics (MA); education (MA); English language (MA); English literature (MA); environmental policy planning (MSES); financial economics (MAFE); geology (MS); history (MA); mathematics (MA, MS); Middle Eastern studies (MA); philosophy (MA); physics (MS); political studies (MA); psychology (MA); public administration (MA); sociology (MA); statistics (MA, MS). Part-time programs available. *Degree requirements:* For master's, one foreign language, comprehensive exam, thesis (for some programs). *Entrance requirements:* For master's, GRE, letter of recommendation. Additional exam requirements/recommendations for international students: Required—TOEFL (minimum score 600 paper-based; 250 computer-based; 100 iBT), IELTS (minimum score 7.5). *Faculty research:* String theory and supergravity; computer graphics; algebra and number theory; popular Arabic literature; marine and freshwater biology; integrating science, math and technology.

American University of Sharjah, Graduate Programs, Sharjah, United Arab Emirates. Offers business (EMBA, GEMPA, MBA); chemical engineering (MS Ch E); civil engineering (MSCE); computer engineering (MS); electrical engineering (MSEE); mechanical engineering (MSME); mechatronics engineering (MS); public administration (MPA); teaching English to speakers of other languages (MA); translation and interpreting (MA); urban planning (MUP). Part-time and evening/weekend programs available. *Faculty:* 59 full-time (4 women), 5 part-time/adjunct (1 woman). *Students:* 101 full-time (44 women), 218 part-time (95 women). Average age 27. 184 applicants, 83% accepted, 92 enrolled. In 2009, 97 master's awarded. *Entrance requirements:* For master's, GMAT (MBA). Additional exam requirements/recommendations for international students: Required—TOEFL (minimum score 550 paper-based; 213 computer-based; 80 iBT), TWE (minimum score 5). *Application deadline:* For fall admission, 7/30 priority date for domestic students, 7/15 priority date for international students; for spring admission, 12/31 priority date for domestic students, 12/16 for international students. Applications are processed on a rolling basis. Application fee: $300. Electronic applications accepted. Tuition charges are reported in United Arab Emirates dirhams. *Expenses:* Tuition: Part-time 3250 United Arab Emirates dirhams per credit hour. *Financial support:* In 2009–10, 63 students received support, including 28 research assistantships with tuition reimbursements available, 35 teaching assistantships with tuition reimbursements available. *Faculty research:* Chemical engineering, civil engineering, computer engineering, electrical engineering, linguistics, translation. *Unit head:* Ghada S. Sami, Admissions Manager, 971-65151006 Ext. 1006, Fax: 971-65151020, E-mail: graduateadmission@aus.edu. *Application contact:* Ghada S. Sami, Admissions Manager, 971-65151006 Ext. 1006, Fax: 971-65151020, E-mail: graduateadmission@aus.edu.

Andrew Jackson University, Jeffrey D. Rubenstein College of Criminal Justice, Program in Public Administration, Birmingham, AL 35244. Offers MPA. Part-time and evening/weekend programs available. Postbaccalaureate distance learning degree programs offered (no on-campus study). *Entrance requirements:* For master's, course work in calculus, statistics. Additional exam requirements/recommendations for international students: Required—TOEFL (minimum score 550 paper-based; 213 computer-based). Electronic applications accepted.

Angelo State University, College of Graduate Studies, College of Liberal and Fine Arts, Department of Political Science and Criminal Justice, San Angelo, TX 76909. Offers public administration (MPA). Part-time and evening/weekend programs available. *Faculty:* 3 full-time (0 women). *Students:* 2 full-time (1 woman), 4 part-time (2 women); includes 3 minority (all Hispanic Americans). Average age 26. 2 applicants, 100% accepted, 2 enrolled. In 2009, 3 master's awarded. *Degree requirements:* For master's, comprehensive exam. *Entrance requirements:* For master's, GRE General Test. Additional exam requirements/recommendations for international students: Required—TOEFL or IELTS. *Application deadline:* For fall admission, 7/15 priority date for domestic students, 6/10 for international students; for spring admission, 12/1 priority date for domestic students, 11/1 for international students. Applications are processed on a rolling basis. Application fee: $40 ($50 for international students). Electronic applications accepted. *Expenses:* Tuition, state resident: full-time $3396; part-time $142 per credit hour. Tuition, nonresident: full-time $10,152; part-time $423 per credit hour. Required fees: $1786; $36.25 per credit hour. $494 per semester. Full-time tuition and fees vary according to course load, degree level and program. *Financial support:* Career-related internships or fieldwork, Federal Work-Study, and scholarships/grants available. Support available to part-time students. Financial award application deadline: 3/1; financial award applicants

Public Administration

Angelo State University (continued)
required to submit FAFSA. *Unit head:* Dr. Edward C. Olson, Department Head, 325-942-2262 Ext. 275, Fax: 325-942-2307, E-mail: ed.olson@angelo.edu. *Application contact:* Dr. Jack Barbour, Graduate Advisor, 325-942-2262 Ext. 282, Fax: 325-942-2307, E-mail: jack.barbour@angelo.edu.

Anna Maria College, Graduate Division, Program in Public Administration, Paxton, MA 01612. Offers MPA.

Appalachian State University, Cratis D. Williams Graduate School, Department of Government and Justice Studies, Boone, NC 28608. Offers criminal justice (MS); political science (MA), including American government, environmental politics and policy analysis, international relations; public administration (MPA), including public management, town, city and county management. Part-time programs available. Postbaccalaureate distance learning degree programs offered (no on-campus study). *Faculty:* 27 full-time (5 women), 12 part-time/adjunct (1 woman). *Students:* 65 full-time (26 women), 62 part-time (22 women); includes 6 minority (5 African Americans, 1 American Indian/Alaska Native), 1 international. 100 applicants, 93% accepted, 53 enrolled. In 2009, 45 master's awarded. *Degree requirements:* For master's, variable foreign language requirement, comprehensive exam, thesis optional. *Entrance requirements:* For master's, GRE General Test, 3 letters of recommendation. Additional exam requirements/recommendations for international students: Required—TOEFL (minimum score 570 paper-based; 230 computer-based; 79 iBT), IELTS (minimum score 6.5). *Application deadline:* For fall admission, 7/1 for domestic students, 2/1 for international students; for spring admission, 11/1 for domestic students, 7/1 for international students. Applications are processed on a rolling basis. Application fee: $50. Electronic applications accepted. *Expenses:* Tuition, state resident: full-time $2960. Tuition, nonresident: full-time $14,051. Required fees: $2320. *Financial support:* In 2009–10, 20 research assistantships (averaging $8,000 per year) were awarded; fellowships, teaching assistantships, career-related internships or fieldwork, Federal Work-Study, scholarships/grants, and unspecified assistantships also available. Financial award application deadline: 4/1; financial award applicants required to submit FAFSA. *Faculty research:* Campaign finance, emerging democracies, bureaucratic politics, judicial behavior, administration of justice. Total annual research expenditures: $320,000. *Unit head:* Dr. Brian Ellison, Chairperson, 828-262-3085, E-mail: ellisonba@appstate.edu. *Application contact:* Sandy Krause, Director of Admissions and Recruiting, 828-262-2130, Fax: 828-262-2709, E-mail: krausesl@appstate.edu.

Argosy University, Chicago, College of Business, Chicago, IL 60601. Offers accounting (DBA); customized professional concentration (MBA, DBA); finance (MBA); fraud examination (MBA); global business sustainability (DBA); healthcare administration (MBA); information systems (DBA); information systems management (MBA); international business (MBA, DBA); management (MBA, MSM, DBA); marketing (MBA, DBA); organizational leadership (Ed D); public administration (MBA); sustainable management (MBA). Postbaccalaureate distance learning degree programs offered (minimal on-campus study).

Argosy University, Dallas, College of Business, Farmers Branch, TX 75244. Offers accounting (DBA, AGC); corporate compliance (MBA, Graduate Certificate); customized professional concentration (MBA); finance (MBA, Graduate Certificate); fraud examination (MBA, Graduate Certificate); global business sustainability (DBA, AGC); healthcare administration (Graduate Certificate); healthcare management (MBA); information systems (MBA, DBA, AGC); information systems management (Graduate Certificate); international business (MBA, DBA, AGC, Graduate Certificate); management (MBA, DBA, AGC, Graduate Certificate); marketing (MBA, DBA, AGC, Graduate Certificate); public administration (MBA, Graduate Certificate); sustainable management (MBA, Graduate Certificate).

Argosy University, Denver, College of Business, Denver, CO 80231. Offers accounting (DBA); corporate compliance (MBA); customized professional concentration (MBA, DBA); finance (MBA); fraud examination (MBA); global business sustainability (DBA); healthcare administration (MBA); information systems (DBA); information systems management (MBA); international business (MBA, DBA); management (MBA, MSM, DBA); marketing (MBA, DBA); organizational leadership (Ed D); public administration (MBA); sustainable management (MBA).

Argosy University, Inland Empire, College of Business, San Bernardino, CA 92408. Offers accounting (DBA); corporate compliance (MBA); customized professional concentration (MBA, DBA); finance (MBA); fraud examination (MBA); global business sustainability (DBA); healthcare administration (MBA); information systems (DBA); information systems management (MBA); international business (MBA, DBA); management (MBA, MSM, DBA); marketing (MBA, DBA); organizational leadership (Ed D); public administration (MBA); sustainable management (MBA).

Argosy University, Los Angeles, College of Business, Santa Monica, CA 90045. Offers accounting (DBA); corporate compliance (MBA); customized professional concentration (MBA, DBA); finance (MBA); fraud examination (MBA); global business sustainability (DBA); healthcare administration (MBA); information systems (DBA); information systems management (MBA); international business (MBA, DBA); management (MBA, MSM, DBA); marketing (MBA, DBA); organizational leadership (Ed D); public administration (MBA); sustainable management (MBA).

Argosy University, Orange County, College of Business, Orange, CA 92868. Offers accounting (DBA, Adv C); corporate compliance (MBA); customized professional concentration (MBA, DBA); finance (MBA, Certificate); fraud examination (MBA); global business sustainability (DBA); healthcare administration (MBA, Certificate); information systems (DBA, Adv C, Certificate); information systems management (MBA); international business (MBA, DBA, Adv C, Certificate); management (MBA, MSM, DBA, Adv C); marketing (MBA, DBA, Adv C, Certificate); organizational leadership (Ed D); public administration (MBA, Certificate); sustainable management (MBA).

Argosy University, Phoenix, College of Business, Phoenix, AZ 85021. Offers accounting (DBA); corporate compliance (MBA); customized professional concentration (MBA, DBA); finance (MBA); fraud examination (MBA); global business sustainability (DBA); healthcare administration (MBA); information systems (DBA); information systems management (MBA); international business (MBA, DBA); management (MBA, DBA); marketing (MBA, DBA); public administration (MBA); sustainable management (MBA).

Argosy University, Salt Lake City, College of Business, Draper, UT 84020. Offers accounting (DBA); corporate compliance (MBA); customized professional concentration (MBA, DBA); finance (MBA); fraud examination (MBA); global business sustainability (DBA); healthcare administration (MBA); information systems (DBA); information systems management (MBA); international business (MBA, DBA); management (MBA, DBA); marketing (MBA, DBA); public administration (MBA); sustainable management (MBA).

Argosy University, San Diego, College of Business, San Diego, CA 92108. Offers accounting (DBA); corporate compliance (MBA); customized professional concentration (MBA, DBA); finance (MBA); fraud examination (MBA); global business sustainability (DBA); information systems (DBA); information systems management (MBA); international business (MBA, DBA); management (MBA, MSM, DBA); marketing (MBA, DBA); organizational leadership (Ed D); public administration (MBA).

Argosy University, San Francisco Bay Area, College of Business, Alameda, CA 94501. Offers accounting (DBA); corporate compliance (MBA); customized professional concentration (MBA, DBA); finance (MBA); fraud examination (MBA); global business sustainability (DBA); healthcare administration (MBA); information systems (DBA); information systems management (MBA); international business (MBA, DBA); management (MBA, MSM, DBA); marketing (MBA, DBA); organizational leadership (Ed D); public administration (MBA); sustainable management (MBA).

Argosy University, Sarasota, College of Business, Sarasota, FL 34235. Offers accounting (DBA, Adv C); corporate compliance (MBA, DBA, Certificate); customized professional concentration (MBA, DBA); finance (MBA, Certificate); fraud examination (MBA, Certificate); global business sustainability (DBA, Adv C); healthcare administration (MBA, Certificate); information systems (DBA, Adv C, Certificate); information systems management (MBA); international business (MBA, DBA, Adv C, Certificate); management (MBA, MSM, DBA, Adv C, Certificate); marketing (MBA, DBA, Adv C, Certificate); organizational leadership (Ed D); public administration (MBA, Certificate); sustainable management (MBA, Certificate).

Argosy University, Schaumburg, College of Business, Schaumburg, IL 60173-5403. Offers accounting (DBA, Adv C); customized professional concentration (MBA, DBA); finance (MBA, Certificate); fraud examination (MBA); global business sustainability (DBA); healthcare administration (MBA, Certificate); information systems (DBA, Adv C, Certificate); information systems management (MBA); international business (MBA, DBA, Adv C, Certificate); management (MBA, MSM, DBA, Adv C, Certificate); marketing (MBA, DBA, Adv C, Certificate); organizational leadership (Ed D); public administration (MBA); sustainable management (MBA).

Argosy University, Seattle, College of Business, Seattle, WA 98121. Offers accounting (DBA); corporate compliance (MBA); customized professional concentration (MBA, DBA); finance (MBA); fraud examination (MBA); global business sustainability (DBA); healthcare administration (MBA); information systems (DBA); information systems management (MBA); international business (MBA, DBA); management (MBA, MSM, DBA); marketing (MBA, DBA); organizational leadership (Ed D); public administration (MBA); sustainable management (MBA).

Argosy University, Tampa, College of Business, Tampa, FL 33607. Offers accounting (DBA); corporate compliance (MBA); customized professional concentration (MBA, DBA); finance (MBA); fraud examination (MBA); global business sustainability (DBA); healthcare administration (MBA); information systems (DBA); information systems management (MBA); international business (MBA, DBA); management (MBA, MSM, DBA); marketing (MBA, DBA); organizational leadership (Ed D); public administration (MBA); sustainable management (MBA).

Argosy University, Twin Cities, College of Business, Eagan, MN 55121. Offers accounting (DBA); customized professional concentration (MBA, DBA); finance (MBA); fraud examination (MBA); global business sustainability (DBA); healthcare administration (MBA); information systems (DBA); information systems management (MBA); international business (MBA, DBA); management (MBA, MSM, DBA); marketing (MBA, DBA); organizational leadership (Ed D); public administration (MBA); sustainable management (MBA).

Argosy University, Washington DC, College of Business, Arlington, VA 22209. Offers accounting (DBA); customized professional concentration (MBA, DBA); finance (MBA); fraud examination (MBA); global business sustainability (DBA); healthcare administration (MBA); information systems (DBA); information systems management (MBA); international business (MBA, DBA, Certificate); management (MBA, MSM, DBA); marketing (MBA, DBA, Certificate); organizational leadership (Ed D); public administration (MBA); sustainable management (MBA).

Arkansas State University—Jonesboro, Graduate School, College of Humanities and Social Sciences, Department of Political Science, Jonesboro, State University, AR 72467. Offers political science (MA); political science education (SCCT); public administration (MPA). *Accreditation:* NASPAA (one or more programs are accredited). Part-time programs available. *Faculty:* 8 full-time (3 women), 1 (woman) part-time/adjunct. *Students:* 24 full-time (8 women), 21 part-time (11 women); includes 12 minority (11 African Americans, 1 American Indian/Alaska Native), 7 international. Average age 32. 27 applicants, 89% accepted, 21 enrolled. In 2009, 17 master's awarded. *Degree requirements:* For master's, comprehensive exam, thesis or alternative; for SCCT, comprehensive exam. *Entrance requirements:* For master's, GRE General Test or MAT, GMAT, appropriate bachelor's degree, letters of recommendation; for SCCT, GRE General Test or MAT, GMAT, interview, master's degree, official transcript, letters of recommendation, immunization records. Additional exam requirements/recommendations for international students: Required—TOEFL (minimum score 550 paper-based; 213 computer-based; 79 iBT), IELTS (minimum score 6). *Application deadline:* For fall admission, 7/1 for domestic and international students; for spring admission, 11/15 for domestic students, 11/13 for international students. Applications are processed on a rolling basis. Application fee: $30 ($40 for international students). Electronic applications accepted. *Expenses:* Tuition, state resident: full-time $3744; part-time $208 per credit hour. Tuition, nonresident: full-time $9540; part-time $530 per credit hour. Required fees: $896; $47 per credit hour. $25 per term. One-time fee: $50. Tuition and fees vary according to course load and program. *Financial support:* In 2009–10, 11 students received support; teaching assistantships, career-related internships or fieldwork, scholarships/grants, and unspecified assistantships available. Financial award application deadline: 7/1; financial award applicants required to submit FAFSA. *Unit head:* Dr. Richard Wang, Chair, 870-972-3048, Fax: 870-972-2720, E-mail: rwang@astate.edu. *Application contact:* Dr. Andrew Sustich, Dean of the Graduate School, 870-972-3029, Fax: 870-972-3857, E-mail: sustich@astate.edu.

Auburn University, Graduate School, College of Liberal Arts, Department of Political Science, Program in Public Administration, Auburn University, AL 36849. Offers MPA, PhD, MPA/MCP. *Accreditation:* NASPAA (one or more programs are accredited). Part-time programs available. *Faculty:* 21 full-time (5 women), 5 part-time/adjunct (1 woman). *Students:* 27 full-time (14 women), 43 part-time (22 women); includes 14 minority (12 African Americans, 1 Asian American or Pacific Islander, 1 Hispanic American), 6 international. Average age 35. 58 applicants, 53% accepted, 14 enrolled. In 2009, 20 master's, 6 doctorates awarded. *Degree requirements:* For master's, internship or research project; for doctorate, thesis/dissertation. *Entrance requirements:* For master's, GRE General Test, sample of written work; for doctorate, GRE General Test. *Application deadline:* For fall admission, 7/7 for domestic students; for spring admission, 11/24 for domestic students. Applications are processed on a rolling basis. Application fee: $50 ($60 for international students). Electronic applications accepted. *Expenses:* Tuition, state resident: full-time $6240. Tuition, nonresident: full-time $18,720. International tuition: $18,938 full-time. Required fees: $492. Tuition and fees vary according to course load, program and reciprocity agreements. *Financial support:* Fellowships, research assistantships, teaching assistantships, career-related internships or fieldwork and Federal Work-Study available. Support available to part-time students. Financial award application deadline: 3/15; financial award applicants required to submit FAFSA. *Faculty research:* Privatization studies, policy evolution, water resources, election administration. *Unit head:* Dr. Caleb Clark, Head, 334-844-5371. *Application contact:* Dr. George Flowers, Dean of the Graduate School, 334-844-2125.

Auburn University Montgomery, School of Sciences, Department of Public Administration and Political Science, Montgomery, AL 36124-4023. Offers MPA, MPS, PhD. *Accreditation:* NASPAA (one or more programs are accredited). Part-time and evening/weekend programs available. *Faculty:* 6 full-time (1 woman), 4 part-time/adjunct (1 woman). *Students:* 31 full-time (22 women), 118 part-time (79 women); includes 68 minority (60 African Americans, 5 Asian Americans or Pacific Islanders, 3 Hispanic Americans), 3 international. Average age 32. In 2009, 22 master's awarded. *Degree requirements:* For master's, comprehensive exam; for doctorate, thesis/dissertation. *Entrance requirements:* For master's, GRE General Test or MAT; for doctorate, GRE General Test. *Application deadline:* Applications are processed on a rolling basis. Electronic applications accepted. *Expenses:* Tuition, state resident: full-time $2841; part-time $225 per credit hour. Tuition, nonresident: full-time $8241; part-time $675 per credit hour. Required fees: $282; $8 per hour. $45 per term. *Financial support:* In 2009–10, 1 research assistantship was awarded; career-related internships or fieldwork and scholarships/grants also available. Support available to part-time students. Financial award application deadline: 3/1; financial award applicants required to submit FAFSA. *Unit head:* Dr. Thomas Vocino, Head, 334-244-3696, Fax: 334-244-3826, E-mail: vocino@mail.aum.edu. *Application contact:* Dr. Glen Ray, Acting Graduate Coordinator, 334-244-3590, Fax: 334-244-3826, E-mail: gray@mail.aum.edu.

Ball State University, Graduate School, College of Sciences and Humanities, Department of Political Science, Program in Public Administration, Muncie, IN 47306-1099. Offers MPA. *Entrance requirements:* For master's, GRE General Test. *Faculty research:* Employment training programs, personnel and labor relations, planning.

Barry University, School of Adult and Continuing Education, Program in Public Administration, Miami Shores, FL 33161-6695. Offers MPA. Part-time and evening/weekend programs available. *Entrance requirements:* For master's, GMAT, GRE or MAT, recommendations. Electronic applications accepted.

Baylor University, Graduate School, College of Arts and Sciences, Department of Political Science, Waco, TX 76798. Offers international studies (MA); political science (MA, PhD); public policy and administration (MPPA); JD/MPPA. *Students:* 28 full-time (8 women), 1 part-time (0 women), 3 international. In 2009, 5 master's, 1 doctorate awarded. *Entrance requirements:* For master's, GRE General Test. *Application deadline:* Applications are processed on a rolling basis. Application fee: $25. *Financial support:* Research assistantships, career-related internships or fieldwork, Federal Work-Study, and institutionally sponsored loans available. Financial award application deadline: 3/1. *Unit head:* Dr. David Corey, Graduate Program Director, 254-710-3161, Fax: 254-710-3122, E-mail: david_d_corey@baylor.edu. *Application contact:* Jenice Langston, Administrative Assistant, 254-710-3161, Fax: 254-710-3870, E-mail: jenice_langston@baylor.edu.

Belhaven University, School of Business, Jackson, MS 39202-1789. Offers business administration (MBA); leadership (MSL); public administration (MPA). MBA program also offered in Houston, TX, Memphis, TN and Orlando, FL. Evening/weekend programs available. *Faculty:* 13 full-time (3 women), 17 part-time/adjunct (2 women). *Students:* 246 full-time (165 women), 21 part-time (15 women); includes 185 minority (166 African Americans, 11 American Indian/Alaska Native, 2 Asian Americans or Pacific Islanders, 6 Hispanic Americans). Average age 36. 222 applicants, 70% accepted, 111 enrolled. In 2009, 60 master's awarded. *Degree requirements:* For master's, comprehensive exam (for some programs), thesis (for some programs). *Entrance requirements:* For master's, GMAT, GRE General Test or MAT, minimum GPA of 2.8. *Application deadline:* Applications are processed on a rolling basis. Application fee: $25. Electronic applications accepted. *Expenses:* Tuition: Full-time $8730; part-time $485 per credit hour. Required fees: $1260; $70 per credit hour. Tuition and fees vary according to campus/location. *Financial support:* Applicants required to submit FAFSA. *Unit head:* Dr. Ralph Mason, Dean, 601-968-8949, Fax: 601-968-8951, E-mail: cmason@belhaven.edu. *Application contact:* Dr. Audrey Kelleher, Vice President of Adult and Graduate Marketing and Development, 407-804-1424, Fax: 407-620-5210, E-mail: akelleher@belhaven.edu.

Bellevue University, Graduate School, Bellevue, NE 68005-3098. Offers acquisition and contract management (MS); business administration (MBA); clinical counseling (MS); computer information systems (MS); healthcare administration (MA, MHA, MS), including healthcare administration (MHA), human services (MA, MS); human capital management (MS, PhD); instructional design and development (MS); leadership (MA); management (MA); management information systems (MS); organizational performance (MS); public administration (MPA); public health (MPH); security management (MS). Part-time and evening/weekend programs available. Postbaccalaureate distance learning degree programs offered (no on-campus study). *Degree requirements:* For master's, thesis or project. *Entrance requirements:* For master's, minimum GPA of 2.5 in last 60 hours. Additional exam requirements/recommendations for international students: Required—TOEFL (minimum score 538 paper-based; 200 computer-based).

Bernard M. Baruch College of the City University of New York, School of Public Affairs, Program in Public Administration, New York, NY 10010-5585. Offers nonprofit administration (MPA); public management (MPA); MS/MPA. *Accreditation:* NASPAA. Part-time and evening/weekend programs available. *Degree requirements:* For master's, thesis, capstone. *Entrance requirements:* For master's, GRE General Test. Additional exam requirements/recommendations for international students: Required—TOEFL (minimum score 625 paper-based; 263 computer-based; 106 iBT). Electronic applications accepted. *Expenses:* Contact institution. *Faculty research:* Urbanization, population and poverty in the developing world, housing and community development, labor unions and housing, government-nongovernment relations, immigration policy, social network analysis, cross-sectoral governance, comparative healthcare systems, program evaluation, social welfare policy, health outcomes, educational policy and leadership, transnationalism, infant health, welfare reform, racial/ethnic disparities in health, urban politics, homelessness, race and ethnic relations.

Birmingham-Southern College, Program in Public and Private Management, Birmingham, AL 35254. Offers MPPM. *Accreditation:* AACSB. Part-time and evening/weekend programs available. *Degree requirements:* For master's, thesis optional. *Entrance requirements:* For master's, GMAT, GRE, or MAT.

Boise State University, Graduate College, College of Social Sciences and Public Affairs, Department of Public Policy and Administration, Boise, ID 83725-0399. Offers environmental and natural resources policy and administration (MPA); general public administration (MPA); state and local government policy and administration (MPA). *Accreditation:* NASPAA. Part-time programs available. *Degree requirements:* For master's, comprehensive exam, directed research project, internship. *Entrance requirements:* For master's, GRE General Test, minimum GPA of 3.0. Additional exam requirements/recommendations for international students: Required—TOEFL. Electronic applications accepted. *Expenses:* Tuition, state resident: full-time $3106; part-time $209 per credit. Tuition, nonresident: part-time $284 per credit.

Boston University, School of Management, Master of Business Administration Program, Boston, MA 02215. Offers entrepreneurship (MBA); finance (MBA); health sector management (MBA); international management (MBA); marketing (MBA); operations and technology management (MBA); public and nonprofit management (MBA); strategy and business analysis (MBA); JD/MBA; MBA/MA; MBA/MPH; MBA/MS; MBA/MSIS; MS/MBA. Part-time and evening/weekend programs available. *Faculty:* 119 full-time (31 women), 99 part-time/adjunct (30 women). *Students:* 326 full-time (138 women), 677 part-time (257 women); includes 149 minority (13 African Americans, 119 Asian Americans or Pacific Islanders, 17 Hispanic Americans), 149 international. Average age 30. 1,617 applicants, 38% accepted, 317 enrolled. In 2009, 284 master's awarded. *Entrance requirements:* For master's, GMAT, resume, 2 letters of recommendation. Additional exam requirements/recommendations for international students: Required—TOEFL or IELTS. *Application deadline:* For fall admission, 3/15 for domestic and international students; for spring admission, 11/15 for domestic students. Application fee: $125. Electronic applications accepted. *Expenses:* Tuition: Full-time $37,910; part-time $1184 per credit hour. Required fees: $386; $40 per semester. Part-time tuition and fees vary according to class time, course level, degree level and program. *Financial support:* Career-related internships or fieldwork, Federal Work-Study, institutionally sponsored loans, and scholarships/grants available. Support available to part-time students. Financial award applicants required to submit FAFSA. *Unit head:* Katherine Nolan, Assistant Dean, Graduate Programs, 617-353-4157, Fax: 617-353-5003, E-mail: mba@bu.edu. *Application contact:* Hayden Estrada, Assistant Dean, Admissions, 617-353-2670, Fax: 617-353-7368, E-mail: mba@bu.edu.

Bowie State University, Graduate Programs, Program in Public Administration, Bowie, MD 20715-9465. Offers MPA. Part-time and evening/weekend programs available. *Degree requirements:* For master's, comprehensive exam. *Entrance requirements:* For master's, minimum undergraduate GPA of 2.5. Electronic applications accepted.

Bowling Green State University, Graduate College, College of Arts and Sciences, Department of Political Science, Program in Public Administration, Bowling Green, OH 43403. Offers MPA. *Degree requirements:* For master's, comprehensive exam or thesis, experiential paper for all non-thesis students. *Entrance requirements:* For master's, GRE General Test. Additional exam requirements/recommendations for international students: Required—TOEFL. Electronic applications accepted. *Faculty research:* Public sector labor relations, administrative law, sexual harassment and violence in the public workplace.

Bridgewater State University, School of Graduate Studies, School of Arts and Sciences, Department of Political Science, Program in Public Administration, Bridgewater, MA 02325-0001. Offers MPA. *Accreditation:* NASPAA. *Entrance requirements:* For master's, GRE General Test.

Brigham Young University, Graduate Studies, Marriott School of Management, Executive Master of Public Administration Program, Provo, UT 84602. Offers EMPA, JD/MPA. *Accreditation:* NASPAA (one or more programs are accredited). Part-time and evening/weekend programs available. *Faculty:* 8 full-time (1 woman), 4 part-time/adjunct (0 women). *Students:* 139 part-time (49 women); includes 17 minority (2 African Americans, 3 American Indian/Alaska Native, 6 Asian Americans or Pacific Islanders, 6 Hispanic Americans). Average age 37. 69 applicants, 75% accepted, 49 enrolled. In 2009, 38 master's awarded. *Application deadline:* For fall admission, 5/1 for domestic students. Application fee: $50. Electronic applications accepted. *Expenses:* Contact institution. *Financial support:* In 2009–10, 11 students received support. Application deadline: 6/15. *Unit head:* Dr. David W. Hart, Director, 801-422-7391, Fax: 801-422-0311, E-mail: mpa@byu.edu. *Application contact:* Catherine L. Cooper, Director of Student Services, 801-422-9173, Fax: 801-422-0311, E-mail: mpa@byu.edu.

Brigham Young University, Graduate Studies, Marriott School of Management, Master of Public Administration Program, Provo, UT 84602. Offers finance (MPA); human resources (MPA); local government (MPA); nonprofit management (MPA); JD/MPA. *Faculty:* 10 full-time (4 women), 18 part-time/adjunct (1 woman). *Students:* 128 full-time (54 women); includes 26 minority (3 African Americans, 13 Asian Americans or Pacific Islanders, 10 Hispanic Americans). Average age 27. 136 applicants, 66% accepted, 62 enrolled. In 2009, 53 master's awarded. *Entrance requirements:* For master's, GRE, GMAT, minimum GPA of 3.0. Additional exam requirements/recommendations for international students: Required—TOEFL (minimum score 580 paper-based; 85 iBT), IELTS (minimum score 7). *Application deadline:* For fall admission, 2/1 for domestic and international students. Application fee: $50. Electronic applications accepted. *Expenses:* Tuition: Full-time $5580; part-time $301 per credit hour. Tuition and fees vary according to student's religious affiliation. *Financial support:* In 2009–10, 96 students received support. Career-related internships or fieldwork and scholarships/grants available. Financial award application deadline: 4/15; financial award applicants required to submit FAFSA. *Faculty research:* Taxes, budgeting, nonprofit, ethics, decision modeling, work balance, organizational behavior. *Unit head:* Dr. David W. Hart, Director, 801-422-4221, Fax: 801-422-0311, E-mail: mpa@byu.edu. *Application contact:* Catherine Cooper, Director of Student Services, E-mail: mpa@byu.edu.

California Baptist University, Program in Public Administration, Riverside, CA 92504-3206. Offers MPA. Part-time programs available. *Faculty:* 3 full-time (1 woman), 1 (woman) part-time/adjunct. *Students:* 26 full-time (13 women), 24 part-time (14 women); includes 24 minority (13 African Americans, 2 Asian Americans or Pacific Islanders, 9 Hispanic Americans), 5 international. 32 applicants, 66% accepted, 16 enrolled. In 2009, 6 master's awarded. *Degree requirements:* For master's, thesis. *Entrance requirements:* For master's, minimum GPA of 2.75. Additional exam requirements/recommendations for international students: Required—TOEFL (minimum score 575 paper-based; 230 computer-based; 89 iBT). *Application deadline:* For fall admission, 8/1 priority date for domestic students, 7/1 for international students; for spring admission, 12/1 priority date for domestic students, 10/15 for international students. Applications are processed on a rolling basis. Application fee: $45. Electronic applications accepted. *Expenses:* Tuition: Full-time $8352; part-time $464 per semester hour. Required fees: $125 per semester. Tuition and fees vary according to course load, campus/location and program. *Financial support:* Federal Work-Study and scholarships/grants available. Support available to part-time students. Financial award applicants required to submit FAFSA. *Unit head:* Dr. Patricia Kircher, Director, 951-343-4306, Fax: 951-343-4661, E-mail: pkircher@calbaptist.edu. *Application contact:* Gail Ronveaux, Dean of Graduate Enrollment, 951-343-5045, Fax: 951-343-5095, E-mail: graduateadmissions@calbaptist.edu.

California Lutheran University, Graduate Studies, Program in Public Policy and Administration, Thousand Oaks, CA 91360-2787. Offers MPPA. *Degree requirements:* For master's, comprehensive exam, thesis or project, internship. *Entrance requirements:* For master's, GMAT or GRE General Test, interview, minimum GPA of 3.0. *Expenses:* Contact institution.

California State Polytechnic University, Pomona, Academic Affairs, College of Letters, Arts, and Social Sciences, Program in Public Administration, Pomona, CA 91768-2557. Offers MPA. *Accreditation:* NASPAA. Part-time programs available. *Students:* 11 full-time (4 women), 63 part-time (38 women); includes 50 minority (10 African Americans, 12 Asian Americans or Pacific Islanders, 28 Hispanic Americans), 2 international. Average age 32. 60 applicants, 35% accepted, 15 enrolled. In 2009, 7 master's awarded. *Degree requirements:* For master's, thesis or alternative. *Entrance requirements:* For master's, GRE General Test. *Application deadline:* For fall admission, 5/1 priority date for domestic students; for winter admission, 10/15 priority date for domestic students; for spring admission, 1/20 priority date for domestic students. Applications are processed on a rolling basis. Application fee: $55. Electronic applications accepted. *Expenses:* Tuition, nonresident: full-time $6696; part-time $248 per credit. Required fees: $5487; $3237 per term. Tuition and fees vary according to course load, degree level and program. *Unit head:* Dr. Sandra M. Emerson, Director, 909-869-3879, E-mail: smemerson@csupomona.edu. *Application contact:* Scott J. Duncan, Director, Admissions, 909-869-3258, Fax: 909-869-4529, E-mail: sjduncan@csupomona.edu.

California State University, Bakersfield, Division of Graduate Studies, School of Business and Public Administration, Program in Public Administration, Bakersfield, CA 93311. Offers MPA. *Accreditation:* NASPAA. *Degree requirements:* For master's, thesis or alternative. *Entrance requirements:* For master's, GRE, minimum GPA of 2.75.

California State University, Chico, Graduate School, College of Behavioral and Social Sciences, Department of Political Science, Program in Public Administration, Chico, CA 95929-0722. Offers health administration (MPA); local government management (MPA); public administration (MPA). *Accreditation:* NASPAA. Part-time programs available. *Students:* 21 full-time (7 women), 26 part-time (13 women); includes 18 minority (4 African Americans, 1 American Indian/Alaska Native, 5 Asian Americans or Pacific Islanders, 8 Hispanic Americans), 4 international. Average age 31. 44 applicants, 91% accepted, 19 enrolled. In 2009, 10 master's awarded. *Entrance requirements:* For master's, 2 letters of recommendation. Additional exam requirements/recommendations for international students: Required—TOEFL (minimum score 550 paper-based; 213 computer-based; 80 iBT), IELTS (minimum score 6.5). *Application deadline:* For fall admission, 3/1 priority date for domestic students, 3/1 for international students; for spring admission, 9/15 priority date for domestic students, 9/15 for international students. Applications are processed on a rolling basis. Application fee: $55. Electronic applications accepted. *Financial support:* Fellowships, career-related internships or fieldwork available. *Unit head:* Dr. Donna Kemp, Graduate Coordinator, 530-898-5734. *Application contact:* Dr. Donna Kemp, Graduate Coordinator, 530-898-5734.

California State University, Dominguez Hills, College of Business Administration and Public Policy, Program in Public Administration, Carson, CA 90747-0001. Offers MPA. *Accreditation:* NASPAA. Part-time and evening/weekend programs available. Postbaccalaureate distance learning degree programs offered (no on-campus study). *Faculty:* 4 full-time (all women), 8 part-time/adjunct (4 women). *Students:* 60 full-time (42 women), 168 part-time (114 women); includes 140 minority (90 African Americans, 2 American Indian/Alaska Native, 20 Asian Americans or Pacific Islanders, 28 Hispanic Americans), 8 international. Average age 36. 100 applicants, 32% accepted, 14 enrolled. In 2009, 90 master's awarded. *Degree requirements:* For master's, thesis or alternative, capstone project. *Entrance requirements:* For master's, GRE, minimum GPA of 2.75. Additional exam requirements/recommendations for international students: Required—TOEFL (minimum score 550 paper-based; 213 computer-based; 79 iBT). *Application deadline:* For fall admission, 4/1 for domestic and international students; for spring admission, 11/1 for domestic students, 10/1 for international students. Application fee: $55. *Expenses:* Tuition, nonresident: full-time $6696; part-time $372 per unit. Required fees: $5946; $1752 per semester. *Faculty research:* Applied public management. *Unit head:* Dr. Kaye Bragg, Interim Chair, 310-243-2356, E-mail: kbragg@csudh.edu. *Application contact:* Eileen Hall, Graduate Advisor, 310-243-3465, E-mail: ehall@csudh.edu.

California State University, East Bay, Academic Programs and Graduate Studies, College of Letters, Arts, and Social Sciences, Department of Public Affairs and Administration, Hayward,

Public Administration

California State University, East Bay (continued)
CA 94542-3000. Offers health care administration (MS); public administration (MPA). Part-time and evening/weekend programs available. *Faculty:* 8 full-time (4 women), 9 part-time/adjunct (1 woman). *Students:* 48 full-time (30 women), 241 part-time (162 women); includes 147 minority (54 African Americans, 1 American Indian/Alaska Native, 67 Asian Americans or Pacific Islanders, 25 Hispanic Americans), 38 international. Average age 34. 266 applicants, 58% accepted, 100 enrolled. In 2009, 92 master's awarded. *Degree requirements:* For master's, comprehensive exam or thesis. *Entrance requirements:* For master's, minimum GPA of 2.5. Additional exam requirements/recommendations for international students: Required—TOEFL (minimum score 550 paper-based; 213 computer-based). *Application deadline:* For fall admission, 4/15 for domestic students. Application fee: $55. Electronic applications accepted. *Financial support:* Fellowships, teaching assistantships, career-related internships or fieldwork, Federal Work-Study, institutionally sponsored loans, and scholarships/grants available. Support available to part-time students. Financial award application deadline: 3/1; financial award applicants required to submit FAFSA. *Unit head:* Prof. Toni Fogarty, Chair, 510-885-2268, Fax: 510-885-3726, E-mail: toni.fogarty@csueastbay.edu. *Application contact:* Donna Wiley, Interim Associate Director, 510-885-2928, Fax: 510-885-4777, E-mail: donna.wiley@csueastbay.edu.

California State University, Fresno, Division of Graduate Studies, College of Social Sciences, Department of Political Science, Program in Public Administration, Fresno, CA 93740-8027. Offers MPA. *Accreditation:* NASPAA. Part-time and evening/weekend programs available. *Degree requirements:* For master's, thesis or alternative. *Entrance requirements:* For master's, GRE General Test or GMAT, minimum GPA of 3.0. Additional exam requirements/recommendations for international students: Required—TOEFL. Electronic applications accepted.

California State University, Fullerton, Graduate Studies, College of Humanities and Social Sciences, Division of Politics, Administration, and Justice, Fullerton, CA 92834-9480. Offers political science (MA); public administration (MPA). *Accreditation:* NASPAA (one or more programs are accredited). Part-time programs available. *Students:* 28 full-time (17 women), 144 part-time (68 women); includes 89 minority (5 African Americans, 1 American Indian/Alaska Native, 33 Asian Americans or Pacific Islanders, 50 Hispanic Americans), 3 international. Average age 30. 165 applicants, 47% accepted, 46 enrolled. In 2009, 62 master's awarded. *Degree requirements:* For master's, comprehensive exam, project or thesis. *Entrance requirements:* For master's, minimum GPA of 2.5 in last 60 units of course work, 12 units of course work in social sciences. Application fee: $55. *Expenses:* Tuition, nonresident: full-time $11,160; part-time $373 per credit. Required fees: $1440 per term. Tuition and fees vary according to course load, degree level and program. *Financial support:* Career-related internships or fieldwork, Federal Work-Study, institutionally sponsored loans, and scholarships/grants available. Support available to part-time students. Financial award application deadline: 3/1; financial award applicants required to submit FAFSA. *Faculty research:* Emergency management plans. *Unit head:* Dr. Phil Gianos, Chair, 657-278-3521. *Application contact:* Admissions/Applications, 657-278-2371.

California State University, Long Beach, Graduate Studies, College of Health and Human Services, Graduate Center for Public Policy and Administration, Long Beach, CA 90840. Offers MPA. *Accreditation:* NASPAA. Part-time and evening/weekend programs available. *Faculty:* 14 full-time (6 women), 2 part-time/adjunct (0 women). *Students:* 71 full-time (47 women), 166 part-time (100 women); includes 150 minority (25 African Americans, 3 American Indian/Alaska Native, 47 Asian Americans or Pacific Islanders, 75 Hispanic Americans), 6 international. Average age 31. 199 applicants, 78% accepted, 121 enrolled. *Degree requirements:* For master's, comprehensive exam. *Entrance requirements:* For master's, minimum GPA of 2.75. *Application deadline:* For fall admission, 7/1 for domestic students. Applications are processed on a rolling basis. Application fee: $55. Electronic applications accepted. *Expenses:* Required fees: $1802 per semester. Part-time tuition and fees vary according to course load. *Financial support:* Fellowships, career-related internships or fieldwork, Federal Work-Study, institutionally sponsored loans, and scholarships/grants available. Financial award application deadline: 3/2. *Faculty research:* Transportation access, air quality controls, coastal issues, intergovernmental relations. *Unit head:* Dr. Walter Frank Baber, Director, 562-985-4178, Fax: 562-985-4672, E-mail: wbaber@csulb.edu. *Application contact:* Dr. Walter Frank Baber, Director, 562-985-4178, Fax: 562-985-4672, E-mail: wbaber@csulb.edu.

California State University, Los Angeles, Graduate Studies, College of Natural and Social Sciences, Department of Political Science, Los Angeles, CA 90032-8530. Offers political science (MA); public administration (MS). Part-time and evening/weekend programs available. *Faculty:* 5 full-time (1 woman), 4 part-time/adjunct (2 women). *Students:* 13 full-time (5 women), 110 part-time (69 women); includes 69 minority (7 African Americans, 12 Asian Americans or Pacific Islanders, 50 Hispanic Americans), 14 international. Average age 31. 73 applicants, 100% accepted, 28 enrolled. In 2009, 20 master's awarded. *Degree requirements:* For master's, comprehensive exam or thesis. *Entrance requirements:* Additional exam requirements/recommendations for international students: Required—TOEFL (minimum score 500 paper-based; 173 computer-based). *Application deadline:* For fall admission, 5/1 for domestic and international students. Applications are processed on a rolling basis. Application fee: $55. Electronic applications accepted. *Financial support:* Career-related internships or fieldwork and Federal Work-Study available. Support available to part-time students. Financial award application deadline: 3/1. *Faculty research:* Government; public policy and law; international, political, and economic relations; comparative politics. *Unit head:* Dr. Scott Bowman, Chair, 323-343-2248, Fax: 323-343-6452, E-mail: sbowman@calstatela.edu. *Application contact:* Dr. Cheryl L. Ney, Associate Vice President for Academic Affairs and Dean of Graduate Studies, 323-343-3820, Fax: 323-343-5653, E-mail: cney@cslanet.calstatela.edu.

California State University, Northridge, Graduate Studies, The Tseng College of Extended Learning, Northridge, CA 91330. Offers knowledge management (MKM); public administration (MPA); taxation (MS). *Entrance requirements:* For master's, GRE (if cumulative undergraduate GPA less than 3.0). *Unit head:* Joyce Feucht-Haviar, Dean, 866-873-6439. *Application contact:* Joyce Feucht-Haviar, Dean, 866-873-6439.

California State University, Sacramento, Graduate Studies, College of Social Sciences and Interdisciplinary Studies, Program in Public Policy and Administration, Sacramento, CA 95819. Offers MPPA. Part-time programs available. *Degree requirements:* For master's, thesis or alternative, writing proficiency exam. *Entrance requirements:* For master's, GRE General Test. Additional exam requirements/recommendations for international students: Required—TOEFL. Electronic applications accepted.

California State University, San Bernardino, Graduate Studies, College of Business and Public Administration, Program in Public Administration, San Bernardino, CA 92407-2397. Offers MPA. *Accreditation:* NASPAA. Part-time and evening/weekend programs available. *Faculty:* 6 full-time (2 women), 3 part-time/adjunct (1 woman). *Students:* 138 full-time (77 women), 79 part-time (50 women); includes 115 minority (36 African Americans, 1 American Indian/Alaska Native, 9 Asian Americans or Pacific Islanders, 69 Hispanic Americans), 11 international. Average age 34. 179 applicants, 83% accepted, 92 enrolled. In 2009, 36 master's awarded. *Degree requirements:* For master's, comprehensive exam, advancement to candidacy. *Application deadline:* For fall admission, 8/31 priority date for domestic students. Applications are processed on a rolling basis. Application fee: $55. *Financial support:* Career-related internships or fieldwork, Federal Work-Study, and institutionally sponsored loans available. Support available to part-time students. Financial award application deadline: 3/1. *Unit head:* Dr. Montgomery Vanwart, Director, 909-537-5758, Fax: 909-537-7517, E-mail: mvanwart@csusb.edu. *Application contact:* Olivia Rosas, Director of Admissions, 909-537-7577, Fax: 909-537-7034, E-mail: orosas@csusb.edu.

California State University, Stanislaus, College of Humanities and Social Sciences, Department of Politics and Public Administration, Turlock, CA 95382. Offers public administration (MPA). *Accreditation:* NASPAA. Part-time and evening/weekend programs available. *Degree requirements:* For master's, comprehensive exam, thesis or alternative. *Entrance requirements:* For master's, minimum GPA of 2.7, 3 letters of reference. Additional exam requirements/recommendations for international students: Required—TOEFL (minimum score 550 paper-based; 213 computer-based), ELPT (minimum score: 954). Electronic applications accepted. *Faculty research:* Blogging in the Middle East, incumbency and electoral competitiveness, legislative acceptance of gubernatorial budget proposals.

Capella University, School of Public Service Leadership, Minneapolis, MN 55402. Offers criminal justice (MS, PhD); emergency management (MS, PhD); general human services (MS, PhD); general public administration (MPA, DPA); gerontology (MS); health care administration (MS, PhD); health management and policy (MSPH); management of nonprofit agencies (MS, PhD); nurse educator (MS); public safety leadership (MS, PhD); social and community services (MS, PhD); social behavioral sciences (MSPH).

Carleton University, Faculty of Graduate Studies, Faculty of Public Affairs and Management, School of Public Policy and Administration, Ottawa, ON K1S 5B6, Canada. Offers public administration (MA, DPA); public policy (PhD). Part-time programs available. *Degree requirements:* For master's, thesis optional; for doctorate, one foreign language, comprehensive exam, thesis/dissertation. *Entrance requirements:* For master's, GRE, honors degree; for doctorate, master's degree. Additional exam requirements/recommendations for international students: Required—TOEFL. *Faculty research:* Canadian public administration and policy, development administration, public policy analysis, public management.

Carnegie Mellon University, H. John Heinz III College, School of Public Policy and Management, Program in Public Management, Pittsburgh, PA 15213-3891. Offers MPM. Part-time and evening/weekend programs available. *Degree requirements:* For master's, internship.

Central Michigan University, Central Michigan University Off-Campus Programs, Program in Administration, Mount Pleasant, MI 48859. Offers acquisitions administration (MSA, Certificate); general administration (MSA, Certificate); health services administration (MSA, Certificate); human resources administration (MSA, Certificate); information resource management (MSA, Certificate); international administration (MSA, Certificate); leadership (MSA, Certificate); public administration (MSA, Certificate); vehicle design and manufacturing administration (MSA, Certificate). Part-time and evening/weekend programs available. Postbaccalaureate distance learning degree programs offered (no on-campus study). *Students:* Average age 38. *Entrance requirements:* For master's, minimum GPA of 2.7 in major. *Application deadline:* Applications are processed on a rolling basis. Application fee: $50. Electronic applications accepted. *Financial support:* Scholarships/grants available. Support available to part-time students. Financial award applicants required to submit FAFSA. *Unit head:* Dr. Nana Korsah, Director, MSA Programs, 989-774-6525, E-mail: korsa1na@cmich.edu. *Application contact:* 877-268-4636, E-mail: cmuoffcampus@cmich.edu.

Central Michigan University, Central Michigan University Off-Campus Programs, Program in Public Administration, Mount Pleasant, MI 48859. Offers public management (MPA); state and local government (MPA). Part-time and evening/weekend programs available. *Entrance requirements:* For master's, minimum GPA of 2.8. Additional exam requirements/recommendations for international students: Required—TOEFL. Electronic applications accepted. *Financial support:* Scholarships/grants available. Support available to part-time students. *Unit head:* Dr. Lawrence Sych, Program Director, 989-774-3316, E-mail: sych1l@cmich.edu. *Application contact:* 877-268-4636, E-mail: cmuoffcampus@cmich.edu.

Central Michigan University, College of Graduate Studies, College of Humanities and Social and Behavioral Sciences, Department of Political Science, Program in Public Administration, Mount Pleasant, MI 48859. Offers professional development in public administration (Graduate Certificate); public administration (MPA), including cognate courses option; public management (MPA); state and local government (MPA). Part-time programs available. *Degree requirements:* For master's, thesis or alternative. Electronic applications accepted.

Central Michigan University, College of Graduate Studies, Interdisciplinary Administration Programs, Mount Pleasant, MI 48859. Offers acquisitions administration (MSA, Graduate Certificate); general administration (MSA, Graduate Certificate); health services administration (MSA, Graduate Certificate); human resource administration (Graduate Certificate); human resources administration (MSA); information resource management (MSA, Graduate Certificate); international administration (MSA, Graduate Certificate); leadership (MSA); organizational communication (MSA, Graduate Certificate); public administration (MSA, Graduate Certificate); recreation and park administration (MSA); sport administration (MSA). *Accreditation:* AACSB. Part-time and evening/weekend programs available. Postbaccalaureate distance learning degree programs offered (no on-campus study). *Degree requirements:* For master's, thesis or alternative. *Entrance requirements:* For master's, bachelor's degree with minimum GPA of 2.7. Electronic applications accepted. *Faculty research:* Interdisciplinary studies in acquisitions administration, health services administration, sport administration, recreation and park administration, and international administration.

Cheyney University of Pennsylvania, School of Education and Professional Studies, Program in Public Administration, Cheyney, PA 19319. Offers MPA.

City College of the City University of New York, Graduate School, College of Liberal Arts and Science, Division of Social Science, New York, NY 10031-9198. Offers economics (MA); international relations (MA); psychology (MA, PhD), including clinical psychology (PhD), experimental cognition (PhD), general psychology (MA), mental health counseling (MA); public service management (MPA); sociology (MA). Part-time programs available. *Students:* 39 full-time (29 women), 37 part-time (26 women); includes 35 minority (13 African Americans, 10 Asian Americans or Pacific Islanders, 12 Hispanic Americans), 19 international. 207 applicants, 64% accepted. In 2009, 75 master's awarded. *Entrance requirements:* For master's, GRE. Additional exam requirements/recommendations for international students: Required—TOEFL (minimum score 500 paper-based; 61 iBT). *Application deadline:* For fall admission, 3/15 priority date for domestic and international students; for spring admission, 11/15 priority date for domestic and international students. Applications are processed on a rolling basis. Application fee: $125. Electronic applications accepted. *Financial support:* Fellowships, research assistantships, teaching assistantships, career-related internships or fieldwork, Federal Work-Study, institutionally sponsored loans, scholarships/grants, and tuition waivers (full and partial) available. Support available to part-time students. Financial award applicants required to submit FAFSA. *Unit head:* Marilyn Hoskin, Dean, 212-650-5967, E-mail: mhoskin@ccny.cuny.edu. *Application contact:* Marilyn Hoskin, Dean, 212-650-5967, E-mail: mhoskin@ccny.cuny.edu.

Clark Atlanta University, School of Arts and Sciences, Department of Public Administration, Atlanta, GA 30314. Offers MPA. *Accreditation:* NASPAA. Part-time programs available. *Faculty:* 3 full-time (1 woman), 1 (woman) part-time/adjunct. *Students:* 13 full-time (8 women), 26 part-time (20 women); includes 31 minority (all African Americans), 1 international. Average age 28. 10 applicants, 90% accepted, 6 enrolled. In 2009, 7 master's awarded. *Degree requirements:* For master's, one foreign language, thesis or alternative. *Entrance requirements:* For master's, GRE General Test, minimum GPA of 2.5. Additional exam requirements/recommendations for international students: Required—TOEFL (minimum score 500 paper-based; 173 computer-based). *Application deadline:* For fall admission, 4/1 for domestic and international students; for spring admission, 11/1 for domestic and international students. Applications are processed on a rolling basis. Application fee: $40 ($55 for international students). *Expenses:* Tuition: Full-time $12,240; part-time $680 per credit hour. Required fees: $710; $355 per semester. *Financial support:* Scholarships/grants and unspecified assistantships available. Financial award application deadline: 4/30; financial award applicants required to submit FAFSA. *Faculty research:* Nutrition education, Africa. *Unit head:* Dr. Ron Finnell, Chairperson, 404-880-6651, E-mail: rfinnell@cau.edu. *Application contact:* Michelle Clark-Davis, Graduate Program Admissions, 404-880-6605, E-mail: cauadmissions@cau.edu.

Clark University, Graduate School, College of Professional and Continuing Education, Program in Public Administration, Worcester, MA 01610-1477. Offers MPA, Certificate. Part-time and evening/weekend programs available. *Students:* 23 full-time (14 women), 29 part-time (23 women); includes 5 minority (2 African Americans, 2 Asian Americans or Pacific Islanders, 1 Hispanic American), 4 international. Average age 31. 29 applicants, 100% accepted, 23 enrolled. In 2009, 34 master's awarded. *Degree requirements:* For master's, thesis optional. *Entrance requirements:* For master's, GMAT or GRE General Test. *Application deadline:* Applications are processed on a rolling basis. Application fee: $50. Electronic applications accepted. *Expenses:* Tuition: Full-time $34,900; part-time $4362.50 per course. *Financial support:* Career-related internships or fieldwork available. Support available to part-time students. *Unit head:* Max E. Hess, Director of Graduate Studies, 508-793-7217, Fax: 508-793-7232. *Application contact:* Julia Parent, Director of Marketing, Communications, and Admissions, 508-793-7217, Fax: 508-793-7232, E-mail: jparent@clarku.edu.

Cleveland State University, College of Graduate Studies, Maxine Goodman Levin College of Urban Affairs, Program in Public Administration, Cleveland, OH 44115. Offers geographic information systems (Certificate); local and urban management (Certificate); non-profit management (Certificate); public administration (MPA); urban real estate development (Certificate); JD/MPA. *Accreditation:* NASPAA. Part-time and evening/weekend programs available. *Degree requirements:* For master's, thesis or alternative, capstone course. *Entrance requirements:* For master's, GRE General Test (minimum 40th percentile verbal and quantitative, 4.0 writing), minimum GPA of 3.0. Additional exam requirements/recommendations for international students: Required—TOEFL (minimum score 525 paper-based; 197 computer-based; 65 iBT). Electronic applications accepted. *Faculty research:* Health care administration, public management, economic development, city management, nonprofit management.

The College at Brockport, State University of New York, School of Education and Human Services, Department of Public Administration, Brockport, NY 14420-2997. Offers arts administration (AGC); nonprofit management (AGC); public administration (MPA), including general public administration, health care management, nonprofit management, public safety. *Accreditation:* NASPAA. Part-time and evening/weekend programs available. *Students:* 25 full-time (18 women), 91 part-time (72 women); includes 18 minority (12 African Americans, 3 Asian Americans or Pacific Islanders, 3 Hispanic Americans). 42 applicants, 95% accepted, 33 enrolled. In 2009, 30 master's awarded. *Degree requirements:* For master's, thesis or alternative. *Entrance requirements:* For master's, GRE or minimum GPA of 3.0, letters of recommendation, statement of objectives. Additional exam requirements/recommendations for international students: Required—TOEFL (minimum score 550 paper-based; 213 computer-based; 79 iBT). *Application deadline:* For fall admission, 3/1 priority date for domestic and international students; for spring admission, 10/1 priority date for domestic and international students. Application fee: $50. Electronic applications accepted. *Expenses:* Tuition, state resident: full-time $8370; part-time $349 per credit. Tuition, nonresident: full-time $13,250; part-time $522 per credit. *Financial support:* In 2009–10, 1 fellowship with full tuition reimbursement (averaging $7,500 per year) was awarded; Federal Work-Study, scholarships/grants, and unspecified assistantships also available. Support available to part-time students. Financial award application deadline: 3/15; financial award applicants required to submit FAFSA. *Faculty research:* E-government, performance management, nonprofits and policy implementation, Medicaid and disabilities. *Unit head:* Dr. James Fatula, Chairperson, 585-395-2375, Fax: 585-395-2172, E-mail: jfatula@brockport.edu. *Application contact:* Dr. James Fatual, Chairperson, 585-395-2375, Fax: 585-395-2172, E-mail: jfatula@brockport.edu.

College of Charleston, Graduate School, School of Humanities and Social Sciences, Program in Public Administration, Charleston, SC 29424-0001. Offers MPA. *Accreditation:* NASPAA. Part-time programs available. *Faculty:* 12 full-time (6 women), 8 part-time/adjunct (4 women). *Students:* 28 full-time (21 women), 24 part-time (18 women); includes 5 minority (3 African Americans, 2 Hispanic Americans). Average age 27. 38 applicants, 68% accepted, 20 enrolled. In 2009, 22 master's awarded. *Degree requirements:* For master's, internship, capstone seminar. *Entrance requirements:* For master's, GRE General Test, previous course work in statistics, 3 letters of recommendation, minimum GPA of 3.0. Additional exam requirements/recommendations for international students: Required—TOEFL. *Application deadline:* For fall admission, 7/1 for domestic students; for spring admission, 11/1 for domestic students. Applications are processed on a rolling basis. Application fee: $45. Electronic applications accepted. *Financial support:* In 2009–10, 6 research assistantships (averaging $12,400 per year) were awarded; career-related internships or fieldwork, Federal Work-Study, scholarships/grants, and unspecified assistantships also available. Support available to part-time students. Financial award application deadline: 4/1; financial award applicants required to submit FAFSA. *Faculty research:* Local government, environmental policy, budgeting, ethics. *Unit head:* Dr. Kendra Stewart, Acting Director, 843-953-5724, Fax: 843-953-8140, E-mail: stewartk@cofc.edu. *Application contact:* Susan Hallatt, Director of Graduate Admissions, 843-953-5614, Fax: 843-953-1434, E-mail: hallatts@cofc.edu.

College of Saint Elizabeth, Program in Justice Studies, Morristown, NJ 07960-6989. Offers justice administration and public service (MA). Part-time and evening/weekend programs available. *Faculty:* 1 full-time (0 women). *Students:* 1 (woman) full-time, 8 part-time (5 women); includes 4 minority (all African Americans). Average age 34. 10 applicants, 80% accepted, 7 enrolled. *Expenses:* Tuition: Part-time $797 per credit hour. Required fees: $65 per credit hour. *Unit head:* Dr. James Ford. *Application contact:* Donna Tatarka, Dean of Admission, 973-290-4705, Fax: 973-290-4710, E-mail: dtatarka@cse.edu.

Columbia University, School of International and Public Affairs, Program in Public Policy and Administration, New York, NY 10027. Offers MPA, JD/MPA, MPA/MS, MPH/MPA. *Entrance requirements:* For master's, GRE General Test. Additional exam requirements/recommendations for international students: Required—TOEFL (minimum score 600 paper-based; 250 computer-based; 100 iBT). Electronic applications accepted.

Columbus State University, Graduate Studies, College of Letters and Sciences, Master of Public Administration Program, Columbus, GA 31907-5645. Offers public administration (MPA), including government administration, health services administration, justice administration. Part-time and evening/weekend programs available. *Faculty:* 12 full-time (4 women), 12 part-time/adjunct (0 women). *Students:* 113 full-time (43 women), 209 part-time (63 women); includes 98 minority (86 African Americans, 4 American Indian/Alaska Native, 1 Asian American or Pacific Islander, 7 Hispanic Americans), 1 international. Average age 41. 84 applicants, 88% accepted, 58 enrolled. In 2009, 130 master's awarded. *Entrance requirements:* For master's, GRE General Test, minimum GPA of 2.75. Additional exam requirements/recommendations for international students: Required—TOEFL (minimum score 550 paper-based; 213 computer-based; 79 iBT). *Application deadline:* For fall admission, 5/1 priority date for domestic students, 5/1 for international students; for spring admission, 11/1 for domestic and international students. Applications are processed on a rolling basis. Application fee: $30. Electronic applications accepted. *Financial support:* In 2009–10, 71 students received support, including 6 research assistantships with partial tuition reimbursements available (averaging $3,000 per year); career-related internships or fieldwork, Federal Work-Study, institutionally sponsored loans, scholarships/grants, tuition waivers (partial), and unspecified assistantships also available. Support available to part-time students. Financial award application deadline: 5/1; financial award applicants required to submit FAFSA. *Unit head:* Dr. William Chappell, Program Director, 706-569-2891, E-mail: chappell_bill@colstate.edu. *Application contact:* Katie Thornton, Graduate Admissions Specialist, 706-568-2035, Fax: 706-568-2462, E-mail: thornton_katie@colstate.edu.

Concordia University, School of Graduate Studies, Faculty of Arts and Science, Department of Political Science, Montréal, QC H3G 1M8, Canada. Offers political science (PhD); public policy and public administration (MA), including geography. *Degree requirements:* For master's, one foreign language, comprehensive exam, thesis optional, internship. *Entrance requirements:* For master's, honors degree or equivalent. Additional exam requirements/recommendations for international students: Required—TOEFL. *Faculty research:* International public policy and administration, Quebec public administration, public policy and social/political theory, geography and public policy, public administration and decision making.

Concordia University Wisconsin, Graduate Programs, School of Business and Legal Studies, MBA Program, Mequon, WI 53097-2402. Offers finance (MBA); health care administration (MBA); human resource management (MBA); international business (MBA); international business-bilingual English/Chinese (MBA); management (MBA); management information systems (MBA); managerial communications (MBA); marketing (MBA); public administration (MBA); risk management (MBA). Postbaccalaureate distance learning degree programs offered (minimal on-campus study). *Degree requirements:* For master's, comprehensive exam, thesis or alternative. *Entrance requirements:* Additional exam requirements/recommendations for international students: Required—TOEFL. *Expenses:* Contact institution.

Cumberland University, Program in Public Service Administration, Lebanon, TN 37087. Offers MS. Part-time and evening/weekend programs available. *Degree requirements:* For master's, comprehensive exam. *Entrance requirements:* For master's, MAT, 3 letters of recommendation. Additional exam requirements/recommendations for international students: Required—TOEFL (minimum score 500 paper-based; 173 computer-based).

Dalhousie University, Faculty of Management, School of Public Administration, Halifax, NS B3H 3J5, Canada. Offers management (MPA); public administration (MPA, GDPA); LL B/MPA; MLIS/MPA. Part-time programs available. *Faculty:* 9 full-time (1 woman), 6 part-time/adjunct (1 woman). *Students:* 59 full-time (36 women), 25 part-time (13 women). 58 applicants, 79% accepted. *Entrance requirements:* For master's, GMAT. Additional exam requirements/recommendations for international students: Required—TOEFL, IELTS, CANTEST, CAEL, or Michigan English Language Assessment Battery. *Application deadline:* Applications are processed on a rolling basis. Application fee: $70. Electronic applications accepted. *Expenses:* Contact institution. *Financial support:* Fellowships, teaching assistantships, career-related internships or fieldwork available. *Faculty research:* Municipal management, policy and program management, environmental policy, economic and social policy, business and government. *Unit head:* Fazley Siddiq, Director, 902-494-8802, Fax: 902-494-7023, E-mail: dalmpa@dal.ca. *Application contact:* Cecilia MacDonald, Graduate Coordinator, 902-494-3743, Fax: 902-494-7023, E-mail: dalmpa@dal.ca.

DePaul University, School of Public Service, Chicago, IL 60604. Offers financial administration management (Certificate); health administration (Certificate); health law and policy (MS); international public services (MS); leadership and policy studies (MS); metropolitan planning (Certificate); public administration (MPA); public service management (MS), including association management, fundraising and philanthropy, healthcare administration, higher education administration, metropolitan planning; public services (Certificate); JD/MS. Part-time and evening/weekend programs available. Postbaccalaureate distance learning degree programs offered (minimal on-campus study). *Faculty:* 14 full-time (3 women), 43 part-time/adjunct (24 women). *Students:* 283 full-time (206 women), 298 part-time (208 women); includes 196 minority (112 African Americans, 1 American Indian/Alaska Native, 30 Asian Americans or Pacific Islanders, 53 Hispanic Americans), 18 international. Average age 26. 162 applicants, 100% accepted, 94 enrolled. In 2009, 108 master's awarded. *Degree requirements:* For master's, thesis or integrative seminar. *Entrance requirements:* For master's, minimum GPA of 2.7. Additional exam requirements/recommendations for international students: Required—TOEFL (minimum score 550 paper-based; 213 computer-based; 80 iBT), IELTS (minimum score 6.5). *Application deadline:* Applications are processed on a rolling basis. Application fee: $40. Electronic applications accepted. *Expenses:* Tuition: Full-time $37,525; part-time $620 per credit hour. *Financial support:* In 2009–10, 60 students received support, including 3 research assistantships with full tuition reimbursements available (averaging $7,000 per year); career-related internships or fieldwork, Federal Work-Study, institutionally sponsored loans, scholarships/grants, tuition waivers (partial), and unspecified assistantships also available. Support available to part-time students. Financial award application deadline: 7/1; financial award applicants required to submit FAFSA. *Faculty research:* Government financing, transportation, leadership, health care, volunteerism and organizational behavior, non-profit organizations. Total annual research expenditures: $20,000. *Unit head:* Dr. J. Patrick Murphy, Director, 312-362-5608, Fax: 312-362-5506, E-mail: jpmurphy@depaul.edu. *Application contact:* Megan B. Balderston, Director of Admissions and Marketing, 312-362-5565, Fax: 312-362-5506, E-mail: pubserv@depaul.edu.

DeVry University, Keller Graduate School of Management, Downers Grove, IL 60515. Offers accounting and financial management (MAFM); business administration (MBA); human resources management (MHRM); information systems management (MISM); network and communications management (MNCM); project management (MPM); public administration (MPA).

Drake University, College of Business and Public Administration, Des Moines, IA 50311-4516. Offers M Acc, MBA, MFM, MPA, JD/MBA, JD/MPA, Pharm D/MBA, Pharm D/MPA. *Accreditation:* AACSB. Part-time and evening/weekend programs available. *Faculty:* 18 full-time (4 women), 5 part-time/adjunct (0 women). *Students:* 59 full-time (22 women), 379 part-time (200 women); includes 16 African Americans, 14 Asian Americans or Pacific Islanders, 4 Hispanic Americans, 21 international. Average age 31. 269 applicants, 61% accepted, 116 enrolled. In 2009, 188 master's awarded. *Degree requirements:* For master's, comprehensive exam (for some programs), thesis (for some programs), internships. *Entrance requirements:* For master's, GMAT, letters of recommendation, resume. Additional exam requirements/recommendations for international students: Required—TOEFL (minimum score 550 paper-based; 213 computer-based). *Application deadline:* For fall admission, 8/15 priority date for domestic students; for winter admission, 12/20 priority date for domestic students; for spring admission, 12/1 priority date for domestic students. Applications are processed on a rolling basis. Application fee: $25. Electronic applications accepted. *Expenses:* Contact institution. *Financial support:* Fellowships with tuition reimbursements, teaching assistantships, career-related internships or fieldwork and institutionally sponsored loans available. Support available to part-time students. Financial award application deadline: 3/1; financial award applicants required to submit FAFSA. *Faculty research:* Venture capital, online commerce, professional ethics, process improvement, project management. *Unit head:* Dr. Charles Edwards, Dean, 515-271-2871, Fax: 515-271-4518, E-mail: charles.edwards@drake.edu. *Application contact:* Danette Kenne, Director of Graduate Programs, 515-271-2188, Fax: 515-271-4518, E-mail: cbpa.gradprograms@drake.edu.

Duquesne University, Graduate School of Liberal Arts, Graduate Center for Social and Public Policy, Pittsburgh, PA 15282-0001. Offers conflict resolution and peace studies (Certificate); social and public policy (MA, Certificate). Part-time and evening/weekend programs available. *Faculty:* 15 full-time (3 women), 1 (woman) part-time/adjunct. *Students:* 40 full-time (26 women), 14 part-time (8 women); includes 5 minority (3 African Americans, 2 Hispanic Americans), 10 international. Average age 27. 31 applicants, 100% accepted, 19 enrolled. In 2009, 13 master's awarded. *Degree requirements:* For master's, thesis. *Entrance requirements:* For master's, GRE General Test. Additional exam requirements/recommendations for international students: Required—TOEFL. *Application deadline:* For fall admission, 4/30 priority date for domestic and international students; for spring admission, 11/1 priority date for domestic and international students. Applications are processed on a rolling basis. Electronic applications accepted. *Expenses:* Tuition: Part-time $851 per credit. Required fees: $81 per credit. *Financial support:* In 2009–10, 20 students received support, including 12 research assistantships with full and partial tuition reimbursements available (averaging $9,000 per year), 4 teaching assistantships with full and partial tuition reimbursements available (averaging $9,000 per year); career-related internships or fieldwork, institutionally sponsored loans, scholarships/grants, tuition waivers (full and partial), and unspecified assistantships also available. Support available to part-time students. Financial award application deadline: 5/1. *Faculty research:* Program evaluation, environmental policy, criminal justice policy, health care policy. Total annual research expenditures: $30,000. *Unit head:* Dr. Joseph Yenerall, Director, 412-396-6485, Fax: 412-396-5265, E-mail: socialpolicy@duq.edu. *Application contact:* Dr. Joseph Yenerall, Assistant to the Dean, 412-396-6485.

East Carolina University, Graduate School, Thomas Harriot College of Arts and Sciences, Department of Political Science, Greenville, NC 27858-4353. Offers public administration (MPA). *Accreditation:* NASPAA. Part-time and evening/weekend programs available. *Degree*

Public Administration

East Carolina University (continued)

requirements: For master's, one foreign language, comprehensive exam. *Entrance requirements:* For master's, GRE General Test. Additional exam requirements/recommendations for international students: Required—TOEFL.

Eastern Kentucky University, The Graduate School, College of Arts and Sciences, Department of Government, Program in General Public Administration, Richmond, KY 40475-3102. Offers community development (MPA); community health administration (MPA); general public administration (MPA). *Accreditation:* NASPAA. Part-time and evening/weekend programs available. *Entrance requirements:* For master's, GRE General Test, minimum GPA of 2.5.

Eastern Michigan University, Graduate School, College of Arts and Sciences, Department of Political Science, Programs in Public Administration, Ypsilanti, MI 48197. Offers local government management (Graduate Certificate); management of public healthcare services (Graduate Certificate); public administration (MPA, Graduate Certificate); public budget management (Graduate Certificate); public land planning (Graduate Certificate); public management (Graduate Certificate); public personnel management (Graduate Certificate); public policy analysis (Graduate Certificate). *Accreditation:* NASPAA. *Students:* 18 full-time (7 women), 130 part-time (72 women); includes 53 minority (46 African Americans, 2 American Indian/Alaska Native, 1 Asian American or Pacific Islander, 4 Hispanic Americans), 5 international. Average age 34. In 2009, 17 master's, 37 other advanced degrees awarded. Application fee: $35. Tuition and fees vary according to course level. *Unit head:* Dr. Joseph Ohren, Program Director, 734-487-2522, Fax: 734-487-3340, E-mail: joseph.ohren@emich.edu. *Application contact:* Dr. Sukru Koyluoglu, Program Coordinator, 734-487-0063, Fax: 734-487-3340, E-mail: sukru.koyuoglu@emich.edu.

Eastern Washington University, Graduate Studies, College of Business and Public Administration, Program in Public Administration, Cheney, WA 99004-2431. Offers MPA, MBA/MPA, MPA/MSW, MPA/MURP. Part-time and evening/weekend programs available. *Degree requirements:* For master's, comprehensive exam, thesis optional. *Entrance requirements:* For master's, minimum GPA of 3.0. *Expenses:* Tuition, state resident: full-time $7476; part-time $249 per quarter hour. Tuition, nonresident: full-time $18,030; part-time $601 per quarter hour. Required fees: $3.50 per quarter hour. $142 per quarter.

The Evergreen State College, Graduate Programs, Program in Public Administration, Olympia, WA 98505. Offers MPA, MES/MPA. Part-time and evening/weekend programs available. *Faculty:* 5 full-time (2 women), 7 part-time/adjunct (3 women). *Students:* 45 full-time (32 women), 94 part-time (69 women); includes 45 minority (9 African Americans, 24 American Indian/Alaska Native, 4 Asian Americans or Pacific Islanders, 8 Hispanic Americans). Average age 37. 107 applicants, 66% accepted, 56 enrolled. In 2009, 40 master's awarded. *Degree requirements:* For master's, 6 credit capstone course or 8 credit thesis. *Entrance requirements:* For master's, minimum GPA of 3.0 in last 90 quarter hours toward BA/BS; 4 quarter credits in statistics within past 5 years; evidence of writing, analytical, and general communication skills at appropriate level for graduate study. Additional exam requirements/recommendations for international students: Required—TOEFL (minimum score 600 paper-based; 250 computer-based; 100 iBT). *Application deadline:* For fall admission, 3/3 priority date for domestic and international students. Applications are processed on a rolling basis. Application fee: $50. Electronic applications accepted. *Expenses:* Contact institution. *Financial support:* In 2009–10, 8 students received support, including 8 fellowships (averaging $1,619 per year); career-related internships or fieldwork, Federal Work-Study, scholarships/grants, tuition waivers (partial), and unspecified assistantships also available. Support available to part-time students. Financial award application deadline: 3/15; financial award applicants required to submit FAFSA. *Faculty research:* Fair housing, democratic governance, energy/public/environmental policy, tribal/community/economic development, tribal governance, nonprofit administration, international administration, organizational theory, management science. *Unit head:* Dr. Cheryl Simrell King, MPA Program Director, 360-867-5541, E-mail: kingcs@evergreen.edu. *Application contact:* Randee Gibbons, Associate MPA Program Director, 360-867-6554, E-mail: gibbonsr@evergreen.edu.

Fairleigh Dickinson University, College at Florham, Anthony J. Petrocelli College of Continuing Studies, Public Administration Institute, Program in Public Administration, Madison, NJ 07940-1099. Offers MPA. *Students:* 1 (woman) full-time, all international. Average age 24. In 2009, 1 master's awarded. Application fee: $40. *Unit head:* Dr. William Roberts, Head, 973-443-8500. *Application contact:* Susan Brooman, University Director, Graduate Admissions, 973-443-8905, Fax: 973-443-8088, E-mail: grad@fdu.edu.

Fairleigh Dickinson University, Metropolitan Campus, Anthony J. Petrocelli College of Continuing Studies, Public Administration Institute, Program in Public Administration, Teaneck, NJ 07666-1914. Offers MPA, Certificate. *Students:* 126 full-time (65 women), 139 part-time (77 women), 111 international. Average age 33. 222 applicants, 86% accepted, 68 enrolled. In 2009, 65 master's awarded. *Application deadline:* Applications are processed on a rolling basis. Application fee: $40. *Unit head:* Dr. William Roberts, Director, 201-692-2000. *Application contact:* Dr. William Roberts, Director, 201-692-2000.

Florida Agricultural and Mechanical University, Division of Graduate Studies, Research, and Continuing Education, College of Arts and Sciences; Division of History and Political Sciences, Program in Applied Social Science, Tallahassee, FL 32307-3200. Offers African American history (MASS); criminal justice (MASS); economics (MASS); history (MASS); political science (MASS); public administration (MASS); public management (MASS); social work (MASS); sociology (MASS). Part-time programs available. *Faculty:* 17 full-time (2 women). *Students:* 54 full-time (42 women), 4 part-time (2 women); includes 57 minority (all African Americans). In 2009, 14 master's awarded. *Degree requirements:* For master's, thesis optional. *Entrance requirements:* For master's, GRE General Test, minimum GPA of 3.0. *Application deadline:* For fall admission, 5/18 for domestic students, 12/18 for international students; for spring admission, 11/12 for domestic students, 5/12 for international students. Application fee: $20. *Financial support:* Fellowships, research assistantships, career-related internships or fieldwork, Federal Work-Study, and tuition waivers (full) available. Financial award application deadline: 4/1. *Faculty research:* Southern history, black history, election trends, presidential history. *Unit head:* Dr. Gary Paul, Director, 850-599-3447. *Application contact:* Dr. Chanta M. Haywood, Dean of Graduate Studies, Research, and Continuing Education, 850-599-3315, Fax: 850-599-3727.

Florida Atlantic University, College of Architecture, Urban and Public Affairs, School of Public Administration, Boca Raton, FL 33431-0991. Offers MNM, MPA, PhD. *Accreditation:* NASPAA (one or more programs are accredited). Part-time and evening/weekend programs available. *Faculty:* 10 full-time (3 women), 6 part-time/adjunct (0 women). *Students:* 29 full-time (14 women), 94 part-time (56 women); includes 39 minority (28 African Americans, 1 Asian American or Pacific Islander, 10 Hispanic Americans), 7 international. Average age 35. 120 applicants, 56% accepted, 32 enrolled. In 2009, 24 master's, 1 doctorate awarded. *Degree requirements:* For master's, thesis optional; for doctorate, comprehensive exam, thesis/dissertation. *Entrance requirements:* For master's, GRE General Test, minimum GPA of 3.0; for doctorate, GRE General Test, faculty reference, scholarly writing samples, letters of recommendation. Additional exam requirements/recommendations for international students: Required—TOEFL. *Application deadline:* For fall admission, 7/1 priority date for domestic students, 2/15 for international students; for spring admission, 11/1 for domestic students, 7/15 for international students. Applications are processed on a rolling basis. Application fee: $30. *Expenses:* Tuition, state resident: full-time $7055; part-time $293.94 per credit hour. Tuition, nonresident: full-time $22,096; part-time $920.66 per credit hour. *Financial support:* Fellowships with full tuition reimbursements, research assistantships with partial tuition reimbursements, teaching assistantships with partial tuition reimbursements, career-related internships or fieldwork, Federal Work-Study, institutionally sponsored loans, and tuition waivers (partial) available. Support available to part-time students. Financial award application deadline: 4/1. *Faculty research:* Public finance and budgeting, public management, evaluation, criminal justice, postmodern public administration. *Unit head:* Dr. Hugh T. Miller, Director, 954-762-5650, Fax: 954-762-5693, E-mail: hmiller@fau.edu. *Application contact:* Dr. Hugh T. Miller, Director, 954-762-5650, Fax: 954-762-5693, E-mail: hmiller@fau.edu.

Florida Gulf Coast University, College of Professional Studies, Program in Public Administration, Fort Myers, FL 33965-6565. Offers criminal justice (MPA); environmental policy (MPA); general public administration (MPA); management (MPA). *Accreditation:* NASPAA. Part-time programs available. *Faculty:* 32 full-time (11 women), 29 part-time/adjunct (12 women). *Students:* 49 full-time (30 women), 19 part-time (12 women); includes 13 minority (4 African Americans, 2 Asian Americans or Pacific Islanders, 7 Hispanic Americans). Average age 35. 34 applicants, 68% accepted, 19 enrolled. In 2009, 14 master's awarded. *Entrance requirements:* For master's, GRE General Test, MAT, minimum GPA of 3.0. Additional exam requirements/recommendations for international students: Required—TOEFL (minimum score 550 paper-based; 213 computer-based). *Application deadline:* For fall admission, 7/1 priority date for domestic students; for spring admission, 11/15 for domestic students. Applications are processed on a rolling basis. Application fee: $30. Electronic applications accepted. *Financial support:* In 2009–10, 5 research assistantships were awarded; career-related internships or fieldwork and tuition waivers (full and partial) also available. Support available to part-time students. *Faculty research:* Personnel, public policy, public finance, housing policy. *Unit head:* Terry Busson, Chair, 239-590-7704, E-mail: tbusson@fgcu.edu. *Application contact:* Roger Green, Information Contact, 239-590-7838, Fax: 239-590-7846.

Florida Institute of Technology, Graduate Programs, College of Business, Extended Studies Division, Melbourne, FL 32901-6975. Offers acquisition and contract management (PMBA); business administration (PMBA); computer information systems (MS); e-business (PMBA); human resource management (PMBA); human resources management (MS); logistics management (MS), including humanitarian and disaster relief logistics; management (MS), including acquisition and contract management, e-business, human resource management, information systems, logistics management, management, transportation management; material acquisition management (MS); project management (MS), including information systems, operations research; public administration (MPA); quality management (MS); space management (MS); space systems (MS); systems management (MS), including information systems, operations research, systems management. Part-time and evening/weekend programs available. Postbaccalaureate distance learning degree programs offered (no on-campus study). *Faculty:* 12 full-time (3 women), 117 part-time/adjunct (20 women). *Students:* 74 full-time (32 women), 1,041 part-time (484 women); includes 343 minority (240 African Americans, 12 American Indian/Alaska Native, 44 Asian Americans or Pacific Islanders, 47 Hispanic Americans), 22 international. Average age 35. 520 applicants, 72% accepted, 279 enrolled. In 2009, 509 master's awarded. *Degree requirements:* For master's, capstone course. *Entrance requirements:* For master's, GMAT or resume showing 8 years of supervised experience, minimum GPA of 3.0, 2 letters of recommendation, resume. Additional exam requirements/recommendations for international students: Required—TOEFL (minimum score 550 paper-based; 213 computer-based; 79 iBT). *Application deadline:* For fall admission, 4/1 for international students; for spring admission, 9/30 for international students. Applications are processed on a rolling basis. Application fee: $50. Electronic applications accepted. *Expenses:* Tuition: Part-time $1015 per credit. Tuition and fees vary according to campus/location and program. *Financial support:* Application deadline: 3/1. *Unit head:* Dr. Clifford Bragdon, Dean, 321-674-8821, Fax: 321-674-7597, E-mail: cbragdon@fit.edu. *Application contact:* Carolyn Farrior, Director of Graduate Admissions Online Learning and Off Campus Programs, 321-674-7118, Fax: 321-674-8216, E-mail: cfarrior@fit.edu.

Florida International University, College of Arts and Sciences, Department of Public Administration, Miami, FL 33199. Offers public administration (MPA); public management (PhD). *Accreditation:* NASPAA (one or more programs are accredited). Part-time and evening/weekend programs available. *Faculty:* 12 full-time (5 women). *Students:* 94 full-time (65 women), 162 part-time (104 women); includes 203 minority (71 African Americans, 1 American Indian/Alaska Native, 5 Asian Americans or Pacific Islanders, 126 Hispanic Americans), 5 international. Average age 32. 136 applicants, 62% accepted, 83 enrolled. In 2009, 64 master's, 3 doctorates awarded. *Degree requirements:* For doctorate, comprehensive exam, thesis/dissertation. *Entrance requirements:* For master's, minimum undergraduate GPA of 3.0 in upper-level coursework, 1 letter of recommendation, letter of intent; for doctorate, GRE, minimum undergraduate GPA of 3.0 in upper-level coursework, 3 letters of recommendation, samples of scholarly written work, interview (when student lives within 50 miles of campus). Additional exam requirements/recommendations for international students: Required—TOEFL (minimum score 550 paper-based; 80 iBT). *Application deadline:* For fall admission, 6/1 for domestic students, 4/1 for international students; for spring admission, 10/1 for domestic students, 9/1 for international students. Applications are processed on a rolling basis. Application fee: $30. Electronic applications accepted. *Expenses:* Tuition, state resident: full-time $8008; part-time $4004 per year. Tuition, nonresident: full-time $20,104; part-time $10,052 per year. Required fees: $298; $149 per term. *Financial support:* Institutionally sponsored loans and scholarships/grants available. Financial award application deadline: 3/1; financial award applicants required to submit FAFSA. *Unit head:* Dr. Meredith Newman, Chair, 305-348-5890, Fax: 305-348-5848, E-mail: meredith.newman@fiu.edu. *Application contact:* Liga Replogle, Student Services Coordinator, 305-348-5890, Fax: 305-348-5848, E-mail: liga.replogle@fiu.edu.

Florida State University, The Graduate School, College of Social Sciences and Public Policy, Reubin O'D. Askew School of Public Administration and Policy, Tallahassee, FL 32306-2250. Offers MPA, PhD, Certificate, JD/MPA, MPA/MSC, MPA/MSP, MPA/MSW. *Accreditation:* NASPAA (one or more programs are accredited). Part-time and evening/weekend programs available. *Faculty:* 11 full-time (1 woman), 6 part-time/adjunct (3 women). *Students:* 66 full-time (23 women), 114 part-time (53 women); includes 51 minority (29 African Americans, 1 American Indian/Alaska Native, 7 Asian Americans or Pacific Islanders, 14 Hispanic Americans), 40 international. Average age 25. 157 applicants, 80% accepted, 48 enrolled. In 2009, 44 master's, 8 doctorates awarded. *Degree requirements:* For master's, action report; for doctorate, comprehensive exam, thesis/dissertation. *Entrance requirements:* For master's, GRE General Test (minimum score 1000), GMAT, MAT, minimum undergraduate upper-division GPA of 3.0; for doctorate, GRE General Test (minimum score of 1000); GMAT; MAT, minimum undergraduate GPA of 3.0, graduate 3.5. Additional exam requirements/recommendations for international students: Required—TOEFL (minimum score 550 paper-based; 213 computer-based; 80 iBT), IELTS (minimum score 6.5), Michigan English Language Assessment Battery (minimum score 77). *Application deadline:* For fall admission, 7/1 for domestic students, 5/1 for international students; for spring admission, 11/1 for domestic students; 9/1 for international students. Applications are processed on a rolling basis. Application fee: $30. Electronic applications accepted. *Expenses:* Tuition, state resident: full-time $7413. Tuition, nonresident: full-time $22,567. *Financial support:* In 2009–10, 38 students received support, including 10 fellowships with full tuition reimbursements available (averaging $15,000 per year), 24 research assistantships with full tuition reimbursements available (averaging $13,000 per year), 4 teaching assistantships with full tuition reimbursements available (averaging $10,000 per year); career-related internships or fieldwork, Federal Work-Study, institutionally sponsored loans, scholarships/grants, tuition waivers (full), and unspecified assistantships also available. Support available to part-time students. Financial award application deadline: 2/1. *Faculty research:* Financial management, human resource management, policy, strategic management, organizations, nonprofit management. *Unit head:* Dr. William Earle Klay, Director, 850-644-3525, Fax: 850-644-7617, E-mail: eklay@fsu.edu. *Application contact:* Velda Williams, Academic Program Specialist, 850-644-3060, Fax: 850-644-7617, E-mail: vwilliams3@fsu.edu.

Framingham State College, Division of Graduate and Continuing Education, Program in Public Administration, Framingham, MA 01701-9101. Offers MA. Part-time and evening/weekend programs available.

Gannon University, School of Graduate Studies, College of Engineering and Business, School of Business, Program in Public Administration, Erie, PA 16541-0001. Offers MPA, Certificate. Part-time and evening/weekend programs available. *Students:* 14 full-time (2 women), 20 part-time (10 women); includes 4 minority (3 African Americans, 1 Hispanic American), 3 international. Average age 31. 28 applicants, 96% accepted, 4 enrolled. In 2009, 10 master's awarded. *Degree requirements:* For master's, thesis or alternative, research project. *Entrance requirements:* For master's, GRE. Additional exam requirements/recommendations for international students: Required—TOEFL (minimum score 79 iBT). *Application deadline:* Applications are processed on a rolling basis. Application fee: $25. Electronic applications accepted. *Expenses:* Tuition: Full-time $13,590; part-time $755 per credit. Required fees: $524; $17 per credit. Tuition and fees vary according to course load, degree level, campus/location and program. *Financial support:* Career-related internships or fieldwork, scholarships/grants, and unspecified assistantships available. Support available to part-time students. Financial award application deadline: 7/1; financial award applicants required to submit FAFSA. *Unit head:* Dr. Rick Prokop, Co-Director, 814-871-7576, E-mail: prokop001@gannon.edu. *Application contact:* Kara Morgan, Assistant Director of Graduate Admissions, 814-871-5831, Fax: 814-871-5827, E-mail: graduate@gannon.edu.

George Mason University, College of Humanities and Social Sciences, Department of Public and International Affairs, Fairfax, VA 22030. Offers association management (Certificate); biodefense (MS, PhD); critical analysis and strategic responses to terrorism (Certificate); nonprofit management (Certificate); political science (MA, PhD); public administration (MPA); public management (Certificate). *Accreditation:* NASPAA (one or more programs are accredited). *Faculty:* 37 full-time (14 women), 34 part-time/adjunct (7 women). *Students:* 115 full-time (62 women), 323 part-time (182 women); includes 60 minority (29 African Americans, 1 American Indian/Alaska Native, 18 Asian Americans or Pacific Islanders, 12 Hispanic Americans), 21 international. Average age 31. 458 applicants, 60% accepted, 129 enrolled. In 2009, 147 master's, 2 doctorates, 6 other advanced degrees awarded. *Entrance requirements:* For master's, GRE General Test, minimum GPA of 3.0 in last 60 hours of course work. Additional exam requirements/recommendations for international students: Required—TOEFL. *Application deadline:* For fall admission, 3/1 priority date for domestic students; for spring admission, 10/15 for domestic students. Application fee: $75. Electronic applications accepted. *Expenses:* Tuition, state resident: full-time $7568; part-time $315.33 per credit hour. Tuition, nonresident: full-time $21,704; part-time $904.33 per credit hour. Required fees: $2184; $91 per credit hour. *Financial support:* In 2009–10, 27 students received support, including 3 fellowships with full tuition reimbursements available (averaging $18,000 per year), 10 research assistantships with full and partial tuition reimbursements available (averaging $11,033 per year), 14 teaching assistantships with full and partial tuition reimbursements available (averaging $9,213 per year); Federal Work-Study, scholarships/grants, unspecified assistantships, and health care benefits (full-time research or teaching assistantship recipients) also available. Support available to part-time students. Financial award application deadline: 3/1; financial award applicants required to submit FAFSA. *Faculty research:* The Rehnquist Court and economic liberties; intersection of economic development with high-tech industry, telecommunications, and entrepreneurism; political economy of development; violence, terrorism and U.S. foreign policy; international security issues. Total annual research expenditures: $429,868. *Unit head:* Dr. Robert Dudley, Chair, 703-993-1400, Fax: 703-993-1399, E-mail: rdudley@gmu.edu. *Application contact:* Peg Koback, Information Contact, 703-993-9466, E-mail: mkoback@gmu.edu.

The George Washington University, Columbian College of Arts and Sciences, Trachtenberg School of Public Policy and Public Administration, Washington, DC 20052. Offers public administration (MPA), including budget and public finance, federal policy, politics, and management, international development management, managing public organizations, managing state and local governments, nonprofit management, policy analysis and evaluation, public administration, public-private policy and management; public policy (MA, MPP), including environmental and resource policy (MA), philosophy and social policy (MA), women's studies (MA); public policy and administration (PhD); JD/MPP; MPA/JD; PhD/MPP. Part-time and evening/weekend programs available. *Faculty:* 35 full-time (12 women), 19 part-time/adjunct (10 women). *Students:* 187 full-time (114 women), 232 part-time (151 women); includes 62 minority (15 African Americans, 3 American Indian/Alaska Native, 29 Asian Americans or Pacific Islanders, 15 Hispanic Americans), 23 international. Average age 26. 913 applicants, 56% accepted, 186 enrolled. In 2009, 106 master's, 9 doctorates awarded. *Degree requirements:* For doctorate, thesis/dissertation, general exam. *Entrance requirements:* For master's, GRE General Test, minimum GPA of 3.0; for doctorate, GRE General Test, interview, minimum GPA of 3.0. Additional exam requirements/recommendations for international students: Required—TOEFL (minimum score 600 paper-based; 250 computer-based; 100 iBT). *Application deadline:* For fall admission, 1/15 priority date for domestic and international students; for spring admission, 10/1 priority date for domestic students, 9/1 priority date for international students. Applications are processed on a rolling basis. Application fee: $60. Electronic applications accepted. *Financial support:* In 2009–10, 87 students received support; fellowships, research assistantships, teaching assistantships, institutionally sponsored loans available. Financial award application deadline: 1/15. *Unit head:* Dr. Kathyrn E. Newcomer, Director, 202-994-3959, Fax: 202-994-3959, E-mail: newcomer@gwu.edu. *Application contact:* Information Contact, 202-994-6295, Fax: 202-994-6295, E-mail: tspppa@gwu.edu.

Georgia College & State University, Graduate School, College of Arts and Sciences, Department of Government and Sociology, Program in Public Administration, Milledgeville, GA 31061. Offers MPA. *Accreditation:* NASPAA. Part-time and evening/weekend programs available. *Students:* 27 full-time (17 women), 65 part-time (38 women); includes 31 minority (25 African Americans, 3 Asian Americans or Pacific Islanders, 3 Hispanic Americans), 1 international. Average age 29. 47 applicants, 87% accepted, 32 enrolled. In 2009, 25 master's awarded. *Degree requirements:* For master's, thesis optional, capstone project or internship. *Entrance requirements:* For master's, GRE or MAT. Additional exam requirements/recommendations for international students: Recommended—TOEFL (minimum score 550 paper-based; 213 computer-based; 79 iBT), IELTS. *Application deadline:* For fall admission, 8/1 for domestic students; for spring admission, 11/15 for domestic students. Applications are processed on a rolling basis. Application fee: $40. Electronic applications accepted. *Expenses:* Tuition, area resident: Part-time $241 per credit hour. Tuition, state resident: full-time $4338. Tuition, nonresident: full-time $17,352; part-time $964 per credit hour. Required fees: $609 per semester. Tuition and fees vary according to course load and campus/location. *Financial support:* In 2009–10, 10 research assistantships were awarded; career-related internships or fieldwork and unspecified assistantships also available. Support available to part-time students. Financial award application deadline: 3/1; financial award applicants required to submit FAFSA. *Unit head:* Dr. Jerry Herbel, Graduate Coordinator, 478-445-7393, E-mail: jerry.herbel@gcsu.edu. *Application contact:* Dr. Jerry Herbel, Graduate Coordinator, 478-445-7393, E-mail: jerry.herbel@gcsu.edu.

Georgia Southern University, Jack N. Averitt College of Graduate Studies, College of Liberal Arts and Social Sciences, Department of Political Science, Program in Public Administration, Statesboro, GA 30460. Offers MPA. *Accreditation:* NASPAA. Part-time and evening/weekend programs available. *Students:* 29 full-time (18 women), 13 part-time (9 women); includes 12 minority (10 African Americans, 2 Hispanic Americans), 2 international. Average age 26. 20 applicants, 95% accepted, 17 enrolled. In 2009, 14 master's awarded. *Degree requirements:* For master's, comprehensive exam, internship, terminal exam. *Entrance requirements:* For master's, GRE General Test, minimum GPA of 2.5, resume, undergraduate major appropriate to field, letters of reference. Additional exam requirements/recommendations for international students: Required—TOEFL (minimum score 550 paper-based; 213 computer-based; 80 iBT). *Application deadline:* For fall admission, 3/1 priority date for domestic and international students; for spring admission, 10/1 priority date for domestic students, 10/1 for international students. Applications are processed on a rolling basis. Application fee: $50. Electronic applications accepted. *Expenses:* Tuition, state resident: full-time $5040; part-time $210 per credit hour. Tuition, nonresident: full-time $20,136; part-time $839 per credit hour. Required fees: $1644. *Financial support:* In 2009–10, 32 students received support, including research assistantships with partial tuition reimbursements available (averaging $7,200 per year), teaching assistantships with partial tuition reimbursements available (averaging $7,200 per year); career-related internships or fieldwork, Federal Work-Study, scholarships/grants, tuition waivers (partial), and unspecified assistantships also available. Support available to part-time students. Financial award application deadline: 4/15; financial award applicants required to submit FAFSA. *Faculty research:* Comparative public administration, equal employment policies, gangs, environmental policy, AIDS policy. *Unit head:* Dr. Richard Pacelle, Chair, 912-478-5698, Fax: 912-478-5348, E-mail: rpacelle@georgiasouthern.edu. *Application contact:* Dr. Charles Ziglar, Coordinator for Graduate Student Recruitment, 912-478-5635, Fax: 912-478-0740, E-mail: gradadmissions@georgiasouthern.edu.

Georgia State University, Andrew Young School of Policy Studies, Department of Public Management and Policy, Atlanta, GA 30303. Offers disaster management (Certificate); nonprofit management (Certificate); planning and economic development (Certificate); public administration (MPA), including criminal justice, management and finance, nonprofit management, planning and economic development, policy analysis and evaluation, public health; public policy (MPP, PhD), including disaster policy (MPP), nonprofit policy (MPP), planning and economic development policy (MPP), public finance policy (MPP), social policy (MPP); JD/MPA. *Accreditation:* NASPAA (one or more programs are accredited). Part-time and evening/weekend programs available. Terminal master's awarded for partial completion of doctoral program. *Degree requirements:* For master's, thesis optional; for doctorate, comprehensive exam, thesis/dissertation. *Entrance requirements:* For master's and doctorate, GRE General Test. Additional exam requirements/recommendations for international students: Required—TOEFL. Electronic applications accepted. *Faculty research:* Public management, policy analysis, public finance, planning and economic development, nonprofit leadership and policy.

Governors State University, College of Business and Public Administration, Program in Public Administration, University Park, IL 60466-0975. Offers MPA. *Accreditation:* NASPAA. Part-time and evening/weekend programs available. *Degree requirements:* For master's, comprehensive exam, thesis or alternative, internship or previous work in field. *Entrance requirements:* For master's, minimum GPA of 2.5. *Faculty research:* State and local politics.

Grambling State University, School of Graduate Studies and Research, College of Arts and Sciences, Program in Public Administration, Grambling, LA 71270. Offers health service administration (MPA); human resource management (MPA); public management (MPA); state and local government (MPA). *Accreditation:* NASPAA. Part-time programs available. *Faculty:* 5 full-time (2 women), 2 part-time/adjunct (0 women). *Students:* 25 full-time (16 women), 14 part-time (12 women); includes 32 minority (all African Americans), 5 international. Average age 29. 30 applicants, 53% accepted, 11 enrolled. In 2009, 12 master's awarded. *Degree requirements:* For master's, comprehensive exam (for some programs), thesis optional. *Entrance requirements:* For master's, GRE, minimum GPA of 2.75 on last degree. Additional exam requirements/recommendations for international students: Required—TOEFL (minimum score 500 paper-based; 173 computer-based; 61 iBT). *Application deadline:* For fall admission, 7/1 for domestic and international students; for spring admission, 12/1 for domestic and international students. Applications are processed on a rolling basis. Application fee: $20 ($30 for international students). Electronic applications accepted. *Expenses:* Tuition, state resident: full-time $2610. Tuition, nonresident: full-time $2610. *Financial support:* In 2009–10, 6 research assistantships (averaging $5,958 per year) were awarded; health care benefits, tuition waivers (full), and unspecified assistantships also available. Financial award application deadline: 5/31. *Unit head:* Dr. Rose Harris, Director, 318-274-2310, Fax: 318-274-3427, E-mail: harrisr@gram.edu. *Application contact:* Sarah Dennis, Admissions Coordinator, 318-274-2319, Fax: 318-274-3427, E-mail: denniss@alpha0.gram.edu.

Grand Valley State University, College of Community and Public Service, School of Public and Nonprofit Administration, Allendale, MI 49401-9403. Offers MHA, MPA. *Accreditation:* NASPAA. Part-time and evening/weekend programs available. *Faculty:* 12 full-time (4 women), 5 part-time/adjunct (1 woman). *Students:* 77 full-time (46 women), 127 part-time (82 women); includes 36 minority (21 African Americans, 1 American Indian/Alaska Native, 4 Asian Americans or Pacific Islanders, 10 Hispanic Americans), 10 international. Average age 31. 99 applicants, 93% accepted, 63 enrolled. In 2009, 65 master's awarded. *Application deadline:* For fall admission, 5/1 priority date for domestic students; for winter admission, 11/1 priority date for domestic students. Applications are processed on a rolling basis. Application fee: $30. Electronic applications accepted. *Expenses:* Tuition, state resident: part-time $471 per credit hour. Tuition, nonresident: part-time $646 per credit hour. Tuition and fees vary according to course level. *Financial support:* In 2009–10, 28 students received support, including 22 fellowships (averaging $1,965 per year), 30 research assistantships with partial tuition reimbursements available (averaging $8,000 per year); career-related internships or fieldwork, Federal Work-Study, scholarships/grants, and unspecified assistantships also available. Financial award application deadline: 5/1. *Faculty research:* Comparative urban systems, ethics and public management, local economic development, public and nonprofit boards and governance. *Unit head:* Dr. Mark Hoffman, Director, 616-331-6575, Fax: 616-331-7120, E-mail: hoffman@gvsu.edu. *Application contact:* Tracey James-Heer, Associate Director for Graduate Recruitment, 616-331-2025, Fax: 616-486-6476, E-mail: james-ht@gvsu.edu.

Hamline University, School of Business, St. Paul, MN 55104-1284. Offers business (MBA); nonprofit management (MNM); public administration (MPA, DPA); JD/MANM; JD/MAPA; JD/MBA; LL M/MPA. Part-time and evening/weekend programs available. *Faculty:* 22 full-time (8 women), 39 part-time/adjunct (9 women). *Students:* 531 full-time (255 women), 154 part-time (87 women); includes 99 minority (55 African Americans, 6 American Indian/Alaska Native, 29 Asian Americans or Pacific Islanders, 9 Hispanic Americans), 76 international. Average age 33. 385 applicants, 72% accepted, 240 enrolled. In 2009, 228 master's, 1 doctorate awarded. *Degree requirements:* For master's, thesis (for some programs); for doctorate, comprehensive exam, thesis/dissertation. *Entrance requirements:* For master's, curriculum vitae, letters of recommendation, writing sample; for doctorate, personal statement, curriculum vitae, official transcripts, letters of recommendation, writing sample. Additional exam requirements/recommendations for international students: Required—TOEFL (minimum score 550 paper-based; 213 computer-based; 80 iBT). *Application deadline:* For fall admission, 8/15 priority date for domestic and international students; for spring admission, 1/15 for domestic students, 1/15 priority date for international students. Applications are processed on a rolling basis. Application fee: $0. Electronic applications accepted. *Expenses:* Tuition: Full-time $6816; part-time $426 per credit. Required fees: $6 per credit. One-time fee: $205. Tuition and fees vary according to degree level, campus/location and program. *Financial support:* In 2009–10, 14 students received support. Federal Work-Study and scholarships/grants available. Support available to part-time students. Financial award applicants required to submit FAFSA. *Faculty research:* Liberal arts based business programs, experiential learning, organizational process/politics, gender differences, social equity. *Unit head:* Dr. Julian Schuster, Dean, 651-523-2284, Fax: 651-523-3098, E-mail: jschuster01@hamline.edu. *Application contact:* Rae A. Lenway, Director, Graduate Recruitment and Admission, 651-523-2900, Fax: 651-523-3058, E-mail: rlenway@hamline.edu.

Harrisburg University of Science and Technology, Program in Project Management, Harrisburg, PA 17101. Offers construction services specialization (MS); governmental services specialization (MS); information technology specialization (MS). Part-time and evening/weekend programs available. *Faculty:* 1 full-time (0 women), 3 part-time/adjunct (0 women). *Students:* 1 full-time (0 women), 21 part-time (4 women); includes 5 minority (2 African Americans, 3 Asian Americans or Pacific Islanders), 2 international. Average age 30. 26 applicants, 92% accepted, 22 enrolled. In 2009, 3 master's awarded. *Entrance requirements:* For master's, BS, BBA. Additional exam requirements/recommendations for international students: Required—TOEFL (minimum score 520 paper-based; 200 computer-based; 80 iBT). *Application deadline:* For fall admission, 8/1 priority date for domestic students, 7/1 priority date for international students. Applications are processed on a rolling basis. Application fee: $0. Electronic applications accepted. *Expenses:* Tuition: Full-time $18,000; part-time $650 per semester hour. *Financial support:* In 2009–10, 7 students received support. Scholarships/grants available. Financial award applicants required to submit FAFSA. *Unit head:* Dr. Amjad Umar, Director and Professor, 717-901-5141, Fax: 717-901-3141, E-mail: aumar@

Public Administration

Harrisburg University of Science and Technology (continued)

harrisburgu.edu. *Application contact:* Julie Cullings, Information Contact, 717-901-5163, Fax: 717-901-3163, E-mail: admissions@harrisburgu.edu.

Harvard University, John F. Kennedy School of Government, Lucius N. Littauer Mid-Career Program in Public Administration, Cambridge, MA 02138. Offers MPA. *Students:* 204 full-time (79 women), 8 part-time (4 women); includes 29 minority (11 African Americans, 2 American Indian/Alaska Native, 8 Asian Americans or Pacific Islanders, 8 Hispanic Americans), 104 international. Average age 40. 568 applicants, 58% accepted, 208 enrolled. In 2009, 196 master's awarded. *Entrance requirements:* For master's, GMAT or GRE General Test, minimum 7 years of professional experience. Additional exam requirements/recommendations for international students: Required—TOEFL (minimum score 600 paper-based; 250 computer-based; 100 iBT), TWE. *Application deadline:* For fall admission, 3/6 for domestic students. Applications are processed on a rolling basis. Application fee: $80. Electronic applications accepted. *Expenses:* Contact institution. *Financial support:* Fellowships, Federal Work-Study, institutionally sponsored loans, scholarships/grants, health care benefits, and unspecified assistantships available. Financial award application deadline: 3/26; financial award applicants required to submit CSS PROFILE or FAFSA. *Unit head:* Robin Engel, Director, 617-496-1100, E-mail: robin_engel@harvard.edu. *Application contact:* 617-495-1155, E-mail: admissions@hks.harvard.edu.

Harvard University, John F. Kennedy School of Government, Master in Public Administration/International Development Program, Cambridge, MA 02138. Offers MPAID. *Students:* 141 full-time (52 women), 5 part-time (2 women); includes 12 minority (9 Asian Americans or Pacific Islanders, 3 Hispanic Americans), 98 international. Average age 29. 349 applicants, 30% accepted, 76 enrolled. In 2009, 52 master's awarded. *Entrance requirements:* For master's, GMAT or GRE General Test (joint Business School applicants), one course each in microeconomics and macroeconomics; two college-level calculus courses (one must contain multivariable calculus); bachelor's degree; 2-3 years of professional experience in development (strongly encouraged). Additional exam requirements/recommendations for international students: Required—TOEFL (minimum score 600 paper-based; 250 computer-based; 100 iBT). *Application deadline:* For fall admission, 1/2 for domestic students. Application fee: $80. Electronic applications accepted. *Expenses:* Tuition: Full-time $33,696. Required fees: $1126. Full-time tuition and fees vary according to program. *Financial support:* Fellowships, research assistantships, teaching assistantships, career-related internships or fieldwork, Federal Work-Study, institutionally sponsored loans, scholarships/grants, health care benefits, and unspecified assistantships available. Financial award application deadline: 2/6; financial award applicants required to submit CSS PROFILE or FAFSA. *Unit head:* Carol Finney, Director, 617-495-7799, E-mail: carol_finney@harvard.edu. *Application contact:* 617-495-2133, E-mail: mpaid_program@hks.harvard.edu.

Harvard University, John F. Kennedy School of Government, Two-year Program in Public Administration, Cambridge, MA 02138. Offers MPA. *Students:* 137 full-time (37 women), 29 part-time (9 women); includes 39 minority (6 African Americans, 1 American Indian/Alaska Native, 22 Asian Americans or Pacific Islanders, 10 Hispanic Americans), 69 international. Average age 31. 168 applicants, 61% accepted, 78 enrolled. In 2009, 70 master's awarded. *Entrance requirements:* For master's, GMAT or GRE General Test, minimum of 3 years of work experience, relevant graduate work. Additional exam requirements/recommendations for international students: Required—TOEFL (minimum score 600 paper-based; 250 computer-based; 100 iBT), TWE. *Application deadline:* For fall admission, 1/4 for domestic students. Application fee: $80. Electronic applications accepted. *Expenses:* Tuition: Full-time $33,696. Required fees: $1126. Full-time tuition and fees vary according to program. *Financial support:* Fellowships, research assistantships, teaching assistantships, career-related internships or fieldwork, Federal Work-Study, institutionally sponsored loans, scholarships/grants, health care benefits, and unspecified assistantships available. Financial award application deadline: 2/6; financial award applicants required to submit CSS PROFILE or FAFSA. *Unit head:* Robin Engel, Director, 617-496-1100, E-mail: robin_engel@harvard.edu. *Application contact:* 617-495-1155.

Hodges University, Graduate Programs, Naples, FL 34119. Offers business administration (MBA); computer information technology (MS); criminal justice (MCJ); education (MPS); information systems management (MIS); interdisciplinary (MPS); law (MPS); management (MSM); professional studies (MPS); psychology (MPS); public administration (MPA). Part-time and evening/weekend programs available. Postbaccalaureate distance learning degree programs offered (no on-campus study). *Faculty:* 14 full-time (4 women), 4 part-time/adjunct (3 women). *Students:* 37 full-time (28 women), 217 part-time (142 women); includes 76 minority (35 African Americans, 5 Asian Americans or Pacific Islanders, 36 Hispanic Americans). Average age 36. 92 applicants, 91% accepted, 81 enrolled. In 2009, 92 master's awarded. *Degree requirements:* For master's, comprehensive exam (for some programs), thesis (for some programs). *Entrance requirements:* For master's, in-house entrance exam. *Application deadline:* Applications are processed on a rolling basis. Application fee: $50. Electronic applications accepted. *Expenses:* Tuition: Full-time $16,605; part-time $615 per credit hour. Required fees: $570. *Financial support:* In 2009–10, 200 students received support. Federal Work-Study and scholarships/grants available. Financial award application deadline: 7/9; financial award applicants required to submit FAFSA. *Unit head:* Terry McMahan, President, 239-513-1122, Fax: 239-598-6253, E-mail: tmcmahan@hodges.edu. *Application contact:* Rita Lampus, Vice President of Student Enrollment Management, 239-513-1122, Fax: 239-598-6253, E-mail: rlampus@hodges.edu.

Hood College, Graduate School, Department of Economics and Management, Frederick, MD 21701-8575. Offers accounting (MBA); administration and management (MBA); finance (MBA); human resource management (MBA); information systems (MBA); marketing (MBA); public management (MBA). Part-time and evening/weekend programs available. *Faculty:* 5 full-time (1 woman), 9 part-time/adjunct (1 woman). *Students:* 21 full-time (16 women), 166 part-time (85 women); includes 33 minority (18 African Americans, 8 Asian Americans or Pacific Islanders, 7 Hispanic Americans), 15 international. Average age 32. 47 applicants, 87% accepted, 32 enrolled. In 2009, 31 master's awarded. *Degree requirements:* For master's, capstone/final research project. *Entrance requirements:* For master's, minimum GPA of 2.75, resume, letters of recommendation. *Application deadline:* For fall admission, 7/15 for domestic and international students; for spring admission, 12/15 for domestic and international students. Applications are processed on a rolling basis. Application fee: $35. Electronic applications accepted. *Expenses:* Tuition: Full-time $6480; part-time $360 per credit. Required fees: $100; $50 per term. *Financial support:* Applicants required to submit FAFSA. *Faculty research:* Corporate strategy and sustainable competitive advantages, business ethics, entrepreneurship, investments management, economic development. *Unit head:* Dr. Anita Jose, Program Director, 301-696-3691, Fax: 301-696-3597, E-mail: jose@hood.edu. *Application contact:* Dr. Allen P. Flora, Dean of Graduate School, 301-696-3811, Fax: 301-696-3597, E-mail: gofurther@hood.edu.

Howard University, Graduate School, Department of Political Science, Program in Public Administration, Washington, DC 20059-0002. Offers MAPA. *Accreditation:* NASPAA. Part-time programs available. *Degree requirements:* For master's, comprehensive exam. *Entrance requirements:* For master's, GRE General Test, minimum GPA of 3.0.

Idaho State University, Office of Graduate Studies, College of Arts and Sciences, Department of Political Science, Program in Public Administration, Pocatello, ID 83209-8073. Offers MPA. Part-time programs available. *Students:* 15 full-time (7 women), 14 part-time (9 women). Average age 35. In 2009, 7 master's awarded. *Degree requirements:* For master's, comprehensive exam, thesis optional, public service internship. *Entrance requirements:* For master's, GRE General Test, course work in humanities and social sciences, 3 letters of recommendation. Additional exam requirements/recommendations for international students: Required—TOEFL (minimum score 550 paper-based; 213 computer-based; 80 iBT). *Application deadline:* For fall admission, 7/1 for domestic students, 6/1 for international students; for spring admission, 12/1 for domestic students, 11/1 for international students. Applications are processed on a rolling basis. Application fee: $55. Electronic applications accepted. *Expenses:* Tuition, state resident: full-time $3318; part-time $297 per credit hour. Tuition, nonresident: full-time $13,120; part-time $437 per credit hour. Required fees: $2530. Tuition and fees vary according to program. *Financial support:* Teaching assistantships with full and partial tuition reimbursements, career-related internships or fieldwork, Federal Work-Study, institutionally sponsored loans, scholarships/grants, health care benefits, and unspecified assistantships available. Support available to part-time students. Financial award application deadline: 1/1; financial award applicants required to submit FAFSA. *Faculty research:* Constitutional law, policy theory, public administration, international affairs. *Unit head:* Dr. Wayne Gabardi, Chairman, 208-282-4536, Fax: 208-282-4833, E-mail: gabawayn@isu.edu. *Application contact:* Tami Carson, Graduate School Technical Records Specialist, 208-282-2150, Fax: 208-282-4847, E-mail: carstami@isu.edu.

Illinois Institute of Technology, Graduate College, College of Science and Letters, Department of Social Sciences, Chicago, IL 60616-3793. Offers nonprofit management (MPA); public administration (MPA); public safety and crisis management (MPA); JD/MPA; MBA/MPA. Part-time and evening/weekend programs available. *Faculty:* 10 full-time (2 women), 14 part-time/adjunct (2 women). *Students:* 69 full-time (31 women), 43 part-time (26 women); includes 15 minority (12 African Americans, 3 Hispanic Americans), 71 international. Average age 33. 160 applicants, 84% accepted, 66 enrolled. In 2009, 71 master's awarded. *Degree requirements:* For master's, comprehensive exam, capstone course (practicum). *Entrance requirements:* For master's, minimum undergraduate GPA of 3.0, 2 letters of recommendation. Additional exam requirements/recommendations for international students: Required—TOEFL (minimum score 523 paper-based; 70 iBT). *Application deadline:* For fall admission, 5/1 for domestic and international students; for spring admission, 10/15 for domestic and international students. Applications are processed on a rolling basis. Application fee: $50. Electronic applications accepted. *Expenses:* Tuition: Full-time $17,550; part-time $888 per credit hour. Required fees: $850; $7.50 per credit hour. One-time fee: $50 full-time. Full-time tuition and fees vary according to program. *Financial support:* Federal Work-Study, institutionally sponsored loans, scholarships/grants, and health care benefits available. Support available to part-time students. Financial award applicants required to submit FAFSA. *Faculty research:* Comparative public administration and policy, migration and ethnic politics, social dimension and impact of science and technology, urban politics, urban ethnography. *Unit head:* Dr. Patrick R. Ireland, Professor and Chairman, 312-567-5128, Fax: 312-567-6821, E-mail: socscience@iit.edu. *Application contact:* Lawerence Ruffolo, Assistant Director, Graduate Program in Public Administration, 312-906-5197, Fax: 312-906-5199, E-mail: lruffolo@kentlaw.edu.

Illinois Institute of Technology, Stuart School of Business, Program in Public Administration, Chicago, IL 60616-3793. Offers MPA, JD/MPA, MBA/MPA. Part-time and evening/weekend programs available. *Faculty:* 10 full-time (2 women), 14 part-time/adjunct (2 women). *Students:* 69 full-time (31 women), 43 part-time (26 women); includes 15 minority (12 African Americans, 3 Hispanic Americans), 71 international. Average age 33. 160 applicants, 84% accepted, 66 enrolled. In 2009, 71 master's awarded. *Degree requirements:* For master's, capstone course (practicum). *Entrance requirements:* For master's, minimum undergraduate GPA of 3.0, 2 letters of recommendation. Additional exam requirements/recommendations for international students: Required—TOEFL (minimum score 575 paper-based; 233 computer-based; 90 iBT). *Application deadline:* For fall admission, 8/1 for domestic students, 5/1 for international students; for spring admission, 12/15 for domestic students, 10/15 for international students. Applications are processed on a rolling basis. Application fee: $40. Electronic applications accepted. *Expenses:* Tuition: Full-time $17,550; part-time $888 per credit hour. Required fees: $850; $7.50 per credit hour. One-time fee: $50 full-time. Full-time tuition and fees vary according to program. *Financial support:* Federal Work-Study, institutionally sponsored loans, scholarships/grants, and health care benefits available. Support available to part-time students. Financial award applicants required to submit FAFSA. *Faculty research:* Comparative public administration and policy, migration and ethnic politics, social dimension and impact of science and technology, urban politics, urban ethnography. *Unit head:* Dr. Calia Rolanda, Dean, 312-906-5181, E-mail: rcalia@stuart.iit.edu. *Application contact:* Dr. Calia Rolanda, Dean, 312-906-5181, E-mail: rcalia@stuart.iit.edu.

Indiana State University, School of Graduate Studies, College of Arts and Sciences, Department of Political Science, Terre Haute, IN 47809. Offers political science (MA, MS); public administration (MPA). *Degree requirements:* For master's, thesis (for some programs). *Entrance requirements:* For master's, GRE or minimum undergraduate GPA of 2.75, 18 semester hours of course work in political science. Additional exam requirements/recommendations for international students: Required—TOEFL (minimum score 550 paper-based). Electronic applications accepted.

Indiana University Bloomington, School of Public and Environmental Affairs, Public Affairs Programs, Bloomington, IN 47405-7000. Offers comparative and international affairs (MPA); economic development (MPA); energy (MPA); environmental policy and natural resource management (MPA); information systems (MPA); local government management (MPA); nonprofit management (MPA); policy analysis (MPA); public financial administration (MPA); public management (MPA); sustainability and sustainable development (MPA); JD/MPA; MPA/MA; MPA/MIS; MPA/MLS; MSES/MPA. *Accreditation:* NASPAA (one or more programs are accredited). Part-time programs available. *Faculty:* 75 full-time (22 women), 91 part-time/adjunct (24 women). *Students:* 389 full-time (222 women), 45 part-time (24 women); includes 38 minority (18 African Americans, 1 American Indian/Alaska Native, 12 Asian Americans or Pacific Islanders, 7 Hispanic Americans), 72 international. Average age 26. 474 applicants, 206 enrolled. In 2009, 190 master's, 11 doctorates, 3 other advanced degrees awarded. Terminal master's awarded for partial completion of doctoral program. *Degree requirements:* For master's, thesis optional; for doctorate, comprehensive exam, thesis/dissertation or alternative, A thesis is required for the Public Affairs and Public Policy degree. *Entrance requirements:* For master's, GRE, LSAT (if also applying for the Law School), 3 letters of recommendation, resume or curriculum vitae; for doctorate, GRE General Test. Additional exam requirements/recommendations for international students: Required—TOEFL (minimum score 590 paper-based; 243 computer-based; 96 iBT). *Application deadline:* For fall admission, 2/1 priority date for domestic students, 12/1 priority date for international students; for spring admission, 9/1 for international students. Application fee: $55 ($65 for international students). Electronic applications accepted. *Financial support:* Fellowships with full tuition reimbursements, research assistantships with partial tuition reimbursements, teaching assistantships with partial tuition reimbursements, career-related internships or fieldwork, Federal Work-Study, institutionally sponsored loans, unspecified assistantships, and Service Corps programs available. Financial award application deadline: 2/1; financial award applicants required to submit FAFSA. *Faculty research:* Comparative and international affairs, environmental policy and resource management, policy analysis, public finance, public management, urban management, nonprofit management. *Unit head:* Dean John Graham, Dean, School of Public and Environmental Affairs, 812-855-1432, E-mail: grahamjd@indiana.edu. *Application contact:* Jennifer Medlin, Assistant Director of Admissions and Financial Aid, 812-855-3784, Fax: 812-856-3665, E-mail: jlmedlin@indiana.edu.

See Close-Up on page 1189.

Indiana University Kokomo, School of Public and Environmental Affairs, Kokomo, IN 46904-9003. Offers public management (MS, Graduate Certificate). *Students:* 18 full-time (11 women), 18 part-time (12 women); includes 8 minority (5 African Americans, 1 American Indian/Alaska Native, 2 Hispanic Americans). Average age 37. In 2009, 1 other advanced degree awarded. *Application deadline:* For fall admission, 8/1 priority date for domestic students; for spring admission, 12/9 priority date for domestic students. Application fee: $40 ($50 for international students). *Unit head:* Dr. Robert Dibie, Assistant Dean, 765-455-9417, Fax: 765-455-9537, E-mail: iuadmis@iuk.edu. *Application contact:* Susan Wilson, Information Contact, 765-455-9330.

Indiana University Northwest, School of Public and Environmental Affairs, Gary, IN 46408-1197. Offers criminal justice (MPA); environmental affairs (Graduate Certificate); health services administration (MPA); human services administration (MPA); nonprofit management (Graduate Certificate); public management (MPA, Graduate Certificate). *Accreditation:* NASPAA (one or more programs are accredited). Part-time programs available. *Faculty:* 5 full-time (3 women). *Students:* 19 full-time (14 women), 121 part-time (100 women); includes 100 minority (84 African Americans, 1 American Indian/Alaska Native, 1 Asian American or Pacific Islander, 14 Hispanic Americans). Average age 39. In 2009, 29 master's, 27 other advanced degrees awarded. *Entrance requirements:* For master's, GRE General Test or GMAT, letters of recommendation. *Application deadline:* For fall admission, 8/15 priority date for domestic students. Applications are processed on a rolling basis. Application fee: $25. *Financial support:* Career-related internships or fieldwork, Federal Work-Study, and tuition waivers (partial) available. Support available to part-time students. Financial award application deadline: 3/1. *Faculty research:* Employment in income security policies, evidence in criminal justice, equal employment law, social welfare policy and welfare reform, public finance in developing countries. *Unit head:* George Assibey-Mensah, Interim Dean/Division Director, 219-980-6695, Fax: 219-980-6737. *Application contact:* Sandra Hall Smith, Secretary, 219-980-6695, Fax: 219-980-6737, E-mail: shsmith@iun.edu.

Indiana University–Purdue University Indianapolis, School of Public and Environmental Affairs, Indianapolis, IN 46202-2896. Offers health administration (MHA); public affairs (MPA), including criminal justice, environmental management, nonprofit management, policy analysis, public management; JD/MHA; MBA/MHA; MLS/NMC; MLS/PMC; MSN/MHA. *Accreditation:* CAHME (one or more programs are accredited); NASPAA. Part-time and evening/weekend programs available. *Faculty:* 17 full-time (6 women). *Students:* 126 full-time (71 women), 283 part-time (164 women); includes 58 minority (29 African Americans, 1 American Indian/Alaska Native, 17 Asian Americans or Pacific Islanders, 11 Hispanic Americans), 20 international. Average age 33. 255 applicants, 77% accepted, 136 enrolled. In 2009, 77 master's awarded. *Entrance requirements:* For master's, GRE General Test, minimum GPA of 3.0 (preferred). Additional exam requirements/recommendations for international students: Required—TOEFL. *Application deadline:* For fall admission, 7/15 priority date for domestic students; for spring admission, 11/15 for domestic students. Applications are processed on a rolling basis. Application fee: $55 ($65 for international students). *Financial support:* In 2009–10, 11 fellowships with full and partial tuition reimbursements (averaging $5,890 per year), 10 teaching assistantships (averaging $9,900 per year) were awarded; research assistantships with full and partial tuition reimbursements, career-related internships or fieldwork, Federal Work-Study, institutionally sponsored loans, and scholarships/grants also available. Support available to part-time students. Financial award application deadline: 3/1. *Faculty research:* Economic development, water and air quality, ethics, financing, organization design and structure. Total annual research expenditures: $1.9 million. *Unit head:* Dr. Greg Lindsey, Associate Dean, 317-274-4656, Fax: 317-274-5153. *Application contact:* 317-274-4656, Fax: 317-274-5153, E-mail: speainfo@speanet.iupui.edu.

Indiana University South Bend, School of Public and Environmental Affairs, South Bend, IN 46634-7111. Offers health systems administration and policy (MPA); health systems management (Certificate); nonprofit management (Certificate); public and community services administration and policy (MPA); public management (Certificate); urban affairs (Certificate). *Accreditation:* NASPAA. Part-time and evening/weekend programs available. *Faculty:* 4 full-time (1 woman). *Students:* 18 part-time (13 women); includes 3 minority (2 African Americans, 1 Hispanic American). Average age 40. In 2009, 9 master's awarded. *Entrance requirements:* For master's, GRE General Test, minimum undergraduate GPA of 2.5. *Application deadline:* For fall admission, 7/1 priority date for domestic students; for spring admission, 11/1 for domestic students. Applications are processed on a rolling basis. Application fee: $46 ($58 for international students). *Financial support:* Fellowships, research assistantships, career-related internships or fieldwork, Federal Work-Study, and institutionally sponsored loans available. Support available to part-time students. Financial award application deadline: 3/1; financial award applicants required to submit FAFSA. *Unit head:* Leda M. Hall, Dean, 574-520-4803. *Application contact:* Leda M. Hall, Dean, 574-520-4803.

Institute of Public Administration, Programs in Public Administration, Dublin, Ireland. Offers healthcare management (MA); local government management (MA); public management (MA, Diploma).

Instituto Tecnológico y de Estudios Superiores de Monterrey, Campus Ciudad Juárez, Program in Applied Public Management, Ciudad Juárez, Mexico. Offers MPM.

Iowa State University of Science and Technology, Graduate College, College of Liberal Arts and Sciences, Department of Political Science, Ames, IA 50011. Offers political science (MA); public administration (MPA); JD/MA. *Accreditation:* NASPAA. *Faculty:* 12 full-time (3 women), 5 part-time/adjunct (3 women). *Students:* 32 full-time (16 women), 40 part-time (17 women); includes 4 minority (all Asian Americans or Pacific Islanders), 11 international. 38 applicants, 79% accepted, 20 enrolled. In 2009, 15 master's awarded. *Degree requirements:* For master's, thesis (for some programs). *Entrance requirements:* For master's, GRE General Test, GMAT or LSAT. Additional exam requirements/recommendations for international students: Required—TOEFL (minimum score 570 paper-based; 80 iBT) or IELTS (minimum score 6.5). *Application deadline:* For fall admission, 1/1 priority date for domestic and international students; for spring admission, 10/1 for domestic and international students. Applications are processed on a rolling basis. Application fee: $40 ($90 for international students). Electronic applications accepted. *Expenses:* Tuition, state resident: full-time $6716. Tuition, nonresident: full-time $8908. Tuition and fees vary according to course level, course load, program and student level. *Financial support:* In 2009–10, 17 research assistantships with full and partial tuition reimbursements (averaging $13,500 per year), 2 teaching assistantships with full and partial tuition reimbursements (averaging $13,990 per year) were awarded; fellowships, scholarships/grants, health care benefits, and unspecified assistantships also available. *Unit head:* Dr. James M. McCormick, Chair, 515-294-8682, Fax: 515-294-1003, E-mail: polsc@iastate.edu. *Application contact:* Dr. Mack Shelley, Director of Graduate Education, 515-294-1075, E-mail: polsci@iastate.edu.

Jackson State University, Graduate School, School of Liberal Arts, Department of Public Policy and Administration, Jackson, MS 39217. Offers MPPA, PhD. *Accreditation:* NASPAA (one or more programs are accredited). Evening/weekend programs available. *Degree requirements:* For master's, comprehensive exam, thesis optional; for doctorate, comprehensive exam, thesis/dissertation. *Entrance requirements:* For master's, GRE General Test; for doctorate, GRE, GMAT, MAT. Additional exam requirements/recommendations for international students: Required—TOEFL.

James Madison University, The Graduate School, College of Arts and Letters, Department of Political Science, Program in Public Administration, Harrisonburg, VA 22807. Offers MPA. Part-time programs available. *Students:* 14 full-time (6 women), 28 part-time (13 women); includes 1 minority (Asian American or Pacific Islander), 1 international. Average age 27. In 2009, 9 master's awarded. *Degree requirements:* For master's, comprehensive exam. *Entrance requirements:* For master's, GMAT or GRE General Test. Additional exam requirements/recommendations for international students: Required—TOEFL. *Application deadline:* For fall admission, 5/1 priority date for domestic students; for spring admission, 9/1 priority date for domestic students. Applications are processed on a rolling basis. Application fee: $55. Electronic applications accepted. *Expenses:* Tuition, area resident: Part-time $305 per credit hour. Tuition, state resident: part-time $305 per credit hour. Tuition, nonresident: part-time $890 per credit hour. *Financial support:* In 2009–10, 9 students received support. Application deadline: 3/1. *Unit head:* Dr. Jessica Adolino, Department Chair, 540-568-6149, E-mail: adolinjr@jmu.edu. *Application contact:* Dr. B. Douglas Skelley, Director, 540-568-6149, E-mail: skellebd@jmu.edu.

John Jay College of Criminal Justice of the City University of New York, Graduate Studies, Program in Public Administration, New York, NY 10019-1093. Offers MPA. *Accreditation:* NASPAA. Part-time and evening/weekend programs available. *Degree requirements:* For master's, thesis or alternative. *Entrance requirements:* For master's, minimum B average. Additional exam requirements/recommendations for international students: Required—TOEFL (minimum score 500 paper-based; 173 computer-based).

Kansas State University, Graduate School, College of Arts and Sciences, Department of Political Science, Manhattan, KS 66506. Offers political science (MA), including international service, political science; public administration (MPA). Part-time programs available. *Faculty:* 16 full-time (4 women). *Students:* 41 full-time (18 women), 6 part-time (3 women); includes 6 minority (3 American Indian/Alaska Native, 3 Asian Americans or Pacific Islanders), 6 international. Average age 28. 37 applicants, 81% accepted, 30 enrolled. In 2009, 19 master's awarded. *Degree requirements:* For master's, thesis or alternative. *Entrance requirements:* For master's, GRE (recommended), minimum GPA of 3.0. Additional exam requirements/recommendations for international students: Required—TOEFL (minimum score 550 paper-based; 213 computer-based). *Application deadline:* For fall admission, 2/1 priority date for domestic and international students; for spring admission, 8/1 priority date for domestic and international students. Applications are processed on a rolling basis. Application fee: $40 ($55 for international students). Electronic applications accepted. *Financial support:* In 2009–10, 3 research assistantships (averaging $20,126 per year), 9 teaching assistantships with tuition reimbursements (averaging $10,500 per year) were awarded; fellowships, career-related internships or fieldwork, Federal Work-Study, institutionally sponsored loans, and scholarships/grants also available. Support available to part-time students. Financial award application deadline: 3/1; financial award applicants required to submit FAFSA. *Faculty research:* Armed conflict, civil military relations, comparative public administration and policy, electoral competition, legislative studies. Total annual research expenditures: $30,909. *Unit head:* Jeff Pickering, Head, 785-532-0454, Fax: 785-532-2339, E-mail: jjp@ksu.edu. *Application contact:* James Franke, Director, 785-532-0451, Fax: 785-532-2339, E-mail: jfranke@ksu.edu.

Kean University, College of Business and Public Administration, Program in Public Administration, Union, NJ 07083. Offers environmental management (MPA); health services administration (MPA); non-profit management (MPA); public administration (MPA). *Accreditation:* NASPAA. Part-time and evening/weekend programs available. *Faculty:* 8 full-time (4 women). *Students:* 48 full-time (33 women), 92 part-time (53 women); includes 85 minority (62 African Americans, 9 Asian Americans or Pacific Islanders, 14 Hispanic Americans), 9 international. Average age 31. 80 applicants, 74% accepted, 34 enrolled. In 2009, 49 master's awarded. *Degree requirements:* For master's, thesis, internship, research seminar. *Entrance requirements:* For master's, minimum GPA of 3.0, 2 letters of recommendation, interview. *Application deadline:* For fall admission, 5/1 for domestic students; for spring admission, 11/1 for domestic students. Application fee: $60 ($150 for international students). Electronic applications accepted. *Expenses:* Tuition, state resident: full-time $10,440; part-time $435 per credit. Tuition, nonresident: full-time $14,160; part-time $590 per credit. Required fees: $2642; $110 per credit. Part-time tuition and fees vary according to course load and degree level. *Financial support:* In 2009–10, 10 research assistantships with full tuition reimbursements (averaging $3,263 per year) were awarded; unspecified assistantships also available. *Unit head:* Dr. Patricia Moore, Program Coordinator, 908-737-4300, E-mail: pmoore@kean.edu. *Application contact:* Steven Koch, Pre-Admissions Coordinator, 908-737-5924, Fax: 908-737-5965, E-mail: skoch@kean.edu.

Kean University, College of Natural, Applied and Health Sciences, Program in Nursing and Public Administration, Union, NJ 07083. Offers MSN/MPA. *Accreditation:* NLN. Part-time and evening/weekend programs available. *Faculty:* 7 full-time (all women). *Students:* 6 part-time (5 women); includes 5 minority (all African Americans). Average age 40. 8 applicants, 88% accepted, 3 enrolled. *Application deadline:* For fall admission, 5/1 for domestic students; for spring admission, 11/1 for domestic students. Application fee: $60 ($150 for international students). Electronic applications accepted. *Expenses:* Tuition, state resident: full-time $10,440; part-time $435 per credit. Tuition, nonresident: full-time $14,160; part-time $590 per credit. Required fees: $2642; $110 per credit. Part-time tuition and fees vary according to course load and degree level. *Financial support:* Research assistantships with full tuition reimbursements, unspecified assistantships available. *Unit head:* Dr. Estelle Pisani, Program Coordinator, 908-737-3390, E-mail: episani@kean.edu. *Application contact:* Dorothy Rowe, Pre-Admissions Coordinator, 908-737-5928, Fax: 908-737-5965, E-mail: drowe@kean.edu.

Kennesaw State University, College of Humanities and Social Sciences, Program in Public Administration, Kennesaw, GA 30144-5591. Offers MPA. *Accreditation:* NASPAA. Part-time and evening/weekend programs available. *Faculty:* 11 full-time (7 women), 4 part-time/adjunct (1 woman). *Students:* 43 full-time (26 women), 49 part-time (37 women); includes 33 minority (29 African Americans, 1 Asian American or Pacific Islander, 3 Hispanic Americans), 9 international. Average age 30. 54 applicants, 57% accepted, 22 enrolled. In 2009, 47 master's awarded. *Entrance requirements:* For master's, GRE General Test, minimum GPA of 2.75. Additional exam requirements/recommendations for international students: Required—TOEFL (minimum score 550 paper-based; 213 computer-based; 80 iBT), IELTS (minimum score 6). *Application deadline:* For fall admission, 8/1 for domestic and international students; for winter admission, 12/1 for domestic and international students; for spring admission, 5/1 for domestic students, 8/1 for international students. Applications are processed on a rolling basis. Application fee: $60. Electronic applications accepted. *Expenses:* Tuition, state resident: full-time $2341; part-time $196 per credit hour. Tuition, nonresident: full-time $9396; part-time $783 per credit hour. Required fees: $573 per semester. *Financial support:* In 2009–10, 2 research assistantships with full tuition reimbursements (averaging $15,000 per year) were awarded; Federal Work-Study also available. Support available to part-time students. Financial award application deadline: 6/15; financial award applicants required to submit FAFSA. *Unit head:* Dr. Andrew Ewoh, Director, 770-423-6246, E-mail: aewoh@kennesaw.edu. *Application contact:* Vilma Marquez, Admissions Counselor, 770-420-4377, Fax: 770-423-6885, E-mail: ksugrad@kennesaw.edu.

Kent State University, College of Arts and Sciences, Department of Political Science, Program in Public Administration, Kent, OH 44242-0001. Offers MPA. *Accreditation:* NASPAA. *Degree requirements:* For master's, thesis optional, public sector internship. *Entrance requirements:* For master's, GRE General Test, minimum GPA of 2.75. Additional exam requirements/recommendations for international students: Required—TOEFL. Electronic applications accepted.

Kentucky State University, College of Professional Studies, Frankfort, KY 40601. Offers business administration (MBA), including accounting, finance, management, marketing; public administration (MPA), including human resource management, international administration and development, management information systems, nonprofit management; special education (MA). Part-time and evening/weekend programs available. Postbaccalaureate distance learning degree programs offered (minimal on-campus study). *Faculty:* 11 full-time (3 women), 2 part-time/adjunct (both women). *Students:* 79 full-time (51 women), 66 part-time (34 women); includes 88 minority (85 African Americans, 2 Asian Americans or Pacific Islanders, 1 Hispanic American), 4 international. Average age 34. 92 applicants, 75% accepted, 52 enrolled. In 2009, 32 master's awarded. *Degree requirements:* For master's, comprehensive exam, thesis optional. *Entrance requirements:* For master's, GMAT, GRE. Additional exam requirements/recommendations for international students: Required—TOEFL (minimum score 525 paper-based; 173 computer-based). *Application deadline:* For fall admission, 7/1 priority date for domestic students, 4/15 priority date for international students; for spring admission, 11/15 priority date for domestic students, 8/1 priority date for international students. Applications are processed on a rolling basis. Application fee: $30 ($100 for international students). Electronic applications accepted. *Expenses:* Tuition, state resident: full-time $5634; part-time $313 per credit hour. Tuition, nonresident: full-time $14,598; part-time $811 per credit hour. Required fees: $450; $25 per credit hour. *Financial support:* In 2009–10, 113 students received support, including 4 research assistantships (averaging $14,035 per year); career-related internships or fieldwork, scholarships/grants, tuition waivers (partial), and unspecified assistantships also available. Financial award application deadline: 4/15; financial award applicants required to submit FAFSA. *Unit head:* Dr. Gashaw Lake, Dean, College of Professional Studies, 502-597-6105, Fax: 502-597-6715, E-mail: gashaw.lake@kysu.edu. *Application contact:* Cedric Cunningham, Administrative Assistant, Office of Graduate Studies, 502-597-6536, E-mail: cedric.cunningham@kysu.edu.

Public Administration

Kutztown University of Pennsylvania, College of Liberal Arts and Sciences, Program in Public Administration, Kutztown, PA 19530-0730. Offers MPA. Part-time and evening/weekend programs available. *Faculty:* 2 full-time (1 woman). *Students:* 7 full-time (3 women), 20 part-time (12 women); includes 4 minority (3 African Americans, 1 American Indian/Alaska Native), 1 international. Average age 30. 34 applicants, 56% accepted, 13 enrolled. In 2009, 3 master's awarded. *Degree requirements:* For master's, comprehensive exam, thesis optional. *Entrance requirements:* For master's, GRE General Test. Additional exam requirements/recommendations for international students: Required—TOEFL. *Application deadline:* For fall admission, 8/15 priority date for domestic and international students; for spring admission, 12/15 priority date for domestic and international students. Applications are processed on a rolling basis. Application fee: $35. Electronic applications accepted. *Expenses:* Tuition, state resident: full-time $6666; part-time $370 per credit. Tuition, nonresident: full-time $10,666; part-time $593 per credit. Required fees: $62 per credit. $60 per semester. *Financial support:* Career-related internships or fieldwork, Federal Work-Study, scholarships/grants, and unspecified assistantships available. Financial award application deadline: 3/1; financial award applicants required to submit FAFSA. *Faculty research:* Structure of code enforcement offices in smaller developing communities. *Unit head:* Dr. Kristin Bremer, Chairperson, 610-683-4449, Fax: 610-683-4603, E-mail: bremer@kutztown.edu. *Application contact:* Kelly D. Burr, Associate Director, Graduate Admissions, 610-683-4200, Fax: 610-683-1393, E-mail: graduate@kutztown.edu.

Lamar University, College of Graduate Studies, College of Arts and Sciences, Department of Political Science, Beaumont, TX 77710. Offers public administration (MPA). Part-time programs available. *Faculty:* 3 full-time (1 woman). *Students:* 8 full-time (3 women), 6 part-time (1 woman); includes 5 minority (2 African Americans, 1 Asian American or Pacific Islander, 2 Hispanic Americans), 1 international. Average age 26. 18 applicants, 56% accepted, 8 enrolled. In 2009, 4 master's awarded. *Entrance requirements:* For master's, GRE General Test. Additional exam requirements/recommendations for international students: Required—TOEFL. *Application deadline:* For fall admission, 8/1 for domestic students; for spring admission, 12/1 for domestic students. Applications are processed on a rolling basis. Application fee: $25 ($50 for international students). *Financial support:* Fellowships, research assistantships, teaching assistantships, career-related internships or fieldwork, Federal Work-Study, and institutionally sponsored loans available. Financial award application deadline: 4/1. *Faculty research:* Political activities of administrators, administrative response to Hurricane Rita, budgeting, environmental politics, urban planning. *Unit head:* Dr. Glenn Utter, Chair, 409-880-8526, Fax: 409-880-8710. *Application contact:* Dr. Terri Davis, Director, 409-880-8533, Fax: 409-880-1710, E-mail: davistb@hal.lamar.edu.

Lewis University, College of Arts and Sciences, Program in Organizational Leadership, Romeoville, IL 60446. Offers higher education/student services (MA); organizational management (MA); public administration (MA); training and development (MA). Part-time and evening/weekend programs available. *Faculty:* 2 full-time (0 women), 9 part-time/adjunct (2 women). *Students:* 24 full-time (11 women), 111 part-time (91 women); includes 42 minority (33 African Americans, 1 American Indian/Alaska Native, 1 Asian American or Pacific Islander, 7 Hispanic Americans), 1 international. Average age 38. In 2009, 41 master's awarded. *Entrance requirements:* For master's, bachelor's degree, at least 25 years of age, minimum of 3 years of work experience, minimum GPA of 3.0, letter of recommendation, interview. Additional exam requirements/recommendations for international students: Required—TOEFL (minimum score 550 paper-based; 213 computer-based). *Application deadline:* For fall admission, 5/1 priority date for international students; for spring admission, 11/15 priority date for international students. Applications are processed on a rolling basis. Application fee: $40. Electronic applications accepted. *Expenses:* Tuition: Full-time $6480; part-time $720 per credit. One-time fee: $40. Tuition and fees vary according to course load, degree level and program. *Financial support:* Federal Work-Study, scholarships/grants, tuition waivers, and unspecified assistantships available. Financial award application deadline: 5/1; financial award applicants required to submit FAFSA. *Unit head:* Dr. Rich Walsh, Director, 815-838-0500, E-mail: walshri@lewisu.edu. *Application contact:* Bernadette Valderrama, Information Contact, 815-838-0500 Ext. 5629.

Lincoln University, School of Graduate Studies and Continuing Education, Jefferson City, MO 65102. Offers business administration (MBA), including accounting, entrepreneurship, management, public administration and policy; educational leadership (Ed S), including elementary leadership, secondary leadership, superintendency; guidance and counseling (M Ed), including community/agency counseling, elementary school, secondary school; history (MA); school administration and supervision (M Ed), including elementary school administration, secondary school administration, special education administration; school teaching (M Ed), including elementary school teaching, secondary school teaching; social science (MA), including history, political science, sociology; sociology (MA); sociology/criminal justice (MA). Part-time and evening/weekend programs available. *Students:* 52 full-time (27 women), 146 part-time (107 women); includes 40 minority (39 African Americans, 1 Asian American or Pacific Islander), 15 international. Average age 35. 76 applicants, 95% accepted, 46 enrolled. In 2009, 60 master's, 6 other advanced degrees awarded. *Degree requirements:* For master's and Ed S, comprehensive exam, thesis optional. *Entrance requirements:* For master's and Ed S, GRE, MAT or GMAT, minimum GPA of 2.75 in major, 2.5 overall; 3 letters of recommendation; minimum C average in English composition; personal statement of purpose. Additional exam requirements/recommendations for international students: Required—TOEFL (minimum score 500 paper-based; 173 computer-based; 61 iBT). *Application deadline:* For fall admission, 7/1 priority date for domestic and international students; for spring admission, 12/1 priority date for domestic and international students. Applications are processed on a rolling basis. Application fee: $20. *Expenses:* Tuition, state resident: full-time $4185; part-time $232.50 per credit hour. Tuition, nonresident: full-time $7767; part-time $431.50 per credit hour. Required fees: $270; $15 per credit hour. $20 per term. *Financial support:* Federal Work-Study and scholarships/grants available. Financial award application deadline: 4/1; financial award applicants required to submit FAFSA. *Faculty research:* Suicide prevention. *Unit head:* Dr. Linda S. Bickel, Dean, 573-681-5247, Fax: 573-681-5106, E-mail: gradschool@lincolnu.edu. *Application contact:* Irasema Steck, Administrative Assistant, 573-681-5247, Fax: 573-681-5106, E-mail: gradschool@lincolnu.edu.

Lindenwood University, Graduate Programs, School of Business and Entrepreneurship, St. Charles, MO 63301-1695. Offers accounting (MBA, MS); business administration (MBA); entrepreneurial studies (MBA, MS); finance (MBA, MS); human resource management (MBA); human resources (MS); international business (MBA, MS); management (MBA, MS); management information systems (MBA, MS); marketing (MBA, MS); public management (MBA, MS); sport management (MA). Part-time and evening/weekend programs available. *Faculty:* 20 full-time (8 women), 17 part-time/adjunct (5 women). *Students:* 129 full-time (60 women), 138 part-time (61 women); includes 15 minority (11 African Americans, 2 Asian Americans or Pacific Islanders, 2 Hispanic Americans), 84 international. Average age 28. 149 applicants, 73 enrolled. In 2009, 142 master's awarded. *Degree requirements:* For master's, comprehensive exam (for some programs), thesis (for some programs). *Entrance requirements:* For master's, interview, minimum GPA of 3.0, letter of recommendation. Additional exam requirements/recommendations for international students: Required—TOEFL (minimum score 550 paper-based; 213 computer-based; 80 iBT). *Application deadline:* For fall admission, 7/30 priority date for domestic students, 9/16 priority date for international students; for winter admission, 12/19 priority date for domestic students, 12/17 priority date for international students; for spring admission, 2/25 priority date for domestic students, 2/11 priority date for international students. Applications are processed on a rolling basis. Application fee: $30 ($100 for international students). Electronic applications accepted. *Expenses:* Tuition: Full-time $12,960; part-time $370 per credit hour. Required fees: $340. One-time fee: $30 full-time. Tuition and fees vary according to course level and course load. *Financial support:* In 2009–10, 209 students received support. Career-related internships or fieldwork, Federal Work-Study, institutionally sponsored loans, and tuition waivers (partial) available. Financial award application deadline: 6/30; financial award applicants required to submit FAFSA. *Unit head:* Ed Morris, Dean of Management, 636-949-4832, E-mail: emorris@lindenwood.edu. *Application contact:* Brett Barger, Dean of Evening Admissions and Extension Campuses, 636-949-4934, Fax: 636-949-4109, E-mail: adultadmissions@lindenwood.edu.

Long Island University, Brooklyn Campus, School of Business, Public Administration and Information Sciences, Program in Public Administration, Brooklyn, NY 11201-8423. Offers MPA. *Accreditation:* NASPAA. Part-time and evening/weekend programs available. *Entrance requirements:* For master's, GMAT or GRE Subject Test, 2 letters of recommendation. Additional exam requirements/recommendations for international students: Required—TOEFL (minimum score 500 paper-based; 173 computer-based). Electronic applications accepted.

Long Island University, C.W. Post Campus, College of Management, Department of Health Care and Public Administration, Brookville, NY 11548-1300. Offers gerontology (Certificate); health care administration (MPA); health care administration/gerontology (MPA); nonprofit management (MPA, Certificate); public administration (MPA). *Accreditation:* NASPAA (one or more programs are accredited). Part-time and evening/weekend programs available. *Degree requirements:* For master's, thesis. *Entrance requirements:* For master's, GMAT, minimum GPA of 2.5; for Certificate, minimum GPA of 2.5. Electronic applications accepted. *Faculty research:* Critical issues in sexuality, social work in religious communities, gerontological social work.

Long Island University, Rockland Graduate Campus, Graduate School, Programs in Health and Public Administration, Orangeburg, NY 10962. Offers gerontology (Advanced Certificate); health administration (MPA); public administration (MPA). *Faculty:* 1 full-time (0 women), 5 part-time/adjunct (3 women). *Students:* 2 full-time (1 woman), 25 part-time (19 women). In 2009, 8 master's awarded. *Entrance requirements:* For master's, GRE General Test. *Application deadline:* Applications are processed on a rolling basis. Application fee: $30. *Expenses:* Tuition: Part-time $930 per credit. Required fees: $200 per semester. *Financial support:* Applicants required to submit FAFSA. *Unit head:* Prof. Patricia Latona, Program Director, 845-359-7200 Ext. 5410, Fax: 845-359-7248, E-mail: patricia.latona@liu.edu. *Application contact:* Peter S. Reiner, Director of Admissions and Marketing, 845-359-7200, Fax: 845-359-7248, E-mail: peter.reiner@liu.edu.

Louisiana State University and Agricultural and Mechanical College, Graduate School, E. J. Ourso College of Business, Public Administration Institute, Baton Rouge, LA 70803. Offers MPA, JD/MPA. Part-time programs available. *Faculty:* 7 full-time (2 women). *Students:* 45 full-time (32 women), 52 part-time (31 women). Average age 29. 80 applicants, 90% accepted, 53 enrolled. In 2009, 44 master's awarded. *Degree requirements:* For master's, comprehensive exam. *Entrance requirements:* For master's, GRE General Test, minimum GPA of 3.0. Additional exam requirements/recommendations for international students: Required—TOEFL (minimum score 550 paper-based; 213 computer-based; 79 iBT) or IELTS (minimum score 6.5). *Application deadline:* For fall admission, 1/25 priority date for domestic students, 5/15 for international students; for spring admission, 10/15 for international students. Applications are processed on a rolling basis. Application fee: $50 ($70 for international students). Electronic applications accepted. *Financial support:* In 2009–10, 96 students received support, including 5 research assistantships with full and partial tuition reimbursements available (averaging $12,480 per year), 5 teaching assistantships with partial tuition reimbursements available (averaging $10,700 per year); Federal Work-Study, scholarships/grants, health care benefits, and unspecified assistantships also available. Support available to part-time students. Financial award applicants required to submit FAFSA. *Faculty research:* Policy analysis, health care policy, financial and budget analysis. Total annual research expenditures: $42,514. *Unit head:* Dr. James A. Richardson, Director, 225-578-6745, Fax: 225-578-9078, E-mail: parich@lsu.edu. *Application contact:* Dr. James A. Richardson, Director, 225-578-6745, Fax: 225-578-9078, E-mail: parich@lsu.edu.

Louisiana State University and Agricultural and Mechanical College, Graduate School, Manship School of Mass Communication, Baton Rouge, LA 70803. Offers MMC, PhD. *Accreditation:* ACEJMC. Part-time programs available. Postbaccalaureate distance learning degree programs offered (minimal on-campus study). *Faculty:* 25 full-time (11 women). *Students:* 54 full-time (36 women), 19 part-time (15 women); includes 16 minority (12 African Americans, 2 American Indian/Alaska Native, 2 Hispanic Americans), 8 international. Average age 31. 107 applicants, 40% accepted, 26 enrolled. In 2009, 11 master's, 4 doctorates awarded. *Degree requirements:* For master's, thesis; for doctorate, thesis/dissertation. *Entrance requirements:* For master's, GRE General Test, minimum GPA of 3.0. Additional exam requirements/recommendations for international students: Required—TOEFL (minimum score 550 paper-based; 213 computer-based; 79 iBT) or IELTS (minimum score 6.5). *Application deadline:* For fall admission, 1/25 priority date for domestic students, 5/15 for international students; for spring admission, 10/15 for international students. Applications are processed on a rolling basis. Application fee: $50 ($70 for international students). Electronic applications accepted. *Financial support:* In 2009–10, 55 students received support, including 2 fellowships (averaging $29,476 per year), 32 research assistantships with full and partial tuition reimbursements available (averaging $15,234 per year), 7 teaching assistantships with full and partial tuition reimbursements available (averaging $16,671 per year); career-related internships or fieldwork, Federal Work-Study, institutionally sponsored loans, scholarships/grants, health care benefits, tuition waivers (full and partial), and unspecified assistantships also available. Support available to part-time students. Financial award application deadline: 3/1; financial award applicants required to submit FAFSA. *Faculty research:* Media effects, political communication, new media technologies, persuasive communication, journalism processes and practice. Total annual research expenditures: $38,772. *Unit head:* Dr. John Maxwell Hamilton, Dean, 225-578-2002, Fax: 225-578-2125, E-mail: jhamilt@lsu.edu. *Application contact:* Dr. Amy L. Reynolds, Associate Dean of Graduate Studies and Research, 225-578-9294, Fax: 225-578-2125, E-mail: defleur@lsu.edu.

Marist College, Graduate Programs, School of Management, Program in Public Administration, Poughkeepsie, NY 12601-1387. Offers MPA. Part-time and evening/weekend programs available. Postbaccalaureate distance learning degree programs offered (no on-campus study). *Entrance requirements:* For master's, GRE General Test, resume. Additional exam requirements/recommendations for international students: Required—TOEFL (minimum score 550 paper-based; 213 computer-based; 80 iBT); Recommended—IELTS (minimum score 6.5). Electronic applications accepted. *Expenses:* Tuition: Full-time $12,510; part-time $695 per credit hour. *Faculty research:* Public policy analysis, health administration.

Marquette University, Graduate School, Program in Public Service, Milwaukee, WI 53201-1881. Offers MAPS. *Faculty:* 2 full-time (0 women). *Students:* 21 full-time (14 women), 125 part-time (81 women); includes 30 minority (22 African Americans, 1 American Indian/Alaska Native, 2 Asian Americans or Pacific Islanders, 5 Hispanic Americans), 1 international. Average age 38. 83 applicants, 82% accepted, 32 enrolled. In 2009, 30 master's awarded. *Unit head:* Dr. Johnette Caulfield, Adjunct Assistant Professor and Director of Graduate Programs, 414-288-5556, E-mail: jay.caulfield@marquette.edu. *Application contact:* Erin Fox, Assistant Director for Recruitment, 414-288-5319, Fax: 414-288-1902, E-mail: erin.fox@marquette.edu.

Marylhurst University, Department of Business Administration, Marylhurst, OR 97036-0261. Offers finance (MBA); general management (MBA); government policy and administration (MBA); green development (MBA); health care management (MBA); marketing (MBA); natural and organic resources (MBA); nonprofit management (MBA); organizational behavior (MBA); real estate (MBA); renewable energy (MBA); sustainable business (MBA). Part-time and evening/weekend programs available. Postbaccalaureate distance learning degree programs offered (no on-campus study). *Faculty:* 2 full-time (1 woman), 28 part-time/adjunct (5 women). *Students:* 30 full-time (12 women), 627 part-time (323 women); includes 79 minority (28 African Americans, 3 American Indian/Alaska Native, 17 Asian Americans or Pacific Islanders, 31 Hispanic Americans), 9 international. Average age 37. 299 applicants, 80% accepted, 209 enrolled. In 2009, 193 master's awarded. *Degree requirements:* For master's, comprehensive exam, capstone course. *Entrance requirements:* For master's, GMAT (if GPA less than 3.0 and fewer than 5 years of work experience), interview, resume, 2 letters of recommendation. Additional exam requirements/recommendations for international students: Recommended—

TOEFL (minimum score 550 paper-based; 213 computer-based; 80 iBT). *Application deadline:* For fall admission, 9/11 priority date for domestic and international students; for winter admission, 12/15 priority date for domestic and international students; for spring admission, 3/17 priority date for domestic and international students. Applications are processed on a rolling basis. Application fee: $40 ($50 for international students). Electronic applications accepted. *Financial support:* Scholarships/grants available. Support available to part-time students. Financial award applicants required to submit FAFSA. *Unit head:* Bob Hanks, Director of Business and Real Estate Programs, 503-636-8141, Fax: 503-697-5597, E-mail: mba@marylhurst.edu. *Application contact:* Kathleen Schneff, Admissions Specialist, 800-634-9982 Ext. 3322, Fax: 503-635-6585, E-mail: admissions@marylhurst.edu.

Marywood University, Academic Affairs, College of Health and Human Services, Department of Nursing and Public Administration, Program in Public Administration, Scranton, PA 18509-1598. Offers nonprofit management (MPA). *Students:* 3 full-time (0 women), 13 part-time (9 women). Average age 30. In 2009, 9 master's awarded. *Entrance requirements:* Additional exam requirements/recommendations for international students: Required—TOEFL (minimum score 550 paper-based; 213 computer-based; 79 iBT). *Application deadline:* For fall admission, 4/1 priority date for domestic students, 3/31 priority date for international students; for spring admission, 11/1 priority date for domestic students, 8/31 priority date for international students. Applications are processed on a rolling basis. Application fee: $35. Electronic applications accepted. *Expenses:* Tuition: Part-time $715 per credit. Required fees: $270 per semester. Tuition and fees vary according to degree level, campus/location and program. *Financial support:* Career-related internships or fieldwork, scholarships/grants, and unspecified assistantships available. Support available to part-time students. Financial award application deadline: 6/30; financial award applicants required to submit FAFSA. *Unit head:* Dr. Katrina Maurer, Co-Chairperson, 570-348-6275, E-mail: maurer@marywood.edu. *Application contact:* Tammy Manka, Assistant Director of Graduate Admissions, 866-279-9663, E-mail: tmanka@marywood.edu.

McMaster University, School of Graduate Studies, Faculty of Social Sciences, Department of Political Science, Hamilton, ON L8S 4M2, Canada. Offers international relations (PhD); political science (MA); public and the global economy (MA); public policy (PhD); public policy and administration (MA). Part-time programs available. *Degree requirements:* For master's, thesis or alternative. *Entrance requirements:* For master's, minimum B+ average. Additional exam requirements/recommendations for international students: Required—TOEFL (minimum score 580 paper-based; 237 computer-based). *Faculty research:* Organizational theory, internationalization of public policy, water resource policies, political interest intermediation, comparative politics.

Metropolitan College of New York, Program in Public Administration, New York, NY 10013. Offers MPA. Evening/weekend programs available. *Degree requirements:* For master's, thesis. *Entrance requirements:* For master's, appropriate work experience, interview, minimum GPA of 2.7, internship or job in administrative setting. Additional exam requirements/recommendations for international students: Required—TOEFL (minimum score 600 paper-based; 220 computer-based). Electronic applications accepted. *Expenses:* Contact institution. *Faculty research:* Transnational politics and culture, women and social policy, confidentiality in the human services, concepts of marginality, ethics in social policy.

Metropolitan State University, College of Management, St. Paul, MN 55106-5000. Offers business administration (MBA); information assurance security (Graduate Certificate); information management (MMIS); MIS generalist (Graduate Certificate); MIS systems analysis and design (Graduate Certificate); nonprofit management (MPNA); project management (Graduate Certificate); public administration (MPNA); systems management (MMIS). Part-time and evening/weekend programs available. *Degree requirements:* For master's, thesis optional, computer language (MMIS). *Entrance requirements:* For master's, GMAT (MBA), resume. Additional exam requirements/recommendations for international students: Required—TOEFL (minimum score 550 paper-based; 213 computer-based). *Expenses:* Tuition, state resident: full-time $5520; part-time $276 per credit hour. Tuition, nonresident: full-time $11,040; part-time $552 per credit hour. Required fees: $209; $10 per credit hour. Tuition and fees vary according to degree level. *Faculty research:* Yugoslav economic system, workers' cooperatives, participative management and job enrichment, global business systems.

Mid-America Christian University, Program in Public Administration, Oklahoma City, OK 73170-4504. Offers MA. *Entrance requirements:* For master's, bachelor's degree from a regionally accredited college or university, minimum overall cumulative GPA of 2.75 of bachelor course work. Additional exam requirements/recommendations for international students: Required—TOEFL (minimum score 550 paper-based; 213 computer-based).

Midwestern State University, Graduate Studies, College of Health Sciences and Human Services, Program in Health Services and Public Administration, Wichita Falls, TX 76308. Offers health services administration (MHA); public administration (MPA); public administration (administrative justice) (MPA); public administration (health services administration) with certificate (MPA); public administration (health services) (MPA). Part-time and evening/weekend programs available. *Degree requirements:* For master's, comprehensive exam, thesis. *Entrance requirements:* For master's, GRE. Additional exam requirements/recommendations for international students: Required—TOEFL (minimum score 550 paper-based; 213 computer-based). Electronic applications accepted. *Expenses:* Tuition, state resident: full-time $1620; part-time $90 per credit hour. Tuition, nonresident: full-time $2160; part-time $120 per credit hour. International tuition: $7506 full-time. Required fees: $3068.80; $145.60 per credit hour. $179 per semester.

Minnesota State University Mankato, College of Graduate Studies, College of Social and Behavioral Sciences, Department of Political Science and Law Enforcement, Program in Public Administration, Mankato, MN 56001. Offers MPA, MAPA/MA. *Students:* 23 full-time (10 women), 45 part-time (20 women). *Degree requirements:* For master's, one foreign language, comprehensive exam, thesis or alternative. *Entrance requirements:* For master's, minimum GPA of 3.0 during previous 2 years. Additional exam requirements/recommendations for international students: Required—TOEFL. *Application deadline:* For fall admission, 3/1 priority date for domestic students. Applications are processed on a rolling basis. Application fee: $40. Electronic applications accepted. *Expenses:* Tuition, state resident: full-time $5364. Tuition, nonresident: full-time $8314. *Financial support:* Research assistantships with full tuition reimbursements, teaching assistantships with full tuition reimbursements, unspecified assistantships available. Financial award application deadline: 3/15; financial award applicants required to submit FAFSA. *Unit head:* Dr. Scott Granberg-Rademacker, Graduate Coordinator, 507-389-6939. *Application contact:* 507-389-2321, E-mail: grad@mnsu.edu.

Minnesota State University Moorhead, Graduate Studies, College of Social and Natural Sciences, Program in Public, Human Services, and Health Administration, Moorhead, MN 56563-0002. Offers MS. Part-time and evening/weekend programs available. *Degree requirements:* For master's, final oral exam, final project paper or thesis. *Entrance requirements:* For master's, GRE General Test, minimum GPA of 2.75. Additional exam requirements/recommendations for international students: Required—TOEFL (minimum score 550 paper-based; 213 computer-based). Electronic applications accepted.

Mississippi State University, College of Arts and Sciences, Department of Political Science and Public Administration, Mississippi State, MS 39762. Offers political science (MA); public policy and administration (MPPA, PhD). *Accreditation:* NASPAA (one or more programs are accredited). Evening/weekend programs available. Postbaccalaureate distance learning degree programs offered (no on-campus study). *Faculty:* 14 full-time (4 women). *Students:* 67 full-time (35 women), 44 part-time (33 women); includes 40 minority (37 African Americans, 1 American Indian/Alaska Native, 2 Asian Americans or Pacific Islanders), 4 international. Average age 30. 85 applicants, 60% accepted, 39 enrolled. In 2009, 28 master's, 2 doctorates awarded. *Degree requirements:* For master's, thesis optional, comprehensive oral or written exam; for doctorate, thesis/dissertation, comprehensive oral and written exam. *Entrance requirements:* For master's, GRE, minimum GPA of 3.0 on the last two years of undergraduate courses or graduate work; for doctorate, GRE General Test, minimum graduate GPA of 3.35. Additional exam requirements/recommendations for international students: Required—TOEFL (minimum score 600 paper-based; 250 computer-based; 100 iBT); Recommended—IELTS (minimum score 7.5). *Application deadline:* For fall admission, 8/1 priority date for domestic students, 5/1 for international students; for spring admission, 12/1 priority date for domestic students, 9/1 for international students. Applications are processed on a rolling basis. Application fee: $40. Electronic applications accepted. *Expenses:* Tuition, state resident: full-time $2575.50; part-time $286.25 per credit hour. Tuition, nonresident: full-time $6510; part-time $723.50 per credit hour. Tuition and fees vary according to course load. *Financial support:* In 2009–10, 5 research assistantships (averaging $14,451 per year), 6 teaching assistantships with full tuition reimbursements (averaging $9,030 per year) were awarded; Federal Work-Study, institutionally sponsored loans, scholarships/grants, and unspecified assistantships also available. Financial award application deadline: 4/15. *Faculty research:* American politics, international relations, state and local government, comparative government, public administration. Total annual research expenditures: $879,000. *Unit head:* Dr. KC Morrison, Department Head, 662-325-2711, Fax: 662-325-2716, E-mail: kcmorrison@ps.msstate.edu. *Application contact:* Dr. Doug Goodman, Associate Professor and Graduate Coordinator, 662-325-7856, Fax: 662-325-2716, E-mail: dg114@ps.msstate.edu.

Missouri State University, Graduate College, College of Humanities and Public Affairs, Department of Political Science, Program in Public Administration, Springfield, MO 65897. Offers MPA. *Accreditation:* NASPAA. Part-time programs available. *Students:* 18 full-time (6 women), 10 part-time (4 women); includes 1 minority (Asian American or Pacific Islander), 2 international. Average age 28. 11 applicants, 73% accepted, 2 enrolled. In 2009, 18 master's awarded. *Degree requirements:* For master's, comprehensive exam, thesis or alternative, internship. *Entrance requirements:* For master's, GRE, minimum GPA of 3.0. Additional exam requirements/recommendations for international students: Required—TOEFL (minimum score 550 paper-based; 213 computer-based; 79 iBT). *Application deadline:* For fall admission, 7/20 priority date for domestic students, 5/1 for international students; for spring admission, 12/20 priority date for domestic students, 9/1 for international students. Applications are processed on a rolling basis. Application fee: $35 ($50 for international students). Electronic applications accepted. *Expenses:* Tuition, state resident: full-time $3852; part-time $214 per credit hour. Tuition, nonresident: full-time $7524; part-time $418 per credit hour. Required fees: $696; $172 per semester. Tuition and fees vary according to course level, course load, degree level and program. *Financial support:* In 2009–10, 1 research assistantship with full tuition reimbursement (averaging $7,340 per year) was awarded; career-related internships or fieldwork, Federal Work-Study, institutionally sponsored loans, scholarships/grants, and unspecified assistantships also available. Support available to part-time students. Financial award application deadline: 3/31; financial award applicants required to submit FAFSA. *Faculty research:* Public management, environmental policy, health care policy, law and religion. *Unit head:* Dr. Kant Patel, Graduate Director, 417-836-6925, Fax: 417-836-6655, E-mail: kantpatel@missouristate.edu. *Application contact:* Eric Eckert, Coordinator of Graduate Admissions and Recruitment, 417-836-5331, Fax: 417-836-6200, E-mail: ericeckert@missouristate.edu.

Missouri State University, Graduate College, Interdisciplinary Program in Administrative Studies, Springfield, MO 65897. Offers applied communication (MS); criminal justice (MS); environmental management (MS); project management (MS); sports management (MS). Part-time and evening/weekend programs available. Postbaccalaureate distance learning degree programs offered (no on-campus study). *Students:* 17 full-time (11 women), 60 part-time (26 women); includes 6 minority (4 African Americans, 1 Asian American or Pacific Islander, 1 Hispanic American), 2 international. Average age 35. 24 applicants, 100% accepted, 19 enrolled. In 2009, 16 master's awarded. *Degree requirements:* For master's, comprehensive exam, thesis or alternative. *Entrance requirements:* For master's, GRE, GMAT, 3 years of work experience. Additional exam requirements/recommendations for international students: Required—TOEFL (minimum score 550 paper-based; 213 computer-based; 79 iBT). *Application deadline:* For fall admission, 7/20 priority date for domestic students; for spring admission, 12/20 priority date for domestic students. Applications are processed on a rolling basis. Application fee: $35 ($50 for international students). Electronic applications accepted. *Expenses:* Tuition, state resident: full-time $3852; part-time $214 per credit hour. Tuition, nonresident: full-time $7524; part-time $418 per credit hour. Required fees: $696; $172 per semester. Tuition and fees vary according to course level, course load, degree level and program. *Financial support:* In 2009–10, 1 teaching assistantship with full tuition reimbursement (averaging $7,340 per year) was awarded; career-related internships or fieldwork, Federal Work-Study, institutionally sponsored loans, scholarships/grants, and unspecified assistantships also available. Support available to part-time students. Financial award application deadline: 3/31; financial award applicants required to submit FAFSA. *Unit head:* John Bourhis, Director, 417-836-6390, E-mail: johnbourhis@missouristate.edu. *Application contact:* Eric Eckert, Coordinator of Graduate Admissions and Recruitment, 417-836-5331, Fax: 417-836-6200, E-mail: ericeckert@missouristate.edu.

Montana State University, College of Graduate Studies, College of Letters and Science, Department of Political Science, Bozeman, MT 59717. Offers public administration (MPA). Part-time programs available. *Faculty:* 7 full-time (4 women), 1 part-time/adjunct (0 women). *Students:* 13 full-time (7 women), 17 part-time (11 women), 2 international. Average age 29. 16 applicants, 69% accepted, 11 enrolled. In 2009, 8 master's awarded. *Degree requirements:* For master's, comprehensive exam, thesis (for some programs). *Entrance requirements:* For master's, GRE General Test. Additional exam requirements/recommendations for international students: Required—TOEFL (minimum score 550 paper-based; 213 computer-based). *Application deadline:* For fall admission, 7/15 priority date for domestic students, 5/15 priority date for international students; for spring admission, 12/1 priority date for domestic students, 10/1 priority date for international students. Applications are processed on a rolling basis. Application fee: $30. Electronic applications accepted. *Expenses:* Tuition, state resident: full-time $5635; part-time $3492 per year. Tuition, nonresident: full-time $17,212; part-time $7865.10 per year. Required fees: $1441; $153.15 per credit. Tuition and fees vary according to course load and program. *Financial support:* In 2009–10, 2 students received support; research assistantships, teaching assistantships, tuition waivers (full and partial) and unspecified assistantships available. Financial award application deadline: 3/1; financial award applicants required to submit FAFSA. *Faculty research:* National resource policy, political economy of agriculture, qualitative methods, and organizational theory. Total annual research expenditures: $206,710. *Unit head:* Dr. Jerry Johnson, Head, 406-994-5164, Fax: 406-994-6692, E-mail: jdj@montana.edu. *Application contact:* Dr. Carl A. Fox, Vice Provost for Graduate Education, 406-994-4145, Fax: 406-994-7433, E-mail: gradstudy@montana.edu.

Montana State University Billings, College of Arts and Sciences, Program in Public Administration, Billings, MT 59101-0298. Offers MPA.

Monterey Institute of International Studies, Graduate School of International Policy and Management, Program in International Public Administration, Monterey, CA 93940-2691. Offers MPA. *Students:* 75 full-time (57 women), 3 part-time (all women); includes 22 minority (9 African Americans, 10 Asian Americans or Pacific Islanders, 3 Hispanic Americans), 14 international. Average age 27. In 2009, 37 master's awarded. *Degree requirements:* For master's, one foreign language. *Entrance requirements:* For master's, minimum GPA of 3.0, proficiency in a foreign language. Additional exam requirements/recommendations for international students: Required—TOEFL (minimum score 550 paper-based; 213 computer-based; 80 iBT). *Application deadline:* For fall admission, 3/15 priority date for domestic and international students; for spring admission, 10/1 priority date for domestic and international students. Applications are processed on a rolling basis. Application fee: $50. Electronic applications accepted. *Expenses:* Tuition: Full-time $31,000; part-time $1500 per credit. Required fees: $56. *Financial support:* Career-related internships or fieldwork, Federal Work-Study, and institutionally sponsored loans available. Support available to part-time students. Financial award application deadline: 3/15; financial award applicants required to submit FAFSA. *Application contact:* 831-647-4123, Fax: 831-647-6405, E-mail: admit@miis.edu.

See Close-Up on page 853.

Public Administration

Morehead State University, Graduate Programs, Institute for Regional Analysis and Public Policy, Morehead, KY 40351. Offers public administration (MPA). *Faculty:* 2 full-time (1 woman), 1 part-time/adjunct (0 women). *Students:* 18 full-time (9 women), 7 part-time (6 women); includes 2 minority (both African Americans). Average age 28. 49 applicants, 31% accepted, 10 enrolled. In 2009, 6 master's awarded. *Entrance requirements:* For master's, GRE. Additional exam requirements/recommendations for international students: Required—TOEFL (minimum score 500 paper-based). *Application deadline:* For fall admission, 8/1 priority date for domestic and international students; for spring admission, 12/1 priority date for domestic and international students. Applications are processed on a rolling basis. Application fee: $30. Electronic applications accepted. *Expenses:* Tuition, state resident: full-time $6318; part-time $351 per credit hour. Tuition, nonresident: full-time $15,804; part-time $878 per credit hour. *Financial support:* In 2009–10, 10 teaching assistantships (averaging $6,000 per year) were awarded. Financial award application deadline: 3/15. *Unit head:* Dr. David Rudy, Dean, 606-783-5419, Fax: 606-783-5092, E-mail: d.rudy@moreheadstate.edu. *Application contact:* Michelle Barber, Graduate Recruitment and Retention Assistant Director, 606-783-5127, Fax: 606-783-5061, E-mail: m.barber@moreheadstate.edu.

National University, Academic Affairs, College of Letters and Sciences, Department of Professional Studies, La Jolla, CA 92037-1011. Offers forensic science (MFS), including criminalistics and investigation; public administration (MPA), including alternative dispute resolution, human resource management, organizational leadership, public finance. Part-time and evening/weekend programs available. Postbaccalaureate distance learning degree programs offered (no on-campus study). *Faculty:* 5 full-time (3 women), 27 part-time/adjunct (7 women). *Students:* 167 full-time (95 women), 246 part-time (133 women); includes 188 minority (71 African Americans, 2 American Indian/Alaska Native, 41 Asian Americans or Pacific Islanders, 74 Hispanic Americans). Average age 38. 284 applicants, 100% accepted, 206 enrolled. In 2009, 104 master's awarded. *Degree requirements:* For master's, thesis. *Entrance requirements:* For master's, interview, minimum GPA of 2.5. Additional exam requirements/recommendations for international students: Required—TOEFL (minimum score 550 paper-based; 213 computer-based; 79 iBT), IELTS (minimum score 6). *Application deadline:* Applications are processed on a rolling basis. Application fee: $60 ($65 for international students). Electronic applications accepted. *Expenses:* Tuition: Part-time $338 per quarter hour. *Financial support:* Career-related internships or fieldwork, institutionally sponsored loans, scholarships/grants, and tuition waivers (partial) available. Support available to part-time students. Financial award application deadline: 6/30; financial award applicants required to submit FAFSA. *Unit head:* Chandrika M. Kelso, Associate Professor and Chair, 858-642-8433, Fax: 858-642-8715, E-mail: ckelso@nu.edu. *Application contact:* Dominick Giovanniello, Associate Regional Dean—San Diego, 800-NAT-UNIV, Fax: 858-541-7792, E-mail: dgiovann@nu.edu.

National University of Singapore, Lee Kuan Yew School of Public Policy, Singapore, Singapore. Offers MPA, MPM, MPP, PhD.

New York University, Robert F. Wagner Graduate School of Public Service, Program in Public Administration, New York, NY 10012-1019. Offers public administration (PhD); public and nonprofit management and policy (MPA, Advanced Certificate), including developmental administration (Advanced Certificate), financial management and public finance, human resources management (Advanced Certificate), international administration (Advanced Certificate), management (MPA), management for public and nonprofit organizations (Advanced Certificate), public policy analysis, quantitative analysis and computer applications (Advanced Certificate), urban public policy (Advanced Certificate); JD/MPA; MBA/MPA; MPA/MA. *Accreditation:* NASPAA (one or more programs are accredited). Part-time and evening/weekend programs available. *Faculty:* 31 full-time (13 women), 33 part-time/adjunct (16 women). *Students:* 363 full-time (270 women), 228 part-time (171 women); includes 146 minority (46 African Americans, 64 Asian Americans or Pacific Islanders, 36 Hispanic Americans), 76 international. Average age 28. 1,117 applicants, 57% accepted, 225 enrolled. In 2009, 236 master's, 3 doctorates awarded. *Degree requirements:* For master's, thesis or alternative, capstone/end event; for doctorate, one foreign language, thesis/dissertation. *Entrance requirements:* For master's, minimum undergraduate GPA of 3.0; for doctorate, GMAT or GRE General Test, minimum GPA of 3.5. Additional exam requirements/recommendations for international students: Required—TOEFL (minimum score 600 paper-based; 250 computer-based; 100 iBT), TWE (minimum score 4). *Application deadline:* For fall admission, 6/1 for domestic students, 1/15 for international students; for spring admission, 11/15 for domestic students, 10/1 for international students. Applications are processed on a rolling basis. Application fee: $80. Electronic applications accepted. *Expenses:* Contact institution. *Financial support:* In 2009–10, 155 students received support, including 150 fellowships (averaging $11,335 per year), 5 research assistantships with full tuition reimbursements available (averaging $22,440 per year); career-related internships or fieldwork, Federal Work-Study, institutionally sponsored loans, scholarships/grants, health care benefits, and unspecified assistantships also available. Support available to part-time students. Financial award application deadline: 12/1; financial award applicants required to submit FAFSA. *Unit head:* Katty Jones, Director, Program Services, 212-998-7411, Fax: 212-995-4164, E-mail: katty.jones@nyu.edu. *Application contact:* Christopher Alexander, Administrative Aide, Enrollment, 212-998-7414, Fax: 212-995-4611, E-mail: wagner.admissions@nyu.edu.

North Carolina Central University, Division of Academic Affairs, College of Behavioral and Social Sciences, Department of Public Administration, Durham, NC 27707-3129. Offers MPA. Part-time and evening/weekend programs available. *Degree requirements:* For master's, one foreign language, comprehensive exam, thesis or alternative. *Entrance requirements:* For master's, GRE, minimum GPA of 3.0 in major, 2.5 overall. Additional exam requirements/recommendations for international students: Required—TOEFL. *Faculty research:* Racial diversity and community policing, economic development, issues in urban transportation.

North Carolina State University, Graduate School, College of Humanities and Social Sciences, School of Public and International Affairs, Program in Public Administration, Raleigh, NC 27695. Offers MPA, PhD. *Accreditation:* NASPAA. *Degree requirements:* For master's, thesis optional; for doctorate, thesis/dissertation. *Entrance requirements:* For master's, GRE General Test, minimum GPA of 3.0 during previous 2 years; for doctorate, GRE General Test. Electronic applications accepted. *Faculty research:* Public budgeting, human resources, public information technology, nonprofit management, environmental policy.

Northeastern University, College of Social Sciences and Humanities, Department of Political Science, Boston, MA 02115-5096. Offers political science (MA); public administration (MPA, Certificate), including development administration (MPA), health administration and policy (MPA), state and local government (MPA), urban studies (Certificate); public and international affairs (PhD). Part-time and evening/weekend programs available. *Faculty:* 22 full-time (4 women), 10 part-time/adjunct (1 woman). *Students:* 10 full-time (3 women), 62 part-time (28 women); includes 7 minority (2 African Americans, 2 American Indian/Alaska Native, 2 Asian Americans or Pacific Islanders, 1 Hispanic American), 11 international. Average age 30. 129 applicants, 69% accepted, 24 enrolled. In 2009, 28 master's, 3 doctorates awarded. *Degree requirements:* For master's, thesis optional; for doctorate, thesis/dissertation. *Entrance requirements:* For master's, GRE General Test. Additional exam requirements/recommendations for international students: Required—TOEFL. *Application deadline:* Applications are processed on a rolling basis. Application fee: $50. *Financial support:* In 2009–10, 12 fellowships, 3 research assistantships with tuition reimbursements, 18 teaching assistantships with tuition reimbursements (averaging $14,035 per year) were awarded; career-related internships or fieldwork, Federal Work-Study, tuition waivers (full and partial), and unspecified assistantships also available. Support available to part-time students. Financial award application deadline: 2/1; financial award applicants required to submit FAFSA. *Faculty research:* Presidency, public opinion, Congress, democratization, national identity. *Unit head:* Dr. John Portz, Chair, 617-373-2796, Fax: 617-373-5311, E-mail: gradpolisci@neu.edu. *Application contact:* Brynn Thompson, Graduate Programs Assistant, 617-373-4404, Fax: 617-373-5311, E-mail: gradpolisci@neu.edu.

Northeastern University, College of Social Sciences and Humanities, Program in Public Administration, Boston, MA 02115-5096. Offers development administration (MPA); health administration and policy (MPA); state and local government (MPA); urban studies (Certificate). *Accreditation:* NASPAA (one or more programs are accredited). Part-time and evening/weekend programs available. *Faculty:* 22 full-time (4 women), 10 part-time/adjunct (1 woman). *Students:* 49 full-time (26 women), 28 part-time (18 women); includes 8 African Americans, 1 Asian American or Pacific Islander, 1 Hispanic American, 14 international. 102 applicants, 52% accepted, 26 enrolled. In 2009, 11 master's awarded. *Degree requirements:* For master's, thesis optional. *Entrance requirements:* For master's, GRE General Test. Additional exam requirements/recommendations for international students: Required—TOEFL. *Application deadline:* For fall admission, 2/1 priority date for domestic students, 5/1 for international students. Applications are processed on a rolling basis. Application fee: $50. *Financial support:* In 2009–10, 2 research assistantships with tuition reimbursements (averaging $14,035 per year) were awarded; teaching assistantships with tuition reimbursements, career-related internships or fieldwork, Federal Work-Study, tuition waivers (full and partial), and unspecified assistantships also available. Support available to part-time students. Financial award application deadline: 2/1; financial award applicants required to submit FAFSA. *Faculty research:* National health care, Third World development, leadership and ethics, science and technology, budgeting. *Unit head:* Dr. Ronald D. Hedlund, Graduate Coordinator, 617-373-2796, Fax: 617-373-5311, E-mail: gradpolisci@neu.edu. *Application contact:* Brynn Thompson, Graduate Programs Assistant, 617-373-4404, Fax: 617-373-5311, E-mail: gradpolisci@neu.edu.

Northern Arizona University, Graduate College, College of Social and Behavioral Sciences, Department of Politics and International Affairs, Program in Political Science, Flagstaff, AZ 86011. Offers political science (MA, PhD); public management (Certificate). *Faculty:* 23 full-time (9 women). *Students:* 25 full-time (12 women), 18 part-time (9 women); includes 12 minority (2 African Americans, 2 American Indian/Alaska Native, 2 Asian Americans or Pacific Islanders, 6 Hispanic Americans), 5 international. Average age 35. 29 applicants, 76% accepted, 15 enrolled. In 2009, 4 master's, 2 doctorates awarded. *Degree requirements:* For master's, thesis optional; for doctorate, one foreign language, thesis/dissertation. *Entrance requirements:* For master's, minimum GPA of 3.0; for doctorate, GRE General Test. Additional exam requirements/recommendations for international students: Required—TOEFL (minimum score 550 paper-based; 213 computer-based; 80 iBT), IELTS (minimum score 7), or a bachelor's degree from an English-speaking university and demonstrated proficiency. *Application deadline:* For fall admission, 2/15 priority date for domestic students. Applications are processed on a rolling basis. Application fee: $65. Electronic applications accepted. *Financial support:* In 2009–10, 12 teaching assistantships with partial tuition reimbursements (averaging $11,300 per year) were awarded; tuition waivers (full and partial) also available. Financial award application deadline: 3/30. *Unit head:* Dr. Lori Poloni-Staudinger, Graduate Coordinator, 928-523-6546, E-mail: lori.poloni-staudinger@nau.edu. *Application contact:* Susan Bemus, Secretary, 928-523-6979, E-mail: political.science@nau.edu.

Northern Arizona University, Graduate College, College of Social and Behavioral Sciences, Department of Politics and International Affairs, Program in Public Administration, Flagstaff, AZ 86011. Offers public administration (MPA); public management (Certificate). *Faculty:* 23 full-time (9 women). *Students:* 6 full-time (3 women), 25 part-time (21 women); includes 8 minority (1 African American, 3 American Indian/Alaska Native, 4 Hispanic Americans), 1 international. Average age 35. 23 applicants, 70% accepted, 11 enrolled. In 2009, 11 master's awarded. *Degree requirements:* For master's, comprehensive exam (for some programs), thesis optional, internship. *Entrance requirements:* For master's, GRE (minimum 70th percentile in each testing area preferred). Additional exam requirements/recommendations for international students: Required—TOEFL (minimum score 550 paper-based; 213 computer-based; 80 iBT), IELTS (minimum score 7), or a bachelor's degree from an English-speaking university and demonstrated proficiency. *Application deadline:* For fall admission, 2/1 priority date for domestic students, 9/1 priority date for international students; for spring admission, 10/15 priority date for domestic students. Applications are processed on a rolling basis. Application fee: $65. Electronic applications accepted. *Financial support:* Career-related internships or fieldwork, Federal Work-Study, and tuition waivers (full and partial) available. Financial award application deadline: 3/30; financial award applicants required to submit FAFSA. *Unit head:* Dr. Fred Solop, Chair, 928-523-0339, Fax: 928-523-6777, E-mail: fred.solop@nau.edu. *Application contact:* Dr. Lori Poloni-Staudinger, Coordinator, 928-523-6546, Fax: 928-523-6777, E-mail: lori.poloni-staudinger@nau.edu.

Northern Illinois University, Graduate School, College of Liberal Arts and Sciences, Department of Political Science, Division of Public Administration, De Kalb, IL 60115-2854. Offers MPA. *Accreditation:* NASPAA. Part-time and evening/weekend programs available. *Faculty:* 5 full-time (1 woman), 3 part-time/adjunct (1 woman). *Students:* 39 full-time (14 women), 40 part-time (9 women); includes 5 minority (all African Americans), 2 international. Average age 31. 59 applicants, 69% accepted, 26 enrolled. In 2009, 25 master's awarded. *Degree requirements:* For master's, comprehensive exam, internship, research paper. *Entrance requirements:* For master's, GRE General Test, minimum GPA of 2.75, 9 hours in social science. Additional exam requirements/recommendations for international students: Required—TOEFL (minimum score 550 paper-based; 213 computer-based). *Application deadline:* For fall admission, 3/1 priority date for domestic students, 5/1 for international students; for spring admission, 10/1 priority date for domestic students, 10/1 for international students. Applications are processed on a rolling basis. Application fee: $30. Electronic applications accepted. *Expenses:* Tuition, state resident: full-time $6576; part-time $274 per credit hour. Tuition, nonresident: full-time $13,152; part-time $548 per credit hour. Required fees: $1813; $75.53 per credit hour. Part-time tuition and fees vary according to course load. *Financial support:* Fellowships with full tuition reimbursements, research assistantships with full tuition reimbursements, teaching assistantships, career-related internships or fieldwork, Federal Work-Study, scholarships/grants, tuition waivers (full), and unspecified assistantships available. Support available to part-time students. Financial award applicants required to submit FAFSA. *Faculty research:* Urban service and management, manpower public policy, performance appraisal, bureaucratic politics. *Unit head:* Dr. Gerald Gabris, Acting Director, 815-753-6140, Fax: 815-753-2539, E-mail: ggabris@niu.edu. *Application contact:* Samantha Fisher, Program Coordinator, 815-753-6149, E-mail: samfisher@niu.edu.

Northern Kentucky University, Office of Graduate Programs, College of Arts and Sciences, Program in Public Administration, Highland Heights, KY 41099. Offers non-profit management (Certificate); public administration (MPA). *Accreditation:* NASPAA. Part-time and evening/weekend programs available. *Students:* 6 full-time (2 women), 87 part-time (46 women); includes 12 minority (9 African Americans, 3 Hispanic Americans), 1 international. Average age 35. 54 applicants, 67% accepted, 28 enrolled. In 2009, 21 master's, 10 other advanced degrees awarded. *Degree requirements:* For master's, capstone. *Entrance requirements:* For master's, GRE, GMAT or MAT, 2 letters of recommendation, writing sample, minimum GPA of 2.75, 2 supportive letters, resume, portfolio demonstrating professional activities. Additional exam requirements/recommendations for international students: Required—TOEFL (minimum score 550 paper-based; 213 computer-based; 79 iBT); Recommended—IELTS (minimum score 6.5). *Application deadline:* For fall admission, 7/1 priority date for domestic students, 6/1 for international students; for spring admission, 12/1 priority date for domestic students, 10/1 for international students. Applications are processed on a rolling basis. Application fee: $40. Electronic applications accepted. *Expenses:* Tuition, state resident: full-time $6912; part-time $384 per credit hour. Tuition, nonresident: full-time $12,150; part-time $675 per credit hour. Tuition and fees vary according to course load, program and reciprocity agreements. *Financial support:* Unspecified assistantships available. Financial award applicants required to submit FAFSA. *Faculty research:* Non-profit management, human resource management, local government, budgeting and finance, urban planning. *Unit head:* Dr. Shamima Ahmed, Director, 859-572-6402, Fax: 859-572-6184, E-mail: ahmed@nku.edu. *Application contact:* Beth Devantier, MPA Coordinator, 859-572-5326, Fax: 859-572-6184, E-mail: devantier@nku.edu.

Northern Michigan University, College of Graduate Studies, College of Arts and Sciences, Department of Political Science and Public Administration, Marquette, MI 49855-5301. Offers public administration (MPA). Part-time programs available. *Degree requirements:* For master's, thesis or alternative. *Entrance requirements:* For master's, minimum GPA of 3.0.

North Georgia College & State University, Graduate Studies, Program in Public Administration, Dahlonega, GA 30597. Offers MPA. Part-time and evening/weekend programs available. Postbaccalaureate distance learning degree programs offered. *Degree requirements:* For master's, thesis optional, internship. *Entrance requirements:* For master's, GMAT or GRE General Test, minimum undergraduate GPA of 2.75, 3 letters of recommendation. Electronic applications accepted.

Northwestern University, School of Continuing Studies, Program in Public Policy and Administration, Evanston, IL 60208. Offers MA. Postbaccalaureate distance learning degree programs offered.

Norwich University, School of Graduate and Continuing Studies, Program in Public Administration, Northfield, VT 05663. Offers MPA. Evening/weekend programs available. *Faculty:* 12 part-time/adjunct (5 women). *Students:* 190 full-time (74 women); includes 20 minority (10 African Americans, 3 American Indian/Alaska Native, 2 Asian Americans or Pacific Islanders, 5 Hispanic Americans). Average age 37. 210 applicants, 98% accepted, 190 enrolled. In 2009, 57 master's awarded. *Entrance requirements:* Additional exam requirements/recommendations for international students: Required—TOEFL (minimum score 550 paper-based; 212 computer-based; 83 iBT). *Application deadline:* For fall admission, 8/10 for domestic and international students; for winter admission, 11/7 for domestic and international students; for spring admission, 2/6 for domestic and international students. Application fee: $50. Full-time tuition and fees vary according to course level and course load. *Financial support:* Scholarships/grants available. Financial award applicants required to submit FAFSA. *Unit head:* Donal Hartman, Program Director, 802-485-2567, Fax: 802-485-2533, E-mail: dhartman@norwich.edu. *Application contact:* Chris Ormsby, Administrative Director, 802-485-2567, Fax: 802-485-2533, E-mail: cormsby@norwich.edu.

Notre Dame de Namur University, Division of Academic Affairs, School of Business and Management, Department of Public Administration, Belmont, CA 94002-1908. Offers human resource management (MPA); public administration (MPA); public affairs administration (MPA). Part-time and evening/weekend programs available. *Faculty:* 2 full-time (1 woman), 4 part-time/adjunct (2 women). *Students:* 2 full-time (both women), 30 part-time (25 women); includes 18 minority (2 African Americans, 1 Asian American or Pacific Islander, 15 Hispanic Americans), 1 international. Average age 31. 20 applicants, 100% accepted, 11 enrolled. In 2009, 7 master's awarded. *Entrance requirements:* For master's, interview, minimum GPA of 2.5. Additional exam requirements/recommendations for international students: Required—TOEFL (minimum score 550 paper-based; 213 computer-based; 79 iBT). *Application deadline:* For fall admission, 8/1 priority date for domestic students; for spring admission, 12/1 priority date for domestic students. Applications are processed on a rolling basis. Application fee: $60. Electronic applications accepted. *Expenses:* Tuition: Part-time $720 per credit. Required fees: $35 per semester hour. *Financial support:* Career-related internships or fieldwork available. Support available to part-time students. Financial award applicants required to submit FAFSA. *Unit head:* Henry Roth, Director, 650-508-3721, E-mail: hroth@ndnu.edu. *Application contact:* Candace Hallmark, Associate Director of Admissions, 650-508-3592, Fax: 650-508-3426, E-mail: grad.admit@ndnu.edu.

Nova Southeastern University, H. Wayne Huizenga School of Business and Entrepreneurship, Program in Public Administration, Fort Lauderdale, FL 33314-7796. Offers MPA. Part-time and evening/weekend programs available. Postbaccalaureate distance learning degree programs offered (minimal on-campus study). *Faculty:* 2 full-time (0 women), 10 part-time/adjunct (1 woman). *Students:* 13 full-time (9 women), 167 part-time (126 women); includes 140 minority (107 African Americans, 3 Asian Americans or Pacific Islanders, 30 Hispanic Americans), 1 international. Average age 35. 85 applicants, 60% accepted, 29 enrolled. In 2009, 63 master's awarded. *Degree requirements:* For master's, thesis or alternative. *Entrance requirements:* For master's, work experience. Additional exam requirements/recommendations for international students: Required—TOEFL (minimum score 550 paper-based; 213 computer-based; 79 iBT), IELTS (minimum score 6). *Application deadline:* For fall admission, 8/15 priority date for domestic students, 8/15 for international students; for winter admission, 12/10 for domestic and international students; for spring admission, 2/10 for domestic and international students. Applications are processed on a rolling basis. Application fee: $50. Electronic applications accepted. *Financial support:* Career-related internships or fieldwork, Federal Work-Study, and institutionally sponsored loans available. Financial award applicants required to submit FAFSA. *Unit head:* Steve Harvey, Assistant Dean of Program Administration, 954-262-5047, Fax: 954-262-3829, E-mail: harvey@nsu.nova.edu. *Application contact:* Karen Goldberg, Associate Director of Recruitment and Special Events, 954-262-5039, Fax: 954-262-3822, E-mail: karen@nova.edu.

Oakland University, Graduate Study and Lifelong Learning, College of Arts and Sciences, Department of Political Science, Rochester, MI 48309-4401. Offers public administration (MPA). *Accreditation:* NASPAA. Part-time and evening/weekend programs available. *Entrance requirements:* For master's, minimum GPA of 3.0 for unconditional admission. Additional exam requirements/recommendations for international students: Required—TOEFL (minimum score 550 paper-based; 213 computer-based). Electronic applications accepted.

Ohio University, Graduate College, College of Arts and Sciences, Department of Political Science, Athens, OH 45701-2979. Offers political science (MA); public administration (MPA). Part-time and evening/weekend programs available. *Faculty:* 24 full-time (8 women). *Students:* 98 full-time (50 women), 11 part-time (2 women); includes 10 minority (7 African Americans, 1 Asian American or Pacific Islander, 2 Hispanic Americans), 19 international. 116 applicants, 83% accepted, 51 enrolled. In 2009, 32 master's awarded. *Degree requirements:* For master's, comprehensive exam, thesis or alternative. *Entrance requirements:* For master's, GRE General Test, minimum GPA of 3.0. Additional exam requirements/recommendations for international students: Required—TOEFL (minimum score 550 paper-based; 80 iBT) or IELTS Academic (minimum score 6.5). *Application deadline:* For fall admission, 2/15 priority date for domestic and international students. Applications are processed on a rolling basis. Application fee: $50 ($55 for international students). Electronic applications accepted. *Expenses:* Tuition, state resident: full-time $7839; part-time $323 per quarter hour. Tuition, nonresident: full-time $15,831; part-time $654 per quarter hour. Required fees: $2931. *Financial support:* Research assistantships with full tuition reimbursements, teaching assistantships with full tuition reimbursements, career-related internships or fieldwork, Federal Work-Study, institutionally sponsored loans, and tuition waivers (partial) available. Financial award application deadline: 2/15. *Faculty research:* International relations, Latin American politics, public policy, economic development, political theory. *Unit head:* Dr. John Gilliom, Chair, 740-593-4368, Fax: 740-593-0394. *Application contact:* Dr. Judith Millesen, Graduate Director, 740-593-4381, Fax: 740-593-0394.

Old Dominion University, College of Business and Public Administration, Doctoral Program in Public Administration and Urban Policy, Norfolk, VA 23529. Offers PhD. Part-time and evening/weekend programs available. *Faculty:* 7 full-time (1 woman), 3 part-time/adjunct (2 women). *Students:* 11 full-time (9 women), 13 part-time (5 women); includes 7 minority (6 African Americans, 1 Asian American or Pacific Islander), 4 international. Average age 37. 19 applicants, 42% accepted, 6 enrolled. In 2009, 4 doctorates awarded. *Degree requirements:* For doctorate, comprehensive exam, thesis/dissertation. *Entrance requirements:* For doctorate, GMAT, GRE General Test, master's degree, minimum graduate GPA of 3.25. Additional exam requirements/recommendations for international students: Required—TOEFL (minimum score 550 paper-based; 213 computer-based; 79 iBT). *Application deadline:* For fall admission, 3/15 priority date for domestic and international students. Application fee: $50. Electronic applications accepted. *Expenses:* Tuition, state resident: full-time $8112; part-time $338 per credit. Tuition, nonresident: full-time $20,256; part-time $844 per credit. Required fees: $119 per semester. One-time fee: $50. *Financial support:* In 2009–10, 10 students received support, including 2 fellowships with partial tuition reimbursements available (averaging $15,000 per year), 6 research assistantships with partial tuition reimbursements available (averaging $13,000 per year); teaching assistantships. Financial award application deadline: 3/15; financial award applicants required to submit FAFSA. *Faculty research:* Educational needs and program development, policy analysis and administration, excellence norms for cooperative education programs. Total annual research expenditures: $60,000. *Unit head:* Dr. John C. Morris, Graduate Program Director, 757-683-3961, Fax: 757-683-4886, E-mail: jcmorris@odu.edu. *Application contact:* Megan S. Jones, Graduate Program Manager, 757-683-3961, Fax: 757-683-4886, E-mail: mmjones@odu.edu.

Old Dominion University, College of Business and Public Administration, Master's Program in Business Administration, Norfolk, VA 23529. Offers business and economic forecasting (MBA); financial analysis and valuation (MBA); information technology and enterprise integration (MBA); international business (MBA); maritime and port management (MBA); public administration (MBA). *Accreditation:* AACSB. Part-time and evening/weekend programs available. *Faculty:* 66 full-time (15 women), 6 part-time/adjunct (1 woman). *Students:* 81 full-time (27 women), 198 part-time (92 women); includes 46 minority (25 African Americans, 1 American Indian/Alaska Native, 13 Asian Americans or Pacific Islanders, 7 Hispanic Americans), 31 international. Average age 30. 169 applicants, 52% accepted, 61 enrolled. In 2009, 81 master's awarded. *Entrance requirements:* For master's, GMAT, letters of reference, resume, coursework in calculus. Additional exam requirements/recommendations for international students: Required—TOEFL (minimum score 550 paper-based; 213 computer-based; 80 iBT). *Application deadline:* For fall admission, 6/1 priority date for domestic students, 4/15 priority date for international students; for spring admission, 11/1 priority date for domestic students, 10/1 priority date for international students. Applications are processed on a rolling basis. Application fee: $50. Electronic applications accepted. *Expenses:* Tuition, state resident: full-time $8112; part-time $338 per credit. Tuition, nonresident: full-time $20,256; part-time $844 per credit. Required fees: $119 per semester. One-time fee: $50. *Financial support:* In 2009–10, 46 students received support, including 31 research assistantships with partial tuition reimbursements available (averaging $7,000 per year), 3 teaching assistantships with partial tuition reimbursements available (averaging $6,300 per year); career-related internships or fieldwork, scholarships/grants, and unspecified assistantships also available. Support available to part-time students. Financial award application deadline: 2/15; financial award applicants required to submit FAFSA. *Faculty research:* International business, buyer behavior, financial markets, strategy, operations research. *Unit head:* Dr. Bruce Rubin, Graduate Program Director, 757-683-3585, E-mail: mbainfo@odu.edu. *Application contact:* Shanna Wood, MBA Program Manager, 757-683-3585, Fax: 757-683-5750, E-mail: mbainfo@odu.edu.

Old Dominion University, College of Business and Public Administration, Program in Public Administration, Norfolk, VA 23529. Offers MPA. *Accreditation:* NASPAA. Part-time and evening/weekend programs available. *Faculty:* 7 full-time (1 woman), 10 part-time/adjunct (7 women). *Students:* 24 full-time (21 women), 99 part-time (63 women); includes 41 minority (37 African Americans, 1 American Indian/Alaska Native, 3 Asian Americans or Pacific Islanders), 4 international. Average age 33. 56 applicants, 88% accepted, 37 enrolled. In 2009, 37 master's awarded. *Degree requirements:* For master's, thesis optional, capstone seminar. *Entrance requirements:* For master's, GRE. Additional exam requirements/recommendations for international students: Required—TOEFL (minimum score 550 paper-based; 213 computer-based; 79 iBT). *Application deadline:* For fall admission, 7/15 for domestic students; for spring admission, 11/15 for domestic students. Applications are processed on a rolling basis. Application fee: $50. Electronic applications accepted. *Expenses:* Tuition, state resident: full-time $8112; part-time $338 per credit. Tuition, nonresident: full-time $20,256; part-time $844 per credit. Required fees: $119 per semester. One-time fee: $50. *Financial support:* In 2009–10, 7 students received support, including 4 research assistantships with partial tuition reimbursements available (averaging $6,400 per year); fellowships, teaching assistantships also available. Financial award application deadline: 2/15; financial award applicants required to submit FAFSA. *Faculty research:* Environmental administration, personnel policy analysis, urban administration. *Unit head:* Dr. William M. Leavitt, Graduate Program Director, 757-683-5695, Fax: 757-683-5639, E-mail: padmgpd@odu.edu. *Application contact:* Megan S. Jones, Graduate Program Manager, 757-683-3961, Fax: 757-683-4886, E-mail: mmjones@odu.edu.

Pace University, Dyson College of Arts and Sciences, Department of Public Administration, New York, NY 10038. Offers environmental management (MPA); government management (MPA); health care administration (MPA); management for public safety and homeland security (MA); nonprofit management (MPA); JD/MPA. Offered at White Plains, NY location only. Part-time and evening/weekend programs available. *Faculty:* 4 full-time, 6 part-time/adjunct. *Students:* 52 full-time (31 women), 75 part-time (49 women); includes 47 minority (28 African Americans, 1 American Indian/Alaska Native, 1 Asian American or Pacific Islander, 17 Hispanic Americans), 8 international. Average age 30. 75 applicants, 100% accepted, 43 enrolled. In 2009, 38 master's awarded. *Degree requirements:* For master's, capstone project. *Entrance requirements:* For master's, GRE General Test. Additional exam requirements/recommendations for international students: Required—TOEFL. *Application deadline:* For fall admission, 8/1 priority date for domestic students; for spring admission, 12/1 priority date for domestic students. Applications are processed on a rolling basis. Application fee: $70. Electronic applications accepted. *Expenses:* Tuition: Part-time $954 per credit. Tuition and fees vary according to course load, degree level and program. *Financial support:* Research assistantships, career-related internships or fieldwork, Federal Work-Study, and tuition waivers (partial) available. Support available to part-time students. Financial award applicants required to submit FAFSA. *Unit head:* Dr. Farrokh Hormozi, Chairperson, 914-422-4285, E-mail: fhormozi@pace.edu. *Application contact:* Joanna Broda, Director of Admissions, 914-422-4283, Fax: 914 422-4287, E-mail: gradwp@pace.edu.

Park University, College of Graduate and Professional Studies, Kansas City, MO 54105. Offers adult education (M Ed); at-risk students (M Ed); disaster and emergency management (MPA); educational administration (M Ed); entrepreneurship (MBA); general business (MBA); general education (M Ed); government/business relations (MPA); healthcare/services management (MBA, MPA); international business (MBA); K-12 certification (MAT); management information systems (MBA); management of information systems (MPA); middle school certification (MAT); multi-cultural education (M Ed); nonprofit management (MPA); public management (MPA); school law (M Ed); secondary school certification (MAT); special education (M Ed). Part-time and evening/weekend programs available. Postbaccalaureate distance learning degree programs offered (no on-campus study). *Degree requirements:* For master's, comprehensive exam, thesis (for some programs). *Entrance requirements:* For master's, GRE, GMAT, teacher certification (M Ed). Additional exam requirements/recommendations for international students: Required—TOEFL (minimum score 550 paper-based). Electronic applications accepted. *Faculty research:* Literacy, leadership, brain based research, multicultural education, diversity.

Pepperdine University, School of Public Policy, Malibu, CA 90263. Offers American politics (MPP); economics (MPP); international relations (MPP); public policy (MPP); state and local policy (MPP). *Faculty:* 7 full-time (2 women), 5 part-time/adjunct (0 women). *Students:* 117 full-time (62 women), 5 part-time (3 women); includes 30 minority (7 African Americans, 1 American Indian/Alaska Native, 10 Asian Americans or Pacific Islanders, 12 Hispanic Americans), 9 international. In 2009, 27 master's awarded. *Entrance requirements:* For master's, GRE, 2 letters of recommendation, resume. Additional exam requirements/recommendations for international students: Required—TOEFL. *Application deadline:* For fall admission, 4/15 for domestic students. Applications are processed on a rolling basis. Electronic applications accepted. *Expenses:* Tuition: Full-time $37,516; part-time $1310 per unit. Required fees: $80. *Financial support:* Research assistantships, teaching assistantships, institutionally sponsored loans and scholarships/grants available. Financial award application deadline: 5/1; financial award applicants required to submit FAFSA. *Unit head:* Dr. James R. Wilburn, Dean, 310-506-7490, Fax: 310-506-7494, E-mail: james.wilburn@pepperdine.edu. *Application contact:* Melinda E. van Hemert, Director of Recruitment and Career Services, 310-506-7492, Fax: 310-506-7494, E-mail: melinda.vanhemert@pepperdine.edu.

Pontifical Catholic University of Puerto Rico, Institute of Graduate Studies in Behavioral Science and Community Affairs, Program in Public Administration, Ponce, PR 00717-0777.

Public Administration

Pontifical Catholic University of Puerto Rico (continued)
Offers MA. Part-time and evening/weekend programs available. *Degree requirements:* For master's, thesis. *Entrance requirements:* For master's, EXADEP, 3 letters of recommendation, interview, minimum GPA of 2.75.

Portland State University, Graduate Studies, College of Urban and Public Affairs, Hatfield School of Government, Division of Public Administration, Portland, OR 97207-0751. Offers public administration (MPA); public administration and policy (PhD). *Accreditation:* NASPAA (one or more programs are accredited). Part-time and evening/weekend programs available. *Degree requirements:* For master's, internship (MPA), practicum (MPH); for doctorate, comprehensive exam, thesis/dissertation, residency. *Entrance requirements:* For master's, GRE, minimum GPA of 3.0 in upper-division course work or 2.75 overall, 3 recommendation forms, resume; for doctorate, GRE General Test, minimum GPA of 2.75. Additional exam requirements/recommendations for international students: Required—TOEFL (minimum score 550 paper-based; 213 computer-based). *Faculty research:* Public budgeting, program evaluation, nonprofit management, natural resources policy and administration.

Regent University, Graduate School, Robertson School of Government, Virginia Beach, VA 23464. Offers american government (MA); global politics (MA); health care policy and administration (MA); international politics (MA); law and public policy (MA); Mid-East Politics (MA); political leadership and management (MA); political management (MA); political theory (MA); public administration (MA); public policy (MA); terrorism and homeland defense (MA); world economies and political development (MA); JD/MA; M Div/MA; M Ed/MA; MBA/MA. Part-time and evening/weekend programs available. Postbaccalaureate distance learning degree programs offered (minimal on-campus study). *Faculty:* 6 full-time (2 women), 11 part-time/adjunct (1 woman). *Students:* 77 full-time (55 women), 65 part-time (36 women); includes 47 minority (38 African Americans, 2 Asian Americans or Pacific Islanders, 7 Hispanic Americans), 4 international. Average age 30. 131 applicants, 65% accepted, 54 enrolled. In 2009, 51 master's awarded. *Degree requirements:* For master's, thesis optional, internship. *Entrance requirements:* For master's, GRE General Test or LSAT, minimum undergraduate GPA of 3.0, writing sample, resume, interview, references. Additional exam requirements/recommendations for international students: Required—TOEFL (minimum score 577 paper-based; 233 computer-based). *Application deadline:* For fall admission, 5/1 priority date for domestic students; for spring admission, 11/1 priority date for domestic students. Applications are processed on a rolling basis. Application fee: $50. Electronic applications accepted. *Expenses:* Contact institution. *Financial support:* In 2009–10, 130 students received support. Career-related internships or fieldwork, scholarships/grants, tuition waivers (full and partial), and unspecified assistantships available. Support available to part-time students. Financial award application deadline: 9/1; financial award applicants required to submit FAFSA. *Faculty research:* Education reform, political character issues, social capital concerns, administrative ethics, Biblical law and public policy. *Unit head:* Dr. Charles W. Dunn, Dean, 757-352-4322, Fax: 757-352-4643, E-mail: cwdunn@regent.edu. *Application contact:* Matthew Chadwick, Director of Admissions, 800-373-5504, Fax: 757-352-4381, E-mail: admissions@regent.edu.

Rhode Island College, School of Graduate Studies, Faculty of Arts and Sciences, Department of Political Science, Providence, RI 02908-1991. Offers public administration (MPA). Part-time and evening/weekend programs available. *Faculty:* 1 full-time (0 women). *Entrance requirements:* Additional exam requirements/recommendations for international students: Recommended—TOEFL (minimum score 550 paper-based; 213 computer-based; 79 iBT). *Application deadline:* For fall admission, 4/1 for domestic students; for spring admission, 11/1 for domestic students. Applications are processed on a rolling basis. *Expenses:* Tuition, state resident: full-time $7440; part-time $310 per credit hour. Tuition, nonresident: full-time $14,784; part-time $616 per credit hour. Required fees: $552; $20 per credit. $70 per term. *Financial support:* Career-related internships or fieldwork, Federal Work-Study, scholarships/grants, health care benefits, and unspecified assistantships available. Support available to part-time students. Financial award application deadline: 5/15; financial award applicants required to submit FAFSA. *Unit head:* Dr. Thomas Schmeling, Chair, 401-456-8056. *Application contact:* Graduate Studies, 401-456-8700.

Roger Williams University, Feinstein College of Arts and Sciences, Program in Public Administration, Bristol, RI 02809. Offers MPA. Part-time and evening/weekend programs available. Postbaccalaureate distance learning degree programs offered (minimal on-campus study). *Degree requirements:* For master's, internship/research project. *Entrance requirements:* For master's, 2 letters of recommendation, curriculum vitae/resume. Additional exam requirements/recommendations for international students: Recommended—IELTS. Electronic applications accepted. *Expenses:* Contact institution.

Roosevelt University, Graduate Division, College of Arts and Sciences, Department of Political Science and Public Administration, Program in Public Administration, Chicago, IL 60605. Offers MPA. Part-time and evening/weekend programs available. *Degree requirements:* For master's, thesis optional. *Entrance requirements:* For master's, minimum undergraduate GPA of 3.0. *Faculty research:* Health policy issues, environmental policy, local government administration.

Rutgers, The State University of New Jersey, Camden, Graduate School of Arts and Sciences, Department of Public Policy and Administration, Camden, NJ 08102-1401. Offers education policy and leadership (MPA); international public service and development (MPA); public management (MPA); JD/MPA; MPA/MA. *Accreditation:* NASPAA. Part-time and evening/weekend programs available. *Degree requirements:* For master's, directed study, research workshop. *Entrance requirements:* For master's, GRE General Test, GMAT or LSAT, 3 letters of recommendation; resume. Additional exam requirements/recommendations for international students: Required—TOEFL (minimum score 550 paper-based; 213 computer-based), IELTS. Electronic applications accepted. *Faculty research:* Nonprofit management, county and municipal administration, health and human services, government communication, administrative law, educational finance.

Rutgers, The State University of New Jersey, Newark, Graduate School, Program in Public Administration, Newark, NJ 07102. Offers health care administration (MPA); human resources administration (MPA); public administration (PhD); public management (MPA); public policy analysis (MPA); urban systems and issues (MPA). *Accreditation:* NASPAA (one or more programs are accredited). Part-time and evening/weekend programs available. *Degree requirements:* For master's, comprehensive exam, thesis or alternative; for doctorate, thesis/dissertation. *Entrance requirements:* For master's, GRE, minimum undergraduate B average; for doctorate, GRE, MPA, minimum B average. Electronic applications accepted. *Faculty research:* Government finance, municipal and state government, public productivity.

Sage Graduate School, Graduate School, School of Management, Troy, NY 12180-4115. Offers business administration (MBA), including business strategy, finance, human resources, marketing; health services administration (MS, Certificate), including dietetic internship (Certificate), gerontology (MS); organizational management (MS), including public administration; JD/MBA. Part-time and evening/weekend programs available. *Faculty:* 4 full-time (2 women), 6 part-time/adjunct (0 women). *Students:* 23 full-time (20 women), 136 part-time (94 women); includes 25 minority (13 African Americans, 2 Asian Americans or Pacific Islanders, 10 Hispanic Americans), 2 international. Average age 31. 101 applicants, 59% accepted, 44 enrolled. In 2009, 39 master's awarded. *Entrance requirements:* For master's, minimum GPA of 2.75. Additional exam requirements/recommendations for international students: Required—TOEFL (minimum score 550 paper-based; 213 computer-based). *Application deadline:* Applications are processed on a rolling basis. Application fee: $40. *Expenses:* Tuition: Full-time $10,620; part-time $590 per credit hour. *Financial support:* Fellowships, research assistantships, Federal Work-Study, scholarships/grants, and unspecified assistantships available. Support available to part-time students. Financial award application deadline: 3/1; financial award applicants required to submit FAFSA. *Unit head:* Daniel Robeson, Chair, Management Department, 518-292-1770, Fax: 518-292-5414, E-mail: robesd@sage.edu. *Application contact:* Wendy D. Diefendorf, Director of Graduate and Adult Admission, 518-244-2443, Fax: 518-244-6880, E-mail: diefew@sage.edu.

Saginaw Valley State University, College of Arts and Behavioral Sciences, Program in Administrative Science, University Center, MI 48710. Offers MA. Part-time and evening/weekend programs available. *Students:* 12 full-time (7 women), 48 part-time (33 women); includes 12 minority (7 African Americans, 1 American Indian/Alaska Native, 1 Asian American or Pacific Islander, 3 Hispanic Americans), 1 international. Average age 36. 31 applicants, 84% accepted, 16 enrolled. In 2009, 22 master's awarded. *Degree requirements:* For master's, thesis optional. *Entrance requirements:* For master's, minimum GPA of 3.0 in social sciences, 2.75 overall. Additional exam requirements/recommendations for international students: Required—TOEFL. *Application deadline:* Applications are processed on a rolling basis. Application fee: $25. Electronic applications accepted. *Financial support:* In 2009–10, 2 fellowships with partial tuition reimbursements, 1 research assistantship with full tuition reimbursement (averaging $5,000 per year) were awarded; Federal Work-Study also available. Support available to part-time students. Financial award application deadline: 4/1; financial award applicants required to submit FAFSA. *Unit head:* Mark Nicol, Coordinator/Instructor of Political Science, 989-964-2605, E-mail: nlnicol@svsu.edu. *Application contact:* Mark Nicol, Coordinator/Instructor of Political Science, 989-964-2605, E-mail: nlnicol@svsu.edu.

St. Edward's University, School of Management and Business, Program in Human Services, Austin, TX 78704. Offers administration (Certificate); conflict resolution (Certificate); family mediation (Certificate); human services (MA), including administration, conflict resolution, human resource management, organization development and training, social and psychological services; mediation (Certificate); organization development and training (Certificate). Part-time and evening/weekend programs available. *Students:* 4 full-time (3 women), 51 part-time (43 women); includes 24 minority (9 African Americans, 2 Asian Americans or Pacific Islanders, 13 Hispanic Americans). Average age 34. 23 applicants, 96% accepted, 18 enrolled. In 2009, 19 master's awarded. *Degree requirements:* For master's, minimum of 24 resident hours. *Entrance requirements:* For master's, GRE General Test, GMAT, minimum GPA of 2.75 in last 60 hours of course work. Additional exam requirements/recommendations for international students: Required—TOEFL (minimum score 550 paper-based; 213 computer-based; 79 iBT) or IELTS (minimum score 6). *Application deadline:* For fall admission, 7/1 for domestic and international students; for spring admission, 11/1 for domestic and international students. Applications are processed on a rolling basis. Application fee: $45 ($50 for international students). Electronic applications accepted. *Expenses:* Tuition: Full-time $14,922; part-time $829 per credit hour. Required fees: $50 per trimester. Full-time tuition and fees vary according to course load and program. *Financial support:* In 2009–10, 2 students received support. Scholarships/grants available. *Faculty research:* Leadership development, organizational management, public policy. *Unit head:* Dr. Constance D. Porter, Director, 512-416-5827, Fax: 512-448-8492, E-mail: constanp@stedwards.edu. *Application contact:* Kay L. Arnold, Assistant Director of Admissions, 512-233-1636, Fax: 512-428-1032, E-mail: kayla@stedwards.edu.

Saint Louis University, Graduate School, College of Education and Public Service and Graduate School, Department of Public Policy Studies, St. Louis, MO 63103-2097. Offers geographic information systems (Certificate); organizational development (Certificate); public administration (MAPA); public policy analysis (PhD); urban affairs (MAUA); urban planning and real estate development (MUPRED). *Accreditation:* NASPAA. Part-time programs available. *Degree requirements:* For master's, comprehensive exam (for some programs), thesis (for some programs); for doctorate, comprehensive exam, thesis/dissertation, preliminary exams. *Entrance requirements:* For master's, GMAT, GRE General Test, or LSAT, letters of recommendation, resume; for doctorate, GMAT, GRE General Test, or LSAT, letters of recommendation, resumé, interview, transcripts, goal statement. Additional exam requirements/recommendations for international students: Required—TOEFL (minimum score 525 paper-based; 194 computer-based). Electronic applications accepted. *Faculty research:* Urban politics, brown fields, e-government, and administration, evaluation research, community development, electronic government and governance.

St. Mary's University, Graduate School, Department of Political Science, Program in Public Administration, San Antonio, TX 78228-8507. Offers inter-American administration (MPA); public management (MPA); JD/MPA. Part-time programs available. Postbaccalaureate distance learning degree programs offered (no on-campus study). *Degree requirements:* For master's, comprehensive exam, internship. *Entrance requirements:* For master's, GRE General Test. Additional exam requirements/recommendations for international students: Required—TOEFL (minimum score 550 paper-based; 213 computer-based; 80 iBT). Electronic applications accepted. *Expenses:* Tuition: Full-time $8004. Required fees: $536. One-time fee: $5 full-time. Full-time tuition and fees vary according to program. *Faculty research:* Voting rights, natural resources, urban policy.

St. Thomas University, School of Business, Department of Management, Miami Gardens, FL 33054-6459. Offers accounting (MBA); general management (MSM, Certificate); health management (MBA, MSM, Certificate); human resource management (MBA, MSM, Certificate); international business (MBA, MIB, MSM, Certificate); justice administration (MSM, Certificate); management accounting (MSM, Certificate); public management (MSM, Certificate); sports administration (MS). Part-time and evening/weekend programs available. *Degree requirements:* For master's, comprehensive exam. *Entrance requirements:* For master's, interview, minimum GPA of 3.0 or GMAT. Additional exam requirements/recommendations for international students: Required—TOEFL (minimum score 550 paper-based; 213 computer-based; 79 iBT). Electronic applications accepted.

Sam Houston State University, College of Humanities and Social Sciences, Department of Political Science, Huntsville, TX 77341. Offers political science (MA); public administration (MPA). Evening/weekend programs available. *Faculty:* 8 full-time (5 women). *Students:* 6 full-time (4 women), 23 part-time (14 women); includes 3 minority (1 Asian American or Pacific Islander, 2 Hispanic Americans), 4 international. Average age 31. 18 applicants, 94% accepted, 13 enrolled. In 2009, 9 master's awarded. *Degree requirements:* For master's, thesis or alternative. *Entrance requirements:* For master's, GRE General Test. Additional exam requirements/recommendations for international students: Required—TOEFL (minimum score 550 paper-based; 213 computer-based; 79 iBT). *Application deadline:* For fall admission, 8/1 for domestic students; for spring admission, 12/1 for domestic students. Applications are processed on a rolling basis. Application fee: $20. *Expenses:* Tuition, state resident: full-time $3690; part-time $205 per credit hour. Tuition, nonresident: full-time $8676; part-time $482 per credit hour. Required fees: $1474. Tuition and fees vary according to course load and campus/location. *Financial support:* Research assistantships, teaching assistantships, career-related internships or fieldwork and institutionally sponsored loans available. Support available to part-time students. Financial award application deadline: 5/31; financial award applicants required to submit FAFSA. *Unit head:* Dr. Rhonda Callaway, Chair, 936-294-4108, Fax: 936-294-4172, E-mail: rlc005@shsu.edu. *Application contact:* Dr. Tamara Waggener, Advisor, 936-294-1466, E-mail: pol_taw@shsu.edu.

San Diego State University, Graduate and Research Affairs, College of Professional Studies and Fine Arts, School of Public Affairs, Program in Public Administration, San Diego, CA 92182. Offers MPA. *Accreditation:* NASPAA. Part-time programs available. *Entrance requirements:* For master's, GRE General Test, 2 letters of reference. Additional exam requirements/recommendations for international students: Required—TOEFL. Electronic applications accepted.

San Francisco State University, Division of Graduate Studies, College of Behavioral and Social Sciences, Public Administration Program, San Francisco, CA 94132-1722. Offers integrated and collaborative services (MPA); nonprofit administration (MPA); policy analysis (MPA); public management (MPA); urban administration (MPA). *Accreditation:* NASPAA.

San Jose State University, Graduate Studies and Research, College of Social Sciences, Department of Political Science, San Jose, CA 95192-0001. Offers public administration (MPA). *Accreditation:* NASPAA. Part-time and evening/weekend programs available. *Students:*

29 full-time (20 women), 64 part-time (36 women); includes 49 minority (8 African Americans, 1 American Indian/Alaska Native, 19 Asian Americans or Pacific Islanders, 21 Hispanic Americans), 1 international. Average age 31. 104 applicants, 31% accepted, 18 enrolled. In 2009, 20 master's awarded. *Degree requirements:* For master's, comprehensive exam, thesis or alternative. *Entrance requirements:* For master's, GRE Subject Test. Additional exam requirements/recommendations for international students: Required—TOEFL (minimum score 575 paper-based). *Application deadline:* For fall admission, 6/29 for domestic students; for spring admission, 11/30 for domestic students. Applications are processed on a rolling basis. Application fee: $59. Electronic applications accepted. *Financial support:* Career-related internships or fieldwork, Federal Work-Study, institutionally sponsored loans, scholarships/grants, and tuition waivers (partial) available. Support available to part-time students. Financial award applicants required to submit FAFSA. *Faculty research:* Modern political philosophy, international relations in the Middle East, public policy, American public policy, political parties and political reform. *Unit head:* Dr. James Brent, Chair, 408-924-5572, Fax: 408-924-5556, E-mail: jcbrent@email.sjsu.edu. *Application contact:* Dr. Frances Edwards, MPA Director, 408-924-5559.

Savannah State University, Master of Public Administration Program, Savannah, GA 31404. Offers MPA. *Accreditation:* NASPAA. Part-time programs available. *Faculty:* 5 full-time (2 women). *Students:* 11 full-time (5 women), 14 part-time (13 women); includes 23 African Americans. In 2009, 7 master's awarded. *Degree requirements:* For master's, major paper, oral exam, public service internship. *Entrance requirements:* For master's, GRE General Test. Additional exam requirements/recommendations for international students: Required—TOEFL. *Application deadline:* For fall admission, 7/1 priority date for domestic students, 7/1 for international students; for spring admission, 10/31 priority date for domestic students, 10/1 for international students. Applications are processed on a rolling basis. Application fee: $20. *Expenses:* Tuition, state resident: full-time $3662; part-time $153 per credit hour. Tuition, nonresident: full-time $14,648. Required fees: $450 per term. *Financial support:* Career-related internships or fieldwork, Federal Work-Study, institutionally sponsored loans, scholarships/grants, and unspecified assistantships available. Financial award applicants required to submit FAFSA. *Faculty research:* Community development, human resources, leadership, conflict resolution. *Unit head:* Dr. Sametria McFall, Interim Chair, 912-358-3221, E-mail: gompa @ savannahstate.edu. *Application contact:* Dr. Emily Crawford, Interim Dean of Graduate Studies, 912-356-2244, Fax: 912-356-2299, E-mail: crawford@savannahstate.edu.

Seattle University, College of Arts and Sciences, Institute of Public Service, Seattle, WA 98122-1090. Offers MPA. *Accreditation:* NASPAA. *Degree requirements:* For master's, thesis or alternative. *Entrance requirements:* For master's, minimum GPA of 3.0, 1 year work experience. *Faculty research:* Housing, experiential learning, citizenship education.

Seton Hall University, College of Arts and Sciences, Department of Public and Healthcare Administration, South Orange, NJ 07079-2697. Offers healthcare administration (MHA, Graduate Certificate); public administration (MPA, Graduate Certificate), including health policy and management (MPA), nonprofit organization management, public service: leadership, governance, and policy. *Accreditation:* NASPAA. Part-time and evening/weekend programs available. Postbaccalaureate distance learning degree programs offered (minimal on-campus study). *Faculty:* 7 full-time (4 women), 6 part-time/adjunct (2 women). *Students:* 60 full-time (35 women), 100 part-time (60 women); includes 58 minority (36 African Americans, 2 American Indian/Alaska Native, 16 Asian Americans or Pacific Islanders, 4 Hispanic Americans), 5 international. Average age 32. 95 applicants, 88% accepted, 51 enrolled. In 2009, 33 master's awarded. *Degree requirements:* For master's, thesis or alternative, internship or practicum. *Entrance requirements:* Additional exam requirements/recommendations for international students: Required—TOEFL. *Application deadline:* For fall admission, 7/1 priority date for domestic and international students; for spring admission, 11/1 priority date for domestic and international students. Applications are processed on a rolling basis. Application fee: $50. Electronic applications accepted. *Financial support:* Research assistantships, career-related internships or fieldwork, Federal Work-Study, scholarships/grants, and unspecified assistantships available. Financial award applicants required to submit FAFSA. *Unit head:* Dr. Matthew Hale, Chair, 973-761-9510, Fax: 973-275-2463, E-mail: halematt@shu.edu. *Application contact:* Dr. Matthew Hale, Chair, 973-761-9510, Fax: 973-275-2463, E-mail: halematt@shu.edu.

Shenandoah University, School of Education and Human Development, Winchester, VA 22601-5195. Offers administrative leadership (D Ed); advanced professional teaching English to speakers of other languages (Certificate); education (MSE); elementary education (Certificate); middle school education (Certificate); organizational leadership (MS); professional studies (Certificate); professional studies (for initial teacher licensure) (Certificate); professional studies (for special education teacher licensure) (Certificate); professional studies (for VA licensure reading specialists) (Certificate); professional studies (for VA licensure) (Certificate); professional teaching English to speakers of other languages (Certificate); public management (Certificate); school reform (Certificate); secondary education (Certificate). *Accreditation:* Teacher Education Accreditation Council. Part-time and evening/weekend programs available. Postbaccalaureate distance learning degree programs offered (minimal on-campus study). *Faculty:* 13 full-time (7 women), 27 part-time/adjunct (20 women). *Students:* 11 full-time (8 women), 382 part-time (276 women); includes 35 minority (17 African Americans, 1 American Indian/Alaska Native, 6 Asian Americans or Pacific Islanders, 11 Hispanic Americans), 4 international. Average age 39. 272 applicants, 95% accepted, 218 enrolled. In 2009, 103 master's, 2 doctorates awarded. *Degree requirements:* For master's, comprehensive exam (for some programs), thesis (for some programs), internship; for doctorate, comprehensive exam, thesis/dissertation; for Certificate, full time teaching in area for 1 year. *Entrance requirements:* For master's, minimum GPA of 3.0 or satisfactory GRE, 3 letters of recommendation, valid teaching license, essay; for doctorate, minimum GPA of 3.5 in master's, 3 years of teaching experience, 3 letters of recommendation, writing samples; for Certificate, minimum undergraduate GPA of 3.0, essay, 3 letters of recommendation. Additional exam requirements/recommendations for international students: Required—TOEFL (minimum score 550 paper-based; 213 computer-based; 79 iBT), IELTS (minimum score 6.5). *Application deadline:* For fall admission, 7/1 for domestic and international students; for spring admission, 10/15 for domestic and international students. Application fee: $30. Electronic applications accepted. *Expenses:* Tuition: Full-time $11,925; part-time $695 per credit. Required fees: $400 per semester. *Financial support:* Application deadline: 3/15. *Unit head:* Dr. Steven E. Humphries, Dean, 540-535-3574, E-mail: shumphri@su.edu. *Application contact:* David Anthony, Dean of Admissions, 540-665-4581, Fax: 540-665-4627, E-mail: admit@su.edu.

Shippensburg University of Pennsylvania, School of Graduate Studies, College of Arts and Sciences, Department of Political Science, Shippensburg, PA 17257-2299. Offers public administration (MPA). Part-time and evening/weekend programs available. *Degree requirements:* For master's, thesis or internship, candidacy. *Entrance requirements:* For master's, GRE or MAT (if GPA less than 2.75), 6 credits of course work in political science or public administration. Additional exam requirements/recommendations for international students: Required—TOEFL (minimum score 560 paper-based; 220 computer-based); Recommended—IELTS (minimum score 6). Electronic applications accepted.

Sojourner-Douglass College, Graduate Program, Baltimore, MD 21205-1814. Offers human services (MASS); public administration (MASS); urban education (reading) (MASS). Part-time and evening/weekend programs available. *Degree requirements:* For master's, comprehensive exam, written proposal oral defense. *Entrance requirements:* For master's, Graduate Examination.

Sonoma State University, School of Social Sciences, Department of Political Science, Rohnert Park, CA 94928. Offers public administration (MPA). Part-time and evening/weekend programs available. *Faculty:* 2 full-time (0 women), 1 (woman) part-time/adjunct. *Students:* 6 full-time (1 woman), 45 part-time (31 women); includes 7 minority (1 African American, 3 Asian Americans or Pacific Islanders, 3 Hispanic Americans). Average age 34. 25 applicants, 76% accepted, 7 enrolled. In 2009, 12 master's awarded. *Degree requirements:* For master's, thesis or alternative. *Entrance requirements:* For master's, GRE General Test, minimum GPA of 3.0. Additional exam requirements/recommendations for international students: Required—TOEFL (minimum score 500 paper-based; 173 computer-based). *Application deadline:* For fall admission, 11/30 for domestic students; for spring admission, 8/31 for domestic students. Application fee: $55. *Expenses:* Tuition, nonresident: full-time $11,160. Required fees: $6226. Full-time tuition and fees vary according to course load. *Financial support:* Research assistantships, teaching assistantships, career-related internships or fieldwork and Federal Work-Study available. Support available to part-time students. Financial award application deadline: 3/2; financial award applicants required to submit FAFSA. *Unit head:* Dr. Diane Parness, Chair, 707-664-2179. *Application contact:* Dr. Donald Dixon, Graduate Program Coordinator, 707-664-2179, Fax: 707-664-3920, E-mail: dixon@sonoma.edu.

Southeast Missouri State University, School of Graduate Studies, Department of Political Science, Philosophy and Religion, Cape Girardeau, MO 63701-4799. Offers public administration (MPA). Part-time and evening/weekend programs available. *Degree requirements:* For master's, internship or thesis. *Entrance requirements:* For master's, minimum undergraduate GPA of 2.7. Additional exam requirements/recommendations for international students: Required—TOEFL (minimum score 550 paper-based; 213 computer-based); Recommended—IELTS (minimum score 6). Electronic applications accepted. *Expenses:* Tuition, state resident: full-time $4266; part-time $237 per credit hour. Tuition, nonresident: full-time $7506; part-time $417 per credit hour. Required fees: $427; $427. *Faculty research:* American political institutions, state and local government, non-profit management.

Southern Arkansas University–Magnolia, Graduate Programs, Magnolia, AR 71753. Offers agriculture (MS); business administration (MBA); computer and information sciences (MS); counseling (MS); education (M Ed), including counseling and development, curriculum and instruction emphasis, educational administration and supervision, elementary education, middle level emphasis, reading emphasis, secondary education, TESOL emphasis; kinesiology (MS); library media and information specialist (M Ed); mental health and clinical counseling (MS); public administration (EMPA); school counseling (M Ed); teaching (MAT). *Accreditation:* NCATE. Part-time and evening/weekend programs available. *Faculty:* 43 full-time (24 women), 12 part-time/adjunct (7 women). *Students:* 116 full-time (78 women), 333 part-time (255 women); includes 105 minority (98 African Americans, 3 American Indian/Alaska Native, 3 Asian Americans or Pacific Islanders, 1 Hispanic American), 11 international. Average age 33. In 2009, 88 master's awarded. *Degree requirements:* For master's, comprehensive exam, thesis optional. *Entrance requirements:* For master's, GRE, MAT or GMAT, minimum GPA of 2.75. *Application deadline:* For fall admission, 8/15 for domestic students; for winter admission, 1/8 for domestic students; for spring admission, 1/8 for domestic students. Applications are processed on a rolling basis. Application fee: $0. *Expenses:* Tuition, state resident: full-time $3798; part-time $211 per hour. Tuition, nonresident: full-time $5580; part-time $310 per hour. Required fees: $584. *Financial support:* Career-related internships or fieldwork, Federal Work-Study, scholarships/grants, tuition waivers (full), and unspecified assistantships available. Financial award applicants required to submit FAFSA. *Faculty research:* Alternative certification for teachers, supervision of instruction, instructional leadership, counseling. *Unit head:* Dr. Kim Bloss, Dean, Graduate Studies, 870-235-4150, Fax: 870-235-5227, E-mail: kkbloss@saumag.edu. *Application contact:* Dr. Kim Bloss, Dean, Graduate Studies, 870-235-4150, Fax: 870-235-5227, E-mail: kkbloss@saumag.edu.

Southern Illinois University Carbondale, Graduate School, College of Liberal Arts, Department of Political Science, Public Administration Program, Carbondale, IL 62901-4701. Offers MPA, JD/MPA. *Accreditation:* NASPAA. Part-time programs available. *Degree requirements:* For master's, thesis or alternative. *Entrance requirements:* For master's, minimum GPA of 2.7. Additional exam requirements/recommendations for international students: Required—TOEFL. *Faculty research:* Natural resources and environmental management, intergovernmental relations, state mandates, rural administration, economic development policy, nonprofit management.

Southern Illinois University Edwardsville, Graduate Studies and Research, College of Arts and Sciences, Department of Public Administration and Policy Analysis, Edwardsville, IL 62026-0001. Offers MPA. *Accreditation:* NASPAA. Part-time and evening/weekend programs available. *Faculty:* 5 full-time (1 woman). *Students:* 59 full-time (34 women), 84 part-time (51 women); includes 62 minority (52 African Americans, 1 American Indian/Alaska Native, 3 Asian Americans or Pacific Islanders, 6 Hispanic Americans), 14 international. Average age 26. 98 applicants, 66% accepted. In 2009, 27 master's awarded. *Degree requirements:* For master's, comprehensive exam, thesis or alternative, final exam. *Entrance requirements:* Additional exam requirements/recommendations for international students: Required—TOEFL (minimum score 550 paper-based; 213 computer-based; 79 iBT), IELTS (minimum score 6.5). *Application deadline:* For fall admission, 7/23 for domestic students, 6/1 for international students; for spring admission, 12/11 for domestic students, 10/1 for international students. Applications are processed on a rolling basis. Application fee: $30. Electronic applications accepted. *Expenses:* Tuition, state resident: part-time $1252.50 per semester. Tuition, nonresident: part-time $3131.25 per semester. Required fees: $586.85 per semester. Tuition and fees vary according to course load. *Financial support:* In 2009–10, 1 research assistantship with full tuition reimbursement (averaging $8,064 per year), 32 teaching assistantships with full tuition reimbursements (averaging $8,064 per year) were awarded; fellowships with full tuition reimbursements, career-related internships or fieldwork, Federal Work-Study, institutionally sponsored loans, scholarships/grants, traineeships, and unspecified assistantships also available. Support available to part-time students. Financial award application deadline: 3/1; financial award applicants required to submit FAFSA. *Unit head:* Dr. T. R. Carr, Chair, 618-650-3762, E-mail: tcarr@siue.edu. *Application contact:* Dr. Drew Dolan, Program Director, 618-650-3762, E-mail: ddolan@siue.edu.

Southern University and Agricultural and Mechanical College, Graduate School, Nelson Mandela School of Public Policy and Urban Affairs, Department of Public Administration, Baton Rouge, LA 70813. Offers MPA. *Accreditation:* NASPAA. Part-time and evening/weekend programs available. *Degree requirements:* For master's, thesis. *Entrance requirements:* For master's, GRE General Test. Additional exam requirements/recommendations for international students: Required—TOEFL (minimum score 525 paper-based; 193 computer-based). *Faculty research:* Fiscal policy, public finance policy and practitioner interests; minority politics, healthcare and political economy.

Southern Utah University, College of Humanities and Social Sciences, Program in Public Administration, Cedar City, UT 84720-2498. Offers MS. *Faculty:* 2 full-time (0 women), 5 part-time/adjunct (1 woman). *Students:* 4 full-time (1 woman), 29 part-time (10 women); includes 1 African American, 2 Asian Americans or Pacific Islanders, 3 Hispanic Americans. 20 applicants, 95% accepted, 16 enrolled. In 2009, 7 master's awarded. *Application deadline:* Applications are processed on a rolling basis. Application fee: $50 ($65 for international students). Electronic applications accepted. *Unit head:* Dr. James McDonald, Dean, 435-586-7898, Fax: 435-865-8193, E-mail: mcdonaldj@suu.edu. *Application contact:* Sandi Levy, Administrative Assistant, 435-865-8420, Fax: 435-586-1925.

State University of New York at Binghamton, Graduate School, College of Community and Public Affairs, Department of Public Administration, Binghamton, NY 13902-6000. Offers MPA. *Students:* 52 full-time (30 women), 32 part-time (21 women); includes 12 minority (8 African Americans, 1 American Indian/Alaska Native, 3 Hispanic Americans), 7 international. Average age 30. 83 applicants, 65% accepted, 27 enrolled. In 2009, 25 master's awarded. Application fee: $60. *Financial support:* In 2009–10, 7 students received support, including teaching assistantships with full tuition reimbursements available (averaging $10,000 per year); career-related internships or fieldwork, Federal Work-Study, institutionally sponsored loans, scholarships/grants, health care benefits, and unspecified assistantships also available. Financial award application deadline: 2/15; financial award applicants required to submit FAFSA. *Unit head:* Dr. Nadia Rubaii-Barrett, Chairperson, 607-777-9172, E-mail: nbarrett@binghamton.edu. *Application contact:* Victoria Williams, Recruiting and Admissions Coordinator, 607-777-2151, Fax: 607-777-2501, E-mail: vwilliam@binghamton.edu.

Public Administration

Stephen F. Austin State University, Graduate School, College of Liberal Arts, Department of Political Science and Geography, Nacogdoches, TX 75962. Offers public administration (MPA). *Degree requirements:* For master's, thesis optional. *Entrance requirements:* For master's, GRE General Test. Additional exam requirements/recommendations for international students: Required—TOEFL.

Strayer University, Graduate Studies, Washington, DC 20005-2603. Offers accounting (MS); acquisition (MBA); business administration (MBA); communications technology (MS); educational management (M Ed); finance (MBA); health services administration (MHSA); hospitality and tourism management (MBA); human resource management (MBA); information systems (MS), including computer security management, decision support system management, enterprise resource management, network management, software engineering management, systems development management; management (MBA); management information systems (MS); marketing (MBA); professional accounting (MS), including accounting information systems, controllership, taxation; public administration (MPA); supply chain management (MBA); technology in education (M Ed). Programs also offered at campus locations in Birmingham, AL; Chamblee, GA; Cobb County, GA; Morrow, GA; White Marsh, MD; Charleston, SC; Columbia, SC; Greensboro, NC; Greenville, SC; Lexington, KY; Louisville, KY; Nashville, TN; North Raleigh, NC; Washington, DC. Part-time and evening/weekend programs available. Postbaccalaureate distance learning degree programs offered (minimal on-campus study). *Degree requirements:* For master's, thesis. *Entrance requirements:* For master's, GMAT, GRE General Test, bachelor's degree from an accredited college or university, minimum undergraduate GPA of 2.75. Electronic applications accepted.

Suffolk University, Sawyer Business School, Department of Public Administration, Boston, MA 02108-2770. Offers nonprofit management (MPA); public administration (CASPA); state and local government (MPA); JD/MPA; MPA/MS. *Accreditation:* NASPAA (one or more programs are accredited). Part-time and evening/weekend programs available. *Faculty:* 9 full-time (4 women), 9 part-time/adjunct (2 women). *Students:* 32 full-time (22 women), 106 part-time (65 women); includes 17 minority (9 African Americans, 1 American Indian/Alaska Native, 2 Asian Americans or Pacific Islanders, 5 Hispanic Americans), 9 international. Average age 31. 89 applicants, 83% accepted, 40 enrolled. In 2009, 57 master's awarded. *Entrance requirements:* Additional exam requirements/recommendations for international students: Required—TOEFL (minimum score 550 paper-based; 213 computer-based; 80 iBT). *Application deadline:* For fall admission, 6/15 priority date for domestic students, 6/15 for international students; for spring admission, 11/1 priority date for domestic students, 11/1 for international students. Applications are processed on a rolling basis. Application fee: $50. Electronic applications accepted. *Expenses:* Contact institution. *Financial support:* In 2009–10, 94 students received support, including 56 fellowships with full and partial tuition reimbursements available (averaging $8,017 per year); career-related internships or fieldwork and Federal Work-Study also available. Support available to part-time students. Financial award application deadline: 4/1; financial award applicants required to submit FAFSA. *Faculty research:* Local government, health care, federal policy, mental health, HIV/AIDS. *Unit head:* Dr. Doug Snow, Chair, 617-573-8330, Fax: 617-227-4618, E-mail: dsnow@suffolk.edu. *Application contact:* Judith Reynolds, Director of Graduate Admissions, 617-573-8302, Fax: 617-305-1733, E-mail: grad.admission@suffolk.edu.

Sul Ross State University, School of Arts and Sciences, Department of Behavioral and Social Sciences, Program in Public Administration, Alpine, TX 79832. Offers MA. Part-time and evening/weekend programs available. *Entrance requirements:* For master's, GRE General Test, minimum GPA of 2.5 in last 60 hours of undergraduate work. *Faculty research:* Local government, state government, personnel, volunteer fire departments, rural health.

Syracuse University, Maxwell School of Citizenship and Public Affairs, International Relations/Public Administration Joint Program, Syracuse, NY 13244. Offers MPA/MA. *Students:* 27 full-time (15 women), 2 part-time (1 woman); includes 10 minority (4 African Americans, 3 Asian Americans or Pacific Islanders, 3 Hispanic Americans), 3 international. Average age 26. 141 applicants, 65% accepted, 19 enrolled. *Entrance requirements:* Additional exam requirements/recommendations for international students: Required—TOEFL (minimum score 100 iBT). *Application deadline:* For fall admission, 2/1 priority date for domestic and international students. Application fee: $75. Electronic applications accepted. *Expenses:* Tuition: Full-time $26,808; part-time $1117 per credit. Required fees: $1024. *Financial support:* Fellowships with tuition reimbursements, research assistantships with tuition reimbursements, teaching assistantships with tuition reimbursements available. Financial award application deadline: 1/1; financial award applicants required to submit FAFSA. *Unit head:* Donald Planty, Chair and Ambassador, 315-443-2306. *Application contact:* Nell Bartkowiak, Director, International Relations, 315-443-9340, E-mail: nsbartko@syr.edu.

Syracuse University, Maxwell School of Citizenship and Public Affairs, Program in Public Administration, Syracuse, NY 13244. Offers EMPA, MPA, PhD, CAS, MPA/MA. *Accreditation:* NASPAA (one or more programs are accredited). Part-time programs available. *Students:* 172 full-time (71 women), 42 part-time (22 women); includes 30 minority (13 African Americans, 1 American Indian/Alaska Native, 10 Asian Americans or Pacific Islanders, 6 Hispanic Americans), 72 international. Average age 32. 568 applicants, 58% accepted, 137 enrolled. In 2009, 266 master's, 1 doctorate, 2 other advanced degrees awarded. *Degree requirements:* For doctorate, comprehensive exam, thesis/dissertation. *Entrance requirements:* For master's, GRE General Test (MPA), 7 years of work experience (EMPA); for doctorate, GRE General Test. Additional exam requirements/recommendations for international students: Required—TOEFL (minimum score 100 iBT). *Application deadline:* For fall admission, 2/1 priority date for domestic and international students. Application fee: $75. Electronic applications accepted. *Expenses:* Tuition: Full-time $26,808; part-time $1117 per credit. Required fees: $1024. *Financial support:* Fellowships with full tuition reimbursements, research assistantships with full and partial tuition reimbursements, teaching assistantships with full tuition reimbursements, scholarships/grants, tuition waivers (partial), and unspecified assistantships available. Financial award application deadline: 1/1; financial award applicants required to submit FAFSA. *Unit head:* Dr. Stuart Bretschneider, Chair, 315-443-4000, Fax: 315-443-5330, E-mail: sibretsc@syr.edu. *Application contact:* Christine Omolino, Associate Director, 315-443-3712, Fax: 315-443-5330, E-mail: comolino@syr.edu.

Syracuse University, Maxwell School of Citizenship and Public Affairs, Program in Public Management and Policy, Syracuse, NY 13244. Offers CAS. *Entrance requirements:* Additional exam requirements/recommendations for international students: Required—TOEFL (minimum score 100 iBT). *Application deadline:* For fall admission, 2/1 priority date for domestic and international students. Application fee: $75. Electronic applications accepted. *Expenses:* Tuition: Full-time $26,808; part-time $1117 per credit. Required fees: $1024. *Unit head:* Margaret Lane, Director, Executive Education, 315-443-28708, Fax: 315-443-3385, E-mail: meland@syr.edu. *Application contact:* Margaret Lane, Director, Executive Education, 315-443-28708, Fax: 315-443-3385, E-mail: meland@syr.edu.

Tennessee State University, The School of Graduate Studies and Research, Institute of Government, Nashville, TN 37209-1561. Offers public administration (MPA, PhD). *Accreditation:* NASPAA (one or more programs are accredited). Part-time and evening/weekend programs available. *Degree requirements:* For master's, comprehensive exam, thesis optional; for doctorate, comprehensive exam, thesis/dissertation. *Entrance requirements:* For master's, GRE General Test, minimum GPA of 2.5, writing sample; for doctorate, GRE General Test, minimum GPA of 3.25, writing sample. *Faculty research:* Total quality management and process improvement, national health care policy and administration, starting non-profit ventures, public service ethics, state education financing across the U.S. public.

Texas A&M International University, Office of Graduate Studies and Research, College of Arts and Sciences, Department of Social Sciences, Laredo, TX 78041-1900. Offers history (MA); political science (MA); public administration (MPA). *Faculty:* 9 full-time (3 women). *Students:* 11 full-time (4 women), 52 part-time (25 women); includes 61 minority (all Hispanic Americans), 2 international. Average age 32. 37 applicants. In 2009, 15 master's awarded. *Degree requirements:* For master's, thesis (for some programs). *Entrance requirements:* For master's, GRE General Test. Additional exam requirements/recommendations for international students: Required—TOEFL (minimum score 550 paper-based; 213 computer-based). *Application deadline:* For fall admission, 4/30 priority date for domestic students; for spring admission, 11/30 for domestic students. Applications are processed on a rolling basis. Application fee: $25. *Financial support:* In 2009–10, 14 students received support, including 2 research assistantships, 3 teaching assistantships. Financial award application deadline: 11/1. *Unit head:* Dr. Mohammed Ben-Ruwin, Chair, 956-328-2632, E-mail: mbenruwin@tamiu.edu. *Application contact:* Rosie Espinoza-Dickinson, Director of Admissions, 956-326-2200, Fax: 956-326-2199, E-mail: enroll@tamiu.edu.

Texas A&M University, George Bush School of Government and Public Service, College Station, TX 77843. Offers advanced international affairs (Certificate); homeland security (Certificate); international affairs (MPIA), including international economics and development, national security affairs; nonprofit management (Certificate); public service and administration (MPSA), including public management, public policy analysis. *Accreditation:* NASPAA. *Faculty:* 51. *Students:* 209 full-time (97 women), 93 part-time (43 women); includes 48 minority (15 African Americans, 5 Asian Americans or Pacific Islanders, 28 Hispanic Americans), 19 international. Average age 24. In 2009, 87 master's awarded. *Degree requirements:* For master's, summer internship. *Entrance requirements:* For master's, GRE (preferred) or GMAT. *Application deadline:* For fall admission, 1/24 for domestic and international students. Application fee: $50 ($75 for international students). Electronic applications accepted. *Expenses:* Tuition, state resident: full-time $3991; part-time $221.74 per credit hour. Tuition, nonresident: full-time $9049; part-time $502.74 per credit hour. *Financial support:* In 2009–10, fellowships (averaging $11,000 per year), research assistantships (averaging $11,250 per year) were awarded; career-related internships or fieldwork, Federal Work-Study, and institutionally sponsored loans also available. Financial award application deadline: 2/1; financial award applicants required to submit FAFSA. *Faculty research:* Public policy, presidential studies, public leadership, economic policy, social policy. *Unit head:* A. Benton Cocanougher, Interim Dean, 979-862-8842, E-mail: bushschool@tamu.edu. *Application contact:* Kathryn Meyer, Recruitment and Placement Officer, 979-458-4767, Fax: 979-845-4155, E-mail: admissions@bushschool.tamu.edu.

Texas A&M University–Corpus Christi, Graduate Studies and Research, College of Liberal Arts, Corpus Christi, TX 78412-5503. Offers English (MA); history (MA); psychology (MA); public administration (MPA); studio arts (MA, MFA). Part-time and evening/weekend programs available. *Degree requirements:* For master's, comprehensive exam, thesis (for some programs). *Entrance requirements:* For master's, GRE General Test. Additional exam requirements/recommendations for international students: Required—TOEFL. Electronic applications accepted.

Texas Southern University, School of Public Affairs, Program in Public Administration, Houston, TX 77004-4584. Offers MPA. *Faculty:* 7 full-time (2 women), 4 part-time/adjunct (0 women). *Students:* 57 full-time (35 women), 20 part-time (16 women); includes 65 African Americans, 2 Asian Americans or Pacific Islanders, 2 Hispanic Americans, 1 international. Average age 30. 38 applicants, 100% accepted, 33 enrolled. In 2009, 19 master's awarded. *Degree requirements:* For master's, comprehensive exam, thesis optional. *Entrance requirements:* For master's, GRE General Test, minimum GPA of 2.5. Additional exam requirements/recommendations for international students: Required—TOEFL. *Application deadline:* For fall admission, 7/1 for domestic and international students; for spring admission, 11/1 for domestic and international students. Applications are processed on a rolling basis. Application fee: $50 ($75 for international students). Electronic applications accepted. *Expenses:* Tuition, state resident: full-time $1805; part-time $100 per credit hour. Tuition, nonresident: full-time $6470; part-time $343 per credit hour. Tuition and fees vary according to course level, course load and degree level. *Financial support:* In 2009–10, 1 research assistantship (averaging $4,000 per year), 7 teaching assistantships (averaging $6,600 per year) were awarded; fellowships, career-related internships or fieldwork, scholarships/grants, and unspecified assistantships also available. Financial award application deadline: 5/1. *Unit head:* Dr. Franklin Jones, Chair, 713-313-7313, E-mail: jones_fd@tsu.edu. *Application contact:* Dr. Franklin Jones, Chair, 713-313-7313, E-mail: jones_fd@tsu.edu.

Texas State University–San Marcos, Graduate School, College of Liberal Arts, Department of Political Science, Program in Public Administration, San Marcos, TX 78666. Offers MPA. *Accreditation:* NASPAA. Part-time and evening/weekend programs available. *Faculty:* 9 full-time (4 women). *Students:* 44 full-time (23 women), 125 part-time (60 women); includes 75 minority (25 African Americans, 2 American Indian/Alaska Native, 3 Asian Americans or Pacific Islanders, 45 Hispanic Americans), 1 international. Average age 30. 62 applicants, 97% accepted, 47 enrolled. In 2009, 30 master's awarded. *Degree requirements:* For master's, comprehensive exam, applied research project. *Entrance requirements:* For master's, GRE General Test, minimum GPA of 2.75 in last 60 hours of course work. Additional exam requirements/recommendations for international students: Required—TOEFL (minimum score 550 paper-based; 213 computer-based), TWE. *Application deadline:* For fall admission, 6/15 priority date for domestic students, 6/1 priority date for international students; for spring admission, 10/15 priority date for domestic students, 10/1 priority date for international students. Applications are processed on a rolling basis. Application fee: $40 ($90 for international students). Electronic applications accepted. *Expenses:* Tuition, state resident: full-time $5784; part-time $241 per credit hour. Tuition, nonresident: part-time $551 per credit hour. Required fees: $1728; $48 per credit hour. $306. Tuition and fees vary according to course load. *Financial support:* In 2009–10, 69 students received support, including 6 teaching assistantships (averaging $5,217 per year); research assistantships, career-related internships or fieldwork, Federal Work-Study, and institutionally sponsored loans also available. Support available to part-time students. Financial award application deadline: 4/1; financial award applicants required to submit FAFSA. *Faculty research:* Ethics in public management, total quality management in government, Texas state budgeting, pragmatism and public administration, minority economic development. *Unit head:* Dr. Patricia Shields, Graduate Advisor, 512-245-2143, Fax: 512-245-7815, E-mail: ps07@txstate.edu. *Application contact:* Dr. J. Michael Willoughby, Dean of Graduate School, 512-245-2581, Fax: 512-245-8365, E-mail: gradcollege@txstate.edu.

Texas Tech University, Graduate School, College of Arts and Sciences, Department of Political Science, Lubbock, TX 79409. Offers political science (MA, PhD); public administration (MPA); JD/MPA; MPA/MA. *Accreditation:* NASPAA (one or more programs are accredited). Part-time programs available. *Faculty:* 13 full-time (3 women). *Students:* 62 full-time (28 women), 16 part-time (4 women); includes 14 minority (1 African American, 2 American Indian/Alaska Native, 2 Asian Americans or Pacific Islanders, 9 Hispanic Americans), 12 international. Average age 28. 103 applicants, 53% accepted, 23 enrolled. In 2009, 29 master's, 1 doctorate awarded. *Degree requirements:* For master's, thesis or alternative; for doctorate, thesis/dissertation. *Entrance requirements:* For master's and doctorate, GRE General Test. Additional exam requirements/recommendations for international students: Required—TOEFL (minimum score 550 paper-based; 213 computer-based). *Application deadline:* For fall admission, 3/1 priority date for international students; for spring admission, 11/1 priority date for international students. Applications are processed on a rolling basis. Application fee: $50 ($75 for international students). Electronic applications accepted. *Expenses:* Tuition, state resident: full-time $5100; part-time $213 per credit hour. Tuition, nonresident: full-time $11,748; part-time $490 per credit hour. Required fees: $2298; $50 per credit hour. $555 per semester. *Financial support:* In 2009–10, 7 teaching assistantships with partial tuition reimbursements (averaging $14,691 per year) were awarded; research assistantships with partial tuition reimbursements, Federal Work-Study and institutionally sponsored loans also available. Support available to part-time students. Financial award application deadline: 4/15; financial award applicants required to submit FAFSA. *Faculty research:* State politics, American institutions and behavior, Asian politics, international and comparative political relations and economics, public administration and organizations. Total annual research expenditures: $18,150. *Unit head:* Dr. Dennis Patterson, Chair, 806-742-3121, Fax: 806-742-0850, E-mail: dennis.patterson@ttu.edu. *Application contact:* Dr. Frank Thames, Associate Chair, 806-742-4049, Fax: 806-742-0850, E-mail: frank.thames@ttu.edu.

Thomas Edison State College, School of Business and Management, Program in Public Service Leadership, Trenton, NJ 08608-1176. Offers Graduate Certificate. Part-time programs available. Postbaccalaureate distance learning degree programs offered (no on-campus study). *Entrance requirements:* Additional exam requirements/recommendations for international students: Required—TOEFL (minimum score 550 paper-based; 213 computer-based; 79 iBT). *Application deadline:* For fall admission, 8/15 priority date for domestic and international students; for winter admission, 11/15 priority date for domestic and international students; for spring admission, 2/15 priority date for domestic and international students. Applications are processed on a rolling basis. Application fee: $75. Electronic applications accepted. *Expenses:* Tuition, area resident: Part-time $479 per credit. Tuition, state resident: part-time $479 per credit. Tuition, nonresident: part-time $479 per credit. *Financial support:* Applicants required to submit FAFSA. *Unit head:* Dr. Joseph Santora, Dean, School of Business and Management, 609-984-1130, Fax: 609-984-3898, E-mail: infor@tesc.edu. *Application contact:* David Hoftiezer, Director of Admissions, 888-442-8372, Fax: 609-984-8447, E-mail: admissions@tesc.edu.

Troy University, Graduate School, College of Arts and Sciences, Program in Public Administration, Troy, AL 36082. Offers education (MPA); environmental management (MPA); government contracting (MPA); health care administration (MPA); justice administration (MPA); management information systems (MPA); national security affairs (MPA); nonprofit management (MPA); public human resources management (MPA); public management (MPA). *Accreditation:* NASPAA. Part-time and evening/weekend programs available. Postbaccalaureate distance learning degree programs offered (no on-campus study). *Students:* 239 full-time (161 women), 652 part-time (416 women); includes 596 minority (547 African Americans, 11 American Indian/Alaska Native, 6 Asian Americans or Pacific Islanders, 32 Hispanic Americans). Average age 34. 415 applicants, 80% accepted. In 2009, 247 master's awarded. *Degree requirements:* For master's, capstone course, research methodologies course. *Entrance requirements:* For master's, GRE, MAT or GMAT, minimum undergraduate GPA of 2.5, letter of recommendation. Additional exam requirements/recommendations for international students: Required—TOEFL (minimum score 523 paper-based; 193 computer-based; 70 iBT), IELTS (minimum score 6). *Application deadline:* Applications are processed on a rolling basis. Application fee: $50. Electronic applications accepted. *Financial support:* Available to part-time students. Applicants required to submit FAFSA. *Unit head:* Dr. Ellen Rosell, Chairman, 334-670-3758, Fax: 334-670-5647, E-mail: erosell@troy.edu. *Application contact:* Brenda K. Campbell, Director of Graduate Admissions, 334-670-3178, Fax: 334-670-3733, E-mail: bcamp@troy.edu.

Troy University, Graduate School, College of Business, Program in Management, Troy, AL 36082. Offers healthcare management (MSM); human resources management (MSM); information systems (MSM); international hospitality management (MSM); international management (MSM); leadership and organizational effectiveness (MSM); public management (MS, MSM). *Accreditation:* ACBSP. Evening/weekend programs available. *Students:* 193 full-time (130 women), 575 part-time (374 women); includes 473 minority (417 African Americans, 12 American Indian/Alaska Native, 20 Asian Americans or Pacific Islanders, 24 Hispanic Americans). Average age 35. 275 applicants, 91% accepted. In 2009, 332 master's awarded. *Degree requirements:* For master's, thesis or alternative. *Entrance requirements:* For master's, GMAT (minimum score 500) or GRE General Test (minimum score 900), minimum GPA of 2.5; letter of recommendation. Additional exam requirements/recommendations for international students: Required—TOEFL (minimum score 523 paper-based; 193 computer-based; 70 iBT), IELTS, or ACT Compass ESL (minimum score 270 on Listening, Reading, and Grammar with no individual score below 85 and a minimum score of 8 out of 12 on writing test). *Application deadline:* Applications are processed on a rolling basis. Application fee: $50. Electronic applications accepted. *Expenses:* Contact institution. *Unit head:* Dr. Henry M. Findley, Interim Chair/Professor, 334-670-3271, Fax: 334-670-3599, E-mail: hfindley@troy.edu. *Application contact:* Brenda K. Campbell, Director of Graduate Admissions, 334-670-3178, Fax: 334-670-3733, E-mail: bcamp@troy.edu.

Troy University, Graduate School, College of Education, Program in Postsecondary Education, Troy, AL 36082. Offers adult education (M Ed); biology (M Ed); criminal justice (M Ed); english (M Ed); foundations of education (M Ed); general science (M Ed); higher education administration (M Ed); history (M Ed); instructional technology (M Ed); mathematics (M Ed); music industry (M Ed); physical fitness (M Ed); political science (M Ed); public administration (M Ed); social science (M Ed); teaching english (M Ed). Also offered through the University College. *Accreditation:* NCATE. Part-time and evening/weekend programs available. *Students:* 267 full-time (192 women), 381 part-time (293 women); includes 326 minority (309 African Americans, 4 American Indian/Alaska Native, 5 Asian Americans or Pacific Islanders, 8 Hispanic Americans). Average age 34. 343 applicants, 90% accepted. In 2009, 480 master's awarded. *Degree requirements:* For master's, comprehensive exam, thesis. *Entrance requirements:* For master's, MAT (minimum score 385), minimum GPA of 2.5. Additional exam requirements/recommendations for international students: Required—TOEFL (minimum score 523 paper-based; 193 computer-based; 70 iBT), IELTS, or ACT Compass ESL (minimum score 270 on Listening, Reading, and Grammar with no individual score below 85 and a minimum score of 8 out of 12 on writing test). *Application deadline:* Applications are processed on a rolling basis. Application fee: $50. Electronic applications accepted. *Financial support:* Available to part-time students. Applicants required to submit FAFSA. *Unit head:* Dr. Andrew Creamer, Chair, 334-670-3350, E-mail: drcreamer@troy.edu. *Application contact:* Brenda K. Campbell, Director of Graduate Admissions, 334-670-3178, Fax: 334-670-3733, E-mail: bcamp@troy.edu.

Tufts University, Graduate School of Arts and Sciences, Graduate Certificate Programs, Program Evaluation Program, Medford, MA 02155. Offers Certificate. Part-time and evening/weekend programs available. Electronic applications accepted. *Expenses:* Contact institution.

TUI University, College of Business Administration, Program in Business Administration, Cypress, CA 90630. Offers business administration (PhD); conflict and negotiation management (MBA); criminal justice administration (MBA); entrepreneurship (MBA); finance (MBA); general management (MBA); government accounting (MBA); human resource management (MBA); information security and digital assurance management (MBA); information technology management (MBA); international business (MBA); logistics management (MBA); marketing (MBA); project management (MBA); public management (MBA); quality management (MBA); strategic leadership (MBA). Part-time and evening/weekend programs available. Postbaccalaureate distance learning degree programs offered (no on-campus study). *Degree requirements:* For doctorate, comprehensive exam, thesis/dissertation, defense of dissertation. *Entrance requirements:* For master's, minimum GPA of 2.5 (students with GPA 3.0 or greater may transfer up to 30% of graduate level credits); for doctorate, minimum GPA of 3.4, curriculum vitae, course work in research methods or statistics. Additional exam requirements/recommendations for international students: Required—TOEFL. Electronic applications accepted.

Université de Moncton, Faculty of Arts and Social Sciences, Department of Public Administration, Moncton, NB E1A 3E9, Canada. Offers MPA, LL B/MPA. Part-time and evening/weekend programs available. *Degree requirements:* For master's, one foreign language. *Entrance requirements:* For master's, minimum GPA of 3.0. *Faculty research:* Public sector reform, privatization, economic modeling, public policy.

Université du Québec à Montréal, Graduate Programs, Program in Urban Analysis and Management, Montréal, QC H3C 3P8, Canada. Offers MA. Part-time programs available. *Entrance requirements:* For master's, appropriate bachelor's degree or equivalent and proficiency in French.

Université du Québec, École nationale d'administration publique, Graduate Program in Public Administration, Diploma Program in Public Administration, Quebec, QC G1K 9E5, Canada. Offers Diploma.

Université du Québec, École nationale d'administration publique, Graduate Program in Public Administration, Doctorate Program in Public Administration, Quebec, QC G1K 9E5, Canada. Offers PhD.

University at Albany, State University of New York, Nelson A. Rockefeller College of Public Affairs and Policy, Department of Public Administration and Policy, Albany, NY 12222-0001. Offers administrative behavior (PhD); comparative and development administration (MPA, PhD); human resources (MPA); legislative administration (MPA); nonprofit leadership and management (Certificate); planning and policy analysis (CAS); policy analysis (MPA); program analysis and evaluation (PhD); public affairs and policy (MA); public finance (MPA, PhD); public management (MPA, PhD); women and public policy (Certificate); JD/MPA. *Accreditation:* NASPAA (one or more programs are accredited). *Degree requirements:* For doctorate, one foreign language, thesis/dissertation. *Entrance requirements:* For doctorate, GRE General Test. Additional exam requirements/recommendations for international students: Required—TOEFL (minimum score 550 paper-based; 213 computer-based). Electronic applications accepted.

The University of Akron, Graduate School, Buchtel College of Arts and Sciences, Department of Public Administration and Urban Studies, Program in Public Administration, Akron, OH 44325. Offers MPA, JD/MPA. *Accreditation:* NASPAA. *Students:* 52 full-time (23 women), 39 part-time (26 women); includes 23 minority (20 African Americans, 3 Asian Americans or Pacific Islanders), 16 international. Average age 35. 48 applicants, 92% accepted, 34 enrolled. In 2009, 24 master's awarded. *Degree requirements:* For master's, thesis optional. *Entrance requirements:* For master's, GRE, GMAT, LSAT, MAT (if undergraduate cumulative GPA less than 3.0), minimum GPA of 3.0, resume, letters of recommendation. Additional exam requirements/recommendations for international students: Required—TOEFL (minimum score 550 paper-based; 213 computer-based; 79 iBT), Michigan English Language Assessment Battery. *Application deadline:* For fall admission, 4/1 for domestic and international students; for spring admission, 11/15 for domestic and international students. Applications are processed on a rolling basis. Application fee: $30 ($40 for international students). Electronic applications accepted. *Expenses:* Tuition, state resident: full-time $6570; part-time $365 per credit hour. Tuition, nonresident: full-time $11,250; part-time $625 per credit hour. *Unit head:* Dr. Raymond Cox, Chair, 330-972-7616, E-mail: rcox@uakron.edu. *Application contact:* Dr. RaJade Berry, Information Contact, 330-972-5407, E-mail: rmberry@uakron.edu.

The University of Alabama, Graduate School, College of Arts and Sciences, Department of Political Science, Tuscaloosa, AL 35487. Offers political science (MA, PhD); public administration (MPA). Part-time programs available. *Faculty:* 15 full-time (4 women). *Students:* 50 full-time (18 women), 13 part-time (7 women); includes 12 minority (6 African Americans, 1 American Indian/Alaska Native, 2 Asian Americans or Pacific Islanders, 3 Hispanic Americans), 6 international. Average age 29. 70 applicants, 44% accepted, 21 enrolled. In 2009, 3 master's, 3 doctorates awarded. Terminal master's awarded for partial completion of doctoral program. *Median time to degree:* Of those who began their doctoral program in fall 2001, 100% received their degree in 8 years or less. *Degree requirements:* For master's, thesis optional; for doctorate, comprehensive exam, thesis/dissertation. *Entrance requirements:* For master's and doctorate, GRE (minimum score: 1000), minimum undergraduate GPA of 3.0. Additional exam requirements/recommendations for international students: Required—TOEFL. *Application deadline:* For fall admission, 6/30 for domestic and international students; for spring admission, 10/15 for domestic and international students. Applications are processed on a rolling basis. Application fee: $50 ($60 for international students). Electronic applications accepted. *Expenses:* Tuition, state resident: full-time $7000. Tuition, nonresident: full-time $19,200. *Financial support:* In 2009–10, 15 students received support, including teaching assistantships with full tuition reimbursements available (averaging $10,908 per year); fellowships, career-related internships or fieldwork and Federal Work-Study also available. Financial award application deadline: 2/15. *Faculty research:* American politics, comparative politics, international relations, public administration, political theory. Total annual research expenditures: $20,223. *Unit head:* Dr. Carol A. Cassel, Chair and Professor, 205-348-5981, Fax: 205-348-5298, E-mail: ccassel@tenhoor.as.ua.edu. *Application contact:* Dr. Joseph Smith, Graduate Advisor, 205-348-3806, Fax: 205-348-5248, E-mail: josmith@bama.ua.edu.

The University of Alabama at Birmingham, College of Arts and Sciences, Program in Public Administration, Birmingham, AL 35294. Offers MPA. *Accreditation:* NASPAA. *Entrance requirements:* For master's, GRE General Test or MAT. Electronic applications accepted.

University of Alaska Anchorage, College of Business and Public Policy, Program in Public Administration, Anchorage, AK 99508. Offers MPA. Part-time programs available. *Degree requirements:* For master's, comprehensive exam, thesis or alternative, capstone project. *Entrance requirements:* For master's, GRE General Test. Additional exam requirements/recommendations for international students: Required—TOEFL (minimum score 550 paper-based; 213 computer-based). *Faculty research:* Policy analysis, policy and administration issues in the North, hypothetical government policies, public management in health care.

University of Alaska Southeast, Graduate Programs, Program in Public Administration, Juneau, AK 99801. Offers MPA. Part-time and evening/weekend programs available. Postbaccalaureate distance learning degree programs offered (no on-campus study). *Degree requirements:* For master's, capstone course or thesis. *Entrance requirements:* For master's, minimum GPA of 3.0, curriculum vitae, letters of reference. Electronic applications accepted. *Faculty research:* Democratic governance, public administrative theory, local government.

The University of Arizona, Graduate College, Eller College of Management, School of Public Administration and Policy, Tucson, AZ 85721. Offers public administration (MPA); public administration and policy (PhD). *Accreditation:* NASPAA. *Students:* 37 full-time (18 women), 23 part-time (13 women); includes 10 minority (1 African American, 1 American Indian/Alaska Native, 2 Asian Americans or Pacific Islanders, 6 Hispanic Americans), 3 international. Average age 29. 76 applicants, 70% accepted, 27 enrolled. In 2009, 23 master's awarded. *Degree requirements:* For master's, internship of 400 hours; for doctorate, comprehensive exam, thesis/dissertation. *Entrance requirements:* For doctorate, GMAT or GRE, minimum graduate GPA of 3.5, letter of interest, 3 letters of recommendation, resume. Additional exam requirements/recommendations for international students: Required—TOEFL (minimum score 650 paper-based; 280 computer-based; 115 iBT). *Application deadline:* For fall admission, 2/15 priority date for domestic students, 2/15 for international students. Applications are processed on a rolling basis. Application fee: $75. Electronic applications accepted. *Expenses:* Contact institution. *Financial support:* In 2009–10, 1 research assistantship with full tuition reimbursement (averaging $9,429 per year) was awarded; teaching assistantships with full tuition reimbursements, career-related internships or fieldwork, scholarships/grants, health care benefits, tuition waivers (full and partial), and unspecified assistantships also available. Financial award application deadline: 4/15. Total annual research expenditures: $18,581. *Unit head:* Dr. H. Brinton Milward, Director, 520-621-7476, Fax: 520-626-5549, E-mail: bmilward@eller.arizona.edu. *Application contact:* Pamela Adams, Administrative Associate, 520-621-3128, Fax: 520-621-5549.

University of Arkansas, Graduate School, J. William Fulbright College of Arts and Sciences, Department of Political Science, Program in Public Administration, Fayetteville, AR 72701-1201. Offers MPA. *Students:* 15 full-time (6 women), 10 part-time (7 women); includes 4 minority (2 African Americans, 1 Asian American or Pacific Islander, 1 Hispanic American), 4 international. 21 applicants, 29% accepted. In 2009, 8 master's awarded. *Degree requirements:* For master's, comprehensive exam, thesis or alternative. *Entrance requirements:* For master's, GRE General Test. Application fee: $40 ($50 for international students). *Expenses:* Tuition, state resident: full-time $7355; part-time $356.58 per hour. Tuition, nonresident: full-time $17,401; part-time $775.17 per hour. Required fees: $1203. *Financial support:* In 2009–10, 1 research assistantship was awarded; fellowships with tuition reimbursements, teaching assistantships, career-related internships or fieldwork and Federal Work-Study also available. Support available to part-time students. Financial award application deadline: 4/1; financial award applicants required to submit FAFSA. *Unit head:* Dr. Margaret Reid, Graduate Coordinator, 479-575-3356, Fax: 479-575-6432, E-mail: mreid@uark.edu. *Application contact:* Dr. Andrew Dowdle, Graduate Coordinator, 479-575-3356, Fax: 479-575-6432, E-mail: adowdle@uark.edu.

University of Arkansas at Little Rock, Graduate School, College of Professional Studies, Program in Public Administration, Little Rock, AR 72204-1099. Offers MPA. *Accreditation:*

Public Administration

University of Arkansas at Little Rock (continued)
NASPAA. Part-time and evening/weekend programs available. *Degree requirements:* For master's, comprehensive exam. *Entrance requirements:* For master's, GRE General Test or MAT, minimum GPA of 2.7. *Faculty research:* State and local administration, nonprofit management.

University of Baltimore, Graduate School, The Yale Gordon College of Liberal Arts, Doctoral Program in Public Administration, Baltimore, MD 21201-5779. Offers DPA. Part-time and evening/weekend programs available. *Degree requirements:* For doctorate, thesis/dissertation. *Entrance requirements:* For doctorate, GRE. Additional exam requirements/recommendations for international students: Required—TOEFL.

University of Baltimore, Graduate School, The Yale Gordon College of Liberal Arts, Master's Program in Public Administration, Baltimore, MD 21201-5779. Offers MPA, JD/MPA. *Accreditation:* NASPAA. Part-time and evening/weekend programs available. Postbaccalaureate distance learning degree programs offered (minimal on-campus study). *Entrance requirements:* For master's, interview, minimum GPA of 3.0. Additional exam requirements/recommendations for international students: Required—TOEFL (minimum score 550 paper-based; 213 computer-based). Electronic applications accepted. *Expenses:* Contact institution. *Faculty research:* Welfare policy, public administration ethics, bureaucratic politics, public sector budgeting, program evaluation.

University of Central Florida, College of Health and Public Affairs, Department of Public Administration, Orlando, FL 32816. Offers emergency management and homeland security (Certificate); non-profit management (MNM, Certificate); public administration (MPA, Certificate); urban and regional planning (Certificate). *Accreditation:* NASPAA. Part-time and evening/weekend programs available. *Faculty:* 11 full-time (2 women), 6 part-time/adjunct (1 woman). *Students:* 68 full-time (45 women), 235 part-time (166 women); includes 105 minority (64 African Americans, 10 Asian Americans or Pacific Islanders, 31 Hispanic Americans), 7 international. Average age 31. 184 applicants, 75% accepted, 95 enrolled. In 2009, 80 master's, 36 other advanced degrees awarded. *Degree requirements:* For master's, comprehensive exam, thesis or alternative, research report. *Entrance requirements:* For master's, GRE General Test. *Application deadline:* For fall admission, 7/1 for domestic students; for spring admission, 12/1 for domestic students. Application fee: $30. Electronic applications accepted. *Expenses:* Tuition, state resident: part-time $306.31 per credit hour. Tuition, nonresident: part-time $1099.01 per credit hour. Part-time tuition and fees vary according to degree level and program. *Financial support:* In 2009–10, 8 students received support, including 4 fellowships with partial tuition reimbursements available (averaging $10,000 per year), 2 research assistantships with partial tuition reimbursements available (averaging $3,100 per year), 3 teaching assistantships with partial tuition reimbursements available (averaging $5,200 per year); career-related internships or fieldwork, Federal Work-Study, institutionally sponsored loans, tuition waivers (partial), and unspecified assistantships also available. Financial award application deadline: 3/1; financial award applicants required to submit FAFSA. *Unit head:* Dr. MaryAnn Feldheim, Chair, 407-823-3693, Fax: 407-823-5651. *Application contact:* Dr. MaryAnn Feldheim, Chair, 407-823-3693, Fax: 407-823-5651.

University of Colorado at Colorado Springs, Graduate School, Graduate School of Public Affairs, Colorado Springs, CO 80933-7150. Offers criminal justice (MCJ); public administration (MPA). *Accreditation:* NASPAA. Part-time and evening/weekend programs available. *Faculty:* 7 full-time (2 women). *Students:* 36 full-time (19 women), 43 part-time (30 women); includes 14 minority (3 African Americans, 4 Asian Americans or Pacific Islanders, 7 Hispanic Americans). Average age 36. 34 applicants, 82% accepted, 24 enrolled. In 2009, 15 master's awarded. *Degree requirements:* For master's, internship (if no experience), capstone project. *Entrance requirements:* For master's, GRE General Test, GMAT, LSAT, minimum GPA of 3.0. *Application deadline:* For fall admission, 6/1 priority date for domestic students; for spring admission, 11/1 for domestic students. Applications are processed on a rolling basis. Application fee: $60 ($75 for international students). *Expenses:* Contact institution. *Financial support:* Career-related internships or fieldwork, Federal Work-Study, and scholarships/grants available. Support available to part-time students. Financial award application deadline: 3/1; financial award applicants required to submit FAFSA. *Unit head:* Dr. Terry Schwartz, Dean, 719-255-4047, Fax: 719-255-4183, E-mail: tschwart@uccs.edu. *Application contact:* Mary Lou Kartis, Program Assistant, 719-255-4182, Fax: 719-255-4183, E-mail: mkartis@uccs.edu.

University of Colorado Denver, Graduate School of Public Affairs, Program in Public Administration, Denver, CO 80217-3364. Offers MPA. *Accreditation:* NASPAA. Part-time and evening/weekend programs available. Postbaccalaureate distance learning degree programs offered. *Students:* 60 full-time (29 women), 254 part-time (157 women); includes 46 minority (14 African Americans, 1 American Indian/Alaska Native, 4 Asian Americans or Pacific Islanders, 27 Hispanic Americans), 18 international. 206 applicants, 80% accepted, 95 enrolled. In 2009, 128 master's awarded. *Degree requirements:* For master's, research paper. *Entrance requirements:* For master's, GRE General Test or minimum GPA of 3.0. Additional exam requirements/recommendations for international students: Required—TOEFL (minimum score 500 paper-based). *Application deadline:* For fall admission, 6/1 priority date for domestic students, 12/1 priority date for international students; for spring admission, 11/1 for domestic students, 5/1 for international students. Applications are processed on a rolling basis. Application fee: $50 ($60 for international students). *Financial support:* In 2009–10, 24 fellowships with partial tuition reimbursements, 20 research assistantships with partial tuition reimbursements, 13 teaching assistantships with partial tuition reimbursements were awarded; career-related internships or fieldwork, Federal Work-Study, institutionally sponsored loans, and scholarships/grants also available. Support available to part-time students. Financial award application deadline: 4/1; financial award applicants required to submit FAFSA. *Unit head:* Dr. Mary Guy, Program Director, 303-315-2007, Fax: 303-315-2229, E-mail: mary.guy@ucdenver.edu. *Application contact:* Antoinette Sandoval, Student Service Specialist, 303-315-2487, Fax: 303-315-2229, E-mail: antoinette.sandoval@ucdenver.edu.

University of Connecticut, Graduate School, College of Liberal Arts and Sciences, Department of Public Policy, Field of Public Administration, Storrs, CT 06269. Offers nonprofit management (Graduate Certificate); public administration (MPA); public financial management (Graduate Certificate); JD/MPA; MPA/MSW. *Accreditation:* NASPAA. *Faculty:* 10 full-time (4 women). *Students:* 45 full-time (29 women), 37 part-time (11 women); includes 12 minority (4 African Americans, 1 Asian American or Pacific Islander, 7 Hispanic Americans), 5 international. Average age 31. 79 applicants, 38% accepted, 29 enrolled. In 2009, 31 master's, 21 other advanced degrees awarded. *Degree requirements:* For master's, comprehensive exam, internship. *Entrance requirements:* For master's, GRE General Test. Additional exam requirements/recommendations for international students: Required—TOEFL (minimum score 550 paper-based; 213 computer-based). *Application deadline:* For fall admission, 2/1 priority date for domestic and international students; for spring admission, 11/1 for domestic students, 10/1 for international students. Applications are processed on a rolling basis. Application fee: $55. Electronic applications accepted. *Expenses:* Tuition, state resident: full-time $4725; part-time $525 per credit. Tuition, nonresident: full-time $12,267; part-time $1363 per credit. Required fees: $346 per semester. Tuition and fees vary according to course load. *Financial support:* In 2009–10, 23 research assistantships with full tuition reimbursements, 1 teaching assistantship with full tuition reimbursement were awarded; career-related internships or fieldwork, Federal Work-Study, scholarships/grants, health care benefits, and unspecified assistantships also available. Financial award application deadline: 2/1; financial award applicants required to submit FAFSA. *Unit head:* William Simonsen, Chairperson, 860-570-9045, E-mail: william.simonsen@uconn.edu. *Application contact:* Valerie Rogers, Program Director, 860-570-9047, Fax: 860-570-9114, E-mail: valerie.rogers@uconn.edu.

University of Dayton, Graduate School, College of Arts and Sciences, Program in Public Administration, Dayton, OH 45469-1300. Offers MPA. *Accreditation:* NASPAA. Part-time and evening/weekend programs available. *Faculty:* 5 full-time (2 women), 5 part-time/adjunct (2 women). *Students:* 24 full-time (17 women), 20 part-time (11 women); includes 8 minority (5 African Americans, 2 Asian Americans or Pacific Islanders, 1 Hispanic American), 1 international. Average age 31. 27 applicants, 56% accepted, 10 enrolled. In 2009, 18 master's awarded. *Degree requirements:* For master's, internship or public service project. *Entrance requirements:* For master's, GRE General Test. Additional exam requirements/recommendations for international students: Required—TOEFL (minimum score 550 paper-based; 213 computer-based; 80 iBT). *Application deadline:* For fall admission, 4/1 priority date for domestic students, 3/1 priority date for international students; for winter admission, 7/1 priority date for international students; for spring admission, 1/1 priority date for international students. Applications are processed on a rolling basis. Application fee: $0 ($50 for international students). Electronic applications accepted. *Expenses:* Tuition: Full-time $8412; part-time $701 per credit hour. Required fees: $325; $65 per course. $25 per semester. Tuition and fees vary according to course load, degree level and program. *Financial support:* In 2009–10, 3 research assistantships with full tuition reimbursements (averaging $9,500 per year) were awarded; career-related internships or fieldwork, institutionally sponsored loans, health care benefits, and unspecified assistantships also available. Financial award applicants required to submit FAFSA. *Faculty research:* Ethics, leadership, state government, environmental policy, welfare reforms, state legislatures. *Unit head:* Dr. Grant Neeley, Director, MPA Program, 937-229-3626, Fax: 937-229-1400, E-mail: grant.neeley@notes.udayton.edu. *Application contact:* Graduate Admissions, 937-229-4411, Fax: 937-229-4729, E-mail: gradadmission@udayton.edu.

University of Delaware, College of Human Services, Education and Public Policy, School of Urban Affairs and Public Policy, Program in Public Administration, Newark, DE 19716. Offers MPA. *Accreditation:* NASPAA. Part-time and evening/weekend programs available. *Degree requirements:* For master's, internship or thesis. *Entrance requirements:* For master's, GRE General Test. Additional exam requirements/recommendations for international students: Required—TOEFL. Electronic applications accepted. *Faculty research:* State and local management, community development and nonprofit leadership, drug and alcohol epidemiology, fiscal and financial policy, transportation impacts and management.

See Close-Up on page 1193.

University of Evansville, Center for Adult Education, Evansville, IN 47722. Offers public service administration (MS). Part-time and evening/weekend programs available. *Faculty:* 4 full-time (2 women), 5 part-time/adjunct (3 women). *Students:* 72 full-time (50 women); includes 3 minority (all African Americans), 1 international. Average age 37. 33 applicants, 100% accepted, 28 enrolled. In 2009, 31 master's awarded. *Entrance requirements:* For master's, GRE or MAT, minimum undergraduate GPA of 3.0, resume, minimum of 3 years work experience, 2 letters of reference. Additional exam requirements/recommendations for international students: Required—TOEFL (minimum score 527 paper-based; 71 iBT). *Application deadline:* For fall admission, 7/15 priority date for domestic students; for spring admission, 11/30 priority date for domestic students. Applications are processed on a rolling basis. Application fee: $35. *Expenses:* Tuition: Full-time $7470. Tuition and fees vary according to course load, degree level and program. *Financial support:* In 2009–10, 12 students received support. Application deadline: 6/1. *Unit head:* Carla S. Doty, Director of Continuing Education, 812-488-2981, Fax: 812-488-2432, E-mail: cd39@evansville.edu. *Application contact:* Carla S. Doty, Director of Continuing Education, 812-488-2981, Fax: 812-488-2432, E-mail: cd39@evansville.edu.

The University of Findlay, Graduate and Professional Studies, College of Business, Findlay, OH 45840-3653. Offers financial management (MBA); human resource management (MBA); international management (MBA); management (MBA); marketing (MBA); public management (MBA). Part-time and evening/weekend programs available. Postbaccalaureate distance learning degree programs offered (no on-campus study). *Degree requirements:* For master's, thesis, cumulative project. *Entrance requirements:* For master's, GMAT, minimum undergraduate GPA of 3.0 in last 64 hours of course work. Additional exam requirements/recommendations for international students: Required—TOEFL (minimum score 550 paper-based; 213 computer-based; 80 iBT). Electronic applications accepted. *Expenses:* Contact institution. *Faculty research:* Health care management, operations and logistics management.

University of Georgia, School of Public and International Affairs, Department of Public Administration and Policy, Athens, GA 30602. Offers public administration (MPA, PhD). *Accreditation:* NASPAA (one or more programs are accredited). *Faculty:* 16 full-time (3 women), 1 part-time/adjunct (0 women). *Students:* 125 full-time (63 women), 42 part-time (26 women); includes 20 African Americans, 2 Asian Americans or Pacific Islanders, 5 Hispanic Americans, 16 international. 225 applicants, 44% accepted, 65 enrolled. In 2009, 46 master's, 10 doctorates awarded. *Degree requirements:* For master's, internship; for doctorate, thesis/dissertation. *Entrance requirements:* For master's and doctorate, GRE General Test. *Application deadline:* For fall admission, 7/1 priority date for domestic students; for spring admission, 11/15 for domestic students. Application fee: $50. Electronic applications accepted. *Expenses:* Tuition, state resident: full-time $6000; part-time $250 per credit hour. Tuition, nonresident: full-time $20,904; part-time $871 per credit hour. Required fees: $730 per semester. *Financial support:* Fellowships, research assistantships, teaching assistantships, unspecified assistantships available. *Unit head:* Dr. J. Edward Kellough, Head, 706-542-0488, Fax: 706-583-0610, E-mail: kellough@uga.edu. *Application contact:* Dr. Vicky M. Wilkins, Graduate Coordinator, 706-542-2648, Fax: 706-583-0610, E-mail: vwilkins@uga.edu.

University of Guam, Office of Graduate Studies, School of Business and Public Administration, Public Administration Program, Mangilao, GU 96923. Offers MPA. *Entrance requirements:* For master's, GRE General Test. Additional exam requirements/recommendations for international students: Required—TOEFL.

University of Guelph, Graduate Program Services, College of Social and Applied Human Sciences, Department of Political Science, Guelph, ON N1G 2W1, Canada. Offers comparative politics (MA); international development (MA); political science (MA); public policy and public administration (MA); the Americas (Canada emphasis) (MA). MA in public policy and public administration offered in collaboration with Department of Political Science of McMaster University. *Degree requirements:* For master's, thesis or paper. *Entrance requirements:* For master's, minimum B average during previous 2 years of course work, 4 year Honours Degree in Political Science. Additional exam requirements/recommendations for international students: Required—TOEFL. Electronic applications accepted. *Faculty research:* Political ethics, constitutional power.

University of Hawaii at Manoa, Graduate Division, College of Social Sciences, Department of Public Administration, Honolulu, HI 96822. Offers MPA, Graduate Certificate. Part-time programs available. *Faculty:* 8 full-time (2 women). *Students:* 28 full-time (17 women), 24 part-time (14 women); includes 23 minority (1 African American, 22 Asian Americans or Pacific Islanders), 10 international. Average age 33. 76 applicants, 58% accepted, 35 enrolled. In 2009, 26 master's awarded. *Degree requirements:* For master's, thesis optional, practicum. *Entrance requirements:* Additional exam requirements/recommendations for international students: Required—TOEFL (minimum score 540 paper-based; 207 computer-based; 76 iBT), IELTS (minimum score 5). *Application deadline:* For fall admission, 3/1 for domestic and international students. Application fee: $60. *Expenses:* Tuition, state resident: full-time $8900; part-time $372 per credit. Tuition, nonresident: full-time $21,400; part-time $898 per credit. Required fees: $207 per semester. *Financial support:* In 2009–10, 4 students received support, including 11 fellowships (averaging $2,662 per year), 1 teaching assistantship (averaging $14,382 per year); career-related internships or fieldwork, Federal Work-Study, institutionally sponsored loans, and tuition waivers (full and partial) also available. Support available to part-time students. *Faculty research:* Public sector finance and the budget process, collaboration between sectors, organizational problem solving and communication processes, system reform in government organizations, public policy analysis. *Application contact:* Richard Pratt, Graduate Chair, 808-956-8260, Fax: 808-956-9571, E-mail: pratt@hawaii.edu.

University of Idaho, College of Graduate Studies, College of Letters, Arts and Social Sciences, Department of Political Science and Public Affairs Research, Program in Public Administration, Moscow, ID 83844-2282. Offers MPA. *Students:* 2 full-time, 10 part-time. In

2009, 7 master's awarded. *Entrance requirements:* For master's, minimum GPA of 2.8. *Application deadline:* For fall admission, 8/1 for domestic students; for spring admission, 12/15 for domestic students. Application fee: $55 ($60 for international students). *Expenses:* Tuition, state resident: full-time $6120. Tuition, nonresident: full-time $17,712. *Financial support:* Application deadline: 2/15. *Unit head:* Dr. Donald Wayne Crowley, Chair, 208-885-6328. *Application contact:* Dr. Donald Wayne Crowley, Chair, 208-885-6328.

University of Illinois at Chicago, Graduate College, College of Urban Planning and Public Affairs, Program in Public Administration, Chicago, IL 60607-7128. Offers MPA, PhD. *Accreditation:* NASPAA (one or more programs are accredited). Part-time and evening/weekend programs available. Terminal master's awarded for partial completion of doctoral program. *Degree requirements:* For master's, internship/project. *Entrance requirements:* For master's, GRE General Test, minimum GPA of 3.0. Additional exam requirements/recommendations for international students: Required—TOEFL. Electronic applications accepted. *Faculty research:* Public management, economic development, public personnel.

University of Illinois at Springfield, Graduate Programs, College of Public Affairs and Administration, Program in Public Administration, Springfield, IL 62703-5407. Offers MPA, DPA. *Accreditation:* NASPAA. Part-time and evening/weekend programs available. Postbaccalaureate distance learning degree programs offered (no on-campus study). *Faculty:* 6 full-time (3 women), 5 part-time/adjunct (2 women). *Students:* 51 full-time (31 women), 136 part-time (70 women); includes 42 minority (31 African Americans, 8 Asian Americans or Pacific Islanders, 3 Hispanic Americans), 4 international. Average age 34. 182 applicants, 46% accepted, 73 enrolled. In 2009, 57 master's, 6 doctorates awarded. *Degree requirements:* For master's, thesis or seminar; for doctorate, comprehensive exam, thesis/dissertation. *Entrance requirements:* For master's, minimum undergraduate GPA of 2.5, resume, career goals statement; for doctorate, GRE, minimum graduate GPA of 3.25; writing sample; 3 letters of reference; interview. Additional exam requirements/recommendations for international students: Required—TOEFL (minimum score 550 paper-based; 213 computer-based). Application fee: $50 ($60 for international students). Electronic applications accepted. *Expenses:* Tuition, state resident: full-time $6390; part-time $266.25 per credit hour. Tuition, nonresident: full-time $14,226; part-time $592.75 per credit hour. Required fees: $2044; $14.36 per credit hour. $722.50 per term. *Financial support:* In 2009–10, research assistantships with full tuition reimbursements (averaging $8,109 per year), teaching assistantships with full tuition reimbursements (averaging $8,109 per year) were awarded; career-related internships or fieldwork, Federal Work-Study, scholarships/grants, health care benefits, and unspecified assistantships also available. Support available to part-time students. Financial award application deadline: 11/15; financial award applicants required to submit FAFSA. *Unit head:* Dr. Will Miller, Program Administrator, 217-206-8361, E-mail: wmill3@uis.edu. *Application contact:* Dr. Will Miller, Program Administrator, 217-206-8361, E-mail: wmill3@uis.edu.

The University of Kansas, Graduate Studies, College of Liberal Arts and Sciences, Department of Public Administration, Lawrence, KS 66045-3129. Offers MPA, PhD, JD/MPA, MUP/MPA. *Accreditation:* NASPAA. Part-time and evening/weekend programs available. *Faculty:* 10 full-time (5 women). *Students:* 31 full-time (13 women), 112 part-time (55 women); includes 16 minority (9 African Americans, 1 Asian American or Pacific Islander, 6 Hispanic Americans), 4 international. Average age 35. 103 applicants, 52% accepted, 40 enrolled. In 2009, 46 master's awarded. Terminal master's awarded for partial completion of doctoral program. *Degree requirements:* For master's, comprehensive exam; for doctorate, comprehensive exam, thesis/dissertation. *Entrance requirements:* For master's and doctorate, GRE General Test. Additional exam requirements/recommendations for international students: Required—TOEFL. *Application deadline:* For fall admission, 7/1 for domestic students, 5/1 for international students; for spring admission, 11/15 for domestic students, 10/1 for international students. Application fee: $45 ($55 for international students). Electronic applications accepted. *Expenses:* Tuition, state resident: full-time $6492; part-time $270.50 per credit hour. Tuition, nonresident: full-time $15,510; part-time $646.25 per credit hour. Required fees: $847; $70.56 per credit hour. Tuition and fees vary according to course load and program. *Financial support:* Fellowships, research assistantships with full and partial tuition reimbursements, teaching assistantships with full and partial tuition reimbursements, career-related internships or fieldwork, institutionally sponsored loans, scholarships/grants, and unspecified assistantships available. Financial award application deadline: 2/1. *Faculty research:* Local government, administrative ethics, non-profit management, policy studies, law and public administration, finance, budgeting. *Unit head:* Marilu Goodyear, Chair, 785-864-3527, Fax: 785-864-5208, E-mail: padept@ku.edu. *Application contact:* Ray Hummert, Administrative Director, 785-864-9097, Fax: 785-864-5208, E-mail: rhummert@ku.edu.

University of Kentucky, Graduate School, Program in Public Administration, Lexington, KY 40506-0032. Offers MPA, MPP, PhD. *Accreditation:* NASPAA (one or more programs are accredited). *Degree requirements:* For master's, comprehensive exam; for doctorate, comprehensive exam, thesis/dissertation. *Entrance requirements:* For master's, GMAT or GRE General Test, minimum undergraduate GPA of 2.75; for doctorate, GMAT or GRE General Test, minimum graduate GPA of 3.0. Additional exam requirements/recommendations for international students: Required—TOEFL (minimum score 550 paper-based; 213 computer-based). Electronic applications accepted. *Faculty research:* Public financial management, education finance and policy, health finance and policy, welfare policy, program evaluation.

University of La Verne, College of Business and Public Management, Doctoral Program in Public Administration, La Verne, CA 91750-4443. Offers DPA. Part-time programs available. *Faculty:* 22 full-time (11 women), 41 part-time/adjunct (8 women). *Students:* 62 full-time (30 women), 47 part-time (21 women); includes 60 minority (26 African Americans, 11 Asian Americans or Pacific Islanders, 23 Hispanic Americans), 8 international. Average age 43. In 2009, 12 doctorates awarded. *Degree requirements:* For doctorate, thesis/dissertation. *Entrance requirements:* For doctorate, MAT, GMAT or GRE, minimum undergraduate GPA of 3.25, interview, 3 letters of recommendation. Additional exam requirements/recommendations for international students: Required—TOEFL (minimum score 550 paper-based; 213 computer-based). Application fee: $75. *Expenses:* Contact institution. *Financial support:* Institutionally sponsored loans available. Financial award application deadline: 3/2; financial award applicants required to submit FAFSA. *Unit head:* Dr. Suzanne Beaumaster, Chairperson, 909-593-3511 Ext. 4817, E-mail: sbeaumaster@laverne.edu. *Application contact:* Erma Cross, Program and Admission Specialist, 909-593-3511 Ext. 4948, Fax: 909-392-2761, E-mail: ecross@laverne.edu.

University of La Verne, College of Business and Public Management, Master's Program in Public Administration, La Verne, CA 91750-4443. Offers MPA. *Accreditation:* NASPAA. Part-time programs available. *Faculty:* 22 full-time (11 women), 41 part-time/adjunct (8 women). *Students:* 27 full-time (15 women), 50 part-time (35 women); includes 48 minority (5 African Americans, 6 Asian Americans or Pacific Islanders, 37 Hispanic Americans). Average age 31. In 2009, 21 master's awarded. *Entrance requirements:* For master's, minimum undergraduate GPA of 2.75, 2 letters of recommendation, resume. Additional exam requirements/recommendations for international students: Required—TOEFL (minimum score 550 paper-based; 213 computer-based). *Application deadline:* Applications are processed on a rolling basis. Application fee: $50. *Expenses:* Contact institution. *Financial support:* Fellowships, research assistantships available. Financial award application deadline: 3/2; financial award applicants required to submit FAFSA. *Unit head:* Dr. Jack Meek, Chairperson, 909-593-3511 Ext. 4941, E-mail: jmeek@laverne.edu. *Application contact:* Connie Hamlow, Program and Admission Specialist, 909-593-3511 Ext. 4819, Fax: 909-392-2761, E-mail: cbpm@laverne.edu.

University of Louisville, Graduate School, College of Arts and Sciences, Department of Urban and Public Affairs, Louisville, KY 40208. Offers public administration (MPA), including human resources management, non-profit management, public policy and administration; urban and public affairs (PhD), including urban planning and development, urban policy and administration; urban planning (MUP), including administration of planning organizations, housing and community development, land use and environmental planning, spatial analysis. Part-time and evening/weekend programs available. *Faculty:* 22 full-time (7 women), 8 part-time/adjunct (1 woman). *Students:* 67 full-time (32 women), 35 part-time (20 women); includes 13 minority (10 African Americans, 1 Asian American or Pacific Islander, 2 Hispanic Americans), 6 international. Average age 31. 107 applicants, 57% accepted, 40 enrolled. In 2009, 25 master's, 5 doctorates awarded. Terminal master's awarded for partial completion of doctoral program. *Degree requirements:* For master's, internship; for doctorate, comprehensive exam, thesis/dissertation. *Entrance requirements:* For master's, GRE General Test, minimum GPA of 3.0; for doctorate, GRE General Test, master's degree in appropriate field. Additional exam requirements/recommendations for international students: Required—TOEFL (minimum score 550 paper-based; 213 computer-based; 79 iBT). *Application deadline:* For fall admission, 7/15 for domestic students; for spring admission, 11/15 for domestic students. Applications are processed on a rolling basis. Application fee: $50. Electronic applications accepted. *Financial support:* In 2009–10, 26 students received support; fellowships, research assistantships, health care benefits available. *Unit head:* Dr. David Simpson, Chair, 502-852-8019, Fax: 502-852-4558, E-mail: dave.simpson@louisville.edu. *Application contact:* Patty Sarley, Graduate Student Advisor, 502-852-7914, Fax: 502-852-4558, E-mail: plclea01@louisville.edu.

University of Maine, Graduate School, College of Business, Public Policy and Health, Department of Public Administration, Orono, ME 04469. Offers MPA, PhD. *Accreditation:* NASPAA. Part-time and evening/weekend programs available. *Faculty:* 4 full-time (1 woman), 4 part-time/adjunct (2 women). *Students:* 23 full-time (12 women), 12 part-time (7 women); includes 4 minority (all American Indian/Alaska Native), 2 international. Average age 36. 22 applicants, 77% accepted, 13 enrolled. In 2009, 9 master's awarded. *Entrance requirements:* For master's, GMAT or GRE General Test. Additional exam requirements/recommendations for international students: Required—TOEFL. *Application deadline:* Applications are processed on a rolling basis. Application fee: $65. Electronic applications accepted. *Financial support:* In 2009–10, 1 teaching assistantship with tuition reimbursement (averaging $12,790 per year) was awarded; career-related internships or fieldwork, Federal Work-Study, institutionally sponsored loans, tuition waivers (full and partial), and unspecified assistantships also available. Support available to part-time students. Financial award application deadline: 3/1. *Faculty research:* Organization theory, personnel administration, public budgeting and finance, policy analysis, environmental policy, community policy and development. *Unit head:* Dr. Carolyn Ball, Chairperson, 207-581-4142, Fax: 207-581-3039. *Application contact:* Scott G. Delcourt, Associate Dean of the Graduate School, 207-581-3291, Fax: 207-581-3232, E-mail: graduate@maine.edu.

See Display on page 1138.

University of Management and Technology, Program in Management, Arlington, VA 22209. Offers acquisition management (MS, AC); general management (MS); project management (MS, AC); public administration (MPA, MS, AC). Part-time and evening/weekend programs available. Postbaccalaureate distance learning degree programs offered (no on-campus study). *Entrance requirements:* For master's, 3 recommendations, resume. Additional exam requirements/recommendations for international students: Required—TOEFL (minimum score 550 paper-based; 213 computer-based). Electronic applications accepted.

University of Manitoba, Faculty of Graduate Studies, Faculty of Arts, Department of Political Studies, Program in Public Administration, Winnipeg, MB R3T 2N2, Canada. Offers MPA. *Degree requirements:* For master's, thesis or alternative.

University of Maryland, College Park, Academic Affairs, Joint Program in Business and Management/Public Policy, College Park, MD 20742. Offers MBA/MPM. *Accreditation:* AACSB. *Students:* 10 full-time (2 women), 2 part-time (1 woman); includes 2 minority (both Asian Americans or Pacific Islanders), 1 international. 26 applicants, 31% accepted, 8 enrolled. *Application deadline:* For fall admission, 12/15 for domestic students, 2/1 for international students; for spring admission, 10/15 for domestic students, 6/1 for international students. Applications are processed on a rolling basis. Application fee: $60. Electronic applications accepted. *Expenses:* Tuition, area resident: Part-time $471 per credit hour. Tuition, state resident: part-time $471 per credit hour. Tuition, nonresident: part-time $1016 per credit hour. Required fees: $337.04 per term. *Financial support:* In 2009–10, 6 teaching assistantships (averaging $15,006 per year) were awarded; fellowships, research assistantships also available. Financial award applicants required to submit FAFSA. *Unit head:* Dr. Charles Caramello, Dean of the Graduate School, 301-405-0358, Fax: 301-314-9305, E-mail: ccaramel@umd.edu. *Application contact:* Dean of Graduate School, 301-405-0376, Fax: 301-314-9305.

University of Maryland, College Park, Academic Affairs, School of Public Policy, Joint Program in Public Policy/Law, College Park, MD 20742. Offers JD/MPM. *Students:* 3 full-time (2 women), 1 (woman) part-time. 14 applicants, 71% accepted, 2 enrolled. *Application deadline:* For fall admission, 4/1 for domestic students, 2/1 for international students; for spring admission, 10/15 for domestic students, 6/1 for international students. Applications are processed on a rolling basis. Application fee: $60. Electronic applications accepted. *Expenses:* Tuition, area resident: Part-time $471 per credit hour. Tuition, state resident: part-time $471 per credit hour. Tuition, nonresident: part-time $1016 per credit hour. Required fees: $337.04 per term. *Financial support:* In 2009–10, 1 teaching assistantship (averaging $14,000 per year) was awarded; fellowships also available. Financial award applicants required to submit FAFSA. *Application contact:* Dean of Graduate School, 301-405-0376, Fax: 301-314-9305.

University of Maryland, College Park, Academic Affairs, School of Public Policy, Public Management Program, College Park, MD 20742. Offers MPM. *Accreditation:* NASPAA. *Students:* 61 full-time (15 women), 82 part-time (26 women); includes 15 minority (5 African Americans, 6 Asian Americans or Pacific Islanders, 4 Hispanic Americans), 108 international. 92 applicants, 68% accepted, 47 enrolled. In 2009, 18 master's awarded. *Degree requirements:* For master's, internship. *Entrance requirements:* For master's, GRE General Test, minimum GPA of 3.0. Additional exam requirements/recommendations for international students: Required—TOEFL. *Application deadline:* For fall admission, 4/1 for domestic students, 2/1 for international students; for spring admission, 10/15 for domestic students, 6/1 for international students. Applications are processed on a rolling basis. Application fee: $60. Electronic applications accepted. *Expenses:* Tuition, area resident: Part-time $471 per credit hour. Tuition, state resident: part-time $471 per credit hour. Tuition, nonresident: part-time $1016 per credit hour. Required fees: $337.04 per term. *Financial support:* In 2009–10, 2 teaching assistantships (averaging $14,803 per year) were awarded; fellowships also available. Financial award applicants required to submit FAFSA. *Faculty research:* International security, economic policy, financial management, social policy. *Unit head:* Donald Kettl, Dean, 301-405-6356, E-mail: kettl@umd.edu. *Application contact:* Dean of Graduate School, 301-405-0376, Fax: 301-314-9305.

University of Massachusetts Amherst, Graduate School, College of Social and Behavioral Sciences, Center for Public Policy and Administration, Amherst, MA 01003. Offers MPPA. Part-time programs available. *Students:* 31 full-time (21 women), 11 part-time (9 women); includes 3 minority (1 African American, 1 Asian American or Pacific Islander, 1 Hispanic American), 10 international. Average age 33. 80 applicants, 69% accepted, 16 enrolled. In 2009, 18 master's awarded. *Degree requirements:* For master's, thesis or alternative. *Entrance requirements:* For master's, GRE General Test. Additional exam requirements/recommendations for international students: Required—TOEFL (minimum score 550 paper-based; 213 computer-based; 80 iBT), IELTS (minimum score 6.5). *Application deadline:* For fall admission, 2/1 for domestic and international students. Applications are processed on a rolling basis. Application fee: $50 ($65 for international students). Electronic applications accepted. *Expenses:* Tuition, state resident: full-time $2640; part-time $110 per credit. Tuition, nonresident: full-time $9936; part-time $414 per credit. Tuition and fees vary according to course load. *Financial support:* Fellowships, research assistantships, teaching assistantships, career-related internships or fieldwork, Federal Work-Study, scholarships/grants, traineeships, health care benefits, tuition waivers (full), and unspecified assistantships available. Support available to part-time students. Financial award application deadline: 2/1. *Unit head:* Dr. M. V. Lee Badgett, Graduate Program Director, 413-545-3956, Fax: 413-545-1108. *Application contact:* Jean M. Ames, Supervisor of Admissions, 413-545-0722, Fax: 413-577-0010, E-mail: gradadm@grad.umass.edu.

Public Administration

University of Memphis, Graduate School, College of Arts and Sciences, Division of Public and Nonprofit Administration, Memphis, TN 38152. Offers nonprofit administration (MPA); public management and policy (MPA); urban management and planning (MPA). *Accreditation:* NASPAA. Part-time and evening/weekend programs available. *Faculty:* 5 full-time (2 women), 1 (woman) part-time/adjunct. *Students:* 17 full-time (11 women), 39 part-time (28 women); includes 32 minority (31 African Americans, 1 Hispanic American), 1 international. Average age 34. 32 applicants, 88% accepted, 9 enrolled. In 2009, 17 master's awarded. *Degree requirements:* For master's, comprehensive exam, thesis or alternative, internship. *Entrance requirements:* For master's, GRE General Test, GMAT, or MAT, minimum GPA of 3.0. *Application deadline:* For fall admission, 8/1 for domestic students; for spring admission, 12/1 for domestic students. Applications are processed on a rolling basis. Application fee: $35 ($60 for international students). *Expenses:* Tuition, state resident: full-time $6246; part-time $347 per credit hour. Tuition, nonresident: full-time $15,894; part-time $883 per credit hour. Required fees: $1160. Full-time tuition and fees vary according to course load, degree level and program. *Financial support:* In 2009–10, 37 students received support; fellowships, research assistantships with full tuition reimbursements available, career-related internships or fieldwork, Federal Work-Study, scholarships/grants, and unspecified assistantships available. Support available to part-time students. Financial award application deadline: 2/15; financial award applicants required to submit FAFSA. *Faculty research:* Nonprofit organization governance, local government management, community collaboration, urban problems, accountability. *Unit head:* Dr. Dorothy Norris-Tirrell, Director, 901-678-3360, Fax: 901-678-2981, E-mail: dnrrstrr@memphis.edu. *Application contact:* Dr. Charles Menifield, Graduate Admissions Coordinator, 901-678-3360, Fax: 901-678-2981, E-mail: cmenifld@memphis.edu.

University of Michigan–Dearborn, College of Arts, Sciences, and Letters, Master of Public Administration Program, Dearborn, MI 48128. Offers assessment and evaluation (Certificate); nonprofit leadership (Certificate); public administration (MPA). Part-time and evening/weekend programs available. *Faculty:* 3 full-time (1 woman), 9 part-time/adjunct (2 women). *Students:* 13 full-time (10 women), 67 part-time (43 women); includes 20 minority (16 African Americans, 1 American Indian/Alaska Native, 2 Asian Americans or Pacific Islanders, 1 Hispanic American). Average age 35. 30 applicants, 90% accepted, 24 enrolled. In 2009, 36 master's awarded. *Degree requirements:* For master's, assessment seminar. *Entrance requirements:* For master's, GRE or minimum undergraduate GPA of 3.0, 3 letters of recommendation. Additional exam requirements/recommendations for international students: Required—TOEFL, TWE. *Application deadline:* For fall admission, 8/1 for domestic students, 4/1 for international students; for winter admission, 12/1 for domestic students, 11/1 for international students; for spring admission, 4/1 for domestic students, 3/1 for international students. Applications are processed on a rolling basis. Application fee: $60. *Expenses:* Tuition, area resident: Part-time $504.10 per credit hour. Tuition, state resident: part-time $504.10 per credit hour. Tuition, nonresident: part-time $957.90 per credit hour. *Financial support:* Career-related internships or fieldwork and Federal Work-Study available. Support available to part-time students. Financial award applicants required to submit FAFSA. *Faculty research:* Federal, state, and local agency management; independent sector management; educational administration. *Unit head:* Dr. Trevor Thrall, Director, 313-593-5282, Fax: 313-583-6700, E-mail: atthrall@umich.edu. *Application contact:* Carol Ligienza, Graduate Programs Coordinator, 313-593-1183, Fax: 313-583-6700, E-mail: caslgrad@umd.umich.edu.

University of Michigan–Flint, Graduate Programs, Program in Public Administration, Flint, MI 48502-1950. Offers MPA. Part-time programs available. *Faculty:* 11 full-time (3 women), 4 part-time/adjunct (1 woman). *Students:* 25 full-time (13 women), 159 part-time (100 women); includes 34 minority (30 African Americans, 1 American Indian/Alaska Native, 3 Hispanic Americans), 10 international. Average age 34. 103 applicants, 76% accepted, 58 enrolled. In 2009, 49 master's awarded. *Degree requirements:* For master's, thesis or alternative, internship. *Entrance requirements:* For master's, minimum GPA of 3.0, 1 course each in American government, microeconomics and statistics. Additional exam requirements/recommendations for international students: Required—TOEFL (minimum score 550 paper-based; 220 computer-based), IELTS (minimum score 6.5). *Application deadline:* For fall admission, 8/1 for domestic students, 5/1 for international students; for winter admission, 11/15 for domestic students, 9/1 for international students; for spring admission, 3/15 for domestic students, 1/1 for international students. Application fee: $55. Electronic applications accepted. *Expenses:* Contact institution. *Financial support:* Career-related internships or fieldwork, Federal Work-Study, and scholarships/grants available. Support available to part-time students. Financial award application deadline: 6/1; financial award applicants required to submit FAFSA. *Unit head:* Dr. Albert Price, Director, 810-762-3470, E-mail: acprice@umflint.edu. *Application contact:* Bradley T. Maki, Director of Graduate Admissions, 810-762-3171, Fax: 810-766-6789, E-mail: bmaki@umflint.edu.

University of Missouri–Kansas City, Henry W. Bloch School of Business and Public Administration, Kansas City, MO 64110-2499. Offers accounting (MS); business administration (MBA); entrepreneurship and innovation (PhD); public affairs (MPA, PhD); JD/MBA; LL M/MPA. PhD (interdisciplinary) offered through the School of Graduate Studies. *Accreditation:* AACSB; NASPAA. Part-time and evening/weekend programs available. *Faculty:* 43 full-time (14 women), 22 part-time/adjunct (7 women). *Students:* 234 full-time (108 women), 437 part-time (193 women); includes 79 minority (33 African Americans, 27 Asian Americans or Pacific Islanders, 19 Hispanic Americans), 51 international. Average age 30. 387 applicants, 65% accepted, 222 enrolled. In 2009, 240 master's awarded. Terminal master's awarded for partial completion of doctoral program. *Entrance requirements:* For master's, GMAT, GRE, 2 writing essays, 2 references and support of employer; for doctorate, GRE, minimum GPA of 3.0. Additional exam requirements/recommendations for international students: Required—TOEFL (minimum score 550 paper-based; 213 computer-based; 80 iBT). *Application deadline:* For fall admission, 5/1 priority date for domestic and international students; for spring admission, 10/1 priority date for domestic and international students. Applications are processed on a rolling basis. Application fee: $45 ($50 for international students). Electronic applications accepted. *Expenses:* Tuition, state resident: full-time $5378; part-time $299 per credit hour. Tuition, nonresident: full-time $13,881; part-time $771 per credit hour. Required fees: $641; $71 per credit hour. Tuition and fees vary according to course load and program. *Financial support:* In 2009–10, 18 research assistantships with partial tuition reimbursements (averaging $8,766 per year), 5 teaching assistantships with partial tuition reimbursements (averaging $8,430 per year) were awarded; career-related internships or fieldwork, Federal Work-Study, institutionally sponsored loans, scholarships/grants, tuition waivers (full and partial), and unspecified assistantships also available. Support available to part-time students. Financial award application deadline: 3/1; financial award applicants required to submit FAFSA. *Faculty research:* Entrepreneurship, finance, non-profit, risk management. Total annual research expenditures: $751,788. *Unit head:* Dr. Teng-Kee Tan, Dean, 816-235-2215, Fax: 816-235-2206. *Application contact:* 816-235-1111, E-mail: admit@umkc.edu.

University of Missouri–St. Louis, College of Arts and Sciences, Department of Political Science, St. Louis, MO 63121. Offers American politics (MA); comparative politics (MA); international politics (MA); political process and behavior (MA); political science (PhD); public administration and public policy (MA); urban and regional politics (MA). Part-time and evening/weekend programs available. *Faculty:* 19 full-time (7 women), 1 (woman) part-time/adjunct. *Students:* 12 full-time (7 women), 35 part-time (17 women); includes 12 minority (8 African Americans, 1 American Indian/Alaska Native, 3 Asian Americans or Pacific Islanders), 2 international. Average age 35. 30 applicants, 57% accepted, 9 enrolled. In 2009, 6 master's, 2 doctorates awarded. Terminal master's awarded for partial completion of doctoral program. *Degree requirements:* For master's, thesis optional; for doctorate, thesis/dissertation. *Entrance requirements:* For master's, GRE General Test, 2 letters of recommendation; for doctorate,

GRE General Test, 3 letters of recommendation. Additional exam requirements/recommendations for international students: Required—TOEFL (minimum score 550 paper-based; 213 computer-based). *Application deadline:* For fall admission, 2/15 priority date for domestic and international students; for spring admission, 10/15 priority date for domestic and international students. Applications are processed on a rolling basis. Application fee: $35 ($40 for international students). Electronic applications accepted. *Expenses:* Tuition, state resident: full-time $5377; part-time $297.70 per credit hour. Tuition, nonresident: full-time $13,882; part-time $771.20 per credit hour. Required fees: $220; $12.20 per credit hour. One-time fee: $12. Tuition and fees vary according to course level, campus/location and program. *Financial support:* In 2009–10, 10 research assistantships with full and partial tuition reimbursements (averaging $10,800 per year), 5 teaching assistantships with full and partial tuition reimbursements (averaging $10,800 per year) were awarded; fellowships, career-related internships or fieldwork also available. Support available to part-time students. Financial award application deadline: 3/15; financial award applicants required to submit FAFSA. *Faculty research:* Public policy, urban politics and administration, American government. *Unit head:* Dr. Barbara Graham, Director of Graduate Studies, 314-516-5522, Fax: 314-516-5268, E-mail: umslpolisci@umsl.edu. *Application contact:* 314-516-5458, Fax: 314-516-6996, E-mail: gradadm@umsl.edu.

University of Missouri–St. Louis, Graduate School, Program in Public Policy Administration, St. Louis, MO 63121. Offers health policy (MPPA); local government management (MPPA); managing human resources and organization (MPPA); nonprofit organization management (MPPA); nonprofit organization management and leadership (Certificate); policy research and analysis (MPPA). *Accreditation:* NASPAA. Part-time and evening/weekend programs available. *Faculty:* 7 full-time (4 women), 6 part-time/adjunct (1 woman). *Students:* 20 full-time (8 women), 69 part-time (45 women); includes 13 minority (11 African Americans, 2 Hispanic Americans), 8 international. Average age 31. 85 applicants, 58% accepted, 28 enrolled. In 2009, 12 master's, 34 Certificates awarded. *Degree requirements:* For master's, exit project. *Entrance requirements:* For master's, 3 letters of recommendation. Additional exam requirements/recommendations for international students: Required—TOEFL (minimum score 550 paper-based; 213 computer-based). *Application deadline:* For fall admission, 7/1 priority date for domestic and international students; for spring admission, 12/1 priority date for domestic and international students. Applications are processed on a rolling basis. Application fee: $35 ($40 for international students). Electronic applications accepted. *Expenses:* Tuition, state resident: full-time $5377; part-time $297.70 per credit hour. Tuition, nonresident: full-time $13,882; part-time $771.20 per credit hour. Required fees: $220; $12.20 per credit hour. One-time fee: $12. Tuition and fees vary according to course level, campus/location and program. *Financial support:* In 2009–10, 2 research assistantships with full and partial tuition reimbursements (averaging $12,000 per year) were awarded; career-related internships or fieldwork also available. Financial award application deadline: 4/1; financial award applicants required to submit FAFSA. *Faculty research:* Urban policy, public finance, evaluation. *Unit head:* Dr. Brady Baybeck, Director, 314-516-5145, Fax: 314-516-5210, E-mail: baybeck@umsl.edu. *Application contact:* 314-516-5458, Fax: 314-516-6996, E-mail: gradadm@umsl.edu.

The University of Montana, Graduate School, College of Arts and Sciences, Department of Political Science, Program in Public Administration, Missoula, MT 59812-0002. Offers MPA, JD/MPA. *Degree requirements:* For master's, professional paper. *Entrance requirements:* For master's, GRE General Test.

University of Nebraska at Omaha, Graduate Studies, College of Public Affairs and Community Service, School of Public Administration, Omaha, NE 68182. Offers public administration (MPA, PhD); public management (Certificate); urban studies (MS). *Accreditation:* NASPAA (one or more programs are accredited). Part-time and evening/weekend programs available. Postbaccalaureate distance learning degree programs offered (no on-campus study). *Faculty:* 19 full-time (6 women). *Students:* 30 full-time (13 women), 187 part-time (90 women); includes 17 minority (13 African Americans, 2 Asian Americans or Pacific Islanders, 2 Hispanic Americans), 9 international. Average age 33. 157 applicants, 54% accepted, 66 enrolled. In 2009, 56 master's, 1 doctorate awarded. *Degree requirements:* For master's, comprehensive exam (for some programs), thesis (for some programs); for doctorate, comprehensive exam, thesis/dissertation. *Entrance requirements:* For master's, GRE General Test, minimum GPA of 3.0, letters of recommendation; for doctorate, GRE General Test, master's degree, minimum graduate GPA of 3.35, resume. Additional exam requirements/recommendations for international students: Required—TOEFL (minimum score 550 paper-based; 213 computer-based; 80 iBT). *Application deadline:* For fall admission, 6/1 for domestic students; for spring admission, 10/1 for domestic students. Applications are processed on a rolling basis. Application fee: $45. Electronic applications accepted. *Financial support:* In 2009–10, 76 students received support; research assistantships with tuition reimbursements available, career-related internships or fieldwork, Federal Work-Study, institutionally sponsored loans, scholarships/grants, tuition waivers (partial), and unspecified assistantships available. Support available to part-time students. Financial award application deadline: 3/1. *Unit head:* Dr. John Bartle, Director, 402-554-2625. *Application contact:* Penny Harmoney, Director, Graduate Studies, 402-554-2341, Fax: 402-554-3143, E-mail: graduate@unomaha.edu.

University of Nevada, Las Vegas, Graduate College, Greenspun College of Urban Affairs, Department of Environmental Studies, Las Vegas, NV 89154-4030. Offers crisis and emergency management (MS); environmental science (MS, PhD); non-profit management (Certificate); public administration (MPA); public affairs (PhD). Part-time programs available. *Faculty:* 6 full-time (2 women). *Students:* 39 full-time (18 women), 145 part-time (79 women); includes 47 minority (22 African Americans, 4 American Indian/Alaska Native, 3 Asian Americans or Pacific Islanders, 18 Hispanic Americans), 7 international. Average age 39. 16 applicants, 31% accepted, 2 enrolled. In 2009, 50 master's, 3 doctorates, 27 other advanced degrees awarded. *Degree requirements:* For master's, comprehensive exam (for some programs), thesis; for doctorate, comprehensive exam (for some programs), thesis/dissertation. *Entrance requirements:* Additional exam requirements/recommendations for international students: Required—TOEFL (minimum score 550 paper-based; 213 computer-based; 80 iBT), IELTS (minimum score 7). *Application deadline:* For fall admission, 6/1 priority date for domestic students, 2/15 priority date for international students; for spring admission, 11/15 priority date for domestic students, 10/1 for international students. Applications are processed on a rolling basis. Application fee: $60 ($95 for international students). Electronic applications accepted. *Financial support:* In 2009–10, 9 students received support, including 6 research assistantships with partial tuition reimbursements available (averaging $13,850 per year), 3 teaching assistantships with partial tuition reimbursements available (averaging $10,666 per year); institutionally sponsored loans, scholarships/grants, health care benefits, and unspecified assistantships also available. Financial award application deadline: 3/1. *Faculty research:* Environmental chemistry, environmental policy and management. *Unit head:* Dr. Ed Weber, Chair/ Associate Professor, 702-895-4440, Fax: 702-895-4436, E-mail: edward.weber@unlv.edu. *Application contact:* Graduate College Admissions Evaluator, 702-895-3320, Fax: 702-895-4180, E-mail: gradcollege@unlv.edu.

University of Nevada, Las Vegas, Graduate College, Greenspun College of Urban Affairs, Department of Public Administration, Las Vegas, NV 89154-6026. Offers crisis and emergency management (MS); non-profit management (Certificate); public administration (MPA); public affairs (PhD); public management (Certificate). *Accreditation:* NASPAA. Part-time and evening/weekend programs available. *Faculty:* 5 full-time (3 women), 2 part-time/adjunct (1 woman). *Students:* 30 full-time (12 women), 129 part-time (70 women); includes 39 minority (21 African Americans, 4 Asian Americans or Pacific Islanders, 14 Hispanic Americans), 3 international. Average age 38. 95 applicants, 76% accepted, 53 enrolled. In 2009, 48 master's, 28 other advanced degrees awarded. *Degree requirements:* For master's, comprehensive exam, professional paper. *Entrance requirements:* For master's, GRE General Test, GMAT or LSAT. Additional exam requirements/recommendations for international students: Required—TOEFL (minimum score 550 paper-based; 213 computer-based; 80 iBT), IELTS (minimum score 7). *Application deadline:* For fall admission, 6/1 priority date for domestic students, 5/1 for international students; for spring admission, 11/1 priority date for domestic students, 10/1 for international students. Applications are processed on a rolling basis. Application fee: $60 ($95 for international students). Electronic applications accepted. *Financial support:* In 2009–10, 8 students received support, including 6 research assistantships with partial tuition reimbursements available (averaging $12,333 per year), 2 teaching assistantships with partial tuition reimbursements available (averaging $12,000 per year); institutionally sponsored loans, scholarships/grants, health care benefits, and unspecified assistantships also available. Financial award application deadline: 3/1. *Faculty research:* Emergency and crisis management, homeland security, public and non-profit management, public policy, policy analysis and evaluation. *Unit head:* Dr. Anna Lukemeyer, Chair/ Associate Professor, 702-895-4828, Fax: 702-895-1813, E-mail: anna.lukemeyer@unlv.edu. *Application contact:* Graduate College Admissions Evaluator, 702-895-3320, Fax: 702-895-4180, E-mail: gradcollege@unlv.edu.

University of Nevada, Reno, Graduate School, College of Liberal Arts, Department of Political Science, Program in Public Administration and Policy, Reno, NV 89557. Offers public administration (MPA). *Degree requirements:* For master's, comprehensive exam, oral exam/thesis or professional paper. *Entrance requirements:* For master's, GRE General Test, GMAT, or LSAT, minimum GPA of 2.75. Additional exam requirements/recommendations for international students: Required—TOEFL (minimum score 500 paper-based; 173 computer-based; 61 iBT), IELTS (minimum score 6). Electronic applications accepted. *Faculty research:* Administrative processes and problems, public policy issues.

University of New Brunswick Fredericton, School of Graduate Studies, Faculty of Business Administration, Fredericton, NB E3B 5A3, Canada. Offers business administration (MBA); engineering management (MBA); entrepreneurship (MBA); sports and recreation management (MBA); MBA/LL B. Part-time programs available. *Faculty:* 37 full-time (13 women). *Students:* 27 full-time (10 women), 51 part-time (25 women). In 2009, 72 master's awarded. *Degree requirements:* For master's, thesis optional. *Entrance requirements:* For master's, GMAT (550 minimum score), minimum GPA of 3.0; 3-5 years work experience. Additional exam requirements/recommendations for international students: Required—TOEFL (minimum score 580 paper-based; 92 iBT), IELTS (minimum score 7), TOEFL or IELTS. *Application deadline:* For fall admission, 3/1 priority date for domestic students. Applications are processed on a rolling basis. Application fee: $50 Canadian dollars. Tuition and fees charges are reported in Canadian dollars. *Expenses:* Tuition, area resident: Full-time $5562 Canadian dollars; part-time $2781 Canadian dollars per year. Required fees: $49.75 Canadian dollars per term. *Financial support:* In 2009–10, 4 research assistantships (averaging $4,500 per year), 11 teaching assistantships (averaging $2,250 per year) were awarded. *Faculty research:* Strategic management, entrepreneurship, investment practices, marketing and supply chain management, operations management. *Unit head:* Judy Roy, Director of Graduate Studies, 506-458-7307, Fax: 506-453-3561, E-mail: jroy@unb.ca. *Application contact:* Marilyn Davis, Acting Graduate Secretary, 506-453-4766, Fax: 506-453-3561, E-mail: mbacontact@unb.ca.

University of New Hampshire, Center for Graduate and Professional Studies, Manchester, NH 03101. Offers business administration (MBA); counseling (M Ed); education (M Ed, MAT); educational administration and supervision (M Ed, CAGS); industrial statistics (Certificate); public administration (MPA); public health (MPH, Certificate); social work (MSW). Part-time and evening/weekend programs available. *Students:* 86 full-time (57 women), 150 part-time (87 women); includes 13 minority (3 African Americans, 6 Asian Americans or Pacific Islanders, 4 Hispanic Americans), 7 international. 127 applicants, 73% accepted, 60 enrolled. In 2009, 81 master's, 5 other advanced degrees awarded. *Degree requirements:* For master's, thesis or alternative. *Entrance requirements:* Additional exam requirements/recommendations for international students: Required—TOEFL (minimum score 550 paper-based; 213 computer-based; 80 iBT), TOEIC, TSE. *Application deadline:* For fall admission, 6/1 for domestic students, 4/1 for international students; for spring admission, 12/1 for domestic students. Applications are processed on a rolling basis. Application fee: $65. Electronic applications accepted. *Expenses:* Tuition, state resident: full-time $10,380; part-time $577 per credit hour. Tuition, nonresident: full-time $24,350; part-time $1002 per credit hour. Required fees: $1550; $387.50 per semester. Tuition and fees vary according to course load and program. *Financial support:* In 2009–10, 20 students received support, including 1 fellowship, 1 teaching assistantship; research assistantships, Federal Work-Study, scholarships/grants, health care benefits, and unspecified assistantships also available. Support available to part-time students. Financial award application deadline: 3/1; financial award applicants required to submit FAFSA. *Unit head:* Kate Ferreira, Director, 603-641-4313, E-mail: unhm.gradcenter@unh.edu. *Application contact:* Graduate Admissions Office, 603-862-3000, Fax: 603-862-0275, E-mail: grad.school@unh.edu.

University of New Hampshire, Graduate School, College of Liberal Arts, Department of Political Science, Program in Public Administration, Durham, NH 03824. Offers MPA. Part-time programs available. *Faculty:* 15 full-time. *Students:* 9 full-time (4 women), 31 part-time (16 women), 1 international. Average age 35. 19 applicants, 89% accepted, 8 enrolled. In 2009, 17 master's awarded. *Entrance requirements:* For master's, GMAT or GRE General Test. Additional exam requirements/recommendations for international students: Required—TOEFL (minimum score 550 paper-based; 213 computer-based; 80 iBT). *Application deadline:* For fall admission, 6/1 priority date for domestic students, 4/1 for international students; for spring admission, 12/1 for domestic students. Applications are processed on a rolling basis. Application fee: $65. Electronic applications accepted. *Expenses:* Tuition, state resident: full-time $10,380; part-time $577 per credit hour. Tuition, nonresident: full-time $24,350; part-time $1002 per credit hour. Required fees: $1550; $387.50 per semester. Tuition and fees vary according to course load and program. *Financial support:* In 2009–10, 1 student received support; fellowships, research assistantships, teaching assistantships, career-related internships or fieldwork, Federal Work-Study, scholarships/grants, and tuition waivers (full and partial) available. Support available to part-time students. Financial award application deadline: 2/15. *Unit head:* Dr. Dante Scala, Chairperson, 603-862-3225. *Application contact:* Janis Marshal, Administrative Assistant, 603-862-1750, E-mail: mpa.ma.political.science.grad@unh.edu.

University of New Haven, Graduate School, Henry C. Lee College of Criminal Justice and Forensic Sciences, National Security and Public Safety Program, West Haven, CT 06516-1916. Offers information protection and security (MS); national security (Certificate); national security administration (Certificate). Part-time and evening/weekend programs available. *Faculty:* 8 full-time (2 women), 5 part-time/adjunct (0 women). *Students:* 34 full-time (10 women), 39 part-time (21 women); includes 19 minority (4 African Americans, 1 American Indian/Alaska Native, 4 Asian Americans or Pacific Islanders, 10 Hispanic Americans), 4 international. Average age 32. 39 applicants, 100% accepted, 33 enrolled. In 2009, 51 master's, 5 other advanced degrees awarded. *Entrance requirements:* Additional exam requirements/recommendations for international students: Required—TOEFL (minimum score 520 paper-based; 190 computer-based; 70 iBT); Recommended—IELTS (minimum score 5.5). *Application deadline:* For fall admission, 5/31 for international students; for winter admission, 10/15 for international students; for spring admission, 1/15 for international students. Applications are processed on a rolling basis. Application fee: $50. Electronic applications accepted. *Expenses:* Tuition: Part-time $700 per credit. Required fees: $45 per term. One-time fee: $390 part-time. *Financial support:* Research assistantships with partial tuition reimbursements, teaching assistantships with partial tuition reimbursements, career-related internships or fieldwork, Federal Work-Study, scholarships/grants, tuition waivers, and unspecified assistantships available. Support available to part-time students. Financial award applicants required to submit FAFSA. *Unit head:* Dr. William L. Tafoya, Dean, 203-932-7260. *Application contact:* Eloise Gormley, Director of Graduate Admissions, 203-932-7449, Fax: 203-932-7137, E-mail: gradinfo@newhaven.edu.

University of New Haven, Graduate School, Henry C. Lee College of Criminal Justice and Forensic Sciences, Program in Fire Science, West Haven, CT 06516-1916. Offers emergency management (Certificate); fire administration (MS); fire science technology (Certificate); fire/arson investigation (MS, Certificate); forensic science/fire science (Certificate); public safety management (MS); public safety management (Certificate). Part-time and evening/weekend programs available. *Faculty:* 2 full-time (0 women). *Students:* 14 part-time (4 women); includes 1 minority (Hispanic American), 1 international. Average age 33. 6 applicants, 83% accepted, 3 enrolled. In 2009, 6 master's, 4 other advanced degrees awarded. *Degree requirements:* For master's, thesis or alternative. *Entrance requirements:* Additional exam requirements/

Public Administration

University of New Haven (continued)
recommendations for international students: Required—TOEFL (minimum score 520 paper-based; 190 computer-based; 70 iBT); Recommended—IELTS (minimum score 5.5). *Application deadline:* For fall admission, 5/31 for international students; for winter admission, 10/15 for international students; for spring admission, 1/15 for international students. Applications are processed on a rolling basis. Application fee: $50. Electronic applications accepted. *Expenses:* Tuition: Part-time $700 per credit. Required fees: $45 per term. One-time fee: $390 part-time. *Financial support:* Research assistantships with partial tuition reimbursements, teaching assistantships with partial tuition reimbursements, career-related internships or fieldwork, Federal Work-Study, scholarships/grants, tuition waivers, and unspecified assistantships available. Support available to part-time students. Financial award applicants required to submit FAFSA. *Unit head:* Robert E. Massicotte, Director, 203-932-7424. *Application contact:* Eloise Gormley, Director of Graduate Admissions, 203-932-7449, Fax: 203-932-7137, E-mail: gradinfo@newhaven.edu.

University of New Haven, Graduate School, School of Business, Program in Public Administration, West Haven, CT 06516-1916. Offers personnel and labor relations (MPA); public administration (MPA, Certificate), including city management (MPA), community-clinical services (MPA), health care management (MPA), long-term health care (MPA), personnel and labor relations (MPA), public administration (Certificate), public management (Certificate), public personnel management (Certificate); MBA/MPA. Part-time and evening/weekend programs available. *Faculty:* 3 full-time (1 woman), 11 part-time/adjunct (5 women). *Students:* 17 full-time (9 women), 26 part-time (14 women); includes 11 minority (9 African Americans, 1 Asian American or Pacific Islander, 1 Hispanic American), 1 international. Average age 35. 35 applicants, 94% accepted, 8 enrolled. In 2009, 9 master's, 12 other advanced degrees awarded. *Degree requirements:* For master's, thesis or alternative. *Entrance requirements:* Additional exam requirements/recommendations for international students: Required—TOEFL (minimum score 520 paper-based; 190 computer-based; 70 iBT); Recommended—IELTS (minimum score 5.5). *Application deadline:* For fall admission, 5/31 for international students; for winter admission, 10/15 for international students; for spring admission, 1/15 for international students. Applications are processed on a rolling basis. Application fee: $50. Electronic applications accepted. *Expenses:* Contact institution. *Financial support:* Research assistantships with partial tuition reimbursements, teaching assistantships with partial tuition reimbursements, career-related internships or fieldwork, Federal Work-Study, scholarships/grants, tuition waivers, and unspecified assistantships available. Support available to part-time students. Financial award application deadline: 5/1; financial award applicants required to submit FAFSA. *Unit head:* Charles Coleman, Chairman, 203-932-7375. *Application contact:* Eloise Gormley, Director of Graduate Admissions, 203-932-7449, Fax: 203-932-7137, E-mail: gradinfo@newhaven.edu.

University of New Mexico, Graduate School, School of Public Administration, Albuquerque, NM 87131-2039. Offers MPA, JD/MPA, MPA/MCRP, MSN/MPA. *Accreditation:* NASPAA (one or more programs are accredited). Part-time and evening/weekend programs available. Postbaccalaureate distance learning degree programs offered (no on-campus study). *Faculty:* 10 full-time (4 women), 4 part-time/adjunct (1 woman). *Students:* 68 full-time (39 women), 134 part-time (87 women); includes 121 minority (11 African Americans, 31 American Indian/Alaska Native, 5 Asian Americans or Pacific Islanders, 74 Hispanic Americans), 8 international. Average age 36. 85 applicants, 69% accepted, 50 enrolled. In 2009, 18 master's awarded. *Degree requirements:* For master's, thesis optional, professional paper. *Entrance requirements:* For master's, minimum GPA of 3.0, 3 letters of recommendation, resume, letter of intent. Additional exam requirements/recommendations for international students: Required—TOEFL (minimum score 520 paper-based; 190 computer-based; 68 iBT). *Application deadline:* For fall admission, 6/1 for domestic students, 3/1 for international students; for spring admission, 11/1 for domestic students, 8/1 for international students. Application fee: $50. Electronic applications accepted. *Expenses:* Tuition, state resident: full-time $2099; part-time $233.20 per credit hour. Tuition, nonresident: full-time $6650. Required fees: $25 per semester. Tuition and fees vary according to course load, program and reciprocity agreements. *Financial support:* In 2009–10, 45 students received support, including 5 fellowships with tuition reimbursements available (averaging $5,000 per year), 5 research assistantships with tuition reimbursements available (averaging $13,500 per year); career-related internships or fieldwork, scholarships/grants, health care benefits, and unspecified assistantships also available. Financial award application deadline: 3/31; financial award applicants required to submit FAFSA. *Faculty research:* Human resources, health care policy and management, privatization, program evaluation, comparative administration, budget and finance. Total annual research expenditures: $65,961. *Unit head:* Dr. Uday Desai, Director, 505-277-1092, Fax: 505-277-2529, E-mail: ucdesai@unm.edu. *Application contact:* Kristen L. Cole, Department Administrator, 505-277-9196, Fax: 505-277-2529, E-mail: klcole@unm.edu.

University of New Orleans, Graduate School, College of Liberal Arts, Department of Political Science, Program in Public Administration, New Orleans, LA 70148. Offers MPA. *Degree requirements:* For master's, thesis. *Entrance requirements:* For master's, GRE General Test. Additional exam requirements/recommendations for international students: Required—TOEFL (minimum score 550 paper-based; 213 computer-based; 79 iBT). Electronic applications accepted.

The University of North Carolina at Chapel Hill, Graduate School, College of Arts and Sciences, Master of Public Administration Program, Chapel Hill, NC 27599. Offers MPA, JD/MPA, MPA/MRP, MPA/MSW. *Accreditation:* NASPAA. *Degree requirements:* For master's, comprehensive exam. *Entrance requirements:* For master's, GRE General Test, minimum GPA of 3.0. Additional exam requirements/recommendations for international students: Required—TOEFL. Electronic applications accepted. *Faculty research:* Local government management, nonprofit management.

The University of North Carolina at Charlotte, Graduate School, College of Arts and Sciences, Department of Political Science, Charlotte, NC 28223-0001. Offers public administration (MPA); public policy (PhD). *Accreditation:* NASPAA. Part-time and evening/weekend programs available. *Faculty:* 20 full-time (7 women), 3 part-time/adjunct (1 woman). *Students:* 45 full-time (29 women), 50 part-time (28 women); includes 14 African Americans, 1 Hispanic American, 13 international. Average age 32. 81 applicants, 65% accepted, 24 enrolled. In 2009, 13 master's, 12 doctorates awarded. *Entrance requirements:* For master's, GRE General Test or MAT, minimum GPA of 3.0 in undergraduate major, 2.75 overall. Additional exam requirements/recommendations for international students: Required—TOEFL (minimum score 557 paper-based; 220 computer-based; 83 iBT). *Application deadline:* For fall admission, 7/1 for domestic students, 5/1 for international students; for spring admission, 11/1 for domestic students, 10/1 for international students. Applications are processed on a rolling basis. Application fee: $55. Electronic applications accepted. *Financial support:* In 2009–10, 13 students received support, including 5 research assistantships (averaging $10,889 per year), 8 teaching assistantships (averaging $9,562 per year); career-related internships or fieldwork, Federal Work-Study, institutionally sponsored loans, scholarships/grants, and unspecified assistantships also available. Support available to part-time students. Financial award application deadline: 4/1; financial award applicants required to submit FAFSA. *Faculty research:* Terrorism, public administration, nonprofit and arts administration, educational policy, social policy. Total annual research expenditures: $224,272. *Unit head:* Dr. Theodore S. Arrington, Chair, 704-687-2571, Fax: 704-687-3497, E-mail: tarrngtn@uncc.edu. *Application contact:* Kathy B. Giddings, Director of Graduate Admissions, 704-687-5503, Fax: 704-687-3279, E-mail: gradadm@uncc.edu.

The University of North Carolina at Pembroke, Graduate Studies, Public Administration Program, Pembroke, NC 28372-1510. Offers MPA. Part-time and evening/weekend programs available. *Degree requirements:* For master's, comprehensive exam, thesis optional. *Entrance requirements:* For master's, GRE General Test or MAT, minimum GPA of 3.0 in major, 2.5 overall; interview. Additional exam requirements/recommendations for international students: Required—TOEFL.

The University of North Carolina Wilmington, College of Arts and Sciences, Department of Public and International Affairs, Wilmington, NC 28403-3297. Offers MPA. *Accreditation:* NASPAA. Part-time programs available. *Degree requirements:* For master's, comprehensive exam, thesis or alternative, practicum. *Entrance requirements:* For master's, GRE, GMAT. Additional exam requirements/recommendations for international students: Required—TOEFL (minimum score 550 paper-based; 217 computer-based; 79 iBT), IELTS (minimum score 6.5).

University of North Dakota, Graduate School, College of Business and Public Administration, Department of Public Administration, Grand Forks, ND 58202. Offers MPA. *Accreditation:* NASPAA. Part-time programs available. Postbaccalaureate distance learning degree programs offered (minimal on-campus study). *Degree requirements:* For master's, comprehensive exam, thesis or alternative, final exam. *Entrance requirements:* For master's, GRE General Test, GMAT or LSAT, minimum GPA of 3.0. Additional exam requirements/recommendations for international students: Required—TOEFL (minimum score 550 paper-based; 213 computer-based; 79 iBT), IELTS (minimum score 6.5). Electronic applications accepted.

University of North Florida, College of Arts and Sciences, Department of Political Science and Public Administration, Jacksonville, FL 32224. Offers public administration (MPA). *Accreditation:* NASPAA. Part-time programs available. *Faculty:* 8 full-time (1 woman). *Students:* 28 full-time (13 women), 63 part-time (35 women); includes 31 minority (16 African Americans, 8 Asian Americans or Pacific Islanders, 7 Hispanic Americans). Average age 29. 44 applicants, 59% accepted, 17 enrolled. In 2009, 19 master's awarded. *Degree requirements:* For master's, thesis or alternative, internship. *Entrance requirements:* For master's, GRE General Test or minimum GPA of 3.0 in last 60 hours, 2 letters of recommendation, interview. Additional exam requirements/recommendations for international students: Required—TOEFL (minimum score 500 paper-based; 173 computer-based). *Application deadline:* For fall admission, 7/1 priority date for domestic students, 5/1 for international students; for spring admission, 11/1 priority date for domestic students, 10/1 for international students. Applications are processed on a rolling basis. Application fee: $30. Electronic applications accepted. *Expenses:* Tuition, state resident: full-time $6649.20; part-time $277.05 per credit hour. Tuition, nonresident: full-time $22,970; part-time $957.08 per credit hour. Required fees: $985; $41.03 per credit hour. *Financial support:* In 2009–10, 52 students received support. Career-related internships or fieldwork, Federal Work-Study, and tuition waivers (partial) available. Support available to part-time students. Financial award application deadline: 4/1; financial award applicants required to submit FAFSA. *Faculty research:* America's usage of the Internet, use of information communication technologies by educators and children. Total annual research expenditures: $20,839. *Unit head:* Dr. Matthew T. Corrigan, Chair, 904-620-2977, Fax: 904-620-2979, E-mail: mcorriga@unf.edu. *Application contact:* Dr. Patrick Plumlee, Director, 904-620-2977, Fax: 907-620-2979, E-mail: pplumlee@unf.edu.

University of North Texas, Robert B. Toulouse School of Graduate Studies, College of Public Affairs and Community Service, Department of Public Administration, Denton, TX 76203. Offers public administration (MPA); public administration and management (PhD). *Accreditation:* NASPAA. Part-time and evening/weekend programs available. *Degree requirements:* For master's, comprehensive exam, thesis optional, paid internship; for doctorate, comprehensive exam, thesis/dissertation. *Entrance requirements:* For master's, GRE General Test or GMAT, minimum GPA of 3.0 on last 60 hours; for doctorate, GRE General Test, minimum GPA of 3.2 on last 60 hours. Additional exam requirements/recommendations for international students: Required—TOEFL (minimum score 550 paper-based; 213 computer-based; 79 iBT), proof of English language proficiency required for non-native English speakers. *Application deadline:* Applications are processed on a rolling basis. Application fee: $50 ($75 for international students). Electronic applications accepted. *Expenses:* Tuition, state resident: full-time $4298; part-time $239 per contact hour. Tuition, nonresident: full-time $9878; part-time $549 per contact hour. Required fees: $265 per contact hour. *Financial support:* Fellowships with partial tuition reimbursements, research assistantships with partial tuition reimbursements, teaching assistantships with partial tuition reimbursements, career-related internships or fieldwork, Federal Work-Study, institutionally sponsored loans, and tuition waivers (full and partial) available. Support available to part-time students. Financial award applicants required to submit FAFSA. *Faculty research:* Municipal management, government financial management, public/private cooperation, emergency administration and planning, nonprofit management.

University of Oklahoma, Graduate College, College of Arts and Sciences, Department of Political Science, Program in Public Administration, Norman, OK 73019-0390. Offers MPA. Part-time and evening/weekend programs available. *Students:* 47 full-time (21 women), 234 part-time (100 women); includes 104 minority (51 African Americans, 18 American Indian/Alaska Native, 17 Asian Americans or Pacific Islanders, 18 Hispanic Americans), 5 international. 84 applicants, 96% accepted, 68 enrolled. In 2009, 76 master's awarded. Terminal master's awarded for partial completion of doctoral program. *Entrance requirements:* For master's, minimum GPA of 2.75 or GRE. Additional exam requirements/recommendations for international students: Required—TOEFL (minimum score 600 paper-based). *Application deadline:* For fall admission, 4/1 for domestic and international students; for spring admission, 11/1 for domestic students, 9/1 for international students. Application fee: $40 ($90 for international students). Electronic applications accepted. *Expenses:* Tuition, state resident: full-time $3744; part-time $156 per credit hour. Tuition, nonresident: full-time $13,577; part-time $565.70 per credit hour. Required fees: $2415; $90.10 per credit hour. *Financial support:* In 2009–10, 79 students received support. Career-related internships or fieldwork available. *Faculty research:* Public policy, public management, health policy, financial management, program evaluation, non-profit. *Application contact:* Debbie Deering, Assistant to the Director and Academic Counselor, 405-325-6432, Fax: 405-325-3733, E-mail: ddeering@ou.edu.

University of Ottawa, Faculty of Graduate and Postdoctoral Studies, Interdisciplinary Programs, Ottawa, ON K1N 6N5, Canada. Offers e-business (Certificate); e-commerce (Certificate); finance (Certificate); health services and policies research (Diploma); population health (PhD); population health risk assessment and management (Certificate); public management and governance (Certificate); systems science (Certificate).

University of Pennsylvania, School of Arts and Sciences, Fels Institute of Government, Philadelphia, PA 19104. Offers MGA. Part-time and evening/weekend programs available. *Students:* 49 full-time (26 women), 70 part-time (43 women); includes 7 minority (5 African Americans, 1 Asian American or Pacific Islander, 1 Hispanic American), 9 international. 252 applicants, 40% accepted, 55 enrolled. In 2009, 66 master's awarded. *Entrance requirements:* For master's, GRE. Additional exam requirements/recommendations for international students: Required—TOEFL or IELTS. *Application deadline:* For fall admission, 1/15 for domestic students. Applications are processed on a rolling basis. Application fee: $70. *Expenses:* Tuition: Full-time $25,660; part-time $4758 per course. Required fees: $2152; $270 per course. Tuition and fees vary according to course load, degree level and program. *Financial support:* Fellowships, institutionally sponsored loans and scholarships/grants available. Financial award application deadline: 1/15; financial award applicants required to submit FAFSA. *Unit head:* David B. Thornburgh, Director, 215-898-2600. *Application contact:* Ilene Ford, Administrative Coordinator, 215-898-2600, Fax: 215-898-6238, E-mail: felsinstitute@sas.upenn.edu.

See Close-Up on page 1195.

University of Phoenix, John Sperling School of Business, College of Graduate Business and Management, Phoenix, AZ 85034-7209. Offers accountancy (MSA); accounting (MBA); business administration (MBA); global management (MBA); human resources management (MBA, MM); management (MM); marketing (MBA); public administration (MBA, MM). *Accreditation:* ACBSP. Evening/weekend programs available. Postbaccalaureate distance learning degree programs offered. *Degree requirements:* For master's, thesis (for some programs). *Entrance requirements:* For master's, 3 years of work experience, minimum undergraduate GPA of 3.0. Additional exam requirements/recommendations for international students: Required—TOEFL (minimum score 550 paper-based; 213 computer-based; 79 iBT). Electronic applications accepted.

University of Phoenix–Atlanta Campus, John Sperling School of Business, College of Graduate Business and Management, Sandy Springs, GA 30350-4153. Offers accounting (MBA); business administration (MBA); global management (MBA); human resources management (MBA, MM); management (MM); marketing (MBA); public administration (MM). Evening/weekend programs available. Postbaccalaureate distance learning degree programs offered. *Degree requirements:* For master's, thesis (for some programs). *Entrance requirements:* For master's, minimum undergraduate GPA of 3.0, 3 years of work experience. Additional exam requirements/recommendations for international students: Required—TOEFL (minimum score 550 paper-based; 213 computer-based; 79 iBT).

University of Phoenix–Augusta Campus, College of Graduate Business and Management, Augusta, GA 30909-4583. Offers accounting (MBA); business administration (MBA); business and management (MBA, MM); global management (MBA); human resources management (MBA, MM); management (MM); marketing (MBA); public administration (MBA, MM). Postbaccalaureate distance learning degree programs offered.

University of Phoenix–Austin Campus, College of Graduate Business and Management, Austin, TX 78759. Offers accounting (MBA); business administration (MBA); business and management (MBA); e-business (MBA); global management (MBA); human resources management (MBA, MM); management (MM); marketing (MBA); public administration (MBA). Postbaccalaureate distance learning degree programs offered.

University of Phoenix–Bay Area Campus, John Sperling School of Business, College of Graduate Business and Management, Pleasanton, CA 94588-3677. Offers accounting (MBA); business administration (MBA); global management (MBA); human resources management (MBA, MM); marketing (MBA); public administration (MBA, MM). Evening/weekend programs available. Postbaccalaureate distance learning degree programs offered (no on-campus study). *Degree requirements:* For master's, thesis (for some programs). *Entrance requirements:* For master's, minimum undergraduate GPA of 3.0, 3 years of work experience. Additional exam requirements/recommendations for international students: Required—TOEFL (minimum score 550 paper-based; 213 computer-based; 79 iBT). Electronic applications accepted.

University of Phoenix–Birmingham Campus, College of Graduate Business and Management, Birmingham, AL 35244. Offers accounting (MBA); business administration (MBA); global management (MBA); human resources management (MBA, MM); management (MM); marketing (MBA); public administration (MM).

University of Phoenix–Central Florida Campus, John Sperling School of Business, College of Graduate Business and Management, Maitland, FL 32751-7057. Offers accounting (MBA); business administration (MBA); business and management (MM); global management (MBA); human resources management (MBA, MM); management (MM); marketing (MBA); public administration (MBA, MM). Evening/weekend programs available. *Degree requirements:* For master's, thesis (for some programs). *Entrance requirements:* For master's, minimum undergraduate GPA of 3.0, 3 years work experience. Additional exam requirements/recommendations for international students: Required—TOEFL (minimum score 550 paper-based; 213 computer-based; 79 iBT). Electronic applications accepted.

University of Phoenix–Central Valley Campus, College of Graduate Business and Management, Fresno, CA 93720-1562. Offers accounting (MBA); business administration (MBA); global management (MBA); human resources management (MBA, MM); management (MM); marketing (MBA); public administration (MBA, MM).

University of Phoenix–Chattanooga Campus, College of Graduate Business and Management, Chattanooga, TN 37421-3707. Offers accounting (MBA); business administration (MBA); business and management (MBA); global management (MBA); human resources management (MBA, MM); management (MM); marketing (MBA); public administration (MBA, MM). Postbaccalaureate distance learning degree programs offered.

University of Phoenix–Cheyenne Campus, College of Graduate Business and Management, Cheyenne, WY 82009. Offers global management (MBA); human resources management (MBA, MM); management (MM); marketing (MBA); public administration (MBA, MM). Postbaccalaureate distance learning degree programs offered.

University of Phoenix–Cincinnati Campus, John Sperling School of Business, College of Graduate Business and Management, West Chester, OH 45069-4875. Offers accounting (MBA); business administration (MBA); global management (MBA); human resources management (MBA, MM); management (MM); marketing (MBA); public administration (MM). Evening/weekend programs available. *Degree requirements:* For master's, thesis (for some programs). *Entrance requirements:* For master's, minimum undergraduate GPA of 3.0, 3 years of work experience. Additional exam requirements/recommendations for international students: Required—TOEFL (minimum score 550 paper-based; 213 computer-based; 79 iBT). Electronic applications accepted.

University of Phoenix–Cleveland Campus, John Sperling School of Business, College of Graduate Business and Management, Independence, OH 44131-2194. Offers accounting (MBA); business administration (MBA); global management (MBA); human resources management (MBA, MM); management (MM); marketing (MBA); public administration (MBA, MM). Evening/weekend programs available. Postbaccalaureate distance learning degree programs offered (no on-campus study). *Degree requirements:* For master's, thesis (for some programs). *Entrance requirements:* For master's, minimum undergraduate GPA of 3.0, 3 years of work experience. Additional exam requirements/recommendations for international students: Required—TOEFL (minimum score 550 paper-based; 213 computer-based; 79 iBT). Electronic applications accepted.

University of Phoenix–Columbus Georgia Campus, John Sperling School of Business, College of Graduate Business and Management, Columbus, GA 31904-6321. Offers accounting (MBA); business administration (MBA); global management (MBA); human resources management (MBA, MM); management (MM); marketing (MBA); public administration (MBA). Evening/weekend programs available. *Degree requirements:* For master's, thesis (for some programs). *Entrance requirements:* For master's, minimum undergraduate GPA of 3.0, 3 years of work experience. Additional exam requirements/recommendations for international students: Required—TOEFL (minimum score 550 paper-based; 213 computer-based; 79 iBT). Electronic applications accepted.

University of Phoenix–Columbus Ohio Campus, John Sperling School of Business, College of Graduate Business and Management, Columbus, OH 43240-4032. Offers accounting (MBA); business administration (MBA); global management (MBA); human resources management (MBA, MM); management (MM); marketing (MBA); public administration (MM). Evening/weekend programs available. Postbaccalaureate distance learning degree programs offered. *Degree requirements:* For master's, thesis (for some programs). *Entrance requirements:* For master's, minimum undergraduate GPA of 3.0, 3 years of work experience. Additional exam requirements/recommendations for international students: Required—TOEFL (minimum score 550 paper-based; 213 computer-based; 79 iBT). Electronic applications accepted.

University of Phoenix–Dallas Campus, John Sperling School of Business, College of Graduate Business and Management, Dallas, TX 75251-2009. Offers accounting (MBA); business administration (MBA); global management (MBA); human resources management (MBA, MM); management (MM); marketing (MBA); public administration (MBA, MM). Evening/weekend programs available. Postbaccalaureate distance learning degree programs offered. *Degree requirements:* For master's, thesis (for some programs). *Entrance requirements:* For master's, 3 years of work experience, minimum undergraduate GPA of 3.0. Additional exam requirements/recommendations for international students: Required—TOEFL (minimum score 550 paper-based; 213 computer-based; 79 iBT). Electronic applications accepted.

University of Phoenix–Denver Campus, John Sperling School of Business, College of Graduate Business and Management, Lone Tree, CO 80124-5453. Offers accountancy (MSA); accounting (MBA); business administration (MBA); e-business (MBA); global management (MBA); human resources management (MBA, MM); management (MM); marketing (MBA); public administration (MBA, MM). Evening/weekend programs available. Postbaccalaureate distance learning degree programs offered. *Degree requirements:* For master's, thesis (for some programs). *Entrance requirements:* For master's, minimum undergraduate GPA of 3.0, 3 years work experience. Additional exam requirements/recommendations for international students: Required—TOEFL (minimum score 550 paper-based; 213 computer-based; 79 iBT). Electronic applications accepted.

University of Phoenix–Des Moines Campus, College of Graduate Business and Management, Des Moines, IA 50266. Offers accounting (MBA); business administration (MBA); global management (MBA); human resources management (MBA, MM); management (MM); marketing (MBA); public administration (MBA, MM). Postbaccalaureate distance learning degree programs offered.

University of Phoenix–Eastern Washington Campus, John Sperling School of Business, College of Graduate Business and Management, Spokane Valley, WA 99212-2531. Offers accounting (MBA); business administration (MBA); human resources management (MBA); marketing (MBA); public administration (MBA). Evening/weekend programs available. *Degree requirements:* For master's, thesis (for some programs). *Entrance requirements:* For master's, minimum undergraduate GPA of 3.0, 3 years of work experience. Additional exam requirements/recommendations for international students: Required—TOEFL (minimum score 550 paper-based; 213 computer-based; 79 iBT). Electronic applications accepted.

University of Phoenix–Harrisburg Campus, College of Graduate Business and Management, Harrisburg, PA 17112. Offers accounting (MBA); business administration (MBA); business and management (MBA); global management (MBA); human resources management (MBA, MM); management (MM); marketing (MBA); public administration (MBA, MM). Postbaccalaureate distance learning degree programs offered.

University of Phoenix–Hawaii Campus, John Sperling School of Business, College of Graduate Business and Management, Honolulu, HI 96813-4317. Offers accounting (MBA); business administration (MBA); global management (MBA); human resources management (MBA, MM); management (MM); marketing (MBA); public administration (MBA, MM). Evening/weekend programs available. *Degree requirements:* For master's, thesis (for some programs). *Entrance requirements:* For master's, minimum undergraduate GPA of 3.0, 3 years of work experience. Additional exam requirements/recommendations for international students: Required—TOEFL (minimum score 550 paper-based; 213 computer-based; 79 iBT). Electronic applications accepted.

University of Phoenix–Houston Campus, John Sperling School of Business, College of Graduate Business and Management, Houston, TX 77079-2004. Offers accounting (MBA); business administration (MBA); global management (MBA); human resources management (MBA, MM); management (MM); marketing (MBA); public administration (MBA, MM). Evening/weekend programs available. Postbaccalaureate distance learning degree programs offered. *Degree requirements:* For master's, thesis (for some programs). *Entrance requirements:* For master's, 3 years of work experience, minimum undergraduate GPA of 3.0. Additional exam requirements/recommendations for international students: Required—TOEFL (minimum score 550 paper-based; 213 computer-based; 79 iBT). Electronic applications accepted.

University of Phoenix–Idaho Campus, John Sperling School of Business, College of Graduate Business and Management, Meridian, ID 83642-3014. Offers accounting (MBA); administration (MBA); global management (MBA); human resources management (MBA, MM); management (MM); marketing (MBA); public administration (MM). Evening/weekend programs available. Postbaccalaureate distance learning degree programs offered. *Degree requirements:* For master's, thesis (for some programs). *Entrance requirements:* For master's, 3 years of work experience, minimum undergraduate GPA of 3.0. Additional exam requirements/recommendations for international students: Required—TOEFL (minimum score 550 paper-based; 213 computer-based). Electronic applications accepted.

University of Phoenix–Indianapolis Campus, John Sperling School of Business, College of Graduate Business and Management, Indianapolis, IN 46250-932. Offers accounting (MBA); business administration (MBA); global management (MBA); human resources management (MBA, MM); management (MM); marketing (MBA); public administration (MM). Evening/weekend programs available. *Degree requirements:* For master's, thesis (for some programs). *Entrance requirements:* For master's, minimum undergraduate GPA of 3.0, 3 years of work experience. Additional exam requirements/recommendations for international students: Required—TOEFL (minimum score 550 paper-based; 213 computer-based). Electronic applications accepted.

University of Phoenix–Jersey City Campus, College of Graduate Business and Management, Jersey City, NJ 07310. Offers accounting (MBA); business administration (MBA); global management (MBA); human resources management (MBA, MM); management (MM); marketing (MBA); public administration (MBA, MM).

University of Phoenix–Kansas City Campus, John Sperling School of Business, College of Graduate Business and Management, Kansas City, MO 64131-4517. Offers accounting (MBA); business administration (MBA); global management (MBA); human resources management (MBA, MM); management (MM); marketing (MBA); public administration (MBA). Evening/weekend programs available. *Degree requirements:* For master's, thesis (for some programs). *Entrance requirements:* For master's, minimum undergraduate GPA of 3.0, 3 years of work experience. Additional exam requirements/recommendations for international students: Required—TOEFL (minimum score 550 paper-based; 213 computer-based). Electronic applications accepted.

University of Phoenix–Las Vegas Campus, John Sperling School of Business, College of Graduate Business and Management, Las Vegas, NV 89128. Offers accounting (MBA); business administration (MBA); global management (MBA); human resources management (MBA, MM); management (MM); marketing (MBA); public administration (MM). Evening/weekend programs available. Postbaccalaureate distance learning degree programs offered (no on-campus study). *Degree requirements:* For master's, thesis (for some programs). *Entrance requirements:* For master's, minimum undergraduate GPA of 3.0, 3 years of work experience. Additional exam requirements/recommendations for international students: Required—TOEFL (minimum score 550 paper-based; 213 computer-based; 79 iBT). Electronic applications accepted.

University of Phoenix–Louisiana Campus, John Sperling School of Business, College of Graduate Business and Management, Metairie, LA 70001-2082. Offers accounting (MBA); business administration (MBA); global management (MBA); human resources management (MBA, MM); management (MM); marketing (MBA); public administration (MBA). Evening/weekend programs available. *Degree requirements:* For master's, thesis (for some programs). *Entrance requirements:* For master's, minimum undergraduate GPA of 3.0, 3 years work experience. Additional exam requirements/recommendations for international students: Required—TOEFL (minimum score 550 paper-based; 213 computer-based; 79 iBT). Electronic applications accepted.

University of Phoenix–Madison Campus, College of Graduate Business and Management, Madison, WI 53718-2416. Offers accounting (MBA); business and management (MBA); e-business (MBA); global management (MBA); human resources management (MBA, MM); management (MM); marketing (MBA); public administration (MBA).

University of Phoenix–Madison Campus, John Sperling School of Business, College of Graduate Business and Management, Madison, WI 53718-2416. Offers accounting (MBA); administration (MBA); global management (MBA); human resources management (MBA); management (MM); marketing (MBA); public administration (MBA). Evening/weekend programs

Public Administration

University of Phoenix–Madison Campus (continued)
available. *Degree requirements:* For master's, thesis (for some programs). *Entrance requirements:* For master's, 3 years of work experience, minimum undergraduate GPA of 3.0. Additional exam requirements/recommendations for international students: Required—TOEFL (minimum score 550 paper-based; 213 computer-based; 79 iBT). Electronic applications accepted.

University of Phoenix–Maryland Campus, John Sperling School of Business, College of Graduate Business and Management, Columbia, MD 21045-5424. Offers accounting (MBA); business administration (MBA); e-business (MBA); global management (MBA); human resources management (MBA, MM); management (MM); marketing (MBA); public administration (MBA, MM). Evening/weekend programs available. *Degree requirements:* For master's, thesis (for some programs). *Entrance requirements:* For master's, minimum undergraduate GPA of 3.0, 3 years of work experience. Additional exam requirements/recommendations for international students: Required—TOEFL (minimum score 550 paper-based; 213 computer-based; 79 iBT). Electronic applications accepted.

University of Phoenix–Memphis Campus, College of Graduate Business and Management, Cordova, TN 38018. Offers accounting (MBA); business and management (MBA); e-business (MBA); global management (MBA); human resources management (MBA, MM); management (MM); marketing (MBA); public administration (MBA, MM).

University of Phoenix–Minneapolis/St. Louis Park Campus, College of Graduate Business and Management, St. Louis Park, MN 55426. Offers accounting (MBA); business administration (MBA); global management (MBA); human resources management (MBA); management (MM); marketing (MBA); public administration (MBA).

University of Phoenix–Northern Nevada Campus, College of Graduate Business and Management, Reno, NV 89521-5862. Offers accounting (MBA); business administration (MBA); global management (MBA); human resources management (MBA, MM); management (MM); marketing (MBA); public administration (MBA, MM).

University of Phoenix–Northern Virginia Campus, College of Graduate Business and Management, Reston, VA 20190. Offers accounting (MBA); business administration (MBA); e-business (MBA); global management (MBA); human resources management (MBA, MM); management (MM); marketing (MBA); public administration (MBA).

University of Phoenix–North Florida Campus, John Sperling School of Business, College of Graduate Business and Management, Jacksonville, FL 32216-0959. Offers accounting (MBA); business administration (MBA); global management (MBA); human resources management (MBA, MM); management (MM); marketing (MBA); public administration (MBA, MM). Evening/weekend programs available. *Degree requirements:* For master's, thesis (for some programs). *Entrance requirements:* For master's, minimum undergraduate GPA of 3.0, 3 years work experience. Additional exam requirements/recommendations for international students: Required—TOEFL (minimum score 550 paper-based; 213 computer-based; 79 iBT). Electronic applications accepted.

University of Phoenix–Northwest Arkansas Campus, College of Graduate Business and Management, Rogers, AR 72756-9615. Offers accounting (MBA); business and management (MBA); global management (MBA); human resources management (MBA, MM); management (MM); marketing (MBA); public administration (MBA, MM).

University of Phoenix–Omaha Campus, College of Graduate Business and Management, Omaha, NE 68154-5240. Offers accounting (MBA); business and management (MBA); global management (MBA); human resources management (MBA, MM); management (MM); marketing (MBA); public administration (MBA, MM).

University of Phoenix–Oregon Campus, The John Sperling School of Business, College of Graduate Business and Management, Tigard, OR 97223. Offers accounting (MBA); business administration (MBA); global management (MBA); human resource management (MM); human resources management (MBA); management (MM); marketing (MBA); public administration (MM). Evening/weekend programs available. *Degree requirements:* For master's, thesis (for some programs). *Entrance requirements:* For master's, minimum undergraduate GPA of 3.0, 3 years of work experience. Additional exam requirements/recommendations for international students: Required—TOEFL (minimum score 550 paper-based; 213 computer-based; 79 iBT). Electronic applications accepted.

University of Phoenix–Philadelphia Campus, The John Sperling School of Business, College of Graduate Business and Management, Wayne, PA 19087-2121. Offers accounting (MBA); business administration (MBA); global management (MBA); human resources management (MBA, MM); management (MM); marketing (MBA); public administration (MM). Evening/weekend programs available. *Degree requirements:* For master's, thesis (for some programs). *Entrance requirements:* For master's, minimum undergraduate GPA of 3.0, 3 years work experience. Additional exam requirements/recommendations for international students: Required—TOEFL (minimum score 550 paper-based; 213 computer-based; 79 iBT). Electronic applications accepted.

University of Phoenix–Pittsburgh Campus, John Sperling School of Business, College of Graduate Business and Management, Pittsburgh, PA 15276. Offers accounting (MBA); business administration (MBA); global management (MBA); human resources management (MBA, MM); management (MM); marketing (MBA); public administration (MBA, MM). Evening/weekend programs available. *Degree requirements:* For master's, thesis (for some programs). *Entrance requirements:* For master's, minimum undergraduate GPA of 3.0, 3 years work experience. Additional exam requirements/recommendations for international students: Required—TOEFL (minimum score 550 paper-based; 213 computer-based; 79 iBT). Electronic applications accepted.

University of Phoenix–Richmond Campus, John Sperling School of Business, College of Graduate Business and Management, Richmond, VA 23230. Offers accounting (MBA); business administration (MBA); global management (MBA); human resources management (MBA, MM); management (MM); marketing (MBA); public administration (MBA, MM). Evening/weekend programs available. *Degree requirements:* For master's, thesis (for some programs). *Entrance requirements:* For master's, minimum undergraduate GPA of 3.0, 3 years work experience. Additional exam requirements/recommendations for international students: Required—TOEFL (minimum score 550 paper-based; 213 computer-based; 79 iBT). Electronic applications accepted.

University of Phoenix–Sacramento Valley Campus, John Sperling School of Business, College of Graduate Business and Management, Sacramento, CA 95833-3632. Offers accounting (MBA); business administration (MBA); global management (MBA); human resources management (MBA, MM); management (MM); marketing (MBA); public administration (MBA, MM). Evening/weekend programs available. *Degree requirements:* For master's, thesis (for some programs). *Entrance requirements:* For master's, minimum undergraduate GPA of 3.0, 3 years work experience. Additional exam requirements/recommendations for international students: Required—TOEFL (minimum score 550 paper-based; 213 computer-based; 79 iBT). Electronic applications accepted.

University of Phoenix–St. Louis Campus, John Sperling School of Business, College of Graduate Business and Management, St. Louis, MO 63043-4828. Offers accounting (MBA); business administration (MBA); global management (MBA); human resources management (MBA, MM); management (MM); marketing (MBA); public administration (MM). Evening/weekend programs available. *Degree requirements:* For master's, thesis (for some programs). *Entrance requirements:* For master's, 3 years of work experience, minimum undergraduate GPA of 3.0. Additional exam requirements/recommendations for international students: Required—TOEFL (minimum score 550 paper-based; 213 computer-based; 79 iBT). Electronic applications accepted.

University of Phoenix–San Antonio Campus, College of Graduate Business and Management, San Antonio, TX 78230. Offers accounting (MBA); business administration (MBA); e-business (MBA); global management (MBA); human resources management (MBA, MM); management (MM); marketing (MBA); public administration (MBA, MM).

University of Phoenix–San Diego Campus, John Sperling School of Business, College of Graduate Business and Management, San Diego, CA 92123. Offers accounting (MBA); business administration (MBA); global management (MBA); human resources management (MBA, MM); management (MM); marketing (MBA); public administration (MBA). Evening/weekend programs available. *Degree requirements:* For master's, thesis (for some programs). *Entrance requirements:* For master's, 3 years of work experience, minimum undergraduate GPA of 3.0. Additional exam requirements/recommendations for international students: Required—TOEFL (minimum score 550 paper-based; 213 computer-based; 79 iBT). Electronic applications accepted.

University of Phoenix–Savannah Campus, College of Graduate Business and Management, Savannah, GA 31405-7400. Offers accounting (MBA); business administration (MBA); global management (MBA); human resources management (MBA, MM); management (MM); marketing (MBA); public administration (MBA, MM).

University of Phoenix–Southern California Campus, John Sperling School of Business, College of Graduate Business and Management, Costa Mesa, CA 92626. Offers accounting (MBA); business administration (MBA); global management (MBA); human resources management (MBA, MM); management (MM); marketing (MBA); public administration (MBA, MM). Evening/weekend programs available. *Degree requirements:* For master's, thesis (for some programs). *Entrance requirements:* For master's, minimum undergraduate GPA of 3.0, 3 years work experience. Additional exam requirements/recommendations for international students: Required—TOEFL (minimum score 550 paper-based; 213 computer-based; 79 iBT). Electronic applications accepted.

University of Phoenix–Southern Colorado Campus, John Sperling School of Business, College of Graduate Business and Management, Colorado Springs, CO 80919-2335. Offers accounting (MBA); business administration (MBA); global management (MBA); human resources management (MBA, MM); management (MM); marketing (MBA); public administration (MM). Evening/weekend programs available. *Degree requirements:* For master's, thesis (for some programs). *Entrance requirements:* For master's, minimum undergraduate GPA of 3.0, 3 years of work experience. Additional exam requirements/recommendations for international students: Required—TOEFL (minimum score 550 paper-based; 213 computer-based; 79 iBT). Electronic applications accepted.

University of Phoenix–South Florida Campus, John Sperling School of Business, College of Graduate Business and Management, Fort Lauderdale, FL 33309. Offers accounting (MBA); business administration (MBA); global management (MBA); human resource management (MBA); human resources management (MM); management (MM); marketing (MBA); public administration (MBA, MM). Evening/weekend programs available. *Degree requirements:* For master's, thesis (for some programs). *Entrance requirements:* For master's, minimum undergraduate GPA of 3.0, 3 years work experience. Additional exam requirements/recommendations for international students: Required—TOEFL (minimum score 550 paper-based; 213 computer-based; 79 iBT). Electronic applications accepted.

University of Phoenix–Springfield Campus, College of Graduate Business and Management, Springfield, MO 65804-7211. Offers accounting (MBA); business administration (MBA); global management (MBA); human resources management (MBA, MM); management (MM); marketing (MBA); public administration (MBA, MM).

University of Phoenix–Western Washington Campus, College of Graduate Business and Management, Tukwila, WA 98188. Offers accounting (MBA); business and management (MBA, MM); global management (MBA); human resources management (MBA, MM); marketing (MBA); public administration (MBA, MM). Evening/weekend programs available. *Degree requirements:* For master's, thesis (for some programs). *Entrance requirements:* For master's, minimum undergraduate GPA of 3.0, 3 years of work experience. Additional exam requirements/recommendations for international students: Required—TOEFL (minimum score 550 paper-based; 213 computer-based; 79 iBT). Electronic applications accepted.

University of Phoenix–West Florida Campus, The John Sperling School of Business, College of Graduate Business and Management, Temple Terrace, FL 33637. Offers accounting (MBA); business administration (MBA); global management (MBA); human resources management (MBA, MM); management (MM); marketing (MBA); public administration (MBA, MM). Evening/weekend programs available. *Degree requirements:* For master's, thesis (for some programs). *Entrance requirements:* For master's, 3 years of work experience, minimum undergraduate GPA of 3.0. Additional exam requirements/recommendations for international students: Required—TOEFL (minimum score 550 paper-based; 213 computer-based; 79 iBT). Electronic applications accepted.

University of Pittsburgh, Graduate School of Public and International Affairs, Division of Public and Urban Affairs, Pittsburgh, PA 15260. Offers policy research and analysis (MPA); public and nonprofit management (MPA); urban and regional affairs (MPA); JD/MPA; MPA/MPIA; MPH/MPA; MSIS/MPA; MSW/MPA. Part-time and evening/weekend programs available. *Faculty:* 28 full-time (8 women), 56 part-time/adjunct (20 women). *Students:* 46 full-time (28 women), 19 part-time (13 women); includes 11 minority (9 African Americans, 1 Asian American or Pacific Islander, 1 Hispanic American), 3 international. Average age 25. 93 applicants, 92% accepted, 30 enrolled. In 2009, 32 master's awarded. *Degree requirements:* For master's, thesis optional, internship, capstone seminar. *Entrance requirements:* For master's, GRE General Test, 3 letters of recommendation, resume, minimum GPA of 3.2. Additional exam requirements/recommendations for international students: Required—TOEFL (minimum score 550 paper-based; 213 computer-based; 80 iBT), TWE (minimum score 4); Recommended—IELTS (minimum score 7). *Application deadline:* For fall admission, 2/1 for domestic students, 1/15 for international students; for spring admission, 11/1 for domestic students, 8/1 for international students. Application fee: $50. *Expenses:* Tuition, state resident: full-time $16,402; part-time $665 per credit. Tuition, nonresident: full-time $28,694; part-time $1175 per credit. Required fees: $690; $175 per term. Tuition and fees vary according to program. *Financial support:* In 2009–10, 22 students received support, including 2 fellowships (averaging $20,000 per year); scholarships/grants, tuition waivers (full and partial), and unspecified assistantships also available. Financial award application deadline: 2/1. *Faculty research:* Disaster response management, government regulation of health and safety risks, comparative regional governance, non-profit management, environmental policy, housing policy, strategic management. Total annual research expenditures: $357,117. *Unit head:* Dr. David Y. Miller, Director, 412-648-7606, Fax: 412-648-2605, E-mail: dymiller@pitt.edu. *Application contact:* Elizabeth A. Hruby, Graduate Enrollment Counselor, 412-648-7640, Fax: 412-648-7641, E-mail: eah44@pitt.edu.

University of Pittsburgh, Graduate School of Public and International Affairs, Doctoral Program in Public and International Affairs, Pittsburgh, PA 15260. Offers development policy (PhD); foreign and security policy (PhD); international political economy (PhD); public administration (PhD); public policy (PhD). *Accreditation:* NASPAA. Part-time programs available. *Faculty:* 28 full-time (8 women), 56 part-time/adjunct (20 women). *Students:* 11 full-time (4 women), 27 part-time (16 women); includes 4 minority (2 African Americans, 1 Asian American or Pacific Islander, 1 Hispanic American), 7 international. Average age 30. 63 applicants, 14% accepted, 5 enrolled. In 2009, 9 doctorates awarded. *Degree requirements:* For doctorate, comprehensive exam, thesis/dissertation. *Entrance requirements:* For doctorate, GRE, 3 letters of recommendation, resume, minimum GPA of 3.0, writing sample. Additional exam requirements/recommendations for international students: Required—TOEFL (minimum score 600 paper-based; 250 computer-based; 100 iBT), TWE (minimum score 4); Recommended—IELTS (minimum score 7). *Application deadline:* For fall admission, 2/1 for domestic students, 1/15 for international students. Application fee: $50. Electronic applications accepted. *Expenses:* Tuition, state resident: full-time $16,402; part-time $665 per credit. Tuition, nonresident: full-time $28,694; part-time $1175 per credit. Required fees: $690; $175 per term. Tuition and fees vary according to program. *Financial support:* In 2009–10, 17 students received support, including 6 fellowships (averaging $34,925 per year); scholarships/grants, tuition waivers (full and partial), and unspecified assistantships also available. Financial award application deadline: 2/1. *Faculty research:* International political economy, international development, public administration, public policy, foreign policy, international security policy. Total annual research expenditures: $357,117. *Unit head:* Dr. Kevin P. Kearns, Program Coordinator, 412-648-7621, Fax: 412-648-2605, E-mail: kkearns@pitt.edu. *Application contact:* Julie Korade, Program Administrator/Graduate Enrollment Counselor, 412-648-7640, Fax: 412-648-7641, E-mail: korade@pitt.edu.

University of Puerto Rico, Río Piedras, College of Social Sciences, School of Public Administration, San Juan, PR 00931-3300. Offers MPA. Part-time programs available. *Degree requirements:* For master's, comprehensive exam, thesis. *Entrance requirements:* For master's, GRE or PAEG, interview, minimum GPA of 3.0, letter of recommendation.

University of Regina, Faculty of Graduate Studies and Research, Johnson-Shoyama Graduate School of Public Policy, Regina, SK S4S 0A2, Canada. Offers economic analysis for public policy (Master's Certificate); non-profit management (Master's Certificate); public management (MPA, Master's Certificate); public policy (MPA, PhD, Master's Certificate). Part-time and evening/weekend programs available. *Faculty:* 6 full-time (3 women). *Students:* 51 full-time (24 women), 71 part-time (39 women). 113 applicants, 89% accepted. In 2009, 51 master's awarded. *Entrance requirements:* Additional exam requirements/recommendations for international students: Required—TOEFL (minimum score 580 paper-based; 237 computer-based; 80 iBT). *Application deadline:* Applications are processed on a rolling basis. Application fee: $90 ($100 for international students). Electronic applications accepted. *Expenses:* Contact institution. *Financial support:* In 2009–10, 7 fellowships (averaging $19,000 per year), 2 research assistantships (averaging $16,910 per year), 11 teaching assistantships (averaging $6,650 per year) were awarded. Financial award application deadline: 6/15. *Faculty research:* Public administration and policy. *Unit head:* Dr. Sylvain Charlebois, Associate Dean, 306-585-2695, E-mail: sylvain.charlebois@uregina.ca. *Application contact:* Elaine Groenendyk, Information Contact, 306-585-5462, E-mail: elaine.groenendyk@uregina.ca.

University of Rhode Island, Graduate School, College of Arts and Sciences, Department of Political Science, Kingston, RI 02881. Offers political science (MA), including American politics, comparative government, international relations, public policy; public policy and administration (MPA); MLIS/MPA. Part-time programs available. *Faculty:* 10 full-time (4 women), 1 part-time/adjunct (0 women). *Students:* 17 full-time (11 women), 44 part-time (28 women); includes 9 minority (4 African Americans, 1 Asian American or Pacific Islander, 4 Hispanic Americans). In 2009, 29 master's awarded. *Degree requirements:* For master's, comprehensive exam (for some programs), thesis optional. *Entrance requirements:* For master's, GRE, GMAT or MAT, 2 letters of recommendation. Additional exam requirements/recommendations for international students: Required—TOEFL (minimum score 550 paper-based; 213 computer-based). *Application deadline:* For fall admission, 2/1 for international students; for spring admission, 7/15 for international students. Application fee: $65. Electronic applications accepted. *Expenses:* Tuition, state resident: full-time $8828; part-time $490 per credit hour. Tuition, nonresident: full-time $22,100; part-time $1228 per credit hour. Required fees: $1118; $57 per semester. Tuition and fees vary according to program. *Financial support:* In 2009–10, 4 teaching assistantships with full tuition reimbursements (averaging $13,894 per year) were awarded. Financial award applicants required to submit FAFSA. *Unit head:* Dr. Gerry Tyler, Chairperson, 401-874-4053, Fax: 401-874-4072, E-mail: gtyler@uri.edu. *Application contact:* Dr. Gerry Tyler, Chairperson, 401-874-4053, Fax: 401-874-4072, E-mail: gtyler@uri.edu.

University of San Francisco, School of Business and Professional Studies, Program in Public Administration, Concentration in Public Administration, San Francisco, CA 94117-1080. Offers MPA. Part-time and evening/weekend programs available. *Faculty:* 3 full-time (1 woman), 4 part-time/adjunct (all women). *Students:* 71 full-time (43 women), 2 part-time (both women); includes 38 minority (10 African Americans, 1 American Indian/Alaska Native, 15 Asian Americans or Pacific Islanders, 12 Hispanic Americans). Average age 34. 68 applicants, 84% accepted, 39 enrolled. In 2009, 29 master's awarded. *Entrance requirements:* For master's, minimum GPA of 3.0. Application fee: $55 ($65 for international students). *Expenses:* Tuition: Full-time $19,710; part-time $1095 per unit. Part-time tuition and fees vary according to degree level, campus/location and program. *Financial support:* In 2009–10, 57 students received support. Application deadline: 3/2. *Unit head:* Dr. Maurice Penner, Director, 415-422-2142. *Application contact:* 415-422-6000, E-mail: graduate@usfca.edu.

University of South Africa, College of Economic and Management Sciences, Pretoria, South Africa. Offers accounting (D Admin, D Com); accounting science (DA); auditing (D Admin, D Com); business administration (M Tech); business economics (D Admin); business leadership (DBL); business management (D Admin, D Com); economic management analysis (M Tech); economics (D Admin, D Com, PhD); human resource development (M Tech); industrial psychology (D Admin, D Com, PhD); logistics (D Com); marketing (M Tech); public administration (D Admin, D Com, DPA, PhD); public management (M Tech); quantitative management (D Admin, D Com); real estate (M Tech); statistics (D Admin, PhD); tourism management (D Admin, D Com); transport economics (D Admin, D Com).

University of South Alabama, Graduate School, College of Arts and Sciences, Department of Political Science and Criminal Justice, Mobile, AL 36688-0002. Offers public administration (MPA). Part-time and evening/weekend programs available. *Degree requirements:* For master's, comprehensive exam, thesis optional. *Entrance requirements:* For master's, GRE, minimum GPA of 3.0. *Expenses:* Tuition, state resident: part-time $218 per contact hour. Required fees: $1102 per year.

University of South Carolina, The Graduate School, College of Arts and Sciences, Department of Political Science, Program in Public Administration, Columbia, SC 29208. Offers MPA, JD/MPA, MSW/MPA. *Accreditation:* NASPAA. Part-time and evening/weekend programs available. *Degree requirements:* For master's, capstone seminar. *Entrance requirements:* For master's, GRE General Test, minimum GPA of 3.0. Additional exam requirements/recommendations for international students: Required—TOEFL. Electronic applications accepted. *Faculty research:* Public policy, organizational theory, personnel administration, budgeting, finance.

The University of South Dakota, Graduate School, College of Arts and Sciences, Department of Political Science, Vermillion, SD 57069-2390. Offers American political institutions (PhD); political science (MA); public administration (MPA, PhD); public policy (PhD); JD/MA; JD/MPA. *Accreditation:* NASPAA (one or more programs are accredited). Part-time programs available. Postbaccalaureate distance learning degree programs offered. *Degree requirements:* For master's, comprehensive exam, thesis (for some programs). *Entrance requirements:* For master's, GRE or LSAT (MPA), GRE General Test (MA), minimum GPA of 2.7. Additional exam requirements/recommendations for international students: Required—TOEFL (minimum score 550 paper-based; 213 computer-based; 79 iBT). Electronic applications accepted.

University of Southern California, Graduate School, School of Policy, Planning, and Development, Doctor of Philosophy in Policy, Planning, and Development Program, Los Angeles, CA 90089. Offers PhD. *Faculty:* 51 full-time (12 women), 74 part-time/adjunct (26 women). *Students:* 16 full-time (10 women), 1 part-time (0 women); includes 4 minority (2 Asian Americans or Pacific Islanders, 2 Hispanic Americans), 9 international. 84 applicants, 17% accepted, 8 enrolled. In 2009, 14 doctorates awarded. *Degree requirements:* For doctorate, thesis/dissertation. *Entrance requirements:* For doctorate, GRE. Additional exam requirements/recommendations for international students: Required—TOEFL (minimum score 600 paper-based; 250 computer-based; 100 iBT). *Application deadline:* For fall admission, 12/1 for domestic and international students. Application fee: $85. Electronic applications accepted. *Expenses:* Tuition: Full-time $25,980; part-time $1315 per unit. Required fees: $554. One-time fee: $35 full-time. Full-time tuition and fees vary according to degree level and program. *Financial support:* In 2009–10, 60 research assistantships with full tuition reimbursements (averaging $12,812 per year) were awarded; scholarships/grants and tuition waivers (full and partial) also available. Financial award application deadline: 12/1. *Faculty research:* Governance: effective institutions, leadership, management, healthy urban and place development, sustainability, community, public policy and planning, societal problem solving and analysis. Total annual research expenditures: $5 million. *Unit head:* Dr. Jack H. Knott, Dean, 213-740-0350, Fax: 213-740-5379, E-mail: jhknott@usc.edu. *Application contact:* Marisol R. Gonzalez, Director of Recruitment and Admission, 213-740-0550, Fax: 213-740-7573, E-mail: marisolr@usc.edu.

University of Southern California, Graduate School, School of Policy, Planning, and Development, Master of Public Administration Program, Los Angeles, CA 90089. Offers MPA, MPA/JD, MPA/M Pl, MPA/MA, MPA/MAJCS, MPA/MS, MPA/MSW. *Accreditation:* NASPAA (one or more programs are accredited). Part-time and evening/weekend programs available. *Faculty:* 51 full-time (12 women), 74 part-time/adjunct (26 women). *Students:* 146 full-time (93 women), 46 part-time (27 women); includes 80 minority (11 African Americans, 31 Asian Americans or Pacific Islanders, 38 Hispanic Americans), 24 international. 264 applicants, 75% accepted, 103 enrolled. In 2009, 71 master's awarded. *Degree requirements:* For master's, internship. *Entrance requirements:* For master's, GRE or GMAT. Additional exam requirements/recommendations for international students: Required—TOEFL (minimum score 600 paper-based; 250 computer-based; 100 iBT). *Application deadline:* For fall admission, 12/15 priority date for domestic and international students. Applications are processed on a rolling basis. Application fee: $85. Electronic applications accepted. *Expenses:* Tuition: Full-time $25,980; part-time $1315 per unit. Required fees: $554. One-time fee: $35 full-time. Full-time tuition and fees vary according to degree level and program. *Financial support:* In 2009–10, 119 students received support, including 6 research assistantships with tuition reimbursements available (averaging $11,161 per year); scholarships/grants and tuition waivers (full and partial) also available. Financial award application deadline: 12/15. *Faculty research:* Collaborative governance and decision making, nonprofit management, environmental management, institutional analysis, local government, civic engagement. Total annual research expenditures: $5 million. *Unit head:* Dr. Juliet Musso, Director, 213-740-0636, Fax: 213-740-1801, E-mail: musso@usc.edu. *Application contact:* Marisol R. Gonzalez, Director of Recruitment and Admission, 213-740-0550, Fax: 213-740-7573, E-mail: marisolr@usc.edu.

University of Southern Indiana, Graduate Studies, College of Liberal Arts, Program in Public Administration, Evansville, IN 47712-3590. Offers MPA. Part-time and evening/weekend programs available. *Faculty:* 3 full-time (1 woman). *Students:* 20 part-time (14 women); includes 3 minority (1 African American, 1 American Indian/Alaska Native, 1 Asian American or Pacific Islander). Average age 34. 9 applicants, 100% accepted, 5 enrolled. In 2009, 4 master's awarded. *Entrance requirements:* For master's, GMAT or GRE, 2 letters of reference, analytical writing sample, minimum GPA of 2.7. Additional exam requirements/recommendations for international students: Required—TOEFL (minimum score 550 paper-based; 213 computer-based; 79 iBT), IELTS (minimum score 6). *Application deadline:* For fall admission, 8/15 priority date for domestic students, 3/1 priority date for international students. Applications are processed on a rolling basis. Application fee: $25. Electronic applications accepted. *Expenses:* Tuition, state resident: full-time $4592; part-time $255 per credit hour. Tuition, nonresident: full-time $9060; part-time $503 per credit hour. Required fees: $220; $22.75 per term. Tuition and fees vary according to course load and reciprocity agreements. *Financial support:* In 2009–10, 12 students received support. Federal Work-Study, scholarships/grants, tuition waivers (full and partial), and unspecified assistantships available. Financial award application deadline: 3/1; financial award applicants required to submit FAFSA. *Unit head:* Dr. Mary Morris, Director, 812-461-5207, E-mail: mhmorris@usi.edu. *Application contact:* Dr. Mary Morris, Director, 812-461-5207, E-mail: mhmorris@usi.edu.

University of South Florida, Graduate School, College of Arts and Sciences, Department of Government and International Affairs, Tampa, FL 33620-9951. Offers Latin American Caribbean and Latino Studies (MA); government (PhD); political science (MA); public administration (MPA). Part-time and evening/weekend programs available. *Faculty:* 19 full-time (4 women), 1 (woman) part-time/adjunct. *Students:* 31 full-time (16 women), 76 part-time (37 women); includes 28 minority (16 African Americans, 1 American Indian/Alaska Native, 4 Asian Americans or Pacific Islanders, 7 Hispanic Americans), 3 international. Average age 32. 126 applicants, 38% accepted, 24 enrolled. In 2009, 28 master's awarded. *Degree requirements:* For master's, comprehensive exam, thesis; for doctorate, comprehensive exam, thesis/dissertation. *Entrance requirements:* For master's, GRE (minimum score 470 verbal, 470 quantitative), minimum GPA of 3.0 in last 60 hours of course work. Additional exam requirements/recommendations for international students: Required—TOEFL (minimum score 550 paper-based; 213 computer-based). *Application deadline:* For fall admission, 2/15 for domestic students, 1/2 for international students; for spring admission, 10/15 for domestic students, 6/1 for international students. Applications are processed on a rolling basis. Application fee: $30. Electronic applications accepted. *Financial support:* In 2009–10, teaching assistantships with tuition reimbursements (averaging $24,000 per year); unspecified assistantships also available. Financial award application deadline: 4/1. *Unit head:* Dr. Mohsen Milani, Chairperson, 813-974-2384, Fax: 813-974-0832, E-mail: milani@chuma1.cas.usf.edu. *Application contact:* Dr. Stephen Tauber, Graduate Coordinator, 813-974-0781, Fax: 813-974-0832, E-mail: stauber@chuma1.cas.usf.edu.

The University of Tennessee, Graduate School, College of Arts and Sciences, Department of Political Science, Program in Public Administration, Knoxville, TN 37996. Offers MPA, JD/MPA. *Accreditation:* NASPAA. Part-time programs available. *Degree requirements:* For master's, thesis or alternative. *Entrance requirements:* For master's, GRE General Test, minimum GPA of 2.7. Additional exam requirements/recommendations for international students: Required—TOEFL. Electronic applications accepted. *Expenses:* Tuition, state resident: full-time $6826; part-time $380 per semester hour. Tuition, nonresident: full-time $21,844; part-time $1147 per semester hour. Tuition and fees vary according to program.

The University of Tennessee at Chattanooga, Graduate School, College of Arts and Sciences, Department of Political Science, Chattanooga, TN 37403. Offers local government management (MPA); non profit management (MPA); public administration (MPA); public administration and non-profit management (Postbaccalaureate Certificate). Part-time and evening/weekend programs available. *Faculty:* 4 full-time (0 women). *Students:* 21 full-time (10 women), 23 part-time (12 women); includes 6 minority (3 African Americans, 2 Asian Americans or Pacific Islanders, 1 Hispanic American). Average age 29. 18 applicants, 89% accepted, 10 enrolled. In 2009, 13 master's awarded. *Degree requirements:* For master's, comprehensive exam, thesis or alternative, internship. *Entrance requirements:* For master's, GRE General Test. Additional exam requirements/recommendations for international students: Required—TOEFL (minimum score 550 paper-based; 213 computer-based; 79 iBT), IELTS (minimum score 6). *Application deadline:* For fall admission, 8/1 priority date for domestic students, 6/1 for international students; for spring admission, 12/1 priority date for domestic students, 10/1 for international students. Applications are processed on a rolling basis. Application fee: $35. Electronic applications accepted. *Expenses:* Tuition, state resident: full-time $5404; part-time $300 per credit hour. Tuition, nonresident: full-time $16,702; part-time $928 per credit hour. Required fees: $1150; $130 per credit hour. *Financial support:* In 2009–10, 6 research assistantships with full and partial tuition reimbursements (averaging $5,500 per year) were awarded; career-related internships or fieldwork, scholarships/grants, and unspecified assistantships also available. Support available to part-time students. *Faculty research:* Organizational cultures and renewal, management theory, public policy, policy analysis, nonprofit organization. Total annual research expenditures: $35,240. *Unit head:* Dr. Fouad M. Moughrabi, Head, 423-425-4281, Fax: 423-425-2373, E-mail: fouad-moughrabi@utc.edu. *Application contact:*

Public Administration

The University of Tennessee at Chattanooga (continued)
Dr. Stephanie Bellar, Dean of Graduate Studies, 423-425-4666, Fax: 423-425-5223, E-mail: stephanie-bellar@utc.edu.

The University of Texas at Arlington, Graduate School, School of Urban and Public Affairs, Program in Public Administration, Arlington, TX 76019. Offers MPA. *Accreditation:* NASPAA. Part-time and evening/weekend programs available. *Students:* 76 full-time (42 women), 103 part-time (59 women); includes 74 minority (38 African Americans, 1 American Indian/Alaska Native, 8 Asian Americans or Pacific Islanders, 27 Hispanic Americans), 2 international. 111 applicants, 96% accepted, 52 enrolled. In 2009, 48 master's awarded. *Degree requirements:* For master's, comprehensive exam, thesis or alternative. *Entrance requirements:* For master's, GRE General Test. Additional exam requirements/recommendations for international students: Required—TOEFL (minimum score 550 paper-based; 213 computer-based). *Application deadline:* For fall admission, 6/16 for domestic students. Application fee: $35 ($50 for international students). *Financial support:* In 2009–10, 1 research assistantship (averaging $750 per year) was awarded; fellowships, career-related internships or fieldwork also available. Financial award application deadline: 6/1; financial award applicants required to submit FAFSA. *Faculty research:* Environment, statistics, public administration, social welfare, economic development, economics, budgeting, planning. Total annual research expenditures: $53,550. *Unit head:* Dr. Alejandro Rodriguez, Graduate Advisor, 817-272-3357, Fax: 817-272-5008. *Application contact:* Linda Slaughter, Administrative Clerk, 817-272-3071, Fax: 817-272-5008, E-mail: slaughter@uta.edu.

The University of Texas at Brownsville, Graduate Studies, College of Liberal Arts, Program in Public Policy and Management, Brownsville, TX 78520-4991. Offers MPPM. *Degree requirements:* For master's, thesis. *Entrance requirements:* For master's, GRE, 2 letters of recommendation.

The University of Texas at Dallas, School of Management, Programs in Management Science, Richardson, TX 75080. Offers accounting (PhD); decision sciences (PhD); finance (PhD); management strategy and public policy (PhD); marketing (PhD); organizational behavior (PhD). *Accreditation:* AACSB. Part-time and evening/weekend programs available. *Faculty:* 12 full-time (3 women). *Students:* 72 full-time (23 women), 12 part-time (6 women); includes 10 minority (all Asian Americans or Pacific Islanders), 63 international. Average age 34. 173 applicants, 12% accepted, 7 enrolled. In 2009, 8 doctorates awarded. *Degree requirements:* For doctorate, thesis/dissertation. *Entrance requirements:* For doctorate, GMAT, minimum GPA of 3.0. Additional exam requirements/recommendations for international students: Required—TOEFL (minimum score 550 paper-based; 213 computer-based). *Application deadline:* For fall admission, 7/15 for domestic students, 5/1 priority date for international students; for spring admission, 11/15 for domestic students, 9/1 priority date for international students. Applications are processed on a rolling basis. Application fee: $50 ($100 for international students). Electronic applications accepted. *Expenses:* Tuition, state resident: full-time $11,068; part-time $461 per credit hour. Tuition, nonresident: full-time $21,178; part-time $882 per credit hour. Tuition and fees vary according to course load. *Financial support:* In 2009–10, 1 research assistantship with full tuition reimbursement (averaging $13,050 per year), 43 teaching assistantships with full tuition reimbursements (averaging $14,795 per year) were awarded; fellowships, career-related internships or fieldwork, Federal Work-Study, institutionally sponsored loans, scholarships/grants, and unspecified assistantships also available. Support available to part-time students. Financial award application deadline: 4/30; financial award applicants required to submit FAFSA. *Faculty research:* Empirical generalizations in marketing, diffusion of generations of technology, stochastic brand-choice theory, acceptance of trade deals by supermarkets, nonparametric estimations of market share response. *Unit head:* Dr. Sumit Sarkar, Program Director, 972-883-2745, Fax: 972-883-5977, E-mail: som-phd.@utdallas.edu. *Application contact:* James Parker, Assistant Director, 972-883-5842, E-mail: jparker@utdallas.edu.

The University of Texas at El Paso, Graduate School, Institute for Policy and Economic Development, El Paso, TX 79968-0001. Offers border administration (Certificate); homeland security (Certificate); intelligence and national security (MS, Certificate); leadership studies (MA); public administration (MPA). *Accreditation:* NASPAA. Part-time and evening/weekend programs available. *Students:* 187 (57 women); includes 124 minority (19 African Americans, 1 American Indian/Alaska Native, 5 Asian Americans or Pacific Islanders, 99 Hispanic Americans), 5 international. 142 applicants, 77% accepted. In 2009, 76 master's awarded. *Degree requirements:* For master's, thesis optional. *Entrance requirements:* For master's, GRE, Statement of Purpose, Letters of Recommendation. Additional exam requirements/recommendations for international students: Required—TOEFL; Recommended—IELTS. *Application deadline:* For fall admission, 8/1 for domestic students, 3/1 for international students; for spring admission, 10/1 for domestic students, 9/1 for international students. Applications are processed on a rolling basis. Application fee: $45 ($80 for international students). Electronic applications accepted. *Financial support:* Fellowships with partial tuition reimbursements, research assistantships with partial tuition reimbursements, teaching assistantships with partial tuition reimbursements, institutionally sponsored loans, scholarships/grants, health care benefits, tuition waivers (partial), and unspecified assistantships available. Support available to part-time students. Financial award application deadline: 3/15; financial award applicants required to submit FAFSA. *Unit head:* Dr. Dennis Soden, Director, 915-747-7974, Fax: 915-747-7948, E-mail: desoden@utep.edu. *Application contact:* Dr. Patricia D. Witherspoon, Dean of the Graduate School, 915-747-5491, Fax: 915-747-5788, E-mail: withersp@utep.edu.

The University of Texas at San Antonio, College of Public Policy, Department of Public Administration, San Antonio, TX 78249-0617. Offers MPA. *Accreditation:* NASPAA. Part-time and evening/weekend programs available. *Faculty:* 8 full-time (4 women), 1 part-time/adjunct (0 women). *Students:* 40 full-time (26 women), 115 part-time (77 women); includes 100 minority (14 African Americans, 2 American Indian/Alaska Native, 4 Asian Americans or Pacific Islanders, 80 Hispanic Americans), 2 international. Average age 31. 62 applicants, 84% accepted, 38 enrolled. In 2009, 23 master's awarded. *Degree requirements:* For master's, comprehensive exam (for some programs), thesis (for some programs). *Entrance requirements:* For master's, GMAT or GRE General Test, undergraduate course work in American government, economics, and research methods; minimum GPA of 3.0 on last 60 hours. Additional exam requirements/recommendations for international students: Required—TOEFL (minimum score 500 paper-based; 173 computer-based; 61 iBT), IELTS (minimum score 5). *Application deadline:* For fall admission, 7/1 for domestic students, 4/1 for international students; for spring admission, 11/1 for domestic students, 9/1 for international students. Applications are processed on a rolling basis. Application fee: $45 ($80 for international students). Electronic applications accepted. *Expenses:* Tuition, state resident: full-time $3975; part-time $221 per contact hour. Tuition, nonresident: full-time $13,947; part-time $775 per contact hour. Required fees: $1853. *Financial support:* In 2009–10, 14 students received support, including 13 research assistantships (averaging $10,792 per year); career-related internships or fieldwork, scholarships/grants, tuition waivers, and unspecified assistantships also available. Support available to part-time students. *Faculty research:* Politics-administration relationship process models for decision making, homeland decurity, bureaucratic politics, institutional determinants of public policy. Total annual research expenditures: $11,307. *Unit head:* Dr. Jerrell Coggburn, Chair, 210-458-2501, Fax: 210-458-2536, E-mail: jcoggburn@utsa.edu. *Application contact:* Francine S. Romero, Graduate Advisor, 210-458-2630, E-mail: francine.romero@utsa.edu.

The University of Texas at Tyler, College of Arts and Sciences, Department of Social Sciences, Tyler, TX 75799-0001. Offers criminal justice (MS); public administration (MPA); sociology (MS). Part-time and evening/weekend programs available. *Faculty:* 10 full-time (2 women). *Students:* 7 full-time (3 women), 21 part-time (14 women); includes 8 minority (5 African Americans, 2 American Indian/Alaska Native, 1 Asian American or Pacific Islander), 2 international. Average age 30. 6 applicants, 100% accepted, 6 enrolled. In 2009, 10 master's awarded. *Degree requirements:* For master's, comprehensive exam, thesis optional. *Entrance requirements:* For master's, GRE General Test, minimum GPA of 3.0. Additional exam requirements/recommendations for international students: Required—TOEFL (minimum score 79 computer-based). *Application deadline:* For fall admission, 8/17 priority date for domestic students, 7/1 priority date for international students; for spring admission, 12/21 priority date for domestic students, 11/1 priority date for international students. Applications are processed on a rolling basis. Application fee: $25 ($50 for international students). *Expenses:* Tuition, state resident: part-time $665 per semester hour. Tuition, nonresident: part-time $942 per semester hour. Part-time tuition and fees vary according to degree level and program. *Financial support:* In 2009–10, 1 fellowship (averaging $1,000 per year), 2 research assistantships, 2 teaching assistantships were awarded; career-related internships or fieldwork, Federal Work-Study, and scholarships/grants also available. Support available to part-time students. Financial award application deadline: 7/1; financial award applicants required to submit FAFSA. *Faculty research:* Urban segregation, minority business, violent crime, gender discrimination. *Unit head:* Dr. Ken Wink, Chair, 903-566-7434, Fax: 903-565-5537, E-mail: kwink@mail.uttyl.edu. *Application contact:* Dr. Ken Wink.

The University of Texas–Pan American, College of Social and Behavioral Sciences, Program in Public Administration, Edinburg, TX 78539. Offers MPA. Part-time and evening/weekend programs available. *Degree requirements:* For master's, comprehensive exam (for some programs), thesis optional. *Entrance requirements:* For master's, GRE General Test. Additional exam requirements/recommendations for international students: Required—TOEFL. Electronic applications accepted. *Expenses:* Tuition, state resident: full-time $3630.60; part-time $201.70 per credit hour. Tuition, nonresident: full-time $8617; part-time $478.70 per credit hour. Required fees: $806.50. *Faculty research:* Immigration policy reform, agriculture food policy, social service delivery systems, community development, social welfare policy reform, urban/city management.

University of the District of Columbia, School of Business and Public Administration, Program in Public Administration, Washington, DC 20008-1175. Offers MPA. Part-time and evening/weekend programs available. *Students:* 13 full-time (9 women), 14 part-time (7 women); includes 15 minority (13 African Americans, 1 Asian American or Pacific Islander, 1 Hispanic American). Average age 30. 21 applicants, 43% accepted. In 2009, 4 master's awarded. *Degree requirements:* For master's, comprehensive exam, thesis optional. *Entrance requirements:* For master's, GMAT or GRE General Test, writing proficiency exam. *Application deadline:* For fall admission, 6/15 priority date for domestic students; for spring admission, 11/1 for domestic students. Applications are processed on a rolling basis. Application fee: $20. *Expenses:* Tuition, state resident: full-time $7580. Tuition, nonresident: full-time $14,580. Required fees: $620. *Financial support:* Career-related internships or fieldwork and Federal Work-Study available. *Faculty research:* Government management, public personnel management, urban management, management information systems, public financial management. *Unit head:* Dr. Hany Makhlouf, Chairperson, 202-274-7037. *Application contact:* Ann Marie Waterman, Associate Vice President of Admission, Recruitment and Financial Aid, 202-274-6069.

University of the Virgin Islands, Graduate Programs, Division of Humanities and Social Sciences, Saint Thomas, VI 00802-9990. Offers MPA. Part-time and evening/weekend programs available. *Degree requirements:* For master's, comprehensive exam, thesis or alternative. *Entrance requirements:* For master's, GMAT, GRE, minimum GPA of 2.5. Additional exam requirements/recommendations for international students: Required—TOEFL (minimum score 550 paper-based; 213 computer-based). *Faculty research:* Ethical issues of arbitration, spiritual leadership, accountability.

The University of Toledo, College of Graduate Studies, College of Arts and Sciences, Department of Political Science and Public Administration, Program in Public Administration, Toledo, OH 43606-3390. Offers health care policy (MPA); healthcare policy (Certificate); municipal administration (MPA, Certificate); public administration (MPA). *Accreditation:* NASPAA. *Degree requirements:* For master's, internship. *Entrance requirements:* For master's, GRE General Test, minimum GPA of 3.0. Electronic applications accepted. *Faculty research:* Economic development, health administration, personnel, budgeting, urban administration.

University of Utah, The Graduate School, College of Social and Behavioral Science, Department of Political Science, Program in Public Administration, Salt Lake City, UT 84112. Offers Exec MPA, MPA, JD/MPA, MHA/MPA, MPA/Ed D, MPA/MPH, MPA/MSW, MPA/PhD. *Accreditation:* NASPAA (one or more programs are accredited). Part-time and evening/weekend programs available. *Students:* 81 full-time (36 women), 88 part-time (42 women); includes 17 minority (2 African Americans, 2 American Indian/Alaska Native, 6 Asian Americans or Pacific Islanders, 7 Hispanic Americans), 28 international. Average age 34. 145 applicants, 68% accepted, 85 enrolled. In 2009, 73 master's awarded. *Degree requirements:* For master's, internship, thesis or research paper. *Entrance requirements:* For master's, GMAT, GRE General Test, LSAT, MAT, minimum GPA of 3.2. Additional exam requirements/recommendations for international students: Required—TOEFL (minimum score 580 paper-based; 237 computer-based; 92 iBT). *Application deadline:* For fall admission, 2/15 priority date for domestic and international students. Application fee: $55 ($65 for international students). *Expenses:* Contact institution. *Financial support:* In 2009–10, 14 students received support; research assistantships with full tuition reimbursements available, career-related internships or fieldwork available. Financial award application deadline: 3/15; financial award applicants required to submit FAFSA. *Faculty research:* Non-profit organizations, health policy, environmental policy, law and legal, human resource management, local government, e-government, conflict resolution, organization theory and behavior. *Unit head:* Dr. Richard Green, MPA Program Director, 801-581-6781, E-mail: rick.green@cppa.utah.edu. *Application contact:* Melissa Hall, Program Manager, 801-585-7985, Fax: 801-585-6492, E-mail: melissa.hall@cppa.utah.edu.

University of Vermont, Graduate College, College of Agriculture and Life Sciences, Department of Community Development and Applied Economics, Program in Public Administration, Burlington, VT 05405. Offers MPA. *Students:* 41 (24 women); includes 5 minority (4 Asian Americans or Pacific Islanders, 1 Hispanic American). 40 applicants, 88% accepted, 14 enrolled. In 2009, 9 master's awarded. *Entrance requirements:* For master's, GRE General Test. Additional exam requirements/recommendations for international students: Required—TOEFL (minimum score 550 paper-based; 213 computer-based; 80 iBT). *Application deadline:* For fall admission, 4/1 priority date for domestic students. Applications are processed on a rolling basis. Application fee: $40. Electronic applications accepted. *Expenses:* Tuition, state resident: part-time $508 per credit hour. Tuition, nonresident: part-time $1281 per credit hour. *Financial support:* Fellowships, teaching assistantships available. Financial award application deadline: 3/1. *Unit head:* Dr. Chris Koliba, Coordinator, 802-656-2606. *Application contact:* Dr. Chris Koliba, Coordinator, 802-656-2606.

University of Victoria, Faculty of Graduate Studies, Faculty of Human and Social Development, School of Public Administration, Victoria, BC V8W 2Y2, Canada. Offers dispute resolution (MADR); public administration (MPA, PhD); MPA/LL B. Part-time and evening/weekend programs available. Postbaccalaureate distance learning degree programs offered. *Degree requirements:* For master's, thesis (for some programs), report; for doctorate, thesis/dissertation, candidacy exam. *Entrance requirements:* For master's, GMAT or GRE General Test, professional resume; for doctorate, GMAT or GRE General Test. Additional exam requirements/recommendations for international students: Required—TOEFL (minimum score 610 paper-based; 255 computer-based). Electronic applications accepted. *Faculty research:* Policy analysis, local government, performance management, energy markets, labor markets.

University of Washington, Graduate School, Daniel J. Evans School of Public Affairs, Seattle, WA 98195. Offers public administration (MPA); public policy and management (PhD); JD/MPA; MPA/MAIS; MPA/MPH; MPA/MS; MPA/MUP. *Accreditation:* NASPAA. Part-time and evening/weekend programs available. *Degree requirements:* For master's, thesis, internship or cooperative experience. *Entrance requirements:* For master's and doctorate, GRE General Test, minimum GPA of 3.0. Additional exam requirements/recommendations for international students: Required—TOEFL (minimum score 580 paper-based; 237 computer-based; 92 iBT). Electronic applications accepted. *Faculty research:* Environmental policy, education and social policy, nonprofit management, international affairs, urban and regional development.

University of West Florida, College of Arts and Sciences: Arts, Department of Government, Pensacola, FL 32514-5750. Offers political science (MA), including public administration, security and diplomacy. Part-time and evening/weekend programs available. *Faculty:* 2 full-time (0 women), 1 part-time/adjunct (0 women). *Students:* 6 full-time (1 woman), 8 part-time (3 women); includes 3 minority (all Hispanic Americans). Average age 31. 12 applicants, 67% accepted, 5 enrolled. In 2009, 9 master's awarded. *Degree requirements:* For master's, thesis or alternative. *Entrance requirements:* For master's, GRE General Test, minimum GPA of 3.0. Additional exam requirements/recommendations for international students: Required—TOEFL (minimum score 550 paper-based; 213 computer-based). *Application deadline:* For fall admission, 6/1 for domestic students, 5/15 for international students; for spring admission, 11/1 for domestic students, 10/1 for international students. Applications are processed on a rolling basis. Application fee: $30. *Expenses:* Tuition, state resident: full-time $4982; part-time $260 per credit hour. Tuition, nonresident: full-time $20,059; part-time $919 per credit hour. Required fees: $1247; $52 per credit hour. *Financial support:* In 2009–10, 1 teaching assistantship with partial tuition reimbursement (averaging $5,000 per year) was awarded; unspecified assistantships also available. Financial award application deadline: 4/15; financial award applicants required to submit FAFSA. *Faculty research:* Political campaigns, elections, law enforcement, growth management. *Unit head:* Dr. Alfred Cuzan, Chairperson, 850-474-2337, E-mail: govt@uwf.edu. *Application contact:* Terry McCray, Assistant Director of Graduate Admissions, 850-473-7718, Fax: 850-473-7714, E-mail: gradadmissions@uwf.edu.

University of West Florida, College of Professional Studies, Department of Professional and Community Leadership, Program in Administration, Pensacola, FL 32514-5750. Offers acquisition and contract administration (MSA); biomedical/pharmaceutical (MSA); criminal justice administration (MSA); database administration (MSA); education leadership (MSA); healthcare administration (MSA); human performance technology (MSA); leadership (MSA); nursing administration (MSA); public administration (MSA); software engineering administration (MSA). Part-time and evening/weekend programs available. Postbaccalaureate distance learning degree programs offered (no on-campus study). *Students:* 33 full-time (21 women), 168 part-time (97 women); includes 53 minority (32 African Americans, 2 American Indian/Alaska Native, 5 Asian Americans or Pacific Islanders, 14 Hispanic Americans), 1 international. Average age 34. 103 applicants, 74% accepted, 64 enrolled. In 2009, 47 master's awarded. *Entrance requirements:* For master's, GRE General Test, letter of intent, names of references. Additional exam requirements/recommendations for international students: Required—TOEFL (minimum score 550 paper-based; 213 computer-based). *Application deadline:* For fall admission, 6/1 for domestic students, 5/15 for international students; for spring admission, 11/1 for domestic students, 10/1 for international students. Applications are processed on a rolling basis. Application fee: $30. *Expenses:* Tuition, state resident: full-time $4982; part-time $260 per credit hour. Tuition, nonresident: full-time $20,059; part-time $919 per credit hour. Required fees: $1247; $52 per credit hour. *Financial support:* Unspecified assistantships available. Financial award application deadline: 4/15; financial award applicants required to submit FAFSA. *Unit head:* Dr. Karen Rasmussen, Chairperson, 850-474-2301, Fax: 850-474-2804. *Application contact:* Terry McCray, Assistant Director of Graduate Admissions, 850-473-7718, Fax: 850-473-7714, E-mail: gradadmissions@uwf.edu.

University of West Georgia, Graduate School, College of Arts and Sciences, Department of Political Science and Planning, Carrollton, GA 30118. Offers public administration (MPA); public management (Certificate); rural and small town planning (MS). *Accreditation:* NASPAA (one or more programs are accredited). Part-time programs available. *Faculty:* 11 full-time (1 woman). *Students:* 17 full-time (10 women), 17 part-time (8 women); includes 11 minority (9 African Americans, 2 Asian Americans or Pacific Islanders), 2 international. Average age 29. 16 applicants, 69% accepted, 3 enrolled. In 2009, 11 master's, 2 other advanced degrees awarded. *Degree requirements:* For master's, exit paper. *Entrance requirements:* For master's, GRE General Test. Additional exam requirements/recommendations for international students: Required—TOEFL. *Application deadline:* For fall admission, 7/17 priority date for domestic students; for spring admission, 11/20 for domestic students. Applications are processed on a rolling basis. Application fee: $30. Electronic applications accepted. *Expenses:* Tuition, state resident: full-time $2952; part-time $164 per semester hour. Tuition, nonresident: full-time $11,808; part-time $656 per semester hour. Required fees: $42.90 per semester hour. $307 per semester. Tuition and fees vary according to course load. *Financial support:* In 2009–10, 4 students received support, including 4 research assistantships with partial tuition reimbursements available (averaging $3,000 per year); career-related internships or fieldwork and unspecified assistantships also available. Support available to part-time students. Financial award application deadline: 7/1; financial award applicants required to submit FAFSA. *Faculty research:* State and local government, environmental health, administrative studies. *Unit head:* Dr. Robert M. Schaefer, Chair, 678-839-6504, Fax: 678-839-5009, E-mail: rschaefe@westga.edu. *Application contact:* Dr. Charles W. Clark, Dean, 678-839-6419, E-mail: cclark@westga.edu.

The University of Winnipeg, Graduate Studies, Program in Public Administration, Winnipeg, MB R3B 2E9, Canada. Offers MPA. Part-time programs available. *Degree requirements:* For master's, comprehensive exam, thesis optional. *Entrance requirements:* For master's, minimum GPA of 3.0 in last 60 credit hours. *Faculty research:* Policy evaluation, federalism, administrative innovation, administrative ethics, economic development/administration.

University of Wisconsin–Milwaukee, Graduate School, College of Letters and Sciences, Interdepartmental Program in Public Administration, Milwaukee, WI 53201-0413. Offers MPA, MPA/MUP. Part-time programs available. *Faculty:* 11 full-time (2 women). *Students:* 25 full-time (4 women), 17 part-time (6 women); includes 1 minority (African American). Average age 33. 27 applicants, 74% accepted, 8 enrolled. In 2009, 17 master's awarded. *Degree requirements:* For master's, thesis or alternative. *Entrance requirements:* For master's, GRE General Test, minimum GPA of 3.0. Additional exam requirements/recommendations for international students: Required—TOEFL (minimum score 550 paper-based; 79 iBT), IELTS (minimum score 6.5). *Application deadline:* For fall admission, 1/1 priority date for domestic students; for spring admission, 9/1 for domestic students. Applications are processed on a rolling basis. Application fee: $45 ($75 for international students). *Expenses:* Tuition, state resident: full-time $8800. Tuition, nonresident: full-time $20,760. Tuition and fees vary according to program and reciprocity agreements. *Financial support:* Career-related internships or fieldwork and unspecified assistantships available. Support available to part-time students. Financial award application deadline: 4/15. *Unit head:* Douglas Ihrke, Director, 414-229-4209, Fax: 414-229-5021, E-mail: dihrke@uwm.edu. *Application contact:* General Information Contact, 414-229-4982, Fax: 414-229-6967, E-mail: gradschool@uwm.edu.

University of Wisconsin–Oshkosh, The Office of Graduate Studies, College of Letters and Science, Department of Public Administration, Oshkosh, WI 54901. Offers general agency (MPA); health care (MPA). Part-time and evening/weekend programs available. *Degree requirements:* For master's, thesis or alternative. *Entrance requirements:* For master's, public service-related experience, resume, sample of written work. Additional exam requirements/recommendations for international students: Required—TOEFL (minimum score 550 paper-based; 213 computer-based; 79 iBT). Electronic applications accepted. *Faculty research:* Drug policy, local government state revenues and expenditures, health care regulation.

University of Wyoming, College of Arts and Sciences, Department of Political Science, Program in Public Administration, Laramie, WY 82070. Offers MPA. Part-time programs available. Postbaccalaureate distance learning degree programs offered (minimal on-campus study). *Degree requirements:* For master's, comprehensive exam (for some programs), thesis (for some programs). *Entrance requirements:* For master's, GRE General Test, minimum GPA of 3.0. Additional exam requirements/recommendations for international students: Required—TOEFL (minimum score 525 paper-based; 195 computer-based). Electronic applications accepted. *Faculty research:* Public policy, public ethics, administrative theory, natural resource policy.

Upper Iowa University, Online Master's Programs, Fayette, IA 52142-1857. Offers accounting (MBA); corporate financial management (MBA); global business (MBA); health and human services (MPA); higher education administration (MHEA); homeland security (MPA); human resources management (MBA); justice administration (MPA); organizational development (MBA); public personnel management (MPA); quality management (MBA). MBA also available at Madison, WI campus. Part-time programs available. Postbaccalaureate distance learning degree programs offered (no on-campus study). *Faculty:* 3 full-time (0 women), 66 part-time/adjunct (27 women). *Students:* 723 full-time (442 women). *Degree requirements:* For master's, research project. *Entrance requirements:* For master's, GMAT, GRE, or minimum GPA of 2.7 during last 60 hours. Additional exam requirements/recommendations for international students: Required—TOEFL (minimum score 570 paper-based; 230 computer-based). *Application deadline:* Applications are processed on a rolling basis. Application fee: $50. Electronic applications accepted. *Expenses:* Tuition: Full-time $6948; part-time $386 per credit hour. *Financial support:* Available to part-time students. Applicants required to submit FAFSA. *Faculty research:* Total quality management, CQI, teams, organization culture and climate, management. *Application contact:* David Hannum, Admissions Advisor, 800-603-3756, E-mail: hannumd@uiu.edu.

Villanova University, Graduate School of Liberal Arts and Sciences, Department of Political Science, Program in Public Administration, Villanova, PA 19085-1699. Offers MPA. Part-time and evening/weekend programs available. *Students:* 17 full-time (11 women), 29 part-time (11 women); includes 3 minority (1 African American, 1 Asian American or Pacific Islander, 1 Hispanic American), 2 international. Average age 32. 29 applicants, 90% accepted, 10 enrolled. In 2009, 12 master's awarded. *Degree requirements:* For master's, comprehensive exam. *Entrance requirements:* For master's, GRE General Test, minimum GPA of 3.0. Additional exam requirements/recommendations for international students: Required—TOEFL. *Application deadline:* For fall admission, 3/1 priority date for domestic and international students; for spring admission, 11/15 priority date for domestic and international students. Applications are processed on a rolling basis. Application fee: $50. Electronic applications accepted. *Expenses:* Tuition: Part-time $630 per credit. Required fees: $60 per credit. Part-time tuition and fees vary according to degree level and program. *Financial support:* Career-related internships or fieldwork and scholarships/grants available. Financial award application deadline: 3/15; financial award applicants required to submit FAFSA. *Unit head:* Dr. Markus Kreuzer, Director, 610-519-4710. *Application contact:* Dr. Adele Lindenmeyr.

See Close-Up on page 857.

Virginia Commonwealth University, Graduate School, College of Humanities and Sciences, Wilder School of Government and Public Affairs, Department of Political Science and Public Administration, Richmond, VA 23284-9005. Offers political science and public administration (MPA); public management (CPM). *Accreditation:* NASPAA (one or more programs are accredited). Part-time programs available. *Entrance requirements:* For master's, GRE General Test. *Faculty research:* Public human resources management, financial management, executive management, policy analysis, local government management.

Virginia Polytechnic Institute and State University, Graduate School, College of Architecture and Urban Studies, Center for Public Administration and Policy, Blacksburg, VA 24061. Offers MPA, PhD. *Accreditation:* NASPAA (one or more programs are accredited). *Students:* 54 full-time (22 women), 93 part-time (33 women); includes 39 minority (1 African American, 11 American Indian/Alaska Native, 25 Asian Americans or Pacific Islanders, 2 Hispanic Americans), 3 international. Average age 36. 75 applicants, 77% accepted, 28 enrolled. In 2009, 26 master's, 12 doctorates awarded. *Entrance requirements:* For master's and doctorate, GRE, GMAT. Additional exam requirements/recommendations for international students: Required—TOEFL (minimum score 550 paper-based; 213 computer-based). *Application deadline:* For fall admission, 5/15 for international students; for spring admission, 10/15 for international students. Applications are processed on a rolling basis. Application fee: $65. Electronic applications accepted. *Expenses:* Tuition, area resident: Full-time $10,228; part-time $459 per credit hour. Tuition, nonresident: full-time $17,892; part-time $865 per credit hour. Required fees: $1966; $451 per semester. *Financial support:* Career-related internships or fieldwork, Federal Work-Study, scholarships/grants, and unspecified assistantships available. Financial award application deadline: 1/15. *Faculty research:* Public administration theory, strategic management, ethics, the Constitution, computer-assisted creativity. *Unit head:* Dr. Laura S. Jensen, Dean, 540-231-5197, Fax: 540-231-7067, E-mail: jensen7@vt.edu. *Application contact:* Anne Khademian, Information Contact, 703-706-8119, Fax: 540-231-7067, E-mail: akhademi@vt.edu.

Walden University, Graduate Programs, School of Public Policy and Administration, Minneapolis, MN 55401. Offers general program (MPA); government management (Post-baccalaureate Certificate); health policy (MPA); homeland security policy (MPA); interdisciplinary policy studies (MPA); law and public policy (MPA); local government management for sustainable communities (MPA); nonprofit management (Postbaccalaureate Certificate); nonprofit management and leadership (MPA, MS); policy analysis (MPA); public management and leadership (MPA); public policy and administration (PhD), including criminal justice, health services, homeland security policy and coordination, international nongovernmental organizations, law and public policy, local government management for sustainable communities, nonprofit management and leadership, public management and leadership, public policy, public safety management, terrorism, mediation, and peace; terrorism, mediation, and peace (MPA). Part-time and evening/weekend programs available. Postbaccalaureate distance learning degree programs offered (minimal on-campus study). *Faculty:* 7 full-time, 62 part-time/adjunct. *Students:* 1,468 full-time (941 women), 233 part-time (162 women); includes 852 minority (761 African Americans, 9 American Indian/Alaska Native, 19 Asian Americans or Pacific Islanders, 63 Hispanic Americans), 53 international. Average age 40. In 2009, 173 master's, 13 doctorates awarded. *Degree requirements:* For doctorate, thesis/dissertation, residency. *Entrance requirements:* For master's, bachelor's degree or equivalent in related field, minimum GPA of 2.5; for doctorate, master's degree or equivalent in related field; minimum GPA of 3.0; official transcripts; three years of related professional/academic experience (preferred); access to computer and Internet. Additional exam requirements/recommendations for international students: Required—TOEFL (minimum score 550 paper-based; 213 computer-based), IELTS (minimum score 6.5), or Michigan English Language Assessment Battery (minimum score 82). *Application deadline:* Applications are processed on a rolling basis. Application fee: $50. Electronic applications accepted. *Expenses:* Tuition: Full-time $13,665; part-time $560 per credit. Required fees: $1375. Tuition and fees vary according to course load, degree level and program. *Financial support:* In 2009–10, 207 students received support; fellowships with tuition reimbursements available, Federal Work-Study, scholarships/grants, unspecified assistantships, and family tuition reduction, active duty/veteran tuition reduction, group tuition reduction, interest-free payment plans available. Support available to part-time students. Financial award applicants required to submit FAFSA. *Unit head:* Dr. Mark Gordon, Associate Dean, 800-925-3368. *Application contact:* Jennifer Hall, Director of Enrollment, 866-4-WALDEN, E-mail: info@waldenu.edu.

Washington Adventist University, Program in Public Administration, Takoma Park, MD 20912. Offers MPA. Part-time programs available. *Students:* 1 (woman) full-time, 8 part-time (6 women); includes 6 African Americans. *Application deadline:* Applications are processed on a rolling basis. *Financial support:* Applicants required to submit FAFSA. *Unit head:* Dr. Davenia Lea, Dean, School of Graduate and Professional Studies, 301-891-4464, E-mail: dlea@wau.edu. *Application contact:* Dr. Davenia Lea, Dean, School of Graduate and Professional Studies, 301-891-4464, E-mail: dlea@wau.edu.

Wayland Baptist University, Graduate Programs, Program in Counseling, Plainview, TX 79072-6998. Offers counseling (MA); government administration (MPA); homeland security (MPA); justice administration (MPA). Part-time and evening/weekend programs available. Postbaccalaureate distance learning degree programs offered. *Faculty:* 9 full-time (2 women). *Students:* 71 part-time (58 women); includes 16 minority (5 African Americans, 1 American Indian/Alaska Native, 10 Hispanic Americans). Average age 34. 21 applicants, 90% accepted, 11 enrolled. In 2009, 16 master's awarded. *Degree requirements:* For master's, comprehensive exam. *Entrance requirements:* For master's, GRE, MAT. Additional exam requirements/recommendations for international students: Required—TOEFL (minimum score 500 paper-

Public Administration

Wayland Baptist University (continued)

based; 173 computer-based; 61 iBT). *Application deadline:* Applications are processed on a rolling basis. Application fee: $50. Electronic applications accepted. *Expenses:* Tuition: Full-time $5796; part-time $322 per credit hour. Required fees: $782; $9 per credit hour. $60 per semester. Tuition and fees vary according to course load and campus/location. *Financial support:* Federal Work-Study, institutionally sponsored loans, and scholarships/grants available. Support available to part-time students. Financial award application deadline: 5/1; financial award applicants required to submit FAFSA. *Unit head:* Dr. Estelle Owens, Chairman, 806-291-1171, Fax: 806-291-1972, E-mail: owensest@wbu.edu. *Application contact:* Amanda Stanton, Graduate Studies, 806-291-3423, Fax: 806-291-1950, E-mail: stanton@wbu.edu.

Wayne State University, College of Liberal Arts and Sciences, Department of Political Science, Program in Public Administration, Detroit, MI 48202. Offers criminal justice (MPA); public administration (MPA). *Accreditation:* NASPAA. Evening/weekend programs available. *Entrance requirements:* For master's, GRE General Test. Additional exam requirements/recommendations for international students: Required—TOEFL (minimum score 550 paper-based; 213 computer-based); Recommended—TWE (minimum score 6). Electronic applications accepted. *Faculty research:* Urban politics, urban education, state administration.

Webster University, George Herbert Walker School of Business and Technology, Department of Management, St. Louis, MO 63119-3194. Offers business and organizational security management (MA); computer resources and information management (MA); environmental management (MS); government contracting (Certificate); health care management (MA); health services management (MA); human resources development (MA); human resources management (MA); management (DM); management and leadership (MA); marketing (MA); nonprofit management (Certificate); procurement and acquisitions management (MA); public administration (MA); quality management (MA); space systems operations management (MS); telecommunications management (MA). Part-time and evening/weekend programs available. Postbaccalaureate distance learning degree programs offered (no on-campus study). *Faculty:* 16 full-time, 781 part-time/adjunct. *Students:* 1,369 full-time (610 women), 5,182 part-time (3,047 women); includes 3,460 minority (2,835 African Americans, 38 American Indian/Alaska Native, 169 Asian Americans or Pacific Islanders, 418 Hispanic Americans), 80 international. Average age 37. In 2009, 2,491 master's, 13 doctorates, 68 other advanced degrees awarded. *Degree requirements:* For master's, thesis (for some programs); for doctorate, thesis/dissertation, written exam. *Entrance requirements:* For doctorate, GMAT, 3 years of work experience, MBA. Additional exam requirements/recommendations for international students: Required—TOEFL. *Application deadline:* Applications are processed on a rolling basis. Application fee: $25 ($50 for international students). *Expenses:* Tuition: Part-time $565 per credit hour. Tuition and fees vary according to degree level, campus/location and program. *Financial support:* Federal Work-Study available. Support available to part-time students. Financial award application deadline: 4/1; financial award applicants required to submit FAFSA. *Unit head:* Jim Brasfield, Chair, 314-961-2660 Ext. 7063, Fax: 314-968-7077, E-mail: mgtchair@webster.edu. *Application contact:* Matt Nolan, Assoc. V.P.—Enrollment Management / Dean of Admissions, Fax: 314-968-7116, E-mail: gadmit@webster.edu.

West Chester University of Pennsylvania, Office of Graduate Studies, College of Business and Public Affairs, Department of Political Science, West Chester, PA 19383. Offers administration (Certificate); human resource management (MSA, Certificate); individualized (MSA); non profit administration (Certificate); nonprofit administration (MSA); public administration (MSA); training and development (MSA). Part-time and evening/weekend programs available. *Students:* 3 full-time (2 women), 42 part-time (31 women); includes 8 minority (6 African Americans, 2 Hispanic Americans), 2 international. Average age 28. 28 applicants, 96% accepted, 11 enrolled. In 2009, 12 master's awarded. *Degree requirements:* For master's, comprehensive exam (for some programs). *Entrance requirements:* For master's, GMAT, GRE General Test, or MAT; for Certificate, GMAT, GRE General Test, or MAT, statement of professional goals, resume, two letters of reference. Additional exam requirements/recommendations for international students: Required—TOEFL (minimum score 550 paper-based; 213 computer-based; 80 iBT). *Application deadline:* For fall admission, 4/15 priority date for domestic students, 3/15 for international students; for spring admission, 10/15 for domestic students, 9/1 for international students. Applications are processed on a rolling basis. Application fee: $35. Electronic applications accepted. *Expenses:* Tuition, state resident: full-time $6666; part-time $370 per credit. Tuition, nonresident: full-time $10,666; part-time $593 per credit. Required fees: $122.56 per credit. *Financial support:* In 2009–10, 5 research assistantships with full and partial tuition reimbursements (averaging $5,000 per year) were awarded; unspecified assistantships also available. Support available to part-time students. Financial award application deadline: 2/15; financial award applicants required to submit FAFSA. *Unit head:* Dr. Christopher Fiorentino, Dean, College of Business and Public Affairs, 610-436-2930, E-mail: cfiorentino@wcupa.edu. *Application contact:* Dr. Lorraine Bernotsky, Graduate Coordinator, 610-738-0576, E-mail: lbernotsky@wcupa.edu.

Western Illinois University, School of Graduate Studies, College of Arts and Sciences, Department of Political Science, Macomb, IL 61455-1390. Offers political science (MA); public and non-profit management (Certificate). Part-time programs available. *Students:* 22 full-time (9 women), 3 part-time (1 woman); includes 4 minority (2 African Americans, 2 Hispanic Americans), 6 international. Average age 26. 20 applicants, 70% accepted. In 2009, 10 master's, 1 other advanced degree awarded. *Degree requirements:* For master's, comprehensive exam, thesis or alternative. *Entrance requirements:* Additional exam requirements/recommendations for international students: Required—TOEFL (minimum score 550 paper-based; 213 computer-based; 80 iBT). *Application deadline:* Applications are processed on a rolling basis. Application fee: $30. Electronic applications accepted. *Expenses:* Tuition, state resident: full-time $4486; part-time $249.21 per credit hour. Tuition, nonresident: full-time $8972; part-time $498.42 per credit hour. Required fees: $72.62 per credit hour. *Financial support:* In 2009–10, 15 students received support, including 15 research assistantships with full tuition reimbursements available (averaging $7,280 per year). Financial award applicants required to submit FAFSA. *Unit head:* Dr. Richard Hardy, Chairperson, 309-298-1055. *Application contact:* Evelyn Hoing, Assistant Director of Graduate Studies, 309-298-1806, Fax: 309-298-2345, E-mail: grad-office@wiu.edu.

Western International University, Graduate Programs in Business, Master of Public Administration Program, Phoenix, AZ 85021-2718. Offers MPA. Part-time and evening/weekend programs available. Postbaccalaureate distance learning degree programs offered (no on-campus study). *Faculty:* 27 part-time/adjunct (6 women). *Students:* 46 full-time (33 women); includes 14 minority (8 African Americans, 2 Asian Americans or Pacific Islanders, 4 Hispanic Americans). Average age 39. In 2009, 19 master's awarded. *Entrance requirements:* For master's, minimum GPA of 2.75. Additional exam requirements/recommendations for international students: Required—TOEFL (minimum score 550 paper-based; 213 computer-based; 79 iBT), TWE (minimum score 5), or IELTS (minimum score 6.5). *Application deadline:* Applications are processed on a rolling basis. Application fee: $25. Electronic applications accepted. *Expenses:* Tuition: Full-time $12,600. One-time fee: $25 full-time. *Financial support:* Applicants required to submit FAFSA. *Unit head:* Dr. Deborah DeSimone, Department Chair, 602-429-1135, E-mail: deborah.desimone@west.edu. *Application contact:* Karen Janitell, Director of Enrollment, 602-943-2311 Ext. 1063, Fax: 602-371-8637, E-mail: karen.janitell@wintu.edu.

Western Michigan University, Graduate College, College of Arts and Sciences, Department of Political Science, Program in Development Administration, Kalamazoo, MI 49008. Offers MDA.

Western Michigan University, Graduate College, College of Arts and Sciences, School of Public Affairs and Administration, Kalamazoo, MI 49008. Offers health care administration (Graduate Certificate); nonprofit leadership and administration (Graduate Certificate); public administration (MPA, PhD). *Accreditation:* NASPAA (one or more programs are accredited). *Degree requirements:* For doctorate, thesis/dissertation, oral exams. *Entrance requirements:* For doctorate, GRE General Test.

West Virginia University, Eberly College of Arts and Sciences, School of Applied Social Sciences, Division of Public Administration, Morgantown, WV 26506. Offers legal studies (MLS); public administration (MPA); JD/MPA; MSW/MPA. *Accreditation:* NASPAA. Part-time programs available. *Degree requirements:* For master's, internship. *Entrance requirements:* For master's, GRE General Test, minimum GPA of 2.75. Additional exam requirements/recommendations for international students: Required—TOEFL. Electronic applications accepted. *Faculty research:* Public management and organization, conflict resolution, work satisfaction, health administration, social policy and welfare.

Wichita State University, Graduate School, Fairmount College of Liberal Arts and Sciences, Hugo Wall School of Urban and Public Affairs, Wichita, KS 67260. Offers public administration (MPA). *Accreditation:* NASPAA. Part-time programs available. *Expenses:* Tuition, state resident: full-time $4247; part-time $235.95 per credit hour. Tuition, nonresident: full-time $11,171; part-time $620.60 per credit hour. Required fees: $34; $3.60 per credit hour. $17 per term. Tuition and fees vary according to campus/location and program. *Unit head:* Dr. John D. Wong, Interim Director, 316-978-7240, Fax: 316-978-6533, E-mail: john.wong@wichita.edu. *Application contact:* Dr. John D. Wong, Interim Director, 316-978-7240, Fax: 316-978-6533, E-mail: john.wong@wichita.edu.

Widener University, College of Arts and Sciences, Program in Public Administration, Chester, PA 19013-5792. Offers MPA, Psy D/MPA. Part-time and evening/weekend programs available. *Faculty:* 1 full-time (0 women), 3 part-time/adjunct (0 women). *Students:* 1 (woman) full-time, 21 part-time (14 women); includes 6 minority (5 African Americans, 1 Asian American or Pacific Islander). Average age 31. 21 applicants, 86% accepted. In 2009, 9 master's awarded. *Degree requirements:* For master's, thesis or comprehensive exam. *Entrance requirements:* For master's, minimum undergraduate GPA of 3.0. *Application deadline:* For fall admission, 8/1 priority date for domestic students; for spring admission, 12/1 priority date for domestic students. Applications are processed on a rolling basis. Application fee: $25 ($300 for international students). Electronic applications accepted. *Expenses:* Contact institution. *Financial support:* In 2009–10, 8 students received support. Career-related internships or fieldwork and institutionally sponsored loans available. Support available to part-time students. Financial award application deadline: 5/1. *Faculty research:* Intergovernmental relations, nonprofit organizations, public policy, political economy, bureaucratic politics. *Unit head:* Dr. James E. Vike, Director, 610-499-1120, Fax: 610-499-4603, E-mail: james.vike@widener.edu. *Application contact:* Christine M. Weist, Assistant to Associate Provost for Graduate Studies, 610-499-4351, Fax: 610-499-4277, E-mail: christine.m.weist@widener.edu.

Wilmington University, College of Business, New Castle, DE 19720-6491. Offers business administration (MBA); finance (MBA); health care administration (MBA, MS); homeland security (MBA, MS); human resource management (MS); management (MS); management information systems (MBA); organizational leadership (MS); public administration (MS); transportation and logistics (MBA, MS). Part-time and evening/weekend programs available. *Entrance requirements:* Additional exam requirements/recommendations for international students: Required—TOEFL (minimum score 500 paper-based; 173 computer-based). Electronic applications accepted.

Wright State University, School of Graduate Studies, College of Liberal Arts, Department of Urban Affairs and Geography, Dayton, OH 45435. Offers public administration (MPA). *Accreditation:* NASPAA. *Degree requirements:* For master's, thesis optional. *Entrance requirements:* For master's, interview, minimum GPA of 2.7. Additional exam requirements/recommendations for international students: Required—TOEFL. *Faculty research:* Strategic planning, economic development, housing and public management.

York University, Faculty of Graduate Studies, Atkinson Faculty of Liberal and Professional Studies, Program in Public Policy, Administration and Law, Toronto, ON M3J 1P3, Canada. Offers MPPAL.

York University, Faculty of Graduate Studies, Schulich School of Business, Toronto, ON M3J 1P3, Canada. Offers administration (PhD); business (MBA); finance (MF); international business (IMBA); public administration (MPA); MBA/JD; MBA/MA; MBA/MFA. Part-time and evening/weekend programs available. *Degree requirements:* For master's, advanced proficiency in a second language, work term (IMBA); for doctorate, comprehensive exam, thesis/dissertation. *Entrance requirements:* For master's, GMAT, minimum GPA of 3.0; for doctorate, GMAT, minimum GPA of 3.3. Electronic applications accepted.

Public Affairs

American University, School of Communication, Program in Journalism and Public Affairs, Washington, DC 20016-8001. Offers broadcast journalism (MA), including economic communication, international journalism, public policy journalism; interactive journalism (MA); news media studies (MA); print journalism (MA), including economic communication, international journalism, public policy journalism. *Accreditation:* ACEJMC. Part-time and evening/weekend programs available. *Faculty:* 13 full-time (5 women), 4 part-time/adjunct (all women). *Students:* 24 full-time (16 women). 190 applicants, 63% accepted. In 2009, 40 master's awarded. *Degree requirements:* For master's, comprehensive exam, thesis or alternative. *Entrance requirements:* For master's, GRE General Test. Additional exam requirements/recommendations for international students: Required—TOEFL (minimum score 600 paper-based; 250 computer-based). *Application deadline:* For fall admission, 2/1 priority date for domestic students, 4/1 priority date for international students. Applications are processed on a rolling basis. Application fee: $50. Electronic applications accepted. *Expenses:* Tuition: Full-time $22,266; part-time $1237 per credit hour. Required fees: $430. Tuition and fees vary according to program. *Financial support:* In 2009–10, 3 fellowships with partial tuition reimbursements (averaging $27,000 per year), 14 research assistantships with tuition reimbursements (averaging $7,000 per year), 3 teaching assistantships with tuition reimbursements (averaging $7,000 per year) were awarded; career-related internships or fieldwork, Federal Work-Study, institutionally sponsored loans, scholarships/grants, tuition waivers (partial), and unspecified assistantships also available. Financial award application deadline: 2/1. *Faculty research:* Government and media effects of journalistic practices and policies, race and gender and the media, investigative reporting, computer assisted reporting. *Unit head:* Wendell Cochran, Division Director, 202-885-2075. *Application contact:* Sharmeen Ahsan-Bracciale, Graduate Admissions Office, 202-885-2040, Fax: 202-885-2019, E-mail: sharmeen@american.edu.

See Close-Up on page 673.

Arizona State University, Graduate College, College of Public Programs, School of Public Affairs, Tempe, AZ 85287. Offers MPA, MPP, PhD, MPA/MSW. *Accreditation:* NASPAA (one or more programs are accredited). *Degree requirements:* For doctorate, thesis/dissertation. *Entrance requirements:* For master's, GRE.

Clemson University, Graduate School, Program in International Family and Community Studies, Clemson, SC 29634. Offers PhD. *Faculty:* 6 full-time (3 women), 3 part-time/adjunct (all women). *Students:* 15 full-time (14 women), 2 part-time (1 woman); includes 2 minority (1 African American, 1 Asian American or Pacific Islander), 8 international. Average age 32. 4 applicants, 50% accepted, 2 enrolled. *Degree requirements:* For doctorate, thesis/dissertation. *Entrance requirements:* For doctorate, GRE General Test. Additional exam requirements/recommendations for international students: Required—TOEFL. *Application deadline:* Applications are processed on a rolling basis. Application fee: $70 ($80 for international students). Electronic applications accepted. *Expenses:* Contact institution. *Financial support:* In 2009–10, 14 students received support, including 3 fellowships with full and partial tuition reimbursements available (averaging $15,000 per year), 14 research assistantships with partial tuition reimbursements available (averaging $19,677 per year); career-related internships or fieldwork, institutionally sponsored loans, scholarships/grants, health care benefits, and unspecified assistantships also available. Support available to part-time students. Total annual research expenditures: $3.2 million. *Unit head:* Dr. Gary B. Melton, Director, 964-656-6271. *Application contact:* Information Contact, 861-656-3195, E-mail: gradapp@clemson.edu.

Concordia University, School of Graduate Studies, Faculty of Arts and Science, School of Community and Public Affairs, Montréal, QC H3G 1M8, Canada. Offers community economic development (Diploma).

Cornell University, Graduate School, Graduate Fields of Arts and Sciences, Field of Public Affairs, Ithaca, NY 14853-0001. Offers public affairs (MPA); public policy (MPA). *Faculty:* 116 full-time (32 women). *Students:* 188 full-time (100 women); includes 29 minority (13 African Americans, 10 Asian Americans or Pacific Islanders, 6 Hispanic Americans), 98 international. Average age 27. 348 applicants, 67% accepted, 110 enrolled. In 2009, 69 master's awarded. *Degree requirements:* For master's, thesis, research project, paper. *Entrance requirements:* For master's, GRE General Test, 2 letters of recommendation. Additional exam requirements/recommendations for international students: Required—TOEFL (minimum score 550 paper-based; 213 computer-based; 77 iBT). *Application deadline:* Applications are processed on a rolling basis. Application fee: $70. Electronic applications accepted. *Expenses:* Tuition: Full-time $29,500. Required fees: $70. Full-time tuition and fees vary according to degree level, program and student level. *Financial support:* In 2009–10, 9 students received support, including 4 fellowships with full tuition reimbursements available, 1 research assistantship with full tuition reimbursement available; teaching assistantships with full tuition reimbursements available, institutionally sponsored loans, scholarships/grants, health care benefits, tuition waivers (full and partial), and unspecified assistantships also available. Financial award applicants required to submit FAFSA. *Unit head:* Director of Graduate Studies, 607-255-8018, Fax: 607-255-5240. *Application contact:* Graduate Field Assistant, 607-255-8018, Fax: 607-255-5240, E-mail: cipa@cornell.edu.

See Close-Up on page 1181.

DePaul University, School of Public Service, Chicago, IL 60604. Offers financial administration management (Certificate); health administration (Certificate); health law and policy (MS); international public services (MS); leadership and policy studies (MS); metropolitan planning (Certificate); public administration (MPA); public service management (MS), including association management, fundraising and philanthropy, healthcare administration, higher education administration, metropolitan planning; public services (Certificate); JD/MS. Part-time and evening/weekend programs available. Postbaccalaureate distance learning degree programs offered (minimal on-campus study). *Faculty:* 14 full-time (3 women), 43 part-time/adjunct (24 women). *Students:* 283 full-time (206 women), 298 part-time (208 women); includes 196 minority (112 African Americans, 1 American Indian/Alaska Native, 30 Asian Americans or Pacific Islanders, 53 Hispanic Americans), 18 international. Average age 26. 162 applicants, 100% accepted, 94 enrolled. In 2009, 108 master's awarded. *Degree requirements:* For master's, thesis or integrative seminar. *Entrance requirements:* For master's, minimum GPA of 2.7. Additional exam requirements/recommendations for international students: Required—TOEFL (minimum score 550 paper-based; 213 computer-based; 80 iBT), IELTS (minimum score 6.5). *Application deadline:* Applications are processed on a rolling basis. Application fee: $40. Electronic applications accepted. *Expenses:* Tuition: Full-time $37,525; part-time $620 per credit hour. *Financial support:* In 2009–10, 60 students received support, including 3 research assistantships with full tuition reimbursements available (averaging $7,000 per year); career-related internships or fieldwork, Federal Work-Study, institutionally sponsored loans, scholarships/grants, tuition waivers (partial), and unspecified assistantships also available. Support available to part-time students. Financial award application deadline: 7/1; financial award applicants required to submit FAFSA. *Faculty research:* Government financing, transportation, leadership, health care, volunteerism and organizational behavior, non-profit organizations. Total annual research expenditures: $20,000. *Unit head:* Dr. J. Patrick Murphy, Director, 312-362-5608, Fax: 312-362-5506, E-mail: jpmurphy@depaul.edu. *Application contact:* Megan B. Balderston, Director of Admissions and Marketing, 312-362-5565, Fax: 312-362-5506, E-mail: pubserv@depaul.edu.

George Mason University, College of Humanities and Social Sciences, Department of Public and International Affairs, Fairfax, VA 22030. Offers association management (Certificate); biodefense (MS, PhD); critical analysis and strategic responses to terrorism (Certificate); nonprofit management (Certificate); political science (MA, PhD); public administration (MPA); public management (Certificate). *Accreditation:* NASPAA (one or more programs are accredited). *Faculty:* 37 full-time (14 women), 34 part-time/adjunct (7 women). *Students:* 115 full-time (62 women), 323 part-time (182 women); includes 60 minority (29 African Americans, 1 American Indian/Alaska Native, 18 Asian Americans or Pacific Islanders, 12 Hispanic Americans), 21 international. Average age 31. 458 applicants, 60% accepted, 129 enrolled. In 2009, 147 master's, 2 doctorates, 6 other advanced degrees awarded. *Entrance requirements:* For master's, GRE General Test, minimum GPA of 3.0 in last 60 hours of course work. Additional exam requirements/recommendations for international students: Required—TOEFL. *Application deadline:* For fall admission, 3/1 priority date for domestic students; for spring admission, 10/15 for domestic students. Application fee: $75. Electronic applications accepted. *Expenses:* Tuition, state resident: full-time $7568; part-time $315.33 per credit hour. Tuition, nonresident: full-time $21,704; part-time $904.33 per credit hour. Required fees: $2184; $91 per credit hour. *Financial support:* In 2009–10, 27 students received support, including 3 fellowships with full tuition reimbursements available (averaging $18,000 per year), 10 research assistantships with full and partial tuition reimbursements available (averaging $11,033 per year), 14 teaching assistantships with full and partial tuition reimbursements available (averaging $9,213 per year); Federal Work-Study, scholarships/grants, unspecified assistantships, and health care benefits (full-time research or teaching assistantship recipients) also available. Support available to part-time students. Financial award application deadline: 3/1; financial award applicants required to submit FAFSA. *Faculty research:* The Rehnquist Court and economic liberties; intersection of economic development with high-tech industry, telecommunications, and entrepreneurism; political economy of development; violence, terrorism and U.S. foreign policy; international security issues. Total annual research expenditures: $429,868. *Unit head:* Dr. Robert Dudley, Chair, 703-993-1400, Fax: 703-993-1399, E-mail: rdudley@gmu.edu. *Application contact:* Peg Koback, Information Contact, 703-993-9466, E-mail: mkoback@gmu.edu.

The George Washington University, Columbian College of Arts and Sciences, School of Media and Public Affairs, Washington, DC 20052. Offers MA. *Faculty:* 22 full-time (6 women), 20 part-time/adjunct (4 women). *Students:* 17 full-time (11 women), 10 part-time (8 women); includes 3 minority (1 American Indian/Alaska Native, 1 Asian American or Pacific Islander, 1 Hispanic American), 5 international. Average age 26. 106 applicants, 56% accepted, 14 enrolled. In 2009, 22 master's awarded. *Degree requirements:* For master's, thesis optional. *Entrance requirements:* For master's, GRE General Test. Additional exam requirements/recommendations for international students: Required—TOEFL (minimum score 550 paper-based; 213 computer-based; 80 iBT). *Application deadline:* For fall admission, 4/1 priority date for domestic students, 1/15 priority date for international students; for spring admission, 10/1 priority date for domestic students, 9/1 priority date for international students. Applications are processed on a rolling basis. Application fee: $60. Electronic applications accepted. *Financial support:* In 2009–10, fellowships with tuition reimbursements (averaging $10,000 per year), teaching assistantships with tuition reimbursements (averaging $5,000 per year) were awarded. Financial award application deadline: 1/15. *Unit head:* Lee W. Huebner, Director, 202-994-6227, E-mail: huebner@gwu.edu. *Application contact:* Information Contact, 202-994-6227, Fax: 202-994-5806, E-mail: smpa@gwu.edu.

Indiana University Bloomington, School of Public and Environmental Affairs, Public Affairs Programs, Bloomington, IN 47405-7000. Offers comparative and international affairs (MPA); economic development (MPA); energy (MPA); environmental policy and natural resource management (MPA); information systems (MPA); local government management (MPA); nonprofit management (MPA); policy analysis (MPA); public financial administration (MPA); public management (MPA); sustainability and sustainable development (MPA); JD/MPA; MPA/MA; MPA/MIS; MPA/MLS; MSES/MPA. *Accreditation:* NASPAA (one or more programs are accredited). Part-time programs available. *Faculty:* 75 full-time (22 women), 91 part-time/adjunct (24 women). *Students:* 389 full-time (222 women), 45 part-time (24 women); includes 38 minority (18 African Americans, 1 American Indian/Alaska Native, 12 Asian Americans or Pacific Islanders, 7 Hispanic Americans), 72 international. Average age 26. 474 applicants, 206 enrolled. In 2009, 190 master's, 11 doctorates, 3 other advanced degrees awarded. Terminal master's awarded for partial completion of doctoral program. *Degree requirements:* For master's, thesis optional; for doctorate, comprehensive exam, thesis/dissertation or alternative, A thesis is required for the Public Affairs and Public Policy degree. *Entrance requirements:* For master's, GRE, LSAT (if also applying for the Law School), 3 letters of recommendation, resume or curriculum vitae; for doctorate, GRE General Test. Additional exam requirements/recommendations for international students: Required—TOEFL (minimum score 590 paper-based; 243 computer-based; 96 iBT). *Application deadline:* For fall admission, 2/1 priority date for domestic students, 12/1 priority date for international students; for spring admission, 9/1 for international students. Application fee: $55 ($65 for international students). Electronic applications accepted. *Financial support:* Fellowships with full tuition reimbursements, research assistantships with partial tuition reimbursements, teaching assistantships with partial tuition reimbursements, career-related internships or fieldwork, Federal Work-Study, institutionally sponsored loans, unspecified assistantships, and Service Corps programs available. Financial award application deadline: 2/1; financial award applicants required to submit FAFSA. *Faculty research:* Comparative and international affairs, environmental policy and resource management, policy analysis, public finance, public management, urban management, nonprofit management. *Unit head:* Dean John Graham, Dean, School of Public and Environmental Affairs, 812-855-1432, E-mail: grahamjd@indiana.edu. *Application contact:* Jennifer Medlin, Assistant Director of Admissions and Financial Aid, 812-855-3784, Fax: 812-856-3665, E-mail: jlmedlin@indiana.edu.

See Close-Up on page 1189.

Indiana University Northwest, School of Public and Environmental Affairs, Gary, IN 46408-1197. Offers criminal justice (MPA); environmental affairs (Graduate Certificate); health services administration (MPA); human services administration (MPA); nonprofit management (Graduate Certificate); public management (MPA, Graduate Certificate). *Accreditation:* NASPAA (one or more programs are accredited). Part-time programs available. *Faculty:* 5 full-time (3 women). *Students:* 19 full-time (14 women), 121 part-time (100 women); includes 100 minority (84 African Americans, 1 American Indian/Alaska Native, 1 Asian American or Pacific Islander, 14 Hispanic Americans). Average age 39. In 2009, 29 master's, 27 other advanced degrees awarded. *Entrance requirements:* For master's, GRE General Test or GMAT, letters of recommendation. *Application deadline:* For fall admission, 8/15 priority date for domestic students. Applications are processed on a rolling basis. Application fee: $25. *Financial support:* Career-related internships or fieldwork, Federal Work-Study, and tuition waivers (partial) available. Support available to part-time students. Financial award application deadline: 3/1. *Faculty research:* Employment in income security policies, evidence in criminal justice, equal employment law, social welfare policy and welfare reform, public finance in developing countries. *Unit head:* George Assibey-Mensah, Interim Dean/Division Director, 219-980-6695, Fax: 219-980-6737. *Application contact:* Sandra Hall Smith, Secretary, 219-980-6695, Fax: 219-980-6737, E-mail: shsmith@iun.edu.

Indiana University of Pennsylvania, School of Graduate Studies and Research, College of Humanities and Social Sciences, Department of Political Science, Program in Public Affairs, Indiana, PA 15705-1087. Offers MA. Part-time programs available. *Faculty:* 5 full-time (3 women). *Students:* 8 full-time (1 woman), 3 part-time (2 women), 5 international. Average age 34. 15 applicants, 47% accepted, 4 enrolled. In 2009, 5 master's awarded. *Degree requirements:* For master's, thesis optional. *Entrance requirements:* For master's, GRE, 2 letters of recommendation. Additional exam requirements/recommendations for international students: Required—TOEFL. *Application deadline:* For fall admission, 7/1 priority date for domestic students; for spring admission, 11/1 for domestic students. Applications are processed on a rolling basis. Application fee: $40. *Expenses:* Tuition, state resident: full-time $6666; part-time $370 per credit hour. Tuition, nonresident: full-time $10,666; part-time $593 per credit hour. Required fees: $813 per semester. *Financial support:* In 2009–10, 8 research assistantships with full and partial tuition reimbursements (averaging $3,400 per year) were awarded. Financial award application deadline: 3/15; financial award applicants required to submit FAFSA. *Unit head:* Dr. Susan Martin, Graduate Coordinator, 724-357-2776, E-mail: susan.martin@iup.edu. *Application contact:* Dr. David Chambers, Graduate Coordinator, 724-357-2776, E-mail: chambers@iup.edu.

Indiana University–Purdue University Fort Wayne, Division of Public and Environmental Affairs, Fort Wayne, IN 46805-1499. Offers public affairs (MPA); public management (MPM, Certificate). *Accreditation:* NASPAA (one or more programs are accredited). Part-time programs available. *Faculty:* 9 full-time (3 women). *Students:* 16 full-time (9 women), 28 part-time (18 women); includes 2 minority (both African Americans), 4 international. Average age 30. 18 applicants, 89% accepted, 15 enrolled. In 2009, 10 master's, 3 Certificates awarded. *Degree requirements:* For master's, internship. *Entrance requirements:* For master's, GRE General Test or GMAT, minimum GPA of 3.0, 3 letters of reference. Additional exam requirements/recommendations for international students: Required—TOEFL (minimum score 550 paper-based; 213 computer-based; 77 iBT). *Application deadline:* Applications are processed on a rolling basis. Application fee: $55. *Expenses:* Tuition, state resident: full-time $4595; part-time $255 per credit. Tuition, nonresident: full-time $10,963; part-time $609 per credit. Required fees: $528; $29.35 per credit. Tuition and fees vary according to course load. *Financial support:* Career-related internships or fieldwork and scholarships/grants available. Support available to part-time students. Financial award application deadline: 3/1; financial award applicants required to submit FAFSA. *Faculty research:* Physician assisted suicide, charters, juvenile offenders, retirement. *Unit head:* Dr. Jane Grant, Chair, 260-481-6349, Fax: 260-481-6346, E-mail: grant@ipfw.edu. *Application contact:* Dr. Brian L. Fife, Director of Graduate Studies, 260-481-6961, Fax: 260-481-6346, E-mail: fifeb@ipfw.edu.

Indiana University–Purdue University Indianapolis, School of Public and Environmental Affairs, Indianapolis, IN 46202-2896. Offers health administration (MHA); public affairs (MPA), including criminal justice, environmental management, nonprofit management, policy analysis, public management; JD/MHA; MBA/MHA; MLS/NMC; MLS/PMC; MSN/MHA. *Accreditation:* CAHME (one or more programs are accredited); NASPAA. Part-time and evening/weekend programs available. *Faculty:* 17 full-time (6 women). *Students:* 126 full-time (71 women), 283 part-time (164 women); includes 58 minority (29 African Americans, 1 American Indian/Alaska Native, 17 Asian Americans or Pacific Islanders, 11 Hispanic Americans), 20 international. Average age 33. 255 applicants, 77% accepted, 136 enrolled. In 2009, 77 master's awarded. *Entrance requirements:* For master's, GRE General Test, minimum GPA of 3.0 (preferred). Additional exam requirements/recommendations for international students: Required—TOEFL.

Public Affairs

Indiana University–Purdue University Indianapolis (continued)
Application deadline: For fall admission, 7/15 priority date for domestic students; for spring admission, 11/15 for domestic students. Applications are processed on a rolling basis. Application fee: $55 ($65 for international students). *Financial support:* In 2009–10, 11 fellowships with full and partial tuition reimbursements (averaging $5,890 per year), 10 teaching assistantships (averaging $9,900 per year) were awarded; research assistantships with full and partial tuition reimbursements, career-related internships or fieldwork, Federal Work-Study, institutionally sponsored loans, and scholarships/grants also available. Support available to part-time students. Financial award application deadline: 3/1. *Faculty research:* Economic development, water and air quality, ethics, financing, organization design and structure. Total annual research expenditures: $1.9 million. *Unit head:* Dr. Greg Lindsey, Associate Dean, 317-274-4656, Fax: 317-274-5153. *Application contact:* 317-274-4656, Fax: 317-274-5153, E-mail: speainfo@speanet.iupui.edu.

Indiana University South Bend, School of Public and Environmental Affairs, South Bend, IN 46634-7111. Offers health systems administration and policy (MPA); health systems management (Certificate); nonprofit management (Certificate); public and community services administration and policy (MPA); public management (Certificate); urban affairs (Certificate). *Accreditation:* NASPAA. Part-time and evening/weekend programs available. *Faculty:* 4 full-time (1 woman). *Students:* 18 part-time (13 women); includes 3 minority (2 African Americans, 1 Hispanic American). Average age 40. In 2009, 9 master's awarded. *Entrance requirements:* For master's, GRE General Test, minimum undergraduate GPA of 2.5. *Application deadline:* For fall admission, 7/1 priority date for domestic students; for spring admission, 11/1 for domestic students. Applications are processed on a rolling basis. Application fee: $46 ($58 for international students). *Financial support:* Fellowships, research assistantships, career-related internships or fieldwork, Federal Work-Study, and institutionally sponsored loans available. Support available to part-time students. Financial award application deadline: 3/1; financial award applicants required to submit FAFSA. *Unit head:* Leda M. Hall, Dean, 574-520-4803. *Application contact:* Leda M. Hall, Dean, 574-520-4803.

The Institute of World Politics, Graduate Programs in National Security, Intelligence, and International Affairs, Washington, DC 20036. Offers American foreign policy (Certificate); comparative political culture (Certificate); counterintelligence (Certificate); democracy building (Certificate); intelligence (Certificate); international politics (Certificate); national security affairs (Certificate); public diplomacy and political warfare (Certificate); statecraft and national security affairs (MA); statecraft and world politics (MA); strategic intelligence studies (MA). Part-time and evening/weekend programs available. *Degree requirements:* For master's, comprehensive exam, thesis optional. *Entrance requirements:* For master's, GRE General Test. Additional exam requirements/recommendations for international students: Required—TOEFL. Electronic applications accepted. *Faculty research:* Intelligence, national security, statecraft.

Jackson State University, Graduate School, College of Public Service, Jackson, MS 39217. Offers MS. *Degree requirements:* For master's, comprehensive exam. *Entrance requirements:* For master's, GRE General Test. Additional exam requirements/recommendations for international students: Required—TOEFL.

McMaster University, School of Graduate Studies, Faculty of Social Sciences, Department of Political Science, Hamilton, ON L8S 4M2, Canada. Offers international relations (PhD); political science (MA); public and the global economy (MA); public policy (PhD); public policy and administration (MA). Part-time programs available. *Degree requirements:* For master's, thesis or alternative. *Entrance requirements:* For master's, minimum B+ average. Additional exam requirements/recommendations for international students: Required—TOEFL (minimum score 580 paper-based; 237 computer-based). *Faculty research:* Organizational theory, internationalization of public policy, water resource policies, political interest intermediation, comparative politics.

Murray State University, College of Humanities and Fine Arts, Department of Government, Laws and International Affairs, Program in Public Administration, Murray, KY 42071. Offers public affairs (MPA). Part-time programs available. Postbaccalaureate distance learning degree programs offered (minimal on-campus study). *Degree requirements:* For master's, capstone course. *Entrance requirements:* For master's, GRE General Test. Additional exam requirements/recommendations for international students: Required—TOEFL.

National University of Singapore, Lee Kuan Yew School of Public Policy, Singapore, Singapore. Offers MPA, MPM, MPP, PhD.

New Mexico Highlands University, Graduate Studies, College of Arts and Sciences, Program in Public Affairs, Las Vegas, NM 87701. Offers applied sociology (MA). Program is interdisciplinary. *Degree requirements:* For master's, comprehensive exam, thesis or alternative. *Entrance requirements:* For master's, minimum undergraduate GPA of 3.0. Additional exam requirements/recommendations for international students: Required—TOEFL (minimum score 540 paper-based; 207 computer-based).

Northeastern University, College of Social Sciences and Humanities, Department of Political Science, Boston, MA 02115-5096. Offers political science (MA); public administration (MPA, Certificate), including development administration (MPA), health administration and policy (MPA), state and local government (MPA), urban studies (Certificate); public and international affairs (PhD). Part-time and evening/weekend programs available. *Faculty:* 22 full-time (4 women), 10 part-time/adjunct (1 woman). *Students:* 10 full-time (3 women), 62 part-time (28 women); includes 7 minority (2 African Americans, 2 American Indian/Alaska Native, 2 Asian Americans or Pacific Islanders, 1 Hispanic American), 11 international. Average age 30. 129 applicants, 69% accepted, 24 enrolled. In 2009, 28 master's, 3 doctorates awarded. *Degree requirements:* For master's, thesis optional; for doctorate, thesis/dissertation. *Entrance requirements:* For master's, GRE General Test. Additional exam requirements/recommendations for international students: Required—TOEFL. *Application deadline:* Applications are processed on a rolling basis. Application fee: $50. *Financial support:* In 2009–10, 12 fellowships, 3 research assistantships with tuition reimbursements, 18 teaching assistantships with tuition reimbursements (averaging $14,035 per year) were awarded; career-related internships or fieldwork, Federal Work-Study, tuition waivers (full and partial), and unspecified assistantships also available. Support available to part-time students. Financial award application deadline: 2/1; financial award applicants required to submit FAFSA. *Faculty research:* Presidency, public opinion, Congress, democratization, national identity. *Unit head:* Dr. John Portz, Chair, 617-373-2796, Fax: 617-373-5311, E-mail: gradpolisci@neu.edu. *Application contact:* Brynn Thompson, Graduate Programs Assistant, 617-373-4404, Fax: 617-373-5311, E-mail: gradpolisci@neu.edu.

Notre Dame de Namur University, Division of Academic Affairs, School of Business and Management, Department of Public Administration, Belmont, CA 94002-1908. Offers human resource management (MPA); public administration (MPA); public affairs administration (MPA). Part-time and evening/weekend programs available. *Faculty:* 2 full-time (1 woman), 4 part-time/adjunct (2 women). *Students:* 2 full-time (both women), 30 part-time (25 women); includes 18 minority (2 African Americans, 1 Asian American or Pacific Islander, 15 Hispanic Americans), 1 international. Average age 31. 20 applicants, 100% accepted, 11 enrolled. In 2009, 7 master's awarded. *Entrance requirements:* For master's, interview, minimum GPA of 2.5. Additional exam requirements/recommendations for international students: Required—TOEFL (minimum score 550 paper-based; 213 computer-based; 79 iBT). *Application deadline:* For fall admission, 8/1 priority date for domestic students; for spring admission, 12/1 priority date for domestic students. Applications are processed on a rolling basis. Application fee: $60. Electronic applications accepted. *Expenses:* Tuition: Part-time $720 per credit. Required fees: $35 per semester hour. *Financial support:* Career-related internships or fieldwork available. Support available to part-time students. Financial award applicants required to submit FAFSA. *Unit head:* Henry Roth, Director, 650-508-3721, E-mail: hroth@ndnu.edu. *Application contact:* Candace Hallmark, Associate Director of Admissions, 650-508-3592, Fax: 650-508-3426, E-mail: grad.admit@ndnu.edu.

The Ohio State University, John Glenn School of Public Affairs, Columbus, OH 43210. Offers MA, MPA, PhD. *Accreditation:* NASPAA (one or more programs are accredited). Part-time programs available. *Faculty:* 14. *Students:* 36 full-time (17 women), 32 part-time (15 women); includes 9 minority (7 African Americans, 1 Asian American or Pacific Islander, 1 Hispanic American), 6 international. Average age 28. In 2009, 11 master's, 20 doctorates awarded. *Degree requirements:* For doctorate, thesis/dissertation. *Entrance requirements:* For master's, GMAT, GRE General Test (MPA), minimum GPA of 3.0 (MA); for doctorate, GRE General Test. Additional exam requirements/recommendations for international students: Recommended—TOEFL (minimum score 573 paper-based; 230 computer-based). *Application deadline:* For fall admission, 8/15 priority date for domestic students, 7/1 priority date for international students; for winter admission, 12/1 priority date for domestic students, 11/1 priority date for international students; for spring admission, 3/1 priority date for domestic students, 2/1 priority date for international students. Applications are processed on a rolling basis. Application fee: $40 ($50 for international students). Electronic applications accepted. *Expenses:* Tuition, state resident: full-time $10,683. Tuition, nonresident: full-time $25,923. Tuition and fees vary according to course load and program. *Financial support:* Fellowships, research assistantships, teaching assistantships, Federal Work-Study, institutionally sponsored loans, and unspecified assistantships available. Support available to part-time students. *Unit head:* Charles R. Wise, Graduate Studies Committee Chair, 614-292-8696, Fax: 614-292-4868, E-mail: wise.983@osu.edu. *Application contact:* 614-292-9444, Fax: 614-292-3895, E-mail: domestic.grad@osu.edu.

Park University, College of Graduate and Professional Studies, Kansas City, MO 54105. Offers adult education (M Ed); at-risk students (M Ed); disaster and emergency management (MPA); educational administration (M Ed); entrepreneurship (MBA); general business (MBA); general education (M Ed); government/business relations (MPA); healthcare/services management (MBA, MPA); international business (MBA); K-12 certification (MAT); management information systems (MBA); management of information systems (MPA); middle school certification (MAT); multi-cultural education (M Ed); nonprofit management (MPA); public management (MPA); school law (M Ed); secondary school certification (MAT); special education (M Ed). Part-time and evening/weekend programs available. Postbaccalaureate distance learning degree programs offered (no on-campus study). *Degree requirements:* For master's, comprehensive exam, thesis (for some programs). *Entrance requirements:* For master's, GRE, GMAT, teacher certification (M Ed). Additional exam requirements/recommendations for international students: Required—TOEFL (minimum score 550 paper-based). Electronic applications accepted. *Faculty research:* Literacy, leadership, brain based research, multicultural education, diversity.

Penn State Harrisburg, Graduate School, School of Public Affairs, Middletown, PA 17057-4898. Offers MA, MHA, MPA, PhD, MPA/JD. *Unit head:* Dr. Steven A. Peterson, Director, 717-948-6154, E-mail: sap12@psu.edu. *Application contact:* Robert Coffman, Director of Admissions, 717-948-6250, Fax: 717-948-6325, E-mail: ric1@psu.edu.

Princeton University, Graduate School, Program in Population Studies, Princeton, NJ 08544-1019. Offers demography (PhD, Certificate); economics and demography (PhD); public affairs and demography (PhD); sociology and demography (PhD). *Degree requirements:* For doctorate, thesis/dissertation. *Entrance requirements:* For doctorate, GRE General Test. Additional exam requirements/recommendations for international students: Required—TOEFL (minimum score 600 paper-based; 250 computer-based). Electronic applications accepted. *Faculty research:* Models, fertility, infant and child mortality, migration.

Princeton University, Graduate School, Woodrow Wilson School of Public and International Affairs, Princeton, NJ 08544-1019. Offers public affairs (MPA, PhD); public policy (MPP); JD/MPA. Terminal master's awarded for partial completion of doctoral program. *Degree requirements:* For master's, internship; for doctorate, one foreign language, thesis/dissertation. *Entrance requirements:* For master's, GRE General Test, original policy memo; for doctorate, GRE General Test. Additional exam requirements/recommendations for international students: Required—TOEFL (minimum score 600 paper-based; 250 computer-based). Electronic applications accepted.

Texas A&M University, George Bush School of Government and Public Service, College Station, TX 77843. Offers advanced international affairs (Certificate); homeland security (Certificate); international affairs (MPIA), including international economics and development, national security affairs; nonprofit management (Certificate); public service and administration (MPSA), including public management, public policy analysis. *Accreditation:* NASPAA. *Faculty:* 51. *Students:* 209 full-time (97 women), 93 part-time (43 women); includes 48 minority (15 African Americans, 5 Asian Americans or Pacific Islanders, 28 Hispanic Americans), 19 international. Average age 24. In 2009, 87 master's awarded. *Degree requirements:* For master's, summer internship. *Entrance requirements:* For master's, GRE (preferred) or GMAT. *Application deadline:* For fall admission, 1/24 for domestic and international students. Application fee: $50 ($75 for international students). Electronic applications accepted. *Expenses:* Tuition, state resident: full-time $3991; part-time $221.74 per credit hour. Tuition, nonresident: full-time $9049; part-time $502.74 per credit hour. *Financial support:* In 2009–10, fellowships (averaging $11,000 per year), research assistantships (averaging $11,250 per year) were awarded; career-related internships or fieldwork, Federal Work-Study, and institutionally sponsored loans also available. Financial award application deadline: 2/1; financial award applicants required to submit FAFSA. *Faculty research:* Public policy, presidential studies, public leadership, economic policy, social policy. *Unit head:* A. Benton Cocanougher, Interim Dean, 979-862-8842, E-mail: bushschool@tamu.edu. *Application contact:* Kathryn Meyer, Recruitment and Placement Officer, 979-458-4767, Fax: 979-845-4155, E-mail: admissions@bushschool.tamu.edu.

The University of Alabama in Huntsville, School of Graduate Studies, College of Liberal Arts, Program in Public Affairs, Huntsville, AL 35899. Offers MA. Part-time and evening/weekend programs available. *Faculty:* 5 full-time (4 women), 2 part-time/adjunct (0 women). *Students:* 11 full-time (8 women), 20 part-time (11 women); includes 6 minority (5 African Americans, 1 Asian American or Pacific Islander), 2 international. Average age 29. 30 applicants, 77% accepted, 20 enrolled. In 2009, 9 master's awarded. *Degree requirements:* For master's, comprehensive exam, thesis or alternative, oral and written exams. *Entrance requirements:* For master's, GRE General Test, minimum GPA of 3.0. Additional exam requirements/recommendations for international students: Required—TOEFL (minimum score 500 paper-based; 173 computer-based; 62 iBT). *Application deadline:* For fall admission, 7/15 for domestic students, 4/1 for international students; for spring admission, 11/30 for domestic students, 9/1 for international students. Applications are processed on a rolling basis. Application fee: $40 ($50 for international students). Electronic applications accepted. *Expenses:* Tuition, state resident: part-time $355.75 per credit hour. Tuition, nonresident: part-time $847.10 per credit hour. Required fees: $210.80 per semester. Tuition and fees vary according to course load and program. *Financial support:* In 2009–10, 5 students received support, including 1 research assistantship (averaging $7,484 per year); career-related internships or fieldwork, Federal Work-Study, institutionally sponsored loans, scholarships/grants, health care benefits, and unspecified assistantships also available. Support available to part-time students. Financial award application deadline: 4/1; financial award applicants required to submit FAFSA. *Faculty research:* Public policy, public management professions, intergovernmental relations, international politics. Total annual research expenditures: $104,673. *Unit head:* Dr. Kathleen H. Hawk, Chair, Political Science and Sociology, 256-824-2315, Fax: 256-824-6949, E-mail: hawkk@email.uah.edu. *Application contact:* Kathy Biggs, Graduate Studies Admissions Manager, 256-824-6199, Fax: 256-824-6405, E-mail: deangrad@uah.edu.

University of Arkansas at Little Rock, Graduate School, Clinton School of Public Service, Little Rock, AR 72204-1099. Offers MPS, Graduate Certificate.

University of Central Florida, College of Health and Public Affairs, Program in Public Affairs, Orlando, FL 32816. Offers PhD. Part-time and evening/weekend programs available. *Students:* 45 full-time (21 women), 42 part-time (22 women); includes 11 minority (4 African Americans, 1 Asian American or Pacific Islander, 6 Hispanic Americans), 16 international. Average age 38. 39 applicants, 64% accepted, 18 enrolled. In 2009, 6 doctorates awarded. *Degree requirements:*

For doctorate, thesis/dissertation, candidacy and qualifying exams. *Entrance requirements:* For doctorate, GRE General Test or minimum GPA of 3.0 during final 60 hours. Additional exam requirements/recommendations for international students: Required—TOEFL. *Application deadline:* For fall admission, 2/7 priority date for domestic students. Application fee: $30. Electronic applications accepted. *Expenses:* Tuition, state resident: part-time $306.31 per credit hour. Tuition, nonresident: part-time $1099.01 per credit hour. Part-time tuition and fees vary according to degree level and program. *Financial support:* In 2009–10, 24 students received support, including 11 fellowships with partial tuition reimbursements available (averaging $6,500 per year), 4 research assistantships with partial tuition reimbursements available (averaging $109 per year), 15 teaching assistantships with partial tuition reimbursements available (averaging $550 per year); career-related internships or fieldwork, Federal Work-Study, institutionally sponsored loans, tuition waivers (partial), and unspecified assistantships also available. Financial award application deadline: 3/1; financial award applicants required to submit FAFSA. *Unit head:* Dr. Thomas T. Wan, Director, 407-823-0172, Fax: 407-823-4895, E-mail: twan@mail.ucf.edu. *Application contact:* Dr. Thomas T. Wan, Director, 407-823-0172, Fax: 407-823-4895, E-mail: twan@mail.ucf.edu.

University of Colorado at Colorado Springs, Graduate School, Graduate School of Public Affairs, Colorado Springs, CO 80933-7150. Offers criminal justice (MCJ); public administration (MPA). *Accreditation:* NASPAA. Part-time and evening/weekend programs available. *Faculty:* 7 full-time (2 women). *Students:* 36 full-time (19 women), 43 part-time (30 women); includes 14 minority (3 African Americans, 4 Asian Americans or Pacific Islanders, 7 Hispanic Americans). Average age 36. 34 applicants, 82% accepted, 24 enrolled. In 2009, 15 master's awarded. *Degree requirements:* For master's, internship (if no experience), capstone project. *Entrance requirements:* For master's, GRE General Test, GMAT, LSAT, minimum GPA of 3.0. *Application deadline:* For fall admission, 6/1 priority date for domestic students; for spring admission, 11/1 for domestic students. Applications are processed on a rolling basis. Application fee: $60 ($75 for international students). *Expenses:* Contact institution. *Financial support:* Career-related internships or fieldwork, Federal Work-Study, and scholarships/grants available. Support available to part-time students. Financial award application deadline: 3/1; financial award applicants required to submit FAFSA. *Unit head:* Dr. Terry Schwartz, Dean, 719-255-4047, Fax: 719-255-4183, E-mail: tschwart@uccs.edu. *Application contact:* Mary Lou Kartis, Program Assistant, 719-255-4182, Fax: 719-255-4183, E-mail: mkartis@uccs.edu.

University of Colorado Denver, Graduate School of Public Affairs, Program in Public Affairs, Denver, CO 80217-3364. Offers PhD. Part-time and evening/weekend programs available. *Students:* 16 full-time (8 women), 90 part-time (48 women); includes 4 minority (1 African American, 2 Asian Americans or Pacific Islanders, 1 Hispanic American), 4 international. 48 applicants, 33% accepted, 13 enrolled. In 2009, 3 doctorates awarded. *Degree requirements:* For doctorate, comprehensive exam, thesis/dissertation. *Entrance requirements:* For doctorate, GRE General Test. Additional exam requirements/recommendations for international students: Required—TOEFL (minimum score 500 paper-based). *Application deadline:* For fall admission, 4/1 for domestic students, 10/1 for international students. Application fee: $50 ($60 for international students). *Financial support:* In 2009–10, 26 fellowships were awarded; research assistantships, teaching assistantships, career-related internships or fieldwork, Federal Work-Study, and institutionally sponsored loans also available. Support available to part-time students. Financial award application deadline: 4/1; financial award applicants required to submit FAFSA. *Unit head:* Paul Teske, Director, 303-315-2805, Fax: 303-315-2229, E-mail: paul.teske@ucdenver.edu. *Application contact:* Antoinette Sandoval, Student Service Specialist, 303-315-2487, Fax: 303-315-2229, E-mail: antoinette.sandoval@ucdenver.edu.

University of Florida, Graduate School, College of Liberal Arts and Sciences, Department of Political Science, Gainesville, FL 32611. Offers international development policy and administration (MA, Certificate); international relations (MA, MAT); political campaigning (MA, Certificate); political science (MA, MAT, PhD); public affairs (MA, Certificate); JD/MA. Part-time programs available. Terminal master's awarded for partial completion of doctoral program. *Degree requirements:* For master's, variable foreign language requirement, thesis or alternative; for doctorate, variable foreign language requirement, thesis/dissertation. *Entrance requirements:* For master's and doctorate, GRE General Test, minimum GPA of 3.0. Additional exam requirements/recommendations for international students: Required—TOEFL (minimum score 550 paper-based; 213 computer-based). Electronic applications accepted. *Faculty research:* U.S. political development, religion and politics, environmental politics and policy, developing societies, international relations.

University of Idaho, College of Graduate Studies, College of Letters, Arts and Social Sciences, Department of Political Science and Public Affairs Research, Moscow, ID 83844-2282. Offers political science (MA, PhD); public administration (MPA). *Faculty:* 7 full-time, 1 part-time/adjunct. *Students:* 10 full-time (5 women), 16 part-time (5 women). In 2009, 9 master's, 1 doctorate awarded. *Degree requirements:* For doctorate, thesis/dissertation. *Entrance requirements:* For master's, minimum GPA of 2.8; for doctorate, minimum undergraduate GPA of 2.8, 3.0 graduate. *Application deadline:* For fall admission, 8/1 for domestic students; for spring admission, 12/15 for domestic students. Application fee: $55 ($60 for international students). *Expenses:* Tuition, state resident: full-time $6120. Tuition, nonresident: full-time $17,712. *Financial support:* Research assistantships, teaching assistantships available. Financial award application deadline: 2/15. *Unit head:* Dr. Donald W. Crowley, Chair, 208-885-6328. *Application contact:* Dr. Donald W. Crowley, Chair, 208-885-6328.

University of Louisville, Graduate School, College of Arts and Sciences, Department of Urban and Public Affairs, Louisville, KY 40208. Offers public administration (MPA), including human resources management, non-profit management, public policy and administration; urban and public affairs (PhD), including urban planning and development, urban policy and administration; urban planning (MUP), including administration of planning organizations, housing and community development, land use and environmental planning, spatial analysis. Part-time and evening/weekend programs available. *Faculty:* 22 full-time (7 women), 8 part-time/adjunct (1 woman). *Students:* 67 full-time (32 women), 35 part-time (20 women); includes 13 minority (10 African Americans, 1 Asian American or Pacific Islander, 2 Hispanic Americans), 6 international. Average age 31. 107 applicants, 57% accepted, 40 enrolled. In 2009, 25 master's, 5 doctorates awarded. Terminal master's awarded for partial completion of doctoral program. *Degree requirements:* For master's, internship; for doctorate, comprehensive exam, thesis/dissertation. *Entrance requirements:* For master's, GRE General Test, minimum GPA of 3.0; for doctorate, GRE General Test, master's degree in appropriate field. Additional exam requirements/recommendations for international students: Required—TOEFL (minimum score 550 paper-based; 213 computer-based; 79 iBT). *Application deadline:* For fall admission, 7/15 for domestic students; for spring admission, 11/15 for domestic students. Applications are processed on a rolling basis. Application fee: $50. Electronic applications accepted. *Financial support:* In 2009–10, 26 students received support; fellowships, research assistantships, health care benefits available. *Unit head:* Dr. David Simpson, Chair, 502-852-8019, Fax: 502-852-4558, E-mail: dave.simpson@louisville.edu. *Application contact:* Patty Sarley, Graduate Student Advisor, 502-852-7914, Fax: 502-852-4558, E-mail: plclea01@louisville.edu.

University of Massachusetts Boston, Office of Graduate Studies, John W. McCormack Graduate School of Policy Studies, Program in Public Affairs, Boston, MA 02125-3393. Offers MS. Part-time and evening/weekend programs available. *Degree requirements:* For master's, final project. *Entrance requirements:* For master's, GRE General Test or MAT, minimum GPA of 2.75. *Faculty research:* Leadership and policy implementation, public management, disability; human services and sound policy.

University of Minnesota, Twin Cities Campus, Graduate School, Hubert H. Humphrey Institute of Public Affairs, Program in Public Affairs, Minneapolis, MN 55455-0213. Offers MPA. *Accreditation:* NASPAA. Part-time and evening/weekend programs available. *Faculty:* 33 full-time (14 women), 29 part-time/adjunct (15 women). *Students:* 5 full-time (2 women), 135 part-time (92 women); includes 31 minority (18 African Americans, 2 American Indian/Alaska Native, 6 Asian Americans or Pacific Islanders, 5 Hispanic Americans), 5 international. Average age 41. 83 applicants, 65% accepted, 40 enrolled. In 2009, 52 master's awarded. *Entrance requirements:* For master's, 10 years of work experience, minimum undergraduate GPA of 3.0. Additional exam requirements/recommendations for international students: Required—TOEFL (minimum score 600 paper-based; 250 computer-based; 100 iBT). *Application deadline:* For fall admission, 4/1 priority date for domestic students, 4/1 for international students; for spring admission, 10/15 for domestic and international students. Applications are processed on a rolling basis. Application fee: $55 ($75 for international students). Electronic applications accepted. *Expenses:* Contact institution. *Financial support:* In 2009–10, 6 students received support, including research assistantships with full and partial tuition reimbursements available (averaging $5,270 per year), teaching assistantships with full and partial tuition reimbursements available (averaging $5,270 per year); career-related internships or fieldwork, Federal Work-Study, scholarships/grants, health care benefits, tuition waivers (full and partial), and unspecified assistantships also available. Support available to part-time students. Financial award application deadline: 4/1. *Faculty research:* Public and non-profit leadership and management, social policy, urban and regional planning, economic and community development, foreign policy and international affairs. Total annual research expenditures: $5.1 million. *Unit head:* Dr. Gary DeCramer, Head, 612-624-3800, Fax: 612-626-0002, E-mail: hhhadmit@umn.edu. *Application contact:* Julie Harrold, Director of Admissions, 612-626-7229, Fax: 612-626-0002, E-mail: hhhadmit@umn.edu.

University of Missouri, Graduate School, Harry S Truman School of Public Affairs, Columbia, MO 65211. Offers MPA. *Accreditation:* NASPAA. *Entrance requirements:* For master's, GRE General Test, minimum GPA of 3.0. Additional exam requirements/recommendations for international students: Required—TOEFL (minimum score 550 paper-based; 213 computer-based; 79 iBT).

University of Missouri–Kansas City, Henry W. Bloch School of Business and Public Administration, Kansas City, MO 64110-2499. Offers accounting (MS); business administration (MBA); entrepreneurship and innovation (PhD); public affairs (MPA, PhD); JD/MBA; LL M/MPA. PhD (interdisciplinary) offered through the School of Graduate Studies. *Accreditation:* AACSB; NASPAA. Part-time and evening/weekend programs available. *Faculty:* 43 full-time (14 women), 22 part-time/adjunct (7 women). *Students:* 234 full-time (108 women), 437 part-time (193 women); includes 79 minority (33 African Americans, 27 Asian Americans or Pacific Islanders, 19 Hispanic Americans), 51 international. Average age 30. 387 applicants, 65% accepted, 222 enrolled. In 2009, 240 master's awarded. Terminal master's awarded for partial completion of doctoral program. *Entrance requirements:* For master's, GMAT, GRE, 2 writing essays, 2 references and support of employer; for doctorate, GRE, minimum GPA of 3.0. Additional exam requirements/recommendations for international students: Required—TOEFL (minimum score 550 paper-based; 213 computer-based; 80 iBT). *Application deadline:* For fall admission, 5/1 priority date for domestic and international students; for spring admission, 10/1 priority date for domestic and international students. Applications are processed on a rolling basis. Application fee: $45 ($50 for international students). Electronic applications accepted. *Expenses:* Tuition, state resident: full-time $5378; part-time $299 per credit hour. Tuition, nonresident: full-time $13,881; part-time $771 per credit hour. Required fees: $641; $71 per credit hour. Tuition and fees vary according to course load and program. *Financial support:* In 2009–10, 18 research assistantships with partial tuition reimbursements (averaging $8,766 per year), 5 teaching assistantships with partial tuition reimbursements (averaging $8,430 per year) were awarded; career-related internships or fieldwork, Federal Work-Study, institutionally sponsored loans, scholarships/grants, tuition waivers (full and partial), and unspecified assistantships also available. Support available to part-time students. Financial award application deadline: 3/1; financial award applicants required to submit FAFSA. *Faculty research:* Entrepreneurship, finance, non-profit, risk management. Total annual research expenditures: $751,788. *Unit head:* Dr. Teng-Kee Tan, Dean, 816-235-2215, Fax: 816-235-2206. *Application contact:* 816-235-1111, E-mail: admit@umkc.edu.

University of Nevada, Las Vegas, Graduate College, Greenspun College of Urban Affairs, Department of Environmental Studies, Las Vegas, NV 89154-4030. Offers crisis and emergency management (MS); environmental science (MS, PhD); non-profit management (Certificate); public administration (MPA); public affairs (PhD). Part-time programs available. *Faculty:* 6 full-time (2 women). *Students:* 39 full-time (18 women), 145 part-time (79 women); includes 47 minority (22 African Americans, 4 American Indian/Alaska Native, 3 Asian Americans or Pacific Islanders, 18 Hispanic Americans), 7 international. Average age 39. 16 applicants, 31% accepted, 2 enrolled. In 2009, 50 master's, 3 doctorates, 27 other advanced degrees awarded. *Degree requirements:* For master's, comprehensive exam (for some programs), thesis; for doctorate, comprehensive exam (for some programs), thesis/dissertation. *Entrance requirements:* Additional exam requirements/recommendations for international students: Required—TOEFL (minimum score 550 paper-based; 213 computer-based; 80 iBT), IELTS (minimum score 7). *Application deadline:* For fall admission, 6/1 priority date for domestic students, 2/15 priority date for international students; for spring admission, 11/15 priority date for domestic students, 10/1 for international students. Applications are processed on a rolling basis. Application fee: $60 ($95 for international students). Electronic applications accepted. *Financial support:* In 2009–10, 9 students received support, including 6 research assistantships with partial tuition reimbursements available (averaging $13,850 per year), 3 teaching assistantships with partial tuition reimbursements available (averaging $10,666 per year); institutionally sponsored loans, scholarships/grants, health care benefits, and unspecified assistantships also available. Financial award application deadline: 3/1. *Faculty research:* Environmental chemistry, environmental policy and management. *Unit head:* Dr. Ed Weber, Chair/ Associate Professor, 702-895-4440, Fax: 702-895-4436, E-mail: edward.weber@unlv.edu. *Application contact:* Graduate College Admissions Evaluator, 702-895-3320, Fax: 702-895-4180, E-mail: gradcollege@unlv.edu.

University of Nevada, Las Vegas, Graduate College, Greenspun College of Urban Affairs, Department of Public Administration, Las Vegas, NV 89154-6026. Offers crisis and emergency management (MS); non-profit management (Certificate); public administration (MPA); public affairs (PhD); public management (Certificate). *Accreditation:* NASPAA. Part-time and evening/weekend programs available. *Faculty:* 5 full-time (3 women), 2 part-time/adjunct (1 woman). *Students:* 30 full-time (12 women), 129 part-time (70 women); includes 39 minority (21 African Americans, 4 Asian Americans or Pacific Islanders, 14 Hispanic Americans), 3 international. Average age 38. 95 applicants, 76% accepted, 53 enrolled. In 2009, 48 master's, 28 other advanced degrees awarded. *Degree requirements:* For master's, comprehensive exam, professional paper. *Entrance requirements:* For master's, GRE General Test, GMAT or LSAT. Additional exam requirements/recommendations for international students: Required—TOEFL (minimum score 550 paper-based; 213 computer-based; 80 iBT), IELTS (minimum score 7). *Application deadline:* For fall admission, 6/1 priority date for domestic students, 5/1 for international students; for spring admission, 11/1 priority date for domestic students, 10/1 for international students. Applications are processed on a rolling basis. Application fee: $60 ($95 for international students). Electronic applications accepted. *Financial support:* In 2009–10, 8 students received support, including 6 research assistantships with partial tuition reimbursements available (averaging $12,333 per year), 2 teaching assistantships with partial tuition reimbursements available (averaging $12,000 per year); institutionally sponsored loans, scholarships/grants, health care benefits, and unspecified assistantships also available. Financial award application deadline: 3/1. *Faculty research:* Emergency and crisis management, homeland security, public and non-profit management, public policy, policy analysis and evaluation. *Unit head:* Dr. Anna Lukemeyer, Chair/ Associate Professor, 702-895-4828, Fax: 702-895-1813, E-mail: anna.lukemeyer@unlv.edu. *Application contact:* Graduate College Admissions Evaluator, 702-895-3320, Fax: 702-895-4180, E-mail: gradcollege@unlv.edu.

The University of North Carolina at Greensboro, Graduate School, College of Arts and Sciences, Department of Political Science, Greensboro, NC 27412-5001. Offers nonprofit management (Certificate); public affairs (MPA); urban and economic development (Certificate). *Accreditation:* NASPAA. *Degree requirements:* For master's, comprehensive exam. *Entrance requirements:* For master's, GRE General Test. Additional exam requirements/recommendations for international students: Required—TOEFL. Electronic applications accepted. *Faculty research:* U.S. Constitution, Canadian parliament, public management, ethical challenge of public service.

Public Affairs

University of San Francisco, College of Arts and Sciences, Graduate Program in Public Affairs and Practical Politics, San Francisco, CA 94117-1080. Offers MPA. *Degree requirements:* For master's, internship, capstone project. *Expenses:* Tuition: Full-time $19,710; part-time $1095 per unit. Part-time tuition and fees vary according to degree level, campus/location and program. *Financial support:* Scholarships/grants available. *Unit head:* Prof. Corey Cook, Program Advisor, 415-422-5101. *Application contact:* Information Contact, 415-422-5135, Fax: 415-422-2217, E-mail: asgraduate@usfca.edu.

University of Saskatchewan, College of Graduate Studies and Research, School of Public Policy, Saskatoon, SK S7N 5A2, Canada. Offers MIT, MPA, MPP, PhD. Tuition and fees charges are reported in Canadian dollars. *Expenses:* Tuition, area resident: Full-time $3000 Canadian dollars; part-time $500 Canadian dollars per term. Required fees: $700 Canadian dollars; $100 Canadian dollars per term.

The University of Texas at Arlington, Graduate School, School of Urban and Public Affairs, Program in Urban and Public Affairs, Arlington, TX 76019. Offers PhD. Part-time and evening/weekend programs available. *Students:* 11 full-time (6 women), 22 part-time (13 women); includes 15 minority (10 African Americans, 2 Asian Americans or Pacific Islanders, 3 Hispanic Americans), 1 international. Average age 30. 27 applicants, 78% accepted, 18 enrolled. *Degree requirements:* For doctorate, comprehensive exam, thesis/dissertation. *Entrance requirements:* For doctorate, GRE General Test. *Application deadline:* For fall admission, 6/16 for domestic students. Application fee: $35 ($50 for international students). *Financial support:* In 2009–10, 4 fellowships (averaging $1,000 per year), 6 research assistantships (averaging $4,500 per year) were awarded. Financial award application deadline: 6/1; financial award applicants required to submit FAFSA. *Faculty research:* Environment urban policy personnel, research theoretical foundations, urban problems. *Unit head:* Dr. Rod Hissong, Graduate Adviser, 817-272-3350, Fax: 817-272-5008, E-mail: hissong@uta.edu. *Application contact:* Linda Slaughter, Administrative Clerk, 817-272-3071, Fax: 817-272-5008, E-mail: slaughter@uta.edu.

The University of Texas at Austin, Graduate School, Lyndon B. Johnson School of Public Affairs, Austin, TX 78712-1111. Offers global policy studies (MGPS); public affairs (MP Aff); public policy (PhD); JD/MP Aff; MBA/MP Aff; MP Aff/MA; MP Aff/MSE. *Accreditation:* NASPAA (one or more programs are accredited). Part-time programs available. *Degree requirements:* For master's, thesis, summer internship; for doctorate, thesis/dissertation. *Entrance requirements:* For master's, GRE General Test; for doctorate, GRE General Test, master's degree in policy-related field. Additional exam requirements/recommendations for international students: Required—TOEFL. Electronic applications accepted. *Faculty research:* Human resource development, health and social policy, philanthropy and community service, ethical leadership, urban and international policy, science and technology policy.

The University of Texas at Dallas, School of Economic, Political and Policy Sciences, Program in Public Affairs, Richardson, TX 75080. Offers MPA, PhD. *Accreditation:* NASPAA. Part-time and evening/weekend programs available. *Faculty:* 7 full-time (2 women), 4 part-time/adjunct (1 woman). *Students:* 44 full-time (22 women), 119 part-time (53 women); includes 47 minority (26 African Americans, 5 Asian Americans or Pacific Islanders, 16 Hispanic Americans), 18 international. Average age 37. 65 applicants, 52% accepted, 22 enrolled. In 2009, 33 master's, 14 doctorates awarded. *Degree requirements:* For master's, internship; for doctorate, thesis/dissertation. *Entrance requirements:* For master's and doctorate, GRE General Test, minimum GPA of 3.0 in upper-level course work in field. Additional exam requirements/recommendations for international students: Required—TOEFL (minimum score 550 paper-based; 213 computer-based). *Application deadline:* For fall admission, 7/15 for domestic students, 5/1 priority date for international students; for spring admission, 11/15 for domestic students, 9/1 priority date for international students. Applications are processed on a rolling basis. Application fee: $50 ($100 for international students). Electronic applications accepted. *Expenses:* Tuition, state resident: full-time $11,068; part-time $461 per credit hour. Tuition, nonresident: full-time $21,178; part-time $882 per credit hour. Tuition and fees vary according to course load. *Financial support:* In 2009–10, 2 research assistantships with full tuition reimbursements (averaging $12,310 per year), 7 teaching assistantships with full tuition reimbursements (averaging $11,314 per year) were awarded; fellowships, career-related internships or fieldwork, Federal Work-Study, institutionally sponsored loans, and scholarships/grants also available. Support available to part-time students. Financial award application deadline: 4/30; financial award applicants required to submit FAFSA. *Faculty research:* Juvenile justice programs, program evaluation and outcome measurement, Hispanic American retention in educational institutions. *Unit head:* Dr. L. Douglas Kiel, Program Head, 972-883-2019, Fax: 972-883-2735, E-mail: dkiel@utdallas.edu. *Application contact:* Dr. Richard Scotch, Director, 972-883-2922, Fax: 972-883-2735, E-mail: richard.scotch@utdallas.edu.

See Close-Up on page 759.

University of Washington, Graduate School, Daniel J. Evans School of Public Affairs, Seattle, WA 98195. Offers public administration (MPA); public policy and management (PhD); JD/MPA; MPA/MAIS; MPA/MPH; MPA/MS; MPA/MUP. *Accreditation:* NASPAA. Part-time and evening/weekend programs available. *Degree requirements:* For master's, thesis, internship or cooperative experience. *Entrance requirements:* For master's and doctorate, GRE General Test, minimum GPA of 3.0. Additional exam requirements/recommendations for international students: Required—TOEFL (minimum score 580 paper-based; 237 computer-based; 92 iBT). Electronic applications accepted. *Faculty research:* Environmental policy, education and social policy, nonprofit management, international affairs, urban and regional development.

University of Waterloo, Graduate Studies, Faculty of Arts, Department of Anthropology, Waterloo, ON N2L 3G1, Canada. Offers anthropology (MA); public issues (MA). *Entrance requirements:* Additional exam requirements/recommendations for international students: Required—TOEFL. Electronic applications accepted. *Faculty research:* Applied socio-cultural anthropology and archaeology.

University of Wisconsin–Madison, Graduate School, College of Letters and Science, Public Policy and Administration Program, Robert M. La Follette School of Public Affairs, Madison, WI 53706-1380. Offers international public affairs (MPIA); public affairs (MPA). Part-time programs available. *Entrance requirements:* For master's, GRE General Test. Additional exam requirements/recommendations for international students: Required—TOEFL (minimum score 650 paper-based; 280 computer-based). Electronic applications accepted. *Expenses:* Tuition, state resident: part-time $594 per credit. Tuition, nonresident: part-time $1504 per credit. Required fees: $65 per credit. Tuition and fees vary according to course load, program and reciprocity agreements. *Faculty research:* Social policy, personnel, economic development, tax and budget, environmental regulations.

Virginia Commonwealth University, Graduate School, College of Humanities and Sciences, Wilder School of Government and Public Affairs, Richmond, VA 23284-9005. Offers MA, MPA, MS, MURP, PhD, CASR, CCJA, CPM, CURP, Certificate, Graduate Certificate, JD/MURP, MSW/Certificate.

Virginia Polytechnic Institute and State University, Graduate School, College of Architecture and Urban Studies, School of Public and International Affairs, Blacksburg, VA 24061. Offers environmental planning and policy (MURP); government and international affairs (MPIA); housing, community and economic development (MURP); international development planning (MURP); land use and physical planning (MURP); planning, governance and globalization (PhD), including environmental planning and landscape analysis, physical planning and urban design, public and international affairs, urban and environmental design and planning; urban and regional planning (MURP). *Accreditation:* ACSP. *Faculty:* 27 full-time (11 women), 2 part-time/adjunct (1 woman). *Students:* 73 full-time (51 women), 65 part-time (39 women); includes 15 minority (4 African Americans, 1 American Indian/Alaska Native, 6 Asian Americans or Pacific Islanders, 4 Hispanic Americans), 10 international. Average age 29. 86 applicants, 67% accepted, 40 enrolled. In 2009, 26 master's, 1 doctorate awarded. *Entrance requirements:* Additional exam requirements/recommendations for international students: Required—TOEFL (minimum score 550 paper-based; 213 computer-based). *Application deadline:* For fall admission, 5/15 for international students; for spring admission, 10/15 for international students. Applications are processed on a rolling basis. Application fee: $45. Electronic applications accepted. *Financial support:* In 2009–10, 1 teaching assistantship with full tuition reimbursement (averaging $5,560 per year) was awarded; career-related internships or fieldwork, Federal Work-Study, scholarships/grants, and unspecified assistantships also available. Financial award application deadline: 4/1. *Faculty research:* Design theory, environmental planning, town planning, transportation planning. *Unit head:* Dr. John Randolph, Dean, 540-231-6971, Fax: 540-231-9938, E-mail: energy@vt.edu. *Application contact:* Krystal D. Wright, Information Contact, 540-231-*5683, Fax: 540-231-9938, E-mail: garch@vt.edu.

Washington State University Vancouver, Graduate Programs, Program in Public Affairs, Vancouver, WA 98686. Offers MPA. Part-time and evening/weekend programs available. *Faculty:* 6. *Students:* 2 full-time (both women), 20 part-time (13 women); includes 1 American Indian/Alaska Native, 1 Hispanic American, 1 international. *Degree requirements:* For master's, comprehensive exam, thesis (for some programs). *Entrance requirements:* For master's, GRE, minimum GPA of 3.0, resume, 3 references. Additional exam requirements/recommendations for international students: Required—TOEFL (minimum score 550 paper-based; 213 computer-based). *Application deadline:* For fall admission, 1/10 priority date for domestic students, 1/10 for international students; for spring admission, 7/1 priority date for domestic students, 7/1 for international students. Application fee: $50. *Expenses:* Tuition, state resident: full-time $4228; part-time $423 per credit. Tuition, nonresident: full-time $10,322; part-time $1032 per credit. *Financial support:* Federal Work-Study and unspecified assistantships available. Financial award application deadline: 2/15. *Unit head:* Dr. Dana Baker, Director, 360-546-9125, Fax: 360-546-9074, E-mail: bakerdl@vancouver.wsu.edu. *Application contact:* Marie Loudermilk, 360-546-9640, E-mail: loudermilk@vancouver.wsu.edu.

West Chester University of Pennsylvania, Office of Graduate Studies, College of Business and Public Affairs, West Chester, PA 19383. Offers MA, MBA, MS, MSA, MSW, Certificate. Part-time and evening/weekend programs available. *Students:* 66 full-time (50 women), 228 part-time (126 women); includes 47 minority (31 African Americans, 1 American Indian/Alaska Native, 8 Asian Americans or Pacific Islanders, 7 Hispanic Americans), 4 international. Average age 29. 255 applicants, 90% accepted, 124 enrolled. In 2009, 108 master's, 16 other advanced degrees awarded. *Degree requirements:* For master's, comprehensive exam, thesis (for some programs). *Entrance requirements:* Additional exam requirements/recommendations for international students: Required—TOEFL (minimum score 550 paper-based; 213 computer-based; 80 iBT). *Application deadline:* For fall admission, 4/15 priority date for domestic students, 3/15 for international students; for spring admission, 10/15 for domestic students, 9/1 for international students. Applications are processed on a rolling basis. Application fee: $35. Electronic applications accepted. *Expenses:* Tuition, state resident: full-time $6666; part-time $370 per credit. Tuition, nonresident: full-time $10,666; part-time $593 per credit. Required fees: $122.56 per credit. *Financial support:* In 2009–10, 21 research assistantships with full and partial tuition reimbursements (averaging $5,000 per year) were awarded; career-related internships or fieldwork and unspecified assistantships also available. Support available to part-time students. Financial award application deadline: 2/15; financial award applicants required to submit FAFSA. *Unit head:* Dr. Christopher Fiorentino, Dean, 610-436-2824, E-mail: cfiorentino@wcupa.edu. *Application contact:* Office of Graduate Studies, 610-436-2943, Fax: 610-436-2763, E-mail: gradstudy@wcupa.edu.

Western Carolina University, Graduate School, College of Arts and Sciences, Department of Political Science and Public Affairs, Cullowhee, NC 28723. Offers MPA. Part-time and evening/weekend programs available. *Students:* 24 full-time (11 women), 28 part-time (10 women). Average age 31. 29 applicants, 76% accepted, 17 enrolled. In 2009, 17 master's awarded. *Degree requirements:* For master's, comprehensive exam. *Entrance requirements:* For master's, GRE General Test, appropriate undergraduate degree, 3 letters of recommendation. Additional exam requirements/recommendations for international students: Required—TOEFL (minimum score 550 paper-based; 270 computer-based; 79 iBT). *Application deadline:* For fall admission, 5/1 priority date for domestic students; for spring admission, 9/1 priority date for domestic students. Applications are processed on a rolling basis. Application fee: $45. *Financial support:* In 2009–10, 2 fellowships (averaging $500 per year), 9 research assistantships with full and partial tuition reimbursements (averaging $6,222 per year) were awarded; teaching assistantships with full and partial tuition reimbursements, career-related internships or fieldwork, institutionally sponsored loans, scholarships/grants, and unspecified assistantships also available. Financial award application deadline: 3/31; financial award applicants required to submit FAFSA. *Faculty research:* Press-government relations, comparative governments, gender in politics, Latin American political systems, foreign policy, trust in government, zoning. *Unit head:* Dr. Gibbs Knotts, Director, 828-227-7475, Fax: 828-227-7502, E-mail: gknotts@email.wcu.edu. *Application contact:* Admissions Specialist for Public Affairs, 828-227-7398, Fax: 828-227-7480, E-mail: gradsch@email.wcu.edu.

Western Michigan University, Graduate College, College of Arts and Sciences, School of Public Affairs and Administration, Kalamazoo, MI 49008. Offers health care administration (Graduate Certificate); nonprofit leadership and administration (Graduate Certificate); public administration (MPA, PhD). *Accreditation:* NASPAA (one or more programs are accredited). *Degree requirements:* For doctorate, thesis/dissertation, oral exams. *Entrance requirements:* For doctorate, GRE General Test.

York University, Faculty of Graduate Studies, Glendon College, Program in Public and International Affairs, Toronto, ON M3J 1P3, Canada. Offers MA.

Public Policy

Albany State University, College of Arts and Humanities, Department of History, Political Science and Public Administration, Albany, GA 31705-2717. Offers community and economic development administration (MPA); criminal justice administration (MPA); fiscal management (MPA); general management (MPA); health administration and policy (MPA); human resources management (MPA); public policy (MPA); water resource management and policy (MPA). *Accreditation:* NASPAA. *Students:* 17 full-time (11 women), 43 part-time (29 women); includes 57 minority (56 African Americans, 1 Asian American or Pacific Islander). Average age 34. 21 applicants, 100% accepted, 17 enrolled. In 2009, 17 master's awarded. *Entrance requirements:* For master's, Graduate Record Examination (GRE) or Miller Analogies Test (MAT). *Application deadline:* For fall admission, 11/16 for domestic students, 9/16 for international students; for spring admission, 4/19 for domestic students, 2/19 for international students. Applications are processed on a rolling basis. Application fee: $20. Electronic applications accepted. *Expenses:* Tuition, state resident: full-time $2970; part-time $162 per credit hour. Tuition, nonresident: full-time $12,168; part-time $676 per credit hour. Required fees: $962; $75 per credit hour. *Financial support:* Application deadline: 6/30. *Faculty research:* Public policy, strategic public human resources and human capital management, diversity management in the public sector and collective bargaining and labor relations in the public sector, e-government and public sector information systems, public administration pedagogy and business process modeling simulation, funded research- community development, non profit organizations, civic engagement and civic participation, health care disparities among minorities and poverty. Total annual research expenditures: $26,000. *Unit head:* Dr. Peter Ngwafu, Director, 229-430-4873, Fax: 229-430-7895, E-mail: peter.ngwafu@asurams.edu. *Application contact:* Nicole Lane, Interim Graduate Admissions Officer, 229-430-4862, Fax: 229-430-6398, E-mail: nicole.lane@asurams.edu.

American University, School of Public Affairs, Department of Public Administration, Program in Public Policy, Washington, DC 20016-8070. Offers MPP, MPP/JD, MPP/LLM. *Students:* 97 full-time (61 women), 32 part-time (26 women); includes 30 minority (15 African Americans, 11 Asian Americans or Pacific Islanders, 4 Hispanic Americans), 4 international. Average age 25. In 2009, 57 master's awarded. *Degree requirements:* For master's, comprehensive exam. *Entrance requirements:* For master's, GRE, 2 recommendations. Additional exam requirements/recommendations for international students: Required—TOEFL. *Application deadline:* For fall admission, 2/1 for domestic students; for spring admission, 11/1 for domestic students. Application fee: $55. *Expenses:* Tuition: Full-time $22,266; part-time $1237 per credit hour. Required fees: $430. Tuition and fees vary according to program. *Financial support:* Application deadline: 2/1.

The American University in Cairo, Graduate Studies and Research, School of Humanities and Social Sciences, Program in Public Policy and Administration, Cairo, Egypt. Offers MA, Diploma.

The American University of Paris, Graduate Programs, Paris, France. Offers cross-cultural and sustainable business management (MA); cultural translation (MA); global communications (MA); global communications and civil society (MA); international affairs, conflict resolution and civil society development (MA); Middle East and Islamic studies (MA); Middle East and Islamic studies and international affairs (MA); public policy and international affairs (MA); public policy and international law (MA). *Faculty:* 14 full-time (3 women). *Students:* 143 full-time (109 women). 71 applicants, 92% accepted, 34 enrolled. *Degree requirements:* For master's, thesis. *Entrance requirements:* For master's, minimum undergraduate GPA of 3.0. *Application deadline:* For fall admission, 4/15 priority date for international students; for spring admission, 11/15 priority date for international students. Applications are processed on a rolling basis. Application fee: $75. Tuition charges are reported in euros. *Expenses:* Tuition: Full-time 23,460 euros. *Financial support:* Scholarships/grants available. Financial award applicants required to submit FAFSA. *Unit head:* Celeste Schenk, President, 33 1-40620659, E-mail: president@aup.fr. *Application contact:* International Admissions Counselor, 33 1-40620720, Fax: 33 1-47053432, E-mail: admissions@aup.edu.

Arizona State University, Sandra Day O'Connor College of Law, Tempe, AZ 85287-7906. Offers biotechnology and genomics (LL M); law (JD); legal studies (MLS); tribal policy, law and government (LL M); JD/MBA; JD/MD; JD/PhD. *Accreditation:* ABA. *Faculty:* 57 full-time (20 women), 46 part-time/adjunct (12 women). *Students:* 591 full-time (258 women), 35 part-time (21 women); includes 131 minority (12 African Americans, 41 American Indian/Alaska Native, 19 Asian Americans or Pacific Islanders, 59 Hispanic Americans), 16 international. Average age 27. 2,400 applicants, 28% accepted, 184 enrolled. In 2009, 177 first professional degrees awarded. *Degree requirements:* For JD, comprehensive exam, paper. *Entrance requirements:* For JD, LSAT; for master's, bachelor's degree; JD (for LL M). Additional exam requirements/recommendations for international students: Required—TOEFL (minimum score 550 paper-based; 213 computer-based; 80 iBT). *Application deadline:* For fall admission, 11/15 priority date for domestic and international students; for spring admission, 2/1 for domestic and international students. Applications are processed on a rolling basis. Application fee: $60. Electronic applications accepted. *Expenses:* Contact institution. *Financial support:* In 2009–10, 490 students received support; research assistantships, teaching assistantships, career-related internships or fieldwork, Federal Work-Study, institutionally sponsored loans, scholarships/grants, tuition waivers (full and partial), and unspecified assistantships available. Financial award application deadline: 3/5; financial award applicants required to submit FAFSA. *Faculty research:* Emerging technologies and the law, Indian law, law and philosophy, international law, intellectual property. Total annual research expenditures: $514,610. *Unit head:* Dean Paul Schiff Berman, Dean and Foundation Professor of Law, 480-965-6188, Fax: 480-965-6521, E-mail: paul.berman@asu.edu. *Application contact:* Chitra Damania, Director of Operations, 480-965-1474, Fax: 480-727-7930, E-mail: law.admissions@asu.edu.

Baylor University, Graduate School, College of Arts and Sciences, Department of Political Science, Waco, TX 76798. Offers international studies (MA); political science (MA, PhD); public policy and administration (MPPA); JD/MPPA. *Students:* 28 full-time (8 women), 1 part-time (0 women), 3 international. In 2009, 5 master's, 1 doctorate awarded. *Entrance requirements:* For master's, GRE General Test. *Application deadline:* Applications are processed on a rolling basis. Application fee: $25. *Financial support:* Research assistantships, career-related internships or fieldwork, Federal Work-Study, and institutionally sponsored loans available. Financial award application deadline: 3/1. *Unit head:* Dr. David Corey, Graduate Program Director, 254-710-3161, Fax: 254-710-3122, E-mail: david_d_corey@baylor.edu. *Application contact:* Jenice Langston, Administrative Assistant, 254-710-3161, Fax: 254-710-3870, E-mail: jenice_langston@baylor.edu.

Boise State University, Graduate College, College of Social Sciences and Public Affairs, Department of Public Policy and Administration, Boise, ID 83725-0399. Offers environmental and natural resources policy and administration (MPA); general public administration (MPA); state and local government policy and administration (MPA). *Accreditation:* NASPAA. Part-time programs available. *Degree requirements:* For master's, comprehensive exam, directed research project, internship. *Entrance requirements:* For master's, GRE General Test, minimum GPA of 3.0. Additional exam requirements/recommendations for international students: Required—TOEFL. Electronic applications accepted. *Expenses:* Tuition, state resident: full-time $3106; part-time $209 per credit. Tuition, nonresident: part-time $284 per credit.

Brandeis University, Graduate School of Arts and Sciences, Joint Master's Programs in Women's and Gender Studies, Waltham, MA 02454-9110. Offers anthropology and women's and gender studies (MA); English and women's and gender studies (MA); music and women's and gender studies (MA); Near Eastern and Judaic studies and women's and gender studies (MA); public policy and women's and gender studies (MA); sociology and women's and gender studies (MA); sustainable international development and women's/gender studies (MA). Part-time programs available. *Faculty:* 18 full-time (17 women), 2 part-time/adjunct (both women). *Students:* 17 full-time (15 women), 4 international. Average age 25. 35 applicants, 49% accepted, 6 enrolled. In 2009, 8 master's awarded. *Degree requirements:* For master's, thesis. *Entrance requirements:* For master's, GRE, sample of written work, resume. Additional exam requirements/recommendations for international students: Required—TOEFL (minimum score 600 paper-based; 250 computer-based; 100 iBT); Recommended—IELTS (minimum score 7). *Application deadline:* For fall admission, 1/15 for domestic students. Application fee: $75. Electronic applications accepted. *Financial support:* In 2009–10, 6 students received support, including 2 fellowships with partial tuition reimbursements available (averaging $4,450 per year), 1 teaching assistantship with partial tuition reimbursement available (averaging $3,200 per year); research assistantships, scholarships/grants and tuition waivers (full and partial) also available. Support available to part-time students. Financial award application deadline: 4/15; financial award applicants required to submit FAFSA. *Unit head:* Prof. James Mandrell, Chair, 781-736-3042, Fax: 781-736-3044, E-mail: mandrell@brandeis.edu. *Application contact:* Kathryn Dalton, Program Administrator, 781-736-3045, Fax: 781-736-3044, E-mail: daltonka@brandeis.edu.

Brandeis University, The Heller School for Social Policy and Management, Program in Public Policy, Waltham, MA 02454-9110. Offers aging (MPP); behavioral health (MPP); children, youth and families (MPP); general social policy (MPP); health (MPP); poverty alleviation and development (MPP). Part-time programs available. *Entrance requirements:* Additional exam requirements/recommendations for international students: Required—TOEFL (minimum score 600 paper-based). Electronic applications accepted. *Faculty research:* Health policy, child and family policy, mental health policy, disability policy, aging policy, substance abuse, work, inequality and social change.

Brigham Young University, Graduate Studies, College of Family, Home, and Social Sciences, Department of Political Science–Public Policy, Provo, UT 84602. Offers MPP, JD/MPP. *Faculty:* 4 full-time (0 women), 3 part-time/adjunct (1 woman). *Students:* 16 full-time (7 women); includes 4 minority (1 African American, 1 American Indian/Alaska Native, 1 Asian American or Pacific Islander, 1 Hispanic American). Average age 26. 31 applicants, 58% accepted, 9 enrolled. In 2009, 4 master's awarded. *Degree requirements:* For master's, internship. *Entrance requirements:* For master's, GRE. Additional exam requirements/recommendations for international students: Required—TOEFL (minimum score 580 paper-based; 237 computer-based; 85 iBT). *Application deadline:* For fall admission, 3/1 priority date for domestic and international students. Application fee: $50. Electronic applications accepted. *Expenses:* Tuition: Full-time $5580; part-time $301 per credit hour. Tuition and fees vary according to student's religious affiliation. *Financial support:* In 2009–10, 13 students received support, including 7 research assistantships with full and partial tuition reimbursements available (averaging $2,456 per year), 1 teaching assistantship with full and partial tuition reimbursement available (averaging $2,500 per year); fellowships also available. Financial award application deadline: 3/1. *Faculty research:* Welfare, environment, and health policy issues; U. S. elections. *Unit head:* Dr. Sven E. Wilson, Graduate Program Director, 801-422-9018, Fax: 801-422-0224, E-mail: sven_wilson@byu.edu. *Application contact:* Jessica A. McArthur, Graduate Secretary, 801-422-7146, Fax: 801-422-0224, E-mail: publicpolicy@byu.edu.

Brock University, Faculty of Graduate Studies, Faculty of Social Sciences, Program in Political Science, St. Catharines, ON L2S 3A1, Canada. Offers Canadian politics (MA); comparative politics (MA); international relations (MA); political theory or philosophy (MA); public policy (MA). Part-time programs available. *Degree requirements:* For master's, thesis optional. *Entrance requirements:* For master's, honors degree. Additional exam requirements/recommendations for international students: Required—TOEFL (minimum score 550 paper-based; 213 computer-based; 80 iBT), IELTS (minimum score 6.5), TWE (minimum score 4). Electronic applications accepted. *Faculty research:* Public administration reform, economic and social justice, politics of societies, Canadian politics, international relations.

Brooklyn College of the City University of New York, Division of Graduate Studies, Department of Political Science, Brooklyn, NY 11210-2889. Offers international affairs (MA); political science (MA, PhD); political science, urban policy and administration (MA). Part-time and evening/weekend programs available. *Students:* 24 full-time (13 women), 168 part-time (98 women); includes 99 minority (70 African Americans, 13 Asian Americans or Pacific Islanders, 16 Hispanic Americans), 29 international. Average age 30. 123 applicants, 87% accepted, 79 enrolled. In 2009, 46 master's awarded. *Degree requirements:* For master's, comprehensive exam (for some programs), thesis or alternative, foreign language exam (for international affairs program). *Entrance requirements:* For master's, 2 letters of recommendation, personal statement. Additional exam requirements/recommendations for international students: Required—TOEFL (minimum score 500 paper-based; 173 computer-based; 61 iBT). *Application deadline:* For fall admission, 5/1 for domestic and international students; for spring admission, 12/12 for domestic students, 11/1 for international students. *Expenses:* Tuition, area resident: Full-time $7360; part-time $310 per credit hour. Tuition, state resident: full-time $7360; part-time $310 per credit hour. Tuition, nonresident: full-time $13,800; part-time $575 per credit hour. International tuition: $13,800 full-time. Required fees: $140.10 per semester. *Financial support:* Career-related internships or fieldwork and Federal Work-Study available. Support available to part-time students. Financial award application deadline: 5/1; financial award applicants required to submit FAFSA. *Faculty research:* Ethics and politics, politics of criminal justice, Western Europe, international law and politics, labor politics. *Unit head:* Dr. Noel Anderson, Acting Chairperson, 718-951-5306, E-mail: anderson@brooklyn.cuny.edu. *Application contact:* Hernan Sierra, Graduate Admissions Coordinator, 718-951-4536, Fax: 718-951-4506, E-mail: grads@brooklyn.cuny.edu.

Brown University, Graduate School, A. Alfred Taubman Center for Public Policy and American Institutions, Providence, RI 02912. Offers MPA, MPP. *Entrance requirements:* For master's, GRE, 3 letters of recommendation. Additional exam requirements/recommendations for international students: Required—TOEFL.

California Lutheran University, Graduate Studies, Program in Public Policy and Administration, Thousand Oaks, CA 91360-2787. Offers MPPA. *Degree requirements:* For master's, comprehensive exam, thesis or project, internship. *Entrance requirements:* For master's, GMAT or GRE General Test, interview, minimum GPA of 3.0. *Expenses:* Contact institution.

California State University, Long Beach, Graduate Studies, College of Health and Human Services, Graduate Center for Public Policy and Administration, Long Beach, CA 90840. Offers MPA. *Accreditation:* NASPAA. Part-time and evening/weekend programs available. *Faculty:* 14 full-time (6 women), 2 part-time/adjunct (0 women). *Students:* 71 full-time (47 women), 166 part-time (100 women); includes 150 minority (25 African Americans, 3 American Indian/Alaska Native, 47 Asian Americans or Pacific Islanders, 75 Hispanic Americans), 6 international. Average age 31. 199 applicants, 78% accepted, 121 enrolled. *Degree requirements:* For master's, comprehensive exam. *Entrance requirements:* For master's, minimum GPA of 2.75. *Application deadline:* For fall admission, 7/1 for domestic students. Applications are processed on a rolling basis. Application fee: $55. Electronic applications accepted. *Expenses:* Required fees: $1802 per semester. Part-time tuition and fees vary according to course load. *Financial support:* Fellowships, career-related internships or fieldwork, Federal Work-Study, institutionally sponsored loans, and scholarships/grants available. Financial award application deadline: 3/2. *Faculty research:* Transportation access, air quality controls, coastal issues, intergovernmental relations. *Unit head:* Dr. Walter Frank Baber, Director, 562-985-4178, Fax: 562-985-4672, E-mail: wbaber@csulb.edu. *Application contact:* Dr. Walter Frank Baber, Director, 562-985-4178, Fax: 562-985-4672, E-mail: wbaber@csulb.edu.

California State University, Monterey Bay, College of Professional Studies, Health, Human Services and Public Policy Department, Seaside, CA 93955-8001. Offers public policy (MPP). Part-time programs available. *Degree requirements:* For master's, internship. *Entrance requirements:* For master's, GRE, curriculum vitae, recommendations. Additional exam

Public Policy

California State University, Monterey Bay (continued)
requirements/recommendations for international students: Required—TOEFL (minimum score 525 paper-based; 213 computer-based; 71 iBT). Electronic applications accepted. *Faculty research:* Social policy, health policy, politics and government.

California State University, Sacramento, Graduate Studies, College of Social Sciences and Interdisciplinary Studies, Program in Public Policy and Administration, Sacramento, CA 95819. Offers MPPA. Part-time programs available. *Degree requirements:* For master's, thesis or alternative, writing proficiency exam. *Entrance requirements:* For master's, GRE General Test. Additional exam requirements/recommendations for international students: Required—TOEFL. Electronic applications accepted.

Carleton University, Faculty of Graduate Studies, Faculty of Public Affairs and Management, School of Public Policy and Administration, Ottawa, ON K1S 5B6, Canada. Offers public administration (MA, DPA); public policy (PhD). Part-time programs available. *Degree requirements:* For master's, thesis optional; for doctorate, one foreign language, comprehensive exam, thesis/dissertation. *Entrance requirements:* For master's, GRE, honors degree; for doctorate, master's degree. Additional exam requirements/recommendations for international students: Required—TOEFL. *Faculty research:* Canadian public administration and policy, development administration, public policy analysis, public management.

Carnegie Mellon University, College of Humanities and Social Sciences, Department of Statistics, Pittsburgh, PA 15213-3891. Offers machine learning and statistics (PhD); mathematical finance (PhD); statistics (MS, PhD), including applied statistics (PhD), computational statistics (PhD), theoretical statistics (PhD); statistics and public policy (PhD). Terminal master's awarded for partial completion of doctoral program. *Degree requirements:* For doctorate, comprehensive exam, thesis/dissertation. *Entrance requirements:* For master's and doctorate, GRE General Test. Additional exam requirements/recommendations for international students: Required—TOEFL. *Faculty research:* Stochastic processes, Bayesian statistics, statistical computing, decision theory, psychiatric statistics.

Carnegie Mellon University, H. John Heinz III College, School of Public Policy and Management, Program in Public Policy and Management–Australia, Adelaide, PA 5000, Australia. Offers MS.

Carnegie Mellon University, H. John Heinz III College, School of Public Policy and Management and Tepper School of Business, Programs in Public Policy and Management, Pittsburgh, PA 15213-3891. Offers MS, PhD, JD/MS, M Div/MS. *Degree requirements:* For master's, internship. *Entrance requirements:* For master's, GMAT or GRE General Test, previous course work in pre-calculus and statistics. Electronic applications accepted.

Central European University, Graduate Studies, School of Social Sciences and Humanities, Budapest, Hungary. Offers economics (MA, PhD); gender studies (MA, PhD); international relations and European studies (MA, PhD); mathematics and its applications (MS, PhD); medieval studies (MA, PhD); nationalism studies (MA, PhD); philosophy (MA, PhD); political science (MA, PhD); public policy (MA, PhD); sociology and social anthropology (MA, PhD). Terminal master's awarded for partial completion of doctoral program. *Degree requirements:* For master's, one foreign language, thesis; for doctorate, one foreign language, comprehensive exam, thesis/dissertation. *Entrance requirements:* For master's, interview; for doctorate, GRE, CEU subject test, interview. Additional exam requirements/recommendations for international students: Required—TOEFL (minimum score 570 paper-based; 230 computer-based). Electronic applications accepted. *Faculty research:* Civil society, fiscal decentralization, party politics, political philosophy (especially Liberalism, theory of Democracy).

Claremont Graduate University, Graduate Programs, Program in Public Policy and Evaluation, Claremont, CA 91711-6160. Offers MA. In 2009, 1 master's awarded. *Entrance requirements:* For master's, GRE General Test. Additional exam requirements/recommendations for international students: Required—TOEFL (minimum score 550 paper-based; 213 computer-based; 80 iBT). *Application deadline:* For fall admission, 2/1 priority date for domestic students. Application fee: $60. Electronic applications accepted. *Expenses:* Tuition: Full-time $35,046; part-time $1524 per credit. Required fees: $161 per semester. *Financial support:* Fellowships, Federal Work-Study, institutionally sponsored loans, and scholarships/grants available. Support available to part-time students. Financial award application deadline: 2/15; financial award applicants required to submit FAFSA. *Unit head:* Jean Schroedel, Dean, 909-621-8696, Fax: 909-621-8545, E-mail: jean.schroedel@cgu.edu. *Application contact:* Lesa Hiben, Recruiter and Admissions Coordinator, 909-621-8699, Fax: 909-621-7545, E-mail: lesa.hiben@cgu.edu.

Claremont Graduate University, Graduate Programs, School of Politics and Economics, Department of Economics, Claremont, CA 91711-6160. Offers business and financial economics (MA, PhD); economic development (Certificate); economics (PhD); industrial organization (PhD); international and development economics (PhD); international economics policy and development (MA); international money and finance (PhD); neuroeconomics (PhD); political economy and public policy (MA); public choice and public economics (PhD); MBA/PhD. Part-time programs available. *Faculty:* 5 full-time (0 women), 1 part-time/adjunct (0 women). *Students:* 103 full-time (25 women), 7 part-time (3 women); includes 16 minority (1 African American, 9 Asian Americans or Pacific Islanders, 6 Hispanic Americans), 62 international. Average age 33. In 2009, 15 master's, 8 doctorates awarded. *Entrance requirements:* For master's and doctorate, GRE General Test or GMAT. Additional exam requirements/recommendations for international students: Required—TOEFL (minimum score 550 paper-based; 213 computer-based; 80 iBT). *Application deadline:* For fall admission, 2/1 priority date for domestic students. Applications are processed on a rolling basis. Application fee: $60. Electronic applications accepted. *Expenses:* Tuition: Full-time $35,046; part-time $1524 per credit. Required fees: $161 per semester. *Financial support:* Fellowships, research assistantships, teaching assistantships, Federal Work-Study, institutionally sponsored loans, and scholarships/grants available. Support available to part-time students. Financial award application deadline: 2/15; financial award applicants required to submit FAFSA. *Faculty research:* International and financial economics, law and economics, regulation, public choice economics. *Unit head:* Paul Zak, Chair, 909-621-8788, Fax: 909-621-8545, E-mail: paul.zak@cgu.edu. *Application contact:* Lesa Hiben, Admissions Coordinator, 909-621-8699, Fax: 909-621-7545, E-mail: lesa.hiben@cga.edu.

Claremont Graduate University, Graduate Programs, School of Politics and Economics, Department of Politics and Policy, Claremont, CA 91711-6160. Offers American politics (MA, PhD); comparative politics (PhD); international political economy (MA); international studies (MA); political philosophy (PhD); political science (PhD); politics, economics and business (MA); public policy (MA, PhD); world politics (PhD); MBA/PhD. Part-time programs available. *Faculty:* 8 full-time (3 women), 4 part-time/adjunct (0 women). *Students:* 163 full-time (68 women), 16 part-time (7 women); includes 29 minority (6 African Americans, 8 Asian Americans or Pacific Islanders, 15 Hispanic Americans), 40 international. Average age 32. In 2009, 23 master's, 19 doctorates awarded. Terminal master's awarded for partial completion of doctoral program. *Entrance requirements:* For master's and doctorate, GRE General Test. Additional exam requirements/recommendations for international students: Required—TOEFL (minimum score 550 paper-based; 213 computer-based; 80 iBT). *Application deadline:* For fall admission, 2/1 priority date for domestic students. Applications are processed on a rolling basis. Application fee: $60. Electronic applications accepted. *Expenses:* Tuition: Full-time $35,046; part-time $1524 per credit. Required fees: $161 per semester. *Financial support:* Fellowships, research assistantships, teaching assistantships, Federal Work-Study, institutionally sponsored loans, and scholarships/grants available. Support available to part-time students. Financial award application deadline: 2/15; financial award applicants required to submit FAFSA. *Faculty research:* Environmental policy, international debt, global democratization, Third World development, public sector discrimination. *Unit head:* Jennifer Merolla, Chair, 909-621-8696, Fax: 909-621-8545, E-mail: jennifer.merolla@cgu.edu. *Application contact:* Lesa Hiben, Admissions Coordinator, 909-621-8699, Fax: 909-621-7545, E-mail: lesa.hiben@cga.edu.

The College of William and Mary, Faculty of Arts and Sciences, Thomas Jefferson Program in Public Policy, Williamsburg, VA 23187-8795. Offers MPP, JD/MPP, MBA/MPP, MS/MPP. *Faculty:* 2 full-time (1 woman), 15 part-time/adjunct (5 women). *Students:* 42 full-time (25 women); includes 5 minority (1 African American, 2 Asian Americans or Pacific Islanders, 2 Hispanic Americans), 5 international. Average age 25. 98 applicants, 51% accepted, 17 enrolled. In 2009, 15 master's awarded. *Entrance requirements:* For master's, GRE General Test. Additional exam requirements/recommendations for international students: Required—TOEFL (minimum score 600 paper-based; 100 iBT). *Application deadline:* For fall admission, 2/15 priority date for domestic and international students. Application fee: $45. Electronic applications accepted. *Expenses:* Tuition, state resident: full-time $6400; part-time $315 per credit hour. Tuition, nonresident: full-time $19,720; part-time $840 per credit hour. Required fees: $4114. *Financial support:* In 2009–10, 30 research assistantships with partial tuition reimbursements (averaging $6,000 per year), 15 teaching assistantships with partial tuition reimbursements (averaging $7,000 per year) were awarded; career-related internships or fieldwork and unspecified assistantships also available. Financial award application deadline: 2/15; financial award applicants required to submit FAFSA. *Faculty research:* Social policy, technology policy, international development, health care policy, environmental policy. Total annual research expenditures: $81,043. *Unit head:* Dr. Eric Jensen, Director, 757-221-2384, Fax: 757-221-2390. *Application contact:* Sophie Correll, Administrative Assistant, 757-221-2368, Fax: 757-221-2390, E-mail: sbcorr@wm.edu.

Columbia University, School of International and Public Affairs, Program in Public Policy and Administration, New York, NY 10027. Offers MPA, JD/MPA, MPA/MS, MPH/MPA. *Entrance requirements:* For master's, GRE General Test. Additional exam requirements/recommendations for international students: Required—TOEFL (minimum score 600 paper-based; 250 computer-based; 100 iBT). Electronic applications accepted.

Concordia University, School of Graduate Studies, Faculty of Arts and Science, Department of Political Science, Montréal, QC H3G 1M8, Canada. Offers political science (PhD); public policy and public administration (MA), including geography. *Degree requirements:* For master's, one foreign language, comprehensive exam, thesis optional, internship. *Entrance requirements:* For master's, honors degree or equivalent. Additional exam requirements/recommendations for international students: Required—TOEFL. *Faculty research:* International public policy and administration, Quebec public administration, public policy and social/political theory, geography and public policy, public administration and decision making.

Cornell University, Graduate School, Graduate Fields of Arts and Sciences, Field of Government, Ithaca, NY 14853-0001. Offers American politics (PhD); comparative politics (PhD); international relations (PhD); political methodology (PhD); political thought (PhD); public policy (PhD). *Faculty:* 58 full-time (19 women). *Students:* 65 full-time (35 women); includes 9 minority (1 African American, 1 American Indian/Alaska Native, 2 Asian Americans or Pacific Islanders, 5 Hispanic Americans), 20 international. Average age 29. 317 applicants, 7% accepted, 11 enrolled. In 2009, 14 doctorates awarded. *Degree requirements:* For doctorate, comprehensive exam, thesis/dissertation. *Entrance requirements:* For doctorate, GRE General Test, sample of written work, 3 letters of recommendation. Additional exam requirements/recommendations for international students: Required—TOEFL (minimum score 550 paper-based; 213 computer-based; 77 iBT). *Application deadline:* For fall admission, 1/15 for domestic students. Application fee: $70. Electronic applications accepted. *Expenses:* Tuition: Full-time $29,500. Required fees: $70. Full-time tuition and fees vary according to degree level, program and student level. *Financial support:* In 2009–10, 60 students received support, including 10 fellowships with full tuition reimbursements available; research assistantships with full tuition reimbursements available, teaching assistantships with full tuition reimbursements available, institutionally sponsored loans, scholarships/grants, health care benefits, tuition waivers (full and partial), and unspecified assistantships also available. Financial award applicants required to submit FAFSA. *Faculty research:* Political theory, American politics, comparative politics, international relations, methodology. *Unit head:* Director of Graduate Studies, 607-255-3567, Fax: 607-255-4530. *Application contact:* Graduate Field Assistant, 607-255-3567, Fax: 607-255-4530, E-mail: cu_govt@cornell.edu.

Cornell University, Graduate School, Graduate Fields of Human Ecology, Field of Policy Analysis and Management, Ithaca, NY 14853-0001. Offers consumer policy (PhD); evaluation (PhD); family and social welfare policy (PhD); health administration (MHA); health management and policy (PhD). *Faculty:* 40 full-time (17 women). *Students:* 51 full-time (27 women); includes 13 minority (4 African Americans, 8 Asian Americans or Pacific Islanders, 1 Hispanic American), 7 international. Average age 26. 130 applicants, 38% accepted, 31 enrolled. In 2009, 25 master's, 5 doctorates awarded. *Degree requirements:* For master's, thesis; for doctorate, thesis/dissertation. *Entrance requirements:* For master's, GRE General Test or GMAT, 2 letters of recommendation; for doctorate, GRE General Test, 2 letters of recommendation. Additional exam requirements/recommendations for international students: Required—TOEFL (minimum score 550 paper-based; 213 computer-based; 77 iBT). *Application deadline:* For fall admission, 1/15 for domestic students. Application fee: $70. Electronic applications accepted. *Expenses:* Tuition: Full-time $29,500. Required fees: $70. Full-time tuition and fees vary according to degree level, program and student level. *Financial support:* In 2009–10, 17 students received support, including 1 fellowship with full and partial tuition reimbursement available, 8 teaching assistantships with full and partial tuition reimbursements available; research assistantships with full and partial tuition reimbursements available, institutionally sponsored loans, scholarships/grants, health care benefits, tuition waivers (full and partial), and unspecified assistantships also available. Financial award applicants required to submit FAFSA. *Faculty research:* Health policy, family policy, social welfare policy, program evaluation, consumer policy. *Unit head:* Director of Graduate Studies, 607-255-7772. *Application contact:* Graduate Field Assistant, 607-255-7772, Fax: 607-255-4071, E-mail: pam_phd@cornell.edu.

DePaul University, School of Public Service, Chicago, IL 60604. Offers financial administration management (Certificate); health administration (Certificate); health law and policy (MS); international public services (MS); leadership and policy studies (MS); metropolitan planning (Certificate); public administration (MPA); public service management (MS), including association management, fundraising and philanthropy, healthcare administration, higher education administration, metropolitan planning; public services (Certificate); JD/MS. Part-time and evening/weekend programs available. Postbaccalaureate distance learning degree programs offered (minimal on-campus study). *Faculty:* 14 full-time (3 women), 43 part-time/adjunct (24 women). *Students:* 283 full-time (206 women), 298 part-time (208 women); includes 196 minority (112 African Americans, 1 American Indian/Alaska Native, 30 Asian Americans or Pacific Islanders, 53 Hispanic Americans), 18 international. Average age 26. 162 applicants, 100% accepted, 94 enrolled. In 2009, 108 master's awarded. *Degree requirements:* For master's, thesis or integrative seminar. *Entrance requirements:* For master's, minimum GPA of 2.7. Additional exam requirements/recommendations for international students: Required—TOEFL (minimum score 550 paper-based; 213 computer-based; 80 iBT), IELTS (minimum score 6.5). *Application deadline:* Applications are processed on a rolling basis. Application fee: $40. Electronic applications accepted. *Expenses:* Tuition: Full-time $37,525; part-time $620 per credit hour. *Financial support:* In 2009–10, 60 students received support, including 3 research assistantships with full tuition reimbursements available (averaging $7,000 per year); career-related internships or fieldwork, Federal Work-Study, institutionally sponsored loans, scholarships/grants, tuition waivers (partial), and unspecified assistantships also available. Support available to part-time students. Financial award application deadline: 7/1; financial award applicants required to submit FAFSA. *Faculty research:* Government financing, transportation, leadership, health care, volunteerism and organizational behavior, non-profit organizations. Total annual research expenditures: $20,000. *Unit head:* Dr. J. Patrick Murphy, Director, 312-362-5608, Fax: 312-362-5506, E-mail: jpmurphy@depaul.edu. *Application contact:* Megan B. Balderston, Director of Admissions and Marketing, 312-362-5565, Fax: 312-362-5506, E-mail: pubserv@depaul.edu.

Duke University, Graduate School, Duke Sanford Institute of Public Policy, Durham, NC 27708-0243. Offers AM, MPP, PhD, Certificate, JD/AM, JD/MPP, MBA/AM, MBA/MPP, MD/AM,

MEM/MPP, MF/MPP. *Faculty:* 43 full-time, 17 part-time/adjunct. *Students:* 109 full-time (73 women); includes 17 minority (7 African Americans, 4 Asian Americans or Pacific Islanders, 6 Hispanic Americans), 15 international. 501 applicants, 34% accepted, 64 enrolled. In 2009, 45 master's awarded. *Entrance requirements:* For master's and doctorate, GRE General Test. Additional exam requirements/recommendations for international students: Required—TOEFL, IELTS. *Application deadline:* For fall admission, 12/8 priority date for domestic students, 12/8 for international students. Application fee: $75. Electronic applications accepted. *Financial support:* Fellowships, research assistantships, teaching assistantships, career-related internships or fieldwork and Federal Work-Study available. Financial award application deadline: 12/31. *Unit head:* Elizabeth Frankenberg, Director, 919-613-9311, Fax: 919-684-3702, E-mail: mppadmit@duke.edu. *Application contact:* Information Contact, 919-613-9205, E-mail: mppadmit@duke.edu.

Duquesne University, Graduate School of Liberal Arts, Graduate Center for Social and Public Policy, Pittsburgh, PA 15282-0001. Offers conflict resolution and peace studies (Certificate); social and public policy (MA, Certificate). Part-time and evening/weekend programs available. *Faculty:* 15 full-time (3 women), 1 (woman) part-time/adjunct. *Students:* 40 full-time (26 women), 14 part-time (8 women); includes 5 minority (3 African Americans, 2 Hispanic Americans), 10 international. Average age 27. 31 applicants, 100% accepted, 19 enrolled. In 2009, 13 master's awarded. *Degree requirements:* For master's, thesis. *Entrance requirements:* For master's, GRE General Test. Additional exam requirements/recommendations for international students: Required—TOEFL. *Application deadline:* For fall admission, 4/30 priority date for domestic and international students; for spring admission, 11/1 priority date for domestic and international students. Applications are processed on a rolling basis. Electronic applications accepted. *Expenses:* Tuition: Part-time $851 per credit. Required fees: $81 per credit. *Financial support:* In 2009–10, 20 students received support, including 12 research assistantships with full and partial tuition reimbursements available (averaging $9,000 per year), 4 teaching assistantships with full and partial tuition reimbursements available (averaging $9,000 per year); career-related internships or fieldwork, institutionally sponsored loans, scholarships/grants, tuition waivers (full and partial), and unspecified assistantships also available. Support available to part-time students. Financial award application deadline: 5/1. *Faculty research:* Program evaluation, environmental policy, criminal justice policy, health care policy. Total annual research expenditures: $30,000. *Unit head:* Dr. Joseph Yenerall, Director, 412-396-6485, Fax: 412-396-5265, E-mail: socialpolicy@duq.edu. *Application contact:* Dr. Joseph Yenerall, Assistant to the Dean, 412-396-6485.

Eastern Michigan University, Graduate School, College of Arts and Sciences, Department of Political Science, Programs in Public Administration, Ypsilanti, MI 48197. Offers local government management (Graduate Certificate); management of public healthcare services (Graduate Certificate); public administration (MPA, Graduate Certificate); public budget management (Graduate Certificate); public land planning (Graduate Certificate); public management (Graduate Certificate); public personnel management (Graduate Certificate); public policy analysis (Graduate Certificate). *Accreditation:* NASPAA. *Students:* 18 full-time (7 women), 130 part-time (72 women); includes 53 minority (46 African Americans, 2 American Indian/Alaska Native, 1 Asian American or Pacific Islander, 4 Hispanic Americans), 5 international. Average age 34. In 2009, 17 master's, 37 other advanced degrees awarded. Application fee: $35. Tuition and fees vary according to course level. *Unit head:* Dr. Joseph Ohren, Program Director, 734-487-2522, Fax: 734-487-3340, E-mail: joseph.ohren@emich.edu. *Application contact:* Dr. Sukru Koyluoglu, Program Coordinator, 734-487-0063, Fax: 734-487-3340, E-mail: sukru.koyuoglu@emich.edu.

Florida State University, The Graduate School, College of Social Sciences and Public Policy, Reubin O'D. Askew School of Public Administration and Policy, Tallahassee, FL 32306-2250. Offers MPA, PhD, Certificate, JD/MPA, MPA/MSC, MPA/MSP, MPA/MSW. *Accreditation:* NASPAA (one or more programs are accredited). Part-time and evening/weekend programs available. *Faculty:* 11 full-time (1 woman), 6 part-time/adjunct (3 women). *Students:* 66 full-time (23 women), 114 part-time (53 women); includes 51 minority (29 African Americans, 1 American Indian/Alaska Native, 7 Asian Americans or Pacific Islanders, 14 Hispanic Americans), 40 international. Average age 25. 157 applicants, 80% accepted, 48 enrolled. In 2009, 44 master's, 8 doctorates awarded. *Degree requirements:* For master's, action report; for doctorate, comprehensive exam, thesis/dissertation. *Entrance requirements:* For master's, GRE General Test (minimum score 1000), GMAT, MAT, minimum undergraduate upper-division GPA of 3.0; for doctorate, GRE General Test (minimum score of 1000); GMAT; MAT, minimum undergraduate GPA of 3.0, graduate 3.5. Additional exam requirements/recommendations for international students: Required—TOEFL (minimum score 550 paper-based; 213 computer-based; 80 iBT), IELTS (minimum score 6.5), Michigan English Language Assessment Battery (minimum score 77). *Application deadline:* For fall admission, 7/1 for domestic students, 5/1 for international students; for spring admission, 11/1 for domestic students, 9/1 for international students. Applications are processed on a rolling basis. Application fee: $30. Electronic applications accepted. *Expenses:* Tuition, state resident: full-time $7413. Tuition, nonresident: full-time $22,567. *Financial support:* In 2009–10, 38 students received support, including 10 fellowships with full tuition reimbursements available (averaging $15,000 per year), 24 research assistantships with full tuition reimbursements available (averaging $13,000 per year), 4 teaching assistantships with full tuition reimbursements available (averaging $10,000 per year); career-related internships or fieldwork, Federal Work-Study, institutionally sponsored loans, scholarships/grants, tuition waivers (full), and unspecified assistantships also available. Support available to part-time students. Financial award application deadline: 2/1. *Faculty research:* Financial management, human resource management, policy, strategic management, organizations, nonprofit management. *Unit head:* Dr. William Earle Klay, Director, 850-644-3525, Fax: 850-644-7617, E-mail: eklay@fsu.edu. *Application contact:* Velda Williams, Academic Program Specialist, 850-644-3060, Fax: 850-644-7617, E-mail: vwilliams3@fsu.edu.

Frederick S. Pardee RAND Graduate School, Program in Policy Analysis, Santa Monica, CA 90407-2138. Offers PhD. *Degree requirements:* For doctorate, comprehensive exam, thesis/dissertation. *Entrance requirements:* For doctorate, GMAT or GRE General Test. Additional exam requirements/recommendations for international students: Required—TOEFL. Electronic applications accepted. *Faculty research:* Education, defense policy, health, labor and population, justice.

George Mason University, School of Public Policy, Program in Public Policy, Arlington, VA 22201. Offers MPP, PhD. Part-time programs available. *Faculty:* 61 full-time (14 women), 30 part-time/adjunct (4 women). *Students:* 149 full-time, 369 part-time; includes 51 minority (15 African Americans, 17 Asian Americans or Pacific Islanders, 19 Hispanic Americans), 68 international. Average age 31. 410 applicants, 67% accepted, 147 enrolled. In 2009, 105 master's, 14 doctorates awarded. *Degree requirements:* For master's, thesis or alternative; for doctorate, comprehensive exam, thesis/dissertation. *Entrance requirements:* For master's, GRE exam is required only for students seeking merit-based scholarship consideration, minimum GPA of 3.0, resume, 2 letters of recommendation, goals statement; for doctorate, GMAT or GRE General Test, resume, writing sample, 2 letters of recommendation. Additional exam requirements/recommendations for international students: Required—TOEFL. *Application deadline:* For fall admission, 6/1 priority date for domestic students, 5/1 priority date for international students; for spring admission, 12/1 priority date for domestic students, 11/1 priority date for international students. Applications are processed on a rolling basis. Application fee: $60. Electronic applications accepted. *Expenses:* Contact institution. *Financial support:* In 2009–10, 24 research assistantships with full tuition reimbursements (averaging $16,000 per year) were awarded; career-related internships or fieldwork, Federal Work-Study, scholarships/grants, health care benefits, tuition waivers (partial), and unspecified assistantships also available. Support available to part-time students. Financial award application deadline: 3/1; financial award applicants required to submit FAFSA. *Unit head:* Dr. Catherine Rudder, Director of MPP Program, 703-993-8099, E-mail: spp@gmu.edu. *Application contact:* Leslie Metzger Levin, Assistant Dean of Graduate Admissions and Marketing, 703-993-8099, Fax: 703-993-4876, E-mail: lmetzger@gmu.edu.

See Close-Up on page 1185.

Georgetown University, Graduate School of Arts and Sciences, The Georgetown Public Policy Institute, Washington, DC 20057. Offers MPM, MPP, MBA/MPP, MPP/JD, MPP/MA, MPP/MS, MPP/PhD. *Entrance requirements:* For master's, GRE General Test, minimum B average. Additional exam requirements/recommendations for international students: Required—TOEFL. *Faculty research:* Social policy, government, private sector.

Georgetown University, Graduate School of Arts and Sciences, School of Continuing Studies, Washington, DC 20057. Offers American studies (MALS); Catholic studies (MALS); classical civilizations (MALS); ethics and the professions (MALS); human resources management (MPS); humanities (MALS); individualized study (MALS); international affairs (MALS); Islam and Muslim-Christian relations (MALS); journalism (MPS); liberal studies (DLS); literature and society (MALS); medieval and early modern European studies (MALS); public relations (MPS); real estate (MPS); religious studies (MALS); social and public policy (MALS); sports industry management (MPS); the theory and practice of American democracy (MALS); visual culture (MALS). *Entrance requirements:* Additional exam requirements/recommendations for international students: Required—TOEFL.

The George Washington University, Columbian College of Arts and Sciences, Trachtenberg School of Public Policy and Public Administration, Washington, DC 20052. Offers public administration (MPA), including budget and public finance, federal policy, politics, and management, international development management, managing public organizations, managing state and local governments, nonprofit management, policy analysis and evaluation, public administration, public-private policy and management; public policy (MA, MPP), including environmental and resource policy (MA), philosophy and social policy (MA), women's studies (MA); public policy and administration (PhD); JD/MPP; MPA/JD; PhD/MPP. Part-time and evening/weekend programs available. *Faculty:* 35 full-time (12 women), 19 part-time/adjunct (10 women). *Students:* 187 full-time (114 women), 232 part-time (151 women); includes 62 minority (15 African Americans, 3 American Indian/Alaska Native, 29 Asian Americans or Pacific Islanders, 15 Hispanic Americans), 23 international. Average age 26. 913 applicants, 56% accepted, 186 enrolled. In 2009, 106 master's, 9 doctorates awarded. *Degree requirements:* For doctorate, thesis/dissertation, general exam. *Entrance requirements:* For master's, GRE General Test, minimum GPA of 3.0; for doctorate, GRE General Test, interview, minimum GPA of 3.0. Additional exam requirements/recommendations for international students: Required—TOEFL (minimum score 600 paper-based; 250 computer-based; 100 iBT). *Application deadline:* For fall admission, 1/15 priority date for domestic and international students; for spring admission, 10/1 priority date for domestic students, 9/1 priority date for international students. Applications are processed on a rolling basis. Application fee: $60. Electronic applications accepted. *Financial support:* In 2009–10, 87 students received support; fellowships, research assistantships, teaching assistantships, institutionally sponsored loans available. Financial award application deadline: 1/15. *Unit head:* Dr. Kathryn E. Newcomer, Director, 202-994-3959, Fax: 202-994-3959, E-mail: newcomer@gwu.edu. *Application contact:* Information Contact, 202-994-6295, Fax: 202-994-6295, E-mail: tspppa@gwu.edu.

The George Washington University, School of Business, Department of Strategic Management and Public Policy, Washington, DC 20052. Offers MBA, PhD. Part-time and evening/weekend programs available. *Faculty:* 14 full-time (3 women), 3 part-time/adjunct (1 woman). *Students:* 199 full-time (89 women); includes 25 minority (7 African Americans, 1 American Indian/Alaska Native, 15 Asian Americans or Pacific Islanders, 2 Hispanic Americans), 55 international. Average age 28. 529 applicants, 53% accepted. In 2009, 110 master's awarded. *Degree requirements:* For doctorate, thesis/dissertation. *Entrance requirements:* For master's, GMAT; for doctorate, GMAT or GRE. Additional exam requirements/recommendations for international students: Required—TOEFL. *Application deadline:* For fall admission, 4/1 priority date for domestic students; for spring admission, 10/1 for domestic students. Applications are processed on a rolling basis. Application fee: $60. *Financial support:* In 2009–10, 1 student received support; fellowships, teaching assistantships, career-related internships or fieldwork, Federal Work-Study, and institutionally sponsored loans available. Financial award application deadline: 4/1. *Unit head:* Dr. Mark Starik, Chair, 202-994-6677, E-mail: starik@gwu.edu. *Application contact:* Kristin Williams, Assistant Vice President for Graduate and Special Enrollment Management, 202-994-0467, Fax: 202-994-0371, E-mail: ksw@gwu.edu.

Georgia Institute of Technology, Graduate Studies and Research, Ivan Allen College of Policy and International Affairs, School of Public Policy, Atlanta, GA 30332-0001. Offers MS Pub P, PhD. Part-time programs available. *Degree requirements:* For master's, professional paper or thesis. *Entrance requirements:* Additional exam requirements/recommendations for international students: Required—TOEFL. Electronic applications accepted. *Faculty research:* National/regional science and technology policy, environmental policy, urban policy and planning, telecommunications policy.

Georgia State University, Andrew Young School of Policy Studies, Department of Public Management and Policy, Atlanta, GA 30303. Offers disaster management (Certificate); nonprofit management (Certificate); planning and economic development (Certificate); public administration (MPA), including criminal justice, management and finance, nonprofit management, planning and economic development, policy analysis and evaluation, public health; public policy (MPP, PhD), including disaster policy (MPP), nonprofit policy (MPP), planning and economic development policy (MPP), public finance policy (MPP), social policy (MPP); JD/MPA. *Accreditation:* NASPAA (one or more programs are accredited). Part-time and evening/weekend programs available. Terminal master's awarded for partial completion of doctoral program. *Degree requirements:* For master's, thesis optional; for doctorate, comprehensive exam, thesis/dissertation. *Entrance requirements:* For master's and doctorate, GRE General Test. Additional exam requirements/recommendations for international students: Required—TOEFL. Electronic applications accepted. *Faculty research:* Public management, policy analysis, public finance, planning and economic development, nonprofit leadership and policy.

Graduate School and University Center of the City University of New York, Graduate Studies, Interdisciplinary Studies, New York, NY 10016-4039. Offers language in social context (PhD); medieval studies (PhD); public policy (MA, PhD); urban studies (MA, PhD); women's studies (MA, PhD). Terminal master's awarded for partial completion of doctoral program. *Degree requirements:* For master's, thesis; for doctorate, comprehensive exam, thesis/dissertation. *Entrance requirements:* For master's and doctorate, GRE General Test.

Harvard University, Graduate School of Arts and Sciences and John F. Kennedy School of Government, Committee on Public Policy, Cambridge, MA 02138. Offers PhD. *Degree requirements:* For doctorate, thesis/dissertation, exams. *Entrance requirements:* For doctorate, GRE General Test or GMAT, Harvard MPP degree. Additional exam requirements/recommendations for international students: Required—TOEFL. *Expenses:* Tuition: Full-time $33,696. Required fees: $1126. Full-time tuition and fees vary according to program.

Harvard University, Graduate School of Arts and Sciences, Program in Social Policy, Cambridge, MA 02138. Offers PhD. *Expenses:* Tuition: Full-time $33,696. Required fees: $1126. Full-time tuition and fees vary according to program.

Harvard University, John F. Kennedy School of Government, Doctoral Programs in Government, Cambridge, MA 02138. Offers political economy and government (PhD); public policy (PhD). *Students:* 16 full-time (7 women); includes 1 minority (Asian American or Pacific Islander), 3 international. Average age 28. 173 applicants, 9% accepted, 12 enrolled. *Degree requirements:* For doctorate, comprehensive exam, thesis/dissertation. *Entrance requirements:* For doctorate, GRE General Test, course work in macroeconomics, multi-variable calculus. Additional exam requirements/recommendations for international students: Required—TOEFL (minimum score 600 paper-based; 250 computer-based; 100 iBT), TWE. *Application deadline:* For fall admission, 12/4 for domestic students. Application fee: $80. Electronic applications accepted. *Expenses:* Tuition: Full-time $33,696. Required fees: $1126. Full-time tuition and fees vary according to program. *Financial support:* Fellowships, research assistantships, teaching assistantships, Federal Work-Study, institutionally sponsored loans, scholarships/grants, health care benefits, and unspecified assistantships available. *Unit head:* Nicole Tateosian, Director, 617-495-1190,

Public Policy

Harvard University (continued)

E-mail: nicole_tateosian@harvard.edu. *Application contact:* Nicole Tateosian, Director, 617-495-1190, E-mail: nicole_tateosian@harvard.edu.

Harvard University, John F. Kennedy School of Government, Program in Public Policy, Cambridge, MA 02138. Offers public policy (MPP); public policy and urban planning (MPPUP); JD/MPP; MBA/MPP; MD/MPP. *Accreditation:* NASPAA. *Students:* 406 full-time (199 women), 20 part-time (10 women); includes 114 minority (29 African Americans, 9 American Indian/Alaska Native, 45 Asian Americans or Pacific Islanders, 31 Hispanic Americans), 104 international. Average age 27. 1,670 applicants, 23% accepted, 216 enrolled. In 2009, 190 master's awarded. *Entrance requirements:* For master's, GMAT or GRE General Test. Additional exam requirements/recommendations for international students: Required—TOEFL (minimum score 600 paper-based; 250 computer-based; 100 iBT), TWE. *Application deadline:* For fall admission, 1/2 for domestic students. Application fee: $80. Electronic applications accepted. *Expenses:* Tuition: Full-time $33,696. Required fees: $1126. Full-time tuition and fees vary according to program. *Financial support:* Fellowships, research assistantships, teaching assistantships, career-related internships or fieldwork, Federal Work-Study, institutionally sponsored loans, scholarships/grants, health care benefits, and unspecified assistantships available. Financial award application deadline: 2/6; financial award applicants required to submit CSS PROFILE or FAFSA. *Unit head:* Debra Isaacson, Director, 617-496-8382, E-mail: debra_isaacson@harvard.edu. *Application contact:* 617-495-1155.

Indiana University Bloomington, Kelley School of Business, Department of Business Economics and Public Policy, Bloomington, IN 47405-7000. Offers PhD. *Faculty:* 8 full-time (1 woman), 1 part-time/adjunct (0 women). *Students:* 20 applicants, 10% accepted, 2 enrolled. In 2009, 2 doctorates awarded. *Degree requirements:* For doctorate, comprehensive exam, thesis/dissertation. *Entrance requirements:* For doctorate, GRE or GMAT, bachelor's degree. Additional exam requirements/recommendations for international students: Required—TOEFL (minimum score 630 paper-based; 267 computer-based; 80 iBT). *Financial support:* Fellowships with full tuition reimbursements available. *Faculty research:* Industrial organization, pricing, environmental regulation and policy, information economics, economics of law and organization. *Unit head:* Dr. John W. Maxwell, Professor, 812-855-9219, Fax: 812-855-3354, E-mail: jwmax@indiana.edu. *Application contact:* Dr. Michael R. Baye, Bert Elwert Professor of Business Economics, 812-855-9219, Fax: 812-855-3354, E-mail: mbaye@indiana.edu.

Indiana University Bloomington, School of Public and Environmental Affairs, Public Affairs Programs, Bloomington, IN 47405-7000. Offers comparative and international affairs (MPA); economic development (MPA); energy (MPA); environmental policy and natural resource management (MPA); information systems (MPA); local government management (MPA); nonprofit management (MPA); policy analysis (MPA); public financial administration (MPA); public management (MPA); sustainability and sustainable development (MPA); JD/MPA; MPA/MA; MPA/MIS; MPA/MLS; MSES/MPA. *Accreditation:* NASPAA (one or more programs are accredited). Part-time programs available. *Faculty:* 75 full-time (22 women), 91 part-time/adjunct (24 women). *Students:* 389 full-time (222 women), 45 part-time (24 women); includes 38 minority (18 African Americans, 1 American Indian/Alaska Native, 12 Asian Americans or Pacific Islanders, 7 Hispanic Americans), 72 international. Average age 26. 474 applicants, 206 enrolled. In 2009, 190 master's, 11 doctorates, 3 other advanced degrees awarded. Terminal master's awarded for partial completion of doctoral program. *Degree requirements:* For master's, thesis optional; for doctorate, comprehensive exam, thesis/dissertation or alternative, A thesis is required for the Public Affairs and Public Policy degree. *Entrance requirements:* For master's, GRE, LSAT (if also applying for the Law School), 3 letters of recommendation, resume or curriculum vitae; for doctorate, GRE General Test. Additional exam requirements/recommendations for international students: Required—TOEFL (minimum score 590 paper-based; 243 computer-based; 96 iBT). *Application deadline:* For fall admission, 2/1 priority date for domestic students, 12/1 priority date for international students; for spring admission, 9/1 for international students. Application fee: $55 ($65 for international students). Electronic applications accepted. *Financial support:* Fellowships with full tuition reimbursements, research assistantships with partial tuition reimbursements, teaching assistantships with partial tuition reimbursements, career-related internships or fieldwork, Federal Work-Study, institutionally sponsored loans, unspecified assistantships, and Service Corps programs available. Financial award application deadline: 2/1; financial award applicants required to submit FAFSA. *Faculty research:* Comparative and international affairs, environmental policy and resource management, policy analysis, public finance, public management, urban management, nonprofit management. *Unit head:* Dean John Graham, Dean, School of Public and Environmental Affairs, 812-855-1432, E-mail: grahamjd@indiana.edu. *Application contact:* Jennifer Medlin, Assistant Director of Admissions and Financial Aid, 812-855-3784, Fax: 812-856-3665, E-mail: jlmedlin@indiana.edu.

See Close-Up on page 1189.

Indiana University–Purdue University Indianapolis, School of Public and Environmental Affairs, Indianapolis, IN 46202-2896. Offers health administration (MHA); public affairs (MPA), including criminal justice, environmental management, nonprofit management, policy analysis, public management; JD/MHA; MBA/MHA; MLS/NMC; MLS/PMC; MSN/MHA. *Accreditation:* CAHME (one or more programs are accredited); NASPAA. Part-time and evening/weekend programs available. *Faculty:* 17 full-time (6 women). *Students:* 126 full-time (71 women), 283 part-time (164 women); includes 58 minority (29 African Americans, 1 American Indian/Alaska Native, 17 Asian Americans or Pacific Islanders, 11 Hispanic Americans), 20 international. Average age 33. 255 applicants, 77% accepted, 136 enrolled. In 2009, 77 master's awarded. *Entrance requirements:* For master's, GRE General Test, minimum GPA of 3.0 (preferred). Additional exam requirements/recommendations for international students: Required—TOEFL. *Application deadline:* For fall admission, 7/15 priority date for domestic students; for spring admission, 11/15 for domestic students. Applications are processed on a rolling basis. Application fee: $55 ($65 for international students). *Financial support:* In 2009–10, 11 fellowships with full and partial tuition reimbursements (averaging $5,890 per year), 10 teaching assistantships (averaging $9,900 per year) were awarded; research assistantships with full and partial tuition reimbursements, career-related internships or fieldwork, Federal Work-Study, institutionally sponsored loans, and scholarships/grants also available. Support available to part-time students. Financial award application deadline: 3/1. *Faculty research:* Economic development, water and air quality, ethics, financing, organization design and structure. Total annual research expenditures: $1.9 million. *Unit head:* Dr. Greg Lindsey, Associate Dean, 317-274-4656, Fax: 317-274-5153. *Application contact:* 317-274-4656, Fax: 317-274-5153, E-mail: speainfo@speanet.iupui.edu.

The Institute of World Politics, Graduate Programs in National Security, Intelligence, and International Affairs, Washington, DC 20036. Offers American foreign policy (Certificate); comparative political culture (Certificate); counterintelligence (Certificate); democracy building (Certificate); intelligence (Certificate); international politics (Certificate); national security affairs (Certificate); public diplomacy and political warfare (Certificate); statecraft and national security affairs (MA); statecraft and world politics (MA); strategic intelligence studies (MA). Part-time and evening/weekend programs available. *Degree requirements:* For master's, comprehensive exam, thesis optional. *Entrance requirements:* For master's, GRE General Test. Additional exam requirements/recommendations for international students: Required—TOEFL. Electronic applications accepted. *Faculty research:* Intelligence, national security, statecraft.

Jackson State University, Graduate School, School of Liberal Arts, Department of Public Policy and Administration, Jackson, MS 39217. Offers MPPA, PhD. *Accreditation:* NASPAA (one or more programs are accredited). Evening/weekend programs available. *Degree requirements:* For master's, comprehensive exam, thesis optional; for doctorate, comprehensive exam, thesis/dissertation. *Entrance requirements:* For master's, GRE General Test; for doctorate, GRE, GMAT, MAT. Additional exam requirements/recommendations for international students: Required—TOEFL.

John Jay College of Criminal Justice of the City University of New York, Graduate Studies, Programs in Criminal Justice, New York, NY 10019-1093. Offers criminal justice (MA, PhD); criminology and deviance (PhD); forensic psychology (PhD); forensic science (PhD); law and philosophy (PhD); organizational behavior (PhD); public policy (PhD). Part-time and evening/weekend programs available. Terminal master's awarded for partial completion of doctoral program. *Degree requirements:* For master's, thesis or alternative; for doctorate, one foreign language, thesis/dissertation. *Entrance requirements:* For master's, GRE General Test, minimum B average; for doctorate, GRE General Test. Additional exam requirements/recommendations for international students: Required—TOEFL (minimum score 500 paper-based; 173 computer-based).

The Johns Hopkins University, Zanvyl Krieger School of Arts and Sciences, Institute for Public Policy, Baltimore, MD 21218-2699. Offers MA. *Faculty:* 7 full-time (4 women), 7 part-time/adjunct (3 women). *Students:* 59 full-time (40 women); includes 11 minority (2 African Americans, 8 Asian Americans or Pacific Islanders, 1 Hispanic American), 10 international. Average age 28. 210 applicants, 43% accepted, 45 enrolled. In 2009, 35 master's awarded. *Degree requirements:* For master's, thesis optional, summer internship. *Entrance requirements:* For master's, GRE General Test. Additional exam requirements/recommendations for international students: Required—TOEFL (minimum score 600 paper-based; 250 computer-based; 100 iBT), IELTS (minimum score 7). *Application deadline:* For fall admission, 1/15 for domestic and international students. Application fee: $75. Electronic applications accepted. *Financial support:* In 2009–10, 50 students received support. Career-related internships or fieldwork, Federal Work-Study, and unspecified assistantships available. Financial award application deadline: 4/15; financial award applicants required to submit FAFSA. *Faculty research:* Housing, criminal justice, human capital investment, nonprofit sector, public finance and infrastructure. *Unit head:* Dr. Carey C. Borkoski, Assistant Director of the Graduate Program, 410-516-4624, Fax: 410-516-8233, E-mail: cborkoski@jhu.edu. *Application contact:* Dr. Carey Borkoski, Assistant Director, 410-516-4624, Fax: 410-516-8233, E-mail: cborkoski@jhu.edu.

See Display on page 1155 and Close-Up on page 1191.

Kent State University, College of Arts and Sciences, Department of Political Science, Kent, OH 44242-0001. Offers political science (MA); public administration (MPA); public policy (PhD). Part-time programs available. Postbaccalaureate distance learning degree programs offered. *Degree requirements:* For master's, thesis optional; for doctorate, 2 foreign languages, thesis/dissertation. *Entrance requirements:* For master's, GRE General Test, minimum GPA of 2.75; for doctorate, GRE General Test, minimum GPA of 3.0. Additional exam requirements/recommendations for international students: Required—TOEFL. Electronic applications accepted.

Lincoln University, School of Graduate Studies and Continuing Education, Jefferson City, MO 65102. Offers business administration (MBA), including accounting, entrepreneurship, management, public administration and policy; educational leadership (Ed S), including elementary leadership, secondary leadership, superintendency; guidance and counseling (M Ed), including community/agency counseling, elementary school, secondary school; history (MA); school administration and supervision (M Ed), including elementary school administration, secondary school administration, special education administration; school teaching (M Ed), including elementary school teaching, secondary school teaching; social science (MA), including history, political science, sociology; sociology (MA); sociology/criminal justice (MA). Part-time and evening/weekend programs available. *Students:* 52 full-time (27 women), 146 part-time (107 women); includes 40 minority (39 African Americans, 1 Asian American or Pacific Islander), 15 international. Average age 35. 76 applicants, 95% accepted, 46 enrolled. In 2009, 60 master's, 6 other advanced degrees awarded. *Degree requirements:* For master's and Ed S, comprehensive exam, thesis optional. *Entrance requirements:* For master's and Ed S, GRE, MAT or GMAT, minimum GPA of 2.75 in major, 2.5 overall; 3 letters of recommendation; minimum C average in English composition; personal statement of purpose. Additional exam requirements/recommendations for international students: Required—TOEFL (minimum score 500 paper-based; 173 computer-based; 61 iBT). *Application deadline:* For fall admission, 7/1 priority date for domestic and international students; for spring admission, 12/1 priority date for domestic and international students. Applications are processed on a rolling basis. Application fee: $20. *Expenses:* Tuition, state resident: full-time $4185; part-time $232.50 per credit hour. Tuition, nonresident: full-time $7767; part-time $431.50 per credit hour. Required fees: $270; $15 per credit hour. $20 per term. *Financial support:* Federal Work-Study and scholarships/grants available. Financial award application deadline: 4/1; financial award applicants required to submit FAFSA. *Faculty research:* Suicide prevention. *Unit head:* Dr. Linda S. Bickel, Dean, 573-681-5247, Fax: 573-681-5106, E-mail: gradschool@lincolnu.edu. *Application contact:* Irasema Steck, Administrative Assistant, 573-681-5247, Fax: 573-681-5106, E-mail: gradschool@lincolnu.edu.

Marylhurst University, Department of Business Administration, Marylhurst, OR 97036-0261. Offers finance (MBA); general management (MBA); government policy and administration (MBA); green development (MBA); health care management (MBA); marketing (MBA); natural and organic resources (MBA); nonprofit management (MBA); organizational behavior (MBA); real estate (MBA); renewable energy (MBA); sustainable business (MBA). Part-time and evening/weekend programs available. Postbaccalaureate distance learning degree programs offered (no on-campus study). *Faculty:* 2 full-time (1 woman), 28 part-time/adjunct (5 women). *Students:* 30 full-time (12 women), 627 part-time (323 women); includes 79 minority (28 African Americans, 3 American Indian/Alaska Native, 17 Asian Americans or Pacific Islanders, 31 Hispanic Americans), 9 international. Average age 37. 299 applicants, 80% accepted, 209 enrolled. In 2009, 193 master's awarded. *Degree requirements:* For master's, comprehensive exam, capstone course. *Entrance requirements:* For master's, GMAT (if GPA less than 3.0 and fewer than 5 years of work experience), interview, resume, 2 letters of recommendation. Additional exam requirements/recommendations for international students: Recommended—TOEFL (minimum score 550 paper-based; 213 computer-based; 80 iBT). *Application deadline:* For fall admission, 9/11 priority date for domestic and international students; for winter admission, 12/15 priority date for domestic and international students; for spring admission, 3/17 priority date for domestic and international students. Applications are processed on a rolling basis. Application fee: $40 ($50 for international students). Electronic applications accepted. *Financial support:* Scholarships/grants available. Support available to part-time students. Financial award applicants required to submit FAFSA. *Unit head:* Bob Hanks, Director of Business and Real Estate Programs, 503-636-8141, Fax: 503-697-5597, E-mail: mba@marylhurst.edu. *Application contact:* Kathleen Schneff, Admissions Specialist, 800-634-9982 Ext. 3322, Fax: 503-635-6585, E-mail: admissions@marylhurst.edu.

McMaster University, School of Graduate Studies, Faculty of Social Sciences, Department of Political Science, Hamilton, ON L8S 4M2, Canada. Offers international relations (PhD); political science (MA); public and the global economy (MA); public policy (PhD); public policy and administration (MA). Part-time programs available. *Degree requirements:* For master's, thesis or alternative. *Entrance requirements:* For master's, minimum B+ average. Additional exam requirements/recommendations for international students: Required—TOEFL (minimum score 580 paper-based; 237 computer-based). *Faculty research:* Organizational theory, internationalization of public policy, water resource policies, political interest intermediation, comparative politics.

Mills College, Graduate Studies, Program in Public Policy, Oakland, CA 94613-1000. Offers MPP. *Faculty:* 2 full-time (1 woman), 2 part-time/adjunct (0 women). *Students:* 28 full-time (all women), 1 (woman) part-time; includes 8 minority (3 African Americans, 1 American Indian/Alaska Native, 4 Asian Americans or Pacific Islanders). Average age 32. 43 applicants, 84% accepted, 20 enrolled. In 2009, 4 master's awarded. *Degree requirements:* For master's, thesis. *Application deadline:* For fall admission, 2/1 priority date for domestic and international students. Application fee: $50. *Expenses:* Tuition: Full-time $26,326; part-time $6584 per course. Required fees: $896. One-time fee: $896 part-time. Tuition and fees vary according to program. *Financial support:* In 2009–10, 25 students received support, including 25 fellowships (averaging $7,374 per year), 2 teaching assistantships (averaging $1,875 per year); scholarships/grants also available. Financial award applicants required to submit FAFSA. *Unit* *head:* Carol Chetkovich, Director, 510-430-3370, E-mail: cchetkov@mills.edu. *Application contact:* Jessica King, Graduate Admission Specialist, 510-430-3305, Fax: 510-430-2159, E-mail: grad-studies@mills.edu.

Mississippi State University, College of Arts and Sciences, Department of Political Science and Public Administration, Mississippi State, MS 39762. Offers political science (MA); public policy and administration (MPPA, PhD). *Accreditation:* NASPAA (one or more programs are accredited). Evening/weekend programs available. Postbaccalaureate distance learning degree programs offered (no on-campus study). *Faculty:* 14 full-time (4 women). *Students:* 67 full-time (35 women), 44 part-time (33 women); includes 40 minority (37 African Americans, 1 American Indian/Alaska Native, 2 Asian Americans or Pacific Islanders), 4 international. Average age 30. 85 applicants, 60% accepted, 39 enrolled. In 2009, 28 master's, 2 doctorates awarded. *Degree requirements:* For master's, thesis optional, comprehensive oral or written exam; for doctorate, thesis/dissertation, comprehensive oral and written exam. *Entrance requirements:* For master's, GRE, minimum GPA of 3.0 on the last two years of undergraduate courses or graduate work; for doctorate, GRE General Test, minimum graduate GPA of 3.35. Additional exam requirements/recommendations for international students: Required—TOEFL (minimum score 600 paper-based; 250 computer-based; 100 iBT); Recommended—IELTS (minimum score 7.5). *Application deadline:* For fall admission, 8/1 priority date for domestic students, 5/1 for international students; for spring admission, 12/1 priority date for domestic students, 9/1 for international students. Applications are processed on a rolling basis. Application fee: $40. Electronic applications accepted. *Expenses:* Tuition, state resident: full-time $2575.50; part-time $286.25 per credit hour. Tuition, nonresident: full-time $6510; part-time $723.50 per credit hour. Tuition and fees vary according to course load. *Financial support:* In 2009–10, 5 research assistantships (averaging $14,451 per year), 6 teaching assistantships with full tuition reimbursements (averaging $9,030 per year) were awarded; Federal Work-Study, institutionally sponsored loans, scholarships/grants, and unspecified assistantships also available. Financial award application deadline: 4/15. *Faculty research:* American politics, international relations, state and local government, comparative government, public administration. Total annual research expenditures: $879,000. *Unit head:* Dr. KC Morrison, Department Head, 662-325-2711, Fax: 662-325-2716, E-mail: kcmorrison@ps.msstate.edu. *Application contact:* Dr. Doug Goodman, Associate Professor and Graduate Coordinator, 662-325-7856, Fax: 662-325-2716, E-mail: dg114@ps.msstate.edu.

Monmouth University, Graduate School, Department of Public Policy, West Long Branch, NJ 07764-1898. Offers MA. Part-time and evening/weekend programs available. *Faculty:* 7 full-time (3 women). *Students:* 17 full-time (7 women), 21 part-time (12 women); includes 9 minority (5 African Americans, 4 Hispanic Americans). Average age 28. 16 applicants, 100% accepted, 11 enrolled. In 2009, 14 master's awarded. *Entrance requirements:* For master's, minimum overall GPA of 2.75. Additional exam requirements/recommendations for international students: Required—TOEFL (minimum score 550 paper-based; 213 computer-based; 79 iBT), IELTS (minimum score 5), Michigan English Language Assessment Battery (minimum score 77), Cambridge A, B, C. *Application deadline:* For fall admission, 7/15 for domestic students, 6/1 for international students; for spring admission, 11/15 for domestic students, 11/1 for international students. Application fee: $50. *Expenses:* Tuition: Part-time $773 per credit. Required fees: $157 per semester. *Financial support:* In 2009–10, 31 students received support, including 24 fellowships (averaging $1,544 per year), 3 research assistantships (averaging $5,334 per year); career-related internships or fieldwork, scholarships/grants, and unspecified assistantships also available. Support available to part-time students. Financial award applicants required to submit FAFSA. *Faculty research:* Political theory, international relations and comparative politics, globalization, politics of language, family sociology, race-class-gender studies, U.S. Senate and impact of domestic politics on U.S. foreign policy. *Unit head:* Dr. Joseph Patten, Program Director, 732-263-5742, E-mail: jpatten@monmouth.edu. *Application contact:* Kevin Roane, Director, Office of Graduate Admission, 732-571-3452, Fax: 732-263-5123, E-mail: gradadm@monmouth.edu.

Morehead State University, Graduate Programs, College of Business and Public Affairs, School of Public Affairs, Morehead, KY 40351. Offers public policy (MPA). Part-time and evening/weekend programs available. *Faculty:* 5 full-time (1 woman), 4 part-time/adjunct (1 woman). *Students:* 21 full-time (11 women), 6 part-time (4 women); includes 1 minority (Asian American or Pacific Islander). Average age 26. 17 applicants. In 2009, 6 master's awarded. *Degree requirements:* For master's, comprehensive exam, thesis. *Entrance requirements:* For master's, GRE, thesis (two-page paper to be used as writing sample on personal, education or career goals). Additional exam requirements/recommendations for international students: Required—TOEFL (minimum score 500 paper-based; 173 computer-based). *Application deadline:* For fall admission, 8/1 priority date for domestic and international students; for spring admission, 12/1 priority date for domestic and international students. Applications are processed on a rolling basis. Application fee: $30. Electronic applications accepted. *Expenses:* Tuition, state resident: full-time $6318; part-time $351 per credit hour. Tuition, nonresident: full-time $15,804; part-time $878 per credit hour. *Financial support:* In 2009–10, 10 research assistantships (averaging $10,000 per year) were awarded; career-related internships or fieldwork, Federal Work-Study, and unspecified assistantships also available. Financial award application deadline: 3/15; financial award applicants required to submit FAFSA. *Unit head:* Dr. Michael Hail, Interim Associate Dean, 606-783-5419, E-mail: m.hail@moreheadstate.edu. *Application contact:* Michelle Barber, Graduate Recruitment and Retention Assistant Director, 606-783-5127, Fax: 606-783-5061, E-mail: m.barber@moreheadstate.edu.

National-Louis University, College of Arts and Sciences, Program in Public Policy, Chicago, IL 60603. Offers MA. *Expenses:* Tuition: Full-time $17,160; part-time $715 per semester hour. Tuition and fees vary according to course load, degree level, campus/location and program.

National University of Singapore, Lee Kuan Yew School of Public Policy, Singapore, Singapore. Offers MPA, MPM, MPP, PhD.

New England College, Program in Public Policy, Henniker, NH 03242-3293. Offers MA. Part-time and evening/weekend programs available. Postbaccalaureate distance learning degree programs offered (no on-campus study). *Degree requirements:* For master's, thesis. *Entrance requirements:* Additional exam requirements/recommendations for international students: Recommended—TOEFL (minimum score 600 paper-based). Electronic applications accepted.

The New School: A University, Milano The New School for Management and Urban Policy, Program in Public and Urban Policy, New York, NY 10011. Offers PhD. Part-time and evening/weekend programs available. *Faculty:* 8 full-time (2 women). *Students:* 29 full-time (18 women), 14 part-time (10 women); includes 15 minority (7 African Americans, 2 American Indian/Alaska Native, 4 Asian Americans or Pacific Islanders, 2 Hispanic Americans), 10 international. Average age 40. 48 applicants, 23% accepted, 4 enrolled. In 2009, 1 doctorate awarded. *Degree requirements:* For doctorate, thesis/dissertation, qualifying exams. *Entrance requirements:* For doctorate, GRE General Test, MA in political science, urban policy or public policy. Additional exam requirements/recommendations for international students: Required—TOEFL (minimum score 600 paper-based; 250 computer-based; 100 iBT). *Application deadline:* For fall admission, 3/1 priority date for domestic and international students; for spring admission, 10/1 priority date for domestic and international students. Applications are processed on a rolling basis. Application fee: $50. Electronic applications accepted. *Financial support:* Fellowships, Federal Work-Study, scholarships/grants, and tuition waivers (full and partial) available. Support available to part-time students. Financial award application deadline: 3/1; financial award applicants required to submit FAFSA. *Unit head:* Dr. David Howell, Director, 212-229-5400 Ext. 1416, Fax: 212-229-5904, E-mail: howell@newschool.edu. *Application contact:* Merida Escandon, Director of Admissions, 212-229-5462 Ext. 1108, Fax: 212-229-5354, E-mail: milanoadmissions@newschool.edu.

Northeastern University, College of Social Sciences and Humanities, Program in Law, Policy, and Society, Boston, MA 02115-5096. Offers MS, PhD, JD/PhD. Part-time and evening/

Public Policy

Northeastern University (continued)

weekend programs available. *Faculty:* 33 full-time (18 women), 18 part-time/adjunct (6 women). *Students:* 42 full-time (22 women), 28 part-time (13 women); includes 3 African Americans, 2 Asian Americans or Pacific Islanders, 2 Hispanic Americans, 10 international. Average age 40. 56 applicants, 41% accepted, 12 enrolled. *Degree requirements:* For master's, comprehensive exam; for doctorate, comprehensive exam, thesis/dissertation. *Entrance requirements:* For master's, GRE General Test; for doctorate, GRE General Test or LSAT. Additional exam requirements/recommendations for international students: Required—TOEFL. *Application deadline:* For fall admission, 2/1 for domestic students. Application fee: $50. *Financial support:* In 2009–10, teaching assistantships with tuition reimbursements (averaging $14,035 per year); fellowships with tuition reimbursements, research assistantships with tuition reimbursements, tuition waivers (full and partial) and unspecified assistantships also available. Financial award application deadline: 2/1; financial award applicants required to submit FAFSA. *Faculty research:* Policy issues in health, crime, and labor; urban studies; education; law and environmental issues; economic development, international trade and law. *Unit head:* Dr. Joan Fitzgerald, Director, 617-373-3644, Fax: 617-373-4691, E-mail: jo.fitzgerald@neu.edu. *Application contact:* Dr. Joan Fitzgerald, Director, 617-373-3644, Fax: 617-373-4691, E-mail: jo.fitzgerald@neu.edu.

Northwestern University, The Graduate School, School of Education and Social Policy, Program in Human Development and Social Policy, Evanston, IL 60208. Offers PhD. Admissions and degrees offered through The Graduate School. *Faculty:* 12 full-time (5 women), 7 part-time/adjunct (2 women). *Students:* 30 full-time (28 women); includes 8 minority (4 African Americans, 4 Asian Americans or Pacific Islanders), 1 international. Average age 30. 70 applicants, 13% accepted, 5 enrolled. In 2009, 4 doctorates awarded. *Degree requirements:* For doctorate, comprehensive exam, thesis/dissertation. *Entrance requirements:* For doctorate, GRE General Test. Additional exam requirements/recommendations for international students: Required—TOEFL (minimum score 600 paper-based; 250 computer-based; 100 iBT). *Application deadline:* For fall admission, 12/31 priority date for domestic and international students. Application fee: $75. Electronic applications accepted. *Financial support:* In 2009–10, 26 students received support, including 8 fellowships with full tuition reimbursements available, 15 research assistantships with full tuition reimbursements available, 3 teaching assistantships with full tuition reimbursements available; institutionally sponsored loans, scholarships/grants, health care benefits, and unspecified assistantships also available. Financial award application deadline: 12/31; financial award applicants required to submit FAFSA. *Faculty research:* Individual development and the personal narrative; the life course and culture; development, intervention and culture; the life course and policy; analysis of policy effects on lives. *Unit head:* Prof. Barton J. Hirsch, Coordinator, Program in Human Development and Social Policy, 847-491-4418, Fax: 847-491-8999, E-mail: bhirsch@northwestern.edu. *Application contact:* Erika Arlene Chavez, Program Assistant, 847-491-4329, Fax: 847-491-8999, E-mail: e-chavez@northwestern.edu.

Northwestern University, School of Continuing Studies, Program in Public Policy and Administration, Evanston, IL 60208. Offers MA. Postbaccalaureate distance learning degree programs offered.

Pepperdine University, School of Public Policy, Malibu, CA 90263. Offers American politics (MPP); economics (MPP); international relations (MPP); public policy (MPP); state and local policy (MPP). *Faculty:* 7 full-time (2 women), 5 part-time/adjunct (0 women). *Students:* 117 full-time (62 women), 5 part-time (3 women); includes 30 minority (7 African Americans, 1 American Indian/Alaska Native, 10 Asian Americans or Pacific Islanders, 12 Hispanic Americans), 9 international. In 2009, 27 master's awarded. *Entrance requirements:* For master's, GRE, 2 letters of recommendation, resume. Additional exam requirements/recommendations for international students: Required—TOEFL. *Application deadline:* For fall admission, 4/15 for domestic students. Applications are processed on a rolling basis. Electronic applications accepted. *Expenses:* Tuition: Full-time $37,516; part-time $1310 per unit. Required fees: $80. *Financial support:* Research assistantships, teaching assistantships, institutionally sponsored loans and scholarships/grants available. Financial award application deadline: 5/1; financial award applicants required to submit FAFSA. *Unit head:* Dr. James R. Wilburn, Dean, 310-506-7490, Fax: 310-506-7494, E-mail: james.wilburn@pepperdine.edu. *Application contact:* Melinda E. van Hemert, Director of Recruitment and Career Services, 310-506-7492, Fax: 310-506-7494, E-mail: melinda.vanhemert@pepperdine.edu.

Princeton University, Graduate School, Woodrow Wilson School of Public and International Affairs, Princeton, NJ 08544-1019. Offers public affairs (MPA, PhD); public policy (MPP); JD/MPA. Terminal master's awarded for partial completion of doctoral program. *Degree requirements:* For master's, internship; for doctorate, one foreign language, thesis/dissertation. *Entrance requirements:* For master's, GRE General Test, original policy memo; for doctorate, GRE General Test. Additional exam requirements/recommendations for international students: Required—TOEFL (minimum score 600 paper-based; 250 computer-based). Electronic applications accepted.

Queen's University at Kingston, School of Graduate Studies and Research, School of Policy Studies, Kingston, ON K7L 3N6, Canada. Offers MIR, MPA. Part-time programs available. *Entrance requirements:* For master's, minimum B+ average. Additional exam requirements/recommendations for international students: Required—TOEFL. *Faculty research:* Public management, social policy, defense management, health policy, the third sector.

Regent University, Graduate School, Robertson School of Government, Virginia Beach, VA 23464. Offers american government (MA); global politics (MA); health care policy and administration (MA); international politics (MA); law and public policy (MA); Mid-East Politics (MA); political leadership and management (MA); political management (MA); political theory (MA); public administration (MA); public policy (MA); terrorism and homeland defense (MA); world economies and political development (MA); JD/MA; M Div/MA; M Ed/MA; MBA/MA. Part-time and evening/weekend programs available. Postbaccalaureate distance learning degree programs offered (minimal on-campus study). *Faculty:* 6 full-time (2 women), 11 part-time/adjunct (1 woman). *Students:* 77 full-time (55 women), 65 part-time (36 women); includes 47 minority (38 African Americans, 2 Asian Americans or Pacific Islanders, 7 Hispanic Americans), 4 international. Average age 30. 131 applicants, 65% accepted, 54 enrolled. In 2009, 51 master's awarded. *Degree requirements:* For master's, thesis optional, internship. *Entrance requirements:* For master's, GRE General Test or LSAT, minimum undergraduate GPA of 3.0, writing sample, resume, interview, references. Additional exam requirements/recommendations for international students: Required—TOEFL (minimum score 577 paper-based; 233 computer-based). *Application deadline:* For fall admission, 5/1 priority date for domestic students; for spring admission, 11/1 priority date for domestic students. Applications are processed on a rolling basis. Application fee: $50. Electronic applications accepted. *Expenses:* Contact institution. *Financial support:* In 2009–10, 130 students received support. Career-related internships or fieldwork, scholarships/grants, tuition waivers (full and partial), and unspecified assistantships available. Support available to part-time students. Financial award application deadline: 9/1; financial award applicants required to submit FAFSA. *Faculty research:* Education reform, political character issues, social capital concerns, administrative ethics, Biblical law and public policy. *Unit head:* Dr. Charles W. Dunn, Dean, 757-352-4322, Fax: 757-352-4643, E-mail: cwdunn@regent.edu. *Application contact:* Matthew Chadwick, Director of Admissions, 800-373-5504, Fax: 757-352-4381, E-mail: admissions@regent.edu.

Rochester Institute of Technology, Graduate Enrollment Services, College of Liberal Arts, Department of Science, Technology and Society/Public Policy, Rochester, NY 14623-5603. Offers science, technology and public policy (MS). Part-time programs available. *Students:* 14 full-time (5 women), 3 part-time (2 women); includes 3 minority (2 African Americans, 1 Asian American or Pacific Islander), 2 international. Average age 28. 18 applicants, 89% accepted, 4 enrolled. In 2009, 8 master's awarded. *Degree requirements:* For master's, thesis. *Entrance requirements:* For master's, GRE General Test, minimum GPA of 3.0. Additional exam requirements/recommendations for international students: Required—TOEFL (minimum score 570 paper-based; 230 computer-based; 88 iBT), or IELTS (minimum score 6.5). *Application deadline:* For fall admission, 2/15 priority date for domestic and international students; for winter admission, 11/1 for domestic and international students; for spring admission, 2/1 for domestic and international students. Applications are processed on a rolling basis. Application fee: $50. Electronic applications accepted. *Expenses:* Tuition: Full-time $31,533; part-time $876 per credit hour. Required fees: $210. *Financial support:* In 2009–10, 9 students received support; research assistantships with partial tuition reimbursements available, teaching assistantships with partial tuition reimbursements available, career-related internships or fieldwork, scholarships/grants, and unspecified assistantships available. Support available to part-time students. Financial award applicants required to submit FAFSA. *Faculty research:* Environmental policy, information and communications policy, energy policy, biotechnology policy. *Unit head:* Dr. James Winebrake, Chair, 585-475-4648, Fax: 585-475-2510, E-mail: james.winebrake@rit.edu. *Application contact:* Diane Ellison, Assistant Vice President, Graduate Enrollment Services, 585-475-2229, Fax: 585-475-7164, E-mail: gradinfo@rit.edu.

Rutgers, The State University of New Jersey, Camden, Graduate School of Arts and Sciences, Department of Public Policy and Administration, Camden, NJ 08102-1401. Offers education policy and leadership (MPA); international public service and development (MPA); public management (MPA); JD/MPA; MPA/MA. *Accreditation:* NASPAA. Part-time and evening/weekend programs available. *Degree requirements:* For master's, directed study, research workshop. *Entrance requirements:* For master's, GRE General Test, GMAT or LSAT, 3 letters of recommendation; resume. Additional exam requirements/recommendations for international students: Required—TOEFL (minimum score 550 paper-based; 213 computer-based), IELTS. Electronic applications accepted. *Faculty research:* Nonprofit management, county and municipal administration, health and human services, government communication, administrative law, educational finance.

Rutgers, The State University of New Jersey, Newark, Graduate School, Program in Public Administration, Newark, NJ 07102. Offers health care administration (MPA); human resources administration (MPA); public administration (PhD); public management (MPA); public policy analysis (MPA); urban systems and issues (MPA). *Accreditation:* NASPAA (one or more programs are accredited). Part-time and evening/weekend programs available. *Degree requirements:* For master's, comprehensive exam, thesis or alternative; for doctorate, thesis/dissertation. *Entrance requirements:* For master's, GRE, minimum undergraduate B average; for doctorate, GRE, MPA, minimum B average. Electronic applications accepted. *Faculty research:* Government finance, municipal and state government, public productivity.

Rutgers, The State University of New Jersey, New Brunswick, Edward J. Bloustein School of Planning and Public Policy, Program in Planning and Public Policy, Piscataway, NJ 08854-8097. Offers PhD. Part-time programs available. *Degree requirements:* For doctorate, comprehensive exam, thesis/dissertation. *Entrance requirements:* For doctorate, GRE, master's degree. Additional exam requirements/recommendations for international students: Required—TOEFL (minimum score 575 paper-based; 245 computer-based). Electronic applications accepted. *Faculty research:* Housing and community development, land use and transportation, politics and policy analysis, urban and regional economics, international development.

Rutgers, The State University of New Jersey, New Brunswick, Edward J. Bloustein School of Planning and Public Policy, Program in Public Policy, Piscataway, NJ 08854-8097. Offers MPAP, MPP, JD/MPAP, MBA/MPAP, MCRP/MPP. Part-time and evening/weekend programs available. *Entrance requirements:* For master's, GRE General Test or LSAT. Electronic applications accepted. *Faculty research:* Public finance, legislative process, public opinion, economics and public policy, campaigning.

Saint Louis University, Graduate School, College of Education and Public Service and Graduate School, Department of Public Policy Studies, St. Louis, MO 63103-2097. Offers geographic information systems (Certificate); organizational development (Certificate); public administration (MAPA); public policy analysis (PhD); urban affairs (MAUA); urban planning and real estate development (MUPRED). *Accreditation:* NASPAA. Part-time programs available. *Degree requirements:* For master's, comprehensive exam (for some programs), thesis (for some programs); for doctorate, comprehensive exam, thesis/dissertation, preliminary exams. *Entrance requirements:* For master's, GMAT, GRE General Test, or LSAT, letters of recommendation, resume; for doctorate, GMAT, GRE General Test, or LSAT, letters of recommendation, resumé, interview, transcripts, goal statement. Additional exam requirements/recommendations for international students: Required—TOEFL (minimum score 525 paper-based; 194 computer-based). Electronic applications accepted. *Faculty research:* Urban politics, brown fields, e-government, and administration, evaluation research, community development, electronic government and governance.

San Francisco State University, Division of Graduate Studies, College of Behavioral and Social Sciences, Public Administration Program, San Francisco, CA 94132-1722. Offers integrated and collaborative services (MPA); nonprofit administration (MPA); policy analysis (MPA); public management (MPA); urban administration (MPA). *Accreditation:* NASPAA.

Seton Hall University, College of Arts and Sciences, Department of Public and Healthcare Administration, Program in Public Administration, South Orange, NJ 07079-2697. Offers nonprofit organization management (MPA). *Accreditation:* NASPAA. Part-time and evening/weekend programs available. *Faculty:* 5 full-time (3 women), 1 part-time/adjunct (0 women). *Students:* 29 full-time (22 women), 19 part-time (11 women); includes 18 minority (10 African Americans, 1 American Indian/Alaska Native, 6 Asian Americans or Pacific Islanders, 1 Hispanic American), 2 international. Average age 31. 44 applicants, 91% accepted, 19 enrolled. In 2009, 7 master's awarded. *Degree requirements:* For master's, thesis or alternative, internship or practicum. *Entrance requirements:* Additional exam requirements/recommendations for international students: Required—TOEFL. *Application deadline:* For fall admission, 7/1 priority date for domestic students; for spring admission, 11/1 priority date for domestic students. Applications are processed on a rolling basis. Application fee: $50. *Financial support:* Research assistantships, career-related internships or fieldwork, Federal Work-Study, scholarships/grants, and unspecified assistantships available. Financial award applicants required to submit FAFSA. *Unit head:* Dr. Matthew Hale, Chair, 973-761-9510, Fax: 973-275-2463, E-mail: halematt@shu.edu. *Application contact:* Dr. Matthew Hale, Chair, 973-761-9510, Fax: 973-275-2463, E-mail: halematt@shu.edu.

Simon Fraser University, Graduate Studies, Faculty of Arts and Social Sciences, Public Policy Program, Burnaby, BC V5A 1S6, Canada. Offers MPP. *Degree requirements:* For master's, internship. *Entrance requirements:* For master's, GRE, 3 letters of reference, resume, minimum undergraduate GPA of 3.0. Additional exam requirements/recommendations for international students: Required—TOEFL (minimum score 570 paper-based; 230 computer-based), TWE (minimum score 5). Electronic applications accepted.

Southern New Hampshire University, School of Community Economic Development, Manchester, NH 03106-1045. Offers MA, MBA, MS, PhD. Part-time and evening/weekend programs available. *Degree requirements:* For master's, thesis or alternative, community project; for doctorate, comprehensive exam, thesis/dissertation, community project. *Entrance requirements:* For master's, 2 years of work experience, minimum GPA of 3.0, 2 letters of recommendation, review; for doctorate, 2 years of work experience, minimum GPA of 3.5, 3 letters of recommendation, research samples. Additional exam requirements/recommendations for international students: Required—TOEFL (minimum score 550 paper-based; 300 computer-based; 70 iBT). Electronic applications accepted. *Expenses:* Contact institution.

Southern University and Agricultural and Mechanical College, Graduate School, Nelson Mandela School of Public Policy and Urban Affairs, Program in Public Policy, Baton Rouge, LA 70813. Offers PhD. *Degree requirements:* For doctorate, comprehensive exam, thesis/dissertation. *Entrance requirements:* For doctorate, GRE General Test. Additional exam requirements/recommendations for international students: Required—TOEFL (minimum score 525 paper-based; 193 computer-based).

State University of New York at Binghamton, Graduate School, School of Arts and Sciences, Department of Political Science, Binghamton, NY 13902-6000. Offers political science (MA, PhD); public policy (MA, PhD). *Faculty:* 13 full-time (4 women), 1 part-time/adjunct (0 women). *Students:* 30 full-time (8 women), 21 part-time (12 women); includes 3 minority (all African Americans), 20 international. Average age 29. 56 applicants, 55% accepted, 11 enrolled. In 2009, 9 master's, 3 doctorates awarded. Terminal master's awarded for partial completion of doctoral program. *Degree requirements:* For master's, thesis or alternative, written exam; for doctorate, 2 foreign languages, thesis/dissertation, written exam. *Entrance requirements:* For master's and doctorate, GRE General Test, GRE Subject Test. Additional exam requirements/recommendations for international students: Required—TOEFL (minimum score 550 paper-based; 213 computer-based; 80 iBT). *Application deadline:* For fall admission, 2/15 priority date for domestic and international students. Applications are processed on a rolling basis. Application fee: $60. Electronic applications accepted. *Financial support:* In 2009–10, 30 students received support, including 1 fellowship with full tuition reimbursement available (averaging $15,000 per year), 3 research assistantships with full tuition reimbursements available (averaging $15,000 per year), 19 teaching assistantships with full tuition reimbursements available (averaging $15,000 per year); career-related internships or fieldwork, Federal Work-Study, institutionally sponsored loans, scholarships/grants, health care benefits, tuition waivers (full), and unspecified assistantships also available. Financial award application deadline: 2/15; financial award applicants required to submit FAFSA. *Unit head:* Dr. Benjamin Fordham, Chairperson, 607-777-4398, E-mail: bfordham@binghamton.edu. *Application contact:* Victoria Williams, Recruiting and Admissions Coordinator, 607-777-2151, Fax: 607-777-2501, E-mail: vwilliam@binghamton.edu.

State University of New York Empire State College, Graduate Studies, Program in Business and Policy Studies, Saratoga Springs, NY 12866-4391. Offers MA. Part-time and evening/weekend programs available. Postbaccalaureate distance learning degree programs offered (minimal on-campus study). *Degree requirements:* For master's, thesis, exam. *Entrance requirements:* For master's, proficiency in statistics. Additional exam requirements/recommendations for international students: Required—TOEFL (minimum score 600 paper-based; 280 computer-based). Electronic applications accepted. *Faculty research:* Business history, applied business statistics, labor/management relations, American social problems and business, effect of government economic policies on business.

State University of New York Empire State College, Graduate Studies, Program in Social Policy, Saratoga Springs, NY 12866-4391. Offers MA. Part-time and evening/weekend programs available. Postbaccalaureate distance learning degree programs offered (minimal on-campus study). *Degree requirements:* For master's, thesis, exam. *Entrance requirements:* Additional exam requirements/recommendations for international students: Required—TOEFL (minimum score 600 paper-based; 250 computer-based). Electronic applications accepted. *Faculty research:* Study of culture, society and mass communications, urban culture and policy, social decision making processes.

Stony Brook University, State University of New York, Graduate School, College of Arts and Sciences, Department of Political Science, Program in Public Policy and Urban Development, Stony Brook, NY 11794. Offers MA. *Expenses:* Tuition, state resident: full-time $8370; part-time $349 per credit. Tuition, nonresident: full-time $13,250; part-time $552 per credit. Required fees: $933.

Suffolk University, College of Arts and Sciences, Program in Ethics and Public Policy, Boston, MA 02108-2770. Offers MS. Part-time and evening/weekend programs available. *Faculty:* 2 full-time (0 women). *Students:* 7 full-time (3 women), 10 part-time (5 women), 10 international. Average age 26. 27 applicants, 74% accepted, 10 enrolled. In 2009, 1 master's awarded. *Degree requirements:* For master's, internship or thesis. *Entrance requirements:* For master's, GRE General Test, MAT, GMAT, statement of professional goals, official transcripts, 2 letters of recommendation, resume. Additional exam requirements/recommendations for international students: Required—TOEFL (minimum score 550 paper-based; 213 computer-based; 80 iBT). *Application deadline:* For fall and spring admission, 6/15 priority date for domestic and international students. Applications are processed on a rolling basis. Application fee: $50. Electronic applications accepted. *Expenses:* Contact institution. *Financial support:* In 2009–10, 15 students received support, including 134 fellowships (averaging $3,665 per year); career-related internships or fieldwork, Federal Work-Study, institutionally sponsored loans, and unspecified assistantships also available. Support available to part-time students. Financial award application deadline: 4/1; financial award applicants required to submit FAFSA. *Faculty research:* History of philosophy, ethics, political philosophy, continental philosophy and phenomenology, applied ethics. *Unit head:* Dr. Greg Fried, Chair of Philosophy Department, 617-573-8109, E-mail: gfried@suffolk.edu. *Application contact:* Judith Reynolds, Director of Graduate Admissions, 617-573-8302, Fax: 617-305-1733, E-mail: grad.admission@suffolk.edu.

Syracuse University, Maxwell School of Citizenship and Public Affairs, Program in Public Management and Policy, Syracuse, NY 13244. Offers CAS. *Entrance requirements:* Additional exam requirements/recommendations for international students: Required—TOEFL (minimum score 100 iBT). *Application deadline:* For fall admission, 2/1 priority date for domestic and international students. Application fee: $75. Electronic applications accepted. *Expenses:* Tuition: Full-time $26,808; part-time $1117 per credit. Required fees: $1024. *Unit head:* Margaret Lane, Director, Executive Education, 315-443-28708, Fax: 315-443-3385, E-mail: meland@syr.edu. *Application contact:* Margaret Lane, Director, Executive Education, 315-443-28708, Fax: 315-443-3385, E-mail: meland@syr.edu.

Texas A&M University, George Bush School of Government and Public Service, College Station, TX 77843. Offers advanced international affairs (Certificate); homeland security (Certificate); international affairs (MPIA), including international economics and development, national security affairs; nonprofit management (Certificate); public service and administration (MPSA), including public management, public policy analysis. *Accreditation:* NASPAA. *Faculty:* 51. *Students:* 209 full-time (97 women), 93 part-time (43 women); includes 48 minority (15 African Americans, 5 Asian Americans or Pacific Islanders, 28 Hispanic Americans), 19 international. Average age 24. In 2009, 87 master's awarded. *Degree requirements:* For master's, summer internship. *Entrance requirements:* For master's, GRE (preferred) or GMAT. *Application deadline:* For fall admission, 1/24 for domestic and international students. Application fee: $50 ($75 for international students). Electronic applications accepted. *Expenses:* Tuition, state resident: full-time $3991; part-time $221.74 per credit hour. Tuition, nonresident: full-time $9049; part-time $502.74 per credit hour. *Financial support:* In 2009–10, fellowships (averaging $11,000 per year), research assistantships (averaging $11,250 per year) were awarded; career-related internships or fieldwork, Federal Work-Study, and institutionally sponsored loans also available. Financial award application deadline: 2/1; financial award applicants required to submit FAFSA. *Faculty research:* Public policy, presidential studies, public leadership, economic policy, social policy. *Unit head:* A. Benton Cocanougher, Interim Dean, 979-862-8842, E-mail: bushschool@tamu.edu. *Application contact:* Kathryn Meyer, Recruitment and Placement Officer, 979-458-4767, Fax: 979-845-4155, E-mail: admissions@bushschool.tamu.edu.

Trinity College, Graduate Programs, Program in Public Policy Studies, Hartford, CT 06106-3100. Offers MA. Part-time and evening/weekend programs available. *Faculty:* 4 full-time (1 woman), 4 part-time/adjunct (1 woman). *Students:* 48 part-time (27 women); includes 9 minority (3 African Americans, 3 Asian Americans or Pacific Islanders, 3 Hispanic Americans). Average age 38. In 2009, 10 master's awarded. *Degree requirements:* For master's, thesis optional, departmental qualifying exam. *Entrance requirements:* For master's, minimum GPA of 3.0. *Application deadline:* For fall admission, 4/15 for domestic students; for spring admission, 11/15 for domestic students. Application fee: $50. *Expenses:* Tuition: Part-time $1700 per course. One-time fee: $75 full-time. *Financial support:* Fellowships, tuition waivers (full) available. Support available to part-time students. Financial award application deadline: 4/1. *Unit head:* Dr. W. Miller Brown, Graduate Director, 860-297-2416. *Application contact:* Nicola Dawkins, Program Manager for Graduate Studies, 860-297-2151, Fax: 860-297-5179, E-mail: nicola.dawkins@trincoll.edu.

Tufts University, Graduate School of Arts and Sciences, Department of Urban and Environmental Policy and Planning, Medford, MA 02155. Offers community development (MA); environmental policy (MA); health and human welfare (MA); housing policy (MA); international environment/development policy (MA); public policy (MPP); MA/MS; MALD/MA. *Accreditation:* ACSP (one or more programs are accredited). Part-time programs available. *Faculty:* 11 full-time, 9 part-time/adjunct. *Students:* 133 (83 women); includes 26 minority (15 African Americans, 5 Asian Americans or Pacific Islanders, 6 Hispanic Americans), 2 international. Average age 27. 200 applicants, 63% accepted, 53 enrolled. In 2009, 44 master's awarded. *Degree requirements:* For master's, thesis, internship. *Entrance requirements:* For master's, GRE General Test. Additional exam requirements/recommendations for international students: Required—TOEFL (minimum score 550 paper-based; 213 computer-based; 80 iBT). *Application deadline:* For fall admission, 1/15 for domestic students, 12/15 for international students. Applications are processed on a rolling basis. Application fee: $75. Electronic applications accepted. *Expenses:* Contact institution. *Financial support:* Teaching assistantships with partial tuition reimbursements, career-related internships or fieldwork, Federal Work-Study, scholarships/grants, tuition waivers (partial), and unspecified assistantships available. Support available to part-time students. Financial award application deadline: 1/15; financial award applicants required to submit FAFSA. *Unit head:* Julian Agyeman, Chair, 617-627-3394, Fax: 617-627-3377. *Application contact:* Ann Urosevich, Department Administrator, 617-627-3394.

Union Institute & University, Master of Arts Program–Online, Montpelier, VT 05602. Offers creativity studies (MA); education (MA); health and wellness (MA); history and culture (MA); leadership, public policy, and social issues (MA); literature and writing (MA); psychology (MA). Part-time programs available. Postbaccalaureate distance learning degree programs offered (no on-campus study). *Faculty:* 3 full-time (1 woman), 16 part-time/adjunct (11 women). *Students:* 27 full-time (23 women), 113 part-time (84 women); includes 30 minority (22 African Americans, 2 American Indian/Alaska Native, 1 Asian American or Pacific Islander, 5 Hispanic Americans). Average age 40. In 2009, 26 master's awarded. *Degree requirements:* For master's, thesis. *Application deadline:* Applications are processed on a rolling basis. Application fee: $50. Electronic applications accepted. *Expenses:* Contact institution. *Financial support:* Career-related internships or fieldwork and tuition waivers available. Financial award applicants required to submit FAFSA. *Unit head:* Dr. Brian Webb, Program Director, 802-828-8777, E-mail: brian.webb@tui.edu. *Application contact:* Kathleen Murphy, Interim Director of Admissions—Montpelier, 888-828-8575, E-mail: admissions@myunion.edu.

Union Institute & University, PhD Program in Interdisciplinary Studies, Cincinnati, OH 45206-1925. Offers public policy and social change (PhD), including Martin Luther King studies. Postbaccalaureate distance learning degree programs offered (minimal on-campus study). *Faculty:* 4 full-time (1 woman), 15 part-time/adjunct (9 women). *Students:* 77 full-time (45 women), 7 part-time (4 women); includes 34 minority (31 African Americans, 3 Hispanic Americans). Average age 45. In 2009, 3 doctorates awarded. *Degree requirements:* For doctorate, comprehensive exam, thesis/dissertation. *Entrance requirements:* For doctorate, master's degree, letters of recommendation, interview. *Application deadline:* Applications are processed on a rolling basis. Application fee: $50. Tuition and fees vary according to course load, degree level, campus/location and program. *Financial support:* Federal Work-Study, scholarships/grants, and tuition waivers (partial) available. Financial award application deadline: 5/1; financial award applicants required to submit FAFSA. *Unit head:* Dr. Larry Preston, Dean, 513-861-6400 Ext. 1151, E-mail: larry.preston@tui.edu. *Application contact:* Dr. Larry Preston, Dean, 513-861-6400 Ext. 1151, E-mail: larry.preston@tui.edu.

Universidad Autonoma de Guadalajara, Graduate Programs, Guadalajara, Mexico. Offers administrative law and justice (LL M); advertising and corporate communications (MA); architecture (M Arch); business (MBA); computational science (MCC); education (Ed M, Ed D); English-Spanish translation (MA); fiscal law (MA); integrated management of digital animation (MA); international business (MIB); international corporate law (LL M); internet technologies (MS); labor health (MS); manufacturing systems (MMS); philosophy (MA, PhD); power electronics (MS); quality systems (MQS); renewable energy (MS); social evaluation of projects (MBA); strategic market research (MBA); teaching mathematics (MA).

Universidad Central del Este, Graduate School, San Pedro de Macoris, Dominican Republic. Offers administration (M Ad); dentistry (DMD); development of educational and social policies (PhD); environmental engineering (ME); financial management (M Ad); higher education (M Ed); human resources (M Ad); public health (MPH). *Entrance requirements:* For master's, letters of recommendation.

Universidad del Este, Graduate School, Carolina, PR 00984. Offers accounting (MBA); adult education (M Ed); agribusiness (MBA); bilingual education (M Ed); criminal justice and criminology (MA); early education (M Ed); elementary education (M Ed); human resources (MBA); information security management (MBA); information technology and Web business development (MBA); management (MBA); public policy (MPA); social work (MA), including clinical social work; special education (M Ed); strategic leadership (MBA); teaching English (M Ed); teaching Spanish (M Ed).

Université de Montréal, Faculty of Arts and Sciences, Programs in Societies, Public Policies and Health, Montréal, QC H3C 3J7, Canada.

University at Albany, State University of New York, Nelson A. Rockefeller College of Public Affairs and Policy, Department of Public Administration and Policy, Albany, NY 12222-0001. Offers administrative behavior (PhD); comparative and development administration (MPA, PhD); human resources (MPA); legislative administration (MPA); nonprofit leadership and management (Certificate); planning and policy analysis (CAS); policy analysis (MPA); program analysis and evaluation (PhD); public affairs and policy (MA); public finance (MPA, PhD); public management (MPA, PhD); women and public policy (Certificate); JD/MPA. *Accreditation:* NASPAA (one or more programs are accredited). *Degree requirements:* For doctorate, one foreign language, thesis/dissertation. *Entrance requirements:* For doctorate, GRE General Test. Additional exam requirements/recommendations for international students: Required—TOEFL (minimum score 550 paper-based; 213 computer-based). Electronic applications accepted.

The University of Arizona, Graduate College, Eller College of Management, School of Public Administration and Policy, Tucson, AZ 85721. Offers public administration (MPA); public administration and policy (PhD). *Accreditation:* NASPAA. *Students:* 37 full-time (18 women), 23 part-time (13 women); includes 10 minority (1 African American, 1 American Indian/Alaska Native, 2 Asian Americans or Pacific Islanders, 6 Hispanic Americans), 3 international. Average age 29. 76 applicants, 70% accepted, 27 enrolled. In 2009, 23 master's awarded. *Degree requirements:* For master's, internship of 400 hours; for doctorate, comprehensive exam, thesis/dissertation. *Entrance requirements:* For doctorate, GMAT or GRE, minimum graduate GPA of 3.5, letter of interest, 3 letters of recommendation, resume. Additional exam requirements/recommendations for international students: Required—TOEFL (minimum score 650 paper-based; 280 computer-based; 115 iBT). *Application deadline:* For fall admission, 2/15 priority date for domestic students, 2/15 for international students. Applications are processed on a rolling basis. Application fee: $75. Electronic applications accepted. *Expenses:* Contact institution. *Financial support:* In 2009–10, 1 research assistantship with full tuition reimbursement (averaging $9,429 per year) was awarded; teaching assistantships with full tuition reimbursements, career-related internships or fieldwork, scholarships/grants, health care benefits, tuition waivers (full and partial), and unspecified assistantships also available. Financial award application deadline: 4/15. Total annual research expenditures: $18,581. *Unit head:* Dr. H. Brinton Milward, Director, 520-621-7476, Fax: 520-626-5549, E-mail: bmilward@eller.arizona.edu. *Application contact:* Pamela Adams, Administrative Associate, 520-621-3128, Fax: 520-621-5549.

Public Policy

University of Arkansas, Graduate School, Interdisciplinary Program in Public Policy, Fayetteville, AR 72701-1201. Offers PhD. *Students:* 14 full-time (8 women), 52 part-time (33 women); includes 18 minority (14 African Americans, 1 American Indian/Alaska Native, 1 Asian American or Pacific Islander, 2 Hispanic Americans), 11 international. In 2009, 12 doctorates awarded. *Degree requirements:* For doctorate, thesis/dissertation. Application fee: $40 ($50 for international students). *Expenses:* Tuition, state resident: full-time $7355; part-time $356.58 per hour. Tuition, nonresident: full-time $17,401; part-time $775.17 per hour. Required fees: $1203. *Financial support:* In 2009–10, 1 fellowship with tuition reimbursement, 9 research assistantships were awarded; teaching assistantships. Financial award application deadline: 4/1; financial award applicants required to submit FAFSA. *Unit head:* Dr. Brinck Kerr, Head, 479-575-3356, Fax: 479-575-5908, E-mail: jbkerr@uark.edu. *Application contact:* Graduate Admissions, 479-575-6246, Fax: 479-575-5908, E-mail: gradinfo@uark.edu.

University of California, Berkeley, Graduate Division, Graduate School of Public Policy, Berkeley, CA 94720-1500. Offers MPP, PhD, JD/MPP, MPP/MA, MPP/MPH, MPP/MS. *Students:* 166 full-time (89 women); includes 45 minority (13 African Americans, 3 American Indian/Alaska Native, 14 Asian Americans or Pacific Islanders, 15 Hispanic Americans), 30 international. Average age 29. 649 applicants, 73 enrolled. In 2009, 76 master's, 1 doctorate awarded. *Degree requirements:* For doctorate, thesis/dissertation, qualifying exam. *Entrance requirements:* For master's and doctorate, GRE General Test, minimum GPA of 3.0, 3 letters of recommendation. *Application deadline:* For fall admission, 12/15 for domestic students. Application fee: $70 ($90 for international students). *Financial support:* Fellowships, research assistantships, teaching assistantships, unspecified assistantships available. *Unit head:* Prof. Henry Brady, Dean, 510-642-4670, E-mail: gsppadm@berkeley.edu. *Application contact:* Jalilah LaBrie, Student Affairs Officer, 510-642-4670, Fax: 510-643-9657, E-mail: gsppadm@berkeley.edu.

University of California, Berkeley, Graduate Division, Haas School of Business, PhD in Business Administration Program, Berkeley, CA 94720-1500. Offers accounting (PhD); business and public policy (PhD); finance (PhD); management of organizations (PhD); marketing (PhD); operations management (PhD); real estate (PhD). *Accreditation:* AACSB. *Faculty:* 80 full-time (20 women), 130 part-time/adjunct (22 women). *Students:* 82 full-time (23 women); includes 22 minority (18 Asian Americans or Pacific Islanders, 4 Hispanic Americans), 29 international. Average age 30. 511 applicants, 5% accepted, 16 enrolled. In 2009, 8 doctorates awarded. *Degree requirements:* For doctorate, comprehensive exam, thesis/dissertation, oral exam, written preliminary exams. *Entrance requirements:* For doctorate, GMAT or GRE, minimum GPA of 3.0 in undergraduate and graduate coursework. Additional exam requirements/recommendations for international students: Required—TOEFL (minimum score 570 paper-based; 230 computer-based; 68 iBT), IELTS (minimum score 7). *Application deadline:* For fall admission, 12/10 for domestic and international students. Application fee: $70 ($90 for international students). Electronic applications accepted. *Financial support:* Fellowships with full and partial tuition reimbursements, research assistantships with full and partial tuition reimbursements, teaching assistantships with full and partial tuition reimbursements, career-related internships or fieldwork, Federal Work-Study, scholarships/grants, health care benefits, tuition waivers (full), unspecified assistantships, and transit pass, travel grants available. Financial award application deadline: 12/10; financial award applicants required to submit FAFSA. *Faculty research:* Accounting, business and public policy, finance, management of organizations, marketing, operations and information technology management, real estate. *Unit head:* Sunil Dutta, Director, 510-642-1229, Fax: 510-643-4255, E-mail: kimg@haas.berkeley.edu. *Application contact:* Kim Guilfoyle, Director, Student Affairs, 510-642-3944, Fax: 510-643-4255, E-mail: kimg@haas.berkeley.edu.

University of California, Los Angeles, Graduate Division, School of Public Affairs, Program in Public Policy, Los Angeles, CA 90095. Offers MPP. *Entrance requirements:* For master's, GRE General Test, minimum GPA of 3.0. Additional exam requirements/recommendations for international students: Required—TOEFL. Electronic applications accepted.

University of Chicago, Irving B. Harris Graduate School of Public Policy Studies, Chicago, IL 60637-1513. Offers environmental science and policy (MS); public policy studies (AM, MPP, PhD); JD/MPP; MBA/MPP; MPP/M Div; MPP/MA. Part-time programs available. *Degree requirements:* For doctorate, thesis/dissertation. *Entrance requirements:* Additional exam requirements/recommendations for international students: Required—TOEFL. Electronic applications accepted. *Expenses:* Contact institution. *Faculty research:* Family and child policy, international security, health policy, social policy.

University of Colorado at Boulder, Graduate School, College of Arts and Sciences, Department of Political Science, Boulder, CO 80309. Offers international affairs (MA); political science (MA, PhD); public policy (MA). *Faculty:* 25 full-time (8 women). *Students:* 55 full-time (27 women), 8 part-time (5 women); includes 7 minority (2 American Indian/Alaska Native, 1 Asian American or Pacific Islander, 4 Hispanic Americans), 6 international. Average age 30. 179 applicants, 9% accepted, 13 enrolled. In 2009, 12 master's, 7 doctorates awarded. Terminal master's awarded for partial completion of doctoral program. *Degree requirements:* For master's, comprehensive exam, thesis; for doctorate, one foreign language, thesis/dissertation. *Entrance requirements:* For master's, GRE General Test, minimum undergraduate GPA of 3.0; for doctorate, GRE General Test, minimum GPA of 3.5 (undergraduate), 3.0 (graduate). *Application deadline:* For fall admission, 12/31 priority date for domestic students, 12/31 for international students. Application fee: $50 ($60 for international students). *Financial support:* In 2009–10, 10 fellowships (averaging $2,060 per year), 41 research assistantships (averaging $12,087 per year) were awarded; Federal Work-Study also available. Financial award application deadline: 12/31. *Faculty research:* American government and politics, comparative politics, international relations, public policy, law and politics, political philosophy, empirical theory and methodology. Total annual research expenditures: $180,188.

University of Delaware, College of Human Services, Education and Public Policy, Center for Energy and Environmental Policy, Program in Urban Affairs and Public Policy, Newark, DE 19716. Offers community development and nonprofit leadership (MA); energy and environmental policy (MA); governance, planning and management (PhD); historic preservation (MA); social and urban policy (PhD); technology, environment and society (PhD). Part-time programs available. Terminal master's awarded for partial completion of doctoral program. *Degree requirements:* For master's, analytical paper or thesis; for doctorate, thesis/dissertation. *Entrance requirements:* For master's, GRE General Test, minimum GPA of 3.0; for doctorate, GRE General Test, minimum GPA of 3.5. Additional exam requirements/recommendations for international students: Required—TOEFL. Electronic applications accepted. *Faculty research:* Political economy; social policy analysis; technology and society; historic preservation; urban policy.

See Close-Up on page 1193.

University of Denver, Division of Arts, Humanities and Social Sciences, Department of Public Policy, Denver, CO 80208. Offers MPP. *Faculty:* 3 full-time (0 women), 3 part-time/adjunct (2 women). *Students:* 24 full-time (14 women), 4 part-time (3 women); includes 3 minority (1 American Indian/Alaska Native, 1 Asian American or Pacific Islander, 1 Hispanic American). Average age 30. 38 applicants, 95% accepted, 20 enrolled. In 2009, 11 master's awarded. *Application deadline:* Applications are processed on a rolling basis. Application fee: $50. Electronic applications accepted. *Expenses:* Tuition: Full-time $34,596; part-time $961 per quarter hour. Required fees: $4 per quarter hour. Tuition and fees vary according to course load, campus/location and program. *Financial support:* In 2009–10, 1 research assistantship with full and partial tuition reimbursement (averaging $2,600 per year), 2 teaching assistantships with full and partial tuition reimbursements (averaging $2,600 per year) were awarded. *Unit head:* Richard Caldwell, Director, 303-871-2468. *Application contact:* Information Contact, 303-871-2468, E-mail: ipps@du.edu.

University of Georgia, School of Public and International Affairs, Department of Public Administration and Policy, Athens, GA 30602. Offers public administration (MPA, PhD). *Accreditation:* NASPAA (one or more programs are accredited). *Faculty:* 16 full-time (3 women), 1 part-time/adjunct (0 women). *Students:* 125 full-time (63 women), 42 part-time (26 women); includes 20 African Americans, 2 Asian Americans or Pacific Islanders, 5 Hispanic Americans, 16 international. 225 applicants, 44% accepted, 65 enrolled. In 2009, 46 master's, 10 doctorates awarded. *Degree requirements:* For master's, internship; for doctorate, thesis/dissertation. *Entrance requirements:* For master's and doctorate, GRE General Test. *Application deadline:* For fall admission, 7/1 priority date for domestic students; for spring admission, 11/15 for domestic students. Application fee: $50. Electronic applications accepted. *Expenses:* Tuition, state resident: full-time $6000; part-time $250 per credit hour. Tuition, nonresident: full-time $20,904; part-time $871 per credit hour. Required fees: $730 per semester. *Financial support:* Fellowships, research assistantships, teaching assistantships, unspecified assistantships available. *Unit head:* Dr. J. Edward Kellough, Head, 706-542-0488, Fax: 706-583-0610, E-mail: kellough@uga.edu. *Application contact:* Dr. Vicky M. Wilkins, Graduate Coordinator, 706-542-2648, Fax: 706-583-0610, E-mail: vwilkins@uga.edu.

University of Guelph, Graduate Program Services, College of Social and Applied Human Sciences, Department of Political Science, Guelph, ON N1G 2W1, Canada. Offers comparative politics (MA); international development (MA); political science (MA); public policy and public administration (MA); the Americas (Canada emphasis) (MA). MA in public policy and public administration offered in collaboration with Department of Political Science of McMaster University. *Degree requirements:* For master's, thesis or paper. *Entrance requirements:* For master's, minimum B average during previous 2 years of course work, 4 year Honours Degree in Political Science. Additional exam requirements/recommendations for international students: Required—TOEFL. Electronic applications accepted. *Faculty research:* Political ethics, constitutional power.

University of Hawaii at Manoa, Graduate Division, College of Social Sciences, Public Policy Center, Honolulu, HI 96822. Offers Graduate Certificate. Part-time programs available. *Faculty:* 1 (woman) full-time, 2 part-time/adjunct (1 woman). *Students:* 3 full-time (1 woman), 1 (woman) part-time, 1 international. Average age 27. 2 applicants, 50% accepted, 1 enrolled. In 2009, 4 Graduate Certificates awarded. *Entrance requirements:* Additional exam requirements/recommendations for international students: Required—TOEFL (minimum score 500 paper-based; 173 computer-based; 61 iBT), IELTS (minimum score 5). *Application deadline:* For fall admission, 3/1 for domestic students, 2/1 for international students. Application fee: $60. *Expenses:* Tuition, state resident: full-time $8900; part-time $372 per credit. Tuition, nonresident: full-time $21,400; part-time $898 per credit. Required fees: $207 per semester. *Financial support:* In 2009–10, 1 student received support, including 2 fellowships (averaging $5,157 per year), 2 research assistantships (averaging $21,363 per year). *Application contact:* Susan Chandler, Interim Director, 808-956-4237, Fax: 808-956-0950, E-mail: chandler@hawaii.edu.

University of Louisville, Graduate School, College of Arts and Sciences, Department of Urban and Public Affairs, Louisville, KY 40208. Offers public administration (MPA), including human resources management, non-profit management, public policy and administration; urban and public affairs (PhD), including urban planning and development, urban policy and administration; urban planning (MUP), including administration of planning organizations, housing and community development, land use and environmental planning, spatial analysis. Part-time and evening/weekend programs available. *Faculty:* 22 full-time (7 women), 8 part-time/adjunct (1 woman). *Students:* 67 full-time (32 women), 35 part-time (20 women); includes 13 minority (10 African Americans, 1 Asian American or Pacific Islander, 2 Hispanic Americans), 6 international. Average age 31. 107 applicants, 57% accepted, 40 enrolled. In 2009, 25 master's, 5 doctorates awarded. Terminal master's awarded for partial completion of doctoral program. *Degree requirements:* For master's, internship; for doctorate, comprehensive exam, thesis/dissertation. *Entrance requirements:* For master's, GRE General Test, minimum GPA of 3.0; for doctorate, GRE General Test, master's degree in appropriate field. Additional exam requirements/recommendations for international students: Required—TOEFL (minimum score 550 paper-based; 213 computer-based; 79 iBT). *Application deadline:* For fall admission, 7/15 for domestic students; for spring admission, 11/15 for domestic students. Applications are processed on a rolling basis. Application fee: $50. Electronic applications accepted. *Financial support:* In 2009–10, 26 students received support; fellowships, research assistantships, health care benefits available. *Unit head:* Dr. David Simpson, Chair, 502-852-8019, Fax: 502-852-4558, E-mail: dave.simpson@louisville.edu. *Application contact:* Patty Sarley, Graduate Student Advisor, 502-852-7914, Fax: 502-852-4558, E-mail: plclea01@louisville.edu.

University of Maryland, Baltimore County, Graduate School, College of Arts, Humanities and Social Sciences, Department of Economics, Program in Economic Policy Analysis, Baltimore, MD 21250. Offers MA. Part-time and evening/weekend programs available. *Faculty:* 25 full-time (9 women), 2 part-time/adjunct (0 women). *Students:* 14 full-time (7 women), 11 part-time (2 women); includes 7 minority (2 African Americans, 1 American Indian/Alaska Native, 2 Asian Americans or Pacific Islanders, 2 Hispanic Americans), 6 international. Average age 27. 24 applicants, 67% accepted, 11 enrolled. In 2009, 9 master's awarded. *Degree requirements:* For master's, comprehensive exam, capstone research project. *Entrance requirements:* For master's, GRE General Test, undergraduate coursework in economic theory, econometrics, calculus. Additional exam requirements/recommendations for international students: Required—TOEFL. *Application deadline:* For fall admission, 7/1 priority date for domestic students, 3/1 priority date for international students; for spring admission, 1/1 priority date for domestic students, 9/15 priority date for international students. Applications are processed on a rolling basis. Application fee: $45. Electronic applications accepted. *Financial support:* In 2009–10, 4 students received support, including 5 research assistantships with full and partial tuition reimbursements available (averaging $11,324 per year); Federal Work-Study, health care benefits, tuition waivers (full and partial), and unspecified assistantships also available. Support available to part-time students. Financial award application deadline: 4/15; financial award applicants required to submit FAFSA. *Faculty research:* International trade policy analysis, health and hospital policy evaluation, environmental policy analysis, economics of education, economic growth and development. Total annual research expenditures: $50,000. *Unit head:* Dr. David F. Mitch, Professor of Economics and Graduate Director, Fax: 410-455-1054, E-mail: mitch@umbc.edu. *Application contact:* Dr. David F. Mitch, Professor of Economics and Graduate Director, Fax: 410-455-1054, E-mail: mitch@umbc.edu.

University of Maryland, Baltimore County, Graduate School, College of Arts, Humanities and Social Sciences, Department of Public Policy, Program in Public Policy, Baltimore, MD 21250. Offers economics (PhD); education (MPP, PhD); evaluation (MPP); health (MPP, PhD); legal (MPP, PhD); management (MPP, PhD); urban (MPP, PhD). Part-time and evening/weekend programs available. *Faculty:* 40 full-time (12 women), 2 part-time/adjunct (1 woman). *Students:* 57 full-time (34 women), 114 part-time (61 women); includes 47 minority (26 African Americans, 21 Hispanic Americans). Average age 33. 89 applicants, 47% accepted, 24 enrolled. In 2009, 12 master's, 5 doctorates awarded. Terminal master's awarded for partial completion of doctoral program. *Degree requirements:* For master's, thesis optional, public analysis paper; for doctorate, comprehensive exam, thesis/dissertation, comprehensive and field qualifying exams. *Entrance requirements:* For master's, GRE General Test, 3 academic letters of reference, transcripts, resume; for doctorate, GRE General Test, 3 academic letters of reference, transcripts, resume, research paper. Additional exam requirements/recommendations for international students: Required—TOEFL (minimum score 550 paper-based; 213 computer-based; 80 iBT). *Application deadline:* For fall admission, 1/15 priority date for domestic students, 1/1 priority date for international students; for spring admission, 11/1 priority date for domestic students, 5/1 priority date for international students. Applications are processed on a rolling basis. Application fee: $50. Electronic applications accepted. *Financial support:* In 2009–10, 32 students received support, including 1 fellowship (averaging $3,000 per year), 17 research assistantships with full tuition reimbursements available (averaging $17,400 per year); career-related internships or fieldwork, Federal Work-Study, scholarships/grants, health care benefits, and unspecified assistantships also available. Support available to part-time students. Financial award application deadline: 2/1; financial award applicants required to submit FAFSA. *Faculty research:* Health policy, education policy, urban policy, public management, evaluation and analytical method. *Unit head:* Dr. Donald Norris, Chair,

410-455-1455, E-mail: norris@umbc.edu. *Application contact:* Sally F. Helms, Administrator of Academic Affairs, 410-455-3202, Fax: 410-455-1172, E-mail: gradposi@umbc.edu.

University of Maryland, College Park, Academic Affairs, A. James Clark School of Engineering and School of Public Policy, Program in Engineering and Public Policy, College Park, MD 20742. Offers MS. *Students:* 4 full-time (1 woman), 8 part-time (4 women); includes 4 minority (2 African Americans, 2 Hispanic Americans), 1 international. 31 applicants, 58% accepted, 3 enrolled. In 2009, 3 master's awarded. *Application deadline:* For fall admission, 4/1 for domestic students, 2/1 for international students; for spring admission, 10/15 for domestic students, 6/1 for international students. Application fee: $60. *Expenses:* Tuition, area resident: Part-time $471 per credit hour. Tuition, state resident: part-time $471 per credit hour. Tuition, nonresident: part-time $1016 per credit hour. Required fees: $337.04 per term. *Financial support:* In 2009–10, 2 teaching assistantships (averaging $15,909 per year) were awarded. *Unit head:* Dr. Steven Gabriel, Co-Director, 301-405-6331, E-mail: mepp@umd.edu. *Application contact:* Dr., Dean of the Graduate School, 301-405-0376, Fax: 301-314-9305, E-mail: ccaramel@umd.edu.

University of Maryland, College Park, Academic Affairs, School of Public Policy, Policy Studies Program, College Park, MD 20742. Offers PhD. *Students:* 35 full-time (15 women), 15 part-time (5 women); includes 3 minority (2 Asian Americans or Pacific Islanders, 1 Hispanic American), 20 international. 125 applicants, 11% accepted, 8 enrolled. In 2009, 2 doctorates awarded. *Degree requirements:* For doctorate, comprehensive exam, thesis/dissertation, written and oral exams. *Entrance requirements:* For doctorate, GRE General Test, writing sample. *Application deadline:* For fall admission, 4/1 for domestic students, 2/1 for international students. Applications are processed on a rolling basis. Application fee: $60. Electronic applications accepted. *Expenses:* Tuition, area resident: Part-time $471 per credit hour. Tuition, state resident: part-time $471 per credit hour. Tuition, nonresident: part-time $1016 per credit hour. Required fees: $337.04 per term. *Financial support:* In 2009–10, 5 fellowships with partial tuition reimbursements (averaging $10,867 per year), 1 research assistantship (averaging $17,776 per year), 18 teaching assistantships (averaging $15,416 per year) were awarded. Financial award applicants required to submit FAFSA. *Application contact:* Dean of Graduate School, 301-405-0376, Fax: 301-314-9305.

University of Maryland, College Park, Academic Affairs, School of Public Policy, Programs in Public Policy, College Park, MD 20742. Offers MPP, JD/MPP. *Accreditation:* NASPAA. *Students:* 154 full-time (79 women), 21 part-time (14 women); includes 25 minority (9 African Americans, 8 Asian Americans or Pacific Islanders, 8 Hispanic Americans), 27 international. 547 applicants, 54% accepted, 88 enrolled. In 2009, 56 master's awarded. *Entrance requirements:* Additional exam requirements/recommendations for international students: Required—TOEFL. *Application deadline:* For fall admission, 4/1 for domestic students, 2/1 for international students; for spring admission, 10/15 for domestic students, 6/1 for international students. Applications are processed on a rolling basis. Application fee: $60. Electronic applications accepted. *Expenses:* Tuition, area resident: Part-time $471 per credit hour. Tuition, state resident: part-time $471 per credit hour. Tuition, nonresident: part-time $1016 per credit hour. Required fees: $337.04 per term. *Financial support:* In 2009–10, 7 fellowships (averaging $12,277 per year), 1 research assistantship (averaging $19,445 per year), 81 teaching assistantships (averaging $14,989 per year) were awarded. *Application contact:* Dean of Graduate School, 301-405-0376, Fax: 301-314-9305.

University of Massachusetts Amherst, Graduate School, College of Social and Behavioral Sciences, Center for Public Policy and Administration, Amherst, MA 01003. Offers MPPA. Part-time programs available. *Students:* 31 full-time (21 women), 11 part-time (9 women); includes 3 minority (1 African American, 1 Asian American or Pacific Islander, 1 Hispanic American), 10 international. Average age 33. 80 applicants, 69% accepted, 16 enrolled. In 2009, 18 master's awarded. *Degree requirements:* For master's, thesis or alternative. *Entrance requirements:* For master's, GRE General Test. Additional exam requirements/recommendations for international students: Required—TOEFL (minimum score 550 paper-based; 213 computer-based; 80 iBT), IELTS (minimum score 6.5). *Application deadline:* For fall admission, 2/1 for domestic and international students. Applications are processed on a rolling basis. Application fee: $50 ($65 for international students). Electronic applications accepted. *Expenses:* Tuition, state resident: full-time $2640; part-time $110 per credit. Tuition, nonresident: full-time $9936; part-time $414 per credit. Tuition and fees vary according to course load. *Financial support:* Fellowships, research assistantships, teaching assistantships, career-related internships or fieldwork, Federal Work-Study, scholarships/grants, traineeships, health care benefits, tuition waivers (full), and unspecified assistantships available. Support available to part-time students. Financial award application deadline: 2/1. *Unit head:* Dr. M. V. Lee Badgett, Graduate Program Director, 413-545-3956, Fax: 413-545-1108. *Application contact:* Jean M. Ames, Supervisor of Admissions, 413-545-0722, Fax: 413-577-0010, E-mail: gradadm@grad.umass.edu.

University of Massachusetts Amherst, Graduate School, Interdisciplinary Programs, Program in Public Policy and Business Administration, Amherst, MA 01003. Offers MPPA/MBA. Part-time programs available. *Students:* 4 full-time (3 women). Average age 27. 12 applicants, 42% accepted, 2 enrolled. *Entrance requirements:* Additional exam requirements/recommendations for international students: Required—TOEFL (minimum score 600 paper-based; 250 computer-based; 100 iBT), IELTS (minimum score 7). *Application deadline:* For fall admission, 2/1 for domestic and international students. Applications are processed on a rolling basis. Application fee: $50 ($65 for international students). Electronic applications accepted. *Expenses:* Tuition, state resident: full-time $2640; part-time $110 per credit. Tuition, nonresident: full-time $9936; part-time $414 per credit. Tuition and fees vary according to course load. *Financial support:* Career-related internships or fieldwork, Federal Work-Study, scholarships/grants, traineeships, health care benefits, tuition waivers (full), and unspecified assistantships available. Support available to part-time students. Financial award application deadline: 2/1. *Unit head:* Dr. M. V. Lee Badgett, Graduate Program Director, 413-545-3956, Fax: 413-545-1108. *Application contact:* Jean M. Ames, Supervisor of Admissions, 413-545-0722, Fax: 413-577-0010, E-mail: gradadm@grad.umass.edu.

University of Massachusetts Boston, Office of Graduate Studies, John W. McCormack Graduate School of Policy Studies, Program in Public Policy, Boston, MA 02125-3393. Offers PhD. Evening/weekend programs available. *Degree requirements:* For doctorate, comprehensive exam, thesis/dissertation, practicum, oral exam. *Entrance requirements:* For doctorate, GRE General Test. *Faculty research:* Political economy, public managerial control, healthcare policy, planning and public policy theory, economic development.

University of Massachusetts Dartmouth, Graduate School, School of Education, Public Policy, and Civic Engagement, Department of Public Policy, North Dartmouth, MA 02747-2300. Offers environmental policy (Postbaccalaureate Certificate); public policy (MPP). Part-time programs available. Postbaccalaureate distance learning degree programs offered. *Faculty:* 4 full-time (1 woman). *Students:* 12 full-time (8 women), 28 part-time (16 women); includes 5 minority (all African Americans). Average age 35. 26 applicants, 92% accepted, 13 enrolled. In 2009, 9 master's awarded. *Entrance requirements:* For master's, GRE or GMAT. Additional exam requirements/recommendations for international students: Required—TOEFL (minimum score 500 paper-based; 213 computer-based). *Application deadline:* For fall admission, 4/20 for domestic students, 2/20 for international students; for spring admission, 11/15 for domestic students, 9/15 for international students. Applications are processed on a rolling basis. Application fee: $40 ($60 for international students). Electronic applications accepted. *Expenses:* Tuition, state resident: full-time $2071; part-time $86.29 per credit. Tuition, nonresident: full-time $8099; part-time $337.46 per credit. Required fees: $9446. Tuition and fees vary according to class time, course load and reciprocity agreements. *Financial support:* In 2009–10, 3 research assistantships with full tuition reimbursements (averaging $5,333 per year) were awarded; Federal Work-Study and unspecified assistantships also available. Support available to part-time students. Financial award application deadline: 3/1. *Faculty research:* International human rights, international political economy, gender and politics. Total annual research expenditures: $128,000. *Unit head:* Dr. Michael Goodmon, 508-990-9660, E-mail: mgoodmon@umassd.edu. *Application contact:* Elan Turcotte-Shamski, Graduate Admissions Officer, 508-999-8604, Fax: 508-999-8183, E-mail: graduate@umassd.edu.

University of Memphis, Graduate School, College of Arts and Sciences, Division of Public and Nonprofit Administration, Memphis, TN 38152. Offers nonprofit administration (MPA); public management and policy (MPA); urban management and planning (MPA). *Accreditation:* NASPAA. Part-time and evening/weekend programs available. *Faculty:* 5 full-time (2 women), 1 (woman) part-time/adjunct. *Students:* 17 full-time (11 women), 39 part-time (28 women); includes 32 minority (31 African Americans, 1 Hispanic American), 1 international. Average age 34. 32 applicants, 88% accepted, 9 enrolled. In 2009, 17 master's awarded. *Degree requirements:* For master's, comprehensive exam, thesis or alternative, internship. *Entrance requirements:* For master's, GRE General Test, GMAT, or MAT, minimum GPA of 3.0. *Application deadline:* For fall admission, 8/1 for domestic students; for spring admission, 12/1 for domestic students. Applications are processed on a rolling basis. Application fee: $35 ($60 for international students). *Expenses:* Tuition, state resident: full-time $6246; part-time $347 per credit hour. Tuition, nonresident: full-time $15,894; part-time $883 per credit hour. Required fees: $1160. Full-time tuition and fees vary according to course load, degree level and program. *Financial support:* In 2009–10, 37 students received support; fellowships, research assistantships with full tuition reimbursements available, career-related internships or fieldwork, Federal Work-Study, scholarships/grants, and unspecified assistantships available. Support available to part-time students. Financial award application deadline: 2/15; financial award applicants required to submit FAFSA. *Faculty research:* Nonprofit organization governance, local government management, community collaboration, urban problems, accountability. *Unit head:* Dr. Dorothy Norris-Tirrell, Director, 901-678-3360, Fax: 901-678-2981, E-mail: dnrrstrr@memphis.edu. *Application contact:* Dr. Charles Menifield, Graduate Admissions Coordinator, 901-678-3360, Fax: 901-678-2981, E-mail: cmenifld@memphis.edu.

University of Michigan, Horace H. Rackham School of Graduate Studies, College of Literature, Science, and the Arts, Department of Economics, Ann Arbor, MI 48109. Offers applied economics (AM); economics (AM, PhD); public policy and economics (PhD); social work and economics (PhD); JD/PhD; MPP/AM. *Faculty:* 57 full-time (9 women). *Students:* 168 full-time (55 women); includes 23 minority (3 African Americans, 17 Asian Americans or Pacific Islanders, 3 Hispanic Americans), 55 international. Average age 27. 596 applicants, 23% accepted, 34 enrolled. In 2009, 42 master's, 21 doctorates awarded. Terminal master's awarded for partial completion of doctoral program. *Degree requirements:* For doctorate, oral defense of dissertation, preliminary exam. *Entrance requirements:* For master's and doctorate, GRE General Test. Additional exam requirements/recommendations for international students: Required—TOEFL (minimum score 600 paper-based; 250 computer-based; 100 iBT). *Application deadline:* For fall admission, 12/15 for domestic and international students. Application fee: $60 ($75 for international students). Electronic applications accepted. *Expenses:* Tuition, state resident: full-time $17,286; part-time $1099 per credit hour. Tuition, nonresident: full-time $34,944; part-time $2080 per credit hour. Required fees: $95 per semester. Tuition and fees vary according to course load, degree level and program. *Financial support:* In 2009–10, 118 students received support, including 40 fellowships with full tuition reimbursements available (averaging $16,000 per year), 18 research assistantships with full tuition reimbursements available (averaging $16,696 per year), 60 teaching assistantships with full tuition reimbursements available (averaging $16,696 per year); career-related internships or fieldwork and traineeships also available. Financial award application deadline: 12/15. *Faculty research:* Economic and econometrical analysis, industrial organization, international trade, public finance, development, health, labor, population standard, macro, theory. *Unit head:* Prof. Linda Tesar, Chair, 734-763-2254, Fax: 734-764-2769, E-mail: ltesar@umich.edu. *Application contact:* Prof. David Lam, Director of Graduate Studies, 734-763-9237, Fax: 734-764-2769, E-mail: davidl@umich.edu.

University of Michigan, Horace H. Rackham School of Graduate Studies, College of Literature, Science, and the Arts, Department of Sociology, Ann Arbor, MI 48109. Offers public policy and sociology (PhD); social work and sociology (PhD); sociology (PhD); women's studies and sociology (PhD). *Faculty:* 37 full-time (16 women), 9 part-time/adjunct (2 women). *Students:* 102 full-time (69 women); includes 27 minority (8 African Americans, 10 Asian Americans or Pacific Islanders, 9 Hispanic Americans), 20 international. Average age 33. 287 applicants, 8% accepted, 9 enrolled. In 2009, 12 doctorates awarded. *Degree requirements:* For doctorate, comprehensive exam, thesis/dissertation, oral defense of dissertation, preliminary exam. *Entrance requirements:* For doctorate, GRE General Test, letters of recommendation, writing sample. Additional exam requirements/recommendations for international students: Required—TOEFL (minimum score 560 paper-based; 220 computer-based; 84 iBT). *Application deadline:* For fall admission, 12/15 for domestic and international students. Application fee: $60 ($75 for international students). Electronic applications accepted. *Expenses:* Tuition, state resident: full-time $17,286; part-time $1099 per credit hour. Tuition, nonresident: full-time $34,944; part-time $2080 per credit hour. Required fees: $95 per semester. Tuition and fees vary according to course load, degree level and program. *Financial support:* In 2009–10, 40 students received support, including 20 fellowships with tuition reimbursements available (averaging $16,000 per year), 50 teaching assistantships with tuition reimbursements available (averaging $16,000 per year); health care benefits also available. *Faculty research:* Power, history and social change; gender and sexuality; race and ethnicity; economic sociology; social demography. Total annual research expenditures: $269,377. *Unit head:* Howard Kimeldorf, Chair, 734-764-5554, Fax: 734-763-6887, E-mail: hkimel@umich.edu. *Application contact:* Jeannie Loughry, Graduate Program Coordinator, 734-647-4428, Fax: 734-763-6887, E-mail: sociology.graduate.program@umich.edu.

University of Michigan, Horace H. Rackham School of Graduate Studies, Gerald R. Ford School of Public Policy, Ann Arbor, MI 48109. Offers MPA, MPP, PhD, JD/MPP, MBA/MPP, MD/MPP, MHSA/MPP, MPH/MPP, MPP/AM, MPP/MA, MPP/MIS, MPP/MS, MPP/MUP, MSW/MPP. Part-time programs available. *Faculty:* 41 full-time (13 women), 17 part-time/adjunct (6 women). *Students:* 231 full-time (110 women); includes 52 minority (17 African Americans, 3 American Indian/Alaska Native, 22 Asian Americans or Pacific Islanders, 10 Hispanic Americans), 35 international. Average age 27. 642 applicants, 52% accepted, 102 enrolled. In 2009, 82 master's, 3 doctorates awarded. *Entrance requirements:* For master's, GRE. Additional exam requirements/recommendations for international students: Required—TOEFL (minimum score 600 paper-based; 250 computer-based; 100 iBT). *Application deadline:* For fall admission, 1/15 priority date for domestic students, 1/15 for international students. Application fee: $60 ($75 for international students). Electronic applications accepted. *Expenses:* Tuition, state resident: full-time $17,286; part-time $1099 per credit hour. Tuition, nonresident: full-time $34,944; part-time $2080 per credit hour. Required fees: $95 per semester. Tuition and fees vary according to course load, degree level and program. *Financial support:* In 2009–10, 104 fellowships, 30 teaching assistantships with tuition reimbursements were awarded; career-related internships or fieldwork and Federal Work-Study also available. Financial award applicants required to submit FAFSA. *Faculty research:* U.S. social policy; international economic policy; quantitative policy analysis; environmental policy; health policy. *Unit head:* Dr. Susan M. Collins, Dean, 734-764-3490. *Application contact:* Beth Soboleski, Director, Admissions and Recruiting, 734-764-0453, Fax: 734-647-7486, E-mail: fspp-admissions@umich.edu.

University of Michigan–Dearborn, College of Arts, Sciences, and Letters, Master of Public Policy Program, Dearborn, MI 48128. Offers MPP. Part-time and evening/weekend programs available. *Faculty:* 3 full-time (0 women). *Students:* 17 full-time (11 women), 11 part-time (4 women); includes 6 minority (3 African Americans, 1 Asian American or Pacific Islander, 2 Hispanic Americans). Average age 31. 8 applicants, 88% accepted, 7 enrolled. In 2009, 3 master's awarded. *Entrance requirements:* For master's, GRE, 2 letters of recommendation. Additional exam requirements/recommendations for international students: Required—TOEFL (minimum score 560 paper-based; 220 computer-based). *Application deadline:* For fall admission, 8/1 for domestic students, 4/1 for international students; for winter admission, 12/1 for domestic students, 11/1 for international students; for spring admission, 4/1 for domestic students, 3/1 for international students. Application fee: $60 ($75 for international students). *Expenses:* Tuition, area resident: Part-time $504.10 per credit hour. Tuition, state resident: part-time $504.10 per credit hour. Tuition, nonresident: part-time $957.90 per credit hour. *Faculty*

Public Policy

University of Michigan–Dearborn (continued)

research: Peace and conflict studies, courts and public policy, public policy and the media. *Unit head:* Dr. Trevor Thrall, Director, 313-593-5282, Fax: 313-583-6700, E-mail: atthrall@umd.umich.edu. *Application contact:* Carol Ligienza, Graduate Program Coordinator, CASL Graduate Programs, 313-593-1183, Fax: 313-583-6700, E-mail: caslgrad@umd.umich.edu.

University of Minnesota, Twin Cities Campus, Graduate School, Hubert H. Humphrey Institute of Public Affairs, Program in Public Policy, Minneapolis, MN 55455-0213. Offers advanced policy analysis methods (MPP); economic and community development (MPP); foreign policy (MPP); public and nonprofit leadership and management (MPP); science technology and environmental policy (MPP); social policy (MPP); women and public policy (MPP); JD/MPP; MPP/MS; MSW/MPP. Part-time programs available. *Faculty:* 33 full-time (14 women), 29 part-time/adjunct (15 women). *Students:* 165 full-time (107 women), 74 part-time (44 women); includes 41 minority (11 African Americans, 24 Asian Americans or Pacific Islanders, 6 Hispanic Americans). Average age 26. 345 applicants, 71% accepted, 109 enrolled. In 2009, 91 master's awarded. *Degree requirements:* For master's, thesis or alternative, internship or equivalent work experience. *Entrance requirements:* For master's, GRE General Test, minimum undergraduate GPA of 3.0. Additional exam requirements/recommendations for international students: Required—TOEFL (minimum score 600 paper-based; 250 computer-based; 100 iBT). *Application deadline:* For fall admission, 4/1 for domestic and international students. Applications are processed on a rolling basis. Application fee: $55 ($75 for international students). Electronic applications accepted. *Financial support:* In 2009–10, 77 students received support, including fellowships with full and partial tuition reimbursements available (averaging $8,500 per year), research assistantships with full and partial tuition reimbursements available (averaging $5,270 per year), teaching assistantships with full and partial tuition reimbursements available (averaging $5,270 per year); career-related internships or fieldwork, Federal Work-Study, scholarships/grants, health care benefits, tuition waivers (full and partial), and unspecified assistantships also available. Financial award application deadline: 1/5. *Faculty research:* Social policy, public and non-profit management and leadership, community and economic development, foreign policy and international affairs, women and public policy. Total annual research expenditures: $5.1 million. *Unit head:* Dr. Maria Hanratty, Head, 612-624-3800, Fax: 612-626-0002, E-mail: hhhadmit@umn.edu. *Application contact:* Julie Harrold, Director of Admissions, 612-626-7229, Fax: 612-626-0002, E-mail: hhhadmit@umn.edu.

University of Missouri–St. Louis, College of Arts and Sciences, Department of Political Science, St. Louis, MO 63121. Offers American politics (MA); comparative politics (MA); international politics (MA); political process and behavior (MA); political science (PhD); public administration and public policy (MA); urban and regional politics (MA). Part-time and evening/weekend programs available. *Faculty:* 19 full-time (7 women), 1 (woman) part-time/adjunct. *Students:* 12 full-time (7 women), 35 part-time (17 women); includes 12 minority (8 African Americans, 1 American Indian/Alaska Native, 3 Asian Americans or Pacific Islanders), 2 international. Average age 35. 30 applicants, 57% accepted, 9 enrolled. In 2009, 6 master's, 2 doctorates awarded. Terminal master's awarded for partial completion of doctoral program. *Degree requirements:* For master's, thesis optional; for doctorate, thesis/dissertation. *Entrance requirements:* For master's, GRE General Test, 2 letters of recommendation; for doctorate, GRE General Test, 3 letters of recommendation. Additional exam requirements/recommendations for international students: Required—TOEFL (minimum score 550 paper-based; 213 computer-based). *Application deadline:* For fall admission, 2/15 priority date for domestic and international students; for spring admission, 10/15 priority date for domestic and international students. Applications are processed on a rolling basis. Application fee: $35 ($40 for international students). Electronic applications accepted. *Expenses:* Tuition, state resident: full-time $5377; part-time $297.70 per credit hour. Tuition, nonresident: full-time $13,882; part-time $771.20 per credit hour. Required fees: $220; $12.20 per credit hour. One-time fee: $12. Tuition and fees vary according to course level, campus/location and program. *Financial support:* In 2009–10, 10 research assistantships with full and partial tuition reimbursements (averaging $10,800 per year), 5 teaching assistantships with full and partial tuition reimbursements (averaging $10,800 per year) were awarded; fellowships, career-related internships or fieldwork also available. Support available to part-time students. Financial award application deadline: 3/15; financial award applicants required to submit FAFSA. *Faculty research:* Public policy, urban politics and administration, American government. *Unit head:* Dr. Barbara Graham, Director of Graduate Studies, 314-516-5522, Fax: 314-516-5268, E-mail: umslpolisci@umsl.edu. *Application contact:* 314-516-5458, Fax: 314-516-6996, E-mail: gradadm@umsl.edu.

University of Missouri–St. Louis, Graduate School, Program in Public Policy Administration, St. Louis, MO 63121. Offers health policy (MPPA); local government management (MPPA); managing human resources and organization (MPPA); nonprofit organization management (MPPA); nonprofit organization management and leadership (Certificate); policy research and analysis (MPPA). *Accreditation:* NASPAA. Part-time and evening/weekend programs available. *Faculty:* 7 full-time (4 women), 6 part-time/adjunct (1 woman). *Students:* 20 full-time (8 women), 69 part-time (45 women); includes 13 minority (11 African Americans, 2 Hispanic Americans), 8 international. Average age 31. 85 applicants, 58% accepted, 28 enrolled. In 2009, 12 master's, 34 Certificates awarded. *Degree requirements:* For master's, exit project. *Entrance requirements:* For master's, 3 letters of recommendation. Additional exam requirements/recommendations for international students: Required—TOEFL (minimum score 550 paper-based; 213 computer-based). *Application deadline:* For fall admission, 7/1 priority date for domestic and international students; for spring admission, 12/1 priority date for domestic and international students. Applications are processed on a rolling basis. Application fee: $35 ($40 for international students). Electronic applications accepted. *Expenses:* Tuition, state resident: full-time $5377; part-time $297.70 per credit hour. Tuition, nonresident: full-time $13,882; part-time $771.20 per credit hour. Required fees: $220; $12.20 per credit hour. One-time fee: $12. Tuition and fees vary according to course level, campus/location and program. *Financial support:* In 2009–10, 2 research assistantships with full and partial tuition reimbursements (averaging $12,000 per year) were awarded; career-related internships or fieldwork also available. Financial award application deadline: 4/1; financial award applicants required to submit FAFSA. *Faculty research:* Urban policy, public finance, evaluation. *Unit head:* Dr. Brady Baybeck, Director, 314-516-5145, Fax: 314-516-5210, E-mail: baybeck@umsl.edu. *Application contact:* 314-516-5458, Fax: 314-516-6996, E-mail: gradadm@umsl.edu.

University of Nebraska–Lincoln, Graduate College, College of Arts and Sciences, Department of Political Science, Lincoln, NE 68588. Offers political science (MA, PhD); public policy analysis (Graduate Certificate). *Degree requirements:* For master's, thesis optional; for doctorate, variable foreign language requirement, comprehensive exam, thesis/dissertation. *Entrance requirements:* For master's and doctorate, GRE General Test, writing sample. Additional exam requirements/recommendations for international students: Required—TOEFL (minimum score 600 paper-based; 250 computer-based). Electronic applications accepted. *Faculty research:* Public policy; comparative politics; international relations; political theory, behavior, and methodology; American politics.

University of Nevada, Las Vegas, Graduate College, College of Liberal Arts, Department of Political Science, Program in Ethics and Policy Studies, Las Vegas, NV 89154-5029. Offers MA. Part-time programs available. *Faculty:* 2 full-time (0 women), 2 part-time/adjunct (both women). *Students:* 9 part-time (2 women); includes 6 minority (1 African American, 1 American Indian/Alaska Native, 2 Asian Americans or Pacific Islanders, 2 Hispanic Americans). Average age 35. 1 applicant, 0% accepted, 0 enrolled. In 2009, 1 master's awarded. *Degree requirements:* For master's, thesis. *Entrance requirements:* For master's, GRE General Test. Additional exam requirements/recommendations for international students: Required—TOEFL (minimum score 550 paper-based; 213 computer-based; 80 iBT), IELTS (minimum score 7). *Application deadline:* For fall admission, 2/1 priority date for domestic and international students; for spring admission, 10/1 priority date for domestic and international students. Applications are processed on a rolling basis. Application fee: $60 ($95 for international students). Electronic applications accepted. *Financial support:* Institutionally sponsored loans, scholarships/grants, health care benefits, and unspecified assistantships available. Financial award application deadline: 3/1. *Faculty research:* Immigration and crime policy, ancient and contemporary political theory. *Unit head:* Dr. Mehran Tamadonfar, Chair/ Associate Professor, 702-895-5258, Fax: 702-895-1065, E-mail: mehran.tamadonfar@unlv.edu. *Application contact:* Graduate College Admissions Evaluator, 702-895-3320, Fax: 702-895-4180, E-mail: gradcollege@unlv.edu.

University of New Brunswick Fredericton, School of Graduate Studies, Policy Studies Program, Fredericton, NB E3B 5A3, Canada. Offers people, property and alternative dispute resolution (M Phil); philosophy politics and economics (M Phil); sustainable development (M Phil). Part-time programs available. *Faculty:* 6 full-time (2 women), 13 part-time/adjunct (2 women). *Students:* 8 full-time (3 women), 5 part-time (3 women). In 2009, 7 master's awarded. *Degree requirements:* For master's, thesis, report. *Entrance requirements:* For master's, minimum GPA of 3.5, BA; BA Honours. Additional exam requirements/recommendations for international students: Required—TOEFL (minimum score 600 paper-based; 250 computer-based; 100 iBT), TWE (minimum score 4), or IELTS (minimum score 7). Application fee: $50 Canadian dollars. Tuition and fees charges are reported in Canadian dollars. *Expenses:* Tuition, area resident: Full-time $5562 Canadian dollars; part-time $2781 Canadian dollars per year. Required fees: $49.75 Canadian dollars per term. *Financial support:* In 2009–10, 5 research assistantships (averaging $5,600 per year), 2 teaching assistantships (averaging $4,400 per year) were awarded. *Unit head:* Dr. Linda Eyre, Dean of Graduate Studies, 506-447-3044, Fax: 506-453-4817, E-mail: gradidst@unb.ca. *Application contact:* Janet Amurault, Graduate Secretary, 506-458-7558, Fax: 506-453-4817, E-mail: jamiraul@unb.ca.

The University of North Carolina at Chapel Hill, Graduate School, Department of Public Policy, Chapel Hill, NC 27599. Offers PhD. *Degree requirements:* For doctorate, thesis/dissertation. *Entrance requirements:* For doctorate, GRE General Test. Electronic applications accepted. *Faculty research:* Environmental policy; energy policy; economic development and science and technology policy; social policy; welfare, education and low-income communities.

The University of North Carolina at Charlotte, Graduate School, College of Arts and Sciences, Department of Political Science, Charlotte, NC 28223-0001. Offers public administration (MPA); public policy (PhD). *Accreditation:* NASPAA. Part-time and evening/weekend programs available. *Faculty:* 20 full-time (7 women), 3 part-time/adjunct (1 woman). *Students:* 45 full-time (29 women), 50 part-time (28 women); includes 14 African Americans, 1 Hispanic American, 13 international. Average age 32. 81 applicants, 65% accepted, 24 enrolled. In 2009, 13 master's, 12 doctorates awarded. *Entrance requirements:* For master's, GRE General Test or MAT, minimum GPA of 3.0 in undergraduate major, 2.75 overall. Additional exam requirements/recommendations for international students: Required—TOEFL (minimum score 557 paper-based; 220 computer-based; 83 iBT). *Application deadline:* For fall admission, 7/1 for domestic students, 5/1 for international students; for spring admission, 11/1 for domestic students, 10/1 for international students. Applications are processed on a rolling basis. Application fee: $55. Electronic applications accepted. *Financial support:* In 2009–10, 13 students received support, including 5 research assistantships (averaging $10,889 per year), 8 teaching assistantships (averaging $9,562 per year); career-related internships or fieldwork, Federal Work-Study, institutionally sponsored loans, scholarships/grants, and unspecified assistantships also available. Support available to part-time students. Financial award application deadline: 4/1; financial award applicants required to submit FAFSA. *Faculty research:* Terrorism, public administration, nonprofit and arts administration, educational policy, social policy. Total annual research expenditures: $224,272. *Unit head:* Dr. Theodore S. Arrington, Chair, 704-687-2571, Fax: 704-687-3497, E-mail: tarrngtn@uncc.edu. *Application contact:* Kathy B. Giddings, Director of Graduate Admissions, 704-687-5503, Fax: 704-687-3279, E-mail: gradadm@uncc.edu.

The University of North Carolina at Charlotte, Graduate School, College of Arts and Sciences, Program in Public Policy, Charlotte, NC 28223-0001. Offers PhD. Part-time and evening/weekend programs available. *Faculty:* 20 full-time (7 women), 3 part-time/adjunct (1 woman). *Students:* 18 full-time (13 women), 14 part-time (9 women); includes 1 minority (African American), 11 international. Average age 37. 21 applicants, 67% accepted, 6 enrolled. In 2009, 12 doctorates awarded. *Degree requirements:* For doctorate, comprehensive exam. *Entrance requirements:* For doctorate, GRE General Test. Additional exam requirements/recommendations for international students: Required—TOEFL (minimum score 557 paper-based; 220 computer-based; 83 iBT). *Application deadline:* For fall admission, 12/1 for domestic and international students. Applications are processed on a rolling basis. Application fee: $55. Electronic applications accepted. *Financial support:* In 2009–10, 12 students received support, including 6 research assistantships (averaging $13,850 per year), 6 teaching assistantships (averaging $10,833 per year); career-related internships or fieldwork, Federal Work-Study, institutionally sponsored loans, scholarships/grants, and unspecified assistantships also available. Support available to part-time students. Financial award application deadline: 4/1; financial award applicants required to submit FAFSA. *Unit head:* Dr. David A. Swindell, Director, 704-687-4519, Fax: 704-687-4771, E-mail: daswinde@.uncc.edu. *Application contact:* Kathy B. Giddings, Director of Graduate Admissions, 704-687-5503, Fax: 704-687-3279, E-mail: gradadm@uncc.edu.

University of Northern Iowa, Graduate College, Program in Public Policy, Cedar Falls, IA 50614. Offers MPP. Part-time programs available. *Students:* 16 full-time (4 women), 4 part-time (3 women); includes 3 minority (all African Americans), 3 international. 33 applicants, 76% accepted, 16 enrolled. In 2009, 10 master's awarded. *Degree requirements:* For master's, comprehensive exam (for some programs). *Entrance requirements:* For master's, minimum GPA of 3.0. Additional exam requirements/recommendations for international students: Required—TOEFL (minimum score 500 paper-based; 180 computer-based; 61 iBT). *Application deadline:* For fall admission, 3/1 priority date for domestic students. Applications are processed on a rolling basis. Application fee: $30 ($50 for international students). Electronic applications accepted. *Financial support:* Career-related internships or fieldwork, Federal Work-Study, institutionally sponsored loans, tuition waivers (full), and unspecified assistantships available. Financial award application deadline: 2/1. *Unit head:* Dr. Richard Allen Hays, Director/Professor, 319-273-2910, Fax: 319-273-7126, E-mail: allen.hays@uni.edu. *Application contact:* Laurie S. Russell, Record Analyst, 319-273-2623, Fax: 319-273-6792, E-mail: laurie.russell@uni.edu.

University of Oregon, Graduate School, School of Architecture and Allied Arts, Department of Planning, Public Policy, and Management, Program in Public Policy and Management, Eugene, OR 97403. Offers MA, MPA, MS. *Accreditation:* NASPAA. Part-time and evening/weekend programs available. *Degree requirements:* For master's, thesis. *Entrance requirements:* For master's, minimum GPA of 3.0. Additional exam requirements/recommendations for international students: Required—TOEFL. *Faculty research:* Community economic development, families in poverty, health services.

University of Pennsylvania, Wharton School, Department of Business and Public Policy, Philadelphia, PA 19104. Offers MBA, PhD. *Degree requirements:* For doctorate, thesis/dissertation. *Entrance requirements:* For doctorate, GRE General Test. *Expenses:* Tuition: Full-time $25,660; part-time $4758 per course. Required fees: $2152; $270 per course. Tuition and fees vary according to course load, degree level and program. *Faculty research:* International policy, business and government, regulation, urban development and policy, transportation.

University of Pittsburgh, Graduate School of Public and International Affairs, Division of Public and Urban Affairs, Pittsburgh, PA 15260. Offers policy research and analysis (MPA); public and nonprofit management (MPA); urban and regional affairs (MPA); JD/MPA; MPA/MPIA; MPH/MPA; MSIS/MPA; MSW/MPA. Part-time and evening/weekend programs available. *Faculty:* 28 full-time (8 women), 56 part-time/adjunct (20 women). *Students:* 46 full-time (28 women), 19 part-time (13 women); includes 11 minority (9 African Americans, 1 Asian American or Pacific Islander, 1 Hispanic American), 3 international. Average age 25. 93 applicants, 92% accepted, 30 enrolled. In 2009, 32 master's awarded. *Degree requirements:* For master's, thesis optional, internship, capstone seminar. *Entrance requirements:* For master's, GRE General Test, 3 letters of recommendation, resume, minimum GPA of 3.2. Additional exam requirements/recommendations for international students: Required—TOEFL (minimum score 550 paper-based; 213 computer-based; 80 iBT), TWE (minimum score 4); Recommended—IELTS (minimum score 7). *Application deadline:* For fall admission, 2/1 for domestic students, 1/15 for international students; for spring admission, 11/1 for domestic students, 8/1 for international students. Application fee: $50. *Expenses:* Tuition, state resident: full-time $16,402; part-time $665 per credit. Tuition, nonresident: full-time $28,694; part-time $1175 per credit. Required fees: $690; $175 per term. Tuition and fees vary according to program. *Financial support:* In 2009–10, 22 students received support, including 2 fellowships (averaging $20,000 per year); scholarships/grants, tuition waivers (full and partial), and unspecified assistantships also available. Financial award application deadline: 2/1. *Faculty research:* Disaster response management, government regulation of health and safety risks, comparative regional governance, non-profit management, environmental policy, housing policy, strategic management. Total annual research expenditures: $357,117. *Unit head:* Dr. David Y. Miller, Director, 412-648-7606, Fax: 412-648-2605, E-mail: dymiller@pitt.edu. *Application contact:* Elizabeth A. Hruby, Graduate Enrollment Counselor, 412-648-7640, Fax: 412-648-7641, E-mail: eah44@pitt.edu.

University of Pittsburgh, Graduate School of Public and International Affairs, Doctoral Program in Public and International Affairs, Pittsburgh, PA 15260. Offers development policy (PhD); foreign and security policy (PhD); international political economy (PhD); public administration (PhD); public policy (PhD). *Accreditation:* NASPAA. Part-time programs available. *Faculty:* 28 full-time (8 women), 56 part-time/adjunct (20 women). *Students:* 11 full-time (4 women), 27 part-time (16 women); includes 4 minority (2 African Americans, 1 Asian American or Pacific Islander, 1 Hispanic American), 7 international. Average age 30. 63 applicants, 14% accepted, 5 enrolled. In 2009, 9 doctorates awarded. *Degree requirements:* For doctorate, comprehensive exam, thesis/dissertation. *Entrance requirements:* For doctorate, GRE, 3 letters of recommendation, resume, minimum GPA of 3.0, writing sample. Additional exam requirements/recommendations for international students: Required—TOEFL (minimum score 600 paper-based; 250 computer-based; 100 iBT), TWE (minimum score 4); Recommended—IELTS (minimum score 7). *Application deadline:* For fall admission, 2/1 for domestic students, 1/15 for international students. Application fee: $50. Electronic applications accepted. *Expenses:* Tuition, state resident: full-time $16,402; part-time $665 per credit. Tuition, nonresident: full-time $28,694; part-time $1175 per credit. Required fees: $690; $175 per term. Tuition and fees vary according to program. *Financial support:* In 2009–10, 17 students received support, including 6 fellowships (averaging $34,925 per year); scholarships/grants, tuition waivers (full and partial), and unspecified assistantships also available. Financial award application deadline: 2/1. *Faculty research:* International political economy, international development, public administration, public policy, foreign policy, international security policy. Total annual research expenditures: $357,117. *Unit head:* Dr. Kevin P. Kearns, Program Coordinator, 412-648-7621, Fax: 412-648-2605, E-mail: kkearns@pitt.edu. *Application contact:* Julie Korade, Program Administrator/Graduate Enrollment Counselor, 412-648-7640, Fax: 412-648-7641, E-mail: korade@pitt.edu.

University of Pittsburgh, Graduate School of Public and International Affairs, Public Policy and Management Program for Mid-Career Professionals, Pittsburgh, PA 15260. Offers development planning (MPPM); international development (MPPM); international political economy (MPPM); international security studies (MPPM); management of non profit organizations (MPPM); metropolitan management and regional development (MPPM); policy analysis and evaluation (MPPM). Part-time programs available. *Faculty:* 28 full-time (8 women), 56 part-time/adjunct (20 women). *Students:* 3 full-time (0 women), 39 part-time (21 women); includes 2 minority (both African Americans), 1 international. Average age 38. 48 applicants, 75% accepted, 19 enrolled. In 2009, 17 master's awarded. *Degree requirements:* For master's, thesis optional, capstone seminar. *Entrance requirements:* For master's, 2 letters of recommendation, resume, 5 years of supervisory or budgetary experience. Additional exam requirements/recommendations for international students: Required—TOEFL (minimum score 600 paper-based; 250 computer-based; 100 iBT), TWE (minimum score 4); Recommended—IELTS (minimum score 7). *Application deadline:* For fall admission, 6/1 priority date for domestic students, 2/15 for international students; for spring admission, 1/1 priority date for domestic students, 8/1 for international students. Applications are processed on a rolling basis. Application fee: $50. Electronic applications accepted. *Expenses:* Tuition, state resident: full-time $16,402; part-time $665 per credit. Tuition, nonresident: full-time $28,694; part-time $1175 per credit. Required fees: $690; $175 per term. Tuition and fees vary according to program. *Financial support:* In 2009–10, 10 students received support. Institutionally sponsored loans, scholarships/grants, and tuition waivers (partial) available. Support available to part-time students. Financial award application deadline: 2/1. *Faculty research:* Nonprofit management, urban and regional affairs, policy analysis and evaluation, security and intelligence studies, global political economy, nongovernmental organizations, civil society, development planning and environmental sustainability, human security. Total annual research expenditures: $357,117. *Unit head:* Dr. George Dougherty, Director, Executive Education, 412-648-7603, Fax: 412-648-2605, E-mail: gwdjr@pitt.edu. *Application contact:* Michael T. Rizzi, Associate Director of Student Services, 412-648-7640, Fax: 412-648-7641, E-mail: rizzim@pitt.edu.

University of Regina, Faculty of Graduate Studies and Research, Johnson-Shoyama Graduate School of Public Policy, Regina, SK S4S 0A2, Canada. Offers economic analysis for public policy (Master's Certificate); non-profit management (Master's Certificate); public management (MPA, Master's Certificate); public policy (MPA, PhD, Master's Certificate). Part-time and evening/weekend programs available. *Faculty:* 6 full-time (3 women). *Students:* 51 full-time (24 women), 71 part-time (39 women). 113 applicants, 89% accepted. In 2009, 51 master's awarded. *Entrance requirements:* Additional exam requirements/recommendations for international students: Required—TOEFL (minimum score 580 paper-based; 237 computer-based; 80 iBT). *Application deadline:* Applications are processed on a rolling basis. Application fee: $90 ($100 for international students). Electronic applications accepted. *Expenses:* Contact institution. *Financial support:* In 2009–10, 7 fellowships (averaging $19,000 per year), 2 research assistantships (averaging $16,910 per year), 11 teaching assistantships (averaging $6,650 per year) were awarded. Financial award application deadline: 6/15. *Faculty research:* Public administration and policy. *Unit head:* Dr. Sylvain Charlebois, Associate Dean, 306-585-2695, E-mail: sylvain.charlebois@uregina.ca. *Application contact:* Elaine Groenendyk, Information Contact, 306-585-5462, E-mail: elaine.groenendyk@uregina.ca.

University of Rhode Island, Graduate School, College of Arts and Sciences, Department of Political Science, Kingston, RI 02881. Offers political science (MA), including American politics, comparative government, international relations, public policy; public policy and administration (MPA); MLIS/MPA. Part-time programs available. *Faculty:* 10 full-time (4 women), 1 part-time/adjunct (0 women). *Students:* 17 full-time (11 women), 44 part-time (28 women); includes 9 minority (4 African Americans, 1 Asian American or Pacific Islander, 4 Hispanic Americans). In 2009, 29 master's awarded. *Degree requirements:* For master's, comprehensive exam (for some programs), thesis optional. *Entrance requirements:* For master's, GRE, GMAT or MAT, 2 letters of recommendation. Additional exam requirements/recommendations for international students: Required—TOEFL (minimum score 550 paper-based; 213 computer-based). *Application deadline:* For fall admission, 2/1 for international students; for spring admission, 7/15 for international students. Application fee: $65. Electronic applications accepted. *Expenses:* Tuition, state resident: full-time $8828; part-time $490 per credit hour. Tuition, nonresident: full-time $22,100; part-time $1228 per credit hour. Required fees: $1118; $57 per semester. Tuition and fees vary according to program. *Financial support:* In 2009–10, 4 teaching assistantships with full tuition reimbursements (averaging $13,894 per year) were awarded. Financial award applicants required to submit FAFSA. *Unit head:* Dr. Gerry Tyler, Chairperson, 401-874-4053, Fax: 401-874-4072, E-mail: gtyler@uri.edu. *Application contact:* Dr. Gerry Tyler, Chairperson, 401-874-4053, Fax: 401-874-4072, E-mail: gtyler@uri.edu.

University of Saskatchewan, College of Graduate Studies and Research, School of Public Policy, Saskatoon, SK S7N 5A2, Canada. Offers MIT, MPA, MPP, PhD. Tuition and fees charges are reported in Canadian dollars. *Expenses:* Tuition, area resident: Full-time $3000 Canadian dollars; part-time $500 Canadian dollars per term. Required fees: $700 Canadian dollars; $100 Canadian dollars per term.

University of Southern California, Graduate School, School of Policy, Planning, and Development, Public Policy Programs, Los Angeles, CA 90089. Offers MPP, Graduate Certificate, M Pl/MPP, MPP/JD. Part-time programs available. *Faculty:* 51 full-time (12 women), 74 part-time/adjunct (26 women). *Students:* 99 full-time (55 women), 3 part-time (1 woman); includes 50 minority (8 African Americans, 20 Asian Americans or Pacific Islanders, 22 Hispanic Americans), 9 international. 248 applicants, 70% accepted, 57 enrolled. In 2009, 32 master's, 1 other advanced degree awarded. *Degree requirements:* For master's, thesis. *Entrance requirements:* For master's, GRE. Additional exam requirements/recommendations for international students: Required—TOEFL (minimum score 600 paper-based; 250 computer-based; 100 iBT). *Application deadline:* For fall admission, 12/15 priority date for domestic and international students; for spring admission, 11/1 for domestic and international students. Applications are processed on a rolling basis. Application fee: $85. Electronic applications accepted. *Expenses:* Tuition: Full-time $25,980; part-time $1315 per unit. Required fees: $554. One-time fee: $35 full-time. Full-time tuition and fees vary according to degree level and program. *Financial support:* In 2009–10, 56 students received support, including 2 research assistantships with tuition reimbursements available (averaging $16,742 per year); scholarships/grants and tuition waivers (full and partial) also available. Financial award application deadline: 12/15. *Faculty research:* Urban political economy, community and economic development, environmental policy, transportation policy, housing policy. Total annual research expenditures: $5 million. *Unit head:* Dr. Juliet Musso, Director of Master of Public Policy, 213-740-0636, Fax: 213-740-7573, E-mail: musso@usc.edu. *Application contact:* Marisol R. Gonzalez, Director, Recruitment and Admission, 213-740-0550, Fax: 213-740-7573, E-mail: marisolr@usc.edu.

University of Southern Maine, Edmund S. Muskie School of Public Service, Doctoral Program in Public Policy, Portland, ME 04104-9300. Offers PhD. Applicants accepted in odd numbered years only. Part-time and evening/weekend programs available. *Degree requirements:* For doctorate, comprehensive exam, thesis/dissertation. *Entrance requirements:* For doctorate, GRE. Additional exam requirements/recommendations for international students: Required—TOEFL. Electronic applications accepted. *Faculty research:* Health policy, community planning and development, education policy, environmental policy.

University of Southern Maine, Edmund S. Muskie School of Public Service, Program in Public Policy and Management, Portland, ME 04104-9300. Offers child and family policy (Certificate); non-profit management (Certificate); public policy and management (MPPM); JD/MPPM. *Accreditation:* NASPAA. Part-time and evening/weekend programs available. Postbaccalaureate distance learning degree programs offered (minimal on-campus study). *Degree requirements:* For master's, thesis, capstone project, field experience. *Entrance requirements:* For master's, GRE General Test or LSAT. Additional exam requirements/recommendations for international students: Required—TOEFL. Electronic applications accepted. *Faculty research:* Sustainable communities, juvenile justice, program management, nonprofit management.

The University of Texas at Austin, Graduate School, Lyndon B. Johnson School of Public Affairs, Austin, TX 78712-1111. Offers global policy studies (MGPS); public affairs (MP Aff); public policy (PhD); JD/MP Aff; MBA/MP Aff; MP Aff/MA; MP Aff/MSE. *Accreditation:* NASPAA (one or more programs are accredited). Part-time programs available. *Degree requirements:* For master's, thesis, summer internship; for doctorate, thesis/dissertation. *Entrance requirements:* For master's, GRE General Test; for doctorate, GRE General Test, master's degree in policy-related field. Additional exam requirements/recommendations for international students: Required—TOEFL. Electronic applications accepted. *Faculty research:* Human resource development, health and social policy, philanthropy and community service, ethical leadership, urban and international policy, science and technology policy.

The University of Texas at Brownsville, Graduate Studies, College of Liberal Arts, Program in Public Policy and Management, Brownsville, TX 78520-4991. Offers MPPM. *Degree requirements:* For master's, thesis. *Entrance requirements:* For master's, GRE, 2 letters of recommendation.

The University of Texas at Dallas, School of Economic, Political and Policy Sciences, Program in Public Policy and Political Economy, Richardson, TX 75080. Offers international political economy (MS); public policy (MPP); public policy and political economy (PhD). Part-time and evening/weekend programs available. *Faculty:* 16 full-time (4 women). *Students:* 49 full-time (25 women), 45 part-time (19 women); includes 28 minority (12 African Americans, 10 Asian Americans or Pacific Islanders, 6 Hispanic Americans), 19 international. Average age 36. 59 applicants, 68% accepted, 31 enrolled. In 2009, 5 master's, 8 doctorates awarded. *Degree requirements:* For doctorate, thesis/dissertation. *Entrance requirements:* For master's and doctorate, GRE General Test, minimum GPA of 3.0 in upper-level course work in field. Additional exam requirements/recommendations for international students: Required—TOEFL (minimum score 550 paper-based; 213 computer-based). *Application deadline:* For fall admission, 7/15 for domestic students, 5/1 priority date for international students; for spring admission, 11/15 for domestic students, 9/1 priority date for international students. Applications are processed on a rolling basis. Application fee: $50 ($100 for international students). Electronic applications accepted. *Expenses:* Tuition, state resident: full-time $11,068; part-time $461 per credit hour. Tuition, nonresident: full-time $21,178; part-time $882 per credit hour. Tuition and fees vary according to course load. *Financial support:* In 2009–10, 5 research assistantships with full tuition reimbursements (averaging $12,690 per year), 11 teaching assistantships with full tuition reimbursements (averaging $11,905 per year) were awarded; fellowships, career-related internships or fieldwork, Federal Work-Study, institutionally sponsored loans, and scholarships/grants also available. Support available to part-time students. Financial award application deadline: 4/30; financial award applicants required to submit FAFSA. *Faculty research:* New leadership development, gender and leadership, globalization and leadership opportunities in democracy. *Unit head:* Dr. Sheila Amin Gutierrez de Pineres, Program Head, 972-883-6228, Fax: 972-883-2735, E-mail: pineres@utdallas.edu. *Application contact:* Dr. Marie I. Chevrier, Associate Program Head, 972-883-2727, Fax: 972-883-2735, E-mail: chevrier@utdallas.edu.

See Close-Up on page 759.

The University of Texas at Dallas, School of Management, Programs in Management Science, Richardson, TX 75080. Offers accounting (PhD); decision sciences (PhD); finance (PhD); management strategy and public policy (PhD); marketing (PhD); organizational behavior (PhD). *Accreditation:* AACSB. Part-time and evening/weekend programs available. *Faculty:* 12 full-time (3 women). *Students:* 72 full-time (23 women), 12 part-time (6 women); includes 10 minority (all Asian Americans or Pacific Islanders), 63 international. Average age 34. 173 applicants, 12% accepted, 7 enrolled. In 2009, 8 doctorates awarded. *Degree requirements:* For doctorate, thesis/dissertation. *Entrance requirements:* For doctorate, GMAT, minimum GPA of 3.0. Additional exam requirements/recommendations for international students: Required—TOEFL (minimum score 550 paper-based; 213 computer-based). *Application deadline:* For fall admission, 7/15 for domestic students, 5/1 priority date for international students; for spring admission, 11/15 for domestic students, 9/1 priority date for international students. Applications are processed on a rolling basis. Application fee: $50 ($100 for international students). Electronic applications accepted. *Expenses:* Tuition, state resident: full-time $11,068; part-time $461 per credit hour. Tuition, nonresident: full-time $21,178; part-time $882 per credit hour. Tuition and fees vary according to course load. *Financial support:* In 2009–10, 1 research assistantship with full tuition reimbursement (averaging $13,050 per year), 43 teaching assistantships with full tuition reimbursements (averaging $14,795 per year) were awarded; fellowships, career-related internships or fieldwork, Federal Work-Study, institutionally sponsored loans, scholarships/grants, and unspecified assistantships also available. Support available to part-time students. Financial award application deadline: 4/30; financial award applicants required to submit FAFSA. *Faculty research:* Empirical generalizations in marketing, diffusion of generations of technology, stochastic brand-choice theory, acceptance of trade deals by supermarkets, nonparametric estimations of market share response. *Unit head:* Dr.

Public Policy

The University of Texas at Dallas (continued)
Sumit Sarkar, Program Director, 972-883-2745, Fax: 972-883-5977, E-mail: som-phd.@utdallas.edu. *Application contact:* James Parker, Assistant Director, 972-883-5842, E-mail: jparker@utdallas.edu.

The University of Texas at El Paso, Graduate School, Institute for Policy and Economic Development, El Paso, TX 79968-0001. Offers border administration (Certificate); homeland security (Certificate); intelligence and national security (MS, Certificate); leadership studies (MA); public administration (MPA). *Accreditation:* NASPAA. Part-time and evening/weekend programs available. *Students:* 187 (57 women); includes 124 minority (19 African Americans, 1 American Indian/Alaska Native, 5 Asian Americans or Pacific Islanders, 99 Hispanic Americans), 5 international. 142 applicants, 77% accepted. In 2009, 76 master's awarded. *Degree requirements:* For master's, thesis optional. *Entrance requirements:* For master's, GRE, Statement of Purpose, Letters of Recommendation. Additional exam requirements/recommendations for international students: Required—TOEFL; Recommended—IELTS. *Application deadline:* For fall admission, 8/1 for domestic students, 3/1 for international students; for spring admission, 10/1 for domestic students, 9/1 for international students. Applications are processed on a rolling basis. Application fee: $45 ($80 for international students). Electronic applications accepted. *Financial support:* Fellowships with partial tuition reimbursements, research assistantships with partial tuition reimbursements, teaching assistantships with partial tuition reimbursements, institutionally sponsored loans, scholarships/grants, health care benefits, tuition waivers (partial), and unspecified assistantships available. Support available to part-time students. Financial award application deadline: 3/15; financial award applicants required to submit FAFSA. *Unit head:* Dr. Dennis Soden, Director, 915-747-7974, Fax: 915-747-7948, E-mail: desoden@utep.edu. *Application contact:* Dr. Patricia D. Witherspoon, Dean of the Graduate School, 915-747-5491, Fax: 915-747-5788, E-mail: withersp@utep.edu.

University of the Pacific, McGeorge School of Law, Sacramento, CA 95817. Offers advocacy (JD); criminal justice (JD); experiential law teaching (LL M); intellectual property (JD); international legal studies (JD); international water resources law (LL M, JSD); law (JD); public law and policy (JD); public policy and law (LL M); tax (JD); transnational business practice (LL M); JD/MBA; JD/MPPA. *Accreditation:* ABA. Part-time and evening/weekend programs available. *Faculty:* 55 full-time (24 women), 57 part-time/adjunct (18 women). *Students:* 697 full-time (343 women), 377 part-time (197 women); includes 301 minority (33 African Americans, 11 American Indian/Alaska Native, 163 Asian Americans or Pacific Islanders, 94 Hispanic Americans). Average age 24. 2,659 applicants, 43% accepted, 236 enrolled. In 2009, 254 first professional degrees, 51 master's awarded. *Degree requirements:* For master's, thesis (for some programs); for doctorate, thesis/dissertation. *Entrance requirements:* For JD, LSAT; for master's, JD; for doctorate, LL M. Additional exam requirements/recommendations for international students: Required—TOEFL (minimum score 600 paper-based; 250 computer-based; 100 iBT). *Application deadline:* For fall admission, 3/15 priority date for domestic students. Applications are processed on a rolling basis. Application fee: $50. Electronic applications accepted. *Expenses:* Contact institution. *Financial support:* In 2009–10, 887 students received support, including 1 fellowship, 114 research assistantships (averaging $1,839 per year), 12 teaching assistantships (averaging $953 per year); career-related internships or fieldwork, Federal Work-Study, institutionally sponsored loans, and scholarships/grants also available. Support available to part-time students. Financial award applicants required to submit FAFSA. *Faculty research:* International legal studies, public policy and law, advocacy, intellectual property law, taxation, criminal law. *Unit head:* Elizabeth Rindskopf Parker, Dean, 916-739-7151, E-mail: elizabeth@pacific.edu. *Application contact:* 916-739-7105, Fax: 916-739-7301, E-mail: mcgeorge@pacific.edu.

University of Tulsa, College of Law, Tulsa, OK 74104. Offers American Indian and indigenous law (LL M); American law for foreign lawyers (LL M); comparative and international law (Certificate); entrepreneurial law (Certificate); health law (Certificate); law (JD); Native American law (Certificate); public policy (Certificate); resources, energy, and environmental law (Certificate); JD/M Tax; JD/MA; JD/MBA; JD/MS; JD/MSF. *Accreditation:* ABA. Part-time programs available. *Faculty:* 29 full-time (14 women), 24 part-time/adjunct (8 women). *Students:* 382 full-time (148 women), 40 part-time (16 women); includes 68 minority (4 African Americans, 40 American Indian/Alaska Native, 12 Asian Americans or Pacific Islanders, 12 Hispanic Americans), 1 international. Average age 28. 1,304 applicants, 51% accepted, 140 enrolled. In 2009, 149 first professional degrees, 1 master's awarded. *Entrance requirements:* For JD, LSAT, BS or BA from accredited college/university; for master's, JD or equivalent from non-US university. Additional exam requirements/recommendations for international students: Required—TOEFL (minimum score 570 paper-based; 230 computer-based; 90 iBT), IELTS (minimum score 7). *Application deadline:* For fall admission, 2/1 priority date for domestic and international students. Applications are processed on a rolling basis. Application fee: $30. Electronic applications accepted. *Expenses:* Contact institution. *Financial support:* In 2009–10, 176 students received support. Career-related internships or fieldwork, Federal Work-Study, and scholarships/grants available. Support available to part-time students. Financial award applicants required to submit FAFSA. *Faculty research:* International law, Native American law, criminal law, commercial speech, copyright law. *Unit head:* Janet Levit, Dean, 918-631-2400, Fax: 918-631-3126, E-mail: janet-levit@utulsa.edu. *Application contact:* April M. Fox, Assistant Dean of Admissions and Financial Aid, 918-631-2406, Fax: 918-631-3630, E-mail: april-fox@utulsa.edu.

University of Virginia, Frank Batten Sr. School of Leadership and Public Policy, Program in Public Policy, Charlottesville, VA 22903. Offers MPP. *Students:* 29 full-time (20 women), 1 part-time (0 women); includes 5 minority (2 African Americans, 2 Asian Americans or Pacific Islanders, 1 Hispanic American), 1 international. Average age 22. In 2009, 24 master's awarded. *Application deadline:* For fall admission, 2/20 for domestic and international students. Application fee: $60. *Unit head:* Dr. Harry Harding, Dean, 434-924-0812, Fax: 434-243-2318. *Application contact:* Edith Simms, Director of Admissions and Student Affairs, 434-243-4383, Fax: 434-243-2318, E-mail: els8a@virginia.edu.

University of Washington, Graduate School, Daniel J. Evans School of Public Affairs, Seattle, WA 98195. Offers public administration (MPA); public policy and management (PhD); JD/MPA; MPA/MAIS; MPA/MPH; MPA/MS; MPA/MUP. *Accreditation:* NASPAA. Part-time and evening/weekend programs available. *Degree requirements:* For master's, thesis, internship or cooperative experience. *Entrance requirements:* For master's and doctorate, GRE General Test, minimum GPA of 3.0. Additional exam requirements/recommendations for international students: Required—TOEFL (minimum score 580 paper-based; 237 computer-based; 92 iBT). Electronic applications accepted. *Faculty research:* Environmental policy, education and social policy, nonprofit management, international affairs, urban and regional development.

University of Washington, Bothell, Program in Policy Studies, Bothell, WA 98011-8246. Offers MA. Evening/weekend programs available. *Faculty:* 9 full-time (4 women), 2 part-time/adjunct (both women). *Students:* 38 full-time (24 women), 11 part-time (6 women); includes 12 minority (4 African Americans, 7 Asian Americans or Pacific Islanders, 1 Hispanic American), 2 international. Average age 32. 38 applicants, 74% accepted, 20 enrolled. In 2009, 15 master's awarded. *Degree requirements:* For master's, thesis. *Entrance requirements:* For master's, GRE, 100-level statistics and micro-economics courses. Additional exam requirements/recommendations for international students: Required—TOEFL. *Application deadline:* For fall admission, 3/1 for domestic and international students. Application fee: $65. Electronic applications accepted. *Expenses:* Tuition, state resident: full-time $10,160; part-time $484 per credit hour. Tuition, nonresident: full-time $23,500; part-time $1120 per credit hour. Required fees: $567; $21.50 per credit hour. Tuition and fees vary according to course load and program. *Financial support:* In 2009–10, 9 students received support, including 5 fellowships (averaging $1,000 per year), 1 research assistantship (averaging $1,000 per year); Federal Work-Study and unspecified assistantships also available. Financial award applicants required to submit FAFSA. *Faculty research:* Policy studies, cultural studies, cultural and environmental politics, disability studies, public policy. *Unit head:* Prof. Bruce Burgett, Director, 425-352-5452, Fax: 425-352-3462, E-mail: bburgett@uwb.edu. *Application contact:* Andrew Brusletten, Program Manager, 425-352-5427, Fax: 425-352-3462, E-mail: abrusletten@uwb.edu.

Vanderbilt University, Graduate School, Program in Community Research and Action, Nashville, TN 37240-1001. Offers MS, PhD. *Faculty:* 33 full-time (14 women). *Students:* 23 full-time (11 women); includes 4 minority (all African Americans), 3 international. Average age 31. 67 applicants, 13% accepted, 4 enrolled. In 2009, 4 master's, 4 doctorates awarded. *Degree requirements:* For master's, thesis; for doctorate, thesis/dissertation, internship, fundable grant proposal. *Entrance requirements:* For doctorate, GRE General Test. Additional exam requirements/recommendations for international students: Required—TOEFL (minimum score 570 paper-based; 230 computer-based; 88 iBT). *Application deadline:* For fall admission, 12/31 for domestic and international students. Application fee: $0. Electronic applications accepted. *Financial support:* Fellowships with tuition reimbursements, research assistantships with full tuition reimbursements, teaching assistantships with full tuition reimbursements, Federal Work-Study, institutionally sponsored loans, scholarships/grants, traineeships, and health care benefits available. Financial award application deadline: 1/15; financial award applicants required to submit CSS PROFILE or FAFSA. *Faculty research:* Applied psychological research, community theory, mental health, public policy, race dynamics. *Unit head:* Joseph Cunningham, Chair, 615-322-6881, Fax: 615-343-2661, E-mail: joe.cunningham@vanderbilt.edu. *Application contact:* Paul Dokecki, Director of Graduate Studies, 615-322-6881, E-mail: paul.r.dokecki@vanderbilt.edu.

Virginia Commonwealth University, Graduate School, College of Humanities and Sciences, Wilder School of Government and Public Affairs, Center for Public Policy, Richmond, VA 23284-9005. Offers public policy and administration (PhD). *Degree requirements:* For doctorate, thesis/dissertation. *Entrance requirements:* For doctorate, GMAT, GRE General Test, LSAT, or MAT.

Virginia Polytechnic Institute and State University, Graduate School, College of Architecture and Urban Studies, Center for Public Administration and Policy, Blacksburg, VA 24061. Offers MPA, PhD. *Accreditation:* NASPAA (one or more programs are accredited). *Students:* 54 full-time (22 women), 93 part-time (33 women); includes 39 minority (1 African American, 11 American Indian/Alaska Native, 25 Asian Americans or Pacific Islanders, 2 Hispanic Americans), 3 international. Average age 36. 75 applicants, 77% accepted, 28 enrolled. In 2009, 26 master's, 12 doctorates awarded. *Entrance requirements:* For master's and doctorate, GRE, GMAT. Additional exam requirements/recommendations for international students: Required—TOEFL (minimum score 550 paper-based; 213 computer-based). *Application deadline:* For fall admission, 5/15 for international students; for spring admission, 10/15 for international students. Applications are processed on a rolling basis. Application fee: $65. Electronic applications accepted. *Expenses:* Tuition, area resident: Full-time $10,228; part-time $459 per credit hour. Tuition, nonresident: full-time $17,892; part-time $865 per credit hour. Required fees: $1966; $451 per semester. *Financial support:* Career-related internships or fieldwork, Federal Work-Study, scholarships/grants, and unspecified assistantships available. Financial award application deadline: 1/15. *Faculty research:* Public administration theory, strategic management, ethics, the Constitution, computer-assisted creativity. *Unit head:* Dr. Laura S. Jensen, Dean, 540-231-5197, Fax: 540-231-7067, E-mail: jensen7@vt.edu. *Application contact:* Anne Khademian, Information Contact, 703-706-8119, Fax: 540-231-7067, E-mail: akhademi@vt.edu.

Virginia Polytechnic Institute and State University, Graduate School, College of Science, Program in Biomedical Technology Development and Management, Blacksburg, VA 24061. Offers MS.

Walden University, Graduate Programs, School of Counseling and Social Service, Minneapolis, MN 55401. Offers counselor education and supervision (PhD), including consultation, counseling and social change, forensic mental health counseling, general program, nonprofit management and leadership, trauma and crisis; human services (PhD), including clinical social work, counseling, criminal justice, family studies and intervention strategies, general program, human services administration, self-designed, social policy analysis and planning; marriage, couple, and family counseling (MS), including forensic counseling, trauma and crisis counseling; mental health counseling (MS), including forensic counseling. Part-time and evening/weekend programs available. Postbaccalaureate distance learning degree programs offered (minimal on-campus study). *Faculty:* 13 full-time, 78 part-time/adjunct. *Students:* 1,932 full-time (1,624 women), 210 part-time (181 women); includes 945 minority (817 African Americans, 24 American Indian/Alaska Native, 24 Asian Americans or Pacific Islanders, 80 Hispanic Americans), 34 international. Average age 39. In 2009, 55 master's, 5 doctorates awarded. *Degree requirements:* For master's, residency (for some programs); for doctorate, thesis/dissertation, residency. *Entrance requirements:* For master's, bachelor's degree or equivalent in related field, minimum GPA of 2.5; for doctorate, master's degree or equivalent in related field; minimum GPA of 3.0; official transcripts; three years' related professional/academic experience (preferred); access to computer and Internet. Additional exam requirements/recommendations for international students: Required—TOEFL (minimum score 550 paper-based; 213 computer-based), IELTS (minimum score 6.5), or Michigan English Language Assessment Battery (minimum score 82). *Application deadline:* Applications are processed on a rolling basis. Application fee: $50. Electronic applications accepted. *Expenses:* Tuition: Full-time $13,665; part-time $560 per credit. Required fees: $1375. Tuition and fees vary according to course load, degree level and program. *Financial support:* In 2009–10, 200 students received support; fellowships, Federal Work-Study, scholarships/grants, unspecified assistantships, and family tuition reduction, active duty/veteran tuition reduction, group tuition reduction, interest-free payment plans available. Support available to part-time students. Financial award applicants required to submit FAFSA. *Unit head:* Dr. Savitri Dixon-Saxon, Associate Dean, 800-925-3368. *Application contact:* Jennifer Hall, Director of Enrollment, 866-4-WALDEN, E-mail: info@waldenu.edu.

Walden University, Graduate Programs, School of Public Policy and Administration, Minneapolis, MN 55401. Offers general program (MPA); government management (Postbaccalaureate Certificate); health policy (MPA); homeland security policy (MPA); interdisciplinary policy studies (MPA); law and public policy (MPA); local government management for sustainable communities (MPA); nonprofit management (Postbaccalaureate Certificate); nonprofit management and leadership (MPA, MS); policy analysis (MPA); public management and leadership (MPA); public policy and administration (PhD), including criminal justice, health services, homeland security policy and coordination, international nongovernmental organizations, law and public policy, local government management for sustainable communities, nonprofit management and leadership, public management and leadership, public policy, public safety management, terrorism, mediation, and peace; terrorism, mediation, and peace (MPA). Part-time and evening/weekend programs available. Postbaccalaureate distance learning degree programs offered (minimal on-campus study). *Faculty:* 7 full-time, 62 part-time/adjunct. *Students:* 1,468 full-time (941 women), 233 part-time (162 women); includes 852 minority (761 African Americans, 9 American Indian/Alaska Native, 19 Asian Americans or Pacific Islanders, 63 Hispanic Americans), 53 international. Average age 40. In 2009, 173 master's, 13 doctorates awarded. *Degree requirements:* For doctorate, thesis/dissertation, residency. *Entrance requirements:* For master's, bachelor's degree or equivalent in related field, minimum GPA of 2.5; for doctorate, master's degree or equivalent in related field; minimum GPA of 3.0; official transcripts; three years of related professional/academic experience (preferred); access to computer and Internet. Additional exam requirements/recommendations for international students: Required—TOEFL (minimum score 550 paper-based; 213 computer-based), IELTS (minimum score 6.5), or Michigan English Language Assessment Battery (minimum score 82). *Application deadline:* Applications are processed on a rolling basis. Application fee: $50. Electronic applications accepted. *Expenses:* Tuition: Full-time $13,665; part-time $560 per credit. Required fees: $1375. Tuition and fees vary according to course load, degree level and program. *Financial support:* In 2009–10, 207 students received support; fellowships with tuition reimbursements available, Federal Work-Study, scholarships/grants, unspecified assistantships, and family tuition reduction, active duty/veteran tuition reduction, group tuition reduction, interest-free payment plans available. Support available to part-time students. Financial award applicants required to submit FAFSA. *Unit head:* Dr. Mark Gordon, Associate Dean, 800-925-3368. *Application contact:* Jennifer Hall, Director of Enrollment, 866-4-WALDEN, E-mail: info@waldenu.edu.

Washington State University, Graduate School, College of Liberal Arts, Department of Sociology, Pullman, WA 99164. Offers crime and deviance (MA, PhD); environments, community and demographics (MA, PhD); institutions and social organizations (MA, PhD); political sociology (MA, PhD); social inequality (MA, PhD); social psychology and life course (MA, PhD). Terminal master's awarded for partial completion of doctoral program. *Degree requirements:* For master's, thesis; for doctorate, comprehensive exam, thesis/dissertation. *Entrance requirements:* For master's, GRE General Test, minimum GPA of 3.0; for doctorate, GRE General Test, MA in sociology, minimum GPA of 3.0. Additional exam requirements/recommendations for international students: Required—TOEFL (minimum score 550 paper-based). Electronic applications accepted. *Faculty research:* Crime/deviance, environmental sociology, social inequality, social psychology, gender.

Washington University in St. Louis, Graduate School of Arts and Sciences, Department of Political Science, Program in Political Economy and Public Policy, St. Louis, MO 63130-4899. Offers MA. *Degree requirements:* For master's, thesis or alternative. *Entrance requirements:* For master's, GRE General Test. Electronic applications accepted.

West Virginia University, Eberly College of Arts and Sciences, Department of Political Science, Morgantown, WV 26506. Offers American public policy and politics (MA); international and comparative public policy and politics (MA); political science (PhD); public policy analysis (PhD). Terminal master's awarded for partial completion of doctoral program. *Degree requirements:* For master's, thesis optional; for doctorate, comprehensive exam, thesis/dissertation. *Entrance requirements:* For master's, GRE General Test, minimum GPA of 2.75; for doctorate, GRE General Test, minimum GPA of 3.0. Additional exam requirements/recommendations for international students: Required—TOEFL. *Faculty research:* Public policy, research methods, foreign policy analysis, judicial politics, environmental and energy policy.

Wilfrid Laurier University, Faculty of Graduate Studies, Faculty of Arts and School of Business and Economics, International Public Policy Program, Waterloo, ON N2L 3C5, Canada. Offers MIPP. *Entrance requirements:* For master's, honours BA with minimum B average. Additional exam requirements/recommendations for international students: Required—TOEFL (minimum score 230 computer-based; 89 iBT). Electronic applications accepted. *Faculty research:* International environmental policy, international economic relations, human security, global governance.

William Paterson University of New Jersey, College of the Humanities and Social Sciences, Wayne, NJ 07470-8420. Offers clinical and counseling psychology (MA); English (MA); history (MA); public policy and international affairs (MA); sociology (MA). Part-time and evening/weekend programs available. *Students:* 39 full-time (22 women), 123 part-time (90 women); includes 42 minority (11 African Americans, 5 Asian Americans or Pacific Islanders, 26 Hispanic Americans), 2 international. *Application deadline:* Applications are processed on a rolling basis. Application fee: $50. Electronic applications accepted. *Financial support:* In 2009–10, 13 students received support; research assistantships with full tuition reimbursements available, teaching assistantships with full tuition reimbursements available, unspecified assistantships available. Support available to part-time students. Financial award application deadline: 4/1; financial award applicants required to submit FAFSA. *Unit head:* Dr. Kara Rabbitt, Dean, College of Humanities and Social Sciences, 973-720-2180, Fax: 973-720-2955, E-mail: rabbittk@wpunj.edu. *Application contact:* Tinu Adeniran, Assistant Director, Graduate Admissions, 973-720-2764, Fax: 973-720-2035, E-mail: adenirant@wpunj.edu.

York University, Faculty of Graduate Studies, Atkinson Faculty of Liberal and Professional Studies, Program in Public Policy, Administration and Law, Toronto, ON M3J 1P3, Canada. Offers MPPAL.

Rural Planning and Studies

Brandon University, Department of Rural Development, Brandon, MB R7A 6A9, Canada. Offers MRD, Diploma. *Degree requirements:* For master's, thesis. *Entrance requirements:* For master's, minimum GPA of 3.0, 2 letters of reference. Additional exam requirements/recommendations for international students: Required—TOEFL (minimum score 580 paper-based). Electronic applications accepted. *Faculty research:* Regional development, healthy communities, economic impact analysis, rural tourism, resource management.

California State University, Chico, Graduate School, College of Behavioral and Social Sciences, Department of Geography and Planning, Program in Rural and Town Planning, Chico, CA 95929-0722. Offers MA. Part-time programs available. *Students:* 3 full-time (all women), 1 part-time (0 women). Average age 35. 7 applicants, 43% accepted, 2 enrolled. *Entrance requirements:* For master's, GRE, 2 letters of recommendation. Additional exam requirements/recommendations for international students: Required—TOEFL (minimum score 550 paper-based; 213 computer-based; 80 iBT), IELTS (minimum score 6.5). *Application deadline:* For fall admission, 3/1 priority date for domestic students, 3/1 for international students; for spring admission, 9/15 priority date for domestic students, 9/15 for international students. Applications are processed on a rolling basis. Application fee: $55. Electronic applications accepted. *Unit head:* Dr. Dean Fairbanks, Graduate Coordinator, 530-898-5780. *Application contact:* Dr. Paul Melcon, Graduate Coordinator, 530-898-6871.

Concordia University, School of Graduate Studies, John Molson School of Business, Montréal, QC H3G 1M8, Canada. Offers administration (M Sc, Diploma); aviation management (Certificate, Diploma); business administration (MBA, UA Undergraduate Associate, PhD), including international aviation (UA Undergraduate Associate); chartered accountancy (Diploma); community organizational development (Certificate); event management and fundraising (Certificate); executive business administration (EMBA); investment management (Diploma); investment management option (MBA); management accounting (Certificate); management of healthcare organizations (Certificate); sport administration (Diploma). *Accreditation:* AACSB. Part-time and evening/weekend programs available. *Degree requirements:* For master's, one foreign language, thesis (for some programs), research project; for doctorate, one foreign language, thesis/dissertation; for other advanced degree, one foreign language. *Entrance requirements:* For master's and doctorate, GMAT. Additional exam requirements/recommendations for international students: Required—TOEFL. *Expenses:* Contact institution. *Faculty research:* General business, capital markets, international business.

Cornell University, Graduate School, Graduate Fields of Agriculture and Life Sciences, Field of International Agriculture and Rural Development, Ithaca, NY 14853-0001. Offers international agriculture and development (MPS). *Faculty:* 53 full-time (10 women). *Students:* 15 full-time (7 women); includes 5 minority (1 American Indian/Alaska Native, 2 Asian Americans or Pacific Islanders, 2 Hispanic Americans), 3 international. Average age 34. 23 applicants, 52% accepted, 6 enrolled. In 2009, 25 master's awarded. *Degree requirements:* For master's, project paper. *Entrance requirements:* For master's, GRE General Test (recommended), 2 years of development experience, 2 letters of recommendation. Additional exam requirements/recommendations for international students: Required—TOEFL (minimum score 550 paper-based; 213 computer-based; 77 iBT). *Application deadline:* For fall admission, 3/1 for domestic students. Application fee: $70. Electronic applications accepted. *Expenses:* Tuition: Full-time $29,500. Required fees: $70. Full-time tuition and fees vary according to degree level, program and student level. *Financial support:* In 2009–10, 4 students received support; fellowships with full tuition reimbursements available, research assistantships with full tuition reimbursements available, teaching assistantships with full tuition reimbursements available, institutionally sponsored loans, scholarships/grants, health care benefits, tuition waivers (full and partial), and unspecified assistantships available. Financial award applicants required to submit FAFSA. *Unit head:* Director of Graduate Studies, 607-255-3037, Fax: 607-255-1005. *Application contact:* Graduate Field Assistant, 607-255-3035, Fax: 607-255-1005, E-mail: mpsiard@cornell.edu.

Dalhousie University, Faculty of Architecture and Planning, School of Planning, Halifax, NS B3J 2X4, Canada. Offers M Eng, M Plan, MPS. *Degree requirements:* For master's, thesis. *Entrance requirements:* Additional exam requirements/recommendations for international students: Required—TOEFL, IELTS, CANTEST, CAEL, or Michigan English Language Assessment Battery. *Application deadline:* For fall admission, 6/1 priority date for domestic students, 4/1 for international students; for winter admission, 11/15 for domestic students, 8/31 for international students; for spring admission, 1/28 for domestic students, 12/31 for international students. Applications are processed on a rolling basis. Application fee: $70. Electronic applications accepted. *Financial support:* Career-related internships or fieldwork and scholarships/grants available. *Unit head:* Carol Madden, Director, 902-494-3260, Fax: 902-423-6672, E-mail: plan.office@dal.ca. *Application contact:* Frank Palermo, Graduate Coordinator, 902-494-3978, Fax: 902-423-6672, E-mail: frank.palermo@dal.ca.

Iowa State University of Science and Technology, Graduate College, College of Liberal Arts and Sciences, Department of History, Ames, IA 50011. Offers agricultural history and rural studies (PhD); history (MA); history of technology and science (MA, PhD). *Faculty:* 20 full-time (6 women). *Students:* 26 full-time (8 women), 10 part-time (5 women); includes 1 minority (Hispanic American), 2 international. 25 applicants, 84% accepted, 11 enrolled. In 2009, 6 master's, 4 doctorates awarded. *Degree requirements:* For master's, thesis or alternative; for doctorate, thesis/dissertation. *Entrance requirements:* For master's and doctorate, GRE General Test. Additional exam requirements/recommendations for international students: Required—TOEFL (minimum score 600 paper-based; 79 iBT) or IELTS (minimum score 7). *Application deadline:* For fall admission, 1/15 priority date for domestic and international students. Applications are processed on a rolling basis. Application fee: $40 ($90 for international students). Electronic applications accepted. *Expenses:* Tuition, state resident: full-time $6716. Tuition, nonresident: full-time $8908. Tuition and fees vary according to course level, course load, program and student level. *Financial support:* In 2009–10, 2 research assistantships with full and partial tuition reimbursements (averaging $13,770 per year), 19 teaching assistantships with full and partial tuition reimbursements (averaging $13,500 per year) were awarded; scholarships/grants, health care benefits, and unspecified assistantships also available. *Unit head:* Dr. Charles Dobbs, Chair, 515-294-7266, Fax: 515-294-6390, E-mail: cdobbs@iastate.edu. *Application contact:* Dr. Pamela Riney-Kehrberg, Information Contact, 515-294-1451, Fax: 515-294-6390.

Université Laval, Faculty of Agricultural and Food Sciences, Program in Integrated Rural Development, Québec, QC G1K 7P4, Canada. Offers Diploma. *Entrance requirements:* For degree, good knowledge of French. Electronic applications accepted.

University of Alaska Fairbanks, College of Rural and Community Development, Department of Alaska Native and Rural Development, Fairbanks, AK 99775. Offers rural development (MA). Part-time programs available. Postbaccalaureate distance learning degree programs offered. *Faculty:* 2 full-time (both women). *Students:* 9 full-time (8 women), 20 part-time (17 women); includes 12 minority (11 American Indian/Alaska Native, 1 Asian American or Pacific Islander). Average age 40. 16 applicants, 75% accepted, 10 enrolled. In 2009, 4 master's awarded. *Degree requirements:* For master's, comprehensive exam, thesis or alternative. *Entrance requirements:* Additional exam requirements/recommendations for international students: Required—TOEFL (minimum score 550 paper-based; 213 computer-based; 80 iBT). *Application deadline:* For fall admission, 6/1 for domestic students, 3/1 for international students; for spring admission, 10/15 for domestic students, 9/1 for international students. Applications are processed on a rolling basis. Application fee: $60. Electronic applications accepted. *Expenses:* Tuition, state resident: full-time $7584; part-time $316 per credit. Tuition, nonresident: full-time $15,504; part-time $646 per credit. Required fees: $23 per credit. $135 per semester. Tuition and fees vary according to course level, course load and reciprocity agreements. *Financial support:* Fellowships, Federal Work-Study, scholarships/grants, and health care benefits available. Support available to part-time students. Financial award application deadline: 2/15; financial award applicants required to submit FAFSA. *Faculty research:* International indigenous leadership development, interrelationships between rural communities and global economy. *Unit head:* Gordon Pullar, Director, 907-474-6528, Fax: 907-474-6325, E-mail: fydanrd@uaf.edu. *Application contact:* Gordon Pullar, Director, 907-474-6528, Fax: 907-474-6325, E-mail: fydanrd@uaf.edu.

University of Guelph, Graduate Program Services, Ontario Agricultural College, School of Environmental Design and Rural Development, Interdisciplinary Program in Rural Studies, Guelph, ON N1G 2W1, Canada. Offers PhD. Offered in cooperation with the Department of Food, Agricultural and Resource Economics, and the Department of Geography. Part-time programs available. *Degree requirements:* For doctorate, thesis/dissertation, qualifying exam. *Entrance requirements:* Additional exam requirements/recommendations for international students: Required—TOEFL (minimum score 600 paper-based; 218 computer-based), IELTS (minimum score 7). Electronic applications accepted. *Faculty research:* Sustainable rural communities, human resource development, rural planning and development.

University of Guelph, Graduate Program Services, Ontario Agricultural College, School of Environmental Design and Rural Development, Program in Capacity Development and Extension, Guelph, ON N1G 2W1, Canada. Offers M Sc. Part-time programs available. *Degree requirements:* For master's, thesis optional. *Entrance requirements:* For master's, minimum B-average in previous 2 years of course work. Additional exam requirements/recommendations for international students: Required—TOEFL (minimum score 550 paper-based; 213 computer-based; 89 iBT), IELTS (minimum score 6.5). Electronic applications accepted. *Faculty research:* Adult learning in non-formal settings, communication technology for remote areas, rural quality of life.

University of Guelph, Graduate Program Services, Ontario Agricultural College, School of Environmental Design and Rural Development, Program in Rural Planning and Development, Guelph, ON N1G 2W1, Canada. Offers international rural planning and development (M Sc); rural planning and development in Canada (M Sc). M Sc offered in cooperation with Departments of Food, Agricultural and Resource Economics; Geography; Land Resource Science; and others by arrangement. Part-time programs available. *Degree requirements:* For master's, thesis or alternative. *Entrance requirements:* For master's, minimum B- average during previous 2 years of course work. Additional exam requirements/recommendations for international students: Required—TOEFL (minimum score 550 paper-based; 213 computer-based), IELTS (minimum score 6.5). Electronic applications accepted. *Faculty research:* Canadian and international rural planning, resource and economic development, tourism.

The University of Montana, Graduate School, College of Arts and Sciences, Department of Geography, Missoula, MT 59812-0002. Offers geography (MA), including cartography and

Rural Planning and Studies

The University of Montana (continued)
GIS, community and environmental planning. *Entrance requirements:* For master's, GRE General Test. Additional exam requirements/recommendations for international students: Required—TOEFL.

University of West Georgia, Graduate School, College of Arts and Sciences, Department of Political Science and Planning, Carrollton, GA 30118. Offers public administration (MPA); public management (Certificate); rural and small town planning (MS). *Accreditation:* NASPAA (one or more programs are accredited). Part-time programs available. *Faculty:* 11 full-time (1 woman). *Students:* 17 full-time (10 women), 17 part-time (8 women); includes 11 minority (9 African Americans, 2 Asian Americans or Pacific Islanders), 2 international. Average age 29. 16 applicants, 69% accepted, 3 enrolled. In 2009, 11 master's, 2 other advanced degrees awarded. *Degree requirements:* For master's, exit paper. *Entrance requirements:* For master's, GRE General Test. Additional exam requirements/recommendations for international students: Required—TOEFL. *Application deadline:* For fall admission, 7/17 priority date for domestic students; for spring admission, 11/20 for domestic students. Applications are processed on a rolling basis. Application fee: $30. Electronic applications accepted. *Expenses:* Tuition, state resident: full-time $2952; part-time $164 per semester hour. Tuition, nonresident: full-time $11,808; part-time $656 per semester hour. Required fees: $42.90 per semester hour. $307 per semester. Tuition and fees vary according to course load. *Financial support:* In 2009–10, 4 students received support, including 4 research assistantships with partial tuition reimbursements available (averaging $3,000 per year); career-related internships or fieldwork and unspecified assistantships also available. Support available to part-time students. Financial award application deadline: 7/1; financial award applicants required to submit FAFSA. *Faculty research:* State and local government, environmental health, administrative studies. *Unit head:* Dr. Robert M. Schaefer, Chair, 678-839-6504, Fax: 678-839-5009, E-mail: rschaefe@westga.edu. *Application contact:* Dr. Charles W. Clark, Dean, 678-839-6419, E-mail: cclark@westga.edu.

University of Wyoming, College of Arts and Sciences, Department of Geography, Program in Rural Planning and Natural Resources, Laramie, WY 82070. Offers community and regional planning and natural resources (MP). *Degree requirements:* For master's, thesis or alternative. *Entrance requirements:* For master's, GRE General Test, minimum GPA of 3.0. Additional exam requirements/recommendations for international students: Required—TOEFL. *Faculty research:* Rural and small town planning, public land management.

Virginia Polytechnic Institute and State University, Graduate School, College of Architecture and Urban Studies, School of Public and International Affairs, Blacksburg, VA 24061. Offers environmental planning and policy (MURP); government and international affairs (MPIA); housing, community and economic development (MURP); international development planning (MURP); land use and physical planning (MURP); planning, governance and globalization (PhD), including environmental planning and landscape analysis, physical planning and urban design, public and international affairs, urban and environmental design and planning; urban and regional planning (MURP). *Accreditation:* ACSP. *Faculty:* 27 full-time (11 women), 2 part-time/adjunct (1 woman). *Students:* 73 full-time (51 women), 65 part-time (39 women); includes 15 minority (4 African Americans, 1 American Indian/Alaska Native, 6 Asian Americans or Pacific Islanders, 4 Hispanic Americans), 10 international. Average age 29. 86 applicants, 67% accepted, 40 enrolled. In 2009, 26 master's, 1 doctorate awarded. *Entrance requirements:* Additional exam requirements/recommendations for international students: Required—TOEFL (minimum score 550 paper-based; 213 computer-based). *Application deadline:* For fall admission, 5/15 for international students; for spring admission, 10/15 for international students. Applications are processed on a rolling basis. Application fee: $45. Electronic applications accepted. *Financial support:* In 2009–10, 1 teaching assistantship with full tuition reimbursement (averaging $5,560 per year) was awarded; career-related internships or fieldwork, Federal Work-Study, scholarships/grants, and unspecified assistantships also available. Financial award application deadline: 4/1. *Faculty research:* Design theory, environmental planning, town planning, transportation planning. *Unit head:* Dr. John Randolph, Dean, 540-231-6971, Fax: 540-231-9938, E-mail: energy@vt.edu. *Application contact:* Krystal D. Wright, Information Contact, 540-231-*5683, Fax: 540-231-9938, E-mail: garch@vt.edu.

Sustainable Development

American University, School of International Service, Washington, DC 20016-8071. Offers comparative and regional studies (Certificate); cross-cultural communication (Certificate); development management (MS); ethics, peace, and global affairs (MA); European studies (Certificate); global environmental policy (MA, Certificate); international affairs (MA), including comparative and regional studies, environmental policy, international economic policy, international politics, natural resources and sustainable development, U.S. foreign policy; international communication (MA, Certificate); international development (MA, Certificate); international development management (Certificate); international economic policy (Certificate); international economic relations (Certificate); international media (MA); international peace and conflict resolution (MA, Certificate); international relations (PhD); international service (MIS); peace building (Certificate); the Americas (Certificate); United States foreign policy (Certificate); JD/MA. Part-time and evening/weekend programs available. *Faculty:* 98 full-time (42 women), 48 part-time/adjunct (13 women). *Students:* 565 full-time (349 women), 329 part-time (189 women); includes 128 minority (44 African Americans, 2 American Indian/Alaska Native, 37 Asian Americans or Pacific Islanders, 45 Hispanic Americans), 102 international. Average age 27. 2,034 applicants, 63% accepted, 344 enrolled. In 2009, 326 master's, 6 doctorates, 9 other advanced degrees awarded. Terminal master's awarded for partial completion of doctoral program. *Degree requirements:* For master's, one foreign language, comprehensive exam, thesis or alternative; for doctorate, one foreign language, comprehensive exam, thesis/dissertation, research practicum; for Certificate, minimum 15 credit hours related course work. *Entrance requirements:* For master's, GRE, 24 credits of course work in related social sciences, minimum GPA of 3.5, 2 letters of recommendation, bachelor's degree, resume; for doctorate, GRE, 2 letters of recommendation, 24 credits in related social sciences; for Certificate, bachelor's degree. Additional exam requirements/recommendations for international students: Required—TOEFL (minimum score 600 paper-based; 250 computer-based; 100 iBT). *Application deadline:* For fall admission, 1/15 priority date for domestic students; for spring admission, 10/1 priority date for domestic students. Applications are processed on a rolling basis. Application fee: $50. *Expenses:* Tuition: Full-time $22,266; part-time $1237 per credit hour. Required fees: $430. Tuition and fees vary according to program. *Financial support:* Career-related internships or fieldwork, Federal Work-Study, and institutionally sponsored loans available. Financial award application deadline: 1/15. *Faculty research:* International intellectual property, international environmental issues, international law and legal order, international telecommunications/technology, international sustainable development. *Unit head:* Dr. Louis W. Goodman, Dean, 202-885-1600, Fax: 202-885-2494. *Application contact:* Yasmin Quianzon, Director of Graduate Admissions and Financial Aid, 202-885-2496, Fax: 202-885-1109.

See Close-Up on page 849.

Appalachian State University, Cratis D. Williams Graduate School, Center for Appalachian Studies, Boone, NC 28608. Offers culture (MA); music (MA); sustainable development (MA). Part-time programs available. *Faculty:* 14 full-time (5 women). *Students:* 24 full-time (18 women), 4 part-time (3 women). 20 applicants, 75% accepted, 10 enrolled. In 2009, 12 master's awarded. *Degree requirements:* For master's, one foreign language, comprehensive exam, thesis optional. *Entrance requirements:* For master's, GRE General Test, 3 letters of recommendation. Additional exam requirements/recommendations for international students: Required—TOEFL (minimum score 570 paper-based; 230 computer-based; 79 iBT), IELTS (minimum score 6.5). *Application deadline:* For fall admission, 7/1 for domestic students, 2/1 for international students; for spring admission, 11/1 for domestic students, 7/1 for international students. Applications are processed on a rolling basis. Application fee: $50. Electronic applications accepted. *Expenses:* Tuition, state resident: full-time $2960. Tuition, nonresident: full-time $14,051. Required fees: $2320. *Financial support:* In 2009–10, 8 research assistantships (averaging $8,000 per year) were awarded; fellowships, teaching assistantships, career-related internships or fieldwork, Federal Work-Study, scholarships/grants, and unspecified assistantships also available. Financial award application deadline: 4/1; financial award applicants required to submit FAFSA. *Faculty research:* Appalachian culture, sustainable development, Appalachian music. Total annual research expenditures: $11,250. *Unit head:* Dr. Pat Beaver, Center Director, 828-262-2550, E-mail: beaverpd@appstate.edu. *Application contact:* Dr. Katherine Ledford, Graduate Program Director, 828-262-4089, E-mail: ledfordke@appstate.edu.

Arizona State University, Graduate College, School of Sustainability, Tempe, AZ 85287. Offers MA, MS, PhD.

Brandeis University, Graduate School of Arts and Sciences, Program in Coexistence and Conflict and Sustainable International Development, Waltham, MA 02454-9110. Offers MA/MA.

Brandeis University, The Heller School for Social Policy and Management, Program in Nonprofit Management, Waltham, MA 02454-9110. Offers aging services management (MBA); child, youth, and family management (MBA); health care management (MBA); social impact management (MBA); social policy and management (MBA); sustainable development (MBA); MBA/MA. *Accreditation:* AACSB. Part-time and evening/weekend programs available. *Degree requirements:* For master's, team consulting project. *Entrance requirements:* For master's, GMAT. Additional exam requirements/recommendations for international students: Required—TOEFL (minimum score 600 paper-based). Electronic applications accepted. *Expenses:* Contact institution. *Faculty research:* Health care, child and family, elder and disabled services, general human services.

Brandeis University, The Heller School for Social Policy and Management, Program in Sustainable International Development, Waltham, MA 02454-9110. Offers international development (MA); sustainable development (MA). *Degree requirements:* For master's, 2nd year fieldwork or internship. *Entrance requirements:* For master's, 3 letters of recommendation, curriculum vitae or resume. Additional exam requirements/recommendations for international students: Required—TOEFL, IELTS. Electronic applications accepted. *Expenses:* Contact institution. *Faculty research:* Water resource management, human rights, biosphere management, rural development, public policy and governance.

California State University, Stanislaus, College of Natural Sciences, Department of Biological Sciences, Turlock, CA 95382. Offers ecology and sustainability (MS); genetic counseling (MS); marine sciences (MS). Part-time programs available. *Degree requirements:* For master's, thesis. *Entrance requirements:* For master's, GRE General Test, GRE Subject Test, minimum GPA of 3.0, 3 letters of reference. Additional exam requirements/recommendations for international students: Required—TOEFL (minimum score 550 paper-based; 213 computer-based). Electronic applications accepted. *Faculty research:* Long-term smoking and pregnancy rate, vertebrate paleobiology, terrestrial animals, benthic invertebrates of central California coastline.

City College of the City University of New York, Graduate School, Program in Sustainability in the Urban Environment, New York, NY 10031-9198. Offers MS. *Degree requirements:* For master's, capstone project.

Clark University, Graduate School, Department of International Development, Community, and Environment, Worchester, MA 01610-1477. Offers community development and planning (MA); environmental science and policy (MA); geographic information science for development and environment (MA); international development and social change (MA); MA/MBA. *Faculty:* 17 full-time (10 women), 4 part-time/adjunct (2 women). *Students:* 134 full-time (80 women), 40 part-time (28 women); includes 13 minority (8 African Americans, 2 Asian Americans or Pacific Islanders, 3 Hispanic Americans), 64 international. Average age 27. 327 applicants, 79% accepted, 106 enrolled. In 2009, 84 master's awarded. *Degree requirements:* For master's, thesis. *Entrance requirements:* For master's, 3 references, resume or curriculum vitae. Additional exam requirements/recommendations for international students: Required—TOEFL (minimum score 575 paper-based; 233 computer-based; 90 iBT) or IELTS (minimum score 6.5). *Application deadline:* For fall admission, 1/15 for domestic students. Application fee: $50. *Expenses:* Tuition: Full-time $34,900; part-time $4362.50 per course. *Financial support:* Fellowships, institutionally sponsored loans and scholarships/grants available. *Faculty research:* Community action research, gender analysis, land-use planning, geographic information systems, HIV and AIDS, global health and social justice, environmental health, climate change and sustainability. Total annual research expenditures: $2.3 million. *Unit head:* Dr. William F. Fisher, Director, 508-421-3765, Fax: 508-793-8820, E-mail: wfisher@clarku.edu. *Application contact:* Paula Hall, Department of International Development, Community, and Environment Graduate Admissions Office, 508-793-7201, Fax: 508-793-8820, E-mail: idce@clarku.edu.

Columbia University, Graduate School of Arts and Sciences, Program in Climate and Society, New York, NY 10027. Offers MA.

Columbia University, Graduate School of Arts and Sciences, Program in Sustainable Development, New York, NY 10027. Offers PhD.

Columbia University, School of International and Public Affairs, Program in Development Practice, New York, NY 10027. Offers MPA. Offered through The Earth Institute.

Dominican University of California, Graduate Programs, School of Business and Leadership, Green Business Administration Program, San Rafael, CA 94901-2298. Offers sustainable development (MBA). *Entrance requirements:* Additional exam requirements/recommendations for international students: Required—TOEFL (minimum score 550 paper-based; 213 computer-based).

Florida Atlantic University, College of Architecture, Urban and Public Affairs, School of Urban and Regional Planning, Boca Raton, FL 33431-0991. Offers economic development and tourism (Certificate); environmental planning (Certificate); sustainable community planning (Certificate); urban and regional planning (MURP); visual planning technology (Certificate). *Accreditation:* ACSP. Part-time and evening/weekend programs available. *Faculty:* 8 full-time (6 women), 1 (woman) part-time/adjunct. *Students:* 28 full-time (17 women), 12 part-time (4 women); includes 11 minority (2 African Americans, 1 Asian American or Pacific Islander, 8 Hispanic Americans), 3 international. Average age 31. 70 applicants, 47% accepted, 7 enrolled. In 2009, 14 master's awarded. *Entrance requirements:* For master's, GRE General Test, minimum GPA of 3.0. Additional exam requirements/recommendations for international students:

Required—TOEFL. *Application deadline:* For fall admission, 7/1 priority date for domestic students, 2/15 for international students; for spring admission, 11/1 priority date for domestic students, 7/15 for international students. Applications are processed on a rolling basis. Application fee: $30. *Expenses:* Tuition, state resident: full-time $7055; part-time $293.94 per credit hour. Tuition, nonresident: full-time $22,096; part-time $920.66 per credit hour. *Financial support:* Fellowships with full tuition reimbursements, research assistantships, career-related internships or fieldwork, Federal Work-Study, institutionally sponsored loans, and tuition waivers (partial) available. Financial award application deadline: 4/1. *Faculty research:* Growth management, urban design, computer applications/geographical information systems, environmental planning. *Unit head:* Dr. Jaap Vos, Chair, 954-762-5653, Fax: 954-762-5673, E-mail: jvos@fau.edu. *Application contact:* Dr. Jaap Vos, Chair, 954-762-5653, Fax: 954-762-5673, E-mail: jvos@fau.edu.

George Mason University, Volgenau School of Information Technology and Engineering, Department of Civil, Environmental, and Infrastructure Engineering, Fairfax, VA 22030. Offers civil and infrastructure engineering (MS, PhD); civil infrastructure and security engineering (Certificate); leading technical enterprises (Certificate); sustainability and the environment (Certificate); water resources engineering (Certificate). Part-time and evening/weekend programs available. *Faculty:* 9 full-time (3 women), 15 part-time/adjunct (0 women). *Students:* 19 full-time (3 women), 61 part-time (18 women); includes 16 minority (5 African Americans, 7 Asian Americans or Pacific Islanders, 4 Hispanic Americans), 8 international. Average age 33. 102 applicants, 58% accepted, 43 enrolled. In 2009, 13 master's, 2 other advanced degrees awarded. *Degree requirements:* For master's, thesis (for some programs), 30 credits, departmental seminars; for doctorate, thesis/dissertation, qualifying exams. *Entrance requirements:* For master's, GRE or GMAT. Additional exam requirements/recommendations for international students: Required—TOEFL (minimum score 575 paper-based; 230 computer-based; 88 iBT). *Application deadline:* For fall admission, 3/15 priority date for domestic students, 3/15 for international students; for spring admission, 11/1 for domestic students, 10/1 for international students. Application fee: $75. Electronic applications accepted. *Expenses:* Tuition, state resident: full-time $7568; part-time $315.33 per credit hour. Tuition, nonresident: full-time $21,704; part-time $904.33 per credit hour. Required fees: $2184; $91 per credit hour. *Financial support:* In 2009–10, 12 students received support, including 2 research assistantships with full and partial tuition reimbursements available (averaging $15,000 per year), 10 teaching assistantships with full and partial tuition reimbursements available (averaging $4,557 per year); career-related internships or fieldwork, scholarships/grants, unspecified assistantships, and health care benefits (full-time research or teaching assistantship recipients) also available. Support available to part-time students. Financial award application deadline: 3/1; financial award applicants required to submit FAFSA. *Faculty research:* Evolutionary design, infrastructure security, intelligent transportation systems, national transportation networks, water quality modeling. Total annual research expenditures: $67,461. *Unit head:* Dr. Michael Bronzini, Chair, 703-993-1504, Fax: 703-993-1521. *Application contact:* Lisa Nolder, Graduate Student Services Director, 703-993-1499, E-mail: snolder@gmu.edu.

Hawai'i Pacific University, College of Natural and Computational Sciences, Program in Global Leadership and Sustainable Development, Honolulu, HI 96813. Offers MA. Part-time and evening/weekend programs available. *Faculty:* 3 full-time (0 women). *Students:* 45 full-time (24 women), 21 part-time (12 women); includes 16 minority (4 African Americans, 6 Asian Americans or Pacific Islanders, 6 Hispanic Americans), 23 international. Average age 30. 52 applicants, 92% accepted, 24 enrolled. In 2009, 12 master's awarded. *Degree requirements:* For master's, thesis. *Entrance requirements:* Additional exam requirements/recommendations for international students: Recommended—TOEFL (minimum score 550 paper-based; 213 computer-based; 80 iBT), TWE (minimum score 5). *Application deadline:* For fall admission, 2/15 priority date for domestic students; for spring admission, 10/15 priority date for domestic students. Applications are processed on a rolling basis. Application fee: $50. Electronic applications accepted. *Expenses:* Tuition: Full-time $12,600; part-time $700 per credit hour. Tuition and fees vary according to program. *Financial support:* Career-related internships or fieldwork, Federal Work-Study, scholarships/grants, and unspecified assistantships available. Support available to part-time students. Financial award application deadline: 3/1; financial award applicants required to submit FAFSA. *Unit head:* Dr. Gordon Jones, Dean, 808-544-1181, Fax: 808-544-0247, E-mail: gjones@hpu.edu. *Application contact:* Danny Lam, Assistant Director of Graduate Admissions, 808-544-1135, Fax: 808-544-0280, E-mail: graduate@hpu.edu.

See Close-Up on page 1187.

HEC Montreal, School of Business Administration, Diploma Programs in Administration, Program in Management and Sustainable Development, Montréal, QC H3T 2A7, Canada. Offers Diploma. Part-time programs available. *Students:* 20 full-time (9 women), 66 part-time (35 women). 88 applicants, 72% accepted, 46 enrolled. In 2009, 13 Diplomas awarded. *Degree requirements:* For Diploma, one foreign language. *Application deadline:* For fall admission, 5/15 for domestic and international students. Application fee: $77. Tuition and fees charges are reported in Canadian dollars. *Expenses:* Tuition, area resident: Part-time $65.60 Canadian dollars per credit. Tuition, state resident: full-time $2361.60 Canadian dollars; part-time $183.36 Canadian dollars per credit. Tuition, nonresident: full-time $6601 Canadian dollars; part-time $448.13 Canadian dollars per credit. International tuition: $16,132.68 Canadian dollars full-time. Required fees: $1254.15 Canadian dollars; $28.99 Canadian dollars per course. $91.68 Canadian dollars per term. Tuition and fees vary according to degree level and program. *Financial support:* Research assistantships, teaching assistantships available. Financial award application deadline: 10/2. *Unit head:* Louise Cote, Director, 514-340-6205, Fax: 514-340-5640, E-mail: louise.cote@hec.ca. *Application contact:* Marie Deshaies, Senior Student Advisor, 514-340-6135, Fax: 514-340-6411, E-mail: marie.deshaies@hec.ca.

Instituto Centroamericano de Administración de Empresas, Graduate Programs, La Garita, Costa Rica. Offers agribusiness (MIAM); business administration (EMBA); economics and finance (MBA); industry and technology (MBA); sustainable development (MBA). *Degree requirements:* For master's, comprehensive exam, essay. *Entrance requirements:* For master's, GMAT or GRE General Test, fluency in Spanish, interview, letters of recommendation, minimum 1 year of work experience. Electronic applications accepted. *Faculty research:* Competitiveness, production.

Iowa State University of Science and Technology, Graduate College, Interdisciplinary Programs, Program in Sustainable Agriculture, Ames, IA 50011. Offers MS, PhD. *Students:* 26 full-time (16 women), 7 part-time (3 women); includes 2 minority (1 Asian American or Pacific Islander, 1 Hispanic American), 7 international. In 2009, 5 master's, 1 doctorate awarded. *Degree requirements:* For master's, thesis or alternative; for doctorate, thesis/dissertation. *Entrance requirements:* For master's and doctorate, GRE General Test. Additional exam requirements/recommendations for international students: Required—TOEFL (minimum score 570 paper-based; 80 iBT) or IELTS (minimum score 6.5). *Application deadline:* For fall admission, 2/1 for domestic and international students; for spring admission, 6/1 priority date for domestic and international students. Application fee: $40 ($90 for international students). *Expenses:* Tuition, state resident: full-time $6716. Tuition, nonresident: full-time $8908. Tuition and fees vary according to course level, course load, program and student level. *Financial support:* In 2009–10, 23 research assistantships with full and partial tuition reimbursements (averaging $15,870 per year), 3 teaching assistantships with full and partial tuition reimbursements (averaging $15,860 per year) were awarded. *Unit head:* Dr. Mary Wiedenhoeft, Chair, Supervising Committee, 515-294-6518, E-mail: gpsa@iastate.edu. *Application contact:* Charles Sauer, Information Contact, 515-294-6518, E-mail: gpsa@iastate.edu.

Lesley University, Graduate School of Arts and Social Sciences, Program in Urban Environmental Leadership, Cambridge, MA 02138-2790. Offers MA. *Entrance requirements:* For master's, 2 letters of recommendation, interview.

Marylhurst University, Department of Business Administration, Marylhurst, OR 97036-0261. Offers finance (MBA); general management (MBA); government policy and administration (MBA); green development (MBA); health care management (MBA); marketing (MBA); natural and organic resources (MBA); nonprofit management (MBA); organizational behavior (MBA); real estate (MBA); renewable energy (MBA); sustainable business (MBA). Part-time and evening/weekend programs available. Postbaccalaureate distance learning degree programs offered (no on-campus study). *Faculty:* 2 full-time (1 woman), 28 part-time/adjunct (5 women). *Students:* 30 full-time (12 women), 627 part-time (323 women); includes 79 minority (28 African Americans, 3 American Indian/Alaska Native, 17 Asian Americans or Pacific Islanders, 31 Hispanic Americans), 9 international. Average age 37. 299 applicants, 80% accepted, 209 enrolled. In 2009, 193 master's awarded. *Degree requirements:* For master's, comprehensive exam, capstone course. *Entrance requirements:* For master's, GMAT (if GPA less than 3.0 and fewer than 5 years of work experience), interview, resume, 2 letters of recommendation. Additional exam requirements/recommendations for international students: Recommended—TOEFL (minimum score 550 paper-based; 213 computer-based; 80 iBT). *Application deadline:* For fall admission, 9/11 priority date for domestic and international students; for winter admission, 12/15 priority date for domestic and international students; for spring admission, 3/17 priority date for domestic and international students. Applications are processed on a rolling basis. Application fee: $40 ($50 for international students). Electronic applications accepted. *Financial support:* Scholarships/grants available. Support available to part-time students. Financial award applicants required to submit FAFSA. *Unit head:* Bob Hanks, Director of Business and Real Estate Programs, 503-636-8141, Fax: 503-697-5597, E-mail: mba@marylhurst.edu. *Application contact:* Kathleen Schneff, Admissions Specialist, 800-634-9982 Ext. 3322, Fax: 503-635-6585, E-mail: admissions@marylhurst.edu.

Michigan Technological University, Graduate School, Sustainable Futures Institute, Houghton, MI 49931. Offers sustainability (Certificate). Part-time programs available.

Minneapolis College of Art and Design, Certificate Programs, Minneapolis, MN 55404-4347. Offers design (Certificate); fine arts (Certificate); graphic design (Certificate); media (Certificate); sustainable design (Certificate). Part-time programs available. Postbaccalaureate distance learning degree programs offered. *Faculty:* 42 full-time (29 women). *Students:* 4 full-time (2 women), 22 part-time (19 women). Average age 24. In 2009, 15 Certificates awarded. *Degree requirements:* For Certificate, final project. *Entrance requirements:* For degree, resume, portfolio, letter of recommendation. Additional exam requirements/recommendations for international students: Required—TOEFL (minimum score 550 paper-based; 213 computer-based; 79 iBT). *Application deadline:* For fall admission, 1/15 for domestic and international students; for spring admission, 10/15 for domestic and international students. Application fee: $50. Electronic applications accepted. *Expenses:* Tuition: Full-time $29,500; part-time $985 per credit. Required fees: $100. *Financial support:* Career-related internships or fieldwork and scholarships/grants available. Financial award application deadline: 3/15; financial award applicants required to submit FAFSA. *Faculty research:* Visual arts. *Unit head:* Howard Oransky, Director of Continuing Studies, 612-874-3778, E-mail: howard_oransky@mcad.edu. *Application contact:* Howard Oransky, Director of Continuing Studies, 612-874-3778, Fax: 612-874-3701, E-mail: howard_oransky@mcad.edu.

New York School of Interior Design, Program in Sustainable Interior Environments, New York, NY 10021-5110. Offers MPS. In 2009, 1 master's awarded. *Entrance requirements:* For master's, first-professional degree in interior design, architecture, or a closely related field; portfolio. Additional exam requirements/recommendations for international students: Required—TOEFL (minimum score 550 paper-based; 213 computer-based; 79 iBT). *Application deadline:* For fall admission, 3/1 priority date for domestic students, 3/1 for international students; for spring admission, 10/1 priority date for domestic students, 10/1 for international students. Applications are processed on a rolling basis. Application fee: $50 ($75 for international students). Electronic applications accepted. *Expenses:* Tuition: Full-time $24,250. *Financial support:* Research assistantships, Federal Work-Study available. Financial award applicants required to submit FAFSA. *Application contact:* Scott Ageloff, Dean, 212-472-1500 Ext. 301, Fax: 212-288-6577, E-mail: sageloff@nysid.edu.

Northern Arizona University, Graduate College, College of Social and Behavioral Sciences, Program in Sustainable Communities, Flagstaff, AZ 86011. Offers MA. Part-time programs available. *Faculty:* 1 (woman) full-time. *Students:* 31 full-time (21 women), 18 part-time (12 women); includes 4 minority (2 American Indian/Alaska Native, 2 Hispanic Americans). Average age 40. 42 applicants, 17% accepted, 5 enrolled. In 2009, 11 master's awarded. *Degree requirements:* For master's, thesis. *Entrance requirements:* For master's, minimum GPA of 3.0. Additional exam requirements/recommendations for international students: Required—TOEFL (minimum score 550 paper-based; 213 computer-based; 80 iBT), IELTS (minimum score 7), or a bachelor's degree from an English-speaking university and demonstrated proficiency. *Application deadline:* For fall admission, 3/15 priority date for domestic students, 9/1 priority date for international students. Applications are processed on a rolling basis. Application fee: $65. Electronic applications accepted. *Financial support:* In 2009–10, 1 research assistantship was awarded. Support available to part-time students. Financial award application deadline: 3/30. *Unit head:* Dr. Sandra Lubarsky, Director, 928-523-2382, Fax: 928-523-6777, E-mail: sandra.lubarsky@nau.edu. *Application contact:* Dr. Sandra Lubarsky, Director, 928-523-2382, Fax: 928-523-6777, E-mail: sandra.lubarsky@nau.edu.

Philadelphia University, School of Architecture, Program in Sustainable Design, Philadelphia, PA 19144. Offers MS.

Rensselaer Polytechnic Institute, Graduate School, School of Humanities and Social Sciences, Department of Science and Technology Studies, Troy, NY 12180-3590. Offers design studies (MS, PhD); policy studies (MS, PhD); science studies (MS, PhD); sustainability studies (MS, PhD); technology studies (MS, PhD). Part-time programs available. *Faculty:* 16 full-time (6 women). *Students:* 21 full-time (8 women), 3 part-time (1 woman); includes 6 Asian Americans or Pacific Islanders. Average age 27. 19 applicants, 42% accepted, 5 enrolled. In 2009, 1 master's, 9 doctorates awarded. Terminal master's awarded for partial completion of doctoral program. *Degree requirements:* For master's, thesis (for some programs); for doctorate, comprehensive exam, thesis/dissertation. *Entrance requirements:* For master's and doctorate, GRE General Test. Additional exam requirements/recommendations for international students: Required—TOEFL (minimum score 600 paper-based; 250 computer-based). *Application deadline:* For fall admission, 1/15 priority date for domestic students, 1/15 for international students. Applications are processed on a rolling basis. Application fee: $75. Electronic applications accepted. *Expenses:* Tuition: Full-time $38,100. *Financial support:* In 2009–10, 22 students received support, including 5 fellowships (averaging $22,000 per year), 1 research assistantship with full tuition reimbursement available (averaging $16,500 per year), 10 teaching assistantships with full tuition reimbursements available (averaging $16,500 per year); career-related internships or fieldwork, institutionally sponsored loans, and tuition waivers (partial) also available. Financial award application deadline: 1/15. *Faculty research:* Communities and technology, social dimensions of IT and biotechnology, ethics and policy, design. Total annual research expenditures: $75,000. *Unit head:* Dr. Sharon Anderson-Gold, Chair, 518-276-8837, Fax: 518-276-2659, E-mail: anders@rpi.edu. *Application contact:* Dr. Edward J. Woodhouse, Director of Graduate Studies, 518-276-8506, Fax: 518-276-2659, E-mail: woodhouse@rpi.edu.

Rochester Institute of Technology, Graduate Enrollment Services, Golisano Institute for Sustainability, Rochester, NY 14623-5603. Offers PhD. *Students:* 12 full-time (8 women), 7 international. Average age 30. 28 applicants, 29% accepted, 7 enrolled. *Entrance requirements:* Additional exam requirements/recommendations for international students: Required—TOEFL (minimum score 600 paper-based; 250 computer-based; 100 iBT), or IELTS (minimum score 6.5). *Application deadline:* For fall admission, 1/15 priority date for domestic and international students. Application fee: $50. *Expenses:* Tuition: Full-time $31,533; part-time $876 per credit hour. Required fees: $210. *Financial support:* In 2009–10, 12 students received support. *Faculty research:* GIS National Center for Remanufacturing and Resource Recovery, the Center for Sustainable Production, the Center for Sustainable Mobility, the Systems Modernization and Sustainment Center, the New York State Pollution Prevention Institute, the NanoPower Research Labs. *Unit head:* Dr. Nabil Nasr, Assistant Provost and Director, 585-

Sustainable Development

Rochester Institute of Technology (continued)
475-2602, E-mail: info@sustainability.rit.edu. *Application contact:* Diane Ellison, Assistant Vice President, Graduate Enrollment Services, 585-475-2229, Fax: 585-475-7164, E-mail: gradinfo@rit.edu.

Saybrook University, Graduate College of Psychology and Humanistic Studies, San Francisco, CA 94111-1920. Offers clinical psychology (Psy D); human science (MA, PhD), including consciousness and spirituality, humanistic and transpersonal psychology, integrative health studies, organizational systems, social transformation, transformative social change (MA); organizational systems (MA, PhD), including consciousness and spirituality, humanistic and transpersonal psychology, integrative health studies, leadership of sustainable systems (MA), organizational systems, social transformation; psychology (MA, PhD), including clinical psychology (PhD), consciousness and spirituality, creativity studies (MA), humanistic and transpersonal psychology, integrative health studies, Jungian studies, marriage and family therapy (MA), organizational systems, social transformation. Postbaccalaureate distance learning degree programs offered (minimal on-campus study). Terminal master's awarded for partial completion of doctoral program. *Degree requirements:* For master's, thesis or alternative; for doctorate, thesis/dissertation. Electronic applications accepted. *Faculty research:* Humanistic theory, health studies, organizational systems, consciousness and spirituality, social transformation.

SIT Graduate Institute, Graduate Programs, Master's Programs in Intercultural Service, Leadership, and Management, Brattleboro, VT 05302-0676. Offers conflict transformation (MA); intercultural service, leadership, and management (MA); international education (MA); management (MS); social justice in intercultural relations (MA); sustainable development (MA). Postbaccalaureate distance learning degree programs offered (minimal on-campus study). *Degree requirements:* For master's, one foreign language, thesis. *Entrance requirements:* For master's, 3 letters of reference. Additional exam requirements/recommendations for international students: Required—TOEFL. *Faculty research:* Intercultural communication, conflict resolution, advising and training, world issues, international business.

Slippery Rock University of Pennsylvania, Graduate Studies (Recruitment), College of Health, Environment, and Science, Department of Geography, Geology, and the Environment, Slippery Rock, PA 16057-1383. Offers sustainable systems (MS). *Degree requirements:* For master's, thesis, internship. *Entrance requirements:* For master's, GRE General Test, MAT, minimum GPA of 2.75 (3.0 for initial certification programs). Additional exam requirements/recommendations for international students: Required—TOEFL (minimum score 550 paper-based; 213 computer-based). *Application deadline:* For fall admission, 3/1 priority date for domestic students, 5/1 priority date for international students; for spring admission, 11/1 priority date for domestic students, 9/1 priority date for international students. Applications are processed on a rolling basis. Application fee: $25 ($30 for international students). Electronic applications accepted. *Expenses:* Tuition, state resident: full-time $6666; part-time $370 per credit. Tuition, nonresident: full-time $10,666; part-time $593 per credit. Required fees: $2184; $182 per credit. *Financial support:* Career-related internships or fieldwork, institutionally sponsored loans, scholarships/grants, and unspecified assistantships available. Support available to part-time students. Financial award application deadline: 5/1; financial award applicants required to submit FAFSA. *Unit head:* Dr. Langdon Smith, Coordinator, 724-738-2389, Fax: 724-738-4217, E-mail: langdon.smith@sru.edu. *Application contact:* Angela Piverotto, Director of Graduate Admissions, 724-738-2051, Fax: 724-738-2146, E-mail: graduate.admissions@sru.edu.

University of Alaska Fairbanks, School of Natural Resources and Agricultural Sciences, Fairbanks, AK 99775-7140. Offers natural resource and sustainability (PhD); natural resource management (MS); natural resource management and geography (MS). Part-time programs available. *Faculty:* 20 full-time (3 women), 2 part-time/adjunct (1 woman). *Students:* 31 full-time (21 women), 18 part-time (7 women); includes 2 minority (1 American Indian/Alaska Native, 1 Asian American or Pacific Islander), 5 international. Average age 32. 49 applicants, 45% accepted, 16 enrolled. In 2009, 7 master's, 3 doctorates awarded. *Degree requirements:* For master's, comprehensive exam, thesis or alternative. *Entrance requirements:* For master's, GRE General Test. Additional exam requirements/recommendations for international students: Required—TOEFL (minimum score 550 paper-based; 213 computer-based). *Application deadline:* For fall admission, 6/1 for domestic students, 3/1 for international students; for spring admission, 10/15 for domestic students, 9/1 for international students. Applications are processed on a rolling basis. Application fee: $60. Electronic applications accepted. *Expenses:* Tuition, state resident: full-time $7584; part-time $316 per credit. Tuition, nonresident: full-time $15,504; part-time $646 per credit. Required fees: $23 per credit. $135 per semester. Tuition and fees vary according to course level, course load and reciprocity agreements. *Financial support:* In 2009–10, 16 research assistantships (averaging $10,412 per year), 2 teaching assistantships (averaging $9,472 per year) were awarded; fellowships, career-related internships or fieldwork, Federal Work-Study, scholarships/grants, health care benefits, and unspecified assistantships also available. Support available to part-time students. Financial award application deadline: 2/15; financial award applicants required to submit FAFSA. *Faculty research:* Conservation biology, soil/water conservation, land use policy and planning in the arctic and subarctic, forest ecosystem management, subarctic agricultural production. Total annual research expenditures: $5.8 million. *Unit head:* Dr. Carol E. Lewis, Dean, 907-474-7083, Fax: 907-474-6567, E-mail: fysnras@uaf.edu. *Application contact:* Veazey David, Director of Enrollment Management, 907-474-5276, Fax: 907-474-6567, E-mail: dave.veazey@alaska.edu.

University of California, Berkeley, UC Berkeley Extension, Certificate Programs in Sustainability Studies, Berkeley, CA 94720-1500. Offers leadership in sustainability and environmental management (Professional Certificate); solar energy and green building (Professional Certificate); sustainable design (Professional Certificate). *Unit head:* Diana Wu, Dean, 510-642-4181. *Application contact:* Sustainability Studies, 510-642-4151, E-mail: course@unex.berkeley.edu.

University of Connecticut, Graduate School, Center for Continuing Studies, Program in Humanitarian Services Administration, Storrs, CT 06269. Offers MPS. Postbaccalaureate distance learning degree programs offered. *Students:* 3 full-time (all women), 21 part-time (12 women); includes 3 minority (2 African Americans, 1 Hispanic American), 4 international. Average age 37. 12 applicants, 58% accepted, 6 enrolled. In 2009, 3 master's awarded. *Entrance requirements:* For master's, minimum GPA of 3.0 or greater than 3.0 for the last 2 years of study; 3 letters of reference. Additional exam requirements/recommendations for international students: Required—TOEFL (minimum score 540 paper-based; 207 computer-based). *Application deadline:* Applications are processed on a rolling basis. *Expenses:* Tuition, state resident: full-time $4725; part-time $525 per credit. Tuition, nonresident: full-time $12,267; part-time $1363 per credit. Required fees: $346 per semester. Tuition and fees vary according to course load. *Financial support:* Fellowships, unspecified assistantships available. Financial award application deadline: 5/1; financial award applicants required to submit FAFSA.

University of Georgia, Graduate School, School of Ecology, Athens, GA 30602. Offers conservation ecology and sustainable development (MS); ecology (MS, PhD). *Faculty:* 21 full-time (6 women), 7 part-time/adjunct (2 women). *Students:* 59 full-time (33 women), 22 part-time (11 women); includes 4 minority (1 African American, 3 Hispanic Americans), 3 international. 138 applicants, 19% accepted, 21 enrolled. In 2009, 13 master's, 10 doctorates awarded. *Degree requirements:* For master's, thesis; for doctorate, one foreign language, thesis/dissertation. *Entrance requirements:* For master's and doctorate, GRE General Test. *Application deadline:* For fall admission, 7/1 priority date for domestic students; for spring admission, 11/15 for domestic students. Application fee: $50. Electronic applications accepted. *Expenses:* Tuition, state resident: full-time $6000; part-time $250 per credit hour. Tuition, nonresident: full-time $20,904; part-time $871 per credit hour. Required fees: $730 per semester. *Financial support:* Fellowships, research assistantships, teaching assistantships, unspecified assistantships available. *Unit head:* Dr. John L. Gittleman, Dean, 706-542-2968, Fax: 706-542-4819, E-mail: ecohead@uga.edu. *Application contact:* Dr. C. Ronald Carroll, Graduate Coordinator, 706-338-1366, Fax: 706-542-4819, E-mail: rcarroll@uga.edu.

University of Maryland, College Park, Academic Affairs, College of Chemical and Life Sciences, Department of Biology, Program in Sustainable Development and Conservation Biology, College Park, MD 20742. Offers MS. Part-time and evening/weekend programs available. *Students:* 21 full-time (12 women), 6 part-time (5 women); includes 1 minority (Hispanic American), 5 international. 55 applicants, 33% accepted, 12 enrolled. In 2009, 14 master's awarded. *Degree requirements:* For master's, internship, scholarly paper. *Entrance requirements:* For master's, GRE General Test, minimum GPA of 3.0, 3 letters of recommendation. *Application deadline:* For fall admission, 2/15 priority date for domestic students, 2/1 for international students. Applications are processed on a rolling basis. Application fee: $60. Electronic applications accepted. *Expenses:* Tuition, area resident: Part-time $471 per credit hour. Tuition, state resident: part-time $471 per credit hour. Tuition, nonresident: part-time $1016 per credit hour. Required fees: $337.04 per term. *Financial support:* In 2009–10, 1 research assistantship (averaging $18,519 per year), 16 teaching assistantships (averaging $18,653 per year) were awarded; fellowships also available. Financial award application deadline: 2/1; financial award applicants required to submit FAFSA. *Faculty research:* Biodiversity, global change, conservation. *Unit head:* Dr. David W. Inouye, Director, 301-405-9358, Fax: 301-314-9358, E-mail: inouye@umd.edu. *Application contact:* Dean of Graduate School, 301-405-0358, Fax: 301-314-9305.

University of Massachusetts Lowell, James B. Francis College of Engineering, Department of Civil and Environmental Engineering, Lowell, MA 01854-2881. Offers civil and environmental engineering (MS Eng, Certificate); environmental engineering (D Eng); environmental studies (MSES, PhD, Certificate), including environmental engineering (MSES), environmental studies (PhD, Certificate); sustainable infrastructure for developing nations (Certificate). Part-time programs available. *Degree requirements:* For master's, thesis optional. *Entrance requirements:* For master's, GRE General Test. *Faculty research:* Bridge design, traffic control, groundwater remediation, pile capacity.

University of Michigan, School of Natural Resources and Environment, Program in Natural Resources and Environment, Ann Arbor, MI 48109. Offers aquatic sciences: research and management (MS); behavior, education and communication (MS); conservation biology (MS); environmental informatics (MS); environmental justice (MS); environmental policy and planning (MS); natural resources and environment (PhD); sustainable systems (MS); terrestrial ecosystems (MS); MS/AM; MS/JD; MS/MBA. *Students:* Average age 27. In 2009, 87 master's, 14 doctorates awarded. Terminal master's awarded for partial completion of doctoral program. *Degree requirements:* For master's, practicum or group project; for doctorate, comprehensive exam, thesis/dissertation, oral defense of dissertation, preliminary exam. *Entrance requirements:* For master's, GRE General Test; for doctorate, GRE General Test, master's degree. Additional exam requirements/recommendations for international students: Required—TOEFL (minimum score 560 paper-based; 220 computer-based; 84 iBT). *Application deadline:* For fall admission, 1/5 priority date for domestic and international students. Applications are processed on a rolling basis. Application fee: $60 ($75 for international students). Electronic applications accepted. *Expenses:* Tuition, state resident: full-time $17,286; part-time $1099 per credit hour. Tuition, nonresident: full-time $34,944; part-time $2080 per credit hour. Required fees: $95 per semester. Tuition and fees vary according to course load, degree level and program. *Financial support:* Fellowships with tuition reimbursements, research assistantships with tuition reimbursements, teaching assistantships with tuition reimbursements, career-related internships or fieldwork, Federal Work-Study, institutionally sponsored loans, scholarships/grants, health care benefits, and unspecified assistantships available. Support available to part-time students. Financial award application deadline: 1/5; financial award applicants required to submit FAFSA. *Faculty research:* Stream ecology, plant-insect interactions, fish biology, resource control and reproductive success, remote sensing. *Application contact:* Graduate Admissions Team, 734-764-6453, Fax: 734-936-2195, E-mail: snre.admissions@umich.edu.

University of New Brunswick Fredericton, School of Graduate Studies, Policy Studies Program, Fredericton, NB E3B 5A3, Canada. Offers people, property and alternative dispute resolution (M Phil); philosophy politics and economics (M Phil); sustainable development (M Phil). Part-time programs available. *Faculty:* 6 full-time (2 women), 13 part-time/adjunct (2 women). *Students:* 8 full-time (3 women), 5 part-time (3 women). In 2009, 7 master's awarded. *Degree requirements:* For master's, thesis, report. *Entrance requirements:* For master's, minimum GPA of 3.5, BA; BA Honours. Additional exam requirements/recommendations for international students: Required—TOEFL (minimum score 600 paper-based; 250 computer-based; 100 iBT), TWE (minimum score 4), or IELTS (minimum score 7). Application fee: $50 Canadian dollars. Tuition and fees charges are reported in Canadian dollars. *Expenses:* Tuition, area resident: Full-time $5562 Canadian dollars; part-time $2781 Canadian dollars per year. Required fees: $49.75 Canadian dollars per term. *Financial support:* In 2009–10, 5 research assistantships (averaging $5,600 per year), 2 teaching assistantships (averaging $4,400 per year) were awarded. *Unit head:* Dr. Linda Eyre, Dean of Graduate Studies, 506-447-3044, Fax: 506-453-4817, E-mail: gradidst@unb.ca. *Application contact:* Janet Amurault, Graduate Secretary, 506-458-7558, Fax: 506-453-4817, E-mail: jamiraul@unb.ca.

University of Southern California, Graduate School, School of Policy, Planning, and Development, Master of Planning Program, Los Angeles, CA 90089. Offers sustainable cities (Graduate Certificate); transportation systems (Graduate Certificate); urban planning (M Pl); M Arch/M Pl; M Pl/MA; M Pl/MS; M Pl/MSW; MBA/M Pl; ML Arch/M Pl; MPA/M Pl. Part-time programs available. *Faculty:* 51 full-time (12 women), 74 part-time/adjunct (26 women). *Students:* 84 full-time (50 women), 6 part-time (4 women); includes 38 minority (5 African Americans, 21 Asian Americans or Pacific Islanders, 12 Hispanic Americans), 12 international. 260 applicants, 60% accepted, 62 enrolled. In 2009, 40 master's awarded. *Degree requirements:* For master's, comprehensive exam, internship. *Entrance requirements:* For master's, GRE or GMAT. Additional exam requirements/recommendations for international students: Required—TOEFL (minimum score 600 paper-based; 250 computer-based; 100 iBT). *Application deadline:* For fall admission, 12/15 priority date for domestic and international students; for spring admission, 11/1 for domestic students, 10/1 for international students. Application fee: $85. Electronic applications accepted. *Expenses:* Tuition: Full-time $25,980; part-time $1315 per unit. Required fees: $554. One-time fee: $35 full-time. Full-time tuition and fees vary according to degree level and program. *Financial support:* In 2009–10, 72 students received support, including 2 research assistantships with tuition reimbursements available (averaging $9,566 per year); scholarships/grants and tuition waivers (full and partial) also available. *Faculty research:* Transportation and infrastructure, comparative international development, healthy communities, social economic development, sustainable community planning. Total annual research expenditures: $5 million. *Unit head:* Dr. Tridib Banerjee, Dean, 213-740-4724, Fax: 213-740-1801, E-mail: tbanerje@usc.edu. *Application contact:* Marisol R. Gonzalez, Director of Recruitment and Admission, 213-740-0550, Fax: 213-740-7573, E-mail: marisolr@usc.edu.

University of Southern California, Graduate School, Viterbi School of Engineering, Sonny Astani Department of Civil Engineering, Los Angeles, CA 90089. Offers applied mechanics (MS); civil engineering (MS, PhD); computer-aided engineering (ME, Graduate Certificate); construction management (MCM); engineering technology commercialization (Graduate Certificate); environmental engineering (MS, PhD); environmental quality management (ME); structural design (ME); sustainable cities (Graduate Certificate); transportation systems (Graduate Certificate). Part-time programs available. Postbaccalaureate distance learning degree programs offered (no on-campus study). *Faculty:* 16 full-time (2 women), 35 part-time/adjunct (5 women). *Students:* 165 full-time (48 women), 65 part-time (16 women); includes 54 minority (40 Asian Americans or Pacific Islanders, 14 Hispanic Americans), 108 international. 451 applicants, 41% accepted, 73 enrolled. In 2009, 74 master's, 10 doctorates awarded. Terminal master's awarded for partial completion of doctoral program. *Degree requirements:* For doctorate, thesis/dissertation. *Entrance requirements:* For master's, GRE General Test; for doctorate, General GRE. *Application deadline:* For fall admission, 3/1 priority date for domestic and international students; for spring admission, 10/1 priority date for domestic and international students. Applications are processed on a rolling basis. Application fee: $85. Electronic applications accepted. *Expenses:* Tuition: Full-time $25,980; part-time $1315 per unit. Required fees: $554. One-time fee: $35 full-time. Full-time tuition and fees vary according to degree level and program. *Financial support:* In 2009–10, fellowships with full tuition reimbursements (averaging $30,000 per year), research assistantships with full tuition reimbursements (averaging $19,250 per year), teaching assistantships with full tuition reimbursements (averaging $19,250 per year) were awarded; career-related internships or fieldwork, scholarships/grants, health care benefits, and unspecified assistantships also available. Financial award application deadline: 12/1; financial award applicants required to submit CSS PROFILE or FAFSA. *Faculty research:* Geotechnical engineering, transportation engineering, structural engineering, construction management, environmental engineering, water resources. Total annual research expenditures: $4.2 million. *Unit head:* Dr. Jean-Pierre Bardet, Chair, 213-740-0609, Fax: 213-744-1426, E-mail: bardet@usc.edu. *Application contact:* Jennifer A. Gerson, Director of Student Services, 213-740-0573, Fax: 213-740-8662, E-mail: jgerson@usc.edu.

University of Washington, Graduate School, College of Forest Resources, Seattle, WA 98195. Offers bioresource science and engineering (MS, PhD); environmental horticulture (MEH); environmental horticulture and urban forestry (MS, PhD); forest ecology (MS, PhD); forest management (MFR); forest soils (MS, PhD); forest systems and bioenergy (MS, PhD); restoration ecology (MS, PhD); social sciences (MS, PhD); sustainable resource management (MS, PhD); wildlife science (MS, PhD); MFR/MAIS; MPA/MS. *Accreditation:* SAF. *Degree requirements:* For master's, thesis (for some programs); for doctorate, comprehensive exam (for some programs), thesis/dissertation. *Entrance requirements:* For master's and doctorate, GRE, minimum GPA of 3.0. Additional exam requirements/recommendations for international students: Required—TOEFL. Electronic applications accepted. *Faculty research:* Ecosystem analysis, silviculture and forest protection, paper science and engineering, environmental horticulture and urban forestry, natural resource policy and economics.

University of Washington, Graduate School, School of Law, Seattle, WA 98195-3020. Offers Asian law (LL M, PhD); intellectual property law and policy (LL M); law (JD); law of sustainable international development (LL M); taxation (LL M); JD/LL M; JD/MA; JD/MAIS; JD/MBA; JD/MPA; JD/MS; JD/PhD. *Accreditation:* ABA. *Degree requirements:* For master's, thesis; for doctorate, thesis/dissertation. *Entrance requirements:* For JD, LSAT; for master's, language proficiency (LL M in Asian law). Additional exam requirements/recommendations for international students: Required—TOEFL. *Expenses:* Contact institution. *Faculty research:* Asian, international and comparative law, intellectual property law, health law, environmental law, taxation.

The University of Western Ontario, Faculty of Graduate Studies, Physical Sciences Division, Department of Earth Sciences, London, ON N6A 5B8, Canada. Offers environment and sustainability (MES); geology (M Sc, PhD); geology and environmental science (M Sc, PhD); geophysics (M Sc, PhD); geophysics and environmental science (M Sc, PhD). *Degree requirements:* For master's, thesis; for doctorate, thesis/dissertation, qualifying exam. *Entrance requirements:* For master's, honors in B Sc; for doctorate, M Sc. Additional exam requirements/recommendations for international students: Required—TOEFL. *Faculty research:* Geophysics, geochemistry, paleontology, sedimentology/stratigraphy, glaciology/quaternary.

University of Wisconsin–Madison, Graduate School, Gaylord Nelson Institute for Environmental Studies, Conservation Biology and Sustainable Development Program, Madison, WI 53706-1380. Offers MS. Part-time programs available. *Degree requirements:* For master's, thesis or alternative, exit seminar. *Entrance requirements:* For master's, GRE General Test. Additional exam requirements/recommendations for international students: Required—TOEFL (minimum score 550 paper-based; 213 computer-based; 79 iBT). Electronic applications accepted. *Expenses:* Tuition, state resident: part-time $594 per credit. Tuition, nonresident: part-time $1504 per credit. Required fees: $65 per credit. Tuition and fees vary according to course load, program and reciprocity agreements. *Faculty research:* Ornithology, forestry, sociology, rural sociology, plant ecology.

Walden University, Graduate Programs, School of Public Policy and Administration, Minneapolis, MN 55401. Offers general program (MPA); government management (Postbaccalaureate Certificate); health policy (MPA); homeland security policy (MPA); interdisciplinary policy studies (MPA); law and public policy (MPA); local government management for sustainable communities (MPA); nonprofit management (Postbaccalaureate Certificate); nonprofit management and leadership (MPA, MS); policy analysis (MPA); public management and leadership (MPA); public policy and administration (PhD), including criminal justice, health services, homeland security policy and coordination, international nongovernmental organizations, law and public policy, local government management for sustainable communities, nonprofit management and leadership, public management and leadership, public policy, public safety management, terrorism, mediation, and peace; terrorism, mediation, and peace (MPA). Part-time and evening/weekend programs available. Postbaccalaureate distance learning degree programs offered (minimal on-campus study). *Faculty:* 7 full-time, 62 part-time/adjunct. *Students:* 1,468 full-time (941 women), 233 part-time (162 women); includes 852 minority (761 African Americans, 9 American Indian/Alaska Native, 19 Asian Americans or Pacific Islanders, 63 Hispanic Americans), 53 international. Average age 40. In 2009, 173 master's, 13 doctorates awarded. *Degree requirements:* For doctorate, thesis/dissertation, residency. *Entrance requirements:* For master's, bachelor's degree or equivalent in related field, minimum GPA of 2.5; for doctorate, master's degree or equivalent in related field; minimum GPA of 3.0; official transcripts; three years of related professional/academic experience (preferred); access to computer and Internet. Additional exam requirements/recommendations for international students: Required—TOEFL (minimum score 550 paper-based; 213 computer-based), IELTS (minimum score 6.5), or Michigan English Language Assessment Battery (minimum score 82). *Application deadline:* Applications are processed on a rolling basis. Application fee: $50. Electronic applications accepted. *Expenses:* Tuition: Full-time $13,665; part-time $560 per credit. Required fees: $1375. Tuition and fees vary according to course load, degree level and program. *Financial support:* In 2009–10, 207 students received support; fellowships with tuition reimbursements available, Federal Work-Study, scholarships/grants, unspecified assistantships, and family tuition reduction, active duty/veteran tuition reduction, group tuition reduction, interest-free payment plans available. Support available to part-time students. Financial award applicants required to submit FAFSA. *Unit head:* Dr. Mark Gordon, Associate Dean, 800-925-3368. *Application contact:* Jennifer Hall, Director of Enrollment, 866-4-WALDEN, E-mail: info@waldenu.edu.

Wayne State University, College of Engineering, Program in Sustainable Engineering, Detroit, MI 48202. Offers Certificate.

West Chester University of Pennsylvania, Office of Graduate Studies, College of Education, Department of Professional and Secondary Education, West Chester, PA 19383. Offers education for sustainability (Certificate); entrepreneurial education (Certificate); secondary education (M Ed, Teaching Certificate); teaching and learning with technology (Certificate). Part-time and evening/weekend programs available. *Students:* 4 full-time (3 women), 39 part-time (27 women); includes 2 minority (both Asian Americans or Pacific Islanders). Average age 30. 33 applicants, 97% accepted, 16 enrolled. In 2009, 13 master's, 3 other advanced degrees awarded. *Degree requirements:* For master's, comprehensive exam, thesis (for some programs). *Entrance requirements:* For master's, GRE or MAT, teaching certificate. Additional exam requirements/recommendations for international students: Required—TOEFL (minimum score 550 paper-based; 213 computer-based; 80 iBT). *Application deadline:* For fall admission, 4/15 priority date for domestic students, 3/15 for international students; for spring admission, 10/15 priority date for domestic students, 9/1 for international students. Applications are processed on a rolling basis. Application fee: $35. Electronic applications accepted. *Expenses:* Tuition, state resident: full-time $6666; part-time $370 per credit. Tuition, nonresident: full-time $10,666; part-time $593 per credit. Required fees: $122.56 per credit. *Financial support:* In 2009–10, research assistantships with full and partial tuition reimbursements (averaging $5,000 per year); unspecified assistantships also available. Support available to part-time students. Financial award application deadline: 2/15; financial award applicants required to submit FAFSA. *Faculty research:* Technology integration: preparing our teachers for the twenty-first century. *Unit head:* Dr. John Kinslow, Chair, 610-436-3108, E-mail: jkinslow@wcupa.edu. *Application contact:* Dr. Cynthia Haggard, Graduate Coordinator, 610-436-6934, E-mail: chaggard@wcupa.edu.

Western Illinois University, School of Graduate Studies, College of Arts and Sciences, Department of Geography, Macomb, IL 61455-1390. Offers community development (Certificate); environmental GIS (Certificate); geography (MA). Part-time programs available. *Students:* 13 full-time (5 women), 5 part-time (2 women); includes 3 minority (1 African American, 2 Asian Americans or Pacific Islanders), 2 international. Average age 32. 9 applicants, 67% accepted. In 2009, 9 master's, 7 other advanced degrees awarded. *Degree requirements:* For master's, thesis or alternative. *Entrance requirements:* Additional exam requirements/recommendations for international students: Required—TOEFL (minimum score 550 paper-based; 213 computer-based; 80 iBT). *Application deadline:* Applications are processed on a rolling basis. Application fee: $30. Electronic applications accepted. *Expenses:* Tuition, state resident: full-time $4486; part-time $249.21 per credit hour. Tuition, nonresident: full-time $8972; part-time $498.42 per credit hour. Required fees: $72.62 per credit hour. *Financial support:* In 2009–10, 9 students received support, including 9 research assistantships with full tuition reimbursements available (averaging $7,280 per year). Financial award applicants required to submit FAFSA. *Unit head:* Dr. Sam Thompson, Chairperson, 309-298-1648. *Application contact:* Evelyn Hoing, Assistant Director of Graduate Studies, 309-298-1806, Fax: 309-298-2345, E-mail: grad-office@wiu.edu.

West Virginia University, Davis College of Agriculture, Forestry and Consumer Sciences, Division of Resource Management and Sustainable Development, Program in Resource Management and Sustainable Development, Morgantown, WV 26506. Offers PhD. Part-time programs available. *Degree requirements:* For doctorate, thesis/dissertation. *Entrance requirements:* For doctorate, GRE General Test. Additional exam requirements/recommendations for international students: Required—TOEFL.

Urban and Regional Planning

Alabama Agricultural and Mechanical University, School of Graduate Studies, School of Agricultural and Environmental Sciences, Department of Community Planning and Urban Studies, Huntsville, AL 35811. Offers urban and regional planning (MURP). *Accreditation:* ACSP. Part-time and evening/weekend programs available. *Degree requirements:* For master's, comprehensive exam. *Entrance requirements:* For master's, GRE General Test. Additional exam requirements/recommendations for international students: Required—TOEFL (minimum score 500 paper-based; 173 computer-based; 61 iBT). Electronic applications accepted. *Faculty research:* Urban and rural research, needs assessment and community trends through analysis of social indicators, fiscal impact studies, rural transportation, health care.

American University of Beirut, Graduate Programs, Faculty of Engineering and Architecture, Beirut, Lebanon. Offers civil engineering (ME, PhD); electrical and computer engineering (ME, PhD); engineering management (MEM); environmental and water resources (ME); environmental and water resources engineering (PhD); environmental technology (MSES); mechanical engineering (ME, PhD); urban design (MUD); urban planning and policy (MUP). Part-time programs available. *Degree requirements:* For master's, one foreign language, comprehensive exam, thesis (for some programs); for doctorate, one foreign language, comprehensive exam, thesis/dissertation, publications. *Entrance requirements:* For master's, letters of recommendation; for doctorate, letters of recommendation, master's degree, transcripts, curriculum vitae, interview. Additional exam requirements/recommendations for international students: Required—TOEFL (minimum score 600 paper-based; 250 computer-based; 100 iBT), IELTS (minimum score 7.5). Electronic applications accepted.

American University of Sharjah, Graduate Programs, Sharjah, United Arab Emirates. Offers business (EMBA, GEMPA, MBA); chemical engineering (MS Ch E); civil engineering (MSCE); computer engineering (MS); electrical engineering (MSEE); mechanical engineering (MSME); mechatronics engineering (MS); public administration (MPA); teaching English to speakers of other languages (MA); translation and interpreting (MA); urban planning (MUP). Part-time and evening/weekend programs available. *Faculty:* 59 full-time (4 women), 5 part-time/adjunct (1 woman). *Students:* 101 full-time (44 women), 218 part-time (95 women). Average age 27. 184 applicants, 83% accepted, 92 enrolled. In 2009, 97 master's awarded. *Entrance requirements:* For master's, GMAT (MBA). Additional exam requirements/recommendations for international students: Required—TOEFL (minimum score 550 paper-based; 213 computer-based; 80 iBT), TWE (minimum score 5). *Application deadline:* For fall admission, 7/30 priority date for domestic students, 7/15 priority date for international students; for spring admission, 12/31 priority date for domestic students, 12/16 for international students. Applications are processed on a rolling basis. Application fee: $300. Electronic applications accepted. Tuition charges are reported in United Arab Emirates dirhams. *Expenses:* Tuition: Part-time 3250 United Arab Emirates dirhams per credit hour. *Financial support:* In 2009–10, 63 students received support, including 28 research assistantships with tuition reimbursements available, 35 teaching assistantships with tuition reimbursements available. *Faculty research:* Chemical engineering, civil engineering, computer engineering, electrical engineering, linguistics, translation. *Unit head:* Ghada S. Sami, Admissions Manager, 971-65151006 Ext. 1006, Fax: 971-65151020, E-mail: graduateadmission@aus.edu. *Application contact:* Ghada S. Sami, Admissions Manager, 971-65151006 Ext. 1006, Fax: 971-65151020, E-mail: graduateadmission@aus.edu.

Arizona State University, Graduate College, College of Design, School of Planning, Tempe, AZ 85287. Offers MUEP. *Accreditation:* ACSP. *Entrance requirements:* For master's, GRE General Test.

Arizona State University, Graduate College, College of Public Programs, School of Community Resources and Development, Tempe, AZ 85287. Offers community resources and development (PhD); nonprofit studies (MNpS); recreation and tourism studies (MS). *Degree requirements:* For master's, thesis or alternative.

Auburn University, Graduate School, College of Architecture, Design, and Construction, Program in Community Planning, Auburn University, AL 36849. Offers MCP, MPA/MCP. *Accreditation:* ACSP. Part-time programs available. *Faculty:* 9 full-time (3 women). *Students:* 24 full-time (13 women), 6 part-time (3 women); includes 5 minority (all African Americans), 2 international. Average age 26. 39 applicants, 62% accepted, 10 enrolled. In 2009, 7 master's awarded. *Degree requirements:* For master's, oral exam, project. *Entrance requirements:* For master's, GRE General Test. *Application deadline:* For fall admission, 7/7 for domestic students; for spring admission, 11/24 for domestic students. Applications are processed on a rolling basis. Application fee: $50 ($60 for international students). Electronic applications accepted. *Expenses:* Tuition, state resident: full-time $6240. Tuition, nonresident: full-time $18,720. International tuition: $18,938 full-time. Required fees: $492. Tuition and fees vary according to course load, program and reciprocity agreements. *Financial support:* Federal Work-Study available. Support available to part-time students. Financial award application deadline: 3/15;

Urban and Regional Planning

Auburn University (continued)
financial award applicants required to submit FAFSA. *Unit head:* Dr. John J. Pittari, Chair, 334-844-4516. *Application contact:* Dr. George Flowers, Dean of the Graduate School, 334-844-2125.

Ball State University, Graduate School, College of Architecture and Planning, Department of Urban Planning, Muncie, IN 47306-1099. Offers MURP. *Accreditation:* ACSP. *Degree requirements:* For master's, thesis. *Entrance requirements:* For master's, writing sample. *Faculty research:* Computer-assisted land-use analysis.

Boston University, Metropolitan College, Program in City Planning, Boston, MA 02215. Offers MCP. Part-time and evening/weekend programs available. *Faculty:* 2 full-time (0 women), 20 part-time/adjunct (5 women). *Students:* 9 full-time (5 women), 29 part-time (17 women); includes 6 minority (2 African Americans, 2 Asian Americans or Pacific Islanders, 2 Hispanic Americans), 4 international. Average age 28. 22 applicants, 82% accepted, 12 enrolled. In 2009, 6 master's awarded. *Entrance requirements:* Additional exam requirements/recommendations for international students: Required—TOEFL (minimum score 590 paper-based; 243 computer-based; 84 iBT). *Application deadline:* For fall admission, 7/15 priority date for domestic and international students; for spring admission, 12/15 priority date for domestic students, 11/15 priority date for international students. Applications are processed on a rolling basis. Application fee: $70. Electronic applications accepted. *Expenses:* Tuition: Full-time $37,910; part-time $1184 per credit hour. Required fees: $386; $40 per semester. Part-time tuition and fees vary according to class time, course level, degree level and program. *Financial support:* In 2009–10, 6 research assistantships with full and partial tuition reimbursements were awarded; career-related internships or fieldwork, institutionally sponsored loans, tuition waivers (partial), and unspecified assistantships also available. Support available to part-time students. Financial award application deadline: 6/15; financial award applicants required to submit FAFSA. *Faculty research:* Housing, community development and land use planning, environmental management and planning, international comparative development planning. *Unit head:* Dr. Daniel P. LeClair, Chair, 617-353-3025, Fax: 617-358-3595, E-mail: dleclair@bu.edu. *Application contact:* Dr. Enrique R. Silva, Professor and Faculty Coordinator, 617-358-3264, Fax: 617-358-3595, E-mail: ersilva@bu.edu.

California Polytechnic State University, San Luis Obispo, College of Architecture and Environmental Design, Department of City and Regional Planning, San Luis Obispo, CA 93407. Offers MCRP, MCRP/MS. *Accreditation:* ACSP. Part-time programs available. *Faculty:* 9 full-time (3 women), 1 part-time/adjunct (0 women). *Students:* 42 full-time (21 women), 1 (woman) part-time; includes 8 minority (4 Asian Americans or Pacific Islanders, 4 Hispanic Americans). Average age 26. 109 applicants, 55% accepted, 25 enrolled. In 2009, 14 master's awarded. *Degree requirements:* For master's, thesis. *Entrance requirements:* For master's, GRE, minimum GPA of 3.0 in last 90 quarter units. Additional exam requirements/recommendations for international students: Required—TOEFL (minimum score 550 paper-based; 213 computer-based), or IELTS (minimum score 6). *Application deadline:* For fall admission, 2/1 for domestic students, 11/30 for international students; for winter admission, 11/1 for domestic students, 6/30 for international students. Applications are processed on a rolling basis. Application fee: $55. Electronic applications accepted. *Expenses:* Tuition, nonresident: full-time $11,160; part-time $248 per unit. Required fees: $7134; $1553 per quarter. *Financial support:* Research assistantships, career-related internships or fieldwork, Federal Work-Study, institutionally sponsored loans, and unspecified assistantships available. Support available to part-time students. Financial award application deadline: 3/2; financial award applicants required to submit FAFSA. *Faculty research:* Natural hazards, housing, small town and rural planning, planning implementation, subdivision site design, transportation. *Unit head:* Dr. Michael Boswell, Graduate Coordinator, 805-756-2496, Fax: 805-756-1340, E-mail: mboswell@calpoly.edu. *Application contact:* Dr. Michael Boswell, Graduate Coordinator, 805-756-2496, Fax: 805-756-1340, E-mail: mboswell@calpoly.edu.

California State Polytechnic University, Pomona, Academic Affairs, College of Environmental Design, Program in Urban and Regional Planning, Pomona, CA 91768-2557. Offers MURP. *Accreditation:* ACSP. Part-time programs available. *Students:* 39 full-time (13 women), 42 part-time (22 women); includes 38 minority (5 African Americans, 16 Asian Americans or Pacific Islanders, 17 Hispanic Americans), 4 international. Average age 30. 119 applicants, 36% accepted, 24 enrolled. In 2009, 13 master's awarded. *Degree requirements:* For master's, thesis or alternative. *Entrance requirements:* For master's, GRE General Test. *Application deadline:* For fall admission, 5/1 priority date for domestic students; for winter admission, 10/15 priority date for domestic students; for spring admission, 1/20 priority date for domestic students. Applications are processed on a rolling basis. Application fee: $55. Electronic applications accepted. *Expenses:* Tuition, nonresident: full-time $6696; part-time $248 per credit. Required fees: $5487; $3237 per term. Tuition and fees vary according to course load, degree level and program. *Financial support:* Career-related internships or fieldwork, Federal Work-Study, and institutionally sponsored loans available. Support available to part-time students. Financial award application deadline: 3/2; financial award applicants required to submit FAFSA. *Unit head:* Herschel H. Farberow, Graduate Coordinator, 909-869-2716, Fax: 909-869-4688, E-mail: hfarberow@csupomona.edu. *Application contact:* Scott J. Duncan, Director, Admissions, 909-869-3258, Fax: 909-869-4529, E-mail: sjduncan@csupomona.edu.

California State University, Chico, Graduate School, College of Behavioral and Social Sciences, Department of Geography and Planning, Program in Rural and Town Planning, Chico, CA 95929-0722. Offers MA. Part-time programs available. *Students:* 3 full-time (all women), 1 part-time (0 women). Average age 35. 7 applicants, 43% accepted, 2 enrolled. *Entrance requirements:* For master's, GRE, 2 letters of recommendation. Additional exam requirements/recommendations for international students: Required—TOEFL (minimum score 550 paper-based; 213 computer-based; 80 iBT), IELTS (minimum score 6.5). *Application deadline:* For fall admission, 3/1 priority date for domestic students, 3/1 for international students; for spring admission, 9/15 priority date for domestic students, 9/15 for international students. Applications are processed on a rolling basis. Application fee: $55. Electronic applications accepted. *Unit head:* Dr. Dean Fairbanks, Graduate Coordinator, 530-898-5780. *Application contact:* Dr. Paul Melcon, Graduate Coordinator, 530-898-6871.

The Catholic University of America, School of Architecture and Planning, Washington, DC 20064. Offers cultural studies/sacred space (M Arch); design technologies (M Arch); digital media (M Arch); urban design (M Arch). Part-time programs available. *Faculty:* 20 full-time (7 women), 34 part-time/adjunct (4 women). *Students:* 110 full-time (46 women), 37 part-time (16 women); includes 40 minority (12 African Americans, 11 Asian Americans or Pacific Islanders, 17 Hispanic Americans), 9 international. Average age 27. 154 applicants, 80% accepted, 55 enrolled. In 2009, 39 master's awarded. *Degree requirements:* For master's, thesis. *Entrance requirements:* For master's, GRE (minimum score: 1000), minimum GPA of 2.8, portfolio, statement of purpose, official copies of academic transcripts, three letters of recommendation. Additional exam requirements/recommendations for international students: Required—TOEFL (minimum score 580 paper-based; 237 computer-based). *Application deadline:* For fall admission, 1/15 priority date for domestic students, 1/15 for international students; for spring admission, 10/15 priority date for domestic students, 10/15 for international students. Applications are processed on a rolling basis. Application fee: $55. Electronic applications accepted. *Expenses:* Contact institution. *Financial support:* Fellowships, research assistantships, teaching assistantships, Federal Work-Study, scholarships/grants, tuition waivers (full and partial), and unspecified assistantships available. Financial award application deadline: 2/1; financial award applicants required to submit FAFSA. *Faculty research:* Architectural history, cultural studies/scared space, design technologies, digital media, real estate development, urban design. *Unit head:* Randall Ott, Dean, 202-319-5784, Fax: 202-319-2023, E-mail: ott@cua.edu. *Application contact:* Julie Schwing, Director of Graduate Admissions, 202-319-5057, Fax: 202-319-6533, E-mail: cua-admissions@cua.edu.

Clark University, Graduate School, Department of International Development, Community, and Environment, Program in Community Development and Planning, Worcester, MA 01610-1477. Offers MA, MA/MBA. *Faculty:* 3 full-time (1 woman), 1 (woman) part-time/adjunct. *Students:* 18 full-time (11 women), 18 part-time (12 women); includes 4 minority (1 African American, 1 Asian American or Pacific Islander, 2 Hispanic Americans), 4 international. Average age 25. 44 applicants, 84% accepted, 24 enrolled. In 2009, 16 master's awarded. *Degree requirements:* For master's, thesis. *Entrance requirements:* For master's, 3 references, resume or curriculum vitae. Additional exam requirements/recommendations for international students: Required—TOEFL (minimum score 575 paper-based; 233 computer-based; 90 iBT) or IELTS (minimum score 6.5). *Application deadline:* For fall admission, 1/15 for domestic students. Application fee: $50. *Expenses:* Tuition: Full-time $34,900; part-time $4362.50 per course. *Financial support:* Fellowships, institutionally sponsored loans and scholarships/grants available. *Faculty research:* Urban revitalization, youth and gang violence, using GIS to assess the location and need for community &'healthy&"; amenities, systemic education reform, housing for disabled residents, economic development in neighborhood planning. *Unit head:* Dr. William F. Fisher, Director, 508-421-3765, Fax: 508-793-8820, E-mail: wfisher@clarku.edu. *Application contact:* Paula Hall, Department of International Development, Community, and Environment Graduate Admissions Office, 508-793-7201, Fax: 508-793-8820, E-mail: idce@clarku.edu.

Clemson University, Graduate School, College of Architecture, Arts, and Humanities, Department of Planning and Landscape Architecture, Program in City and Regional Planning, Clemson, SC 29634. Offers developmental planning (MCRP). *Students:* 42 full-time (18 women), 3 part-time (2 women); includes 3 minority (2 African Americans, 1 Hispanic American), 6 international. Average age 27. 49 applicants, 69% accepted, 23 enrolled. In 2009, 10 master's awarded. *Degree requirements:* For master's, departmental paper or thesis. *Entrance requirements:* For master's, GRE General Test. Additional exam requirements/recommendations for international students: Required—TOEFL. *Application deadline:* For fall admission, 2/15 priority date for domestic and international students. Applications are processed on a rolling basis. Application fee: $70 ($80 for international students). Electronic applications accepted. *Expenses:* Tuition, state resident: full-time $8684; part-time $528 per credit hour. Tuition, nonresident: full-time $15,330; part-time $1078 per credit hour. Required fees: $736; $37 per semester. Part-time tuition and fees vary according to course load and program. *Financial support:* In 2009–10, 33 students received support; fellowships with full and partial tuition reimbursements available, research assistantships with partial tuition reimbursements available, teaching assistantships with partial tuition reimbursements available, career-related internships or fieldwork, Federal Work-Study, institutionally sponsored loans, scholarships/grants, health care benefits, and unspecified assistantships available. Financial award application deadline: 4/15; financial award applicants required to submit FAFSA. *Faculty research:* Coastal planning, regional economic development, health care access. *Unit head:* Dr. Elaine M. Worzala, Chair, 864-656-3657, Fax: 864-656-0204, E-mail: eworzal@clemson.edu. *Application contact:* Dr. Barry C. Nocks, Director, 864-656-3926, Fax: 864-656-7519, E-mail: nocks2@clemson.edu.

Cleveland State University, College of Graduate Studies, Maxine Goodman Levin College of Urban Affairs, Program in Urban Planning, Design, and Development, Cleveland, OH 44115. Offers geographic information systems (Certificate); local and urban management (Certificate); urban economic development (Certificate); urban planning, design, and development (MUPDD); urban real estate development and finance (Certificate); JD/MUPDD. *Accreditation:* ACSP. Part-time and evening/weekend programs available. *Degree requirements:* For master's, project or thesis. *Entrance requirements:* For master's, GRE General Test (minimum 50th percentile verbal and quantitative, 4.0 analytical writing), minimum GPA of 3.0. Additional exam requirements/recommendations for international students: Required—TOEFL (minimum score 525 paper-based; 197 computer-based; 65 iBT). Electronic applications accepted. *Faculty research:* Housing and neighborhood development, urban housing policy, environmental sustainability, economic development.

Columbia University, Graduate School of Architecture, Planning, and Preservation, Program in Urban Planning, New York, NY 10027. Offers MS, PhD, JD/MS, M Arch/MS, MBA/MS, MIA/MS, MPH/MS, MS/MS. PhD offered through the Graduate School of Arts and Sciences. *Accreditation:* ACSP (one or more programs are accredited). *Degree requirements:* For master's, thesis. *Entrance requirements:* For master's, GRE General Test.

Concordia University, School of Graduate Studies, Faculty of Arts and Science, School of Community and Public Affairs, Montréal, QC H3G 1M8, Canada. Offers community economic development (Diploma).

Cornell University, Graduate School, Graduate Fields of Architecture, Art and Planning, Field of City and Regional Planning, Ithaca, NY 14853-0001. Offers city and regional planning (MRP, PhD); environmental planning and design (MRP, PhD); historic preservation planning (MA); international development planning (MRP, PhD); planning theory and systems analysis (MRP, PhD); regional economics and development planning (MRP, PhD); regional science (MRP, PhD); social and health systems planning (MRP, PhD); urban and regional theory (MRP, PhD); urban planning history (MRP, PhD). *Accreditation:* ACSP (one or more programs are accredited). *Faculty:* 32 full-time (11 women). *Students:* 127 full-time (70 women); includes 19 minority (5 African Americans, 8 Asian Americans or Pacific Islanders, 6 Hispanic Americans), 22 international. Average age 30. 331 applicants, 46% accepted, 68 enrolled. In 2009, 50 master's, 4 doctorates awarded. *Degree requirements:* For master's, thesis (MA); for doctorate, comprehensive exam, thesis/dissertation. *Entrance requirements:* For master's and doctorate, GRE General Test, 2 letters of recommendation. Additional exam requirements/recommendations for international students: Required—TOEFL (minimum score 600 paper-based; 250 computer-based; 77 iBT). *Application deadline:* For fall admission, 1/10 for domestic students. Application fee: $70. Electronic applications accepted. *Expenses:* Tuition: Full-time $29,500. Required fees: $70. Full-time tuition and fees vary according to degree level, program and student level. *Financial support:* In 2009–10, 24 students received support, including 3 teaching assistantships with full tuition reimbursements available; fellowships with full tuition reimbursements available, research assistantships with full tuition reimbursements available, institutionally sponsored loans, scholarships/grants, health care benefits, tuition waivers (full and partial), and unspecified assistantships also available. Financial award applicants required to submit FAFSA. *Faculty research:* Land use planning, economic development, international development, historic preservation, community development. *Unit head:* Director of Graduate Studies, 607-255-6848, Fax: 607-255-1971. *Application contact:* Graduate Field Assistant, 607-255-6848, Fax: 607-255-1971, E-mail: crp_admissions@cornell.edu.

Cornell University, Graduate School, Graduate Fields of Architecture, Art and Planning, Field of Regional Science, Ithaca, NY 14853-0001. Offers environmental studies (MA, MS, PhD); international spatial problems (MA, MS, PhD); location theory (MA, MS, PhD); multiregional economic analysis (MA, MS, PhD); peace science (MA, MS, PhD); planning methods (MA, MS, PhD); urban and regional economics (MA, MS, PhD). *Faculty:* 22 full-time (5 women). *Students:* 21 full-time (8 women); includes 2 minority (1 African American, 1 Asian American or Pacific Islander), 18 international. Average age 35. 15 applicants, 53% accepted, 4 enrolled. In 2009, 1 master's, 4 doctorates awarded. Terminal master's awarded for partial completion of doctoral program. *Degree requirements:* For master's, thesis; for doctorate, comprehensive exam, thesis/dissertation. *Entrance requirements:* For master's and doctorate, GRE General Test, 2 letters of recommendation. Additional exam requirements/recommendations for international students: Required—TOEFL (minimum score 600 paper-based; 250 computer-based; 77 iBT). *Application deadline:* For fall admission, 1/15 priority date for domestic students. Application fee: $70. Electronic applications accepted. *Expenses:* Tuition: Full-time $29,500. Required fees: $70. Full-time tuition and fees vary according to degree level, program and student level. *Financial support:* In 2009–10, 7 students received support; fellowships with full tuition reimbursements available, research assistantships with full tuition reimbursements available, teaching assistantships with full tuition reimbursements available, institutionally sponsored loans, scholarships/grants, health care benefits, tuition waivers (full and partial), and unspecified assistantships available. Financial award applicants required to submit FAFSA. *Faculty research:* Urban and regional growth, spatial economics, formation of spatial patterns by socioeconomic systems, non-linear dynamics and complex systems, environmental-economic systems. *Unit head:* Director of Graduate Studies, 607-255-6848, Fax: 607-255-1971. *Application contact:* Graduate Field Assistant, 607-255-6848, Fax: 607-255-1971, E-mail: regsci@cornell.edu.

Dalhousie University, Faculty of Architecture and Planning, School of Planning, Halifax, NS B3J 2X4, Canada. Offers M Eng, M Plan, MPS. *Degree requirements:* For master's, thesis. *Entrance requirements:* Additional exam requirements/recommendations for international students: Required—TOEFL, IELTS, CANTEST, CAEL, or Michigan English Language Assessment Battery. *Application deadline:* For fall admission, 6/1 priority date for domestic students, 4/1 for international students; for winter admission, 11/15 for domestic students, 8/31 for international students; for spring admission, 1/28 for domestic students, 12/31 for international students. Applications are processed on a rolling basis. Application fee: $70. Electronic applications accepted. *Financial support:* Career-related internships or fieldwork and scholarships/grants available. *Unit head:* Carol Madden, Director, 902-494-3260, Fax: 902-423-6672, E-mail: plan.office@dal.ca. *Application contact:* Frank Palermo, Graduate Coordinator, 902-494-3978, Fax: 902-423-6672, E-mail: frank.palermo@dal.ca.

Delta State University, Graduate Programs, College of Arts and Sciences, Division of Social Sciences, Program in Community Development, Cleveland, MS 38733-0001. Offers MS. Part-time programs available. *Degree requirements:* For master's, thesis or alternative. *Expenses:* Tuition, state resident: full-time $4450; part-time $247 per credit hour. Tuition, nonresident: full-time $11,520; part-time $640 per credit hour.

DePaul University, School of Public Service, Chicago, IL 60604. Offers financial administration management (Certificate); health administration (Certificate); health law and policy (MS); international public services (MS); leadership and policy studies (MS); metropolitan planning (Certificate); public administration (MPA); public service management (MS), including association management, fundraising and philanthropy, healthcare administration, higher education administration, metropolitan planning; public services (Certificate); JD/MS. Part-time and evening/weekend programs available. Postbaccalaureate distance learning degree programs offered (minimal on-campus study). *Faculty:* 14 full-time (3 women), 43 part-time/adjunct (24 women). *Students:* 283 full-time (206 women), 298 part-time (208 women); includes 196 minority (112 African Americans, 1 American Indian/Alaska Native, 30 Asian Americans or Pacific Islanders, 53 Hispanic Americans), 18 international. Average age 26. 162 applicants, 100% accepted, 94 enrolled. In 2009, 108 master's awarded. *Degree requirements:* For master's, thesis or integrative seminar. *Entrance requirements:* For master's, minimum GPA of 2.7. Additional exam requirements/recommendations for international students: Required—TOEFL (minimum score 550 paper-based; 213 computer-based; 80 iBT), IELTS (minimum score 6.5). *Application deadline:* Applications are processed on a rolling basis. Application fee: $40. Electronic applications accepted. *Expenses:* Tuition: Full-time $37,525; part-time $620 per credit hour. *Financial support:* In 2009–10, 60 students received support, including 3 research assistantships with full tuition reimbursements available (averaging $7,000 per year); career-related internships or fieldwork, Federal Work-Study, institutionally sponsored loans, scholarships/grants, tuition waivers (partial), and unspecified assistantships also available. Support available to part-time students. Financial award application deadline: 7/1; financial award applicants required to submit FAFSA. *Faculty research:* Government financing, transportation, leadership, health care, volunteerism and organizational behavior, non-profit organizations. Total annual research expenditures: $20,000. *Unit head:* Dr. J. Patrick Murphy, Director, 312-362-5608, Fax: 312-362-5506, E-mail: jpmurphy@depaul.edu. *Application contact:* Megan B. Balderston, Director of Admissions and Marketing, 312-362-5565, Fax: 312-362-5506, E-mail: pubserv@depaul.edu.

Eastern Kentucky University, The Graduate School, College of Arts and Sciences, Department of Government, Program in General Public Administration, Richmond, KY 40475-3102. Offers community development (MPA); community health administration (MPA); general public administration (MPA). *Accreditation:* NASPAA. Part-time and evening/weekend programs available. *Entrance requirements:* For master's, GRE General Test, minimum GPA of 2.5.

Eastern Michigan University, Graduate School, College of Arts and Sciences, Department of Geography and Geology, Program in Urban and Regional Planning, Ypsilanti, MI 48197. Offers MS. *Accreditation:* ACSP. *Students:* 6 full-time (4 women), 9 part-time (4 women); includes 4 minority (2 African Americans, 2 American Indian/Alaska Native), 1 international. Average age 32.Application fee: $35. Tuition and fees vary according to course level. *Application contact:* Dr. Norman Tyler, Program Advisor, 734-487-8656, Fax: 734-487-6979, E-mail: norman.tyler@emich.edu.

Eastern Michigan University, Graduate School, College of Arts and Sciences, Department of Political Science, Programs in Public Administration, Ypsilanti, MI 48197. Offers local government management (Graduate Certificate); management of public healthcare services (Graduate Certificate); public administration (MPA, Graduate Certificate); public budget management (Graduate Certificate); public land planning (Graduate Certificate); public management (Graduate Certificate); public personnel management (Graduate Certificate); public policy analysis (Graduate Certificate). *Accreditation:* NASPAA. *Students:* 18 full-time (7 women), 130 part-time (72 women); includes 53 minority (46 African Americans, 2 American Indian/Alaska Native, 1 Asian American or Pacific Islander, 4 Hispanic Americans), 5 international. Average age 34. In 2009, 17 master's, 37 other advanced degrees awarded. Application fee: $35. Tuition and fees vary according to course level. *Unit head:* Dr. Joseph Ohren, Program Director, 734-487-2522, Fax: 734-487-3340, E-mail: joseph.ohren@emich.edu. *Application contact:* Dr. Sukru Koyluoglu, Program Coordinator, 734-487-0063, Fax: 734-487-3340, E-mail: sukru.koyuoglu@emich.edu.

Eastern University, School for Social Change, St. Davids, PA 19087-3696. Offers urban studies (MA), including arts in transformation, community development, youth leadership.

Eastern University, School of Leadership and Development, St. Davids, PA 19087-3696. Offers economic development (MBA), including international development, urban development (MA, MBA); international development (MA), including global development, urban development (MA, MBA); nonprofit management (MS); organizational leadership (MA); M Div/MBA. Part-time and evening/weekend programs available. *Degree requirements:* For master's, thesis (for some programs). *Entrance requirements:* For master's, GMAT (MBA), minimum GPA of 2.5. *Expenses:* Contact institution. *Faculty research:* Micro-level economic development, China welfare and economic development, macroethics, micro- and macro-level economic development in transitional economics, organizational effectiveness.

Eastern Washington University, Graduate Studies, College of Business and Public Administration, Program in Urban and Regional Planning, Cheney, WA 99004-2431. Offers MURP, MPA/MURP. *Accreditation:* ACSP. *Degree requirements:* For master's, comprehensive exam, thesis or alternative. *Entrance requirements:* For master's, minimum GPA of 3.0. *Expenses:* Tuition, state resident: full-time $7476; part-time $249 per quarter hour. Tuition, nonresident: full-time $18,030; part-time $601 per quarter hour. Required fees: $3.50 per quarter hour. $142 per quarter.

East Tennessee State University, School of Graduate Studies, College of Business and Technology, Department of Economics, Finance, and Urban Studies, Johnson City, TN 37614. Offers city management (MCM); community development (MPM); general administration (MPM); municipal service management (MPM); urban and regional economic development (MPM); urban and regional planning (MPM). *Degree requirements:* For master's, internship, oral defense of thesis, research report. *Entrance requirements:* For master's, GRE General Test, minimum GPA of 3.0. Additional exam requirements/recommendations for international students: Required—TOEFL (minimum score 550 paper-based; 213 computer-based).

Florida Atlantic University, College of Architecture, Urban and Public Affairs, School of Urban and Regional Planning, Boca Raton, FL 33431-0991. Offers economic development and tourism (Certificate); environmental planning (Certificate); sustainable community planning (Certificate); urban and regional planning (MURP); visual planning technology (Certificate). *Accreditation:* ACSP. Part-time and evening/weekend programs available. *Faculty:* 8 full-time (6 women), 1 (woman) part-time/adjunct. *Students:* 28 full-time (17 women), 12 part-time (4 women); includes 11 minority (2 African Americans, 1 Asian American or Pacific Islander, 8 Hispanic Americans), 3 international. Average age 31. 70 applicants, 47% accepted, 7 enrolled. In 2009, 14 master's awarded. *Entrance requirements:* For master's, GRE General Test, minimum GPA of 3.0. Additional exam requirements/recommendations for international students: Required—TOEFL. *Application deadline:* For fall admission, 7/1 priority date for domestic students, 2/15 for international students; for spring admission, 11/1 priority date for domestic students, 7/15 for international students. Applications are processed on a rolling basis. Application fee: $30. *Expenses:* Tuition, state resident: full-time $7055; part-time $293.94 per credit hour. Tuition, nonresident: full-time $22,096; part-time $920.66 per credit hour. *Financial support:* Fellowships with full tuition reimbursements, research assistantships, career-related internships or fieldwork, Federal Work-Study, institutionally sponsored loans, and tuition waivers (partial) available. Financial award application deadline: 4/1. *Faculty research:* Growth management, urban design, computer applications/geographical information systems, environmental planning. *Unit head:* Dr. Jaap Vos, Chair, 954-762-5653, Fax: 954-762-5673, E-mail: jvos@fau.edu. *Application contact:* Dr. Jaap Vos, Chair, 954-762-5653, Fax: 954-762-5673, E-mail: jvos@fau.edu.

Florida State University, The Graduate School, College of Social Sciences and Public Policy, Department of Urban and Regional Planning, Tallahassee, FL 32306. Offers MSP, PhD, JD/MSP, MA/MSP, MPA/MSP. *Accreditation:* ACSP (one or more programs are accredited). Part-time programs available. *Faculty:* 11 full-time (4 women), 4 part-time/adjunct (0 women). *Students:* 108 full-time (47 women), 26 part-time (10 women); includes 35 minority (14 African Americans, 3 American Indian/Alaska Native, 9 Asian Americans or Pacific Islanders, 9 Hispanic Americans), 8 international. Average age 27. 118 applicants, 64% accepted, 55 enrolled. In 2009, 47 master's, 2 doctorates awarded. *Degree requirements:* For master's, capstone project, internship; for doctorate, thesis/dissertation. *Entrance requirements:* For master's and doctorate, GRE General Test, minimum GPA of 3.0. Additional exam requirements/recommendations for international students: Required—TOEFL (minimum score 550 paper-based; 213 computer-based; 80 iBT); Recommended—IELTS. *Application deadline:* For fall admission, 2/15 priority date for domestic students, 11/15 priority date for international students; for spring admission, 11/1 for domestic students, 9/1 for international students. Applications are processed on a rolling basis. Application fee: $30. Electronic applications accepted. *Expenses:* Tuition, state resident: full-time $7413. Tuition, nonresident: full-time $22,567. *Financial support:* In 2009–10, 36 students received support, including 1 fellowship with full tuition reimbursement available (averaging $19,000 per year), 28 research assistantships with full tuition reimbursements available (averaging $7,000 per year), 6 teaching assistantships with full tuition reimbursements available (averaging $13,500 per year); career-related internships or fieldwork, Federal Work-Study, institutionally sponsored loans, and tuition waivers (partial) also available. Financial award application deadline: 2/15; financial award applicants required to submit FAFSA. *Faculty research:* Growth management, environmental planning, developing countries, transportation, sustainable and healthy communities. Total annual research expenditures: $950,000. *Unit head:* Dr. Timothy S. Chapin, Chairperson, 850-644-4510, Fax: 850-645-4841, E-mail: tchapin@fsu.edu. *Application contact:* Cynthia E. Brown, Admissions Coordinator, 850-644-4510, Fax: 850-645-4841, E-mail: durp@coss.fsu.edu.

Georgia Institute of Technology, Graduate Studies and Research, College of Architecture, City and Regional Planning Program, Atlanta, GA 30332-0001. Offers city and regional planning (PhD); economic development (MCRP); environmental planning and management (MCRP); geographic information systems (MCRP); land and community development (MCRP); land use planning (MCRP); transportation (MCRP); urban design (MCRP); MCP/MSCE. *Accreditation:* ACSP. *Degree requirements:* For master's, thesis, internship. *Entrance requirements:* For master's, GRE General Test, minimum GPA of 2.7. Additional exam requirements/recommendations for international students: Required—TOEFL. Electronic applications accepted.

Georgia State University, Andrew Young School of Policy Studies, Department of Public Management and Policy, Atlanta, GA 30303. Offers disaster management (Certificate); nonprofit management (Certificate); planning and economic development (Certificate); public administration (MPA), including criminal justice, management and finance, nonprofit management, planning and economic development, policy analysis and evaluation, public health; public policy (MPP, PhD), including disaster policy (MPP), nonprofit policy (MPP), planning and economic development policy (MPP), public finance policy (MPP), social policy (MPP); JD/MPA. *Accreditation:* NASPAA (one or more programs are accredited). Part-time and evening/weekend programs available. Terminal master's awarded for partial completion of doctoral program. *Degree requirements:* For master's, thesis optional; for doctorate, comprehensive exam, thesis/dissertation. *Entrance requirements:* For master's and doctorate, GRE General Test. Additional exam requirements/recommendations for international students: Required—TOEFL. Electronic applications accepted. *Faculty research:* Public management, policy analysis, public finance, planning and economic development, nonprofit leadership and policy.

Harvard University, Graduate School of Arts and Sciences, Committee on Architecture, Landscape Architecture, and Urban Planning, Cambridge, MA 02138. Offers architecture (PhD); landscape architecture (PhD); urban planning (PhD). *Degree requirements:* For doctorate, one foreign language, thesis/dissertation, oral exam. *Entrance requirements:* For doctorate, GRE General Test. Additional exam requirements/recommendations for international students: Required—TOEFL. *Expenses:* Tuition: Full-time $33,696. Required fees: $1126. Full-time tuition and fees vary according to program.

Harvard University, Graduate School of Design, Department of Urban Planning and Design, Cambridge, MA 02138. Offers urban planning (MUP); urban planning and design (MAUD, MLAUD). *Accreditation:* ACSP (one or more programs are accredited). *Faculty:* 5 full-time (2 women), 31 part-time/adjunct (6 women). *Students:* 110 full-time (45 women); includes 19 minority (3 African Americans, 1 American Indian/Alaska Native, 11 Asian Americans or Pacific Islanders, 4 Hispanic Americans), 42 international. Average age 29. In 2009, 59 master's awarded. *Entrance requirements:* For master's, GRE General Test. Additional exam requirements/recommendations for international students: Required—TOEFL (minimum score 600 paper-based; 250 computer-based; 104 iBT). *Application deadline:* For fall admission, 1/14 for domestic and international students. Application fee: $85. Electronic applications accepted. *Expenses:* Tuition: Full-time $33,696. Required fees: $1126. Full-time tuition and fees vary according to program. *Financial support:* Federal Work-Study and scholarships/grants available. Financial award application deadline: 2/4; financial award applicants required to submit FAFSA. *Unit head:* Rahul Mehrotra, Chair, 617-495-2521. *Application contact:* Gail Gustafson, Director of Admissions, 617-495-5453, Fax: 617-495-8949, E-mail: ggustafson@gsd.harvard.edu.

Harvard University, John F. Kennedy School of Government, Program in Public Policy, Cambridge, MA 02138. Offers public policy (MPP); public policy and urban planning (MPPUP); JD/MPP; MBA/MPP; MD/MPP. *Accreditation:* NASPAA. *Students:* 406 full-time (199 women), 20 part-time (10 women); includes 114 minority (29 African Americans, 9 American Indian/Alaska Native, 45 Asian Americans or Pacific Islanders, 31 Hispanic Americans), 104 international. Average age 27. 1,670 applicants, 23% accepted, 216 enrolled. In 2009, 190 master's awarded. *Entrance requirements:* For master's, GMAT or GRE General Test. Additional exam requirements/recommendations for international students: Required—TOEFL (minimum score 600 paper-based; 250 computer-based; 100 iBT), TWE. *Application deadline:* For fall admission, 1/2 for domestic students. Application fee: $80. Electronic applications accepted. *Expenses:* Tuition: Full-time $33,696. Required fees: $1126. Full-time tuition and fees vary according to program. *Financial support:* Fellowships, research assistantships, teaching assistantships, career-related internships or fieldwork, Federal Work-Study, institutionally sponsored loans, scholarships/grants, health care benefits, and unspecified assistantships available. Financial award application deadline: 2/6; financial award applicants required to submit CSS PROFILE or FAFSA. *Unit head:* Debra Isaacson, Director, 617-496-8382, E-mail: debra_isaacson@harvard.edu. *Application contact:* 617-495-1155.

Urban and Regional Planning

Hunter College of the City University of New York, Graduate School, School of Arts and Sciences, Department of Urban Affairs and Planning, Program in Urban Planning, New York, NY 10021-5085. Offers MUP, JD/MUP. *Accreditation:* ACSP. Part-time programs available. *Faculty:* 13 full-time (5 women), 12 part-time/adjunct (5 women). *Students:* 58 full-time (25 women), 55 part-time (24 women); includes 22 minority (9 African Americans, 2 American Indian/Alaska Native, 5 Asian Americans or Pacific Islanders, 6 Hispanic Americans). Average age 30. 167 applicants, 38% accepted, 37 enrolled. *Degree requirements:* For master's, planning studio and internship. *Entrance requirements:* For master's, minimum 12 credits of course work in social sciences, 2 letters of recommendation. Additional exam requirements/recommendations for international students: Required—TOEFL. *Application deadline:* For fall admission, 4/1 for domestic students, 2/1 for international students; for spring admission, 11/1 for domestic students, 9/1 for international students. Application fee: $125. *Expenses:* Tuition, state resident: full-time $7360; part-time $310 per credit. Required fees: $250 per semester. *Financial support:* In 2009–10, 4 fellowships with full tuition reimbursements (averaging $9,000 per year), 10 teaching assistantships (averaging $1,200 per year) were awarded; research assistantships, career-related internships or fieldwork, Federal Work-Study, and tuition waivers (partial) also available. Support available to part-time students. *Faculty research:* Community and economic development, transportation planning and policy, geographic information systems, housing, land use. *Unit head:* Dr. Lynn McCormick, Director, 212-772-5733, Fax: 212-772-5593, E-mail: lmccormi@hunter.cuny.edu. *Application contact:* William Zlata, Director for Graduate Admissions, 212-772-4482, Fax: 212-650-3336, E-mail: admissions@hunter.cuny.edu.

Iowa State University of Science and Technology, Graduate College, College of Design, Department of Community and Regional Planning, Ames, IA 50011. Offers community and regional planning (MCRP); transportation (MS); M Arch/MCRP; MBA/MCRP; MCRP/MLA; MCRP/MPA. *Accreditation:* ACSP (one or more programs are accredited). Part-time programs available. *Faculty:* 11 full-time (3 women), 1 part-time/adjunct (0 women). *Students:* 21 full-time (11 women), 13 part-time (7 women); includes 2 minority (both African Americans), 6 international. Average age 31. 34 applicants, 71% accepted, 14 enrolled. In 2009, 10 master's awarded. *Degree requirements:* For master's, thesis or alternative. *Entrance requirements:* For master's, GRE General Test. Additional exam requirements/recommendations for international students: Required—TOEFL (minimum score 550 paper-based; 213 computer-based; 79 iBT) or IELTS (minimum score 6.5). *Application deadline:* For fall admission, 1/1 priority date for domestic and international students. Applications are processed on a rolling basis. Application fee: $40 ($90 for international students). Electronic applications accepted. *Expenses:* Tuition, state resident: full-time $6716. Tuition, nonresident: full-time $8908. Tuition and fees vary according to course level, course load, program and student level. *Financial support:* In 2009–10, 11 teaching assistantships with full and partial tuition reimbursements (averaging $7,210 per year) were awarded; research assistantships with full and partial tuition reimbursements, career-related internships or fieldwork, institutionally sponsored loans, tuition waivers (partial), and unspecified assistantships also available. Support available to part-time students. Financial award application deadline: 2/1; financial award applicants required to submit FAFSA. *Faculty research:* Economic development, housing, land use, geographic information systems planning in developing nations, regional and community revitalization, transportation planning in developing countries. *Unit head:* Dr. Douglas Johnston, Chair, 515-294-8958, Fax: 515-294-2348, E-mail: landarch@iastate.edu. *Application contact:* Dr. Francis Owusu, Director of Graduate Education, 515-294-7769, E-mail: crp@iastate.edu.

Jackson State University, Graduate School, School of Liberal Arts, Department of Urban and Regional Planning, Jackson, MS 39217. Offers MS. *Degree requirements:* For master's, comprehensive exam. *Entrance requirements:* For master's, GRE General Test. Additional exam requirements/recommendations for international students: Required—TOEFL.

Kansas State University, Graduate School, College of Architecture, Planning and Design, Department of Interior Architecture and Product Design, Manhattan, KS 66506. Offers regional and community planning (MRCP). *Accreditation:* ACSP. Part-time and evening/weekend programs available. Postbaccalaureate distance learning degree programs offered (minimal on-campus study). *Faculty:* 11 full-time (3 women). *Students:* 29 full-time (25 women); includes 4 minority (1 African American, 3 Hispanic Americans). Average age 22. 29 applicants, 100% accepted, 29 enrolled. In 2009, 32 master's awarded. *Degree requirements:* For master's, thesis, oral exam. *Entrance requirements:* For master's, minimum GPA of 3.0, portfolio. Additional exam requirements/recommendations for international students: Required—TOEFL (minimum score 600 paper-based). *Application deadline:* For fall admission, 2/1 priority date for domestic and international students; for spring admission, 8/1 priority date for domestic and international students. Applications are processed on a rolling basis. Application fee: $80. Electronic applications accepted. *Financial support:* Research assistantships, teaching assistantships with full tuition reimbursements, career-related internships or fieldwork, Federal Work-Study, institutionally sponsored loans, and scholarships/grants available. Support available to part-time students. Financial award application deadline: 3/1; financial award applicants required to submit FAFSA. *Faculty research:* Planning interior spaces for exhibition; residential and commercial spaces; design of objects such as furniture, lighting, equipment, finishing treatments and accessories. *Unit head:* Lorraine Cutler, Head, 785-532-5992, Fax: 785-532-6722, E-mail: lcutler@ksu.edu. *Application contact:* Neal Hubbell, Director, 785-532-5992, Fax: 785-532-6722, E-mail: nhubbel@ksu.edu.

Lesley University, Graduate School of Arts and Social Sciences, Program in Urban Environmental Leadership, Cambridge, MA 02138-2790. Offers MA. *Entrance requirements:* For master's, 2 letters of recommendation, interview.

Loyola University Chicago, Institute of Pastoral Studies, Program in Social Justice and Community Development, Chicago, IL 60660. Offers MA, Certificate. *Students:* 33 full-time (24 women), 5 part-time (4 women); includes 7 minority (5 African Americans, 2 Hispanic Americans), 1 international. Average age 30. 19 applicants, 100% accepted, 14 enrolled. In 2009, 16 master's awarded. *Degree requirements:* For master's, internship. *Expenses:* Tuition: Full-time $14,220; part-time $790 per credit hour. Required fees: $60 per semester hour. Tuition and fees vary according to program. *Unit head:* Dr. Robert A. Ludwig. *Application contact:* Randy Gibbons, Administrative Assistant, 312-915-7450, Fax: 312-915-7410, E-mail: rgibbon@luc.edu.

Massachusetts Institute of Technology, School of Architecture and Planning, Department of Urban Studies and Planning, Cambridge, MA 02139-4307. Offers city planning (MCP); urban and regional planning (PhD); urban and regional studies (PhD); urban studies and planning (SM). *Accreditation:* ACSP (one or more programs are accredited). *Faculty:* 29 full-time (11 women). *Students:* 207 full-time (118 women); includes 44 minority (9 African Americans, 2 American Indian/Alaska Native, 19 Asian Americans or Pacific Islanders, 14 Hispanic Americans), 62 international. Average age 29. 575 applicants, 19% accepted, 78 enrolled. In 2009, 93 master's, 7 doctorates awarded. Terminal master's awarded for partial completion of doctoral program. *Degree requirements:* For master's, thesis; for doctorate, comprehensive exam, thesis/dissertation. *Entrance requirements:* For master's, GRE General Test; for doctorate, GRE General Test—minimum score required: 1200 (V&Q) combined; 5.0 analytical writing. Additional exam requirements/recommendations for international students: Required—TOEFL (minimum score 600 paper-based; 250 computer-based; 100 iBT) or IELTS (minimum score 7); Recommended—TWE. *Application deadline:* For fall admission, 1/3 for domestic and international students. Application fee: $75. Electronic applications accepted. *Expenses:* Tuition: Full-time $37,510; part-time $585 per unit. Required fees: $272. *Financial support:* In 2009–10, 176 students received support, including 74 fellowships with tuition reimbursements available (averaging $20,544 per year), 65 research assistantships with tuition reimbursements available (averaging $20,932 per year), 16 teaching assistantships with tuition reimbursements available (averaging $28,535 per year); career-related internships or fieldwork, Federal Work-Study, institutionally sponsored loans, scholarships/grants, health care benefits, and unspecified assistantships also available. *Faculty research:* City design and sustainable urban development, housing, environment and energy policy and planning, international development and regional planning, community and economic development, urban and geographic information systems. Total annual research expenditures: $1.9 million. *Unit head:* Prof. Amy Glasmeier, Department Head, 617-253-1907, Fax: 617-253-2654, E-mail: duspinfo@mit.edu. *Application contact:* Graduate Admissions, 617-253-9403, Fax: 617-253-2654, E-mail: duspapply@mit.edu.

McGill University, Faculty of Graduate and Postdoctoral Studies, Faculty of Engineering, School of Urban Planning, Montréal, QC H3A 2T5, Canada. Offers environmental planning (MUP); housing (MUP); transportation (MUP); urban design (MUP); urban planning, policy and design (PhD).

Michigan State University, The Graduate School, College of Agriculture and Natural Resources and College of Social Science, School of Planning, Design and Construction, East Lansing, MI 48824. Offers construction management (MS, PhD); environmental design (MA); interior design and facilities management (MA); international planning studies (MIPS); urban and regional planning (MURP). *Faculty:* 25 full-time (12 women). *Students:* 56 full-time (21 women), 25 part-time (12 women); includes 4 minority (1 African American, 2 Asian Americans or Pacific Islanders, 1 Hispanic American), 53 international. Average age 30. 122 applicants, 57% accepted. In 2009, 34 degrees awarded. *Degree requirements:* For master's, thesis or alternative. *Entrance requirements:* Additional exam requirements/recommendations for international students: Required—TOEFL. *Application deadline:* Applications are processed on a rolling basis. Electronic applications accepted. *Financial support:* In 2009–10, 16 research assistantships with tuition reimbursements (averaging $13,001 per year), 2 teaching assistantships with tuition reimbursements (averaging $13,599 per year) were awarded. Total annual research expenditures: $281,011. *Unit head:* Dr. Scott G. Witter, Director, 517-432-6379, Fax: 517-432-8108, E-mail: witter@msu.edu. *Application contact:* Dawn Brown, Graduate Secretary, 517-432-3393, Fax: 517-432-3772, E-mail: browndaw@msu.edu.

Minnesota State University Mankato, College of Graduate Studies, College of Social and Behavioral Sciences, Department of Urban and Regional Studies, Mankato, MN 56001. Offers local government management (Certificate); urban and regional studies (MA); urban planning (MA, Certificate); MAPA/MA. *Students:* 16 full-time (2 women), 19 part-time (9 women). *Degree requirements:* For master's, one foreign language, comprehensive exam, thesis or alternative. *Entrance requirements:* For master's, minimum GPA of 3.0 during previous 2 years, 2 letters of recommendation. Additional exam requirements/recommendations for international students: Required—TOEFL. *Application deadline:* For fall admission, 7/1 priority date for domestic students; for spring admission, 11/1 for domestic students. Applications are processed on a rolling basis. Application fee: $40. Electronic applications accepted. *Expenses:* Tuition, state resident: full-time $5364. Tuition, nonresident: full-time $8314. *Financial support:* Fellowships with partial tuition reimbursements, research assistantships with full tuition reimbursements, teaching assistantships with full tuition reimbursements, career-related internships or fieldwork, Federal Work-Study, institutionally sponsored loans, and unspecified assistantships available. Support available to part-time students. Financial award application deadline: 3/15; financial award applicants required to submit FAFSA. *Unit head:* Dr. Anthony Filipovitch, Chairperson, 507-389-1714. *Application contact:* 507-389-2321, E-mail: grad@mnsu.edu.

Missouri State University, Graduate College, College of Natural and Applied Sciences, Department of Geography, Geology, and Planning, Springfield, MO 65897. Offers geospatial sciences (MS); natural and applied science (MNAS), including geography, geology and planning; secondary education (MS Ed), including earth science, geography. *Accreditation:* ACSP. Part-time and evening/weekend programs available. *Faculty:* 20 full-time (4 women). *Students:* 19 full-time (10 women), 12 part-time (5 women); includes 1 minority (American Indian/Alaska Native), 1 international. Average age 29. 19 applicants, 100% accepted, 13 enrolled. In 2009, 4 master's awarded. *Degree requirements:* For master's, comprehensive exam, thesis (for some programs). *Entrance requirements:* For master's, GRE General Test (MS, MNAS), minimum undergraduate GPA of 3.0 (MS, MNAS), 9-12 teacher certification (MS Ed). Additional exam requirements/recommendations for international students: Required—TOEFL (minimum score 550 paper-based; 213 computer-based; 79 iBT). *Application deadline:* For fall admission, 7/20 priority date for domestic students, 5/1 for international students; for spring admission, 12/20 priority date for domestic students, 9/1 for international students. Applications are processed on a rolling basis. Application fee: $35 ($50 for international students). Electronic applications accepted. *Expenses:* Tuition, state resident: full-time $3852; part-time $214 per credit hour. Tuition, nonresident: full-time $7524; part-time $418 per credit hour. Required fees: $696; $172 per semester. Tuition and fees vary according to course level, course load, degree level and program. *Financial support:* In 2009–10, 7 research assistantships with full tuition reimbursements (averaging $8,933 per year), 8 teaching assistantships with full tuition reimbursements (averaging $8,236 per year) were awarded; career-related internships or fieldwork, Federal Work-Study, institutionally sponsored loans, scholarships/grants, and unspecified assistantships also available. Financial award application deadline: 3/31; financial award applicants required to submit FAFSA. *Faculty research:* Stratigraphy and ancient meteorite impacts, environmental geochemistry of karst, hyperspectral image processing, water quality, small town planning. *Unit head:* Dr. Thomas Plymate, Head, 417-836-5800, Fax: 417-836-6934, E-mail: tomplymate@missouristate.edu. *Application contact:* Eric Eckert, Coordinator of Graduate Admissions and Recruitment, 417-836-5331, Fax: 417-836-6200, E-mail: ericeckert@missouristate.edu.

Montclair State University, The Graduate School, College of Humanities and Social Sciences, Department of Anthropology, Montclair, NJ 07043-1624. Offers community development (Certificate). Part-time and evening/weekend programs available. *Faculty:* 8 full-time (4 women), 13 part-time/adjunct (9 women). *Students:* 3 part-time (2 women). Average age 40. 5 applicants, 100% accepted, 3 enrolled. *Entrance requirements:* Additional exam requirements/recommendations for international students: Required—TOEFL (minimum score 83 computer-based), or IELTS. *Expenses:* Tuition, area resident: Part-time $486.74 per credit. Tuition, state resident: part-time $486.74 per credit. Tuition, nonresident: part-time $751.34 per credit. Tuition and fees vary according to degree level and program. *Financial support:* In 2009–10, 2 research assistantships with full tuition reimbursements (averaging $7,000 per year) were awarded; Federal Work-Study, scholarships/grants, and unspecified assistantships also available. Support available to part-time students. Financial award application deadline: 3/1; financial award applicants required to submit FAFSA. *Unit head:* Dr. Kenneth Brook, Chairperson, 973-655-4119, E-mail: brookk@mail.montclair.edu. *Application contact:* Amy Aiello, Director of Graduate Admissions and Operations, 973-655-5147, Fax: 973-655-7869, E-mail: graduate.school@montclair.edu.

Morgan State University, School of Graduate Studies, Institute of Architecture and Planning, Program in City and Regional Planning, Baltimore, MD 21251. Offers MCRP. *Accreditation:* ACSP. *Degree requirements:* For master's, thesis. *Entrance requirements:* Additional exam requirements/recommendations for international students: Required—TOEFL (minimum score 550 paper-based; 213 computer-based). *Faculty research:* Nonprofit organizations, community development, urban design, transportation, international planning.

New York University, Robert F. Wagner Graduate School of Public Service, Program in Urban Planning, New York, NY 10012-1019. Offers housing (Advanced Certificate); public economics (Advanced Certificate); quantitative analysis and computer applications for policy and planning (Advanced Certificate); urban planning (MUP); JD/MUP. *Accreditation:* ACSP (one or more programs are accredited). Part-time and evening/weekend programs available. *Faculty:* 8 full-time (4 women), 13 part-time/adjunct (4 women). *Students:* 83 full-time (49 women), 54 part-time (25 women); includes 24 minority (7 African Americans, 11 Asian Americans or Pacific Islanders, 6 Hispanic Americans), 14 international. Average age 28. 271 applicants, 56% accepted, 52 enrolled. In 2009, 37 master's awarded. *Degree requirements:* For master's, thesis or alternative, end event workshop. *Entrance requirements:* For master's, minimum undergraduate GPA of 3.0. Additional exam requirements/recommendations for international students: Required—TOEFL (minimum score 600 paper-based; 250 computer-based; 100 iBT), TWE (minimum score 4). *Application deadline:* For fall admission, 6/1 for domestic students, 1/15 for international students; for spring admission, 11/15 for domestic students, 10/1 for international students. Applications are processed on a rolling basis. Application fee: $80. Electronic applications accepted. *Expenses:* Tuition: Full-time $30,528; part-time $1272 per credit. Required fees: $2177. *Financial support:* In 2009–10, 24 students received support, including 23 fellowships (averaging $9,572 per year), 1 research assistantship with full tuition reimbursement available (averaging $22,440 per year); career-related internships or fieldwork, Federal Work-Study, institutionally sponsored loans, scholarships/grants, health care benefits, and unspecified assistantships also available. Support available to part-time students. Financial award application deadline: 12/1; financial award applicants required to submit FAFSA. *Unit head:* Prof. Ingrid Gould Ellen, Director of the Planning Program, 212-998-7533, Fax: 212-995-4164, E-mail: ingrid.ellen@nyu.edu. *Application contact:* Christopher Alexander, Administrative Aide, Enrollment, 212-998-7414, Fax: 212-995-4611, E-mail: wagner.admissions@nyu.edu.

Northeastern University, College of Social Sciences and Humanities, School of Public Policy and Urban Affairs, Boston, MA 02115-5096. Offers urban and regional policy (MURP). Part-time and evening/weekend programs available. *Faculty:* 5 full-time (2 women). *Students:* 4 full-time (3 women), 4 part-time (2 women). 15 applicants, 60% accepted, 8 enrolled. *Entrance requirements:* For master's, GRE. Additional exam requirements/recommendations for international students: Required—TOEFL. *Application deadline:* For fall admission, 2/1 priority date for domestic and international students. Applications are processed on a rolling basis. Application fee: $50. Electronic applications accepted. *Financial support:* Federal Work-Study, scholarships/grants, and tuition waivers available. Financial award application deadline: 3/1; financial award applicants required to submit FAFSA. *Unit head:* Dr. Laurie Dopkins, Graduate Coordinator, 617-373-2889, E-mail: murp@neu.edu. *Application contact:* Jo-Anne Dickinson, Graduate Admissions Contact, 617-373-5990, Fax: 617-373-7281, E-mail: gsas@neu.edu.

The Ohio State University, Graduate School, College of Engineering, Austin E. Knowlton School of Architecture, Program in City and Regional Planning, Columbus, OH 43210. Offers MCRP, PhD. *Accreditation:* ACSP (one or more programs are accredited). *Faculty:* 11. *Students:* 77 full-time (35 women), 19 part-time (8 women); includes 17 minority (12 African Americans, 3 Asian Americans or Pacific Islanders, 2 Hispanic Americans), 21 international. Average age 28. In 2009, 49 master's, 3 doctorates awarded. *Degree requirements:* For master's, thesis optional; for doctorate, thesis/dissertation. *Entrance requirements:* Additional exam requirements/recommendations for international students: Required—TOEFL (minimum score 600 paper-based; 250 computer-based). *Application deadline:* For fall admission, 8/15 priority date for domestic students, 7/1 priority date for international students; for winter admission, 12/1 priority date for domestic students, 11/1 priority date for international students; for spring admission, 3/1 priority date for domestic students, 2/1 priority date for international students. Applications are processed on a rolling basis. Application fee: $40 ($50 for international students). Electronic applications accepted. *Expenses:* Tuition, state resident: full-time $10,683. Tuition, nonresident: full-time $25,923. Tuition and fees vary according to course load and program. *Financial support:* Fellowships, research assistantships, Federal Work-Study, institutionally sponsored loans, and unspecified assistantships available. Support available to part-time students. *Unit head:* Jennifer Evans-Cowley, Section Head, 614-292-5427, Fax: 614-292-7106, E-mail: cowley.11@osu.edu. *Application contact:* 614-292-9444, Fax: 614-292-3895, E-mail: domestic.grad@osu.edu.

Portland State University, Graduate Studies, College of Urban and Public Affairs, Nohad A. Toulan School of Urban Studies and Planning, Program in Urban and Regional Planning, Portland, OR 97207-0751. Offers MURP. *Accreditation:* ACSP. Part-time programs available. *Entrance requirements:* For master's, minimum GPA of 2.75, 3 letters of recommendation. Additional exam requirements/recommendations for international students: Required—TOEFL (minimum score 550 paper-based; 213 computer-based). *Faculty research:* Policy planning and administration, community development, land-use and environment, transportation, urban and regional analysis.

Pratt Institute, School of Architecture, Program in City and Regional Planning, Brooklyn, NY 11205-3899. Offers MSCRP. *Accreditation:* ACSP. Part-time programs available. *Faculty:* 2 full-time (1 woman), 9 part-time/adjunct (3 women). *Students:* 57 full-time (31 women), 11 part-time (8 women); includes 15 minority (8 African Americans, 4 Asian Americans or Pacific Islanders, 3 Hispanic Americans), 3 international. Average age 28. 121 applicants, 56% accepted, 29 enrolled. In 2009, 12 master's awarded. *Degree requirements:* For master's, thesis. *Entrance requirements:* For master's, writing sample, bachelor's degree, transcripts, letters of recommendation, portfolio. Additional exam requirements/recommendations for international students: Required—TOEFL (minimum score 550 paper-based; 213 computer-based; 79 iBT). *Application deadline:* For fall admission, 1/5 for domestic and international students; for spring admission, 10/1 for domestic and international students. Applications are processed on a rolling basis. Application fee: $50 ($90 for international students). Electronic applications accepted. *Expenses:* Tuition: Full-time $22,734. Required fees: $1280. *Financial support:* Career-related internships or fieldwork, Federal Work-Study, institutionally sponsored loans, scholarships/grants, health care benefits, and unspecified assistantships available. Support available to part-time students. Financial award application deadline: 2/1; financial award applicants required to submit FAFSA. *Faculty research:* Advocacy planning, community development, comprehensive physical planning, transportation planning, real estate development. *Unit head:* John Shapiro, Chairperson, 718-399-4391, E-mail: jshapir6@pratt.edu. *Application contact:* Young Hah, Director of Graduate Admissions, 718-636-3683, Fax: 718-399-4242, E-mail: yhah@pratt.edu.

See Close-Up on page 145.

Pratt Institute, School of Architecture, Program in Urban Environmental Systems Management, Brooklyn, NY 11205-3899. Offers MS. Part-time programs available. *Faculty:* 5 part-time/adjunct (3 women). *Students:* 25 full-time (16 women), 10 part-time (4 women); includes 9 minority (2 African Americans, 1 Asian American or Pacific Islander, 6 Hispanic Americans), 2 international. Average age 31. 52 applicants, 94% accepted, 17 enrolled. In 2009, 2 master's awarded. *Degree requirements:* For master's, thesis. *Entrance requirements:* For master's, portfolio or writing sample, letters of recommendation. Additional exam requirements/recommendations for international students: Required—TOEFL (minimum score 550 paper-based; 213 computer-based; 79 iBT). *Application deadline:* For fall admission, 1/5 for domestic and international students; for spring admission, 10/1 for domestic and international students. Application fee: $50 ($90 for international students). Electronic applications accepted. *Expenses:* Tuition: Full-time $22,734. Required fees: $1280. *Financial support:* Career-related internships or fieldwork, Federal Work-Study, institutionally sponsored loans, scholarships/grants, and unspecified assistantships available. Support available to part-time students. Financial award application deadline: 2/1; financial award applicants required to submit FAFSA. *Unit head:* Eva Hanhardt, Chairperson, 718-399-4391, E-mail: ehanhard@pratt.edu. *Application contact:* Young Hah, Director of Graduate Admissions, 718-636-3683, Fax: 718-399-4242, E-mail: yhah@pratt.edu.

See Close-Up on page 145.

Queen's University at Kingston, School of Graduate Studies and Research, School of Urban and Regional Planning, Kingston, ON K7L 3N6, Canada. Offers M Pl. Part-time programs available. *Degree requirements:* For master's, thesis optional. *Entrance requirements:* Additional exam requirements/recommendations for international students: Required—TOEFL (minimum score 580 paper-based; 237 computer-based). *Faculty research:* Housing, real estate development, human services, environmental services, land use planning.

Rutgers, The State University of New Jersey, New Brunswick, Edward J. Bloustein School of Planning and Public Policy, Program in Planning and Public Policy, Piscataway, NJ 08854-8097. Offers PhD. Part-time programs available. *Degree requirements:* For doctorate, comprehensive exam, thesis/dissertation. *Entrance requirements:* For doctorate, GRE, master's degree. Additional exam requirements/recommendations for international students: Required—TOEFL (minimum score 575 paper-based; 245 computer-based). Electronic applications accepted. *Faculty research:* Housing and community development, land use and transportation, politics and policy analysis, urban and regional economics, international development.

Rutgers, The State University of New Jersey, New Brunswick, Edward J. Bloustein School of Planning and Public Policy, Program in Urban Planning and Policy Development, Piscataway, NJ 08854-8097. Offers MCRP, MCRS, PhD, JD/MCRP, MBA/MCRP. *Accreditation:* ACSP (one or more programs are accredited). Part-time and evening/weekend programs available. Terminal master's awarded for partial completion of doctoral program. *Degree requirements:* For master's, thesis optional; for doctorate, thesis/dissertation. *Entrance requirements:* For master's and doctorate, GRE General Test. Electronic applications accepted. *Faculty research:* Land use, transportation, housing, regional economic development, urban redevelopment, developing countries.

San Diego State University, Graduate and Research Affairs, College of Professional Studies and Fine Arts, School of Public Affairs, Program in City Planning, San Diego, CA 92182. Offers MCP. Part-time programs available. *Entrance requirements:* For master's, GRE General Test. Additional exam requirements/recommendations for international students: Required—TOEFL. Electronic applications accepted. *Faculty research:* Community development, housing, sustainable development, visioning.

San Jose State University, Graduate Studies and Research, College of Social Sciences, Department of Urban and Regional Planning, San Jose, CA 95192-0001. Offers MUP, Certificate. *Accreditation:* ACSP. Part-time programs available. *Students:* 79 full-time (44 women), 52 part-time (30 women); includes 49 minority (7 African Americans, 27 Asian Americans or Pacific Islanders, 15 Hispanic Americans), 11 international. Average age 30. 110 applicants, 35% accepted, 32 enrolled. In 2009, 32 master's awarded. *Degree requirements:* For master's, comprehensive exam, thesis or alternative. *Entrance requirements:* For master's, GRE, minimum GPA of 3.0. *Application deadline:* For fall admission, 6/29 for domestic students; for spring admission, 11/30 for domestic students. Applications are processed on a rolling basis. Application fee: $59. Electronic applications accepted. *Financial support:* Teaching assistantships, career-related internships or fieldwork, Federal Work-Study, and institutionally sponsored loans available. Financial award application deadline: 5/31; financial award applicants required to submit FAFSA. *Faculty research:* Retirement communities, planning and problems, women in suburbia, influence on urban development, Taiwanese urban development issues. *Unit head:* Dayana Salazar, Chair, 408-924-5854, Fax: 408-924-5872. *Application contact:* Dayana Salazar, Chair, 408-924-5854, Fax: 408-924-5872.

State University of New York College of Environmental Science and Forestry, Department of Landscape Architecture, Syracuse, NY 13210-2779. Offers community design and planning (MLA, MS); cultural landscape studies and conservation (MLA, MS); landscape and urban ecology (MLA, MS). *Accreditation:* ASLA (one or more programs are accredited). *Degree requirements:* For master's, comprehensive exam (for some programs), thesis (for some programs). *Entrance requirements:* For master's, GRE General Test, minimum GPA of 3.0. Additional exam requirements/recommendations for international students: Required—TOEFL (paper-based 550, computer-based 213, iBT 80) or IELTS (6) or STEP Aiken (Grade 1). *Faculty research:* Site analysis and design, city and regional planning, community environments.

State University of New York College of Environmental Science and Forestry, Program in Environmental Science, Syracuse, NY 13210-2779. Offers environmental and community land planning (MPS, MS, PhD); environmental and natural resources policy (PhD); environmental communication and participatory processes (MPS, MS, PhD); environmental policy and democratic processes (MPS, MS, PhD); environmental systems and risk management (MPS, MS, PhD); water and wetland resource studies (MPS, MS, PhD). Part-time programs available. *Degree requirements:* For master's, thesis (for some programs); for doctorate, comprehensive exam, thesis/dissertation. *Entrance requirements:* For master's and doctorate, GRE General Test, minimum GPA of 3.0. Additional exam requirements/recommendations for international students: Required—TOEFL (minimum score 550 paper-based; 213 computer-based; 80 iBT), IELTS (minimum score 6). *Faculty research:* Environmental education/communications, water resources, land resources, waste management.

Temple University, Ambler College, Department of Community and Regional Planning, Philadelphia, PA 19122-6096. Offers MS. Program offered at Ambler Campus. Part-time and evening/weekend programs available. *Entrance requirements:* For master's, GRE or GMAT, 2 letters of recommendation, minimum undergraduate GPA of 3.0. Additional exam requirements/recommendations for international students: Required—TOEFL (minimum score 550 paper-based; 213 computer-based; 79 iBT).

Texas A&M University, College of Architecture, Department of Landscape Architecture and Urban Planning, College Station, TX 77843. Offers land development (MSLD); landscape architecture (MLA); urban and regional science (PhD); urban planning (MUP). *Accreditation:* ACSP (one or more programs are accredited); ASLA (one or more programs are accredited). *Faculty:* 28. *Students:* 159 full-time (60 women), 17 part-time (10 women); includes 15 minority (5 African Americans, 1 American Indian/Alaska Native, 1 Asian American or Pacific Islander, 8 Hispanic Americans), 97 international. Average age 31. In 2009, 50 master's, 9 doctorates awarded. Terminal master's awarded for partial completion of doctoral program. *Degree requirements:* For master's, thesis optional, professional internship; for doctorate, comprehensive exam, thesis/dissertation, methods statistics seminar. *Entrance requirements:* For master's, GMAT or GRE General Test, portfolio (MLA), minimum GPA of 3.0; for doctorate, GMAT or GRE General Test. Additional exam requirements/recommendations for international students: Required—TOEFL. *Application deadline:* For fall admission, 2/1 priority date for domestic students; for spring admission, 8/1 for domestic students. Applications are processed on a rolling basis. Application fee: $50 ($75 for international students). Electronic applications accepted. *Expenses:* Tuition, state resident: full-time $3991; part-time $221.74 per credit hour. Tuition, nonresident: full-time $9049; part-time $502.74 per credit hour. *Financial support:* In 2009–10, fellowships with tuition reimbursements (averaging $1,000 per year), research assistantships with partial tuition reimbursements (averaging $8,100 per year), teaching assistantships with partial tuition reimbursements (averaging $11,250 per year) were awarded; career-related internships or fieldwork, institutionally sponsored loans, and scholarships/grants also available. Financial award application deadline: 4/1; financial award applicants required to submit FAFSA. *Faculty research:* Erosion control/water quality, geographic information systems/spatial information technology, transport hazards, international sustainable development. *Unit head:* Head, 979-845-1019, Fax: 979-862-1784. *Application contact:* Graduate Office, 979-845-6582, Fax: 979-845-4491, E-mail: t-morris@tamu.edu.

Texas Southern University, School of Public Affairs, Program in Urban Planning and Environmental Policy, Houston, TX 77004-4584. Offers MS, PhD. *Accreditation:* ACSP. Part-time and evening/weekend programs available. *Faculty:* 3 full-time (1 woman). *Students:* 36 full-time (20 women), 28 part-time (13 women); includes 52 minority (49 African Americans, 3 Hispanic Americans), 5 international. Average age 40. 24 applicants, 100% accepted, 18 enrolled. In 2009, 4 master's, 1 doctorate awarded. *Degree requirements:* For master's, comprehensive exam, thesis optional. *Entrance requirements:* For master's, GRE General Test, minimum GPA of 2.5. Additional exam requirements/recommendations for international students: Required—TOEFL. *Application deadline:* For fall admission, 7/1 priority date for domestic students, 7/1 for international students; for spring admission, 11/1 for domestic and international students. Applications are processed on a rolling basis. Application fee: $50 ($75 for international students). Electronic applications accepted. *Expenses:* Tuition, state resident: full-time $1805; part-time $100 per credit hour. Tuition, nonresident: full-time $6470; part-time $343 per credit hour. Tuition and fees vary according to course level, course load and degree level. *Financial support:* In 2009–10, 14 research assistantships (averaging $6,793 per year), 4 teaching assistantships (averaging $3,250 per year) were awarded; fellowships, career-related internships or fieldwork, Federal Work-Study, and institutionally sponsored loans also available. Financial award application deadline: 5/1; financial award applicants required to submit FAFSA. *Unit head:* Dr. Walter McCoy, Interim Chair, 713-313-7312, E-mail: mccoy_wj@tsu.edu. *Application contact:* Brenda Randell, Secretary, 713-313-7405, E-mail: randell_bj@tsu.edu.

Urban and Regional Planning

Tufts University, Graduate School of Arts and Sciences, Department of Urban and Environmental Policy and Planning, Medford, MA 02155. Offers community development (MA); environmental policy (MA); health and human welfare (MA); housing policy (MA); international environment/development policy (MA); public policy (MPP); MA/MS; MALD/MA. *Accreditation:* ACSP (one or more programs are accredited). Part-time programs available. *Faculty:* 11 full-time, 9 part-time/adjunct. *Students:* 133 (83 women); includes 26 minority (15 African Americans, 5 Asian Americans or Pacific Islanders, 6 Hispanic Americans), 2 international. Average age 27. 200 applicants, 63% accepted, 53 enrolled. In 2009, 44 master's awarded. *Degree requirements:* For master's, thesis, internship. *Entrance requirements:* For master's, GRE General Test. Additional exam requirements/recommendations for international students: Required—TOEFL (minimum score 550 paper-based; 213 computer-based; 80 iBT). *Application deadline:* For fall admission, 1/15 for domestic students, 12/15 for international students. Applications are processed on a rolling basis. Application fee: $75. Electronic applications accepted. *Expenses:* Contact institution. *Financial support:* Teaching assistantships with partial tuition reimbursements, career-related internships or fieldwork, Federal Work-Study, scholarships/grants, tuition waivers (partial), and unspecified assistantships available. Support available to part-time students. Financial award application deadline: 1/15; financial award applicants required to submit FAFSA. *Unit head:* Julian Agyeman, Chair, 617-627-3394, Fax: 617-627-3377. *Application contact:* Ann Urosevich, Department Administrator, 617-627-3394.

Université du Québec à Rimouski, Graduate Programs, Program in Regional Development, Rimouski, QC G5L 3A1, Canada. Offers MA, PhD, Diploma. Part-time programs available. *Degree requirements:* For master's, thesis. *Entrance requirements:* For master's, appropriate bachelor's degree, proficiency in French.

Université du Québec en Outaouais, Graduate Programs, Program in Regional Development, Gatineau, QC J8X 3X7, Canada. Offers MA.

Université Laval, Faculty of Architecture, Planning and Visual Arts, Department of Regional Planning, Programs in Planning and Regional Development, Québec, QC G1K 7P4, Canada. Offers MATDR, PhD. Terminal master's awarded for partial completion of doctoral program. *Degree requirements:* For master's, thesis (for some programs); for doctorate, comprehensive exam, thesis/dissertation. *Entrance requirements:* For master's and doctorate, knowledge of French and English. Electronic applications accepted.

University at Albany, State University of New York, College of Arts and Sciences, Department of Geography and Planning, Program in Regional Planning, Albany, NY 12222-0001. Offers MRP. *Accreditation:* ACSP. Part-time programs available. *Degree requirements:* For master's, thesis optional. *Entrance requirements:* Additional exam requirements/recommendations for international students: Required—TOEFL (minimum score 550 paper-based; 213 computer-based). Electronic applications accepted. *Faculty research:* Urban planning, Third World development, political and social aspects of planning, urban housing and employment, environmental planning.

University at Buffalo, the State University of New York, Graduate School, School of Architecture and Planning, Department of Urban and Regional Planning, Buffalo, NY 14260. Offers MUP, JD/MUP, M Arch/MUP. *Accreditation:* ACSP. Part-time programs available. *Faculty:* 13 full-time (3 women), 8 part-time/adjunct (2 women). *Students:* 77 full-time (36 women), 19 part-time (11 women); includes 15 minority (13 African Americans, 2 Hispanic Americans), 16 international. Average age 28. 147 applicants, 62% accepted, 39 enrolled. In 2009, 39 master's awarded. *Degree requirements:* For master's, thesis or alternative, project. *Entrance requirements:* For master's, minimum GPA of 3.0, resume, 3 letters of recommendation. Additional exam requirements/recommendations for international students: Required—TOEFL (minimum score 550 paper-based; 213 computer-based; 79 iBT), or IELTS (minimum score 6.5). *Application deadline:* For fall admission, 3/1 priority date for domestic and international students; for spring admission, 10/31 priority date for domestic students, 10/1 priority date for international students. Applications are processed on a rolling basis. Application fee: $75. Electronic applications accepted. *Financial support:* In 2009–10, 3 fellowships with full tuition reimbursements (averaging $9,600 per year), 15 research assistantships with full and partial tuition reimbursements (averaging $5,044 per year), 9 teaching assistantships with partial tuition reimbursements (averaging $6,400 per year) were awarded; career-related internships or fieldwork, Federal Work-Study, institutionally sponsored loans, scholarships/grants, health care benefits, tuition waivers (partial), and unspecified assistantships also available. Support available to part-time students. Financial award application deadline: 3/1; financial award applicants required to submit FAFSA. *Faculty research:* Community development and urban management, economic and international development, environmental and land use planning, GIS and spatial modeling, urban design and physical planning. Total annual research expenditures: $341,108. *Unit head:* Dr. Niraj Verma, Professor and Chair, 716-829-2133 Ext. 109, Fax: 716-829-3256, E-mail: nverma@buffalo.edu. *Application contact:* Donna M. Rogalski, Assistant to the Chair, 716-829-2133 Ext. 109, Fax: 716-829-3256, E-mail: dmr1@buffalo.edu.

The University of Akron, Graduate School, Buchtel College of Arts and Sciences, Department of Geography and Planning, Program in Urban Planning, Akron, OH 44325. Offers MA. *Students:* 13 full-time (4 women), 1 (woman) part-time, 5 international. Average age 27. 11 applicants, 91% accepted, 8 enrolled. In 2009, 3 master's awarded. *Degree requirements:* For master's, thesis optional. *Entrance requirements:* For master's, 2 letters of recommendation. Additional exam requirements/recommendations for international students: Required—TOEFL (minimum score 550 paper-based; 213 computer-based; 79 iBT). *Application deadline:* Applications are processed on a rolling basis. Application fee: $30 ($40 for international students). Electronic applications accepted. *Expenses:* Tuition, state resident: full-time $6570; part-time $365 per credit hour. Tuition, nonresident: full-time $11,250; part-time $625 per credit hour. *Unit head:* Dr. Linda Barrett, Graduate Director, 330-972-6120. *Application contact:* Dr. Linda Barrett, Graduate Director, 330-972-6120.

The University of Arizona, College of Architecture and Landscape Architecture, Planning Program, Tucson, AZ 85721. Offers MS. *Accreditation:* ACSP. *Faculty:* 1. *Students:* 18 full-time (8 women), 8 part-time (5 women); includes 2 African Americans, 3 Hispanic Americans. Average age 33. 20 applicants, 75% accepted, 6 enrolled. In 2009, 19 master's awarded. *Entrance requirements:* For master's, GRE, 3 letters of recommendation, letter of intent. Additional exam requirements/recommendations for international students: Required—TOEFL (minimum score 573 paper-based; 233 computer-based; 80 iBT). *Application deadline:* For fall admission, 2/1 for domestic students, 12/1 for international students; for spring admission, 10/1 for domestic students, 6/1 for international students. Application fee: $75. Electronic applications accepted. *Expenses:* Tuition, state resident: full-time $9028. Tuition, nonresident: full-time $24,890. *Financial support:* In 2009–10, 1 teaching assistantship (averaging $10,184 per year) was awarded; health care benefits and unspecified assistantships also available. Total annual research expenditures: $3,040. *Unit head:* Dr. John Paul Jones, Department Head, 520-621-1652, Fax: 520-621-2889, E-mail: jpjones@email.arizona.edu. *Application contact:* Debi Romero, 520-621-1004, Fax: 520-626-6448, E-mail: dab@ul.arizona.edu.

The University of British Columbia, School of Community and Regional Planning, Vancouver, BC V6T 1Z1, Canada. Offers M Sc P, MAP, PhD. *Accreditation:* ACSP (one or more programs are accredited). *Degree requirements:* For master's, thesis; for doctorate, thesis/dissertation, oral exam. *Entrance requirements:* For master's, GRE (recommended); for doctorate, MCRP or equivalent. Additional exam requirements/recommendations for international students: Required—TOEFL (minimum score 600 paper-based; 250 computer-based). Electronic applications accepted. *Faculty research:* Natural resources management, international development, urban spatial, urban policy and community development planning.

University of California, Berkeley, Graduate Division, College of Environmental Design, Department of City and Regional Planning, Berkeley, CA 94720-1500. Offers MCP, PhD, JD/MCP, M Arch/MCP, MCP/MPH, MCP/MS, MLA/MCP. *Accreditation:* ACSP. *Students:* 129 full-time (67 women). Average age 30. 423 applicants, 43 enrolled. In 2009, 40 master's, 9 doctorates awarded. *Degree requirements:* For master's, professional project or thesis; for doctorate, thesis/dissertation, qualifying exam. *Entrance requirements:* For master's and doctorate, GRE General Test, minimum GPA of 3.0, 3 letters of recommendation. Additional exam requirements/recommendations for international students: Required—TOEFL. *Application deadline:* For fall admission, 12/5 for domestic students. Application fee: $70 ($90 for international students). *Financial support:* Fellowships, research assistantships, teaching assistantships available. *Faculty research:* Housing and project development, physical planning and design, community and economic development, geographic information systems, transportation. *Unit head:* Prof. Karen Christensen, 510-642-3256, Fax: 510-642-1641. *Application contact:* Yeri Caesar-Kaptoech, Student Affairs Officer, 510-643-9440, Fax: 510-642-1641, E-mail: dcrpgrad@berkeley.edu.

University of California, Davis, Graduate Studies, Graduate Group in Community Development, Davis, CA 95616. Offers MS. *Degree requirements:* For master's, comprehensive exam (for some programs), thesis (for some programs). *Entrance requirements:* For master's, GRE General Test, minimum GPA of 3.0. Additional exam requirements/recommendations for international students: Required—TOEFL (minimum score 550 paper-based; 213 computer-based). Electronic applications accepted. *Faculty research:* Globalization; community economic change; urban and regional development; community planning design and sustainability; race, ethnic, and gender roles; community organization and political mobilization.

University of California, Irvine, Office of Graduate Studies, School of Social Ecology, Department of Planning, Policy and Design, Irvine, CA 92697. Offers planning, policy and design (PhD); urban and regional planning (MURP). *Accreditation:* ACSP (one or more programs are accredited). *Faculty:* 19 full-time (6 women), 10 part-time/adjunct (3 women). *Students:* 113 full-time (71 women), 1 part-time (0 women); includes 33 minority (1 African American, 1 American Indian/Alaska Native, 18 Asian Americans or Pacific Islanders, 13 Hispanic Americans), 25 international. Average age 32. 240 applicants, 60% accepted, 53 enrolled. In 2009, 42 master's, 7 doctorates awarded. *Degree requirements:* For doctorate, thesis/dissertation, research project. *Entrance requirements:* For master's and doctorate, GRE General Test, minimum GPA of 3.0. Additional exam requirements/recommendations for international students: Required—TOEFL (minimum score 550 paper-based; 213 computer-based). *Application deadline:* For fall admission, 1/15 priority date for domestic and international students. Application fee: $70 ($90 for international students). Electronic applications accepted. *Financial support:* Fellowships with tuition reimbursements, research assistantships with full tuition reimbursements, teaching assistantships with tuition reimbursements, institutionally sponsored loans, traineeships, health care benefits, and unspecified assistantships available. Financial award application deadline: 1/15; financial award applicants required to submit FAFSA. *Faculty research:* Community and social policy, economic development, land-use and growth management, transportation planning, environmental policy. Total annual research expenditures: $1.5 million. *Unit head:* Marlon G. Boarnet, Chair, 949-824-7695, E-mail: mgboarne@uci.edu. *Application contact:* Janet Gallagher, Academic Coordinator, 949-824-9849, Fax: 949-824-8566, E-mail: ppd@uci.edu.

University of California, Los Angeles, Graduate Division, School of Public Affairs, Department of Urban Planning, Los Angeles, CA 90095-1656. Offers MA, PhD, JD/MA, MA/MA, MBA/MA. *Accreditation:* ACSP (one or more programs are accredited). *Degree requirements:* For master's, comprehensive exam or thesis; for doctorate, thesis/dissertation, oral and written qualifying exams. *Entrance requirements:* For master's, GRE General Test (recommended); for doctorate, GRE General Test, master's degree in urban planning or related field. Additional exam requirements/recommendations for international students: Required—TOEFL. Electronic applications accepted. *Faculty research:* Industrial hazards, political economy of South and Southeast Asia, historic preservation, flexible production in U.S. and Western Europe, land-use controls.

University of Central Florida, College of Health and Public Affairs, Department of Public Administration, Orlando, FL 32816. Offers emergency management and homeland security (Certificate); non-profit management (MNM, Certificate); public administration (MPA, Certificate); urban and regional planning (Certificate). *Accreditation:* NASPAA. Part-time and evening/weekend programs available. *Faculty:* 11 full-time (2 women), 6 part-time/adjunct (1 woman). *Students:* 68 full-time (45 women), 235 part-time (166 women); includes 105 minority (64 African Americans, 10 Asian Americans or Pacific Islanders, 31 Hispanic Americans), 7 international. Average age 31. 184 applicants, 75% accepted, 95 enrolled. In 2009, 80 master's, 36 other advanced degrees awarded. *Degree requirements:* For master's, comprehensive exam, thesis or alternative, research report. *Entrance requirements:* For master's, GRE General Test. *Application deadline:* For fall admission, 7/1 for domestic students; for spring admission, 12/1 for domestic students. Application fee: $30. Electronic applications accepted. *Expenses:* Tuition, state resident: part-time $306.31 per credit hour. Tuition, nonresident: part-time $1099.01 per credit hour. Part-time tuition and fees vary according to degree level and program. *Financial support:* In 2009–10, 8 students received support, including 4 fellowships with partial tuition reimbursements available (averaging $10,000 per year), 2 research assistantships with partial tuition reimbursements available (averaging $3,100 per year), 3 teaching assistantships with partial tuition reimbursements available (averaging $5,200 per year); career-related internships or fieldwork, Federal Work-Study, institutionally sponsored loans, tuition waivers (partial), and unspecified assistantships also available. Financial award application deadline: 3/1; financial award applicants required to submit FAFSA. *Unit head:* Dr. MaryAnn Feldheim, Chair, 407-823-3693, Fax: 407-823-5651. *Application contact:* Dr. MaryAnn Feldheim, Chair, 407-823-3693, Fax: 407-823-5651.

University of Cincinnati, Graduate School, College of Design, Architecture, Art, and Planning, School of Planning, Program in Community Planning, Cincinnati, OH 45221. Offers MCP, JD/MCP. *Accreditation:* ACSP. *Degree requirements:* For master's, thesis. *Entrance requirements:* For master's, GRE General Test. Additional exam requirements/recommendations for international students: Required—TOEFL.

University of Colorado Denver, College of Architecture and Planning, Program in Design and Planning, Denver, CO 80217-3364. Offers PhD. Part-time programs available. *Students:* 10 full-time (6 women), 28 part-time (15 women); includes 5 minority (2 African Americans, 1 Asian American or Pacific Islander, 2 Hispanic Americans), 7 international. 52 applicants, 19% accepted, 7 enrolled. In 2009, 5 doctorates awarded. *Degree requirements:* For doctorate, thesis/dissertation. *Entrance requirements:* For doctorate, GRE, minimum undergraduate GPA of 3.0, graduate 3.5. Additional exam requirements/recommendations for international students: Required—TOEFL. *Application deadline:* For fall admission, 2/15 for domestic students; for spring admission, 10/1 for domestic students. Applications are processed on a rolling basis. Application fee: $50 ($75 for international students). *Expenses:* Contact institution. *Financial support:* Fellowships with partial tuition reimbursements, research assistantships, teaching assistantships, career-related internships or fieldwork, Federal Work-Study, institutionally sponsored loans, scholarships/grants, and tuition waivers (full and partial) available. Support available to part-time students. Financial award application deadline: 2/15; financial award applicants required to submit FAFSA. *Faculty research:* Land use and environmental planning and design; design and planning processes and practices; history, theory, and criticism of the built environment. *Unit head:* Dr. Kevin Krizek, Director, 303-556-3282, Fax: 303-556-3687, E-mail: kevin.krizek@colorado.edu. *Application contact:* Michael Harper, Administrative Coordinator, 303-556-6042, Fax: 303-556-3687, E-mail: michael.t.harper@ucdenver.edu.

University of Colorado Denver, College of Architecture and Planning, Program in Urban and Regional Planning, Denver, CO 80217-3364. Offers MURP. *Accreditation:* ACSP. Part-time programs available. *Students:* 109 full-time (44 women), 34 part-time (13 women); includes 14 minority (2 African Americans, 1 American Indian/Alaska Native, 4 Asian Americans or Pacific Islanders, 7 Hispanic Americans), 9 international. 139 applicants, 82% accepted, 61 enrolled. In 2009, 38 master's awarded. *Degree requirements:* For master's, thesis optional. *Entrance requirements:* For master's, GRE or minimum GPA of 3.0, writing sample, resume. Additional exam requirements/recommendations for international students: Required—TOEFL (minimum score 550 paper-based; 213 computer-based). *Application deadline:* For fall admission, 3/15 for domestic students; for spring admission, 10/1 for domestic students. Application fee: $50

($75 for international students). *Financial support:* Teaching assistantships, career-related internships or fieldwork, Federal Work-Study, institutionally sponsored loans, and scholarships/grants available. Financial award application deadline: 3/1; financial award applicants required to submit FAFSA. *Faculty research:* Physical planning, environmental planning, economic development planning. *Unit head:* Tom Clark, Chair, 303-556-3296, Fax: 303-492-6163, E-mail: tom.clark@cudenver.edu. *Application contact:* Jenny Richardson, Administrative Assistant II, 303-492-8010, Fax: 303-556-3687, E-mail: jenny.richardson@colorado.edu.

University of Florida, Graduate School, College of Design, Construction and Planning, Department of Urban and Regional Planning, Gainesville, FL 32611. Offers MAURP, PhD, JD/MAURP. *Accreditation:* ACSP (one or more programs are accredited). *Degree requirements:* For master's, thesis. *Entrance requirements:* For master's, GRE General Test, minimum GPA of 3.0. Additional exam requirements/recommendations for international students: Required—TOEFL. Electronic applications accepted. *Faculty research:* Planning and information systems, urban and environmental design, community and economic development, transportation and growth management.

University of Hawaii at Manoa, Graduate Division, College of Social Sciences, Department of Urban and Regional Planning, Honolulu, HI 96822. Offers community planning and social policy (MURP); disaster preparedness and emergency management (Graduate Certificate); environmental planning and management (MURP); land use and infrastructure planning (MURP); urban and regional planning (PhD, Graduate Certificate); urban and regional planning in Asia and Pacific (MURP). *Accreditation:* ACSP. Part-time programs available. *Faculty:* 19 full-time (6 women), 17 part-time/adjunct (3 women). *Students:* 51 full-time (26 women), 45 part-time (22 women); includes 28 minority (1 American Indian/Alaska Native, 26 Asian Americans or Pacific Islanders, 1 Hispanic American), 25 international. Average age 32. 67 applicants, 66% accepted, 21 enrolled. In 2009, 27 master's, 4 doctorates, 1 other advanced degree awarded. *Entrance requirements:* For master's, GRE General Test, minimum GPA of 3.0; for doctorate, GRE General Test. Additional exam requirements/recommendations for international students: Required—TOEFL (minimum score 500 paper-based; 173 computer-based; 61 iBT), IELTS (minimum score 5). *Application deadline:* For fall admission, 3/1 for domestic and international students; for spring admission, 9/1 for domestic and international students. Application fee: $60. *Expenses:* Tuition, state resident: full-time $8900; part-time $372 per credit. Tuition, nonresident: full-time $21,400; part-time $898 per credit. Required fees: $207 per semester. *Financial support:* In 2009–10, 4 students received support, including 8 fellowships (averaging $1,625 per year), 23 research assistantships (averaging $16,551 per year), 1 teaching assistantship (averaging $15,558 per year); career-related internships or fieldwork, Federal Work-Study, institutionally sponsored loans, and tuition waivers (full) also available. Total annual research expenditures: $423,000. *Application contact:* Dolores Foley, Graduate Chair, 808-956-7381, Fax: 808-956-6870, E-mail: dolores@hawaii.edu.

University of Idaho, College of Graduate Studies, Department of Bioregional Planning and Community Design, Moscow, ID 83844-2282. Offers bioregional planning (MS). *Faculty:* 3 full-time, 1 part-time/adjunct. *Students:* 9 full-time, 1 part-time. *Expenses:* Tuition, state resident: full-time $6120. Tuition, nonresident: full-time $17,712. *Faculty research:* Environment and behavior interaction, geographic trade, design development, economic development, natural resource policy. *Unit head:* Mark Hoversten, Dean, 208-885-7448, E-mail: bioregionalplanning@uidaho.edu. *Application contact:* Mark Hoversten, Dean, 208-885-7448, E-mail: bioregionalplanning@uidaho.edu.

University of Illinois at Chicago, Graduate College, College of Urban Planning and Public Affairs, Program in Urban Planning and Policy, Chicago, IL 60607-7128. Offers MUPP, PhD. *Accreditation:* ACSP (one or more programs are accredited). Part-time programs available. *Degree requirements:* For master's, thesis or alternative, internship; for doctorate, thesis/dissertation. *Entrance requirements:* For master's and doctorate, GRE General Test, minimum GPA of 2.75, writing sample. Additional exam requirements/recommendations for international students: Required—TOEFL. Electronic applications accepted.

University of Illinois at Urbana–Champaign, Graduate College, College of Fine and Applied Arts, Department of Urban and Regional Planning, Champaign, IL 61820. Offers regional planning (PhD); urban planning (MUP); JD/MUP; M Arch/MUP. *Accreditation:* ACSP (one or more programs are accredited). *Faculty:* 12 full-time (4 women). *Students:* 70 full-time (34 women), 10 part-time (7 women); includes 15 minority (10 African Americans, 3 Asian Americans or Pacific Islanders, 2 Hispanic Americans), 24 international. 165 applicants, 27% accepted, 25 enrolled. In 2009, 22 master's, 3 doctorates awarded. *Entrance requirements:* For master's and doctorate, GRE, minimum GPA of 3.0. Additional exam requirements/recommendations for international students: Required—TOEFL (minimum score 610 paper-based; 253 computer-based; 102 iBT). *Application deadline:* Applications are processed on a rolling basis. Application fee: $60 ($75 for international students). Electronic applications accepted. *Financial support:* In 2009–10, 12 fellowships, 42 research assistantships, 23 teaching assistantships were awarded; tuition waivers (full and partial) also available. *Faculty research:* Environmental impact, economic development, firmation technology, planning systems, housing, community participation. *Unit head:* Edward Feser, Head, 217-244-6767, Fax: 217-244-1717, E-mail: feser@illinois.edu. *Application contact:* Jane Terry, Admissions and Records Officer II, 217-244-5401, Fax: 217-244-1717, E-mail: jterry2@illinois.edu.

The University of Iowa, Graduate College, Program in Urban and Regional Planning, Iowa City, IA 52242-1316. Offers MA, MS, JD/MA, MHA/MA, MHA/MS, MS/MA, MS/MS, MSW/MA, MSW/MS. *Accreditation:* ACSP. *Degree requirements:* For master's, thesis optional, portfolio. *Entrance requirements:* For master's, GRE General Test, minimum GPA of 3.0. Additional exam requirements/recommendations for international students: Required—TOEFL (minimum score 600 paper-based; 250 computer-based; 100 iBT). Electronic applications accepted.

The University of Kansas, Graduate Studies, School of Architecture, Design, and Planning, Program in Urban Planning, Lawrence, KS 66045. Offers MUP, JD/MUP, M Arch/MUP, MUP/MA, MUP/MPA. *Accreditation:* ACSP. Part-time programs available. *Faculty:* 5 full-time (2 women), 6 part-time/adjunct (0 women). *Students:* 31 full-time (9 women), 5 part-time (2 women); includes 5 minority (3 African Americans, 2 Hispanic Americans), 1 international. Average age 27. 50 applicants, 68% accepted, 17 enrolled. In 2009, 23 master's awarded. *Degree requirements:* For master's, comprehensive exam, thesis or alternative. *Entrance requirements:* For master's, GRE. Additional exam requirements/recommendations for international students: Required—TOEFL (minimum score 570 paper-based; 230 computer-based). *Application deadline:* For fall admission, 7/1 for domestic students, 6/1 for international students; for spring admission, 12/1 for domestic students, 11/1 for international students. Applications are processed on a rolling basis. Application fee: $45 ($55 for international students). Electronic applications accepted. *Expenses:* Tuition, state resident: full-time $6492; part-time $270.50 per credit hour. Tuition, nonresident: full-time $15,510; part-time $646.25 per credit hour. Required fees: $847; $70.56 per credit hour. Tuition and fees vary according to course load and program. *Financial support:* Fellowships, research assistantships with partial tuition reimbursements, career-related internships or fieldwork available. Financial award application deadline: 2/1. *Faculty research:* Environmental land use, housing and economic development, community development and transportation, urban mass transportation, urban sprawl. *Unit head:* James M. Mayo, Chair, 785-864-4184, Fax: 785-864-5301, E-mail: jimmayo@ku.edu. *Application contact:* Pat Owens, Administrative Specialist, 785-864-4184, Fax: 785-864-5301, E-mail: ubpl@ku.edu.

University of Louisville, Graduate School, College of Arts and Sciences, Department of Urban and Public Affairs, Louisville, KY 40208. Offers public administration (MPA), including human resources management, non-profit management, public policy and administration; urban and public affairs (PhD), including urban planning and development, urban policy and administration; urban planning (MUP), including administration of planning organizations, housing and community development, land use and environmental planning, spatial analysis. Part-time and evening/weekend programs available. *Faculty:* 22 full-time (7 women), 8 part-time/adjunct (1 woman). *Students:* 67 full-time (32 women), 35 part-time (20 women); includes 13 minority (10 African Americans, 1 Asian American or Pacific Islander, 2 Hispanic Americans), 6 international. Average age 31. 107 applicants, 57% accepted, 40 enrolled. In 2009, 25 master's, 5 doctorates awarded. Terminal master's awarded for partial completion of doctoral program. *Degree requirements:* For master's, internship; for doctorate, comprehensive exam, thesis/dissertation. *Entrance requirements:* For master's, GRE General Test, minimum GPA of 3.0; for doctorate, GRE General Test, master's degree in appropriate field. Additional exam requirements/recommendations for international students: Required—TOEFL (minimum score 550 paper-based; 213 computer-based; 79 iBT). *Application deadline:* For fall admission, 7/15 for domestic students; for spring admission, 11/15 for domestic students. Applications are processed on a rolling basis. Application fee: $50. Electronic applications accepted. *Financial support:* In 2009–10, 26 students received support; fellowships, research assistantships, health care benefits available. *Unit head:* Dr. David Simpson, Chair, 502-852-8019, Fax: 502-852-4558, E-mail: dave.simpson@louisville.edu. *Application contact:* Patty Sarley, Graduate Student Advisor, 502-852-7914, Fax: 502-852-4558, E-mail: plclea01@louisville.edu.

University of Manitoba, Faculty of Graduate Studies, Faculty of Architecture, Department of City Planning, Winnipeg, MB R3T 2N2, Canada. Offers MCP. *Degree requirements:* For master's, thesis.

University of Maryland, College Park, Academic Affairs, School of Architecture, Planning and Preservation, Program in Urban Studies and Planning, College Park, MD 20742. Offers urban and regional planning/design (PhD); urban studies and planning (MCP); M Arch/MCP. *Accreditation:* ACSP. Part-time and evening/weekend programs available. *Faculty:* 8 full-time (2 women), 2 part-time/adjunct (0 women). *Students:* 60 full-time (36 women), 18 part-time (13 women); includes 10 minority (9 African Americans, 1 Hispanic American), 9 international. 208 applicants, 39% accepted, 30 enrolled. In 2009, 25 master's, 3 doctorates awarded. *Entrance requirements:* For master's and doctorate, GRE General Test, minimum GPA of 3.0, 3 letters of recommendation. Additional exam requirements/recommendations for international students: Required—TOEFL. *Application deadline:* For fall admission, 12/15 for domestic and international students; for spring admission, 6/1 for international students. Applications are processed on a rolling basis. Application fee: $60. Electronic applications accepted. *Expenses:* Tuition, area resident: Part-time $471 per credit hour. Tuition, state resident: part-time $471 per credit hour. Tuition, nonresident: part-time $1016 per credit hour. Required fees: $337.04 per term. *Financial support:* In 2009–10, 3 fellowships with partial tuition reimbursements (averaging $10,017 per year), 36 teaching assistantships with tuition reimbursements (averaging $15,762 per year) were awarded; research assistantships, Federal Work-Study and scholarships/grants also available. Support available to part-time students. Financial award applicants required to submit FAFSA. *Faculty research:* Policy analysis, urban planning, program planning and management, economic development planning. Total annual research expenditures: $28,437. *Unit head:* James R. Cohen, Director, 301-405-6795, Fax: 301-314-9583, E-mail: jimcohen@umd.edu. *Application contact:* Dean of Graduate School, 301-405-0358.

University of Massachusetts Amherst, Graduate School, College of Social and Behavioral Sciences, Department of Landscape Architecture and Regional Planning, Program in Landscape Architecture and Regional Planning, Amherst, MA 01003. Offers MLA/MRP. *Accreditation:* ACSP; ASLA. Part-time programs available. *Students:* 8 full-time (6 women), 2 international. Average age 30. 10 applicants, 80% accepted, 3 enrolled. *Entrance requirements:* Additional exam requirements/recommendations for international students: Required—TOEFL (minimum score 550 paper-based; 213 computer-based; 80 iBT), IELTS (minimum score 6.5). *Application deadline:* For fall admission, 2/1 for domestic and international students. Applications are processed on a rolling basis. Application fee: $50 ($65 for international students). Electronic applications accepted. *Expenses:* Tuition, state resident: full-time $2640; part-time $110 per credit. Tuition, nonresident: full-time $9936; part-time $414 per credit. Tuition and fees vary according to course load. *Financial support:* Fellowships, research assistantships, teaching assistantships, career-related internships or fieldwork, Federal Work-Study, scholarships/grants, traineeships, health care benefits, tuition waivers (full), and unspecified assistantships available. Support available to part-time students. Financial award application deadline: 2/1. *Unit head:* Dr. Robert L. Ryan, Graduate Program Director, 413-545-2266, Fax: 413-545-1772. *Application contact:* Jean M. Ames, Supervisor of Admissions, 413-545-0721, Fax: 413-577-0010, E-mail: gradadm@grad.umass.edu.

University of Massachusetts Amherst, Graduate School, College of Social and Behavioral Sciences, Department of Landscape Architecture and Regional Planning, Program in Regional Planning, Amherst, MA 01003. Offers MRP, PhD, MLA/MRP. *Accreditation:* ACSP (one or more programs are accredited). Part-time programs available. *Students:* 40 full-time (23 women), 14 part-time (9 women); includes 6 minority (2 African Americans, 3 Asian Americans or Pacific Islanders, 1 Hispanic American), 9 international. Average age 31. 74 applicants, 69% accepted, 22 enrolled. In 2009, 12 master's, 1 doctorate awarded. Terminal master's awarded for partial completion of doctoral program. *Degree requirements:* For master's, thesis or alternative; for doctorate, comprehensive exam, thesis/dissertation. *Entrance requirements:* For master's and doctorate, GRE General Test. Additional exam requirements/recommendations for international students: Required—TOEFL (minimum score 550 paper-based; 213 computer-based; 80 iBT), IELTS (minimum score 6.5). *Application deadline:* For fall admission, 2/1 for domestic and international students; for spring admission, 10/1 for domestic and international students. Applications are processed on a rolling basis. Application fee: $50 ($65 for international students). Electronic applications accepted. *Expenses:* Tuition, state resident: full-time $2640; part-time $110 per credit. Tuition, nonresident: full-time $9936; part-time $414 per credit. Tuition and fees vary according to course load. *Financial support:* Fellowships, research assistantships, teaching assistantships, career-related internships or fieldwork, Federal Work-Study, scholarships/grants, traineeships, health care benefits, tuition waivers (full), and unspecified assistantships available. Support available to part-time students. Financial award application deadline: 2/1. *Unit head:* Dr. Mark T. Hamin, Graduate Program Director, 413-545-2266, Fax: 413-545-1772. *Application contact:* Jean M. Ames, Supervisor of Admissions, 413-545-0722, Fax: 413-577-0010, E-mail: gradadm@grad.umass.edu.

University of Memphis, Graduate School, College of Arts and Sciences, Division of City and Regional Planning, Memphis, TN 38152. Offers MCRP. *Accreditation:* ACSP. *Faculty:* 4 full-time (2 women), 1 part-time/adjunct (0 women). *Students:* 14 full-time (5 women), 13 part-time (5 women); includes 6 minority (all African Americans). Average age 30. 20 applicants, 95% accepted, 9 enrolled. In 2009, 6 master's awarded. *Degree requirements:* For master's, comprehensive exam, thesis. *Entrance requirements:* For master's, GRE General Test. *Application deadline:* For fall admission, 7/1 for domestic students; for spring admission, 12/1 for domestic students. Applications are processed on a rolling basis. Application fee: $35 ($60 for international students). *Expenses:* Tuition, state resident: full-time $6246; part-time $347 per credit hour. Tuition, nonresident: full-time $15,894; part-time $883 per credit hour. Required fees: $1160. Full-time tuition and fees vary according to course load, degree level and program. *Financial support:* In 2009–10, 14 students received support; research assistantships with full tuition reimbursements available, career-related internships or fieldwork, Federal Work-Study, scholarships/grants, and unspecified assistantships available. Financial award application deadline: 2/15; financial award applicants required to submit FAFSA. *Faculty research:* Growth planning, site design, economic development, housing, smart growth. *Unit head:* Kenneth Reardon, Director and Coordinator of Graduate Studies in Planning, 901-678-2161, Fax: 901-678-4162, E-mail: kreardon@memphis.edu. *Application contact:* Kenneth Reardon, Director and Coordinator of Graduate Studies in Planning, 901-678-2161, Fax: 901-678-4162, E-mail: kreardon@memphis.edu.

University of Memphis, Graduate School, College of Arts and Sciences, Division of Public and Nonprofit Administration, Memphis, TN 38152. Offers nonprofit administration (MPA); public management and policy (MPA); urban management and planning (MPA). *Accreditation:* NASPAA. Part-time and evening/weekend programs available. *Faculty:* 5 full-time (2 women), 1 (woman) part-time/adjunct. *Students:* 17 full-time (11 women), 39 part-time (28 women); includes 32 minority (31 African Americans, 1 Hispanic American), 1 international. Average age 34. 32 applicants, 88% accepted, 9 enrolled. In 2009, 17 master's awarded. *Degree requirements:* For master's, comprehensive exam, thesis or alternative, internship. *Entrance*

Urban and Regional Planning

University of Memphis (continued)

requirements: For master's, GRE General Test, GMAT, or MAT, minimum GPA of 3.0. *Application deadline:* For fall admission, 8/1 for domestic students; for spring admission, 12/1 for domestic students. Applications are processed on a rolling basis. Application fee: $35 ($60 for international students). *Expenses:* Tuition, state resident: full-time $6246; part-time $347 per credit hour. Tuition, nonresident: full-time $15,894; part-time $883 per credit hour. Required fees: $1160. Full-time tuition and fees vary according to course load, degree level and program. *Financial support:* In 2009–10, 37 students received support; fellowships, research assistantships with full tuition reimbursements available, career-related internships or fieldwork, Federal Work-Study, scholarships/grants, and unspecified assistantships available. Support available to part-time students. Financial award application deadline: 2/15; financial award applicants required to submit FAFSA. *Faculty research:* Nonprofit organization governance, local government management, community collaboration, urban problems, accountability. *Unit head:* Dr. Dorothy Norris-Tirrell, Director, 901-678-3360, Fax: 901-678-2981, E-mail: dnrrstrr@memphis.edu. *Application contact:* Dr. Charles Menifield, Graduate Admissions Coordinator, 901-678-3360, Fax: 901-678-2981, E-mail: cmenifld@memphis.edu.

University of Michigan, Taubman College of Architecture and Urban Planning, Urban and Regional Planning PhD Program, Ann Arbor, MI 48109. Offers PhD. Offered through the Horace H. Rackham School of Graduate Studies. *Degree requirements:* For doctorate, comprehensive exam, thesis/dissertation, 1 interdisciplinary paper, 2 preliminary exams, oral defense of dissertation. *Entrance requirements:* For doctorate, GRE General Test. Additional exam requirements/recommendations for international students: Required—TOEFL (minimum score 560 paper-based; 220 computer-based; 100 iBT). Electronic applications accepted. *Expenses:* Contact institution. *Faculty research:* Urban and regional planning, community and economic development, transportation planning and geological information systems, environmental planning, the built environment, international development and planning.

University of Michigan, Taubman College of Architecture and Urban Planning, Urban and Regional Planning Program, Ann Arbor, MI 48109. Offers real estate development (Certificate); urban planning (MUP); JD/MUP; M Arch/MUP; MBA/MUP; MLA/MUP; MPP/MUP. Offered through the Horace H. Rackham School of Graduate Studies; students in the Certificate program must either be currently enrolled in a graduate program or have earned a master's or PhD degree within the last five years. *Accreditation:* ACSP (one or more programs are accredited). Part-time programs available. *Degree requirements:* For master's, thesis or alternative, professional project, capstone studio. *Entrance requirements:* For master's, GRE General Test, LSAT or GMAT. Additional exam requirements/recommendations for international students: Required—TOEFL (minimum score 600 paper-based; 250 computer-based; 100 iBT). Electronic applications accepted. *Expenses:* Tuition, state resident: full-time $17,286; part-time $1099 per credit hour. Tuition, nonresident: full-time $34,944; part-time $2080 per credit hour. Required fees: $95 per semester. Tuition and fees vary according to course load, degree level and program. *Faculty research:* Housing community and economic development; transportation planning; physical planning and urban design; planning in developing countries; land use and environmental planning.

University of Minnesota, Twin Cities Campus, Graduate School, Hubert H. Humphrey Institute of Public Affairs, Program in Urban and Regional Planning, Minneapolis, MN 55455-0213. Offers environmental planning (MURP); housing and community development (MURP); land use and urban design (MURP); regional, economic and workforce development (MURP); transportation planning (MURP); JD/MURP; MURP/MLA; MURP/MS. *Accreditation:* ACSP (one or more programs are accredited). Part-time programs available. *Faculty:* 33 full-time (14 women), 29 part-time/adjunct (15 women). *Students:* 78 full-time (33 women), 26 part-time (9 women); includes 11 minority (3 African Americans, 8 Asian Americans or Pacific Islanders), 6 international. Average age 26. 136 applicants, 65% accepted, 47 enrolled. In 2009, 63 master's awarded. *Degree requirements:* For master's, thesis or alternative, internship or equivalent work experience. *Entrance requirements:* For master's, GRE General Test, minimum undergraduate GPA of 3.0. Additional exam requirements/recommendations for international students: Required—TOEFL (minimum score 600 paper-based; 250 computer-based; 100 iBT). *Application deadline:* For fall admission, 4/1 for domestic and international students. Applications are processed on a rolling basis. Application fee: $75 ($95 for international students). Electronic applications accepted. *Financial support:* In 2009–10, 26 students received support, including fellowships with full and partial tuition reimbursements available (averaging $8,500 per year), research assistantships with full and partial tuition reimbursements available (averaging $5,270 per year), teaching assistantships with full and partial tuition reimbursements available (averaging $5,270 per year); career-related internships or fieldwork, Federal Work-Study, scholarships/grants, health care benefits, tuition waivers (full and partial), and unspecified assistantships also available. Financial award application deadline: 1/5. *Faculty research:* Policy planning, resource allocation planning, regulatory planning, program planning, project planning. Total annual research expenditures: $5.1 million. *Unit head:* Dr. Ragui Assaad, Head, 612-624-3800, Fax: 612-626-0002, E-mail: hhhadmit@umn.edu. *Application contact:* Julie Harrold, Director of Admissions, 612-626-7229, Fax: 612-626-0002, E-mail: hhhadmit@umn.edu.

University of Nebraska–Lincoln, Graduate College, College of Agricultural Sciences and Natural Resources, Department of Agricultural Economics, Lincoln, NE 68588. Offers agribusiness (MBA); agricultural economics (MS, PhD); community development (M Ag). *Degree requirements:* For master's, thesis optional; for doctorate, comprehensive exam, thesis/dissertation. *Entrance requirements:* For master's and doctorate, GRE General Test. Additional exam requirements/recommendations for international students: Required—TOEFL (minimum score 550 paper-based; 213 computer-based). Electronic applications accepted. *Faculty research:* Marketing and agribusiness, production economics, resource law, international trade and development, rural policy and revitalization.

University of Nebraska–Lincoln, Graduate College, College of Architecture, Department of Community and Regional Planning, Lincoln, NE 68588. Offers MCRP, JD/MCRP, M Arch/MCRP, MCRP/MSCE. *Accreditation:* ACSP. *Degree requirements:* For master's, thesis optional. *Entrance requirements:* For master's, GRE General Test. Additional exam requirements/recommendations for international students: Required—TOEFL (minimum score 550 paper-based; 213 computer-based). Electronic applications accepted. *Faculty research:* Economic development, community development and improvement, social planning, land use planning, physical planning, environmental planning.

University of New Haven, Graduate School, School of Business, Program in Public Administration, West Haven, CT 06516-1916. Offers personnel and labor relations (MPA); public administration (MPA, Certificate), including city management (MPA), community-clinical services (MPA), health care management (MPA), long-term health care (MPA), personnel and labor relations (MPA), public administration (Certificate), public management (Certificate), public personnel management (Certificate); MBA/MPA. Part-time and evening/weekend programs available. *Faculty:* 3 full-time (1 woman), 11 part-time/adjunct (5 women). *Students:* 17 full-time (9 women), 26 part-time (14 women); includes 11 minority (9 African Americans, 1 Asian American or Pacific Islander, 1 Hispanic American), 1 international. Average age 35. 35 applicants, 94% accepted, 8 enrolled. In 2009, 9 master's, 12 other advanced degrees awarded. *Degree requirements:* For master's, thesis or alternative. *Entrance requirements:* Additional exam requirements/recommendations for international students: Required—TOEFL (minimum score 520 paper-based; 190 computer-based; 70 iBT); Recommended—IELTS (minimum score 5.5). *Application deadline:* For fall admission, 5/31 for international students; for winter admission, 10/15 for international students; for spring admission, 1/15 for international students. Applications are processed on a rolling basis. Application fee: $50. Electronic applications accepted. *Expenses:* Contact institution. *Financial support:* Research assistantships with partial tuition reimbursements, teaching assistantships with partial tuition reimbursements, career-related internships or fieldwork, Federal Work-Study, scholarships/grants, tuition waivers, and unspecified assistantships available. Support available to part-time students. Financial award application deadline: 5/1; financial award applicants required to submit FAFSA. *Unit head:* Charles Coleman, Chairman, 203-932-7375. *Application contact:* Eloise Gormley, Director of Graduate Admissions, 203-932-7449, Fax: 203-932-7137, E-mail: gradinfo@newhaven.edu.

University of New Mexico, Graduate School, School of Architecture and Planning, Program in Community and Regional Planning, Albuquerque, NM 87131-2039. Offers MCRP, MCRP/MA, MPA/MCRP. *Accreditation:* ACSP. Part-time programs available. *Faculty:* 1 (woman) part-time/adjunct. *Students:* 51 full-time (28 women), 35 part-time (24 women); includes 35 minority (1 African American, 15 American Indian/Alaska Native, 2 Asian Americans or Pacific Islanders, 17 Hispanic Americans), 4 international. Average age 32. 60 applicants, 63% accepted, 27 enrolled. In 2009, 10 master's awarded. *Degree requirements:* For master's, thesis. *Entrance requirements:* For master's, minimum GPA of 3.0 in last two years of graduate study, 3 letters of recommendation, letter of intent, resume, copies of all official transcripts. Additional exam requirements/recommendations for international students: Required—TOEFL (minimum score 550 paper-based; 213 computer-based). *Application deadline:* For fall admission, 1/30 priority date for domestic students; for spring admission, 10/15 for domestic students. Application fee: $50. Electronic applications accepted. *Expenses:* Tuition, state resident: full-time $2099; part-time $233.20 per credit hour. Tuition, nonresident: full-time $6650. Required fees: $25 per semester. Tuition and fees vary according to course load, program and reciprocity agreements. *Financial support:* In 2009–10, 21 students received support, including 1 fellowship (averaging $2,700 per year), 1 research assistantship with partial tuition reimbursement available (averaging $7,278 per year), 2 teaching assistantships with partial tuition reimbursements available (averaging $3,300 per year); career-related internships or fieldwork, Federal Work-Study, institutionally sponsored loans, scholarships/grants, health care benefits, tuition waivers (full), and unspecified assistantships also available. Support available to part-time students. Financial award application deadline: 3/1; financial award applicants required to submit FAFSA. *Faculty research:* Community development, urban and ecological design, land economics, community-based planning, environmental dispute resolution, environmental justice, indigenous planning, watershed management. *Unit head:* Dr. Teresa L. Cordova, Program Director, 505-277-3922, Fax: 505-277-0076, E-mail: tcordova@unm.edu. *Application contact:* Beth Rowe, Senior Academic Advisor, 505-277-1303, Fax: 505-277-0076, E-mail: erowe@unm.edu.

University of New Orleans, Graduate School, College of Liberal Arts, School of Urban Planning and Regional Studies, Program in Urban and Regional Planning, New Orleans, LA 70148. Offers MURP. *Accreditation:* ACSP. *Degree requirements:* For master's, thesis. *Entrance requirements:* For master's, GRE General Test. Additional exam requirements/recommendations for international students: Required—TOEFL (minimum score 550 paper-based; 213 computer-based; 79 iBT). Electronic applications accepted. *Faculty research:* Urban economic development, environmental planning and analysis, social and cultural change.

The University of North Carolina at Chapel Hill, Graduate School, College of Arts and Sciences, Department of City and Regional Planning, Chapel Hill, NC 27599. Offers city and regional planning (MCRP); planning (PhD); public policy analysis (PhD); JD/MCRP; MBA/MCRP; MPA/MCRP. *Accreditation:* ACSP (one or more programs are accredited). *Faculty:* 16 full-time (5 women), 6 part-time/adjunct (1 woman). *Students:* 108 full-time (58 women); includes 20 minority (6 African Americans, 11 Asian Americans or Pacific Islanders, 3 Hispanic Americans). Average age 27. 242 applicants, 52% accepted, 57 enrolled. In 2009, 46 master's, 1 doctorate awarded. *Degree requirements:* For master's, project; for doctorate, comprehensive exam, thesis/dissertation. *Entrance requirements:* For master's and doctorate, GRE General Test. Additional exam requirements/recommendations for international students: Required—TOEFL (minimum score 550 paper-based; 213 computer-based). *Application deadline:* For fall admission, 1/1 priority date for domestic students, 12/1 priority date for international students; for spring admission, 3/15 for domestic and international students. Applications are processed on a rolling basis. Application fee: $73. Electronic applications accepted. *Financial support:* In 2009–10, 54 students received support, including 4 fellowships with full tuition reimbursements available (averaging $20,000 per year), 21 research assistantships with full tuition reimbursements available (averaging $10,000 per year), 29 teaching assistantships with full and partial tuition reimbursements available (averaging $10,700 per year); career-related internships or fieldwork, Federal Work-Study, scholarships/grants, traineeships, health care benefits, and unspecified assistantships also available. Financial award application deadline: 1/1; financial award applicants required to submit FAFSA. *Faculty research:* Developing areas, transportation, affordable housing, growth management, coastal zone management. *Unit head:* Dr. Emil E. Malizla, Chairman, 919-962-4759, Fax: 919-962-5206, E-mail: malizia@email.unc.edu. *Application contact:* Carolyn Turner, Student Services Manager, 919-962-4784, Fax: 919-962-5206, E-mail: turnerc@email.unc.edu.

University of Oklahoma, Graduate College, College of Architecture, Division of Regional and City Planning, Norman, OK 73019-0390. Offers MRCP, MRCP/MLA. *Accreditation:* ACSP (one or more programs are accredited). Part-time programs available. *Faculty:* 3 full-time (1 woman). *Students:* 29 full-time (18 women), 3 part-time (1 woman); includes 4 minority (2 African Americans, 2 American Indian/Alaska Native), 10 international. 16 applicants, 88% accepted, 9 enrolled. In 2009, 8 master's awarded. *Degree requirements:* For master's, thesis or alternative, portfolio, project. *Entrance requirements:* For master's, GRE General Test, appropriate bachelor's degree, portfolio. Additional exam requirements/recommendations for international students: Required—TOEFL (minimum score 550 paper-based; 213 computer-based). *Application deadline:* For fall admission, 4/1 for domestic and international students; for spring admission, 11/1 for domestic students, 9/1 for international students. Applications are processed on a rolling basis. Application fee: $40 ($90 for international students). Electronic applications accepted. *Expenses:* Tuition, state resident: full-time $3744; part-time $156 per credit hour. Tuition, nonresident: full-time $13,577; part-time $565.70 per credit hour. Required fees: $2415; $90.10 per credit hour. *Financial support:* In 2009–10, 25 students received support, including 4 research assistantships with partial tuition reimbursements available (averaging $10,565 per year); career-related internships or fieldwork, Federal Work-Study, institutionally sponsored loans, scholarships/grants, health care benefits, tuition waivers (partial), and unspecified assistantships also available. Support available to part-time students. Financial award applicants required to submit FAFSA. *Faculty research:* Transportation planning, economic development, urban design, city and regional planning. *Unit head:* Bob Goins, Interim Director, Institute for Quality Communities, 405-325-1696, Fax: 405-325-7558, E-mail: bobgoins@ou.edu. *Application contact:* Terry Patterson, Professor/Graduate Liaison, 405-325-3869, Fax: 405-325-7558, E-mail: tpatterson@ou.edu.

University of Oregon, Graduate School, School of Architecture and Allied Arts, Department of Planning, Public Policy, and Management, Program in Community and Regional Planning, Eugene, OR 97403. Offers MCRP. *Accreditation:* ACSP. Part-time programs available. *Degree requirements:* For master's, thesis or alternative. *Entrance requirements:* For master's, minimum GPA of 3.0. Additional exam requirements/recommendations for international students: Required—TOEFL. *Faculty research:* Community economic development, tourism, families in poverty.

University of Pennsylvania, School of Design, Department of City and Regional Planning, Philadelphia, PA 19104. Offers MCP, PhD, Certificate, MSE/MCP. *Accreditation:* ACSP (one or more programs are accredited). *Faculty:* 15 full-time (5 women), 4 part-time/adjunct (0 women). *Students:* 157 full-time (82 women), 43 part-time (24 women); includes 22 minority (13 African Americans, 1 American Indian/Alaska Native, 2 Asian Americans or Pacific Islanders, 6 Hispanic Americans), 23 international. 56 applicants, 9% accepted, 3 enrolled. In 2009, 74 master's, 1 doctorate awarded. *Degree requirements:* For doctorate, thesis/dissertation. *Entrance requirements:* For master's and doctorate, GRE General Test. Additional exam requirements/recommendations for international students: Required—TOEFL. *Application deadline:* For fall admission, 1/2 priority date for domestic students. Application fee: $70. *Expenses:* Tuition: Full-time $25,660; part-time $4758 per course. Required fees: $2152; $270 per course. Tuition and fees vary according to course load, degree level and program. *Financial support:* Fellowships, research assistantships, teaching assistantships, institutionally sponsored loans, scholarships/grants, traineeships, health care benefits, and unspecified assistantships available. *Faculty research:* Growth management, transportation planning, urban simulation modeling, housing, development planning.

See Close-Up on page 147.

University of Pennsylvania, School of Design, Program in Landscape Architecture and Regional Planning, Philadelphia, PA 19104. Offers landscape architecture and regional planning (MLA); landscape studies (Certificate). *Accreditation:* ASLA (one or more programs are accredited). Part-time programs available. *Faculty:* 4 full-time (2 women), 6 part-time/adjunct (2 women). *Students:* 106 full-time (70 women), 2 part-time (both women); includes 9 minority (2 African Americans, 1 American Indian/Alaska Native, 5 Asian Americans or Pacific Islanders, 1 Hispanic American), 33 international. 244 applicants, 50% accepted, 50 enrolled. In 2009, 33 master's, 3 Certificates awarded. *Degree requirements:* For master's, thesis optional. *Entrance requirements:* For master's, GRE, portfolio. Additional exam requirements/recommendations for international students: Required—TOEFL. *Application deadline:* For fall admission, 1/2 priority date for domestic students. Application fee: $70. *Expenses:* Tuition: Full-time $25,660; part-time $4758 per course. Required fees: $2152; $270 per course. Tuition and fees vary according to course load, degree level and program. *Financial support:* Fellowships, research assistantships, teaching assistantships, career-related internships or fieldwork, Federal Work-Study, and institutionally sponsored loans available. Financial award applicants required to submit FAFSA. *Faculty research:* Early landscape architecture, natural distribution through landslides, urban gardens, landscape registration, watershed studies.

See Close-Up on page 147.

University of Pittsburgh, Graduate School of Public and International Affairs, Division of International Development, Pittsburgh, PA 15260. Offers development planning and environmental sustainability (MID); human security (MID); nongovernmental organizations and civil society (MID); MID/JD; MID/MBA; MID/MPH; MID/MPIA; MID/MSIS; MID/MSW. Part-time programs available. *Faculty:* 28 full-time (8 women), 56 part-time/adjunct (20 women). *Students:* 47 full-time (34 women), 4 part-time (3 women); includes 8 minority (3 African Americans, 2 Asian Americans or Pacific Islanders, 3 Hispanic Americans), 4 international. Average age 25. 123 applicants, 87% accepted, 37 enrolled. In 2009, 26 master's awarded. *Degree requirements:* For master's, thesis optional, internship, capstone seminar. *Entrance requirements:* For master's, GRE General Test, 3 letters of recommendation, minimum GPA of 3.2. Additional exam requirements/recommendations for international students: Required—TOEFL (minimum score 550 paper-based; 213 computer-based; 80 iBT), TWE (minimum score 4); Recommended—IELTS (minimum score 7). *Application deadline:* For fall admission, 2/1 for domestic students, 1/5 for international students; for spring admission, 11/1 for domestic students, 8/1 for international students. Application fee: $50. Electronic applications accepted. *Expenses:* Tuition, state resident: full-time $16,402; part-time $665 per credit. Tuition, nonresident: full-time $28,694; part-time $1175 per credit. Required fees: $690; $175 per term. Tuition and fees vary according to program. *Financial support:* In 2009–10, 27 students received support, including 4 fellowships (averaging $30,000 per year); scholarships/grants, tuition waivers (full and partial), and unspecified assistantships also available. Financial award application deadline: 2/1. *Faculty research:* Nongovernmental organizations, religion and civil society, international development, development economics and policy, human rights and development, humanitarian intervention, ethnic conflict and civil war, post-conflict peace building, corruption and transnational governance, civil society and public affairs, political constraints on rural development. Total annual research expenditures: $357,117. *Unit head:* Dr. Louis Picard, Director, 412-648-7659, Fax: 412-648-2605, E-mail: picard@pitt.edu. *Application contact:* Elizabeth Hruby, Graduate Enrollment Counselor, 412-648-7640, Fax: 412-648-7641, E-mail: eah44@pitt.edu.

University of Pittsburgh, Graduate School of Public and International Affairs, Division of Public and Urban Affairs, Pittsburgh, PA 15260. Offers policy research and analysis (MPA); public and nonprofit management (MPA); urban and regional affairs (MPA); JD/MPA; MPA/MPIA; MPH/MPA; MSIS/MPA; MSW/MPA. Part-time and evening/weekend programs available. *Faculty:* 28 full-time (8 women), 56 part-time/adjunct (20 women). *Students:* 46 full-time (28 women), 19 part-time (13 women); includes 11 minority (9 African Americans, 1 Asian American or Pacific Islander, 1 Hispanic American), 3 international. Average age 25. 93 applicants, 92% accepted, 30 enrolled. In 2009, 32 master's awarded. *Degree requirements:* For master's, thesis optional, internship, capstone seminar. *Entrance requirements:* For master's, GRE General Test, 3 letters of recommendation, resume, minimum GPA of 3.2. Additional exam requirements/recommendations for international students: Required—TOEFL (minimum score 550 paper-based; 213 computer-based; 80 iBT), TWE (minimum score 4); Recommended—IELTS (minimum score 7). *Application deadline:* For fall admission, 2/1 for domestic students, 1/15 for international students; for spring admission, 11/1 for domestic students, 8/1 for international students. Application fee: $50. *Expenses:* Tuition, state resident: full-time $16,402; part-time $665 per credit. Tuition, nonresident: full-time $28,694; part-time $1175 per credit. Required fees: $690; $175 per term. Tuition and fees vary according to program. *Financial support:* In 2009–10, 22 students received support, including 2 fellowships (averaging $20,000 per year); scholarships/grants, tuition waivers (full and partial), and unspecified assistantships also available. Financial award application deadline: 2/1. *Faculty research:* Disaster response management, government regulation of health and safety risks, comparative regional governance, non-profit management, environmental policy, housing policy, strategic management. Total annual research expenditures: $357,117. *Unit head:* Dr. David Y. Miller, Director, 412-648-7606, Fax: 412-648-2605, E-mail: dymiller@pitt.edu. *Application contact:* Elizabeth A. Hruby, Graduate Enrollment Counselor, 412-648-7640, Fax: 412-648-7641, E-mail: eah44@pitt.edu.

University of Puerto Rico, Río Piedras, Graduate School of Planning, San Juan, PR 00931-3300. Offers MP. *Accreditation:* ACSP. Part-time programs available. *Degree requirements:* For master's, comprehensive exam, thesis, planning project defense. *Entrance requirements:* For master's, PAEG, GRE, minimum GPA of 3.0, 2 letters of recommendation. *Faculty research:* Municipalities, historic Atlas, Puerto Rico, economic future.

University of Southern California, Graduate School, School of Policy, Planning, and Development, Doctor of Philosophy in Policy, Planning, and Development Program, Los Angeles, CA 90089. Offers PhD. *Faculty:* 51 full-time (12 women), 74 part-time/adjunct (26 women). *Students:* 16 full-time (10 women), 1 part-time (0 women); includes 4 minority (2 Asian Americans or Pacific Islanders, 2 Hispanic Americans), 9 international. 84 applicants, 17% accepted, 8 enrolled. In 2009, 14 doctorates awarded. *Degree requirements:* For doctorate, thesis/dissertation. *Entrance requirements:* For doctorate, GRE. Additional exam requirements/recommendations for international students: Required—TOEFL (minimum score 600 paper-based; 250 computer-based; 100 iBT). *Application deadline:* For fall admission, 12/1 for domestic and international students. Application fee: $85. Electronic applications accepted. *Expenses:* Tuition: Full-time $25,980; part-time $1315 per unit. Required fees: $554. One-time fee: $35 full-time. Full-time tuition and fees vary according to degree level and program. *Financial support:* In 2009–10, 60 research assistantships with full tuition reimbursements (averaging $12,812 per year) were awarded; scholarships/grants and tuition waivers (full and partial) also available. Financial award application deadline: 12/1. *Faculty research:* Governance: effective institutions, leadership, management, healthy urban and place development, sustainability, community, public policy and planning, societal problem solving and analysis. Total annual research expenditures: $5 million. *Unit head:* Dr. Jack H. Knott, Dean, 213-740-0350, Fax: 213-740-5379, E-mail: jhknott@usc.edu. *Application contact:* Marisol R. Gonzalez, Director of Recruitment and Admission, 213-740-0550, Fax: 213-740-7573, E-mail: marisolr@usc.edu.

University of Southern California, Graduate School, School of Policy, Planning, and Development, Doctor of Policy, Planning, and Development Program, Los Angeles, CA 90089. Offers DPPD. Part-time programs available. *Faculty:* 51 full-time (12 women), 74 part-time/adjunct (26 women). *Students:* 48 full-time (25 women), 1 (woman) part-time; includes 4 minority (3 Asian Americans or Pacific Islanders, 1 Hispanic American), 32 international. 30 applicants, 40% accepted, 10 enrolled. In 2009, 3 doctorates awarded. *Degree requirements:* For doctorate, thesis/dissertation, project. *Entrance requirements:* Additional exam requirements/recommendations for international students: Required—TOEFL (minimum score 600 paper-based; 250 computer-based; 100 iBT). *Application deadline:* For fall admission, 2/1 priority date for domestic and international students. Application fee: $85. Electronic applications accepted. *Expenses:* Tuition: Full-time $25,980; part-time $1315 per unit. Required fees: $554. One-time fee: $35 full-time. Full-time tuition and fees vary according to degree level and program. *Faculty research:* Governance: effective institutions, leadership, management, healthy urban and place development, sustainability, community, public policy and planning, societal problem solving and analysis. Total annual research expenditures: $5 million. *Unit head:* Dr. Richard Callahan, Director, 916-442-6911, Fax: 916-444-7712, E-mail: rcallaha@usc.edu. *Application contact:* Marisol R. Gonzalez, Director of Recruitment and Admission, 213-740-0550, Fax: 213-740-7573, E-mail: marisolr@usc.edu.

University of Southern California, Graduate School, School of Policy, Planning, and Development, Master of Planning Program, Los Angeles, CA 90089. Offers sustainable cities (Graduate Certificate); transportation systems (Graduate Certificate); urban planning (M Pl); M Arch/M Pl; M Pl/MA; M Pl/MS; M Pl/MSW; MBA/M Pl; ML Arch/M Pl; MPA/M Pl. Part-time programs available. *Faculty:* 51 full-time (12 women), 74 part-time/adjunct (26 women). *Students:* 84 full-time (50 women), 6 part-time (4 women); includes 38 minority (5 African Americans, 21 Asian Americans or Pacific Islanders, 12 Hispanic Americans), 12 international. 260 applicants, 60% accepted, 62 enrolled. In 2009, 40 master's awarded. *Degree requirements:* For master's, comprehensive exam, internship. *Entrance requirements:* For master's, GRE or GMAT. Additional exam requirements/recommendations for international students: Required—TOEFL (minimum score 600 paper-based; 250 computer-based; 100 iBT). *Application deadline:* For fall admission, 12/15 priority date for domestic and international students; for spring admission, 11/1 for domestic students, 10/1 for international students. Application fee: $85. Electronic applications accepted. *Expenses:* Tuition: Full-time $25,980; part-time $1315 per unit. Required fees: $554. One-time fee: $35 full-time. Full-time tuition and fees vary according to degree level and program. *Financial support:* In 2009–10, 72 students received support, including 2 research assistantships with tuition reimbursements available (averaging $9,566 per year); scholarships/grants and tuition waivers (full and partial) also available. *Faculty research:* Transportation and infrastructure, comparative international development, healthy communities, social economic development, sustainable community planning. Total annual research expenditures: $5 million. *Unit head:* Dr. Tridib Banerjee, Dean, 213-740-4724, Fax: 213-740-1801, E-mail: tbanerje@usc.edu. *Application contact:* Marisol R. Gonzalez, Director of Recruitment and Admission, 213-740-0550, Fax: 213-740-7573, E-mail: marisolr@usc.edu.

University of Southern Maine, Edmund S. Muskie School of Public Service, Program in Community Planning and Development, Portland, ME 04104-9300. Offers MCPD, Certificate, JD/MCPD. Part-time and evening/weekend programs available. *Degree requirements:* For master's, thesis, capstone project, field experience. *Entrance requirements:* For master's, GRE General Test or LSAT. Additional exam requirements/recommendations for international students: Required—TOEFL. Electronic applications accepted. *Faculty research:* Sustainable communities, ego system management, economic and environmental tradeoffs.

The University of Texas at Arlington, Graduate School, School of Urban and Public Affairs, Program in City and Regional Planning, Arlington, TX 76019. Offers MCRP, M Arch/MCRP. *Accreditation:* ACSP. Part-time and evening/weekend programs available. *Students:* 34 full-time (15 women), 29 part-time (11 women); includes 13 minority (2 African Americans, 1 American Indian/Alaska Native, 3 Asian Americans or Pacific Islanders, 7 Hispanic Americans), 11 international. Average age 35. 32 applicants, 100% accepted, 13 enrolled. In 2009, 15 master's awarded. *Degree requirements:* For master's, thesis or alternative. *Entrance requirements:* For master's, GRE General Test. Additional exam requirements/recommendations for international students: Required—TOEFL (minimum score 550 paper-based; 213 computer-based). *Application deadline:* For fall admission, 6/16 for domestic students. Application fee: $35 ($50 for international students). *Financial support:* Fellowships, research assistantships, career-related internships or fieldwork available. Financial award application deadline: 6/1; financial award applicants required to submit FAFSA. *Faculty research:* Urban structure, GIS environmental resolutions, qualitative methods, JTS housing, planning history/theory. Total annual research expenditures: $30,453. *Unit head:* Dr. Enid Arvidson, Graduate Adviser, 817-272-3349, Fax: 817-272-5008. *Application contact:* Linda Slaughter, Administrative Clerk, 817-272-3071, Fax: 817-272-5008, E-mail: slaughter@uta.edu.

The University of Texas at Arlington, Graduate School, School of Urban and Public Affairs, Urban and Public Affairs Division, Arlington, TX 76019. Offers MA, MSSW/MA. Part-time and evening/weekend programs available. *Students:* 16 full-time (8 women), 54 part-time (22 women); includes 22 minority (16 African Americans, 1 Asian American or Pacific Islander, 5 Hispanic Americans), 11 international. Average age 25. 10 applicants, 100% accepted, 7 enrolled. In 2009, 3 master's awarded. *Degree requirements:* For master's, thesis or alternative. *Entrance requirements:* For master's, GRE General Test. Additional exam requirements/recommendations for international students: Required—TOEFL (minimum score 550 paper-based; 213 computer-based). *Application deadline:* For fall admission, 6/16 for domestic students. Application fee: $35 ($50 for international students). *Financial support:* In 2009–10, 1 research assistantship (averaging $750 per year) was awarded; fellowships, career-related internships or fieldwork also available. Financial award application deadline: 6/1; financial award applicants required to submit FAFSA. *Faculty research:* Personnel, non-profit organizational change, welfare policy, urban research. Total annual research expenditures: $33,080. *Unit head:* Dr. Edith Barrett, Graduate Adviser, 817-272-3285, Fax: 817-272-5008, E-mail: ebarrett@uta.edu. *Application contact:* Linda Slaughter, Administrative Clerk, 817-272-3071, Fax: 817-272-5008, E-mail: slaughter@uta.edu.

The University of Texas at Austin, Graduate School, School of Architecture, Program in Community and Regional Planning, Austin, TX 78712-1111. Offers MSCRP, PhD, JD/MSCRP, MSCRP/MA, MSCRP/PhD. *Accreditation:* ACSP. *Degree requirements:* For master's, thesis; for doctorate, thesis/dissertation. *Entrance requirements:* For master's and doctorate, GRE General Test. Electronic applications accepted.

The University of Toledo, College of Graduate Studies, College of Arts and Sciences, Department of Geography and Planning, Toledo, OH 43606-3390. Offers geographic information systems and applied geographics (Certificate); geography (MA); planning (MA). Part-time programs available. *Degree requirements:* For master's, thesis. *Entrance requirements:* For master's, GRE General Test. Electronic applications accepted.

University of Toronto, School of Graduate Studies, Social Sciences Division, Department of Geography, Program in Planning, Toronto, ON M5S 1A1, Canada. Offers M Sc Pl, PhD. Part-time programs available. *Degree requirements:* For master's, summer internship. *Entrance requirements:* For master's, bachelor's degree in planning, geography, social science or a closely related professional field, minimum B+ average in final year, 3 letters of reference. *Expenses:* Contact institution.

University of Utah, The Graduate School, College of Architecture and Planning, Department of City and Metropolitan Planning, Salt Lake City, UT 84112. Offers city and metropolitan planning (MS); metropolitan planning, policy and design (PhD). Part-time programs available. *Faculty:* 16 full-time (4 women), 4 part-time/adjunct (0 women). *Students:* 29 full-time (7 women), 15 part-time (6 women), 2 international. Average age 31. 46 applicants, 80% accepted, 24 enrolled. *Degree requirements:* For master's, thesis or alternative, comprehensive project. *Entrance requirements:* For master's, GRE, minimum undergraduate GPA of 3.0; for doctorate, GRE. Additional exam requirements/recommendations for international students: Required—TOEFL (minimum score 500 paper-based; 173 computer-based). *Application deadline:* For fall admission, 4/1 for domestic and international students; for spring admission, 10/1 for domestic students. Applications are processed on a rolling basis. Application fee: $55 ($65 for international students). Electronic applications accepted. *Expenses:* Contact institution. *Financial support:* In 2009–10, 29 fellowships with full tuition reimbursements, 3 research assistantships

Urban and Regional Planning

University of Utah (continued)
with full tuition reimbursements, 29 teaching assistantships with partial tuition reimbursements were awarded; career-related internships or fieldwork, Federal Work-Study, and scholarships/grants also available. Financial award application deadline: 2/1; financial award applicants required to submit FAFSA. *Faculty research:* History, design, acoustics, photography, structures, architecture of American West, architectural communications and representation, impact of technology. *Unit head:* Thomas W. Sanchez, Chair, 801-585-9354, E-mail: tom.sanchez@utah.edu. *Application contact:* Jeanette Benson, Admissions Advisor, 801-581-8255, Fax: 801-581-8217, E-mail: benson@arch.utah.edu.

University of Virginia, School of Architecture, Department of Urban and Environmental Planning, Charlottesville, VA 22903. Offers MUEP, JD/MUEP. *Accreditation:* ACSP (one or more programs are accredited). *Faculty:* 7 full-time (3 women). *Students:* 42 full-time (25 women); includes 1 minority (African American), 3 international. Average age 26. 137 applicants, 55% accepted, 20 enrolled. In 2009, 20 master's awarded. *Entrance requirements:* For master's, GRE General Test, previous course work in statistics, 3 letters of recommendation. Additional exam requirements/recommendations for international students: Required—TOEFL (minimum score 600 paper-based; 250 computer-based; 90 iBT). *Application deadline:* For fall admission, 1/16 for domestic and international students. Applications are processed on a rolling basis. Application fee: $60. Electronic applications accepted. *Financial support:* Applicants required to submit FAFSA. *Faculty research:* Urban development, land use, environment, policy analysis, historic preservation. *Unit head:* Daphne Spain, Chair, 434-924-1339, Fax: 434-982-2678, E-mail: dgs4g@virginia.edu. *Application contact:* Graduate Admissions Officer, 434-924-6442, Fax: 434-982-2678, E-mail: arch-admissions@virginia.edu.

University of Washington, Graduate School, College of Built Environments, Department of Urban Design and Planning, Seattle, WA 98195. Offers strategic planning for critical infrastructures (MSCPI); urban design and planning (PhD); urban planning (MUP). *Accreditation:* ACSP (one or more programs are accredited). *Degree requirements:* For master's, thesis or alternative; for doctorate, thesis/dissertation. *Entrance requirements:* For master's and doctorate, GRE General Test, minimum GPA of 3.0. Additional exam requirements/recommendations for international students: Required—TOEFL. *Faculty research:* Land-use and growth management, urban form and travel behavior, geographic information systems/remote sensing, historic preservation, urban ecology and environmental planning.

University of Waterloo, Graduate Studies, Faculty of Environmental Studies, Program in Local Economic Development, Waterloo, ON N2L 3G1, Canada. Offers MAES. Part-time programs available. *Degree requirements:* For master's, internship, research paper. Electronic applications accepted.

University of Waterloo, Graduate Studies, Faculty of Environmental Studies, School of Planning, Waterloo, ON N2L 3G1, Canada. Offers MA, MAES, MES, PhD. Part-time programs available. *Degree requirements:* For master's, thesis (for some programs); for doctorate, comprehensive exam, thesis/dissertation. *Entrance requirements:* For master's, honors degree, minimum B+ average; for doctorate, master's degree, minimum A- average, resume. Additional exam requirements/recommendations for international students: Required—TOEFL, TWE. Electronic applications accepted. *Faculty research:* Environmental planning, planning for resource development, urban planning and information systems, social planning, urban design.

University of Wisconsin–Madison, Graduate School, College of Letters and Science and College of Agricultural and Life Sciences, Department of Urban and Regional Planning, Madison, WI 53706-1380. Offers MS, PhD. *Accreditation:* ACSP (one or more programs are accredited). Part-time programs available. *Degree requirements:* For master's, thesis optional, internship; for doctorate, thesis/dissertation, 3 preliminary exams. *Entrance requirements:* For master's, GRE, minimum GPA of 3.0, previous course work in statistics; for doctorate, 1 year of experience, master's degree in related field. Electronic applications accepted. *Expenses:* Tuition, state resident: part-time $594 per credit. Tuition, nonresident: part-time $1504 per credit. Required fees: $65 per credit. Tuition and fees vary according to course load, program and reciprocity agreements. *Faculty research:* Land use, environmental planning, community development, economic development planning.

University of Wisconsin–Milwaukee, Graduate School, School of Architecture and Urban Planning, Department of Urban Planning, Milwaukee, WI 53201-0413. Offers geographic information systems (Certificate); real estate development (Certificate); urban planning (MUP); M Arch/MUP; MPA/MUP; MUP/MS. *Accreditation:* ACSP. Part-time programs available. *Faculty:* 4 full-time (1 woman). *Students:* 29 full-time (11 women), 5 part-time (3 women), 2 international. Average age 28. 52 applicants, 71% accepted, 13 enrolled. In 2009, 22 master's awarded. *Degree requirements:* For master's, comprehensive exam, thesis or alternative. *Entrance requirements:* For master's, GRE General Test. Additional exam requirements/recommendations for international students: Required—TOEFL (minimum score 550 paper-based; 213 computer-based; 79 iBT), IELTS (minimum score 6.5). *Application deadline:* For fall admission, 1/1 priority date for domestic students; for spring admission, 9/1 for domestic students. Applications are processed on a rolling basis. Application fee: $45 ($75 for international students). *Expenses:* Tuition, state resident: full-time $8800. Tuition, nonresident: full-time $20,760. Tuition and fees vary according to program and reciprocity agreements. *Financial support:* In 2009–10, 3 teaching assistantships were awarded; career-related internships or fieldwork and unspecified assistantships also available. Support available to part-time students. Financial award application deadline: 4/15. Total annual research expenditures: $4,667. *Unit head:* Joan Simuncak, Representative, 414-229-4015, Fax: 414-229-6976, E-mail: joanarch@uwm.edu. *Application contact:* General Information Contact, 414-229-4982, Fax: 414-229-6967, E-mail: gradschool@uwm.edu.

Utah State University, School of Graduate Studies, College of Humanities, Arts and Social Sciences, Department of Landscape Architecture and Environmental Planning, Logan, UT 84322. Offers bioregional planning (MS); landscape architecture (MLA). *Accreditation:* ASLA (one or more programs are accredited). *Degree requirements:* For master's, thesis. *Entrance requirements:* For master's, GRE General Test, minimum GPA of 3.0. Additional exam requirements/recommendations for international students: Required—TOEFL. *Faculty research:* Visual resource management, planning for wildlife, agricultural land preservation, watershed planning, community planning and design.

Utah State University, School of Graduate Studies, College of Natural Resources, Department of Environment and Society, Logan, UT 84322. Offers bioregional planning (MS); geography (MA, MS); human dimensions of ecosystem science and management (MS, PhD); recreation resource management (MS, PhD). *Degree requirements:* For master's, comprehensive exam, thesis (for some programs). *Entrance requirements:* For master's and doctorate, GRE General Test, minimum GPA of 3.0. Additional exam requirements/recommendations for international students: Required—TOEFL. Electronic applications accepted. *Faculty research:* Geographic information systems/geographic and environmental education, bioregional planning, natural resource and environmental policy, outdoor recreation and tourism, natural resource and environmental management.

Vanderbilt University, Peabody College, Department of Human and Organizational Development, Nashville, TN 37240-1001. Offers community development and action (M Ed); human development counseling (M Ed). *Accreditation:* ACA; NCATE. Part-time programs available. *Faculty:* 29 full-time (14 women), 27 part-time/adjunct (19 women). *Students:* 88 full-time (82 women), 7 part-time (all women); includes 16 minority (11 African Americans, 1 Asian American or Pacific Islander, 4 Hispanic Americans), 1 international. Average age 27. 141 applicants, 57% accepted, 56 enrolled. In 2009, 31 master's awarded. *Degree requirements:* For master's, comprehensive exam, thesis optional. *Entrance requirements:* For master's, GRE General Test, MAT. Additional exam requirements/recommendations for international students: Required—TOEFL (minimum score 550 paper-based; 213 computer-based). *Application deadline:* For fall admission, 12/31 priority date for domestic and international students; for spring admission, 11/1 priority date for domestic and international students. Applications are processed on a rolling basis. Application fee: $0. Electronic applications accepted. *Financial support:* In 2009–10, 86 students received support, including 31 research assistantships with full and partial tuition reimbursements available, 20 teaching assistantships with full and partial tuition reimbursements available; fellowships with full and partial tuition reimbursements available, Federal Work-Study, institutionally sponsored loans, scholarships/grants, tuition waivers (partial), and unspecified assistantships also available. Support available to part-time students. Financial award application deadline: 2/1; financial award applicants required to submit FAFSA. *Faculty research:* Community psychology, community development and urban policy, counseling and mental health services, organizational development and institutional change; youth physical and behavioral health in schools and communities. *Unit head:* Dr. Marybeth Shinn, Chair, 615-322-6881, Fax: 615-322-1141, E-mail: marybeth.shinn@vanderbilt.edu. *Application contact:* Sherrie Lane, Office Assistant, 615-322-8484, Fax: 615-322-1141, E-mail: sherrie.a.lane@vanderbilt.edu.

Virginia Commonwealth University, Graduate School, College of Humanities and Sciences, Wilder School of Government and Public Affairs, Department of Urban Studies and Planning, Program in Planning Information Systems, Richmond, VA 23284-9005. Offers Certificate.

Virginia Commonwealth University, Graduate School, College of Humanities and Sciences, Wilder School of Government and Public Affairs, Department of Urban Studies and Planning, Program in Urban and Regional Planning, Richmond, VA 23284-9005. Offers MURP, JD/MURP. *Degree requirements:* For master's, thesis optional, internship. *Entrance requirements:* For master's, GRE General Test or LSAT, minimum GPA of 2.7.

Virginia Polytechnic Institute and State University, Graduate School, College of Architecture and Urban Studies, School of Public and International Affairs, Blacksburg, VA 24061. Offers environmental planning and policy (MURP); government and international affairs (MPIA); housing, community and economic development (MURP); international development planning (MURP); land use and physical planning (MURP); planning, governance and globalization (PhD), including environmental planning and landscape analysis, physical planning and urban design, public and international affairs, urban and environmental design and planning; urban and regional planning (MURP). *Accreditation:* ACSP. *Faculty:* 27 full-time (11 women), 2 part-time/adjunct (1 woman). *Students:* 73 full-time (51 women), 65 part-time (39 women); includes 15 minority (4 African Americans, 1 American Indian/Alaska Native, 6 Asian Americans or Pacific Islanders, 4 Hispanic Americans), 10 international. Average age 29. 86 applicants, 67% accepted, 40 enrolled. In 2009, 26 master's, 1 doctorate awarded. *Entrance requirements:* Additional exam requirements/recommendations for international students: Required—TOEFL (minimum score 550 paper-based; 213 computer-based). *Application deadline:* For fall admission, 5/15 for international students; for spring admission, 10/15 for international students. Applications are processed on a rolling basis. Application fee: $45. Electronic applications accepted. *Financial support:* In 2009–10, 1 teaching assistantship with full tuition reimbursement (averaging $5,560 per year) was awarded; career-related internships or fieldwork, Federal Work-Study, scholarships/grants, and unspecified assistantships also available. Financial award application deadline: 4/1. *Faculty research:* Design theory, environmental planning, town planning, transportation planning. *Unit head:* Dr. John Randolph, Dean, 540-231-6971, Fax: 540-231-9938, E-mail: energy@vt.edu. *Application contact:* Krystal D. Wright, Information Contact, 540-231-*5683, Fax: 540-231-9938, E-mail: garch@vt.edu.

Wayne State University, College of Liberal Arts and Sciences, Department of Geography and Urban Planning, Detroit, MI 48202. Offers geography (MA); urban planning (MUP). Evening/weekend programs available. *Entrance requirements:* For master's, minimum 3.0 GPA, 2 letters of recommendation. Additional exam requirements/recommendations for international students: Required—TOEFL (minimum score 550 paper-based; 213 computer-based); Recommended—TWE (minimum score 6). Electronic applications accepted. *Faculty research:* Housing and community development, urban and regional economic development, urban development and land use, transportation policy and planning, environmental policy and planning.

Wayne State University, College of Liberal Arts and Sciences, Program in Urban Planning, Detroit, MI 48202. Offers MUP. *Accreditation:* ACSP. Evening/weekend programs available. *Degree requirements:* For master's, thesis. *Entrance requirements:* Additional exam requirements/recommendations for international students: Required—TOEFL (minimum score 550 paper-based; 213 computer-based); Recommended—TWE (minimum score 6). Electronic applications accepted.

West Chester University of Pennsylvania, Office of Graduate Studies, College of Business and Public Affairs, Department of Geography and Planning, West Chester, PA 19383. Offers geographic technology (Certificate); geography (MA); regional planning (MSA). Part-time and evening/weekend programs available. *Students:* 3 full-time (0 women), 27 part-time (9 women); includes 5 minority (3 African Americans, 1 Asian American or Pacific Islander, 1 Hispanic American), 1 international. Average age 28. 13 applicants, 100% accepted, 9 enrolled. In 2009, 11 master's, 5 other advanced degrees awarded. *Degree requirements:* For master's, comprehensive exam, thesis optional. *Entrance requirements:* For master's, GRE, GMAT, or MAT, minimum GPA of 2.8, resume, two letters of recommendation; for Certificate, minimum GPA of 2.8, resume, two letters of recommendation. Additional exam requirements/recommendations for international students: Required—TOEFL (minimum score 550 paper-based; 213 computer-based; 80 iBT). *Application deadline:* For fall admission, 4/15 priority date for domestic students, 3/15 for international students; for spring admission, 10/15 for domestic students, 9/1 for international students. Applications are processed on a rolling basis. Application fee: $35. Electronic applications accepted. *Expenses:* Tuition, state resident: full-time $6666; part-time $370 per credit. Tuition, nonresident: full-time $10,666; part-time $593 per credit. Required fees: $122.56 per credit. *Financial support:* In 2009–10, 6 research assistantships with full and partial tuition reimbursements (averaging $5,000 per year) were awarded; unspecified assistantships also available. Support available to part-time students. Financial award application deadline: 2/15; financial award applicants required to submit FAFSA. *Faculty research:* Environmental education, land use/suburban planning, landscapes of Catalunya. *Unit head:* Dr. Joan Welch, Chair and Graduate Coordinator, 610-436-2940, E-mail: jwelch@wcupa.edu. *Application contact:* Dr. Dottie Ives Dewey, MSA Graduate Coordinator, 610-436-2746, E-mail: divesdewey@wcupa.edu.

West Virginia University, Davis College of Agriculture, Forestry and Consumer Sciences, Division of Resource Management and Sustainable Development, Morgantown, WV 26506. Offers agricultural and extension education (MS, PhD), including agricultural and extension education, teaching vocational-agriculture (MS); agricultural and resource economics (MS); human and community development (PhD); natural resource economics (PhD); resource management (PhD); resource management and sustainable development (PhD). Part-time programs available. *Degree requirements:* For master's, thesis; for doctorate, comprehensive exam, thesis/dissertation. *Entrance requirements:* For master's, GRE General Test. Additional exam requirements/recommendations for international students: Required—TOEFL. *Faculty research:* Environmental economics, energy economics, agriculture.

West Virginia University, Eberly College of Arts and Sciences, Department of Geology and Geography, Program in Geography, Morgantown, WV 26506. Offers energy and environmental resources (MA); geographic information systems (PhD); geography-regional development (PhD); GIS/cartographic analysis (MA); regional development (MA). Part-time programs available. *Degree requirements:* For master's, thesis, oral and written exams; for doctorate, comprehensive exam, thesis/dissertation, oral and written exams. *Entrance requirements:* For master's and doctorate, GRE General Test, minimum GPA of 3.0. Additional exam requirements/recommendations for international students: Required—TOEFL. Electronic applications accepted. *Faculty research:* Space, place and development, geographic information science, environmental geography.

Urban Studies

Boston University, Metropolitan College, Program in Urban Affairs, Boston, MA 02215. Offers MUA. Part-time and evening/weekend programs available. *Faculty:* 5 full-time (1 woman), 23 part-time/adjunct (4 women). *Students:* 1 (woman) full-time, 14 part-time (5 women); includes 5 African Americans, 1 international. Average age 30. In 2009, 10 master's awarded. *Entrance requirements:* Additional exam requirements/recommendations for international students: Required—TOEFL; Recommended—IELTS. *Application deadline:* For fall admission, 7/15 priority date for domestic and international students; for spring admission, 12/15 for domestic students, 11/15 priority date for international students. Applications are processed on a rolling basis. Application fee: $70. Electronic applications accepted. *Expenses:* Tuition: Full-time $37,910; part-time $1184 per credit hour. Required fees: $386; $40 per semester. Part-time tuition and fees vary according to class time, course level, degree level and program. *Financial support:* In 2009–10, 10 students received support, including 10 research assistantships with full and partial tuition reimbursements available; career-related internships or fieldwork, Federal Work-Study, institutionally sponsored loans, tuition waivers (partial), and unspecified assistantships also available. Support available to part-time students. Financial award application deadline: 6/15; financial award applicants required to submit FAFSA. *Faculty research:* Housing, community development and land use planning, environmental management and planning, international comparative development planning. *Unit head:* Dr. Daniel P. LeClair, Chair, 617-353-3025, Fax: 617-358-3595, E-mail: dleclair@bu.edu. *Application contact:* Dr. Enrique Silvia, Assistant Professor, 617-358-2364, E-mail: ersilva@bu.edu.

Brooklyn College of the City University of New York, Division of Graduate Studies, Department of Political Science, Brooklyn, NY 11210-2889. Offers international affairs (MA); political science (MA, PhD); political science, urban policy and administration (MA). Part-time and evening/weekend programs available. *Students:* 24 full-time (13 women), 168 part-time (98 women); includes 99 minority (70 African Americans, 13 Asian Americans or Pacific Islanders, 16 Hispanic Americans), 29 international. Average age 30. 123 applicants, 87% accepted, 79 enrolled. In 2009, 46 master's awarded. *Degree requirements:* For master's, comprehensive exam (for some programs), thesis or alternative, foreign language exam (for international affairs program). *Entrance requirements:* For master's, 2 letters of recommendation, personal statement. Additional exam requirements/recommendations for international students: Required—TOEFL (minimum score 500 paper-based; 173 computer-based; 61 iBT). *Application deadline:* For fall admission, 5/1 for domestic and international students; for spring admission, 12/12 for domestic students, 11/1 for international students. *Expenses:* Tuition, area resident: Full-time $7360; part-time $310 per credit hour. Tuition, state resident: full-time $7360; part-time $310 per credit hour. Tuition, nonresident: full-time $13,800; part-time $575 per credit hour. International tuition: $13,800 full-time. Required fees: $140.10 per semester. *Financial support:* Career-related internships or fieldwork and Federal Work-Study available. Support available to part-time students. Financial award application deadline: 5/1; financial award applicants required to submit FAFSA. *Faculty research:* Ethics and politics, politics of criminal justice, Western Europe, international law and politics, labor politics. *Unit head:* Dr. Noel Anderson, Acting Chairperson, 718-951-5306, E-mail: anderson@brooklyn.cuny.edu. *Application contact:* Hernan Sierra, Graduate Admissions Coordinator, 718-951-4536, Fax: 718-951-4506, E-mail: grads@brooklyn.cuny.edu.

Cleveland State University, College of Graduate Studies, Maxine Goodman Levin College of Urban Affairs, Program in Urban Studies, Cleveland, OH 44115. Offers geographic information systems (Certificate); local and urban management (Certificate); nonprofit management (Certificate); urban economic development (Certificate); urban real estate development and finance (Certificate); urban studies (MS); urban studies and public affairs (PhD). Part-time and evening/weekend programs available. *Degree requirements:* For master's, thesis or alternative, exit project, capstone course; for doctorate, comprehensive exam, thesis/dissertation. *Entrance requirements:* For master's, GRE General Test, minimum GPA of 3.0; for doctorate, GRE General Test, minimum GPA of 3.5. Additional exam requirements/recommendations for international students: Required—TOEFL (minimum score 525 paper-based; 197 computer-based; 65 iBT). Electronic applications accepted. *Faculty research:* Environmental issues, economic development, urban and public policy, public management.

Concordia University, School of Graduate Studies, Faculty of Arts and Science, Department of Geography, Planning and Environment, Montréal, QC H3G 1M8, Canada. Offers environmental impact assessment (Diploma); geography, urban and environmental studies (M Sc).

Eastern University, School for Social Change, St. Davids, PA 19087-3696. Offers urban studies (MA), including arts in transformation, community development, youth leadership.

East Tennessee State University, School of Graduate Studies, College of Business and Technology, Department of Economics, Finance, and Urban Studies, Johnson City, TN 37614. Offers city management (MCM); community development (MPM); general administration (MPM); municipal service management (MPM); urban and regional economic development (MPM); urban and regional planning (MPM). *Degree requirements:* For master's, internship, oral defense of thesis, research report. *Entrance requirements:* For master's, GRE General Test, minimum GPA of 3.0. Additional exam requirements/recommendations for international students: Required—TOEFL (minimum score 550 paper-based; 213 computer-based).

Fordham University, Graduate School of Arts and Sciences, Program in Urban Studies, New York, NY 10458. Offers MA. *Students:* 4 part-time (3 women); includes 2 minority (1 Asian American or Pacific Islander, 1 Hispanic American). 5 applicants, 100% accepted, 2 enrolled. *Degree requirements:* For master's, internship or field work, research project. *Unit head:* Dr. Rosemary Wakeman, Director, 212-636-7359, E-mail: rwakeman@fordham.edu. *Application contact:* Charlene Dundie, Director of Graduate Admissions, 718-817-4420, Fax: 718-817-3566, E-mail: dundie@fordham.edu.

Graduate School and University Center of the City University of New York, Graduate Studies, Interdisciplinary Studies, New York, NY 10016-4039. Offers language in social context (PhD); medieval studies (PhD); public policy (MA, PhD); urban studies (MA, PhD); women's studies (MA, PhD). Terminal master's awarded for partial completion of doctoral program. *Degree requirements:* For master's, thesis; for doctorate, comprehensive exam, thesis/dissertation. *Entrance requirements:* For master's and doctorate, GRE General Test.

Hunter College of the City University of New York, Graduate School, School of Arts and Sciences, Department of Urban Affairs and Planning, Program in Urban Affairs, New York, NY 10021-5085. Offers urban studies/affairs (MS). Part-time programs available. *Faculty:* 13 full-time (5 women), 12 part-time/adjunct (5 women). *Students:* 15 full-time (8 women), 65 part-time (46 women); includes 30 minority (12 African Americans, 6 Asian Americans or Pacific Islanders, 12 Hispanic Americans). Average age 33. 90 applicants, 64% accepted, 30 enrolled. In 2009, 59 master's awarded. *Degree requirements:* For master's, thesis or alternative, 2 formal reports, internship. *Entrance requirements:* For master's, minimum 12 credits of course work in social sciences. Additional exam requirements/recommendations for international students: Required—TOEFL. *Application deadline:* For fall admission, 4/1 priority date for domestic students, 2/1 for international students; for spring admission, 11/1 priority date for domestic students, 9/1 for international students. Applications are processed on a rolling basis. Application fee: $125. *Expenses:* Tuition, state resident: full-time $7360; part-time $310 per credit. Required fees: $250 per semester. *Financial support:* Fellowships, research assistantships, teaching assistantships, career-related internships or fieldwork, Federal Work-Study, scholarships/grants, and unspecified assistantships available. *Faculty research:* Women, tourism, youth, immigration, employment. *Unit head:* Dr. Jill Simone Gross, Director, 212-772-5600, Fax: 212-772-5593, E-mail: igross@hunter.cuny.edu. *Application contact:* William Zlata, Director for Graduate Admissions, 212-772-4482, Fax: 212-650-3336, E-mail: admissions@hunter.cuny.edu.

Long Island University, Brooklyn Campus, Richard L. Conolly College of Liberal Arts and Sciences, Department of Urban Studies, Brooklyn, NY 11201-8423. Offers MA. Part-time and evening/weekend programs available. *Degree requirements:* For master's, thesis or alternative. *Entrance requirements:* For master's, 2 letters of recommendation. Additional exam requirements/recommendations for international students: Required—TOEFL (minimum score 500 paper-based; 173 computer-based). Electronic applications accepted.

Loyola University Chicago, Graduate School, Department of Sociology, Chicago, IL 60660. Offers applied sociology (MA); sociology (MA, PhD); urban studies (MA). Part-time and evening/weekend programs available. *Faculty:* 14 full-time (7 women), 3 part-time/adjunct (2 women). *Students:* 66 full-time (44 women), 15 part-time (9 women); includes 15 minority (8 African Americans, 5 Asian Americans or Pacific Islanders, 2 Hispanic Americans), 6 international. Average age 33. 113 applicants, 42% accepted, 20 enrolled. In 2009, 5 master's, 4 doctorates awarded. Terminal master's awarded for partial completion of doctoral program. *Degree requirements:* For master's, thesis or alternative; for doctorate, comprehensive exam, thesis/dissertation. *Entrance requirements:* For master's and doctorate, GRE General Test. Additional exam requirements/recommendations for international students: Required—TOEFL. *Application deadline:* For winter admission, 2/1 for domestic and international students. Electronic applications accepted. *Expenses:* Tuition: Full-time $14,220; part-time $790 per credit hour. Required fees: $60 per semester hour. Tuition and fees vary according to program. *Financial support:* In 2009–10, 35 students received support, including 10 fellowships with full tuition reimbursements available (averaging $14,000 per year), 5 research assistantships with full tuition reimbursements available (averaging $14,000 per year), 9 teaching assistantships with full tuition reimbursements available (averaging $14,000 per year); career-related internships or fieldwork, Federal Work-Study, tuition waivers (full), and unspecified assistantships also available. Financial award application deadline: 2/1; financial award applicants required to submit FAFSA. *Faculty research:* Religion, knowledge, culture, urban and social policy. Total annual research expenditures: $160,000. *Unit head:* Dr. Rhys Williams, Chair, 773-508-3459, Fax: 773-508-7099, E-mail: rwilliams7s@luc.edu. *Application contact:* Dr. Anne Figert, Graduate Program Director, 773-508-3431, Fax: 773-508-7099, E-mail: afigert@luc.edu.

Massachusetts Institute of Technology, School of Architecture and Planning, Department of Urban Studies and Planning, Cambridge, MA 02139-4307. Offers city planning (MCP); urban and regional planning (PhD); urban and regional studies (PhD); urban studies and planning (SM). *Accreditation:* ACSP (one or more programs are accredited). *Faculty:* 29 full-time (11 women). *Students:* 207 full-time (118 women); includes 44 minority (9 African Americans, 2 American Indian/Alaska Native, 19 Asian Americans or Pacific Islanders, 14 Hispanic Americans), 62 international. Average age 29. 575 applicants, 19% accepted, 78 enrolled. In 2009, 93 master's, 7 doctorates awarded. Terminal master's awarded for partial completion of doctoral program. *Degree requirements:* For master's, thesis; for doctorate, comprehensive exam, thesis/dissertation. *Entrance requirements:* For master's, GRE General Test; for doctorate, GRE General Test—minimum score required: 1200 (V&Q) combined; 5.0 analytical writing. Additional exam requirements/recommendations for international students: Required—TOEFL (minimum score 600 paper-based; 250 computer-based; 100 iBT) or IELTS (minimum score 7); Recommended—TWE. *Application deadline:* For fall admission, 1/3 for domestic and international students. Application fee: $75. Electronic applications accepted. *Expenses:* Tuition: Full-time $37,510; part-time $585 per unit. Required fees: $272. *Financial support:* In 2009–10, 176 students received support, including 74 fellowships with tuition reimbursements available (averaging $20,544 per year), 65 research assistantships with tuition reimbursements available (averaging $20,932 per year), 16 teaching assistantships with tuition reimbursements available (averaging $28,535 per year); career-related internships or fieldwork, Federal Work-Study, institutionally sponsored loans, scholarships/grants, health care benefits, and unspecified assistantships also available. *Faculty research:* City design and sustainable urban development, housing, environment and energy policy and planning, international development and regional planning, community and economic development, urban and geographic information systems. Total annual research expenditures: $1.9 million. *Unit head:* Prof. Amy Glasmeier, Department Head, 617-253-1907, Fax: 617-253-2654, E-mail: duspinfo@mit.edu. *Application contact:* Graduate Admissions, 617-253-9403, Fax: 617-253-2654, E-mail: duspapply@mit.edu.

Minnesota State University Mankato, College of Graduate Studies, College of Social and Behavioral Sciences, Department of Urban and Regional Studies, Mankato, MN 56001. Offers local government management (Certificate); urban and regional studies (MA); urban planning (MA, Certificate); MAPA/MA. *Students:* 16 full-time (2 women), 19 part-time (9 women). *Degree requirements:* For master's, one foreign language, comprehensive exam, thesis or alternative. *Entrance requirements:* For master's, minimum GPA of 3.0 during previous 2 years, 2 letters of recommendation. Additional exam requirements/recommendations for international students: Required—TOEFL. *Application deadline:* For fall admission, 7/1 priority date for domestic students; for spring admission, 11/1 for domestic students. Applications are processed on a rolling basis. Application fee: $40. Electronic applications accepted. *Expenses:* Tuition, state resident: full-time $5364. Tuition, nonresident: full-time $8314. *Financial support:* Fellowships with partial tuition reimbursements, research assistantships with full tuition reimbursements, teaching assistantships with full tuition reimbursements, career-related internships or fieldwork, Federal Work-Study, institutionally sponsored loans, and unspecified assistantships available. Support available to part-time students. Financial award application deadline: 3/15; financial award applicants required to submit FAFSA. *Unit head:* Dr. Anthony Filipovitch, Chairperson, 507-389-1714. *Application contact:* 507-389-2321, E-mail: grad@mnsu.edu.

Moody Bible Institute, Graduate School, Chicago, IL 60610-3284. Offers biblical studies (MABS, Graduate Certificate); intercultural studies (MAIS, Graduate Certificate); ministry (M Div, M Min); spiritual formation and discipleship (MASF, Graduate Certificate); urban studies (MA, Graduate Certificate). Part-time programs available. *Degree requirements:* For master's, 2 foreign languages, fieldwork (MABS); colloquium, field research project (MA Min). *Entrance requirements:* For master's, 30 hours in Bible/theology, 2 years of ministry experience (MA Min).

New Jersey City University, Graduate Studies and Continuing Education, Debra Cannon Partridge Wolfe College of Education, Department of Educational Leadership, Jersey City, NJ 07305-1597. Offers basics and urban studies (MA); bilingual/bicultural education and English as a second language (MA); educational administration and supervision (MA). Part-time and evening/weekend programs available. *Faculty:* 3. *Students:* 27 full-time (18 women), 187 part-time (115 women); includes 77 minority (18 African Americans, 6 Asian Americans or Pacific Islanders, 53 Hispanic Americans), 16 international. Average age 34. In 2009, 121 master's awarded. *Entrance requirements:* For master's, GRE General Test or MAT. Additional exam requirements/recommendations for international students: Required—TOEFL. *Application deadline:* For fall admission, 8/1 priority date for domestic students; for spring admission, 12/1 for domestic students. Applications are processed on a rolling basis. Application fee: $0. *Expenses:* Tuition, area resident: Part-time $456.75 per credit. Tuition, nonresident: part-time $842.55 per credit. Required fees: $65 per term. *Financial support:* Fellowships, teaching assistantships, career-related internships or fieldwork and unspecified assistantships available. *Unit head:* Dr. Susan Phifer, Chairperson, 201-200-3012, E-mail: sphifer@njcu.edu. *Application contact:* Dr. Susan Phifer, Chairperson, 201-200-3012, E-mail: sphifer@njcu.edu.

New Jersey Institute of Technology, Office of Graduate Studies, School of Architecture, Program in Urban Systems, Newark, NJ 07102. Offers PhD. Part-time and evening/weekend programs available. *Entrance requirements:* Additional exam requirements/recommendations

Urban Studies

New Jersey Institute of Technology (continued)
for international students: Required—TOEFL (minimum score 550 paper-based; 213 computer-based; 79 iBT). Electronic applications accepted.

The New School: A University, Milano The New School for Management and Urban Policy, Program in Urban Policy Analysis and Management, 72 5th Avenue, NY 10011. Offers MS. *Accreditation:* NASPAA. Part-time programs available. *Faculty:* 3 full-time (2 women). *Students:* 105 full-time (71 women), 69 part-time (50 women); includes 60 minority (29 African Americans, 12 Asian Americans or Pacific Islanders, 19 Hispanic Americans), 10 international. Average age 29. In 2009, 42 master's awarded. *Degree requirements:* For master's, thesis. *Entrance requirements:* For master's, interview. Additional exam requirements/recommendations for international students: Required—TOEFL (minimum score 600 paper-based; 250 computer-based; 100 iBT). *Application deadline:* For fall admission, 3/1 priority date for domestic and international students; for spring admission, 10/1 priority date for domestic and international students. Applications are processed on a rolling basis. Application fee: $50. Electronic applications accepted. *Financial support:* Fellowships, Federal Work-Study, scholarships/grants, and tuition waivers (full and partial) available. Support available to part-time students. Financial award application deadline: 3/1; financial award applicants required to submit FAFSA. *Faculty research:* Community and economic development, national urban policy, social welfare policy, management of low-income housing, race and gender issues. *Unit head:* Dr. Alex F. Schwartz, Chair, 212-229-5400 Ext. 1415, Fax: 212-229-5404, E-mail: schwartz@newschool.edu. *Application contact:* Merida Escandon, Director of Admissions, 212-229-5462 Ext. 1108, Fax: 212-229-5354, E-mail: milanoadmissions@newschool.edu.

Norfolk State University, School of Graduate Studies, School of Liberal Arts, Department of Sociology, Program in Urban Affairs, Norfolk, VA 23504. Offers MA. Part-time programs available. *Degree requirements:* For master's, thesis. *Entrance requirements:* For master's, minimum GPA of 2.5.

Northeastern University, College of Social Sciences and Humanities, Department of Political Science, Boston, MA 02115-5096. Offers political science (MA); public administration (MPA, Certificate), including development administration (MPA), health administration and policy (MPA), state and local government (MPA), urban studies (Certificate); public and international affairs (PhD). Part-time and evening/weekend programs available. *Faculty:* 22 full-time (4 women), 10 part-time/adjunct (1 woman). *Students:* 10 full-time (3 women), 62 part-time (28 women); includes 7 minority (2 African Americans, 2 American Indian/Alaska Native, 2 Asian Americans or Pacific Islanders, 1 Hispanic American), 11 international. Average age 30. 129 applicants, 69% accepted, 24 enrolled. In 2009, 28 master's, 3 doctorates awarded. *Degree requirements:* For master's, thesis optional; for doctorate, thesis/dissertation. *Entrance requirements:* For master's, GRE General Test. Additional exam requirements/recommendations for international students: Required—TOEFL. *Application deadline:* Applications are processed on a rolling basis. Application fee: $50. *Financial support:* In 2009–10, 12 fellowships, 3 research assistantships with tuition reimbursements, 18 teaching assistantships with tuition reimbursements (averaging $14,035 per year) were awarded; career-related internships or fieldwork, Federal Work-Study, tuition waivers (full and partial), and unspecified assistantships also available. Support available to part-time students. Financial award application deadline: 2/1; financial award applicants required to submit FAFSA. *Faculty research:* Presidency, public opinion, Congress, democratization, national identity. *Unit head:* Dr. John Portz, Chair, 617-373-2796, Fax: 617-373-5311, E-mail: gradpolisci@neu.edu. *Application contact:* Brynn Thompson, Graduate Programs Assistant, 617-373-4404, Fax: 617-373-5311, E-mail: gradpolisci@neu.edu.

Northeastern University, College of Social Sciences and Humanities, Program in Public Administration, Boston, MA 02115-5096. Offers development administration (MPA); health administration and policy (MPA); state and local government (MPA); urban studies (Certificate). *Accreditation:* NASPAA (one or more programs are accredited). Part-time and evening/weekend programs available. *Faculty:* 22 full-time (4 women), 10 part-time/adjunct (1 woman). *Students:* 49 full-time (26 women), 28 part-time (18 women); includes 8 African Americans, 1 Asian American or Pacific Islander, 1 Hispanic American, 14 international. 102 applicants, 52% accepted, 26 enrolled. In 2009, 11 master's awarded. *Degree requirements:* For master's, thesis optional. *Entrance requirements:* For master's, GRE General Test. Additional exam requirements/recommendations for international students: Required—TOEFL. *Application deadline:* For fall admission, 2/1 priority date for domestic students, 5/1 for international students. Applications are processed on a rolling basis. Application fee: $50. *Financial support:* In 2009–10, 2 research assistantships with tuition reimbursements (averaging $14,035 per year) were awarded; teaching assistantships with tuition reimbursements, career-related internships or fieldwork, Federal Work-Study, tuition waivers (full and partial), and unspecified assistantships also available. Support available to part-time students. Financial award application deadline: 2/1; financial award applicants required to submit FAFSA. *Faculty research:* National health care, Third World development, leadership and ethics, science and technology, budgeting. *Unit head:* Dr. Ronald D. Hedlund, Graduate Coordinator, 617-373-2796, Fax: 617-373-5311, E-mail: gradpolisci@neu.edu. *Application contact:* Brynn Thompson, Graduate Programs Assistant, 617-373-4404, Fax: 617-373-5311, E-mail: gradpolisci@neu.edu.

Old Dominion University, College of Business and Public Administration, Doctoral Program in Public Administration and Urban Policy, Norfolk, VA 23529. Offers PhD. Part-time and evening/weekend programs available. *Faculty:* 7 full-time (1 woman), 3 part-time/adjunct (2 women). *Students:* 11 full-time (9 women), 13 part-time (5 women); includes 7 minority (6 African Americans, 1 Asian American or Pacific Islander), 4 international. Average age 37. 19 applicants, 42% accepted, 6 enrolled. In 2009, 4 doctorates awarded. *Degree requirements:* For doctorate, comprehensive exam, thesis/dissertation. *Entrance requirements:* For doctorate, GMAT, GRE General Test, master's degree, minimum graduate GPA of 3.25. Additional exam requirements/recommendations for international students: Required—TOEFL (minimum score 550 paper-based; 213 computer-based; 79 iBT). *Application deadline:* For fall admission, 3/15 priority date for domestic and international students. Application fee: $50. Electronic applications accepted. *Expenses:* Tuition, state resident: full-time $8112; part-time $338 per credit. Tuition, nonresident: full-time $20,256; part-time $844 per credit. Required fees: $119 per semester. One-time fee: $50. *Financial support:* In 2009–10, 10 students received support, including 2 fellowships with partial tuition reimbursements available (averaging $15,000 per year), 6 research assistantships with partial tuition reimbursements available (averaging $13,000 per year); teaching assistantships. Financial award application deadline: 3/15; financial award applicants required to submit FAFSA. *Faculty research:* Educational needs and program development, policy analysis and administration, excellence norms for cooperative education programs. Total annual research expenditures: $60,000. *Unit head:* Dr. John C. Morris, Graduate Program Director, 757-683-3961, Fax: 757-683-4886, E-mail: jcmorris@odu.edu. *Application contact:* Megan S. Jones, Graduate Program Manager, 757-683-3961, Fax: 757-683-4886, E-mail: mmjones@odu.edu.

Portland State University, Graduate Studies, College of Urban and Public Affairs, Nohad A. Toulan School of Urban Studies and Planning, Program in Urban Studies, Portland, OR 97207-0751. Offers MUS, PhD. *Degree requirements:* For doctorate, comprehensive exam, thesis/dissertation, residency. *Entrance requirements:* For master's, GRE General Test, minimum GPA of 2.75, 3 letters of recommendation; for doctorate, GRE General Test, minimum GPA of 2.75. Additional exam requirements/recommendations for international students: Required—TOEFL (minimum score 550 paper-based; 213 computer-based).

Queens College of the City University of New York, Division of Graduate Studies, Social Science Division, Department of Urban Studies, Flushing, NY 11367-1597. Offers MA. Part-time and evening/weekend programs available. *Faculty:* 12 full-time (4 women). *Students:* 17 full-time (11 women), 162 part-time (118 women). 177 applicants, 56% accepted, 89 enrolled. In 2009, 81 master's awarded. *Degree requirements:* For master's, thesis. *Entrance requirements:* For master's, minimum GPA of 3.0. Additional exam requirements/recommendations for international students: Required—TOEFL. *Application deadline:* For fall admission, 4/1 for domestic students; for spring admission, 11/1 for domestic students. Applications are processed on a rolling basis. Application fee: $125. *Expenses:* Tuition, state resident: full-time $7360; part-time $310 per credit. Tuition, nonresident: part-time $575 per credit. One-time fee: $195.25 full-time; $145.25 part-time. *Financial support:* Career-related internships or fieldwork, Federal Work-Study, institutionally sponsored loans, and tuition waivers (partial) available. Support available to part-time students. Financial award application deadline: 4/1; financial award applicants required to submit FAFSA. *Faculty research:* Housing abandonment, industrial rehabilitation of Long Island City, health facilities in Queens County. *Unit head:* Dr. Leonard S. Rodberg, Chairperson, 718-997-5130. *Application contact:* Dr. William Muraskin, Graduate Adviser, 718-997-5130, E-mail: william_muraskin@qc.edu.

Rutgers, The State University of New Jersey, Newark, Graduate School, Program in Public Administration, Newark, NJ 07102. Offers health care administration (MPA); human resources administration (MPA); public administration (PhD); public management (MPA); public policy analysis (MPA); urban systems and issues (MPA). *Accreditation:* NASPAA (one or more programs are accredited). Part-time and evening/weekend programs available. *Degree requirements:* For master's, comprehensive exam, thesis or alternative; for doctorate, thesis/dissertation. *Entrance requirements:* For master's, GRE, minimum undergraduate B average; for doctorate, GRE, MPA, minimum B average. Electronic applications accepted. *Faculty research:* Government finance, municipal and state government, public productivity.

Rutgers, The State University of New Jersey, Newark, Graduate School, Program in Urban Systems, Newark, NJ 07102. Offers PhD.

Saint Louis University, Graduate School, College of Education and Public Service and Graduate School, Department of Public Policy Studies, St. Louis, MO 63103-2097. Offers geographic information systems (Certificate); organizational development (Certificate); public administration (MAPA); public policy analysis (PhD); urban affairs (MAUA); urban planning and real estate development (MUPRED). *Accreditation:* NASPAA. Part-time programs available. *Degree requirements:* For master's, comprehensive exam (for some programs), thesis (for some programs); for doctorate, comprehensive exam, thesis/dissertation, preliminary exams. *Entrance requirements:* For master's, GMAT, GRE General Test, or LSAT, letters of recommendation, resume; for doctorate, GMAT, GRE General Test, or LSAT, letters of recommendation, resumé, interview, transcripts, goal statement. Additional exam requirements/recommendations for international students: Required—TOEFL (minimum score 525 paper-based; 194 computer-based). Electronic applications accepted. *Faculty research:* Urban politics, brown fields, e-government, and administration, evaluation research, community development, electronic government and governance.

San Francisco Art Institute, Graduate Program, Department of Urban Studies, San Francisco, CA 94133. Offers MA. *Entrance requirements:* Additional exam requirements/recommendations for international students: Required—TOEFL (minimum score 580 paper-based; 237 computer-based). Electronic applications accepted.

Savannah State University, Master of Science in Urban Studies and Planning Program, Savannah, GA 31404. Offers MS. Part-time programs available. *Faculty:* 1 (woman) full-time, 5 part-time/adjunct (0 women). *Students:* 9 full-time (5 women), 5 part-time (3 women); includes 13 African Americans, 1 Hispanic American. In 2009, 7 master's awarded. *Degree requirements:* For master's, thesis optional. *Entrance requirements:* For master's, GRE. Additional exam requirements/recommendations for international students: Required—TOEFL. *Application deadline:* For fall admission, 7/1 priority date for domestic students, 5/15 for international students; for spring admission, 10/31 priority date for domestic students, 10/1 for international students. Applications are processed on a rolling basis. Application fee: $20. *Expenses:* Tuition, state resident: full-time $3662; part-time $153 per credit hour. Tuition, nonresident: full-time $14,648. Required fees: $450 per term. *Financial support:* In 2009–10, 5 students received support, including 1 fellowship (averaging $1,000 per year), 2 research assistantships (averaging $2,000 per year); career-related internships or fieldwork, Federal Work-Study, institutionally sponsored loans, and scholarships/grants also available. Support available to part-time students. Financial award applicants required to submit FAFSA. *Faculty research:* Transportation, political effectiveness, labor, sociology, criminal justice, waste management. *Unit head:* Larry Stokes, Assistant Vice President of Academic Affairs and Chair, 912-356-2204, E-mail: stokesl@savannahstate.edu. *Application contact:* Dr. Rukmana Deden, Graduate Coordinator, 912-356-2983, E-mail: rukmanad@savannahstate.edu.

Simon Fraser University, Graduate Studies, Faculty of Arts and Social Sciences, Urban Studies Program, Burnaby, BC V5A 1S6, Canada. Offers MUS, Graduate Diploma. *Degree requirements:* For master's, project.

Southern Connecticut State University, School of Graduate Studies, School of Arts and Sciences, Program in Urban Studies, New Haven, CT 06515-1355. Offers MS, MSW/MS. Part-time and evening/weekend programs available. *Students:* 8 full-time (7 women), 19 part-time (10 women); includes 14 minority (10 African Americans, 4 Hispanic Americans). 21 applicants, 57% accepted, 12 enrolled. In 2009, 9 master's awarded. *Degree requirements:* For master's, thesis or alternative. *Entrance requirements:* For master's, interview, minimum QPA of 2.5. *Application deadline:* For fall admission, 7/15 priority date for domestic students. Applications are processed on a rolling basis. Application fee: $50. Electronic applications accepted. Tuition and fees vary according to program. *Financial support:* Career-related internships or fieldwork available. Financial award application deadline: 4/15; financial award applicants required to submit FAFSA. *Unit head:* Dr. Eric West, Interim Chair of Geography, 203-392-6693, E-mail: weste1@southernct.edu. *Application contact:* Dr. Eric West, Graduate Coordinator, 203-392-6693.

Temple University, Graduate School, College of Liberal Arts, Department of Geography and Urban Studies, Philadelphia, PA 19122-6096. Offers geography (MA); urban studies (MA). *Degree requirements:* For master's, comprehensive exam, thesis or alternative. *Entrance requirements:* For master's, GRE General Test, minimum GPA of 3.0. Additional exam requirements/recommendations for international students: Required—TOEFL (minimum score 550 paper-based; 213 computer-based; 79 iBT). Electronic applications accepted. *Faculty research:* Environmental issues, urban political economy, poverty and unemployment, neighborhood development, African and Asian urbanization, housing, computer cartography.

Tufts University, Graduate School of Arts and Sciences, Department of Urban and Environmental Policy and Planning, Medford, MA 02155. Offers community development (MA); environmental policy (MA); health and human welfare (MA); housing policy (MA); international environment/development policy (MA); public policy (MPP); MA/MS; MALD/MA. *Accreditation:* ACSP (one or more programs are accredited). Part-time programs available. *Faculty:* 11 full-time, 9 part-time/adjunct. *Students:* 133 (83 women); includes 26 minority (15 African Americans, 5 Asian Americans or Pacific Islanders, 6 Hispanic Americans), 2 international. Average age 27. 200 applicants, 63% accepted, 53 enrolled. In 2009, 44 master's awarded. *Degree requirements:* For master's, thesis, internship. *Entrance requirements:* For master's, GRE General Test. Additional exam requirements/recommendations for international students: Required—TOEFL (minimum score 550 paper-based; 213 computer-based; 80 iBT). *Application deadline:* For fall admission, 1/15 for domestic students, 12/15 for international students. Applications are processed on a rolling basis. Application fee: $75. Electronic applications accepted. *Expenses:* Contact institution. *Financial support:* Teaching assistantships with partial tuition reimbursements, career-related internships or fieldwork, Federal Work-Study, scholarships/grants, tuition waivers (partial), and unspecified assistantships available. Support available to part-time students. Financial award application deadline: 1/15; financial award applicants required to submit FAFSA. *Unit head:* Julian Agyeman, Chair, 617-627-3394, Fax: 617-627-3377. *Application contact:* Ann Urosevich, Department Administrator, 617-627-3394.

Université du Québec à Montréal, Graduate Programs, Program in Urban Analysis and Management, Montréal, QC H3C 3P8, Canada. Offers MA. Part-time programs available. *Entrance requirements:* For master's, appropriate bachelor's degree or equivalent and proficiency in French.

Université du Québec à Montréal, Graduate Programs, Program in Urban Studies, Montréal, QC H3C 3P8, Canada. Offers MA, PhD. Part-time programs available. *Degree requirements:* For doctorate, thesis/dissertation. *Entrance requirements:* For doctorate, appropriate master's degree or equivalent, proficiency in French.

Université du Québec, École nationale d'administration publique, Graduate Program in Public Administration, Program in Urban Analysis and Management, Quebec, QC G1K 9E5, Canada. Offers MAGU. Part-time programs available. *Entrance requirements:* For master's, appropriate bachelor's degree, proficiency in French.

Université du Québec, Institut National de la Recherche Scientifique, Graduate Programs, Research Center—Urbanization, Culture and Society, Québec, QC G1K 9A9, Canada. Offers demography (M Sc, PhD); research and public action (M Sc); urban studies (M Sc, PhD). Programs given in French. Part-time programs available. *Faculty:* 36. *Students:* 153 full-time (95 women), 22 part-time (10 women), 26 international. Average age 33. In 2009, 5 master's, 1 doctorate awarded. *Degree requirements:* For master's, thesis optional; for doctorate, thesis/dissertation. *Entrance requirements:* For master's, appropriate bachelor's degree, proficiency in French; for doctorate, appropriate master's degree, proficiency in French. *Application deadline:* For fall admission, 3/30 for domestic and international students; for winter admission, 11/1 for domestic and international students. Application fee: $30. *Financial support:* Fellowships, research assistantships, teaching assistantships available. *Faculty research:* Regional space, urban and metropolitan space, micro-urban space. *Unit head:* Johanne Charbonneau, Director, 514-499-4001, Fax: 514-499-4065, E-mail: johanne.charbonneau@ucs.inrs.ca. *Application contact:* Yvonne Boisvert, Registrar, 418-654-3861, Fax: 418-654-3858, E-mail: registrariat@adm.inrs.ca.

University at Albany, State University of New York, College of Arts and Sciences, Department of Sociology, Albany, NY 12222-0001. Offers demography (Certificate); sociology (MA, PhD); urban policy (Certificate). Terminal master's awarded for partial completion of doctoral program. *Degree requirements:* For master's, thesis; for doctorate, thesis/dissertation, 2 specialization exams, research tool. *Entrance requirements:* For master's and doctorate, GRE General Test. Additional exam requirements/recommendations for international students: Required—TOEFL (minimum score 213 computer-based). Electronic applications accepted. *Faculty research:* Gender and equality, crime and deviance, aging, work and organizations, social demography.

The University of Akron, Graduate School, Buchtel College of Arts and Sciences, Department of Public Administration and Urban Studies, Program in Urban Studies, Akron, OH 44325. Offers urban studies (MA); urban studies and public affairs (PhD). *Students:* 4 full-time (all women), 13 part-time (10 women); includes 8 minority (all African Americans), 1 international. Average age 40. 19 applicants, 68% accepted, 10 enrolled. In 2009, 2 master's, 4 doctorates awarded. *Degree requirements:* For master's, thesis optional; for doctorate, one foreign language, comprehensive exam, thesis/dissertation. *Entrance requirements:* For master's, GRE, GMAT, LSAT, MAT (if undergraduate cumulative GPA less than 3.0), minimum GPA of 3.0, resume, letters of recommendation; for doctorate, GRE General Test, writing sample, minimum graduate GPA of 3.5, letters of recommendation, personal statement. Additional exam requirements/recommendations for international students: Required—TOEFL (minimum score 550 paper-based; 213 computer-based; 79 iBT). *Application deadline:* For fall admission, 7/1 priority date for domestic and international students; for spring admission, 11/15 priority date for domestic students, 11/14 priority date for international students. Applications are processed on a rolling basis. Application fee: $30 ($40 for international students). Electronic applications accepted. *Expenses:* Tuition, state resident: full-time $6570; part-time $365 per credit hour. Tuition, nonresident: full-time $11,250; part-time $625 per credit hour. *Unit head:* Dr. Raymond Cox, Chair, 330-972-7616, E-mail: rcox@uakron.edu. *Application contact:* Dr. Raymond Cox, Chair, 330-972-7616, E-mail: rcox@uakron.edu.

University of California, Irvine, Office of Graduate Studies, School of Social Ecology, Department of Planning, Policy and Design, Irvine, CA 92697. Offers planning, policy and design (PhD); urban and regional planning (MURP). *Accreditation:* ACSP (one or more programs are accredited). *Faculty:* 19 full-time (6 women), 10 part-time/adjunct (3 women). *Students:* 113 full-time (71 women), 1 part-time (0 women); includes 33 minority (1 African American, 1 American Indian/Alaska Native, 18 Asian Americans or Pacific Islanders, 13 Hispanic Americans), 25 international. Average age 32. 240 applicants, 60% accepted, 53 enrolled. In 2009, 42 master's, 7 doctorates awarded. *Degree requirements:* For doctorate, thesis/dissertation, research project. *Entrance requirements:* For master's and doctorate, GRE General Test, minimum GPA of 3.0. Additional exam requirements/recommendations for international students: Required—TOEFL (minimum score 550 paper-based; 213 computer-based). *Application deadline:* For fall admission, 1/15 priority date for domestic and international students. Application fee: $70 ($90 for international students). Electronic applications accepted. *Financial support:* Fellowships with tuition reimbursements, research assistantships with full tuition reimbursements, teaching assistantships with tuition reimbursements, institutionally sponsored loans, traineeships, health care benefits, and unspecified assistantships available. Financial award application deadline: 1/15; financial award applicants required to submit FAFSA. *Faculty research:* Community and social policy, economic development, land-use and growth management, transportation planning, environmental policy. Total annual research expenditures: $1.5 million. *Unit head:* Marlon G. Boarnet, Chair, 949-824-7695, E-mail: mgboarne@uci.edu. *Application contact:* Janet Gallagher, Academic Coordinator, 949-824-9849, Fax: 949-824-8566, E-mail: ppd@uci.edu.

University of Central Oklahoma, College of Graduate Studies and Research, College of Liberal Arts, Department of Political Science, Program in Urban Affairs, Edmond, OK 73034-5209. Offers MA. Part-time programs available. *Entrance requirements:* Additional exam requirements/recommendations for international students: Required—TOEFL (minimum score 550 paper-based; 213 computer-based). Electronic applications accepted. *Expenses:* Tuition, state resident: full-time $4128; part-time $172 per credit hour. Tuition, nonresident: full-time $10,373; part-time $432.20 per credit hour. Required fees: $433.20; $18.05 per credit hour.

University of Delaware, College of Human Services, Education and Public Policy, Center for Energy and Environmental Policy, Program in Urban Affairs and Public Policy, Newark, DE 19716. Offers community development and nonprofit leadership (MA); energy and environmental policy (MA); governance, planning and management (PhD); historic preservation (MA); social and urban policy (PhD); technology, environment and society (PhD). Part-time programs available. Terminal master's awarded for partial completion of doctoral program. *Degree requirements:* For master's, analytical paper or thesis; for doctorate, thesis/dissertation. *Entrance requirements:* For master's, GRE General Test, minimum GPA of 3.0; for doctorate, GRE General Test, minimum GPA of 3.5. Additional exam requirements/recommendations for international students: Required—TOEFL. Electronic applications accepted. *Faculty research:* Political economy; social policy analysis; technology and society; historic preservation; urban policy.

See Close-Up on page 1193.

University of Lethbridge, School of Graduate Studies, Lethbridge, AB T1K 3M4, Canada. Offers accounting (MScM); addictions counseling (M Sc); agricultural biotechnology (M Sc); agricultural studies (M Sc, MA); anthropology (MA); archaeology (MA); art (MA, MFA); biochemistry (M Sc); biological sciences (M Sc); biomolecular science (PhD); biosystems and biodiversity (PhD); Canadian studies (MA); chemistry (M Sc); computer science (M Sc); computer science and geographical information science (M Sc); counseling psychology (M Ed); dramatic arts (MA); earth, space, and physical science (PhD); economics (MA); educational leadership (M Ed); English (MA); environmental science (M Sc); evolution and behavior (PhD); exercise science (M Sc); finance (MScM); French (MA); French/German (MA); French/Spanish (MA); general education (M Ed); general management (MScM); geography (M Sc, MA); German (MA); health science (M Sc); health sciences (MA); history (MA); human resource management and labour relations (MScM); individualized multidisciplinary (M Sc, MA); information systems (MScM); international management (MScM); kinesiology (M Sc, MA); management (M Sc, MA); marketing (MScM); mathematics (M Sc); music (M Mus, MA); Native American studies (MA); neuroscience (M Sc, PhD); new media (MA); nursing (M Sc); philosophy (MA); physics (M Sc); policy and strategy (MScM); political science (MA); psychology (M Sc, MA); religious studies (MA); social sciences (MA); sociology (MA); theatre and dramatic arts (MFA); theoretical and computational science (PhD); urban and regional studies (MA); women's studies (MA). Part-time and evening/weekend programs available. *Degree requirements:* For doctorate, comprehensive exam, thesis/dissertation. *Entrance requirements:* For master's, GMAT (M Sc in management), bachelor's degree in related field, minimum GPA of 3.0 during previous 20 graded semester courses, 2 years teaching or related experience (M Ed); for doctorate, master's degree, minimum graduate GPA of 3.5. Additional exam requirements/recommendations for international students: Required—TOEFL. *Faculty research:* Movement and brain plasticity, gibberellin physiology, photosynthesis, carbon cycling, molecular properties of main-group ring components.

University of Louisville, Graduate School, College of Arts and Sciences, Department of Urban and Public Affairs, Louisville, KY 40208. Offers public administration (MPA), including human resources management, non-profit management, public policy and administration; urban and public affairs (PhD), including urban planning and development, urban policy and administration; urban planning (MUP), including administration of planning organizations, housing and community development, land use and environmental planning, spatial analysis. Part-time and evening/weekend programs available. *Faculty:* 22 full-time (7 women), 8 part-time/adjunct (1 woman). *Students:* 67 full-time (32 women), 35 part-time (20 women); includes 13 minority (10 African Americans, 1 Asian American or Pacific Islander, 2 Hispanic Americans), 6 international. Average age 31. 107 applicants, 57% accepted, 40 enrolled. In 2009, 25 master's, 5 doctorates awarded. Terminal master's awarded for partial completion of doctoral program. *Degree requirements:* For master's, internship; for doctorate, comprehensive exam, thesis/dissertation. *Entrance requirements:* For master's, GRE General Test, minimum GPA of 3.0; for doctorate, GRE General Test, master's degree in appropriate field. Additional exam requirements/recommendations for international students: Required—TOEFL (minimum score 550 paper-based; 213 computer-based; 79 iBT). *Application deadline:* For fall admission, 7/15 for domestic students; for spring admission, 11/15 for domestic students. Applications are processed on a rolling basis. Application fee: $50. Electronic applications accepted. *Financial support:* In 2009–10, 26 students received support; fellowships, research assistantships, health care benefits available. *Unit head:* Dr. David Simpson, Chair, 502-852-8019, Fax: 502-852-4558, E-mail: dave.simpson@louisville.edu. *Application contact:* Patty Sarley, Graduate Student Advisor, 502-852-7914, Fax: 502-852-4558, E-mail: plclea01@louisville.edu.

University of Maryland, Baltimore County, Graduate School, College of Arts, Humanities and Social Sciences, Department of Public Policy, Program in Public Policy, Baltimore, MD 21250. Offers economics (PhD); education (MPP, PhD); evaluation (MPP); health (MPP, PhD); legal (MPP, PhD); management (MPP, PhD); urban (MPP, PhD). Part-time and evening/weekend programs available. *Faculty:* 40 full-time (12 women), 2 part-time/adjunct (1 woman). *Students:* 57 full-time (34 women), 114 part-time (61 women); includes 47 minority (26 African Americans, 21 Hispanic Americans). Average age 33. 89 applicants, 47% accepted, 24 enrolled. In 2009, 12 master's, 5 doctorates awarded. Terminal master's awarded for partial completion of doctoral program. *Degree requirements:* For master's, thesis optional, public analysis paper; for doctorate, comprehensive exam, thesis/dissertation, comprehensive and field qualifying exams. *Entrance requirements:* For master's, GRE General Test, 3 academic letters of reference, transcripts, resume; for doctorate, GRE General Test, 3 academic letters of reference, transcripts, resume, research paper. Additional exam requirements/recommendations for international students: Required—TOEFL (minimum score 550 paper-based; 213 computer-based; 80 iBT). *Application deadline:* For fall admission, 1/1 priority date for domestic students, 1/1 priority date for international students; for spring admission, 11/1 priority date for domestic students, 5/1 priority date for international students. Applications are processed on a rolling basis. Application fee: $50. Electronic applications accepted. *Financial support:* In 2009–10, 32 students received support, including 1 fellowship (averaging $3,000 per year), 17 research assistantships with full tuition reimbursements available (averaging $17,400 per year); career-related internships or fieldwork, Federal Work-Study, scholarships/grants, health care benefits, and unspecified assistantships also available. Support available to part-time students. Financial award application deadline: 2/1; financial award applicants required to submit FAFSA. *Faculty research:* Health policy, education policy, urban policy, public management, evaluation and analytical method. *Unit head:* Dr. Donald Norris, Chair, 410-455-1455, E-mail: norris@umbc.edu. *Application contact:* Sally F. Helms, Administrator of Academic Affairs, 410-455-3202, Fax: 410-455-1172, E-mail: gradposi@umbc.edu.

University of New Orleans, Graduate School, College of Liberal Arts, School of Urban Planning and Regional Studies, Program in Urban Studies, New Orleans, LA 70148. Offers MS, PhD. *Degree requirements:* For master's, thesis; for doctorate, thesis/dissertation. *Entrance requirements:* For master's, GRE General Test. Additional exam requirements/recommendations for international students: Required—TOEFL (minimum score 550 paper-based; 213 computer-based; 79 iBT). Electronic applications accepted. *Faculty research:* Urban economic development, environmental planning and analysis, social and cultural change.

University of Oklahoma—Tulsa, Urban Design Studio, Tulsa, OK 74135-2512. Offers architectural urban studies (MS); urban design (M Arch).

University of Wisconsin–Milwaukee, Graduate School, College of Letters and Sciences, Department of History, Milwaukee, WI 53201-0413. Offers global history (PhD); history (MA); modern studies (PhD); urban history (PhD); MLIS/MA. Part-time programs available. *Faculty:* 33 full-time (16 women). *Students:* 44 full-time (22 women), 41 part-time (19 women); includes 9 minority (2 African Americans, 2 American Indian/Alaska Native, 1 Asian American or Pacific Islander, 4 Hispanic Americans), 1 international. Average age 31. 74 applicants, 58% accepted, 11 enrolled. In 2009, 28 master's, 1 doctorate awarded. *Degree requirements:* For master's, comprehensive exam, thesis or alternative; for doctorate, thesis/dissertation. *Entrance requirements:* For master's and doctorate, GRE General Test. Additional exam requirements/recommendations for international students: Required—TOEFL (minimum score 550 paper-based; 79 iBT), IELTS (minimum score 6.5). *Application deadline:* For fall admission, 1/1 priority date for domestic students; for spring admission, 9/1 for domestic students. Applications are processed on a rolling basis. Application fee: $45 ($75 for international students). *Expenses:* Tuition, state resident: full-time $8800. Tuition, nonresident: full-time $20,760. Tuition and fees vary according to program and reciprocity agreements. *Financial support:* In 2009–10, 23 teaching assistantships were awarded; career-related internships or fieldwork and unspecified assistantships also available. Support available to part-time students. Financial award application deadline: 4/15. Total annual research expenditures: $7,605. *Unit head:* Joe Austin, Representative, 414-229-4361, Fax: 414-229-2435, E-mail: jaustin@uwm.edu. *Application contact:* General Information Contact, 414-229-4982, Fax: 414-229-6967, E-mail: gradschool@uwm.edu.

University of Wisconsin–Milwaukee, Graduate School, College of Letters and Sciences, Interdepartmental Program in Urban Studies, Milwaukee, WI 53201-0413. Offers MS, PhD, MLIS/MS. *Faculty:* 32 full-time (13 women). *Students:* 21 full-time (11 women), 32 part-time

Urban Studies

University of Wisconsin–Milwaukee (continued)
(19 women); includes 12 minority (7 African Americans, 1 American Indian/Alaska Native, 1 Asian American or Pacific Islander, 3 Hispanic Americans), 3 international. Average age 39. 27 applicants, 56% accepted, 2 enrolled. In 2009, 9 master's, 3 doctorates awarded. *Degree requirements:* For master's, thesis or alternative; for doctorate, thesis/dissertation. *Entrance requirements:* For doctorate, GRE General Test. Additional exam requirements/recommendations for international students: Required—TOEFL (minimum score 550 paper-based; 79 iBT), IELTS (minimum score 6.5). *Application deadline:* For fall admission, 1/1 priority date for domestic students; for spring admission, 9/1 for domestic students. Applications are processed on a rolling basis. Application fee: $45 ($75 for international students). *Expenses:* Tuition, state resident: full-time $8800. Tuition, nonresident: full-time $20,760. Tuition and fees vary according to program and reciprocity agreements. *Financial support:* In 2009–10, 4 teaching assistantships were awarded; career-related internships or fieldwork and unspecified assistantships also available. Support available to part-time students. Financial award application deadline: 4/15. *Unit head:* Amanda Seligman, Representative, 414-229-4751, Fax: 414-229-4266, E-mail: seligman@uwm.edu. *Application contact:* General Information Contact, 414-229-4982, Fax: 414-229-6967, E-mail: gradschool@uwm.edu.

Wright State University, School of Graduate Studies, College of Liberal Arts, Department of Urban Affairs and Geography, Dayton, OH 45435. Offers public administration (MPA). *Accreditation:* NASPAA. *Degree requirements:* For master's, thesis optional. *Entrance requirements:* For master's, interview, minimum GPA of 2.7. Additional exam requirements/recommendations for international students: Required—TOEFL. *Faculty research:* Strategic planning, economic development, housing and public management.

Cornell University
Cornell Institute for Public Affairs

CORNELL UNIVERSITY

Cornell Institute for Public Affairs

Program of Study

The Cornell Institute for Public Affairs (CIPA) offers a two-year program of graduate professional studies leading to a Master of Public Administration (M.P.A.) degree. The interdisciplinary nature of this M.P.A. program is one of its distinguishing features. CIPA students, called "fellows," have the flexibility to design individualized plans of study using faculty resources from across the University.

The program consists of sixteen courses; CIPA fellows typically take four courses per semester for four semesters. Although the M.P.A. program offers a basic structure for study, each CIPA fellow works closely with a faculty adviser to design an individualized program based on his or her specific area of interest. Courses may be taken through the program in any department or college in the university.

To develop a foundation of basic concepts and capabilities for the study of public policy, CIPA fellows take three courses in each of the following three subject areas: administration, politics, and public policy; economics and public finance; and quantitative analysis.

Concentration course work enables students to focus on a specific area of public policy study. Fellows choose their course of study—domestic or international—from a broad range of options: environmental policy; finance and fiscal policy; government, politics, and policy studies; human rights and social justice; international development studies; public and nonprofit management; science and technology policy; and social policy.

Experiential learning is an integral component of CIPA's educational strategy, and a practical experience such as an internship is a requirement for obtaining the M.P.A. degree. Internships allow students to apply training in a practical environment and establish contacts for permanent employment. CIPA fellows also have the opportunity to gain professional experience off-campus, while taking a semester of courses for credit through Cornell in Rome, the Cornell-Nepal Study Program, and the CIPA Washington, D.C. externship semester. Fellows may also fulfill the practical experience requirement by participating in the Public Service Exchange, a unique service learning partnership with local nonprofit and government agencies.

As a culmination of studies, all fellows are required to develop and complete a professional writing project, which typically grows out of their area of concentration. There are three options for completing this writing requirement: a capstone project, a professional report, or a master's thesis. For the capstone project, second-year fellows enroll in a semester-long capstone workshop course and complete a consulting project for a real-world client, that culminates with a written proposal. The second option—the professional report—is similar to the capstone, but is done independently. A fellow undertakes an experiential project on behalf of a "client," such as a public, private, or nonprofit organization, and works on solving a problem in policy analysis or program evaluation. The third professional writing option is the formal thesis, which is a substantial, independent research paper offering an original contribution to the field of public affairs. It requires a fellow to pose a policy problem, review and summarize previous efforts to address this problem, and propose an alternate solution.

CIPA fellows may elect to combine their M.P.A. study program with complementary degree study, such as a J.D. from Cornell Law School, an M.B.A. from the Johnson School of Management, an M.M.H. from the Hotel School, or an M.R.P. in the field of city and regional planning.

Research Facilities

Cornell is a major research university with significant derivative policy interests in natural and physical sciences, nutrition, genetics, engineering, computer and social sciences, health, education, consumer policy, art, architecture, and the humanities. Separate interdisciplinary work centers on the environment, international studies and development, and international food and agriculture. Programs on infrastructure, education, family development, and health administration provide valuable resources for fellows.

The University has an excellent library system, including nineteen libraries with more than 5 million volumes, 600,000 periodical titles, and extensive microfilm and other materials.

Financial Aid

The Cornell Institute for Public Affairs provides some funding to more than 80 percent of its students. The Institute itself, however, is unable to provide anyone with full support. CIPA fellows often win support from Fulbright, Truman, and World Bank fellowships. Applicants are encouraged to explore all available sources of external funding, including grants that may be provided by current employers. Because funding decisions are made on a first-come, first-served basis, those seeking funding should submit their application by the end of January.

Cost of Study

The estimated total cost of tuition and fees for full-time fellows for the 2010–11 academic year is $39,450. The estimated cost of books and materials is approximately $1500.

Living and Housing Costs

Living expenses for single students range from $1700 to $1800 per month, including room, meals, and personal expenses but excluding travel. There are many housing options for CIPA fellows. Some University housing is available exclusively to students in graduate and professional programs. Non-University housing includes apartment complexes, multiple-unit houses, single-unit houses, individual rooms, and cooperative living units. A listing of off-campus housing options is available from Cornell's Housing Office.

Student Group

Enrollment in the CIPA two-year M.P.A. program ranges between 200 and 240 full-time students. In general, the program has similar numbers of men and women, and about 35 to 40 percent of the fellows are international. Of the total CIPA population, about half study international relations, policy, or development, while the remainder pursue a wide variety of domestic policy interests, from social policy to national security policy to environmental policy.

Student Outcomes

CIPA employs a full-time professional development specialist who provides career advisement and assistance in locating employment and internships. Professional development at CIPA also includes the cultivation of an extensive network of alumni in the public, private, nonprofit, and academic sectors. Historically, more than 95 percent of CIPA graduates find employment within six months of graduation. Recent organizations that have employed CIPA alumni include the World Bank, the United Nations (UN), the United States Agency for International Development (USAID), the Environmental Protection Agency (EPA), Deloitte and Touche, Goldman Sachs, and Booz Allen Hamilton, Inc. International fellows often return to their countries of origin to work in high-level leadership posts in government and industry. Some CIPA alumni choose to continue their graduate studies in J.D. or Ph.D. programs.

Location

Cornell is located in Tompkins County in the heart of New York's Finger Lakes region, with pristine lakes, waterfalls, and multiple state parks. The area has more than beauty to recommend it. People who like to be outdoors thrive at Cornell. Nearby are opportunities for skiing, swimming, hiking, sailing, and mountain biking. Ithaca may be small and rural, but it also has an urban sophistication and an intellectual dynamism.

The University and The Institute

The Cornell Institute for Public Affairs is an autonomous, University-wide program designed to build on Cornell's legendary commitment to an education "which shall combine the practical with the liberal education." Cornell has offered the M.P.A. degree since 1946, originally through the Johnson Graduate School of Management, and since 1989 through the broader Cornell Institute for Public Affairs. CIPA's current alumni network includes graduates of both programs.

Applying

Admission to CIPA is selective. A committee of faculty members evaluates individual applications based on the overall academic record; GRE scores; English language skills (applicants for whom English is a second language will need to obtain the following minimum scores on the Internet-based test version of the TOEFL: writing 20, listening 15, reading 20, and speaking 22); potential for public-policy leadership as evidenced by professional work and community, extracurricular, or other relevant experience (students should include a copy of their most recent resume); and letters of recommendation. Applicants should also include an extensive written statement of purpose in which they address why they are applying to the program, their personal and/or professional experience that led to their interest in Cornell's M.P.A. program, their future goals (how they intend to put their M.P.A. degree to use), and examples of volunteer work, positions of responsibility, and any other life experiences contributing to their interest in public policy. The committee looks for sound analytic preparation and instruction or prior professional work experience in fields relevant to public affairs, such as economics, politics, public administration, planning, sociology, and law. CIPA has a rolling admissions policy; however, decisions concerning CIPA funding are made on a first-come, first-served basis, so students who wish to be considered should complete their applications by January 30.

Correspondence and Information

To request additional information:
Cornell Institute for Public Affairs
294 Caldwell Hall
Cornell University
Ithaca, New York 14853-2602

Phone: 607-255-8018
Fax: 607-255-5240
E-mail: cipa@cornell.edu
Web site: http://www.cipa.cornell.edu

Cornell University

THE FACULTY AND THEIR RESEARCH

The program offers great depth and flexibility. It is not confined to a single school or college but spans the entire University. More than 100 faculty members in the field of public affairs from a diverse cross section of schools, departments, and programs, welcome CIPA fellows into their courses and serve on thesis committees. Within this group, 14 members serve as Core Faculty, providing instruction in core foundation course work.

The Core Faculty

Norman Uphoff, CIPA Interim Director and Professor in the Department of Government.
Nancy Brooks, CIPA Director of Graduate Studies and Visiting Associate Professor in the Department of City and Regional Planning.
Richard Booth, Professor in the Department of City and Regional Planning.
Nancy Chau, Associate Professor in the Department of Applied Economics and Management.
Ralph D. Christy, Director of the Cornell International Institute for Food, Agriculture, and Development, and Professor of Emerging Markets.
Kieran Donaghy, Professor and Chair for the Department of City and Regional Planning.
Gary Fields, John P. Windmuller Chair in International and Comparative Labor in the School of Industrial and Labor Relations.
Robert Harris Jr., Director of the Africana Studies and Research Center and Professor of African-American History.
Neema Kudva, Assistant Professor in the Department of City and Regional Planning.
Daniel (Pete) Loucks, Professor in the Department of Civil and Environmental Engineering.
Theodore J. Lowi, John L. Senior Professor of American Institutions in the Department of Government.
Kathryn S. March, Professor in the Departments of Anthropology and Feminist, Gender, and Sexuality Studies.
Per Pinstrup-Andersen, J. Thomas Clark Professor of Entrepreneurship and H. E. Babcock Professor of Food, Nutrition, and Public Policy.
Jerome M. Ziegler, Professor Emeritus in the Department of Policy Analysis and Management.

Cornell University ILR School

CORNELL UNIVERSITY

ILR School

Programs of Study

Cornell University and the ILR School are world-renowned global institutions that have earned a reputation for excellence. The School's graduate degree programs provide a broad-based foundation with a specific, intense focus on the interaction between people and organizations in the workplace. ILR's unique depth and breadth sets it apart from other programs. No other educational institution has graduate programs in workplace studies that are as comprehensive, or the number of faculty teaching and doing research on workplace issues in one school. The curriculum is thorough, rigorous, and comprehensive, combining experience and theory in innovative ways. ILR studies many areas that shape the working world and contribute to an organization's success in a global economy. These include human resource management; labor-management relations; labor economics; organizational behavior; international and comparative labor; labor relations, labor law, and history; conflict resolution; management development; diversity management; employment and disability; and social statistics. ILR was the first school to develop a graduate degree program in the study of employment and workplace issues, and its advanced degrees are considered among the best in the world.

ILR offers five top-ranked and highly regarded graduate degree programs. The **Master of Industrial and Labor Relations (M.I.L.R.)** is a two-year, professional, career-focused degree for those interested in putting their education into practice. The M.I.L.R. is specifically for students preparing to enter the workforce or professionals who wish to enhance their education and skills. The **Master of Industrial and Labor Relations/Master of Business Administration (M.I.L.R./M.B.A.)** is a dual-degree program offered jointly by the ILR School and the Johnson School at Cornell, giving graduates a powerful double credential highly valued by employers. The **Master of Industrial and Labor Relations/Master in Management** is a global three-year dual degree that allows students the opportunity for an international experience that will advance their career goals and increase their marketability worldwide with degrees from ILR and ESCP Europe, which includes five fully integrated campuses in Paris, London, Madrid, Berlin, and Torino. The **Master of Science and the Doctor of Philosophy (M.S./Ph.D.)** are excellent for students considering academic or research careers. The ILR graduate field is multidisciplinary, focusing broadly on work and employment relationships from a variety of social science perspectives, including political science, history, sociology, psychology, and economics. Students applying to the M.S./Ph.D. program apply to one of four ILR departments: organizational behavior; human resource studies; labor relations, law, and history; or international and comparative labor. The **Master of Professional Studies in Industrial and Labor Relations (M.P.S.)** is designed for individuals who are already practitioners and want to expand or advance into a specific competency or upgrade their skills and understanding.

Candidates for the M.I.L.R. degree come from a variety of backgrounds and are interested in preparing for positions in human resource management, labor relations (including collective bargaining), and public policy. The M.I.L.R. reflects the need of future practitioners to become broadly familiar with all major aspects of the field and to become particularly competent in one of five areas: human resources and organizations, collective representation, dispute resolution, international and comparative labor, or labor-market policy. Students complete a minimum of 48 credits in courses and seminars, including required courses in collective bargaining, labor economics, labor and employment law, human resource management, organizational behavior, and statistics. Students have a great deal of flexibility in choosing courses in addition to their required core courses. Courses offered by the ILR School and the thirteen other colleges at Cornell provide opportunity for cross-disciplinary work. Some candidates with a law (J.D.) or M.B.A. degree may be able to obtain an M.I.L.R. degree in two semesters. The M.P.S. degree is limited to individuals with professionally related work experience who wish to update their knowledge of current practices. Applicants for this degree are often sponsored by their governments or organizations. Degree requirements include course work and an M.P.S. project. Students may choose to study part-time in New York City in the M.P.S. New York program or full-time in residence on the Ithaca campus. M.S. and Ph.D. candidates select major and minor subjects from the following areas: collective bargaining, labor law, and labor history; organizational behavior; human resource studies; and international and comparative labor. Minor subjects can also include social statistics and labor economics. Minor subjects in fields outside ILR are encouraged. Each candidate's program is supervised by a special committee of faculty members chosen by the candidate. The average M.S. program requires two years; the doctoral program typically takes an additional three years.

Research Facilities

The ILR School's Catherwood Library, with more than 232,000 volumes, is regarded as the world's most comprehensive source of information on work, employment, and labor issues. Catherwood's Kheel Center for Labor-Management Documentation and Archives ranks as one of three major centers of its type in the country. Catherwood is one of seventeen libraries constituting the Cornell University Library, ranked as one of the ten largest academic research libraries in the United States, with more than 7 million printed volumes, 65,000 journal and newspaper subscriptions, and more than 40,000 networked electronic databases available to users. Networked computer facilities in Catherwood and in other campus libraries are provided for graduate students, and a rapidly expanding array of electronic and full-text resources is available for use outside of the library. Catherwood's programs and services are aimed at providing easy access to its outstanding collections. Library staff members offer seminars and individualized training to acquaint graduate students with the research potential of Catherwood's print and electronic holdings.

Financial Aid

A small number of fellowships may be awarded on a competitive basis by Cornell University and the ILR School for students interested in the M.I.L.R., M.P.S., or dual-degree programs. In addition, the School awards a limited number of merit-based teaching or research assistantships to qualified students in their second year of study in the M.I.L.R. degree program. Tuition scholarships are also granted to graduate assistants. Assistantships require 15–20 hours of work each week in the School's instructional, research, or extension programs. Funding is guaranteed for students accepted in the M.S./Ph.D. programs.

Cost of Study

Tuition is $25,815 for the 2010–11 academic year for both state residents and out-of-state students in the M.I.L.R. and M.P.S. degree programs. Tuition for the M.S./Ph.D. programs for 2010–11 is $20,800. Books cost between $900 and $1200 per year; there is also a thesis fee.

Living and Housing Costs

Budgets for single students to live at a modest comfort level average $1200 per month. Married students should expect greater expenses. The largest variable is rent; both University and private housing are available to graduate students.

Student Group

The population of graduate students at Cornell is more than 6,000, representing all regions of the United States and many other countries. Candidates for the M.I.L.R. degree, approximately half of the 180 graduate students in ILR, have a wide variety of academic and employment backgrounds. M.I.L.R. candidates generally choose professional careers, while Ph.D. candidates usually aim for academic appointments.

Student Outcomes

Most students have job offers before graduation, even in tough economies. ILR graduates work in every region of the United States and around the world in business, manufacturing, consulting, technology, not-for-profit, unions, government, and other sectors. The ILR Office of Career Services provides a wide variety of services, including individual advising, workshops, resume reviews, career fairs, networking assistance, job listings, and practice interviews to help students explore their career options and develop effective job-search strategies. The office manages an on-campus recruitment program, with representatives of numerous corporations, labor unions, government agencies, and labor law firms interviewing students for positions in human resources and labor relations. The office also cultivates contacts with alumni and others working in the field. Further career information is available from the Office of Career Services, 201 Ives Hall, Cornell University (phone: 607-255-7816; Web site: http://www.ilr.cornell.edu/careerservices/). A few of the leading employers of M.I.L.R. degree recipients are the AFL-CIO, American Express Company, Citigroup, Dell, General Electric, General Mills, Honeywell, IBM, Microsoft, the National Labor Relations Board (NLRB), and Shell Oil Company. The mean salary for a recent M.I.L.R. graduating class was approximately $78,262. The mean salary for recent M.I.L.R. graduates choosing the corporate sector was $80,880, with a mean signing bonus of $10,611. Those recently completing doctoral degree programs found employment at such places as Cornell, Washington University, the London School of Business, the University of Delaware, Cardiff University in Wales, the University of Michigan, Harvard Business School, and the U.S. Bureau of Labor Statistics.

Location

Ithaca is a university town of nearly 40,000, set in the center of the beautiful Finger Lakes region of upstate New York. The area is rich in outdoor recreational resources for swimming, skiing, and boating. Cornell and neighboring Ithaca College as well as community groups in the creative and performing arts contribute to a lively and diverse cultural life that includes plays, concerts, opera, ballet, and lectures.

The University

The Cornell tradition of graduate education recognizes that each student has different needs, strengths, and goals, and the University makes every effort to accommodate students' specific requirements and incomes. Every member of the social science faculties at Cornell is a potential resource to each ILR graduate student, whatever the field of study, providing intellectual resources that are extensive and cross college boundaries. Distinguished scholars in economics, sociology, and psychology can be found in ILR as well as in appropriate fields in the College of Arts and Sciences, the College of Human Ecology, and the Johnson School of Management; in other professional fields, such as developmental sociology, child development and family relations, agricultural economics, and business law; and in research institutes such as the Southeast Asia and Latin American Centers.

Applying

While a strong background in the social sciences is both appropriate and helpful for advanced work at ILR, those with different backgrounds (engineering, law, business) regularly enroll. The deadline for fall admission is January 1; for spring admission, the deadline is October 15. Ph.D. candidates generally undertake master's thesis research before entering the Ph.D. program. Exceptionally well-qualified applicants may be admitted directly to the doctoral program with only a bachelor's degree. All applicants must take the General Test of the Graduate Record Examinations (GRE) or the Graduate Management Admission Test (GMAT). International students are also required to take the Test of English as a Foreign Language (TOEFL).

Correspondence and Information

ILR Graduate Programs Office
ILR School
218 Ives Hall
Cornell University
Ithaca, New York 14853-3901

Phone: 607-255-1522
E-mail: ilrgradapplicant@cornell.edu
Web site: http://www.ilr.cornell.edu/graddegreeprograms

Cornell University

THE FACULTY

The graduate faculty members at Cornell's ILR School represent a wide spectrum of the social and behavioral sciences—cultural anthropology, economics, history, law, political science, psychology, social psychology, sociology, and statistics—offering courses, advising, consulting, directing research activities, and sharing research opportunities. In addition, students may take courses from and select as advisers other Cornell faculty members in the social sciences, the humanities, mathematics, and engineering.

Department of Labor Relations, Law, and History

Lee H. Adler, Senior Extension Associate; J.D., Golden Gate. Law.
Kate Brofenbrenner, Senior Lecturer and Director of Labor Education Research; Ph.D., Cornell. Labor and industrial relations.
Alex Colvin, Associate Professor; Ph.D., Cornell.
Lance Compa, Senior Lecturer; J.D., Yale. Law.
Maria L. Cook, Associate Professor; Ph.D., Berkeley. Political science.
Jefferson Cowie, Associate Professor; Ph.D., North Carolina at Chapel Hill. History.
Ileen A. DeVault, Professor; Ph.D., Yale. History.
Rebecca Givan, Assistant Professor; Ph.D., Northwestern. Political science.
Michael E. Gold, Associate Professor; J.D., Stanford. Law.
Kate Griffith, Assistant Professor; J.D., NYU. Law.
James A. Gross, Professor; Ph.D., Wisconsin. Labor economics and industrial relations.
Richard W. Hurd, Professor; Ph.D., Vanderbilt. Economics.
Lawrence Kahn, Professor; Ph.D., Berkeley. Economics.
Harry C. Katz, Jack Sheinkman Professor in Collective Bargaining and Dean of the ILR School; Ph.D., Berkeley. Economics.
Sarosh C. Kuruvilla, Professor; Ph.D., Iowa. Business administration.
Risa L. Lieberwitz, Professor; J.D., Florida. Law.
David B. Lipsky, Professor; Ph.D., MIT. Economics.
Nicholas Salvatore, Maurice and Hinda Neufeld Founders Professorship in Industrial and Labor Relations; Ph.D., Berkeley. History.
Ronald L. Seeber, Professor; Ph.D., Illinois. Labor and industrial relations.
Lowell Turner, Professor; Ph.D., Berkeley. Political science.

Department of Human Resource Studies

Rosemary Batt, Professor and Alice Cook Professor of Women and Work; Ph.D., MIT. Human resources.
Bradford Bell, Associate Professor; Ph.D., Michigan State. Organizational psychology.
John H. Bishop, Associate Professor; Ph.D., Michigan. Economics.
Diane Burton, Associate Professor, Ph.D., Stanford. Sociology.
Christopher Collins, Associate Professor; Ph.D., Maryland. Organizational behavior.
Lisa Dragoni, Assistant Professor; Ph.D., Maryland. Organizational behavior and human resource management.
Lee D. Dyer, Professor; Ph.D., Wisconsin. Personnel.
Kevin F. Hallock, Professor; Ph.D., Princeton. Economics.
John Hausknecht, Assistant Professor; Ph.D., Penn State. Industrial and organizational psychology.
Beth Livingston, Assistant Professor, Ph.D., Florida. Organizational behavior/management.
Lisa Hisae Nishii, Assistant Professor; Ph.D., Maryland. Organizational psychology.
Patrick M. Wright, Professor; Ph.D., Michigan State. Business administration.

Department of International and Comparative Labor Relations

Rosemary Batt, Professor and Alice Cook Professor of Women and Work; Ph.D., MIT. Human resources.
John H. Bishop, Associate Professor; Ph.D., Michigan. Economics.
George Boyer, Professor; Ph.D., Wisconsin. Economics.
Alex Colvin, Associate Professor; Ph.D., Cornell. Collective bargaining and conflict resolution.
Lance Compa, Senior Lecturer; J.D., Yale. Law.
Maria L. Cook, Associate Professor; Ph.D., Berkeley. Political science.
Gary S. Fields, Professor; Ph.D., Michigan. Economics.
James A. Gross, Professor; Ph.D., Wisconsin. Labor economics and industrial relations.
Sarosh C. Kuruvilla, Professor; Ph.D., Iowa. Industrial relations.
Lisa Hisae Nishii, Assistant Professor; Ph.D., Maryland. Organizational psychology.
Lowell Turner, Professor; Ph.D., Berkeley. Political science.

Department of Labor Economics

John M. Abowd, Edmund Ezra Day Professor of Industrial and Labor Relations; Ph.D., Chicago. Economics.
Francine D. Blau, Frances Perkins Professor of Industrial and Labor Relations; Ph.D., Harvard. Economics.
George R. Boyer, Professor; Ph.D., Wisconsin. Economics.
Ronald Ehrenberg, Irving M. Ives Professor of Industrial and Labor Relations; Ph.D., Northwestern. Economics.
Gary S. Fields, Professor; Ph.D., Michigan. Economics.
Matthew Freedman, Assistant Professor, Ph.D., Maryland, College Park. Economics.
Kevin F. Hallock, Professor; Ph.D., Princeton. Economics.
Robert M. Hutchens, Professor; Ph.D., Wisconsin. Economics.
Kirabo Jackson, Assistant Professor; Ph.D., Harvard, Economics.
George H. Jakubson, Associate Professor; Ph.D., Wisconsin. Economics.
Lawrence M. Kahn, Professor; Ph.D., Berkeley. Economics.
Robert S. Smith, Professor; Ph.D., Stanford. Economics.

Department of Organizational Behavior

Samuel B. Bacharach, Jean McKelvey-Alice Grant Professor of Labor Management Relations; Ph.D., Wisconsin. Sociology.
Marya Besharov, Assistant Professor; Ph.D., Harvard, Organizational behavior.
Jack Goncalo, Assistant Professor; Ph.D., Berkeley. Business administration.
Tove H. Hammer, Professor; Ph.D., Maryland. Industrial organizational psychology.
Edward J. Lawler, Martin P. Catherwood Professor of Industrial and Labor Relations; Ph.D., Wisconsin. Sociology.
Brian Rubineau, Assistant Professor; Ph.D., MIT. Organization studies and economic sociology.
William J. Sonnenstuhl, Associate Professor; Ph.D., NYU. Sociology.
Pamela S. Tolbert, Professor; Ph.D., UCLA. Sociology.
Michele Williams, Assistant Professor; Ph.D., Michigan. Organizational behavior.

Department of Social Statistics

John A. Bunge, Associate Professor; Ph.D., Ohio. Statistics.
Thomas J. DiCiccio, Associate Professor; Ph.D., Waterloo. Statistics.
Paul F. Velleman, Associate Professor; Ph.D., Princeton. Statistics.
Martin T. Wells, Associate Professor; Ph.D., Berkeley. Mathematics.

ILR School at Cornell's Ives Hall.

GEORGE MASON UNIVERSITY

School of Public Policy

Programs of Study

The School of Public Policy (SPP) at George Mason University seeks to prepare its graduates for positions of responsibility in academic institutions, industry, government, and profit and not-for-profit institutions dedicated to the improvement of both the substance and the processes of public policymaking in the United States and abroad. SPP offers the following degree programs: Doctor of Philosophy (Ph.D.) in public policy; Master of Public Policy (M.P.P.); Master of Arts (M.A.) in international commerce and policy; Master of Arts (M.A.) in transportation policy, operations, and logistics; Master of Science (M.S.) in organization development and knowledge management; and Master of Science in new professional studies: peace operations. In conjunction with the master's programs, SPP offers certificate programs in specialized areas of study including culture and values in social policy, global trade management, and national security and public policy.

The School's programs, led by a distinguished faculty, focus on the interplay of culture, organizations, and technology in a quest to find alternative approaches to public policy decisions and policymaking. Teaching and research is focused on, but not limited to, six themes: Governance; International Commerce and Policy; Entrepreneurship; Regional and Economic Development; Science and Technology Policy; and Culture and Values.

The Ph.D. in Public Policy program is distinctive in its emphasis on the combined influence of technology, culture, and institutions on public policy. To investigate the policy issues associated with substantive policy areas, students develop an in-depth understanding of American institutions, values, and culture; competence in research methods and advanced analytical methodologies; and a comparative, international perspective. The M.P.P. provides a degree for aspiring or experienced professionals who seek career advancement through cutting-edge education and training in policy analysis and development in increasingly technical and global environments. Professional certificates are also offered with this program. The M.A. in International Commerce and Policy program is an interdisciplinary course of study that prepares students for careers in the new global economy. Unlike traditional M.B.A. and international affairs programs, the degree is focused on international economic issues such as global trade and investment. Professional certificates are also offered with this program. The M.A. in Transportation Policy, Operations, and Logistics program is designed for students and practicing professionals engaged in planning, regulating, managing, and operating transportation facilities and services. The M.S. in Organization Development and Knowledge Management program is run in an executive format and is designed for professionals with several years of work experience. It provides students with the conceptual tools and practical guidance to foster organizational change. The Peace Operations program offers candidates a focused degree in various aspects of the planning, regulation, management, and conduct of peace operations.

Research Facilities

George Mason University (GMU) Libraries comprise the Fenwick and Johnson Center Libraries on the Fairfax campus and the Arlington and Prince William campus libraries. Fenwick is the main research library and offers access to a large number of electronic resources in addition to more than 600,000 volumes. GMU provides students with e-mail and Internet access and is a member of the Washington Regional Library Consortium, giving students access to 4 million volumes. In addition to research facilities on campus, GMU is a short distance from major research facilities in the Washington, D.C., area, including the Library of Congress, the National Archives, and numerous governmental agencies. Students may visit the GMU Libraries' Web site for more information (http://library.gmu.edu).

SPP's research centers include the Center for Regional Analysis; the International Center for Applied Studies in Information Technology; the Center for Science and Technology Policy; the Center for Transportation Policy, Operations, and Logistics; the Center for the Study of International Medical Policies and Practices; the State Economic Development Center; the Center for Entrepreneurship and Public Policy; the Center for Global Policy; the Center for Aerospace Policy Research; the Terrorism, Transnational Crime, and Corruption Center (TraCCC); the Transportation and Economic Development Research Center; and the Mason Enterprise Center.

Financial Aid

Full-time Ph.D. candidates are eligible for graduate research assistantships. These assistantships offer a stipend of $19,000 and also include tuition waivers. Financial assistance is granted to master's candidates on a limited basis.

Cost of Study

For the 2009–10 academic year, tuition and fees were $573 per credit hour for in-state students and $1062 for out-of-state students.

Living and Housing Costs

The cost of living in the northern Virginia/Washington, D.C., area is comparable to that in most major metropolitan centers. Limited on-campus graduate student housing is available on the Fairfax campus; no on-campus housing is available on the Arlington campus. Most graduate students choose to live off campus.

Student Group

In fall 2009, SPP enrolled 969 students in its various graduate programs. Fifty-three percent were women, 12 percent were members of minority groups, and 11 percent were international students. Fifteen percent were enrolled in the Ph.D. program, and 85 percent were enrolled in the various master's programs. Sixty-eight percent enrolled part-time, while 32 percent enrolled full-time.

Student Outcomes

Upon completion of degree requirements, graduates find employment in academic institutions, federal and state agencies and departments, international businesses and banks, law firms, consulting firms, think tanks, and not-for-profit organizations. Many international students return home to work in the public and private sectors. SPP provides career advisement, internship, and placement support for all students.

Location

Located in Northern Virginia, George Mason is only 15 miles from all the resources of the National Capital Region and the Washington metropolitan area. Washington's libraries, galleries, and museums; Virginia's historic sites; and Fairfax County's high-technology firms are easily accessible. George Mason's 5.2-acre Arlington Campus, which is home to most SPP master's programs, is just minutes to Washington, D.C., by Metrorail.

Applying

Application deadlines for the master's and certificate programs are June 1 for fall and December 1 for spring. International applicant deadlines are one month prior to these dates. For Ph.D. applicants, fall application deadlines are February 1 for international students and March 1 for domestic students. For the spring term, Ph.D. application deadlines are October 1 for international applicants and November 1 for domestic applicants. Students should note that funding is only awarded to full-time Ph.D. students beginning their study in the fall term. All applicants must submit a graduate application and fee, all official university transcripts, a written goals statement, a professional resume, two letters of recommendation, and a writing sample (Ph.D. applicants only). GRE or GMAT scores are required for all Ph.D. candidates and for master's degree applicants who are seeking merit-based funding consideration. International applicants must also submit a TOEFL score. Students should visit http://policy.gmu.edu/admissions for more specific information on application requirements for both the master's and Ph.D. degree programs.

Correspondence and Information

Graduate Admissions
School of Public Policy
George Mason University
3401 Fairfax Drive, MS 3B1
Arlington, Virginia 22201

Phone: 703-993-8099
Fax: 703-993-4876
E-mail: spp@gmu.edu
Web site: http://policy.gmu.edu

George Mason University

CORE FACULTY

Administrative Faculty

Kingsley E. Haynes, University Professor and Dean; Ph.D., Johns Hopkins, 1971.
James H. Finkelstein, Professor and Vice Dean for Administration; Ph.D., Ohio State, 1980.
Jonathan L. Gifford, Professor, Associate Dean for Research, and Program Director for the Transportation, Operations, and Logistics M.A. program; Ph.D., Berkeley, 1983.
Matthys van Schaik, Associate Dean for Academic Affairs; Ph.D., South Carolina, 1995.

The Faculty and Their Research

Zoltan J. Acs, University Professor; Ph.D., The New School, 1980. Mathematical economics, microeconomics, macroeconomics, managerial economics and public policy, the global economic environment, technology management, entrepreneurship and innovation, new venture creation, global and domestic business environment, global and domestic business environment–Web, basic economics–Web.
Mark S. Addleson, Associate Professor; Ph.D., Witwatersrand, 1992. Knowledge management, organizational change, learning organizations, methodology of social inquiry, Austrian economics.
Katrin B. Anacker, Assistant Professor; Ph.D., Ohio State, 2006. City and regional planning, housing, housing policy, urban policy, race and public policy, real estate markets, statistical methods, qualitative methods, research writing.
David J. Armor, Professor of Public Policy; Ph.D., Harvard, 1966. Education policy, military manpower, family policy, welfare policy, civil rights/race relations policy (desegregation, affirmative action), methodology (statistical analysis, survey design).
Philip E. Auerswald, Assistant Professor; Ph.D., Washington (Seattle), 1999. Innovation, entrepreneurship, economics of security, energy policy.
Ann Baker, Associate Professor; Ph.D., Case Western Reserve, 1995. Organization change, group and organization communication to promote innovation, knowledge management, cross-cultural communication.
Kenneth J. Button, University Professor; Ph.D., Loughborough (England), 1981. Transportation economics, transport planning, economics of privatization and regulation, environmental economics, regional economics, urban economics.
Janine Davidson, Assistant Professor of National and Global Security; Ph.D., South Carolina, 2005. International Security, U.S. foreign policy, civil and ethnic conflict, weak and failed states, terrorism.
Desmond Dinan, Professor of Public Policy and Jean Monnet Chair; Ph.D., National University of Ireland, 1985. Global governance; European Union institutions, history, and historiography.
Michael K. Fauntroy, Assistant Professor of Public Policy; Ph.D., Howard, 2001. American government and politics, political parties, race and public policy, civil rights policy, urban policy, District of Columbia governance.
Allison M. Frendak-Blume, Assistant Professor of Public Policy; Ph.D., George Mason, 2004. International peacekeeping, stability and reconstruction operations, post-conflict peacebuilding, conflict analysis and resolution, international supervisory/administrative regimes, U.S. foreign policy, Balkans, Russia/former Soviet Union.
A. Lee Fritschler, Professor of Public Policy; Ph.D., Syracuse, 1965. U.S. national government (executive branch), relationship between the institutions of government, accountability, regulation, federalism, public management, science and public policy, higher education policy, U.S. Postal Service, communications policy.
Stephen S. Fuller, Dwight Schar Faculty Chair and University Professor of Public Policy and Regional Development; Ph.D., Cornell, 1969. Regional economic development; urban development; housing; urban planning; demographics; development of the Washington D.C. area; economic analysis; labor force; forecasting—population, income, employment, real estate development; economic and fiscal impact analyses; economic development in developing countries.
Jonathan L. Gifford, Professor of Public Policy, Associate Dean for Research, and Director, Transportation, Policy, Operations, and Logistics Program; Ph.D., Berkeley, 1983. Transportation policy and planning, infrastructure policy and planning, urban and metropolitan planning and land use, technology standards and public policy, transportation and regional development policy, transportation finance and privatization.
Jack A. Goldstone, Virginia E. Hazel and John T. Hazel, Jr. Professor of Public Policy; Ph.D., Harvard, 1981. Democratization, civil conflict, state failure and reconstruction, long-term social change, sources of economic growth.
David M. Hart, Associate Professor; Ph.D., MIT, 1995. Science and technology policy; business and politics; lobbying and representation; U.S. public policy process; U.S. policy history, especially business, economic, and political history; international migration; entrepreneurship; global governance.
Kingsley E. Haynes, Ruth D. and John T. Hazel M.D. Endowed Chair and Eminent Scholar, Professor and Dean, School of Public Policy; Ph.D., Johns Hopkins, 1971. Regional economic development, infrastructure and transportation policy, resource planning and policy analysis.
Jack C. High, Professor of Public Policy, Economics, and Social Learning; Ph.D., UCLA, 1980. Economic regulation, economic growth, economic history, international trade and investment, international institutions.
Christopher T. Hill, Professor of Public Policy and Technology and Director, Public Policy Doctoral Program; Ph.D., Wisconsin–Madison, 1969. Science, technology, and innovation policy (U.S. and international); climate change policy; research management in higher education, government, and industry.
Andrew Hughes Hallett, Professor of Public Policy and Economics; D.Phil., Oxford, 1976. Open economy macroeconomics; policy coordination and exchange rate management; monetary integration (monetary and fiscal union in Europe); political economy models; fiscal policy; regionalism, policy choice, and reform; the theory of economic policy and institutional design; dynamic games and bargaining models; risk and decisions under uncertainty; commodity markets, financial policy, and strategic trade policy; numerical methods in economics.
Jessica Heineman-Pieper, Assistant Professor of Public Policy; Ph.D., Chicago, 2005. Psychology and the conceptual foundations of science, philosophy of the social sciences, deep democracy, post-development studies, applied ethics, transformation, leadership.
Michael R. Kelley, Professor of Telecommunications; Ph.D., Catholic University, 1970. Telecommunications policy, polices for managing scarce radio frequency spectrum, government organizations and their approach to managing a variety of public assets (oil, gas, fishing, hunting, etc.).
Naoru Koizumi, Assistant Professor; Ph.D. (regional science), Pennsylvania, 2002; Ph.D. (environmental and preventive medicine), Hyogo Medical College, (Japan), 2005. Stochastic modeling, simulation of health care systems, applied statistics in health care, spatial statistics and applications of geographic information systems in public health
Todd M. La Porte, Associate Professor; Ph.D., Yale, 1989. Technologies and organizations; technology and society; technology and politics; technology in politics; technology assessment and policy analysis; information and communications technologies; energy technologies; digital government, both worldwide and in the U.S.; comparative political and economic systems, particularly European; critical infrastructures; large technical systems; high reliability organizations and organizational failure; organization studies; public management and public administration; qualitative methods; data collection methodologies; extreme events; disaster studies; emergency management; space weather.
Siona R. Listokin, Assistant Professor; Ph.D., Berkeley, 2007. Public finance, political economy, retirement and welfare policy, public management, private regulation.
Stuart S. Malawer, Distinguished Service Professor of Law and International Trade; Ph.D., Pennsylvania, 1976; Diploma, Hague Academy of International Law, 1971; J.D., Cornell, 1967. U.S. trade law, U.S. and global trade politics, international trade relations, World Trade Organization, national security law and policy.
Jeremy D. Mayer, Associate Professor and Director, Master of Public Policy Program; Ph.D., Georgetown, 1996. Public opinion, racial politics, foreign policy, presidential elections, statistical methods, survey methods, media politics.
Connie L. McNeely, Associate Professor of Public Policy; Ph.D., Stanford, 1990. Culture and policy; states and society; international development; complex organizations and institutional analysis; comparative education; race, ethnicity, and nations; gender; social theory.
Arnauld Nicogossian, Distinguished Research Professor; M.D., Teheran, 1964; M.S., Ohio State, 1972. Public health policy, program/project management, strategic planning and execution of research and development, global public health and preventative medicine, aerospace medicine, internal medicine.
Todd Olmstead, Assistant Professor; Ph.D., Harvard, 2000. Public policy, health policy, transportation policy, health services research, operations research, statistics, program evaluation.
Wayne D. Perry, Professor of Public Policy and Operations Research; Ph.D., Carnegie Mellon, 1975. Science and technology, defense, international security and arms control, health care, operations research/management science, statistical models, stochastic processes, managerial economics and econometrics, policy analysis, cost-benefit analysis.
John E. Petersen, Professor of Public Policy; Ph.D., Pennsylvania, 1967. Public finance (government finance), both domestic (state, local, federal) and international; international finance and financial institutions.
James P. Pfiffner, University Professor of Public Policy; Ph.D., Wisconsin–Madison, 1975. The presidency, Congress, American national government and policy process, public administration.
Ramkishen S. Rajan, Associate Professor of Public Policy; Ph.D., Claremont, 2000. International economics (open economy macroeconomics, finance, and trade) with particular reference to Asia.
Kenneth A. Reinert, Professor of Public Policy and Director, International Commerce and Policy Program; Ph.D., Maryland, College Park, 1988. International trade policy, international development policy, multilateral development organizations, foreign direct investment.
Hilton L. Root, Professor of Public Policy; Ph.D., Michigan, 1983. International economics; international finance; international development; developing nations; political economy of the design and implementation of development policy, economic policy reform; North-South relations and Asian-Pacific affairs.
Mark J. Rozell, Professor of Public Policy; Ph.D., Virginia, 1987. The presidency, media and politics, religion and politics.
Catherine Rudder, Professor of Public Policy; Ph.D., Ohio State, 1973. American political institutions and politics, Congress, tax policy making, self-regulation, governance, non-profit institutions.
Stephen R. Ruth, Professor; Ph.D., Pennsylvania, 1971. Policy approaches for technology-based learning interventions, information technology diffusion in developing nations, religious/theological issues in public policy formulation, strategic issues in knowledge management implementation.
Laurie A. Schintler, Associate Professor of Public Policy; Ph.D., Illinois at Urbana-Champaign, 1996. Critical infrastructure, transportation, quantitative methods, regional development, geographic information systems.
William Schneider, Hirst Chair in Public Policy; Ph.D., Harvard, 1972. Political science; American politics; public opinion and public policy; news media and public affairs; polling and vote analysis; interviewing and fieldwork; comparative elections and politics; ideology and political movements; presidential politics; race, religion, and gender; the politics of foreign policy and national security.
Louise Shelley, Professor of Public Policy; Ph.D., Pennsylvania, 1977. Transnational crime; terrorism; corruption; human trafficking; illicit trade; Soviet successor states.
Rainer Sommer, Associate Professor of Public Policy and Enterprise Engineering; Ph.D., Columbia Pacific (software engineering), 1991; Ph.D., George Mason (information technology), 1998. Enterprise systems, strategic planning and telecommunications.
Roger R. Stough, Vice President for Research and Economic Development; President, George Mason Intellectual Properties; NOVA Endowed Chair and Professor of Public Policy; Ph.D., Johns Hopkins, 1978. Regional economic development policy and analysis, information technology policy, transportation policy, entrepreneurship.
Tojo J. Thatchenkery, Professor of Organization Development and Director, Organization Development and Knowledge Management; Ph.D., Case Western Reserve, 1994. Organizational learning and development; appreciative intelligence; knowledge management; ethnicity, social capital, and organizational mobility; information communication technology and development of Southeast Asia.
Susan Tolchin, University Professor; Ph.D., NYU, 1968. Public policy theory, federal government (U.S.), federal regulation, ethics.
Matthys van Schaik, Associate Dean for Academic Affairs; Ph.D., South Carolina, 1995. International commerce and research methods.
Janine R. Wedel, Professor; Ph.D., Berkeley, 1985. Governance and privatization of policy, corruption and the state, foreign aid, social networks, eastern Europe, anthropology of public policy.

Selected Affiliated Faculty

Kevin Avruch, Professor of Anthropology; Ph.D., California, San Diego, 1978.
Timothy J. Conlan, Associate Professor of Government and Politics; Ph.D., Harvard, 1981.
George L. Donahue, Professor of Systems Engineering and Operations Research; Ph.D., Oklahoma State, 1972.
Robert L. Dudley, Associate Professor of Government and Politics; Ph.D., Northern Illinois.
Gregory A. Guagnano, Associate Professor of Sociology; Ph.D., California, Davis, 1986.
Hugh Heclo, Robinson Professor of Public Affairs; Ph.D., Yale, 1970.
James T. Hennessey, Chief of Staff; Ph.D., George Mason, 1997.
Julianne G. Mahler, Associate Professor of Government and Politics; Ph.D., SUNY at Buffalo, 1976.
John Paden, Robinson Professor of International Studies; Ph.D., Harvard, 1968.
Priscilla M. Regan, Associate Professor of Government and Politics; Ph.D., Cornell, 1981.
Joseph A. Scimecca, Professor of Sociology; Ph.D., NYU, 1972.
Martin Jay Sherwin, Professor of History; Ph.D., UCLA, 1971.
Edgar H. Sibley, University of Professor of Information and Software Engineering; Sc.D., MIT, 1967.

Instructional and Research Faculty

Brien Benson, Research Associate Professor; Ph.D., George Mason, 1998.
George Cook, Affiliate Professor; A.B., George Washington, 1957.
David F. Davis, Assistant Research Professor; M.S., Naval Postgraduate School, 1981.
Robert L. Deitz, Distinguished Visiting Professor, CIA Officer In Residence; M.P.A., Princeton (Wilson), 1972; J.D. Harvard, 1975.
Michael V. Hayden, Distinguished Visiting Professor; M.A., Duquesne, 1969.
Desmond J. Lugg, Distinguished Research Professor; M.D., Adelaide, 1974.
Monty Marshall, Research Professor; Ph.D., Iowa, 1996.
Arthur S. Melmed, Research Professor; M.S.E.E., Columbia, 1956.
James L. Narel, Academic Director, Peace Operations Policy Program, School of Public Policy; Ph.D., George Mason, 2007.
James Riggle, Research Associate Professor; Ph.D., George Mason, 2002.
Charles Robb, Distinguished Professor of Law and Public Policy; J.D., Virginia, 1973.

HAWAI'I PACIFIC UNIVERSITY

Master of Arts in Global Leadership and Sustainable Development

Program of Study

Hawai'i Pacific University's (HPU's) Master of Arts in Global Leadership and Sustainable Development (M.A./GLSD) program is designed to prepare students to lead change initiatives in a globalizing world that is increasingly characterized by chaos, complexity, and change. Students learn simultaneously to search for the underlying causes of global environmental, economic, and social problems and how to design and lead responses that produce sustainable outcomes for current and future generations.

Faculty members who teach in the M.A./GLSD program combine impressive academic credentials, stature in their professional disciplines, and years of actual business and consulting experience. Many have extensive international experience and therefore welcome the diversity that HPU's students bring to the classroom. Graduate students have the benefit of learning from adjunct professors who are part of the local business community—managing partners, vice presidents, and presidents from a wide variety of companies and organizations, both domestic and international. All program faculty members are dedicated to making the HPU experience edifying, challenging, and enjoyable for the student.

The M.A./GLSD is designed to prepare students to become leaders in all types of organizations, including multinational, governmental, and not-for-profit organizations. The program concentrates on teaching relevant interdisciplinary theories and tools to help professionals succeed in today's fast-paced global economy.

Research Facilities

To support graduate studies, HPU's Meader and Atherton Libraries offer more than 110,000 bound volumes, 350,000 microfiche items, and periodical subscriptions to 1,500 print titles and 30,000 electronic journals. Databases of public and state university libraries, legislative information, and business-oriented statistical data are also available in the library or online. Students can access HPU's library databases, course information, their academic information, and an e-mail account through Pipeline, the University's internal Web site for students. The University's accessible on-campus computer center houses more than 100 computers with specialized software to support graduate academic programs. HPU also provides free Wi-Fi service so students can have wireless access to Pipeline resources anywhere on campus using laptops. A significant number of online courses are available as well.

Financial Aid

The University participates in all federal financial aid programs designated for graduate students. These programs provide aid in the form of subsidized (need-based) and unsubsidized (non-need-based) Federal Stafford Student Loans. Through these loans, funds may be available to cover a student's entire cost of education. To apply for aid, students must submit the Free Application for Federal Student Aid (FAFSA) beginning January 1. Mailing of student award letters usually begins by the end of March. The University also offers several types of institutional graduate scholarships to new full-time, degree-seeking students. The Graduate Trustee Scholarship provides $6000 for two semesters, the Graduate Dean Scholarship provides $4000 for two semesters, and the Graduate Kokua Scholarship provides $2000 for two semesters. Priority consideration is given to those students who apply by the deadline.

Cost of Study

Tuition for graduate students enrolled in fall and spring semesters is determined on a per-credit basis; full-time status for a graduate student is nine credits. Tuition for the optional winter and summer sessions is also determined on a per-credit basis. The estimated minimum funds needed for a nine-month academic year (September to May) based on 2010–11 school year expenses is $26,459. For the 2010–11 academic year, full-time tuition is $12,600 for most graduate degree programs, including the M.A./GLSD program. Books, supplies, and transportation cost $1885, and health insurance costs $880.

Living and Housing Costs

Most graduate students live in off-campus housing. The cost to live in off-campus apartments is approximately $11,094 for a double occupancy room.

Student Group

University enrollment currently stands at more than 8,200. HPU is one of the most culturally diverse universities in America with students from all 50 U.S. states and more than 100 countries.

Location

Hawai'i Pacific combines the excitement of an urban, downtown campus with the serenity of a residential campus. The main campus is ideally located in downtown Honolulu, the business and financial center of the Pacific. The downtown campus comprises six buildings in the center of Honolulu's business district and is home to the College of Business Administration and the College of Humanities and Social Sciences. Eight miles away, situated on 135 acres in Kaneohe, the windward Hawai'i Loa campus is the site of the College of Nursing and Health Sciences and the College of Natural and Computational Sciences. HPU is affiliated with the Oceanic Institute, an applied aquaculture research facility located on a 56-acre site at Makapu'u Point on the windward coast of Oahu, Hawaii. Students can conveniently travel between the three sites using the HPU shuttle service. There are also eight military campus programs located at Pearl Harbor, Barbers Point, Hickam Air Force Base, Schofield Barracks, Fort Shafter, Tripler Army Medical Center, Kaneohe Marine Corps Air Station, and Camp Smith.

The University

HPU is a private, nonprofit university with approximately 8,200 students. Founded in 1965, HPU prides itself on maintaining strong academic programs, small class sizes, individual attention to students, and a diverse faculty and student population. HPU is recognized as a "Best in the West" college by Princeton Review and a "Best Buy" by *Barron's* business magazine. HPU offers more than fifty acclaimed undergraduate programs and thirteen distinguished graduate programs. The University has a faculty of more than 500, a student-faculty ratio of 15:1, and an average class size of fewer than 20 students. A wide range of counseling and other student support services are available. There are more than seventy student organizations on campus, including the Graduate Student Organization.

Applying

Students must have a baccalaureate degree from an accredited college or university in the United States or an equivalent degree from another country. Applicants should complete and forward a Graduate Admissions Application, send in the $50 nonrefundable application fee, have official transcripts sent from all colleges or universities previously attended, and forward two letters of recommendation. A resume and a personal statement about the applicant's academic and career goals are required. Applicants who have taken the Graduate Record Examination (GRE) should have their scores sent directly to the Graduate Admissions Office. International students should submit scores from a recognized English proficiency test, such as the TOEFL. Admissions decisions are made on a rolling basis, and applicants are notified between one and two weeks after all documents have been submitted. Applicants are encouraged to submit their applications online.

Correspondence and Information

Graduate Admissions
Hawai'i Pacific University
1164 Bishop Street, Suite 911
Honolulu, Hawaii 96813

Phone: 808-544-1135
866-GRAD-HPU (toll-free)
Fax: 808-544-0280
E-mail: graduate@hpu.edu
Web site: http://www.hpu.edu/hpumaglsd

Hawaiʻi Pacific University

THE FACULTY AND THEIR RESEARCH

Cheryl Crozier-Garcia, Assistant Professor of Human Resource Management; Ph.D., Walden.
Gerald W. Glover, Professor of Organizational Change; Ph.D., Florida.
John Gutrich, Associate Professor of Environmental Sciences; Ph.D., Ohio State.
Gordon Jones, Professor of Computer Science and Information Systems; Ph.D., New Mexico.
Margo Kitts, Associate Professor of Humanities/Religious Studies; Ph.D., Berkeley.
Ernesto Lucas, Associate Professor of Economics; Ph.D., Hawaii.
Daniel Morgan, Instructor of Sociology; M.A., Miami (Florida).
Regina Ostergaard-Klem, Adjunct Professor of Mathematics; Ph.D., Johns Hopkins.
Catherine Sajna, Assistant Professor of English; M.A., Hawaii at Manoa.
Richard Ward, Associate Professor of Organizational Change; Ed.D., USC.
Arthur Whatley, Professor of Management; Ph.D., North Texas.
Larry Zimmerman, Assistant Professor of Organizational Change; Ph.D., Nebraska–Lincoln.

SCHOOL OF PUBLIC AND ENVIRONMENTAL AFFAIRS
INDIANA UNIVERSITY

INDIANA UNIVERSITY BLOOMINGTON

School of Public and Environmental Affairs
Public Affairs Graduate Programs

Programs of Study

The School of Public and Environmental Affairs (SPEA) offers graduate degree programs leading to the Master of Public Affairs (M.P.A.), the Ph.D. in public policy, and the Ph.D. in public affairs.

The two-year, 48-credit hour M.P.A. degree is an interdisciplinary program that equips students with a combination of skills for professional careers in government, nonprofit, and private sectors. The program consists of four components: a core curriculum, a concentration area, an experiential component, and sufficient electives and/or prior professional experience. The core courses include public management, statistical analysis, public management economics, law and public affairs, public finance and budgeting, and a capstone project in public and environmental affairs. Many SPEA students choose to pursue more than one concentration. The M.P.A. concentration areas are comparative and international affairs, economic development, environmental policy and natural resource management, information systems, local government management, nonprofit management, policy analysis, public financial administration, public management, and SPEA's latest addition, sustainable development. To integrate their academic training into a practical framework, students are required to complete an internship or a significant research project in order to satisfy the experiential component of the M.P.A. program. The capstone project serves as the culmination to a student's academic training. Capstone projects are normally a semester-long, detailed analysis of a policy or management issue, often undertaken for a real-world client in the public or nonprofit sector.

M.P.A. joint-degree programs are offered with SPEA's Master of Science in Environmental Science (M.S.E.S.) and Indiana University's Departments of African American and African Diaspora Studies, African Studies, Central Eurasian Studies, East Asian Studies, Latin American and Caribbean Studies, Russian and East European Studies, and West European Studies, as well as the schools of library and information science, law, and journalism.

The Ph.D. in public affairs is designed to prepare scholars for research and teaching in the multidisciplinary field of public policy and management. The program emphasizes the study of public management and organization, policy analysis, and public finance. The joint Ph.D. in public policy is a collaborative venture with Indiana University's Department of Political Science. This program emphasizes study of the public policy process. Students explore issues regarding policy analysis, government institutions, political behavior, and public affairs.

Research Facilities

Complementing SPEA's own resources, Indiana University maintains eight nationally prominent area studies centers and sixty language programs to facilitate international research and career interests. SPEA has affiliations with several research centers on both the Bloomington and Indianapolis campuses, including the Transportation Research Center; the Institute for Family and Social Responsibility; the Environmental Science Research Center; the Indiana University Research and Teaching Preserve; the Center for the Study of Institutions, Population, and Environmental Change; the Indiana University Public Policy Institute; and the Center for Urban Policy and Environment.

SPEA houses its own newly renovated Information Commons, which provides convenient access to individual and group workstations, student-focused services that support individual and collaborative learning and research, and access to rich library resources shared with the Kelley School of Business. The Indiana University Bloomington Libraries have been recognized by peers as the top university library in the country, according to the Association of College and Research Libraries, 2010.

Financial Aid

Departmental assistance for qualified students is awarded on a competitive basis determined by merit. Awards include fellowships, scholarships, and teaching and research assistantships. Prospective students may apply for merit-based awards by checking the appropriate box on the admission application form. Students may apply for need-based aid through the University Office of Student Financial Assistance (OSFA).

SPEA hosts a one-of-a-kind, collaborative program called Service Corps, which enables M.P.A. and M.S.E.S. students to apply their classroom learning directly to the field in both the public and nonprofit sectors. Service Corps is a financial aid mechanism that offers students real-world experience working in an array of governmental and nonprofit agencies while concurrently pursuing their academic plans. The program is a partnership among the University, SPEA, and a number of valued external stakeholders in the community and region. Students are selected for participation during the merit aid allocation process.

Cost of Study

In-state residents pay $391.55 per credit hour and nonresidents pay $850.33 per credit hour for master's programs in 2010–11.

Living and Housing Costs

The 1,200 on-campus apartments for graduate students range in monthly rent from $519 for a furnished efficiency to $1119 for an unfurnished three-bedroom apartment. Rates include all utilities as well as local telephone service, cable TV, and Internet connection. A variety of off-campus apartments are available near the University. Rents are generally inexpensive, with the average two-bedroom unit renting for $550 to $800 per month. A free campus bus runs to most apartments in the area, providing easy access to SPEA and many other areas of Bloomington.

Student Groups

About 314 students are enrolled in the M.P.A. program, with 77 students pursuing the joint M.P.A./M.S.E.S. program, and 75 students are enrolled in the Ph.D. programs in public affairs or public policy. About 8 percent of these students are international, more than one half are women, and more than 10 percent are members of underrepresented populations.

SPEA recognizes service in AmeriCorps, Teach for America, and Peace Corps. These volunteers receive a waiver of the experiential component which is a part of the academic design and a reduction of the total number of credit hours required for degree completion. SPEA also hosts both Peace Corps Fellows/U.S.A., and Master's International (MI) programs. Peace Corps and MI Fellows receive a competitive merit aid package in addition to the benefits described above.

Student Outcomes

SPEA maintains an outstanding placement record, attributed to a well-rounded curriculum, national prestige, and strong alumni support. Within six months of the close of the 2008–09 academic year, approximately 76 percent of students responding to SPEA's annual employment survey indicated that they had procured full-time professional positions or were continuing their education. The SPEA Office of Career Services (OCS) is staffed with professionals who assist graduate students with all of their career development needs. The services offered to students include individual career counseling; on-campus recruiting; a Web-based job listing service, SPEACareers.com; a wide range of employer information sessions; alumni mentoring; user-friendly Web-based career resources; and an extensive career resource library. With so many resources at their disposal, SPEA students annually compete for many of the most prestigious and competitive positions in federal and state government and top-tier nonprofits and foundations. SPEA students are also top candidates for positions with top consulting firms like Booz Allen Hamilton, Crowe Chizek, Deloitte, and Grant Thornton. Some examples of other recent placements include the World Bank, the Environmental Protection Agency, the Department of State, the National Forest Service, the Government Accountability Office, the National Institutes of Health, the National Oceanographic and Atmospheric Institute, the Millennium Challenge Corporation, the Nature Conservancy, the Corporation for National and Community Service, the Bill and Melinda Gates Foundation, the Indiana Department of Environmental Management, the Indiana Office of Management and Budget, and the Indiana Department of Transportation.

Additionally, SPEA typically has 5–15 M.P.A. students selected as finalists for the Presidential Management Fellowship Program (PMF), one of the most selective federal programs for graduate students pursuing careers with the federal government.

Location

Bloomington, a college town of 110,000 people, was chosen as one of the top ten college towns in America for its "rich mixture of atmospherics and academia" by Edward Fiske, former education editor of the *New York Times*. It is a culturally vibrant community settled among southern Indiana's rolling hills, just 45 miles south of Indianapolis, the state capital. Mild winters and warm summers are ideal for outdoor recreation in the two state forests, one national forest, three state parks, and an array of lakes and streams that surround Bloomington.

The University and The School

Established in 1820, Indiana University has more than 7,500 graduate students and more than 38,000 students total enrolled on the Bloomington campus. SPEA is the top-ranked graduate program on campus. Fifty-five other academic departments are ranked in the top 20 in the country, including music, business, biology, foreign languages, political science, and chemistry. Attractions include nearly 1,000 musical performances each year, with eight full-length operas and professional Broadway plays; the IU Art Museum, designed by I. M. Pei, with more than 30,000 art objects; fifty campus and community volunteer agencies; more than 700 student sports clubs and organizations; two indoor student recreational facilities; and Big Ten athletics. SPEA, founded in 1972, was the first school to combine public management, policy, and administration with the environmental sciences.

Applying

Application files must include the SPEA Admission Application form, transcripts, GRE General Test scores, and three letters of recommendation. Priority is given to applications received by February 1. Students applying for awards must submit a complete application file by the priority deadline, February 1. School visits are encouraged. Applicants can also access the School's Web site at http://www.spea.indiana.edu.

Correspondence and Information

For master's programs:
Master's Program Office
SPEA 260
Indiana University
Bloomington, Indiana 47405
Phone: 812-855-2840
800-765-7755 (toll-free, domestic only)
E-mail: speainfo@indiana.edu
Web site: http://www.spea.indiana.edu

For doctoral programs:
Ph.D. Programs Office
SPEA 441
Indiana University
Bloomington, Indiana 47405
Phone: 812-855-2457
800-765-7755 (toll-free, domestic only)
E-mail: speainfo@indiana.edu
Web site: http://www.spea.indiana.edu

Indiana University Bloomington

THE FACULTY AND THEIR RESEARCH

Osita G. Afoaku, Ph.D., Washington State, 1991. Human rights, sustainable development, democratization, and state reconstruction in Africa; U.S.-African/Third World relations; UN Security Council reform.
David B. Audretsch, Ph.D., Wisconsin, 1980. Economics policy, entrepreneurship, innovation, globalization, regional economic policy, industrial restructuring and government policy, small enterprises in Europe and the United States.
Matthew R. Auer, Ph.D., Yale, 1996. Intersection of foreign aid and sustainable development, international forest politics, energy efficiency, environmental education.
James Barnes, J.D., Harvard, 1967. Environmental law, domestic and international environmental policy, ethics and the public official, mediation and alternative dispute resolution, law and public policy.
Lisa Blomgren Bingham, J.D., Connecticut, 1979. Collaborative governance, comparative governance, dispute resolution, dispute system design, mediation, administrative law, labor and employment law.
Anthony A. Blasingame, Ph.D., Maryland, College Park, 2002. Public finance, labor economics, poverty, U.S. political economy.
Melissa A. L. Clark, M.S., Indiana, 1999. Aquatic and terrestrial habitats, Indiana Clean Lakes Program, water resources and water quality.
Christopher B. Craft, Ph.D., North Carolina State, 1987. Wetland restoration and ecosystem development; wetlands and water quality; wetlands and climate change, including carbon sequestration and peat accretion.
Michael A. Edwards, Ph.D., North Dakota State, 1999. Atmospheric chemistry research: mechanistic studies of terpenes reacting with ozone, future regulation of hydrogen storage materials.
Sergio Fernandez, Ph.D., Georgia, 2004. Public management and organization theory, privatization and contracting out, public-sector leadership, organizational change.
Burnell C. Fischer, Ph.D., Purdue, 1974. Forestry, particularly silviculture and urban forestry; growth and development of Central Hardwood forest stands and response to various silvicultural practices; community and urban forestry issues; forest resources policy and state government management; human factors relating to forests and forest products, particularly with regard to collaborative forestry.
Beth Gazley, Ph.D., Georgia, 2004. Nonprofit management and governance, volunteerism, collaboration, intersectoral relations and the role of the voluntary sector in emergency planning.
David Good, Ph.D., Pennsylvania, 1985. Quantitative policy modeling, productivity measurement in public and regulated industries, urban policy analysis.
John D. Graham, Ph.D., Carnegie Mellon, 1983. Government reform, energy and the environment, the future of the automobile in both developed and developing countries.
Kirsten Grønbjerg, Ph.D., Chicago, 1974. Nonprofit and public sector relationships, examining scope and community dimensions of the Indiana nonprofit sector, the American welfare system, nonprofit funding relations, nonprofit data sources.
Hendrik M. Haitjema, Ph.D., Minnesota, 1982. Groundwater flow modeling, including regional groundwater flow systems, conjunctive surface-water and groundwater flow modeling, 3-D groundwater flow, and saltwater intrusion problems, with emphasis on application of analytic functions to modeling groundwater flow, specifically analytic-element method.
Diane S. Henshel, Ph.D., Washington (St. Louis), 1987. Sublethal health effects of environmental pollutants, especially pollutant effects on the developing organism, including the effects of polychlorinated dibenzo-p-dioxins (PCDDs) and related congeners on the developing nervous system of birds exposed in the wild and under controlled laboratory conditions.
Monika Herzig, D.M.E., Indiana, 1997. Touring jazz pianist, concert promotion, music industry, jazz education.
Ronald Hites, Ph.D., MIT, 1968. Applying organic analytical chemistry techniques to the analysis of trace levels of toxic pollutants, such as polychlorinated biphenyls and pesticides, with focus on understanding behavior of these compounds in the atmosphere and in the Great Lakes.
Christopher Hunt, M.A., Cambridge, 1961. Programming and presentation of the performing and visual arts and entertainment.
Chaman Jain, Ph.D., Indiana, 1975. Governmental and non-profit accounting and reporting, financial management in nonprofit organizations, governmental budgeting and finance, financial (corporate) management.
Craig Johnson, Ph.D., SUNY at Albany, 1993. Capital markets and financial intermediation, financial management, public budgeting and finance, financing e-government, financing economic development, environmental and infrastructure finance.
William W. Jones, M.S., Wisconsin–Madison, 1977. Lake and watershed management, especially diagnosing lake and watershed water-quality problems; preparing management plans to address problems identified; stream ecology; Caribbean coral reef ecology and underwater archaeology; certified lake manager (CLM).
Haeil Jung, Ph.D., Chicago, 2009. Applied econometrics and program evaluation, crime policy, public policy for low-income families.
Kerry Krutilla, Ph.D., Duke, 1988. Theory and practice of benefit-cost analysis, environmental policy analysis, program evaluation of environmental programs, natural resource management in developing countries.
Marc L. Lame, Ph.D., Arizona State, 1992. Implementation of integrated pest-management programs in schools and day-care facilities.
Leslie Lenkowsky, Ph.D., Harvard, 1982. Nonprofits and public policy, civil society in comparative perspective, institutional grant makers, volunteering and civic engagement, education and social welfare policy, social entrepreneurship.
Joyce Y. Man, Ph.D., Johns Hopkins, 1993. Public finance, urban and regional economics, international trade, economic development, public budgeting and financial management.
Eugene B. McGregor Jr., Ph.D., Syracuse, 1968. Interaction of public policy, organizational structure, and management practice; the relationship between education and economic development; impact of information technology on structure and management of public and nonprofit enterprise.
Michael McGuire, Ph.D., Indiana, 1995. Intergovernmental and interorganizational collaboration and networks, federalism and intergovernmental relations, public management, emergency management.
Vicky J. Meretsky, Ph.D., Arizona, 1995. Ecology and management of rare species, biocomplexity, landscape-level species and community conservation, temporal patterns in biodiversity, integrating ecosystem research and endangered species management within adaptive management.
John L. Mikesell, Ph.D., Illinois, 1969. Governmental finance, especially questions of policy and administration of sales and property taxation; state lotteries; public budgeting; public finance in countries of the former Soviet Union.
Alfredo Minetti, Ph.D., Indiana, 2007. Social dynamics of music: how music groups organize themselves, their social aesthetics, how they foster creativity, how different music styles and genres are embodied by individuals, audience development, and arts organizations.
Ashlyn Aiko Nelson, Ph.D., Stanford, 2005. Housing finance, education finance, education policy, the mortgage crisis.
Patrick O'Meara, Ph.D., Indiana, 1970. Comparative politics and development, Southern African politics, ethics and politics.
Clinton V. Oster Jr., Ph.D., Harvard, 1978. Aviation safety, airline economics and competition policy, international aviation, aviation infrastructure, environmental and natural resource policy, government regulation, business-government relations.
Elinor Ostrom, Ph.D., UCLA, 1965. How institutional rules affect the structure of action situations within which individuals face incentives, make choices, and jointly affect each other; problems involving collective goods and common-pool resource systems; how various types of institutions enhance or detract from the capabilities of individuals to achieve equitable, workable, efficient solutions.
James Perry, Ph.D., Syracuse, 1974. Public service motivation, government and civil service reform, public management, public human resource management, national and community service, performance-related pay, public organizational behavior.
Flynn W. Picardal, Ph.D., Arizona, 1992. Bioremediation, environmental microbiology, and biogeochemistry, with a focus on the microbial reduction of iron oxides and nitrate, transformation of metals and chlorinated hydrocarbons, and combined microbial-geochemical interactions.
Maureen A. Pirog, Ph.D., Pennsylvania, 1981. Poverty and income maintenance, child support enforcement, welfare reform, adolescent parenting.
Orville W. Powell, M.P.A., Penn State, 1963. Local government and the U.S. Constitution.
J. C. Randolph, Ph.D., Carleton (Ottawa), 1972. Forest ecology; ecological aspects of global environmental change, with particular interests in forestry and agriculture; applications of geographic information systems (GIS) and remote sensing in environmental and natural resources management; landscape ecology and regional-scale modeling; physiological ecology of woody plants and of small mammals.
David A. Reingold, Ph.D., Chicago, 1996. Urban poverty, economic development, social welfare policy, low-income housing policy and government performance.
Terri L. Renner, M.B.A., Indiana, 1985. Financial management, information systems, entrepreneurship.
Rafael Reuveny, Ph.D., Indiana, 1997. International political economy; globalization; rise and fall of major powers; political conflict and how it interacts with international trade, democracy, and the environment; sustainable development; Middle East political economy.
Edwardo L. Rhodes, Ph.D., Carnegie Mellon, 1978. Public policy analysis, particularly public-sector applications of management science in the evaluation and assessment of the efficiency or organization performance of public activities, including environmental and natural resource policy implementation.
Kenneth R. Richards, J.D./Ph.D., Pennsylvania, 1997. Domestic and international climate change policy, environmental policy implementation, carbon sequestration economics and law, energy law, U.S. Forest Service organizational design and management.
Evan J. Ringquist, Ph.D., Wisconsin–Madison, 1990. Public policy (environmental, energy, natural resources, and regulation), research methodology, American political institutions.
Justin Ross, Ph.D., West Virginia, 2007. Public economics, urban/regional economics, spatial econometrics, applied microeconomics, quantile regressions, public finance, political economy, game theory.
Todd V. Royer, Ph.D., Idaho State, 1999. Aquatic biogeochemistry, water resources, nutrient and carbon cycling in streams and rivers, water quality and nutrient standards.
Barry Rubin, Ph.D., Wisconsin–Madison, 1977. Urban and regional economic development and impact analysis, quantitative analysis of local government management and labor relations issues, statistics and quantitative methods, econometric modeling, public management information systems, strategic planning and management.
Michael Rushton, Ph.D., British Columbia, 1990. Cultural economics, policy and administration, nonprofit and public organizations and management, tax policy, government funding for the arts and other policies toward nonprofit organizations, cultural districts, the relationships between the arts and economic growth.
Yue (Jen) Shang, Ph.D., Indiana, 2008. Nonprofit marketing, marketing communications for nonprofit organizations, donor behavior, fund development, philanthropic psychology.
Joseph Shaw, Ph.D., Kentucky, 2001. Environmental toxicology, comparative physiology, functional genomics.
Nan Stager, M.S., Indiana, 1978. Mediation, negotiation, alternative dispute resolution, public input processes.
Philip S. Stevens, Ph.D., Harvard, 1990. Characterization of chemical mechanisms that influence regional air quality and global climate change.
Anh Tran, Ph.D., Harvard, 2009. Economic and public administration policies for developing countries, evaluation of public policies and social programs.
Terry Usrey, M.S., Indiana, 1983. E-government, information technology policy, information technology management.
Henry K. Wakhungu, Ph.D., Indiana, 2004. Development of growth simulation models for sustainable management of indigenous community forests; experimental designs in tropical forestry research; how preservice teachers conceptualize mathematics (philosophically), indexed with mathematics learning and teaching.
Jeffrey R. White, Ph.D., Syracuse, 1984. Environmental biogeochemistry, aquatic chemistry, limnology.
Lois R. Wise, Ph.D., Indiana, 1982. Public management and employment policies and practices.
Wenli Yan, Ph.D., Kentucky, 2008. Public and nonprofit financial management, state and local finance, quantitative methods.
C. Kurt Zorn, Ph.D., Syracuse, 1981. State and local finance, transportation safety, economic development, gaming policy.

JOHNS HOPKINS Institute for Policy Studies

THE JOHNS HOPKINS UNIVERSITY

Institute for Policy Studies

Program of Study

Johns Hopkins University offers a Master of Arts degree in public policy (MPP). This two-year public policy program prepares graduates for professional careers in private as well as public organizations involved with solving societal problems. Graduates are equipped for responsible positions around the world that deal with the analysis of public problems and the development and implementation of solutions to meet them. By design, the program is kept small to nurture mentoring relationships between students and faculty members. Core courses are taught primarily by Institute faculty members. The number of ongoing policy research projects at the Institute creates a wealth of opportunities for students, including research assistantships. Extensive faculty member–student interaction in seminars and with faculty research and student thesis research enriches the students' experience and prepares them thoroughly for professional careers.

The curriculum consists of four basic components: a set of core analytical courses, a set of substantive policy courses in an area of specialization, an internship, and the opportunity to write a thesis. The program features a curriculum combining strong analytical courses and a focus on the evolving concept of citizenship and the moral dimensions of policy choice; location within a University-based research institute; easy access to Washington, D.C., and significant opportunities to learn firsthand about the policy process; attention to the role of private as well as public institutions in coping with public problems, with a special emphasis on nonprofit organizations; and opportunities for interaction with international fellows in residence at the Institute.

Students generally take most core courses and some electives during the first year, followed by an internship during the summer. Areas of concentration include health policy, social policy, urban policy, international affairs, nonprofit sector, human resource policy, education policy, and the environment.

Research Facilities

All resources of Johns Hopkins University System are available to policy studies students, including the Schools of Arts and Sciences, Engineering, Advanced International Studies (SAIS), Public Health, and the Carey School of Business. The library includes more than 2.1 million volumes, more than 1.2 million microforms, and more than 13,000 serial subscriptions. The Government Publications/Maps/Law Library provides a full range of services for accessing and utilizing an extensive collection of publications of the U.S. government, the UN and other international agencies, and state and local governments. The University has been a depository for U.S. government publications since 1882 and currently selects approximately 50 percent of the items offered to depository libraries. The computer facility includes two central systems: a VAX/VMS and Silicon Graphics SGI with UNIX. Students have access to several on-campus computer labs; in addition, the Institute maintains a computer lab for its own students. Students are assigned study carrels at the Institute or University libraries.

Financial Aid

Institute financial aid is awarded to graduate students who demonstrate intellectual promise in the field of policy studies through past academic performance, GRE test scores, previous relevant work experience, and a personal statement. The Institute awards tuition remissions and research fellowships. Students may also apply for available special fellowships. Low-interest loans and work-study assignments are awarded by the Financial Aid Office of Johns Hopkins University. Research fellowships pay $14 to $16 an hour for 15 to 20 hours of work per week.

Cost of Study

Tuition for 2010–11 is $40,680. There is a one-time matriculation fee of $500. Annual book expenses are estimated to be $1200.

Living and Housing Costs

Cost of living was estimated at $16,000 for 2009–10. Students generally live in privately arranged apartments or shared houses close to the campus. Rents range from $550 to $1200 a month. University meal plans are available.

Student Group

About 1,400 graduate students are in residence at Hopkins' main campus. There are currently 94 students in the Policy Studies Program and 5 students in the International Fellows Programs at the Institute for Policy Studies. Students come from all parts of the U.S.; some either have lived abroad or are international students. Approximately two thirds of all students are women, and one fifth are members of minority groups. Most students have prior work experience.

Student Outcomes

Graduates of the MPP Program are generally middle- to upper-level employees in all levels of government and in private and nonprofit organizations. In addition, some graduates have enrolled in Ph.D. programs. Typical jobs include program officer for a philanthropic foundation, policy or research analyst at a research institute or government agency, and executive director of a nonprofit organization. Recent graduates are working at the U.S. Office of Management and Budget, Mathematica Policy Research, World Bank, the Urban Institute, Pepsi Corporation, Charles Mott Foundation, U.S. General Accounting Office, Public/Private Ventures, and Enterprise Foundation.

Location

The Institute for Policy Studies is located on the 140-acre rolling wooded Homewood campus, about 3 miles north of the Inner Harbor of downtown Baltimore. The campus is 1 mile from the Amtrak train station; 40 miles from Washington, D.C.; 30 miles from Annapolis; and about 15 miles from the Chesapeake Bay.

The University and The Institute

Johns Hopkins University has a reputation as a world-renowned center of scholarship and research. The relatively small student body yields a favorable student-faculty ratio. Students are encouraged to think for themselves in an environment that fosters independence and creativity. The Institute for Policy Studies is a group of political scientists, economists, policy analysts, and policy practitioners who seek to improve the response of government and private institutions to the challenges of poverty and disadvantage, urban and regional economic change, human resource investment, and environmental degradation. The Institute carries out its work through a combination of policy-oriented research; seminars, briefings, and other public education efforts; and formal training of policy professionals in this country and abroad.

Applying

The deadline for applying to the Institute for Policy Studies is January 15. The application fee is $60. Applications for student loan and work-study programs must be submitted separately to the Office of Student Financial Services by April 1. Successful applicants generally have a college grade point average of at least 3.0 on a 4.0 scale. GRE General Test scores are required, and a score of at least 600 on each section is preferred. Students are encouraged to visit the Institute, but interviews are not required.

Correspondence and Information

Master of Arts in Public Policy
Institute for Policy Studies
The Johns Hopkins University
3400 North Charles Street, Wyman Park Building, 5th Floor
Baltimore, Maryland 21218

Phone: 410-516-4624
Fax: 410-516-8233
E-mail: mpp@jhu.edu
Web site: http://ips.jhu.edu/pub/Why-A-Hopkins-MPP

The Johns Hopkins University

THE FACULTY AND THEIR RESEARCH

David M. Altschuler, Principal Research Scientist, Associate Professor of Mental Hygiene, Public Health Adjunct, and Adjunct Associate Professor of Sociology; Ph.D., Chicago, 1983. Project director and co–principal investigator on a federally funded research and training project that has developed a model of intensive aftercare for the high-risk juvenile parolee being released from secure correctional facilities; chair of Baltimore Mayor's Working Group on drug policy reform. Current research interests: juvenile justice sanctioning and aftercare; community-based delinquency program design, implementation, and assessment; privatization in corrections; drug involvement and crime among inner-city youth.

John J. Boland, Professor of Geography and Environmental Engineering; Ph.D., Johns Hopkins, 1973. Current research interests: environment and public utility economics, water resource management, environmental policy.

Senator Benjamin L. Cardin, Distinguished Lecturer; J.D., Maryland, 1967. Member of the U.S. Senate, Maryland. Policy interests: ethics, political process, and human resource policy.

Andrew Cherlin, Benjamin H. Griswold III Professor of Public Policy in the Department of Sociology; Ph.D., UCLA, 1976. Current research interests: sociology of the family, social policy and demography.

Matthew A. Crenson, Professor of Political Science; Ph.D., Chicago, 1969. Current research interests: political origins of American welfare policy.

Ruth R. Faden, Philip Franklin Wagley Professor of Biomedical Ethics at the Bioethics Institute and Professor of Health Policy and Management at the School of Public Health; Ph.D., Berkeley, 1976. Current research interests: ethics and health policy management.

Bernard Guyer, Professor and Chair of Maternal and Child Health Policy at the School of Public Health; M.D., Rochester, 1970. Current research interests: maternal and child health policy, practice, and finance; childhood injury prevention; child development; childhood immunization.

Robert Moffitt, Professor of Economics; Ph.D., Brown, 1975. Current research interests: labor economics, econometrics, public finance, population economics.

Vicente Navarro, Professor of Health Policy and of Sociology; Ph.D., Johns Hopkins, 1968. Current research interests: international study of public policy, health and social policy.

Sandra J. Newman, Director of the Center on Housing, Neighborhoods, and Communities and Professor of Policy Studies (joint appointments in sociology, health policy, and management; geography and environmental engineering); Ph.D., NYU, 1973. Member of Board of Directors, Center for Housing Policy, National Foundation for Affordable Housing Solutions; Associate Editor, *Housing Policy Debate*. Current research interests: long-term effects of housing assistance on children and families, implications of welfare reform for housing, living conditions of America's disabled, low-income rental housing market dynamics.

Marion Pines, Senior Fellow and Director of the Institute's Sar Levitan Center for Social Policy Studies; B.A., Goucher. Chair of interagency team managing policy, planning, implementation, and evaluation of statewide high school dropout prevention project. Current research interests: at-risk populations, development of education alternatives, welfare reform policies, employment strategies for youth and adults, service integration model targeted at families.

Lester M. Salamon, Founding Director of the Institute for Policy Studies and Director of its Center for Civil Society Studies and Professor of Political Science; Ph.D., Harvard, 1971. Vice Chair of the International Society for Third-Sector Research. Current research interests: alternative instruments of government action; social welfare policy; scope, structure, and role of the private nonprofit sector in the United States and overseas; human capital investment policy.

Curt Ventriss, Visiting Professor, Ph.D., USC, 1980. Current research interests: ethics and public policy, environmental issues.

Aerial view of the parklike Homewood campus with old Baltimore neighborhood in the background, the Institute for Policy Studies at the far left, and the Eisenhower Library in the center across from the ellipse.

UNIVERSITY OF DELAWARE

School of Urban Affairs and Public Policy

Programs of Study

The School of Urban Affairs and Public Policy offers three graduate degree programs: a Master of Public Administration (M.P.A.), a Master of Arts (M.A.) in urban affairs and public policy, and a Ph.D. in urban affairs and public policy.

The M.P.A. is a 42- or 45-credit, two-year professional degree program that prepares students for leadership positions in public affairs. The M.P.A. program is accredited by the National Association of Schools of Public Affairs and Administration (NASPAA). Students can choose from four options for specializations: nonprofit management, public management, policy and program development, or a student-designed specialization.

The M.A. and Ph.D. in urban affairs and public policy programs are ranked among the top nine programs in the United States. The M.A. is a 36-credit degree program designed for students who are interested in pursuing policy analysis and planning–related careers. The program extends over two years and may include a thesis, an analytical paper, or an internship. M.A. students may specialize in such areas as community development and nonprofit leadership; energy, environment, and equity; historic preservation; and urban and regional planning. The Ph.D. is a research-oriented interdisciplinary degree intended for students who have completed master's-level work in urban affairs and public policy or other related social science fields. First-year doctoral seminars are followed by study in a specialization that leads to the preparation of the dissertation proposal. Most students conduct dissertation research in the areas of technology, environment, and society; governance planning and management; social and urban policy; public administration; and urban affairs. All doctoral students collaborate with faculty and staff members on regional, national, and international research on critical urban and policy issues.

The School offers a nationally recognized internship program that places students in paid professional positions in international, national, state, and local government. All students in the School are eligible; the internship is a requirement for preservice M.P.A. students.

Research Facilities

The School is centrally located in its own building, with its own classrooms, student offices, and computer/GIS facilities. One of the most distinguishing characteristics of the School of Urban Affairs and Public Policy is the integration of theory and practice through applied research projects with the affiliated research and public service centers. Most full-time students are awarded research assistantships on projects in these centers.

The Center for Applied Demography and Survey Research provides demographic and survey data and information on important public issues to researchers and policy makers at all levels (http://www.cadsr.udel.edu). The Center for Community Research and Service helps public, nonprofit, and private organizations in Delaware to design, implement, and evaluate policies and programs that address the needs of low- and moderate-income families and communities related to economic development, housing, and social services. The center also focuses on issues that are vital to the physical and emotional well-being of the world's population. These questions concern the delivery and financing of health care and the outcomes of health care provided (http://www.udel.edu/CCRS). The Center for Historic Architecture and Design focuses on shaping historic preservation planning and policy, reconstructing historic landscapes, documenting threatened historic properties, and advocating for the preservation of historic resources (http://www.udel.edu/CHAD). The Institute for Public Administration links the resources of the University of Delaware (UD) with the management and policy information needs of public and nonprofit organizations (http://www.ipa.udel.edu).

Financial Aid

The School has competitive financial aid programs, including fellowships, research assistantships, and scholarships. Aid is awarded on merit and is limited by the various restrictions established by the sources of aid. Stipends for 2010–11 are $15,500 for the full academic year. Additional special assistantships, fellowships, and internships are available to students through the University Graduate Scholar's Program, for both newly admitted and graduate students currently enrolled. Awards are competitive and are based on many criteria, including challenging social, economic, educational, cultural, or other life circumstances; academic achievements; first generation graduate student status; and/or need as determined by federal income guidelines (FAFSA). Funds are also available through the Delaware Legislative Fellows Program.

Cost of Study

In 2010–11, tuition for full-time graduate students is $24,240 per academic year. Part-time students are charged on a per-credit basis. (The 2010–11 rate is $1347 per credit.) Full-time matriculated students are automatically assessed nonrefundable fees of $486 for health and $232 for student-sponsored activities.

Living and Housing Costs

The University provides some graduate apartments, and there is plenty of off-campus housing in the surrounding community in many price ranges. For more information, students should contact the Housing Assignment Services Office (302-831-2491; http://www.udel.edu/has).

Student Group

The School has 74 students in the M.P.A. program, 53 in the M.A. program, and 49 in the Ph.D. program.

Student Outcomes

Graduates find career positions in government and nonprofit organizations and occasionally in the private sector with consulting firms. With UD's proximity to Washington, D.C.; Philadelphia; and New York, many graduates pursue positions in nearby metropolitan areas, as well as positions in state and local government in the region and in the nation. Several recent graduates have been successful in the highly competitive federal Presidential Management Fellowship Program.

Location

Located midway between Philadelphia and Baltimore, the main campus of the University of Delaware is in Newark, conveniently near New York City; Washington, D.C.; and the seashore. A community of 30,000, with a vibrant Main Street of coffeehouses, restaurants, and small shops, Newark is about 14 miles from Wilmington, Delaware's largest city.

The University

The University is a comprehensive land-, sea-, space-, and urban-grant institution of higher education with an enrollment of 3,634 graduate students in 2009–10. The University offers seventy-nine programs leading to a master's degree and thirty-nine programs leading to a doctoral degree. In 2010, the University awarded 251 doctoral degrees and 727 master's degrees.

Applying

The School welcomes informal inquiries. Students seeking financial aid or admission to the Ph.D. program should apply by February 1. For the master's programs, candidates must have an undergraduate GPA above 3.0 (on a 4.0 scale). Admission to the Ph.D. program requires a master's degree with at least a 3.5 GPA. A combined GRE score above 1000 on the math and verbal portions of the exam is normally expected. Complete applications contain three letters of recommendation, a personal statement of academic and career objectives (for the Ph.D., a 1,000-word statement of the applicant's research interest as well), and academic transcripts. For nonnative speakers of English, a demonstrated proficiency in English is required, with a TOEFL score of at least 550 (213 on the computer-based test).

Correspondence and Information

School of Urban Affairs and Public Policy Admissions
University of Delaware
Newark, Delaware 19716-7310
Phone: 302-831-1687
Fax: 302-831-3296
E-mail: suapp@udel.edu
Web site: http://www.udel.edu/suapp

University of Delaware

THE FACULTY AND THEIR RESEARCH

At the core of the School of Urban Affairs and Public Policy are the dedicated faculty members, who are challenging teachers, seasoned researchers, and experienced practitioners. With interdisciplinary backgrounds as skilled executives, managers, and community leaders, they bring practical experience to the classroom and successfully blend a solid academic base with stimulating practical experience.

David L. Ames, Professor and Director, Center for Historic Architecture and Design; Ph.D., Clark, 1969; ACIP. Historic preservation, urban geography, urban and regional planning.
Maria P. Aristigueta, Professor; Director, School of Urban Affairs and Public Policy; and Senior Policy Fellow, Institute for Public Administration; D.P.A., USC, 1997. Administrative behavior, performance management, policy analysis, strategic management.
Deborah A. Auger, Associate Professor and Policy Fellow, Center for Community Research and Service; Ph.D., MIT, 1988. Public policy and administration, nonprofit management, state and local government, U.S. social policy.
Karen A. Curtis, Associate Professor and Policy Scientist, Center for Community Research and Service; Ph.D., Temple, 1984. Nonprofit leadership and management, applied research and public policy analysis, qualitative methods, social and economic opportunity.
Kathryn G. Denhardt, Professor and Policy Scientist, Center for Community Research and Service; Ph.D., Kansas, 1984. Collaborative decision making and conflict resolution, human resources management, ethics in public service.
Robert B. Denhardt, Visiting Scholar; Ph.D., Kentucky, 1968. Public sector management, strategic planning and public productivity.
Bernard L. Dworsky, Assistant Professor and Policy Scientist, Institute for Public Administration; M.A., Delaware, 1971. Water resources management, planning.
James P. Flynn, Assistant Professor; Director, M.P.A. Program; and Associate Policy Scientist, Institute for Public Administration; Ed.D., Delaware, 1998. Personnel administration, quality improvement initiatives, educational governance, legislative management, professional development, human resources management.
Edward J. Freel, Instructor and Policy Scientist, Institute for Public Administration; M.Ed., Delaware, 1975. Civic education, learning initiatives, public administration.
Audrey L. Helfman, Associate Professor and Interim Director, Leadership Program; Ph.D., Delaware, 1993. Personnel administration, organizational theory, legislative management, public fiscal analysis, data systems, analytic methods.
Raheemah Jabbar-Bey, Assistant Professor and Assistant Policy Specialist, Center for Community Research and Service; M.A., New Hampshire, 1996. Community and economic development planning, organizational capacity building of nonprofits, urban policy analysis.
Eric D. Jacobson, Associate Professor and Assistant Director, Institute for Public Administration; M.P.A., Delaware, 1981. Public economics, health policy, employee compensation and benefits, tourism development and research, analytical methods.
Janet B. Johnson, Associate Professor, Department of Political Science and International Relations and Senior Research Associate, Center for Energy and Environmental Policy; Ph.D., Cornell, 1978. Subnational politics, environmental policy, research methods, public policy analysis.
Jonathan Justice, Associate Professor; Ph.D., Rutgers, 2003. Public financial management, nongovernmental public administration, urban policy and administration.
Gerald Kauffman, Instructor and Director, Water Resources Agency; M.P.A., Delaware, 2003. Watershed policy, planning, and management; water resources government and finance; water resources engineering; hydrology and hydraulics.
Jerome R. Lewis, Associate Professor and Director, Institute for Public Administration; Ph.D., NYU, 1968. Public administration, personnel management, urban planning, political leadership.
John G. McNutt, Professor and Policy Fellow, Center for Community Research and Service; Ph.D., Tennessee, 1991. Technology, nonprofit management, advocacy and government relations, community organization and planning.
Anthony E. Middlebrooks, Associate Professor; Ph.D., Wisconsin, 1999. Leadership formation and development, creativity and leadership, service and social justice, research methods.
James L. Morrison, Professor; Ed.D., Temple, 1971. Telecommunications and consumer policy, consumer environmental issues, consumer protection.
Audrey J. Noble, Assistant Professor and Director, Public Policy Program; Ph.D., Arizona State, 1994. Qualitative research and evaluation.
Edward J. O'Donnell, Instructor and Senior Policy Advisor, Institute for Public Administration; M.Ed., West Chester, 1975. Growth management, transportation/infrastructure planning, comprehensive planning.
Marian Lief Palley, Professor, Department of Political Science and International Relations; Ph.D., NYU, 1966. American politics and public policy, intergovernmental relations, health and welfare policy.
Steven W. Peuquet, Associate Professor and Director, Center for Community Research and Service; Ph.D., Pennsylvania, 1996. Strategic planning, housing, homelessness, electronic community networks, public policy analysis and evaluation.
Jeffrey A. Raffel, Charles P. Messick Professor of Public Administration and Faculty Associate, Institute for Public Administration; Ph.D., MIT, 1972. Educational policy, policy analysis, urban management.
Edward C. Ratledge, Associate Professor and Director, Center for Applied Demography and Survey Research; M.A., Delaware, 1972. Management information systems, econometrics, criminal justice systems.
Daniel Rich, Professor; Ph.D., MIT, 1972. Public policy and public management.
Breck Robinson, Associate Professor and Associate Professor, Institute for Public Administration; Ph.D., Tennessee, 1994. Financial institutions, public policy, real estate finance.
Rebecca Sheppard, Assistant Professor and Associate Director, Center of Historic Architecture and Design; Ph.D. Delaware, 2009. Historic preservation planning, history of rural landscapes and the built environment, landscape preservation.
Paul L. Solano, Associate Professor; Ph.D., Maryland, 1978. Financial administration and public finance, political economy, health economics.
Karen F. Stein, Associate Professor; Ph.D., Delaware, 1984. Domestic elder abuse and neglect, leadership studies, consumer and family economic policy analysis.
Richard T. Sylves, Professor, Department of Political Science and International Relations, and Fellow, Center for Energy and Environmental Policy; Ph.D., Illinois at Urbana-Champaign, 1977. Energy policy, disaster policy.
Douglas F. Tuttle, Instructor; Internship Coordinator; and Policy Scientist, Institute for Public Administration; M.P.A., Delaware, 1990. State and local government personnel development, strategic planning, emergency service planning and public service quality assessment.
Leland Ware, Louis L. Redding Chair for the Study of Law and Public Policy; J.D., Boston College, 1973. Employment discrimination law, civil rights law, civil procedure.
Robert Warren, Professor and Senior Research Associate, Institute for Public Administration; Ph.D., UCLA, 1964. Urban and regional government, telecommunications policy, urban planning and development, cultural theory.
Margaret G. Wilder, Professor; Ph.D., Michigan, 1983. Community development policy and organizations; economic development policy and planning; housing problems and policy; race, gender, and economic mobility.
Devona E. G. Williams, Assistant Professor; Ph.D., Delaware, 1992. Entrepreneurship, small business growth and development, women in leadership, community development.
Danilo Yanich, Associate Professor; Director, Urban Affairs and Public Policy Program; and Associate Policy Scientist, Center for Community Research and Service; Ph.D., Delaware, 1980. Criminal justice policy, media and public policy, international comparative governance.

UNIVERSITY OF PENNSYLVANIA

Fels Institute of Government
Master of Governmental Administration Program

Programs of Study

Penn's Fels Institute of Government is proud to educate students who have a commitment to public service and help them prepare to provide results-oriented leadership to public and nonprofit organizations.

Fels offers a Master of Governmental Administration (M.G.A.) that is comparable to a Master of Public Administration. It also offers five-course graduate-level certificates in economic development and growth, nonprofit administration, politics, and public finance. The certificates can be obtained either as a concentration within the M.G.A. or as a stand-alone diploma.

The twelve-course M.G.A. is offered in full-time and part-time formats and consists of eight core courses (required) and four elective courses. Full-time students take the eight core courses during the week, part-time students take the eight core courses on Saturdays, and students in both formats commingle for their four electives, which are available on weekdays, weeknights, and Saturdays.

Students have the option of taking their elective courses at Fels or other graduate programs within the University of Pennsylvania. Students can also seek approval to transfer, as electives, up to four courses taken in graduate programs outside of Penn before, during, or after their time in the M.G.A. program. In addition to the certificates, Fels students often create informal concentrations (for example, city planning, education policy, environmental studies, transportation) through careful selection of their courses. Other students cover a broader range of subject matter in their electives.

The standard full-time course sequence includes three courses per semester for two academic years with summers off for internships, although some students accelerate the program by taking four courses per semester to finish in a year and a half. Part-time students typically take two courses per semester while working full-time and complete the program in two calendar years, including summers. Some executive students, however, reduce their course load in certain semesters in order to balance the program with their other responsibilities.

Fels offers the possibility of earning dual graduate degrees in the following areas: the M.G.A./J.D. with Penn Law School, the M.G.A./ M.S.Ed. with the Graduate School of Education, the M.G.A./M.S.W. or M.G.A/M.S.S.P. with the School of Social Policy and Practice, the M.G.A./M.C.P. with City Planning Program/School of Design, the M.G.A./M.B.E. with the Bioethics Program, the M.G.A./M.E.S. with the Environmental Studies Program, and the M.G.A./M.S.E. with the School of Engineering. Dual-degree students are granted some flexibility in their course sequencing as needed.

The certificate programs consist of a mix of core and elective courses. Certifcates in economic development and growth, and public finance also have an additional microeconomics prerequisite. Students may take one elective at another graduate school at Penn.

Research Facilities

The Fels Institute occupies the home of the late industrialist and philanthropist, Samuel S. Fels. Built in 1937, the Fels residence has been adapted for academic use in a way that maintains its original character. Fels offers wireless computer access and is equipped with two small computer labs that provide online access to a range of information resources, including the extensive electronic holdings of the Penn library. In addition, Fels students have access to the vast resources offered by the University of Pennsylvania.

Financial Aid

Students in the M.G.A. program rely upon a combination of funding sources to finance their education at Fels. Merit-based scholarships are provided to full-time and part-time students with an average award representing 25 percent of tuition. Additional support comes from Federal Stafford Student Loans, Federal Perkins Loans, and University work-study opportunities. Most full-time students also seek out part-time internships or jobs that pay from $10 to $20 per hour.

Cost of Study

The 2010–11 cost per course for tuition and fees is $5028. Students are billed each semester based on the number of classes they are taking. Students must carry health insurance, which they can purchase through the University for $2632 per year.

Living and Housing Costs

Housing is readily available near campus as well as elsewhere in the city. The cost of living in Philadelphia tends to be lower than other major U.S. cities, and many graduate students live off campus. Housing is available at widely varying rates depending on location and size, from about $500 per month to share an apartment or house with roommates to $800 or more for studio/one-bedroom apartments.

Student Group

The Fels Institute enrolls approximately 130 students who are evenly split between the full-time and part-time formats. Fels students represent a full range of diversity by age, race, gender, politics, nationality, and geography. Most full-time students bring at least two years of full-time work experience on campaigns, in government, and for nonprofits. Some have served in national service programs such as Teach for America, Peace Corps, and AmeriCorps, or have spent time in the private sector. International students comprise approximately 20 percent of the class and include Fulbright fellows, Thouron fellows, and seasoned government employees. A few students with excellent internship and volunteer experience are accepted directly after completing their bachelor's degree. Part-time students bring slightly more professional experience—generally five to seven years or more—and most work full-time while studying at Fels.

Student Outcomes

In 2009, 50 percent of graduates were employed in government/politics, 30 percent in the nonprofit sector, and 20 percent in the private sector, with an emphasis on firms that service the public sector. Fels alumni work across the public spectrum in political jobs as elected officials and campaign managers; public finance positions in government, bond-rating agencies, and investment banks; and leadership positions at all levels of government, in more than 100 nonprofit organizations, and at management consulting, lobbying, and political consulting firms.

Location

The Fels Institute is located just west of Center City Philadelphia, in the northwest corner of the Penn campus at the intersection of Walnut and 39th Streets. Fels is a short walk to trolley, subway, and intercity train lines that provide easy access to downtown; the airport; the New Jersey shore; Harrisburg; Washington, D.C.; New York City; and the rest of the Northeast corridor.

The University

A member of the Ivy League and one of the world's leading universities, Penn is renowned for its graduate schools, faculty, research centers, and institutes. Conveniently situated on a beautiful urban campus, Penn offers an abundance of multidisciplinary and cross-school educational programs with exceptional opportunities for individually tailored graduate education. It also offers students all the amenities of a 20,000 student university.

Applying

Inquiries should be made directly to the Fels Institute. Full-time students are admitted primarily for the fall semester, with a few students admitted for the spring semester if space permits. In order to receive full financial aid consideration, full-time applicants should apply by January 15. Executive students are admitted each term and should apply by July 1 for the fall term; by November 1 for the spring term; and by March 1 for the summer term.

Correspondence and Information

Admissions Office
Fels Institute of Government
University of Pennsylvania
3814 Walnut Street
Philadelphia, Pennsylvania 19104-6197
Phone: 215-746-6684
Fax: 215-898-6238
E-mail: felsinstitute@sas.upenn.edu
Web site: http://www.fels.upenn.edu

University of Pennsylvania

THE FACULTY

David Thornburgh, Executive Director, Fels Institute of Government.
Leigh Botwinik, Director of Graduate Education, Fels Institute of Government.
Allison Brummel, Director of Research and Consulting, Fels Institute of Government.
Peter A. Angelides, Vice President and Director, Econsult Corporation.
Arthur C. Benedict, Principal, Benedict Associates.
Concetta Anne Bencivenga, Chief Financial Officer and Vice President of Finance, Please Touch Museum.
John DiIulio, Frederic Fox Leadership Professor and Faculty Director and Co-Chair of the Director's Advisory Group, Robert A. Fox Leadership Program, University of Pennsylvania.
E. Michael Golda, Chief Technologist, Machinery Research and Engineering Department, Naval Sea Systems Command Carderock Division, Philadelphia.
Tine Hansen-Turton, Executive Director, National Nursing Centers Consortium.
James E. Hartling, Founding Partner, Urban Partners.
John Hawkins, Senior Lobbyist, S. R. Wojdak & Associates.
James F. Kenney, Councilman at Large, City of Philadelphia.
John Kromer, Fels Senior Consultant, former Director of the Office of Housing and Community Development, City of Philadelphia.
Janice F. Madden, Professor of Regional Science, Sociology, Urban Studies, and Real Estate, University of Pennsylvania.
Marjorie Margolies, Fels Senior Fellow and CEO, Women's Campaign International; former member of Congress.
Deirdre Martinez, Director, Fels Public Policy Internship Program.
Brett H. Mandel, Executive Director, National Education Technology Funding Corp.
Brett Matteo, Partner and Managing Director, Public Financial Management, Inc.
Stephanie Maurer, Deputy Auditor General for Performance Audits, Pennsylvania Department of the Auditor General.
John J. Mulhern, Fels Senior Fellow, Adjunct Associate Professor of Classical Studies and Government Administration.
Stephen P. Mullin, Senior Vice President and Principal, Econsult Corporation.
Michael Nadol, Managing Director, Public Financial Management.
Jack H. Nagel, Associate Dean for Graduate Studies, School of Arts and Sciences.
Eric C. Neiderman, Product Manager for Inspection Technologies, Transportation Security Administration.
Robert A. Nixon, Lobbyist and Public Affairs Adviser, Princeton Public Affairs Group.
Leroy D. Nunery, Deputy Superintendent, School District of Philadelphia.
Folasade Olanipekun-Lewis, Deputy Director for Finance and Administration, Commerce Department, City of Philadelphia.
Robert W. Pearson, Senior Fellow, Fels Institute of Government.
Gerald L. Perrins, Regional Economist, U.S. Bureau of Labor Statistics.
Hon. Edward G. Rendell, Governor of the Commonwealth of Pennsylvania.
Ramin Sedehi, Vice Dean, School of Arts and Sciences, University of Pennsylvania.
Wayne A. Smith, President and CEO, Delaware Healthcare Association; former House Majority Leader, Delaware General Assembly.
Nicholas D. Torres, President of Congreso de Latinos Unidos.
Daniel Velazquez-Nunez, Manager, Deloitte & Touche.
Eric J. Weinberg, Chief Operating Officer, Guggenheim Venture Partners.

Section 26
Social Sciences

This section contains a directory of institutions offering graduate work in social sciences. Additional information about programs listed in the directory but not augmented by an in-depth entry may be obtained by writing directly to the dean of a graduate school or chair of a department at the address given in the directory.

For programs offering related work, see also in this book *Area and Cultural Studies, Communication and Media, Criminology and Forensics, Economics, Geography, Family and Consumer Sciences, Political Science and International Affairs, Psychology and Counseling,* and *Sociology, Anthropology, and Archaeology.*

CONTENTS

Program Directory

Social Sciences 1198

Social Sciences

Arizona State University, Graduate College, College of Liberal Arts and Sciences, Division of Social Sciences, Tempe, AZ 85287. Offers MA, MAS, MS, PhD, PhD/JD.

Arkansas Tech University, Graduate College, College of Arts and Humanities, Russellville, AR 72801. Offers communication (MLA); English (M Ed, MA); fine arts (MLA); history (MA); multi-media journalism (MA); psychology (MS); social science (MLA); Spanish (MA, MLA); teaching English as a second language (MA, MLA). Part-time programs available. *Students:* 39 full-time (30 women), 80 part-time (63 women); includes 11 minority (3 African Americans, 1 American Indian/Alaska Native, 1 Asian American or Pacific Islander, 6 Hispanic Americans), 23 international. Average age 33. In 2009, 70 master's awarded. *Degree requirements:* For master's, comprehensive exam (for some programs), thesis (for some programs), project. *Entrance requirements:* For master's, GRE General Test or MAT. Additional exam requirements/recommendations for international students: Required—TOEFL (minimum score 550 paper-based; 213 computer-based; 79 iBT), IELTS (minimum score 6). *Application deadline:* For fall admission, 3/1 priority date for domestic students, 5/1 priority date for international students; for spring admission, 10/1 priority date for domestic and international students. Applications are processed on a rolling basis. Application fee: $0 ($50 for international students). Electronic applications accepted. *Expenses:* Tuition, state resident: full-time $3438; part-time $191 per hour. Tuition, nonresident: full-time $6876; part-time $382 per hour. Required fees: $482; $9 per credit hour. $140 per semester. Tuition and fees vary according to course load. *Financial support:* In 2009–10, teaching assistantships with full tuition reimbursements (averaging $4,000 per year); research assistantships, career-related internships or fieldwork, Federal Work-Study, scholarships/grants, health care benefits, and unspecified assistantships also available. Support available to part-time students. Financial award application deadline: 4/15; financial award applicants required to submit FAFSA. *Unit head:* Dr. Micheal Tarver, Dean, 479-968-0274, Fax: 479-964-0812, E-mail: mtarver@atu.edu. *Application contact:* Dr. Mary B. Gunter, Dean of Graduate College, 479-968-0398, Fax: 479-964-0542, E-mail: graduate.school@atu.edu.

Ball State University, Graduate School, College of Sciences and Humanities, Program in Social Sciences, Muncie, IN 47306-1099. Offers MA.

California Institute of Technology, Division of the Humanities and Social Sciences, Social Science Program, Pasadena, CA 91125-0001. Offers MS, PhD. Terminal master's awarded for partial completion of doctoral program. *Degree requirements:* For doctorate, thesis/dissertation. *Entrance requirements:* For doctorate, GRE General Test. Additional exam requirements/recommendations for international students: Required—TOEFL (minimum score 600 paper-based; 250 computer-based); Recommended—TWE. Electronic applications accepted. *Faculty research:* Individual and group decision making, experimental social science, political science, quantitative history, behavioral economics and neuroscience.

California State University, Chico, Graduate School, College of Behavioral and Social Sciences, Social Science Program, Chico, CA 95929-0722. Offers social science (MA); social science education (MA). *Students:* 8 full-time (6 women), 12 part-time (8 women); includes 4 minority (1 Asian American or Pacific Islander, 3 Hispanic Americans), 1 international. Average age 34. 16 applicants, 88% accepted, 7 enrolled. In 2009, 4 master's awarded. *Degree requirements:* For master's, thesis or alternative. *Entrance requirements:* For master's, GRE General Test or MAT. Additional exam requirements/recommendations for international students: Required—TOEFL (minimum score 550 paper-based; 213 computer-based; 80 iBT), IELTS (minimum score 6.5). *Application deadline:* For fall admission, 3/1 priority date for domestic students, 3/1 for international students; for spring admission, 9/15 priority date for domestic students, 9/15 for international students. Applications are processed on a rolling basis. Application fee: $55. Electronic applications accepted. *Financial support:* Fellowships, teaching assistantships available. *Unit head:* Dr. Gwen Sheldon, Graduate Coordinator, 530-895-5204. *Application contact:* School of Graduate, International, and Interdisciplinary Studies, 530-898-6880, Fax: 530-898-6889, E-mail: grin@csuchico.edu.

California State University, San Bernardino, Graduate Studies, College of Social and Behavioral Sciences, Program in Social Sciences, San Bernardino, CA 92407-2397. Offers MA. *Faculty:* 10 full-time (3 women), 3 part-time/adjunct (0 women). *Students:* 35 full-time (24 women), 26 part-time (17 women); includes 30 minority (14 African Americans, 16 Hispanic Americans), 2 international. Average age 33. 47 applicants, 64% accepted, 21 enrolled. In 2009, 5 master's awarded. *Degree requirements:* For master's, comprehensive exam or thesis. *Entrance requirements:* For master's, writing exam, minimum GPA of 3.5 in major, 2.5 overall. *Application deadline:* For fall admission, 8/31 priority date for domestic students. Application fee: $55. *Financial support:* Fellowships, research assistantships, teaching assistantships, career-related internships or fieldwork, Federal Work-Study, and institutionally sponsored loans available. Financial award application deadline: 5/1. *Unit head:* Dr. Jamal Nassar, Dean, 909-537-7500, Fax: 909-537-7645, E-mail: jnassar@csusb.edu. *Application contact:* Olivia Rosas, Director of Admissions, 909-537-7577, Fax: 909-537-7034, E-mail: orosas@csusb.edu.

California University of Pennsylvania, School of Graduate Studies and Research, College of Liberal Arts, Department of Sociology/Criminal Justice, California, PA 15419-1394. Offers social science—criminal justice (MA). Part-time and evening/weekend programs available. *Degree requirements:* For master's, comprehensive exam, thesis optional. *Entrance requirements:* For master's, MAT, minimum GPA of 3.0. Additional exam requirements/recommendations for international students: Required—TOEFL (minimum score 550 paper-based; 213 computer-based; 80 iBT). Electronic applications accepted. *Faculty research:* Ethics and law, ethics in police practice, law and morality, police policy, St. Thomas Aquinas and crime.

Campbellsville University, College of Arts and Sciences, Campbellsville, KY 42718-2799. Offers social science (MA). Part-time programs available. *Degree requirements:* For master's, comprehensive exam. *Entrance requirements:* For master's, GRE General Test, LSAT, minimum GPA of 2.9. Electronic applications accepted. *Expenses:* Tuition: Full-time $6750; part-time $375 per credit hour.

Carnegie Mellon University, College of Humanities and Social Sciences, Department of Social and Decision Sciences, Pittsburgh, PA 15213-3891. Offers behavioral decision research (PhD); behavioral decision research and psychology (PhD); social and decision science (PhD); strategy, entrepreneurship, and technological change (PhD). Terminal master's awarded for partial completion of doctoral program. *Degree requirements:* For doctorate, comprehensive exam, thesis/dissertation, research paper. *Entrance requirements:* For doctorate, GRE General Test. Additional exam requirements/recommendations for international students: Required—TOEFL. Electronic applications accepted. *Faculty research:* Organization theory, political science, sociology, technology studies.

Central European University, Graduate Studies, School of Social Sciences and Humanities, Budapest, Hungary. Offers economics (MA, PhD); gender studies (MA, PhD); international relations and European studies (MA, PhD); mathematics and its applications (MS, PhD); medieval studies (MA, PhD); nationalism studies (MA, PhD); philosophy (MA, PhD); political science (MA, PhD); public policy (MA, PhD); sociology and social anthropology (MA, PhD). Terminal master's awarded for partial completion of doctoral program. *Degree requirements:* For master's, one foreign language, thesis; for doctorate, one foreign language, comprehensive exam, thesis/dissertation. *Entrance requirements:* For master's, interview; for doctorate, GRE, CEU subject test, interview. Additional exam requirements/recommendations for international students: Required—TOEFL (minimum score 570 paper-based; 230 computer-based). Electronic applications accepted. *Faculty research:* Civil society, fiscal decentralization, party politics, political philosophy (especially Liberalism, theory of Democracy).

The Citadel, The Military College of South Carolina, Citadel Graduate College, Department of Political Science and Criminal Justice, Charleston, SC 29409. Offers social science (MA). Part-time and evening/weekend programs available. *Faculty:* 3 full-time (1 woman). *Students:* 4 full-time (3 women), 20 part-time (7 women); includes 4 minority (3 African Americans, 1 Hispanic American), 1 international. Average age 32. In 2009, 8 master's awarded. *Entrance requirements:* For master's, GRE (minimum score 900) or MAT (minimum score 396). Additional exam requirements/recommendations for international students: Required—TOEFL (minimum score 550 paper-based; 213 computer-based). *Application deadline:* Applications are processed on a rolling basis. Application fee: $30. Electronic applications accepted. *Expenses:* Tuition, state resident: part-time $400 per credit hour. Tuition, nonresident: part-time $657 per credit hour. Required fees: $40 per term. *Financial support:* Health care benefits and unspecified assistantships available. Support available to part-time students. Financial award application deadline: 7/1; financial award applicants required to submit FAFSA. *Unit head:* Dr. Gardel M. Feurtado, Department Head, 843-953-2037, Fax: 843-953-5066, E-mail: gardel.feurtado@citadel.edu. *Application contact:* Dr. Terry M. Mays, Associate Professor, 843-953-5069, Fax: 843-953-5069, E-mail: terry.mays@citadel.edu.

Clemson University, Graduate School, Program in International Family and Community Studies, Clemson, SC 29634. Offers PhD. *Faculty:* 6 full-time (3 women), 3 part-time/adjunct (all women). *Students:* 15 full-time (14 women), 2 part-time (1 woman); includes 2 minority (1 African American, 1 Asian American or Pacific Islander), 8 international. Average age 32. 4 applicants, 50% accepted, 2 enrolled. *Degree requirements:* For doctorate, thesis/dissertation. *Entrance requirements:* For doctorate, GRE General Test. Additional exam requirements/recommendations for international students: Required—TOEFL. *Application deadline:* Applications are processed on a rolling basis. Application fee: $70 ($80 for international students). Electronic applications accepted. *Expenses:* Contact institution. *Financial support:* In 2009–10, 14 students received support, including 3 fellowships with full and partial tuition reimbursements available (averaging $15,000 per year), 14 research assistantships with partial tuition reimbursements available (averaging $19,677 per year); career-related internships or fieldwork, institutionally sponsored loans, scholarships/grants, health care benefits, and unspecified assistantships also available. Support available to part-time students. Total annual research expenditures: $3.2 million. *Unit head:* Dr. Gary B. Melton, Director, 964-656-6271. *Application contact:* Information Contact, 861-656-3195, E-mail: gradapp@clemson.edu.

College of the Humanities and the Sciences, Harrison Middleton University, Graduate Program, Tempe, AZ 85282. Offers education (MA, Ed D); humanities (MA); imaginative literature (MA); interdisciplinary studies (DA); jurisprudence (MA); natural science (MA); philosophy and religion (MA); social science (MA). Part-time and evening/weekend programs available. Post-baccalaureate distance learning degree programs offered (no on-campus study). *Faculty:* 17 full-time (7 women), 14 part-time/adjunct (6 women). *Students:* 49 full-time (18 women). In 2009, 4 master's awarded. *Application deadline:* Applications are processed on a rolling basis. Application fee: $50. Electronic applications accepted. *Application contact:* Deborah Deacon, Dean of Graduate Studies, 877-248-6724, Fax: 800-762-1622, E-mail: ddeacon@chumsci.edu.

Columbia University, Graduate School of Arts and Sciences, Program in Quantitative Methods in the Social Sciences, New York, NY 10027. Offers MA. Part-time programs available.

Eastern Michigan University, Graduate School, College of Arts and Sciences, Department of History and Philosophy, Programs in Social Sciences, Ypsilanti, MI 48197. Offers social science (MA, Graduate Certificate); social science and American culture (MLS). Part-time and evening/weekend programs available. Postbaccalaureate distance learning degree programs offered (minimal on-campus study). *Students:* 7 full-time (3 women), 23 part-time (14 women); includes 2 minority (1 African American, 1 Asian American or Pacific Islander), 2 international. Average age 32. In 2009, 10 master's awarded. *Degree requirements:* For master's, thesis optional. *Entrance requirements:* Additional exam requirements/recommendations for international students: Required—TOEFL. *Application deadline:* Applications are processed on a rolling basis. Application fee: $35. Tuition and fees vary according to course level. *Financial support:* Fellowships, research assistantships with full tuition reimbursements, teaching assistantships with full tuition reimbursements, career-related internships or fieldwork, Federal Work-Study, institutionally sponsored loans, scholarships/grants, tuition waivers (partial), and unspecified assistantships available. Support available to part-time students. Financial award applicants required to submit FAFSA. *Application contact:* Dr. Ronald Delph, Coordinator, 734-487-0053, Fax: 734-487-6835, E-mail: rdelph@emich.edu.

Edinboro University of Pennsylvania, School of Graduate Studies and Research, School of Liberal Arts, Department of History and Anthropology, Edinboro, PA 16444. Offers social sciences (MA). Part-time and evening/weekend programs available. *Faculty:* 6 full-time (3 women). *Students:* 24 full-time (9 women), 10 part-time (3 women); includes 4 minority (3 African Americans, 1 Hispanic American). Average age 33. In 2009, 2 master's awarded. *Degree requirements:* For master's, thesis or alternative, competency exam. *Entrance requirements:* For master's, GRE or MAT, minimum QPA of 2.5. *Application deadline:* Applications are processed on a rolling basis. Application fee: $30. Electronic applications accepted. *Expenses:* Tuition, state resident: full-time $6666; part-time $370 per credit. Tuition, nonresident: full-time $10,666; part-time $593 per credit. Required fees: $2206.28. One-time fee: $204 part-time. *Financial support:* In 2009–10, 10 research assistantships with full and partial tuition reimbursements (averaging $4,050 per year) were awarded; career-related internships or fieldwork, Federal Work-Study, institutionally sponsored loans, scholarships/grants, and unspecified assistantships also available. Support available to part-time students. Financial award application deadline: 2/15; financial award applicants required to submit FAFSA. *Unit head:* Dr. Jerra Jenrette, Chairperson, 814-732-1225, E-mail: jjenrette@edinboro.edu. *Application contact:* Dr. R. Scott Baldwin, Dean, 814-732-2752, Fax: 814-732-2268, E-mail: sbaldwin@edinboro.edu.

Florida Agricultural and Mechanical University, Division of Graduate Studies, Research, and Continuing Education, College of Arts and Sciences, Division of History and Political Sciences, Program in Applied Social Science, Tallahassee, FL 32307-3200. Offers African American history (MASS); criminal justice (MASS); economics (MASS); history (MASS); political science (MASS); public administration (MASS); public management (MASS); social work (MASS); sociology (MASS). Part-time programs available. *Faculty:* 17 full-time (2 women). *Students:* 54 full-time (42 women), 4 part-time (2 women); includes 57 minority (all African Americans). In 2009, 14 master's awarded. *Degree requirements:* For master's, thesis optional. *Entrance requirements:* For master's, GRE General Test, minimum GPA of 3.0. *Application deadline:* For fall admission, 5/18 for domestic students, 12/18 for international students; for spring admission, 11/12 for domestic students, 5/12 for international students. Application fee: $20. *Financial support:* Fellowships, research assistantships, career-related internships or fieldwork, Federal Work-Study, and tuition waivers (full) available. Financial award application deadline: 4/1. *Faculty research:* Southern history, black history, election trends, presidential history. *Unit head:* Dr. Gary Paul, Director, 850-599-3447. *Application contact:* Dr. Chanta M. Haywood, Dean of Graduate Studies, Research, and Continuing Education, 850-599-3315, Fax: 850-599-3727.

George Mason University, College of Science, Fairfax, VA 22030. Offers biodefense (MS, PhD); bioinformatics and computational biology (MS, PhD, Certificate); biology (MS, PhD), including bioinformatics (MS), ecology, systematics and evolution (MS), interpretive biology (MS), molecular and cellular biology (MS), molecular and microbiology (PhD), organismal biology (MS); chemistry and biochemistry (MS), including chemistry; climate dynamics (PhD); computational and data sciences (MS, PhD, Certificate); computational social science (PhD); computational techniques and applications (Certificate); earth systems and geoinformation sciences (MS, PhD, Certificate); environmental science and policy (MS, PhD); geography (MS), including geographic and cartographic sciences; mathematical sciences (MS, PhD), including mathematics; nanotechnology and nanoscience (Certificate); neuroscience (PhD); physical sciences (PhD); physics and astronomy (MS), including applied and engineering physics; remote sensing and earth image processing (Certificate). Part-time and evening/weekend programs available. *Degree requirements:* For doctorate, comprehensive exam, thesis/dissertation. *Entrance requirements:* For master's and doctorate, GRE General Test, minimum GPA of 3.0 in last 60 hours. Additional exam requirements/recommendations for international students: Required—TOEFL. Electronic applications accepted. *Expenses:* Tuition, state resident: full-time $7568; part-time $315.33 per credit hour. Tuition, nonresident: full-time $21,704; part-time $904.33 per credit hour. Required fees: $2184; $91 per credit hour. *Faculty research:* Space sciences and astrophysics, fluid dynamics, materials modeling and simulation, bioinformatics, global changes and statistics.

Graduate Theological Union, Graduate Programs, Berkeley, CA 94709-1212. Offers art and religion (MA, PhD, Th D); biblical languages (MA); Biblical studies (PhD, Th D); biblical studies (MA); Buddhist studies (MA); Christian spirituality (MA, PhD, Th D); cultural and historical studies of religions (MA, PhD, Th D); ethics and social theory (PhD, Th D); history (MA, PhD, Th D); homiletics (MA, PhD, Th D); interdisciplinary studies (PhD, Th D); Jewish studies (MA, PhD, Th D, Certificate); liturgical studies (MA, PhD, Th D); Near Eastern religions (PhD, Th D); Orthodox Christian studies (MA); religion and psychology (MA, PhD, Th D); religion and society/ethics and social theory (MA); systematic and philosophical theology (MA, PhD, Th D). *Accreditation:* ATS. Terminal master's awarded for partial completion of doctoral program. *Degree requirements:* For master's, one foreign language, thesis; for doctorate, one foreign language, comprehensive exam, thesis/dissertation. *Entrance requirements:* For master's, GRE General Test; for doctorate, GRE General Test, MA or M Div. Additional exam requirements/recommendations for international students: Required—TOEFL. Electronic applications accepted.

Hollins University, Graduate Programs, Program in Liberal Studies, Roanoke, VA 24020-1603. Offers humanities (MALS); interdisciplinary studies (MALS); justice and legal studies (MALS); liberal studies (CAS); social science (MALS); visual and performing arts (MALS). Part-time and evening/weekend programs available. *Faculty:* 7 full-time (1 woman), 4 part-time/adjunct (2 women). *Students:* 23 full-time (22 women), 73 part-time (57 women); includes 15 minority (13 African Americans, 2 Asian Americans or Pacific Islanders), 4 international. Average age 39. 31 applicants, 94% accepted, 25 enrolled. In 2009, 30 master's awarded. *Degree requirements:* For master's, thesis. *Entrance requirements:* For master's, letters of recommendation, interview. Additional exam requirements/recommendations for international students: Required—TOEFL (minimum score 550 paper-based; 213 computer-based; 79 iBT). *Application deadline:* For fall admission, 7/1 priority date for domestic and international students; for spring admission, 12/10 priority date for domestic and international students. Applications are processed on a rolling basis. Application fee: $40. Electronic applications accepted. *Expenses:* Tuition: Full-time $27,780; part-time $295 per contact hour. Required fees: $280; $70 per unit. Part-time tuition and fees vary according to course load and program. *Financial support:* In 2009–10, 31 students received support, including 2 fellowships (averaging $902 per year); Federal Work-Study and scholarships/grants also available. Support available to part-time students. Financial award application deadline: 7/15; financial award applicants required to submit FAFSA. *Faculty research:* Elderly blacks, film, feminist economics, US voting patterns, Wagner, diversity. *Unit head:* Dr. Edward A. Lynch, Director, 540-362-6475, Fax: 540-362-6288, E-mail: elynch@hollins.edu. *Application contact:* Cathy S. Koon, Manager of Graduate Services, 540-362-6326, Fax: 540-362-6288, E-mail: ckoon@hollins.edu.

Humboldt State University, Graduate Studies, College of Arts, Humanities, and Social Sciences, Program in Environment and Community, Arcata, CA 95521-8299. Offers MA. *Students:* 26 full-time (22 women), 5 part-time (3 women); includes 3 minority (1 American Indian/Alaska Native, 1 Asian American or Pacific Islander, 1 Hispanic American). Average age 33. 53 applicants, 51% accepted, 16 enrolled. In 2009, 6 master's awarded. *Degree requirements:* For master's, thesis or alternative, qualifying exam. *Entrance requirements:* For master's, minimum GPA of 2.5, 3 letters of recommendation. Additional exam requirements/recommendations for international students: Required—TOEFL (minimum score 500 paper-based; 173 computer-based). *Application deadline:* For fall admission, 3/15 for domestic and international students. Applications are processed on a rolling basis. Application fee: $55. *Expenses:* Tuition, nonresident: full-time $8928. Required fees: $6102. Tuition and fees vary according to program. *Financial support:* Application deadline: 3/1. *Faculty research:* Geography, political science, ethnic studies, anthropology, economics. *Unit head:* Dr. John Meyer, Chair, 707-826-4494, Fax: 707-826-4496, E-mail: jmm7001@humboldt.edu. *Application contact:* Dr. Mark Baker, Coordinator, 717-826-3907, Fax: 717-826-4496, E-mail: jb141@humboldt.edu.

Indiana University Bloomington, Maurer School of Law, Bloomington, IN 47405-7000. Offers comparative law (MCL); juridical science (SJD); law (JD, LL M); law and social sciences (PhD); legal studies (Certificate); JD/MA; JD/MBA; JD/MLS; JD/MPA; JD/MS; JD/MSES. PhD offered through University Graduate School. *Accreditation:* ABA. *Faculty:* 72 full-time (28 women), 14 part-time/adjunct (4 women). *Students:* 675 full-time (274 women), 42 part-time (16 women); includes 103 minority (45 African Americans, 32 Asian Americans or Pacific Islanders, 26 Hispanic Americans), 110 international. Average age 27. 1,273 applicants, 73% accepted, 209 enrolled. In 2009, 198 first professional degrees, 66 master's, 10 doctorates, 2 other advanced degrees awarded. *Degree requirements:* For master's, thesis or practicum; for doctorate, thesis/dissertation (for some programs); for JD, research seminar. *Entrance requirements:* For JD, LSAT; for master's, LSAT, 3 letters of recommendation, law degree or license to practice; for doctorate, LSAT, 3 letters of recommendation, LL M or JD. Additional exam requirements/recommendations for international students: Required—TOEFL (minimum score 560 paper-based; 213 computer-based; 80 iBT). *Application deadline:* For fall admission, 3/1 priority date for domestic and international students. Applications are processed on a rolling basis. Application fee: $55 ($65 for international students). Electronic applications accepted. *Financial support:* In 2009–10, 301 students received support, including 278 fellowships (averaging $16,000 per year), 1 research assistantship (averaging $15,217 per year), 2 teaching assistantships (averaging $14,000 per year); career-related internships or fieldwork, Federal Work-Study, institutionally sponsored loans, scholarships/grants, health care benefits, and unspecified assistantships also available. Financial award application deadline: 3/1; financial award applicants required to submit FAFSA. *Faculty research:* Environmental risk assessment and policy analysis, information privacy and security, judicial independence, accountability, ethics. Total annual research expenditures: $1.4 million. *Unit head:* Lauren K. Robel, Dean, 812-855-8885, Fax: 812-855-7057, E-mail: lrobel@indiana.edu. *Application contact:* Kelly M. Compton, Director of Admissions, 812-855-2704, Fax: 812-855-0555, E-mail: kmcompto@indiana.edu.

The Johns Hopkins University, Bloomberg School of Public Health, Department of Health, Behavior and Society, Baltimore, MD 21218-2699. Offers genetic counseling (Sc M); health education and health communication (MHS); social and behavioral sciences (Dr PH, PhD, Sc D); social factors in health (MHS). *Faculty:* 43 full-time (30 women), 59 part-time/adjunct (40 women). *Students:* 100 full-time (89 women), 4 part-time (3 women); includes 28 minority (13 African Americans, 12 Asian Americans or Pacific Islanders, 3 Hispanic Americans), 13 international. Average age 29. 227 applicants, 31% accepted, 26 enrolled. In 2009, 25 master's, 8 doctorates awarded. *Degree requirements:* For master's, comprehensive exam (for some programs), thesis (for some programs); for doctorate, comprehensive exam, thesis/dissertation. *Entrance requirements:* For master's, GRE, curriculum vitae, 3 letters of recommendation; for doctorate, GRE, transcripts, curriculum vitae, statement, 3 recommendation letters. Additional exam requirements/recommendations for international students: Required—TOEFL (minimum score 600 paper-based; 250 computer-based; 100 iBT). *Application deadline:* For fall admission, 12/1 for domestic and international students. Applications are processed on a rolling basis. Application fee: $45. Electronic applications accepted. *Financial support:* In 2009–10, 96 students received support, including 17 fellowships with tuition reimbursements available (averaging $23,634 per year), 30 research assistantships (averaging $7,800 per year), 25 teaching assistantships (averaging $2,759 per year); career-related internships or fieldwork, Federal Work-Study, scholarships/grants, traineeships, health care benefits, unspecified assistantships, and stipends also available. Financial award application deadline: 3/15. *Faculty research:* Social determinants of health, and structural- and community-level inventions to improve health; communication and health education; behavioral and social aspects of genetic counseling. Total annual research expenditures: $6.3 million. *Unit head:* Georgean Smith, Administrator, 410-502-3715, Fax: 410-502-4333, E-mail: gcsmith@jhsph.edu. *Application contact:* Barbara W. Diehl, Senior Academic Program Coordinator, 410-502-4415, Fax: 410-502-4333, E-mail: bdiehl@jhsph.edu.

Lincoln University, School of Graduate Studies and Continuing Education, Jefferson City, MO 65102. Offers business administration (MBA), including accounting, entrepreneurship, management, public administration and policy; educational leadership (Ed S), including elementary leadership, secondary leadership, superintendency; guidance and counseling (M Ed), including community/agency counseling, elementary school, secondary school; history (MA); school administration and supervision (M Ed), including elementary school administration, secondary school administration, special education administration; school teaching (M Ed), including elementary school teaching, secondary school teaching; social science (MA), including history, political science, sociology; sociology (MA); sociology/criminal justice (MA). Part-time and evening/weekend programs available. *Students:* 52 full-time (27 women), 146 part-time (107 women); includes 40 minority (39 African Americans, 1 Asian American or Pacific Islander), 15 international. Average age 35. 76 applicants, 95% accepted, 46 enrolled. In 2009, 60 master's, 6 other advanced degrees awarded. *Degree requirements:* For master's and Ed S, comprehensive exam, thesis optional. *Entrance requirements:* For master's and Ed S, GRE, MAT or GMAT, minimum GPA of 2.75 in major, 2.5 overall; 3 letters of recommendation; minimum C average in English composition; personal statement of purpose. Additional exam requirements/recommendations for international students: Required—TOEFL (minimum score 500 paper-based; 173 computer-based; 61 iBT). *Application deadline:* For fall admission, 7/1 priority date for domestic and international students; for spring admission, 12/1 priority date for domestic and international students. Applications are processed on a rolling basis. Application fee: $20. *Expenses:* Tuition, state resident: full-time $4185; part-time $232.50 per credit hour. Tuition, nonresident: full-time $7767; part-time $431.50 per credit hour. Required fees: $270; $15 per credit hour. $20 per term. *Financial support:* Federal Work-Study and scholarships/grants available. Financial award application deadline: 4/1; financial award applicants required to submit FAFSA. *Faculty research:* Suicide prevention. *Unit head:* Dr. Linda S. Bickel, Dean, 573-681-5247, Fax: 573-681-5106, E-mail: gradschool@lincolnu.edu. *Application contact:* Irasema Steck, Administrative Assistant, 573-681-5247, Fax: 573-681-5106, E-mail: gradschool@lincolnu.edu.

Long Island University, Brooklyn Campus, Richard L. Conolly College of Liberal Arts and Sciences, Program in Social Science, Brooklyn, NY 11201-8423. Offers history (MS); United Nations studies (Certificate). Part-time and evening/weekend programs available. *Entrance requirements:* For master's, 2 letters of recommendation. Additional exam requirements/recommendations for international students: Required—TOEFL (minimum score 500 paper-based; 173 computer-based). Electronic applications accepted.

Long Island University, C.W. Post Campus, School of Education, Department of Curriculum and Instruction, Brookville, NY 11548-1300. Offers adolescence education (MS); adolescence education: biology (MS); adolescence education: earth science (MS); adolescence education: English (MS); adolescence education: mathematics (MS); adolescence education: social studies (MS); adolescence education: Spanish (MS); art education (MS); bilingual education (MS); childhood education (MS); early childhood education (MS); middle childhood education (MS); music education (MS); teaching English to speakers of other languages (MS). Part-time and evening/weekend programs available. *Degree requirements:* For master's, comprehensive exam or thesis, student teaching. *Entrance requirements:* For master's, minimum GPA of 2.75 in major, 2.5 overall. Electronic applications accepted. *Faculty research:* Ethics and education, teaching strategies.

Massachusetts Institute of Technology, School of Humanities, Arts, and Social Sciences, Program in Science, Technology, and Society, Cambridge, MA 02139-4307. Offers history, anthropology, and science, technology and society (PhD). *Faculty:* 13 full-time (5 women). *Students:* 28 full-time (16 women); includes 3 minority (1 African American, 2 American Indian/Alaska Native), 7 international. Average age 30. 92 applicants, 4% accepted, 4 enrolled. In 2009, 5 doctorates awarded. *Degree requirements:* For doctorate, comprehensive exam, thesis/dissertation. *Entrance requirements:* For doctorate, GRE General Test. Additional exam requirements/recommendations for international students: Required—TOEFL (minimum score 577 paper-based; 233 computer-based; 90 iBT), IELTS (minimum score 7). *Application deadline:* For fall admission, 1/1 for domestic and international students. Application fee: $75. Electronic applications accepted. *Financial support:* In 2009–10, 26 students received support, including 19 fellowships with tuition reimbursements available (averaging $27,275 per year), 6 teaching assistantships with tuition reimbursements available (averaging $30,736 per year); research assistantships, Federal Work-Study, institutionally sponsored loans, scholarships/grants, traineeships, health care benefits, and unspecified assistantships also available. *Faculty research:* History of science, history of technology, sociology of science and technology, anthropology of science and technology, science, technology, and society. Total annual research expenditures: $543,000. *Unit head:* Prof. David A. Mindell, Director, 617-253-4062, Fax: 617-258-8118, E-mail: stsprogram@mit.edu. *Application contact:* Karen Gardner, Academic Administrator, 617-253-9759, Fax: 617-258-8118, E-mail: hasts@mit.edu.

Middle Tennessee State University, College of Graduate Studies, University College, Murfreesboro, TN 37132. Offers MPS. Part-time and evening/weekend programs available. Postbaccalaureate distance learning degree programs offered. *Students:* 1 (woman) full-time, 65 part-time (41 women); includes 13 minority (12 African Americans, 1 Hispanic American). 41 applicants, 78% accepted, 32 enrolled. In 2009, 4 master's awarded. *Entrance requirements:* Additional exam requirements/recommendations for international students: Required—TOEFL (minimum score 525 paper-based; 195 computer-based; 71 iBT) or IELTS (minimum score 6). *Application deadline:* For fall admission, 6/1 for domestic and international students. Applications are processed on a rolling basis. Application fee: $25 ($30 for international students). *Expenses:* Tuition, state resident: full-time $4404. Tuition, nonresident: full-time $10,956. *Financial support:* In 2009–10, 4 students received support. Application deadline: 5/1. *Unit head:* Dr. David Gotcher, Program Advisor, 615-904-8042, E-mail: dgotcher@mtsu.edu. *Application contact:* Dr. Michael Allen, Dean and Vice Provost for Research, 615-898-2840, Fax: 615-904-8020, E-mail: mallen@mtsu.edu.

Mississippi College, Graduate School, College of Arts and Sciences, School of Humanities and Social Sciences, Department of History, Political Science, Administration of Justice, and Paralegal Studies, Clinton, MS 39058. Offers administration of justice (MSS); history (M Ed, MA, MSS); paralegal studies (Certificate); political science (MSS); social sciences (M Ed, MSS). Part-time programs available. *Faculty:* 4 full-time (0 women), 5 part-time/adjunct (1 woman). *Students:* 10 full-time (5 women), 27 part-time (10 women); includes 8 minority (all African Americans), 1 international. Average age 32. In 2009, 12 master's awarded. *Degree requirements:* For master's, one foreign language, comprehensive exam, thesis (for some programs). *Entrance requirements:* For master's, GRE or NTE, minimum GPA of 2.5. Additional exam requirements/recommendations for international students: Recommended—IELTS. *Application deadline:* For fall admission, 8/15 priority date for domestic students. Applications are processed on a rolling basis. Application fee: $30. Electronic applications accepted. *Expenses:* Tuition: Part-time $452 per credit hour. Required fees: $101 per semester. Tuition and fees vary according to degree level, campus/location, program and student level. *Financial support:* Teaching assistantships, Federal Work-Study, scholarships/grants, and unspecified assistantships available. Support available to part-time students. Financial award application deadline: 4/1; financial award applicants required to submit FAFSA. *Unit head:* Dr. Kirk Ford, Chair, 601-925-3326, E-mail: ford@mc.edu. *Application contact:* Elnora Lewis, Secretary, 601-925-3225, Fax: 601-925-3889, E-mail: lewis09@mc.edu.

Montclair State University, The Graduate School, College of Education and Human Services, Department of Curriculum and Teaching, Montclair, NJ 07043-1624. Offers education (M Ed); educational technology (M Ed); learning disabled teacher consultant (Certificate); school library media specialist (Certificate); teaching (MAT, Certificate), including art (MAT), biological science

Social Sciences

Montclair State University (continued)
(MAT), early childhood education (P-3) (MAT), earth science (MAT), elementary education (K-8) (MAT), English (MAT), French (MAT), health and physical education (MAT), health education (MAT), home economics (MAT), mathematics (MAT), music (MAT), physical education (MAT), physical science (MAT), social studies (MAT), Spanish (MAT), teacher of ESL (MAT), teacher of students with disabilities (MAT). Part-time and evening/weekend programs available. *Faculty:* 17 full-time (12 women), 29 part-time/adjunct (21 women). *Students:* 124 full-time (63 women), 174 part-time (126 women). Average age 31. 112 applicants, 69% accepted, 59 enrolled. In 2009, 179 master's, 2 other advanced degrees awarded. *Degree requirements:* For master's, comprehensive exam, field experience. *Entrance requirements:* For master's, GRE, 2 letters of recommendation. Additional exam requirements/recommendations for international students: Required—TOEFL (minimum score 83 computer-based), or IELTS. *Application deadline:* For fall admission, 2/15 for domestic and international students; for spring admission, 9/15 for domestic and international students. Applications are processed on a rolling basis. Application fee: $60. Electronic applications accepted. *Expenses:* Tuition, area resident: Part-time $486.74 per credit. Tuition, state resident: part-time $486.74 per credit. Tuition, nonresident: part-time $751.34 per credit. Tuition and fees vary according to degree level and program. *Financial support:* In 2009–10, 12 research assistantships with full tuition reimbursements (averaging $7,000 per year) were awarded; Federal Work-Study, scholarships/grants, and unspecified assistantships also available. Support available to part-time students. Financial award application deadline: 3/1; financial award applicants required to submit FAFSA. *Unit head:* Dr. David Schwarzer, Chairperson, 973-655-5187. *Application contact:* Amy Aiello, Director of Graduate Admissions and Operations, 973-655-5147, Fax: 973-655-7869, E-mail: graduate.school@montclair.edu.

The New School: A University, The New School for Social Research, New York, NY 10003. Offers M Phil, MA, MS, DS Sc, PhD. Part-time and evening/weekend programs available. *Faculty:* 71 full-time (31 women), 15 part-time/adjunct (1 woman). *Students:* 785 full-time (394 women), 277 part-time (157 women); includes 156 minority (45 African Americans, 2 American Indian/Alaska Native, 47 Asian Americans or Pacific Islanders, 62 Hispanic Americans), 293 international. Average age 31. 1,109 applicants, 73% accepted, 246 enrolled. In 2009, 213 master's, 56 doctorates awarded. Terminal master's awarded for partial completion of doctoral program. *Degree requirements:* For master's, variable foreign language requirement, exam or thesis; for doctorate, variable foreign language requirement, comprehensive exam, thesis/dissertation, qualifying exam. *Entrance requirements:* For master's, GRE General Test; for doctorate, GRE General Test, MA. Additional exam requirements/recommendations for international students: Required—TOEFL (minimum score 600 paper-based; 250 computer-based; 100 iBT). *Application deadline:* For fall admission, 1/17 priority date for domestic and international students; for spring admission, 10/15 priority date for domestic and international students. Applications are processed on a rolling basis. Application fee: $50. Electronic applications accepted. *Expenses:* Contact institution. *Financial support:* Fellowships, research assistantships, teaching assistantships, Federal Work-Study, scholarships/grants, tuition waivers (full and partial), and unspecified assistantships available. Support available to part-time students. Financial award application deadline: 3/1; financial award applicants required to submit FAFSA. *Faculty research:* Civil society and democracy, international movements of refugees, minority use of health services, memory, morality and genetics. *Unit head:* Dr. Michael Schober, Dean, 212-229-5777, E-mail: schober@newschool.edu. *Application contact:* Robert MacDonald, Director of Admissions, 212-229-5710 Ext. 3007, Fax: 212-989-7102, E-mail: macdonar@newschool.edu.

New York University, Graduate School of Arts and Science, Program in Trauma and Violence Transdisciplinary Studies, New York, NY 10012-1019. Offers MA, Advanced Certificate. *Students:* 4 full-time (all women), 8 part-time (7 women); includes 1 minority (Asian American or Pacific Islander). Average age 26. 8 applicants, 100% accepted, 6 enrolled. In 2009, 6 master's awarded. *Entrance requirements:* Additional exam requirements/recommendations for international students: Required—TOEFL. *Application deadline:* For fall admission, 4/15 priority date for domestic students; for spring admission, 11/1 priority date for domestic students. Application fee: $90. *Expenses:* Tuition: Full-time $30,528; part-time $1272 per credit. Required fees: $2177. *Financial support:* Application deadline: 4/14. *Unit head:* Judie Alpert, Co-Director, 212-998-8655, Fax: 212-995-4370, E-mail: tvts.info@nyu.edu. *Application contact:* Avital Ronell, Co-Director, 212-998-8655, Fax: 212-995-4370, E-mail: tvts.info@nyu.edu.

North Dakota State University, College of Graduate and Interdisciplinary Studies, College of Arts, Humanities and Social Sciences, Department of Sociology, Anthropology, and Emergency Management, Fargo, ND 58108. Offers emergency management (MS, PhD); social science (MA, MS); sociology (MS). Part-time programs available. *Faculty:* 8 full-time (3 women), 5 part-time/adjunct (2 women). *Students:* 35 full-time (17 women), 15 part-time (9 women); includes 5 minority (2 African Americans, 1 American Indian/Alaska Native, 1 Asian American or Pacific Islander, 1 Hispanic American), 2 international. Average age 27. 15 applicants, 60% accepted, 7 enrolled. In 2009, 9 master's awarded. *Degree requirements:* For master's, thesis; for doctorate, comprehensive exam, thesis/dissertation. *Entrance requirements:* For master's, GRE (emergency management), course work in sociology, minimum GPA of 3.2; for doctorate, GRE, minimum GPA of 3.2. Additional exam requirements/recommendations for international students: Required—TOEFL. *Application deadline:* For fall admission, 4/1 priority date for domestic students. Applications are processed on a rolling basis. Application fee: $45 ($60 for international students). *Financial support:* In 2009–10, 7 research assistantships with full tuition reimbursements (averaging $6,156 per year), 7 teaching assistantships with full tuition reimbursements (averaging $3,078 per year) were awarded; fellowships, career-related internships or fieldwork, Federal Work-Study, institutionally sponsored loans, and tuition waivers (full) also available. Support available to part-time students. Financial award application deadline: 4/15. *Faculty research:* Medical sociology, demography, ethnology, archaeology. Total annual research expenditures: $75,000. *Unit head:* Dr. Daniel J. Klenow, Chair, 701-231-8657, Fax: 701-231-1047, E-mail: daniel.klenow@ndsu.edu. *Application contact:* Dr. Daniel J. Klenow, Chair, 701-231-8657, Fax: 701-231-1047, E-mail: daniel.klenow@ndsu.edu.

Northwestern University, The Graduate School, Interdepartmental Programs, Program in Mathematical Methods in Social Science, Evanston, IL 60208. Offers MS.

Northwestern University, The Graduate School, Program in Law and Social Science, Evanston, IL 60208. Offers Certificate. *Degree requirements:* For Certificate, research project. *Faculty research:* Law and social science.

Nova Southeastern University, Graduate School of Humanities and Social Sciences, Department of Multi-Disciplinary Studies, Fort Lauderdale, FL 33314-7796. Offers college student affairs (MS); cross-disciplinary studies (MA). Part-time programs available. Postbaccalaureate distance learning degree programs offered (minimal on-campus study). *Faculty:* 1 (woman) full-time. *Students:* 12 full-time (9 women), 37 part-time (32 women); includes 20 African Americans, 9 Hispanic Americans, 1 international. In 2009, 15 master's awarded. *Degree requirements:* For master's, comprehensive exam, thesis optional, portfolio. *Entrance requirements:* For master's, interview, minimum GPA of 3.0. Additional exam requirements/recommendations for international students: Required—TOEFL. *Application deadline:* For fall admission, 7/1 priority date for domestic and international students; for winter admission, 11/1 priority date for domestic and international students; for spring admission, 3/1 priority date for domestic and international students. Applications are processed on a rolling basis. Electronic applications accepted. *Financial support:* Research assistantships, career-related internships or fieldwork, Federal Work-Study, institutionally sponsored loans, and scholarships/grants available. Financial award applicants required to submit CSS PROFILE. *Unit head:* Dr. Judith McKay, Chair, 954-262-3060, Fax: 954-262-3893, E-mail: mckayj@nsu.nova.edu. *Application contact:* Marcia Arango, Student Recruitment Coordinator, 954-262-3006, Fax: 954-262-3968, E-mail: marango@nsu.nova.edu.

Nyack College, Alliance Graduate School of Counseling, School of Social and Behavioral Sciences, Nyack, NY 10960-3698. Offers counseling (MA). *Degree requirements:* For master's, thesis (for some programs).

Ohio University, Graduate College, College of Arts and Sciences, Program in Social Sciences, Athens, OH 45701-2979. Offers MSS. Part-time and evening/weekend programs available. *Students:* 4 full-time (2 women), 34 part-time (17 women); includes 1 minority (African American). Average age 39. 9 applicants, 67% accepted, 4 enrolled. *Degree requirements:* For master's, oral exam. *Entrance requirements:* For master's, minimum GPA of 2.75. Additional exam requirements/recommendations for international students: Required—TOEFL (minimum score 600 paper-based; 220 computer-based). Application fee: $50 ($55 for international students). Electronic applications accepted. *Expenses:* Tuition, state resident: full-time $7839; part-time $323 per quarter hour. Tuition, nonresident: full-time $15,831; part-time $654 per quarter hour. Required fees: $2931. *Financial support:* Institutionally sponsored loans available. Financial award application deadline: 3/15; financial award applicants required to submit FAFSA. *Unit head:* Dr. Marvin Fletcher, Coordinator, 740-593-2969, E-mail: mfletcher1@ohiou.edu. *Application contact:* Graduate Admissions, 740-593-2800, Fax: 740-593-4625, E-mail: graduate@ohio.edu.

Queens College of the City University of New York, Division of Graduate Studies, Social Science Division, Program in Social Sciences, Flushing, NY 11367-1597. Offers MASS. Part-time and evening/weekend programs available. *Students:* 6 part-time (3 women). *Degree requirements:* For master's, thesis. *Entrance requirements:* For master's, minimum GPA of 3.0. Additional exam requirements/recommendations for international students: Required—TOEFL. *Application deadline:* For fall admission, 4/1 for domestic students; for spring admission, 11/1 for domestic students. Applications are processed on a rolling basis. Application fee: $125. *Expenses:* Tuition, state resident: full-time $7360; part-time $310 per credit. Tuition, nonresident: part-time $575 per credit. One-time fee: $195.25 full-time; $145.25 part-time. *Financial support:* Career-related internships or fieldwork, Federal Work-Study, institutionally sponsored loans, and tuition waivers (partial) available. Support available to part-time students. Financial award application deadline: 4/1; financial award applicants required to submit FAFSA. *Unit head:* Dr. Martin Hanlon, Graduate Adviser, 718-997-5510, E-mail: martin_hanlon@qc.edu. *Application contact:* Mario Caruso, Director of Graduate Admissions, 718-997-5200, Fax: 718-997-5193, E-mail: graduate_admissions@qc.edu.

Regis University, College for Professional Studies, MA Program, Denver, CO 80221-1099. Offers criminology (MA); fine arts administration (Certificate); language and communication (MA); mediation (Certificate); psychology (MA); self-designed major (MA); social justice, peace, and reconciliation (Certificate); social science (MA); technical communication (Certificate). Program also offered in Henderson and Las Vegas (Summerlin), NV. Part-time and evening/weekend programs available. Postbaccalaureate distance learning degree programs offered (minimal on-campus study). *Degree requirements:* For master's, thesis, research project. *Entrance requirements:* For master's, resume, recommendations. Additional exam requirements/recommendations for international students: Required—TOEFL (minimum score 213 computer-based), TWE (minimum score 5). Electronic applications accepted. *Expenses:* Contact institution. *Faculty research:* Independent/nonresidential graduate study: new methods and models, adult learning and the capstone experience, Goal Setting, behavior of Adult students, Innovative Studies for Community Colleges.

St. Edward's University, New College, Program in Liberal Arts, Austin, TX 78704. Offers global issues (MLA); humanities (MLA); liberal arts (Certificate); social sciences (MLA). Part-time and evening/weekend programs available. *Students:* 3 full-time (2 women), 85 part-time (60 women); includes 21 minority (3 African Americans, 2 Asian Americans or Pacific Islanders, 16 Hispanic Americans), 1 international. Average age 34. 34 applicants, 88% accepted, 23 enrolled. In 2009, 23 master's awarded. *Degree requirements:* For master's, minimum of 24 resident hours. *Entrance requirements:* For master's, minimum GPA of 2.75 in last 60 hours of course work, interview. Additional exam requirements/recommendations for international students: Required—TOEFL (minimum score 550 paper-based; 213 computer-based; 79 iBT) or IELTS (minimum score 6). *Application deadline:* For fall admission, 7/1 for domestic and international students; for spring admission, 11/1 for domestic and international students. Applications are processed on a rolling basis. Application fee: $45 ($50 for international students). Electronic applications accepted. *Expenses:* Tuition: Full-time $14,922; part-time $829 per credit hour. Required fees: $50 per trimester. Full-time tuition and fees vary according to course load and program. *Financial support:* In 2009–10, 2 students received support. Scholarships/grants available. *Unit head:* Dr. H. Ramsey Fowler, Director, 512-448-8648, Fax: 512-448-8492, E-mail: ramseyf@stewards.edu. *Application contact:* Kay L. Arnold, Assistant Director of Admissions, 512-233-1636, Fax: 512-428-1032, E-mail: kayla@stedwards.edu.

Southern University and Agricultural and Mechanical College, Graduate School, College of Arts and Humanities, Department of History, Baton Rouge, LA 70813. Offers social sciences (MA). Part-time programs available. *Degree requirements:* For master's, thesis. *Entrance requirements:* For master's, GRE General Test. Additional exam requirements/recommendations for international students: Required—TOEFL (minimum score 525 paper-based; 193 computer-based).

Stony Brook University, State University of New York, School of Professional Development, Stony Brook, NY 11794. Offers biology-grade 7-12 (MAT); chemistry-grade 7-12 (MAT); coaching (Graduate Certificate); computer integrated engineering (Graduate Certificate); earth science-grade 7-12 (MAT); educational computing (Graduate Certificate); educational leadership (Advanced Certificate); English-grade 7-12 (MAT); environmental management (Graduate Certificate); environmental/occupational health and safety (Graduate Certificate); French-grade 7-12 (MAT); German-grade 7-12 (MAT); human resource management (Graduate Certificate); information systems management (Graduate Certificate); Italian-grade 7-12 (MAT); liberal studies (MA); mathematics-grade 7-12 (MAT); operation research (Graduate Certificate); physics-grade 7-12 (MAT); school administration and supervision (Graduate Certificate); school building leadership (Graduate Certificate); school district administration (Graduate Certificate); school district business leadership (Advanced Certificate); school district leadership (Graduate Certificate); social science and the professions (MPS), including environmental waste management, human resource management; social studies-grade 7-12 (MAT); Spanish-grade 7-12 (MAT); waste management (Graduate Certificate). Part-time and evening/weekend programs available. Postbaccalaureate distance learning degree programs offered. *Faculty:* 5 full-time (3 women), 131 part-time/adjunct (53 women). *Students:* 317 full-time (187 women), 1,200 part-time (773 women); includes 187 minority (77 African Americans, 2 American Indian/Alaska Native, 22 Asian Americans or Pacific Islanders, 86 Hispanic Americans), 11 international. Average age 28. In 2009, 597 master's, 234 other advanced degrees awarded. *Degree requirements:* For master's, one foreign language, thesis or alternative. *Application deadline:* Applications are processed on a rolling basis. Application fee: $62. *Expenses:* Tuition, state resident: full-time $8370; part-time $349 per credit. Tuition, nonresident: full-time $13,250; part-time $552 per credit. Required fees: $933. *Financial support:* Fellowships, research assistantships, teaching assistantships, career-related internships or fieldwork available. Support available to part-time students. *Unit head:* Dr. Paul J. Edelson, Dean, 631-632-7052, Fax: 631-632-9046, E-mail: paul.edelson@stonybrook.edu. *Application contact:* Dr. Paul J. Edelson, Dean, 631-632-7052, Fax: 631-632-9046, E-mail: paul.edelson@stonybrook.edu.

Syracuse University, Maxwell School of Citizenship and Public Affairs, Program in Social Sciences, Syracuse, NY 13244. Offers MS Sc, PhD. Part-time and evening/weekend programs available. Postbaccalaureate distance learning degree programs offered. *Students:* 34 full-time (21 women), 64 part-time (33 women); includes 13 minority (5 African Americans, 2 American Indian/Alaska Native, 2 Asian Americans or Pacific Islanders, 4 Hispanic Americans), 12 international. Average age 40. 37 applicants, 68% accepted, 11 enrolled. In 2009, 7 master's, 3 doctorates awarded. *Degree requirements:* For doctorate, thesis/dissertation. *Entrance requirements:* For doctorate, GRE General Test. Additional exam requirements/recommendations for international students: Required—TOEFL (minimum score 100 iBT). *Application deadline:* For fall admission, 3/15 priority date for domestic and international students. Application fee: $75. Electronic applications accepted. *Expenses:* Tuition: Full-time $26,808; part-time $1117 per credit. Required fees: $1024. *Financial support:* Fellowships with tuition reimbursements, research assistantships with tuition reimbursements, teaching assistantships with full and partial tuition reimbursements, tuition waivers (partial) available. Financial award application deadline: 1/1. *Unit head:* Dr. Vernon Greene, Chair, 315-443-2275, Fax: 315-443-1463, E-mail: vgreene@maxwell.syr.edu. *Application contact:* Mary Olszewski, Information Contact, 315-443-2275, E-mail: mtolszew@maxwell.syr.edu.

Texas A&M International University, Office of Graduate Studies and Research, College of Arts and Sciences, Department of Social Sciences, Laredo, TX 78041-1900. Offers history (MA); political science (MA), public administration (MPA). *Faculty:* 9 full-time (3 women). *Students:* 11 full-time (4 women), 52 part-time (25 women); includes 61 minority (all Hispanic Americans), 2 international. Average age 32. 37 applicants. In 2009, 15 master's awarded. *Degree requirements:* For master's, thesis (for some programs). *Entrance requirements:* For master's, GRE General Test. Additional exam requirements/recommendations for international students: Required—TOEFL (minimum score 550 paper-based; 213 computer-based). *Application deadline:* For fall admission, 4/30 priority date for domestic students; for spring admission, 11/30 for domestic students. Applications are processed on a rolling basis. Application fee: $25. *Financial support:* In 2009–10, 14 students received support, including 2 research assistantships, 3 teaching assistantships. Financial award application deadline: 11/1. *Unit head:* Dr. Mohammed Ben-Ruwin, Chair, 956-328-2632, E-mail: mbenruwin@tamiu.edu. *Application contact:* Rosie Espinoza-Dickinson, Director of Admissions, 956-326-2200, Fax: 956-326-2199, E-mail: enroll@tamiu.edu.

Texas A&M University–Commerce, Graduate School, College of Arts and Sciences, Department of History, Commerce, TX 75429-3011. Offers history (MA, MS); social sciences (M Ed, MS). Part-time programs available. *Degree requirements:* For master's, comprehensive exam, thesis (for some programs). *Entrance requirements:* For master's, GRE General Test. Electronic applications accepted. *Faculty research:* American foreign policy, colonial America, Texas politics, Medieval England.

Towson University, College of Graduate Studies and Research, Program in Social Science, Towson, MD 21252-0001. Offers MS. Part-time and evening/weekend programs available. *Entrance requirements:* For master's, minimum GPA of 3.0, 3 letters of recommendation, letter of intent. Additional exam requirements/recommendations for international students: Required—TOEFL. Electronic applications accepted. *Faculty research:* Race and ethnicity, diplomatic history, sociology methodology, central Asian geography.

University of Atlanta, Graduate Programs, Atlanta, GA 30360. Offers business (MS); business administration (Exec MBA, MBA, DBA); computer science (MS); educational leadership (MS, Ed D); health administration (MS); healthcare administration (D Sc, Graduate Certificate); information technology for management (Graduate Certificate); international project management (Graduate Certificate); law (JD); project management (Graduate Certificate); social science (MS). Postbaccalaureate distance learning degree programs offered.

University of California, Irvine, Office of Graduate Studies, School of Social Sciences, Irvine, CA 92697. Offers MA, PhD. *Students:* 363 full-time (161 women), 9 part-time (3 women); includes 99 minority (4 African Americans, 1 American Indian/Alaska Native, 55 Asian Americans or Pacific Islanders, 39 Hispanic Americans), 43 international. Average age 29. 798 applicants, 23% accepted, 84 enrolled. In 2009, 68 master's, 51 doctorates awarded. *Degree requirements:* For doctorate, thesis/dissertation. *Entrance requirements:* For master's, GRE, minimum GPA of 3.0; for doctorate, GRE General Test, minimum GPA of 3.0. Additional exam requirements/recommendations for international students: Required—TOEFL (minimum score 550 paper-based; 213 computer-based). *Application deadline:* For fall admission, 1/15 priority date for domestic students, 1/15 for international students. Applications are processed on a rolling basis. Application fee: $70 ($90 for international students). Electronic applications accepted. *Financial support:* Fellowships, research assistantships with full tuition reimbursements, teaching assistantships, institutionally sponsored loans, traineeships, health care benefits, and unspecified assistantships available. Financial award application deadline: 3/1; financial award applicants required to submit FAFSA. *Faculty research:* Mathematical modeling of perception and cognitive processes, economic analysis of transportation, impact of society's political system on its economy, exploration of authority structures and inequality in society. *Unit head:* Barbara Anne Dosher, Dean, 949-824-7373, E-mail: bdosher@uci.edu. *Application contact:* Diane Enriquez, Graduate Counselor, 949-824-5924, Fax: 949-824-3548, E-mail: dmvargas@uci.edu.

University of California, Merced, Division of Graduate Studies, School of Social Sciences, Humanities and Arts, Merced, CA 95343. Offers social and cognitive sciences (MA, PhD); world cultures (MA, PhD). *Expenses:* Tuition, nonresident: full-time $15,102. Required fees: $10,919.

University of California, Santa Cruz, Division of Graduate Studies, Division of Humanities, Program in the History of Consciousness, Santa Cruz, CA 95064. Offers PhD. *Degree requirements:* For doctorate, one foreign language, thesis/dissertation, qualifying exam. *Entrance requirements:* Additional exam requirements/recommendations for international students: Required—TOEFL (minimum score 550 paper-based; 220 computer-based). *Faculty research:* Interdisciplinary humanities and social sciences, political theory, cultural theory, feminist studies, literary theory.

University of Chicago, Division of Social Sciences, Committee on Social Thought, Chicago, IL 60637-1513. Offers PhD. *Students:* 61. In 2009, 3 doctorates awarded. *Degree requirements:* For doctorate, one foreign language, thesis/dissertation, exam. *Entrance requirements:* For doctorate, GRE General Test. Additional exam requirements/recommendations for international students: Required—TOEFL, IELTS (minimum score 7). *Application deadline:* For fall admission, 12/15 for domestic and international students. Application fee: $55. Electronic applications accepted. *Financial support:* Fellowships, teaching assistantships, Federal Work-Study, institutionally sponsored loans, scholarships/grants, traineeships, health care benefits, and unspecified assistantships available. Financial award application deadline: 12/15; financial award applicants required to submit FAFSA. *Unit head:* Prof. Robert Pippin, Chair, 773-702-8410. *Application contact:* Office of the Dean of Students, 773-702-8415.

University of Chicago, Division of Social Sciences, Master of Arts Program in the Social Sciences, Chicago, IL 60637-1513. Offers AM. Part-time programs available. *Students:* 191. In 2009, 152 master's awarded. *Degree requirements:* For master's, thesis. *Entrance requirements:* For master's, GRE General Test. Additional exam requirements/recommendations for international students: Required—TOEFL. *Application deadline:* For fall admission, 1/4 for domestic and international students. Application fee: $55. Electronic applications accepted. *Financial support:* Fellowships, Federal Work-Study, institutionally sponsored loans, and scholarships/grants available. Financial award application deadline: 1/4; financial award applicants required to submit FAFSA. *Unit head:* Prof. John J. MacAloon, Director, 773-702-8316. *Application contact:* Office of the Dean of Students, 773-702-8415.

University of Colorado Denver, College of Liberal Arts and Sciences, Program in Social Science, Denver, CO 80217-3364. Offers MSS. Part-time and evening/weekend programs available. *Students:* 11 full-time (8 women), 39 part-time (29 women); includes 9 minority (1 African American, 2 American Indian/Alaska Native, 1 Asian American or Pacific Islander, 5 Hispanic Americans). 19 applicants, 68% accepted, 9 enrolled. In 2009, 11 master's awarded. *Degree requirements:* For master's, thesis or alternative. *Entrance requirements:* For master's, GRE General Test, 18 hours of course work in social science, interview, minimum GPA of 2.75. Additional exam requirements/recommendations for international students: Required—TOEFL (minimum score 525 paper-based; 197 computer-based). *Application deadline:* For fall admission, 5/15 for domestic students; for spring admission, 10/15 for domestic students. Applications are processed on a rolling basis. Application fee: $50 ($75 for international students). Electronic applications accepted. *Financial support:* Research assistantships, teaching assistantships, Federal Work-Study available. Financial award application deadline: 3/1; financial award applicants required to submit FAFSA. *Unit head:* Myra Bookman, Director, 303-556-2496, Fax: 303-556-8100, E-mail: myra.bookman@ucdenver.edu. *Application contact:* Myra Bookman, Director, 303-556-2496, Fax: 303-556-8100, E-mail: myra.bookman@ucdenver.edu.

University of Florida, Graduate School, College of Public Health and Health Professions and College of Medicine, Programs in Public Health, Gainesville, FL 32611. Offers biostatistics (MPH); environmental health (MPH); epidemiology (MPH); public health management and policy (MPH); public health practice (MPH); social and behavioral sciences (MPH). *Entrance requirements:* For master's, GRE General Test, minimum GPA of 3.0. Additional exam requirements/recommendations for international students: Required—TOEFL (minimum score 550 paper-based; 213 computer-based).

University of Idaho, College of Graduate Studies, College of Natural Resources, Department of Conservation Social Sciences, Moscow, ID 83844-2282. Offers MS. *Faculty:* 10 full-time, 1 part-time/adjunct. *Students:* 20 full-time (12 women), 19 part-time (11 women). In 2009, 15 master's awarded. *Entrance requirements:* For master's, minimum GPA of 2.8. *Application deadline:* For fall admission, 8/1 for domestic students; for spring admission, 12/15 for domestic students. Application fee: $55 ($60 for international students). *Expenses:* Tuition, state resident: full-time $6120. Tuition, nonresident: full-time $17,712. *Financial support:* Research assistantships, teaching assistantships available. Financial award application deadline: 2/15. *Faculty research:* Parks, wilderness and protected areas policy, planning and management, recreation and tourism planning, urban and community forestry, resource-based tourism, ecotourism, human dimensions of ecosystem management. *Unit head:* Dr. Thomas M. Gorman, Acting Dean, 208-885-7911. *Application contact:* Dr. Thomas M. Gorman, Acting Dean, 208-885-7911.

University of Illinois at Springfield, Graduate Programs, College of Education and Human Services, Program in Human Services, Springfield, IL 62703-5407. Offers alcoholism and substance abuse (MA); child and family services (MA); gerontology (MA); social services administration (MA). Part-time and evening/weekend programs available. Postbaccalaureate distance learning degree programs offered (no on-campus study). *Faculty:* 4 full-time (3 women), 1 (woman) part-time/adjunct. *Students:* 34 full-time (32 women), 91 part-time (76 women); includes 34 minority (31 African Americans, 1 American Indian/Alaska Native, 1 Asian American or Pacific Islander, 1 Hispanic American), 1 international. Average age 36. 76 applicants, 54% accepted, 33 enrolled. In 2009, 20 master's awarded. *Degree requirements:* For master's, internship; project or thesis. *Entrance requirements:* For master's, minimum undergraduate GPA of 3.0, 2 letters of recommendation. Additional exam requirements/recommendations for international students: Required—TOEFL (minimum score 500 paper-based; 176 computer-based; 61 iBT). Application fee: $50 ($60 for international students). Electronic applications accepted. *Expenses:* Tuition, state resident: full-time $6390; part-time $266.25 per credit hour. Tuition, nonresident: full-time $14,226; part-time $592.75 per credit hour. Required fees: $2044; $14.36 per credit hour. $722.50 per term. *Financial support:* In 2009–10, research assistantships with full tuition reimbursements (averaging $8,109 per year), teaching assistantships with full tuition reimbursements (averaging $8,109 per year) were awarded; career-related internships or fieldwork, scholarships/grants, health care benefits, and unspecified assistantships also available. Support available to part-time students. Financial award application deadline: 11/15. *Unit head:* Dr. Carolyn Peck, Program Administrator, 217-206-7577, Fax: 217-206-6775, E-mail: peck.carolyn@uis.edu. *Application contact:* Dr. Lynn Pardie, Office of Graduate Studies, 800-252-8533, Fax: 217-206-7623, E-mail: pardie.lynn@uis.edu.

The University of Kansas, Graduate Studies, College of Liberal Arts and Sciences, Department of Applied Behavioral Science, Lawrence, KS 66045. Offers applied behavioral science (MA); behavioral psychology (PhD). *Faculty:* 17. *Students:* 53 full-time (37 women), 2 part-time (both women); includes 4 minority (1 African American, 2 Asian Americans or Pacific Islanders, 1 Hispanic American), 4 international. Average age 32. 57 applicants, 25% accepted, 10 enrolled. In 2009, 3 master's, 4 doctorates awarded. Terminal master's awarded for partial completion of doctoral program. *Degree requirements:* For master's, thesis; for doctorate, comprehensive exam, thesis/dissertation, comprehensive oral and written exams, journal reviews. *Entrance requirements:* For master's and doctorate, departmental application, curriculum vitae, 3 letters of recommendation. Additional exam requirements/recommendations for international students: Required—TOEFL. *Application deadline:* For fall admission, 12/15 priority date for domestic and international students. Applications are processed on a rolling basis. Application fee: $45 ($55 for international students). Electronic applications accepted. *Expenses:* Tuition, state resident: full-time $6492; part-time $270.50 per credit hour. Tuition, nonresident: full-time $15,510; part-time $646.25 per credit hour. Required fees: $847; $70.56 per credit hour. Tuition and fees vary according to course load and program. *Financial support:* Fellowships, research assistantships with full and partial tuition reimbursements, teaching assistantships with full and partial tuition reimbursements, career-related internships or fieldwork, traineeships, tuition waivers (full), and unspecified assistantships available. Financial award application deadline: 12/15; financial award applicants required to submit CSS PROFILE or FAFSA. *Faculty research:* Early childhood, developmental disabilities, community health and development, adults with disabilities, applied behavior analysis. *Unit head:* Dr. Edward K. Morris, Chair, 785-864-4840, Fax: 785-864-5202, E-mail: ekm@ku.edu. *Application contact:* Dr. Gregory J. Madden, Graduate Director, 785-864-4840, Fax: 785-864-5202, E-mail: gmadden@ku.edu.

University of Lethbridge, School of Graduate Studies, Lethbridge, AB T1K 3M4, Canada. Offers accounting (MScM); addictions counseling (M Sc); agricultural biotechnology (M Sc); agricultural studies (M Sc, MA); anthropology (MA); archaeology (MA); art (MA, MFA); biochemistry (M Sc); biological sciences (M Sc); biomolecular science (PhD); biosystems and biodiversity (PhD); Canadian studies (MA); chemistry (M Sc); computer science (M Sc); computer science and geographical information science (M Sc); counseling psychology (M Ed); dramatic arts (MA); earth, space, and physical science (PhD); economics (MA); educational leadership (M Ed); English (MA); environmental science (M Sc); evolution and behavior (PhD); exercise science (M Sc); finance (MScM); French (MA); French/German (MA); French/Spanish (MA); general education (M Ed); general management (MScM); geography (M Sc, MA); German (MA); health science (M Sc); health sciences (MA); history (MA); human resource management and labour relations (MScM); individualized multidisciplinary (M Sc, MA); information systems (MScM); international management (MScM); kinesiology (M Sc, MA); management (M Sc, MA); marketing (MScM); mathematics (M Sc); music (M Mus, MA); Native American studies (MA); neuroscience (M Sc, PhD); new media (MA); nursing (M Sc); philosophy (MA); physics (M Sc); policy and strategy (MScM); political science (MA); psychology (M Sc, MA); religious studies (MA); social sciences (MA); sociology (MA); theatre and dramatic arts (MFA); theoretical and computational science (PhD); urban and regional studies (MA); women's studies (MA). Part-time and evening/weekend programs available. *Degree requirements:* For doctorate, comprehensive exam, thesis/dissertation. *Entrance requirements:* For master's, GMAT (M Sc in management), bachelor's degree in related field, minimum GPA of 3.0 during previous 20 graded semester courses, 2 years teaching or related experience (M Ed); for doctorate, master's degree, minimum graduate GPA of 3.5. Additional exam requirements/recommendations for international students: Required—TOEFL. *Faculty research:* Movement and brain plasticity, gibberellin physiology, photosynthesis, carbon cycling, molecular properties of main-group ring components.

University of Maryland, Baltimore County, Graduate School, Program in Gerontology, Baltimore, MD 21201. Offers aging policy for the elderly (PhD); epidemiology of aging (PhD); social, cultural, and behavioral sciences (PhD). Part-time programs available. *Faculty:* 19 part-time/adjunct (13 women). *Students:* 18 full-time (14 women), 8 part-time (all women); includes 7 minority (5 African Americans, 2 Asian Americans or Pacific Islanders). Average age 34. 26 applicants, 19% accepted, 4 enrolled. In 2009, 3 doctorates awarded. *Degree requirements:* For doctorate, comprehensive exam, thesis/dissertation. *Entrance requirements:* For doctorate, GRE General Test. Additional exam requirements/recommendations for international students: Required—TOEFL, TWE. *Application deadline:* For spring admission, 1/15 for domestic and international students. Application fee: $45. Electronic applications accepted. *Financial support:* In 2009–10, 6 fellowships with full tuition reimbursements (averaging $22,314 per year), 5 research assistantships with full tuition reimbursements (averaging $21,008 per year) were awarded; teaching assistantships with full tuition reimbursements, career-related internships or fieldwork, scholarships/grants, traineeships, health care benefits, tuition waivers

Social Sciences

University of Maryland, Baltimore County (continued)

(partial), and unspecified assistantships also available. Financial award application deadline: 2/1; financial award applicants required to submit FAFSA. *Faculty research:* Aging and health policy, behavioral aspects of aging, caregiving, LTC, epidemiology of aging. Total annual research expenditures: $39.5 million. *Unit head:* Dr. Leslie Morgan, Co-Director, 410-455-2074, Fax: 410-455-1154, E-mail: lmorgan@umbc.edu. *Application contact:* Justine Golden, Academic Coordinator, 410-706-4926, Fax: 410-706-4433, E-mail: jgold002@umaryland.edu.

University of Memphis, Graduate School, School of Public Health, Memphis, TN 38152. Offers biostatistics (MPH); environmental health (MPH); epidemiology (MPH); health systems management (MPH); public health (MHA); social and behavioral sciences (MPH). Part-time and evening/weekend programs available. Postbaccalaureate distance learning degree programs offered. *Faculty:* 5 full-time (2 women), 4 part-time/adjunct (2 women). *Students:* 45 full-time (23 women), 29 part-time (14 women); includes 19 African Americans, 6 Asian Americans or Pacific Islanders, 2 Hispanic Americans, 7 international. Average age 32. 57 applicants, 70% accepted, 22 enrolled. In 2009, 17 master's awarded. *Degree requirements:* For master's, comprehensive exam, thesis. *Entrance requirements:* For master's, GRE, MAT, DAT, GMAT or LSAT, letters of recommendation. Additional exam requirements/recommendations for international students: Required—TOEFL. *Application deadline:* For fall admission, 11/1 for domestic students; for spring admission, 4/1 for domestic students. Application fee: $35 ($60 for international students). Electronic applications accepted. *Expenses:* Tuition, state resident: full-time $6246; part-time $347 per credit hour. Tuition, nonresident: full-time $15,894; part-time $883 per credit hour. Required fees: $1160. Full-time tuition and fees vary according to course load, degree level and program. *Financial support:* In 2009–10, 46 students received support; research assistantships with full tuition reimbursements available, Federal Work-Study, scholarships/grants, and unspecified assistantships available. Financial award application deadline: 2/15; financial award applicants required to submit FAFSA. *Faculty research:* Health and medical savings accounts, adoption rates, health informatics, Telehealth technologies, biostatistics, environmental health, epidemiology, health systems management, social and behavioral sciences. *Unit head:* Dr. Lisa M. Klesges, Director, 901-678-4637, E-mail: lmklsges@memphis.edu. *Application contact:* Dr. Lisa M. Klesges, Director, 901-678-4637, E-mail: lmklsges@memphis.edu.

University of Michigan, School of Social Work, Interdisciplinary Program in Social Work and Social Science, Ann Arbor, MI 48109. Offers PhD. Offered through the Horace H. Rackham School of Graduate Studies. *Faculty:* 51 full-time (23 women), 47 part-time/adjunct (32 women). *Students:* 79 full-time (67 women); includes 17 minority (7 African Americans, 2 American Indian/Alaska Native, 8 Hispanic Americans), 16 international. Average age 31. 114 applicants, 12% accepted, 13 enrolled. In 2009, 4 doctorates awarded. *Degree requirements:* For doctorate, thesis/dissertation, oral defense of dissertation, preliminary exam. *Entrance requirements:* For doctorate, GRE General Test. Additional exam requirements/recommendations for international students: Required—TOEFL. *Application deadline:* For fall admission, 12/1 for domestic and international students. Application fee: $60 ($75 for international students). *Expenses:* Tuition, state resident: full-time $17,286; part-time $1099 per credit hour. Tuition, nonresident: full-time $34,944; part-time $2080 per credit hour. Required fees: $95 per semester. Tuition and fees vary according to course load, degree level and program. *Financial support:* In 2009–10, 68 students received support, including 29 fellowships with full tuition reimbursements available (averaging $15,000 per year), 12 research assistantships with full tuition reimbursements available (averaging $16,600 per year), 27 teaching assistantships with full tuition reimbursements available (averaging $16,600 per year); career-related internships or fieldwork, Federal Work-Study, scholarships/grants, traineeships, and tuition waivers (full and partial) also available. Financial award application deadline: 12/1; financial award applicants required to submit FAFSA. *Faculty research:* Substance abuse, child welfare, mental health, poverty, aging. Total annual research expenditures: $7.1 million. *Unit head:* Dr. Berit Ingersoll-Dayton, Director, 734-763-5768, Fax: 734-615-3192, E-mail: bid@umich.edu. *Application contact:* Graduate Coordinator, E-mail: ssw.phd.info@umich.edu.

University of Michigan–Flint, College of Arts and Sciences, Program in Social Sciences, Flint, MI 48502-1950. Offers MA. Part-time programs available. *Faculty:* 4 full-time (3 women). *Students:* 9 full-time (7 women), 36 part-time (24 women); includes 10 minority (8 African Americans, 1 American Indian/Alaska Native, 1 Asian American or Pacific Islander). Average age 35. 24 applicants, 67% accepted, 10 enrolled. In 2009, 9 master's awarded. *Entrance requirements:* Additional exam requirements/recommendations for international students: Required—TOEFL (minimum score 560 paper-based; 220 computer-based; 84 iBT), IELTS (minimum score 6.5). *Application deadline:* For fall admission, 8/1 for domestic students, 5/1 priority date for international students; for winter admission, 11/15 for domestic students, 9/1 priority date for international students; for spring admission, 3/15 for domestic students, 1/1 priority date for international students. Application fee: $55. *Expenses:* Contact institution. *Financial support:* Federal Work-Study, scholarships/grants, and unspecified assistantships available. Support available to part-time students. Financial award application deadline: 6/1; financial award applicants required to submit FAFSA. *Unit head:* Dr. Adam Lutzker, Program Director, 810-762-3280, Fax: 810-766-6789, E-mail: alutzker@umflint.edu. *Application contact:* Bradley T. Maki, Director of Graduate Admissions, 810-762-3171, Fax: 810-766-6789, E-mail: bmaki@umflint.edu.

University of Northern Iowa, Graduate College, College of Social and Behavioral Sciences, Department of Social Science, Cedar Falls, IA 50614. Offers MA. *Students:* 19 part-time (7 women). *Entrance requirements:* For master's, minimum GPA of 3.0. Additional exam requirements/recommendations for international students: Required—TOEFL (minimum score 500 paper-based; 180 computer-based; 61 iBT). Application fee: $30 ($50 for international students). *Unit head:* Dr. Philip Mauceri, Dean/Professor, 319-273-2221, Fax: 319-273-2222, E-mail: philip.mauceri@uni.edu. *Application contact:* Laurie S. Russell, Record Analyst, 319-273-2623, Fax: 319-273-6792, E-mail: laurie.russell@uni.edu.

University of Regina, Faculty of Graduate Studies and Research, Faculty of Arts, Department of Sociology and Social Studies, Regina, SK S4S 0A2, Canada. Offers social studies (MA, PhD); sociology (MA, PhD). *Faculty:* 12 full-time (5 women), 1 part-time/adjunct (0 women). *Students:* 13 full-time (10 women), 4 part-time (1 woman). 7 applicants, 86% accepted. In 2009, 4 master's awarded. *Degree requirements:* For master's, thesis. *Entrance requirements:* Additional exam requirements/recommendations for international students: Required—TOEFL (minimum score 580 paper-based; 237 computer-based; 80 iBT). *Application deadline:* Applications are processed on a rolling basis. Application fee: $90 ($100 for international students). Electronic applications accepted. *Financial support:* In 2009–10, 4 fellowships (averaging $19,000 per year), 3 research assistantships (averaging $16,910 per year), 5 teaching assistantships (averaging $6,650 per year) were awarded; scholarships/grants also available. Financial award application deadline: 6/15. *Faculty research:* Social justice; development and the environment; knowledge, technology, and society. *Unit head:* Dr. John Conway, Head, 306-585-4052, Fax: 306-585-4815, E-mail: john.conway@uregina.ca. *Application contact:* Dr. Henry Chow, Graduate Program Coordinator, 306-585-5604, Fax: 306-585-4815, E-mail: henry.chow@uregina.ca.

The University of Texas at Tyler, College of Arts and Sciences, Department of Social Sciences, Tyler, TX 75799-0001. Offers criminal justice (MS); public administration (MPA); sociology (MS). Part-time and evening/weekend programs available. *Faculty:* 10 full-time (2 women). *Students:* 7 full-time (3 women), 21 part-time (14 women); includes 8 minority (5 African Americans, 2 American Indian/Alaska Native, 1 Asian American or Pacific Islander), 2 international. Average age 30. 6 applicants, 100% accepted, 6 enrolled. In 2009, 10 master's awarded. *Degree requirements:* For master's, comprehensive exam, thesis optional. *Entrance requirements:* For master's, GRE General Test, minimum GPA of 3.0. Additional exam requirements/recommendations for international students: Required—TOEFL (minimum score 79 computer-based). *Application deadline:* For fall admission, 8/17 priority date for domestic students, 7/1 priority date for international students; for spring admission, 12/21 priority date for domestic students, 11/1 priority date for international students. Applications are processed on a rolling basis. Application fee: $25 ($50 for international students). *Expenses:* Tuition, state resident: part-time $665 per semester hour. Tuition, nonresident: part-time $942 per semester hour. Part-time tuition and fees vary according to degree level and program. *Financial support:* In 2009–10, 1 fellowship (averaging $1,000 per year), 2 research assistantships, 2 teaching assistantships were awarded; career-related internships or fieldwork, Federal Work-Study, and scholarships/grants also available. Support available to part-time students. Financial award application deadline: 7/1; financial award applicants required to submit FAFSA. *Faculty research:* Urban segregation, minority business, violent crime, gender discrimination. *Unit head:* Dr. Ken Wink, Chair, 903-566-7434, Fax: 903-565-5537, E-mail: kwink@mail.uttyl.edu. *Application contact:* Dr. Ken Wink.

University of Washington, Graduate School, School of Public Health, Department of Health Services, Seattle, WA 98195. Offers bioinformatics (PhD); cancer prevention and control (PhD); clinical research (MS); community oriented public health practice (MPH); economics or finance (PhD); evaluation sciences (PhD); executive program (MHA); health behavior and health promotion (PhD); health care and population health research (MPH); health policy analysis and process (PhD); health policy and analysis and process (MPH); health services (MS, PhD); health services administration (EMHA, MHA); in residence program (MHA); occupational health (PhD); population health and social determinants (PhD); social and behavioral sciences (MPH); sociology and demography (PhD); JD/MHA; MHA/MBA; MHA/MD; MHA/MPA; MPH/JD; MPH/MD; MPH/MN; MPH/MPA; MPH/MSD; MPH/MSW; MPH/PhD. Part-time and evening/weekend programs available. Postbaccalaureate distance learning degree programs offered (minimal on-campus study). *Faculty:* 52 full-time (24 women), 60 part-time/adjunct (28 women). *Students:* 104 full-time (83 women), 100 part-time (76 women); includes 21 minority (6 African Americans, 1 American Indian/Alaska Native, 11 Asian Americans or Pacific Islanders, 3 Hispanic Americans), 6 international. Average age 34. 375 applicants, 17% accepted, 24 enrolled. In 2009, 33 master's awarded. Terminal master's awarded for partial completion of doctoral program. *Degree requirements:* For master's, thesis (for some programs), practicum (MPH); for doctorate, comprehensive exam, thesis/dissertation. *Entrance requirements:* For master's and doctorate, GRE General Test, minimum GPA of 3.0. Additional exam requirements/recommendations for international students: Required—TOEFL. *Application deadline:* For fall admission, 1/15 for domestic students, 11/1 for international students. Application fee: 50 Albanian leks. Electronic applications accepted. *Financial support:* In 2009–10, 64 students received support, including 10 fellowships with full and partial tuition reimbursements available (averaging $21,000 per year), 10 research assistantships with full and partial tuition reimbursements available (averaging $18,000 per year), 3 teaching assistantships with full and partial tuition reimbursements available (averaging $18,000 per year); career-related internships or fieldwork, Federal Work-Study, institutionally sponsored loans, and traineeships also available. Financial award application deadline: 2/28; financial award applicants required to submit FAFSA. *Faculty research:* Health promotion and disease prevention, maternal and child health, health services research design, program evaluation, health policy. Total annual research expenditures: $10.5 million. *Unit head:* Dr. Larry Kessler, Chair, 206-543-616-2930. *Application contact:* Kitty A. Andert, MPH/MS/PhD Program Manager, 206-616-2926, Fax: 206-543-3964, E-mail: kitander@u.washington.edu.

University of Wisconsin–Madison, Development Studies Program, Madison, WI 53706-1380. Offers PhD. *Expenses:* Tuition, state resident: part-time $594 per credit. Tuition, nonresident: part-time $1504 per credit. Required fees: $65 per credit. Tuition and fees vary according to course load, program and reciprocity agreements.

Worcester Polytechnic Institute, Graduate Studies and Research, Department of Social Science and Policy Studies, Worcester, MA 01609-2280. Offers interdisciplinary social science (PhD); system dynamics (MS, Graduate Certificate). Part-time and evening/weekend programs available. Postbaccalaureate distance learning degree programs offered (no on-campus study). *Faculty:* 3 full-time (0 women), 2 part-time/adjunct (0 women). *Students:* 12 part-time (11 women). 13 applicants, 85% accepted, 5 enrolled. In 2009, 2 master's awarded. *Entrance requirements:* For master's, GRE General Test, 3 letters of recommendation. Additional exam requirements/recommendations for international students: Required—TOEFL (minimum score 550 paper-based; 213 computer-based; 79 iBT), IELTS (minimum score 6.5). *Application deadline:* For fall admission, 1/15 priority date for domestic students, 1/15 for international students; for spring admission, 10/15 priority date for domestic students, 10/15 for international students. Applications are processed on a rolling basis. Application fee: $70. Electronic applications accepted. *Financial support:* Career-related internships or fieldwork, institutionally sponsored loans, scholarships/grants, and unspecified assistantships available. Financial award application deadline: 1/15. *Faculty research:* Sustainable development, information economics, judgment and decision making, learning science, system dynamics, social simulation, political economies. *Unit head:* Dr. James K. Doyle, Head, 508-831-5296, Fax: 508-831-5896, E-mail: doyle@wpi.edu. *Application contact:* Dr. Oleg Pavlov, Graduate Coordinator, 508-831-5296, Fax: 508-831-5896, E-mail: opavlov@wpi.edu.

Worcester Polytechnic Institute, Graduate Studies and Research, Programs in Interdisciplinary Studies, Worcester, MA 01609-2280. Offers bioscience administration (MS); impact engineering (MS); manufacturing engineering management (MS); power systems management (MS); social science (PhD); systems modeling (MS). Part-time and evening/weekend programs available. *Faculty:* 1 part-time/adjunct (0 women). *Students:* 3 full-time (1 woman), 126 part-time (24 women). 184 applicants, 68% accepted, 100 enrolled. In 2009, 19 master's awarded. *Degree requirements:* For master's, thesis; for doctorate, comprehensive exam, thesis/dissertation. *Entrance requirements:* For master's and doctorate, 3 letters of recommendation. Additional exam requirements/recommendations for international students: Required—TOEFL (minimum score 550 paper-based; 213 computer-based; 79 iBT), IELTS (minimum score 6.5). *Application deadline:* For fall admission, 1/15 priority date for domestic students; for spring admission, 10/15 priority date for domestic students. Application fee: $70. *Financial support:* Institutionally sponsored loans, scholarships/grants, and unspecified assistantships available. Financial award application deadline: 1/15. *Unit head:* Dr. Fred J. Looft, Head, 508-831-5231, Fax: 508-831-5491, E-mail: fjlooft@wpi.edu. *Application contact:* Lynne Dougherty, Administrative Assistant, 508-831-5301, Fax: 508-831-5717, E-mail: grad@wpi.edu.

Yale University, School of Medicine, School of Public Health, New Haven, CT 06520. Offers biostatistics (MPH, MS, PhD); chronic disease epidemiology (MPH, PhD); environmental health sciences (MPH, PhD); epidemiology of microbial diseases (MPH, PhD); health management (MPH); health policy and administration (MPH, PhD); social and behavioral sciences (MPH); MBA/MPH; MD/MPH; MPH/MA; MSN/MPH. MS and PhD offered through the Graduate School. Part-time programs available. Terminal master's awarded for partial completion of doctoral program. *Degree requirements:* For master's, thesis, internship; for doctorate, comprehensive exam, thesis/dissertation, residency. *Entrance requirements:* For master's, GMAT, GRE, or MCAT, previous undergraduate course work in mathematics and science; for doctorate, GRE General Test. Additional exam requirements/recommendations for international students: Required—TOEFL. Electronic applications accepted. *Expenses:* Contact institution. *Faculty research:* Genetic and emerging infections epidemiology, virology, cost/quality, vector biology, quantitative methods.

York University, Faculty of Graduate Studies, Faculty of Arts, Program in International Development Studies, Toronto, ON M3J 1P3, Canada. Offers MA.

Section 27
Sociology, Anthropology, and Archaeology

This section contains a directory of institutions offering graduate work in sociology, anthropology, and archaeology, followed by an in-depth entry submitted by an institution that chose to prepare a detailed program description. Additional information about programs listed in the directory but not augmented by an in-depth entry may be obtained by writing directly to the dean of a graduate school or chair of a department at the address given in the directory.

For programs offering related work, see also in this book *Area and Cultural Studies, Art and Art History, History, Humanities, Language and Literature,* and *Psychology and Counseling.*

CONTENTS

Program Directories

Anthropology 1204
Applied Social Research 1217
Archaeology 1217
Biological Anthropology 1222
Demography and Population Studies 1222
Rural Sociology 1224
Sociology 1224
Survey Methodology 1243

Close-Up

Texas A&M University 1245

See also:

The University of Texas at Dallas—Economic, Political, and Policy Sciences 759

Anthropology

American University, College of Arts and Sciences, Department of Anthropology, Washington, DC 20016-8003. Offers anthropology (PhD); public anthropology (MA, Certificate). Part-time and evening/weekend programs available. *Faculty:* 15 full-time (7 women), 4 part-time/adjunct (2 women). *Students:* 39 full-time (29 women), 60 part-time (41 women); includes 23 minority (12 African Americans, 6 Asian Americans or Pacific Islanders, 5 Hispanic Americans), 11 international. Average age 31. 71 applicants, 59% accepted, 19 enrolled. In 2009, 6 master's, 7 doctorates awarded. Terminal master's awarded for partial completion of doctoral program. *Degree requirements:* For master's, comprehensive exam, thesis or alternative; for doctorate, 2 foreign languages, comprehensive exam, thesis/dissertation. *Entrance requirements:* For master's, GRE, sample of written work; for doctorate, GRE, sample of written work, personal statement. Additional exam requirements/recommendations for international students: Required—TOEFL. *Application deadline:* For fall admission, 2/1 for domestic students; for spring admission, 10/1 for domestic students. Application fee: $80. *Expenses:* Tuition: Full-time $22,266; part-time $1237 per credit hour. Required fees: $430. Tuition and fees vary according to program. *Financial support:* Fellowships, research assistantships with full and partial tuition reimbursements, teaching assistantships with full and partial tuition reimbursements, career-related internships or fieldwork, Federal Work-Study, institutionally sponsored loans, and unspecified assistantships available. Support available to part-time students. Financial award application deadline: 1/15. *Faculty research:* Poverty and race, lesbian and gay studies, class and culture, developing countries. *Unit head:* Dr. William Leap, Chair, 202-885-1831, Fax: 202-885-1837. *Application contact:* Dr. William Leap, Chair, 202-885-1831, Fax: 202-885-1837.

The American University in Cairo, Graduate Studies and Research, School of Humanities and Social Sciences, Department of Sociology, Anthropology, Psychology, and Egyptology, Cairo, Egypt. Offers sociology and anthropology (MA). *Degree requirements:* For master's, one foreign language, thesis. *Entrance requirements:* Additional exam requirements/recommendations for international students: Required—English entrance exam and/or TOEFL. Electronic applications accepted. *Faculty research:* Development, gender, sociopolitical economic formulations, social science indigenization, Arab world.

American University of Beirut, Graduate Programs, Faculty of Arts and Sciences, Beirut, Lebanon. Offers anthropology (MA); Arabic language and literature (MA); archaeology (MA); biology (MS); chemistry (MS); computer science (MS); economics (MA); education (MA); English language (MA); English literature (MA); environmental policy planning (MSES); financial economics (MAFE); geology (MS); history (MA); mathematics (MA, MS); Middle Eastern studies (MA); philosophy (MA); physics (MS); political studies (MA); psychology (MA); public administration (MA); sociology (MA); statistics (MA, MS). Part-time programs available. *Degree requirements:* For master's, one foreign language, comprehensive exam, thesis (for some programs). *Entrance requirements:* For master's, GRE, letter of recommendation. Additional exam requirements/recommendations for international students: Required—TOEFL (minimum score 600 paper-based; 250 computer-based; 100 iBT), IELTS (minimum score 7.5). *Faculty research:* String theory and supergravity; computer graphics; algebra and number theory; popular Arabic literature; marine and freshwater biology; integrating science, math and technology.

Arizona State University, Graduate College, College of Liberal Arts and Sciences, Division of Social Sciences, School of Human Evolution and Social Change, Tempe, AZ 85287. Offers anthropology (PhD); applied mathematics for the life and social sciences (PhD); environmental social science (PhD); museum studies in anthropology (MA); social science and health (PhD). *Degree requirements:* For master's, thesis or alternative; for doctorate, thesis/dissertation. *Entrance requirements:* For master's and doctorate, GRE.

Ball State University, Graduate School, College of Sciences and Humanities, Department of Anthropology, Muncie, IN 47306-1099. Offers MA. *Entrance requirements:* For master's, GRE General Test, resume.

Boston University, Graduate School of Arts and Sciences, Department of Anthropology, Boston, MA 02215. Offers anthropology (PhD); applied anthropology (MA). *Students:* 33 full-time (20 women), 2 part-time (both women); includes 3 minority (1 African American, 2 Asian Americans or Pacific Islanders), 13 international. Average age 32. 81 applicants, 14% accepted, 4 enrolled. In 2009, 7 doctorates awarded. Terminal master's awarded for partial completion of doctoral program. *Degree requirements:* For master's, one foreign language, thesis or alternative; for doctorate, one foreign language, thesis/dissertation. *Entrance requirements:* For master's and doctorate, GRE General Test, 2 letters of recommendation. Additional exam requirements/recommendations for international students: Required—TOEFL (minimum score 550 paper-based; 213 computer-based). *Application deadline:* For fall admission, 1/1 for domestic and international students. Application fee: $70. *Expenses:* Tuition: Full-time $37,910; part-time $1184 per credit hour. Required fees: $386; $40 per semester. Part-time tuition and fees vary according to class time, course level, degree level and program. *Financial support:* In 2009–10, 15 students received support, including 3 fellowships with full tuition reimbursements available (averaging $18,900 per year), 7 teaching assistantships with full tuition reimbursements available (averaging $18,400 per year); Federal Work-Study and unspecified assistantships also available. Support available to part-time students. Financial award application deadline: 1/1; financial award applicants required to submit FAFSA. *Unit head:* Robert Weller, Chairman, 617-353-2195, Fax: 617-353-2610, E-mail: rpweller@bu.edu. *Application contact:* Mark Palmer, Administrator, 617-353-2195, Fax: 617-353-2610, E-mail: palmerm@bu.edu.

Brandeis University, Graduate School of Arts and Sciences, Department of Anthropology, Waltham, MA 02454. Offers anthropology (MA, PhD); anthropology and women's and gender studies (MA). Part-time programs available. *Faculty:* 9 full-time (4 women), 1 part-time/adjunct (0 women). *Students:* 39 full-time (25 women), 2 part-time (1 woman); includes 5 minority (1 Asian American or Pacific Islander, 4 Hispanic Americans), 13 international. Average age 34. 68 applicants, 44% accepted, 12 enrolled. In 2009, 12 master's awarded. Terminal master's awarded for partial completion of doctoral program. *Degree requirements:* For master's, thesis; for doctorate, one foreign language, comprehensive exam, thesis/dissertation. *Entrance requirements:* For master's, GRE General Test (recommended), sample of written work, resume, letters of recommendation; for doctorate, GRE General Test, sample of written work, resume, letters of recommendation. Additional exam requirements/recommendations for international students: Required—TOEFL (minimum score 600 paper-based; 250 computer-based; 100 iBT); Recommended—IELTS (minimum score 7). *Application deadline:* For fall admission, 1/15 for domestic students. Applications are processed on a rolling basis. Application fee: $75. Electronic applications accepted. *Financial support:* In 2009–10, 23 students received support, including 12 fellowships with full tuition reimbursements available (averaging $20,000 per year), 11 teaching assistantships with partial tuition reimbursements available (averaging $3,200 per year); research assistantships with partial tuition reimbursements available, career-related internships or fieldwork, scholarships/grants, health care benefits, tuition waivers (full and partial), and unspecified assistantships also available. Support available to part-time students. Financial award application deadline: 4/15; financial award applicants required to submit FAFSA. *Faculty research:* Technology and culture, comparative methods, economic anthropology, gender studies, semiotic anthropology. *Unit head:* Dr. Elizabeth Ferry, Associate Professor/Director of Graduate Studies, 781-736-2210, Fax: 781-736-2232, E-mail: ferry@brandeis.edu. *Application contact:* Laurel Carpenter, Academic Administrator, 781-736-2210, Fax: 781-736-2232, E-mail: lcarpenter@brandeis.edu.

Brigham Young University, Graduate Studies, College of Family, Home, and Social Sciences, Department of Anthropology, Provo, UT 84602-1001. Offers MA. *Faculty:* 9 full-time (1 woman). *Students:* 9 full-time (all women), 9 part-time (6 women). Average age 28. 11 applicants, 55% accepted, 6 enrolled. In 2009, 2 master's awarded. *Degree requirements:* For master's, comprehensive exam, thesis. *Entrance requirements:* For master's, GRE General Test, minimum GPA of 3.0 in last 60 hours. Additional exam requirements/recommendations for international students: Required—TOEFL (minimum score 580 paper-based; 237 computer-based). *Application deadline:* For fall admission, 2/1 for domestic and international students. Application fee: $50. Electronic applications accepted. *Expenses:* Tuition: Full-time $5580; part-time $301 per credit hour. Tuition and fees vary according to student's religious affiliation. *Financial support:* In 2009–10, 17 students received support, including 10 research assistantships (averaging $7,000 per year), 2 teaching assistantships (averaging $7,000 per year); fellowships, career-related internships or fieldwork, institutionally sponsored loans, and tuition waivers (partial) also available. Financial award application deadline: 3/1; financial award applicants required to submit FAFSA. *Faculty research:* Archaeology of the Southwest, Near East, and Mesoamerica; Mayan glyphs. Total annual research expenditures: $51,800. *Unit head:* Dr. Charles W. Nuckolls, Chair, 801-422-3058, Fax: 801-422-0021, E-mail: david_crandall@byu.edu. *Application contact:* Dr. Cynthia S. Finlayson, Graduate Coordinator, 801-422-5628, Fax: 801-422-0021, E-mail: calderfin@aol.com.

Brown University, Graduate School, Department of Anthropology, Providence, RI 02912. Offers anthropology (AM, PhD); museum studies (AM). *Degree requirements:* For doctorate, one foreign language, thesis/dissertation, preliminary exam.

California Institute of Integral Studies, School of Consciousness and Transformation, San Francisco, CA 94103. Offers creative inquiry (MFA); cultural anthropology and social transformation (MA); East-West psychology (MA, PhD); integrative health studies (MA); philosophy and religion (MA, PhD), including Asian and comparative studies, philosophy, cosmology, and consciousness, women's spirituality; social and cultural anthropology (PhD); transformative leadership (MA); transformative studies (PhD); writing and consciousness (MFA). Part-time and evening/weekend programs available. Postbaccalaureate distance learning degree programs offered (minimal on-campus study). *Students:* 334 full-time (218 women), 126 part-time (77 women); includes 116 minority (40 African Americans, 4 American Indian/Alaska Native, 42 Asian Americans or Pacific Islanders, 30 Hispanic Americans). Average age 38. 265 applicants, 90% accepted, 149 enrolled. In 2009, 64 master's, 22 doctorates awarded. Terminal master's awarded for partial completion of doctoral program. *Degree requirements:* For master's, comprehensive exam (for some programs), thesis optional; for doctorate, comprehensive exam, thesis/dissertation, 1 foreign language (Asian comparative studies). *Entrance requirements:* For master's, minimum GPA of 3.0, letters of recommendation, writing sample; for doctorate, master's degree, minimum GPA of 3.0, letters of recommendation, writing sample. Additional exam requirements/recommendations for international students: Required—TOEFL. *Application deadline:* For fall admission, 2/1 priority date for domestic and international students; for spring admission, 10/15 priority date for domestic and international students. Applications are processed on a rolling basis. Application fee: $65. Electronic applications accepted. *Expenses:* Tuition: Full-time $15,300; part-time $850 per credit hour. Required fees: $110 per semester. Tuition and fees vary according to degree level. *Financial support:* In 2009–10, 330 students received support; research assistantships, teaching assistantships, career-related internships or fieldwork, Federal Work-Study, scholarships/grants, and tuition waivers (partial) available. Support available to part-time students. Financial award application deadline: 4/15; financial award applicants required to submit FAFSA. *Faculty research:* Altered states of consciousness, dreams, cosmology, postcolonial studies, integrative health studies. *Application contact:* Allyson Werner, Associate Director of Admissions, 415-575-6155, Fax: 415-575-1268.

California State University, Bakersfield, Division of Graduate Studies, School of Humanities and Social Sciences, Program in Anthropology, Bakersfield, CA 93311. Offers MA. *Degree requirements:* For master's, thesis optional. *Entrance requirements:* For master's, GRE, minimum GPA of 2.5, 3 letters of recommendation. Additional exam requirements/recommendations for international students: Required—TOEFL (minimum score 550 paper-based; 213 computer-based). *Faculty research:* Human services, social science teaching.

California State University, Chico, Graduate School, College of Behavioral and Social Sciences, Department of Anthropology, Chico, CA 95929-0722. Offers museum studies (MA). *Students:* 14 full-time (12 women), 16 part-time (12 women); includes 3 minority (1 Asian American or Pacific Islander, 2 Hispanic Americans), 1 international. Average age 32. 37 applicants, 38% accepted, 10 enrolled. In 2009, 6 master's awarded. *Degree requirements:* For master's, thesis. *Entrance requirements:* For master's, GRE General Test, 2 letters of recommendation. Additional exam requirements/recommendations for international students: Required—TOEFL (minimum score 550 paper-based; 213 computer-based; 80 iBT), IELTS (minimum score 6.5). *Application deadline:* For fall admission, 1/15 for domestic students, 3/1 for international students. Application fee: $55. Electronic applications accepted. *Financial support:* Fellowships, career-related internships or fieldwork available. *Unit head:* Dr. William Collins, Graduate Coordinator, 530-898-4953. *Application contact:* Dr. William Collins, Graduate Coordinator, 530-898-4953.

California State University, East Bay, Academic Programs and Graduate Studies, College of Letters, Arts, and Social Sciences, Department of Anthropology, Hayward, CA 94542-3000. Offers MA. Part-time programs available. *Faculty:* 7 full-time (2 women). *Students:* 7 full-time (5 women), 15 part-time (6 women); includes 2 minority (1 African American, 1 Asian American or Pacific Islander). Average age 37. 15 applicants, 67% accepted, 9 enrolled. In 2009, 5 master's awarded. *Degree requirements:* For master's, one foreign language, comprehensive exam, thesis. *Entrance requirements:* For master's, minimum GPA of 2.5 during previous 2 years of course work. Additional exam requirements/recommendations for international students: Required—TOEFL (minimum score 550 paper-based; 213 computer-based). *Application deadline:* For fall admission, 6/30 for domestic and international students; for spring admission, 11/30 for domestic students. Applications are processed on a rolling basis. Application fee: $55. Electronic applications accepted. *Financial support:* Fellowships, teaching assistantships, career-related internships or fieldwork, Federal Work-Study, institutionally sponsored loans, and scholarships/grants available. Support available to part-time students. Financial award application deadline: 3/1; financial award applicants required to submit FAFSA. *Unit head:* Prof. Laurie Price, Graduate Coordinator, 510-885-4367, Fax: 510-885-3353, E-mail: laurie.price@csueastbay.edu. *Application contact:* Donna Wiley, Interim Associate Director, 510-885-2928, Fax: 510-885-4777, E-mail: donna.wiley@csueastbay.edu.

California State University, Fullerton, Graduate Studies, College of Humanities and Social Sciences, Department of Anthropology, Fullerton, CA 92834-9480. Offers MA. Part-time programs available. *Students:* 31 full-time (17 women), 39 part-time (22 women); includes 20 minority (2 African Americans, 2 American Indian/Alaska Native, 4 Asian Americans or Pacific Islanders, 12 Hispanic Americans), 2 international. Average age 31. 66 applicants, 59% accepted, 34 enrolled. In 2009, 18 master's awarded. *Degree requirements:* For master's, project or thesis. *Entrance requirements:* For master's, minimum GPA of 2.5 in last 60 hours of course work. Application fee: $55. *Expenses:* Tuition, nonresident: full-time $11,160; part-time $373 per credit. Required fees: $1440 per term. Tuition and fees vary according to course load, degree level and program. *Financial support:* Career-related internships or fieldwork, Federal Work-Study, institutionally sponsored loans, and scholarships/grants available. Support available to part-time students. Financial award application deadline: 3/1; financial award applicants required to submit FAFSA. *Unit head:* Dr. John Bedell, Chair, 657-278-3626. *Application contact:* Admissions/Applications, 657-278-2371.

California State University, Long Beach, Graduate Studies, College of Liberal Arts, Department of Anthropology, Long Beach, CA 90840. Offers anthropology (MA); applied anthropology (MA). Part-time programs available. *Faculty:* 7 full-time (4 women), 1 part-time/adjunct (0 women). *Students:* 15 full-time (13 women), 17 part-time (10 women); includes 11 minority (1 African American, 4 Asian Americans or Pacific Islanders, 6 Hispanic Americans). Average age 31. 34 applicants, 38% accepted, 11 enrolled. *Degree requirements:* For master's, one foreign language, comprehensive exam or thesis. *Application deadline:* For fall admission, 4/15 for domestic students. Applications are processed on a rolling basis. Application fee: $55. Electronic applications accepted. *Expenses:* Required fees: $1802 per semester. Part-time tuition and fees vary according to course load. *Financial support:* Research assistantships, Federal Work-Study, institutionally sponsored loans, and scholarships/grants available. Financial award application deadline: 3/2. *Faculty research:* Archeology of California, Fiji, and Ireland; cultures of American Indian and Mexico. *Unit head:* Dr. Barbara LeMaster, Chair, 562-985-5171, Fax: 562-985-4379. *Application contact:* Dr. Ron Loewe, Graduate Advisor, 562-985-5034, Fax: 562-985-4379, E-mail: rloewe@csulb.edu.

California State University, Los Angeles, Graduate Studies, College of Natural and Social Sciences, Department of Anthropology, Los Angeles, CA 90032-8530. Offers MA. Part-time and evening/weekend programs available. *Faculty:* 2 full-time (1 woman), 4 part-time/adjunct (3 women). *Students:* 28 full-time (23 women), 48 part-time (29 women); includes 24 minority (5 African Americans, 5 Asian Americans or Pacific Islanders, 14 Hispanic Americans), 4 international. Average age 32. 40 applicants, 100% accepted, 14 enrolled. In 2009, 8 master's awarded. *Degree requirements:* For master's, one foreign language, comprehensive exam or thesis. *Entrance requirements:* Additional exam requirements/recommendations for international students: Required—TOEFL (minimum score 500 paper-based; 173 computer-based). *Application deadline:* For fall admission, 5/1 for domestic and international students. Applications are processed on a rolling basis. Application fee: $55. *Financial support:* Federal Work-Study available. Support available to part-time students. Financial award application deadline: 3/1. *Faculty research:* Archaeology, folklore, petroglyphs, symbolism, medical anthropology. *Unit head:* Dr. Rene Vellanoweth, Chair, 323-343-2440, Fax: 323-343-2446, E-mail: rvellan@calstatela.edu. *Application contact:* Dr. Cheryl L. Ney, Associate Vice President for Academic Affairs and Dean of Graduate Studies, 323-343-3820, Fax: 323-343-5653, E-mail: cney@cslanet.calstatela.edu.

California State University, Northridge, Graduate Studies, College of Social and Behavioral Sciences, Department of Anthropology, Northridge, CA 91330. Offers general anthropology (MA); public archaeology (MA). *Faculty:* 7 full-time (5 women), 6 part-time/adjunct (1 woman). *Students:* 15 full-time (10 women), 28 part-time (14 women); includes 1 African American, 2 Asian Americans or Pacific Islanders, 8 Hispanic Americans. Average age 35. 22 applicants, 55% accepted, 9 enrolled. In 2009, 2 master's awarded. *Degree requirements:* For master's, thesis or alternative. *Entrance requirements:* For master's, GRE General Test or minimum GPA of 3.0. Additional exam requirements/recommendations for international students: Required—TOEFL. *Application deadline:* For fall admission, 11/30 for domestic students. Application fee: $55. *Financial support:* Career-related internships or fieldwork, Federal Work-Study, and institutionally sponsored loans available. Financial award application deadline: 3/1. *Unit head:* Sabina Magliocco, Chair, 818-677-3331. *Application contact:* Dr. Cathy L. Costin, Graduate Adviser, 818-677-3324.

California State University, Sacramento, Graduate Studies, College of Social Sciences and Interdisciplinary Studies, Department of Anthropology, Sacramento, CA 95819. Offers MA. Part-time programs available. *Degree requirements:* For master's, thesis, departmental qualifying exam, writing proficiency exam. *Entrance requirements:* For master's, minimum GPA of 3.0 during previous 2 years. Additional exam requirements/recommendations for international students: Required—TOEFL. Electronic applications accepted.

Carleton University, Faculty of Graduate Studies, Faculty of Arts and Social Sciences, Department of Sociology and Anthropology, Program in Anthropology, Ottawa, ON K1S 5B6, Canada. Offers MA. *Degree requirements:* For master's, comprehensive exam, thesis optional. *Entrance requirements:* For master's, honors degree. Additional exam requirements/recommendations for international students: Required—TOEFL. *Faculty research:* Culture, symbols and mind, anthropology of signs and symbols, Indigenous studies, anthropology of development and underdevelopment.

Case Western Reserve University, Frances Payne Bolton School of Nursing and Department of Anthropology, Nursing/Anthropology Program, Cleveland, OH 44106. Offers MSN/MA.

Case Western Reserve University, School of Graduate Studies, Department of Anthropology, Cleveland, OH 44106. Offers MA, PhD, MD/MA, MD/PhD, MPH/MA, MSN/MA, PhD/MPH. Part-time programs available. *Faculty:* 10 full-time (5 women), 11 part-time/adjunct (4 women). *Students:* 30 full-time (25 women), 2 part-time (both women); includes 4 minority (1 African American, 3 Asian Americans or Pacific Islanders), 2 international. Average age 30. 41 applicants, 34% accepted, 10 enrolled. In 2009, 5 master's awarded. Terminal master's awarded for partial completion of doctoral program. *Degree requirements:* For master's, comprehensive exam, thesis optional; for doctorate, one foreign language, thesis/dissertation. *Entrance requirements:* For master's and doctorate, GRE General Test. Additional exam requirements/recommendations for international students: Required—TOEFL (minimum score 550 paper-based; 213 computer-based; 79 iBT). *Application deadline:* For fall admission, 3/1 priority date for domestic students. Applications are processed on a rolling basis. Application fee: $50. Electronic applications accepted. *Financial support:* Research assistantships with tuition reimbursements, teaching assistantships with tuition reimbursements, career-related internships or fieldwork and Federal Work-Study available. Support available to part-time students. Financial award application deadline: 2/15; financial award applicants required to submit FAFSA. *Faculty research:* Medical anthropology, psychological anthropology, cross-cultural aging, physical anthropology, international health. *Unit head:* Lawrence P. Greksa, Chairman, 216-368-2259, Fax: 216-368-5334, E-mail: lawrence.greksa@case.edu. *Application contact:* Kathleen Dowdell, Department Assistant, 216-368-2264, Fax: 216-368-5334, E-mail: kathleen.dowdell@case.edu.

The Catholic University of America, School of Arts and Sciences, Department of Anthropology, Washington, DC 20064. Offers MA. Part-time programs available. *Faculty:* 5 full-time (3 women), 1 part-time/adjunct (0 women). *Students:* 3 full-time (all women), 6 part-time (3 women); includes 1 minority (Asian American or Pacific Islander). Average age 40. 9 applicants, 67% accepted, 1 enrolled. In 2009, 2 master's awarded. *Degree requirements:* For master's, one foreign language, comprehensive exam, thesis or alternative. *Entrance requirements:* For master's, GRE General Test, statement of purpose, official copies of academic transcripts, three letters of recommendation. Additional exam requirements/recommendations for international students: Required—TOEFL (minimum score 580 paper-based; 237 computer-based). *Application deadline:* For fall admission, 8/1 priority date for domestic students, 7/15 for international students; for spring admission, 12/1 priority date for domestic students, 10/15 for international students. Applications are processed on a rolling basis. Application fee: $55. Electronic applications accepted. *Expenses:* Tuition: Full-time $31,740; part-time $1245 per credit hour. Required fees: $50; $25 per semester hour. One-time fee: $425. *Financial support:* Fellowships, research assistantships, teaching assistantships, Federal Work-Study, scholarships/grants, tuition waivers (full and partial), and unspecified assistantships available. Financial award application deadline: 2/1; financial award applicants required to submit FAFSA. *Faculty research:* Medical and applied anthropology, ethnopsychology, Latin American studies, ceramic analysis, economics and ecological anthropology. *Unit head:* Dr. Jon W. Anderson, Chair, 202-319-5080, Fax: 202-319-4782, E-mail: anderson@cua.edu. *Application contact:* Julie Schwing, Director of Graduate Admissions, 202-319-5057, Fax: 202-319-6533, E-mail: cua-admissions@cua.edu.

Central European University, Graduate Studies, School of Social Sciences and Humanities, Budapest, Hungary. Offers economics (MA, PhD); gender studies (MA, PhD); international relations and European studies (MA, PhD); mathematics and its applications (MS, PhD); medieval studies (MA, PhD); nationalism studies (MA, PhD); philosophy (MA, PhD); political science (MA, PhD); public policy (MA, PhD); sociology and social anthropology (MA, PhD). Terminal master's awarded for partial completion of doctoral program. *Degree requirements:* For master's, one foreign language, thesis; for doctorate, one foreign language, comprehensive exam, thesis/dissertation. *Entrance requirements:* For master's, interview; for doctorate, GRE, CEU subject test, interview. Additional exam requirements/recommendations for international students: Required—TOEFL (minimum score 570 paper-based; 230 computer-based). Electronic applications accepted. *Faculty research:* Civil society, fiscal decentralization, party politics, political philosophy (especially Liberalism, theory of Democracy).

The College of William and Mary, Faculty of Arts and Sciences, Department of Anthropology, Williamsburg, VA 23187-8795. Offers MA, PhD. *Students:* 33 full-time (23 women), 3 part-time (2 women); includes 5 minority (1 African American, 2 American Indian/Alaska Native, 2 Hispanic Americans), 3 international. Average age 31. 82 applicants, 29% accepted, 5 enrolled. In 2009, 7 master's, 1 doctorate awarded. Terminal master's awarded for partial completion of doctoral program. *Degree requirements:* For master's, thesis, fieldwork; for doctorate, one foreign language, comprehensive exam, thesis/dissertation, fieldwork. *Entrance requirements:* For master's and doctorate, GRE, course work in anthropology or history. Additional exam requirements/recommendations for international students: Required—TOEFL. *Application deadline:* For fall admission, 1/15 for domestic and international students. Application fee: $45. Electronic applications accepted. *Expenses:* Tuition, state resident: full-time $6400; part-time $315 per credit hour. Tuition, nonresident: full-time $19,720; part-time $840 per credit hour. Required fees: $4114. *Financial support:* Research assistantships with full tuition reimbursements, teaching assistantships with full tuition reimbursements, career-related internships or fieldwork, institutionally sponsored loans, and scholarships/grants available. Financial award application deadline: 1/15; financial award applicants required to submit FAFSA. *Faculty research:* Historical archaeology, comparative colonialism, biocultural anthropology, African diaspora, historical archaeology of native America. Total annual research expenditures: $584,616. *Unit head:* Dr. Katie Bragdon, Chair, 757-221-1067, Fax: 757-221-1066, E-mail: bkbrag@wm.edu. *Application contact:* Dr. Martin D. Gallivan, Director of Graduate Studies, 757-221-3622, Fax: 757-221-1066, E-mail: mdgall@wm.edu.

Colorado State University, Graduate School, College of Liberal Arts, Department of Anthropology, Fort Collins, CO 80523-1787. Offers MA. Part-time programs available. *Faculty:* 12 full-time (7 women). *Students:* 24 full-time (19 women), 32 part-time (21 women); includes 1 minority (Hispanic American). Average age 30. 47 applicants, 55% accepted, 16 enrolled. In 2009, 9 master's awarded. *Degree requirements:* For master's, variable foreign language requirement, comprehensive exam, thesis (for some programs), oral exam. *Entrance requirements:* For master's, GRE General Test, minimum GPA of 3.0, BA/BS. Additional exam requirements/recommendations for international students: Required—TOEFL. *Application deadline:* For fall admission, 2/15 priority date for domestic and international students. Applications are processed on a rolling basis. Application fee: $50. Electronic applications accepted. *Expenses:* Tuition, state resident: full-time $6434; part-time $359.10 per credit. Tuition, nonresident: full-time $18,116; part-time $1006.45 per credit. Required fees: $1496; $83 per credit. *Financial support:* In 2009–10, 12 students received support, including 12 teaching assistantships with full tuition reimbursements available (averaging $11,588 per year); fellowships, research assistantships with full tuition reimbursements available, career-related internships or fieldwork, Federal Work-Study, scholarships/grants, and unspecified assistantships also available. Financial award application deadline: 3/1; financial award applicants required to submit FAFSA. *Faculty research:* Archaeology, cultural anthropology, biological anthropology, globalizational development, human ecology. Total annual research expenditures: $77,919. *Unit head:* Dr. Kathleen A. Galvin, Chair, 970-491-5784, Fax: 970-491-7597, E-mail: kathleen.galvin@colostate.edu. *Application contact:* Dr. Ann L. Magennis, Graduate Program Coordinator and Associate Professor, 970-491-5966, Fax: 970-491-7597, E-mail: ann.magennis@colostate.edu.

Columbia University, Graduate School of Arts and Sciences, Division of Social Sciences, Department of Anthropology, New York, NY 10027. Offers M Phil, MA, PhD, JD/MA, JD/PhD. Part-time programs available. *Degree requirements:* For master's, one foreign language, 2 research papers; for doctorate, 2 foreign languages, thesis/dissertation. *Entrance requirements:* For master's and doctorate, GRE General Test. Additional exam requirements/recommendations for international students: Required—TOEFL. *Faculty research:* Archaeology, physical anthropology, cultural and linguistic anthropology.

Concordia University, School of Graduate Studies, Faculty of Arts and Science, Department of Sociology and Anthropology, Montréal, QC H3G 1M8, Canada. Offers social and cultural anthropology (MA); sociology (MA). *Degree requirements:* For master's, comprehensive exam or thesis. *Entrance requirements:* For master's, honors degree in sociology or equivalent. *Faculty research:* Community and ethnic relations, popular culture, regional development in Canada, industrial and social movements, social problems and policies.

Cornell University, Graduate School, Graduate Fields of Arts and Sciences, Field of Anthropology, Ithaca, NY 14853-0001. Offers archaeological anthropology (PhD); biological anthropology (PhD); sociocultural anthropology (PhD). *Faculty:* 32 full-time (12 women). *Students:* 55 full-time (37 women); includes 11 minority (4 African Americans, 1 American Indian/Alaska Native, 2 Asian Americans or Pacific Islanders, 4 Hispanic Americans), 17 international. Average age 32. 111 applicants, 10% accepted, 8 enrolled. In 2009, 5 doctorates awarded. *Degree requirements:* For doctorate, one foreign language, comprehensive exam, thesis/dissertation, teaching experience. *Entrance requirements:* For doctorate, GRE General Test, 3 letters of recommendation, sample of written work. Additional exam requirements/recommendations for international students: Required—TOEFL (minimum score 550 paper-based; 213 computer-based; 77 iBT). *Application deadline:* For fall admission, 1/1 for domestic students. Application fee: $70. Electronic applications accepted. *Expenses:* Tuition: Full-time $29,500. Required fees: $70. Full-time tuition and fees vary according to degree level, program and student level. *Financial support:* In 2009–10, 47 students received support, including 5 fellowships with full tuition reimbursements available, 2 research assistantships with full tuition reimbursements available, 1 teaching assistantship with full tuition reimbursement available; institutionally sponsored loans, scholarships/grants, health care benefits, tuition waivers (full and partial), and unspecified assistantships also available. Financial award applicants required to submit FAFSA. *Faculty research:* Culture, engaged anthropology, political economy, area studies: Asia, Americas, Europe; interdisciplinary and ethnic studies: Asian-American studies. *Unit head:* Director of Graduate Studies, 607-255-6768. *Application contact:* Graduate Field Assistant, 607-255-6768, E-mail: graduate_anthropology@cornell.edu.

Dalhousie University, Faculty of Arts and Social Science, Department of Sociology and Social Anthropology, Halifax, NS B3H 4R2, Canada. Offers social anthropology (MA, PhD); sociology (MA, PhD). In 2009, 8 master's awarded. *Entrance requirements:* Additional exam requirements/recommendations for international students: Required—TOEFL, IELTS, CANTEST, CAEL, or Michigan English Language Assessment Battery. *Application deadline:* For fall admission, 6/1 for domestic students, 4/1 for international students; for winter admission, 10/31 for domestic students, 8/31 for international students; for spring admission, 2/28 for domestic students, 12/31 for international students. Application fee: $70. Electronic applications accepted. *Financial support:* Career-related internships or fieldwork, scholarships/grants, and health care benefits available. *Faculty research:* Social inequality and social injustice; work, industry, and development (regional and international perspectives); health and illness. *Unit head:* Dr. Emma Whelan, Graduate Coordinator, 902-494-6752, Fax: 902-494-2897, E-mail: sosagrad@dal.ca. *Application contact:* Rachelle Fox, Graduate Administrator, 902-494-6593, Fax: 902-494-2897, E-mail: sosagrad@is.dal.ca.

Duke University, Graduate School, Department of Cultural Anthropology, Durham, NC 27708. Offers physical anthropology (PhD), including comparative morphology of human and non-human primates, primate social behavior; social/cultural anthropology (PhD); JD/AM. *Faculty:* 13 full-time. *Students:* 32 full-time (22 women); includes 9 minority (5 African Americans, 2 Asian Americans or Pacific Islanders, 2 Hispanic Americans), 12 international. 102 applicants, 15% accepted, 5 enrolled. In 2009, 1 doctorate awarded. *Degree requirements:* For doctorate, one foreign language, thesis/dissertation. *Entrance requirements:* For doctorate, GRE General Test. Additional exam requirements/recommendations for international students: Required—TOEFL (minimum score 550 paper-based; 213 computer-based; 83 iBT), IELTS (minimum score 7). *Application deadline:* For fall admission, 12/8 priority date for domestic and international students. Application fee: $75. *Financial support:* Fellowships, research assistant-

Anthropology

Duke University (continued)

ships, teaching assistantships, Federal Work-Study available. Financial award application deadline: 12/31. *Unit head:* Louise Meintjes, Director of Graduate Studies, Fax: 919-681-8483, E-mail: hfrancis@duke.edu. *Application contact:* Cynthia Roberts, Associate Dean for Enrollment Services, 919-684-3913, E-mail: grad-admissions@duke.edu.

East Carolina University, Graduate School, Thomas Harriot College of Arts and Sciences, Department of Anthropology, Greenville, NC 27858-4353. Offers MA. Part-time programs available. *Degree requirements:* For master's, one foreign language, comprehensive exam, thesis. *Entrance requirements:* For master's, GRE General Test. Additional exam requirements/recommendations for international students: Required—TOEFL.

Eastern New Mexico University, Graduate School, College of Liberal Arts and Sciences, Department of Anthropology and Applied Archaeology, Portales, NM 88130. Offers anthropology (MA). Part-time programs available. *Faculty:* 4 full-time (2 women). *Students:* 3 full-time (1 woman), 41 part-time (24 women); includes 4 minority (1 American Indian/Alaska Native, 3 Hispanic Americans). Average age 31. 19 applicants, 68% accepted, 9 enrolled. In 2009, 4 master's awarded. *Degree requirements:* For master's, variable foreign language requirement, comprehensive exam, thesis. *Entrance requirements:* For master's, minimum GPA of 2.7, letters of recommendation, curriculum vitae, writing sample. Additional exam requirements/recommendations for international students: Required—TOEFL (minimum score 550 paper-based; 213 computer-based; 79 iBT), IELTS (minimum score 6). *Application deadline:* For fall admission, 7/20 priority date for domestic students, 6/20 priority date for international students. Applications are processed on a rolling basis. Application fee: $10. Electronic applications accepted. *Expenses:* Tuition, state resident: full-time $2922; part-time $121.75 per credit hour. Tuition, nonresident: full-time $8454; part-time $352.25 per credit hour. Required fees: $1038; $43.25 per credit hour. *Financial support:* In 2009–10, 3 fellowships (averaging $5,312 per year), 19 research assistantships with full tuition reimbursements (averaging $4,250 per year), 1 teaching assistantship with full tuition reimbursement (averaging $4,250 per year) were awarded; career-related internships or fieldwork and unspecified assistantships also available. Support available to part-time students. Financial award applicants required to submit FAFSA. *Faculty research:* Paleobotany, remote sensing, conservation archaeology, obsidian hydration. *Unit head:* Dr. David Batten, Graduate Coordinator, 575-562-2750, E-mail: david.batten@enmu.edu. *Application contact:* Dr. David Batten, Graduate Coordinator, 575-562-2750, E-mail: david.batten@enmu.edu.

Emory University, Graduate School of Arts and Sciences, Department of Anthropology, Atlanta, GA 30322-1100. Offers PhD. *Degree requirements:* For doctorate, thesis/dissertation, qualifying exams. *Entrance requirements:* For doctorate, GRE General Test. Additional exam requirements/recommendations for international students: Required—TOEFL. Electronic applications accepted. *Faculty research:* Primate behavioral ecology, comparative human biology, human growth and development, medical anthropology, globalization, gender and sexuality.

Florida Atlantic University, Dorothy F. Schmidt College of Arts and Letters, Department of Anthropology, Boca Raton, FL 33431-0991. Offers MA. Part-time programs available. *Faculty:* 7 full-time (3 women), 4 part-time/adjunct (2 women). *Students:* 17 full-time (12 women), 16 part-time (12 women); includes 5 minority (1 African American, 1 Asian American or Pacific Islander, 3 Hispanic Americans). Average age 31. 14 applicants, 79% accepted, 5 enrolled. In 2009, 6 master's awarded. *Degree requirements:* For master's, one foreign language, thesis. *Entrance requirements:* For master's, GRE General Test, minimum GPA of 3.0. Additional exam requirements/recommendations for international students: Required—TOEFL. *Application deadline:* For fall admission, 7/1 priority date for domestic students, 2/15 for international students; for spring admission, 11/1 for domestic students, 7/15 for international students. Applications are processed on a rolling basis. Application fee: $30. Electronic applications accepted. *Expenses:* Tuition, state resident: full-time $7055; part-time $293.94 per credit hour. Tuition, nonresident: full-time $22,096; part-time $920.66 per credit hour. *Financial support:* Fellowships, research assistantships with tuition reimbursements, teaching assistantships with tuition reimbursements, Federal Work-Study and unspecified assistantships available. *Faculty research:* Archaeological, ethnological, ethnographical, osteological, paleoanthropological, and zoo-archaeological research. *Unit head:* Dr. Michael S. Harris, Chairman, 561-297-3233, Fax: 561-297-0084, E-mail: mharris@fau.edu. *Application contact:* Dr. Emily Stockard, Associate Dean, 561-297-2817, Fax: 561-297-2744, E-mail: stockard@fau.edu.

George Mason University, College of Humanities and Social Sciences, Department of Sociology and Anthropology, Fairfax, VA 22030. Offers anthropology (MA); sociology (MA, PhD). *Faculty:* 26 full-time (12 women), 7 part-time/adjunct (4 women). *Students:* 23 full-time (16 women), 69 part-time (51 women); includes 17 minority (8 African Americans, 2 Asian Americans or Pacific Islanders, 7 Hispanic Americans), 2 international. Average age 32. 87 applicants, 57% accepted, 24 enrolled. In 2009, 5 master's awarded. *Degree requirements:* For master's, thesis; for doctorate, comprehensive exam, thesis/dissertation. *Entrance requirements:* For doctorate, GRE. Additional exam requirements/recommendations for international students: Required—TOEFL. *Application deadline:* For fall admission, 3/1 priority date for domestic students; for spring admission, 10/1 for domestic students. Applications are processed on a rolling basis. Application fee: $75. Electronic applications accepted. *Expenses:* Tuition, state resident: full-time $7568; part-time $315.33 per credit hour. Tuition, nonresident: full-time $21,704; part-time $904.33 per credit hour. Required fees: $2184; $91 per credit hour. *Financial support:* In 2009–10, 15 students received support, including 2 fellowships with full tuition reimbursements available (averaging $18,000 per year), 4 research assistantships with full and partial tuition reimbursements available (averaging $13,219 per year), 10 teaching assistantships with full and partial tuition reimbursements available (averaging $6,018 per year); Federal Work-Study, scholarships/grants, unspecified assistantships, and health care benefits (full-time research or teaching assistantship recipients) also available. Support available to part-time students. Financial award application deadline: 3/1. *Faculty research:* Africa, American teenagers, black entrepreneur, human rights, gambling. Total annual research expenditures: $59,230. *Unit head:* Dr. Susan Trencher, Chair, 703-993-1429, E-mail: strenche@gmu.edu. *Application contact:* Amy Best, Associate Professor/Graduate Coordinator, 703-993-1426, E-mail: abest@gmu.edu.

The George Washington University, Columbian College of Arts and Sciences, Department of Anthropology, Washington, DC 20052. Offers anthropology (MA); folklife (MA); hominid paleobiology (MS, PhD); international development (MA). Part-time and evening/weekend programs available. *Faculty:* 13 full-time (4 women), 11 part-time/adjunct (5 women). *Students:* 32 full-time (26 women), 8 part-time (7 women); includes 6 minority (1 African American, 3 Asian Americans or Pacific Islanders, 2 Hispanic Americans), 1 international. Average age 25. 67 applicants, 79% accepted, 27 enrolled. In 2009, 19 master's awarded. *Degree requirements:* For master's, one foreign language, comprehensive exam, thesis or alternative. *Entrance requirements:* For master's, GRE General Test, minimum GPA of 3.0. Additional exam requirements/recommendations for international students: Required—TOEFL (minimum score 550 paper-based; 213 computer-based; 80 iBT). *Application deadline:* For fall admission, 1/15 priority date for international students; for spring admission, 9/15 priority date for domestic students, 9/1 priority date for international students. Applications are processed on a rolling basis. Application fee: $60. Electronic applications accepted. *Financial support:* In 2009–10, 8 students received support; fellowships, teaching assistantships, career-related internships or fieldwork and Federal Work-Study available. Financial award application deadline: 1/15. *Unit head:* Catherine J. Allen, Chair, 202-994-7545, E-mail: kitallen@gwu.edu. *Application contact:* Information Contact, 202-994-6075, E-mail: anth@gwu.edu.

Georgia State University, College of Arts and Sciences, Department of Anthropology, Atlanta, GA 30302. Offers MA. Part-time programs available. *Degree requirements:* For master's, one foreign language, thesis or alternative, exam. *Entrance requirements:* For master's, GRE General Test, departmental supplemental form. Additional exam requirements/recommendations for international students: Required—TOEFL. Electronic applications accepted. *Faculty research:* Latin America, medical anthropology, urban anthropology.

Graduate School and University Center of the City University of New York, Graduate Studies, Program in Anthropology, New York, NY 10016-4039. Offers anthropological linguistics (PhD); archaeology (PhD); cultural anthropology (PhD); physical anthropology (PhD). *Faculty:* 39 full-time (14 women). *Students:* 166 full-time (95 women), 1 (woman) part-time; includes 40 minority (13 African Americans, 1 American Indian/Alaska Native, 9 Asian Americans or Pacific Islanders, 17 Hispanic Americans), 25 international. Average age 33. 165 applicants, 27% accepted, 22 enrolled. In 2009, 13 doctorates awarded. *Degree requirements:* For doctorate, one foreign language, thesis/dissertation. *Entrance requirements:* For doctorate, GRE General Test. Additional exam requirements/recommendations for international students: Required—TOEFL. *Application deadline:* For fall admission, 1/8 priority date for domestic students. Application fee: $125. Electronic applications accepted. *Financial support:* In 2009–10, 111 students received support, including 88 fellowships, 16 research assistantships, 10 teaching assistantships; career-related internships or fieldwork, Federal Work-Study, institutionally sponsored loans, and tuition waivers (full and partial) also available. Financial award application deadline: 2/1; financial award applicants required to submit FAFSA. *Unit head:* Dr. Louise Lennihan, Executive Officer, 212-817-8006, Fax: 212-817-1501, E-mail: anthro@gc.cuny.edu. *Application contact:* Information Contact, 212-817-8005, Fax: 212-817-1501, E-mail: anthro@gc.cuny.edu.

Harvard University, Graduate School of Arts and Sciences, Committee on Middle Eastern Studies, Cambridge, MA 02138. Offers anthropology and Middle Eastern studies (PhD); economics and Middle Eastern studies (PhD); fine arts and Middle Eastern studies (PhD); history and Middle Eastern studies (PhD); regional studies–Middle East (AM). Terminal master's awarded for partial completion of doctoral program. *Degree requirements:* For master's, one foreign language; for doctorate, 2 foreign languages, thesis/dissertation. *Entrance requirements:* For master's, GRE General Test; for doctorate, GRE General Test, 1 year of course work in Middle Eastern regional studies, proficiency in a related language. Additional exam requirements/recommendations for international students: Required—TOEFL. *Expenses:* Tuition: Full-time $33,696. Required fees: $1126. Full-time tuition and fees vary according to program.

Harvard University, Graduate School of Arts and Sciences, Department of Anthropology, Cambridge, MA 02138. Offers archaeology (PhD); biological anthropology (PhD); legal anthropology (AM); medical anthropology (AM); social anthropology (AM, PhD); social change and development (AM). Terminal master's awarded for partial completion of doctoral program. *Degree requirements:* For master's, 2 foreign languages, thesis (for some programs); for doctorate, 2 foreign languages, thesis/dissertation, laboratory and/or fieldwork; general, qualifying, or special exams. *Entrance requirements:* For master's and doctorate, GRE General Test. Additional exam requirements/recommendations for international students: Required—TOEFL. *Expenses:* Tuition: Full-time $33,696. Required fees: $1126. Full-time tuition and fees vary according to program.

Hunter College of the City University of New York, Graduate School, School of Arts and Sciences, Department of Anthropology, New York, NY 10021-5085. Offers MA. Part-time and evening/weekend programs available. *Faculty:* 6 full-time (1 woman), 2 part-time/adjunct (both women). *Students:* 2 full-time (both women), 43 part-time (26 women); includes 10 minority (2 American Indian/Alaska Native, 2 Asian Americans or Pacific Islanders, 6 Hispanic Americans). Average age 32. 55 applicants, 45% accepted, 13 enrolled. In 2009, 16 master's awarded. *Degree requirements:* For master's, comprehensive exam, thesis, language or statistics exam. *Entrance requirements:* For master's, GRE General Test, minimum 9 credits of course work in anthropology or a related field. Additional exam requirements/recommendations for international students: Required—TOEFL. *Application deadline:* For fall admission, 4/1 for domestic students, 2/1 for international students; for spring admission, 11/1 for domestic students, 9/1 for international students. Application fee: $125. *Expenses:* Tuition, state resident: full-time $7360; part-time $310 per credit. Required fees: $250 per semester. *Financial support:* Research assistantships, tuition waivers (full and partial) available. *Faculty research:* Primatology, human ecology, archeology, political anthropology, primate and human evolution. *Unit head:* Gregory A. Johnson, Chair, 212-772-5652, Fax: 212-772-5410, E-mail: gjohnson@hunter.cuny.edu. *Application contact:* William Zlata, Director for Graduate Admissions, 212-772-4482, Fax: 212-650-3336, E-mail: admissions@hunter.cuny.edu.

Idaho State University, Office of Graduate Studies, College of Arts and Sciences, Department of Anthropology, Pocatello, ID 83209-8005. Offers MA, MS. Part-time programs available. *Faculty:* 6 full-time (2 women), 1 (woman) part-time/adjunct. *Students:* 15 full-time (10 women), 6 part-time (2 women); includes 4 minority (3 American Indian/Alaska Native, 1 Hispanic American). Average age 39. In 2009, 7 master's awarded. *Degree requirements:* For master's, one foreign language, comprehensive exam, thesis, 4 semesters foreign language, oral defense. *Entrance requirements:* For master's, GRE General Test, GMAT or MAT, minimum GPA of 3.0 in all upper-division classes, 3 letters of recommendation. Additional exam requirements/recommendations for international students: Required—TOEFL (minimum score 550 paper-based; 213 computer-based; 80 iBT). *Application deadline:* For fall admission, 7/1 for domestic students, 6/1 for international students; for spring admission, 12/1 for domestic students, 11/1 for international students. Applications are processed on a rolling basis. Application fee: $55. Electronic applications accepted. *Expenses:* Tuition, state resident: full-time $3318; part-time $297 per credit hour. Tuition, nonresident: full-time $13,120; part-time $437 per credit hour. Required fees: $2530. Tuition and fees vary according to program. *Financial support:* In 2009–10, 2 research assistantships with full and partial tuition reimbursements (averaging $7,051 per year), 2 teaching assistantships with full and partial tuition reimbursements (averaging $10,841 per year) were awarded; career-related internships or fieldwork, Federal Work-Study, institutionally sponsored loans, scholarships/grants, health care benefits, tuition waivers (full and partial), and unspecified assistantships also available. Support available to part-time students. Financial award application deadline: 1/1; financial award applicants required to submit FAFSA. *Faculty research:* Native American studies: health care, language/ethnopoetics, prehistory, art, resource environmental management. *Unit head:* Dr. Ernst Lohse, Chairman, 208-282-2629, Fax: 208-282-4741, E-mail: lohserne@isu.edu. *Application contact:* Tami Carson, Graduate School Technical Records Specialist, 208-282-2150, Fax: 208-282-4847, E-mail: carstami@isu.edu.

Indiana University Bloomington, University Graduate School, College of Arts and Sciences, Department of Anthropology, Bloomington, IN 47405-7000. Offers MA, PhD. *Faculty:* 26 full-time (16 women), 25 part-time/adjunct (9 women). *Students:* 135 full-time (91 women); includes 21 minority (3 African Americans, 6 American Indian/Alaska Native, 3 Asian Americans or Pacific Islanders, 9 Hispanic Americans), 10 international. Average age 32. 174 applicants, 26% accepted, 22 enrolled. In 2009, 13 master's, 7 doctorates awarded. Terminal master's awarded for partial completion of doctoral program. *Degree requirements:* For master's, thesis or alternative; for doctorate, one foreign language, comprehensive exam, thesis/dissertation. *Entrance requirements:* For master's and doctorate, GRE General Test, minimum GPA of 3.0. Additional exam requirements/recommendations for international students: Required—TOEFL (minimum score 550 paper-based; 213 computer-based; 79 iBT). *Application deadline:* For fall admission, 1/15 for domestic and international students. Application fee: $55 ($65 for international students). Electronic applications accepted. *Financial support:* In 2009–10, 85 students received support; fellowships with full tuition reimbursements available, research assistantships with full tuition reimbursements available, teaching assistantships with full tuition reimbursements available, Federal Work-Study, scholarships/grants, health care benefits, and unspecified assistantships available. Financial award application deadline: 2/15; financial award applicants required to submit FAFSA. *Faculty research:* Ecologic and economic development, symbolism, arts/dance, paleoarchaeology, bioanthropology. Total annual research expenditures: $22.7 million. *Unit head:* Dr. Eduardo S. Brondizio, Chair, 812-855-2555, Fax: 812-855-4358, E-mail: ebrondiz@indiana.edu. *Application contact:* Debra Wilkerson, Secretary, 812-855-1203, Fax: 812-855-4358, E-mail: dwilkers@indiana.edu.

Iowa State University of Science and Technology, Graduate College, College of Liberal Arts and Sciences, Department of Anthropology, Ames, IA 50011. Offers MA. *Faculty:* 7 full-time (3 women), 2 part-time/adjunct (both women). *Students:* 13 full-time (12 women), 4 part-time (all women); includes 1 minority (African American), 2 international. 15 applicants, 40% accepted, 5 enrolled. In 2009, 5 master's awarded. *Degree requirements:* For master's, thesis. *Entrance requirements:* For master's, GRE General Test. Additional exam requirements/recommendations for international students: Required—TOEFL (minimum score 550 paper-based; 79 iBT) or IELTS (minimum score 6.5). *Application deadline:* For fall admission, 1/15 priority date for domestic and international students; for spring admission, 10/1 for domestic and international students. Applications are processed on a rolling basis. Application fee: $40 ($90 for international students). Electronic applications accepted. *Expenses:* Tuition, state resident: full-time $6716. Tuition, nonresident: full-time $8908. Tuition and fees vary according to course level, course load, program and student level. *Financial support:* In 2009–10, 1 research assistantship with full and partial tuition reimbursement (averaging $14,000 per year), 8 teaching assistantships with full and partial tuition reimbursements (averaging $14,800 per year) were awarded; fellowships, scholarships/grants, health care benefits, and unspecified assistantships also available. *Unit head:* Dr. R. Paul Lasley, Interim Chair, 515-294-8212, Fax: 515-294-1708, E-mail: anthgrad@iastate.edu. *Application contact:* Dr. Jill Pruetz, Director of Graduate Education, 515-294-7139, E-mail: anthgrade@iastate.edu.

The Johns Hopkins University, Zanvyl Krieger School of Arts and Sciences, Department of Anthropology, Baltimore, MD 21218-2699. Offers PhD. *Faculty:* 10 full-time (7 women), 1 part-time/adjunct (0 women). *Students:* 18 full-time (12 women), 12 international. Average age 30. 102 applicants, 4% accepted, 4 enrolled. In 2009, 3 doctorates awarded. *Degree requirements:* For doctorate, one foreign language, thesis/dissertation. *Entrance requirements:* For doctorate, GRE General Test. Additional exam requirements/recommendations for international students: Required—TOEFL, IELTS. *Application deadline:* For fall admission, 1/11 for domestic and international students. Application fee: $75. Electronic applications accepted. *Financial support:* In 2009–10, 12 fellowships with full and partial tuition reimbursements (averaging $17,500 per year), 10 teaching assistantships with full and partial tuition reimbursements (averaging $17,500 per year) were awarded; research assistantships, career-related internships or fieldwork, Federal Work-Study, and institutionally sponsored loans also available. Financial award application deadline: 4/15; financial award applicants required to submit FAFSA. *Faculty research:* Social and cultural anthropology of complex societies, gender politics, economic anthropology, religion. Total annual research expenditures: $117,673. *Unit head:* Dr. Jane I. Guyer, Chair, 410-516-7272, Fax: 410-516-6080, E-mail: jiguyer@jhu.edu. *Application contact:* Richard Helman, Admissions Coordinator, 410-516-7271, Fax: 410-516-6080, E-mail: rhelman@jhu.edu.

Kent State University, College of Arts and Sciences, Department of Anthropology, Kent, OH 44242-0001. Offers MA. *Degree requirements:* For master's, thesis. *Entrance requirements:* For master's, GRE General Test, minimum GPA of 3.0. Additional exam requirements/recommendations for international students: Required—TOEFL. Electronic applications accepted.

Louisiana State University and Agricultural and Mechanical College, Graduate School, College of Arts and Sciences, Department of Geography and Anthropology, Baton Rouge, LA 70803. Offers anthropology (MA); geography (MA, MS, PhD). Part-time programs available. *Faculty:* 30 full-time (11 women), 1 part-time/adjunct (0 women). *Students:* 63 full-time (32 women), 25 part-time (14 women); includes 4 minority (1 African American, 3 Hispanic Americans), 19 international. Average age 31. 68 applicants, 71% accepted, 15 enrolled. In 2009, 8 master's, 5 doctorates awarded. Terminal master's awarded for partial completion of doctoral program. *Degree requirements:* For master's, 2 foreign languages, thesis (for some programs); for doctorate, 2 foreign languages, thesis/dissertation. *Entrance requirements:* For master's and doctorate, GRE General Test, minimum GPA of 3.0. Additional exam requirements/recommendations for international students: Required—TOEFL (minimum score 550 paper-based; 213 computer-based; 79 iBT) or IELTS (minimum score 6.5). *Application deadline:* For fall admission, 1/25 priority date for domestic students, 5/15 for international students; for spring admission, 10/15 for international students. Applications are processed on a rolling basis. Application fee: $50 ($70 for international students). Electronic applications accepted. *Financial support:* In 2009–10, 73 students received support, including 2 fellowships with full tuition reimbursements available (averaging $33,473 per year), 17 research assistantships with full and partial tuition reimbursements available (averaging $16,266 per year), 30 teaching assistantships with full and partial tuition reimbursements available (averaging $13,013 per year); career-related internships or fieldwork, health care benefits, and unspecified assistantships also available. Financial award application deadline: 3/1; financial award applicants required to submit FAFSA. *Faculty research:* Cultural, coastal, climate, geographic information systems-geography, cultural, linguistics, archaeology-anthropology. Total annual research expenditures: $731,204. *Unit head:* Dr. Patrick A. Hesp, Chair, 225-578-5942, Fax: 225-578-4420, E-mail: gachair@lsu.edu. *Application contact:* Dr. Helen Regis, Graduate Adviser, 225-578-6171, Fax: 225-578-4420, E-mail: hregis1@lsu.edu.

McGill University, Faculty of Graduate and Postdoctoral Studies, Faculty of Arts, Department of Anthropology, Montréal, QC H3A 2T5, Canada. Offers anthropology (MA, PhD); medical anthropology (MA).

McGill University, Faculty of Graduate and Postdoctoral Studies, Faculty of Medicine, Department of Social Studies in Medicine, Montréal, QC H3A 2T5, Canada. Offers medical anthropology (MA, PhD); medical history (MA, PhD); medical sociology (MA, PhD).

McMaster University, School of Graduate Studies, Faculty of Social Sciences, Department of Anthropology, Hamilton, ON L8S 4M2, Canada. Offers MA, PhD. Part-time programs available. *Degree requirements:* For master's, thesis or alternative; for doctorate, one foreign language, comprehensive exam, thesis/dissertation, fieldwork. *Entrance requirements:* Additional exam requirements/recommendations for international students: Required—TOEFL (minimum score 580 paper-based; 237 computer-based). *Faculty research:* Medical anthropology, contemporary ethnography in an interdisciplinary perspective, archaeological and social theory, linguistics, folklore.

Memorial University of Newfoundland, School of Graduate Studies, Department of Anthropology, St. John's, NL A1C 5S7, Canada. Offers archaeology and physical anthropology (MA, PhD); social and cultural anthropology (MA, PhD). Part-time programs available. *Degree requirements:* For master's, thesis (for some programs); for doctorate, comprehensive exam, thesis/dissertation, oral defense of thesis. *Entrance requirements:* For master's, 2nd class degree in related field. Electronic applications accepted. *Faculty research:* Early European settlements, ethnoarchaeology, economic/political anthropology, land claims and aboriginal rights, marine anthropology.

Michigan State University, The Graduate School, College of Social Science, Department of Anthropology, East Lansing, MI 48824. Offers anthropology (MA, PhD); professional applications in anthropology (MA). *Faculty:* 21 full-time (12 women). *Students:* 77 full-time (59 women), 10 part-time (6 women); includes 18 minority (6 African Americans, 2 American Indian/Alaska Native, 4 Asian Americans or Pacific Islanders, 6 Hispanic Americans), 4 international. Average age 31. 101 applicants, 27% accepted. In 2009, 32 master's, 6 doctorates awarded. Terminal master's awarded for partial completion of doctoral program. *Degree requirements:* For master's, comprehensive exam (for some programs); for doctorate, annual evaluation. *Entrance requirements:* Additional exam requirements/recommendations for international students: Required—TOEFL. Electronic applications accepted. *Expenses:* Tuition, state resident: part-time $478.25 per credit hour. Tuition, nonresident: part-time $966.50 per credit hour. Part-time tuition and fees vary according to program. *Financial support:* In 2009–10, 14 research assistantships with tuition reimbursements (averaging $6,691 per year), 24 teaching assistantships with tuition reimbursements (averaging $6,264 per year) were awarded. Total annual research expenditures: $368,422. *Unit head:* Dr. Jodie O'Gorman, Acting Chairperson, 517-353-2950, Fax: 517-432-2363, E-mail: ogorman@msu.edu. *Application contact:* Nancy Jean Smith, Graduate Secretary, 517-432-1445, Fax: 517-432-2363, E-mail: anthropology@ssc.msu.edu.

Minnesota State University Mankato, College of Graduate Studies, College of Social and Behavioral Sciences, Department of Anthropology, Mankato, MN 56001. Offers MS. Part-time programs available. *Students:* 4 full-time (all women), 10 part-time (7 women). *Degree requirements:* For master's, comprehensive exam. *Entrance requirements:* For master's, minimum undergraduate GPA of 3.0 in last 2 years of course work. Additional exam requirements/recommendations for international students: Required—TOEFL. *Application deadline:* For fall admission, 7/1 priority date for domestic students; for spring admission, 11/1 for domestic students. Applications are processed on a rolling basis. Application fee: $40. Electronic applications accepted. *Expenses:* Tuition, state resident: full-time $5364. Tuition, nonresident: full-time $8314. *Financial support:* Unspecified assistantships available. Financial award application deadline: 3/15; financial award applicants required to submit FAFSA. *Unit head:* Dr. Paul Brown, Chair, 507-389-6504, Fax: 507-389-6769, E-mail: paul.brown@mnsu.edu. *Application contact:* 507-389-2321, E-mail: grad@mnsu.edu.

Mississippi State University, College of Arts and Sciences, Department of Anthropology and Middle Eastern Cultures, Mississippi State, MS 39762. Offers applied anthropology (MA). Part-time programs available. *Faculty:* 6 full-time (1 woman). *Students:* 13 full-time (3 women), 10 part-time (4 women); includes 1 minority (African American), 1 international. Average age 28. 11 applicants, 82% accepted, 6 enrolled. In 2009, 4 master's awarded. *Degree requirements:* For master's, thesis. *Entrance requirements:* For master's, GRE, minimum GPA of 3.0 on last 60 hours of undergraduate courses. Additional exam requirements/recommendations for international students: Required—TOEFL (minimum score 475 paper-based; 153 computer-based; 53 iBT); Recommended—IELTS (minimum score 4.5). *Application deadline:* For fall admission, 4/15 priority date for domestic students, 4/15 for international students; for spring admission, 11/1 priority date for domestic students, 9/1 for international students. Applications are processed on a rolling basis. Application fee: $40. Electronic applications accepted. *Expenses:* Tuition, state resident: full-time $2575.50; part-time $286.25 per credit hour. Tuition, nonresident: full-time $6510; part-time $723.50 per credit hour. Tuition and fees vary according to course load. *Financial support:* In 2009–10, 5 research assistantships with full and partial tuition reimbursements (averaging $8,923 per year), 3 teaching assistantships with full and partial tuition reimbursements (averaging $8,766 per year) were awarded; Federal Work-Study, institutionally sponsored loans, scholarships/grants, and unspecified assistantships also available. Financial award application deadline: 3/15; financial award applicants required to submit FAFSA. *Faculty research:* Archaeology and bioarchaeology, environmental archaeology, cultural archaeology, research projects in Southeastern archaeology and bioarchaeology. *Unit head:* Dr. Paul F. Jacobs, Professor and Department Head, 662-325-7525, Fax: 662-325-8690, E-mail: pfj1@ra.msstate.edu. *Application contact:* Dr. Evan Peacock, Associate Professor/Graduate Coordinator, 662-325-1663, Fax: 662-325-1967, E-mail: peacock@anthro.msstate.edu.

Missouri State University, Graduate College, College of Humanities and Public Affairs, Department of Sociology, Anthropology, and Criminology, Springfield, MO 65897. Offers applied anthropology (MS); criminology (MS). Part-time programs available. *Faculty:* 20 full-time (6 women). *Students:* 31 full-time (10 women), 21 part-time (14 women); includes 4 minority (3 Asian Americans or Pacific Islanders, 1 Hispanic American). Average age 28. 25 applicants, 96% accepted, 19 enrolled. In 2009, 8 master's awarded. *Degree requirements:* For master's, comprehensive exam. *Entrance requirements:* For master's, GRE, minimum GPA of 3.0. Additional exam requirements/recommendations for international students: Required—TOEFL (minimum score 550 paper-based; 213 computer-based; 79 iBT). *Application deadline:* For fall admission, 7/20 priority date for domestic students, 5/1 for international students; for spring admission, 12/20 priority date for domestic students, 9/1 for international students. Applications are processed on a rolling basis. Application fee: $35 ($50 for international students). Electronic applications accepted. *Expenses:* Tuition, state resident: full-time $3852; part-time $214 per credit hour. Tuition, nonresident: full-time $7524; part-time $418 per credit hour. Required fees: $696; $172 per semester. Tuition and fees vary according to course level, course load, degree level and program. *Financial support:* Federal Work-Study, institutionally sponsored loans, scholarships/grants, and unspecified assistantships available. Financial award application deadline: 3/31; financial award applicants required to submit FAFSA. *Faculty research:* Youth delinquency, social theory, linguistic anthropology, forensic anthropology, homeland security. *Unit head:* Dr. Karl Kunkel, Head, 417-836-5640, Fax: 417-836-6416, E-mail: karlkunkel@missouristate.edu. *Application contact:* Eric Eckert, Coordinator of Admissions and Recruitment, 417-836-5331, Fax: 417-836-6888, E-mail: ericeckert@missouristate.edu.

Montclair State University, The Graduate School, College of Humanities and Social Sciences, Department of Anthropology, Montclair, NJ 07043-1624. Offers community development (Certificate). Part-time and evening/weekend programs available. *Faculty:* 8 full-time (4 women), 13 part-time/adjunct (9 women). *Students:* 3 part-time (2 women). Average age 40. 5 applicants, 100% accepted, 3 enrolled. *Entrance requirements:* Additional exam requirements/recommendations for international students: Required—TOEFL (minimum score 83 computer-based), or IELTS. *Expenses:* Tuition, area resident: Part-time $486.74 per credit. Tuition, state resident: part-time $486.74 per credit. Tuition, nonresident: part-time $751.34 per credit. Tuition and fees vary according to degree level and program. *Financial support:* In 2009–10, 2 research assistantships with full tuition reimbursements (averaging $7,000 per year) were awarded; Federal Work-Study, scholarships/grants, and unspecified assistantships also available. Support available to part-time students. Financial award application deadline: 3/1; financial award applicants required to submit FAFSA. *Unit head:* Dr. Kenneth Brook, Chairperson, 973-655-4119, E-mail: brookk@mail.montclair.edu. *Application contact:* Amy Aiello, Director of Graduate Admissions and Operations, 973-655-5147, Fax: 973-655-7869, E-mail: graduate.school@montclair.edu.

New Mexico Highlands University, Graduate Studies, College of Arts and Sciences, Program in Southwest Studies, Las Vegas, NM 87701. Offers anthropology (MA). Program is interdisciplinary. Part-time programs available. *Degree requirements:* For master's, comprehensive exam, thesis or alternative. *Entrance requirements:* For master's, minimum undergraduate GPA of 3.0. Additional exam requirements/recommendations for international students: Required—TOEFL (minimum score 540 paper-based; 207 computer-based).

New Mexico State University, Graduate School, College of Arts and Sciences, Department of Sociology and Anthropology, Las Cruces, NM 88003-8001. Offers anthropology (MA); sociology (MA). Part-time programs available. *Faculty:* 23 full-time (17 women), 4 part-time/adjunct (2 women). *Students:* 44 full-time (28 women), 81 part-time (57 women); includes 35 minority (6 African Americans, 5 American Indian/Alaska Native, 1 Asian American or Pacific Islander, 23 Hispanic Americans), 4 international. Average age 33. 79 applicants, 92% accepted, 40 enrolled. In 2009, 28 master's awarded. *Degree requirements:* For master's, comprehensive exam (for some programs), thesis (for some programs). *Entrance requirements:* For master's, undergraduate research methods and statistics. Additional exam requirements/recommendations for international students: Required—TOEFL. *Application deadline:* For fall admission, 2/15 priority date for domestic students; for spring admission, 10/15 priority date for domestic students. Applications are processed on a rolling basis. Application fee: $30 ($50 for international students). Electronic applications accepted. *Expenses:* Tuition, state resident: full-time $4080; part-time $223 per credit. Tuition, nonresident: full-time $14,256; part-time $647 per credit. Required fees: $1278; $639 per semester. *Financial support:* In 2009–10, 11 students received support, including 19 teaching assistantships with partial tuition reimbursements available (averaging $10,484 per year); fellowships, research assistantships with partial tuition reimbursements available, career-related internships or fieldwork, Federal Work-Study, and health care benefits also available. Support available to part-time students. Financial award application deadline: 2/15. *Faculty research:* Native American culture and society, Latin America and border studies, prehistoric and historic archaeology, medical anthropology, applied anthropology, gender and sexualities, globalization, rural sociology, delinquency and criminology, sociology of education, sociology of sport. *Unit head:* Dr. Miriam Chaiken, Head, 575-646-2826, Fax: 575-646-3725, E-mail: mchaiken@nmsu.edu. *Application contact:* Coordinator.

The New School: A University, The New School for Social Research, Department of Anthropology, New York, NY 10003. Offers M Phil, MA, DS Sc, PhD. Part-time and evening/

Anthropology

The New School: A University (continued)
weekend programs available. *Faculty:* 9 full-time (5 women). *Students:* 56 full-time (35 women), 12 part-time (10 women); includes 13 minority (2 African Americans, 1 American Indian/Alaska Native, 7 Asian Americans or Pacific Islanders, 3 Hispanic Americans), 15 international. Average age 29. 88 applicants, 74% accepted, 22 enrolled. In 2009, 13 master's, 4 doctorates awarded. Terminal master's awarded for partial completion of doctoral program. *Degree requirements:* For master's, comprehensive exam; for doctorate, one foreign language, comprehensive exam, thesis/dissertation, 30 credits, including three proseminars. *Entrance requirements:* For master's, GRE General Test; for doctorate, GRE General Test, MA in anthropology. Additional exam requirements/recommendations for international students: Required—TOEFL (minimum score 600 paper-based; 250 computer-based; 100 iBT). *Application deadline:* For fall admission, 1/17 priority date for domestic and international students; for spring admission, 10/15 priority date for domestic and international students. Applications are processed on a rolling basis. Application fee: $50. Electronic applications accepted. *Financial support:* Fellowships, research assistantships, teaching assistantships, Federal Work-Study, scholarships/grants, tuition waivers (full and partial), and unspecified assistantships available. Support available to part-time students. Financial award application deadline: 3/1; financial award applicants required to submit FAFSA. *Faculty research:* Critical theory; modern social and cultural systems; race, class, gender. *Unit head:* Dr. Hugh Raffles, Chair, 212-229-5757 Ext. 3025, E-mail: rafflesh@newschool.edu. *Application contact:* Robert MacDonald, Director of Admissions, 212-229-5710 Ext. 3007, Fax: 212-989-7102, E-mail: macdonar@newschool.edu.

New York University, Graduate School of Arts and Science, Department of Anthropology, New York, NY 10012-1019. Offers anthropology (MA, PhD), including archaeological anthropology, linguistic anthropology, physical anthropology, socio-cultural anthropology; anthropology and French studies (PhD); MA/Advanced Certificate; PhD/Advanced Certificate. Part-time programs available. *Faculty:* 22 full-time, 13 part-time/adjunct. *Students:* 84 full-time (54 women); includes 10 minority (5 Asian Americans or Pacific Islanders, 5 Hispanic Americans), 24 international. Average age 30. 380 applicants, 5% accepted, 14 enrolled. In 2009, 11 master's, 10 doctorates awarded. *Degree requirements:* For master's, thesis; for doctorate, one foreign language, comprehensive exam, thesis/dissertation. *Entrance requirements:* For master's, GRE General Test; for doctorate, GRE General Test, MA or equivalent. Additional exam requirements/recommendations for international students: Required—TOEFL. *Application deadline:* For fall admission, 1/4 priority date for domestic students. Application fee: $90. *Expenses:* Tuition: Full-time $30,528; part-time $1272 per credit. Required fees: $2177. *Financial support:* Fellowships with tuition reimbursements, research assistantships with tuition reimbursements, teaching assistantships with tuition reimbursements, career-related internships or fieldwork, Federal Work-Study, institutionally sponsored loans, scholarships/grants, health care benefits, and unspecified assistantships available. Financial award application deadline: 1/4; financial award applicants required to submit FAFSA. *Faculty research:* Sociocultural anthropology, archaeology, biological anthropology, linguistic anthropology. *Unit head:* Fred Myers, Chair, 212-998-8550, Fax: 212-995-4014, E-mail: anthropology@nyu.edu. *Application contact:* Susan Carol-Rogers, Director of Graduate Studies, 212-998-8550, Fax: 212-995-4014, E-mail: anthropology@nyu.edu.

North Carolina State University, Graduate School, College of Humanities and Social Sciences, Department of Sociology and Anthropology, Program in Anthropology, Raleigh, NC 27695. Offers bioarchaeology (MA); cultural anthropology (MA); environmental anthropology (MA).

Northern Arizona University, Graduate College, College of Social and Behavioral Sciences, Department of Anthropology, Flagstaff, AZ 86011. Offers archaeology (MA); cultural anthropology (MA); linguistic anthropology (MA). *Faculty:* 17 full-time (7 women). *Students:* 45 full-time (30 women), 19 part-time (11 women); includes 11 minority (5 American Indian/Alaska Native, 1 Asian American or Pacific Islander, 5 Hispanic Americans). Average age 35. 502 applicants, 12% accepted, 52 enrolled. In 2009, 47 master's awarded. *Degree requirements:* For master's, thesis (for some programs), internship paper. *Entrance requirements:* For master's, 18 undergraduate hours in anthropology. Additional exam requirements/recommendations for international students: Required—TOEFL (minimum score 550 paper-based; 213 computer-based; 80 iBT), IELTS (minimum score 7), or a bachelor's degree from an English-speaking university and demonstrated proficiency. *Application deadline:* For fall admission, 2/15 priority date for domestic students, 9/1 priority date for international students. Applications are processed on a rolling basis. Application fee: $65. Electronic applications accepted. *Financial support:* In 2009–10, 11 teaching assistantships with partial tuition reimbursements (averaging $10,439 per year) were awarded; career-related internships or fieldwork, Federal Work-Study, health care benefits, tuition waivers (full and partial), and unspecified assistantships also available. Support available to part-time students. Financial award application deadline: 3/30; financial award applicants required to submit FAFSA. *Faculty research:* Economic development, culture change, ethnohistory, archaeology of the Southwest, small town networks and HIV. Total annual research expenditures: $594,266. *Unit head:* Dr. Robert Trotter, Chair, 928-523-4521, Fax: 928-523-9135, E-mail: robert.trotter@nau.edu. *Application contact:* Dr. Cathy Small, Coordinator, 928-523-1090, Fax: 928-523-9135, E-mail: cathy.small@nau.edu.

Northern Illinois University, Graduate School, College of Liberal Arts and Sciences, Department of Anthropology, De Kalb, IL 60115-2854. Offers MA. Part-time programs available. *Faculty:* 12 full-time (6 women). *Students:* 15 full-time (7 women), 31 part-time (20 women); includes 6 minority (1 African American, 1 American Indian/Alaska Native, 3 Asian Americans or Pacific Islanders, 1 Hispanic American), 5 international. Average age 29. 32 applicants, 66% accepted, 13 enrolled. In 2009, 10 master's awarded. *Degree requirements:* For master's, one foreign language, comprehensive exam, thesis optional. *Entrance requirements:* For master's, GRE General Test, minimum GPA of 2.75, 15 hours of course work in anthropology, course work in statistics. Additional exam requirements/recommendations for international students: Required—TOEFL (minimum score 550 paper-based; 213 computer-based). *Application deadline:* For fall admission, 6/1 for domestic students, 5/1 for international students; for spring admission, 11/1 for domestic students, 10/1 for international students. Applications are processed on a rolling basis. Application fee: $30. Electronic applications accepted. *Expenses:* Tuition, state resident: full-time $6576; part-time $274 per credit hour. Tuition, nonresident: full-time $13,152; part-time $548 per credit hour. Required fees: $1813; $75.53 per credit hour. Part-time tuition and fees vary according to course load. *Financial support:* In 2009–10, 17 teaching assistantships with full tuition reimbursements were awarded; fellowships with full tuition reimbursements, research assistantships with full tuition reimbursements, career-related internships or fieldwork, Federal Work-Study, scholarships/grants, tuition waivers (full), and unspecified assistantships also available. Support available to part-time students. Financial award applicants required to submit FAFSA. *Faculty research:* Linguistic anthropology of Oceania, Mayan languages, human paleontology, primate evolution, dental anthropology. *Unit head:* Dr. Judy Ledgerwood, Chair, 815-753-0246, Fax: 815-753-7027, E-mail: jledgerw@niu.edu. *Application contact:* Graduate School Office, 815-753-0395, E-mail: gradsch@niu.edu.

Northwestern University, The Graduate School, Judd A. and Marjorie Weinberg College of Arts and Sciences, Department of Anthropology, Evanston, IL 60208. Offers PhD, JD/PhD. Admissions and degrees offered through The Graduate School. *Degree requirements:* For doctorate, thesis/dissertation. *Entrance requirements:* For doctorate, GRE General Test. Additional exam requirements/recommendations for international students: Required—TOEFL. Electronic applications accepted. *Faculty research:* Archaeology of complex societies, gender, political/urban anthropology, linguistic anthropology, African studies.

The Ohio State University, Graduate School, College of Social and Behavioral Sciences, School of Social and Behavioral Science, Department of Anthropology, Columbus, OH 43210. Offers MA, PhD. *Faculty:* 31. *Students:* 34 full-time (21 women), 25 part-time (20 women); includes 8 minority (1 African American, 2 Asian Americans or Pacific Islanders, 5 Hispanic Americans), 4 international. Average age 29. In 2009, 6 master's, 5 doctorates awarded. *Degree requirements:* For master's, thesis optional; for doctorate, one foreign language, thesis/dissertation. *Entrance requirements:* For master's and doctorate, GRE General Test. Additional exam requirements/recommendations for international students: Required—TOEFL (minimum score 600 paper-based; 250 computer-based). *Application deadline:* For fall admission, 8/15 priority date for domestic students, 7/1 priority date for international students; for winter admission, 12/1 priority date for domestic students, 11/1 priority date for international students; for spring admission, 3/1 priority date for domestic students, 2/1 priority date for international students. Applications are processed on a rolling basis. Application fee: $40 ($50 for international students). Electronic applications accepted. *Expenses:* Tuition, state resident: full-time $10,683. Tuition, nonresident: full-time $25,923. Tuition and fees vary according to course load and program. *Financial support:* Fellowships, research assistantships, teaching assistantships, Federal Work-Study, institutionally sponsored loans, and unspecified assistantships available. Support available to part-time students. *Unit head:* Jeffrey K. McKee, Graduate Studies Committee Chair, 614-292-4117, Fax: 614-292-2435, E-mail: mckee.95@osu.edu. *Application contact:* 614-292-9444, Fax: 614-292-3895, E-mail: domestic.grad@osu.edu.

Oregon State University, Graduate School, College of Liberal Arts, Department of Anthropology, Corvallis, OR 97331. Offers anthropology (MAIS); applied anthropology (MA). *Faculty:* 7 full-time (3 women), 3 part-time/adjunct (2 women). *Students:* 29 full-time (18 women), 3 part-time (1 woman); includes 5 minority (2 American Indian/Alaska Native, 2 Asian Americans or Pacific Islanders, 1 Hispanic American). Average age 28. In 2009, 10 master's awarded. *Degree requirements:* For master's, one foreign language, thesis. *Entrance requirements:* For master's, minimum GPA of 3.0 in last 90 hours. Additional exam requirements/recommendations for international students: Required—TOEFL. *Application deadline:* For fall admission, 3/1 for domestic students. Applications are processed on a rolling basis. Application fee: $50. *Expenses:* Tuition, state resident: full-time $9774; part-time $362 per credit. Tuition, nonresident: full-time $15,849; part-time $587 per credit. Required fees: $1639. Full-time tuition and fees vary according to course load and program. *Financial support:* Research assistantships, teaching assistantships, career-related internships or fieldwork, Federal Work-Study, and institutionally sponsored loans available. Support available to part-time students. Financial award application deadline: 2/1. *Faculty research:* Historical anthropology; first American studies; Japanese, Asian, South Pacific, and Native American cultures; business anthropology. *Unit head:* Dr. David McMurray, Chair, 541-737-4515, Fax: 541-737-3650, E-mail: david.mcmurray@oregonstate.edu. *Application contact:* Dr. David McMurray, Chair, 541-737-4515, Fax: 541-737-3650, E-mail: david.mcmurray@oregonstate.edu.

Penn State University Park, Graduate School, College of the Liberal Arts, Department of Anthropology, State College, University Park, PA 16802-1503. Offers MA, PhD.

Portland State University, Graduate Studies, College of Liberal Arts and Sciences, Department of Anthropology, Portland, OR 97207-0751. Offers MA. *Degree requirements:* For master's, one foreign language, thesis. *Entrance requirements:* For master's, GRE General Test, minimum GPA of 3.25 in upper-division anthropology course work, 3.0 overall; 3 letters of recommendation. Additional exam requirements/recommendations for international students: Required—TOEFL. *Faculty research:* Forensic anthropology, Northwest Coast prehistory, Native Americans, applied anthropology, urban anthropology.

Portland State University, Graduate Studies, Systems Science Program, Portland, OR 97207-0751. Offers computational intelligence (Certificate); computer modeling and simulation (Certificate); systems science (MS); systems science/anthropology (PhD); systems science/business administration (PhD); systems science/civil engineering (PhD); systems science/economics (PhD); systems science/engineering management (PhD); systems science/general (PhD); systems science/mathematical sciences (PhD); systems science/mechanical engineering (PhD); systems science/psychology (PhD); systems science/sociology (PhD). *Degree requirements:* For doctorate, variable foreign language requirement, thesis/dissertation. *Entrance requirements:* For master's, 2 letters of recommendation; for doctorate, GMAT, GRE General Test, minimum undergraduate GPA of 3.0. Additional exam requirements/recommendations for international students: Required—TOEFL. *Faculty research:* Systems theory and methodology, artificial intelligence neural networks, information theory, nonlinear dynamics/chaos, modeling and simulation.

Princeton University, Graduate School, Department of Anthropology, Princeton, NJ 08544-1019. Offers PhD. *Degree requirements:* For doctorate, variable foreign language requirement, thesis/dissertation. *Entrance requirements:* For doctorate, GRE General Test, sample of written work. Additional exam requirements/recommendations for international students: Required—TOEFL (minimum score 600 paper-based; 250 computer-based). Electronic applications accepted. *Faculty research:* Symbolic anthropology, social theory, gender studies, law and society, political and social anthropology.

Purdue University, Graduate School, College of Liberal Arts, Department of Sociology and Anthropology, West Lafayette, IN 47907. Offers anthropology (MS, PhD); sociology (MS, PhD). Terminal master's awarded for partial completion of doctoral program. *Degree requirements:* For doctorate, thesis/dissertation. *Entrance requirements:* For master's and doctorate, GRE General Test. Additional exam requirements/recommendations for international students: Required—TOEFL, TWE. Electronic applications accepted. *Faculty research:* Communiversity survey project, risk, fear, constrained behavior, archaeological services.

Rice University, Graduate Programs, School of Social Sciences, Department of Anthropology, Houston, TX 77251-1892. Offers social-cultural anthropology (MA); archaeology (MA, PhD); social-cultural anthropology (PhD). *Faculty:* 10 full-time (5 women). *Students:* 30 full-time (18 women); includes 1 minority (African American), 11 international. 26 applicants, 12% accepted, 3 enrolled.Terminal master's awarded for partial completion of doctoral program. *Degree requirements:* For master's, one foreign language, 3 major papers, dissertation proposal and language exam or thesis; for doctorate, one foreign language, thesis/dissertation. *Entrance requirements:* For master's, Research Proposal; for doctorate, none, Research Proposal. Additional exam requirements/recommendations for international students: Required—TOEFL (minimum score 90 iBT). *Application deadline:* For fall admission, 1/15 for domestic and international students. Application fee: $75. Electronic applications accepted. *Financial support:* In 2009–10, 19 students received support, including 14 fellowships (averaging $16,000 per year); scholarships/grants, health care benefits, and tuition waivers also available. Financial award application deadline: 1/15. *Unit head:* Dr. Eugenia Georges, Professor and Chair, 713-348-3390, Fax: 713-348-5455, E-mail: nia@rice.edu. *Application contact:* Dr. James D. Faubion, Professor and Director of Graduate Studies, 713-348-3384, Fax: 713-348-5455, E-mail: jdf@rice.edu.

Roosevelt University, Graduate Division, College of Arts and Sciences, Department of Sociology and Anthropology, Chicago, IL 60605. Offers anthropology (MA); sociology (MA). Part-time and evening/weekend programs available. *Degree requirements:* For master's, comprehensive exam, thesis. *Faculty research:* Social theory, urban sociology, gerontology, social organizations.

Rutgers, The State University of New Jersey, New Brunswick, Graduate School-New Brunswick, Program in Anthropology, Piscataway, NJ 08854-8097. Offers MA, PhD. Terminal master's awarded for partial completion of doctoral program. *Degree requirements:* For master's, thesis or alternative; for doctorate, comprehensive exam, thesis/dissertation. *Entrance requirements:* For master's and doctorate, GRE General Test, writing sample. Additional exam requirements/recommendations for international students: Required—TOEFL. Electronic applications accepted. *Faculty research:* Human evolution, lithic technology, behavioral ecology, ethnicity, gender.

San Diego State University, Graduate and Research Affairs, College of Arts and Letters, Department of Anthropology, San Diego, CA 92182. Offers MA. *Degree requirements:* For master's, one foreign language, thesis. *Entrance requirements:* For master's, GRE General Test, 3 letters of recommendation, typed writing sample. Additional exam requirements/

recommendations for international students: Required—TOEFL. Electronic applications accepted. *Faculty research:* Meso-American archaeology, cognitive anthropology, ethnomusicology, primate conservation, biomedical anthropology.

San Francisco State University, Division of Graduate Studies, College of Behavioral and Social Sciences, Department of Anthropology, San Francisco, CA 94132-1722. Offers MA. *Faculty research:* Immigration, ethnicity, urban anthropology, Californian and Latin American archaeology.

San Jose State University, Graduate Studies and Research, College of Social Sciences, Department of Anthropology, San Jose, CA 95192-0001. Offers applied anthropology (MA). *Students:* 14 full-time (11 women), 8 part-time (4 women); includes 9 minority (1 African American, 3 Asian Americans or Pacific Islanders, 5 Hispanic Americans), 2 international. Average age 32. 21 applicants. In 2009, 3 master's awarded. *Entrance requirements:* For master's, curriculum vitae or resume, official transcripts, 2 letters of reference. *Application deadline:* For fall admission, 5/30 for domestic students. *Unit head:* Chuck Darrah, Chair, 408-924-5314, Fax: 408-924-5348. *Application contact:* Chuck Darrah, Chair, 408-924-5314, Fax: 408-924-5348.

Simon Fraser University, Graduate Studies, Faculty of Arts and Social Sciences, Department of Sociology and Anthropology, Burnaby, BC V5A 1S6, Canada. Offers anthropology (MA, PhD); sociology (MA, PhD). *Degree requirements:* For master's, thesis (for some programs); for doctorate, thesis/dissertation. *Entrance requirements:* For master's and doctorate, minimum GPA of 3.25. Additional exam requirements/recommendations for international students: Required—TOEFL or IELTS. *Faculty research:* Sociology theory, social and cultural anthropology, political sociology, religion and society, Canadian native peoples.

Sonoma State University, School of Social Sciences, Program in Cultural Resources Management, Rohnert Park, CA 94928. Offers MA. Part-time programs available. *Faculty:* 3 full-time (1 woman). *Students:* 31 part-time (23 women); includes 2 minority (1 Asian American or Pacific Islander, 1 Hispanic American), 1 international. Average age 31. 25 applicants, 36% accepted, 5 enrolled. In 2009, 3 master's awarded. *Degree requirements:* For master's, thesis. *Entrance requirements:* For master's, minimum GPA of 3.0. Additional exam requirements/recommendations for international students: Required—TOEFL (minimum score 500 paper-based; 173 computer-based). *Application deadline:* For fall admission, 1/31 for domestic students. Application fee: $55. *Expenses:* Tuition, nonresident: full-time $11,160. Required fees: $6226. Full-time tuition and fees vary according to course load. *Financial support:* Career-related internships or fieldwork, scholarships/grants, traineeships, and unspecified assistantships available. Financial award application deadline: 3/2; financial award applicants required to submit FAFSA. *Unit head:* Dr. John D. Wingard, Chair, Anthropology Department, 707-664-2319, Fax: 707-664-2505, E-mail: john.wingard@sonoma.edu. *Application contact:* Margaret Purser, Coordinator, 707-664-3164, Fax: 707-664-2505, E-mail: margaret.purser@sonoma.edu.

Southern Illinois University Carbondale, Graduate School, College of Liberal Arts, Department of Anthropology, Carbondale, IL 62901-4701. Offers MA, PhD. *Degree requirements:* For master's, one foreign language, thesis; for doctorate, one foreign language, thesis/dissertation. *Entrance requirements:* For master's, GRE General Test, minimum GPA of 2.7; for doctorate, GRE General Test, minimum GPA of 3.25. Additional exam requirements/recommendations for international students: Required—TOEFL. *Faculty research:* Archaeology, human variability, evolution, cultural ecology, social anthropology.

Southern Methodist University, Dedman College, Department of Anthropology, Dallas, TX 75205. Offers anthropology (PhD); medical anthropology (MA). *Faculty:* 14 full-time (8 women), 5 part-time/adjunct (2 women). *Students:* 14 full-time (11 women), 38 part-time (19 women); includes 6 minority (all Hispanic Americans), 4 international. Average age 33. 21 applicants, 29% accepted, 6 enrolled. In 2009, 8 master's, 5 doctorates awarded. Terminal master's awarded for partial completion of doctoral program. *Degree requirements:* For master's, one foreign language, comprehensive exam, thesis or alternative; for doctorate, one foreign language, comprehensive exam, thesis/dissertation, qualifying exam, defense of dissertation. *Entrance requirements:* For master's and doctorate, GRE General Test, minimum GPA of 3.0. Additional exam requirements/recommendations for international students: Required—TOEFL (minimum score 550 paper-based). *Application deadline:* For fall admission, 2/1 priority date for domestic students; for spring admission, 11/30 priority date for domestic students. Applications are processed on a rolling basis. Application fee: $60. *Financial support:* In 2009–10, 1 fellowship with full and partial tuition reimbursement (averaging $16,000 per year), 3 research assistantships with full tuition reimbursements (averaging $16,000 per year), 4 teaching assistantships with full tuition reimbursements (averaging $16,000 per year) were awarded; Federal Work-Study, institutionally sponsored loans, scholarships/grants, traineeships, tuition waivers (full), and unspecified assistantships also available. Financial award application deadline: 3/1; financial award applicants required to submit FAFSA. *Faculty research:* Health and gender, Paleoindians, Mesoamerica, American southwest, migration and ethnicity. Total annual research expenditures: $300,000. *Unit head:* Pamela Carter Hogan, Administrative Assistant to the Chair, 214-768-4152, Fax: 214-768-2906, E-mail: phogan@smu.edu. *Application contact:* Dr. Caroline Brettell, Director of Graduate Studies, 214-768-4254, Fax: 214-768-2906, E-mail: trick@smu.edu.

Stanford University, School of Humanities and Sciences, Department of Anthropological Sciences, Stanford, CA 94305-9991. Offers MA, MS, PhD. Terminal master's awarded for partial completion of doctoral program. *Degree requirements:* For master's, thesis; for doctorate, one foreign language, thesis/dissertation. *Entrance requirements:* For master's and doctorate, GRE General Test. Additional exam requirements/recommendations for international students: Required—TOEFL. Electronic applications accepted. *Expenses:* Tuition: Full-time $37,380; part-time $2760 per quarter. Required fees: $501.

Stanford University, School of Humanities and Sciences, Department of Cultural and Social Anthropology, Stanford, CA 94305-9991. Offers MA, PhD. Terminal master's awarded for partial completion of doctoral program. *Degree requirements:* For master's, thesis; for doctorate, one foreign language, thesis/dissertation. *Entrance requirements:* For master's and doctorate, GRE General Test. Additional exam requirements/recommendations for international students: Required—TOEFL. Electronic applications accepted. *Expenses:* Tuition: Full-time $37,380; part-time $2760 per quarter. Required fees: $501.

State University of New York at Binghamton, Graduate School, School of Arts and Sciences, Department of Anthropology, Binghamton, NY 13902-6000. Offers MA, PhD. Part-time programs available. *Faculty:* 17 full-time (6 women), 4 part-time/adjunct (1 woman). *Students:* 56 full-time (43 women), 84 part-time (55 women); includes 14 minority (3 African Americans, 2 American Indian/Alaska Native, 4 Asian Americans or Pacific Islanders, 5 Hispanic Americans), 23 international. Average age 32. 88 applicants, 64% accepted, 29 enrolled. In 2009, 23 master's, 8 doctorates awarded. Terminal master's awarded for partial completion of doctoral program. *Degree requirements:* For master's, one foreign language, thesis or alternative, written exam; for doctorate, variable foreign language requirement, thesis/dissertation, oral exam. *Entrance requirements:* For master's and doctorate, GRE General Test, GRE Subject Test. Additional exam requirements/recommendations for international students: Required—TOEFL (minimum score 550 paper-based; 213 computer-based; 80 iBT). *Application deadline:* For fall admission, 4/15 priority date for domestic and international students. Applications are processed on a rolling basis. Application fee: $60. Electronic applications accepted. *Financial support:* In 2009–10, 49 students received support, including 6 fellowships with full tuition reimbursements available (averaging $1,500 per year), 5 research assistantships with full tuition reimbursements available (averaging $15,000 per year), 27 teaching assistantships with full tuition reimbursements available (averaging $15,000 per year); career-related internships or fieldwork, Federal Work-Study, institutionally sponsored loans, scholarships/grants, health care benefits, and unspecified assistantships also available. Financial award application deadline: 2/15; financial award applicants required to submit FAFSA. *Unit head:* Dr. Thomas Wilson, Chairperson, 607-777-2738, E-mail: twilson@binghamton.edu. *Application contact:* Victoria Williams, Recruiting and Admissions Coordinator, 607-777-2151, Fax: 607-777-2501, E-mail: vwilliam@binghamton.edu.

Stony Brook University, State University of New York, Graduate School, College of Arts and Sciences, Department of Anthropology, Stony Brook, NY 11794. Offers MA, PhD. *Faculty:* 13 full-time (5 women), 3 part-time/adjunct (all women). *Students:* 42 full-time (31 women), 3 part-time (1 woman); includes 3 minority (1 African American, 2 Asian Americans or Pacific Islanders), 13 international. Average age 30. 81 applicants, 16% accepted. In 2009, 3 master's, 3 doctorates awarded. *Degree requirements:* For master's, thesis, fieldwork; for doctorate, one foreign language, thesis/dissertation, fieldwork. *Entrance requirements:* For master's and doctorate, GRE General Test. Additional exam requirements/recommendations for international students: Required—TOEFL. *Application deadline:* For fall admission, 1/15 for domestic students. Application fee: $60. *Expenses:* Tuition, state resident: full-time $8370; part-time $349 per credit. Tuition, nonresident: full-time $13,250; part-time $552 per credit. Required fees: $933. *Financial support:* In 2009–10, 2 research assistantships, 23 teaching assistantships were awarded; fellowships, career-related internships or fieldwork also available. *Faculty research:* Social and cultural anthropology, cultural history and archaeology, physical anthropology. Total annual research expenditures: $615,356. *Unit head:* Prof. Diane M. Doran-Sheehy, Chair, 631-632-9445, E-mail: diane.doran@stonybrook.edu. *Application contact:* Dr. Elizabeth Stone, Director, 631-632-7627, Fax: 631-632-9165, E-mail: elizabeth.stone@stonybrook.edu.

Syracuse University, Maxwell School of Citizenship and Public Affairs, Program in Anthropology, Syracuse, NY 13244. Offers MA, PhD. *Students:* 49 full-time (31 women), 21 part-time (11 women); includes 5 minority (2 Asian Americans or Pacific Islanders, 3 Hispanic Americans), 19 international. Average age 32. 61 applicants, 25% accepted, 5 enrolled. In 2009, 11 master's, 1 doctorate awarded. *Degree requirements:* For master's, thesis or alternative; for doctorate, one foreign language, thesis/dissertation. *Entrance requirements:* For master's and doctorate, GRE General Test. Additional exam requirements/recommendations for international students: Required—TOEFL (minimum score 100 iBT). *Application deadline:* For fall admission, 12/15 priority date for domestic and international students. Application fee: $75. Electronic applications accepted. *Expenses:* Tuition: Full-time $26,808; part-time $1117 per credit. Required fees: $1024. *Financial support:* Fellowships with full tuition reimbursements, research assistantships with tuition reimbursements, teaching assistantships with full and partial tuition reimbursements available. Financial award application deadline: 1/1. *Unit head:* Dr. Christopher DeCorse, Chair, 315-443-4647, Fax: 315-443-4860. *Application contact:* Kristina Ashley, Recruiting Contact, 315-443-2200, E-mail: krashley@syr.edu.

Teachers College, Columbia University, Graduate Faculty of Education, Department of International and Transcultural Studies, Program in Anthropology, New York, NY 10027-6696. Offers Ed M, MA, Ed D, PhD. *Faculty:* 4 full-time (0 women). *Students:* 20 full-time (16 women), 58 part-time (42 women); includes 25 minority (7 African Americans, 16 Asian Americans or Pacific Islanders, 2 Hispanic Americans), 9 international. Average age 32. 49 applicants, 71% accepted, 21 enrolled. In 2009, 11 master's, 5 doctorates awarded. *Degree requirements:* For doctorate, variable foreign language requirement, thesis/dissertation. *Entrance requirements:* For master's and doctorate, GRE General Test. *Application deadline:* For fall admission, 5/15 for domestic students; for spring admission, 12/1 for domestic students. Application fee: $65. *Financial support:* Career-related internships or fieldwork, Federal Work-Study, institutionally sponsored loans, and tuition waivers (full and partial) available. Support available to part-time students. Financial award application deadline: 2/1. *Faculty research:* African studies, sociocultural change, education in the developing world, human development in social and cultural contexts, culture and communication theory. *Unit head:* Dr. George Bond, Chair, 212-678-3947. *Application contact:* Deanna Ghozati, Assistant Director of Admission, 212-678-4018, Fax: 212-678-4171, E-mail: ghozati@tc.edu.

Teachers College, Columbia University, Graduate Faculty of Education, Department of International and Transcultural Studies, Program in Anthropology and Education, New York, NY 10027-6696. Offers Ed M, MA, Ed D, PhD.

Temple University, Graduate School, College of Liberal Arts, Department of Anthropology, Philadelphia, PA 19122-6096. Offers PhD. Part-time and evening/weekend programs available. Terminal master's awarded for partial completion of doctoral program. *Degree requirements:* For doctorate, 2 foreign languages, thesis/dissertation. *Entrance requirements:* For doctorate, GRE General Test, minimum GPA of 3.0. Additional exam requirements/recommendations for international students: Required—TOEFL (minimum score 550 paper-based; 213 computer-based; 79 iBT). Electronic applications accepted. *Faculty research:* Political economy, biocultural adaptation, visual anthropology, critical urban anthropology, archaeology.

Texas A&M University, College of Liberal Arts, Department of Anthropology, College Station, TX 77843. Offers MA, PhD. *Faculty:* 23. *Students:* 75 full-time (44 women), 38 part-time (21 women); includes 8 minority (3 Asian Americans or Pacific Islanders, 5 Hispanic Americans), 11 international. Average age 33. In 2009, 15 master's, 4 doctorates awarded. *Degree requirements:* For doctorate, thesis/dissertation. *Entrance requirements:* For master's and doctorate, GRE General Test. Additional exam requirements/recommendations for international students: Required—TOEFL. Application fee: $50 ($75 for international students). *Expenses:* Tuition, state resident: full-time $3991; part-time $221.74 per credit hour. Tuition, nonresident: full-time $9049; part-time $502.74 per credit hour. *Financial support:* Fellowships, research assistantships, teaching assistantships, career-related internships or fieldwork, Federal Work-Study, and institutionally sponsored loans available. Financial award application deadline: 4/1; financial award applicants required to submit FAFSA. *Faculty research:* Nautical archaeology, archaeological conservation, archaeological palynology, paleoethnobotany, folklore. *Unit head:* Dr. Donny Hamilton, Head, 979-845-6355, E-mail: dlhamilton@tamu.edu. *Application contact:* Karen Taylor, Assistant Advisor, 979-845-9333, Fax: 979-845-4070.

Texas State University–San Marcos, Graduate School, College of Liberal Arts, Department of Anthropology, San Marcos, TX 78666. Offers MA. *Faculty:* 14 full-time (6 women). *Students:* 32 full-time (23 women), 16 part-time (9 women); includes 9 minority (2 African Americans, 1 American Indian/Alaska Native, 6 Hispanic Americans), 1 international. Average age 29. 77 applicants, 30% accepted, 19 enrolled. In 2009, 10 master's awarded. *Degree requirements:* For master's, comprehensive exam, thesis. *Entrance requirements:* For master's, GRE (minimum score 1000 verbal and quantitative preferred), minimum GPA of 3.0 in last 60 undergraduate hours. Additional exam requirements/recommendations for international students: Required—TOEFL (minimum score 550 paper-based; 213 computer-based). *Application deadline:* For fall admission, 3/15 for domestic and international students. Applications are processed on a rolling basis. Application fee: $40 ($90 for international students). Electronic applications accepted. *Expenses:* Tuition, state resident: full-time $5784; part-time $241 per credit hour. Tuition, nonresident: part-time $551 per credit hour. Required fees: $1728; $48 per credit hour. $306. Tuition and fees vary according to course load. *Financial support:* In 2009–10, 40 students received support, including 1 research assistantship (averaging $4,928 per year), 20 teaching assistantships (averaging $1,863 per year). Financial award application deadline: 4/1; financial award applicants required to submit FAFSA. *Faculty research:* Reu Site Guatemala, Zatopeck Site, Excavation S. Africa, Wilson Pottery Site, El Camino Real Survey, Highland Mesoamerica. Total annual research expenditures: $314,842. *Unit head:* Dr. Jon McGee, Chair, 512-245-8272, E-mail: rm08@txstate.edu. *Application contact:* Dr. J. Michael Willoughby, Dean of Graduate School, 512-245-2581, Fax: 512-245-8365, E-mail: gradcollege@txstate.edu.

Texas Tech University, Graduate School, College of Arts and Sciences, Department of Sociology, Anthropology and Social Work, Lubbock, TX 79409. Offers anthropology (MA); sociology (MA). Part-time programs available. *Faculty:* 17 full-time (7 women). *Students:* 20 full-time (13 women), 15 part-time (7 women); includes 10 minority (3 African Americans, 2 Asian Americans or Pacific Islanders, 5 Hispanic Americans), 1 international. Average age 29. 29 applicants, 69% accepted, 11 enrolled. In 2009, 8 master's awarded. *Degree requirements:* For master's, one foreign language, thesis or alternative. *Entrance requirements:* For master's, GRE General Test. Additional exam requirements/recommendations for international students:

Anthropology

Texas Tech University (continued)

Required—TOEFL (minimum score 550 paper-based; 213 computer-based). *Application deadline:* For fall admission, 3/1 priority date for international students; for spring admission, 11/1 priority date for international students. Applications are processed on a rolling basis. Application fee: $50 ($75 for international students). Electronic applications accepted. *Expenses:* Tuition, state resident: full-time $5100; part-time $213 per credit hour. Tuition, nonresident: full-time $11,748; part-time $490 per credit hour. Required fees: $2298; $50 per credit hour. $555 per semester. *Financial support:* In 2009–10, 23 students received support, including 6 teaching assistantships with partial tuition reimbursements available (averaging $13,012 per year); research assistantships with partial tuition reimbursements available, Federal Work-Study and institutionally sponsored loans also available. Support available to part-time students. Financial award application deadline: 4/15; financial award applicants required to submit FAFSA. *Faculty research:* Sociology theory, research methods, physical and forensic anthropology, Texas archaeology, Mayan archaeology. *Unit head:* Dr. Jeffrey Payne Williams, Chair and Professor, 806-742-2400, Fax: 806-742-1088, E-mail: jeff.williams@ttu.edu. *Application contact:* Dr. Yung-Mei Tsai, Sociology Graduate Program Director, 806-742-2400, Fax: 806-742-1088, E-mail: yung.mei.tsai@ttu.edu.

Trent University, Graduate Studies, Program in Anthropology, Peterborough, ON K9J 7B8, Canada. Offers MA. Part-time programs available. *Degree requirements:* For master's, thesis. *Entrance requirements:* For master's, honors degree. *Faculty research:* Paleoecology, trade and fortification networks, pre-Columbian art.

Tulane University, School of Liberal Arts, Department of Anthropology, New Orleans, LA 70118-5669. Offers MA, PhD. Terminal master's awarded for partial completion of doctoral program. *Degree requirements:* For master's, one foreign language, thesis; for doctorate, 2 foreign languages, thesis/dissertation. *Entrance requirements:* For master's, GRE General Test, minimum B average in undergraduate course work; for doctorate, GRE General Test. Additional exam requirements/recommendations for international students: Required—TOEFL. Electronic applications accepted. *Faculty research:* Linguistics, physical anthropology, sociocultural archaeology, Mesoamerica.

Universidad de las Américas–Puebla, Division of Graduate Studies, School of Social Sciences, Program in Anthropology, Puebla, Mexico. Offers anthropology (MA); archaeology (MA). Part-time and evening/weekend programs available. *Degree requirements:* For master's, one foreign language, thesis. *Entrance requirements:* For master's, bachelor's degree in anthropology or equivalent. *Faculty research:* Archaeology, ethnography, and ethnohistory of Mesoamerica.

Université de Montréal, Faculty of Arts and Sciences, Department of Anthropology, Montréal, QC H3C 3J7, Canada. Offers M Sc, PhD. Part-time programs available. *Degree requirements:* For master's, thesis; for doctorate, thesis/dissertation, general exam. Electronic applications accepted. *Faculty research:* Archaeology, ethnolinguistics, ethnology.

Université Laval, Faculty of Social Sciences, Department of Anthropology, Programs in Anthropology, Québec, QC G1K 7P4, Canada. Offers MA, PhD. Terminal master's awarded for partial completion of doctoral program. *Degree requirements:* For master's, thesis; for doctorate, thesis/dissertation. *Entrance requirements:* For master's, knowledge of French, interview; for doctorate, knowledge of French, comprehensive of written English, knowledge of a third language. Electronic applications accepted.

University at Albany, State University of New York, College of Arts and Sciences, Department of Anthropology, Albany, NY 12222-0001. Offers MA, PhD. Terminal master's awarded for partial completion of doctoral program. *Degree requirements:* For master's, comprehensive exam, thesis; for doctorate, 2 foreign languages, thesis/dissertation, field exams. *Entrance requirements:* For master's and doctorate, GRE. Additional exam requirements/recommendations for international students: Required—TOEFL (minimum score 550 paper-based; 213 computer-based). Electronic applications accepted. *Faculty research:* Economic and ecological anthropology; language, culture, and cognition; symbolic and interpretive anthropology; human evolution, morphology, demography, and medical anthropology; spatial and settlement archaeology.

University at Buffalo, the State University of New York, Graduate School, College of Arts and Sciences, Department of Anthropology, Buffalo, NY 14260. Offers MA, PhD. *Faculty:* 17 full-time (8 women), 5 part-time/adjunct (0 women). *Students:* 96 full-time (63 women), 14 part-time (8 women); includes 10 minority (2 African Americans, 1 American Indian/Alaska Native, 2 Asian Americans or Pacific Islanders, 5 Hispanic Americans), 7 international. Average age 31. 76 applicants, 47% accepted, 28 enrolled. In 2009, 14 master's, 5 doctorates awarded. Terminal master's awarded for partial completion of doctoral program. *Degree requirements:* For master's, project; for doctorate, one foreign language, thesis/dissertation, exam. *Entrance requirements:* For master's, GRE General Test, minimum GPA of 3.0; for doctorate, GRE General Test, minimum GPA of 3.2. Additional exam requirements/recommendations for international students: Required—TOEFL (minimum score 600 paper-based; 250 computer-based; 79 iBT). *Application deadline:* For fall admission, 1/18 priority date for domestic and international students; for winter admission, 5/1 for domestic students, 3/15 for international students. Applications are processed on a rolling basis. Application fee: $50. Electronic applications accepted. *Financial support:* In 2009–10, 7 fellowships with full tuition reimbursements (averaging $19,616 per year), 14 teaching assistantships with full tuition reimbursements (averaging $13,616 per year) were awarded; career-related internships or fieldwork, Federal Work-Study, and institutionally sponsored loans also available. Financial award application deadline: 1/18; financial award applicants required to submit FAFSA. *Faculty research:* Old and New World archaeology, medical anthropology, primatology/human biology, cognition. Total annual research expenditures: $800,000. *Unit head:* Dr. Donald Pollock, Chair, 716-645-2414, Fax: 716-645-3808. *Application contact:* Margaret M. Kasprzyk, Graduate Coordinator, 716-645-2414 Ext. 104, Fax: 716-645-3808, E-mail: mmk22@buffalo.edu.

The University of Alabama, Graduate School, College of Arts and Sciences, Department of Anthropology, Tuscaloosa, AL 35487. Offers MA, PhD. *Faculty:* 10 full-time (2 women), 1 part-time/adjunct (0 women). *Students:* 31 full-time (19 women), 5 part-time (4 women); includes 4 minority (1 Asian American or Pacific Islander, 3 Hispanic Americans). Average age 27. 31 applicants, 35% accepted, 9 enrolled. In 2009, 7 master's, 2 doctorates awarded. *Degree requirements:* For master's, one foreign language, comprehensive exam, thesis optional; for doctorate, one foreign language, comprehensive exam, thesis/dissertation. *Entrance requirements:* For master's, GRE; for doctorate, GRE, MA in anthropology. *Application deadline:* For fall admission, 1/31 for domestic and international students. Application fee: $50 ($60 for international students). *Expenses:* Tuition, state resident: full-time $7000. Tuition, nonresident: full-time $19,200. *Financial support:* In 2009–10, 25 students received support, including 4 fellowships with full tuition reimbursements available (averaging $15,000 per year), 1 research assistantship with full tuition reimbursement available (averaging $12,258 per year), 20 teaching assistantships with full tuition reimbursements available (averaging $12,258 per year); Federal Work-Study and health care benefits also available. Financial award application deadline: 1/31. *Faculty research:* Medical anthropology, Southeastern archaeology, physical and cultural anthropology. Total annual research expenditures: $41,314. *Unit head:* Dr. Michael D. Murphy, Chairman/Professor, 205-348-1953, Fax: 205-348-7937, E-mail: mdmurphy@ua.edu. *Application contact:* Dr. Ian Brown, Professor and Director of Graduate Studies, 205-348-9758, Fax: 205-348-7937, E-mail: ibrown@bama.ua.edu.

The University of Alabama at Birmingham, College of Arts and Sciences, Program in Anthropology, Birmingham, AL 35294. Offers MA. *Degree requirements:* For master's, one foreign language. *Entrance requirements:* For master's, GRE General Test. Electronic applications accepted. *Faculty research:* Ethnicity, medical anthropology, primate conservation, pastoral systems, Southeastern archaeology.

University of Alaska Anchorage, College of Arts and Sciences, Department of Anthropology, Anchorage, AK 99508. Offers MA. *Degree requirements:* For master's, comprehensive exam, thesis (for some programs), practicum. *Entrance requirements:* For master's, GRE General Test. Additional exam requirements/recommendations for international students: Required—TOEFL (minimum score 550 paper-based; 213 computer-based).

University of Alaska Fairbanks, College of Liberal Arts, Department of Anthropology, Fairbanks, AK 99775-7720. Offers MA, PhD. Part-time programs available. *Faculty:* 11 full-time (2 women), 2 part-time/adjunct (0 women). *Students:* 9 full-time (1 woman), 3 part-time (1 woman). Average age 39. 24 applicants, 58% accepted. In 2009, 5 master's, 6 doctorates awarded. Terminal master's awarded for partial completion of doctoral program. *Degree requirements:* For master's, one foreign language, comprehensive exam, thesis, oral defense; for doctorate, 2 foreign languages, comprehensive exam, thesis/dissertation, oral defense. *Entrance requirements:* For master's and doctorate, GRE General Test. Additional exam requirements/recommendations for international students: Required—TOEFL (minimum score 550 paper-based; 213 computer-based; 80 iBT). *Application deadline:* For fall admission, 6/1 for domestic students, 3/1 for international students; for spring admission, 10/15 for domestic students, 9/1 for international students. Applications are processed on a rolling basis. Application fee: $60. Electronic applications accepted. *Expenses:* Tuition, state resident: full-time $7584; part-time $316 per credit. Tuition, nonresident: full-time $15,504; part-time $646 per credit. Required fees: $23 per credit. $135 per semester. Tuition and fees vary according to course level, course load and reciprocity agreements. *Financial support:* In 2009–10, 1 fellowship (averaging $13,500 per year), 5 research assistantships (averaging $12,448 per year), 11 teaching assistantships (averaging $7,955 per year) were awarded; Federal Work-Study, scholarships/grants, health care benefits, and unspecified assistantships also available. Support available to part-time students. Financial award application deadline: 7/1; financial award applicants required to submit FAFSA. *Faculty research:* Circumpolar archaeology and population biology; rural subsistence; arctic physical, biological and social anthropology; arctic ethnohistory; arctic linguistics. *Unit head:* Dr. Maribeth Murray, Department Chair, 907-474-7288, Fax: 907-474-7453, E-mail: fyanth@uaf.edu. *Application contact:* Dr. Maribeth Murray, Department Chair, 907-474-7288, Fax: 907-474-7453, E-mail: fyanth@uaf.edu.

University of Alberta, Faculty of Graduate Studies and Research, Department of Anthropology, Edmonton, AB T6G 2E1, Canada. Offers MA, PhD. *Faculty:* 16 full-time (6 women), 20 part-time/adjunct (8 women). *Students:* 61 full-time (34 women), 12 part-time (10 women), 7 international. 66 applicants, 20% accepted, 12 enrolled. In 2009, 11 master's, 3 doctorates awarded. *Degree requirements:* For master's, thesis; for doctorate, one foreign language, thesis/dissertation. *Entrance requirements:* For master's and doctorate, minimum GPA of 7.0 on a 9.0 scale in last 2 years. Additional exam requirements/recommendations for international students: Required—TOEFL. *Application deadline:* For fall admission, 1/15 for domestic students. Application fee: $0. Tuition and fees charges are reported in Canadian dollars. *Expenses:* Tuition, area resident: Full-time $4626 Canadian dollars; part-time $99.72 Canadian dollars per unit. International tuition: $8216 Canadian dollars full-time. Required fees: $3590 Canadian dollars; $99.72 Canadian dollars per unit. $215 Canadian dollars per term. *Financial support:* In 2009–10, 53 students received support, including 10 fellowships, 6 research assistantships, 11 teaching assistantships; career-related internships or fieldwork and scholarships/grants also available. *Faculty research:* Cultural anthropology of North America, South East Asia; physical anthropology in osteology, forensic primatology; archaeology of North America, South America, Old World/Africa. *Unit head:* Dr. Nancy Lovell, Acting Chair, 780-492-2368, Fax: 780-492-5273. *Application contact:* Gail Mathew, Secretary, 780-492-2368, Fax: 780-492-1526, E-mail: anthgrad@ualberta.ca.

The University of Arizona, Graduate College, College of Social and Behavioral Sciences, Department of Anthropology, Tucson, AZ 85721. Offers MA, PhD. Part-time programs available. *Faculty:* 30 full-time (15 women). *Students:* 40 full-time (26 women), 100 part-time (56 women); includes 10 minority (2 American Indian/Alaska Native, 3 Asian Americans or Pacific Islanders, 5 Hispanic Americans), 31 international. Average age 34. 179 applicants, 18% accepted, 14 enrolled. In 2009, 16 master's, 13 doctorates awarded. Terminal master's awarded for partial completion of doctoral program. *Degree requirements:* For master's, thesis or alternative; for doctorate, one foreign language, thesis/dissertation. *Entrance requirements:* For master's and doctorate, GRE General Test, minimum GPA of 3.5, 2 letters of recommendation. Additional exam requirements/recommendations for international students: Required—TOEFL (minimum score 550 paper-based; 213 computer-based; 79 iBT). *Application deadline:* For fall admission, 3/1 for domestic and international students. Applications are processed on a rolling basis. Application fee: $65. Electronic applications accepted. *Expenses:* Tuition, state resident: full-time $9028. Tuition, nonresident: full-time $24,890. *Financial support:* In 2009–10, 18 research assistantships (averaging $16,027 per year), 32 teaching assistantships with full tuition reimbursements (averaging $15,169 per year) were awarded; career-related internships or fieldwork, Federal Work-Study, institutionally sponsored loans, scholarships/grants, health care benefits, tuition waivers (full and partial), and unspecified assistantships also available. *Faculty research:* Archaeology of pre-Han China, cultural ecology, health and illness-related behavior, interaction of linguistic and social processes, human growth and development under stress. Total annual research expenditures: $1.8 million. *Unit head:* Dr. Barbara J. Mills, Department Head, 520-621-6298, Fax: 520-621-2088, E-mail: bmills@u.arizona.edu. *Application contact:* Ann Samuelson, 520-626-6027, Fax: 520-621-2088, E-mail: anns@email.arizona.edu.

University of Arkansas, Graduate School, J. William Fulbright College of Arts and Sciences, Department of Anthropology, Fayetteville, AR 72701-1201. Offers MA, PhD. Part-time and evening/weekend programs available. *Students:* 15 full-time (8 women), 35 part-time (19 women); includes 4 minority (2 American Indian/Alaska Native, 1 Asian American or Pacific Islander, 1 Hispanic American), 2 international. In 2009, 4 master's, 2 doctorates awarded. *Degree requirements:* For master's, comprehensive exam. *Entrance requirements:* For master's, GRE General Test, minimum GPA of 3.0; for doctorate, GRE General Test. Application fee: $40 ($50 for international students). *Expenses:* Tuition, state resident: full-time $7355; part-time $356.58 per hour. Tuition, nonresident: full-time $17,401; part-time $775.17 per hour. Required fees: $1203. *Financial support:* In 2009–10, 8 fellowships with tuition reimbursements, 4 research assistantships, 15 teaching assistantships were awarded; career-related internships or fieldwork and Federal Work-Study also available. Support available to part-time students. Financial award application deadline: 4/1; financial award applicants required to submit FAFSA. *Unit head:* Dr. Peter Ungar, Department Chairperson, 479-575-2508, Fax: 479-575-6595, E-mail: pungar@uark.edu. *Application contact:* Dr. Mary Jo Schneider, Graduate Coordinator, 479-575-2508, Fax: 479-575-6595, E-mail: maryjo@uark.edu.

The University of British Columbia, Faculty of Arts, Department of Anthropology, Vancouver, BC V6T 1Z1, Canada. Offers MA, PhD. *Degree requirements:* For master's, thesis; for doctorate, comprehensive exam, thesis/dissertation. *Entrance requirements:* For master's, BA in anthropology or equivalent with minimum B+ average in upper level courses; for doctorate, MA in anthropology or equivalent. Additional exam requirements/recommendations for international students: Required—TOEFL (minimum score 600 paper-based; 250 computer-based; 80 iBT). Electronic applications accepted. *Faculty research:* Cultures of North America, East Asia, Oceania; museum studies; archaeology.

University of Calgary, Faculty of Graduate Studies, Faculty of Social Sciences, Department of Anthropology, Calgary, AB T2N 1N4, Canada. Offers MA, PhD. *Degree requirements:* For master's, thesis; for doctorate, one foreign language, comprehensive exam, thesis/dissertation, candidacy exam. *Entrance requirements:* Additional exam requirements/recommendations for international students: Required—TOEFL. *Faculty research:* Primatology, culture and society, biosocial anthropology, political anthropology, evolutionary theory.

University of California, Berkeley, Graduate Division, College of Letters and Science, Department of Anthropology, Program in Anthropology, Berkeley, CA 94720-1500. Offers PhD. *Students:* 104 full-time (57 women). Average age 31. 347 applicants, 11 enrolled. In 2009, 12 doctorates awarded. *Degree requirements:* For doctorate, thesis/dissertation. *Entrance* *requirements:* For doctorate, GRE General Test, minimum GPA of 3.0, 3 letters of recommendation. Additional exam requirements/recommendations for international students: Required—TOEFL. *Application deadline:* For fall admission, 12/15 for domestic students. Application fee: $70 ($90 for international students). *Financial support:* Unspecified assistantships available. *Unit head:* Prof. Rosemary Joyce, Chair, 510-642-3392, Fax: 510-643-8557, E-mail: anthro_chair@berkeley.edu. *Application contact:* Ned Garrett, Student Affairs Officer, 510-642-3406, Fax: 510-643-8557, E-mail: ned@berkeley.edu.

University of California, Berkeley, Graduate Division, College of Letters and Science, Department of Anthropology, Program in Medical Anthropology, Berkeley, CA 94720-1500. Offers PhD. *Students:* 17 full-time (10 women). Average age 33. 47 applicants, 3 enrolled. In 2009, 2 doctorates awarded. *Degree requirements:* For doctorate, thesis/dissertation. *Entrance requirements:* For doctorate, GRE General Test, minimum GPA of 3.0, 3 letters of recommendation. Additional exam requirements/recommendations for international students: Required—TOEFL. *Application deadline:* For fall admission, 12/15 for domestic students. Application fee: $70 ($90 for international students). *Financial support:* Unspecified assistantships available. *Unit head:* Prof. Nancy Scheper-Hughes, Chair, 510-642-3392, E-mail: ch_anthropology@ls.berkeley.edu. *Application contact:* Ned Garrett, Student Affairs Officer, 510-642-3406, Fax: 510-643-8557, E-mail: ned@berkeley.edu.

University of California, Davis, Graduate Studies, Program in Anthropology, Davis, CA 95616. Offers MA, PhD. Terminal master's awarded for partial completion of doctoral program. *Degree requirements:* For master's, one foreign language; for doctorate, one foreign language, thesis/dissertation. *Entrance requirements:* For master's and doctorate, GRE General Test, minimum GPA of 3.0. Additional exam requirements/recommendations for international students: Required—TOEFL (minimum score 550 paper-based; 213 computer-based). Electronic applications accepted. *Faculty research:* Archaeology, linguistics, biological and sociocultural anthropology.

University of California, Irvine, Office of Graduate Studies, School of Social Sciences, Department of Anthropology, Irvine, CA 92697. Offers MA, PhD. *Students:* 43 full-time (26 women), 1 (woman) part-time; includes 8 Asian Americans or Pacific Islanders, 4 Hispanic Americans, 6 international. Average age 29. 94 applicants, 17% accepted, 9 enrolled. In 2009, 7 master's, 6 doctorates awarded. *Degree requirements:* For doctorate, thesis/dissertation. *Entrance requirements:* For master's, GRE, minimum GPA of 3.0; for doctorate, GRE General Test, minimum GPA of 3.0. Additional exam requirements/recommendations for international students: Required—TOEFL (minimum score 550 paper-based; 213 computer-based). *Application deadline:* For fall admission, 1/15 priority date for domestic and international students. Applications are processed on a rolling basis. Application fee: $70 ($90 for international students). Electronic applications accepted. *Financial support:* Fellowships, research assistantships with full tuition reimbursements, teaching assistantships, institutionally sponsored loans, traineeships, health care benefits, and unspecified assistantships available. Financial award application deadline: 3/1; financial award applicants required to submit FAFSA. *Faculty research:* Cognitive anthropology, sociology of culture, social structure, family and gender. *Unit head:* Michael L. Burton, Chair, 949-824-7208, E-mail: mlburton@uci.edu. *Application contact:* Victoria Bernal, Graduate Advisor, 949-824-3137, Fax: 949-824-4717, E-mail: vbernal@uci.edu.

University of California, Los Angeles, Graduate Division, College of Letters and Science, Department of Anthropology, Los Angeles, CA 90095. Offers MA, PhD. *Students:* 72 full-time (53 women); includes 7 minority (2 African Americans, 2 Asian Americans or Pacific Islanders, 3 Hispanic Americans), 7 international. Average age 30. 172 applicants, 3% accepted, 5 enrolled. In 2009, 9 master's, 7 doctorates awarded. Terminal master's awarded for partial completion of doctoral program. *Degree requirements:* For master's, thesis; for doctorate, thesis/dissertation, oral and written qualifying exams. *Entrance requirements:* For master's, GRE General Test, minimum GPA of 3.0, sample of research writing, 3 letters of recommendation; for doctorate, GRE General Test, minimum undergraduate GPA of 3.0, sample of research writing, 3 letters of recommendation. *Application deadline:* For fall admission, 12/15 for domestic students. Application fee: $60 ($80 for international students). Electronic applications accepted. *Financial support:* In 2009–10, 42 fellowships with full and partial tuition reimbursements, 23 research assistantships with full and partial tuition reimbursements, 37 teaching assistantships with full and partial tuition reimbursements were awarded; Federal Work-Study, institutionally sponsored loans, scholarships/grants, health care benefits, tuition waivers (full and partial), and unspecified assistantships also available. Financial award application deadline: 3/1; financial award applicants required to submit FAFSA. *Unit head:* Dr. Carole Browner, Chair, 310-825-4119. *Application contact:* Department Office, 310-825-2511, E-mail: awalters@anthro.ucla.edu.

University of California, Riverside, Graduate Division, Department of Anthropology, Riverside, CA 92521-0102. Offers MA, MS, PhD. Part-time programs available. Terminal master's awarded for partial completion of doctoral program. *Degree requirements:* For master's, comprehensive exams or thesis; for doctorate, one foreign language, comprehensive exam, thesis/dissertation, qualifying exams. *Entrance requirements:* For master's and doctorate, GRE General Test, sample of written work, minimum GPA of 3.2, 3 letters of recommendation. Additional exam requirements/recommendations for international students: Required—TOEFL (minimum score 550 paper-based; 213 computer-based; 80 iBT). Electronic applications accepted. *Faculty research:* Transnational processes, border communities, political and cultural ecology, Mesoamerican and Western US archaeology, applied anthropology.

University of California, San Diego, Office of Graduate Studies, Department of Anthropology, La Jolla, CA 92093. Offers PhD. *Degree requirements:* For doctorate, thesis/dissertation. *Entrance requirements:* For doctorate, GRE General Test. Electronic applications accepted.

University of California, San Diego, Office of Graduate Studies, Interdisciplinary Program in Cognitive Science, La Jolla, CA 92093. Offers cognitive science/anthropology (PhD); cognitive science/communication (PhD); cognitive science/computer science and engineering (PhD); cognitive science/linguistics (PhD); cognitive science/neuroscience (PhD); cognitive science/philosophy (PhD); cognitive science/psychology (PhD); cognitive science/sociology (PhD). Admissions offered through affiliated departments. *Degree requirements:* For doctorate, thesis/dissertation. *Entrance requirements:* For doctorate, GRE General Test, acceptance into one of the eight participating departments. *Faculty research:* Language and cognition, philosophy of mind, visual perception, biological anthropology, sociolinguistics.

University of California, San Francisco, Graduate Division, Program in Medical Anthropology, San Francisco, CA 94143. Offers PhD. *Degree requirements:* For doctorate, one foreign language, thesis/dissertation, 3 field statements. *Entrance requirements:* For doctorate, GRE General Test, master's degree in anthropology or a related social or health science. *Faculty research:* Ethnicity, gender, aging, international health, health policy.

University of California, Santa Barbara, Graduate Division, College of Letters and Sciences, Division of Social Sciences, Department of Anthropology, Santa Barbara, CA 93106-3210. Offers European archaeology (MA); global studies (PhD); North American archeology (MA); sociocultural anthropology (MA); South American archaeology (MA); MA/PhD. *Faculty:* 13 full-time (2 women), 2 part-time/adjunct (both women). *Students:* 57 full-time (36 women). Average age 31. 64 applicants, 41% accepted, 11 enrolled. In 2009, 7 master's, 3 doctorates awarded. Terminal master's awarded for partial completion of doctoral program. *Degree requirements:* For master's, comprehensive exam, thesis; for doctorate, comprehensive exam, thesis/dissertation. *Entrance requirements:* For master's, GRE General Test, sample of written work, 3 letters of recommendation, resume/curriculum vitae; for doctorate, GRE General Test, sample of written work, 3 letters of recommendation, statement of purpose, personal achievements/contributions statement, resume/curriculum vitae, transcripts for post-secondary institutions attended. Additional exam requirements/recommendations for international students: Required—TOEFL (minimum score 550 paper-based; 213 computer-based; 80 iBT) or IELTS (minimum score 7). *Application deadline:* For fall admission, 12/1 for domestic and international students. Application fee: $70 ($90 for international students). Electronic applications accepted. *Financial support:* In 2009–10, 51 students received support, including 47 fellowships with full and partial tuition reimbursements available (averaging $4,000 per year), 9 research assistantships with full and partial tuition reimbursements available (averaging $7,400 per year), 30 teaching assistantships with partial tuition reimbursements available (averaging $10,500 per year); career-related internships or fieldwork, Federal Work-Study, institutionally sponsored loans, scholarships/grants, traineeships, health care benefits, and unspecified assistantships also available. Financial award application deadline: 3/1; financial award applicants required to submit FAFSA. *Faculty research:* Archaeology, bioarchaeology, biosocial anthropology, evolutionary ecology, evolutionary psychology, sociocultural anthropology. *Unit head:* Prof. Katharina Schreiber, Chair, 805-893-2519, Fax: 805-893-8707, E-mail: kschreiber@anth.ucsb.edu. *Application contact:* Robin Roe, Graduate Program Assistant, 805-893-2516, Fax: 805-893-8707, E-mail: roe@anth.ucsb.edu.

University of California, Santa Cruz, Division of Graduate Studies, Division of Social Sciences, Program in Anthropology, Santa Cruz, CA 95064. Offers anthropological archaeology (PhD); cultural anthropology (PhD). *Degree requirements:* For doctorate, thesis/dissertation, qualifying exam. *Entrance requirements:* For doctorate, GRE General Test. *Faculty research:* Culture and power, women's roles, AIDS, folklore.

University of Central Florida, College of Sciences, Department of Anthropology, Orlando, FL 32816. Offers MA. *Faculty:* 16 full-time (7 women), 2 part-time/adjunct (1 woman). *Students:* 33 full-time (20 women), 23 part-time (17 women); includes 9 minority (3 African Americans, 1 Asian American or Pacific Islander, 5 Hispanic Americans), 2 international. Average age 30. 39 applicants, 59% accepted, 18 enrolled. In 2009, 11 master's awarded. *Expenses:* Tuition, state resident: part-time $306.31 per credit hour. Tuition, nonresident: part-time $1099.01 per credit hour. Part-time tuition and fees vary according to degree level and program. *Financial support:* In 2009–10, 22 students received support, including 2 fellowships with partial tuition reimbursements available (averaging $10,000 per year), 2 research assistantships with partial tuition reimbursements available (averaging $9,300 per year), 19 teaching assistantships with full tuition reimbursements available (averaging $6,000 per year). *Unit head:* Dr. Arlen Chase, Chair, 407-823-2227, Fax: 407-823-3498, E-mail: achase@mail.ucf.edu. *Application contact:* Dr. Arlen Chase, Chair, 407-823-2227, Fax: 407-823-3498, E-mail: achase@mail.ucf.edu.

University of Chicago, Division of Social Sciences, Department of Anthropology, Chicago, IL 60637-1513. Offers PhD. *Students:* 201. In 2009, 15 doctorates awarded. *Degree requirements:* For doctorate, 2 foreign languages, thesis/dissertation, exams. *Entrance requirements:* For doctorate, GRE General Test. Additional exam requirements/recommendations for international students: Required—TOEFL, IELTS (minimum score 7). *Application deadline:* For fall admission, 12/10 for domestic and international students. Application fee: $55. Electronic applications accepted. *Financial support:* Fellowships, teaching assistantships, Federal Work-Study, institutionally sponsored loans, scholarships/grants, traineeships, health care benefits, and unspecified assistantships available. Financial award application deadline: 12/10; financial award applicants required to submit FAFSA. *Unit head:* Prof. Judith Farquhar, Chair, 773-702-8551. *Application contact:* Office of the Dean of Students, 773-702-8415.

University of Chicago, Division of the Humanities, Department of Linguistics, Chicago, IL 60637-1513. Offers anthropology and linguistics (PhD); linguistics (AM, PhD). Terminal master's awarded for partial completion of doctoral program. *Degree requirements:* For master's, one foreign language, thesis; for doctorate, 2 foreign languages, thesis/dissertation. *Entrance requirements:* For master's and doctorate, GRE General Test. Additional exam requirements/recommendations for international students: Required—TOEFL.

University of Cincinnati, Graduate School, McMicken College of Arts and Sciences, Department of Anthropology, Cincinnati, OH 45221. Offers MA. Part-time programs available. *Degree requirements:* For master's, thesis or alternative. *Entrance requirements:* For master's, GRE General Test. Additional exam requirements/recommendations for international students: Required—TOEFL; Recommended—TWE. Electronic applications accepted. *Faculty research:* Medical anthropology, Mayan prehistory, southwestern U.S. prehistory, skeletal biology and paleoanthropology; immigrants; Mexico.

University of Colorado at Boulder, Graduate School, College of Arts and Sciences, Department of Anthropology, Boulder, CO 80309. Offers MA, PhD. *Faculty:* 20 full-time (7 women). *Students:* 53 full-time (35 women), 20 part-time (12 women); includes 10 minority (1 American Indian/Alaska Native, 2 Asian Americans or Pacific Islanders, 7 Hispanic Americans), 4 international. Average age 31. 82 applicants, 24% accepted, 17 enrolled. In 2009, 8 master's, 2 doctorates awarded. *Degree requirements:* For master's, comprehensive exam, thesis or alternative; for doctorate, one foreign language, thesis/dissertation. *Entrance requirements:* For master's, GRE General Test, minimum undergraduate GPA of 3.0; for doctorate, GRE General Test, minimum undergraduate GPA of 3.0, master's degree in anthropology. *Application deadline:* For fall admission, 1/15 for domestic students, 12/1 for international students. Applications are processed on a rolling basis. Application fee: $50 ($60 for international students). Electronic applications accepted. *Financial support:* In 2009–10, 18 fellowships (averaging $4,283 per year), 18 research assistantships (averaging $4,514 per year) were awarded; tuition waivers (full) also available. Financial award application deadline: 1/15. *Faculty research:* Archaeology of ancient Mayan, plains Indians; skeletal biology of ancient Nubians; human biology of modern people of the Amazon; paleontology of early primates. Total annual research expenditures: $484,848.

University of Colorado Denver, College of Liberal Arts and Sciences, Department of Anthropology, Denver, CO 80217-3364. Offers MA. Part-time and evening/weekend programs available. *Students:* 7 full-time (5 women), 28 part-time (24 women); includes 2 minority (1 African American, 1 Hispanic American). 39 applicants, 72% accepted, 11 enrolled. In 2009, 11 master's awarded. *Degree requirements:* For master's, comprehensive exam, thesis or alternative. *Entrance requirements:* For master's, GRE General Test, minor in anthropology. Additional exam requirements/recommendations for international students: Required—TOEFL (minimum score 525 paper-based; 197 computer-based). *Application deadline:* For fall admission, 2/15 for domestic students. Applications are processed on a rolling basis. Application fee: $50 ($75 for international students). Electronic applications accepted. *Financial support:* Research assistantships, teaching assistantships, Federal Work-Study available. Financial award application deadline: 4/1; financial award applicants required to submit FAFSA. *Unit head:* Dr. Steve P. Koester, Chair, 303-556-6795, Fax: 303-556-8501, E-mail: steve.koester@ucdenver.edu. *Application contact:* Connie Turner, Program Assistant, 303-556-3554, Fax: 303-556-8501, E-mail: connie.turner@ucdenver.edu.

University of Connecticut, Graduate School, College of Liberal Arts and Sciences, Department of Anthropology, Storrs, CT 06269. Offers MA, PhD. *Faculty:* 18 full-time (8 women). *Students:* 36 full-time (18 women), 17 part-time (13 women); includes 8 minority (4 African Americans, 1 American Indian/Alaska Native, 1 Asian American or Pacific Islander, 2 Hispanic Americans), 3 international. Average age 33. 66 applicants, 9% accepted, 6 enrolled. In 2009, 8 master's, 6 doctorates awarded. Terminal master's awarded for partial completion of doctoral program. *Degree requirements:* For master's, comprehensive exam; for doctorate, thesis/dissertation. *Entrance requirements:* For master's and doctorate, GRE General Test. Additional exam requirements/recommendations for international students: Required—TOEFL (minimum score 550 paper-based; 213 computer-based). *Application deadline:* For fall admission, 2/1 priority date for domestic and international students; for spring admission, 11/1 for domestic students, 10/1 for international students. Applications are processed on a rolling basis. Application fee: $55. Electronic applications accepted. *Expenses:* Tuition, state resident: full-time $4725; part-time $525 per credit. Tuition, nonresident: full-time $12,267; part-time $1363 per credit. Required fees: $346 per semester. Tuition and fees vary according to course load. *Financial support:* In 2009–10, 5 research assistantships with full tuition reimbursements, 29 teaching assistantships with full tuition reimbursements were awarded; fellowships, Federal Work-Study, scholarships/grants, health care benefits, and unspecified assistantships also available. Financial award application deadline: 2/1; financial award applicants required to submit FAFSA.

Anthropology

University of Connecticut (continued)

Unit head: John J. Manning, Head, 860-486-0074, Fax: 860-486-1719, E-mail: john.manning@uconn.edu. *Application contact:* Kevin McBride, Chairperson, 860-486-4511, Fax: 860-486-1719, E-mail: kmcbride@mptn.org.

University of Denver, Division of Arts, Humanities and Social Sciences, Department of Anthropology, Denver, CO 80208. Offers MA. Part-time programs available. *Faculty:* 7 full-time (4 women), 1 (woman) part-time/adjunct. *Students:* 5 full-time (4 women), 15 part-time (all women); includes 4 minority (1 African American, 1 American Indian/Alaska Native, 2 Hispanic Americans), 1 international. Average age 27. 31 applicants, 55% accepted, 8 enrolled. In 2009, 6 master's awarded. *Degree requirements:* For master's, thesis or alternative, 1 foreign language or quantitative methods. *Entrance requirements:* For master's, GRE. Additional exam requirements/recommendations for international students: Required—TOEFL. *Application deadline:* Applications are processed on a rolling basis. Application fee: $50. Electronic applications accepted. *Expenses:* Tuition: Full-time $34,596; part-time $961 per quarter hour. Required fees: $4 per quarter hour. Tuition and fees vary according to course load, campus/location and program. *Financial support:* In 2009–10, 12 teaching assistantships with full and partial tuition reimbursements (averaging $4,000 per year) were awarded; career-related internships or fieldwork, Federal Work-Study, institutionally sponsored loans, and scholarships/grants also available. Support available to part-time students. Financial award application deadline: 2/20; financial award applicants required to submit FAFSA. *Faculty research:* Gender, class, race, ground-penetrating radar, archaeology. Total annual research expenditures: $10,000. *Unit head:* Dr. Richard Clemmer-Smith, Chairperson, 303-871-2406. *Application contact:* Jeff Quinlisk, Assistant to Chair, 303-871-2677, E-mail: anth02@du.edu.

University of Florida, Graduate School, College of Liberal Arts and Sciences, Department of Anthropology, Gainesville, FL 32611. Offers MA, PhD, JD/MA. Part-time programs available. *Degree requirements:* For master's, thesis optional; for doctorate, thesis/dissertation. *Entrance requirements:* For master's and doctorate, GRE General Test, minimum GPA of 3.2. Additional exam requirements/recommendations for international students: Required—TOEFL (minimum score 550 paper-based; 213 computer-based). Electronic applications accepted. *Faculty research:* Social and cultural anthropology, archaeology, anthropological linguistics, physical anthropology.

University of Georgia, Graduate School, College of Arts and Sciences, Department of Anthropology, Athens, GA 30602. Offers anthropology (MA, PhD); archaeological resource management (MS). *Faculty:* 13 full-time (4 women). *Students:* 47 full-time (25 women), 11 part-time (5 women); includes 5 minority (1 African American, 1 American Indian/Alaska Native, 1 Asian American or Pacific Islander, 2 Hispanic Americans). 78 applicants, 26% accepted, 11 enrolled. In 2009, 6 master's, 7 doctorates awarded. *Degree requirements:* For master's, one foreign language, thesis; for doctorate, one foreign language, thesis/dissertation. *Entrance requirements:* For master's and doctorate, GRE General Test. *Application deadline:* For fall admission, 7/1 priority date for domestic students; for spring admission, 11/15 for domestic students. Application fee: $50. Electronic applications accepted. *Expenses:* Tuition, state resident: full-time $6000; part-time $250 per credit hour. Tuition, nonresident: full-time $20,904; part-time $871 per credit hour. Required fees: $730 per semester. *Financial support:* Fellowships, research assistantships, teaching assistantships, unspecified assistantships available. *Unit head:* Dr. Ervan G. Garrison, Head, 706-542-1479, Fax: 706-542-3998, E-mail: egarriso@uga.edu. *Application contact:* Dr. Elizabeth J. Reitz, Graduate Coordinator, 706-542-1464, Fax: 706-542-3998, E-mail: ereitz@uga.edu.

University of Guelph, Graduate Program Services, College of Social and Applied Human Sciences, Department of Sociology and Anthropology, Guelph, ON N1G 2W1, Canada. Offers anthropology (MA); crime and criminal justice policy (MA); sociology (MA, PhD). *Degree requirements:* For master's, thesis or major paper; for doctorate, comprehensive exam, thesis/dissertation. *Entrance requirements:* For master's, minimum B+ average during previous 2 years of course work, honors BA or equivalent; for doctorate, must have an MA in Sociology, must have 80% or higher in graduate level studies. Additional exam requirements/recommendations for international students: Required—TOEFL (minimum score 550 paper-based; 213 computer-based; 89 iBT), IELTS (minimum score 6.5), TOEFL or IELTS. Electronic applications accepted. *Faculty research:* Rural and development sociology; education, employment, and the workplace; race, ethnicity, and native studies; criminology and deviance; social psychology.

University of Hawaii at Manoa, Graduate Division, College of Social Sciences, Department of Anthropology, Honolulu, HI 96822. Offers MA, PhD. Part-time programs available. *Faculty:* 29 full-time (7 women), 22 part-time/adjunct (7 women). *Students:* 67 full-time (42 women), 20 part-time (13 women); includes 23 minority (20 Asian Americans or Pacific Islanders, 3 Hispanic Americans), 22 international. Average age 31. 125 applicants, 26% accepted, 16 enrolled. In 2009, 12 master's, 3 doctorates awarded. *Degree requirements:* For master's, thesis optional; for doctorate, comprehensive exam, thesis/dissertation. *Entrance requirements:* For master's and doctorate, GRE General Test. Additional exam requirements/recommendations for international students: Required—TOEFL (minimum score 560 paper-based; 220 computer-based; 83 iBT), IELTS (minimum score 5). *Application deadline:* For fall admission, 1/15 for domestic and international students. Application fee: $60. *Expenses:* Tuition, state resident: full-time $8900; part-time $372 per credit. Tuition, nonresident: full-time $21,400; part-time $898 per credit. Required fees: $207 per semester. *Financial support:* In 2009–10, 1 student received support, including 23 fellowships (averaging $5,293 per year), 3 research assistantships (averaging $11,224 per year), 11 teaching assistantships (averaging $15,023 per year); Federal Work-Study, institutionally sponsored loans, and tuition waivers (full) also available. Financial award application deadline: 3/1; financial award applicants required to submit FAFSA. *Faculty research:* Evolution of social complexity, ethnopharmacology, social interaction, faunal analysis, human ecology. Total annual research expenditures: $464,951. *Application contact:* Dr. Jacob Bilmes, Graduate Chairperson, 808-956-7153, Fax: 808-956-4893, E-mail: bilmes@hawaii.edu.

University of Houston, College of Liberal Arts and Social Sciences, Department of Anthropology, Houston, TX 77204. Offers MA. Part-time and evening/weekend programs available. *Faculty:* 5 full-time (3 women), 4 part-time/adjunct (1 woman). *Students:* 11 full-time (10 women), 18 part-time (13 women); includes 7 minority (3 African Americans, 4 Hispanic Americans), 1 international. Average age 34. 8 applicants, 63% accepted, 3 enrolled. In 2009, 4 master's awarded. *Degree requirements:* For master's, comprehensive exam, thesis. *Entrance requirements:* For master's, GRE General Test (minimum 500 verbal, 500 quanititative). Additional exam requirements/recommendations for international students: Required—TOEFL. *Application deadline:* For fall admission, 2/28 for domestic and international students. Application fee: $0 ($75 for international students). Electronic applications accepted. *Expenses:* Tuition, state resident: full-time $7676; part-time $320 per credit hour. Tuition, nonresident: full-time $14,324; part-time $597 per credit hour. Required fees: $3034. *Financial support:* In 2009–10, 2 research assistantships with full tuition reimbursements (averaging $8,800 per year), 7 teaching assistantships with full tuition reimbursements (averaging $8,800 per year) were awarded; career-related internships or fieldwork, Federal Work-Study, institutionally sponsored loans, scholarships/grants, health care benefits, and unspecified assistantships also available. Support available to part-time students. Financial award application deadline: 2/1. *Unit head:* Dr. Norris Lang, Chairperson, 713-743-3780, Fax: 713-743-3798, E-mail: nlang@uh.edu. *Application contact:* Dr. Rebecca Storey, Associate Professor, 713-743-3786, Fax: 713-743-4287, E-mail: rstorey@uh.edu.

University of Idaho, College of Graduate Studies, College of Letters, Arts and Social Sciences, Department of Sociology, Anthropology and Justice Studies, Program in Anthropology, Moscow, ID 83844-2282. Offers MA. *Students:* 13 full-time, 11 part-time. In 2009, 8 master's awarded. *Degree requirements:* For master's, one foreign language, thesis (for some programs). *Entrance requirements:* For master's, minimum GPA of 2.8. *Application deadline:* For fall admission, 8/1 for domestic students; for spring admission, 12/15 for domestic students. Application fee: $55 ($60 for international students). *Expenses:* Tuition, state resident: full-time $6120. Tuition, nonresident: full-time $17,712. *Financial support:* Research assistantships, teaching assistantships available. Financial award application deadline: 2/15. *Unit head:* Dr. Donald E Tyler, Chair, 208-885-6751. *Application contact:* Dr. Donald E. Tyler, Chair, 208-885-6752.

University of Illinois at Chicago, Graduate College, College of Liberal Arts and Sciences, Department of Anthropology, Chicago, IL 60607-7128. Offers anthropology (MA, PhD); environmental and urban geography (MA), including environmental studies, urban geography. Part-time programs available. *Degree requirements:* For doctorate, comprehensive exam. *Entrance requirements:* For master's and doctorate, minimum GPA of 2.75. Additional exam requirements/recommendations for international students: Required—TOEFL. Electronic applications accepted. *Faculty research:* Archaeological, physical, and cultural anthropology.

University of Illinois at Urbana–Champaign, Graduate College, College of Liberal Arts and Sciences, Department of Anthropology, Champaign, IL 61820. Offers MA, PhD. *Faculty:* 27 full-time (12 women), 1 (woman) part-time/adjunct. *Students:* 49 full-time (27 women), 16 part-time (13 women); includes 14 minority (2 African Americans, 4 Asian Americans or Pacific Islanders, 8 Hispanic Americans), 17 international. 92 applicants, 10% accepted, 7 enrolled. In 2009, 4 master's, 7 doctorates awarded. Terminal master's awarded for partial completion of doctoral program. *Entrance requirements:* For master's and doctorate, GRE General Test, minimum GPA of 3.0. Additional exam requirements/recommendations for international students: Required—TOEFL (minimum score 550 paper-based; 213 computer-based). *Application deadline:* Applications are processed on a rolling basis. Application fee: $60 ($75 for international students). Electronic applications accepted. *Financial support:* In 2009–10, 17 fellowships, 20 research assistantships, 30 teaching assistantships were awarded; tuition waivers (full and partial) also available. *Unit head:* Steven R. Leigh, Head, 217-333-3616, Fax: 217-244-3490, E-mail: sleigh@illinois.edu. *Application contact:* Elizabeth M. Spears, Office Support Specialist, 217-244-0296, Fax: 217-244-3490, E-mail: espears@illinois.edu.

The University of Iowa, Graduate College, College of Liberal Arts and Sciences, Department of Anthropology, Iowa City, IA 52242-1316. Offers MA, PhD. *Degree requirements:* For master's, thesis optional, exam; for doctorate, comprehensive exam, thesis/dissertation. *Entrance requirements:* For master's and doctorate, GRE General Test, minimum GPA of 3.0. Additional exam requirements/recommendations for international students: Required—TOEFL (minimum score 550 paper-based; 213 computer-based; 81 iBT). Electronic applications accepted.

The University of Kansas, Graduate Studies, College of Liberal Arts and Sciences, Department of Anthropology, Lawrence, KS 66045. Offers MA, PhD. *Faculty:* 14 full-time (5 women), 6 part-time/adjunct (1 woman). *Students:* 52 full-time (32 women), 14 part-time (7 women); includes 6 minority (2 American Indian/Alaska Native, 3 Asian Americans or Pacific Islanders, 1 Hispanic American), 7 international. Average age 29. 49 applicants, 61% accepted, 20 enrolled. In 2009, 5 master's, 5 doctorates awarded. *Degree requirements:* For master's, comprehensive exam (for some programs), thesis; for doctorate, one foreign language, comprehensive exam, thesis/dissertation. *Entrance requirements:* For master's, minimum GPA of 3.2; for doctorate, minimum GPA of 3.5. Additional exam requirements/recommendations for international students: Required—TOEFL. *Application deadline:* For fall admission, 1/5 for domestic and international students. Application fee: $45 ($55 for international students). Electronic applications accepted. *Expenses:* Tuition, state resident: full-time $6492; part-time $270.50 per credit hour. Tuition, nonresident: full-time $15,510; part-time $646.25 per credit hour. Required fees: $847; $70.56 per credit hour. Tuition and fees vary according to course load and program. *Financial support:* Fellowships with full tuition reimbursements, research assistantships with full and partial tuition reimbursements, teaching assistantships with full and partial tuition reimbursements, career-related internships or fieldwork, institutionally sponsored loans, and unspecified assistantships available. Financial award application deadline: 1/5; financial award applicants required to submit FAFSA. *Faculty research:* Theoretical and applied anthropology; old and new world archaeology; endangered language documentation and revitalization; bio-cultural medical anthropology; anthropological/molecular genetics; Latin American, African, Asian, European and North American anthropology. *Unit head:* Jane W. Gibson, Acting Chair, 785-864-4103, Fax: 785-864-5224, E-mail: jwgc@ku.edu. *Application contact:* Donald D. Stull, Graduate Coordinator, 785-864-4103, Fax: 785-864-5224, E-mail: stull@ku.edu.

University of Kentucky, Graduate School, College of Arts and Sciences, Program in Anthropology, Lexington, KY 40506-0032. Offers MA, PhD. Part-time programs available. *Degree requirements:* For master's, comprehensive exam, thesis optional; for doctorate, one foreign language, comprehensive exam, thesis/dissertation. *Entrance requirements:* For master's, GRE General Test, minimum undergraduate GPA of 2.75; for doctorate, GRE General Test, minimum graduate GPA of 3.0. Additional exam requirements/recommendations for international students: Required—TOEFL (minimum score 550 paper-based; 213 computer-based). Electronic applications accepted. *Faculty research:* Applied social anthropology, developmental change, medical anthropology, culture history, ethnohistory.

University of Lethbridge, School of Graduate Studies, Lethbridge, AB T1K 3M4, Canada. Offers accounting (MScM); addictions counseling (M Sc); agricultural biotechnology (M Sc); agricultural studies (M Sc, MA); anthropology (MA); archaeology (MA); art (MA, MFA); biochemistry (M Sc); biological sciences (M Sc); biomolecular science (PhD); biosystems and biodiversity (PhD); Canadian studies (MA); chemistry (M Sc); computer science (M Sc); computer science and geographical information science (M Sc); counseling psychology (M Ed); dramatic arts (MA); earth, space, and physical science (PhD); economics (MA); educational leadership (M Ed); English (MA); environmental science (M Sc); evolution and behavior (PhD); exercise science (M Sc); finance (MScM); French (MA); French/German (MA); French/Spanish (MA); general education (M Ed); general management (MScM); geography (M Sc, MA); German (MA); health science (M Sc); health sciences (MA); history (MA); human resource management and labour relations (MScM); individualized multidisciplinary (M Sc, MA); information systems (MScM); international management (MScM); kinesiology (M Sc, MA); management (M Sc, MA); marketing (MScM); mathematics (M Sc); music (M Mus, MA); Native American studies (MA); neuroscience (M Sc, PhD); new media (MA); nursing (M Sc); philosophy (MA); physics (M Sc); policy and strategy (MScM); political science (MA); psychology (M Sc, MA); religious studies (MA); social sciences (MA); sociology (MA); theatre and dramatic arts (MFA); theoretical and computational science (PhD); urban and regional studies (MA); women's studies (MA). Part-time and evening/weekend programs available. *Degree requirements:* For doctorate, comprehensive exam, thesis/dissertation. *Entrance requirements:* For master's, GMAT (M Sc in management), bachelor's degree in related field, minimum GPA of 3.0 during previous 20 graded semester courses, 2 years teaching or related experience (M Ed); for doctorate, master's degree, minimum graduate GPA of 3.5. Additional exam requirements/recommendations for international students: Required—TOEFL. *Faculty research:* Movement and brain plasticity, gibberellin physiology, photosynthesis, carbon cycling, molecular properties of main-group ring components.

University of Louisville, Graduate School, College of Arts and Sciences, Department of Anthropology, Louisville, KY 40292-0001. Offers MA. *Students:* 3 full-time (2 women), 4 part-time (2 women); includes 1 minority (Asian American or Pacific Islander). Average age 32. 12 applicants, 83% accepted, 7 enrolled. *Unit head:* Dr. Julie Peteet, Chair, E-mail: jmpete01@louisville.edu. *Application contact:* Libby Leggett, Director, Graduate Admissions, 502-852-3101, Fax: 502-852-6536, E-mail: gradadm@louisville.edu.

University of Manitoba, Faculty of Graduate Studies, Faculty of Arts, Department of Anthropology, Winnipeg, MB R3T 2N2, Canada. Offers MA, PhD. *Degree requirements:* For master's, thesis or alternative.

University of Maryland, College Park, Academic Affairs, College of Behavioral and Social Sciences, Department of Anthropology, College Park, MD 20742. Offers applied anthropology (MAA). Part-time and evening/weekend programs available. *Faculty:* 15 full-time (6 women), 6 part-time/adjunct (3 women). *Students:* 30 full-time (23 women), 6 part-time (4 women); includes 5 minority (1 American Indian/Alaska Native, 1 Asian American or Pacific Islander, 3 Hispanic Americans). 112 applicants, 28% accepted, 16 enrolled. In 2009, 12 master's awarded. *Degree requirements:* For master's, internship. *Entrance requirements:* For master's, GRE General Test, minimum GPA of 3.0, 3 letters of recommendation. Additional exam requirements/recommendations for international students: Required—TOEFL. *Application deadline:* For fall admission, 12/15 for domestic and international students. Applications are processed on a rolling basis. Application fee: $60. Electronic applications accepted. *Expenses:* Tuition, area resident: Part-time $471 per credit hour. Tuition, state resident: part-time $471 per credit hour. Tuition, nonresident: part-time $1016 per credit hour. Required fees: $337.04 per term. *Financial support:* In 2009–10, 7 fellowships with full and partial tuition reimbursements (averaging $14,450 per year), 20 teaching assistantships with tuition reimbursements (averaging $15,051 per year) were awarded; research assistantships, Federal Work-Study and scholarships/grants also available. Support available to part-time students. Financial award applicants required to submit FAFSA. *Faculty research:* Archaeology, human biodiversity, cultural and resource management. Total annual research expenditures: $258,578. *Unit head:* Dr. Paul Shackel, Chair, 301-405-1423, E-mail: pshackel@umd.edu. *Application contact:* Dean of Graduate School, 301-405-0358, Fax: 301-314-9305.

University of Massachusetts Amherst, Graduate School, College of Social and Behavioral Sciences, Department of Anthropology, Amherst, MA 01003. Offers MA, PhD. Part-time programs available. *Faculty:* 22 full-time (11 women). *Students:* 53 full-time (42 women), 22 part-time (18 women); includes 21 minority (7 African Americans, 4 American Indian/Alaska Native, 3 Asian Americans or Pacific Islanders, 7 Hispanic Americans), 6 international. Average age 35. 112 applicants, 13% accepted, 10 enrolled. In 2009, 2 master's, 5 doctorates awarded. Terminal master's awarded for partial completion of doctoral program. *Degree requirements:* For master's, thesis or alternative; for doctorate, comprehensive exam, thesis/dissertation. *Entrance requirements:* Additional exam requirements/recommendations for international students: Required—TOEFL (minimum score 550 paper-based; 213 computer-based; 80 iBT), IELTS (minimum score 6.5). *Application deadline:* For fall admission, 1/2 for domestic and international students. Applications are processed on a rolling basis. Application fee: $50 ($65 for international students). Electronic applications accepted. *Expenses:* Tuition, state resident: full-time $2640; part-time $110 per credit. Tuition, nonresident: full-time $9936; part-time $414 per credit. Tuition and fees vary according to course load. *Financial support:* In 2009–10, 10 research assistantships with full tuition reimbursements (averaging $8,752 per year), 30 teaching assistantships with full tuition reimbursements (averaging $10,029 per year) were awarded; fellowships, career-related internships or fieldwork, Federal Work-Study, scholarships/grants, traineeships, health care benefits, tuition waivers (full), and unspecified assistantships also available. Support available to part-time students. Financial award application deadline: 1/2. *Unit head:* Dr. Martin Wobst, Graduate Program Director, 413-545-0935, Fax: 413-545-9494. *Application contact:* Jean M. Ames, Supervisor of Admissions, 413-545-0722, Fax: 413-577-0010, E-mail: gradadm@grad.umass.edu.

University of Memphis, Graduate School, College of Arts and Sciences, Department of Anthropology, Memphis, TN 38152. Offers medical anthropology (MA); urban anthropology (MA). Part-time programs available. *Faculty:* 6 full-time (4 women), 2 part-time/adjunct (1 woman). *Students:* 26 full-time (24 women), 3 part-time (all women); includes 3 minority (all African Americans). Average age 27. 23 applicants, 83% accepted, 10 enrolled. In 2009, 7 master's awarded. *Degree requirements:* For master's, comprehensive exam, practicum. *Entrance requirements:* For master's, GRE General Test. *Application deadline:* For fall admission, 11/1 priority date for domestic students; for spring admission, 4/1 priority date for domestic students. Application fee: $35 ($60 for international students). Electronic applications accepted. *Expenses:* Tuition, state resident: full-time $6246; part-time $347 per credit hour. Tuition, nonresident: full-time $15,894; part-time $883 per credit hour. Required fees: $1160. Full-time tuition and fees vary according to course load, degree level and program. *Financial support:* In 2009–10, 27 students received support; fellowships, research assistantships with full tuition reimbursements available, teaching assistantships with full tuition reimbursements available, career-related internships or fieldwork, Federal Work-Study, scholarships/grants, and unspecified assistantships available. Financial award application deadline: 2/15; financial award applicants required to submit FAFSA. *Faculty research:* Community development, medical anthropology, environmental justice, health disparities, cultural identity and heritage. *Unit head:* Dr. Ruth Beth Finerman, Chair, 901-678-3334, Fax: 901-678-2069, E-mail: finerman@memphis.edu. *Application contact:* Dr. Charles Williams, Coordinator of Graduate Studies, 901-678-3333, Fax: 901-678-0827, E-mail: cwilliam@memphis.edu.

University of Michigan, Horace H. Rackham School of Graduate Studies, College of Literature, Science, and the Arts, Department of Anthropology, Ann Arbor, MI 48109. Offers PhD. *Faculty:* 40 full-time (19 women), 8 part-time/adjunct (4 women). *Students:* 94 full-time (63 women); includes 13 minority (1 African American, 5 Asian Americans or Pacific Islanders, 7 Hispanic Americans), 13 international. Average age 27. 241 applicants, 14% accepted, 17 enrolled. In 2009, 10 doctorates awarded. *Degree requirements:* For doctorate, one foreign language, comprehensive exam, thesis/dissertation, oral defense of dissertation, preliminary exam. *Entrance requirements:* For doctorate, GRE General Test. Additional exam requirements/recommendations for international students: Required—TOEFL (minimum score 560 paper-based; 220 computer-based; 84 iBT). *Application deadline:* For fall admission, 12/15 for domestic and international students. Application fee: $60 ($75 for international students). Electronic applications accepted. *Expenses:* Tuition, state resident: full-time $17,286; part-time $1099 per credit hour. Tuition, nonresident: full-time $34,944; part-time $2080 per credit hour. Required fees: $95 per semester. Tuition and fees vary according to course load, degree level and program. *Financial support:* In 2009–10, 31 students received support, including 40 fellowships with full tuition reimbursements available (averaging $16,000 per year), 10 research assistantships with full tuition reimbursements available (averaging $16,700 per year), 44 teaching assistantships with full tuition reimbursements available (averaging $16,700 per year); institutionally sponsored loans, scholarships/grants, traineeships, and health care benefits also available. Financial award application deadline: 3/1; financial award applicants required to submit FAFSA. *Faculty research:* Kinship and behavior in wild chimpanzees, paleontological research in the Lower Miocene of Northeast Uganda, long-term fitness consequences of wild chimpanzee behavior, social movements. Total annual research expenditures: $136,094. *Unit head:* Dr. Thomas Fricke, Chair, 734-764-7274, Fax: 734-763-6077. *Application contact:* Jessica Greenwald, Graduate Admissions Coordinator, 734-936-7933, Fax: 734-763-6077, E-mail: greenjes@umich.edu.

University of Michigan, Horace H. Rackham School of Graduate Studies, College of Literature, Science, and the Arts, Doctoral Program in Anthropology and History, Ann Arbor, MI 48109. Offers PhD. *Faculty:* 64 full-time (27 women). *Students:* 35 full-time (15 women); includes 7 minority (2 African Americans, 2 Asian Americans or Pacific Islanders, 3 Hispanic Americans), 15 international. Average age 32. 45 applicants, 20% accepted, 2 enrolled. In 2009, 4 doctorates awarded. *Degree requirements:* For doctorate, 2 foreign languages, thesis/dissertation, oral defense of dissertation, preliminary exam. *Entrance requirements:* For doctorate, GRE General Test, writing sample. Additional exam requirements/recommendations for international students: Required—TOEFL. *Application deadline:* For fall admission, 12/1 for domestic and international students. Application fee: $65 ($75 for international students). Electronic applications accepted. *Expenses:* Tuition, state resident: full-time $17,286; part-time $1099 per credit hour. Tuition, nonresident: full-time $34,944; part-time $2080 per credit hour. Required fees: $95 per semester. Tuition and fees vary according to course load, degree level and program. *Financial support:* In 2009–10, 29 students received support, including 14 fellowships with full and partial tuition reimbursements available (averaging $16,500 per year), 12 teaching assistantships with full tuition reimbursements available (averaging $19,300 per year); research assistantships with full tuition reimbursements available, institutionally sponsored loans and scholarships/grants also available. Financial award application deadline: 3/1. *Faculty research:* Historical anthropology. *Unit head:* Prof. Paul Christopher Johnson, Director, 734-764-1817. *Application contact:* Diana Y. Denney, Graduate Program Coordinator, 734-764-2559, Fax: 734-647-4881, E-mail: dianad@umich.edu.

University of Minnesota, Duluth, Graduate School, College of Liberal Arts, Department of Sociology/Anthropology, Duluth, MN 55812-2496. Offers criminology (MA); liberal studies (MLS). Part-time programs available. *Degree requirements:* For master's, thesis or alternative. *Entrance requirements:* For master's, interview, minimum GPA of 3.0, letters of recommendation. Additional exam requirements/recommendations for international students: Required—TOEFL. *Faculty research:* Nature of knowledge, philosophy of science, ecology, cultural studies, language.

University of Minnesota, Twin Cities Campus, Graduate School, College of Liberal Arts, Department of Anthropology, Minneapolis, MN 55455-0213. Offers MA, PhD. Terminal master's awarded for partial completion of doctoral program. *Degree requirements:* For master's, thesis or alternative; for doctorate, one foreign language, thesis/dissertation. *Entrance requirements:* For master's and doctorate, GRE. Additional exam requirements/recommendations for international students: Required—TOEFL. Electronic applications accepted. *Faculty research:* Psychological anthropology, gender and feminist anthropology, economic anthropology, Latin America, the Pacific.

University of Mississippi, Graduate School, College of Liberal Arts, Department of Sociology and Anthropology, Oxford, University, MS 38677. Offers anthropology (MA); sociology (MA, MSS). *Faculty:* 19 full-time (8 women), 8 part-time/adjunct (4 women). *Students:* 23 full-time (13 women), 3 part-time (1 woman); includes 4 minority (3 African Americans, 1 American Indian/Alaska Native), 3 international. In 2009, 4 master's awarded. *Degree requirements:* For master's, thesis (for some programs). *Entrance requirements:* For master's, GRE General Test, minimum GPA of 3.0. Additional exam requirements/recommendations for international students: Required—TOEFL. *Application deadline:* For fall admission, 4/1 for domestic students; for spring admission, 10/1 for domestic students. Applications are processed on a rolling basis. Application fee: $25. Electronic applications accepted. *Financial support:* Scholarships/grants available. Financial award application deadline: 3/1; financial award applicants required to submit FAFSA. *Unit head:* Dr. Kirsten A. Dellinger, Chairman, 662-915-7421, Fax: 662-915-5372, E-mail: kdelling@olemiss.edu. *Application contact:* Dr. Christy M. Wyandt, Associate Dean, 662-915-7474, Fax: 662-915-7577, E-mail: cwyandt@olemiss.edu.

University of Missouri, Graduate School, College of Arts and Sciences, Department of Anthropology, Columbia, MO 65211. Offers MA, PhD. *Faculty:* 11 full-time (4 women), 3 part-time/adjunct (1 woman). *Students:* 12 full-time (8 women), 28 part-time (16 women); includes 1 minority (Asian American or Pacific Islander). Average age 31. 34 applicants, 56% accepted, 7 enrolled. In 2009, 3 master's, 2 doctorates awarded. *Degree requirements:* For master's, thesis (for some programs); for doctorate, one foreign language, comprehensive exam, thesis/dissertation. *Entrance requirements:* For master's, GRE General Test (minimum score 1000 verbal and quantitative), minimum GPA of 3.25 in last 60 hours and in all anthropology courses; for doctorate, GRE General Test; V+Q = 1000, minimum GPA of 3.5 in previous graduate work. Additional exam requirements/recommendations for international students: Required—TOEFL (minimum score 500 paper-based; 173 computer-based; 61 iBT), IELTS (minimum score 5.5). *Application deadline:* For fall admission, 1/10 priority date for domestic students; for winter admission, 10/15 for domestic students. Applications are processed on a rolling basis. Application fee: $45 ($60 for international students). Electronic applications accepted. *Financial support:* In 2009–10, 2 fellowships with full tuition reimbursements, 5 research assistantships with full tuition reimbursements, 16 teaching assistantships with full tuition reimbursements were awarded; institutionally sponsored loans, health care benefits, and unspecified assistantships also available. *Faculty research:* Social/cultural anthropology, biological anthropology, archaeology. *Unit head:* Dr. R. Lee Lyman, Department Chair, E-mail: lymanr@missouri.edu. *Application contact:* Gail Lawrence, 573-882-4731, E-mail: lawrenceag@missouri.edu.

The University of Montana, Graduate School, College of Arts and Sciences, Department of Anthropology, Missoula, MT 59812-0002. Offers anthropology (MA); cultural heritage (MA); cultural heritage studies (PhD); forensic anthropology (MA); historical anthropology (PhD); linguistics (MA). *Degree requirements:* For master's, thesis (for some programs). *Entrance requirements:* For master's, GRE General Test. Additional exam requirements/recommendations for international students: Required—TOEFL. *Faculty research:* Historical preservation, plateau plains archaeology and ethnohistory.

University of Nebraska–Lincoln, Graduate College, College of Arts and Sciences, Department of Anthropology and Geography, Program in Anthropology, Lincoln, NE 68588. Offers MA. *Degree requirements:* For master's, thesis optional. *Entrance requirements:* For master's, GRE General Test. Additional exam requirements/recommendations for international students: Required—TOEFL (minimum score 500 paper-based; 173 computer-based). Electronic applications accepted. *Faculty research:* Cultural, archaeologic, linguistic, and physical anthropology.

University of Nevada, Las Vegas, Graduate College, College of Liberal Arts, Department of Anthropology and Ethnic Studies, Las Vegas, NV 89154-5003. Offers anthropology (MA, PhD). Part-time programs available. *Faculty:* 14 full-time (7 women). *Students:* 19 full-time (14 women), 22 part-time (16 women); includes 2 minority (1 Asian American or Pacific Islander, 1 Hispanic American), 1 international. Average age 36. 45 applicants, 36% accepted, 9 enrolled. In 2009, 5 master's, 2 doctorates awarded. *Degree requirements:* For master's, thesis, oral defense of thesis; for doctorate, comprehensive exam, thesis/dissertation, oral defense of dissertation. *Entrance requirements:* For master's and doctorate, GRE General Test. Additional exam requirements/recommendations for international students: Required—TOEFL (minimum score 550 paper-based; 213 computer-based; 80 iBT), IELTS (minimum score 7). *Application deadline:* For fall admission, 2/1 priority date for domestic and international students. Applications are processed on a rolling basis. Application fee: $60 ($95 for international students). Electronic applications accepted. *Financial support:* In 2009–10, 15 students received support, including 15 teaching assistantships with partial tuition reimbursements available (averaging $10,800 per year); institutionally sponsored loans, scholarships/grants, health care benefits, and unspecified assistantships also available. Financial award application deadline: 3/1. *Faculty research:* Cross-cultural comparisons, evolution of humans, diet and disease, violence, sex. *Unit head:* Dr. Alan Simmons, Chair/ Professor, 702-895-3512, Fax: 702-8985-4823, E-mail: simmonsa@unlv.nevada.edu. *Application contact:* Graduate College Admissions Evaluator, 702-895-3320, Fax: 702-895-4180, E-mail: gradcollege@unlv.edu.

University of Nevada, Reno, Graduate School, College of Liberal Arts, Department of Anthropology, Reno, NV 89557. Offers MA, PhD. Terminal master's awarded for partial completion of doctoral program. *Degree requirements:* For master's, thesis; for doctorate, thesis/dissertation. *Entrance requirements:* For master's, GRE, minimum GPA of 2.75; for doctorate, GRE, minimum GPA of 3.0. Additional exam requirements/recommendations for international students: Required—TOEFL (minimum score 500 paper-based; 173 computer-based; 61 iBT), IELTS (minimum score 6). Electronic applications accepted. *Faculty research:* Ethnology, linguistics, cultural/medical/religious/ethnic relations, ecological anthropology, historical anthropology.

University of New Brunswick Fredericton, School of Graduate Studies, Faculty of Arts, Department of Anthropology, Fredericton, NB E3B 5A3, Canada. Offers MA. Part-time programs available. *Faculty:* 6 full-time (5 women), 4 part-time/adjunct (1 woman). *Students:* 12 full-time (7 women). *Degree requirements:* For master's, thesis, proposal. *Entrance requirements:* For master's, minimum GPA of 3.7. Additional exam requirements/recommendations for international students: Required—TOEFL. *Application deadline:* 1/31 for domestic and international students. Application fee: $50 Canadian dollars. Tuition and fees charges are reported in Canadian dollars. *Expenses:* Tuition, area resident: Full-time $5562 Canadian dollars; part-time $2781 Canadian dollars per year. Required fees: $49.75 Canadian dollars per term. *Financial support:* In 2009–10, 3 fellowships (averaging $9,709 per year), 5 research assistantships (averaging $7,214 per year), 5 teaching assistantships (averaging $3,600 per year) were awarded. *Faculty research:* Latin America, anthropology of education, community-based fisheries, biomedical anthropology, archaeology of the Maritimes. *Unit head:* Susan Blair, Director of

Anthropology

University of New Brunswick Fredericton (continued)
Graduate Studies, 506-458-7929, Fax: 506-453-5071, E-mail: sblair@unb.ca. *Application contact:* Misty Cormier, Graduate Secretary, 506-453-4975, Fax: 506-453-5071, E-mail: mistyc@unb.ca.

University of New Mexico, Graduate School, College of Arts and Sciences, Department of Anthropology, Albuquerque, NM 87131-2039. Offers MA, MS, PhD. *Faculty:* 26 full-time (10 women), 6 part-time/adjunct (3 women). *Students:* 108 full-time (64 women), 38 part-time (30 women); includes 23 minority (3 American Indian/Alaska Native, 3 Asian Americans or Pacific Islanders, 17 Hispanic Americans), 9 international. Average age 33. 104 applicants, 31% accepted, 19 enrolled. In 2009, 13 master's, 11 doctorates awarded. Terminal master's awarded for partial completion of doctoral program. *Degree requirements:* For master's, comprehensive exam (for some programs), thesis or alternative, 3 exams; for doctorate, one foreign language, comprehensive exam, thesis/dissertation, proposal, oral defense, skill and/or second language. *Entrance requirements:* For master's and doctorate, GRE General Test, 3 letters of recommendation, letter of interest, transcripts. Additional exam requirements/recommendations for international students: Required—TOEFL (minimum score 550 paper-based; 213 computer-based), IELTS (minimum score 7). *Application deadline:* For fall admission, 1/7 for domestic and international students. Application fee: $50. Electronic applications accepted. *Expenses:* Tuition, state resident: full-time $2099; part-time $233.20 per credit hour. Tuition, nonresident: full-time $6650. Required fees: $25 per semester. Tuition and fees vary according to course load, program and reciprocity agreements. *Financial support:* In 2009–10, 78 students received support, including 32 fellowships (averaging $14,000 per year), 10 research assistantships with partial tuition reimbursements available (averaging $14,000 per year), 25 teaching assistantships with partial tuition reimbursements available (averaging $14,000 per year); career-related internships or fieldwork, Federal Work-Study, institutionally sponsored loans, scholarships/grants, traineeships, health care benefits, tuition waivers (partial), and unspecified assistantships also available. Support available to part-time students. Financial award application deadline: 3/1; financial award applicants required to submit FAFSA. *Faculty research:* Ethnology, archaeology, evolutionary anthropology, environment, water and land use, gender and social frameworks, Greater Southwest, Latin America, political economy, public anthropology. Total annual research expenditures: $1.2 million. *Unit head:* Michael W. Graves, Chair, 505-277-4524, Fax: 505-277-0874, E-mail: mwgraves@unm.edu. *Application contact:* Erika E. Gerety, Program Advisement Coordinator, 505-277-2732, Fax: 505-277-0874, E-mail: erika@unm.edu.

The University of North Carolina at Chapel Hill, Graduate School, College of Arts and Sciences, Department of Anthropology, Chapel Hill, NC 27599-3115. Offers MA, PhD. Terminal master's awarded for partial completion of doctoral program. *Degree requirements:* For master's, variable foreign language requirement, thesis; for doctorate, variable foreign language requirement, comprehensive exam, thesis/dissertation. *Entrance requirements:* For master's and doctorate, GRE General Test, minimum GPA of 3.0. Additional exam requirements/recommendations for international students: Required—TOEFL. Electronic applications accepted. *Faculty research:* Archeology, ecology and evolution, medical anthropology, social systems, anthropology of meaning.

University of North Texas, Robert B. Toulouse School of Graduate Studies, College of Public Affairs and Community Service, Department of Anthropology, Denton, TX 76203. Offers applied anthropology (MA, MS). Part-time and evening/weekend programs available. *Degree requirements:* For master's, practicum. *Entrance requirements:* For master's, GRE General Test. Additional exam requirements/recommendations for international students: Required—proof of English language proficiency required for non-native English speakers; Recommended—TOEFL (minimum score 550 paper-based; 213 computer-based; 79 iBT). *Application deadline:* Applications are processed on a rolling basis. Application fee: $50 ($75 for international students). Electronic applications accepted. *Expenses:* Tuition, state resident: full-time $4298; part-time $239 per contact hour. Tuition, nonresident: full-time $9878; part-time $549 per contact hour. Required fees: $265 per contact hour. *Financial support:* Research assistantships, teaching assistantships, career-related internships or fieldwork, Federal Work-Study, and scholarships/grants available. Financial award applicants required to submit FAFSA. *Faculty research:* Cross-cultural/bilingual education in schools, globalization in work teams/business culture, environmental anthropology. *Application contact:* Graduate Adviser, 940-565-4160, Fax: 940-369-7833, E-mail: lhenry@unt.edu.

University of Oklahoma, Graduate College, College of Arts and Sciences, Department of Anthropology, Norman, OK 73019. Offers MA, PhD. Part-time programs available. *Faculty:* 26 full-time (11 women), 1 part-time/adjunct (0 women). *Students:* 44 full-time (22 women), 19 part-time (12 women); includes 10 minority (5 American Indian/Alaska Native, 2 Asian Americans or Pacific Islanders, 3 Hispanic Americans), 1 international. 28 applicants, 68% accepted, 13 enrolled. In 2009, 8 master's, 6 doctorates awarded. Terminal master's awarded for partial completion of doctoral program. *Degree requirements:* For master's, thesis; for doctorate, thesis/dissertation, departmental qualifying exam. *Entrance requirements:* For master's, GRE, BA with 12 hours in anthropology. Additional exam requirements/recommendations for international students: Required—TOEFL (minimum score 550 paper-based; 213 computer-based). *Application deadline:* For fall admission, 4/1 for domestic and international students; for spring admission, 11/1 for domestic students, 9/1 for international students. Applications are processed on a rolling basis. Application fee: $40 ($90 for international students). Electronic applications accepted. *Expenses:* Tuition, state resident: full-time $3744; part-time $156 per credit hour. Tuition, nonresident: full-time $13,577; part-time $565.70 per credit hour. Required fees: $2415; $90.10 per credit hour. *Financial support:* In 2009–10, 58 students received support, including 5 fellowships (averaging $4,500 per year), 2 research assistantships with partial tuition reimbursements available (averaging $13,423 per year), 22 teaching assistantships with partial tuition reimbursements available (averaging $13,764 per year); career-related internships or fieldwork, Federal Work-Study, scholarships/grants, health care benefits, and unspecified assistantships also available. Financial award applicants required to submit FAFSA. *Faculty research:* Sociocultural anthropology, archeology, linguistics, Native America, biology/medical anthropology, applied anthropological linguistics. Total annual research expenditures: $1 million. *Unit head:* Dr. Pat Gilman, Chair, 405-325-3261, Fax: 405-325-7386, E-mail: pgilman@ou.edu. *Application contact:* Keli Mitchell, Staff Assistant, 405-325-3261, Fax: 405-325-7386, E-mail: keli@ou.edu.

University of Oregon, Graduate School, College of Arts and Sciences, Department of Anthropology, Eugene, OR 97403. Offers MA, MS, PhD. Terminal master's awarded for partial completion of doctoral program. *Degree requirements:* For master's, one foreign language; for doctorate, 2 foreign languages, thesis/dissertation. *Entrance requirements:* For master's and doctorate, GRE General Test. Additional exam requirements/recommendations for international students: Required—TOEFL. *Faculty research:* Prehistory, primatology, cultural anthropology of Native Americans, human evolution, Africa.

University of Ottawa, Faculty of Graduate and Postdoctoral Studies, Faculty of Social Sciences, Department of Sociology and Anthropology, Ottawa, ON K1N 6N5, Canada. Offers MA. *Degree requirements:* For master's, thesis or alternative. *Entrance requirements:* For master's, honors bachelor's degree or equivalent, minimum B average. Electronic applications accepted. *Faculty research:* Inter-ethnic relations, development, political policies.

University of Pennsylvania, School of Arts and Sciences, Graduate Group in Anthropology, Philadelphia, PA 19104. Offers AM, MS, PhD. *Faculty:* 26 full-time (11 women), 17 part-time/adjunct (10 women). *Students:* 48 full-time (26 women), 26 part-time (19 women); includes 6 minority (1 African American, 2 Asian Americans or Pacific Islanders, 3 Hispanic Americans), 8 international. 221 applicants, 8% accepted, 13 enrolled. In 2009, 15 master's, 20 doctorates awarded. Terminal master's awarded for partial completion of doctoral program. *Degree requirements:* For master's, thesis, final exam; for doctorate, one foreign language, thesis/dissertation, fieldwork, preliminary and final exams. *Entrance requirements:* For doctorate, GRE General Test. Additional exam requirements/recommendations for international students: Required—TOEFL. *Application deadline:* For fall admission, 12/1 priority date for domestic students. Application fee: $70. *Expenses:* Tuition: Full-time $25,660; part-time $4758 per course. Required fees: $2152; $270 per course. Tuition and fees vary according to course load, degree level and program. *Financial support:* Fellowships, teaching assistantships, institutionally sponsored loans, scholarships/grants, traineeships, health care benefits, and unspecified assistantships available. Financial award application deadline: 12/15.

University of Pittsburgh, School of Arts and Sciences, Department of Anthropology, Pittsburgh, PA 15260. Offers MA, PhD. Part-time programs available. *Faculty:* 19 full-time (6 women), 2 part-time/adjunct (1 woman). *Students:* 70 full-time (39 women), 3 part-time (2 women); includes 3 minority (1 African American, 2 Hispanic Americans), 25 international. 123 applicants, 11% accepted, 12 enrolled. In 2009, 2 master's, 8 doctorates awarded. *Degree requirements:* For master's, one foreign language, thesis or alternative; for doctorate, one foreign language, thesis/dissertation. *Entrance requirements:* For master's and doctorate, GRE General Test. Additional exam requirements/recommendations for international students: Required—TOEFL (minimum score 550 paper-based; 213 computer-based), IELTS (minimum score 5.5). *Application deadline:* For fall admission, 1/7 priority date for domestic and international students. Applications are processed on a rolling basis. Application fee: $50. Electronic applications accepted. *Expenses:* Tuition, state resident: full-time $16,402; part-time $665 per credit. Tuition, nonresident: full-time $28,694; part-time $1175 per credit. Required fees: $690; $175 per term. Tuition and fees vary according to program. *Financial support:* In 2009–10, 56 students received support, including 25 fellowships with full tuition reimbursements available (averaging $17,972 per year), 29 teaching assistantships with full tuition reimbursements available (averaging $15,065 per year); research assistantships with full tuition reimbursements available, career-related internships or fieldwork, Federal Work-Study, scholarships/grants, health care benefits, tuition waivers (full and partial), and unspecified assistantships also available. Support available to part-time students. Financial award application deadline: 1/7. *Faculty research:* Conflict studies; ethnicity, nationalism, and the state; origins of complex societies; Latin American archaeology; human evolutionary biology. Total annual research expenditures: $41,672. *Unit head:* Dr. Joseph S. Alter, Chair, 412-648-7530, Fax: 412-648-7535, E-mail: jsalter@pitt.edu. *Application contact:* Phyllis J. Deasy, Graduate Coordinator, 412-648-7504, Fax: 412-648-7535, E-mail: pdeasy@pitt.edu.

University of Regina, Faculty of Graduate Studies and Research, Faculty of Arts, Department of Anthropology, Regina, SK S4S 0A2, Canada. Offers MA. Part-time programs available. *Faculty:* 4 full-time (1 woman). *Students:* 2 applicants, 100% accepted. *Degree requirements:* For master's, thesis. *Entrance requirements:* For master's, writing sample. Additional exam requirements/recommendations for international students: Required—TOEFL (minimum score 580 paper-based; 237 computer-based; 80 iBT). *Application deadline:* Applications are processed on a rolling basis. Application fee: $90 ($100 for international students). Electronic applications accepted. *Financial support:* Fellowships, research assistantships, teaching assistantships, scholarships/grants available. Financial award application deadline: 6/15. *Unit head:* Dr. Tobias Sperlich, Graduate Program Coordinator, 306-585-4770, Fax: 306-585-4773, E-mail: tobias.sperlich@uregina.ca. *Application contact:* Dr. Tobias Sperlich, Graduate Program Coordinator, 306-585-4770, Fax: 306-585-4773, E-mail: tobias.sperlich@uregina.ca.

University of Saskatchewan, College of Graduate Studies and Research, College of Arts and Sciences, Department of Religious Studies and Anthropology, Saskatoon, SK S7N 5A2, Canada. Offers MA. *Faculty:* 20. *Students:* 1. *Degree requirements:* For master's, thesis. *Entrance requirements:* Additional exam requirements/recommendations for international students: Required—TOEFL (minimum score 80 iBT); Recommended—IELTS (minimum score 6.5). *Application deadline:* Applications are processed on a rolling basis. Application fee: $75. Electronic applications accepted. Tuition and fees charges are reported in Canadian dollars. *Expenses:* Tuition, area resident: Full-time $3000 Canadian dollars; part-time $500 Canadian dollars per term. Required fees: $700 Canadian dollars; $100 Canadian dollars per term. *Financial support:* Fellowships, research assistantships, teaching assistantships available. Financial award application deadline: 1/31. *Unit head:* Dr. Baj Sinha, Head, 306-966-4258, E-mail: baj.sinha@usask.ca. *Application contact:* Dr. Mary Beavis, Graduate Chair, 306-966-4258, E-mail: mary.beavis@usas.ca.

University of South Africa, College of Human Sciences, Pretoria, South Africa. Offers adult education (M Ed); African languages (MA, PhD); African politics (MA, PhD); Afrikaans (MA, PhD); ancient history (MA, PhD); ancient Near Eastern studies (MA, PhD); anthropology (MA, PhD); applied linguistics (MA); Arabic (MA, PhD); archaeology (MA); art history (MA); Biblical archaeology (MA); Biblical studies (M Th, D Th, PhD); Christian spirituality (M Th, D Th); church history (M Th, D Th); classical studies (MA, PhD); clinical psychology (MA); communication (MA, PhD); comparative education (M Ed, Ed D); consulting psychology (D Admin, D Com, PhD); curriculum studies (M Ed, Ed D); development studies (M Admin, MA, D Admin, PhD); didactics (M Ed, Ed D); education (M Tech); education management (M Ed, Ed D); educational psychology (M Ed); English (MA); environmental education (M Ed); French (MA, PhD); German (MA, PhD); Greek (MA); guidance and counseling (M Ed); health studies (MA, PhD), including health sciences education (MA), health services management (MA), medical and surgical nursing science (critical care general) (MA), midwifery and neonatal nursing science (MA), trauma and emergency care (MA); history (MA, PhD); history of education (Ed D); inclusive education (M Ed, Ed D); information and communications technology policy and regulation (MA); information science (MA, MIS, PhD); international politics (MA, PhD); Islamic studies (MA, PhD); Italian (MA, PhD); Judaica (MA, PhD); linguistics (MA, PhD); mathematical education (M Ed); mathematics education (MA); missiology (M Th, D Th); modern Hebrew (MA, PhD); musicology (MA, MMus, D Mus, PhD); natural science education (M Ed); New Testament (M Th, D Th); Old Testament (D Th); pastoral therapy (M Th, D Th); philosophy (MA); philosophy of education (M Ed, Ed D); politics (MA, PhD); Portuguese (MA, PhD); practical theology (M Th, D Th); psychology (MA, MS, PhD); psychology of education (M Ed, Ed D); public health (MA); religious studies (MA, D Th, PhD); Romance languages (MA); Russian (MA, PhD); Semitic languages (MA, PhD); social behavior studies in HIV/AIDS (MA); social science (mental health) (MA); social science in development studies (MA); social science in psychology (MA); social science in social work (MA); social science in sociology (MA); social work (MSW, DSW, PhD); socio-education (M Ed, Ed D); sociolinguistics (MA); sociology (MA, PhD); Spanish (MA, PhD); systematic theology (M Th, D Th); TESOL (teaching English to speakers of other languages) (MA); theological ethics (M Th, D Th); theory of literature (MA, PhD); urban ministries (D Th); urban ministry (M Th).

University of South Carolina, The Graduate School, College of Arts and Sciences, Department of Anthropology, Columbia, SC 29208. Offers MA, PhD. Terminal master's awarded for partial completion of doctoral program. *Degree requirements:* For master's, comprehensive exam, thesis; for doctorate, comprehensive exam, thesis/dissertation. *Entrance requirements:* For master's and doctorate, GRE General Test, letters of reference. Additional exam requirements/recommendations for international students: Required—TOEFL. Electronic applications accepted. *Faculty research:* Biocultural anthropology, archaeology, cultural anthropology.

University of Southern Mississippi, Graduate School, College of Arts and Letters, Department of Anthropology and Sociology, Hattiesburg, MS 39406-0001. Offers anthropology (MA). Part-time programs available. *Faculty:* 8 full-time (5 women). *Students:* 14 full-time (11 women), 7 part-time (5 women). Average age 33. 8 applicants, 63% accepted, 3 enrolled. *Degree requirements:* For master's, one foreign language, comprehensive exam, thesis. *Entrance requirements:* For master's, GRE General Test, minimum GPA of 2.75 in last 2 years, 3.0 in field of study. Additional exam requirements/recommendations for international students: Required—TOEFL. *Application deadline:* For fall admission, 3/15 priority date for domestic students, 3/1 for international students. Applications are processed on a rolling basis. Application fee: $35. *Expenses:* Tuition, state resident: full-time $5096; part-time $284 per hour. Tuition, nonresident: full-time $13,052; part-time $726 per hour. Required fees: $402. Tuition and fees vary according to course level and course load. *Financial support:* In 2009–10, 8 research assistantships with full tuition reimbursements (averaging $7,500 per year), 6 teaching assistantships with full tuition reimbursements (averaging $7,500 per year) were awarded; career-related internships or fieldwork, Federal Work-Study, institutionally sponsored loans, scholarships/

grants, and unspecified assistantships also available. Financial award application deadline: 3/15; financial award applicants required to submit FAFSA. *Faculty research:* Archaeology of North America, historic archaeology, bioarchaeology, ethnography of Europe, ethnography of Africa. *Unit head:* Dr. James Flanagan, Chair, 601-266-4306, Fax: 601-266-6373. *Application contact:* Dr. Marie Danforth, Graduate Coordinator, 601-266-4306, Fax: 601-266-6373, E-mail: marie.danforth@usm.edu.

University of South Florida, Graduate School, College of Arts and Sciences, Department of Anthropology, Tampa, FL 33620-9951. Offers applied anthropology (MA, PhD). Part-time programs available. *Faculty:* 18 full-time (13 women), 1 (woman) part-time/adjunct. *Students:* 93 full-time (59 women), 64 part-time (44 women); includes 39 minority (15 African Americans, 2 American Indian/Alaska Native, 4 Asian Americans or Pacific Islanders, 18 Hispanic Americans), 7 international. Average age 32. 179 applicants, 27% accepted, 33 enrolled. In 2009, 10 master's, 6 doctorates awarded. *Degree requirements:* For master's, comprehensive exam, thesis; for doctorate, one foreign language, comprehensive exam, thesis/dissertation. *Entrance requirements:* For master's and doctorate, GRE General Test, minimum GPA of 3.2, 3 letters of recommendation. Additional exam requirements/recommendations for international students: Required—TOEFL (minimum score 550 paper-based; 213 computer-based). *Application deadline:* For fall admission, 1/15 for domestic students, 1/2 for international students. Application fee: $30. Electronic applications accepted. *Financial support:* In 2009–10, teaching assistantships with partial tuition reimbursements (averaging $23,963 per year); scholarships/grants and tuition waivers (partial) also available. Financial award application deadline: 1/15; financial award applicants required to submit FAFSA. *Faculty research:* Population genetics, biomedical anthropology, archaeology and culture resource management in the Americas, urban community issues, media and education. Total annual research expenditures: $2.2 million. *Unit head:* Dr. Elizabeth Bird, Chairperson, 813-974-0802, Fax: 813-974-2668, E-mail: ebird@cas.usf.edu. *Application contact:* Nancy Romero-Daza, Director, 813-974-1205, Fax: 813-974-2668, E-mail: daza@cas.usf.edu.

The University of Tennessee, Graduate School, College of Arts and Sciences, Department of Anthropology, Knoxville, TN 37996. Offers archaeology (MA, PhD); biological anthropology (MA, PhD); cultural anthropology (MA, PhD); zoo-archaeology (MA, PhD). *Degree requirements:* For master's, thesis; for doctorate, one foreign language, thesis/dissertation. *Entrance requirements:* For master's and doctorate, GRE General Test, minimum GPA of 2.7. Additional exam requirements/recommendations for international students: Required—TOEFL. Electronic applications accepted. *Expenses:* Tuition, state resident: full-time $6826; part-time $380 per semester hour. Tuition, nonresident: full-time $21,844; part-time $1147 per semester hour. Tuition and fees vary according to program.

The University of Texas at Arlington, Graduate School, College of Liberal Arts, Department of Sociology and Anthropology, Program in Anthropology, Arlington, TX 76019. Offers MA. Part-time and evening/weekend programs available. *Degree requirements:* For master's, comprehensive exam, thesis or alternative. *Entrance requirements:* For master's, GRE General Test, minimum GPA of 3.0, 3 letters of recommendation. Additional exam requirements/recommendations for international students: Required—TOEFL (minimum score 550 paper-based; 213 computer-based).

The University of Texas at Austin, Graduate School, College of Liberal Arts, Department of Anthropology, Austin, TX 78712-1111. Offers archaeology (MA, PhD); folklore and public culture (MA, PhD); linguistic anthropology (MA, PhD); physical anthropology (MA, PhD); social anthropology (MA, PhD). Part-time programs available. Terminal master's awarded for partial completion of doctoral program. *Degree requirements:* For master's, thesis; for doctorate, one foreign language, thesis/dissertation. *Entrance requirements:* For master's and doctorate, GRE General Test. Additional exam requirements/recommendations for international students: Required—TOEFL. Electronic applications accepted.

The University of Texas at San Antonio, College of Liberal and Fine Arts, Department of Anthropology, San Antonio, TX 78249-0617. Offers MA, PhD. Part-time programs available. *Faculty:* 7 full-time (4 women). *Students:* 13 full-time (9 women), 29 part-time (21 women); includes 11 minority (2 African Americans, 1 Asian American or Pacific Islander, 8 Hispanic Americans), 4 international. Average age 30. 20 applicants, 85% accepted, 13 enrolled. In 2009, 4 master's awarded. *Degree requirements:* For master's, one foreign language, comprehensive exam (for some programs), thesis (for some programs); for doctorate, comprehensive exam (for some programs), thesis/dissertation (for some programs). *Entrance requirements:* For master's, GRE General Test, minimum GPA of 3.0 during last 60 hours, 18 hours in major field; for doctorate, GRE. Additional exam requirements/recommendations for international students: Required—TOEFL (minimum score 500 paper-based; 173 computer-based; 61 iBT), IELTS (minimum score 5). *Application deadline:* For fall admission, 7/1 for domestic students, 4/1 for international students; for spring admission, 11/1 for domestic students, 9/1 for international students. Applications are processed on a rolling basis. Application fee: $45 ($80 for international students). Electronic applications accepted. *Expenses:* Tuition, state resident: full-time $3975; part-time $221 per contact hour. Tuition, nonresident: full-time $13,947; part-time $775 per contact hour. Required fees: $1853. *Financial support:* In 2009–10, 15 students received support, including 4 research assistantships (averaging $11,471 per year), 17 teaching assistantships (averaging $8,332 per year); career-related internships or fieldwork, scholarships/grants, and unspecified assistantships also available. Support available to part-time students. *Faculty research:* Archaeology, ethnohistory, American social history, borderlands history, history of imperialism. Total annual research expenditures: $244,303. *Unit head:* Dr. James McDonald, Interim Chair, 210-458-4673, Fax: 210-458-5728, E-mail: jmcdonald@utsa.edu. *Application contact:* Dr. James McDonald, Interim Chair, 210-458-4673, Fax: 210-458-5728, E-mail: jmcdonald@utsa.edu.

University of Toronto, School of Graduate Studies, Social Sciences Division, Department of Anthropology, Toronto, ON M5S 1A1, Canada. Offers M Sc, MA, PhD. Part-time programs available. *Degree requirements:* For master's, research paper; for doctorate, one foreign language, thesis/dissertation, language exam, thesis defense. *Entrance requirements:* For master's, minimum B+ average, 5 full-year anthropology courses, 2 letters of reference, resume; for doctorate, minimum B+ average, master's degree in relevant area, resumé, 2 letters of reference. Additional exam requirements/recommendations for international students: Required—TOEFL (minimum score 580 paper-based), TWE (minimum score 5), Michigan English Language Assessment Battery (minimum score: 85), IELTS (minimum score: 7) or COPE (minimum score: 4).

University of Tulsa, Graduate School, College of Arts and Sciences, Department of Anthropology, Tulsa, OK 74104-3189. Offers MA, JD/MA. Part-time programs available. *Faculty:* 6 full-time (0 women). *Students:* 5 full-time (all women), 3 part-time (2 women); includes 1 minority (American Indian/Alaska Native). Average age 29. 7 applicants, 71% accepted, 2 enrolled. In 2009, 3 master's awarded. *Degree requirements:* For master's, thesis (for some programs). *Entrance requirements:* For master's, GRE General Test. Additional exam requirements/recommendations for international students: Required—TOEFL (minimum score 575 paper-based; 231 computer-based; 91 iBT), IELTS (minimum score 6.5). *Application deadline:* Applications are processed on a rolling basis. Application fee: $40. Electronic applications accepted. *Expenses:* Tuition: Full-time $16,182; part-time $899 per credit hour. Required fees: $4 per credit hour. Tuition and fees vary according to course load. *Financial support:* In 2009–10, 5 students received support, including 1 research assistantship with full and partial tuition reimbursement available (averaging $11,594 per year), 4 teaching assistantships with full and partial tuition reimbursements available (averaging $11,718 per year); fellowships with full and partial tuition reimbursements available, career-related internships or fieldwork, Federal Work-Study, scholarships/grants, health care benefits, tuition waivers (full and partial), and unspecified assistantships also available. Support available to part-time students. Financial award application deadline: 2/1; financial award applicants required to submit FAFSA. *Faculty research:* Archaeology, cultural anthropology, Native American studies. Total annual research expenditures: $33,817. *Unit head:* Dr. Lamont Lindstrom, Chairperson, 918-631-2888, Fax: 918-631-2540, E-mail: lamont-lindstrom@utulsa.edu. *Application contact:* Dr. George Odell, Advisor, 918-631-3082, Fax: 918-631-2540, E-mail: george-odell@utulsa.edu.

University of Utah, The Graduate School, College of Humanities, Program in Middle East Studies, Salt Lake City, UT 84112. Offers anthropology (MA); Arabic (MA, PhD); Arabic and linguistics (MA, PhD); Hebrew (MA); history (MA, PhD); Persian (MA, PhD); political science (MA, PhD); Turkish (MA). *Students:* 24 full-time (8 women), 19 part-time (9 women), 13 international. Average age 33. 33 applicants, 48% accepted, 10 enrolled. In 2009, 8 master's, 2 doctorates awarded. Terminal master's awarded for partial completion of doctoral program. *Degree requirements:* For master's, 2 foreign languages, comprehensive exam, thesis optional; for doctorate, 3 foreign languages, comprehensive exam, thesis/dissertation. *Entrance requirements:* For master's, GRE General Test, minimum GPA of 3.2; for doctorate, GRE General Test, MA in Middle East studies or equivalent, minimum GPA of 3.2. Additional exam requirements/recommendations for international students: Required—TOEFL (minimum score 580 paper-based; 237 computer-based; 92 iBT). *Application deadline:* For fall admission, 1/15 priority date for domestic and international students; for spring admission, 9/15 priority date for domestic and international students. Application fee: $55 ($65 for international students). Electronic applications accepted. *Expenses:* Tuition, state resident: full-time $4004; part-time $1674 per semester. Tuition, nonresident: full-time $14,134; part-time $5915 per semester. Required fees: $324 per semester. Tuition and fees vary according to course load, degree level and program. *Financial support:* In 2009–10, 19 students received support, including 15 fellowships with full tuition reimbursements available (averaging $14,000 per year), 3 teaching assistantships with full tuition reimbursements available (averaging $12,000 per year); unspecified assistantships also available. Financial award application deadline: 1/15. *Faculty research:* Arabic linguistics; Islamic studies; Middle Eastern history; political science; Judaic studies; anthropology; Arabic, Persian, Hebrew, and Turkish language and literature. *Unit head:* Dr. Bahman Baktiari, Director, 801-581-6181, Fax: 801-581-6183, E-mail: b.baktiari@utah.edu. *Application contact:* Peter von Sivers, Director of Graduate Studies, 801-581-9028, Fax: 801-581-6183, E-mail: peter.vonsivers@utah.edu.

University of Utah, The Graduate School, College of Social and Behavioral Science, Department of Anthropology, Salt Lake City, UT 84112. Offers M Phil, MA, MS, PhD. Part-time programs available. *Faculty:* 15 full-time (4 women), 2 part-time/adjunct (1 woman). *Students:* 25 full-time (13 women), 14 part-time (6 women), 1 international. Average age 32. 68 applicants, 24% accepted, 10 enrolled. In 2009, 9 master's, 4 doctorates awarded. *Degree requirements:* For master's, comprehensive exam, thesis optional; for doctorate, comprehensive exam (for some programs), thesis/dissertation. *Entrance requirements:* For master's, GRE General Test, minimum undergraduate GPA of 3.0; for doctorate, GRE General Test. Additional exam requirements/recommendations for international students: Required—TOEFL (minimum score 500 paper-based; 173 computer-based). *Application deadline:* For fall admission, 1/15 for domestic and international students. Application fee: $55 ($65 for international students). Electronic applications accepted. *Expenses:* Tuition, state resident: full-time $4004; part-time $1674 per semester. Tuition, nonresident: full-time $14,134; part-time $5915 per semester. Required fees: $324 per semester. Tuition and fees vary according to course load, degree level and program. *Financial support:* In 2009–10, 18 students received support, including 3 research assistantships with full tuition reimbursements available (averaging $15,000 per year), 15 teaching assistantships with full tuition reimbursements available (averaging $11,000 per year); fellowships with full tuition reimbursements available, career-related internships or fieldwork, health care benefits, and unspecified assistantships also available. Financial award application deadline: 2/15. *Faculty research:* Evolutionary ecology, anthropological genetics, hunter-gatherers, North American archaeology. Total annual research expenditures: $285,073. *Unit head:* Dr. Elizabeth A. Cashdan, Chair, 801-581-6251, Fax: 801-581-6252, E-mail: cashdan@anthro.utah.edu. *Application contact:* Ursula E. Hanly, Administrative Assistant, 801-581-6251, Fax: 801-581-6252, E-mail: ursula@anthro.utah.edu.

University of Victoria, Faculty of Graduate Studies, Faculty of Social Sciences, Department of Anthropology, Victoria, BC V8W 2Y2, Canada. Offers MA. Part-time programs available. *Degree requirements:* For master's, comprehensive exam (for some programs), thesis (for some programs). *Entrance requirements:* For master's, minimum B+ average in last 2 years of undergraduate course work, writing sample. Additional exam requirements/recommendations for international students: Required—TOEFL (minimum score 575 paper-based; 233 computer-based), IELTS (minimum score 7).

University of Virginia, College and Graduate School of Arts and Sciences, Department of Anthropology, Charlottesville, VA 22903. Offers MA, PhD. *Faculty:* 24 full-time (12 women). *Students:* 48 full-time (31 women), 2 part-time (0 women); includes 8 minority (3 African Americans, 1 American Indian/Alaska Native, 2 Asian Americans or Pacific Islanders, 2 Hispanic Americans), 7 international. Average age 31. 73 applicants, 15% accepted, 5 enrolled. In 2009, 7 master's, 1 doctorate awarded. *Degree requirements:* For master's, one foreign language, thesis; for doctorate, 2 foreign languages, thesis/dissertation. *Entrance requirements:* For master's and doctorate, GRE General Test, GRE Subject Test, 3 letters of recommendation. Additional exam requirements/recommendations for international students: Required—TOEFL (minimum score 600 paper-based; 250 computer-based; 90 iBT), IELTS (minimum score 7). *Application deadline:* For fall admission, 12/15 for domestic and international students. Applications are processed on a rolling basis. Application fee: $60. Electronic applications accepted. *Financial support:* Application deadline: 3/15. *Unit head:* Susan McKinnon, Chair, 434-924-7044, Fax: 434-924-1350. *Application contact:* Susan McKinnon, Chair, 434-924-7044, Fax: 434-924-1350.

University of Washington, Graduate School, College of Arts and Sciences, Department of Anthropology, Seattle, WA 98195. Offers MA, PhD. *Faculty:* 25 full-time (15 women), 16 part-time/adjunct (7 women). *Students:* 71 full-time (46 women), 15 part-time (11 women); includes 23 minority (5 African Americans, 5 American Indian/Alaska Native, 5 Asian Americans or Pacific Islanders, 8 Hispanic Americans), 11 international. Average age 32. 155 applicants, 19% accepted, 11 enrolled. In 2009, 18 master's, 11 doctorates awarded. Terminal master's awarded for partial completion of doctoral program. *Degree requirements:* For master's, one foreign language, comprehensive exam (for some programs), thesis optional; for doctorate, one foreign language, comprehensive exam (for some programs), thesis/dissertation. *Entrance requirements:* For doctorate, GRE General Test, minimum GPA of 3.4. Additional exam requirements/recommendations for international students: Required—TOEFL. *Application deadline:* For fall admission, 12/15 for domestic students, 11/1 for international students. Application fee: $65. Electronic applications accepted. *Financial support:* In 2009–10, 3 fellowships with full tuition reimbursements (averaging $12,000 per year), 4 research assistantships with full tuition reimbursements (averaging $13,000 per year), 20 teaching assistantships with full tuition reimbursements (averaging $13,000 per year) were awarded; Federal Work-Study, institutionally sponsored loans, scholarships/grants, traineeships, health care benefits, and unspecified assistantships also available. Financial award application deadline: 1/15; financial award applicants required to submit FAFSA. *Faculty research:* Sociocultural anthropology, biocultural anthropology, archaeology, environmental anthropology, medical anthropology. *Unit head:* Prof. Bettina Shell-Duncan, Chair, 206-543-9607, Fax: 206-543-3285, E-mail: bsd@u.washington.edu. *Application contact:* Catherine M. Zeigler, Graduate Program Assistant, 206-685-1562, Fax: 206-543-3285, E-mail: gradanth@u.washington.edu.

University of Waterloo, Graduate Studies, Faculty of Arts, Department of Anthropology, Waterloo, ON N2L 3G1, Canada. Offers anthropology (MA); public issues (MA). *Entrance requirements:* Additional exam requirements/recommendations for international students: Required—TOEFL. Electronic applications accepted. *Faculty research:* Applied socio-cultural anthropology and archaeology.

The University of Western Ontario, Faculty of Graduate Studies, Social Sciences Division, Department of Anthropology, London, ON N6A 5B8, Canada. Offers MA, PhD. *Degree requirements:* For master's, thesis; for doctorate, thesis/dissertation. *Entrance requirements:* For master's, minimum B average, honors BA. Additional exam requirements/recommendations

Anthropology

The University of Western Ontario (continued)

for international students: Required—TOEFL. Electronic applications accepted. *Faculty research:* Sociocultural anthropology, bioarchaeology, linguistics.

University of West Florida, College of Arts and Sciences: Arts, Division of Anthropology and Archaeology, Pensacola, FL 32514-5750. Offers anthropology (MA); historical archaeology (MA); maritime studies (MA). *Faculty:* 7 full-time (2 women). *Students:* 40 full-time (24 women), 20 part-time (15 women); includes 8 minority (2 African Americans, 2 Asian Americans or Pacific Islanders, 4 Hispanic Americans). Average age 28. 59 applicants, 54% accepted, 20 enrolled. In 2009, 10 master's awarded. *Degree requirements:* For master's, internship or thesis. *Entrance requirements:* For master's, GRE, bachelor's degree in anthropology, minimum GPA of 3.0, 3 letters of recommendation, writing sample. Additional exam requirements/recommendations for international students: Required—TOEFL (minimum score 550 paper-based; 213 computer-based). *Application deadline:* For fall admission, 6/1 for domestic students, 5/15 for international students; for spring admission, 11/1 for domestic students, 10/1 for international students. Application fee: $30. *Expenses:* Tuition, state resident: full-time $4982; part-time $260 per credit hour. Tuition, nonresident: full-time $20,059; part-time $919 per credit hour. Required fees: $1247; $52 per credit hour. *Financial support:* In 2009–10, 10 research assistantships with partial tuition reimbursements (averaging $3,760 per year), 7 teaching assistantships with partial tuition reimbursements (averaging $3,938 per year) were awarded; unspecified assistantships also available. Financial award application deadline: 4/15; financial award applicants required to submit FAFSA. *Unit head:* Dr. John Bratten, Interim Chair, 850-857-6278, E-mail: anthropology@uwf.edu. *Application contact:* Terry McCray, Assistant Director of Graduate Admissions, 850-473-7718, Fax: 850-473-7714, E-mail: gradadmissions@uwf.edu.

University of Wisconsin–Madison, Graduate School, College of Letters and Science, Department of Anthropology, Madison, WI 53706-1380. Offers archaeology (PhD); biological anthropology (PhD); cultural anthropology (PhD). Terminal master's awarded for partial completion of doctoral program. *Degree requirements:* For doctorate, thesis/dissertation. *Entrance requirements:* For doctorate, qualifying exam. Electronic applications accepted. *Expenses:* Tuition, state resident: part-time $594 per credit. Tuition, nonresident: part-time $1504 per credit. Required fees: $65 per credit. Tuition and fees vary according to course load, program and reciprocity agreements. *Faculty research:* Archaeology, biological, anthropology, cultural anthropology.

University of Wisconsin–Milwaukee, Graduate School, College of Letters and Sciences, Department of Anthropology, Milwaukee, WI 53201-0413. Offers anthropology (PhD); museum studies (Certificate). *Faculty:* 18 full-time (8 women). *Students:* 50 full-time (32 women), 44 part-time (36 women); includes 9 minority (2 African Americans, 3 American Indian/Alaska Native, 2 Asian Americans or Pacific Islanders, 2 Hispanic Americans), 2 international. Average age 33. 54 applicants, 76% accepted, 11 enrolled. In 2009, 11 master's, 1 doctorate awarded. *Degree requirements:* For master's, thesis or alternative; for doctorate, one foreign language, thesis/dissertation, departmental qualifying exam. *Entrance requirements:* For master's, GRE; for doctorate, GRE, minimum GPA of 3.0, master's degree. Additional exam requirements/recommendations for international students: Required—TOEFL (minimum score 550 paper-based; 79 iBT), IELTS (minimum score 6.5). *Application deadline:* For fall admission, 1/1 priority date for domestic students; for spring admission, 9/1 for domestic students. Applications are processed on a rolling basis. Application fee: $45 ($75 for international students). *Expenses:* Tuition, state resident: full-time $8800. Tuition, nonresident: full-time $20,760. Tuition and fees vary according to program and reciprocity agreements. *Financial support:* In 2009–10, 19 teaching assistantships were awarded; fellowships, research assistantships, career-related internships or fieldwork and unspecified assistantships also available. Support available to part-time students. Financial award application deadline: 4/15. Total annual research expenditures: $224,571. *Unit head:* J. Patrick Gray, Chair, 414-229-4822, Fax: 414-229-5848, E-mail: jpgray@uwm.edu. *Application contact:* General Information Contact, 414-229-4982, Fax: 414-229-6967, E-mail: gradschool@uwm.edu.

University of Wyoming, College of Arts and Sciences, Department of Anthropology, Laramie, WY 82070. Offers MA, PhD. Part-time programs available. Terminal master's awarded for partial completion of doctoral program. *Degree requirements:* For master's, one foreign language, comprehensive exam, thesis optional; for doctorate, one foreign language, comprehensive exam, thesis/dissertation. *Entrance requirements:* For master's and doctorate, GRE General Test, minimum GPA of 3.0. Electronic applications accepted. *Faculty research:* Paleo-Indian archaeology, osteology, faunal analysis, lithic analysis, hunter-gatherers.

Vanderbilt University, Graduate School, Department of Anthropology, Nashville, TN 37240-1001. Offers MA, PhD. *Faculty:* 14 full-time (4 women). *Students:* 29 full-time (17 women); includes 1 minority (Hispanic American), 5 international. Average age 30. 64 applicants, 8% accepted, 4 enrolled. In 2009, 1 master's, 1 doctorate awarded. *Degree requirements:* For master's, comprehensive exam, thesis or alternative; for doctorate, one foreign language, comprehensive exam, thesis/dissertation, general, qualifying, and final exams. *Entrance requirements:* For master's and doctorate, GRE General Test. Additional exam requirements/recommendations for international students: Required—TOEFL (minimum score 570 paper-based; 230 computer-based; 88 iBT). *Application deadline:* For fall admission, 1/15 for domestic and international students. Application fee: $0. Electronic applications accepted. *Financial support:* Fellowships with full and partial tuition reimbursements, research assistantships with full tuition reimbursements, teaching assistantships with full tuition reimbursements, career-related internships or fieldwork, Federal Work-Study, institutionally sponsored loans, scholarships/grants, and health care benefits available. Financial award application deadline: 1/15; financial award applicants required to submit CSS PROFILE or FAFSA. *Faculty research:* Archaeology, ethnohistory and ethnography, epigraphy, conflict theory, Latin America. *Unit head:* Dr. Lesley Gill, Chair, 615-343-6120, Fax: 615-343-0230. *Application contact:* Dr. John W. Janusek, Director of Graduate Studies, 615-343-6120, Fax: 615-343-0230, E-mail: anthropology@vanderbilt.edu.

Washington State University, Graduate School, College of Liberal Arts, Department of Anthropology, Pullman, WA 99164. Offers archaeology (MA, PhD); cultural anthropology (MA, PhD); evolutionary anthropology (MA, PhD). Part-time programs available. *Faculty:* 20. *Students:* 59 full-time (36 women), 11 part-time (7 women); includes 6 minority (1 African American, 4 Asian Americans or Pacific Islanders, 1 Hispanic American), 3 international. Average age 32. 93 applicants, 35% accepted, 15 enrolled. In 2009, 14 master's, 5 doctorates awarded. *Degree requirements:* For master's, comprehensive exam (for some programs), thesis, oral exam; for doctorate, comprehensive exam, thesis/dissertation, qualifying exam, oral exam and written exam. *Entrance requirements:* For master's, GRE General Test, curriculum vitae, 3 references; for doctorate, GRE General Test, To apply, submit the online Graduate School application, current curriculum vitae, statement of your educational and professional goals, official transcripts of all post-secondary education, contact information of three references, and official GRE scores. Additional exam requirements/recommendations for international students: Required—TOEFL (minimum score 550 paper-based; 213 computer-based), IELTS. *Application deadline:* For fall admission, 1/10 priority date for domestic and international students; for spring admission, 7/1 priority date for domestic and international students. Applications are processed on a rolling basis. Application fee: $50. Electronic applications accepted. *Financial support:* In 2009–10, 5 research assistantships with full tuition reimbursements (averaging $13,917 per year), 34 teaching assistantships with full tuition reimbursements (averaging $13,056 per year) were awarded; fellowships, Federal Work-Study, scholarships/grants, health care benefits, and tuition waivers (partial) also available. Support available to part-time students. Financial award application deadline: 2/15; financial award applicants required to submit FAFSA. *Faculty research:* Western North America, including Alaska; international development; psychological anthropology; cultural ecology; medical anthropology; power and gender; evolutionary psychology; behavioral ecology; evolutionary cultural anthropology; evolutionary archaeology; paleoanthropology. Total annual research expenditures: $791,000. *Unit head:* Dr. William Andrefsky, Chair, 509-335-3441, Fax: 509-335-3999, E-mail: jmstrunk@wsu.edu. *Application contact:* Graduate School Admissions, 800-GRADWSU, Fax: 509-335-1949, E-mail: gradsch@wsu.edu.

Washington University in St. Louis, Graduate School of Arts and Sciences, Department of Anthropology, St. Louis, MO 63130-4899. Offers PhD. Terminal master's awarded for partial completion of doctoral program. *Degree requirements:* For doctorate, thesis/dissertation. *Entrance requirements:* For doctorate, GRE General Test. Additional exam requirements/recommendations for international students: Required—TOEFL. Electronic applications accepted. *Faculty research:* Archaeology; physical anthropology; primate studies; sociocultural anthropology; medical anthropology.

Wayne State University, College of Liberal Arts and Sciences, Department of Anthropology, Detroit, MI 48202. Offers MA, PhD. *Degree requirements:* For master's, one foreign language, thesis; for doctorate, one foreign language, thesis/dissertation. *Entrance requirements:* Additional exam requirements/recommendations for international students: Required—TOEFL (minimum score 550 paper-based; 213 computer-based); Recommended—TWE (minimum score 6). Electronic applications accepted. *Faculty research:* Business anthropology and organizational culture, African and African-American religions, medical anthropology, skeletal epidemiology and forensic anthropology, Latin American anthropology and archaeology.

West Chester University of Pennsylvania, Office of Graduate Studies, College of Arts and Sciences, Department of Anthropology and Sociology, West Chester, PA 19383. Offers gerontology (Certificate); long term health care (MSA). Part-time and evening/weekend programs available. *Students:* 1 (woman) full-time, 2 part-time (both women). Average age 38. 4 applicants, 100% accepted, 1 enrolled. *Degree requirements:* For master's, comprehensive exam. *Entrance requirements:* For master's, MAT, GRE, or GMAT, interview, resume, 2 letters of reference. Additional exam requirements/recommendations for international students: Required—TOEFL (minimum score 550 paper-based; 213 computer-based; 80 iBT). *Application deadline:* For fall admission, 4/15 priority date for domestic students, 3/15 for international students; for spring admission, 10/15 for domestic students, 9/1 for international students. Applications are processed on a rolling basis. Application fee: $35. Electronic applications accepted. *Expenses:* Tuition, state resident: full-time $6666; part-time $370 per credit. Tuition, nonresident: full-time $10,666; part-time $593 per credit. Required fees: $122.56 per credit. *Financial support:* In 2009–10, research assistantships with full tuition reimbursements (averaging $5,000 per year); unspecified assistantships also available. Support available to part-time students. Financial award application deadline: 2/15; financial award applicants required to submit FAFSA. *Faculty research:* West African communities in the U.S., life long learning-distance education, comparative religions. *Unit head:* Dr. Douglas McConatha, Chair and Graduate Coordinator, 610-436-2556, E-mail: dmcconatha@wcupa.edu. *Application contact:* Dr. Douglas McConatha, Chair and Graduate Coordinator, 610-436-2556, E-mail: dmcconatha@wcupa.edu.

Western Kentucky University, Graduate Studies, Potter College of Arts and Letters, Department of Folk Studies and Anthropology, Bowling Green, KY 42101. Offers folk studies (MA). *Degree requirements:* For master's, comprehensive exam, thesis optional, written exam. *Entrance requirements:* For master's, GRE General Test, minimum GPA of 3.0. Additional exam requirements/recommendations for international students: Required—TOEFL (minimum score 555 paper-based; 213 computer-based; 79 iBT). *Expenses:* Tuition, state resident: full-time $4160; part-time $416 per credit hour. Tuition, nonresident: full-time $9550; part-time $506 per credit hour. Tuition and fees vary according to campus/location and reciprocity agreements. *Faculty research:* Public folklore, folklore and education, vernacular belief, music and culture, historic presentation.

Western Michigan University, Graduate College, College of Arts and Sciences, Department of Anthropology, Kalamazoo, MI 49008. Offers MA. *Degree requirements:* For master's, comprehensive exam, thesis, written exams.

Western Washington University, Graduate School, College of Humanities and Social Sciences, Department of Anthropology, Bellingham, WA 98225-5996. Offers MA. Part-time programs available. *Degree requirements:* For master's, thesis. *Entrance requirements:* For master's, GRE General Test, minimum GPA of 3.0 in last 60 semester hours or last 90 quarter hours. Additional exam requirements/recommendations for international students: Required—TOEFL (minimum score 567 paper-based; 227 computer-based). Electronic applications accepted. *Faculty research:* Peoples and culture of the Pacific Rim; prehistory of North America; applied health; community-based action research; globalization and human rights.

Wichita State University, Graduate School, Fairmount College of Liberal Arts and Sciences, Department of Anthropology, Wichita, KS 67260. Offers MA. Part-time programs available. *Students:* 22 applicants. *Entrance requirements:* For master's, minimum GPA of 2.75 in last 60 hours and 3.0 in anthropology. *Expenses:* Tuition, state resident: full-time $4247; part-time $235.95 per credit hour. Tuition, nonresident: full-time $11,171; part-time $620.60 per credit hour. Required fees: $34; $3.60 per credit hour. $17 per term. Tuition and fees vary according to campus/location and program. *Unit head:* Dr. Peer H. Moore-Jansen, Chair, 316-978-3195, E-mail: pmojan@wichita.edu. *Application contact:* Dr. Peer H. Moore-Jansen, Chair, 316-978-3195, E-mail: pmojan@wichita.edu.

Yale University, Graduate School of Arts and Sciences, Department of Anthropology, New Haven, CT 06520. Offers M Phil, MA, PhD. *Degree requirements:* For doctorate, thesis/dissertation. *Entrance requirements:* For master's and doctorate, GRE General Test. *Faculty research:* Linguistics, national identity.

York University, Faculty of Graduate Studies, Faculty of Arts, Program in Social Anthropology, Toronto, ON M3J 1P3, Canada. Offers MA, PhD. Part-time programs available. *Degree requirements:* For master's, thesis or alternative; for doctorate, comprehensive exam, thesis/dissertation. Electronic applications accepted.

Applied Social Research

American University, College of Arts and Sciences, Department of Sociology, Washington, DC 22016-8072. Offers social research (Certificate); sociology (MA). Part-time and evening/weekend programs available. *Faculty:* 14 full-time (9 women), 4 part-time/adjunct (3 women). *Students:* 11 full-time (10 women), 32 part-time (25 women); includes 19 minority (14 African Americans, 1 American Indian/Alaska Native, 1 Asian American or Pacific Islander, 3 Hispanic Americans), 2 international. Average age 37. 22 applicants, 77% accepted, 5 enrolled. In 2009, 10 master's awarded. *Degree requirements:* For master's, comprehensive exam, thesis or alternative, tool of research examination. *Entrance requirements:* For master's, GRE; for Certificate, bachelor's degree. Additional exam requirements/recommendations for international students: Required—TOEFL. *Application deadline:* For fall admission, 2/1 for domestic students. Application fee: $80. *Expenses:* Tuition: Full-time $22,266; part-time $1237 per credit hour. Required fees: $430. Tuition and fees vary according to program. *Financial support:* Fellowships, research assistantships with full and partial tuition reimbursements, teaching assistantships with full and partial tuition reimbursements, career-related internships or fieldwork, Federal Work-Study, institutionally sponsored loans, tuition waivers (full and partial), and unspecified assistantships available. Support available to part-time students. Financial award application deadline: 2/1; financial award applicants required to submit FAFSA. *Faculty research:* Gender, race, development, applied social policy, political economy. *Unit head:* Dr. John Philip Drysdale, Chair, 202-885-2488, Fax: 202-885-2477, E-mail: drysdale@american.edu. *Application contact:* Dr. John Philip Drysdale, Chair, 202-885-2488, Fax: 202-885-2477, E-mail: drysdale@american.edu.

California State University, Dominguez Hills, College of Natural and Behavioral Sciences, Program in Sociology, Carson, CA 90747-0001. Offers social research (Certificate); sociology (MA). Part-time and evening/weekend programs available. *Faculty:* 10 full-time (6 women), 2 part-time/adjunct (1 woman). *Students:* 41 full-time (31 women), 37 part-time (25 women); includes 62 minority (42 African Americans, 3 Asian Americans or Pacific Islanders, 17 Hispanic Americans). Average age 37. 58 applicants, 78% accepted, 26 enrolled. In 2009, 29 master's awarded. *Degree requirements:* For master's, comprehensive exam, thesis. *Entrance requirements:* For master's and Certificate, minimum GPA of 2.85. *Application deadline:* For fall admission, 6/1 for domestic students. Application fee: $55. *Expenses:* Tuition, nonresident: full-time $6696; part-time $372 per unit. Required fees: $5946; $1752 per semester. *Faculty research:* Community studies, social movements, criminology. *Unit head:* Dr. Clare Weber, Chair, 310-243-3458, E-mail: cweber@csudh.edu. *Application contact:* Dr. Gayle Ball-Parker, Director of Admissions, 310-243-3645, E-mail: gball@csudh.edu.

Concordia University, School of Theology, Irvine, CA 92612-3299. Offers Christian leadership (MA); research in theology (MA); theology and culture (MA). Part-time and evening/weekend programs available. Postbaccalaureate distance learning degree programs offered (no on-campus study). *Faculty:* 9 full-time (2 women). *Students:* 32 full-time (4 women), 8 part-time (3 women); includes 5 minority (1 African American, 1 Asian American or Pacific Islander, 3 Hispanic Americans), 3 international. Average age 36. 7 applicants, 100% accepted, 5 enrolled. In 2009, 10 master's awarded. *Degree requirements:* For master's, project/thesis or vicarage. *Entrance requirements:* For master's, 2 references, interview. Additional exam requirements/recommendations for international students: Required—TOEFL. *Application deadline:* For fall admission, 7/1 priority date for domestic students, 6/1 for international students; for spring admission, 11/30 priority date for domestic students, 10/1 for international students. Applications are processed on a rolling basis. Application fee: $50 ($125 for international students). Electronic applications accepted. *Expenses:* Contact institution. *Financial support:* In 2009–10, 34 students received support. Scholarships/grants available. Financial award applicants required to submit FAFSA. *Unit head:* Rev. Dr. James Bachman, Dean, School of Theology Graduate Studies, 949-854-8002 Ext. 1751, E-mail: james.bachman@cui.edu. *Application contact:* Carrie Donohoe, Christ College Program Coordinator, 949-854-8002 Ext. 1407, E-mail: carrie.donohoe@cui.edu.

Hofstra University, College of Liberal Arts and Sciences, Department of Sociology, Hempstead, NY 11549. Offers applied social research and policy analysis (MA). Part-time and evening/weekend programs available. *Faculty:* 6 full-time (3 women). *Students:* 7 full-time (5 women); includes 2 minority (both African Americans), 2 international. Average age 26. 5 applicants, 100% accepted, 3 enrolled. *Degree requirements:* For master's, comprehensive exam, thesis optional, internship. *Entrance requirements:* For master's, GRE, interview, minimum GPA of 3.0. Additional exam requirements/recommendations for international students: Required—TOEFL (minimum score 550 paper-based; 213 computer-based; 80 iBT). *Application deadline:* Applications are processed on a rolling basis. Application fee: $60. Electronic applications accepted. *Expenses:* Tuition: Full-time $16,200; part-time $900 per credit hour. Required fees: $970; $145 per term. Tuition and fees vary according to program. *Financial support:* In 2009–10, 5 students received support, including 2 fellowships with full and partial tuition reimbursements available (averaging $2,500 per year), 3 research assistantships with full and partial tuition reimbursements available (averaging $7,231 per year); Federal Work-Study, institutionally sponsored loans, scholarships/grants, tuition waivers (full and partial), and unspecified assistantships also available. Support available to part-time students. Financial award applicants required to submit FAFSA. *Faculty research:* Housing policy, immigration, labor economic policy, education policy, health care policy. Total annual research expenditures: $100,000. *Unit head:* Dr. Marc Silver, Program Director, 516-463-5640, Fax: 516-463-6250, E-mail: socmls@hofstra.edu. *Application contact:* Carol Drummer, Dean of Graduate Admissions, 516-463-4876, Fax: 516-463-4664, E-mail: gradstudent@hofstra.edu.

Hunter College of the City University of New York, Graduate School, School of Arts and Sciences, Department of Sociology, Program in Applied Social Research, New York, NY 10021-5085. Offers MS. Part-time and evening/weekend programs available. *Faculty:* 5 full-time (1 woman), 3 part-time/adjunct (2 women). *Students:* 12 full-time (7 women), 23 part-time (18 women); includes 8 minority (3 African Americans, 3 Asian Americans or Pacific Islanders, 2 Hispanic Americans). Average age 29. 28 applicants, 71% accepted, 14 enrolled. In 2009, 20 master's awarded. *Degree requirements:* For master's, internship, research reports. *Entrance requirements:* For master's, GRE General Test or GMAT, 3 credits of course work in statistics, research methods, background in sociology or related social science. Additional exam requirements/recommendations for international students: Required—TOEFL. *Application deadline:* For fall admission, 4/1 for domestic students, 2/1 for international students; for spring admission, 11/1 for domestic students, 9/1 for international students. Applications are processed on a rolling basis. Application fee: $125. *Expenses:* Tuition, state resident: full-time $7360; part-time $310 per credit. Required fees: $250 per semester. *Financial support:* Fellowships, research assistantships, teaching assistantships, career-related internships or fieldwork, Federal Work-Study, institutionally sponsored loans, scholarships/grants, and tuition waivers (full and partial) available. Support available to part-time students. *Faculty research:* Consumer behavior, new electronic media, voting behavior, policy analysis, sociomedicine. *Unit head:* Dr. Joong-Hwan Oh, Director, 212-772-5643, E-mail: goh@hunter.cuny.edu. *Application contact:* Prof. Howard Lune, Advisor, 212-772-5641, Fax: 212-772-5581, E-mail: hlune@hunter.cuny.edu.

Laurentian University, School of Graduate Studies and Research, Programme in Sociology, Sudbury, ON P3E 2C6, Canada. Offers applied social research (MA). Part-time programs available. *Entrance requirements:* For master's, honors degree in sociology or equivalent. *Faculty research:* Work foundations, managing AIDS organization, tracking laid-off mine workers.

The New School: A University, The New School for Social Research, New York, NY 10003. Offers M Phil, MA, MS, DS Sc, PhD. Part-time and evening/weekend programs available. *Faculty:* 71 full-time (31 women), 15 part-time/adjunct (1 woman). *Students:* 785 full-time (394 women), 277 part-time (157 women); includes 156 minority (45 African Americans, 2 American Indian/Alaska Native, 47 Asian Americans or Pacific Islanders, 62 Hispanic Americans), 293 international. Average age 31. 1,109 applicants, 73% accepted, 246 enrolled. In 2009, 213 master's, 56 doctorates awarded. Terminal master's awarded for partial completion of doctoral program. *Degree requirements:* For master's, variable foreign language requirement, exam or thesis; for doctorate, variable foreign language requirement, comprehensive exam, thesis/dissertation, qualifying exam. *Entrance requirements:* For master's, GRE General Test; for doctorate, GRE General Test, MA. Additional exam requirements/recommendations for international students: Required—TOEFL (minimum score 600 paper-based; 250 computer-based; 100 iBT). *Application deadline:* For fall admission, 1/17 priority date for domestic and international students; for spring admission, 10/15 priority date for domestic and international students. Applications are processed on a rolling basis. Application fee: $50. Electronic applications accepted. *Expenses:* Contact institution. *Financial support:* Fellowships, research assistantships, teaching assistantships, Federal Work-Study, scholarships/grants, tuition waivers (full and partial), and unspecified assistantships available. Support available to part-time students. Financial award application deadline: 3/1; financial award applicants required to submit FAFSA. *Faculty research:* Civil society and democracy, international movements of refugees, minority use of health services, memory, morality and genetics. *Unit head:* Dr. Michael Schober, Dean, 212-229-5777, E-mail: schober@newschool.edu. *Application contact:* Robert MacDonald, Director of Admissions, 212-229-5710 Ext. 3007, Fax: 212-989-7102, E-mail: macdonar@newschool.edu.

Portland State University, Graduate Studies, Graduate School of Social Work, Portland, OR 97207-0751. Offers social work (MSW); social work and social research (PhD). *Accreditation:* CSWE (one or more programs are accredited). Part-time programs available. *Degree requirements:* For doctorate, comprehensive exam, thesis/dissertation, residency. *Entrance requirements:* For master's, minimum GPA of 3.0 in upper-division course work or 2.75 overall; for doctorate, GRE General Test, 4 references. Additional exam requirements/recommendations for international students: Required—TOEFL (minimum score 550 paper-based; 213 computer-based). *Faculty research:* Child welfare; child mental health; social welfare policies and services; work, family, and dependent care; adult mental health.

University of California, Los Angeles, Graduate Division, School of Public Affairs, Los Angeles, CA 90095. Offers MA, MPP, MSW, PhD, JD/MA, JD/MSW, MA/MA, MBA/MA, MD/PhD. *Accreditation:* CSWE. *Degree requirements:* For doctorate, thesis/dissertation, oral and written qualifying exams. *Entrance requirements:* For master's, minimum GPA of 3.0; for doctorate, minimum undergraduate GPA of 3.0. Additional exam requirements/recommendations for international students: Required—TOEFL. Electronic applications accepted.

Virginia Commonwealth University, Graduate School, College of Humanities and Sciences, Wilder School of Government and Public Affairs, Department of Sociology, Richmond, VA 23284-9005. Offers applied social research (CASR); gender violence intervention (Certificate); sociology (MS); MSW/Certificate. *Degree requirements:* For master's, thesis optional. *Entrance requirements:* For master's, GRE General Test.

West Virginia University, Eberly College of Arts and Sciences, School of Applied Social Sciences, Department of Sociology, Morgantown, WV 26506. Offers applied social research (MA). Part-time programs available. *Degree requirements:* For master's, thesis or alternative. *Entrance requirements:* For master's, GRE General Test, minimum GPA of 2.75. Additional exam requirements/recommendations for international students: Required—TOEFL. *Faculty research:* Applied sociology, stratification, social/complex organization, research methodology criminology.

Archaeology

American University of Beirut, Graduate Programs, Faculty of Arts and Sciences, Beirut, Lebanon. Offers anthropology (MA); Arabic language and literature (MA); archaeology (MA); biology (MS); chemistry (MS); computer science (MS); economics (MA); education (MA); English language (MA); English literature (MA); environmental policy planning (MSES); financial economics (MAFE); geology (MS); history (MA); mathematics (MA, MS); Middle Eastern studies (MA); philosophy (MA); physics (MS); political studies (MA); psychology (MA); public administration (MA); sociology (MA); statistics (MA, MS). Part-time programs available. *Degree requirements:* For master's, one foreign language, comprehensive exam, thesis (for some programs). *Entrance requirements:* For master's, GRE, letter of recommendation. Additional exam requirements/recommendations for international students: Required—TOEFL (minimum score 600 paper-based; 250 computer-based; 100 iBT), IELTS (minimum score 7.5). *Faculty research:* String theory and supergravity; computer graphics; algebra and number theory; popular Arabic literature; marine and freshwater biology; integrating science, math and technology.

Boston University, Graduate School of Arts and Sciences, Department of Archaeology, Boston, MA 02215. Offers archaeological heritage management (MA); archaeology (MA, PhD); geoarchaeology (MA). *Students:* 54 full-time (30 women), 4 part-time (2 women); includes 3 minority (1 African American, 1 Asian American or Pacific Islander, 1 Hispanic American), 6 international. Average age 30. 107 applicants, 30% accepted, 9 enrolled. In 2009, 2 master's, 4 doctorates awarded. Terminal master's awarded for partial completion of doctoral program. *Degree requirements:* For master's, one foreign language, comprehensive exam, thesis or alternative; for doctorate, 2 foreign languages, comprehensive exam, thesis/dissertation. *Entrance requirements:* For master's, GRE General Test, 3 letters of recommendation; for doctorate, GRE General Test, scholarly writing sample, 3 letters of recommendation. Additional exam requirements/recommendations for international students: Required—TOEFL (minimum score 550 paper-based; 213 computer-based). *Application deadline:* For fall admission, 1/15 for domestic and international students. Application fee: $70. *Expenses:* Tuition: Full-time $37,910; part-time $1184 per credit hour. Required fees: $386; $40 per semester. Part-time tuition and fees vary according to class time, course level, degree level and program. *Financial support:* In 2009–10, 26 students received support, including 2 fellowships with full tuition reimbursements available (averaging $18,900 per year), 1 research assistantship with full tuition reimbursement available (averaging $18,400 per year), 7 teaching assistantships with full tuition reimbursements available (averaging $18,400 per year); career-related internships or fieldwork, Federal Work-Study, and unspecified assistantships also available. Support available to part-time students. Financial award application deadline: 1/15; financial award applicants required to submit FAFSA. *Unit head:* Ricardo Elia, Chairman, 617-353-3415, Fax: 617-353-6800, E-mail: elia@bu.edu. *Application contact:* Evelyn Labree, Department Administrator, 617-358-1640, Fax: 617-353-6800, E-mail: labree@bu.edu.

Archaeology

Brown University, Graduate School, Department of Egyptology and Ancient Western Asian Studies, Providence, RI 02912. Offers AM, PhD. *Degree requirements:* For master's, one foreign language, thesis, final exam; for doctorate, 2 foreign languages, comprehensive exam, thesis/dissertation. *Entrance requirements:* For master's and doctorate, GRE General Test.

Brown University, Graduate School, Joukowsky Institute for Archaeology and the Ancient World, Providence, RI 02912. Offers PhD. *Degree requirements:* For doctorate, thesis/dissertation.

Bryn Mawr College, Graduate School of Arts and Sciences, Department of Classical and Near Eastern Archaeology, Bryn Mawr, PA 19010-2899. Offers MA, PhD. Part-time programs available. *Degree requirements:* For master's, 2 foreign languages, thesis; for doctorate, 3 foreign languages, comprehensive exam, thesis/dissertation. *Entrance requirements:* For master's and doctorate, GRE General Test. Additional exam requirements/recommendations for international students: Required—TOEFL (minimum score 600 paper-based; 250 computer-based). *Expenses:* Tuition: Full-time $31,340. Required fees: $430.

California State University, Northridge, Graduate Studies, College of Social and Behavioral Sciences, Department of Anthropology, Northridge, CA 91330. Offers general anthropology (MA); public archaeology (MA). *Faculty:* 7 full-time (5 women), 6 part-time/adjunct (1 woman). *Students:* 15 full-time (10 women), 28 part-time (14 women); includes 1 African American, 2 Asian Americans or Pacific Islanders, 8 Hispanic Americans. Average age 35. 22 applicants, 55% accepted, 9 enrolled. In 2009, 2 master's awarded. *Degree requirements:* For master's, thesis or alternative. *Entrance requirements:* For master's, GRE General Test or minimum GPA of 3.0. Additional exam requirements/recommendations for international students: Required—TOEFL. *Application deadline:* For fall admission, 11/30 for domestic students. Application fee: $55. *Financial support:* Career-related internships or fieldwork, Federal Work-Study, and institutionally sponsored loans available. Financial award application deadline: 3/1. *Unit head:* Sabina Magliocco, Chair, 818-677-3331. *Application contact:* Dr. Cathy L. Costin, Graduate Adviser, 818-677-3324.

Columbia University, Graduate School of Arts and Sciences, Division of Humanities, Department of Art History and Archaeology, New York, NY 10027. Offers archaeology (M Phil, MA, PhD); art history and archaeology (M Phil, MA, PhD); modern art (MA). *Degree requirements:* For master's, 2 foreign languages, thesis; for doctorate, 3 foreign languages, thesis/dissertation. *Entrance requirements:* For master's and doctorate, GRE General Test. Additional exam requirements/recommendations for international students: Required—TOEFL.

Cornell University, Graduate School, Graduate Fields of Arts and Sciences, Field of Archaeology, Ithaca, NY 14853-0001. Offers environmental archaeology (MA); historical archaeology (MA); Latin American archaeology (MA); medieval archaeology (MA); Mediterranean and Near Eastern archaeology (MA); Stone Age archaeology (MA). *Faculty:* 13 full-time (3 women). *Students:* 7 full-time (5 women). Average age 25. 20 applicants, 35% accepted, 4 enrolled. *Degree requirements:* For master's, one foreign language, thesis. *Entrance requirements:* For master's, GRE General Test, 3 letters of recommendation, sample of written work. Additional exam requirements/recommendations for international students: Required—TOEFL (minimum score 550 paper-based; 213 computer-based; 77 iBT). *Application deadline:* For fall admission, 1/15 for domestic students. Application fee: $70. Electronic applications accepted. *Expenses:* Tuition: Full-time $29,500. Required fees: $70. Full-time tuition and fees vary according to degree level, program and student level. *Financial support:* In 2009–10, 4 students received support; fellowships with full tuition reimbursements available, research assistantships with full tuition reimbursements available, teaching assistantships with full tuition reimbursements available, institutionally sponsored loans, scholarships/grants, health care benefits, tuition waivers (full and partial), and unspecified assistantships available. Financial award applicants required to submit FAFSA. *Faculty research:* Anatolia, Lydia, Sardis, classical and Hellenistic Greece; science in archaeology; North American Indians; Stone Age Africa; Maya trade. *Unit head:* Director of Graduate Studies, 607-255-6768, E-mail: blj7@cornell.edu. *Application contact:* Graduate Field Assistant, 607-255-6768, E-mail: dsd6@cornell.edu.

Cornell University, Graduate School, Graduate Fields of Arts and Sciences, Field of History of Art, Archaeology and Visual Studies, Ithaca, NY 14853. Offers American art (PhD); ancient art and archaeology (PhD); Asian art (PhD); baroque art (PhD); medieval art (PhD); modern art (PhD); Renaissance art (PhD); Southeast Asian art (PhD); theory and criticism (PhD). *Faculty:* 23 full-time (14 women). *Students:* 20 full-time (18 women); includes 4 minority (1 African American, 1 American Indian/Alaska Native, 1 Asian American or Pacific Islander, 1 Hispanic American), 5 international. Average age 35. 73 applicants. In 2009, 3 doctorates awarded. *Degree requirements:* For doctorate, one foreign language, comprehensive exam, thesis/dissertation, general exams in 3 areas. *Entrance requirements:* For doctorate, GRE General Test, sample of written work, 3 letters of recommendation. Additional exam requirements/recommendations for international students: Required—TOEFL (minimum score 550 paper-based; 213 computer-based; 77 iBT). *Application deadline:* For fall admission, 1/15 for domestic students. Application fee: $70. Electronic applications accepted. *Expenses:* Tuition: Full-time $29,500. Required fees: $70. Full-time tuition and fees vary according to degree level, program and student level. *Financial support:* In 2009–10, 17 students received support, including 3 fellowships with full tuition reimbursements available; research assistantships with full tuition reimbursements available, teaching assistantships with full tuition reimbursements available, institutionally sponsored loans, scholarships/grants, health care benefits, tuition waivers (full and partial), and unspecified assistantships also available. Financial award applicants required to submit FAFSA. *Unit head:* Director of Graduate Studies, 607-255-4905, Fax: 607-255-0566, E-mail: art_history@cornell.edu. *Application contact:* Graduate Field Assistant, 607-255-4905, Fax: 607-255-0566, E-mail: art_history@cornell.edu.

Florida State University, The Graduate School, College of Arts and Sciences, Department of Classics, Tallahassee, FL 32306-1510. Offers classical archaeology (MA); classical civilization (MA); classics (MA, PhD), including archaeology (PhD), literature and languages (PhD); Greek (MA); Greek and Latin (MA); Latin (MA). Part-time programs available. *Faculty:* 13 full-time (3 women), 1 (woman) part-time/adjunct. *Students:* 43 full-time (21 women); includes 2 Asian Americans or Pacific Islanders. Average age 24. 52 applicants, 67% accepted, 16 enrolled. In 2009, 15 master's, 1 doctorate awarded. Terminal master's awarded for partial completion of doctoral program. *Degree requirements:* For master's, one foreign language, comprehensive exam (for some programs), thesis (for some programs); for doctorate, 2 foreign languages, comprehensive exam, thesis/dissertation. *Entrance requirements:* For master's, GRE General Test, minimum GPA of 3.0; for doctorate, GRE General Test. Additional exam requirements/recommendations for international students: Required—TOEFL. *Application deadline:* For fall admission, 1/15 priority date for domestic students, 2/15 for international students. Applications are processed on a rolling basis. Application fee: $30. Electronic applications accepted. *Expenses:* Tuition, state resident: full-time $7413. Tuition, nonresident: full-time $22,567. *Financial support:* In 2009–10, 42 students received support, including 2 fellowships with full tuition reimbursements available (averaging $18,000 per year), 2 research assistantships with full tuition reimbursements available (averaging $10,000 per year), 28 teaching assistantships with full tuition reimbursements available (averaging $10,000 per year); Federal Work-Study, institutionally sponsored loans, and tuition waivers (full and partial) also available. Support available to part-time students. Financial award application deadline: 1/15; financial award applicants required to submit FAFSA. *Faculty research:* Greek and Latin literature, classical archaeology, history, Roman religion. Total annual research expenditures: $100,000. *Unit head:* Dr. Daniel J. Pullen, Chairman, 850-644-0304, Fax: 850-644-4073, E-mail: dpullen@fsu.edu. *Application contact:* Dr. Nancy de Grummond, Admissions Director, 850-644-0305, Fax: 850-644-0303, E-mail: ndegrummond@fsu.edu.

Gordon-Conwell Theological Seminary, Graduate and Professional Programs, South Hamilton, MA 01982. Offers Biblical languages (MABL); church history (MACH); counseling (MACO); ministry (D Min); missions/evangelism (MAME); New Testament (MANT); Old Testament (MAOT); religion (MAR); theology (M Div, MATH, Th M, Th D). *Accreditation:* ACIPE; ATS (one or more programs are accredited). Part-time and evening/weekend programs available. *Degree requirements:* For master's, one foreign language, thesis optional; for doctorate, 2 foreign languages, thesis/dissertation; for M Div, 2 foreign languages. *Entrance requirements:* For M Div and master's, minimum GPA of 2.5; for doctorate, minimum GPA of 3.0.

Graduate School and University Center of the City University of New York, Graduate Studies, Program in Anthropology, New York, NY 10016-4039. Offers anthropological linguistics (PhD); archaeology (PhD); cultural anthropology (PhD); physical anthropology (PhD). *Faculty:* 39 full-time (14 women). *Students:* 166 full-time (95 women), 1 (woman) part-time; includes 40 minority (13 African Americans, 1 American Indian/Alaska Native, 9 Asian Americans or Pacific Islanders, 17 Hispanic Americans), 25 international. Average age 33. 165 applicants, 27% accepted, 22 enrolled. In 2009, 13 doctorates awarded. *Degree requirements:* For doctorate, one foreign language, thesis/dissertation. *Entrance requirements:* For doctorate, GRE General Test. Additional exam requirements/recommendations for international students: Required—TOEFL. *Application deadline:* For fall admission, 1/8 priority date for domestic students. Application fee: $125. Electronic applications accepted. *Financial support:* In 2009–10, 111 students received support, including 88 fellowships, 16 research assistantships, 10 teaching assistantships; career-related internships or fieldwork, Federal Work-Study, institutionally sponsored loans, and tuition waivers (full and partial) also available. Financial award application deadline: 2/1; financial award applicants required to submit FAFSA. *Unit head:* Dr. Louise Lennihan, Executive Officer, 212-817-8006, Fax: 212-817-1501, E-mail: anthro@gc.cuny.edu. *Application contact:* Information Contact, 212-817-8005, Fax: 212-817-1501, E-mail: anthro@gc.cuny.edu.

Harvard University, Graduate School of Arts and Sciences, Department of Anthropology, Cambridge, MA 02138. Offers archaeology (PhD); biological anthropology (PhD); legal anthropology (AM); medical anthropology (AM); social anthropology (AM, PhD); social change and development (AM). Terminal master's awarded for partial completion of doctoral program. *Degree requirements:* For master's, 2 foreign languages, thesis (for some programs); for doctorate, 2 foreign languages, thesis/dissertation, laboratory and/or fieldwork; general, qualifying, or special exams. *Entrance requirements:* For master's and doctorate, GRE General Test. Additional exam requirements/recommendations for international students: Required—TOEFL. *Expenses:* Tuition: Full-time $33,696. Required fees: $1126. Full-time tuition and fees vary according to program.

Harvard University, Graduate School of Arts and Sciences, Department of Near Eastern Languages and Civilizations, Cambridge, MA 02138. Offers Akkadian and Sumerian (AM, PhD); Arabic (AM, PhD); Armenian (AM, PhD); biblical history (AM, PhD); Hebrew (AM, PhD); Indo-Muslim culture (AM, PhD); Iranian (AM, PhD); Jewish history and literature (AM, PhD); Persian (AM, PhD); Semitic philology (AM, PhD); Syro-Palestinian archaeology (AM, PhD); Turkish (AM, PhD). *Degree requirements:* For doctorate, variable foreign language requirement, thesis/dissertation, general exams. *Entrance requirements:* For master's, GRE General Test; for doctorate, GRE General Test, proficiency in a Near Eastern language. Additional exam requirements/recommendations for international students: Required—TOEFL. *Expenses:* Tuition: Full-time $33,696. Required fees: $1126. Full-time tuition and fees vary according to program.

Harvard University, Graduate School of Arts and Sciences, Department of the Classics, Cambridge, MA 02138. Offers Byzantine Greek (PhD); classical archaeology (PhD); classical philology (PhD); classical philosophy (PhD); medieval Latin (PhD). *Degree requirements:* For doctorate, 4 foreign languages, thesis/dissertation, preliminary and special exams. *Entrance requirements:* For doctorate, GRE General Test. Additional exam requirements/recommendations for international students: Required—TOEFL. *Expenses:* Tuition: Full-time $33,696. Required fees: $1126. Full-time tuition and fees vary according to program.

Illinois State University, Graduate School, College of Arts and Sciences, Department of Sociology, Program in Historical Archaeology, Normal, IL 61790-2200. Offers MA, MS.

Indiana University of Pennsylvania, School of Graduate Studies and Research, College of Humanities and Social Sciences, Department of Anthropology, Indiana, PA 15705-1087. Offers applied archaeology (MA). *Faculty:* 5 full-time (2 women). *Students:* 16 full-time (8 women), 1 (woman) part-time; includes 1 American Indian/Alaska Native. Average age 30. 30 applicants, 57% accepted, 17 enrolled. *Degree requirements:* For master's, thesis and/or internship. *Application deadline:* Applications are processed on a rolling basis. Application fee: $40. Electronic applications accepted. *Expenses:* Tuition, state resident: full-time $6666; part-time $370 per credit hour. Tuition, nonresident: full-time $10,666; part-time $593 per credit hour. Required fees: $813 per semester. *Financial support:* In 2009–10, 1 fellowship (averaging $500 per year), 6 research assistantships (averaging $3,230 per year) were awarded; unspecified assistantships also available. Financial award application deadline: 3/15. *Unit head:* Dr. Phillip Neusius, Chair, 724-357-2841, Fax: 724-357-7637, E-mail: phillip.neusius@iup.edu. *Application contact:* Dr. Phillip Neusius, Chair, 724-357-2841, Fax: 724-357-7637, E-mail: phillip.neusius@iup.edu.

Massachusetts Institute of Technology, School of Engineering, Department of Materials Science and Engineering, Cambridge, MA 02139-4307. Offers archaeological materials (PhD, Sc D); bio- and polymeric materials (PhD, Sc D); electronic, photonic and magnetic materials (PhD, Sc D); emerging, fundamental and computational studies in materials science (Sc D); materials emerging, fundamental, and computational studies in materials science (PhD); materials engineering (Mat E); materials science and engineering (M Eng, SM, PhD, Sc D); metallurgical engineering (Met E); structural and environmental materials (PhD, Sc D); SM/MBA. *Faculty:* 36 full-time (8 women). *Students:* 222 full-time (62 women); includes 32 minority (3 African Americans, 21 Asian Americans or Pacific Islanders, 8 Hispanic Americans), 125 international. Average age 26. 459 applicants, 23% accepted, 63 enrolled. In 2009, 35 master's, 28 doctorates awarded. Terminal master's awarded for partial completion of doctoral program. *Degree requirements:* For master's and other advanced degree, thesis; for doctorate, comprehensive exam, thesis/dissertation. *Entrance requirements:* For master's and doctorate, GRE General Test. Additional exam requirements/recommendations for international students: Required—IELTS (minimum score 5.5); Recommended—TOEFL (minimum score 577 paper-based; 233 computer-based; 90 iBT). *Application deadline:* For fall admission, 1/1 for domestic and international students. Application fee: $75. Electronic applications accepted. *Financial support:* In 2009–10, 222 students received support, including 55 fellowships with tuition reimbursements available (averaging $22,387 per year), 135 research assistantships with tuition reimbursements available (averaging $27,287 per year), 10 teaching assistantships with tuition reimbursements available (averaging $30,736 per year); career-related internships or fieldwork, Federal Work-Study, institutionally sponsored loans, scholarships/grants, health care benefits, and unspecified assistantships also available. *Faculty research:* Thermodynamics and kinetics of phase transformations, structure of all materials classes: metals, ceramics, semiconductors, polymers, biomaterials, influence of processing on materials structure, structure, property relationships (electrical, magnetic, optical, mechanical). Total annual research expenditures: $22.6 million. *Unit head:* Prof. Edwin L. Thomas, Department Head, 617-253-3300, Fax: 617-252-1775. *Application contact:* Angelita Mireles, Graduate Admissions, 617-253-3302, E-mail: dmse-admissions@mit.edu.

Memorial University of Newfoundland, School of Graduate Studies, Department of Anthropology, St. John's, NL A1C 5S7, Canada. Offers archaeology and physical anthropology (MA, PhD); social and cultural anthropology (MA, PhD). Part-time programs available. *Degree requirements:* For master's, thesis (for some programs); for doctorate, comprehensive exam, thesis/dissertation, oral defense of thesis. *Entrance requirements:* For master's, 2nd class degree in related field. Electronic applications accepted. *Faculty research:* Early European settlements, ethnoarchaeology, economic/political anthropology, land claims and aboriginal rights, marine anthropology.

Michigan Technological University, Graduate School, College of Sciences and Arts, Department of Social Sciences, Program in Industrial Archaeology, Houghton, MI 49931. Offers MS. Part-time programs available. *Degree requirements:* For master's, comprehensive exam, thesis. *Entrance requirements:* For master's, GRE. Additional exam requirements/recommendations for international students: Required—TOEFL (minimum score 550 paper-based; 213 computer-based). Electronic applications accepted.

Michigan Technological University, Graduate School, College of Sciences and Arts, Department of Social Sciences, Program in Industrial Heritage and Archeology, Houghton, MI 49931. Offers PhD. Part-time programs available. *Degree requirements:* For doctorate, comprehensive exam, thesis/dissertation. *Entrance requirements:* Additional exam requirements/recommendations for international students: Required—TOEFL (minimum score 550 paper-based; 213 computer-based). Electronic applications accepted.

Midwestern Baptist Theological Seminary, Graduate and Professional Programs, Kansas City, MO 64118-4697. Offers Biblical archaeology (MA); Biblical languages (MA); Christian education (M Div, MACE); Christian foundations—lay ministry (Graduate Certificate); collegiate ministries (M Div); counseling (MA); educational ministry (D Ed Min); international church planting (M Div); ministry (M Div, D Min); North American church planting (M Div); sacred music (MCM); urban ministry (M Div); worship leadership (M Div); youth ministry (M Div). *Accreditation:* ATS. Part-time programs available. Postbaccalaureate distance learning degree programs offered (minimal on-campus study). *Degree requirements:* For doctorate, thesis/dissertation; for M Div, 2 foreign languages. *Entrance requirements:* For doctorate, MAT. Electronic applications accepted. *Faculty research:* Ministerial studies, Biblical and theological studies, missions, counseling.

New York University, Graduate School of Arts and Science, Institute of Fine Arts, Program in Art History and Archaeology, New York, NY 10012-1019. Offers architectural studies (PhD); art history and archaeology (MA, PhD); classical art and archaeology (PhD); curatorial studies (PhD); East and South Asian art (PhD); Near Eastern art and archaeology (PhD); MA/Diploma; PhD/Certificate. Part-time programs available. *Students:* 193 full-time (151 women), 86 part-time (70 women); includes 23 minority (16 Asian Americans or Pacific Islanders, 7 Hispanic Americans), 26 international. Average age 32. 318 applicants, 28% accepted, 39 enrolled. In 2009, 38 master's, 18 doctorates awarded. Terminal master's awarded for partial completion of doctoral program. *Degree requirements:* For master's, 2 foreign languages, thesis or alternative, 2 qualifying papers; for doctorate, 2 foreign languages, thesis/dissertation. *Entrance requirements:* For master's, GRE General Test; for doctorate, GRE General Test, MA. Additional exam requirements/recommendations for international students: Required—TOEFL. *Application deadline:* For fall admission, 12/18 for domestic students. Application fee: $90. *Expenses:* Tuition: Full-time $30,528; part-time $1272 per credit. Required fees: $2177. *Financial support:* Fellowships with tuition reimbursements, research assistantships with tuition reimbursements, teaching assistantships with tuition reimbursements, career-related internships or fieldwork, Federal Work-Study, and institutionally sponsored loans available. Financial award application deadline: 12/18; financial award applicants required to submit FAFSA. *Unit head:* Patricia Rubin, Chair, 212-992-5800, Fax: 212-992-5807, E-mail: ifa.program@nyu.edu. *Application contact:* Priscilla Saucek, Director of Graduate Studies, 212-992-5800, Fax: 212-992-5807, E-mail: ifa.program@nyu.edu.

Northern Arizona University, Graduate College, College of Social and Behavioral Sciences, Department of Anthropology, Flagstaff, AZ 86011. Offers archaeology (MA); cultural anthropology (MA); linguistic anthropology (MA). *Faculty:* 17 full-time (7 women). *Students:* 45 full-time (30 women), 19 part-time (11 women); includes 11 minority (5 American Indian/Alaska Native, 1 Asian American or Pacific Islander, 5 Hispanic Americans). Average age 35. 502 applicants, 12% accepted, 52 enrolled. In 2009, 47 master's awarded. *Degree requirements:* For master's, thesis (for some programs), internship paper. *Entrance requirements:* For master's, 18 undergraduate hours in anthropology. Additional exam requirements/recommendations for international students: Required—TOEFL (minimum score 550 paper-based; 213 computer-based; 80 iBT), IELTS (minimum score 7), or a bachelor's degree from an English-speaking university and demonstrated proficiency. *Application deadline:* For fall admission, 2/15 priority date for domestic students, 9/1 priority date for international students. Applications are processed on a rolling basis. Application fee: $65. Electronic applications accepted. *Financial support:* In 2009–10, 11 teaching assistantships with partial tuition reimbursements (averaging $10,439 per year) were awarded; career-related internships or fieldwork, Federal Work-Study, health care benefits, tuition waivers (full and partial), and unspecified assistantships also available. Support available to part-time students. Financial award application deadline: 3/30; financial award applicants required to submit FAFSA. *Faculty research:* Economic development, culture change, ethnohistory, archaeology of the Southwest, small town networks and HIV. Total annual research expenditures: $594,266. *Unit head:* Dr. Robert Trotter, Chair, 928-523-4521, Fax: 928-523-9135, E-mail: robert.trotter@nau.edu. *Application contact:* Dr. Cathy Small, Coordinator, 928-523-1090, Fax: 928-523-9135, E-mail: cathy.small@nau.edu.

Northwestern State University of Louisiana, Graduate Studies and Research, Program in Heritage Resources, Natchitoches, LA 71497. Offers MA. *Degree requirements:* For master's, comprehensive exam, thesis or alternative. *Entrance requirements:* For master's, GRE General Test, minimum undergraduate GPA of 2.5.

Princeton University, Graduate School, Department of Art and Archaeology, Princeton, NJ 08544-1019. Offers classical art and archaeology (PhD); East Asian art and archaeology (PhD). *Degree requirements:* For doctorate, 2 foreign languages, thesis/dissertation. *Entrance requirements:* For doctorate, GRE General Test. Additional exam requirements/recommendations for international students: Required—TOEFL (minimum score 600 paper-based; 250 computer-based). Electronic applications accepted.

Rice University, Graduate Programs, School of Social Sciences, Department of Anthropology, Houston, TX 77251-1892. Offers social-cultural anthropology (MA); archaeology (MA, PhD); social-cultural anthropology (PhD). *Faculty:* 10 full-time (5 women). *Students:* 30 full-time (18 women); includes 1 minority (African American), 11 international. 26 applicants, 12% accepted, 3 enrolled.Terminal master's awarded for partial completion of doctoral program. *Degree requirements:* For master's, one foreign language, 3 major papers, dissertation proposal and language exam or thesis; for doctorate, one foreign language, thesis/dissertation. *Entrance requirements:* For master's, Research Proposal; for doctorate, none, Research Proposal. Additional exam requirements/recommendations for international students: Required—TOEFL (minimum score 90 iBT). *Application deadline:* For fall admission, 1/15 for domestic and international students. Application fee: $75. Electronic applications accepted. *Financial support:* In 2009–10, 19 students received support, including 14 fellowships (averaging $16,000 per year); scholarships/grants, health care benefits, and tuition waivers also available. Financial award application deadline: 1/15. *Unit head:* Dr. Eugenia Georges, Professor and Chair, 713-348-3390, Fax: 713-348-5455, E-mail: nia@rice.edu. *Application contact:* Dr. James D. Faubion, Professor and Director of Graduate Studies, 713-348-3384, Fax: 713-348-5455, E-mail: jdf@rice.edu.

St. Cloud State University, School of Graduate Studies, College of Social Sciences, Program in Cultural Resource Management Archeology, St. Cloud, MN 56301-4498. Offers MS. *Students:* 13 full-time (3 women), 7 part-time (3 women); includes 1 minority (American Indian/Alaska Native). 10 applicants, 100% accepted, 0 enrolled. *Entrance requirements:* For master's, GRE General Test, minimum GPA of 2.75. Additional exam requirements/recommendations for international students: Required—Michigan English Language Assessment Battery; Recommended—TOEFL (minimum score 550 paper-based; 213 computer-based). *Application deadline:* For fall admission, 6/1 for domestic students, 4/1 for international students. Application fee: $35. *Unit head:* Dr. Mark Muniz, Coordinator, 320-308-4162, E-mail: mpmuniz@stcloudstate.edu. *Application contact:* Linda Lou Krueger, School of Graduate Studies, 320-308-2113, Fax: 320-308-5371, E-mail: lekrueger@stcloudstate.edu.

Simon Fraser University, Graduate Studies, Faculty of Arts and Social Sciences, Department of Archaeology, Burnaby, BC V5A 1S6, Canada. Offers MA, PhD. *Degree requirements:* For master's, one foreign language, thesis; for doctorate, one foreign language, thesis/dissertation. *Entrance requirements:* For master's, minimum GPA of 3.0; for doctorate, minimum GPA of 3.5. Additional exam requirements/recommendations for international students: Required—TOEFL or IELTS. *Faculty research:* Ethnology, archaeometry, zooarchaeology, primate behavior, forensic anthropology.

Temple Baptist Seminary, Program in Theology, Chattanooga, TN 37404-3530. Offers biblical languages (M Div); Biblical studies (MABS); Christian education (MACE); English Bible û language tools (M Div); theology (MM, D Min). Part-time and evening/weekend programs available. Postbaccalaureate distance learning degree programs offered (minimal on-campus study). *Degree requirements:* For doctorate, thesis/dissertation; for M Div, proficiency in Greek and Hebrew. *Entrance requirements:* For doctorate, minimum GPA of 3.0, M Div.

Trinity International University, Trinity Evangelical Divinity School, Deerfield, IL 60015-1284. Offers Biblical and Near Eastern archaeology and languages (MA); Christian studies (MA, Certificate); Christian thought (MA); church history (MA, Th M); congregational ministry: pastor-teacher (M Div); congregational ministry: team ministry (M Div); counseling ministries (MA); counseling psychology (MA); cross-cultural ministry (M Div); educational studies (PhD); evangelism (MA); history of Christianity in America (MA); intercultural studies (MA, PhD); leadership and ministry management (D Min); military chaplaincy (D Min); ministry (MA); mission and evangelism (Th M); missions and evangelism (D Min); New Testament (MA, Th M); Old Testament (Th M); Old Testament and Semitic languages (MA); pastoral care (M Div); pastoral care and counseling (D Min); pastoral counseling and psychology (Th M); pastoral theology (Th M); philosophy of religion (MA); preaching (D Min); religion (MA); research ministry (M Div); systematic theology (Th M); theological studies (PhD); urban ministry (MA). *Accreditation:* ATS (one or more programs are accredited). Part-time programs available. Postbaccalaureate distance learning degree programs offered (minimal on-campus study). *Degree requirements:* For master's, comprehensive exam, thesis, fieldwork; for doctorate, comprehensive exam (for some programs), thesis/dissertation; for M Div, 2 foreign languages, fieldwork; for Certificate, comprehensive exam, integrative papers. *Entrance requirements:* For M Div, GRE, MAT; for master's, GRE, MAT, minimum cumulative undergraduate GPA of 3.0; for doctorate, GRE, minimum cumulative graduate GPA of 3.2; for Certificate, GRE, MAT, minimum undergraduate GPA of 2.5. Additional exam requirements/recommendations for international students: Required—TOEFL (minimum score 580 paper-based; 237 computer-based), TWE (minimum score 4). Electronic applications accepted.

Tufts University, Graduate School of Arts and Sciences, Department of Classics, Medford, MA 02155. Offers classical archaeology (MA); classics (MA). Part-time programs available. *Faculty:* 7 full-time, 4 part-time/adjunct. *Students:* 12 full-time (7 women). Average age 27. 22 applicants, 68% accepted, 5 enrolled. In 2009, 7 master's awarded. *Degree requirements:* For master's, 2 foreign languages, comprehensive exam, thesis or alternative. *Entrance requirements:* For master's, GRE General Test, writing sample. Additional exam requirements/recommendations for international students: Required—TOEFL (minimum score 550 paper-based; 213 computer-based; 80 iBT). *Application deadline:* For fall admission, 2/15 for domestic students, 12/15 for international students; for spring admission, 10/15 for domestic students, 9/15 for international students. Applications are processed on a rolling basis. Application fee: $75. Electronic applications accepted. *Expenses:* Tuition: Full-time $38,096; part-time $3962 per credit. Required fees: $686; $40 per year. Tuition and fees vary according to course level, course load, degree level, program and student level. *Financial support:* Teaching assistantships with full and partial tuition reimbursements, Federal Work-Study, scholarships/grants, tuition waivers (partial), and unspecified assistantships available. Financial award application deadline: 2/15; financial award applicants required to submit FAFSA. *Unit head:* Gregory Crane, Chair, 617-627-3213. *Application contact:* David J. Proctor, Information Contact, 617-627-3213.

Universidad de las Américas–Puebla, Division of Graduate Studies, School of Social Sciences, Program in Anthropology, Puebla, Mexico. Offers anthropology (MA); archaeology (MA). Part-time and evening/weekend programs available. *Degree requirements:* For master's, one foreign language, thesis. *Entrance requirements:* For master's, bachelor's degree in anthropology or equivalent. *Faculty research:* Archaeology, ethnography, and ethnohistory of Mesoamerica.

Université Laval, Faculty of Letters, Department of History, Programs in Archaeology, Québec, QC G1K 7P4, Canada. Offers MA, PhD. Terminal master's awarded for partial completion of doctoral program. *Degree requirements:* For master's, thesis; for doctorate, comprehensive exam, thesis/dissertation. *Entrance requirements:* For master's and doctorate, English test, knowledge of French. Electronic applications accepted.

University of Alberta, Faculty of Graduate Studies and Research, Department of History and Classics, Edmonton, AB T6G 2E1, Canada. Offers ancient history (PhD); classical archaeology (MA, PhD); classical literature (PhD); classics (MA); history (MA, PhD). Part-time and evening/weekend programs available. *Faculty:* 40 full-time (11 women), 30 part-time/adjunct (12 women). *Students:* 47 full-time (18 women), 31 part-time (16 women). 73 applicants, 51% accepted, 22 enrolled. In 2009, 13 master's, 6 doctorates awarded. *Degree requirements:* For master's, one foreign language, thesis (for some programs); for doctorate, one foreign language, thesis/dissertation. *Entrance requirements:* For master's, minimum B+ average; for doctorate, minimum A- average. Additional exam requirements/recommendations for international students: Required—TOEFL (minimum score 580 paper-based; 237 computer-based). *Application deadline:* For fall admission, 1/15 for domestic and international students. Electronic applications accepted. Tuition and fees charges are reported in Canadian dollars. *Expenses:* Tuition, area resident: Full-time $4626 Canadian dollars; part-time $99.72 Canadian dollars per unit. International tuition: $8216 Canadian dollars full-time. Required fees: $3590 Canadian dollars; $99.72 Canadian dollars per unit. $215 Canadian dollars per term. *Financial support:* In 2009–10, fellowships with full tuition reimbursements (averaging $20,000 per year), research assistantships with partial tuition reimbursements (averaging $10,000 per year), teaching assistantships with partial tuition reimbursements (averaging $10,000 per year) were awarded; scholarships/grants, health care benefits, and unspecified assistantships also available. Financial award application deadline: 1/15. *Faculty research:* Western Canada, classical archaeology, Britain, Eastern Europe, East Asia. Total annual research expenditures: $96,000. *Unit head:* Dr. Christopher C. Mackay, Graduate Chair, 780-492-2698, Fax: 780-492-9125. *Application contact:* Lydia A. Dugbazah, Graduate Secretary, 780-492-2698, Fax: 780-492-9125, E-mail: gradstud@ualberta.ca.

The University of British Columbia, Faculty of Arts and Faculty of Graduate Studies, Department of Classical, Near Eastern and Religious Studies, Programmes in Classics, Vancouver, BC V6T 1Z1, Canada. Offers ancient culture, religion, and ethnicity (MA); classical and near eastern archaeology (MA); classics (MA, PhD). Part-time programs available. *Degree requirements:* For master's, 2 foreign languages, thesis or comprehensive exam; for doctorate, 2 foreign languages, comprehensive exam, thesis/dissertation. *Entrance requirements:* For doctorate, MA. Additional exam requirements/recommendations for international students: Required—TOEFL (minimum score 600 paper-based; 250 computer-based), IELTS (minimum score 7.5). Electronic applications accepted. *Faculty research:* Classical archaeology, ancient historians, late antiquity, ancient prose fiction, epigraphy.

University of Calgary, Faculty of Graduate Studies, Faculty of Social Sciences, Department of Archaeology, Calgary, AB T2N 1N4, Canada. Offers MA, PhD. *Degree requirements:* For master's, thesis; for doctorate, one foreign language, thesis/dissertation, candidacy exam. *Entrance requirements:* For master's, BA or B Sc in anthropology or archaeology; for doctorate, MA in anthropology or archaeology. Additional exam requirements/recommendations for international students: Required—TOEFL. Electronic applications accepted. *Faculty research:* Prehistory, ethnoarchaeology, Africa, Latin America, biological anthropology.

University of California, Berkeley, Graduate Division, College of Letters and Science, Department of Classics, Program in Classical Archaeology, Berkeley, CA 94720-1500. Offers MA, PhD. *Faculty:* 2 full-time. *Students:* 5 full-time (2 women). Average age 29. 10 applicants, 1 enrolled. In 2009, 1 master's, 1 doctorate awarded. *Degree requirements:* For master's, one

Archaeology

University of California, Berkeley (continued)

foreign language, thesis, exams; for doctorate, 2 foreign languages, thesis/dissertation, qualifying exam. *Entrance requirements:* For master's and doctorate, GRE General Test, minimum GPA of 3.0, 3 letters of recommendation. Additional exam requirements/recommendations for international students: Required—TOEFL (minimum score 570 paper-based; 230 computer-based), TWE. *Application deadline:* For fall admission, 12/15 for domestic students. Application fee: $70 ($90 for international students). *Financial support:* Fellowships, research assistantships, teaching assistantships, unspecified assistantships available. *Unit head:* Prof. Leslie Kurke, Chair, 510-642-4218, E-mail: ch_classics@ls.berkeley.edu. *Application contact:* Valerie Brown, Secretary, 510-642-4218, Fax: 510-643-2959, E-mail: casmaoff@berkeley.edu.

University of California, Berkeley, Graduate Division, College of Letters and Science, Group in Ancient History and Mediterranean Archaeology, Berkeley, CA 94720-1500. Offers MA, PhD. *Students:* 19 full-time (5 women). Average age 30. 41 applicants, 2 enrolled. In 2009, 3 master's, 2 doctorates awarded. *Degree requirements:* For master's, one foreign language, exam or thesis; for doctorate, 2 foreign languages, thesis/dissertation, qualifying exam. *Entrance requirements:* For master's and doctorate, GRE General Test, minimum GPA of 3.0, 3 letters of recommendation. Additional exam requirements/recommendations for international students: Required—TOEFL (minimum score 570 paper-based; 230 computer-based), TWE. *Application deadline:* For fall admission, 12/15 for domestic students. Application fee: $70 ($90 for international students). *Financial support:* Fellowships, research assistantships, teaching assistantships, career-related internships or fieldwork and unspecified assistantships available. *Unit head:* Prof. Andrew Stewart, Chair, 510-643-8741, E-mail: casmaadm@berkeley.edu. *Application contact:* Janet A. Yonan, Student Affairs Officer, 510-643-8741, Fax: 510-643-2959, E-mail: casmaadm@berkeley.edu.

University of California, Los Angeles, Graduate Division, College of Letters and Science, Program in Archaeology, Los Angeles, CA 90095. Offers MA, PhD. *Students:* 23 full-time (16 women); includes 3 minority (1 African American, 2 Asian Americans or Pacific Islanders), 3 international. Average age 28. 62 applicants, 18% accepted, 4 enrolled. In 2009, 5 master's awarded. *Degree requirements:* For master's, one foreign language, comprehensive exam, comprehensive core exam, paper, field experience; for doctorate, 2 foreign languages, thesis/dissertation, oral and written qualifying exams. *Entrance requirements:* For master's, GRE General Test, minimum GPA of 3.0, sample of research writing; for doctorate, GRE General Test, minimum undergraduate GPA of 3.0, sample of research writing, ability to read 1 foreign language. *Application deadline:* For fall admission, 12/15 for domestic and international students. Application fee: $70 ($90 for international students). Electronic applications accepted. *Financial support:* In 2009–10, 14 fellowships with full and partial tuition reimbursements, 4 research assistantships with full and partial tuition reimbursements, 14 teaching assistantships with full and partial tuition reimbursements were awarded; Federal Work-Study, institutionally sponsored loans, scholarships/grants, health care benefits, tuition waivers (full and partial), and unspecified assistantships also available. Financial award application deadline: 3/1; financial award applicants required to submit FAFSA. *Unit head:* Dr. Richard Lesure, Chair, 310-825-4169. *Application contact:* Department Office, 310-825-4169, E-mail: evgenia@ioa.ucla.edu.

University of California, Santa Barbara, Graduate Division, College of Letters and Sciences, Division of Social Sciences, Department of Anthropology, Santa Barbara, CA 93106-3210. Offers European archaeology (MA); global studies (PhD); North American archeology (MA); sociocultural anthropology (MA); South American archaeology (MA); MA/PhD. *Faculty:* 13 full-time (2 women), 2 part-time/adjunct (both women). *Students:* 57 full-time (36 women). Average age 31. 64 applicants, 41% accepted, 11 enrolled. In 2009, 7 master's, 3 doctorates awarded. Terminal master's awarded for partial completion of doctoral program. *Degree requirements:* For master's, comprehensive exam, thesis; for doctorate, comprehensive exam, thesis/dissertation. *Entrance requirements:* For master's, GRE General Test, sample of written work, 3 letters of recommendation, resume/curriculum vitae; for doctorate, GRE General Test, sample of written work, 3 letters of recommendation, statement of purpose, personal achievements/contributions statement, resume/curriculum vitae, transcripts for post-secondary institutions attended. Additional exam requirements/recommendations for international students: Required—TOEFL (minimum score 550 paper-based; 213 computer-based; 80 iBT) or IELTS (minimum score 7). *Application deadline:* For fall admission, 12/1 for domestic and international students. Application fee: $70 ($90 for international students). Electronic applications accepted. *Financial support:* In 2009–10, 51 students received support, including 47 fellowships with full and partial tuition reimbursements available (averaging $4,000 per year), 9 research assistantships with full and partial tuition reimbursements available (averaging $7,400 per year), 30 teaching assistantships with partial tuition reimbursements available (averaging $10,500 per year); career-related internships or fieldwork, Federal Work-Study, institutionally sponsored loans, scholarships/grants, traineeships, health care benefits, and unspecified assistantships also available. Financial award application deadline: 3/1; financial award applicants required to submit FAFSA. *Faculty research:* Archaeology, bioarchaeology, biosocial anthropology, evolutionary ecology, evolutionary psychology, sociocultural anthropology. *Unit head:* Prof. Katharina Schreiber, Chair, 805-893-2519, Fax: 805-893-8707, E-mail: kschreiber@anth.ucsb.edu. *Application contact:* Robin Roe, Graduate Program Assistant, 805-893-2516, Fax: 805-893-8707, E-mail: roe@anth.ucsb.edu.

University of California, Santa Cruz, Division of Graduate Studies, Division of Social Sciences, Program in Anthropology, Santa Cruz, CA 95064. Offers anthropological archaeology (PhD); cultural anthropology (PhD). *Degree requirements:* For doctorate, thesis/dissertation, qualifying exam. *Entrance requirements:* For doctorate, GRE General Test. *Faculty research:* Culture and power, women's roles, AIDS, folklore.

University of Chicago, Division of the Humanities, Department of Classics, Chicago, IL 60637-1513. Offers ancient philosophy (AM, PhD); classical archaeology (AM, PhD); classical languages and literatures (AM, PhD). Terminal master's awarded for partial completion of doctoral program. *Degree requirements:* For master's, one foreign language, thesis; for doctorate, 2 foreign languages, thesis/dissertation. *Entrance requirements:* For master's and doctorate, GRE General Test. Additional exam requirements/recommendations for international students: Required—TOEFL.

University of Georgia, Graduate School, College of Arts and Sciences, Department of Anthropology, Athens, GA 30602. Offers anthropology (MA, PhD); archaeological resource management (MS). *Faculty:* 13 full-time (4 women). *Students:* 47 full-time (25 women), 11 part-time (5 women); includes 5 minority (1 African American, 1 American Indian/Alaska Native, 1 Asian American or Pacific Islander, 2 Hispanic Americans). 78 applicants, 26% accepted, 11 enrolled. In 2009, 6 master's, 7 doctorates awarded. *Degree requirements:* For master's, one foreign language, thesis; for doctorate, one foreign language, thesis/dissertation. *Entrance requirements:* For master's and doctorate, GRE General Test. *Application deadline:* For fall admission, 7/1 priority date for domestic students; for spring admission, 11/15 for domestic students. Application fee: $50. Electronic applications accepted. *Expenses:* Tuition, state resident: full-time $6000; part-time $250 per credit hour. Tuition, nonresident: full-time $20,904; part-time $871 per credit hour. Required fees: $730 per semester. *Financial support:* Fellowships, research assistantships, teaching assistantships, unspecified assistantships available. *Unit head:* Dr. Ervan G. Garrison, Head, 706-542-1479, Fax: 706-542-3998, E-mail: egarriso@uga.edu. *Application contact:* Dr. Elizabeth J. Reitz, Graduate Coordinator, 706-542-1464, Fax: 706-542-3998, E-mail: ereitz@uga.edu.

University of Lethbridge, School of Graduate Studies, Lethbridge, AB T1K 3M4, Canada. Offers accounting (MScM); addictions counseling (M Sc); agricultural biotechnology (M Sc); agricultural studies (M Sc, MA); anthropology (MA); archaeology (MA); art (MA, MFA); biochemistry (M Sc); biological sciences (M Sc); biomolecular science (PhD); biosystems and biodiversity (PhD); Canadian studies (MA); chemistry (M Sc); computer science (M Sc); computer science and geographical information science (M Sc); counseling psychology (M Ed); dramatic arts (MA); earth, space, and physical science (PhD); economics (MA); educational leadership (M Ed); English (MA); environmental science (M Sc); evolution and behavior (PhD); exercise science (M Sc); finance (MScM); French (MA); French/German (MA); French/Spanish (MA); general education (M Ed); general management (MScM); geography (M Sc, MA); German (MA); health science (M Sc); health sciences (MA); history (MA); human resource management and labour relations (MScM); individualized multidisciplinary (M Sc, MA); information systems (MScM); international management (MScM); kinesiology (M Sc, MA); management (M Sc, MA); marketing (MScM); mathematics (M Sc); music (M Mus, MA); Native American studies (MA); neuroscience (M Sc, PhD); new media (MA); nursing (M Sc); philosophy (MA); physics (M Sc); policy and strategy (MScM); political science (MA); psychology (M Sc, MA); religious studies (MA); social sciences (MA); sociology (MA); theatre and dramatic arts (MFA); theoretical and computational science (PhD); urban and regional studies (MA); women's studies (MA). Part-time and evening/weekend programs available. *Degree requirements:* For doctorate, comprehensive exam, thesis/dissertation. *Entrance requirements:* For master's, GMAT (M Sc in management), bachelor's degree in related field, minimum GPA of 3.0 during previous 20 graded semester courses, 2 years teaching or related experience (M Ed); for doctorate, master's degree, minimum graduate GPA of 3.5. Additional exam requirements/recommendations for international students: Required—TOEFL. *Faculty research:* Movement and brain plasticity, gibberellin physiology, photosynthesis, carbon cycling, molecular properties of main-group ring components.

University of Massachusetts Boston, Office of Graduate Studies, College of Liberal Arts, Program in History, Track in Historical Archaeology, Boston, MA 02125-3393. Offers MA. Part-time and evening/weekend programs available. *Degree requirements:* For master's, thesis, oral exams, practicum. *Entrance requirements:* For master's, GRE General Test, minimum GPA of 2.75. *Faculty research:* New World Colonialism, New England archeology, historical and urban archeology, archeological botany, ethnology.

University of Memphis, Graduate School, College of Communication and Fine Arts, Department of Art, Memphis, TN 38152. Offers art (Graduate Certificate); art history (MA), including Egyptian art and archaeology, general art history; ceramics (MFA); graphic design (MFA); interior design (MFA); painting (MFA); printmaking/photography (MFA); sculpture (MFA). *Accreditation:* NASAD (one or more programs are accredited). *Faculty:* 20 full-time (7 women), 4 part-time/adjunct (2 women). *Students:* 39 full-time (26 women), 10 part-time (8 women); includes 4 African Americans, 1 Asian American or Pacific Islander, 1 international. Average age 29. 44 applicants, 77% accepted, 22 enrolled. In 2009, 16 master's, 5 other advanced degrees awarded. *Degree requirements:* For master's, 2 foreign languages, comprehensive exam, thesis. *Entrance requirements:* For master's, GRE General Test or MAT, portfolio (MFA). *Application deadline:* For fall admission, 8/1 for domestic students; for spring admission, 12/1 for domestic students. Applications are processed on a rolling basis. Application fee: $35 ($60 for international students). *Expenses:* Tuition, state resident: full-time $6246; part-time $347 per credit hour. Tuition, nonresident: full-time $15,894; part-time $883 per credit hour. Required fees: $1160. Full-time tuition and fees vary according to course load, degree level and program. *Financial support:* In 2009–10, 38 students received support; research assistantships with full tuition reimbursements available, teaching assistantships with full tuition reimbursements available, Federal Work-Study, scholarships/grants, and unspecified assistantships available. Financial award application deadline: 2/15; financial award applicants required to submit FAFSA. *Faculty research:* Online collaborative learning, advanced art history studies, electronic publishing/design, studio arts, architectural studies. *Unit head:* Prof. Richard Lou, Chair, 901-678-2216, Fax: 901-678-2735, E-mail: gmyatt@memphis.edu. *Application contact:* Greely Myat, Graduate Studies Coordinator, 901-678-2650.

University of Michigan, Horace H. Rackham School of Graduate Studies, College of Literature, Science, and the Arts, Interdepartmental Program in Classical Art and Archaeology, Ann Arbor, MI 48109. Offers PhD. *Faculty:* 20 full-time. *Students:* 28 full-time (16 women); includes 3 minority (2 Asian Americans or Pacific Islanders, 1 Hispanic American), 4 international. Average age 28. 48 applicants, 10% accepted, 5 enrolled. In 2009, 3 doctorates awarded. *Degree requirements:* For doctorate, 4 foreign languages, comprehensive exam, thesis/dissertation, preliminary exam. *Entrance requirements:* For doctorate, GRE General Test. Additional exam requirements/recommendations for international students: Required—TOEFL (minimum score 560 paper-based; 220 computer-based). *Application deadline:* For fall admission, 1/1 for domestic and international students. Applications are processed on a rolling basis. Application fee: $60 ($75 for international students). Electronic applications accepted. *Expenses:* Tuition, state resident: full-time $17,286; part-time $1099 per credit hour. Tuition, nonresident: full-time $34,944; part-time $2080 per credit hour. Required fees: $95 per semester. Tuition and fees vary according to course load, degree level and program. *Financial support:* In 2009–10, 24 students received support, including 14 fellowships with full tuition reimbursements available (averaging $17,000 per year), 1 research assistantship with full tuition reimbursement available (averaging $16,694 per year), 8 teaching assistantships with full tuition reimbursements available (averaging $16,694 per year); career-related internships or fieldwork and health care benefits also available. Financial award application deadline: 4/15. *Faculty research:* Greek art and archaeology, roman art and archaeology, near eastern art and archaeology, archaeological theory and methodology. Total annual research expenditures: $34,240. *Unit head:* Prof. Christopher Ratte, Director, 734-936-3888, Fax: 734-763-8976, E-mail: ratte@umich.edu. *Application contact:* Alex Zwinak, Graduate Coordinator, 734-764-6323, Fax: 734-763-8976, E-mail: ipcaa.office@umich.edu.

University of Minnesota, Twin Cities Campus, Graduate School, College of Liberal Arts, Department of Classical and Near Eastern Studies, Minneapolis, MN 55455-0213. Offers ancient and medieval art and archaeology (MA, PhD); classics (MA, PhD); Greek (MA, PhD); Latin (MA, PhD); religions in antiquity (MA). Part-time programs available. *Faculty:* 22 full-time (6 women). *Students:* 24 full-time (10 women), 1 part-time (0 women), 1 international. Average age 29. 40 applicants, 20% accepted, 4 enrolled. In 2009, 5 master's awarded. Terminal master's awarded for partial completion of doctoral program. *Degree requirements:* For master's, 2 foreign languages, comprehensive exam, thesis or alternative; for doctorate, variable foreign language requirement, comprehensive exam, thesis/dissertation. *Entrance requirements:* For master's and doctorate, GRE, 3 letters of recommendation, department application, writing sample, copies of transcripts, personal statement. Additional exam requirements/recommendations for international students: Required—TOEFL. *Application deadline:* For fall admission, 1/4 priority date for domestic and international students. Application fee: $50 ($75 for international students). Electronic applications accepted. *Financial support:* In 2009–10, 24 students received support, including 2 fellowships with full tuition reimbursements available (averaging $22,500 per year), 2 research assistantships with partial tuition reimbursements available (averaging $7,000 per year), 20 teaching assistantships with full tuition reimbursements available (averaging $14,000 per year); career-related internships or fieldwork, Federal Work-Study, institutionally sponsored loans, health care benefits, and tuition waivers (full and partial) also available. Support available to part-time students. Financial award application deadline: 1/4. *Faculty research:* Greek and Latin literature, religions in antiquity, ancient Near East. *Unit head:* Christopher Nappa, Chair, 612-625-624-6339, Fax: 612-624-4894, E-mail: cnappa@umn.edu. *Application contact:* Victoria H. Keller, Administrative Specialist, 612-625-8371, Fax: 612-624-4894, E-mail: kell0801@umn.edu.

University of Missouri, Graduate School, College of Arts and Sciences, Department of Art History and Archaeology, Columbia, MO 65211. Offers MA, PhD. *Faculty:* 10 full-time (5 women). *Students:* 16 full-time (14 women), 15 part-time (8 women), 3 international. Average age 31. 30 applicants, 37% accepted, 9 enrolled. In 2009, 4 master's awarded. Terminal master's awarded for partial completion of doctoral program. *Degree requirements:* For master's, 2 foreign languages, thesis; for doctorate, 2 foreign languages, thesis/dissertation. *Entrance requirements:* For master's, GRE General Test (minimum score 1000 verbal and quantitative, 4.5 analytical), minimum GPA of 3.0; min GPA of 3.3 in major field; at least 3 semesters in appropriate foreign language; for doctorate, GRE General Test, minimum GPA of 3.0; MA or equiv in art history or classical archaeology; MA thesis. Additional exam requirements/recommendations for international students: Required—TOEFL (minimum score 500 paper-based; 173 computer-based; 61 iBT), IELTS (minimum score 5.5). *Application deadline:* For fall admission, 1/18 priority date for domestic students. Applications are processed on a rolling basis. Application fee: $45 ($60 for international students). Electronic applications accepted. *Financial support:* In 2009–10, 4 fellowships with full tuition reimbursements, 13 research assistantships with full tuition reimbursements, 5 teaching assistantships with full tuition reimbursements were awarded; institutionally sponsored loans, health care benefits, and unspecified assistantships also available. *Unit head:* Dr. Anne Rufdloff Stanton, Department Chair, E-mail: stantona@missouri.edu. *Application contact:* Linda Garrison, 573-882-2757, E-mail: garrisonl@missouri.edu.

University of Nebraska–Lincoln, Graduate College, College of Arts and Sciences, Department of Anthropology and Geography, Lincoln, NE 68588. Offers anthropology (MA); geography (MA, PhD); professional archaeology (MA). *Degree requirements:* For master's, thesis optional. *Entrance requirements:* For master's, GRE General Test. Additional exam requirements/recommendations for international students: Required—TOEFL. Electronic applications accepted.

The University of North Carolina at Chapel Hill, Graduate School, College of Arts and Sciences, Department of Classics, Chapel Hill, NC 27599. Offers classical archaeology (MA, PhD); classics (MA, PhD). Terminal master's awarded for partial completion of doctoral program. *Degree requirements:* For master's, one foreign language, comprehensive exam, thesis; for doctorate, 2 foreign languages, comprehensive exam, thesis/dissertation. *Entrance requirements:* For master's and doctorate, GRE General Test, minimum GPA of 3.0. Electronic applications accepted.

University of Pennsylvania, School of Arts and Sciences, Graduate Group in Art and Archaeology of the Mediterranean World, Philadelphia, PA 19104. Offers AM, PhD. Part-time programs available. *Faculty:* 16 full-time (7 women), 2 part-time/adjunct (1 woman). *Students:* 17 full-time (12 women), 5 part-time (4 women); includes 1 minority (Asian American or Pacific Islander), 5 international. 58 applicants, 14% accepted, 2 enrolled. In 2009, 1 master's, 1 doctorate awarded. Terminal master's awarded for partial completion of doctoral program. *Degree requirements:* For master's, 3 foreign languages, thesis, Greek or Latin exam, German and French or Italian exam; for doctorate, 4 foreign languages, thesis/dissertation, Greek or Latin exam, 2nd ancient language exam, German and French or Italian exam. *Entrance requirements:* For master's and doctorate, GRE General Test, knowledge of Greek or Latin and either French, German, or Italian. Additional exam requirements/recommendations for international students: Required—TOEFL. *Application deadline:* For fall admission, 12/1 priority date for domestic students. Application fee: $70. Electronic applications accepted. *Expenses:* Tuition: Full-time $25,660; part-time $4758 per course. Required fees: $2152; $270 per course. Tuition and fees vary according to course load, degree level and program. *Financial support:* Fellowships, institutionally sponsored loans, scholarships/grants, traineeships, health care benefits, and unspecified assistantships available. Financial award application deadline: 12/15.

University of Saskatchewan, College of Graduate Studies and Research, College of Arts and Sciences, Department of Archaeology, Saskatoon, SK S7N 5A2, Canada. Offers MA, PhD. Part-time programs available. *Faculty:* 18. *Students:* 29. In 2009, 5 master's awarded. *Degree requirements:* For master's, thesis; for doctorate, comprehensive exam (for some programs), thesis/dissertation. *Entrance requirements:* Additional exam requirements/recommendations for international students: Required—TOEFL (minimum score 80 iBT); Recommended—IELTS (minimum score 6.5). *Application deadline:* For fall admission, 7/1 priority date for domestic students. Applications are processed on a rolling basis. Application fee: $75. Tuition and fees charges are reported in Canadian dollars. *Expenses:* Tuition, area resident: Full-time $3000 Canadian dollars; part-time $500 Canadian dollars per term. Required fees: $700 Canadian dollars; $100 Canadian dollars per term. *Financial support:* Fellowships, research assistantships, teaching assistantships available. Financial award application deadline: 1/31. *Unit head:* Dr. David Meyer, Head, 306-966-4181, Fax: 306-966-5640, E-mail: david.meyer@usask.ca. *Application contact:* Dr. Margaret Kennedy, Graduate Chair, 306-966-4181, Fax: 306-966-5640, E-mail: marg.kennedy@usask.ca.

University of South Africa, College of Human Sciences, Pretoria, South Africa. Offers adult education (M Ed); African languages (MA, PhD); African politics (MA, PhD); Afrikaans (MA, PhD); ancient history (MA, PhD); ancient Near Eastern studies (MA, PhD); anthropology (MA, PhD); applied linguistics (MA); Arabic (MA, PhD); archaeology (MA); art history (MA); Biblical archaeology (MA); Biblical studies (M Th, D Th, PhD); Christian spirituality (M Th, D Th); church history (M Th, D Th); classical studies (MA, PhD); clinical psychology (MA); communication (MA, PhD); comparative education (M Ed, Ed D); consulting psychology (D Admin, D Com, PhD); curriculum studies (M Ed, Ed D); development studies (M Admin, MA, D Admin, PhD); didactics (M Ed, Ed D); education (M Tech); education management (M Ed, Ed D); educational psychology (M Ed); English (MA); environmental education (M Ed); French (MA, PhD); German (MA, PhD); Greek (MA); guidance and counseling (M Ed); health studies (MA, PhD), including health sciences education (MA), health services management (MA), medical and surgical nursing science (critical care general) (MA), midwifery and neonatal nursing science (MA), trauma and emergency care (MA); history (MA, PhD); history of education (Ed D); inclusive education (M Ed, Ed D); information and communications technology policy and regulation (MA); information science (MA, MIS, PhD); international politics (MA, PhD); Islamic studies (MA, PhD); Italian (MA, PhD); Judaica (MA, PhD); linguistics (MA, PhD); mathematical education (M Ed); mathematics education (MA); missiology (M Th, D Th); modern Hebrew (MA, PhD); musicology (MA, MMus, D Mus, PhD); natural science education (M Ed); New Testament (M Th, D Th); Old Testament (D Th); pastoral therapy (M Th, D Th); philosophy (MA); philosophy of education (M Ed, Ed D); politics (MA, PhD); Portuguese (MA, PhD); practical theology (M Th, D Th); psychology (MA, MS, PhD); psychology of education (M Ed, Ed D); public health (MA); religious studies (MA, D Th, PhD); Romance languages (MA); Russian (MA, PhD); Semitic languages (MA, PhD); social behavior studies in HIV/AIDS (MA); social science (mental health) (MA); social science in development studies (MA); social science in psychology (MA); social science in social work (MA); social science in sociology (MA); social work (MSW, DSW, PhD); socio-education (M Ed, Ed D); sociolinguistics (MA); sociology (MA, PhD); Spanish (MA, PhD); systematic theology (M Th, D Th); TESOL (teaching English to speakers of other languages) (MA); theological ethics (M Th, D Th); theory of literature (MA, PhD); urban ministries (D Th); urban ministry (M Th).

The University of Tennessee, Graduate School, College of Arts and Sciences, Department of Anthropology, Knoxville, TN 37996. Offers archaeology (MA, PhD); biological anthropology (MA, PhD); cultural anthropology (MA, PhD); zoo-archaeology (MA, PhD). *Degree requirements:* For master's, thesis; for doctorate, one foreign language, thesis/dissertation. *Entrance requirements:* For master's and doctorate, GRE General Test, minimum GPA of 2.7. Additional exam requirements/recommendations for international students: Required—TOEFL. Electronic applications accepted. *Expenses:* Tuition, state resident: full-time $6826; part-time $380 per semester hour. Tuition, nonresident: full-time $21,844; part-time $1147 per semester hour. Tuition and fees vary according to program.

The University of Texas at Austin, Graduate School, College of Liberal Arts, Department of Anthropology, Austin, TX 78712-1111. Offers archaeology (MA, PhD); folklore and public culture (MA, PhD); linguistic anthropology (MA, PhD); physical anthropology (MA, PhD); social anthropology (MA, PhD). Part-time programs available. Terminal master's awarded for partial completion of doctoral program. *Degree requirements:* For master's, thesis; for doctorate, one foreign language, thesis/dissertation. *Entrance requirements:* For master's and doctorate, GRE General Test. Additional exam requirements/recommendations for international students: Required—TOEFL. Electronic applications accepted.

University of Virginia, College and Graduate School of Arts and Sciences, McIntire Department of Art, Charlottesville, VA 22904-4130. Offers classical art and archaeology (MA, PhD); history of art and architecture (MA, PhD). *Degree requirements:* For master's, one foreign language, thesis, defense; for doctorate, 2 foreign languages, comprehensive exam, thesis/dissertation, defense. *Entrance requirements:* For master's and doctorate, GRE General Test, writing sample. Additional exam requirements/recommendations for international students: Recommended—TOEFL (minimum score 600 paper-based; 250 computer-based; 90 iBT), IELTS (minimum score 7). Electronic applications accepted. *Faculty research:* Classical art, renaissance art and architecture, American material culture.

University of West Florida, College of Arts and Sciences: Arts, Division of Anthropology and Archaeology, Pensacola, FL 32514-5750. Offers anthropology (MA); historical archaeology (MA); maritime studies (MA). *Faculty:* 7 full-time (2 women). *Students:* 40 full-time (24 women), 20 part-time (15 women); includes 8 minority (2 African Americans, 2 Asian Americans or Pacific Islanders, 4 Hispanic Americans). Average age 28. 59 applicants, 54% accepted, 20 enrolled. In 2009, 10 master's awarded. *Degree requirements:* For master's, internship or thesis. *Entrance requirements:* For master's, GRE, bachelor's degree in anthropology, minimum GPA of 3.0, 3 letters of recommendation, writing sample. Additional exam requirements/recommendations for international students: Required—TOEFL (minimum score 550 paper-based; 213 computer-based). *Application deadline:* For fall admission, 6/1 for domestic students, 5/15 for international students; for spring admission, 11/1 for domestic students, 10/1 for international students. Application fee: $30. *Expenses:* Tuition, state resident: full-time $4982; part-time $260 per credit hour. Tuition, nonresident: full-time $20,059; part-time $919 per credit hour. Required fees: $1247; $52 per credit hour. *Financial support:* In 2009–10, 10 research assistantships with partial tuition reimbursements (averaging $3,760 per year), 7 teaching assistantships with partial tuition reimbursements (averaging $3,938 per year) were awarded; unspecified assistantships also available. Financial award application deadline: 4/15; financial award applicants required to submit FAFSA. *Unit head:* Dr. John Bratten, Interim Chair, 850-857-6278, E-mail: anthropology@uwf.edu. *Application contact:* Terry McCray, Assistant Director of Graduate Admissions, 850-473-7718, Fax: 850-473-7714, E-mail: gradadmissions@uwf.edu.

University of Wisconsin–Madison, Graduate School, College of Letters and Science, Department of Anthropology, Madison, WI 53706-1380. Offers archaeology (PhD); biological anthropology (PhD); cultural anthropology (PhD). Terminal master's awarded for partial completion of doctoral program. *Degree requirements:* For doctorate, thesis/dissertation. *Entrance requirements:* For doctorate, qualifying exam. Electronic applications accepted. *Expenses:* Tuition, state resident: part-time $594 per credit. Tuition, nonresident: part-time $1504 per credit. Required fees: $65 per credit. Tuition and fees vary according to course load, program and reciprocity agreements. *Faculty research:* Archaeology, biological, anthropology, cultural anthropology.

Washington State University, Graduate School, College of Liberal Arts, Department of Anthropology, Pullman, WA 99164. Offers archaeology (MA, PhD); cultural anthropology (MA, PhD); evolutionary anthropology (MA, PhD). Part-time programs available. *Faculty:* 20. *Students:* 59 full-time (36 women), 11 part-time (7 women); includes 6 minority (1 African American, 4 Asian Americans or Pacific Islanders, 1 Hispanic American), 3 international. Average age 32. 93 applicants, 35% accepted, 15 enrolled. In 2009, 14 master's, 5 doctorates awarded. *Degree requirements:* For master's, comprehensive exam (for some programs), thesis, oral exam; for doctorate, comprehensive exam, thesis/dissertation, qualifying exam, oral exam and written exam. *Entrance requirements:* For master's, GRE General Test, curriculum vitae, 3 references; for doctorate, GRE General Test, To apply, submit the online Graduate School application, current curriculum vitae, statement of your educational and professional goals, official transcripts of all post-secondary education, contact information of three references, and official GRE scores. Additional exam requirements/recommendations for international students: Required—TOEFL (minimum score 550 paper-based; 213 computer-based), IELTS. *Application deadline:* For fall admission, 1/10 priority date for domestic and international students; for spring admission, 7/1 priority date for domestic and international students. Applications are processed on a rolling basis. Application fee: $50. Electronic applications accepted. *Financial support:* In 2009–10, 5 research assistantships with full tuition reimbursements (averaging $13,917 per year), 34 teaching assistantships with full tuition reimbursements (averaging $13,056 per year) were awarded; fellowships, Federal Work-Study, scholarships/grants, health care benefits, and tuition waivers (partial) also available. Support available to part-time students. Financial award application deadline: 2/15; financial award applicants required to submit FAFSA. *Faculty research:* Western North America, including Alaska; international development; psychological anthropology; cultural ecology; medical anthropology; power and gender; evolutionary psychology; behavioral ecology; evolutionary cultural anthropology; evolutionary archaeology; paleoanthropology. Total annual research expenditures: $791,000. *Unit head:* Dr. William Andrefsky, Chair, 509-335-3441, Fax: 509-335-3999, E-mail: jmstrunk@wsu.edu. *Application contact:* Graduate School Admissions, 800-GRADWSU, Fax: 509-335-1949, E-mail: gradsch@wsu.edu.

Washington University in St. Louis, Graduate School of Arts and Sciences, Department of Art History and Archaeology, St. Louis, MO 63130-4899. Offers art history (MA, PhD); classical archaeology (MA, PhD). *Degree requirements:* For doctorate, 2 foreign languages, comprehensive exam, thesis/dissertation. *Entrance requirements:* For master's and doctorate, GRE General Test, sample of written work. Electronic applications accepted.

Wheaton College, Graduate School, Department of Biblical and Theological Studies, Program in Biblical Archaeology, Wheaton, IL 60187-5593. Offers MA. *Degree requirements:* For master's, thesis or alternative, semester of study in Israel. *Entrance requirements:* For master's, GRE General Test or MAT. Electronic applications accepted.

Wilfrid Laurier University, Faculty of Graduate Studies, Faculty of Arts, Department of Archaeology and Classical Studies, Waterloo, ON N2L 3C5, Canada. Offers MA. *Degree requirements:* For master's, thesis optional. *Entrance requirements:* For master's, minimum B+ average in last two undergraduate years (exclusive of first year level courses in those years). Additional exam requirements/recommendations for international students: Required—TOEFL.

Yale University, Graduate School of Arts and Sciences, Department of Near Eastern Languages and Civilizations, New Haven, CT 06520. Offers Arabic and Islamic studies (MA, PhD); archaeology of the ancient Near East (MA, PhD); Assyriology (MA, PhD); Egyptology (MA, PhD); Graeco-Arabic studies (MA, PhD); Northwest Semitic, Bible, comparative Semitics (MA, PhD). *Degree requirements:* For doctorate, 2 foreign languages, thesis/dissertation. *Entrance requirements:* For doctorate, GRE General Test.

Yale University, Graduate School of Arts and Sciences, Interdisciplinary Program in Archaeological Studies, New Haven, CT 06520. Offers MA. *Degree requirements:* For master's, thesis. *Entrance requirements:* For master's, GRE General Test.

Biological Anthropology

Duke University, Graduate School, Department of Biological Anthropology and Anatomy, Durham, NC 27710. Offers cellular and molecular biology (PhD); gross anatomy and physical anthropology (PhD), including comparative morphology of human and non-human primates, primate social behavior, vertebrate paleontology; neuroanatomy (PhD). *Faculty:* 8 full-time. *Students:* 14 full-time (9 women); includes 2 minority (1 African American, 1 Hispanic American), 1 international. 39 applicants, 15% accepted, 4 enrolled. In 2009, 4 doctorates awarded. *Degree requirements:* For doctorate, one foreign language, thesis/dissertation. *Entrance requirements:* For doctorate, GRE General Test. Additional exam requirements/recommendations for international students: Required—TOEFL (minimum score 550 paper-based; 213 computer-based; 83 iBT), IELTS (minimum score 7). *Application deadline:* For fall admission, 12/8 priority date for domestic and international students. Application fee: $75. Electronic applications accepted. *Financial support:* Fellowships, teaching assistantships, Federal Work-Study available. Financial award application deadline: 12/31. *Unit head:* Daniel Schmitt, Director of Graduate Studies, 919-684-5664, Fax: 919-684-4124, E-mail: mlsquire@duke.edu. *Application contact:* Cynthia Robertson, Associate Dean for Enrollment Services, 919-684-3913, E-mail: grad-admissions@duke.edu.

Kent State University, School of Biomedical Sciences, Program in Biological Anthropology, Kent, OH 44242-0001. Offers PhD. Offered in cooperation with Northeastern Ohio Universities College of Medicine. *Degree requirements:* For doctorate, thesis/dissertation. *Entrance requirements:* For doctorate, GRE General Test, MA/MS in anthropology or one of the biological science disciplines, letter of recommendation. Electronic applications accepted. *Faculty research:* Human evolution, paleodemography, orofacial anatomy, osteology, primate behavior.

Mercyhurst College, Graduate Program, Program in Forensic and Biological Anthropology, Erie, PA 16546. Offers MS. *Entrance requirements:* For master's, GRE or MAT, undergraduate degree in related field, interview. Additional exam requirements/recommendations for international students: Required—TOEFL.

Demography and Population Studies

The American University in Cairo, Center for Migration and Refugee Studies, Cairo, Egypt. Offers forced migration and refugee studies (Diploma); migration and refugee studies (MA).

Bowling Green State University, Graduate College, College of Arts and Sciences, Department of Sociology, Bowling Green, OH 43403. Offers demography and population studies (MA); social psychology (MA); sociology (PhD). Part-time programs available. *Degree requirements:* For master's, thesis or alternative; for doctorate, comprehensive exam, thesis/dissertation. *Entrance requirements:* For master's and doctorate, GRE General Test. Additional exam requirements/recommendations for international students: Required—TOEFL. Electronic applications accepted. *Faculty research:* Applied demography, criminology and deviance, family studies, population studies, social psychology.

Cornell University, Graduate School, Graduate Fields of Agriculture and Life Sciences, Field of Development Sociology, Ithaca, NY 14853-0001. Offers community and regional society (MS); community and regional sociology (MPS, PhD); methods of social research (MPS, MS, PhD); population and development (MPS, MS, PhD); rural and environmental sociology (MPS, MS, PhD); state, economy, and society (MPS, MS, PhD). *Faculty:* 23 full-time (6 women). *Students:* 44 full-time (29 women); includes 6 minority (1 African American, 2 American Indian/Alaska Native, 2 Asian Americans or Pacific Islanders, 1 Hispanic American), 16 international. Average age 34. 59 applicants, 19% accepted, 7 enrolled. In 2009, 4 master's, 4 doctorates awarded. *Degree requirements:* For doctorate, comprehensive exam, thesis/dissertation. *Entrance requirements:* For master's and doctorate, GRE General Test, 3 letters of recommendation. Additional exam requirements/recommendations for international students: Required—TOEFL (minimum score 550 paper-based; 213 computer-based; 77 iBT). *Application deadline:* For fall admission, 1/15 priority date for domestic students. Application fee: $60. Electronic applications accepted. *Expenses:* Tuition: Full-time $29,500. Required fees: $70. Full-time tuition and fees vary according to degree level, program and student level. *Financial support:* In 2009–10, 25 students received support, including 2 fellowships with full tuition reimbursements available, 1 research assistantship with full tuition reimbursement available, 1 teaching assistantship with full tuition reimbursement available; institutionally sponsored loans, scholarships/grants, health care benefits, tuition waivers (full and partial), and unspecified assistantships also available. Financial award applicants required to submit FAFSA. *Faculty research:* Demography (population and development), environmental sociology, international and rural community development, political economy and ecology, sustainable agriculture. *Unit head:* Director of Graduate Studies, 607-255-3092, Fax: 607-254-2896. *Application contact:* Graduate Field Assistant, 607-255-3092, Fax: 607-254-2896, E-mail: devsoc@cornell.edu.

Cornell University, Graduate School, Graduate Fields of Arts and Sciences, Field of International Development, Ithaca, NY 14853-0001. Offers development policy (MPS); international nutrition (MPS); international planning (MPS); international population (MPS); science and technology policy (MPS). *Faculty:* 54 full-time (18 women). *Students:* 1 (woman) full-time, all international. Average age 33. 31 applicants, 42% accepted, 1 enrolled. In 2009, 15 master's awarded. *Degree requirements:* For master's, project paper. *Entrance requirements:* For master's, GRE General Test (recommended), 2 academic recommendations, 2 years of development experience. Additional exam requirements/recommendations for international students: Required—TOEFL (minimum score 77 iBT). *Application deadline:* Applications are processed on a rolling basis. Application fee: $70. Electronic applications accepted. *Expenses:* Tuition: Full-time $29,500. Required fees: $70. Full-time tuition and fees vary according to degree level, program and student level. *Financial support:* In 2009–10, 1 student received support; fellowships with full tuition reimbursements available, research assistantships with full tuition reimbursements available, teaching assistantships with full tuition reimbursements available, institutionally sponsored loans, scholarships/grants, health care benefits, tuition waivers (full and partial), and unspecified assistantships available. Financial award applicants required to submit FAFSA. *Faculty research:* Development policy, international nutrition, international planning, science and technology policy, international population. *Unit head:* Director of Graduate Studies, 607-255-3037, Fax: 607-255-1005. *Application contact:* Graduate Field Assistant, 607-255-0831, Fax: 607-255-1005, E-mail: mpsid@cornell.edu.

Emory University, Rollins School of Public Health, Hubert Department of Global Health, Atlanta, GA 30322-1100. Offers global demography (MSPH); global environmental health (MPH); public nutrition (MSPH). *Accreditation:* CEPH. Part-time programs available. *Degree requirements:* For master's, thesis, practicum. *Entrance requirements:* For master's, GRE General Test. Additional exam requirements/recommendations for international students: Required—TOEFL (minimum score 550 paper-based; 213 computer-based; 80 iBT). Electronic applications accepted.

Florida State University, The Graduate School, College of Social Sciences and Public Policy, Center for Demography and Population Health, Tallahassee, FL 32306-2240. Offers MS. *Faculty:* 14 full-time (6 women). *Students:* 18 full-time (10 women), 1 part-time (0 women); includes 2 minority (1 African American, 1 Hispanic American), 1 international. Average age 24. 27 applicants, 85% accepted, 15 enrolled. In 2009, 7 master's awarded. *Degree requirements:* For master's, thesis or alternative. *Entrance requirements:* For master's, GRE General Test, minimum upper division GPA of 3.0. Additional exam requirements/recommendations for international students: Required—TOEFL (minimum score 550 paper-based; 213 computer-based; 80 iBT). *Application deadline:* For fall admission, 7/1 for domestic and international students. Applications are processed on a rolling basis. Application fee: $30. Electronic applications accepted. *Expenses:* Tuition, state resident: full-time $7413. Tuition, nonresident: full-time $22,567. *Financial support:* Career-related internships or fieldwork, Federal Work-Study, and institutionally sponsored loans available. Financial award application deadline: 1/31; financial award applicants required to submit FAFSA. *Faculty research:* Health, aging, immigration, mortality, family. Total annual research expenditures: $222,000. *Unit head:* Dr. Isaac Eberstein, Director, 850-644-7108, Fax: 850-644-8818, E-mail: ieberstn@fsu.edu. *Application contact:* Dr. Isaac Eberstein, Director, 850-644-7108, Fax: 850-644-8818, E-mail: ieberstn@fsu.edu.

Harvard University, School of Public Health, Department of Global Health and Population, Boston, MA 02115-6096. Offers SM, DPH, SD. Part-time programs available. *Faculty:* 35 full-time (8 women), 11 part-time/adjunct (2 women). *Students:* 93 full-time, 4 part-time; includes 14 minority (3 African Americans, 11 Asian Americans or Pacific Islanders), 37 international. Average age 30. 256 applicants, 24% accepted, 32 enrolled. In 2009, 22 master's, 7 doctorates awarded. *Degree requirements:* For master's, thesis; for doctorate, thesis/dissertation, qualifying exam. *Entrance requirements:* For master's and doctorate, GRE. Additional exam requirements/recommendations for international students: Required—TOEFL (minimum score 595 paper-based; 240 computer-based; 95 iBT); Recommended—IELTS (minimum score 7). *Application deadline:* For fall admission, 12/15 for domestic and international students. Application fee: $115. Electronic applications accepted. *Expenses:* Tuition: Full-time $33,696. Required fees: $1126. Full-time tuition and fees vary according to program. *Financial support:* Fellowships, research assistantships, teaching assistantships, Federal Work-Study, scholarships/grants, traineeships, tuition waivers (partial), and unspecified assistantships available. Support available to part-time students. Financial award application deadline: 2/8; financial award applicants required to submit FAFSA. *Faculty research:* International health policy, economics, reproductive health, ecology. *Unit head:* Dr. David Bloom, Chair, 617-432-1232, Fax: 617-432-6733, E-mail: dbloom@hsph.harvard.edu. *Application contact:* Vincent W. James, Director of Admissions, 617-432-1031, Fax: 617-432-7080, E-mail: admisofc@hsph.harvard.edu.

The Johns Hopkins University, Bloomberg School of Public Health, Department of Population, Family and Reproductive Health, Baltimore, MD 21205. Offers child and adolescent health and development (Dr PH, PhD); demography (MHS); population and health (Dr PH, PhD); population, family and reproductive health (MHS); reproductive, perinatal women's health (Dr PH, PhD). Part-time programs available. *Faculty:* 35 full-time (24 women), 40 part-time/adjunct (25 women). *Students:* 89 full-time (79 women), 1 (woman) part-time; includes 25 minority (4 African Americans, 1 American Indian/Alaska Native, 13 Asian Americans or Pacific Islanders, 7 Hispanic Americans), 15 international. Average age 30. 150 applicants, 40% accepted, 33 enrolled. In 2009, 21 master's, 10 doctorates awarded. *Degree requirements:* For master's, essay, fieldwork; for doctorate, thesis/dissertation, 1 year full-time residency, oral and written exams. *Entrance requirements:* For master's, GRE General Test, 3 letters of recommendation, curriculum vitae; for doctorate, GRE General Test, TOEFL (International students), 3 letters of recommendation, curriculum vitae. Additional exam requirements/recommendations for international students: Required—TOEFL (minimum score 600 paper-based; 250 computer-based). *Application deadline:* For fall admission, 1/2 for domestic and international students. Applications are processed on a rolling basis. Application fee: $45. Electronic applications accepted. *Financial support:* In 2009–10, 89 students received support, including 13 fellowships with full and partial tuition reimbursements available (averaging $51,144 per year), 6 research assistantships (averaging $5,760 per year), 10 teaching assistantships (averaging $1,136 per year); Federal Work-Study, institutionally sponsored loans, scholarships/grants, traineeships, health care benefits, and stipends also available. Support available to part-time students. Financial award application deadline: 3/15; financial award applicants required to submit FAFSA. *Faculty research:* Child and adolescent health and development, population and health and reproductive, perinatal and women's health. Total annual research expenditures: $18.8 million. *Unit head:* Dr. Robert Blum, Chair, 410-955-3384, Fax: 410-955-2303, E-mail: rblum@jhsph.edu. *Application contact:* Lauren Ferretti, Academic Coordinator, 410-614-6676, Fax: 410-955-2303, E-mail: lferrett@jhsph.edu.

Penn State University Park, Graduate School, Intercollege Graduate Programs, State College, University Park, PA 16802-1503. Offers acoustics (M Eng, MS, PhD); bioengineering (MS, PhD); biogeochemistry (dual) (PhD); business administration (MBA); cell and developmental biology (PhD); demography (dual) (MA); ecology (MS, PhD); environmental pollution control (MEPC, MS); genetics (MS, PhD); human dimensions of natural resources and the environment (dual) (MA, MS, PhD); immunology and infectious diseases (MS); integrative biosciences (MS, PhD), including integrative biosciences; materials science and engineering (PhD); operations research (dual) (M Eng, MA, MS, PhD); physiology (MS, PhD); plant physiology (MS, PhD); quality and manufacturing management (MMM). *Students:* 371 full-time (157 women), 22 part-time (7 women). Average age 27. 1,074 applicants, 18% accepted, 130 enrolled. *Entrance requirements:* Additional exam requirements/recommendations for international students: Required—TOEFL (minimum score 550 paper-based; 213 computer-based; 80 iBT). *Application deadline:* Applications are processed on a rolling basis. Application fee: $45. Electronic applications accepted. *Financial support:* Fellowships, research assistantships, teaching assistantships available. Financial award applicants required to submit FAFSA. *Unit head:* Dr. Regina Vasilatos-Younken, Senior Associate Dean, 814-865-2516, Fax: 814-863-4627, E-mail: rxv@psu.edu. *Application contact:* Cynthia E. Nicosia, Director, Graduate Enrollment Services, 814-865-1795, Fax: 814-865-4627, E-mail: cey1@psu.edu.

Princeton University, Graduate School, Department of Sociology, Princeton, NJ 08544-1019. Offers sociology (PhD); sociology and demography (PhD). *Degree requirements:* For doctorate, variable foreign language requirement, thesis/dissertation. *Entrance requirements:* For doctorate, GRE General Test, GRE Subject Test (recommended), sample of written work. Additional exam requirements/recommendations for international students: Required—TOEFL (minimum score 600 paper-based; 250 computer-based). Electronic applications accepted.

Princeton University, Graduate School, Program in Population Studies, Princeton, NJ 08544-1019. Offers demography (PhD, Certificate); economics and demography (PhD); public affairs and demography (PhD); sociology and demography (PhD). *Degree requirements:* For doctorate, thesis/dissertation. *Entrance requirements:* For doctorate, GRE General Test. Additional exam requirements/recommendations for international students: Required—TOEFL (minimum score 600 paper-based; 250 computer-based). Electronic applications accepted. *Faculty research:* Models, fertility, infant and child mortality, migration.

Université de Montréal, Faculty of Arts and Sciences, Department of Demography, Montréal, QC H3C 3J7, Canada. Offers M Sc, PhD. Terminal master's awarded for partial completion of doctoral program. *Degree requirements:* For master's, one foreign language, thesis; for doctorate, one foreign language, thesis/dissertation, general exam. *Entrance requirements:* For master's, minimum GPA of 2.7. Electronic applications accepted. *Faculty research:* Historical demography, population and development, ethnic and linguistic groups, aging of population, family demography.

Université du Québec, Institut National de la Recherche Scientifique, Graduate Programs, Research Center—Urbanization, Culture and Society, Québec, QC G1K 9A9, Canada. Offers demography (M Sc, PhD); research and public action (M Sc); urban studies (M Sc, PhD). Programs given in French. Part-time programs available. *Faculty:* 36. *Students:* 153 full-time (95 women), 22 part-time (10 women), 26 international. Average age 33. In 2009, 5 master's, 1 doctorate awarded. *Degree requirements:* For master's, thesis optional; for doctorate, thesis/dissertation. *Entrance requirements:* For master's, appropriate bachelor's degree, proficiency in French; for doctorate, appropriate master's degree, proficiency in French. *Application deadline:* For fall admission, 3/30 for domestic and international students; for winter admission, 11/1 for domestic and international students. Application fee: $30. *Financial support:* Fellowships, research assistantships, teaching assistantships available. *Faculty research:* Regional space, urban and metropolitan space, micro-urban space. *Unit head:* Johanne Charbonneau, Director, 514-499-4001, Fax: 514-499-4065, E-mail: johanne.charbonneau@ucs.inrs.ca. *Application contact:* Yvonne Boisvert, Registrar, 418-654-3861, Fax: 418-654-3858, E-mail: registrariat@adm.inrs.ca.

University at Albany, State University of New York, College of Arts and Sciences, Department of Sociology, Albany, NY 12222-0001. Offers demography (Certificate); sociology (MA, PhD); urban policy (Certificate). Terminal master's awarded for partial completion of doctoral program. *Degree requirements:* For master's, thesis; for doctorate, thesis/dissertation, 2 specialization exams, research tool. *Entrance requirements:* For master's and doctorate, GRE General Test. Additional exam requirements/recommendations for international students: Required—TOEFL (minimum score 213 computer-based). Electronic applications accepted. *Faculty research:* Gender and equality, crime and deviance, aging, work and organizations, social demography.

University of Alberta, Faculty of Graduate Studies and Research, Department of Sociology, Edmonton, AB T6G 2E1, Canada. Offers criminal justice (MA); demography (MA, PhD); sociology (MA, PhD). Part-time programs available. *Faculty:* 30 full-time (6 women), 8 part-time/adjunct (2 women). *Students:* 50 full-time (33 women), 33 part-time (21 women). 77 applicants, 34% accepted. In 2009, 8 master's, 11 doctorates awarded. *Degree requirements:* For master's, thesis (for some programs); for doctorate, thesis/dissertation. *Application deadline:* For fall admission, 3/1 for domestic students. Application fee: $60. Tuition and fees charges are reported in Canadian dollars. *Expenses:* Tuition, area resident: Full-time $4626 Canadian dollars; part-time $99.72 Canadian dollars per unit. International tuition: $8216 Canadian dollars full-time. Required fees: $3590 Canadian dollars; $99.72 Canadian dollars per unit. $215 Canadian dollars per term. *Financial support:* In 2009–10, 49 students received support, including 9 fellowships, 9 research assistantships, 17 teaching assistantships; career-related internships or fieldwork and scholarships/grants also available. Support available to part-time students. Financial award application deadline: 3/1. *Faculty research:* Criminology, knowledge and culture, methods and theory, population studies, stratification. *Unit head:* Dr. W. A. Johnston, Graduate Coordinator, 780-492-5236, Fax: 403-492-7196. *Application contact:* F. L. Van Reede, Graduate Program Coordinator, 403-492-5236, Fax: 403-492-7196, E-mail: socgrad2@ualberta.ca.

University of California, Berkeley, Graduate Division, College of Letters and Science, Department of Demography, Berkeley, CA 94720-1500. Offers PhD. *Students:* 16 full-time (11 women). Average age 30. 22 applicants, 4 enrolled. *Degree requirements:* For doctorate, thesis/dissertation, qualifying exam. *Entrance requirements:* For doctorate, GRE General Test, minimum GPA of 3.0, 3 letters of recommendation. *Application deadline:* For fall admission, 12/14 for domestic students. Application fee: $70 ($90 for international students). *Financial support:* Fellowships with full and partial tuition reimbursements, research assistantships with full and partial tuition reimbursements, teaching assistantships with full and partial tuition reimbursements, unspecified assistantships available. *Unit head:* Prof. Michael Hout, Chair, 510-643-6874, E-mail: mikehout@berkeley.edu. *Application contact:* Monique Marie Verrier, Student Affairs Officer, 510-642-9800, Fax: 510-643-8558, E-mail: applications@demog.berkeley.edu.

University of California, Berkeley, Graduate Division, College of Letters and Science, Group in Sociology and Demography, Berkeley, CA 94720-1500. Offers MA, PhD. *Students:* 4 full-time (3 women). Average age 30. 9 applicants, 0 enrolled. *Degree requirements:* For doctorate, thesis/dissertation, qualifying exam. *Entrance requirements:* For master's and doctorate, GRE General Test, minimum GPA of 3.0, 3 letters of recommendation. *Application deadline:* For fall admission, 12/14 for domestic students. Application fee: $70 ($90 for international students). Electronic applications accepted. *Financial support:* Fellowships with full and partial tuition reimbursements, research assistantships with full and partial tuition reimbursements, teaching assistantships with full and partial tuition reimbursements, traineeships and unspecified assistantships available. *Unit head:* Prof. Mike Hout, Chair, 510-642-9800, E-mail: mikehout@berkeley.edu. *Application contact:* Monique Marie Verrier, Student Affairs Officer, 510-642-9800, Fax: 510-643-8558, E-mail: applications@demog.berkeley.edu.

University of California, Irvine, Office of Graduate Studies, School of Social Sciences and School of Social Ecology, Program in Demographic and Social Analysis, Irvine, CA 92697. Offers MA. *Students:* 15 full-time (12 women); includes 4 Asian Americans or Pacific Islanders, 4 Hispanic Americans, 2 international. Average age 25. 27 applicants, 74% accepted, 15 enrolled. In 2009, 18 master's awarded. *Entrance requirements:* For master's, GRE, minimum GPA of 3.0. Additional exam requirements/recommendations for international students: Required—TOEFL (minimum score 550 paper-based; 213 computer-based). *Application deadline:* For fall admission, 1/15 priority date for domestic and international students. Application fee: $70 ($90 for international students). *Financial support:* Application deadline: 3/1. *Unit head:* Ken Chew, Graduate Director, 949-824-6990, E-mail: chew@uci.edu. *Application contact:* Diane Enriquez, Graduate Counselor, 949-824-5924, Fax: 949-824-3548, E-mail: dmvargas@uci.edu.

University of Guelph, Ontario Veterinary College and Graduate Program Services, Graduate Programs in Veterinary Sciences, Department of Population Medicine, Guelph, ON N1G 2W1, Canada. Offers epidemiology (M Sc, DV Sc, PhD); health management (DV Sc); population medicine and health management (M Sc); swine health management (M Sc); theriogenology (M Sc, DV Sc). *Degree requirements:* For master's, thesis; for doctorate, comprehensive exam, thesis/dissertation. *Entrance requirements:* Additional exam requirements/recommendations for international students: Required—TOEFL.

University of Hawaii at Manoa, John A. Burns School of Medicine, Department of Public Health Sciences and Epidemiology, Global Health and Population Studies Program, Honolulu, HI 96822. Offers Graduate Certificate. Part-time programs available. *Students:* 6 full-time (5 women), 1 (woman) part-time, 5 international. In 2009, 1 Graduate Certificate awarded. *Entrance requirements:* For degree, GRE General Test. Additional exam requirements/recommendations for international students: Required—TOEFL (minimum score 500 paper-based; 173 computer-based; 61 iBT), IELTS (minimum score 5). *Application deadline:* For fall admission, 3/1 for domestic and international students; for spring admission, 9/1 for domestic and international students. Application fee: $60. *Expenses:* Tuition, state resident: full-time $8900; part-time $372 per credit. Tuition, nonresident: full-time $21,400; part-time $898 per credit. Required fees: $207 per semester. *Financial support:* In 2009–10, 1 fellowship (averaging $372 per year), 1 research assistantship (averaging $18,198 per year) were awarded. *Application contact:* Andrew Mason, Information Contact, 808-956-7551, Fax: 808-956-7738, E-mail: popstudy@hawaii.edu.

University of Pennsylvania, School of Arts and Sciences, Graduate Group in Demography, Philadelphia, PA 19104. Offers AM, PhD. *Faculty:* 40 full-time (16 women), 9 part-time/adjunct (5 women). *Students:* 26 full-time (15 women); includes 4 minority (1 African American, 3 Asian Americans or Pacific Islanders), 9 international. 31 applicants, 29% accepted, 9 enrolled. In 2009, 2 master's, 4 doctorates awarded. Terminal master's awarded for partial completion of doctoral program. *Degree requirements:* For master's, thesis or alternative; for doctorate, thesis/dissertation. *Entrance requirements:* For master's and doctorate, GRE General Test. Additional exam requirements/recommendations for international students: Required—TOEFL. *Application deadline:* For fall admission, 12/1 priority date for domestic students. Application fee: $70. Electronic applications accepted. *Expenses:* Tuition: Full-time $25,660; part-time $4758 per course. Required fees: $2152; $270 per course. Tuition and fees vary according to course load, degree level and program. *Financial support:* Fellowships, research assistantships, institutionally sponsored loans, scholarships/grants, traineeships, health care benefits, and unspecified assistantships available. Financial award application deadline: 12/15.

University of Puerto Rico, Medical Sciences Campus, Graduate School of Public Health, Program in Demography, San Juan, PR 00936-5067. Offers MS. Part-time programs available. *Degree requirements:* For master's, thesis. *Entrance requirements:* For master's, GRE, previous course work in algebra and statistics.

The University of Texas at San Antonio, College of Public Policy, Department of Demography and Organizational Studies, San Antonio, TX 78249-0617. Offers applied demography (PhD). Part-time and evening/weekend programs available. *Faculty:* 7 full-time (2 women). *Students:* 16 full-time (7 women), 16 part-time (13 women); includes 16 minority (3 Asian Americans or Pacific Islanders, 13 Hispanic Americans), 7 international. Average age 37. 9 applicants, 100% accepted, 9 enrolled. *Entrance requirements:* For doctorate, GRE. Additional exam requirements/recommendations for international students: Required—TOEFL (minimum score 500 paper-based; 173 computer-based; 61 iBT), IELTS (minimum score 5). *Application deadline:* For fall admission, 7/1 for domestic students, 4/1 for international students; for spring admission, 11/1 for domestic students, 9/1 for international students. Applications are processed on a rolling basis. Application fee: $45 ($80 for international students). Electronic applications accepted. *Expenses:* Tuition, state resident: full-time $3975; part-time $221 per contact hour. Tuition, nonresident: full-time $13,947; part-time $775 per contact hour. Required fees: $1853. *Financial support:* In 2009–10, 1 student received support, including 24 research assistantships (averaging $15,500 per year); career-related internships or fieldwork, scholarships/grants, tuition waivers, and unspecified assistantships also available. Support available to part-time students. *Faculty research:* Health disparities, immigration, population estimates and projections, rural development and fertility change, spatial inequality. Total annual research expenditures: $13,776. *Unit head:* Dr. Mary A. Zey, Chair, 210-458-6570, E-mail: mary.zey@utsa.edu. *Application contact:* Karl Eschbach, Graduate Advisor, 210-458-6798, E-mail: karl.eschbach@utsa.edu.

University of Washington, Graduate School, School of Public Health, Department of Health Services, Seattle, WA 98195. Offers bioinformatics (PhD); cancer prevention and control (PhD); clinical research (MS); community oriented public health practice (MPH); economics or finance (PhD); evaluation sciences (PhD); executive program (MHA); health behavior and health promotion (PhD); health care and population health research (MPH); health policy analysis and process (PhD); health policy and analysis and process (MPH); health services (MS, PhD); health services administration (EMHA, MHA); in residence program (MHA); occupational health (PhD); population health and social determinants (PhD); social and behavioral sciences (MPH); sociology and demography (PhD); JD/MHA; MHA/MBA; MHA/MD; MHA/MPA; MPH/JD; MPH/MD; MPH/MN; MPH/MPA; MPH/MSD; MPH/MSW; MPH/PhD. Part-time and evening/weekend programs available. Postbaccalaureate distance learning degree programs offered (minimal on-campus study). *Faculty:* 52 full-time (24 women), 60 part-time/adjunct (28 women). *Students:* 104 full-time (83 women), 100 part-time (76 women); includes 21 minority (6 African Americans, 1 American Indian/Alaska Native, 11 Asian Americans or Pacific Islanders, 3 Hispanic Americans), 6 international. Average age 34. 375 applicants, 17% accepted, 24 enrolled. In 2009, 33 master's awarded. Terminal master's awarded for partial completion of doctoral program. *Degree requirements:* For master's, thesis (for some programs), practicum (MPH); for doctorate, comprehensive exam, thesis/dissertation. *Entrance requirements:* For master's and doctorate, GRE General Test, minimum GPA of 3.0. Additional exam requirements/recommendations for international students: Required—TOEFL. *Application deadline:* For fall admission, 1/15 for domestic students, 11/1 for international students. Application fee: 50 Albanian leks. Electronic applications accepted. *Financial support:* In 2009–10, 64 students received support, including 10 fellowships with full and partial tuition reimbursements available (averaging $21,000 per year), 10 research assistantships with full and partial tuition reimbursements available (averaging $18,000 per year), 3 teaching assistantships with full and partial tuition reimbursements available (averaging $18,000 per year); career-related internships or fieldwork, Federal Work-Study, institutionally sponsored loans, and traineeships also available. Financial award application deadline: 2/28; financial award applicants required to submit FAFSA. *Faculty research:* Health promotion and disease prevention, maternal and child health, health services research design, program evaluation, health policy. Total annual research expenditures: $10.5 million. *Unit head:* Dr. Larry Kessler, Chair, 206-543-616-2930. *Application contact:* Kitty A. Andert, MPH/MS/PhD Program Manager, 206-616-2926, Fax: 206-543-3964, E-mail: kitander@u.washington.edu.

Washington State University, Graduate School, College of Liberal Arts, Department of Sociology, Pullman, WA 99164. Offers crime and deviance (MA, PhD); environments, community and demographics (MA, PhD); institutions and social organizations (MA, PhD); political sociology (MA, PhD); social inequality (MA, PhD); social psychology and life course (MA, PhD). Terminal master's awarded for partial completion of doctoral program. *Degree requirements:* For master's, thesis; for doctorate, comprehensive exam, thesis/dissertation. *Entrance requirements:* For master's, GRE General Test, minimum GPA of 3.0; for doctorate, GRE General Test, MA in sociology, minimum GPA of 3.0. Additional exam requirements/recommendations for international students: Required—TOEFL (minimum score 550 paper-based). Electronic applications accepted. *Faculty research:* Crime/deviance, environmental sociology, social inequality, social psychology, gender.

Rural Sociology

Auburn University, Graduate School, Interdepartmental Programs, Graduate Programs in Sociology and Rural Sociology, Auburn University, AL 36849. Offers rural sociology (MS); sociology (MA, MS). Part-time programs available. *Faculty:* 33 full-time (12 women), 1 (woman) part-time/adjunct. *Students:* 6 full-time (5 women), 5 part-time (3 women); includes 1 minority (Asian American or Pacific Islander), 3 international. Average age 27. 15 applicants, 20% accepted, 2 enrolled. In 2009, 4 master's awarded. *Degree requirements:* For master's, thesis, computer language (MS), foreign language (MA). *Entrance requirements:* For master's, GRE General Test. *Application deadline:* For fall admission, 7/7 for domestic students; for spring admission, 11/24 for domestic students. Applications are processed on a rolling basis. Application fee: $50 ($60 for international students). *Expenses:* Tuition, state resident: full-time $6240. Tuition, nonresident: full-time $18,720. International tuition: $18,938 full-time. Required fees: $492. Tuition and fees vary according to course load, program and reciprocity agreements. *Financial support:* Research assistantships, teaching assistantships available. Financial award application deadline: 3/15; financial award applicants required to submit FAFSA. *Unit head:* Dr. Kelly Alley, Interim Chair, 334-844-5049. *Application contact:* Dr. George Flowers, Dean of the Graduate School, 334-844-4700.

Cornell University, Graduate School, Graduate Fields of Agriculture and Life Sciences, Field of Development Sociology, Ithaca, NY 14853-0001. Offers community and regional society (MS); community and regional sociology (MPS, PhD); methods of social research (MPS, MS, PhD); population and development (MPS, MS, PhD); rural and environmental sociology (MPS, MS, PhD); state, economy, and society (MPS, MS, PhD). *Faculty:* 23 full-time (6 women). *Students:* 44 full-time (29 women); includes 6 minority (1 African American, 2 American Indian/Alaska Native, 2 Asian Americans or Pacific Islanders, 1 Hispanic American), 16 international. Average age 34. 59 applicants, 19% accepted, 7 enrolled. In 2009, 4 master's, 4 doctorates awarded. *Degree requirements:* For doctorate, comprehensive exam, thesis/dissertation. *Entrance requirements:* For master's and doctorate, GRE General Test, 3 letters of recommendation. Additional exam requirements/recommendations for international students: Required—TOEFL (minimum score 550 paper-based; 213 computer-based; 77 iBT). *Application deadline:* For fall admission, 1/15 priority date for domestic students. Application fee: $60. Electronic applications accepted. *Expenses:* Tuition: Full-time $29,500. Required fees: $70. Full-time tuition and fees vary according to degree level, program and student level. *Financial support:* In 2009–10, 25 students received support, including 2 fellowships with full tuition reimbursements available, 1 research assistantship with full tuition reimbursement available, 1 teaching assistantship with full tuition reimbursement available; institutionally sponsored loans, scholarships/grants, health care benefits, tuition waivers (full and partial), and unspecified assistantships also available. Financial award applicants required to submit FAFSA. *Faculty research:* Demography (population and development), environmental sociology, international and rural community development, political economy and ecology, sustainable agriculture. *Unit head:* Director of Graduate Studies, 607-255-3092, Fax: 607-254-2896. *Application contact:* Graduate Field Assistant, 607-255-3092, Fax: 607-254-2896, E-mail: devsoc@cornell.edu.

Iowa State University of Science and Technology, Graduate College, College of Liberal Arts and Sciences, Department of Sociology and College of Agriculture, Program in Rural Sociology, Ames, IA 50011. Offers MS, PhD. *Faculty:* 13 full-time (7 women), 1 (woman) part-time/adjunct. *Students:* 11 full-time (6 women), 9 part-time (6 women); includes 1 minority (Hispanic American), 5 international. 3 applicants, 100% accepted, 2 enrolled. In 2009, 2 master's, 2 doctorates awarded. *Degree requirements:* For master's, thesis; for doctorate, thesis/dissertation. *Entrance requirements:* For master's, GRE General Test; for doctorate, GRE General Test, master's degree. Additional exam requirements/recommendations for international students: Required—TOEFL (minimum score 550 paper-based; 79 iBT) or IELTS (minimum score 6.5). *Application deadline:* For fall admission, 1/10 priority date for domestic and international students; for spring admission, 10/1 for domestic and international students. Application fee: $40 ($90 for international students). Electronic applications accepted. *Expenses:* Tuition, state resident: full-time $6716. Tuition, nonresident: full-time $8908. Tuition and fees vary according to course level, course load, program and student level. *Financial support:* In 2009–10, 3 research assistantships with full and partial tuition reimbursements (averaging $16,200 per year), 1 teaching assistantship with partial tuition reimbursement (averaging $15,700 per year) were awarded; scholarships/grants, health care benefits, and unspecified assistantships also available. *Unit head:* Dr. R. Paul Lasley, Chair, 515-294-2506, Fax: 515-294-8312, E-mail: sociology@iastate.edu. *Application contact:* Dr. Stephen Sapp, Director of Graduate Education, 515-294-1403, E-mail: sociology@iastate.edu.

The Ohio State University, Graduate School, College of Food, Agricultural, and Environmental Sciences, Department of Agricultural, Environmental, and Development Economics, Columbus, OH 43210. Offers agricultural economics and rural sociology (MS, PhD). *Faculty:* 32. *Students:* 62 full-time (30 women), 7 part-time (3 women); includes 3 minority (all Asian Americans or Pacific Islanders), 39 international. Average age 27. In 2009, 15 master's, 6 doctorates awarded. *Degree requirements:* For master's, thesis optional; for doctorate, thesis/dissertation. *Entrance requirements:* For master's and doctorate, GRE General Test. Additional exam requirements/recommendations for international students: Required—TOEFL (minimum score 550 paper-based; 213 computer-based) or IELTS (minimum score 7) or Michigan English Language Assessment Battery (minimum score 92). *Application deadline:* For fall admission, 8/15 priority date for domestic students, 7/1 priority date for international students; for winter admission, 12/1 priority date for domestic students, 11/1 priority date for international students; for spring admission, 3/1 priority date for domestic students, 2/1 priority date for international students. Applications are processed on a rolling basis. Application fee: $40 ($50 for international students). Electronic applications accepted. *Expenses:* Tuition, state resident: full-time $10,683. Tuition, nonresident: full-time $25,923. Tuition and fees vary according to course load and program. *Financial support:* Fellowships, research assistantships, teaching assistantships, Federal Work-Study and institutionally sponsored loans available. Support available to part-time students. *Unit head:* Mario Miranda, Graduate Studies Committee Chair, E-mail: miranda.4@osu.edu. *Application contact:* Graduate Admissions, 614-292-9444, Fax: 614-292-3895, E-mail: domestic.grad@osu.edu.

The Ohio State University, Graduate School, College of Food, Agricultural, and Environmental Sciences, Department of Rural Sociology, Columbus, OH 43210. Offers MS, PhD. *Students:* 14 full-time (10 women), 5 part-time (4 women); includes 3 minority (2 African Americans, 1 Hispanic American), 3 international. Average age 31. In 2009, 6 doctorates awarded. *Entrance requirements:* For master's and doctorate, GRE or GMAT. *Application deadline:* Applications are processed on a rolling basis. Application fee: $40 ($50 for international students). Electronic applications accepted. *Expenses:* Tuition, state resident: full-time $10,683. Tuition, nonresident: full-time $25,923. Tuition and fees vary according to course load and program. *Unit head:* Linda M. Lobao, Graduate Studies Committee Chair, 614-292-6394, Fax: 614-292-7007, E-mail: lobao.1@osu.edu. *Application contact:* Graduate Admissions, 614-292-9444, Fax: 614-292-3985, E-mail: domestic.grad@osu.edu.

Penn State University Park, Graduate School, College of Agricultural Sciences, Department of Agricultural Economics and Rural Sociology, State College, University Park, PA 16802-1503. Offers MPS, MS, PhD.

South Dakota State University, Graduate School, College of Agriculture and Biological Sciences, Department of Rural Sociology, Brookings, SD 57007. Offers rural sociology (MS); sociology (PhD). Part-time programs available. Postbaccalaureate distance learning degree programs offered. *Degree requirements:* For master's, comprehensive exam (for some programs), thesis, oral and written exams; for doctorate, comprehensive exam, thesis/dissertation, preliminary oral and written exams. *Entrance requirements:* Additional exam requirements/recommendations for international students: Required—TOEFL (minimum score 550 paper-based; 213 computer-based; 79 iBT). *Faculty research:* Demography, rural families, rural development, Native Americans, rural poverty, sociology of agriculture.

University of Alberta, Faculty of Graduate Studies and Research, Department of Rural Economy, Edmonton, AB T6G 2E1, Canada. Offers agricultural economics (M Ag, M Sc, PhD); forest economics (M Ag, M Sc, PhD); rural sociology (M Ag, M Sc); MBA/M Ag. Part-time programs available. *Faculty:* 13 full-time (1 woman), 6 part-time/adjunct (0 women). *Students:* 31 full-time (13 women), 21 part-time (11 women). Average age 25. 35 applicants, 83% accepted. In 2009, 10 master's, 2 doctorates awarded. *Degree requirements:* For doctorate, thesis/dissertation. *Entrance requirements:* Additional exam requirements/recommendations for international students: Required—TOEFL. Application fee: $60. Tuition and fees charges are reported in Canadian dollars. *Expenses:* Tuition, area resident: Full-time $4626.24 Canadian dollars; part-time $99.72 Canadian dollars per unit. International tuition: $8216 Canadian dollars full-time. Required fees: $3589.92 Canadian dollars; $99.72 Canadian dollars per unit. $215 Canadian dollars per term. *Financial support:* In 2009–10, 4 fellowships, 12 research assistantships, 2 teaching assistantships were awarded; scholarships/grants also available. *Faculty research:* Agroforestry, development, extension education, marketing and trade, natural resources and environment, policy, production economics. Total annual research expenditures: $850,000. *Unit head:* Dr. V. Adamowicz, Graduate Coordinator, 403-492-4225, Fax: 403-492-0268. *Application contact:* Liz Bruce, Graduate Secretary, 780-492-4225, Fax: 780-492-0268, E-mail: rural.economy@ualberta.ca.

University of Missouri, Graduate School, College of Agriculture, Food and Natural Resources, Department of Rural Sociology, Columbia, MO 65211. Offers MS, PhD. Part-time programs available. *Faculty:* 6 full-time (2 women), 6 part-time/adjunct (2 women). *Students:* 9 full-time (3 women), 14 part-time (10 women); includes 4 minority (3 African Americans, 1 American Indian/Alaska Native), 7 international. Average age 40. 14 applicants, 43% accepted, 4 enrolled. In 2009, 2 master's awarded. *Degree requirements:* For doctorate, comprehensive exam, thesis/dissertation. *Entrance requirements:* For master's and doctorate, GRE General Test, minimum GPA of 3.0. Additional exam requirements/recommendations for international students: Required—TOEFL (minimum score 570 paper-based; 233 computer-based; 89 iBT). *Application deadline:* Applications are processed on a rolling basis. Application fee: $45 ($60 for international students). Electronic applications accepted. *Financial support:* Fellowships with tuition reimbursements, research assistantships with tuition reimbursements, teaching assistantships with tuition reimbursements, institutionally sponsored loans available. *Unit head:* Dr. Mike Nolan, Department Chair, E-mail: nolanm@missouri.edu. *Application contact:* Carol Swaim, 573-882-7451, E-mail: swaimc@missouri.edu.

The University of Montana, Graduate School, College of Arts and Sciences, Department of Sociology, Missoula, MT 59812-0002. Offers criminology (MA); rural and environmental change (MA); sociology (MA). *Entrance requirements:* For master's, GRE General Test. Additional exam requirements/recommendations for international students: Required—TOEFL. *Faculty research:* Housing, homelessness, hunger, infant mortality, work safety.

University of Wisconsin–Madison, Graduate School, College of Letters and Science, Department of Sociology, Madison, WI 53706-1380. Offers rural sociology (MS); sociology (MS, PhD). Part-time programs available. Terminal master's awarded for partial completion of doctoral program. *Degree requirements:* For master's, thesis, oral exam; for doctorate, thesis/dissertation, preliminary and final oral exams, 4 seminars. *Entrance requirements:* For master's and doctorate, GRE General Test. Additional exam requirements/recommendations for international students: Required—TOEFL. Electronic applications accepted. *Expenses:* Tuition, state resident: part-time $594 per credit. Tuition, nonresident: part-time $1504 per credit. Required fees: $65 per credit. Tuition and fees vary according to course load, program and reciprocity agreements.

Sociology

Acadia University, Faculty of Arts, Department of Sociology, Wolfville, NS B4P 2R6, Canada. Offers MA. *Faculty:* 6 full-time (3 women). *Students:* 7 full-time (4 women), 2 part-time (both women). Average age 25. 9 applicants, 78% accepted, 7 enrolled. In 2009, 4 master's awarded. *Degree requirements:* For master's, thesis. *Entrance requirements:* For master's, honors degree, minimum GPA of 3.25. Additional exam requirements/recommendations for international students: Required—TOEFL (minimum score 580 paper-based; 237 computer-based; 93 iBT), IELTS (minimum score 6.5). *Application deadline:* For fall admission, 2/1 for domestic students. Applications are processed on a rolling basis. Application fee: $50. *Financial support:* Research assistantships, teaching assistantships, unspecified assistantships available. Financial award application deadline: 2/1. *Faculty research:* Atlantic cultures, class analysis, gender and women's studies, religion, symbolism, development studies. *Unit head:* Dr. Jim Sacouman, Head, 902-585-1494, Fax: 902-585-1769, E-mail: jim.sacouman@acadiau.ca. *Application contact:* Karen Turner, Administrative Secretary, 902-585-1493, Fax: 902-585-1769, E-mail: karen.turner@acadiau.ca.

American University, College of Arts and Sciences, Department of Sociology, Washington, DC 22016-8072. Offers social research (Certificate); sociology (MA). Part-time and evening/weekend programs available. *Faculty:* 14 full-time (9 women), 4 part-time/adjunct (3 women). *Students:* 11 full-time (10 women), 32 part-time (25 women); includes 19 minority (14 African Americans, 1 American Indian/Alaska Native, 1 Asian American or Pacific Islander, 3 Hispanic Americans), 2 international. Average age 37. 22 applicants, 77% accepted, 5 enrolled. In 2009, 10 master's awarded. *Degree requirements:* For master's, comprehensive exam, thesis or alternative, tool of research examination. *Entrance requirements:* For master's, GRE; for Certificate, bachelor's degree. Additional exam requirements/recommendations for international students: Required—TOEFL. *Application deadline:* For fall admission, 2/1 for domestic students. Application fee: $80. *Expenses:* Tuition: Full-time $22,266; part-time $1237 per credit hour. Required fees: $430. Tuition and fees vary according to program. *Financial support:* Fellowships, research assistantships with full and partial tuition reimbursements, teaching assistantships with full and partial tuition reimbursements, career-related internships or fieldwork, Federal Work-Study, institutionally sponsored loans, tuition waivers (full and partial), and unspecified assistantships available. Support available to part-time students. Financial award application deadline: 2/1; financial award applicants required to submit FAFSA. *Faculty research:* Gender, race, development, applied social policy, political economy. *Unit head:* Dr. John Philip Drysdale, Chair, 202-885-2488, Fax: 202-885-2477, E-mail: drysdale@american.edu. *Application contact:* Dr. John Philip Drysdale, Chair, 202-885-2488, Fax: 202-885-2477, E-mail: drysdale@american.edu.

The American University in Cairo, Graduate Studies and Research, School of Humanities and Social Sciences, Department of Sociology, Anthropology, Psychology, and Egyptology, Cairo, Egypt. Offers sociology and anthropology (MA). *Degree requirements:* For master's, one foreign language, thesis. *Entrance requirements:* Additional exam requirements/recommendations for international students: Required—English entrance exam and/or TOEFL. Electronic applications accepted. *Faculty research:* Development, gender, sociopolitical economic formulations, social science indigenization, Arab world.

American University of Beirut, Graduate Programs, Faculty of Arts and Sciences, Beirut, Lebanon. Offers anthropology (MA); Arabic language and literature (MA); archaeology (MA); biology (MS); chemistry (MS); computer science (MS); economics (MA); education (MA); English language (MA); English literature (MA); environmental policy planning (MSES); financial economics (MAFE); geology (MS); history (MA); mathematics (MA, MS); Middle Eastern studies (MA); philosophy (MA); physics (MS); political studies (MA); psychology (MA); public administration (MA); sociology (MA); statistics (MA, MS). Part-time programs available. *Degree requirements:* For master's, one foreign language, comprehensive exam, thesis (for some programs). *Entrance requirements:* For master's, GRE, letter of recommendation. Additional exam requirements/recommendations for international students: Required—TOEFL (minimum score 600 paper-based; 250 computer-based; 100 iBT), IELTS (minimum score 7.5). *Faculty research:* String theory and supergravity; computer graphics; algebra and number theory; popular Arabic literature; marine and freshwater biology; integrating science, math and technology.

Arizona State University, Graduate College, College of Liberal Arts and Sciences, Division of Social Sciences, School of Social and Family Dynamics, Tempe, AZ 85287. Offers family and human development (MS, PhD); infant-family practice (MAS); marriage and family therapy (MAS); sociology (MA, PhD). *Degree requirements:* For master's, thesis or alternative; for doctorate, thesis/dissertation. *Entrance requirements:* For master's and doctorate, GRE.

Arkansas State University—Jonesboro, Graduate School, College of Humanities and Social Sciences, Department of Criminology, Sociology, and Geography, Jonesboro, State University, AR 72467. Offers criminal justice (MA, Certificate); sociology (MA); sociology education (SCCT). Part-time programs available. *Faculty:* 7 full-time (4 women). *Students:* 9 full-time (7 women), 32 part-time (23 women); includes 15 minority (all African Americans). Average age 33. 29 applicants, 59% accepted, 12 enrolled. In 2009, 7 master's awarded. *Degree requirements:* For master's, one foreign language, comprehensive exam, thesis or alternative; for other advanced degree, comprehensive exam. *Entrance requirements:* For master's, GRE General Test or MAT, appropriate bachelor's degree, letters of recommendation; for other advanced degree, GRE General Test or MAT, interview, master's degree, official transcript, immunization records. Additional exam requirements/recommendations for international students: Required—TOEFL (minimum score 550 paper-based; 213 computer-based; 79 iBT), IELTS (minimum score 6). *Application deadline:* For fall admission, 7/1 for domestic and international students; for spring admission, 11/15 for domestic students, 11/13 for international students. Applications are processed on a rolling basis. Application fee: $30 ($40 for international students). Electronic applications accepted. *Expenses:* Tuition, state resident: full-time $3744; part-time $208 per credit hour. Tuition, nonresident: full-time $9540; part-time $530 per credit hour. Required fees: $896; $47 per credit hour. $25 per term. One-time fee: $50. Tuition and fees vary according to course load and program. *Financial support:* In 2009–10, 8 students received support. Career-related internships or fieldwork, scholarships/grants, and unspecified assistantships available. Financial award application deadline: 7/1; financial award applicants required to submit FAFSA. *Unit head:* Dr. Anthony Troy Adams, Chair, 870-972-3705, Fax: 870-972-3694, E-mail: aadams@astate.edu. *Application contact:* Dr. Andrew Sustich, Dean of the Graduate School, 870-972-3029, Fax: 870-972-3857, E-mail: sustich@astate.edu.

Auburn University, Graduate School, Interdepartmental Programs, Graduate Programs in Sociology and Rural Sociology, Auburn University, AL 36849. Offers rural sociology (MS); sociology (MA, MS). Part-time programs available. *Faculty:* 33 full-time (12 women), 1 (woman) part-time/adjunct. *Students:* 6 full-time (5 women), 5 part-time (3 women); includes 1 minority (Asian American or Pacific Islander), 3 international. Average age 27. 15 applicants, 20% accepted, 2 enrolled. In 2009, 4 master's awarded. *Degree requirements:* For master's, thesis, computer language (MS), foreign language (MA). *Entrance requirements:* For master's, GRE General Test. *Application deadline:* For fall admission, 7/7 for domestic students; for spring admission, 11/24 for domestic students. Applications are processed on a rolling basis. Application fee: $50 ($60 for international students). *Expenses:* Tuition, state resident: full-time $6240. Tuition, nonresident: full-time $18,720. International tuition: $18,938 full-time. Required fees: $492. Tuition and fees vary according to course load, program and reciprocity agreements. *Financial support:* Research assistantships, teaching assistantships available. Financial award application deadline: 3/15; financial award applicants required to submit FAFSA. *Unit head:* Dr. Kelly Alley, Interim Chair, 334-844-5049. *Application contact:* Dr. George Flowers, Dean of the Graduate School, 334-844-4700.

Ball State University, Graduate School, College of Sciences and Humanities, Department of Sociology, Muncie, IN 47306-1099. Offers MA. *Entrance requirements:* For master's, GRE General Test. *Faculty research:* Retention policies for secondary education, community mental health.

Baylor University, Graduate School, College of Arts and Sciences, Department of Sociology and Anthropology, Waco, TX 76798. Offers applied sociology (PhD); sociology (MA). *Students:* 25 full-time (11 women); includes 1 minority (African American), 1 international. In 2009, 2 master's, 5 doctorates awarded. *Entrance requirements:* For master's and doctorate, GRE General Test. *Application deadline:* For fall admission, 8/1 for domestic students. Applications are processed on a rolling basis. Application fee: $25. *Financial support:* Research assistantships, teaching assistantships, career-related internships or fieldwork, Federal Work-Study, and institutionally sponsored loans available. *Faculty research:* Community studies, thanatology, sociology of education. *Unit head:* Dr. Roby Driskell, Graduate Program Director, 254-710-3362, Fax: 254-710-3809, E-mail: robyn_driskell@baylor.edu. *Application contact:* Sharon Sloan, Administrative Assistant, 254-710-1165, Fax: 254-710-3870, E-mail: sharon_sloan@baylor.edu.

Boston College, Graduate School of Arts and Sciences, Department of Sociology, Chestnut Hill, MA 02467-3800. Offers MA, PhD, MBA/MA, MBA/PhD. Part-time programs available. *Students:* 48 full-time (31 women), 7 part-time (4 women); includes 7 minority (2 African Americans, 3 Asian Americans or Pacific Islanders, 2 Hispanic Americans), 7 international. 189 applicants, 38% accepted, 19 enrolled. In 2009, 4 master's, 6 doctorates awarded. Terminal master's awarded for partial completion of doctoral program. *Degree requirements:* For master's, thesis optional; for doctorate, thesis/dissertation. *Entrance requirements:* For master's and doctorate, GRE General Test. Additional exam requirements/recommendations for international students: Required—TOEFL (minimum score 600 paper-based; 250 computer-based; 100 iBT). *Application deadline:* For fall admission, 1/2 for domestic students. Application fee: $70. Electronic applications accepted. *Financial support:* Fellowships with full tuition reimbursements, research assistantships with full tuition reimbursements, teaching assistantships with full tuition reimbursements, Federal Work-Study available. Support available to part-time students. Financial award application deadline: 3/1; financial award applicants required to submit FAFSA. *Faculty research:* Sociological theory, social economy, social psychology, political sociology, development modernization. *Unit head:* Dr. Juliet Schor, Chairperson, 617-552-4056. *Application contact:* Dr. Sarah Babb, Graduate Program Director, 617-552-2930, E-mail: sarah.babb@bc.edu.

Boston University, Graduate School of Arts and Sciences, Department of Sociology, Boston, MA 02215. Offers MA, PhD. *Students:* 20 full-time (14 women), 5 part-time (1 woman); includes 2 minority (1 Asian American or Pacific Islander, 1 Hispanic American), 5 international. Average age 32. 113 applicants, 19% accepted, 6 enrolled. In 2009, 2 doctorates awarded. Terminal master's awarded for partial completion of doctoral program. *Degree requirements:* For master's, one foreign language, comprehensive exam, thesis; for doctorate, one foreign language, comprehensive exam, thesis/dissertation. *Entrance requirements:* For master's, GRE General Test, sample of written work, 3 letters of recommendation; for doctorate, GRE General Test or MAT, sample of written work, 3 letters of recommendation. Additional exam requirements/recommendations for international students: Required—TOEFL (minimum score 550 paper-based; 213 computer-based). *Application deadline:* For fall admission, 1/15 for domestic and international students. Application fee: $70. Electronic applications accepted. *Expenses:* Tuition: Full-time $37,910; part-time $1184 per credit hour. Required fees: $386; $40 per semester. Part-time tuition and fees vary according to class time, course level, degree level and program. *Financial support:* In 2009–10, 9 students received support, including 1 fellowship with full tuition reimbursement available (averaging $18,900 per year), 1 research assistantship with full tuition reimbursement available (averaging $18,400 per year), 4 teaching assistantships with full tuition reimbursements available (averaging $18,400 per year); career-related internships or fieldwork, Federal Work-Study, and scholarships/grants also available. Support available to part-time students. Financial award application deadline: 1/15; financial award applicants required to submit FAFSA. *Unit head:* Nancy Ammerman, Chairman, 617-358-0634, Fax: 617-353-4837, E-mail: nta@bu.edu. *Application contact:* Vivienne Pustell, Department Administrator, 617-353-2594, Fax: 617-353-4837, E-mail: vivienne@bu.edu.

Bowling Green State University, Graduate College, College of Arts and Sciences, Department of Sociology, Bowling Green, OH 43403. Offers demography and population studies (MA); social psychology (MA); sociology (PhD). Part-time programs available. *Degree requirements:* For master's, thesis or alternative; for doctorate, comprehensive exam, thesis/dissertation. *Entrance requirements:* For master's and doctorate, GRE General Test. Additional exam requirements/recommendations for international students: Required—TOEFL. Electronic applications accepted. *Faculty research:* Applied demography, criminology and deviance, family studies, population studies, social psychology.

Brandeis University, Graduate School of Arts and Sciences, Department of Sociology, Waltham, MA 02454-9110. Offers Near Eastern and Judaic studies and sociology (PhD); social policy and sociology (PhD); sociology (MA, PhD); sociology and women's and gender studies (MA). Part-time programs available. *Faculty:* 10 full-time (6 women), 1 part-time/adjunct (0 women). *Students:* 22 full-time (17 women), 3 part-time (all women); includes 6 minority (2 African Americans, 2 Asian Americans or Pacific Islanders, 2 Hispanic Americans), 4 international. Average age 33. 73 applicants, 14% accepted, 5 enrolled. In 2009, 2 master's, 3 doctorates awarded. Terminal master's awarded for partial completion of doctoral program. *Degree requirements:* For master's, thesis; for doctorate, thesis/dissertation. *Entrance requirements:* For master's, GRE, resume, letters of recommendation; for doctorate, GRE, writing sample, resume, letters of recommendation. Additional exam requirements/recommendations for international students: Required—TOEFL (minimum score 600 paper-based; 250 computer-based; 100 iBT); Recommended—IELTS (minimum score 7). *Application deadline:* For fall admission, 1/15 for domestic and international students. Application fee: $75. Electronic applications accepted. *Financial support:* In 2009–10, 12 students received support, including 13 fellowships with full tuition reimbursements available (averaging $20,000 per year), 1 teaching assistantship with partial tuition reimbursement available (averaging $3,200 per year); scholarships/grants, health care benefits, and tuition waivers (full and partial) also available. Support available to part-time students. Financial award application deadline: 4/15; financial award applicants required to submit FAFSA. *Faculty research:* Social theory and cultural studies; feminist sociology; political sociology; sociology of medicine, health and health care; comparative social structures. *Unit head:* Dr. David Cunningham, Co-Chair, Graduate Committee, 781-736-2631, Fax: 781-736-2653, E-mail: dcunning@brandeis.edu. *Application contact:* Cheryl Hansen, Graduate Program Administrator, 781-736-2631, Fax: 781-736-2653, E-mail: chansen@brandeis.edu.

Brigham Young University, Graduate Studies, College of Family, Home, and Social Sciences, Department of Sociology, Provo, UT 84602. Offers MS. *Faculty:* 17 full-time (5 women), 2 part-time/adjunct (1 woman). *Students:* 24 full-time (10 women), 1 (woman) part-time; includes 2 minority (1 African American, 1 Asian American or Pacific Islander). Average age 29. 17 applicants, 76% accepted, 11 enrolled. In 2009, 10 master's awarded. Terminal master's awarded for partial completion of doctoral program. *Degree requirements:* For master's, thesis. *Entrance requirements:* For master's, GRE General Test, minimum GPA of 3.0 in last 60 hours, writing sample, bachelor's degree in sociology or related field, 3 letters of recommendation, Honor Code commitment. Additional exam requirements/recommendations for international students: Required—TOEFL. *Application deadline:* For fall admission, 2/1 for domestic students. Application fee: $50. Electronic applications accepted. *Expenses:* Tuition: Full-time $5580; part-time $301 per credit hour. Tuition and fees vary according to student's religious affiliation. *Financial support:* In 2009–10, 9 research assistantships (averaging $15,750 per year), 9 teaching assistantships (averaging $15,750 per year) were awarded; institutionally sponsored loans and unspecified assistantships also available. Financial award application deadline: 2/1. *Faculty research:* Demography, race and ethnicity, gender, rural and community, international development, comparative family. Total annual research expenditures: $33,500. *Unit head:* Dr. Renata Forste, Department Chair, 801-422-3146, Fax: 801-422-0625, E-mail: renata_forste@byu.edu. *Application contact:* Dr. Carol J. Ward, Graduate Coordinator, 801-422-3047, Fax: 801-422-0625, E-mail: carol.ward@byu.edu.

Brock University, Faculty of Graduate Studies, Faculty of Social Sciences, Program in Critical Sociology, St. Catharines, ON L2S 3A1, Canada. Offers MA.

Brooklyn College of the City University of New York, Division of Graduate Studies, Department of Sociology, Brooklyn, NY 11210-2889. Offers MA, PhD. Part-time and evening/weekend programs available. *Students:* 34 part-time (25 women); includes 23 minority (14 African Americans, 5 Asian Americans or Pacific Islanders, 4 Hispanic Americans), 1 international. Average age 33. 28 applicants, 57% accepted, 7 enrolled. In 2009, 16 master's awarded. *Degree requirements:* For master's, comprehensive exam or research essay. *Entrance requirements:* For master's, 12 upper-level credits in sociology, 2 letters of recommendation, essay. Additional exam requirements/recommendations for international students: Required—TOEFL (minimum score 500 paper-based; 173 computer-based; 61 iBT). *Application deadline:* For fall admission, 3/1 priority date for domestic students, 2/1 priority date for international students; for spring admission, 11/1 priority date for domestic students, 10/1 priority date for international students. Applications are processed on a rolling basis. Application fee: $125. Electronic applications accepted. *Expenses:* Tuition, area resident: Full-time $7360; part-time $310 per credit hour. Tuition, state resident: full-time $7360; part-time $310 per credit hour. Tuition, nonresident: full-time $13,800; part-time $575 per credit hour. International tuition: $13,800 full-time. Required fees: $140.10 per semester. *Financial support:* Career-related internships or fieldwork, Federal Work-Study, institutionally sponsored loans, and scholarships/grants available. Support available to part-time students. Financial award application deadline: 5/1; financial award applicants required to submit FAFSA. *Faculty research:* Urbanization, religion, family, gender, research methods. *Unit head:* Dr. Kenneth Gould, Chairperson, 718-951-5314, E-mail: kgould@brooklyn.cuny.edu. *Application contact:* Hernan Sierra, Graduate Admissions Coordinator, 718-951-4536, Fax: 718-951-4506, E-mail: grads@brooklyn.cuny.edu.

Brown University, Graduate School, Department of Sociology, Program in Sociology, Providence, RI 02912. Offers AM, PhD. *Degree requirements:* For master's, thesis; for doctorate, thesis/dissertation, oral exam. *Entrance requirements:* For master's and doctorate, GRE General Test.

California State University, Bakersfield, Division of Graduate Studies, School of Humanities and Social Sciences, Program in Sociology, Bakersfield, CA 93311. Offers MA.

California State University, Dominguez Hills, College of Natural and Behavioral Sciences, Program in Sociology, Carson, CA 90747-0001. Offers social research (Certificate); sociology (MA). Part-time and evening/weekend programs available. *Faculty:* 10 full-time (6 women), 2 part-time/adjunct (1 woman). *Students:* 41 full-time (31 women), 37 part-time (25 women); includes 62 minority (42 African Americans, 3 Asian Americans or Pacific Islanders, 17 Hispanic Americans). Average age 37. 58 applicants, 78% accepted, 26 enrolled. In 2009, 29 master's

Sociology

California State University, Dominguez Hills (continued)
awarded. *Degree requirements:* For master's, comprehensive exam, thesis. *Entrance requirements:* For master's and Certificate, minimum GPA of 2.85. *Application deadline:* For fall admission, 6/1 for domestic students. Application fee: $55. *Expenses:* Tuition, nonresident: full-time $6696; part-time $372 per unit. Required fees: $5946; $1752 per semester. *Faculty research:* Community studies, social movements, criminology. *Unit head:* Dr. Clare Weber, Chair, 310-243-3458, E-mail: cweber@csudh.edu. *Application contact:* Dr. Gayle Ball-Parker, Director of Admissions, 310-243-3645, E-mail: gball@csudh.edu.

California State University, Fullerton, Graduate Studies, College of Humanities and Social Sciences, Department of Sociology, Fullerton, CA 92834-9480. Offers MA. Part-time programs available. *Students:* 21 full-time (17 women), 30 part-time (18 women); includes 15 minority (2 African Americans, 5 Asian Americans or Pacific Islanders, 8 Hispanic Americans), 1 international. Average age 29. 56 applicants, 50% accepted, 15 enrolled. In 2009, 6 master's awarded. *Degree requirements:* For master's, thesis. *Entrance requirements:* For master's, minimum GPA of 3.0 in sociology, 2.5 in last 60 units. Application fee: $55. *Expenses:* Tuition, nonresident: full-time $11,160; part-time $373 per credit. Required fees: $1440 per term. Tuition and fees vary according to course load, degree level and program. *Financial support:* Career-related internships or fieldwork, Federal Work-Study, institutionally sponsored loans, and scholarships/grants available. Support available to part-time students. Financial award application deadline: 3/1; financial award applicants required to submit FAFSA. *Faculty research:* Gerontology wellness clinic. *Unit head:* Dr. Dennis Berg, Chair, 657-278-3531. *Application contact:* Admissions/Applications, 657-278-2371.

California State University, Los Angeles, Graduate Studies, College of Natural and Social Sciences, Department of Sociology, Los Angeles, CA 90032-8530. Offers MA. Part-time and evening/weekend programs available. *Faculty:* 5 full-time (3 women), 4 part-time/adjunct (1 woman). *Students:* 15 full-time (5 women), 53 part-time (32 women); includes 52 minority (9 African Americans, 1 American Indian/Alaska Native, 6 Asian Americans or Pacific Islanders, 36 Hispanic Americans), 2 international. Average age 31. 47 applicants, 100% accepted, 19 enrolled. In 2009, 9 master's awarded. *Degree requirements:* For master's, comprehensive exam or thesis. *Entrance requirements:* For master's, minimum GPA of 2.5 in last 90 units of course work. Additional exam requirements/recommendations for international students: Required—TOEFL (minimum score 500 paper-based; 173 computer-based). *Application deadline:* For fall admission, 5/1 for domestic and international students. Applications are processed on a rolling basis. Application fee: $55. Electronic applications accepted. *Financial support:* Federal Work-Study available. Support available to part-time students. Financial award application deadline: 3/1. *Faculty research:* Criminal and delinquent careers, family and sex, ethnic minorities, demographic trends, human socialization and aging. *Unit head:* Dr. Steven L. Gordon, Chair, 323-343-2200, Fax: 323-343-5155, E-mail: sgordon@calstatela.edu. *Application contact:* Dr. Cheryl L. Ney, Associate Vice President for Academic Affairs and Dean of Graduate Studies, 323-343-3820, Fax: 323-343-5653, E-mail: cney@cslanet.calstatela.edu.

California State University, Northridge, Graduate Studies, College of Social and Behavioral Sciences, Department of Sociology, Northridge, CA 91330. Offers MA. *Accreditation:* CSWE. Part-time and evening/weekend programs available. *Faculty:* 20 full-time (9 women), 25 part-time/adjunct (15 women). *Students:* 143 full-time (123 women), 61 part-time (50 women); includes 104 minority (17 African Americans, 2 American Indian/Alaska Native, 17 Asian Americans or Pacific Islanders, 68 Hispanic Americans), 4 international. Average age 30. 356 applicants, 32% accepted, 91 enrolled. In 2009, 51 master's awarded. *Degree requirements:* For master's, thesis or alternative. *Entrance requirements:* For master's, GRE General Test. Additional exam requirements/recommendations for international students: Required—TOEFL. *Application deadline:* For fall admission, 3/27 for domestic students; for spring admission, 10/17 for domestic students. Application fee: $55. *Financial support:* Career-related internships or fieldwork, Federal Work-Study, and institutionally sponsored loans available. Support available to part-time students. Financial award application deadline: 3/1. *Faculty research:* Crime and corrections, relationships between adult children and parents. *Unit head:* Dr. Herman DeBose, Chair, 818-677-3591. *Application contact:* Dr. David Boyns, Graduate Advisor, 818-677-6803.

California State University, Sacramento, Graduate Studies, College of Social Sciences and Interdisciplinary Studies, Department of Sociology, Sacramento, CA 95819. Offers MA. Part-time programs available. *Degree requirements:* For master's, thesis or alternative, writing proficiency exam. *Entrance requirements:* For master's, minimum GPA of 3.0 during previous 2 years. Additional exam requirements/recommendations for international students: Required—TOEFL. Electronic applications accepted.

California State University, San Marcos, College of Arts and Sciences, Program in Sociological Practice, San Marcos, CA 92096-0001. Offers MA. *Degree requirements:* For master's, thesis. *Entrance requirements:* For master's, GRE General Test (recommended), minimum GPA of 3.0 in last 60 units of undergraduate study, minimum GPA of 3.0 in upper division sociology courses. *Faculty research:* Organized crime, juvenile detention, counseling services for minorities, mental-health facilities.

Carleton University, Faculty of Graduate Studies, Faculty of Arts and Social Sciences, Department of Sociology and Anthropology, Program in Sociology, Ottawa, ON K1S 5B6, Canada. Offers MA, PhD. *Degree requirements:* For master's, thesis optional; for doctorate, one foreign language, comprehensive exam, thesis/dissertation. *Entrance requirements:* For master's, honors degree; for doctorate, master's degree. Additional exam requirements/recommendations for international students: Required—TOEFL. *Faculty research:* Canadian society and policy, inequality and mobility, race/ethnic relations, cultural studies, gender studies.

Case Western Reserve University, School of Graduate Studies, Department of Sociology, Cleveland, OH 44106. Offers MA, PhD. *Faculty:* 8 full-time (4 women). *Students:* 32 full-time (24 women); includes 3 minority (2 African Americans, 1 Asian American or Pacific Islander), 3 international. Average age 33. 10 applicants, 70% accepted, 6 enrolled. In 2009, 1 master's, 1 doctorate awarded. Terminal master's awarded for partial completion of doctoral program. *Degree requirements:* For master's, comprehensive exam; for doctorate, comprehensive exam, thesis/dissertation. *Entrance requirements:* For master's, GRE, Writing Sample; for doctorate, GRE, Writing sample. Additional exam requirements/recommendations for international students: Required—TOEFL (minimum score 550 paper-based; 213 computer-based; 79 iBT). *Application deadline:* For fall admission, 2/1 priority date for domestic students. Applications are processed on a rolling basis. Application fee: $50. Electronic applications accepted. *Financial support:* Fellowships, research assistantships, teaching assistantships, tuition waivers (full and partial) available. Financial award application deadline: 2/15. *Faculty research:* Sociology of aging and the life course, medical sociology, population and individual health, social inequality, and family sociology. *Unit head:* Dr. Dale Dannefer, Chair, 216-368-2700, Fax: 216-368-2676, E-mail: dale.dannefer@case.edu. *Application contact:* Brian Gran, Graduate Director, 216-368-2700, Fax: 216-368-2676, E-mail: brian.gran@case.edu.

The Catholic University of America, School of Arts and Sciences, Department of Sociology, Washington, DC 20064. Offers MA. Part-time programs available. *Faculty:* 4 full-time (1 woman), 4 part-time/adjunct (0 women). *Students:* 3 full-time (2 women), 3 part-time (1 woman), 2 international. Average age 36. 10 applicants, 50% accepted, 1 enrolled. In 2009, 2 master's awarded. *Degree requirements:* For master's, comprehensive exam, thesis or alternative. *Entrance requirements:* For master's, GRE General Test, statement of purpose, official copies of academic transcripts, three letters of recommendation. Additional exam requirements/recommendations for international students: Required—TOEFL (minimum score 580 paper-based; 237 computer-based). *Application deadline:* For fall admission, 8/1 priority date for domestic students, 7/15 for international students; for spring admission, 12/1 priority date for domestic students, 10/15 for international students. Applications are processed on a rolling basis. Application fee: $55. Electronic applications accepted. *Expenses:* Tuition: Full-time $31,740; part-time $1245 per credit hour. Required fees: $50; $25 per semester hour. One-time fee: $425. *Financial support:* Fellowships, research assistantships, teaching assistantships, Federal Work-Study, scholarships/grants, tuition waivers (full and partial), and unspecified assistantships available. Financial award application deadline: 2/1; financial award applicants required to submit FAFSA. *Faculty research:* Social movements, gender structure, political sociology, race and ethnic relations, evaluation methodologies. Total annual research expenditures: $79,339. *Unit head:* Dr. Bronislaw Misztal, Chair, 202-319-5445, Fax: 202-319-4980, E-mail: misztal@cua.edu. *Application contact:* Julie Schwing, Director of Graduate Admissions, 202-319-5057, Fax: 202-319-6533, E-mail: cua-admissions@cua.edu.

Central European University, Graduate Studies, School of Social Sciences and Humanities, Budapest, Hungary. Offers economics (MA, PhD); gender studies (MA, PhD); international relations and European studies (MA, PhD); mathematics and its applications (MS, PhD); medieval studies (MA, PhD); nationalism studies (MA, PhD); philosophy (MA, PhD); political science (MA, PhD); public policy (MA, PhD); sociology and social anthropology (MA, PhD). Terminal master's awarded for partial completion of doctoral program. *Degree requirements:* For master's, one foreign language, thesis; for doctorate, one foreign language, comprehensive exam, thesis/dissertation. *Entrance requirements:* For master's, interview; for doctorate, GRE, CEU subject test, interview. Additional exam requirements/recommendations for international students: Required—TOEFL (minimum score 570 paper-based; 230 computer-based). Electronic applications accepted. *Faculty research:* Civil society, fiscal decentralization, party politics, political philosophy (especially Liberalism, theory of Democracy).

City College of the City University of New York, Graduate School, College of Liberal Arts and Science, Division of Social Science, Department of Sociology, New York, NY 10031-9198. Offers MA. *Degree requirements:* For master's, one foreign language, comprehensive exam, thesis. *Entrance requirements:* Additional exam requirements/recommendations for international students: Required—TOEFL (minimum score 500 paper-based; 61 iBT). Electronic applications accepted. *Faculty research:* Urban sociology, criminology and deviance, race and ethnicity.

Clark Atlanta University, School of Arts and Sciences, Department of Sociology, Atlanta, GA 30314. Offers MA. Part-time programs available. *Faculty:* 2 full-time (1 woman). *Students:* 4 full-time (2 women); all minorities (all African Americans). Average age 26. 5 applicants, 80% accepted, 2 enrolled. In 2009, 1 master's awarded. *Degree requirements:* For master's, one foreign language, comprehensive exam, thesis. *Entrance requirements:* For master's, GRE General Test, minimum GPA of 2.5. Additional exam requirements/recommendations for international students: Required—TOEFL (minimum score 500 paper-based; 173 computer-based). *Application deadline:* For fall admission, 4/1 for domestic and international students; for spring admission, 11/1 for domestic and international students. Applications are processed on a rolling basis. Application fee: $40 ($55 for international students). Electronic applications accepted. *Expenses:* Tuition: Full-time $12,240; part-time $680 per credit hour. Required fees: $710; $355 per semester. *Financial support:* Scholarships/grants and unspecified assistantships available. Financial award application deadline: 4/30; financial award applicants required to submit FAFSA. *Faculty research:* Gerontology, geriatric education. *Unit head:* Dr. Sandra Taylor, Chairperson, 404-880-8681, E-mail: staylor@cau.edu. *Application contact:* Michelle Clark-Davis, Graduate Program Admissions, 404-880-6605, E-mail: cauadmissions@cau.edu.

Clemson University, Graduate School, College of Business and Behavioral Science, Department of Sociology and Anthropology, Clemson, SC 29634. Offers applied sociology (MS). Part-time programs available. *Faculty:* 15 full-time (10 women). *Students:* 12 full-time (9 women), 7 part-time (5 women); includes 3 minority (1 African American, 1 Asian American or Pacific Islander, 1 Hispanic American), 4 international. Average age 25. 14 applicants, 71% accepted, 6 enrolled. In 2009, 4 master's awarded. *Degree requirements:* For master's, thesis. *Entrance requirements:* For master's, GRE General Test, minimum GPA of 3.0. Additional exam requirements/recommendations for international students: Required—TOEFL. *Application deadline:* For fall admission, 3/15 priority date for domestic students. Applications are processed on a rolling basis. Application fee: $70 ($80 for international students). Electronic applications accepted. *Expenses:* Contact institution. *Financial support:* In 2009–10, 9 students received support, including 8 teaching assistantships with partial tuition reimbursements available (averaging $10,000 per year); fellowships with full and partial tuition reimbursements available, research assistantships with partial tuition reimbursements available, career-related internships or fieldwork, institutionally sponsored loans, scholarships/grants, health care benefits, and unspecified assistantships also available. Support available to part-time students. Financial award application deadline: 3/15; financial award applicants required to submit FAFSA. *Faculty research:* Organizational and industrial sociology, inequality, sexual abuse and police-community relations, homelessness, emotions. Total annual research expenditures: $133,073. *Unit head:* Dr. Kinly Sturkie, Chair, 864-656-3820, E-mail: dkstr@clemson.edu. *Application contact:* Dr. Brenda Vander Mey, Graduate Coordinator, 864-656-3821, Fax: 864-656-1252, E-mail: vanmey@clemson.edu.

Cleveland State University, College of Graduate Studies, College of Liberal Arts and Social Sciences, Department of Sociology, Cleveland, OH 44115. Offers MA. Part-time and evening/weekend programs available. *Entrance requirements:* For master's, minimum GPA of 3.0. Additional exam requirements/recommendations for international students: Required—TOEFL (minimum score 525 paper-based; 197 computer-based). Electronic applications accepted. *Faculty research:* Criminology, research methods, theory, symbolic interaction.

Colorado State University, Graduate School, College of Liberal Arts, Department of Sociology, Fort Collins, CO 80523-1784. Offers MA, PhD. *Faculty:* 14 full-time (5 women). *Students:* 20 full-time (9 women), 21 part-time (13 women); includes 2 minority (1 Asian American or Pacific Islander, 1 Hispanic American), 1 international. Average age 33. 47 applicants, 28% accepted, 8 enrolled. In 2009, 3 master's, 1 doctorate awarded. *Degree requirements:* For master's, variable foreign language requirement, comprehensive exam (for some programs), thesis (for some programs); for doctorate, variable foreign language requirement, comprehensive exam, thesis/dissertation (for some programs). *Entrance requirements:* For master's, GRE General Test, minimum GPA of 3.0; BA coursework in sociology, letters of recommendation; for doctorate, GRE General Test, minimum GPA of 3.0; BA, MA coursework in sociology, letters of recommendation, statement of purpose. Additional exam requirements/recommendations for international students: Required—TOEFL (minimum score 550 paper-based; 220 computer-based). *Application deadline:* For fall admission, 1/15 priority date for domestic and international students. Applications are processed on a rolling basis. Application fee: $50. Electronic applications accepted. *Expenses:* Tuition, state resident: full-time $6434; part-time $359.10 per credit. Tuition, nonresident: full-time $18,116; part-time $1006.45 per credit. Required fees: $1496; $83 per credit. *Financial support:* In 2009–10, 26 students received support, including 4 research assistantships (averaging $12,670 per year), 22 teaching assistantships (averaging $12,084 per year); career-related internships or fieldwork, Federal Work-Study, institutionally sponsored loans, scholarships/grants, traineeships, and unspecified assistantships also available. Financial award application deadline: 3/1; financial award applicants required to submit FAFSA. *Faculty research:* Sociology policy analysis, environmental impact, criminology, community development, rural and natural resources. Total annual research expenditures: $221,854. *Unit head:* Dr. Jack Brouillette, Chairman, 970-491-6805, Fax: 970-491-2191, E-mail: jack.brouillette@colostate.edu. *Application contact:* Betty Burkett, Administrative Assistant, 970-491-6044, Fax: 970-491-2191, E-mail: elizabeth.burkett@colostate.edu.

Columbia University, Graduate School of Arts and Sciences, Division of Social Sciences, Department of Sociology, New York, NY 10027. Offers M Phil, MA, PhD, JD/MA, JD/PhD. *Degree requirements:* For master's, 2 research papers; for doctorate, one foreign language, thesis/dissertation. *Entrance requirements:* For master's and doctorate, GRE General Test. Additional exam requirements/recommendations for international students: Required—TOEFL. *Faculty research:* Urban and political studies, sociology of knowledge, organizations.

Concordia University, School of Graduate Studies, Faculty of Arts and Science, Department of Sociology and Anthropology, Montréal, QC H3G 1M8, Canada. Offers social and cultural anthropology (MA); sociology (MA). *Degree requirements:* For master's, comprehensive exam or thesis. *Entrance requirements:* For master's, honors degree in sociology or equivalent. *Faculty research:* Community and ethnic relations, popular culture, regional development in Canada, industrial and social movements, social problems and policies.

Cornell University, Graduate School, Graduate Fields of Agriculture and Life Sciences, Field of Development Sociology, Ithaca, NY 14853-0001. Offers community and regional society (MS); community and regional sociology (MPS, PhD); methods of social research (MPS, MS, PhD); population and development (MPS, MS, PhD); rural and environmental sociology (MPS, MS, PhD); state, economy, and society (MPS, MS, PhD). *Faculty:* 23 full-time (6 women). *Students:* 44 full-time (29 women); includes 6 minority (1 African American, 2 American Indian/Alaska Native, 2 Asian Americans or Pacific Islanders, 1 Hispanic American), 16 international. Average age 34. 59 applicants, 19% accepted, 7 enrolled. In 2009, 4 master's, 4 doctorates awarded. *Degree requirements:* For doctorate, comprehensive exam, thesis/dissertation. *Entrance requirements:* For master's and doctorate, GRE General Test, 3 letters of recommendation. Additional exam requirements/recommendations for international students: Required—TOEFL (minimum score 550 paper-based; 213 computer-based; 77 iBT). *Application deadline:* For fall admission, 1/15 priority date for domestic students. Application fee: $60. Electronic applications accepted. *Expenses:* Tuition: Full-time $29,500. Required fees: $70. Full-time tuition and fees vary according to degree level, program and student level. *Financial support:* In 2009–10, 25 students received support, including 2 fellowships with full tuition reimbursements available, 1 research assistantship with full tuition reimbursement available, 1 teaching assistantship with full tuition reimbursement available; institutionally sponsored loans, scholarships/grants, health care benefits, tuition waivers (full and partial), and unspecified assistantships also available. Financial award applicants required to submit FAFSA. *Faculty research:* Demography (population and development), environmental sociology, international and rural community development, political economy and ecology, sustainable agriculture. *Unit head:* Director of Graduate Studies, 607-255-3092, Fax: 607-254-2896. *Application contact:* Graduate Field Assistant, 607-255-3092, Fax: 607-254-2896, E-mail: devsoc@cornell.edu.

Cornell University, Graduate School, Graduate Fields of Arts and Sciences, Field of Sociology, Ithaca, NY 14853-0001. Offers economy and society (MA, PhD); gender and life course (MA, PhD); methodology (MA, PhD); organizations (MA, PhD); policy analysis (MA, PhD); political sociology/social movements (MA, PhD); racial and ethnic relations (MA, PhD); social networks (MA, PhD); social psychology (MA, PhD); social stratification (MA, PhD). *Faculty:* 41 full-time (17 women). *Students:* 39 full-time (19 women); includes 4 minority (all Asian Americans or Pacific Islanders), 10 international. Average age 31. 153 applicants, 8% accepted, 7 enrolled. In 2009, 2 master's, 2 doctorates awarded. Terminal master's awarded for partial completion of doctoral program. *Degree requirements:* For master's, thesis; for doctorate, thesis/dissertation, 1 year of teaching experience. *Entrance requirements:* For master's and doctorate, GRE General Test, 2 letters of recommendation, writing sample. Additional exam requirements/recommendations for international students: Required—TOEFL (minimum score 550 paper-based; 213 computer-based; 77 iBT). *Application deadline:* For fall admission, 1/15 for domestic students. Application fee: $70. Electronic applications accepted. *Expenses:* Tuition: Full-time $29,500. Required fees: $70. Full-time tuition and fees vary according to degree level, program and student level. *Financial support:* In 2009–10, 32 students received support, including 6 fellowships with full tuition reimbursements available; research assistantships with full tuition reimbursements available, teaching assistantships with full tuition reimbursements available, institutionally sponsored loans, scholarships/grants, health care benefits, tuition waivers (full and partial), and unspecified assistantships also available. Financial award applicants required to submit FAFSA. *Faculty research:* Comparative societal analysis, work and family, simulations, social class and mobility, racial segregation and inequality. *Unit head:* Director of Graduate Studies, 607-255-4266. *Application contact:* Graduate Field Assistant, 607-255-4266, E-mail: sociology@cornell.edu.

Dalhousie University, Faculty of Arts and Social Science, Department of Sociology and Social Anthropology, Halifax, NS B3H 4R2, Canada. Offers social anthropology (MA, PhD); sociology (MA, PhD). In 2009, 8 master's awarded. *Entrance requirements:* Additional exam requirements/recommendations for international students: Required—TOEFL, IELTS, CANTEST, CAEL, or Michigan English Language Assessment Battery. *Application deadline:* For fall admission, 6/1 for domestic students, 4/1 for international students; for winter admission, 10/31 for domestic students, 8/31 for international students; for spring admission, 2/28 for domestic students, 12/31 for international students. Application fee: $70. Electronic applications accepted. *Financial support:* Career-related internships or fieldwork, scholarships/grants, and health care benefits available. *Faculty research:* Social inequality and social injustice; work, industry, and development (regional and international perspectives); health and illness. *Unit head:* Dr. Emma Whelan, Graduate Coordinator, 902-494-6752, Fax: 902-494-2897, E-mail: sosagrad@dal.ca. *Application contact:* Rachelle Fox, Graduate Administrator, 902-494-6593, Fax: 902-494-2897, E-mail: sosagrad@is.dal.ca.

DePaul University, College of Liberal Arts and Sciences, Department of Sociology, Chicago, IL 60614. Offers MA. Part-time and evening/weekend programs available. *Faculty:* 21 full-time (12 women), 4 part-time/adjunct (2 women). *Students:* 43 full-time (34 women), 35 part-time (22 women); includes 33 minority (20 African Americans, 6 Asian Americans or Pacific Islanders, 7 Hispanic Americans), 1 international. Average age 28. 44 applicants, 84% accepted, 30 enrolled. In 2009, 17 master's awarded. *Degree requirements:* For master's, thesis or alternative, essay, research project. *Entrance requirements:* Additional exam requirements/recommendations for international students: Required—TOEFL. *Application deadline:* For fall admission, 8/25 priority date for domestic students; for winter admission, 12/15 priority date for domestic students; for spring admission, 3/15 priority date for domestic students. Applications are processed on a rolling basis. Application fee: $25. Electronic applications accepted. *Expenses:* Tuition: Full-time $37,525; part-time $620 per credit hour. *Financial support:* In 2009–10, 8 students received support, including 1 research assistantship with full tuition reimbursement available (averaging $7,000 per year); career-related internships or fieldwork, tuition waivers (partial), and tuition remissions also available. Financial award application deadline: 6/15. *Faculty research:* Law and society, urban sociology, race/ethnicity, health, social inequality. *Unit head:* Dr. Roberta Garner, Chairperson, 773-325-7823, Fax: 773-325-7821, E-mail: rgarner@depaul.edu. *Application contact:* Dr. Shu-Ju Ada Cheng, Graduate Program Director, 773-325-4856, Fax: 773-325-7821, E-mail: scheng1@depaul.edu.

Duke University, Graduate School, Department of Sociology, Durham, NC 27708. Offers AM, PhD. *Faculty:* 20 full-time. *Students:* 49 full-time (27 women); includes 10 minority (4 African Americans, 1 Asian American or Pacific Islander, 5 Hispanic Americans), 11 international. 138 applicants, 9% accepted, 6 enrolled. In 2009, 8 master's, 6 doctorates awarded. Terminal master's awarded for partial completion of doctoral program. *Degree requirements:* For doctorate, thesis/dissertation. *Entrance requirements:* For master's and doctorate, GRE General Test. Additional exam requirements/recommendations for international students: Required—TOEFL (minimum score 550 paper-based; 213 computer-based; 83 iBT), IELTS (minimum score 7). *Application deadline:* For fall admission, 12/8 priority date for domestic and international students. Application fee: $75. Electronic applications accepted. *Financial support:* Fellowships, research assistantships, teaching assistantships, Federal Work-Study available. Financial award application deadline: 12/31. *Unit head:* Moody James, Director of Graduate Studies, 919-660-5650, Fax: 919-660-5623, E-mail: jmoody77@soc.duke.edu. *Application contact:* Cynthia Robertson, Associate Dean for Enrollment Services, 919-684-3913, E-mail: grad-admissions@duke.edu.

East Carolina University, Graduate School, Thomas Harriot College of Arts and Sciences, Department of Sociology, Greenville, NC 27858-4353. Offers MA. Part-time and evening/weekend programs available. *Degree requirements:* For master's, one foreign language, comprehensive exam, thesis. *Entrance requirements:* For master's, GRE General Test. Additional exam requirements/recommendations for international students: Required—TOEFL.

Eastern Michigan University, Graduate School, College of Arts and Sciences, Department of Sociology, Anthropology and Criminology, Programs in Sociology, Ypsilanti, MI 48197. Offers schools, society and violence (MA); sociology (MA); sociology—family specialty (MA). *Students:* 6 full-time (4 women), 14 part-time (11 women); includes 9 minority (7 African Americans, 2 Hispanic Americans), 1 international. Average age 31. In 2009, 6 master's awarded. Application fee: $35. Tuition and fees vary according to course level. *Application contact:* Dr. Robert Orrange, Advisor, 734-487-0012, Fax: 734-487-9666, E-mail: rorrange@emich.edu.

East Tennessee State University, School of Graduate Studies, College of Arts and Sciences, Department of Sociology and Anthropology, Johnson City, TN 37614. Offers applied sociology (MA); general sociology (MA). Part-time and evening/weekend programs available. *Degree requirements:* For master's, comprehensive exam, thesis or alternative, internship. *Entrance requirements:* For master's, GRE General Test, minimum GPA of 3.0 in major. Additional exam requirements/recommendations for international students: Required—TOEFL (minimum score 550 paper-based; 213 computer-based). *Faculty research:* Biosociology and sex differences, political change in Latin America, medical beliefs and practices in southern Appalachia, Scottish-Irish traditions and Appalachia culture.

Emory University, Graduate School of Arts and Sciences, Department of Sociology, Atlanta, GA 30322-1100. Offers MA, PhD. Terminal master's awarded for partial completion of doctoral program. *Degree requirements:* For master's, thesis optional; for doctorate, comprehensive exam, thesis/dissertation, 2 preliminary exams, research paper, paper presentation. *Entrance requirements:* For doctorate, GRE General Test, minimum GPA of 3.0. Additional exam requirements/recommendations for international students: Required—TOEFL. Electronic applications accepted. *Faculty research:* Political economy and global analysis, culture, social psychology, criminology, stratification.

Fayetteville State University, Graduate School, Program in Sociology, Fayetteville, NC 28301-4298. Offers MA. Part-time and evening/weekend programs available. *Faculty:* 4 full-time (1 woman). *Students:* 8 part-time (7 women); includes 6 minority (all African Americans). Average age 35. In 2009, 2 master's awarded. *Degree requirements:* For master's, comprehensive exam, internship. *Application deadline:* For fall admission, 4/15 for domestic students; for spring admission, 10/15 for domestic students. Applications are processed on a rolling basis. Application fee: $35. Electronic applications accepted. *Unit head:* Dr. Kwaku Twumasi-Ankrah, Chairperson, 910-672-1122, E-mail: kankrah@uncfsu.edu. *Application contact:* Katrina Hoffman, Associate Vice-Chancellor for Enrollment Management, 910-672-1374, Fax: 910-672-1470, E-mail: khoffma1@uncfsu.edu.

Florida Agricultural and Mechanical University, Division of Graduate Studies, Research, and Continuing Education, College of Arts and Sciences, Division of History and Political Sciences, Program in Applied Social Science, Tallahassee, FL 32307-3200. Offers African American history (MASS); criminal justice (MASS); economics (MASS); history (MASS); political science (MASS); public administration (MASS); public management (MASS); social work (MASS); sociology (MASS). Part-time programs available. *Faculty:* 17 full-time (2 women). *Students:* 54 full-time (42 women), 4 part-time (2 women); includes 57 minority (all African Americans). In 2009, 14 master's awarded. *Degree requirements:* For master's, thesis optional. *Entrance requirements:* For master's, GRE General Test, minimum GPA of 3.0. *Application deadline:* For fall admission, 5/18 for domestic students, 12/18 for international students; for spring admission, 11/12 for domestic students, 5/12 for international students. Application fee: $20. *Financial support:* Fellowships, research assistantships, career-related internships or fieldwork, Federal Work-Study, and tuition waivers (full) available. Financial award application deadline: 4/1. *Faculty research:* Southern history, black history, election trends, presidential history. *Unit head:* Dr. Gary Paul, Director, 850-599-3447. *Application contact:* Dr. Chanta M. Haywood, Dean of Graduate Studies, Research, and Continuing Education, 850-599-3315, Fax: 850-599-3727.

Florida Atlantic University, Dorothy F. Schmidt College of Arts and Letters, Department of Sociology, Boca Raton, FL 33431-0991. Offers MA. Part-time and evening/weekend programs available. *Faculty:* 15 full-time (8 women), 3 part-time/adjunct (1 woman). *Students:* 11 full-time (7 women), 5 part-time (4 women); includes 2 minority (1 African American, 1 Hispanic American). Average age 30. 18 applicants, 44% accepted, 2 enrolled. In 2009, 10 master's awarded. *Degree requirements:* For master's, thesis optional. *Entrance requirements:* For master's, GRE General Test, minimum GPA of 3.0. Additional exam requirements/recommendations for international students: Required—TOEFL. *Application deadline:* For fall admission, 5/1 priority date for domestic and international students. Applications are processed on a rolling basis. Application fee: $30. Electronic applications accepted. *Expenses:* Tuition, state resident: full-time $7055; part-time $293.94 per credit hour. Tuition, nonresident: full-time $22,096; part-time $920.66 per credit hour. *Financial support:* Teaching assistantships with tuition reimbursements, Federal Work-Study available. *Faculty research:* Gender/race/class, globalization, theory, social control, social movements. *Unit head:* Dr. Farshad A. Araghi, Chair and Associate Professor, 561-297-0261, Fax: 561-297-2511, E-mail: araghi@fau.edu. *Application contact:* Dr. Ann Branaman, Associate Professor, 561-297-3278, Fax: 561-297-2511, E-mail: branaman@fau.edu.

Florida International University, College of Arts and Sciences, Department of Global and Sociocultural Studies, Miami, FL 33199. Offers comparative sociology (MA, PhD). Part-time and evening/weekend programs available. *Faculty:* 22 full-time (12 women), 1 part-time/adjunct (0 women). *Students:* 28 full-time (22 women), 21 part-time (17 women); includes 20 minority (7 African Americans, 1 American Indian/Alaska Native, 12 Hispanic Americans), 10 international. Average age 30. 39 applicants, 38% accepted, 15 enrolled. In 2009, 12 master's, 3 doctorates awarded. *Degree requirements:* For master's, thesis; for doctorate, comprehensive exam, thesis/dissertation. *Entrance requirements:* For master's, GRE General Test, 3 letters of recommendation; minimum undergraduate GPA of 3.25, 3.5 GPA on any previous graduate work; written examples of academic or other relevant professional work; for doctorate, GRE General Test, Letter of intent, 3 letters of recommendation; minimum undergraduate GPA of 3.25, 3.5 GPA on any previous graduate work; Written examples of academic or other relevant professional work. Additional exam requirements/recommendations for international students: Required—TOEFL (minimum score 550 paper-based; 80 iBT). *Application deadline:* For fall admission, 6/1 for domestic students, 4/1 for international students; for spring admission, 10/1 for domestic students, 9/1 for international students. Applications are processed on a rolling basis. Application fee: $30. Electronic applications accepted. *Expenses:* Tuition, state resident: full-time $8008; part-time $4004 per year. Tuition, nonresident: full-time $20,104; part-time $10,052 per year. Required fees: $298; $149 per term. *Financial support:* Institutionally sponsored loans and scholarships/grants available. Financial award application deadline: 3/1; financial award applicants required to submit FAFSA. *Unit head:* Dr. Rod Neumann, Chair, 305-348-2247, Fax: 305-348-3605, E-mail: roderick.neumann@fiu.edu. *Application contact:* Dr. Kathleen Martin, Graduate Program Director, 305-348-2247, Fax: 305-348-7441, E-mail: kathleen.martin@fiu.edu.

Florida State University, The Graduate School, College of Social Sciences and Public Policy, Department of Sociology, Tallahassee, FL 32306. Offers MA, MS, PhD. *Faculty:* 21 full-time (10 women). *Students:* 47 full-time (30 women), 16 part-time (11 women); includes 12 minority (7 African Americans, 1 American Indian/Alaska Native, 1 Asian American or Pacific Islander, 3 Hispanic Americans), 4 international. Average age 27. 55 applicants, 36% accepted, 12 enrolled. In 2009, 8 master's, 5 doctorates awarded. *Degree requirements:* For doctorate, comprehensive exam, thesis/dissertation. *Entrance requirements:* For master's and doctorate, GRE General Test, minimum GPA of 3.0. Additional exam requirements/recommendations for international students: Required—TOEFL (minimum score 550 paper-based; 213 computer-based). *Application deadline:* For fall admission, 1/10 priority date for domestic students. Applications are processed on a rolling basis. Application fee: $30. Electronic applications accepted. *Expenses:* Tuition, state resident: full-time $7413. Tuition, nonresident: full-time $22,567. *Financial support:* In 2009–10, 43 students received support, including 5 fellowships with full tuition reimbursements available (averaging $17,700 per year), 6 research assistantships with full tuition reimbursements available (averaging $14,000 per year), 35 teaching assistantships with full tuition reimbursements available (averaging $14,000 per year);

Sociology

Florida State University (continued)

institutionally sponsored loans, scholarships/grants, health care benefits, and unspecified assistantships also available. Financial award application deadline: 1/10; financial award applicants required to submit FAFSA. *Faculty research:* Inequality (gender/race), demography, social psychology, health and aging. Total annual research expenditures: $249,000. *Unit head:* Dr. Isaac Eberstein, Chair, 850-644-6416, Fax: 850-644-6208, E-mail: ieberstn@fsu.edu. *Application contact:* Dr. John Taylor, Graduate Program Director, 850-644-7109, Fax: 850-644-6208, E-mail: jrtaylor@fsu.edu.

Fordham University, Graduate School of Arts and Sciences, Department of Sociology, New York, NY 10458. Offers MA. Part-time and evening/weekend programs available. *Faculty:* 21 full-time (10 women). *Students:* 8 full-time (5 women), 22 part-time (11 women); includes 7 minority (4 African Americans, 3 Hispanic Americans), 2 international. Average age 35. 25 applicants, 64% accepted, 4 enrolled. In 2009, 3 master's awarded. Terminal master's awarded for partial completion of doctoral program. *Degree requirements:* For master's, comprehensive exam. *Entrance requirements:* For master's, GRE General Test. Additional exam requirements/recommendations for international students: Required—TOEFL (minimum score 600 paper-based; 250 computer-based). *Application deadline:* For fall admission, 1/4 priority date for domestic students; for spring admission, 11/1 for domestic students. Application fee: $70. Electronic applications accepted. *Financial support:* In 2009–10, 8 students received support, including 2 fellowships with tuition reimbursements available (averaging $19,600 per year), 6 research assistantships with tuition reimbursements available (averaging $18,400 per year); career-related internships or fieldwork, Federal Work-Study, institutionally sponsored loans, tuition waivers (full and partial), and unspecified assistantships also available. Financial award application deadline: 1/4; financial award applicants required to submit FAFSA. *Faculty research:* Social demography, immigration, crime and deviance, religion. *Unit head:* Dr. Greta Gilbertson, Acting Chair, 718-817-3850, Fax: 718-817-3846, E-mail: gilbertson@fordham.edu. *Application contact:* Charlene Dundie, Director of Graduate Admissions, 718-817-4420, Fax: 718-817-3566, E-mail: dundie@fordham.edu.

George Mason University, College of Humanities and Social Sciences, Department of Sociology and Anthropology, Fairfax, VA 22030. Offers anthropology (MA); sociology (MA, PhD). *Faculty:* 26 full-time (12 women), 7 part-time/adjunct (4 women). *Students:* 23 full-time (16 women), 69 part-time (51 women); includes 17 minority (8 African Americans, 2 Asian Americans or Pacific Islanders, 7 Hispanic Americans), 2 international. Average age 32. 87 applicants, 57% accepted, 24 enrolled. In 2009, 5 master's awarded. *Degree requirements:* For master's, thesis; for doctorate, comprehensive exam, thesis/dissertation. *Entrance requirements:* For doctorate, GRE. Additional exam requirements/recommendations for international students: Required—TOEFL. *Application deadline:* For fall admission, 3/1 priority date for domestic students; for spring admission, 10/1 for domestic students. Applications are processed on a rolling basis. Application fee: $75. Electronic applications accepted. *Expenses:* Tuition, state resident: full-time $7568; part-time $315.33 per credit hour. Tuition, nonresident: full-time $21,704; part-time $904.33 per credit hour. Required fees: $2184; $91 per credit hour. *Financial support:* In 2009–10, 15 students received support, including 2 fellowships with full tuition reimbursements available (averaging $18,000 per year), 4 research assistantships with full and partial tuition reimbursements available (averaging $13,219 per year), 10 teaching assistantships with full and partial tuition reimbursements available (averaging $6,018 per year); Federal Work-Study, scholarships/grants, unspecified assistantships, and health care benefits (full-time research or teaching assistantship recipients) also available. Support available to part-time students. Financial award application deadline: 3/1. *Faculty research:* Africa, American teenagers, black entrepreneur, human rights, gambling. Total annual research expenditures: $59,230. *Unit head:* Dr. Susan Trencher, Chair, 703-993-1429, E-mail: strenche@gmu.edu. *Application contact:* Amy Best, Associate Professor/Graduate Coordinator, 703-993-1426, E-mail: abest@gmu.edu.

The George Washington University, Columbian College of Arts and Sciences, Department of Sociology, Washington, DC 20052. Offers criminology (MA); sociology (MA). Part-time and evening/weekend programs available. *Faculty:* 11 full-time (7 women), 27 part-time/adjunct (11 women). *Students:* 14 full-time (11 women), 11 part-time (9 women); includes 6 minority (1 African American, 1 American Indian/Alaska Native, 1 Asian American or Pacific Islander, 3 Hispanic Americans), 1 international. Average age 26. 36 applicants, 50% accepted, 9 enrolled. In 2009, 8 master's awarded. *Degree requirements:* For master's, comprehensive exam, thesis or alternative. *Entrance requirements:* For master's, GRE General Test, minimum GPA of 3.0. Additional exam requirements/recommendations for international students: Required—TOEFL (minimum score 550 paper-based; 213 computer-based; 80 iBT). *Application deadline:* For fall admission, 6/1 priority date for domestic students, 1/15 priority date for international students; for spring admission, 11/1 priority date for domestic students, 9/1 priority date for international students. Applications are processed on a rolling basis. Application fee: $60. Electronic applications accepted. *Financial support:* In 2009–10, 7 students received support; fellowships with full tuition reimbursements available, teaching assistantships with tuition reimbursements available, career-related internships or fieldwork, Federal Work-Study, and tuition waivers available. Financial award application deadline: 1/15. *Unit head:* Dr. Steven Tuch, Chair, 202-994-7466, E-mail: steven.tuch@gwu.edu. *Application contact:* Information Contact, 202-994-6345, Fax: 202-994-3239, E-mail: soc@gwu.edu.

Georgia Southern University, Jack N. Averitt College of Graduate Studies, College of Liberal Arts and Social Sciences, Department of Sociology and Anthropology, Statesboro, GA 30460. Offers MA. Part-time and evening/weekend programs available. *Students:* 18 full-time (9 women), 10 part-time (5 women); includes 6 minority (3 African Americans, 1 American Indian/Alaska Native, 2 Hispanic Americans). Average age 30. 17 applicants, 94% accepted, 11 enrolled. In 2009, 14 master's awarded. *Degree requirements:* For master's, thesis optional. *Entrance requirements:* For master's, GRE General Test. Additional exam requirements/recommendations for international students: Required—TOEFL (minimum score 550 paper-based; 213 computer-based; 80 iBT). *Application deadline:* For fall admission, 3/1 priority date for domestic and international students; for spring admission, 10/1 priority date for domestic students, 10/1 for international students. Applications are processed on a rolling basis. Application fee: $50. Electronic applications accepted. *Expenses:* Tuition, state resident: full-time $5040; part-time $210 per credit hour. Tuition, nonresident: full-time $20,136; part-time $839 per credit hour. Required fees: $1644. *Financial support:* In 2009–10, 23 students received support, including research assistantships with partial tuition reimbursements available (averaging $7,200 per year), teaching assistantships with partial tuition reimbursements available (averaging $7,200 per year); career-related internships or fieldwork, Federal Work-Study, scholarships/grants, tuition waivers (partial), and unspecified assistantships also available. Support available to part-time students. Financial award application deadline: 4/15; financial award applicants required to submit FAFSA. *Faculty research:* Compliance archeology, cultural anthropology, historical interpretation, international relations, sociological practice, social psychology. *Unit head:* Dr. Peggy Hargis, Chair, 912-478-5443, Fax: 912-478-0703, E-mail: har_agga@georgiasouthern.edu. *Application contact:* Dr. Charles Ziglar, Coordinator for Graduate Student Recruitment, 912-478-5635, Fax: 912-478-0740, E-mail: gradadmissions@georgiasouthern.edu.

Georgia State University, College of Arts and Sciences, Department of Sociology, Atlanta, GA 30302-3083. Offers MA, PhD. Part-time and evening/weekend programs available. Terminal master's awarded for partial completion of doctoral program. *Degree requirements:* For master's, thesis; for doctorate, comprehensive exam, thesis/dissertation. *Entrance requirements:* For master's, GRE General Test, departmental supplemental form, letters of recommendation; for doctorate, GRE General Test, departmental supplemental form, writing sample, letters of recommendation. Additional exam requirements/recommendations for international students: Required—TOEFL. Electronic applications accepted. *Faculty research:* Family, health, and life course; gender and sexuality; race and urban studies.

Graduate School and University Center of the City University of New York, Graduate Studies, Program in Sociology, New York, NY 10016-4039. Offers PhD. *Faculty:* 69 full-time (15 women). *Students:* 155 full-time (96 women), 2 part-time (1 woman); includes 26 minority (12 African Americans, 1 American Indian/Alaska Native, 7 Asian Americans or Pacific Islanders, 6 Hispanic Americans), 23 international. Average age 34. 142 applicants, 46% accepted, 23 enrolled. In 2009, 13 doctorates awarded. *Degree requirements:* For doctorate, one foreign language, thesis/dissertation. *Entrance requirements:* For doctorate, GRE General Test, writing sample. Additional exam requirements/recommendations for international students: Required—TOEFL. *Application deadline:* For fall admission, 12/15 for domestic students. Application fee: $125. Electronic applications accepted. *Financial support:* In 2009–10, 129 students received support, including 98 fellowships, 13 research assistantships, 8 teaching assistantships; career-related internships or fieldwork, Federal Work-Study, institutionally sponsored loans, and tuition waivers (full and partial) also available. Financial award application deadline: 2/1; financial award applicants required to submit FAFSA. *Unit head:* Dr. Philip Kasinitz, Executive Officer, 212-817-8783, Fax: 212-817-1536, E-mail: pkasinitz@gc.cuny.edu. *Application contact:* Les Gribben, Director of Admissions, 212-817-7470, Fax: 212-817-1624, E-mail: lgribben@gc.cuny.edu.

Harvard University, Graduate School of Arts and Sciences, Department of Sociology, Cambridge, MA 02138. Offers PhD. *Degree requirements:* For doctorate, thesis/dissertation, oral exams in 2 subfields. *Entrance requirements:* For doctorate, GRE General Test. Additional exam requirements/recommendations for international students: Required—TOEFL. *Expenses:* Tuition: Full-time $33,696. Required fees: $1126. Full-time tuition and fees vary according to program. *Faculty research:* Sociological theory, political theories, quantitative approaches to methodology.

Hofstra University, College of Liberal Arts and Sciences, Department of Sociology, Hempstead, NY 11549. Offers applied social research and policy analysis (MA). Part-time and evening/weekend programs available. *Faculty:* 6 full-time (3 women). *Students:* 7 full-time (5 women); includes 2 minority (both African Americans), 2 international. Average age 26. 5 applicants, 100% accepted, 3 enrolled. *Degree requirements:* For master's, comprehensive exam, thesis optional, internship. *Entrance requirements:* For master's, GRE, interview, minimum GPA of 3.0. Additional exam requirements/recommendations for international students: Required—TOEFL (minimum score 550 paper-based; 213 computer-based; 80 iBT). *Application deadline:* Applications are processed on a rolling basis. Application fee: $60. Electronic applications accepted. *Expenses:* Tuition: Full-time $16,200; part-time $900 per credit hour. Required fees: $970; $145 per term. Tuition and fees vary according to program. *Financial support:* In 2009–10, 5 students received support, including 2 fellowships with full and partial tuition reimbursements available (averaging $2,500 per year), 3 research assistantships with full and partial tuition reimbursements available (averaging $7,231 per year); Federal Work-Study, institutionally sponsored loans, scholarships/grants, tuition waivers (full and partial), and unspecified assistantships also available. Support available to part-time students. Financial award applicants required to submit FAFSA. *Faculty research:* Housing policy, immigration, labor economic policy, education policy, health care policy. Total annual research expenditures: $100,000. *Unit head:* Dr. Marc Silver, Program Director, 516-463-5640, Fax: 516-463-6250, E-mail: socmls@hofstra.edu. *Application contact:* Carol Drummer, Dean of Graduate Admissions, 516-463-4876, Fax: 516-463-4664, E-mail: gradstudent@hofstra.edu.

Howard University, Graduate School, Department of Health, Human Performance and Leisure Studies, Washington, DC 20059-0002. Offers exercise physiology (MS); health education (MS); sports studies (MS), including sociology of sports, sports management; urban recreation (MS), including leisure studies. Part-time and evening/weekend programs available. *Degree requirements:* For master's, comprehensive exam, thesis. *Entrance requirements:* For master's, BS in human performance or related field. Electronic applications accepted. *Faculty research:* Health promotion, cardiovascular hypertension, physical activity, sport and human rights issues.

Howard University, Graduate School, Department of Sociology and Anthropology, Washington, DC 20059-0002. Offers sociology (MA, PhD). Part-time and evening/weekend programs available. *Degree requirements:* For master's, thesis; for doctorate, one foreign language, comprehensive exam, thesis/dissertation, RCR, writing exam. *Entrance requirements:* For master's, GRE General Test, minimum GPA of 3.0; for doctorate, GRE General Test, minimum GPA of 3.5. Additional exam requirements/recommendations for international students: Required—TOEFL. Electronic applications accepted. *Faculty research:* Medical sociology; criminology; race, class and gender; urban sociology.

Humboldt State University, Graduate Studies, College of Arts, Humanities, and Social Sciences, Department of Sociology, Arcata, CA 95521-8299. Offers MA. *Students:* 16 full-time (11 women), 7 part-time (2 women); includes 4 minority (1 African American, 1 American Indian/Alaska Native, 2 Hispanic Americans). Average age 33. 21 applicants, 81% accepted, 10 enrolled. In 2009, 7 master's awarded. *Degree requirements:* For master's, thesis or alternative, qualifying exam. *Entrance requirements:* For master's, minimum GPA of 2.5, 3 letters of recommendation. Additional exam requirements/recommendations for international students: Required—TOEFL (minimum score 500 paper-based; 173 computer-based). *Application deadline:* For fall admission, 3/15 for domestic students; for spring admission, 11/15 for domestic students. Applications are processed on a rolling basis. Application fee: $55. *Expenses:* Tuition, nonresident: full-time $8928. Required fees: $6102. Tuition and fees vary according to program. *Financial support:* Application deadline: 3/1. *Faculty research:* Sociology of women political activists, environmental dispute resolution, prosocial behavior. *Unit head:* Dr. Mary Virnoche, Chair, 707-826-4569, Fax: 707-826-4418, E-mail: mv23@humboldt.edu. *Application contact:* Dr. Jennifer Eichstedt, Coordinator, 707-826-4949, Fax: 707-826-4418, E-mail: jle7001@humboldt.edu.

Hunter College of the City University of New York, Graduate School, School of Arts and Sciences, Department of Sociology, New York, NY 10021-5085. Offers applied social research (MS). *Faculty:* 5 full-time (1 woman), 3 part-time/adjunct (2 women). *Students:* 12 full-time (7 women), 25 part-time (19 women); includes 5 minority (1 African American, 2 Asian Americans or Pacific Islanders, 2 Hispanic Americans). Average age 30. 28 applicants, 71% accepted, 14 enrolled. In 2009, 20 master's awarded. *Degree requirements:* For master's, internship. *Entrance requirements:* For master's, GRE General Test or GMAT, 3 credits of course work in statistics, 2 letters of recommendation. Additional exam requirements/recommendations for international students: Required—TOEFL. *Application deadline:* For fall admission, 4/1 for domestic students, 2/1 for international students; for spring admission, 11/1 for domestic students, 9/1 for international students. Application fee: $125. *Expenses:* Tuition, state resident: full-time $7360; part-time $310 per credit. Required fees: $250 per semester. *Financial support:* Federal Work-Study and tuition waivers (partial) available. Support available to part-time students. *Unit head:* Dr. Robert Perinbanayagaia, Chairperson, 212-772-5585, Fax: 212-772-5645, E-mail: rperinba@hunter.cuny.edu. *Application contact:* Dr. Joong-Hwan Oh, Graduate Adviser, 212-772-5643.

Idaho State University, Office of Graduate Studies, College of Arts and Sciences, Department of Sociology, Pocatello, ID 83209-8114. Offers MA. Part-time programs available. *Faculty:* 7 full-time (3 women). *Students:* 10 full-time (4 women), 7 part-time (4 women); includes 3 minority (2 African Americans, 1 Hispanic American), 1 international. Average age 36. *Degree requirements:* For master's, comprehensive exam, thesis, oral defense of thesis. *Entrance requirements:* For master's, GRE General Test (minimum 40th percentile in one of 3 sections), minimum undergraduate GPA of 3.0, 3 letters of recommendation. Additional exam requirements/recommendations for international students: Required—TOEFL (minimum score 550 paper-based; 213 computer-based; 80 iBT). *Application deadline:* For fall admission, 7/1 for domestic students, 6/1 for international students; for spring admission, 12/1 for domestic students, 11/1 for international students. Applications are processed on a rolling basis. Application fee: $55. Electronic applications accepted. *Expenses:* Tuition, state resident: full-time $3318; part-time $297 per credit hour. Tuition, nonresident: full-time $13,120; part-time $437 per credit hour. Required fees: $2530. Tuition and fees vary according to program. *Financial support:* In 2009–10, 1 research assistantship with full and partial tuition reimbursement (averaging $10,121 per year), 5 teaching assistantships with full and partial tuition reimbursements (averaging $10,841 per year) were awarded; career-related internships or fieldwork, Federal Work-Study, institutionally sponsored loans, scholarships/grants, health care benefits, tuition waivers (full and partial), and unspecified assistantships also available. Support available to part-time students. Financial award application deadline: 1/1; financial award applicants required to submit FAFSA. *Faculty research:* Terrorism, social organization, family social work. *Unit head:* Dr. Ann Hunter, Chairperson, 208-282-2170, Fax: 208-282-4733, E-mail: soccj@isu.edu. *Application contact:* Tami Carson, Graduate School Technical Records Specialist, 208-282-2150, Fax: 208-282-4847, E-mail: carstami@isu.edu.

Illinois State University, Graduate School, College of Arts and Sciences, Department of Sociology, Normal, IL 61790-2200. Offers historical archaeology (MA, MS); sociology (MA, MS). *Degree requirements:* For master's, thesis. *Entrance requirements:* For master's, GRE General Test, GRE Subject Test, minimum GPA of 2.4 in last 60 hours of course work. *Faculty research:* Japanese Saturday school (Kato).

Indiana University Bloomington, University Graduate School, College of Arts and Sciences, Department of Sociology, Bloomington, IN 47405-7000. Offers MA, PhD. *Faculty:* 18 full-time (9 women). *Students:* 91 full-time (55 women), 1 (woman) part-time; includes 23 minority (15 African Americans, 3 Asian Americans or Pacific Islanders, 5 Hispanic Americans), 8 international. Average age 29. 152 applicants, 13% accepted, 12 enrolled. In 2009, 10 master's, 7 doctorates awarded. Terminal master's awarded for partial completion of doctoral program. *Degree requirements:* For master's, thesis; for doctorate, comprehensive exam, thesis/dissertation. *Entrance requirements:* For master's and doctorate, GRE General Test. Additional exam requirements/recommendations for international students: Required—TOEFL. *Application deadline:* For fall admission, 1/15 for domestic students, 12/1 for international students. Application fee: $55 ($65 for international students). Electronic applications accepted. *Financial support:* In 2009–10, 74 students received support, including 13 fellowships with full tuition reimbursements available (averaging $17,500 per year), 5 research assistantships with full tuition reimbursements available (averaging $15,600 per year), 36 teaching assistantships with full tuition reimbursements available (averaging $13,470 per year); scholarships/grants, health care benefits, and unspecified assistantships also available. Financial award application deadline: 1/15; financial award applicants required to submit FAFSA. *Faculty research:* Social psychology, political sociology, sociological research methods, stratification/mobility, education. *Unit head:* Prof. Eliza Pavalko, Professor, 812-855-7629, Fax: 812-855-0781, E-mail: epavalko@indiana.edu. *Application contact:* Shana Bergen, Information Contact, 812-855-2924, E-mail: sbergen@indiana.edu.

Indiana University of Pennsylvania, School of Graduate Studies and Research, College of Humanities and Social Sciences, Department of Sociology, Program in Sociology, Indiana, PA 15705-1087. Offers MA. Part-time programs available. *Faculty:* 5 full-time (2 women). *Students:* 19 full-time (15 women), 4 part-time (2 women); includes 1 minority (Hispanic American). Average age 28. 21 applicants, 67% accepted, 11 enrolled. In 2009, 11 master's awarded. *Degree requirements:* For master's, thesis optional. *Entrance requirements:* For master's, GRE, 2 letters of recommendation. Additional exam requirements/recommendations for international students: Required—TOEFL. *Application deadline:* For fall admission, 7/1 priority date for domestic students; for spring admission, 11/1 for domestic students. Applications are processed on a rolling basis. Application fee: $40. *Expenses:* Tuition, state resident: full-time $6666; part-time $370 per credit hour. Tuition, nonresident: full-time $10,666; part-time $593 per credit hour. Required fees: $813 per semester. *Financial support:* In 2009–10, 9 research assistantships (averaging $5,421 per year) were awarded. Financial award application deadline: 3/15; financial award applicants required to submit FAFSA. *Unit head:* Dr. Valerie Gunter, Graduate Coordinator, 724-357-3931, E-mail: valeriegunter@iup.edu. *Application contact:* Dr. Valerie Gunter, Graduate Coordinator, 724-357-3931, E-mail: valeriegunter@iup.edu.

Indiana University–Purdue University Fort Wayne, College of Arts and Sciences, Department of Sociology, Fort Wayne, IN 46805-1499. Offers sociological practice (MA). Part-time programs available. *Faculty:* 10 full-time (3 women). *Students:* 11 part-time (7 women); includes 3 minority (all African Americans). Average age 37. 2 applicants, 100% accepted, 1 enrolled. In 2009, 1 master's awarded. *Degree requirements:* For master's, practicum. *Entrance requirements:* For master's, minimum GPA of 3.0, 3 letters of recommendation, essay, interview. Additional exam requirements/recommendations for international students: Required—TOEFL (minimum score 550 paper-based; 213 computer-based; 77 iBT). *Application deadline:* For fall admission, 8/1 for domestic students; for spring admission, 11/1 priority date for domestic students. Applications are processed on a rolling basis. Application fee: $50. *Expenses:* Tuition, state resident: full-time $4595; part-time $255 per credit. Tuition, nonresident: full-time $10,963; part-time $609 per credit. Required fees: $528; $29.35 per credit. Tuition and fees vary according to course load. *Financial support:* In 2009–10, 2 teaching assistantships with partial tuition reimbursements (averaging $12,740 per year) were awarded; scholarships/grants and unspecified assistantships also available. Support available to part-time students. Financial award application deadline: 3/1; financial award applicants required to submit FAFSA. *Faculty research:* Non-compliant youths, tattoo meanings, homelessness, globalization. *Unit head:* Dr. Peter Iadicola, Chair, 260-481-6572, Fax: 260-481-0474, E-mail: iadicola@ipfw.edu. *Application contact:* Dr. Anson Shupe, Graduate Program Director, 260-481-6667, Fax: 260-481-0474, E-mail: shupe@ipfw.edu.

Indiana University–Purdue University Indianapolis, School of Liberal Arts, Department of Sociology, Indianapolis, IN 46202-2896. Offers family/gender studies (MA); medical sociology (MA); work/occupations (MA). *Faculty:* 17 full-time (8 women). *Students:* 13 full-time (8 women), 10 part-time (8 women), 3 international. Average age 29. 26 applicants, 73% accepted, 12 enrolled. In 2009, 5 master's awarded. Application fee: $55 ($65 for international students). *Financial support:* In 2009–10, 2 fellowships (averaging $9,500 per year), 2 teaching assistantships (averaging $6,309 per year) were awarded. *Unit head:* Carrie Foote, Director of Graduate Studies, 317-274-8981, E-mail: sociology@iupui.edu. *Application contact:* Director of Research and Graduate Programs, 317-274-8305.

Iowa State University of Science and Technology, Graduate College, College of Liberal Arts and Sciences, Department of Sociology, Ames, IA 50011. Offers rural sociology (MS, PhD); sociology (MS, PhD). *Faculty:* 33 full-time (17 women). *Students:* 44 full-time (29 women), 24 part-time (15 women); includes 5 minority (2 African Americans, 2 Asian Americans or Pacific Islanders, 1 Hispanic American), 17 international. 39 applicants, 67% accepted, 4 enrolled. In 2009, 4 master's, 6 doctorates awarded. *Degree requirements:* For master's, thesis; for doctorate, thesis/dissertation. *Entrance requirements:* For master's and doctorate, GRE General Test. Additional exam requirements/recommendations for international students: Required—TOEFL (minimum score 550 paper-based; 79 iBT) or IELTS (minimum score 6.5). *Application deadline:* For fall admission, 1/10 priority date for domestic and international students; for spring admission, 10/1 for domestic and international students. Application fee: $40 ($90 for international students). Electronic applications accepted. *Expenses:* Tuition, state resident: full-time $6716. Tuition, nonresident: full-time $8908. Tuition and fees vary according to course level, course load, program and student level. *Financial support:* In 2009–10, 12 research assistantships with full and partial tuition reimbursements (averaging $16,200 per year), 14 teaching assistantships with full and partial tuition reimbursements (averaging $15,700 per year) were awarded; fellowships, scholarships/grants, health care benefits, and unspecified assistantships also available. *Unit head:* Dr. R. Paul Lasley, Chair, 515-294-2506, Fax: 515-294-8312, E-mail: sociology@iastate.edu. *Application contact:* Dr. Stephen Sapp, Director of Graduate Education, 515-294-1403, E-mail: sociology@iastate.edu.

Jackson State University, Graduate School, School of Liberal Arts, Department of Sociology, Jackson, MS 39217. Offers MA. Part-time and evening/weekend programs available. *Degree requirements:* For master's, comprehensive exam, thesis or alternative. *Entrance requirements:* For master's, GRE General Test. Additional exam requirements/recommendations for international students: Required—TOEFL.

The Johns Hopkins University, Zanvyl Krieger School of Arts and Sciences, Department of Sociology, Baltimore, MD 21218-2699. Offers PhD. *Faculty:* 11 full-time (6 women), 3 part-time/adjunct (2 women). *Students:* 29 full-time (16 women); includes 3 minority (1 African American, 1 Asian American or Pacific Islander, 1 Hispanic American), 10 international. Average age 29. 116 applicants, 13% accepted, 8 enrolled. In 2009, 3 doctorates awarded. *Degree requirements:* For doctorate, one foreign language, thesis/dissertation. *Entrance requirements:* For doctorate, GRE General Test. Additional exam requirements/recommendations for international students: Required—TOEFL (minimum score 600 paper-based; 250 computer-based; 100 iBT), IELTS; Recommended—TWE. *Application deadline:* For fall admission, 1/4 for domestic and international students. Application fee: $75. Electronic applications accepted. *Financial support:* In 2009–10, 2 fellowships with full tuition reimbursements (averaging $15,000 per year), 13 research assistantships with full tuition reimbursements (averaging $15,000 per year), 16 teaching assistantships with full tuition reimbursements (averaging $15,000 per year) were awarded; institutionally sponsored loans, health care benefits, and tuition waivers (partial) also available. Financial award applicants required to submit CSS PROFILE or FAFSA. *Faculty research:* Education, immigration, race and gender, world systems, social policy. Total annual research expenditures: $599,554. *Unit head:* Dr. Andrew Cherlin, Chair, 410-410-516-2370, Fax: 410-516-7590, E-mail: cherlin@jhu.edu. *Application contact:* Linda Burkhardt, Academic Program Coordinator, 410-516-7627, Fax: 410-516-7590, E-mail: lindab@jhu.edu.

Kansas State University, Graduate School, College of Arts and Sciences, Department of Sociology, Anthropology and Social Work, Manhattan, KS 66506. Offers sociology (MA, PhD). Part-time programs available. *Faculty:* 22 full-time (12 women), 4 part-time/adjunct (1 woman). *Students:* 43 full-time (22 women), 12 part-time (7 women); includes 7 minority (4 African Americans, 1 Asian American or Pacific Islander, 2 Hispanic Americans), 9 international. Average age 32. 31 applicants, 84% accepted, 16 enrolled. In 2009, 4 master's awarded. *Degree requirements:* For master's, thesis or alternative; for doctorate, thesis/dissertation. *Entrance requirements:* For master's, GRE, minimum undergraduate GPA of 3.0; for doctorate, master's degree in sociology. Additional exam requirements/recommendations for international students: Required—TOEFL (minimum score 550 paper-based; 213 computer-based). *Application deadline:* For fall admission, 2/1 priority date for domestic and international students; for spring admission, 8/1 priority date for domestic and international students. Applications are processed on a rolling basis. Application fee: $40 ($55 for international students). Electronic applications accepted. *Financial support:* In 2009–10, 7 research assistantships (averaging $15,758 per year), 18 teaching assistantships with full tuition reimbursements (averaging $10,716 per year) were awarded; institutionally sponsored loans and scholarships/grants also available. Support available to part-time students. Financial award application deadline: 3/1; financial award applicants required to submit FAFSA. *Faculty research:* Rural development, sex and gender, criminology/delinquency, international development/globalization, political sociology/social movements. Total annual research expenditures: $41.2 million. *Unit head:* Betsy Cauble, Head, 785-532-6865, Fax: 785-532-6978, E-mail: bcauble@ksu.edu. *Application contact:* Gerad Middendorf, Director, 785-532-4960, Fax: 785-532-6978, E-mail: middendo@ksu.edu.

Kean University, College of Humanities and Social Sciences, Program in Sociology and Social Justice, Union, NJ 07083. Offers MA. *Faculty:* 13 full-time (6 women). *Students:* 7 full-time (5 women), 17 part-time (14 women); includes 12 minority (6 African Americans, 1 Asian American or Pacific Islander, 5 Hispanic Americans), 1 international. Average age 34. 16 applicants, 81% accepted, 10 enrolled. *Degree requirements:* For master's, comprehensive exam, thesis, practicum. *Entrance requirements:* For master's, GRE (may be waived if cumulative undergraduate GPA is 3.7 or higher), minimum GPA of 3.0, 2 letters of recommendation, interview, official transcripts from all institutions attended. *Application deadline:* For fall admission, 5/1 for domestic students; for spring admission, 11/1 for domestic students. Application fee: $60 ($150 for international students). Electronic applications accepted. *Expenses:* Tuition, state resident: full-time $10,440; part-time $435 per credit. Tuition, nonresident: full-time $14,160; part-time $590 per credit. Required fees: $2642; $110 per credit. Part-time tuition and fees vary according to course load and degree level. *Financial support:* Research assistantships with full tuition reimbursements, unspecified assistantships available. *Unit head:* Dr. Jose Sanchez, Program Coordinator, 908-737-4050, E-mail: jsanchez@kean.edu. *Application contact:* Steven Koch, Pre-Admissions Coordinator, 908-737-5924, Fax: 908-737-5965, E-mail: skoch@kean.edu.

Kent State University, College of Arts and Sciences, Department of Sociology, Kent, OH 44242-0001. Offers MA, PhD. Part-time programs available. *Degree requirements:* For master's, thesis optional, monograph option; for doctorate, comprehensive exam, thesis/dissertation. *Entrance requirements:* For master's, GRE General Test or MAT, minimum GPA of 2.75; for doctorate, GRE, minimum GPA of 3.0. Additional exam requirements/recommendations for international students: Required—TOEFL. Electronic applications accepted. *Faculty research:* Medical sociology, social psychology, social inequalities.

Lakehead University, Graduate Studies, Faculty of Social Sciences and Humanities, Department of Sociology, Thunder Bay, ON P7B 5E1, Canada. Offers gerontology (MA); health services and policy research (MA); sociology (MA); women's studies (MA). Part-time and evening/weekend programs available. *Degree requirements:* For master's, research project or thesis. *Entrance requirements:* For master's, minimum B average. Additional exam requirements/recommendations for international students: Required—TOEFL. *Faculty research:* Sociology of medicine, cultural and social change, health human resources, gerontology, women's studies.

Laurentian University, School of Graduate Studies and Research, Programme in Sociology, Sudbury, ON P3E 2C6, Canada. Offers applied social research (MA). Part-time programs available. *Entrance requirements:* For master's, honors degree in sociology or equivalent. *Faculty research:* Work foundations, managing AIDS organization, tracking laid-off mine workers.

Lehigh University, College of Arts and Sciences, Department of Sociology and Anthropology, Bethlehem, PA 18015. Offers sociology (MA). Part-time programs available. *Faculty:* 13 full-time (6 women). *Students:* 11 full-time (7 women); includes 2 minority (1 African American, 1 Asian American or Pacific Islander). Average age 25. 16 applicants, 63% accepted, 6 enrolled. In 2009, 10 master's awarded. *Degree requirements:* For master's, comprehensive exam, thesis optional. *Entrance requirements:* For master's, GRE General Test. Additional exam requirements/recommendations for international students: Required—TOEFL (minimum score 650 paper-based; 94 iBT). *Application deadline:* For fall admission, 1/15 priority date for domestic and international students. Application fee: $65. Electronic applications accepted. *Financial support:* In 2009–10, 10 students received support, including 4 fellowships with full tuition reimbursements available, 6 teaching assistantships with full tuition reimbursements available; research assistantships with full tuition reimbursements available, career-related internships or fieldwork, Federal Work Study, institutionally sponsored loans, scholarships/grants, tuition waivers (full and partial), and unspecified assistantships also available. Support available to part-time students. Financial award application deadline: 1/15. *Faculty research:* Juvenile delinquency, parent-child relations, urban sociology, medical sociology, policy studies. Total annual research expenditures: $296,025. *Unit head:* Dr. Judith N. Lasker, Chair and NEH Distinguished Professor, 610-758-3811, Fax: 610-758-6552, E-mail: judith.lasker@lehigh.edu. *Application contact:* Prof. James McIntosh, Graduate Coordinator, 610-758-3809, Fax: 610-758-6552, E-mail: ijm1@lehigh.edu.

Lincoln University, School of Graduate Studies and Continuing Education, Jefferson City, MO 65102. Offers business administration (MBA), including accounting, entrepreneurship, management, public administration and policy; educational leadership (Ed S), including elementary leadership, secondary leadership, superintendency; guidance and counseling (M Ed), including community/agency counseling, elementary school, secondary school; history (MA); school administration and supervision (M Ed), including elementary school administration, secondary school administration, special education administration; school teaching (M Ed), including elementary school teaching, secondary school teaching; social science (MA), including history, political science, sociology; sociology (MA); sociology/criminal justice (MA). Part-time and evening/weekend programs available. *Students:* 52 full-time (27 women), 146 part-time

Sociology

Lincoln University (continued)
(107 women); includes 40 minority (39 African Americans, 1 Asian American or Pacific Islander), 15 international. Average age 35. 76 applicants, 95% accepted, 46 enrolled. In 2009, 60 master's, 6 other advanced degrees awarded. *Degree requirements:* For master's and Ed S, comprehensive exam, thesis optional. *Entrance requirements:* For master's and Ed S, GRE, MAT or GMAT, minimum GPA of 2.75 in major, 2.5 overall; 3 letters of recommendation; minimum C average in English composition; personal statement of purpose. Additional exam requirements/recommendations for international students: Required—TOEFL (minimum score 500 paper-based; 173 computer-based; 61 iBT). *Application deadline:* For fall admission, 7/1 priority date for domestic and international students; for spring admission, 12/1 priority date for domestic and international students. Applications are processed on a rolling basis. Application fee: $20. *Expenses:* Tuition, state resident: full-time $4185; part-time $232.50 per credit hour. Tuition, nonresident: full-time $7767; part-time $431.50 per credit hour. Required fees: $270; $15 per credit hour. $20 per term. *Financial support:* Federal Work-Study and scholarships/grants available. Financial award application deadline: 4/1; financial award applicants required to submit FAFSA. *Faculty research:* Suicide prevention. *Unit head:* Dr. Linda S. Bickel, Dean, 573-681-5247, Fax: 573-681-5106, E-mail: gradschool@lincolnu.edu. *Application contact:* Irasema Steck, Administrative Assistant, 573-681-5247, Fax: 573-681-5106, E-mail: gradschool@lincolnu.edu.

Louisiana State University and Agricultural and Mechanical College, Graduate School, College of Arts and Sciences, Department of Sociology, Baton Rouge, LA 70803. Offers MA, PhD. Part-time programs available. *Faculty:* 16 full-time (4 women). *Students:* 34 full-time (18 women), 3 part-time (all women); includes 7 minority (6 African Americans, 1 Asian American or Pacific Islander), 3 international. Average age 30. 22 applicants, 82% accepted, 7 enrolled. In 2009, 2 master's, 5 doctorates awarded. Terminal master's awarded for partial completion of doctoral program. *Degree requirements:* For master's, comprehensive exam, thesis; for doctorate, comprehensive exam, thesis/dissertation. *Entrance requirements:* For master's and doctorate, GRE General Test, minimum GPA of 3.0. Additional exam requirements/recommendations for international students: Required—TOEFL (minimum score 550 paper-based; 213 computer-based; 79 iBT) or IELTS (minimum score 6.5). *Application deadline:* For fall admission, 1/31 priority date for domestic students, 3/31 for international students; for spring admission, 10/15 for international students. Applications are processed on a rolling basis. Application fee: $50 ($70 for international students). Electronic applications accepted. *Financial support:* In 2009–10, 36 students received support, including 5 fellowships (averaging $24,087 per year), 6 research assistantships with partial tuition reimbursements available (averaging $16,583 per year), 20 teaching assistantships with partial tuition reimbursements available (averaging $11,650 per year); Federal Work-Study, scholarships/grants, health care benefits, tuition waivers (full and partial), and unspecified assistantships also available. Support available to part-time students. Financial award application deadline: 3/1; financial award applicants required to submit FAFSA. *Faculty research:* Family, stratification, demography, rural sociology, criminology. Total annual research expenditures: $416,871. *Unit head:* Dr. William Bankston, Chair, 225-578-1645, Fax: 225-578-5102, E-mail: sobank@lsu.edu. *Application contact:* Dr. Yoshinori Kamo, Graduate Adviser, 225-578-5311, Fax: 225-578-5102.

Loyola University Chicago, Graduate School, Department of Sociology, Chicago, IL 60660. Offers applied sociology (MA); sociology (MA, PhD); urban studies (MA). Part-time and evening/weekend programs available. *Faculty:* 14 full-time (7 women), 3 part-time/adjunct (2 women). *Students:* 66 full-time (44 women), 15 part-time (9 women); includes 15 minority (8 African Americans, 5 Asian Americans or Pacific Islanders, 2 Hispanic Americans), 6 international. Average age 33. 113 applicants, 42% accepted, 20 enrolled. In 2009, 5 master's, 4 doctorates awarded. Terminal master's awarded for partial completion of doctoral program. *Degree requirements:* For master's, thesis or alternative; for doctorate, comprehensive exam, thesis/dissertation. *Entrance requirements:* For master's and doctorate, GRE General Test. Additional exam requirements/recommendations for international students: Required—TOEFL. *Application deadline:* For winter admission, 2/1 for domestic and international students. Electronic applications accepted. *Expenses:* Tuition: Full-time $14,220; part-time $790 per credit hour. Required fees: $60 per semester hour. Tuition and fees vary according to program. *Financial support:* In 2009–10, 35 students received support, including 10 fellowships with full tuition reimbursements available (averaging $14,000 per year), 5 research assistantships with full tuition reimbursements available (averaging $14,000 per year), 9 teaching assistantships with full tuition reimbursements available (averaging $14,000 per year); career-related internships or fieldwork, Federal Work-Study, tuition waivers (full), and unspecified assistantships also available. Financial award application deadline: 2/1; financial award applicants required to submit FAFSA. *Faculty research:* Religion, knowledge, culture, urban and social policy. Total annual research expenditures: $160,000. *Unit head:* Dr. Rhys Williams, Chair, 773-508-3459, Fax: 773-508-7099, E-mail: rwilliams7s@luc.edu. *Application contact:* Dr. Anne Figert, Graduate Program Director, 773-508-3431, Fax: 773-508-7099, E-mail: afigert@luc.edu.

Marshall University, Academic Affairs Division, College of Liberal Arts, Department of Sociology and Anthropology, Huntington, WV 25755. Offers sociology (MA). *Faculty:* 7 full-time (2 women), 1 (woman) part-time/adjunct. *Students:* 14 full-time (6 women), 1 (woman) part-time; includes 1 minority (African American), 1 international. Average age 28. In 2009, 4 master's awarded. *Degree requirements:* For master's, thesis optional. Application fee: $40. *Unit head:* Dr. Anders Lind-Laursen, Chairperson, 304-696-6700, E-mail: sociology@marshall.edu. *Application contact:* Graduate Admissions, 304-746-1900, Fax: 304-746-1902, E-mail: services@marshall.edu.

McGill University, Faculty of Graduate and Postdoctoral Studies, Faculty of Arts, Department of Sociology, Montréal, QC H3A 2T5, Canada. Offers medical sociology (MA); neo-tropical environment (MA); social statistics (MA); sociology (MA, PhD, Diploma).

McGill University, Faculty of Graduate and Postdoctoral Studies, Faculty of Medicine, Department of Social Studies in Medicine, Montréal, QC H3A 2T5, Canada. Offers medical anthropology (MA, PhD); medical history (MA, PhD); medical sociology (MA, PhD).

McMaster University, School of Graduate Studies, Faculty of Social Sciences, Department of Sociology, Hamilton, ON L8S 4M2, Canada. Offers MA, PhD. Part-time programs available. *Degree requirements:* For master's, thesis; for doctorate, comprehensive exam, thesis/dissertation. *Entrance requirements:* For master's and doctorate, minimum B+ average. Additional exam requirements/recommendations for international students: Required—TOEFL (minimum score 580 paper-based; 237 computer-based). *Faculty research:* Socialization and conversion, ethnic relations, international migration, racism, social implications of the Internet.

Memorial University of Newfoundland, School of Graduate Studies, Department of Sociology, St. John's, NL A1C 5S7, Canada. Offers gender (PhD); maritime sociology (PhD); sociology (M Phil, MA); work and development (PhD). Part-time programs available. *Degree requirements:* For master's, comprehensive exam, thesis optional, program journal (M Phil); for doctorate, one foreign language, comprehensive exam, thesis/dissertation, oral defense of thesis. *Entrance requirements:* For master's, 2nd class degree from university of recognized standing in area of study; for doctorate, MA, M Phil, or equivalent. Electronic applications accepted. *Faculty research:* Work and development, gender, maritime sociology.

Michigan State University, The Graduate School, College of Social Science, Department of Sociology, East Lansing, MI 48824. Offers MA, PhD. Part-time programs available. *Faculty:* 25 full-time (12 women). *Students:* 57 full-time (39 women), 6 part-time (4 women); includes 17 minority (10 African Americans, 2 Asian Americans or Pacific Islanders, 5 Hispanic Americans), 16 international. Average age 32. 72 applicants, 43% accepted. In 2009, 5 master's, 4 doctorates awarded. *Entrance requirements:* Additional exam requirements/recommendations for international students: Required—TOEFL (minimum score 550 paper-based; 213 computer-based), Michigan State University ELT (minimum score 85), Michigan Michigan English Language Assessment Battery (minimum score 83). Electronic applications accepted. *Expenses:* Tuition, state resident: part-time $478.25 per credit hour. Tuition, nonresident: part-time $966.50 per credit hour. Part-time tuition and fees vary according to program. *Financial support:* In 2009–10, 19 research assistantships with tuition reimbursements (averaging $6,496 per year), 16 teaching assistantships with tuition reimbursements (averaging $5,953 per year) were awarded. Total annual research expenditures: $699,642. *Unit head:* Dr. Janet L. Bokemeier, Chairperson, 517-355-6632, Fax: 517-432-2856, E-mail: bokemeie@msu.edu. *Application contact:* Tammy Spangler, Graduate Program Secretary, 517-355-6634, Fax: 517-432-2856, E-mail: soc@msu.edu.

Middle Tennessee State University, College of Graduate Studies, College of Liberal Arts, Department of Sociology and Anthropology, Murfreesboro, TN 37132. Offers sociology (MA). Part-time and evening/weekend programs available. Postbaccalaureate distance learning degree programs offered. *Faculty:* 12 full-time (6 women). *Students:* 2 full-time (1 woman), 30 part-time (21 women); includes 6 minority (3 African Americans, 2 Asian Americans or Pacific Islanders, 1 Hispanic American). Average age 26. 14 applicants, 64% accepted, 9 enrolled. In 2009, 4 master's awarded. *Degree requirements:* For master's, comprehensive exam, thesis. *Entrance requirements:* For master's, GRE. Additional exam requirements/recommendations for international students: Required—TOEFL (minimum score 525 paper-based; 195 computer-based; 71 iBT) or IELTS (minimum score 6). *Application deadline:* For fall admission, 6/1 for domestic and international students. Applications are processed on a rolling basis. Application fee: $25 ($30 for international students). Electronic applications accepted. *Expenses:* Tuition, state resident: full-time $4404. Tuition, nonresident: full-time $10,956. *Financial support:* In 2009–10, 8 students received support. Institutionally sponsored loans available. Support available to part-time students. Financial award application deadline: 5/1; financial award applicants required to submit FAFSA. *Faculty research:* Applied sociology, crime/deviance, aging/social gerontology, social organization, social psychology. *Unit head:* Dr. Jackie Eller, Interim Chair, 615-898-2509, Fax: 615-898-5428, E-mail: jaeller@mtsu.edu. *Application contact:* Dr. Michael Allen, Dean and Vice Provost for Research, 615-898-2840, Fax: 615-904-8020, E-mail: mallen@mtsu.edu.

Minnesota State University Mankato, College of Graduate Studies, College of Social and Behavioral Sciences, Department of Sociology and Corrections, Mankato, MN 56001. Offers sociology (MA); sociology: corrections (MS); sociology: human services planning and administration (MS). Part-time programs available. *Students:* 10 full-time (5 women), 41 part-time (25 women). *Degree requirements:* For master's, comprehensive exam, thesis or alternative. *Entrance requirements:* For master's, minimum GPA of 3.0 during previous 2 years, 3 letters of reference, resume. Additional exam requirements/recommendations for international students: Required—TOEFL. *Application deadline:* For fall admission, 7/1 priority date for domestic students; for spring admission, 11/1 for domestic students. Applications are processed on a rolling basis. Application fee: $40. Electronic applications accepted. *Expenses:* Tuition, state resident: full-time $5364. Tuition, nonresident: full-time $8314. *Financial support:* Research assistantships with full tuition reimbursements, teaching assistantships with full tuition reimbursements, career-related internships or fieldwork, Federal Work-Study, institutionally sponsored loans, and unspecified assistantships available. Support available to part-time students. Financial award application deadline: 3/15; financial award applicants required to submit FAFSA. *Faculty research:* Women's suffrage movements. *Unit head:* Dr. Barbara Keating, Chairperson, 507-389-1561. *Application contact:* 507-389-2321, E-mail: grad@mnsu.edu.

Mississippi State University, College of Arts and Sciences, Department of Sociology, Mississippi State, MS 39762. Offers MS, PhD. Part-time programs available. *Faculty:* 12 full-time (5 women), 1 part-time/adjunct (0 women). *Students:* 28 full-time (17 women), 18 part-time (12 women); includes 13 minority (9 African Americans, 1 American Indian/Alaska Native, 2 Asian Americans or Pacific Islanders, 1 Hispanic American), 6 international. Average age 31. 21 applicants, 57% accepted, 8 enrolled. In 2009, 11 master's, 3 doctorates awarded. *Degree requirements:* For master's, thesis optional, comprehensive oral or written exam; for doctorate, thesis/dissertation, comprehensive oral and written exam. *Entrance requirements:* For master's, minimum GPA of 3.0 on last two years of undergraduate courses or GRE; academic writing sample; for doctorate, GRE, academic writing sample. Additional exam requirements/recommendations for international students: Required—TOEFL (minimum score 550 paper-based). *Application deadline:* For fall admission, 4/15 priority date for domestic students, 5/1 for international students; for spring admission, 10/15 priority date for domestic students, 9/1 for international students. Applications are processed on a rolling basis. Application fee: $40. Electronic applications accepted. *Expenses:* Tuition, state resident: full-time $2575.50; part-time $286.25 per credit hour. Tuition, nonresident: full-time $6510; part-time $723.50 per credit hour. Tuition and fees vary according to course load. *Financial support:* In 2009–10, 14 research assistantships (averaging $9,607 per year), 13 teaching assistantships with tuition reimbursements (averaging $10,086 per year) were awarded; Federal Work-Study, institutionally sponsored loans, scholarships/grants, and unspecified assistantships also available. Financial award application deadline: 3/15; financial award applicants required to submit FAFSA. *Faculty research:* Community and regional development, criminology, natural resource development, family sociology, gender. Total annual research expenditures: $1.3 million. *Unit head:* Dr. R. Gregory Dunaway, Head, 662-325-2495, Fax: 662-325-4564, E-mail: dunaway@soc.msstate.edu. *Application contact:* Dr. Lynne Cossman, Graduate Coordinator, 662-325-2495, Fax: 662-325-4564, E-mail: sociology@soc.msstate.edu.

Montclair State University, The Graduate School, College of Humanities and Social Sciences, Department of Sociology, Montclair, NJ 07043-1624. Offers applied sociology (MA). Part-time and evening/weekend programs available. *Faculty:* 15 part-time/adjunct (3 women). In 2009, 1 master's awarded. *Degree requirements:* For master's, comprehensive exam, comprehensive project, internship. *Entrance requirements:* For master's, GRE General Test, 2 letters of recommendation. Additional exam requirements/recommendations for international students: Required—TOEFL (minimum score 83 computer-based), or IELTS. *Application deadline:* For fall admission, 6/1 for international students; for spring admission, 10/1 for international students. Applications are processed on a rolling basis. Application fee: $60. Electronic applications accepted. *Expenses:* Tuition, area resident: Part-time $486.74 per credit. Tuition, state resident: part-time $486.74 per credit. Tuition, nonresident: part-time $751.34 per credit. Tuition and fees vary according to degree level and program. *Financial support:* Federal Work-Study and scholarships/grants available. Support available to part-time students. Financial award application deadline: 3/1; financial award applicants required to submit FAFSA. *Unit head:* Dr. Jay Livingston, Chairperson, 973-655-4131. *Application contact:* Amy Aiello, Associate Director of Admissions, 973-655-5147, Fax: 973-655-7869, E-mail: graduate.school@montclair.edu.

Morehead State University, Graduate Programs, Caudill College of Arts, Humanities and Social Sciences, Department of Sociology, Social Work and Criminology, Morehead, KY 40351. Offers criminology (MA); general sociology (MA); gerontology (MA); sociology regional analysis (MA); sociology/chemical dependency (MA). Part-time and evening/weekend programs available. *Faculty:* 6 full-time (3 women), 1 (woman) part-time/adjunct. *Students:* 14 full-time (11 women), 18 part-time (12 women). Average age 34. 27 applicants, 78% accepted, 14 enrolled. In 2009, 5 master's awarded. *Degree requirements:* For master's, comprehensive exam, thesis (for some programs). *Entrance requirements:* For master's, GRE General Test, minimum GPA of 3.0 in sociology, 2.75 overall; 18 hours of course work in sociology, writing sample. Additional exam requirements/recommendations for international students: Required—TOEFL (minimum score 500 paper-based; 173 computer-based). *Application deadline:* For fall admission, 8/1 priority date for domestic and international students; for spring admission, 12/1 priority date for domestic and international students. Applications are processed on a rolling basis. Application fee: $30. Electronic applications accepted. *Expenses:* Tuition, state resident: full-time $6318; part-time $351 per credit hour. Tuition, nonresident: full-time $15,804; part-time $878 per credit hour. *Financial support:* In 2009–10, 4 teaching assistantships (averaging $10,000 per year) were awarded; career-related internships or fieldwork, Federal Work-Study, and unspecified assistantships also available. Financial award application deadline: 3/15; financial award applicants required to submit FAFSA. *Faculty research:* Death and dying; aging, drinking, and drugs; economic development; adult children of alcoholics. *Unit head:* Dr. Clarenda Phillips, Department Chair, 606-783-2434, Fax: 606-783-5070, E-mail: c.phillips@

moreheadstate.edu. *Application contact:* Michelle Barber, Graduate Recruitment and Retention Assistant Director, 606-783-5127, Fax: 606-783-5061, E-mail: m.barber@moreheadstate.edu.

Morgan State University, School of Graduate Studies, College of Liberal Arts, Department of Sociology and Anthropology, Baltimore, MD 21251. Offers sociology (MA, MS). Part-time and evening/weekend programs available. *Degree requirements:* For master's, comprehensive exam. *Entrance requirements:* Additional exam requirements/recommendations for international students: Required—TOEFL (minimum score 550 paper-based; 213 computer-based). *Faculty research:* Domestic violence, homelessness, social movements, marriage and family.

New Mexico Highlands University, Graduate Studies, College of Arts and Sciences, Program in Public Affairs, Las Vegas, NM 87701. Offers applied sociology (MA). Program is interdisciplinary. *Degree requirements:* For master's, comprehensive exam, thesis or alternative. *Entrance requirements:* For master's, minimum undergraduate GPA of 3.0. Additional exam requirements/recommendations for international students: Required—TOEFL (minimum score 540 paper-based; 207 computer-based).

New Mexico State University, Graduate School, College of Arts and Sciences, Department of Sociology and Anthropology, Las Cruces, NM 88003-8001. Offers anthropology (MA); sociology (MA). Part-time programs available. *Faculty:* 23 full-time (17 women), 4 part-time/adjunct (2 women). *Students:* 44 full-time (28 women), 81 part-time (57 women); includes 35 minority (6 African Americans, 5 American Indian/Alaska Native, 1 Asian American or Pacific Islander, 23 Hispanic Americans), 4 international. Average age 33. 79 applicants, 92% accepted, 40 enrolled. In 2009, 28 master's awarded. *Degree requirements:* For master's, comprehensive exam (for some programs), thesis (for some programs). *Entrance requirements:* For master's, undergraduate research methods and statistics. Additional exam requirements/recommendations for international students: Required—TOEFL. *Application deadline:* For fall admission, 2/15 priority date for domestic students; for spring admission, 10/15 priority date for domestic students. Applications are processed on a rolling basis. Application fee: $30 ($50 for international students). Electronic applications accepted. *Expenses:* Tuition, state resident: full-time $4080; part-time $223 per credit. Tuition, nonresident: full-time $14,256; part-time $647 per credit. Required fees: $1278; $639 per semester. *Financial support:* In 2009–10, 11 students received support, including 19 teaching assistantships with partial tuition reimbursements available (averaging $10,484 per year); fellowships, research assistantships with partial tuition reimbursements available, career-related internships or fieldwork, Federal Work-Study, and health care benefits also available. Support available to part-time students. Financial award application deadline: 2/15. *Faculty research:* Native American culture and society, Latin America and border studies, prehistoric and historic archaeology, medical anthropology, applied anthropology, gender and sexualities, globalization, rural sociology, delinquency and criminology, sociology of education, sociology of sport. *Unit head:* Dr. Miriam Chaiken, Head, 575-646-2826, Fax: 575-646-3725, E-mail: mchaiken@nmsu.edu. *Application contact:* Coordinator.

The New School: A University, The New School for Social Research, Department of Sociology, New York, NY 10003. Offers sociology (MA, DS Sc, PhD); sociology and historical studies (MA, PhD). Part-time and evening/weekend programs available. *Faculty:* 12 full-time (5 women). *Students:* 145 full-time (81 women), 18 part-time (10 women); includes 22 minority (11 African Americans, 3 Asian Americans or Pacific Islanders, 8 Hispanic Americans), 62 international. Average age 34. 145 applicants, 68% accepted, 28 enrolled. In 2009, 24 master's, 7 doctorates awarded. Terminal master's awarded for partial completion of doctoral program. *Degree requirements:* For master's, exam; for doctorate, one foreign language, thesis/dissertation, qualifying exam. *Entrance requirements:* For master's, GRE General Test; for doctorate, GRE General Test, MA. Additional exam requirements/recommendations for international students: Required—TOEFL (minimum score 600 paper-based; 250 computer-based; 100 iBT). *Application deadline:* For fall admission, 1/17 priority date for domestic and international students; for spring admission, 10/15 priority date for domestic and international students. Applications are processed on a rolling basis. Application fee: $50. Electronic applications accepted. *Financial support:* Fellowships, research assistantships, teaching assistantships, Federal Work-Study, scholarships/grants, tuition waivers (full and partial), and unspecified assistantships available. Support available to part-time students. Financial award application deadline: 3/1; financial award applicants required to submit FAFSA. *Faculty research:* Media, culture, urban sociology, democratic transitions, critical theory. *Unit head:* Dr. Eiko Ikegami, Chair, 212-229-5737 Ext. 4925, E-mail: ikegame1@newschool.edu. *Application contact:* Robert MacDonald, Director of Admissions, 212-229-5710 Ext. 3007, Fax: 212-989-7102, E-mail: macdonar@newschool.edu.

New York University, Graduate School of Arts and Science, Department of Sociology, New York, NY 10012-1019. Offers French studies and sociology (PhD); sociology (MA, PhD); JD/MA. Part-time programs available. *Faculty:* 27 full-time (9 women), 1 part-time/adjunct (0 women). *Students:* 62 full-time (29 women), 10 part-time (9 women); includes 14 minority (6 African Americans, 4 Asian Americans or Pacific Islanders, 4 Hispanic Americans), 11 international. Average age 30. 371 applicants, 6% accepted, 12 enrolled. In 2009, 6 master's, 6 doctorates awarded. Terminal master's awarded for partial completion of doctoral program. *Degree requirements:* For master's, thesis or alternative; for doctorate, comprehensive exam, thesis/dissertation. *Entrance requirements:* For master's and doctorate, GRE General Test. Additional exam requirements/recommendations for international students: Required—TOEFL. *Application deadline:* For fall admission, 1/4 priority date for domestic students. Application fee: $90. *Expenses:* Tuition: Full-time $30,528; part-time $1272 per credit. Required fees: $2177. *Financial support:* Fellowships with tuition reimbursements, research assistantships with tuition reimbursements, teaching assistantships with tuition reimbursements, Federal Work-Study, institutionally sponsored loans, scholarships/grants, health care benefits, and unspecified assistantships available. Financial award application deadline: 1/4; financial award applicants required to submit FAFSA. *Faculty research:* Political sociology and social movements; gender and inequality; deviance, law, and crime; education; stratification and theory. *Unit head:* Jeff Manza, Chair, 212-998-8340, Fax: 212-995-4140, E-mail: gsas.sociology.info@nyu.edu. *Application contact:* Eric Klinenberg, Director of Graduate Studies, 212-998-8340, Fax: 212-995-4140, E-mail: gsas.sociology.info@nyu.edu.

New York University, Steinhardt School of Culture, Education, and Human Development, Department of Humanities and Social Sciences in the Professions, Program in Sociology of Education, New York, NY 10012-1019. Offers education and social policy (MA); sociology of education (MA, PhD), including education policy (MA), social and cultural studies of education (MA). Part-time programs available. *Students:* 16 full-time (14 women), 7 part-time (4 women); includes 3 minority (1 African American, 1 American Indian/Alaska Native, 1 Hispanic American), 3 international. Average age 27. 35 applicants, 57% accepted, 6 enrolled. In 2009, 6 master's awarded. *Degree requirements:* For master's, thesis (for some programs); for doctorate, thesis/dissertation. *Entrance requirements:* For master's, letters of recommendation; for doctorate, GRE General Test, interview. Additional exam requirements/recommendations for international students: Required—TOEFL. *Application deadline:* For fall admission, 12/15 priority date for domestic and international students; for spring admission, 11/1 for domestic and international students. Applications are processed on a rolling basis. Application fee: $75. Electronic applications accepted. *Expenses:* Tuition: Full-time $30,528; part-time $1272 per credit. Required fees: $2177. *Financial support:* Fellowships with full and partial tuition reimbursements, Federal Work-Study, institutionally sponsored loans, scholarships/grants, and tuition waivers (partial) available. Support available to part-time students. Financial award application deadline: 2/1; financial award applicants required to submit FAFSA. *Faculty research:* Legal and institutional environments of schools; social inequality; high school reform and achievement; urban schooling, economics and education, educational policy. *Unit head:* Dr. Floyd M. Hammack, Program Director, 212-998-5542, Fax: 212-995-4832, E-mail: fmhl@nyu.edu. *Application contact:* 212-998-5030, Fax: 212-995-4328, E-mail: steinhardt.gradadmissions@nyu.edu.

Norfolk State University, School of Graduate Studies, School of Liberal Arts, Department of Sociology, Program in Applied Sociology, Norfolk, VA 23504. Offers MS. Part-time programs available.

North Carolina Central University, Division of Academic Affairs, College of Behavioral and Social Sciences, Department of Sociology, Durham, NC 27707-3129. Offers MA. Part-time and evening/weekend programs available. *Degree requirements:* For master's, one foreign language, comprehensive exam, thesis. *Entrance requirements:* For master's, GRE, minimum GPA of 3.0 in major, 2.5 overall. Additional exam requirements/recommendations for international students: Required—TOEFL. *Faculty research:* Urban demography, family, statistical methods.

North Carolina State University, Graduate School, College of Humanities and Social Sciences, Department of Sociology and Anthropology, Program in Sociology, Raleigh, NC 27695. Offers M Soc, MS, PhD. Part-time programs available. *Degree requirements:* For master's, practicum (M Soc), thesis (MS); for doctorate, comprehensive exam, thesis/dissertation. *Entrance requirements:* For master's and doctorate, GRE General Test, sample of written work. Electronic applications accepted. *Faculty research:* Inequity: gender, race and class; crime and social control; work and organizations; rural sociology; family and intimate relations.

North Dakota State University, College of Graduate and Interdisciplinary Studies, College of Arts, Humanities and Social Sciences, Department of Sociology, Anthropology, and Emergency Management, Fargo, ND 58108. Offers emergency management (MS, PhD); social science (MA, MS); sociology (MS). Part-time programs available. *Faculty:* 8 full-time (3 women), 5 part-time/adjunct (2 women). *Students:* 35 full-time (17 women), 15 part-time (9 women); includes 5 minority (2 African Americans, 1 American Indian/Alaska Native, 1 Asian American or Pacific Islander, 1 Hispanic American), 2 international. Average age 27. 15 applicants, 60% accepted, 7 enrolled. In 2009, 9 master's awarded. *Degree requirements:* For master's, thesis; for doctorate, comprehensive exam, thesis/dissertation. *Entrance requirements:* For master's, GRE (emergency management), course work in sociology, minimum GPA of 3.2; for doctorate, GRE, minimum GPA of 3.2. Additional exam requirements/recommendations for international students: Required—TOEFL. *Application deadline:* For fall admission, 4/1 priority date for domestic students. Applications are processed on a rolling basis. Application fee: $45 ($60 for international students). *Financial support:* In 2009–10, 7 research assistantships with full tuition reimbursements (averaging $6,156 per year), 7 teaching assistantships with full tuition reimbursements (averaging $3,078 per year) were awarded; fellowships, career-related internships or fieldwork, Federal Work-Study, institutionally sponsored loans, and tuition waivers (full) also available. Support available to part-time students. Financial award application deadline: 4/15. *Faculty research:* Medical sociology, demography, ethnology, archaeology. Total annual research expenditures: $75,000. *Unit head:* Dr. Daniel J. Klenow, Chair, 701-231-8657, Fax: 701-231-1047, E-mail: daniel.klenow@ndsu.edu. *Application contact:* Dr. Daniel J. Klenow, Chair, 701-231-8657, Fax: 701-231-1047, E-mail: daniel.klenow@ndsu.edu.

Northeastern University, College of Social Sciences and Humanities, Department of Sociology and Anthropology, Boston, MA 02115-5096. Offers sociology (MA, PhD). Part-time programs available. *Faculty:* 24 full-time (11 women), 6 part-time/adjunct (5 women). *Students:* 54 full-time (40 women), 1 (woman) part-time; includes 1 African American, 1 Asian American or Pacific Islander, 4 Hispanic Americans, 4 international. 108 applicants, 28% accepted, 16 enrolled. In 2009, 4 master's, 2 doctorates awarded. *Degree requirements:* For master's, thesis; for doctorate, thesis/dissertation, teaching tutorial. *Entrance requirements:* For master's and doctorate, GRE General Test or MAT. Additional exam requirements/recommendations for international students: Required—TOEFL. *Application deadline:* For fall admission, 2/1 for domestic students. Application fee: $50. *Financial support:* In 2009–10, 14 teaching assistantships with tuition reimbursements (averaging $14,035 per year) were awarded; fellowships, research assistantships with tuition reimbursements, career-related internships or fieldwork, tuition waivers (full and partial), and unspecified assistantships also available. Financial award application deadline: 2/1; financial award applicants required to submit FAFSA. *Faculty research:* Globalization and international studies, urban affairs, social justice. *Unit head:* Dr. Steven Vallas, Acting Chair, 617-373-2686, Fax: 617-373-2688, E-mail: gradsoc@neu.edu. *Application contact:* Graduate Programs Assistant, 617-373-2686, Fax: 617-373-2688, E-mail: gradsoc@neu.edu.

Northern Arizona University, Graduate College, College of Social and Behavioral Sciences, Department of Sociology and Social Work, Flagstaff, AZ 86011. Offers applied sociology (MA); sociology (MA). Part-time programs available. *Faculty:* 20 full-time (11 women). *Students:* 21 full-time (13 women), 7 part-time (4 women); includes 7 minority (2 African Americans, 2 American Indian/Alaska Native, 1 Asian American or Pacific Islander, 2 Hispanic Americans), 1 international. Average age 33. 22 applicants, 77% accepted, 11 enrolled. In 2009, 5 master's awarded. *Degree requirements:* For master's, thesis or internship. *Entrance requirements:* For master's, minimum GPA of 3.0. Additional exam requirements/recommendations for international students: Required—TOEFL (minimum score 550 paper-based; 213 computer-based; 80 iBT), IELTS (minimum score 7), or a bachelor's degree from an English-speaking university and demonstrated proficiency. *Application deadline:* For fall admission, 2/15 priority date for domestic students, 9/1 priority date for international students. Applications are processed on a rolling basis. Application fee: $65. Electronic applications accepted. *Financial support:* In 2009–10, 8 teaching assistantships (averaging $10,439 per year) were awarded; career-related internships or fieldwork, Federal Work-Study, and tuition waivers (full and partial) also available. Financial award application deadline: 3/30. *Faculty research:* Demography, death and dying, criminology, social policy, divorce. *Unit head:* Dr. Kooros Mohit Mahmoudi, Chair, 928-523-6554, Fax: 928-523-6777, E-mail: kooros.mahmoudi@nau.edu. *Application contact:* Dr. Janine Minkler, Coordinator, 928-523-7482, Fax: 928-523-6777, E-mail: janine.minkler@nau.edu.

Northern Illinois University, Graduate School, College of Liberal Arts and Sciences, Department of Sociology, De Kalb, IL 60115-2854. Offers MA. Part-time programs available. *Faculty:* 14 full-time (3 women). *Students:* 14 full-time (9 women), 13 part-time (9 women); includes 3 minority (1 African American, 1 Asian American or Pacific Islander, 1 Hispanic American), 1 international. Average age 28. 31 applicants, 58% accepted, 12 enrolled. In 2009, 8 master's awarded. *Degree requirements:* For master's, comprehensive exam, thesis optional. *Entrance requirements:* For master's, GRE General Test, minimum GPA of 2.75; course work in social theory, social methods, and statistics. Additional exam requirements/recommendations for international students: Required—TOEFL (minimum score 550 paper-based; 213 computer-based). *Application deadline:* For fall admission, 6/1 for domestic students, 5/1 for international students; for spring admission, 11/1 for domestic students, 10/1 for international students. Applications are processed on a rolling basis. Application fee: $30. Electronic applications accepted. *Expenses:* Tuition, state resident: full-time $6576; part-time $274 per credit hour. Tuition, nonresident: full-time $13,152; part-time $548 per credit hour. Required fees: $1813; $75.53 per credit hour. Part-time tuition and fees vary according to course load. *Financial support:* In 2009–10, 22 research assistantships with full tuition reimbursements were awarded; fellowships with full tuition reimbursements, teaching assistantships with full tuition reimbursements, career-related internships or fieldwork, Federal Work-Study, scholarships/grants, tuition waivers (full), and unspecified assistantships also available. Support available to part-time students. Financial award applicants required to submit FAFSA. *Faculty research:* Welfare reform, interpersonal disputes, multicultural education, race and ethnicism, social control. *Unit head:* Dr. William Minor, Chair, 815-753-1194, Fax: 815-753-6302, E-mail: bminor@niu.edu. *Application contact:* Dr. William Minor, Chair, 815-753-1194, Fax: 815-753-6302, E-mail: bminor@niu.edu.

Northwestern University, The Graduate School, Interdepartmental Programs and Kellogg School of Management, Program in Management and Organizations and Sociology, Evanston, IL 60208. Offers PhD. Program requires admission to both The Graduate School and the Kellogg Graduate School of Management. *Degree requirements:* For doctorate, comprehensive exam, thesis/dissertation. *Entrance requirements:* For doctorate, GRE General Test. Additional exam requirements/recommendations for international students: Required—TOEFL. Electronic applications accepted. *Faculty research:* Strategic alliances and organizational competitiveness, institutional change and the information of industries, social capital and the creation of financial capital, negotiation, organizational networks, diversity.

Sociology

Northwestern University, The Graduate School, Judd A. and Marjorie Weinberg College of Arts and Sciences, Department of Sociology, Evanston, IL 60208. Offers PhD, JD/PhD. Admissions and degrees offered through The Graduate School. *Degree requirements:* For doctorate, thesis/dissertation. *Entrance requirements:* For doctorate, GRE General Test. Additional exam requirements/recommendations for international students: Required—TOEFL. Electronic applications accepted. *Faculty research:* Sociology of culture, social organizations, social inequality, comparative/historical sociology, economic sociology.

The Ohio State University, Graduate School, College of Social and Behavioral Sciences, School of Social and Behavioral Science, Department of Sociology, Columbus, OH 43210. Offers MA, PhD. *Faculty:* 41. *Students:* 44 full-time (23 women), 32 part-time (21 women); includes 15 minority (8 African Americans, 4 Asian Americans or Pacific Islanders, 3 Hispanic Americans), 5 international. Average age 29. In 2009, 20 master's, 3 doctorates awarded. *Degree requirements:* For master's, thesis; for doctorate, thesis/dissertation. *Entrance requirements:* For master's and doctorate, GRE General Test. Additional exam requirements/recommendations for international students: Required—TOEFL (minimum score 600 paper-based; 250 computer-based). *Application deadline:* For fall admission, 8/15 priority date for domestic students, 7/1 priority date for international students; for winter admission, 12/1 priority date for domestic students, 11/1 priority date for international students; for spring admission, 3/1 priority date for domestic students, 2/1 priority date for international students. Applications are processed on a rolling basis. Application fee: $40 ($50 for international students). Electronic applications accepted. *Expenses:* Tuition, state resident: full-time $10,683. Tuition, nonresident: full-time $25,923. Tuition and fees vary according to course load and program. *Financial support:* Fellowships, research assistantships, teaching assistantships, Federal Work-Study and institutionally sponsored loans available. Support available to part-time students. *Unit head:* Dana Haynie, Graduate Studies Committee Chair, 614-292-8432, Fax: 614-292-6687, E-mail: haynie.7@osu.edu. *Application contact:* 614-292-9444, Fax: 614-292-3895, E-mail: domestic.grad@osu.edu.

Ohio University, Graduate College, College of Arts and Sciences, Department of Sociology and Anthropology, Athens, OH 45701-2979. Offers sociology (MA). Part-time programs available. *Faculty:* 17 full-time (8 women). *Students:* 27 full-time (15 women), 4 part-time (3 women); includes 3 minority (1 African American, 1 Asian American or Pacific Islander, 1 Hispanic American), 4 international. 24 applicants, 79% accepted, 15 enrolled. In 2009, 9 master's awarded. *Degree requirements:* For master's, thesis or alternative. *Entrance requirements:* For master's, minimum GPA of 3.0; minimum of 20 hours in sociology including statistics, theory, and research methods. Additional exam requirements/recommendations for international students: Required—TOEFL (minimum score 550 paper-based; 80 iBT) or IELTS Academic (minimum score 6.5). *Application deadline:* For fall admission, 6/1 for domestic students, 3/1 priority date for international students; for winter admission, 10/1 for domestic and international students; for spring admission, 1/1 for domestic and international students. Application fee: $50 ($55 for international students). Electronic applications accepted. *Expenses:* Tuition, state resident: full-time $7839; part-time $323 per quarter hour. Tuition, nonresident: full-time $15,831; part-time $654 per quarter hour. Required fees: $2931. *Financial support:* Research assistantships with full and partial tuition reimbursements, teaching assistantships with full tuition reimbursements, career-related internships or fieldwork, Federal Work-Study, and unspecified assistantships available. Financial award application deadline: 3/1. *Faculty research:* Criminology/deviance, gender studies, inequality, social psychology and rural poverty. *Unit head:* Dr. Leon Anderson, Department Chair, 740-593-1381, Fax: 740-593-1365, E-mail: andersoe@ohio.edu. *Application contact:* Dr. Cynthia D. Anderson, Graduate Chair, 740-593-1385, Fax: 740-593-1365, E-mail: andersc2@ohio.edu.

Oklahoma City University, Petree College of Arts and Sciences, Division of Sociology and Justice Studies, Oklahoma City, OK 73106-1402. Offers applied sociology (MA), including nonprofit leadership; criminal justice (MCJ). Part-time and evening/weekend programs available. *Faculty:* 4 full-time (1 woman), 3 part-time/adjunct (2 women). *Students:* 11 full-time (8 women), 4 part-time (3 women); includes 3 minority (all African Americans), 1 international. Average age 31. 9 applicants, 89% accepted. In 2009, 7 master's awarded. *Degree requirements:* For master's, thesis optional. *Entrance requirements:* For master's, minimum GPA of 3.0, two letters of recommendation. Additional exam requirements/recommendations for international students: Required—TOEFL (minimum score 550 paper-based). *Application deadline:* For fall admission, 8/22 for domestic students; for spring admission, 1/15 for domestic students. Applications are processed on a rolling basis. Application fee: $30 ($70 for international students). *Expenses:* Contact institution. *Financial support:* Fellowships with partial tuition reimbursements, career-related internships or fieldwork available. Financial award application deadline: 8/1; financial award applicants required to submit FAFSA. *Faculty research:* Victims, police, corrections, security, women and crime. *Unit head:* Dr. Jody Horn, Director, 405-208-5247, Fax: 405-208-5447, E-mail: jhorn@okcu.edu. *Application contact:* Michelle Lockhart, Director, Admissions, 800-633-7242, Fax: 405-208-5916, E-mail: gadmissions@okcu.edu.

Oklahoma State University, College of Arts and Sciences, Department of Sociology, Stillwater, OK 74078. Offers sociology (MS, PhD). *Faculty:* 14 full-time (4 women), 2 part-time/adjunct (both women). *Students:* 10 full-time (5 women), 22 part-time (13 women); includes 4 minority (2 African Americans, 2 American Indian/Alaska Native), 3 international. Average age 35. 46 applicants, 35% accepted, 7 enrolled. In 2009, 3 master's, 1 doctorate awarded. *Degree requirements:* For master's, thesis; for doctorate, comprehensive exam, thesis/dissertation. *Entrance requirements:* For master's and doctorate, GRE General Test. Additional exam requirements/recommendations for international students: Required—TOEFL (minimum score 550 paper-based; 79 iBT). *Application deadline:* For fall admission, 3/1 priority date for international students; for spring admission, 8/1 priority date for international students. Applications are processed on a rolling basis. Application fee: $40 ($75 for international students). Electronic applications accepted. *Expenses:* Tuition, state resident: full-time $3716; part-time $154.85 per credit hour. Tuition, nonresident: full-time $14,448; part-time $602 per credit hour. Required fees: $1772; $73.85 per credit hour. One-time fee: $50. Tuition and fees vary according to course load and campus/location. *Financial support:* In 2009–10, 3 research assistantships (averaging $10,825 per year), 24 teaching assistantships (averaging $14,447 per year) were awarded; career-related internships or fieldwork, Federal Work-Study, scholarships/grants, health care benefits, tuition waivers (partial), and unspecified assistantships also available. Support available to part-time students. Financial award application deadline: 3/1; financial award applicants required to submit FAFSA. *Faculty research:* Criminology/correction/legal issues; race, ethnicity, and gender in American society; environmental conflict and population problems; international comparative research; social change and social movement in American culture. *Unit head:* Dr. Duane Gill, Head, 405-744-6105, Fax: 405-744-5780. *Application contact:* Dr. Gordon Emslie, Dean, 405-744-6368, Fax: 405-744-0355, E-mail: grad-i@okstate.edu.

Old Dominion University, College of Arts and Letters, Program in Applied Sociology, Norfolk, VA 23529. Offers MA. Part-time and evening/weekend programs available. *Faculty:* 15 full-time (10 women), 1 part-time/adjunct (0 women). *Students:* 7 full-time (5 women), 28 part-time (20 women); includes 10 minority (9 African Americans, 1 Asian American or Pacific Islander), 1 international. Average age 28. 26 applicants, 65% accepted, 12 enrolled. In 2009, 8 master's awarded. *Degree requirements:* For master's, thesis. *Entrance requirements:* For master's, GRE General Test, minimum GPA of 3.0, 12 credits in criminal justice, sociology, or women's studies. Additional exam requirements/recommendations for international students: Required—TOEFL. *Application deadline:* For fall admission, 5/1 for domestic and international students; for spring admission, 11/1 for domestic students, 10/1 for international students. Application fee: $40. Electronic applications accepted. *Expenses:* Tuition, state resident: full-time $8112; part-time $338 per credit. Tuition, nonresident: full-time $20,256; part-time $844 per credit. Required fees: $119 per semester. One-time fee: $50. *Financial support:* In 2009–10, fellowships (averaging $2,000 per year), 2 research assistantships with partial tuition reimbursements (averaging $8,000 per year), 2 teaching assistantships with partial tuition reimbursements (averaging $8,000 per year) were awarded; career-related internships or fieldwork, scholarships/grants, and unspecified assistantships also available. Financial award application deadline: 2/15; financial award applicants required to submit CSS PROFILE or FAFSA. *Faculty research:* Quantitative methodology, theory, family, gender/class/race, crime. Total annual research expenditures: $350,000. *Unit head:* Dr. Dianne Carmody, Graduate Program Director, 757-683-6801, Fax: 757-683-5634, E-mail: dcarmody@odu.edu. *Application contact:* Dr. Dianne Carmody, Graduate Program Director, 757-683-6801, Fax: 757-683-5634, E-mail: dcarmody@odu.edu.

Penn State University Park, Graduate School, College of the Liberal Arts, Department of Sociology, State College, University Park, PA 16802-1503. Offers MA, PhD. *Unit head:* Dr. John D. McCarthy, Head, 814-863-8260, Fax: 814-863-7216, E-mail: jxm516@psu.edu. *Application contact:* Cynthia E. Nicosia, Director, Graduate Enrollment Services, 814-865-1795, Fax: 814-865-4627, E-mail: cey1@psu.edu.

Portland State University, Graduate Studies, College of Liberal Arts and Sciences, Department of Sociology, Portland, OR 97207-0751. Offers MA, MS, PhD. Part-time programs available. *Degree requirements:* For master's, variable foreign language requirement, thesis, written exam; for doctorate, thesis/dissertation. *Entrance requirements:* For master's, GRE General Test, GRE Subject Test, minimum GPA of 3.0 in upper-division course work or 2.75 overall, 3 letters of recommendation. Additional exam requirements/recommendations for international students: Required—TOEFL (minimum score 550 paper-based; 213 computer-based). *Faculty research:* Urban sociology, gender and class, development, social change, race/ethnic/minority relations.

Portland State University, Graduate Studies, Systems Science Program, Portland, OR 97207-0751. Offers computational intelligence (Certificate); computer modeling and simulation (Certificate); systems science (MS); systems science/anthropology (PhD); systems science/business administration (PhD); systems science/civil engineering (PhD); systems science/economics (PhD); systems science/engineering management (PhD); systems science/general (PhD); systems science/mathematical sciences (PhD); systems science/mechanical engineering (PhD); systems science/psychology (PhD); systems science/sociology (PhD). *Degree requirements:* For doctorate, variable foreign language requirement, thesis/dissertation. *Entrance requirements:* For master's, 2 letters of recommendation; for doctorate, GMAT, GRE General Test, minimum undergraduate GPA of 3.0. Additional exam requirements/recommendations for international students: Required—TOEFL. *Faculty research:* Systems theory and methodology, artificial intelligence neural networks, information theory, nonlinear dynamics/chaos, modeling and simulation.

Prairie View A&M University, College of Arts and Sciences, Division of Social Work, Behavioral and Political Science, Prairie View, TX 77446-0519. Offers sociology (MA). Part-time and evening/weekend programs available. *Faculty:* 3 full-time (2 women), 1 part-time/adjunct (0 women). *Students:* 4 full-time (3 women), 11 part-time (9 women); all minorities (13 African Americans, 1 Asian American or Pacific Islander, 1 Hispanic American). Average age 30. 5 applicants, 100% accepted, 5 enrolled. In 2009, 7 master's awarded. *Degree requirements:* For master's, comprehensive exam, thesis optional. *Entrance requirements:* For master's, GRE General Test. *Application deadline:* Applications are processed on a rolling basis. Application fee: $50. *Expenses:* Tuition, state resident: full-time $2200. Tuition, nonresident: full-time $5600. Required fees: $1720. Tuition and fees vary according to course load. *Financial support:* Federal Work-Study and institutionally sponsored loans available. Financial award application deadline: 4/1; financial award applicants required to submit FAFSA. *Faculty research:* Criminology, political sociology, sociology of education, gender, race, African-American mental health, global development-social movements, African-American status attainment. *Unit head:* Dr. Walle Engedayehu, Division Head, 936-261-3200, Fax: 936-261-3229, E-mail: waengedayehu@pvamu.edu. *Application contact:* Dr. Walle Engedayehu, Division Head, 936-261-3200, Fax: 936-261-3229, E-mail: waengedayehu@pvamu.edu.

Princeton University, Graduate School, Department of Sociology, Princeton, NJ 08544-1019. Offers sociology (PhD); sociology and demography (PhD). *Degree requirements:* For doctorate, variable foreign language requirement, thesis/dissertation. *Entrance requirements:* For doctorate, GRE General Test, GRE Subject Test (recommended), sample of written work. Additional exam requirements/recommendations for international students: Required—TOEFL (minimum score 600 paper-based; 250 computer-based). Electronic applications accepted.

Princeton University, Graduate School, Program in Population Studies, Princeton, NJ 08544-1019. Offers demography (PhD, Certificate); economics and demography (PhD); public affairs and demography (PhD); sociology and demography (PhD). *Degree requirements:* For doctorate, thesis/dissertation. *Entrance requirements:* For doctorate, GRE General Test. Additional exam requirements/recommendations for international students: Required—TOEFL (minimum score 600 paper-based; 250 computer-based). Electronic applications accepted. *Faculty research:* Models, fertility, infant and child mortality, migration.

Purdue University, Graduate School, College of Liberal Arts, Department of Sociology and Anthropology, West Lafayette, IN 47907. Offers anthropology (MS, PhD); sociology (MS, PhD). Terminal master's awarded for partial completion of doctoral program. *Degree requirements:* For doctorate, thesis/dissertation. *Entrance requirements:* For master's and doctorate, GRE General Test. Additional exam requirements/recommendations for international students: Required—TOEFL, TWE. Electronic applications accepted. *Faculty research:* Communiversity survey project, risk, fear, constrained behavior, archaeological services.

Queens College of the City University of New York, Division of Graduate Studies, Social Science Division, Department of Sociology, Flushing, NY 11367-1597. Offers MA. Part-time and evening/weekend programs available. *Faculty:* 26 full-time (9 women). *Students:* 12 full-time (9 women), 32 part-time (23 women). 41 applicants, 78% accepted, 26 enrolled. In 2009, 21 master's awarded. *Degree requirements:* For master's, thesis optional. *Entrance requirements:* For master's, minimum GPA of 3.0. Additional exam requirements/recommendations for international students: Required—TOEFL. *Application deadline:* For fall admission, 4/1 for domestic students; for spring admission, 11/1 for domestic students. Applications are processed on a rolling basis. Application fee: $125. *Expenses:* Tuition, state resident: full-time $7360; part-time $310 per credit. Tuition, nonresident: part-time $575 per credit. One-time fee: $195.25 full-time; $145.25 part-time. *Financial support:* Career-related internships or fieldwork, Federal Work-Study, institutionally sponsored loans, and tuition waivers (partial) available. Support available to part-time students. Financial award application deadline: 4/1; financial award applicants required to submit FAFSA. *Unit head:* Dr. Andrew Beveridge, Chairperson, 718-997-2800. *Application contact:* Mario Caruso, Director of Graduate Admissions, 718-997-5200, Fax: 718-997-5193, E-mail: graduate_admissions@qc.edu.

Queen's University at Kingston, School of Graduate Studies and Research, Faculty of Arts and Sciences, Department of Sociology, Kingston, ON K7L 3N6, Canada. Offers communication and Information technology (MA, PhD); feminist sociology (MA, PhD); socio-legal studies (MA, PhD); sociological theory (MA, PhD). Part-time programs available. *Degree requirements:* For master's, thesis; for doctorate, comprehensive exam, thesis/dissertation. *Entrance requirements:* For master's, honors bachelors degree in sociology; for doctorate, honors bachelors degree, masters degree in sociology. Additional exam requirements/recommendations for international students: Required—TOEFL. *Faculty research:* Social change and modernization, social control, deviance and criminology, surveillance.

Rice University, Graduate Programs, School of Social Sciences, Department of Sociology, Houston, TX 77251-1892. Offers PhD.

Roosevelt University, Graduate Division, College of Arts and Sciences, Department of Sociology and Anthropology, Chicago, IL 60605. Offers anthropology (MA); sociology (MA). Part-time and evening/weekend programs available. *Degree requirements:* For master's, comprehensive exam, thesis. *Faculty research:* Social theory, urban sociology, gerontology, social organizations.

Rutgers, The State University of New Jersey, New Brunswick, Graduate School-New Brunswick, Program in Sociology, Piscataway, NJ 08854-8097. Offers MA, PhD. Terminal master's awarded for partial completion of doctoral program. *Degree requirements:* For master's, qualifying paper; for doctorate, thesis/dissertation, qualifying exam, qualifying papers. *Entrance requirements:* For master's, GRE General Test; for doctorate, GRE General Test, sample of written work. Additional exam requirements/recommendations for international students: Required—TOEFL. Electronic applications accepted. *Faculty research:* Comparative-historical, sex and gender, organizations and work, culture and cognition, economics, occupations/professions, religion.

St. John's University, St. John's College of Liberal Arts and Sciences, Department of Sociology and Anthropology, Queens, NY 11439. Offers criminology and justice (MA); sociology (MA). Part-time and evening/weekend programs available. *Students:* 39 full-time (24 women), 25 part-time (16 women); includes 34 minority (16 African Americans, 7 Asian Americans or Pacific Islanders, 11 Hispanic Americans), 5 international. Average age 27. 67 applicants, 58% accepted, 31 enrolled. In 2009, 36 master's awarded. *Degree requirements:* For master's, comprehensive exam, thesis optional. *Entrance requirements:* For master's, 18 undergraduate credits in social services, minimum GPA of 3.0. Additional exam requirements/recommendations for international students: Required—TOEFL (minimum score 500 paper-based; 173 computer-based; 61 iBT), IELTS (minimum score 5.5). *Application deadline:* For fall admission, 5/1 priority date for domestic and international students; for spring admission, 11/1 priority date for domestic and international students. Applications are processed on a rolling basis. Application fee: $70. Electronic applications accepted. *Expenses:* Tuition: Full-time $16,290; part-time $905 per credit. Required fees: $300; $150 per semester. Tuition and fees vary according to program. *Financial support:* Research assistantships, career-related internships or fieldwork and scholarships/grants available. Support available to part-time students. Financial award application deadline: 3/1; financial award applicants required to submit FAFSA. *Faculty research:* Community studies and gentrification, global financial crisis, insurance fraud, globalization, immigration and human rights. *Unit head:* Dr. Dawn Esposito, Chair, 718-990-5667, E-mail: espositd@stjohns.edu. *Application contact:* Kathleen Davis, Director of Graduate Admission, 718-990-2790, Fax: 718-990-5686, E-mail: gradhelp@stjohns.edu.

Sam Houston State University, College of Humanities and Social Sciences, Department of Sociology, Huntsville, TX 77341. Offers MA. Part-time programs available. *Faculty:* 7 full-time (5 women). *Students:* 4 full-time (all women), 7 part-time (3 women); includes 4 minority (1 Asian American or Pacific Islander, 3 Hispanic Americans), 2 international. Average age 26. 4 applicants, 100% accepted, 4 enrolled. In 2009, 3 master's awarded. *Degree requirements:* For master's, thesis optional. *Entrance requirements:* For master's, GRE General Test. Additional exam requirements/recommendations for international students: Required—TOEFL (minimum score 550 paper-based; 213 computer-based; 79 iBT). *Application deadline:* For fall admission, 8/1 for domestic students; for spring admission, 12/1 for domestic students. Applications are processed on a rolling basis. Application fee: $20. *Expenses:* Tuition, state resident: full-time $3690; part-time $205 per credit hour. Tuition, nonresident: full-time $8676; part-time $482 per credit hour. Required fees: $1474. Tuition and fees vary according to course load and campus/location. *Financial support:* Teaching assistantships, Federal Work-Study available. Support available to part-time students. Financial award application deadline: 5/31; financial award applicants required to submit FAFSA. *Unit head:* Dr. Alessandro Bonanno, Chair, 936-294-1488, Fax: 963-294-3573, E-mail: soc_aab@shsu.edu. *Application contact:* Dr. Gene Theodori, Director of Graduate Studies, 936-294-4143, E-mail: glt002@shsu.edu.

San Diego State University, Graduate and Research Affairs, College of Arts and Letters, Department of Sociology, San Diego, CA 92182. Offers MA. *Degree requirements:* For master's, thesis. *Entrance requirements:* For master's, GRE General Test, 3 letters of recommendation, writing sample. Additional exam requirements/recommendations for international students: Required—TOEFL. Electronic applications accepted. *Faculty research:* The homeless and mentally ill, medical data relating to the homeless.

San Jose State University, Graduate Studies and Research, College of Social Sciences, Department of Sociology, San Jose, CA 95192-0001. Offers MA. Part-time and evening/weekend programs available. *Students:* 7 full-time (3 women), 24 part-time (17 women); includes 20 minority (2 African Americans, 1 American Indian/Alaska Native, 6 Asian Americans or Pacific Islanders, 11 Hispanic Americans), 1 international. Average age 28. 37 applicants, 43% accepted, 7 enrolled. In 2009, 2 master's awarded. *Degree requirements:* For master's, comprehensive exams or thesis. *Entrance requirements:* For master's, GRE Subject Test, minimum GPA of 3.0. *Application deadline:* For fall admission, 6/29 for domestic students; for spring admission, 11/30 for domestic students. Applications are processed on a rolling basis. Application fee: $59. Electronic applications accepted. *Financial support:* Teaching assistantships, career-related internships or fieldwork, Federal Work-Study, and institutionally sponsored loans available. Financial award application deadline: 3/1; financial award applicants required to submit FAFSA. *Faculty research:* Theory construction, sexuality, sociology of the media, social causes of stress, social change. *Unit head:* Yoko Baba, Chair, 408-924-5320, Fax: 408-924-5322. *Application contact:* Preston Rudy, Graduate Advisor, 408-924-5333, E-mail: porudy@sjsu.edu.

Shippensburg University of Pennsylvania, School of Graduate Studies, College of Arts and Sciences, Department of Sociology and Anthropology, Shippensburg, PA 17257-2299. Offers organizational development and leadership (MS), including business, communications, education, environmental management, higher education, historical administration, individual and organizational development, public organizations, social structures and organizations. Part-time and evening/weekend programs available. *Degree requirements:* For master's, capstone experience. *Entrance requirements:* For master's, interview (if GPA less than 2.75), resume. Additional exam requirements/recommendations for international students: Required—TOEFL (minimum score 560 paper-based; 220 computer-based); Recommended—IELTS (minimum score 6). Electronic applications accepted.

Simon Fraser University, Graduate Studies, Faculty of Arts and Social Sciences, Department of Sociology and Anthropology, Burnaby, BC V5A 1S6, Canada. Offers anthropology (MA, PhD); sociology (MA, PhD). *Degree requirements:* For master's, thesis (for some programs); for doctorate, thesis/dissertation. *Entrance requirements:* For master's and doctorate, minimum GPA of 3.25. Additional exam requirements/recommendations for international students: Required—TOEFL or IELTS. *Faculty research:* Sociology theory, social and cultural anthropology, political sociology, religion and society, Canadian native peoples.

Southeastern Louisiana University, College of Arts, Humanities and Social Sciences, Department of Sociology and Criminal Justice, Hammond, LA 70402. Offers applied sociology (MS). Part-time and evening/weekend programs available. *Faculty:* 5 full-time (1 woman). *Students:* 19 full-time (16 women), 9 part-time (8 women); includes 11 minority (all African Americans). Average age 28. 11 applicants, 91% accepted, 5 enrolled. In 2009, 13 master's awarded. *Degree requirements:* For master's, comprehensive exam, thesis or alternative. *Entrance requirements:* For master's, GRE General Test (verbal and quantitative), bachelor's degree in sociology, social work, criminal justice or related social science; minimum GPA of 3.0. Additional exam requirements/recommendations for international students: Required—TOEFL (minimum score 500 paper-based; 173 computer-based; 61 iBT). *Application deadline:* For fall admission, 7/15 priority date for domestic students, 6/1 priority date for international students; for spring admission, 12/1 priority date for domestic students, 10/1 priority date for international students. Application fee: $20 ($30 for international students). *Expenses:* Tuition, state resident: full-time $3086; part-time $225 per credit hour. Tuition, nonresident: part-time $529 per credit hour. Required fees: $1195. Tuition and fees vary according to course level and course load. *Financial support:* In 2009–10, 6 students received support, including 6 research assistantships (averaging $9,367 per year); Federal Work-Study, institutionally sponsored loans, scholarships/grants, and administrative assistantships also available. Support available to part-time students. Financial award application deadline: 5/1; financial award applicants required to submit FAFSA. *Faculty research:* Community development, population and migration trends, environmental sociology, homicide and crime mapping, race and gender in the justice system. *Unit head:* Dr. Kenneth Bolton, Department Head, 985-549-2110, Fax: 985-549-5961, E-mail: kbolton@selu.edu. *Application contact:* Sandra Meyers, Graduate Admissions Analyst, 985-549-5620, Fax: 985-549-5632, E-mail: admissions@selu.edu.

Southern Connecticut State University, School of Graduate Studies, School of Arts and Sciences, Department of Sociology, New Haven, CT 06515-1355. Offers MS. Part-time and evening/weekend programs available. *Faculty:* 5 full-time, 1 part-time/adjunct. *Students:* 9 full-time (7 women), 19 part-time (12 women); includes 8 minority (5 African Americans, 1 American Indian/Alaska Native, 1 Asian American or Pacific Islander, 1 Hispanic American). 14 applicants, 93% accepted, 10 enrolled. In 2009, 6 master's awarded. *Degree requirements:* For master's, thesis or alternative. *Entrance requirements:* For master's, interview. *Application deadline:* For fall admission, 7/15 priority date for domestic students. Applications are processed on a rolling basis. Application fee: $50. Electronic applications accepted. Tuition and fees vary according to program. *Financial support:* Application deadline: 4/15. *Unit head:* Dr. Jon Bloch, Chairperson, 203-392-5685, Fax: 203-392-5670, E-mail: blochj1@southernct.edu. *Application contact:* Dr. Jessica Kenty-Drane, Graduate Coordinator, 203-392-5689, Fax: 203-392-5670, E-mail: kentydranej1@southernct.edu.

Southern Illinois University Carbondale, Graduate School, College of Liberal Arts, Department of Sociology, Carbondale, IL 62901-4701. Offers MA, PhD. Part-time programs available. *Degree requirements:* For master's, thesis; for doctorate, thesis/dissertation. *Entrance requirements:* For master's, minimum GPA of 2.7; for doctorate, minimum GPA of 3.25. Additional exam requirements/recommendations for international students: Required—TOEFL. *Faculty research:* Deviance, family, social stratification, social change, theory methodology, culture.

Southern Illinois University Edwardsville, Graduate Studies and Research, College of Arts and Sciences, Department of Sociology and Criminal Justice Studies, Edwardsville, IL 62026-0001. Offers sociology (MA). Part-time programs available. *Faculty:* 13 full-time (8 women). *Students:* 1 full-time (0 women), 21 part-time (16 women); includes 3 minority (2 African Americans, 1 Hispanic American), 1 international. Average age 26. 24 applicants, 54% accepted. In 2009, 3 master's awarded. *Degree requirements:* For master's, internship or thesis. *Entrance requirements:* Additional exam requirements/recommendations for international students: Required—TOEFL (minimum score 550 paper-based; 213 computer-based; 79 iBT), IELTS (minimum score 6.5). *Application deadline:* For fall admission, 7/10 for domestic students; for spring admission, 11/15 for domestic students. Application fee: $30. Electronic applications accepted. *Expenses:* Tuition, state resident: part-time $1252.50 per semester. Tuition, nonresident: part-time $3131.25 per semester. Required fees: $586.85 per semester. Tuition and fees vary according to course load. *Financial support:* In 2009–10, 11 teaching assistantships with full tuition reimbursements (averaging $8,064 per year) were awarded; fellowships with full tuition reimbursements, research assistantships with full tuition reimbursements, career-related internships or fieldwork, Federal Work-Study, institutionally sponsored loans, scholarships/grants, traineeships, and unspecified assistantships also available. Support available to part-time students. Financial award application deadline: 3/1; financial award applicants required to submit FAFSA. *Unit head:* Dr. David Kauzlarich, Chair, 618-650-3713, E-mail: dkauzla@siue.edu. *Application contact:* Dr. Florence Maatita, Program Director, 618-650-3287, E-mail: fmaatit@siue.edu.

Stanford University, School of Humanities and Sciences, Department of Sociology, Stanford, CA 94305-9991. Offers PhD. *Degree requirements:* For doctorate, thesis/dissertation, oral exam. *Entrance requirements:* For doctorate, GRE General Test. Additional exam requirements/recommendations for international students: Required—TOEFL. Electronic applications accepted. *Expenses:* Tuition: Full-time $37,380; part-time $2760 per quarter. Required fees: $501.

State University of New York at Binghamton, Graduate School, School of Arts and Sciences, Department of Sociology, Binghamton, NY 13902-6000. Offers MA, PhD. *Faculty:* 13 full-time (4 women), 11 part-time/adjunct (4 women). *Students:* 25 full-time (9 women), 47 part-time (20 women); includes 13 minority (5 African Americans, 5 Asian Americans or Pacific Islanders, 3 Hispanic Americans), 33 international. Average age 34. 43 applicants, 65% accepted, 8 enrolled. In 2009, 1 master's, 5 doctorates awarded. Terminal master's awarded for partial completion of doctoral program. *Degree requirements:* For doctorate, thesis/dissertation. *Entrance requirements:* For master's and doctorate, GRE General Test, GRE Subject Test. Additional exam requirements/recommendations for international students: Required—TOEFL (minimum score 550 paper-based; 213 computer-based; 80 iBT). *Application deadline:* For fall admission, 1/15 priority date for domestic and international students. Applications are processed on a rolling basis. Application fee: $60. Electronic applications accepted. *Financial support:* In 2009–10, 26 students received support, including 3 fellowships with full tuition reimbursements available (averaging $14,700 per year), 19 teaching assistantships with full tuition reimbursements available (averaging $14,700 per year); research assistantships with full tuition reimbursements available, career-related internships or fieldwork, Federal Work-Study, institutionally sponsored loans, scholarships/grants, health care benefits, and unspecified assistantships also available. Financial award application deadline: 2/15; financial award applicants required to submit FAFSA. *Unit head:* Dr. Ravi Palat, Chairperson, 607-777-4756, E-mail: palat@binghamton.edu. *Application contact:* Victoria Williams, Recruiting and Admissions Coordinator, 607-777-2151, Fax: 607-777-2501, E-mail: vwilliam@binghamton.edu.

State University of New York Institute of Technology, School of Arts and Sciences, Program in Applied Sociology, Utica, NY 13504-3050. Offers MS. Part-time and evening/weekend programs available. *Degree requirements:* For master's, thesis or project. *Entrance requirements:* For master's, minimum GPA of 3.0, letters of recommendation (3). Additional exam requirements/recommendations for international students: Required—TOEFL (minimum score 550 paper-based; 213 computer-based). *Faculty research:* Family violence, race/class/gender, prisoner re-entry, drug abuse, information technology applications.

Stony Brook University, State University of New York, Graduate School, College of Arts and Sciences, Department of Sociology, Stony Brook, NY 11794. Offers MA, PhD. *Faculty:* 16 full-time (3 women). *Students:* 49 full-time (29 women), 5 part-time (all women); includes 6 minority (2 African Americans, 3 Asian Americans or Pacific Islanders, 1 Hispanic American), 18 international. Average age 33. 83 applicants, 25% accepted. In 2009, 5 master's, 5 doctorates awarded. *Degree requirements:* For doctorate, thesis/dissertation, comprehensive exam or professional papers, field exam, teaching practicum. *Entrance requirements:* For doctorate, GRE General Test, minimum GPA of 3.0. Additional exam requirements/recommendations for international students: Required—TOEFL. *Application deadline:* For fall admission, 1/15 for domestic students. Application fee: $60. *Expenses:* Tuition, state resident: full-time $8370; part-time $349 per credit. Tuition, nonresident: full-time $13,250; part-time $552 per credit. Required fees: $933. *Financial support:* In 2009–10, 4 research assistantships, 37 teaching assistantships were awarded; fellowships also available. *Faculty research:* Deviant behavior, history of sociology/social thought, marriage and family sociology, political sociology. Total annual research expenditures: $58,745. *Unit head:* Dr. Ian Roxborough, Chair, 631-632-7700, Fax: 631-632-8203, E-mail: ian.roxborough@stonybrook.edu. *Application contact:* Dr. Timothy P. Moran, Director, 631-632-7700, Fax: 631-632-8203, E-mail: tpmoran@notes.cc.sunysb.edu.

Syracuse University, Maxwell School of Citizenship and Public Affairs, Program in Sociology, Syracuse, NY 13244. Offers MA, PhD. *Students:* 28 full-time (23 women), 10 part-time (all women); includes 10 minority (8 African Americans, 2 Hispanic Americans), 10 international. Average age 32. 28 applicants, 36% accepted, 3 enrolled. In 2009, 6 master's, 4 doctorates awarded. *Degree requirements:* For master's, thesis optional; for doctorate, thesis/dissertation. *Entrance requirements:* For master's and doctorate, GRE General Test. Additional exam requirements/recommendations for international students: Required—TOEFL (minimum score 100 iBT). *Application deadline:* For fall admission, 2/1 priority date for domestic and international students. Application fee: $75. Electronic applications accepted. *Expenses:* Tuition: Full-time $26,808; part-time $1117 per credit. Required fees: $1024. *Financial support:* Fel-

Sociology

Syracuse University (continued)

lowships with full tuition reimbursements, research assistantships with tuition reimbursements, teaching assistantships with full and partial tuition reimbursements, tuition waivers (full and partial) and unspecified assistantships available. Financial award application deadline: 1/1. *Faculty research:* Qualitative methods and feminist methods, inequality studies, aging and the life course. *Unit head:* Dr. Prema Kurien, Graduate Chair, 315-443-2347, Fax: 315-443-4597, E-mail: sociology@maxwell.syr.edu. *Application contact:* Janet Coria, Recruiting Contact, 315-443-2347, E-mail: jmcoria@syr.edu.

Teachers College, Columbia University, Graduate Faculty of Education, Department of Human Development, Program in Sociology and Education, New York, NY 10027-6696. Offers Ed M, MA, Ed D, PhD. *Faculty:* 3 full-time (1 woman). *Students:* 17 full-time (13 women), 54 part-time (42 women); includes 45 minority (28 African Americans, 9 Asian Americans or Pacific Islanders, 8 Hispanic Americans), 2 international. Average age 28. 60 applicants, 85% accepted, 25 enrolled. In 2009, 12 master's awarded. *Degree requirements:* For doctorate, thesis/dissertation. *Entrance requirements:* For master's, GRE (Ed M); for doctorate, GRE. *Application deadline:* For fall admission, 5/15 for domestic students. Application fee: $65. *Financial support:* Career-related internships or fieldwork, Federal Work-Study, institutionally sponsored loans, and tuition waivers (full and partial) available. Support available to part-time students. Financial award application deadline: 2/1. *Faculty research:* Stratification, race and evaluation, desegregation of schools and communities, quantitative research. *Application contact:* Melba Remice, Assistant Director of Admission, 212-678-4035, Fax: 212-678-4171, E-mail: ms2545@columbia.edu.

Temple University, Graduate School, College of Liberal Arts, Department of Sociology, Philadelphia, PA 19122-6096. Offers MA, PhD. Part-time and evening/weekend programs available. Terminal master's awarded for partial completion of doctoral program. *Degree requirements:* For doctorate, thesis/dissertation. *Entrance requirements:* For master's and doctorate, GRE General Test, minimum GPA of 3.0. Additional exam requirements/recommendations for international students: Required—TOEFL (minimum score 550 paper-based; 213 computer-based; 79 iBT). Electronic applications accepted. *Faculty research:* International development, race-ethnicity-gender inequality, urban structure, political economy.

Texas A&M International University, Office of Graduate Studies and Research, College of Arts and Sciences, Department of Behavioral, Applied Sciences, and Criminal Justice, Laredo, TX 78041-1900. Offers counseling psychology (MACP); criminal justice (MS); psychology (MS); sociology (MA). *Faculty:* 8 full-time (3 women), 1 part-time/adjunct (0 women). *Students:* 13 full-time (8 women), 88 part-time (63 women); includes 94 minority (1 African American, 93 Hispanic Americans). Average age 30. 68 applicants, 69% accepted, 47 enrolled. In 2009, 14 master's awarded. *Degree requirements:* For master's, thesis (for some programs). *Entrance requirements:* For master's, GRE General Test. Additional exam requirements/recommendations for international students: Required—TOEFL (minimum score 550 paper-based; 213 computer-based). *Application deadline:* For fall admission, 4/30 priority date for domestic students; for spring admission, 11/30 for domestic students. Applications are processed on a rolling basis. Application fee: $25. *Financial support:* In 2009–10, 17 students received support, including 3 research assistantships, 1 teaching assistantship. Financial award application deadline: 11/1. *Unit head:* Dr. Roberto Heredia, Chair, 956-326-2637, Fax: 956-326-2459, E-mail: rheredia@tamiu.edu. *Application contact:* Rosie Espinoza-Dickinson, Director of Admissions, 956-326-2200, Fax: 956-326-2199, E-mail: enroll@tamiu.edu.

Texas A&M University, College of Liberal Arts, Department of Sociology, College Station, TX 77843. Offers MS, PhD. *Faculty:* 19. *Students:* 79 full-time (45 women), 32 part-time (24 women); includes 60 minority (23 African Americans, 2 American Indian/Alaska Native, 6 Asian Americans or Pacific Islanders, 29 Hispanic Americans), 10 international. Average age 32. In 2009, 7 master's, 8 doctorates awarded. *Degree requirements:* For master's, thesis or alternative; for doctorate, thesis/dissertation. *Entrance requirements:* For master's and doctorate, GRE General Test. Additional exam requirements/recommendations for international students: Required—TOEFL. *Application deadline:* For fall admission, 1/15 priority date for domestic students; for winter admission, 11/1 priority date for domestic students. Applications are processed on a rolling basis. Application fee: $50 ($75 for international students). Electronic applications accepted. *Expenses:* Tuition, state resident: full-time $3991; part-time $221.74 per credit hour. Tuition, nonresident: full-time $9049; part-time $502.74 per credit hour. *Financial support:* In 2009–10, fellowships (averaging $12,000 per year), research assistantships (averaging $9,795 per year), teaching assistantships (averaging $9,795 per year) were awarded; institutionally sponsored loans and unspecified assistantships also available. Financial award application deadline: 1/15; financial award applicants required to submit FAFSA. *Faculty research:* Crime, deviance, and law; culture; demography and human ecology; political and economic sociology; racial and ethnic relations; social psychology; Latino sociology; gender; Asian studies. *Unit head:* Mark Fossett, Head, 979-845-5133, Fax: 979-862-4057, E-mail: m-fossett@tamu.edu. *Application contact:* Dr. Kathryn Henderson, Graduate Advisor, 979-845-9706, Fax: 979-862-4057, E-mail: hendrsn@acs.tamu.edu.

See Close-Up on page 1245.

Texas A&M University–Commerce, Graduate School, College of Arts and Sciences, Department of Sociology and Criminal Justice, Commerce, TX 75429-3011. Offers sociology (MA, MS). Part-time programs available. *Degree requirements:* For master's, comprehensive exam, thesis (for some programs). *Entrance requirements:* For master's, GRE General Test. *Faculty research:* Marriage and family, drugs and society, criminal justice, delinquency.

Texas A&M University–Kingsville, College of Graduate Studies, College of Arts and Sciences, Department of Psychology and Sociology, Kingsville, TX 78363. Offers gerontology (MS); psychology (MA, MS); sociology (MA, MS). Part-time and evening/weekend programs available. *Degree requirements:* For master's, comprehensive exam, thesis or alternative. *Entrance requirements:* For master's, GRE General Test, minimum GPA of 2.5. Additional exam requirements/recommendations for international students: Required—TOEFL. *Faculty research:* Hispanic female voting behavior, attitudes toward criminal justice, immigration of aged into south Texas, folk medicine.

Texas Southern University, College of Liberal Arts and Behavioral Sciences, Department of Sociology, Houston, TX 77004-4584. Offers MA. Part-time and evening/weekend programs available. *Faculty:* 4 full-time (2 women), 1 part-time/adjunct (0 women). *Students:* 7 full-time (5 women), 16 part-time (13 women); includes 22 African Americans. Average age 34. 13 applicants, 92% accepted, 9 enrolled. In 2009, 4 master's awarded. *Degree requirements:* For master's, comprehensive exam, thesis. *Entrance requirements:* For master's, GRE General Test, minimum GPA of 2.5. Additional exam requirements/recommendations for international students: Required—TOEFL. *Application deadline:* For fall admission, 7/1 for domestic and international students; for spring admission, 11/1 for domestic and international students. Applications are processed on a rolling basis. Application fee: $50 ($75 for international students). Electronic applications accepted. *Expenses:* Tuition, state resident: full-time $1805; part-time $100 per credit hour. Tuition, nonresident: full-time $6470; part-time $343 per credit hour. Tuition and fees vary according to course level, course load and degree level. *Financial support:* Teaching assistantships, scholarships/grants and unspecified assistantships available. Financial award application deadline: 5/1. *Faculty research:* Sociocultural systems, ethnic and regional studies, community sociology. *Unit head:* Dr. Earl Wright, Head, 713-313-4438. *Application contact:* Dr. Gregory Maddox, Interim Dean of the Graduate School, 713-313-7011 Ext. 4410, Fax: 713-639-1876, E-mail: maddox_gh@tsu.edu.

Texas State University–San Marcos, Graduate School, College of Liberal Arts, Department of Sociology, San Marcos, TX 78666. Offers MA, MS. Part-time and evening/weekend programs available. *Faculty:* 12 full-time (7 women), 1 part-time/adjunct (0 women). *Students:* 17 full-time (11 women), 25 part-time (15 women); includes 15 minority (4 African Americans, 11 Hispanic Americans). Average age 30. 18 applicants, 72% accepted, 10 enrolled. In 2009, 12 master's awarded. *Degree requirements:* For master's, comprehensive exam, thesis (for some programs). *Entrance requirements:* For master's, minimum GPA of 3.0 in last 60 hours of course work, 3 letters of reference, letter of intent, personal interview. Additional exam requirements/recommendations for international students: Required—TOEFL (minimum score 550 paper-based; 213 computer-based). *Application deadline:* For fall admission, 6/15 priority date for domestic students, 6/1 priority date for international students; for spring admission, 10/15 priority date for domestic students, 10/1 priority date for international students. Applications are processed on a rolling basis. Application fee: $40 ($90 for international students). Electronic applications accepted. *Expenses:* Tuition, state resident: full-time $5784; part-time $241 per credit hour. Tuition, nonresident: part-time $551 per credit hour. Required fees: $1728; $48 per credit hour. $306. Tuition and fees vary according to course load. *Financial support:* In 2009–10, 22 students received support, including 1 research assistantship (averaging $5,362 per year), 14 teaching assistantships (averaging $5,313 per year); career-related internships or fieldwork, Federal Work-Study, and institutionally sponsored loans also available. Support available to part-time students. Financial award application deadline: 4/1; financial award applicants required to submit FAFSA. *Unit head:* Dr. Susan Day, Chair, 512-245-2113, Fax: 512-245-8362, E-mail: sd01@txstate.edu. *Application contact:* Dr. J. Michael Willoughby, Dean of Graduate School, 512-245-2581, Fax: 512-245-8365, E-mail: gradcollege@txstate.edu.

Texas State University–San Marcos, Graduate School, Interdisciplinary Studies Program in Applied Sociology, San Marcos, TX 78666. Offers MAIS. Part-time and evening/weekend programs available. *Students:* 1 applicant, 100% accepted, 0 enrolled. *Degree requirements:* For master's, comprehensive exam. *Entrance requirements:* For master's, minimum GPA of 3.0 on last 60 hours of undergraduate work, 3 letters of reference, letter of intent. Additional exam requirements/recommendations for international students: Required—TOEFL (minimum score 550 paper-based; 213 computer-based). *Application deadline:* For fall admission, 6/15 priority date for domestic students; for spring admission, 10/15 priority date for domestic students. Applications are processed on a rolling basis. Application fee: $40 ($90 for international students). Electronic applications accepted. *Expenses:* Tuition, state resident: full-time $5784; part-time $241 per credit hour. Tuition, nonresident: part-time $551 per credit hour. Required fees: $1728; $48 per credit hour. $306. Tuition and fees vary according to course load. *Financial support:* Teaching assistantships available. Financial award application deadline: 4/1; financial award applicants required to submit FAFSA. *Unit head:* Dr. Audwin Anderson, Head, 512-245-2113, E-mail: aa04@txstate.edu. *Application contact:* Dr. J. Michael Willoughby, Dean of Graduate School, 512-245-2581, Fax: 512-245-8365, E-mail: gradcollege@txstate.edu.

Texas Tech University, Graduate School, College of Arts and Sciences, Department of Sociology, Anthropology and Social Work, Lubbock, TX 79409. Offers anthropology (MA); sociology (MA). Part-time programs available. *Faculty:* 17 full-time (7 women). *Students:* 20 full-time (13 women), 15 part-time (7 women); includes 10 minority (3 African Americans, 2 Asian Americans or Pacific Islanders, 5 Hispanic Americans), 1 international. Average age 29. 29 applicants, 69% accepted, 11 enrolled. In 2009, 8 master's awarded. *Degree requirements:* For master's, one foreign language, thesis or alternative. *Entrance requirements:* For master's, GRE General Test. Additional exam requirements/recommendations for international students: Required—TOEFL (minimum score 550 paper-based; 213 computer-based). *Application deadline:* For fall admission, 3/1 priority date for international students; for spring admission, 11/1 priority date for international students. Applications are processed on a rolling basis. Application fee: $50 ($75 for international students). Electronic applications accepted. *Expenses:* Tuition, state resident: full-time $5100; part-time $213 per credit hour. Tuition, nonresident: full-time $11,748; part-time $490 per credit hour. Required fees: $2298; $50 per credit hour. $555 per semester. *Financial support:* In 2009–10, 23 students received support, including 6 teaching assistantships with partial tuition reimbursements available (averaging $13,012 per year); research assistantships with partial tuition reimbursements available, Federal Work-Study and institutionally sponsored loans also available. Support available to part-time students. Financial award application deadline: 4/15; financial award applicants required to submit FAFSA. *Faculty research:* Sociology theory, research methods, physical and forensic anthropology, Texas archaeology, Mayan archaeology. *Unit head:* Dr. Jeffrey Payne Williams, Chair and Professor, 806-742-2400, Fax: 806-742-1088, E-mail: jeff.williams@ttu.edu. *Application contact:* Dr. Yung-Mei Tsai, Sociology Graduate Program Director, 806-742-2400, Fax: 806-742-1088, E-mail: yung.mei.tsai@ttu.edu.

Texas Woman's University, Graduate School, College of Arts and Sciences, Department of Sociology and Social Work, Denton, TX 76201. Offers sociology (MA, PhD). Evening/weekend programs available. *Faculty:* 7 full-time (4 women), 2 part-time/adjunct (0 women). *Students:* 6 full-time (4 women), 30 part-time (24 women); includes 13 minority (10 African Americans, 3 Hispanic Americans), 7 international. Average age 37. 10 applicants, 90% accepted, 6 enrolled. In 2009, 3 master's awarded. Terminal master's awarded for partial completion of doctoral program. *Degree requirements:* For master's, thesis; for doctorate, one foreign language, comprehensive exam, thesis/dissertation. *Entrance requirements:* For master's, minimum GPA of 3.0, 2 letters of reference; for doctorate, GRE General Test, minimum 12 hours course work in sociology (including graduate statistics and research methods), 3 letters of reference, minimum GPA of 3.5, 2-3 page statement of intent. Additional exam requirements/recommendations for international students: Required—TOEFL (minimum score 550 paper-based; 213 computer-based; 79 iBT). *Application deadline:* For fall admission, 7/1 priority date for domestic students, 3/1 for international students; for spring admission, 12/1 priority date for domestic students, 7/1 for international students. Applications are processed on a rolling basis. Application fee: $50. Electronic applications accepted. *Expenses:* Tuition, state resident: full-time $3564; part-time $198 per credit hour. Tuition, nonresident: full-time $8550; part-time $475 per credit hour. Required fees: $69.26 per credit hour. Tuition and fees vary according to course load. *Financial support:* In 2009–10, 16 students received support, including 6 research assistantships (averaging $10,746 per year), 10 teaching assistantships (averaging $10,746 per year); career-related internships or fieldwork, Federal Work-Study, institutionally sponsored loans, scholarships/grants, traineeships, health care benefits, and unspecified assistantships also available. Support available to part-time students. Financial award application deadline: 3/1; financial award applicants required to submit FAFSA. *Faculty research:* Pre-impact evaluation planning for families of law enforcement, disasters, criminology, immigration, sociological theory, race/ethnicity, culture of breast cancer. *Unit head:* Dr. James Williams, Chair, 940-898-2052, Fax: 940-898-2067, E-mail: jwilliams2@twu.edu. *Application contact:* Samuel Wheeler, Assistant Director of Admissions, 940-898-3188, Fax: 940-898-3081, E-mail: wheelersr@twu.edu.

Tulane University, School of Liberal Arts, Department of Sociology, New Orleans, LA 70118-5669. Offers MA, PhD. Terminal master's awarded for partial completion of doctoral program. *Degree requirements:* For master's, thesis; for doctorate, thesis/dissertation, preliminary exams. *Entrance requirements:* For master's, GRE General Test, minimum B average in undergraduate course work; for doctorate, GRE General Test. Additional exam requirements/recommendations for international students: Required—TOEFL. Electronic applications accepted.

Université de Montréal, Faculty of Arts and Sciences, Department of Sociology, Montréal, QC H3C 3J7, Canada. Offers M Sc, PhD. *Degree requirements:* For master's, thesis; for doctorate, thesis/dissertation, general exam. *Entrance requirements:* For master's, minimum GPA of 3.0; for doctorate, minimum GPA of 3.5, proficiency in French. Electronic applications accepted. *Faculty research:* Sociological theory, economy, state and social movements, work, social politics and health.

Université du Québec à Montréal, Graduate Programs, Program in Social Intervention, Montréal, QC H3C 3P8, Canada. Offers MA. Part-time programs available. *Degree requirements:* For master's, thesis. *Entrance requirements:* For master's, appropriate bachelor's degree or equivalent, proficiency in French.

Université du Québec à Montréal, Graduate Programs, Program in Sociology, Montréal, QC H3C 3P8, Canada. Offers MA, PhD. Part-time programs available. *Degree requirements:* For master's, thesis optional; for doctorate, thesis/dissertation. *Entrance requirements:* For master's, appropriate bachelor's degree or equivalent, proficiency in French; for doctorate, appropriate master's degree or equivalent, proficiency in French.

Université Laval, Faculty of Social Sciences, Department of Sociology, Programs in Sociology, Québec, QC G1K 7P4, Canada. Offers MA, PhD. Terminal master's awarded for partial completion of doctoral program. *Degree requirements:* For master's, thesis; for doctorate, comprehensive exam, thesis/dissertation. *Entrance requirements:* For master's, English exam (comprehension of written English), French exam (for some), knowledge of French; for doctorate, English exam (comprehension of written English), French exam may be required, knowledge of French. Electronic applications accepted.

University at Albany, State University of New York, College of Arts and Sciences, Department of Communication, Albany, NY 12222-0001. Offers communication (MA); sociology and communication (PhD). Part-time programs available. *Degree requirements:* For master's, comprehensive exam, thesis or alternative; for doctorate, comprehensive exam, thesis/dissertation. *Entrance requirements:* For master's, minimum GPA of 3.0; for doctorate, GRE, minimum GPA of 3.0. Additional exam requirements/recommendations for international students: Required—TOEFL (minimum score 550 paper-based; 213 computer-based). Electronic applications accepted. *Faculty research:* Language and social interaction, campaign communication, media agenda-setting, high-speed management, organizational boundary-spanning.

University at Albany, State University of New York, College of Arts and Sciences, Department of Sociology, Albany, NY 12222-0001. Offers demography (Certificate); sociology (MA, PhD); urban policy (Certificate). Terminal master's awarded for partial completion of doctoral program. *Degree requirements:* For master's, thesis; for doctorate, thesis/dissertation, 2 specialization exams, research tool. *Entrance requirements:* For master's and doctorate, GRE General Test. Additional exam requirements/recommendations for international students: Required—TOEFL (minimum score 213 computer-based). Electronic applications accepted. *Faculty research:* Gender and equality, crime and deviance, aging, work and organizations, social demography.

University at Buffalo, the State University of New York, Graduate School, College of Arts and Sciences, Department of Sociology, Buffalo, NY 14260. Offers MA, PhD. Part-time programs available. *Faculty:* 16 full-time (6 women), 4 part-time/adjunct (1 woman). *Students:* 37 full-time (18 women), 15 part-time (10 women); includes 5 minority (4 African Americans, 1 Hispanic American), 11 international. Average age 26. 57 applicants, 42% accepted, 4 enrolled. In 2009, 8 master's, 1 doctorate awarded. Terminal master's awarded for partial completion of doctoral program. *Degree requirements:* For master's, project or thesis; for doctorate, thesis/dissertation, qualifying paper. *Entrance requirements:* For master's and doctorate, GRE General Test. Additional exam requirements/recommendations for international students: Required—TOEFL (minimum score 550 paper-based; 213 computer-based; 79 iBT). *Application deadline:* For fall admission, 2/1 priority date for domestic and international students. Applications are processed on a rolling basis. Application fee: $75. Electronic applications accepted. *Financial support:* In 2009–10, 16 students received support, including 3 fellowships with full tuition reimbursements available (averaging $16,400 per year), 1 research assistantship (averaging $8,000 per year), 16 teaching assistantships with full tuition reimbursements available (averaging $13,460 per year); Federal Work-Study and unspecified assistantships also available. Financial award application deadline: 10/5; financial award applicants required to submit FAFSA. *Faculty research:* Theory, culture, sociology of law/criminology, urban sociology, family. Total annual research expenditures: $102,000. *Unit head:* Dr. Robert Granfield, Chair, 716-645-8462, Fax: 716-645-3934, E-mail: rgranfie@buffalo.edu. *Application contact:* Dr. Robert Adelman, Director of Graduate Studies, 716-645-8478, Fax: 716-645-3934, E-mail: adelman4@buffalo.edu.

The University of Akron, Graduate School, Buchtel College of Arts and Sciences, Department of Sociology, Akron, OH 44325. Offers MA, PhD. Part-time programs available. *Faculty:* 13 full-time (5 women), 5 part-time/adjunct (3 women). *Students:* 27 full-time (20 women), 11 part-time (9 women); includes 6 minority (all African Americans), 2 international. Average age 33. 22 applicants, 59% accepted, 8 enrolled. In 2009, 5 master's, 3 doctorates awarded. Terminal master's awarded for partial completion of doctoral program. *Degree requirements:* For master's, thesis optional, oral defense of thesis, paper or oral exam; for doctorate, one foreign language, comprehensive exam, thesis/dissertation. *Entrance requirements:* For master's, GRE General Test, minimum GPA of 3.0, letters of recommendation, writing sample; for doctorate, GRE General Test, minimum GPA of 3.5, letters of recommendation, writing sample, statement of purpose. Additional exam requirements/recommendations for international students: Required—TOEFL (minimum score 575 paper-based; 234 computer-based). *Application deadline:* For fall admission, 1/15 priority date for domestic and international students. Application fee: $30 ($40 for international students). Electronic applications accepted. *Expenses:* Tuition, state resident: full-time $6570; part-time $365 per credit hour. Tuition, nonresident: full-time $11,250; part-time $625 per credit hour. *Financial support:* In 2009–10, 25 teaching assistantships with full tuition reimbursements were awarded; career-related internships or fieldwork and Federal Work-Study also available. *Faculty research:* Medical sociology, inequality, social psychology, criminology, mental health. Total annual research expenditures: $752,857. *Unit head:* Dr. Kathy Feltey, Interim Chair, 330-972-8082, E-mail: kfeltey@uakron.edu. *Application contact:* Dr. Rebecca Erickson, Director of Graduate Studies, 330-972-5157, E-mail: rericks@uakron.edu.

The University of Alabama at Birmingham, College of Arts and Sciences, Program in Sociology, Birmingham, AL 35294. Offers MA. Evening/weekend programs available. *Degree requirements:* For master's, thesis or alternative. *Entrance requirements:* For master's, GRE General Test or MAT. Electronic applications accepted. *Faculty research:* Gerontology, applied sociology, urban sociology.

University of Alberta, Faculty of Graduate Studies and Research, Department of Sociology, Edmonton, AB T6G 2E1, Canada. Offers criminal justice (MA); demography (MA, PhD); sociology (MA, PhD). Part-time programs available. *Faculty:* 30 full-time (6 women), 8 part-time/adjunct (2 women). *Students:* 50 full-time (33 women), 33 part-time (21 women). 77 applicants, 34% accepted. In 2009, 8 master's, 11 doctorates awarded. *Degree requirements:* For master's, thesis (for some programs); for doctorate, thesis/dissertation. *Application deadline:* For fall admission, 3/1 for domestic students. Application fee: $60. Tuition and fees charges are reported in Canadian dollars. *Expenses:* Tuition, area resident: Full-time $4626 Canadian dollars; part-time $99.72 Canadian dollars per unit. International tuition: $8216 Canadian dollars full-time. Required fees: $3590 Canadian dollars; $99.72 Canadian dollars per unit. $215 Canadian dollars per term. *Financial support:* In 2009–10, 49 students received support, including 9 fellowships, 9 research assistantships, 17 teaching assistantships; career-related internships or fieldwork and scholarships/grants also available. Support available to part-time students. Financial award application deadline: 3/1. *Faculty research:* Criminology, knowledge and culture, methods and theory, population studies, stratification. *Unit head:* Dr. W. A. Johnston, Graduate Coordinator, 780-492-5236, Fax: 403-492-7196. *Application contact:* F. L. Van Reede, Graduate Program Coordinator, 403-492-5236, Fax: 403-492-7196, E-mail: socgrad2@ualberta.ca.

The University of Arizona, Graduate College, College of Social and Behavioral Sciences, Department of Sociology, Tucson, AZ 85721. Offers PhD. *Faculty:* 17. *Students:* 30 full-time (19 women), 27 part-time (12 women); includes 8 minority (1 African American, 1 Asian American or Pacific Islander, 6 Hispanic Americans), 4 international. Average age 30. 90 applicants, 7% accepted, 5 enrolled. In 2009, 10 doctorates awarded. *Degree requirements:* For doctorate, thesis/dissertation, 2 preliminary exams. *Entrance requirements:* For doctorate, GRE General Test, 3 letters of recommendation, writing samples. Additional exam requirements/recommendations for international students: Required—TOEFL (minimum score 630 paper-based; 267 computer-based). *Application deadline:* For fall admission, 1/15 for domestic and international students. Applications are processed on a rolling basis. Application fee: $65. Electronic applications accepted. *Expenses:* Tuition, state resident: full-time $9028. Tuition, nonresident: full-time $24,890. *Financial support:* In 2009–10, 1 research assistantship with full tuition reimbursement (averaging $15,698 per year), 46 teaching assistantships with full tuition reimbursements (averaging $15,404 per year) were awarded; institutionally sponsored loans, scholarships/grants, health care benefits, tuition waivers (full), and unspecified assistantships also available. Financial award application deadline: 1/15; financial award applicants required to submit FAFSA. *Faculty research:* Organizations, social psychology, social movement, stratification, religion. Total annual research expenditures: $168,595. *Unit head:* Dr. Albert J. Bergesen, Head, 520-621-3303, Fax: 520-621-9875, E-mail: albert@u.arizona.edu. *Application contact:* Vienna Marum, Information Contact, 520-621-5057, Fax: 520-621-9875, E-mail: vienna@u.arizona.edu.

University of Arkansas, Graduate School, J. William Fulbright College of Arts and Sciences, Department of Sociology, Fayetteville, AR 72701-1201. Offers MA. Part-time programs available. *Students:* 7 full-time (3 women), 14 part-time (11 women); includes 5 minority (2 African Americans, 1 American Indian/Alaska Native, 2 Hispanic Americans), 1 international. In 2009, 10 master's awarded. *Degree requirements:* For master's, thesis. Application fee: $40 ($50 for international students). *Expenses:* Tuition, state resident: full-time $7355; part-time $356.58 per hour. Tuition, nonresident: full-time $17,401; part-time $775.17 per hour. Required fees: $1203. *Financial support:* In 2009–10, 6 research assistantships, 9 teaching assistantships were awarded; fellowships with tuition reimbursements, career-related internships or fieldwork and Federal Work-Study also available. Support available to part-time students. Financial award application deadline: 4/1; financial award applicants required to submit FAFSA. *Unit head:* Dr. Brent Smith, Department Chairperson, 479-575-3206, Fax: 479-575-7981, E-mail: bls@uark.edu. *Application contact:* Dr. Anna Zajicek, Graduate Coordinator, 479-575-5149, Fax: 479-575-7981, E-mail: azajicek@uark.edu.

The University of British Columbia, Faculty of Arts, Department of Sociology, Vancouver, BC V6T 1Z1, Canada. Offers MA, PhD. *Degree requirements:* For master's, thesis; for doctorate, comprehensive exam, thesis/dissertation. *Entrance requirements:* For master's, BA in sociology or equivalent with minimum B+ average in upper level courses; for doctorate, master's degree in sociology or equivalent. Additional exam requirements/recommendations for international students: Required—TOEFL (minimum score 600 paper-based; 250 computer-based). Electronic applications accepted. *Faculty research:* Social and cultural theories and methods; gender, race, class and sexuality; environment economy and development politics; law and social movements.

University of Calgary, Faculty of Graduate Studies, Faculty of Social Sciences, Department of Sociology, Calgary, AB T2N 1N4, Canada. Offers MA, PhD. Terminal master's awarded for partial completion of doctoral program. *Degree requirements:* For master's, thesis, prospectus; for doctorate, comprehensive exam, thesis/dissertation, oral and written candidacy exams, prospectus, qualifying paper. *Entrance requirements:* For master's, minimum GPA of 3.2; for doctorate, minimum GPA of 3.5. Additional exam requirements/recommendations for international students: Required—TOEFL or IELTS. Electronic applications accepted. *Faculty research:* Deviance, gender, medical, religion, ethnicity.

University of California, Berkeley, Graduate Division, College of Letters and Science, Department of Sociology, Berkeley, CA 94720-1500. Offers PhD. *Faculty:* 16 full-time, 9 part-time/adjunct. *Students:* 133 full-time (71 women). Average age 31. 362 applicants, 16 enrolled. In 2009, 13 doctorates awarded. *Degree requirements:* For doctorate, thesis/dissertation, qualifying exam. *Entrance requirements:* For doctorate, GRE General Test, minimum GPA of 3.0, sample of academic written work, 3 letters of recommendation. Additional exam requirements/recommendations for international students: Required—TOEFL (minimum score 570 paper-based; 230 computer-based) or IELTS. *Application deadline:* For fall admission, 12/12 for domestic students. Application fee: $70 ($90 for international students). Electronic applications accepted. *Financial support:* Fellowships with full tuition reimbursements, research assistantships with partial tuition reimbursements, teaching assistantships with partial tuition reimbursements, Federal Work-Study, institutionally sponsored loans, and unspecified assistantships available. Financial award applicants required to submit FAFSA. *Faculty research:* Race, gender, political, stratification theory. *Unit head:* Prof. Trond Petersen, Chair, 510-642-4766, E-mail: sociology@berkeley.edu. *Application contact:* Information Contact, 510-642-1445, E-mail: socgrad_admit@berkeley.edu.

University of California, Davis, Graduate Studies, Program in Sociology, Davis, CA 95616. Offers MA, PhD. Terminal master's awarded for partial completion of doctoral program. *Degree requirements:* For master's, written exam; for doctorate, thesis/dissertation, professional paper, qualifying exam. *Entrance requirements:* For master's and doctorate, GRE General Test, minimum GPA of 3.0, writing sample. Additional exam requirements/recommendations for international students: Required—TOEFL (minimum score 550 paper-based; 213 computer-based). Electronic applications accepted. *Faculty research:* Collective behavior, social movements, comparative sociology, historical sociology, culture development, inequality.

University of California, Irvine, Office of Graduate Studies, School of Social Sciences, Department of Sociology, Irvine, CA 92697. Offers social networks (PhD); social networks-social science (MA); social science (MA, PhD); sociology and social relations-social science (MA, PhD). *Students:* 76 full-time (40 women), 1 part-time (0 women); includes 24 minority (1 African American, 1 American Indian/Alaska Native, 10 Asian Americans or Pacific Islanders, 12 Hispanic Americans). Average age 29. 156 applicants, 20% accepted, 12 enrolled. In 2009, 7 master's, 9 doctorates awarded. *Degree requirements:* For doctorate, thesis/dissertation. *Entrance requirements:* For master's and doctorate, GRE General Test, minimum GPA of 3.0. *Application deadline:* For fall admission, 1/15 priority date for domestic students, 1/15 for international students. Applications are processed on a rolling basis. Application fee: $70 ($90 for international students). Electronic applications accepted. *Financial support:* Fellowships, research assistantships with full tuition reimbursements, teaching assistantships, institutionally sponsored loans, traineeships, health care benefits, and unspecified assistantships available. Financial award application deadline: 3/1; financial award applicants required to submit FAFSA. *Faculty research:* Cognitive anthropology, sociology of culture, social structure, family and gender. *Unit head:* Calvin Morrill, Chair, 949-824-6460, E-mail: calvin@uci.edu. *Application contact:* Diane Enriquez, Graduate Counselor, 949-824-5924, Fax: 949-824-3548, E-mail: dmvargas@uci.edu.

University of California, Los Angeles, Graduate Division, College of Letters and Science, Department of Sociology, Los Angeles, CA 90095. Offers MA, PhD. *Students:* 94 full-time (53 women); includes 25 minority (3 African Americans, 9 Asian Americans or Pacific Islanders, 13 Hispanic Americans), 15 international. Average age 29. 223 applicants, 17% accepted, 10 enrolled. In 2009, 20 master's, 16 doctorates awarded. Terminal master's awarded for partial completion of doctoral program. *Degree requirements:* For master's, thesis or alternative, final paper; for doctorate, thesis/dissertation, oral and written qualifying exams. *Entrance requirements:* For master's, GRE General Test, minimum GPA of 3.0, sample of work; for doctorate, GRE General Test, minimum undergraduate GPA of 3.0, sample of work. Additional exam requirements/recommendations for international students: Required—TOEFL. *Application deadline:* For fall admission, 12/1 for domestic and international students. Application fee: $70 ($90 for international students). Electronic applications accepted. *Financial support:* In 2009–10, 78 fellowships with full and partial tuition reimbursements, 41 research assistantships with full and partial tuition reimbursements, 54 teaching assistantships with full and partial tuition reimbursements were awarded; Federal Work-Study, institutionally sponsored loans, scholarships/grants, health care benefits, tuition waivers (full and partial), and unspecified assistantships also available. Financial award application deadline: 3/1; financial award applicants required to submit FAFSA. *Unit head:* Dr. Roy William, Chair, 310-825-8044. *Application contact:* Department Office, 310-825-1026, E-mail: dietrich@soc.ucla.edu.

University of California, Riverside, Graduate Division, Department of Sociology, Riverside, CA 92521-0102. Offers MA, PhD. *Faculty:* 22 full-time (7 women). *Students:* 71 full-time (36 women); includes 24 minority (5 African Americans, 2 American Indian/Alaska Native, 10 Asian Americans or Pacific Islanders, 7 Hispanic Americans), 3 international. Average age 31. 80 applicants, 33% accepted, 14 enrolled. In 2009, 3 master's, 6 doctorates awarded. *Degree requirements:* For doctorate, thesis/dissertation, 1 quarter of teaching experience, professional paper. *Entrance requirements:* For doctorate, GRE General Test, minimum GPA of 3.2. Additional

Sociology

University of California, Riverside (continued)
exam requirements/recommendations for international students: Required—TOEFL (minimum score 550 paper-based; 213 computer-based; 80 iBT). *Application deadline:* For fall admission, 3/1 for domestic students, 2/1 for international students. Application fee: $80 ($100 for international students). Electronic applications accepted. *Financial support:* In 2009–10, 17 students received support, including fellowships with tuition reimbursements available (averaging $12,000 per year), teaching assistantships with partial tuition reimbursements available (averaging $16,500 per year); research assistantships, career-related internships or fieldwork, institutionally sponsored loans, health care benefits, and tuition waivers (full and partial) also available. Financial award application deadline: 2/1; financial award applicants required to submit FAFSA. *Faculty research:* Crime/deviance, race/ethnic relations, family/gender, political economy/globalization, theory. *Unit head:* Dr. Adalberto Aguirre, Chair, 951-827-5507, Fax: 951-827-3330, E-mail: adalberto.aguirre@ucr.edu. *Application contact:* Anna M. Wire, Graduate Program Assistant, 951-827-5445, Fax: 951-827-3330, E-mail: socgrad@ucr.edu.

University of California, San Diego, Office of Graduate Studies, Department of Sociology, La Jolla, CA 92093. Offers science studies (PhD); sociology (PhD). *Degree requirements:* For doctorate, thesis/dissertation. *Entrance requirements:* For doctorate, GRE General Test. Electronic applications accepted.

University of California, San Diego, Office of Graduate Studies, Interdisciplinary Program in Cognitive Science, La Jolla, CA 92093. Offers cognitive science/anthropology (PhD); cognitive science/communication (PhD); cognitive science/computer science and engineering (PhD); cognitive science/linguistics (PhD); cognitive science/neuroscience (PhD); cognitive science/philosophy (PhD); cognitive science/psychology (PhD); cognitive science/sociology (PhD). Admissions offered through affiliated departments. *Degree requirements:* For doctorate, thesis/dissertation. *Entrance requirements:* For doctorate, GRE General Test, acceptance into one of the eight participating departments. *Faculty research:* Language and cognition, philosophy of mind, visual perception, biological anthropology, sociolinguistics.

University of California, San Francisco, Graduate Division, School of Nursing, Department of Social and Behavioral Sciences, San Francisco, CA 94143. Offers sociology (PhD). *Degree requirements:* For doctorate, one foreign language, thesis/dissertation. *Entrance requirements:* For doctorate, GRE General Test. *Faculty research:* Urban social relations; sociology of women's role in healing; sociology of work, occupations, and professions.

University of California, Santa Barbara, Graduate Division, College of Letters and Sciences, Division of Social Sciences, Department of Sociology, Santa Barbara, CA 93106-9430. Offers global studies (PhD); human development (PhD); language, interaction and social organization (PhD); technology and society (PhD); women's studies (PhD); MA/PhD. *Faculty:* 35 full-time (14 women). *Students:* 77 full-time (50 women). Average age 30. 155 applicants, 9% accepted, 8 enrolled. In 2009, 10 doctorates awarded. Terminal master's awarded for partial completion of doctoral program. *Degree requirements:* For doctorate, comprehensive exam, thesis/dissertation. *Entrance requirements:* For doctorate, GRE General Test, sample of written work, 3 letters of recommendation, resume/curriculum vitae. Additional exam requirements/recommendations for international students: Required—TOEFL (minimum score 550 paper-based; 213 computer-based; 80 iBT), or IELTS. *Application deadline:* For fall admission, 12/10 for domestic students. Application fee: $70 ($90 for international students). Electronic applications accepted. *Financial support:* In 2009–10, 69 students received support, including 50 fellowships with full tuition reimbursements available (averaging $7,900 per year), 6 research assistantships with full and partial tuition reimbursements available (averaging $2,600 per year), 53 teaching assistantships with partial tuition reimbursements available (averaging $9,200 per year); career-related internships or fieldwork, Federal Work-Study, institutionally sponsored loans, scholarships/grants, health care benefits, and unspecified assistantships also available. Financial award applicants required to submit FAFSA. *Faculty research:* Conversation analysis, social movements, human sexuality, urban sociology, race and ethnic relations. *Unit head:* Prof. Verta Taylor, Chair, 805-893-3118, Fax: 805-893-3324, E-mail: grad-soc@soc.ucsb.edu. *Application contact:* Ra Thea, Graduate Staff Advisor, 805-893-3328, Fax: 805-893-3324, E-mail: grad-soc@soc.ucsb.edu.

University of California, Santa Cruz, Division of Graduate Studies, Division of Social Sciences, Program in Sociology, Santa Cruz, CA 95064. Offers PhD. *Degree requirements:* For doctorate, thesis/dissertation, qualifying exam. *Entrance requirements:* For doctorate, GRE General Test. *Faculty research:* Marxism, feminism, ethnic studies, social theory.

University of Central Florida, College of Sciences, Department of Sociology, Orlando, FL 32816. Offers applied sociology (MA); Maya studies (Certificate); sociology (PhD). Part-time and evening/weekend programs available. *Faculty:* 18 full-time (10 women), 2 part-time/adjunct (1 woman). *Students:* 47 full-time (37 women), 16 part-time (9 women); includes 15 minority (6 African Americans, 1 Asian American or Pacific Islander, 8 Hispanic Americans), 1 international. Average age 30. 49 applicants, 73% accepted, 20 enrolled. In 2009, 16 master's, 4 doctorates, 4 other advanced degrees awarded. *Degree requirements:* For master's, comprehensive written exam or thesis. *Entrance requirements:* For master's, GRE General Test, minimum GPA of 3.0 in last 60 hours of course work. Additional exam requirements/recommendations for international students: Required—TOEFL. *Application deadline:* For fall admission, 7/15 for domestic students; for spring admission, 12/1 for domestic students. Application fee: $30. Electronic applications accepted. *Expenses:* Tuition, state resident: part-time $306.31 per credit hour. Tuition, nonresident: part-time $1099.01 per credit hour. Part-time tuition and fees vary according to degree level and program. *Financial support:* In 2009–10, 31 students received support, including 13 fellowships with partial tuition reimbursements available (averaging $5,800 per year), 2 research assistantships with partial tuition reimbursements available (averaging $4,900 per year), 26 teaching assistantships with partial tuition reimbursements available (averaging $9,700 per year); career-related internships or fieldwork, Federal Work-Study, institutionally sponsored loans, tuition waivers (partial), and unspecified assistantships also available. Financial award application deadline: 3/1; financial award applicants required to submit FAFSA. *Faculty research:* Religious subcultures, attitudes toward abortion, population, sport research, stratification. *Unit head:* Dr. Jay Corzine, Chair, 407-823-2227, Fax: 407-823-5156, E-mail: hcorzine@mail.ucf.edu. *Application contact:* Dr. Jay Corzine, Chair, 407-823-2227, Fax: 407-823-5156, E-mail: hcorzine@mail.ucf.edu.

University of Central Missouri, The Graduate School, College of Health and Human Services, Warrensburg, MO 64093. Offers criminal justice (MS); industrial hygiene (MS); occupational safety management (MS); physical education/exercise and sport science (MS); rural family nursing (MS); social gerontology (MS); sociology (MA); speech language pathology and audiology (MS). *Accreditation:* NCATE. Part-time programs available. Postbaccalaureate distance learning degree programs offered. *Faculty:* 53. *Students:* 169 full-time (107 women), 364 part-time (210 women); includes 65 minority (46 African Americans, 1 American Indian/Alaska Native, 5 Asian Americans or Pacific Islanders, 13 Hispanic Americans), 27 international. Average age 32. 236 applicants, 92% accepted, 211 enrolled. In 2009, 153 master's awarded. *Entrance requirements:* Additional exam requirements/recommendations for international students: Required—TOEFL (minimum score 550 paper-based; 79 computer-based). *Application deadline:* For fall admission, 6/1 priority date for domestic students, 5/1 for international students; for spring admission, 10/1 priority date for domestic students, 10/1 for international students. Applications are processed on a rolling basis. Application fee: $30 ($75 for international students). Electronic applications accepted. *Expenses:* Tuition, area resident: Part-time $245.80 per credit hour. Tuition, nonresident: part-time $491.60 per credit hour. Required fees: $24.20 per credit hour. Full-time tuition and fees vary according to course load, degree level, campus/location and reciprocity agreements. *Financial support:* Research assistantships with full and partial tuition reimbursements, teaching assistantships with full and partial tuition reimbursements, career-related internships or fieldwork, Federal Work-Study, scholarships/grants, and administrative and laboratory assistantships available. Support available to part-time students. Financial award application deadline: 3/1; financial award applicants required to submit FAFSA. *Unit head:* Dr. Rick Sluder, Dean, 660-543-4245, Fax: 660-543-4167, E-mail: sluder@ucmo.edu. *Application contact:* Laurie Delap, Admissions Coordinator, 660-543-4621, Fax: 660-543-4778, E-mail: gradinfo@ucmo.edu.

University of Chicago, Division of Social Sciences, Department of Sociology, Chicago, IL 60637-1513. Offers PhD. *Students:* 140. In 2009, 10 doctorates awarded. *Degree requirements:* For doctorate, one foreign language, thesis/dissertation, 2 field exams. *Entrance requirements:* For doctorate, GRE General Test. Additional exam requirements/recommendations for international students: Required—TOEFL, IELTS (minimum score 7). *Application deadline:* For fall admission, 12/10 for domestic and international students. Application fee: $55. Electronic applications accepted. *Financial support:* Fellowships, research assistantships, teaching assistantships, Federal Work-Study, institutionally sponsored loans, scholarships/grants, traineeships, health care benefits, and unspecified assistantships available. Financial award application deadline: 12/10; financial award applicants required to submit FAFSA. *Unit head:* Prof. Kazuo Yamaguchi, Chair, 773-702-8677. *Application contact:* Office of the Dean of Students, 773-702-8415, E-mail: admissions@ssd.uchicago.edu.

University of Cincinnati, Graduate School, McMicken College of Arts and Sciences, Department of Sociology, Cincinnati, OH 45221. Offers MA, PhD. Part-time programs available. *Degree requirements:* For master's, thesis; for doctorate, thesis/dissertation. *Entrance requirements:* For master's and doctorate, GRE General Test. Additional exam requirements/recommendations for international students: Required—TOEFL. Electronic applications accepted. *Faculty research:* Work and family, race and urban, health and medicine, social psychology.

University of Colorado at Boulder, Graduate School, College of Arts and Sciences, Department of Sociology, Boulder, CO 80309. Offers PhD. *Faculty:* 22 full-time (14 women). *Students:* 53 full-time (31 women), 13 part-time (10 women); includes 7 minority (3 African Americans, 2 Asian Americans or Pacific Islanders, 2 Hispanic Americans), 6 international. Average age 31. 107 applicants, 8% accepted, 9 enrolled. In 2009, 7 doctorates awarded. *Degree requirements:* For doctorate, comprehensive exam, thesis/dissertation. *Entrance requirements:* For doctorate, GRE General Test, GRE Subject Test, minimum undergraduate GPA of 2.75. *Application deadline:* For fall admission, 1/1 for domestic students, 12/1 for international students. Application fee: $50 ($60 for international students). *Financial support:* In 2009–10, 17 fellowships (averaging $1,388 per year), 29 research assistantships (averaging $8,451 per year) were awarded; Federal Work-Study, institutionally sponsored loans, and scholarships/grants also available. Support available to part-time students. Financial award application deadline: 1/1; financial award applicants required to submit FAFSA. *Faculty research:* Criminology, social control, law delinquency and deviance, population, health studies, gender relations, social stratification, race relations, the environment, institutions and international systems. Total annual research expenditures: $3.6 million.

University of Colorado at Colorado Springs, Graduate School, College of Letters, Arts and Sciences, Department of Sociology, Colorado Springs, CO 80933-7150. Offers MA. Part-time programs available. *Faculty:* 12 full-time (10 women). *Students:* 21 full-time (14 women), 13 part-time (8 women); includes 6 minority (1 African American, 1 American Indian/Alaska Native, 1 Asian American or Pacific Islander, 3 Hispanic Americans). Average age 33. 24 applicants, 88% accepted, 14 enrolled. In 2009, 8 master's awarded. *Degree requirements:* For master's, thesis optional. *Entrance requirements:* For master's, GRE, minimum GPA of 2.75. *Application deadline:* For fall admission, 7/1 priority date for domestic students; for spring admission, 11/1 for domestic students. Applications are processed on a rolling basis. Application fee: $60 ($75 for international students). *Expenses:* Tuition, state resident: full-time $8922; part-time $639 per credit hour. Tuition, nonresident: full-time $19,372; part-time $1154 per credit hour. Tuition and fees vary according to course level, course load, degree level, program, reciprocity agreements and student level. *Financial support:* Teaching assistantships, career-related internships or fieldwork, Federal Work-Study, and scholarships/grants available. Support available to part-time students. Financial award application deadline: 3/1; financial award applicants required to submit FAFSA. *Faculty research:* Environmental justice, gender, race and ethnicity, sport and popular culture, youth and deviant behavior. *Unit head:* Dr. Lynda Dickson, Chair, 719-255-4142, Fax: 719-255-4450, E-mail: ldickson@uccs.edu. *Application contact:* Rosemary Kelbel, Program Assistant, 719-255-4153, Fax: 719-255-4450, E-mail: rkelbel@uccs.edu.

University of Colorado Denver, College of Liberal Arts and Sciences, Department of Sociology, Denver, CO 80217-3364. Offers MA. Part-time and evening/weekend programs available. *Students:* 7 full-time (4 women), 12 part-time (9 women); includes 2 minority (1 Asian American or Pacific Islander, 1 Hispanic American). 24 applicants, 50% accepted, 6 enrolled. In 2009, 4 master's awarded. *Degree requirements:* For master's, thesis or alternative. *Entrance requirements:* For master's, GRE. *Application deadline:* For fall admission, 6/1 for domestic students; for spring admission, 11/1 for domestic students. Applications are processed on a rolling basis. Application fee: $50 ($75 for international students). Electronic applications accepted. *Financial support:* Research assistantships, teaching assistantships, Federal Work-Study, institutionally sponsored loans, and scholarships/grants available. Financial award application deadline: 4/1; financial award applicants required to submit FAFSA. *Unit head:* Dr. Sharon Araji, Chair, 303-315-2144, Fax: 303-315-2149, E-mail: sharon.araji@ucdenver.edu. *Application contact:* Rachel Watson, Program Assistant, 303-315-2148, Fax: 303-315-2149, E-mail: rachel.watson@ucdenver.edu.

University of Connecticut, Graduate School, College of Liberal Arts and Sciences, Department of Sociology, Storrs, CT 06269. Offers MA, PhD. *Faculty:* 26 full-time (10 women). *Students:* 56 full-time (37 women), 3 part-time (all women); includes 10 minority (5 African Americans, 3 Asian Americans or Pacific Islanders, 2 Hispanic Americans), 8 international. Average age 30. 53 applicants, 13% accepted, 6 enrolled. In 2009, 7 master's, 6 doctorates awarded. Terminal master's awarded for partial completion of doctoral program. *Degree requirements:* For master's, comprehensive exam; for doctorate, thesis/dissertation. *Entrance requirements:* For master's and doctorate, GRE General Test. Additional exam requirements/recommendations for international students: Required—TOEFL (minimum score 550 paper-based; 213 computer-based). *Application deadline:* For fall admission, 2/1 priority date for domestic and international students; for spring admission, 11/1 for domestic students, 10/1 for international students. Applications are processed on a rolling basis. Application fee: $55. Electronic applications accepted. *Expenses:* Tuition, state resident: full-time $4725; part-time $525 per credit. Tuition, nonresident: full-time $12,267; part-time $1363 per credit. Required fees: $346 per semester. Tuition and fees vary according to course load. *Financial support:* In 2009–10, 6 research assistantships with full tuition reimbursements, 50 teaching assistantships with full tuition reimbursements were awarded; fellowships, Federal Work-Study, scholarships/grants, health care benefits, and unspecified assistantships also available. Financial award application deadline: 2/1; financial award applicants required to submit FAFSA. *Unit head:* Davita Glasberg, Head, 860-486-5504, Fax: 860-486-6356, E-mail: davita.glasberg@uconn.edu. *Application contact:* Nancy Naples, Chairperson, 860-486-3049, Fax: 860-486-6356, E-mail: nancy.naples@uconn.edu.

University of Delaware, College of Arts and Sciences, Department of Sociology and Criminology, Newark, DE 19716. Offers criminology (MA, PhD); sociology (MA, PhD). *Degree requirements:* For master's, thesis; for doctorate, comprehensive exam, thesis/dissertation. *Entrance requirements:* For master's and doctorate, GRE, 3 letters of recommendation. Additional exam requirements/recommendations for international students: Required—TOEFL. Electronic applications accepted. *Faculty research:* Sex and gender, criminology/deviance, theory, methods, collective behavior.

University of Florida, Graduate School, College of Liberal Arts and Sciences, Department of Sociology, Gainesville, FL 32611. Offers MA, PhD, JD/MA. *Degree requirements:* For master's, thesis optional; for doctorate, thesis/dissertation. *Entrance requirements:* For master's and doctorate, GRE General Test, minimum GPA of 3.0. Additional exam requirements/recommendations for international students: Required—TOEFL (minimum score 550 paper-based; 213 computer-based). Electronic applications accepted. *Faculty research:* Sociology of the family, social gerontology, criminology and deviance, race ethnicity.

University of Georgia, Graduate School, College of Arts and Sciences, Department of Sociology, Athens, GA 30602. Offers MA, PhD. *Faculty:* 17 full-time (6 women). *Students:* 28 full-time (16 women), 5 part-time (all women); includes 1 minority (African American), 3 international. 56 applicants, 32% accepted, 9 enrolled. In 2009, 4 master's, 5 doctorates awarded. *Degree requirements:* For master's, thesis; for doctorate, thesis/dissertation. *Entrance requirements:* For master's and doctorate, GRE General Test. Additional exam requirements/recommendations for international students: Required—TOEFL. *Application deadline:* For fall admission, 2/1 priority date for domestic students, 1/1 for international students. Application fee: $50. Electronic applications accepted. *Expenses:* Tuition, state resident: full-time $6000; part-time $250 per credit hour. Tuition, nonresident: full-time $20,904; part-time $871 per credit hour. Required fees: $730 per semester. *Financial support:* In 2009–10, 16 students received support, including teaching assistantships with full tuition reimbursements available (averaging $12,220 per year); research assistantships, unspecified assistantships also available. Financial award application deadline: 1/1. *Faculty research:* Race, deviance, gender, culture. *Unit head:* Dr. William Finlay, Head, 706-542-3195, Fax: 706-542-4320, E-mail: wfinlay@uga.edu. *Application contact:* Dr. Jody Clay-Warner, Graduate Coordinator, 706-542-3212, Fax: 706-542-4320, E-mail: jclayw@uga.edu.

University of Guelph, Graduate Program Services, College of Social and Applied Human Sciences, Department of Sociology and Anthropology, Guelph, ON N1G 2W1, Canada. Offers anthropology (MA); crime and criminal justice policy (MA); sociology (MA, PhD). *Degree requirements:* For master's, thesis or major paper; for doctorate, comprehensive exam, thesis/dissertation. *Entrance requirements:* For master's, minimum B+ average during previous 2 years of course work, honors BA or equivalent; for doctorate, must have an MA in Sociology, must have 80% or higher in graduate level studies. Additional exam requirements/recommendations for international students: Required—TOEFL (minimum score 550 paper-based; 213 computer-based; 89 iBT), IELTS (minimum score 6.5), TOEFL or IELTS. Electronic applications accepted. *Faculty research:* Rural and development sociology; education, employment, and the workplace; race, ethnicity, and native studies; criminology and deviance; social psychology.

University of Hawaii at Manoa, Graduate Division, College of Social Sciences, Department of Sociology, Honolulu, HI 96822. Offers sociology (MA, PhD). Part-time programs available. *Faculty:* 23 full-time (9 women), 8 part-time/adjunct (4 women). *Students:* 47 full-time (28 women), 13 part-time (8 women); includes 14 minority (13 Asian Americans or Pacific Islanders, 1 Hispanic American), 28 international. Average age 32. 40 applicants, 68% accepted, 15 enrolled. In 2009, 6 master's, 2 doctorates awarded. *Degree requirements:* For master's, thesis optional; for doctorate, comprehensive exam, thesis/dissertation. *Entrance requirements:* For master's and doctorate, GRE General Test. Additional exam requirements/recommendations for international students: Required—TOEFL (minimum score 500 paper-based; 173 computer-based; 61 iBT), IELTS (minimum score 5). *Application deadline:* For fall admission, 2/1 for domestic and international students; for spring admission, 9/1 for domestic students, 8/15 for international students. Applications are processed on a rolling basis. Application fee: $60. *Expenses:* Tuition, state resident: full-time $8900; part-time $372 per credit. Tuition, nonresident: full-time $21,400; part-time $898 per credit. Required fees: $207 per semester. *Financial support:* In 2009–10, 1 student received support, including 8 fellowships (averaging $2,207 per year), 10 research assistantships (averaging $18,424 per year), 11 teaching assistantships (averaging $15,451 per year); Federal Work-Study, institutionally sponsored loans, and tuition waivers (full and partial) also available. *Faculty research:* Comparative sociology of Asia; population studies; crime, law, and deviance; health; aging and medical sociology. Total annual research expenditures: $1.1 million. *Application contact:* Patricia Steinhoff, Graduate Chair, 808-956-7693, Fax: 808-956-3707, E-mail: steinhof@hawaii.edu.

University of Houston, College of Liberal Arts and Social Sciences, Department of Sociology, Houston, TX 77204. Offers MA. Part-time and evening/weekend programs available. *Faculty:* 9 full-time (5 women). *Students:* 16 full-time (13 women), 13 part-time (10 women); includes 15 minority (5 African Americans, 3 Asian Americans or Pacific Islanders, 7 Hispanic Americans), 6 international. Average age 32. 18 applicants, 50% accepted, 7 enrolled. In 2009, 10 master's awarded. *Degree requirements:* For master's, thesis optional. *Entrance requirements:* For master's, GRE (minimim score 1000), minimum GPA of 3.0; letters of recommendation, resume. Additional exam requirements/recommendations for international students: Required—TOEFL (minimum score 550 paper-based; 79 iBT), IELTS. *Application deadline:* For fall admission, 4/15 for domestic students, 4/1 for international students; for spring admission, 11/15 for domestic students. Application fee: $75 for international students. Electronic applications accepted. *Expenses:* Tuition, state resident: full-time $7676; part-time $320 per credit hour. Tuition, nonresident: full-time $14,324; part-time $597 per credit hour. Required fees: $3034. *Financial support:* In 2009–10, 2 fellowships with full tuition reimbursements (averaging $8,800 per year), 2 research assistantships with full tuition reimbursements (averaging $8,800 per year), 10 teaching assistantships with full tuition reimbursements (averaging $8,800 per year) were awarded; career-related internships or fieldwork, Federal Work-Study, institutionally sponsored loans, scholarships/grants, health care benefits, and unspecified assistantships also available. Support available to part-time students. Financial award application deadline: 2/1; financial award applicants required to submit FAFSA. *Faculty research:* Immigration, public education, HIV/AIDS. *Unit head:* Dr. Joseph Kotarba, Chairperson, 713-743-3954, Fax: 713-743-3943, E-mail: jkotarba@uh.edu. *Application contact:* Dr. Joseph Kotarba, Chairperson, 713-743-3954, Fax: 713-743-3943, E-mail: jkotarba@uh.edu.

University of Houston–Clear Lake, School of Human Sciences and Humanities, Programs in Human Sciences, Houston, TX 77058-1098. Offers behavioral sciences (MA), including criminology, cross cultural studies, general psychology, sociology; clinical psychology (MA); criminology (MA); cross cultural studies (MA); family therapy (MA); fitness and human performance (MA); school psychology (MA). *Accreditation:* AAMFT/COAMFTE. Part-time and evening/weekend programs available. Postbaccalaureate distance learning degree programs offered (minimal on-campus study). *Degree requirements:* For master's, thesis or alternative. *Entrance requirements:* For master's, GRE General Test. Additional exam requirements/recommendations for international students: Required—TOEFL (minimum score 550 paper-based; 213 computer-based). Electronic applications accepted. *Faculty research:* Smoking cessation, adolescent sexuality, white collar crime, serial murder, human factors/human computer interaction.

University of Illinois at Chicago, Graduate College, College of Liberal Arts and Sciences, Department of Sociology, Chicago, IL 60607-7128. Offers MA, PhD. Terminal master's awarded for partial completion of doctoral program. *Degree requirements:* For master's, comprehensive exam, thesis; for doctorate, thesis/dissertation, qualifying exam. *Entrance requirements:* For master's and doctorate, GRE General Test, minimum GPA of 3.0. Additional exam requirements/recommendations for international students: Required—TOEFL. Electronic applications accepted. *Faculty research:* Social psychology, social organization, applied sociology, demography and human ecology.

University of Illinois at Urbana–Champaign, Graduate College, College of Liberal Arts and Sciences, Department of Sociology, Champaign, IL 61820. Offers MA, PhD. *Faculty:* 11 full-time (6 women), 2 part-time/adjunct (1 woman). *Students:* 29 full-time (17 women), 21 part-time (13 women); includes 14 minority (6 African Americans, 5 Asian Americans or Pacific Islanders, 3 Hispanic Americans), 18 international. 53 applicants, 30% accepted, 15 enrolled. In 2009, 1 master's, 6 doctorates awarded. *Entrance requirements:* For doctorate, GRE, minimum GPA of 3.0; writing sample. Additional exam requirements/recommendations for international students: Required—TOEFL (minimum score 79 iBT). *Application deadline:* Applications are processed on a rolling basis. Application fee: $60 ($75 for international students). Electronic applications accepted. *Financial support:* In 2009–10, 12 fellowships, 9 research assistantships, 32 teaching assistantships were awarded; tuition waivers (full and partial) also available. *Unit head:* Anna-Maria Marshall, Head, 217-333-1950, Fax: 217-333-5225, E-mail: amarshll@illinois.edu. *Application contact:* Shari Day, Office Manager, 217-244-1809, Fax: 217-333-5225, E-mail: shariday@illinois.edu.

University of Indianapolis, Graduate Programs, College of Arts and Sciences, Department of Social Sciences, Indianapolis, IN 46227-3697. Offers applied sociology (MA). Part-time and evening/weekend programs available. *Faculty:* 4 full-time (2 women), 1 (woman) part-time/adjunct. *Students:* 6 full-time (all women), 9 part-time (5 women); includes 3 minority (all African Americans), 4 international. Average age 29. *Degree requirements:* For master's, thesis optional. *Entrance requirements:* For master's, GRE Subject Test, minimum GPA of 3.0, letter of intent, 3 letters of recommendation. Additional exam requirements/recommendations for international students: Required—TOEFL (minimum score 550 paper-based; 213 computer-based). *Application deadline:* Applications are processed on a rolling basis. Application fee: $30. Electronic applications accepted. *Financial support:* Federal Work-Study, scholarships/grants, tuition waivers (full and partial), and unspecified assistantships available. Support available to part-time students. Financial award application deadline: 5/1; financial award applicants required to submit FAFSA. *Unit head:* Dr. James Pennell, Chair, 317-788-3535, Fax: 317-788-3480, E-mail: jpennell@uindy.edu. *Application contact:* Dr. James Pennell, Chair, 317-788-3535, Fax: 317-788-3480, E-mail: jpennell@uindy.edu.

The University of Iowa, Graduate College, College of Liberal Arts and Sciences, Department of Sociology, Iowa City, IA 52242-1316. Offers MA, PhD. *Degree requirements:* For master's, thesis optional, exam; for doctorate, comprehensive exam, thesis/dissertation. *Entrance requirements:* For master's and doctorate, GRE General Test, minimum GPA of 3.0. Additional exam requirements/recommendations for international students: Required—TOEFL (minimum score 600 paper-based; 250 computer-based; 100 iBT). Electronic applications accepted.

The University of Kansas, Graduate Studies, College of Liberal Arts and Sciences, Department of Sociology, Lawrence, KS 66045. Offers MA, PhD. Part-time programs available. *Faculty:* 14 full-time (8 women), 6 part-time/adjunct (4 women). *Students:* 33 full-time (19 women), 5 part-time (2 women); includes 1 minority (Asian American or Pacific Islander), 4 international. Average age 30. 43 applicants, 63% accepted, 7 enrolled. In 2009, 10 master's, 3 doctorates awarded. *Degree requirements:* For master's, thesis; for doctorate, comprehensive exam, thesis/dissertation. *Entrance requirements:* For master's and doctorate, GRE General Test. Additional exam requirements/recommendations for international students: Required—TOEFL (minimum score 530 paper-based; 200 computer-based) or IELTS (minimum score 6). *Application deadline:* For fall admission, 12/15 priority date for domestic and international students; for spring admission, 10/15 for domestic and international students. Applications are processed on a rolling basis. Application fee: $45 ($55 for international students). Electronic applications accepted. *Expenses:* Tuition, state resident: full-time $6492; part-time $270.50 per credit hour. Tuition, nonresident: full-time $15,510; part-time $646.25 per credit hour. Required fees: $847; $70.56 per credit hour. Tuition and fees vary according to course load and program. *Financial support:* Fellowships with full tuition reimbursements, research assistantships with full tuition reimbursements, teaching assistantships with full and partial tuition reimbursements, unspecified assistantships available. Financial award application deadline: 12/15. *Faculty research:* Comparative/historical sociology, sex and gender, social movements, social theory, medical sociology. *Unit head:* William G. Staples, Chair, 785-864-4111, Fax: 785-864-5280. *Application contact:* Eric Hanley, Graduate Director, 785-864-4111, Fax: 785-864-5280, E-mail: hanley@ku.edu.

University of Kentucky, Graduate School, College of Arts and Sciences, Program in Sociology, Lexington, KY 40506-0032. Offers MA, PhD. Part-time programs available. *Degree requirements:* For master's, comprehensive exam, thesis optional; for doctorate, comprehensive exam, thesis/dissertation. *Entrance requirements:* For master's, GRE General Test, minimum undergraduate GPA of 2.75; for doctorate, GRE General Test, minimum graduate GPA of 3.0. Additional exam requirements/recommendations for international students: Required—TOEFL (minimum score 550 paper-based; 213 computer-based). Electronic applications accepted. *Faculty research:* Work organizations, social inequalities, rural sociology, criminology/deviance, medical sociology.

University of Lethbridge, School of Graduate Studies, Lethbridge, AB T1K 3M4, Canada. Offers accounting (MScM); addictions counseling (M Sc); agricultural biotechnology (M Sc); agricultural studies (M Sc, MA); anthropology (MA); archaeology (MA); art (MA, MFA); biochemistry (M Sc); biological sciences (M Sc); biomolecular science (PhD); biosystems and biodiversity (PhD); Canadian studies (MA); chemistry (M Sc); computer science (M Sc); computer science and geographical information science (M Sc); counseling psychology (M Ed); dramatic arts (MA); earth, space, and physical science (PhD); economics (MA); educational leadership (M Ed); English (MA); environmental science (M Sc); evolution and behavior (PhD); exercise science (M Sc); finance (MScM); French (MA); French/German (MA); French/Spanish (MA); general education (M Ed); general management (MScM); geography (M Sc, MA); German (MA); health science (M Sc); health sciences (MA); history (MA); human resource management and labour relations (MScM); individualized multidisciplinary (M Sc, MA); information systems (MScM); international management (MScM); kinesiology (M Sc, MA); management (M Sc, MA); marketing (MScM); mathematics (M Sc); music (M Mus, MA); Native American studies (MA); neuroscience (M Sc, PhD); new media (MA); nursing (M Sc); philosophy (MA); physics (M Sc); policy and strategy (MScM); political science (MA); psychology (M Sc, MA); religious studies (MA); social sciences (MA); sociology (MA); theatre and dramatic arts (MFA); theoretical and computational science (PhD); urban and regional studies (MA); women's studies (MA). Part-time and evening/weekend programs available. *Degree requirements:* For doctorate, comprehensive exam, thesis/dissertation. *Entrance requirements:* For master's, GMAT (M Sc in management), bachelor's degree in related field, minimum GPA of 3.0 during previous 20 graded semester courses, 2 years teaching or related experience (M Ed); for doctorate, master's degree, minimum graduate GPA of 3.5. Additional exam requirements/recommendations for international students: Required—TOEFL. *Faculty research:* Movement and brain plasticity, gibberellin physiology, photosynthesis, carbon cycling, molecular properties of main-group ring components.

University of Louisville, Graduate School, College of Arts and Sciences, Department of Sociology, Louisville, KY 40292. Offers MA. Part-time and evening/weekend programs available. *Faculty:* 17 full-time (9 women). *Students:* 10 full-time (6 women), 12 part-time (7 women); includes 5 minority (all African Americans), 1 international. Average age 30. 15 applicants, 47% accepted, 5 enrolled. In 2009, 2 master's awarded. *Degree requirements:* For master's, thesis or practicum. *Entrance requirements:* For master's, GRE General Test. Additional exam requirements/recommendations for international students: Required—TOEFL. *Application deadline:* For fall admission, 6/1 priority date for domestic students, 6/1 for international students; for spring admission, 10/1 priority date for domestic students, 10/1 for international students. Applications are processed on a rolling basis. Application fee: $50. Electronic applications accepted. *Financial support:* In 2009–10, 4 students received support, including 6 teaching assistantships with full tuition reimbursements available. *Faculty research:* Crime/corrections, gender/sexuality, medicine/health, education, urban. *Unit head:* Dr. L. Allen Furr, Chair, 502-852-8022, Fax: 502-852-0099, E-mail: allenfur@louisville.edu. *Application contact:* Libby Leggett, Director, Graduate Admissions, 502-852-3101, Fax: 502-852-6536, E-mail: gradadm@louisville.edu.

University of Manitoba, Faculty of Graduate Studies, Faculty of Arts, Department of Sociology, Winnipeg, MB R3T 2N2, Canada. Offers MA, PhD. *Degree requirements:* For master's, thesis.

University of Maryland, Baltimore County, Graduate School, College of Arts, Humanities and Social Sciences, Department of Sociology and Anthropology, Baltimore, MD 21250. Offers applied sociology (MA, Postbaccalaureate Certificate), including applied sociology (MA), nonprofit sector (Postbaccalaureate Certificate). Part-time and evening/weekend programs available. *Faculty:* 16 full-time (9 women), 3 part-time/adjunct (all women). *Students:* 25 full-time (21 women), 39 part-time (29 women); includes 23 minority (15 African Americans, 1 American Indian/Alaska Native, 6 Asian Americans or Pacific Islanders, 1 Hispanic American), 1 international. Average age 32. 37 applicants, 78% accepted, 20 enrolled. In 2009, 26 master's awarded. *Degree requirements:* For master's, thesis or alternative. *Entrance requirements:* For master's, minimum GPA of 3.0, undergraduate statistics course. Additional exam

Sociology

University of Maryland, Baltimore County (continued)
requirements/recommendations for international students: Required—TOEFL. *Application deadline:* For fall admission, 7/15 for domestic students; for spring admission, 12/15 for domestic students. Applications are processed on a rolling basis. Application fee: $70. Electronic applications accepted. *Financial support:* In 2009–10, 11 students received support, including 7 research assistantships with full and partial tuition reimbursements available (averaging $12,500 per year), 4 teaching assistantships with full and partial tuition reimbursements available (averaging $12,500 per year); scholarships/grants, health care benefits, unspecified assistantships, and tuition remission also available. Financial award application deadline: 2/14; financial award applicants required to submit FAFSA. *Faculty research:* Sociology of aging, medical sociology, migration. *Unit head:* Dr. J. Kevin Eckert, Chairperson, 410-455-2076, Fax: 410-455-1154, E-mail: eckert@umbc.edu. *Application contact:* Dr. William G. Rothstein, Director, 410-455-2078, Fax: 410-455-1154, E-mail: rothstei@umbc.edu.

University of Maryland, College Park, Academic Affairs, College of Behavioral and Social Sciences, Department of Sociology, College Park, MD 20742. Offers MA, PhD. *Faculty:* 26 full-time (10 women), 6 part-time/adjunct (3 women). *Students:* 75 full-time (45 women), 4 part-time (3 women); includes 13 minority (7 African Americans, 3 Asian Americans or Pacific Islanders, 3 Hispanic Americans), 15 international. 172 applicants, 22% accepted, 16 enrolled. In 2009, 17 master's, 9 doctorates awarded. *Degree requirements:* For master's, thesis; for doctorate, thesis/dissertation, 2 qualifying exams. *Entrance requirements:* For master's, GRE General Test, minimum GPA of 3.0, 3 letters of recommendation; for doctorate, GRE General Test, 3 letters of recommendation. Additional exam requirements/recommendations for international students: Required—TOEFL. *Application deadline:* For fall admission, 2/15 for domestic students, 2/1 for international students. Applications are processed on a rolling basis. Application fee: $60. Electronic applications accepted. *Expenses:* Tuition, area resident: Part-time $471 per credit hour. Tuition, state resident: part-time $471 per credit hour. Tuition, nonresident: part-time $1016 per credit hour. Required fees: $337.04 per term. *Financial support:* In 2009–10, 6 fellowships with full and partial tuition reimbursements (averaging $12,642 per year), 1 research assistantship (averaging $17,642 per year), 59 teaching assistantships with tuition reimbursements (averaging $15,885 per year) were awarded; Federal Work-Study and scholarships/grants also available. Support available to part-time students. Financial award applicants required to submit FAFSA. *Faculty research:* Social psychology, sociology of work, sociology of the military, population studies, stratification. Total annual research expenditures: $1 million. *Unit head:* Dr. Reeve Vannerman, Chair, 301-405-6892, Fax: 301-314-6892, E-mail: reeve@umd.edu. *Application contact:* Dean of Graduate School, 301-405-0358, Fax: 301-314-9305.

University of Massachusetts Amherst, Graduate School, College of Social and Behavioral Sciences, Department of Sociology, Amherst, MA 01003. Offers MA, PhD. Part-time programs available. *Faculty:* 31 full-time (15 women). *Students:* 47 full-time (33 women), 27 part-time (18 women); includes 15 minority (5 African Americans, 2 Asian Americans or Pacific Islanders, 8 Hispanic Americans), 19 international. Average age 31. 137 applicants, 15% accepted, 9 enrolled. In 2009, 3 master's, 3 doctorates awarded. Terminal master's awarded for partial completion of doctoral program. *Degree requirements:* For master's, thesis or alternative; for doctorate, comprehensive exam, thesis/dissertation. *Entrance requirements:* For master's and doctorate, GRE General Test, writing sample, 3 letters of recommendation. Additional exam requirements/recommendations for international students: Required—TOEFL (minimum score 550 paper-based; 213 computer-based; 80 iBT), IELTS (minimum score 6.5). *Application deadline:* For fall admission, 1/15 for domestic and international students. Applications are processed on a rolling basis. Application fee: $50 ($65 for international students). Electronic applications accepted. *Expenses:* Tuition, state resident: full-time $2640; part-time $110 per credit. Tuition, nonresident: full-time $9936; part-time $414 per credit. Tuition and fees vary according to course load. *Financial support:* In 2009–10, 11 research assistantships with full tuition reimbursements (averaging $8,659 per year), 42 teaching assistantships with full tuition reimbursements (averaging $12,188 per year) were awarded; fellowships, career-related internships or fieldwork, Federal Work-Study, scholarships/grants, traineeships, health care benefits, tuition waivers (full), and unspecified assistantships also available. Support available to part-time students. Financial award application deadline: 1/15. *Unit head:* Dr. Sanjiv Gupta, Graduate Program Director, 413-545-4057, Fax: 413-545-3204. *Application contact:* Jean M. Ames, Supervisor of Admissions, 413-545-0722, Fax: 413-577-0010, E-mail: gradadm@grad.umass.edu.

University of Massachusetts Boston, Office of Graduate Studies, College of Liberal Arts, Program in Applied Sociology, Boston, MA 02125-3393. Offers MA. Part-time and evening/weekend programs available. *Degree requirements:* For master's, comprehensive exam, thesis. *Entrance requirements:* For master's, GRE or MAT, minimum GPA of 2.75. *Faculty research:* Sociology of education, social deviance and control, women and development, race and ethnic group relations, criminology.

University of Massachusetts Lowell, College of Arts and Sciences, Department of Regional Economic and Social Development, Lowell, MA 01854-2881. Offers MA, Graduate Certificate. Part-time programs available. *Entrance requirements:* For master's, GRE. Electronic applications accepted.

University of Memphis, Graduate School, College of Arts and Sciences, Department of Sociology, Memphis, TN 38152. Offers MA. Part-time programs available. *Faculty:* 6 full-time (3 women). *Students:* 10 full-time (8 women), 4 part-time (2 women); includes 1 minority (African American). Average age 33. 9 applicants, 89% accepted, 1 enrolled. In 2009, 4 master's awarded. *Degree requirements:* For master's, comprehensive exam, thesis (for some programs). *Entrance requirements:* For master's, GRE General Test, 12 undergraduate hours in sociology. Additional exam requirements/recommendations for international students: Required—TOEFL (minimum score 550 paper-based; 213 computer-based). *Application deadline:* For fall admission, 7/1 for domestic students, 5/1 for international students; for spring admission, 12/1 for domestic students, 9/15 for international students. Applications are processed on a rolling basis. Application fee: $35 ($60 for international students). Electronic applications accepted. *Expenses:* Tuition, state resident: full-time $6246; part-time $347 per credit hour. Tuition, nonresident: full-time $15,894; part-time $883 per credit hour. Required fees: $1160. Full-time tuition and fees vary according to course load, degree level and program. *Financial support:* In 2009–10, 12 students received support, including 9 research assistantships with full tuition reimbursements available (averaging $9,600 per year), 1 teaching assistantship with full tuition reimbursement available (averaging $6,000 per year); Federal Work-Study, scholarships/grants, and unspecified assistantships also available. Financial award application deadline: 2/15; financial award applicants required to submit FAFSA. *Faculty research:* Globalization, medical, inequality, religion, urban. *Unit head:* Dr. Martin Levin, Chair, 901-678-2611, Fax: 901-678-2525. *Application contact:* Dr. Larry Petersen, Professor and Graduate Coordinator, 901-678-3341, Fax: 901-678-2525, E-mail: lpetersn@memphis.edu.

University of Miami, Graduate School, College of Arts and Sciences, Department of Sociology, Coral Gables, FL 33124. Offers MA, PhD. Part-time programs available. Terminal master's awarded for partial completion of doctoral program. *Degree requirements:* For master's, thesis; for doctorate, comprehensive exam, thesis/dissertation. *Entrance requirements:* For master's and doctorate, GRE General Test. Additional exam requirements/recommendations for international students: Required—TOEFL (minimum score 515 paper-based; 213 computer-based). Electronic applications accepted. *Faculty research:* Crime, violence, mental health, ethnic relations, health.

University of Michigan, Horace H. Rackham School of Graduate Studies, College of Literature, Science, and the Arts, Department of Sociology, Ann Arbor, MI 48109. Offers public policy and sociology (PhD); social work and sociology (PhD); sociology (PhD); women's studies and sociology (PhD). *Faculty:* 37 full-time (16 women), 9 part-time/adjunct (2 women). *Students:* 102 full-time (69 women); includes 27 minority (8 African Americans, 10 Asian Americans or Pacific Islanders, 9 Hispanic Americans), 20 international. Average age 33. 287 applicants, 8% accepted, 9 enrolled. In 2009, 12 doctorates awarded. *Degree requirements:* For doctorate, comprehensive exam, thesis/dissertation, oral defense of dissertation, preliminary exam. *Entrance requirements:* For doctorate, GRE General Test, letters of recommendation, writing sample. Additional exam requirements/recommendations for international students: Required—TOEFL (minimum score 560 paper-based; 220 computer-based; 84 iBT). *Application deadline:* For fall admission, 12/15 for domestic and international students. Application fee: $60 ($75 for international students). Electronic applications accepted. *Expenses:* Tuition, state resident: full-time $17,286; part-time $1099 per credit hour. Tuition, nonresident: full-time $34,944; part-time $2080 per credit hour. Required fees: $95 per semester. Tuition and fees vary according to course load, degree level and program. *Financial support:* In 2009–10, 40 students received support, including 20 fellowships with tuition reimbursements available (averaging $16,000 per year), 50 teaching assistantships with tuition reimbursements available (averaging $16,000 per year); health care benefits also available. *Faculty research:* Power, history and social change; gender and sexuality; race and ethnicity; economic sociology; social demography. Total annual research expenditures: $269,377. *Unit head:* Howard Kimeldorf, Chair, 734-764-5554, Fax: 734-763-6887, E-mail: hkimel@umich.edu. *Application contact:* Jeannie Loughry, Graduate Program Coordinator, 734-647-4428, Fax: 734-763-6887, E-mail: sociology.graduate.program@umich.edu.

University of Michigan, Horace H. Rackham School of Graduate Studies, College of Literature, Science, and the Arts, Department of Women's Studies, Ann Arbor, MI 48109. Offers English and women's studies (PhD); history and women's studies (PhD); lesbian, gay, bisexual, transgender, queer (LGBTQ) studies (Certificate); psychology and women's studies (PhD); sociology and women's studies (PhD); women's studies (Certificate). *Faculty:* 74 full-time (68 women). *Students:* 68 full-time (63 women); includes 21 minority (7 African Americans, 1 American Indian/Alaska Native, 8 Asian Americans or Pacific Islanders, 5 Hispanic Americans), 12 international. Average age 31. 119 applicants, 9% accepted, 7 enrolled. In 2009, 5 doctorates, 8 other advanced degrees awarded. *Degree requirements:* For doctorate, variable foreign language requirement, comprehensive exam (for some programs), thesis/dissertation. *Entrance requirements:* For doctorate, GRE General Test, previous undergraduate course work in women's studies. *Application deadline:* For fall admission, 12/1 for domestic and international students. Application fee: $60 ($75 for international students). Electronic applications accepted. *Expenses:* Tuition, state resident: full-time $17,286; part-time $1099 per credit hour. Tuition, nonresident: full-time $34,944; part-time $2080 per credit hour. Required fees: $95 per semester. Tuition and fees vary according to course load, degree level and program. *Financial support:* In 2009–10, 34 students received support, including 19 fellowships with full tuition reimbursements available (averaging $16,000 per year), 15 teaching assistantships with full and partial tuition reimbursements available (averaging $16,135 per year); career-related internships or fieldwork, institutionally sponsored loans, scholarships/grants, traineeships, health care benefits, and unspecified assistantships also available. *Faculty research:* Gender issues; LGBTQ studies; sexuality; women and science; global feminism. *Unit head:* Anne Herrmann, Chair, 734-763-2047, Fax: 734-647-4943, E-mail: anneh@umich.edu. *Application contact:* Aimee Germain, Graduate Program Coordinator, 734-763-2047, Fax: 734-647-4943, E-mail: wsdgradInquiry@umich.edu.

University of Minnesota, Duluth, Graduate School, College of Liberal Arts, Department of Sociology/Anthropology, Duluth, MN 55812-2496. Offers criminology (MA); liberal studies (MLS). Part-time programs available. *Degree requirements:* For master's, thesis or alternative. *Entrance requirements:* For master's, interview, minimum GPA of 3.0, letters of recommendation. Additional exam requirements/recommendations for international students: Required—TOEFL. *Faculty research:* Nature of knowledge, philosophy of science, ecology, cultural studies, language.

University of Minnesota, Twin Cities Campus, Graduate School, College of Liberal Arts, Department of Sociology, Minneapolis, MN 55455-0213. Offers MA, PhD. *Faculty:* 31 full-time (14 women), 1 part-time/adjunct (0 women). *Students:* 88 full-time (54 women); includes 14 minority (3 African Americans, 1 American Indian/Alaska Native, 4 Asian Americans or Pacific Islanders, 6 Hispanic Americans), 18 international. Average age 31. 110 applicants, 13% accepted, 11 enrolled. In 2009, 1 master's, 6 doctorates awarded. Terminal master's awarded for partial completion of doctoral program. *Degree requirements:* For master's, thesis optional; for doctorate, thesis/dissertation, preliminary written exam & oral defense, prospectus hearing, dissertation, & final oral defense. *Entrance requirements:* For doctorate, GRE General Test, Bachelor degree (official transcripts), 3.0 or higher GPA (on 4.0 scale), personal statement, three letters of recommendation, writing sample. Additional exam requirements/recommendations for international students: Required—TOEFL (minimum score 550 paper-based; 79 iBT). *Application deadline:* For fall admission, 12/1 for domestic and international students. Application fee: $75 ($95 for international students). Electronic applications accepted. *Financial support:* In 2009–10, 16 fellowships with full tuition reimbursements (averaging $22,000 per year), 17 research assistantships with full tuition reimbursements (averaging $18,700 per year), 30 teaching assistantships with full tuition reimbursements (averaging $14,500 per year) were awarded; career-related internships or fieldwork, Federal Work-Study, scholarships/grants, traineeships, health care benefits, and unspecified assistantships also available. Financial award application deadline: 12/1. *Faculty research:* Organizations, work, and markets; inequality: race, class, and gender; law, crime and deviance; family and life course; political sociology and social movements. *Unit head:* Dr. Christopher Uggen, Chair, 612-624-4300, Fax: 612-624-7020, E-mail: uggen001@umn.edu. *Application contact:* Robert Fox, Graduate Program Associate, 612-624-2093, Fax: 612-624-7020, E-mail: soc@umn.edu.

University of Mississippi, Graduate School, College of Liberal Arts, Department of Sociology and Anthropology, Oxford, University, MS 38677. Offers anthropology (MA); sociology (MA, MSS). *Faculty:* 19 full-time (8 women), 8 part-time/adjunct (4 women). *Students:* 23 full-time (13 women), 3 part-time (1 woman); includes 4 minority (3 African Americans, 1 American Indian/Alaska Native), 3 international. In 2009, 4 master's awarded. *Degree requirements:* For master's, thesis (for some programs). *Entrance requirements:* For master's, GRE General Test, minimum GPA of 3.0. Additional exam requirements/recommendations for international students: Required—TOEFL. *Application deadline:* For fall admission, 4/1 for domestic students; for spring admission, 10/1 for domestic students. Applications are processed on a rolling basis. Application fee: $25. Electronic applications accepted. *Financial support:* Scholarships/grants available. Financial award application deadline: 3/1; financial award applicants required to submit FAFSA. *Unit head:* Dr. Kirsten A. Dellinger, Chairman, 662-915-7421, Fax: 662-915-5372, E-mail: kdelling@olemiss.edu. *Application contact:* Dr. Christy M. Wyandt, Associate Dean, 662-915-7474, Fax: 662-915-7577, E-mail: cwyandt@olemiss.edu.

University of Missouri, Graduate School, College of Arts and Sciences, Department of Sociology, Columbia, MO 65211. Offers MA, PhD. *Faculty:* 14 full-time (6 women), 5 part-time/adjunct (2 women). *Students:* 20 full-time (9 women), 36 part-time (16 women); includes 10 minority (3 African Americans, 2 American Indian/Alaska Native, 1 Asian American or Pacific Islander, 4 Hispanic Americans), 6 international. Average age 33. 41 applicants, 39% accepted, 8 enrolled. In 2009, 3 master's awarded. *Degree requirements:* For doctorate, one foreign language, comprehensive exam, thesis/dissertation. *Entrance requirements:* For master's and doctorate, GRE General Test, minimum GPA of 3.0; 15 hours of undergraduate sociology with a grade of B or better, including one course in sociological theory and a basic statistics course. Additional exam requirements/recommendations for international students: Required—TOEFL (minimum score 500 paper-based; 173 computer-based; 61 iBT). *Application deadline:* For fall admission, 1/15 priority date for domestic students. Applications are processed on a rolling basis. Application fee: $45 ($60 for international students). Electronic applications accepted. *Financial support:* In 2009–10, 9 fellowships with full tuition reimbursements, 2 research assistantships with full tuition reimbursements, 31 teaching assistantships with full tuition reimbursements were awarded; institutionally sponsored loans, health care benefits, and unspecified assistantships also available. *Faculty research:* Culture and identity; political and economic institutions and social movements; social control and deviance; social inequalities. *Unit head:* Dr. Jay Gubrium, Department Chair, 573-882-8331, E-mail: gubriumj@missouri.edu.

Application contact: Mary Oakes, Administrative Assistant, 573-882-7163, E-mail: oakesm@missouri.edu.

University of Missouri–Kansas City, College of Arts and Sciences, Department of Sociology, Kansas City, MO 64110-2499. Offers MA, PhD. PhD (interdisciplinary) offered through the School of Graduate Studies. Part-time and evening/weekend programs available. *Faculty:* 13 full-time (7 women), 2 part-time/adjunct (both women). *Students:* 5 full-time (4 women), 9 part-time (7 women); includes 3 minority (2 African Americans, 1 Hispanic American), 2 international. Average age 33. 14 applicants, 50% accepted, 5 enrolled. In 2009, 3 master's awarded. *Degree requirements:* For master's, thesis optional. *Entrance requirements:* For master's, GRE, minimum GPA of 3.0 in major, 2.7 overall. Additional exam requirements/recommendations for international students: Required—TOEFL (minimum score 550 paper-based; 213 computer-based; 80 iBT). *Application deadline:* For fall admission, 3/1 for domestic and international students; for spring admission, 11/1 for domestic and international students. Applications are processed on a rolling basis. Application fee: $45 ($50 for international students). Electronic applications accepted. *Expenses:* Tuition, state resident: full-time $5378; part-time $299 per credit hour. Tuition, nonresident: full-time $13,881; part-time $771 per credit hour. Required fees: $641; $71 per credit hour. Tuition and fees vary according to course load and program. *Financial support:* In 2009–10, 1 research assistantship with full tuition reimbursement (averaging $12,000 per year), 4 teaching assistantships with full and partial tuition reimbursements (averaging $12,000 per year) were awarded; career-related internships or fieldwork, Federal Work-Study, institutionally sponsored loans, and tuition waivers (partial) also available. Support available to part-time students. Financial award application deadline: 3/1; financial award applicants required to submit FAFSA. *Faculty research:* Gerontology, religious movements, urban community and neighborhoods. Total annual research expenditures: $64,644. *Unit head:* Dr. Linda Breytspraak, Chairperson, 816-235-2514, Fax: 816-235-1117. *Application contact:* Dr. Deborah Smith, Graduate Advisor, 816-235-2529, Fax: 816-235-1117, E-mail: smithde@umkc.edu.

The University of Montana, Graduate School, College of Arts and Sciences, Department of Sociology, Missoula, MT 59812-0002. Offers criminology (MA); rural and environmental change (MA); sociology (MA). *Entrance requirements:* For master's, GRE General Test. Additional exam requirements/recommendations for international students: Required—TOEFL. *Faculty research:* Housing, homelessness, hunger, infant mortality, work safety.

University of Nebraska–Lincoln, Graduate College, College of Arts and Sciences, Department of Sociology, Lincoln, NE 68588. Offers MA, PhD. *Degree requirements:* For master's, thesis optional; for doctorate, comprehensive exam, thesis/dissertation. *Entrance requirements:* For master's and doctorate, GRE General Test, writing sample. Additional exam requirements/recommendations for international students: Required—TOEFL (minimum score 550 paper-based; 213 computer-based). Electronic applications accepted. *Faculty research:* Family, deviance and social control, ethnic studies, inequality (gender, race, and class).

University of Nevada, Las Vegas, Graduate College, College of Liberal Arts, Department of Sociology, Las Vegas, NV 89154-5003. Offers MA, PhD. Part-time programs available. *Faculty:* 13 full-time (4 women). *Students:* 29 full-time (19 women), 13 part-time (7 women); includes 7 minority (6 African Americans, 1 Hispanic American), 2 international. Average age 37. 33 applicants, 45% accepted, 11 enrolled. In 2009, 5 master's, 2 doctorates awarded. *Degree requirements:* For master's, thesis, oral exams; for doctorate, comprehensive exam, thesis/dissertation, oral exams. *Entrance requirements:* For master's and doctorate, GRE General Test. Additional exam requirements/recommendations for international students: Required—TOEFL (minimum score 550 paper-based; 213 computer-based), IELTS (minimum score 7). *Application deadline:* For fall admission, 2/1 priority date for domestic and international students. Applications are processed on a rolling basis. Application fee: $60 ($95 for international students). Electronic applications accepted. *Financial support:* In 2009–10, 28 students received support, including 12 research assistantships with partial tuition reimbursements available (averaging $12,125 per year), 16 teaching assistantships with partial tuition reimbursements available (averaging $12,000 per year); institutionally sponsored loans, scholarships/grants, health care benefits, and unspecified assistantships also available. Financial award application deadline: 3/1. *Faculty research:* Gaming behavior and gaming addiction; environment, social and economic sustainability in Las Vegas; U.S. white power movement and social movements; relevance of gender and age in work and family life; the sex industry. *Unit head:* Dr. Andy Fontana, Chair/ Professor, 702-895-3322, Fax: 702-895-4800, E-mail: andrea.fontana@unlv.edu. *Application contact:* Graduate College Admissions Evaluator, 702-895-3320, Fax: 702-895-4180, E-mail: gradcollege@unlv.edu.

University of Nevada, Reno, Graduate School, College of Liberal Arts, School of Social Research and Justice Studies, Department of Sociology, Reno, NV 89557. Offers MA. *Degree requirements:* For master's, thesis optional. *Entrance requirements:* For master's, GRE General Test, minimum GPA of 2.75. Additional exam requirements/recommendations for international students: Required—TOEFL (minimum score 500 paper-based; 173 computer-based; 61 iBT), IELTS (minimum score 6). Electronic applications accepted. *Faculty research:* Statistics, politics and economics, religion and law, industry, theory stratification.

University of New Brunswick Fredericton, School of Graduate Studies, Faculty of Arts, Department of Sociology, Fredericton, NB E3B 5A3, Canada. Offers MA, PhD. Part-time programs available. *Faculty:* 10 full-time (6 women), 8 part-time/adjunct (5 women). *Students:* 21 full-time (14 women), 4 part-time (2 women). In 2009, 4 master's, 2 doctorates awarded. *Degree requirements:* For master's, thesis; for doctorate, comprehensive exam, thesis/dissertation, 6 courses. *Entrance requirements:* For master's, minimum GPA of 3.5; for doctorate, minimum GPA of 3.0, MA in sociology with thesis or equivalent, curriculum vitae, statement of interest about interview research. Additional exam requirements/recommendations for international students: Required—TOEFL (minimum score 650 paper-based). *Application deadline:* For fall admission, 3/1 priority date for domestic students. Application fee: $50 Canadian dollars. Tuition and fees charges are reported in Canadian dollars. *Expenses:* Tuition, area resident: Full-time $5562 Canadian dollars; part-time $2781 Canadian dollars per year. Required fees: $49.75 Canadian dollars per term. *Financial support:* In 2009–10, 7 teaching assistantships with full tuition reimbursements (averaging $17,000 per year) were awarded. *Faculty research:* Social policy; media, communication and culture, family and domestic violence; sociology of health and health care. *Unit head:* Dr. Gary Bowden, Director of Graduate Studies, 506-452-6217, Fax: 506-453-4659, E-mail: glb@unb.ca. *Application contact:* Joyce Smith, Acting Graduate Secretary, 506-458-7474, Fax: 506-453-4659, E-mail: socio@unb.ca.

University of New Hampshire, Graduate School, College of Liberal Arts, Department of Sociology, Durham, NH 03824. Offers MA, PhD. Part-time programs available. *Faculty:* 12 full-time. *Students:* 31 full-time (24 women), 9 part-time (8 women); includes 5 minority (2 African Americans, 1 American Indian/Alaska Native, 2 Hispanic Americans), 3 international. Average age 32. 34 applicants, 74% accepted, 9 enrolled. In 2009, 3 master's, 1 doctorate awarded. *Degree requirements:* For master's, thesis; for doctorate, one foreign language, thesis/dissertation. *Entrance requirements:* For master's and doctorate, GRE General Test. Additional exam requirements/recommendations for international students: Required—TOEFL (minimum score 550 paper-based; 213 computer-based; 80 iBT). *Application deadline:* For fall admission, 4/1 priority date for domestic students, 4/1 for international students; for spring admission, 12/1 for domestic students. Applications are processed on a rolling basis. Application fee: $65. Electronic applications accepted. *Expenses:* Tuition, state resident: full-time $10,380; part-time $577 per credit hour. Tuition, nonresident: full-time $24,350; part-time $1002 per credit hour. Required fees: $1550; $387.50 per semester. Tuition and fees vary according to course load and program. *Financial support:* In 2009–10, 27 students received support, including 5 fellowships, 3 research assistantships, 18 teaching assistantships; career-related internships or fieldwork, Federal Work-Study, scholarships/grants, and tuition waivers (full and partial) also available. Support available to part-time students. Financial award application deadline: 2/15. *Faculty research:* Deviance, conflict and control, social psychology, comparative institutional analysis, family. *Unit head:* Dr. Michele Dillon, Chairperson, 603-862-1814. *Application contact:* Deena Peschke, Administrative Assistant, 603-862-2500, E-mail: sociology.dept@unh.edu.

University of New Mexico, Graduate School, College of Arts and Sciences, Department of Sociology, Albuquerque, NM 87131-2039. Offers MA, PhD. Part-time programs available. *Faculty:* 19 full-time (8 women), 8 part-time/adjunct (4 women). *Students:* 32 full-time (17 women), 7 part-time (5 women); includes 8 minority (1 African American, 1 American Indian/Alaska Native, 6 Hispanic Americans), 3 international. Average age 34. 26 applicants, 58% accepted, 7 enrolled. In 2009, 2 master's, 5 doctorates awarded. Terminal master's awarded for partial completion of doctoral program. *Degree requirements:* For master's, thesis; for doctorate, comprehensive exam, thesis/dissertation. *Entrance requirements:* For master's and doctorate, GRE General Test, 2 writing samples, 3 letters of reference, letter of intent. Additional exam requirements/recommendations for international students: Required—TOEFL. *Application deadline:* For fall admission, 2/1 for domestic and international students; for spring admission, 9/30 for domestic and international students. Application fee: $50. Electronic applications accepted. *Expenses:* Tuition, state resident: full-time $2099; part-time $233.20 per credit hour. Tuition, nonresident: full-time $6650. Required fees: $25 per semester. Tuition and fees vary according to course load, program and reciprocity agreements. *Financial support:* In 2009–10, 20 students received support, including 16 teaching assistantships with partial tuition reimbursements available (averaging $12,510 per year); research assistantships, institutionally sponsored loans, scholarships/grants, health care benefits, tuition waivers (partial), and unspecified assistantships also available. Support available to part-time students. Financial award applicants required to submit FAFSA. *Faculty research:* Criminology/deviance, gender, Latin American/comparative sociology, political sociology, race and ethnicity, social movements, religion, social welfare, work/organizations. Total annual research expenditures: $696,099. *Unit head:* Dr. Beverly Burris, Chair, 505-277-2501, Fax: 505-277-8805, E-mail: bburris@unm.edu. *Application contact:* Karen Majors, Chair, Graduate Committee, 505-277-2501, Fax: 505-277-8805, E-mail: majors@unm.edu.

University of New Orleans, Graduate School, College of Liberal Arts, Department of Sociology, New Orleans, LA 70148. Offers MA. Part-time and evening/weekend programs available. *Degree requirements:* For master's, thesis (for some programs). *Entrance requirements:* For master's, GRE General Test. Additional exam requirements/recommendations for international students: Required—TOEFL (minimum score 550 paper-based; 213 computer-based; 79 iBT). Electronic applications accepted. *Faculty research:* Environment and gender.

The University of North Carolina at Chapel Hill, Graduate School, College of Arts and Sciences, Department of Sociology, Chapel Hill, NC 27599. Offers MA, PhD. *Degree requirements:* For master's, comprehensive exam, thesis; for doctorate, comprehensive exam, thesis/dissertation. *Entrance requirements:* For master's and doctorate, GRE General Test, minimum GPA of 3.0. Additional exam requirements/recommendations for international students: Required—TOEFL (minimum score 550 paper-based; 213 computer-based). Electronic applications accepted. *Faculty research:* Comparative historical, work/organizations, religion, demography, stratification.

The University of North Carolina at Charlotte, Graduate School, College of Arts and Sciences, Department of Sociology, Charlotte, NC 28223-0001. Offers MA. Part-time and evening/weekend programs available. *Faculty:* 18 full-time (10 women). *Students:* 10 full-time (8 women), 5 part-time (4 women); includes 5 minority (2 African Americans, 3 Asian Americans or Pacific Islanders). Average age 31. 14 applicants, 57% accepted, 3 enrolled. In 2009, 9 master's awarded. *Degree requirements:* For master's, thesis or comprehensive exam. *Entrance requirements:* For master's, GRE or MAT, minimum GPA of 3.0 in last 2 years, 2.75 overall. Additional exam requirements/recommendations for international students: Required—TOEFL (minimum score 557 paper-based; 220 computer-based; 83 iBT). *Application deadline:* For fall admission, 7/1 for domestic students, 5/1 for international students; for spring admission, 11/1 for domestic students, 10/1 for international students. Applications are processed on a rolling basis. Application fee: $55. Electronic applications accepted. *Financial support:* In 2009–10, 7 students received support, including 3 research assistantships (averaging $10,739 per year), 4 teaching assistantships (averaging $9,500 per year); career-related internships or fieldwork, Federal Work-Study, institutionally sponsored loans, scholarships/grants, and unspecified assistantships also available. Support available to part-time students. Financial award application deadline: 4/1; financial award applicants required to submit FAFSA. *Faculty research:* Social psychology, sociology of education, social gerontology, quantitative methodology, medical sociology. Total annual research expenditures: $82,232. *Unit head:* Dr. Lisa Rachotte, Chair, 704-687-2288, Fax: 704-687-3091, E-mail: lrashott@uncc.edu. *Application contact:* Kathy B. Giddings, Director of Graduate Admissions, 704-687-5503, Fax: 704-687-3279, E-mail: gradadm@uncc.edu.

The University of North Carolina at Greensboro, Graduate School, College of Arts and Sciences, Department of Sociology, Greensboro, NC 27412-5001. Offers criminology (MA); sociology (MA). Part-time programs available. *Degree requirements:* For master's, comprehensive exam, thesis. *Entrance requirements:* For master's, GRE General Test. Additional exam requirements/recommendations for international students: Required—TOEFL. Electronic applications accepted.

The University of North Carolina Wilmington, College of Arts and Sciences, Department of Sociology and Criminology, Wilmington, NC 28403-3297. Offers criminology (MA); public sociology (MA). *Degree requirements:* For master's, comprehensive exam, thesis or internship. *Entrance requirements:* Additional exam requirements/recommendations for international students: Required—TOEFL (minimum score 550 paper-based; 217 computer-based; 79 iBT), IELTS (minimum score 6.5). Electronic applications accepted.

University of North Dakota, Graduate School, College of Arts and Sciences, Department of Sociology, Grand Forks, ND 58202. Offers MA. *Degree requirements:* For master's, thesis, final examination. *Entrance requirements:* For master's, minimum GPA of 3.0. Additional exam requirements/recommendations for international students: Required—TOEFL (minimum score 550 paper-based; 213 computer-based; 79 iBT), IELTS (minimum score 6.5). Electronic applications accepted. *Faculty research:* Criminal justice studies, social psychology, research methods, corrections, social theory.

University of Northern Colorado, Graduate School, College of Humanities and Social Sciences, School of Social Sciences, Program in Social Sciences, Greeley, CO 80639. Offers clinical sociology (MA). Part-time programs available. *Faculty:* 23 full-time (9 women). *Students:* 10 full-time (6 women), 5 part-time (4 women); includes 3 minority (1 African American, 1 American Indian/Alaska Native, 1 Hispanic American), 1 international. Average age 32. 14 applicants, 64% accepted, 7 enrolled. In 2009, 5 master's awarded. *Degree requirements:* For master's, comprehensive exam. *Entrance requirements:* For master's, 2 letters of recommendation. *Application deadline:* Applications are processed on a rolling basis. Application fee: $50 ($60 for international students). Electronic applications accepted. *Expenses:* Tuition, state resident: full-time $5770; part-time $320.55 per credit hour. Tuition, nonresident: full-time $13,847; part-time $769.27 per credit hour. Required fees: $948.78; $52.72 per credit. *Financial support:* In 2009–10, 3 teaching assistantships (averaging $2,849 per year) were awarded; fellowships, research assistantships, unspecified assistantships also available. Financial award application deadline: 3/1; financial award applicants required to submit FAFSA. *Unit head:* Dr. David Musick, Program Coordinator, 970-351-2315, Fax: 970-351-1527. *Application contact:* Linda Sisson, Graduate Student Admission Coordinator, 970-351-1807, Fax: 970-351-2371, E-mail: linda.sisson@unco.edu.

University of Northern Iowa, Graduate College, College of Social and Behavioral Sciences, Department of Sociology, Anthropology and Criminology, Cedar Falls, IA 50614. Offers criminology (MA); sociology (MA). Part-time and evening/weekend programs available. *Students:* 16 full-time (12 women), 1 (woman) part-time; includes 2 minority (both American Indian/Alaska Native). 22 applicants, 59% accepted, 7 enrolled. In 2009, 2 master's awarded. *Degree*

Sociology

University of Northern Iowa (continued)

requirements: For master's, thesis. *Entrance requirements:* For master's, minimum GPA of 3.0. Additional exam requirements/recommendations for international students: Required—TOEFL (minimum score 500 paper-based; 180 computer-based; 61 iBT). *Application deadline:* For fall admission, 8/1 priority date for domestic students. Applications are processed on a rolling basis. Application fee: $30 ($50 for international students). Electronic applications accepted. *Financial support:* Career-related internships or fieldwork, Federal Work-Study, scholarships/grants, and tuition waivers (full and partial) available. Support available to part-time students. Financial award application deadline: 2/1. *Unit head:* Dr. Kent Sandstrom, Department Head/Professor, 319-273-2786, Fax: 319-273-7104, E-mail: kent.sandstrom@uni.edu. *Application contact:* Laurie S. Russell, Record Analyst, 319-273-2623, Fax: 319-273-6792, E-mail: laurie.russell@uni.edu.

University of North Texas, Robert B. Toulouse School of Graduate Studies, College of Public Affairs and Community Service, Department of Sociology, Denton, TX 76203-5017. Offers global and comparative (PhD); health and illness (PhD); social stratification and inequality (PhD); sociology (MA, MS). Terminal master's awarded for partial completion of doctoral program. *Degree requirements:* For master's, variable foreign language requirement, comprehensive exam, thesis (for some programs); for doctorate, variable foreign language requirement, comprehensive exam, thesis/dissertation. *Entrance requirements:* For master's, GRE General Test, 4 letters of recommendation; for doctorate, GRE General Test, master's degree, 4 letters of recommendation. Additional exam requirements/recommendations for international students: Required—TOEFL (minimum score 550 paper-based; 213 computer-based; 79 iBT), proof of English language proficiency required for non-native English speakers. *Application deadline:* Applications are processed on a rolling basis. Application fee: $50 ($75 for international students). Electronic applications accepted. *Expenses:* Tuition, state resident: full-time $4298; part-time $239 per contact hour. Tuition, nonresident: full-time $9878; part-time $549 per contact hour. Required fees: $265 per contact hour. *Financial support:* Fellowships, research assistantships, teaching assistantships, career-related internships or fieldwork, Federal Work-Study, institutionally sponsored loans, scholarships/grants, health care benefits, tuition waivers (partial), and unspecified assistantships available. Support available to part-time students. Financial award applicants required to submit FAFSA. *Faculty research:* Health and illness, social inequality, globalization and development, family. *Application contact:* Graduate Adviser, 940-565-2296, Fax: 940-369-7035, E-mail: seward@unt.edu.

University of Notre Dame, Graduate School, College of Arts and Letters, Division of Social Science, Department of Sociology, Notre Dame, IN 46556. Offers PhD. *Degree requirements:* For doctorate, thesis/dissertation, 2 area specialty exams. *Entrance requirements:* For doctorate, GRE General Test, GRE Subject Test (strongly recommended). Additional exam requirements/recommendations for international students: Required—TOEFL (minimum score 600 paper-based; 250 computer-based; 80 iBT). Electronic applications accepted. *Faculty research:* Cultural sociology, development, family, education, historical/comparative sociology.

University of Oklahoma, Graduate College, College of Arts and Sciences, Department of Sociology, Norman, OK 73019. Offers MA, PhD. Part-time programs available. *Faculty:* 16 full-time (9 women). *Students:* 34 full-time (23 women), 7 part-time (all women); includes 10 minority (4 African Americans, 1 American Indian/Alaska Native, 3 Asian Americans or Pacific Islanders, 2 Hispanic Americans), 2 international. 25 applicants, 36% accepted, 9 enrolled. In 2009, 5 master's, 4 doctorates awarded. Terminal master's awarded for partial completion of doctoral program. *Degree requirements:* For master's, thesis or alternative; for doctorate, thesis/dissertation, general exams, qualifying exam. *Entrance requirements:* For master's and doctorate, GRE General Test, 3 letters of recommendation. Additional exam requirements/recommendations for international students: Required—TOEFL (minimum score 550 paper-based; 213 computer-based). *Application deadline:* For fall admission, 2/15 priority date for domestic students, 2/15 for international students; for spring admission, 11/1 for domestic students, 9/1 for international students. Applications are processed on a rolling basis. Application fee: $40 ($90 for international students). Electronic applications accepted. *Expenses:* Tuition, state resident: full-time $3744; part-time $156 per credit hour. Tuition, nonresident: full-time $13,577; part-time $565.70 per credit hour. Required fees: $2415; $90.10 per credit hour. *Financial support:* In 2009–10, 37 students received support, including 2 fellowships with full tuition reimbursements available (averaging $3,750 per year), 35 teaching assistantships with partial tuition reimbursements available (averaging $13,848 per year); unspecified assistantships also available. Financial award application deadline: 3/15; financial award applicants required to submit FAFSA. *Faculty research:* Criminology, sociology of gender, sociology of family, social stratification, demography. Total annual research expenditures: $35,997. *Unit head:* Dr. Craig St. John, Chair, 405-325-1751, Fax: 405-325-7825, E-mail: cstjohn@ou.edu. *Application contact:* Dr. Amy Kroska, Associate Professor and Graduate Advisor, 405-325-1751, Fax: 405-325-7825, E-mail: amykroska@ou.edu.

University of Oregon, Graduate School, College of Arts and Sciences, Department of Sociology, Eugene, OR 97403. Offers MA, MS, PhD. Part-time programs available. Terminal master's awarded for partial completion of doctoral program. *Degree requirements:* For doctorate, thesis/dissertation. *Entrance requirements:* For master's and doctorate, GRE General Test, minimum GPA of 3.0. Additional exam requirements/recommendations for international students: Required—TOEFL. *Faculty research:* Criminology, environment, gender, labor, political economy.

University of Ottawa, Faculty of Graduate and Postdoctoral Studies, Faculty of Social Sciences, Department of Sociology and Anthropology, Ottawa, ON K1N 6N5, Canada. Offers MA. *Degree requirements:* For master's, thesis or alternative. *Entrance requirements:* For master's, honors bachelor's degree or equivalent, minimum B average. Electronic applications accepted. *Faculty research:* Inter-ethnic relations, development, political policies.

University of Pennsylvania, School of Arts and Sciences, Graduate Group in Sociology, Philadelphia, PA 19104. Offers AM, PhD. *Faculty:* 40 full-time (16 women), 9 part-time/adjunct (5 women). *Students:* 46 full-time (33 women), 3 part-time (all women); includes 5 minority (3 African Americans, 2 Asian Americans or Pacific Islanders), 8 international. 213 applicants, 9% accepted, 11 enrolled. In 2009, 4 master's, 6 doctorates awarded. Terminal master's awarded for partial completion of doctoral program. *Degree requirements:* For master's, thesis or alternative; for doctorate, one foreign language, thesis/dissertation. *Entrance requirements:* For master's and doctorate, GRE General Test. Additional exam requirements/recommendations for international students: Required—TOEFL. *Application deadline:* For fall admission, 12/1 priority date for domestic students. Application fee: $70. Electronic applications accepted. *Expenses:* Tuition: Full-time $25,660; part-time $4758 per course. Required fees: $2152; $270 per course. Tuition and fees vary according to course load, degree level and program. *Financial support:* Fellowships, teaching assistantships, institutionally sponsored loans, scholarships/grants, traineeships, health care benefits, and unspecified assistantships available. Financial award application deadline: 12/15.

University of Pittsburgh, School of Arts and Sciences, Department of Sociology, Pittsburgh, PA 15260. Offers MA, PhD. Part-time programs available. *Faculty:* 11 full-time (7 women), 4 part-time/adjunct (2 women). *Students:* 30 full-time (19 women), 2 part-time (1 woman); includes 9 minority (3 African Americans, 1 American Indian/Alaska Native, 3 Asian Americans or Pacific Islanders, 2 Hispanic Americans), 11 international. Average age 28. 93 applicants, 11% accepted, 10 enrolled. In 2009, 1 master's awarded. Terminal master's awarded for partial completion of doctoral program. *Degree requirements:* For master's, thesis; for doctorate, comprehensive exam, thesis/dissertation, preliminary exam. *Entrance requirements:* For master's and doctorate, GRE General Test, writing sample. Additional exam requirements/recommendations for international students: Required—TOEFL (minimum score 550 paper-based; 213 computer-based). *Application deadline:* For fall admission, 1/15 priority date for domestic and international students. Applications are processed on a rolling basis. Application fee: $50. Electronic applications accepted. *Expenses:* Tuition, state resident: full-time $16,402; part-time $665 per credit. Tuition, nonresident: full-time $28,694; part-time $1175 per credit. Required fees: $690; $175 per term. Tuition and fees vary according to program. *Financial support:* In 2009–10, 3 fellowships with full tuition reimbursements, 1 research assistantship with full tuition reimbursement, 19 teaching assistantships with full tuition reimbursements were awarded; scholarships/grants, health care benefits, tuition waivers (partial), and unspecified assistantships also available. Financial award application deadline: 1/15. *Faculty research:* Collective behavior/social movements, comparative sociology/historical sociology, cultural sociology, political sociology, qualitative methodology, quantitative methodology, sex and gender, social change, theory. Total annual research expenditures: $165,785. *Unit head:* Dr. Kathleen Blee, Chairman, 412-648-7584, Fax: 412-648-2799, E-mail: jm2@pitt.edu. *Application contact:* Terri Reich, Graduate Administrator, 412-648-7585, Fax: 412-648-2799, E-mail: tareich@pitt.edu.

University of Puerto Rico, Río Piedras, College of Social Sciences, Department of Sociology, San Juan, PR 00931-3300. Offers MA. *Degree requirements:* For master's, comprehensive exam, thesis. *Entrance requirements:* For master's, GRE or PAEG, interview, minimum GPA of 3.0, letter of recommendation.

University of Regina, Faculty of Graduate Studies and Research, Faculty of Arts, Department of Philosophy, Regina, SK S4S 0A2, Canada. Offers philosophy (MA); social and political thought (MA). *Faculty:* 9 full-time (3 women). *Students:* 1 (woman) full-time, 2 part-time (0 women). 2 applicants, 50% accepted. *Degree requirements:* For master's, thesis. *Entrance requirements:* Additional exam requirements/recommendations for international students: Required—TOEFL (minimum score 580 paper-based; 237 computer-based; 80 iBT). *Application deadline:* Applications are processed on a rolling basis. Application fee: $90 ($100 for international students). Electronic applications accepted. *Financial support:* Fellowships, research assistantships, teaching assistantships, scholarships/grants available. Financial award application deadline: 6/15. *Faculty research:* History of philosophy, ethics, aesthetics, metaphysics, epistemology. *Unit head:* Dr. Eldon Soifer, Head, 306-585-4301, Fax: 306-585-4827, E-mail: eldon.soifer@uregina.ca. *Application contact:* Dr. Eldon Soifer, Head, 306-585-4301, Fax: 306-585-4827, E-mail: eldon.soifer@uregina.ca.

University of Regina, Faculty of Graduate Studies and Research, Faculty of Arts, Department of Sociology and Social Studies, Regina, SK S4S 0A2, Canada. Offers social studies (MA, PhD); sociology (MA, PhD). *Faculty:* 12 full-time (5 women), 1 part-time/adjunct (0 women). *Students:* 13 full-time (10 women), 4 part-time (1 woman). 7 applicants, 86% accepted. In 2009, 4 master's awarded. *Degree requirements:* For master's, thesis. *Entrance requirements:* Additional exam requirements/recommendations for international students: Required—TOEFL (minimum score 580 paper-based; 237 computer-based; 80 iBT). *Application deadline:* Applications are processed on a rolling basis. Application fee: $90 ($100 for international students). Electronic applications accepted. *Financial support:* In 2009–10, 4 fellowships (averaging $19,000 per year), 3 research assistantships (averaging $16,910 per year), 5 teaching assistantships (averaging $6,650 per year) were awarded; scholarships/grants also available. Financial award application deadline: 6/15. *Faculty research:* Social justice; development and the environment; knowledge, technology, and society. *Unit head:* Dr. John Conway, Head, 306-585-4052, Fax: 306-585-4815, E-mail: john.conway@uregina.ca. *Application contact:* Dr. Henry Chow, Graduate Program Coordinator, 306-585-5604, Fax: 306-585-4815, E-mail: henry.chow@uregina.ca.

University of Saskatchewan, College of Graduate Studies and Research, College of Arts and Sciences, Department of Sociology, Saskatoon, SK S7N 5A2, Canada. Offers MA, PhD. *Faculty:* 25. *Students:* 47. In 2009, 9 master's, 3 doctorates awarded. *Degree requirements:* For master's, thesis; for doctorate, comprehensive exam (for some programs), thesis/dissertation. *Entrance requirements:* Additional exam requirements/recommendations for international students: Required—TOEFL (minimum score 80 iBT); Recommended—IELTS (minimum score 6.5). *Application deadline:* For fall admission, 7/1 priority date for domestic students. Applications are processed on a rolling basis. Application fee: $75. Electronic applications accepted. Tuition and fees charges are reported in Canadian dollars. *Expenses:* Tuition, area resident: Full-time $3000 Canadian dollars; part-time $500 Canadian dollars per term. Required fees: $700 Canadian dollars; $100 Canadian dollars per term. *Financial support:* Fellowships, research assistantships, teaching assistantships available. Financial award application deadline: 1/31. *Unit head:* Dr. Terry Wotherspoon, Head, 306-966-6925, Fax: 306-966-6950, E-mail: terry.wotherspoon@usask.ca. *Application contact:* Dr. Patricia Monture, Graduate Chair, 306-966-6984, Fax: 306-966-6950, E-mail: patricia.monture@usask.ca.

University of South Africa, College of Human Sciences, Pretoria, South Africa. Offers adult education (M Ed); African languages (MA, PhD); African politics (MA, PhD); Afrikaans (MA, PhD); ancient history (MA, PhD); ancient Near Eastern studies (MA, PhD); anthropology (MA, PhD); applied linguistics (MA); Arabic (MA, PhD); archaeology (MA); art history (MA); Biblical archaeology (MA); Biblical studies (M Th, D Th, PhD); Christian spirituality (M Th, D Th); church history (M Th, D Th); classical studies (MA, PhD); clinical psychology (MA); communication (MA, PhD); comparative education (M Ed, Ed D); consulting psychology (D Admin, D Com, PhD); curriculum studies (M Ed, Ed D); development studies (M Admin, MA, D Admin, PhD); didactics (M Ed, Ed D); education (M Tech); education management (M Ed, Ed D); educational psychology (M Ed); English (MA); environmental education (M Ed); French (MA, PhD); German (MA, PhD); Greek (MA); guidance and counseling (M Ed); health studies (MA, PhD), including health sciences education (MA), health services management (MA), medical and surgical nursing science (critical care general) (MA), midwifery and neonatal nursing science (MA), trauma and emergency care (MA); history (MA, PhD); history of education (Ed D); inclusive education (M Ed, Ed D); information and communications technology policy and regulation (MA); information science (MA, MIS, PhD); international politics (MA, PhD); Islamic studies (MA, PhD); Italian (MA, PhD); Judaica (MA, PhD); linguistics (MA, PhD); mathematical education (M Ed); mathematics education (MA); missiology (M Th, D Th); modern Hebrew (MA, PhD); musicology (MA, MMus, D Mus, PhD); natural science education (M Ed); New Testament (M Th, D Th); Old Testament (D Th); pastoral therapy (M Th, D Th); philosophy (MA); philosophy of education (M Ed, Ed D); politics (MA, PhD); Portuguese (MA, PhD); practical theology (M Th, D Th); psychology (MA, MS, PhD); psychology of education (M Ed, Ed D); public health (MA); religious studies (MA, D Th, PhD); Romance languages (MA); Russian (MA, PhD); Semitic languages (MA, PhD); social behavior studies in HIV/AIDS (MA); social science (mental health) (MA); social science in development studies (MA); social science in psychology (MA); social science in social work (MA); social science in sociology (MA); social work (MSW, DSW, PhD); socio-education (M Ed, Ed D); sociolinguistics (MA); sociology (MA, PhD); Spanish (MA, PhD); systematic theology (M Th, D Th); TESOL (teaching English to speakers of other languages) (MA); theological ethics (M Th, D Th); theory of literature (MA, PhD); urban ministries (D Th); urban ministry (M Th).

University of South Alabama, Graduate School, College of Arts and Sciences, Department of Sociology, Anthropology and Social Work, Mobile, AL 36688-0002. Offers sociology (MA). Part-time and evening/weekend programs available. *Degree requirements:* For master's, comprehensive exam, thesis optional. *Entrance requirements:* For master's, GRE General Test, minimum GPA of 3.0. *Expenses:* Tuition, state resident: part-time $218 per contact hour. Required fees: $1102 per year. *Faculty research:* Cultural adaptation.

University of South Carolina, The Graduate School, College of Arts and Sciences, Department of Sociology, Columbia, SC 29208. Offers MA, PhD. Part-time programs available. Terminal master's awarded for partial completion of doctoral program. *Degree requirements:* For master's, thesis; for doctorate, comprehensive exam, thesis/dissertation. *Entrance requirements:* For master's and doctorate, GRE General Test. Additional exam requirements/recommendations for international students: Required—TOEFL (minimum score 570 paper-based; 230 computer-based; 75 iBT). Electronic applications accepted. *Faculty research:* Social psychology, social inequality.

University of Southern California, Graduate School, College of Letters, Arts and Sciences, Department of Sociology, Los Angeles, CA 90089. Offers PhD. *Faculty:* 39 full-time (22 women). *Students:* 39 full-time (22 women); includes 13 minority (1 African American, 1 American Indian/Alaska Native, 4 Asian Americans or Pacific Islanders, 7 Hispanic Americans),

8 international. 73 applicants, 14% accepted, 7 enrolled. In 2009, 6 doctorates awarded. *Degree requirements:* For doctorate, comprehensive exam, thesis/dissertation. *Entrance requirements:* For doctorate, GRE, TOEFL. *Application deadline:* For fall admission, 12/1 for domestic and international students. Application fee: $85. Electronic applications accepted. *Expenses:* Tuition: Full-time $25,980; part-time $1315 per unit. Required fees: $554. One-time fee: $35 full-time. Full-time tuition and fees vary according to degree level and program. *Financial support:* In 2009–10, 29 students received support, including 11 fellowships (averaging $21,000 per year), 3 research assistantships (averaging $19,000 per year), 15 teaching assistantships with tuition reimbursements available (averaging $19,000 per year); tuition waivers also available. Financial award application deadline: 12/1; financial award applicants required to submit CSS PROFILE or FAFSA. *Faculty research:* Family, immigration, gender, culture, race. *Application contact:* Stachelle L. Overland, Student Service Coordinator II, 213-740-8851, Fax: 213-740-3535, E-mail: overland@usc.edu.

University of South Florida, Graduate School, College of Arts and Sciences, Department of Sociology, Tampa, FL 33620-9951. Offers MA, PhD. Part-time programs available. *Faculty:* 7 full-time (4 women). *Students:* 15 full-time (10 women), 3 part-time (all women); includes 4 minority (1 African American, 2 Asian Americans or Pacific Islanders, 1 Hispanic American). Average age 32. 51 applicants, 33% accepted, 12 enrolled. In 2009, 11 master's awarded. *Degree requirements:* For master's, comprehensive exam, thesis; for doctorate, comprehensive exam, thesis/dissertation. *Entrance requirements:* For master's, GRE General Test, minimum GPA of 3.0 in last 60 hours. Additional exam requirements/recommendations for international students: Required—TOEFL (minimum score 550 paper-based; 213 computer-based). *Application deadline:* For fall admission, 2/15 priority date for domestic students, 1/2 priority date for international students; for spring admission, 10/15 for domestic students, 6/1 priority date for international students. Application fee: $30. Electronic applications accepted. *Financial support:* In 2009–10, teaching assistantships with tuition reimbursements (averaging $25,194 per year); unspecified assistantships also available. Financial award application deadline: 3/1. Total annual research expenditures: $194,740. *Unit head:* Dr. Maralee Mayberry, Chairperson, 813-974-2241, Fax: 813-974-6455, E-mail: mayberry@chuma1.cas.usf.edu. *Application contact:* Dr. Donileen R. Loseke, Program Director, 813-974-2517, Fax: 813-974-6455, E-mail: dloseke@cas.usf.edu.

The University of Tennessee, Graduate School, College of Arts and Sciences, Department of Sociology, Knoxville, TN 37996. Offers criminology (MA, PhD); energy, environment, and resource policy (MA, PhD); political economy (MA, PhD). Part-time programs available. *Degree requirements:* For master's, thesis or alternative; for doctorate, thesis/dissertation. *Entrance requirements:* For master's, GRE General Test, minimum GPA of 3.0; for doctorate, GRE General Test, minimum GPA of 3.5. Additional exam requirements/recommendations for international students: Required—TOEFL. Electronic applications accepted. *Expenses:* Tuition, state resident: full-time $6826; part-time $380 per semester hour. Tuition, nonresident: full-time $21,844; part-time $1147 per semester hour. Tuition and fees vary according to program.

The University of Texas at Arlington, Graduate School, College of Liberal Arts, Department of Sociology and Anthropology, Program in Sociology, Arlington, TX 76019. Offers MA. Part-time and evening/weekend programs available. *Students:* 5 full-time (1 woman), 16 part-time (11 women); includes 10 minority (4 African Americans, 3 Asian Americans or Pacific Islanders, 3 Hispanic Americans), 2 international. 9 applicants, 89% accepted, 5 enrolled. In 2009, 5 master's awarded. *Degree requirements:* For master's, comprehensive exam, thesis or alternative. *Entrance requirements:* For master's, GRE General Test, 12 hours of undergraduate course work in sociology. Additional exam requirements/recommendations for international students: Required—TOEFL (minimum score 550 paper-based; 213 computer-based). *Application deadline:* For fall admission, 6/16 for domestic students. Applications are processed on a rolling basis. Application fee: $35 ($50 for international students). *Financial support:* In 2009–10, 4 teaching assistantships (averaging $9,000 per year) were awarded; research assistantships, Federal Work-Study also available. Financial award application deadline: 4/1. *Application contact:* Dr. Joel Ryan, Graduate Advisor, 817-272-2661, Fax: 817-272-3759, E-mail: jcryan@uta.edu.

The University of Texas at Austin, Graduate School, College of Liberal Arts, Department of Sociology, Austin, TX 78712-1111. Offers MA, PhD. *Degree requirements:* For master's, thesis; for doctorate, thesis/dissertation. *Entrance requirements:* For master's and doctorate, GRE General Test. Additional exam requirements/recommendations for international students: Required—TOEFL. Electronic applications accepted. *Faculty research:* Criminology, demography, Latin America, health, political sociology.

The University of Texas at Dallas, School of Economic, Political and Policy Sciences, Program in Sociology, Richardson, TX 75080. Offers applied sociology (MS). *Faculty:* 3 full-time (0 women). *Students:* 3 full-time (2 women), 6 part-time (4 women), 1 international. Average age 36. 2 applicants, 50% accepted, 1 enrolled. In 2009, 10 master's awarded. *Degree requirements:* For master's, internship. *Entrance requirements:* For master's, GRE General Test, minimum GPA of 3.0 in upper-level coursework in field. Additional exam requirements/recommendations for international students: Required—TOEFL (minimum score 550 paper-based; 213 computer-based). *Application deadline:* For fall admission, 7/15 for domestic students, 5/1 priority date for international students; for spring admission, 11/15 for domestic students, 9/1 priority date for international students. Applications are processed on a rolling basis. Application fee: $50 ($100 for international students). Electronic applications accepted. *Expenses:* Tuition, state resident: full-time $11,068; part-time $461 per credit hour. Tuition, nonresident: full-time $21,178; part-time $882 per credit hour. Tuition and fees vary according to course load. *Financial support:* Fellowships, research assistantships, teaching assistantships, career-related internships or fieldwork, Federal Work-Study, institutionally sponsored loans, and scholarships/grants available. Support available to part-time students. Financial award application deadline: 4/30. *Faculty research:* Social impact of alcohol in Latino families, reading one-to-one, AmeriCorps, neighborhood evaluations. *Unit head:* Dr. Jennifer Holmes, Interim Program Head, 972-883-6843, Fax: 972-883-2735, E-mail: jholmes@utdallas.edu. *Application contact:* Judy C. Robertson, Administrative Assistant, 972-883-6406, Fax: 972-883-2735, E-mail: judy.robertson@utdallas.edu.

See Close-Up on page 759.

The University of Texas at El Paso, Graduate School, College of Liberal Arts, Department of Sociology and Anthropology, El Paso, TX 79968-0001. Offers Latin American and border studies (MA, Certificate); sociology (MA). Part-time and evening/weekend programs available. *Degree requirements:* For master's, thesis optional. *Entrance requirements:* For master's, GRE General Test, minimum GPA of 3.0. Additional exam requirements/recommendations for international students: Required—TOEFL. Electronic applications accepted.

The University of Texas at San Antonio, College of Liberal and Fine Arts, Department of Sociology, San Antonio, TX 78249-0617. Offers MS. Part-time and evening/weekend programs available. *Faculty:* 7 full-time (1 woman). *Students:* 13 full-time (6 women), 35 part-time (21 women); includes 26 minority (8 African Americans, 2 Asian Americans or Pacific Islanders, 16 Hispanic Americans), 2 international. Average age 33. 24 applicants, 88% accepted, 17 enrolled. In 2009, 6 master's awarded. *Degree requirements:* For master's, comprehensive exam (for some programs), thesis (for some programs). *Entrance requirements:* For master's, GRE General Test, undergraduate course work in sociology or related areas. Additional exam requirements/recommendations for international students: Required—TOEFL (minimum score 500 paper-based; 173 computer-based; 61 iBT), IELTS (minimum score 5). *Application deadline:* For fall admission, 7/1 for domestic students, 4/1 for international students; for spring admission, 11/1 for domestic students, 9/1 for international students. Applications are processed on a rolling basis. Application fee: $45 ($80 for international students). Electronic applications accepted. *Expenses:* Tuition, state resident: full-time $3975; part-time $221 per contact hour. Tuition, nonresident: full-time $13,947; part-time $775 per contact hour. Required fees: $1853. *Financial support:* In 2009–10, 2 students received support, including 11 research assistantships (averaging $11,194 per year); career-related internships or fieldwork, scholarships/grants, and unspecified assistantships also available. Support available to part-time students. *Faculty research:* Social welfare and social policy, violent behavior and homicide, migration and immigration to the U.S./Mexico border, educational experiences of Latino children, sociology of marriage and family. Total annual research expenditures: $21,348. *Unit head:* Dr. Raquel R. Marquez, Chair, 210-458-5606, Fax: 210-458-4629, E-mail: raquel.marquez@utsa.edu. *Application contact:* Gabriel Acevedo, Graduate Advisor, 210-458-6469, E-mail: gabriel.acevedo@utsa.edu.

The University of Texas at Tyler, College of Arts and Sciences, Department of Social Sciences, Tyler, TX 75799-0001. Offers criminal justice (MS); public administration (MPA); sociology (MS). Part-time and evening/weekend programs available. *Faculty:* 10 full-time (2 women). *Students:* 7 full-time (3 women), 21 part-time (14 women); includes 8 minority (5 African Americans, 2 American Indian/Alaska Native, 1 Asian American or Pacific Islander), 2 international. Average age 30. 6 applicants, 100% accepted, 6 enrolled. In 2009, 10 master's awarded. *Degree requirements:* For master's, comprehensive exam, thesis optional. *Entrance requirements:* For master's, GRE General Test, minimum GPA of 3.0. Additional exam requirements/recommendations for international students: Required—TOEFL (minimum score 79 computer-based). *Application deadline:* For fall admission, 8/17 priority date for domestic students, 7/1 priority date for international students; for spring admission, 12/21 priority date for domestic students, 11/1 priority date for international students. Applications are processed on a rolling basis. Application fee: $25 ($50 for international students). *Expenses:* Tuition, state resident: part-time $665 per semester hour. Tuition, nonresident: part-time $942 per semester hour. Part-time tuition and fees vary according to degree level and program. *Financial support:* In 2009–10, 1 fellowship (averaging $1,000 per year), 2 research assistantships, 2 teaching assistantships were awarded; career-related internships or fieldwork, Federal Work-Study, and scholarships/grants also available. Support available to part-time students. Financial award application deadline: 7/1; financial award applicants required to submit FAFSA. *Faculty research:* Urban segregation, minority business, violent crime, gender discrimination. *Unit head:* Dr. Ken Wink, Chair, 903-566-7434, Fax: 903-565-5537, E-mail: kwink@mail.uttyl.edu. *Application contact:* Dr. Ken Wink.

The University of Texas–Pan American, College of Social and Behavioral Sciences, Department of Sociology, Edinburg, TX 78539. Offers MS. Part-time programs available. *Degree requirements:* For master's, thesis or journal article. *Entrance requirements:* For master's, minimum GPA of 3.0, BS of BA in sociology or social science. Additional exam requirements/recommendations for international students: Required—TOEFL (minimum score 500 paper-based). *Expenses:* Tuition, state resident: full-time $3630.60; part-time $201.70 per credit hour. Tuition, nonresident: full-time $8617; part-time $478.70 per credit hour. Required fees: $806.50. *Faculty research:* Border studies, U.S.-Mexico issues, Mexican-American peoples, aging and gerontology.

The University of Toledo, College of Graduate Studies, College of Arts and Sciences, Department of Sociology and Anthropology, Toledo, OH 43606-3390. Offers sociology (MA). Part-time programs available. *Degree requirements:* For master's, thesis or alternative. Electronic applications accepted. *Faculty research:* Medical and social gerontology, population, social movements, socioeconomic development, corporations and work, race and ethnicity.

University of Toronto, School of Graduate Studies, Social Sciences Division, Department of Sociology, Toronto, ON M5S 1A1, Canada. Offers M Ed, MA, Ed D, PhD. Part-time programs available. *Degree requirements:* For doctorate, thesis/dissertation. *Entrance requirements:* For master's, GRE (for applicants from non-Canadian universities, recommended for those from Canadian universities), 5 full-year courses in sociology, basic research and statistical skills; 2 letters of reference; for doctorate, GRE (required for applicants from non-Canadian universities; recommended for those from Canadian universities), MA in sociology, minimum A–average, 2 letters of reference.

University of Utah, The Graduate School, College of Social and Behavioral Science, Department of Sociology, Salt Lake City, UT 84112-1107. Offers M Stat, MA, MS, PhD. *Faculty:* 11 full-time (6 women), 3 part-time/adjunct (1 woman). *Students:* 17 full-time (9 women), 4 part-time (2 women), 6 international. Average age 30. 32 applicants, 41% accepted, 7 enrolled. In 2009, 1 doctorate awarded. *Degree requirements:* For master's, thesis; for doctorate, comprehensive exam, thesis/dissertation. *Entrance requirements:* For master's and doctorate, GRE, minimum undergraduate GPA of 3.0. Additional exam requirements/recommendations for international students: Required—TOEFL (minimum score 500 paper-based; 173 computer-based). *Application deadline:* For fall admission, 2/1 priority date for domestic and international students. Applications are processed on a rolling basis. Application fee: $55 ($65 for international students). *Expenses:* Tuition, state resident: full-time $4004; part-time $1674 per semester. Tuition, nonresident: full-time $14,134; part-time $5915 per semester. Required fees: $324 per semester. Tuition and fees vary according to course load, degree level and program. *Financial support:* In 2009–10, 3 fellowships (averaging $11,000 per year), 2 research assistantships with partial tuition reimbursements (averaging $11,500 per year), 10 teaching assistantships with full tuition reimbursements (averaging $11,500 per year) were awarded; Federal Work-Study, scholarships/grants, health care benefits, tuition waivers, and departmental waivers also available. Support available to part-time students. Financial award application deadline: 4/1; financial award applicants required to submit FAFSA. *Faculty research:* Comparative international sociology, population and health, criminology, diversity, demography. Total annual research expenditures: $48,448. *Unit head:* Dr. Jeffrey Kentor, Chair, 801-581-6153, Fax: 801-585-3784, E-mail: kentor@soc.utah.edu. *Application contact:* Dr. Ming Wen, Director of Graduate Studies, 801-581-6153, Fax: 801-585-3784, E-mail: ming.wen@soc.utah.edu.

University of Utah, The Graduate School, Interdepartmental Program in Statistics, Salt Lake City, UT 84112-1107. Offers biostatistics (MST); business (MST); econometrics (MST); educational psychology (MST); mathematics (MST); sociology (MST); statistics (M Stat). Part-time programs available. *Students:* 25 full-time (11 women), 15 part-time (6 women); includes 4 minority (3 Asian Americans or Pacific Islanders, 1 Hispanic American), 12 international. Average age 30. 59 applicants, 44% accepted, 12 enrolled. In 2009, 15 master's awarded. *Degree requirements:* For master's, comprehensive exam, projects. *Entrance requirements:* For master's, GMAT (business), GRE General Test (sociology and educational psychology), minimum GPA of 3.0; course work in calculus, matrix theory, statistics. Additional exam requirements/recommendations for international students: Required—TOEFL (minimum score 500 paper-based; 173 computer-based). *Application deadline:* For fall admission, 7/1 for domestic students, 4/1 for international students. Applications are processed on a rolling basis. Application fee: $55 ($65 for international students). *Expenses:* Tuition, state resident: full-time $4004; part-time $1674 per semester. Tuition, nonresident: full-time $14,134; part-time $5915 per semester. Required fees: $324 per semester. Tuition and fees vary according to course load, degree level and program. *Financial support:* Career-related internships or fieldwork available. *Faculty research:* Biostatistics, management, economics, educational psychology, mathematics. *Unit head:* Tariq Mughal, Chair, University Statistics Committee, 801-585-9547, E-mail: tariaq.mughal@business.utah.edu. *Application contact:* Laura Egbert, MSTAT Program Coordinator, 801-585-6853, E-mail: laura.demattia@utah.edu.

University of Victoria, Faculty of Graduate Studies, Faculty of Social Sciences, Department of Sociology, Victoria, BC V8W 2Y2, Canada. Offers MA, PhD. PhD by special arrangement. Part-time programs available. *Degree requirements:* For master's, thesis; for doctorate, thesis/dissertation, candidacy exam. *Entrance requirements:* For master's, minimum B+ average. Additional exam requirements/recommendations for international students: Required—TOEFL (minimum score 575 paper-based; 233 computer-based), IELTS (minimum score 7), TWE (minimum score 4). *Faculty research:* Social and political thought, social justice, health and aging, globalization and social psychology.

University of Virginia, College and Graduate School of Arts and Sciences, Department of Sociology, Charlottesville, VA 22903. Offers MA, PhD, JD/MA. *Faculty:* 19 full-time (8 women). *Students:* 46 full-time (21 women); includes 2 minority (1 African American, 1 Asian American

Sociology

University of Virginia (continued)

or Pacific Islander), 13 international. Average age 29. 83 applicants, 29% accepted, 7 enrolled. In 2009, 11 master's, 7 doctorates awarded. *Degree requirements:* For master's, thesis; for doctorate, comprehensive exam, thesis/dissertation. *Entrance requirements:* For master's and doctorate, GRE General Test, GRE Subject Test, 2 letters of recommendation. Additional exam requirements/recommendations for international students: Required—TOEFL (minimum score 600 paper-based; 250 computer-based; 90 iBT), IELTS (minimum score 7). *Application deadline:* For fall admission, 1/1 for domestic and international students. Applications are processed on a rolling basis. Application fee: $60. Electronic applications accepted. *Financial support:* Applicants required to submit FAFSA. *Unit head:* Krishan Kumar, Chair, 434-924-7293, Fax: 434-924-7028, E-mail: sociology@virginia.edu. *Application contact:* Paul Kingston, Director, Graduate Admissions Committee, 434-924-6521, E-mail: pwk@virginia.edu.

University of Washington, Graduate School, College of Arts and Sciences, Department of Sociology, Seattle, WA 98195. Offers MA, PhD. *Degree requirements:* For master's, thesis; for doctorate, thesis/dissertation. *Entrance requirements:* For master's and doctorate, GRE General Test, minimum GPA of 3.0. Additional exam requirements/recommendations for international students: Required—TOEFL. Electronic applications accepted. *Faculty research:* Demography, criminology, social psychology, race/ethnicity/inequality, family.

University of Washington, Graduate School, School of Public Health, Department of Health Services, Seattle, WA 98195. Offers bioinformatics (PhD); cancer prevention and control (PhD); clinical research (MS); community oriented public health practice (MPH); economics or finance (PhD); evaluation sciences (PhD); executive program (MHA); health behavior and health promotion (PhD); health care and population health research (MPH); health policy analysis and process (PhD); health policy and analysis and process (MPH); health services (MS, PhD); health services administration (EMHA, MHA); in residence program (MHA); occupational health (PhD); population health and social determinants (PhD); social and behavioral sciences (MPH); sociology and demography (PhD); JD/MHA; MHA/MBA; MHA/MD; MHA/MPA; MPH/JD; MPH/MD; MPH/MN; MPH/MPA; MPH/MSD; MPH/MSW; MPH/PhD. Part-time and evening/weekend programs available. Postbaccalaureate distance learning degree programs offered (minimal on-campus study). *Faculty:* 52 full-time (24 women), 60 part-time/adjunct (28 women). *Students:* 104 full-time (83 women), 100 part-time (76 women); includes 21 minority (6 African Americans, 1 American Indian/Alaska Native, 11 Asian Americans or Pacific Islanders, 3 Hispanic Americans), 6 international. Average age 34. 375 applicants, 17% accepted, 24 enrolled. In 2009, 33 master's awarded. Terminal master's awarded for partial completion of doctoral program. *Degree requirements:* For master's, thesis (for some programs), practicum (MPH); for doctorate, comprehensive exam, thesis/dissertation. *Entrance requirements:* For master's and doctorate, GRE General Test, minimum GPA of 3.0. Additional exam requirements/recommendations for international students: Required—TOEFL. *Application deadline:* For fall admission, 1/15 for domestic students, 11/1 for international students. Application fee: 50 Albanian leks. Electronic applications accepted. *Financial support:* In 2009–10, 64 students received support, including 10 fellowships with full and partial tuition reimbursements available (averaging $21,000 per year), 10 research assistantships with full and partial tuition reimbursements available (averaging $18,000 per year), 3 teaching assistantships with full and partial tuition reimbursements available (averaging $18,000 per year); career-related internships or fieldwork, Federal Work-Study, institutionally sponsored loans, and traineeships also available. Financial award application deadline: 2/28; financial award applicants required to submit FAFSA. *Faculty research:* Health promotion and disease prevention, maternal and child health, health services research design, program evaluation, health policy. Total annual research expenditures: $10.5 million. *Unit head:* Dr. Larry Kessler, Chair, 206-543-616-2930. *Application contact:* Kitty A. Andert, MPH/MS/PhD Program Manager, 206-616-2926, Fax: 206-543-3964, E-mail: kitander@u.washington.edu.

University of Waterloo, Graduate Studies, Faculty of Arts, Department of Sociology, Waterloo, ON N2L 3G1, Canada. Offers MA, PhD. Part-time programs available. *Degree requirements:* For master's, thesis (for some programs); for doctorate, one foreign language, thesis/dissertation. *Entrance requirements:* For master's, honors degree, minimum B+ average, resume, writing sample; for doctorate, master's degree, minimum A- average, resumé, writing sample. Additional exam requirements/recommendations for international students: Required—TOEFL, TWE. Electronic applications accepted. *Faculty research:* Theory, methods, stratification deviance, political sociology.

The University of Western Ontario, Faculty of Graduate Studies, Social Sciences Division, Department of Sociology, London, ON N6A 5B8, Canada. Offers MA, PhD. Terminal master's awarded for partial completion of doctoral program. *Degree requirements:* For master's, thesis (for some programs); for doctorate, one foreign language, comprehensive exam, thesis/dissertation. *Entrance requirements:* For master's, minimum B+ average, honors degree; for doctorate, minimum A- average. Additional exam requirements/recommendations for international students: Required—TOEFL. Electronic applications accepted. *Faculty research:* Social demography, class and change, health and aging, theory, methods.

University of West Florida, College of Professional Studies, Division of Health, Leisure, and Exercise Science, Community Health Education, Pensacola, FL 32514-5750. Offers aging studies (MS); promotion and worksite wellness (MS); psycho-social (MS). Part-time and evening/weekend programs available. *Faculty:* 2 full-time (1 woman), 1 (woman) part-time/adjunct. *Students:* 7 full-time (6 women), 7 part-time (all women); includes 4 minority (1 African American, 1 American Indian/Alaska Native, 1 Asian American or Pacific Islander, 1 Hispanic American), 1 international. Average age 34. 7 applicants, 86% accepted, 5 enrolled. In 2009, 13 master's awarded. *Degree requirements:* For master's, thesis or alternative. *Entrance requirements:* For master's, GRE General Test, minimum GPA of 3.0. Additional exam requirements/recommendations for international students: Required—TOEFL (minimum score 550 paper-based; 213 computer-based). *Application deadline:* For fall admission, 6/1 for domestic students, 5/15 for international students; for spring admission, 11/1 for domestic students, 10/1 for international students. Applications are processed on a rolling basis. Application fee: $30. *Expenses:* Tuition, state resident: full-time $4982; part-time $260 per credit hour. Tuition, nonresident: full-time $20,059; part-time $919 per credit hour. Required fees: $1247; $52 per credit hour. *Financial support:* Research assistantships, teaching assistantships, unspecified assistantships available. *Unit head:* Dr. John Todorovich, Chairperson, 850-473-7248, Fax: 850-474-2106. *Application contact:* Terry McCray, Assistant Director of Graduate Admissions, 850-473-7718, Fax: 850-473-7714, E-mail: gradadmissions@uwf.edu.

University of West Georgia, Graduate School, College of Arts and Sciences, Department of Sociology and Criminology, Carrollton, GA 30118. Offers criminology (MA); sociology (MA). Part-time and evening/weekend programs available. *Faculty:* 13 full-time (5 women), 5 part-time/adjunct (4 women). *Students:* 11 full-time (6 women), 8 part-time (4 women); includes 2 minority (both African Americans). Average age 30. 11 applicants, 82% accepted, 1 enrolled. In 2009, 3 master's awarded. *Degree requirements:* For master's, one foreign language, comprehensive exam (for some programs), thesis (for some programs). *Entrance requirements:* For master's, GRE General Test, minimum GPA of 2.5, references, intellectual biography. Additional exam requirements/recommendations for international students: Required—TOEFL. *Application deadline:* For fall admission, 7/17 for domestic students; for spring admission, 11/20 for domestic students. Applications are processed on a rolling basis. Application fee: $30. Electronic applications accepted. *Expenses:* Tuition, state resident: full-time $2952; part-time $164 per semester hour. Tuition, nonresident: full-time $11,808; part-time $656 per semester hour. Required fees: $42.90 per semester hour. $307 per semester. Tuition and fees vary according to course load. *Financial support:* In 2009–10, 8 students received support, including 7 research assistantships with full tuition reimbursements available (averaging $6,000 per year); career-related internships or fieldwork, scholarships/grants, and unspecified assistantships also available. Financial award application deadline: 7/1; financial award applicants required to submit FAFSA. *Faculty research:* Criminology, gangs, courts, policing, ethics, women's studies, methods. *Unit head:* Dr. N. Jane McCandless, Chair, 678-839-6505, Fax: 678-839-6506, E-mail: jmccandl@westga.edu. *Application contact:* Dr. Charles W. Clark, Dean, 678-839-6508, E-mail: cclark@westga.edu.

University of Windsor, Faculty of Graduate Studies, Faculty of Arts and Social Sciences, Department of Sociology and Anthropology, Windsor, ON N9B 3P4, Canada. Offers criminology (MA); sociology (MA); sociology-social justice (PhD). Part-time programs available. *Degree requirements:* For master's, thesis; for doctorate, comprehensive exam, thesis/dissertation. *Entrance requirements:* For master's, minimum B+ average; for doctorate, writing sample, minimum B+ average. Additional exam requirements/recommendations for international students: Required—TOEFL (minimum score 560 paper-based; 220 computer-based). Electronic applications accepted. *Faculty research:* Power and social change; criminology/deviance; social psychology; comparative development; race and ethnic relations; family, sex, and gender, social justice.

University of Wisconsin–Madison, Graduate School, College of Letters and Science, Department of Sociology, Madison, WI 53706-1380. Offers rural sociology (MS); sociology (MS, PhD). Part-time programs available. Terminal master's awarded for partial completion of doctoral program. *Degree requirements:* For master's, thesis, oral exam; for doctorate, thesis/dissertation, preliminary and final oral exams, 4 seminars. *Entrance requirements:* For master's and doctorate, GRE General Test. Additional exam requirements/recommendations for international students: Required—TOEFL. Electronic applications accepted. *Expenses:* Tuition, state resident: part-time $594 per credit. Tuition, nonresident: part-time $1504 per credit. Required fees: $65 per credit. Tuition and fees vary according to course load, program and reciprocity agreements.

University of Wisconsin–Milwaukee, Graduate School, College of Letters and Sciences, Department of Sociology, Milwaukee, WI 53201-0413. Offers MA. Part-time programs available. *Faculty:* 17 full-time (8 women). *Students:* 18 full-time (12 women), 17 part-time (13 women); includes 7 minority (2 African Americans, 1 Asian American or Pacific Islander, 4 Hispanic Americans), 2 international. Average age 30. 26 applicants, 62% accepted, 10 enrolled. In 2009, 16 master's awarded. *Degree requirements:* For master's, thesis. *Entrance requirements:* For master's, GRE. *Application deadline:* For fall admission, 1/1 priority date for domestic students; for spring admission, 9/1 for domestic students. Applications are processed on a rolling basis. Application fee: $45 ($75 for international students). *Expenses:* Tuition, state resident: full-time $8800. Tuition, nonresident: full-time $20,760. Tuition and fees vary according to program and reciprocity agreements. *Financial support:* In 2009–10, 16 teaching assistantships were awarded; career-related internships or fieldwork and unspecified assistantships also available. Support available to part-time students. Financial award application deadline: 4/15. Total annual research expenditures: $47,408. *Unit head:* Pat Rubio Goldsmith, Representative, 414-229-6945, Fax: 847-673-4122, E-mail: goldsmit@uwm.edu. *Application contact:* General Information Contact, 414-229-4982, Fax: 414-229-6967, E-mail: gradschool@uwm.edu.

University of Wyoming, College of Arts and Sciences, Department of Sociology, Laramie, WY 82070. Offers MA. Part-time programs available. *Degree requirements:* For master's, thesis. *Entrance requirements:* For master's, GRE General Test, minimum GPA of 3.0. Additional exam requirements/recommendations for international students: Required—TOEFL (minimum score 525 paper-based). Electronic applications accepted. *Faculty research:* Gender, theory, international studies, law, social inequality.

Utah State University, School of Graduate Studies, College of Humanities, Arts and Social Sciences, Department of Sociology, Logan, UT 84322. Offers MA, MS, MSS, PhD. *Degree requirements:* For master's, thesis; for doctorate, comprehensive exam, thesis/dissertation. *Entrance requirements:* For master's, GRE General Test, minimum GPA of 3.0, recommendation letters; for doctorate, GRE General Test, minimum GPA of 3.0, recommendation letters, transcripts, personal statement, MS degree. Additional exam requirements/recommendations for international students: Required—TOEFL; Recommended—TWE. *Faculty research:* Demography, environmental/natural resource sociology, rural community change, international development, health studies.

Valdosta State University, Graduate School, Department of Sociology, Anthropology, and Criminal Justice, Valdosta, GA 31698. Offers criminal justice (MS); marriage and family therapy (MS); sociology (MS). *Accreditation:* AAMFT/COAMFTE. Part-time and evening/weekend programs available. *Degree requirements:* For master's, thesis or alternative, comprehensive written and/or oral exams. *Entrance requirements:* For master's, GRE General Test or MAT (sociology, marriage and family therapy), minimum GPA of 2.5. Additional exam requirements/recommendations for international students: Required—TOEFL (minimum score 523 paper-based; 193 computer-based). Electronic applications accepted. *Faculty research:* Police-civilian ride-along project.

Vanderbilt University, Graduate School, Department of Sociology, Nashville, TN 37240-1001. Offers MA, PhD. *Faculty:* 28 full-time (12 women). *Students:* 25 full-time (17 women), 2 part-time (0 women); includes 5 minority (3 African Americans, 2 Hispanic Americans), 4 international. Average age 29. 126 applicants, 13% accepted, 8 enrolled. In 2009, 5 master's, 3 doctorates awarded. *Degree requirements:* For master's, thesis; for doctorate, comprehensive exam, thesis/dissertation, area, qualifying, and final exams. *Entrance requirements:* For master's and doctorate, GRE General Test. Additional exam requirements/recommendations for international students: Required—TOEFL (minimum score 570 paper-based; 230 computer-based; 88 iBT). *Application deadline:* For fall admission, 1/15 for domestic and international students. Application fee: $0. Electronic applications accepted. *Financial support:* Fellowships with full tuition reimbursements, research assistantships, teaching assistantships with full tuition reimbursements, Federal Work-Study, institutionally sponsored loans, scholarships/grants, and health care benefits available. Financial award application deadline: 1/15; financial award applicants required to submit CSS PROFILE or FAFSA. *Faculty research:* Criminology; cultural sociology; gender, race, and ethics relations; deviant behavior and social control. *Unit head:* Katharine M. Donato, Chair, 615-322-7626, Fax: 615-322-7505, E-mail: katharine.donato@vanderbilt.edu. *Application contact:* Holly McCammon, Director of Graduate Studies, 615-322-7626, Fax: 615-322-7505, E-mail: dgs-soc@vanderbilt.edu.

Virginia Commonwealth University, Graduate School, College of Humanities and Sciences, Wilder School of Government and Public Affairs, Department of Sociology, Program in Sociology, Richmond, VA 23284-9005. Offers MS. *Degree requirements:* For master's, thesis optional. *Entrance requirements:* For master's, GRE General Test.

Virginia Polytechnic Institute and State University, Graduate School, College of Liberal Arts and Human Sciences, Department of Sociology, Blacksburg, VA 24061. Offers MS, PhD. *Faculty:* 26 full-time (11 women), 1 (woman) part-time/adjunct. *Students:* 43 full-time (26 women), 7 part-time (4 women); includes 15 minority (1 American Indian/Alaska Native, 12 Asian Americans or Pacific Islanders, 2 Hispanic Americans), 3 international. Average age 33. 22 applicants, 45% accepted, 8 enrolled. In 2009, 8 master's, 5 doctorates awarded. *Entrance requirements:* For master's and doctorate, GRE, GMAT. Additional exam requirements/recommendations for international students: Required—TOEFL (minimum score 550 paper-based; 213 computer-based). *Application deadline:* For fall admission, 5/15 for international students; for spring admission, 10/15 for international students. Applications are processed on a rolling basis. Application fee: $65. Electronic applications accepted. *Expenses:* Tuition, area resident: Full-time $10,228; part-time $459 per credit hour. Tuition, nonresident: full-time $17,892; part-time $865 per credit hour. Required fees: $1966; $451 per semester. *Financial support:* In 2009–10, 17 teaching assistantships with full tuition reimbursements (averaging $10,575 per year) were awarded; career-related internships or fieldwork, Federal Work-Study, scholarships/grants, and unspecified assistantships also available. Financial award application deadline: 1/15. *Faculty research:* Science and technology, deviance and criminology, social psychology, social organization, demography. Total annual research expenditures: $69,119. *Unit head:* Dr. John W. Ryan, Dean, 540-231-6878, Fax: 540-231-3860, E-mail: johnryan@

vt.edu. *Application contact:* Jim Hawdon, Information Contact, 540-231-7476, Fax: 540-231-3860, E-mail: hawdonj@vt.edu.

Washington State University, Graduate School, College of Liberal Arts, Department of Sociology, Pullman, WA 99164. Offers crime and deviance (MA, PhD); environments, community and demographics (MA, PhD); institutions and social organizations (MA, PhD); political sociology (MA, PhD); social inequality (MA, PhD); social psychology and life course (MA, PhD). Terminal master's awarded for partial completion of doctoral program. *Degree requirements:* For master's, thesis; for doctorate, comprehensive exam, thesis/dissertation. *Entrance requirements:* For master's, GRE General Test, minimum GPA of 3.0; for doctorate, GRE General Test, MA in sociology, minimum GPA of 3.0. Additional exam requirements/recommendations for international students: Required—TOEFL (minimum score 550 paper-based). Electronic applications accepted. *Faculty research:* Crime/deviance, environmental sociology, social inequality, social psychology, gender.

Wayne State University, College of Liberal Arts and Sciences, Department of Sociology, Detroit, MI 48202. Offers MA, PhD. *Degree requirements:* For master's, thesis optional; for doctorate, thesis/dissertation. *Entrance requirements:* For master's, GRE General Test, GRE Subject Test, minimum GPA of 3.3; letters of reference; writing sample; for doctorate, GRE General Test, GRE Subject Test, minimum GPA of 3.5 in master's work; letters of reference. Additional exam requirements/recommendations for international students: Required—TOEFL (minimum score 550 paper-based; 213 computer-based); Recommended—TWE (minimum score 6). Electronic applications accepted. *Faculty research:* Social deviance, family, social inequality, medical sociology.

West Chester University of Pennsylvania, Office of Graduate Studies, College of Arts and Sciences, Department of Anthropology and Sociology, West Chester, PA 19383. Offers gerontology (Certificate); long term health care (MSA). Part-time and evening/weekend programs available. *Students:* 1 (woman) full-time, 2 part-time (both women). Average age 38. 4 applicants, 100% accepted, 1 enrolled. *Degree requirements:* For master's, comprehensive exam. *Entrance requirements:* For master's, MAT, GRE, or GMAT, interview, resume, 2 letters of reference. Additional exam requirements/recommendations for international students: Required—TOEFL (minimum score 550 paper-based; 213 computer-based; 80 iBT). *Application deadline:* For fall admission, 4/15 priority date for domestic students, 3/15 for international students; for spring admission, 10/15 for domestic students, 9/1 for international students. Applications are processed on a rolling basis. Application fee: $35. Electronic applications accepted. *Expenses:* Tuition, state resident: full-time $6666; part-time $370 per credit. Tuition, nonresident: full-time $10,666; part-time $593 per credit. Required fees: $122.56 per credit. *Financial support:* In 2009–10, research assistantships with full tuition reimbursements (averaging $5,000 per year); unspecified assistantships also available. Support available to part-time students. Financial award application deadline: 2/15; financial award applicants required to submit FAFSA. *Faculty research:* West African communities in the U.S., life long learning-distance education, comparative religions. *Unit head:* Dr. Douglas McConatha, Chair and Graduate Coordinator, 610-436-2556, E-mail: dmcconatha@wcupa.edu. *Application contact:* Dr. Douglas McConatha, Chair and Graduate Coordinator, 610-436-2556, E-mail: dmcconatha@wcupa.edu.

Western Illinois University, School of Graduate Studies, College of Arts and Sciences, Department of Sociology and Anthropology, Macomb, IL 61455-1390. Offers sociology (MA). Part-time programs available. *Students:* 24 full-time (16 women), 7 part-time (5 women); includes 7 minority (5 African Americans, 1 American Indian/Alaska Native, 1 Hispanic American), 2 international. Average age 28. 23 applicants, 83% accepted. In 2009, 7 master's awarded. *Degree requirements:* For master's, thesis or alternative. *Entrance requirements:* Additional exam requirements/recommendations for international students: Required—TOEFL (minimum score 550 paper-based; 213 computer-based; 80 iBT). *Application deadline:* Applications are processed on a rolling basis. Application fee: $30. Electronic applications accepted. *Expenses:* Tuition, state resident: full-time $4486; part-time $249.21 per credit hour. Tuition, nonresident: full-time $8972; part-time $498.42 per credit hour. Required fees: $72.62 per credit hour. *Financial support:* In 2009–10, 14 students received support, including 13 research assistantships with full tuition reimbursements available (averaging $7,280 per year), 1 teaching assistantship with full tuition reimbursement available (averaging $8,400 per year). Financial award applicants required to submit FAFSA. *Unit head:* Dr. John Wozniak, Chairperson, 309-298-1056. *Application contact:* Evelyn Hoing, Assistant Director of Graduate Studies, 309-298-1806, Fax: 309-298-2345, E-mail: grad-office@wiu.edu.

Western Kentucky University, Graduate Studies, Potter College of Arts and Letters, Department of Sociology, Bowling Green, KY 42101. Offers MA. *Degree requirements:* For master's, comprehensive exam, thesis optional, final exam. *Entrance requirements:* For master's, GRE General Test, minimum GPA of 3.0. Additional exam requirements/recommendations for international students: Required—TOEFL (minimum score 555 paper-based; 213 computer-based; 79 iBT). *Expenses:* Tuition, state resident: full-time $4160; part-time $416 per credit hour. Tuition, nonresident: full-time $9550; part-time $506 per credit hour. Tuition and fees vary according to campus/location and reciprocity agreements. *Faculty research:* Criminology/delinquency, quantitative and survey research methodology, occupations/professions, sex and gender, demography.

Western Michigan University, Graduate College, College of Arts and Sciences, Department of Sociology, Kalamazoo, MI 49008. Offers MA, PhD. *Degree requirements:* For master's, thesis, oral exams; for doctorate, one foreign language, thesis/dissertation, oral exams, written exams. *Entrance requirements:* For doctorate, GRE General Test.

West Virginia University, Eberly College of Arts and Sciences, School of Applied Social Sciences, Department of Sociology, Morgantown, WV 26506. Offers applied social research (MA). Part-time programs available. *Degree requirements:* For master's, thesis or alternative. *Entrance requirements:* For master's, GRE General Test, minimum GPA of 2.75. Additional exam requirements/recommendations for international students: Required—TOEFL. *Faculty research:* Applied sociology, stratification, social/complex organization, research methodology criminology.

Wichita State University, Graduate School, Fairmount College of Liberal Arts and Sciences, Department of Sociology, Wichita, KS 67260. Offers MA. Part-time programs available. *Expenses:* Tuition, state resident: full-time $4247; part-time $235.95 per credit hour. Tuition, nonresident: full-time $11,171; part-time $620.60 per credit hour. Required fees: $34; $3.60 per credit hour. $17 per term. Tuition and fees vary according to campus/location and program. *Unit head:* Dr. Ronald R. Matson, Chair, 316-978-3280, Fax: 316-978-3281, E-mail: ron.matson@wichita.edu. *Application contact:* Dr. Ronald R. Matson, Chair, 316-978-3280, Fax: 316-978-3281, E-mail: ron.matson@wichita.edu.

Wilfrid Laurier University, Faculty of Graduate Studies, Faculty of Arts, Department of Sociology, Waterloo, ON N2L 3C5, Canada. Offers MA. *Entrance requirements:* For master's, honours BA with a minimum average of B+ with a major in sociology. Additional exam requirements/recommendations for international students: Required—TOEFL (minimum score 230 computer-based; 89 iBT). Electronic applications accepted. *Faculty research:* Internationalization, migration and human rights, health, families, and well-being.

William Paterson University of New Jersey, College of the Humanities and Social Sciences, Wayne, NJ 07470-8420. Offers clinical and counseling psychology (MA); English (MA); history (MA); public policy and international affairs (MA); sociology (MA). Part-time and evening/weekend programs available. *Students:* 39 full-time (22 women), 123 part-time (90 women); includes 42 minority (11 African Americans, 5 Asian Americans or Pacific Islanders, 26 Hispanic Americans), 2 international. *Application deadline:* Applications are processed on a rolling basis. Application fee: $50. Electronic applications accepted. *Financial support:* In 2009–10, 13 students received support; research assistantships with full tuition reimbursements available, teaching assistantships with full tuition reimbursements available, unspecified assistantships available. Support available to part-time students. Financial award application deadline: 4/1; financial award applicants required to submit FAFSA. *Unit head:* Dr. Kara Rabbitt, Dean. College of Humanities and Social Sciences, 973-720-2180, Fax: 973-720-2955, E-mail: rabbittk@wpunj.edu. *Application contact:* Tinu Adeniran, Assistant Director, Graduate Admissions, 973-720-2764, Fax: 973-720-2035, E-mail: adenirant@wpunj.edu.

Yale University, Graduate School of Arts and Sciences, Department of Sociology, New Haven, CT 06520. Offers comparative and historical sociology (PhD); cultural sociology and social theory (PhD); social stratification and the life course (PhD). *Degree requirements:* For doctorate, thesis/dissertation. *Entrance requirements:* For doctorate, GRE General Test.

York University, Faculty of Graduate Studies, Faculty of Arts, Program in Social and Political Thought, Toronto, ON M3J 1P3, Canada. Offers MA, PhD. Part-time programs available. *Degree requirements:* For master's, one foreign language, thesis or alternative, oral exams; for doctorate, one foreign language, comprehensive exam, thesis/dissertation. Electronic applications accepted.

York University, Faculty of Graduate Studies, Faculty of Arts, Program in Sociology, Toronto, ON M3J 1P3, Canada. Offers MA, PhD. Part-time programs available. *Degree requirements:* For master's, thesis or alternative; for doctorate, one foreign language, comprehensive exam, thesis/dissertation, analytical paper. Electronic applications accepted.

Survey Methodology

University of Maryland, College Park, Academic Affairs, College of Behavioral and Social Sciences, Joint Program in Survey Methodology, College Park, MD 20742. Offers MS, PhD. *Faculty:* 3 full-time (2 women), 1 part-time/adjunct (0 women). *Students:* 18 full-time (11 women), 22 part-time (16 women); includes 6 minority (4 African Americans, 2 Asian Americans or Pacific Islanders), 4 international. 38 applicants, 42% accepted, 10 enrolled. In 2009, 11 master's, 3 doctorates awarded. *Degree requirements:* For master's, thesis (for some programs), scholarly paper; for doctorate, thesis/dissertation. *Entrance requirements:* For master's, GRE General Test (recommended), minimum GPA of 3.0, 3 letters of recommendation; for doctorate, GRE General Test, minimum GPA of 3.0, 3 letters of recommendation. *Application deadline:* For fall admission, 1/15 for domestic and international students. Applications are processed on a rolling basis. Application fee: $60. Electronic applications accepted. *Expenses:* Tuition, area resident: Part-time $471 per credit hour. Tuition, state resident: part-time $471 per credit hour. Tuition, nonresident: part-time $1016 per credit hour. Required fees: $337.04 per term. *Financial support:* In 2009–10, 1 fellowship with partial tuition reimbursement (averaging $11,304 per year), 4 research assistantships with tuition reimbursements (averaging $16,168 per year), 8 teaching assistantships (averaging $14,630 per year) were awarded; Federal Work-Study also available. Support available to part-time students. Financial award applicants required to submit FAFSA. Total annual research expenditures: $1.6 million. *Unit head:* Roger Tourangeau, Director, 301-314-7911, Fax: 301-314-7912, E-mail: rtourang@umd.edu. *Application contact:* Dean of Graduate School, 301-405-0358, Fax: 301-314-9305.

University of Michigan, Horace H. Rackham School of Graduate Studies, Program in Survey Methodology, Ann Arbor, MI 48109. Offers MS, PhD, Certificate. Part-time programs available. Terminal master's awarded for partial completion of doctoral program. *Degree requirements:* For master's, internships; for doctorate, comprehensive exam, thesis/dissertation. *Entrance requirements:* For master's and doctorate, GRE, 3 letters of recommendation; for Certificate, current enrollment in a graduate degree program at University of Michigan or have completed one within past 5 years. Additional exam requirements/recommendations for international students: Required—TOEFL (minimum score 560 paper-based; 220 computer-based). Electronic applications accepted. *Expenses:* Contact institution. *Faculty research:* Survey methodology, statistics, psychology, sociology, social psychology.

University of Nebraska–Lincoln, Graduate College, Interdepartmental Area of Survey Research and Methodology, Lincoln, NE 68588. Offers MS, PhD. *Degree requirements:* For master's, comprehensive exam. *Entrance requirements:* For master's, GRE General Test or GMAT. Additional exam requirements/recommendations for international students: Required—TOEFL (minimum score 550 paper-based; 213 computer-based). Electronic applications accepted. *Faculty research:* Survey research and data analysis.

TEXAS A&M UNIVERSITY

Department of Sociology

Programs of Study

The Department of Sociology prepares students for careers in teaching and research in higher education and private and public sectors. The Department offers a broad-based curriculum with excellent opportunities for advanced training in the following areas of faculty expertise and research: culture; demography; law, deviance, and social control; political and economic sociology; race, class, and gender; and social psychology. The program is relatively large, with more than 90 students, but with 33 tenured and tenure-track faculty members, it has a favorable student-faculty ratio (under 3:1). Thus, students have many opportunities to work on faculty research projects and develop research programs under close faculty supervision.

For students with a bachelor's degree, the graduate program is designed to facilitate completion of both the master's and doctoral degrees within five years. The master's degree requires 34 hours of course work (including 8 research hours for the thesis) and can be completed in two years. For students who have completed (or entered with) the master's degree, the Ph.D. requires an additional 64 hours of course work, of which 18 to 32 hours may be research hours. Doctoral students take preliminary examinations in two specialty areas within the discipline usually after approximately two years in the program. They also undertake a dissertation project that extends the boundaries of the discipline. In most cases, the Ph.D. can be completed in three years from the master's.

Research Facilities

Texas A&M has ample resources to support graduate student research and training. The University maintains a major research library system and is home to the George Bush Presidential Library. The Department maintains a computer lab to augment the computing facilities maintained by the University. The Department also houses the Laboratory for the Study of Social Deviance, which oversees a major longitudinal study supported by the National Institute on Drug Abuse (NIDA) to encourage study of youth socialization, deviance, and the self. Numerous other institutes and centers offer opportunities for specialized sociological study, including the Mexican American and U.S. Latino Research Center (MALRC), the China Archives, the Racial and Ethnic Studies Institute (RESI), and the Center for Presidential Studies (a major national depository of public opinion poll data).

Financial Aid

Most students in the program receive financial assistance in various forms including Department scholarships, University fellowships, Department assistantships, research assistantships on faculty grants, and assistantships in various units around the University. Departmental assistantships are awarded competitively each year. Department assistants work 20 hours per week for the academic year, receiving a nine-month stipend of $1350 per month, or $12,150 annually, for master's students or $1450–$1550 per month, or $13,050–$13,950 annually, for doctoral students. University-level fellowships offer stipends at even higher levels. Funded students also receive tuition waivers, fee assistance payments, and University-funded health insurance. Students receiving scholarships receive out-of-state tuition waivers.

Cost of Study

Tuition is $221.74 per credit hour for residents and $502.74 per credit hour for nonresidents. Students awarded assistantships or university fellowships receive tuition waivers.

Living and Housing Costs

The cost of living in Bryan–College Station is low compared with most metropolitan areas. Options for on-campus housing are limited, but off-campus housing is abundant and moderately priced. For information, students should contact the Off-Campus Housing Office (979-845-1741).

Student Group

This past year, the Department had a diverse group of more than 90 graduate students. Approximately, 80 percent are in residence and enrolled full-time. About 65 percent were women, about 40 percent were members of racial or ethnic minority groups, and about 15 percent were international students. Professional placements vary based on student accomplishments. In general, graduates place well; most are employed full-time in universities, colleges, and public and private research agencies within a year of formal graduation.

Location

Bryan–College Station is located 100 miles northwest of Houston, 150 miles south of Dallas–Fort Worth, and 100 miles east of Austin. It is easily accessible by air on American or Continental airlines. With a population of 175,000, the twin-cities area is notable for the diversity of its ethnic and religious communities and for the range of cultural activities it supports, including blues and bluegrass, classical musical concerts, opera, ballet, local and visiting theatrical productions, art galleries, sports, and more. Resting in the Brazos River valley, the city has a pleasant geography of gently rolling hills, abundant trees, ready access to excellent public park and camping facilities, and a mild climate.

The University and The College

Texas A&M is a large, public, land-grant institution with a diverse student body of more than 48,000. Founded in 1876, it has a long tradition of excellence in scientific research. Rapidly expanding since its founding in the early 1970s, the College of Liberal Arts has become the second-largest college in the University and is home to nationally recognized faculty members in the humanities and social sciences. College growth has been accompanied by the rising prominence of its graduate programs and the expansion of the University's library holdings and other facilities supporting advanced research and scholarship.

Applying

Applications for fall semester admission are accepted from those with bachelor's degrees (or higher) and should be sent as early as possible. Completed applications received by January 1 are assured full consideration for financial aid, fellowships, assistantships, and scholarships. Funding decisions begin in January and funding may be unavailable for applications received after January 1. All applications are evaluated on an individual basis. Successful applicants typically have all or most of the following characteristics: an A or B average in relevant course work, a strong commitment to a professional career in sociology, strong letters of reference from professional sociologists, and scores in the top half of the GRE General Test.

Correspondence and Information

William A. McIntosh
Department of Sociology
Texas A&M University
4351 TAMU
College Station, Texas 77843-4351
Phone: 979-845-8525 or 5133
E-mail: socadvisor@tamu.edu
w-mcintosh@tamu.edu
Web site: http://sociweb.tamu.edu

Texas A&M University

TENURED AND TENURE-TRACK FACULTY

In recent decades, the Department has grown in size, nearly doubling its tenured and tenure-track faculty, and in reputation. The faculty members are recognized nationally and internationally for their contributions in sociological research, scholarship, service, and graduate and undergraduate teaching.

Jeff Ackerman, Assistant Professor; Ph.D., Penn State, 2003. Criminology, deviance, sociology of law, quantitative methods.
Paul Almeida, Assistant Professor; Ph.D., California, Riverside, 2001. Social movements, political sociology, social inequality, Latin America, environmental sociology.
James Burk, Professor; Ph.D., Chicago, 1982. Social control, theory, political sociology.
Samuel Cohn, Professor; Ph.D., Michigan, 1981. Work and labor markets, industrial sociology, economy and society.
Ben Crouch, Professor; Ph.D., Southern Illinois at Carbondale, 1971. Criminology/delinquency, deviant behavior/social disorganization.
Ashley Currier, Assistant Professor; Ph.D., Pittsburgh, 2007. Social movements, sexualities, gender, Southern Africa, qualitative methods.
Joe Feagin, Professor; Ph.D., Harvard, 1966. Race and ethnic relations, gender relations, urban political economy.
Nadia Flores, Assistant Professor; Ph.D., Pennsylvania, 2005. Demography, economic sociology, economics, sociology of immigration, international migration, urban sociology.
Mark A. Fossett, Professor; Ph.D., Texas at Austin, 1983. Race/ethnic/minority relations, stratification/mobility, urban sociology.
Holly Foster, Assistant Professor; Ph.D., Toronto, 2002. Crime, deviance, life course, quantitative methods.
Sarah Nicole Gatson, Associate Professor; Ph.D., Northwestern, 1999. Race/ethnic/minority relations, law and society, cultural sociology.
Kathryn Henderson, Associate Professor; Ph.D., California, San Diego, 1991. Science and technology, cultural sociology, qualitative methodology.
Stuart Hysom, Assistant Professor; Ph.D., Emory, 2003. Social psychology, group processes, theory construction.
Joseph O. Jewell, Associate Professor; Ph.D., UCLA, 1998. Race/ethnic/minority relations, history of sociology/sociological thought, education.
Howard B. Kaplan, Professor; Ph.D., NYU, 1958. Social psychology, deviant behavior/social disorganization, mental health.
Verna M. Keith, Professor; Ph.D., Kentucky, 1982. Medical sociology, mental health, race/ethnicity, health disparities.
Dongxiao Liu, Assistant Professor; Ph.D., Harvard, 2007. Political sociology, social movements, comparative and historical, gender, China.
Robert Mackin, Assistant Professor; Ph.D., Wisconsin–Madison, 2005. Political sociology, sociology of religion, comparative/historical sociology, qualitative methods.
Reuben A. Buford May, Associate Professor, Ph.D., Chicago, 1996. Race and culture, sociology of sport, sociology of the everyday, urban ethnography.
William A. McIntosh, Professor; Ph.D., Iowa State, 1975. Sociology of food and nutrition, culture, medical sociology, social change.
Stjepan Mestrovic, Professor; Ph.D., Syracuse, 1982. Theory, religion, political sociology.
Wendy L. Moore, Assistant Professor; Ph.D., Minnesota, 2005. American race relations; critical race theory; intersections of race, class, and gender.
Edward Murguia, Associate Professor; Ph.D., Texas at Austin, 1978. Race/ethnic/minority relations, family.
Hiroshi Ono, Assistant Professor; Ph.D., Chicago, 1999. Economic sociology, social stratification and inequality, labor markets, organizations.
Dudley Poston, Professor; Ph.D., Oregon, 1968. Demography, human ecology, sex and gender.
Harland Prechel, Professor; Ph.D., Kansas, 1986. Comparative sociology/macrosociology, political sociology, formal and complex social organization.
Rogelio Saenz, Professor; Ph.D., Iowa State, 1986. Demography, Latina/Latino sociology, rural sociology.
David Sciulli, Professor; Ph.D., Columbia, 1983. Law and society, political sociology, theory.
Jane Sell, Professor; Ph.D., Washington State, 1979. Small groups, social psychology.
Kazuko Suzuki, Assistant Professor; Ph.D., Princeton, 2003. International migration, racial and ethnic relations, gender, Asian/Asian-American studies.
Nancy Plankey Vadela, Assistant Professor; Ph.D., Wisconsin–Madison, 2004. Development and social chance, Latin America, sociology of work, gender, social movements, qualitative methods.
Zulema Valdez, Assistant Professor; Ph.D., UCLA, 2002. Race and ethnic relations, economic sociology, immigration, Latina/Latino sociology.
Wenquan (Charles) Zhang, Assistant Professor; Ph.D., SUNY at Albany, 2004. Immigration, secondary migration, spatial assimilation and stratification, spatial econometrics and GIS.
Lu Zheng, Assistant Professor; Ph.D., Stanford, 2007. Institutions and organizations, economic sociology, stratification and mobility, China studies.

Affiliated and Joint Appointments

George Rogers, Professor of Urban Planning; Ph.D., Pittsburgh, 1983. Environmental sociology, science and technology, formal and complex social organization.
John Thomas, Professor of Recreation, Park, and Tourism Sciences; Ph.D., Texas A&M, 1979. Quantitative methodology, applied sociology, evaluation research.

Emeritus Faculty

Jon Alston, Ph.D., Texas at Austin, 1971. Religion, formal and complex social organization.
Barbara Finlay, Ph.D., Florida, 1976. Quantitative, family demography.
Jerry Gaston, Ph.D., Yale, 1969. Science and technology, education.
Bardin Nelson, Ph.D., LSU, 1950. Social psychology, theory aging/social gerontology.
Albert Schaffer, Ph.D., North Carolina at Chapel Hill, 1957. Urban sociology community, theory.

APPENDIXES

Institutional Changes Since the 2010 Edition

Following is an alphabetical listing of institutions that have recently closed, merged with other institutions, or changed their names or status. In the case of a name change, the former name appears first, followed by the new name.

Agnes Scott College (Decatur, GA): no longer offers graduate degrees

American Graduate School of International Relations and Diplomacy (Paris, France): name changed to American Graduate School in Paris

Antioch University McGregor (Yellow Springs, OH): name changed to Antioch University Midwest

Arizona State University at the Downtown Phoenix Campus (Phoenix, AZ): will be included with main campus Arizona State University (Tempe, AZ) by request from the institution

Arizona State University at the Polytechnic Campus (Mesa, AZ): will be included with main campus Arizona State University (Tempe, AZ) by request from the institution

Arizona State University at the West campus (Phoenix, AZ): [will be included with main campus Arizona State University (Tempe, AZ) by request from the institution

Arkansas State University (State University, AR): name changed to Arkansas State University–Jonesboro

Asbury College (Wilmore, KY): name changed to Asbury University

Australasian College of Health Sciences (Portland, OR): name changed to American College of Healthcare Sciences

Baker College Center for Graduate Studies (Flint, MI): name changed to Baker College Center for Graduate Studies–Online

Baltimore Hebrew University (Baltimore, MD): now a unit of Towson University (Towson, MD)

Beacon University (Columbus, GA): closed

Belhaven College (Jackson, MS): name changed to Belhaven University

Beth Benjamin Academy of Connecticut (Stamford, CT): no longer offers graduate degrees

Bethel College (McKenzie, TN): name changed to Bethel University

Bridgewater State College (Bridgewater, MA): name changed to Bridgewater State University

British American College London (London, United Kingdom): name changed to Regent's American College London

The Chicago School of Professional Psychology: Downtown Los Angeles Campus (Los Angeles, CA): name changed to The Chicago School of Professional Psychology at Downtown Los Angeles

The Chicago School of Professional Psychology: Grayslake Campus (Grayslake, IL): name changed to The Chicago School of Professional Psychology at Grayslake

The Cleveland Institute of Art (Cleveland, OH): no longer offers graduate degrees

Coleman College (San Diego, CA): name changed to Coleman University

Columbia Union College (Takoma Park, MD): name changed to Washington Adventist University

Dell'Arte School of Physical Theatre (Blue Lake, CA): name changed to Dell'Arte International School of Physical Theatre

DeVry University (San Francisco, CA): closed

Fitchburg State College (Fitchburg, MA): name changed to Fitchburg State University

George Meany Center for Labor Studies–The National Labor College (Silver Spring, MD): name changed to National Labor College

Hebrew Theological College (Skokie, IL): no longer offers graduate degrees

International University in Geneva (Geneva, Switzerland): no longer accredited by agency recognized by USDE or CHEA

Joint Military Intelligence College (Washington, DC): name changed to National Defense Intelligence College

Kent State University, Stark Campus (Canton, OH): name changed to Kent State University at Stark

Lancaster Bible College (Lancaster, PA): name changed to Lancaster Bible College & Graduate School

Leadership Institute of Seattle (Kenmore, WA): is now part of Saybrook University (San Francisco, CA)

New England School of Law (Boston, MA): name changed to New England Law-Boston

Otterbein College (Westerville, OH): name changed to Otterbein University

Pepperdine University (Los Angeles, CA): will be included with Pepperdine University (Malibu, CA) by request from the institution

The Protestant Episcopal Theological Seminary in Virginia (Alexandria, VA): name changed to Virginia Theological Seminary

Reinhardt College (Waleska, GA): name changed to Reinhardt University

Robert Morris College (Chicago, IL): name changed to Robert Morris University Illinois

St. Petersburg Theological Seminary (St. Petersburg, FL): no longer accredited by agency recognized by USDE or CHEA

Saybrook Graduate School and Research Center (San Francisco, CA): name changed to Saybrook University

Shorter College (Rome, GA): name changed to Shorter University

Southeastern University (Washington, DC): closed

Southern New England School of Law (North Dartmouth, MA): is now part of University of Massachusetts Dartmouth (North Dartmouth, MA)

Trinity Episcopal School for Ministry (Ambridge, PA): name changed to Trinity School for Ministry

University of Missouri–Columbia (Columbia, MO): name changed to University of Missouri

University of Phoenix–Renton Learning Center (Renton, WA): name changed to University of Phoenix–Western Washington Campus

University of Phoenix–Wisconsin Campus (Brookfield, WI): now listed as University of Phoenix–Madison Campus (Madison, WI)

West Liberty State University (West Liberty, WV): name changed to West Liberty University

World Medicine Institute: College of Acupuncture and Herbal Medicine (Honolulu, HI): name changed to World Medicine Institute of Acupuncture and Herbal Medicine

Abbreviations Used in the Guides

The following list includes abbreviations of degree names used in the profiles in the 2011 edition of the guides. Because some degrees (e.g., Doctor of Education) can be abbreviated in more than one way (e.g., D.Ed. or Ed.D.), and because the abbreviations used in the guides reflect the preferences of the individual colleges and universities, the list may include two or more abbreviations for a single degree.

Degrees

A Mus D	Doctor of Musical Arts
AC	Advanced Certificate
AD	Artist's Diploma Doctor of Arts
ADP	Artist's Diploma
Adv C	Advanced Certificate
Adv M	Advanced Master
AGC	Advanced Graduate Certificate
AGSC	Advanced Graduate Specialist Certificate
ALM	Master of Liberal Arts
AM	Master of Arts
AMBA	Accelerated Master of Business Administration
AMRS	Master of Arts in Religious Studies
APC	Advanced Professional Certificate
App Sc	Applied Scientist
App Sc D	Doctor of Applied Science
Au D	Doctor of Audiology
B Th	Bachelor of Theology
CAES	Certificate of Advanced Educational Specialization
CAGS	Certificate of Advanced Graduate Studies
CAL	Certificate in Applied Linguistics
CALS	Certificate of Advanced Liberal Studies
CAMS	Certificate of Advanced Management Studies
CAPS	Certificate of Advanced Professional Studies
CAS	Certificate of Advanced Studies
CASPA	Certificate of Advanced Study in Public Administration
CASR	Certificate in Advanced Social Research
CATS	Certificate of Achievement in Theological Studies
CBHS	Certificate in Basic Health Sciences
CBS	Graduate Certificate in Biblical Studies
CCJA	Certificate in Criminal Justice Administration
CCSA	Certificate in Catholic School Administration
CCTS	Certificate in Clinical and Translational Science
CE	Civil Engineer
CEM	Certificate of Environmental Management
CET	Certificate in Educational Technologies
CGS	Certificate of Graduate Studies
Ch E	Chemical Engineer
CM	Certificate in Management
CMH	Certificate in Medical Humanities
CMM	Master of Church Ministries
CMS	Certificate in Ministerial Studies
CNM	Certificate in Nonprofit Management
CP	Certificate in Performance
CPASF	Certificate Program for Advanced Study in Finance
CPC	Certificate in Professional Counseling Certificate in Publication and Communication
CPH	Certificate in Public Health
CPM	Certificate in Public Management
CPS	Certificate of Professional Studies
CScD	Doctor of Clinical Science
CSD	Certificate in Spiritual Direction
CSS	Certificate of Special Studies
CTS	Certificate of Theological Studies
CURP	Certificate in Urban and Regional Planning
D Admin	Doctor of Administration
D Arch	Doctor of Architecture
D Com	Doctor of Commerce
D Div	Doctor of Divinity
D Ed	Doctor of Education
D Ed Min	Doctor of Educational Ministry
D Eng	Doctor of Engineering
D Engr	Doctor of Engineering
D Env	Doctor of Environment
D Env M	Doctor of Environmental Management
D Law	Doctor of Law
D Litt	Doctor of Letters
D Med Sc	Doctor of Medical Science
D Min	Doctor of Ministry
D Miss	Doctor of Missiology
D Mus	Doctor of Music
D Mus A	Doctor of Musical Arts
D Phil	Doctor of Philosophy

D Ps	Doctor of Psychology
D Sc	Doctor of Science
D Sc D	Doctor of Science in Dentistry
D Sc IS	Doctor of Science in Information Systems
D Sc PA	Doctor of Science in Physician Assistant Studies
D Th	Doctor of Theology
D Th P	Doctor of Practical Theology
DA	Doctor of Accounting Doctor of Arts
DA Ed	Doctor of Arts in Education
DAH	Doctor of Arts in Humanities
DAOM	Doctorate in Acupuncture and Oriental Medicine
DAST	Diploma of Advanced Studies in Teaching
DBA	Doctor of Business Administration
DBL	Doctor of Business Leadership
DBS	Doctor of Buddhist Studies
DC	Doctor of Chiropractic
DCC	Doctor of Computer Science
DCD	Doctor of Communications Design
DCL	Doctor of Civil Law Doctor of Comparative Law
DCM	Doctor of Church Music
DCN	Doctor of Clinical Nutrition
DCS	Doctor of Computer Science
DDN	Diplôme du Droit Notarial
DDS	Doctor of Dental Surgery
DE	Doctor of Education Doctor of Engineering
DED	Doctor of Economic Development
DEIT	Doctor of Educational Innovation and Technology
DEL	Doctor of Executive Leadership
DEM	Doctor of Educational Ministry
DEPD	Diplôme Études Spécialisées
DES	Doctor of Engineering Science
DESS	Diplôme Études Supérieures Spécialisées
DFA	Doctor of Fine Arts
DGP	Diploma in Graduate and Professional Studies
DH Ed	Doctor of Health Education
DH Sc	Doctor of Health Sciences
DHA	Doctor of Health Administration
DHCE	Doctor of Health Care Ethics
DHL	Doctor of Hebrew Letters Doctor of Hebrew Literature
DHS	Doctor of Health Science Doctor of Human Services
DHSc	Doctor of Health Science
Dip CS	Diploma in Christian Studies
DIT	Doctor of Industrial Technology
DJ Ed	Doctor of Jewish Education
DJS	Doctor of Jewish Studies
DLS	Doctor of Liberal Studies
DM	Doctor of Management Doctor of Music
DMA	Doctor of Musical Arts
DMD	Doctor of Dental Medicine
DME	Doctor of Manufacturing Management Doctor of Music Education
DMEd	Doctor of Music Education
DMFT	Doctor of Marital and Family Therapy
DMH	Doctor of Medical Humanities
DML	Doctor of Modern Languages
DMM	Doctor of Music Ministry
DMP	Doctorate in Medical Physics
DMPNA	Doctor of Management Practice in Nurse Anesthesia
DN Sc	Doctor of Nursing Science
DNAP	Doctor of Nurse Anesthesia Practice
DNP	Doctor of Nursing Practice
DNS	Doctor of Nursing Science
DO	Doctor of Osteopathy
DPA	Doctor of Public Administration
DPC	Doctor of Pastoral Counseling
DPDS	Doctor of Planning and Development Studies
DPH	Doctor of Public Health
DPM	Doctor of Plant Medicine Doctor of Podiatric Medicine
DPPD	Doctor of Policy, Planning, and Development
DPS	Doctor of Professional Studies
DPT	Doctor of Physical Therapy
DPTSc	Doctor of Physical Therapy Science
Dr DES	Doctor of Design
Dr PH	Doctor of Public Health
Dr Sc PT	Doctor of Science in Physical Therapy
DRSc	Doctor of Regulatory Science
DS	Doctor of Science
DS Sc	Doctor of Social Science
DSJS	Doctor of Science in Jewish Studies

DSL	Doctor of Strategic Leadership
DSN	Doctor of Science in Nursing
DSW	Doctor of Social Work
DTL	Doctor of Talmudic Law
DV Sc	Doctor of Veterinary Science
DVM	Doctor of Veterinary Medicine
EAA	Engineer in Aeronautics and Astronautics
ECS	Engineer in Computer Science
Ed D	Doctor of Education
Ed DCT	Doctor of Education in College Teaching
Ed M	Master of Education
Ed S	Specialist in Education
Ed Sp	Specialist in Education
Ed Sp PTE	Specialist in Education in Professional Technical Education
EDM	Executive Doctorate in Management
EDSPC	Education Specialist
EE	Electrical Engineer
EJD	Executive Juris Doctor
EMBA	Executive Master of Business Administration
EMFA	Executive Master of Forensic Accounting
EMHA	Executive Master of Health Administration
EMIB	Executive Master of International Business
EML	Executive Master of Leadership
EMPA	Executive Master of Public Administration Executive Master of Public Affairs
EMS	Executive Master of Science
EMTM	Executive Master of Technology Management
Eng	Engineer
Eng Sc D	Doctor of Engineering Science
Engr	Engineer
Ex Doc	Executive Doctor of Pharmacy
Exec Ed D	Executive Doctor of Education
Exec MBA	Executive Master of Business Administration
Exec MPA	Executive Master of Public Administration
Exec MPH	Executive Master of Public Health
Exec MS	Executive Master of Science
G Dip	Graduate Diploma
GBC	Graduate Business Certificate
GCE	Graduate Certificate in Education
GDM	Graduate Diploma in Management
GDPA	Graduate Diploma in Public Administration
GDRE	Graduate Diploma in Religious Education
GEMBA	Global Executive Master of Business Administration
GEMPA	Gulf Executive Master of Public Administration
GM Acc	Graduate Master of Accountancy
GMBA	Global Master of Business Administration
GPD	Graduate Performance Diploma
GSS	Graduate Special Certificate for Students in Special Situations
IEMBA	International Executive Master of Business Administration
IM Acc	Integrated Master of Accountancy
IMA	Interdisciplinary Master of Arts
IMBA	International Master of Business Administration
IMES	International Masters in Environmental Studies
Ingeniero	Engineer
JCD	Doctor of Canon Law
JCL	Licentiate in Canon Law
JD	Juris Doctor
JSD	Doctor of Juridical Science Doctor of Jurisprudence Doctor of the Science of Law
JSM	Master of Science of Law
L Th	Licenciate in Theology
LL B	Bachelor of Laws
LL CM	Master of Laws in Comparative Law
LL D	Doctor of Laws
LL M	Master of Laws
LL M in Tax	Master of Laws in Taxation
LL M CL	Master of Laws (Common Law)
LL M/MBA	Master of Laws/Master of Business Administration
LL M/MNM	Master of Laws/Master of Nonprofit Management
M Ac	Master of Accountancy Master of Accounting Master of Acupuncture
M Ac OM	Master of Acupuncture and Oriental Medicine
M Acc	Master of Accountancy Master of Accounting
M Acct	Master of Accountancy Master of Accounting
M Accy	Master of Accountancy
M Actg	Master of Accounting
M Acy	Master of Accountancy
M Ad	Master of Administration
M Ad Ed	Master of Adult Education
M Adm	Master of Administration

M Adm Mgt	Master of Administrative Management
M Admin	Master of Administration
M ADU	Master of Architectural Design and Urbanism
M Adv	Master of Advertising
M Aero E	Master of Aerospace Engineering
M AEST	Master of Applied Environmental Science and Technology
M Ag	Master of Agriculture
M Ag Ed	Master of Agricultural Education
M Agr	Master of Agriculture
M Anesth Ed	Master of Anesthesiology Education
M App Comp Sc	Master of Applied Computer Science
M App St	Master of Applied Statistics
M Appl Stat	Master of Applied Statistics
M Aq	Master of Aquaculture
M Ar	Master of Architecture
M Arc	Master of Architecture
M Arch	Master of Architecture
M Arch I	Master of Architecture I
M Arch II	Master of Architecture II
M Arch E	Master of Architectural Engineering
M Arch H	Master of Architectural History
M Bioethics	Master in Bioethics
M Biomath	Master of Biomathematics
M Ch	Master of Chemistry
M Ch E	Master of Chemical Engineering
M Chem	Master of Chemistry
M Cl D	Master of Clinical Dentistry
M Cl Sc	Master of Clinical Science
M Comp E	Master of Computer Engineering
M Comp Sc	Master of Computer Science
M Coun	Master of Counseling
M Dent	Master of Dentistry
M Dent Sc	Master of Dental Sciences
M Des	Master of Design
M Des S	Master of Design Studies
M Div	Master of Divinity
M Ec	Master of Economics
M Econ	Master of Economics
M Ed	Master of Education
M Ed T	Master of Education in Teaching
M En	Master of Engineering Master of Environmental Science
M En S	Master of Environmental Sciences
M Eng	Master of Engineering
M Eng Mgt	Master of Engineering Management
M Engr	Master of Engineering
M Env	Master of Environment
M Env Des	Master of Environmental Design
M Env E	Master of Environmental Engineering
M Env Sc	Master of Environmental Science
M Fin	Master of Finance
M Geo E	Master of Geological Engineering
M Geoenv E	Master of Geoenvironmental Engineering
M Geog	Master of Geography
M Hum	Master of Humanities
M Hum Svcs	Master of Human Services
M IBD	Master of Integrated Building Delivery
M IDST	Master's in Interdisciplinary Studies
M Kin	Master of Kinesiology
M Land Arch	Master of Landscape Architecture
M Litt	Master of Letters
M Man	Master of Management
M Mat SE	Master of Material Science and Engineering
M Math	Master of Mathematics
M Med Sc	Master of Medical Science
M Mgmt	Master of Management
M Mgt	Master of Management
M Min	Master of Ministries
M Mtl E	Master of Materials Engineering
M Mu	Master of Music
M Mus	Master of Music
M Mus Ed	Master of Music Education
M Music	Master of Music
M Nat Sci	Master of Natural Science
M Oc E	Master of Oceanographic Engineering
M Pet E	Master of Petroleum Engineering
M Pharm	Master of Pharmacy
M Phil	Master of Philosophy
M Phil F	Master of Philosophical Foundations
M Pl	Master of Planning
M Plan	Master of Planning
M Pol	Master of Political Science
M Pr Met	Master of Professional Meteorology
M Prob S	Master of Probability and Statistics

M Psych	Master of Psychology
M Pub	Master of Publishing
M Rel	Master of Religion
M Sc	Master of Science
M Sc A	Master of Science (Applied)
M Sc AHN	Master of Science in Applied Human Nutrition
M Sc BMC	Master of Science in Biomedical Communications
M Sc CS	Master of Science in Computer Science
M Sc E	Master of Science in Engineering
M Sc Eng	Master of Science in Engineering
M Sc Engr	Master of Science in Engineering
M Sc F	Master of Science in Forestry
M Sc FE	Master of Science in Forest Engineering
M Sc Geogr	Master of Science in Geography
M Sc N	Master of Science in Nursing
M Sc OT	Master of Science in Occupational Therapy
M Sc P	Master of Science in Planning
M Sc Pl	Master of Science in Planning
M Sc PT	Master of Science in Physical Therapy
M Sc T	Master of Science in Teaching
M SEM	Master of Sustainable Environmental Management
M Serv Soc	Master of Social Service
M Soc	Master of Sociology
M Sp Ed	Master of Special Education
M Stat	Master of Statistics
M Sw En	Master of Software Engineering
M Sys Sc	Master of Systems Science
M Tax	Master of Taxation
M Tech	Master of Technology
M Th	Master of Theology
M Tox	Master of Toxicology
M Trans E	Master of Transportation Engineering
M Urb	Master of Urban Planning
M Vet Sc	Master of Veterinary Science
MA	Master of Administration Master of Arts
MA Comm	Master of Arts in Communication
MA Ed	Master of Arts in Education
MA Ed Ad	Master of Arts in Educational Administration
MA Ext	Master of Agricultural Extension
MA Islamic	Master of Arts in Islamic Studies
MA Military Studies	Master of Arts in Military Studies
MA Min	Master of Arts in Ministry
MA Miss	Master of Arts in Missiology
MA Past St	Master of Arts in Pastoral Studies
MA Ph	Master of Arts in Philosophy
MA Psych	Master of Arts in Psychology
MA Sc	Master of Applied Science
MA Sp	Master of Arts (Spirituality)
MA Strategic Intelligence	Master of Arts in Strategic Intelligence
MA Th	Master of Arts in Theology
MA-R	Master of Arts (Research)
MAA	Master of Administrative Arts Master of Applied Anthropology Master of Applied Arts Master of Arts in Administration
MAAAP	Master of Arts Administration and Policy
MAAE	Master of Arts in Art Education
MAAT	Master of Arts in Applied Theology Master of Arts in Art Therapy
MAB	Master of Agribusiness
MABC	Master of Arts in Biblical Counseling Master of Arts in Business Communication
MABE	Master of Arts in Bible Exposition
MABL	Master of Arts in Biblical Languages
MABM	Master of Agribusiness Management
MABS	Master of Arts in Biblical Studies
MABT	Master of Arts in Bible Teaching
MAC	Master of Accountancy Master of Accounting Master of Arts in Communication Master of Arts in Counseling
MACC	Master of Arts in Accountancy Master of Arts in Christian Counseling Master of Arts in Clinical Counseling
MACCM	Master of Arts in Church and Community Ministry
MACCT	Master of Accounting
MACE	Master of Arts in Christian Education
MACFM	Master of Arts in Children's and Family Ministry
MACH	Master of Arts in Church History
MACIS	Master of Accounting and Information Systems
MACJ	Master of Arts in Criminal Justice
MACL	Master of Arts in Christian Leadership

MACM	Master of Arts in Christian Ministries Master of Arts in Christian Ministry Master of Arts in Church Music Master of Arts in Counseling Ministries
MACN	Master of Arts in Counseling
MACO	Master of Arts in Counseling
MAcOM	Master of Acupuncture and Oriental Medicine
MACP	Master of Arts in Counseling Psychology
MACS	Master of Arts in Catholic Studies
MACSE	Master of Arts in Christian School Education
MACT	Master of Arts in Christian Thought Master of Arts in Communications and Technology
MAD	Master in Educational Institution Administration Master of Art and Design
MADR	Master of Arts in Dispute Resolution
MADS	Master of Animal and Dairy Science Master of Applied Disability Studies
MAE	Master of Aerospace Engineering Master of Agricultural Economics Master of Agricultural Education Master of Architectural Engineering Master of Art Education Master of Arts in Education Master of Arts in English Master of Automotive Engineering
MAECMS	Master of Aerospace Engineering in Composite Materials and Structures
MAEd	Master of Arts Education
MAEL	Master of Arts in Educational Leadership
MAEM	Master of Arts in Educational Ministries
MAEN	Master of Arts in English
MAEP	Master of Arts in Economic Policy
MAES	Master of Arts in Environmental Sciences
MAESL	Master of Arts in English as a Second Language
MAET	Master of Arts in English Teaching
MAF	Master of Arts in Finance
MAFE	Master of Arts in Financial Economics
MAFLL	Master of Arts in Foreign Language and Literature
MAFM	Master of Accounting and Financial Management
MAFS	Master of Arts in Family Studies
MAG	Master of Applied Geography
MAGU	Master of Urban Analysis and Management
MAH	Master of Arts in Humanities
MAHA	Master of Arts in Humanitarian Assistance Master of Arts in Humanitarian Studies
MAHCM	Master of Arts in Health Care Mission
MAHG	Master of American History and Government
MAHL	Master of Arts in Hebrew Letters
MAHN	Master of Applied Human Nutrition
MAHSR	Master of Applied Health Services Research
MAIA	Master of Arts in International Administration
MAIB	Master of Arts in International Business
MAICS	Master of Arts in Intercultural Studies
MAIDM	Master of Arts in Interior Design and Merchandising
MAIH	Master of Arts in Interdisciplinary Humanities
MAIPCR	Master of Arts in International Peace and Conflict Management
MAIR	Master of Arts in Industrial Relations
MAIS	Master of Arts in Intercultural Studies Master of Arts in Interdisciplinary Studies Master of Arts in International Studies
MAIT	Master of Administration in Information Technology Master of Applied Information Technology
MAJ	Master of Arts in Journalism
MAJ Ed	Master of Arts in Jewish Education
MAJCS	Master of Arts in Jewish Communal Service
MAJE	Master of Arts in Jewish Education
MAJS	Master of Arts in Jewish Studies
MAL	Master in Agricultural Leadership
MALA	Master of Arts in Liberal Arts
MALD	Master of Arts in Law and Diplomacy
MALED	Master of Arts in Literacy Education
MALER	Master of Arts in Labor and Employment Relations
MALM	Master of Applied Leadership and Management Master of Arts in Leadership Evangelical Mobilization
MALP	Master of Arts in Language Pedagogy
MALPS	Master of Arts in Liberal and Professional Studies
MALS	Master of Arts in Liberal Studies
MALT	Master of Arts in Learning and Teaching
MAM	Master of Acquisition Management Master of Agriculture and Management Master of Applied Mathematics Master of Arts in Management Master of Arts in Ministry Master of Arts Management Master of Avian Medicine
MAMB	Master of Applied Molecular Biology
MAMC	Master of Arts in Mass Communication Master of Arts in Ministry and Culture Master of Arts in Ministry for a Multicultural Church
MAME	Master of Arts in Missions/Evangelism

MAMFC	Master of Arts in Marriage and Family Counseling
MAMFCC	Master of Arts in Marriage, Family, and Child Counseling
MAMFT	Master of Arts in Marriage and Family Therapy
MAMM	Master of Arts in Ministry Management
MAMS	Master of Applied Mathematical Sciences Master of Arts in Ministerial Studies Master of Arts in Ministry and Spirituality
MAMT	Master of Arts in Mathematics Teaching
MAN	Master of Applied Nutrition
MANP	Master of Applied Natural Products
MANT	Master of Arts in New Testament
MAOM	Master of Acupuncture and Oriental Medicine Master of Arts in Organizational Management
MAOT	Master of Arts in Old Testament
MAP	Master of Applied Psychology Master of Arts in Planning Master of Public Administration Masters of Psychology
MAP Min	Master of Arts in Pastoral Ministry
MAPA	Master of Arts in Public Administration
MAPC	Master of Arts in Pastoral Counseling
MAPE	Master of Arts in Political Economy
MAPL	Master of Arts in Pastoral Leadership
MAPM	Master of Arts in Pastoral Ministry Master of Arts in Pastoral Music Master of Arts in Practical Ministry
MAPP	Master of Arts in Public Policy
MAPPS	Master of Arts in Asia Pacific Policy Studies
MAPS	Master of Arts in Pastoral Counseling/Spiritual Formation Master of Arts in Pastoral Studies Master of Arts in Public Service
MAPT	Master of Practical Theology
MAPW	Master of Arts in Professional Writing
MAR	Master of Arts in Religion
Mar Eng	Marine Engineer
MARC	Master of Arts in Rehabilitation Counseling
MARE	Master of Arts in Religious Education
MARL	Master of Arts in Religious Leadership
MARS	Master of Arts in Religious Studies
MAS	Master of Accounting Science Master of Actuarial Science Master of Administrative Science Master of Advanced Study Master of Aeronautical Science Master of American Studies Master of Applied Science Master of Applied Statistics Master of Architectural Studies Master of Archival Studies
MASA	Master of Advanced Studies in Architecture
MASD	Master of Arts in Spiritual Direction
MASE	Master of Arts in Special Education
MASF	Master of Arts in Spiritual Formation
MASJ	Master of Arts in Systems of Justice
MASL	Master of Arts in School Leadership
MASLA	Master of Advanced Studies in Landscape Architecture
MASM	Master of Aging Services Management Master of Arts in Specialized Ministries
MASP	Master of Applied Social Psychology Master of Arts in School Psychology
MASPAA	Master of Arts in Sports and Athletic Administration
MASS	Master of Applied Social Science Master of Arts in Social Science
MAST	Master of Arts in Science Teaching
MASW	Master of Aboriginal Social Work
MAT	Master of Arts in Teaching Master of Arts in Theology Master of Athletic Training Masters in Administration of Telecommunications
Mat E	Materials Engineer
MATCM	Master of Acupuncture and Traditional Chinese Medicine
MATDE	Master of Arts in Theology, Development, and Evangelism
MATDR	Master of Territorial Management and Regional Development
MATE	Master of Arts for the Teaching of English
MATESL	Master of Arts in Teaching English as a Second Language
MATESOL	Master of Arts in Teaching English to Speakers of Other Languages
MATF	Master of Arts in Teaching English as a Foreign Language/Intercultural Studies
MATFL	Master of Arts in Teaching Foreign Language
MATH	Master of Arts in Therapy
MATI	Master of Administration of Information Technology

MATL	Master of Arts in Teaching of Languages Master of Arts in Transformational Leadership
MATM	Master of Arts in Teaching of Mathematics
MATS	Master of Arts in Theological Studies Master of Arts in Transforming Spirituality
MATSL	Master of Arts in Teaching a Second Language
MAUA	Master of Arts in Urban Affairs
MAUD	Master of Arts in Urban Design
MAURP	Master of Arts in Urban and Regional Planning
MAW	Master of Arts in Worship
MAWL	Master of Arts in Worship Leadership
MAWSHP	Master of Arts in Worship
MAYM	Master of Arts in Youth Ministry
MB	Master of Bioinformatics
MBA	Master of Business Administration
MBA-EP	Master of Business Administration–Experienced Professionals
MBAA	Master of Business Administration in Aviation
MBAE	Master of Biological and Agricultural Engineering Master of Biosystems and Agricultural Engineering
MBAH	Master of Business Administration in Health
MBAi	Master of Business Administration–International
MBAICT	Master of Business Administration in Information and Communication Technology
MBAPA	Master of Business Administration–Physician Assistant
MBATM	Master of Business Administration in Technology Management
MBC	Master of Building Construction
MBE	Master of Bilingual Education Master of Bioengineering Master of Biological Engineering Master of Biomedical Engineering Master of Business and Engineering Master of Business Economics Master of Business Education
MBET	Master of Business, Entrepreneurship and Technology
MBiotech	Master of Biotechnology
MBIT	Master of Business Information Technology
MBL	Master of Business Law Master of Business Leadership
MBLE	Master in Business Logistics Engineering
MBMI	Master of Biomedical Imaging and Signals
MBMSE	Master of Business Management and Software Engineering
MBS	Master of Behavioral Science Master of Biblical Studies Master of Biological Science Master of Biomedical Sciences Master of Bioscience Master of Building Science
MBSI	Master of Business Information Science
MBT	Master of Biblical and Theological Studies Master of Biomedical Technology Master of Biotechnology Master of Business Taxation
MC	Master of Communication Master of Counseling Master of Cybersecurity
MC Ed	Master of Continuing Education
MC Sc	Master of Computer Science
MCA	Master of Arts in Applied Criminology Master of Commercial Aviation
MCAM	Master of Computational and Applied Mathematics
MCC	Master of Computer Science
MCCS	Master of Crop and Soil Sciences
MCD	Master of Communications Disorders Master of Community Development
MCE	Master in Electronic Commerce Master of Christian Education Master of Civil Engineering Master of Control Engineering
MCEM	Master of Construction Engineering Management
MCH	Master of Chemical Engineering
MCHE	Master of Chemical Engineering
MCIS	Master of Communication and Information Studies Master of Computer and Information Science Master of Computer Information Systems
MCIT	Master of Computer and Information Technology
MCJ	Master of Criminal Justice
MCJA	Master of Criminal Justice Administration
MCL	Master in Communication Leadership Master of Canon Law Master of Comparative Law
MCM	Master of Christian Ministry Master of Church Music Master of City Management Master of Communication Management Master of Community Medicine Master of Construction Management Master of Contract Management Masters of Corporate Media

MCMS	Master of Clinical Medical Science
MCP	Master in Science Master of City Planning Master of Community Planning Master of Counseling Psychology Master of Cytopathology Practice
MCPC	Master of Arts in Chaplaincy and Pastoral Care
MCPD	Master of Community Planning and Development
MCRP	Master of City and Regional Planning
MCRS	Master of City and Regional Studies
MCS	Master of Christian Studies Master of Clinical Science Master of Combined Sciences Master of Communication Studies Master of Computer Science Master of Consumer Science
MCSE	Master of Computer Science and Engineering
MCSL	Master of Catholic School Leadership
MCSM	Master of Construction Science/Management
MCST	Master of Science in Computer Science and Information Technology
MCTP	Master of Communication Technology and Policy
MCTS	Master of Clinical and Translational Science
MCVS	Master of Cardiovascular Science
MD	Doctor of Medicine
MDA	Master of Development Administration Master of Dietetic Administration
MDB	Master of Design-Build
MDE	Master of Developmental Economics Master of Distance Education Master of the Education of the Deaf
MDH	Master of Dental Hygiene
MDM	Master of Digital Media
MDP	Master of Development Practice
MDR	Master of Dispute Resolution
MDS	Master of Dental Surgery
ME	Master of Education Master of Engineering Master of Entrepreneurship Master of Evangelism
ME Sc	Master of Engineering Science
MEA	Master of Educational Administration Master of Engineering Administration
MEAP	Master of Environmental Administration and Planning
MEBT	Master in Electronic Business Technologies
MEC	Master of Electronic Commerce
MECE	Master of Electrical and Computer Engineering
Mech E	Mechanical Engineer
MED	Master of Education of the Deaf
MEDS	Master of Environmental Design Studies
MEE	Master in Education Master of Electrical Engineering Master of Energy Engineering Master of Environmental Engineering
MEEM	Master of Environmental Engineering and Management
MEENE	Master of Engineering in Environmental Engineering
MEEP	Master of Environmental and Energy Policy
MEERM	Master of Earth and Environmental Resource Management
MEH	Master in Humanistic Studies Master of Environmental Horticulture
MEHS	Master of Environmental Health and Safety
MEIM	Master of Entertainment Industry Management
MEL	Master of Educational Leadership Master of English Literature
MELP	Master of Environmental Law and Policy
MEM	Master of Ecosystem Management Master of Electricity Markets Master of Engineering Management Master of Environmental Management Master of Marketing
MEME	Master of Engineering in Manufacturing Engineering Master of Engineering in Mechanical Engineering
MEMS	Master of Engineering in Manufacturing Systems
MENG	Master of Arts in English
MENVEGR	Master of Environmental Engineering
MEP	Master of Engineering Physics
MEPC	Master of Environmental Pollution Control
MEPD	Master of Education–Professional Development Master of Environmental Planning and Design
MEPM	Master of Environmental Protection Management
MER	Master of Employment Relations
MES	Master of Education and Science Master of Engineering Science Master of Environmenta and Sustainability Master of Environmental Science Master of Environmental Studies Master of Environmental Systems Master of Special Education
MESM	Master of Environmental Science and Management
MET	Master of Education in Teaching Master of Educational Technology Master of Engineering Technology Master of Entertainment Technology Master of Environmental Toxicology
Met E	Metallurgical Engineer

METM	Master of Engineering and Technology Management
MF	Master of Finance Master of Forestry
MFA	Master of Financial Administration Master of Fine Arts
MFAM	Master in Food Animal Medicine
MFAS	Master of Fisheries and Aquatic Science
MFAW	Master of Fine Arts in Writing
MFC	Master of Forest Conservation
MFCS	Master of Family and Consumer Sciences
MFE	Master of Financial Economics Master of Financial Engineering Master of Forest Engineering
MFG	Master of Functional Genomics
MFHD	Master of Family and Human Development
MFM	Master of Financial Mathematics
MFMS	Masters in Food Microbiology and Safety
MFPE	Master of Food Process Engineering
MFR	Master of Forest Resources
MFRC	Master of Forest Resources and Conservation
MFS	Master of Food Science Master of Forensic Sciences Master of Forest Science Master of Forest Studies Master of French Studies
MFSA	Master of Forensic Sciences Administration
MFST	Master of Food Safety and Technology
MFT	Master of Family Therapy Master of Food Technology
MFWB	Master of Fishery and Wildlife Biology
MFWCB	Master of Fish, Wildlife and Conservation Biology
MFWS	Master of Fisheries and Wildlife Sciences
MFYCS	Master of Family, Youth and Community Sciences
MG	Master of Genetics
MGA	Master of Governmental Administration
MGD	Master of Graphic Design
MGE	Master of Gas Engineering Master of Geotechnical Engineering
MGEM	Master of Global Entrepreneurship and Management
MGH	Master of Geriatric Health
MGIS	Master of Geographic Information Science Master of Geographic Information Systems
MGM	Master of Global Management
MGP	Master of Gestion de Projet
MGPS	Master of Global Policy Studies
MGS	Master of Gerontological Studies Master of Global Studies
MH	Master of Humanities
MH Ed	Master of Health Education
MH Sc	Master of Health Sciences
MHA	Master of Health Administration Master of Healthcare Administration Master of Hospital Administration Master of Hospitality Administration
MHAD	Master of Health Administration
MHB	Master of Human Behavior
MHCA	Master of Health Care Administration
MHCI	Master of Human-Computer Interaction
MHCL	Master of Health Care Leadership
MHE	Master of Health Education Master of Human Ecology
MHE Ed	Master of Home Economics Education
MHEA	Masters of Higher Education Administration
MHHS	Master of Health and Human Services
MHI	Master of Health Informatics Master of Healthcare Innovation
MHIIM	Master of Health Informatics and Information Management
MHIS	Master of Health Information Systems
MHK	Master of Human Kinetics
MHL	Master of Hebrew Literature
MHMS	Master of Health Management Systems
MHP	Master of Health Physics Master of Heritage Preservation Master of Historic Preservation
MHPA	Master of Heath Policy and Administration
MHPE	Master of Health Professions Education
MHR	Master of Human Resources
MHRD	Master in Human Resource Development
MHRIR	Master of Human Resources and Industrial Relations
MHRLR	Master of Human Resources and Labor Relations
MHRM	Master of Human Resources Management
MHS	Master of Health Science Master of Health Sciences Master of Health Studies Master of Hispanic Studies Master of Human Services Master of Humanistic Studies
MHSA	Master of Health Services Administration
MHSM	Master of Health Sector Management Master of Health Systems Management
MI	Master of Instruction

MI Arch	Master of Interior Architecture
MI St	Master of Information Studies
MIA	Master of Interior Architecture Master of International Affairs
MIAA	Master of International Affairs and Administration
MIAM	Master of International Agribusiness Management
MIB	Master of International Business
MIBA	Master of International Business Administration
MICM	Master of International Construction Management
MID	Master of Industrial Design Master of Industrial Distribution Master of Interior Design Master of International Development
MIE	Master of Industrial Engineering
MIH	Master of Integrative Health
MIHTM	Master of International Hospitality and Tourism Management
MIJ	Master of International Journalism
MILR	Master of Industrial and Labor Relations
MiM	Master in Management
MIM	Master of Industrial Management Master of Information Management Master of International Management
MIMLAE	Master of International Management for Latin American Executives
MIMS	Master of Information Management and Systems Master of Integrated Manufacturing Systems
MIP	Master of Infrastructure Planning Master of Intellectual Property
MIPER	Master of International Political Economy of Resources
MIPP	Master of International Policy and Practice Master of International Public Policy
MIPS	Master of International Planning Studies
MIR	Master of Industrial Relations Master of International Relations
MIS	Master of Industrial Statistics Master of Information Science Master of Information Systems Master of Integrated Science Master of Interdisciplinary Studies Master of International Service Master of International Studies
MISE	Master of Industrial and Systems Engineering
MISKM	Master of Information Sciences and Knowledge Management
MISM	Master of Information Systems Management
MIT	Master in Teaching Master of Industrial Technology Master of Information Technology Master of Initial Teaching Master of International Trade Master of Internet Technology
MITA	Master of Information Technology Administration
MITM	Master of International Technology Management
MITO	Master of Industrial Technology and Operations
MJ	Master of Journalism Master of Jurisprudence
MJ Ed	Master of Jewish Education
MJA	Master of Justice Administration
MJM	Master of Justice Management
MJS	Master of Judicial Studies Master of Juridical Science
MKM	Master of Knowledge Management
ML	Master of Latin
ML Arch	Master of Landscape Architecture
MLA	Master of Landscape Architecture Master of Liberal Arts
MLAS	Master of Laboratory Animal Science Master of Liberal Arts and Sciences
MLAUD	Master of Landscape Architecture in Urban Development
MLD	Master of Leadership Development Master of Leadership Studies
MLE	Master of Applied Linguistics and Exegesis
MLER	Master of Labor and Employment Relations
MLERE	Master of Land Economics and Real Estate
MLHR	Master of Labor and Human Resources
MLI	Master of Legal Institutions
MLI Sc	Master of Library and Information Science
MLIS	Master of Library and Information Science Master of Library and Information Studies
MLM	Master of Library Media
MLOS	Masters in Leadership and Organizational Studies
MLRHR	Master of Labor Relations and Human Resources
MLS	Master of Leadership Studies Master of Legal Studies Master of Liberal Studies Master of Library Science Master of Life Sciences
MLSP	Master of Law and Social Policy
MLT	Master of Language Technologies

MM	Master of Management Master of Ministry Master of Missiology Master of Music
MM Ed	Master of Music Education
MM Sc	Master of Medical Science
MM St	Master of Museum Studies
MMA	Master of Marine Affairs Master of Media Arts Master of Musical Arts
MMAE	Master of Mechanical and Aerospace Engineering
MMAS	Master of Military Art and Science
MMB	Master of Microbial Biotechnology
MMBA	Managerial Master of Business Administration
MMC	Master of Manufacturing Competitiveness Master of Mass Communications Master of Music Conducting
MMCM	Master of Music in Church Music
MMCSS	Masters of Mathematical Computational and Statistical Sciences
MME	Master of Manufacturing Engineering Master of Mathematics Education Master of Mathematics for Educators Master of Mechanical Engineering Master of Medical Engineering Master of Mining Engineering Master of Music Education
MMF	Master of Mathematical Finance
MMFT	Master of Marriage and Family Therapy
MMG	Master of Management
MMH	Master of Management in Hospitality Master of Medical Humanities
MMI	Master of Management of Innovation
MMIS	Master of Management Information Systems
MMM	Master of Manufacturing Management Master of Marine Management Master of Medical Management
MMME	Master of Metallurgical and Materials Engineering
MMP	Master of Management Practice Master of Marine Policy Master of Medical Physics Master of Music Performance
MMPA	Master of Management and Professional Accounting
MMQM	Master of Manufacturing Quality Management
MMR	Master of Marketing Research
MMRM	Master of Marine Resources Management
MMS	Master of Management Science Master of Management Studies Master of Manufacturing Systems Master of Marine Studies Master of Materials Science Master of Medical Science Master of Medieval Studies Master of Modern Studies
MMSE	Master of Manufacturing Systems Engineering
MMSM	Master of Music in Sacred Music
MMT	Master in Marketing Master of Management Master of Music Teaching Master of Music Therapy Masters in Marketing Technology
MMus	Master of Music
MN	Master of Nursing Master of Nutrition
MN NP	Master of Nursing in Nurse Practitioner
MNA	Master of Nonprofit Administration Master of Nurse Anesthesia
MNAL	Master of Nonprofit Administration and Leadership
MNAS	Master of Natural and Applied Science
MNCM	Master of Network and Communications Management
MNE	Master of Network Engineering Master of Nuclear Engineering
MNL	Master in International Business for Latin America
MNM	Master of Nonprofit Management
MNO	Master of Nonprofit Organization
MNPL	Master of Not-for-Profit Leadership
MNPS	Master of New Professional Studies
MNpS	Master of Nonprofit Studies
MNR	Master of Natural Resources
MNRES	Master of Natural Resources and Environmental Studies
MNRM	Master of Natural Resource Management
MNRS	Master of Natural Resource Stewardship
MNS	Master of Natural Science
MO	Master of Oceanography
MOD	Master of Organizational Development
MOGS	Master of Oil and Gas Studies
MOH	Master of Occupational Health
MOL	Master of Organizational Leadership
MOM	Master of Oriental Medicine
MOR	Master of Operations Research

MOT	Master of Occupational Therapy
MP	Master of Physiology Master of Planning
MP Ac	Master of Professional Accountancy
MP Acc	Master of Professional Accountancy Master of Professional Accounting Master of Public Accounting
MP Aff	Master of Public Affairs
MP Th	Master of Pastoral Theology
MPA	Master of Physician Assistant Master of Professional Accountancy Master of Professional Accounting Master of Public Administration Master of Public Affairs
MPAC	Masters in Professional Accounting
MPAID	Master of Public Administration and International Development
MPAP	Master of Physician Assistant Practice Master of Public Affairs and Politics
MPAS	Master of Physician Assistant Science Master of Physician Assistant Studies Master of Public Art Studies
MPC	Master of Pastoral Counseling Master of Professional Communication Master of Professional Counseling
MPD	Master of Product Development Master of Public Diplomacy
MPDS	Master of Planning and Development Studies
MPE	Master of Physical Education Master of Power Engineering
MPEM	Master of Project Engineering and Management
MPH	Master of Public Health
MPHE	Master of Public Health Education
MPHTM	Master of Public Health and Tropical Medicine
MPIA	Master of Public and International Affairs Master Program in International Affairs
MPM	Master of Pastoral Ministry Master of Pest Management Master of Policy Management Master of Practical Ministries Master of Project Management Master of Public Management
MPNA	Master of Public and Nonprofit Administration
MPOD	Master of Positive Organizational Development
MPP	Master of Public Policy
MPPA	Master of Public Policy Administration Master of Public Policy and Administration
MPPAL	Master of Public Policy, Administration and Law
MPPM	Master of Public and Private Management Master of Public Policy and Management
MPPPM	Master of Plant Protection and Pest Management
MPPUP	Master of Public Policy and Urban Planning
MPRTM	Master of Parks, Recreation, and Tourism Management
MPS	Master of Pastoral Studies Master of Perfusion Science Master of Planning Studies Master of Political Science Master of Preservation Studies Master of Professional Studies Master of Public Service
MPSA	Master of Public Service Administration
MPSRE	Master of Professional Studies in Real Estate
MPT	Master of Pastoral Theology Master of Physical Therapy
MPVM	Master of Preventive Veterinary Medicine
MPW	Master of Professional Writing Master of Public Works
MQF	Master of Quantitative Finance
MQM	Master of Quality Management
MQS	Master of Quality Systems
MR	Master of Recreation Master of Retailing
MRA	Master in Research Administration
MRC	Master of Rehabilitation Counseling
MRCP	Master of Regional and City Planning Master of Regional and Community Planning
MRD	Master of Rural Development
MRE	Master of Religious Education
MRED	Master of Real Estate Development
MREM	Master of Resource and Environmental Management
MRLS	Master of Resources Law Studies
MRM	Master of Resources Management
MRP	Master of Regional Planning
MRS	Master of Religious Studies
MRSc	Master of Rehabilitation Science
MS	Master of Science
MS Cmp E	Master of Science in Computer Engineering
MS Kin	Master of Science in Kinesiology
MS Acct	Master of Science in Accounting
MS Accy	Master of Science in Accountancy
MS Aero E	Master of Science in Aerospace Engineering
MS Ag	Master of Science in Agriculture
MS Arch	Master of Science in Architecture
MS Arch St	Master of Science in Architectural Studies

MS Bio E	Master of Science in Bioengineering Master of Science in Biomedical Engineering
MS Bm E	Master of Science in Biomedical Engineering
MS Ch E	Master of Science in Chemical Engineering
MS Chem	Master of Science in Chemistry
MS Cp E	Master of Science in Computer Engineering
MS Eco	Master of Science in Economics
MS Econ	Master of Science in Economics
MS Ed	Master of Science in Education
MS El	Master of Science in Educational Leadership and Administration
MS En E	Master of Science in Environmental Engineering
MS Eng	Master of Science in Engineering
MS Engr	Master of Science in Engineering
MS Env E	Master of Science in Environmental Engineering
MS Exp Surg	Master of Science in Experimental Surgery
MS Int A	Master of Science in International Affairs
MS Mat E	Master of Science in Materials Engineering
MS Mat SE	Master of Science in Material Science and Engineering
MS Met E	Master of Science in Metallurgical Engineering
MS Metr	Master of Science in Meteorology
MS Mgt	Master of Science in Management
MS Min	Master of Science in Mining
MS Min E	Master of Science in Mining Engineering
MS Mt E	Master of Science in Materials Engineering
MS Otal	Master of Science in Otalrynology
MS Pet E	Master of Science in Petroleum Engineering
MS Phys	Master of Science in Physics
MS Phys Op	Master of Science in Physiological Optics
MS Poly	Master of Science in Polymers
MS Psy	Master of Science in Psychology
MS Pub P	Master of Science in Public Policy
MS Sc	Master of Science in Social Science
MS Sp Ed	Master of Science in Special Education
MS Stat	Master of Science in Statistics
MS Surg	Master of Science in Surgery
MS Tax	Master of Science in Taxation
MS Tc E	Master of Science in Telecommunications Engineering
MS-R	Master of Science (Research)
MSA	Master of School Administration Master of Science Administration Master of Science in Accountancy Master of Science in Accounting Master of Science in Administration Master of Science in Aeronautics Master of Science in Agriculture Master of Science in Anesthesia Master of Science in Architecture Master of Science in Aviation Master of Sports Administration
MSA Phy	Master of Science in Applied Physics
MSAA	Master of Science in Astronautics and Aeronautics
MSAAE	Master of Science in Aeronautical and Astronautical Engineering
MSABE	Master of Science in Agricultural and Biological Engineering
MSAC	Master of Science in Acupuncture
MSACC	Master of Science in Accounting
MSaCS	Master of Science in Applied Computer Science
MSAE	Master of Science in Aeronautical Engineering Master of Science in Aerospace Engineering Master of Science in Applied Economics Master of Science in Applied Engineering Master of Science in Architectural Engineering Master of Science in Art Education
MSAL	Master of Sport Administration and Leadership
MSAM	Master of Science in Applied Mathematics
MSANR	Master of Science in Agriculture and Natural Resources Systems Management
MSAPM	Master of Security Analysis and Portfolio Management
MSAS	Master of Science in Applied Statistics Master of Science in Architectural Studies
MSAT	Master of Science in Accounting and Taxation Master of Science in Advanced Technology Master of Science in Athletic Training
MSAUS	Master of Science in Architectural Urban Studies
MSB	Master of Science in Bible Master of Science in Business
MSBA	Master of Science in Business Administration
MSBAE	Master of Science in Biological and Agricultural Engineering Master of Science in Biosystems and Agricultural Engineering
MSBC	Master of Science in Building Construction
MSBE	Master of Science in Biological Engineering Master of Science in Biomedical Engineering
MSBENG	Master of Science in Bioengineering

MSBIT	Master of Science in Business Information Technology
MSBM	Master of Sport Business Management
MSBME	Master of Science in Biomedical Engineering
MSBMS	Master of Science in Basic Medical Science
MSBS	Master of Science in Biomedical Sciences
MSC	Master of Science in Commerce Master of Science in Communication Master of Science in Computers Master of Science in Counseling Master of Science in Criminology
MSCA	Master of Science in Construction Administration
MSCC	Master of Science in Christian Counseling Master of Science in Community Counseling
MSCD	Master of Science in Communication Disorders Master of Science in Community Development
MSCE	Master of Science in Civil Engineering Master of Science in Clinical Epidemiology Master of Science in Computer Engineering Master of Science in Continuing Education
MSCEE	Master of Science in Civil and Environmental Engineering
MSCF	Master of Science in Computational Finance
MSChE	Master of Science in Chemical Engineering
MSCI	Master of Science in Clinical Investigation Master of Science in Curriculum and Instruction
MSCIS	Master of Science in Computer and Information Systems Master of Science in Computer Information Science Master of Science in Computer Information Systems
MSCIT	Master of Science in Computer Information Technology
MSCJ	Master of Science in Criminal Justice
MSCJA	Master of Science in Criminal Justice Administration
MSCJS	Master of Science in Crime and Justice Studies
MSCL	Master of Science in Collaborative Leadership
MSCLS	Master of Science in Clinical Laboratory Studies
MSCM	Master of Science in Conflict Management Master of Science in Construction Management
MScM	Master of Science in Management
MSCM	Master of Supply Chain Management
MSCP	Master of Science in Clinical Psychology Master of Science in Computer Engineering Master of Science in Counseling Psychology
MSCPE	Master of Science in Computer Engineering
MSCPharm	Master of Science in Pharmacy
MSCPI	Master in Strategic Planning for Critical Infrastructures
MSCRP	Master of Science in City and Regional Planning Master of Science in Community and Regional Planning
MSCS	Master of Science in Clinical Science Master of Science in Computer Science
MSCSD	Master of Science in Communication Sciences and Disorders
MSCSE	Master of Science in Computer Science and Engineering
MSCTE	Master of Science in Career and Technical Education
MSD	Master of Science in Dentistry Master of Science in Design Master of Science in Dietetics
MSDD	Master of Software Design and Development
MSDM	Master of Design Methods
MSDR	Master of Dispute Resolution
MSE	Master of Science Education Master of Science in Economics Master of Science in Education Master of Science in Engineering Master of Science in Engineering Management Master of Software Engineering Master of Special Education Master of Structural Engineering
MSECE	Master of Science in Electrical and Computer Engineering
MSED	Master of Sustainable Economic Development
MSEE	Master of Science in Electrical Engineering Master of Science in Environmental Engineering
MSEH	Master of Science in Environmental Health
MSEL	Master of Science in Educational Leadership Master of Science in Executive Leadership
MSEM	Master of Science in Engineering Management Master of Science in Engineering Mechanics Master of Science in Environmental Management
MSENE	Master of Science in Environmental Engineering
MSEO	Master of Science in Electro-Optics
MSEP	Master of Science in Economic Policy Master of Science in Engineering Physics
MSEPA	Masters of Science in Economics and Policy Analysis
MSES	Master of Science in Embedded Software Engineering Master of Science in Engineering Science Master of Science in Environmental Science Master of Science in Environmental Studies

MSESM	Master of Science in Engineering Science and Mechanics
MSET	Master of Science in Education in Educational Technology Master of Science in Engineering Technology
MSETM	Master of Science in Environmental Technology Management
MSEV	Master of Science in Environmental Engineering
MSEVH	Master of Science in Environmental Health and Safety
MSF	Master of Science in Finance Master of Science in Forestry
MSFA	Master of Science in Financial Analysis
MSFAM	Master of Science in Family Studies
MSFCS	Master of Science in Family and Consumer Science
MSFE	Master of Science in Financial Engineering
MSFOR	Master of Science in Forestry
MSFP	Master of Science in Financial Planning
MSFS	Master of Science in Financial Sciences Master of Science in Forensic Science
MSFSB	Master of Science in Financial Services and Banking
MSFT	Master of Science in Family Therapy
MSGC	Master of Science in Genetic Counseling
MSGL	Master of Science in Global Leadership
MSH	Master of Science in Health Master of Science in Hospice
MSHA	Master of Science in Health Administration
MSHCA	Master of Science in Health Care Administration
MSHCI	Master of Science in Human Computer Interaction
MSHCPM	Master of Science in Health Care Policy and Management
MSHE	Master of Science in Health Education
MSHES	Master of Science in Human Environmental Sciences
MSHFID	Master of Science in Human Factors in Information Design
MSHFS	Master of Science in Human Factors and Systems
MSHI	Master of Science in Health Informatics
MSHP	Master of Science in Health Professions Master of Science in Health Promotion
MSHR	Master of Science in Human Resources
MSHRL	Master of Science in Human Resource Leadership
MSHRM	Master of Science in Human Resource Management
MSHROD	Master of Science in Human Resources and Organizational Development
MSHS	Master of Science in Health Science Master of Science in Health Services Master of Science in Health Systems Master of Science in Homeland Security
MSHT	Master of Science in History of Technology
MSI	Master of Science in Instruction
MSIA	Master of Science in Industrial Administration Master of Science in Information Assurance and Computer Security
MSIB	Master of Science in International Business
MSIDM	Master of Science in Interior Design and Merchandising
MSIDT	Master of Science in Information Design and Technology
MSIE	Master of Science in Industrial Engineering Master of Science in International Economics
MSIEM	Master of Science in Information Engineering and Management
MSIID	Master of Science in Information and Instructional Design
MSIM	Master of Science in Information Management Master of Science in International Management Master of Science in Investment Management
MSIMC	Master of Science in Integrated Marketing Communications
MSIR	Master of Science in Industrial Relations
MSIS	Master of Science in Information Science Master of Science in Information Systems Master of Science in Interdisciplinary Studies
MSISE	Master of Science in Infrastructure Systems Engineering
MSISM	Master of Science in Information Systems Management
MSISPM	Master of Science in Information Security Policy and Management
MSIST	Master of Science in Information Systems Technology
MSIT	Master of Science in Industrial Technology Master of Science in Information Technology Master of Science in Instructional Technology
MSITM	Master of Science in Information Technology Management
MSJ	Master of Science in Journalism Master of Science in Jurisprudence
MSJE	Master of Science in Jewish Education
MSJFP	Master of Science in Juvenile Forensic Psychology
MSJJ	Master of Science in Juvenile Justice
MSJPS	Master of Science in Justice and Public Safety

MSJS	Master of Science in Jewish Studies
MSK	Master of Science in Kinesiology
MSKM	Master of Science in Knowledge Management
MSL	Master of School Leadership Master of Science in Leadership Master of Science in Limnology Master of Strategic Leadership Master of Studies in Law
MSLA	Master of Science in Landscape Architecture Master of Science in Legal Administration
MSLD	Master of Science in Land Development
MSLS	Master of Science in Legal Studies Master of Science in Library Science
MSLSCM	Master of Science in Logistics and Supply Chain Management
MSLT	Master of Second Language Teaching
MSM	Master of Sacred Ministry Master of Sacred Music Master of School Mathematics Master of Science in Management Master of Science in Mathematics Master of Science in Organization Management Master of Security Management
MSMA	Master of Science in Marketing Analysis
MSMAE	Master of Science in Materials Engineering
MSMC	Master of Science in Mass Communications
MSME	Master of Science in Mathematics Education Master of Science in Mechanical Engineering
MSMFE	Master of Science in Manufacturing Engineering
MSMFT	Master of Science in Marriage and Family Therapy
MSMIS	Master of Science in Management Information Systems
MSMIT	Master of Science in Management and Information Technology
MSMM	Master of Science in Manufacturing Management
MSMO	Master of Science in Manufacturing Operations
MSMOT	Master of Science in Management of Technology
MSMS	Master of Science in Management Science Master of Science in Medical Sciences
MSMSE	Master of Science in Manufacturing Systems Engineering Master of Science in Material Science and Engineering Master of Science in Mathematics and Science Education
MSMT	Master of Science in Management and Technology Master of Science in Medical Technology
MSMus	Master of Sacred Music
MSN	Master of Science in Nursing
MSN-R	Master of Science in Nursing (Research)
MSNA	Master of Science in Nurse Anesthesia
MSNE	Master of Science in Nuclear Engineering
MSNED	Master of Science in Nurse Education
MSNM	Master of Science in Nonprofit Management
MSNS	Master of Science in Natural Science Master's of Science in Nutritional Science
MSOD	Master of Science in Organizational Development
MSOEE	Master of Science in Outdoor and Environmental Education
MSOES	Master of Science in Occupational Ergonomics and Safety
MSOH	Master of Science in Occupational Health
MSOL	Master of Science in Organizational Leadership
MSOM	Master of Science in Operations Management Master of Science in Organization and Management Master of Science in Oriental Medicine
MSOR	Master of Science in Operations Research
MSOT	Master of Science in Occupational Technology Master of Science in Occupational Therapy
MSP	Master of Science in Pharmacy Master of Science in Planning Master of Science in Psychology Master of Speech Pathology
MSPA	Master of Science in Physician Assistant Master of Science in Professional Accountancy
MSPAS	Master of Science in Physician Assistant Studies
MSPC	Master of Science in Professional Communications Master of Science in Professional Counseling
MSPE	Master of Science in Petroleum Engineering
MSPG	Master of Science in Psychology
MSPH	Master of Science in Public Health
MSPHR	Master of Science in Pharmacy
MSPM	Master of Science in Professional Management Master of Science in Project Management
MSPNGE	Master of Science in Petroleum and Natural Gas Engineering
MSPS	Master of Science in Pharmaceutical Science Master of Science in Political Science Master of Science in Psychological Services
MSPT	Master of Science in Physical Therapy
MSpVM	Master of Specialized Veterinary Medicine
MSR	Master of Science in Radiology Master of Science in Reading
MSRA	Master of Science in Recreation Administration
MSRC	Master of Science in Resource Conservation

MSRE	Master of Science in Real Estate Master of Science in Religious Education
MSRED	Master of Science in Real Estate Development
MSRLS	Master of Science in Recreation and Leisure Studies
MSRMP	Master of Science in Radiological Medical Physics
MSRS	Master of Science in Rehabilitation Science
MSS	Master of Science in Software Master of Social Science Master of Social Services Master of Software Systems Master of Sports Science Master of Strategic Studies
MSSA	Master of Science in Social Administration
MSSCP	Master of Science in Science Content and Process
MSSE	Master of Science in Software Engineering Master of Science in Space Education Master of Science in Special Education
MSSEM	Master of Science in Systems and Engineering Management
MSSI	Master of Science in Security Informatics Master of Science in Strategic Intelligence
MSSL	Master of Science in Strategic Leadership
MSSLP	Master of Science in Speech-Language Pathology
MSSM	Master of Science in Sports Medicine
MSSP	Master of Science in Social Policy
MSSPA	Master of Science in Student Personnel Administration
MSSS	Master of Science in Safety Science Master of Science in Systems Science
MSST	Master of Science in Security Technologies
MSSW	Master of Science in Social Work
MSSWE	Master of Science in Software Engineering
MST	Master of Science and Technology Master of Science in Taxation Master of Science in Teaching Master of Science in Technology Master of Science in Telecommunications Master of Science Teaching
MSTC	Master of Science in Technical Communication Master of Science in Telecommunications
MSTCM	Master of Science in Traditional Chinese Medicine
MSTE	Master of Science in Telecommunications Engineering Master of Science in Transportation Engineering
MSTM	Master of Science in Technical Management
MSTOM	Master of Science in Traditional Oriental Medicine
MSUD	Master of Science in Urban Design
MSW	Master of Social Work
MSWE	Master of Software Engineering
MSWREE	Master of Science in Water Resources and Environmental Engineering
MSX	Master of Science in Exercise Science
MT	Master of Taxation Master of Teaching Master of Technology Master of Textiles
MTA	Master of Tax Accounting Master of Teaching Arts Master of Tourism Administration
MTCM	Master of Traditional Chinese Medicine
MTD	Master of Training and Development
MTE	Master in Educational Technology Master of Teacher Education
MTESOL	Master in Teaching English to Speakers of Other Languages
MTHM	Master of Tourism and Hospitality Management
MTI	Master of Information Technology
MTIM	Masters of Trust and Investment Management
MTL	Master of Talmudic Law
MTM	Master of Technology Management Master of Telecommunications Management Master of the Teaching of Mathematics
MTMH	Master of Tropical Medicine and Hygiene
MTOM	Master of Traditional Oriental Medicine
MTP	Master of Transpersonal Psychology
MTPC	Master of Technical and Professional Communication
MTS	Master of Theological Studies
MTSC	Master of Technical and Scientific Communication
MTSE	Master of Telecommunications and Software Engineering
MTT	Master in Technology Management
MTX	Master of Taxation
MUA	Master of Urban Affairs
MUD	Master of Urban Design
MUEP	Master of Urban and Environmental Planning
MUP	Master of Urban Planning
MUPDD	Master of Urban Planning, Design, and Development
MUPP	Master of Urban Planning and Policy
MUPRED	Masters of Urban Planning and Real Estate Development
MURP	Master of Urban and Regional Planning Master of Urban and Rural Planning

MUS	Master of Urban Studies
MVM	Master of VLSI and microelectronics
MVP	Master of Voice Pedagogy
MVPH	Master of Veterinary Public Health
MVS	Master of Visual Studies
MWC	Master of Wildlife Conservation
MWE	Master in Welding Engineering
MWPS	Master of Wood and Paper Science
MWR	Master of Water Resources
MWS	Master of Women's Studies
MZS	Master of Zoological Science
Nav Arch	Naval Architecture
Naval E	Naval Engineer
ND	Doctor of Naturopathic Medicine
NE	Nuclear Engineer
Nuc E	Nuclear Engineer
OD	Doctor of Optometry
OTD	Doctor of Occupational Therapy
PBME	Professional Master of Biomedical Engineering
PD	Professional Diploma
PGC	Post-Graduate Certificate
PGD	Postgraduate Diploma
Ph L	Licentiate of Philosophy
Pharm D	Doctor of Pharmacy
PhD	Doctor of Philosophy
PhD Otal	Doctor of Philosophy in Otalrynology
Phd Surg	Doctor of Philosophy in Surgery
PhDEE	Doctor of Philosophy in Electrical Engineering
PM Sc	Professional Master of Science
PMBA	Professional Master of Business Administration
PMC	Post Master Certificate
PMD	Post-Master's Diploma
PMS	Professional Master of Science Professional Master's Degree
Post-Doctoral MS	Post-Doctoral Master of Science
PPDPT	Postprofessional Doctor of Physical Therapy
PSM	Professional Master of Science Professional Science Master's
Psy D	Doctor of Psychology
Psy M	Master of Psychology
Psy S	Specialist in Psychology
Psya D	Doctor of Psychoanalysis
Re Dir	Director of Recreation
Rh D	Doctor of Rehabilitation
S Psy S	Specialist in Psychological Services
Sc D	Doctor of Science
Sc M	Master of Science
SCCT	Specialist in Community College Teaching
ScDPT	Doctor of Physical Therapy Science
SD	Doctor of Science Specialist Degree
SJD	Doctor of Juridical Science
SLPD	Doctor of Speech-Language Pathology
SLS	Specialist in Library Science
SM	Master of Science
SM Arch S	Master of Science in Architectural Studies
SM Vis S	Master of Science in Visual Studies
SMBT	Master of Science in Building Technology
SP	Specialist Degree
Sp C	Specialist in Counseling
Sp Ed	Specialist in Education
Sp LIS	Specialist in Library and Information Science
SPA	Specialist in Arts
SPCM	Special in Church Music
Spec	Specialist's Certificate
Spec M	Specialist in Music
SPEM	Special in Educational Ministries
SPS	School Psychology Specialist
Spt	Specialist Degree
SPTH	Special in Theology
SSP	Specialist in School Psychology
STB	Bachelor of Sacred Theology
STD	Doctor of Sacred Theology
STL	Licentiate of Sacred Theology
STM	Master of Sacred Theology
TDPT	Transitional Doctor of Physical Therapy
Th D	Doctor of Theology
Th M	Master of Theology
VMD	Doctor of Veterinary Medicine
WEMBA	Weekend Executive Master of Business Administration
XMA	Executive Master of Arts
XMBA	Executive Master of Business Administration

INDEXES

Close-Ups and Displays

Adler School of Professional Psychology
Psychology 1047
American University
Communication 673
International Service 849
Argosy University, Atlanta
Psychology and Behavioral Sciences 1049
Argosy University, Chicago
Psychology and Behavioral Sciences 1051
Argosy University, Dallas
Psychology and Behavioral Sciences 1053
Argosy University, Denver
Psychology and Behavioral Sciences 1055
Argosy University, Hawai'i
Psychology and Behavioral Sciences 1057
Argosy University, Inland Empire
Psychology and Behavioral Sciences 1059
Argosy University, Los Angeles
Psychology and Behavioral Sciences 1061
Argosy University, Nashville
Psychology and Behavioral Sciences 1063
Argosy University, Orange County
Psychology and Behavioral Sciences 1065
Argosy University, Phoenix
Psychology and Behavioral Sciences 1067
Argosy University, Salt Lake City
Psychology and Behavioral Sciences 1069
Argosy University, San Diego
Psychology and Behavioral Sciences 1071
Argosy University, San Francisco Bay Area
Psychology and Behavioral Sciences 1073
Argosy University, Sarasota
Psychology and Behavioral Sciences 1075
Argosy University, Schaumburg
Psychology and Behavioral Sciences 1077
Argosy University, Seattle
Psychology and Behavioral Sciences 1079
Argosy University, Tampa
Psychology and Behavioral Sciences 1081
Argosy University, Twin Cities
Psychology and Behavioral Sciences 1083
Argosy University, Washington DC
Psychology and Behavioral Sciences 1085
Art Center College of Design
Art and Design 113
Auburn University
English 417
Bard Graduate Center for Studies in the Decorative Arts, Design, and Culture
Decorative Arts, Design, and Culture 191
Boston University
Communication 675
Columbia University
Film, Theater Arts, Visual Arts, and Writing 261
Cornell University
Industrial and Labor Relations 1183
Public Affairs 1181
CUNY Graduate School of Journalism
Journalism 677
Fashion Institute of Technology
Fashion and Textile Studies 115
Felician College
Counseling Psychology 1087
Florida Institute of Technology
Psychology 1089
George Mason University
Art History 193
Public Policy 1185
Hawai'i Pacific University
Communication 679
Diplomacy and Military Studies Program 809
Global Leadership and Sustainable Development 1187
Illinois Institute of Technology
Architecture 143
Architecture (Display) 125
Indiana University Bloomington
Public Affairs 1189
The Jewish Theological Seminary
Graduate Studies 511
Rabbinical Studies 513
The Johns Hopkins University
Public Policy 1191
Public Policy (Display) 1155
Memphis College of Art
Studio Practice and Art Education 195
Miami International University of Art & Design
Art and Design 117
Missouri State University
Global Studies 851
Global Studies (Display) 817
Monterey Institute of International Studies
International Policy Studies 853
Translation and Interpretation 437
New York University
Individualized Study 551
Northwestern University
English (Display) 350
Nova Southeastern University
Criminal Justice 721
Philadelphia College of Osteopathic Medicine
Psychology 1091
Point Park University
Journalism and Mass Communication 681
Pratt Institute
Architecture 145
Art and Design 119
Rutgers, The State University of New Jersey, Newark
Psychology and Counseling 1093
Rutgers, The State University of New Jersey, New Brunswick
Industrial Relations and Human Resources (Display) 1117
Saint Louis University–Madrid Campus
Spanish Language and Literature and English 419
St. Mary's Seminary and University
Religious Studies (Display) 503
Seton Hall University
Diplomacy and International Relations 855
South University (AL)
Counseling 1097
South University (FL)
Counseling 1105
South University (GA)
Counseling 1101
South University (SC)
Counseling 1095

South University (VA)
Counseling 1099, 1103
Syracuse University
Communications 683
Communications (Display) 622
Texas A&M University
Sociology 1245
University of California, Riverside
Economics (Display) 747
University of Delaware
Urban Affairs and Public Policy 1193
University of Maine
Public Administration (Display) 1138
University of Pennsylvania
Design 147
Government 1195
University of Rochester
Art and Art History 197
University of Southern California
Communication and Journalism 685
Communication and Journalism (Display) 629
The University of Texas at Dallas
Economic, Political, and Policy Sciences 759
The University of the Arts
Graduate Studies 199
Villanova University
English 421
Hispanic Studies 607
History 303
Political Science 857
Psychology 1107
Theology 515

Directories and Subject Areas

Following is an alphabetical listing of directories and subject areas. Also listed are cross-references for subject area names not used in the directory structure of the guides, for example, "Arabic (*see* Near and Middle Eastern Languages)."

Graduate Programs in the Humanities, Arts & Social Sciences

Addictions/Substance Abuse Counseling
Administration (*see* Arts Administration; Public Administration)
African-American Studies
African Languages and Literatures (*see* African Studies)
African Studies
Agribusiness (*see* Agricultural Economics and Agribusiness)
Agricultural Economics and Agribusiness
Alcohol Abuse Counseling (*see* Addictions/Substance Abuse Counseling)
American Indian/Native American Studies
American Studies
Anthropology
Applied Arts and Design—General
Applied Economics
Applied History (*see* Public History)
Applied Social Research
Arabic (*see* Near and Middle Eastern Languages)
Arab Studies (*see* Near and Middle Eastern Studies)
Archaeology
Architectural History
Architecture
Archives Administration (*see* Public History)
Area and Cultural Studies (*see* African-American Studies; African Studies; American Indian/Native American Studies; American Studies; Asian-American Studies; Asian Studies; Canadian Studies; Cultural Studies; East European and Russian Studies; Ethnic Studies; Folklore; Gender Studies; Hispanic Studies; Holocaust Studies; Jewish Studies; Latin American Studies; Near and Middle Eastern Studies; Northern Studies; Pacific Area/Pacific Rim Studies; Western European Studies; Women's Studies)
Art/Fine Arts
Art History
Arts Administration
Arts Journalism
Art Therapy
Asian-American Studies
Asian Languages
Asian Studies
Behavioral Sciences (*see* Psychology)
Bible Studies (*see* Religion; Theology)
Biological Anthropology
Black Studies (*see* African-American Studies)
Broadcasting (*see* Communication; Film, Television, and Video Production)
Broadcast Journalism
Building Science
Canadian Studies
Celtic Languages
Ceramics (*see* Art/Fine Arts)
Child and Family Studies
Child Development
Chinese
Chinese Studies (*see* Asian Languages; Asian Studies)
Christian Studies (*see* Missions and Missiology; Religion; Theology)
Cinema (*see* Film, Television, and Video Production)
City and Regional Planning (*see* Urban and Regional Planning)
Classical Languages and Literatures (*see* Classics)
Classics
Clinical Psychology
Clothing and Textiles
Cognitive Psychology (*see* Psychology—General; Cognitive Sciences)
Cognitive Sciences
Communication—General
Community Affairs (*see* Urban and Regional Planning; Urban Studies)
Community Planning (*see* Architecture; Environmental Design; Urban and Regional Planning; Urban Design; Urban Studies)
Community Psychology (*see* Social Psychology)
Comparative and Interdisciplinary Arts
Comparative Literature
Composition (*see* Music)
Computer Art and Design
Conflict Resolution and Mediation/Peace Studies
Consumer Economics
Corporate and Organizational Communication
Corrections (*see* Criminal Justice and Criminology)
Counseling (*see* Counseling Psychology; Pastoral Ministry and Counseling)
Counseling Psychology
Crafts (*see* Art/Fine Arts)
Creative Arts Therapies (*see* Art Therapy; Therapies—Dance, Drama, and Music)
Criminal Justice and Criminology
Cultural Studies
Dance
Decorative Arts
Demography and Population Studies
Design (*see* Applied Arts and Design; Architecture; Art/Fine Arts; Environmental Design; Graphic Design; Industrial Design; Interior Design; Textile Design; Urban Design)
Developmental Psychology
Diplomacy (*see* International Affairs)
Disability Studies
Drama Therapy (*see* Therapies—Dance, Drama, and Music)
Dramatic Arts (*see* Theater)
Drawing (*see* Art/Fine Arts)
Drug Abuse Counseling (*see* Addictions/Substance Abuse Counseling)

Drug and Alcohol Abuse Counseling (*see* Addictions/Substance Abuse Counseling)
East Asian Studies (*see* Asian Studies)
East European and Russian Studies
Economic Development
Economics
Educational Theater (*see* Theater; Therapies—Dance, Drama, and Music)
Emergency Management
English
Environmental Design
Ethics
Ethnic Studies
Ethnomusicology (*see* Music)
Experimental Psychology
Family and Consumer Sciences—General
Family Studies (*see* Child and Family Studies)
Family Therapy (*see* Child and Family Studies; Clinical Psychology; Counseling Psychology; Marriage and Family Therapy)
Filmmaking (*see* Film, Television, and Video Production)
Film Studies (*see* Film, Television, and Video Production)
Film, Television, and Video Production
Film, Television, and Video Theory and Criticism
Fine Arts (*see* Art/Fine Arts)
Folklore
Foreign Languages (*see* specific language)
Foreign Service (*see* International Affairs; International Development)
Forensic Psychology
Forensic Sciences
Forensics (*see* Speech and Interpersonal Communication)
French
Gender Studies
General Studies (*see* Liberal Studies)
Genetic Counseling
Geographic Information Systems
Geography
German
Gerontology
Graphic Design
Greek (*see* Classics)
Health Communication
Health Psychology
Hebrew (*see* Near and Middle Eastern Languages)
Hebrew Studies (*see* Jewish Studies)
Hispanic Studies
Historic Preservation
History
History of Art (*see* Art History)
History of Medicine
History of Science and Technology
Holocaust and Genocide Studies
Home Economics (*see* Family and Consumer Sciences—General)
Homeland Security
Household Economics, Sciences, and Management (*see* Family and Consumer Sciences—General)
Human Development
Humanities
Illustration
Industrial and Labor Relations
Industrial and Organizational Psychology
Industrial Design
Interdisciplinary Studies
Interior Design
International Affairs
International Development
International Economics
International Service (*see* International Affairs; International Development)
International Trade Policy
Internet and Interactive Multimedia
Interpersonal Communication (*see* Speech and Interpersonal Communication)
Interpretation (*see* Translation and Interpretation)
Islamic Studies (*see* Near and Middle Eastern Studies; Religion)
Italian
Japanese
Japanese Studies (*see* Asian Languages; Asian Studies; Japanese)
Jewelry (*see* Art/Fine Arts)
Jewish Studies
Journalism
Judaic Studies (*see* Jewish Studies; Religion)
Labor Relations (*see* Industrial and Labor Relations)
Landscape Architecture
Latin American Studies
Latin (*see* Classics)
Law Enforcement (*see* Criminal Justice and Criminology)
Liberal Studies
Lighting Design
Linguistics
Literature (*see* Classics; Comparative Literature; specific language)
Marriage and Family Therapy
Mass Communication
Media Studies
Medical Illustration
Medieval and Renaissance Studies
Metalsmithing (*see* Art/Fine Arts)
Middle Eastern Studies (*see* Near and Middle Eastern Studies)
Military and Defense Studies
Mineral Economics
Ministry (*see* Pastoral Ministry and Counseling; Theology)
Missions and Missiology
Motion Pictures (*see* Film, Television, and Video Production)
Museum Studies
Music
Musicology (*see* Music)
Music Therapy (*see* Therapies—Dance, Drama, and Music)
National Security
Native American Studies (*see* American Indian/Native American Studies)
Near and Middle Eastern Languages
Near and Middle Eastern Studies

Near Environment (*see* Family and Consumer Sciences)
Northern Studies
Organizational Psychology (*see* Industrial and Organizational Psychology)
Oriental Languages (*see* Asian Languages)
Oriental Studies (*see* Asian Studies)
Pacific Area/Pacific Rim Studies
Painting (*see* Art/Fine Arts)
Pastoral Ministry and Counseling
Philanthropic Studies
Philosophy
Photography
Playwriting (*see* Theater; Writing)
Policy Studies (*see* Public Policy)
Political Science
Population Studies (*see* Demography and Population Studies)
Portuguese
Printmaking (*see* Art/Fine Arts)
Product Design (*see* Industrial Design)
Psychoanalysis and Psychotherapy
Psychology—General
Public Administration
Public Affairs
Public History
Public Policy
Public Speaking (*see* Mass Communication; Rhetoric; Speech and Interpersonal Communication)
Publishing
Regional Planning (*see* Architecture; Urban and Regional Planning; Urban Design; Urban Studies)
Rehabilitation Counseling
Religion
Renaissance Studies (*see* Medieval and Renaissance Studies)
Rhetoric
Romance Languages
Romance Literatures (*see* Romance Languages)
Rural Planning and Studies
Rural Sociology
Russian
Scandinavian Languages
School Psychology
Sculpture (*see* Art/Fine Arts)
Security Administration (*see* Criminal Justice and Criminology)
Slavic Languages
Slavic Studies (*see* East European and Russian Studies; Slavic Languages)
Social Psychology
Social Sciences
Sociology
Southeast Asian Studies (*see* Asian Studies)
Soviet Studies (*see* East European and Russian Studies; Russian)
Spanish
Speech and Interpersonal Communication
Sport Psychology
Studio Art (*see* Art/Fine Arts)
Substance Abuse Counseling (*see* Addictions/Substance Abuse Counseling)
Survey Methodology
Sustainable Development
Technical Communication
Technical Writing
Telecommunications (*see* Film, Television, and Video Production)
Television (*see* Film, Television, and Video Production)
Textile Design
Textiles (*see* Clothing and Textiles; Textile Design)
Thanatology
Theater
Theater Arts (*see* Theater)
Theology
Therapies—Dance, Drama, and Music
Translation and Interpretation
Transpersonal and Humanistic Psychology
Urban and Regional Planning
Urban Design
Urban Planning (*see* Architecture; Urban and Regional Planning; Urban Design; Urban Studies)
Urban Studies
Video (*see* Film, Television, and Video Production)
Visual Arts (*see* Applied Arts and Design; Art/Fine Arts; Film, Television, and Video Production; Graphic Design; Illustration; Photography)
Western European Studies
Women's Studies
World Wide Web (*see* Internet and Interactive Multimedia)
Writing

Graduate Programs in the Biological Sciences

Anatomy
Animal Behavior
Bacteriology
Behavioral Sciences (*see* Biopsychology; Neuroscience; Zoology)
Biochemistry
Biological and Biomedical Sciences—General
Biological Chemistry (*see* Biochemistry)
Biological Oceanography (*see* Marine Biology)
Biophysics
Biopsychology
Botany
Breeding (*see* Botany; Plant Biology; Genetics)
Cancer Biology/Oncology
Cardiovascular Sciences
Cell Biology
Cellular Physiology (*see* Cell Biology; Physiology)
Computational Biology
Conservation (*see* Conservation Biology; Environmental Biology)
Conservation Biology
Crop Sciences (*see* Botany; Plant Biology)
Cytology (*see* Cell Biology)

Developmental Biology
Dietetics (*see* Nutrition)
Ecology
Embryology (*see* Developmental Biology)
Endocrinology (*see* Physiology)
Entomology
Environmental Biology
Evolutionary Biology
Foods (*see* Nutrition)
Genetics
Genomic Sciences
Histology (*see* Anatomy; Cell Biology)
Human Genetics
Immunology
Infectious Diseases
Laboratory Medicine (*see* Immunology; Microbiology; Pathology)
Life Sciences (*see* Biological and Biomedical Sciences)
Marine Biology
Medical Microbiology
Medical Sciences (*see* Biological and Biomedical Sciences)
Medical Science Training Programs (*see* Biological and Biomedical Sciences)
Microbiology
Molecular Biology
Molecular Biophysics
Molecular Genetics
Molecular Medicine
Molecular Pathogenesis
Molecular Pathology
Molecular Pharmacology
Molecular Physiology
Molecular Toxicology
Neural Sciences (*see* Biopsychology; Neurobiology; Neuroscience)
Neurobiology
Neuroendocrinology (*see* Biopsychology; Neurobiology; Neuroscience; Physiology)
Neuropharmacology (*see* Biopsychology; Neurobiology; Neuroscience; Pharmacology)
Neurophysiology (*see* Biopsychology; Neurobiology; Neuroscience; Physiology)
Neuroscience
Nutrition
Oncology (*see* Cancer Biology/Oncology)
Organismal Biology (*see* Biological and Biomedical Sciences; Zoology)
Parasitology
Pathobiology
Pathology
Pharmacology
Photobiology of Cells and Organelles (*see* Botany; Cell Biology; Plant Biology)
Physiological Optics (*see* Physiology)
Physiology
Plant Biology
Plant Molecular Biology
Plant Pathology
Plant Physiology
Pomology (*see* Botany; Plant Biology)
Psychobiology (*see* Biopsychology)
Psychopharmacology (*see* Biopsychology; Neuroscience; Pharmacology)
Radiation Biology
Reproductive Biology
Sociobiology (*see* Evolutionary Biology)
Structural Biology
Systems Biology
Teratology
Theoretical Biology (*see* Biological and Biomedical Sciences)
Therapeutics (*see* Pharmacology)
Toxicology
Translational Biology
Tropical Medicine (*see* Parasitology)
Virology
Wildlife Biology (*see* Zoology)
Zoology

Graduate Programs in the Physical Sciences, Mathematics, Agricultural Sciences, the Environment & Natural Resources

Acoustics
Agricultural Sciences
Agronomy and Soil Sciences
Analytical Chemistry
Animal Sciences
Applied Mathematics
Applied Physics
Applied Statistics
Aquaculture
Astronomy
Astrophysical Sciences (*see* Astrophysics; Atmospheric Sciences; Meteorology; Planetary and Space Sciences)
Astrophysics
Atmospheric Sciences
Biological Oceanography (*see* Marine Affairs; Marine Sciences; Oceanography)
Biomathematics
Biometry
Biostatistics
Chemical Physics
Chemistry
Computational Sciences
Condensed Matter Physics
Dairy Science (*see* Animal Sciences)
Earth Sciences (*see* Geosciences)
Environmental Management and Policy
Environmental Sciences
Environmental Studies (*see* Environmental Management and Policy)
Experimental Statistics (*see* Statistics)

Fish, Game, and Wildlife Management
Food Science and Technology
Forestry
General Science (*see* specific topics)
Geochemistry
Geodetic Sciences
Geological Engineering (*see* Geology)
Geological Sciences (*see* Geology)
Geology
Geophysical Fluid Dynamics (*see* Geophysics)
Geophysics
Geosciences
Horticulture
Hydrogeology
Hydrology
Inorganic Chemistry
Limnology
Marine Affairs
Marine Geology
Marine Sciences
Marine Studies (*see* Marine Affairs; Marine Geology; Marine Sciences; Oceanography)
Mathematical and Computational Finance
Mathematical Physics
Mathematical Statistics (*see* Applied Statistics; Statistics)
Mathematics
Meteorology
Mineralogy
Natural Resource Management (*see* Environmental Management and Policy; Natural Resources)
Natural Resources
Nuclear Physics (*see* Physics)
Ocean Engineering (*see* Marine Affairs; Marine Geology; Marine Sciences; Oceanography)
Oceanography
Optical Sciences
Optical Technologies (*see* Optical Sciences)
Optics (*see* Applied Physics; Optical Sciences; Physics)
Organic Chemistry
Paleontology
Paper Chemistry (*see* Chemistry)
Photonics
Physical Chemistry
Physics
Planetary and Space Sciences
Plant Sciences
Plasma Physics
Poultry Science (*see* Animal Sciences)
Radiological Physics (*see* Physics)
Range Management (*see* Range Science)
Range Science
Resource Management (*see* Environmental Management and Policy; Natural Resources)
Solid-Earth Sciences (*see* Geosciences)
Space Sciences (*see* Planetary and Space Sciences)
Statistics
Theoretical Chemistry
Theoretical Physics
Viticulture and Enology
Water Resources

Graduate Programs in Engineering & Applied Sciences

Aeronautical Engineering (*see* Aerospace/Aeronautical Engineering)
Aerospace/Aeronautical Engineering
Aerospace Studies (*see* Aerospace/Aeronautical Engineering)
Agricultural Engineering
Applied Mechanics (*see* Mechanics)
Applied Science and Technology
Architectural Engineering
Artificial Intelligence/Robotics
Astronautical Engineering (*see* Aerospace/Aeronautical Engineering)
Automotive Engineering
Aviation
Biochemical Engineering
Bioengineering
Bioinformatics
Biological Engineering (*see* Bioengineering)
Biomedical Engineering
Biosystems Engineering
Biotechnology
Ceramic Engineering (*see* Ceramic Sciences and Engineering)
Ceramic Sciences and Engineering
Ceramics (*see* Ceramic Sciences and Engineering)
Chemical Engineering
Civil Engineering
Computer and Information Systems Security
Computer Engineering
Computer Science
Computing Technology (*see* Computer Science)
Construction Engineering
Construction Management
Database Systems
Electrical Engineering
Electronic Materials
Electronics Engineering (*see* Electrical Engineering)
Energy and Power Engineering
Energy Management and Policy
Engineering and Applied Sciences
Engineering and Public Affairs (*see* Technology and Public Policy)
Engineering and Public Policy (*see* Energy Management and Policy; Technology and Public Policy)
Engineering Design
Engineering Management
Engineering Mechanics (*see* Mechanics)
Engineering Metallurgy (*see* Metallurgical Engineering and Metallurgy)
Engineering Physics

Environmental Design (*see* Environmental Engineering)
Environmental Engineering
Ergonomics and Human Factors
Financial Engineering
Fire Protection Engineering
Food Engineering (*see* Agricultural Engineering)
Game Design and Development
Gas Engineering (*see* Petroleum Engineering)
Geological Engineering
Geophysics Engineering (*see* Geological Engineering)
Geotechnical Engineering
Hazardous Materials Management
Health Informatics
Health Systems (*see* Safety Engineering; Systems Engineering)
Highway Engineering (*see* Transportation and Highway Engineering)
Human-Computer Interaction
Human Factors (*see* Ergonomics and Human Factors)
Hydraulics
Hydrology (*see* Water Resources Engineering)
Industrial Engineering (*see* Industrial/Management Engineering)
Industrial/Management Engineering
Information Science
Internet Engineering
Macromolecular Science (*see* Polymer Science and Engineering)
Management Engineering (*see* Engineering Management; Industrial/Management Engineering)
Management of Technology
Manufacturing Engineering
Marine Engineering (*see* Civil Engineering)
Materials Engineering
Materials Sciences
Mechanical Engineering
Mechanics
Medical Informatics
Metallurgical Engineering and Metallurgy
Metallurgy (*see* Metallurgical Engineering and Metallurgy)
Mineral/Mining Engineering
Nanotechnology
Nuclear Engineering
Ocean Engineering
Operations Research
Paper and Pulp Engineering
Petroleum Engineering
Pharmaceutical Engineering
Plastics Engineering (*see* Polymer Science and Engineering)
Polymer Science and Engineering
Public Policy (*see* Energy Management and Policy; Technology and Public Policy)
Reliability Engineering
Robotics (*see* Artificial Intelligence/Robotics)
Safety Engineering
Software Engineering
Solid-State Sciences (*see* Materials Sciences)
Structural Engineering
Surveying Science and Engineering
Systems Analysis (*see* Systems Engineering)
Systems Engineering
Systems Science
Technology and Public Policy
Telecommunications
Telecommunications Management
Textile Sciences and Engineering
Textiles (*see* Textile Sciences and Engineering)
Transportation and Highway Engineering
Urban Systems Engineering (*see* Systems Engineering)
Waste Management (*see* Hazardous Materials Management)
Water Resources Engineering

Graduate Programs in Business, Education, Health, Information Studies, Law & Social Work

Accounting
Actuarial Science
Acupuncture and Oriental Medicine
Acute Care/Critical Care Nursing
Administration (*see* Business Administration and Management; Educational Administration; Health Services Management and Hospital Administration; Industrial and Manufacturing Management; Nursing and Healthcare Administration; Pharmaceutical Administration; Sports Management)
Adult Education
Adult Nursing
Advanced Practice Nursing (*see* Family Nurse Practitioner Studies)
Advertising and Public Relations
Agricultural Education
Alcohol Abuse Counseling (*see* Counselor Education)
Allied Health—General
Allied Health Professions (*see* Clinical Laboratory Sciences/Medical Technology; Clinical Research; Communication Disorders; Dental Hygiene; Emergency Medical Services; Occupational Therapy; Physical Therapy; Physician Assistant Studies; Rehabilitation Sciences)
Allopathic Medicine
Anesthesiologist Assistant Studies
Art Education
Athletics Administration (*see* Kinesiology and Movement Studies)
Athletic Training and Sports Medicine
Audiology (*see* Communication Disorders)
Aviation Management
Banking (*see* Finance and Banking)
Bioethics
Business Administration and Management—General
Business Education
Child-Care Nursing (*see* Maternal and Child/Neonatal Nursing)
Chiropractic
Clinical Laboratory Sciences/Medical Technology
Clinical Research
Communication Disorders
Community College Education
Community Health

Community Health Nursing
Computer Education
Continuing Education (*see* Adult Education)
Counseling (*see* Counselor Education)
Counselor Education
Curriculum and Instruction
Dental and Oral Surgery (*see* Oral and Dental Sciences)
Dental Assistant Studies (*see* Dental Hygiene)
Dental Hygiene
Dental Services (*see* Dental Hygiene)
Dentistry
Developmental Education
Distance Education Development
Drug Abuse Counseling (*see* Counselor Education)
Early Childhood Education
Educational Leadership and Administration
Educational Measurement and Evaluation
Educational Media/Instructional Technology
Educational Policy
Educational Psychology
Education—General
Education of the Blind (*see* Special Education)
Education of the Deaf (*see* Special Education)
Education of the Gifted
Education of the Hearing Impaired (*see* Special Education)
Education of the Learning Disabled (*see* Special Education)
Education of the Mentally Retarded (*see* Special Education)
Education of the Physically Handicapped (*see* Special Education)
Education of Students with Severe/Multiple Disabilities
Education of the Visually Handicapped (*see* Special Education)
Electronic Commerce
Elementary Education
Emergency Medical Services
English as a Second Language
English Education
Entertainment Management
Entrepreneurship
Environmental and Occupational Health
Environmental Education
Environmental Law
Epidemiology
Exercise and Sports Science
Exercise Physiology (*see* Kinesiology and Movement Studies)
Facilities and Entertainment Management
Family Nurse Practitioner Studies
Finance and Banking
Food Services Management (*see* Hospitality Management)
Foreign Languages Education
Forensic Nursing
Foundations and Philosophy of Education
Gerontological Nursing
Guidance and Counseling (*see* Counselor Education)
Health Education
Health Law
Health Physics/Radiological Health
Health Promotion
Health-Related Professions (*see* individual allied health professions)
Health Services Management and Hospital Administration
Health Services Research
Hearing Sciences (*see* Communication Disorders)
Higher Education
HIV/AIDS Nursing
Home Economics Education
Hospice Nursing
Hospital Administration (*see* Health Services Management and Hospital Administration)
Hospitality Management
Hotel Management (*see* Travel and Tourism)
Human Resources Development
Human Resources Management
Human Services
Industrial Administration (*see* Industrial and Manufacturing Management)
Industrial and Manufacturing Management
Industrial Education (*see* Vocational and Technical Education)
Industrial Hygiene
Information Studies
Instructional Technology (*see* Educational Media/Instructional Technology)
Insurance
International and Comparative Education
International Business
International Commerce (*see* International Business)
International Economics (*see* International Business)
International Health
International Trade (*see* International Business)
Investment and Securities (*see* Business Administration and Management; Finance and Banking; Investment Management)
Investment Management
Junior College Education (*see* Community College Education)
Kinesiology and Movement Studies
Laboratory Medicine (*see* Clinical Laboratory Sciences/Medical Technology)
Law
Legal and Justice Studies
Leisure Services (*see* Recreation and Park Management)
Leisure Studies
Library Science
Logistics
Management (*see* Business Administration and Management)
Management Information Systems
Management Strategy and Policy
Marketing
Marketing Research
Maternal and Child Health
Maternal and Child/Neonatal Nursing
Mathematics Education
Medical Imaging
Medical Nursing (*see* Medical/Surgical Nursing)
Medical Physics
Medical/Surgical Nursing
Medical Technology (*see* Clinical Laboratory Sciences/Medical Technology)

Medicinal and Pharmaceutical Chemistry
Medicinal Chemistry (*see* Medicinal and Pharmaceutical Chemistry)
Medicine (*see* Allopathic Medicine; Naturopathic Medicine; Osteopathic Medicine; Podiatric Medicine)
Middle School Education
Midwifery (*see* Nurse Midwifery)
Movement Studies (*see* Kinesiology and Movement Studies)
Multilingual and Multicultural Education
Museum Education
Music Education
Naturopathic Medicine
Nonprofit Management
Nuclear Medical Technology (*see* Clinical Laboratory Sciences/Medical Technology)
Nurse Anesthesia
Nurse Midwifery
Nurse Practitioner Studies (*see* Family Nurse Practitioner Studies)
Nursery School Education (*see* Early Childhood Education)
Nursing Administration (*see* Nursing and Healthcare Administration)
Nursing and Healthcare Administration
Nursing Education
Nursing—General
Nursing Informatics
Occupational Education (*see* Vocational and Technical Education)
Occupational Health (*see* Environmental and Occupational Health; Occupational Health Nursing)
Occupational Health Nursing
Occupational Therapy
Oncology Nursing
Optometry
Oral and Dental Sciences
Oral Biology (*see* Oral and Dental Sciences)
Oral Pathology (*see* Oral and Dental Sciences)
Organizational Behavior
Organizational Management
Oriental Medicine and Acupuncture (*see* Acupuncture and Oriental Medicine)
Orthodontics (*see* Oral and Dental Sciences)
Osteopathic Medicine
Parks Administration (*see* Recreation and Park Management)
Pediatric Nursing
Pedontics (*see* Oral and Dental Sciences)
Perfusion
Personnel (*see* Human Resources Development; Human Resources Management; Organizational Behavior; Organizational Management; Student Affairs)
Pharmaceutical Administration
Pharmaceutical Chemistry (*see* Medicinal and Pharmaceutical Chemistry)
Pharmaceutical Sciences
Pharmacy
Philosophy of Education (*see* Foundations and Philosophy of Education)
Physical Education
Physical Therapy
Physician Assistant Studies
Physiological Optics (*see* Vision Sciences)
Podiatric Medicine
Preventive Medicine (*see* Community Health and Public Health)
Project Management
Psychiatric Nursing
Public Health—General
Public Health Nursing (*see* Community Health Nursing)
Public Relations (*see* Advertising and Public Relations)
Quality Management
Quantitative Analysis
Radiological Health (*see* Health Physics/Radiological Health)
Reading Education
Real Estate
Recreation and Park Management
Recreation Therapy (*see* Recreation and Park Management)
Rehabilitation Sciences
Rehabilitation Therapy (*see* Physical Therapy)
Religious Education
Remedial Education (*see* Special Education)
Restaurant Administration (*see* Hospitality Management)
School Nursing
Science Education
Secondary Education
Social Sciences Education
Social Studies Education (*see* Social Sciences Education)
Social Work
Special Education
Speech-Language Pathology and Audiology (*see* Communication Disorders)
Sports Management
Sports Medicine (*see* Athletic Training and Sports Medicine)
Sports Psychology and Sociology (*see* Kinesiology and Movement Studies)
Student Affairs
Substance Abuse Counseling (*see* Counselor Education)
Supply Chain Management
Surgical Nursing (*see* Medical/Surgical Nursing)
Sustainability Management
Systems Management (*see* Management Information Systems)
Taxation
Teacher Education (*see* specific subject areas)
Teaching English as a Second Language (*see* English as a Second Language)
Technical Education (*see* Vocational and Technical Education)
Teratology (*see* Environmental and Occupational Health)
Therapeutics (*see* Pharmaceutical Sciences; Pharmacy)
Transcultural Nursing
Transportation Management
Travel and Tourism
Urban Education
Veterinary Medicine
Veterinary Sciences
Vision Sciences
Vocational and Technical Education
Vocational Counseling (*see* Counselor Education)
Women's Health Nursing

Directories and Subject Areas in This Book

Addictions/Substance Abuse Counseling 900
Administration (*see* Arts Administration; Public Administration)
African-American Studies 556
African Languages and Literatures (*see* African Studies)
African Studies 558
Agribusiness (*see* Agricultural Economics and Agribusiness)
Agricultural Economics and Agribusiness 724
Alcohol Abuse Counseling (*see* Addictions/Substance Abuse Counseling)
American Indian/Native American Studies 560
American Studies 561
Anthropology 1204
Applied Arts and Design—General 86
Applied Economics 729
Applied History (*see* Public History)
Applied Social Research 1217
Arabic (*see* Near and Middle Eastern Languages)
Arab Studies (*see* Near and Middle Eastern Studies)
Archaeology 1217
Architectural History 122
Architecture 122
Archives Administration (*see* Public History)
Area and Cultural Studies (*see* African-American Studies; African Studies; American Indian/Native American Studies; American Studies; Asian-American Studies; Asian Studies; Canadian Studies; Cultural Studies; East European and Russian Studies; Ethnic Studies; Folklore; Gender Studies; Hispanic Studies; Holocaust Studies; Jewish Studies; Latin American Studies; Near and Middle Eastern Studies; Northern Studies; Pacific Area/Pacific Rim Studies; Western European Studies; Women's Studies)
Art/Fine Arts 150
Art History 170
Arts Administration 180
Arts Journalism 632
Art Therapy 183
Asian-American Studies 567
Asian Languages 320
Asian Studies 567
Behavioral Sciences (*see* Psychology)
Bible Studies (*see* Religion; Theology)
Biological Anthropology 1222
Black Studies (*see* African-American Studies)
Broadcasting (*see* Communication; Film, Television, and Video Production)
Broadcast Journalism 632
Building Science 131
Canadian Studies 573
Celtic Languages 322
Ceramics (*see* Art/Fine Arts)
Child and Family Studies 766
Child Development 774
Chinese 322
Chinese Studies (*see* Asian Languages; Asian Studies)
Christian Studies (*see* Missions and Missiology; Religion; Theology)
Cinema (*see* Film, Television, and Video Production)
City and Regional Planning (*see* Urban and Regional Planning)
Classical Languages and Literatures (*see* Classics)
Classics 323
Clinical Psychology 904
Clothing and Textiles 776
Cognitive Psychology (*see* Psychology—General; Cognitive Sciences)
Cognitive Sciences 925
Communication—General 610
Community Affairs (*see* Urban and Regional Planning; Urban Studies)
Community Planning (*see* Architecture; Environmental Design; Urban and Regional Planning; Urban Design; Urban Studies)
Community Psychology (*see* Social Psychology)
Comparative and Interdisciplinary Arts 202
Comparative Literature 330
Composition (*see* Music)
Computer Art and Design 90
Conflict Resolution and Mediation/Peace Studies 688
Consumer Economics 778
Corporate and Organizational Communication 633
Corrections (*see* Criminal Justice and Criminology)
Counseling (*see* Counseling Psychology; Pastoral Ministry and Counseling)
Counseling Psychology 931
Crafts (*see* Art/Fine Arts)
Creative Arts Therapies (*see* Art Therapy; Therapies—Dance, Drama, and Music)
Criminal Justice and Criminology 696
Cultural Studies 574
Dance 214
Decorative Arts 185
Demography and Population Studies 1222
Design (*see* Applied Arts and Design; Architecture; Art/Fine Arts; Environmental Design; Graphic Design; Industrial Design; Interior Design; Textile Design; Urban Design)
Developmental Psychology 956
Diplomacy (*see* International Affairs)
Disability Studies 1110
Drama Therapy (*see* Therapies—Dance, Drama, and Music)
Dramatic Arts (*see* Theater)
Drawing (*see* Art/Fine Arts)
Drug Abuse Counseling (*see* Addictions/Substance Abuse Counseling)
Drug and Alcohol Abuse Counseling (*see* Addictions/Substance Abuse Counseling)
East Asian Studies (*see* Asian Studies)
East European and Russian Studies 578
Economic Development 732
Economics 735
Educational Theater (*see* Theater; Therapies—Dance, Drama, and Music)
Emergency Management 1110
English 336

Environmental Design 132
Ethics 440
Ethnic Studies 579
Ethnomusicology (*see* Music)
Experimental Psychology 961
Family and Consumer Sciences—General 762
Family Studies (*see* Child and Family Studies)
Family Therapy (*see* Child and Family Studies; Clinical Psychology; Counseling Psychology; Marriage and Family Therapy)
Filmmaking (*see* Film, Television, and Video Production)
Film Studies (*see* Film, Television, and Video Production)
Film, Television, and Video Production 204
Film, Television, and Video Theory and Criticism 210
Fine Arts (*see* Art/Fine Arts)
Folklore 580
Foreign Languages (*see* specific language)
Foreign Service (*see* International Affairs; International Development)
Forensic Psychology 968
Forensic Sciences 717
Forensics (*see* Speech and Interpersonal Communication)
French 369
Gender Studies 581
General Studies (*see* Liberal Studies)
Genetic Counseling 970
Geographic Information Systems 790
Geography 794
German 380
Gerontology 781
Graphic Design 95
Greek (*see* Classics)
Health Communication 638
Health Psychology 971
Hebrew (*see* Near and Middle Eastern Languages)
Hebrew Studies (*see* Jewish Studies)
Hispanic Studies 583
Historic Preservation 133
History 266
History of Art (*see* Art History)
History of Medicine 294
History of Science and Technology 294
Holocaust and Genocide Studies 585
Home Economics (*see* Family and Consumer Sciences—General)
Homeland Security 1113
Household Economics, Sciences, and Management (*see* Family and Consumer Sciences—General)
Human Development 975
Humanities 306
Illustration 99
Industrial and Labor Relations 1115
Industrial and Organizational Psychology 983
Industrial Design 100
Interdisciplinary Studies 540
Interior Design 101
International Affairs 812
International Development 824
International Economics 756
International Service (*see* International Affairs; International Development)
International Trade Policy 826
Internet and Interactive Multimedia 639
Interpersonal Communication (*see* Speech and Interpersonal Communication)
Interpretation (*see* Translation and Interpretation)
Islamic Studies (*see* Near and Middle Eastern Studies; Religion)
Italian 387
Japanese 390
Japanese Studies (*see* Asian Languages; Asian Studies; Japanese)
Jewelry (*see* Art/Fine Arts)
Jewish Studies 586
Journalism 642
Judaic Studies (*see* Jewish Studies; Religion)
Labor Relations (*see* Industrial and Labor Relations)
Landscape Architecture 135
Latin American Studies 589
Latin (*see* Classics)
Law Enforcement (*see* Criminal Justice and Criminology)
Liberal Studies 310
Lighting Design 139
Linguistics 424
Literature (*see* Classics; Comparative Literature; specific language)
Marriage and Family Therapy 992
Mass Communication 648
Media Studies 654
Medical Illustration 105
Medieval and Renaissance Studies 296
Metalsmithing (*see* Art/Fine Arts)
Middle Eastern Studies (*see* Near and Middle Eastern Studies)
Military and Defense Studies 806
Mineral Economics 757
Ministry (*see* Pastoral Ministry and Counseling; Theology)
Missions and Missiology 458
Motion Pictures (*see* Film, Television, and Video Production)
Museum Studies 186
Music 217
Musicology (*see* Music)
Music Therapy (*see* Therapies—Dance, Drama, and Music)
National Security 807
Native American Studies (*see* American Indian/Native American Studies)
Near and Middle Eastern Languages 392
Near and Middle Eastern Studies 592
Near Environment (*see* Family and Consumer Sciences)
Northern Studies 596
Organizational Psychology (*see* Industrial and Organizational Psychology)
Oriental Languages (*see* Asian Languages)
Oriental Studies (*see* Asian Studies)
Pacific Area/Pacific Rim Studies 596
Painting (*see* Art/Fine Arts)
Pastoral Ministry and Counseling 461
Philanthropic Studies 1118
Philosophy 442
Photography 105
Playwriting (*see* Theater; Writing)
Policy Studies (*see* Public Policy)
Political Science 827
Population Studies (*see* Demography and Population Studies)

Portuguese 394
Printmaking (*see* Art/Fine Arts)
Product Design (*see* Industrial Design)
Psychoanalysis and Psychotherapy 1005
Psychology—General 860
Public Administration 1119
Public Affairs 1146
Public History 299
Public Policy 1151
Public Speaking (*see* Mass Communication; Rhetoric; Speech and Interpersonal Communication)
Publishing 661
Regional Planning (*see* Architecture; Urban and Regional Planning; Urban Design; Urban Studies)
Rehabilitation Counseling 1005
Religion 475
Renaissance Studies (*see* Medieval and Renaissance Studies)
Rhetoric 662
Romance Languages 396
Romance Literatures (*see* Romance Languages)
Rural Planning and Studies 1163
Rural Sociology 1224
Russian 398
Scandinavian Languages 400
School Psychology 1012
Sculpture (*see* Art/Fine Arts)
Security Administration (*see* Criminal Justice and Criminology)
Slavic Languages 401
Slavic Studies (*see* East European and Russian Studies; Slavic Languages)
Social Psychology 1031
Social Sciences 1198
Sociology 1224
Southeast Asian Studies (*see* Asian Studies)
Soviet Studies (*see* East European and Russian Studies; Russian)
Spanish 403
Speech and Interpersonal Communication 666
Sport Psychology 1043
Studio Art (*see* Art/Fine Arts)
Substance Abuse Counseling (*see* Addictions/Substance Abuse Counseling)
Survey Methodology 1243
Sustainable Development 1164
Technical Communication 671
Technical Writing 518
Telecommunications (*see* Film, Television, and Video Production)
Television (*see* Film, Television, and Video Production)
Textile Design 110
Textiles (*see* Clothing and Textiles; Textile Design)
Thanatology 1045
Theater 245
Theater Arts (*see* Theater)
Theology 487
Therapies—Dance, Drama, and Music 258
Translation and Interpretation 435
Transpersonal and Humanistic Psychology 1045
Urban and Regional Planning 1167
Urban Design 140
Urban Planning (*see* Architecture; Urban and Regional Planning; Urban Design; Urban Studies)
Urban Studies 1177
Video (*see* Film, Television, and Video Production)
Visual Arts (*see* Applied Arts and Design; Art/Fine Arts; Film, Television, and Video Production; Graphic Design; Illustration; Photography)
Western European Studies 597
Women's Studies 599
World Wide Web (*see* Internet and Interactive Multimedia)
Writing 519

NOTES

NOTES

NOTES

NOTES